Wine Spectator's

Ultimate Guide To Buying Wine

7TH EDITION

WINE SPECTATOR PRESS
A DIVISION OF M. SHANKEN COMMUNICATIONS, INC.
New York

Contents

J.L. Bulcao

Introduction

Get acquainted with *Wine Spectator's* tasting system, and learn several ways to get the most for your wine-buying dollar.

A handy list of wineries and wines from all over the world that regularly offer good quality for $12 or less.

Argentina
Australia
Chile
France
Italy
Spain
United States

Geared especially to the collector, this listing gathers the best wines from recent vintages of eight of the world's most prestigious wine types.

The Main Listings: Wines by Country and Producer

Following a general introduction to the wines of each country—complete with maps of the major wine regions—you'll find *Wine Spectator*'s ratings and release or auction prices for more than 40,000 wines, plus the many tasting notes that describe a wine's special character.

Sara Matthews

Find the exact page number in the main listings on which each winery's ratings begin.

Pamela Reed

Wine Spectator's Ultimate Guide to Buying Wine, Seventh Edition

Publisher Marvin R. Shanken
Editor Michael Moaba
Executive Editor, *Wine Spectator* Thomas Matthews

Editorial Director, Book Division Ann Berkhausen
Copy Editor Alan Richtmyer
Editorial Assistant Grace Check
Writer Ben Giliberti

Tasting Director Bruce Sanderson
Tasting Coordinators James Molesworth, New York; MaryAnn Worobiec, San Francisco
Associate Tasting Coordinators Morgan Rich, New York; Jo Cooke, Italy
Copy Chief Cordelia Macintire

Cover Art Director Bill Jones
Design and Production Sophia Latto
Production Manager Connie McGilvray
Cover Photographs Clockwise from top left: Glenn Oakley; Frank Wing/Photodisc; Rick Mariani; François Poincet/Occit' Media

Wine Spectator's Ultimate Guide to Buying Wine, Seventh Edition

Printed in the United States of America

ISBN: 1-881659-62-3
ISSN: 1058-5729

Published by M. Shanken Communications, Inc.
387 Park Avenue South
New York, NY 10016

San Francisco office:
601 Van Ness Ave., Suite 2032
San Francisco, CA 94102

For subscriptions to *Wine Spectator*, call (800) 752-7799 in the U.S. and Canada, or write
PO Box 50462
Boulder, CO 80322-0462.

Distributed by Running Press Book Publishers
125 South Twenty-Second Street
Philadelphia, PA 19103-4399

Visit our Web site at: **www.winespectator.com**

Foreword

Wine Spectator's Ultimate Guide to Buying Wine is back, now in its seventh edition. As always, our goal is to publish the most authoritative and up-to-date wine information available anywhere. To that end, we've added to and modified some parts of this book to provide you with the most useful and user-friendly wine buying guide on the market.

A new feature entitled Best Value Producers lists the wineries and wines you can count on from year to year to deliver good quality for $12 or less. Our Great Wines section has been refocused to include only the very best wines—those scoring 90 and above—from each of the most recent vintages, plus selected older vintages. And we've added overviews and greatly expanded the wine listings for two major New World wine producers: Argentina and New Zealand.

Wine lovers around the world find the *Ultimate Guide to Buying Wine* an indispensable resource. We want you to be able to use this book at home to plan your wine purchases and take it with you to wine shops when you buy. It's like having at your fingertips the nearly 320 issues of *Wine Spectator* magazine that have been published since 1985, when we began our wine-tasting program in its current form.

The scope of the wines reviewed here is as broad as the charter of *Wine Spectator,* the world's most widely read consumer wine publication, founded in 1976. In exclusive tastings by our senior editors, we rate the best—and the best-selling—wines from California, Bordeaux, Burgundy, Italy, Washington, Germany, and Spain, to mention just a few regions. From Chardonnay and Cabernet Sauvignon, to Champagne and vintage Port, our editors give you their independent views on which are the best wines in each category.

Sara Matthews

Our guide enables you to quickly look up our editors' ratings of over 40,000 of the wines we've reviewed—including tasting notes with descriptions of aromas and flavors for more than 20,000 wines from recent vintages, and advice on whether to drink it now or cellar for a while.

The *Ultimate Guide to Buying Wine,* Seventh Edition, is an incomparable reference for wine consumers and wine-trade members alike. We are always looking for ways to improve it, and we welcome your help. Please contact us with any criticisms or suggestions.

Finally, I invite you to visit us on the World Wide Web—at **www.winespectator.com—**where you'll find additional information about the world of wine, plus feature stories and databases on award-winning restaurants, recipes, hotels, travel, events, and much more.

Marvin R. Shanken
Editor and Publisher

Wine-Buying Strategies

By James Laube

If you're new to wine, you're in for an adventure. Devising a buying strategy can be as simple as choosing a few brands you like and sticking with them, or it can be as complex as collecting verticals of the world's greatest wines or buying wine futures.

For many wine drinkers, maintaining brand loyalty is a tried-and-true way to keep your cellar stocked with reliable wines that suit your taste and budget. More daring collectors expand their hobby of wine collecting into a more sophisticated enterprise. They keep tabs on new wines and vintages from old-guard producers in Bordeaux, Burgundy, Italy, Spain, or Germany, and a watchful eye on up-and-coming producers from the New World, such as California, Oregon, Washington, Australia, New Zealand, Chile, and South Africa.

Regardless of your level of interest in wine, you're in for some fun and challenges. Wine is a living thing and is constantly changing. Every year you'll be presented with a seemingly endless stream of new wines, producers, appellations and vintages. Even when you find a winery or style of wine that appeals to you, your taste will likely change over time, and you'll discover new things that appeal to you. The combination of possibilities is endless.

Rule No. 1 of buying wine is to trust your own taste. No one knows your taste preferences better than you, so it's important to be comfortable deciding which wines appeal to you and which don't. The best advice is to taste a wine by buying a single bottle before you commit to several bottles or a case. The importance of this rule is further magnified for expensive wines. It makes no sense to pay $20, $30 or $40 for a wine you've never tried and might not like. You'll be far happier with your buying decisions if you taste a wine and decide you like it before committing to more bottles. There's a big wine world to choose from, with literally thousands of different wines. Even if your friends or wine critics rave about a wine, there's no guarantee that you'll like it.

Gaining experience with the world's fine wines takes time, but it is a fascinating journey. You're likely to learn as much from your buying mistakes as you will from your triumphs. Part of the fun of wine is learning where and how it's grown and vinified, which food types match well with different wines, and which wine types and vintages improve with cellaring and bottle age.

Before you start buying wine, it's a good idea to assess your needs. How much wine do you drink and on what occasions? Do you want to cellar young wines for drinking in a few years? You may also decide to budget money for your wine hobby so you can determine how much you can realistically afford to spend on wine. For some people it's easy to identify their wine needs. For others it's wiser to plan a strategy before heading to the wine shop. Remember, it's easier to buy a case of wine than it is to drink it.

It's also easy to buy more wine than you realistically need. Buying wine on a whim can be fun, particularly when you spot a special bottle you've been looking for. But fanciful buying also increases the odds that you'll end up with a wine you may not need for which you may have paid too much. Planning ahead allows you to set aside a specific amount of money for buying wine by the case. Many retailers and wineries offer a 10 percent discount for case purchases. Discount stores, however, usually pass along the 10 percent discount on all purchases.

Once you've outlined your needs, you'll need a place to shop. Years ago, about the only source to buy fine wine was the traditional fine-wine merchant. Today, your options abound. You see fine wine in scores of discount chain stores and upscale supermarkets, some of which present a dazzling selection. Retailers have also become more aggressive with sales promotions, selling wine through ads in newspapers and magazines, and via telephone and toll-free "800" numbers. A growing list of retailers publish catalogs, especially during the holiday season, offering hundreds of wines and special gift packages. There are even wine-of-the-month clubs. Once you join, the club selects wines for you and ships them to your home for you to sample.

10 Tips to Better Wine Buying

1. Always taste before you buy. Don't get trapped buying what your friends or critics call the best. Trust your own palate. Taste a bottle before you buy six bottles or a case.

2. Diversify your collection. You may have passions for one kind of wine or another, but variety is the spice of life with wine, so shop around for different styles of wine.

3. Shop for values. Go out of your way to look for best buys to get the most mileage out of your wine dollar.

4. Drink your wines before they get too old. Even the most age-worthy reds from Bordeaux or California reach drinkability in 10 years. You've paid good money for your wines; don't let them slide over the hill.

5. Keep costs in perspective. A few fine wines are expensive, but far too many well-made, reasonably priced wines are ignored because they lack the image and prestige of higher-priced wines.

6. Buy wine by the case. Most retailers give you a 10 percent discount or one bottle free.

7. Beware of last year's superstar. Last year's hero could be this year's goat.

8. Stockpile wine you like so that you don't run out or hesitate to open the last bottle.

9. Investing in futures can be risky business.

10. Assemble your wines with rhyme and reason. Think about your needs before parting with your cash.

Most of the time, though, you'll be purchasing wine at a retail store, so it helps to get to know your local wine stores and merchants, including what kinds of wines they stock and their pricing strategies.

A well-informed retailer is an excellent source of sound buying advice and tips about what's new and interesting in his store. Retailers can also help find special wines that may be hard to find. Some retail stores even do the shopping for their customers. When a special wine comes in, they set aside a few bottles or a case and bill the customer, holding the wine until it's picked up.

While you're visiting wine shops, take special notice of how the wines are stored and if the temperature is cool. Light and heat are enemies of wine. Wine shops that are warm or hot in summer months may not be the best place to buy your wines. It's also wise to examine wine bottles to make sure the fill level is good—up to the neck of the bottle—and that wine hasn't leaked through the cork. If wine leaks out, that means air is getting into the bottle and oxidizing the wine. Avoid bottles with low fills or leaks.

James Suckling

As wine gets costlier, it makes greater sense to develop a buying strategy. One fun way to defray costs and taste a broad selection of wines is to join a club or group that tastes wines regularly. This way you can spread out some of the costs and taste expensive wines such as Château Lafite-Rothschild, Romanée-Conti, Gaja or Château d'Yquem. Each member brings a bottle of wine to the tasting and shares it among six, eight or 12 people. Some wine syndicates even order cases of wines together, which is another way to cut costs (with a 10 percent discount) and broaden your exposure to the world of fine wines.

For those who like to take risks, buying wine futures, where you pay a discounted price in advance of a wine's delivery, is one way to obtain hard-to-get wines, presumably at reduced prices. Buying futures works like this: Young, unbottled wines are sold at discounted prices through retailers or wineries. Once the wine is bottled and ready for sale, it is delivered to the consumer. Most of the time, consumers pay less for futures, and futures can be a good way to obtain hard-to-get wines.

Others buy wine futures for speculation purposes. They hope that the price they pay for futures is sufficiently lower than the price will be when the wine is released. If that's true, they can resell the wine at a profit. But there are risks in buying futures. The major danger is that you're buying a wine you haven't tried. Unless you're intimately familiar with the producer, vintage or style of wine, you're gambling. You could also pay more for a wine than is necessary. If the economy sours, the price on release may be far less than anticipated, reducing the savings you hoped to achieve. Finally, in buying futures you may tie up your money with one or two producers and miss out on some of the other bargains once that vintage is released. There's also the possibility that your retailer may go out of business before the wine is released, making your wine and your money difficult to recover.

When you're on the road touring wine country, you'll also discover that many wineries have specialty wines or older vintages no longer on the market that they sell only at the winery. Be on the lookout for some of those rarities, but don't necessarily expect to find great bargains. Most wineries give a 10 percent discount on sales, but they mark their wines up to full retail price. You can often find them less expensive at your local retail outlet.

How We Taste Wine

The wine ratings and tasting notes contained in this book are the result of thousands of tastings by the senior editors of *Wine Spectator*. Two types of tastings are used to review wines for the magazine and for this book. First are the weekly blind tastings of newly released wines by our editors in San Francisco and New York. Second are special blind tastings of a particular type or vintage of wine, frequently conducted on location around the world. (A small percentage of the scores in this book, notably those of very old vintages, were not conducted under blind conditions.)

The weekly blind tastings are arranged by our tasting coordinators, who bag and code the wine bottles. They do not participate in the tastings. All capsules and corks are removed from the bottles prior to tasting, and when necessary other efforts are made to conceal the wines' identity from the tasters. Tasters are told only the general type of wine (varietal or region) and the vintage. Price is not taken into account in scoring, although the notes are often edited after the scores are determined to include comments about price and value.

Wines are chosen for tasting from those sent to our offices for review and from wines we purchase at retail. Wines scoring below 70 are automatically retasted under blind conditions from a different bottle. We also retaste many other wines to confirm our impressions.

Wines are scored using *Wine Spectator's* 100-point scale. (See "How to Use These Listings" on page 126 for a fuller explanation.)

Ratings reflect how highly our tasters regard each wine relative to other wines. They are based on both immediate quality and on how good a wine will be when it's at its peak, regardless of how soon that will be.

Wine Spectator **European Bureau Chief James Suckling conducts a blind tasting.**

François Poincet

THE TASTERS

MARVIN R. SHANKEN
EDITOR AND PUBLISHER

Sara Matthews

During the 1970s, wine lover and Wall Street investor Marvin Shanken purchased first the beverage-industry newsletter *Impact* and then *Wine Spectator*—today, the world's largest and most influential wine publication.

Shanken is chairman of M. Shanken Communications, Inc.; publisher of *Cigar Aficionado, Hamptons Country, Food Arts, Market Watch* and *Impact;* and event chairman of the New York and California Wine Experiences.

THOMAS MATTHEWS
EXECUTIVE EDITOR

Tasting beat: Spain

Sara Matthews

Thomas Matthews has been writing for *Wine Spectator* since 1987, when he was a freelance writer living in Bordeaux. Hired full-time in 1988, Matthews served first in the London office, then was reassigned to New York. Promoted to New York Bureau Chief in 1989, he was named Executive Editor in 1999.

Matthews' book about his experiences living and working in Bordeaux, *A Village in the Vineyards,* was published in 1993.

HARVEY STEIMAN
EDITOR AT LARGE

Tasting beat: Australia, New Zealand, Oregon, Washington

Jason Grow

Harvey Steiman tastes and reports on a wide variety of wine types, but his primary areas of responsibility as a critic are Australia and the Pacific Northwest. Steiman joined *Wine Spectator* in 1984, after serving as food and wine editor of the *San Francisco Examiner.* *Wine Spectator* recently published Steiman's *Essentials of Wine,* a comprehensive introduction to wine basics.

JAMES LAUBE
SENIOR EDITOR

Tasting beat: California

James Laube is *Wine Spectator*'s senior expert on the major wine types of California. He has been writing for the magazine since 1980, and joined the staff full-time in 1983.

The second edition of Laube's book *California Wine* was published by *Wine Spectator* in 1999; the first edition won the 1996 James Beard Award for best wine book of the year. His two previous books, *California's Great Cabernets* and *California's Great Chardonnays,* quickly became the most respected references on these topics.

JAMES SUCKLING
SENIOR EDITOR AND
EUROPEAN BUREAU CHIEF

Tasting beat: Bordeaux, Port, Italy

François Poincet

James Suckling joined *Wine Spectator* in 1981 when it was based in San Diego. He moved with the magazine to San Francisco in 1982, and in 1985 was reassigned to Europe. He lived in Paris for two years and in London for 11 years, and now resides in Italy.

Suckling blind-tastes every vintage of Bordeaux twice before it is released and spends more than a month each year in the region. His comprehensive book on collectible Port, *Vintage Port,* has become the Bible among vintage Port aficionados.

PER-HENRIK MANSSON
SENIOR EDITOR

Tasting beat: Burgundy, Rhône

In addition to his tasting and criticism on Burgundy and the Rhône, Per-Henrik Mansson does news and investigative reporting throughout Europe. Mansson joined *Wine Spectator* in 1987 in San Francisco, and has been based in Europe since 1989—first in London, now in Switzerland.

His reviews of red Burgundy helped bring attention to the classic 1990 and excellent 1996 vintages. But he also warned consumers of the much weaker 1992 and 1997 vintages and endured severe criticism from the wine trade for his tough stance.

BRUCE SANDERSON
TASTING DIRECTOR AND SENIOR EDITOR

Tasting beat: Austria, Germany, Alsace, Champagne, Loire

G. Palmisano

Bruce Sanderson joined *Wine Spectator* in 1993 after working for the previous five years as a wine steward and in retail wine sales. He oversees the tasting operations in New York, San Francisco and Europe.

KIM MARCUS
MANAGING EDITOR

Tasting beat: Languedoc-Rousillion, Midi; Portugal

John Harding

Kim Marcus joined the *Wine Spectator* staff in 1988 in San Francisco and was reassigned to New York in 1993. He has been a regular taster since 1990. He also authors regular tasting reports on great wine values.

Vintage Charts

The best guarantee of satisfaction in evaluating a wine for purchase is the quality behind the producer's name. Once you've picked a producer with a track record for quality, often the next question is, "Which vintage should I buy?" Knowing the relative merits of each vintage can help you make more informed buying decisions.

This section presents our qualitative ratings—using *Wine Spectator's* 100-point scale—of vintages in the world's major wine regions for the past 10 or more years. The ratings have been updated according to ongoing wine evaluations by our senior editors. For each year listed you will find the score, a comment on the characteristics of that vintage or its wines and our drinkability recommendation.

Wine Spectator's 100-Point Scale

95-100 — Classic; a great wine

90-94 — Outstanding; a wine of superior character and style

80-89 — Good to Very Good; a wine with special qualities

70-79 — Average; a drinkable wine that may have minor flaws

60-69 — Below Average; drinkable but not recommended

50-59 — Poor; undrinkable, not recommended

Vintage charts are, by necessity, general in nature. Vintage ratings listed here are averages for region and year. A score range indicates that wines were tasted as barrel samples. Many good wines are produced in "bad" years, just as bad wines are produced in "good" years. Use our vintage charts as a general guide to overall quality.

FRANCE | ALSACE

Vintage	Score	Rating	Comment	Drinkability
1998	89*	Very Good	Rich, balanced wines; some botrytis due to Oct. rains	Drink or hold
1997	89	Very Good	Rich, ripe, precocious wines; high yields, little botrytis; top Rieslings superb	Drink or hold
1996	92	Outstanding	Aromatic, racy, complex and long-lived; little botrytis	Drink or hold
1995	90	Outstanding	Small crop due to rot, but rich, vibrant Rieslings; uneven for other varietals and late-harvest wines	Drink or hold
1994	91	Outstanding	Rainy Sept., but top producers made excellent dry wines and great late-harvest wines	Drink or hold
1993	87	Very Good	Rainy year, but ripe grapes; intense, steely wines	Drink
1992	84	Good	A huge crop; producers who limited yields made solid wines	Drink
1991	77	Average	Harvest rains hurt quality; some late-harvest success	Drink
1990	93	Outstanding	Exceptionally ripe year; stunning Rieslings, some fine late-harvest wines	Drink or hold
1989	96	Classic	A ripe year; rich, round wines and superb late-harvest wines	Drink or hold
1988	95	Classic	Excellent balance; firm and opulent	Drink

*Some wines from top producers not yet tasted.

FRANCE | RED BORDEAUX

Vintage	Score	Rating	Comment	Drinkability
1999	82–86*	Good	Weak year overall; balanced, fruity, firm reds from top estates only*	Not Released
1998	85–89*	Very Good	Monumental in Pomerol; excellent in St.-Emilion, Pessac-Léognan, Sauternes; variable quality, tannic in Médoc *	Not Released
1997	81	Good	Pleasant, light and fruity clarets with lovely perfumes; superb Sauternes	Drink
1996	87	Very Good	Stick to the Médoc for aromatic, firm and medium-bodied wines; most other districts taste diluted	Drink or hold
1995	95	Classic	Warm, wonderful reds with opulent fruit and velvety tannins; harmonious and beautiful	Hold
1994	85	Very Good	Medium-bodied, with good fruit, firm tannins	Drink or hold
1993	82	Good	Good color, perfumy, fruity and balanced	Drink
1992	72	Average	Light, simple and often diluted; early-maturing	Drink
1991	72	Average	Lean, tough and light; stick to top names	Drink
1990	97	Classic	Opulent, well-structured and harmonious	Hold
1989	98	Classic	Bold, dramatic fruit character; tannic and long-aging	Hold
1988	93	Outstanding	Typical structure; racy, fruity wines, firm tannins; best in Pessac-Léognan, Pomerol, Pauillac	Drink or hold
1987	76	Average	Delicate, ripe yet diluted	Drink
1986	95	Classic	Powerful, intense and tannic; best in Médoc	Hold
1985	93	Outstanding	Balanced, supple and fruity; defines finesse	Drink or hold
1984	70	Average	Unripe, astringent and dry; most fading	Drink

1983	86	Very Good	Rich and ripe in fruit and tannins; some overly tannic	Drink
1982	95	Classic	Intense ripe fruit and generous in style; plenty of round tannins; St.-Julien and St.-Emilion stand out	Drink or hold
1970	91	Outstanding	Excellent all-around vintage; structured, lots of fruit	Drink or hold
1961	99	Classic	Best since 1945; great concentration and structure	Drink or hold

* Preliminary analysis based on barrel samples.

France | Red Burgundy

Vintage	Score	Rating	Comment	Drinkability
1998	89	Very Good	Uneven; stick to top domaines. Côte de Nuits better than Côte de Beaune; best show dark color, focused fruit, massive but ripe tannins. Decant	Drink or hold
1997	83	Good	Ripe, round Pinots; low in natural acidity, short on lively fruit flavors and finish	Drink
1996	95	Classic	Impressively vibrant and balanced; dark in color, high in acidity, with focused berry flavors, ripe tannins; large crop produced some diluted wines	Drink or hold
1995	88	Very Good	Stick to Côte de Nuits: best are elegant but firm, with ripe fruit and refined tannins; many Côte de Beaune wines weak	Hold
1994	81	Good	Uneven quality; tough and rustic, but the best wines have good fruit to balance the firm tannins; stick to top estates	Drink
1993	91	Outstanding	Top domaines made exuberant, racy, balanced wines	Drink or hold
1992	79	Average	Pleasant at best, diluted and light at worst	Drink
1991	86	Very Good	Uneven quality, but many ripe wines have improved as tannins soften and they flesh out	Drink
1990	98	Classic	Classic balance, formidable fruit and ripe tannins	Drink or hold
1989	90	Outstanding	Seductive and succulent on release, but these low-acid wines have not aged well in many cases; many have peaked	Drink
1988	90	Outstanding	Still a question mark. Muscular and firm; some losing fruit, others improving	Drink or hold
1978	92	Outstanding	Best wines have extraordinary richness and finesse	Drink or hold

France | White Burgundy

Vintage	Score	Rating	Comment	Drinkability
1998	88	Very Good	Delicious, early-drinking, fruity	Drink or hold
1997	88	Very Good	Best are pleasant, supple; uneven in Côte d'Or	Drink or hold
1996	95	Classic	Still improving. Elegant, racy, with well-defined, pure, clean flavors; best to cellar for years, otherwise decant	Drink or hold
1995	93	Outstanding	Rich, thick and generous, concentrated, with good aging potential	Drink or hold
1994	87	Very Good	Charming, soft, honeyed Chardonnays; aging fast	Drink
1993	82	Good	Austere, lean; best are elegant	Drink
1992	89	Very Good	Balanced; great finesse, lovely fruit; best still improving	Drink or hold

1991	85	Very Good	Fruity, charming, delicious now	Drink
1990	92	Outstanding	Racy, graceful, minerally; some are peaking	Drink
1989	92	Outstanding	Rich, opulent; some taste hot, alcoholic, but best should still improve	Drink or hold
1988	86	Very Good	Have stayed very firm, hard and ungenerous	Drink
1986	92	Outstanding	Seductive, opulent and honeyed for years; now peaking	Drink
1985	94	Outstanding	Bold, powerful yet elegant; some remain youthful	Drink

FRANCE | CHAMPAGNE

Vintage	Score	Rating	Comment	Drinkability
1995	90–95*	Outstanding	Potentially outstanding*	Drink or hold
1994	80–84*	Good	Not a vintage year for most*	Drink
1993	87	Very Good	Bright and lively, especially blanc de blancs	Drink or hold
1992	82	Good	Soft and mature in style	Drink
1991	79	Average	Fair quality; few vintage bottlings	Drink
1990	95	Classic	Fine balance and full flavor	Drink or hold
1989	90	Outstanding	Extremely ripe and generous	Drink or hold
1988	93	Outstanding	Outstanding, beautifully balanced	Drink or hold
1987	81	Good	Acceptable, but few vintage bottlings	Drink
1986	86	Very Good	Very good quality, lean in style	Drink
1985	96	Classic	Superb balance, great structure and flavor	Drink or hold
1984	79	Average	Unexceptional quality; large harvest	Drink
1983	83	Good	Good, pleasant Champagnes	Drink
1982	94	Outstanding	Rich, complex, with abundant flavor	Drink
1979	91	Outstanding	Classy, elegant, aging well	Drink
1976	88	Very Good	Ripe, opulent year	Drink
1975	92	Outstanding	Bold but balanced Champagnes	Drink

*Preliminary rating based on a limited sampling; many wines of the vintage not yet released.

FRANCE | NORTHERN RHÔNE (RED AND WHITE)

Vintage	Score	Rating	Comment	Drinkability
1998	88–92*	Very Good–Outstanding	Barrel samples are elegant, fruity, balanced*	Not Released
1997	86	Very Good	Round, supple; best are pleasant	Drink or hold
1996	91	Outstanding	Refined, balanced, elegant Syrahs; super Hermitage, St.-Joseph; racy whites	Hold
1995	91	Outstanding	Red wines offer concentration and typicity; whites are very good to outstanding	Drink or hold
1994	88	Very Good	Concentrated, chewy reds; best will be long-agers	Drink or hold
1993	75	Average	Wet harvest left many wines diluted	Drink
1992	78	Average	Light year for early drinking	Drink
1991	89	Very Good	Elegant, with fine tannins and silky fruit; early maturing	Drink or hold

1990	97	Classic	Massive and rich, with loads of tannin and fruit	Hold
1989	92	Outstanding	Round and opulent, with great texture and backbone	Hold
1988	90	Outstanding	Solid and tough; excellent aging potential	Hold
1987	85	Very Good	Soft and short, but drinking well	Drink
1986	87	Very Good	Tannic and medium-bodied, very firm; starting to come around	Drink
1985	90	Outstanding	Rich, round, loads of fruit	Drink

Other noteworthy vintages: 1983, 1978

*Preliminary analysis based on barrel samples and/or a limited sampling.

FRANCE | SOUTHERN RHÔNE (RED AND WHITE)

Vintage	Score	Rating	Comment	Drinkability
1998	91–95*	Outstanding	Dense and rich, blockbuster reds with ripe tannins*	Not Released
1997	81	Good	Soft, easy, early-drinking reds and whites	Drink or hold
1996	80	Good	Light, fruity, pleasant, early-drinking reds; some excellent whites	Drink
1995	88	Very Good	Intense, tannic, ripe reds and rich whites; cellar reds, drink whites	Drink or hold
1994	86	Very Good	Less consistent than northern appellations; only top wines need aging	Drink or hold
1993	78	Average	Inconsistent; best are balanced	Drink
1992	74	Average	Diluted, lean; few successful wines	Drink
1991	73	Average	Most wines hard and green	Drink
1990	95	Classic	Massive wines with great concentration	Hold
1989	96	Classic	Hot year with average crop; powerful, concentrated; reds built for aging	Hold
1988	90	Outstanding	Dry and temperate year; balanced wines with focused fruit and firm backbone	Hold
1987	75	Average	Wet weather with rot prevalent; light, fruity wines, some lacking character	Drink
1986	88	Very Good	Racy wines with plenty of steely tannins and clean fruit; underrated	Hold
1985	86	Very Good	Ripe and exuberant, with loads of fruit that's evolving quickly	Drink or hold

*Preliminary analysis based on barrel samples and/or a limited sampling.

FRANCE | SAUTERNES

Vintage	Score	Rating	Comment	Drinkability
1997	92	Outstanding	Superb Sauternes	Drink or hold
1996	89	Very Good	Best since 1992	Drink or hold
1995	87	Very Good	Uneven quality; many are tannic, a few winners	Drink or hold
1992	72	Average	Light, straightforward, diluted and medium sweet	Drink
1991	77	Average	Moderately sweet, attractive aperitif wines	Drink
1990	89	Very Good	Fabulous balance; rich and racy, with power and elegance	Hold
1989	98	Classic	Incredibly rich, with lots of botrytis; built for aging	Hold
1988	93	Outstanding	Extremely fine and firm, well balanced and concentrated	Hold
1987	79	Average	Clean, appealing, with little botrytis	Drink

Wine Spectator's Vintage Chart

PLEASE DETACH ALONG PERFORATIONS AND FOLD TO WALLET SIZE

Wine Spectator

VINTAGE CHART

(Updated September 2000)

Vintage charts are, by necessity, general in nature. Vintage ratings listed here are averages for region and year. For each current vintage and any exceptional older year, you will find our score and drinkability rating. A score range indicates that most wines of the vintage are not yet released.

100-Point Scale	
95-100	Classic
90-94	Outstanding
80-89	Good to Very Good
70-79	Average
60-69	Below Average
50-59	Poor

WHITE WINE AND CHAMPAGNE

FRANCE/ALSACE

Vintage	Score	Drinkability
1998	89	Drink/Hold
1997	89	Drink/Hold
1996	92	Drink/Hold
1995	90	Drink/Hold
1994	91	Drink/Hold
1993	87	Drink
1992	84	Drink
1990	93	Drink/Hold
1989	96	Drink/Hold

FRANCE/BURGUNDY WHITE

Vintage	Score	Drinkability
1998	88	Drink/Hold
1997	88	Drink/Hold
1996	95	Drink/Hold
1995	93	Drink/Hold
1994	87	Drink
1993	82	Drink
1992	89	Drink/Hold
1991	85	Drink
1990	92	Drink
1989	92	Drink/Hold
1986	92	Drink
1985	94	Drink/Hold

FRANCE/CHAMPAGNE

Vintage	Score	Drinkability
1995	90-95	Drink/Hold
1994	80-84	Drink
1993	87	Drink/Hold
1992	82	Drink
1991	79	Drink
1990	95	Drink/Hold
1989	90	Drink/Hold
1988	93	Drink/Hold
1986	86	Drink
1985	96	Drink/Hold
1982	94	Drink
1979	91	Drink

FRANCE/SAUTERNES

Vintage	Score	Drinkability
1997	92	Drink/Hold
1996	89	Drink/Hold
1990	97	Hold
1989	98	Hold
1988	93	Hold
1986	90	Hold
1985	85	Drink
1983	95	Drink/Hold

GERMANY/RIESLING

Vintage	Score	Drinkability
1998	89	Drink/Hold
1997	88	Drink/Hold
1996	89	Drink/Hold
1995	88	Drink
1994	86	Drink/Hold
1993	89	Drink/Hold
1992	88	Drink/Hold
1991	85	Drink/Hold
1990	97	Hold
1989	92	Drink/Hold
1988	93	Drink
1986	86	Drink
1985	87	Drink
1983	93	Drink/Hold
1979	88	Drink
1976	96	Drink

CALIFORNIA/CHARDONNAY

Vintage	Score	Drinkability
1998	85	Drink/Hold
1997	96	Drink/Hold
1996	97	Drink/Hold
1995	97	Drink/Hold
1994	95	Drink/Hold
1993	88	Drink
1992	93	Drink
1991	92	Drink
1990	92	Drink
1989	85	Drink
1988	89	Drink
1987	85	Drink
1986	91	Drink

RED WINE AND PORT

Vintage	Score	Drinkability
FRANCE/BORDEAUX RED		
1999	82-86	Not Released
1998	85-89	Not Released
1997	81	Drink
1996	87	Drink/Hold
1995	95	Hold
1994	85	Drink/Hold
1993	82	Drink
1992	72	Drink
1991	72	Drink
1990	97	Hold
1989	98	Hold
1988	93	Drink/Hold
1986	95	Hold
1985	93	Drink/Hold
1983	86	Drink
1982	95	Drink/Hold
1975	85	Drink/Hold
1970	91	Drink/Hold
1961	99	Drink/Hold
FRANCE/BURGUNDY RED		
1998	89	Drink/Hold
1997	83	Drink/Hold
1996	95	Drink/Hold
1995	88	Hold
1994	81	Drink/Hold
1993	91	Hold
1992	79	Drink
1991	86	Drink
1990	98	Drink/Hold
1989	93	Drink
1988	90	Drink/Hold
1985	93	Drink
FRANCE/NORTHERN RHÔNE		
1998	88-92	Not Released
1997	86	Drink/Hold
1996	91	Hold
1995	91	Drink/Hold
1994	88	Drink/Hold
1993	75	Drink
1992	78	Drink
1991	89	Drink/Hold
1990	97	Hold
1989	92	Hold
1988	90	Drink/Hold
1986	87	Drink
1985	90	Drink
FRANCE/SOUTHERN RHÔNE		
1998	91-95	Not Released
1997	81	Drink/Hold
1996	80	Drink
1995	88	Drink/Hold
1994	86	Drink/Hold
1993	78	Drink
1990	95	Hold
1989	96	Hold
1988	90	Drink/Hold
1986	88	Drink/Hold
ITALY/BRUNELLO		
1995	91	Drink/Hold
1994	82	Drink
1993	90	Drink/Hold
1992	76	Drink
1991	84	Drink/Hold
1990	98	Drink/Hold
1989	80	Drink
1988	94	Drink/Hold
1986	85	Drink/Hold
1985	94	Drink/Hold
ITALY/OTHER TUSCAN		
1998	87-91	Not Released
1997	99	Drink/Hold
1996	87	Drink/Hold
1995	88	Drink/Hold
1994	86	Drink/Hold
1993	84	Drink
1992	77	Drink
1991	81	Drink
1990	98	Drink/Hold
1988	96	Drink/Hold
ITALY/PIEDMONT		
1997	91-95	Not Released
1996	93-97	Hold
1995	89	Drink/Hold
1994	77	Drink
1993	87	Drink/Hold
1992	76	Drink
1991	77	Drink
1990	97	Hold
1989	97	Hold
1988	90	Drink/Hold
1985	94	Drink/Hold
1982	90	Drink/Hold
PORTUGAL/VINTAGE PORT		
1997	96	Hold
1995	90	Hold
1994	99	Hold
1992	94	Hold
1991	93	Hold
1987	88	Drink/Hold
1985	93	Drink/Hold
1983	92	Hold
1980	87	Drink/Hold
1977	97	Hold
1970	95	Drink/Hold
1967	88	Drink
1966	93	Drink/Hold
1963	98	Drink/Hold
CALIFORNIA/CABERNET		
1999	90-94	Not Released
1998	88-92	Not Released
1997	98	Hold
1996	94	Hold
1995	95	Hold
1994	96	Hold
1993	90	Drink/Hold
1992	93	Hold
1991	94	Hold
1990	95	Drink/Hold
1989	84	Drink
1988	82	Drink
1987	96	Drink
1986	95	Drink
1985	97	Drink
1984	94	Drink
1978	93	Drink
CALIFORNIA/MERLOT		
1998	84	Drink/Hold
1997	88	Drink/Hold
1996	88	Drink/Hold
1995	87	Drink/Hold
1994	92	Drink/Hold
1993	83	Drink/Hold
1992	89	Drink/Hold
1990	90	Drink/Hold
1987	91	Drink
CALIFORNIA/PINOT NOIR		
1998	84	Drink
1997	88	Hold
1996	87	Drink/Hold
1995	92	Drink/Hold
1994	95	Drink/Hold
1992	92	Drink/Hold
1991	91	Drink
1990	92	Drink/Hold
CALIFORNIA/ZINFANDEL		
1998	83	Drink
1997	95	Drink/Hold
1996	87	Drink/Hold
1995	95	Drink/Hold
1994	96	Drink/Hold
1992	93	Drink/Hold
1991	92	Drink/Hold
1990	93	Drink/Hold

Wine Spectator's Vintage Chart

PLEASE DETACH ALONG PERFORATIONS AND FOLD TO WALLET SIZE

■ ■ ■ ■

1986	90	Outstanding	Harmonious, charming, focused and honeyed; lively acidity	Hold
1985	79	Average	Little botrytis character; clean and sweet	Drink
1984	68	Below Average	A few good wines; a wet, difficult harvest	Drink
1983	95	Classic	Intense, complex and stylish; abundant botrytis character	Drink or hold
1982	77	Average	Mostly fat, alcoholic and sweet	Drink or hold
1981	83	Good	Medium richness; finely balanced wines	Drink
1980	82	Good	Good year; balanced, lightly botrytized wines	Drink

Germany

Vintage	Score	Rating	Comment	Drinkability
1998	89	Very Good	Ripe, sleek, crisp wines. Fine dry wines, especially in the Pfalz; exciting ice wines	Drink or hold
1997	88	Very Good	Pure, clear wines with lower acidity and little botrytis; best in Mosel-Saar-Ruwer	Drink or hold
1996	89	Very Good	Extremely late harvest; stunning in Rheingau; stick to top producers. Perfumed, ripe and high in acidity; ageworthy	Drink or hold
1995	88	Very Good	Top estates made best wines; aromatic, fruity, with harmonious acidity	Drink
1994	86	Very Good	Solid quality, high acidity, medium extract; focus on top estates	Drink or hold
1993	89	Very Good	Great surprise; plenty of fruit, acidity and character; stick to top estates	Drink or hold
1992	88	Very Good	Uneven quality; some late-harvest, botrytized classics, but many soft, diluted wines	Drink or hold
1991	85	Very Good	Crisp, racy acidity, but uneven quality	Drink or hold
1990	97	Classic	Powerful, great acidity and extract, harmonious	Hold
1989	92	Outstanding	Outstanding for botrytized, late-harvest wines, but others tough and unexceptional	Drink or hold
1988	93	Outstanding	Balanced, firm; best from middle Mosel	Drink
1987	83	Good	Fresh, light, high acidity, surprisingly good	Drink
1986	86	Very Good	Aromatic, elegant; best from Pfalz	Drink
1985	87	Very Good	Racy, well structured; some problems in Rheingau, Pfalz	Drink
1983	93	Outstanding	Very fruity, ripe, round; little botrytis	Drink

Italy | Piedmont Reds

Vintage	Score	Rating	Comment	Drinkability
1997	91–95*	Outstanding	Superripe, opulent Barolos and Barbarescos; dense Barberas*	Not Released/ Drink or hold
1996	93–97*	Outstanding–Classic	Could rival or exceed '90 and '89; structured, ripe, racy Barolos; refined Barbarescos*	Not Released/ Hold
1995	89	Very Good	Hail and uneven weather led to dry tannins in some wines, but dozens of Barolos and Barbarescos of surprisingly good quality	Drink or hold
1994	77	Average	Barbarescos show spice, modest fruit; lack concentration; some Barolos offer decent fruit and complexity	Drink

1993	87	Very Good	Some are delicious and fruity, with supple tannins	Drink or hold
1992	76	Average	Diluted; many estates didn't bottle	Drink
1991	77	Average	Mostly light, some pleasant; a few very good wines	Drink
1990	97	Classic	Firm, ripe and long-aging	Hold
1989	97	Classic	Ripe, opulent and supple	Hold
1988	90	Outstanding	Firm, focused and generous	Drink or hold
1987	83	Good	Light, but with pretty fruit	Drink
1986	86	Very Good	Soft and generous	Drink or hold
1985	94	Outstanding	Rich, ripe, concentrated and elegant	Drink or hold
1984	80	Good	Light style, spicy and fruity	Drink
1983	75	Average	Very light, sometimes thin	Drink
1982	90	Outstanding	Powerful, tannic and long-lived	Drink or hold
1981	73	Average	Light; mature now	Drink
1980	70	Average	Very light; some are thin	Drink
1979	86	Very Good	Supple and flavorful	Drink or hold
1978	90	Outstanding	Firm and classically built	Drink or hold

Other outstanding vintages: 1974, 1971, 1967, 1964, 1961.

*Preliminary rating and comments based on barrel samples and/or limited sampling.

Italy | Brunello

Vintage	Score	Rating	Comment	Drinkability
1995	91	Outstanding	Plenty of fruit and ripe tannins; ageworthy; top names best	Drink or hold
1994	82	Good	Pleasant, aromatic wines for near-term enjoyment	Drink
1993	90	Outstanding	Harmonious, well structured, with fine tannins, fresh fruit	Drink or hold
1992	76	Average	Aromatic, light and diluted; slightly unripe	Drink
1991	84	Good	Perfumed and fruity, with fresh tannins and good structure; some diluted	Drink or hold
1990	98	Classic	Super structure; powerful and ripe, yet balanced	Drink or hold
1989	80	Good	Light, aromatic and fresh	Drink
1988	94	Outstanding	Rich and harmonious, with outstanding structure	Drink or hold
1987	81	Good	Lean and aromatic, with delicate fruit	Drink
1986	85	Very Good	Medium weight; better than expected, with firm tannins	Drink or hold
1985	94	Outstanding	Superripe, concentrated and powerful; some wines overdone	Drink or hold
1984	72	Average	Light, diluted and weak	Drink
1983	88	Very Good	Well rounded, with luscious fruit and good tannins	Drink

Italy | Chianti and Super Tuscan Reds

Vintage	Score	Rating	Comment	Drinkability
1998	87-91*	Very Good–Outstanding	Ripe, balanced; some slightly diluted, Bolgheri superb	Not released
1997	99	Classic	Bold, super-ripe, well-structured yet balanced and harmonious	Drink or hold

1996	87	Very Good	Perfumed reds with fine tannins. Some diluted. Bolgheri outstanding	Drink or hold
1995	88	Very Good	Fruity, well-structured, with lively acidity, long finish	Drink or hold
1994	86	Very Good	Aromatic, soft-textured and easy to drink	Drink or hold
1993	84	Good	Fresh, clean and perfumed; firm tannins, crisp acidity	Drink
1992	77	Average	Very light, very diluted; buy only the best names	Drink
1991	81	Good	Delicate, aromatic; fresh wines for early drinking	Drink
1990	98	Classic	Concentrated, highly extracted, with firm tannins and fresh acidity	Drink or hold
1989	79	Average	Some light, pleasant wines; others very diluted	Drink
1988	96	Classic	Balanced, with excellent concentration, firm acidity and fine tannins	Drink or hold
1987	82	Good	Variable quality, but some good surprises	Drink
1986	86	Very Good	Slightly lean but solid wines, with good fruit	Drink
1985	95	Classic	Hot, superripe year; big, rich wines, with lots of fruit	Drink
1984	75	Average	Light, difficult vintage; most wines insipid	Drink
1983	88	Very Good	Pretty wines, with good intensity and backbone	Drink
1982	90	Outstanding	Very ripe fruit, with plenty of tannins; rich, round wines	Drink

*Preliminary rating and comments based on barrel samples and/or limited sampling; many wines not yet bottled.

PORTUGAL I VINTAGE PORT

Vintage	Score	Rating	Comment	Drinkability
1997	96	Classic	Aromatic, with powerful tannins and a complement of ripe fruit*	Hold
1995	90	Outstanding	Extremely fruity; well structured with fine tannins, good length	Hold
1994	99	Classic	Classic vintage, superlative structure, fabulous harmony	Hold
1992	94	Outstanding	Concentrated, tannic and fruity; best are classics	Hold
1991	93	Outstanding	Racy, harmonious, rich	Hold
1987	88	Very Good	Balanced and elegant, with good finesse	Hold
1985	93	Outstanding	Opulent and intense, but some variability	Drink or hold
1983	92	Outstanding	Powerful, tannic and age-worthy	Hold
1982	84	Good	Sweet and raisiny; unbalanced	Drink or hold
1980	87	Very Good	Solid and well structured, with focused fruit	Drink or hold
1978	84	Good	Fruity, soft and ready	Drink
1977	97	Classic	Tough, tannic and complex; ageless	Hold
1975	80	Good	Light and one-dimensional, but fruity	Drink
1970	95	Classic	Harmonious and well structured, with intense fruit	Drink or hold
1967	88	Very Good	Focused fruit; angular and elegant	Drink
1966	93	Outstanding	Iron backbone; fresh, with good concentration	Drink or hold
1963	98	Classic	Copious fruit; forceful and extremely age-worthy	Drink or hold
1960	87	Very Good	Balanced, sweet and elegant; at its peak	Drink

* Preliminary analysis based on barrel samples.

United States | California Cabernet Sauvignon

Vintage	Score	Rating	Comment	Drinkability
1999	90-94*	Outstanding	Small crop, very rich and complex out of barrel	Not Released
1998	88-92*	Very Good–Outstanding	Highly variable, but may surprise; being selective is key*	Not Released
1997	98	Classic	Grand wine, deep and potent, surpassing 1994 for best of decade	Hold
1996	94	Outstanding	Ripe, complex, elegant and supple	Hold
1995	95	Classic	Rich, complex and flavorful	Hold
1994	96	Classic	Ripe, dark, high extract; supple tannins	Hold
1993	90	Outstanding	Variable, some excellent wines	Drink or hold
1992	93	Outstanding	Supple, rich, fruity, with soft tannins	Hold
1991	94	Outstanding	Intense, tannic, age-worthy; best in Napa	Hold
1990	95	Classic	Ripe, supple, complex; best in Napa	Drink or hold
1989	84	Good	Austere, tannic, uneven quality	Drink
1988	82	Good	Lean, crisp and mostly simple	Drink
1987	96	Classic	Deep, rich, complex, tannic; best in Napa	Drink
1986	95	Classic	Classic structure, tight, age-worthy	Drink
1985	97	Classic	California's finest; elegant, rich, stylish	Drink
1984	94	Outstanding	Rich, fruity, opulent; peaking now	Drink
1983	81	Good	Lean, tannic, uneven quality; fading	Drink
1982	78	Average	Austere, lean, uneven quality; fading	Drink
1981	85	Very Good	Supple, charming, balanced early on	Drink
1980	84	Good	Ripe, firm; fading now	Drink
1979	88	Very Good	Austere but age-worthy; most have peaked	Drink
1978	93	Outstanding	Ripe, flavorful, complex; past prime	Drink

*Preliminary analysis based on barrel samples and/or a limited sampling.

United States | California Chardonnay

Vintage	Score	Rating	Comment	Drinkability
1998	85	Very Good	Atypically lean and austere; for fans of high acidity	Drink or hold
1997	96	Classic	Grand; very ripe, complex, flavorful wines	Drink or hold
1996	97	Classic	Tremendous flavors, finesse and concentration	Drink or hold
1995	97	Classic	Great depth, richness, complexity and finesse	Drink or hold
1994	95	Classic	Lots of superb wines; uniformly ripe, rich, complex	Drink
1993	88	Very Good	Variable quality; some fruity wines, some lean wines	Drink
1992	93	Outstanding	Elegant and flavorful, with fine depth	Drink
1991	92	Outstanding	Intense, ripe, complex and balanced	Drink
1990	92	Outstanding	Ripe, rich and concentrated, with fine depth	Drink

United States | California Merlot

Vintage	Score	Rating	Comment	Drinkability
1998	84*	Good	Variable quality; lighter style	Drink or hold
1997	89	Very Good	Huge crop; ripe flavors, but mixed quality	Drink or hold
1996	88	Very Good	Austere, tannic, variable quality; a few gems	Drink or hold
1995	87	Very Good	Uneven quality; many are tannic; a few winners	Drink or hold
1994	92	Outstanding	Best since '90; complex, age-worthy	Drink or hold
1993	83	Good	Variable quality, with a few stars	Drink or hold
1992	89	Very Good	Best wines are complex, well-balanced	Drink or hold
1991	88	Very Good	Ripe, large crop, well-balanced	Drink or hold
1990	90	Outstanding	Ripe and complex; best since '87	Drink or hold
1989	84	Good	Large crop; uneven quality	Drink
1988	86	Very Good	Small crop; fruity and balanced	Drink
1987	91	Outstanding	Rich and complex; best of decade	Drink

*Preliminary rating; many wines not yet released.

United States | California Zinfandel

Vintage	Score	Rating	Comment	Drinkability
1998	83	Good	Tough, cool year; mostly lean, simple wines	Drink
1997	90	Outstanding	Best were ripe and potent, though quality varied	Drink or hold
1996	87	Very Good	Variable quality; best are well-balanced	Drink or hold
1995	95	Classic	Brilliant fruit; ripe, complex, intense, balanced	Drink or hold
1994	96	Classic	Dark, rich, intense, complex; classy	Drink or hold
1993	88	Very Good	Fruity, complex, fine balance	Drink or hold
1992	93	Outstanding	Very ripe, opulent and complex	Drink or hold
1991	92	Outstanding	Ripe, elegant, complex	Drink or hold
1990	93	Outstanding	Rich, complex and concentrated	Drink or hold
1989	82	Good	Huge crop; uneven quality, tannic	Drink
1988	84	Good	Uneven crop; forward-balanced wines	Drink
1987	92	Outstanding	Bright, rich and complex	Drink
1986	91	Outstanding	Firm, intense, tannic yet age-worthy	Drink
1985	93	Outstanding	Wonderful balance and harmony	Drink
1984	88	Very Good	Ripe, opulent and complex	Drink
1983	79	Average	Uneven quality, tannic, average	Drink
1982	82	Good	Tight and firm, but uneven quality	Drink
1981	85	Very Good	Ripe, fruity, early-drinking	Drink
1980	82	Good	Hot harvest; uneven quality	Drink

United States | California Pinot Noir

Vintage	Score	Rating	Comment	Drinkability
1998	84	Good	Light colors, modest flavors, simple wines	Drink
1997	88	Very Good	Austere, tannic but balanced, with appealing flavors	Drink or hold
1996	87	Very Good	Uneven quality; most are lean, tannic; best early	Drink or hold
1995	92	Outstanding	Elegant, fruity, complex, balanced	Drink or hold
1994	95	Classic	Best ever; dark, rich, flavorful	Drink
1993	86	Very Good	Light in color and body, but appealing	Drink
1992	92	Outstanding	Ripe and fruity, best in Russian River	Drink
1991	91	Outstanding	Complex and concentrated; best in Russian River	Drink
1990	92	Outstanding	Rich, complex and concentrated	Drink

United States | Oregon Pinot Noir

Vintage	Score	Rating	Comment	Drinkability
1997	84	Good	Light, often watery; best wines fleshing out nicely	Drink or hold
1996	87	Very Good	Light, but generally ripe; most wines on the tannic side	Hold
1995	81	Good	Some successes, but many wines hollow, short	Drink or hold
1994	92	Outstanding	Very ripe, exotic wines dominate the vintage	Drink or hold
1993	85	Very Good	Uneven, but the best wines are elegant	Drink
1992	90	Outstanding	Underrated by many; numerous opulent wines	Drink
1991	86	Very Good	Generally ripe flavors; starting to fade	Drink

The Top 100

Every year since 1988 the editors of *Wine Spectator* have choosen 100 of the most exciting wines from the thousands reviewed to present our Top 100 Wines of the Year in the December 31 issue. All of the wines considered for our Top 100 were evaluated in blind tastings in our offices or on location in Europe. The result each year is 100 wine choices that would make for splendid drinking for even the toughest wine critic.

We could have simply given you a list of the highest-scoring wines, but that would only be part of the story. A wine's score simply reflects how good it is, regardless of price or where it comes from. Many of the most exciting wines we review are worth special attention because they represent a unique style or make a real contribution to the great diversity that makes wine so much fun. Absolute quality is only one component of this "excitement factor." Listed below are some additional criteria that we consider.

Overall Value

We expect more of higher-priced wines. A $100 Bordeaux has to carry an extremely high rating to make the Top 100. Conversely, a $10 Cabernet Sauvignon could make the Top 100 with a lower score.

Relative Value within Type

The Top 100 favors highly rated wines that are priced below average for their type. For example, a $25 Chassagne-Montrachet is a good relative value. A $25 Chilean Chardonnay is not.

Availability

Overall, the Top 100 favors wines that are not in extemely short supply. However, some wines made in tiny quantities, such as *cru* Burgundies, were so highly rated and reasonably priced in their categories that we decided they are well worth searching for. We made exceptions to the rule for wines such as these.

Rarity of Excellence within Type

We like to find outstanding wines in categories that don't usually produce outstanding quality. For example, the best Sauvignon Blanc may make the list while a Chardonnay with the same score and price may not, because we find fewer outstanding Sauvignon Blancs.

In the following pages are the Top 100 rankings for every year from 1999 back through 1988.

Top 100: Best Wines Released in 1999

RANK	SCORE	PRICE*	WINE
1	95	$28	**CHATEAU ST. JEAN** Cabernet Sauvignon Sonoma County Cinq Cépages **1996**
2	96	$125	**OPUS ONE** Napa Valley **1996**
3	96	$38	**ISOLE E OLENA** Toscana Cepparello **1997**
4	95	$45	**KISTLER** Chardonnay Sonoma Valley Durell Vineyard **1996**
5	96	$55	**PETER MICHAEL** Les Pavots Knights Valley **1996**
6	96	$50	**PAHLMEYER** Chardonnay Napa Valley **1997**
7	97	$60	**BAROSSA VALLEY ESTATE** Shiraz Barossa Valley E&E Black Pepper **1996**
8	95	$71	**CHATEAU MONTROSE** St.-Estèphe **1996**
9	95	$100	**ROBERT MONDAVI** Cabernet Sauvignon Napa Valley Reserve **1996**
10	95	$75	**CHATEAU COS-D'ESTOURNEL** St.-Estèphe **1996**
11	95	$70	**BOLLINGER** Brut Champagne Grande Année **1990**
12	97	$58	**ARGIANO** Toscana Solengo **1997**
13	99	$120	**BRYANT FAMILY** Cabernet Sauvignon Napa Valley **1996**
14	97	$232	**CHATEAU LATOUR** Pauillac **1996**
15	94	$17	**CHATEAU DE CHAMIREY** Mercurey White **1997**
16	94	$20	**CHAIN OF PONDS** Chardonnay Adelaide Hills **1997**
17	93	$24	**STONESTREET** Chardonnay Sonoma County **1997**
18	93	$25	**RIDGE** Geyserville Sonoma County **1996**
19	97	$65	**COMTE ARMAND** Pommard Clos des Epeneaux **1996**
20	92	$22	**LANDMARK** Chardonnay Sonoma-Santa Barbara-Monterey Counties Overlook **1997**
21	92	$23	**FERRARI-CARANO** Chardonnay Alexander Valley **1997**
22	93	$18	**VERGET** Pouilly-Fuissé Tête de Cuvée **1997**
23	93	$25	**BEAULIEU VINEYARD** Chardonnay Carneros Reserve **1997**
24	92	$20	**PETER LEHMANN** Clancy's Barossa **1997**
25	96	$165	**PENFOLDS** Shiraz South Australia Grange **1994**

RANK	SCORE	PRICE*	WINE
26	97	$85	**CASTELLO DEI RAMPOLLA** Toscana Vigna d'Alceo **1997**
27	97	$200	**GAJA** Barbaresco Sorì San Lorenzo **1996**
28	92	$23	**FONTODI** Chianti Classico **1997**
29	93	$22	**LOUIS JADOT** Santenay Clos de Malte **1996**
30	93	$36	**BERINGER** Chardonnay Napa Valley Private Reserve **1997**
31	94	$29	**LEASINGHAM** Shiraz Clare Valley Classic Clare **1996**
32	94	$21	**DR. PAULY-BERGWEILER** Riesling Spätlese Mosel-Saar-Ruwer Wehlener Sonnenuhr **1997**
33	93	$30	**A. LONG-DEPAQUIT** Chablis Vaillons **1997**
34	96	$32	**ROGER CAILLOT** Meursault La Barre Dessus Clos Marguerite **1996**
35	92	$30	**PRIDE** Merlot Napa Valley **1997**
36	93	$38	**ROEDERER ESTATE** Brut Anderson Valley L'Ermitage **1993**
37	94	$45	**FLORA SPRINGS** Trilogy Napa Valley **1996**
38	94	$50	**STERLING** Cabernet Sauvignon Napa Valley Reserve **1996**
39	91	$20	**ST. FRANCIS** Zinfandel Sonoma County Old Vines **1997**
40	91	$11	**COLUMBIA CREST** Chardonnay Columbia Valley Estate Series **1997**
41	93	$30	**TRIMBACH** Riesling Alsace Cuvée Frédéric Émile **1995**
42	92	$18	**CLOUDY BAY** Sauvignon Blanc Marlborough **1998**
43	91	$17	**MOUNT EDEN** Chardonnay Edna Valley MacGregor Vineyard **1997**
44	92	$25	**THE HESS COLLECTION** Cabernet Sauvignon Napa Valley **1995**
45	91	$12	**ST. SUPERY** Sauvignon Blanc Napa Valley **1998**
46	92	$30	**GIOVANNI SORDO** Barolo **1995**
47	93	$34	**CASTELLO DI LILLIANO** Colli della Toscana Centrale Anagallis **1997**
48	94	$52	**J. MOREAU & FILS** Chablis Les Clos **1997**
49	94	$40	**ROBERT CHEVILLON** Nuits-St.-Georges Les Chaignots **1996**

*PRICE ON RELEASE

■ ■ ■ ■

Top 100: Best Wines Released in 1999

RANK	SCORE	PRICE*	WINE
50	91	$30	**MOUNT VEEDER** Cabernet Sauvignon Napa Valley **1996**
51	92	$20	**ST. FRANCIS** Chardonnay Sonoma Valley Reserve **1997**
52	90	$9	**GEYSER PEAK** Sauvignon Blanc Sonoma County **1998**
53	90	$9	**REDBANK** Chardonnay Victoria Long Paddock **1997**
54	91	$22	**ROSEMOUNT** Cabernet Sauvignon Coonawarra Show Reserve **1996**
55	92	$16	**LINCOURT** Chardonnay Santa Barbara County **1997**
56	92	$25	**CHATEAU STE. MICHELLE** Chardonnay Columbia Valley Cold Creek Vineyard **1997**
57	92	$28	**SENORIO DE SAN VICENTE** Tempranillo Rioja **1996**
58	91	$15	**GREG NORMAN ESTATES** Cabernet-Merlot Coonawarra **1996**
59	91	$19	**KENDALL-JACKSON** Chardonnay Santa Maria Valley Camelot Vineyard Single Vineyard Series **1996**
60	90	$17	**SONOMA-CUTRER** Chardonnay Sonoma Coast Russian River Ranches **1997**
61	91	$18	**STEELE** Chardonnay California Steele Cuvée **1997**
62	92	$35	**BEAULIEU VINEYARD** Tapestry Reserve Napa Valley **1996**
63	91	$20	**GLORIA FERRER** Chardonnay Carneros **1997**
64	90	$23	**RAYMOND** Cabernet Sauvignon Napa Valley Reserve **1997**
65	92	$35	**BODEGAS Y VINEDOS ALION** Ribera del Duero Reserva **1995**
66	90	$22	**CHATEAU POUJEAUX** Moulis **1996**
67	92	$51	**CHATEAU LYNCH-BAGES** Pauillac **1996**
68	92	$51	**PICHON-LONGUEVILLE-BARON** Pauillac **1996**
69	91	$22	**FATTORIA DI FELSINA** Chianti Classico Berardenga **1997**
70	90	$25	**ALVARO PALACIOS** Priorat Les Terrasses **1996**
71	91	$33	**POMMERY** Brut Champagne Royal Apanage **NV**
72	91	$28	**WHITEHALL LANE** Cabernet Sauvignon Napa Valley **1997**
73	90	$10	**BABICH** Sauvignon Blanc Marlborough **1998**
74	91	$15	**VOCORET & FILS** Chablis **1997**
75	90	$18	**BERNARDUS** Chardonnay Monterey County **1997**
76	92	$20	**DOMAINE CLAVEL** Coteaux du Languedoc La Copa Santa **1996**
77	93	$20	**REICHSGRAF VON KESSELSTATT** Riesling Spätlese Mosel-Saar-Ruwer Scharzhofberger **1997**
78	90	$23	**MASSANDRA** Pinot Gris Crimea 2 Year Old **NV**
79	90	$13	**CHATEAU SOUVERAIN** Chardonnay Sonoma County **1997**
80	90	$18	**THE HESS COLLECTION** Chardonnay Napa Valley **1997**
81	90	$20	**LA GRANJA NUESTRA SENORA DE REMELLURI** Rioja **1996**
82	90	$16	**DAVID BRUCE** Pinot Noir Central Coast **1997**
83	90	$17	**BYRON** Chardonnay Santa Maria Valley **1997**
84	91	$23	**CHATEAU CANTEMERLE** Haut-Médoc **1996**
85	90	$18	**KING ESTATE** Pinot Gris Oregon Reserve **1997**
86	90	$23	**SANFORD** Pinot Noir Santa Barbara County **1997**
87	90	$12	**COOPERS CREEK** Chardonnay Gisborne **1998**
88	91	$15	**GRANT BURGE** Shiraz Barossa Filsell **1996**
89	90	$17	**FINCA ALLENDE** Rioja **1996**
90	90	$9	**RENZO MASI** Toscana Erta e China **1997**
91	90	$10	**BALTHASAR RESS** Riesling Kabinett Rheingau Hattenheimer Schützenhaus **1997**
92	90	$17	**GEORGES DUBOEUF** Pouilly-Fuissé Élevé en Fût de Chêne **1997**
93	90	$20	**TE MATA** Cabernet-Merlot Hawkes Bay **1998**
94	90	$20	**WOLFBERGER** Riesling Alsace Cuvée des Seigneurs **1995**
95	91	$21	**THELEMA** Chardonnay Stellenbosch **1997**
96	90	$25	**CHATEAU D'ISSAN** Margaux **1996**
97	92	$17	**ELVIO COGNO** Dolcetto d'Alba Vigna del Mandorlo **1998**
98	90	$12	**DR. BÜRKLIN-WOLF** Riesling Kabinett Pfalz Forster **1997**
99	92	$35	**MUMM CUVEE NAPA DVX** Napa Valley **1995**
100	90	$22	**ZIND-HUMBRECHT** Pinot d'Alsace Alsace **1997**

*PRICE ON RELEASE

Top 100: Best Wines Released in 1998

RANK	SCORE	PRICE*	WINE
			TOP 50 RED WINES
1	97	$95	**CHATEAU DUCRU-BEAUCAILLOU** St.-Julien **1995**
2	100	$350	**CHATEAU MARGAUX** Margaux **1995**
3	96	$35	**A. CLAPE** Cornas **1996**
4	95	$60	**CHATEAU CLERC MILON** Pauillac **1995**
5	95	$60	**WHITEHALL LANE** Cabernet Sauvignon Napa Valley Reserve **1995**
6	96	$75	**CHATEAU CALON-SEGUR** St.-Estèphe **1995**
7	96	$100	**DIAMOND CREEK** Cabernet Sauvignon Napa Valley Red Rock Terrace **1995**
8	95	$52	**ARGIANO** Toscana Solengo **1996**
9	95	$75	**BERINGER** Cabernet Sauvignon Napa Valley Private Reserve **1994**
10	94	$35	**BODEGAS Y VINEDOS ALION** Ribera del Duero Reserva **1994**
11	96	$100	**GROTH** Cabernet Sauvignon Napa Valley Reserve **1994**
12	97	$160	**CHATEAU TROTANOY** Pomerol **1995**
13	97	$275	**CHATEAU LAFITE ROTHSCHILD** Pauillac **1995**
14	93	$17	**ALAIN GRAILLOT** Crozes-Hermitage **1996**
15	94	$40	**CHATEAU PONTET-CANET** Pauillac **1995**
16	95	$75	**ARAUJO** Cabernet Sauvignon Napa Valley Eisele Vineyard **1995**
17	94	$80	**ROBERT MONDAVI** Cabernet Sauvignon Napa Valley Reserve **1995**
18	95	$120	**PENFOLDS** Shiraz South Australia Grange **1993**
19	96	$190	**GAJA** Barbaresco Sorì San Lorenzo **1995**
20	97	$100	**BRYANT FAMILY** Cabernet Sauvignon Napa Valley **1995**
21	95	$40	**TURLEY** Zinfandel Napa Valley Hayne Vineyard **1996**
22	96	$78	**MEO-CAMUZET** Vosne-Romanée Les Chaumes **1996**
23	98	$300	**DOMAINE DE LA ROMANEE-CONTI** Richebourg **1995**
24	96	$110	**HARLAN ESTATE** Napa Valley **1995**
25	94	$40	**JEAN-PAUL & JEAN-LUC JAMET** Côte-Rôtie **1996**
26	97	$260	**ALVARO PALACIOS** Priorat L'Ermita **1995**
27	93	$30	**SHAFER** Cabernet Sauvignon Stags Leap District **1995**
28	93	$19	**BENI DI BATASIOLO** Barbaresco **1995**
29	92	$30	**CHATEAU D'ARMAILHAC** Pauillac **1995**
30	92	$24	**BODEGAS ALEJANDRO FERNANDEZ** Ribera del Duero Pesquera Crianza **1995**
31	93	$35	**SAINTSBURY** Pinot Noir Carneros Reserve **1995**
32	93	$32	**DOMAINE BRUSSET** Gigondas Les Hauts de Montmirail **1996**
33	93	$33	**DOMAINE PEYRE ROSE** Syrah Coteaux du Languedoc Clos Léone **1994**
34	93	$45	**CASTELLO BANFI** Toscana Summus **1995**
35	92	$28	**WOODWARD CANYON** Cabernet Sauvignon Washington Canoe Ridge Vineyard Artist Series #4 **1995**
36	93	$40	**GIACOMO BOLOGNA** Barbera d'Asti Ai Suma **1996**
37	90	$12	**CHATEAU FERRANDE** Graves **1995**
38	91	$24	**NIEBAUM-COPPOLA** Zinfandel Napa Valley Edizione Pennino **1995**
39	91	$25	**CARPINETO** Cabernet Sauvignon Toscana Farnito **1996**
40	91	$30	**BEAULIEU VINEYARD** Pinot Noir Carneros Reserve **1995**
41	93	$63	**LUCE** Toscana Luce della Vite **1995**
42	91	$12	**CHATEAU ST.-GERMAIN** Coteaux du Languedoc **1995**
43	90	$13	**HIJOS DE ANTONIO BARCELO** Ribera del Duero Viña Mayor Reserva **1994**
44	90	$16	**FATTORIA MONSANTO** Chianti Classico Riserva **1995**
45	91	$25	**MARIMAR TORRES** Pinot Noir Sonoma County Green Valley Don Miguel Vineyard **1995**
46	91	$27	**JOSEPH PHELPS** Merlot Napa Valley **1995**
47	90	$25	**QUPE** Syrah Santa Barbara County Bien Nacido Reserve **1996**
48	90	$19	**LOUIS JADOT** Moulin-à-Vent Château des Jacques **1996**
49	90	$25	**PINE RIDGE** Merlot Napa Valley Crimson Creek **1996**
50	90	$24	**COLUMBIA** Syrah Yakima Valley Red Willow Vineyard David Lake Signature Series **1995**

*PRICE ON RELEASE

Top 100: Best Wines Released in 1998

RANK	SCORE	PRICE*	WINE
			Top 40 White and Sparkling Wines
1	99	$85	**DOMAINE LAROCHE** Chablis Les Clos **1996**
2	95	$32	**BERINGER** Chardonnay Napa Valley Private Reserve **1996**
3	96	$82	**DOMAINE LEFLAIVE** Puligny-Montrachet Clavoillon **1995**
4	95	$25	**JEAN-MARC BROCARD** Chablis Beauregard **1996**
5	94	$42	**KISTLER** Chardonnay Russian River Valley Vine Hill Vineyard **1995**
6	94	$35	**DIDIER DAGUENEAU** Pouilly-Fumé Pur Sang **1996**
7	95	$40	**CHÂTEAU DE BEAUCASTEL** Châteauneuf-du-Pape White **1997**
8	95	$45	**VERGET** Puligny-Montrachet Les Enseignères **1996**
9	93	$28	**CHALK HILL** Chardonnay Chalk Hill **1996**
10	94	$27	**LA CHABLISIENNE** Chablis Les Fourchaumes **1996**
11	93	$30	**TALBOTT** Chardonnay Monterey Sleepy Hollow Vineyard **1995**
12	97	$48	**CHARLES HEIDSIECK** Brut Champagne **1990**
13	95	$80	**BONNEAU DU MARTRAY** Corton-Charlemagne **1996**
14	92	$14	**MERIDIAN** Chardonnay Edna Valley Coastal Reserve **1996**
15	95	$50	**DELAMOTTE** Brut Blanc de Blancs Champagne **1990**
16	94	$29	**PATZ & HALL** Chardonnay Napa Valley **1996**
17	93	$29	**SIMI** Chardonnay Sonoma County Reserve **1995**
18	92	$21	**LANDMARK** Chardonnay Sonoma County Overlook **1996**
19	92	$22	**MURE** Riesling Alsace Grand Cru Vorbourg Clos St.-Landelin **1996**
20	91	$13	**VOSS** Sauvignon Blanc Napa Valley **1997**
21	91	$14	**CAYMUS** Sauvignon Blanc Napa Valley **1996**
22	91	$16	**MOUNT EDEN** Chardonnay Edna Valley MacGregor Vineyard **1996**
23	91	$18	**CLOUDY BAY** Sauvignon Blanc Marlborough **1997**
24	91	$18	**BERNARDUS** Chardonnay Monterey County 1996
25	90	$13	**CHATEAU SOUVERAIN** Chardonnay Sonoma County **1996**
26	91	$16	**PLANTAGENET** Chardonnay Western Australia Omrah Unoaked **1997**
27	91	$30	**BOLLINGER** Brut Champagne Special Cuvée **NV**
28	90	$14	**SHAW & SMITH** Sauvignon Blanc South Australia **1996**
29	93	$29	**CAVE DE TAIN L'HERMITAGE** Hermitage White Les Nobles Rives **1996**
30	93	$34	**FERRARI-CARANO** Chardonnay Napa & Sonoma Counties Reserve **1995**
31	91	$20	**VILLA MT. EDEN** Chardonnay Santa Maria Valley Bien Nacido Vineyard Grand Reserve **1996**
32	91	$21	**JACQUES BURRIER** Pouilly-Fuissé Château de Beauregard **1996**
33	92	$26	**CHATEAU STE. MICHELLE** Chardonnay Columbia Valley Cold Creek Vineyard **1996**
34	93	$58	**TRIMBACH** Riesling Alsace Clos Ste.-Hune **1992**
35	90	$15	**FRANCISCAN OAKVILLE ESTATE** Chardonnay Napa Valley **1996**
36	90	$16	**MUMM** Cuvée Napa Brut Napa Valley Prestige **NV**
37	91	$20	**ARGYLE** Chardonnay Willamette Valley Reserve **1995**
38	90	$17	**ROEDERER ESTATE** Brut Anderson Valley **NV**
39	90	$16	**ORLANDO** Chardonnay Padthaway St. Hilary **1996**
40	90	$17	**PASCAL JOLIVET** Sancerre **1996**
			Top 10 Dessert Wines
1	95	$35	**DOMAINE DES BAUMARD** Quarts de Chaume **1996**
2	98	$100	**KRACHER** Chardonnay Trockenbeerenauslese Neusiedlersee Nouvelle Vague No. 13 **1995** (375ml)
3	99	$450	**CHATEAU PAJZOS** Tokay Esszencia **1993** (500ml)
4	95	$60	**QUINTA DO VESUVIO** Vintage Port **1995**
5	95	$55	**DOLCE** Late Harvest California **1994** (375ml)
6	94	$32	**DISZNO´KO** Tokay Aszú 5 Puttonyos **1993** (500ml)
7	94	$15	**YALUMBA** Museum Muscat Victoria Museum Release **NV** (375ml)
8	92	$33	**WARRE** Vintage Port Quinta da Cavadinha **1995**
9	92	$39	**FONSECA** Vintage Port Guimaraens **1995**
10	92	$39	**TAYLOR FLADGATE** Vintage Port Quinya de Vargellas **1995**

* PRICE ON RELEASE

Top 100: Best Wines Released in 1997

RANK	SCORE	PRICE*	WINE
1	100	$55	**FONSECA** Vintage Port **1994**
1	100	$55	**TAYLOR FLADGATE** Vintage Port **1994**
3	96	$70	**JOSEPH PHELPS** Insignia Napa Valley **1994**
4	96	$60	**ARAUJO** Cabernet Sauvignon Napa Valley Eisele Vineyard **1994**
5	95	$30	**ROBERT MONDAVI** Chardonnay Napa Valley Reserve **1994**
6	97	$160	**CHATEAU D'YQUEM** Sauternes **1990**
7	94	$17	**CLOUDY BAY** Sauvignon Blanc Marlborough **1996**
8	95	$25	**BODEGAS REYES** Ribera del Duero Teófilo Reyes **1994**
9	95	$36	**CAYMUS** Cabernet Sauvignon Napa Valley **1994**
10	93	$30	**SAINTSBURY** Chardonnay Carneros Reserve **1995**
11	94	$29	**BERINGER** Chardonnay Napa Valley Private Reserve **1995**
12	94	$75	**DOMINUS ESTATE** Napa Valley Napanook Vineyard **1994**
13	94	$90	**OPUS ONE** Napa Valley **1994**
14	98	$35	**DOMAINE DES BAUMARD** Quarts de Chaume **1995**
15	95	$45	**WARRE** Vintage Port 1994
16	95	$35	**DIDIER DAGUENEAU** Pouilly-Fumé Pur Sang **1995**
17	93	$18	**MERRYVALE** Chardonnay Napa Valley Starmont **1995**
18	97	$60	**JACQUES PRIEUR** Puligny-Montrachet Les Combettes **1995**
19	95	$47	**DENIS MORTET** Gevrey-Chambertin En Motrot **1995**
20	93	$75	**PAUL JABOULET AÎNÉ** Hermitage La Chapelle **1995**
21	94	$31	**ALLEGRINI** Amarone della Valpolicella Classico Superiore **1990**
22	95	$30	**MARTINEZ** Vintage Port **1994**
23	94	$45	**LEONETTI** Cabernet Sauvignon Columbia Valley **1994**
24	94	$60	**SHAFER** Cabernet Sauvignon Stags Leap District Hillside Select **1993**
25	96	$100	**CASTELLO DI AMA** Vigna l'Apparita **1993**
26	95	$60	**BODEGAS ALEJANDRO FERNANDEZ** Ribera del Duero Pesquera Janus Reserva **1994**
27	94	$60	**J.L. CHAVE** Hermitage **1994**
28	94	$60	**TRIMBACH** Riesling Alsace Clos Ste.-Hune **1991**
29	94	$18	**JEAN-PAUL DROIN** Chablis Montée de Tonnerre **1996**
30	94	$35	**VERGET** Puligny-Montrachet Les Enseignères **1995**
31	93	$24	**CHALK HILL** Chardonnay Chalk Hill **1995**
32	94	$30	**MATANZAS CREEK** Chardonnay Sonoma Valley **1995**
33	94	$35	**PETER MICHAEL** Les Pavots Knights Valley **1994**
34	93	$30	**VIADER** Napa Valley **1994**
35	93	$70	**BONNEAU DU MARTRAY** Corton-Charlemagne **1995**
36	94	$125	**ALDO CONTERNO** Barolo Cicala **1993**
37	93	$115	**CHÂTEAU LAFITE ROTHSCHILD** Pauillac **1994**
38	92	$16	**ESTANCIA** Meritage Red Alexander Valley **1994**
39	93	$29	**GÉRARD CHAVY** Puligny-Montrachet **1995**
40	92	$18	**VILLA MT. EDEN** Chardonnay California Grand Reserve **1995**
41	93	$85	**CHÂTEAU CLINET** Pomerol **1994**
42	92	$43	**MATANZAS CREEK** Merlot Sonoma Valley **1994**
43	92	$21	**FERRARI-CARANO** Chardonnay Alexander Valley **1995**
44	92	$15	**ALAIN GRAILLOT** Crozes-Hermitage 1995
45	91	$12	**ROSEMOUNT** Shiraz South Eastern Australia **1996**
46	92	$12	**LOLONIS** Zinfandel Mendocino County **1994**
47	93	$40	**ROSEMOUNT** Syrah McLaren Vale Balmoral **1994**
48	92	$23	**RIDGE** Lytton Springs Dry Creek Valley **1995**
49	93	$115	**CHÂTEAU HAUT-BRION** Pessac-Léognan **1994**
50	92	$25	**CAKEBREAD** Cabernet Sauvignon Napa Valley **1994**

*PRICE ON RELEASE

Top 100: Best Wines Released in 1997

RANK	SCORE	PRICE*	WINE
51	92	$24	**ROCHIOLI** Pinot Noir Russian River Valley **1995**
52	92	$13	**RABBIT RIDGE** Sangiovese Sonoma County Coniglio Selezione **1994**
53	92	$15	**FLORA SPRINGS** Sangiovese Napa Valley **1995**
54	92	$35	**FATTORIA DI FELSINA** Chianti Classico Rancia Riserva **1994**
55	93	$45	**COSTERS DEL SIURANA** Priorat Clos de L'Obac **1995**
56	91	$14	**COLUMBIA CREST** Chardonnay Columbia Valley Estate Series **1995**
57	92	$28	**GRGICH HILLS** Chardonnay Napa Valley **1995**
58	92	$15	**CHARLES KRUG** Merlot Napa Valley Peter Mondavi Family **1995**
59	92	$85	**CHATEAU L'ANGÉLUS** St.-Emilion **1994**
60	92	$21	**ROEDERER ESTATE** Brut Rosé Anderson Valley **NV**
61	91	$16	**THE HESS COLLECTION** Chardonnay Napa Valley **1995**
62	91	$20	**BERINGER** Cabernet Sauvignon Knights Valley **1994**
63	92	$45	**PENFOLDS** Cabernet Sauvignon South Australia Bin 707 **1993**
64	91	$15	**LOCKWOOD** Chardonnay Monterey **1995**
65	91	$18	**SANFORD** Chardonnay Santa Barbara County **1995**
66	92	$25	**SONOMA-CUTRER** Chardonnay Sonoma Coast The Cutrer Vineyard **1994**
67	93	$15	**BONNY DOON** Muscat California Vin de Glacière **1996** (375 ml)
68	93	$18	**PETER LEHMANN** Clancy's Gold Preference Barossa Valley **1994**
69	91	$20	**KANONKOP** Pinotage Stellenbosch **1995**
70	91	$33	**E. GUIGAL** Côte-Rôtie Côtes Brune et Blonde **1993**
71	91	$40	**HENRIOT** Brut Champagne Millésimé **1989**
72	92	$61	**DOMAINE WEINBACH** Riesling Alsace Grand Cru Schlossberg Cuvée Ste.-Cathérine **1996**
73	90	$11	**KURT DARTING** Riesling Kabinett Pfalz Ungsteiner Bettelhaus **1996**
74	90	$11	**COLUMBIA CREST** Cabernet Sauvignon Columbia Valley **1994**
75	90	$15	**BEAULIEU VINEYARD** Cabernet Sauvignon Rutherford **1994**
76	91	$13	**BEAULIEU VINEYARD** Zinfandel Napa Valley **1995**
77	91	$13	**LEASINGHAM** Shiraz Clare Valley Domain **1995**
78	92	$40	**LOUIS CARILLON** Puligny-Montrachet **1995**
79	92	$35	**VINCENT GIRARDIN** Volnay Clos des Chênes **1995**
80	90	$18	**STEELE** Pinot Noir Carneros **1995**
81	91	$19	**BODEGAS ISMAEL ARROYO** Ribera del Duero Val Sotillo Crianza **1994**
82	90	$15	**DRY CREEK** Chardonnay Sonoma County **1995**
83	91	$15	**GHISLAINE & JEAN-HUGUES GOISOT** Chardonnay Bourgogne Côtes d'Auxerre Corps de Garde **1995**
84	90	$14	**RAYMOND** Chardonnay Napa Valley Reserve **1995**
85	90	$17	**CONDADO DE HAZA** Ribera del Duero **1995**
86	90	$15	**CASA LAPOSTOLLE** Merlot Rapel Valley Cuvée Alexandre **1995**
87	90	$18	**CHATEAU ST. JEAN** Merlot Sonoma County **1994**
88	91	$45	**CHATEAU COS-D'ESTOURNEL** St.-Estèphe **1994**
89	90	$17	**PASCAL JOLIVET** Sancerre **1995**
90	90	$9	**GIESEN** Sauvignon Blanc Marlborough **1996**
91	90	$12	**MARKHAM** Sauvignon Blanc Napa Valley **1996**
92	92	$15	**MARKHAM** Cabernet Sauvignon Napa Valley **1994**
93	91	$25	**CHÂTEAU BOUSCASSÉ** Madiran Vieilles Vignes **1995**
94	90	$13	**RABBIT RIDGE** Zinfandel Sonoma County **1995**
95	91	$30	**MONTAUDON** Brut Champagne **NV**
96	91	$30	**CATTIER** Brut Champagne Antique **NV**
97	90	$17	**BYRON** Pinot Noir Santa Barbara County **1995**
98	90	$19	**ROBERT WEIL** Riesling Kabinett Rheingau **1996**
99	90	$7	**HOGUE** White Riesling Late Harvest Columbia Valley **1996**
100	91	$23	**TRUCHARD** Pinot Noir Carneros **1995**

*PRICE ON RELEASE

■ ■ ■ ■

Top 100: Best Wines Released in 1996

RANK	SCORE	PRICE*	WINE
1	95	$20	**BERINGER** Chardonnay Napa Valley Private Reserve **1994**
2	98	$70	**GROTH** Cabernet Sauvignon Napa Valley Reserve **1992**
3	93	$20	**CHALK HILL** Chardonnay Chalk Hill **1994**
4	93	$22	**HENSCHKE** Shiraz-Cabernet-Malbec Eden Valley Barossa Valley Keyneton Estate **1993**
5	93	$23	**SHAFER** Chardonnay Napa Valley Carneros Red Shoulder Ranch **1994**
6	93	$29	**KUMEU RIVER** Chardonnay Kumeu **1994**
7	92	$13	**LINDEMANS** Chardonnay Padthaway **1994**
8	92	$16	**GALLO-SONOMA** Chardonnay Russian River Valley Laguna Ranch Vineyard **1994**
9	92	$15	**ALAIN GRAILLOT** Crozes-Hermitage **1994**
10	92	$27	**ARROWOOD** Cabernet Sauvignon Sonoma County **1993**
11	92	$30	**CHÂTEAU CANON-LA GAFFELIÈRE** St.-Emilion **1993**
12	91	$16	**CONCHA Y TORO** Cabernet Sauvignon Maipo Puente Alto Vineyard Don Melchor Private Reserve **1993**
13	92	$18	**CHATEAU ST. JEAN** Chardonnay Alexander Valley Belle Terre Vineyards **1994**
14	92	$18	**STEELE** Chardonnay California **1994**
15	95	$34	**NIEPOORT** Tawny Port Colheita **1983**
16	91	$12	**CHATEAU SOUVERAIN** Chardonnay Sonoma County **1994**
17	91	$17	**FERRARI-CARANO** Fumé Blanc Sonoma County Reserve **1995**
18	92	$12	**CHATEAU REYNELLA** Shiraz McLaren Vale Basket Pressed **1994**
19	95	$25	**SAINTSBURY** Chardonnay Carneros Reserve **1994**
20	94	$20	**HARDYS** Shiraz Padthaway-McLaren Vale-Clare Valley Eileen Hardy **1993**
21	94	$40	**LEONETTI** Merlot Washington **1994**
22	93	$45	**SILVER OAK** Cabernet Sauvignon Napa Valley **1992**
23	94	$19	**TRUCHARD** Chardonnay Napa Valley Carneros **1994**
24	94	$25	**BROADLEY** Pinot Noir Oregon Claudia's Choice **1994**
25	93	$28	**BYRON** Chardonnay Santa Maria Valley Estate **1993**
26	93	$40	**SIMI** Cabernet Sauvignon Alexander Valley Reserve **1992**
27	93	$50	**SILVER OAK** Cabernet Sauvignon Napa Valley Bonny's Vineyard **1991**
28	93	$28	**DE BORTOLI** Sémillon Australia Noble One **1993** (375ml)
29	97	$84	**CAMPOGIOVANNI** Brunello di Montalcino Vigna del Quercione Riserva **1990**
30	96	$27	**TURLEY** Zinfandel Napa Valley Hayne Vineyard **1994**
31	96	$34	**HENSCHKE** Shiraz Keyneton Mount Edelstone **1993**
32	96	$48	**ROCHIOLI** Pinot Noir Russian River Valley West Block Reserve **1994**
33	96	$60	**CHÂTEAU PAPE CLÉMENT** Pessac-Léognan White **1994**
34	95	$38	**CHATEAU ST. JEAN** Cabernet Sauvignon Sonoma County Reserve **1990**
35	92	$22	**LINDEMANS** Cabernet Sauvignon Coonawarra St. George Vineyard **1991**
36	92	$24	**ST. FRANCIS** Merlot Sonoma Valley Reserve Estate **1992**
37	91	$14	**PAUL JABOULET** Aîné Crozes-Hermitage Les Jalets **1994**
38	91	$18	**PENFOLDS** Shiraz South Australia Kalimna Bin 28 **1993**
39	91	$18	**BOLLA** Amarone della Valpolicella Classico **1988**
40	95	$52	**ARGIANO** Brunello di Montalcino Riserva **1990**
41	95	$100	**CASTELLO BANFI** Brunello di Montalcino Poggio all'Oro Riserva **1990**
42	95	$110	**PENFOLDS** Shiraz South Australia Grange **1991**
43	94	$32	**JEAN GRIVOT** Vosne-Romanée Les Beaux Monts **1993**
44	94	$50	**CHÂTEAU LA FLEUR DE GAY** Pomerol **1993**
45	92	$16	**VILLA MT. EDEN** Chardonnay Napa Valley Grand Reserve **1994**
46	92	$16	**TYRRELL'S** Pinot Chardonnay Hunter Valley Vat 47 **1994**
47	93	$14	**NAVARRO** White Riesling Late Harvest Anderson Valley Sweet **1994**
48	93	$19	**ROBERT BIALE** Zinfandel Napa Valley Aldo's Vineyard Proprietor's Series **1994**
49	93	$27	**ST. HALLETT** Shiraz Barossa Old Block **1993**

*PRICE ON RELEASE

Top 100: Best Wines Released in 1996

RANK	SCORE	PRICE*	WINE
50	93	$40	**MICHEL COLIN-DELÉGER** Chassagne-Montrachet En Remilly **1994**
51	93	$40	**BEAUX FRÈRES** Pinot Noir Yamhill County Beaux Frères Vineyard **1994**
52	93	$75	**POGGIO ANTICO** Brunello di Montalcino Riserva **1990**
53	92	$19	**SADDLEBACK** Cabernet Sauvignon Napa Valley **1993**
54	92	$20	**ROSENBLUM** Zinfandel Mount Veeder Brandlin Ranch **1994**
55	92	$29	**TRIMBACH** Riesling Alsace Cuvée Frédéric Emile **1992**
56	92	$30	**MARQUIS D'ANGERVILLE** Volnay Premier Cru **1993**
57	92	$31	**QUILCEDA CREEK** Cabernet Sauvignon Washington **1992**
58	92	$46	**LOUIS ROEDERER** Brut Champagne **1990**
59	91	$16	**LANDMARK** Chardonnay Sonoma County Overlook **1994**
60	91	$16	**CARMENET** Chardonnay Sonoma Valley Carneros Sangiacomo Vineyard **1993**
61	91	$15	**MCGUIGAN BROTHERS** Cabernet Sauvignon Australia Personal Reserve **1993**
62	91	$16	**MITCHELTON** Chardonnay Victoria Reserve **1994**
63	91	$16	**ROBERT MONDAVI** Zinfandel Napa Valley **1994**
64	91	$17	**CASTELLO BANFI** Chardonnay Tuscany Fontanelle **1993**
65	91	$18	**STEELE** Zinfandel Mendocino Du Pratt Vineyard **1993**
66	91	$20	**RIDGE** Geyserville Sonoma County **1994**
67	91	$15	**VALETTE** Mâcon-Chaintré Vieilles Vignes **1994**
68	91	$22	**CHATEAU ST. JEAN** Cabernet Sauvignon Sonoma County Cinq Cépages **1993**
69	91	$22	**JEAN-PIERRE GROSSOT** Chablis Les Fourneaux **1994**
70	90	$10	**MARTINELLI** Gewürztraminer Russian River Valley **1995**
71	90	$10	**TALTARNI** Sauvignon Blanc Victoria **1995**
72	90	$10	**VOSS** Sauvignon Blanc Napa Valley **1995**
73	90	$11	**BERINGER** Chardonnay Napa Valley **1994**
74	90	$11	**CHATEAU ST. JEAN** Chardonnay Sonoma County **1994**
75	90	$12	**DECOY** Migration Red Napa Valley **1993**
76	90	$12	**J. LOHR** Chardonnay Monterey Riverstone **1994**
77	90	$12	**WYNNS** Chardonnay Coonawarra **1994**
78	90	$12	**SILVAN RIDGE** Early Muscat Oregon Semi-Sparkling **1994**
79	90	$13	**FRANCISCAN** Chardonnay Napa Valley Oakville Estate Barrel Fermented **1994**
80	90	$14	**PETER LEHMANN** Cabernet Sauvignon Barossa **1993**
81	90	$14	**CHATEAU ST. JEAN** Merlot Sonoma County **1993**
82	90	$14	**CHALK HILL** Sauvignon Blanc Chalk Hill **1994**
83	90	$15	**BERNARDUS** Chardonnay Monterey County **1994**
84	90	$15	**CASA LAPOSTOLLE** Merlot Rapel Valley Cuvée Alexandre **1994**
85	90	$15	**GREENWOOD RIDGE** Zinfandel Sonoma County Scherrer Vineyards **1994**
86	90	$16	**CHÂTEAU D'OLIVIER** Pessac-Léognan White **1994**
87	91	$25	**CHÂTEAU LA LOUVIÈRE** Pessac-Léognan White **1994**
88	91	$25	**CAYMUS** Cabernet Sauvignon Napa Valley **1993**
89	90	$16	**SAXENBURG** Shiraz Stellenbosch Private Collection **1993**
90	90	$17	**RAYMOND** Cabernet Sauvignon Napa Valley Reserve **1993**
91	90	$18	**DOMAINES SCHLUMBERGER** Gewürztraminer Alsace Fleur de Guebwiller **1993**
92	90	$18	**WATERBROOK** Merlot Columbia Valley **1993**
93	90	$18	**HEDGES** Cabernet Sauvignon Columbia Valley Three Vineyards at Red Mountain **1994**
94	90	$18	**KUNDE** Viognier Sonoma Valley **1995**
95	90	$19	**GARY FARRELL** Pinot Noir Russian River Valley **1994**
96	90	$20	**STEELE** Pinot Noir Santa Barbara County Bien Nacido Vineyard **1994**
97	90	$21	**PANTHER CREEK** Pinot Noir Willamette Valley Reserve **1993**
98	90	$21	**KEN WRIGHT** Pinot Noir Willamette Valley **1994**
99	90	$22	**ALION** Ribera del Duero **1992**
100	90	$30	**DRAPPIER** Brut Champagne Carte Blanche **NV**

*PRICE ON RELEASE

Top 100: Best Wines Released in 1995

RANK	SCORE	PRICE*	WINE
1	97	$100	**PENFOLDS** Shiraz South Australia Grange **1990**
2	99	$100	**CAYMUS** Cabernet Sauvignon Napa Valley Special Selection **1991**
3	94	$18	**THE HESS COLLECTION** Cabernet Sauvignon Napa Valley **1992**
4	96	$45	**FONSECA** Vintage Port **1992**
5	96	$140	**COMTE GEORGES DE VOGÜÉ** Musigny Cuvée Vieilles Vignes **1993**
6	94	$13	**ZACA MESA** Syrah Santa Barbara County Zaca Vineyards **1993**
7	95	$43	**CAMPOGIOVANNI** Brunello di Montalcino **1990**
8	94	$40	**KISTLER** Chardonnay Sonoma Valley Kistler Vineyard **1992**
9	95	$45	**BERINGER** Cabernet Sauvignon Napa Valley Private Reserve **1992**
10	96	$27	**TRIMBACH** Riesling Alsace Cuvée Frédéric Emile **1990**
11	95	$22	**TURLEY** Zinfandel Napa Valley Hayne Vineyard **1993**
12	98	$60	**ALTESINO** Brunello di Montalcino Montosoli **1990**
13	97	$150	**E. GUIGAL** Côte-Rôtie La Landonne **1991**
14	96	$40	**ARAUJO** California Cabernet Sauvignon Eisele Vineyard **1992**
15	97	$90	**DANIEL RION** Clos Vougeot **1993**
16	96	$28	**ARROWOOD** California White Riesling Late Harvest Russian River Valley Oak Meadow Vineyard Special Select **1993** (375ml)
17	96	$40	**FLORA SPRINGS** Cabernet Sauvignon Napa Valley Rutherford Reserve **1992**
18	95	$37	**TAYLOR FLADGATE** Vintage Port **1992**
19	94	$30	**LEWIS** Cabernet Sauvignon Napa Valley Oakville Ranch **1992**
20	93	$30	**ANDERSON'S** Conn Valley Cabernet Sauvignon Napa Valley Estate Reserve **1992**
21	93	$45	**FAR NIENTE** Cabernet Sauvignon Napa Valley **1992**
22	95	$72	**CAPARZO** Brunello di Montalcino Vigna la Casa **1990**
23	96	$185	**LEROY** Volnay-Santenots **1993**
24	93	$9	**CHATEAU STE. MICHELLE** Washington White Riesling Late Harvest Columbia Valley Chateau Reserve **1991** (375ml)
25	93	$30	**JEAN-MARC BOILLOT** Volnay **1993**
26	94	$15	**BONNY DOON** California Muscat Canelli Vin de Glacière **1994** (375ml)
27	94	$26	**MONTICELLO** Chardonnay Napa Valley Corley Estate Reserve **1992**
28	93	$44	**MONTHELIE-DOUHAIRET** Volnay En Champans **1993**
29	92	$16	**PENFOLDS** South Australia Cabernet-Shiraz Bin 389 **1992**
30	93	$18	**RABBIT RIDGE** Zinfandel Sonoma Country San Lorenzo Reserve **1993**
31	92	$17	**A. RAFANELLI** Cabernet Sauvignon Dry Creek Valley **1992**
32	92	$18	**ROMBAUER** Chardonnay Carneros **1993**
33	92	$20	**BERINGER** Chardonnay Napa Valley Private Reserve **1993**
34	94	$27	**MASTROJANNI** Brunello di Montalcino **1990**
35	94	$49	**QUINTA DO VESÚVIO** Vintage Port **1992**
36	93	$28	**WHITEHALL LANE** Cabernet Sauvignon Napa Valley Morisoli Vineyard **1992**
37	91	$20	**GROTH** Cabernet Sauvignon Napa Valley **1992**
38	93	$60	**MÉO-CAMUZET** Nuits-St.-Georges Aux Murgers **1993**
39	93	$30	**FORMAN** Cabernet Sauvignon Napa Valley **1992**
40	93	$45	**SHAFER** Cabernet Sauvignon Stags Leap District Hillside Select **1991**
41	93	$55	**DOMINUS** Napa Valley Napanook Vineyard **1991**
42	93	$30	**ETUDE** Cabernet Sauvignon Napa Valley **1992**
43	92	$29	**BERINGER** Merlot Howell Mountain Bancroft Ranch **1992**
44	92	$30	**CHATEAU MONTELENA** Cabernet Sauvignon Napa Valley The Montelena Estate **1991**
45	92	$40	**PENFOLDS** Cabernet Sauvignon South Australia Bin 707 **1992**
46	93	$59	**ORNELLAIA** Masseto **1992**
47	92	$20	**ALION** Ribera del Duero Reserva **1991**
48	91	$17	**MARKHAM** Chardonnay Napa Valley Barrel Fermented **1993**
49	93	$30	**CASTELLO BANFI** Brunello di Montalcino **1990**

*PRICE ON RELEASE

Top 100: Best Wines Released in 1995

RANK	SCORE	PRICE*	WINE
50	93	$42	**OLIVIER LEFLAIVE FRÈRES** Volnay Frémiets **1993**
51	91	$23	**MATANZAS CREEK** Chardonnay Sonoma Valley **1993**
52	92	$25	**ARROWOOD** Cabernet Sauvignon Sonoma County **1992**
53	93	$54	**CONTI COSTANTI** Brunello di Montalcino **1990**
54	91	$16	**BODEGAS ESMERALDA** Cabernet Sauvignon Mendoza Agrelo Vineyard Catena **1992**
55	92	$180	**BODEGAS VEGA SICILIA** Ribera del Duero Unico Reserva **1970**
56	92	$65	**DOMAINE LEFLAIVE** Puligny-Montrachet Clavaillon **1992**
57	92	$35	**DOMAINE ZIND-HUMBRECHT** Gewürztraminer Grand Cru Goldert **1993**
58	92	$35	**HENSCHKE** Cabernet Sauvignon Eden Valley Cyril Henschke **1991**
59	92	$20	**RIDGE** California Chardonnay Santa Cruz Mountains **1992**
60	91	$15	**GLORIA FERRER** Chardonnay Carneros **1993**
61	92	$27	**KUMEU RIVER** Chardonnay Kumeu **1993**
62	91	$17	**CAYMUS** California Conundrum **1994**
63	91	$12	**MARIENBERG** Shiraz McLaren Vale **1992**
64	92	$35	**SIMI** Cabernet Sauvignon Alexander Valley Reserve **1991**
65	91	$19	**CHALK HILL** Chardonnay Chalk Hill **1993**
66	91	$20	**FERRARI-CARANO** Chardonnay Alexander Valley **1993**
67	91	$30	**EL MOLINO** Pinot Noir Napa Valley **1992**
68	92	$68	**MONGEARD-MUGNERET** Echezeaux Vieilles Vignes **1993**
69	92	$21	**STONESTREET** Chardonnay Sonoma County **1993**
70	92	$45	**NOZZOLE** Il Pareto **1993**
71	92	$28	**ROSEMOUNT** Chardonnay Hunter Valley Roxburgh **1991**
72	91	$12	**KIONA** Merlot Columbia Valley **1992**
73	90	$11	**MARQUÉS DE RISCAL** Rioja Riserva **1989**
74	90	$10	**ROSEMOUNT** Shiraz South Australia **1994**
75	91	$29	**LEONETTI WASHINGTON** Merlot **1992**
76	91	$32	**SILVER OAK** Cabernet Sauvignon Alexander Valley **1991**
77	91	$30	**MATANZAS CREEK** Merlot Alexander Valley **1993**
78	91	$55	**ROBERT MONDAVI** Cabernet Sauvignon, Napa Valley Reserve **1992**
79	91	$20	**RIDGE** Zinfandel Blend Sonoma County Geyserville **1993**
80	90	$12	**FRANCISCAN** Chardonnay Napa Valley Oakville Estate Barrel Fermented **1993**
81	91	$37	**RUINART** Champagne R de Ruinart **NV**
82	91	$25	**TALBOTT** Chardonnay Monterey **1992**
83	91	$30	**HENSCHKE** Shiraz Keyneton Mount Edelstone **1992**
84	91	$18	**ST. FRANCIS** Zinfandel Sonoma Valley Old Vines **1993**
85	91	$20	**MARIMAR TORRES** Chardonnay Sonoma County Green Valley Don Miguel **1992**
86	90	$25	**CHATEAU STE. MICHELLE** Chardonnay Columbia Valley Cold Creek Vineyard **1993**
87	90	$15	**FERRARI-CARANO** Fumé Blanc Sonoma County Reserve **1994**
88	90	$18	**FONTODI** Chianti Classico Riserva **1991**
89	90	$14	**E. & J. GALLO** Zinfandel Dry Creek Valley Frei Ranch Vineyard Gallo **1990**
90	90	$20	**GLEN CARLOU** Chardonnay Paarl **1994**
91	90	$15	**GREEN & RED** Zinfandel Napa Valley Chiles Mill Vineyard **1993**
92	90	$18	**HEITZ** Cabernet Sauvignon Napa Valley **1990**
93	90	$32	**LAURENT PERRIER** Champagne Brut L.P. **NV**
94	90	$18	**SIRO PANCENTI** Rosso di Montalcino **1993**
95	90	$18	**SANFORD** Chardonnay Santa Barbara County **1993**
96	90	$18	**STEELE** Pinot Noir Carneros **1993**
97	90	$20	**THELEMA** Cabernet Sauvignon-Merlot Stellenbosch **1992**
98	90	$16	**ROEDERER ESTATE** Anderson Valley Brut **NV**
99	90	$65	**ANTINORI** Solaia **1991**
100	91	$89	**MOËT & CHANDON** Cuvée Dom Pérignon **1988**

*PRICE ON RELEASE

Top 100: Best Wines Released in 1994

RANK	SCORE	PRICE*	WINE
1	98	$75	**CAYMUS** Cabernet Sauvignon Napa Valley Special Selection **1990**
2	98	$135	**E. GUIGAL** Côte-Rôtie La Mouline **1990**
3	97	$33	**FLORA SPRINGS** Cabernet Sauvignon Napa Valley Reserve **1991**
4	96	$25	**LEONETTI** Merlot Washington **1992**
5	93	$20	**FERRARI-CARANO** Chardonnay Alexander Valley **1992**
6	96	$45	**DOMAINE ZIND-HUMBRECHT** Gewürztraminer Alsace Grand Cru Goldert Vendange Tardive **1990**
7	96	$46	**SANDRONE** Barolo Cannubi Boschis **1990**
8	96	$63	**J. L. CHAVE** Hermitage **1990**
9	94	$32	**CROFT** Vintage Port **1991**
10	93	$16	**RIDGE** Zinfandel Sonoma Valley Pagani Ranch Late Picked **1992**
11	96	$40	**CONTERNO FANTINO** Barolo Sorì Ginestra **1990**
12	95	$25	**ST. CLEMENT** Oroppas Napa Valley **1992**
13	95	$29	**LEONETTI** Cabernet Sauvignon Washington **1991**
14	93	$17	**SILVERADO** Cabernet Sauvignon Stags Leap District **1991**
15	93	$20	**CAYMUS** Cabernet Sauvignon Napa Valley **1991**
16	95	$41	**PIO CESARE** Barolo Ornato **1990**
17	94	$35	**GUENOC** Cabernet Sauvignon Napa Valley Beckstoffer Vineyard Reserve **1991**
18	94	$37	**TAYLOR FLADGATE** Vintage Port Quinta de Vargellas **1991**
19	94	$40	**BENI DI BATASIOLO** Barolo La Corda della Briccolina **1990**
20	94	$45	**GROTH** Cabernet Sauvignon Napa Valley Reserve **1990**
21	93	$26	**KISTLER** Chardonnay Sonoma County **1992**
22	93	$29	**WOODWARD CANYON** Cabernet Sauvignon Columbia Valley **1991**
23	93	$30	**PIPER-HEIDSIECK** Brut Rosé Champagne **NV**
24	93	$35	**FONSECA** Vintage Port Guimaraens **1991**
25	93	$35	**E. GUIGAL** Hermitage **1990**
26	93	$38	**VERGET** Puligny-Montrachet Sous le Puits **1992**
27	93	$41	**NOZZOLE** Il Pareto **1990**
28	93	$45	**PAOLO SCAVINO** Barolo Bric dël Fiasc **1990**
29	93	$45	**GRAHAM** Vintage Port **1991**
30	92	$10	**GUNDLACH BUNDSCHU** Zinfandel Sonoma Valley **1992**
31	98	$12	**YALUMBA** Muscat Rutherglen Museum Show Reserve **NV** (375ml)
32	92	$12	**CHATEAU REYNELLA** Fine Old Tawny Port Old Cave **NV**
33	92	$14	**DOMAINE DU CLOSEL** Savennières Cuvée Spéciale **1992**
34	92	$14	**ROBERT MONDAVI** Zinfandel Napa Valley **1992**
35	92	$18	**THE HESS COLLECTION** Cabernet Sauvignon Napa Valley **1991**
36	92	$22	**CHATEAU STE. MICHELLE** Chardonnay Columbia Valley Chateau Reserve **1992**
37	92	$22	**WYNNS** Cabernet Sauvignon Coonawarra John Riddoch Limited Release **1990**
38	92	$23	**BYRON** Chardonnay Santa Barbara County Reserve **1992**
39	94	$60	**CAPARZO** Brunello di Montalcino Vigna la Casa **1988**
40	94	$81	**BOUCHARD PERE & FILS** Chevalier-Montrachet Domaines du Château de Beaune **1992**
41	91	$10	**CAYMUS** Sauvignon Blanc Napa Valley Barrel Fermented **1992**
42	91	$10	**HOGUE** Chardonnay Columbia Valley **1992**
43	91	$11	**GEORGES DUBOEUF** Moulin-à-Vent Aged in Oak **1991**
44	91	$12	**WYNNS** Chardonnay Coonawarra **1992**
45	91	$12	**RAVENSWOOD** Zinfandel Sonoma County **1992**
46	92	$25	**DOMAINES SCHLUMBERGER** Gewürztraminer Alsace Grand Cru Kessler **1989**
47	92	$25	**TRIMBACH** Riesling Alsace Cuvée Frédéric Emile **1989**
48	92	$25	**DR. LOOSEN** Riesling Spätlese Mosel Urziger Würzgarten **1993**
49	92	$25	**DALLA VALLE** Cabernet Sauvignon Napa Valley **1991**

*PRICE ON RELEASE

Top 100: Best Wines Released in 1994

RANK	SCORE	PRICE*	WINE
50	92	$25	**AU BON CLIMAT** Chardonnay Santa Barbara County Bien Nacido Vineyard Le Bouge D'à côté **1992**
51	92	$26	**CASTELLO DI VOLPAIA** Coltassala **1990**
52	92	$28	**ROBERT MONDAVI** Chardonnay Napa Valley Reserve **1992**
53	92	$28	**KUMEU RIVER** Chardonnay Kumeu **1992**
54	92	$30	**KISTLER** Chardonnay Russian River Valley Dutton Ranch **1992**
55	92	$30	**PONZI** Pinot Noir Oregon Reserve **1992**
56	92	$35	**GOULD CAMPBELL** Vintage Port **1991**
57	91	$15	**GLORIA FERRER** Chardonnay Carneros **1992**
58	91	$15	**ST. FRANCIS** Chardonnay Sonoma Valley Estate Reserve **1992**
59	91	$16	**TRUCHARD** Chardonnay Napa Valley Carneros **1992**
60	91	$17	**BERINGER** Chardonnay Napa Valley Private Reserve **1992**
61	91	$18	**PESQUERA** Ribera del Duero Crianza **1991**
62	91	$18	**CUNE** Rioja Viña Real Gran Reserva **1985**
63	91	$19	**CLOUDY BAY** Chardonnay Marlborough **1992**
64	90	$10	**MCWILLIAMS** Chardonnay South Eastern Australia Mount Pleasant **1992**
65	90	$10	**PAUL THOMAS** Chardonnay Columbia Valley **1993**
66	90	$10	**FOREST GLEN** Chardonnay Sonoma County **1992**
67	91	$20	**ROBERT PECOTA** Cabernet Sauvignon Napa Valley Kara's Vineyard **1991**
68	91	$23	**DEHLINGER** Pinot Noir Russian River Valley Reserve **1991**
69	91	$25	**MUMM** Cuvée Napa DVX Napa Valley **1990**
70	91	$25	**AU BON CLIMAT** Pinot Noir Santa Barbara County Bien Nacido Vineyard La Bauge Au-dessus **1991**
71	91	$30	**DOMAINE DROUHIN** Pinot Noir Oregon Laurène **1992**
72	91	$26	**MARCARINI** Barolo Brunate **1990**
73	90	$12	**JACKY JANODET** Morgon **1991**
74	90	$14	**RIDGE** Zinfandel Paso Robles Dusi Ranch **1992**

*PRICE ON RELEASE

RANK	SCORE	PRICE*	WINE
75	90	$14	**E. & J. GALLO** Zinfandel Dry Creek Valley Frei Ranch Vineyard Gallo Sonoma **1990**
76	90	$14	**BODEGAS ISMAEL ARROYO** Ribera del Duero Mesoneros de Castilla Crianza **1990**
77	91	$28	**ALTESINO** Brunello di Montalcino **1988**
78	91	$29	**ARGIANO** Brunello di Montalcino **1988**
79	91	$30	**DAVID BRUCE** Pinot Noir Santa Cruz Mountains Estate Reserve **1990**
80	91	$34	**BEAUX FRERES** Pinot Noir Willamette Valley Unfined and Unfiltered **1992**
81	90	$15	**LUCIEN CROCHET** Sancerre **1992**
82	90	$15	**GREENWOOD** Ridge Pinot Noir Anderson Valley Roederer Estate Vineyards **1992**
83	90	$15	**MARKHAM** Chardonnay Napa Valley Barrel Fermented **1992**
84	90	$15	**A. RAFANELLI** Cabernet Sauvignon Dry Creek Valley Unfiltered **1991**
85	90	$15	**CHATEAU MONTELENA** Cabernet Napa Valley Calistoga Cuvée **1992**
86	90	$16	**DOMAINE DENIS GAUDRY** Pouilly-Fumé Coteaux du Petit Boisgibault **1992**
87	90	$18	**SWANSON** Sangiovese Napa Valley **1992**
88	91	$35	**POGGIO ANTICO** Brunello di Montalcino **1988**
89	90	$16	**ROEDERER ESTATE** Brut Anderson Valley **NV**
90	90	$16	**STEFANO FARINA** Barolo **1989**
91	90	$16	**SEQUOIA GROVE** Cabernet Sauvignon Napa Valley **1990**
92	90	$16	**ST. CLEMENT** Chardonnay Napa Valley Carneros **1992**
93	90	$17	**PUNSET** Barbaresco **1989**
94	91	$39	**ROBERT CHEVILLON** Nuits-St.-Georges Les Vaucrains **1991**
95	90	$18	**GROTH** Cabernet Sauvignon Napa Valley **1991**
96	90	$18	**BELVEDERE** Chardonnay Sonoma County Preferred Stock **1992**
97	90	$18	**ROBERT MONDAVI** Cabernet Sauvignon Napa Valley Unfiltered **1991**
98	90	$19	**ANDREW WILL** Merlot Washington **1992**
99	90	$19	**ROCHIOLI** Pinot Noir Russian River Valley **1991**
100	91	$45	**G. ROUMIER** Bonnes Mares **1991**

Top 100: Best Wines Released in 1993

RANK	SCORE	PRICE*	WINE
1	100	$80	CHATEAU LATOUR Pauillac **1990**
2	96	$60	GAJA Barolo Sperss **1989**
3	97	$40	SILVERADO Cabernet Sauvignon Napa Valley Limited Reserve **1990**
4	94	$14	CHATEAU LA LOUVIERE Pessac-Léognan **1990**
5	95	$83	LOUIS LATOUR Corton-Charlemagne **1990**
6	97	$40	CHATEAU PICHON-LONGUEVILLE Comtesse de Lalande Pauillac **1990**
7	94	$15	MOUNT VEEDER Cabernet Sauvignon Napa Valley **1990**
8	96	$42	ORNELLAIA Tuscany Vino da Tavola **1990**
9	95	$26	CHATEAU LAGRANGE St.-Julien **1990**
10	97	$85	CHATEAU LAFITE-ROTHSCHILD Pauillac **1990**
11	98	$139	GAJA Barbaresco Sorì San Lorenzo **1989**
12	96	$32	CHATEAU LE GAY Pomerol **1990**
13	96	$26	LEONETTI Cabernet Sauvignon Washington **1990**
14	97	$150	E. GUIGAL Côte-Rôtie La Turque **1989**
15	98	$400	CHATEAU PETRUS Pomerol **1990**
16	96	$63	CHATEAU TROTANOY Pomerol **1990**
17	96	$65	CA' DEI GANCIA Barolo Cannubi **1989**
18	95	$25	CHATEAU ST. JEAN Johannisberg Riesling Late Harvest Alexander Valley Special Selection **1989** (375ml)
19	95	$29	CHATEAU GRAND-PUY-LACOSTE Pauillac **1990**
20	95	$30	CHATEAU CANON-LA-GAFFELIERE St.-Emilion **1990**
21	95	$30	CHATEAU LAGRANGE Pomerol **1990**
22	95	$33	CHATEAU CORDEILLAN-BAGES Pauillac **1990**
23	95	$45	PAOLO SCAVINO Barolo Bric dël Fiasc **1989**
24	95	$50	LUCIANO SANDRONE Barolo Cannubi Boschis **1989**

RANK	SCORE	PRICE*	WINE
25	94	$24	CHATEAU LARMANDE St.-Emilion **1990**
26	94	$25	CHATEAU COS-LABORY St.-Estèphe **1990**
27	94	$28	CHATEAU BOURGENEUF Pomerol **1990**
28	94	$28	CHATEAU LA CROIX DE GAY Pomerol **1990**
29	94	$30	BADIA A COLTIBUONO Sangioveto **1988**
30	94	$30	CHATEAU CLERC-MILON Pauillac **1990**
31	94	$32	G. MASCARELLO Barbaresco Marcarini **1988**
32	94	$38	BENI DI BATASIOLO Barolo La Corda della Briccolina **1989**
33	95	$45	CHATEAU BEAUSEJOUR-DUFFAU-LA-GARROSSE St.-Emilion **1990**
34	96	$195	LOUIS LATOUR Montrachet **1990**
35	94	$71	DOMAINE DES COMTES LAFON Meursault Désirée **1990**
36	95	$150	DOMAINE LEFLAIVE Bâtard-Montrachet **1990**
37	93	$20	CHATEAU DE PEZ St.-Estèphe **1990**
38	93	$20	DUCKHORN Cabernet Sauvignon Napa Valley **1990**
39	93	$22	CHATEAU LES ORMES DE PEZ St.-Estèphe **1990**
40	93	$22	CHATEAU SMITH HAUT-LAFITTE Pessac-Léognan **1990**
41	93	$22	CHATEAU PAVIE-DECESSE St.-Emilion **1990**
42	93	$23	PRUNOTTO Barolo **1988**
43	93	$23	WILLIAMS-SELYEM Pinot Noir Russian River Valley **1991**
44	94	$24	PAHLMEYER Chardonnay Napa Valley **1991**
45	93	$24	TALBOTT Chardonnay Monterey **1990**
46	93	$23	DR. LOOSEN Riesling Auslese Mosel Wehlener Sonnenuhr **1992**
47	93	$25	DALLA VALLE Cabernet Sauvignon Napa Valley **1990**
48	93	$31	CHATEAU LEOVILLE-BARTON St.-Julien **1990**
49	93	$31	CHATEAU TALBOT St.-Julien **1990**

*PRICE ON RELEASE

Top 100: Best Wines Released in 1993

RANK	SCORE	PRICE*	WINE
50	94	$80	**VEUVE CLICQUOT** La Grande Dame **1985**
51	94	$80	**DOMAINE DE CHEVALIER** Pessac-Léognan **1989**
52	94	$110	**DOMAINE DE LA ROMANÉE-CONTI** Echézeaux **1990**
53	92	$14	**BYRON** Chardonnay Santa Barbara County **1991**
54	92	$15	**BONNY DOON** Muscat Canelli Vin de Glacière **1992** (375ml)
55	92	$16	**ROSEMOUNT** Syrah Show McLaren Vale Reserve **1990**
56	92	$17	**GUNDERLOCH** Riesling Spätlese Rheinhessen Nackenheimer Rothenberg **1992**
57	92	$18	**CAYMUS** Conundrum **1991**
58	93	$36	**CHATEAU LE BON PASTEUR** Pomerol **1990**
59	93	$37	**RUINART** Brut Champagne R de Ruinart **NV**
60	92	$34	**DOMAINE GUY ROULOT** Meursault Les Tessons Clos de Mon Plaisir **1990**
61	91	$9	**MICHELE CHIARLO** Barbera d'Asti **1990**
62	91	$12	**COLUMBIA** Chardonnay Columbia Valley Woodburne Cuvée **1991**
63	91	$13	**GREENWOOD RIDGE** Zinfandel Sonoma County Scherrer Vineyards **1991**
64	91	$13	**WILLIAM WHEELER** Chardonnay Sonoma County **1991**
65	91	$15	**GUENOC** Meritage Lake County **1990**
66	91	$15	**NAVARRO** Chardonnay Anderson Valley Premiere Reserve **1991**
67	91	$15	**SHAFER** Chardonnay Napa Valley Barrel Select **1991**
68	91	$15	**ROMBAUER** Chardonnay Carneros **1991**
69	91	$15	**MARKHAM** Merlot Napa Valley **1990**
70	91	$16	**ALPHONSE MELLOT** Sancerre Domaine La Moussière **1991**
71	91	$16	**COVEY RUN** Chardonnay Yakima Valley Reserve **1990**
72	91	$18	**RIDGE** Zinfandel Dry Creek Valley Lytton Springs **1991**
73	91	$17	**CHATEAU FONTENIL** Fronsac **1990**
74	91	$17	**DOMAINE DE LA VIELLE JULIENNE** Châteauneuf-du-Pape **1990**
75	91	$17	**CLOS PEGASE** Cabernet Sauvignon Napa Valley **1990**
76	91	$18	**STAG'S LEAP WINE CELLARS** Cabernet Sauvignon Napa Valley **1990**
77	90	$9	**MARKHAM** Sauvignon Blanc Napa Valley **1991**
78	90	$9	**BYRON** Sauvignon Blanc Santa Barbara County **1992**
79	90	$10	**ESTATE WILLIAM BACCALA** Merlot Napa Valley **1990**
80	90	$10	**MEEKER** Zinfandel Dry Creek Valley Gold Leaf Cuvée **1990**
81	90	$11	**CHATEAU SOUVERAIN** Cabernet Sauvignon Alexander Valley **1990**
82	90	$11	**SELBACH-OSTER** Riesling Spätlese Mosel Zeltinger Sonnenuhr **1992**
83	91	$21	**DOMAINE RENE MANUEL** Meursault Clos de la Baronne **1991**
84	91	$25	**LOUIS JADOT** Meursault **1990**
85	92	$23	**MICHELE CHIARLO** Barolo **1988**
86	91	$25	**MARCARINI** Barolo Brunate **1989**
87	90	$13	**FIRESTONE** Chardonnay Santa Ynez Barrel Fermented **1991**
88	90	$13	**BERINGER** Cabernet Sauvignon Knights Valley **1990**
89	90	$14	**ESTANCIA** Meritage Alexander Valley **1990**
90	91	$31	**LOUIS LATOUR** Puligny-Montrachet **1990**
91	91	$33	**E. GUIGAL** Hermitage **1989**
92	91	$35	**PONZI** Pinot Noir Willamette Valley 20th Anniversary Edition **1990**
93	92	$22	**LEONETTI** Merlot Washington **1991**
94	92	$30	**E.&J. GALLO** Chardonnay Northern Sonoma Estate **1991**
95	92	$35	**DRAPPIER** Champagne Carte d'Or **1989**
96	92	$35	**ROEDERER ESTATE** Brut Anderson Valley L'Ermitage **1989**
97	92	$40	**CHATEAU DE BEAUCASTEL** Châteauneuf-du-Pape **1990**
98	90	$16	**PODERE IL PALAZZINO** Chianti Classico **1990**
99	90	$20	**FERRARI-CARANO** Siena Sonoma County **1991**
100	90	$30	**DOMAINE DROUHIN** Pinot Noir **1990**

*PRICE ON RELEASE

Top 100: Best Wines Released in 1992

RANK	SCORE	PRICE*	WINE
1	98	$45	**CHATEAU LONGUEVILLE AU BARON DE BARON-LONGUEVILLE** Pauillac **1989**
2	96	$32	**CHATEAU CLERC-MILON** Pauillac **1989**
3	99	$100	**CHATEAU MARGAUX** Margaux **1989**
4	99	$105	**CHATEAU MOUTON-ROTHSCHILD** Pauillac **1989**
5	100	$140	**COMTE DE VOGUE** Musigny Cuvée Vieilles Vignes **1990**
6	96	$25	**LEONETTI** Cabernet Sauvignon Washington **1989**
7	92	$9	**ROSEMOUNT** Shiraz South Eastern Australia **1990**
8	92	$13	**SELVAPIANA** Chianti Rufina **1990**
9	98	$46	**CHATEAU LYNCH-BAGES** Pauillac **1989**
10	96	$81	**JOSEPH DROUHIN** Charmes-Chambertin **1990**
11	100	$410	**CHATEAU PETRUS** Pomerol **1989**
12	96	$45	**CHATEAU L'EGLISE CLINET** Pomerol **1989**
13	98	$88	**CHATEAU LA FLEUR DE GAY** Pomerol **1989**
14	97	$100	**CHATEAU LATOUR** Pauillac **1989**
15	97	$120	**CHATEAU HAUT-BRION** Pessac-Léognan **1989**
16	98	$150	**E. GUIGAL** Côte-Rôtie La Landonne **1988**
17	96	$125	**GAJA** Barbaresco Sorì San Lorenzo **1988**
18	95	$26	**CHATEAU LARMANDE** St.-Emilion **1989**
19	95	$29	**CHATEAU LAGRANGE** St.-Julien **1989**
20	95	$30	**CHATEAU DE FIEUZAL** Pessac-Léognan **1989**
21	95	$34	**ANSELMI** Recioto di Soave Dei Capitelli **1988**
22	95	$30	**CHATEAU CHASSE-SPLEEN** Moulis **1989**
23	95	$37	**DOMAINE COSTE-CAUMARTIN** Pommard Clos des Boucherottes **1990**
24	95	$40	**CHATEAU BEYCHEVELLE** St.-Julien **1989**
25	95	$32	**CHATEAU CALON-SEGUR** St.-Estèphe **1989**
26	95	$40	**CHATEAU MONTROSE** St.-Estèphe **1989**
27	95	$50	**KENDALL-JACKSON** Cardinale Meritage California **1987**
28	95	$62	**PAUL JABOULET AINE** Hermitage La Chapelle **1990**
29	95	$65	**HEITZ** Cabernet Sauvignon Napa Valley Martha's Vineyard **1987**
30	94	$22	**MADER** Riesling Alsace Rosacker **1990**
31	94	$26	**CHATEAU D'ARMAILLIACQ** Pauillac **1989**
32	94	$28	**CHATEAU LANGOA-BARTON** St.-Julien **1989**
33	92	$11	**PIERRE SPARR TOKAY** Pinot Gris Alsace Cuvée Réserve **1990**
34	92	$12	**CUNE** Rioja Contino Reserva **1982**
35	93	$20	**WILLIAMS-SELYEM** Pinot Noir Russian River Valley **1990**
36	93	$25	**SEQUOIA GROVE** Cabernet Sauvignon Napa Valley Estate Reserve **1989**
37	93	$28	**KISTLER** Chardonnay Sonoma Valley Durell Vineyard Sand Hill **1990**
38	94	$39	**BOUCHARD PERE & FILS** Pommard Premier Cru Domaines du Chateau de Beaune **1990**
39	94	$49	**DOMAINE RAMONET** Chassagne-Montrachet Les Ruchottes **1990**
40	94	$52	**BOUCHARD PERE & FILS** Volnay Caillerets Ancienne Cuvée Carnot Domaine de Château de Beaune **1989**
41	94	$60	**CAYMUS** Cabernet Sauvignon Napa Valley Special Selection **1988**
42	95	$97	**DOM PERIGNON** Champagne **1983**
43	95	$188	**DOMAINE ETIENNE SAUZET** Bâtard Montrachet **1990**
44	92	$16	**MERRYVALE** Cabernet Sauvignon Napa Valley **1989**
44	92	$16	**RAVENSWOOD** Zinfandel Napa Valley Dickerson **1990**
46	92	$17	**FATTORIA DI FELSINA** Chianti Classico Berardenga Riserva **1988**
47	92	$18	**SAN FELICE** Chianti Classico Il Poggio Riserva **1988**
48	92	$19	**KUNDE ESTATE** Chardonnay Sonoma Valley Estate Reserve **1990**
49	92	$20	**SULLIVAN** Merlot Napa Valley **1989**
50	91	$9	**CHATEAU STE. MICHELLE** Sauvignon Blanc Columbia Valley **1990**
52	93	$22	**CHATEAU BOUSCAUT** Pessac-Léognan **1989**
53	93	$22	**CHATEAU MEYNEY** St.-Estèphe **1989**

*PRICE ON RELEASE

Top 100: Best Wines Released in 1992

RANK	SCORE	PRICE*	WINE
54	92	$45	**ARROWOOD** Chardonnay Réserve Spéciale **1990** (1.5 liter)
55	92	$24	**FLORA SPRINGS** Chardonnay Napa Valley Barrel Fermented **1990**
56	92	$27	**WOODWARD CANYON** Cabernet Sauvignon Columbia Valley **1989**
57	92	$28	**ROBERT MONDAVI** Pinot Noir Napa Valley Reserve **1990**
58	92	$28	**CHARLES KRUG** Cabernet Sauvignon Napa Valley Vintage Selection **1986**
59	92	$30	**ROCHIOLI** Pinot Noir Russian River Valley Reserve **1990**
60	93	$35	**MARQUES DE MURRIETA** Rioja Gran Reserva **1975**
61	93	$35	**KENWOOD** Cabernet Sauvignon Sonoma Valley Artist Series **1989**
62	93	$35	**DOMAINE ZIND-HUMBRECHT** Riesling Alsace Brand **1990**
63	92	$15	**HUGEL TOKAY** Pinot Gris Alsace Jubilée **1990**
64	92	$20	**MARQUES DE MURRIETA** Rioja Reserva White **1986**
65	92	$25	**FREEMARK ABBEY** Johannisberg Riesling Late Harvest Napa Valley Edelwein Gold **1991** (375ml)
66	92	$28	**KUMEU RIVER** Chardonnay Kumeu **1991**
67	92	$29	**BLANC DE LYNCH-BAGES** Bordeaux **1990**
68	92	$30	**LOUIS JADOT** Vosne-Romanée **1990**
69	91	$12	**PEACHY CANYON** Zinfandel Paso Robles Westside **1990**
70	91	$12	**FATTORIA DI FELSINA** Chianti Classico Berardenga **1990**
71	91	$13	**WHITE OAK** Zinfandel Dry Creek Valley Saunders Vineyard **1990**
72	91	$14	**MIETZ** Merlot Sonoma County **1989**
73	91	$14	**BENZIGER** Chardonnay Carneros Premiere Vineyard **1990**
74	91	$14	**CONCHA Y TORO** Cabernet Sauvignon Maipo Puente Alto Vineyard Don Melchor Private Reserve **1988**
75	91	$15	**BURGESS** Chardonnay Napa Valley Triere Vineyard **1990**
76	91	$18	**SHAFER** Merlot Napa Valley **1990**
77	91	$19	**HARDY'S** Chardonnay South Australia Eileen Hardy **1999**
78	91	$15	**KENWOOD** Cabernet Sauvignon Sonoma Valley **1989**
79	91	$18	**RODNEY STRONG** Cabernet Sauvignon Northern Sonoma Alexander's Crown Vineyard **1998**
80	91	$10	**CHALK HILL** Late Harvest Sémillon Chalk Hill **1986** (375ml)
81	91	$20	**CAPE MENTELLE** Chardonnay Margaret River **1990**
82	91	$20	**TUALATIN** Chardonnay Willamette Valley Selected Private Reserve **1989**
83	91	$20	**PESQUERA** Ribera del Duero **1989**
84	91	$21	**ALDO CONTERNO** Barbera d'Alba Conca Tre Pile **1989**
85	92	$39	**MACULAN** Cabernet Sauvignon Breganze Fratta **1990**
86	92	$40	**DOMAINE DAUVISSAT-CAMUS** Chablis Les Preuses **1990**
87	91	$27	**HENSCHKE** Shiraz Barossa Ranges Keyneton Hill of Grace **1987**
88	91	$28	**PRODUTTORI DEL BARBARESCO** Barbaresco Seleziốne del Trentennio 30 **1988**
89	91	$28	**M. CHAPOUTIER** Hermitage Monier de la Sizeranne **1990**
90	91	$38	**LOUIS ROEDERER** Brut Premier **NV**
91	91	$32	**JOSEPH DROUHIN** Meursault **1990**
92	90	$10	**BOEGER** Zinfindel El Dorado Walker Vineyard **1990**
93	90	$11	**JOSEPH PHELPS** Gewürztraminer California **1991**
94	90	$11	**FATTORIA LE BOCCE** Chianti Classico **1990**
95	90	$11	**VITICCIO** Chianti Classico **1990**
96	90	$12	**GRGICH HILLS** Fume Blanc Napa Valley **1990**
97	90	$13	**MURPHY-GOODE** Fumé Blanc Alexander Valley Barrel Fermented Reserve **1990**
98	90	$12	**COLUMBIA** Cabernet Sauvignon Columbia Valley **1989**
99	90	$16	**M. CHAPOUTIER** Châteauneuf-du-Pape Le Bernardine **1990**
100	90	$17	**SANFORD** Pinot Noir Santa Barbara County **1990**

*PRICE ON RELEASE

Top 100: Best Wines Released in 1991

RANK	SCORE	PRICE*	WINE
1	97	$35	**CHATEAU DE BEAUCASTEL** Châteauneuf-du-Pape **1989**
2	100	$89	**CHATEAU MOUTON-ROTHSCHILD** Pauillac **1988**
3	98	$60	**CAYMUS** Cabernet Sauvignon Napa Valley Special Selection **1987**
4	96	$26	**CHATEAU LAGRANGE** St.-Julien **1988**
5	98	$60	**SASSICAIA 1988**
6	97	$75	**CHATEAU MARGAUX** Margaux **1988**
7	98	$95	**CHATEAU HAUT-BRION** Pessac-Léognan **1988**
8	95	$30	**CHATEAU MONTELENA** Napa Valley Cabernet Sauvignon **1987**
9	95	$30	**CHATEAU PICHON-BARON** Pauillac **1988**
10	95	$35	**CHATEAU LYNCH-BAGES** Pauillac **1988**
11	95	$34	**DR. BÜRKLIN-WOLF** Riesling Auslese Rheinpfalz Wachenheimer Gerümpel **1989**
12	96	$34	**THE HESS COLLECTION** Cabernet Sauvignon Napa Valley Reserve **1987**
13	96	$60	**DOMAINE D'AUVENAY** Meursault Les Narvaux **1989**
14	96	$65	**CHATEAU PALMER** Margaux **1988**
15	97	$92	**JOSEPH DROUHIN** Corton-Charlemagne **1989**
16	97	$95	**DOMAINE D'AUVENAY** Puligny-Montrachet Les Folatières **1989**
17	96	$97	**LOUIS JADOT** Chambertin Clos de Bèze **1988**
18	95	$30	**DOMAINE DE MARCOUX** Châteauneuf-du-Pape Vieilles Vignes **1989**
19	95	$26	**WOODWARD CANYON** Charbonneau Walla Walla County **1988**
20	94	$17	**THE HESS COLLECTION** Cabernet Sauvignon Napa Valley **1987**
21	94	$18	**CHAPPELLET** Cabernet Sauvignon Napa Valley Signature Reserve **1987**
22	94	$25	**DR. BÜRKLIN-WOLF** Riesling Auslese Rheinpfalz Forster Pechstein **1989**
23	93	$16	**FONTODI** Chianti Classico Riserva **1985**
24	93	$16	**QUAIL RIDGE** Cabernet Sauvignon Napa Valley **1987**
25	92	$12	**MERIDIAN** Cabernet Sauvignon Paso Robles **1988**
26	92	$12	**HOGUE** Merlot Washington **1989**
27	93	$18	**LEONETTI** Merlot Washington **1989**
28	93	$19	**LES CAILLOUX** Châteauneuf-du-Pape **1989**
29	94	$31	**EGON MÜLLER** Riesling Spätlese Mosel-Saar-Ruwer Scharzhofberger **1989**
30	94	$25	**CHATEAU LARRIVET-HAUT-BRION** Pessac-Léognan **1988**
31	94	$26	**CHATEAU CLERC-MILON** Pauillac **1988**
32	94	$27	**CHATEAU PAVIE-DECESSE** St.-Emilion **1988**
33	93	$33	**DOMAINE DANIEL RION** Nuits-St.-Georges Les Lavières **1988**
34	94	$30	**CHATEAU HAUT-BAILLY** Pessac-Léognan **1988**
35	94	$50	**JEAN GROS** Vosne-Romanée Clos de Réas **1988**
36	93	$13	**GEYSER PEAK** Johannisberg Riesling Mendocino County Late Harvest Selected Dried Berry **1990** (375ml)
37	94	$42	**F. CHAUVENET** Meursault Genevrières **1989**
38	95	$55	**CHATEAU COS D'ESTOURNEL** St.-Estèphe **1988**
39	95	$60	**HEITZ** Cabernet Sauvignon Napa Valley Martha's Vineyard **1986**
40	95	$180	**JOSEPH DROUHIN** Montrachet Marquis de Laguiche **1988**
41	94	$36	**DUNN** Cabernet Sauvignon Howell Mountain **1987**
42	94	$40	**BERINGER** Cabernet Sauvignon Napa Valley Private Reserve **1987**
43	95	$91	**DOMAINE MEO-CAMUZET** Vosne-Romanée Au Cros-Parantoux **1989**
44	93	$18	**HOUSE OF NOBILO** Chardonnay Gisborne Tietjen Vineyard Reserve **1989**
45	94	$45	**PHILIPPE PICHON** Condrieu **1989**
46	94	$49	**ORNELLAIA 1988**
47	94	$54	**CHARTRON ET TREBUCHET** Chassagne-Montrachet Les Morgeots **1989**
48	92	$15	**CHATEAU DE MARBUZET** St.-Estèphe **1988**
49	92	$12	**MARKHAM** Chardonnay Napa Valley **1989**
50	92	$33	**LOUIS JADOT** Beaune Bucherottes **1988**
51	92	$17	**CHATEAU LES FIEFS DE LAGRANGE** St.-Julien **1988**

* PRICE ON RELEASE

Top 100: Best Wines Released in 1991

RANK	SCORE	PRICE*	WINE
52	92	$30	**DOMAINE FRANÇOIS LEGROS** Chambolle-Musigny Les Noirots **1989**
53	92	$18	**CHATEAU DE FRANCE** Pessac-Léognan **1988**
54	92	$16	**CHATEAU ST. JEAN** Cabernet Sauvignon Alexander Valley **1987**
55	93	$32	**CA' DEL BOSCO** Maurizio Zanela Signature **1988**
56	93	$18	**REVERE** Chardonnay Napa Valley Reserve **1988**
57	92	$32	**ROSSIGNOL-FEVRIER** Volnay **1988**
58	91	$13	**LATAH CREEK** Cabernet Sauvignon Washington Limited Bottling **1988**
59	92	$32	**CHOPIN-GROFFIER** Vougeot **1988**
60	91	$11	**LATAH CREEK** Merlot Washington Limited Bottling **1989**
61	92	$38	**JOSEPH DROUHIN** Morey St.-Denis Monts-Luisants **1988**
62	93	$55	**POGGIO ANTICO** Brunello di Montalcino Riserva **1985**
63	93	$19	**WOODWARD CANYON** Chardonnay Columbia Valley **1990**
64	93	$32	**ISOLE E OLENA** Cepparello **1988**
65	90	$12	**DOMAINE LE PEU DE LA MORIETTE** Vouvray **1989**
66	93	$24	**WOODWARD CANYON** Cabernet Sauvignon Columbia Valley **1988**
67	94	$55	**CHATEAU DE MEURSAULT** Meursault **1986**
68	93	$45	**PAUL JABOULET AINE** Hermitage La Chapelle **1989**
69	92	$32	**REICHSGRAF VON KESSELSTATT** Riesling Auslese Mosel-Saar-Ruwer Oberemmeler Karlsberg **1989**
70	92	$35	**JOH. JOS. PRÜM** Riesling Auslese Mosel-Saar-Ruwer Wehlener Sonnenuhr **1989**
71	91	$10	**FETZER** Johannisberg Riesling Sonoma County Late Harvest Reserve **1988** (375ml)
72	91	$14	**MERIDIAN** Syrah Paso Robles **1988**
73	91	$13	**ELIO ALTARE** Barbera d'Alba **1989**
74	92	$17	**CLOS DU VAL** Cabernet Sauvignon Stags Leap District **1987**
75	92	$20	**FATTORIA VALTELLINA** Chanti Classico Giorgio Regni Riserva **1985**
76	91	$13	**FONTODI** Chianti Classico **1988**
77	90	$10	**ARTERBERRY** Chardonnay Willamette Valley **1988**
78	91	$13	**VILLA CAFAGGIO** Chianti Classico Riserva **1985**
79	92	$18	**KENWOOD** Cabernet Sauvignon Sonoma Valley Jack London Ranch **1987**
80	93	$26	**GRAHAM** Port Malvedos **1988**
81	93	$23	**CHATEAU HAUT-BAGES-AVEROUS** Pauillac **1988**
82	92	$17	**MONTICELLO** Chardonnay Napa Valley Corley Reserve **1988**
83	91	$8	**ROSEMOUNT** Shiraz Hunter Valley **1989**
84	93	$30	**CALERA** Pinot Noir San Benito County Jensen **1988**
85	91	$12	**PRESTON WINE CELLARS** Chardonnay Washington Barrel Fermented **1989**
86	91	$13	**KUNDE** Chardonay Sonoma Valley **1990**
87	92	$16	**ROSEMOUNT** Chardonnay Hunter Valley Show Reserve **1989**
88	91	$18	**CAYMUS** Conundrum California **1990**
89	92	$20	**CHATEAU MONBRISON** Margaux **1988**
90	92	$28	**SAN FELICE** Brunello di Montalcino Campogiovanni **1986**
91	90	$9	**FLORA SPRINGS** Sauvignon Blanc Napa Valley **1990**
92	91	$24	**IRON HORSE** Brut Sonoma Valley Green Valley Late Disgorged **1986**
93	90	$13	**REICHSGRAF VON KESSELSTATT** Riesling Spätlese Mosel-Saar-Ruwer Scharzhofberger **1989**
94	90	$12	**ROCCHE COSTAMAGNA** Barbera d'Alba **1988**
95	91	$15	**R.H. PHILLIPS** Syrah California EXP **1988**
96	90	$14	**LAR DE LARES** Tierra de Barros Gran Reserva **1982**
97	91	$20	**ACACIA** Pinot Noir Carneros Napa Valley St. Clair **1988**
98	92	$24	**ANDERSON'S CONN VALLEY** Cabernet Sauvignon Napa Valley Estate Reserve **1988**
99	92	$37	**CASTELLO BANFI** Brunello di Montalcino Poggio all'Oro **1985**
100	91	$20	**SCHARFFENBERGER** Blanc de Blancs Mendocino County **1986**

*PRICE ON RELEASE

Top 100: Best Wines Released in 1990

RANK	SCORE	PRICE*	WINE
1	95	$30	**BERINGER** Cabernet Sauvignon Napa Valley Private Reserve **1986**
2	99	$50	**CAYMUS** Cabernet Sauvignon Napa Valley Special Selection **1985**
3	96	$34	**CHARTRON & TREBUCHET** Chassagne-Montrachet Les Morgeots **1988**
4	95	$36	**POGGIO ANTICO** Brunello di Montalcino **1985**
5	98	$60	**HEITZ** Cabernet Sauvignon Napa Valley Martha's Vineyard **1985**
6	97	$68	**OPUS ONE** Napa Valley **1987**
7	95	$35	**DANIEL RION** Nuits-St.-Georges Les Vignes Rondes **1987**
8	98	$24	**JOH. JOS. PRÜM** Riesling Spätlese Wehlener Sonnenuhr (Cask 2) **1988**
9	96	$36	**SPOTTSWOODE** Cabernet Sauvignon Napa Valley **1987**
10	95	$19	**WOODWARD CANYON** Cabernet Sauvignon Columbia Valley **1987**
11	95	$20	**DUCKHORN** Cabernet Sauvignon Napa Valley **1987**
12	96	$18	**C. VON SCHUBERT** Riesling Spätlese Mosel-Saar-Ruwer Maximin Grünhauser Abstberg **1988**
13	95	$24	**WILLIAM HILL** Cabernet Sauvignon Napa Valley Reserve **1987**
14	95	$17	**ZILLIKEN** Riesling Spätlese Mosel-Saar-Ruwer Saarburger Rausch **1988**
15	96	$35	**SILVERADO** Cabernet Sauvignon Napa Valley Limited Reserve **1986**
16	95	$25	**LA JOTA** Cabernet Sauvignon Howell Mountain **1987**
17	96	$45	**BOLLINGER** Brut Champagne Grande Année **1985**
18	95	$30	**DUNN** Cabernet Sauvignon Howell Mountain **1986**
19	95	$30	**GROTH** Cabernet Sauvignon Napa Valley Reserve **1985**
20	96	$81	**EMMANUEL ROUGET** Echézeaux **1988**
21	95	$75	**BODEGAS VEGA SICILIA** Ribera del Duero Unico **1979**
22	95	$19	**DOPFF AU MOULIN** Riesling Alsace Grand Cru Schoenenbourg **1988**
23	94	$20	**ST. FRANCIS** Merlot Sonoma Valley Reserve **1986**
24	94	$22	**CAYMUS** Cabernet Sauvignon Napa Valley Estate Bottled **1986**
25	94	$25	**SANFORD** Chardonnay Santa Barbara County Barrel Select **1988**
26	94	$26	**KISTLER** Chardonnay Sonoma Valley Kistler Estate **1988**
27	94	$35	**GIUSEPPE MASCARELLO & FIGLIO** Barolo Santo Stefano di Perno **1985**
28	94	$34	**SIMI** Cabernet Sauvignon Alexander Valley Reserve **1985**
29	94	$26	**SILVER OAK** Cabernet Sauvignon Napa Valley **1986**
30	93	$15	**CHATEAU LA TOUR MARTILLAC** Pessac-Léognan Blanc **1987**
31	93	$10	**BENZIGER** Cabernet Sauvignon Sonoma County **1987**
32	95	$35	**STERLING** Napa Valley Reserve **1986**
33	94	$38	**JEAN CHARTRON** Puligny-Montrachet Les Folatières **1988**
34	92	$14	**SILVERADO** Cabernet Sauvignon Napa Valley **1987**
35	93	$37	**LANSON** Brut Champagne **1985**
36	91	$14	**SILVERADO** Merlot Napa Valley **1987**
37	92	$15	**FRANCISCAN** Chardonnay Valley Oakville Estate Reserve **1987**
38	91	$8	**LAR DE BARROS** Tierra de Barros Tinto Reserva **1986**
39	90	$8	**ROSEMOUNT** Shiraz Hunter Valley **1988**
40	93	$16	**CAYMUS** Cabernet Sauvignon Napa Valley **1987**
41	93	$18	**FERRARI-CARANO** Chardonnay Alexander Valley **1988**
42	93	$19	**ARGYLE** Chardonnay Oregon Barrel Fermented **1987**
43	93	$19	**MERRYVALE** Chardonnay Napa Valley **1987**
44	92	$11	**RUTHERFORD RANCH** Cabernet Sauvignon Napa Valley **1985**
45	92	$12	**BYRON** Chardonnay Santa Barbara County **1988**
46	93	$23	**FATTORIA DI FELSINA** Chianti Classico Berardenga Vigneto Rancia Riserva **1985**
47	93	$20	**LOUIS M. MARTINI** Cabernet Sauvignon Sonoma Valley Monte Rosso **1987**
48	93	$20	**MAZZOCCO** Cabernet Sauvignon Alexander Valley Claret Style **1987**

*PRICE ON RELEASE

Top 100: Best Wines Released in 1990

RANK	SCORE	PRICE*	WINE
49	96	$26	**SILVER OAK** Cabernet Sauvignon Alexander Valley **1986**
50	93	$29	**DOMAINE LUCIEN GEOFFROY** Gevrey-Chambertin Clos Prieur **1987**
51	94	$48	**CHATEAU MAGDELAINE** St.-Emilion **1986**
52	93	$24	**CLOS DU BOIS** Chardonnay Alexander Valley Winemaker's Reserve **1987**
53	93	$33	**OLIVIER LEFLAIVE FRERES** Puligny-Montrachet **1987**
54	93	$34	**PODERE IL POGGIOLO** Brunello di Montalcino **1985**
55	93	$37	**MICHEL BOUZEREAU & FILS** Meursault Genevrières **1988**
56	93	$40	**CHATEAU ST. JEAN** Chardonnay Alexander Valley Robert Young Vineyard Reserve **1985** (1.5 liter)
57	95	$99	**E. GUIGAL** Côte-Rôtie La Turque **1986**
58	95	$99	**JEAN GROS** Richebourg **1987**
59	94	$76	**GAJA** Cabernet Sauvignon Darmagi **1986**
60	96	$149	**CHATEAU D'YQUEM** Sauternes **1984**
61	92	$18	**WILLIAMS SELYEM** Pinot Noir Sonoma Coast **1988**
62	92	$19	**FATTORIA VITICCIO** Prunaio **1986**
63	91	$12	**SNOQUALMIE** Merlot Columbia Valley Reserve **1987**
64	91	$20	**CAPEZZANA** Ghiaie della Furba **1985**
65	92	$38	**DOMAINE AUFFREY** Chablis Les Clos **1988**
66	92	$41	**DOMAINE DAUVISSAT-CAMUS** Chablis Les Clos **1988**
67	92	$40	**BODEGAS VEGA SICILIA** Ribera del Duero Valbuena 3.° **1985**
68	91	$15	**SAINTSBURY** Pinot Noir Carneros **1988**
69	91	$15	**EDMUNDS ST. JOHN** Les Fleurs du Chaparral Napa Valley **1987**
70	91	$16	**BROWN BROTHERS** Chardonnay King Valley Family Reserve **1987**
71	92	$22	**FREEMARK ABBEY** Johannisberg Riesling Napa Valley Late Harvest Edelwein Gold **1989** (375ml)
72	92	$24	**LUCIANO SANDRONE** Barolo Cannubi Boschis **1985**
73	92	$24	**ELIO ALTARE** Barolo **1985**
74	92	$27	**CLERICO** Barolo Ciabot Mentin Ginestra **1985**
75	92	$26	**PESQUERA** Ribera del Duero Cosecha Propia Reserva **1986**
76	92	$30	**VILLA BANFI** Brunello di Montalcino **1985**
77	91	$18	**BRIDGEHAMPTON** Chardonnay Long Island Grand Vineyard Selection **1988**
78	90	$12	**CLINE** Oakley Cuvée Contra Costa County **1988**
79	91	$15	**TRIMBACH** Riesling Alsace Cuvée Frédéric Emile **1988**
80	91	$19	**SELVAPIANA** Chianti Rufina Vignetto Bucerchiale Riserva **1985**
81	91	$20	**PONZI** Pinot Noir Willamette Valley Reserve **1987**
82	91	$22	**LEONETTI** Cabernet Sauvignon Washington **1987**
83	91	$22	**DOMAINE MUMM** Brut Carneros Winery Lake Cuvée Napa **1987**
84	92	$32	**E. GUIGAL** Hermitage **1986**
85	92	$36	**PRINCE FLORENT DE MERODE** Corton Renardes **1987**
86	92	$37	**CA' ROME** Barbaresco Maria di Brün **1985**
87	90	$8	**SIMI** Sauvignon Blanc Sonoma County **1988**
88	90	$9	**SILVERADO** Sauvignon Blanc Napa Valley **1988**
89	90	$9	**KENDALL-JACKSON** Sauvignon Blanc Lake County Vintner's Reserve **1989**
90	90	$10	**BODEGAS BERBERANA** Rioja Reserva **1985**
91	90	$10	**A. RAFANELLI** Dry Creek Valley Zinfandel **1988**
92	90	$10	**GRGICH HILLS** Fumé Blanc Napa Valley **1988**
93	90	$10	**SNOQUALMIE** Cabernet Sauvignon Columbia Valley **1987**
94	90	$13	**DOMAINE DU GOUT DE CHAULE** Gigondas **1986**
95	90	$14	**VALFIERI** Barolo **1985**
96	90	$12	**LYTTON SPRINGS** Zinfandel Sonoma County **1988**
97	90	$12	**PRODUTTORI DEL BARBARESCO** Barbaresco **1986**
98	90	$15	**J.J. VINCENT** Pouilly-Fuissé **1988**
99	90	$14	**DOMAINES SCHLUMBERGER** Tokay Pinot Gris Alsace Grand Cru Kitterlé **1988**
100	90	$33	**N. JOLY** Savennières Clos de la Coulée de Serrant **1989**

*PRICE ON RELEASE

Top 100: Best Wines Released in 1989

RANK	SCORE	PRICE*	WINE
1	98	$38	**CAYMUS** Cabernet Sauvignon Special Selection **1984**
2	97	$23	**CHATEAU CLERC MILON 1986**
3	97	$40	**HEITZ** Martha's Vineyard **1984**
4	97	$31	**CHATEAU PICHON-BARON 1986**
5	97	$45	**KENDALL-JACKSON** Cardinale **1985**
6	98	$70	**CHATEAU MARGAUX 1986**
7	98	$80	**CHATEAU CHEVAL BLANC 1986**
8	98	$102	**CHATEAU MOUTON-ROTHSCHILD 1986**
9	97	$50	**CHATEAU PICHON-LALANDE 1986**
10	96	$60	**PENFOLDS** Grange Hermitage **1982**
11	98	$195	**DOMAINE DE LA ROMANEE-CONTI** Romanée-St.-Vivant **1986**
12	98	$250	**DOMAINE DE LA ROMANEE-CONTI** La Tâche **1986**
13	95	$15	**JOHNSON TURNBULL** Vineyard Selection 82 **1986**
14	96	$30	**STERLING** Reserve **1985**
15	95	$15	**SEPPELT** Old Trafford Tawny **NV**
16	95	$63	**DOMAINE MEO-CAMUZET** Vosne-Romanée Aux Brûlées **1986**
17	95	$63	**DOMAINE MEO-CAMUZET** Vosne-Romanée au Cros Parantoux **1987**
18	95	$27	**DUNN** Cabernet Sauvignon Napa Valley **1986**
19	95	$29	**CHATEAU LA DOMINIQUE 1986**
20	95	$30	**SPOTTSWOODE** Cabernet Sauvignon **1986**
21	95	$30	**KENWOOD** Artist Series **1986**
22	95	$30	**BERINGER** Cabernet Sauvignon Private Reserve **1985**
23	95	$35	**ROBERT MONDAVI** Cabernet Sauvignon Reserve **1986**
24	94	$13	**LAUREL GLEN** Counterpoint **1987**
25	94	$14	**SILVERADO** Cabernet Sauvignon **1986**
26	94	$15	**CUVAISON** Cabernet Sauvignon **1986**
27	94	$15	**FROG'S LEAP** Cabernet Sauvignon **1987**
28	92	$9	**ROSEMOUNT** Shiraz **1986**
29	92	$9	**CARNEROS CREEK** Fleur de Carneros Pinot Noir **1987**
30	94	$16	**FERRARI-CARANO** Chardonnay **1987**
31	94	$18	**B.R. COHN** Cabernet Sauvignon **1986**
32	94	$18	**DUCKHORN** Cabernet Sauvignon **1986**
33	94	$18	**BUENA VISTA** Cabernet Sauvignon Private Reserve **1985**
34	94	$19	**CLOS RENE 1986**
35	94	$23	**BERINGER** Cabernet Sauvignon Private Reserve **1984**
36	94	$25	**CASTELLARE DI CASTELLINA** I Sodi di San Niccolò **1986**
37	94	$30	**CASTELLO DI AMA** Chianti Classico Vigneto Bellavista **1985**
38	95	$40	**ROBERT MONDAVI** Cabernet Sauvignon Reserve **1985**
39	95	$40	**DIAMOND CREEK** Volcanic Hill **1987**
40	96	$75	**STAG'S LEAP WINE CELLARS** Cask 23 **1985**
41	95	$50	**SASSICAIA 1986**
42	95	$53	**OPUS ONE 1985**
43	94	$70	**GAJA** Cabernet Sauvignon Darmagi **1985**
44	90	$6	**VALLANA** Barbera **1986**
45	90	$7	**SAUSAL** Zinfandel **1986**
46	90	$6	**HOGUE** Johannisberg Riesling Yakima Valley R.S. 1.8 Percent **1988**
47	93	$11	**STRAUSS** Merlot **1986**
48	93	$11	**ROSEMOUNT** Cabernet Sauvignon **1986**
49	93	$13	**GUNDLACH BUNDSCHU** Merlot **1987**
50	93	$14	**MOUNT EDEN** Chardonnay MEV **1987**

*PRICE ON RELEASE

Top 100: Best Wines Released in 1989

RANK	SCORE	PRICE*	WINE
51	93	$15	CHATEAU OLIVIER **1985**
52	93	$16	KEENAN Cabernet Sauvignon **1986**
53	93	$16	SHAFER Cabernet Sauvignon **1986**
54	94	$61	DOM RUINART Blanc de Blancs **1982**
55	93	$19	WOODWARD CANYON Cabernet Sauvignon **1986**
56	93	$19	NAVARRO Gewürtztraminer Late Harvest Sweet Vineyard Selection **1986**
57	93	$20	DOMAINE AUFFRAY Chablis Vaillons **1988**
58	93	$25	ORNELLAIA **1986**
59	92	$10	NALLE Zinfandel **1987**
60	92	$12	LE MASSE Chianti Classico **1985**
61	93	$23	CHATEAU MOUTON-BARON-PHILIPPE **1986**
62	92	$20	WILLIAMS SELYEM Pinot Noir Allen Vineyard **1987**
63	93	$29	KUMEU RIVER Chardonnay **1987**
64	93	$31	BERNARD BURGAUD Côte Rôtie **1986**
65	93	$36	OLIVIER LEFLAIVE Puligny-Montrachet Les Chalumeux **1986**
66	93	$40	JOSEPH PHELPS Insignia **1985**
67	93	$47	DOMAINE DANIEL RION Vosne-Romanée Les Chaumes **1986**
68	91	$10	RAFANELLI Cabernet Sauvignon **1986**
69	90	$9	HESS SELECT Chardonnay **1988**
70	92	$15	DOMAINE RASPAIL-AY Gigondas **1986**
71	92	$15	CHATEAU DE MARBUZET **1986**
72	92	$18	BURGESS Vintage Select **1985**
73	91	$10	KIONA Chardonnay Yakima Valley Barrel Fermented **1987**
74	92	$19	ROBERT MONDAVI Pinot Noir Reserve **1985**
75	92	$20	MATANZAS CREEK Merlot **1986**
76	92	$25	CHATEAU MONTELENA Cabernet Sauvignon **1985**
77	92	$25	CHANSON Beaune Clos des Fèves **1985**
78	92	$30	GUIGAL Côte Rôtie Côtes Brune et Blonde **1985**
79	91	$11	RIDGE Zinfandel Lytton Springs **1987**
80	91	$12	EDMUNDS ST. JOHN Syrah **1986**
81	92	$30	SEAN THACKERAY Syrah Orion **1987**
82	91	$13	M. TRIBAUT Brut Monterey County **1985**
83	91	$14	RIDGE Zinfandel Geyserville **1987**
84	92	$25	KISTLER Chardonnay Sonoma Valley Estate Vineyard **1987**
85	92	$28	FERRARI-CARANO Chardonnay Reserve **1986**
86	90	$10	LATAH CREEK Merlot Limited Bottling **1987**
87	90	$10	CASTELLO DI VOLPAIA Chianti Classico **1985**
88	91	$11	BUENA VISTA Cabernet Sauvignon Carneros **1986**
89	91	$15	TUDAL Cabernet Sauvignon **1986**
90	91	$12	BERNARD PRADEL Cabernet Sauvignon **1985**
91	91	$15	CHATEAU LA LOUVIERE **1986**
92	92	$17	CHATEAU ST.-PIERRE **1986**
93	91	$18	COLUMBIA Cabernet Sauvignon Otis Vineyard **1986**
94	91	$19	PESQUERA Ribera del Duero **1986**
95	90	$8	GRGICH HILLS Riesling **1987**
96	90	$8	FREEMARK ABBEY Riesling **1988**
97	91	$13	SIMI Cabernet Sauvignon **1985**
98	91	$12	COSENTINO Chardonnay **1987**
99	91	$22	ROBERT MONDAVI Pinot Noir Reserve **1986**
100	90	$17	KENDALL-JACKSON Syrah **1987**

*PRICE ON RELEASE

Top 100: Best Wines Released in 1988

RANK	SCORE	PRICE*	WINE
1	97	$37	CHATEAU LYNCH-BAGES **1985**
2	99	$76	CHATEAU MARGAUX **1985**
3	100	$210	DOMAINE DE LA ROMANEE-CONTI Richebourg **1985**
4	98	$49	DOMAINE TOLLOT-BEAUT Corton **1985**
5	97	$94	GAJA Barbaresco Sorì Tildin **1985**
6	96	$21	CASTELLARE I Sodi di San Niccolò **1985**
7	95	$30	LOUIS JADOT Beaune Clos des Ursules **1985**
8	95	$25	SPOTTSWOODE Cabernet Sauvignon Napa Valley **1985**
9	97	$180	CHATEAU D'YQUEM Sauternes **1983**
10	97	$200	JOSEPH DROUHIN Montrachet Marquis de Laguiche **1986**
11	98	$99	LOUIS LATOUR Romanée-St.-Vivant Les Quatre Journaux **1985**
12	98	$200	CHATEAU PETRUS **1985**
13	96	$83	GAJA Barbaresco Costa Russi **1985**
14	96	$83	GAJA Barbaresco Sorì San Lorenzo **1985**
15	95	$40	RIDGE Cabernet Sauvignon Monte Bello **1985**
16	95	$35	CHATEAU BEYCHEVELLE **1985**
17	95	$40	CHATEAU PICHON-LALANDE **1985**
18	95	$50	CHATEAU DUCRU-BEAUCAILLOU **1985**
19	95	$40	DOMAINE DAUVISSAT-CAMUS Chablis Les Clos **1986**
20	95	$45	GAJA Barbaresco **1985**
21	93	$12	FRESCOBALDI Tenuto di Pomino Rosso **1985**
22	92	$14	BONNY DOON Le Cigare Volant **1986**
23	92	$14	KENDALL-JACKSON Syrah Durell Vineyard **1986**
24	92	$16	ANTINORI Chianti Classico Pèppoli **1985**
25	94	$35	TORRES Chardonnay Milmanda Penedès **1987**
26	93	$50	PENFOLDS Grange Hermitage South Australia **1981**
27	94	$75	PESQUERA Janus Reserve **1982**
28	92	$19	SAN FELICE Predicato di Bitùrica **1982**
29	90	$18	BONNY DOON Pinot Noir Oregon Bethel Heights Vineyard **1985**
30	91	$22	CLERICO Arte **1985**
31	94	$16	B.R. COHN Cabernet Sauvignon Olive Hill Vineyard **1985**
32	94	$19	ARROWOOD Cabernet Sauvignon Sonoma County **1985**
33	97	$150	DOMAINE MEO-CAMUZET Richebourg **1985**
34	97	$100	CHATEAU LAFITE-ROTHSCHILD **1985**
35	97	$117	CHATEAU LATOUR **1985**
36	96	$102	CHATEAU HAUT-BRION **1985**
37	98	$225	DOMAINE DE LA ROMANEE-CONTI La Tâche **1985**
38	94	$32	CHATEAU PICHON-BARON **1985**
39	91	$11	CHATEAU MUSAR Lebanon **1980**
40	92	$38	CA' DEL BOSCO Maurizio Zanella Signature Red **1985**
41	95	$20	KENDALL-JACKSON The Proprietor's Cabernet Sauvignon **1985**
42	96	$44	LOUIS JADOT Nuits-St.-Georges Clos des Corvées **1985**
43	96	$49	JAFFELIN Clos de Vougeot **1985**
44	94	$14	FROG'S LEAP Cabernet Sauvignon Napa Valley **1986**
45	94	$15	ROBERT MONDAVI Cabernet Sauvignon Napa Valley **1985**
46	94	$20	DUNN Cabernet Sauvignon Napa Valley **1985**
47	94	$20	CHATEAU MONTELENA Cabernet Sauvignon **1984**
48	95	$48	LOUIS JADOT Bonnes Mares **1985**
49	95	$38	DOMAINE DANIEL RION Vosne-Romanée Beaux-Monts **1985**

*PRICE ON RELEASE

Top 100: Best Wines Released in 1988

RANK	SCORE	PRICE*	WINE
50	95	$50	CHATEAU CLIMENS **1983**
51	95	$62	CHATEAU FIGEAC **1985**
52	95	$70	CHATEAU LA MISSION-HAUT-BRION **1985**
53	94	$50	OPUS ONE **1984**
54	94	$80	BIONDI-SANTI Brunello di Montalcino Riserva **1982**
55	93	$13	FERRARI-CARANO Chardonnay Alexander Valley **1986**
56	93	$14	GIRARD Chardonnay Napa Valley **1986**
57	93	$16	KENDALL-JACKSON Merlot Alexander Valley **1986**
58	93	$23	CHATEAU DU TERTRE **1985**
59	93	$24	POMMERY Champagne Brut **1982**
60	93	$25	PIERRE GELIN Gevrey-Chambertin **1985**
61	93	$35	JABOULET Côte Rôtie Les Jumelles **1985**
62	92	$16	CHATEAU MEYNEY **1985**
63	92	$16	AVIGNONESI Chardonnay Il Marzocco **1986**
64	92	$16	CLOS RENE **1985**
65	92	$17	CHATEAU LARMANDE **1985**
66	93	$25	CHATEAU LA CROIX **1985**
67	93	$30	CHATEAU L'EGLISE CLINET **1985**
68	93	$30	BOLLINGER Champagne Grande Année **1982**
69	94	$52	CHATEAU RIEUSSEC **1983**
70	94	$45	PRINCE FLORENT DE MERODE Pommard Clos de la Palatière **1985**
71	94	$47	MOILLARD Echézeaux **1985**
72	94	$50	JEAN CHARTRON Puligny-Montrachet Clos de la Pucelle **1986**
73	93	$41	CHATEAU RAYAS Châteauneuf-du-Pape Reserve **1985**
74	91	$10	TORRES Sangre de Toro Reserva **1983**
75	90	$8	CASTELLO DEI RAMPOLLA Chianti Classico **1985**
76	93	$20	STERLING Red Table Wine Three Palms Vineyard **1985**
77	95	$93	JEAN-NOEL GAGNARD Bâtard-Montrachet **1986**
78	91	$7	A. RAFANELLI Zinfandel Dry Creek Valley **1986**
79	92	$12	CAYMUS Cabernet Sauvignon Napa Cuvée **1985**
80	92	$10	CORBANS Chardonnay Marlborough New Zealand **1986**
81	91	$10	INGLENOOK Gravion Napa Valley **1986**
82	91	$10	PRESTON Sirah-Syrah Dry Creek Valley **1985**
83	91	$11	INGLENOOK Merlot Reserve Napa Valley **1985**
84	91	$11	WILLM Gewürtztraminer **1985**
85	92	$12	SILVERADO Chardonnay Napa Valley **1986**
86	92	$14	SAINTSBURY Pinot Noir Carneros **1986**
87	92	$14	COSENTINO Cabernet Franc North Coast **1986**
88	90	$6	ANTINORI Chianti Classico Santa Cristina **1985**
89	90	$7	HUSCH Gewürtztraminer Anderson Valley **1987**
90	90	$8	BUENA VISTA Sauvignon Blanc Lake County **1987**
91	90	$8	NAVARRO White Riesling Anderson Valley **1987**
92	90	$8	CHRISTIAN BROTHERS Cabernet Sauvignon **1985**
93	90	$11	SAN FELICE Chianti Classico Riserva Il Grigio **1982**
94	92	$17	CHATEAU ST. JEAN Chardonnay Belle Terre **1986**
95	92	$18	KISTLER Chardonnay Dutton Ranch **1987**
96	91	$15	BERINGER Chardonnay Private Reserve **1986**
97	91	$35	JABOULET Hermitage La Chapelle **1985**
98	90	$9	NALLE Zinfandel Dry Creek Valley **1986**
99	91	$15	ZACA MESA Pinot Noir Reserve Santa Barbara County **1986**
100	93	$75	DOM PERIGNON Champagne **1982**

* PRICE ON RELEASE

Cellar at Viña Santa Rita in the Maipo Valley, Chile.

Best Value Producers

In this section you will find a list, grouped by country, of wineries that have a particular strength in offering good values at very reasonable prices. In order to qualify, a producer needed to have at least three different wines that cost $12 or less, and that scored 80 points or more on *Wine Spectator's* 100-point scale in at least two vintages since 1995.

Note that the list is not limited strictly to "budget wineries." For example, Beringer and Robert Mondavi in California and Antinori in Italy all make several wines that cost far more than $12. But each also offers wines that can be relied on to provide good quality at a modest price.

The names of the wines that met our criteria are listed under each producer. For price and score information on specific vintages of these and other wines, see the Main Listings.

James Suckling

ARGENTINA

ESMERALDA, BODEGAS

Cabernet Sauvignon Mendoza Alamos Ridge
Chardonnay Mendoza Alamos Ridge
Malbec Mendoza Alamos Ridge
Merlot Tupungato Valley Trumpeter

AUSTRALIA

BANROCK STATION

Chardonnay South Eastern Australia Unwooded
Sémillon-Chardonnay South Eastern Australia
Shiraz South Eastern Australia
Shiraz-Cabernet Sauvignon South Eastern Australia
Shiraz-Cabernet South Eastern Australia

BLACK OPAL

Cabernet Sauvignon South Eastern Australia
Cabernet Sauvignon-Merlot South Eastern Australia
Chardonnay South Eastern Australia
Shiraz South Eastern Australia

BLASS, WOLF

Cabernet Sauvignon South Australia Yellow Label
Chardonnay South Australia
Riesling South Australia Gold Label
Shiraz South Australia
Shiraz-Cabernet Sauvignon South Australia Red Label

BULLETIN PLACE

Cabernet Sauvignon South Eastern Australia
Chardonnay South Eastern Australia
Shiraz South Eastern Australia

HARDYS

Cabernet Sauvignon-Shiraz South Eastern Australia Nottage Hill
Chardonnay Padthaway
Chardonnay South Eastern Australia Nottage Hill
Chardonnay South Eastern Australia Signature
Merlot South Eastern Australia Nottage Hill
Shiraz South Eastern Australia Nottage Hill

LINDEMANS

Cabernet Sauvignon South Eastern Australia Bin 45
Chardonnay South Eastern Australia Bin 65
Merlot South Eastern Australia Bin 40
Pinot Noir South Australia Bin 99
Sauvignon Blanc South Eastern Australia Bin 95
Sémillon-Chardonnay South Eastern Australia Bin 77
Shiraz South Australia Bin 50

ORLANDO

Cabernet Sauvignon South Eastern Australia Jacob's Creek
Chardonnay South Eastern Australia Jacob's Creek
Merlot South Eastern Australia Jacob's Creek
Sémillon-Chardonnay South Eastern Australia Jacob's Creek
Shiraz-Cabernet South Eastern Australia Jacob's Creek

OXFORD LANDING

Cabernet Sauvignon-Shiraz South Eastern Australia
Chardonnay South Eastern Australia
Sauvignon Blanc South Australia

PENFOLDS

Chardonnay South Eastern Australia Koonunga Hill
Sémillon-Chardonnay South Australia Koonunga Hill
Shiraz-Cabernet South Australia Koonunga Hill
Shiraz-Mourvèdre South Eastern Australia Bin 2

ROSEMOUNT

Cabernet Sauvignon South Eastern Australia
Chardonnay South Eastern Australia
Grenache-Shiraz South Eastern Australia
Pinot Noir South Eastern Australia
Sauvignon Blanc South Eastern Australia
Sémillon-Chardonnay South Eastern Australia
Shiraz South Eastern Australia
Shiraz-Cabernet South Eastern Australia
Traminer-Riesling South Eastern Australia

SALISBURY

Cabernet Sauvignon Victoria
Chardonnay Victoria
Sauvignon Blanc Victoria

TYRRELL'S

Cabernet Sauvignon-Merlot South Australia Old Winery
Chardonnay South Eastern Australia Old Winery
Chardonnay-Sémillon South Eastern Australia Long Flat
Pinot Noir South Eastern Australia Old Winery
Shiraz South Eastern Australia Old Winery

WYNDHAM ESTATE

Cabernet Sauvignon South Eastern Australia Bin 444
Chardonnay Hunter Valley Oak Cask
Sémillon-Chardonnay South Eastern Australia Bin 777

CHILE

CALITERRA, VIÑA

Cabernet Sauvignon Valle Central
Chardonnay Valle Central
Merlot Valle Central
Sauvignon Blanc Valle Central

CASA LAPOSTOLLE

Cabernet Sauvignon Rapel Valley
Chardonnay Rapel Valley
Merlot Rapel Valley
Sauvignon Blanc Rapel Valley

CONCHA Y TORO

Cabernet Sauvignon Maipo Valley Casillero del Diablo
Cabernet Sauvignon Maipo Valley Trio
Cabernet Sauvignon Valle Central Sunrise
Chardonnay Casablanca Valley Trio
Chardonnay Valle Central Sunrise
Merlot Peumo Valley Trio
Merlot Rapel Valley Casillero del Diablo
Merlot Valle Central Sunrise

ECHEVERRIA

Cabernet Sauvignon Molina
Cabernet Sauvignon Molina Reserva
Chardonnay Molina Unwooded

ERRAZURIZ

Cabernet Sauvignon Aconcagua Valley El Ceibo Estate
Chardonnay Casablanca Valley La Escultura Estate
Sauvignon Blanc Casablanca Valley La Escultura Estate
Sauvignon Blanc Late Harvest Casablanca Valley

MONTES

Cabernet Sauvignon Curicó Valley
Malbec Colchagua Valley
Merlot Curicó Valley Special Cuvée
Sauvignon Blanc Curicó Valley Fumé Blanc

SANTA CAROLINA, VIÑA

Cabernet Sauvignon Maipo Valley Reserva
Chardonnay Maipo Valley Reserva
Merlot Maule Valley Reserva

SANTA RITA

Cabernet Sauvignon Maipo Valley Reserva
Cabernet Sauvignon Rapel Valley 120
Chardonnay Lontué Valley 120
Chardonnay Maipo Valley Reserva
Merlot Lontué Valley 120
Sauvignon Blanc Lontué Valley 120
Sauvignon Blanc Maule Valley Reserva

SEGU OLLE, VIÑA

Cabernet Sauvignon Maule Valley Doña Consuelo
Cabernet Sauvignon-Merlot Maule Valley
Merlot Maule Valley Doña Consuelo

TARAPACA, VIÑA

Cabernet Sauvignon Maipo Valley Reserva
Chardonnay Maipo Valley
Chardonnay Maipo Valley Reserva
Merlot Maipo Valley
Sauvignon Blanc Maipo Valley
Sauvignon Blanc Maipo Valley La Isla Vineyard

UNDURRAGA

Chardonnay Colchagua Valley
Pinot Noir Maipo Valley
Sauvignon Blanc Lontué Valley

VIU MANENT

Cabernet Sauvignon Colchagua Valley
Cabernet Sauvignon Colchagua Valley Reserve
Malbec Colchagua Valley
Malbec Colchagua Valley Reserve
Merlot Colchagua Valley
Sauvignon Blanc Colchagua Valley

WALNUT CREST

Cabernet Sauvignon Rapel Valley
Chardonnay Rapel Valley
Merlot Rapel Valley

FRANCE

CHEREAU-CARRE

Muscadet de Sèvre et Maine Les Vergers
Muscadet de Sèvre et Maine Sur Lie Château de la Gravelle
Muscadet de Sèvre et Maine Sur Lie Château du Coing de St.-Fiacre

DUBOEUF, GEORGES

Beaujolais Château de Buffavent
Beaujolais-Villages Château de Varennes
Beaujolais-Villages Château des Vierres
Beaujolais-Villages Domaine du Granit Bleu
Beaujolais-Villages Flower Label
Brouilly Château de Nervers
Brouilly Domaine de Combillaty
Brouilly Grand Cuvée Flower Label
Chénas Domaine des Darroux
Chiroubles Château de Javernand
Chiroubles Domaine Desmures
Chiroubles Flower Label
Côte de Brouilly Domaine de la Feuillée
Côte de Brouilly Flower Label
Fleurie Flower Label
Juliénas Domaine de la Seigneurie de Juliénas
Juliénas Flower Label
Mâcon-Villages Flower Label
Merlot Vin de Pays d'Oc Flower Label
Morgon Domaine Bellevue
Morgon Flower Label
Morgon Jean Descombes
Moulin-à-Vent Domaine des Rosiers
Régnié Domaine des Buyats
Régnié Domaine du Potet
Régnié Flower Label
St.-Amour Flower Label
St.-Véran Flower Label

JAMELLES, LES

Cabernet Sauvignon Vin de Pays d'Oc
Chardonnay Vin de Pays d'Oc
Merlot Vin de Pays d'Oc

REMEJEANNE, DOMAINE DE LA

Côtes du Rhône Les Arbousiers
Côtes du Rhône Les Chevrefeuilles
Côtes du Rhône Rosé Les Arbousiers
Côtes du Rhône White Les Arbousiers

SAUVION & FILS

Anjou
Muscadet de Sèvre et Maine
Muscadet de Sèvre et Maine Sur Lie Château du Cléray
Saumur-Champigny Les Gravières du Roy
Vouvray

SPARR, PIERRE

Gewürztraminer Alsace Carte d'Or
Pinot Blanc Alsace Diamant d'Alsace Réserve
Pinot Gris Alsace Carte d'Or
Riesling Alsace Carte d'Or

WILLM, ALSACE

Gewürztraminer Alsace
Pinot Blanc Alsace
Pinot Gris Alsace

ITALY

ANTINORI

Orvieto Classico Campogrande
Sangiovese Toscana Santa Cristina
Sauvignon Blanc Umbria Castello della Sala

BORGO MAGREDO

Merlot Grave del Friuli
Pinot Grigio Grave del Friuli
Tocai Friulano Grave del Friuli

CAPPUCCINA, LA

Sauvignon Verona
Soave
Soave Superiore Fontégo

CECCHI

Chianti Classico
Sangiovese Toscana
Vernaccia di San Gimignano

PLOZNER

Chardonnay Grave del Friuli
Pinot Grigio Grave del Friuli
Tocai Friulano Grave del Friuli

VILLA DEL BORGO

Cabernet Sauvignon Grave del Friuli
Merlot Grave del Friuli
Pinot Grigio Grave del Friuli
Sauvignon Grave del Friuli

SPAIN

FARIÑA, BODEGAS

Toro
Toro White Colegiata
Viño de la Tierra de Zamora

NEKEAS, BODEGA

Cabernet Sauvignon-Tempranillo Navarra Vega Sindoa
Chardonnay Navarra Vega Sindoa Barrel Fermented
Chardonnay Navarra Vega Sindoa Cuvée Allier Barrel Fermented
Grenache Navarra Vega Sindoa El Chaparral Old Vines
Merlot Navarra Vega Sindoa
Tempranillo-Merlot Navarra Vega Sindoa
Viura-Chardonnay Navarra Vega Sindoa

TORRES

Chardonnay Penedès Gran Viña Sol
Penedès Gran Sangre de Toro Reserva
Penedès White Viña Esmeralda

VIÑAS DEL VERO

Cabernet Sauvignon Somontano
Chardonnay Somontano Barrel Select
Merlot Somontano

UNITED STATES

BARGETTO, LAWRENCE J. | CALIFORNIA

Chardonnay Central Coast Cypress
Gewürztraminer Monterey County
Gewürztraminer Santa Cruz Mountains Dry

BEAULIEU VINEYARD | CALIFORNIA

Cabernet Sauvignon California Coastal
Merlot California Coastal
Pinot Noir California Beautour
Pinot Noir Carneros Vin Gris Signet Collection
Sauvignon Blanc Napa Valley

BERINGER | CALIFORNIA

Gamay Beaujolais California Nouveau
Sauvignon Blanc Napa Valley
Sauvignon Blanc Napa Valley Appellation Collection
Zinfandel North Coast Appellation Collection

BOGLE | CALIFORNIA

Chardonnay California
Chenin Blanc Clarksburg
Fumé Blanc California
Merlot California
Petite Sirah California
Zinfandel California Old Vine Cuvée

BOOKWALTER | WASHINGTON

Chenin Blanc Washington
Johannisberg Riesling Washington
Riesling Washington Vintner's Select

BRIDGEVIEW | OREGON

Chardonnay Oregon
Chardonnay Oregon Blue Moon
Early Muscat Oregon
Pinot Gris Oregon Cuvée Spéciale
Pinot Noir Oregon

COLUMBIA CREST | WASHINGTON

Cabernet Sauvignon Columbia Valley
Chardonnay Columbia Valley
Chardonnay Columbia Valley Estate Series
Gewürztraminer Columbia Valley
Johannisberg Riesling Columbia Valley
Sauvignon Blanc Columbia Valley
Sauvignon Blanc Columbia Valley Estate Series
Sémillon Columbia Valley
Sémillon-Chardonnay Columbia Valley

COVEY RUN | WASHINGTON

Chardonnay Washington
Chenin Blanc Columbia Valley
Johannisberg Riesling Columbia Valley

DUCK POND | OREGON

Chardonnay Willamette Valley
Pinot Gris Willamette Valley

DUCK POND | WASHINGTON

Cabernet Sauvignon Columbia Valley Fries' Desert Wind Vineyard Wahluke Slope
Chardonnay Columbia Valley
Merlot Columbia Valley Fries' Desert Wind Vineyard Wahluke Slope

ESTANCIA | CALIFORNIA

Cabernet Sauvignon Alexander Valley
Chardonnay Monterey County Pinnacles
Fumé Blanc Monterey County Pinnacles

FETZER | CALIFORNIA

Cabernet Sauvignon California Valley Oaks
Chardonnay California Sundial
Chardonnay Mendocino County Barrel Select
Gewürztraminer California
Sauvignon Blanc California Echo Ridge

FORIS | OREGON

Chardonnay Rogue Valley
Pinot Blanc Rogue Valley
Pinot Gris Rogue Valley

FOX RUN | NEW YORK

Chardonnay Finger Lakes
Chardonnay Finger Lakes Reserve
Riesling Finger Lakes
Riesling Finger Lakes Dry

FRANK, DR. KONSTANTIN | NEW YORK

Chardonnay Finger Lakes
Johannisberg Riesling Finger Lakes Dry
Johannisberg Riesling Finger Lakes Semi-Dry

GALLO OF SONOMA | CALIFORNIA

Chardonnay Russian River Valley
Merlot Sonoma County
Pinot Noir Russian River Valley
Zinfandel Dry Creek Valley

GEYSER PEAK | CALIFORNIA

Chardonnay Sonoma County
Johannisberg Riesling California
Sauvignon Blanc Sonoma County

HOGUE | WASHINGTON

Cabernet-Merlot Columbia Valley
Chardonnay Columbia Valley
Chenin Blanc Columbia Valley
Chenin Blanc Columbia Valley Dry
Fumé Blanc Columbia Valley
Gewürztraminer Columbia Valley
Johannisberg Riesling Columbia Valley
Johannisberg Riesling Columbia Valley Dry
Sémillon Columbia Valley
Sémillon-Chardonnay Columbia Valley
White Riesling Late Harvest Columbia Valley

KIONA | WASHINGTON

Chardonnay Washington
Chenin Blanc Columbia Valley
Lemberger Washington
White Riesling Columbia Valley
White Riesling Columbia Valley Dry

LATAH CREEK | WASHINGTON

Chardonnay Washington
Johannisberg Riesling Washington
Lemberger Washington
Muscat Canelli Washington

MERIDIAN | CALIFORNIA

Cabernet Sauvignon California
Chardonnay Santa Barbara County
Sauvignon Blanc California

MONDAVI, ROBERT | CALIFORNIA

Chardonnay Central Coast Coastal
Fumé Blanc Napa Valley
Merlot Central Coast Coastal
Pinot Noir Central Coast Coastal
Sauvignon Blanc North Coast Coastal

MONTEREY VINEYARD | CALIFORNIA

Cabernet Sauvignon Monterey County
Pinot Noir Monterey County
Sauvignon Blanc Monterey County

MONTEVINA | CALIFORNIA

Barbera Amador County
Sangiovese Amador County
Zinfandel Amador County
Zinfandel Amador County Brioso

NAPA RIDGE | CALIFORNIA

Chardonnay Central Coast Coastal Vines
Chardonnay North Coast Coastal Vines
Pinot Noir North Coast Coastal
Sauvignon Blanc North Coast

PHILLIPS, R.H. | CALIFORNIA

Chardonnay Dunnigan Hills Barrel Cuvée
Chardonnay Dunnigan Hills Toasted Head
Sauvignon Blanc Dunnigan Hills Night Harvest
Viognier Dunnigan Hills EXP

POWERS | Washington

Cabernet Sauvignon Washington
Chardonnay Columbia Valley
Fumé Blanc Columbia Valley
Lemberger Columbia Valley Mercer Ranch Vineyard
Merlot Columbia Valley
Muscat Canelli Columbia Valley

PRESTON | California

Faux Red Dry Creek Valley
Gamay Beaujolais Dry Creek Valley
Sauvignon Blanc Dry Creek Valley Cuvée de Fumé

RABBIT RIDGE | California

Sauvignon Blanc Russian River Valley
Zinfandel Amador County
Zinfandel California Barrel Cuvée

STANDING STONE | New York

Gewürztraminer Finger Lakes
Riesling Finger Lakes
Riesling Finger Lakes Dry

STEVENOT | California

Chardonnay Sierra Foothills
Sauvignon Blanc Calaveras County
Zinfandel Sierra Foothills

TURNING LEAF | California

Cabernet Sauvignon California
Chardonnay Sonoma County Sonoma Reserve
Merlot California
Merlot Sonoma County Sonoma Reserve

VALLEY VIEW | Oregon

Cabernet Sauvignon Rogue Valley
Fumé Blanc Rogue Valley Anna Maria
Merlot Rogue Valley

WASHINGTON HILLS | Washington

Cabernet-Merlot Columbia Valley Varietal Select
Chenin Blanc Columbia Valley Dry Varietal Select
Gewürztraminer Columbia Valley Varietal Select
Johannisberg Riesling Columbia Valley Varietal Select
Sauvignon Blanc Columbia Valley Varietal Select
Sémillon Columbia Valley Varietal Select
White Riesling Columbia Valley Late Harvest Varietal Select
White Riesling Columbia Valley Varietal Select

WILLAMETTE VALLEY | Oregon

Gewürztraminer Oregon
Riesling Oregon
Riesling Oregon Dry

The dramatic Stags Leap escarpment in Napa Valley.

Great Wines

In the following pages you will find *Wine Spectator's* ratings for the very best wines—those that scored 90 or above—from recent vintages of eight prestigious and collectible wine types: red Bordeaux; red and white Burgundy; red wines from the Rhône, Piedmont and Tuscany; vintage Port; and California Cabernet Sauvignon and Cabernet-based blends.

On the principle that even mediocre years produce at least a few wonderful wines, we have provided listings for each of the last three or four available vintages, supplemented by one or more outstanding vintages from the preceding decade. Thus, the red Burgundy, Piedmont and Tuscany sections each include the 1990 vintage, while Bordeaux includes 1988 and 1989 as well.

The wines are organized in descending order of score. Also listed is either the release price or, where available, an average of recent auction prices. The date of the issue of *Wine Spectator* in which the rating was first published is in parentheses.

Richard Gillette

Château Cos-d'Estournel in St.-Estèphe.

Red Bordeaux

Here are *Wine Spectator's* ratings and prices for the best Bordeaux from the five most recent vintages—1993 through 1997—plus the excellent years of 1988, 1989 and 1990. For ratings from years omitted from this section, turn to the main listings, where you will find complete ratings under the château names.

The 1995 vintage created a lot of excitement among Bordeaux drinkers and collectors because it was the first vintage rated outstanding or better in five years. A number of good wines were produced in 1993, '94, '96 and '97, and these can be worthwhile purchases for drinking now and over the next few years, while you're waiting for your 1995s to mature.

"Futures" purchases of the 1998 and 1999 vintages are available, too, but neither of these vintages will be as good as 1995. Based on blind tastings of barrel samples, *Wine Spectator* bureau chief James Suckling rates 1998 at 85-89 points out of 100—although Pomerol, St.-Emilion and Pessac-Léognan are shaping up exceptionally well—and 1999 at 82-86.

1997 Red Bordeaux
Vintage Rating: 81

90 **Château Angélus** St.-Emilion 1997 • $75 • (1/31/2000) • CS

90 **Château Ausone** St.-Emilion 1997 • $203 • (1/31/2000)

90 **Château Beau-Séjour Bécot** St.-Emilion 1997 • $40 • (1/31/2000)

90 **Château de Valandraud** St.-Emilion 1997 • $429 • (1/31/2000)

90 **Château Haut-Brion** Pessac-Léognan 1997 • $132 • (1/31/2000)

90 **Château La Mondotte** St.-Emilion 1997 • $273 • (1/31/2000)

90 **Château Lafite Rothschild** Pauillac 1997 • $137 • (1/31/2000)

90 **Château Margaux** Margaux 1997 • $101 Ⓐ • (1/31/2000)

90 **Château Palmer** Margaux 1997 • $NA • (1/31/2000)

90 **Château Pavie-Decesse** St.-Emilion 1997 • $65 • (1/31/2000)

90 **Château Pétrus** Pomerol 1997 • $457 • (1/31/2000)

90 **Vieux-Château-Certan** Pomerol 1997 • $51 Ⓐ • (1/31/2000)

Key: SS—Spectator Selection. CS—Cellar Selection. HR—Highly Recommended. $NA—Price not available. (BT)—Barrel tasting. Ⓐ—Auction Price.
Dates in parentheses represent the issues in which the ratings were published.

1996 Red Bordeaux
Vintage Rating: 87

97 **Château Latour** Pauillac 1996 • $203 Ⓐ • (1/31/1999) • CS

96 **Château Lafite Rothschild** Pauillac 1996 • $218 Ⓐ • (1/31/1999) • CS

95 **Château Cos-d'Estournel** St.-Estèphe 1996 • $70 Ⓐ • (1/31/1999) • CS

95 **Château Margaux** Margaux 1996 • $257 Ⓐ • (1/31/1999) • CS

95 **Château Montrose** St.-Estèphe 1996 • $62 Ⓐ • (1/31/1999) • CS

94 **Château Mouton-Rothschild** Pauillac 1996 • $188 Ⓐ • (1/31/1999) • CS

92 **Château Ducru-Beaucaillou** St.-Julien 1996 • $92 Ⓐ • (1/31/1999)

92 **Château Léoville Las Cases** St.-Julien 1996 • $143 Ⓐ • (1/01/1999)

92 **Château Lynch-Bages** Pauillac 1996 • $52 Ⓐ • (1/31/1999)

92 **Château Pichon-Longueville-Baron** Pauillac 1996 • $78 Ⓐ • (1/31/1999)

92 **Château Pichon-Longueville-Lalande** Pauillac 1996 • $119 • (1/31/1999)

91 **Château Cantemerle** Haut-Médoc 1996 • $21 Ⓐ • (1/31/1999) • HR

91 **Château Haut-Brion** Pessac-Léognan 1996 • $148 Ⓐ • (1/31/1999)

91 **Château Palmer** Margaux 1996 • $50 Ⓐ • (1/31/1999)

Sara Matthews

■ ■ ■ ■

Red Bordeaux

90 **Château Ausone** St.-Emilion 1996 • $156 Ⓐ • (1/31/1999)

90 **Château Brane-Cantenac** Margaux 1996 • $40 • (1/31/1999)

90 **Château Calon-Ségur** St.-Estèphe 1996 • $47 Ⓐ • (1/31/1999)

90 **Château Caronne-Ste.-Gemme** Haut-Médoc 1996 • $22 • (1/31/1999) • HR

90 **Château Chasse-Spleen** Moulis 1996 • $56 Ⓐ • (1/31/1999) • HR

90 **Château Cheval-Blanc** St.-Emilion 1996 • $156 Ⓐ • (6/30/1999)

90 **Château d'Issan** Margaux 1996 • $25 • (1/31/1999)

90 **Château Grand-Puy-Lacoste** Pauillac 1996 • $56 Ⓐ • (1/31/1999)

90 **Château Gruaud-Larose** St.-Julien 1996 • $34 Ⓐ • (1/31/1999)

90 **Château Haut-Bailly** Pessac-Léognan 1996 • $29 Ⓐ • (1/31/1999)

90 **Château Haut-Marbuzet** St.-Estèphe 1996 • $28 • (1/31/1999)

90 **Château Kirwan** Margaux 1996 • $26 • (1/31/1999)

90 **Château Lafon-Rochet** St.-Estèphe 1996 • $30 • (1/31/1999)

90 **Château Lagrange** St.-Julien 1996 • $37 • (1/31/1999)

90 **Château Langoa Barton** St.-Julien 1996 • $35 Ⓐ • (1/31/1999)

90 **Château L'Église Clinet** Pomerol 1996 • $98 Ⓐ • (4/30/1999)

90 **Château Léoville Barton** St.-Julien 1996 • $48 Ⓐ • (1/31/1999)

90 **Château Pétrus** Pomerol 1996 • $522 Ⓐ • (6/30/1999)

90 **Château Pontet-Canet** Pauillac 1996 • $84 Ⓐ • (1/31/1999)

90 **Château Potensac** Médoc 1996 • $21 Ⓐ • (1/01/1999)

90 **Château Poujeaux** Moulis 1996 • $22 • (1/31/1999)

90 **Château Rauzan-Ségla** Margaux 1996 • $40 Ⓐ • (1/31/1999)

90 **Château Sociando-Mallet** Haut-Médoc 1996 • $31 • (1/31/1999)

90 **Château St.-Pierre** St.-Julien 1996 • $35 • (1/31/1999)

90 **Château Talbot** St.-Julien 1996 • $31 Ⓐ • (1/31/1999)

90 **Clos du Marquis** St.-Julien 1996 • $27 Ⓐ • (1/01/1999)

1995 Red Bordeaux
Vintage Rating: 95

100 **Château Margaux** Margaux 1995 • $279 Ⓐ • (1/31/1998) • CS

98 **Château Lafleur** Pomerol 1995 • $262 Ⓐ • (1/31/2000)

98 **Château Pétrus** Pomerol 1995 • $751 Ⓐ • (1/31/1998) • CS

97 **Château Ducru-Beaucaillou** St.-Julien 1995 • $102 Ⓐ • (1/31/1998) • CS

97 **Château Lafite Rothschild** Pauillac 1995 • $189 Ⓐ • (1/31/1998) • CS

97 **Château Trotanoy** Pomerol 1995 • $75 • (1/31/1998) • HR

96 **Château Calon-Ségur** St.-Estèphe 1995 • $53 Ⓐ • (1/31/1998) • SS

Key: SS—Spectator Selection. CS—Cellar Selection. HR—Highly Recommended. $NA—Price not available. (BT)—Barrel tasting. Ⓐ—Auction Price.
Dates in parentheses represent the issues in which the ratings were published.

96 **Château Certan de May** Pomerol 1995 • $76 Ⓐ • (9/15/1998)

96 **Château L'Église Clinet** Pomerol 1995 • $150 Ⓐ • (4/30/1999)

96 **Château Mouton-Rothschild** Pauillac 1995 • $206 Ⓐ • (1/31/1998) • CS

96 **Château Pichon-Longueville-Lalande** Pauillac 1995 • $75 • (1/31/1998) • CS

95 **Château Ausone** St.-Emilion 1995 • $149 Ⓐ • (1/31/1998) • HR

95 **Château Canon-La Gaffelière** St.-Emilion 1995 • $49 Ⓐ • (1/31/1998)

95 **Château Clerc Milon** Pauillac 1995 • $46 Ⓐ • (1/31/1998) • SS

95 **Château Clinet** Pomerol 1995 • $124 Ⓐ • (1/31/1998)

95 **Château Figeac** St.-Emilion 1995 • $57 Ⓐ • (1/31/1998)

95 **Château Léoville Las Cases** St.-Julien 1995 • $109 Ⓐ • (9/15/1998)

95 **Vieux-Château-Certan** Pomerol 1995 • $58 Ⓐ • (1/31/1998)

94 **Château Angélus** St.-Emilion 1995 • $101 Ⓐ • (1/31/1998)

94 **Château Cheval-Blanc** St.-Emilion 1995 • $167 Ⓐ • (1/31/1998)

94 **Château Ferrière** Margaux 1995 • $53 Ⓐ • (1/31/1998)

94 **Château Haut-Brion** Pessac-Léognan 1995 • $167 Ⓐ • (1/31/1998)

94 **Château La Conseillante** Pomerol 1995 • $64 Ⓐ • (1/31/1998)

94 **Château Latour** Pauillac 1995 • $215 Ⓐ • (1/31/1998) • CS

94 **Château L'Evangile** Pomerol 1995 • $104 Ⓐ • (9/15/1998)

94 **Château Lynch-Bages** Pauillac 1995 • $54 Ⓐ • (1/31/1998)

94 **Château Palmer** Margaux 1995 • $67 Ⓐ • (1/31/1998)

94 **Château Pontet-Canet** Pauillac 1995 • $39 Ⓐ • (1/31/1998) • SS

94 **Château Rauzan-Ségla** Margaux 1995 • $48 Ⓐ • (1/31/1998)

93 **Château Cos-d'Estournel** St.-Estèphe 1995 • $83 Ⓐ • (1/31/1998)

93 **Château de Valandraud** St.-Emilion 1995 • $329 Ⓐ • (1/31/1998)

93 **Château Kirwan** Margaux 1995 • $28 Ⓐ • (1/31/1998)

93 **Château La Gomerie** St.-Emilion 1995 • $100 • (9/15/1998)

93 **Château La Mission-Haut-Brion** Pessac-Léognan 1995 • $65 • (1/31/1998)

93 **Château La Pointe** Pomerol 1995 • $24 Ⓐ • (1/31/1998)

93 **Château Lafon-Rochet** St.-Estèphe 1995 • $34 Ⓐ • (1/31/1998)

93 **Château Langoa Barton** St.-Julien 1995 • $36 Ⓐ • (1/31/1998)

93 **Château Larmande** St.-Emilion 1995 • $31 Ⓐ • (1/31/1998)

93 **Château Le Pin** Pomerol 1995 • $582 Ⓐ • (1/31/1998)

93 **Château Léoville Barton** St.-Julien 1995 • $52 Ⓐ • (1/31/1998)

93 **Château Léoville Poyferré** St.-Julien 1995 • $46 Ⓐ • (1/31/1998)

93 **Château Pavie-Macquin** St.-Emilion 1995 • $32 Ⓐ • (1/31/1998)

93 **Château Siran** Margaux 1995 • $25 • (1/31/1998)

93 **La Petite Eglise** Pomerol 1995 • $55 • (9/15/1998)

93 **Pensées de Lafleur** Pomerol 1995 • $75 • (1/31/1998)

92 **Château Beau-Séjour Bécot** St.-Emilion 1995 • $35 • (9/15/1998)

92 **Château Bourgneuf** Pomerol 1995 • $30 • (1/31/1998)

92 **Château d'Armailhac** Pauillac 1995 • $25 Ⓐ • (1/31/1998)

92 **Château Dauzac** Margaux 1995 • $22 Ⓐ • (1/31/1998)

92 **Château Giscours** Margaux 1995 • $34 Ⓐ • (1/31/1998)

92 **Château Grand-Puy-Lacoste** Pauillac 1995 • $62 Ⓐ • (1/31/1998)

92 **Château Haut-Bailly** Pessac-Léognan 1995 • $32 Ⓐ • (1/31/1998)

92 **Château Lascombes** Margaux 1995 • $25 Ⓐ • (1/31/1998)

92 **Château Monbousquet** St.-Emilion 1995 • $47 Ⓐ • (1/31/1998)

92 **Château Moulin-St.-Georges** St.-Emilion 1995 • $24 • (1/31/1998)

92 **Château Pape Clément** Pessac-Léognan 1995 • $40 Ⓐ • (1/31/1998)

92 **Château Poujeaux** Moulis 1995 • $18 Ⓐ • (1/31/1998)

92 **Château Troplong-Mondot** St.-Emilion 1995 • $54 Ⓐ • (1/31/1998)

91 **Château Beauregard** Pomerol 1995 • $50 • (1/31/1998)

91 **Château Cordeillan-Bages** Pauillac 1995 • $NA • (9/15/1998)

91 **Château de Fieuzal** Pessac-Léognan 1995 • $35 Ⓐ • (1/31/1998)

91 **Château Grand-Pontet** St.-Emilion 1995 • $35 • (9/15/1998)

91 **Château Haut-Marbuzet** St.-Estèphe 1995 • $35 • (1/31/1998)

91 **Château La Serre** St.-Emilion 1995 • $28 • (1/31/1998)

91 **Château Lagrange** St.-Julien 1995 • $30 • (1/31/1998)

91 **Château Le Roc de Cambes** Côtes de Bourg 1995 • $25 • (1/01/1999)

91 **Château Magdelaine** St.-Emilion 1995 • $43 Ⓐ • (1/31/1998)

91 **Château Malescot-St.-Exupéry** Margaux 1995 • $46 Ⓐ • (1/31/1998)

91 **Château Pavie-Decesse** St.-Emilion 1995 • $28 • (1/31/1998)

91 **Château Rauzan-Gassies** Margaux 1995 • $30 • (1/31/1998)

91 **Château Sociando-Mallet** Haut-Médoc 1995 • $32 Ⓐ • (1/31/1998)

91 **Château Taillefer** Pomerol 1995 • $NA • (9/15/1998)

91 **Château Tertre Roteboeuf** St.-Emilion 1995 • $104 Ⓐ • (9/15/1998)

91 **Clos l'Église** Pomerol 1995 • $30 • (1/31/1998)

91 **Les Forts de Latour** Pauillac 1995 • $46 Ⓐ • (1/31/1998)

91 **Pavillon Rouge du Château Margaux** Margaux 1995 • $38 • (1/31/1998)

90 **Carruades de Lafite Rothschild** Pauillac 1995 • $39 Ⓐ • (1/31/1998)

90 **Château Biston-Brillette** Moulis 1995 • $NA • (9/15/1998)

90 **Château Boyd-Cantenac** Margaux 1995 • $NA • (9/15/1998)

90 **Château Canuet** Margaux 1995 • $20 • (1/31/1998)

90 **Château Chasse-Spleen** Moulis 1995 • $26 Ⓐ • (1/31/1998)

90 **Château Dassault** St.-Emilion 1995 • $NA • (9/15/1998)

90 **Château de Camensac** Haut-Médoc 1995 • $28 • (9/15/1998)

90 **Château de Carles** Fronsac 1995 • $15 • (8/31/1998) • HR

90 **Château de Cruzeau** Pessac-Léognan 1995 • $15 • (1/31/1998)

90 **Château Duhart-Milon Rothschild** Pauillac 1995 • $26 Ⓐ • (1/31/1998)

90 **Château Faizeau** Montagne-St.-Emilion Sélection Vieilles Vignes 1995 • $18 • (1/31/1998)

90 **Château Ferrande** Graves 1995 • $12 • (1/31/1998)

90 **Château Fontenil** Fronsac 1995 • $15 • (1/31/1998)

90 **Château Gazin** Pomerol 1995 • $45 • (1/31/1998)

90 **Château Gloria** St.-Julien 1995 • $30 Ⓐ • (1/31/1998)

90 **Château Grand Moulinet** Pomerol 1995 • $20 • (1/31/1998)

90 **Château Grand-Mayne** St.-Emilion 1995 • $29 Ⓐ • (9/15/1998)

90 **Château Guillot-Clauzel** Pomerol 1995 • $NA • (9/15/1998)

90 **Château Haut-Bages-Libéral** Pauillac 1995 • $20 • (1/31/1998)

90 **Château Haut-Batailley** Pauillac 1995 • $30 Ⓐ • (1/31/1998)

90 **Château Haut-Lagrange** Pessac-Léognan 1995 • $20 • (1/31/1998)

90 **Château La Cabanne** Pomerol 1995 • $NA • (9/15/1998)

90 **Château La Cardonne** Médoc 1995 • $18 • (1/31/1998)

90 **Château La Fleur de Gay** Pomerol 1995 • $67 Ⓐ • (1/31/1998)

90 **Château La Garde** Pessac-Léognan 1995 • $15 • (1/31/1998)

90 **Château La Gurgue** Margaux 1995 • $25 • (1/31/1998)

90 **Château Lafleur-Gazin** Pomerol 1995 • $30 • (1/31/1998)

90 **Château Latour Martillac** Pessac-Léognan 1995 • $30 • (9/15/1998)

90 **Château Le Bon-Pasteur** Pomerol 1995 • $38 Ⓐ • (1/31/1998)

90 **Château Le Gay** Pomerol 1995 • $40 • (9/15/1998)

90 **Château L'Enclos** Pomerol 1995 • $40 • (9/15/1998)

90 **Château Marquis de Terme** Margaux 1995 • $30 • (9/15/1998)

90 **Château Moulin Pey-Labrie** Canon-Fronsac 1995 • $18 • (1/31/1998)

90 **Château Prieuré-Lichine** Margaux 1995 • $31 Ⓐ • (1/31/1998)

90 **Château Smith-Haut-Lafitte** Pessac-Léognan 1995 • $38 Ⓐ • (1/31/1998)

90 **Château St.-Pierre** St.-Julien 1995 • $25 • (1/31/1998)

90 **Château Tertre Daugay** St.-Emilion 1995 • $44 • (1/31/1998)

90 **Clos de l'Oratoire** St.-Emilion 1995 • $30 • (1/31/1998)

90 **Clos des Jacobins** St.-Emilion 1995 • $30 • (1/31/1998)

90 **Clos du Marquis** St.-Julien 1995 • $27 Ⓐ • (9/15/1998)

90 **Clos Fourtet** St.-Emilion 1995 • $24 Ⓐ • (1/31/1998)

90 **Domaine de Courteillac** Bordeaux Supérieur 1995 • $18 • (1/31/1998)

1994 Red Bordeaux
Vintage Rating: 85

95 **Château Le Pin** Pomerol 1994 • $347 Ⓐ • (1/31/1997) • CS

94 **Château Haut-Brion** Pessac-Léognan 1994 • $99 Ⓐ • (4/30/1997)

93 **Château Clinet** Pomerol 1994 • $64 (• (1/31/1997) • HR

93 **Château Lafite Rothschild** Pauillac 1994 • $88 Ⓐ • (1/31/1997) • CS

93 **Château Pétrus** Pomerol 1994 • $332 Ⓐ • (1/31/1997) • CS

92 **Château Angélus** St.-Emilion 1994 • $56 Ⓐ • (1/31/1997) • HR

92 **Château Troplong-Mondot** St.-Emilion 1994 • $38 Ⓐ • (1/31/1997)
91 **Château Cheval-Blanc** St.-Emilion 1994 • $80 Ⓐ • (1/31/1997)
91 **Château Cos-d'Estournel** St.-Estèphe 1994 • $50 Ⓐ • (1/31/1997) • HR
91 **Château de Valandraud** St.-Emilion 1994 • $224 Ⓐ • (1/31/1997)
91 **Château Mouton-Rothschild** Pauillac 1994 • $92 Ⓐ • (1/31/1997)
90 **Château Certan de May** Pomerol 1994 • $43 Ⓐ • (1/31/1997)
90 **Château Gazin** Pomerol 1994 • $43 • (1/31/1997)
90 **Château Haut-Bailly** Pessac-Léognan 1994 • $31 Ⓐ • (1/31/1997)
90 **Château La Pointe** Pomerol 1994 • $29 • (1/31/1997) • SS
90 **Château Latour** Pauillac 1994 • $110 Ⓐ • (12/15/1997)
90 **Château Léoville Barton** St.-Julien 1994 • $40 Ⓐ • (1/31/1997) • SS
90 **Château Magdelaine** St.-Emilion 1994 • $25 Ⓐ • (1/31/1997)
90 **Château Margaux** Margaux 1994 • $112 Ⓐ • (1/31/1997)
90 **Château Pavie-Macquin** St.-Emilion 1994 • $27 Ⓐ • (1/31/1997)
90 **Château Rauzan-Ségla** Margaux 1994 • $42 Ⓐ • (1/31/1997)
90 **Château Trotanoy** Pomerol 1994 • $62 • (1/31/1997)
90 **Clos de l'Oratoire** St.-Emilion 1994 • $29 • (1/31/1997)

1993 Red Bordeaux
VINTAGE RATING: 82

95 **Château Pétrus** Pomerol 1993 • $311 Ⓐ • (1/31/1996) • CS
94 **Château La Fleur de Gay** Pomerol 1993 • $34 Ⓐ • (1/31/1996) • CS
92 **Château Canon-La Gaffelière** St.-Emilion 1993 • $30 • (1/31/1996) • HR
91 **Château Haut-Brion** Pessac-Léognan 1993 • $85 Ⓐ • (4/30/1997)
91 **Château Lafleur** Pomerol 1993 • $90 Ⓐ • (1/31/2000)
91 **Château Trotanoy** Pomerol 1993 • $50 • (1/31/1996) • CS
90 **Château Angélus** St.-Emilion 1993 • $52 Ⓐ • (1/31/1996)
90 **Château Cheval-Blanc** St.-Emilion 1993 • $80 Ⓐ • (1/31/1996) • CS
90 **Château Clinet** Pomerol 1993 • $49 Ⓐ • (1/31/1996)
90 **Château Le Pin** Pomerol 1993 • $317 Ⓐ • (1/31/1996)
90 **Château L'Église Clinet** Pomerol 1993 • $44 Ⓐ • (4/30/1999)
90 **Château Margaux** Margaux 1993 • $101 Ⓐ • (1/31/1996)
90 **Château Montrose** St.-Estèphe 1993 • $37 Ⓐ • (1/31/1996)
90 **Château Mouton-Rothschild** Pauillac 1993 • $102 Ⓐ • (1/31/1996)

1990 Red Bordeaux
VINTAGE RATING: 97

100 **Château Latour** Pauillac 1990 • $408 Ⓐ • (3/15/1993)
98 **Château Pétrus** Pomerol 1990 • $1,014 Ⓐ • (3/31/1993)
97 **Château Lafite Rothschild** Pauillac 1990 • $207 Ⓐ • (3/31/1993) • CS
97 **Château Le Pin** Pomerol 1990 • $962 Ⓐ • (3/31/1993)
96 **Château Haut-Brion** Pessac-Léognan 1990 • $216 Ⓐ • (4/30/1997)
96 **Château Le Gay** Pomerol 1990 • $46 Ⓐ • (3/31/1993)
96 **Château Margaux** Margaux 1990 • $396 Ⓐ • (3/31/1993)
96 **Château Trotanoy** Pomerol 1990 • $62 • (3/31/1993)
95 **Château Beauséjour Duffau-Lagarosse** St.-Emilion 1990 • $350 Ⓐ • (3/31/1993)
95 **Château Canon-La Gaffelière** St.-Emilion 1990 • $75 Ⓐ • (3/15/1993) • HR
95 **Château Cordeillan-Bages** Pauillac 1990 • $33 • (3/31/1993)
95 **Château Grand-Puy-Lacoste** Pauillac 1990 • $84 Ⓐ • (3/31/1993)
95 **Château La Fleur de Gay** Pomerol 1990 • $96 Ⓐ • (3/31/1993)
95 **Château La Lagune** Haut-Médoc 1990 • $54 Ⓐ • (10/15/1994)
95 **Château La Mission-Haut-Brion** Pessac-Léognan 1990 • $65 • (3/31/1993)
95 **Château Lafleur** Pomerol 1990 • $508 Ⓐ • (5/15/1994)
95 **Château Lagrange** Pomerol 1990 • $30 • (3/31/1993)
95 **Château Lagrange** St.-Julien 1990 • $26 • (3/31/1993) • SS
95 **Château Mouton-Rothschild** Pauillac 1990 • $163 Ⓐ • (3/31/1993) • CS
94 **Château Ausone** St.-Emilion 1990 • $167 Ⓐ • (3/31/1993)
94 **Château Bourgneuf** Pomerol 1990 • $33 Ⓐ • (3/31/1993)
94 **Château Cheval-Blanc** St.-Emilion 1990 • $387 Ⓐ • (3/31/1999)
94 **Château Clerc Milon** Pauillac 1990 • $60 Ⓐ • (3/31/1993)
94 **Château Cos-Labory** St.-Estèphe 1990 • $40 Ⓐ • (3/31/1993)
94 **Château Fonroque** St.-Emilion 1990 • $28 • (3/31/1993)
94 **Château La Conseillante** Pomerol 1990 • $170 Ⓐ • (3/31/1993)
94 **Château La Croix-de-Gay** Pomerol 1990 • $28 • (3/31/1993)
94 **Château La Louvière** Pessac-Léognan 1990 • $216 Ⓐ • (3/31/1993)
94 **Château Larmande** St.-Emilion 1990 • $57 Ⓐ • (3/31/1993)
94 **Château L'Église Clinet** Pomerol 1990 • $121 Ⓐ • (4/30/1999)
94 **Château Lynch-Bages** Pauillac 1990 • $109 Ⓐ • (3/31/1993)
94 **Château Montrose** St.-Estèphe 1990 • $218 Ⓐ • (3/31/1993)
94 **Château Pavie** St.-Emilion 1990 • $63 Ⓐ • (3/31/1993)
94 **Château Pichon-Longueville-Baron** Pauillac 1990 • $110 Ⓐ • (3/31/1993)
94 **Château Pichon-Longueville-Lalande** Pauillac 1990 • $NA • (11/15/1997)
94 **Clos de l'Oratoire** St.-Emilion 1990 • $28 • (3/31/1993)
94 **Les Forts de Latour** Pauillac 1990 • $89 Ⓐ • (3/31/1993)
93 **Château Angélus** St.-Emilion 1990 • $170 Ⓐ • (3/31/1993)
93 **Château de Pez** St.-Estèphe 1990 • $40 Ⓐ • (3/31/1993)
93 **Château La Tour-Haut-Brion** Pessac-Léognan 1990 • $82 Ⓐ • (3/31/1993)
93 **Château Le Bon-Pasteur** Pomerol 1990 • $60 Ⓐ • (3/31/1993)
93 **Château Léoville Barton** St.-Julien 1990 • $79 Ⓐ • (3/31/1993)
93 **Château Leoville Las Cases** St.-Julien 1990 • $154 Ⓐ • (10/15/1994)

Key: SS—Spectator Selection. CS—Cellar Selection. HR—Highly Recommended. $NA—Price not available. (BT)—Barrel tasting. Ⓐ—Auction Price.
Dates in parentheses represent the issues in which the ratings were published.

93 **Château Les Ormes-de-Pez** St.-Estèphe 1990 • $33 Ⓐ • (3/31/1993)
93 **Château Pavie-Decesse** St.-Emilion 1990 • $22 • (3/31/1993)
93 **Château Pibran** Pauillac 1990 • $25 • (3/31/1993)
93 **Château Smith-Haut-Lafitte** Pessac-Léognan 1990 • $30 Ⓐ • (3/31/1993)
93 **Château Talbot** St.-Julien 1990 • $55 Ⓐ • (3/31/1993)
92 **Château Cantenac-Brown** Margaux 1990 • $38 Ⓐ • (3/31/1993)
92 **Château de Fieuzal** Pessac-Léognan 1990 • $36 Ⓐ • (3/31/1993)
92 **Château Duhart-Milon Rothschild** Pauillac 1990 • $42 Ⓐ • (10/15/1994)
92 **Château Figeac** St.-Emilion 1990 • $123 Ⓐ • (3/31/1993)
92 **Château Giscours** Margaux 1990 • $38 Ⓐ • (3/31/1993)
92 **Château Haut-Marbuzet** St.-Estèphe 1990 • $62 Ⓐ • (3/31/1993)
92 **Château La Grave à Pomerol** Pomerol 1990 • $28 • (3/31/1993)
92 **Château Léoville Poyferré** St.-Julien 1990 • $84 Ⓐ • (3/31/1993)
92 **Château L'Evangile** Pomerol 1990 • $146 Ⓐ • (3/31/1993)
92 **Château Pape Clément** Pessac-Léognan 1990 • $69 Ⓐ • (3/31/1993)
92 **Château Petit-Village** Pomerol 1990 • $83 Ⓐ • (3/31/1993)
92 **Château St.-Pierre** St.-Julien 1990 • $26 • (3/31/1993)
92 **Château Villemaurine** St.-Emilion 1990 • $28 • (3/31/1993)
92 **Domaine de Chevalier** Pessac-Léognan 1990 • $59 Ⓐ • (3/31/1993)
91 **Château Brane-Cantenac** Margaux 1990 • $30 • (3/31/1993)
91 **Château Canon** St.-Emilion 1990 • $56 Ⓐ • (3/31/1993)
91 **Château Certan de May** Pomerol 1990 • $83 Ⓐ • (10/15/1994)
91 **Château de Cruzeau** Pessac-Léognan 1990 • $16 • (3/31/1993)
91 **Château Desmirail** Margaux 1990 • $27 • (3/31/1993)
91 **Château Fontenil** Fronsac 1990 • $17 • (3/31/1993)
91 **Château Franc-Mayne** St.-Emilion 1990 • $23 • (3/31/1993)
91 **Château Haut-Bages-Avérous** Pauillac 1990 • $22 • (3/31/1993)
91 **Château Haut-Corbin** St.-Emilion 1990 • $23 • (3/31/1993)
91 **Château Langoa Barton** St.-Julien 1990 • $27 • (3/31/1993)
91 **Château Latour Martillac** Pessac-Léognan 1990 • $25 • (3/31/1993)
91 **Château Monbrison** Margaux 1990 • $34 Ⓐ • (3/31/1993)
91 **Château Moulin du Cadet** St.-Emilion 1990 • $NA • (3/31/1993)
91 **Château Palmer** Margaux 1990 • $89 Ⓐ • (3/31/1993)
91 **Château Phélan-Ségur** St.-Estèphe 1990 • $43 Ⓐ • (3/31/1993)
91 **Château Pouget** Margaux 1990 • $22 • (3/31/1993)
91 **Château Sociando-Mallet** Haut-Médoc 1990 • $55 Ⓐ • (3/31/1993)
91 **Château Troplong-Mondot** St.-Emilion 1990 • $150 Ⓐ • (3/31/1993)
91 **Château Trottevieille** St.-Emilion 1990 • $48 Ⓐ • (3/31/1993)
90 **Château Beau-Site** St.-Estèphe 1990 • $23 • (3/31/1993)
90 **Château Bélair** St.-Emilion 1990 • $33 • (3/31/1993)
90 **Château Branaire-Ducru** St.-Julien 1990 • $51 Ⓐ • (3/31/1993)
90 **Château Chasse-Spleen** Moulis 1990 • $44 Ⓐ • (3/31/1993)
90 **Château Cos-d'Estournel** St.-Estèphe 1990 • $108 Ⓐ • (3/31/1993)
90 **Château Fonplégade** St.-Emilion 1990 • $25 • (3/31/1993)
90 **Château Gruaud-Larose** St.-Julien 1990 • $70 Ⓐ • (3/31/1993)
90 **Château Kirwan** Margaux 1990 • $28 • (3/31/1993)
90 **Château La Fleur-Pétrus** Pomerol 1990 • $98 Ⓐ • (3/31/1993)
90 **Château Lafleur-Gazin** Pomerol 1990 • $30 • (3/31/1993)
90 **Château Lalande-Borie** St.-Julien 1990 • $19 • (3/31/1993)
90 **Château Larcis-Ducasse** St.-Emilion 1990 • $37 Ⓐ • (3/31/1993)
90 **Château Latour à Pomerol** Pomerol 1990 • $74 Ⓐ • (10/15/1994)
90 **Château Magdelaine** St.-Emilion 1990 • $44 Ⓐ • (3/31/1993)
90 **Château Meyney** St.-Estèphe 1990 • $20 • (3/31/1993)
90 **Château Olivier** Pessac-Léognan 1990 • $19 • (3/31/1993)
90 **Château Petit-Figeac** St.-Emilion 1990 • $24 • (3/31/1993)
90 **Château Siran** Margaux 1990 • $30 Ⓐ • (3/31/1993)
90 **Clos Fourtet** St.-Emilion 1990 • $43 Ⓐ • (3/31/1993)
90 **Tourelles de Longueville** Pauillac 1990 • $22 • (3/31/1993)

1989 Red Bordeaux
Vintage Rating: 98

100 **Château Haut-Brion** Pessac-Léognan 1989 • $395 Ⓐ • (5/31/1999)
100 **Château Pétrus** Pomerol 1989 • $952 Ⓐ • (5/31/1999)
99 **Château Margaux** Margaux 1989 • $194 Ⓐ • (5/31/1999)
98 **Château Lynch-Bages** Pauillac 1989 • $132 Ⓐ • (5/31/1999)
98 **Château Mouton-Rothschild** Pauillac 1989 • $196 Ⓐ • (5/31/1999)
98 **Château Pichon-Longueville-Baron** Pauillac 1989 • $118 Ⓐ • (5/31/1999)
97 **Château Lafleur** Pomerol 1989 • $342 Ⓐ • (5/31/1999)
97 **Château Latour** Pauillac 1989 • $167 Ⓐ • (5/31/1999)
96 **Château Clerc Milon** Pauillac 1989 • $62 Ⓐ • (5/31/1999)
96 **Château La Mission-Haut-Brion** Pessac-Léognan 1989 • $NA • (5/31/1999)
96 **Château L'Église Clinet** Pomerol 1989 • $93 Ⓐ • (4/30/1999)
96 **Domaine de Chevalier** Pessac-Léognan 1989 • $55 Ⓐ • (5/31/1999)
95 **Château Cantemerle** Haut-Médoc 1989 • $58 Ⓐ • (5/31/1999)
95 **Château Cordeillan-Bages** Pauillac 1989 • $NA • (5/31/1999)
95 **Château Cos-d'Estournel** St.-Estèphe 1989 • $83 Ⓐ • (5/31/1999)
95 **Château Le Gay** Pomerol 1989 • $75 Ⓐ • (5/31/1999)
94 **Château Angélus** St.-Emilion 1989 • $138 Ⓐ • (5/31/1999)
94 **Château Brane-Cantenac** Margaux 1989 • $39 Ⓐ • (5/31/1999)
94 **Château Franc-Mayne** St.-Emilion 1989 • $NA • (5/31/1999)
94 **Château La Fleur de Gay** Pomerol 1989 • $116 Ⓐ • (5/31/1999)
94 **Château Lafite Rothschild** Pauillac 1989 • $164 Ⓐ • (5/31/1999)

94 **Château Lagrange** St.-Julien 1989 • $NA • (5/31/1999)

94 **Château Pichon-Longueville-Lalande** Pauillac 1989 • $NA • (5/31/1999)

94 **Tourelles de Longueville** Pauillac 1989 • $27 • (3/15/1992)

93 **Château Ausone** St.-Emilion 1989 • $125 Ⓐ • (5/31/1999)

93 **Château Beychevelle** St.-Julien 1989 • $74 Ⓐ • (5/31/1999)

93 **Château Grand-Puy-Lacoste** Pauillac 1989 • $52 Ⓐ • (5/31/1999)

93 **Château Larmande** St.-Emilion 1989 • $42 Ⓐ • (5/31/1999)

93 **Château L'Arrosée** St.-Emilion 1989 • $46 Ⓐ • (4/30/1992) • HR

93 **Château Meyney** St.-Estèphe 1989 • $46 Ⓐ • (5/31/1999)

93 **Château Montrose** St.-Estèphe 1989 • $92 Ⓐ • (5/31/1999)

93 **Château Palmer** Margaux 1989 • $131 Ⓐ • (5/31/1999)

93 **Château Poujeaux** Moulis 1989 • $35 Ⓐ • (5/31/1999)

93 **Château Tertre Roteboeuf** St.-Emilion 1989 • $NA • (5/31/1999)

93 **Château Troplong-Mondot** St.-Emilion 1989 • $106 Ⓐ • (5/31/1999)

93 **Château Villemaurine** St.-Emilion 1989 • $NA • (5/31/1999)

92 **Château Cheval-Blanc** St.-Emilion 1989 • $160 Ⓐ • (5/31/1999)

92 **Château d'Armailhac** Pauillac 1989 • $63 Ⓐ • (5/31/1999)

92 **Château Durfort-Vivens** Margaux 1989 • $28 • (3/15/1992)

92 **Château Giscours** Margaux 1989 • $43 Ⓐ • (5/31/1999)

92 **Château Grand-Mayne** St.-Emilion 1989 • $45 Ⓐ • (5/31/1999)

92 **Château Haut-Bailly** Pessac-Léognan 1989 • $59 Ⓐ • (5/31/1999)

92 **Château La Fleur-Pétrus** Pomerol 1989 • $90 Ⓐ • (5/31/1999)

92 **Château La Tour-Haut-Brion** Pessac-Léognan 1989 • $77 Ⓐ • (5/31/1999)

92 **Château Langoa Barton** St.-Julien 1989 • $41 Ⓐ • (5/31/1999)

92 **Château Le Pin** Pomerol 1989 • $615 Ⓐ • (5/31/1999)

92 **Château Léoville Barton** St.-Julien 1989 • $65 Ⓐ • (5/31/1999)

92 **Château L'Evangile** Pomerol 1989 • $112 Ⓐ • (5/31/1999)

92 **Château Pibran** Pauillac 1989 • $NA • (5/31/1999)

92 **Château Trotanoy** Pomerol 1989 • $NA • (5/31/1999)

91 **Château Chasse-Spleen** Moulis 1989 • $48 Ⓐ • (5/31/1999)

91 **Château Cos-Labory** St.-Estèphe 1989 • $NA • (5/31/1999)

91 **Château Figeac** St.-Emilion 1989 • $64 Ⓐ • (5/31/1999)

91 **Château Grand-Puy-Ducasse** Pauillac 1989 • $39 Ⓐ • (5/31/1999)

91 **Château Gruaud-Larose** St.-Julien 1989 • $64 Ⓐ • (5/31/1999)

91 **Château Haut-Corbin** St.-Emilion 1989 • $NA • (5/31/1999)

91 **Château La Dominique** St.-Emilion 1989 • $71 Ⓐ • (5/31/1999)

91 **Château La Pointe** Pomerol 1989 • $27 Ⓐ • (5/31/1999)

91 **Château Larcis-Ducasse** St.-Emilion 1989 • $NA • (5/31/1999)

Key: SS—Spectator Selection. CS—Cellar Selection. HR—Highly Recommended. $NA—Price not available. (BT)—Barrel tasting. Ⓐ—Auction Price.
Dates in parentheses represent the issues in which the ratings were published.

91 **Château Magdelaine** St.-Emilion 1989 • $65 Ⓐ • (5/31/1999)

91 **Château Monbrison** Margaux 1989 • $35 Ⓐ • (5/31/1999)

91 **Château Moulin Pey-Labrie** Canon-Fronsac 1989 • $NA • (5/31/1999)

91 **Château Pavie-Decesse** St.-Emilion 1989 • $NA • (5/31/1999)

91 **Château St.-André-Corbin** St.-Georges-St.-Emilion 1989 • $15 • (4/30/1992)

91 **Château St.-Pierre** St.-Julien 1989 • $35 Ⓐ • (5/31/1999)

91 **Les Forts de Latour** Pauillac 1989 • $58 Ⓐ • (3/15/1992)

91 **Vieux-Château-Certan** Pomerol 1989 • $68 Ⓐ • (5/31/1999)

90 **Château Bahans Haut-Brion** Pessac-Léognan 1989 • $76 Ⓐ • (3/15/1992)

90 **Château Beauregard** Pomerol 1989 • $NA • (5/31/1999)

90 **Château Beau-Site** St.-Estèphe 1989 • $NA • (5/31/1999)

90 **Château Bélair** St.-Emilion 1989 • $NA • (5/31/1999)

90 **Château Bourgneuf** Pomerol 1989 • $44 Ⓐ • (5/31/1999)

90 **Château Branaire-Ducru** St.-Julien 1989 • $59 Ⓐ • (5/31/1999)

90 **Château Canon** St.-Emilion 1989 • $62 Ⓐ • (5/31/1999)

90 **Château Cissac** Haut-Médoc 1989 • $26 Ⓐ • (5/31/1999)

90 **Château Citran** Haut-Médoc 1989 • $24 Ⓐ • (5/31/1999)

90 **Château Clarke** Listrac 1989 • $NA • (5/31/1999)

90 **Château de Chantegrive** Graves Cuvée Edouard 1989 • $NA • (5/31/1999)

90 **Château de Malleret** Haut-Médoc 1989 • $NA • (3/15/1992)

90 **Château de Rochemorin** Pessac-Léognan 1989 • $NA • (5/31/1999)

90 **Château du Tertre** Margaux 1989 • $29 • (3/15/1992)

90 **Château Duhart-Milon Rothschild** Pauillac 1989 • $42 Ⓐ • (5/31/1999)

90 **Château Faizeau** Montagne-St.-Emilion Sélection Vieilles Vignes 1989 • $NA • (5/31/1999)

90 **Château Haut-Bages-Avérous** Pauillac 1989 • $26 • (3/15/1992)

90 **Château Haut-Batailley** Pauillac 1989 • $40 Ⓐ • (5/31/1999)

90 **Château Haut-Marbuzet** St.-Estèphe 1989 • $45 Ⓐ • (5/31/1999)

90 **Château La Commanderie** St.-Emilion 1989 • $NA • (5/31/1999)

90 **Château La Conseillante** Pomerol 1989 • $167 Ⓐ • (5/31/1999)

90 **Château La Gurgue** Margaux 1989 • $20 Ⓐ • (5/31/1999)

90 **Château La Lagune** Haut-Médoc 1989 • $49 Ⓐ • (5/31/1999)

90 **Château La Serre** St.-Emilion 1989 • $NA • (5/31/1999)

90 **Château La Tour de Mons** Margaux 1989 • $NA • (5/31/1999)

90 **Château Lafon-Rochet** St.-Estèphe 1989 • $42 Ⓐ • (5/31/1999)

90 **Château Lanessan** Haut-Médoc 1989 • $NA • (5/31/1999)

90 **Château Latour à Pomerol** Pomerol 1989 • $74 Ⓐ • (5/31/1999)

90 **Château Léoville Las Cases** St.-Julien 1989 • $107 Ⓐ • (5/31/1999)

90 **Château Léoville Poyferré** St.-Julien 1989 • $47 Ⓐ • (5/31/1999)

90 **Château Les Ormes-de-Pez** St.-Estèphe 1989 • $42 Ⓐ • (5/31/1999)

90 **Château Liversan** Haut-Médoc 1989 • $NA • (5/31/1999)
90 **Château Malartic-Lagravière** Pessac-Léognan 1989 • $NA • (5/31/1999)
90 **Château Moulin Haut-Laroque** Fronsac 1989 • $NA • (5/31/1999)
90 **Château Pape Clément** Pessac-Léognan 1989 • $42 Ⓐ • (5/31/1999)
90 **Château Pavie** St.-Emilion 1989 • $51 Ⓐ • (5/31/1999)
90 **Château Pavie-Macquin** St.-Emilion 1989 • $50 Ⓐ • (5/31/1999)
90 **Château Pontet-Canet** Pauillac 1989 • $45 Ⓐ • (5/31/1999)
90 **Château Puy-Blanquet** St.-Emilion 1989 • $14 • (3/15/1992)
90 **Château Ramage La Bâtisse** Haut-Médoc 1989 • $NA • (5/31/1999)
90 **Château Rausan-Ségla** Margaux 1989 • $72 Ⓐ • (5/31/1999)
90 **Château Sociando-Mallet** Haut-Médoc 1989 • $46 Ⓐ • (5/31/1999)
90 **Château Verdignan** Haut-Médoc 1989 • $NA • (5/31/1999)
90 **Clos des Jacobins** St.-Emilion 1989 • $34 Ⓐ • (5/31/1999)
90 **Clos Fourtet** St.-Emilion 1989 • $62 Ⓐ • (5/31/1999)

1988 Red Bordeaux
Vintage Rating: 93

98 **Château Haut-Brion** Pessac-Léognan 1988 • $171 Ⓐ • (11/30/1998)
98 **Château Lafleur** Pomerol 1988 • $201 Ⓐ • (1/31/2000)
97 **Château La Fleur de Gay** Pomerol 1988 • $77 Ⓐ • (11/30/1998)
97 **Château Lynch-Bages** Pauillac 1988 • $76 Ⓐ • (11/30/1998)
96 **Château La Mission-Haut-Brion** Pessac-Léognan 1988 • $NA • (11/30/1998)
96 **Château Lagrange** St.-Julien 1988 • $NA • (11/30/1998)
96 **Château Latour** Pauillac 1988 • $128 Ⓐ • (11/30/1998)
95 **Château Cos-d'Estournel** St.-Estèphe 1988 • $70 Ⓐ • (11/30/1998)
95 **Château Margaux** Margaux 1988 • $148 Ⓐ • (11/30/1998)
95 **Château Pichon-Longueville-Baron** Pauillac 1988 • $76 Ⓐ • (11/30/1998)
94 **Château Angélus** St.-Emilion 1988 • $80 Ⓐ • (11/30/1998)
94 **Château Clerc Milon** Pauillac 1988 • $42 Ⓐ • (4/30/1991) • SS
94 **Château Larrivet-Haut-Brion** Pessac-Léognan 1988 • $20 Ⓐ • (4/30/1991)
94 **Château Mouton-Rothschild** Pauillac 1988 • $140 Ⓐ • (11/30/1998)
94 **Château Pavie-Decesse** St.-Emilion 1988 • $27 • (3/31/1991) • HR
94 **Château Pétrus** Pomerol 1988 • $385 Ⓐ • (11/30/1998)
93 **Château Clinet** Pomerol 1988 • $76 Ⓐ • (11/30/1998)
93 **Château Haut-Bages-Avérous** Pauillac 1988 • $20 • (4/30/1991)
93 **Château Tertre Roteboeuf** St.-Emilion 1988 • $105 Ⓐ • (11/30/1998)
93 **Château Trotanoy** Pomerol 1988 • $NA • (11/30/1998)
92 **Château Cheval-Blanc** St.-Emilion 1988 • $124 Ⓐ • (11/30/1998)
92 **Château de France** Pessac-Léognan 1988 • $18 • (2/28/1991) • SS
92 **Château Ducru-Beaucaillou** St.-Julien 1988 • $52 Ⓐ • (4/30/1991)
92 **Château Gruaud-Larose** St.-Julien 1988 • $77 Ⓐ • (11/30/1998)
92 **Château La Fleur-Pétrus** Pomerol 1988 • $56 Ⓐ • (11/30/1998)
92 **Château Le Pin** Pomerol 1988 • $390 Ⓐ • (11/30/1998)
92 **Château Léoville Las Cases** St.-Julien 1988 • $76 Ⓐ • (11/30/1998)
92 **Château Marbuzet** St.-Estèphe 1988 • $22 Ⓐ • (7/15/1991) • SS
92 **Les Fiefs de Lagrange** St.-Julien 1988 • $17 • (4/30/1991)
91 **Château Balestard-La-Tonnelle** St.-Emilion 1988 • $25 • (4/30/1991)
91 **Château Citran** Haut-Médoc 1988 • $22 Ⓐ • (4/30/1991)
91 **Château de Fieuzal** Pessac-Léognan 1988 • $33 • (4/30/1991)
91 **Château Grand-Puy-Lacoste** Pauillac 1988 • $42 Ⓐ • (11/30/1998)
91 **Château La Tour-Haut-Brion** Pessac-Léognan 1988 • $30 • (6/15/1991) • CS
91 **Château Olivier** Pessac-Léognan 1988 • $25 • (2/15/1991) • HR
91 **Château Sociando-Mallet** Haut-Médoc 1988 • $31 Ⓐ • (11/30/1998)
91 **Château Trimoulet** St.-Emilion 1988 • $16 • (6/15/1991) • HR
90 **Château Batailley** Pauillac 1988 • $30 • (4/30/1991)
90 **Château Beauregard** Pomerol 1988 • $36 • (7/31/1991) • HR
90 **Château Beauséjour Duffau-Lagarosse** St.-Emilion 1988 • $NA • (11/30/1998)
90 **Château Beychevelle** St.-Julien 1988 • $47 Ⓐ • (11/30/1998)
90 **Château Bourgneuf** Pomerol 1988 • $19 • (6/30/1991)
90 **Château Canon-La Gaffelière** St.-Emilion 1988 • $48 Ⓐ • (11/30/1998)
90 **Château Dauzac** Margaux 1988 • $20 • (6/30/1991) • HR
90 **Château Gazin** Pomerol 1988 • $NA • (11/30/1998)
90 **Château Haut-Marbuzet** St.-Estèphe 1988 • $37 Ⓐ • (11/30/1998)
90 **Château La Conseillante** Pomerol 1988 • $60 Ⓐ • (11/30/1998)
90 **Château La Gurgue** Margaux 1988 • $34 • (4/30/1991)
90 **Château La Louvière** Pessac-Léognan 1988 • $29 Ⓐ • (11/30/1998)
90 **Château Lafite Rothschild** Pauillac 1988 • $147 Ⓐ • (11/30/1998)
90 **Château Lafleur** Pomerol 1988 • $201 Ⓐ • (11/30/1998)
90 **Château Latour à Pomerol** Pomerol 1988 • $49 Ⓐ • (10/15/1994)
90 **Château Malescot-St.-Exupéry** Margaux 1988 • $NA • (11/30/1998)
90 **Château Monbrison** Margaux 1988 • $29 Ⓐ • (11/30/1998)
90 **Château Mouton-Baronne-Philippe** Pauillac 1988 • $45 Ⓐ • (4/30/1991)
90 **Château Pape Clément** Pessac-Léognan 1988 • $65 Ⓐ • (11/30/1998)
90 **Château Poujeaux** Moulis 1988 • $27 Ⓐ • (11/30/1998)
90 **Château Prieuré-Lichine** Margaux 1988 • $31 Ⓐ • (4/30/1991)
90 **Château Troplong-Mondot** St.-Emilion 1988 • $43 Ⓐ • (11/30/1998)
90 **Clos des Jacobins** St.-Emilion 1988 • $33 Ⓐ • (4/15/1991) • HR

One of Domaine de la Romanée-Conti's vineyards.

Red Burgundy

The highest-scoring wines from five consecutive recent vintages of red Burgundy—1993 through 1997—are listed in this section, with ratings and prices. The classic 1990 vintage is here as well. For ratings of wines from other vintages, see the main listings. (Note that our 1998 red Burgundy tastings were completed too close to publication of this book to be included. *Wine Spectator's* Burgundy expert, Per-Henrik Mansson, gives the overall vintage an 89 rating, but reports that it is uneven, with Côte de Nuits showing better than Côte de Beaune.)

The recent vintage of choice for Burgundy lovers remains 1996. Both 1993 and 1995 produced many great wines, but they are years for which careful shopping is recommended because quality was somewhat uneven. Neither 1994 nor 1997 was a washout, but these two vintages are weaker overall than the other years covered here.

Red Burgundy is generally made in small quantities, and many of the best wines are bought up quickly upon release. But diligent shoppers can find them on sale at retail, at auction and on restaurant wine lists.

1997 Red Burgundy | Vintage Rating: 83

96 **Dominique Laurent** Grands Echézeaux 1997 • $270 • (1/01/2000)

96 **Dominique Laurent** Mazis-Chambertin 1997 • $150 • (1/01/2000)

95 **Domaine des Comtes Lafon** Volnay-Santenots du-Milieu 1997 • $65 • (1/01/2000)

95 **Dominique Laurent** Chambertin-Clos de Bèze 1997 • $270 • (1/01/2000)

95 **Dominique Laurent** Clos de la Roche 1997 • $123 • (1/01/2000)

95 **Dominique Laurent** Corton 1997 • $123 • (1/01/2000)

95 **Dominique Laurent** Vosne-Romanée Les Suchots 1997 • $87 • (1/01/2000)

95 **Philippe Charlopin-Parizot** Charmes-Chambertin 1997 • $92 • (9/30/1999)

94 **Denis Mortet** Chambolle-Musigny Aux Beaux Bruns 1997 • $70 • (9/30/1999) • HR

94 **Dominique Laurent** Charmes-Chambertin 1997 • $120 • (1/01/2000)

94 **Dominique Laurent** Ruchottes-Chambertin 1997 • $166 • (1/01/2000)

93 **Bertrand Ambroise** Nuits-St.-Georges En Rue de Chaux 1997 • $55 • (1/01/2000)

Key: SS—Spectator Selection. CS—Cellar Selection. HR—Highly Recommended. $NA—Price not available. (BT)—Barrel tasting. Ⓐ—Auction Price.
Dates in parentheses represent the issues in which the ratings were published.

93 **Bertrand Ambroise** Nuits-St.-Georges Les Vaucrains 1997 • $60 • (1/01/2000)

93 **Caillot** Pommard 1997 • $NA • (1/01/2000)

93 **Château de la Tour** Clos Vougeot 1997 • $85 • (9/30/1999)

93 **Daniel Rion** Nuits-St.-Georges Aux Vignerondes 1997 • $45 • (9/30/1999) • HR

93 **Domaine Leroy** Clos de la Roche 1997 • $610 • (9/30/1999)

93 **Domaine Leroy** Clos de Vougeot 1997 • $434 • (9/30/1999) • CS

93 **Domaine Leroy** Richebourg 1997 • $610 • (9/30/1999)

93 **Dominique Laurent** Beaune Premier Cru Hospices de Beaune 1997 • $NA • (1/01/2000)

93 **Dominique Laurent** Bonnes Mares 1997 • $270 • (1/01/2000)

93 **Dominique Laurent** Echézeaux 1997 • $150 • (1/01/2000)

93 **Dominique Laurent** Mercurey Les Saumons 1997 • $30 • (9/30/1999)

93 **Henri & Gilles Remoriquet** Nuits-St.-Georges Les Damodes 1997 • $40 • (1/01/2000)

93 **Henri Gouges** Nuits-St.-Georges Clos des Porrets St.-Georges 1997 • $NA • (1/01/2000)

93 **Hubert Lignier** Clos de la Roche 1997 • $150 • (1/01/2000)

93 **Jacques Prieur** Corton Bressandes 1997 • $112 • (9/30/1999)

93 **Jacques Prieur** Musigny 1997 • $170 • (9/30/1999)

93 **Jean-Jacques Confuron** Clos Vougeot 1997 • $135 • (9/30/1999)

Fred Seidman

93 **Michele & Patrice Rion** Chambolle-Musigny Les Cras 1997 • $NA • (9/30/1999)
93 **Mongeard-Mugneret** Richebourg 1997 • $208 • (9/30/1999)
92 **Alain Gras** Auxey-Duresses Vieilles Vignes 1997 • $30 • (9/30/1999)
92 **Comte Georges de Vogüé** Musigny Cuvée Vieilles Vignes 1997 • $250 • (1/01/2000)
92 **Domaine Leroy** Romanée St.-Vivant 1997 • $610 • (9/30/1999)
92 **Domaine Leroy** Vosne-Romanée Les Beaux Monts 1997 • $257 • (9/30/1999)
92 **Henri Gouges** Nuits-St.-Georges Les St.- Georges 1997 • $71 • (1/01/2000)
92 **Hubert Lignier** Gevrey-Chambertin 1997 • $45 • (1/01/2000)
92 **Hubert Lignier** Morey-St.-Denis 1997 • $NA • (1/01/2000)
92 **Jacques Prieur** Beaune Grèves 1997 • $50 • (1/01/2000)
92 **Jacques Prieur** Beaune Grèves 1997 • $NA • (1/01/2000)
92 **Lucien Muzard & Fils** Santenay Gravières 1997 • $29 • (9/30/1999)
92 **René Engel** Vosne-Romanée Les Brûlées 1997 • $NA • (1/01/2000)
91 **Claude Dugat** Gevrey-Chambertin Premier Cru 1997 • $85 • (9/30/1999)
91 **Daniel Rion** Vosne-Romanée Les Beaux Monts 1997 • $49 • (9/30/1999)
91 **Denis Mortet** Gevrey-Chambertin Combe-du-Dessus 1997 • $54 • (9/30/1999)
91 **Domaine Leroy** Nuits-St.-Georges Aux Boudots 1997 • $257 • (9/30/1999)
91 **Dominique Laurent** Beaune Les Grèves 1997 • $40 • (9/30/1999)
91 **G. Roumier** Morey-St.-Denis Clos de la Bussière 1997 • $45 • (1/01/2000)
91 **Henri Gouges** Nuits-St.-Georges 1997 • $40 • (1/01/2000)
91 **Henri Gouges** Nuits-St.-Georges Les Chaignots 1997 • $NA • (1/01/2000)
91 **Jean-Michel Guillon** Gevrey-Chambertin Clos Prieur 1997 • $36 • (9/30/1999)
91 **Jean-Noël Gagnard** Chassagne-Montrachet Red Morgeot 1997 • $28 • (9/30/1999)
91 **Louis Jadot** Savigny-lès-Beaune Les Vergelesses 1997 • $28 • (9/30/1999) • HR
91 **Louis Jadot** Volnay Clos de la Barre 1997 • $44 • (9/30/1999)
91 **Lucien Muzard & Fils** Santenay Champs Claude Vieilles Vignes 1997 • $24 • (9/30/1999)
91 **Monthélie-Douhairet** Monthélie Les Duressees 1997 • $34 • (9/30/1999)
91 **René Engel** Grands Echézeaux 1997 • $NA • (1/01/2000)
91 **Tollot-Beaut & Fils** Corton Bressandes 1997 • $63 • (9/30/1999)
91 **Vincent Girardin** Pommard Les Chaponnières 1997 • $66 • (9/30/1999)
90 **Bertrand Ambroise** Vougeot Les Crâs 1997 • $64 • (1/01/2000)
90 **Bouchard Père & Fils** Bonnes Mares 1997 • $131 • (9/30/1999)
90 **Denis Mortet** Chambertin 1997 • $144 • (9/30/1999)

Key: SS—Spectator Selection. CS—Cellar Selection.
HR—Highly Recommended. $NA—Price not available.
(BT)—Barrel tasting. Ⓐ—Auction Price.
Dates in parentheses represent the issues in which the ratings were published.

90 **Domaine Leroy** Chambolle-Musigny Les Charmes 1997 • $282 • (9/30/1999)
90 **Domaine Leroy** Nuits-St.-Georges Au Bas de Combe 1997 • $115 • (9/30/1999)
90 **Domaine Leroy** Pommard Les Vignots 1997 • $115 • (9/30/1999)
90 **Domaine Leroy** Savigny-lès-Beaune Les Narbantons 1997 • $85 • (9/30/1999)
90 **Domaine Leroy** Vosne-Romanée Les Brûlées 1997 • $257 • (9/30/1999)
90 **Dominique Laurent** Clos Vougeot 1997 • $190 • (1/01/2000)
90 **Dominique Laurent** Vosne-Romanée Les Chaumes 1997 • $91 • (1/01/2000)
90 **Henri Gouges** Nuits-St.-Georges Les Chênes Carteaux 1997 • $52 • (1/01/2000)
90 **Jayer-Gilles** Echézeaux du Dessus 1997 • $155 • (9/30/1999)
90 **Jean Grivot** Vosne-Romanée Les Beaux Monts 1997 • $45 • (9/30/1999)
90 **Jean-Michel Guillon** Gevrey-Chambertin Les Champonnets 1997 • $36 • (9/30/1999)
90 **Louis Jadot** Beaune Clos des Ursules 1997 • $44 • (9/30/1999)
90 **Michel Gros** Nuits-St.-Georges Premier Cru 1997 • $NA • (1/01/2000)
90 **Michel Gros** Vosne-Romanée 1997 • $49 • (9/30/1999)
90 **René Engel** Vosne-Romanée 1997 • $NA • (1/01/2000)
90 **Robert Arnoux** Clos de Vougeot 1997 • $NA • (1/01/2000)
90 **Robert Arnoux** Nuits-St.-Georges Les Corvées Pagets 1997 • $NA • (1/01/2000)
90 **Robert Arnoux** Nuits-St.-Georges Les Poisets 1997 • $NA • (1/01/2000)
90 **Robert Arnoux** Vosne-Romanée Les Suchots 1997 • $NA • (1/01/2000)

1996 Red Burgundy
Vintage Rating: 95

99 **Denis Mortet** Clos Vougeot 1996 • $87 • (9/30/1998)
99 **Jayer-Gilles** Echézeaux du Dessus 1996 • $140 • (9/30/1998)
98 **Claude Dugat** Griotte-Chambertin 1996 • $911 Ⓐ • (5/15/1999)
98 **Domaine de la Romanée-Conti** Romanée-Conti 1996 • $1,754 Ⓐ • (9/30/1999) • CS
98 **Domaine Leroy** Romanée St.-Vivant 1996 • $610 • (9/30/1998)
98 **Jacques Prieur** Corton Bressandes 1996 • $120 • (5/15/1999)
97 **Comte Armand** Pommard Clos des Epeneaux 1996 • $102 Ⓐ • (9/30/1999) • HR
97 **Dominique Laurent** Musigny 1996 • $136 • (9/30/1999)
97 **J. Confuron-Cotetidot** Charmes-Chambertin 1996 • $94 • (5/15/1999)
97 **Philippe Charlopin-Parizot** Clos St.-Denis 1996 • $92 • (9/30/1999)
97 **Sérafin Père & Fils** Charmes-Chambertin 1996 • $120 • (9/30/1998)
96 **Bouchard Père & Fils** Clos Vougeot 1996 • $88 • (9/30/1998)
96 **Comte Georges de Vogüé** Musigny Cuvée Vieilles Vignes 1996 • $336 Ⓐ • (5/15/1999) • CS
96 **Domaine de la Romanée-Conti** La Tâche 1996 • $480 Ⓐ • (9/30/1999) • CS

96 **Dominique Laurent** Chambolle-Musigny Les Charmes 1996 • $100 • (5/15/1999)
96 **Henri & Gilles Remoriquet** Nuits-St.-Georges Les St.-Georges 1996 • $46 • (5/15/1999)
96 **Jacques Prieur** Musigny 1996 • $162 • (9/30/1998) • CS
96 **Louis Jadot** Chambertin-Clos de Bèze 1996 • $105 Ⓐ • (9/30/1998)
96 **Méo-Camuzet** Vosne-Romanée Les Chaumes 1996 • $78 • (9/30/1998)
95 **Denis Mortet** Chambertin 1996 • $125 • (9/30/1998)
95 **Domaine d'Auvenay** Bonnes Mares 1996 • $260 Ⓐ • (9/30/1998)
95 **Domaine de la Romanée-Conti** Richebourg 1996 • $319 Ⓐ • (9/30/1999)
95 **Domaine de la Romanée-Conti** Romanée St.-Vivant 1996 • $192 Ⓐ • (9/30/1999)
95 **Domaine Leroy** Musigny 1996 • $660 • (9/30/1998)
95 **Domaine Leroy** Richebourg 1996 • $610 • (9/30/1998)
95 **Dominique Laurent** Chambertin-Clos de Bèze 1996 • $272 • (5/15/1999)
95 **Forey Père & Fils** Echézeaux 1996 • $70 • (9/30/1999)
95 **Gros Frère & Soeur** Richebourg 1996 • $180 • (5/15/1999)
95 **Henri & Gilles Remoriquet** Nuits-St.-Georges Les Bousselots 1996 • $40 • (5/15/1999)
95 **J. Confuron-Cotetidot** Gevrey-Chambertin Lavaut St.-Jacques 1996 • $61 • (5/15/1999)
95 **Jean-Jacques Confuron** Nuits-St.-Georges Aux Boudots 1996 • $70 • (5/15/1999)
95 **Jean-Jacques Confuron** Romanée St.-Vivant 1996 • $155 • (5/15/1999)
95 **Louis Jadot** Ruchottes-Chambertin 1996 • $96 • (5/15/1999)
95 **Méo-Camuzet** Clos de Vougeot 1996 • $98 • (9/30/1998) • CS
95 **Méo-Camuzet** Richebourg 1996 • $260 • (9/30/1998)
95 **Newman** Latricières-Chambertin 1996 • $95 • (7/31/1999)
95 **Robert Chevillon** Nuits-St.-Georges Les Bousselots 1996 • $40 • (7/31/1999) • HR
95 **Sérafin Père & Fils** Gevrey-Chambertin Vieilles Vignes 1996 • $60 • (9/30/1998)
94 **Bertagna** Chambertin 1996 • $67 • (2/28/1999)
94 **Claude Dugat** Gevrey-Chambertin Lavaux St.-Jacques 1996 • $201 Ⓐ • (9/30/1998)
94 **Claude Dugat** Gevrey-Chambertin Premier Cru 1996 • $80 • (9/30/1998)
94 **Domaine d'Auvenay** Mazis-Chambertin 1996 • $660 • (9/30/1998)
94 **Domaine de la Romanée-Conti** Grands Echézeaux 1996 • $249 Ⓐ • (9/30/1999)
94 **Domaine Leroy** Chambolle-Musigny Les Fremières 1996 • $165 • (9/30/1998)
94 **Domaine Leroy** Latricières-Chambertin 1996 • $610 • (9/30/1998)
94 **Domaine Leroy** Savigny-lès-Beaune Les Narbantons 1996 • $85 • (9/30/1998)
94 **Dominique Laurent** Chambertin 1996 • $134 • (9/30/1999)
94 **Dominique Laurent** Gevrey-Chambertin Clos St.-Jacques 1996 • $52 Ⓐ • (5/15/1999)
94 **Dominique Laurent** Nuits-St.-Georges Les Cailles 1996 • $78 • (5/15/1999)
94 **Emmanuel Rouget** Vosne-Romanée Les Beaumonts 1996 • $101 Ⓐ • (1/01/2000)
94 **Fougeray de Beauclair** Bonnes Mares 1996 • $82 • (9/30/1998)
94 **Henri Gouges** Nuits-St.-Georges Les Pruliers 1996 • $45 • (9/30/1998)
94 **J. Confuron-Cotetidot** Mazis-Chambertin 1996 • $100 • (5/15/1999)
94 **J. Confuron-Cotetidot** Nuits-St.-Georges 1996 • $52 • (5/15/1999)
94 **Jean-Jacques Confuron** Clos Vougeot 1996 • $125 • (5/15/1999)
94 **Louis Jadot** Corton Les Pougets 1996 • $61 • (9/30/1999)
94 **Ponsot** Chapelle-Chambertin 1996 • $150 • (5/15/1999)
94 **Robert Chevillon** Nuits-St.-Georges Les Chaignots 1996 • $58 Ⓐ • (7/31/1999)
94 **Sérafin Père & Fils** Gevrey-Chambertin Le Fonteny 1996 • $75 • (9/30/1998)
94 **Sérafin Père & Fils** Gevrey-Chambertin Les Cazetiers 1996 • $80 • (9/30/1998)
94 **Sérafin Père & Fils** Gevrey-Chambertin Les Corbeaux 1996 • $75 • (9/30/1998)
93 **Bertrand Ambroise** Nuits-St.-Georges Les Vaucrains 1996 • $60 • (9/30/1998)
93 **Bertrand Ambroise** Vougeot Les Crâs 1996 • $60 • (9/30/1998)
93 **Château de la Tour** Clos Vougeot 1996 • $65 • (9/30/1998)
93 **Comte Georges de Vogüé** Chambolle-Musigny Les Amoureuses 1996 • $188 • (5/15/1999)
93 **Denis Bachelet** Gevrey-Chambertin Vieilles Vignes 1996 • $40 • (1/01/2000)
93 **Domaine Leroy** Chambertin 1996 • $660 • (9/30/1998)
93 **Domaine Leroy** Nuits-St.-Georges Aux Boudots 1996 • $261 Ⓐ • (9/30/1998)
93 **Domaine Leroy** Volnay-Santenots 1996 • $180 • (9/30/1998)
93 **Dominique Laurent** Gevrey-Chambertin Les Combottes 1996 • $80 • (5/15/1999)
93 **Doudet-Naudin** Nuits-St.-Georges Les Cailles 1996 • $NA • (1/01/1999)
93 **Drouhin-Laroze** Chambertin-Clos de Bèze 1996 • $93 • (9/30/1998)
93 **G. Roumier** Bonnes Mares 1996 • $147 Ⓐ • (7/31/1999) • CS
93 **J. Confuron-Cotetidot** Chambolle-Musigny 1996 • $50 • (5/15/1999)
93 **J. Confuron-Cotetidot** Vosne-Romanée 1996 • $51 • (5/15/1999)
93 **J. Confuron-Cotetidot** Vosne-Romanée Les Suchots 1996 • $66 • (5/15/1999)
93 **Jacques Prieur** Echézeaux 1996 • $120 • (9/30/1998)
93 **Jean Grivot** Richebourg 1996 • $215 Ⓐ • (9/30/1998)
93 **Jean-Jacques Confuron** Chambolle-Musigny 1996 • $48 • (5/15/1999)
93 **Jean-Marc Boillot** Pommard Rugiens 1996 • $93 • (9/30/1998)
93 **Jean-Marc Millot** Echézeaux 1996 • $90 • (2/28/1999)
93 **Louis Jadot** Bonnes Mares 1996 • $96 • (5/15/1999)
93 **Louis Jadot** Chambolle-Musigny Les Feusselottes 1996 • $54 • (5/15/1999)
93 **Louis Jadot** Chambolle-Musigny Les Fuées 1996 • $54 • (5/15/1999)
93 **Louis Jadot** Clos St.-Denis Domaine André Gagey 1996 • $85 • (5/15/1999)
93 **Louis Jadot** Nuits-St.-Georges Les Boudots 1996 • $54 • (5/15/1999)
93 **Louis Jadot** Santenay Clos de Malte 1996 • $22 • (5/15/1999)
93 **Louis Jadot** Vosne-Romanée Les Suchots 1996 • $57 • (5/15/1999)
93 **Louis Latour** Vosne-Romanée Les Suchots 1996 • $58 • (5/15/1999)

93 **Michel Gros** Nuits-St.-Georges 1996 • $44 • (5/15/1999)
93 **Vincent Girardin** Pommard Clos des Lambots Vieilles Vignes 1996 • $46 • (9/30/1998) • HR
93 **Vincent Girardin** Pommard Les Chanlins Vieilles Vignes 1996 • $59 • (9/30/1998)
92 **Anne & François Gros** Richebourg 1996 • $200 • (9/30/1998)
92 **Bertrand Ambroise** Nuits-St.-Georges Cuvée Vieilles Vignes 1996 • $40 • (9/30/1998) • HR
92 **Bertrand Ambroise** Pommard Les Saussilles 1996 • $45 • (9/30/1998)
92 **Bouchard Père & Fils** Chambertin-Clos de Bèze 1996 • $142 • (9/30/1998)
92 **Bouchard Père & Fils** Gevrey-Chambertin Les Cazetiers 1996 • $75 • (5/15/1999)
92 **Bouchard-Aîné & Fils** Echézeaux 1996 • $80 • (9/30/1998)
92 **Daniel Rion** Nuits-St.-Georges Les Grandes Vignes 1996 • $32 • (9/30/1998)
92 **Daniel Rion** Vosne-Romanée Les Beaux Monts 1996 • $48 • (9/30/1998)
92 **Daniel Rion** Vosne-Romanée Les Chaumes 1996 • $51 • (9/30/1998)
92 **Denis Mortet** Gevrey-Chambertin Les Champeaux 1996 • $62 Ⓐ • (9/30/1998)
92 **Domaine Leroy** Clos de Vougeot 1996 • $263 Ⓐ • (9/30/1998)
92 **Domaine Leroy** Vosne-Romanée Les Beaux Monts 1996 • $328 Ⓐ • (9/30/1998)
92 **Drouhin-Laroze** Musigny 1996 • $260 • (9/30/1998)
92 **Henri & Gilles Remoriquet** Nuits-St.-Georges Les Allots 1996 • $34 • (5/15/1999)
92 **Henri & Gilles Remoriquet** Nuits-St.-Georges Les Damodes 1996 • $40 • (5/15/1999)
92 **Henri Gouges** Nuits-St.-Georges Les St.-Georges 1996 • $53 Ⓐ • (9/30/1998)
92 **Jacques Prieur** Volnay-Santenots Clos des Santenots 1996 • $64 • (9/30/1998)
92 **Jayer-Gilles** Côte de Nuits-Villages 1996 • $45 • (9/30/1998)
92 **Jayer-Gilles** Nuits-St.-Georges Les Hauts Poirets 1996 • $75 • (9/30/1998)
92 **Louis Jadot** Beaune Clos des Couchereaux 1996 • $28 • (5/15/1999)
92 **Louis Jadot** Pommard 1996 • $33 • (5/15/1999) • SS
92 **Louis Latour** Romanée St.-Vivant Les Quatre Journaux 1996 • $175 • (5/15/1999)
92 **Méo-Camuzet** Nuits-St.-Georges Aux Boudots 1996 • $89 • (9/30/1998)
92 **Méo-Camuzet** Vosne-Romanée Aux Brûlées 1996 • $130 • (9/30/1998)
92 **Philippe Charlopin-Parizot** Chambertin 1996 • $105 • (9/30/1999)
92 **Ponsot** Morey-St.-Denis Cuvée des Alouettes 1996 • $33 Ⓐ • (5/15/1999)
92 **Robert Arnoux** Romanée St.-Vivant 1996 • $364 Ⓐ • (9/30/1998)
92 **Robert Chevillon** Nuits-St.-Georges Les Cailles 1996 • $60 • (7/31/1999)
92 **Robert Chevillon** Nuits-St.-Georges Les Perrières 1996 • $40 • (7/31/1999)

Key: SS—Spectator Selection. CS—Cellar Selection. HR—Highly Recommended. $NA—Price not available. (BT)—Barrel tasting. Ⓐ—Auction Price.
Dates in parentheses represent the issues in which the ratings were published.

91 **Bertagna** Clos St.-Denis 1996 • $77 • (2/28/1999)
91 **Comte Georges de Vogüé** Chambolle-Musigny Premier Cru 1996 • $110 • (5/15/1999)
91 **Daniel Rion** Chambolle-Musigny Les Charmes 1996 • $59 • (9/30/1998)
91 **Daniel Rion** Nuits-St.-Georges Les Lavières 1996 • $32 • (9/30/1998)
91 **Daniel Rion** Vosne-Romanée 1996 • $32 • (9/30/1998)
91 **Denis Mortet** Chambolle-Musigny Aux Beaux Bruns 1996 • $63 • (9/30/1998)
91 **Denis Mortet** Gevrey-Chambertin Lavaux St-Jacques 1996 • $63 • (9/30/1998)
91 **Domaine de la Romanée-Conti** Echézeaux 1996 • $173 Ⓐ • (9/30/1999)
91 **Domaine Leroy** Corton Renardes 1996 • $305 • (9/30/1998)
91 **Dominique Laurent** Beaune Grèves 1996 • $80 • (5/15/1999)
91 **Dominique Laurent** Bourgogne Cuvée No. 1 1996 • $28 • (5/15/1999)
91 **Dominique Laurent** Clos Vougeot 1996 • $200 • (5/15/1999)
91 **Dujac** Charmes-Chambertin 1996 • $110 • (7/31/1999)
91 **Guy Castagnier** Clos de la Roche 1996 • $99 • (7/31/1999)
91 **Jacques Prieur** Volnay Champans 1996 • $60 • (9/30/1998)
91 **Jayer-Gilles** Nuits-St.-Georges Les Damodes 1996 • $85 • (9/30/1998)
91 **Jean Boillot** Volnay Les Caillerets 1996 • $66 • (9/30/1998)
91 **Jean Grivot** Clos de Vougeot 1996 • $58 • (9/30/1998)
91 **Jean-Jacques Confuron** Vosne-Romanée Les Beaux Monts 1996 • $70 • (5/15/1999)
91 **Lécheneaut** Chambolle-Musigny Premier Cru 1996 • $65 • (9/30/1998)
91 **Lécheneaut** Clos de la Roche 1996 • $249 Ⓐ • (9/30/1998)
91 **Louis Jadot** Volnay Clos de la Barre 1996 • $37 • (5/15/1999)
91 **Maume** Gevrey-Chambertin En Pallud 1996 • $30 • (1/01/2000)
91 **Méo-Camuzet** Nuits-St.-Georges Aux Murgers 1996 • $89 • (9/30/1998)
91 **Michel Gros** Chambolle-Musigny 1996 • $45 • (5/15/1999)
91 **Michel Gros** Clos Vougeot Le Grand Maupertuis 1996 • $112 • (5/15/1999)
91 **Philippe Charlopin-Parizot** Charmes-Chambertin 1996 • $92 • (9/30/1999)
91 **René Engel** Clos Vougeot 1996 • $72 Ⓐ • (7/31/1999)
91 **Robert Arnoux** Echézeaux 1996 • $66 Ⓐ • (9/30/1998)
90 **A.-F. Gros** Vosne-Romanée Aux Réas 1996 • $54 • (2/28/1999)
90 **Bertagna** Clos de Vougeot 1996 • $89 • (2/28/1999)
90 **Bertrand Ambroise** Clos de Vougeot 1996 • $85 • (9/30/1998)
90 **Bertrand Ambroise** Volnay Santenots Hospices de Beaune Cuvée Jehan de Massol 1996 • $90 • (9/30/1998)
90 **Bonneau du Martray** Corton 1996 • $55 Ⓐ • (9/30/1998)
90 **Bouchard Père & Fils** Bonnes Mares 1996 • $99 • (9/30/1998)
90 **Bouchard Père & Fils** La Romanée Château de Vosne-Romanée 1996 • $180 Ⓐ • (9/30/1998)
90 **Bruno Clair** Savigny-lès-Beaune La Dominode 1996 • $56 • (9/30/1998)

90 **Claude Dugat** Charmes-Chambertin 1996 • $552 Ⓐ • (9/30/1998)
90 **Comte Georges de Vogüé** Bonnes Mares 1996 • $137 Ⓐ • (5/15/1999)
90 **Daniel Rion** Chambolle-Musigny Les Beaux-Bruns 1996 • $48 • (9/30/1998)
90 **Daniel Rion** Nuits-St.-Georges Clos des Argillières 1996 • $49 • (9/30/1998)
90 **Denis Bachelet** Gevrey-Chambertin Les Corbeaux Vieilles Vignes 1996 • $60 • (1/01/2000)
90 **Denis Mortet** Gevrey-Chambertin 1996 • $42 • (9/30/1998)
90 **Denis Mortet** Gevrey-Chambertin En Champs Vieille Vigne 1996 • $53 • (9/30/1998)
90 **Denis Mortet** Gevrey-Chambertin En Motrot 1996 • $48 • (9/30/1998)
90 **Domaine de l'Arlot** Nuits-St.-Georges Clos des Forêts St.-Georges 1996 • $48 • (7/31/1999)
90 **Domaine Leroy** Chambolle-Musigny Les Charmes 1996 • $255 • (9/30/1998)
90 **Domaine Leroy** Nuits-St.-Georges Aux Vignerondes 1996 • $255 • (9/30/1998)
90 **Domaine Leroy** Vosne-Romanée Aux Genaivrières 1996 • $115 • (9/30/1998)
90 **Dominique Laurent** Mazis-Chambertin 1996 • $160 • (5/15/1999)
90 **Drouhin-Laroze** Clos de Vougeot 1996 • $85 • (9/30/1998)
90 **Dujac** Morey-St.-Denis 1996 • $37 Ⓐ • (7/31/1999)
90 **Emmanuel Rouget** Nuits-St.-Georges 1996 • $67 Ⓐ • (7/31/1999)
90 **Fernand & Laurent Pillot** Pommard Rugiens 1996 • $62 • (2/28/1999)
90 **Gros Frère & Soeur** Clos Vougeot Musigni 1996 • $72 • (5/15/1999)
90 **J. Confuron-Cotetidot** Gevrey-Chambertin 1996 • $52 • (5/15/1999)
90 **Jacques Prieur** Chambertin 1996 • $130 • (9/30/1998)
90 **Jacques Prieur** Clos Vougeot 1996 • $90 • (9/30/1998)
90 **Jacques Prieur** Volnay-Santenots 1996 • $58 • (9/30/1998)
90 **Jacques-Frédéric Mugnier** Chambolle-Musigny Les Amoureuses 1996 • $90 • (7/31/1999)
90 **Jean & Jean-Louis Trapet** Chambertin 1996 • $100 • (9/30/1998)
90 **Jean Boillot** Beaune Clos du Roi 1996 • $48 • (9/30/1998)
90 **Jean Grivot** Nuits-St.-Georges Les Boudots 1996 • $47 • (9/30/1998)
90 **Jean Grivot** Vosne-Romanée Les Beaux Monts 1996 • $47 • (9/30/1998)
90 **Jean-Marc Boillot** Beaune Montrevenots 1996 • $36 • (9/30/1998)
90 **Joseph Drouhin** Bonnes Mares 1996 • $118 • (9/30/1998)
90 **Joseph Drouhin** Clos de Vougeot 1996 • $85 • (9/30/1998)
90 **Laurent Roumier** Chambolle-Musigny 1996 • $35 • (9/30/1998)
90 **Lécheneaut** Nuits-St.-Georges Les Cailles 1996 • $82 Ⓐ • (9/30/1998)
90 **Louis Jadot** Clos Vougeot 1996 • $82 Ⓐ • (5/15/1999)
90 **Louis Jadot** Echézeaux 1996 • $96 • (9/30/1999)
90 **Louis Jadot** Savigny-lès-Beaune Aux Guettes 1996 • $25 • (9/30/1999)
90 **Maillard Père & Fils** Corton Renardes 1996 • $55 • (9/30/1998)
90 **Méo-Camuzet** Nuits-St.-Georges 1996 • $49 • (9/30/1998)
90 **Newman** Bonnes Mares 1996 • $99 • (7/31/1999)
90 **Philippe Charlopin-Parizot** Gevrey-Chambertin Cuvée Vieilles Vignes 1996 • $38 • (9/30/1998)
90 **Ponsot** Chambolle-Musigny Les Charmes 1996 • $85 • (5/15/1999)
90 **Ponsot** Clos de la Roche Vieilles Vignes 1996 • $150 Ⓐ • (5/15/1999)
90 **René Bourgeon** Givry 1996 • $NA • (5/15/1999)
90 **René Engel** Echézeaux 1996 • $75 • (7/31/1999)
90 **René Engel** Vosne-Romanée Les Brûlées 1996 • $55 • (7/31/1999)
90 **Robert Arnoux** Clos de Vougeot 1996 • $90 • (9/30/1998)
90 **Robert Arnoux** Vosne-Romanée Les Suchots 1996 • $100 • (9/30/1998)
90 **Rossignol-Février** Volnay Robardelle 1996 • $NA • (1/01/1999)
90 **Vincent Girardin** Pommard Les Grands Epenots Vieilles Vignes 1996 • $70 • (9/30/1998)
90 **Vincent Girardin** Pommard Les Rugiens 1996 • $74 • (9/30/1998)

1995 Red Burgundy
Vintage Rating: 88

98 **Domaine de la Romanée-Conti** Richebourg 1995 • $251 Ⓐ • (8/31/1998) • CS
98 **Domaine de la Romanée-Conti** Romanée-Conti 1995 • $1,650 Ⓐ • (8/31/1998)
98 **Domaine Leroy** Romanée St.-Vivant 1995 • $600 • (11/15/1997) • CS
98 **Dominique Laurent** Mazis-Chambertin 1995 • $144 Ⓐ • (8/31/1998)
97 **Denis Mortet** Chambolle-Musigny Aux Beaux Bruns 1995 • $59 • (11/15/1997) • HR
97 **Gros Frère & Soeur** Richebourg 1995 • $130 • (8/31/1998)
96 **Armand Rousseau** Chambertin 1995 • $167 Ⓐ • (11/15/1997) • HR
96 **Lécheneaut** Chambolle-Musigny Premier Cru 1995 • $60 • (11/15/1997)
96 **Philippe Charlopin-Parizot** Charmes-Chambertin 1995 • $87 • (11/15/1997)
96 **Robert Groffier** Bonnes Mares 1995 • $120 Ⓐ • (1/31/1998)
96 **Sérafin Père & Fils** Charmes-Chambertin 1995 • $95 • (11/15/1997)
95 **Bernard Dugat-Py** Gevrey-Chambertin Coeur de Roy Vieilles Vignes 1995 • $40 • (1/31/1998) • HR
95 **Bouchard Père & Fils** La Romanée Château de Vosne-Romanée 1995 • $210 • (11/15/1997) • HR
95 **Denis Mortet** Clos Vougeot 1995 • $81 • (11/15/1997)
95 **Denis Mortet** Gevrey-Chambertin En Motrot 1995 • $47 • (11/15/1997)
95 **Domaine de la Romanée-Conti** La Tâche 1995 • $349 Ⓐ • (9/30/1999)
95 **Domaine Leroy** Richebourg 1995 • $540 Ⓐ • (11/15/1997)
95 **Frédéric Esmonin** Mazis-Chambertin Hospices de Beaune Cuvée Madeleine Collignon 1995 • $85 • (11/15/1997)
95 **Méo-Camuzet** Richebourg 1995 • $232 Ⓐ • (8/31/1998)
95 **Philippe Charlopin-Parizot** Chambertin 1995 • $95 • (11/15/1997)
95 **Robert Chevillon** Nuits-St.-Georges Les Bousselots 1995 • $35 • (8/31/1998) • HR
95 **Robert Groffier** Chambolle-Musigny Les Sentiers 1995 • $55 • (1/31/1998) • HR
95 **Robert Jayer-Gilles** Echézeaux du Dessus 1995 • $150 • (11/15/1997)

94 **Comte Georges de Vogüé** Chambolle-Musigny Les Amoureuses 1995 • $139 Ⓐ • (11/15/1997)
94 **Dominique Laurent** Chambertin 1995 • $77 • (8/31/1998)
94 **J. Faiveley** Corton Clos des Cortons 1995 • $93 • (8/31/1998) • CS
94 **J. Faiveley** Mazis-Chambertin 1995 • $97 • (11/15/1997)
94 **Jean Grivot** Echézeaux 1995 • $60 • (11/15/1997)
93 **Anne & François Gros** Vosne-Romanée Les Barreaux 1995 • $55 • (11/15/1997)
93 **Claude Dugat** Charmes-Chambertin 1995 • $460 Ⓐ • (11/15/1997)
93 **Denis Mortet** Chambertin 1995 • $115 • (11/15/1997)
93 **Denis Mortet** Gevrey-Chambertin En Champs Vieille Vigne 1995 • $55 • (11/15/1997)
93 **Denis Mortet** Gevrey-Chambertin Lavaux St.-Jacques 1995 • $59 • (11/15/1997)
93 **Domaine d'Auvenay** Bonnes Mares 1995 • $550 • (11/15/1997)
93 **Domaine de la Romanée-Conti** Echézeaux 1995 • $124 Ⓐ • (8/31/1998)
93 **Domaine de la Romanée-Conti** Grands Echézeaux 1995 • $167 Ⓐ • (8/31/1998)
93 **Domaine de la Romanée-Conti** Romanée St.-Vivant 1995 • $169 Ⓐ • (8/31/1998)
93 **Domaine de l'Arlot** Romanée St.-Vivant 1995 • $90 • (8/31/1998)
93 **Domaine Leroy** Nuits-St.-Georges Aux Boudots 1995 • $178 Ⓐ • (11/15/1997)
93 **Dominique Laurent** Bonnes Mares 1995 • $79 • (8/31/1998)
93 **Maume** Mazis-Chambertin 1995 • $60 • (8/31/1998)
93 **Philippe Charlopin-Parizot** Clos St.-Denis 1995 • $80 • (11/15/1997)
93 **René Engel** Grands Echézeaux 1995 • $73 • (8/31/1998)
92 **Anne & François Gros** Clos Vougeot Le Grand Maupertuis 1995 • $80 • (11/15/1997)
92 **Bouchard Père & Fils** Bonnes Mares 1995 • $89 • (11/15/1997)
92 **Chopin-Groffier** Clos Vougeot 1995 • $92 • (11/15/1997)
92 **Daniel Rion** Vosne-Romanée Les Beaux Monts 1995 • $66 • (11/15/1997)
92 **Denis Mortet** Gevrey-Chambertin Au Vellé 1995 • $47 • (11/15/1997)
92 **Denis Mortet** Gevrey-Chambertin Les Champeaux 1995 • $59 • (11/15/1997)
92 **Domaine Leroy** Pommard Les Vignots 1995 • $110 • (11/15/1997)
92 **Domaine Leroy** Vosne-Romanée Les Beaux Monts 1995 • $250 • (11/15/1997)
92 **Louis Jadot** Chambertin-Clos de Bèze 1995 • $96 Ⓐ • (11/15/1997) • CS
92 **Méo-Camuzet** Clos de Vougeot 1995 • $70 Ⓐ • (11/15/1997)
92 **Michel Lafarge** Volnay Clos des Chênes 1995 • $103 • (8/31/1998)
92 **Michele & Patrice Rion** Chambolle-Musigny Les Cras 1995 • $48 • (11/15/1997)
92 **Robert Chevillon** Nuits-St.-Georges Les Chaignots 1995 • $35 • (8/31/1998)

Key: SS—Spectator Selection. CS—Cellar Selection. HR—Highly Recommended. $NA—Price not available. (BT)—Barrel tasting. Ⓐ—Auction Price.
Dates in parentheses represent the issues in which the ratings were published.

92 **Robert Jayer-Gilles** Nuits-St.-Georges Les Hauts Poirets 1995 • $85 • (11/15/1997)
92 **Vincent Girardin** Volnay Clos des Chênes 1995 • $35 • (11/15/1997)
91 **Armand Rousseau** Ruchottes-Chambertin Clos des Ruchottes 1995 • $62 Ⓐ • (11/15/1997)
91 **Bertrand Ambroise** Clos de Vougeot 1995 • $90 • (11/15/1997)
91 **Bruno Clair** Savigny-lès-Beaune La Dominode 1995 • $40 • (11/15/1997)
91 **Comte Armand** Pommard Clos des Epeneaux 1995 • $60 • (8/31/1998)
91 **Comte Georges de Vogüé** Bonnes Mares 1995 • $136 Ⓐ • (11/15/1997)
91 **Daniel Rion** Clos Vougeot 1995 • $99 • (11/15/1997)
91 **Denis Bachelet** Gevrey-Chambertin Vieilles Vignes 1995 • $38 Ⓐ • (1/31/1998)
91 **Denis Mortet** Gevrey-Chambertin 1995 • $42 • (11/15/1997)
91 **Domaine Leroy** Latricières-Chambertin 1995 • $600 • (11/15/1997)
91 **Domaine Thomas-Moillard** Corton Clos du Roi 1995 • $43 • (11/15/1997)
91 **Dominique Laurent** Chambertin-Clos de Bèze 1995 • $79 • (8/31/1998)
91 **Joseph Roty** Charmes-Chambertin Vieilles Vignes 1995 • $170 • (8/31/1998)
91 **Philippe Charlopin-Parizot** Morey-St.-Denis 1995 • $32 • (11/15/1997)
90 **Alain Burguet** Gevrey-Chambertin Les Champeaux 1995 • $55 • (8/31/1998)
90 **Alain Burguet** Gevrey-Chambertin Vieilles Vignes 1995 • $40 • (8/31/1998)
90 **Anne & François Gros** Richebourg 1995 • $170 • (11/15/1997)
90 **Bertrand Ambroise** Corton Le Rognet 1995 • $80 • (11/15/1997)
90 **Bertrand Ambroise** Nuits-St.-Georges Les Vaucrains 1995 • $58 • (11/15/1997)
90 **Coron Père & Fils** Clos de Vougeot 1995 • $63 • (11/15/1997)
90 **Daniel Rion** Nuits-St.-Georges Clos des Argillières 1995 • $66 • (11/15/1997)
90 **Daniel Rion** Nuits-St.-Georges Les Grandes Vignes 1995 • $44 • (11/15/1997)
90 **Daniel Rion** Vosne-Romanée 1995 • $44 • (11/15/1997)
90 **Domaine Leroy** Corton Renardes 1995 • $250 • (11/15/1997)
90 **Domaine Leroy** Gevrey-Chambertin Les Combottes 1995 • $NA • (11/15/1997)
90 **François Lamarche** La Grande Rue 1995 • $98 • (11/15/1997)
90 **J. Faiveley** Clos de la Roche 1995 • $93 • (11/15/1997)
90 **Jean Grivot** Richebourg 1995 • $139 Ⓐ • (11/15/1997)
90 **Jean-Jacques Confuron** Vosne-Romanée Les Beaux Monts 1995 • $70 • (11/15/1997)
90 **Joseph Drouhin** Charmes-Chambertin 1995 • $85 • (11/15/1997)
90 **Joseph Drouhin** Griotte-Chambertin 1995 • $95 • (11/15/1997)
90 **Joseph Drouhin** Musigny 1995 • $110 • (1/31/1998)
90 **Philippe Charlopin-Parizot** Gevrey-Chambertin Cuvée Vieilles Vignes 1995 • $37 • (11/15/1997)
90 **Philippe Charlopin-Parizot** Vosne-Romanée 1995 • $37 • (11/15/1997)
90 **René Engel** Clos Vougeot 1995 • $67 • (8/31/1998)

90 **Robert Groffier** Chambolle-Musigny Les Amoureuses 1995 • $75 • (1/31/1998)
90 **Rossignol-Trapet** Chambertin 1995 • $68 • (11/15/1997)
90 **Sérafin Père & Fils** Gevrey-Chambertin 1995 • $46 • (11/15/1997)
90 **Sérafin Père & Fils** Gevrey-Chambertin Les Cazetiers 1995 • $72 • (11/15/1997)
90 **Tollot-Beaut & Fils** Beaune Clos du Roi 1995 • $40 • (11/15/1997)
90 **Vincent Girardin** Chassagne-Montrachet Red Clos de la Boudriotte 1995 • $30 • (11/15/1997)
90 **Vincent Girardin** Pommard Les Chanlins Vieilles Vignes 1995 • $40 • (11/15/1997)

1994 Red Burgundy
Vintage Rating: 81

97 **Dominique Laurent** Echézeaux 1994 • $75 • (9/30/1997)
96 **Dominique Laurent** Bonnes Mares 1994 • $160 • (9/30/1997)
95 **Philippe Charlopin-Parizot** Clos St.-Denis 1994 • $79 • (11/15/1996)
94 **Anne & François Gros** Clos Vougeot Le Grand Maupertuis 1994 • $59 • (11/15/1996)
94 **Bouchard Père & Fils** La Romanée Château de Vosne-Romanée 1994 • $160 • (11/15/1996)
94 **Dominique Laurent** Chambolle-Musigny Les Sentiers 1994 • $95 • (9/30/1997)
94 **Dominique Laurent** Pommard Epenots 1994 • $95 • (9/30/1997)
93 **Bertrand Ambroise** Clos de Vougeot 1994 • $75 • (11/15/1996)
93 **Domaine d'Auvenay** Bonnes Mares 1994 • $459 • (9/30/1997)
93 **Domaine d'Auvenay** Mazis-Chambertin 1994 • $459 • (9/30/1997)
93 **Domaine Leroy** Romanée St.-Vivant 1994 • $475 • (9/30/1997)
93 **Dominique Laurent** Chambertin-Clos de Bèze 1994 • $53 Ⓐ • (9/30/1997)
93 **Dominique Laurent** Gevrey-Chambertin Lavaux St.-Jacques 1994 • $80 • (9/30/1997)
93 **Gros Frère & Soeur** Richebourg 1994 • $135 • (11/15/1996)
93 **Philippe Charlopin-Parizot** Chambertin 1994 • $92 • (11/15/1996)
93 **Robert Jayer-Gilles** Echézeaux 1994 • $115 • (11/15/1996)
92 **Antonin Rodet** Mazis-Chambertin 1994 • $NA • (11/15/1996)
92 **Bernard Dugat-Py** Gevrey-Chambertin Petite-Chapelle 1994 • $43 • (9/30/1997)
92 **Daniel Rion** Clos Vougeot 1994 • $76 • (11/15/1996)
92 **Domaine des Comtes Lafon** Volnay-Santenots du Milieu 1994 • $55 • (9/30/1997)
92 **Dominique Laurent** Nuits-St.-Georges La Richemone 1994 • $75 • (9/30/1997)
92 **Forey Père & Fils** Echézeaux 1994 • $60 • (11/15/1996)
92 **Georges Mugneret** Ruchottes-Chambertin 1994 • $65 • (12/31/1996) • HR
92 **Louis Jadot** Chapelle-Chambertin 1994 • $56 • (9/30/1997)
92 **Michel Lafarge** Volnay Clos des Chênes 1994 • $70 • (9/30/1997)
92 **Robert Arnoux** Romanée St.-Vivant 1994 • $160 • (11/15/1996)
92 **Vincent Girardin** Pommard Les Chanlins Vieilles Vignes 1994 • $43 • (11/15/1996)
91 **Denis Mortet** Gevrey-Chambertin 1994 • $33 • (11/15/1996)
91 **Doudet-Naudin** Corton Les Maréchaudes Vieilles Vignes 1994 • $60 • (11/15/1996)
91 **Gros Frère & Soeur** Grands Echézeaux 1994 • $83 • (11/15/1996)
91 **Jean Grivot** Richebourg 1994 • $160 • (9/30/1997)
91 **Jean-Jacques Confuron** Romanée St.-Vivant 1994 • $120 • (11/15/1996)
91 **Joseph Drouhin** Chambertin 1994 • $94 • (11/15/1996)
91 **Louis Jadot** Chambertin-Clos de Bèze 1994 • $72 • (11/15/1996)
91 **Louis Jadot** Clos St.-Denis 1994 • $55 • (11/15/1996)
91 **Philippe Charlopin-Parizot** Charmes-Chambertin 1994 • $79 • (11/15/1996)
90 **Anne & François Gros** Richebourg 1994 • $105 Ⓐ • (11/15/1996)
90 **Bertrand Ambroise** Corton Le Rognet 1994 • $60 • (11/15/1996)
90 **Denis Mortet** Chambolle-Musigny Aux Beaux Bruns 1994 • $46 • (11/15/1996)
90 **Domaine de la Romanée-Conti** Richebourg 1994 • $147 Ⓐ • (9/30/1997)
90 **Domaine des Comtes Lafon** Volnay Clos des Chênes 1994 • $55 • (9/30/1997)
90 **Domaine Leroy** Corton Renardes 1994 • $145 • (11/15/1996)
90 **Domaine Leroy** Latricières-Chambertin 1994 • $286 • (11/15/1996)
90 **Domaine Leroy** Richebourg 1994 • $367 • (11/15/1996)
90 **Domaine Thomas-Moillard** Corton Clos du Roi 1994 • $47 • (11/15/1996)
90 **Dominique Laurent** Grands Echézeaux 1994 • $125 • (9/30/1997)
90 **Jean Grivot** Echézeaux 1994 • $50 • (9/30/1997)
90 **Jean-Jacques Confuron** Chambolle-Musigny Premier Cru 1994 • $50 • (11/15/1996)
90 **Jean-Jacques Confuron** Clos de Vougeot 1994 • $80 • (11/15/1996)
90 **Jean-Marc Boillot** Beaune Montrevenots 1994 • $27 • (11/15/1996)
90 **Louis Jadot** Clos Vougeot 1994 • $42 • (11/15/1996)
90 **Méo-Camuzet** Clos de Vougeot 1994 • $50 Ⓐ • (11/15/1996)
90 **Robert Jayer-Gilles** Nuits-St.-Georges Les Damodes 1994 • $70 • (11/15/1996)

1993 Red Burgundy
Vintage Rating: 91

99 **Domaine Leroy** Romanée St.-Vivant 1993 • $500 • (12/15/1996)
98 **Domaine Leroy** Chambertin 1993 • $500 • (12/15/1996)
98 **Domaine Leroy** Musigny 1993 • $500 • (12/15/1996)
98 **Dominique Laurent** Mazis-Chambertin 1993 • $120 Ⓐ • (5/15/1996)
97 **Bertrand Ambroise** Corton Le Rognet 1993 • $75 • (11/15/1995) • CS
97 **Daniel Rion** Clos Vougeot 1993 • $90 • (11/15/1995) • HR
96 **Bertrand Ambroise** Clos de Vougeot 1993 • $90 • (11/15/1995)
96 **Comte Georges de Vogüé** Musigny Cuvée Vieilles Vignes 1993 • $248 Ⓐ • (11/15/1995) • CS
96 **Domaine Leroy** Clos de Vougeot 1993 • $250 • (11/15/1995)

Red Burgundy

96 **Domaine Leroy** Volnay-Santenots 1993 • $185 • (11/15/1995)

96 **Dominique Laurent** Ruchottes-Chambertin 1993 • $117 • (5/15/1996)

96 **Jean Grivot** Richebourg 1993 • $128 • (5/15/1996)

96 **Sérafin Père & Fils** Charmes-Chambertin 1993 • $90 • (11/15/1995)

95 **Anne & François Gros** Clos Vougeot Le Grand Maupertuis 1993 • $55 • (11/15/1995)

95 **Armand Rousseau** Chambertin 1993 • $140 Ⓐ • (9/15/1996)

95 **Domaine Leroy** Latricières-Chambertin 1993 • $325 • (12/15/1996)

95 **Domaine Leroy** Nuits-St.-Georges Aux Vignerondes 1993 • $185 • (11/15/1995)

95 **Domaine Leroy** Richebourg 1993 • $500 • (12/15/1996)

95 **Dominique Laurent** Gevrey-Chambertin Vieilles Vignes 1993 • $NA • (5/15/1996)

95 **Emmanuel Rouget** Echézeaux 1993 • $153 Ⓐ • (5/15/1996)

95 **Emmanuel Rouget** Vosne-Romanée Cros Parantoux 1993 • $184 Ⓐ • (5/15/1996)

95 **Robert Jayer-Gilles** Echézeaux du Dessus 1993 • $135 • (11/15/1995)

94 **Comte Georges de Vogüé** Bonnes Mares 1993 • $86 Ⓐ • (11/15/1995)

94 **Comte Georges de Vogüé** Chambolle-Musigny Les Amoureuses 1993 • $125 • (11/15/1995)

94 **Daniel Rion** Nuits-St.-Georges Aux Vignerondes 1993 • $50 • (11/15/1995)

94 **Denis Mortet** Chambertin 1993 • $115 • (11/15/1995)

94 **Denis Mortet** Clos Vougeot 1993 • $80 • (11/15/1995)

94 **Domaine de la Romanée-Conti** Romanée-Conti 1993 • $1,382 Ⓐ • (5/15/1996) • CS

94 **Domaine Leroy** Clos de la Roche 1993 • $325 • (12/15/1996)

94 **Domaine Leroy** Vosne-Romanée Les Beaux Monts 1993 • $185 • (11/15/1995)

94 **Dominique Laurent** Clos Vougeot 1993 • $NA • (5/15/1996)

94 **Gros Frère & Soeur** Richebourg 1993 • $110 • (11/15/1995)

94 **J. Confuron-Cotetidot** Gevrey-Chambertin 1993 • $NA • (5/15/1996)

94 **Jacques Prieur** Musigny 1993 • $96 Ⓐ • (11/15/1995)

94 **Jean Grivot** Vosne-Romanée Les Beaux Monts 1993 • $32 • (5/15/1996) • HR

94 **Jean Gros** Richebourg 1993 • $160 • (11/15/1995)

94 **Jean-Jacques Confuron** Chambolle-Musigny Premier Cru 1993 • $60 • (11/15/1995) • HR

94 **Jean-Jacques Confuron** Vosne-Romanée Les Beaux Monts 1993 • $63 • (11/15/1995)

94 **Méo-Camuzet** Richebourg 1993 • $175 • (11/15/1995)

94 **Philippe Charlopin-Parizot** Charmes-Chambertin 1993 • $94 • (5/15/1996)

93 **Armand Rousseau** Chambertin-Clos de Bèze 1993 • $1,823 Ⓐ • (9/15/1996)

93 **Armand Rousseau** Ruchottes-Chambertin Clos des Ruchottes 1993 • $67 Ⓐ • (9/15/1996)

93 **Daniel Rion** Nuits-St.-Georges Les Grandes Vignes 1993 • $32 • (11/15/1995)

Key: SS—Spectator Selection. CS—Cellar Selection. HR—Highly Recommended. $NA—Price not available. (BT)—Barrel tasting. Ⓐ—Auction Price.
Dates in parentheses represent the issues in which the ratings were published.

93 **Daniel Rion** Vosne-Romanée Les Chaumes 1993 • $50 • (11/15/1995)

93 **Domaine des Comtes Lafon** Volnay-Santenots du Milieu 1993 • $55 Ⓐ • (5/15/1996)

93 **Domaine Leroy** Vosne-Romanée Les Brûlées 1993 • $185 • (11/15/1995)

93 **Dominique Laurent** Pommard Epenots 1993 • $85 • (5/15/1996)

93 **Dominique Laurent** Pommard Vieilles Vignes 1993 • $48 • (5/15/1996)

93 **Gros Frère & Soeur** Grands Echézeaux 1993 • $69 • (11/15/1995)

93 **Jean-Marc Boillot** Volnay 1993 • $30 • (11/15/1995)

93 **Joseph Drouhin** Corton Les Bressandes 1993 • $70 • (11/15/1995)

93 **Lécheneaut** Chambolle-Musigny Premier Cru 1993 • $68 • (11/15/1995)

93 **Lécheneaut** Nuits-St.-Georges Les Damodes 1993 • $68 • (11/15/1995)

93 **Maurice Ecard** Savigny-lès-Beaune Aux Serpentières 1993 • $25 • (5/15/1996)

93 **Méo-Camuzet** Nuits-St.-Georges Aux Murgers 1993 • $76 Ⓐ • (11/15/1995)

93 **Méo-Camuzet** Vosne-Romanée Aux Brûlées 1993 • $75 • (11/15/1995)

93 **Méo-Camuzet** Vosne-Romanée Les Chaumes 1993 • $50 Ⓐ • (11/15/1995)

93 **Michel Lafarge** Volnay Clos du Château des Ducs 1993 • $65 • (11/15/1995)

93 **Mongeard-Mugneret** Clos de Vougeot 1993 • $71 • (11/15/1995)

93 **Monthélie-Douhairet** Volnay Champans 1993 • $44 • (11/15/1995)

93 **Olivier Leflaive Frères** Volnay Frémiets 1993 • $42 • (11/15/1995)

93 **Robert Arnoux** Romanée St.-Vivant 1993 • $NA • (11/15/1995)

93 **Robert Jayer-Gilles** Nuits-St.-Georges Les Poirets 1993 • $70 • (11/15/1995)

92 **Armand Rousseau** Gevrey-Chambertin Clos St.-Jacques 1993 • $107 Ⓐ • (9/15/1996)

92 **Claude Dugat** Gevrey-Chambertin Lavaux St.-Jacques 1993 • $134 Ⓐ • (11/15/1995)

92 **Daniel Rion** Chambolle-Musigny Les Charmes 1993 • $38 Ⓐ • (11/15/1995)

92 **Daniel Rion** Vosne-Romanée Les Beaux Monts 1993 • $38 Ⓐ • (11/15/1995)

92 **Domaine de la Romanée-Conti** La Tâche 1993 • $338 Ⓐ • (9/30/1999)

92 **Domaine de la Romanée-Conti** Romanée St.-Vivant 1993 • $173 Ⓐ • (5/15/1996)

92 **Domaine de l'Arlot** Nuits-St.-Georges Clos des Forêts St.-Georges 1993 • $43 Ⓐ • (5/15/1996)

92 **Domaine Leroy** Corton Renardes 1993 • $185 • (11/15/1995)

92 **Domaine Leroy** Pommard Les Vignots 1993 • $94 • (11/15/1995)

92 **Forey Père & Fils** Vosne-Romanée Les Gaudichots LD 1993 • $45 • (11/15/1995)

92 **Jacques Prieur** Clos Vougeot 1993 • $54 • (11/15/1995)

92 **Jacques-Frédéric Mugnier** Bonnes Mares 1993 • $90 • (5/15/1996)

92 **Jean & Jean-Louis Trapet** Chambertin 1993 • $NA • (5/15/1996)

92 **Jean Grivot** Clos de Vougeot 1993 • $65 Ⓐ • (5/15/1996) • CS

92 **Jean Grivot** Echézeaux 1993 • $45 • (5/15/1996)

92 **Jean-Marc Boillot** Volnay Pitures 1993 • $11 Ⓐ • (11/15/1995)

92 **Louis Jadot** Clos de Vougeot 1993 • $NA • (11/15/1995)

92 **Louis Jadot** Corton Les Pougets 1993 • $46 • (11/15/1995)

92 **Marquis d'Angerville** Volnay Premier Cru 1993 • $30 • (5/15/1996)

92 **Mongeard-Mugneret** Echézeaux Vieille Vigne 1993 • $60 • (11/15/1995)

92 **Robert Jayer-Gilles** Nuits-St.-Georges Les Damodes 1993 • $85 • (11/15/1995)

92 **Rossignol-Trapet** Latricières-Chambertin 1993 • $64 • (11/15/1995)

92 **Thierry Mortet** Gevrey-Chambertin 1993 • $42 • (9/15/1996)

91 **Anne & François Gros** Richebourg 1993 • $100 • (11/15/1995)

91 **Armand Girardin** Pommard Les Charmots 1993 • $60 • (11/15/1995)

91 **Claude Dugat** Gevrey-Chambertin Premier Cru 1993 • $50 • (11/15/1995)

91 **Denis Mortet** Chambolle-Musigny Aux Beaux Bruns 1993 • $43 • (11/15/1995)

91 **Domaine Leroy** Nuits-St.-Georges Aux Boudots 1993 • $185 • (11/15/1995)

91 **Dujac** Clos St.-Denis 1993 • $79 • (5/15/1996)

91 **Emmanuel Rouget** Vosne-Romanée Les Beaux Monts 1993 • $55 • (5/15/1996)

91 **Forey Père & Fils** Echézeaux 1993 • $45 • (11/15/1995)

91 **Gros Frère & Soeur** Vosne-Romanée 1993 • $35 • (11/15/1995)

91 **J. Faiveley** Chambertin-Clos de Bèze 1993 • $113 • (5/15/1996)

91 **J. Faiveley** Echézeaux 1993 • $56 • (5/15/1996)

91 **Jean Gros** Vosne-Romanée Clos des Réas 1993 • $60 • (11/15/1995)

91 **Joseph Drouhin** Chambertin 1993 • $119 • (11/15/1995)

91 **Laleure-Piot** Corton Bressandes 1993 • $51 • (11/15/1995)

91 **Lécheneaut** Clos de la Roche 1993 • $90 • (11/15/1995)

91 **Lucien Boillot** Pommard Les Fremiers 1993 • $38 • (11/15/1995)

91 **Lucien Boillot** Volnay Les Caillerets 1993 • $38 • (11/15/1995)

91 **Michel Gros** Chambolle-Musigny 1993 • $35 • (11/15/1995)

91 **Mongeard-Mugneret** Echézeaux 1993 • $50 • (11/15/1995)

91 **Pierre Damoy** Chambertin 1993 • $69 • (11/15/1995)

91 **Pierre Damoy** Chambertin-Clos de Bèze 1993 • $84 Ⓐ • (11/15/1995)

91 **Pierre Damoy** Chapelle-Chambertin 1993 • $63 Ⓐ • (11/15/1995)

91 **Robert Arnoux** Clos de Vougeot 1993 • $80 • (11/15/1995)

91 **Sérafin Père & Fils** Gevrey-Chambertin Fonteny 1993 • $65 • (11/15/1995)

91 **Sérafin Père & Fils** Gevrey-Chambertin Les Cazetiers 1993 • $70 • (11/15/1995)

91 **Tollot-Beaut & Fils** Corton 1993 • $57 • (11/15/1995)

90 **Aleth Girardin** Beaune Clos des Mouches 1993 • $48 • (11/15/1995)

90 **Armand Girardin** Pommard Les Epenots 1993 • $60 • (11/15/1995)

90 **Bertagna** Clos St.-Denis 1993 • $71 • (5/15/1996)

90 **Bertrand Ambroise** Nuits-St.-Georges Les Vaucrains 1993 • $65 • (11/15/1995)

90 **Bouchard Père & Fils** La Romanée Château de Vosne-Romanée 1993 • $82 Ⓐ • (11/15/1995)

90 **Claude Dugat** Charmes-Chambertin 1993 • $480 Ⓐ • (11/15/1995)

90 **Claude Dugat** Gevrey-Chambertin 1993 • $40 • (11/15/1995)

90 **Coste-Caumartin** Pommard Les Boucherottes 1993 • $42 • (11/15/1995)

90 **Daniel Rion** Vosne-Romanée 1993 • $32 • (11/15/1995)

90 **Denis Mortet** Gevrey-Chambertin 1993 • $42 • (9/15/1996)

90 **Denis Mortet** Gevrey-Chambertin En Champs Vieille Vigne 1993 • $50 • (11/15/1995)

90 **Denis Mortet** Gevrey-Chambertin En Motrot 1993 • $46 • (11/15/1995)

90 **Denis Mortet** Gevrey-Chambertin Lavaux St.-Jacques 1993 • $58 • (11/15/1995)

90 **Denis Mortet** Gevrey-Chambertin Les Champeaux 1993 • $58 • (11/15/1995)

90 **Domaine de Courcel** Pommard Les Rugiens 1993 • $42 Ⓐ • (11/15/1995)

90 **Domaine de la Romanée-Conti** Echézeaux 1993 • $259 Ⓐ • (5/15/1996)

90 **Domaine de la Romanée-Conti** Richebourg 1993 • $489 Ⓐ • (5/15/1996)

90 **Domaine Leroy** Chambolle-Musigny Les Charmes 1993 • $200 • (11/15/1995)

90 **Emmanuel Rouget** Nuits-St.-Georges 1993 • $NA • (5/15/1996)

90 **Fontaine-Gagnard** Volnay Clos des Chênes 1993 • $43 • (11/15/1995)

90 **Frédéric Esmonin** Ruchottes-Chambertin 1993 • $65 • (11/15/1995)

90 **Geantet-Pansiot** Charmes-Chambertin 1993 • $62 Ⓐ • (5/15/1996)

90 **Geantet-Pansiot** Gevrey-Chambertin Poissenot 1993 • $45 • (5/15/1996)

90 **J. Faiveley** Nuits-St.-Georges Porrets St.-Georges 1993 • $43 • (5/15/1996)

90 **Jacques Prieur** Volnay-Santenots Clos des Santenots 1993 • $37 • (11/15/1995)

90 **Jean Grivot** Nuits-St.-Georges Aux Boudots 1993 • $32 • (5/15/1996)

90 **Jean-Jacques Confuron** Clos Vougeot 1993 • $85 • (11/15/1995)

90 **Jean-Jacques Confuron** Nuits-St.-Georges Les Fleurières LD 1993 • $45 • (11/15/1995)

90 **Jean-Marc Boillot** Pommard Jarolières 1993 • $50 • (11/15/1995)

90 **Jean-Marc Pavelot** Savigny-lès-Beaune Aux Guettes 1993 • $28 • (11/15/1995)

90 **Jean-Marc Pavelot** Savigny-lès-Beaune La Dominode 1993 • $28 • (11/15/1995)

90 **Lécheneaut** Nuits-St.-Georges Premier Cru 1993 • $60 • (11/15/1995)

90 **Louis Jadot** Chambertin-Clos de Bèze 1993 • $50 Ⓐ • (11/15/1995)

90 **Marquis d'Angerville** Volnay Champans 1993 • $29 • (5/15/1996)

90 **Maume** Gevrey-Chambertin 1993 • $NA • (5/15/1996)

90 **Méo-Camuzet** Nuits-St.-Georges Aux Boudots 1993 • $60 • (11/15/1995)

90 **Michele & Patrice Rion** Chambolle-Musigny Les Cras 1993 • $38 • (11/15/1995)

90 **Parent** Corton Les Renardes 1993 • $62 • (11/15/1995)

90 **Philippe Charlopin-Parizot** Clos St.-Denis 1993 • $94 • (5/15/1996)
90 **Philippe Rossignol** Gevrey-Chambertin Les Corbeaux Cuvée Vieilles Vignes 1993 • $NA • (5/15/1996)
90 **Prince Florent de Mérode** Ladoix Les Chaillots 1993 • $17 • (11/15/1995)
90 **Robert Jayer-Gilles** Côte de Nuits-Villages 1993 • $36 • (11/15/1995)
90 **Robert Jayer-Gilles** Hautes-Côtes de Beaune 1993 • $22 • (11/15/1995)
90 **Rossignol-Trapet** Beaune Teurons 1993 • $33 • (11/15/1995)
90 **Rossignol-Trapet** Chambertin 1993 • $77 • (11/15/1995)
90 **Simon Bize & Fils** Aloxe-Corton Le Suchot 1993 • $24 • (5/15/1996)
90 **Tollot-Beaut & Fils** Corton Bressandes 1993 • $57 • (11/15/1995)
90 **Tollot-Beaut & Fils** Savigny-lès-Beaune Les Lavières 1993 • $25 • (11/15/1995)

1990 Red Burgundy
Vintage Rating: 98

99 **Comte Georges de Vogüé** Bonnes Mares 1990 • $234 Ⓐ • (12/15/1992)
99 **Comte Georges de Vogüé** Musigny Cuvée Vieilles Vignes 1990 • $370 Ⓐ • (2/28/1995)
99 **Méo-Camuzet** Vosne-Romanée Cros Parantoux 1990 • $179 Ⓐ • (6/15/1993)
98 **Domaine Leroy** Musigny 1990 • $1073 • (12/15/1996)
97 **Anne & François Gros** Richebourg 1990 • $130 • (12/15/1992)
97 **Christophe Roumier** Ruchottes-Chambertin 1990 • $80 • (12/15/1992)
97 **Daniel Rion** Clos Vougeot 1990 • $100 • (12/15/1992)
97 **Domaine Leroy** Clos de Vougeot 1990 • $290 Ⓐ • (12/15/1992)
97 **Domaine Leroy** Pommard Les Vignots 1990 • $74 • (12/15/1992)
97 **Domaine Leroy** Vosne-Romanée Aux Réas 1990 • $58 • (12/15/1992)
97 **Méo-Camuzet** Richebourg 1990 • $455 Ⓐ • (6/15/1993)
97 **Robert Jayer-Gilles** Echézeaux du Dessus 1990 • $100 • (12/15/1992)
97 **Robert Jayer-Gilles** Nuits-St.-Georges Les Poirets 1990 • $48 • (12/15/1992)
97 **Rossignol-Trapet** Latricières-Chambertin 1990 • $74 Ⓐ • (12/15/1992)
96 **Armand Rousseau** Ruchottes-Chambertin Clos des Ruchottes 1990 • $80 • (12/15/1992)
96 **Domaine Leroy** Chambertin 1990 • $481 • (12/15/1996)
96 **Domaine Leroy** Richebourg 1990 • $472 Ⓐ • (12/15/1996)
96 **G. Roumier** Bonnes Mares 1990 • $247 Ⓐ • (12/15/1992)
96 **Gros Frère & Soeur** Richebourg 1990 • $51 • (12/15/1992)
96 **Joseph Drouhin** Charmes-Chambertin 1990 • $126 Ⓐ • (12/15/1992)
96 **Mommessin** Charmes-Chambertin 1990 • $114 Ⓐ • (12/15/1992)
96 **Tollot-Beaut & Fils** Corton Bressandes 1990 • $40 • (2/28/1995)

Key: SS—Spectator Selection. CS—Cellar Selection. HR—Highly Recommended. $NA—Price not available. (BT)—Barrel tasting. Ⓐ—Auction Price.
Dates in parentheses represent the issues in which the ratings were published.

95 **Anne & François Gros** Clos Vougeot Le Grand Maupertuis 1990 • $75 • (12/15/1992)
95 **Armand Rousseau** Chambertin-Clos de Bèze 1990 • $196 Ⓐ • (12/15/1992)
95 **Coste-Caumartin** Pommard Les Boucherottes 1990 • $37 • (12/15/1992)
95 **Domaine Leroy** Nuits-St.-Georges Aux Allots 1990 • $67 • (12/15/1992)
95 **Domaine Leroy** Nuits-St.-Georges Aux Vignerondes 1990 • $100 • (12/15/1992)
95 **Domaine Leroy** Vosne-Romanée Aux Genaivrières 1990 • $61 • (12/15/1992)
95 **Domaine Leroy** Vosne-Romanée Les Beaux Monts 1990 • $112 • (12/15/1992) • HR
95 **F. Chauvenet** Clos St.-Denis 1990 • $65 • (12/15/1992)
95 **Joseph Drouhin** Musigny 1990 • $129 • (12/15/1992)
95 **Leroy** Pommard Trois Follots 1990 • $863 Ⓐ • (12/15/1992)
95 **Michel Lafarge** Volnay Clos du Château des Ducs 1990 • $75 • (12/15/1992)
95 **Mommessin** Clos de Tart 1990 • $110 Ⓐ • (12/15/1992)
95 **Rossignol-Trapet** Chambertin 1990 • $106 • (12/15/1992)
95 **Rossignol-Trapet** Chapelle-Chambertin 1990 • $83 • (12/15/1992)
94 **A.-F. Gros** Richebourg 1990 • $180 • (12/15/1992)
94 **Bertrand Ambroise** Corton Le Rognet 1990 • $60 • (12/15/1992)
94 **Bouchard Père & Fils** Pommard Premier Cru 1990 • $39 • (12/15/1992)
94 **Château de La Tour** Clos Vougeot 1990 • $45 • (12/15/1992)
94 **Chopin-Groffier** Clos Vougeot 1990 • $70 • (12/15/1992)
94 **Comte Georges de Vogüé** Chambolle-Musigny Les Amoureuses 1990 • $134 Ⓐ • (12/15/1992)
94 **Coste-Caumartin** Pommard 1990 • $28 • (12/15/1992)
94 **Coste-Caumartin** Pommard Les Fremiers 1990 • $32 • (12/15/1992)
94 **Denis Bachelet** Charmes-Chambertin 1990 • $53 • (12/15/1992)
94 **Domaine de la Romanée-Conti** Echézeaux 1990 • $269 Ⓐ • (12/31/1993) • CS
94 **Domaine de la Romanée-Conti** Grands Echézeaux 1990 • $298 Ⓐ • (12/31/1993) • CS
94 **Domaine Leroy** Chambolle-Musigny Les Fremières 1990 • $79 • (12/15/1992)
94 **Domaine Leroy** Clos de la Roche 1990 • $413 • (12/15/1996)
94 **Domaine Leroy** Nuits-St.-Georges Aux Boudots 1990 • $108 • (12/15/1992)
94 **Domaine Leroy** Nuits-St.-Georges Aux Lavières 1990 • $59 • (12/15/1992)
94 **F. Chauvenet** Corton 1990 • $60 • (12/15/1992)
94 **Guy Castagnier** Bonnes Mares 1990 • $NA • (12/15/1992)
94 **Guy Castagnier** Mazy-Chambertin 1990 • $NA • (12/15/1992)
94 **Jean Gros** Richebourg 1990 • $150 • (12/15/1992)
94 **Jean-Marc Boillot** Pommard Jarolières 1990 • $68 Ⓐ • (12/15/1992)
94 **Jean-Marc Boillot** Volnay Pitures 1990 • $55 • (12/15/1992)
94 **Joseph Drouhin** Griotte-Chambertin 1990 • $84 • (12/15/1992)
94 **Méo-Camuzet** Vosne-Romanée Les Chaumes 1990 • $116 Ⓐ • (2/15/1993)
94 **Michel Lafarge** Volnay Clos des Chênes 1990 • $115 Ⓐ • (2/28/1995)

94 **Philippe Charlopin-Parizot** Chambertin 1990 • $90 • (8/31/1992)
94 **Prince Florent de Mérode** Corton Les Renardes 1990 • $54 • (12/15/1992)
94 **Tollot-Beaut & Fils** Corton 1990 • $53 • (12/15/1992)
93 **Armand Rousseau** Mazy-Chambertin 1990 • $75 • (12/15/1992)
93 **Bouchard Père & Fils** Beaune Les Marconnets 1990 • $28 • (12/15/1992)
93 **Bruno Clair** Chambertin-Clos de Bèze 1990 • $70 • (12/15/1992)
93 **Chopin-Groffier** Vougeot 1990 • $44 • (12/15/1992)
93 **Christophe Roumier** Charmes-Chambertin 1990 • $105 • (12/15/1992)
93 **Comte Armand** Pommard Clos des Epeneaux 1990 • $90 Ⓐ • (12/15/1992)
93 **Daniel Rion** Nuits-St.-Georges Clos des Argillières 1990 • $70 • (12/15/1992)
93 **Daniel Rion** Vosne-Romanée Les Chaumes 1990 • $70 • (2/28/1995)
93 **Daniel Senard** Corton En Charlemagne 1990 • $NA • (12/15/1992)
93 **Daniel Senard** Corton Le Clos du Roi 1990 • $55 • (12/15/1992)
93 **Daniel Senard** Corton Les Meix 1990 • $NA • (12/15/1992)
93 **Domaine de la Pousse d'Or** Volnay Clos de la Bousse d'Or 1990 • $86 Ⓐ • (11/30/1992) • CS
93 **Domaine de la Romanée-Conti** La Tâche 1990 • $706 Ⓐ • (9/30/1999)
93 **Domaine de la Romanée-Conti** Romanée-Conti 1990 • $2,725 Ⓐ • (12/31/1993) • CS
93 **Domaine Leroy** Latricières-Chambertin 1990 • $336 Ⓐ • (12/15/1996)
93 **Georges Mugneret** Ruchottes-Chambertin 1990 • $78 • (12/15/1992)
93 **Ghislaine Barthod** Chambolle-Musigny Aux Beaux Bruns 1990 • $50 • (12/15/1992)
93 **Gros Frère & Soeur** Clos Vougeot Musigni 1990 • $72 • (12/15/1992)
93 **Guy Castagnier** Clos St.-Denis 1990 • $NA • (12/15/1992)
93 **J. Faiveley** Chambertin-Clos de Bèze 1990 • $130 • (12/15/1992)
93 **Jaffelin** Romanée St.-Vivant 1990 • $75 • (12/15/1992)
93 **Jean Gros** Vosne-Romanée Clos des Réas 1990 • $48 • (12/15/1992)
93 **Joseph Drouhin** Beaune Clos des Mouches 1990 • $52 • (12/15/1992)
93 **Joseph Drouhin** Bonnes Mares 1990 • $111 Ⓐ • (12/15/1992)
93 **Joseph Drouhin** Chambolle-Musigny Les Amoureuses 1990 • $68 Ⓐ • (12/15/1992)
93 **Joseph Drouhin** Volnay Clos des Chênes 1990 • $42 • (12/15/1992)
93 **Méo-Camuzet** Vosne-Romanée 1990 • $36 • (2/15/1993)
93 **Méo-Camuzet** Vosne-Romanée Aux Brûlées 1990 • $81 • (6/15/1993)
93 **Mugneret-Gibourg** Echézeaux 1990 • $66 • (12/15/1992)
93 **P. Dubreuil-Fontaine Père & Fils** Corton Clos du Roi 1990 • $61 • (12/15/1992)
93 **Philippe Batacchi** Clos de la Roche 1990 • $59 • (12/15/1992)
93 **Philippe Batacchi** Morey-St.-Denis Premier Cru 1990 • $44 • (12/15/1992)
93 **Tollot-Beaut & Fils** Aloxe-Corton 1990 • $38 • (12/15/1992)
92 **Armand Rousseau** Chambertin 1990 • $269 Ⓐ • (12/15/1992)
92 **Armand Rousseau** Clos de la Roche 1990 • $182 Ⓐ • (12/15/1992)
92 **Bouchard Père & Fils** Volnay Taille Pieds 1990 • $50 • (12/15/1992)
92 **Bruno Clair** Gevrey-Chambertin Clos du Fonteny 1990 • $45 • (12/15/1992)
92 **Bruno Clair** Savigny-lès-Beaune La Dominode 1990 • $28 Ⓐ • (12/15/1992)
92 **Daniel Rion** Nuits-St.-Georges Aux Vignerondes 1990 • $70 • (12/15/1992)
92 **Daniel Rion** Nuits-St.-Georges Les Grandes Vignes 1990 • $42 • (12/15/1992)
92 **Daniel Rion** Vosne-Romanée Les Beaux Monts 1990 • $65 Ⓐ • (12/15/1992)
92 **Domaine Leroy** Corton Renardes 1990 • $111 • (12/15/1992)
92 **Domaine Leroy** Gevrey-Chambertin Les Combottes 1990 • $111 • (12/15/1992)
92 **Domaine Leroy** Romanée St.-Vivant 1990 • $405 • (12/15/1996)
92 **Domaine Leroy** Savigny-lès-Beaune Les Narbantons 1990 • $48 • (12/15/1992)
92 **Dujac** Charmes-Chambertin 1990 • $126 Ⓐ • (12/15/1992)
92 **Dujac** Clos de la Roche 1990 • $164 Ⓐ • (12/15/1992)
92 **Dujac** Gevrey-Chambertin Aux Combottes 1990 • $42 Ⓐ • (12/15/1992)
92 **F. Chauvenet** Clos de Vougeot 1990 • $69 • (12/15/1992)
92 **Forey Père & Fils** Echézeaux 1990 • $65 • (12/15/1992)
92 **G. Roumier** Chambolle-Musigny Les Amoureuses 1990 • $55 • (12/15/1992)
92 **G. Roumier** Clos Vougeot 1990 • $65 • (12/15/1992)
92 **Henri Gouges** Nuits-St.-Georges Clos des Porrets St.-Georges 1990 • $58 • (12/15/1992)
92 **Henri Gouges** Nuits-St.-Georges Les St.-Georges 1990 • $39 Ⓐ • (12/15/1992)
92 **Hubert Lignier** Clos de la Roche 1990 • $90 • (12/15/1992)
92 **J. Faiveley** Clos de Vougeot 1990 • $82 • (12/15/1992)
92 **J. Faiveley** Gevrey-Chambertin Les Marchais 1990 • $45 • (12/15/1992)
92 **J. Faiveley** Morey-St.-Denis Clos des Ormes 1990 • $NA • (12/15/1992)
92 **Jaffelin** Charmes-Chambertin 1990 • $55 • (12/15/1992)
92 **Jean-Marc Boillot** Beaune Montrevenots 1990 • $39 • (12/15/1992)
92 **Jean-Marc Boillot** Pommard Les Saussilles 1990 • $48 • (12/15/1992)
92 **Jean-Marc Boillot** Volnay 1990 • $40 • (12/15/1992)
92 **Jean-Marc Pavelot** Savigny-lès-Beaune Aux Guettes 1990 • $33 • (12/15/1992)
92 **Lejeune** Pommard Les Rugiens 1990 • $49 • (12/15/1992)
92 **Louis Jadot** Chambertin-Clos de Bèze 1990 • $164 Ⓐ • (2/28/1995)
92 **Louis Jadot** Vosne-Romanée 1990 • $30 • (12/15/1992)
92 **Mommessin** Volnay Taillepieds 1990 • $23 • (12/15/1992)
92 **Olivier Leflaive Frères** Pommard 1990 • $30 • (12/15/1992)
92 **Olivier Leflaive Frères** Volnay Clos de la Barre 1990 • $36 • (12/15/1992)
92 **Olivier Leflaive Frères** Volnay Frémiets 1990 • $35 • (12/15/1992)
92 **Philippe Charlopin-Parizot** Charmes-Chambertin 1990 • $70 • (8/31/1992)

■ ■ ■ ■

Red Burgundy

92 **Philippe Leclerc** Gevrey-Chambertin Combe au Moine 1990 • $73 Ⓐ • (12/15/1992)

92 **Ponsot** Clos de la Roche Vieilles Vignes 1990 • $280 Ⓐ • (3/15/1993)

92 **Robert Chevillon** Nuits-St.-Georges Les St.-Georges 1990 • $115 Ⓐ • (2/28/1995)

92 **Tollot-Beaut & Fils** Beaune Grèves 1990 • $40 • (12/15/1992)

91 **Bouchard Père & Fils** Corton Le Corton 1990 • $50 • (12/15/1992)

91 **Chopin-Groffier** Nuits-St.-Georges Aux Chaignots 1990 • $40 • (12/15/1992)

91 **Daniel Rion** Vosne-Romanée 1990 • $42 • (12/15/1992)

91 **Denis Bachelet** Gevrey-Chambertin Vieilles Vignes 1990 • $43 • (12/15/1992)

91 **Domaine de la Pousse d'Or** Volnay Les Caillerets Clos des 60 Ouvrées 1990 • $86 Ⓐ • (12/15/1992) • HR

91 **Domaine de la Romanée-Conti** Richebourg 1990 • $454 Ⓐ • (12/31/1993)

91 **Domaine Taupenot-Merme** Charmes-Chambertin 1990 • $58 • (11/30/1994)

91 **Domaine Thomas-Moillard** Beaune Les Grèves 1990 • $40 • (12/15/1992)

91 **Dujac** Echézeaux 1990 • $88 • (12/15/1992)

91 **F. Chauvenet** Echézeaux 1990 • $62 • (12/15/1992)

91 **Georges Mugneret** Clos Vougeot 1990 • $89 • (12/15/1992)

91 **Gros Frère & Soeur** Grands Echézeaux 1990 • $85 • (12/15/1992)

91 **J. Confuron-Cotetidot** Echézeaux 1990 • $65 • (12/15/1992)

91 **J. Confuron-Cotetidot** Nuits-St.-Georges Premier Cru 1990 • $28 • (12/15/1992)

91 **J. Faiveley** Echézeaux 1990 • $82 • (12/15/1992)

91 **J. Faiveley** Mazis-Chambertin 1990 • $89 • (12/15/1992)

91 **J. Faiveley** Nuits-St.-Georges Les Damodes 1990 • $45 • (12/15/1992)

91 **Jacques Germain** Beaune Les Cents Vignes 1990 • $46 • (12/15/1992)

91 **Jacques Germain** Beaune Les Teurons 1990 • $48 • (12/15/1992)

91 **Jacques Germain** Beaune Les Vignes Franches 1990 • $46 • (12/15/1992)

91 **Jaffelin** Gevrey-Chambertin Lavaut St.-Jacques 1990 • $42 • (12/15/1992)

91 **Jean Garaudet** Pommard Les Charmots 1990 • $48 • (8/31/1992)

91 **Joseph Drouhin** Chambertin 1990 • $107 Ⓐ • (12/15/1992)

91 **Joseph Drouhin** Clos de Vougeot 1990 • $71 • (12/15/1992)

91 **Joseph Drouhin** Echézeaux 1990 • $60 Ⓐ • (12/15/1992)

91 **Joseph Drouhin** Gevrey-Chambertin Champeaux 1990 • $70 • (12/15/1992)

91 **Joseph Drouhin** Grands Echézeaux 1990 • $100 • (2/28/1995)

91 **Joseph Drouhin** Pommard Les Epenots 1990 • $43 Ⓐ • (12/15/1992)

91 **Louis Jadot** Beaune Clos des Ursules 1990 • $63 Ⓐ • (12/15/1992)

Key: SS—Spectator Selection. CS—Cellar Selection.
HR—Highly Recommended. $NA—Price not available.
(BT)—Barrel tasting. Ⓐ—Auction Price.
Dates in parentheses represent the issues in which the ratings were published.

91 **Louis Jadot** Bonnes Mares 1990 • $152 Ⓐ • (12/15/1992)

91 **Louis Jadot** Chambolle-Musigny 1990 • $46 Ⓐ • (12/15/1992)

91 **Louis Jadot** Clos Vougeot 1990 • $109 Ⓐ • (12/15/1992)

91 **Louis Jadot** Griotte-Chambertin 1990 • $70 • (12/15/1992)

91 **Méo-Camuzet** Nuits-St.-Georges Aux Boudots 1990 • $96 Ⓐ • (2/15/1993)

91 **Mommessin** Aloxe-Corton 1990 • $20 • (12/15/1992)

91 **Mommessin** Vosne-Romanée Les Suchots 1990 • $35 • (12/15/1992)

91 **Olivier Leflaive Frères** Pommard Les Rugiens 1990 • $35 • (12/15/1992)

91 **P. Dubreuil-Fontaine Père & Fils** Pommard Epenots 1990 • $59 • (12/15/1992)

91 **Philippe Batacchi** Gevrey-Chambertin Les Evosselles 1990 • $32 • (12/15/1992)

91 **Philippe Leclerc** Gevrey-Chambertin Champeaux 1990 • $50 • (12/15/1992)

91 **Ponsot** Morey-St.-Denis 1990 • $68 • (3/15/1993)

91 **Rossignol-Trapet** Beaune Teurons 1990 • $46 • (12/15/1992)

91 **Sérafin Père & Fils** Gevrey-Chambertin Les Cazetiers 1990 • $67 Ⓐ • (12/15/1992)

90 **A.-F. Gros** Echézeaux 1990 • $90 • (12/15/1992)

90 **Alain Burguet** Gevrey-Chambertin Vieilles Vignes 1990 • $51 Ⓐ • (12/15/1992)

90 **Armand Rousseau** Gevrey-Chambertin Clos St.-Jacques 1990 • $184 Ⓐ • (12/15/1992)

90 **Bertrand Ambroise** Nuits-St.-Georges En Rue de Chaux 1990 • $48 • (12/15/1992)

90 **Bertrand Ambroise** Nuits-St.-Georges Les Vaucrains 1990 • $45 • (12/15/1992)

90 **Bouchard Père & Fils** Volnay Caillerets Ancienne Cuvée Carnot 1990 • $37 • (12/15/1992)

90 **Bourée Père & Fils** Clos de la Roche 1990 • $70 • (12/15/1992)

90 **Bourée Père & Fils** Gevrey-Chambertin Le Clos St.-Jacques 1990 • $60 • (12/15/1992)

90 **Bruno Clair** Morey-St.-Denis En la Rue de Vergy 1990 • $29 Ⓐ • (12/15/1992)

90 **Comte Georges de Vogüé** Chambolle-Musigny 1990 • $45 • (12/15/1992)

90 **Daniel Rion** Nuits-St.-Georges Les Pruliers 1990 • $70 • (12/15/1992)

90 **Domaine de la Romanée-Conti** Romanée St.-Vivant 1990 • $295 Ⓐ • (12/31/1993)

90 **Domaine Taupenot-Merme** Chambolle-Musigny 1990 • $22 • (11/30/1994) • HR

90 **Dujac** Clos St.-Denis 1990 • $172 Ⓐ • (12/15/1992)

90 **F. Chauvenet** Gevrey-Chambertin Lavaut St.-Jacques 1990 • $56 • (12/15/1992)

90 **F. Chauvenet** Nuits-St.-Georges Les Pruliers 1990 • $52 • (12/15/1992)

90 **Ghislaine Barthod** Chambolle-Musigny Les Charmes 1990 • $50 • (12/15/1992)

90 **Ghislaine Barthod** Chambolle-Musigny Les Véroilles 1990 • $50 • (12/15/1992)

90 **Guy Castagnier** Clos de la Roche 1990 • $NA • (12/15/1992)

90 **Henri Gouges** Nuits-St.-Georges Les Pruliers 1990 • $58 • (12/15/1992)

90 **J. Faiveley** Corton Clos des Cortons 1990 • $86 • (12/15/1992)

90 **J. Faiveley** Nuits-St.-Georges Aux Chaignots 1990 • $48 • (12/15/1992)

90 **J. Faiveley** Nuits-St.-Georges Clos de la Maréchale 1990 • $44 • (11/30/1992) • HR

90 **J. Faiveley** Nuits-St.-Georges Porrets St.-Georges 1990 • $45 • (12/15/1992)

90 **J. Faiveley** Pommard Les Chaponnières 1990 • $65 • (12/15/1992)

90 **Jaffelin** Beaune Champs Pimont 1990 • $25 • (12/15/1992)

90 **Joseph Drouhin** Volnay 1990 • $33 • (12/15/1992)

90 **Joseph Drouhin** Vosne-Romanée Les Petits Monts 1990 • $NA • (12/15/1992)

90 **Laleure-Piot** Corton Bressandes 1990 • $NA • (12/15/1992)

90 **Laleure-Piot** Pernand-Vergelesses Ile des Vergelesses 1990 • $NA • (12/15/1992)

90 **Louis Jadot** Corton Les Pougets 1990 • $60 Ⓐ • (12/15/1992)

90 **Louis Jadot** Gevrey-Chambertin Le Clos St.-Jacques 1990 • $100 Ⓐ • (12/15/1992)

90 **Louis Jadot** Mazis-Chambertin 1990 • $70 • (12/15/1992)

90 **Louis Jadot** Pommard Les Arvelets 1990 • $42 • (12/15/1992)

90 **Lucien Boillot** Volnay Les Brouillards 1990 • $32 • (12/15/1992)

90 **Méo-Camuzet** Nuits-St.-Georges Aux Murgers 1990 • $68 • (2/15/1993)

90 **Michel Lafarge** Volnay 1990 • $43 • (12/15/1992)

90 **Moillard** Morey-St.-Denis Monts Luisants 1990 • $33 • (12/15/1992)

90 **Mommessin** Beaune Les Cents Vignes 1990 • $20 • (12/15/1992)

90 **Mommessin** Gevrey-Chambertin Lavaut St.-Jacques 1990 • $45 • (12/15/1992)

90 **Mommessin** Nuits-St.-Georges Aux Chaignots 1990 • $29 • (12/15/1992)

90 **Mommessin** Savigny-lès-Beaune 1990 • $14 • (12/15/1992)

90 **Olivier Leflaive Frères** Pommard Les Epenots 1990 • $35 • (12/15/1992)

90 **Paul Pernot** Beaune Les Teurons 1990 • $33 • (4/30/1992)

90 **Philippe Batacchi** Gevrey-Chambertin Les Jeunes Rois 1990 • $38 • (12/15/1992)

90 **Philippe Charlopin-Parizot** Gevrey-Chambertin Cuvée Vieilles Vignes 1990 • $40 • (4/30/1992)

90 **Philippe Leclerc** Gevrey-Chambertin La Platière 1990 • $35 • (12/15/1992)

90 **Prince Florent de Mérode** Corton Le Clos du Roi 1990 • $38 • (12/15/1992)

90 **Prince Florent de Mérode** Pommard Clos de la Platière 1990 • $48 • (12/15/1992)

90 **Robert Jayer-Gilles** Côte de Nuits-Villages 1990 • $34 • (12/15/1992)

90 **Rossignol-Trapet** Gevrey-Chambertin Petite Chapelle 1990 • $61 • (12/15/1992)

90 **Simon Bize & Fils** Savigny-lès-Beaune Aux Vergelesses 1990 • $48 Ⓐ • (12/15/1992)

90 **Simon Bize & Fils** Savigny-lès-Beaune Les Marconnets 1990 • $33 • (12/15/1992)

90 **Tollot-Beaut & Fils** Beaune Clos du Roi 1990 • $48 • (12/15/1992)

90 **Tollot-Beaut & Fils** Savigny-lès-Beaune Les Lavières 1990 • $35 • (12/15/1992)

Louis Latour's vineyard in Corton-Charlemagne.

White Burgundy

Here are *Wine Spectator's* ratings and prices for the wines that scored 90 or above from the four most recent vintages of white Burgundy—1995 through 1998.

Burgundy has had a run of good luck with its white wines lately. The two most recent vintages on sale—1997 and 1998—each merited a solid rating of 88 points (out of 100), although Burgundy expert Per-Henrik Mansson says that 1997 was a bit uneven in the Côte d'Or. And the two vintages before that, the outstanding 1995 and the classic 1996, are showing good aging potential. (Even 1994 is still rated very good, but those wines are not listed here because they are now aging quickly.)

1998 WHITE BURGUNDY | VINTAGE RATING: 88

97 **Jean-Marc Boillot** Bâtard-Montrachet 1998 • $195 • (5/31/2000) • CS

95 **Marc Colin** Montrachet 1998 • $325 • (5/31/2000)

94 **Jean-Marc Boillot** Puligny-Montrachet Les Combettes 1998 • $93 • (5/31/2000)

94 **Joseph Drouhin** Meursault Perrières 1998 • $81 • (5/31/2000)

94 **Marc Colin** Puligny-Montrachet Le Trézin 1998 • $45 • (5/31/2000)

93 **Billaud-Simon** Chablis Les Clos 1998 • $50 • (5/15/2000)

93 **Borgeot** Chassagne-Montrachet Morgeot 1998 • $43 • (5/31/2000)

93 **Jean-Paul Droin** Chablis Montée de Tonnerre 1998 • $30 • (5/15/2000) • HR

93 **Marc Colin** Puligny-Montrachet Les Garennes 1998 • $60 • (5/31/2000)

93 **Michel Colin-Deléger** Chassagne-Montrachet Les Vergers 1998 • $59 • (5/31/2000)

93 **Michel Colin-Deléger** Chevalier-Montrachet 1998 • $166 • (5/31/2000)

93 **R. Ballot-Millot & Fils** Meursault Les Criots 1998 • $43 • (5/31/2000)

Key: SS—Spectator Selection. CS—Cellar Selection. HR—Highly Recommended. $NA—Price not available. (BT)—Barrel tasting. Ⓐ—Auction Price.
Dates in parentheses represent the issues in which the ratings were published.

93 **Vincent Girardin** Bâtard-Montrachet 1998 • $209 • (5/31/2000)

93 **Vincent Girardin** Meursault Les Narvaux 1998 • $52 • (5/31/2000) • HR

93 **William Fèvre** Chablis Valmur 1998 • $69 • (5/15/2000)

92 **Bernard Millot** Meursault La Goutte d'Or 1998 • $45 • (5/31/2000)

92 **Borgeot** Puligny-Montrachet Vieilles Vignes 1998 • $40 • (5/31/2000)

92 **Chartron & Trébuchet** Bâtard-Montrachet 1998 • $175 • (5/31/2000)

92 **Chartron & Trébuchet** Montrachet 1998 • $300 • (5/31/2000)

92 **Fernand & Laurent Pillot** Chassagne-Montrachet Morgeot 1998 • $62 • (5/31/2000)

92 **Gérard Chavy** Puligny-Montrachet Les Perrières 1998 • $48 • (5/31/2000)

92 **Hubert Lamy** St.-Aubin En Remilly 1998 • $NA • (5/31/2000)

92 **Jean Chartron** Puligny-Montrachet Clos du Cailleret 1998 • $85 • (5/31/2000)

92 **Marc Colin** St.-Aubin En Montceau 1998 • $33 • (5/31/2000)

92 **Marc Colin** St.-Aubin En Remilly 1998 • $33 • (5/31/2000) • HR

92 **Marc Colin** St.-Aubin Le Charmois 1998 • $33 • (5/31/2000)

92 **Marc Colin** St.-Aubin Les Combes 1998 • $33 • (5/31/2000)

Tim Stead

92 **Michel Colin-Deléger** St.-Aubin En Charmois 1998 • $34 • (5/31/2000)

91 **Bernard Moreau** Chassagne-Montrachet Morgeot 1998 • $45 • (5/31/2000)

91 **Fernand & Laurent Pillot** Puligny-Montrachet Noyers Brets 1998 • $53 • (5/31/2000)

91 **Jean-Marc Boillot** Puligny-Montrachet La Truffière 1998 • $93 • (5/31/2000)

91 **La Chablisienne** Chablis Mont de Milieu 1998 • $30 • (5/15/2000)

91 **Marc Colin** St.-Aubin La Chatenière 1998 • $33 • (5/31/2000)

91 **Michel Barat** Chablis Mont de Milieu 1998 • $20 • (5/15/2000)

91 **Michel Colin-Deléger** Puligny-Montrachet Les Demoiselles 1998 • $120 • (5/31/2000)

91 **Philippe Chavy** Puligny-Montrachet Les Folatières 1998 • $57 • (5/31/2000)

91 **Verget** Bâtard-Montrachet 1998 • $179 • (5/31/2000)

91 **Vincent Girardin** Savigny-lès-Beaune White Les Vermots-Dessus 1998 • $33 • (5/31/2000)

91 **William Fèvre** Chablis Les Clos 1998 • $80 • (5/15/2000)

90 **A. Long-Depaquit** Chablis Les Lys 1998 • $NA • (5/15/2000)

90 **Bernard Millot** Puligny-Montrachet 1998 • $34 • (5/31/2000)

90 **Billaud-Simon** Chablis Mont de Milieu Vieille Vigne 1998 • $34 • (5/15/2000)

90 **Chartron & Trébuchet** Chassagne-Montrachet Morgeot 1998 • $70 • (5/31/2000)

90 **Chartron & Trébuchet** Meursault Les Charmes 1998 • $75 • (5/31/2000)

90 **Fernand & Laurent Pillot** Chassagne-Montrachet 1998 • $42 • (5/31/2000)

90 **Fernand & Laurent Pillot** Chassagne-Montrachet Grandes Ruchottes 1998 • $80 • (5/31/2000)

90 **Ghislaine & Jean-Hugues Goisot** Sauvignon de St.-Bris 1998 • $14 • (5/15/2000)

90 **Hubert Lamy** St.-Aubin Clos de la Chatenière 1998 • $32 • (5/31/2000)

90 **Jean Chartron** Chevalier-Montrachet Clos des Chevaliers 1998 • $235 • (5/31/2000)

90 **Jean-Marc Brocard** Chablis Vaillons 1998 • $29 • (5/15/2000)

90 **Jean-Paul Droin** Chablis Vaudésir 1998 • $47 • (5/15/2000)

90 **Joseph Drouhin** Beaune Clos des Mouches 1998 • $79 • (5/31/2000)

90 **La Chablisienne** Chablis Grenouilles 1998 • $50 • (5/15/2000)

90 **Louis Carillon** Puligny-Montrachet 1998 • $54 • (5/31/2000)

90 **Louis Michel & Fils** Chablis Les Clos 1998 • $39 • (5/15/2000)

90 **Maillard Père & Fils** Corton White 1998 • $63 • (5/31/2000)

90 **Marc Colin** Chassagne-Montrachet Les Vide-Bourses 1998 • $55 • (5/31/2000)

90 **Maroslavac-Leger** Puligny-Montrachet Les Folatières 1998 • $60 • (5/31/2000)

Key: SS—Spectator Selection. CS—Cellar Selection. HR—Highly Recommended. $NA—Price not available. (BT)—Barrel tasting. Ⓐ—Auction Price.
Dates in parentheses represent the issues in which the ratings were published.

90 **P. Dubreuil-Fontaine Père & Fils** Corton-Charlemagne 1998 • $85 • (5/31/2000)

90 **Thierry Hamelin** Chablis Vau Ligneau 1998 • $22 • (5/15/2000)

90 **Verget** Pouilly-Fuissé Tête de Cuvée 1998 • $28 • (5/31/2000)

90 **Vincent Girardin** Meursault Les Poruzots 1998 • $NA • (5/31/2000)

90 **Vincent Girardin** Puligny-Montrachet Les Enseignères 1998 • $56 • (5/31/2000)

1997 White Burgundy
Vintage Rating: 88

98 **Michel Niellon** Bâtard-Montrachet 1997 • $210 • (9/30/1999)

97 **Domaine d'Auvenay** Meursault Chaumes des Perrières 1997 • $108 • (9/30/1999)

97 **Jacques Prieur** Montrachet 1997 • $460 • (9/30/1999) • CS

96 **Blain-Gagnard** Criots-Bâtard-Montrachet 1997 • $120 • (5/31/1999)

96 **François Raveneau** Chablis Valmur 1997 • $95 • (5/15/2000) • CS

96 **Marc Colin** Montrachet 1997 • $325 • (5/31/1999)

96 **Michel Colin-Deléger** Chevalier-Montrachet 1997 • $160 • (9/30/1999)

96 **Vincent Girardin** Bâtard-Montrachet 1997 • $173 • (5/31/1999)

95 **Domaine d'Auvenay** Auxey-Duresses White 1997 • $76 • (9/30/1999)

95 **Domaine d'Auvenay** Auxey-Duresses White Les Boutonniers 1997 • $76 • (9/30/1999)

95 **Domaine d'Auvenay** Puligny-Montrachet Les Folatières 1997 • $202 • (9/30/1999)

95 **Domaine Laroche** Chablis Les Clos 1997 • $102 • (9/30/1999)

95 **François Raveneau** Chablis Montée de Tonnerre 1997 • $60 • (5/15/2000)

95 **J.-F. Coche-Dury** Puligny-Montrachet Les Enseignères 1997 • $82 • (9/30/1999)

95 **Jean-Marc Brocard** Chablis Les Clos 1997 • $47 • (5/31/1999)

95 **Ramonet** Chassagne-Montrachet Les Vergers 1997 • $58 • (9/30/1999)

95 **René & Vincent Dauvissat** Chablis Les Clos 1997 • $61 • (5/31/1999) • CS

95 **Vincent Girardin** Corton-Charlemagne 1997 • $96 • (5/31/1999)

94 **A. Long-Depaquit** Chablis Moutonne 1997 • $56 • (5/31/1999)

94 **Arnaud Ente** Meursault La Goutte d'Or 1997 • $56 • (9/30/1999) • HR

94 **Billaud-Simon** Chablis Blanchots Vieille Vigne 1997 • $56 • (5/31/1999)

94 **Billaud-Simon** Chablis Les Preuses 1997 • $45 • (5/31/1999)

94 **Caillot** Puligny-Montrachet Les Pucelles 1997 • $80 • (1/01/2000)

94 **Château de Chamirey** Mercurey White 1997 • $17 • (5/31/1999) • SS

94 **Domaine des Comtes Lafon** Montrachet 1997 • $500 • (5/31/2000)

94 **François Raveneau** Chablis Butteaux 1997 • $45 • (5/15/2000)

94 **Guy Amiot** Puligny-Montrachet Les Demoiselles 1997 • $104 • (9/30/1999)

94 **Guy Roulot** Meursault Perrières 1997 • $86 • (9/30/1999)
94 **J. Moreau & Fils** Chablis Les Clos 1997 • $52 • (5/31/1999) • CS
94 **J.-A. Ferret** Pouilly-Fuissé Les Scélés Cuvée Spéciale 1997 • $29 • (5/31/1999)
94 **Jacques Thevenot-Machal** Puligny-Montrachet Les Charmes 1997 • $35 • (5/31/1999)
94 **Jean-Marc Brocard** Chablis Vaugiraut 1997 • $26 • (9/30/1999)
94 **Jean-Noël Gagnard** Bâtard-Montrachet 1997 • $150 • (9/30/1999)
94 **Jean-Paul Droin** Chablis Montée de Tonnerre 1997 • $NA • (5/31/1999)
94 **La Chablisienne** Chablis Blanchot 1997 • $50 • (5/31/1999)
94 **Laleure-Piot** Corton-Charlemagne 1997 • $109 • (5/31/1999)
94 **Latour-Giraud** Puligny-Montrachet Champs Canet 1997 • $55 • (9/30/1999)
94 **Louis Michel & Fils** Chablis Les Clos 1997 • $51 • (5/31/1999)
94 **Michel Colin-Deléger** Bâtard-Montrachet 1997 • $142 • (9/30/1999)
94 **Michel Colin-Deléger** Chassagne-Montrachet La Maltroie 1997 • $56 • (9/30/1999)
94 **Servin** Chablis Les Clos 1997 • $20 • (5/31/1999)
94 **Verget** Chablis Bougros 1997 • $50 • (5/31/1999)
94 **Verget** Chablis Vaillons 1997 • $28 • (5/31/1999)
94 **Vocoret & Fils** Chablis Montmains 1997 • $22 • (5/31/1999)
93 **A. Long-Depaquit** Chablis Vaillons 1997 • $30 • (5/31/1999)
93 **Arnaud Ente** Meursault 1997 • $42 • (9/30/1999)
93 **Bitouzet-Prieur** Meursault Santenots 1997 • $37 • (9/30/1999)
93 **Borgeot** Chassagne-Montrachet Morgeot 1997 • $43 • (5/31/1999)
93 **Borgeot** Santenay White Les Gravières 1997 • $29 • (5/31/1999)
93 **Caillot** Meursault Clos du Cromin 1997 • $39 • (1/01/2000)
93 **Caillot** Puligny-Montrachet Les Folatières 1997 • $60 • (5/31/2000)
93 **Domaine d'Auvenay** Meursault Les Gouttes d'Or 1997 • $220 • (9/30/1999)
93 **Domaine d'Auvenay** Meursault Pré de Manche 1997 • $108 • (9/30/1999)
93 **Domaine des Comtes Lafon** Meursault Charmes 1997 • $100 • (5/31/2000)
93 **Domaine des Comtes Lafon** Meursault Perrières 1997 • $110 • (5/31/2000)
93 **Domaine des Comtes Lafon** Puligny-Montrachet Champ-Gain 1997 • $90 • (5/31/2000)
93 **Domaine Laroche** Chablis Blanchots 1997 • $85 • (9/30/1999)
93 **Domaine Laroche** Chablis Réserve de l'Obédience 1997 • $152 • (9/30/1999)
93 **Domaine Laroche** Chablis Vaillons Vieilles Vignes 1997 • $45 • (5/31/1999)
93 **Domaine Leflaive** Bâtard-Montrachet 1997 • $265 • (9/30/1999)
93 **Domaine Leflaive** Bienvenues-Bâtard-Montrachet 1997 • $255 • (9/30/1999)
93 **Fernand & Laurent Pillot** Chassagne-Montrachet Les Vergers 1997 • $50 • (2/28/1999)
93 **François Raveneau** Chablis Blanchot 1997 • $70 • (5/15/2000)
93 **Guffens-Heynen** Pouilly-Fuissé Clos des Petits-Croux 1997 • $NA • (9/30/1999)
93 **Guy Bocard** Meursault Les Narvaux 1997 • $40 • (9/30/1999)
93 **Guy Roulot** Meursault Les Charmes 1997 • $78 • (9/30/1999)
93 **Guy Roulot** Meursault Les Meix Chavaux 1997 • $47 • (9/30/1999)
93 **Jacques Prieur** Corton-Charlemagne 1997 • $120 • (9/30/1999)
93 **Jean Dauvissat** Chablis Les Preuses 1997 • $55 • (9/30/1999)
93 **Jean-Marc Brocard** Chablis Bougros 1997 • $47 • (5/31/1999)
93 **Jean-Marc Brocard** Chablis Vaucoupin 1997 • $26 • (9/30/1999) • HR
93 **Joseph Drouhin** Chablis Les Clos 1997 • $51 • (9/30/1999)
93 **La Chablisienne** Chablis Bougros 1997 • $47 • (5/31/1999)
93 **La Chablisienne** Chablis Les Clos 1997 • $47 • (5/31/1999)
93 **Louis Carillon** Puligny-Montrachet Les Perrières 1997 • $64 • (9/30/1999)
93 **Louis Jadot** Puligny-Montrachet Clos de la Garenne Duc de Magenta 1997 • $69 • (9/30/1999)
93 **Maillard Père & Fils** Chorey-lès-Beaune White 1997 • $22 • (5/31/1999)
93 **Marc Colin** Puligny-Montrachet Les Garennes 1997 • $55 • (9/30/1999)
93 **Michel Colin-Deléger** Puligny-Montrachet Les Demoiselles 1997 • $120 • (9/30/1999)
93 **Pascal Bouchard** Chablis Blanchot 1997 • $60 • (5/31/1999)
93 **Philippe Chavy** Puligny-Montrachet Les Corvées des Vignes 1997 • $40 • (5/31/1999)
93 **Roger Belland** Chassagne-Montrachet Morgeot-Clos Pitois 1997 • $50 • (9/30/1999)
93 **Verget** Chablis Fourchaume 1997 • $31 • (5/31/1999)
93 **Verget** Pouilly-Fuissé Tête de Cuvée 1997 • $18 • (5/31/1999)
92 **Bernard Morey** Puligny-Montrachet La Truffière 1997 • $47 • (5/31/1999)
92 **Bertrand Ambroise** Bourgogne Hautes-Côtes de Nuits White 1997 • $25 • (5/31/1999)
92 **Bertrand Ambroise** Corton-Charlemagne 1997 • $125 • (9/30/1999)
92 **Borgeot** Chassagne-Montrachet 1997 • $32 • (5/31/1999)
92 **Bruno Clair** Morey-St.-Denis White En la Rue de Vergy 1997 • $47 • (5/31/1999)
92 **Caillot** Santenay White 1997 • $20 • (1/01/2000)
92 **Cordier Père & Fils** Pouilly-Fuissé Au Metertière 1997 • $38 • (5/31/1999)
92 **Domaine Leflaive** Chevalier-Montrachet 1997 • $330 • (9/30/1999)
92 **Domaine Leflaive** Puligny-Montrachet Clavoillon 1997 • $114 • (9/30/1999)
92 **Fernand & Laurent Pillot** Chassagne-Montrachet Morgeot 1997 • $54 • (2/28/1999)
92 **François Raveneau** Chablis Forêt 1997 • $58 • (5/15/2000)
92 **François Raveneau** Chablis Monts Mains 1997 • $45 • (5/15/2000)
92 **Guy Amiot** St.-Aubin En Remilly 1997 • $44 • (9/30/1999)
92 **J.-A. Ferret** Pouilly-Fuissé Le Clos Cuvée Spéciale Tête de Cru 1997 • $37 • (9/30/1999)

■■■■

White Burgundy

92 **J.-F. Coche-Dury** Corton-Charlemagne 1997 • $205 • (9/30/1999)

92 **Jacques Prieur** Chevalier-Montrachet 1997 • $240 • (9/30/1999)

92 **Jean Chartron** Puligny-Montrachet Clos de la Pucelle 1997 • $70 • (5/31/1999)

92 **Jean Chartron** Puligny-Montrachet Clos du Cailleret 1997 • $72 • (5/31/1999)

92 **Jean Dauvissat** Chablis Montmains 1997 • $30 • (9/30/1999)

92 **Jean-Marc Boillot** Puligny-Montrachet Les Pucelles 1997 • $73 • (5/31/1999)

92 **Jean-Marc Brocard** Chablis Montmain 1997 • $26 • (5/31/1999)

92 **Louis Jadot** Meursault Charmes 1997 • $65 • (9/30/1999)

92 **Louis Michel & Fils** Chablis Grenouilles 1997 • $52 • (5/31/1999)

92 **Marc Colin** St.-Aubin Les Cortons 1997 • $35 • (5/31/1999)

92 **Marc Morey** Chassagne-Montrachet En Virondot 1997 • $48 • (9/30/1999)

92 **Michel Coutoux** Chassagne-Montrachet Les Chenevottes 1997 • $58 • (2/28/1999)

92 **Philippe Bouchard** Corton-Charlemagne 1997 • $68 • (5/31/1999)

92 **Prieur-Brunet** Bâtard-Montrachet 1997 • $195 • (9/30/1999)

92 **René & Vincent Dauvissat** Chablis Les Preuses 1997 • $61 • (5/31/1999)

92 **Roger Belland** Criots-Bâtard-Montrachet 1997 • $105 • (9/30/1999)

92 **Saumaize-Michelin** Pouilly-Fuissé Les Ronchevats 1997 • $40 • (5/31/1999)

92 **Saumaize-Michelin** St.-Véran Les Vieilles Vignes 1997 • $22 • (5/31/1999)

92 **Verget** St.-Véran Tête de Cuvée 1997 • $20 • (5/31/1999)

92 **Vincent Girardin** Meursault Les Narvaux 1997 • $47 • (9/30/1999)

92 **Vincent Girardin** Santenay White Le Beaurepaire 1997 • $38 • (5/31/1999)

91 **A. Long-Depaquit** Chablis Les Lys 1997 • $34 • (5/31/1999)

91 **Bernard Moreau** Chassagne-Montrachet Les Chenevottes 1997 • $42 • (5/31/1999)

91 **Bernard Morey** Chassagne-Montrachet Les Caillerets 1997 • $52 • (5/31/1999)

91 **Blain-Gagnard** Bâtard-Montrachet 1997 • $120 • (5/31/1999)

91 **Bouchard Père & Fils** Meursault Genevrières 1997 • $88 • (5/31/1999)

91 **Chartron & Trébuchet** Corton-Charlemagne 1997 • $80 • (5/31/1999)

91 **Domaine d'Auvenay** Auxey-Duresses White Les Clous 1997 • $76 • (9/30/1999)

91 **Domaine du Château de Puligny-Montrachet** St.-Aubin En Remilly 1997 • $30 • (5/31/1999)

91 **Domaine Laroche** Chablis Fourchaumes Vieilles Vignes 1997 • $50 • (5/31/1999)

91 **Domaine Leflaive** Puligny-Montrachet Les Pucelles 1997 • $170 • (9/30/1999)

Key: SS—Spectator Selection. CS—Cellar Selection. HR—Highly Recommended. $NA—Price not available. (BT)—Barrel tasting. Ⓐ—Auction Price.
Dates in parentheses represent the issues in which the ratings were published.

91 **Gérard Chavy** Puligny-Montrachet Les Folatières 1997 • $49 • (5/31/1999)

91 **Guy Amiot** Montrachet 1997 • $348 • (9/30/1999)

91 **J. Moreau & Fils** Chablis Vaillons 1997 • $30 • (5/31/1999)

91 **Jean Boillot** Puligny-Montrachet Les Perrières 1997 • $73 • (5/31/1999)

91 **La Chablisienne** Chablis Côte de Léchet 1997 • $47 • (5/31/1999)

91 **Latour-Giraud** Meursault Poruzots 1997 • $45 • (9/30/1999)

91 **Lupé-Cholet** Chablis Vaillons Château de Viviers 1997 • $34 • (9/30/1999)

91 **Marc Colin** St.-Aubin La Chatenière 1997 • $35 • (5/31/1999)

91 **Marc Morey** Chassagne-Montrachet Les Chenevottes 1997 • $48 • (9/30/1999)

91 **Michel Colin-Deléger** Chassagne-Montrachet Les Chenevottes 1997 • $58 • (9/30/1999)

91 **Michel Colin-Deléger** Chassagne-Montrachet Morgeot 1997 • $56 • (9/30/1999)

91 **Michel Coutoux** Chassagne-Montrachet La Maltroie 1997 • $59 • (2/28/1999)

91 **Michel Morey-Coffinet** Chassagne-Montrachet La Romanée 1997 • $50 • (5/31/1999)

91 **Olivier Leflaive Frères** Meursault Les Tillets 1997 • $NA • (1/01/1999)

91 **Prieur-Brunet** Meursault Chevalières 1997 • $50 • (9/30/1999)

91 **Roger Belland** Puligny-Montrachet Les Champs-Gains 1997 • $53 • (9/30/1999)

91 **Simonnet-Febvre** Chablis Mont de Milieu 1997 • $27 • (5/31/1999)

91 **Vocoret & Fils** Chablis 1997 • $15 • (5/31/1999) • HR

91 **Vocoret & Fils** Chablis Mont de Milieu 1997 • $NA • (5/31/1999)

90 **A. Long-Depaquit** Chablis Blanchot 1997 • $48 • (5/31/1999)

90 **A. Long-Depaquit** Chablis Vaudésir 1997 • $48 • (5/31/1999)

90 **Auvigue & Revel** Pouilly-Fuissé Les Crays 1997 • $22 • (5/31/1999)

90 **Bitouzet-Prieur** Meursault Perrières 1997 • $54 • (9/30/1999)

90 **Caillot** Bourgogne White Les Herbeux 1997 • $15 • (1/01/2000)

90 **Caillot** Meursault Les Tessons 1997 • $39 • (1/01/2000)

90 **Catherine & Pascal Rollet** Pouilly-Fuissé Domaine de la Chapelle Vieilles Vignes 1997 • $21 • (5/31/1999)

90 **Chartron & Trébuchet** Auxey-Duresses White 1997 • $NA • (1/01/1999)

90 **Château de Maligny** Chablis Fourchaume 1997 • $24 • (5/31/1999)

90 **Château des Rontets** Pouilly-Fuissé Les Birbettes Cuvée Vieilles Vignes 1997 • $28 • (9/30/1999)

90 **Château Fuissé** Pouilly-Fuissé Le Clos 1997 • $37 • (5/31/1999)

90 **Claude & Hubert Chavy-Chouet** Puligny-Montrachet Les Enseignères Vieille Vigne 1997 • $45 • (5/31/1999)

90 **Cordier Père & Fils** Pouilly-Fuissé Champs-Murgers 1997 • $33 • (5/31/1999)

90 **Cordier Père & Fils** Pouilly-Fuissé Juliette la Grande 1997 • $65 • (5/31/1999)

90 **Cordier Père & Fils** Pouilly-Fuissé Vieilles Vignes 1997 • $38 • (5/31/1999)

90 **Corinne & Jean-Pierre Grossot** Chablis Les Fourneaux 1997 • $22 • (5/31/1999)

90 **Domaine d'Auvenay** Chevalier-Montrachet 1997 • $686 • (9/30/1999)
90 **Domaine de la Collonge** Pouilly-Fuissé 1997 • $15 • (5/31/1999)
90 **Domaine de la Soufrandise** Pouilly-Fuissé Levrouté Vieilles Vignes 1997 • $25 • (5/31/1999)
90 **Domaine des Comtes Lafon** Meursault Désirée 1997 • $70 • (5/31/2000)
90 **Domaine des Comtes Lafon** Meursault Genevrières 1997 • $100 • (5/31/2000)
90 **Domaine Laroche** Chablis Bougerots 1997 • $NA • (9/30/1999)
90 **Domaine Leflaive** Puligny-Montrachet Les Folatières 1997 • $150 • (9/30/1999)
90 **Emilian Gillet** Mâcon-Viré Quintaine 1997 • $23 • (5/31/1999)
90 **Fontaine-Gagnard** Chassagne-Montrachet Morgeot 1997 • $64 • (5/31/1999)
90 **Fontaine-Gagnard** Criots-Bâtard-Montrachet 1997 • $165 • (5/31/1999)
90 **François Jobard** Meursault Genevrières 1997 • $72 • (5/31/2000)
90 **François Jobard** Meursault Poruzot 1997 • $66 • (5/31/2000)
90 **François Raveneau** Chablis Vaillons 1997 • $45 • (5/15/2000)
90 **Georges Duboeuf** Pouilly-Fuissé Aged in Oak 1997 • $17 • (5/31/1999) • HR
90 **Gérard Chavy** Puligny-Montrachet Les Clavoillons 1997 • $49 • (5/31/1999)
90 **Ghislaine & Jean-Hugues Goisot** Bourgogne Côtes d'Auxerre White Domaine du Corps de Garde 1997 • $17 • (5/31/1999)
90 **Guy Roulot** Meursault Les Luchets 1997 • $47 • (9/30/1999)
90 **Guy Roulot** Meursault Les Vireuils 1997 • $47 • (9/30/1999)
90 **Hubert Lamy** St.-Aubin Clos de la Chatenière 1997 • $25 • (5/31/1999)
90 **Jacques Prieur** Meursault Clos de Mazeray 1997 • $50 • (9/30/1999)
90 **Jayer-Gilles** Hautes-Côtes de Nuits White 1997 • $30 • (9/30/1999)
90 **Jean Boillot** Puligny-Montrachet Les Pucelles 1997 • $83 • (5/31/1999)
90 **Jean-Marc Boillot** Puligny-Montrachet 1997 • $31 Ⓐ • (5/31/1999)
90 **Jean-Marc Brocard** Chablis Beauregard 1997 • $26 • (5/31/1999)
90 **Jean-Marc Brocard** Chablis Fourchaume 1997 • $26 • (5/31/1999)
90 **Jean-Noël Gagnard** Chassagne-Montrachet Les Masures 1997 • $40 • (9/30/1999)
90 **Jean-Paul Droin** Chablis Les Clos 1997 • $45 • (5/31/1999)
90 **Joseph Drouhin** Beaune White Clos des Mouches 1997 • $80 • (5/31/1999)
90 **Joseph Drouhin** Chablis Vaudésir 1997 • $49 • (5/31/1999)
90 **Joseph Drouhin** Rully 1997 • $20 • (5/31/1999)
90 **Labouré-Roi** Meursault Clos des Bouches Chères Domaine René Manuel 1997 • $39 • (9/30/1999)
90 **Latour-Giraud** Meursault Charmes 1997 • $48 • (9/30/1999)
90 **Latour-Giraud** Meursault Clos du Cromin 1997 • $NA • (1/01/1999)
90 **Louis Jadot** Bâtard-Montrachet 1997 • $202 • (9/30/1999)
90 **Louis Jadot** Chevalier-Montrachet Les Demoiselles 1997 • $225 • (9/30/1999)
90 **Louis Jadot** Puligny-Montrachet Les Folatières 1997 • $69 • (9/30/1999)
90 **Louis Max** Chassagne-Montrachet Morgeot 1997 • $75 • (9/30/1999)
90 **Louis Michel & Fils** Chablis Montmain 1997 • $31 • (5/31/1999)
90 **Louis Michel & Fils** Chablis Vaillons 1997 • $31 • (5/31/1999)
90 **Louis Michel & Fils** Chablis Vaudésir 1997 • $50 • (5/31/1999)
90 **Louis Moreau** Chablis Les Fourneaux 1997 • $25 • (9/30/1999)
90 **Lupé-Cholet** Chablis Blanchot Château de Viviers 1997 • $48 • (9/30/1999)
90 **Marc Colin** Chassagne-Montrachet Les Vide-Bourses 1997 • $55 • (5/31/1999)
90 **Marc Colin** St.-Aubin En Remilly 1997 • $35 • (5/31/1999)
90 **Marc Colin** St.-Aubin Le Charmois 1997 • $35 • (5/31/1999)
90 **Michel Barat** Chablis Côte de Léchet 1997 • $19 • (5/31/1999)
90 **Michel Bouzereau & Fils** Meursault Genevrières 1997 • $55 • (5/31/1999)
90 **Michel Colin-Deléger** Chassagne-Montrachet En Remilly 1997 • $58 • (9/30/1999)
90 **Michel Juillot** Mercurey White Les Champs Martins 1997 • $30 • (5/31/1999)
90 **Michel Niellon** Chassagne-Montrachet Les Champgains 1997 • $65 • (9/30/1999)
90 **Olivier Leflaive Frères** Criots-Bâtard-Montrachet 1997 • $175 • (9/30/1999)
90 **Olivier Leflaive Frères** Puligny-Montrachet Les Pucelles 1997 • $80 • (9/30/1999)
90 **P. Dubreuil-Fontaine Père & Fils** Pernand-Vergelesses White Clos Berthet 1997 • $39 • (5/31/1999)
90 **Pascal Bouchard** Chablis Mont de Milieu Vieilles Vignes Grande Réserve 1997 • $52 • (5/31/1999)
90 **Pascal Bouchard** Chablis Vieilles Vignes Grande Réserve 1997 • $30 • (5/31/1999)
90 **Pavelot** Pernand-Vergelesses White 1997 • $28 • (5/31/1999)
90 **Servin** Chablis Montée de Tonnerre 1997 • $20 • (5/31/1999)
90 **Sylvain Mosnier** Chablis Côte de Léchet 1997 • $24 • (5/31/1999)
90 **Verget** Chablis 1997 • $20 • (5/31/1999)
90 **Vincent Girardin** Puligny-Montrachet Les Charmes 1997 • $51 • (5/31/1999)
90 **Vincent Girardin** Santenay White Clos du Beauregard 1997 • $34 • (5/31/1999)
90 **Vincent Girardin** Savigny-lès-Beaune White Les Vermots-Dessus 1997 • $32 • (5/31/1999)

1996 White Burgundy
Vintage Rating: 95

99 **Caillot** Bâtard-Montrachet 1996 • $115 Ⓐ • (5/31/1999)
99 **Domaine des Comtes Lafon** Meursault Genevrières 1996 • $80 • (5/31/1999)
99 **Domaine Laroche** Chablis Les Clos 1996 • $85 • (5/31/1998) • CS
99 **J.-F. Coche-Dury** Corton-Charlemagne 1996 • $1,342 Ⓐ • (5/31/1999)
99 **Marc Colin** Montrachet 1996 • $250 • (5/31/1998)

99 **Michel Colin-Deléger** Bâtard-Montrachet 1996 • $100 • (8/31/1998)
98 **Domaine d'Auvenay** Criots-Bâtard-Montrachet 1996 • $425 • (8/31/1998)
98 **Domaine des Comtes Lafon** Montrachet 1996 • $300 • (5/31/1999)
98 **Domaine Laroche** Chablis Réserve de l'Obédience 1996 • $110 • (5/31/1998)
98 **J. Moreau & Fils** Chablis Les Clos 1996 • $47 • (5/31/1998)
98 **J.-F. Coche-Dury** Meursault Les Perrières 1996 • $138 • (5/31/1999)
98 **Jacques Prieur** Montrachet 1996 • $240 Ⓐ • (8/31/1998)
98 **Jean-Noël Gagnard** Bâtard-Montrachet 1996 • $220 Ⓐ • (8/31/1998) • HR
98 **Joseph Drouhin** Chablis Les Clos 1996 • $50 • (5/31/1998)
98 **Louis Carillon** Bienvenues-Bâtard-Montrachet 1996 • $125 • (5/31/1999)
98 **Verget** Chablis Vaillons 1996 • $48 Ⓐ • (5/31/1998)
97 **Blain-Gagnard** Bâtard-Montrachet 1996 • $110 • (5/31/1998) • CS
97 **Domaine Leflaive** Puligny-Montrachet Les Combettes 1996 • $159 Ⓐ • (5/31/1999)
97 **Jean Chartron** Chevalier-Montrachet Clos des Chevaliers 1996 • $170 • (5/31/1998)
97 **Latour-Giraud** Meursault Genevrières 1996 • $42 • (8/31/1998)
97 **Marc Colin** Bâtard-Montrachet 1996 • $130 • (5/31/1998)
96 **Bernard Morey** Puligny-Montrachet La Truffière 1996 • $69 • (8/31/1998)
96 **Bouchard Père & Fils** Chevalier-Montrachet 1996 • $88 Ⓐ • (5/31/1998)
96 **Caillot** Meursault La Barre Dessus Clos Marguerite 1996 • $32 • (5/31/1999)
96 **Domaine des Comtes Lafon** Meursault Perrières 1996 • $80 • (5/31/1999)
96 **Domaine du Château de Puligny-Montrachet** Chevalier-Montrachet 1996 • $175 • (8/31/1998)
96 **Domaine Laroche** Chablis Blanchots 1996 • $73 • (8/31/1998)
96 **Jean-Marc Boillot** Puligny-Montrachet La Truffière 1996 • $72 • (5/31/1998)
96 **Jean-Paul Droin** Chablis Les Clos 1996 • $40 • (5/31/1998)
96 **Louis Jadot** Meursault Perrières 1996 • $55 • (8/31/1998) • HR
96 **Louis Pinson** Chablis Les Clos 1996 • $35 • (8/31/1998)
96 **Michel Colin-Deléger** Puligny-Montrachet Les Demoiselles 1996 • $100 • (8/31/1998)
96 **Verget** Chablis Fourchaume Vieilles Vignes 1996 • $43 • (8/31/1998)
96 **Verget** Chablis Montée de Tonnerre 1996 • $36 Ⓐ • (5/31/1998)
96 **Verget** Chablis Vaudésir 1996 • $51 • (8/31/1998)
95 **A. Long-Depaquit** Chablis Les Clos 1996 • $37 • (8/31/1998)
95 **A. Long-Depaquit** Chablis Les Preuses 1996 • $35 • (5/31/1998)
95 **Blain-Gagnard** Criots-Bâtard-Montrachet 1996 • $110 • (5/31/1998)

Key: SS—Spectator Selection. CS—Cellar Selection. HR—Highly Recommended. $NA—Price not available. (BT)—Barrel tasting. Ⓐ—Auction Price.
Dates in parentheses represent the issues in which the ratings were published.

95 **Bonneau du Martray** Corton-Charlemagne 1996 • $104 Ⓐ • (8/31/1998)
95 **Bouchard Père & Fils** Corton-Charlemagne 1996 • $110 • (5/31/1998)
95 **Caillot** Meursault Les Tessons 1996 • $34 • (5/31/1999)
95 **Domaine des Comtes Lafon** Meursault Charmes 1996 • $249 Ⓐ • (5/31/1999)
95 **Domaine des Comtes Lafon** Meursault Désirée 1996 • $163 Ⓐ • (5/31/1999)
95 **Domaine du Château de Puligny-Montrachet** Puligny-Montrachet La Garenne 1996 • $58 • (8/31/1998)
95 **Domaine du Château de Puligny-Montrachet** Puligny-Montrachet Les Chalumeaux 1996 • $56 • (8/31/1998)
95 **Domaine du Château de Puligny-Montrachet** Puligny-Montrachet Les Folatières 1996 • $65 • (8/31/1998)
95 **Domaine Leflaive** Puligny-Montrachet Les Folatières 1996 • $100 • (5/31/1999)
95 **Domaine Leflaive** Puligny-Montrachet Les Pucelles 1996 • $125 Ⓐ • (5/31/1999)
95 **Guy Amiot** Puligny-Montrachet Les Demoiselles 1996 • $98 • (5/31/1999)
95 **Guy Roulot** Meursault Perrières 1996 • $75 • (8/31/1998)
95 **J.-F. Coche-Dury** Meursault Les Rougeots 1996 • $158 Ⓐ • (5/31/1999)
95 **J.-F. Coche-Dury** Puligny-Montrachet Les Enseignères 1996 • $82 • (5/31/1999)
95 **Jacques Prieur** Puligny-Montrachet Les Combettes 1996 • $73 • (8/31/1998)
95 **Jean-Marc Boillot** Puligny-Montrachet Les Referts 1996 • $62 • (5/31/1998)
95 **Jean-Marc Brocard** Chablis Beauregard 1996 • $25 • (5/31/1998)
95 **Jean-Paul Droin** Chablis Valmur 1996 • $40 • (5/31/1998)
95 **Jean-Paul Droin** Chablis Vaudésir 1996 • $40 • (5/31/1998)
95 **Joseph Drouhin** Bâtard-Montrachet 1996 • $150 • (8/31/1998)
95 **Larue** Puligny-Montrachet Les Garennes 1996 • $NA • (8/31/1998)
95 **Latour-Giraud** Meursault Perrières 1996 • $45 • (8/31/1998)
95 **Louis Carillon** Puligny-Montrachet Les Perrières 1996 • $64 • (8/31/1998)
95 **Louis Jadot** Corton-Charlemagne 1996 • $100 • (8/31/1998)
95 **Michel Colin-Deléger** Chassagne-Montrachet Morgeot 1996 • $67 Ⓐ • (8/31/1998)
95 **Olivier Leflaive Frères** Meursault Les Perrières 1996 • $65 • (8/31/1998)
95 **Patrick Javillier** Meursault Cuvée Tête de Murger 1996 • $70 • (5/31/1999)
95 **Rémi Jobard** Meursault Les Charmes 1996 • $59 • (8/31/1998)
95 **René & Vincent Dauvissat** Chablis Les Clos 1996 • $61 • (8/31/1998)
95 **Roger Belland** Criots-Bâtard-Montrachet 1996 • $90 • (5/31/1998)
95 **Verget** Puligny-Montrachet Les Enseignères 1996 • $64 Ⓐ • (8/31/1998)
95 **Vincent Girardin** Meursault Les Perrières 1996 • $65 • (5/31/1998)
94 **A. Long-Depaquit** Chablis Moutonne 1996 • $50 • (8/31/1998)
94 **Albert Grivault** Meursault Perrières 1996 • $48 Ⓐ • (5/31/1998)
94 **Bertagna** Vougeot White 1996 • $55 • (1/01/1999)

94 **Billaud-Simon** Chablis Les Clos 1996 • $NA • (5/31/1998)

94 **Caillot** Meursault Clos du Cromin 1996 • $30 • (5/31/1999)

94 **Caillot** Puligny-Montrachet Les Folatières 1996 • $53 • (5/31/1999)

94 **Cordier Père & Fils** Pouilly-Fuissé Vieilles Vignes 1996 • $29 • (5/31/1998)

94 **Domaine des Comtes Lafon** Meursault 1996 • $86 Ⓐ • (5/31/1999)

94 **Domaine des Malandes** Chablis Côte de Léchet 1996 • $17 • (5/31/1998)

94 **Domaine Laroche** Chablis Fourchaumes 1996 • $40 • (5/31/1998)

94 **Domaine Laroche** Chablis Vaillons 1996 • $40 • (8/31/1998)

94 **Étienne Sauzet** Montrachet 1996 • $440 • (8/31/1998)

94 **François d'Allaines** Chassagne-Montrachet Les Champsgains 1996 • $NA • (9/30/1999)

94 **François Raveneau** Chablis Blanchot 1996 • $80 • (1/01/2000)

94 **Guffens-Heynen** Mâcon-Pierreclos 1996 • $NA • (8/31/1998)

94 **Guffens-Heynen** Mâcon-Pierreclos Le Chavigne 1996 • $25 • (8/31/1998)

94 **Guy Amiot** Chassagne-Montrachet Les Vergers 1996 • $54 • (5/31/1999)

94 **Jean Dauvissat** Chablis Vaillons 1996 • $25 • (5/31/1998)

94 **Jean Pillot** Chevalier-Montrachet 1996 • $150 • (5/31/1998)

94 **Jean-Marc Boillot** Puligny-Montrachet Les Combettes 1996 • $72 • (5/31/1998)

94 **Jean-Marc Boillot** Puligny-Montrachet Les Pucelles 1996 • $62 • (5/31/1998)

94 **Jean-Paul Droin** Chablis Montée de Tonnerre 1996 • $18 • (8/31/1997)

94 **Jean-Paul Droin** Chablis Montmains 1996 • $23 • (5/31/1998)

94 **Jean-Paul Droin** Chablis Vaillons 1996 • $23 • (5/31/1998)

94 **Jean-Paul Droin** Chablis Vosgros 1996 • $23 • (5/31/1998)

94 **La Chablisienne** Chablis Bougros 1996 • $42 • (5/31/1998)

94 **La Chablisienne** Chablis Fourchaume 1996 • $27 • (5/31/1998)

94 **La Chablisienne** Chablis Montée de Tonnerre 1996 • $27 • (5/31/1998)

94 **La Chablisienne** Chablis Valmur 1996 • $42 • (5/31/1998)

94 **Louis Michel & Fils** Chablis Les Clos 1996 • $46 • (5/31/1998)

94 **Michel Barat** Chablis Côte de Léchet 1996 • $15 • (5/31/1998)

94 **Michel Barat** Chablis Les Fourneaux 1996 • $18 • (8/31/1998)

94 **Michel Barat** Chablis Mont de Milieu 1996 • $15 • (5/31/1998)

94 **Michel Juillot** Corton-Charlemagne 1996 • $72 Ⓐ • (5/31/1998)

94 **Olivier Leflaive Frères** Corton-Charlemagne 1996 • $61 Ⓐ • (5/31/1999)

94 **Prieur-Brunet** Meursault Charmes 1996 • $45 • (8/31/1998)

94 **René Monnier** Puligny-Montrachet Les Folatières 1996 • $NA • (8/31/1998)

94 **Verget** Chablis Valmur 1996 • $86 Ⓐ • (8/31/1998)

94 **Vincent Girardin** Corton-Charlemagne 1996 • $83 • (5/31/1998)

93 **Antonin Guyon** Meursault Charmes-Dessus 1996 • $50 • (8/31/1998)

93 **Bernard Morey** Chassagne-Montrachet Morgeot 1996 • $47 • (8/31/1998)

93 **Billaud-Simon** Chablis Montée de Tonnerre 1996 • $24 • (5/31/1998)

93 **Borgeot** Santenay White Les Gravières 1996 • $26 • (5/31/1998)

93 **Bouchard Père & Fils** Meursault Genevrières 1996 • $66 • (8/31/1998)

93 **Château de Maligny** Chablis Fourchaume 1996 • $25 • (8/31/1997)

93 **Demessey** Puligny-Montrachet Le Cailleret 1996 • $42 • (8/31/1998)

93 **Domaine d'Auvenay** Meursault Les Narvaux 1996 • $189 • (8/31/1998)

93 **Domaine Laroche** Chablis Vaudevey 1996 • $40 • (8/31/1998)

93 **Domaine Leflaive** Bâtard-Montrachet 1996 • $258 Ⓐ • (5/31/1999)

93 **Domaine Leflaive** Puligny-Montrachet 1996 • $56 • (5/31/1999)

93 **Fontaine-Gagnard** Criots-Bâtard-Montrachet 1996 • $148 • (5/31/1998)

93 **Fontaine-Gagnard** Montrachet 1996 • $335 • (5/31/1998)

93 **François Raveneau** Chablis Valmur 1996 • $80 • (1/01/2000)

93 **J. Moreau & Fils** Chablis Valmur 1996 • $46 • (5/31/1998)

93 **J.-F. Coche-Dury** Meursault Caillerets 1996 • $92 • (5/31/1999)

93 **Jean Pillot** Chassagne-Montrachet Morgeot 1996 • $40 • (5/31/1998)

93 **Jean-Marc Boillot** Meursault 1996 • $39 • (5/31/1998)

93 **Jean-Marc Boillot** Puligny-Montrachet Les Folatières 1996 • $56 • (5/31/1998)

93 **Jean-Marc Brocard** Chablis Bougros 1996 • $45 • (5/31/1998)

93 **Jean-Marc Brocard** Chablis Fourchaume 1996 • $25 • (5/31/1998)

93 **Jean-Marc Brocard** Chablis Les Clos 1996 • $45 • (5/31/1998)

93 **Jean-Noël Gagnard** Chassagne-Montrachet Les Caillerets 1996 • $77 Ⓐ • (8/31/1998)

93 **Jean-Noël Gagnard** Chassagne-Montrachet Les Chenevottes 1996 • $NA • (8/31/1998)

93 **Joseph Drouhin** Chablis Domaine de Vaudon 1996 • $20 • (5/31/1998)

93 **La Chablisienne** Chablis Beauroy 1996 • $42 • (8/31/1998)

93 **La Chablisienne** Chablis Montmain 1996 • $25 • (5/31/1998)

93 **La Chablisienne** Chablis Premier Cru Vieilles Vignes 1996 • $25 • (5/31/1998)

93 **La Chablisienne** Chablis Vaillon 1996 • $25 • (5/31/1998)

93 **Laleure-Piot** Corton-Charlemagne 1996 • $96 • (5/31/1998)

93 **Lamblin & Fils** Chablis Vaillon 1996 • $12 • (5/31/1999)

93 **Latour-Giraud** Meursault Charmes 1996 • $42 • (8/31/1998)

93 **Louis Jadot** Puligny-Montrachet Clos de la Garenne Duc de Magenta 1996 • $60 • (8/31/1998)

93 **Louis Michel & Fils** Chablis Montée de Tonnerre 1996 • $30 • (5/31/1998)

93 **Louis Michel & Fils** Chablis Montmain 1996 • $31 • (8/31/1998)

93 **Louis Pinson** Chablis Mont de Milieu 1996 • $22 • (5/31/1998)

93 **Lupé-Cholet** Chablis Blanchot Château de Viviers 1996 • $44 • (5/31/1998)

93 **Lupé-Cholet** Chablis Vaillons Château de Viviers 1996 • $26 • (5/31/1998)

93 **Marc Colin** St.-Aubin Le Charmois 1996 • $35 • (5/31/1998)

93 **Marc Colin** St.-Aubin Les Combes 1996 • $35 • (5/31/1998)

93 **Marc Morey** Chassagne-Montrachet Les Vergers 1996 • $48 • (5/31/1998)

93 **Maroslavac-Leger** Puligny-Montrachet Les Folatières 1996 • $50 • (5/31/1998)

93 **Michel Barat** Chablis Vaillons 1996 • $15 • (5/31/1998)

93 **Michel Bouzereau & Fils** Meursault Genevrières 1996 • $NA • (5/31/1998)

93 **Michel Colin-Deléger** Chevalier-Montrachet 1996 • $115 • (8/31/1998)

93 **Michel Colin-Deléger** Puligny-Montrachet La Truffière 1996 • $58 • (8/31/1998)

93 **Monthélie-Douhairet** Meursault Les Santenots 1996 • $53 • (5/31/1998)

93 **Olivier Leflaive Frères** Meursault Charmes 1996 • $56 • (8/31/1998)

93 **Olivier Leflaive Frères** Puligny-Montrachet Champ Gain 1996 • $52 • (5/31/1999)

93 **Pascal Bouchard** Chablis Vaudésir 1996 • $44 • (5/31/1998)

93 **Patrick Javillier** Meursault Clos du Cromin 1996 • $44 • (5/31/1999)

93 **Pierre Matrot** Meursault Perrières 1996 • $50 • (5/31/1999)

93 **Rémi Jobard** Meursault Les Genevrières 1996 • $55 • (5/31/1998)

93 **René & Vincent Dauvissat** Chablis La Forest 1996 • $35 • (8/31/1998)

93 **René & Vincent Dauvissat** Chablis Séchet 1996 • $35 • (8/31/1998)

93 **René Monnier** Meursault Charmes 1996 • $NA • (8/31/1998)

93 **Verget** Bâtard-Montrachet 1996 • $219 Ⓐ • (8/31/1998)

93 **Verget** Chablis Bougros 1996 • $80 Ⓐ • (8/31/1998)

93 **Verget** Pouilly-Fuissé Tête de Cuvée 1996 • $15 • (5/31/1998) • HR

93 **Vincent Girardin** Chassagne-Montrachet Morgeot Vieilles Vignes 1996 • $NA • (5/31/1998)

93 **Vincent Girardin** Meursault Les Narvaux 1996 • $42 • (5/31/1998)

92 **A. Long-Depaquit** Chablis 1996 • $17 • (8/31/1998)

92 **A. Long-Depaquit** Chablis Blanchot 1996 • $36 • (8/31/1998)

92 **A. Long-Depaquit** Chablis Vaillons 1996 • $25 • (5/31/1998)

92 **Albert Grivault** Meursault Clos des Perrières 1996 • $60 • (5/31/1998)

92 **Bernard Morey** Chassagne-Montrachet Les Embrazées 1996 • $37 Ⓐ • (8/31/1998)

92 **Billaud-Simon** Chablis Blanchots Vieille Vigne 1996 • $60 • (5/31/1998)

92 **Bouchard Père & Fils** Beaune White Premier Cru 1996 • $38 • (5/31/1998)

Key: SS—Spectator Selection. CS—Cellar Selection. HR—Highly Recommended. $NA—Price not available. (BT)—Barrel tasting. Ⓐ—Auction Price.
Dates in parentheses represent the issues in which the ratings were published.

92 **Bouchard Père & Fils** Puligny-Montrachet Les Pucelles 1996 • $68 • (5/31/1998)

92 **Bzikot Père & Fils** Puligny-Montrachet Les Folatières 1996 • $40 • (8/31/1998)

92 **Château de la Maltroye** Chassagne-Montrachet Grandes Ruchottes 1996 • $50 • (5/31/1998)

92 **Claude & Hubert Chavy-Chouet** Puligny-Montrachet Les Enseignères 1996 • $45 • (5/31/1998)

92 **Corsin** Pouilly-Fuissé 1996 • $23 • (5/31/1998)

92 **Domaine d'Auvenay** Meursault Les Gouttes d'Or 1996 • $185 • (8/31/1998)

92 **Domaine du Château de Puligny-Montrachet** Meursault 1996 • $26 • (5/31/1998)

92 **Etienne Boileau** Chablis Montée de Tonnerre 1996 • $25 • (5/31/1998)

92 **François d'Allaines** Mâcon La Roche Vineuse 1996 • $NA • (5/31/1998)

92 **Gérard Chavy** Puligny-Montrachet Les Perrières 1996 • $40 • (5/31/1998)

92 **Ghislaine & Jean-Hugues Goisot** Sauvignon de St.-Bris Domaine du Corps de Garde 1996 • $14 • (5/31/1998)

92 **Guffens-Heynen** Pouilly-Fuissé Vinians L'Année Louise 1996 • $NA • (8/31/1998)

92 **Guy Roulot** Meursault Les Charmes 1996 • $75 • (8/31/1998)

92 **Guy Roulot** Meursault Les Luchets 1996 • $50 • (8/31/1998)

92 **Guy Roulot** Meursault Les Meix Chavaux 1996 • $50 • (8/31/1998)

92 **Henri Clerc & Fils** Chevalier-Montrachet 1996 • $120 • (5/31/1998)

92 **Hubert Lamy** Chassagne-Montrachet Les Macherelles 1996 • $38 • (5/31/1998)

92 **Hubert Lamy** St.-Aubin Clos de la Chatenière 1996 • $22 • (5/31/1998)

92 **Hubert Lamy** St.-Aubin En Remilly 1996 • $22 • (5/31/1998)

92 **Hubert Lamy** St.-Aubin Les Murgers des Dents de Chien 1996 • $28 • (5/31/1998)

92 **Jacques Burrier** Pouilly-Fuissé Château de Beauregard Cuvée Prestige 1996 • $21 • (5/31/1998)

92 **Jacques Prieur** Meursault Clos de Mazeray 1996 • $50 • (8/31/1998)

92 **Jean Dauvissat** Chablis 1996 • $18 • (5/31/1998)

92 **Jean Dauvissat** Chablis Séchet 1996 • $23 • (5/31/1998)

92 **Jean-Claude Courtault** Chablis 1996 • $NA • (8/31/1997)

92 **Joseph Drouhin** Corton-Charlemagne 1996 • $92 • (5/31/1998)

92 **Joseph Drouhin** Puligny-Montrachet Clos de la Garenne 1996 • $65 • (5/31/1998)

92 **Lamblin & Fils** Chablis Fourchaume 1996 • $NA • (8/31/1997)

92 **Lupé-Cholet** Chablis Château de Viviers 1996 • $18 • (5/31/1998)

92 **Lupé-Cholet** Chablis Vaucoupin Château de Viviers 1996 • $25 • (5/31/1998)

92 **Marc Colin** Chassagne-Montrachet Les Encégnières 1996 • $45 • (8/31/1998)

92 **Prieur-Brunet** Meursault Chevalières 1996 • $40 • (8/31/1998)

92 **Simonnet-Febvre** Chablis Fourchaume 1996 • $23 • (5/31/1998)

92 **Tollot-Beaut & Fils** Corton-Charlemagne 1996 • $90 • (8/31/1998)

92 **Vincent Girardin** Savigny-lès-Beaune White Les Vermots-Dessus 1996 • $28 • (5/31/1998)

92 **William Fèvre** Chablis Montée de Tonnerre 1996 • $22 • (5/31/1998)

91 **Bernard Légland** Chablis Montmains 1996 • $24 • (5/31/1998)

91 **Billaud-Simon** Chablis Mont de Milieu 1996 • $24 • (5/31/1998)

91 **Billaud-Simon** Chablis Mont de Milieu Vieille Vigne 1996 • $27 • (5/31/1998)

91 **Blain-Gagnard** Chassagne-Montrachet Morgeot 1996 • $36 Ⓐ • (5/31/1998)

91 **Bouchard Père & Fils** Bâtard-Montrachet 1996 • $150 • (8/31/1998)

91 **Bouchard Père & Fils** Puligny-Montrachet Les Chalumeaux 1996 • $50 • (5/31/1998)

91 **Château Fuissé** Pouilly-Fuissé Vieilles Vignes 1996 • $49 • (5/31/1998)

91 **Corsin** Mâcon-Villages 1996 • $13 • (8/31/1997)

91 **Domaine Leflaive** Bienvenues-Bâtard-Montrachet 1996 • $148 Ⓐ • (5/31/1999)

91 **Fontaine-Gagnard** Bâtard-Montrachet 1996 • $148 • (5/31/1998)

91 **François Raveneau** Chablis Montée de Tonnerre 1996 • $60 • (1/01/2000)

91 **Ghislaine & Jean-Hugues Goisot** Bourgogne Aligoté Domaine du Corps de Garde 1996 • $14 • (5/31/1998)

91 **Hubert Lamy** St.-Aubin Les Frionnes 1996 • $20 • (5/31/1998)

91 **J.-A. Ferret** Pouilly-Fuissé Les Scélés 1996 • $26 • (5/31/1998)

91 **Jacques Burrier** Pouilly-Fuissé Château de Beauregard 1996 • $21 • (5/31/1998)

91 **Jean Dauvissat** Chablis Montmains 1996 • $28 • (8/31/1998)

91 **Jean-Marc Boillot** Montagny Premier Cru 1996 • $20 • (5/31/1998)

91 **Jean-Marc Brocard** Bourgogne White sur Kimmeridjien 1996 • $15 • (8/31/1997)

91 **Jean-Marc Brocard** Chablis Vieilles Vignes Domaine Ste.-Claire 1996 • $21 • (8/31/1997)

91 **Latour-Giraud** Meursault Bouchères 1996 • $35 • (8/31/1998)

91 **Louis Jadot** Puligny-Montrachet 1996 • $38 • (8/31/1998)

91 **Louis Latour** Corton-Charlemagne 1996 • $112 Ⓐ • (5/31/1999)

91 **Marc Colin** Chassagne-Montrachet Les Caillerets 1996 • $50 • (5/31/1998)

91 **Marc Morey** Chassagne-Montrachet Les Chenevottes 1996 • $44 • (5/31/1998)

91 **Marc Morey** Chassagne-Montrachet Morgeot 1996 • $50 • (5/31/1998)

91 **Maroslavac-Leger** Meursault Les Murgers 1996 • $36 • (5/31/1998)

91 **Michel Bouzereau & Fils** Meursault Les Grands Charrons 1996 • $36 • (5/31/1998)

91 **Michel Bouzereau & Fils** Puligny-Montrachet Les Champs Gains 1996 • $55 • (5/31/1998)

91 **Michel Morey-Coffinet** Chassagne-Montrachet La Romanée 1996 • $47 • (5/31/1998)

91 **Parent** Corton White 1996 • $100 • (2/28/1999)

91 **Pascal Bouchard** Chablis Blanchot 1996 • $44 • (5/31/1998)

91 **Ramonet** Chassagne-Montrachet Les Vergers 1996 • $60 • (5/31/1999)

91 **Ramonet** Chassagne-Montrachet Morgeot 1996 • $67 Ⓐ • (5/31/1999)

91 **Rémi Jobard** Meursault Les Chevalières 1996 • $40 • (8/31/1998)

91 **Rémi Jobard** Meursault Sous La Velle 1996 • $35 • (5/31/1998)

91 **René Monnier** Meursault Le Limozin 1996 • $NA • (8/31/1998)

91 **Simonnet-Febvre** Chablis 1996 • $15 • (8/31/1997)

91 **Verget** Chablis 1996 • $20 • (5/31/1998)

91 **Verget** St.-Aubin Premier Cru 1996 • $29 Ⓐ • (5/31/1998)

90 **A. Long-Depaquit** Chablis Les Beugnons 1996 • $25 • (5/31/1998)

90 **Bernard Morey** Chassagne-Montrachet Les Caillerets 1996 • $44 Ⓐ • (8/31/1998)

90 **Bernard Morey** St.-Aubin Les Charmois 1996 • $33 • (8/31/1998)

90 **Bertrand Ambroise** Corton-Charlemagne 1996 • $NA • (8/31/1998)

90 **Billaud-Simon** Chablis Fourchaume 1996 • $26 • (5/31/1998)

90 **Billaud-Simon** Chablis Tête d'Or 1996 • $20 • (8/31/1998)

90 **Blain-Gagnard** Chassagne-Montrachet Caillerets 1996 • $45 • (8/31/1998)

90 **Bouchard Père & Fils** Beaune White Clos St.-Landry 1996 • $50 • (5/31/1998)

90 **Bouchard Père & Fils** Chassagne-Montrachet 1996 • $39 • (5/31/1998)

90 **Bouchard Père & Fils** Meursault 1996 • $35 • (5/31/1998)

90 **Bouchard Père & Fils** Montrachet 1996 • $320 • (8/31/1998)

90 **Bouchard Père & Fils** Puligny-Montrachet Les Folatières 1996 • $55 • (5/31/1998)

90 **Chartron & Trébuchet** St.-Aubin La Chatenière 1996 • $25 • (5/31/1998)

90 **Claude & Hubert Chavy-Chouet** Puligny-Montrachet Hameau de Blagny Vieille Vigne 1996 • $60 • (5/31/1998)

90 **Cordier Père & Fils** Pouilly-Fuissé Au Metertière 1996 • $32 • (5/31/1998)

90 **Corinne & Jean-Pierre Grossot** Chablis Les Fourneaux 1996 • $22 • (5/31/1998)

90 **Corinne & Jean-Pierre Grossot** Chablis Vaucoupin 1996 • $25 • (5/31/1998)

90 **Daniel Barraud** Pouilly-Fuissé La Verchère 1996 • $25 • (5/31/1998)

90 **Demessey** Pernand-Vergelesses White Sous le Bois de Noël et Belles Filles 1996 • $19 • (5/31/1998)

90 **Domaine d'Auvenay** Auxey-Duresses White Les Boutonniers 1996 • $60 • (8/31/1998)

90 **Domaine d'Auvenay** Meursault 1996 • $98 • (8/31/1998)

90 **Domaine de la Bongran** Mâcon-Clessé Quintaine Cuvée Tradition 1996 • $25 • (5/31/1998)

90 **Domaine Leflaive** Chevalier-Montrachet 1996 • $191 Ⓐ • (5/31/1999)

90 **Domaine Leflaive** Puligny-Montrachet Clavoillon 1996 • $86 Ⓐ • (5/31/1999)

90 **Étienne Sauzet** Puligny-Montrachet Les Combettes 1996 • $105 Ⓐ • (8/31/1998)

90 **Fontaine-Gagnard** Chassagne-Montrachet Clos St.-Jean Clos Les Murées 1996 • $60 • (5/31/1998)

90 **Fontaine-Gagnard** Chassagne-Montrachet Les Caillerets 1996 • $60 • (5/31/1998)

90 **Francine & Olivier Savary** Chablis 1996 • $22 • (8/31/1997)

90 **François Jobard** Meursault Genevrières 1996 • $60 Ⓐ • (5/31/1999)

90 **Gérard Chavy** Puligny-Montrachet 1996 • $45 • (8/31/1998)

90 **Gilbert Picq** Chablis Vosgros 1996 • $22 • (5/31/1998)
90 **Guy Bocard** Meursault Sous la Velle 1996 • $30 • (8/31/1998)
90 **H. & P. Jacqueson** Rully La Pucelle 1996 • $20 • (5/31/1998)
90 **Jacques Prieur** Beaune White Clos de la Féguine 1996 • $54 • (8/31/1998)
90 **Jacques Prieur** Meursault Perrières 1996 • $92 • (8/31/1998)
90 **Jean Chartron** Puligny-Montrachet Clos du Cailleret 1996 • $60 • (5/31/1998)
90 **Jean Pillot** Chassagne-Montrachet Les Champs-Gain 1996 • $38 • (5/31/1998)
90 **Jean Pillot** Chassagne-Montrachet Les Chenevottes 1996 • $35 • (5/31/1998)
90 **Jean-Claude Thévenet** Mâcon-Pierreclos 1996 • $13 • (8/31/1997)
90 **Jean-Marc Boillot** Rully Grésigny 1996 • $21 • (5/31/1998)
90 **Jean-Marc Brocard** Petit Chablis 1996 • $18 • (8/31/1997)
90 **Jean-Noël Gagnard** Chassagne-Montrachet 1996 • $23 • (8/31/1998)
90 **Jean-Noël Gagnard** Chassagne-Montrachet Premier Cru 1996 • $45 • (8/31/1998)
90 **Joseph Drouhin** Beaune White Clos des Mouches 1996 • $78 • (5/31/1998)
90 **Joseph Drouhin** Chablis Premier Cru 1996 • $25 • (8/31/1997) • SS
90 **Joseph Matrot** Meursault-Blagny 1996 • $46 • (5/31/1999)
90 **Latour-Giraud** Meursault Clos du Cromin 1996 • $30 • (8/31/1998)
90 **Latour-Giraud** Meursault Cuvée Charles Maxime 1996 • $32 • (8/31/1998)
90 **Louis Carillon** Puligny-Montrachet Les Champs Canet 1996 • $77 Ⓐ • (8/31/1998)
90 **Louis Latour** Montrachet 1996 • $218 Ⓐ • (5/31/1999)
90 **Maillard Père & Fils** Corton White 1996 • $50 • (8/31/1998)
90 **Marc Colin** Puligny-Montrachet Les Garennes 1996 • $50 • (5/31/1998)
90 **Marc Colin** St.-Aubin En Remilly 1996 • $35 • (5/31/1998)
90 **Marc Colin** St.-Aubin La Chatenière 1996 • $35 • (5/31/1998)
90 **Marc Colin** St.-Aubin Les Cortons 1996 • $35 • (5/31/1998)
90 **Marc Morey** Chassagne-Montrachet 1996 • $32 • (5/31/1998)
90 **Marc Morey** Chassagne-Montrachet En Virondot 1996 • $44 • (5/31/1998)
90 **Maroslavac-Leger** Puligny-Montrachet Les Combettes 1996 • $50 • (5/31/1998)
90 **Michel Bouzereau & Fils** Meursault Le Limozin 1996 • $NA • (5/31/1998)
90 **Michel Bouzereau & Fils** Meursault Les Charmes-Dessus 1996 • $NA • (5/31/1998)
90 **Michel Colin-Deléger** St.-Aubin Les Combes 1996 • $27 • (8/31/1998)
90 **Michel Niellon** Chassagne-Montrachet Clos de la Maltroie 1996 • $91 Ⓐ • (8/31/1998)
90 **Michel Niellon** Chassagne-Montrachet Clos St.-Jean 1996 • $77 Ⓐ • (8/31/1998)

Key: SS—Spectator Selection. CS—Cellar Selection.
HR—Highly Recommended. $NA—Price not available.
(BT)—Barrel tasting. Ⓐ—Auction Price.
Dates in parentheses represent the issues in which the ratings were published.

90 **Michel Niellon** Chassagne-Montrachet Les Champgains 1996 • $60 • (8/31/1998)
90 **Olivier Leflaive Frères** Meursault 1996 • $42 • (8/31/1998)
90 **Olivier Leflaive Frères** Puligny-Montrachet Les Folatières 1996 • $62 • (5/31/1999)
90 **Pascal Bouchard** Chablis Les Clos 1996 • $44 • (5/31/1998)
90 **Paul Garaudet** Meursault Vieille Vigne 1996 • $32 • (5/31/1998)
90 **Pierre Labet** Beaune White Clos des Monsnières 1996 • $33 • (5/31/1998)
90 **Ramonet** Chassagne-Montrachet Boudriotte 1996 • $48 Ⓐ • (5/31/1999)
90 **Rapet Père & Fils** Corton-Charlemagne 1996 • $79 • (5/31/1998)
90 **Rémi Jobard** Bourgogne White 1996 • $20 • (5/31/1998)
90 **Rémi Jobard** Meursault Le Poruzot-Dessus 1996 • $52 • (5/31/1998)
90 **René Monnier** Puligny-Montrachet 1996 • $NA • (8/31/1998)
90 **Servin** Chablis Bougros 1996 • $42 • (5/31/1998)
90 **Servin** Chablis Les Clos 1996 • $45 • (5/31/1998)
90 **Servin** Chablis Montée de Tonnerre 1996 • $26 • (5/31/1998)
90 **Thierry Hamelin** Chablis 1996 • $17 • (8/31/1997)
90 **Thierry Hamelin** Petit Chablis 1996 • $14 • (8/31/1997)
90 **Verget** Corton-Charlemagne 1996 • $122 Ⓐ • (8/31/1998)
90 **Verget** Meursault Les Charmes Cuvée Vieilles Vignes 1996 • $75 • (8/31/1998)
90 **Verget** St.-Véran 1996 • $13 • (5/31/1998)
90 **Vessigaud Père & Fils** Pouilly-Fuissé Vieilles Vignes 1996 • $27 • (5/31/1998)

1995 White Burgundy
Vintage Rating: 93

100 **Domaine Leflaive** Chevalier-Montrachet 1995 • $174 Ⓐ • (8/31/1998) • HR
99 **Domaine d'Auvenay** Chevalier-Montrachet 1995 • $492 • (8/31/1997) • HR
99 **Jacques Prieur** Montrachet 1995 • $360 Ⓐ • (8/31/1997) • HR
99 **Verget** Bâtard-Montrachet 1995 • $180 • (5/31/1997)
98 **Domaine d'Auvenay** Criots-Bâtard-Montrachet 1995 • $498 • (8/31/1997)
98 **Domaine d'Auvenay** Puligny-Montrachet Les Folatières 1995 • $133 • (8/31/1997)
98 **Domaine des Comtes Lafon** Montrachet 1995 • $400 • (5/31/1998)
98 **Domaine Leflaive** Bienvenues-Bâtard-Montrachet 1995 • $153 Ⓐ • (8/31/1998)
98 **Étienne Sauzet** Chevalier-Montrachet 1995 • $267 Ⓐ • (8/31/1997)
98 **J.-F. Coche-Dury** Corton-Charlemagne 1995 • $175 • (5/31/1998)
98 **Louis Latour** Chevalier-Montrachet Les Demoiselles 1995 • $186 • (8/31/1997)
98 **Marc Colin** Montrachet 1995 • $273 Ⓐ • (5/31/1997)
98 **P. Dubreuil-Fontaine Père & Fils** Corton-Charlemagne 1995 • $74 • (5/31/1997)
98 **Ramonet** Montrachet 1995 • $486 Ⓐ • (8/31/1998)
98 **Rapet Père & Fils** Corton-Charlemagne 1995 • $NA • (5/31/1997)

97 **Domaine d'Auvenay** Meursault Les Narvaux 1995 • $155 • (8/31/1997)

97 **Domaine des Comtes Lafon** Meursault Charmes 1995 • $80 • (5/31/1998)

97 **Domaine Leflaive** Puligny-Montrachet Les Folatières 1995 • $46 Ⓐ • (8/31/1998)

97 **Étienne Sauzet** Montrachet 1995 • $440 • (8/31/1998)

97 **J.-F. Coche-Dury** Meursault Les Perrières 1995 • $130 • (5/31/1998)

97 **Jacques Prieur** Puligny-Montrachet Les Combettes 1995 • $60 • (8/31/1997)

97 **Latour-Giraud** Meursault Genevrières 1995 • $NA • (8/31/1997)

97 **Ramonet** Chassagne-Montrachet Les Grandes Ruchottes 1995 • $70 • (8/31/1997)

96 **Antonin Guyon** Corton-Charlemagne 1995 • $105 Ⓐ • (5/31/1997)

96 **Domaine Leflaive** Puligny-Montrachet Clavoillon 1995 • $82 • (8/31/1998)

96 **Étienne Sauzet** Bienvenues-Bâtard-Montrachet 1995 • $185 • (8/31/1997)

96 **François Jobard** Meursault Genevrières 1995 • $76 Ⓐ • (8/31/1998)

96 **Jacques Prieur** Meursault Perrières 1995 • $80 • (8/31/1997)

96 **Jacques Thevenot-Machal** Meursault Charmes 1995 • $30 • (8/31/1997)

96 **Jean-Noël Gagnard** Chassagne-Montrachet Clos de la Maltroye 1995 • $55 • (8/31/1997)

96 **Marius Delarche Père & Fils** Corton-Charlemagne 1995 • $NA • (5/31/1997)

95 **Domaine des Comtes Lafon** Meursault Perrières 1995 • $307 Ⓐ • (5/31/1998)

95 **Étienne Sauzet** Bâtard-Montrachet 1995 • $266 Ⓐ • (8/31/1997)

95 **François Jobard** Meursault Poruzot 1995 • $65 • (8/31/1998)

95 **Guy Roulot** Meursault Les Charmes 1995 • $80 • (8/31/1997)

95 **Guy Roulot** Meursault Perrières 1995 • $62 Ⓐ • (8/31/1997)

95 **Jacques Prieur** Chevalier-Montrachet 1995 • $175 • (8/31/1997)

95 **Jean-Marc Boillot** Puligny-Montrachet Champ-Canet 1995 • $58 • (8/31/1997)

95 **Jean-Marc Boillot** Puligny-Montrachet La Truffière 1995 • $74 • (5/31/1997)

95 **Louis Jadot** Montrachet 1995 • $268 Ⓐ • (8/31/1998)

95 **Louis Latour** Bâtard-Montrachet 1995 • $157 • (8/31/1997)

95 **Marc Morey** Puligny-Montrachet Les Pucelles 1995 • $45 • (5/31/1997)

95 **Maroslavac-Leger** Puligny-Montrachet Les Combettes 1995 • $40 • (8/31/1997)

95 **Michel Bouzereau & Fils** Puligny-Montrachet Les Champs Gains 1995 • $50 • (5/31/1997)

95 **Michel Niellon** Chassagne-Montrachet Les Champgains 1995 • $50 • (8/31/1997)

95 **Michel Niellon** Chevalier-Montrachet 1995 • $130 • (8/31/1997)

95 **Ramonet** Chassagne-Montrachet Les Caillerets 1995 • $45 • (5/31/1997)

95 **Roger Caillot** Bâtard-Montrachet 1995 • $92 • (8/31/1997)

94 **Charles & Rémi Jobard** Meursault Le Porusot-Dessus 1995 • $45 • (5/31/1997)

94 **Domaine de la Bongran** Mâcon-Clessé Quintaine Cuvée Tradition 1995 • $25 • (5/31/1998)

94 **Domaine des Comtes Lafon** Meursault Clos de la Barre 1995 • $77 Ⓐ • (5/31/1998)

94 **Étienne Sauzet** Puligny-Montrachet Les Combettes 1995 • $112 • (8/31/1997)

94 **Étienne Sauzet** Puligny-Montrachet Les Perrières 1995 • $54 Ⓐ • (8/31/1997)

94 **Guffens-Heynen** Pouilly-Fuissé Premier Jus 1995 • $40 • (8/31/1998)

94 **Guy Roulot** Meursault Les Tessons Clos de Mon Plaisir 1995 • $50 • (5/31/1998)

94 **Jean Pillot** Chassagne-Montrachet Les Champs-Gain 1995 • $35 • (5/31/1997)

94 **Jean-Marc Boillot** Puligny-Montrachet Les Combettes 1995 • $75 • (8/31/1997)

94 **Joseph Drouhin** Meursault Perrières 1995 • $60 • (5/31/1997)

94 **Laurent Clerc** Puligny-Montrachet Les Folatières 1995 • $45 • (5/31/1997) • HR

94 **Louis Jadot** Corton-Charlemagne 1995 • $91 Ⓐ • (8/31/1997)

94 **Louis Jadot** Puligny-Montrachet Clos de la Garenne Duc de Magenta 1995 • $91 Ⓐ • (8/31/1997)

94 **Louis Latour** Montrachet 1995 • $213 Ⓐ • (8/31/1998)

94 **Michel Colin-Deléger** Chassagne-Montrachet En Remilly 1995 • $50 • (5/31/1997)

94 **Roger Caillot** Meursault Le Limozin 1995 • $32 • (8/31/1997)

94 **Saumaize-Michelin** St.-Véran Poncetys 1995 • $20 • (5/31/1998)

94 **Tollot-Beaut & Fils** Corton-Charlemagne 1995 • $77 Ⓐ • (8/31/1997)

94 **Valette** Pouilly-Fuissé Le Clos de Monsieur Noly Vieilles Vignes Reserve 1995 • $70 • (5/31/1999)

94 **Verget** Chassagne-Montrachet La Maltroie Cuvée Vieilles Vignes 1995 • $44 • (8/31/1997)

94 **Verget** Puligny-Montrachet Les Enseignères 1995 • $21 Ⓐ • (5/31/1997)

93 **Antonin Rodet** Corton-Charlemagne 1995 • $75 • (5/31/1997)

93 **Blain-Gagnard** Chassagne-Montrachet La Boudriotte 1995 • $45 • (8/31/1997)

93 **Bonneau du Martray** Corton-Charlemagne 1995 • $75 Ⓐ • (8/31/1997)

93 **Charles & Rémi Jobard** Meursault Les Genevrières 1995 • $47 • (5/31/1997)

93 **Domaine de Roally** Mâcon-Viré 1995 • $23 • (5/31/1997)

93 **Domaine des Comtes Lafon** Meursault 1995 • $134 Ⓐ • (5/31/1998)

93 **Domaine des Comtes Lafon** Meursault Désirée 1995 • $NA • (5/31/1998)

93 **Domaine des Comtes Lafon** Puligny-Montrachet Champ-Gain 1995 • $NA • (5/31/1998)

93 **Domaine du Château de Puligny-Montrachet** Meursault Les Perrières 1995 • $36 • (1/31/1998)

93 **Domaine du Château de Puligny-Montrachet** Meursault Les Poruzots 1995 • $42 • (1/31/1998)

93 **Domaine du Château de Puligny-Montrachet** Montrachet 1995 • $NA • (8/31/1998)

93 **Étienne Sauzet** Puligny-Montrachet Champ Canet 1995 • $147 Ⓐ • (8/31/1997)

93 **Étienne Sauzet** Puligny-Montrachet La Garenne 1995 • $87 • (8/31/1997)

93 **Étienne Sauzet** Puligny-Montrachet Les Referts 1995 • $67 Ⓐ • (8/31/1997)

93 **François Jobard** Meursault En la Barre 1995 • $45 • (8/31/1998)

93 **Gérard Chavy** Puligny-Montrachet 1995 • $29 • (5/31/1997) • HR

93 **Gérard Chavy** Puligny-Montrachet Les Clavoillons 1995 • $35 • (5/31/1997)

93 **Gérard Chavy** Puligny-Montrachet Les Perrières 1995 • $35 • (5/31/1997)

93 **Guy Roulot** Meursault Les Luchets 1995 • $45 • (5/31/1997)

93 **Guy Roulot** Meursault Les Tessons Clos de Mon Plaisir 1995 • $50 • (8/31/1997)

93 **Henri Clerc & Fils** Chevalier-Montrachet 1995 • $110 • (5/31/1997)

93 **J.-F. Coche-Dury** Meursault Les Rougeots 1995 • $164 Ⓐ • (5/31/1998)

93 **Jean-Marc Boillot** Bâtard-Montrachet 1995 • $131 • (5/31/1997)

93 **Jean-Noël Gagnard** Chassagne-Montrachet Les Caillerets 1995 • $31 Ⓐ • (8/31/1997)

93 **Jean-Noël Gagnard** Chassagne-Montrachet Les Chenevottes 1995 • $65 • (8/31/1997)

93 **Joseph Drouhin** Montrachet Marquis de Laguiche 1995 • $282 Ⓐ • (8/31/1997)

93 **Joseph Matrot** Meursault-Blagny 1995 • $46 • (8/31/1997)

93 **Latour-Giraud** Meursault Perrières 1995 • $NA • (5/31/1997)

93 **Louis Carillon** Puligny-Montrachet Les Champs Canet 1995 • $57 • (8/31/1997)

93 **Louis Jadot** Criots-Bâtard-Montrachet 1995 • $135 • (8/31/1997)

93 **Louis Latour** Corton-Charlemagne 1995 • $91 Ⓐ • (8/31/1997) • CS

93 **Marc Colin** Chassagne-Montrachet Les Champs-Gains 1995 • $50 • (5/31/1997)

93 **Maroslavac-Leger** Puligny-Montrachet Les Folatières 1995 • $40 • (8/31/1997)

93 **Michel Colin-Deléger** Chassagne-Montrachet Les Chaumées 1995 • $44 Ⓐ • (5/31/1997)

93 **Ramonet** Chassagne-Montrachet 1995 • $40 • (8/31/1997)

93 **Ramonet** Chassagne-Montrachet Boudriotte 1995 • $50 • (8/31/1997)

93 **Roger Caillot** Puligny-Montrachet Les Folatières 1995 • $45 • (8/31/1997)

93 **Roux Père & Fils** Chassagne-Montrachet Les Macherelles 1995 • $35 • (5/31/1997)

93 **Verget** Chassagne-Montrachet Morgeot Cuvée Vieilles Vignes 1995 • $46 • (8/31/1997)

93 **Verget** Meursault Les Poruzots 1995 • $50 • (5/31/1997)

92 **Bernard Moreau** Chassagne-Montrachet Morgeot 1995 • $35 • (5/31/1997)

92 **Bouchard Père & Fils** Beaune White Premier Cru 1995 • $38 • (8/31/1997)

92 **Bouchard Père & Fils** Montrachet 1995 • $320 • (8/31/1997)

92 **Château de Chamirey** Mercurey White 1995 • $18 • (8/31/1997)

92 **Cordier Père & Fils** Pouilly-Fuissé Lot No. 2 1995 • $25 • (5/31/1997)

92 **Domaine Leflaive** Bourgogne White 1995 • $36 • (8/31/1998)

92 **Étienne Sauzet** Chassagne-Montrachet 1995 • $53 • (8/31/1997)

Key: SS—Spectator Selection. CS—Cellar Selection. HR—Highly Recommended. $NA—Price not available. (BT)—Barrel tasting. Ⓐ—Auction Price.
Dates in parentheses represent the issues in which the ratings were published.

92 **Étienne Sauzet** Puligny-Montrachet 1995 • $55 • (8/31/1997)

92 **François Raveneau** Chablis Blanchot 1995 • $80 • (1/01/1999)

92 **François Raveneau** Chablis Butteaux 1995 • $72 Ⓐ • (1/01/1999)

92 **Guy Amiot** Chassagne-Montrachet Clos St.-Jean 1995 • $40 • (8/31/1997)

92 **Guy Bocard** Meursault Charmes 1995 • $NA • (8/31/1997)

92 **Jacques Thevenot-Machal** Puligny-Montrachet Les Folatières 1995 • $30 • (8/31/1997)

92 **Jean Pillot** Chassagne-Montrachet Les Chenevottes 1995 • $33 • (5/31/1997)

92 **Jean-Marc Boillot** Puligny-Montrachet 1995 • $41 • (8/31/1997)

92 **Jean-Marc Boillot** Puligny-Montrachet Les Referts 1995 • $58 • (5/31/1997)

92 **Joseph Matrot** Puligny-Montrachet Les Chalumeaux 1995 • $44 • (5/31/1997)

92 **Louis Carillon** Puligny-Montrachet 1995 • $40 • (5/31/1997)

92 **Louis Carillon** Puligny-Montrachet Les Perrières 1995 • $53 • (8/31/1997)

92 **Louis Jadot** Chevalier-Montrachet Les Demoiselles 1995 • $192 Ⓐ • (8/31/1997)

92 **Louis Jadot** Puligny-Montrachet Les Folatières 1995 • $51 • (8/31/1997)

92 **Louis Latour** Puligny-Montrachet Les Folatières 1995 • $56 • (8/31/1997)

92 **Michel Bouzereau & Fils** Meursault Les Charmes-Dessus 1995 • $50 • (5/31/1997)

92 **Michel Colin-Deléger** Puligny-Montrachet La Truffière 1995 • $58 Ⓐ • (5/31/1997)

92 **Michel Morey-Coffinet** Chassagne-Montrachet La Romanée 1995 • $45 • (8/31/1997)

92 **Olivier Leflaive Frères** Criots-Bâtard-Montrachet 1995 • $125 • (8/31/1997)

92 **Olivier Leflaive Frères** Montrachet 1995 • $270 • (8/31/1997)

92 **Prieur-Brunet** Meursault Chevalières 1995 • $36 • (8/31/1997)

92 **Ramonet** Chassagne-Montrachet Les Vergers 1995 • $50 • (5/31/1997)

92 **Ramonet** Puligny-Montrachet Champ Canet 1995 • $70 • (8/31/1997)

92 **Roger Caillot** Meursault La Barre Dessus Clos Marguerite 1995 • $32 • (8/31/1997)

92 **Valette** Pouilly-Fuissé Clos Reyssié Réserve Particulière 1995 • $40 • (5/31/1997)

92 **Verget** Chablis Montée de Tonnerre 1995 • $29 • (6/15/1997) • HR

91 **Blain-Gagnard** Chassagne-Montrachet Caillerets 1995 • $42 Ⓐ • (5/31/1997)

91 **Bouchard Père & Fils** Meursault Genevrières 1995 • $66 • (5/31/1997)

91 **Bruno Clair** Morey-St.-Denis White En la Rue de Vergy 1995 • $49 • (5/31/1997)

91 **Château Fuissé** Pouilly-Fuissé Vieilles Vignes 1995 • $48 • (5/31/1997)

91 **Domaine d'Auvenay** Auxey-Duresses White 1995 • $56 • (8/31/1997)

91 **Domaine Leflaive** Puligny-Montrachet Les Pucelles 1995 • $67 Ⓐ • (8/31/1998)

91 **Gérard Chavy** Puligny-Montrachet Les Folatières 1995 • $35 • (5/31/1997)

91 **Ghislaine & Jean-Hugues Goisot** Bourgogne Côtes d'Auxerre White Domaine du Corps de Garde 1995 • $15 • (6/15/1997)

91 **Guffens-Heynen** Mâcon-Pierreclos Le Chavigne 1995 • $20 • (5/31/1997)

91 **J.-A. Ferret** Pouilly-Fuissé Les Ménétrières 1995 • $41 • (5/31/1998)

91 **Jacques Prieur** Beaune White Clos de la Féguine 1995 • $45 • (8/31/1997)

91 **Jean-Marc Brocard** Chablis Bougros 1995 • $43 • (6/15/1997)

91 **Louis Michel & Fils** Chablis Grenouilles 1995 • $46 • (6/15/1997)

91 **Marc Colin** Puligny-Montrachet Les Garennes 1995 • $50 • (5/31/1997)

91 **Maroslavac-Leger** Meursault Les Murgers 1995 • $28 • (8/31/1997)

91 **Michel Bouzereau & Fils** Meursault Les Grands Charrons 1995 • $40 • (5/31/1997)

91 **Michel Colin-Deléger** Chassagne-Montrachet Les Chenevottes 1995 • $50 • (5/31/1997)

91 **Michel Colin-Deléger** Chassagne-Montrachet Les Vergers 1995 • $42 Ⓐ • (8/31/1997)

91 **Olivier Leflaive Frères** Meursault Charmes 1995 • $62 • (8/31/1997)

91 **Olivier Leflaive Frères** Puligny-Montrachet Champ Gain 1995 • $52 • (8/31/1997)

91 **Patrick Javillier** Meursault Clos du Cromin Cuvée Spéciale Mise Tardive 1995 • $40 • (8/31/1997)

91 **Paul Garaudet** Monthélie White Les Champs Fulliot 1995 • $23 • (5/31/1997)

91 **R. Ballot-Millot & Fils** Meursault Genevrières 1995 • $50 • (5/31/1997)

91 **Roux Père & Fils** Puligny-Montrachet Les Enseignères 1995 • $38 • (5/31/1997)

91 **Verget** Chablis Valmur 1995 • $168 Ⓐ • (6/15/1997)

91 **Verget** Meursault Les Casse-Têtes 1995 • $35 • (5/31/1997)

91 **Verget** Meursault Les Charmes Cuvée Vieilles Vignes 1995 • $65 • (5/31/1997)

90 **Albert Grivault** Meursault Clos des Perrières 1995 • $62 • (5/31/1997)

90 **Albert Grivault** Meursault Les Perrières 1995 • $46 • (5/31/1997)

90 **Antonin Rodet** Chassagne-Montrachet La Grande Montagne 1995 • $54 • (5/31/1997)

90 **Bernard Moreau** Chassagne-Montrachet Les Chenevottes 1995 • $35 • (5/31/1997)

90 **Billaud-Simon** Chablis Vaudésir 1995 • $36 • (6/15/1997)

90 **Bouchard Père & Fils** Corton-Charlemagne 1995 • $110 • (8/31/1997)

90 **Charles & Rémi Jobard** Meursault Les Chevalières 1995 • $35 • (5/31/1997)

90 **Charles & Rémi Jobard** Meursault Sous la Velle 1995 • $33 • (5/31/1997)

90 **Corinne & Jean-Pierre Grossot** Chablis Vaucoupin 1995 • $24 • (6/15/1997)

90 **Demessey** Chassagne-Montrachet Morgeot 1995 • $39 • (5/31/1997)

90 **Domaine de la Romanée-Conti** Montrachet 1995 • $907 Ⓐ • (8/31/1998)

90 **Domaine du Château de Puligny-Montrachet** Monthélie White 1995 • $20 • (1/31/1998)

90 **Domaine du Château de Puligny-Montrachet** Puligny-Montrachet 1995 • $32 • (8/31/1997)

90 **Domaine du Château de Puligny-Montrachet** Puligny-Montrachet Les Folatières 1995 • $48 • (1/31/1998)

90 **François Raveneau** Chablis Montée de Tonnerre 1995 • $65 • (8/31/1998)

90 **Gagnard-Delagrange** Montrachet 1995 • $NA • (8/31/1998)

90 **Ghislaine & Jean-Hugues Goisot** Sauvignon de St.-Bris Domaine du Corps de Garde 1995 • $14 • (6/15/1997)

90 **Guffens-Heynen** Pouilly-Fuissé 1995 • $34 • (5/31/1998)

90 **Guy Bocard** Meursault Limozin 1995 • $NA • (5/31/1997)

90 **Guy Roulot** Bourgogne White 1995 • $20 • (8/31/1997)

90 **Guy Roulot** Meursault Les Meix Chavaux 1995 • $45 • (5/31/1997)

90 **Guy Roulot** Meursault Les Vireuils 1995 • $45 • (5/31/1997)

90 **Henri Clerc & Fils** Meursault-Blagny Sous le Dos d'Ane 1995 • $50 • (8/31/1997)

90 **Henry Lamy** St.-Aubin En Remilly 1995 • $22 • (5/31/1997)

90 **Jacques Prieur** Corton-Charlemagne 1995 • $90 • (8/31/1997)

90 **Jacques Prieur** Meursault Clos de Mazeray 1995 • $42 • (8/31/1997)

90 **Jacques Thevenot-Machal** Puligny-Montrachet 1995 • $25 • (8/31/1997)

90 **Jean Pillot** Chassagne-Montrachet Morgeot 1995 • $38 • (5/31/1997)

90 **Jean Pillot** Puligny-Montrachet 1995 • $30 • (5/31/1997)

90 **Jean-Pierre Diconne** Meursault Clos des Luchets 1995 • $NA • (5/31/1997)

90 **Joseph Drouhin** Beaune White Clos des Mouches 1995 • $70 • (8/31/1997)

90 **Joseph Drouhin** Chassagne-Montrachet Marquis de Laguiche 1995 • $65 • (8/31/1997)

90 **Joseph Matrot** Meursault Charmes 1995 • $NA • (5/31/1997)

90 **La Chablisienne** Chablis Grenouilles Château Grenouilles 1995 • $NA • (6/15/1997)

90 **La Chablisienne** Chablis Mont de Milieu 1995 • $30 • (6/15/1997)

90 **Louis Jadot** St.-Aubin 1995 • $21 • (8/31/1997)

90 **Louis Latour** Chassagne-Montrachet Morgeot 1995 • $43 • (8/31/1997)

90 **Louis Latour** Meursault 1995 • $30 • (5/31/1997)

90 **Louis Latour** Meursault Les Charmes 1995 • $52 • (8/31/1997)

90 **Louis Latour** Meursault Les Gouttes d'Or 1995 • $49 • (8/31/1997)

90 **Louis Latour** Meursault-Blagny Château de Blagny 1995 • $42 • (5/31/1997)

90 **Louis Latour** Puligny-Montrachet La Garenne 1995 • $49 • (8/31/1997)

90 **Louis Pinson** Chablis Mont de Milieu 1995 • $23 • (6/15/1997)

90 **Marc Morey** Chassagne-Montrachet En Virondot 1995 • $45 • (5/31/1997)

90 **Michel Colin-Deléger** Chassagne-Montrachet Morgeot 1995 • $50 • (8/31/1997)

90 **Michel Morey-Coffinet** Chassagne-Montrachet 1995 • $32 • (8/31/1997)

90 **Michel Niellon** Chassagne-Montrachet Clos de la Maltroie 1995 • $50 • (8/31/1997)

90 **Olivier Leflaive Frères** Chassagne-Montrachet Morgeot 1995 • $52 • (8/31/1997)

90 **Olivier Leflaive Frères** Mercurey White 1995 • $16 • (8/31/1997)

90 **Olivier Leflaive Frères** Meursault 1995 • $41 • (8/31/1997)

90 **Olivier Leflaive Frères** Puligny-Montrachet Les Folatières 1995 • $62 • (8/31/1997)

90 **Patrick Javillier** Meursault Les Charmes 1995 • $50 • (8/31/1997)

90 **Patrick Javillier** Meursault Les Narvaux 1995 • $NA • (5/31/1997)

90 **Patrick Javillier** Puligny-Montrachet Les Levrons 1995 • $45 • (8/31/1998)

90 **Pierre Matrot** Puligny-Montrachet Les Combettes 1995 • $50 • (5/31/1997)

90 **R. Ballot-Millot & Fils** Meursault 1995 • $35 • (5/31/1997)

90 **René & Vincent Dauvissat** Chablis Séchet 1995 • $32 • (6/15/1997)

90 **René Monnier** Meursault Les Chevalières 1995 • $NA • (8/31/1997)

90 **Roger Caillot** Meursault Les Tessons 1995 • $31 • (8/31/1997)

90 **Roger Caillot** Puligny-Montrachet Les Pucelles 1995 • $68 • (8/31/1997)

90 **Roux Père & Fils** Meursault Clos des Porusots 1995 • $32 • (5/31/1997)

90 **Servin** Chablis Montée de Tonnerre 1995 • $17 • (6/15/1997)

90 **Tollot-Beaut & Fils** Bourgogne White 1995 • $20 • (8/31/1997)

90 **Vocoret & Fils** Chablis Blanchot 1995 • $40 • (6/15/1997)

Red Rhône

In this section you will find ratings for the best Rhône wines from five vintages: the last four consecutive years that have been fully released—1994 through 1997—plus the classic 1990 vintage.

The Rhône Valley is long enough—over 125 miles from end to end—that its northern and southern halves possess different geographies and climates, and therefore experience different growing conditions. Sometimes quite different; see for example the 1996 vintage, which *Wine Spectator* rated 91 for the northern Rhône but only 80 for the south. (Hence the prevalence of Hermitage, St.-Joseph and Côte-Rôtie on the 1996 list below, with scarcely a Châteauneuf-du-Pape among them.)

In fact, throughout most of the 1990s, northern Rhône wines held at least a slight edge over their southern counterparts. But that may finally be about to change. Based on preliminary tastings, senior editor Per-Henrik Mansson predicts that 1998 will be an outstanding year for the southern Rhône, making it the best vintage there since 1990.

1997 Red Rhône

Vintage Ratings: North, 86; South, 81

94 **Tardieu-Laurent** Côte-Rôtie 1997 • $70 • (11/30/1999) • HR

93 **Noël Verset** Cornas 1997 • $35 • (1/01/2000)

93 **Tardieu-Laurent** Crozes-Hermitage Vieilles Vignes 1997 • $NA • (12/15/1999)

93 **Tardieu-Laurent** Hermitage 1997 • $72 • (11/30/1999)

92 **A. Clape** Cornas 1997 • $42 • (12/15/1999) • CS

92 **Delas** Hermitage Les Bessards 1997 • $NA • (11/30/1999)

91 **Château La Nerthe** Châteauneuf-du-Pape Cuvée des Cadettes 1997 • $75 • (12/15/1999)

91 **Domaine du Vieux Télégraphe** Châteauneuf-du-Pape Vieux Mas des Papes 1997 • $30 • (8/31/1999) • HR

91 **Michel Ferraton** Hermitage Les Miaux 1997 • $NA • (11/30/1999)

91 **Tardieu-Laurent** St.-Joseph Vieilles Vignes 1997 • $32 • (12/15/1999)

90 **Cave de Tain l'Hermitage** St.-Joseph Les Nobles Rives 1997 • $15 • (11/15/1998)

90 **Château Gigognan** Châteauneuf-du-Pape Clos du Roi 1997 • $27 • (12/15/1999)

Key: SS—Spectator Selection. CS—Cellar Selection. HR—Highly Recommended. $NA—Price not available. (BT)—Barrel tasting. Ⓐ—Auction Price.
Dates in parentheses represent the issues in which the ratings were published.

90 **Château Valcombe** Côtes du Ventoux La Sereine 1997 • $24 • (12/15/1999)

90 **Delas** Côte-Rôtie La Landonne 1997 • $NA • (11/30/1999)

90 **Domaine Brusset** Côtes du Rhône-Villages Cairanne Côteaux des Travers 1997 • $13 • (11/15/1998)

90 **Domaine Courbis** Cornas Les Eygats 1997 • $35 • (12/15/1999)

90 **Domaine de la Janasse** Châteauneuf-du-Pape Chaupin 1997 • $35 • (8/31/1999)

90 **Domaine de la Mordorée** Châteauneuf-du-Pape 1997 • $45 • (8/31/1999)

90 **Gilles Robin** Crozes-Hermitage Cuvée Albéric Bouvet 1997 • $19 • (12/15/1999)

90 **Michel Bernard** Lirac Domaine des Muretins Elevé en Barriques 1997 • $12 • (11/15/1998)

90 **Paul Coulon & Fils** Châteauneuf-du-Pape Boisrenard 1997 • $55 • (8/31/1999)

90 **Pierre Usseglio & Fils** Châteauneuf-du-Pape 1997 • $22 • (12/15/1999)

1996 Red Rhône

Vintage Ratings: North, 91; South, 80

98 **M. Chapoutier** Ermitage L'Ermite 1996 • $190 • (11/15/1998) • HR

96 **A. Clape** Cornas 1996 • $35 • (10/15/1998) • CS

96 **Alain Voge** Cornas Cuvée Vieilles Vignes 1996 • $40 • (10/15/1998)

95 **Domaine Courbis** Cornas La Sabarotte 1996 • $26 • (10/15/1998) • HR

95 **Domaine du Colombier** Hermitage 1996 • $55 • (9/15/1998)
95 **Eric & Joël Durand** Cornas 1996 • $25 • (10/15/1998)
95 **M. Chapoutier** Ermitage Le Méal 1996 • $170 • (11/15/1998)
95 **M. Chapoutier** Hermitage La Sizeranne 1996 • $25 Ⓐ • (11/15/1998)
94 **Bernard Chave** Hermitage 1996 • $39 • (11/15/1998)
94 **Domaine de la Mordorée** Châteauneuf-du-Pape Cuvée de la Reine des Bois 1996 • $50 • (9/30/1998)
94 **François Villard** Côte-Rôtie La Brocarde 1996 • $40 • (11/15/1998)
94 **Jean-Paul & Jean-Luc Jamet** Côte-Rôtie 1996 • $40 • (11/15/1998)
94 **M. Chapoutier** Ermitage Le Pavillon 1996 • $170 • (11/15/1998)
94 **Paul Jaboulet Aîné** Hermitage La Chapelle 1996 • $57 Ⓐ • (12/15/1999)
94 **Tardieu-Laurent** Hermitage 1996 • $66 • (9/15/1999)
94 **Thierry Allemand** Cornas Chaillot 1996 • $30 • (11/15/1998)
93 **Alain Graillot** Crozes-Hermitage 1996 • $17 • (11/15/1998) • SS
93 **André Perret** St.-Joseph Les Grisières 1996 • $24 • (11/15/1998)
93 **Domaine Brusset** Gigondas Les Hauts de Montmirail 1996 • $32 • (10/15/1998) • HR
93 **Domaine Courbis** St.-Joseph Les Royes 1996 • $15 • (11/15/1998)
93 **Domaine du Monteillet** St.-Joseph Cuvée de Papy 1996 • $23 • (11/15/1998)
93 **Jean-Louis Chave** Hermitage 1996 • $57 Ⓐ • (9/15/1999) • CS
93 **Jean-Michel Gérin** Côte-Rôtie Les Grandes Places 1996 • $75 • (9/15/1998)
93 **Yves Cuilleron** St.-Joseph Les Serines 1996 • $35 • (11/15/1998)
92 **Alain Graillot** Hermitage 1996 • $60 • (11/15/1998)
92 **Alain Graillot** St.-Joseph 1996 • $20 • (11/15/1998)
92 **Bernard Burgaud** Côte-Rôtie 1996 • $40 • (9/15/1998)
92 **Domaine Desmeure** Hermitage Domaine de Remizières Cuvée Emilie 1996 • $38 • (11/15/1998)
92 **Eric & Joël Durand** St.-Joseph 1996 • $20 • (11/15/1998)
92 **Michel Bernard** Châteauneuf-du-Pape La Réserve des Pontifes 1996 • $36 • (9/30/1998)
92 **Paul Coulon & Fils** Châteauneuf-du-Pape Boisrenard 1996 • $48 • (9/30/1998)
92 **Thierry Allemand** Cornas Reynard 1996 • $33 • (11/15/1998)
92 **Yves Cuilleron** St.-Joseph L'Amarybelle Cuvée Prestige 1996 • $24 • (11/15/1998)
91 **Alain Graillot** Crozes-Hermitage La Guiraude 1996 • $25 • (10/15/1998)
91 **Delas** Côte-Rôtie Seigneur de Maugiron 1996 • $35 • (9/15/1998)
91 **Delas** Hermitage 1996 • $35 • (9/15/1998)
91 **Domaine Chèze** St.-Joseph Cuvée Ro-Rée 1996 • $15 • (11/15/1998)
91 **Jean-Michel Gérin** Côte-Rôtie Champin Le Seigneur 1996 • $40 • (9/15/1998)

Key: SS—Spectator Selection. CS—Cellar Selection.
HR—Highly Recommended. $NA—Price not available.
(BT)—Barrel tasting. Ⓐ—Auction Price.
Dates in parentheses represent the issues in which the ratings were published.

91 **M. Chapoutier** Côte-Rôtie La Mordorée 1996 • $84 Ⓐ • (11/15/1998)
91 **Pierre Gonon** St.-Joseph 1996 • $23 • (11/15/1998)
91 **R. Rostaing** Côte-Rôtie Côte Blonde 1996 • $45 • (9/15/1999)
91 **Tardieu-Laurent** Cornas Vieilles Vignes 1996 • $56 • (8/31/1999)
90 **A. Clape** Côtes du Rhône Cuvée Spéciale 1996 • $19 • (12/15/1999)
90 **André Perret** St.-Joseph 1996 • $20 • (11/15/1998)
90 **Bosquet des Papes** Châteauneuf-du-Pape 1996 • $25 • (11/15/1998)
90 **Domaine Combier** Crozes-Hermitage Clos des Grives 1996 • $40 • (10/15/1998)
90 **Domaine Courbis** Cornas Champelrose 1996 • $21 • (11/15/1998)
90 **Gérard Charvin** Châteauneuf-du-Pape 1996 • $28 • (11/15/1998)
90 **M. Chapoutier** Crozes-Hermitage Les Meysonniers 1996 • $19 • (10/15/1998)
90 **Mathilde & Yves Gangloff** Côte-Rôtie 1996 • $65 • (12/15/1999)
90 **Mathilde & Yves Gangloff** Côte-Rôtie La Barbarine 1996 • $50 • (12/15/1999)
90 **Michel Ogier** Côte-Rôtie 1996 • $38 • (11/15/1998)
90 **Paul Jaboulet Aîné** Cornas Domaine de St.-Pierre 1996 • $52 • (10/15/1998)
90 **Yves Cuilleron** Côte-Rôtie Coteau de Bassenon 1996 • $35 • (9/15/1998)

1995 Red Rhône

Vintage Ratings: North, 91; South, 88

98 **Jean-Louis Chave** Ermitage Cathelin 1995 • $455 Ⓐ • (9/15/1998)
96 **Domaine de Villeneuve** Châteauneuf-du-Pape Les Vieilles Vignes 1995 • $NA • (9/30/1998)
96 **Thierry Allemand** Cornas Reynard 1995 • $32 • (11/15/1998) • CS
95 **Château de Beaucastel** Châteauneuf-du-Pape Hommage à Jacques Perrin Grande Cuvée 1995 • $237 Ⓐ • (11/15/1998) • HR
95 **E. Guigal** Côte-Rôtie La Mouline 1995 • $216 Ⓐ • (1/01/2000)
95 **Tardieu-Laurent** Cornas Vieilles Vignes 1995 • $53 • (10/15/1997)
95 **Thierry Allemand** Cornas Chaillot 1995 • $29 • (11/15/1998)
94 **Domaine Roger Sabon & Fils** Châteauneuf-du-Pape Cuvée Prestige 1995 • $30 • (1/01/2000)
94 **E. Guigal** Côte-Rôtie La Landonne 1995 • $98 Ⓐ • (11/30/1999) • CS
94 **E. Guigal** Côte-Rôtie La Turque 1995 • $264 Ⓐ • (11/30/1999)
94 **M. Chapoutier** Ermitage Le Pavillon 1995 • $195 Ⓐ • (10/15/1997)
93 **Bernard Faurie** Hermitage Meal 1995 • $60 • (1/01/1998)
93 **Château de la Gardine** Châteauneuf-du-Pape Cuvée des Générations 1995 • $78 • (10/15/1997)
93 **Château La Nerthe** Châteauneuf-du-Pape Cuvée des Cadettes 1995 • $50 • (9/30/1998) • HR
93 **Domaine Courbis** Cornas La Sabarotte 1995 • $29 • (10/15/1997)
93 **Mathilde & Yves Gangloff** Côte-Rôtie La Barbarine 1995 • $50 • (11/30/1999)
93 **Tardieu-Laurent** Châteauneuf-du-Pape 1995 • $40 • (10/15/1997)

92 **Alain Graillot** Crozes-Hermitage 1995 • $15 • (10/15/1997)
92 **Alain Voge** Cornas Cuvée Vieilles Vignes 1995 • $40 • (11/15/1998)
92 **Bernard Burgaud** Côte-Rôtie 1995 • $38 • (10/15/1997)
92 **Cave de Tain l'Hermitage** Cornas Les Nobles Rives 1995 • $15 • (11/15/1998)
92 **Cave de Tain l'Hermitage** Hermitage Les Nobles Rives 1995 • $29 • (11/15/1998)
92 **Château de Beaucastel** Châteauneuf-du-Pape 1995 • $41 Ⓐ • (11/15/1998)
92 **Domaine des Espiers** Gigondas Cuvée Tradition 1995 • $NA • (10/15/1998)
92 **François Villard** Côte-Rôtie La Brocarde 1995 • $35 • (10/15/1997)
92 **Paul Coulon & Fils** Châteauneuf-du-Pape Boisrenard 1995 • $45 • (10/15/1997)
92 **Tardieu-Laurent** Gigondas Vieilles Vignes 1995 • $40 • (10/15/1997)
91 **A. Clape** Cornas 1995 • $36 • (10/15/1997)
91 **Alain Graillot** St.-Joseph 1995 • $19 • (10/15/1997)
91 **Château Rayas** Châteauneuf-du-Pape Réservé 1995 • $NA • (12/15/1999)
91 **Jean-Michel Gérin** Côte-Rôtie Les Grandes Places 1995 • $69 • (10/15/1997)
91 **Les Cailloux** Châteauneuf-du-Pape Cuvée Centenaire 1995 • $80 • (11/15/1998)
91 **R. Rostaing** Côte-Rôtie La Landonne 1995 • $75 • (11/15/1998)
91 **Tardieu-Laurent** Hermitage 1995 • $61 • (10/15/1997)
91 **Tardieu-Laurent** Vacqueyras 1995 • $23 • (10/15/1997)
90 **Domaine du Grand Tinel** Châteauneuf-du-Pape 1995 • $17 • (11/15/1998)
90 **Domaine du Trapadis** Côtes du Rhône-Villages Rasteau Prestige 1995 • $17 • (9/15/1997)
90 **E. Guigal** Côte-Rôtie Brune et Blonde de Guigal 1995 • $35 • (11/30/1999) • SS
90 **Jean-Louis Chave** Hermitage 1995 • $97 Ⓐ • (9/15/1998) • HR
90 **Jean-Luc Colombo** Châteauneuf-du-Pape Les Bartavelles 1995 • $40 • (9/30/1998)
90 **Jean-Michel Gérin** Côte-Rôtie Champin Le Seigneur 1995 • $40 • (10/15/1997)
90 **M. Chapoutier** Côte-Rôtie La Mordorée 1995 • $109 Ⓐ • (10/15/1997)
90 **M. Chapoutier** Gigondas 1995 • $22 • (10/15/1997)
90 **Marie-France Masson** Côtes du Rhône-Villages Rasteau Cuvée Paul Emile 1995 • $14 • (11/15/1998)
90 **Paul Jaboulet Aîné** Crozes-Hermitage Domaine de Thalabert 1995 • $28 Ⓐ • (1/01/1998)
90 **Paul Jaboulet Aîné** Hermitage Le Pied de la Côte 1995 • $33 • (10/15/1997)
90 **Tardieu-Laurent** Côtes du Rhône Cuvée Guy Louis 1995 • $25 • (10/15/1997)
90 **Tardieu-Laurent** Côtes du Rhône Guy Louis 1995 • $25 • (10/15/1997)
90 **Tardieu-Laurent** Crozes-Hermitage Vieilles Vignes 1995 • $23 • (10/15/1997)
90 **Tardieu-Laurent** St.-Joseph Vieilles Vignes 1995 • $45 • (10/15/1997)

1994 Red Rhône

Vintage Ratings: North, 88; South, 86

94 **E. Guigal** Côte-Rôtie La Mouline 1994 • $150 • (9/15/1998) • CS
94 **Jean-Louis Chave** Hermitage 1994 • $60 Ⓐ • (4/30/1997) • CS
93 **Noël & Joël Durand** St.-Joseph Les Côteaux 1994 • $15 • (10/15/1997)
92 **Alain Graillot** Crozes-Hermitage 1994 • $15 • (11/30/1996) • HR
92 **Bernard Faurie** Hermitage 1994 • $40 • (1/01/1998)
92 **Château La Nerthe** Châteauneuf-du-Pape Cuvée des Cadettes 1994 • $50 • (10/15/1997)
92 **Jean-Michel Gérin** Côte-Rôtie Les Grandes Places 1994 • $56 • (11/30/1996)
92 **M. Chapoutier** Crozes-Hermitage Les Varonniers 1994 • $55 • (10/15/1997)
91 **Château de la Gardine** Châteauneuf-du-Pape Cuvée des Générations 1994 • $60 • (10/15/1997)
91 **Delas** Crozes-Hermitage Les Launes 1994 • $13 • (10/15/1997)
91 **Domaine Combier** Crozes-Hermitage Clos des Grives 1994 • $35 • (11/30/1996)
91 **Jean-Paul & Jean-Luc Jamet** Côte-Rôtie 1994 • $36 • (10/15/1997)
91 **Noël & Joël Durand** Cornas 1994 • $20 • (10/15/1997)
91 **Paul Jaboulet Aîné** Crozes-Hermitage Les Jalets 1994 • $14 • (11/30/1996) • HR
91 **Paul Jaboulet Aîné** St.-Joseph Le Grand Pompée 1994 • $21 • (11/30/1996)
90 **Alain Graillot** Crozes-Hermitage La Guiraude 1994 • $20 • (11/30/1996)
90 **Alain Graillot** Hermitage 1994 • $43 • (11/30/1996)
90 **Bernard Burgaud** Côte-Rôtie 1994 • $38 • (10/15/1997)
90 **Bosquet des Papes** Châteauneuf-du-Pape 1994 • $25 • (10/15/1997)
90 **Delas** Hermitage Les Bessards 1994 • $65 • (9/15/1997)
90 **Domaine Brusset** Gigondas Les Hauts de Montmirail 1994 • $24 • (10/15/1997)
90 **E. Guigal** Côte-Rôtie La Landonne 1994 • $145 Ⓐ • (9/15/1998)
90 **E. Guigal** Côte-Rôtie La Turque 1994 • $150 • (9/15/1998)
90 **Jean-Luc Colombo** Cornas Cuvée X 1994 • $NA • (10/15/1997)
90 **Jean-Michel Gérin** Côte-Rôtie Champin-Junior 1994 • $38 • (11/30/1996)
90 **M. Chapoutier** Ermitage Le Pavillon 1994 • $91 Ⓐ • (4/30/1997)
90 **M. Chapoutier** Hermitage La Sizeranne 1994 • $42 • (4/30/1997)
90 **Paul Jaboulet Aîné** Crozes-Hermitage Domaine de Thalabert 1994 • $18 Ⓐ • (12/15/1996)
90 **Yves Cuilleron** Côte-Rôtie Coteau de Bassenon 1994 • $35 • (11/30/1996)

1990 Red Rhône

Vintage Ratings: North, 97; South, 95

98 **E. Guigal** Côte-Rôtie La Mouline 1990 • $306 Ⓐ • (11/15/1995)
97 **E. Guigal** Côte-Rôtie La Landonne 1990 • $295 Ⓐ • (11/15/1995)
97 **Paul Jaboulet Aîné** Hermitage La Chapelle 1990 • $223 Ⓐ • (12/15/1999)
96 **Jean-Louis Chave** Hermitage 1990 • $198 Ⓐ • (5/31/1994) • CS
95 **E. Guigal** Côte-Rôtie La Turque 1990 • $323 Ⓐ • (11/15/1995)
94 **Château de Fonsalette** Côtes du Rhône Réservé 1990 • $NA • (1/01/1999)
94 **Château Rayas** Châteauneuf-du-Pape Réservé 1990 • $525 Ⓐ • (12/15/1999)

94 **E. Guigal** Côte-Rôtie Brune et Blonde La Pommière 1990 • $NA • (11/15/1995)

93 **Belle Père & Fils** Hermitage 1990 • $46 • (4/15/1993)

93 **E. Guigal** Hermitage 1990 • $99 Ⓐ • (5/31/1994) • CS

93 **Les Cailloux** Châteauneuf-du-Pape Cuvée Centenaire 1990 • $45 • (4/15/1993)

92 **Château de Beaucastel** Châteauneuf-du-Pape 1990 • $87 Ⓐ • (3/15/1993) • HR

92 **Domaine Combier** Crozes-Hermitage Clos des Grives 1990 • $20 • (4/15/1993)

92 **J. Vidal-Fleury** Côte-Rôtie Côte Blonde La Chatillonne 1990 • $42 • (5/31/1994)

92 **Jean-Paul & Jean-Luc Jamet** Côte-Rôtie 1990 • $39 • (5/31/1994)

91 **Bernard Burgaud** Côte-Rôtie 1990 • $37 • (4/15/1993)

91 **Château Mont-Redon** Châteauneuf-du-Pape 1990 • $23 • (9/30/1993)

91 **Clusel Roch** Côte-Rôtie Les Grandes Places 1990 • $50 • (5/31/1994)

91 **Delas** Hermitage Cuvée Marquise de la Tourette 1990 • $30 • (11/30/1996)

91 **Domaine de la Vieille Julienne** Châteauneuf-du-Pape 1990 • $17 • (4/15/1993)

91 **Lyliane Saugère** Hermitage La Côte des Seigneurs 1990 • $26 • (4/15/1994) • HR

91 **M. Chapoutier** Côte-Rôtie La Mordorée 1990 • $169 Ⓐ • (5/31/1994)

91 **M. Chapoutier** Hermitage Monier de la Sizeranne 1990 • $58 Ⓐ • (8/31/1992)

90 **Alain Graillot** Hermitage 1990 • $45 • (5/31/1994)

90 **Belle Père & Fils** Crozes-Hermitage 1990 • $20 • (2/28/1993) • HR

90 **E. Guigal** Côte-Rôtie Brune et Blonde 1990 • $40 Ⓐ • (11/15/1995)

90 **M. Chapoutier** Châteauneuf-du-Pape La Bernardine 1990 • $40 Ⓐ • (8/31/1992) • SS

90 **M. Chapoutier** Côte-Rôtie Brune et Blonde 1990 • $35 • (11/15/1992)

90 **Paul Coulon & Fils** Châteauneuf-du-Pape Domaine de Beaurenard 1990 • $19 • (11/15/1992) • HR

90 **Paul Jaboulet Aîné** Vacqueyras 1990 • $14 • (9/30/1995)

Piedmont Red

Red wines from the Piedmont area of Italy have just enjoyed three excellent years in a row. Both the 1996 and 1997 vintages are rated outstanding to classic, with many rich, ripe, intensely flavored wines to offer. (*Wine Spectator's* tastings for these vintages had not quite been completed at press time, which is why the overall vintage ratings are still given as a range of scores. So many wines scoring 90 or above had already been tasted, however, that we decided to list them here.)

The preceding vintage, 1995, was somewhat more uneven, but still produced dozens of very fine Barolos and Barbarescos. And for a featured earlier vintage, we chose the classic 1990, which not only received a spectacular 97 rating but is so long-aging that our recommendation is still to hold onto rather than drink these wines.

For ratings from years omitted from this section, see the main listings.

1997 Piedmont Red
Vintage Rating: 91-95*

94 **Luciano Sandrone** Barbera d'Alba 1997 • $23 • (9/15/1999)

93 **Albino Rocca** Barbera d'Alba Gepin 1997 • $23 • (9/15/1999)

93 **Roberto Ferraris** Barbera d'Asti Nobbio 1997 • $16 • (11/15/1999)

92 **Cordero di Montezemolo** Barbera d'Alba Monfalletto 1997 • $16 • (10/31/1998)

92 **Crissante Alessandria** Rugé 1997 • $32 • (11/15/1999)

92 **Giacomo Ascheri** Barbera d'Alba Vigna Fontanelle 1997 • $12 • (10/31/1998)

91 **Elvio Cogno** Barbera d'Alba Bricco del Merlo 1997 • $32 • (9/15/1999)

91 **Giuseppe Cortese** Dolcetto d'Alba Trifolera 1997 • $13 • (10/31/1998)

90 **Agostino Pavia & Figli** Barbera d'Asti La Marescialla 1997 • $18 • (11/15/1999)

90 **Andrea Oberto** Barbera d'Alba Vigneto Boiolo 1997 • $18 • (9/15/1999)

90 **Armando Parusso** Barbera d'Alba Ornati 1997 • $22 • (10/31/1998)

Key: SS—Spectator Selection. CS—Cellar Selection. HR—Highly Recommended. $NA—Price not available. (BT)—Barrel tasting. Ⓐ—Auction Price.
Dates in parentheses represent the issues in which the ratings were published.

90 **Carlo Giacosa** Barbera d'Alba Lina 1997 • $28 • (9/15/1999)

90 **Ca'Viola** Dolcetto d'Alba Barturot 1997 • $18 • (11/15/1999)

90 **Il Vino dei Padri** Barbera d'Asti 1997 • $13 • (10/31/1998)

90 **Vietti** Barbera d'Asti Tre Vigne 1997 • $18 • (11/15/1999)

1996 Piedmont Red
Vintage Rating: 93-97*

97 **Gaja** Barbaresco Costa Russi 1996 • $180 • (10/31/1999)

97 **Gaja** Barbaresco Sorì San Lorenzo 1996 • $200 • (10/31/1999) • CS

95 **Bruno Giacosa** Barbaresco Santo Stefano di Neive 1996 • $100 • (8/31/1999) • CS

95 **Fiorenzo Nada** Langhe Seifile 1996 • $60 • (11/15/1999)

95 **Fontanabianca** Barbaresco Sorì Burdin 1996 • $45 • (8/31/1999)

95 **Gaja** Barbaresco Sorì Tildìn 1996 • $200 • (10/31/1999) • CS

95 **Moccagatta** Barbaresco Basarin 1996 • $42 • (8/31/1999)

95 **Moccagatta** Barbaresco Vigna Cole 1996 • $48 • (8/31/1999)

94 **Ceretto** La Bernardina Monsordo Red 1996 • $50 • (11/15/1999)

94 **Fiorenzo Nada** Barbaresco 1996 • $53 • (10/31/1999)

94 **Michele Chiarlo** Barbaresco Rabajà 1996 • $79 • (8/31/1999)

Mick Rock

94 **Rocche dei Manzoni** Langhe Quatr Nas 1996 • $NA • (11/15/1999)
93 **Bruno Giacosa** Barbaresco 1996 • $65 • (8/31/1999)
93 **Carlo Giacosa** Barbaresco Narin 1996 • $35 • (8/31/1999)
93 **Ca'Viola** Langhe Bric du Luv 1996 • $35 • (11/15/1999)
93 **Ceretto** Barbaresco Fasêt 1996 • $70 • (8/31/1999)
93 **Ceretto** Cabernet Sauvignon Langhe La Bernardina Da Uve 1996 • $60 • (11/15/1999)
93 **Fratelli Brovia** Dolcetto d'Alba Solatio Brovia 1996 • $26 • (10/31/1998)
93 **Giacomo Bologna** Barbera d'Asti Ai Suma 1996 • $40 Ⓐ • (10/31/1998)
93 **Moccagatta** Barbaresco Bric Balin 1996 • $45 • (8/31/1999)
92 **Albino Rocca** Barbaresco Vigneto Brich Ronchi 1996 • $53 • (10/31/1999)
92 **Albino Rocca** Dolcetto d'Alba Vignalunga 1996 • $15 • (10/31/1997)
92 **Armando Parusso** Langhe Red Bricco Rovella 1996 • $32 • (10/31/1998)
92 **Bertelli** Barbera d'Asti Montetusa 1996 • $NA • (10/31/1998)
92 **Bertelli** Barbera d'Asti San Antonio Vieilles Vignes 1996 • $45 • (10/31/1998)
92 **Cascina Bongiovanni** Langhe Falletto 1996 • $40 • (11/15/1999)
92 **Coppo** Barbera d'Asti Pomorosso 1996 • $48 • (11/15/1999)
92 **Giovanni Viberti** Barbera d'Alba Bricco Airoli 1996 • $25 • (10/31/1998)
92 **Marchesi di Gresy** Barbaresco Gaiun Martinenga 1996 • $75 • (10/31/1999)
92 **Rocche dei Manzoni** Bricco Manzoni 1996 • $NA • (11/15/1999)
92 **Sant'Agata** Barbera d'Asti Superiore Cavalé 1996 • $23 • (11/15/1999)
92 **Varaldo** Barbaresco Bricco Libero 1996 • $60 • (10/31/1999)
91 **Albino Rocca** Barbera d'Alba Gepin 1996 • $21 • (10/31/1998)
91 **Aldo & Riccardo Seghesio** Barbera d'Alba Vigneto della Chiesa 1996 • $15 • (10/31/1998)
91 **Aldo Conterno** Barbera d'Alba 1996 • $27 • (10/31/1998)
91 **Aldo Conterno** Nebbiolo delle Langhe Il Favot 1996 • $45 • (10/31/1998)
91 **Ceretto** Barbaresco Asij 1996 • $42 • (8/31/1999)
91 **G.D. Vajra** Dolcetto d'Alba Coste & Fossati 1996 • $20 • (10/31/1997)
91 **Giuseppe Rivetti & Figli** Barbaresco Vigneto Gallina Vürsù 1996 • $60 • (10/31/1999)
91 **Marco & Vittorio Adriano** Barbaresco 1996 • $30 • (10/31/1999)
91 **Paitin** Dolcetto d'Alba Sorì Paitin 1996 • $14 • (10/31/1997)
91 **Prunotto** Barbera d'Asti Costamiòle 1996 • $56 • (11/15/1999)
91 **Vietti** Barbaresco Masseria 1996 • $45 • (10/31/1999)
91 **Vietti** Barbera d'Asti La Crena 1996 • $25 • (11/15/1999)
90 **Ca' del Re** Barbera d'Alba 1996 • $10 • (10/31/1997)

Key: SS—Spectator Selection. CS—Cellar Selection. HR—Highly Recommended. $NA—Price not available. (BT)—Barrel tasting. Ⓐ—Auction Price.
Dates in parentheses represent the issues in which the ratings were published.

90 **Ca' Romé di Romano Marengo** Barbaresco 1996 • $55 • (10/31/1999)
90 **Cappellano** Langhe Augusto 1996 • $NA • (10/31/1998)
90 **Ceretto** Barbaresco Asili 1996 • $105 • (8/31/1999)
90 **Cordero di Montezemolo** Barbera d'Alba Monfalletto 1996 • $18 • (10/31/1998)
90 **Gaja** Barbaresco 1996 • $120 • (10/31/1999)
90 **Luigi Einaudi** Dolcetto di Dogliani Vigna Tecc 1996 • $16 • (10/31/1998)
90 **Paolo Scavino** Dolcetto d'Alba Vigneto dël Fiasc 1996 • $17 • (10/31/1997)
90 **Sottimano** Barbaresco Fausoni Vigna del Salto 1996 • $40 • (8/31/1999)

1995 Piedmont Red
Vintage Rating: 89

96 **Gaja** Barbaresco Costa Russi 1995 • $190 • (10/31/1998)
96 **Gaja** Barbaresco Sorì San Lorenzo 1995 • $190 • (10/31/1998)
95 **Ceretto** Cabernet Sauvignon Langhe La Bernardina Da Uve 1995 • $50 • (10/31/1998)
95 **Gaja** Cabernet Sauvignon Darmagi 1995 • $NA • (10/31/1998)
94 **Aldo & Riccardo Seghesio** Barolo Vigneto La Villa 1995 • $48 • (11/15/1999)
94 **Armando Parusso** Barolo Bussia Vigna Munie 1995 • $53 • (11/15/1999)
94 **Azelia** Barolo Bricco Fiasco 1995 • $58 • (11/15/1999)
94 **Ceretto** Barolo Brunate 1995 • $70 • (11/15/1999)
94 **Gaja** Barbaresco 1995 • $115 Ⓐ • (10/31/1998)
94 **Gaja** Barolo Sperss 1995 • $135 • (11/15/1999)
94 **Luigi Einaudi** Barolo Costa Grimaldi 1995 • $52 • (11/15/1999)
94 **Paolo Conterno** Barolo Ginestra 1995 • $75 • (11/15/1999)
94 **Paolo Scavino** Barolo Rocche dell'Annunziata 1995 • $80 • (11/15/1999)
93 **Andrea Oberto** Barolo Vigneto Rocche 1995 • $42 • (11/15/1999)
93 **Beni di Batasiolo** Barbaresco 1995 • $19 • (10/31/1998)
93 **Ceretto** Barolo Bricco Rocche 1995 • $140 • (11/15/1999)
93 **Ceretto** La Bernardina Monsordo Red 1995 • $50 • (10/31/1998)
93 **Moccagatta** Barbaresco Bric Balin 1995 • $35 • (10/31/1998)
93 **Paolo Scavino** Barolo Bric dël Fiasc 1995 • $68 • (11/15/1999)
93 **Pio Cesare** Barbaresco Il Bricco 1995 • $NA • (11/15/1999)
93 **Punset** Barbaresco 1995 • $35 • (10/31/1998)
93 **Rocche dei Manzoni** Barolo Vigna Big 1995 • $75 • (11/15/1999)
93 **Rocche dei Manzoni** Barolo Vigna Cappella di S. Stefano 1995 • $85 • (11/15/1999)
93 **Scrimaglio** Barbaresco Bricco Loreto 1995 • $32 • (8/31/1999) • HR
93 **Vietti** Barolo Brunate 1995 • $60 • (11/15/1999)
92 **Ceretto** Barolo Prapò 1995 • $70 • (11/15/1999)
92 **Domenico Clerico** Barolo Pajana 1995 • $60 • (11/15/1999)
92 **Giovanni Sordo** Barolo 1995 • $30 • (11/15/1999)
92 **Paitin** Barbaresco Sorì Paitin 1995 • $37 • (10/31/1998)
92 **Paolo Scavino** Barolo Cannubi 1995 • $68 • (11/15/1999)

92 **Pira** Barolo Cannubi 1995 • $70 • (11/15/1999)
92 **Vietti** Barolo Rocche 1995 • $65 • (11/15/1999)
91 **Alfredo & Giovanni Roagna** Barbaresco 1995 • $44 • (10/31/1998)
91 **Armando Parusso** Barolo Bussia Vigna Rocche 1995 • $60 • (11/15/1999)
91 **Armando Parusso** Langhe Red Bricco Rovella 1995 • $30 • (10/31/1998)
91 **Conterno-Fantino** Barolo Sorì Ginestra 1995 • $61 • (11/15/1999)
91 **Manora** Barbera del Monferrato Collezione 1995 • $12 • (10/31/1998)
91 **Paolo Scavino** Barbera d'Alba Affinato in Carati 1995 • $35 • (10/31/1998)
91 **Pelissero** Barbaresco Vanotu 1995 • $48 • (9/15/1998)
91 **Stefano Farina** Barbaresco 1995 • $24 • (9/15/1998)
91 **Vietti** Barbaresco Masseria 1995 • $55 • (9/15/1998)
90 **Aldo Conterno** Barolo Vigna Cicala 1995 • $105 • (11/15/1999)
90 **Attilio Ghisolfi** Barolo Bricco Visette 1995 • $38 • (11/15/1999)
90 **Bertelli** St. Marsan 1995 • $45 • (10/31/1997)
90 **Bruno Giacosa** Barbaresco Santo Stefano di Neive 1995 • $115 • (9/15/1998)
90 **Bruno Rocca** Barbaresco Coparossa 1995 • $40 • (9/15/1998)
90 **Bruno Rocca** Barbaresco Rabajà 1995 • $44 • (9/15/1998)
90 **Cascina Bongiovanni** Dolcetto d'Alba 1995 • $18 • (10/31/1997)
90 **Ciabot Berton** Barolo Roggeri 1995 • $46 • (11/15/1999)
90 **Fontanabianca** Barbaresco Sorì Burdin 1995 • $34 • (9/15/1998)
90 **Marchesi di Gresy** Langhe Virtus 1995 • $27 • (10/31/1998)
90 **Michele Chiarlo** Barbaresco Rabajà 1995 • $65 • (9/15/1998)
90 **Pietro Barbero** Barbera d'Asti La Vignassa 1995 • $35 • (10/31/1998)
90 **Pio Cesare** Barolo Ornato 1995 • $NA • (11/15/1999)
90 **Vietti** Barolo Lazzarito 1995 • $60 • (11/15/1999)

1990 Piedmont Red
Vintage Rating: 97

100 **Gaja** Barbaresco Sorì Tildìn 1990 • $295 Ⓐ • (10/31/1993)
98 **Gaja** Barbaresco Costa Russi 1990 • $225 Ⓐ • (10/31/1993)
98 **Luciano Sandrone** Barolo Le Vigne 1990 • $NA • (10/31/1994)
96 **Conterno-Fantino** Barolo Sorì Ginestra 1990 • $40 • (10/31/1994)
96 **Gaja** Barbaresco Sorì San Lorenzo 1990 • $380 Ⓐ • (10/31/1993)
96 **Luciano Sandrone** Barolo Cannubi Boschis 1990 • $274 Ⓐ • (10/31/1994)
95 **Pio Cesare** Barolo Ornato 1990 • $41 • (10/31/1994)
94 **Beni di Batasiolo** Barolo La Corda della Briccolina 1990 • $40 • (10/31/1994)
94 **Gaja** Barbaresco 1990 • $165 Ⓐ • (10/31/1993)
93 **Conterno-Fantino** Barolo Vigna del Gris 1990 • $36 • (10/31/1994)
93 **Elio Altare** Barolo Vigneto Arborina 1990 • $115 Ⓐ • (10/31/1994)
93 **Gancia** Barolo Cannubi Ca' dei Gancia 1990 • $65 • (10/31/1994)
93 **Michele Chiarlo** Barolo Cerequio 1990 • $56 • (10/31/1994)
93 **Moccagatta** Barbaresco Bric Balin 1990 • $31 • (10/31/1993)
93 **Paolo Scavino** Barolo Bric dël Fiasc 1990 • $86 Ⓐ • (10/31/1994)
93 **Paolo Scavino** Barolo Cannubi 1990 • $115 Ⓐ • (10/31/1994)
92 **Aldo Conterno** Barolo Vigna Colonello 1990 • $120 Ⓐ • (10/31/1994)
92 **Bruno Giacosa** Barbaresco Asili 1990 • $NA • (10/31/1994)
92 **Corino** Barbera d'Alba Vigna Pozzo 1990 • $30 • (11/15/1993)
92 **Gigi Rosso** Barolo Arione Sôrì dell'Ulivo 1990 • $NA • (10/31/1996)
92 **Michele Chiarlo** Barolo Brunate 1990 • $47 • (10/31/1994)
91 **Aldo Conterno** Barbera d'Alba Conca Tre Pile 1990 • $22 • (4/30/1993)
91 **Armando Parusso** Barbera d'Alba Bricco di Pugnana 1990 • $20 • (10/15/1993)
91 **Cordero di Montezemolo** Barolo Enrico VI 1990 • $40 • (10/31/1994)
91 **Corino** Barolo Vigneto Rocche 1990 • $45 • (10/31/1994)
91 **Gianni Gagliardo** Barolo Preve 1990 • $35 • (10/31/1995)
91 **Marcarini** Barolo Brunate 1990 • $26 • (10/31/1994)
91 **Michele Chiarlo** Barbera d'Asti 1990 • $9 • (10/15/1993)
91 **Renato Ratti** Barolo Marcenasco 1990 • $36 • (10/31/1994)
90 **Aldo Conterno** Barolo Granbussia 1990 • $120 • (10/31/1995)
90 **Armando Parusso** Barolo 1990 • $27 • (10/31/1994)
90 **Coppo** Barbera d'Asti Pomorosso 1990 • $33 • (10/31/1994)
90 **Corino** Barolo Vigna Giachini 1990 • $81 Ⓐ • (10/31/1994)
90 **Domenico Clerico** Barolo Briccoto Bussia 1990 • $40 • (10/31/1994)
90 **Domenico Clerico** Barolo Pajana 1990 • $115 Ⓐ • (10/31/1994)
90 **Giovanni Manzone** Barbera d'Alba Gramolere 1990 • $19 • (11/15/1993)
90 **Giuseppe Cappellano** Barolo Gabutti 1990 • $42 • (10/31/1995)
90 **Marchesi di Gresy** Barbaresco Camp Gros Martinenga 1990 • $60 • (10/31/1993)
90 **Michele Chiarlo** Barbaresco Rabajà 1990 • $48 • (10/31/1994)
90 **Michele Chiarlo** Barolo Vigna Rionda di Serralunga 1990 • $47 • (10/31/1994)
90 **Moccagatta** Barbaresco Basarin 1990 • $26 • (10/31/1993)
90 **Paolo Scavino** Barolo Rocche dell'Annunziata Riserva 1990 • $65 • (10/31/1995)
90 **Rocche Costamagna** Barolo Vigna San Francesco 1990 • $NA • (10/31/1994)
90 **Rocche dei Manzoni** Barolo Vigna d'La Roul Riserva 1990 • $NA • (10/31/1995)

Chianti Classico's Castello di Brolio.

Tuscan Red

The highest-scoring Tuscan wines (primarily super Tuscans and Chiantis) from the three most recently released vintages—1995, 1996 and 1997—are found in this section, together with a look back at the classic 1990s.

The next great Tuscan vintage was a long time in coming. The vintages of the early- to mid-1990s ranged in quality from the decidedly average 1992 (77 points out of 100) to the very good 1995 and 1996. Then the 1997 vintage burst upon the scene like a thunderclap. *Wine Spectator's* expert on Tuscan wines, James Suckling, gives it a rating of 99—the region's vintage of the century. The bad news about the 1997s: many of the wines cost about twice as much as their 1990 counterparts did on release.

For ratings of wines from vintages not covered here, see the main listings.

1997 Tuscan Red | Vintage Rating: 99

97 **Argiano** Toscana Solengo 1997 • $115 Ⓐ • (11/30/1999) • HR

97 **Castello dei Rampolla** Toscana Vigna d'Alceo 1997 • $85 • (11/30/1999)

97 **Tua Rita** Toscana Redigaffi 1997 • $100 • (11/30/1999)

96 **Antinori** Bolgheri Guado al Tasso Tenuta Belvedere 1997 • $52 • (6/15/2000)

96 **Fattoria di Manzano** Syrah Toscana Podere il Bosco 1997 • $63 • (11/30/1999)

96 **Isole e Olena** Toscana Cepparello 1997 • $38 • (11/30/1999)

96 **Marchesi de' Frescobaldi** Merlot Toscana Castelgiocondo Lamaione 1997 • $NA • (11/30/1999)

95 **Antinori** Toscana Tignanello 1997 • $51 • (6/15/2000) • CS

95 **Dievole** Toscana Duemila Dievole 1997 • $175 • (11/30/1999)

95 **Fattoria Le Pupille** Toscana Saffredi 1997 • $80 • (11/30/1999) • HR

95 **Villa Cafaggio** Toscana Cortaccio 1997 • $50 • (6/15/2000)

95 **Villa Cafaggio** Toscana San Martino 1997 • $50 • (6/15/2000) • CS

Key: SS—Spectator Selection. CS—Cellar Selection. HR—Highly Recommended. $NA—Price not available. (BT)—Barrel tasting. Ⓐ—Auction Price.
Dates in parentheses represent the issues in which the ratings were published.

94 **Fattoria Petrolo** Toscana Galatrona 1997 • $50 • (11/30/1999)

94 **Fattoria Petrolo** Toscana Torrione 1997 • $42 • (11/30/1999)

93 **Castello di Lilliano** Colli della Toscana Centrale Anagallis 1997 • $34 • (11/30/1999)

93 **Fattoria Montellori** Toscana Salamartano 1997 • $43 • (11/30/1999)

93 **Riecine** Toscana La Gioia 1997 • $53 • (11/30/1999)

93 **Tenuta di Trinoro** Toscana 1997 • $130 • (11/30/1999)

92 **Antico Podere Gagliole** Toscana 1997 • $60 • (11/30/1999)

92 **Castello di Verrazzano** Toscana Sassello 1997 • $50 • (11/30/1999)

92 **Eredi Fuligni** Toscana Rosso San Jacopo 1997 • $35 • (11/30/1999)

92 **Fattoria Le Pupille** Morellino di Scansano Poggio Valente 1997 • $38 • (11/30/1999)

92 **Fattoria Poggiopiano** Toscana Rosso di Sera 1997 • $44 • (11/30/1999)

92 **Fontodi** Chianti Classico 1997 • $23 • (11/30/1999) • SS

92 **La Massa** Chianti Classico Giorgio Primo 1997 • $49 • (11/30/1999)

92 **Podere Poggio Scalette** Alta Valle della Greve Il Carbonaione 1997 • $60 • (11/30/1999)

92 **San Fabiano Calcinaia** Toscana Cerviolo Red 1997 • $36 • (11/30/1999)

92 **Tenuta Valdipiatta** Toscana Trincerone 1997 • $33 • (11/30/1999)

James Suckling

91 **Capezzana** Carmignano Conte Contini Bonacossi 1997 • $22 • (11/30/1999)

91 **Capezzana** Toscana Ghiaie della Furba 1997 • $50 • (11/30/1999)

91 **Castello di Ama** Chianti Classico 1997 • $35 • (11/30/1999)

91 **Cecchi** Toscana Spargolo 1997 • $38 • (11/30/1999)

91 **Fattoria di Felsina** Chianti Classico Berardenga 1997 • $22 • (11/30/1999) • SS

91 **Fattoria Le Pupille** Morellino di Scansano Riserva 1997 • $19 • (5/31/2000) • HR

91 **La Rampa di Fugnano** Colli della Toscana Centrale Gisele 1997 • $45 • (11/30/1999)

91 **Le Corti** Chianti Classico Don Tommaso 1997 • $35 • (11/30/1999)

91 **Marchesi de' Frescobaldi** Chianti Rufina Montesodi 1997 • $50 • (11/30/1999)

91 **Michele Satta** Toscana Vigna al Cavaliere 1997 • $45 • (11/30/1999)

91 **Podere Salicutti** Rosso di Montalcino 1997 • $26 • (9/15/1999)

91 **Poggerino** Toscana Primamateria 1997 • $120 • (11/30/1999)

91 **Tenuta di Valgiano** Toscana Scasso dei Cesari 1997 • $28 • (11/30/1999)

90 **Agricola Querciabella** Chianti Classico 1997 • $20 • (11/30/1999) • SS

90 **Casaloste** Chianti Classico 1997 • $25 • (11/30/1999)

90 **Cecchi** Toscana La Gavina 1997 • $NA • (11/30/1999)

90 **Collelungo** Chianti Classico Roveto 1997 • $45 • (11/30/1999)

90 **Conti Costanti** Rosso di Montalcino Calbello 1997 • $30 • (9/15/1999)

90 **Erik Banti** Toscana Annoprimo 1997 • $25 • (11/30/1999)

90 **Fattoria del Cerro** Merlot Toscana Poggio Golo 1997 • $NA • (1/01/2000)

90 **Fattoria di Petroio** Chianti Classico 1997 • $10 • (11/30/1999)

90 **Fattoria La Ripa** Colli della Toscana Centrale Santa Brigida 1997 • $21 • (11/30/1999)

90 **Guicciardini Strozzi** Toscana Selvascura 1997 • $40 • (11/30/1999)

90 **Guicciardini Strozzi** Toscana Sòdole 1997 • $70 • (11/30/1999)

90 **Marchesi Pancrazi** Pinot Nero Toscana Villa di Bagnolo 1997 • $39 • (11/30/1999)

90 **Renzo Masi** Toscana Erta e China 1997 • $9 • (11/30/1999)

90 **Riecine** Chianti Classico 1997 • $23 • (11/30/1999)

90 **Siro Pacenti** Rosso di Montalcino 1997 • $25 • (9/15/1999)

90 **Tenuta di Ghizzano** Toscana Veneroso 1997 • $28 • (11/30/1999)

90 **Tua Rita** Toscana Giusto di Notri 1997 • $75 • (11/30/1999)

90 **Villa La Selva** Colli della Toscana Centrale Felciaia 1997 • $24 • (5/31/2000) • HR

Key: SS—Spectator Selection. CS—Cellar Selection. HR—Highly Recommended. $NA—Price not available. (BT)—Barrel tasting. Ⓐ—Auction Price.

Dates in parentheses represent the issues in which the ratings were published.

1996 Tuscan Red
Vintage Rating: 87

95 **Argiano** Toscana Solengo 1996 • $115 Ⓐ • (12/15/1998) • CS

95 **Castello dei Rampolla** Toscana Vigna d'Alceo 1996 • $NA • (12/15/1998)

95 **Tenuta dell'Ornellaia** Toscana Masseto 1996 • $201 • (11/30/1999)

94 **Antinori** Bolgheri Superiore Guado al Tasso Tenuta Belvedere 1996 • $52 • (11/30/1999) • HR

94 **Tenuta dell'Ornellaia** Bolgheri Ornellaia 1996 • $74 • (11/30/1999)

93 **Tua Rita** Toscana Redigaffi 1996 • $70 • (12/15/1998)

92 **Castello di Ama** Toscana Vigna l'Apparita 1996 • $146 • (11/30/1999)

91 **Castello dei Rampolla** Toscana Sammarco 1996 • $65 • (11/30/1999)

91 **Fattoria Petrolo** Toscana Torrione 1996 • $40 • (11/30/1999)

91 **Grattamacco** Bolgheri Superiore 1996 • $45 • (11/30/1999)

91 **Gualdo del Re** Toscana Federico Primo 1996 • $30 • (11/30/1999)

91 **Isole e Olena** Cabernet Sauvignon Toscana Collezione de Marchi 1996 • $40 • (11/30/1999)

91 **Podere Poggio Scalette** Toscana Il Carbonaione 1996 • $55 • (12/15/1998)

91 **Poliziano** Vino Nobile di Montepulciano Vigna Asinone 1996 • $NA • (11/30/1999)

91 **Tenuta del Terriccio** Toscana Lupicaia 1996 • $85 • (12/15/1998)

91 **Tenuta San Guido** Bolgheri-Sassicaia Sassicaia 1996 • $110 • (11/30/1999)

91 **Tua Rita** Toscana Giusto di Notri 1996 • $50 • (12/15/1998)

90 **Antico Podere Gagliole** Colli della Toscana Centrale 1996 • $42 • (12/15/1998)

90 **Antinori** Toscana Solaia 1996 • $90 • (11/30/1999) • CS

90 **Avignonesi** Toscana Grifi 1996 • $45 • (11/30/1999)

90 **Avignonesi** Toscana Toro Desiderio 1996 • $63 • (11/30/1999)

90 **Brolio** Toscana Casalferro 1996 • $37 • (11/30/1999)

90 **Capezzana** Carmignano Conte Contini Bonacossi 1996 • $NA • (12/15/1998)

90 **Castello Banfi** Cabernet Sauvignon Sant'Antimo 1996 • $33 • (11/30/1999)

90 **Castello della Paneretta** Toscana 1596-1996 1996 • $36 • (5/31/2000)

90 **Castello della Paneretta** Toscana Terrine 1996 • $26 • (5/31/2000)

90 **Fattoria Montellori** Toscana Salamartano 1996 • $44 • (11/30/1999)

90 **Fattoria Poggiopiano** Toscana Rosso di Sera 1996 • $22 • (12/15/1998)

90 **Fontodi** Colli della Toscana Centrale Flaccianello 1996 • $50 • (11/30/1999)

90 **Gualdo del Re** Val di Cornia Suvereto Riserva 1996 • $28 • (11/30/1999)

90 **Isole e Olena** Toscana Cepparello 1996 • $45 • (12/15/1998)

90 **La Lastra** Toscana Rovaio 1996 • $30 • (11/30/1999)

90 **Le Macchiole** Bolgheri Scrio 1996 • $75 • (11/30/1999)

90 **Marchesi de' Frescobaldi** Cabernet Sauvignon Toscana Mormoreto 1996 • $47 • (11/30/1999)

90 **Marchesi de' Frescobaldi** Chianti Rufina Montesodi 1996 • $47 • (12/15/1998)

90 **Marchesi de' Frescobaldi** Merlot Toscana Castelgiocondo Lamaione 1996 • $45 • (11/30/1999)
90 **Mazzei** Toscana Siepi 1996 • $66 • (11/30/1999)
90 **Montevertine** Le Pergole Torte 1996 • $73 • (11/30/1999)
90 **Podere La Cappella** Toscana Corbezzolo 1996 • $36 • (11/30/1999)
90 **Poliziano** Vino Nobile di Montepulciano 1996 • $NA • (11/30/1999)
90 **Riecine** Toscana La Gioia 1996 • $53 • (11/30/1999)
90 **Rocca di Castagnoli** Cabernet Sauvignon Toscana Buriano 1996 • $40 • (11/30/1999)
90 **San Fabiano Calcinaia** Toscana Cerviolo Red 1996 • $32 • (12/15/1998)

1995 Tuscan Red
Vintage Rating: 88

95 **Tenuta dell'Ornellaia** Toscana Masseto 1995 • $150 • (12/15/1998)
94 **Argiano** Toscana Solengo 1995 • $117 Ⓐ • (12/31/1997) • HR
94 **Casanova di Neri** Brunello di Montalcino Tenuta Nuova 1995 • $49 • (6/30/2000) • HR
93 **Agricola Querciabella** Toscana Camartina 1995 • $55 • (11/30/1999)
93 **Castello Banfi** Toscana Summus 1995 • $45 • (12/15/1998) • CS
93 **Castello dei Rampolla** Toscana Sammarco 1995 • $NA • (12/15/1998)
93 **Eredi Fuligni** Brunello di Montalcino Vigneti dei Cottimelli 1995 • $60 • (6/30/2000)
93 **Gorelli** Brunello di Montalcino 1995 • $53 • (6/30/2000)
93 **Luce** Toscana Luce della Vite 1995 • $63 • (12/15/1998)
93 **Podere Poggio Scalette** Toscana Il Carbonaione 1995 • $55 • (12/15/1998)
92 **Antico Podere Gagliole** Colli della Toscana Centrale 1995 • $33 • (12/15/1998)
92 **Castello di Ama** Toscana Vigna l'Apparita 1995 • $200 • (12/15/1998)
92 **Conti Costanti** Brunello di Montalcino 1995 • $61 • (6/30/2000)
92 **Fattoria di Manzano** Toscana Podere il Bosco 1995 • $NA • (9/30/1997)
92 **Fontodi** Colli della Toscana Centrale Flaccianello 1995 • $50 • (12/15/1998)
92 **La Fortuna** Brunello di Montalcino 1995 • $59 • (6/30/2000)
92 **Montevertine** Le Pergole Torte 1995 • $NA • (11/30/1999)
92 **Siro Pacenti** Brunello di Montalcino 1995 • $50 • (6/30/2000)
92 **Villa Poggio Salvi** Brunello di Montalcino 1995 • $55 • (6/30/2000)
91 **Caparzo** Brunello di Montalcino La Casa 1995 • $85 • (6/30/2000) • CS
91 **Carpineto** Cabernet Sauvignon Toscana Farnito 1995 • $25 • (12/15/1998)
91 **Castello Banfi** Cabernet Sauvignon Toscana Tavernelle 1995 • $32 • (12/15/1998)
91 **Castello Banfi** Merlot Toscana Mandrielle 1995 • $32 • (12/15/1998)
91 **Castello Romitorio** Brunello di Montalcino 1995 • $38 • (6/30/2000)
91 **Centolani** Brunello di Montalcino Tenuta Friggiali 1995 • $54 • (6/30/2000)
91 **Fattoria Le Pupille** Toscana Saffredi 1995 • $34 • (12/15/1998)
91 **Fontodi** Syrah Colli della Toscana Centrale Case Via 1995 • $40 • (12/15/1998)
91 **Isole e Olena** Toscana Cepparello 1995 • $33 Ⓐ • (9/30/1997)
91 **Le Macchiole** Toscana Messorio 1995 • $95 • (12/15/1998)
91 **Marchesi de' Frescobaldi** Brunello di Montalcino Castelgiocondo 1995 • $55 • (6/30/2000)
91 **Marchesi de' Frescobaldi** Merlot Toscana Castelgiocondo Lamaione 1995 • $42 • (12/15/1998)
91 **Poderi Boscarelli** Vino Nobile di Montepulciano Vigna del Nocio 1995 • $37 • (12/15/1998)
91 **San Felice** Chianti Classico Poggio Rosso Riserva 1995 • $30 • (12/15/1998)
91 **Silvio Nardi** Brunello di Montalcino Vigneto Manichiara 1995 • $66 • (6/30/2000)
91 **Solaria** Brunello di Montalcino 1995 • $NA • (6/30/2000)
91 **Tenuta dell'Ornellaia** Bolgheri Ornellaia 1995 • $65 • (12/15/1998)
90 **Antinori** Brunello di Montalcino Pian delle Vigne 1995 • $50 • (6/30/2000)
90 **Antinori** Toscana Solaia 1995 • $129 Ⓐ • (12/15/1998)
90 **Avignonesi** Toscana Grifi 1995 • $45 • (12/15/1998)
90 **Avignonesi-Capannelle** Toscana 50 & 50 1995 • $99 • (11/30/1999)
90 **Caparzo** Brunello di Montalcino 1995 • $55 • (6/30/2000)
90 **Castellare di Castellina** Colli della Toscana Centrale Coniale 1995 • $32 • (11/30/1999)
90 **Castellare di Castellina** Colli della Toscana Centrale I Sodi di San Niccolò 1995 • $45 • (11/30/1999)
90 **Castello della Paneretta** Toscana 1596-1996 1995 • $40 • (12/15/1998)
90 **Castello di Ama** Chianti Classico Bellavista Riserva 1995 • $30 Ⓐ • (12/15/1998)
90 **Castello di Lilliano** Colli della Toscana Centrale Vignacatena 1995 • $38 • (12/15/1998)
90 **Col d'Orcia** Olmaia 1995 • $48 • (11/30/1999)
90 **E. Roberto Cosimi** Rosso di Montalcino Il Poggiolo Sassello 1995 • $19 • (9/30/1997)
90 **Fattoria Corzano e Paterno** Toscana Il Corzano 1995 • $32 • (12/15/1998)
90 **Fattoria dei Barbi** Brunello di Montalcino 1995 • $45 • (6/30/2000)
90 **Fattoria del Cerro** Sangiovese Toscana Manero 1995 • $NA • (1/01/2000)
90 **Fattoria del Cerro** Vino Nobile di Montepulciano Vigneto Antica Chiusina 1995 • $35 • (11/30/1999)
90 **Fattoria di Felsina** Chianti Classico Berardenga Rancia Riserva 1995 • $32 • (12/15/1998)
90 **Fattoria di Felsina** Toscana Fontalloro 1995 • $NA • (11/30/1999)
90 **Fattoria Le Pupille** Morellino di Scansano Riserva 1995 • $17 • (12/15/1998)
90 **Fattoria Monsanto** Chianti Classico Riserva 1995 • $16 • (12/15/1998)
90 **Fattoria Petrolo** Toscana Galatrona 1995 • $50 • (12/15/1998)
90 **Fattoria Petrolo** Toscana Torrione 1995 • $38 • (12/15/1998)
90 **Fontodi** Chianti Classico Riserva 1995 • $28 • (12/15/1998)
90 **Fontodi** Chianti Classico Vigna del Sorbo Riserva 1995 • $42 • (12/15/1998)
90 **Grattamacco** Bolgheri 1995 • $40 • (12/15/1998)
90 **Isole e Olena** Cabernet Sauvignon Toscana Collezione de Marchi 1995 • $40 • (12/15/1998)

90 **La Fornace** Brunello di Montalcino 1995 • $45 • (6/30/2000)
90 **La Palazzetta** Brunello di Montalcino 1995 • $68 • (6/30/2000)
90 **Lambardi** Brunello di Montalcino 1995 • $48 • (6/30/2000)
90 **Montecalvi** Alta Valle della Greve 1995 • $36 • (10/31/1997)
90 **Podere Capaccia** Colli della Toscana Centrale Querciagrande 1995 • $NA • (11/30/1999)
90 **Poggerino** Chianti Classico Bugialla Riserva 1995 • $50 • (12/15/1998)
90 **Poggio Bonelli** Toscana Tramonto d'Oca Red 1995 • $28 • (12/15/1998)
90 **Poliziano** Vino Nobile di Montepulciano Vigna Asinone 1995 • $42 • (12/15/1998)
90 **Riecine** Chianti Classico Riserva 1995 • $35 • (12/15/1998)
90 **Riecine** Toscana La Gioia 1995 • $45 • (12/15/1998)
90 **Rietine** Colli della Toscana Centrale Tiziano 1995 • $16 • (11/30/1999)
90 **Ruffino** Toscana Cabreo Il Borgo 1995 • $28 • (9/30/1997)
90 **Sesti** Brunello di Montalcino 1995 • $NA • (6/30/2000)
90 **Tenuta del Terriccio** Toscana Lupicaia 1995 • $NA • (12/15/1998)
90 **Tenuta San Guido** Bolgheri-Sassicaia Sassicaia 1995 • $95 • (12/15/1998)
90 **Villa Cafaggio** Toscana Cortaccio 1995 • $45 • (12/15/1998)
90 **Villa Monte Rico** Toscana 1995 • $30 • (12/15/1998)

1990 Tuscan Red
Vintage Rating: 98

98 **Altesino** Brunello di Montalcino Montosoli 1990 • $137 Ⓐ • (10/31/1995)
97 **Antinori** Toscana Solaia 1990 • $202 Ⓐ • (2/28/1995) • CS
97 **Campogiovanni** Brunello di Montalcino Vigna del Quercione Riserva 1990 • $84 • (11/30/1996)
96 **Col d'Orcia** Olmaia 1990 • $19 • (2/28/1995)
96 **Nozzole** Toscana Il Pareto 1990 • $41 • (1/01/1994)
96 **Tenuta dell'Ornellaia** Bolgheri Ornellaia 1990 • $42 • (11/15/1993)
95 **Argiano** Brunello di Montalcino Riserva 1990 • $134 Ⓐ • (11/30/1996) • CS
95 **Campogiovanni** Brunello di Montalcino 1990 • $33 • (10/31/1995)
95 **Caparzo** Brunello di Montalcino La Casa 1990 • $113 Ⓐ • (10/31/1995) • CS
95 **Castello Banfi** Brunello di Montalcino Poggio all'Oro Riserva 1990 • $123 Ⓐ • (11/30/1996)
95 **Castello di Ama** Chianti Classico Bellavista Riserva 1990 • $NA • (9/30/1997)
95 **Isole e Olena** Cabernet Sauvignon Tuscany Collezione de Marchi 1990 • $30 • (10/31/1993)
95 **Montevertine** Le Pergole Torte Riserva 1990 • $NA • (11/30/1999)
94 **La Chiesa di S. Restituta** Red 1990 • $NA • (10/31/1993)
94 **Mastrojanni** Brunello di Montalcino 1990 • $27 • (10/31/1995)

Key: SS—Spectator Selection. CS—Cellar Selection. HR—Highly Recommended. $NA—Price not available. (BT)—Barrel tasting. Ⓐ—Auction Price.
Dates in parentheses represent the issues in which the ratings were published.

94 **Vignamaggio** Tuscany 1990 • $NA • (10/31/1993)
93 **Caparzo** Brunello di Montalcino Riserva 1990 • $115 Ⓐ • (11/30/1996)
93 **Carpineto** Toscana Farnito 1990 • $18 • (10/31/1993)
93 **Casanova di Neri** Brunello di Montalcino Cerreto Alto Riserva 1990 • $72 • (11/30/1996)
93 **Castello Banfi** Brunello di Montalcino 1990 • $80 Ⓐ • (10/31/1995)
93 **Castello di Ama** Chianti Classico Bertinga 1990 • $34 • (2/28/1995) • HR
93 **Castello di Ama** Chianti Classico La Casuccia 1990 • $38 • (2/28/1995)
93 **Ciacci Piccolomini D'Aragona** Brunello di Montalcino 1990 • $35 • (10/31/1995)
93 **Conti Costanti** Brunello di Montalcino 1990 • $54 • (10/31/1995)
93 **Conti Costanti** Brunello di Montalcino Riserva 1990 • $75 • (11/30/1996)
93 **E. Roberto Cosimi** Brunello di Montalcino Il Poggiolo Sassello Riserva 1990 • $70 • (11/30/1996)
93 **Fattoria di Felsina** Chianti Classico Berardenga Rancia Riserva 1990 • $28 • (2/28/1995) • SS
93 **Fattoria Le Filigare** Toscana Podere Le Rocce 1990 • $NA • (10/31/1993)
93 **Fontodi** Syrah Colli della Toscana Centrale Case Via 1990 • $28 • (10/31/1993)
93 **Giorgio Regni** Chianti Classico Riserva 1990 • $25 • (2/28/1995)
93 **Giorgio Regni** Toscana Convivio 1990 • $NA • (10/31/1993)
93 **Grattamacco** Tuscany 1990 • $NA • (10/31/1993)
93 **Isole e Olena** Toscana Cepparello 1990 • $30 • (10/31/1993)
93 **Montevertine** Le Pergole Torte 1990 • $NA • (11/30/1999)
93 **Podere Il Palazzino** Grosso Sanese 1990 • $35 • (10/31/1993) • HR
93 **Poggio Antico** Brunello di Montalcino Riserva 1990 • $101 Ⓐ • (11/30/1996)
93 **Ruffino** Brunello di Montalcino Tenuta Il Greppone Mazzi Riserva 1990 • $50 • (11/30/1996)
93 **Tenuta San Guido** Sassicaia 1990 • $90 • (7/31/1996)
93 **Valdicava** Brunello di Montalcino Madonna del Piano Riserva 1990 • $NA • (11/30/1996)
92 **Antinori** Chianti Classico Badia a Passignano 1990 • $NA • (10/31/1993)
92 **Antinori** Toscana Tignanello 1990 • $149 Ⓐ • (2/28/1995) • CS
92 **Biondi-Santi** Brunello di Montalcino Riserva 1990 • $230 • (11/30/1996)
92 **Castello Banfi** Toscana Summus 1990 • $40 • (10/31/1993)
92 **Castello di Ama** Vigna l'Apparita 1990 • $169 Ⓐ • (10/31/1993) • HR
92 **Castello di Verrazzano** Toscana Sassello 1990 • $NA • (10/31/1993)
92 **Castello di Volpaia** Coltassala 1990 • $26 • (11/30/1994) • SS
92 **E. Roberto Cosimi** Brunello di Montalcino Il Poggiolo Riserva 1990 • $55 • (11/30/1996)
92 **Marchesi de' Frescobaldi** Brunello di Montalcino Castelgiocondo 1990 • $30 • (10/31/1995)
92 **Poggerino** Chianti Classico Bugialla Riserva 1990 • $NA • (9/30/1997)
92 **Ruffino** Toscana Cabreo Il Borgo 1990 • $NA • (10/31/1993)
92 **San Felice** Chianti Classico Poggio Rosso Riserva 1990 • $24 • (9/30/1997)

92 **Selvapiana** Chianti Rufina 1990 • $13 • (9/15/1992)

92 **Siro Pacenti** Brunello di Montalcino 1990 • $36 • (10/31/1995)

92 **Soldera** Brunello di Montalcino Case Basse Riserva 1990 • $273 Ⓐ • (11/30/1996)

91 **Avignonesi** Toscana Grifi 1990 • $36 • (2/28/1995) • CS

91 **Caparzo** Brunello di Montalcino 1990 • $93 Ⓐ • (10/31/1995)

91 **Castello dei Rampolla** Toscana Sammarco 1990 • $94 Ⓐ • (10/31/1995)

91 **Castello di Fonterutoli** Brancaia 1990 • $24 • (10/31/1993)

91 **Castello di Vicchiomaggio** Toscana Ripa delle More 1990 • $NA • (10/31/1993)

91 **Colle Bereto** Il Cénno 1990 • $27 • (12/31/1995)

91 **Eredi Fuligni** Brunello di Montalcino Vigneti dei Cottimelli Riserva 1990 • $75 • (11/30/1996)

91 **Fattoria dei Barbi** Brunello di Montalcino Riserva 1990 • $49 • (11/30/1996)

91 **Fattoria dei Barbi** Brunello di Montalcino Vigna del Fiore Riserva 1990 • $68 • (11/30/1996)

91 **Fattoria di Felsina** Chianti Classico Berardenga 1990 • $12 • (9/15/1992)

91 **Fattoria di Felsina** Toscana Fontalloro 1990 • $38 • (2/28/1995)

91 **Fontodi** Chianti Classico Vigna del Sorbo Riserva 1990 • $27 • (2/28/1995)

91 **Il Poggione** Brunello di Montalcino Riserva 1990 • $47 • (11/30/1996)

91 **Isole e Olena** Toscana Cepparello 1990 • $51 Ⓐ • (11/15/1993)

91 **La Gerla** Brunello di Montalcino Riserva 1990 • $37 • (11/30/1996)

91 **La Massa** Chianti Classico Giorgio Primo Riserva 1990 • $17 • (2/28/1995)

91 **Mastrojanni** Brunello di Montalcino Riserva 1990 • $90 • (11/30/1996)

91 **Poggerino** Bugialla 1990 • $20 • (10/31/1993)

91 **Poggerino** Chianti Classico 1990 • $14 • (9/15/1992)

91 **Poggio Antico** Brunello di Montalcino 1990 • $85 Ⓐ • (10/31/1995)

91 **Poggio San Polo** Brunello di Montalcino Riserva 1990 • $70 • (11/30/1996)

91 **San Felice** Toscana Vigorello 1990 • $NA • (10/31/1993)

91 **Selvapiana** Chianti Rufina Bucerchiale Riserva 1990 • $20 • (9/30/1997)

91 **Vignavecchia** Canvalle 1990 • $NA • (10/31/1993)

91 **Villa Cafaggio** Toscana Cortaccio 1990 • $32 • (10/31/1993)

91 **Villa Poggio Salvi** Brunello di Montalcino 1990 • $45 • (10/31/1995)

90 **Argiano** Brunello di Montalcino 1990 • $77 Ⓐ • (10/31/1995)

90 **Carobbio** Chianti Classico 1990 • $NA • (10/31/1993)

90 **Casanova di Neri** Brunello di Montalcino 1990 • $33 • (10/31/1995)

90 **Castello di Ama** Chianti Classico San Lorenzo 1990 • $34 • (2/28/1995)

90 **Castello di Cacchiano** Toscana RF 1990 • $25 • (2/28/1995)

90 **Eredi Fuligni** Brunello di Montalcino Vigneti dei Cottimelli 1990 • $46 • (10/31/1995)

90 **Fattoria di Felsina** Chianti Classico Berardenga Riserva 1990 • $18 • (2/28/1995)

90 **Fattoria Le Bocce** Chianti Classico 1990 • $11 • (9/15/1992) • HR

90 **Fattoria Petrolo** Toscana Torrione 1990 • $NA • (10/31/1993)

90 **Fontodi** Colli della Toscana Centrale Flaccianello 1990 • $NA • (11/15/1993)

90 **Giorgio Regni** Chianti Classico 1990 • $NA • (10/31/1993)

90 **Isole e Olena** Chianti Classico 1990 • $12 • (9/15/1992)

90 **La Sala** Colli della Toscana Centrale Campo all'Abero 1990 • $NA • (2/28/1995)

90 **Lisini** Brunello di Montalcino Ugolaia Riserva 1990 • $99 • (11/30/1996)

90 **Luciani** Brunello di Montalcino Riserva 1990 • $50 • (11/30/1996)

90 **Marchesi de' Frescobaldi** Chianti Rufina Montesodi 1990 • $NA • (9/30/1997)

90 **Melini** Toscana I Coltri Vigna 2 1990 • $20 • (12/31/1995)

90 **Podere Il Palazzino** Chianti Classico 1990 • $16 • (10/31/1993)

90 **Riecine** Toscana La Gioia 1990 • $45 • (10/31/1995)

90 **Rocca di Castagnoli** Toscana Stielle 1990 • $33 • (10/31/1995)

90 **Siro Pacenti** Brunello di Montalcino Riserva 1990 • $40 • (11/30/1996)

90 **Tenuta dell'Ornellaia** Toscana Masseto 1990 • $235 • (10/31/1993)

90 **Terrabianca** Chianti Classico Scassino 1990 • $13 • (9/15/1992)

90 **Vignamaggio** Chianti Classico 1990 • $13 • (9/15/1992)

90 **Viticcio** Chianti Classico 1990 • $11 • (9/15/1992) • SS

90 **Viticcio** Prunaio 1990 • $34 • (10/31/1993)

The wide terraces of Quinta do Noval in the Pinhão Valley.

Vintage Port

Here are our ratings and prices for the vintage Ports that scored 90 or better from seven "declared" vintages: 1997, 1994, 1991 and 1985—the four most recent declared vintages that *Wine Spectator* rates outstanding or better—plus the classic 1977, 1970 and 1963.

The decade of the 1990s has been an exceptional one for Port. First of all, 1994 is proving to be one of the vintages of the century. Our Port expert, James Suckling, rates it 99, and *Wine Spectator* named the 1994 Taylor and 1994 Fonseca as twin Wines of the Year for 1997.

In addition, because Port houses are traditionally extremely reluctant to declare two vintages in a row, neither 1992 nor 1995 was generally declared, despite the fact that both years produced many outstanding wines. (In fact, James Suckling gives 1992 an overall rating of 94—one point higher than the "declared" 1991 vintage.) This makes vintage-style Ports from 1992 and 1995 an excellent value for consumers, especially as compared to the sky-high prices for the renowned 1994s and the limited-production 1997s.

See the main listings for ratings and prices of vintage-character and single quinta Ports from these and many other years.

1997 Vintage Port

Vintage Rating: 96

98 **Niepoort** Vintage Port 1997 • $45 • (2/29/2000) • CS
97 **Quinta do Noval** Vintage Port 1997 • $85 • (2/29/2000)
95 **Delaforce** Vintage Port Quinta da Corte 1997 • $78 • (2/29/2000)
94 **Taylor Fladgate** Vintage Port 1997 • $83 • (2/29/2000)
94 **Warre** Vintage Port 1997 • $55 • (2/29/2000)
90-94 **Dow** Vintage Port 1997 • $NA • (12/31/1999) • (BT)
93 **Cálem** Vintage Port 1997 • $67 • (2/29/2000)
92 **Croft** Vintage Port Quinta da Roêda 1997 • $83 • (2/29/2000)
92 **Sandeman** Vintage Port Vau Vintage 1997 • $42 • (2/29/2000)
91 **Ferreira** Vintage Port 1997 • $49 • (2/29/2000)
91 **Fonseca** Vintage Port 1997 • $83 • (2/29/2000)
91 **Quinta do Noval** Vintage Port Quinto do Silval 1997 • $50 • (2/29/2000)
90 **Gould Campbell** Vintage Port 1997 • $45 • (2/29/2000)
90 **Graham** Vintage Port 1997 • $78 • (2/29/2000)
90 **Quarles Harris** Vintage Port 1997 • $NA • (2/29/2000)

Key: SS—Spectator Selection. CS—Cellar Selection. HR—Highly Recommended. $NA—Price not available. (BT)—Barrel tasting. Ⓐ—Auction Price.
Dates in parentheses represent the issues in which the ratings were published.

90 **Quinta do Crasto** Vintage Port 1997 • $56 • (2/29/2000)
90 **Quinta do Passadouro** Vintage Port 1997 • $45 • (2/29/2000)
90 **Quinta do Vale Dona Maria** Vintage Port 1997 • $50 • (2/29/2000)
90 **Quinta do Vesuvio** Vintage Port 1997 • $80 • (2/29/2000)
90 **Smith Woodhouse** Vintage Port 1997 • $50 • (2/29/2000)

1994 Vintage Port

Vintage Rating: 99

100 **Fonseca** Vintage Port 1994 • $132 Ⓐ • (4/30/1997) • CS
100 **Quinta do Noval** Vintage Port Nacional 1994 • $739 Ⓐ • (4/30/1997) • CS
100 **Taylor Fladgate** Vintage Port 1994 • $120 Ⓐ • (4/30/1997) • CS
97 **Dow** Vintage Port 1994 • $57 Ⓐ • (12/31/1999)
97 **Martinez** Vintage Port Quinta da Eira Velha 1994 • $30 • (4/30/1997)
96 **Croft** Vintage Port 1994 • $37 Ⓐ • (4/30/1997)
96 **Quinta do Vesuvio** Vintage Port 1994 • $35 Ⓐ • (4/30/1997)
95 **Graham** Vintage Port 1994 • $68 Ⓐ • (4/30/1997)
95 **Martinez** Vintage Port 1994 • $30 • (4/30/1997)
95 **Quinta do Noval** Vintage Port 1994 • $50 • (4/30/1997)
95 **Warre** Vintage Port 1994 • $44 Ⓐ • (4/30/1997)
93 **Churchill** Vintage Port 1994 • $35 • (4/30/1997)
93 **Quinta do Crasto** Vintage Port 1994 • $35 • (4/30/1997)

92 **Cockburn** Vintage Port 1994 • $22 Ⓐ • (4/30/1997)
92 **Delaforce** Vintage Port 1994 • $18 Ⓐ • (4/30/1997)
92 **Gould Campbell** Vintage Port 1994 • $55 • (4/30/1997)
91 **Niepoort** Vintage Port 1994 • $45 • (4/30/1997)
91 **Osborne** Vintage Port 1994 • $30 • (4/30/1997)

1991 Vintage Port
Vintage Rating: 93

94 **Croft** Vintage Port 1991 • $30 Ⓐ • (7/31/1994)
94 **Taylor Fladgate** Vintage Port Quinta de Vargellas 1991 • $NA • (7/31/1994)
93 **Fonseca** Vintage Port 1991 • $NA • (7/31/1994)
93 **Fonseca** Vintage Port Guimaraens 1991 • $35 • (7/31/1994)
93 **Graham** Vintage Port 1991 • $37 Ⓐ • (7/31/1994)
93 **Quinta do Noval** Vintage Port Nacional 1991 • $180 • (6/15/1998) • CS
92 **Gould Campbell** Vintage Port 1991 • $35 • (7/31/1994)
91 **Churchill** Vintage Port 1991 • $35 • (7/31/1994)
91 **Dow** Vintage Port 1991 • $45 Ⓐ • (12/31/1999)
91 **Ferreira** Vintage Port 1991 • $19 • (7/31/1994)
91 **Quinta do Vesuvio** Vintage Port 1991 • $53 Ⓐ • (7/31/1994)
91 **Warre** Vintage Port 1991 • $34 Ⓐ • (7/31/1994)

1985 Vintage Port
Vintage Rating: 93

96 **Graham** Vintage Port 1985 • $42 • (1/01/1989)
95 **Fonseca** Vintage Port 1985 • $32 • (1/01/1989)
95 **Quinta do Noval** Vintage Port Nacional 1985 • $225 • (1/01/1989)
93 **Burmester** Vintage Port 1985 • $25 • (1/01/1989)
92 **Niepoort** Vintage Port 1985 • $44 • (1/01/1989)
91 **Quinta do Noval** Vintage Port 1985 • $NA • (10/31/1988)
91 **Warre** Vintage Port 1985 • $28 • (1/01/1989)
90 **Cockburn** Vintage Port 1985 • $33 • (1/01/1989)
90 **Kopke** Vintage Port 1985 • $25 • (1/01/1989)
90 **Taylor Fladgate** Vintage Port 1985 • $40 • (1/01/1989)

1977 Vintage Port
Vintage Rating: 97

100 **Fonseca** Vintage Port 1977 • $16 • (1/01/1989)
98 **Taylor Fladgate** Vintage Port 1977 • $70 • (1/01/1989)
94 **Dow** Vintage Port 1977 • $NA • (12/31/1999)
93 **Gould Campbell** Vintage Port 1977 • $11 • (1/01/1989)
92 **Warre** Vintage Port 1977 • $32 • (1/01/1989)
90 **Graham** Vintage Port 1977 • $58 • (1/01/1989)

1970 Vintage Port
Vintage Rating: 95

98 **Quinta do Noval** Vintage Port Nacional 1970 • $300 • (1/01/1989)
98 **Taylor Fladgate** Vintage Port 1970 • $70 • (1/01/1989)
96 **Fonseca** Vintage Port 1970 • $65 • (1/01/1989)
94 **Dow** Vintage Port 1970 • $NA • (12/31/1999)
94 **Graham** Vintage Port 1970 • $72 • (1/01/1989)
93 **Niepoort** Vintage Port 1970 • $55 • (1/01/1989)
92 **Rebello-Valente** Vintage Port 1970 • $50 • (1/01/1989)

1963 Vintage Port
Vintage Rating: 98

100 **Quinta do Noval** Vintage Port Nacional 1963 • $600 • (1/01/1989)
98 **Fonseca** Vintage Port 1963 • $162 • (1/01/1989)
97 **Graham** Vintage Port 1963 • $150 • (1/01/1989)
97 **Taylor Fladgate** Vintage Port 1963 • $140 • (1/01/1989)
96 **Sandeman** Vintage Port 1963 • $39 • (7/15/1990)
93 **Delaforce** Vintage Port 1963 • $35 • (1/01/1989)
92 **Dow** Vintage Port 1963 • $NA • (12/31/1999)
92 **Warre** Vintage Port 1963 • $65 • (1/01/1989)
91 **Croft** Vintage Port 1963 • $52 • (1/01/1989)
90 **Niepoort** Vintage Port 1963 • $90 • (1/01/1989)

California Cabernet

In this section we list *Wine Spectator's* ratings and prices for the best wines from the last seven consecutive vintages—1990 through 1996—of California Cabernet Sauvignon and Bordeaux-style blends.

Why seven consecutive years? Because each of those vintages is rated outstanding or classic (although 1993 was slightly more variable than the other years). Furthermore, in the judgment of *Wine Spectator* critic James Laube, 1997 will not only prove to be a classic vintage but will rival 1994 as the vintage of the decade. (Final tastings of the 1997 vintage were not completed in time for publication.) And based on barrel tastings, Laube predicts that even 1998 may achieve an outstanding rating, though it is clearly not as good as 1997.

All of which makes the 1990s the most extraordinary decade in the history of California Cabernet.

1996 CALIFORNIA CABERNET | VINTAGE RATING: 94

99 **Bryant Family** Cabernet Sauvignon Napa Valley 1996 • $440 Ⓐ • (10/15/1999) • HR

98 **Dalla Valle** Maya Napa Valley 1996 • $420 Ⓐ • (11/15/1999) • CS

97 **Harlan Estate** Napa Valley 1996 • $125 • (11/15/1999) • CS

96 **Opus One** Napa Valley 1996 • $132 Ⓐ • (2/29/2000)

96 **Peter Michael** Les Pavots Knights Valley 1996 • $163 Ⓐ • (6/30/1999) • HR

96 **Screaming Eagle** Cabernet Sauvignon Napa Valley 1996 • $1,120 Ⓐ • (11/15/1999)

95 **Chateau St. Jean** Cabernet Sauvignon Sonoma County Cinq Cépages 1996 • $28 • (11/15/1999) • SS

95 **Dalla Valle** Cabernet Sauvignon Napa Valley 1996 • $113 Ⓐ • (11/15/1999)

95 **David Arthur** Cabernet Sauvignon Napa Valley Elevation 1147 1996 • $75 • (5/15/1999)

95 **Dunn** Cabernet Sauvignon Howell Mountain 1996 • $50 • (10/15/1999) • CS

95 **Elyse** Cabernet Sauvignon Napa Valley Tietjen Vineyard 1996 • $37 • (1/31/2000)

95 **Lokoya** Cabernet Sauvignon Napa Valley Diamond Mountain 1996 • $100 • (11/15/1999)

Key: SS—Spectator Selection. CS—Cellar Selection. HR—Highly Recommended. $NA—Price not available. (BT)—Barrel tasting. Ⓐ—Auction Price.
Dates in parentheses represent the issues in which the ratings were published.

95 **Lokoya** Cabernet Sauvignon Rutherford 1996 • $115 Ⓐ • (11/15/1999)

95 **Martin Ray** Cabernet Sauvignon Napa Valley Diamond Mountain Vineyard 1996 • $50 • (11/15/1999)

95 **Peju** Cabernet Sauvignon Napa Valley Reserve 1996 • $75 • (11/15/1999)

95 **Robert Mondavi** Cabernet Sauvignon Napa Valley Reserve 1996 • $72 Ⓐ • (11/15/1999) • HR

94 **Araujo** Cabernet Sauvignon Napa Valley Eisele Vineyard 1996 • $264 Ⓐ • (11/15/1999) • HR

94 **Bacio Divino** Cabernet-Sangiovese-Petite Sirah-Merlot Napa Valley 1996 • $57 Ⓐ • (11/15/1999)

94 **Beaulieu Vineyard** Cabernet Sauvignon Rutherford Clone 6 Signet Collection 1996 • $100 • (11/15/1999)

94 **Colgin** Cabernet Sauvignon Napa Valley Herb Lamb Vineyard 1996 • $520 Ⓐ • (10/31/1999) • CS

94 **Cornerstone** Cabernet Sauvignon Howell Mountain Beatty Ranch 1996 • $45 • (10/31/1999)

94 **David Arthur** Cabernet Sauvignon Napa Valley 1996 • $45 • (5/15/1999) • HR

94 **Diamond Creek** Cabernet Sauvignon Napa Valley Red Rock Terrace Microclimate 3 1996 • $150 • (12/31/1998) • CS

94 **E. & J. Gallo** Cabernet Sauvignon Northern Sonoma 1996 • $65 • (10/31/1999)

94 **Flora Springs** Trilogy Napa Valley 1996 • $45 • (7/31/1999) • CS

94 **Lokoya** Cabernet Sauvignon Mount Veeder 1996 • $100 • (11/15/1999)

94 **Pride** Cabernet Sauvignon Napa Valley Reserve 1996 • $216 Ⓐ • (10/31/1999)

94 **Sterling** Cabernet Sauvignon Napa Valley Reserve 1996 • $50 • (10/31/1999) • CS

94 **Vine Cliff** Cabernet Sauvignon Oakville Estate 1996 • $44 • (11/15/1999)

94 **Whitehall Lane** Cabernet Sauvignon Napa Valley Leonardini Vineyard 1996 • $60 • (11/15/1999)

93 **B.R. Cohn** Cabernet Sauvignon Sonoma Valley Olive Hill Estate Vineyards Special Selection 1996 • $80 • (8/31/1999)

93 **Barnett** Cabernet Sauvignon Spring Mountain District Rattlesnake Hill 1996 • $60 • (4/30/1999)

93 **Benziger** Cabernet Sauvignon Sonoma Mountain Reserve 1996 • $35 • (10/31/1999)

93 **Cardinale** Red Napa-Sonoma Counties 1996 • $100 • (11/15/1999)

93 **Herzog** Cabernet Sauvignon Napa Valley Special Reserve 1996 • $30 • (6/15/1999) • HR

93 **Jones Family** Cabernet Sauvignon Napa Valley 1996 • $50 • (11/15/1999)

93 **Joseph Phelps** Cabernet Sauvignon Napa Valley Backus Vineyard 1996 • $95 • (10/31/1999)

93 **Joseph Phelps** Insignia Napa Valley 1996 • $96 Ⓐ • (8/31/1999)

93 **La Jota** Cabernet Sauvignon Howell Mountain 15th Anniversary Release 1996 • $82 Ⓐ • (4/30/1999)

93 **Merryvale** Cabernet Sauvignon Napa Valley Reserve 1996 • $35 • (10/15/1999)

93 **Miner** Cabernet Sauvignon Napa Valley Oakville 1996 • $50 • (7/31/1999)

93 **Pahlmeyer** Napa Valley 1996 • $134 Ⓐ • (11/15/1999)

93 **Philip Togni** Cabernet Sauvignon Napa Valley 1996 • $81 Ⓐ • (5/15/1999)

93 **Pine Ridge** Cabernet Sauvignon Howell Mountain 1996 • $40 • (5/15/1999)

93 **Shafer** Cabernet Sauvignon Stags Leap District Hillside Select 1996 • $NA • (11/15/1999)

93 **Spottswoode** Cabernet Sauvignon Napa Valley 1996 • $73 Ⓐ • (10/31/1999) • CS

93 **St. Francis** Cabernet Sauvignon Sonoma Valley Reserve 1996 • $39 • (10/15/1999)

93 **Stonestreet** Legacy Alexander Valley 1996 • $85 • (7/31/1999)

93 **Whitehall Lane** Cabernet Sauvignon Napa Valley Reserve 1996 • $48 • (11/15/1999)

92 **Andrus** Napa Valley Reserve 1996 • $95 • (8/31/1999)

92 **Arns** Cabernet Sauvignon Napa Valley 1996 • $50 • (10/31/1999)

92 **B.R. Cohn** Cabernet Sauvignon Sonoma Valley Olive Hill Estate Vineyards 1996 • $35 • (8/31/1999)

92 **Beaulieu Vineyard** Cabernet Sauvignon Napa Valley Georges de Latour Private Reserve 1996 • $75 • (11/15/1999)

92 **Beaulieu Vineyard** Tapestry Reserve Napa Valley 1996 • $35 • (10/15/1999) • SS

92 **Carmenet** Meritage Sonoma Valley Moon Mountain Reserve 1996 • $39 • (11/15/1999)

92 **Chateau Montelena** Cabernet Sauvignon Napa Valley The Montelena Estate 1996 • $NA • (11/15/1999)

92 **Clos du Bois** Cabernet Sauvignon Alexander Valley Briarcrest Vineyard 1996 • $36 • (10/15/1999)

Key: SS—Spectator Selection. CS—Cellar Selection.
HR—Highly Recommended. $NA—Price not available.
(BT)—Barrel tasting. Ⓐ—Auction Price.
Dates in parentheses represent the issues in which the ratings were published.

92 **Clos du Bois** Cabernet Sauvignon Alexander Valley Winemaker's Reserve 1996 • $50 • (11/15/1999)

92 **Constant** Cabernet-Merlot-Cabernet Franc Napa Valley Diamond Mountain Vineyard 1996 • $100 • (11/15/1999)

92 **Cornerstone** Cabernet Sauvignon Howell Mountain Black Sears 1996 • $44 • (10/31/1999)

92 **Del Dotto** Cabernet Sauvignon Napa Valley 1996 • $49 • (10/15/1999)

92 **Diamond Creek** Cabernet Sauvignon Napa Valley Lake 1996 • $345 Ⓐ • (12/31/1998) • CS

92 **Diamond Creek** Cabernet Sauvignon Napa Valley Red Rock Terrace 1996 • $86 Ⓐ • (12/31/1998) • CS

92 **Diamond Creek** Cabernet Sauvignon Napa Valley Volcanic Hill 1996 • $100 • (12/31/1998) • CS

92 **Dominus Estate** Napa Valley Napanook Vineyard 1996 • $106 Ⓐ • (8/31/1999) • CS

92 **Elyse** Cabernet Sauvignon Napa Valley Morisoli Vineyard 1996 • $45 • (1/31/2000)

92 **Emilio's Terrace** Cabernet Sauvignon Napa Valley Reserve 1996 • $40 • (8/31/1999)

92 **Etude** Cabernet Sauvignon Napa Valley 1996 • $50 • (4/30/2000) • CS

92 **Fife** Cabernet Sauvignon Spring Mountain District Reserve 1996 • $40 • (11/15/1999)

92 **Flora Springs** Cabernet Sauvignon Rutherford Hillside Reserve 1996 • $70 • (10/31/1999)

92 **Forman** Cabernet Sauvignon Napa Valley 1996 • $45 • (11/15/1999)

92 **Herzog** Cabernet Sauvignon Alexander Valley Special Edition 1996 • $40 • (6/15/1999)

92 **Herzog** Cabernet Sauvignon Alexander Valley Special Reserve 1996 • $26 • (6/15/1999)

92 **Joseph Phelps** Cabernet Sauvignon Napa Valley 1996 • $30 • (5/15/1999) • SS

92 **Lewis** Cabernet Sauvignon Napa Valley Reserve 1996 • $48 Ⓐ • (3/31/1999)

92 **Lokoya** Cabernet Sauvignon Howell Mountain 1996 • $100 • (11/15/1999)

92 **Oakford** Cabernet Sauvignon Oakville 1996 • $70 • (8/31/1999)

92 **Pine Ridge** Cabernet Sauvignon Stags Leap District 1996 • $40 • (2/28/1999)

92 **Raymond** Cabernet Sauvignon Napa Valley Generations 1996 • $50 • (11/15/1999)

92 **Reverie** Cabernet Sauvignon Napa Valley 1996 • $43 • (11/15/1999)

92 **Robert Craig** Affinity Napa Valley 1996 • $40 • (4/30/1999) • CS

92 **Robert Craig** Cabernet Sauvignon Mount Veeder 1996 • $40 • (8/31/1999)

92 **Seavey** Cabernet Sauvignon Napa Valley 1996 • $48 • (10/31/1999)

92 **Sherwin Family** Cabernet Sauvignon Spring Mountain District 1996 • $52 • (2/29/2000)

92 **Signorello** Cabernet Sauvignon Napa Valley Founder's Reserve 1996 • $75 • (9/15/1999)

92 **Stag's Leap Wine Cellars** Cabernet Sauvignon Napa Valley S.L.V. 1996 • $100 • (11/15/1999)

92 **Terraces** Cabernet Sauvignon Napa Valley 1996 • $50 • (10/31/1999)

92 **Truchard** Cabernet Sauvignon Napa Valley Carneros 1996 • $32 • (10/15/1999)

92 **Villa Mt. Eden** Cabernet Sauvignon Mendocino Signature Series 1996 • $52 • (11/15/1999)

92 **von Strasser** Cabernet Sauvignon Napa Valley Diamond Mountain 1996 • $29 Ⓐ • (11/15/1999)

91 **August Briggs** Cabernet Sauvignon Napa Valley 1996 • $35 • (4/30/1999)

91 **Barbour** Cabernet Sauvignon Napa Valley 1996 • $115 Ⓐ • (2/28/1999)

91 **Clos Pegase** Cabernet Sauvignon Napa Valley 1996 • $26 • (4/30/1999)

91 **Corison** Cabernet Sauvignon Napa Valley Kronos Vineyard 1996 • $85 • (10/31/1999)

91 **Cosentino** M. Coz Meritage Napa Valley 1996 • $80 • (10/15/1999)

91 **David Arthur** Meritagio Napa Valley 1996 • $38 • (5/15/1999)

91 **Diamond Creek** Cabernet Sauvignon Napa Valley Gravelly Meadow 1996 • $100 • (12/31/1998) • CS

91 **Dunn** Cabernet Sauvignon Napa Valley 1996 • $45 • (10/15/1999)

91 **Far Niente** Cabernet Sauvignon Napa Valley 1996 • $77 • (6/15/1999) • CS

91 **Fisher** Cabernet Sauvignon Napa Valley Lamb Vineyard 1996 • $60 • (9/30/1999)

91 **Fisher** Coach Insignia Napa County 1996 • $30 • (2/28/1999)

91 **Harrison** Cabernet Sauvignon Napa Valley 1996 • $42 • (10/31/1998)

91 **Hartwell** Cabernet Sauvignon Stags Leap District Grace Vineyard 1996 • $65 • (6/15/1999)

91 **La Jota** Cabernet Sauvignon Howell Mountain Selection 1996 • $34 • (4/30/1999)

91 **Merryvale** Profile Napa Valley 1996 • $75 • (11/15/1999)

91 **Mount Veeder** Cabernet Sauvignon Napa Valley 1996 • $30 • (10/31/1999) • SS

91 **Paradigm** Cabernet Sauvignon Oakville 1996 • $44 • (10/15/1999)

91 **Pine Ridge** Epitome Stags Leap District 1996 • $95 • (11/15/1999)

91 **Quintessa** Rutherford 1996 • $90 • (4/30/2000)

91 **Regusci** Cabernet Sauvignon Stags Leap District 1996 • $42 • (9/15/1999)

91 **Robert Craig** Cabernet Sauvignon Howell Mountain 1996 • $40 • (10/15/1999)

91 **Schug** Cabernet Sauvignon Sonoma Valley Heritage Reserve 1996 • $40 • (11/15/1999)

91 **Swanson** Cabernet Sauvignon Napa Valley 1996 • $30 • (10/31/1999)

90 **A. Rafanelli** Cabernet Sauvignon Dry Creek Valley 1996 • $26 • (8/31/1999)

90 **Anderson's Conn Valley** Cabernet Sauvignon Napa Valley Estate Reserve 1996 • $48 • (11/15/1999)

90 **Caymus** Cabernet Sauvignon Napa Valley 1996 • $58 Ⓐ • (1/31/2000)

90 **Chimney Rock** Cabernet Sauvignon Napa Valley 1996 • $30 • (4/30/1999)

90 **Clos Pegase** Hommage Artist Series Reserve Napa Valley 1996 • $60 • (11/15/1999)

90 **Corison** Cabernet Sauvignon Napa Valley Tenth Anniversary 1996 • $45 • (9/30/1999)

90 **De Loach** Cabernet Sauvignon Russian River Valley O.F.S. 1996 • $36 • (10/15/1999)

90 **Estancia** Meritage Alexander Valley 1996 • $30 • (10/15/1999) • SS

90 **Franciscan Oakville Estate** Magnificat Napa Valley 1996 • $35 • (10/15/1999)

90 **Geyser Peak** Cabernet Sauvignon Alexander Valley Reserve 1996 • $32 • (11/15/1999)

90 **Hartwell** Cabernet Sauvignon Stags Leap District Sunshine Vineyard 1996 • $55 • (9/15/1999)

90 **Karl Lawrence** Cabernet Sauvignon Napa Valley 1996 • $30 • (10/15/1999)

90 **Kendall-Jackson** Cabernet Sauvignon California Grand Reserve 1996 • $74 • (11/15/1999)

90 **La Sirena** Cabernet Sauvignon Napa Valley 1996 • $75 • (11/15/1999)

90 **Merryvale** Cabernet Sauvignon Napa Valley Hillside 1996 • $20 • (12/15/1998)

90 **Paoletti** Cabernet Sauvignon Napa Valley 1996 • $39 • (9/30/1999)

90 **Pezzi King** Cabernet Sauvignon Dry Creek Valley 1996 • $26 • (4/30/1999)

90 **PlumpJack** Cabernet Sauvignon Oakville 1996 • $32 • (6/15/1999)

90 **Ristow** Cabernet Sauvignon Napa Valley Quinta de Pedras Vineyard 1996 • $45 • (10/31/1999)

90 **Robert Mondavi** Cabernet Sauvignon Napa Valley 30th Anniversary 1996 • $150 • (6/30/2000)

90 **Robert Mondavi** Cabernet Sauvignon Oakville 1996 • $45 • (9/15/1999)

90 **Robert Mondavi** Cabernet Sauvignon Stags Leap District 1996 • $45 • (11/15/1999)

90 **Rombauer** Cabernet Sauvignon Napa Valley 1996 • $30 • (11/15/1999)

90 **S. Anderson** Cabernet Sauvignon Stags Leap District Richard Chambers Vineyard 1996 • $65 • (11/15/1999)

90 **Saddleback** Cabernet Sauvignon Napa Valley 1996 • $32 • (6/15/1999)

90 **Silverado Vineyards** Cabernet Sauvignon Stags Leap District Disney Family Vineyard 1996 • $50 • (11/15/1999)

90 **Spring Mountain** Miravalle-La Perla-Chevalier Napa Valley Red 1996 • $45 • (11/15/1999)

90 **Staglin** Cabernet Sauvignon Rutherford 1996 • $50 • (8/31/1999)

90 **Stonestreet** Cabernet Sauvignon Alexander Valley Christopher's Vineyard Alexander Mountain Estate 1996 • $60 • (11/15/1999)

90 **White Cottage** Cabernet Sauvignon Howell Mountain 1996 • $40 • (10/15/1999)

1995 California Cabernet
Vintage Rating: 95

97 **Bryant Family** Cabernet Sauvignon Napa Valley 1995 • $393 Ⓐ • (8/31/1998) • CS

97 **Caymus** Cabernet Sauvignon Napa Valley Special Selection 1995 • $145 Ⓐ • (6/30/1999) • CS

97 **Lokoya** Cabernet Sauvignon Rutherford 1995 • $135 Ⓐ • (11/15/1998) • HR

96 **Diamond Creek** Cabernet Sauvignon Napa Valley Gravelly Meadow 1995 • $75 • (6/15/1998)

96 **Diamond Creek** Cabernet Sauvignon Napa Valley Red Rock Terrace 1995 • $75 • (6/15/1998)

96 **Harlan Estate** Napa Valley 1995 • $420 Ⓐ • (11/15/1998) • CS

96 **Screaming Eagle** Cabernet Sauvignon Napa Valley 1995 • $1,126 Ⓐ • (11/15/1998) • CS

95 **Araujo** Cabernet Sauvignon Napa Valley Eisele Vineyard 1995 • $323 Ⓐ • (10/31/1998) • CS

95 **Dalla Valle** Maya Napa Valley 1995 • $458 Ⓐ • (11/15/1998)

95 **Groth** Cabernet Sauvignon Napa Valley Reserve 1995 • $115 Ⓐ • (8/31/1999) • CS

95 **Martin Ray** Cabernet Sauvignon Napa Valley Diamond Mountain 1995 • $45 • (7/31/1998)

95 **Opus One** Napa Valley 1995 • $142 Ⓐ • (2/29/2000)

95 **Silverado Vineyards** Cabernet Sauvignon Napa Valley Limited Reserve 1995 • $76 Ⓐ • (11/15/1998)

95 **Whitehall Lane** Cabernet Sauvignon Napa Valley Reserve 1995 • $40 • (11/15/1998) • HR

94 **Arrowood** Cabernet Sauvignon Sonoma County Réserve Spéciale 1995 • $75 • (11/15/1999)

94 **Beringer** Cabernet Sauvignon Napa Valley St. Helena Home Vineyard 1995 • $85 • (10/31/1999)

94 **Beringer** Cabernet Sauvignon Napa Valley State Lane Vineyard 1995 • $85 • (10/31/1999)

94 **Colgin** Cabernet Sauvignon Napa Valley Herb Lamb Vineyard 1995 • $561 Ⓐ • (11/15/1998)

94 **Constant** Cabernet-Merlot-Cabernet Franc Napa Valley Diamond Mountain Vineyard 1995 • $95 • (11/15/1999)

94 **Dalla Valle** Cabernet Sauvignon Napa Valley 1995 • $101 Ⓐ • (11/15/1998)

94 **Diamond Creek** Cabernet Sauvignon Napa Valley Volcanic Hill 1995 • $125 Ⓐ • (6/15/1998)

94 **Robert Mondavi** Cabernet Sauvignon Napa Valley Reserve 1995 • $61 Ⓐ • (7/31/1998)

94 **Stag's Leap Wine Cellars** Cask 23 Napa Valley 1995 • $120 • (11/15/1998)

94 **Sterling** Reserve Napa Valley 1995 • $50 • (4/30/1999) • CS

94 **Villa Mt. Eden** Cabernet Sauvignon Mendocino Signature Series 1995 • $45 • (11/15/1998)

93 **Altamura** Cabernet Sauvignon Napa Valley 1995 • $40 • (5/31/1999)

93 **Beringer** Cabernet Sauvignon Howell Mountain Bancroft Ranch 1995 • $100 • (10/31/1999)

93 **Clos Du Val** Cabernet Sauvignon Napa Valley Reserve 1995 • $65 • (11/15/1999)

93 **Dunn** Cabernet Sauvignon Howell Mountain 1995 • $82 Ⓐ • (4/30/1999) • CS

93 **Herzog** Cabernet Sauvignon Alexander Valley Special Edition 1995 • $46 • (9/30/1998)

93 **Joseph Phelps** Insignia Napa Valley 1995 • $90 Ⓐ • (10/31/1998) • CS

93 **Lewis** Cabernet Sauvignon Napa Valley Reserve 1995 • $40 • (5/15/1998) • HR

93 **Paradigm** Cabernet Sauvignon Oakville 1995 • $40 • (11/15/1998)

93 **Peter Michael** Les Pavots Knights Valley 1995 • $50 • (7/31/1998)

93 **Pride** Cabernet Sauvignon Napa Valley Reserve 1995 • $70 • (11/30/1998)

93 **Shafer** Cabernet Sauvignon Stags Leap District 1995 • $30 • (8/31/1998)

93 **Signorello** Cabernet Sauvignon Napa Valley 1995 • $30 • (7/31/1998)

93 **Signorello** Cabernet Sauvignon Napa Valley Founder's Reserve 1995 • $55 • (7/31/1998)

93 **Simi** Cabernet Sauvignon Sonoma County Reserve 1995 • $45 • (11/15/1999)

93 **Snowden** Cabernet Sauvignon Napa Valley 1995 • $57 Ⓐ • (10/31/1999) • HR

93 **Spottswoode** Cabernet Sauvignon Napa Valley 1995 • $69 Ⓐ • (10/31/1998) • CS

93 **St. Clement** Oroppas Napa Valley 1995 • $35 • (8/31/1997)

93 **Stag's Leap Wine Cellars** Cabernet Sauvignon Napa Valley Fay 1995 • $70 • (10/31/1998)

93 **Stag's Leap Wine Cellars** Cabernet Sauvignon Napa Valley S.L.V. 1995 • $70 • (11/15/1998)

Key: SS—Spectator Selection. CS—Cellar Selection. HR—Highly Recommended. $NA—Price not available. (BT)—Barrel tasting. Ⓐ—Auction Price.
Dates in parentheses represent the issues in which the ratings were published.

93 **Truchard** Cabernet Sauvignon Napa Valley Carneros Reserve 1995 • $55 • (10/31/1999)

93 **von Strasser** Cabernet Sauvignon Napa Valley Diamond Mountain 1995 • $36 • (7/31/1998)

92 **Barbour** Cabernet Sauvignon Napa Valley 1995 • $50 • (2/28/1999)

92 **Beaulieu Vineyard** Cabernet Sauvignon Rutherford Clone 4 Signet Collection 1995 • $100 • (10/31/1998)

92 **Beringer** Cabernet Sauvignon Howell Mountain Tre Colline Vineyard 1995 • $85 • (10/31/1999)

92 **Beringer** Cabernet Sauvignon Napa Valley Private Reserve 1995 • $75 • (4/30/2000) • CS

92 **Cardinale** Red Napa-Alexander Valleys 1995 • $70 • (7/31/1998)

92 **Caymus** Cabernet Sauvignon Napa Valley 1995 • $86 Ⓐ • (8/31/1998)

92 **Chateau Montelena** Cabernet Sauvignon Napa Valley The Montelena Estate 1995 • $85 • (11/15/1999)

92 **Clos du Bois** Cabernet Sauvignon Alexander Valley Winemaker's Reserve 1995 • $50 • (11/15/1998)

92 **Del Dotto** Cabernet Sauvignon Napa Valley 1995 • $43 • (11/15/1998)

92 **Etude** Cabernet Sauvignon Napa Valley 1995 • $40 • (1/31/1999)

92 **Far Niente** Cabernet Sauvignon Napa Valley 1995 • $70 • (6/30/1998) • HR

92 **Freemark Abbey** Cabernet Sauvignon Napa Valley Cabernet Bosché Bosché Estate 1995 • $50 • (10/31/1999)

92 **Geyser Peak** Cabernet Sauvignon Alexander Valley Bin 2 1995 • $100 • (11/15/1999)

92 **Grace Family** Cabernet Sauvignon Napa Valley 1995 • $475 • (6/15/1998)

92 **Hartwell** Cabernet Sauvignon Stags Leap District Sunshine Vineyard 1995 • $90 Ⓐ • (5/15/1998)

92 **Lokoya** Cabernet Sauvignon Mount Veeder 1995 • $199 Ⓐ • (11/15/1998)

92 **Mount Veeder** Reserve Napa Valley 1995 • $50 • (11/15/1999)

92 **Niebaum-Coppola** Rubicon Rutherford 1995 • $80 • (6/15/1999) • CS

92 **Oakville Ranch** Cabernet Sauvignon Napa Valley 1995 • $35 • (11/15/1998)

92 **Pahlmeyer** Napa Valley 1995 • $73 Ⓐ • (10/31/1998)

92 **Pine Ridge** Andrus Reserve Napa Valley 1995 • $85 • (6/30/1998)

92 **PlumpJack** Cabernet Sauvignon Napa Valley McWilliam's Mt. Eden Vineyard 1995 • $30 • (11/15/1997)

92 **PlumpJack** Cabernet Sauvignon Napa Valley McWilliam's Mt. Eden Vineyard Reserve 1995 • $65 • (11/15/1997)

92 **Quintessa** Rutherford 1995 • $90 • (1/31/1999) • HR

92 **Reverie** Special Reserve Napa Valley 1995 • $75 • (6/15/1999)

92 **Ridge** Monte Bello Santa Cruz Mountains 1995 • $100 • (10/31/1998) • CS

92 **Seavey** Cabernet Sauvignon Napa Valley 1995 • $46 Ⓐ • (10/31/1998)

92 **Shafer** Cabernet Sauvignon Stags Leap District Hillside Select 1995 • $213 Ⓐ • (10/31/1998) • CS

92 **St. Francis** Cabernet Sauvignon Sonoma Valley Reserve 1995 • $29 • (10/31/1998) • SS

92 **Staglin** Cabernet Sauvignon Rutherford 1995 • $43 • (8/31/1998) • HR

92 **Stonestreet** Cabernet Sauvignon Alexander Valley Alexander Mountain Estate Three Block 1995 • $60 • (2/28/1999)

92 **Swanson** Alexis Napa Valley 1995 • $40 • (12/15/1997) • HR

92 **Terraces** Cabernet Sauvignon Napa Valley 1995 • $50 • (4/30/1999)

92 **The Hess Collection** Cabernet Sauvignon Napa Valley 1995 • $25 • (5/15/1999)

92 **Tom Eddy** Cabernet Sauvignon Napa Valley 1995 • $60 • (4/30/1999)

92 **Viader** Napa Valley 1995 • $33 • (1/31/1998) • HR

92 **Vine Cliff** Cabernet Sauvignon Napa Valley 1995 • $38 • (10/31/1998)

92 **Whitehall Lane** Cabernet Sauvignon Napa Valley Leonardini Vineyard 1995 • $50 • (11/15/1998)

92 **ZD Wines** Cabernet Sauvignon Napa Valley Reserve 1995 • $60 • (4/30/1999)

91 **Arns** Cabernet Sauvignon Napa Valley 1995 • $40 • (12/15/1998)

91 **B.R. Cohn** Cabernet Sauvignon Sonoma Valley Olive Hill Estate Vineyards 1995 • $35 • (7/31/1998)

91 **Bacio Divino** Cabernet-Sangiovese-Petite Sirah Napa Valley 1995 • $72 Ⓐ • (10/31/1998)

91 **Beaulieu Vineyard** Tapestry Reserve Napa Valley 1995 • $30 • (11/30/1998) • SS

91 **Behrens & Hitchcock** Cabernet Sauvignon Napa Valley TLK Ranch 1995 • $30 • (11/15/1998)

91 **Beringer** Cabernet Sauvignon Knights Valley Appellation Collection 1995 • $22 • (6/15/1998)

91 **Chateau Souverain** Cabernet Sauvignon Alexander Valley Library Reserve 1995 • $45 • (6/15/1999)

91 **Chateau St. Jean** Cabernet Sauvignon Sonoma County Cinq Cépages 1995 • $24 • (10/31/1998) • SS

91 **Clos du Bois** Cabernet Sauvignon Alexander Valley Briarcrest Vineyard 1995 • $30 • (11/15/1998)

91 **Clos du Bois** Marlstone Vineyard Alexander Valley 1995 • $30 • (11/15/1998)

91 **Cosentino** Cabernet Sauvignon Napa Valley Reserve 1995 • $50 • (10/31/1998)

91 **Del Dotto** Giovanni's Tuscan Reserve Napa Valley 1995 • $30 • (11/15/1998)

91 **Delectus** Cabernet Sauvignon Napa Valley 1995 • $42 • (7/31/1998)

91 **Forman** Cabernet Sauvignon Napa Valley 1995 • $49 Ⓐ • (6/30/1998)

91 **Girard** Cabernet Sauvignon Napa Valley 1995 • $30 • (2/28/1999) • CS

91 **Grgich Hills** Cabernet Sauvignon Napa Valley 1995 • $45 • (11/15/1998)

91 **Joseph Phelps** Cabernet Sauvignon Napa Valley 1995 • $27 • (6/30/1998) • SS

91 **Joseph Phelps** Cabernet Sauvignon Napa Valley Backus Vineyard 1995 • $75 • (3/31/1999)

91 **Merryvale** Cabernet Sauvignon Napa Valley Reserve 1995 • $30 • (10/31/1998)

91 **Merryvale** Profile Napa Valley 1995 • $65 • (11/15/1998)

91 **Pride** Cabernet Sauvignon Napa Valley 1995 • $24 • (11/30/1997) • HR

91 **Robert Craig** Affinity Napa Valley 1995 • $34 • (6/15/1998) • CS

91 **Robert Craig** Cabernet Sauvignon Howell Mountain 1995 • $34 • (10/31/1998)

91 **Robert Craig** Cabernet Sauvignon Mount Veeder 1995 • $34 • (8/31/1998)

91 **S. Anderson** Cabernet Sauvignon Stags Leap District Richard Chambers Vineyard 1995 • $65 • (10/31/1998)

91 **Saddleback** Cabernet Sauvignon Napa Valley 1995 • $27 • (8/31/1998)

91 **Silver Oak** Cabernet Sauvignon Napa Valley 1995 • $75 • (4/30/2000)

91 **Stonestreet** Cabernet Sauvignon Alexander Valley 1995 • $34 • (8/31/1998)

91 **Stonestreet** Legacy Alexander Valley 1995 • $65 • (11/15/1998)

91 **Swanson** Cabernet Sauvignon Napa Valley 1995 • $26 • (7/31/1998)

91 **Truchard** Cabernet Sauvignon Napa Valley Carneros 1995 • $27 • (11/15/1998)

91 **ZD Wines** Cabernet Sauvignon Napa Valley 1995 • $32 • (5/15/1998)

90 **Alexander Valley Vineyards** Cyrus Alexander Valley 1995 • $35 • (2/29/2000)

90 **B.R. Cohn** Cabernet Sauvignon Sonoma Valley Olive Hill Estate Vineyards Special Selection 1995 • $80 • (6/15/1998)

90 **Cakebread** Cabernet Sauvignon Napa Valley Benchland Select 1995 • $65 • (12/31/1998)

90 **Carmenet** Meritage Sonoma Valley Moon Mountain Estate Reserve 1995 • $40 • (11/15/1998)

90 **Chateau Potelle** Cabernet Sauvignon Mount Veeder V.G.S. 1995 • $50 • (10/31/1999)

90 **Chimney Rock** Cabernet Sauvignon Napa Valley 1995 • $28 • (5/15/1998) • SS

90 **Cornerstone** Cabernet Sauvignon Napa Valley 1995 • $39 • (11/15/1998)

90 **Fife** Cabernet Sauvignon Napa Valley Estate Vineyard 1995 • $24 • (5/15/1998)

90 **Flora Springs** Cabernet Sauvignon Rutherford Hillside Reserve 1995 • $58 Ⓐ • (10/31/1998)

90 **Frank-Rombauer** Cabernet Sauvignon Rutherford Frank-Rombauer Larkmead Cellars 1995 • $50 • (6/15/1999)

90 **Galante** Cabernet Sauvignon Carmel Valley Blackjack Pasture 1995 • $30 • (11/15/1998)

90 **Geyser Peak** Reserve Alexandre Alexander Valley 1995 • $28 • (8/31/1998)

90 **Groth** Cabernet Sauvignon Napa Valley 1995 • $45 Ⓐ • (10/31/1998)

90 **Heitz** Cabernet Sauvignon Napa Valley 1995 • $27 • (1/31/2000)

90 **Hendry Ranch** Cabernet Sauvignon Napa Valley Block 8 1995 • $24 • (5/15/1998)

90 **Judd's Hill** Cabernet Sauvignon Napa Valley 1995 • $32 • (10/31/1998)

90 **Kendall-Jackson** Cabernet Sauvignon California Grand Reserve 1995 • $50 • (10/31/1998)

90 **Lockwood** Cabernet Sauvignon Monterey Partners' Reserve 1995 • $22 • (11/15/1998)

90 **Long** Cabernet Sauvignon Napa Valley 1995 • $40 • (3/31/1998)

90 **Mount Veeder** Cabernet Sauvignon Napa Valley 1995 • $30 • (11/15/1998)

90 **Murphy-Goode** Cabernet Sauvignon Alexander Valley Brenda Block Reserve 1995 • $35 • (10/31/1998)

90 **Oakford** Cabernet Sauvignon Oakville 1995 • $50 • (1/31/1999)

90 **Pine Ridge** Cabernet Sauvignon Stags Leap District 1995 • $38 • (6/15/1998)

90 **Robert Mondavi** Cabernet Sauvignon Napa Valley 1995 • $22 • (8/31/1998) • SS

90 **Robert Pecota** Cabernet Sauvignon Napa Valley Kara's Vineyard 1995 • $25 • (5/31/1998)

90 **Silver Oak** Cabernet Sauvignon Alexander Valley 1995 • $72 Ⓐ • (10/15/1999) • CS

90 **St. Clement** Cabernet Sauvignon Howell Mountain 1995 • $45 • (10/31/1998)

90 **St. Clement** Cabernet Sauvignon Napa Valley 1995 • $26 • (10/31/1998)

90 **Steele** Cabernet Sauvignon Anderson Valley 1995 • $26 • (2/28/1999)

90 **White Cottage** Cabernet Sauvignon Howell Mountain 1995 • $40 • (11/15/1998)

1994 California Cabernet
Vintage Rating: 96

97 **Beringer** Cabernet Sauvignon Howell Mountain Bancroft Vineyard 1994 • $85 • (10/31/1997)

97 **Opus One** Napa Valley 1994 • $166 Ⓐ • (2/29/2000)

96 **Abreu** Cabernet Sauvignon Napa Valley Madrona Ranch 1994 • $201 Ⓐ • (1/01/1999)

96 **Araujo** Cabernet Sauvignon Napa Valley Eisele Vineyard 1994 • $346 Ⓐ • (10/15/1997) • HR

96 **Flora Springs** Cabernet Sauvignon Rutherford Hillside Reserve 1994 • $96 Ⓐ • (10/15/1997) • HR

96 **Groth** Cabernet Sauvignon Napa Valley Reserve 1994 • $189 Ⓐ • (5/15/1998) • CS

96 **Joseph Phelps** Insignia Napa Valley 1994 • $134 Ⓐ • (9/30/1997) • CS

95 **Beringer** Cabernet Sauvignon Napa Valley Private Reserve 1994 • $87 Ⓐ • (10/15/1998) • CS

95 **Caymus** Cabernet Sauvignon Napa Valley 1994 • $87 Ⓐ • (5/31/1997) • CS

95 **Caymus** Cabernet Sauvignon Napa Valley Special Selection 1994 • $178 Ⓐ • (12/31/1997) • CS

95 **Chateau Montelena** Cabernet Sauvignon Napa Valley The Montelena Estate 1994 • $40 • (11/15/1999)

95 **Colgin** Cabernet Sauvignon Napa Valley Herb Lamb Vineyard 1994 • $515 Ⓐ • (7/31/1997) • HR

95 **Dalla Valle** Maya Napa Valley 1994 • $484 Ⓐ • (10/31/1997) • HR

95 **Harlan Estate** Napa Valley 1994 • $454 Ⓐ • (5/15/1998) • CS

95 **Screaming Eagle** Cabernet Sauvignon Napa Valley 1994 • $1,244 Ⓐ • (10/31/1997)

95 **Shafer** Cabernet Sauvignon Stags Leap District Hillside Select 1994 • $250 Ⓐ • (10/15/1997)

94 **Arrowood** Cabernet Sauvignon Sonoma County Réserve Spéciale 1994 • $50 • (7/31/1998)

94 **Bryant Family** Cabernet Sauvignon Napa Valley 1994 • $409 Ⓐ • (11/30/1997)

94 **Dominus Estate** Napa Valley Napanook Vineyard 1994 • $148 Ⓐ • (7/31/1997) • CS

94 **Grace Family** Cabernet Sauvignon Napa Valley 1994 • $471 Ⓐ • (5/31/1997) • CS

94 **Hartwell** Cabernet Sauvignon Stags Leap District Grace Vineyard 1994 • $63 • (11/30/1997)

94 **Lewis** Cabernet Sauvignon Napa Valley Reserve 1994 • $56 Ⓐ • (6/15/1997) • HR

94 **Livingston** Cabernet Sauvignon Napa Valley Moffett Vineyard 1994 • $36 • (10/31/1997) • HR

94 **Peter Michael** Les Pavots Knights Valley 1994 • $127 Ⓐ • (8/31/1997) • CS

94 **Robert Craig** Affinity Napa Valley 1994 • $28 • (8/31/1997) • HR

94 **Robert Craig** Cabernet Sauvignon Mount Veeder 1994 • $28 • (11/15/1997)

94 **Robert Mondavi** Cabernet Sauvignon Napa Valley Reserve 1994 • $81 Ⓐ • (7/31/1997) • CS

93 **Beaulieu Vineyard** Cabernet Sauvignon Rutherford Clone 6 Signet Collection 1994 • $100 • (11/15/1997)

Key: SS—Spectator Selection. CS—Cellar Selection. HR—Highly Recommended. $NA—Price not available. (BT)—Barrel tasting. Ⓐ—Auction Price.
Dates in parentheses represent the issues in which the ratings were published.

93 **Chateau Souverain** Cabernet Sauvignon Alexander Valley Winemaker's Reserve 1994 • $30 • (10/15/1997)

93 **Cornerstone** Cabernet Sauvignon Howell Mountain Beatty Ranch 1994 • $35 • (10/31/1997)

93 **Dalla Valle** Cabernet Sauvignon Napa Valley 1994 • $105 Ⓐ • (10/31/1997) • CS

93 **Diamond Creek** Cabernet Sauvignon Napa Valley Gravelly Meadow 1994 • $NA • (6/15/1998)

93 **Diamond Creek** Cabernet Sauvignon Napa Valley Lake 1994 • $230 Ⓐ • (6/15/1998)

93 **Diamond Creek** Cabernet Sauvignon Napa Valley Red Rock Terrace Microclimate 2 1994 • $NA • (6/15/1998)

93 **Etude** Cabernet Sauvignon Napa Valley 1994 • $43 Ⓐ • (9/30/1997)

93 **Ferrari-Carano** Trésor Reserve Sonoma County 1994 • $65 • (10/15/1999)

93 **Girard** Cabernet Sauvignon Napa Valley Reserve 1994 • $40 • (11/15/1997)

93 **Guenoc** Cabernet Sauvignon Napa Valley Beckstoffer IV Vineyard Reserve 1994 • $40 • (10/31/1997)

93 **Harrison** Cabernet Sauvignon Napa Valley 1994 • $33 • (7/31/1997) • HR

93 **Kenwood** Cabernet Sauvignon Sonoma Valley Artist Series 20th Anniversary 1994 • $65 • (11/15/1998)

93 **La Jota** Cabernet Sauvignon Howell Mountain 13th Anniversary Release 1994 • $46 • (4/30/1997)

93 **Liparita** Cabernet Sauvignon Howell Mountain 1994 • $32 • (5/15/1998) • HR

93 **Pine Ridge** Andrus Reserve Napa Valley 1994 • $85 • (7/31/1997)

93 **Raymond** Cabernet Sauvignon Napa Valley Generations 1994 • $38 Ⓐ • (10/31/1997) • SS

93 **Ridge** Monte Bello Santa Cruz Mountains 1994 • $100 • (9/30/1997)

93 **Rockland** Cabernet Sauvignon Napa Valley 1994 • $30 • (11/15/1996)

93 **Silverado Vineyards** Cabernet Sauvignon Napa Valley Limited Reserve 1994 • $96 Ⓐ • (11/30/1997) • HR

93 **Simi** Cabernet Sauvignon Sonoma County Reserve 1994 • $47 • (11/30/1998) • CS

93 **St. Francis** Cabernet Sauvignon Sonoma Valley Reserve 1994 • $29 Ⓐ • (10/15/1997) • SS

93 **Stag's Leap Wine Cellars** Cask 23 Napa Valley 1994 • $134 Ⓐ • (3/31/1998) • CS

93 **Stonestreet** Legacy Alexander Valley 1994 • $106 Ⓐ • (10/15/1997) • HR

93 **Viader** Napa Valley 1994 • $30 • (5/31/1997)

93 **White Cottage** Cabernet Sauvignon Howell Mountain 1994 • $96 Ⓐ • (10/15/1997)

92 **Behrens & Hitchcock** Cabernet Sauvignon Napa Valley Staglin Vineyard 1994 • $28 • (11/30/1997)

92 **Beringer** Cabernet Sauvignon Napa Valley Chabot Vineyard 1994 • $85 • (10/31/1997)

92 **Beringer** Cabernet Sauvignon Napa Valley Marston Vineyard 1994 • $85 • (10/31/1997)

92 **Cakebread** Cabernet Sauvignon Napa Valley 1994 • $25 • (7/31/1997) • SS

92 **Chateau St. Jean** Cabernet Sauvignon Sonoma County Reserve 1994 • $60 • (11/15/1999)

92 **Clark-Claudon** Cabernet Sauvignon Napa Valley 1994 • $45 • (5/31/1997)

92 **Cuvaison** Cabernet Sauvignon Napa Valley ATS 1994 • $50 • (4/30/1998)

92 **Del Dotto** Cabernet Sauvignon Napa Valley 1994 • $42 • (10/31/1997)

92 **E. & J. Gallo** Cabernet Sauvignon Northern Sonoma Estate Bottled 1994 • $55 • (11/15/1998)

92 **Estancia** Meritage Alexander Valley 1994 • $16 • (5/15/1997) • SS

92 **Fisher** Cabernet Sauvignon Napa Valley Lamb Vineyard 1994 • $53 Ⓐ • (10/31/1997)

92 **Forman** Cabernet Sauvignon Napa Valley 1994 • $62 Ⓐ • (5/31/1997)

92 **Justin** Isosceles Paso Robles 1994 • $33 • (10/31/1997)

92 **Markham** Cabernet Sauvignon Napa Valley 1994 • $15 • (10/31/1997) • SS

92 **Niebaum-Coppola** Rubicon Rutherford 1994 • $65 • (6/15/1998) • CS

92 **Pahlmeyer** Napa Valley 1994 • $83 Ⓐ • (11/30/1996) • HR

92 **Paradigm** Cabernet Sauvignon Napa Valley Oakville 1994 • $30 • (9/30/1997)

92 **Peju** Cabernet Sauvignon Napa Valley HB Vineyard 1994 • $55 • (10/31/1997)

92 **Pine Ridge** Cabernet Sauvignon Stags Leap District 1994 • $35 • (10/31/1997)

92 **Spottswoode** Cabernet Sauvignon Napa Valley 1994 • $81 Ⓐ • (10/15/1997)

92 **St. Clement** Cabernet Sauvignon Howell Mountain White Cottage Ranch 1994 • $45 • (9/30/1997)

92 **Stag's Leap Wine Cellars** Cabernet Sauvignon Napa Valley Fay 1994 • $50 • (3/31/1998) • CS

92 **Villa Mt. Eden** Cabernet Sauvignon Mendocino Signature Series 1994 • $50 • (10/31/1997)

92 **von Strasser** Cabernet Sauvignon Napa Valley Diamond Mountain 1994 • $31 Ⓐ • (10/31/1997)

92 **Whitehall Lane** Cabernet Sauvignon Rutherford Morisoli Vineyard Reserve 1994 • $62 Ⓐ • (9/30/1997)

91 **Altamura** Cabernet Sauvignon Napa Valley 1994 • $33 • (12/15/1997)

91 **Anderson's Conn Valley** Cabernet Sauvignon Napa Valley Estate Reserve 1994 • $27 Ⓐ • (10/15/1997)

91 **Arrowood** Cabernet Sauvignon Sonoma County 1994 • $55 Ⓐ • (10/15/1997)

91 **Beaulieu Vineyard** Tapestry Reserve Napa Valley 1994 • $20 • (10/31/1997) • SS

91 **Beringer** Cabernet Sauvignon Knights Valley 1994 • $20 • (7/31/1997) • SS

91 **Chateau Souverain** Cabernet Sauvignon Alexander Valley Library Reserve 1994 • $45 • (10/31/1998)

91 **Chateau St. Jean** Cabernet Sauvignon Sonoma County Cinq Cépages 1994 • $24 • (9/30/1997) • SS

91 **Chimney Rock** Cabernet Sauvignon Stags Leap District Reserve 1994 • $50 • (10/15/1997)

91 **Clos Du Val** Cabernet Sauvignon Napa Valley Reserve 1994 • $53 • (10/31/1998)

91 **Cosentino** M. Coz Meritage Napa Valley 1994 • $34 Ⓐ • (11/15/1997)

91 **Dehlinger** Cabernet Sauvignon Russian River Valley 1994 • $25 • (9/30/1997)

91 **Diamond Creek** Cabernet Sauvignon Napa Valley Red Rock Terrace 1994 • $NA • (6/15/1998)

91 **Diamond Creek** Cabernet Sauvignon Napa Valley Volcanic Hill 1994 • $NA • (6/15/1998)

91 **Dunn** Cabernet Sauvignon Howell Mountain 1994 • $105 Ⓐ • (5/15/1998) • CS

91 **Far Niente** Cabernet Sauvignon Napa Valley 1994 • $55 • (2/28/1997)

91 **Freemark Abbey** Cabernet Bosché Bosché Estate Napa Valley 1994 • $44 • (11/15/1998)

91 **Galleron** Cabernet Sauvignon Napa Valley 1994 • $50 • (9/30/1997)

91 **Gallo of Sonoma** Cabernet Sauvignon Dry Creek Valley Frei Ranch Vineyard 1994 • $18 • (10/31/1998) • SS

91 **Geyser Peak** Reserve Alexandre Alexander Valley 1994 • $28 • (10/31/1997)

91 **Grgich Hills** Cabernet Sauvignon Napa Valley Yountville Selection 1994 • $65 • (12/31/1998)

91 **Lambert Bridge** Crane Creek Cuvée Dry Creek Valley 1994 • $28 • (11/15/1997)

91 **Merryvale** Profile Napa Valley 1994 • $48 Ⓐ • (10/31/1998)

91 **Oakford** Cabernet Sauvignon Oakville 1994 • $45 • (10/31/1998)

91 **Paul Hobbs** Cabernet Sauvignon Howell Mountain Liparita Vineyard 1994 • $45 • (10/31/1997)

91 **Pride** Cabernet Sauvignon Napa Valley Reserve 1994 • $65 • (3/31/1998)

91 **Quintessa** Rutherford Napa Valley 1994 • $70 • (11/30/1997)

91 **S. Anderson** Cabernet Sauvignon Stags Leap District Richard Chambers Vineyard 1994 • $53 Ⓐ • (10/31/1997)

91 **Saddleback** Cabernet Sauvignon Napa Valley 1994 • $23 • (9/30/1997)

91 **Silver Oak** Cabernet Sauvignon Napa Valley 1994 • $103 Ⓐ • (10/31/1998)

91 **Snowden** Cabernet Sauvignon Napa Valley 1994 • $40 • (11/15/1998)

91 **St. Clement** Cabernet Sauvignon Napa Valley 1994 • $27 • (7/31/1997)

91 **St. Clement** Oroppas Napa Valley 1994 • $30 • (11/15/1996)

91 **Stag's Leap Wine Cellars** Cabernet Sauvignon Napa Valley S.L.V. 1994 • $50 • (11/30/1997) • CS

91 **Steele** Cabernet Sauvignon Anderson Valley 1994 • $24 • (12/15/1997)

91 **Stonestreet** Cabernet Sauvignon Alexander Valley 1994 • $35 • (10/31/1997)

91 **Swanson** Alexis Napa Valley 1994 • $33 • (3/31/1997)

91 **Swanson** Cabernet Sauvignon Napa Valley 1994 • $24 • (7/31/1997)

91 **Terraces** Cabernet Sauvignon Napa Valley 1994 • $50 • (10/31/1998)

91 **Truchard** Cabernet Sauvignon Napa Valley Carneros 1994 • $24 • (9/30/1997)

91 **Truchard** Cabernet Sauvignon Napa Valley Carneros Reserve 1994 • $48 • (10/15/1998)

91 **Venezia** Cabernet Sauvignon Alexander Valley Meola Vineyards 1994 • $25 • (5/15/1997)

90 **Beaulieu Vineyard** Cabernet Sauvignon Napa Valley Rutherford 1994 • $15 • (7/31/1997) • SS

90 **Benziger** Cabernet Sauvignon Sonoma County Five Bordeaux Varietals 1994 • $14 • (4/30/1997) • SS

90 **Beringer** Alluvium Knights Valley Red 1994 • $25 • (3/31/1998)

90 **Bernardus** Marinus Carmel Valley 1994 • $30 • (4/30/1997)

90 **Buehler** Cabernet Sauvignon Napa Valley Estate 1994 • $35 • (11/15/1997)

90 **Chateau Potelle** Cabernet Sauvignon Mount Veeder V.G.S. 1994 • $39 • (3/31/1999)

90 **Chimney Rock** Cabernet Sauvignon Napa Valley 1994 • $24 • (7/31/1997)

90 **Clos du Bois** Marlstone Vineyard Alexander Valley 1994 • $25 • (5/15/1998)

90 **Clos Pegase** Homage Artist Series Reserve Cabernet Sauvignon Napa Valley 1994 • $40 • (9/30/1997)

90 **Cronin** Concerto Stags Leap District Robinson Vineyard 1994 • $23 • (4/30/1998)

90 **David Coffaro** Estate Cuvée Dry Creek Valley Coffaro Estate Vineyard Old Vines 1994 • $16 • (9/15/1996)

90 **De Loach** Cabernet Sauvignon Russian River Valley O.F.S. 1994 • $28 • (9/30/1997)

90 **Duckhorn** Cabernet Sauvignon Napa Valley 1994 • $67 Ⓐ • (5/31/1997)

90 **Flora Springs** Trilogy Napa Valley 1994 • $33 • (10/15/1997)

90 **Guenoc** Cabernet Sauvignon Napa Valley Bella Vista Vineyard Reserve 1994 • $26 • (9/30/1997)

90 **Guenoc** Langtry Meritage Red Napa Valley 1994 • $41 • (9/30/1997)

90 **La Jota** Cabernet Sauvignon Howell Mountain Selection 1994 • $77 Ⓐ • (5/15/1997)

90 **Long** Cabernet Sauvignon Napa Valley 1994 • $35 • (1/31/1997)

90 **Moraga** Red Bel Air 1994 • $55 • (5/15/1998)

90 **Philip Togni** Cabernet Sauvignon Napa Valley 1994 • $89 Ⓐ • (11/15/1996)

90 **Pine Ridge** Cabernet Sauvignon Howell Mountain 1994 • $35 • (10/31/1997)

90 **Pride** Cabernet Sauvignon Napa Valley 1994 • $58 Ⓐ • (10/31/1997)

90 **Robert Craig** Cabernet Sauvignon Howell Mountain 1994 • $28 • (11/30/1997)

90 **Robert Mondavi** Cabernet Sauvignon Napa Valley 1994 • $22 • (11/15/1997)

90 **Rocking Horse** Cabernet Sauvignon Napa Valley Garvey Family Vineyard 1994 • $24 • (11/30/1997)

90 **Rombauer** Cabernet Sauvignon Napa Valley Diamond Mountain Selection 1994 • $50 • (11/15/1997)

90 **Rosenthal-The Malibu Estate** Cabernet Sauvignon Malibu-Newton Canyon 1994 • $25 • (5/15/1998)

90 **Sebastiani** Cabernet Sauvignon Sonoma Valley Cherryblock Old Vines 1994 • $35 • (10/31/1998)

90 **Signorello** Cabernet Sauvignon Napa Valley Founder's Reserve 1994 • $55 • (9/30/1997)

90 **Sonoma Creek** Cabernet Sauvignon Sonoma Valley Rancho Salina Vineyard 1994 • $28 • (10/31/1997)

90 **Spring Mountain** Napa Valley 1994 • $36 • (4/30/1998)

90 **Staglin** Cabernet Sauvignon Rutherford 1994 • $40 • (6/15/1997)

90 **The Hess Collection** Cabernet Sauvignon Napa Valley Reserve 1994 • $45 • (10/31/1998)

90 **Tom Eddy** Cabernet Sauvignon Napa Valley 1994 • $50 • (5/15/1998)

90 **Vine Cliff** Cabernet Sauvignon Napa Valley Oakville Estate 1994 • $36 • (10/15/1997)

90 **Vineyard 29** Cabernet Sauvignon Napa Valley 1994 • $163 Ⓐ • (9/30/1997)

90 **ZD Wines** Cabernet Sauvignon Napa Valley Reserve 1994 • $55 • (5/15/1998)

1993 California Cabernet
Vintage Rating: 90

96 **Colgin** Cabernet Sauvignon Napa Valley Herb Lamb Vineyard 1993 • $355 Ⓐ • (11/15/1996)

96 **Dalla Valle** Maya Napa Valley 1993 • $407 Ⓐ • (11/15/1996) • CS

94 **Chateau Montelena** Cabernet Sauvignon Napa Valley The Montelena Estate 1993 • $40 • (11/15/1999)

Key: SS—Spectator Selection. CS—Cellar Selection. HR—Highly Recommended. $NA—Price not available. (BT)—Barrel tasting. Ⓐ—Auction Price.
Dates in parentheses represent the issues in which the ratings were published.

94 **Shafer** Cabernet Sauvignon Stags Leap District Hillside Select 1993 • $110 Ⓐ • (10/31/1997) • CS

93 **Araujo** Cabernet Sauvignon Napa Valley Eisele Vineyard 1993 • $249 Ⓐ • (11/15/1996) • CS

93 **Arns** Cabernet Sauvignon Napa Valley 1993 • $30 • (4/30/1997)

93 **Beringer** Cabernet Sauvignon Napa Valley Private Reserve 1993 • $69 Ⓐ • (5/31/1997) • CS

93 **Chateau St. Jean** Cabernet Sauvignon Sonoma County Reserve 1993 • $47 • (11/15/1998)

93 **Conn Creek** Anthology Napa Valley 1993 • $30 • (11/15/1996)

93 **Cornerstone** Cabernet Sauvignon Howell Mountain Beatty Ranch 1993 • $33 • (4/30/1996)

93 **Harlan Estate** Napa Valley 1993 • $277 Ⓐ • (10/15/1997)

93 **Opus One** Napa Valley 1993 • $141 Ⓐ • (2/29/2000)

92 **Altamura** Cabernet Sauvignon Napa Valley 1993 • $25 • (2/28/1997)

92 **Arrowood** Cabernet Sauvignon Sonoma County 1993 • $27 • (11/15/1996) • SS

92 **Arrowood** Cabernet Sauvignon Sonoma County Réserve Spéciale 1993 • $38 • (12/31/1996)

92 **Del Dotto** Cabernet Sauvignon Napa Valley 1993 • $30 • (4/30/1997)

92 **Ferrari-Carano** Trésor Reserve Sonoma County 1993 • $55 • (11/15/1998)

92 **Freemark Abbey** Cabernet Bosché Bosché Estate Napa Valley 1993 • $35 • (6/30/1998) • CS

92 **Heitz** Cabernet Sauvignon Napa Valley Trailside Vineyard 1993 • $48 • (8/31/1998) • CS

92 **Justin** Cabernet Sauvignon San Luis Obispo County 1993 • $20 • (4/30/1997) • HR

92 **Saddleback** Cabernet Sauvignon Napa Valley 1993 • $19 • (5/31/1996)

92 **Snowden** Cabernet Sauvignon Napa Valley 1993 • $35 • (7/31/1997)

92 **St. Clement** Oroppas Napa Valley 1993 • $30 • (10/31/1995) • HR

92 **Tay** Cabernet Sauvignon Napa Valley 1993 • $35 • (4/30/1996)

91 **Caymus** Cabernet Sauvignon Napa Valley 1993 • $58 Ⓐ • (11/15/1996) • SS

91 **Chateau Souverain** Cabernet Sauvignon Alexander Valley Library Reserve 1993 • $40 • (11/15/1996)

91 **Chateau St. Jean** Cabernet Sauvignon Sonoma County Cinq Cépages 1993 • $22 • (11/15/1996) • SS

91 **Clos Du Val** Cabernet Sauvignon Napa Valley Reserve 1993 • $50 • (10/31/1997)

91 **Cosentino** Cabernet Sauvignon Napa Valley Reserve 1993 • $35 • (11/15/1996)

91 **Cosentino** The Poet Meritage Napa Valley 1993 • $26 • (11/15/1996)

91 **Franciscan Oakville Estate** Meritage Magnificat Napa Valley 1993 • $20 • (11/15/1996)

91 **Heitz** Cabernet Sauvignon Napa Valley Bella Oaks Vineyard 1993 • $28 • (5/15/1998) • CS

91 **Kathryn Kennedy** Cabernet Sauvignon Santa Cruz Mountains 1993 • $70 • (10/31/1997)

91 **La Jota** Cabernet Sauvignon Howell Mountain 12th Anniversary Release 1993 • $72 Ⓐ • (4/30/1996)

91 **Moraga** Red Bel Air 1993 • $50 • (7/31/1997)

91 **Pahlmeyer** Napa Valley 1993 • $36 • (5/31/1996) • CS

91 **Screaming Eagle** Cabernet Sauvignon Napa Valley 1993 • $1,094 Ⓐ • (12/31/1996)

91 **Stag's Leap Wine Cellars** Cabernet Sauvignon Napa Valley Fay 1993 • $40 • (11/15/1996)

91 **Terraces** Cabernet Sauvignon Napa Valley 1993 • $40 • (11/30/1997)

91 **Whitehall Lane** Cabernet Sauvignon Napa Valley Morisoli Vineyard Reserve 1993 • $30 • (11/15/1996)

90 **Adelaida** Cabernet Sauvignon San Luis Obispo County 1993 • $19 • (8/31/1997)

90 **Anderson's Conn Valley** Cabernet Sauvignon Napa Valley Estate Reserve 1993 • $35 • (11/15/1996)

90 **B.R. Cohn** Cabernet Sauvignon Sonoma Valley Olive Hill Vineyard 1993 • $32 • (4/30/1996)

90 **Beringer** Cabernet Sauvignon Napa Valley Chabot Vineyard 1993 • $100 • (6/15/1998)

90 **Buena Vista** Cabernet Sauvignon Carneros Grand Reserve 1993 • $26 • (8/31/1997)

90 **Chateau Souverain** Cabernet Sauvignon Alexander Valley Winemaker's Reserve 1993 • $30 • (11/15/1996)

90 **Chimney Rock** Cabernet Sauvignon Stags Leap District Reserve 1993 • $40 • (11/30/1996)

90 **Clark-Claudon** Cabernet Sauvignon Napa Valley 1993 • $50 • (12/15/1996)

90 **Decoy** Migration Napa Valley Red 1993 • $12 • (2/29/1996) • SS

90 **Dunn** Cabernet Sauvignon Howell Mountain 1993 • $33 • (4/30/1997)

90 **E. & J. Gallo** Cabernet Sauvignon Northern Sonoma Estate Bottled 1993 • $24 Ⓐ • (10/31/1997)

90 **Estancia** Meritage Alexander Valley 1993 • $15 • (3/31/1997) • SS

90 **Etude** Cabernet Sauvignon Napa Valley 1993 • $30 • (11/15/1996)

90 **Ferrari-Carano** Siena Sonoma County 1993 • $24 • (11/30/1995) • HR

90 **Fife** Cabernet Sauvignon Spring Mountain Reserve 1993 • $28 • (11/15/1996)

90 **Fisher** Cabernet Sauvignon Napa Valley Lamb Vineyard 1993 • $45 • (11/15/1996)

90 **Fisher** Cabernet Sauvignon Sonoma County Wedding Vineyard 1993 • $33 • (11/15/1996)

90 **Flora Springs** Cabernet Sauvignon Napa Valley Rutherford Reserve 1993 • $45 • (11/15/1996)

90 **Jarvis** Lake William Napa Valley 1993 • $45 • (11/30/1996)

90 **Joseph Phelps** Insignia Napa Valley 1993 • $70 Ⓐ • (10/15/1996) • HR

90 **Kenwood** Cabernet Sauvignon Sonoma Valley Artist Series 1993 • $50 • (10/31/1997) • CS

90 **Martin Brothers** Etrusco Paso Robles 1993 • $16 • (12/15/1995)

90 **Mount Veeder** Reserve Napa Valley 1993 • $40 • (8/31/1997)

90 **Murrieta's Well** Vendimia Livermore Valley Red 1993 • $28 • (4/30/1997)

90 **Niebaum-Coppola** Rubicon Rutherford 1993 • $55 • (5/15/1998)

90 **Peter Michael** Les Pavots Knights Valley 1993 • $35 • (9/30/1996) • CS

90 **Pride** Cabernet Sauvignon Napa Valley 1993 • $22 • (9/15/1996)

90 **Raymond** Cabernet Sauvignon Napa Valley Reserve 1993 • $17 • (4/30/1996)

90 **Robert Craig** Cabernet Sauvignon Mount Veeder 1993 • $25 • (10/15/1995)

90 **Robert Mondavi** Cabernet Sauvignon Napa Valley Reserve 1993 • $54 Ⓐ • (11/30/1996) • CS

90 **S. Anderson** Cabernet Sauvignon Stags Leap District Richard Chambers Vineyard 1993 • $38 Ⓐ • (11/30/1996)

90 **Silver Oak** Cabernet Sauvignon Alexander Valley 1993 • $70 Ⓐ • (9/30/1997) • CS

90 **Silverado Vineyards** Cabernet Sauvignon Napa Valley Limited Reserve 1993 • $81 Ⓐ • (2/28/1997)

90 **Spottswoode** Cabernet Sauvignon Napa Valley 1993 • $51 Ⓐ • (11/15/1996)

90 **St. Clement** Cabernet Sauvignon Howell Mountain White Cottage Ranch 1993 • $45 • (11/15/1996)

90 **St. Francis** Cabernet Sauvignon Sonoma Valley Reserve 1993 • $29 • (12/15/1996)

90 **Stag's Leap Wine Cellars** Cabernet Sauvignon Napa Valley S.L.V. 1993 • $40 • (11/15/1996)

90 **Steele** Cabernet Sauvignon Anderson Valley 1993 • $22 • (4/30/1996)

90 **The Hess Collection** Cabernet Sauvignon Napa Valley Reserve 1993 • $58 Ⓐ • (5/15/1998)

90 **Tom Eddy** Cabernet Sauvignon Napa Valley 1993 • $40 • (10/31/1997)

90 **Truchard** Cabernet Sauvignon Napa Valley Carneros 1993 • $22 • (11/15/1996)

90 **Vine Cliff** Cabernet Sauvignon Napa Valley Oakville Estate 1993 • $30 • (11/15/1996)

1992 California Cabernet
Vintage Rating: 93

98 **Groth** Cabernet Sauvignon Napa Valley Reserve 1992 • $166 Ⓐ • (4/30/1996) • CS

96 **Araujo** Cabernet Sauvignon Napa Valley Eisele Vineyard 1992 • $234 Ⓐ • (11/15/1995) • CS

96 **Flora Springs** Cabernet Sauvignon Napa Valley Rutherford Reserve 1992 • $40 • (11/15/1995) • HR

95 **Beringer** Cabernet Sauvignon Napa Valley Private Reserve 1992 • $86 Ⓐ • (11/15/1995) • CS

95 **St. Clement** Oroppas Napa Valley 1992 • $25 • (9/30/1994) • CS

94 **Dalla Valle** Maya Napa Valley 1992 • $416 Ⓐ • (12/15/1995)

94 **Diamond Creek** Cabernet Sauvignon Napa Valley Lake 1992 • $311 Ⓐ • (6/15/1998)

94 **Lewis** Cabernet Sauvignon Napa Valley Oakville Ranch 1992 • $30 • (11/30/1995) • HR

94 **Screaming Eagle** Cabernet Sauvignon Napa Valley 1992 • $1,079 Ⓐ • (2/29/1996)

94 **Stag's Leap Wine Cellars** Cask 23 Napa Valley 1992 • $121 Ⓐ • (12/15/1995) • CS

94 **The Hess Collection** Cabernet Sauvignon Napa Valley 1992 • $30 Ⓐ • (11/15/1995) • SS

93 **Abreu** Cabernet Sauvignon Napa Valley Madrona Ranch 1992 • $95 Ⓐ • (1/01/1998)

93 **Anderson's Conn Valley** Cabernet Sauvignon Napa Valley Estate Reserve 1992 • $29 Ⓐ • (11/15/1995) • HR

93 **Beringer** Cabernet Sauvignon Napa Valley Chabot Vineyard 1992 • $100 • (12/15/1996)

93 **Cronin** Concerto Stags Leap District Robinson Vineyard 1992 • $17 • (4/30/1996)

93 **Etude** Cabernet Sauvignon Napa Valley 1992 • $30 • (11/30/1995) • HR

93 **Far Niente** Cabernet Sauvignon Napa Valley 1992 • $45 • (11/15/1995) • HR

93 **Forman** Cabernet Sauvignon Napa Valley 1992 • $27 Ⓐ • (6/15/1995) • CS

93 **Freemark Abbey** Cabernet Sauvignon Napa Valley Bosché 1992 • $32 • (9/30/1997) • CS

93 **Heitz** Cabernet Sauvignon Napa Valley Martha's Vineyard 1992 • $79 Ⓐ • (5/31/1997) • CS

93 **Paul Hobbs** Cabernet Sauvignon Napa Valley Carneros Hyde Vineyard 1992 • $30 • (12/15/1995) • HR

93 **Shafer** Cabernet Sauvignon Stags Leap District Hillside Select 1992 • $133 Ⓐ • (11/15/1996) • HR

93 **Silver Oak** Cabernet Sauvignon Napa Valley 1992 • $98 Ⓐ • (11/15/1996) • CS

93 **Simi** Cabernet Sauvignon Alexander Valley Reserve 1992 • $40 • (11/15/1996) • CS

93 **Whitehall Lane** Cabernet Sauvignon Napa Valley Morisoli Vineyard 1992 • $28 • (10/15/1995) • HR

92 **A. Rafanelli** Cabernet Sauvignon Dry Creek Valley 1992 • $17 • (9/30/1995) • SS

92 **Altamura** Cabernet Sauvignon Napa Valley 1992 • $28 • (8/31/1996) • HR

92 **Arrowood** Cabernet Sauvignon Sonoma County 1992 • $36 Ⓐ • (11/15/1995) • HR

92 **Arrowood** Cabernet Sauvignon Sonoma County Réserve Spéciale 1992 • $35 • (12/15/1995) • HR

92 **Caymus** Cabernet Sauvignon Napa Valley Special Selection 1992 • $136 Ⓐ • (5/15/1996) • CS

92 **Chateau Montelena** Cabernet Sauvignon Napa Valley The Montelena Estate 1972-1992 Anniversary 1992 • $36 • (11/15/1999)

92 **Chateau St. Jean** Cabernet Sauvignon Sonoma County Reserve 1992 • $45 • (9/30/1997)

92 **Chimney Rock** Reserve Stags Leap District 1992 • $30 • (12/15/1995)

92 **Colgin** Cabernet Sauvignon Napa Valley Herb Lamb Vineyard 1992 • $348 Ⓐ • (10/15/1995) • HR

92 **Corison** Cabernet Sauvignon Napa Valley 1992 • $28 • (11/30/1995) • CS

92 **Cosentino** M. Coz Meritage Napa Valley 1992 • $45 • (12/15/1995)

92 **Dalla Valle** Cabernet Sauvignon Napa Valley 1992 • $95 Ⓐ • (12/15/1995) • CS

92 **Diamond Creek** Cabernet Sauvignon Napa Valley Gravelly Meadow 1992 • $78 Ⓐ • (6/15/1998)

92 **Diamond Creek** Cabernet Sauvignon Napa Valley Volcanic Hill 1992 • $72 Ⓐ • (6/15/1998)

92 **E. & J. Gallo** Cabernet Sauvignon Northern Sonoma Estate Bottled 1992 • $45 • (11/15/1996)

92 **Flora Springs** Trilogy Napa Valley 1992 • $27 • (11/30/1995) • CS

92 **Justin** Isosceles Reserve San Luis Obispo County 1992 • $25 • (12/15/1995) • HR

92 **Niebaum-Coppola** Rubicon Rutherford 1992 • $50 • (5/31/1997)

92 **Opus One** Napa Valley 1992 • $149 Ⓐ • (2/29/2000)

92 **St. Francis** Cabernet Sauvignon Sonoma County Reserve 1992 • $24 • (11/30/1995) • HR

92 **Stonestreet** Legacy Alexander Valley 1992 • $35 • (9/30/1995) • CS

92 **Villa Mt. Eden** Cabernet Sauvignon Mendocino Signature Series 1992 • $45 • (3/31/1995) • HR

92 **Whitehall Lane** Cabernet Sauvignon Napa Valley Reserve 1992 • $23 • (10/15/1995) • HR

91 **Diamond Creek** Cabernet Sauvignon Napa Valley Red Rock Terrace 1992 • $77 Ⓐ • (6/15/1998)

91 **Elan** Cabernet Sauvignon Atlas Peak 1992 • $30 • (11/30/1997)

91 **Ferrari-Carano** Reserve Red Sonoma County 1992 • $47 • (9/30/1997)

91 **Groth** Cabernet Sauvignon Napa Valley 1992 • $20 • (9/30/1995) • CS

Key: SS—Spectator Selection. CS—Cellar Selection. HR—Highly Recommended. $NA—Price not available. (BT)—Barrel tasting. Ⓐ—Auction Price.
Dates in parentheses represent the issues in which the ratings were published.

91 **Harlan Estate** Napa Valley 1992 • $285 Ⓐ • (11/15/1996)

91 **Judd's Hill** Cabernet Sauvignon Napa Valley 1992 • $26 • (12/15/1995)

91 **Kendall-Jackson** Cabernet Sauvignon California Grand Reserve 1992 • $35 • (11/30/1995)

91 **Kenwood** Cabernet Sauvignon Sonoma Valley Artist Series 1992 • $31 Ⓐ • (12/15/1996)

91 **Peju** Cabernet Sauvignon Napa Valley HB Vineyard 1992 • $35 • (12/15/1995)

91 **Philip Togni** Cabernet Sauvignon Napa Valley 1992 • $76 Ⓐ • (11/15/1994) • CS

91 **Pine Ridge** Cabernet Sauvignon Napa Valley Rutherford Cuvée 1992 • $16 • (11/15/1995) • SS

91 **Ridge** Monte Bello Santa Cruz Mountains 1992 • $80 • (11/15/1996) • CS

91 **Robert Mondavi** Cabernet Sauvignon Napa Valley Oakville District 1992 • $28 • (12/15/1995)

91 **Robert Mondavi** Cabernet Sauvignon Napa Valley Reserve 1992 • $58 Ⓐ • (7/31/1995) • CS

91 **Shafer** Cabernet Sauvignon Stags Leap District 1992 • $22 • (9/30/1995) • CS

91 **Staglin** Cabernet Sauvignon Napa Valley 1992 • $28 • (12/15/1995)

91 **Stag's Leap Wine Cellars** Cabernet Sauvignon Napa Valley Fay 1992 • $56 Ⓐ • (12/15/1995) • CS

91 **Stonestreet** Cabernet Sauvignon Alexander Valley 1992 • $25 • (10/31/1995) • HR

90 **Burgess** Cabernet Sauvignon Napa Valley Vintage Selection 1992 • $22 • (11/15/1996) • SS

90 **Chateau Montelena** Cabernet Sauvignon Napa Valley Calistoga Cuvée 1992 • $15 • (11/15/1994) • SS

90 **Conn Creek** Anthology Napa Valley 1992 • $30 • (12/15/1995)

90 **Cornerstone** Cabernet Sauvignon Howell Mountain Beatty Ranch 1992 • $33 • (12/15/1995)

90 **Diamond Creek** Cabernet Sauvignon Napa Valley Gravelly Meadow-Lake 1992 • $NA • (6/15/1998)

90 **Duckhorn** Cabernet Sauvignon Napa Valley 1992 • $24 • (10/31/1995) • SS

90 **Guenoc** Cabernet Sauvignon Napa Valley Beckstoffer IV Vineyard Reserve 1992 • $40 • (12/15/1995)

90 **Guenoc** Cabernet Sauvignon Napa Valley Bella Vista Vineyard Reserve 1992 • $25 • (12/15/1995)

90 **Gundlach Bundschu** Cabernet Sauvignon Sonoma Valley Rhinefarm Vineyards Vintage Reserve 1992 • $30 • (11/15/1996)

90 **Harrison** Cabernet Sauvignon Napa Valley 1992 • $33 • (11/15/1995)

90 **Hartwell** Cabernet Sauvignon Stags Leap District 1992 • $50 • (11/15/1995)

90 **Heitz** Cabernet Sauvignon Napa Valley Trailside Vineyard 1992 • $48 • (9/30/1997)

90 **Jarvis** Cabernet Sauvignon Napa Valley 1992 • $72 Ⓐ • (8/31/1995)

90 **Joseph Phelps** Insignia Napa Valley 1992 • $74 Ⓐ • (9/30/1995) • CS

90 **Mount Eden** Cabernet Sauvignon Santa Cruz Mountains Old Vine Reserve 1992 • $35 • (6/15/1996)

90 **Oakville Ranch** Cabernet Sauvignon Napa Valley 1992 • $24 • (12/15/1995)

90 **Peter Michael** Les Pavots Cabernet Sauvignon Knights Valley 1992 • $53 Ⓐ • (12/15/1995)

90 **Pine Ridge** Cabernet Sauvignon Stags Leap District 1992 • $31 • (12/15/1995)

90 **Raymond** Cabernet Sauvignon Napa Valley Private Reserve 1992 • $26 • (11/15/1996)

90 **Sequoia Grove** Cabernet Sauvignon Napa Valley 1992 • $18 • (7/31/1995) • SS

90 **Signorello** Cabernet Sauvignon Napa Valley Founder's Reserve 1992 • $32 • (9/15/1995) • CS

90 **Silver Oak** Cabernet Sauvignon Alexander Valley 1992 • $87 Ⓐ • (11/15/1996)

90 **Silverado Vineyards** Cabernet Sauvignon Napa Valley 1992 • $19 • (3/31/1995) • SS

90 **Spottswoode** Cabernet Sauvignon Napa Valley 1992 • $78 Ⓐ • (11/30/1995) • CS

90 **St. Clement** Cabernet Sauvignon Napa Valley 1992 • $24 • (10/31/1995)

90 **Swanson** Cabernet Sauvignon Napa Valley 1992 • $22 • (12/15/1995)

90 **The Hess Collection** Cabernet Sauvignon Napa Valley Reserve 1992 • $39 • (11/15/1996)

90 **Thomas Fogarty** Cabernet Sauvignon Napa Valley Vallerga Vineyards 1992 • $25 • (4/30/1996)

90 **Zia** Cabernet Sauvignon Napa Valley 1992 • $24 • (4/30/1996)

1991 California Cabernet
Vintage Rating: 94

99 **Caymus** Cabernet Sauvignon Napa Valley Special Selection 1991 • $187 Ⓐ • (4/15/1995) • CS

97 **Chateau Montelena** Cabernet Sauvignon Napa Valley The Montelena Estate 1991 • $40 • (11/15/1999)

97 **Flora Springs** Cabernet Sauvignon Napa Valley Reserve 1991 • $33 • (9/30/1994) • CS

97 **Opus One** Napa Valley 1991 • $174 Ⓐ • (2/29/2000)

95 **Groth** Cabernet Sauvignon Napa Valley Reserve 1991 • $142 Ⓐ • (4/15/1995) • CS

94 **Beringer** Cabernet Sauvignon Napa Valley Private Reserve 1991 • $93 Ⓐ • (3/31/1995) • CS

94 **Diamond Creek** Cabernet Sauvignon Napa Valley Red Rock Terrace 1991 • $25 • (6/15/1998)

94 **Diamond Creek** Cabernet Sauvignon Napa Valley Red Rock Terrace Microclimate 3 1991 • $50 • (11/15/1993) • CS

94 **Guenoc** Cabernet Sauvignon Napa Valley Beckstoffer Vineyard Reserve 1991 • $35 • (9/30/1994) • CS

94 **Martin Ray** Cabernet Sauvignon Napa Valley 1991 • $28 • (11/15/1994) • HR

94 **Spottswoode** Cabernet Sauvignon Napa Valley 1991 • $81 Ⓐ • (12/31/1998)

94 **St. Clement** Oroppas Napa Valley 1991 • $22 • (10/31/1993) • HR

93 **Abreu** Cabernet Sauvignon Napa Valley Madrona Ranch 1991 • $45 • (1/01/1998)

93 **Caymus** Cabernet Sauvignon Napa Valley 1991 • $66 Ⓐ • (11/15/1994) • SS

93 **Conn Creek** Anthology Napa Valley 1991 • $30 • (9/30/1994) • CS

93 **Cornerstone** Cabernet Sauvignon Howell Mountain Beatty Ranch 1991 • $33 • (11/15/1994) • HR

93 **Diamond Creek** Cabernet Sauvignon Napa Valley Volcanic Hill 1991 • $86 Ⓐ • (6/15/1998)

93 **Diamond Creek** Cabernet Sauvignon Napa Valley Volcanic Hill Microclimate 4 1991 • $50 • (11/15/1993) • CS

93 **Dominus Estate** Napa Valley Napanook Vineyard 1991 • $154 Ⓐ • (11/15/1995) • CS

93 **Judd's Hill** Cabernet Sauvignon Napa Valley 1991 • $24 • (9/30/1994) • SS

93 **Newton** Cabernet Sauvignon Napa County 1991 • $NA • (1/01/1997)

93 **Shafer** Cabernet Sauvignon Stags Leap District Hillside Select 1991 • $91 Ⓐ • (11/15/1995) • CS

93 **Silver Oak** Cabernet Sauvignon Napa Valley Bonny's Vineyard 1991 • $101 Ⓐ • (9/15/1996) • CS

93 **Silverado Vineyards** Cabernet Sauvignon Napa Valley Limited Reserve 1991 • $77 Ⓐ • (11/15/1994) • CS

93 **Silverado Vineyards** Cabernet Sauvignon Napa Valley Stags Leap District 1991 • $17 • (4/30/1994) • SS

92 **Chateau St. Jean** Cabernet Sauvignon Sonoma County Reserve 1991 • $39 • (11/15/1996)

92 **Clos du Bois** Cabernet Sauvignon Alexander Valley Winemaker's Reserve 1991 • $30 • (10/15/1994) • CS

92 **Dalla Valle** Cabernet Sauvignon Napa Valley 1991 • $99 Ⓐ • (11/15/1994) • SS

92 **Diamond Creek** Cabernet Sauvignon Napa Valley Gravelly Meadow 1991 • $NA • (6/15/1998)

92 **Diamond Creek** Cabernet Sauvignon Napa Valley Volcanic Hill Microclimate 1991 • $NA • (6/15/1998)

92 **Hartwell** Cabernet Sauvignon Stags Leap District 1991 • $86 Ⓐ • (11/15/1994)

92 **Oakville Ranch** Cabernet Sauvignon Napa Valley Reserve 1991 • $32 • (5/15/1995) • HR

92 **Pride** Cabernet Sauvignon Napa Valley 1991 • $18 • (5/15/1994) • HR

92 **Simi** Cabernet Sauvignon Alexander Valley Reserve 1991 • $53 Ⓐ • (10/15/1995) • HR

92 **Stag's Leap Wine Cellars** Cask 23 Napa Valley 1991 • $157 Ⓐ • (12/31/1994) • CS

92 **The Hess Collection** Cabernet Sauvignon Napa Valley 1991 • $18 • (11/15/1994) • SS

91 **Arrowood** Cabernet Sauvignon Sonoma County 1991 • $25 • (9/30/1994) • SS

91 **B.R. Cohn** Cabernet Sauvignon Sonoma Valley Olive Hill Vineyard 1991 • $28 • (4/15/1995) • HR

91 **Buehler** Cabernet Sauvignon Napa Valley Reserve 1991 • $25 • (9/30/1995)

91 **Chateau Souverain** Cabernet Sauvignon Alexander Valley Winemaker's Reserve 1991 • $14 • (10/31/1994) • HR

91 **Chateau St. Jean** Cabernet Sauvignon Sonoma County Cinq Cépages 1991 • $18 • (11/15/1995) • HR

91 **Dunn** Cabernet Sauvignon Howell Mountain 1991 • $96 Ⓐ • (12/15/1995) • CS

91 **E. & J. Gallo** Cabernet Sauvignon Northern Sonoma Estate Bottled 1991 • $50 • (11/15/1994) • HR

91 **Eberle** Cabernet Sauvignon Paso Robles Reserve 1991 • $35 • (11/15/1997)

91 **Geyser Peak** Reserve Alexandre Alexander Valley 1991 • $30 • (7/31/1994) • CS

91 **Guenoc** Langtry Meritage Red California 1991 • $35 • (9/30/1994) • HR

91 **Heitz** Cabernet Sauvignon Napa Valley Martha's Vineyard 1991 • $75 Ⓐ • (4/30/1996) • CS

91 **Kendall-Jackson** Cardinale Meritage California 1991 • $60 • (12/15/1995)

91 **Niebaum-Coppola** Rubicon Rutherford 1991 • $40 • (9/15/1996) • CS

91 **Oakville Ranch** Cabernet Sauvignon Napa Valley Lewis Select 1991 • $28 • (9/30/1994)

91 **Paul Hobbs** Cabernet Sauvignon Napa Valley Carneros Hyde Vineyard 1991 • $30 • (10/31/1994) • HR

91 **Ridge** Monte Bello Santa Cruz Mountains 1991 • $75 • (11/15/1995) • CS

91 **Robert Pecota** Cabernet Sauvignon Napa Valley Kara's Vineyard 1991 • $20 • (9/15/1994) • HR

91 **Rosenthal-The Malibu Estate** Cabernet Sauvignon California 1991 • $20 • (11/15/1994)

91 **S. Anderson** Cabernet Sauvignon Stags Leap District Richard Chambers Vineyard 1991 • $43 Ⓐ • (12/31/1994) • HR

91 **Sequoia Grove** Cabernet Sauvignon Napa Valley Estate Reserve 1991 • $26 • (7/31/1994)

91 **Silver Oak** Cabernet Sauvignon Alexander Valley 1991 • $86 Ⓐ • (11/15/1995) • HR

91 **Stonestreet** Legacy Alexander Valley 1991 • $35 • (11/15/1994)

91 **The Hess Collection** Cabernet Sauvignon Napa Valley Reserve 1991 • $39 • (4/30/1996)

91 **Viader** Napa Valley 1991 • $28 • (11/15/1994) • HR

90 **A. Rafanelli** Cabernet Sauvignon Dry Creek Valley 1991 • $15 • (9/15/1994) • SS

90 **Araujo** Cabernet Sauvignon Napa Valley Eisele Vineyard 1991 • $259 Ⓐ • (10/15/1994) • CS

90 **Chimney Rock** Elevage Stags Leap District 1991 • $30 • (11/15/1994)

90 **Cosentino** Cabernet Sauvignon Napa Valley Reserve 1991 • $30 • (12/15/1995)

90 **Dalla Valle** Maya Napa Valley 1991 • $368 Ⓐ • (11/15/1994)

90 **Diamond Creek** Cabernet Sauvignon Napa Valley Gravelly Meadow Lake Blend 1991 • $50 • (11/15/1993)

90 **Ferrari-Carano** Reserve Red Sonoma County 1991 • $47 • (11/15/1996)

90 **Ferrari-Carano** Siena Sonoma County 1991 • $20 • (11/15/1993)

90 **Foxen** Cabernet Sauvignon Santa Barbara County 1991 • $20 • (2/28/1994) • HR

90 **Freemark Abbey** Cabernet Sauvignon Napa Valley Bosché 1991 • $24 • (11/30/1996)

90 **Gallo of Sonoma** Cabernet Sauvignon Sonoma County 1991 • $12 • (3/31/1995) • SS

90 **Geyser Peak** Cabernet Sauvignon Alexander Valley Reserve 1991 • $20 • (3/15/1994) • SS

90 **Groth** Cabernet Sauvignon Napa Valley 1991 • $18 • (10/15/1994) • SS

90 **Harlan Estate** Napa Valley 1991 • $334 Ⓐ • (11/30/1995)

90 **Joseph Phelps** Cabernet Sauvignon Napa Valley Backus Vineyard 1991 • $35 • (10/15/1994) • CS

90 **Joseph Phelps** Insignia Napa Valley 1991 • $78 Ⓐ • (5/31/1995) • CS

90 **Kistler** Cabernet Sauvignon Sonoma Valley Kistler Estate Vineyard 1991 • $30 • (6/15/1995) • HR

90 **La Jota** Cabernet Sauvignon Howell Mountain 10th Anniversary Release 1991 • $38 • (6/15/1994) • CS

90 **Laurel Glen** Cabernet Sauvignon Sonoma Mountain Counterpoint 1991 • $15 • (11/30/1993) • SS

90 **Merryvale** Profile Napa Valley 1991 • $36 • (12/15/1995)

90 **Paradigm** Cabernet Sauvignon Napa Valley 1991 • $26 • (11/15/1994)

90 **Peachy Canyon** Cabernet Sauvignon Paso Robles 1991 • $18 • (11/15/1993)

90 **Philip Togni** Cabernet Sauvignon Napa Valley 1991 • $72 Ⓐ • (11/15/1993)

90 **Robert Mondavi** Cabernet Sauvignon Napa Valley Reserve 1991 • $77 Ⓐ • (11/15/1994)

90 **Robert Mondavi** Cabernet Sauvignon Napa Valley Unfiltered 1991 • $18 • (11/15/1994) • SS

90 **Rocking Horse** Cabernet Sauvignon Stags Leap District Robinson Vineyard 1991 • $24 • (3/31/1994) • HR

90 **Rosenblum** Cabernet Sauvignon Napa Valley Holbrook Mitchell Vineyard 1991 • $14 • (10/31/1994) • HR

90 **Saddleback** Cabernet Sauvignon Napa Valley 1991 • $17 • (10/31/1994) • HR

Key: SS—Spectator Selection. CS—Cellar Selection. HR—Highly Recommended. $NA—Price not available. (BT)—Barrel tasting. Ⓐ—Auction Price.
Dates in parentheses represent the issues in which the ratings were published.

90 **Shafer** Cabernet Sauvignon Stags Leap District 1991 • $21 • (8/31/1994) • HR

90 **Signorello** Cabernet Sauvignon Napa Valley Founder's Reserve 1991 • $30 • (9/30/1994)

90 **Silver Oak** Cabernet Sauvignon Napa Valley 1991 • $91 Ⓐ • (11/15/1995)

90 **St. Clement** Cabernet Sauvignon Napa Valley 1991 • $23 • (9/30/1994) • SS

90 **Sterling** Reserve Napa Valley 1991 • $30 • (11/15/1994)

90 **Tom Eddy** Cabernet Sauvignon Napa Valley 1991 • $32 • (4/30/1995)

90 **V. Sattui** Cabernet Sauvignon Napa Valley Mario's Reserve Stock 1991 • $35 • (11/15/1994)

1990 California Cabernet
Vintage Rating: 95

98 **Caymus** Cabernet Sauvignon Napa Valley Special Selection 1990 • $197 Ⓐ • (3/31/1994) • CS

97 **Silverado Vineyards** Cabernet Sauvignon Napa Valley Limited Reserve 1990 • $86 Ⓐ • (10/31/1993) • CS

96 **Opus One** Napa Valley 1990 • $153 Ⓐ • (2/29/2000)

95 **Chateau St. Jean** Cabernet Sauvignon Sonoma County Reserve 1990 • $38 • (4/30/1996) • CS

94 **Chateau Montelena** Cabernet Sauvignon Napa Valley The Montelena Estate 1990 • $30 • (11/15/1999)

94 **Groth** Cabernet Sauvignon Napa Valley Reserve 1990 • $107 Ⓐ • (11/15/1994) • CS

94 **Mount Veeder** Cabernet Sauvignon Napa Valley 1990 • $15 • (10/31/1993) • SS

93 **Cain** Five Napa Valley 1990 • $34 • (9/15/1994) • CS

93 **Dalla Valle** Cabernet Sauvignon Napa Valley 1990 • $80 Ⓐ • (9/30/1993) • HR

93 **Diamond Creek** Cabernet Sauvignon Napa Valley Volcanic Hill 1990 • $NA • (6/15/1998)

93 **Duckhorn** Cabernet Sauvignon Napa Valley 1990 • $65 Ⓐ • (7/31/1993) • CS

93 **E. & J. Gallo** Cabernet Sauvignon Northern Sonoma Estate Bottled 1990 • $60 • (10/31/1993) • CS

93 **Oakville Ranch** Cabernet Sauvignon Napa Valley 1990 • $23 • (10/15/1993) • HR

92 **Beringer** Cabernet Sauvignon Napa Valley Private Reserve 1990 • $88 Ⓐ • (11/15/1994) • CS

92 **Cosentino** M. Coz Meritage Napa Valley 1990 • $45 • (11/15/1993)

92 **Diamond Creek** Cabernet Sauvignon Napa Valley Lake 1990 • $192 Ⓐ • (6/15/1998)

92 **Dunn** Cabernet Sauvignon Napa Valley 1990 • $61 Ⓐ • (11/15/1993) • CS

92 **Guenoc** Cabernet Sauvignon Napa Valley Beckstoffer Vineyard Reserve 1990 • $35 • (11/15/1993) • HR

92 **Mount Veeder** Reserve Napa Valley 1990 • $25 • (9/15/1994) • CS

92 **Philip Togni** Cabernet Sauvignon Napa Valley 1990 • $68 Ⓐ • (11/15/1992)

92 **Signorello** Cabernet Sauvignon Napa Valley Founder's Reserve 1990 • $30 • (10/15/1993)

92 **Stag's Leap Wine Cellars** Cask 23 Napa Valley 1990 • $117 Ⓐ • (10/31/1993) • CS

91 **Arrowood** Cabernet Sauvignon Sonoma County 1990 • $24 • (10/31/1993) • SS

91 **Clos Pegase** Cabernet Sauvignon Napa Valley 1990 • $17 • (11/15/1993) • SS

91 **Corison** Cabernet Sauvignon Napa Valley 1990 • $38 Ⓐ • (10/15/1993) • HR

91 **Dominus Estate** Napa Valley 1990 • $143 Ⓐ • (6/30/1994) • SS

91 **Ferrari-Carano** Reserve Red Sonoma County 1990 • $47 • (11/30/1995)

91 **Guenoc** Langtry Meritage Red Lake County 1990 • $35 • (11/15/1993) • HR

91 **Guenoc** Meritage Red Lake County 1990 • $15 • (11/15/1993) • SS

91 **Harrison** Cabernet Sauvignon Napa Valley Reserve 1990 • $40 • (10/15/1994)

91 **Heitz** Cabernet Sauvignon Napa Valley Trailside Vineyard 1990 • $45 • (10/15/1995) • CS

91 **Kendall-Jackson** Cardinale Meritage California 1990 • $50 • (10/15/1994) • HR

91 **Livingston** Cabernet Sauvignon Napa Valley Moffett Vineyard 1990 • $30 • (11/15/1993) • HR

91 **Robert Mondavi** Cabernet Sauvignon Napa Valley Reserve 1990 • $67 Ⓐ • (10/31/1993) • HR

91 **Rocking Horse** Cabernet Sauvignon Stags Leap District Robinson Vineyard 1990 • $22 • (2/15/1993)

91 **Silver Oak** Cabernet Sauvignon Napa Valley 1990 • $270 Ⓐ • (11/15/1994) • CS

91 **St. Francis** Cabernet Sauvignon Sonoma County Reserve 1990 • $24 • (9/30/1993) • HR

91 **Stag's Leap Wine Cellars** Cabernet Sauvignon Napa Valley 1990 • $18 • (5/15/1993) • SS

91 **Viader** Napa Valley 1990 • $25 • (7/15/1993) • HR

91 **Vichon** Cabernet Sauvignon Stags Leap District 1990 • $24 • (11/15/1993) • HR

90 **A. Rafanelli** Cabernet Sauvignon Dry Creek Valley 1990 • $15 • (9/15/1993) • HR

90 **Anderson's Conn Valley** Cabernet Sauvignon Napa Valley Estate Reserve 1990 • $25 Ⓐ • (11/15/1993)

90 **B.R. Cohn** Cabernet Sauvignon Sonoma Valley Olive Hill Vineyard 1990 • $25 • (11/15/1993)

90 **Beaulieu Vineyard** Cabernet Sauvignon Napa Valley Georges de Latour Private Reserve 1990 • $60 Ⓐ • (2/29/2000)

90 **Beringer** Cabernet Sauvignon Knights Valley 1990 • $13 • (11/15/1993) • SS

90 **Caymus** Cabernet Sauvignon Napa Valley 1990 • $65 Ⓐ • (12/15/1993) • SS

90 **Chateau Souverain** Cabernet Sauvignon Alexander Valley 1990 • $11 • (11/15/1993) • SS

90 **Estancia** Meritage Alexander Valley 1990 • $14 • (10/15/1993) • SS

90 **Gary Farrell** Cabernet Sauvignon Sonoma County Ladi's Vineyard 1990 • $18 • (11/15/1992)

90 **Geyser Peak** Cabernet Sauvignon Alexander Valley Reserve 1990 • $15 • (6/15/1993) • HR

90 **Geyser Peak** Reserve Alexandre Alexander Valley 1990 • $30 • (11/15/1993)

90 **Grace Family** Cabernet Sauvignon Napa Valley 1990 • $311 Ⓐ • (8/31/1993)

90 **Groth** Cabernet Sauvignon Napa Valley 1990 • $17 • (9/30/1993) • SS

90 **Heitz** Cabernet Sauvignon Napa Valley 1990 • $36 Ⓐ • (4/30/1995) • HR

90 **Heitz** Cabernet Sauvignon Napa Valley Martha's Vineyard 1990 • $87 Ⓐ • (4/30/1995) • CS

90 **Kendall-Jackson** Cabernet Sauvignon California Grand Reserve 1990 • $30 • (11/15/1993)

90 **Markham** Cabernet Sauvignon Napa Valley 1990 • $17 • (11/15/1993) • SS

90 **Niebaum-Coppola** Rubicon Napa Valley 1990 • $35 • (12/15/1995)

90 **Pahlmeyer** Caldwell Vineyard Napa Valley 1990 • $54 Ⓐ • (10/15/1993)

90 **Raymond** Meritage Private Reserve Napa Valley 1990 • $40 • (10/31/1994) • HR

90 **Robert Mondavi** Cabernet Sauvignon Napa Valley 1990 • $62 Ⓐ • (10/31/1993) • SS

90 **Rombauer** Le Meilleur du Chai Napa Valley 1990 • $40 • (8/31/1997)

90 **S. Anderson** Cabernet Sauvignon Stags Leap District Richard Chambers Vineyard 1990 • $38 Ⓐ • (11/15/1993)

90 **Sequoia Grove** Cabernet Sauvignon Napa Valley 1990 • $16 • (3/31/1994) • SS

90 **Sequoia Grove** Cabernet Sauvignon Napa Valley Estate Reserve 1990 • $25 • (12/15/1993)

90 **Shafer** Cabernet Sauvignon Stags Leap District 1990 • $52 Ⓐ • (11/15/1993)

90 **Shafer** Cabernet Sauvignon Stags Leap District Hillside Select 1990 • $153 Ⓐ • (12/15/1995)

90 **Silverado Vineyards** Cabernet Sauvignon Napa Valley Stags Leap District 1990 • $17 • (6/30/1993) • HR

90 **Spottswoode** Cabernet Sauvignon Napa Valley 1990 • $103 Ⓐ • (12/31/1998)

90 **St. Clement** Cabernet Sauvignon Napa Valley 1990 • $22 • (10/31/1993)

90 **The Hess Collection** Cabernet Sauvignon Napa Valley 1990 • $18 • (4/15/1994) • CS

90 **The Hess Collection** Cabernet Sauvignon Napa Valley Reserve 1990 • $38 • (11/15/1994)

Wynns Coonawarra Estate
in South Australia.

The Main Listings

Wines by Country and Producer

This is the *Ultimate Guide's* main listings section. Here you will find "nuts-and-bolts" information—producer, appellation, vintage, price, date of rating, and score—on over 40,000 wines reviewed by *Wine Spectator* since 1984. Listings of the more than 20,000 wines tasted between July 1998 and June 2000 also contain descriptive notes that will help you get a sense of what the wine actually tastes like.

Turn the page for detailed information that will help you to understand and make use of our listings.

How to Use These Listings

The wine ratings contained in this guide are taken from the tasting results that have been published in *Wine Spectator* since 1984. While the majority of the ratings in this book are quite recent, some ratings are not as current.

While we feel that these older ratings can be very useful in presenting a vertical representation of a particular wine, or a horizontal representation of a particular vintage in a given region, we also feel the need to caution you to pay particular attention to the date on each of the ratings. This will tell you how current the rating is.

Ratings and tasting notes included here are by *Wine Spectator's* senior editors, and include tastings conducted by an editor as part of the research for one of our Wine Spectator Press books.

Wine Spectator's 100-Point Scale

95-100—Classic; a great wine

90-94—Outstanding; superior character and style

80-89—Good to very good; wine with special qualities

70-79—Average; drinkable wine that may have minor flaws

60-69—Below average; drinkable but not recommended

50-59—Poor; undrinkable, not recommended

There is one other type of rating you will see in this book, primarily in the listings for red Bordeaux and California Cabernet. These are ratings based on barrel tastings. which are tastings conducted on wines before they have been bottled and released for sale. These are, by definition, very preliminary ratings and should be treated as such. Many things can happen to a wine between the time it is tasted in barrel and the time that you purchase it at your local store; wines can improve or decline during that time, and can show signs of poor shipping or storage conditions. Barrel-tasting ratings are indicated by the code (BT) and by a range of scores (e.g. 85-89).

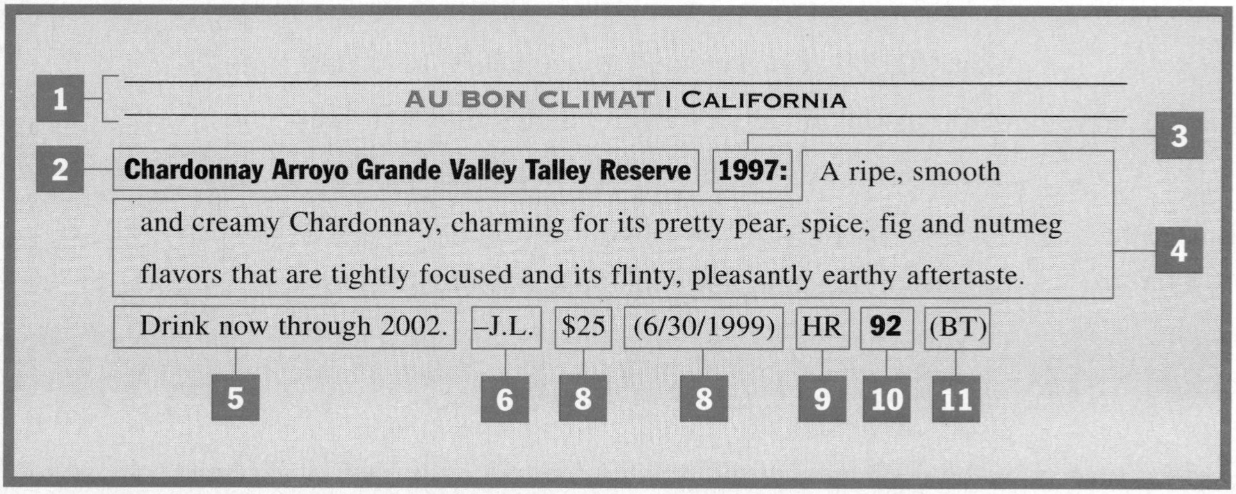

1 AU BON CLIMAT | CALIFORNIA

2 **Chardonnay Arroyo Grande Valley Talley Reserve** 3 **1997:** 4 A ripe, smooth and creamy Chardonnay, charming for its pretty pear, spice, fig and nutmeg flavors that are tightly focused and its flinty, pleasantly earthy aftertaste.

Drink now through 2002. (5) –J.L. (6) $25 (8) (6/30/1999) (8) HR (9) **92** (10) (BT) (11)

The Ratings: Piece by Piece

Because of the very large number of ratings presented here, each wine listing must be as brief as possible. Therefore, we have used abbreviations and shortcuts throughout this book.

A key to these symbols can be found in the lower left-hand corner of every other left-hand page in the main listings. At left is a typical wine listing and an explanation for each of its elements.

1. Producer's Name—The name of the winery or producer. For North American listings, the producer's state or province also appears.

Producers whose names are preceded by "Château," "Domaine," "Bodegas" and the like are listed by the name following these designations. For example, Château Margaux will be listed under "M" as "Margaux, Château." The United States and other English-speaking countries are an exception to this rule, however. (Thus, Chateau St. Jean in California is found under "C.")

Producers' names that include given names are listed alphabetically under the surname. For example, Robert Mondavi will be found under "M" as "Mondavi, Robert."

Producers' names that begin with English and foreign articles such as a, the, de, di, le, la, los, etc., are listed under the main word following the article. Thus, La Vieille Ferme is listed as "Vieille Ferme, La."

Producers' names that begin with "St." or "Ste." are alphabetized as though this word were spelled out. For example, "Saint Laurent, Château" follows "St.-Jovian."

2. Wine Type/Description—Contains the wine type and any varietal name, appellation, or other vineyard or special designation, such as Sonoma Valley or Cask 23.

3. Vintage—The year the wine was harvested and vinified.

4. Tasting Note—The tasting note for the wine, as published in *Wine Spectator* or on our Web site, **www.winespectator.com** (or, in rare cases, in a Wine Spectator Press book). These notes give the tasters' impressions of the wine, and thus present a more complete picture than the score alone.

5. Drinkability—Tasting notes may also include our estimate as to when a wine will be at its best.

6. Taster's Initials—Initials given here tell you which *Wine Spectator* editor wrote the tasting note and assigned the wine's score. The initials used are:

B.S.—Bruce Sanderson
H.S.—Harvey Steiman
J.L.—James Laube
J.S.—James Suckling
K.M.—Kim Marcus
P.M.—Per-Henrik Mansson
T.M.—Thomas Matthews

Notes that appear without taster's initials may have been rated by a tasting panel consisting of more than one editor.

7. Price Data—The wine's price information can come in three distinct forms:

- A simple price, such as $37, signifies the suggested retail price *on release*. Bottle age, scarcity and retailer markup can all influence a wine's price, so please note—**prices will vary.**
- A price followed by the symbol is an average of recent auction prices, for older or collectible wines.
- $NA means that no price data was available; it occurs typically with older wines, very new ones, and wines that are not imported into the U.S.

8. Date Tasted—The date of the issue of *Wine Spectator* in which the rating was first published. Wines are usually tasted within two months prior to this date.

In general, an issue date of the first of the month (e.g. 01/01/2000) indicates a note that was published only on **www.winespectator.com** and has never appeared in the magazine.

9. Special Ratings—The special designations used here are:

SS (Spectator Selection)—*Wine Spectator*'s highest recommendations in a given issue. Not necessarily the highest-scoring wines, they are the wines we think represent the most outstanding values when quality is balanced against price.

CS (Cellar Selection)—The wines we believe are the best candidates for addition to your cellar. We believe these wines will improve most with bottle age, and show the greatest potential as collectibles.

HR (Highly Recommended)—Other noteworthy wines selected from among the highest-scoring wines in a given issue. Price is not a consideration.

10. Score—This is the number, from *Wine Spectator*'s 100-point scale, that represents the taster's evaluation of the wine's quality relative to other wines.

Ratings are based on immediate quality, as well as on how good a wine will be when it's at its peak, regardless of how soon that will be.

A range of scores (90-94, for example) indicates a preliminary rating, and is used in conjunction with a barrel tasting.

11. Barrel Tasting—The code (BT) appearing after a range of scores indicates a barrel tasting, as described on the previous page.

Argentina

Although Argentina is the world's fifth-largest wine producer, less than a quarter of its production can be considered fine wine. Until fairly recently, Argentinean wineries focused on the uncritical domestic market, which accepted tired, oxidized wines of mediocre quality. However, that situation is changing rapidly, as Argentina adjusts its traditional practices and improves its wine in order to serve world markets. The new breed of Argentinean wines combines the best of New World-style fruit with the native flair for round, mellow, structures without excessive tannins.

1. Mendoza
2. San Rafael
3. Lujan de Cuyo
4. Rio Negro
5. La Rioja
6. Catamarca
7. Salta

REGIONS

Argentina's climate bears scant resemblance to that of its western neighbor, Chile, owing to the Andes mountain range, a huge barrier between the two. On the Chilean side, the Pacific ocean imposes a strong maritime effect, with cool breezes and ocean winds. The Argentinean side is much warmer, with less difference in temperature between day and night.

The hot, arid, Mendoza province has almost 75% of the country's 650,000 acres of vines and produces more than 90% of its fine wines, the vast majority of which are red. The abundant snowmelt from the Andes provides pure, clean water for irrigation, but also permits some growers to over-irrigate to get excessively large crops. In recent years, the Lujan de Cujo and San Rafael regions in Mendoza have attracted a significant foreign investment aimed at the production of quality wine. Many vineyards throughout Mendoza are now being planted at cooler, higher elevations to produce wines with better structure.

Although Mendoza dominates production, two smaller regions have carved out niches for themselves. South of Mendoza, in the province of the Rio Negro, average temperatures are quite brisk. Rio Negro produces crisp, almost Médoc-like reds and lively whites. North of Mendoza, the Catamarca, La Rioja and Salta regions produce the country's finest white wines. The vineyards are among the highest in the world (over 5,000 ft elevation). Here, the indigenous Torrontés grape variety produces highly aromatic, sensuous wines.

GRAPE VARIETIES

Most of the country's vineyards were first planted by Spanish and Italian immigrants late in the 19th century, and many important wineries date to that era. Not surprisingly, European grape varieties have been warmly embraced by Argentinean wineries. Chardonnay, Pinot Blanc, Riesling, Sauvignon Blanc and Sémillon have now joined the native Torrontés as quality white

Etchart's Bodega el Paraiso vineyard which lies about 6000 feet above sea level.

Andy Christodolo/Cephas

varieties. As for reds, Pinot Noir, Merlot, Syrah, Sangiovese and Cabernet Sauvignon are now widely planted and are also highly successful.

However, the grape that has attracted the most attention is Malbec. Although used largely as a blending grape in Bordeaux, Malbec truly comes into its own in the soil of Argentina. Many now consider Argentina the premier producer of this often-underrated variety. The best Argentinean Malbecs exhibit the grape's typically robust, meaty feel, along with rich plum and cassis flavors accented by traditional leather notes.

Argentina is successfully making the transition from a rustic past to a promising future. Consumers looking for distinctive character and good value will find much to like among Argentina's diverse offerings.

The Tupungato Valley region of Mendoza with the Andes mountains beyond.

Andy Christodolo/Cephas

AGRICOLA, LA

Cabernet Sauvignon Mendoza Uvas del Sol 1998: Dried cherry and leather flavors turn a bit tarry-tasting on the finish in this murky red.—K.M. • $9 • (3/31/2000) • **76**

Cabernet Sauvignon Mendoza Uvas del Sol 1997: Straightforward and fairly simple, this smooth red shows herbal and cherry flavors, with modest tannins and a short finish.—T.M. • $8 • (2/28/1999) • **78**

Cabernet Sauvignon Mendoza Uvas del Sol 1996: Simple and straightforward, with brown sugar, plum and berry flavors. Drink now.—K.M. • $8 • (9/15/1998) • **80**

Cabernet Sauvignon Mendoza Uvas del Sol Gaucho Reserve 1997: Sweet cherry and prune flavors in this modest red, with tarry notes on the finish.—K.M. • $13 • (3/31/2000) • **78**

Chardonnay Mendoza Uvas del Sol 1998: Rich and smooth, this ripe white shows buttery and light earth flavors. A bit dull, but light, lemony acidity keeps it fresh on the finish. Drink now.—T.M. • $8 • (2/28/1999) • **80**

Chardonnay Mendoza Uvas del Sol 1997: A bit dull, with modest green apple flavors and an earthy finish.—K.M. • $8 • (9/30/1998) • **76**

Malbec Mendoza Uvas del Sol 1998: Shows candied strawberry and rhubarb notes before turning thin on the finish. Tasted twice, with consistent notes.—K.M. • $9 • (3/31/2000) • **74**

Malbec Mendoza Uvas del Sol 1997: Round yet firm, this meaty red wraps gamy, smoky flavors around a firm core of tannins. Though modest in flavor, it has the balance and structure to match well with meat dishes. Drink now.—T.M. • $8 • (3/31/1999) • **80**

Malbec Mendoza Uvas del Sol 1996: A well-focused red, with good coffee, red plum and cassis flavors. Turns just a tad tough on the finish.—K.M. • $8 • (7/31/1998) • **82**

Malbec Mendoza Uvas del Sol 1995 • $8 • (5/15/1998) • **82**

Malbec Mendoza Uvas del Sol Gaucho Reserve 1997: Thin, stewy and volatile, this murky-colored red shows muddled root beer notes before its clumsy finish.—K.M. • $13 • (3/31/2000) • **74**

Malbec-Cabernet Sauvignon Mendoza Uvas del Sol 1997: This rather austere red shows the meaty, gamy flavors of Malbec and the herbal notes and firm tannins of Cabernet. Though lacking in up-front fruit flavors, it has a clean structure that should complement meat dishes. Drink now.—T.M. • $8 • (3/31/1999) • **80**

Malbec-Cabernet Sauvignon Mendoza Uvas del Sol 1996: Ripe-tasting, with brown sugar, plum and spice flavors. Awkward in the end, showing drying tannins on the finish. Drink now.—K.M. • $8 • (9/15/1998) • **79**

Malbec-Cabernet Sauvignon Mendoza Uvas del Sol 1995 • $8 • (5/15/1998) • **85**

Merlot Mendoza Uvas del Sol 1997: Earthy and herbal flavors dominate this light-bodied red. The light tannins turn dry on the herbal finish.—T.M. • $8 • (3/31/1999) • **75**

Merlot Mendoza Uvas del Sol Reserve 1998: Browning in color, with decaying fruit aromas, this lightweight red has cola and brown sugar flavors and a slightly astringent finish. Past its prime.—T.M. • $13 • (3/31/2000) • **77**

Pinot Noir Mendoza Uvas del Sol 1998: Tired and lean, with only faint flavors of cola and spice.—K.M. • $10 • (3/31/2000) • **75**

Pinot Noir Mendoza Uvas del Sol 1997: Fully mature, this light red shows some spicy, earthy flavors characteristic of the varietal, with hints of berry and cherry and very soft tannins. Turns dry on the finish.—T.M. • $9 • (3/31/1999) • **77**

Sangiovese Mendoza Uvas del Sol 1998: Soft and jammy, with good flavors of plum, berry and some cherry, this medium-bodied red then ends on a spicy note. Drink now.—K.M. • $8 • (2/28/1999) • **82**

Sangiovese Mendoza Uvas del Sol 1997: Fresh and fruity, with cherry and spice flavors and brown-sugar notes on the finish. Drink now.—K.M. • $8 • (9/15/1998) • **81**

Tempranillo Mendoza Uvas del Sol 1998: Thick-textured and chewy, with ripe plum and chocolate flavors and moderate tannins. There's plenty of sweet fruit, but low acidity leaves it a bit cloying on the finish.—T.M. • $8 • (3/31/1999) • **79**

Tempranillo Mendoza Uvas del Sol 1997: A chewy red, with berry and plum flavors and a chocolaty finish. Drink now.—K.M. • $8 • (9/15/1998) • **82**

Torrontés Mendoza Uvas del Sol 1998: Pleasant and quaffable, with lovely floral aromas and flavors and plenty of spice besides. Finishes on a nice note of orange peel. Drink now.—K.M. • $8 • (2/28/1999) • **83**

Key: SS—Spectator Selection. CS—Cellar Selection. HR—Highly Recommended. $NA—Price not available. (BT)—Barrel tasting. Ⓐ—Auction Price.
For a key to the tasters' initials, see "How to Use These Listings."
Dates in parentheses represent the issues in which the ratings were published.

Torrontés Mendoza Uvas del Sol 1997: A peachy- and spicy-tasting wine reminiscent of Gewürztraminer. A bit heavy-handed on the finish.—K.M. • $8 • (8/31/1998) • **79**

Torrontés-Chenin Blanc Mendoza Uvas del Sol Argentinian White 1998: Simple, with a perfumed aroma and some modest melon and figlike flavors.—K.M. • $7 • (3/31/1999) • **77**

Torrontés-Chenin Blanc Mendoza Uvas del Sol 1997: The floral aroma and attractive peach and spice flavors are reminiscent of Gewürztraminer. An exuberant white that is crisp and enjoyable. Drink now, well chilled.—K.M. • $7 • (8/31/1998) • **84**

Uvas del Sol Argentinian Red Mendoza 1998: Very light and thin, with fresh, simple berry and cherry flavors, light floral and spicy accents.—T.M. • $7 • (3/31/1999) • **78**

Uvas del Sol Argentinian Red Mendoza 1997: Appealing for its fruitiness, with nice berry and cherry flavors. Fairly light, but effusive. A nice quaffer. A blend of Sangiovese, Bonarda and Malbec. Drink now.—K.M. • $7 • (7/31/1998) • **83**

ALTA VISTA

Malbec Mendoza 1997: Sweet and syrupy, this red offers a thick, jammy texture and very ripe flavors of prune and plum, with accents of coffee and vanilla. Powerful but simple. A new wine from Pomerol's Jean-Michel Arcaute. The better of two samples, with significant bottle variation. Drink now.—K.M. • $12 • (11/15/1999) • **82**

BARRAL & ROCA

Exclusivo Mendoza NV: This Sangiovese blend starts off with berry, spice and leather aromas, but it's light and insipid on the palate.—B.S. • $7 • (9/15/1999) • **76**

Malbec Mendoza 1996: A big, generous red, with ample fruit flavors, a broad texture and full body. It's ripe and hearty, tannic but well balanced. Drink now through 2002. • $8 • (8/31/1999) • **85**

Merlot Mendoza 1996: A bit severe, with a camphorlike aroma and herbal and dried cherry flavors. Past its prime.—K.M. • $8 • (9/15/1999) • **71**

Syrah Mendoza 1996: Shows very sweet blackberry and raspberry jam notes that verge on cloying. Medium-bodied, with a supple finish.—K.M. • $10 • (3/31/2000) • **82**

BIANCHI, VALENTIN

Cabernet Sauvignon Mendoza Elsa's Vineyard 1990 • $5 • (6/15/1994) • **78**

Malbec Mendoza Elsa's Vineyard 1994 • $6 • (2/28/1997) • **82**

Malbec Mendoza Elsa's Vineyard 1992 • $5 • (7/31/1995) • **81**

Malbec Mendoza Elsa's Vineyard 1991 • $6 • (6/15/1994) • **84**

BLUE NUN

Merlot Mendoza 1996: Nice plum and coffee flavors, with an herbal note running through. Smooth, and ready to drink.—K.M. • $6 • (7/31/1998) • **81**

CHATEAU DIANA

Cabernet Sauvignon Mendoza Reserve NV: Showing only a hint of decayed fruit on the nose and palate, this is a thin, dilute, barely vinous offering.—K.M. • $5 • (3/31/2000) • **71**

Chardonnay Mendoza Reserve NV: This buttery white is soft and sweet, but lacks enough fruit and acidity to keep it refreshing.—T.M. • $5 • (3/31/2000) • **78**

Merlot Mendoza Reserve NV: A barely vinous grape flavor quickly turns dilute, then a dry finish takes over.—T.M. • $5 • (3/31/2000) • **75**

COASTAL CELLARS

Chardonnay Mendoza 1997: Starts nicely with good pear, apple and citrus flavors, but turns flabby on the finish.—K.M. • $NA • (9/30/1998) • **79**

COMPASS

Merlot Mendoza 1996: Quite a distinctive red, boasting rich plum and berry flavors and an assertive menthol note. Displays good concentration, with chocolaty tones on the finish. Drink now.—K.M. • $9 • (7/31/1998) • **85**

DOMECQ, BODEGAS

Cabernet Sauvignon Mendoza Balbi Vineyard Reserve 1997: There are sweet cola and licorice flavors in this roughly hewn red, with a slightly murky finish.—B.S. • $13 • (5/31/2000) • **78**

Chardonnay-Sémillon Mendoza Balbi Vineyard 1997: Simple and straightforward, with modest green apple flavors and some earthy notes on the finish. Drink now.—K.M. • $7 • (8/31/1998) • **81**

Malbec Mendoza Balbi Vineyard 1997: Ripe fruit flavor is the strong suit of this generous, easy-drinking red wine. It's medium-bodied, not very tannic and brimming over with cherry and blackberry flavors. Drink now. • $13 • (8/31/1999) • **85**

Malbec-Syrah Mendoza Balbi Vineyard 1998: Thin and lean, this lacks freshness and fruit. Seems stripped of life.—B.S. • $7 • (5/31/2000) • **74**

Malbec-Syrah Mendoza Balbi Vineyard 1997: Check out the price on this red blend from Argentina. Fruity and quite jammy-tasting, with a nice lushness and pleasant chocolate and spice notes, it's a rich medium-bodied wine that would go well with barbecued food. 50 percent Malbec, 50 percent Syrah. Drink now.—K.M. • $7 • (7/31/1998) • **85**

Syrah Mendoza Balbi Vineyard 1998: Candied on the nose, it gives way to a simple cherry cola flavor, with a slight spritz on the finish.—B.S. • $10 • (5/31/2000) • **76**

ESCORIHUELA, BODEGAS

Malbec Mendoza Don Miguel Gascón 1997: This plush red offers ripe black cherry and blackberry flavor, thick and juicy, and oak flavors of vanilla and toast. It has more stuffing than sophistication, but delivers a mouthful of pleasure. Drink now through 2003.—T.M. • $13 • (12/15/1998) • **87**

Viognier Mendoza Don Miguel Gascón 1997: Peach and onion flavors don't offer much in this flabby white.—K.M. • $13 • (12/15/1998) • **76**

ESMERALDA, BODEGAS

Cabernet Sauvignon Argentina Trumpeter 1994 • $8 • (2/28/1997) • **86**

Cabernet Sauvignon Maipú Trumpeter 1995 • $9 • (11/30/1997) • **85**

Cabernet Sauvignon Mendoza Alamos Ridge 1997: A medium-bodied red with some appealing red plum and sweet cherry flavors, with a spicy note on the finish. Drink now.—K.M. • $10 • (10/15/1999) • **83**

Cabernet Sauvignon Mendoza Alamos Ridge 1996: Red plum and leathery flavors dominate this mature tasting red. Tobacco notes chime in on the finish. Drink now.—K.M. • $10 • (1/1/1999) • **80**

Cabernet Sauvignon Mendoza Alamos Ridge 1994 • $9 • (6/15/1997) • **83**

Cabernet Sauvignon Mendoza Catena Agrelo Vineyard 1994 • $16 • (2/28/1997) • **89**

Cabernet Sauvignon Mendoza Catena Agrelo Vineyard 1993 • $16 • (6/30/1996) • **84**

Cabernet Sauvignon Mendoza Catena Agrelo Vineyard 1992 • $16 • (4/30/1995) HR • **91**

Cabernet Sauvignon Mendoza Catena Alta Agrelo Vineyard 1994 • $45 • (2/28/1998) • **89**

Cabernet Sauvignon Mendoza Catena Reserve 1990 • $14 • (5/31/1994) • **85**

Cabernet Sauvignon Mendoza Catena Reserve 1990 • $15 • (3/31/1993) • **84**

Cabernet Sauvignon Mendoza Trumpeter 1992 • $7 • (4/30/1995) • **80**

Cabernet Sauvignon Mendoza Trumpeter 1991 • $10 • (6/15/1994) • **77**

Chardonnay Mendoza Agrelo Vineyards 1997: Ripe and buttery tasting, with baked apple flavors and a twist of orange peel on the finish. Drink now.—K.M. • $17 • (10/15/1999) • **82**

Chardonnay Mendoza Alamos Ridge 1998: The best Argentinean Chardonnay in our current report, and quite affordable as well. It's broad-shouldered in frame, with waxy, toasty aromas and a soft, plush texture carrying the ripe apple and hazelnut flavors through the lengthy, stylish finish. Drink now.—K.M. • $10 • (3/31/2000) • **86**

Chardonnay Mendoza Alamos Ridge 1997: Fairly crisp and well defined, with apple, green pear and some mineral notes. A smooth white that's balanced but has a short finish. Drink now.—K.M. • $10 • (10/15/1999) • **84**

Malbec Mendoza Alamos Ridge 1998: Exuberant, with cassis and toast aromas that give way to a juicy, muscular mouthful of plums, blackberries and spice. Nice chewy texture and grip. Tasted twice, with consistent notes. Drink now.—K.M. • $10 • (3/31/2000) • **86**

Malbec Mendoza Alamos Ridge 1997: A full-bodied red, offering a mix of cherry, plum, leather and cassis flavors and picking up notes of coffee and spice that add richness to the finish. Drink now.—K.M. • $10 • (9/15/1999) • **86**

Malbec Mendoza Alamos Ridge 1995 • $8 • (2/28/1997) • **86**

Malbec Mendoza Catena Alta Lunlunta 1996: This vivid, concentrated red shows how brightly Malbec can shine in Argentina. It has the lush oak and polished texture of the best international-style reds, married to the meaty, smoky, plummy flavors characteristic of this obscure variety. Though slightly dominated by oak at the moment, it should show beautifully with a bit of time in the bottle. Drink through 2010—T.M. • $50 • (3/31/1999) • **92**

Malbec Mendoza Catena Lunlunta Vineyards 1996: Lively and exuberant despite its age, with plenty of sweet cherry and spice flavors. Fairly high-toned, with crisp acidity, and flavors that linger appealingly on the finish. Drink now.—K.M. • $20 • (9/15/1999) • **88**

Malbec Vistalba Trumpeter 1996 • $10 • (5/15/1998) • **82**

Merlot Tupungato Valley Trumpeter 1996 • $10 • (11/30/1997) • **84**

Merlot Tupungato Valley Trumpeter 1995 • $9 • (5/15/1997) • **86**

ETCHART

Cabernet Sauvignon Cafayate 1995: Ripe and soft, this gentle red shows herbal, coffee and cedar flavors, with gentle tannins and little fruit. Has some concentration, but lacks freshness. Drink now.—T.M. • $9 • (2/28/1999) • **80**

Cabernet Sauvignon Mendoza 1995 • $8 • (3/31/1998) • **83**

Cabernet Sauvignon Mendoza Rio de Plata 1996: Light and firm, this straightforward red offers light cherry, herb and toast flavors, with lean tannins and a slightly sweet finish. Balanced and clean. Drink now.—T.M. • $8 • (12/15/1998) • **82**

Chardonnay Cafayate 1997: A big, oaky style, with loads of buttery, creamy notes, also ripe apple and tropical fruit flavors. Finishes with flavors of fresh-baked apple pie. Drink now.—K.M. • $14 • (2/28/1999) • **84**

Chardonnay Mendoza Rio de Plata 1997: Blunt but forceful, this full-bodied white shows toasty oak, ripe apple and pear flavors and firm acidity, integrated but without much subtlety. Can stand up to bold food. Drink now.—T.M. • $8 • (12/15/1998) • **82**

Malbec Mendoza 1993 • $6 • (11/15/1995) • **84**

Malbec Mendoza Rio de Plata 1996: This ripe red shows polish and intensity, with ripe cherry and kirsch flavors, accented by vanilla and licorice, that float across the palate and linger on the finish. Fresh and balanced. Drink now through 2002.—T.M. • $8 • (12/15/1998) • **87**

Malbec-Cabernet Sauvignon Cafayate Arnaldo B. Etchart Reserva 1994: An Argentine original, with appealing flavors of dark plum, brick and espresso. A ripe style, with a supple texture and a long, smoky finish. Polished, with plenty of character. Drink now through 2002.—K.M. • $14 • (2/28/1999) • **86**

Merlot Mendoza 1993 • $6 • (11/15/1995) • **78**

Merlot Mendoza Rio de Plata 1997: Firm and nicely concentrated, with good plum, beet root and herb flavors. Finishes with bittersweet chocolate notes. Good for barbecued foods. Tasted twice, with consistent notes. Drink now.—K.M. • $8 • (12/15/1998) • **83**

Torrontés Cafayate 1997: This solid and intriguing white from Argentina is almost Alsace-like, with a good dose of acidity and delicious flavors of apple, white currant, grapefruit and melon. Makes a nice change of pace—at a no-risk price. Drink now.—K.M. • $9 • (2/28/1999) • **85**

EVOLUNA

Cabernet Sauvignon Mendoza Reserve 1997: Cherry and berry flavors are broad and ripe in this smooth red. Vanilla and toast add sweetness, while the tannins are soft and the acidity low. An easy-drinking wine with just enough grip for food. Drink now.—T.M. • $10 • (12/15/1998) • **84**

Malbec Mendoza Reserve 1997: Strong gamy and earthy aromas and flavors dominate this medium-bodied red.—K.M. • $10 • (3/31/2000) • **78**

Merlot Mendoza Reserve 1997: Seems volatile on the nose, with some muddled prune, plum and coffee notes before the dull, short finish.—T.M. • $10 • (3/31/2000) • **74**

FAZIO, NICOLAS E.

Cabernet Sauvignon Mendoza 1986 • $12 • (4/30/1995) • **71**

Cabernet Sauvignon Mendoza 1980 • $11 • (9/15/1992) • **70**

Malbec Mendoza 1982 • $12 • (7/31/1995) • **83**

Malbec Mendoza 1978 • $12 • (9/15/1992) • **79**

Merlot Rio Negro Fabre Montmayou 1988 • $11 • (11/15/1995) • **82**

FLICHMAN, FINCA

Argenta Mendoza Red 1990 • $6 • (9/30/1994) • **75**

Argenta Mendoza Red 1989 • $5 • (9/15/1992) • **83**

FLICHMAN, FINCA

Argenta Mendoza Red 1988 • $4 • (3/15/1991) • **84**
Cabernet Sauvignon Mendoza 1997: Tired, astringent and muddled with bittersweet chocolate notes. Stewy notes linger on the finish. Past its prime.—K.M. • $8 • (10/15/1999) • **76**
Cabernet Sauvignon Mendoza 1991 • $6 • (4/30/1995) • **74**
Cabernet Sauvignon Mendoza 1989 • $8 • (6/15/1994) • **80**
Cabernet Sauvignon Mendoza Caballero de la Cepa 1991 • $11 • (7/31/1996) • **72**
Cabernet Sauvignon Mendoza Caballero de la Cepa 1990 • $10 • (4/30/1995) • **79**
Cabernet Sauvignon Mendoza Caballero de la Cepa 1989 • $11 • (1/31/1995) • **80**
Cabernet Sauvignon Mendoza Caballero de la Cepa 1987 • $11 • (6/15/1994) • **74**
Cabernet Sauvignon Mendoza Dedicado 1996: A fairly heavy red, with sweet cherry and dark plum flavors, and drying tannins on the finish. Drink now.—K.M. • $20 • (10/15/1999) • **80**
Cabernet Sauvignon Mendoza Proprietors Private Reserve 1990 • $8 • (1/31/1995) • **84**
Cabernet Sauvignon Mendoza Proprietors Private Reserve 1989 • $7 • (6/15/1993) • **81**
Cabernet Sauvignon Mendoza Proprietors Private Reserve 1988 • $7 • (9/15/1992) • **82**
Cabernet Sauvignon Mendoza Reserva 1996: Stewy, rhubarb flavors lead to a muddled finish with dull cardboard notes.—K.M. • $11 • (10/15/1999) • **75**
Chardonnay Mendoza 1998: There is an earthy and minerally streak to this wine, which also has apple and pear flavors. Finishes on a slightly cloying note.—K.M. • $8 • (10/15/1999) • **78**
Malbec Mendoza Reserva 1997: A hearty red, with some nice plum, leather and black cherry flavors, and peppery notes on the finish. Drink now.—K.M. • $11 • (9/15/1999) • **84**
Merlot Mendoza 1998: A bit of acetone on the nose overrides the plum and spice flavors in this muddled red. Tasted twice, with consistent notes.—B.S. • $8 • (9/15/1999) • **73**
Merlot Mendoza Proprietors Private Reserve 1988 • $6 • (3/15/1991) • **66**
Sangiovese Mendoza 1997: Offers modest cherry and leather flavors, but overall it's simple.—B.S. • $8 • (9/15/1999) • **77**
Sangiovese Mendoza 1992 • $6 • (11/15/1995) • **78**
Selection Mendoza Red 1988 • $4 • (3/15/1991) • **79**
Syrah Mendoza 1995: A bit lumbering, with some modestly ripe plum flavors, and dull leather notes on the finish.—K.M. • $8 • (9/15/1999) • **77**
Syrah Mendoza 1991 • $9 • (7/31/1996) • **81**
Syrah Mendoza 1990 • $9 • (4/30/1994) • **84**

GROVE STREET

Malbec Mendoza Barrel Reserve 1996 • $8 • (6/15/1997) • **83**
Merlot Mendoza Barrel Reserve 1996 • $8 • (6/15/1997) • **75**

JAMES, MARCUS

Cabernet Sauvignon Mendoza Special Reserve 1995: This off-beat red shows light, perfumed notes of berry, white chocolate and rose, with soft tannins and a silky texture. Lacks varietal character, but has quirky appeal. Drink now.—T.M. • $5 • (12/15/1998) • **82**
Chardonnay Mendoza Special Reserve 1997: This soft, bland white tastes more of sawdust than fruit, with very light apple flavors and a rather cloying finish.—T.M. • $5 • (12/15/1998) • **75**
Malbec Mendoza Special Reserve 1995: Light, showing candied raspberry and strawberry flavors, with light tannins and enough acidity to balance the fruity sweetness. Not much varietal character.—T.M. • $5 • (12/15/1998) • **77**
Merlot Mendoza Special Reserve 1995: A strong minty, herbal flavor marks this medium-bodied, simple Merlot. • $5 • (12/15/1998) • **78**

LAGARDE, HENRY

Cabernet Sauvignon Mendoza Gold Medal 1985 • $12 • (2/28/1997) • **87**
Malbec Mendoza 1982 • $11 • (2/28/1997) • **84**

Key: SS—Spectator Selection. CS—Cellar Selection. HR—Highly Recommended. $NA—Price not available. (BT)—Barrel tasting. (A)—Auction Price.
For a key to the tasters' initials, see "How to Use These Listings."
Dates in parentheses represent the issues in which the ratings were published.

Merlot Mendoza 1993 • $11 • (5/15/1997) • **85**
Syrah Mendoza 1993 • $12 • (6/15/1997) • **86**

LEWELLYN ESTATES

Cabernet Sauvignon Mendoza 1994: A strange mix of sweet plum and spicy cherry flavors.—K.M. • $4 • (7/31/1998) • **73**
Chardonnay Mendoza 1997: This is dominated by an oniony aroma and flavor that make it harsh and unappealing.—K.M. • $4 • (8/31/1998) • **72**
Merlot Mendoza 1995: A cloying aroma, with candied flavors and a sweet finish. A bit bizarre in the end. —K.M. • $4 • (7/31/1998) • **74**

LURTON, J. & F.

Cabernet Sauvignon Mendoza 1996 • $6 • (9/15/1997) • **85**
Cabernet Sauvignon Mendoza Gran Lurton Reserva 1996: An accessible Cabernet, with good concentration. Delicious dark plum cherry and chocolate flavors, with a spicy, slightly sweet note on the finish.—K.M. • $12 • (7/31/1998) • **85**
Cabernet Sauvignon Mendoza Oak Aged 1998: An overt smoky aroma and stewy flavors don't add up to much.—K.M. • $8 • (3/31/2000) • **75**
Malbec Mendoza 1996 • $6 • (10/15/1997) • **88**
Sauvignon Blanc Mendoza 1999: The light, crisp texture of this white is refreshing, but the citrus and herbal flavors veer into soapiness on the finish and diminish the pleasure.—T.M. • $NA • (3/31/2000) • **79**

MARIPOSA

Cabernet Sauvignon Mendoza 1997: Vivid and refreshing. This lively red shows exuberant grapey and blackberry flavors, with plenty of toasty oak, firm tannins and bright acidity; the elements are balanced and clean. Drink now through 2004.—T.M. • $9 • (2/28/1999) • **85**
Cabernet Sauvignon Mendoza Tapiz 1998: Simple, with red plum and rhubarb flavors. Lingering finish.—K.M. • $11 • (10/15/1999) • **77**
Chardonnay Mendoza 1997: Nothing fancy here, but this wine shows good, straightforward apple and pear character. Medium-bodied, with spicy notes on the finish. Drink now.—K.M. • $9 • (9/30/1998) • **83**
Malbec Mendoza 1997: Fresh, grapey flavors and good balance make this fine for quaffing. Tasted twice, with consistent notes. Drink now. • $9 • (9/30/1998) • **80**
Malbec Mendoza 1996 • $10 • (10/15/1997) • **86**
Malbec Mendoza Tapiz 1998: A light-bodied red, with sweet cherry and cinnamon flavors. Drink now.—K.M. • $10 • (3/31/2000) • **81**
Malbec Mendoza Tapiz Reserve 1997: Deeply colored and highly extracted, this exuberant red shows rich, ripe flavors of blackberry, chocolate and coffee, with a bitter, brambly note adding interest to the finish. Alluring now, it will be better when it settles down a bit. Best after 2000.—T.M. • $15 • (2/28/1999) • **87**
Merlot Mendoza 1997: Ripe and thick, with green olive, red plum and some cherry flavors, finishing on a charry note. Drink now.—K.M. • $9 • (2/28/1999) • **81**
Merlot Mendoza Tapiz 1998: A little sawdust and dill add to the plum note in this soft red; firms up a bit on the finish.—B.S. • $11 • (9/15/1999) • **79**

NAVARRO CORREAS

Cabernet Sauvignon Maipú-Mendoza Colección Privada 1994: Mature, with dried cherry and brick flavors. Smooth and round, with drying herbal notes on the finish. Drink now.—K.M. • $13 • (11/15/1999) • **82**
Cabernet Sauvignon Mendoza Colección Privada 1992 • $12 • (9/15/1997) • **79**
Cabernet Sauvignon Mendoza Colección Privada 1991 • $12 • (6/15/1997) • **77**
Cabernet Sauvignon Mendoza Colección Privada 1990 • $11 • (4/30/1995) • **75**
Cabernet Sauvignon Mendoza Colección Privada 1988 • $12 • (5/31/1994) • **82**
Cabernet Sauvignon Mendoza Colección Privada 1985 • $10 • (3/31/1993) • **79**
Malbec Maipú-Mendoza 1994: A bit stewy-tasting, with dried cherry and rhubarb flavors.—K.M. • $13 • (11/15/1999) • **76**
Malbec Mendoza Russell Vineyard 1993 • $13 • (10/15/1997) • **78**
Malbec Mendoza Russell Vineyard 1992 • $12 • (6/15/1997) • **84**
Malbec Mendoza Russell Vineyard 1991 • $10 • (7/31/1995) • **78**
Malbec Mendoza Russell Vineyard 1988 • $10 • (5/31/1994) • **86**
Malbec Mendoza Russell Vineyard 1987 • $10 • (3/31/1993) • **80**

Pinot Noir Mendoza 1991 • $15 • (9/30/1997) • **71**
Pinot Noir Mendoza 1989 • $11 • (7/31/1994) • **72**
Syrah Mendoza 1994: Round and mature, with residual dried cherry and leather flavors. Finishes with spicy notes. Drink now.—K.M. • $15 • (11/15/1999) • **80**
Syrah Mendoza 1992 • $15 • (9/30/1997) • **84**
Syrah Mendoza 1991 • $12 • (11/15/1995) • **79**

NORTON, BODEGA

Cabernet Sauvignon Mendoza 1995: Ripe, broad and fairly rich, with plum and chocolate flavors and a charred note on the finish. Drink now.—K.M. • $9 • (7/31/1998) • **83**
Cabernet Sauvignon Mendoza 1994 • $9 • (9/30/1997) • **85**
Cabernet Sauvignon Mendoza 1993 • $9 • (2/28/1997) • **81**
Malbec Mendoza 1996: This Argentine red is an impresssive package for so few dollars. It's nicely sculpted and balanced, with ripe, lush flavors of dark plum, cherry and berry that echo with chocolaty notes on the lingering finish. 8,000 cases imported. Drink now.—K.M. • $9 • (7/31/1998) • **86**
Malbec Mendoza 1995 • $9 • (10/15/1997) • **83**
Malbec Mendoza 1994 • $9 • (2/28/1997) • **80**
Merlot Mendoza 1995: Ripe and rich, though a bit rough-hewn, with dark plum and cherry flavors. Finishes with roasted notes.—K.M. • $9 • (7/31/1998) • **83**
Merlot Mendoza 1994 • $9 • (10/31/1997) • **86**
Merlot Mendoza 1993 • $9 • (5/15/1997) • **85**
Privada Mendoza Red 1996: This soft, light-bodied red offers well-balanced flavors of cherries, milk chocolate and herbs, with light yet firm tannins and a clean finish. It's modest, but a fine accompaniment to lighter dishes. Drink now through 2001.—T.M. • $14 • (1/1/1999) • **83**
Privada Mendoza Red 1995 • $13 • (9/30/1997) • **85**
Privada Mendoza Red 1994 • $12 • (2/28/1997) • **85**
Sangiovese Mendoza 1996: This soft red bears little resemblance to Sangiovese, but does offer some plain black cherry and cedar flavors, finishing on a slightly bitter note.—T.M. • $9 • (1/1/1999) • **79**
Sangiovese Mendoza 1995 • $9 • (10/15/1997) • **81**
Sangiovese Mendoza 1994 • $9 • (2/28/1997) • **83**

PATAGONIA, VINA

Chardonnay Mendoza TriVento 1997: This round, simple white has a pleasant waxy texture, light flavors of apple and pear and just enough acidity to keep it lively.—T.M. • $6 • (12/15/1998) • **78**
Malbec Mendoza TriVento 1997: Plump and fruity, this bright red offers black cherry, plum and light vanilla flavors over ripe, round tannins. It's juicy and exuberant, a fine match with grilled foods. Drink now through 2001.—T.M. • $6 • (12/15/1998) • **84**
Syrah Mendoza TriVento 1997: Round and fruity, showing berry and light smoke flavors. True to the varietal, though in a simple style. Drink now.—T.M. • $6 • (12/15/1998) • **82**
Syrah-Malbec Mendoza Reserve 1997: An odd marriage saved from discord by the blandness of the partners, this soft red delivers standard flavors of plum and black cherry, with hints of toast and chocolate. Balanced, fruity and clean. Drink now.—T.M. • $7 • (11/15/1999) • **83**

PROVIAR

Clos du Moulin Mendoza 1985 • $10 • (9/30/1994) • **76**

RAFAEL

Malbec-Tempranillo Mendoza 1997: A rich and ripe red, with delicious plum, chocolate and cassis. Tightly wound, but still enjoyable. Drink now through 2001.—K.M. • $8 • (7/31/1998) • **84**
Sangiovese Mendoza 1997: Rough around the edges, with red cherry and berry flavors and leathery qualities on the finish. Tasted twice, with consistent notes.—K.M. • $8 • (9/15/1998) • **77**
Tempranillo Mendoza 1997: A bit astringent and tired-tasting, with modest plum and spice flavors, but there's an overwhelming roasted note.—K.M. • $6 • (7/31/1998) • **78**
Trebbiano Mendoza 1997: A fresh white, slightly off-dry, with peachy flavors and herbal notes. Finishes on an earthy note. Drink now.—K.M. • $6 • (8/31/1998) • **81**

RURAL, LA

Chardonnay Tupungato Trumpeter 1997: This has modest apple and pear flavors, and a hint of spice on the finish.—K.M. • $9 • (10/15/1999) • **79**
Malbec Vistalba Trumpeter 1997: A good, all-purpose red wine, with generous cherry and plum flavors, medium body, smooth texture and firm balance. Drink now. • $9 • (8/31/1999) • **85**

SANTA ANA

Cabernet Sauvignon Mendoza Reserve 1990 • $5 • (8/31/1995) • **74**

SANTA JULIA

Cabernet Sauvignon Mendoza 1994 • $7 • (7/31/1996) • **75**
Cabernet Sauvignon Mendoza Oak Reserve 1996: Modest spice and dried cherry flavors make for a soft, medium-bodied red. Drink now.—K.M. • $10 • (11/15/1999) • **81**
Cabernet Sauvignon Mendoza Oak Reserve 1993 • $9 • (7/31/1996) • **77**
Cabernet Sauvignon Mendoza Reserva 1997: Light-bodied, with tea and brown sugar flavors and drying tannins on the finish.—B.S. • $10 • (5/31/2000) • **77**
Chardonnay Mendoza 1997: A full-blown style that verges on the decadent. Has a nutty aroma and some interesting ripe, buttery flavors, but comes off a bit unbalanced in the end.—K.M. • $7 • (8/31/1998) • **79**
Malbec Mendoza 1994 • $6 • (7/31/1996) • **86**
Malbec Mendoza Oak Reserve 1996: This has sweet cherry and spice flavors, with coffee and mocha on the finish. Drink now.—K.M. • $10 • (11/15/1999) • **81**
Malbec Mendoza Oak Reserve 1993 • $8 • (7/31/1996) • **82**
Malbec-Cabernet Sauvignon Mendoza 1995 • $7 • (10/15/1997) • **86**
Malbec-Cabernet Sauvignon Mendoza 1994 • $6 • (7/31/1996) • **83**
Merlot Mendoza 1997: An interesting mix of leather, dark plum and spice flavors. Ripe and round, with a lingering finish dominated by roasted notes. Drink now.—K.M. • $7 • (7/31/1998) • **84**
Pinot Noir Mendoza 1996 • $7 • (10/15/1997) • **75**
Sangiovese Mendoza 1997: Light, with berry and spice flavors and a distinctive leathery element. Has a nice grape flavor. Drink now.—K.M. • $6 • (7/31/1998) • **81**
Sangiovese Mendoza Don Alberto 1996 • $7 • (10/15/1997) • **79**
Sauvignon Blanc Mendoza 1997 • $7 • (6/15/1998) • **78**
Syrah Mendoza Don Alberto 1996 • $7 • (10/31/1997) • **87**
Tempranillo Mendoza 1997: Fruity, with nice berry and plum flavors, though a bit simple in the end. Finishes on an earthy note. Drink now.—K.M. • $7 • (7/31/1998) • **80**
Tempranillo Mendoza Don Alberto 1996 • $7 • (10/31/1997) • **82**
Torrontés Mendoza 1997 • $7 • (5/15/1998) • **79**

SONGMEADOW

Merlot Mendoza 1996 • $7 • (5/15/1997) • **81**

TERRA ROSA

Cabernet Sauvignon Mendoza 1997: Root beer and licorice root aromas announce this muddled red, with cola notes, cloying fruit and a tough finish.—K.M. • $10 • (1/1/2000) • **75**

TORINO, MICHEL

Cabernet Sauvignon Cafayate Bodega La Rosa 1996: This round, soft red offers sweet flavors of cooked cherries and plums, with a reviving streak of citrusy acidity. The tannins are firm. Drink now.—T.M. • $7 • (12/15/1998) • **82**
Malbec Cafayate Bodega La Rosa 1996: Check out the price on this fresh and fruity red from Argentina. It offers black cherry and blackberry flavors, ripe and even jammy, with firm tannins and lively acidity. It's focused and firm and can stand up to rich food. Drink now through 2001.—T.M. • $7 • (12/15/1998) • **86**

TOSO, PASCUAL

Cabernet Sauvignon Mendoza 1992 • $8 • (9/30/1995) • **82**
Cabernet Sauvignon Mendoza 1991 • $8 • (6/15/1994) • **78**
Cabernet Sauvignon Mendoza 1990 • $7 • (4/30/1995) • **72**

TOSO, PASCUAL

Cabernet Sauvignon Mendoza 1988 • $7 • (3/15/1991) • **79**
Malbec Mendoza 1994 • $6 • (9/30/1995) • **83**
Malbec Mendoza 1990 • $6 • (5/31/1994) • **74**
Red Mendoza 1994 • $6 • (9/30/1995) • **79**
Red Mendoza 1991 • $6 • (5/31/1994) • **76**

TRAPICHE

Cabernet Sauvignon Mendoza 1994 • $6 • (9/15/1997) • **83**
Cabernet Sauvignon Mendoza 1990 • $8 • (5/31/1994) • **83**
Cabernet Sauvignon Mendoza Fond de Cave 1997: Smoke and cassis notes run through this chewy Cab. Solid, but somewhat one-dimensional. Drink now.—K.M. • $17 • (3/31/2000) • **83**
Cabernet Sauvignon Mendoza Fond de Cave 1996: Medium-bodied with dark plum flavors and coffee-ground notes.—K.M. • $17 • (10/15/1999) • **78**
Cabernet Sauvignon Mendoza Fond de Cave 1991 • $12 • (11/15/1995) • **83**
Cabernet Sauvignon Mendoza Fond de Cave 1990 • $13 • (6/15/1994) • **79**
Cabernet Sauvignon Mendoza Oak Cask 1995: There are some sweet cherry and rhubarb flavors in this red, with some herbal notes on the finish.—K.M. • $10 • (10/15/1999) • **79**
Cabernet Sauvignon Mendoza Oak Cask 1993 • $9 • (9/15/1997) • **87**
Cabernet Sauvignon Mendoza Oak Cask 1991 • $8 • (4/30/1995) • **80**
Cabernet Sauvignon Mendoza Oak Cask 1986 • $10 • (10/15/1991) • **82**
Cabernet Sauvignon Mendoza Reserve 1992 • $6 • (11/15/1995) • **77**
Cabernet Sauvignon Mendoza Reserve 1988 • $7 • (9/15/1992) • **79**
Chardonnay Mendoza 1998: Offers pear and crisp apple flavors, with some buttery and spicy notes on the finish. Drink now.—K.M. • $7 • (10/15/1999) • **81**
Chardonnay Mendoza Fond de Cave 1998: An exaggerated style, with toasty and smoky character and only hints of dried and candied fruit. It's rich and clean, but doesn't bring you back for another sip.—T.M. • $17 • (3/31/2000) • **79**
Chardonnay Mendoza Fond de Cave 1997: A nutty flavor dominates this ripe and simple white, which has some pear and buttery flavors.—K.M. • $17 • (10/15/1999) • **79**
Chardonnay Mendoza Oak Cask 1997: Ripe and fairly smooth with flavors of pear and apple and some smoky notes. Drink now.—K.M. • $10 • (10/15/1999) • **83**
Malbec Mendoza 1998: On the light side, with modest berry and rhubarb flavors.—K.M. • $7 • (3/31/2000) • **78**
Malbec Mendoza 1997: An average-quality red wine that's modestly fruity, very dry and rather tannic. • $7 • (8/31/1999) • **77**
Malbec Mendoza 1995 • $6 • (10/15/1997) • **85**
Malbec Mendoza Oak Cask 1995: It's hard to warm up to this tannic, woody-tasting red wine. It has good fruit flavors underneath, but the coarse texture overwhelms them. • $10 • (8/31/1999) • **79**
Malbec Mendoza Oak Cask 1993 • $9 • (10/15/1997) • **84**
Malbec Mendoza Oak Cask 1991 • $8 • (8/31/1995) • **87**
Malbec Mendoza Oak Cask 1990 • $8 • (5/31/1994) • **86**
Malbec Mendoza Oak Cask 1988 • $8 • (7/15/1991) • **74**
Malbec Mendoza Reserve 1991 • $6 • (7/31/1995) • **78**
Medalla Mendoza Red 1995: This has stewy, plummy flavors and charry notes, with a muddled finish. Cabernet Sauvignon, Merlot and Malbec.—K.M. • $23 • (10/15/1999) • **78**
Medalla Mendoza Red 1994 • $19 • (9/15/1997) • **85**
Medalla Mendoza Red 1991 • $18 • (9/30/1994) • **87**
Merlot-Malbec Mendoza Cuvée de Trapiche 1994 • $4 • (11/15/1995) • **76**
Merlot-Malbec Mendoza Iscay 1997: Smoke, espresso and mint notes dominate the nose in this medium-bodied red, showing Merlot characteristics of plum and raspberry before the Malbec side takes over on the firm, taut finish. The better of two samples, with significant bottle variation. Drink now.—K.M. • $50 • (3/31/2000) • **83**
Pinot Noir Mendoza 1999: Shows candied cherry and cough syrup notes on a medium-bodied frame, finishing on a slightly dusty note.—K.M. • $7 • (3/31/2000) • **79**
Pinot Noir Mendoza 1998: A light red wine with grassy, herbal aromas and flavors. OK as a quaff, but shows little Pinot character. • $7 • (8/31/1999) • **77**
Pinot Noir Mendoza Reserve 1988 • $7 • (9/15/1992) • **80**

Key: SS—Spectator Selection. CS—Cellar Selection. HR—Highly Recommended. $NA—Price not available. (BT)—Barrel tasting. (A)—Auction Price.
For a key to the tasters' initials, see "How to Use These Listings."
Dates in parentheses represent the issues in which the ratings were published.

Sauvignon Blanc Mendoza 1998: This muscular, deep-colored white offers bold flavors of apple, melon and herbs, assertive if a bit clumsy, with an unfortunate whiff of shellac.—T.M. • $7 • (3/31/2000) • **77**
Sauvignon Blanc Mendoza 1997: Tropical and fruit-cocktail flavors dominate this wine, which finishes on a spicy note.—K.M. • $7 • (9/30/1998) • **78**
Syrah Maipú-Mendoza 1996: Ripe and round, with plum, berry and cassis flavors. A little thin in the middle. Finishes on a leathery note. Drink now.—K.M. • $11 • (7/31/1998) • **82**

VINTERRA

Cabernet Sauvignon Mendoza 1997: Ripe and jammy in flavor, with a soft texture, this is a simple wine that's easy to enjoy. Drink now. • $6 • (9/30/1998) • **83**
Chardonnay Mendoza 1997: Forward, with pretty spice, butter and ripe pear flavors. There's a nice elegance and a lingering finish. Drink now.—K.M. • $6 • (10/31/1998) • **85**
Malbec Mendoza 1997: Light and lean, a young, simple berry-flavored red wine. Drink now. • $6 • (9/30/1998) • **78**
Malbec Mendoza 1995 • $6 • (10/15/1997) • **80**
Merlot Mendoza 1997: Bright, clean fruit flavors and a lightly tannic texture make this medium-bodied Merlot appealing. Drink now. • $6 • (9/30/1998) • **82**
Merlot Mendoza 1996 • $6 • (9/30/1997) • **71**

WEINERT, BODEGA Y CAVAS DE

Cabernet Sauvignon Mendoza 1995: This murky, dark brown wine seems tired, with brown sugar and tea notes. Dry, astringent finish. Tasted twice, with consistent notes.—K.M. • $20 • (3/31/2000) • **74**
Cabernet Sauvignon Mendoza 1992 • $17 • (9/15/1997) • **80**
Cabernet Sauvignon Mendoza 1985 • $16 • (4/30/1995) • **80**
Cabernet Sauvignon Mendoza 1983 • $16 • (5/31/1994) • **81**
Carrascal Mendoza Red 1996: Mature, with stewed tomato, mushroom and earth notes. There's some concentrated fruit, but it struggles to push through the rustic style that's not for everyone.—K.M. • $14 • (3/31/2000) • **78**
Carrascal Mendoza Red 1993 • $13 • (9/15/1997) • **78**
Carrascal Mendoza Red 1989 • $10 • (11/15/1995) • **76**
Carrascal Mendoza Red 1988 • $10 • (5/31/1994) • **82**
Carrascal Mendoza Red 1985 • $10 • (3/31/1993) • **75**
Carrascal Mendoza White 1998: Candied orange peel aromas give way to a flaccid wine devoid of freshness or fruit.—K.M. • $14 • (3/31/2000) • **71**
Cavas de Weinert Mendoza Red 1994: There's some fruit, but it fails to push through the rustic mushroom and *sous bois* qualities. Finishes on an astringent note. Tasted twice, with consistent notes.—K.M. • $22 • (3/31/2000) • **74**
Cavas de Weinert Mendoza Red 1992 • $21 • (9/15/1997) • **84**
Cavas de Weinert Mendoza Red 1989 • $17 • (11/15/1995) • **86**
Cavas de Weinert Mendoza Red 1985 • $17 • (5/31/1994) • **83**
Cavas de Weinert Mendoza Red 1983 • $16 • (3/31/1993) • **77**
Malbec Mendoza 1994: Stewy- and pruny-tasting, with smoky notes.—K.M. • $17 • (3/31/2000) • **76**
Malbec Mendoza 1992 • $15 • (10/15/1997) • **85**
Merlot Mendoza 1996: Seeming a bit cooked, this rustic red has a charry, caramelized onion aroma, with mushroom and soggy wood notes. Slightly astringent finish.—T.M. • $17 • (3/31/2000) • **74**
Merlot Mendoza 1993 • $15 • (9/30/1997) • **82**
Merlot Mendoza 1990 • $12 • (9/30/1994) • **72**
Merlot Mendoza 1988 • $13 • (3/31/1993) • **76**

ZUCCARDI, FAMILIA

Cabernet Sauvignon Mendoza Q 1998: Nice polish and ripeness, with concentrated, firm flavors of currant and chocolate. A good job in a tough vintage for Mendoza. Drink now.—B.S. • $20 • (5/31/2000) • **86**
Malbec Mendoza Q 1998: This soft Malbec shows a traditional note of game to go along with the currant, prune and chocolate flavors. Drink now.—B.S. • $20 • (5/31/2000) • **85**

Australia

Quality, not quantity, has become the chief driver of the Australian wine industry today. The most visible evidence of this phenomenon is a recent influx of new offerings from small, quality-oriented winemakers, dubbed "smallmakers" by the Australians. Some of these hand-crafted, highly individual wines come to the United States in lots of less than 100 cases. Though virtually unknown here until a few years ago, these wines have garnered enormous acclaim. Today, Australian wines such as Jasper Hill Shiraz, Leeuwin Estate Chardonnay and Mount Horrock Cordon Cut Riesling have garnered enormous attention. This is an amazing achievement for a country that was focused on bag-in-a-box wines little more than a decade ago.

But not all that is beautiful is small. Australia's well-heeled corporate wineries have also played a major part in the quality revolution. The "Big Four"—Southcorp Wines (Penfolds, Lindemans and others), BRL Hardy, Orlando Wyndham and Mildara-Blass Ltd.—account for about 75% of Australia's world exports. These companies routinely produce wines that rank among the best in Australia. Indeed, Penfolds Grange is still widely regarded as Australia's greatest wine, and has served as the inspiration for many of the smallmakers.

While these developments at the luxury end of the market have vastly upgraded the image of Australian wines, the country is still best known for putting out multitudes of delectable, user-friendly wines at the value end of the price scale. Made in a bold, fruit-forward style that Americans like, Australian wines in this category are stylistically similar to California's. Their flavors tend to be full and hearty, and new oak (often the strongly vanilla-tasting American oak) is frequently employed in their production. Australian winemakers have traditionally relied on blending, not only of different grape varieties but of different regions' wines. Thus, most value-oriented wines carry broad appellations such as "Victoria" or even "South Eastern Australia," which encompasses a region nearly 600 miles wide, and they may also contain several judiciously select-ed grape varieties.

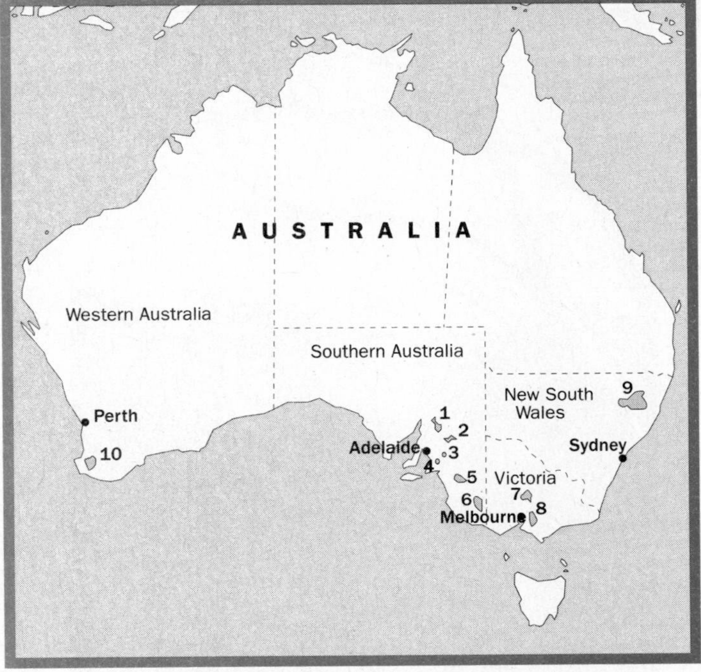

1. Clare Valley
2. Barossa
3. Adelaide Hills
4. McLaren Vale
5. Padthaway
6. Coonawarra
7. Goulburn Valley
8. Yarra Valley
9. Hunter Valley
10. Margaret River

HISTORY OF AUSTRALIAN WINE PRODUCTION

The first vines arrived in Australia with the British Expeditionary Fleet in 1778. However, serious commercial wine production did not begin until the 1890s, in the areas now known as the Barossa Valley, the Hunter Valley and the Yarra Valley. All of these places are located in Southeastern Australia, where the majority of wine production still takes place. Before 1950, Australian wine production focused on fortified wines. A red wine boom in the 1960s was followed by a white wine boom in the 1980s, culminating in the more balanced growth of the present.

Most Australian wineries were established as family enterprises. In recent years, the face of the Australian wine industry has become increasingly corporate, as family wineries have been bought up in a wave of mergers and acquisition by Australian wine, beer and spirits conglomerates. As noted, the Big Four now control about three quarters of exports, while the top 20 companies account for almost 97%. While such developments have been decried in some quarters as leading to a dull uniformity, the reality is less fearsome than the rhetoric. Corporate ownership has provided the financing to modernize wineries and to lavish care upon declining vineyards, vastly improving overall quality. Moreover, by penetrating the tough export markets of Europe and North America, the big corporations have blazed a trail through which the "smallmakers" then followed. All in all, the future of the Australian wine industry looks brighter than ever.

Henschke's Hill of Grace vineyard in Barossa Valley.

AUSTRALIAN GRAPE VARIETIES

As in the U.S., Australia labels most of its wines with varietal names, making them easy to understand. At least 85% of a varietal wine must be made from the single grape variety named on the front label. When more than one variety is named, the order of the names indicates the proportions. For example, Sémillon-Chardonnay has more Sémillon in it, while Chardonnay-Sémillon has more Chardonnay.

In recent years, the workhorse Shiraz (known as Syrah elsewhere) has moved to the forefront among red varieties. Shiraz truly thrives Down Under, producing rich, voluptuous, often age-worthy wines. At the top end, Penfolds Grange, created in the 1950s by the late Max Schubert, the legendary former head of Penfolds winemaking operations, is still the benchmark, (although Jasper Hill Georgia's Paddock, d'Arenberg The Dead Arm, and Hardys Eileen Hardy, among others, have now become serious rivals.) But outstanding, reasonably priced Australian Shiraz is also abundant. Moderately priced Australian Shiraz often exhibit gobs of up-front fruit with smooth, agreeable flavors and light tannins.

The Bordeaux varieties such as Cabernet and Merlot have had a rougher time in Australia, even though their quality can be high. Cabernet-Shiraz blends, which tend to cost less than Cabernet alone, are often fruitier, better-rounded and more popular.

Among the white varietals, Chardonnay has improved markedly of late. While there is still work to be done, the old bugaboo—excessive use of oak—is mostly a memory. Australian Chardonnay now has better acidity and more ripe, tropical fruit character, resulting in more interesting, complex wines at all price levels. Sémillon, Riesling, Gewürztraminer and Sauvignon Blanc are also among the more popular white varieties.

AUSTRALIAN WINE REGIONS

Australia's chief wine regions are South Australia (centered around Adelaide), New South Wales (centered near Sydney), and Victoria (centered near Melbourne). Often wines from all three regions are blended and sold under the catch-all Southeastern Australia denomination. The only other significant wine region is Western Australia, located near Perth on the West Coast. Though its wine quality is high, Western Australia accounts for a relatively small percentage of total production.

South Australia

More than 60 percent of the country's wine production come from the South Australia region, which includes the well-known Barossa Valley, located about 60 kilometers from Adelaide. Barossa is also the headquarters of many of the country's most famous wineries, including Penfolds, Seppelt, Peter Lehmann and Wolf Blass. South Australia is also the source of Penfolds Grange (formerly Grange Hermitage). Made from almost 100 percent Shiraz and always aged in new American oak, it is generally regarded as Australia's greatest red wine.

The chief grape varieties in South Australia are Shiraz and Grenache for reds, and Sémillon and Riesling for whites. Cabernet Sauvignon and Chardonnay, however, are becoming increasingly important, particularly for export markets.

South Australia's finest Cabernet-based reds come from the Coonawarra district, which, like the Médoc in France and Napa Valley, excels in producing ageworthy, well-structured Cabernet Sauvignons. Although Coonawarra's climate is among the coolest in Australia, the key feature of its *terroir* is its unique soil, called *terra rossa*, which consists of a rich layer of rust-colored earth laid over a thick layer of limestone and clay. The cigar-shaped Coonawarra district, only a mile wide and seven miles long, contains the most significant acreage of this prized soil. Wynns, Parker and Bowen Estate are perhaps the most famous wineries located in Coonawarra, but many other wineries, such as Lindemans, Penfolds, Seppelt, and Rosemount, obtain considerable production from the region.

South Australia also boasts what many consider to be Australia's finest white wine district: Padthaway, which is located about 65 miles north of Coonawarra. Padthaway's Chardonnays are particularly distinguished, seeming to combine a California-like generosity with a European-style minerally austerity. The Clare region, north of Adelaide, has developed an excellent reputation for its Riesling and other German varietals.

New South Wales

Although South Australia now outranks it in production, New South Wales was Australia's first important wine region; some of its vineyards date back to the 1820s. While Cabernet Sauvignon and Chardonnay have been extensively planted in New South Wales, Shiraz and Sémillon remain the most distinctive wines of the region.

Hunter Valley, about 100 miles north of Sydney, is the most important wine region of New South Wales. Major Hunter Valley wineries include Tyrell's, McWilliams, Wyndham Estate and Rothbury Estate, all of which have achieved international reputations. Though not widely planted until the 1970s, a subregion called the Upper Hunter Valley seems to have a special facility for producing Chardonnays and Shiraz with vigorous fruit and alcoholic richness.

Victoria

Victoria is not as well-known as the other major Australian wine regions, but its wines can be sensational. Victoria's cool Yarra Valley excels at producing Burgundian-style Pinot Noirs and Chardonnays. Yarra Valley wines often sell at top prices, reflecting the low yields and painstaking production methods typically maintained by the wineries there.

Victoria also excels in the production of sparkling wines, owing to a cool climate that allows the grapes to achieve excellent acidity along with concentrated fruit. Although some of the traditional Champagne grapes, such as Pinot Noir and Chardonnay, are cultivated here, Sémillon is the dominant sparkling wine grape in Victoria. This variety lends Victoria's sparkling wines a unique herbal dimension that is quite appealing. Well-known sparkling wine producers in Victoria include Yellowglen and Seppelt.

Western Australia

Lying on the western coast near Perth, the Western Australia region is far removed geographically from the rest of Australian winemaking. Located at its southwestern extreme is the Margaret River area, Western Australia's most prestigious wine-producing area. With high natural acidity and firm tannins, Margaret River products are considered by many the most European-style wines of Australia. Leading Margaret River producers include Leeuwin Estate and Vasse Felix.

AUSTRALIAN DESSERT WINES

Sweet dessert wines are an Australian specialty. Among the best known is the hazelnut-scented Yalumba Galway Pipe Port, which is similar to a Portuguese tawny, with a bit more almondy sweetness. Hardys Tawny Port Whiskers Blake NV and Chateau Reynella Museum Release are also Ports to seek out. Among late-harvest wines, the pineapple-and butterscotch-scented Peter Lehmann Sémillon Sauternes has proven itself a genuine value through the years. Finally, the island of Tasmania, off the coast of Melbourne, specializes in late-harvest Riesling and Gewürztraminer, both of which combine excellent acidity with well-balanced sweetness.

ABBEY VALE

Cabernet-Merlot Margaret River 1997: Earthy, tarry flavors characterize this firm-textured red, echoing mint and other herbal notes on the chewy finish. Best after 2002.–H.S. • $16 • (11/15/1999) • **83**

Cabernet-Merlot Margaret River 1995 • $20 • (11/30/1997) • **87**

Chardonnay Margaret River 1998: Bright and racy, with zesty, citrusy acidity supporting a range of pretty pear, apple and spice flavors that linger enticingly on the ripe finish. Drink now through 2003.–H.S. • $14 • (11/15/1999) • **88**

Chardonnay Margaret River 1997: A lean style, nicely focused to show off its lemony pear and mineral flavors, finishing with a gentle touch of spicy oak. Drink through 2002–H.S. • $14 • (10/31/1998) • **88**

Merlot-Shiraz Margaret River 1998: Firm and focused, with a distinctive flavor profile that echoes the herb of Merlot and the minty berry notes of Shiraz in a velvety package. Drink now through 2004.–H.S. • $16 • (3/31/2000) • **86**

Merlot-Shiraz Margaret River 1996: Crisp and bright, offering pretty plum and berry flavors with streaks of mint and sage running through. Crisp tannins want a bit of cellaring. Best after 1999.–H.S. • $16 • (10/15/1998) • **85**

Sauvignon Blanc Margaret River 1999: A solid white, redolent of herb, pepper and diesel-fuel overtones to the citrus and apple character. Drink now.–H.S. • $15 • (3/31/2000) • **85**

Sauvignon Blanc Margaret River 1998: A real eye-opener. Fresh, lively and juicy, not high in acidity, this rich mouthful of apricot, pear, passion fruit and light herb flavors remains rich and vibrant on the long finish. Drink now.–H.S. • $15 • (11/15/1999) • **91**

Sauvignon Blanc Margaret River 1997 • $17 • (11/30/1997) • **86**

Verdelho Margaret River 1999: Bright and appealing for its generous apple and delicately herbal flavors, which linger on the silky finish. Drink now.–H.S. • $15 • (3/31/2000) • **86**

Verdelho Margaret River 1998: Silky and bright, with spicy apple and citrus flavors that linger nicely on the round finish. Drink now.–H.S. • $14 • (11/15/1999) • **86**

ADAMS, TIM

Grenache Clare Valley The Fergus 1998: Tight, with a cedary edge to the plum and blueberry flavors. Finishes with a gush of fruit. Drink now through 2005.–J.L. • $22 • (5/31/2000) • **86**

Grenache Clare Valley The Fergus 1997: Light and supple, generous with its plum and spice flavors. Appealing from the first sip. Drink now.–H.S. • $20 • (2/28/1999) • **86**

Grenache Clare Valley The Fergus 1996 • $20 • (4/30/1998) • **85**

Shiraz Clare Valley 1996: Crisp and racy, with pretty currant and mint flavors that remind more of Cabernet than Shiraz, but what the hey, it's tasty. Drink now through 2003.–H.S. • $21 • (2/28/1999) • **87**

Shiraz Clare Valley 1992 • $16 • (11/15/1995) • **83**

ALL SAINTS

Merlot Rutherglen-Victoria Classic Release 1994 • $14 • (5/31/1997) • **85**

ALLANDALE

Chardonnay Hunter River Valley 1997: A supple, generous Chardonnay with a juicy core of pear, pineapple and mineral flavors that echo through the round finish. Drink now through 2002.–H.S. • $16 • (3/31/1999) • **89**

Shiraz Hunter River Valley Matthew 1996 • $17 • (5/15/1998) • **86**

Shiraz Hunter River Valley Matthew 1995 • $12 • (9/30/1997) • **89**

ALLANMERE

Shiraz Hunter Valley 1997: Crisp and generous, this brightly flavorful wine emphasizes its blackberry, leather and black pepper flavors on the firm finish. Flavors last and last. Approachable now. Drink now.–H.S. • $17 • (3/31/1999) • **91**

Verdelho Australia 1998: Fresh and crisp, with straightforward melon and leafy flavors. Drink now.–H.S. • $16 • (3/31/1999) • **81**

Key: SS—Spectator Selection. CS—Cellar Selection. HR—Highly Recommended. $NA—Price not available. (BT)—Barrel tasting. Ⓐ—Auction Price. For a key to the tasters' initials, see "How to Use These Listings."
Dates in parentheses represent the issues in which the ratings were published.

ALLINDA

Sauvignon Blanc Yarra Valley 1997 • $22 • (5/15/1998) • **85**

AMBERLEY

Sémillon-Sauvignon Blanc Margaret River 1999: Strong jalapeño, mineral and lime flavors are intense and focused, with just a twinge of bitterness on the finish. Drink now.–B.S. • $14 • (6/30/2000) • **86**

Shiraz Margaret River 1998: Lean and a bit prickly on the palate, this has chocolate and pepper notes followed by a fairly tart finish. Drink now through 2004.–B.S. • $22 • (6/30/2000) • **83**

ANGOVE'S

Cabernet Sauvignon South Eastern Australia Classic Reserve 1997: Light and velvety, with pretty bayleaf-scented black cherry flavors that finish smooth and simple. Drink now through 2002.–H.S. • $10 • (9/15/1999) • **83**

Cabernet Sauvignon South Eastern Australia Classic Reserve 1996: Soft and supple, with pretty cherry and anise flavors bouncing through the generous finish. Drink now.–H.S. • $10 • (10/15/1998) • **84**

Chardonnay South Eastern Australia Classic Reserve 1998: Silky and generous, with pretty pear and strongly spicy flavors that finish soft. Drink now.–H.S. • $10 • (9/15/1999) • **84**

Chardonnay South Eastern Australia Classic Reserve 1997: Light and fragrant, a pretty white with citrus, pear and vanilla flavors. Nicely proportioned. Drink now.–H.S. • $10 • (11/15/1998) • **85**

Shiraz South Eastern Australia Classic Reserve 1997: Simple and appealing for its pretty plum and blackberry flavors, which sail smoothly on the supple finish. Drink now.–H.S. • $10 • (9/15/1999) • **84**

Shiraz South Eastern Australia Classic Reserve 1996: Smooth and appealing for its round structure and focused berry and licorice flavors. Despite a layer of tannins, drink now for its lively balance.–H.S. • $10 • (10/15/1998) • **85**

ANTIPODEAN

Sauvignon Blanc-Sémillon-Viognier Yarra Valley 1997 • $15 • (6/15/1998) • **84**

Shiraz-Mourvèdre-Grenache-Viognier Barossa 1996 • $15 • (6/15/1998) • **87**

South Australia Red 1997: Ripe, exotic and silky-smooth, with decidedly spicy aromas and flavors. A pretty core of blackberry and plum lingers enticingly. Mourvèdre, Grenache, Shiraz and Viognier. Drink now through 2005.–H.S. • $16 • (6/15/1999) • **88**

South Australia White 1998: Ripe and fragrant, with nice earthy, herbal overtones to the ripe pear and fig flavors. Balanced to show the fruit. A blend of Sémillon, Sauvignon Blanc and Viognier. Drink now through 2002.–H.S. • $16 • (6/15/1999) • **87**

ARMSTRONG

Shiraz Great Western 1997: Flavors of dried wild berry combine with eucalyptus and wax notes in a medium-bodied, fairly lean structure. Drink now through 2005.–B.S. • $29 • (6/30/2000) • **84**

ARROWFIELD

Cabernet Sauvignon Australia Show Reserve 1990 • $15 • (11/30/1992) • **84**

Cabernet Sauvignon Hunter Valley Show Reserve 1995: The earthy, gamy flavors are reminiscent of barley soup or coffee, with enough ripe cherry flavor on the finish to keep this distinctive wine in balance. 250 cases imported. Best after 2001.–H.S. • $20 • (1/31/1999) • **82**

Cabernet Sauvignon Hunter Valley Show Reserve 1991 • $18 • (7/31/1994) • **86**

Cabernet Sauvignon McLaren Vale Show Reserve 1992 • $22 • (4/30/1996) • **87**

Cabernet Sauvignon-Merlot South Eastern Australia 1996: Light and spicy, with pretty raspberry and vanilla flavors gliding through the smooth finish. 450 cases imported. Drink now.–H.S. • $12 • (12/15/1998) • **84**

Cabernet Sauvignon-Merlot South Eastern Australia 1993 • $11 • (6/30/1995) • **81**

Cabernet Sauvignon-Merlot South Eastern Australia 1991 • $10 • (8/31/1994) • **83**

Cabernet-Merlot Australia 1990 • $10 • (3/31/1993) • **84**

Chardonnay South Eastern Australia 1997: Light and simple, with a resiny edge to the pear and caramel flavors.–H.S. • $12 • (12/15/1998) • **77**

Gewürztraminer South Eastern Australia Late Harvest 1993 • $11 • (5/15/1995) • **88**

Rhine Riesling Cowra Late Harvest Show Reserve 1993 • $22/375 ml. • (5/15/1996) • **90**
Shiraz Australia Show Reserve 1990 • $15 • (11/30/1992) • **85**
Shiraz Hunter Valley Show Reserve 1991 • $18 • (9/30/1994) • **89**
Shiraz McLaren Vale Show Reserve 1994: Smooth and generous with its plum, toast and anise flavors, finishing a bit narrow. Drink it with a rare steak. Drink through 2002.–H.S. • $20 • (12/15/1998) • **86**
Shiraz South Eastern Australia 1996: Light and spicy, with earthy black cherry notes bouncing through the chewy finish. Drink now through 2001.–H.S. • $12 • (12/15/1998) • **84**
Shiraz South Eastern Australia 1993 • $11 • (5/15/1995) • **84**
Shiraz South Eastern Australia 1991 • $10 • (9/30/1994) • **82**
Shiraz South Eastern Australia Show Reserve 1992 • $20 • (5/15/1995) • **88**
Shiraz-Cabernet Australia 1990 • $10 • (11/30/1992) • **87**

ARUNDA

Cabernet Sauvignon-Shiraz South Eastern Australia 1990 • $6 • (5/31/1993) • **81**
Chardonnay South Eastern Australia 1998: Fresh, generous, appealing for its mouthfilling apple, pineapple and guava notes that linger nicely on the soft finish. Drink now.–H.S. • $9 • (9/30/1999) • **85**
Shiraz-Cabernet South Eastern Australia 1996 • $9 • (4/30/1997) • **84**

ASHTON HILLS

Obliqua Adelaide Hills 1997: Herb juice, full of bell pepper and black currant leaf.–B.S. • $37 • (6/30/2000) • **76**
Pinot Noir Piccadilly Valley 1998: Ripe and silky, showing spice and plum flavors, medium body and concentration, ending with a touch of heat. Drink now.–B.S. • $40 • (6/30/2000) • **81**

ASHWOOD GROVE

Cabernet Sauvignon Riverina 1991 • $10 • (7/15/1993) • **84**
Cabernet Sauvignon Riverland 1992 • $9 • (6/30/1995) • **83**
River Willow Red Riverland 1991 • $7 • (5/31/1993) • **85**
River Willow White Riverland 1993 • $7 • (6/30/1995) • **73**
Shiraz Riverina 1991 • $9 • (5/31/1993) • **84**
Shiraz Riverland 1993 • $9 • (3/31/1996) • **83**
Shiraz Riverland 1992 • $9 • (6/30/1995) • **83**

AUSTRALIAN DOMAINE WINES

Shiraz Limestone Coast Sheeraz 1998: Bold and intense. Smells and tastes like cough medicine, with tart berry, earth and anise flavors. Drink now.–J.L. • $25 • (6/30/2000) • **80**
The Hattrick McLaren Vale 1998: Beautiful purity to the violet and blackberry aromas, followed by notes of sage and earth, all wrapped in a cloak of lively acidity and firm tannins. Well balanced and promising for the future. Shiraz, Grenache and Cabernet Sauvignon. Best from 2001 through 2005.–B.S. • $46 • (6/30/2000) • **90**

AUSVETIA

Shiraz South Australia 1995: Ripe, round and dripping with berry, cherry and plum flavors, offering gobs of fruit, shaded with hints of coffee and smoke on the long, supple finish. A big, muscular wine that finishes with remarkable finesse. Drink now through 2010.–H.S. • $60 • (9/15/1999) • **93**
Shiraz South Australia 1994 • $60 • (5/15/1998) • **92**

AVALON

Shiraz South Eastern Australia 1999: Vegetal, with a muddled green note and only glimpses of berry flavors.–J.L. • $9 • (6/30/2000) • **77**

BANROCK STATION

Chardonnay South Eastern Australia Unwooded 1999: Light and pretty, with a refreshing tang of citrus and green apple flavor. Drink now.–H.S. • $5 • (12/15/1999) • **82**
Chardonnay South Eastern Australia Unwooded 1998: Fresh, fruity and appealing for its straight-ahead apple flavors balanced nicely with a modest touch of oak. Drink now.–H.S. • $7 • (3/31/1999) • **82**
Chardonnay South Eastern Australia Unwooded 1997 • $7 • (11/30/1997) • **84**
Grenache-Shiraz South Eastern Australia 1999: A pretty rosé, with floral, watermelon and strawberry flavors on a soft frame. Almost sweet. Drink now.–H.S. • $6 • (11/15/1999) • **83**
Riesling South Eastern Australia 1998: Light and refreshing, with a sappy edge to the modest apple flavors. Drink now.–H.S. • $5 • (11/15/1999) • **83**
Sémillon-Chardonnay South Eastern Australia 1999: Fresh and appealing for its ebullient pear and grassy spice flavors, which linger on the round finish. Drink now.–H.S. • $5 • (11/30/1999) • **83**
Sémillon-Chardonnay South Eastern Australia 1998: Offering a generous portion of ripe fig and pear flavors on a supple frame and finishing juicy and soft, just short of sweet, this white blend delivers pleasurable drinking that belies its affordable price. Ready now.–H.S. • $6 • (3/31/1999) • **84**
Sémillon-Chardonnay South Eastern Australia 1997 • $6 • (11/30/1997) • **83**
Shiraz South Eastern Australia 1999: Spicy, with ripe, round raspberry notes and a twang of herbalness on the finish. Drink now.–J.L. • $7 • (6/30/2000) • **86**
Shiraz South Eastern Australia 1998: Need a few bottles, yet minding the budget? This chewy-style Shiraz can be counted on for its nice core of blackberry flavor and solid, lingering finish. Drink now through 2002.–H.S. • $7 • (3/31/1999) • **85**
Shiraz South Eastern Australia 1997 • $7 • (2/28/1998) • **87**
Shiraz-Cabernet South Eastern Australia 1999: Bright and lively, a pretty mouthful of blackberry and currant, finishing with a wild berry edge. Drink now.–H.S. • $6 • (11/30/1999) • **82**
Shiraz-Cabernet South Eastern Australia 1998: Firm in texture, with slightly gritty tannins and a solid core of blackberry and spice. Good with hearty food. Drink now.–H.S. • $6 • (11/30/1998) • **84**
Shiraz-Cabernet South Eastern Australia 1997 • $6 • (5/31/1998) • **88**
Shiraz-Cabernet South Eastern Australia 1996 • $6 • (11/30/1997) • **86**

BAROSSA RIDGE

Shiraz Barossa Valley Old Creek 1998: Enough leather for a pair of shoes. Dense and earthy, with a leathery tobacco streak that turns bitter on the finish.–J.L. • $38 • (6/30/2000) • **77**

BAROSSA VALLEY ESTATE

Cabernet Sauvignon South Australia 1987 • $11 • (1/31/1990) • **83**
Chardonnay Barossa Valley 1999: Ripe, straightforward style of Chardonnay centers around pretty apple and spice flavors which persist on the open-textured finish. Drink now through 2004.–H.S. • $10 • (6/30/2000) • **85**
Chardonnay Barossa Valley Ebenezer 1997: Maturing fast, this has a spicy edge to the pineapple and mineral flavors, hinting at honey on the slightly dry finish. Drink now through 2002.–H.S. • $16 • (11/15/1999) • **85**
Shiraz Barossa Valley 1998: Tight, firm style offers intense, classic blackberry and anise flavors under a layer of chewy tannins. Best after 2002.–H.S. • $10 • (6/30/2000) • **88**
Shiraz Barossa Valley E&E Black Pepper 1997: Distinctively spicy, brimming with prune, pepper and leather aromas and flavors on a rich, supple frame. A towering Barossa Shiraz that keeps ringing beautifully on the finish, and can only deepen with additional cellaring. Drink now through 2012.–H.S. • $65 • (6/30/2000) HR • **94**
Shiraz Barossa Valley E&E Black Pepper 1996: A profound wine, This Australian Shiraz burrows deep into its plush texture to reveal gorgeous flavors of ripe plum, berry and exotic spice, all balanced impressively on an elegant frame. The tannins are refined and well integrated. Approachable already. Best after 2001.–H.S. • $60 • (11/15/1999) HR • **97**
Shiraz Barossa Valley E&E Black Pepper 1995: Ripe, rich and exotic, here's a big mouthful of anise- and pepper-scented black fruit flavors; a gooey wine with layers of character that last nicely on the finish. Firm tannins can use cellaring. Drink through 2005–H.S. • $70 • (3/31/1999) • **91**
Shiraz Barossa Valley E&E Black Pepper 1994 • $60 • (6/15/1997) • **87**
Shiraz Barossa Valley Ebenezer 1997: Firm in texture, with juicy plum, blackberry and rose petal flavors, the fruit echoing enticingly amid the fine-grained tannins on the finish. Appealing already, but it's destined for a long life. Drink now through 2012.–H.S. • $29 • (6/30/2000) • **92**
Shiraz Barossa Valley Ebenezer 1996: A serious red, packed with pepper-shaded plum and black cherry flavors that linger on the firm finish. Has personality and intensity, and should be a beauty for a long time. Best after 2001.–H.S. • $29 • (11/15/1999) • **92**
Shiraz Barossa Valley Ebenezer 1995: Supple and appealing for its balance, this is a rich-textured wine with layers of anise-scented blackberry, earth and spice flavors that echo nicely on the firm finish. Drink now through 2005.–H.S. • $25 • (3/31/1999) • **90**
Shiraz Barossa Valley Ebenezer 1994 • $25 • (5/31/1997) • **88**

BAROSSAVALE

Merlot South Australia 1997: Firm, chewy and focused, showing some ripe berry flavors behind the hard veneer of tannin. Best after 2001.–H.S. • $25 • (9/15/1999) • **83**

BARRATT

Pinot Noir Adelaide Hills Piccadilly Valley 1996 • $21 • (4/30/1998) • **82**

BARRIER REEF

Cabernet Sauvignon South Eastern Australia 1993 • $7 • (10/15/1996) • **84**
Cabernet Sauvignon South Eastern Australia 1992 • $8 • (11/30/1995) • **85**
Cabernet Sauvignon-Shiraz South Eastern Australia 1991 • $7 • (6/30/1993) • **76**

BARRINGTON

Chardonnay Hunter Valley 1997: Fresh and bright, this zingy wine has melon, pineapple and spice flavors that linger on the zesty finish. Drink now through 2002.–H.S. • $15 • (11/15/1999) • **86**
Shiraz-Cabernet-Merlot South Eastern Australia 1998: Smooth, soft and pretty, with nice raspberry and cherry notes floating through the modest structure to make an amiable dinner wine. Drink now.–H.S. • $17 • (11/15/1999) • **83**

BARRY, BRIAN

Cabernet Sauvignon Clare Valley Jud's Hill Vineyard 1996: Lean and herbal, with more mint character than fruit, but it picks up raspberry and tobacco flavors on the supple finish. Best after 2001.–H.S. • $14 • (6/15/1999) • **85**
Cabernet Sauvignon Clare Valley Jud's Hill Vineyard 1994 • $16 • (5/31/1998) • **85**
Shiraz McLaren Vale Special Release 1998: Bright and focused, this juicy Shiraz delivers ripe blackberry and a touch of spice, all backed up by a firm structure. Drink now.–B.S. • $25 • (6/30/2000) • **83**

BARRY, JIM

Cabernet-Malbec Clare Valley McCrae Wood 1996: Firm and chewy, with a gamy edge to the berry and cherry flavors lingering beneath. Picks up a distinctive minty note on the finish. Best from 2001 through 2006.–H.S. • $30 • (9/15/1999) • **87**
Cabernet-Malbec Clare Valley McCrae Wood 1995 • $31 • (6/15/1998) • **85**
Shiraz Clare Valley McCrae Wood 1996: Bright and jazzy, a racy mouthful of raspberry, mineral, blackberry and game flavors that swirl through the fine-textured finish. A stylish wine with power. Best after 2001.–H.S. • $35 • (9/15/1999) • **90**
Shiraz Clare Valley McCrae Wood 1995 • $31 • (6/15/1998) • **88**
Shiraz Clare Valley McCrae Wood 1994 • $30 • (5/31/1997) • **89**
Shiraz Clare Valley The Armagh 1996: A jazzy mouthful, filled with personality, shading its bright plum and blackberry with hints of pepper and herbs, picking up a nice bay leaf note on the generous, firm-textured finish. A hummer already. Best after 2000.–H.S. • $100 • (9/15/1999) • **92**
Shiraz Clare Valley The Armagh 1995 • $91 Ⓐ • (6/15/1998) • **92**
Shiraz Clare Valley The Armagh 1994 • $75 • (5/31/1997) • **91**

BARWANG

Cabernet Sauvignon Australia 1992 • $18 • (9/30/1994) • **89**
Cabernet Sauvignon Coonawarra Regional Selection 1997: On the light side, but it shows nice cherry and currant flavors, with an overlay of herbal notes. Drink now through 2004.–H.S. • $14 • (3/31/2000) • **85**
Cabernet Sauvignon Coonawarra Regional Selection 1996: A lighter, supple style of Cabernet, emphasizing pretty currant flavors and a soft texture that's supported with a touch of lemony acidity on the finish. Drink now.–H.S. • $12 • (2/28/1999) • **84**
Cabernet Sauvignon Hilltops Winemaker's Reserve 1997: Smooth and fruity, with polished herb and cherry notes. Drink now.–J.L. • $20 • (6/30/2000) • **85**
Cabernet Sauvignon New South Wales 1994 • $16 • (4/30/1996) • **88**
Cabernet Sauvignon New South Wales 1993 • $18 • (10/15/1995) • **85**
Cabernet Sauvignon New South Wales Winemaker's Reserve 1996: Tight and chewy, this lean style of Cabernet has earthy, tobacco-scented currant and mint flavors that linger. Drink through 2006.–H.S. • $18 • (11/30/1998) • **87**
Cabernet Sauvignon South Eastern Australia Vintage Selection 1997: Soft and exotic, with spicy, herbal notes exceeding the modest fruit flavors. Drink now.–H.S. • $9 • (2/28/1999) • **81**
Chardonnay South Eastern Australia Regional Selection 1997: Simple and appealing for its generous pear and spice flavors. Drink now.–H.S. • $12 • (1/31/1999) • **81**
Chardonnay South Eastern Australia Vintage Selection 1997: Simple, generous with its citrusy pear and spice flavors on a modest frame. Drink now.–H.S. • $9 • (1/31/1999) • **84**
Shiraz Australia 1991 • $18 • (9/30/1994) • **84**
Shiraz Coonawarra Regional Selection 1997: Light and appealing for its pretty plum and berry flavors that linger nicely on the open-textured finish. Drink now through 2005.–H.S. • $14 • (3/31/2000) • **86**
Shiraz Coonawarra Regional Selection 1996: Firm in texture but packed with flavor, favoring black cherry, black pepper and licorice notes that linger nicely on a crisp frame. Beautifully focused. Drink now.–H.S. • $12 • (2/28/1999) • **87**
Shiraz Hilltops Winemaker's Reserve 1997: Juicy, with plum, leather and tobacco notes, moderate acidity and firm tannins. Mouthwatering finish. Drink now through 2002.–B.S. • $27 • (6/30/2000) • **88**
Shiraz New South Wales 1994 • $16 • (4/30/1996) • **86**
Shiraz New South Wales 1992 • $18 • (11/15/1995) • **85**
Shiraz New South Wales Winemaker's Reserve 1996: Soft and silky, with lovely blackberry, black cherry, spice and vanilla notes and a creamy mouthfeel that invites yet another sip. Just delicious. Drink now through 2001.–H.S. • $18 • (11/30/1998) • **88**
Shiraz South Eastern Australia 1998: Jammy strawberry and white pepper notes are friendly and straightforward. Drink now through 2002.–J.L. • $8 • (6/30/2000) • **83**
Shiraz South Eastern Australia Vintage Selection 1997: Light, soft and appealing for its pretty berry and mineral flavors. Drink now.–H.S. • $9 • (2/28/1999) • **82**

BASEDOW

Bush Vine Grenache Barossa 1995 • $10 • (11/30/1997) • **87**
Chardonnay Barossa 1998: Ripe and spicy. A jazzy mouthful of pear, peach and caramel flavors that lasts on the sleek finish. Drink now.–H.S. • $14 • (9/30/1999) • **87**
Chardonnay Barossa 1997: Ripe and refreshing. A lively mouthful of pear, melon and spice flavors that keep bouncing through the finish.–H.S. • $12 • (10/15/1998) • **87**
Grenache Barossa Bush Vine 1996: Light and fruity, with a spicy edge to the raspberry flavors, all lingering on the firm finish. Drink now.–H.S. • $11 • (10/15/1998) • **84**
Sémillon Barossa Valley 1997: Ripe and generous, this distinctive Australian white has grapefruit and tobacco overtones to its tasty pear and pineapple character. Makes lively drinking at an appealing price. Tempting now. Best after 2001.–H.S. • $11 • (11/15/1999) • **87**
Shiraz Barossa 1997: Smooth and gamy, an earthy wine on a remarkably supple frame, picking up some nice ripe plum and prune notes on the soft, spicy finish. Drink now through 2005.–H.S. • $15 • (9/15/1999) • **86**
Shiraz Barossa 1996: A bright medley of cheerful raspberry and red cherry flavors, shaded with hints of pepper and licorice on the velvety finish. Drink now.–H.S. • $16 • (10/15/1998) • **87**
Shiraz Barossa 1995 • $17 • (11/30/1997) • **85**

BASS PHILLIP

Pinot Noir Victoria 1995 • $35 • (8/31/1997) • **86**
Pinot Noir Victoria Premium 1997: Rich, deep, ripe and concentrated. A gorgeous mouthful of blackberry, currant and spice aromas and flavors that cascade smoothly and gently through the long finish. Has style and intensity. Best after 2000.–H.S. • $79 • (9/30/1999) • **91**
Pinot Noir Victoria Premium 1995 • $55 • (8/31/1997) • **91**
Pinot Noir Victoria Reserve 1995 • $75 • (8/31/1997) • **89**

Key: SS—Spectator Selection. CS—Cellar Selection. HR—Highly Recommended. $NA—Price not available. (BT)—Barrel tasting. Ⓐ—Auction Price. For a key to the tasters' initials, see "How to Use These Listings."
Dates in parentheses represent the issues in which the ratings were published.

BEACON HILL

Sémillon-Chardonnay South Eastern Australia 1998: Light and snappy, with an herbal edge to the bright pear flavors. Drink now.–H.S. • $9 • (11/15/1999) • **82**

Shiraz-Cabernet South Eastern Australia 1998: Ripe and open, with pretty blackberry and cherry flavors that persist on the smooth finish. Drink now through 2006.–H.S. • $9 • (11/15/1999) • **85**

BENJAMIN

Muscat Victoria Museum Reserve NV: Sweet, rich, unctuous, deep and delicious—like opening a spice box while chewing on a mouthful of dried fruit. Deliriously exotic and ripe, hitting extra walnut and pecan notes and finishing satiny-smooth. Drink now.–H.S. • $16/375 ml. • (2/29/2000) • **93**

Tokay Victoria Museum Release NV: Oxidized, with stale pecan pie-like flavors right down to the burnt crust. Still enjoyable, with a range of sweet-tasting, sugary flavors. Drink now through 2006.–J.L. • $16/375 ml. • (6/30/2000) • **89**

Tokay Victoria Museum Reserve NV: Gently spicy, harmonious and supple, with smooth-textured raisin, aromatic spice, dried apricot, dried cherry and even a hint of citrus sneaking in on the long, long finish. Drink now.–H.S. • $16/375 ml. • (2/29/2000) • **92**

BETHANY CREEK

Chardonnay South Eastern Australia 1997: Pleasant apple and grapefruit flavors make this modest white easy to quaff. Drink now.–H.S. • $10 • (3/31/1999) • **82**

Merlot South Eastern Australia 1997: Firm in texture, and its earthy tobacco and berry flavors have little charm.–H.S. • $10 • (3/31/1999) • **78**

Shiraz South Eastern Australia 1996 • $11 • (4/30/1997) • **70**

BIMBADGEN

Cabernet Sauvignon Hunter Valley Estate 1998: Sweaty and musty, with a dry structure and little charm. Tasted twice, with consistent notes.–B.S. • $18 • (6/30/2000) • **75**

BIRCHWOOD

Cabernet Sauvignon Langhorne Creek Twin Rivers 1998: The sweet oak and dill flavors never come to an agreement in this awkward, tannic red.–B.S. • $30 • (6/30/2000) • **79**

BLACK CREEK

Pinot Noir South Eastern Australia 1997: Light, with lean herb, spice and tart berry flavors and a minty finish. Drink now.–J.L. • $8 • (6/30/2000) • **80**

BLACK MARLIN

Shiraz South Eastern Australia 1998: Coarse and on the earthy, herbal side, with tart cranberry flavors and a short finish. Drink now.–J.L. • $9 • (6/30/2000) • **80**

BLACK OPAL

Cabernet Sauvignon South Eastern Australia 1997: Soft and pleasant for its modest level of spicy, grapey flavors. Drink now.–H.S. • $11 • (3/31/1999) • **80**

Cabernet Sauvignon South Eastern Australia 1996 • $11 • (11/30/1997) • **86**

Cabernet Sauvignon South Eastern Australia 1995 • $10 • (1/31/1997) • **80**

Cabernet Sauvignon South Eastern Australia 1994 • $9 • (4/30/1996) • **85**

Cabernet Sauvignon South Eastern Australia 1992 • $10 • (4/30/1994) • **83**

Cabernet Sauvignon South Eastern Australia 1989 • $9 • (11/30/1992) • **78**

Cabernet Sauvignon-Merlot Barossa 1996: Rich and ripe, with spicy cherry and herb flavors emerging and lingering on the smooth palate. Has more up front than on the finish. Drink now through 2005.–H.S. • $16 • (11/15/1999) • **85**

Cabernet Sauvignon-Merlot Coonawarra Reserve 1995 • $16 • (5/15/1997) • **83**

Cabernet Sauvignon-Merlot South Australia Reserve 1994 • $14 • (4/30/1996) • **80**

Cabernet Sauvignon-Merlot South Eastern Australia 1998: Smooth and generous, this simple red has nice blackberry and smoke flavors that have more up front than on the finish. Drink now through 2003.–H.S. • $11 • (11/15/1999) • **83**

Cabernet Sauvignon-Merlot South Eastern Australia 1997: Ripe and flavorful, certainly richer than most comparatively priced bottlings, this enticing red blend is adorned with pretty berry, vanilla and spice notes that linger on the velvety finish. Drink now.–H.S. • $11 • (3/31/1999) • **85**

Cabernet Sauvignon-Merlot South Eastern Australia 1996 • $11 • (11/30/1997) • **82**

Cabernet Sauvignon-Merlot South Eastern Australia 1995 • $10 • (1/31/1997) • **79**

Cabernet Sauvignon-Merlot South Eastern Australia 1994 • $9 • (4/30/1996) • **83**

Cabernet Sauvignon-Merlot South Eastern Australia 1992 • $10 • (4/30/1994) • **81**

Cabernet Sauvignon-Merlot South Eastern Australia 1990 • $9 • (4/15/1993) • **87**

Cabernet Sauvignon-Merlot South Eastern Australia 1989 • $9 • (11/30/1992) • **82**

Chardonnay South Eastern Australia 1998: Bright and appealing for its crisp peach and pear flavors. Drink now.–H.S. • $11 • (2/28/1999) • **82**

Chardonnay South Eastern Australia 1997 • $11 • (3/31/1998) • **85**

Shiraz Barossa 1996: Rich and bright in flavor, with focused berry, plum and spice flavors that ring with a hint of pickle barrel on the finish. Smooth and distinctive, this is very pretty already. Drink now through 2002.–H.S. • $16 • (11/15/1999) • **87**

Shiraz South Eastern Australia 1998: Clove, tea and cherry flavors mingle nicely on a solid frame with a substantial finish. Drink now through 2002.–J.L. • $11 • (6/30/2000) • **83**

Shiraz South Eastern Australia 1997: Smooth and round, generous with its pretty black cherry and coffee flavors. Drink now.–H.S. • $11 • (2/28/1999) • **83**

Shiraz South Eastern Australia 1996 • $11 • (3/31/1998) • **87**

Shiraz South Eastern Australia 1995 • $10 • (2/28/1997) • **84**

Shiraz South Eastern Australia 1994 • $9 • (4/30/1996) • **82**

Shiraz South Eastern Australia 1991 • $10 • (3/31/1994) • **83**

Shiraz South Eastern Australia 1990 • $8 • (11/30/1992) • **80**

BLACK ROCK

Cabernet Sauvignon Coonawarra 1995 • $22 • (11/30/1997) • **87**

BLASS, WOLF

Black Label Cabernet-Shiraz-Merlot Australia 1994: Strives for elegance, the Shiraz feeling leaner and more astringent via the addition of Merlot, offering modest berry and tobacco flavors and a firm finish. Best from 2001 through 2004.–H.S. • $60 • (1/31/1999) • **84**

Black Label Cabernet-Shiraz South Australia Bilyara 1992 • $40 • (7/31/1996) • **89**

Black Label Cabernet-Shiraz South Australia 1987 • $26 • (8/31/1994) • **87**

Black Label Cabernet-Shiraz-Merlot South Australia 1986 • $25 • (5/31/1993) • **90**

Black Label Cabernet-Merlot South Australia 1983 • $25 • (4/30/1989) • **77**

Black Label Cabernet-Shiraz Clare-Barossa Valleys 1982 • $25 • (4/15/1988) • **88**

Black Label Cabernet-Shiraz Australia 1980 • $18 • (7/01/1987) • **89**

Cabernet Sauvignon South Australia President's Selection 1993 • $16 • (6/15/1996) • **87**

Cabernet Sauvignon South Australia President's Selection 1995: Smooth and silky, with exotic licorice and spice overtones to the lithe core of pretty currant flavor, all echoing nicely on the graceful finish. Drink through 2004.–H.S. • $18 • (2/28/1999) • **86**

Cabernet Sauvignon South Australia President's Selection 1994 • $16 • (4/30/1997) • **86**

Cabernet Sauvignon South Australia President's Selection 1989 • $15 • (8/31/1994) • **83**

Cabernet Sauvignon South Australia President's Selection 1987 • $15 • (5/31/1993) • **85**

Cabernet Sauvignon South Australia President's Selection 1986 • $18 • (3/15/1992) • **78**

Cabernet Sauvignon South Australia President's Selection 1983 • $14 • (4/30/1988) • **76**

Cabernet Sauvignon South Australia Yellow Label 1997: Light in texture, with straightforward berry and cedar flavors that echo on the finish. An easy-to-drink style. Drink now.–H.S. • $12 • (2/28/1999) • **83**

Cabernet Sauvignon South Australia Yellow Label 1996 • $12 • (3/31/1998) • **84**

BLASS, WOLF

Cabernet Sauvignon South Australia Yellow Label 1995 • $12 • (5/15/1997) • **83**
Cabernet Sauvignon South Australia Yellow Label 1994 • $11 • (6/15/1996) • **86**
Cabernet Sauvignon South Australia Yellow Label 1992 • $10 • (8/31/1994) • **85**
Cabernet Sauvignon South Australia Yellow Label 1990 • $10 • (5/31/1993) • **86**
Cabernet Sauvignon South Australia Yellow Label 1989 • $10 • (6/30/1993) • **81**
Cabernet Sauvignon South Australia Yellow Label 1988 • $10 • (3/15/1992) • **88**
Cabernet Sauvignon South Australia Yellow Label 1984 • $10 • (4/30/1989) • **78**
Cabernet-Shiraz Langhorne Creek 1981 • $18 • (7/01/1987) • **90**
Chardonnay McLaren Vale Presidents Selection 1997: Fresh, with an appealing core of pear and quince flavors on an open-textured frame. Has some nice spice and resin notes on the finish. Drink now through 2001.–H.S. • $15 • (2/28/1999) • **86**
Chardonnay South Australia 1999: Bright and fruity, offering pretty apple and pear notes on a lively frame. Drink now.–H.S. • $12 • (12/31/1999) • **85**
Chardonnay South Australia 1998: Fresh, fruity and appealing, with a touch of mineral behind the apple and pear flavors. Drink now.–H.S. • $12 • (2/28/1999) • **83**
Chardonnay South Australia 1997 • $12 • (3/31/1998) • **84**
Grenache Clare Valley Old Vine Presidents Selection 1995 • $19 • (11/30/1997) • **87**
Riesling Eden-Clare Valleys Rhine Gold Label 1998: Bright and fresh, a juicy mouthful of green apple, citrus and peach flavors that remain elegant and smooth through the finish. Delicious now, and will improve through 2010.–H.S. • $12 • (1/31/1999) • **89**
Riesling South Australia Gold Label 1999: Soft and generous, vibrant with lime and green apple flavors that linger on the dry finish. Drink now through 2009.–H.S. • $12 • (6/30/2000) • **88**
Shiraz South Australia 1997: Soft and aromatic, a generous mouthful of anise-scented berry, black cherry and prune flavors that linger on the supple finish. Drink now through 2007.–H.S. • $12 • (12/31/1999) • **87**
Shiraz South Australia 1996 • $12 • (5/15/1998) • **87**
Shiraz South Australia President's Selection 1995: Ripe, rich and complex, layered with berry, cherry, tar and dried tomato flavors that power through the solid finish. Has more up front than on the finish, but it's distinctive and velvety. Drink now through 2002.–H.S. • $18 • (2/28/1999) • **87**
Shiraz South Australia Presidents Selection 1994 • $16 • (4/30/1997) • **86**
Shiraz South Australia President's Selection 1990 • $13 • (9/30/1994) • **86**
Shiraz South Australia President's Selection 1988 • $15 • (5/31/1993) • **85**
Shiraz-Cabernet Sauvignon South Australia Red Label 1997: If it's a good-drinking red value you're after, here's your wine. It's supple and refreshingly open-textured, with distinctive, spiced red cherry, blackberry and anise flavors that finish gracefully. Drink now through 2007.–H.S. • $12 • (1/31/2000) • **88**
Shiraz-Cabernet South Australia Red Label 1996 • $NA • (3/31/1998) • **85**
Shiraz-Cabernet South Australia Red Label 1995 • $11 • (1/31/1997) • **85**

BLEASDALE

Cabernet Sauvignon Longhorne Creek 1990 • $9 • (6/30/1995) • **86**
Malbec Langhorne Creek 1992 • $8 • (3/31/1996) • **80**
Shiraz Langhorne Creek 1993 • $8 • (3/31/1996) • **87**
Shiraz Langhorne Creek Bremerview 1997: Begins with herbal notes, then flavors of dried berry and chocolate come through. Just a bit tart and green on the finish. Drink now through 2004.–B.S. • $16 • (6/30/2000) • **85**
Shiraz Langhorne Creek Bremerview 1994 • $11 • (6/15/1997) • **85**
Shiraz Longhorne Creek 1992 • $8 • (5/15/1995) • **87**
Shiraz-Cabernet Sauvignon Langhorne Creek 1992 • $8 • (3/31/1996) • **87**
Shiraz-Cabernet Sauvignon Langhorne Creek 1989 • $7 • (5/31/1993) • **78**

BLUE PYRENEES

Cabernet Sauvignon Australia 1982 • $20 • (5/31/1987) • **89**
Chardonnay Victoria 1998: Bright and lively, this zingy wine has citrusy pear and honey flavors that pick up a sappy edge on the lean finish. Drink now through 2003.–H.S. • $22 • (11/15/1999) • **87**
Estate Red Victoria 1997: Crisp, elegant and balanced to show off its lean core of berry and plum flavors, which linger on the refined finish. Not as rich as some vintages, but nicely done. Cabernet, Merlot and Shiraz. Drink now through 2005.–H.S. • $22 • (5/15/2000) • **87**
Estate Red Victoria 1995 • $24 • (5/15/1998) • **88**

Key: SS—Spectator Selection. CS—Cellar Selection. HR—Highly Recommended. $NA—Price not available. (BT)—Barrel tasting. (A)—Auction Price.
For a key to the tasters' initials, see "How to Use These Listings."
Dates in parentheses represent the issues in which the ratings were published.

Sparkling Australia Midnight Cuvée NV • $26 • (5/31/1998) • **87**

BOOTS

Grenache Barossa Valley 1998: Lean and waxy, with a touch of spice and blueberry. Turns earthy, with an anise edge. Drink now through 2004.–J.L. • $15 • (5/31/2000) • **85**

BOULDER OPAL

Chardonnay South Eastern Australia Malo-Oak 1997: Light and refreshing for its pretty pear and nectarine flavors on a simple, soft frame. Drink now.–H.S. • $14 • (2/28/1999) • **85**

BOUTIQUE

Chardonnay Adelaide Hills The Region 1998: Lean and a bit earthy, with pretty pear and spice notes lingering on the impressive finish. A stylish wine with enough depth to suggest it might improve over the short term. A blend of barrels from five Adelaide Hills wineries. Drink now through 2004.–H.S. • $35 • (11/15/1999) • **88**
Shiraz Australia The Blend 1997: Supple in texture, complex and generous with its raspberry, black cherry and toasty, chocolaty notes meandering through the plush finish. A collaborative blend of Shiraz created by various Australian winemakers. Drink now through 2005.–H.S. • $75 • (5/15/1999) • **90**

BOWEN ESTATE

Cabernet Sauvignon Coonawarra 1992 • $22 • (10/31/1995) • **89**
Red Coonawarra 1992 • $22 • (10/31/1995) • **89**
Shiraz Coonawarra 1996: Crisp and focused, its sharp beam of currant, guava and black pepper flavors remaining supple enough on the finish to make it appealing now. Drink through 2005.–H.S. • $22 • (1/31/1999) • **87**
Shiraz Coonawarra 1995 • $11 • (6/15/1997) • **82**

BOYNTON'S OF BRIGHT

Brut South Eastern Australia NV: Light, bright and fruity, with pretty pear and spice flavors in a refreshing style. Drink now.–H.S. • $23 • (3/31/2000) • **86**

BRANDS LAIRA

Cabernet Sauvignon Coonawarra 1991 • $13 • (9/30/1994) • **84**
Cabernet Sauvignon Coonawarra Laira 1993 • $15 • (6/30/1995) • **87**
Shiraz Coonawarra 1994 • $15 • (4/30/1996) • **90**
Shiraz Coonawarra 1992 • $15 • (6/30/1995) • **84**
Shiraz Coonawarra 1990 • $13 • (10/31/1993) • **86**

BREMERTON

Cabernet-Shiraz-Merlot Langhorne Creek 1997: Shows eucalyptus and waxy notes, with some herbal and chocolate flavors. A bit lean. Drink now through 2002.–B.S. • $20 • (6/30/2000) • **83**
Shiraz Langhorne Creek Y.V. 1997: Ripe, with chocolate, leather and subtle mint notes that show good richness and length through the softly tannic finish. Drink now through 2006.–B.S. • $20 • (6/30/2000) • **87**

BRIAR RIDGE

Cabernet Sauvignon Hunter Valley 1996 • $17 • (5/31/1998) • **83**
Chardonnay Hunter Valley Hand Picked 1997 • $17 • (5/31/1998) • **85**
Shiraz Hunter Valley Old Vines 1996 • $17 • (5/31/1998) • **87**

BRIDGEWATER MILL

Shiraz Australia Millstone 1996: Dense and deep in color, with powerful mint-scented black cherry and anise flavors at the core. Layers of fruit and spice continue to unfold on the firm, smoothly chewy finish, lasting impressively. Drink through 2004.–H.S. • $17 • (8/31/1998) • **90**
Shiraz McLaren Vale Millstone 1993 • $15 • (5/31/1996) • **88**

BRIEN

Shiraz-Cabernet Victoria Family Selection 1996 • $14 • (4/30/1998) • **71**

BROKE FORDWICH

Chardonnay Hunter Valley 1997 • $12 • (6/15/1998) • **86**

BROKENWOOD

Cabernet Sauvignon South Eastern Australia 1990 • $15 • (5/15/1994) • **82**
Sémillon Hunter Valley 1999: Youthful, bright and elegant, showing lots of tart, citrusy flavors, centering on lime and mineral notes that pick up hints of spicy apple on the long finish. Needs time to flesh out. Best after 2002.–H.S. • $18 • (6/30/2000) • **88**
Shiraz Australia 1998: Big and ripe, with spice, leather, blackberry and pepper notes that turn dry and leathery. Drink now.–J.L. • $24 • (6/30/2000) • **86**
Shiraz McLaren Vale-King Valley 1997: Has a firm layer of fine tannins under the bright plum and berry flavors, giving this a raw edge that suggests it needs cellaring. Drink through 2006.–H.S. • $21 • (6/15/1999) • **87**
Shiraz South Eastern Australia 1990 • $15 • (10/31/1993) • **86**

BROWN BROTHERS

Cabernet Sauvignon King Valley Family Selection 1991 • $10 • (6/30/1994) • **80**
Cabernet Sauvignon Victoria Family Selection Reserve 1988 • $17 • (4/30/1995) • **88**
Cabernet Sauvignon Victoria Reserve 1987 • $12 • (9/15/1990) • **83**
Chardonnay Australia Reserve NV • $9 • (5/31/1987) • **86**
Everton Family Selection King Valley Red 1992 • $9 • (6/30/1995) • **85**
Everton Family Selection Victoria Red 1990 • $7 • (3/31/1995) • **81**
Muscat Victoria Lexia Family Selection 1993 • $9 • (5/15/1995) • **87**
Port Victoria Family Selection Wood Matured Reserve NV • $8 • (3/31/1995) • **86**
Shiraz King Valley Family Selection 1991 • $9 • (9/30/1994) • **85**
Shiraz Victoria 1990 • $9 • (5/31/1993) • **82**
Shiraz-Cabernet Sauvignon Victoria 1988 • $9 • (5/31/1993) • **83**
Shiraz-Mondeuse-Cabernet Sauvignon Australia 1983 • $10 • (7/01/1987) • **87**
Tarrango Victoria Red 1993 • $8 • (1/31/1995) • **83**

BROWNS' OF PADTHAWAY

Cabernet Sauvignon Padthaway Family Reserve 1995 • $19 • (5/31/1998) • **87**
Shiraz Padthaway T-Trellis 1995 • $19 • (5/15/1998) • **85**

BUCKELEY'S

Cabernet Sauvignon-Merlot South Australia 1997: This mostly Cabernet blend is firm in texture, with a nice core of ripe blackberry and tobacco flavors that extend into a solid finish. A substantial red—at a price that's hard to beat. Drink now through 2002.–H.S. • $10 • (5/31/1999) • **85**
Chardonnay South Australia 1998: Smooth and ripe, this is a generous mouthful of Chardonnay, its pear, citrus and guava flavors picking up a hint of barrel spice on the polished finish. A winner for both quality and value. Drink now through 2002.–H.S. • $10 • (11/15/1999) • **88**
Chardonnay South Australia 1997: A crisp white, light and lean, with pretty green apple and herb flavors. Drink now.–H.S. • $10 • (3/31/1999) • **83**
Sémillon-Chardonnay South Australia 1998: Bright and jazzy, citrusy, with overtones of pear and nutmeg. Drink now.–H.S. • $10 • (3/31/1999) • **82**
Shiraz South Australia 1998: Fresh, vibrant and gentle, this is appealing for its pretty, youthful strawberry, raspberry and spice flavors that linger nicely on the finish. Drink now through 2004.–H.S. • $10 • (6/30/1999) • **87**

BULLER & SON, R.L.

Cabernet-Shiraz North West Victoria The Magee 1995 • $10 • (1/01/1997) • **78**

BULLETIN PLACE

Cabernet Sauvignon Australia 1994 • $10 • (10/31/1997) • **87**
Cabernet Sauvignon South Eastern Australia 1998: Fresh, almost raw, a jazzy mouthful of berry and currant flavors that persist on the finish. Drink now.–H.S. • $10 • (6/30/1999) • **87**
Chardonnay South Eastern Australia 1998: Fresh, fruity and round, with pretty apple and tropical fruit aromas and flavors that linger, this tasty white is perfect for summer sipping, and its moderate price makes it easy to keep a couple of bottles chilled. Drink now.–H.S. • $9 • (6/15/1999) • **85**
Shiraz Australia 1995 • $10 • (10/31/1997) • **87**
Shiraz South Eastern Australia 1998: Looking for a good-drinking Aussie Shiraz without a cult-label price tag? Try this bottling. It's firm in texture and delivers pretty plum and berry flavors that persist on the fine-grained finish. Drink now through 2002.–H.S. • $10 • (6/30/1999) • **87**
Shiraz South Eastern Australia 1997: Smooth and pretty, this light style of Shiraz has pretty plum and floral flavors. Starts better than it finishes. Drink now.–H.S. • $9 • (6/15/1999) • **84**

BURGE, GRANT

Cabernet Sauvignon Barossa Cameron Vale 1996: Generous with its black cherry and bell pepper flavors, with a raw, animal edge as it develops on the palate. Shows style and harmony on the finish. Drink now through 2004.–H.S. • $12 • (3/31/1999) • **87**
Chardonnay Eden Valley Summer's Gate 1997: Bright and racy, with jazzy citrus, pineapple and honey flavors on a razor's edge of juicy acidity. Needs time to settle down. Drink through 2004.–H.S. • $11 • (6/15/1999) • **87**
Merlot Barossa Hillcot 1996: Firm in texture, with ripe cherry and mint flavors on a modest scale. Best after 2000.–H.S. • $12 • (3/31/1999) • **82**
Sauvignon Blanc Barossa Kraft 1997: Supple in texture, with juicy fig, melon and citrus flavors that remain lively through the finish. Drink now.–H.S. • $10 • (3/31/1999) • **86**
Shiraz Barossa Filsell 1996: Ripe and spicy, here's a generous and focused red from Australia, dripping with blackberry, black cherry, anise and leather flavors that keep pumping through the long finish. Best after 2001.–H.S. • $15 • (3/31/1999) HR • **91**

BURRAMURRA

Cabernet-Merlot Goulburn Valley 1994: Firm and chewy, with a modest level of currant and herb flavors, finishing with a touch of mineral.–H.S. • $30 • (12/15/1998) • **79**

CALLAHAN

Chardonnay Murray Valley 1998: Soft and smooth, with pretty melon and apple flavors on a finish that stops short of being sweet. Drink now.–H.S. • $7 • (9/30/1999) • **80**
Chardonnay Murray Valley 1997: Sturdy and spicy, with more earth than pear flavor scooting through the chunky finish.–H.S. • $7 • (11/30/1998) • **79**
Shiraz Murray Valley 1997: Bright and juicy, with pretty raspberry and cherry flavors on a light frame. Drink now.–H.S. • $9 • (11/30/1998) • **84**
Shiraz South Eastern Australia 1998: When was the last time you saw a very good Aussie Shiraz at so low a price? This one is soft and fruity, with ripe blackberry and cherry flavors that linger on the straightforward finish. Drink now.–H.S. • $8 • (12/15/1999) • **85**

CALLAHAN HILL

Chardonnay Murray Valley 1999: This Chardonnay is light and appealing for its basic sappy melon flavors, which hang on nicely on the fresh finish. Drink now.–H.S. • $6 • (12/15/1999) • **84**
Chardonnay Murray Valley 1998: A light and refreshing, straightforward white with spicy apple notes on the soft finish. Drink now.–H.S. • $6 • (9/30/1999) • **80**
Chardonnay Murray Valley 1997: Smooth and generous, with tropical fruit flavors oozing through the finish. Drink now.–H.S. • $6 • (11/30/1998) • **83**
Shiraz Murray Valley 1998: Firm, almost chewy, with a nice core of vibrant black cherry fruit and a suggestion of oriental spice flavors. Drink now.–H.S. • $8 • (9/30/1999) • **84**
Shiraz-Cabernet Murray Valley 1997: Light and fragrant, with pretty berry and vanilla flavors that linger. Drink now.–H.S. • $7 • (11/30/1998) • **83**

CALLARA

Cabernet Sauvignon South Eastern Australia Reserve Bin 1996: Soft and supple, a pretty red with modest Cabernet flavors. Drink now.–H.S. • $7 • (5/31/1999) • **82**
Chardonnay South Eastern Australia Reserve Bin 1997: Soft and generous with its pineapple, honey and apple flavors, which linger on the smooth finish. Drink now.–H.S. • $7 • (5/31/1999) • **84**

CALLARA

Shiraz South Eastern Australia Reserve Bin 1998: Has a firm edge to the simple, ripe blackberry and spice flavors; just the thing with a nice roast. Drink now.–H.S. • $9 • (9/30/1999) • **82**

CAMPBELLS

Muscat Rutherglen NV: Very sweet and thick, spicy for its dried orange peel and incense flavors, hinting at chocolate on the finish. Drink now.–H.S. • $50/500 ml. • (2/28/1999) • **87**

Muscat Rutherglen NV: Sweet and spicy, this sneaks up on you, starting off with pretty brown sugar notes and adding layers of spice, prune, raisin and fig that linger on the extra-long finish. Not at all harsh. Drink now.–H.S. • $17/375 ml. • (2/29/2000) • **92**

Muscat Rutherglen Old NV • $15 • (7/01/1987) • **92**

Shiraz Rutherglen Bobbie Burns 1996: Earthy, tobacco-scented flavors hint at blackberry through a layer of fine tannins. Not a blockbuster, but geared to mesh with meals. Drink now.–H.S. • $18 • (8/31/1998) • **85**

Tokay Rutherglen NV: Sweet, syrupy and spicy, with a strong current of brown sugar, coffee, tobacco and nutmeg running through the raisin and earth flavors. Drink now.–H.S. • $17/375 ml. • (11/15/1999) • **91**

Tokay Rutherglen Liquid Gold NV: Sweet and syrupy, with flavors reminiscent of maple and molasses. Feels sticky, but it's certainly flavorful. Drink now.–H.S. • $50/500 ml. • (2/28/1999) • **86**

Tokay Rutherglen Old NV • $15 • (7/01/1987) • **91**

CAPE CLAIRAULT

Cabernet Blend Margaret River Cape Red 1996: A crisp texture and dark, licoricelike flavors characterize this distinctive, hard-edged red. Needs time to soften. A blend of Cabernet Sauvignon, Merlot and Cabernet Franc. Best after 2002.–H.S. • $14 • (6/15/1999) • **86**

Cabernet-Merlot Margaret River Jupiter 1997: Has decent berry flavors, but remains green and ungenerous.–B.S. • $18 • (6/30/2000) • **78**

Cape Red Margaret River 1997: Pronounced fresh green bean overtones, but with good focus and depth to the chocolate and black currant flavors. Drink now through 2004.–B.S. • $16 • (6/30/2000) • **84**

The Clairault Margaret River 1996: A streak of distinctly gamy flavors runs through the blackberry and cola notes at the center of this firm-textured red. Needs time in the cellar to come together. Cabernet Sauvignon, Merlot and Cabernet Franc. Best from 2001 through 2005.–H.S. • $35 (5/31/1999) • **87**

CAPE MENTELLE

Cabernet Sauvignon Margaret River 1994: Strives for elegance, with a strong minty-herbal streak running through the mature black cherry and mineral flavors. Approachable now. Drink through 2003.–H.S. • $29 • (2/28/1999) • **83**

Cabernet Sauvignon Margaret River 1993 • $24 • (5/31/1998) • **85**

Cabernet Sauvignon Margaret River 1992 • $20 • (6/15/1996) • **83**

Cabernet Sauvignon Margaret River 1991 • $19 • (10/31/1995) • **77**

Cabernet Sauvignon Margaret River 1988 • $19 • (6/30/1992) • **79**

Cabernet Sauvignon Western Australia 1987 • $19 • (3/31/1991) • **84**

Chardonnay Margaret River 1997: Bright and appealing, with a distinctive array of apple, tropical fruit and candied lime flavors in a fresh style. Flavors remain elegant and refined through the finish. Drink now through 2001.–H.S. • $23 • (2/28/1999) • **88**

Sémillon-Sauvignon Blanc Margaret River 1998: Distinctively green, with herbal, green berry and minty-peppery notes scattered between the layers of citrus and green apple in this lively white. (From the same company that brings us Cloudy Bay of New Zealand.) Drink now.–H.S. • $16 • (5/31/1999) • **86**

Shiraz Margaret River 1996: A solid red, with earthy, herbal notes mixed in with the blackberry flavors. Firm enough to want cellaring. Drink through 2003.–H.S. • $18 • (1/31/1999) • **81**

Shiraz Margaret River 1994 • $15 • (10/31/1996) • **83**

Shiraz Margaret River 1992 • $15 • (10/31/1995) • **85**

Shiraz Margaret River 1989 • $15 • (5/31/1992) • **84**

Shiraz Margaret River 1988 • $15 • (2/28/1991) • **88**

Key: SS—Spectator Selection. CS—Cellar Selection. HR—Highly Recommended. $NA—Price not available. (BT)—Barrel tasting. (A)—Auction Price. For a key to the tasters' initials, see "How to Use These Listings."
Dates in parentheses represent the issues in which the ratings were published.

CAPEL VALE

Shiraz Western Australia 1994 • $14 • (3/31/1996) • **84**

Shiraz Western Australia 1990 • $11 • (5/31/1993) • **70**

CARRAMAR

Chardonnay South Eastern Australia 1998: Light and earthy, with pretty pear and spice notes on a simple frame. Drink now.–H.S. • $10 • (11/15/1999) • **81**

Merlot South Eastern Australia 1998: Lean and chewy, with light but pleasant berry and herb flavors lingering on the finish. Drink through 2002.–H.S. • $10 • (11/15/1999) • **82**

Shiraz South Eastern Australia 1998: Fresh and flavorful, with a pretty plum note echoing on the light-textured finish. Drink now through 2001.–H.S. • $10 • (11/15/1999) • **83**

CASCABEL

et al. McLaren Vale 1998: Ample, showing polish and moderate tannins that support the straightforward plum and blackberry flavors. Grenache, Shiraz and Mourvèdre. Drink now.–B.S. • $22 • (6/30/2000) • **84**

Shiraz Fleurieu Peninsula 1998: Offers floral, spicy aromas, with tasty plum and blackberry notes. Finishes with a peppery edge, turning firm. Drink now.–J.L. • $30 • (6/30/2000) • **86**

CASSEGRAIN

Cabernet Sauvignon Hunter Valley Vintage Selection 1990 • $16 • (6/30/1994) • **87**

Cabernet Sauvignon Pokolbin 1986 • $18 • (3/31/1991) • **83**

Cabernet-Merlot Hastings River 1997: Distinctly herbal, with mint, rosemary and cedar notes running through the firm black currant and plum flavors. Best after 2000.–H.S. • $12 • (11/15/1999) • **87**

Cabernet-Merlot Hastings River 1996 • $15 • (5/31/1998) • **85**

Cabernet-Merlot South Eastern Australia 1988 • $15 • (8/31/1992) • **86**

Cabernet-Shiraz-Merlot Hastings River 1997 • $13 • (5/31/1998) • **82**

Cabernet-Shiraz-Merlot South Eastern Australia 1991 • $8 • (11/30/1993) • **77**

Cabernet-Shiraz-Merlot South Eastern Australia 1988 • $8 • (9/30/1991) • **69**

Chambourcin Hastings Valley 1993 • $13 • (1/31/1995) • **82**

Chambourcin New South Wales 1992 • $12 • (4/30/1994) • **83**

Chambourcin South Eastern Australia 1990 • $12 • (2/15/1992) • **77**

Pinot Noir Hastings River Cellar Selection 1997 • $15 • (5/31/1998) • **87**

Pinot Noir Hastings River Reserve 1997 • $20 • (5/31/1998) • **88**

Pinot Noir New South Wales Morrillon Vineyard 1988 • $20 • (2/29/1992) • **80**

Shiraz Hastings River 1998: Firm, focused and supple, with a minty, herbal edge to the ripe blackberry and licorice flavors. Drink now through 2006.–H.S. • $12 • (11/15/1999) • **88**

Shiraz Hastings River 1997 • $15 • (5/31/1998) • **83**

Shiraz Hastings Valley 1993 • $16 • (3/31/1995) • **88**

Shiraz Hunter Valley Foundation 1989 • $11 • (5/31/1993) • **75**

Shiraz Hunter Valley Vintage Selection 1983 • $18 • (5/31/1993) • **72**

Shiraz New South Wales Black Label 1993 • $16 • (3/31/1995) • **86**

Shiraz Pokolbin Leonard Select Vineyard 1987 • $20 • (3/15/1991) • **87**

Shiraz South Eastern Australia 1988 • $13 • (2/15/1992) • **77**

Shiraz South Eastern Australia Black Label 1989 • $16 • (3/31/1994) • **82**

CEDAR CREEK

Cabernet Sauvignon South Eastern Australia 1998: Light, fruity and supple, with floral-scented grape juice flavors that echo nicely on the soft finish. Drink now.–H.S. • $10/1 liter • (6/15/1999) • **83**

Cabernet Sauvignon South Eastern Australia 1997: Bright and appealing for its forward cherry and plum flavors, nicely shaded with a hint of pepper.–H.S. • $10/1.5 liter • (10/15/1998) • **83**

Cabernet Sauvignon South Eastern Australia Bin 99 1994 • $11/1.5 liter • (4/30/1996) • **72**

Cabernet Sauvignon South Eastern Australia Bin 99 1992 • $6 • (9/30/1994) • **78**

Cabernet Sauvignon South Eastern Australia Bin 99 1990 • $6 • (3/31/1993) • **82**

Chardonnay South Eastern Australia 1998: Fresh and juicy, with pretty pear and peach character and extra hints of mineral and spice. A lot of wine for the price. Drink now.–H.S. • $5 • (1/31/1999) • **84**
Chardonnay South Eastern Australia 1997: Soft and a bit sweet. A simple white with little charm.–H.S. • $10/1.5 liter • (8/31/1998) • **78**
Sémillon-Chardonnay South Eastern Australia 1997: Soft and spicy, with a hint of tobacco sneaking around the sweet apple flavors. Drink now.–H.S. • $10/1.5 liter • (8/31/1998) • **80**
Shiraz South Eastern Australia 1997 • $10/1.5 liter • (5/31/1998) • **81**
Shiraz-Cabernet South Eastern Australia 1997 • $10/1.5 liter • (5/31/1998) • **83**
Shiraz-Cabernet South Eastern Australia Bin 21 1995 • $10/1.5 liter • (4/30/1996) • **75**
Shiraz-Cabernet South Eastern Australia Bin 21 1991 • $5 • (9/30/1994) • **79**
Shiraz-Merlot South Eastern Australia 1997 • $10/1.5 liter • (5/31/1998) • **82**

CHAIN OF PONDS

Cabernet Sauvignon Adelaide Hills Amadeus 1994 • $25 • (4/30/1998) • **89**
Chardonnay Adelaide Hills 1997: A glorious white wine, graceful and harmonious as it layers its vibrant apple, pear, tropical fruit, spice and vanilla flavors and hints at raisin and lemon on the long, long finish. Drink through 2005.–H.S. • $20 • (2/28/1999) HR • **94**
Grenache-Sangiovese Adelaide Hills Novello Rosso 1998: Dry and fruity, with candied strawberry, watermelon and raspberry notes echoing on the light finish. Drink now.–H.S. • $12 • (6/15/1999) • **83**
Grenache-Sangiovese Adelaide Hills Novello Rosso 1997 • $12 • (5/15/1998) • **86**
Sauvignon Blanc-Sémillon Adelaide Hills 1999: Crisp and lemony, accented by grass and melon flavors, this is a straightforward, focused white, with a lingering finish. Drink now.–B.S. • $16 • (6/30/2000) • **85**
Sauvignon Blanc-Sémillon Adelaide Hills 1998: Fresh and soft, appealing for its modest apple and fig flavors that linger on the delicate finish. Drink now.–H.S. • $15 • (2/28/1999) • **85**
Sémillon Adelaide Hills 1997: Harmonious, graceful, youthful white, with a range of flavors that include green apple, green fig and hay. Finishes with crisp acidity. Built to develop with age. Best from 2001 through 2005.–H.S. • $15 • (2/28/1999) • **87**
Shiraz Adelaide Hills Ledge 1997: Dripping with berry and game flavors, this smooth-textured, bright red shows plenty of backbone, personality and style. Approachable now. Drink through 2005.–H.S. • $17 • (9/30/1999) • **91**

CHAMBERS

Muscat Rutherglen Rosewood Vineyards NV • $13/375 ml. • (9/15/1997) • **92**
Muscat Rutherglen Rosewood Vineyards Rare NV • $130/375 ml. • (9/15/1997) • **94**
Muscat Rutherglen Rosewood Vineyards Special NV • $45/375 ml. • (9/15/1997) • **95**
Tokay Rutherglen Rosewood Vineyards NV • $13/375 ml. • (9/15/1997) • **90**
Tokay Rutherglen Rosewood Vineyards Rare NV • $130/375 ml. • (9/15/1997) HR • **98**
Tokay Rutherglen Rosewood Vineyards Special NV • $60/375 ml. • (9/15/1997) • **95**

CHAPEL HILL

Shiraz McLaren Vale 1997: Ripe and glossy, this is full of plum, berry and licorice, with a chewy texture and firm tannins. Fine, lingering finish. Drink now through 2003.–B.S. • $22 • (6/30/2000) • **88**
Shiraz McLaren Vale 1994 • $20 • (5/15/1997) • **91**

CHAPOUTIER, M.

Shiraz Mount Benson 1998: Ripe and oozing with blackberry and boysenberry. Loosely knit, with soft tannins and a modest finish. Drink now.–B.S. • $48 • (6/30/2000) • **84**

CHATEAU REYNELLA

Brut Australia NV • $10 • (5/15/1997) • **84**
Cabernet Sauvignon Coonawarra 1988 • $9 • (4/30/1991) • **86**
Cabernet Sauvignon Coonawarra 1980 • $15 • (5/31/1987) • **84**
Cabernet Sauvignon McLaren Vale 1994 • $12 • (6/30/1996) • **88**
Cabernet Sauvignon McLaren Vale Basket Pressed 1996: Ripe and generous character on an elegant frame. A smooth, warm mouthful of black cherry, herb and cedar flavors that linger on the polished finish. Drink now through 2005.–H.S. • $24 • (3/31/2000) • **88**
Cabernet Sauvignon McLaren Vale Basket Pressed 1995 • $22 • (5/31/1998) • **86**
Cabernet Sauvignon McLaren Vale Basket Pressed 1993 • $12 • (3/31/1996) • **85**
Cabernet Sauvignon McLaren Vale Basket Pressed 1992 • $10 • (6/30/1995) • **86**
Cabernet Sauvignon McLaren Vale Basket Pressed 1991 • $8 • (7/31/1994) • **84**
Cabernet Sauvignon McLaren Vale Basket Pressed 1990 • $10 • (5/15/1994) • **82**
Cabernet-Merlot McLaren Vale 1990 • $8 • (9/30/1994) • **79**
Cabernet-Merlot McLaren Vale Basket Pressed 1996: Crisp and lively, with a bit of a tannic bite to the currant and floral flavors. Best after 2001.–H.S. • $24 • (11/15/1999) • **85**
Cabernet-Merlot McLaren Vale Basket Pressed 1995 • $25 • (3/31/1998) • **88**
Cabernet-Merlot McLaren Vale Basket Pressed 1993 • $10 • (3/31/1996) • **86**
Cabernet-Merlot McLaren Vale Basket Pressed 1992 • $10 • (12/15/1995) • **87**
Chardonnay McLaren Vale 1998: A ripe, generous style of Australian Chardonnay at a gobble-it-up price, offering plenty of pear, honey and spice flavors that linger on the smooth finish. Not a big wine, but a flavorful one. Drink now through 2003.–H.S. • $11 • (12/31/1999) • **87**
Fine Old Tawny Port McLaren Vale Old Cave NV • $15 • (5/31/1997) • **90**
Shiraz McLaren Vale Basket Pressed 1997: Roasted coffee and spice on the nose, with green olive and cherry emerging on the palate. Sinewy and rustic in its tannins, showing personality and length. Drink now through 2003.–B.S. • $24 • (6/30/2000) • **88**
Shiraz McLaren Vale Basket Pressed 1996: Ripe and bright, this is a delicious version of Australia's most popular red variety, with distinctive black pepper, plum and berry flavors that pick up more than a hint of licorice on the lively finish. Fine-grained tannins don't get in the way. Drink now through 2008.–H.S. • $25 • (9/15/1999) HR • **90**
Shiraz McLaren Vale Basket Pressed 1995 • $22 • (5/31/1998) • **88**
Shiraz McLaren Vale Basket Pressed 1994 • $12 • (6/30/1996) HR • **92**
Shiraz McLaren Vale Basket Pressed 1993 • $10 • (3/31/1996) • **86**
Shiraz McLaren Vale Basket Pressed 1991 • $8 • (9/30/1994) • **81**
Tawny Port McLaren Vale Old Cave NV • $15 • (5/15/1996) • **90**
Tawny Port South Australia Old Cave Fine Old NV • $12 • (11/15/1991) • **77**
Vintage Port McLaren Vale 1992 • $13 • (6/30/1995) • **79**

CHATEAU TAHBILK

Cabernet Sauvignon Goulburn Valley 1993 • $14 • (12/31/1996) • **85**
Cabernet Sauvignon Goulburn Valley 1992 • $14 • (8/31/1996) • **85**
Cabernet Sauvignon Goulburn Valley 1990 • $11 • (6/15/1994) • **83**
Cabernet Sauvignon Goulburn Valley 1989 • $12 • (11/30/1992) • **83**
Cabernet Sauvignon Goulburn Valley 1988 • $12 • (3/31/1991) • **87**
Cabernet Sauvignon Goulburn Valley 1987 • $11 • (7/31/1990) • **89**
Cabernet Sauvignon Goulburn Valley 1986 • $10 • (3/31/1989) • **88**
Cabernet Sauvignon Victoria 1990 • $11 • (6/30/1993) • **78**
Shiraz Goulburn Valley 1993 • $14 • (12/31/1996) • **82**
Shiraz Goulburn Valley 1992 • $14 • (8/31/1996) • **86**
Shiraz Goulburn Valley 1991 • $10 • (6/15/1994) • **84**
Shiraz Goulburn Valley 1989 • $11 • (11/30/1992) • **73**
Shiraz Goulburn Valley 1988 • $10 • (2/15/1992) • **82**
Shiraz Goulburn Valley 1987 • $11 • (3/15/1991) • **87**
Shiraz Victoria 1990 • $10 • (5/31/1993) • **84**
Shiraz Victoria 1986 • $10 • (3/31/1989) • **88**

CHATEAU XANADU

Cabernet Sauvignon Margaret River 1996: Supple in texture and generous of flavor, with black currant, tar and earthy notes combining on the round finish. Drink through 2003.–H.S. • $23 • (2/28/1999) • **83**
Cabernet Sauvignon Margaret River Reserve 1995: A sturdy red with distinctive herbal, red pepper overtones to the basic Cabernet flavors. Finishes with firm tannins. Best after 2001.–H.S. • $38 • (2/28/1999) • **83**
Chardonnay Margaret River 1997: Ripe, generous and immensely appealing for its cascade of apple, grapefruit, vanilla and spice flavors that linger beautifully on the wide-open finish. The finish goes on and on, suggesting this wine can improve further in the cellar. Drink now through 2004.–H.S. • $21 • (5/31/1999) • **91**
Sauvignon Blanc-Sémillon Margaret River Secession 1998: A lively mouthful of pear, spice and herb flavors, bright and fresh. Drink now.–H.S. • $15 • (2/28/1999) • **84**
Sémillon Margaret River 1997: Fresh and bright, with straightforward pineapple and mineral flavors. Drink now through 2001.–H.S. • $18 • (2/28/1999) • **84**

CHITTERING

Cabernet-Merlot Western Australia 1996: Smooth and polished, this light, well-manicured style of Cabernet shows plenty of nice currant and herb flavors that linger on the gentle finish. Drink now through 2003.–H.S. • $19 • (1/31/2000) • **85**

Cabernet-Merlot Western Australia 1988 • $18 • (9/30/1991) • **79**

Chardonnay Western Australia 1997: Light in structure but really lively in flavor, with pineapple and citrusy flavors weaving through the long finish. Worth cellaring. Drink now through 2005.–H.S. • $19 • (12/31/1999) • **89**

Sémillon-Sauvignon Blanc Western Australia 1997: Generous with its fig, apple and herb flavors, this manages to combine ripe richness with the twang of Sauvignon flavors for an intriguing wine. Drink now through 2005.–H.S. • $15 • (12/31/1999) • **88**

CIMICKY, CHARLES

Barossa Valley 1995 • $20 • (3/31/1998) • **91**

Cabernet-Merlot-Cabernet Franc Barossa Valley The Red Blend 1997: A stylish wine, ripe and generous. This distinctive mouthful of currant, plum and exotic spices lingers on the supple, mildly chewy finish. Drink now through 2007.–H.S. • $30 • (1/31/2000) • **90**

Grenache Barossa Valley Gnarled Vine 1997: Beautifully focused, generous with its blackberry flavors on a supple frame, and showing just enough firm tannin on the finish to suggest it may develop further with cellaring. Try now through 2003.–H.S. • $24 • (3/31/1999) • **88**

Shiraz Barossa Valley Signature 1997: Smooth, ripe and spicy, with an intriguing layer of dusky spice and dried fruit around the core of generous black cherry and plum flavors. Not as juicy as some, but a real Barossa Shiraz. Drink now through 2012.–H.S. • $30 • (12/31/1999) • **88**

Shiraz Barossa Valley Signature 1996: Dark and dense, with beautiful blackberry and spice flavors shining through the fine layer of tannins. A gentler wine than it seems when first poured. Drink now through 2004.–H.S. • $24 • (3/31/1999) • **88**

Shiraz Barossa Valley Signature 1995 • $20 • (5/15/1998) • **88**

Shiraz Barossa Valley Signature 1994 • $16 • (5/31/1997) • **88**

CLARENDON HILLS

Cabernet Sauvignon Clarendon 1997: Serves up ripe blackberry, boysenberry, anise, cedar and plum flavors, with a touch of herb worked in. Finishes smooth, with moderate tannins. Drink now through 2007.–J.L. • $44 • (6/30/2000) • **88**

Chardonnay Adelaide Hills Norton Summit Vineyard 1997: Tangy, with green pear, pineapple, honey and slightly metallic notes competing for attention on the smooth, open-textured finish. Drink now through 2003.–H.S. • $38 • (6/30/2000) • **85**

Grenache Clarendon Blewitt Springs Vineyard 1995 • $28 • (5/31/1997) • **92**

Grenache Clarendon Blewitt Springs Vineyard Old Vines 1998: Firm, even a bit chewy, with lush berry and spice flavors that linger on the slightly sharp finish. Best from 2001 through 2007.–H.S. • $40 • (6/30/2000) • **88**

Grenache Clarendon Blewitt Springs Vineyard Old Vines 1997: Dripping with wild berry and herb flavors, with layers of earth and spice weaving through. Distinctive and dashing, this should benefit from cellaring. Drink through 2005.–H.S. • $37 • (5/15/1999) • **91**

Grenache Clarendon Blewitt Springs Vineyard Old Vines 1996 • $34 • (4/30/1998) • **88**

Grenache Clarendon Clarendon Vineyard Old Vines 1997: Ripe, round and generous, with plush tannins wrapped around a vibrant core of black cherry and smoky, peppery flavors. Drink now through 2004.–H.S. • $37 • (5/15/1999) • **89**

Grenache Clarendon Clarendon Vineyard Old Vines 1995 • $28 • (6/15/1997) • **89**

Grenache Clarendon Kangarilla Vineyard Old Vines 1998: Rich and velvety yet it remains elegant and refined, generous with its plum, black cherry and gentle leather aromas and flavors, framed with slightly gritty tannins on the finish. Tasted twice, with consistent notes. Drink now through 2005.–H.S. • $40 • (6/30/2000) • **86**

Key: SS—Spectator Selection. CS—Cellar Selection. HR—Highly Recommended. $NA—Price not available. (BT)—Barrel tasting. Ⓐ—Auction Price.
For a key to the tasters' initials, see "How to Use These Listings."
Dates in parentheses represent the issues in which the ratings were published.

Grenache Clarendon Kangarilla Vineyard Old Vines 1997: Bright and spicy, with pretty cherry and raspberry flavors persisting intensely, along with an earthy note, on the firm-textured finish. Drink now through 2004.–H.S. • $37 • (5/15/1999) • **85**

Grenache Clarendon Kangarilla Vineyard Old Vines 1996 • $34 • (4/30/1998) • **88**

Grenache Clarendon Old Vines 1994 • $25 • (12/15/1996) • **90**

Merlot Clarendon 1997: Really ripe and aromatic, this is firmly tannic but generous with its black cherry and currant flavors that persist into the chewy finish. Best after 2001.–H.S. • $41 • (6/15/1999) • **87**

Merlot Clarendon 1995 • $35 • (5/31/1997) • **91**

Shiraz Clarendon 1996 • $38 • (4/30/1998) • **87**

Shiraz Clarendon 1995 • $33 • (6/15/1997) • **92**

Shiraz Clarendon Astralis 1998: Deep, dark and dense, a powerfully concentrated mouthful of cherry, blackberry, plum and exotic spice flavors that linger on the beautifully crafted finish. Stylish and graceful, it also has power. Best from 2003 through 2013.–H.S. • $150 • (6/30/2000) • **93**

Shiraz Clarendon Astralis 1996 • $159 Ⓐ • (4/30/1998) • **92**

Shiraz Clarendon Astralis 1995 • $249 Ⓐ • (6/15/1997) • **95**

Shiraz Clarendon Hickinbotham Vineyard 1998: Bright in flavor, elegant in structure. Well wrapped in fine-grained tannins, but the berry, cherry and spice flavors shine through on the long finish. Best after 2002.–H.S. • $81 • (6/30/2000) • **91**

Shiraz Clarendon Liandra 1998: Firm, almost chewy, with nicely focused blackberry, cherry and mint flavors coming through and lingering nicely on the balanced finish. Best after 2002.–H.S. • $68 • (6/30/2000) • **87**

Shiraz Clarendon Liandra 1997: Firm in texture, almost chewy, with bursts of blueberry, blackberry and anise flavors, plus a hint of chocolate on the finish. Drink now through 2003.–H.S. • $60 • (5/15/1999) • **89**

CLEVELAND

Pinot Noir Australia Macedon Ranges 1996 • $18 • (4/30/1998) • **81**

COCKATOO RIDGE

Cabernet Sauvignon-Merlot South Eastern Australia 1995 • $9 • (12/31/1997) • **81**

Cabernet Sauvignon-Merlot South Eastern Australia 1994 • $9 • (3/31/1996) • **82**

Cabernet Sauvignon-Merlot South Eastern Australia 1993 • $7 • (10/15/1995) • **84**

Cabernet Sauvignon-Merlot South Eastern Australia 1992 • $6 • (5/15/1994) • **84**

Cabernet Sauvignon-Merlot South Eastern Australia 1990 • $7 • (6/30/1992) • **82**

Grenache-Shiraz South Eastern Australia 1996 • $9 • (12/31/1997) • **86**

COCKFIGHTER'S GHOST

Chardonnay Hunter Valley 1997: Lithe and polished, refreshing for its citrus and tropical fruit overtones on a narrow, elegant frame, finishing with a hint of spice. Not a powerful wine, but it has grace and restraint. Drink now through 2003.–H.S. • $18 • (5/31/1999) • **88**

Sémillon Hunter Valley 1998: Reminiscent of wax and lemon curd.–B.S. • $15 • (6/30/2000) • **72**

Shiraz Hunter Valley 1998: Lean and simple, with tart berry, herb and cherry notes. Drink now.–J.L. • $20 • (6/30/2000) • **83**

Shiraz Hunter Valley 1997: Very light, almost ethereal, with gamy, leathery flavors and just enough raspberry and spice notes to make it appealing in a gentle way. Drink now.–H.S. • $20 • (5/15/1999) • **82**

COLDRIDGE

Cabernet Sauvignon-Shiraz South Eastern Australia 1994 • $7 • (6/30/1995) • **82**

Shiraz-Cabernet South Eastern Australia 1993 • $6 • (6/15/1994) • **80**

Shiraz-Cabernet South Eastern Australia 1992 • $6 • (10/31/1993) • **82**

Shiraz-Cabernet Victoria 1989 • $6 • (8/31/1992) • **81**

COLDSTREAM HILLS

Cabernet Sauvignon Lilydale 1987 • $20 • (1/31/1990) • **84**

Cabernet-Merlot-Cabernet Franc Yarra Valley Briarston 1995: Firm and chewy, with an herbal-mushroomy thread running through the hard-edged cherry flavors. Needs cellaring to soften the tannins. Best after 2001.–H.S. • $17 • (3/31/1999) • **86**

Chardonnay Yarra Valley Reserve 1997: Rich in flavor, refined in style, with lovely honey- and spice-scented pear and citrus flavors swirling through the beautifully balanced finish. Elegant already. Drink now through 2003.–H.S. • $26 • (5/31/1999) • **91**

Pinot Noir Yarra Valley 1998: Light and fragrant, a fresh-tasting, youthful Pinot Noir, showing black cherry, vanilla and spice notes on the soft finish. Drink now through 2003.–H.S. • $15 • (6/30/2000) • **84**

Pinot Noir Yarra Valley 1997: Smooth, polished and inviting with its silky texture and beautifully modulated flavors of currant, black cherry and sandalwood, with even a touch of citrus peel on the elegant finish. Drink now through 2002.–H.S. • $17 • (3/31/1999) • **89**

Pinot Noir Yarra Valley 1992 • $15 • (4/30/1994) • **88**

Pinot Noir Yarra Valley Reserve 1998: Firm and focused, generous with its black cherry flavors, with spicy, meaty overtones to the fresh fruit character. Can use time to soften. Drink now through 2005.–H.S. • $22 • (6/30/2000) • **86**

Pinot Noir Yarra Valley Reserve 1997: Supple and silky, generous with its pretty plum, spice and berry flavors. Strives for elegance, but emphasizes the fruit in the flavor spectrum, letting it linger enticingly on the polished finish. Drink now through 2003.–H.S. • $26 • (5/31/1999) • **90**

Sauvignon Blanc Yarra Valley 1998: Light and appealing for its melon and fig flavors, which finish clear and refreshing. Drink now.–H.S. • $15 • (5/31/1999) • **85**

CORIOLE

Cabernet Sauvignon McLaren Vale 1997: Ripe and generous, with blackberry and currant flavors framed by modest oak spice notes, finishing with a layer of fine-grained tannins. Best from 2001 through 2005.–H.S. • $28 • (5/15/2000) • **87**

Cabernet Sauvignon McLaren Vale 1996: Very firm and chewy up front, but the pretty strawberry, currant and mint flavors emerge nicely on the finish. Needs cellaring. Best after 2001.–H.S. • $25 • (3/31/1999) • **86**

Cabernet Sauvignon McLaren Vale 1994 • $20 • (4/30/1997) • **90**

Cabernet Sauvignon McLaren Vale 1993 • $20 • (4/30/1996) • **89**

Cabernet-Merlot McLaren Vale Mary Kathleen 1997: Ripe and generous, this lively mouthful of blackberry, currant, toast and light mint aromas and flavors lingers crisply on the balanced finish. Best after 2000.–H.S. • $40 • (11/15/1999) • **88**

Cabernet-Merlot McLaren Vale Mary Kathleen 1995 • $44 • (5/31/1998) • **86**

Chardonnay McLaren Vale 1997: Ripe and generous, yet pulled together well, with a sappy edge to the light pineapple and citrus flavors. Finishes gracefully. Drink now.–H.S. • $20 • (11/15/1999) • **87**

Grenache McLaren Vale Lalla Rookh Old Vines 1997: Ripe, rich and seductive, this lovely mouthful of currant, berry and spice expands and lingers on the round finish. Drink now through 2006.–H.S. • $24 • (11/15/1999) • **90**

Grenache McLaren Vale Lalla Rookh Old Vines 1996 • $24 • (5/15/1998) • **86**

Redstone Red McLaren Vale 1997: Ripe in flavor and crisp in texture, offering generous blackberry, cherry and anise flavors that pick up hints of herb and pepper on the firm finish. Tannins are well integrated. A blend of Shiraz, Cabernet Sauvignon and Grenache. Best from 2002 through 2007.–H.S. • $20 • (11/15/1999) • **90**

Redstone Red McLaren Vale 1995 • $17 • (9/30/1997) • **88**

Redstone Red McLaren Vale 1994 • $17 • (2/28/1997) • **89**

Redstone Red McLaren Vale 1993 • $15 • (4/30/1996) • **87**

Sangiovese McLaren Vale 1997: Light in color, body and flavor, with a modest level of slightly stalky raspberry and coffee flavors. Drink now through 2003.–H.S. • $20 • (11/15/1999) • **81**

Sangiovese McLaren Vale 1994 • $16 • (4/30/1996) • **86**

Sémillon-Sauvignon Blanc McLaren Vale 1998: Ripe, rich and especially fragrant, with pear, apple and grapefruit aromas and flavors, shaded by hints of herb and coffee at the edges. Drink now through 2008.–H.S. • $18 • (11/15/1999) • **88**

Sémillon-Sauvignon Blanc McLaren Vale 1997 • $17 • (5/15/1998) • **86**

Shiraz McLaren Vale 1997: Firm in texture and generous with its ripe black cherry and spice flavors, this delicious mouthful of fruit character lingers nicely on the rich finish. Drink through 2010.–H.S. • $25 • (11/15/1999) • **91**

Shiraz McLaren Vale 1996 • $25 • (5/15/1998) • **87**

Shiraz McLaren Vale 1995 • $20 • (9/30/1997) • **91**

Shiraz McLaren Vale 1994 • $20 • (2/28/1997) • **88**

Shiraz McLaren Vale 1993 • $20 • (4/30/1996) • **87**

Shiraz McLaren Vale Lloyd Reserve 1996: Ripe, rich and beautifully focused to emphasize the plum, blackberry and spice flavors as they expand across the palate. Texture is like velvet as the fine-grained tannins immerse themselves in the wine. Drink now through 2011.–H.S. • $65 • (5/15/2000) • **90**

Shiraz McLaren Vale Lloyd Reserve 1993 • $36 • (2/28/1997) • **92**

CRABTREE

Riesling Watervale 1999: Showing almond and petrol notes, this comes off as a little heavy and dull.–B.S. • $17 • (6/30/2000) • **79**

Riesling Watervale 1998: Fresh and aromatic, exuberant with its floral, apple, pear and spice flavors that persist engagingly on the finish. Give it some age to develop additional flavor. Try through 2008.–H.S. • $16 • (3/31/1999) • **88**

Shiraz-Cabernet Watervale 1996: Smooth and generous with its earthy, gamy, berry and plum flavors, this round-textured wine is easy going down. Drink now through 2003.–H.S. • $22 • (3/31/1999) • **86**

CRANSWICK

Cabernet Sauvignon Riverina 1991 • $8 • (6/15/1994) • **82**

Shiraz-Cabernet South Eastern Australia 1995 • $8 • (10/31/1996) • **78**

Shiraz-Cabernet South Eastern Australia 1990 • $7 • (5/31/1993) • **82**

Shiraz-Merlot South Eastern Australia 1995 • $8 • (11/30/1996) • **83**

Shiraz-Merlot South Eastern Australia 1990 • $7 • (4/15/1993) • **80**

CRITTENDEN, GARRY

Barbera Victoria 1996 • $19 • (4/30/1998) • **87**

Barbera Victoria i 1997: Firm in texture, veering a bit to the rough side, but the core of berry flavor comes through. Give this time. Best after 2000.–H.S. • $19 • (6/30/1999) • **85**

I Riserva Red King Valley 1995 • $18 • (5/31/1997) • **82**

Sangiovese Victoria 1996 • $19 • (5/15/1998) • **82**

CULLEN

Cabernet-Merlot Margaret River 1996: Generous and open-textured, with distinctive green bean and mint overtones to the basic cherry and currant flavors. Drink now through 2005.–H.S. • $45 • (9/15/1999) • **87**

Cabernet-Merlot Margaret River 1995 • $40 • (5/15/1998) • **88**

Cabernet-Merlot Margaret River 1985 • $15 • (11/15/1987) • **87**

Sauvignon Blanc-Sémillon Margaret River 1997: Smooth and earthy, nicely polished and elegant, but with a vegetal edge to the apple and citrus flavors. Drink now.–H.S. • $30 • (11/15/1999) • **82**

CUPID

Chardonnay South Eastern Australia 1997: Fresh and round, with generous nectarine and mineral flavors that linger on the soft finish. Drink now through 2001.–H.S. • $10 • (6/15/1999) • **84**

DALWHINNIE

Cabernet Sauvignon Victoria 1994 • $40 • (2/28/1997) • **84**

Cabernet Sauvignon Victoria Moonambel 1996: Crisp and lively, appealing for its bright raspberry and red currant flavors shaded with spicy oak. Enticing now. Best after 2000.–H.S. • $42 • (1/31/1999) • **87**

Shiraz Victoria 1994 • $42 • (2/28/1997) • **90**

Shiraz Victoria Moonambel 1996: Crisp and racy, with explosive flavors of raspberry, blackberry, bacon and anise flavors filling in all the nooks and crannies of this tightly packed red. Drink through 2004.–H.S. • $42 • (1/31/1999) • **90**

D'ARENBERG

Cabernet Sauvignon McLaren Vale Coppermine Road 1995 • $40 • (7/31/1997) • **88**

Cabernet Sauvignon McLaren Vale High Trellis 1989 • $8 • (7/15/1993) • **82**

Cabernet Sauvignon McLaren Vale The Coppermine Road 1997: Ripe and nicely focused, with pretty black cherry and currant flavors shining through a thin veil of tannin on the long finish. Worth cellaring. Drink through 2007.–H.S. • $50 • (9/15/1999) • **88**

Cabernet Sauvignon McLaren Vale The Coppermine Road 1996: Flavors jump out of the glass, dripping with raw currant and blackberry notes, but it's a bit rough through the finish. Maybe just needs time. Best from 2001 through 2005.–H.S. • $50 • (8/31/1998) • **87**

Cabernet Sauvignon McLaren Vale The High Trellis 1997: Has a strong earthy-mineral streak weaving through the otherwise attractive ripe plum and currant flavors on a sinewy frame. Drink now through 2003.–H.S. • $16 • (9/15/1999) • **84**

D'ARENBERG

Cabernet Sauvignon McLaren Vale The High Trellis 1995 • $15 • (5/15/1998) • **87**
Cabernet Sauvignon McLaren Vale The High Trellis 1994 • $15 • (7/31/1997) • **87**
Chambourcin McLaren Vale The Peppermint Paddock 1995 • $21 • (7/31/1997) • **86**
Chardonnay McLaren Vale The Olive Grove 1998: Crisp, almost raw, with tangy citrus, green apple and spice flavors that reverberate on the racy finish. Drink through 2005.–H.S. • $15 • (9/15/1999) • **87**
Chardonnay McLaren Vale The Olive Grove 1997: Simple and refreshing for its apple and earthy (yes, olive) flavors, which linger on the finish. Drink now.–H.S. • $15 • (10/15/1998) • **83**
Chardonnay McLaren Vale The Other Side 1997: Dark in color and spicy in flavor, with a soy sauce edge to the ripe melon and citrus flavors. Finishes on a smoky note. Drink now.–H.S. • $35 • (11/15/1999) • **83**
d'Arry's Original McLaren Vale 1998: Rich and full, a lush mouthful of berry and spice with a hint of dried tomato lingering on the finish. Tannins are firm but not intrusive. Best from 2001 through 2005.–H.S. • $NA • (6/30/2000) • **88**
Grenache McLaren Vale The Custodian 1997: Firm and chewy, with charry, toasty blackberry and spice flavors that finish a bit tight. Best after 2001.–H.S. • $23 • (9/15/1999) • **86**
Grenache McLaren Vale The Custodian 1996 • $21 • (7/31/1997) • **86**
Grenache-Shiraz McLaren Vale Ironstone Pressings 1995 • $25 • (7/31/1997) • **87**
Grenache-Shiraz McLaren Vale The Ironstone Pressings 1996: Supple in texture and generous with its spicy, vanilla-scented blackberry and anise flavors, narrowing to fine beam on the finish. Drink now through 2001.–H.S. • $27 • (8/31/1998) • **87**
Grenache-Shiraz-Mourvèdre McLaren Vale The Ironstone Pressings 1997: Ripe and distinctive. Firm in texture, expansive with its blackberry, anise, black pepper and nutmeg flavors that linger on the firm finish. Impressive already. Best from 2001 through 2007.–H.S. • $50 • (9/15/1999) • **90**
Ironstone Pressings Australia 1991 • $15 • (1/31/1995) • **87**
Ironstone Pressings McLaren Vale 1989 • $11 • (5/31/1993) • **86**
Mourvèdre McLaren Vale The Twenty Eight Road 1996 • $22 • (5/15/1998) • **86**
Mourvèdre McLaren Vale The Twenty Eight Road 1995 • $21 • (7/31/1997) • **85**
Nostalgia Very Old Tawny Port NV • $16 • (3/31/1995) • **83**
Red Ochre McLaren Vale 1997: On the lighter side, with pretty berry and dried orange peel aromas, hinting at pepper and vanilla on the smooth finish. Drink now.–H.S. • $9 • (9/15/1999) • **84**
Red Ochre McLaren Vale 1996 • $9 • (6/15/1998) • **87**
Riesling Fleurieu Peninsula The Dry Dam 1997: Fresh and grapey, a generous, open-textured mouthful of fruit and more fruit, finishing dry. Drink now.–H.S. • $15 • (11/15/1998) • **87**
Riesling McLaren Vale The Noble 1997: Sweet, silky and flavorful, balancing its ripe pineapple and cream flavors against the honey and apricot notes swirling in. A delicious wine that unfolds beautifully on the long finish. Drink now through 2007.–H.S. • $27/375 ml. • (9/15/1999) • **91**
Riesling McLaren Vale Noble 1996 • $25/375 ml. • (5/31/1998) • **91**
Sauvignon Blanc Fleurieu Peninsula The Dryland 1997: Light and crisp, with straightforward apple and citrus flavors that finish with a flourish. Drink now.–H.S. • $15 • (10/15/1998) • **85**
Shiraz Australia Old Vine 1990 • $11 • (3/31/1995) • **75**
Shiraz McLaren Vale Old Vine 1989 • $8 • (5/31/1993) • **85**
Shiraz McLaren Vale The Dead Arm 1997: Firm in texture and generous with its bright berry, spice and slightly gamy flavors, nicely focused to display the fruit. Flavors persist impressively on the round finish. Best from 2001 through 2010.–H.S. • $50 • (9/15/1999) • **91**
Shiraz McLaren Vale The Dead Arm 1996: Jammed with flavor; a jazzy mouthful of black cherry, blackberry, beet and anise, nicely wrapped in a light veil of tannin. Flavors burst from this wine, exploding with richness and depth. Drink now through 2005.–H.S. • $50 • (8/31/1998) • **92**
Shiraz McLaren Vale The Dead Arm 1995 • $50 • (7/31/1997) • **92**
Shiraz McLaren Vale The Footbolt Old Vine 1997: Ripe and forward, a generous mouthful of licorice-scented blackberry and plum flavors wrapped in a layer of slightly scratchy tannins. Needs time. Best after 2001.–H.S. • $16 • (9/15/1999) • **87**
Shiraz McLaren Vale The Footbolt Old Vine 1996: Firm and focused, a smaller-scale Shiraz but one with solid blackberry and anise flavors, finishing with an edge of tannin. Drink through 2005.–H.S. • $16 • (8/31/1998) • **83**
Shiraz McLaren Vale The Old Vine 1995 • $15 • (7/31/1997) • **91**

Key: SS—Spectator Selection. CS—Cellar Selection. HR—Highly Recommended. $NA—Price not available. (BT)—Barrel tasting. (A)—Auction Price.
For a key to the tasters' initials, see "How to Use These Listings."
Dates in parentheses represent the issues in which the ratings were published.

Shiraz Port McLaren Vale 1997: Not terribly sweet, but bursting with rich black cherry, blackberry and toast flavors that echo on the smooth finish. Drink now through 2012.–H.S. • $15/375 ml. • (2/29/2000) • **88**
Shiraz-Grenache McLaren Vale d'Arry's Original 1996: Lithe, supple and flavorful, with spicy overtones that add a distinctive cast to the blackberry and black cherry notes. Drink now.–H.S. • $16 • (9/30/1998) • **88**
Shiraz-Grenache McLaren Vale d'Arry's Original 1995 • $15 • (7/31/1997) • **87**
Sparkling Chambourcin McLaren Vale The Peppermint Paddock 1997: Ripe, generous in flavor and lively in structure, like the fizzy red wine that it is, offering berry, cherry and anise flavors. Drink now.–H.S. • $20 • (3/31/2000) • **87**
White Ochre McLaren Vale 1998: Soft in texture, with light, pretty floral and peach flavors. Finishes a bit coarse. Made from Riesling, Chenin Blanc and Sauvignon Blanc. Drink now.–H.S. • $9 • (11/15/1999) • **82**
White Ochre McLaren Vale 1997: Vivid in flavor and refreshing in texture, with pretty peach and floral flavors in profusion. Finishes dry. A blend of Riesling and Crouchen. Drink now.–H.S. • $9 • (11/15/1998) • **86**

DE BORTOLI

Sémillon Australia Noble One 1993 • $28/375 ml. • (6/15/1996) • **93**

DEAKIN

Merlot Victoria 1998: Bright and appealing for its supple berry and cherry flavors, which linger on the open-textured finish. Drink now through 2004.–H.S. • $12 • (3/31/2000) • **87**
Shiraz Victoria 1998: A little lean, with ripe blueberry and raspberry notes and a pretty minty and herbal side. Drink now.–J.L. • $12 • (6/30/2000) • **83**

DENNIS

Cabernet Sauvignon McLaren Vale 1997: Dark and dense in color but lighter in texture, with earthy overtones running through the black fruit character, finishing with mildly chewy tannins. Drink through 2003.–H.S. • $18 • (5/31/1999) • **83**
Shiraz McLaren Vale 1997: Light in texture, with generous berry and tobacco flavors that linger with style. Drink now through 2001.–H.S. • $18 • (5/15/1999) • **86**

DEVIL'S LAIR

Cabernet Sauvignon Margaret River 1992 • $20 • (10/15/1995) • **82**
Margaret River Red Margaret River 1995 • $25 • (2/28/1998) • **83**

DIAMOND RIDGE

Cabernet Sauvignon South Eastern Australia 1998: Light and smooth, with pretty plum and herb flavors that linger on the soft finish. Drink now.–H.S. • $9 • (10/31/1999) • **84**
Chardonnay South Eastern Australia 1998: Smooth in texture, if slightly sweet, with pretty pear and spice flavors. Drink now.–H.S. • $8 • (9/30/1999) • **80**
Chardonnay South Eastern Australia 1997: Soft and generous with its spicy, slightly herbal pear and tropical fruit flavors.–H.S. • $8 • (11/15/1998) • **83**
Merlot South Eastern Australia 1998: Light, smooth and polished, with pretty plum and floral flavors that linger on the velvety finish. Drink now through 2003.–H.S. • $9 • (11/15/1999) • **83**
Merlot South Eastern Australia 1997: Crisp and light, with firm tannins around a modest core of berry and tobacco flavor. Drink now.–H.S. • $9 • (5/31/1999) • **80**
Shiraz South Eastern Australia 1998: Soft and ripe, with nice black cherry and spice flavors on a velvety background. Drink now.–H.S. • $9 • (9/30/1999) • **84**

DRAYTON'S

Cabernet Sauvignon Hunter Valley 1993 • $10 • (10/31/1995) • **84**
Cabernet Sauvignon Hunter Valley 1991 • $10 • (9/30/1994) • **79**
Cabernet-Merlot Hunter Valley 1991 • $10 • (9/30/1994) • **64**
Chardonnay South Eastern Australia 1998: Soft and spicy, offering a distinctive floral character to go along with its basic apple cider notes. Drink now through 2001.–H.S. • $10 • (9/15/1999) • **82**
Chardonnay South Eastern Australia C-6 1998: Light and earthy, with a smoky edge to the thin apple flavors.–H.S. • $8 • (9/30/1999) • **78**

Port Australia Fine Old Pioneer NV • $10 • (3/31/1995) • **82**

Port Hunter Valley Old Tawny Port Log Press NV • $18 • (3/31/1995) • **88**

Shiraz Hunter Valley Bin 5555 1994 • $9 • (12/15/1995) • **73**

Shiraz Hunter Valley Bin 5555 1990 • $10 • (4/15/1994) • **82**

Shiraz Hunter Valley S-5 1994 • $7 • (10/31/1995) • **82**

Shiraz Hunter Valley William 1991 • $23 • (10/31/1995) • **83**

Shiraz Hunter Valley William 1989 • $30 • (9/30/1994) • **85**

Shiraz South Eastern Australia 1998: Smells like a garden shop, with potting soil and mulch overtones to the modest berry flavors. Not to every taste.–H.S. • $10 • (9/30/1999) • **77**

Shiraz South Eastern Australia 1995 • $14 • (4/30/1997) • **82**

Shiraz South Eastern Australia S-5 1998: Soft and appealing with its spicy blackberry and anise flavors, finishing with a layer of fine tannins. Drink now through 2002.–H.S. • $8 • (9/30/1999) • **81**

Shiraz South Eastern Australia S-5 1996 • $8 • (4/30/1997) • **79**

Shiraz South Eastern Australia S-5 1995 • $8 • (4/30/1996) • **84**

Shiraz-Cabernet Sauvignon Hunter Valley Oakey Creek 1993 • $7 • (6/15/1994) • **82**

Verdelho Hunter Valley 1994 • $10 • (10/31/1995) • **83**

DROMANA

Shiraz Mornington Peninsula 1997: Ripe in flavor and round in texture, with refined tannins surrounding a rich core of blackberry, anise and dark plum flavors that linger on the generous finish. Drink now through 2007.–H.S. • $24 • (6/15/1999) • **89**

ECHO POINT

Cabernet Sauvignon South Australia 1997: A bit chewy, but packed with enough plum and currant flavor to make it feel bright and appealing right through the firm finish. Drink now through 2002.–H.S. • $10 • (9/15/1999) • **85**

Chardonnay South Eastern Australia 1998: Smooth and slightly sappy, with a spicy edge to the apple and olive flavors. Drink now.–H.S. • $10 • (9/30/1999) • **82**

Shiraz Langhorne Creek 1997: Lean and lively, with spicy, exotic, earthy overtones to the delicate plum and berry flavors that linger on the gentle finish. Drink now through 2007.–H.S. • $10 • (11/15/1999) • **87**

ELDERTON

Cabernet Sauvignon-Merlot Barossa Valley 1984 • $11 • (4/30/1988) • **86**

Cabernet Sauvignon-Shiraz-Merlot Barossa CSM 1996: Nicely proportioned, with trim plum, blackberry and currant notes. Hints of herb and spice fill in the gaps, gaining richness and depth on the finish. Drink now through 2007.–J.L. • $36 • (6/30/2000) • **90**

Cabernet Sauvignon-Shiraz-Merlot Barossa Valley 1995 • $33 • (4/30/1998) • **88**

Merlot Barossa Valley 1996: More Barossa than Merlot, this plush, juicy wine is very ripe and spicy, with black cherry, smoke and exotic spice flavors swirling through the nicely focused finish. Drink now through 2005.–H.S. • $27 • (6/15/1999) • **90**

Sémillon South Eastern Australia Golden 1996 • $18/375 ml. • (5/31/1997) • **88**

Shiraz Barossa Valley 1997: Refined and bursting with blackberry, licorice and coffee notes, all on a firm, vibrant frame, this red unfolds layer by layer while retaining its harmony and integrity. Great finish. Drink now through 2003.–B.S. • $25 • (6/30/2000) • **92**

Shiraz Barossa Valley 1996: Firm in texture, with ultraripe flavors of blackberry, anise and prune that keep biting on the finish, echoing spicy oak notes. Needs time to soften its hard edges. Best after 2000.–H.S. • $25 • (5/15/1999) • **90**

Shiraz Barossa Valley 1995 • $20 • (6/15/1997) • **91**

Shiraz Barossa Valley Command 1995: Superrich and jammy, with a wonderful array of black cherry, wild berry, sexy toasty oak and spice nuances. The texture is silky-smooth, with a mile-long finish. Drink now through 2008.–J.L. • $60 • (6/30/2000) HR • **95**

Shiraz Barossa Valley Command 1992 • $34 • (12/15/1996) • **94**

EVANS FAMILY WINERY

Shiraz Hunter Valley Howard 1997: Firm in texture and distinctly reflecting its Lower Hunter Valley roots. Earthy, smoky and exotic, dripping with gamy flavors around a supple core of black cherry and black pepper character. Not for everyone, but worth cellaring. Best after 2001.–H.S. • $20 • (6/15/1999) • **87**

EVANS & TATE

Cabernet Sauvignon Margaret River 1996: Firm in texture, with juicy berry and mint flavors that keep pulsing through the fine-grained tannins on the finish. Drink through 2005.–H.S. • $35 • (11/30/1998) • **87**

Cabernet Sauvignon Margaret River 1991 • $14 • (11/15/1993) • **82**

Cabernet-Merlot Australia Barrique 61 1994 • $14 • (4/30/1996) • **88**

Cabernet-Merlot Margaret River Pemberton 1996: Herbal, vegetal, gamy flavors won't please everyone, but there's enough fruit at the core to warrant cellaring to see what happens. Best from 2001 through 2003.–H.S. • $19 • (8/31/1998) • **81**

Cabernet-Merlot Western Australia Barrique 61 1995 • $15 • (10/31/1997) • **83**

Chardonnay Margaret River Perth Hills 1997: Bright and jazzy, with generous apple and peach flavors that remain lively through the clear, fruit-centered finish. Drink now.–H.S. • $19 • (8/31/1998) • **88**

Gnangara Western Australia 1997: Sturdy and simple, with resiny flavors that veer into bitterness on the finish. A blend of Sauvignon Blanc, Sémillon, Chardonnay and Verdelho. Drink now.–H.S. • $12 • (8/31/1998) • **79**

Merlot Australia Margaret River 1992 • $15 • (5/31/1995) • **85**

Merlot Margaret River 1995 • $22 • (11/30/1997) • **86**

Merlot Margaret River 1994 • $16 • (8/31/1996) • **79**

Merlot Margaret River 1992 • $15 • (9/30/1994) • **82**

Merlot Margaret River 1991 • $16 • (4/30/1994) • **70**

Merlot Margaret River 1990 • $15 • (12/15/1993) • **82**

Sauvignon Blanc Margaret River 1997: Juicy and distinctive for its floral, violet-scented pear and passion fruit character, finishing solid. Drink now.–H.S. • $18 • (8/31/1998) • **87**

Shiraz Australia Gnangara 1993 • $10 • (6/30/1995) • **85**

Shiraz Margaret River 1996: Bright and jazzy, with raspberry and blackberry flavors and hints of mint and moss on the finish. Drink through 2003.–H.S. • $35 • (11/30/1998) • **86**

Shiraz Margaret River Hermitage 1991 • $14 • (10/31/1993) • **87**

Shiraz Western Australia Gnangara 1996: Firm in texture and generous with its dark blackberry and cherry flavors. A claret-shaped wine with a nice edge of spiciness on the finish. Drink through 2002.–H.S. • $12 • (8/31/1998) • **87**

Shiraz Western Australia Gnangara 1995 • $15 • (10/31/1997) • **86**

Shiraz-Cabernet Western Australia Gnangara 1992 • $12 • (3/31/1994) • **82**

Shiraz-Cabernet Western Australia Gnangara 1991 • $10 • (11/30/1993) • **80**

EVANS WINE COMPANY

Cabernet Sauvignon King Valley 1998: Round and supple, with bright, open currant and plum flavors that extend into a generous finish. Nice now. Best after 2001.–H.S. • $15 • (6/30/1999) • **88**

Chardonnay King Valley 1998: Has an unusual note of dusky spices that harmonize with fresh apple flavors on a crisp frame. Drink now through 2001.–H.S. • $15 • (6/30/1999) • **86**

Sémillon Hunter Valley 1997 • $12 • (3/31/1998) • **86**

Shiraz King Valley 1998: Firm in texture and generous with its open-throttle plum and blueberry as it persists through the extensive finish. A distinctive Shiraz, more on the crisp side than most Aussie reds. Drink through 2008.–H.S. • $15 • (6/30/1999) • **89**

Shiraz South Eastern Australia 1996 • $15 • (11/15/1997) • **88**

Verdelho Hunter Valley 1997 • $12 • (3/31/1998) • **84**

FERN HILL

Cabernet Sauvignon South Australia 1995: A firm, generous, bright mouthful of polished blueberry, plum and currant, shaded with a light herbal note. Appealing. Drink now through 2001.–H.S. • $16 • (11/15/1998) • **86**

Chardonnay South Australia 1997: Fresh and open-textured, with ebullient pear and citrus flavors, a hint of toast on the soft finish. Drink now.–H.S. • $13 • (11/15/1998) • **85**

Shiraz South Australia 1995: A lovely, almost profuse wine of berry and plum flavors that linger on the racy finish, balancing with a light jolt of acidity. Nice already. Drink now.–H.S. • $16 • (10/15/1998) • **87**

FIDDLERS CREEK

Cabernet-Shiraz Australia 1996: Fresh, appealing for its supple berry and currant flavors, even more so for its smooth texture and pretty finish. Drink now through 2002.–H.S. • $13 • (1/31/1999) • **85**

■ ■ ■ ■

FIDDLERS CREEK

Chardonnay South Eastern Australia 1997: Bright and fresh, with pretty apple and citrus flavors and hints of oaky spice. Drink now.–H.S. • $13 • (1/31/1999) • **83**

FIFTH LEG

Margaret River Red 1998: Has barnyard and leather notes, but with dried berry, chocolate and eucalyptus notes. Drink now through 2004.–B.S. • $15 • (6/30/2000) • **85**
Margaret River Red 1996 • $15 • (2/28/1998) • **85**
Margaret River White 1997 • $15 • (3/31/1998) • **87**

FIVE MILE HOLLOW

Red Table Wine Hastings River 1994 • $12 • (4/30/1996) • **80**
Red Table Wine Hastings Valley 1993 • $12 • (5/31/1995) • **85**
Sémillon-Chardonnay Hastings River 1997 • $13 • (5/31/1998) • **87**
Shiraz-Cabernet-Merlot Australia 1992 • $10 • (9/30/1994) • **85**

FLAME OPAL

Chardonnay South Eastern Australia 1997: Light and appealing for its resiny apple and pear flavors, finishing with hints of fruit cocktail. Drink now.–H.S. • $14 • (2/28/1999) • **84**

FOOTHILLS

Chardonnay Hunter Valley 1997: Has a distinctive profile, offering racy citrus, pear and guava flavors on a crisp frame, finishing with a sense of restraint and nice focus to the flavors. Tasty now, but feels like it can grow with cellaring. Drink now through 2005.–H.S. • $12 • (5/31/1999) • **88**

FOX CREEK

Sparkling Shiraz McLaren Vale Burgundy Vixen NV • $NA • (1/01/1998) • **88**
Shiraz McLaren Vale Reserve 1997: Eccentric and distinctive. Ripe up front, like a Port, with exuberant berry, violet and wet earth flavors. Lacks a little flesh midpalate; dry tannins on the finish. Drink now through 2002.–B.S. • $50 • (6/30/2000) • **89**
Shiraz-Cabernets McLaren Vale J.S.M. 1997: A core of cherry and tobacco gives way to a tannic structure in this lean red. May improve with time. Best from 2001 through 2004.–B.S. • $24 • (6/30/2000) • **85**
Vixen McLaren Vale NV: This sparkling Shiraz blend shows black cherry, mineral and spice notes that have pleasant focus. Drink now.–B.S. • $18 • (6/30/2000) • **83**

FOX RIVER

Chardonnay Australia 1997 • $12 • (6/15/1998) • **84**
Classic Red Australia 1996 • $12 • (6/15/1998) • **87**
Classic Red Western Australia 1995 • $12 • (5/15/1997) • **79**
Pinot Noir Western Australia 1997 • $12 • (6/15/1998) • **80**

FRANKLAND

Olmo's Reward Western Australia 1995: Raucous, with ripe flavors competing with mint, herb and green pepper notes. Chewy, but not as rich as it could be to balance. Best after 2001.–H.S. • $24 • (6/15/1999) • **84**
Olmo's Reward Western Australia 1994 • $24 • (4/30/1998) • **88**
Olmo's Reward Western Australia 1993 • $20 • (6/15/1997) • **84**
Riesling Western Australia Isolation Ridge 1998: Dry and fragrant, generous with its floral, green apple, peach and vaguely minty aromas and flavors, finishing fresh and appealing. Drink now through 2008.–H.S. • $17 • (6/30/2000) • **87**
Shiraz Western Australia Isolation Ridge 1997: Broad, succulent and leathery, displaying licorice, plum and tobacco, solid tannins and a modest finish. Drink now through 2002.–B.S. • $21 • (6/30/2000) • **85**
Shiraz Western Australia Isolation Ridge 1996: Light and fragrant, with pretty plum and currant flavors that keep glowing on the firm finish. Could develop more depth with cellaring. Drink now through 2006.–H.S. • $19 • (6/15/1999) • **89**
Shiraz Western Australia Isolation Ridge 1995 • $19 • (6/30/1998) • **83**
Shiraz Western Australia Isolation Ridge 1994 • $16 • (6/15/1997) • **86**

FROG ROCK

Cabernet Sauvignon Mudgee 1997: This racy, intense red is crisp in texture, offering jazzy plum, berry and spice flavors and hints of exotic herb on the finish. Best from 2001 through 2007.–H.S. • $26 • (6/15/1999) • **87**
Chardonnay Mudgee 1997: Bright and jazzy, very youthful, with sharply focused pineapple, melon and guava flavors that linger on the firm finish. Nice now. Drink now.–H.S. • $24 • (3/31/1999) • **88**
Shiraz Mudgee 1997: Supple and generous with its blackberry, black cherry and spice flavors, finishing soft. Appealing for current drinking. Drink now through 2002.–H.S. • $24 • (3/31/1999) • **87**

GLAETZER

Malbec-Cabernet Sauvignon Barossa Valley 1996: Thick, rich and aromatic, with mint and sage notes hovering around the plush cherry, red plum and spice flavors that linger on the polished finish. Drink now through 2003.–H.S. • $61 • (5/15/2000) • **88**

GLENARA

Cabernet Sauvignon Adelaide Hills 1996: Aromatic, with smoke and fruit, this firm red has pretty blackberry, pepper and floral character that echoes on the smooth finish. Best from 2001 through 2005.–H.S. • $18 • (1/31/2000) • **88**
Cabernet-Merlot Adelaide Hills 1996: A crisp style of Cabernet, with juicy plum and herb flavors on a sleek, jazzy frame, echoing fruit and spice on the gentle finish. Drink now through 2003.–H.S. • $16 • (1/31/2000) • **87**
Shiraz Adelaide Hills 1996: Crisp, jazzy style of Shiraz offering ripe berry and spice flavors around a lively core of citrusy acidity. Appealing for its brightness. Probably best if cellared. Drink through 2008.–H.S. • $16 • (12/31/1999) • **87**

GOUNDREY

Cabernet Sauvignon Mount Barker Reserve 1996: A ripe and distinctive wine, aromatic with spices and chocolate, its supple currant, prune and herbal flavors gliding smoothly to the finish. Best after 2000.–H.S. • $24 • (2/28/1999) • **90**
Cabernet Sauvignon Mount Barker Reserve Selection 1995 • $24 • (6/15/1998) • **90**
Cabernet-Merlot Mount Barker 1997: Light and supple, featuring a distinctive green mint and sage tang to the ripe berry flavors, finishing with fine-grained tannins. Drink now through 2002.–H.S. • $14 • (2/28/1999) • **85**
Cabernet-Merlot Mount Barker 1996 • $14 • (6/15/1998) • **87**
Cabernet-Merlot Mount Barker 1995 • $10 • (5/15/1997) • **81**
Chardonnay Mount Barker Reserve Selection 1997 • $24 • (6/15/1998) • **91**
Chardonnay Mount Barker Unwooded 1998: Bright and appealing for its generous nectarine and spice flavors on a lively frame, finishing smooth. Drink now.–H.S. • $14 • (2/28/1999) • **87**
Chardonnay Mount Barker Unwooded 1997 • $14 • (6/15/1998) • **88**
Chenin Blanc Mount Barker 1998: On the soft side, with lovely pear, floral and spice flavors that expand and persist on the supple finish. Drink now.–H.S. • $14 • (2/28/1999) • **87**
Chenin Blanc Mount Barker 1997 • $14 • (6/15/1998) • **87**
Merlot Mount Barker Reserve 1995 • $25 • (5/15/1997) • **86**
Riesling Mount Barker Reserve Selection 1997 • $20 • (6/15/1998) • **88**
Shiraz Mount Barker Reserve 1995 • $15 • (5/15/1997) • **85**
Shiraz Mount Barker Reserve Selection 1997: Round and velvety, a supple mouthful of gamy black cherry and vanilla flavors that echo nicely on the smooth finish. Drink now through 2006.–H.S. • $24 • (5/15/2000) • **88**
Shiraz Mount Barker Reserve Selection 1996 • $23 • (6/15/1998) • **86**
Shiraz-Grenache Mount Barker 1997: Light and bright, with pretty black cherry and rhubarb flavors that remain crisp and appealing on the finish. Drink now through 2001.–H.S. • $14 • (2/28/1999) • **83**

GRAMP, TIM

Shiraz McLaren Vale 1998: Gorgeous aromas of blackberry, sweet plum and spice mingle with ripe tannins and bright acidity in this intense, balanced

Key: SS—Spectator Selection. CS—Cellar Selection. HR—Highly Recommended. $NA—Price not available. (BT)—Barrel tasting. (A)—Auction Price.
For a key to the tasters' initials, see "How to Use These Listings."
Dates in parentheses represent the issues in which the ratings were published.

red. Picks up chocolate on the palate, ending with sweet fruit. Drink now through 2003.–B.S. • $28 • (6/30/2000) • **87**

GREENOCK CREEK

Cabernet Sauvignon Barossa Valley 1997: A hearty style, with meaty currant, blackberry, cedary oak and firm tannins. Turns chunky, so short-term cellaring may help. Best from 2001 through 2007.–J.L. • $50 • (6/30/2000) • **89**

Cabernet Sauvignon Barossa Valley 1996: Gamy, with metallic green bean flavors that turn murky.–J.L. • $42 • (6/30/2000) • **77**

Grenache Barossa Valley Corner Stone 1998: Smooth and generous, with sweet plum, vanilla, raspberry and tobacco aromas and flavors. Full-bodied, with a touch of heat on the finish. Drink now through 2001.–B.S. • $43 • (6/30/2000) • **87**

Shiraz Barossa Valley Creek Block 1997: Rich and fleshy, with pretty coffee, plum, wild berry and spice notes that are smooth and polished, long and flavorful. Drink now through 2006.–J.L. • $70 • (6/30/2000) • **88**

Shiraz Barossa Valley Seven Acre 1997: Dense and tightly wound, yet doesn't show the range of flavors and expression of the best Shiraz. Still, there's thyme, black cherry and wood notes, with firm tannins on the finish. Drink now through 2003.–B.S. • $65 • (6/30/2000) • **89**

GROSSET

Chardonnay Adelaide Hills Piccadilly 1998: Bright and focused, a lively wine with earthy pear and peach flavors that linger on the lightly toasty finish. Drink now through 2006.–H.S. • $NA • (6/30/2000) • **89**

Chardonnay Adelaide Hills Piccadilly 1997: Very ripe and generous yet balanced on a razor's edge of sharp acidity, with pear, fig and almond flavors that balloon elegantly on the finish. Has style, flavor and finesse in a seductive package. Drink now through 2005.–H.S. • $28 • (6/15/1999) • **91**

Gaia Clare Valley Red 1997: Crisp in texture, with cedary black cherry and spice flavors battling past a layer of scratchy tannins on the finish. Has enough richness to balance. Best after 2002.–H.S. • $32 • (6/30/2000) • **85**

Riesling Clare Valley Polish Hill 1999: Bright and juicy, a snappy mouthful of pear, rose petal and mineral flavors that linger on the intense finish. Remains sleek and focused. Drink now through 2009.–H.S. • $28 • (6/30/2000) • **89**

Riesling Clare Valley Polish Hill 1998: Bright, ripe and bracing, with lemon, apple and floral flavors that remain racy and remarkably expressive through the deftly balanced finish. This bottling has a track record for aging beautifully. Drink now through 2008.–H.S. • $21 • (6/15/1999) • **91**

Riesling Clare Valley Polish Hill 1997 • $21 • (4/30/1998) • **89**

GROVE HILL

Riesling Adelaide Hills Dry Grown 1998: Excessively floral and peppery, like old rose petals. Finishes bitter. Tasted twice, with consistent notes.–H.S. • $24 • (11/15/1999) • **70**

HAMILTON, HUGH

Cabernet Sauvignon McLaren Vale 1996: Firm, chewy and lavishly flavorful, with bay leaf and a slightly metallic edge to the earthy currant and cherry flavors. Flavors linger without a hard edge. Drink now through 2006.–H.S. • $20 • (2/29/2000) • **88**

Shiraz McLaren Vale 1996: Ripe and open-textured, with a layer of fine tannins around a fresh-tasting core of berry and plum flavor. The fruit echoes nicely on the velvety finish. Drink now through 2006.–H.S. • $20 • (2/29/2000) • **87**

HAMILTON, RICHARD

Cabernet Sauvignon Coonawarra Reserve 1994 • $21 • (11/15/1996) • **88**

Grenache-Shiraz McLaren Vale Burton's Vineyard 1995 • $15 • (2/28/1997) • **87**

Grenache-Shiraz McLaren Vale Burton's Vineyard 1994 • $12 • (10/31/1996) • **87**

Merlot McLaren Vale Reserve 1996 • $24 • (4/30/1998) • **86**

Shiraz McLaren Vale Old Vine Reserve 1995 • $23 • (2/28/1997) • **86**

HANWOOD

Cabernet Sauvignon Australia 1993 • $8 • (6/30/1995) • **81**

Cabernet Sauvignon South Eastern Australia 1994 • $7 • (4/30/1996) • **83**

Shiraz South Eastern Australia 1994 • $7 • (4/30/1996) • **81**

HARDYS

Brut Australia Grand Reserve Australian Champagne NV • $8 • (9/15/1994) • **81**

Brut Chardonnay South Eastern Australia Nottage Hill 1997: Goes for elegance by balancing its supple texture and soft flavors of pear, lime and vanilla against a crisp background. A harmonious style, nicely done. Drink now.–H.S. • $9 • (3/31/1999) • **87**

Cabernet Sauvignon Coonawarra 1995 • $18 • (5/31/1998) • **86**

Cabernet Sauvignon Coonawarra 1994 • $11 • (10/15/1996) HR • **88**

Cabernet Sauvignon Coonawarra 1993 • $11 • (3/31/1996) • **86**

Cabernet Sauvignon Coonawarra 1992 • $10 • (6/30/1995) • **87**

Cabernet Sauvignon Coonawarra 1987 • $11 • (7/15/1990) • **81**

Cabernet Sauvignon Coonawarra Collection 1990 • $10 • (6/30/1994) • **88**

Cabernet Sauvignon Coonawarra Regional Collection 1992 • $10 • (8/31/1994) • **89**

Cabernet Sauvignon Coonawarra Regional Collection 1991 • $10 • (6/30/1994) • **84**

Cabernet Sauvignon Coonawarra Thomas Hardy 1994: Ripe and elegant, a refined style of Cabernet that emphasizes open texture and lovely currant, berry and herb flavors. Drink now through 2009.–H.S. • $50 • (12/15/1999) • **89**

Cabernet Sauvignon Coonawarra Thomas Hardy 1993 • $50 • (5/31/1998) • **87**

Cabernet Sauvignon Coonawarra Thomas Hardy 1992 • $45 • (5/31/1997) • **92**

Cabernet Sauvignon Coonawarra Thomas Hardy 1991 • $20 • (3/31/1996) • **89**

Cabernet Sauvignon Coonawarra Thomas Hardy 1989 • $27 • (3/31/1995) • **88**

Cabernet Sauvignon McLaren Vale Collection No. 8 1986 • $11 • (1/31/1989) • **76**

Cabernet Sauvignon South Australia Bird Series 1988 • $8 • (3/15/1992) • **83**

Cabernet Sauvignon South Australia Collection 1989 • $12 • (5/31/1993) • **83**

Cabernet Sauvignon South Australia Collection 1988 • $10 • (2/15/1991) • **83**

Cabernet Sauvignon South Eastern Australia 1994 • $8 • (6/30/1995) • **81**

Cabernet Sauvignon South Eastern Australia Nottage Hill 1992 • $7 • (7/31/1994) • **82**

Cabernet Sauvignon South Eastern Australia Nottage Hill 1990 • $8 • (3/31/1993) • **77**

Cabernet Sauvignon South Australia Nottage Hill 1989 • $8 • (11/30/1992) • **80**

Cabernet Sauvignon-Shiraz South Eastern Australia Bird Series 1990 • $8 • (5/15/1994) • **82**

Cabernet Sauvignon-Shiraz South Eastern Australia Nottage Hill 1999: Simple and plummy, with cherry flavors and a spicy oak frame. Drink now.–J.L. • $7 • (6/30/2000) • **83**

Cabernet Sauvignon-Shiraz South Eastern Australia Nottage Hill 1998: Firm in texture, with pretty blackberry and vanilla flavors lingering on the light, lively finish. Drink now.–H.S. • $7 • (11/15/1999) • **82**

Cabernet Sauvignon-Shiraz South Eastern Australia Nottage Hill 1997: Firm and focused, showing pretty plum and vanilla flavors on a supple frame. Finishes with a sweet note. Drink now.–H.S. • $8 • (11/30/1998) • **83**

Cabernet Sauvignon-Shiraz South Eastern Australia Nottage Hill 1996 • $7 • (6/15/1998) • **83**

Cabernet Sauvignon-Shiraz South Eastern Australia Nottage Hill 1995 • $7 • (5/15/1997) • **84**

Cabernet Sauvignon-Shiraz South Eastern Australia Nottage Hill 1994 • $7 • (4/30/1996) • **86**

Cabernet Sauvignon-Shiraz South Eastern Australia Nottage Hill 1993 • $7 • (4/30/1995) • **85**

Cabernet Sauvignon-Shiraz South Eastern Australia Signature 1995 • $11 • (2/28/1998) • **86**

Chardonnay South Eastern Australia Nottage Hill 1999: Light and bright, with effusive melon and pear flavors that echo nicely on the round finish. Drink now.–H.S. • $6 • (11/15/1999) • **84**

Chardonnay South Eastern Australia Nottage Hill 1998: Bright and refreshing, with lively green apple and citrus flavors that linger a bit on the finish. Drink now.–H.S. • $7 • (3/31/1999) • **84**

Chardonnay South Eastern Australia Nottage Hill 1997 • $7 • (6/15/1998) • **84**

Chardonnay South Eastern Australia Signature 1998: A lively mouthful of fruit that pumps its apple, pear and spice character through the wide-open finish. A big, round wine with flavor to burn. Drink now through 2003.–H.S. • $9 • (11/15/1999) • **87**

Chardonnay South Eastern Australia Signature 1997 • $9 • (2/28/1998) • **87**

Merlot South Eastern Australia Nottage Hill 1998: Light and soft, this pretty red has strawberry and raspberry flavors that linger on the gentle finish. Drink now through 2002.–H.S. • $7 • (11/30/1999) • **83**

Merlot South Eastern Australia Nottage Hill 1997: Light and pretty, with cherry and currant notes and firm tannins on the finish. Drink now.–H.S. • $7 • (3/31/1999) • **83**

Merlot South Eastern Australia Nottage Hill 1996 • $7 • (6/15/1998) • **83**

Merlot South Eastern Australia Nottage Hill 1994 • $8 • (3/31/1996) • **85**

HARDYS

Merlot South Eastern Australia Nottage Hill 1993 • $7 • (5/31/1995) • **86**

Pinot Noir Yarra Valley Signature 1998: Light, supple and pretty for its blackberry flavor that turns into raspberry on the delicate finish. Drink now through 2002.–H.S. • $11 • (12/15/1999) • **83**

Port Australia Tall Ships Tawny Port NV • $10 • (3/31/1995) • **86**

Premium Classic Dry Red South Australia 1988 • $5 • (7/31/1990) • **78**

Shiraz McLaren Vale Bird Series 1991 • $8 • (4/15/1994) • **84**

Shiraz McLaren Vale Bird Series 1990 • $7 • (5/31/1993) • **80**

Shiraz McLaren Vale Bird Series 1988 • $8 • (9/30/1991) • **84**

Shiraz McLaren Vale-Padthaway Eileen Hardy 1996: Smooth and broad, distinctive for the herbal, vegetal notes swirling around the basic blackberry and spice flavors. Not for all tastes, but a red with real personality and style. Drink through 2010.–H.S. • $65 • (11/15/1999) • **91**

Shiraz McLaren Vale-Padthaway Eileen Hardy 1995: Rich in flavor and remarkably focused, this red pinpoints its blackberry, plum, mint and anise flavors as it expands across the palate. Nicely styled to show off the pretty flavors which echo on the firm finish. Drink now.–H.S. • $65 • (9/30/1998) HR • **92**

Shiraz McLaren Vale-Padthaway-Clare Valley Eileen Hardy 1994 • $45 • (5/31/1997) • **90**

Shiraz Padthaway-McLaren Vale-Clare Valley Eileen Hardy 1993 • $20 • (4/30/1996) • **94**

Shiraz South Australia Eileen Hardy 1992 • $20 • (5/15/1995) • **87**

Shiraz South Australia Eileen Hardy 1990 • $20 • (3/31/1994) • **86**

Shiraz South Australia Eileen Hardy 1989 • $20 • (5/31/1993) • **84**

Shiraz South Australia Eileen Hardy 1988 • $19 • (2/15/1992) HR • **91**

Shiraz South Eastern Australia Nottage Hill 1998: Bright, briery flavors show plenty of pizzazz, echoing plum and spice notes on the soft finish. Drink now through 2003.–H.S. • $7 • (11/30/1999) • **84**

Shiraz South Eastern Australia Nottage Hill 1997: A lighter style that strives for delicacy over power, this drink-me-now Shiraz is smooth on the palate, appealing for its pretty plum and spice flavors. Always heartening to find the combo of inexpensive wine and reliable producer. Drink now.–H.S. • $8 • (11/30/1998) • **85**

Shiraz South Eastern Australia Nottage Hill 1995 • $7 • (5/15/1997) • **82**

Shiraz South Eastern Australia Nottage Hill 1994 • $7 • (10/15/1996) • **82**

Shiraz South Eastern Australia Nottage Hill 1993 • $7 • (11/15/1995) • **82**

Shiraz-Cabernet South Eastern Australia Bird Series 1991 • $10 • (9/30/1994) • **83**

Shiraz-Cabernet South Eastern Australia Captain's Selection 1993 • $6 • (9/30/1994) • **83**

Shiraz-Cabernet South Eastern Australia Captain's Selection 1992 • $7 • (9/30/1994) • **76**

Shiraz-Cabernet South Eastern Australia Captain's Selection 1991 • $6 • (5/31/1993) • **84**

Shiraz-Cabernet South Eastern Australia Captain's Selection 1990 • $6 • (6/30/1992) • **82**

Shiraz-Cabernet South Eastern Australia Stamps of Australia 1993 • $7 • (9/30/1994) • **81**

Shiraz-Cabernet South Eastern Australia Stamps of Australia 1992 • $6 • (9/30/1994) • **82**

Sparkling Shiraz Australia NV • $19 • (11/30/1997) • **86**

Tawny Port Australia Tall Ships NV • $11 • (7/31/1990) • **83**

Tawny Port South Australia Whiskers Blake NV • $13 • (5/31/1997) HR • **94**

HASELGROVE

Cabernet Sauvignon South Eastern Australia Sovereign 1996 • $10 • (5/31/1998) • **85**

Cabernet-Merlot-Shiraz McLaren Vale 1996 • $16 • (5/31/1998) • **86**

Chardonnay McLaren Vale 1997 • $13 • (5/15/1998) • **86**

Chardonnay South Eastern Australia Sovereign 1997 • $9 • (5/15/1998) • **84**

Grenache South Eastern Australia Sovereign 1996 • $10 • (5/15/1998) • **84**

Sauvignon Blanc McLaren Vale 1997 • $13 • (5/15/1998) • **86**

Shiraz McLaren Vale H Reserve 1996 • $29 • (5/31/1998) HR • **92**

Shiraz South Australia Sovereign 1997 • $10 • (5/15/1998) • **87**

Sparkling Shiraz McLaren Vale H Garnet SG-4 NV • $20 • (5/31/1998) • **86**

Key: SS—Spectator Selection. CS—Cellar Selection. HR—Highly Recommended. $NA—Price not available. (BT)—Barrel tasting. Ⓐ—Auction Price.
For a key to the tasters' initials, see "How to Use These Listings."
Dates in parentheses represent the issues in which the ratings were published.

HAY SHED HILL

Cabernet Sauvignon Margaret River 1997: Tightly wound, this Cabernet is cedary, with modest cherry and firm, dry tannins. Drink now through 2002.–B.S. • $28 • (6/30/2000) • **83**

Cabernet Sauvignon Margaret River 1996: Earthy and minty aromas, mixed with tomato and currant notes, mark this as a distinctive Cabernet, folding in cedary oak character to make it feel rich and focused enough to develop into something special with cellaring. Best from 2002 through 2008.–H.S. • $28 • (5/31/1999) • **88**

Pitchfork Pink Margaret River 1998: Light and refreshing, with pretty citrus flavors and just a tiny hint of berry to mark it as a rosé. Finishes dry. Drink now.–H.S. • $15 • (6/15/1999) • **85**

Pitchfork White Margaret River 1998: Ripe in flavor and open in texture, this is generous with its pineapple and nectarine, shaded with spicy oak notes on the finish. A blend of Sémillon, Sauvignon Blanc, Chardonnay and Chenin Blanc. Drink now through 2002.–H.S. • $15 • (6/15/1999) • **86**

Sauvignon Blanc Margaret River 1998: Light and refreshing, with modest melon and citrus aromas and flavors. Drink now.–H.S. • $19 • (6/15/1999) • **82**

HEGGIES

Cabernets Australia 1985 • $15 • (3/31/1993) • **84**

Merlot Eden Valley 1995: Ripe and generous. A rich mouthful of black cherry, pepper, herb and spice flavors that linger smoothly on the velvety finish. The seductive style is appealing already. Best after 2001.–H.S. • $22 • (3/31/2000) • **88**

Merlot Eden Valley 1994: Lean and a bit chewy, with modest prune and spice flavors on a firm frame. Drink through 2003–H.S. • $23 • (1/31/1999) • **80**

Merlot Eden Valley 1993 • $15 • (5/31/1997) • **85**

Merlot Eden Valley 1992 • $16 • (6/30/1996) • **80**

Riesling Eden Valley Botrytis 1998: Sweet and generous, with nicely focused honey, pineapple and spice flavors that linger softly on the gentle finish. Drink now through 2007.–H.S. • $15/375 ml. • (2/29/2000) • **88**

Riesling Eden Valley Botrytis 1997 • $16/375 ml. • (6/15/1998) • **94**

Riesling Eden Valley Botrytis 1996 • $14/375 ml. • (5/31/1997) • **92**

Riesling Eden Valley Botrytis Affected 1995 • $15 • (10/31/1996) • **90**

Viognier Eden Valley 1998: Ripe, round and effusive, an explosion of flavor on a silky frame, offering hay, wildflower and spicy overtones to the solid core of pear and grapefruit flavors. Drink now through 2002.–H.S. • $22 • (3/31/2000) • **89**

Viognier Eden Valley 1994 • $15 • (9/30/1995) • **86**

HENRY'S DRIVE

Shiraz Padthaway 1998: Firm, with dense, detailed cedar, coconut, black cherry and blackberry flavors that slowly unfold, revealing subtle nuances, finishing with complex earth notes. Best from 2001 through 2008.–J.L. • $30 • (6/30/2000) • **91**

HENSCHKE

Cabernet Sauvignon Eden Valley Cyril Henschke 1994 • $49 • (6/15/1998) • **92**

Cabernet Sauvignon Eden Valley Cyril Henschke 1993 • $66 • (5/31/1997) • **94**

Cabernet Sauvignon Eden Valley Cyril Henschke 1992 • $36/750 ml. • (4/30/1996) • **92**

Cabernet Sauvignon Eden Valley Cyril Henschke 1990 • $28 • (8/31/1994) • **84**

Cabernet Sauvignon Eden Valley Cyril Henschke 1989 • $23 • (5/31/1993) • **86**

Cabernet Sauvignon Keyneton Cyril Henschke 1991 • $35 • (6/15/1995) CS • **92**

Cabernet Sauvignon Keyneton Cyril Henschke 1988 • $23 • (6/30/1992) • **85**

Cabernet Sauvignon Keyneton Cyril Henschke 1986 • $23 • (9/15/1989) • **91**

Cabernet Sauvignon Keyneton Cyril Henschke 1985 • $21 • (1/31/1989) • **90**

Cabernet Sauvignon Keyneton Cyril Henschke 1984 • $19 • (12/15/1987) • **94**

Cabernet Sauvignon-Merlot-Cabernet Franc Eden Valley Cyril Henschke 1995: An elegant, refined, open-textured red, with plenty of flavor packed into its sleek frame. Echoes of pure plum, berry, mint and tarragon reverberate on the long finish. Drink now through 2010.–H.S. • $80 • (12/15/1999) • **92**

Chardonnay Adelaide Hills Lenswood Vineyard Croft 1997: Soft and supple, with earthy, creamy notes on a rich frame, echoing hints of pear and apple on the smooth finish. Drink now through 2001.–H.S. • $21 • (1/31/1999) • **87**

Chardonnay Eden Valley Barossa Ranges 1997 • $25 • (6/15/1998) • **86**

Chardonnay Eden Valley Cranes 1998: Ripe and generous, a pretty wine, with supple texture and apple, peach, spice and honey notes echoing on the finish. Drink now through 2005.–H.S. • $36 • (12/15/1999) • **89**

Chardonnay Lenswood Lenswood Vineyard Croft Vineyard 1998: Lean and refined, almost crisp in texture, with soft-spoken pear, peach, caramel and toast flavors receding ever so gradually on the finish. Drink now through 2004.–H.S. • $40 • (12/15/1999) • **88**

Grenache-Mourvèdre Barossa Valley Johann's Garden Bush Vine 1997: Ripe and peppery, positively dripping with black cherry, anise and other sweet spice flavors that swirl and linger on the generous finish. Smooth already, this can develop more with further cellaring. Drink now through 2007.–H.S. • $30 • (12/15/1999) • **90**

Johann's Garden Red Barossa Valley 1996 • $30 • (6/15/1998) • **87**

Keyneton Estate Keyneton 1988 • $14 • (6/30/1992) • **82**

Keyneton Estate Keyneton 1985 • $12 • (3/31/1989) • **79**

Keyneton Estate Keyneton 1984 • $12 • (2/15/1988) • **85**

Merlot-Cabernet Lenswood Lenswood Vineyard Abbotts Prayer 1996: Smooth and refined, appealing for its generous mint-tinged blackberry and currant flavors, finishing with polish and surprising intensity. Tannins are integrated. Drink now through 2008.–H.S. • $55 • (12/15/1999) • **90**

Merlot-Cabernet Sauvignon-Cabernet Franc Lenswood Lenswood Vineyard Abbott's Prayer 1995: Lovely, supple, subtle red with silky texture and pretty ripe blackberry, currant, cedar and vanilla flavors that linger on the gentle finish. Not a blockbuster, but a real sweetheart. Drink now through 2005.–H.S. • $57 • (1/31/1999) • **88**

Pinot Noir Lenswood Lenswood Vineyard Giles Vineyard 1997: Polished in texture and ripe in flavor, offering lovely currant, spice and toasty vanilla flavors that linger nicely on the smooth finish. Drink now through 2002.–H.S. • $40 • (12/15/1999) • **87**

Riesling Adelaide Hills Lenswood Vineyard Green's Hill 1997: Dry, bright and flavorful, artfully balanced to emphasize its pretty green apple, floral and spicy flavors. This spot-on Riesling is fun to drink now, but should gain with cellaring. Drink now through 2010.–H.S. • $25 • (1/31/1999) • **89**

Riesling Lenswood Lenswood Vineyard Green's Hill Vineyard 1998: Lively and distinctive, a wide-open dry Riesling, with layers of apple, floral, citrus and pine aromas and flavors that linger enticingly on the finish. Drink now through 2010.–H.S. • $22 • (12/15/1999) • **89**

Sémillon Eden Valley Louis 1998: A supple white, with lovely melon, fig and tobacco flavors that linger nicely on the honey-tinged finish. Tasty now. Best after 2003.–H.S. • $22 • (12/15/1999) • **87**

Sémillon Eden Valley Louis 1997 • $23 • (6/15/1998) • **84**

Shiraz Eden Valley Mount Edelstone Vineyard 1995 • $56 • (6/15/1998) HR • **93**

Shiraz Keyneton Estate 1989 • $15 • (5/31/1993) • **83**

Shiraz Keyneton Hill of Grace 1992 • $197 Ⓐ • (11/15/1997) • **94**

Shiraz Keyneton Hill of Grace 1991 • $157 Ⓐ • (6/30/1995) • **91**

Shiraz Keyneton Hill of Grace 1989 • $167 Ⓐ • (5/31/1993) • **91**

Shiraz Keyneton Hill of Grace 1988 • $162 Ⓐ • (5/31/1992) • **88**

Shiraz Keyneton Hill of Grace 1987 • $119 Ⓐ • (5/31/1992) CS • **91**

Shiraz Keyneton Hill of Grace 1986 • $188 Ⓐ • (9/30/1989) • **87**

Shiraz Keyneton Hill of Grace Keyneton Vineyard 1994: Rich in texture and extraordinarily deep in flavor, a bottomless well of ripe purple plum, black cherry, blackberry, anise and mint flavors that remain round and powerful through the finish, yet maintain a surprisingly elegant feel throughout. Approachable now. Best after 2004.–H.S. • $150 • (12/15/1999) • **95**

Shiraz Keyneton Mount Edelstone 1994 • $48 • (11/15/1997) • **89**

Shiraz Keyneton Mount Edelstone 1993 • $34 • (3/31/1996) CS • **96**

Shiraz Keyneton Mount Edelstone 1992 • $30 • (6/15/1995) SS • **91**

Shiraz Keyneton Mount Edelstone 1991 • $18 • (9/30/1994) • **87**

Shiraz Keyneton Mount Edelstone 1990 • $17 • (5/31/1993) • **84**

Shiraz Keyneton Mount Edelstone 1989 • $17 • (5/31/1992) • **88**

Shiraz Keyneton Mount Edelstone 1988 • $17 • (5/31/1992) HR • **90**

Shiraz Keyneton Mount Edelstone 1987 • $17 • (5/31/1991) • **86**

Shiraz Keyneton Mount Edelstone 1986 • $17 • (10/31/1989) HR • **90**

Shiraz Keyneton Mount Edelstone 1985 • $15 • (3/31/1989) • **81**

Shiraz Keyneton Mount Edelstone 1984 • $14 • (2/15/1988) • **90**

Shiraz Keyneton Mount Edelstone Keyneton Vineyard 1996: Bright and focused in flavor, this lithe red centers around a lovely beam of blackberry and tobacco flavors that linger forever and pick up an interesting gamy note on the refined finish. Has plenty of room to grow. Drink now through 2008.–H.S. • $60 • (12/15/1999) HR • **94**

Shiraz-Cabernet-Malbec Australia Keyneton Estate 1992 • $19 • (6/15/1995) • **86**

Shiraz-Cabernet-Malbec Australia Keyneton Estate 1991 • $12 • (8/31/1994) • **85**

Shiraz-Cabernet-Malbec Eden-Barossa Valleys Keyneton Estate 1994 • $30 • (5/31/1997) • **91**

Shiraz-Cabernet-Malbec Eden Barossa Valleys Keyneton Estate 1993 • $22 • (3/31/1996) HR • **93**

Shiraz-Cabernet-Merlot Barossa Keyneton Estate 1996: This lithe, supple style shows off plenty of pretty plum, berry and vanilla flavors, which pick up floral and spicy notes as the finish firms up. Feels youthful and definitely wants cellaring. Best after 2002.–H.S. • $36 • (12/15/1999) • **90**

Shiraz-Cabernet-Merlot Eden-Barossa Valleys Keyneton Estate 1995 • $36 • (6/15/1998) • **87**

HERMITAGE ROAD

Cabernet Sauvignon Hunter Valley Reserve 1997: Ripe and smoky, a firm-textured, youthful Cabernet that combines pretty berry flavors with tarry, exotic overtones. Drink through 2004.–H.S. • $15 • (2/28/1999) • **85**

Chardonnay Hunter Valley 1998: Ripe and juicy, this is distinctive for its guava, pineapple and citrus flavors on a medium-weight frame. Finish is polished and elegant. Drink now through 2003.–H.S. • $9 • (6/15/1999) • **87**

Chardonnay Hunter Valley Reserve 1997: Aromatic, with earthy, spicy nuances around a core of melon and pineapple, picking up nice honey notes on the long finish. Not a conventional Chardonnay, but it has its charms. Drink now.–H.S. • $15 • (3/31/1999) • **87**

Shiraz Hunter Valley Reserve 1997: Soft in texture, with earthy plum flavors on a supple frame. Not an expansive Shiraz, but feels like it can grow with cellaring. Drink now through 2004.–H.S. • $15 • (2/28/1999) • **86**

Shiraz Limestone Coast Reserve 1998: Crisp and focused, a jazzy wine with delicious black cherry, plum and citrus flavors that pick up hints of mineral and spice on the round finish. Drink now through 2005.–H.S. • $15 • (9/15/1999) • **87**

Shiraz South Australia 1998: Smooth and silky, this lightweight Shiraz has distinctive black cherry and spice flavors that linger enticingly through the generous finish. At this price and score, it's a solid choice when the occasion calls for multiple bottles. Drink now through 2005.–H.S. • $9 • (6/15/1999) • **87**

Shiraz South Eastern Australia 1997 • $10 • (5/15/1998) • **87**

HEWITSON

Mourvèdre Barossa Valley Old Garden 1998: Pretty good intensity, with chocolate, pepper and dried berry flavors framed within slightly dry acid and tannins. Drink now through 2005.–H.S. • $27 • (6/30/2000) • **85**

HIGHBANK

Red Coonawarra Basket Pressed 1997: Tough and raw in texture, with pure, focused plum and currant flavors that emerge and expand on the finish. Promises much but needs cellaring. A blend of 65 percent Cabernet Sauvignon, 23 percent Merlot, 12 percent Cabernet Franc. Best after 2002.–H.S. • $37 • (6/15/1999) • **88**

Red Coonawarra Basket Pressed 1996 • $38 • (4/30/1998) • **86**

HILL OF CONTENT

Grenache-Shiraz Clare Valley Old Vines 1997: Firm in texture, with juicy blackberry and mint aromas and flavors that keep ringing on the finish. Crisp acidity keeps it lively. Best after 2000.–H.S. • $13 • (6/15/1999) • **87**

HILL-SMITH ESTATE

Cabernet-Shiraz Adelaide Hills Terra Rossa Block 1988 • $11 • (11/30/1992) • **81**

Cabernet-Shiraz Eden Valley Terra Rossa Block 1994 • $12 • (5/15/1997) • **86**

Cabernet-Shiraz Eden Valley Terra Rossa Block 1992 • $12 • (5/15/1996) • **87**

HILLSTOWE

Merlot-Cabernet McLaren Vale Buxton 1994 • $15 • (3/31/1998) • **86**

Pinot Noir Adelaide Hills 1991 • $15 • (6/30/1993) • **88**

Pinot Noir Adelaide Hills Udy's Mill 1994 • $19 • (3/31/1998) • **86**

Pinot Noir Yarra Valley 1992 • $21 • (7/31/1994) • **83**

Shiraz McLaren Vale Buxton 1994 • $20 • (3/31/1998) • **87**

HOLLICK

Cabernet Sauvignon Coonawarra 1988 • $14 • (3/15/1992) • **74**

Cabernet Sauvignon Coonawarra Ravenswood 1994: Ripe, juicy and distinctive, this aromatic wine offers real mouthful of currant, blackberry and peppery flavors on a polished, elegant frame. Best after 2000.–H.S. • $45 • (2/28/1999) • **87**

Cabernet-Merlot Coonawarra 1997: Lean and a touch green, with cedar, black currant leaf and tobacco dissipating quickly, while the astringent tannins take over. Drink now through 2002.–B.S. • $20 • (6/30/2000) • **83**

Cabernet-Merlot Coonawarra 1995: Very crisp and racy, with ripe flavors against a steely-acidic backbone. Echoes licorice-scented blackberry and currant notes on the generous finish. Needs time. Best from 2002 through 2010.–H.S. • $20 • (6/30/1999) • **88**

Cabernet-Merlot Coonawarra 1994: Lean and juicy, with peppery currant, tomato and herb flavors on a tight frame. Distinctive, worthy of cellaring to see what develops. Drink through 2004.–H.S. • $23 • (11/15/1998) • **87**

Cabernet-Merlot Coonawarra 1985 • $16 • (5/31/1988) • **72**

Chardonnay Coonawarra 1997: A silky texture and pretty flavors characterize this refined Chardonnay, offering nicely melded honeydew, pear and vanilla flavors that persist on the light finish. Drink now through 2002.–H.S. • $17 • (11/15/1999) • **88**

Chardonnay Coonawarra Reserve 1998: Appley in aroma, then turns a touch tanky. Crisp and firm. Drink now.–B.S. • $17 • (6/30/2000) • **83**

Shiraz Coonawarra Wilgha 1996: Crisp and juicy. A lively mouthful of raspberry and cherry shaded by hints of almond and white pepper. Softens a bit on the finish. Drink now through 2002.–H.S. • $30 • (2/28/1999) • **85**

Shiraz-Cabernet Sauvignon Limestone Coast 1998: Not fleshy, but with fine focus to the aromas of dried berry, raspberry liqueur and chocolate. Dry tannins on the finish. Drink now through 2004.–B.S. • $19 • (6/30/2000) • **86**

HOPE ESTATE

Chardonnay Hunter Valley 1998: Straightforward, fruity and refreshing for its uncomplicated style. Echoes its flavors nicely on the finish. Drink now through 2002.–H.S. • $10 • (12/15/1999) • **86**

Merlot Hunter Valley 1998: Light and smooth, with pretty strawberry and sage flavors that remain soft and pleasant through the finish. Drink now.–H.S. • $13 • (12/15/1999) • **82**

Sémillon-Chardonnay Hunter Valley 1998: Earthy oyster shell aromas and flavors mark this as an oddball.–H.S. • $8 • (12/15/1999) • **78**

Shiraz Hunter Valley 1998: Ripe and spicy, with earthy anise notes weaving through the concentrated plum and currant flavors. Lovable for its generosity. Drink now through 2008.–H.S. • $13 • (12/15/1999) • **89**

Verdelho Hunter Valley 1998: Bright and jazzy, with simple green pear aromas and flavors. Drink now.–H.S. • $8 • (12/15/1999) • **80**

HOUGHTON

Cabernet Sauvignon Frankland River Wildflower Ridge 1988 • $9 • (7/15/1991) • **78**

Cabernet Sauvignon Western Australia Wildflower Ridge 1992 • $8 • (10/31/1995) • **88**

Cabernet Sauvignon Western Australia Wildflower Ridge 1991 • $7 • (9/30/1994) • **82**

Cabernet Sauvignon Western Australia Wildflower Ridge 1990 • $7 • (9/30/1994) • **82**

Shiraz Western Australia Wildflower Ridge 1994 • $8 • (6/30/1996) • **85**

Shiraz Western Australia Wildflower Ridge 1993 • $8 • (10/31/1995) • **84**

Shiraz Western Australia Wildflower Ridge 1991 • $7 • (6/15/1994) • **84**

Shiraz Western Australia Wildflower Ridge 1990 • $9 • (5/31/1993) • **84**

Shiraz Western Australia Wildflower Ridge 1989 • $9 • (11/30/1992) • **83**

HOWARD PARK

Cabernet-Merlot Western Australia 1994 • $48 • (6/15/1997) • **87**

Riesling Western Australia 1997 • $20 • (4/30/1998) • **86**

HUGO

Shiraz McLaren Vale 1996 • $15 • (6/15/1998) • **89**

Shiraz McLaren Vale 1995 • $16 • (9/15/1997) • **84**

Key: SS—Spectator Selection. CS—Cellar Selection. HR—Highly Recommended. $NA—Price not available. (BT)—Barrel tasting. Ⓐ—Auction Price.
For a key to the tasters' initials, see "How to Use These Listings."
Dates in parentheses represent the issues in which the ratings were published.

HUNTER RIDGE

Chardonnay South Eastern Australia Vanessa's Vale 1997: Bright and lemony, with racy acidity balanced against fresh pineapple and pear flavors. Drink now.–H.S. • $8 • (3/31/1999) • **84**

Merlot South Eastern Australia Grand Show Reserve 1997: Has thick texture and firm structure, but strong herb flavors make this an acquired taste.–H.S. • $18 • (3/31/2000) • **78**

Merlot South Eastern Australia Grand Show Reserve 1995 • $17 • (4/30/1997) • **80**

Merlot South Eastern Australia Vanessa's Vale 1997: Firm in texture, with chewy tannins and modest anise-scented cherry flavors. Best after 2000.–H.S. • $8 • (3/31/1999) • **80**

Merlot South Eastern Australia Vanessa's Vale 1996 • $9 • (4/30/1997) • **81**

Merlot South Eastern Australia Vanessa's Vale 1995 • $9 • (3/31/1996) • **87**

Shiraz South Eastern Australia Grand Show Reserve 1997: Straightforward, refreshing red, offering some pretty floral and anise notes around the fresh berry flavors. Drink now.–H.S. • $18 • (5/15/2000) • **83**

Shiraz South Eastern Australia Vanessa's Vale 1997: An appealing red, smooth and soft, with modest berry and spice flavors. Drink now.–H.S. • $8 • (3/31/1999) • **83**

Shiraz South Eastern Australia Vanessa's Vale 1996 • $9 • (4/30/1997) • **79**

Shiraz South Eastern Australia Vanessa's Vale 1995 • $9 • (3/31/1996) • **85**

Tawny Port South Eastern Australia Grand Show NV • $18/500 ml. • (4/30/1997) • **91**

JABIRU

Cabernet Sauvignon Australia 1993 • $8 • (3/31/1995) • **85**

JACOB'S CREEK (ORLANDO)

Cabernet Sauvignon South Eastern Australia 1998: Sour cherry and menthol flavors, finishing with a touch of bitterness.–B.S. • $9 • (6/30/2000) • **79**

Chardonnay Padthaway Reserve 1997: Light, bright and appealing for the earthy mineral overtones to its basic pear and citrus flavors. Drink now through 2002.–H.S. • $14 • (9/15/1999) • **87**

Chardonnay South Eastern Australia 1999: Attention Chardonnay-value hunters: This Aussie version is light, bright and refreshing for its citrusy apple and peach flavors. Go for it. Drink now.–H.S. • $8 • (2/29/2000) • **85**

Merlot South Eastern Australia 1998: Light, fruity and appealing for its juicy plum and berry flavors that echo nicely on the bright finish, this bottling represents good value and availability in a popular category. Drink now.–H.S. • $9 • (3/31/2000) • **85**

Shiraz Barossa Valley Reserve 1997: Waxy, with fine black fruit depth and lingering chocolate notes. Begins with good flesh, then firm tannins kick in through an intense finish. Drink now through 2008.–B.S. • $15 • (6/30/2000) HR • **89**

Shiraz Barossa Valley Reserve 1996: Ripe, generous, almost explosive in the way its berry, black cherry and anise flavors burst over the palate, yet it remains supple and deft through the long finish. Drink now through 2011.–H.S. • $15 • (9/15/1999) • **89**

Shiraz South Eastern Australia 1998: Sturdy and appealing for its bright plum and black cherry character, hinting at mineral notes on the finish. Drink now.–H.S. • $9 • (3/31/2000) • **85**

Shiraz-Cabernet Sauvignon South Eastern Australia 1998: Fresh and appealing for its dark berry and anise flavors on a simple frame, finishing solidly. Try with roast chicken. Drink now.–H.S. • $8 • (2/29/2000) • **84**

JAMIESONS RUN

Cabernet Sauvignon-Merlot-Cabernet Franc Coonawarra Reserve 1995: Velvety, and artfully balanced to show off its currant, pepper and herb flavors, finishing with enough length to suggest cellaring will add depth. Drink through 2005.–H.S. • $50 • (10/15/1998) • **88**

Cabernet Sauvignon-Shiraz Coonawarra 1994 • $9 • (2/28/1997) • **84**

Cabernet Sauvignon-Shiraz-Cabernet Franc Coonawarra 1995 • $11 • (3/31/1998) • **86**

Cabernet Sauvignon-Shiraz-Merlot Coonawarra 1996: Firm and chewy, with a leathery note chiming in among the raspberry and cherry flavors. Has density and length, but needs cellaring to soften. Best after 2001.–H.S. • $10 • (3/31/1999) • **87**

Chardonnay South Australia 1997: Fresh and youthful, this dry white displays nice apple and resin flavors, morphing into a touch of honey on the finish. Drink now.–H.S. • $11 • (3/31/1999) • **85**

Pinot Noir South Eastern Australia 1997 • $11 • (5/15/1998) • **80**

Sauvignon Blanc South Australia 1998: Supple, fresh and generous with its lime-scented apple and herb flavors, finishing with a touch of passion fruit. Drink now.–H.S. • $11 • (3/31/1999) • **85**

Sauvignon Blanc South Eastern Australia 1997 • $11 • (3/31/1998) • **85**

Shiraz-Cabernet Coonawarra 1991 • $10 • (9/30/1994) • **81**

Shiraz-Cabernet Coonawarra 1990 • $10 • (9/30/1994) • **77**

JASPER HILL

Riesling Heathcote Georgia's Paddock 1998: Fresh and appealing for its floral-scented apple and citrus flavors that linger on the soft, dry finish. Drink now through 2008.–H.S. • $25 • (2/29/2000) • **87**

Shiraz Heathcote Georgia's Paddock 1997: Smooth, ripe and plush, an amazingly supple wine with a streak of fine acidity racing through the plum, spice and earth flavors. Like drinking flavored silk. Delicious now. Best after 2001.–H.S. • $59 • (9/15/1999) • **92**

Shiraz Heathcote Georgia's Paddock 1996: Lush, supple and distinctive, offering layers of earthy spice, deep blackberry and black currant, with hints of earth and exotic pepper notes swirling through the finish. Flavors last and last. 99 cases imported. Drink now through 2010.–H.S. • $55 • (8/31/1998) • **93**

Shiraz Heathcote Georgia's Paddock 1995 • $44 • (8/31/1997) HR • **94**

JENKE

Cabernet Sauvignon Barossa 1997: Ripe and chewy, not a broad wine, but nicely focused to show off its spicy, earthy berry and prune flavors that linger on the bright beam of a finish. Drink now through 2010.–H.S. • $20 • (2/29/2000) • **88**

Merlot Barossa 1997: Light and bright, with fine tannins supporting a pretty core of black cherry and spice flavors. Drink now through 2002.–H.S. • $17 • (3/31/1999) • **84**

JINDALEE

Cabernet Sauvignon Murray Darling Region 1998: Ripe and fruity, appealing to drink already, with currant and herb flavors that linger nicely on the lightly chewy finish. Drink through 2002.–H.S. • $9 • (9/15/1999) • **86**

Chardonnay Australia 1997: Soft and silky, with pretty nectarine and spice aromas and flavors that linger gently on the finish. Drink now.–H.S. • $9 • (5/31/1999) • **85**

Chardonnay Murray Darling Region 1998: Soft, bordering on sweet, with a caramel edge to the modest pear flavors.–H.S. • $9 • (9/30/1999) • **79**

Shiraz Australia 1997: Soft and pretty, with nice blackberry flavor and a hint of pepper on the polished finish. Drink now.–H.S. • $NA • (3/31/1999) • **82**

Shiraz Murray Darling Region 1998: With good buys in quality Aussie Shiraz growing scarcer, don't hesitate to grab a few bottles of this version. It's crisp and bright, with an appealing core of light-bodied berry and pepper flavors. Drink now through 2002.–H.S. • $9 • (9/15/1999) • **85**

JONES, TREVOR

Sparkling Shiraz Barossa Valley NV: Straightforward, with sweet chipotle and iron notes. Drink now.–B.S. • $40 • (6/30/2000) • **82**

JOSEPH

Cabernet Sauvignon-Merlot McLaren Vale 1997: Velvety and nicely focused, with pretty berry and herb flavors emerging nicely and lingering under a layer of fine tannins. Made via the Italian method of drying the grapes before fermentation, but it doesn't feel as rich and Portlike as an Italian Amarone. Tasted twice, with consistent notes. Best after 2002.–H.S. • $33 • (6/30/2000) • **87**

KAESLER

Shiraz Barossa Valley Old Vine 1997: Dark, rich and peppery, it packs in lots of wild berry, anise, stewed plum and cherry flavors, gaining finesse and polish on the finish, where it turns chocolaty. Drink now through 2007.–J.L. • $30 • (6/30/2000) • **90**

Shiraz Barossa Valley Old Vine 1996: Bright and jazzy, a vigorous wine with layers of cherry, beet and strawberry shaded with hints of anise and toast, all echoing nicely on the finish. Drink now.–H.S. • $30 • (3/31/1999) • **88**

Shiraz Barossa Valley Old Vine 1995 • $30 • (3/31/1998) • **88**

Shiraz Barossa Valley Old Vine 1994 • $13 • (6/15/1997) • **87**

KANGARILLA ROAD

Cabernet-Cabernet Franc-Malbec McLaren Vale 1997: This firm-textured wine has an earthy, decadent edge to the ripe blackberry and anise flavors. May be a bit short on charm but has plenty of oomph. Best from 2002 through 2007.–H.S. • $18 • (6/30/1999) • **86**

Shiraz McLaren Vale 1997: Firm, almost chewy, with ripe berry and anise flavors that stop just short of gooey on the firm finish. Drink through 2005.–H.S. • $18 • (6/30/1999) • **86**

KANGAROO ISLAND

Cabernet-Merlot Kangaroo Island Florance Premium Release 1996: A strong green streak runs through this firm-textured red, dripping with leather, truffle and olive flavors around a core of black cherry. The flavors aren't for everyone, but it has character. Best after 2000.–H.S. • $16 • (3/31/1999) • **86**

KATHERINE HILLS

Cabernet Sauvignon South Australia 1998: Ripe and open-textured, not especially deep or complex, but it has nice blueberry, currant and cedar flavors. Drink now through 2003.–H.S. • $8 • (3/31/2000) • **84**

KATNOOK

Cabernet Sauvignon Coonawarra 1996: Focused and supple, generous with its pretty currant and black cherry flavors, hinting at tar and herbs on the finish. Tannins are firm but not too tough. Best after 2001.–H.S. • $28 • (2/28/1999) • **88**

Cabernet Sauvignon Coonawarra 1994 • $27 • (5/31/1997) • **87**

Cabernet Sauvignon Coonawarra 1992 • $29 • (11/15/1996) • **87**

Cabernet Sauvignon Coonawarra Odyssey 1994: Supple, polished and generous with its blackberry, currant, mint and spice flavors that linger effortlessly on the smooth finish. Approachable now. Best after 2001.–H.S. • $73 • (3/31/2000) • **89**

Cabernet Sauvignon Coonawarra Odyssey 1992: Mature and generous, its ripe black cherry and herb flavors glowing through the layers of fine-grained tannins. Flavors echo nicely on the finish. Approachable now. Drink through 2005.–H.S. • $29 • (2/28/1999) • **88**

Merlot Coonawarra 1996: Fresh and supple, capturing a range of pretty Merlot flavors from mulberries to currants to mineral to cedar. Graceful, it finishes with smooth texture and balance. Drink now through 2002.–H.S. • $28 • (2/28/1999) • **88**

Merlot Coonawarra 1995 • $28 • (4/30/1998) • **86**

Merlot Coonawarra 1994 • $26 • (2/28/1997) • **86**

Merlot Coonawarra 1993 • $26 • (11/15/1996) • **84**

Sauvignon Blanc Coonawarra 1997: Bright and lively, sporting distinctive passion fruit, pineapple and herb flavors on a racy frame. Drink now.–H.S. • $18 • (2/28/1999) • **87**

KILIKANOON

Shiraz Clare Valley 1997: Ripe, supple, focused and generous with its blackberry, anise, black pepper and vanilla flavors that mingle and linger on the long, velvety finish. Delicious now, with just enough sneaky acidity to keep it lively. Drink now through 2012.–H.S. • $30 • (5/15/2000) • **91**

KILLERBY

Cabernet Sauvignon Western Australia 1998: Firm and compact, with a tight band of cedary currant, coffee, anise and spice, finishing with a glimmer of stewed plum. Tannis are firm and dry. Drink now through 2008.–J.L. • $28 • (6/30/2000) • **87**

Cabernet Sauvignon Western Australia 1997: Firm and chewy, not harsh, but the fine-grained tannins frame a nice bead of smoky blackberry, sage and spice flavors. Drink through 2004.–H.S. • $28 • (5/15/1999) • **88**

Shiraz Western Australia 1998: Dark, with rich, peppery blackberry, wild berry, cedar and sage, turning tight and tannic. Best from 2001 through 2007.–J.L. • $28 • (6/30/2000) • **86**

KILLERBY

Shiraz Western Australia 1997: Medium-weight, smooth, focused and appealing for the distinctive raspberry, nutmeg and cherry notes lingering on the firm finish. Drink now through 2002.–H.S. • $28 • (5/15/1999) • **84**

KILLIBINBIN

Shiraz Langhorne Creek 1997: Gorgeous aromas of spice, fruitcake and plum are set on a rich, lush and vibrant structure that drives the flavors to a satisfying conclusion. Lingering aftertaste of boysenberry. Drink now through 2003.–B.S. • $26 • (6/30/2000) • **90**

KINGSTON ESTATE

Cabernet Sauvignon Riverland 1992 • $10 • (3/31/1996) • **82**
Cabernet Sauvignon South Australia Riverland 1991 • $10 • (7/31/1994) • **85**
Merlot Riverland 1995 • $9 • (5/15/1997) • **80**
Merlot Riverland 1993 • $10 • (3/31/1996) • **84**
Merlot Riverland Reserve 1991 • $15 • (5/15/1997) • **82**
Merlot South Australia Riverland Reserve 1989 • $15 • (9/30/1994) • **83**
Mourvèdre Riverland 1993 • $10 • (3/31/1996) • **83**
Shiraz Riverland 1993 • $10 • (3/31/1996) • **86**
Shiraz South Australia Riverland 1991 • $9 • (9/30/1994) • **84**
Shiraz South Australia Riverland Reserve 1991 • $15 • (1/31/1995) • **85**

KOLTZ

Cabernet Sauvignon McLaren Vale Niseda 1997: Marked by bayleaf and beef notes, it struggles to find riper fruit flavors. Turns tannic and dry. Drink now through 2004.–J.L. • $20 • (5/31/2000) • **82**

KOPPAMURRA

Classic Red South Australia 1997: Firm in texture, with bright, distinctive blackberry, blueberry and plum flavors glowing through a fine layer of tannin. Has a nice layer of dusky spice, too. (Koppamurra is a region near and similar to Coonawarra and Padthaway.) Best after 2000.–H.S. • $20 • (11/15/1999) • **87**

Classic Red South Australia 1996: Firm in texture, with a bite of acidity around the edges. Has pretty raspberry and herbal flavors at the core, with a surprising touch of lime sneaking in on the finish. A blend of Cabernet Sauvignon, Cabernet Franc and Merlot. Best from 2001 through 2007.–H.S. • $20 • (8/31/1998) • **87**

LAKE BREEZE

Bernoota Langhorne Creek 1996: Flavors of Shiraz and Cabernet do a lively dance for preeminence in this crisply focused, flavorful red. Tannins recede into the framework, letting the cherry, berry and coffee notes come to the fore. Drink now through 2008.–H.S. • $19 • (11/15/1999) • **90**

Cabernet Sauvignon Langhorne Creek 1996: Crisp in texture, with fresh, lively raspberry and dusky herb flavors that linger appealingly on the finish. Needs time to soften. Best from 2001 through 2006.–H.S. • $20 • (10/31/1999) • **87**

Cabernet Sauvignon Langhorne Creek Winemaker's Selection 1996: Smooth and generous, with a strong mint note singing in counterpoint to the light plum and sage flavors. Silky and distinctive on the finish. Drink now through 2006.–H.S. • $31 • (10/31/1999) • **89**

Shiraz Langhorne Creek Winemaker's Selection 1996: Ripe, rich and generous, dripping with blackberry, cherry and licorice flavors that firm up a bit in texture as they linger on the finish. Starts off big and finishes with considerable grace. Drink now through 2011.–H.S. • $30 • (11/15/1999) • **93**

LARRIKIN

Shiraz Barossa Valley 1997: Smooth, polished and redolent of spice cake, black cherry and dried berry flavors that linger exotically on the long, elegant finish. Has all its elements in beautiful proportion already. From Mount Langi Ghiran. Drink now through 2010.–H.S. • $25 • (5/15/2000) • **90**

Key: SS—Spectator Selection. CS—Cellar Selection. HR—Highly Recommended. $NA—Price not available. (BT)—Barrel tasting. Ⓐ—Auction Price.
For a key to the tasters' initials, see "How to Use These Listings."
Dates in parentheses represent the issues in which the ratings were published.

LEASINGHAM

Cabernet Sauvignon Clare Valley Classic Clare 1996: Crisp in texture up front, with vibrant blackberry, mint and cedar flavors that linger nicely on the finish, where the tannins are starting to polish up. Best after 2000.–H.S. • $29 • (10/31/1999) • **88**
Cabernet Sauvignon Clare Valley Classic Clare 1995 • $29 • (5/31/1998) • **88**
Cabernet Sauvignon Clare Valley Classic Clare 1992 • $16 • (6/15/1995) • **90**
Cabernet-Malbec Clare Valley Bin 56 1996: Firm in texture, with lively acidity supporting focused blackberry and currant flavors that manage to keep pace with the chewy tannins. Best after 2001.–H.S. • $15 • (11/15/1999) • **85**
Cabernet-Malbec Clare Valley Domaine 1995 • $13 • (10/31/1997) • **82**
Cabernet-Malbec Clare Valley Domaine 1994 • $12 • (10/15/1996) • **87**
Cabernet-Malbec Clare Valley Domaine 1993 • $12 • (3/31/1996) • **80**
Cabernet-Malbec Clare Valley Domaine 1992 • $8 • (6/30/1994) • **89**
Cabernet-Malbec Clare Valley Domaine 1989 • $8 • (8/31/1992) • **82**
Chardonnay Clare Valley Bin 37 1997: Bright and flavorful, this Australian Chardonnay boasts nicely balanced and well-focused flavors of green apple and melon on a robust frame. Quite tasty, and certainly reasonable in price. Drink now through 2001.–H.S. • $10 • (3/31/1999) • **88**
Riesling Clare Valley Bin 7 1998: Crisp and dry, with refreshing grapefruit, apple and floral aromas and flavors that come together smoothly on the welcoming finish. Drink now through 2008.–H.S. • $8 • (11/15/1999) • **87**
Riesling Clare Valley Bin 7 1997: Earthy and mineral flavors show most prominently in this lean, attractive Riesling. Needs time to evolve. Best from 2001 through 2007.–H.S. • $8 • (1/31/1999) • **86**
Shiraz Clare Valley 1992 • $8 • (9/30/1994) • **83**
Shiraz Clare Valley Bin 61 1997: Brimming with brilliant raspberry and plum flavors, this is a pretty Australian red, finishing with a nicely polished texture. The emphasis is on fruit all the way, so it's seductive to drink already, but it will be best after 2002.–H.S. • $15 • (12/15/1999) SS • **90**
Shiraz Clare Valley Bin 61 1996: Built for elegance, this is generous with its tarry black cherry and anise flavors. Finishes with lively acidity and fine-grained tannins. Drink now.–H.S. • $15 • (9/30/1998) • **88**
Shiraz Clare Valley Classic Clare 1996: This firm, beautifully framed, elegantly styled Shiraz fleshes out with berry, plum, white pepper and licorice flavors that last and last on the focused finish. Has style and the ability to age. Drink now through 2011.–H.S. • $29 • (11/15/1999) HR • **94**
Shiraz Clare Valley Classic Clare 1995 • $29 • (5/31/1998) • **90**
Shiraz Clare Valley Classic Clare 1994 • $24 • (11/30/1996) • **93**
Shiraz Clare Valley Classic Clare 1992 • $16 • (6/30/1995) • **86**
Shiraz Clare Valley Domaine 1995 • $13 • (10/31/1997) HR • **91**
Shiraz Clare Valley Domaine 1994 • $13 • (11/30/1996) • **89**
Shiraz Clare Valley Domaine 1993 • $9 • (2/29/1996) • **86**
Shiraz Clare Valley Domaine 1992 • $9 • (6/30/1995) • **85**
Shiraz-Cabernet Sauvignon South Australia Hutt Creek 1991 • $6 • (9/30/1994) • **82**
Shiraz-Cabernet Sauvignon South Australia Hutt Creek 1989 • $6 • (8/31/1992) • **87**

LECONFIELD

Cabernets Coonawarra 1998: Ripe and generous, with a red pepper and earth edge to the blackberry and black cherry flavors. Soft tannins don't get in the way. Drink now through 2008.–H.S. • $30 • (5/15/2000) • **87**

LEEUWIN

Cabernet Sauvignon Margaret River 1995: Ripe and focused, a graceful wine, firm in texture but not rough, showing plenty of pretty black cherry and mint flavors that linger on the smooth finish. Drink now through 2003.–H.S. • $45 • (9/15/1999) • **88**
Cabernet Sauvignon Margaret River 1993 • $35 • (7/31/1997) • **87**
Cabernet Sauvignon Margaret River 1988 • $18 • (7/31/1994) • **84**
Cabernet Sauvignon Margaret River 1983 • $18 • (5/31/1988) • **86**
Cabernet Sauvignon Margaret River 1979 • $20 • (9/15/1989) • **79**
Cabernet Sauvignon Margaret River Art Series 1987 • $20 • (11/30/1992) • **70**
Cabernet Sauvignon Margaret River Redgum Ridge 1990 • $15 • (11/15/1993) • **83**
Pinot Noir Margaret River Art Series 1988 • $20 • (11/30/1992) • **81**
Riesling Margaret River 1998: Very ripe and focused, this lively, generous mouthful of peach, mineral and floral flavors lasts on the long finish. Drink now.–H.S. • $NA • (11/15/1999) • **91**
Riesling Margaret River 1997: Lean and jazzy, with lots of mineral and lime flavors. Has muscle and elegance, but needs time to soften. Best after 2004.–H.S. • $NA • (11/15/1999) • **87**

LEHMANN, PETER

Cabernet Sauvignon Barossa 1997: Firm and dry, with nice, ripe berry notes oozing through the fine-textured tannins. Finishes with a pretty layer of plum, brown sugar and vanilla. Promising stuff. Best after 2001.–H.S. • $20 • (11/15/1999) • **88**

Cabernet Sauvignon Barossa 1996: Supple, generous and ripe. A satiny mouthful of currant, plum and mineral flavors, finishing with a nice touch of sage. Approachable now. Best after 2000.–H.S. • $18 • (3/31/1999) • **89**

Cabernet Sauvignon Barossa Valley 1995 • $17 • (9/30/1997) • **89**

Cabernet Sauvignon Barossa Valley 1994 • $15 • (1/31/1997) • **85**

Cabernet Sauvignon Barossa Valley 1993 • $14 • (4/30/1996) HR • **90**

Cabernet Sauvignon Barossa Valley 1992 • $13 • (6/30/1995) • **80**

Chardonnay Barossa 1997 • $16 • (5/15/1998) • **85**

Clancy's Barossa Red 1998: Entrancing for its pure, focused fruit character, this reputable red centers on blueberry, blackberry and currant that echo beautifully on the long, gorgeous finish. Harmonious and inviting already, it should only gain with cellaring. Drink now through 2010.–H.S. • $25 • (5/15/2000) HR • **92**

Clancy's Barossa Red 1997: A big red, ripe, rich and round, with lots of spicy, earth-scented black cherry and berry flavors, hinting deliciously at chocolate on the smooth finish. This distinctive Shiraz blend is drinkable now, yet has the depth to repay cellaring through 2007.–H.S. • $20 • (3/31/1999) SS • **92**

Clancy's Barossa Red 1996 • $19 • (5/31/1998) • **89**

Clancy's Gold Preference Barossa Valley Red 1995 • $18 • (9/30/1997) • **92**

Clancy's Gold Preference Barossa Valley Red 1994 • $18 • (2/28/1997) • **93**

Clancy's Gold Preference Barossa Valley Red 1992 • $16 • (4/30/1996) • **86**

Clancy's Gold Preference Barossa Valley Red 1991 • $15 • (6/30/1995) • **77**

Mentor Barossa Valley 1995: Rich, round and generous, with spicy, peppery blackberry and currant flavors, gooey texture and a long finish that echoes the fruit. Some earth-anise notes add depth. Cabernet Sauvignon, Malbec and Merlot. Drink now through 2007.–H.S. • $40 • (5/15/2000) • **91**

Mentor Barossa Valley 1994: Ripe and round, this generous mouthful of currant, blackberry and sweet pepper flavors remains round and appealing through the supple finish. Cabernet Sauvignon and Malbec. Drink now through 2004.–H.S. • $40 • (3/31/1999) • **91**

Mentor Barossa Valley 1993 • $32 • (5/31/1998) • **85**

Mentor Barossa Valley 1991 • $35 • (9/30/1996) • **88**

Port Barossa Bin AD 2016 1995 • $20 • (6/15/1998) • **85**

Port Barossa Valley Bin AD 2010 1989 • $15 • (4/15/1995) • **85**

Riesling Eden Valley 1998: Light and pretty, with a sappy edge to the bright apple and citrus flavors. Drink now through 2005.–H.S. • $14 • (11/15/1999) • **85**

Sémillon Barossa 1998: Soft and pretty, with appealing citrus and pear flavors that pick up hints of mint and sage on the supple finish. Drink now through 2008.–H.S. • $13 • (11/15/1999) • **86**

Sémillon Barossa 1997 • $12 • (5/15/1998) • **87**

Sémillon Barossa Botrytis Sauternes 1996 • $16/375 ml. • (11/30/1997) • **88**

Sémillon Barossa Valley Late Harvest Botrytis Sauternes 1995 • $15/375 ml. • (10/15/1996) • **85**

Sémillon Barossa Valley Late Harvest Botrytis Sauternes 1992 • $12/375 ml. • (6/30/1995) • **83**

Shiraz Barossa Eight Songs 1996: Ripe, focused, spicy and generous with its black cherry, anise and peppermint flavors that mingle effortlessly on the long finish. Lovely now. Drink now through 2008.–H.S. • $55 • (5/15/2000) • **90**

Shiraz Barossa Stonewell 1994: Ripe and aromatic, dripping with black cherry, blackberry, licorice and exotic spices, but nicely pulled together to be firm and focused on the long finish. Delicious already. Best after 2002.–H.S. • $60 • (5/15/2000) • **92**

Shiraz Barossa Stonewell 1991 • $36 • (2/28/1997) • **89**

Shiraz Barossa Valley 1997: Smooth and flavorful, focusing its yummy berry and smoke flavors on a firm frame. Approachable now, though the tannins can use softening. Best after 2000.–H.S. • $17 • (11/15/1999) • **87**

Shiraz Barossa Valley 1996 • $15 • (5/15/1998) • **87**

Shiraz Barossa Valley 1995 • $13 • (9/30/1997) • **89**

Shiraz Barossa Valley 1994 • $11 • (9/30/1996) • **87**

Shiraz Barossa Valley 1993 • $10 • (4/30/1996) • **88**

Shiraz Barossa Valley 1992 • $10 • (1/31/1995) • **81**

LENGS & COOTER

Shiraz Clare Valley Old Vines 1997: Dense, ripe and generous, with a strong minty edge to the raspberry, blackberry and currant flavors, finishing with bright acidity and firm, well-integrated tannins. Should age nicely. Best after 2001.–H.S. • $33 • (6/30/2000) • **90**

The Victor Clare Valley Red 1998: Ripe and fragrant, but the flavors pick up a distinctly sour note which pulls it out of balance. Tasted twice, with consistent notes. Drink now.–H.S. • $20 • (6/30/2000) • **78**

LENSWOOD

Cabernets Lenswood 1994 • $25 • (6/15/1997) • **86**

Pinot Noir Lenswood 1996 • $31 • (4/30/1998) • **87**

Pinot Noir Lenswood 1995 • $28 • (5/31/1997) • **83**

Sauvignon Blanc Lenswood 1997 • $21 • (4/30/1998) • **85**

Sémillon Lenswood 1998: Bright and jazzy, silky beneath a veneer of citrusy sharpness, offering lime, almond and fig notes that linger on the finish. Needs time to fill out. Best after 2002.–H.S. • $24 • (6/30/2000) • **86**

Sémillon South Australia 1997: Riper and fruitier than many Sémillons, with pretty citrus and fig flavors that remain rich and vibrant through the crisp finish. Drink now through 2007.–H.S. • $21 • (6/15/1999) • **87**

LEYDENS VALE

Cabernet Sauvignon Victoria 1997: Smooth and nicely open-textured, with pretty black currant and blackberry floating on a light, elegant frame. Finishes with a nice balance of fruit and herb flavors. Drink through 2007.–H.S. • $15 • (11/15/1999) • **87**

Chardonnay Victoria 1998: Light, bright and fruity, with pretty apple, citrus and spice flavors that linger on the gentle finish. Drink now.–H.S. • $15 • (11/15/1999) • **85**

Merlot Victoria 1995 • $20 • (4/30/1998) • **82**

Pinot Noir Victoria 1995 • $20 • (4/30/1998) • **84**

Shiraz Victoria 1997: A bit on the firm side, with a chewy texture around ripe blackberry and licorice flavors that become almost citrusy-tart on the finish. Flavors persist beautifully. Drink with a roast. Drink now through 2007.–H.S. • $15 • (11/15/1999) • **87**

Shiraz Victoria 1996 • $20 • (4/30/1998) • **87**

LILLYPILLY

Noble Harvest Riverina 1996: Smells racy and a bit volatile, with earthy apricot and almond paste flavors that turn vinegary. Waxy aftertaste. Drink now.–J.L. • $23/375 ml. • (6/30/2000) • **83**

LINDEMANS

Cabernet Sauvignon Coonawarra 1986 • $14 • (10/31/1990) • **83**

Cabernet Sauvignon Coonawarra 1985 • $14 • (4/30/1989) • **86**

Cabernet Sauvignon Coonawarra 1984 • $12 • (2/15/1988) • **84**

Cabernet Sauvignon Coonawarra 150 Years Sequicentenary 1990 • $13 • (3/31/1995) • **80**

Cabernet Sauvignon Coonawarra Special Selection 1995 • $15 • (6/30/1998) • **86**

Cabernet Sauvignon Coonawarra Special Selection 1994 • $15 • (5/31/1997) • **88**

Cabernet Sauvignon Coonawarra Special Selection 1993 • $15 • (4/30/1996) • **85**

Cabernet Sauvignon Coonawarra Special Selection 1991 • $13 • (11/30/1995) • **85**

Cabernet Sauvignon Coonawarra St. George 1996: Focused, elegant style emphasizing the pretty currant and berry flavors, hinting at a touch of sage on the firm finish. Drink now through 2006.–H.S. • $28 • (6/30/2000) • **87**

Cabernet Sauvignon Coonawarra St. George Vineyard NV • $15 • (5/31/1987) • **88**

Cabernet Sauvignon Coonawarra St. George Vineyard 1994 • $28 • (5/15/1998) • **89**

Cabernet Sauvignon Coonawarra St. George Vineyard 1993 • $28 • (5/31/1997) • **87**

Cabernet Sauvignon Coonawarra St. George Vineyard 1991 • $22 • (4/30/1996) • **92**

Cabernet Sauvignon Coonawarra St. George Vineyard 1990 • $6 • (11/30/1994) • **72**

Cabernet Sauvignon Coonawarra St. George Vineyard 1986 • $25 • (6/30/1992) • **82**

Cabernet Sauvignon Coonawarra St. George Vineyard 1985 • $21 • (4/30/1989) • **80**

Cabernet Sauvignon Coonawarra St. George Vineyard 1984 • $15 • (1/31/1988) • **88**

Cabernet Sauvignon Coonawarra Vineyard 1990 • $22 • (3/31/1995) • **85**

Cabernet Sauvignon South Eastern Australia Bin 45 1997: A nice, firm red here, nothing particularly Cabernet-like, but worth pouring with pizza or burgers. Drink now.–H.S. • $9 • (3/31/1999) • **82**

LINDEMANS

Cabernet Sauvignon South Eastern Australia Bin 45 1996 • $8 • (3/31/1998) • **83**
Cabernet Sauvignon South Eastern Australia Bin 45 1995 • $8 • (5/31/1997) • **87**
Cabernet Sauvignon South Australia Bin 45 1994 • $7 • (4/30/1996) • **85**
Cabernet Sauvignon South Australia Bin 45 1993 • $7 • (11/30/1995) • **83**
Cabernet Sauvignon South Eastern Australia Bin 45 1992 • $7 • (3/31/1995) • **86**
Cabernet Sauvignon South Eastern Australia Bin 45 1991 • $7 • (4/30/1994) • **82**
Cabernet Sauvignon South Eastern Australia Bin 45 1990 • $7 • (4/15/1993) • **80**
Cabernet Sauvignon South Eastern Australia Bin 45 1989 • $6 • (8/31/1992) • **81**
Cabernet-Merlot Padthaway 1996: A solid red, smooth in texture, with pretty, ripe black cherry, currant and sautéed mushroom flavors in a nice swirl. Drink now.–H.S. • $15 • (1/31/1999) • **86**
Cabernet-Merlot Padthaway 1995 • $15 • (11/15/1997) • **86**
Cabernet-Merlot Padthaway 1994 • $15 • (12/31/1996) • **87**
Cabernet-Merlot South Australia Padthaway 1990 • $13 • (4/15/1993) • **83**
Chardonnay Padthaway 1997: Ripe and generous, this Chardonnay from Australia offers a nice range of oak-spiced pear and nectarine flavors that remain fresh and lively through the finish. Not as effusive as earlier vintages, this year's version is richer in style. Drink now through 2001.–H.S. • $12 • (1/31/1999) HR • **88**
Chardonnay Padthaway Winemaker's Reserve 1997: Rich in texture, with strong nutmeg and black pepper overtones to the peach and honey flavors. Not quite as intense as in years past. Tasted twice, with consistent notes. Drink now.–H.S. • $20 • (6/30/2000) • **87**
Chardonnay Padthaway Winemaker's Reserve 1995 • $25 • (5/15/1998) • **91**
Chardonnay South Eastern Australia Bin 65 1998: Youthful, with a cascade of spicy fig and melon flavors keeping it lively to the finish. Has considerably more going for it than most value-priced Chardonnays, and the case production suggests it shouldn't be hard to find. 650,000 cases imported. Drink now.–H.S. • $8 • (3/31/1999) • **85**
Chardonnay South Eastern Australia Bin 65 1997 • $8 • (3/31/1998) • **85**
Merlot South Eastern Australia Bin 40 1997: Attention Merlot fans. Check out this reasonable priced version, supple and appealing for its minty cherry flavors that linger gently on the finish. Enjoyable now through 2000.–H.S. • $9 • (3/31/1999) • **84**
Merlot South Eastern Australia Bin 40 1996 • $9 • (3/31/1998) • **82**
Merlot South Australia Bin 40 1995 • $7 • (2/28/1997) • **81**
Merlot South Australia Bin 40 1994 • $7 • (3/31/1996) • **82**
Merlot South Australia Bin 40 1993 • $8 • (4/15/1995) • **87**
Merlot South Eastern Australia Bin 40 1992 • $7 • (9/30/1994) • **80**
Merlot South Eastern Australia Reserve 1996: Firm and chewy, but there's enough pretty strawberry and spice flavor to make this balanced and appealing. Drink now.–H.S. • $15 • (1/31/1999) • **82**
Merlot South Australia Reserve 1995 • $15 • (11/15/1997) • **85**
Merlot South Australia Reserve 1993 • $13 • (12/15/1995) • **86**
Pinot Noir Padthaway 1997: Has some lovely Pinot Noir flavors, emphasizing dark cherry, tea and spice. Texture is a bit tough, with firm tannins that persist along with the flavors. Drink now.–H.S. • $15 • (1/31/1999) • **83**
Pinot Noir Padthaway 1996 • $15 • (5/15/1998) • **83**
Pinot Noir Padthaway 1995 • $15 • (5/31/1997) • **86**
Pinot Noir Padthaway 1986 • $12 • (9/15/1989) • **73**
Pinot Noir Padthaway 1984 • $12 • (2/15/1988) • **82**
Pinot Noir South Australia Bin 99 1997: Light and supple, with a chocolaty edge to the simple berry flavors. Drink now.–H.S. • $9 • (1/31/1999) • **82**
Pinot Noir South Australia Bin 99 1996 • $9 • (10/31/1997) • **82**
Pyrus Coonawarra 1996: Tight and trim, with firm tannins and a leathery band of currant and spice. Turns chewy and dry on the finish, so be forewarned. Drink now through 2007.–J.L. • $28 • (6/30/2000) • **86**
Pyrus Coonawarra 1994 • $28 • (5/15/1998) • **88**
Pyrus Coonawarra 1993 • $28 • (5/31/1997) • **87**
Pyrus Coonawarra 1991 • $22 • (4/30/1996) • **87**
Pyrus Coonawarra 1987 • $25 • (5/31/1993) • **84**
Pyrus Coonawarra 1986 • $24 • (7/31/1990) • **78**
Pyrus Coonawarra 1986 • $25 • (6/30/1992) • **77**
Pyrus Coonawarra 1985 • $20 • (5/31/1988) • **87**
Sauvignon Blanc South Australia Bin 95 1999: Refreshing, with tingly acidity and grapefruit notes. Drink now.–B.S. • $8 • (6/30/2000) • **81**
Sauvignon Blanc South Eastern Australia Bin 95 1997: Fresh and fruity but not especially varietal; a pretty wine with modest flavors. Drink now.–H.S. • $8 • (1/31/1999) • **80**
Sémillon-Chardonnay South Eastern Australia Bin 77 1997: Ripe and generous, this offers a round mouthful of pineapple, pear and tobacco flavors on a fat frame, getting crisp on the lemony finish. Drink now through 2002.–H.S. • $8 • (2/28/1999) • **85**
Sémillon Griffith Late Harvest Botrytis 1997: Sweet and ripe, a luscious mouthful of orange, pineapple and honey that remains juicy through the harmonious finish. Needs time to settle in. Best after1999.–H.S. • $11/375 ml. • (11/15/1998) • **88**
Shiraz Barossa Valley 1986 • $12 • (5/15/1989) • **83**
Shiraz Hunter Valley 1987 • $10 • (2/15/1991) • **81**
Shiraz Hunter Valley Bin 9003 1995: Dense, tannic and chewy, with earthy flavors that never show much charm. Tasted twice, with consistent notes. Best after 2003.–H.S. • $15 • (6/30/2000) • **78**
Shiraz Hunter Valley Bin 5910 Lindemans Classic 1980 • $30 • (7/31/1990) • **73**
Shiraz Hunter Valley Bin 4110 Lindemans Classic 1970 • $60 • (9/15/1989) • **89**
Shiraz Hunter Valley Bin 3110 Lindemans Classic 1965 • $95 • (9/15/1989) • **96**
Shiraz Padthaway 1997: Firm, spicy style, focusing on exotic pepper and wild berry aromas and flavors, finishing with hints of mint and a layer of fine-grained tannins. Drink now through 2005.–H.S. • $16 • (6/30/2000) • **86**
Shiraz Padthaway 1996: Ripe and generous, with pure and supple blueberry, plum and blackberry flavors that persist into a round, nicely focused finish. Has a bit of a tannic bite that needs cellaring. 4,354 cases imported. Drink through 2004.–H.S. • $15 • (1/31/1999) • **88**
Shiraz Padthaway 1995 • $15 • (6/30/1998) • **87**
Shiraz Padthaway 1994 • $15 • (5/15/1998) • **89**
Shiraz South Australia Bin 50 1997: Firm in texture, with a roundness to the berry and cherry flavors that linger on the modest finish. Drink now.–H.S. • $9 • (3/31/1999) • **82**
Shiraz South Australia Bin 50 1996 • $8 • (3/31/1998) • **84**
Shiraz South Australia Bin 50 1995 • $7 • (2/28/1997) • **85**
Shiraz South Australia Bin 50 1994 • $8 • (6/30/1996) • **86**
Shiraz South Australia Bin 50 1993 • $7 • (12/15/1995) • **84**
Shiraz South Eastern Australia Bin 50 1992 • $7 • (1/31/1995) • **82**
Shiraz South Eastern Australia Bin 50 1989 • $6 • (5/31/1992) • **80**
Shiraz-Cabernet Coonawarra Limestone Ridge Lindemans Classic 1982 • $38 • (7/31/1990) • **70**
Shiraz-Cabernet Coonawarra Limestone Ridge Vineyard 1996: Rich and complex without excessive weight, beautifully balanced to pack in the anise- and mint-scented black cherry and plum flavors, which arch elegantly through the finish. Drink now through 2010.–H.S. • $28 • (6/30/2000) • **91**
Shiraz-Cabernet Coonawarra Limestone Ridge Vineyard 1994 • $28 • (5/15/1998) • **91**
Shiraz-Cabernet Coonawarra Limestone Ridge Vineyard 1993 • $28 • (5/31/1997) • **94**
Shiraz-Cabernet Coonawarra Limestone Ridge Vineyard 1991 • $22 • (4/30/1996) • **91**
Shiraz-Cabernet Coonawarra Limestone Ridge Vineyard 1990 • $22 • (1/31/1995) • **87**
Shiraz-Cabernet Coonawarra Limestone Ridge Vineyard 1986 • $25 • (6/30/1992) • **86**
Shiraz-Cabernet Coonawarra Limestone Ridge Vineyard 1985 • $21 • (7/31/1989) • **68**
Shiraz-Cabernet Coonawarra Limestone Ridge Vineyard 1984 • $15 • (7/01/1987) • **87**
Shiraz-Cabernet South Eastern Australia Cawarra 1999: Light and fruity, with floral-tinted berry flavors that keep zinging on the lively finish. Drink now.–H.S. • $6 • (6/30/2000) • **84**
Shiraz-Cabernet South Eastern Australia Henry Lindeman 1991 • $6 • (5/31/1993) • **79**
Tawny Port Australia Macquarie Very Special Wood Matured NV • $11 • (7/31/1990) • **84**
Tawny Port Barossa Valley Macquarie Very Special NV • $10 • (4/30/1998) • **88**

LOWE

Cabernet-Merlot Orange Region & Hunter Valley 1997: Firm and chewy in texture, with earthy, minty currant and tobacco flavors. 100 cases imported. Drink now.–H.S. • $17 • (12/15/1998) • **82**
Chardonnay Mudgee 1997: Crisp and refreshing. A jazzy mouthful of citrus, pineapple and apple flavor on a delicate frame. 100 cases imported. Drink now.–H.S. • $20 • (12/15/1998) • **86**

Key: SS—Spectator Selection. CS—Cellar Selection. HR—Highly Recommended. $NA—Price not available. (BT)—Barrel tasting. Ⓐ—Auction Price.
For a key to the tasters' initials, see "How to Use These Listings."
Dates in parentheses represent the issues in which the ratings were published.

Merlot Hunter Valley 1997: Supple in texture, with unusually earthy, floral flavors centering around tobacco and anise notes. 100 cases imported. Drink now.–H.S. • $17 • (12/15/1998) • **82**

Sémillon Hunter Valley 1998: Light and silky, with pretty grapefruit and tobacco flavors emerging on the polished finish. Nice now; best after 2002. 100 cases imported.–H.S. • $20 • (12/15/1998) • **85**

MAGLIERI

Cabernet Sauvignon McLaren Vale 1996: Ripe, polished and generous with its chocolate-tinged black cherry and plum flavors that linger on the sweet, cedary finish. Well-proportioned. Drink through 2005.–H.S. • $21 • (11/15/1998) • **90**

Chardonnay McLaren Vale 1997: Bright and refreshing for its citrusy peach and spice flavors, finishing crisp and juicy. Drink now.–H.S. • $16 • (11/15/1998) • **87**

Sémillon McLaren Vale Ingleburne Estate Unwooded 1997: Bright and flavorful, with citrus and green fig flavors lingering on the finish. Drink now.–H.S. • $13 • (11/30/1998) • **84**

Shiraz McLaren Vale 1996: Dense, dark and chewy, with a glowing core of black cherry and pepper flavors that linger on the rich finish. Solidly built. Drink now.–H.S. • $21 • (11/15/1998) • **91**

Shiraz McLaren Vale Steve Maglieri 1995: Ripe and exotic, with gorgeous black cherry, pepper, licorice and a cascade of spices weaving through the flavor profile. Rich and chewy in texture, not at all harsh, just big and remarkably focused. Best after 2000.–H.S. • $38 • (11/15/1998) • **92**

MAJELLA

Shiraz Coonawarra 1997: Tight and cedary, with a slight green, stalky edge to the earthy berry flavors. Turns tannic. Drink now through 2005.–J.L. • $30 • (6/30/2000) • **85**

MARGAN

Chardonnay Hunter Valley 1998: Smoothly polished, ripe, generous with its honey-scented pear and tropical fruit aromas and flavors, creamy on the long finish. Drink now through 2005.–H.S. • $12 • (12/31/1999) • **88**

Sémillon Hunter Valley 1999: Soft and round, with modest pear and tobacco flavors and tangy citrus notes on a medium frame. Needs time to develop some depth. Drink through 2009.–H.S. • $12 • (12/31/1999) • **86**

Verdelho Hunter Valley 1998: A peppery, distinctly floral set of aromas and flavors run through the basic melon flavors of this soft, pleasant white. Drink now.–H.S. • $12 • (12/31/1999) • **84**

MARIENBERG

Blanc de Noir Australia Nicolle NV: Tart and lively, with a gingery, spicy overtone to the pretty pear and citrus flavors, smoothly effervescent through the finish. Drink now.–H.S. • $15 • (10/15/1999) • **87**

Cabernet Sauvignon McLaren Vale 1992 • $12 • (10/15/1995) • **84**

Cabernet Sauvignon South Australia Reserve 1995: Round and generous, a pretty mouthful of mint-scented black cherry and mineral flavors that linger gently on the smooth finish. Drink now through 2004.–H.S. • $12 • (11/15/1999) • **86**

Cabernet Sauvignon South Eastern Australia Reserve 1994 • $13 • (10/31/1997) • **85**

Cabernet Sauvignon-Mourvèdre-Grenache South Australia Cottage Classic 1996: An unusual red, with herbal, gamy, peppery flavors dominating the modest cherry character. Firm texture needs cellaring. Drink through 2002.–H.S. • $10 • (10/15/1998) • **80**

Chardonnay South Australia Reserve 1997: Ripe and round, with spicy pear and melon flavors that linger nicely on the generous finish. Drink now through 2002.–H.S. • $13 • (11/15/1999) • **87**

Cottage Classic Red South Australia 1995 • $10 • (10/31/1997) • **84**

Sémillon-Sauvignon Blanc-Riesling South Australia Cottage Classic 1997: Fresh and flavorful, with jazzy pear, tobacco and passion fruit flavors that linger on the refreshing finish. Drink now.–H.S. • $9 • (11/30/1998) • **87**

Shiraz McLaren Vale 1993 • $12 • (4/30/1996) • **85**

Shiraz McLaren Vale 1992 • $12 • (10/31/1995) HR • **91**

Shiraz South Australia Reserve 1996: Ripe, smooth and nicely focused, this straight-ahead Shiraz offers berry and spice flavors that linger on the mildly chewy finish. Drink now through 2006.–H.S. • $12 • (11/15/1999) • **87**

Shiraz South Eastern Australia Reserve 1994 • $13 • (10/31/1997) • **85**

MCALISTER

South East Gippsland Red 1994 • $35 • (10/15/1997) • **82**

MCGUIGAN

Cabernet Sauvignon South Eastern Australia Bin 4000 1998: Firm in texture, with pretty currant and raisin flavors that linger. Drink now.–H.S. • $9 • (3/31/1999) • **82**

Cabernet Sauvignon South Eastern Australia Bin 4000 1997 • $9 • (5/31/1998) • **86**

Cabernet Sauvignon South Eastern Australia Personal Reserve 1996 • $20 • (11/30/1997) • **87**

Chardonnay Hunter Valley Bin 7000 1999: Bright and lively, with refreshing star-fruit, pear and citrus flavors that remain juicy through the finish. Drink now.–H.S. • $10 • (12/31/1999) • **86**

Chardonnay South Eastern Australia Bin 7000 1997 • $9 • (5/15/1998) • **83**

Chardonnay South Eastern Australia The Black Label 1998: Simple and fresh, even a little raw-edged, with citrus and pineapple notes holding on the finish. Drink now.–H.S. • $7 • (6/15/1999) • **83**

Merlot South Eastern Australia Bin 3000 1999: Light and fruity, with pretty blueberry and spice flavors more reminiscent of Grenache than of Merlot, but what the heck. It's quaffable. Drink now.–H.S. • $10 • (12/31/1999) • **84**

Merlot South Eastern Australia Bin 3000 1997 • $9 • (5/31/1998) • **84**

Merlot South Eastern Australia The Black Label 1999: Tangy, sweet-tasting berry flavors and a spicy edge. Drink now.–J.L. • $7 • (6/30/2000) • **82**

Sauvignon Blanc South Eastern Australia Bin 8000 1998: Fresh and racy, with lively citrus and passion fruit flavors, and an extra note of apricot sneaking in on the finish. Drink now.–H.S. • $9 • (11/30/1998) • **87**

Sauvignon Blanc South Eastern Australia Bin 8000 1997 • $8 • (3/31/1998) • **80**

Shiraz South Eastern Australia Millenium Bin 2000 1998: Bright and focused, this jazzy Shiraz is brimming with blueberry, blackberry and spice flavors that enlarge and linger on the yummy finish. Certainly a very good bottle for so reasonable a price. Drink now through 2001.–H.S. • $10 • (2/28/1999) • **89**

Shiraz South Eastern Australia Millenium Bin 2000 1997 • $10 • (5/15/1998) • **86**

Shiraz South Eastern Australia Personal Reserve 1996 • $20 • (11/30/1997) • **88**

Shiraz-Grenache South Eastern Australia The Black Label 1997: Supple, generous and pretty, with bright raspberry and spice flavors on a lithe frame. 5,000 cases imported. Drink now.–H.S. • $8 • (11/15/1998) • **85**

MCGUIGAN BROTHERS

Cabernet Sauvignon Australia Personal Reserve 1993 • $15 • (4/30/1996) • **91**

Cabernet Sauvignon South Eastern Australia Bin 4000 1991 • $8 • (6/15/1994) • **80**

Cabernet-Merlot Hunter Valley Shareholders Reserve 1991 • $11 • (2/28/1993) • **86**

Merlot South Eastern Australia Bin 3000 1996 • $9 • (4/30/1997) • **83**

Merlot South Eastern Australia Bin 3000 1995 • $8 • (4/30/1996) • **85**

Merlot South Eastern Australia Bin 3000 Soft Mellow Dry Red 1994 • $9 • (6/30/1996) • **81**

Merlot South Eastern Australia Bin 3000 1993 • $8 • (4/15/1995) • **85**

Sémillon South Eastern Australia Botrytis Personal Reserve 1995 • $11/500 ml. • (4/30/1997) • **88**

Shiraz Hunter Valley Hermitage Personal Reserve 1993 • $15 • (4/30/1996) • **91**

Shiraz South Eastern Australia Black 1994 • $7 • (11/15/1995) • **85**

Shiraz South Eastern Australia Black 1992 • $7 • (10/31/1993) • **83**

Shiraz South Eastern Australia Black 1991 • $7 • (5/31/1993) • **82**

Tawny Port South Eastern Australia Brian McGuigan's Private Reserve NV • $18 • (1/31/1997) • **87**

The Black Label South Eastern Australia 1996 • $8 • (4/30/1997) • **83**

MCLARENS

Sémillon-Chardonnay South Eastern Australia 1992 • $10 • (1/31/1995) • **83**

Shiraz South Eastern Australia 1992 • $8 • (4/15/1994) • **85**

Shiraz South Eastern Australia 1991 • $9 • (11/30/1993) • **87**

Shiraz-Cabernet Sauvignon South Eastern Australia 1992 • $9 • (1/31/1995) • **82**

MCWILLIAM'S

Cabernet Sauvignon Australia Hanwood Estate 1991 • $7 • (12/15/1993) • **82**

Cabernet Sauvignon South Eastern Australia Mount Pleasant 1992 • $10 • (9/30/1994) • **85**

MCWILLIAM'S

Cabernet Sauvignon South Eastern Australia Mount Pleasant 1991 • $10 • (12/15/1993) • **80**
Shiraz Australia Hanwood 1993 • $7 • (9/30/1994) • **77**

MEADOWBANK

Pinot Noir Tasmania 1995 • $19 • (3/31/1998) • **83**

MELTON, CHARLES

Grenache Barossa Valley 1997: Smells exotic, with coconut, maple and berryish flavors that pick up a anise edge. Turns earthy and waxy. Drink now through 2004.–J.L. • $37 • (5/31/2000) • **84**
Grenache Barossa Valley Rosé of Virginia 1997 • $16 • (4/30/1998) • **86**
Nine Popes Barossa Valley 1996 • $45 • (4/30/1998) • **88**
Nine Popes Barossa Valley 1995 • $35 • (4/30/1997) • **92**

MENZIES

Cabernet Sauvignon Coonawarra 1993 • $17 • (5/31/1997) • **84**
Cabernet Sauvignon Coonawarra 1992 • $18 • (11/30/1996) • **90**

MERRILL, GEOFF

Cabernet Sauvignon South Australia 1992 • $24 • (11/30/1996) • **83**
Cabernet Sauvignon-Merlot South Eastern Australia Owen's Estate 1994 • $14 • (10/15/1996) • **78**

MILBURN PARK

Cabernet Sauvignon South Eastern Australia 1997: Soft and supple, a pretty wine with floral and berry flavors on a modest frame. Drink now.–H.S. • $10 • (3/31/1999) • **83**
Cabernet Sauvignon South Eastern Australia 1996 • $9 • (5/31/1998) • **84**
Cabernet Sauvignon Victoria 1995 • $9 • (2/28/1997) • **80**
Cabernet Sauvignon Victoria 1994 • $9 • (3/31/1996) • **85**
Chardonnay South Eastern Australia 1997: Fresh in flavor, supple in texture, with spicy melon notes echoing on the light finish. Drink now.–H.S. • $10 • (3/31/1999) • **83**
Chardonnay South Eastern Australia Reserve 1997 • $9 • (5/31/1998) • **85**
Grenache South Eastern Australia 1997: Very light and fragrant; a delicate mouthful of strawberry and black cherry flavors, deftly packaged. Drink now.–H.S. • $10 • (3/31/1999) • **84**

MIRANDA

Cabernet Sauvignon King & Ovens Valley High Country 1996: Supple and generous, with a distinct layer of vanilla and coffee flavor from oak providing a pretty background for the modest raspberry notes at the center. Drink now through 2002.–H.S. • $10 • (2/28/1999) • **85**
Cabernet Sauvignon Padthaway Barossa Valley Rovalley Ridge Grey Series 1996: Bright and nicely balanced, this snazzy red wine has layers of black cherry, spice, currant and cedar that swirl around on the supple finish. Best after 2002.–H.S. • $12 • (2/28/1999) • **87**
Cabernet-Shiraz South Eastern Australia Mirrool Creek 1997: Soft and pretty, with ripe berry and spice flavors. Smooth and easy to drink. Drink now.–H.S. • $7 • (2/28/1999) • **84**
Chardonnay King Valley High Country 1997: Crisp and bright, with zingy apple and spice flavors that pick up hints of mineral on the finish. Appealing for its freshness. Drink now.–H.S. • $12 • (2/28/1999) • **86**
Chardonnay South Eastern Australia Mirrool Creek 1997: Crisp and refreshing, here's a simple wine with pretty citrus and peach flavors to perk it up. Drink now.–H.S. • $7 • (2/28/1999) • **81**
Merlot King Valley High Country 1997: Crisp, appealing for its racy style, with pretty chocolate and spice nuances to the supple berry flavors. A different style of Aussie Merlot, enjoyable now. Drink now.–H.S. • $10 • (2/28/1999) • **85**
Shiraz Barossa Valley Old Vine Show Reserve 1995: A generous mouthful of ripe black cherry, licorice and gamy flavors, firm in texture but not rough; a focused wine that feels like it can grow with cellaring. Drink through 2005.–H.S. • $15 • (2/28/1999) • **89**
Shiraz Barossa Valley Rovalley Ridge Grey Series 1995: Ripe and spicy, with layers of licorice, black cherry and smoke aromas and flavors folding together to make a tasty drink definitely in the Barossa style. Drink now through 2001.–H.S. • $12 • (2/28/1999) • **87**
Shiraz-Cabernet Eden Valley Show Reserve 1995: Supple and ripe, distinctive for the way it unfolds its licorice-scented blackberry, smoke and black cherry flavors on a smooth background of fine tannins. Drink through 2005.–H.S. • $15 • (2/28/1999) • **88**

MITCHELTON

Cabernet Sauvignon Goulburn Valley 1988 • $13 • (4/15/1991) • **86**
Cabernet Sauvignon Goulburn Valley 1986 • $13 • (1/31/1990) • **73**
Cabernet Sauvignon Goulburn Valley Reserve 1990 • $18 • (3/31/1993) • **82**
Cabernet Sauvignon South Eastern Australia Reserve 1992 • $16 • (1/31/1995) • **80**
Cabernet Sauvignon South Eastern Australia Reserve 1991 • $14 • (11/15/1993) • **81**
Cabernet Sauvignon Victoria 1995: Structured like a claret, with lovely black currant and plum shining through a veil of fine tannins, persisting nicely on the elegant finish. Drink through 2005.–H.S. • $22 • (8/31/1998) • **90**
Cabernet Sauvignon Victoria Reserve 1994 • $20 • (11/30/1996) • **87**
Cabernet Sauvignon Victoria Reserve 1993 • $16 • (11/30/1995) • **90**
Cabernet Sauvignon-Merlot Australia Print Label 1985 • $17 • (1/31/1990) • **78**
Cabernet Sauvignon-Shiraz South Eastern Australia Thomas Mitchell 1995 • $10 • (7/31/1997) • **84**
Cabernet Sauvignon-Shiraz-Cabernet Franc South Eastern Australia Thomas Mitchell 1996: Chewy, with vibrant and appealing, bright spicy berry and anise flavors, this is supple enough to approach now. The pretty flavors linger nicely. Drink now through 2005.–H.S. • $12 • (8/31/1998) • **87**
Cabernet Sauvignon-Shiraz-Cabernet Franc South Eastern Australia Thomas Mitchell 1994 • $10 • (4/30/1996) • **80**
Cabernet Sauvignon-Shiraz-Malbec South Eastern Australia 1992 • $9 • (5/15/1994) • **84**
Cabernet Sauvignon-Shiraz-Merlot South Eastern Australia 1991 • $10 • (11/30/1993) • **82**
Cabernet Sauvignon-Shiraz-Merlot Victoria 1990 • $10 • (8/31/1992) • **87**
Chardonnay South Eastern Australia Thomas Mitchell 1997: A festive mouthful of pure fruit flavor gives this immense appeal. The citrus, green apple and green melon flavors have real zing. Drink now.–H.S. • $12 • (10/15/1998) • **86**
Marsanne Goulburn Valley 1997: Light and fruity, with pretty pear, green fig and floral flavors on a medium-weight frame. Echoes the fruit on the soft finish. Drink now.–H.S. • $17 • (11/15/1998) • **86**
Marsanne South Eastern Australia Thomas Mitchell 1998: Soft and ripe, with pretty pear and orange aromas and flavors, picking up a nice hint of grassiness on the round finish. Drink now.–H.S. • $10 • (6/15/1999) • **85**
MCM Cab Mac Victoria 1992 • $9 • (3/31/1993) • **85**
Shiraz Goulburn Valley 1996: Rich, ripe and distinctively and exotically spicy, offering tiers of berry, black cherry and plum flavors, with a nice hint of licorice on the finish. Delicious already, but feels like it can go on and on. Drink now through 2007.–H.S. • $17 • (6/15/1999) • **90**
Shiraz Goulburn Valley 1995 • $17 • (11/30/1997) • **88**
Shiraz Goulburn Valley 1989 • $8 • (2/15/1992) • **80**
Shiraz Goulburn Valley 1988 • $8 • (3/15/1991) • **86**
Shiraz South Eastern Australia 1993 • $10 • (6/30/1995) • **85**
Shiraz South Eastern Australia Thomas Mitchell 1997: On the lighter side, its fresh plum and allspice flavors making it a distinctive, drink-now red.–H.S. • $12 • (11/15/1998) • **86**
Shiraz South Eastern Australia Thomas Mitchell 1996: Minty character pervades this claret-style red, its chewy texture holding a nice array of earthy blackberry and herbal flavors. Drink through 2002–H.S. • $12 • (8/31/1998) • **86**
Shiraz South Eastern Australia Thomas Mitchell 1995 • $10 • (11/30/1997) • **86**
Shiraz South Eastern Australia Thomas Mitchell 1994 • $10 • (4/30/1996) • **83**
Shiraz Victoria 1991 • $9 • (5/31/1993) • **84**
Shiraz Victoria 1990 • $8 • (11/30/1992) • **84**
Shiraz Victoria Print Label 1995: Bright and generous with its berry and spice flavors, this very pretty mouthful of fruit, vanilla and anise lingers appealingly on the harmonious finish. Drink now through 2001.–H.S. • $46 • (9/30/1998) • **89**
Shiraz Victoria Print Label 1991 • $18 • (9/30/1994) • **87**
Shiraz Victoria Print Label 1990 • $17 • (5/31/1993) • **88**
Shiraz Victoria Reserve 1993 • $16 • (6/30/1996) • **91**
South Eastern Australia 1993 • $10 • (6/30/1995) • **82**

Key: SS—Spectator Selection. CS—Cellar Selection. HR—Highly Recommended. $NA—Price not available. (BT)—Barrel tasting. Ⓐ—Auction Price.
For a key to the tasters' initials, see "How to Use These Listings."
Dates in parentheses represent the issues in which the ratings were published.

Thomas Mitchell South Eastern Australia Red 1998: Earthy, weedy and drying. Cabernet Franc, Shiraz and others.–B.S. • $11 • (6/30/2000) • **75**

MONTROSE

Cabernet Sauvignon Mudgee 1987 • $10 • (2/28/1991) • **81**
Cabernet Sauvignon Mudgee 1984 • $10 • (4/30/1988) • **88**
Cabernet Sauvignon Mudgee Special Reserve 1985 • $16 • (1/31/1990) • **80**
Poet's Corner South Eastern Australia 1991 • $6 • (3/31/1993) • **82**
Shiraz Mudgee 1988 • $9 • (3/15/1991) • **78**
Shiraz Mudgee 1984 • $10 • (7/01/1987) • **87**
Shiraz South Eastern Australia Poet's Corner 1995 • $10 • (5/15/1997) • **84**

MOUNT HORROCKS

Cabernet-Merlot Clare Valley 1997: Perfumed, with violet, blackberry and mint notes encased within brawny, dry tannins. Drink now through 2002.–B.S. • $24 • (6/30/2000) • **81**

Riesling Clare Valley Cordon Cut 1998: Typically sweet and silky, with a gleaming intensity of apricot, pear and resin flavors that finish with a flourish of raisiny spices. Delicious now, but try to keep hands off to see what develops. Drink through 2010.–H.S. • $20/375 ml. • (9/15/1999) • **92**

Riesling Clare Valley Cordon Cut 1997 • $18/375 ml. • (5/31/1998) • **92**
Riesling Watervale Cordon Cut 1996 • $17/375 ml. • (5/31/1997) • **94**

MOUNT LANGI GHIRAN

Cabernet-Merlot Victoria Langi 1996: Spicy, with pepper, coffee and earthy berry flavors that pick up a cedary edge and turn crisp and firm. Drink now through 2006.–J.L. • $39 • (5/31/2000) • **86**

Cabernet-Merlot Victoria Langi 1995: Lean and elegant, firm with tannins but juicy with currant and plum flavors on a medium-weight frame. Flavors linger nicely on the finish. Drink now.–H.S. • $35 • (2/28/1999) • **88**

Cabernet-Merlot Victoria Langi 1994 • $30 • (11/30/1997) • **86**
Cabernet-Merlot Victoria 1993 • $24 • (11/30/1996) • **90**

Riesling Victoria 1998: Fresh and juicy, a jazzy mouthful of crisp lime and green apple flavors that linger on the moderately tart finish. Drink now through 2008.–H.S. • $20 • (6/30/2000) • **87**

Shiraz Victoria 1997: A juxtaposition of lean texture and dense berry and licorice that's ambitious and moderate in length. Drink now through 2002.–B.S. • $46 • (6/30/2000) • **86**

Shiraz Victoria 1994 • $24 • (6/15/1996) • **92**

Shiraz Victoria Langi 1996: Light and airy for a Shiraz, not as brilliantly fruity as previous vintages, with pretty raspberry and sweet leather flavors that dance delicately over the finish. Firm tannins will keep it awhile. Drink now through 2003.–H.S. • $33 • (5/15/1999) • **89**

Shiraz Victoria Langi 1995 • $30 • (7/31/1997) • **91**

Shiraz-Cabernet-Grenache South Eastern Australia Billi Billi Creek 1996: Light in texture but flavorful, this is a solid red with hints of black cherry and black pepper on a firm frame. Drink now through 2002.–H.S. • $21 • (2/28/1999) • **85**

MOUNT MARY

Quintet Red Lilydale 1994 • $65 • (9/30/1997) • **85**

MOUNT PLEASANT

Shiraz Hunter Valley 1993 • $11 • (4/30/1996) • **82**
Shiraz Hunter Valley 1992 • $12 • (11/30/1995) • **83**

MOUNTADAM

Chardonnay Eden Valley 1997: Rich and ripe, but a bitter streak spoils the honeyed pear and caramel flavors for me. Tasted twice, with consistent notes.–H.S. • $24 • (9/30/1999) • **79**

Pinot Noir Eden Valley 1996: Light and herbal, with more tea leaf than fruit flavors; the spicy berry notes on the finish are welcome. Drink now through 2002.–H.S. • $30 • (9/30/1999) • **80**

Pinot Noir Eden Valley 1993 • $26 • (4/30/1996) • **81**
Pinot Noir Eden Valley 1992 • $20 • (7/31/1994) • **88**
Pinot Noir Eden Valley 1988 • $25 • (3/31/1991) • **86**

NINTH ISLAND

Chardonnay Tasmania 1998: Light, crisp and floral, a tangy mouthful of pineapple, earth and mineral flavors that linger on the zingy finish. Not for every taste, but a distinctive wine that should benefit from cellaring. Drink now through 2003.–H.S. • $15 • (5/31/1999) • **86**

Pinot Noir Tasmania 1998: Light and silky, a delicate Pinot with pretty blackberry, plum and floral flavors that echo softly on the gentle finish. Drink through 2003.–H.S. • $15 • (5/31/1999) • **87**

Sauvignon Blanc Tasmania 1998: Fragrant, showing lots of green pepper–scented citrus and apple flavors on a light frame. Distinctly herbal. Drink now.–H.S. • $15 • (6/15/1999) • **86**

NOON'S

Cabernet-Shiraz Langhorne Creek 1995 • $17 • (5/31/1998) • **85**

NORMAN ESTATES, GREG

Cabernet-Merlot Coonawarra 1996: Ripe and supple, with a chocolate and tobacco edge to the lovely berry, currant and herb flavors that linger through the silky finish. Has power and grace. A terrific wine, period, and even better for the price. Drink now through 2008.–H.S. • $15 • (11/15/1999) HR • **91**

Chardonnay Yarra Valley 1998: Smooth in texture and bright in flavor, offering pretty pear, floral and apricot flavors in profusion. Lingers nicely on the finish. Drink now through 2003.–H.S. • $15 • (11/15/1999) • **88**

NORMANS

Cabernet Sauvignon South Australia Bin C106 1995 • $12 • (11/30/1997) • **87**
Cabernet Sauvignon McLaren Vale Chais Clarendon 1995 • $18 • (3/31/1998) • **84**
Cabernet Sauvignon South Australia Chais Clarendon 1991 • $20 • (6/30/1995) • **78**
Cabernet Sauvignon South Australia Chais Clarendon 1989 • $19 • (9/30/1994) • **78**
Cabernet Sauvignon South Australia Family Reserve 1993 • $8 • (5/15/1997) • **83**
Cabernet Sauvignon South Australia Family Reserve 1992 • $10 • (9/30/1994) • **79**
Shiraz McLaren Vale Chais Clarendon 1995 • $18 • (3/31/1998) • **88**
Shiraz South Australia Chais Clarendon 1992 • $20 • (4/15/1995) • **87**
Shiraz South Australia Chais Clarendon 1990 • $19 • (6/15/1994) • **86**
Shiraz South Australia Chandlers Hill 1993 • $8 • (4/15/1995) • **79**
Shiraz South Australia Chandlers Hill 1992 • $8 • (6/15/1994) • **82**
Shiraz South Eastern Australia Lone Gum 1996 • $9 • (3/31/1998) • **84**
Shiraz-Cabernet South Eastern Australia Lone Gum 1996 • $8 • (3/31/1998) • **83**

NURIHANNAM

Shiraz Barossa Barossa Class 1998: A home run. Dense and lively, this packs plum, blackberry and vanilla into a sleek, elegant framework. Really intense, with a long finish. Drink now through 2003.–B.S. • $40 • (6/30/2000) • **92**

O'SHEA, MAURICE

Shiraz Hunter Valley 1993 • $25 • (4/30/1996) • **86**

ORLANDO

Cabernet Sauvignon Coonawarra Jacaranda Ridge 1989 • $35 • (10/31/1995) • **83**
Cabernet Sauvignon Coonawarra St.-Hugo 1993 • $28 • (6/15/1997) • **90**
Cabernet Sauvignon Coonawarra St.-Hugo 1989 • $15 • (12/15/1993) • **86**
Cabernet Sauvignon Coonawarra St.-Hugo 1987 • $15 • (5/31/1991) • **78**
Cabernet Sauvignon Coonawarra St.-Hugo 1985 • $15 • (4/30/1989) • **90**

Cabernet Sauvignon South Eastern Australia Jacob's Creek 1997: Ripe and supple, with currant and blackberry flavors in a generous, round style, hinting at toast on the soft finish. Drink now.–H.S. • $9 • (2/28/1999) • **83**

Cabernet Sauvignon South Eastern Australia Jacob's Creek 1995 • $9 • (5/31/1998) • **85**
Cabernet Sauvignon South Eastern Australia Jacob's Creek 1994 • $8 • (5/15/1997) • **79**

ORLANDO

Cabernet Sauvignon South Eastern Australia Jacob's Creek 1990 • $8 • (12/15/1993) • **78**
Cabernet Sauvignon South Eastern Australia Jacob's Creek 1989 • $7 • (6/30/1992) • **77**
Cabernet Sauvignon South Eastern Australia Jacob's Creek 1988 • $7 • (7/15/1991) • **83**
Chardonnay South Eastern Australia Jacob's Creek 1998: A fresh and lively white, its charm equal to its affordability, with an attractive apricotlike accent to its pear and apple character. Drink now.–H.S. • $9 • (2/28/1999) • **85**
Chardonnay South Eastern Australia Jacob's Creek 1997 • $9 • (5/15/1998) • **85**
Extra Brut Australia Carrington NV • $9 • (3/31/1998) • **84**
Merlot South Eastern Australia Jacob's Creek 1997: Light, with modest tar, cherry and dried orange peel flavors, finishing with a firm touch of tannin. Drink now through 2001.–H.S. • $9 • (2/28/1999) • **80**
Merlot South Eastern Australia Jacob's Creek 1996 • $9 • (5/31/1998) • **83**
Merlot South Eastern Australia Jacob's Creek 1995 • $9 • (5/15/1997) • **80**
Merlot South Eastern Australia Jacob's Creek 1994 • $7 • (3/31/1996) • **80**
Merlot South Eastern Australia Jacob's Creek 1992 • $8 • (9/30/1994) • **77**
Merlot South Eastern Australia Jacob's Creek 1991 • $8 • (12/15/1993) • **81**
Merlot South Eastern Australia Jacob's Creek 1990 • $7 • (6/30/1992) • **79**
Merlot South Eastern Australia Jacob's Creek 1989 • $7 • (9/30/1991) • **82**
Riesling South Eastern Australia Dry 1997 • $9 • (5/31/1998) • **84**
Sémillon-Chardonnay South Eastern Australia Jacob's Creek 1998: Fresh and focused, with pretty lemon, apple and fig flavors on a modest scale. Drink now.–H.S. • $8 • (2/28/1999) • **82**
Sémillon-Chardonnay South Eastern Australia Jacob's Creek 1997 • $9 • (5/15/1998) • **82**
Shiraz Padthaway Lawson's 1992 • $26 • (5/15/1998) • **87**
Shiraz Padthaway Lawson's 1991 • $22 • (2/29/1996) • **89**
Shiraz-Cabernet South Eastern Australia Jacob's Creek 1997: Soft and supple, with open-textured cherry and cola flavors. Drink now.–H.S. • $9 • (2/28/1999) • **82**
Shiraz-Cabernet South Eastern Australia Jacob's Creek 1996 • $9 • (5/31/1998) • **86**
Shiraz-Cabernet South Eastern Australia Jacob's Creek 1995 • $7 • (5/15/1997) • **82**
Shiraz-Cabernet South Eastern Australia Jacob's Creek 1994 • $7 • (3/31/1996) • **82**
Shiraz-Cabernet South Eastern Australia Jacob's Creek 1991 • $8 • (10/31/1993) • **80**
Cabernet-Shiraz South Eastern Australia 1991 • $7 • (4/30/1994) • **81**
Cabernet-Shiraz South Australia 1989 • $7 • (2/29/1992) • **82**
Cabernet-Shiraz South Australia 1988 • $7 • (9/15/1990) • **73**
Chardonnay South Eastern Australia 1998: Light and refreshing, with simple flavors of apple and spice. Drink now.–H.S. • $9 • (2/28/1999) • **82**
Chardonnay South Eastern Australia 1997 • $8 • (12/31/1997) • **86**
Grenache South Australia Yalumba Limited Release 1997: Light in texture, with pretty cherry, spice and smoke flavors that are eerily reminiscent of Chateauneuf-du-Pape. Finishes smooth and silky. Drink now through 2003.–H.S. • $10 • (11/15/1999) • **87**
Merlot South Australia 1998: Light and fragrant, appealing for its modest berry and herb flavors, picking up a pleasant hint of vanilla on the soft finish. Drink now.–H.S. • $8 • (6/30/2000) • **82**
Merlot South Eastern Australia 1997: Light and earthy, with a strong mineral component to the soft black cherry flavors. Drink now.–H.S. • $9 • (2/28/1999) • **82**
Merlot South Eastern Australia 1994 • $7 • (6/30/1996) • **78**
Merlot South Eastern Australia 1993 • $7 • (6/30/1996) • **85**
Merlot South Eastern Australia 1992 • $8 • (9/30/1994) • **78**
Sauvignon Blanc South Australia 1999: Racy, with crisp lemon-lime notes. Drink now.–B.S. • $8 • (6/30/2000) • **82**
Sauvignon Blanc South Australia 1998: Fresh and fruity, with hints of herbs to the apple and pear flavors. Drink now.–H.S. • $9 • (2/28/1999) • **83**
Sauvignon Blanc South Australia 1997 • $9 • (1/31/1998) • **84**
Shiraz South Australia Yalumba Limited Release 1998: On the light side, with pretty plum and vanilla flavors on a soft frame. Drink now.–H.S. • $10 • (11/15/1999) • **83**
Viognier South Australia Yalumba Limited Release 1998: Ripe, round and silky, with lovely flavors that evoke Viognier perfectly. Doesn't feel heavy, just generous with its floral pear and melon flavors. Drink now.–H.S. • $10 • (11/15/1999) • **88**

OWEN'S ESTATE

Cabernet Sauvignon South Eastern Australia 1998: The smooth, polished style emphasizes the pretty currant and berry side of Cabernet, with just a hint of sage on the crisp, refined finish. Drink now through 2003.–H.S. • $15 • (11/30/1999) • **86**
Chardonnay South Eastern Australia 1998: Bright and sappy, with jazzy kiwi and spice flavors that remain refreshing through the finish. Drink now.–H.S. • $12 • (11/30/1999) • **85**
Merlot South Australia 1998: Smooth in texture, a refined style, with lovely berry and spice flavors that echo on the polished finish. Drink now through 2005.–H.S. • $15 • (11/30/1999) • **87**
Sauvignon Blanc South Australia 1998: Soft and silky, with an almost sweet edge to the almond and herb flavors. Finishes tangy, though. Drink now.–H.S. • $12 • (11/30/1999) • **84**
Shiraz South Eastern Australia 1998: Smooth and appealing, a lovely mouthful of plum and blueberry that remains lively on the polished finish. Drink now through 2005.–H.S. • $15 • (11/30/1999) • **88**

OXFORD LANDING

Cabernet-Shiraz South Australia 1998: Bright and flavorful, a charming mouthful of currant, plum and distinctly minty aromas and flavors that all linger effortlessly on the finish. Drink now through 2007.–H.S. • $8 • (6/30/2000) • **85**
Cabernet-Shiraz South Eastern Australia 1997 • $9 • (6/15/1998) • **84**
Cabernet-Shiraz South Eastern Australia 1995 • $8 • (2/28/1997) • **82**
Cabernet-Shiraz South Eastern Australia 1993 • $7 • (11/30/1995) • **85**
Cabernet-Shiraz South Eastern Australia 1992 • $7 • (6/30/1995) • **84**

PARACOMBE

Shiraz Adelaide Hills 1996: Strays into dry, tannic pickle barrel flavors.–J.L. • $28 • (6/30/2000) • **78**

PARINGA

Shiraz Clarendon Individual Vineyard 1999: Firm in texture but lush with spicy berry flavors; a juicy wine that finishes smooth and velvety. Drink now through 2005.–H.S. • $12 • (6/30/2000) • **87**

PARKER COONAWARRA ESTATE

Cabernet Sauvignon Coonawarra Terra Rossa 1996: Chewy and tart, with violet-scented currant, mineral and toast flavors that remain lively through the racy finish. Best from 2001 through 2006.–H.S. • $26 • (3/31/1999) • **89**
Cabernet Sauvignon Coonawarra Terra Rossa 1995 • $25 • (9/30/1997) • **85**
Cabernet Sauvignon Coonawarra Terra Rossa 1994 • $22 • (9/30/1996) • **88**
Cabernet Sauvignon Coonawarra Terra Rossa 1992 • $20 • (3/31/1995) • **74**
Cabernet Sauvignon Coonawarra Terra Rossa 1991 • $22 • (9/30/1994) • **82**
Cabernet Sauvignon Coonawarra Terra Rossa 1989 • $20 • (5/31/1993) • **83**
Terra Rossa First Growth Coonawarra 1996: Firm in texture and beautifully focused, laying out its pretty blackberry, currant, sage and mineral flavors on a bed of fine-grained tannins. Has all the pieces in place, just needs time. Best from 2001 through 2006.–H.S. • $65 • (3/31/1999) • **92**
Terra Rossa First Growth Coonawarra 1994 • $45 • (9/30/1997) • **88**
Terra Rossa First Growth Coonawarra 1993 • $45 • (1/31/1997) • **86**
Terra Rossa First Growth Coonawarra 1991 • $39 • (3/31/1995) • **87**
Terra Rossa First Growth Coonawarra 1990 • $38 • (9/30/1994) • **80**
Terra Rossa First Growth Coonawarra 1989 • $35 • (5/31/1993) • **89**

PARSON'S FLAT

Shiraz-Cabernet Padthaway 1998: Huge, with an inky color and brooding aromas of plum, blackberry and sweet spice married to a silky texture and a full-bodied frame. A tannic raspberry and tobacco finish prevails. Drink now through 2004.–B.S. • $35 • (6/30/2000) • **92**

PASSING CLOUDS

Cabernet Sauvignon Victoria 1996: Firm and focused, with dark berry, herb and meaty flavors that echo nicely on the crisp finish. Needs cellaring. Best after 2001.–H.S. • $25 • (5/15/1999) • **87**

Key: SS—Spectator Selection. CS—Cellar Selection. HR—Highly Recommended. $NA—Price not available. (BT)—Barrel tasting. (A)—Auction Price.
For a key to the tasters' initials, see "How to Use These Listings."
Dates in parentheses represent the issues in which the ratings were published.

Cabernet-Shiraz Victoria 1996: Firm and focused, with a pretty mint and mineral edge to the black cherry and anise flavors. Finishes crisp and refreshing. Best from 2001 through 2007.–H.S. • $25 • (6/15/1999) • **89**

Shiraz-Cabernet Victoria 1996: Lean and racy, this jazzy mouthful of blackberry, mint and toast flavors remains lively through the not-too-tannic finish. Drink through 2005.–H.S. • $25 • (6/15/1999) • **87**

PAULETT

Riesling Clare Valley Dry 1997: A lean white, dry and refreshing, with floral apple and resin flavors. Drink now through 2004.–H.S. • $16 • (3/31/1999) • **85**

PENFOLDS

Cabernet Sauvignon South Australia Bin 407 1997: An acquired taste, this distinctive wine emphasizes earthy, minty flavors over the modest fruit character. Has intensity, range and depth, making it a good candidate for the cellar. Best after 2002.–H.S. • $25 • (6/30/2000) • **87**

Cabernet Sauvignon South Australia Bin 407 1995: Velvety, bordering on chewy, with modest berry and mint flavors that linger on the gentle finish. Drink now through 2001.–H.S. • $17 • (9/30/1998) • **85**

Cabernet Sauvignon South Australia Bin 407 1994 • $39 Ⓐ • (9/15/1997) • **87**

Cabernet Sauvignon South Australia Bin 407 1993 • $50 Ⓐ • (4/30/1996) • **88**

Cabernet Sauvignon South Australia Bin 407 1992 • $16 • (3/31/1996) • **85**

Cabernet Sauvignon South Australia Bin 407 1991 • $16 • (11/30/1994) • **86**

Cabernet Sauvignon South Australia Bin 407 1990 • $62 Ⓐ • (3/31/1993) • **78**

Cabernet Sauvignon South Australia Bin 707 1996: Ripe and rich, with style and tremendous length. Redolent of blackberry, bay leaf and pepper, this supple, generous mouthful of Aussie Cabernet reflects a ton of fruit packed into a big frame. Best from 2004 through 2011.–H.S. • $77 • (1/31/2000) CS • **93**

Cabernet Sauvignon South Australia Bin 707 1994 • $45 • (3/31/1998) • **88**

Cabernet Sauvignon South Australia Bin 707 1993 • $45 • (4/30/1997) • **92**

Cabernet Sauvignon South Australia Bin 707 1992 • $40 • (10/15/1995) CS • **92**

Cabernet Sauvignon South Australia Bin 707 1990 • $40 • (3/31/1995) CS • **92**

Cabernet Sauvignon South Australia Bin 707 1989 • $39 Ⓐ • (5/31/1993) • **85**

Cabernet Sauvignon South Australia Bin 707 1987 • $57 Ⓐ • (5/31/1991) • **83**

Cabernet Sauvignon South Australia Bin 707 1986 • $28 • (9/30/1989) • **90**

Cabernet Sauvignon South Australia Bin 707 1981 • $18 • (7/01/1987) • **90**

Cabernet-Shiraz Clare Valley 1995 • $10 • (5/31/1997) • **84**

Cabernet-Shiraz Coonawarra Bin 920 1990 • $110 • (5/15/1996) • **86**

Cabernet-Shiraz South Australia Bin 389 1997: Ripe and generous in plum and berry flavors if a bit shy on density, finishing by echoing the pretty fruit elegantly. Drink now through 2005.–H.S. • $25 • (6/30/2000) • **88**

Cabernet-Shiraz South Australia Bin 389 1996: Fat and flavorful, This is a richly textured red wine that unfolds its ripe black cherry, blackberry and anise flavors like a thick quilt. Soft, warm and generous, with a sweet, supple finish. Drink now through 2008.–H.S. • $25 • (1/31/2000) SS • **91**

Cabernet-Shiraz South Australia Bin 389 1995: On the firm side, with pretty raspberry and blackberry flavors giving plenty of charm. Drinkable now with hearty food. Drink now.–H.S. • $19 • (9/30/1998) • **88**

Cabernet-Shiraz South Australia Bin 389 1994 • $19 • (9/15/1997) • **86**

Cabernet-Shiraz South Australia Bin 389 1993 • $18 • (4/30/1996) • **87**

Cabernet-Shiraz South Australia Bin 389 1992 • $16 • (11/30/1995) SS • **92**

Cabernet-Shiraz South Australia Bin 389 1991 • $16 • (11/30/1995) • **90**

Cabernet-Shiraz South Australia Bin 389 1990 • $16 • (1/31/1995) • **86**

Cabernet-Shiraz South Australia Bin 389 1989 • $16 • (4/15/1994) • **87**

Cabernet-Shiraz South Australia Bin 389 1988 • $16 • (3/31/1993) • **81**

Cabernet-Shiraz South Australia Bin 389 1987 • $14 • (2/28/1991) • **88**

Cabernet-Shiraz South Australia Bin 389 1986 • $15 • (1/31/1990) • **83**

Cabernet-Shiraz South Australia Bin 389 1985 • $14 • (12/31/1988) • **86**

Cabernet-Shiraz South Australia Bin 389 1983 • $15 • (7/01/1987) • **91**

Chardonnay Adelaide Hills 1997: Particularly refined and elegant, this is deftly balanced, with pear, spice and honey aromas and flavors that linger elegantly. It doesn't feel like a blockbuster, but it keeps going and going convincingly on the finish. Drink now through 2007.–H.S. • $27 • (11/15/1999) • **91**

Chardonnay South Australia The Valleys 1997: A solid white, with fresh pear and spice flavors on a medium-weight frame. Flavors linger gently and appealingly on the finish. Drink now.–H.S. • $12 • (1/31/1999) • **86**

Chardonnay South Eastern Australia Koonunga Hill 1998: Soft, fruity and generous with its peach and apple flavors, picking up a sappy note on the finish. Drink now.–H.S. • $10 • (11/15/1999) • **85**

Chardonnay South Eastern Australia Koonunga Hill 1997 • $9 • (5/15/1998) • **84**

Chardonnay-Sauvignon Blanc Clare Valley Organically Grown Grapes 1993 • $10 • (1/31/1995) • **85**

Grange Shiraz South Australia 1994: A magnificent edifice of a wine, elegant and refined in structure but dripping with flavor—a virtual cascade of plum, black cherry, blackberry, anise, pepper and exotic spices that lingers on the finish; this just doesn't quit. Best after 2002.–H.S. • $190 Ⓐ • (11/30/1999) CS • **96**

Grange Shiraz South Australia 1993: Dark, peppery and earthy overtones add substance to this chewy, remarkably complex red wine. It delivers a ripe core of plum and dried currant, then branches out, hinting at anise and mineral on the finish. Approachable now, but oh what a future this has. Drink now.–H.S. • $154 Ⓐ • (11/15/1998) CS • **95**

Grange Shiraz South Australia 1992 • $178 Ⓐ • (10/15/1997) CS • **94**

Grange Shiraz South Australia 1991 • $211 Ⓐ • (11/30/1996) CS • **95**

Grange Shiraz South Australia 1990 • $323 Ⓐ • (1/31/1997) • **98**

Grange Hermitage South Australia Bin 95 1989 • $214 Ⓐ • (1/31/1995) CS • **96**

Grange Hermitage South Australia Bin 95 1988 • $180 Ⓐ • (1/31/1997) • **91**

Grange Hermitage South Australia Bin 95 1987 • $171 Ⓐ • (1/31/1997) • **90**

Grange Hermitage South Australia Bin 95 1986 • $308 Ⓐ • (1/31/1997) • **98**

Grange Hermitage South Australia Bin 95 1985 • $189 Ⓐ • (1/31/1997) • **94**

Grange Hermitage South Australia Bin 95 1984 • $131 Ⓐ • (1/31/1997) • **91**

Grange Hermitage South Australia Bin 95 1983 • $224 Ⓐ • (1/31/1997) • **90**

Grange Hermitage South Australia Bin 95 1982 • $250 Ⓐ • (1/31/1997) • **92**

Grange Hermitage South Australia Bin 95 1981 • $195 Ⓐ • (1/31/1997) • **89**

Grange Hermitage South Australia Bin 95 1980 • $207 Ⓐ • (1/31/1997) • **93**

Grange Hermitage South Australia Bin 95 1979 • $143 Ⓐ • (1/31/1997) • **94**

Grange Hermitage South Australia Bin 95 1978 • $238 Ⓐ • (1/31/1997) • **83**

Grange Hermitage South Australia Bin 95 1977 • $201 Ⓐ • (1/31/1997) • **90**

Grange Hermitage South Australia Bin 95 1976 • $523 Ⓐ • (1/31/1997) • **93**

Grange Hermitage South Australia Bin 95 1975 • $426 Ⓐ • (1/31/1997) • **87**

Grange Hermitage South Australia Bin 95 1974 • $NA • (1/31/1997) • **90**

Grange Hermitage South Australia Bin 95 1973 • $266 Ⓐ • (1/31/1997) • **87**

Grange Hermitage South Australia Bin 95 1972 • $NA • (1/31/1997) • **88**

Grange Hermitage South Australia Bin 95 1971 • $542 Ⓐ • (1/31/1997) • **92**

Grange Hermitage South Australia Bin 95 1970 • $205 Ⓐ • (1/31/1997) • **89**

Grange Hermitage South Australia Bin 95 1969 • $213 Ⓐ • (1/31/1997) • **86**

Grange Hermitage South Australia Bin 95 1968 • $322 Ⓐ • (1/31/1997) • **85**

Grange Hermitage South Australia Bin 95 1967 • $380 Ⓐ • (1/31/1997) • **91**

Grange Hermitage South Australia Bin 95 1966 • $481 Ⓐ • (1/31/1997) • **87**

Grange Hermitage South Australia Bin 95 1965 • $545 Ⓐ • (1/31/1997) • **88**

Grange Hermitage South Australia Bin 95 1964 • $361 Ⓐ • (1/31/1997) • **86**

Grange Hermitage South Australia Bin 95 1963 • $245 Ⓐ • (1/31/1997) • **89**

Grange Hermitage South Australia Bin 95 1962 • $NA • (1/31/1997) • **87**

Grange Hermitage South Australia Bin 95 1961 • $1,189 Ⓐ • (1/31/1997) • **92**

Grange Hermitage South Australia Bin 95 1960 • $NA • (1/31/1997) • **87**

Grange Hermitage South Australia Bin 95 1959 • $NA • (1/31/1997) • **80**

Grange Hermitage South Australia Bin 95 1958 • $NA • (1/31/1997) • **84**

Grange Hermitage South Australia Bin 95 1957 • $NA • (1/31/1997) • **89**

Grange Hermitage South Australia Bin 95 1956 • $NA • (1/31/1997) • **86**

Grange Hermitage South Australia Bin 95 1955 • $2,222 Ⓐ • (1/31/1997) • **90**

Grenache-Shiraz-Mourvèdre Barossa Valley Old Vine 1994 • $17 • (5/15/1998) • **88**

Sémillon Adelaide Hills 1997: Youthful and fruity, with nice pineapple and citrus flavors and a beguiling hint of passion fruit in the background. Drink now through 2002.–H.S. • $27 • (11/15/1999) • **88**

Port Australia Club NV • $9 • (5/15/1996) • **89**

Riesling Eden Valley Reserve 1999: Youthful, exuberant style emphasizing fresh, almost raw, apple and lime flavors, picking up mineral and floral notes on the dry finish. Drink now through 2009.–H.S. • $18 • (6/30/2000) • **89**

Sémillon-Chardonnay South Australia Koonunga Hill 1997 • $8 • (5/15/1998) • **85**

Sémillon-Chardonnay South Eastern Australia Koonunga Hill 1998: Silky and appealing for its tobacco-scented pear and citrus flavors, and finishing with juicy acidity and a round texture, this white blend from Australia is quite a lovely wine for so modest a price. Drink now through 2002.–H.S. • $8 • (11/15/1999) • **85**

Shiraz Coonawarra Bin 128 1997: Ripe and complex, with firm tannins and a wide range of spice, earth, plum and berry flavors that swirl through the finish. Needs time to smooth the tannins. Best after 2003.–H.S. • $22 • (6/30/2000) • **89**

Shiraz Coonawarra Bin 128 1996: Crisp, almost bright even though it's almost 4 years old, focusing its plum, spice and tobacco flavors on an frame that feels more like Cabernet but tastes like Shiraz. Drink through 2010.–H.S. • $22 • (12/31/1999) • **88**

PENFOLDS

Shiraz Coonawarra Bin 128 1995: Light and airy, with focused blackberry and earth flavors that linger on the austere finish. Drink now.–H.S. • $14 • (9/30/1998) • **86**
Shiraz Coonawarra Bin 128 1994 • $14 • (9/15/1997) • **87**
Shiraz Coonawarra Bin 128 1993 • $14 • (4/30/1996) • **86**
Shiraz Coonawarra Bin 128 1992 • $13 • (11/30/1995) • **88**
Shiraz Coonawarra Bin 128 1990 • $15 • (3/31/1994) • **83**
Shiraz Magill Magill Estate 1996: A very interesting wine, balancing tangy red plum and blueberry flavors with rich chocolate, spice and toast overtones. Long and tasty, this feels like it can grow and grow. Drink now through 2006.–H.S. • $47 • (11/30/1999) • **92**
Shiraz Magill Magill Estate 1994 • $44 • (5/15/1998) • **90**
Shiraz Magill Magill Estate 1993 • $44 • (11/30/1997) • **89**
Shiraz South Australia Kalimna Bin 28 1997: Earthy flavors run through this firm-textured red, but ripe berry and cherry flavors come through on the solid finish. Finish is strong enough to merit cellaring to see what develops. Best from 2002 through 2012.–H.S. • $25 • (6/30/2000) • **88**
Shiraz South Australia Kalimna Bin 28 1996: A beguiling combination of rich, almost decadent flavors on an upright frame that has a nicely buried backbone of acidity and tannin. Nothing is obtrusive, everything is in graceful balance, leaving an ultimate impression of both muscle and flesh. Best after 2002.–H.S. • $25 • (1/31/2000) • **90**
Shiraz South Australia Kalimna Bin 28 1995: Round and velvety, filling its racy frame with pretty berry and spice flavors that linger on the gentle finish. Drink now through 2001.–H.S. • $19 • (9/30/1998) • **88**
Shiraz South Australia Kalimna Bin 28 1994 • $19 • (9/15/1997) • **86**
Shiraz South Australia Kalimna Bin 28 1993 • $18 • (4/30/1996) • **91**
Shiraz South Australia Kalimna Bin 28 1992 • $16 • (11/15/1995) • **85**
Shiraz South Australia Magill Estate Vineyard 1988 • $44 • (5/31/1993) • **85**
Shiraz South Australia Magill Estate Vineyard 1985 • $45 • (7/31/1989) • **87**
Shiraz South Australia St. Henri 1995: Lithe and elegant, a refined style of Shiraz that weaves tobacco and cedar notes smoothly through the mature blackberry, tar and pepper flavors, which linger impressively. Drink now through 2010.–H.S. • $31 • (11/30/1999) • **90**
Shiraz-Cabernet South Australia St. Henri 1994: Firm and chewy, with gritty tannins that still have a grip on the pretty berry flavors beneath, but the chocolate-tinged fruit wins on the finish. Best after 2001.–H.S. • $21 • (3/31/1999) • **87**
Shiraz South Australia St. Henri 1992 • $21 • (4/30/1997) • **88**
Shiraz-Cabernet Sauvignon South Australia Bin 920 1990 • $NA • (1/31/1997) • **92**
Shiraz-Cabernet Sauvignon South Australia Bin 820 1982 • $NA • (1/31/1997) • **88**
Shiraz-Cabernet Sauvignon South Australia Bin 80A 1980 • $98Ⓐ • (1/31/1997) • **92**
Shiraz-Cabernet South Australia Koonunga Hill 1998: Firm and chewy, with a layer of surprisingly scratchy tannins around a nice core of blackberry, currant and peppery flavors. Best after 2002.–H.S. • $11 • (6/30/2000) • **85**
Shiraz-Cabernet Sauvignon South Australia Koonunga Hill 1996: Ripe, silky and plush, with cascades of black cherry, raspberry and anise flavors that keep swirling through the generous finish, this Down Under red blend is much more wine than its moderate price would indicate. Delicious now. Drink through 2005–H.S. • $9 • (8/31/1998) • **88**
Shiraz-Cabernet South Australia Koonunga Hill 1995 • $9 • (7/31/1997) • **83**
Shiraz-Cabernet Sauvignon Australia Koonunga Hill 1994 • $9 • (4/30/1996) • **85**
Shiraz-Cabernet Sauvignon South Australia Koonunga Hill 1993 • $9 • (3/31/1996) • **78**
Shiraz-Cabernet Sauvignon South Australia Koonunga Hill 1992 • $9 • (6/30/1995) • **84**
Shiraz-Cabernet Sauvignon South Australia Koonunga Hill 1991 • $9 • (3/31/1995) • **85**
Shiraz-Cabernet Sauvignon South Australia Koonunga Hill 1990 • $9 • (2/28/1993) • **86**
Shiraz-Mourvèdre South Eastern Australia Bin 2 1998: Dark and spicy, with earthy plum and berry flavors on a firm texture. Flavors linger on the finish, along with slightly scratchy tannins that should soften within a year or two. Drink now through 2004.–H.S. • $11 • (6/30/2000) • **85**
Shiraz-Mourvèdre South Eastern Australia Bin 2 1996 • $9 • (5/15/1998) • **87**
Shiraz-Mourvèdre South Eastern Australia Bin 2 1995 • $9 • (4/30/1997) • **85**
Shiraz-Mourvèdre South Eastern Australia Bin 2 1994 • $10 • (11/15/1996) • **86**

Key: SS—Spectator Selection. CS—Cellar Selection. HR—Highly Recommended. $NA—Price not available. (BT)—Barrel tasting. Ⓐ—Auction Price. For a key to the tasters' initials, see "How to Use These Listings."
Dates in parentheses represent the issues in which the ratings were published.

Shiraz-Mourvèdre-Grenache Barossa Valley Old Vine 1995: Ripe and aromatic, with gamy, anise-scented blackberry and prune flavors on a lean frame. Firm tannins need cellaring. Drink through 2004.–H.S. • $16 • (1/31/1999) • **85**

PENLEY

Cabernet Sauvignon Coonawarra 1995: Ripe, rich and elegant, an aristocratic wine with lovely plum, berry and sage flavors in equal proportions. Tannins are beautifully integrated. Supple enough to drink now, intense enough to cellar. Drink through 2010.–H.S. • $49 • (9/15/1999) • **90**
Cabernet Sauvignon Coonawarra 1994 • $40 • (8/31/1997) • **89**
Cabernet Sauvignon Coonawarra Phoenix 1996: Lean and crisp, with a peppery edge to the modest blackberry and currant flavors. A licorice note adds interest to the tight finish. Best after 2000.–H.S. • $25 • (10/15/1998) • **86**
Cabernet Sauvignon Coonawarra Phoenix 1995 • $23 • (8/31/1997) • **90**
Merlot Coonawarra 1996: The predominant flavors are mint, mint and more mint in this supple red, with plum and berry flavors lurking on the long finish. Drink now through 2003.–H.S. • $29 • (9/15/1999) • **85**
Shiraz Coonawarra Hyland 1997: Lean in structure, almost crisp, with plenty of juicy plum, prune and anise flavors that linger on the firm finish. Tannins need time to resolve. Best after 2002.–H.S. • $NA • (6/30/2000) • **88**
Shiraz-Cabernet South Australia 1995: Folds a nice whiff of Cabernet herb and cedar into the sweet spice and berry of Shiraz, finishing with a rare sense of austerity coupled with ripeness. A wine of some restraint, this needs cellaring. Drink through 2005.–H.S. • $29 • (8/31/1998) • **92**
Shiraz-Cabernet South Australia 1994 • $24 • (8/31/1997) • **91**

PEPPER TREE

Shiraz Hunter Valley-McLaren Vale Hunter Vineyards 1996 • $17 • (5/31/1998) • **86**

PERTARINGA

Cabernet Sauvignon McLaren Vale 1998: Ripe and generous. A lovely mouthful of currant, plum and spice flavors that hang nicely on a broad frame. Approachable now. Best after 2001.–H.S. • $30 • (3/31/2000) • **88**
Shiraz McLaren Vale 1998: Very ripe and generous. A lush, seductive, opulent mouthful of berry, plum and spice flavors that practically tumble over each other before harmonizing on the long finish. Drink now through 2010.–H.S. • $30 • (2/29/2000) • **92**

PETALUMA

Cabernet Sauvignon Coonawarra 1991 • $20 • (4/30/1995) • **88**
Cabernet Sauvignon Coonawarra 1984 • $18 • (5/31/1987) • **91**
Cabernet Sauvignon-Merlot Coonawarra 1995: Ripe, rich and supple, this is an elegant red with layers of black currant, blackberry, mint and sage. Finishes with a graceful balance of fine tannins and fruit. 200 cases imported. Drink through 2005.–H.S. • $30 • (8/31/1998) • **89**
Cabernet Sauvignon-Merlot Coonawarra 1988 • $21 • (12/15/1993) • **85**
Cabernet Sauvignon-Merlot Coonawarra 1986 • $25 • (5/31/1991) • **87**
Cabernet Sauvignon-Merlot Coonawarra 1984 • $18 • (5/31/1987) • **92**
Cabernet-Shiraz Coonawarra 1982 • $16 • (7/01/1987) • **89**
Chardonnay South Australia Piccadilly Valley 1997: Light and crisp, with a metallic edge to the apple, peach and Italian prune flavors, finishing with a bright touch of lemony acidity. Flavors linger enticingly. Drink through 2004.–H.S. • $30 • (2/28/1999) • **88**
Coonawarra Red 1996: Ripe and generous, with lovely, open-textured black currant, black pepper, green olive and spice flavors that linger on the supple finish. Harmonious already. A blend of Cabernet Sauvignon and Merlot. Drink through 2005.–H.S. • $30 • (2/28/1999) • **88**
Coonawarra Red 1994 • $21 • (5/31/1997) • **89**
Riesling South Australia 1998: Bright in flavor, with generous apple, floral and white pepper flavors that round out and linger on the finish. Feels fatter and less steely than usual. Drink now through 2002.–H.S. • $15 • (2/28/1999) • **87**

PETERSONS

Cabernet Sauvignon Mudgee 1998: The crisp style emphasizes the bright blackberry flavors, mineral notes and racy finish. It all balances nicely and bodes well for added depth developing in the cellar. Drink now through 2006.–H.S. • $19 • (3/31/2000) • **87**

Chardonnay Hunter Valley 1998: Broad in texture, ripe in flavor, with generous tropical fruit, pear, honey and spice flavors that come together smoothly on the finish. Drink now through 2002.–H.S. • $19 • (3/31/2000) • **88**

Merlot Mudgee 1998: Supple, generous and round, with pretty strawberry, raspberry and spice flavors that linger gently on the finish. Drink now through 2004.–H.S. • $19 • (3/31/2000) • **88**

Shiraz Hunter Valley 1998: On the light side, but with nice ripe black cherry flavors to go along with the Hunter Valley game and spice. Drink now through 2005.–H.S. • $19 • (3/31/2000) • **85**

PFEIFFER

Cabernet Sauvignon South Eastern Australia 1997: Light and lean for a Cabernet, but offering modest berry and herb flavors. Drink now.–H.S. • $25 • (2/29/2000) • **80**

Shiraz South Eastern Australia 1997: Light in texture, ripe in flavor, appealing all the way around, echoing blackberry and plum flavors on the herbal finish. Drink now.–H.S. • $25 • (3/31/2000) • **84**

PIBBIN

Pinot Noir Adelaide Hills 1995 • $14 • (10/31/1997) • **85**

PIERRO

Chardonnay Margaret River 1998: Unpleasant aromas, but the flavors are palatable, centering around earthy pear notes. Drink now.–J.L. • $44 • (5/31/2000) • **82**

PIKES

Cabernet Sauvignon Clare Valley 1995 • $16 • (5/31/1997) • **87**

Cabernet-Merlot Clare Valley 1998: Crisp in texture, with a strong minty note harmonizing with the modest blackberry and cherry. Finish has some intensity.–H.S. • $21 • (6/30/2000) • **83**

Riesling Clare Valley 1998: Dry and bordering on tart at first, with light apple and mineral aromas and flavors that linger on the gentle finish. Can age nicely. Drink now through 2007.–H.S. • $14 • (6/15/1999) • **88**

Riesling Clare Valley 1997 • $14 • (4/30/1998) • **88**

Sauvignon Blanc Clare Valley 1998: Lean and crisp, with a metallic edge to the pear and grape flavors, hinting at grapefruit on the racy finish. Drink now.–H.S. • $14 • (6/15/1999) • **86**

Shiraz Clare Valley 1998: Compact, with mint, blackberry, leather and pencil lead notes. Turns firm, with dry tannins. Best from 2001 through 2007.–J.L. • $22 • (6/30/2000) • **87**

Shiraz Clare Valley 1997: Crisp in texture and intense in flavor, with ripe berry, cherry and spice flavors that swirl through the chewy finish and keep echoing. A little raucous now, it should soften with cellaring. Best after 2000.–H.S. • $18 • (6/15/1999) • **90**

Shiraz Clare Valley 1995 • $17 • (5/31/1997) • **88**

Shiraz-Grenache-Mourvèdre Clare Valley 1998: Shows off lots of minty, spicy aromatics, then fills in the gaps with blackberry and black cherry, holding its focus. Drink now through 2007.–J.L. • $20 • (6/30/2000) • **88**

PIPERS BROOK

Chardonnay Tasmania 1997: Tart, slightly metallic flavors add an edge to the citrus and pear in this lean, racy wine. Not for all tastes, but try it with oysters. Drink now through 2002.–H.S. • $24 • (5/31/1999) • **85**

Chardonnay Tasmania Summit 1997: Tart and citrusy, with a heavy overlay of spicy oak. Flavors don't seem to mesh well yet, but it could come together with cellaring. Drink through 2008.–H.S. • $43 • (5/31/1999) • **85**

Gewürztraminer Tasmania 1998: Light and fragrant, this dry, pretty wine has modest rose petal accents to the peach and apple flavors. Drink now.–H.S. • $20 • (6/15/1999) • **85**

Opimian Tasmania Red 1997: Dark in color, light in texture, with crisp acidity and modest berry and herb flavors. Starts off better than it finishes. A blend of Cabernet Sauvignon, Cabernet Franc and Merlot. Drink now.–H.S. • $27 • (5/31/1999) • **80**

Pinot Gris Tasmania 1998: Typically crisp for a Tasmanian white, with bright apple and melon flavors on a rough-textured frame. Drink now.–H.S. • $18 • (6/15/1999) • **84**

Pinot Noir Tasmania 1990 • $25 • (2/29/1992) • **81**

Pinot Noir Tasmania Pellion 1998: Shows lots of ripe flavor on a crisp frame. A pretty mouthful of blackberry and black cherry, with hints of pepper and herb around the edges. Drink through 2005.–H.S. • $24 • (6/15/1999) • **87**

Riesling Tasmania 1998: Light and fragrant, with pretty apple pie and spice aromas and flavors, adding floral notes on the finish. Drink now through 2002.–H.S. • $20 • (6/15/1999) • **87**

PIRRAMIMMA

Petit Verdot McLaren Vale 1997: Unusually ripe, rich and supple, almost opulent with its overlay of spicy oak character around a core of generous cherry and currant. Distinctive; after all, how many varietal Petit Verdots are there in the world? Drink now through 2005.–H.S. • $19 • (12/31/1999) • **89**

Shiraz McLaren Vale 1997: Ripe, round and seductive, offering layers of gorgeous blackberry and plum and spicy, sweet oak flavors that swirl through the velvety finish. Impressive already. Best from 2002 through 2012.–H.S. • $19 • (12/31/1999) • **92**

PLANTAGENET

Chardonnay Mount Barker 1998: Nicely balanced to show off its apricot and pear flavors while reining everything in to remain lean and focused. Tasty already. Drink now through 2003.–H.S. • $21 • (11/15/1999) • **89**

Chardonnay Mount Barker 1997: Bright and minerally, with pretty apple and lime notes dancing through the crisp finish. Beautifully put together. Drink now through 2001.–H.S. • $22 • (10/31/1998) • **89**

Chardonnay Western Australia Omrah Unoaked 1999: Crisp and refreshing, with pure lime, green pippen apple and passion fruit flavors. Drink now.–J.L. • $14 • (6/30/2000) • **86**

Chardonnay Western Australia Omrah Unoaked 1998: Fresh and pure, like biting into a fresh green apple, with overtones of lime, pineapple and spice that come into full bloom on the finish. Very nicely done. Drink through 2002.–H.S. • $14 • (6/30/1999) HR • **88**

Chardonnay Western Australia Omrah Unoaked 1997: Bright and sharply focused, this jazzy mouthful of citrus, pear and mineral flavors remains juicy and vivid through the delicate finish. Nice now, but it should fill out with cellaring. Drink through 2005.–H.S. • $16 • (11/15/1998) • **91**

Merlot-Cabernet Franc Mount Barker Omrah 1996: On the light side, with more tobacco and mineral flavors than fruit. Pleasant. Drink now.–H.S. • $16 • (11/15/1998) • **83**

Shiraz Mount Barker 1997: Firm in texture, with earthy, gamy notes adding a touch of distinction to the basic cherry and anise flavors. Finishes with a sense of elegance, making it approachable now.–H.S. • $25 • (11/15/1999) • **89**

Shiraz Mount Barker 1996: Peppery, exotic flavors make this distinctive, with a gooey texture and tarry, pruny, cherrylike flavors persisting through the plush finish. Not for every taste, but it really glows with personality. Drink now through 2005.–H.S. • $25 • (11/15/1998) • **90**

Shiraz Western Australia Omrah 1998: Herb and pepper turn to blackberry and cedar notes. Firms up on the finish, where the tannins weigh in. Drink now through 2004.–J.L. • $17 • (6/30/2000) • **85**

Shiraz Western Australia Omrah 1997: Firm and chewy, with focused black cherry and mint flavors on the finish. Best after 2000.–H.S. • $17 • (2/28/1999) • **82**

PLUNKETT

Cabernet-Merlot Victoria Strathbogie Ranges 1997: Lean and lively, this jazzy red has a minty edge to the modest berry flavors. Drink now.–H.S. • $15 • (1/31/2000) • **84**

Chardonnay Victoria Strathbogie Ranges 1997: Light and refined, with pretty mint-scented apple and honey flavors melding nicely on the silky finish. Drink now through 2004.–H.S. • $15 • (12/31/1999) • **88**

Chardonnay Victoria Strathbogie Ranges Unwooded 1997: Bright in texture, but it tastes like it's been aged in leather pouches—earthy and a little bitter.–H.S. • $18 • (1/31/1999) • **74**

Pinot Noir Victoria Blackwood Ridge 1998: Light and lively, with a lime note sneaking in with the cherry and spice flavors on the finish. Drink now through 2003.–H.S. • $15 • (12/31/1999) • **84**

Shiraz Goulburn Valley Blackwood Ridge 1996: Fresh, appealing for its bright blackberry and raspberry flavors, swirling in hints of pepper and licorice on the finish. Drink now through 2002.–H.S. • $17 • (1/31/1999) • **87**

Shiraz Victoria Blackwood Ridge 1998: A light style of Shiraz that centers its plum, berry and black pepper flavors on a supple, open-textured frame. Immediately appealing. Drink now through 2004.–H.S. • $15 • (1/31/2000) • **87**

POOLE'S ROCK

Chardonnay Hunter Valley 1997: Light and juicy, with earthy flavors and nice hints of fig on a modest frame. Drink now.–H.S. • $25 • (6/15/1999) • **83**

PREECE

Cabernet Sauvignon Goulburn Valley 1990 • $14 • (11/30/1992) • **85**
Cabernet Sauvignon Goulburn Valley 1989 • $13 • (3/15/1992) • **84**
Cabernet Sauvignon South Eastern Australia 1994 • $15 • (10/15/1996) • **85**
Cabernet Sauvignon South Eastern Australia 1993 • $12 • (6/30/1995) • **82**
Cabernet Sauvignon South Eastern Australia 1992 • $12 • (4/30/1994) • **86**
Cabernet Sauvignon Victoria 1995 • $15 • (5/15/1997) • **83**
Merlot Victoria 1995 • $15 • (5/15/1997) • **86**
Merlot Victoria 1994 • $15 • (10/31/1996) • **85**
Sauvignon Blanc Victoria 1998: Light, fresh and appealing for its delicate, straightforward apple and passion fruit flavors. Drink now.–H.S. • $14 • (6/15/1999) • **85**
Shiraz Victoria 1997: This solid red is firm in texture, offering pretty plum and blueberry flavors and fine-grained tannins that promise a good future. Drink now through 2007.–H.S. • $14 • (6/15/1999) • **86**

PUNTERS CORNER

Shiraz Coonawarra 1997: Scents of sweet oak lead off in this cherry- and herb-flavored red. Light and a little awkward, turning firm and dry on the finish.–B.S. • $24 • (6/30/2000) • **78**

QUEEN ADELAIDE

Chardonnay South Eastern Australia 1999: Light and lively, refreshing for its pretty apple and floral aromas and flavors. Drink now.–H.S. • $8 • (9/30/1999) • **83**
Chardonnay South Eastern Australia 1998: Light and bright, with pretty green apple and spice flavors. Drink now.–H.S. • $8 • (3/31/1999) • **82**
Chardonnay South Eastern Australia 1997 • $7 • (5/15/1998) • **85**
Pinot Noir South Australia 1996 • $6 • (5/15/1997) • **82**
Sauvignon Blanc South Eastern Australia 1998: Soft and simple, with hints of earth and herb around the edges.–H.S. • $8 • (3/31/1999) • **79**
Shiraz-Cabernet South Eastern Australia 1995 • $6 • (10/31/1997) • **86**
Shiraz-Cabernet South Eastern Australia 1993 • $6 • (10/15/1995) • **83**
Shiraz-Cabernet South Eastern Australia 1992 • $6 • (6/30/1995) • **82**
Shiraz-Cabernet South Eastern Australia 1991 • $6 • (10/31/1993) • **80**
Spaetlese Lexia South Eastern Australia 1998: Light, sweet and aromatic, with honey, pear and floral flavors competing for attention, folding together harmoniously on the finish. Made from Muscat Gordo Blanco. Drink now through 2004.–H.S. • $8 • (3/31/1999) • **85**

REDBANK

Brut Australia Emily NV • $12 • (5/15/1996) • **85**
Cabernet Sauvignon South Eastern Australia Long Paddock 1986 • $13 • (1/31/1990) • **74**
Cabernet Sauvignon South Eastern Australia Redbank 1986 • $54 • (1/31/1990) • **89**
Cabernet Sauvignon Victoria Redbank 1991 • $37 • (10/15/1995) • **87**
Cabernet Sauvignon-Merlot King Valley Percydale 1998: Open-textured and generous with its currant and black cherry flavors, which linger expressively on the crisp finish. Drink now through 2005.–H.S. • $14 • (5/15/2000) • **86**
Chardonnay Victoria Long Paddock 1998: Light, lively and zingy, with spice, passion fruit and apple flavors lingering on the bright finish. Drink now through 2004.–H.S. • $10 • (12/31/1999) • **87**
Chardonnay Victoria Long Paddock 1997: What a find at this price and score. A lively white, crisp and juicy, with layers of vibrant apple, nectarine, passion fruit and floral flavors that last on the gentle finish. Wonderful now for its freshness. Drink now through 2001.–H.S. • $9 • (2/28/1999) SS • **90**
Sally's Paddock South Eastern Australia Red 1986 • $32 • (1/31/1990) • **86**
Sally's Paddock Victoria Red 1997: Strives for elegance and achieves a sense of refinement, allowing blackberry, toast and herbal flavors to come smoothly through the fine-grained tannins on the finish. Best from 2001 through 2009.–H.S. • $36 • (12/31/1999) • **88**
Sally's Paddock Victoria Red 1993 • $57 • (4/30/1996) • **85**
Shiraz King Valley Fighting Flat 1998: Minty and sleek, with an open-knit texture and a firm structure. Closes up on the finish. Drink now through 2002.–B.S. • $14 • (6/30/2000) • **84**
Shiraz South Eastern Australia Long Paddock 1996 • $12 • (6/30/1997) • **83**
Shiraz South Eastern Australia Long Paddock 1991 • $9 • (11/30/1993) • **82**
Shiraz Victoria Long Paddock 1997: Looking for a pleasurable red that won't break your budget? This Australian Shiraz is supple and generous, its tightly packed black cherry and spice flavors lingering on the velvety finish. Drink now through 2001.–H.S. • $9 • (2/28/1999) • **88**
Shiraz-Cabernet Victoria Long Paddock 1998: Lean, almost austere, but with pretty anise and blackberry flavors riding along the streamlined frame. Best after 2000.–H.S. • $12 • (12/31/1999) • **87**

REYNOLDS

Cabernet Sauvignon Hunter Valley Orange 1997: Firm and chewy, showing some pretty black cherry and herbal flavors on a lean frame. Drink now.–H.S. • $24 • (2/28/1999) • **83**
Cabernet Sauvignon Hunter Valley Orange 1996: Dark, supple and decidedly minty, this is a rich-textured Cabernet with herbal berry flavors that shows more up front than on the finish. The texture is the nicest thing. Drink now through 2002.–H.S. • $24 • (2/28/1999) • **85**
Cabernet Sauvignon Hunter Valley Orange District 1995 • $24 • (6/15/1998) • **83**
Cabernet Sauvignon Hunter Valley Orange District 1994 • $23 • (5/15/1997) • **83**
Cabernet-Merlot Hunter Valley Orange District Yarraman 1995 • $16 • (5/15/1997) • **86**
Cabernet-Merlot Orange & Hunter Districts 1996 • $16 • (6/15/1998) • **85**
Chardonnay Hunter Valley Orange 1997: Soft and generous, open-textured and fresh, with pear and resiny flavors echoing on the finish. Drink now through 2001.–H.S. • $22 • (2/28/1999) • **88**
Chardonnay Hunter Valley Yarraman 1997: Dark gold in color, satiny in texture, with pretty pear and tropical fruit flavors and an overlay of spice and toast. Drink now through 2001.–H.S. • $15 • (2/28/1999) • **87**
Merlot-Cabernet Orange-Hunter Districts Yarraman 1997: Crisp and firm in texture, with focused black currant and tar flavors that linger on the finish. Best after 2000.–H.S. • $16 • (2/28/1999) • **85**
Sémillon Hunter Valley Yarraman 1997: Fresh and open-textured, with aromas and flavors reminiscent of pear, hay and fig. Needs time to come together. Best after 2001.–H.S. • $14 • (2/28/1999) • **85**
Shiraz Hunter Valley Yarraman 1997: Crisp and lively, with pretty flavors of peppery raspberry and strawberry that linger on the gentle finish. A light style for Hunter Valley, and very appealing. Drink now through 2002.–H.S. • $16 • (2/28/1999) • **87**
Shiraz Hunter Valley Yarraman 1995 • $16 • (5/15/1997) • **89**

RICHLAND

Shiraz Riverina Westend 1997: Open in texture, with pretty, ripe black cherry and currant flavors on a round finish. Drink now through 2003.–H.S. • $11 • (6/15/1999) • **84**

RIDDOCH

Shiraz Coonawarra 1996: Firm, mildly chewy, and packed with crisp blackberry, tar and spice flavors that linger on the finish. Tannins need cellar time. Drink through 2005.–H.S. • $18 • (2/28/1999) • **87**
Shiraz Coonawarra 1995 • $18 • (4/30/1998) • **86**

ROBERTSON'S WELL

Cabernet Sauvignon Coonawarra 1995 • $16 • (6/15/1998) • **87**
Cabernet Sauvignon Coonawarra 1994 • $15 • (6/15/1997) • **83**
Cabernet Sauvignon Coonawarra 1994 • $15 • (12/31/1997) • **80**

ROBSON, MURRAY

Chardonnay Hunter Valley 1997 • $24 • (5/15/1998) • **88**
Gewürztraminer Hunter Valley 1997 • $22 • (5/31/1998) • **85**
Sémillon Hunter Valley 1997 • $22 • (5/31/1998) • **86**

Key: SS—Spectator Selection. CS—Cellar Selection. HR—Highly Recommended. $NA—Price not available. (BT)—Barrel tasting. Ⓐ—Auction Price.
For a key to the tasters' initials, see "How to Use These Listings."
Dates in parentheses represent the issues in which the ratings were published.

ROLF, CHRISTA

Shiraz-Grenache Barossa Valley 1998: On the rustic side, this gregarious red hangs its sweet plum, fruitcake and spice flavors on a loosely knit and broad-shouldered frame. Drink now.–B.S. • $25 • (6/30/2000) • **86**

ROSEMOUNT

Cabernet Sauvignon Coonawarra Kirri Billi Vineyard 1986 • $20 • (10/31/1990) • **88**

Cabernet Sauvignon Coonawarra Reserve 1994 • $19 • (10/31/1997) • **88**

Cabernet Sauvignon Coonawarra Show Reserve 1996: Ripe, generous and supple, with pretty plum and currant flavors that persist beautifully on the finish. A bit rough around the edges, which cellaring should soften. Drink now through 2006.–H.S. • $22 • (6/15/1999) • **91**

Cabernet Sauvignon Coonawarra Show Reserve 1994: Firm and chewy, with a rich, vibrant core of vanilla- and spice-scented currant and blackberry flavors. Tannins are present but well integrated, letting the flavors emerge and echo through the finish. A sophisticated, elegant wine that needs cellaring. Best from 2004 through 2009.–H.S. • $17 • (5/15/1999) • **90**

Cabernet Sauvignon Coonawarra Show Reserve 1993 • $17 • (3/31/1996) • **88**

Cabernet Sauvignon Coonawarra Show Reserve 1992 • $17 • (11/30/1995) HR • **93**

Cabernet Sauvignon Coonawarra Show Reserve 1991: Ripe and generous, with a rich core of black cherry and currant under a few layers of firm, slightly hard-edged tannins. High acidity keeps it a youthful wine even at 8 years of age. Best after 2005.–H.S. • $17 • (5/15/1999) • **88**

Cabernet Sauvignon Coonawarra Show Reserve 1990: Minty, earthy notes predominate, a sort of pickle barrel-flavor at the forefront of otherwise pleasant black cherry and cola flavors. Still chewy on the finish. Best after 2003.–H.S. • $16 • (5/15/1999) • **82**

Cabernet Sauvignon Coonawarra Show Reserve 1988: Firm, still quite tannic, with a chewy layer over a still-fresh core of berry and herb flavor. Narrows quite a bit on the finish. Drink now through 2002.–H.S. • $15 • (5/15/1999) • **84**

Cabernet Sauvignon Coonawarra Show Reserve 1987 • $15 • (2/28/1991) • **88**

Cabernet Sauvignon Coonawarra Show Reserve 1986: A lithe, supple mouthful of Cabernet, still showing plenty of youthful currant and blackberry, vibrant and generous without being heavy. Harmonious, with gentle tannins and elegant, persistent flavors echoing on the long finish. Drink now through 2010.–H.S. • $15 • (5/15/1999) • **91**

Cabernet Sauvignon Coonawarra Show Reserve 1985: A lighter-style Cabernet, with pretty black cherry and minty-herb flavors, well-integrated tannins and a nice hint of chocolaty richness on the finish. Drink now. –H.S. • $15 • (5/15/1999) • **88**

Cabernet Sauvignon Coonawarra Show Reserve 1984 • $14 • (2/28/1987) • **86**

Cabernet Sauvignon Coonawarra Show Reserve 1982: A mature Cabernet with high-toned spice, mint, black cherry and cedar flavors, long and velvety. Not a big wine, but focused, intense and very fine. Right there. Drink now.–H.S. • $15 • (5/15/1999) • **90**

Cabernet Sauvignon Hunter Valley 1989 • $10 • (9/30/1991) • **82**

Cabernet Sauvignon Hunter Valley 1988 • $10 • (1/31/1990) • **76**

Cabernet Sauvignon Hunter Valley 1987 • $10 • (7/31/1989) • **83**

Cabernet Sauvignon Hunter Valley 1986 • $11 • (1/31/1989) SS • **93**

Cabernet Sauvignon Orange 1998: Tart, tough and raw; youthful and not pleasing because of its high acidity and hard-edged tannins.–H.S. • $NA • (5/15/1999) (BT) • **975**

Cabernet Sauvignon Orange 1997: Crisp and jazzy, with lively flavors of fresh berry and green herb. Best after 2004.–H.S. • $NA • (5/15/1999) • **83**

Cabernet Sauvignon Orange 1996: Fresh and appealing for its currant and plum flavors on a gentle frame, with modest tannins and high but well-modulated acidity.—Rosemount vertical. Best after 2002.–H.S. • $NA • (5/15/1999) • **86**

Cabernet Sauvignon Orange 1995: Bright and crisp, this jazzy red shows fresh currant and overtones of mint. Appealing for its zest, but how will it age? Best after 2003.–H.S. • $NA • (5/15/1999) • **81**

Cabernet Sauvignon South Eastern Australia 1999: Good concentration, with rich chocolate, dried berry and blackberry notes and firm tannins. Drink now through 2005.–B.S. • $11 • (6/30/2000) • **84**

Cabernet Sauvignon South Eastern Australia 1998: Firm, ripe and generous, a chewy mouthful of blackberry, currant, tar and peppery flavors that linger attractively on the round finish. Drink now through 2003.–H.S. • $11 • (9/15/1999) • **86**

Cabernet Sauvignon South Eastern Australia 1997: Firm in texture but appealing, with ripe currant and blueberry flavors that echo on the ripe finish. Drink now through 2002.–H.S. • $11 • (12/15/1998) • **88**

Cabernet Sauvignon South Eastern Australia 1996 • $11 • (4/30/1998) • **87**

Cabernet Sauvignon South Australia 1995 • $11 • (2/28/1997) • **85**

Cabernet Sauvignon South Australia 1994 • $10 • (10/15/1995) • **84**

Cabernet Sauvignon South Australia 1993 • $10 • (4/30/1995) • **85**

Cabernet Sauvignon South Eastern Australia 1992 • $10 • (7/31/1994) • **83**

Cabernet Sauvignon South Eastern Australia 1991 • $10 • (3/31/1993) • **86**

Cabernet-Merlot South Eastern Australia 1999: Simple, with tangy cranberry flavors and herbal edges. Drink now.–B.S. • $8 • (6/30/2000) • **81**

Cabernet-Merlot-Petit Verdot McLaren Vale Traditional 1997: Dark, ripe and complex, this red blend reveals its depth with layers of ripe plum, blackberry, coffee and earth. Finishes with a wide range of tasty herb flavors and rich, full tannins. Drink now through 2008.–J.L. • $20 • (5/31/2000) HR • **92**

Cabernet-Merlot-Petit Verdot McLaren Vale Traditional 1996: Ripe, round and generous, this beautifully focused mouthful of plum, berry and floral flavors lasts and lasts on the firm-textured finish. Has style and grace, plus intensity. Drink now.–H.S. • $20 • (2/28/1999) • **91**

Cabernet-Merlot-Petit Verdot McLaren Vale Traditional 1995: Firm in texture, with chewy tannins and a layer of juicy berry and herb flavors sneaking through on the finish. Best from 2001 through 2006.–H.S. • $20 • (8/31/1998) • **86**

Chardonnay Hunter Valley Giants Creek 1997: Has the best integration of all the wines tasted here, burying its mouthwatering acidity in layers of soft, supple, spicy flavors. Fig, tobacco and dried apricot notes prevail.—Rosemount vertical. Drink now through 2002 .–H.S. • $15 • (5/15/1999) • **89**

Chardonnay Hunter Valley Roxburgh 1997: Soft and round, with a sense of elegance; a lush mouthful of pineapple, pear, lanolin and earthy notes that linger impressively on the finish. Drink now through 2003.–H.S. • $30 • (6/30/2000) • **88**

Chardonnay Hunter Valley Show Reserve 1998: Bright and distinctive for its spicy elements surrounding a juicy core of pear and nutmeg flavors that remain focused through the round finish. Drink now through 2004.–H.S. • $18 • (2/29/2000) • **89**

Chardonnay Hunter Valley Show Reserve 1997: Fresh and crisp in texture, with pretty apple, passion fruit and mineral flavors on a racy frame. Very Chablis-like; it can stand short-term cellaring. Drink through 2003.–H.S. • $17 • (2/28/1999) • **89**

Chardonnay Hunter Valley Show Reserve 1997: Youthful and exuberant, with appealing pear, fig, floral and honey flavors on a smooth, balanced frame.—Rosemount vertical. Drink now through 2002.–H.S. • $17 • (5/15/1999) • **88**

Chardonnay Orange 1997: Fresh and vigorous, delivering a lively medley of passion fruit, pear and honey flavors, with hints of chestnut on the finish. Drink now.–H.S. • $22 • (5/15/1999) • **88**

Chardonnay South Eastern Australia 1998: Refreshing and lively for its juicy green apple and spice aromas and flavors that linger impressively. Drink now.–H.S. • $10 • (6/15/1999) • **87**

Chardonnay South Eastern Australia 1997 • $10 • (5/15/1998) • **85**

Dry Red Diamond Reserve Hunter Valley 1988 • $7 • (2/28/1990) • **83**

Grenache-Shiraz South Eastern Australia 1999: Fruity, with lots of ripe raspberry flavors and toasty vanilla notes. Focused and tasty, with a lingering finish. Drink now through 2002.–J.L. • $8 • (6/30/2000) • **85**

Grenache-Shiraz South Eastern Australia 1998: Yet another good value from this Down Under winery, this red blend is attractive for its pretty flavors on a supple frame, with juicy black cherry and cinnamon pouring out to make it feel light and seductive. Drink now.–H.S. • $8 • (6/15/1999) • **86**

Grenache-Shiraz South Eastern Australia 1997 • $8 • (5/15/1998) • **84**

Grenache-Shiraz South Eastern Australia 1996 • $8 • (5/15/1997) • **86**

Grenache-Syrah-Mourvèdre McLaren Vale GSM 1997: Rich and distinctive, a bit lighter than most straight Aussie Shirazes but dripping with flavors, corralling a wild range of meaty blackberry, red cherry, black cherry and pepper flavors into a smooth wine of enormous character and depth. Appealing already. Best after 2002.–H.S. • $22 • (1/31/2000) HR • **94**

Grenache-Syrah-Mourvèdre McLaren Vale GSM 1996: Dark and dense, with licorice-scented raspberry jam and cherry flavors swirling around a supple, almost gooey texture. A warm, generous wine with layers of flavor. Drink now through 2005.–H.S. • $18 • (2/28/1999) • **91**

Grenache-Syrah-Mourvèdre McLaren Vale GSM 1995: Lithe and agile, offering juicy berry, plum and spice flavors on a modest frame. Fine-grained tannins need time to subside. Best after 2001.–H.S. • $16 • (5/15/1999) • **87**

Grenache-Syrah-Mourvèdre McLaren Vale GSM 1994: Dense but not heavy, more concentrated in flavor than in aroma, offering delicious raspberry, blackberry and peppery flavors on a racy frame. Delicious stuff, just needs a little more lift on the finish. Drink now through 2003.–H.S. • $15 • (5/15/1999) • **89**

Merlot South Eastern Australia 1998: Currant, oregano and cedar flavors finish with dryness. Drink now.–B.S. • $12 • (6/30/2000) • **80**

ROSEMOUNT

Merlot South Eastern Australia 1992 • $11 • (12/15/1993) • **82**
Pinot Noir Hunter Valley 1989 • $10 • (9/30/1991) • **81**
Pinot Noir Hunter Valley 1985 • $10 • (4/30/1987) • **84**
Pinot Noir Hunter Valley Giants Creek 1987: Earthy, gamy notes have the upper hand on the modest berry flavors in this firmly tannic wine. Lacks a pretty texture.–H.S. • $NA • (5/15/1999) • **75**
Pinot Noir Hunter Valley Show Reserve 1986: Firm tannins persist and acidity intrudes on the delicate cherry and earth flavors. –H.S. • $NA • (5/15/1999) • **75**
Pinot Noir Hunter Valley Show Reserve 1985: Light and silky, with mature woodsy, brown sugar and black cherry flavors in modest proportions. Has a nice sense of sweetness on the finish. Drink now.–H.S. • $NA • (5/15/1999) • **82**
Pinot Noir Hunter Valley Show Reserve 1983: Gamy, medicinal, old-wine flavors, with some black cherry coming through on the finish.–H.S. • $NA • (5/15/1999) • **77**
Pinot Noir Hunter Valley Show Reserve 1982: Earthy, gamy character predominates, with a brown sugar note in the background to make it palatable.–H.S. • $NA • (5/15/1999) • **73**
Pinot Noir South Eastern Australia 1998: Ripe cherry, orange peel and spice flavors are straightforward, appealing and juicy. Drink now.–J.L. • $10 • (6/30/2000) • **84**
Pinot Noir South Eastern Australia 1997: Light and supple, with pretty black cherry and raspberry flavors shaded by hints of tobacco and cocoa. More complete and appealing than many Aussie Pinots. 8,800 cases imported.–H.S. • $10 • (1/31/1999) • **84**
Sauvignon Blanc South Eastern Australia 1999: Appealing, with juicy lemon and spice notes. Tasty and focused. Drink now.–B.S. • $9 • (6/30/2000) • **84**
Sauvignon Blanc South Eastern Australia 1997 • $10 • (6/30/1998) • **84**
Sémillon South Eastern Australia 1997: Fresh and focused, appealing for its clearly articulated melon and apple, picking up scents of tobacco on the zippy finish. Drink now through 2001.–H.S. • $9 • (8/31/1998) • **87**
Sémillon-Chardonnay South Eastern Australia 1998: Ripe, open-textured and aromatic, with minty-herbal notes around a core of pear and pineapple. Refreshing. 85,000 cases imported. Drink now.–H.S. • $8 • (12/15/1998) • **85**
Sémillon-Chardonnay South Eastern Australia 1997 • $8 • (4/30/1998) • **84**
Shiraz Hunter Valley 1989 • $8 • (2/15/1991) SS • **91**
Shiraz Hunter Valley 1988 • $8 • (1/31/1990) SS • **90**
Shiraz McLaren Vale Show Reserve 1996: Firm and ripe, packed with blackberry, plum and mineral flavors that linger impressively on the fine-textured finish. Best after 2000.–H.S. • $23 • (9/15/1999) • **91**
Shiraz South Australia 1995 • $10 • (11/30/1996) SS • **90**
Shiraz South Australia 1994 • $10 • (10/31/1995) SS • **90**
Shiraz South Australia 1993 • $10 • (1/31/1995) • **83**
Shiraz South Eastern Australia 1999: A nice mouthful of berry and plum here, but it thins out some on the finish and the tannins feel a bit coarse. Drink with hearty food. Drink now through 2005.–H.S. • $12 • (6/30/2000) • **87**
Shiraz South Eastern Australia 1998: Count on Rosemount for a winning combinations of quality, value and availability. This Shiraz is polished and silky, featuring sweet blackberry and anise flavors, with a slight bite of pepper on the light finish. Not as big and rich as previous vintages, but seductive nonetheless. Drink now.–H.S. • $11 • (6/15/1999) • **89**
Shiraz South Eastern Australia 1997: Delicious stuff, smooth and appealing for its generous prune, cherry and spice flavors that linger nicely on the easygoing finish. Drink now.–H.S. • $11 • (8/31/1998) • **89**
Shiraz South Eastern Australia 1996 • $12 • (11/30/1997) SS • **91**
Shiraz South Eastern Australia 1992 • $10 • (1/31/1994) SS • **89**
Shiraz South Eastern Australia 1991 • $10 • (4/15/1993) HR • **89**
Shiraz South Eastern Australia 1990 • $9 • (2/15/1992) SS • **92**
Shiraz-Cabernet Mudgee Mountain Blue 1996: Bright, crisp and delicious for its focused berry, currant and herb flavors. Echoes sage and dusky spice on the racy finish. Drink now through 2006.–H.S. • $30 • (6/30/1999) • **88**
Shiraz-Cabernet Mudgee Mountain Blue 1995: Crisp in texture, with chocolate-scented red berry and red plum flavors swirling through the lithe finish. Earthy touches add a little extra to the finish. Drink now through 2001 .–H.S. • $30 • (5/15/1999) • **88**
Shiraz-Cabernet Mudgee Mountain Blue 1994: Bright and appealing for its blueberry and plum flavors on a crisp, elegant frame. Flavors persist impressively on the racy finish. Has a distinctive style and a graceful feel. Drink now through 2001 .–H.S. • $25 • (5/15/1999) • **90**
Shiraz-Cabernet South Eastern Australia 1998: A lively, jazzy mouthful of ripe cherry, plum, floral and spice flavors that nicely echo on the finish. 150,000 cases imported.–H.S. • $9 • (12/15/1998) • **86**
Shiraz-Cabernet South Eastern Australia 1997 • $9 • (2/28/1998) • **86**
Shiraz-Cabernet South Eastern Australia 1996 • $8 • (1/31/1997) • **85**
Shiraz-Cabernet South Eastern Australia 1995 • $10 • (6/15/1996) • **86**
Shiraz-Cabernet South Eastern Australia 1993 • $8 • (6/30/1994) • **85**
Shiraz-Cabernet South Eastern Australia 1992 • $8 • (10/31/1993) • **86**
Shiraz-Cabernet South Eastern Australia 1991 • $7 • (11/30/1992) • **67**
Shiraz-Cabernet South Eastern Australia 1990 • $7 • (7/15/1991) • **84**
Shiraz-Cabernet South Eastern Australia 1989 • $6 • (7/31/1990) • **81**
Syrah McLaren Vale Balmoral 1996: Ripe, round and remarkably generous, this smooth-textured, gleaming red spins out blueberry, blackberry, plum, tobacco and anise flavors that last and last on the pretty finish. One of the more supple examples of Balmoral. Drink now through 2010.–H.S. • $40 • (6/30/1999) HR • **92**
Syrah McLaren Vale Balmoral 1995: Dense in flavor, crisp in structure, with beautifully proportioned blueberry, plum and pepper aromas and flavors. Acidity is a bit livelier than in earlier vintages, but this should be a "wow" wine for years to come. Drink now through 2004.–H.S. • $40 • (5/15/1999) • **90**
Syrah McLaren Vale Balmoral 1994: Ripe, powerful and aristocratic, packing tremendous berry, pepper and cream flavors onto a remarkably elegant structure. Youthful and vibrant, it glows and echoes with flavor and yet feels restrained. Cellar it some more, if you can keep your hands off. Best after 2004.–H.S. • $35 • (5/15/1999) • **93**
Syrah McLaren Vale Balmoral 1993: An elegantly proportioned wine, with velvety texture and warm plum and spice flavors on the finish. Feels ripe and more mature than the '91 or '92. Almost ready. Best from 2000 through 2004.–H.S. • $30 • (5/15/1999) • **88**
Syrah McLaren Vale Balmoral 1992: Smooth, amazingly deep and fragrant, with dark-hued plum, smoke and anise flavors that remain harmonious through the chewy finish. Has an earthy, sexy edge. Drink now through 2005 .–H.S. • $25 • (5/15/1999) • **91**
Syrah McLaren Vale Balmoral 1991: Classically proportioned, this is an elegant, aromatic, rich-textured Shiraz, with dense berry, anise and slightly gamy flavors. Tannins are showing a bit, but it feels like it can go for miles. Drink now through 2006 .–H.S. • $25 • (5/15/1999) • **90**
Syrah McLaren Vale Show Reserve 1991 • $19 • (1/31/1994) SS • **90**
Syrah McLaren Vale Show Reserve 1990 • $16 • (4/15/1993) HR • **92**
Syrah McLaren Vale Show Reserve 1989 • $15 • (2/29/1992) • **89**
Tawny Port South Eastern Australia Solera Aged Old Benson Fine Old Tawny NV: Dark, sweet and exotic—a sexy wine dripping with toffee, incense, Brazil nut, rose petal, caramel and coffee flavors that swirl around the core of black cherry. A fully rounded wine that lingers long after each sip. Extraordinary dessert wine. Drink now.–H.S. • $25/500 ml. • (2/28/1999) • **97**
Traminer-Riesling South Eastern Australia 1998: Distinctly spicy and lightly sweet, this easy-sipping white boasts pretty litchi, honeydew melon and green apple character in abundance, and its modest asking price facilitates giving it a try. Drink now.–H.S. • $8 • (2/28/1999) • **86**
Traminer-Riesling South Eastern Australia 1997 • $8 • (2/28/1998) • **84**

ROSEWOOD

Muscat Australia Liqueur NV • $50 • (7/01/1987) • **91**
Muscat Rutherglen Old Liqueur NV • $40 • (7/01/1987) • **90**
Muscat Rutherglen Special Liqueur NV • $30 • (7/01/1987) • **91**

ROTHBURY

Cabernet Sauvignon South Eastern Australia 1994 • $9 • (6/15/1996) • **84**
Hermitage Hunter Valley 1984 • $10 • (7/01/1987) • **90**
Hermitage Hunter Valley 1983 • $15 • (7/01/1987) • **90**
Pinot Noir Hunter Valley 1983 • $10 • (7/01/1987) • **87**
Pinot Noir Hunter Valley Director's Reserve 1983 • $15 • (7/01/1987) • **89**
Sémillon-Chardonnay Hunter Valley NV • $9 • (5/31/1987) • **87**
Shiraz Hunter Valley Herlstone Vineyard 1986 • $11 • (7/31/1989) • **76**
Shiraz Hunter Valley Herlstone Vineyard 1985 • $11 • (3/31/1989) • **78**
Shiraz Hunter Valley Reserve Bottling 1993 • $20 • (6/30/1996) • **88**
Shiraz South Eastern Australia 1994 • $8 • (5/15/1997) • **87**
Shiraz South Eastern Australia 1993 • $8 • (5/31/1996) • **85**
Shiraz South Eastern Australia 1992 • $9 • (11/30/1994) • **85**
Syrah Hunter Valley 1989 • $12 • (5/31/1993) • **78**

Key: SS—Spectator Selection. CS—Cellar Selection. HR—Highly Recommended. $NA—Price not available. (BT)—Barrel tasting. Ⓐ—Auction Price. For a key to the tasters' initials, see "How to Use These Listings."
Dates in parentheses represent the issues in which the ratings were published.

ROVALLEY RIDGE

Cabernet-Shiraz Barossa Valley Limited Release 1991 • $NA • (6/30/1996) • **85**
Cabernet-Shiraz Eden Valley Show Reserve 1992 • $NA • (1/01/1996) • **92**
Cabernets Barossa Valley 1992 • $NA • (6/30/1996) • **85**
Shiraz Barossa Valley Old Vine Show Reserve 1992 • $NA • (6/30/1996) • **85**
Shiraz Barossa Valley Old Vine Show Reserve 1991 • $18 • (5/15/1995) HR • **92**
Shiraz-Cabernet Eden Valley Show Reserve 1991 • $18 • (6/30/1995) • **82**

RUMBALL, PETER

Shiraz South Eastern Australia Sparkling Special Cuvée SB9 NV • $23 • (3/31/1998) • **89**
Sparkling Shiraz Australia Special Cuvee SB12 NV: A bit cloying, with meaty and spicy overtones. Drink now.–B.S. • $27 • (6/30/2000) • **81**

RYMILL

Cabernet Sauvignon Coonawarra 1996: Firm in texture, with focused black cherry and herb flavors poking through the chewy tannins on the finish and lingering nicely. Best after 2001.–H.S. • $18 • (11/15/1999) • **88**
Cabernet Sauvignon Coonawarra 1995 • $16 • (6/15/1998) • **87**
Merlot-Cabernets Coonawarra 1996: Smooth and silky under a layer of firm tannins, with mint, blackberry and currant flavors lingering on the gentle finish. Drink now through 2005.–H.S. • $13 • (11/15/1999) • **86**
Merlot-Cabernets Coonawarra 1995 • $15 • (6/15/1998) • **80**
Merlot-Cabernets Coonawarra 1994 • $15 • (2/28/1998) • **88**
Shiraz Coonawarra 1996: A strong earth-tobacco component runs through the crisp berry and spice flavors, making it distinctive if not immediately appealing to everyone. Best after 2000.–H.S. • $17 • (11/15/1999) • **87**
Shiraz Coonawarra 1995 • $16 • (6/15/1998) • **88**

SADDLER'S CREEK

Cabernet Sauvignon Australia Bluegrass 1995 • $19 • (11/15/1996) • **88**
Shiraz Australia Marrowbone 1994 • $19 • (11/15/1996) • **87**

ST. HALLETT

Gamekeeper's Reserve Red Barossa 1999: Light and appealing for its pretty berry and spice flavors, finishing with a layer of firm tannins that need time to soften. Best after 2001.–H.S. • $10 • (6/30/2000) • **85**
Gamekeeper's Reserve Red Barossa 1998: Ripe and chewy, packed with raspberry, cooked strawberry, exotic spice and herb flavors that swirl beautifully on
the velvet-lined frame and linger nicely on the finish. Grenache, Touriga, Mourvèdre and Shiraz. Drink now through 2008.–H.S. • $10 • (2/29/2000) • **89**
Gamekeeper's Reserve Red Barossa 1997 • $10 • (6/15/1998) • **88**
Gamekeeper's Reserve Red Barossa 1996 • $10 • (7/31/1997) • **85**
Gamekeeper's Reserve Red Barossa 1994 • $10 • (3/31/1996) • **86**
Poacher's Blend Barossa White 1999: Apple, citrus and spice flavors are clean and refreshing. Drink now.–B.S. • $10 • (6/30/2000) • **84**
Poacher's Blend Barossa White 1997 • $10 • (6/15/1998) • **86**
Shiraz Barossa Blackwell 1996: Light and fragrant, with firm tannins supporting bright berry, plum and vanilla flavors that linger gently on the supple finish. Best with food. Drink now through 2006.–H.S. • $24 • (6/30/2000) • **89**
Shiraz Barossa Faith 1997: Smooth and silky, distinctive for its wild plum and herbal flavors, if a bit short on intensity. Needs no cellaring. Tasted twice, with consistent notes. Drink now.–H.S. • $18 • (6/30/2000) • **86**
Shiraz Barossa Faith 1996 • $33 • (6/15/1998) • **90**
Shiraz Barossa Faith 1995 • $17 • (5/31/1997) • **88**
Shiraz Barossa Faith 1994 • $18 • (4/30/1997) • **88**
Shiraz Barossa Old Block 1995: Ripe and generous, a mouthfilling red with lovely blackberry, anise and smoky tea-leaf aromas and flavors that last impressively. Tannins are well integrated. Best from 2002 through 2010.–H.S. • $40 • (6/30/2000) • **91**
Shiraz Barossa Old Block 1994 • $33 • (6/15/1998) • **91**
Shiraz Barossa Old Block 1993 • $27 • (11/30/1996) HR • **93**
Shiraz Barossa Old Block 1992 • $23 • (3/31/1996) CS • **92**

SALISBURY

Cabernet Sauvignon Victoria 1996 • $8 • (5/31/1998) • **84**
Cabernet Sauvignon Victoria 1995 • $8 • (6/15/1997) • **83**

Chardonnay Victoria 1998: The price is right, the character fresh and appealing in this Down Under Chardonnay, its apricot-scented pear and spice flavors nicely wrapped in a lively package. It has the balance to drink now or can age a few years. Best through 2004.–H.S. • $8 • (11/15/1999) • **87**
Chardonnay Victoria 1997 • $8 • (5/31/1998) • **86**
Sauvignon Blanc Victoria 1997 • $8 • (5/31/1998) • **86**
Shiraz South Eastern Australia 1998: Open-textured and refreshing for its straightforward berry and currant flavors, which persist on the finish. Drink now through 2003.–H.S. • $8 • (11/15/1999) • **86**

SALITAGE

Chardonnay Pemberton Unwooded 1997: Fresh and silky, with lovely apple, apricot and mineral flavors that echo enticingly on the firm finish. Drink now through 2001.–H.S. • $23 • (10/15/1998) • **88**
Pinot Noir Pemberton 1995 • $35 • (7/31/1997) • **80**
Red Pemberton 1996: A round, plummy wine, distinctive for the blueberry and tomato notes adding extra aspects to its cedary, firm-textured profile. Drink now.–H.S. • $40 • (10/15/1998) • **90**
Red Pemberton 1995 • $40 • (7/31/1997) • **88**

SANDALFORD

Cabernet Sauvignon Mount Barker-Margaret River 1997: Lovely green olive, cedar and tobacco aromas take on a black currant note on the palate. Lean yet focused and harmonious, with a lingering finish. Drink now through 2002.–B.S. • $22 • (6/30/2000) • **86**
Cabernet Sauvignon Mount Barker Margaret River 1996: Firm in texture, with focused blackberry and red pepper aromas and flavors, a hint of vinegar on the earthy finish. Drink now.–H.S. • $20 • (2/28/1999) • **84**
Cabernet Sauvignon Mount Barker-Margaret River 1994 • $18 • (5/31/1997) • **88**
Chardonnay Mount Barker-Margaret River 1997: Bright in flavor and polished in texture, with pretty citrus, nectarine and pineapple flavors lingering on the generous finish. Drink now through 2003.–H.S. • $17 • (11/15/1999) • **87**
Shiraz Australia 1995 • $18 • (12/31/1997) • **85**
Shiraz Mount Barker-Margaret River 1996: Crisp in texture, dripping with flavor, with herbal and licorice overtones to the dark, slightly jammy blackberry character. Drink now.–H.S. • $20 • (2/28/1999) • **84**
Shiraz Mount Barker-Margaret River 1997: Ripe and generous, with a strong minty component to the berry and toast flavors. Drink now through 2007.–H.S. • $22 • (11/15/1999) • **86**
Shiraz Mount Barker-Margaret River 1995 • $18 • (6/30/1997) • **85**

SCOTHMANS HILL

Chardonnay Geelong Bellarine Peninsula 1997: This ripe, gooey style of Chardonnay features delicious honey-laced baked apple and spice flavors that harmonize nicely on the long finish, with a layer of crisp acidity. Drink now through 2005.–H.S. • $24 • (6/15/1999) • **90**
Pinot Noir Geelong 1996 • $24 • (4/30/1998) • **83**
Pinot Noir Geelong 1995 • $NA • (1/01/1997) • **85**
Pinot Noir Geelong 1994 • $20 • (12/15/1995) • **87**

SEABROOK & SEABROOK

Merlot McLaren Vale 1997: Smooth and flavorful, with medium-weight blackberry and toasty flavors on a modest frame. Drink now.–H.S. • $23 • (1/31/1999) • **83**

SEAVIEW

Brut South Eastern Australia 1997: Don't let the oh-so-low price make you hesitate—this fresh-tasting sparkling wine offers a richer texture and more spice than most, finishing round and generous with dried pear and toasty flavors. Drink now.–H.S. • $8 • (3/31/1999) • **87**
Cabernet Sauvignon McLaren Vale 1993 • $8 • (3/31/1996) • **85**
Cabernet Sauvignon McLaren Vale Edwards & Chaffey 1996: Firm and chewy, its earthy currant and berry flavors lingering nicely under a layer of fine-grained tannins. Best after 2001.–H.S. • $24 • (6/30/2000) • **85**
Cabernet Sauvignon McLaren Vale Edwards & Chaffey 1994 • $27 • (9/30/1996) • **91**
Cabernet Sauvignon South Australia 1996: On the lighter side, with pretty currant and sage flavors, finishing with a modest bite of tannin. Drink through 2003.–H.S. • $9 • (9/30/1998) • **84**

SEAVIEW

Cabernet Sauvignon South Australia 1995 • $9 • (5/15/1998) • **85**
Cabernet Sauvignon South Australia 1994 • $9 • (9/30/1997) • **86**
Cabernet Sauvignon South Australia 1992 • $8 • (10/31/1995) • **83**
Cabernet Sauvignon South Australia 1989 • $6 • (5/15/1994) • **82**
Cabernet Sauvignon South Australia 1986 • $10 • (7/31/1990) • **88**
Chardonnay McLaren Vale 1997: Hailing from Australia is this pretty white, light and smooth, notable for its floral and pear flavors and appealing echoes of fruit on the finish. Its affordable price is appealing, too. Ready to drink.–H.S. • $9 • (10/15/1998) • **86**
Port Australia Flagship NV • $9 • (11/15/1991) • **79**
Shiraz McLaren Vale 1996 • $9 • (5/15/1998) • **86**
Shiraz McLaren Vale 1994 • $9 • (9/30/1997) • **88**
Shiraz McLaren Vale 1993 • $8 • (3/31/1996) • **85**
Shiraz McLaren Vale 1992 • $8 • (6/30/1996) • **86**
Shiraz McLaren Vale Edwards & Chaffey 1995 • $27 • (5/31/1998) • **88**
Shiraz McLaren Vale Edwards & Chaffey 1994 • $27 • (9/30/1996) HR • **92**
Shiraz South Australia 1987 • $10 • (9/30/1991) • **86**
Shiraz South Eastern Australia 1989 • $6 • (9/30/1994) • **71**
Shiraz-Cabernet South Australia 1991 • $6 • (5/15/1994) • **84**
Sparkling Shiraz-Cabernet South Eastern Australia NV: This red sparkling wine smells and tastes like a dry cherry cola with class. It's smooth-textured, with the spice and fruit of red wine lingering on the finish. Drink now.–H.S. • $14 • (3/31/1999) • **86**

SEPPELT

Amontillado Australia Seppeltsfield Show D.P. 116 NV • $20/375 ml. • (10/15/1996) • **89**
Amontillado Barossa Show D.P. 116 NV • $16/375 ml. • (5/31/1998) • **88**
Brut South Eastern Australia Imperial NV • $10 • (1/31/1990) • **82**
Cabernet Sauvignon Australia Dorrien 1989 • $26 • (6/30/1995) • **83**
Cabernet Sauvignon Barossa Valley Dorrien 1990 • $26 • (3/31/1996) • **89**
Cabernet Sauvignon Barossa Valley Dorrien 1987 • $22 • (3/31/1993) • **85**
Cabernet Sauvignon Barossa Valley Dorrien Vineyard 1992 • $28 • (5/31/1997) • **86**
Cabernet Sauvignon Padthaway Black Label 1988 • $12 • (3/31/1991) • **81**
Cabernet Sauvignon South Australia Black Label 1994 • $11 • (8/31/1996) • **85**
Cabernet Sauvignon South Australia Black Label 1993 • $10 • (4/30/1996) • **80**
Cabernet Sauvignon South Australia Black Label 1992 • $10 • (10/31/1995) HR • **90**
Cabernet Sauvignon South Australia Black Label 1991 • $10 • (7/31/1994) • **86**
Cabernet Sauvignon South Australia Black Label 1990 • $10 • (11/15/1993) • **82**
Cabernet Sauvignon South Australia Reserve Bin 1993 • $8 • (10/31/1995) • **82**
Cabernet Sauvignon South Eastern Australia Black Label 1982 • $13 • (4/01/1986) • **78**
Cabernet Sauvignon South Eastern Australia Reserve Bin 1991 • $8 • (6/15/1994) • **82**
Cabernet Sauvignon South Eastern Australia Reserve Bin 1990 • $8 • (11/15/1993) • **84**
Cabernet Sauvignon South Eastern Australia Reserve Bin 1988 • $9 • (7/15/1991) • **82**
Cabernet Sauvignon South Eastern Australia Terrain Series Black Label 1996: Light, appealing for its pretty berry flavors. Drink now.–H.S. • $11 • (8/31/1998) • **84**
Cabernet Sauvignon Victoria Drumborg 1989 • $30 • (6/30/1995) • **72**
Cabernet Sauvignon Victoria Harpers Range 1994 • $16 • (8/31/1996) • **89**
Cabernet Sauvignon-Shiraz South Australia Classic 1994 • $6 • (4/30/1996) • **79**
Cabernet Sauvignon-Shiraz South Australia Classic 1992 • $6 • (4/15/1995) • **87**
Cabernet Sauvignon-Shiraz South Eastern Australia Classic 1990 • $6 • (11/30/1993) • **76**
Cabernet Sauvignon-Shiraz South Eastern Australia Moyston 1989 • $8 • (11/30/1992) • **79**
Fino Australia Seppeltsfield Show D.P. 117 NV • $20/375 ml. • (10/15/1996) • **85**
Fino Barossa Valley Show D.P. 117 NV • $16/375 ml. • (5/31/1998) • **83**
Muscat Rutherglen Show D.P. 63 NV • $19/375 ml. • (12/31/1997) • **92**
Oloroso Australia Seppeltsfield Show D.P. 38 NV • $20/375 ml. • (10/15/1996) • **88**
Oloroso Barossa Show D.P. 38 NV • $16/375 ml. • (5/31/1998) • **89**
Port Australia Para No. 113 NV • $25 • (11/15/1991) • **83**
Port Barossa Valley Para Port Bin 109 NV • $25 • (2/15/1988) • **92**
Port Barossa Valley Para Port No. 110 NV • $25 • (3/15/1989) • **79**
Sémillon-Chardonnay South Eastern Australia Classic 1997 • $7 • (5/15/1998) • **82**
Shiraz Australia Great Western Vineyards Hermitage 1988 • $25 • (4/15/1995) • **82**
Shiraz South Australia Black Label 1993 • $10 • (4/30/1996) • **87**
Shiraz South Australia Black Label 1990 • $10 • (10/31/1993) • **82**
Shiraz South Australia Black Label 1989 • $10 • (5/31/1993) • **85**
Shiraz South Australia Reserve Bin 1995 • $9 • (5/15/1997) • **81**
Shiraz South Australia Reserve Bin 1994 • $9 • (10/15/1996) • **80**
Shiraz South Australia Reserve Bin 1992 • $7 • (4/15/1995) • **87**
Shiraz South Eastern Australia Black Label 1994 • $11 • (8/31/1996) • **84**
Shiraz South Eastern Australia Black Label 1984 • $12 • (12/31/1988) • **87**
Shiraz South Eastern Australia Black Label 1983 • $10 • (2/15/1988) • **74**
Shiraz South Eastern Australia Reserve Bin 1993 • $8 • (10/31/1995) • **83**
Shiraz South Eastern Australia Reserve Bin 1991 • $8 • (9/30/1994) • **78**
Shiraz South Eastern Australia Reserve Bin 1990 • $8 • (10/31/1993) • **82**
Shiraz South Eastern Australia Reserve Bin 1989 • $9 • (8/31/1992) • **84**
Shiraz Victoria Black Label 1992 • $10 • (10/31/1995) • **87**
Shiraz Victoria Black Label 1988 • $12 • (8/31/1992) • **86**
Shiraz Victoria Chalambar 1994 • $14 • (8/31/1996) • **92**
Shiraz Victoria Great Western Vineyards Hermitage 1988 • $25 • (10/31/1995) • **85**
Tawny Port Australia Old Trafford NV • $15 • (3/15/1989) • **95**
Tawny Port Barossa Valley Mt. Rufus NV • $12 • (2/15/1988) • **78**
Tawny Port Barossa Valley Trafford D.P. 30 NV • $12 • (12/31/1997) • **88**
Tokay Rutherglen Show D.P. 57 NV • $19/375 ml. • (6/30/1998) • **91**

SEVENHILL

Cabernet Sauvignon Clare Valley 1998: Rich in flavor and lively in texture, with broad raspberry, currant and mint flavors gathered together nicely. Pointedly bright acidity on the balanced finish. Drink now through 2007.–H.S. • $30 • (3/31/2000) • **89**
Cabernet Sauvignon Clare Valley 1997: Ripe, with a raw-boned texture that emphasizes chewy tannins and flavors that lean toward blackberry and mineral. Best after 2000.–H.S. • $28 • (3/31/1999) • **85**
Cabernet Sauvignon-Merlot-Cabernet Franc-Malbec Clare Valley St. Ignatius 1997: Very firm, with a tannic grip up front, but there's plenty of raw flavor behind it; has violet-tinged currant and blackberry, and a touch of green pepper on the tart finish. Best after 2000.–H.S. • $30 • (3/31/1999) • **87**
Dry Red Clare Valley 1997: Ripe and distinctive, with eucalyptus and pepper overtones to the solid black cherry flavors, finishing with a firm layer of fine-grained tannins. Best after 2000.–H.S. • $25 • (3/31/1999) • **87**
Port Clare Valley 1988 • $31 • (6/15/1998) • **85**
Riesling Clare Valley 1999: Very fragrant, with floral, honeysuckle, peach and lemon notes. Drink now.–B.S. • $16 • (6/30/2000) • **83**
Riesling Clare Valley 1998: A riot of flavor on a crisp, dry frame, with floral, green apple and slate competing for attention. Should develop more richness with cellaring. Try through 2010.–H.S. • $18 • (3/31/1999) • **87**
Shiraz Clare Valley 1998: Bright, focused and generous with its crisp blackberry and anise flavors that hang nicely on a sleek frame. May develop more nuances with cellaring. Drink now through 2006.–H.S. • $35 • (2/29/2000) • **88**
Shiraz Clare Valley 1997: Bright with acidity, this has blackberry, anise and bittersweet chocolate flavors that fill the mouth and linger on the rich finish. Needs cellaring to settle down. Best from 2002 through 2008.–H.S. • $28 • (3/31/1999) • **89**
Shiraz-Touriga-Malbec Clare Valley 1998: Ripe and gamy, this crisp, focused red has earthy flavors weaving through the dark berry notes. Best from 2001 through 2005.–H.S. • $25 • (2/29/2000) • **87**
St. Ignatius Clare Valley 1998: Firm in texture, with a hard edge to the blackberry, herb, spice and earth flavors that linger on the chewy finish. Best after 2002.–H.S. • $40 • (3/31/2000) • **85**
Tawny Port Clare Valley NV • $23 • (6/15/1998) • **87**
Tokay Clare Valley Liqueur NV • $31 • (6/15/1998) • **92**
Verdelho Clare Valley NV • $31 • (6/15/1998) • **87**

SHARGREN

Australia Sparkling NV: Youthful berry and currant aromas and flavors give the impression of sweetness, but this red sparkler finishes on the dry side, echoing the fruit character. Grenache and Shiraz. Drink now.–H.S. • $10 • (3/31/2000) • **87**

Key: SS—Spectator Selection. CS—Cellar Selection. HR—Highly Recommended. $NA—Price not available. (BT)—Barrel tasting. Ⓐ—Auction Price.
For a key to the tasters' initials, see "How to Use These Listings."
Dates in parentheses represent the issues in which the ratings were published.

AUSTRALIA

SHAW & SMITH

Chardonnay Adelaide Hills 1998: Fresh and appealing for its lively green apple, tropical and citrus flavors that last impressively. Smooth, refreshing finish. Drink now.–H.S. • $16 • (6/15/1999) • **88**

Sauvignon Blanc Adelaide Hills 1999: Bright, juicy and fragrant. A lithe mouthful of pear, passion fruit and citrus flavors that hint at herbs on the long, silky finish. More like a New Zealand Sauvignon Blanc than an Aussie one. Drink now.–H.S. • $17 • (6/30/2000) • **89**

Sauvignon Blanc Adelaide Hills 1998: Crisp, juicy and bright, with distinctive passion fruit and guava flavors. Hints of citrus appear on the generous, gently herbal finish. Drink now.–H.S. • $15 • (6/15/1999) • **88**

Sauvignon Blanc South Australia 1997 • $14 • (5/15/1998) • **88**

SHELDRAKE

Merlot Western Australia 1996 • $16 • (4/30/1998) • **81**

Merlot Western Australia 1995 • $16 • (4/30/1997) • **83**

Shiraz Western Australia 1995 • $13 • (2/28/1997) • **88**

Tawny Port Australia NV • $13 • (2/28/1998) • **88**

SHOTTESBROOKE

Cabernet Sauvignon McLaren Vale 1995: Firm in texture, with straighforward plum and currant flavors persisting on the modest finish. Drink now.–H.S. • $16 • (3/31/1999) • **85**

Chardonnay McLaren Vale 1997: Bright and juicy. A lively mouthful of citrus, apple and spice flavors that keep jumping on the fresh finish. Drink now.–H.S. • $20 • (6/15/1999) • **86**

Shiraz McLaren Vale 1997: Earthy, gamy notes weave through the ripe black cherry and sage flavors of this firm-textured, full-bodied red. Drink now.–H.S. • $17 • (5/15/1999) • **87**

SIENNA RIDGE

Red South Eastern Australia 1994 • $6 • (7/31/1996) • **84**

SINGING CREEK

Red South Eastern Australia 1995 • $6 • (7/31/1996) • **82**

STAFFORD RIDGE

Cabernet Sauvignon-Merlot South Australia Geoff Weaver 1992 • $15 • (5/31/1997) • **84**

STANLEY BROTHERS

Cabernet Sauvignon Barossa Valley Thoroughbred 1997: Firm and chewy, a crisp-textured wine with fine tannins around a lean core of minty berry flavors that echo promisingly on the finish. Best after 2002.–H.S. • $24 • (6/30/2000) • **87**

Cabernet Sauvignon Barossa Valley Thoroughbred 1996: A soft-textured red, with plenty of spicy black cherry, currant and mint aromas and flavors packed into a supple frame. Drink now through 2004.–H.S. • $21 • (5/31/1999) • **88**

Cabernet Sauvignon Barossa Valley Thoroughbred 1995 • $19 • (6/15/1998) • **87**

Sémillon Barossa Valley Full-Sister 1998: Ripe, broad and generous for a young Sémillon, dripping with buttery fig and pepper flavors that linger on the soft finish. Drink now through 2006.–H.S. • $18 • (6/30/2000) • **87**

Shiraz Barossa Valley John Hancock 1997: Deliciously ripe, with boysenberry jam, wild berry and blackberry flavors stacked up. Firming on the finish, with hints of coffee and spice. Drink now through 2007.–J.L. • $24 • (6/30/2000) • **90**

Shiraz Barossa Valley John Hancock 1996: Dark in color, forward in flavor, chunky in texture, with a strong anise and smoke streak running through the cherry and berry flavors. Has plenty of parts, but it's not harmonious yet. Best after 2000.–H.S. • $26 • (11/30/1998) • **81**

STANTON & KILLEEN

Muscat Rutherglen Collectors NV • $48/375 ml. • (4/30/1998) • **87**

Muscat Rutherglen Premium NV • $30/375 ml. • (4/30/1998) • **91**

Tokay Rutherglen Premium NV • $30/375 ml. • (4/30/1998) • **90**

STONEHAVEN

Cabernet Sauvignon Limestone Coast 1997: This crisp style of Cabernet is a bit chewy and dry, but offers nice blackberry and dark currant flavors to balance. Feels like it needs food or a few years to soften. Best from 2001 through 2007.–H.S. • $15 • (2/29/2000) • **85**

Cabernet Sauvignon McLaren Vale Reserve 1996: A solid range of flavors on a velvety background, with nice berry and earthy mushroom notes. Finishes with a touch of bay leaf against the echoing blackberry flavors. Drink now through 2005.–H.S. • $35 • (2/29/2000) • **87**

Chardonnay Adelaide Hills-Padthaway Reserve 1997: Rich, ripe and spicy, a big mouthful of peach, pear and nutmeg flavors that picks up some lovely floral and guava notes on the supple finish. Drink now.–H.S. • $25 • (3/31/2000) • **89**

Chardonnay Limestone Coast 1998: Light, spicy and polished, balancing its focused apple, nutmeg and citrus flavors on a silky frame. Spice and fruit echo on the delicate finish. Drink now through 2003.–H.S. • $15 • (3/31/2000) • **87**

Shiraz Limestone Coast 1997: Polished, refined style, playing out its smoky blackberry and black cherry flavors on a smooth frame; flavors echo gently on the finish. Drink now through 2004.–H.S. • $25 • (3/31/2000) • **87**

Shiraz Padthaway Reserve 1996: Ripe and dense, redolent of black cherry, mineral and anise that ooze through the finish. Has a distinctive range of flavors, including a menthol note on the supple finish. Drink now through 2006.–H.S. • $40 • (3/31/2000) • **88**

STRINGY BRAE

Cabernet Sauvignon Clare Valley 1996: Bright and juicy, with minty berry and leather flavors that remain lively and ripe through the well-modulated finish. Beautifully done. Drink now through 2005.–H.S. • $24 • (5/15/1999) • **88**

Riesling Clare Valley 1998: Light, bright and tasty, with citrus, apple and mineral flavors that linger on the dry, gentle finish. Drink now through 2010.–H.S. • $17 • (11/15/1999) • **87**

Shiraz Clare Valley Mòte Hill Sir Lancelot Reserve Selection 1994: Mature, rich and exotic, though hardly heavy, with pretty floral overtones to the ripe blackberry and anise flavors that echo persistently on the velvety finish. A distinctive, seductive wine. Drink now through 2006.–H.S. • $75 • (5/15/1999) • **94**

STURT, CHARLES

University South Eastern Australia 1995 • $10 • (10/31/1997) • **87**

SUMMERFIELD

Shiraz Victoria Reserve 1997: Big-boned and angular, with moderate blackberry, cherry and plum flavors that struggle against the tough texture. Has substance underneath. Best from 2001 through 2004.–B.S. • $47 • (6/30/2000) • **85**

SUNRISE PEAK

Chardonnay South Eastern Australia 1997: Simple and fruity, with a slightly metallic edge to the pineapple and citrus flavors. Drink now.–H.S. • $9 • (5/31/1999) • **80**

SWANN, MARK

Cabernet Sauvignon South Australia 1990 • $8 • (3/31/1993) • **75**

Cabernet Sauvignon South Australia 1989 • $8 • (3/15/1992) • **81**

Cabernet Sauvignon South Australia Proprietor's Reserve 1988 • $6 • (2/28/1991) • **86**

Gold Vintner's Select Rutherglen NV • $10/375 ml. • (12/31/1988) • **92**

Sauvignon Blanc Australia Proprietor's Reserve NV • $5 • (8/31/1987) • **83**

TALTARNI

Brut Australia Cuvée Brut NV • $16 • (8/31/1992) • **85**

Brut Australia Taché NV: Soft and fragrant, generous with its citrus and watermelon flavors, finishing with an earthy note and a slightly broad texture. Drink now.–H.S. • $19 • (6/30/2000) • **86**

TALTARNI

Cabernet Sauvignon Victoria 1996: Crisp and juicy, lean in structure, showing some mature cherry, herb and spice flavors that linger gently on the finish. Drink now through 2006.–H.S. • $16 • (6/30/2000) • **84**
Cabernet Sauvignon Victoria 1995: Lean and refined, not a powerful Cabernet, but one with nice ripe blackberry and herb flavors lurking in the background. Best after 2001.–H.S. • $16 • (11/15/1999) • **87**
Cabernet Sauvignon Victoria 1994: Smooth and focused, with mint-scented blackberry and cherry flavors at moderate intensity. Has a touch of gaminess on the silky finish. Drink now through 2004.–H.S. • $15 • (9/30/1998) • **87**
Cabernet Sauvignon Victoria 1993 • $15 • (8/31/1997) • **89**
Cabernet Sauvignon Victoria 1992 • $15 • (11/30/1996) • **80**
Cabernet Sauvignon Victoria 1990 • $15 • (4/30/1996) • **89**
Cabernet Sauvignon Victoria 1989 • $15 • (6/30/1995) • **87**
Cabernet Sauvignon Victoria 1988 • $12 • (6/30/1994) • **86**
Cabernet Sauvignon Victoria 1987 • $12 • (8/31/1992) • **80**
Cabernet Sauvignon Victoria 1986 • $10 • (9/30/1991) • **81**
Merlot Victoria 1992 • $15 • (4/30/1996) • **89**
Merlot Victoria 1991 • $15 • (4/15/1995) • **83**
Merlot-Cabernet Franc Victoria 1990 • $13 • (7/31/1994) • **85**
Sauvignon Blanc Victoria 1998: Bright, harmonious and distinctive, with mineral-scented pear and passion fruit flavors lingering on the lively, spicy, peppery finish. Drink now.–H.S. • $13 • (2/28/1999) • **88**
Sauvignon Blanc Victoria 1997 • $13 • (5/15/1998) • **88**
Shiraz Victoria 1997: Lean and spicy, a generous mouthful of herb- and tar-scented blackberry and cherry flavors that linger on the refined finish. Not a blockbuster Shiraz, it goes for elegance and complexity. Drink now through 2010.–H.S. • $16 • (11/15/1999) • **90**
Shiraz Victoria 1996: Elegant in style, balancing its pure blueberry and blackberry flavors on a racy frame, showing pretty spice nuances on the lightish finish. Drink now through 2003.–H.S. • $15 • (2/28/1999) • **88**
Shiraz Victoria 1995 • $16 • (3/31/1998) • **86**
Shiraz Victoria 1993 • $15 • (4/30/1996) • **90**
Shiraz Victoria 1992 • $15 • (3/31/1995) • **89**
Shiraz Victoria 1991 • $13 • (9/30/1994) • **88**
Shiraz Victoria 1990 • $13 • (4/30/1993) • **92**
Shiraz Victoria 1989 • $14 • (8/31/1992) • **88**
Shiraz Victoria 1988 • $14 • (5/31/1992) • **89**
Shiraz Victoria 1987 • $10 • (9/30/1991) • **82**
Shiraz Victoria 1986 • $10 • (10/31/1990) • **84**
Shiraz Victoria 1985 • $10 • (11/30/1988) SS • **91**

TAMBURLAINE

The Chapel Reserve Red Hunter Valley NV • $14 • (9/30/1997) • **80**

TAPESTRY

Shiraz McLaren Vale Bin 338 1997: Black pepper and boysenberry hold court in this medium-bodied, solidly tannic Shiraz. Finishes on the dry, astringent side. Drink now through 2002.–B.S. • $25 • (6/30/2000) • **83**

TARRAWARRA

Pinot Noir Yarra Glen 1989 • $28 • (4/15/1992) • **80**
Pinot Noir Yarra Glen 1988 • $25 • (12/31/1990) • **86**
Pinot Noir Yarra Valley 1991 • $26 • (7/31/1994) • **85**
Pinot Noir Yarra Valley 1990 • $27 • (8/31/1992) • **87**
Pinot Noir Yarra Valley Tunnel Hill 1991 • $15 • (6/30/1993) • **81**

TATACHILLA

Cabernet Sauvignon South Australia Wattle Park 1997: Rich in texture, with lovely blueberry and currant emerging on the supple palate, finishing with fine-grained tannins that can use some cellaring. Drink now through 2005.–H.S. • $10 • (1/31/1999) • **88**
Chardonnay Adelaide Hills 1998: Ripe and rich in flavor, with a remarkably refined frame, this is a lovely mouthful of pear, spice and a hint of mushroom mellowed with a touch of vanilla, all echoing beautifully on the long, elegant finish. Drink now through 2008.–H.S. • $25 • (9/15/1999) • **92**

Key: SS—Spectator Selection. CS—Cellar Selection. HR—Highly Recommended. $NA—Price not available. (BT)—Barrel tasting. Ⓐ—Auction Price.
For a key to the tasters' initials, see "How to Use These Listings."
Dates in parentheses represent the issues in which the ratings were published.

Chardonnay McLaren Vale 1997: Fresh and focused, with pretty pear and spice flavors. Slightly bitter on the finish, but it balances. Drink now.–H.S. • $14 • (1/31/1999) • **82**
Chardonnay South Australia Wattle Park 1998: This pretty white is soft and generous with its spicy pear and citrus flavors. Drink now.–H.S. • $10 • (6/30/1999) • **85**
Grenache-Shiraz McLaren Vale 1997: Dense and chewy, with dark berry and anise flavors that persist into a long, firm, elegant finish that echoes spice and herb notes. Drink through 2005.–H.S. • $14 • (1/31/1999) • **85**
Merlot McLaren Vale Clarendon Vineyard 1997: Light, bright and flavorful, with pretty black cherry and green tobacco notes that remain crisp on the finish. Drink now through 2001.–H.S. • $30 • (6/30/1999) • **82**
Shiraz McLaren Vale 1997: Firm and chewy, this is nicely packed with blackberry, pepper and spice flavors that linger on the refined finish. Tasted twice, with consistent notes. Drink now through 2007.–H.S. • $20 • (5/15/2000) • **88**
Shiraz McLaren Vale 1996: Rich and opulent, focusing its gorgeous blueberry, plum and licorice flavors in a brilliant beam that vibrates and echoes on the polished, generous finish. It lasts and lasts, pouring out the fruit. Drink now through 2002.–H.S. • $17 • (1/31/1999) • **91**
Shiraz McLaren Vale Foundation 1996: Dark and racy, with a sharp edge to the ripe blackberry and plum flavors that remain focused and true through the tough finish. Best after 2001.–H.S. • $40 • (9/15/1999) • **87**
Shiraz McLaren Vale Foundation 1995: Firm in texture, with juicy blackberry and plum flavors at the core, and spice and bay leaf notes around the edges. An elegant wine with a unique style. Drink through 2005.–H.S. • $35 • (1/31/1999) • **87**
Shiraz South Australia Wattle Park 1998: A youthful, vibrant Shiraz, this is almost like a barrel sample it's so fresh, with a raw edge to the plum and berry flavors that linger on the rounded finish. It's drinkable now; reasonably priced, too.–H.S. • $10 • (12/15/1999) • **86**
Shiraz South Australia Wattle Park 1997: Ripe and generous, this smooth-textured red has spicy blueberry and blackberry flavors shaded with anise and smoke on the firm finish. Drink now through 2003.–H.S. • $10 • (1/31/1999) • **85**

TEAL LAKE

Shiraz South Eastern Australia Herzog Selection 1999: Kind of dull, with simple cough drop and cherry flavors and an earthy profile. Kosher.–J.L. • $12 • (6/30/2000) • **78**

TEMPLE BRUER

Cabernet Sauvignon-Merlot-Cabernet Franc South Australia 1989 • $11 • (3/31/1995) • **84**
Grenache South Australia Cornucopia 1997: Firm in texture, with bright cherry and grape flavors that finish with welcome restraint. Best after 2000.–H.S. • $14 • (11/15/1999) • **86**
Grenache South Australia Cornucopia 1994 • $10 • (5/15/1997) • **83**
Merlot Langhorne Creek Reserve 1996: Round and generous in texture, with a strong minty-herbal streak running through the berry flavors. Has style, but not for everyone. Drink now through 2004.–H.S. • $16 • (11/15/1999) • **85**
Shiraz-Malbec Langhorne Creek 1996: Firm in texture, with extra nuances that differentiate it from Shirazes. Nicely packed with ripe blackberry and blueberry flavors that become richer and pick up hints of spice on the long finish. Seductive and approachable. Drink now through 2006.–H.S. • $15 • (11/15/1999) • **89**
Shiraz-Malbec Langhorne Creek 1995: Light and distinctive for its spicy, gamy grace notes that add extra dimension to the plummy flavors. Not your usual Shiraz.–H.S. • $15 • (10/15/1998) • **86**
Shiraz-Malbec Langhorne Creek 1991 • $15 • (6/15/1997) • **87**
Shiraz-Malbec South Australia 1994 • $14 • (4/30/1998) • **85**
Shiraz-Malbec South Australia 1990 • $11 • (1/31/1995) • **80**

THOMAS, WAYNE

Cabernet Sauvignon McLaren Vale 1997: Lean and crisp, with some pretty plum and berry flavors coming through, finishing with a definite touch of sweet oak. Drink now through 2004.–H.S. • $19 • (3/31/1999) • **87**
Shiraz McLaren Vale 1997: Bright and refined in style, with pretty blackberry, plum and earth aromas and flavors, hinting at mineral on the well-modulated finish. Drink now through 2005.–H.S. • $16 • (2/29/2000) • **85**

3 BRIDGES

Sémillon Riverina Golden Mist Botrytis 1997: The golden color and intense aromas and flavors dance lightly over a graceful, almost delicate frame in this sweet wine. Honey, vanilla, fig, apricot and spice notes harmonize beautifully. Tempting and seductive already. Drink now through 2012.–H.S. • $15/375 ml. • (2/29/2000) • **94**

T'GALLANT

Chardonnay Victoria 1997: Bright and refreshing. A lively wine with pretty nectarine, apple and gentle spice flavors that linger on the fresh finish. Drink now.–H.S. • $16 • (8/31/1998) • **88**

Pinot Gris Mornington Peninsula Tribute 1997: Bright and fruity, a simple, sturdy white with nectarine and melon notes.–H.S. • $18 • (8/31/1998) • **84**

TORBRECK

The Steading Barossa Valley 1998: Smooth and generous, a velvety wine with layers of black cherry, blackberry, pepper and spice that linger lightly on the finish. Drink now through 2005.–H.S. • $48 • (6/30/2000) • **88**

TRAEGER, DAVID

Shiraz Victoria 1997: On the crisp side, with a jazzy violet edge to the berry flavors, finishing with a touch of tar. Not tannic, but a bit sharp. Best after 2001.–H.S. • $24 • (11/15/1999) • **88**

TRENTHAM

Cabernet-Merlot Murray River Valley 1996 • $15 • (5/31/1998) • **86**

Shiraz Murray River Valley 1996: Smooth and spicy, with stewed plum and spice flavors on a solid frame. Drink now.–H.S. • $18 • (11/15/1999) • **83**

Taminga Murray River Valley Noble 1996: Lots of Muscat aromas and flavors, with a touch of honey and citrus, all lightly sweet on a firm, slightly bitter framework. Drink now.–B.S. • $10/375 ml. • (6/30/2000) • **84**

TRIO STATION

Cabernet Sauvignon Victoria Three Steps 1998: Light and supple, with pretty berry, beet and chocolate flavors that linger on the gentle finish, lending a sense of elegance. Drink now through 2003.–H.S. • $10 • (11/15/1999) • **85**

Cabernet-Merlot Victoria Reserve 1997: Earthy, herbal flavors dominate the fruit in this distinctive, elegant and highly personalized wine. Not lacking for flavor, it will appeal to those looking for something completely different. Drink through 2007.–H.S. • $19 • (11/15/1999) • **89**

Chardonnay Victoria Three Steps 1998: Bright and spicy, this is lively with citrusy acidity but rich enough in smoky apple and pear notes to keep it in balance. Drink now through 2003.–H.S. • $10 • (11/15/1999) • **87**

Riesling Victoria Three Steps Dry 1998: Dry, fragrant and appealing for its green apple, melon and floral spice flavors that linger extensively on the finish. Drink now through 2005.–H.S. • $12 • (6/15/1999) • **88**

Shiraz-Cabernet Victoria Three Steps 1998: Soft and ripe, with an herbal twist to the gentle black cherry and spice flavors, which linger solidly on the generous finish. Drink through 2005.–H.S. • $12 • (5/15/1999) • **87**

Three Steps Rosé Victoria 1998: Odd aromas of iodine and candy intrude on the freshness of this rosé, but it has strong Cabernet fruit flavor on the dry finish. Not for wimps. Drink now.–H.S. • $12 • (6/15/1999) • **80**

TUCK'S RIDGE

Pinot Noir Mornington Peninsula 1995: Light in color, with earthy, gamy flavors and a delicate thread of floral berry character.–H.S. • $20 • (8/31/1998) • **82**

TURKEY FLAT

Grenache Noir Barossa Valley 1998: Firm in texture, with ripe plum and spice flavors that persist on the grainy finish. Has a little less oomph than a Shiraz, but offers lots of character. Drink now through 2005.–H.S. • $21 • (11/15/1999) • **88**

Grenache Noir Barossa Valley 1997: Smooth and generous, a pretty wine, with solid black cherry and raspberry flavors, hinting at smoke on the slightly chewy finish. Drink through 2004.–H.S. • $21 • (3/31/1999) • **86**

Grenache Noir Barossa Valley 1996 • $20 • (10/15/1997) • **90**

Shiraz Barossa Valley 1997: Ripe but refined in style, this frames the distinctively ripe, licorice-scented plum, blueberry and black cherry flavors with a smooth texture and a sense of restraint on the long finish. Drink now through 2010.–H.S. • $30 • (11/15/1999) • **91**

Shiraz Barossa Valley 1996: A sturdy wine, with a distinctive character that lasts and lasts on the focused finish, this Shiraz from Oz weaves notes of earth and spice through the blueberry and anise flavors that swirl through the firm frame. Drink now through 2005.–H.S. • $27 • (3/31/1999) HR • **93**

Shiraz Barossa Valley 1995 • $28 • (9/15/1997) HR • **93**

TWELVE STAVES

Grenache McLaren Vale 1998: Immediately appealing for its jazzy, jammy cherry and ripe strawberry flavors on a medium frame, generous without generating extra power. Drink now through 2007.–H.S. • $16 • (12/31/1999) • **88**

Grenache McLaren Vale 1997: Firm, almost chewy, dense with floral, raspberry and red cherry flavors that linger on the solid finish. Best after 2000.–H.S. • $18 • (5/15/1999) • **87**

TYRRELL'S

Cabernet Sauvignon South Eastern Australia Old Winery 1992 • $8 • (6/30/1995) • **83**

Cabernet Sauvignon South Eastern Australia Old Winery 1991 • $8 • (11/15/1993) • **80**

Cabernet Sauvignon-Merlot South Australia Old Winery 1997 • $11 • (5/31/1998) • **84**

Cabernet Sauvignon-Merlot South Australia Old Winery 1996 • $10 • (5/15/1997) • **82**

Cabernet Sauvignon-Merlot South Eastern Australia Old Winery 1994 • $8 • (3/31/1996) • **84**

Cabernet Sauvignon-Merlot South Eastern Australia Old Winery 1992 • $8 • (6/30/1995) • **84**

Cabernet Sauvignon-Merlot South Eastern Australia Old Winery 1991 • $8 • (12/15/1993) • **81**

Cabernet Sauvignon-Merlot South Eastern Australia Old Winery 1990 • $9 • (3/31/1993) • **78**

Cabernet-Merlot Australia Old Winery 1988 • $8 • (3/31/1991) • **84**

Chardonnay Hunter Valley Shee-Oak Individual Vineyards 1997 • $25 • (5/31/1998) • **90**

Chardonnay South Eastern Australia Old Winery 1997 • $11 • (5/31/1998) • **87**

Chardonnay-Sémillon South Eastern Australia Long Flat 1997 • $8 • (5/31/1998) • **85**

Dry Red Vat 9 Hunter Valley 1987 • $15 • (4/15/1993) • **81**

Dry Red Winemaker's Selection Vat 9 Hunter River 1984 • $15 • (2/15/1992) • **83**

Long Flat Red South Eastern Australia 1997 • $8 • (5/31/1998) • **84**

Long Flat Red South Eastern Australia 1992 • $6 • (5/31/1995) • **83**

Long Flat Red South Eastern Australia 1991 • $7 • (5/31/1993) • **82**

Long Flat Red South Eastern Australia 1990 • $6 • (8/31/1992) • **84**

Long Flat Red South Eastern Australia 1988 • $7 • (2/15/1992) • **84**

Long Flat White Hunter Valley NV • $4 • (5/31/1987) • **84**

Long Flat White South Eastern Australia 1994 • $6 • (5/31/1995) • **84**

Pinot Chardonnay Hunter Valley Vat 47 1997 • $40 • (5/31/1998) • **89**

Pinot Noir Hunter Valley Eclipse Individual Vineyards 1996 • $25 • (5/31/1998) • **85**

Pinot Noir Hunter Valley Old Winery 1995 • $8 • (4/30/1996) • **84**

Pinot Noir South Eastern Australia Old Winery 1997 • $11 • (5/31/1998) • **83**

Pinot Noir South Eastern Australia Old Winery 1996 • $10 • (5/15/1997) • **82**

Pinot Noir South Eastern Australia Old Winery 1993 • $8 • (6/15/1995) • **88**

Sémillon Hunter Valley Old Winery 1997 • $11 • (5/31/1998) • **85**

Sémillon-Sauvignon Blanc South Eastern Australia Old Winery 1997 • $11 • (5/31/1998) • **86**

Shiraz Hunter Valley Brokenback Individual Vineyards 1996 • $25 • (5/31/1998) • **83**

Shiraz Hunter Valley Dry Red Vat 9 1987 • $10 • (6/15/1994) • **82**

Shiraz Hunter Valley Hunter River Vat 9 1989 • $12 • (6/30/1995) • **77**

Shiraz Hunter Valley Old Winery 1990 • $8 • (6/30/1995) • **83**

Shiraz Hunter Valley Old Winery 1988 • $10 • (5/31/1993) • **77**

Shiraz Hunter Valley Old Winery Premier Selection 1993 • $8 • (2/29/1996) • **86**

Shiraz Hunter Valley Stevens 1994 • $20 • (5/15/1997) • **88**

Shiraz Hunter Valley Vat 9 1994 • $40 • (5/31/1998) • **86**

Shiraz Hunter Valley Vat 9 1993 • $30 • (5/15/1997) • **84**

Shiraz Hunter Valley Vat 9 1991 • $11 • (4/30/1996) • **88**

Shiraz Hunter Valley Vat 9 Aged Release 1990 • $12 • (2/29/1996) • **87**

Shiraz South Australia Moore's Creek 1996 • $8 • (5/15/1998) • **86**

Shiraz South Eastern Australia Old Winery 1996 • $11 • (5/31/1998) • **83**

TYRRELL'S

Shiraz South Eastern Australia Old Winery 1995 • $10 • (5/15/1997) • **83**
Tawny Port Australia 8 Barrels NV • $9 • (5/15/1996) • **87**
Tawny Port Australia 8 Year Old Fine Aged NV • $9 • (6/30/1995) • **81**

VASSE FELIX

Cabernet Sauvignon Margaret River 1995 • $24 • (6/15/1997) • **83**
Cabernet Sauvignon Margaret River 1990 • $14 • (4/30/1994) • **85**
Cabernet-Merlot Margaret River Classic Dry Red 1991 • $12 • (4/30/1994) • **82**
Cabernet-Merlot Western Australia 1995 • $16 • (6/15/1997) • **86**
Shiraz Margaret River 1995 • $26 • (6/15/1997) • **83**

VERITAS

Cabernet-Merlot Barossa Valley 1998: Smooth and nicely refined, offering beautifully focused raspberry, plum and spice flavors that linger nicely on the supple finish. Drink now through 2007.–H.S. • $22 • (6/30/2000) • **88**

Mourvèdre-Grenache Barossa Valley 1998: Fresh and generous, with lively plum, anise and leather aromas and flavors that linger on the velvety finish. Drink now through 2005.–H.S. • $40 • (6/30/2000) • **88**

Shiraz Barossa Valley Hanisch Vineyard 1997: Smooth and velvety, nicely packed with spicy berry, anise and nutmeg flavors, picking up a minty note on the long finish. Less gooey than most Barossa Shirazes, but exceedingly distinctive and elegant. Drink now through 2005.–H.S. • $50 • (6/30/2000) • **91**

Shiraz Barossa Valley Heysen Vineyard 1997: Ripe and focused, not a big wine but offering pure plum and blackberry flavors that ride on a smooth texture, picking up delicate hints of vanilla and spice on the harmonious finish. Drink now through 2007.–H.S. • $35 • (6/30/2000) • **90**

Shiraz-Mourvèdre Barossa Valley Pressings 1997: Soft, ripe and appealing for its elegant structure and pure plum fruit, which lingers on the velvety finish framed with hints of berry and spice. Has plenty of flavor without hitting the palate hard. Drink now through 2007.–H.S. • $40 • (6/30/2000) • **90**

VIRGIN HILLS

Cabernet-Shiraz-Malbec-Merlot Keyneton 1995: Light and silky, with pretty plum flavors and a streak of smoky tea character running through. Flavors are unusual, but persist on the finish. Drink through 2002.–H.S. • $38 • (8/31/1998) • **87**

Red Keyneton 1994 • $33 • (7/31/1997) • **89**

V Victoria 1997: Sleek and silky, strongly marked with herb and cedar notes, with a nice beam of berry and sage flavors that remain prominent on the firm, elegant finish. Needs to soften. Best after 2001.–H.S. • $45 • (11/15/1999) • **87**

VOYAGER ESTATE

Chardonnay Margaret River 1997: Bright, focused, aromatic and impressive for its range of flavor, touching upon pineapple, pear, nutmeg and citrus notes and revealing a grace note of honey on the long finish. A substantial wine, built to age. Drink now through 2010.–H.S. • $27 • (12/31/1999) • **92**

Sauvignon Blanc-Sémillon Margaret River 1998: Tangy and distinctive, this is a soft-textured, brightly flavorful white that offers nice apple, sweet pea and spice aromas and flavors. Drink now.–H.S. • $20 • (12/31/1999) • **86**

Shiraz-Grenache Margaret River 1997: Dark as ink, but neither heavy not heavy-handed, this has nicely focused blackberry and cherry flavors that hint at spice and smoke on the firm finish. Drink now through 2005.–H.S. • $24 • (12/31/1999) • **87**

WAKEFIELD

Cabernet Sauvignon Clare Valley 1994 • $13 • (10/31/1997) • **89**

WALLINGTON

Chardonnay Cowra Nyrang Creek Vineyard 1997: A streak of bracing, citrusy acidity cuts through this otherwise round and generous white that offers pretty pear and hazelnut flavors. Needs food to balance the crispness. Drink now through 2003.–H.S. • $15 • (6/15/1999) • **87**

Key: SS—Spectator Selection. CS—Cellar Selection. HR—Highly Recommended. $NA—Price not available. (BT)—Barrel tasting. Ⓐ—Auction Price.
For a key to the tasters' initials, see "How to Use These Listings."
Dates in parentheses represent the issues in which the ratings were published.

WARRABILLA

Cabernet Sauvignon-Shiraz Victoria Brimin 1997: Smooth and generous, with soft cherry and tobacco flavors. Echoes plum and spice on the finish. Drink now through 2002.–H.S. • $24 • (12/15/1998) • **88**

Chardonnay Victoria 1998: Bright and refreshing for its citrusy pear and Santa Rosa plum flavors, which reverberate nicely on the lively finish. Drink now.–H.S. • $22 • (5/31/1999) • **87**

Chardonnay Victoria 1997: Tries to pack a lot of flavor onto a lean frame, but the flavors tend toward raw wood and lime.–H.S. • $22 • (12/15/1998) • **79**

Merlot King Valley 1997: Pleasantly light and fruity, with pretty currant and plum flavors in modest proportions. Drink now.–H.S. • $27 • (12/15/1998) • **84**

Merlot Victoria Reserve 1998: Ripe, round and generous, with effusive raspberry, blackberry and cherry flavors. It all hangs elegantly on a supple frame, with velvety tannins and hints of spicy oak nicely integrated into the package. Best after 2000.–H.S. • $30 • (5/31/1999) • **90**

Shiraz Victoria 1998: Shows lots of ripe flavor on a crisp frame, offering blackberry, mint and earth notes that linger on the supple finish. Drink now through 2007.–H.S. • $27 • (11/15/1999) • **89**

Shiraz Victoria 1997: Bright and crisp, with tangy blackberry, tar and herb flavors packed into the finish. Drink now.–H.S. • $27 • (12/15/1998) • **86**

WATER WHEEL

Cabernet Sauvignon Bendigo 1996 • $14 • (4/30/1998) • **85**

Chardonnay Bendigo 1998: A distinctive style of Chardonnay emphasizing spicy tobacco notes. Hints of fig and raisin sneak in on the finish, but the main appeal is the spiciness. Drink now.–H.S. • $12 • (3/31/1999) • **86**

Shiraz Bendigo 1997: Flavorful and velvety, a rich mouthful of smoky black cherry and anise flavors that persist nicely on the solid finish. Drink now through 2005.–H.S. • $14 • (11/30/1999) • **89**

Shiraz Bendigo 1996 • $14 • (4/30/1998) • **86**

WEAVER, GEOFF

Chardonnay Lenswood 1997: Simple, with a tart, earthy, herbal edge to the spicy grapefruit and modest pear shadings. Drink now.–J.L. • $29 • (6/30/2000) • **81**

WHISSON LAKE

Pinot Noir Adelaide Hills 1995: Shows maturity already, with a brick color and pretty black cherry and earthy spice flavors, finishing with a fine layer of gritty tannins. Drink now through 2001.–H.S. • $38 • (3/31/1999) • **85**

WHITE, ALICE

Chardonnay South Eastern Australia 1998: Fresh, fruity and open, here's a pretty mouthful of tropical fruit and apple flavors that linger on the soft finish. Drink now.–H.S. • $7 • (9/30/1999) • **86**

Chardonnay South Eastern Australia 1997: A lively, quaffable mouthful of pear, citrus and green melon flavors that echo on the smooth finish, this bright and refreshing Chardonnay is building a reputation as a solid, tasty value. Enjoy now.–H.S. • $7 • (11/30/1998) • **86**

Sémillon-Chardonnay South Eastern Australia 1998: Smooth and generous, with pretty pineapple and pear flavors lingering on the soft finish. Drink now.–H.S. • $7 • (11/15/1999) • **84**

Shiraz South Eastern Australia 1998: Soft and supple, with pretty plum and spice flavors, a candied hint on the finish. Drink now.–H.S. • $8 • (9/30/1999) • **82**

WHITE OPAL

Chardonnay South Eastern Australia Unwooded 1998: Simple and straightforward, soft enough to feel a bit sweet, with modest pear and spice flavors. Drink now.–H.S. • $11 • (2/28/1999) • **80**

WILD DUCK CREEK

Shiraz Heathcote Springflat 1997: A picture of elegance. From the fresh and pure violet, raspberry and dark chocolate aromas and flavors and lithe framework to the lingering finish, this Shiraz shows a restrained style for Australia. Drink now through 2003.–B.S. • $38 • (6/30/2000) • **89**

WILDERNESS

Cabernet-Merlot Hunter Valley 1996: Earthy, gamy flavors weave through this firm, full-bodied, round, ripe red; some pretty plum and raisin notes give balance on the finish. Drink through 2003.–H.S. • $15 • (9/15/1999) • **84**

Chardonnay Hunter Valley Reserve 1997: Ripe, spicy and generous with its orange peel-scented pear and nutmeg flavors, supple and rounded on the finish as the flavors echo nicely. Drink now through 2003.–H.S. • $15 • (9/30/1999) • **87**

Merlot Hunter Valley 1995 • $15 • (10/31/1997) • **77**

Shiraz Hunter Valley 1996: Light and graceful, more delicate than powerful, with pretty raspberry, blackberry and black pepper flavors that linger gently on the finish. Drink now through 2006.–H.S. • $15 • (9/15/1999) • **85**

Shiraz Hunter Valley 1995 • $15 • (10/31/1997) • **79**

WILLESPIE

Cabernet Sauvignon Margaret River 1996: Crisp in structure, turning silky as it spreads out its pretty currant and plum flavors, shaded with bay leaf and herb. Has a solid feel and should develop nicely with cellaring. Drink now through 2006.–H.S. • $25 • (2/29/2000) • **87**

Cabernet Sauvignon Margaret River 1993 • $14 • (10/31/1997) • **87**

Cabernet Sauvignon Margaret River 1990 • $13 • (11/15/1993) • **79**

Cabernet Sauvignon Margaret River 1989 • $13 • (6/30/1993) • **82**

Shiraz Margaret River 1997: A lighter style of Shiraz, this still has plenty of berry and anise flavors packed into it, with hints of mint and mineral on the finish. Drink now through 2003.–H.S. • $25 • (3/31/2000) • **85**

Verdelho Margaret River 1997: A sturdy white wine with earthy apple flavors lingering on the round finish. Drink now.–H.S. • $20 • (3/31/2000) • **82**

WILTON

Sémillon New South Wales Botrytis 1995 • $24/375 ml. • (6/30/1998) • **88**

WIRRA WIRRA

Cabernet Sauvignon McLaren Vale 1984 • $14 • (1/31/1988) • **84**

Cabernet Sauvignon McLaren Vale-Coonawarra The Angelus 1996: Firm and fresh-tasting, with pretty blueberry and currant flavors on a crisp, nicely defined framework. Drink now through 2003.–H.S. • $33 • (2/28/1999) • **86**

Cabernet-Shiraz-Merlot McLaren Vale Church Block 1997: Bright and pretty. A firm-textured, light-structured red with ripe berry and peppery flavors that linger on the finish. Drink now through 2001.–H.S. • $18 • (2/28/1999) • **87**

Cabernet-Shiraz-Merlot McLaren Vale Church Block 1985 • $11 • (3/15/1988) • **89**

Grenache-Shiraz McLaren Vale Original Blend 1997: Supple and generous, though not heavy, with pretty red plum and tarry flavors lingering on the smooth finish. Drink now.–H.S. • $18 • (2/28/1999) • **86**

Shiraz McLaren Vale R.S.W. 1996: Deep, dark, dense and complex, this ripe, complex mouthful of plum, prune, exotic spice and cedar flavors spreads exuberantly across the palate, then lingers on the finish. A powerful wine with great style. Drink through 2010–H.S. • $33 • (2/28/1999) • **92**

WISE

Cabernet Sauvignon Margaret River 1996: Firm in texture, with a solid core of blackberry and currant flavors, shaded with hints of green pepper, mint and tomato among the fine-grained tannins on the finish. Best from 2001 through 2005.–H.S. • $17 • (5/31/1999) • **85**

Chardonnay Western Australia 1997: Ripe and round, with pretty pear, caramel and spice notes echoing on the smooth, polished finish. Touched by oak but not overwhelmed by it. Drink now through 2002.–H.S. • $16 • (5/31/1999) • **89**

Chardonnay Western Australia Aquercus Unwooded 1997: Bright and jazzy, a very pretty wine with focused apple, pear and citrus flavors that keep singing on the lively finish. A touch of earthiness cuts through the finish. Drink now through 2002.–H.S. • $13 • (5/31/1999) • **87**

Chardonnay Western Australia Coat Door 1998: Ripe and generous, with a nice array of pear and spice flavors. A lovely mouthful of freshness that has more Chardonnay fruit up front than on the finish. Drink now.–H.S. • $14 • (5/31/1999) • **85**

Grenache-Shiraz McLaren Vale-Margaret River 1998: Firm, almost astringent, with earthy, sour notes intruding upon a lingering core of blackberry and spice flavors that come through on the lean finish. Tasted twice, with consistent notes. Drink now through 2004.–H.S. • $12 • (6/30/2000) • **80**

Grenache-Shiraz McLaren Vale-Margaret River 1997: Ripe and velvety, with pretty blackberry, mint and anise flavors on a supple frame. 400 cases imported. Drink now through 2002.–H.S. • $14 • (5/15/1999) • **86**

Merlot Western Australia 1997: Earthy, gamy notes weave through the modest blackberry character in this hard-edged red, echoing herbal and gamy flavors. Drink through 2004.–H.S. • $16 • (5/31/1999) • **83**

Old Vines Classic Red Margaret River 1998: Light, supple in texture, with a strong minty-herbal note, almost vegetal, running through the plum and berry. Finishes soft. Tasted twice, with consistent notes. Drink now.–H.S. • $12 • (6/30/2000) • **81**

WOOD PARK

Shiraz-Cabernet Victoria W 1997: Earthy, gamy notes take the forefront over the ripe cherry and berry flavors lurking underneath in this supple red. Drink now through 2007.–H.S. • $15 • (11/15/1999) • **88**

WOODLEY

Shiraz-Cabernet South Eastern Australia Queen Adelaide 1992 • $6 • (6/30/1995) • **82**

Shiraz-Cabernet South Eastern Australia Queen Adelaide 1989 • $7 • (5/31/1993) • **74**

Shiraz-Cabernet South Eastern Australia Queen Adelaide 1988 • $7 • (2/29/1992) • **82**

Tawny Port South Australia Queen Adelaide NV • $7 • (4/15/1995) • **87**

WYNDHAM ESTATE

Brut Australia Cuvée NV • $8 • (5/15/1995) • **86**

Cabernet Sauvignon Hunter Valley Bin 444 1988 • $8 • (6/30/1992) • **80**

Cabernet Sauvignon South Eastern Australia Bin 444 1996: Here's an Aussie red of real value. It's firm in texture, with fruit concentration at the center and enticing echoes of pure plum and currant on the finish. The fine-grained tannins don't get in the way. Drink now.–H.S. • $8 • (10/15/1998) • **85**

Cabernet Sauvignon South Eastern Australia Bin 444 1995 • $10 • (6/15/1997) • **88**

Cabernet Sauvignon South Eastern Australia Bin 444 1993 • $7 • (5/15/1996) • **79**

Cabernet Sauvignon South Eastern Australia Bin 444 1992 • $9 • (11/30/1994) • **84**

Cabernet Sauvignon South Eastern Australia Bin 444 1991 • $7 • (1/31/1995) • **83**

Cabernet Sauvignon-Shiraz South Eastern Australia 1989 • $8 • (6/30/1992) • **76**

Cabernet-Merlot Hunter Valley Bin 888 1990 • $8 • (9/30/1994) • **77**

Chardonnay Hunter Valley Oak Cask 1997: This graceful Chardonnay from Australia is ripe in flavor and crisp in texture, with a creamy feel to the pretty pear, citrus and floral character. Finishes long and elegant. A great buy at this price. Drink now.–H.S. • $10 • (12/15/1998) • **88**

Chardonnay South Eastern Australia Bin 222 1997 • $8 • (6/30/1998) • **82**

Pinot Noir South Eastern Australia Bin 333 1994 • $7 • (5/15/1996) • **85**

Sémillon-Chardonnay South Eastern Australia Bin 777 1997: A smooth-textured and pretty white, with a buttery edge adding dimension to the lemony pear and fig flavors. At so reasonable a price, chill a few bottles for current drinking, while it's fresh.–H.S. • $7 • (10/31/1998) • **85**

Shiraz South Eastern Australia Bin 555 1993 • $8 • (6/15/1996) • **82**

Shiraz South Eastern Australia Bin 555 1991 • $9 • (9/30/1994) • **81**

Shiraz South Eastern Australia Bin 555 1990 • $7 • (2/15/1993) • **85**

Shiraz South Eastern Australia Bin 555 1988 • $8 • (6/30/1992) • **83**

Tawny Port South Eastern Australia George Wyndham Old Tawny NV: It's hard to believe how affordable is the price for this sweet and silky tawny, with pretty coffee and toffee accents around a black cherry core, hinting at tar on the finish. Go for it now.–H.S. • $9 • (2/28/1999) • **88**

WYNN, DAVID

Cabernet Sauvignon Eden Valley 1996 • $14 • (11/30/1997) • **85**

Cabernet Sauvignon Eden Valley 1995 • $12 • (2/28/1997) • **85**

Chardonnay South Eastern Australia 1997: Exuberantly fruity, here's a jazzy mouthful of apricot, apple and passion fruit flavors that linger smoothly on the finish. Drink now.–H.S. • $15 • (8/31/1998) • **87**

Shiraz Eden Valley 1999: Peppery, with blackberry, licorice and earth nuances and a twinge of bitterness on the finish. Drink now through 2002.–J.L. • $12 • (6/30/2000) • **84**

■ ■ ■ ■

WYNN, DAVID

Shiraz Eden Valley Patriarch 1995 • $25 • (11/30/1997) • **89**
Shiraz Eden Valley Patriarch 1994 • $22 • (5/15/1997) • **90**
Shiraz Eden Valley Unwooded 1996 • $12 • (2/28/1997) • **83**
Shiraz South Australia Unwooded 1997: Has a rough edge to its boisterous blackberry, raspberry and sweet leather flavors, lingering on the generous finish. Drink through 2003.–H.S. • $15 • (8/31/1998) • **86**
Shiraz South Eastern Australia 1998: Smooth and flavorful, with pretty dark plum and spice flavors that linger softly on the round finish. Drink now.–H.S. • $15 • (6/30/1999) • **86**
Shiraz South Eastern Australia Patriarch 1993 • $15 • (10/31/1995) • **86**

WYNNS COONAWARRA ESTATE

Cabernet Hermitage Coonawarra 1984 • $10 • (12/31/1988) • **79**
Cabernet Sauvignon Coonawarra 1995 • $14 • (6/15/1998) • **86**
Cabernet Sauvignon Coonawarra 1993 • $12 • (12/15/1996) • **86**
Cabernet Sauvignon Coonawarra 1991 • $12 • (4/30/1995) • **85**
Cabernet Sauvignon Coonawarra 1989 • $12 • (4/30/1994) • **82**
Cabernet Sauvignon Coonawarra 1982 • $15 • (11/30/1988) • **90**
Cabernet Sauvignon Coonawarra Estate 1989 • $12 • (4/15/1993) • **86**
Cabernet Sauvignon Coonawarra John Riddoch 1994: Firm and chewy, this serious mouthful of herb-scented dark cherry and cedar flavors has depth, presence and style. Just needs time. Best after 2001.–H.S. • $40 • (1/31/1999) • **88**
Cabernet Sauvignon Coonawarra John Riddoch 1992 • $40 • (4/30/1996) • **91**
Cabernet Sauvignon Coonawarra John Riddoch Limited 1996: Firm and flavorful, a bit muddled but has blackberry, herb, earth and currant flavors. Tannins wrap around the finish. Needs cellaring. Best from 2002 through 2010.–H.S. • $49 • (6/30/2000) • **85**
Cabernet Sauvignon Coonawarra John Riddoch Limited 1990 • $22 • (11/30/1994) SS • **92**
Cabernet Sauvignon Coonawarra John Riddoch Limited 1988 • $22 • (3/31/1993) • **84**
Cabernet Sauvignon-Shiraz Coonawarra 1990 • $11 • (4/30/1994) • **83**
Cabernet-Shiraz-Merlot Coonawarra 1997: Lean and chewy, with earthy berry flavors up front, but they take some time to reappear on the finish. Has a distinctive range of leathery notes around the fruit. Best after 2001.–H.S. • $11 • (6/30/2000) • **85**
Cabernet-Shiraz-Merlot Coonawarra 1995 • $11 • (6/15/1998) • **83**
Chardonnay Coonawarra 1997 • $12 • (6/15/1998) • **88**
Shiraz Coonawarra 1997: Crisp, zingy style centers around bright plum and berry flavors, supported by lively acidity. All remains harmonious through the finish. Drink now through 2005.–H.S. • $13 • (6/30/2000) • **87**
Shiraz Coonawarra 1996 • $13 • (6/15/1998) • **88**
Shiraz Coonawarra 1993 • $12 • (12/15/1996) • **87**
Shiraz Coonawarra 1992 • $11 • (3/31/1995) • **84**
Shiraz Coonawarra 1991 • $11 • (3/31/1994) • **84**
Shiraz Coonawarra Michael 1993 • $40 • (8/31/1996) • **90**
Shiraz Coonawarra Michael Limited Release 1996: Aromatically generous, with spicy berry notes, bit it seems airy and light on the palate despite some firm tannins on the finish. Might flesh out with time. Tasted twice, with consistent notes. Best after 2001.–H.S. • $49 • (6/30/2000) • **86**

YALUMBA

Brut Australia Angas NV • $10 • (3/31/1996) • **86**
Brut Rosé Australia Angas NV • $9 • (9/30/1994) • **81**
Brut Rosé South Australia Angas NV • $9 • (12/31/1990) • **84**
Brut South Australia Angas NV • $9 • (12/31/1990) • **78**
Cabernet Sauvignon Clare Valley Reserve 1996: Strongly herbal, with generous raspberry and leather aromas and flavors. Solid. Drink now.–H.S. • $25 • (3/31/2000) • **85**
Cabernet Sauvignon Coonawarra Family Reserve 1989 • $9 • (2/28/1993) • **84**
Cabernet Sauvignon Coonawarra The Menzies 1996: Velvety, generous and flavorful, layering harmonious mint, herb, dusky spice and berry. Drink now through 2008.–H.S. • $28 • (12/15/1999) • **90**
Cabernet Sauvignon Coonawarra The Menzies 1995: Firm texture, with gorgeous currant, plum and herbal flavors coursing over the palate, focused, fleshy and elegant. Flavors persist on the wide-open finish. Best after 2000.–H.S. • $28 • (11/30/1998) • **90**

> **Key:** SS—Spectator Selection. CS—Cellar Selection. HR—Highly Recommended. $NA—Price not available. (BT)—Barrel tasting. Ⓐ—Auction Price.
> For a key to the tasters' initials, see "How to Use These Listings."
> **Dates in parentheses represent the issues in which the ratings were published.**

Cabernet Sauvignon Coonawarra The Menzies 1994 • $21 • (2/28/1998) • **86**
Cabernet Sauvignon Coonawarra The Octavius 1988 • $30 • (5/15/1994) • **90**
Cabernet Sauvignon South Australia 1997: Lots of minty flavors that are refreshing, with blackberry and leather notes. Firms up on the tannic finish. Drink now through 2005.–J.L. • $15 • (5/31/2000) • **83**
Cabernet Sauvignon Sparkling Australia Cuvée Two Prestige NV • $15 • (3/31/1996) • **88**
Cabernet Sauvignon-Merlot South Australia Barrel Select Family Reserve 1995 • $12 • (5/31/1997) • **85**
Cabernet Sauvignon-Merlot South Australia Family Reserve 1994 • $12 • (9/30/1996) • **88**
Cabernet-Shiraz Barossa Valley The Signature 1995: Ripe, smooth and generous, a velvety wine, with layers of blackberry, cherry, herb and spice flavors that recede slowly on the finish. Has the finish to encourage cellaring. Drink now through 2010.–H.S. • $40 • (12/15/1999) • **91**
Cabernet-Shiraz Barossa Valley-Coonawarra The Signature 1994: A ripe and intriguing wine, distinctive for its hints of exotic spices swirling around the currant and plum flavors at the core, this red blend is dense and focused, balanced to rein its rich flavors into an elegant form. Firm tannins need cellaring. Best after 2001.–H.S. • $40 • (11/30/1998) CS • **90**
Chardonnay Barossa 1998: Simple if pleasantly fruity, with spicy pear, citrus and light oak shadings. Drink now through 2003.–J.L. • $13 • (5/31/2000) • **86**
Chardonnay Barossa 1997 • $13 • (6/15/1998) • **85**
Grenache Barossa Bush Vine 1997: Rich and complex, with racy cherry, wild berry and spice notes, picking up an anise and mineral flavor that gives it dimension. Drink now through 2005.–J.L. • $14 • (5/31/2000) • **87**
Grenache Barossa Bush Vine 1994 • $12 • (4/30/1996) • **80**
Grenache Barossa Bush Vine Reserve 1995 • $12 • (6/30/1997) • **88**
Muscat Rutherglen Museum Show Reserve NV • $12/375 ml. • (9/15/1994) HR • **98**
Muscat Victoria Museum Release NV • $15/375 ml. • (2/28/1998) HR • **94**
Museum Release Antique Tawny Barossa NV • $15/375 ml. • (2/28/1998) • **92**
Museum Release Old Sweet Wine Barossa NV • $15/375 ml. • (2/28/1998) • **89**
Pinot Noir-Chardonnay Australia Sparkling Cuvée One Prestige NV • $15 • (3/31/1996) • **88**
Port Australia Galway Pipe NV • $19 • (5/31/1996) • **92**
Port Barossa Valley Galway Pipe NV • $18 • (7/31/1994) SS • **92**
Sémillon Barossa Valley Late Harvest Botrytis Sémillon Family Reserve 1994 • $12/375 ml. • (12/31/1995) HR • **94**
Sémillon Barossa Valley Late Harvest Botrytis Sémillon Family Reserve 1993 • $11 • (9/30/1995) • **93**
Sémillon Eden Valley Late Harvest Botrytis Family Reserve 1991 • $10 • (9/15/1994) • **86**
Sémillon South Australia Botrytis Family Reserve 1995 • $13/375 ml. • (10/15/1996) • **89**
Sémillon-Sauvignon Blanc South Australia Botrytis Family Reserve 1996 • $12/375 ml. • (5/31/1997) • **86**
Sémillon-Sauvignon Blanc Griffith-Barossa Botrytis 1997 • $15/375 ml. • (6/15/1998) HR • **91**
Shiraz Barossa Family Reserve 1995 • $12 • (5/31/1997) • **90**
Shiraz Barossa Family Reserve 1994 • $12 • (10/15/1996) • **87**
Shiraz Barossa Growers 1997: Drips with lots of ripe berry and cherry flavors, along with a rich overlay of licorice and smoke on a surprisingly lithe and elegant frame. Tannins are well submerged. Drink now through 2010.–H.S. • $15 • (5/15/2000) • **88**
Shiraz Barossa Reserve 1993: Not as big and gooey as most Barossa Shirazes, but it makes up for it with elegance and style. Flavors are pinpoint Shiraz—dark cherry, blackberry, and gobs of spice—and they come together in a deft finish that emphasizes style over power. Drink now through 2008.–H.S. • $27 • (3/31/2000) • **91**
Shiraz Barossa The Octavius 1995: Firm enough in texture to keep the ripe plum, cherry and anise flavors from becoming too gooey, this one pulls all its parts together into a muscular wine that never gets too heavy. Best after 2001.–H.S. • $80 • (12/15/1999) • **91**
Shiraz Barossa The Octavius 1994: Ripe, broad and spicy, layering its smoke and licorice overtones around a core of soft black cherry and blackberry. Drink now.–H.S. • $60 • (11/30/1998) • **91**
Shiraz Barossa The Octavius 1993 • $40 • (5/31/1997) • **88**
Shiraz Barossa The Octavius Old Vine 1992 • $40 • (11/30/1996) • **92**
Shiraz Barossa Valley Family Reserve 1993 • $10 • (3/31/1996) • **86**
Shiraz Barossa Valley Family Reserve 1991 • $10 • (9/30/1994) • **88**
Shiraz Barossa Valley Family Reserve 1989 • $9 • (11/30/1992) • **86**
Shiraz Clare Valley Reserve 1996: Rich and fleshy, with plum, spice and chocolate flavors supported by a firm, tannic structure. Sweet fruit prevails

on the finish. Well balanced and appealing. Drink now through 2002.–B.S. • $25 • (6/30/2000) • **88**

Tawny Port South Australia Clocktower NV • $10 • (5/15/1996) • **89**

YARRA RIDGE

Cabernet Sauvignon Victoria 1994 • $11 • (1/31/1997) • **83**

Cabernet Sauvignon Yarra Valley 1996 • $12 • (5/15/1998) • **85**

Cabernet Sauvignon Yarra Valley Reserve 1995 • $NA • (3/31/1998) • **86**

Chardonnay Yarra Valley 1997: Fresh, supple and generous, this beautifully proportioned Chardonnay offers a range of flavors on a modest frame; pear, apple, grapefruit and apricot capture the attention at various times, finishing with elegance and grace. Drink now through 2004.–H.S. • $12 • (1/31/1999) • **90**

Pinot Noir Victoria 1996 • $12 • (8/31/1997) • **85**

Pinot Noir Victoria 1995 • $12 • (5/15/1997) • **85**

Pinot Noir Victoria 1993 • $12 • (6/30/1995) • **74**

Pinot Noir Yarra Valley 1997 • $12 • (3/31/1998) • **85**

YARRA VALLEY HILLS

Riesling Yarra Valley Warranwood 1998: Musty, with sour flavors.–B.S. • $18 • (6/30/2000) • **74**

YARRA YERING

Cabernet Sauvignon Coldstream Dry Red Wine No. 1 1984 • $14 • (5/31/1988) • **73**

Dry Red No.1 Yarra Valley 1994 • $40 • (8/31/1997) • **89**

Dry Red No.2 Yarra Valley 1994 • $40 • (8/31/1997) • **89**

Dry Red Wine No. 1 Yarra Valley 1995: Light and focused in flavor, centering on plum and currant flavors that keep echoing on the uncharacteristically pure finish. Very pretty to drink already. Drink now through 2002.–H.S. • $45 • (9/30/1998) • **86**

Pinot Noir Yarra Valley 1995: Elegant and refined, with nicely defined plum and berry flavors, shaded with hints of leather and herb and just a touch of spice on the supple finish. Drink now through 2001.–H.S. • $50 • (9/30/1998) • **88**

Pinot Noir Yarra Valley 1994 • $50 • (8/31/1997) • **85**

Shiraz Yarra Valley Underhill 1995: Distinctively gamy, with a sweet, earthy, decadent feel to the silky berry and smoke flavors. Not a mainstream wine, but it has personality. Drink through 2005.–H.S. • $45 • (8/31/1998) • **86**

Shiraz Yarra Valley Underhill 1994 • $40 • (8/31/1997) • **92**

YARRAMAN

Cabernet-Shiraz Australia Wybong 1994 • $22 • (10/31/1996) • **89**

YARRAMAN ROAD

Cabernet Sauvignon-Shiraz South Eastern Australia 1995 • $20 • (10/15/1997) • **87**

Chardonnay Hunter Valley 1998: Smooth and silky, with a spicy, earthy note running through the pretty pear and delicate herb flavors. Don't wait. Drink now.–H.S. • $20 • (11/15/1999) • **87**

Shiraz South Eastern Australia 1994: Ripe and spicy, this dark wine has a strong tang of licorice shading the basic blackberry flavors. Finishes with a flourish. 800 cases imported. Drink now through 2001.–H.S. • $20 • (12/15/1998) • **88**

YERING STATION

Cabernet Sauvignon Yarra Valley 1998: Firm, with good depth to the dried berry flavors. Dry tannin and chocolate notes on the finish. Drink now through 2003.–B.S. • $22 • (6/30/2000) • **84**

Red Yarra Valley 1995 • $14 • (10/31/1997) • **86**

YERINGBERG

Marsanne-Roussanne Yarra Valley 1997: Soft and fragrant, a pretty medley of pear, floral and almond flavors that last nicely on the finish. Drink now.–H.S. • $35 • (11/15/1998) • **88**

Red Yarra Valley 1995 • $40 • (9/30/1997) • **90**

YUNBAR

Shiraz Barossa Valley Sinners 1998: Tart, with a sour cherry and leather edge, turning bitter.–J.L. • $35 • (6/30/2000) • **78**

Austria

Though long overshadowed by wines from its neighbor-to-the-northwest, Germany, Austrian wines are at long last making some headway with American consumers. Americans have come to recognize that Austrian wines' unique combination of vibrant structure, dense fruit and mineral flavors makes them remarkably versatile matches for menus.

Austrian wines share many similarities with German wines: a predominance of white grapes and a particular strength in sweet wines. However, because of Austria's more southerly location and more varied climate, its range of grapes and wines is notably wider than Germany's.

Austria's "national grape" and most widely planted variety is the versatile Grüner Veltliner, which can be made into light, dry (*Trocken*), even austere table wines, or unctuous sweet wines. Some of the most exciting recent developments in Austrian whites, though, involve Riesling—a probable 19th-century immigrant from Germany—made in both dry and off-dry styles. Other Austrian whites include the unrelated native Welschriesling, Weissburgunder (Pinot Blanc), Grauburgunder (Pinot Gris), Scheurebe (a cross between Riesling and Sylvaner), and Bouvier, which was originally a table grape. The ubiquitous Chardonnay (called Morillon in Austria) has begun to appear, as well, even—astonishingly—in the form of superb botrytized dessert wines.

Red grapes, while in the minority, are found in most of Austria's winegrowing regions. Varieties include the native Zweigelt or Blauer Zweigelt (the grape is a cross between the Austrian specialty St.-Laurent and Blaufränkisch), now sometimes blended with Cabernet Sauvignon; Blaufränkisch, the same grape known in the American Northwest as Lemberger; and Spätburgunder (Pinot Noir) and its likely relative St.-Laurent.

1. Wachau
2. Kremstal
3. Kamptal
4. Neusiedlersee-Hügelland
5. Neusiedlersee

Most Austrian wine labels bear the same quality/ripeness designations as German wines, although the region of Wachau uses its own equivalent system: Qualitätswein = Steinfeder, Kabinett = Federspiel, and Spätlese = Smaragd (a world referring to the emerald color of the tiny lizards that live in the vineyards!)

WINE REGIONS

The winegrowing areas of Austria lie entirely within the eastern third of the country. The northernmost area, Niederösterreich, borders on the Czech and Slovak Republics, and includes the highly respected wine districts of Kamptal, Kremstal and Wachau. These are the source of many of the country's best dry Grüner Veltliners and Rieslings. The style of the latter combines the aromatics of German Riesling and the body of Alsatian versions, yet remains distinctly Austrian.

The capital city of Vienna (Wien) is unique in being the center of its own small viticultural area, and there are even some vines within the city limits.

Neusiedlersee and Neusiedlersee-Hügelland occupy eastern Austria's central latitudes, where numerous shallow lakes and ponds encourage the formation of botrytis practically every year. Most of the

The wine village of Weissenkirchen in Wachau.

Mick Rock/Cephas

extraordinary Beerenauslese and Trockenbeerenauslese dessert wines that have reached the market over the last few years originated here, as does Austria's most traditional sweet wine, Ausbruch Rust.

Further south lies Burgenland, heartland of Austria's red wine industry. The traditional varieties of Blaufränkisch and Blauer Zweigelt are grown in abundance here, but the region is also a hotbed of experimentation with western European "noble" grapes such as Cabernet Sauvignon. The best reds offer plenty of fresh fruit and lively, vibrant structures that complement a wide range of foods. West of Burgenland is Steiermark, source of a wide variety of dry white wines.

ALZINGER

Grüner Veltliner Smaragd Trocken Wachau Dürnsteiner Liebenberg 1997: Elegant and flavorful, this beautifully integrated wine displays the ripeness of the vintage with the mineral and vegetal character of Grüner Veltliner. Still firmly structured, with a lingering aftertaste of peach and mineral. Not imported into the U.S. Drink now through 2005.–B.S. • $NA • (12/31/1998) • **90**

Riesling Smaragd Trocken Wachau Dürnsteiner Höhereck 1998: Splendid. This is thick, rich and creamy, exhibiting passion fruit, lemon curd and grapefruit, with plenty of power and firm structure in reserve. Amazingly, it still seems elegant, in a baroque, Modigliani-esque way. Not imported into the U.S. Best after 2000.–B.S. • $NA • (1/01/2000) • **90**

Riesling Smaragd Trocken Wachau Loibner Loibenberg 1997: There are warm baking-bread and spice components in the aroma and plenty of complexity from the soil in this intense and focused Riesling. All the elements are harmonious, with a disarming clarity that belies its internal structure and concentration. Not imported into the U.S. Drink through 2007–B.S. • $NA • (1/01/1999) • **92**

Riesling Smaragd Trocken Wachau Loibner Steinertal 1998: Exotic and smoky nuances complement the ripe apricot, while citrus aromas and flavors unfold like layers of velvet, punctuated by moderate acidity. Not imported into the U.S. Drink now through 2004.–B.S. • $NA • (1/01/2000) • **90**

ANGERHOF

Chardonnay-Welschriesling Eiswein Neusiedlersee 1997: Very expressive, showing floral and herbal aromas and flavors and a sweet-tart component on the structure. Light on its feet, with moderate intensity and length. Not imported into the U.S. Drink now.–B.S. • $NA/375 ml. • (1/01/2000) • **88**

Muscat Ottonel Trockenbeerenauslese Neusiedlersee 1995 • $NA/375 ml. • (2/28/1998) • **94**

Qualitätswein Trocken Neusiedlersee Grand Select Red 1997: Very ripe, offering mint and plum on a lush, open-knit framework. The firm tannins on the finish sit apart today. May just need a few months to integrate. Contains Zweigelt and Cabernet Sauvignon. Not imported into the U.S. Drink now through 2001.–B.S. • $NA • (1/01/2000) • **86**

Sämling 88 Eiswein Neusiedlersee 1997: Emphatically spicy, evoking cardamom, clove and a strong Muscat character, all on a bright, focused structure that ends on a refreshing citrus note. Not imported into the U.S. Drink now through 2003.–B.S. • $NA/375 ml. • (1/01/2000) • **88**

Sämling 88 Trockenbeerenauslese Neusiedlersee 1995 • $NA/375 ml. • (2/28/1998) • **92**

Scheurebe Trockenbeerenauslese Neusiedlersee 1995: This resonates on the palate with intense concentration and nerve. Orange marmalade aromas give way to a smoky flavor that just keeps coming. Beautifully balanced and long, with a complex aftertaste. Not imported into the U.S. Drink now through 2006.–B.S. • $NA/375 ml. • (1/01/1999) • **90**

Weissburgunder Trockenbeerenauslese Neusiedlersee 1995: Marked by new oak, this TBA exhibits smoke, lemon and vanilla aromas and flavors, scorching acidity and an intense character that leaves it feeling coarse on the finish. A little time should tame it. Not imported into the U.S. Drink through 2005.–B.S. • $NA/375 ml. • (1/01/1999) • **90**

Welschriesling Trockenbeerenauslese Neusiedlersee 1995: Rich and ethereal, its unctuous texture balanced by racy acidity, this complex dessert wine shows apricot, crème brûlée, passion fruit and citrus notes. Very fresh and unevolved, it needs time to integrate the sugar and structure. Not imported into the U.S. Drink through 2010.–B.S. • $NA • (1/01/1999) • **92**

Zweigelt Strohwein Neusiedlersee Vin de Paille Rosé 1995: Light-colored and aromatic. Shows honey and raisin, with some spice accents. Rich and sweet, it's not unlike a white varietal but for the hint of tannin at the end. Not imported into the U.S. Drink now through 2002.–B.S. • $NA/375 ml. • (1/01/1999) • **87**

BERGER, E. & M.

Blauer Zweigelt Qualitätswein Trocken Kremstal Barrique 1994 • $14 • (2/28/1997) • **83**

Key: SS—Spectator Selection. CS—Cellar Selection. HR—Highly Recommended. $NA—Price not available. (BT)—Barrel tasting. Ⓐ—Auction Price.
For a key to the tasters' initials, see "How to Use These Listings."
Dates in parentheses represent the issues in which the ratings were published.

Chardonnay Kabinett Kremstal Gedersdorfer Altmandl 1996 • $NA • (2/28/1998) • **88**

Chardonnay Qualitätswein Kremstal Gedersdorfer Altmandl 1997: A lean, racy style of Chardonnay, with lemon and pie crust flavors. Drink now. –B.S. • $16 • (12/31/1998) • **81**

Chardonnay Qualitätswein Trocken Kremstal Gedersdorfer Altmandl 1998: Delicious. A little trapped carbon dioxide lends spritz, yet underneath there's depth, intensity and rich flavors of apple and brioche, with a mineral element. Very complex, harmonious and long. Not imported into the U.S. Drink through 2004.–B.S. • $NA • (1/01/1999) • **89**

Grüner Veltliner Kabinett Kremstal Gedersdorfer Lössterrassen 1998: A powerful white, combining weight and ample flavors of lanolin, honey and lentil, along with a slight cheesiness associated with promising young wines. Unevolved and full, but well balanced, this should develop nicely with some bottle age. Drink now through 2003.–B.S. • $13 • (8/31/1999) • **89**

Grüner Veltliner Kabinett Kremstal Gedersdorfer Lössterrassen 1996 • $11 • (2/28/1998) • **85**

Grüner Veltliner Kabinett Trocken Kremstal Gedersdorfer Gebling 1998: Distinctive, offering laurel and sage aromas, with flavors like white peach and grapefruit. Rich, yet lacks the balance and intensity of the best Grüners. Drink now.–B.S. • $14 • (12/31/1999) • **83**

Riesling Kabinett Kremstal Gedersdorfer Steingraben + Lissen 1996 • $14 • (2/28/1998) • **87**

Riesling Qualitätswein Halbtrocken Kremstal Gedersdorfer Steingraben 1998: Broad and lush, this offers lime, grapefruit and floral flavors matched to juicy texture. Good balance and length. Drink now through 2002.–B.S. • $18 • (12/31/1999) • **86**

Riesling Qualitätswein Kremstal Gedersdorfer Steingraben 1997: Big and full-bodied, just off dry, bursting with honey, pear and vanilla aromas and flavors. Rich and succulent, it should attract a lot of fans to Austrian Riesling. Finishes slightly coarse. Not imported into the U.S. Drink now through 2003.–B.S. • $NA • (1/01/1999) • **88**

Rivaner Qualitätswein Kremstal Gedersdorfer Im Satzen 1997: A fresh, almost grapey-tasting white that offers good richness and a clean, lemony finish. Appealing, if a little simple. Not imported into the U.S. Drink now.–B.S. • $NA • (1/01/1999) • **82**

Rivaner Trockenbeerenauslese Kremstal 1998: Full of baked apple and cinnamon, with hints of honey and apricot, this is sweet and vibrant, dancing across the palate. The finish comes in waves of apple and citrus. Not imported into the U.S. Drink now through 2003.–B.S. • $50/375 ml. • (1/01/2000) • **89**

BOCKFLIESS

Pinot Blanc Qualitätswein Weinviertel Riede Hochfeld 1996 • $15 • (2/28/1998) • **84**

BRAUNSTEIN, PAUL

Chardonnay Qualitätswein Burgenland Oxhoft 1997: Medium-bodied and spicy, this white offers hints of clove, nutmeg, banana and pineapple. A slight astringency and moderate acidity provide structure. Not imported into the U.S. Drink now.–B.S. • $NA • (1/01/1999) • **83**

Pinot Blanc Qualitätswein Burgenland 1997: Here's a delicious Pinot Blanc offering the stone, nut and peach notes typical of the varietal. Shows fatness midpalate, with lively acidity that prevents it from being heavy. Not imported into the U.S. Drink now.–B.S. • $NA • (1/01/1999) • **85**

Pinot Blanc Qualitätswein Trocken Neusiedlersee-Hügelland 1998: A study in contrasts. Almost viscous in texture, with the underlying tart acidity emerging on the finish. Modest apple and lemon flavors. Not imported into the U.S. Drink through 2004.–B.S. • $NA • (1/01/1999) • **80**

Qualitätswein Trocken Neusiedlersee-Hügelland Oxhoft Red 1997: A lush, vanilla-scented red in a modern style. The blackberry and coffee flavors combine with a medium-bodied, crisp structure, all balanced and enticing. Moderate length. Not imported into the U.S. Drink now through 2002. –B.S. • $NA • (1/01/2000) • **89**

Saint Laurent Qualitätswein Burgenland 1995: Rich and supple, this red displays black currant and leather character, medium body and firm but light tannins. Not imported into the U.S. Drink now through 2002.–B.S. • $NA • (1/01/1999) • **85**

BRUNDLMAYER

Grüner Veltliner Beerenauslese Kamptal Ried Loiser Berg 1995 • $NA • (2/28/1998) • **93**

Grüner Veltliner Kabinett Kamptal Langenloiser Berg-Vogelsang 1997: This fat, ripe wine is full of peach, lentil and mineral flavors that turn dry and slightly austere midpalate. Very good intensity and length, with racy acidity on the finish. Best from 2001 through 2006.–B.S. • $17 • (2/28/1999) • **87**

Grüner Veltliner Qualitätswein Kamptal Alte Reben 1996 • $20 • (2/28/1998) • **87**

Grüner Veltliner Qualitätswein Kamptal Ried Lamm 1997: Seductive. Very concentrated and seamless, offering a rich texture, aromas and flavors of butter, vanilla and lanolin and deceptive acidity to balance all the elements. The aftertaste has a fine resonance on the palate. Not imported into the U.S. Drink now through 2003.–B.S. • $NA • (1/01/1999) • **88**

Grüner Veltliner Qualitätswein Kamptal Ried Lamm 1996 • $20 • (2/28/1998) • **88**

Grüner Veltliner Qualitätswein Trocken Kamptal Alte Reben 1998: Ripe and tropical, showing pineapple and nectarine notes woven into a rich, almost oily texture balanced by bright acidity. A slightly exaggerated, pumped-up Grüner, with just a hint of the grapes' more typical white pepper and tobacco character. Not imported into the U.S. Drink now through 2001.–B.S. • $NA • (12/31/1999) • **89**

Grüner Veltliner Qualitätswein Trocken Kamptal Alte Reben 1997: Much richness, concentration and depth in this Grüner Veltliner, with a pronounced lees character. The chamomile, peach and white pepper flavors are locked in a firm grip of acidity, and a mineral note comes through on the long finish. Needs time. Drink through 2005.–B.S. • $28 • (2/28/1999) • **90**

Grüner Veltliner Qualitätswein Trocken Kamptal L & T 1998: The aromas are a bit muted, but on the palate this is a beauty. Ripe and fat, with good underlying structure. Flavors evoke apricot, sage and tobacco, ending with a mouthwatering citrus sensation. Drink now.–B.S. • $18 • (8/31/1999) • **88**

Grüner Veltliner Qualitätswein Trocken Kamptal Ried Lamm 1998: Exotic. Very ripe, with a touch of botrytis given the apricot, honey aromas and flavors. Moderate acidity keeps it balanced and it finishes dry. Drink now.–B.S. • $39 • (12/31/1999) • **86**

Pinot Noir Qualitätswein Kamptal Cécile 1994 • $NA • (2/28/1998) • **79**

Riesling Beerenauslese Kamptal Zöbinger Heiligenstein 1995 • $NA • (2/28/1998) • **90**

Riesling Qualitätswein Kamptal Zöbinger Heiligenstein Alte Reben 1996 • $32 • (2/28/1998) • **89**

Riesling Qualitätswein Trocken Kamptal Langenloiser Steinmassel 1998: Intriguing. Ripe quince, nettle and Indian spices highlight this lovely Riesling, whose smooth texture and peppery accents carry through to the moderate finish. Drink now through 2003.–B.S. • $27 • (12/31/1999) • **88**

Riesling Qualitätswein Trocken Kamptal Langenloiser Steinmassel 1997: Full of earth and mineral tones, this vibrant white is firmly structured and compact. Needs time to unleash its fruit and personality. Drink through 2004.–B.S. • $21 • (2/28/1999) • **88**

Riesling Qualitätswein Trocken Kamptal Zöbinger Heiligenstein 1998: Wonderful stone and mineral character match the white peach and citrus notes in this intense, high-alcohol white. Turns a bit hot and coarse on the finish. Drink now through 2002.–B.S. • $31 • (12/31/1999) • **87**

Riesling Qualitätswein Trocken Kamptal Zöbinger Heiligenstein 1997: Brilliant Riesling. Floral, peach and orange-peel notes are interwoven with spice and mineral elements in this racy yet intensely flavored beauty. All harmony and finesse, its richness is balanced by refreshing acidity. Fine length. Drink now through 2005.–B.S. • $22 • (2/28/1999) • **90**

Riesling Qualitätswein Trocken Kamptal Zöbinger Heiligenstein Alte Reben 1998: Broad, fat and luscious, bursting with apricot and a licorice flavor, it's so intense, all supported by a firm structure. Complex flavors of tropical fruit and mineral mingle through the long, long finish. Not imported into the U.S. Drink now through 2006.–B.S. • $NA • (4/30/2000) • **92**

Riesling Qualitätswein Trocken Kamptal Zöbinger Heiligenstein Alte Reben 1997: Intense aromas of lime, spice and mineral, with enough flesh to offset a lean, driven character marked by a firm backbone of acidity. It's tightly wound and reserved on the finish, so be patient. Drink through 2005.–B.S. • $33 • (2/28/1999) • **90**

Riesling Qualitätswein Trocken Kamptal Zöbinger Heiligenstein Lyra 1998: A flamboyant, exotic Riesling that shows apricot and passion fruit alongside lime and an orange marmalade note. Full-bodied and velvety, with enough backbone to keep it lively. Tremendous finish. Not imported into the U.S. Drink now through 2007.–B.S. • $NA • (4/30/2000) • **90**

Riesling Qualitätswein Trocken Kamptal Zöbinger Heiligenstein Lyra 1997: Exotic and ripe, bursting with quince and pear, it's rich and intense before finishing on a firm, chalky note. Not imported into the U.S. Drink through 2005.–B.S. • $NA • (1/31/1999) • **91**

Saint Laurent Kamptal Ried Ladner 1993 • $NA • (2/28/1997) • **80**

CHORHERREN KLOSTERNEUBERG

Chardonnay Auslese Lieblich Wien Ried Jungherren Stift Klosterneuberg 1996: Has mature character in the form of slightly gamy and decadent overtones to the apricot flavor. The definite sweetness is backed by lively acidity, though the finish is a bit pinched. Not imported into the U.S. Drink now.–B.S. • $NA • (12/31/1998) • **83**

Chardonnay Auslese Wien Ried Altweingarten 1996 • $22 • (2/28/1998) • **85**

Chardonnay Qualitätswein Trocken Wien Ried Altweingarten Stift Klosterneuberg 1998: An odd juxtaposition of candied fruit flavors and bracing acidity render this white disjointed. Not imported into the U.S.–B.S. • $NA • (1/01/1999) • **78**

Chardonnay Qualitätswein Trocken Wien Ried Altweingarten Stift Klosterneuberg 1997: Slightly tart, with bitter almond augmenting the apple skin flavor. Not imported into the U.S.–B.S. • $NA • (12/31/1998) • **78**

Gewürztraminer Auslese Wien Ried Gebhardin 1996 • $23/500 ml. • (2/28/1998) • **90**

Saint Laurent Qualitätswein Trocken Wien Ried Stiftsbreite Barrique Stift Klosterneuberg 1997: A gorgeous red, from the deep ruby color and dark plum aromas to the rich texture and concentration. Firmly structured, with a mineral note and a spiciness that persist through the long finish. Not imported into the U.S. Drink now through 2002.–B.S. • $NA • (1/01/2000) • **88**

Saint Laurent Qualitätswein Trocken Wien Ried Stiftsbreite Barrique Stift Klosterneuberg 1995: Round and full, with black cherry and herb accents that push the resinous, acetone end of the spectrum. Good concentration and firm tannins. Not imported into the U.S. Drink now.–B.S. • $NA • (12/31/1998) • **82**

Traminer Auslese Wien Ried Gebhardin 1996: Floral and spicy flavors are accented with mineral in this light, airy white. Medium-sweet, with pronounced acidity but not much depth. Drink now.–B.S. • $29 • (2/28/1999) • **84**

Weissburgunder Qualitätswein Wien Ried Kuchelviertel Stift Klosterneuburg 1997: An austere style that shows peach and mineral on a lean, compact framework, with firm acidity. A little more flesh would help the balance. Not imported into the U.S. Drink now through 2001.–B.S. • $NA • (2/28/1999) • **80**

FEILER-ARTINGER

Ruster Ausbruch Neusiedlersee-Hügelland 1996: Refined aromas of honey and apricots continue on the palate in this balanced and elegant sweet white. Lively acidity gives it focus and clarity. An orange note chimes in on the lingering finish. Not imported into the U.S. Drink now through 2006.–B.S. • $NA/375 ml. • (1/01/1999) • **89**

Ruster Ausbruch Neusiedlersee-Hügelland 1995 • $NA/375 ml. • (2/28/1998) • **90**

Ruster Ausbruch Neusiedlersee-Hügelland Pinot Cuvée 1996: A rich, upfront style with soft acidity, this is very applelike, with a herbaceous element that disappears midpalate as a honey flavor emerges, giving way to coconut on the finish. The aftertaste has a candied component. Not imported into the U.S. Drink now through 2002.–B.S. • $NA/375 ml. • (1/01/1999) • **86**

Ruster Ausbruch Neusiedlersee-Hügelland Pinot Cuvée 1995 • $NA/375 ml. • (2/28/1998) • **88**

Traminer Auslese Neusiedlersee 1998: Frankly sweet, exuding honey, apricot, rose and litchi aromas and flavors woven into a swath of velvet. Apricot and litchi linger on the finish. Drink now.–B.S. • $19 • (4/30/2000) • **88**

Weissburgunder Ruster Ausbruch Neusiedlersee-Hügelland Essenz 1995 • $NA/375 ml. • (2/28/1998) • **92**

FREIE WEINGARTNER WACHAU

Grüner Veltliner Smaragd Trocken Wachau Dürnsteiner Kellerberg 1998: Ripe, this '98 offers straightforward pear and marmalade notes, without a lot of structure and length. Tasted twice, with consistent notes. Drink now through 2003.–B.S. • $22 • (4/30/2000) • **86**

Grüner Veltliner Smaragd Trocken Wachau Dürnsteiner Kellerberg 1997: This has the weight and feel of a white Burgundy, but the flavors are almond and lentil, with a hint of residual sweetness balanced by vibrant acidity. Lingering finish. Drink now through 2003.–B.S. • $20 • (12/31/1998) • **88**

Grüner Veltliner Smaragd Trocken Wachau Terrassen Thal 1997: Tightly wound and racy despite the concentration and intensity of peach, violet and citrus, this needs time to unfold and integrate its structure and flavors. Drink through 2007.–B.S. • $15 • (12/31/1998) • **88**

FREIE WEINGARTNER WACHAU

Grüner Veltliner Smaragd Trocken Wachau Weissenkirchner Achleiten 1998: Big and bold, exhibiting anise and almond flavors, with hints of peach and grapefruit. Moderately structured, ending on a licorice note. Drink now through 2004.–B.S. • $27 • (4/30/2000) • **88**

Grüner Veltliner Smaragd Wachau Weissenkirchner Achleiten 1996 • $20 • (2/28/1998) • **86**

Riesling Federspiel Wachau Terrassen Thal 1997: Smells and tastes more like Muscat, with an attractive spicy undercurrent that comes to the fore on the finish. Drink now.–B.S. • $14 • (9/15/1999) • **83**

Riesling Smaragd Trocken Wachau Dürnsteiner Kellerberg 1998: Otherworldly. It's hard to believe these aromas and flavors of licorice, tobacco and Indian spices come from Riesling, yet it's exotic, concentrated, dense and built like a skyscraper. Seemingly impenetrable today, wait until it all comes together. Best from 2002 through 2012.–B.S. • $27 • (3/31/2000) HR • **92**

Riesling Smaragd Trocken Wachau Dürnsteiner Kellerberg 1997: Tantalizing. This starts out so rich and densely textured, one hardly notices the firm, mouthwatering acidity as the quince, apricot and citrus flavors weave through. Just lacks that extra midpalate concentation and length to be outstanding. Drink through 2004.–B.S. • $26 • (2/28/1999) • **89**

Riesling Smaragd Trocken Wachau Loibner Loibenberg 1997: Evocative lime and peach notes introduce this white, like a supercharged Mosel Riesling, but it's medium-bodied, with a stony, broad midpalate and a firm, dry finish. Beautifully made. Drink through 2006.–B.S. • $26 • (2/28/1999) • **90**

Riesling Smaragd Trocken Wachau Spitzer Singerriedel 1998: Multidimensional. Intense aromas of licorice and spice combine with a broad structure and thick texture that feels more like that of a red wine. Closed now, so be patient. Best from 2001 through 2006.–B.S. • $29 • (4/30/2000) • **91**

Riesling Smaragd Trocken Wachau Weissenkirchner Achleiten 1997: Begins with a lively interplay of richness and acidity, spice, peach and stone flavors, then the richness of the '97 vintage takes the lead, only to be outdistanced on the finish by the firm, minerally structure. Young, and only hinting at its great future. Best from 2001 through 2007.–B.S. • $26 • (1/31/1999) HR • **92**

Riesling Smaragd Wachau Weissenkirchner Achleiten 1996 • $28 • (2/28/1998) • **85**

FRITSCH, WEINBERGHOF

Blauer Burgunder Qualitätswein Donauland Ried Kreuzberg-Ruppersthal 1995 • $NA • (2/28/1998) • **74**

Blauer Burgunder Qualitätswein Trocken Donauland P 1997: An overtly oaky style, with a vanilla and smoke overlay to the berry aromas and flavors. Supple and medium-bodied, with a lingering aftertaste. Drink now.–B.S. • $28 • (4/30/2000) • **83**

Blauer Spätburgunder Qualitätswein Trocken Donauland Ried Kreuzberg-Ruppersthal 1994 • $NA • (2/28/1997) • **85**

Foggathal Donauland Red 1995 • $22 • (2/28/1998) • **78**

Foggathal Qualitätswein Trocken Donauland 1994 • $24 • (2/28/1997) • **84**

Grüner Veltliner Kabinett Donauland Ried Zeiselgraben-Mitterstockstall 1996 • $NA • (2/28/1998) • **80**

Grüner Veltliner Qualitätswein Donauland Alte Reben 1997: Sports floral and peach aromas and flavors, with underlying mineral and herb accents. Soft, ripe, round and attractive, finishing on a minerally note. Drink now.–B.S. • $18 • (12/31/1998) • **84**

Grüner Veltliner Qualitätswein Donauland Zeiselgraben 1998: A bit of trapped CO2 gas provides an edge to the texture of this white but may be flattening the aromas and flavors at this stage. It hints at white pepper, celery and lentil, finishing on the sour side.–B.S. • $15 • (8/31/1999) • **78**

Grüner Veltliner Qualitätswein Trocken Donauland Schlossberg P 1998: Peach and earth aromas and flavors mingle in this rich, almost viscous Grüner. Very ripe, it's balanced by a citrus element on the finish. Not imported into the U.S. Drink now.–B.S. • $NA • (1/01/1999) • **84**

Grüner Veltliner Spätlese Donauland 1996 • $19 • (2/28/1998) • **84**

Merlot Qualitätswein Trocken Donauland Kreuzberg-Ruppersthal 1994 • $24 • (2/28/1997) • **84**

Rieslaner Qualitätswein Donauland Perfektion 1997: An austere style that shows medium concentration, this is really more elegant, with a mineral, citrus character. Drink now through 2001.–B.S. • $18 • (2/28/1999) • **86**

Key: SS—Spectator Selection. CS—Cellar Selection. HR—Highly Recommended. $NA—Price not available. (BT)—Barrel tasting. (A)—Auction Price. For a key to the tasters' initials, see "How to Use These Listings." **Dates in parentheses represent the issues in which the ratings were published.**

Riesling Qualitätswein Donauland 1996 • $15 • (2/28/1998) • **87**

Riesling Qualitätswein Trocken Donauland Mordthal 1998: Rich and broad, showing floral, lime and mineral aromas and flavors. Well balanced, with a lingering aftertaste. Very appealing. Drink now.–B.S. • $18 • (12/31/1999) • **86**

Weissburgunder Qualitätswein Trocken Donauland Schlossberg 1998: Seems mature, offering almond, cut apple and earth flavors that start out rich, turn austere and almost tart on the finish. Drink now.–B.S. • $18 • (12/31/1999) • **84**

Weissburgunder-Chardonnay Qualitätswein Donauland Schlossberg-Oberstockstall 1996 • $NA • (2/28/1998) • **85**

Zweigelt Qualitätswein Trocken Donauland 1994 • $13 • (2/28/1997) • **85**

Zweigelt-Cabernet-Merlot Qualitätswein Trocken Donauland Foggathal No. 4 1997: Round and generous, this feels ripe, though there are some dill and bell pepper notes along with the raspberry. Some tannins emerge on the finish. Not imported into the U.S. Drink now.–B.S. • $NA • (1/01/2000) • **85**

GLATZER, W.

Blauer Zweigelt Qualitätswein Carnuntum Dornen Vogel 1996 • $16 • (2/28/1998) • **86**

Blauer Zweigelt Qualitätswein Carnuntum Rieden Cuvée 1996 • $10 • (2/28/1998) • **82**

Blaufränkisch Qualitätswein Carnuntum Reserve 1995 • $14 • (2/28/1998) • **87**

Blaufränkisch Qualitätswein Trocken Carnuntum 1995 • $11 • (2/28/1997) • **82**

Grüner Veltliner Qualitätswein Carnuntum 1996 • $8 • (2/28/1998) • **84**

Qualitätswein Trocken Carnuntum Gotinsprun Red 1997: A Syrah look-alike, this Zweigelt blend delivers inky blackberry flavors, bacon fat, fine concentration and depth and some rough-and-tumble tannins. A hint of new oak rounds it out a little. Great character. Drink now through 2003.–B.S. • $28 • (4/30/2000) • **89**

Weissburgunder Kabinett Carnuntum 1996 • $10 • (2/28/1998) • **85**

Zweigelt Qualitätswein Trocken Carnuntum Dornen Vogel 1995 • $16 • (2/28/1997) • **85**

Zweigelt Qualitätswein Trocken Carnuntum Rieden Cuvée 1995 • $11 • (2/28/1997) • **83**

GOBELSBURG, SCHLOSS

Grüner Veltliner Kabinett Trocken Kamptal Gobelsburger 1998: Typical aromas and flavors of lentil, white pepper and grapefruit with just a hint of botrytis, in a lean, minerally style. Drink now through 2002.–B.S. • $17 • (12/31/1999) • **84**

Grüner Veltliner Landwein Kamptal Messwein NV • $8/1 liter • (2/28/1998) • **79**

Grüner Veltliner Qualitätswein Kamptal Ried Lamm 1996 • $21 • (2/28/1998) • **85**

Grüner Veltliner Qualitätswein Trocken Kamptal Gobelsburger Steinsetz 1998: Broad in character, showing almond and red berry notes combined with an open structure and a short finish. Drink now.–B.S. • $20 • (12/31/1999) • **83**

Grüner Veltliner Qualitätswein Trocken Kamptal Ried Grubb 1998: Wow. Exotic peach, apricot, white pepper and red berry notes marry with the creamy texture in this flavorful white. Interesting juxtaposition of intensity and lightness. Not imported into the U.S. Drink now through 2001.–B.S. • $NA • (1/01/1999) • **89**

Grüner Veltliner Qualitätswein Trocken Kamptal Ried Lamm 1998: Ripe and forward, evoking tropical nuances and a kiss of new oak, this Grüner is expansive and broad in the mouth, offering flavors of vanilla, peach and herbs, with a little white chocolate at the end. Not imported into the U.S. Drink now.–B.S. • $NA • (1/01/1999) • **89**

Grüner Veltliner Qualitätswein Trocken Kamptal Ried Lamm 1997: Forward and appealing, this full-bodied white has loads of apricot, quince and vanilla, backed by crisp, mouth-tingling acidity and an almond aftertaste. Drink now through 2002.–B.S. • $24 • (12/31/1998) • **86**

Grüner Veltliner Qualitätswein Trocken Kamptal Ried Steinsetz 1997: Lentil and tobacco notes, along with quince and mineral, are allied to a firm structure and an almost thick texture. The finish is citrusy and refreshing. Drink now through 2002.–B.S. • $15 • (12/31/1998) • **86**

Riesling Kabinett Kamptal Urgesteins 1997: Firm, spicy and elegant, this white starts off on a floral note before the distinctive spicy character unfolds on the palate. Accents of peach and apple, along with medium weight, offset its taut structure. Drink through 2004.–B.S. • $15 • (2/28/1999) • **88**

Riesling Qualitätswein Trocken Kamptal Alte Reben 1997: Very ripe, showing tropical fruit nuances and a hint of rosemary married to a soft texture.

Good concentration and a bit of heat (alcohol) on the finish. Drink now through 2001.–B.S. • $29 • (2/28/1999) • **88**

Riesling Qualitätswein Trocken Kamptal Kammerner Gaisberg 1998: Focused and intense, with a mealy, cereal and grain flavor along with citrus and mineral. Smooth in texture, it loses focus ever so slightly on the finish. Drink now through 2004.–B.S. • $26 • (12/31/1999) • **88**

Riesling Qualitätswein Trocken Kamptal Ried Gaisberg 1997: Soft and rich, yet with deceptive acidity, this white is full of sweet corn, mineral and a cheesy quality that marks its youth. Broad and concentrated before finishing with a firm mineral note, it needs time. Drink through 2005.–B.S. • $20 • (2/28/1999) • **89**

Riesling Qualitätswein Trocken Kamptal Zöbinger Heiligenstein 1998: A delicious mix of lime, vanilla custard, tropical fruit and mineral is married to a creamy texture in this forceful Riesling. Indian spices peek through on the finish. Not imported into the U.S. Best from 2001 through 2005.–B.S. • $NA • (1/01/2000) • **88**

GRAF HARDEGG

Merlot-Cabernet Qualitätswein Weinviertel Max 1995: If you like cherries, this is your wine. Pure cherry character, though one-dimensional, with a firm tannic underpinning and a hint of vanilla on the finish. Not imported into the U.S. Drink now through 2002.–B.S. • $NA • (1/01/1999) • **84**

Riesling Eiswein Weinviertel Steinbügel-Seefeld 1996 • $29/375 ml. • (2/28/1998) • **89**

Riesling Eiswein Weinviertel Steinbügel-Seefeld 1995 • $25/375 ml. • (2/28/1998) • **92**

Viognier Tafelwein Trocken Austria 1998: Leans toward the bitter side, with peach pit, spice and a musky note mated to a medium-bodied frame and moderate acidity. Not imported into the U.S. Drink now.–B.S. • $NA • (1/01/2000) • **83**

Weissburgunder Qualitätswein Weinviertel Max 1997: This atypical style works well, marrying new oak scents and flavors of clove and vanilla with a rich texture and peach notes, all supported by bright acidity. Not imported into the U.S. Drink now.–B.S. • $NA • (1/01/1999) • **85**

Weissburgunder-Chardonnay Qualitätswein Trocken Weinviertel Max 1998: Lean, dry and crisp, this white combines spicy apple and grapefruit flavors with a sinewy structure. Good depth and intensity. Should come alive with food. Not imported into the U.S. Drink now through 2001.–B.S. • $NA • (1/01/1999) • **84**

GRAFLICH STURGKH'SCHES

Rheinriesling Südoststeiermark 1997: Broad and waxy, this lacks the verve and clarity of Riesling at its best, but offers richness and a soft personality, giving it appeal. Finishes short. Not imported into the U.S. Drink now.–B.S. • $NA • (1/01/1999) • **84**

Weissburgunder Qualitätswein Südoststeiermark 1997: Firm and slightly austere, this Pinot Blanc shows lemon, mineral and apricot flavors underscored by mouthwatering acidity. Best with food. Not imported into the U.S. Drink now.–B.S. • $NA • (1/01/1999) • **82**

GROSS

Grauburgunder Qualitätswein Südsteiermark 1997: A pleasant but simple white, with no particular varietal character.–B.S. • $19 • (2/28/1999) • **78**

Sauvignon Blanc Qualitätswein Südsteiermark Ratscher Nussberg 1997: Barely vinous, this offers almost no varietal character.–B.S. • $30 • (2/28/1999) • **75**

Weissburgunder Qualitätswein Südsteiermark Kittenberg 1997: This rich, balanced white is marked by intriguing aromas of a meadow in springtime, with stone and peach flavors. The finish is crisp and refreshing. Drink now.–B.S. • $19 • (2/28/1999) • **84**

GSELLMANN & GSELLMANN

Qualitätswein Trocken Neusiedlersee Alte Lagen Red 1995 • $16 • (2/28/1998) • **85**

HEINRICH, GERNOT

Blauer Zweigelt Qualitätswein Trocken Neusiedlersee 1997: Dark ruby in color and smelling of black cherry and plum, this has richness and weight along with black fruit character, but the finish is astringent. Overall, lacking in dimension and complexity, but a good effort. Drink now through 2001.–B.S. • $16 • (2/28/1999) • **84**

Blauer Zweigelt Qualitätswein Trocken Neusiedlersee 1996 • $15 • (2/28/1998) • **86**

Blauer Zweigelt Qualitätswein Trocken Neusiedlersee 1994 • $16 • (2/28/1997) • **84**

Blaufränkisch Qualitätswein Trocken Mittelburgenland I. Goldberg 1997: Inky in color, the blackberry and cassis virtually explode from the glass in this soft, quaffable red. Its light tannins and refreshing acidity suggest chilling it slightly. Drink now.–B.S. • $14 • (9/15/1999) • **85**

Blaufränkisch Qualitätswein Trocken Neusiedlersee 1997: Ripe, gamy and broad in its approach, this red shows cherry flavors, with moderate structure and tannin. Firms up a little on the finish, where there's a metallic note. Drink now.–B.S. • $16 • (4/30/2000) • **84**

Blaufränkisch Qualitätswein Trocken Neusiedlersee 1994 • $16 • (2/28/1997) • **84**

Weissburgunder Qualitätswein Trocken Burgenland 1998: Lean and tart, showing only a modicum of lemon and unripe apple notes.–B.S. • $16 • (12/31/1999) • **78**

Weissburgunder Qualitätswein Trocken Burgenland 1997: Ripe and peachy, this straightforward white has moderate concentration and depth. Well balanced, with a modest finish. Drink now.–B.S. • $16 • (2/28/1999) • **83**

Weissburgunder Qualitätswein Trocken Neusiedlersee 1996 • $14 • (2/28/1998) • **82**

HEINRICH, J.

Blaufränkisch Qualitätswein Trocken Mittelburgenland Goldberg 1997: The aromas are muted, yet there's no mistaking the flavor of fresh raspberries on the palate. Lively, frivolous, bursting with charm, with good concentration and structure. Not imported into the U.S. Drink now through 2002.–B.S. • $NA • (1/01/2000) • **88**

Blaufränkisch Qualitätswein Trocken Mittelburgenland Goldberg Exclusiv Selection 1997: Inky in color, full of blackberry, coffee and spice notes. A vibrant, medium-bodied red showing balance and concentration, with a crisp, lingering finish. Not imported into the U.S. Drink now through 2002.–B.S. • $NA • (1/01/2000) • **89**

Cabernet Sauvignon Qualitätswein Trocken Mittelburgenland Exclusiv Selection 1997: An assertive style, boasting plenty of spicy new oak character along with black cherry, cedar and a firm, moderately tannic structure. Appealing for fans of the modern, oaky school. Not imported into the U.S. Drink now through 2002.–B.S. • $NA • (1/01/2000) • **87**

Pinot Noir Qualitätswein Trocken Mittelburgenland Weisses Kreutz 1997: Deeply colored, offering spicy, blackberry character, medium body, fine tannins and a slightly grainy texture. Tasty and modern in style, but if you're looking for a Burgundy stand-in, this isn't for you. Not imported into the U.S. Drink now.–B.S. • $NA • (1/01/2000) • **85**

Qualitätswein Trocken Mittelburgenland Terra O. 1997: Very Cabernet-like, grainy, with plum, black currant and leaflike aromas and flavors, with a lean intensity. Firmly structured, medium-bodied. Good finish. Not imported into the U.S. Drink now.–B.S. • $NA • (1/01/2000) • **86**

Zweigelt Qualitätswein Trocken Mittelburgenland Ried Siglos 1997: Lovely raspberry and black pepper aromas and flavors highlight this smooth, firmly structured Zweigelt. It's medium-bodied, with ripe, mouthcoating tannins. Not imported into the U.S. Drink now through 2001.–B.S. • $NA • (1/01/2000) • **85**

HIEDLER

Chardonnay Qualitätswein Kamptal Kittmannsberg 1997: Broad in texture, this attractive white has good underlying acidity, yet the floral and peach flavors would benefit from a little more focus. Drink now.–B.S. • $24 • (12/31/1998) • **83**

Chardonnay Qualitätswein Kamptal Langenloiser Kittmannsberg 1996 • $22 • (2/28/1998) • **85**

Grüner Veltliner Qualitätswein Kamptal Langenloiser Thal 1996 • $17 • (2/28/1998) • **84**

Grüner Veltliner Qualitätswein Kamptal Vier Weinberge 1996 • $14 • (2/28/1998) • **84**

Grüner Veltliner Qualitätswein Trocken Kamptal Maximum 1998: Terrific Grüner. This wine is light and airy, yet intense and concentrated at the same time, its exotic, complex flavors of apricot, celery, white pepper and grapefruit mingling with the broad profile and firm backbone. Drink now through 2001.–B.S. • $24 • (12/31/1999) HR • **92**

Grüner Veltliner Qualitätswein Trocken Kamptal Maximum 1997: Marzipan aromas and flavors are the dominant theme in this heavy-handed, powerful white. Makes up with intensity for what it lacks in grace and finesse. Drink through 2005.–B.S. • $22 • (12/31/1998) • **87**

HIEDLER

Grüner Veltliner Qualitätswein Trocken Kamptal Thal 1998: Richly textured, this Grüner shows textbook lentil, cereal and grapefruit aromas and flavors, together on a firm framework. Good weight and density. Drink now through 2001.–B.S. • $18 • (12/31/1999) • **88**

Grüner Veltliner Qualitätswein Trocken Kamptal Thal 1997: This shows the grapefruit side of Grüner Veltliner along with a vibrant but tender structure, ending on citrus and mineral notes. Drink now through 2001.–B.S. • $17 • (2/28/1999) • **84**

Grüner Veltliner Qualitätswein Trocken Kamptal Thal Novemberlese 1998: A frank, juicy white, smelling and tasting of lentil, grapefruit and sweet red cherry. Deftly balanced and rich, with a hint of residual sweetness, this is delicious now. Drink now through 2001.–B.S. • $24 • (8/31/1999) • **87**

Grüner Veltliner Qualitätswein Trocken Kamptal Vier Weinberge 1998: Broad, showing almond, licorice and red berry notes, moderate structure and an easygoing profile. Tasted twice, with consistent notes. Drink now.–B.S. • $17 • (12/31/1999) • **83**

Riesling Qualitätswein Halbtrocken Kamptal Maximum 1998: Noticably sweet, delivering apricot, grapefruit and bitter almond aromas and flavors in a moderately firm, round presentation. Drink now through 2003.–B.S. • $31 • (4/30/2000) • **89**

Riesling Qualitätswein Trocken Kamptal Zöbinger Heiligenstein Maximum 1997: Rich and satisfying, this has plenty of ripe peach, pear and stony aromas and flavors; forward and inviting, yet lacks the extra dimension and finish of the best. Drink now through 2002.–B.S. • $25 • (2/28/1999) • **86**

Weissburgunder Qualitätswein Halbtrocken Kamptal Langenloiser Schenkenbichl 1996 • $20 • (2/28/1998) • **82**

Weissburgunder Qualitätswein Trocken Kamptal Maximum 1998: Ripe and smoky, this Pinot Blanc packs plenty of banana, nut and tropical fruit nuances. Full-bodied and dense, with moderate structure. Long, sweet, vanilla and hazelnut finish. Drink now through 2002.–B.S. • $26 • (4/30/2000) • **89**

Weissburgunder Qualitätswein Trocken Kamptal Maximum 1997: A lean, racy Pinot Blanc displaying plenty of mineral and lemon notes. Depth and intensity of flavor are stuffed into the lean framework. Try with food. Drink now through 2002.–B.S. • $26 • (2/28/1999) • **86**

HIRSCH

Grüner Veltliner Qualitätswein Trocken Kamptal Kammerner Heiligenstein 1998: A hint of new oak here, but it works. Butterscotch, vanilla apricot and lemon marry with the round profile and rich texture. What it loses in crispness, it gains in smoothness. Drink now through 2001.–B.S. • $18 • (12/31/1999) • **87**

Grüner Veltliner Qualitätswein Trocken Kamptal Kammerner Heiligenstein Alte Reben 1998: Ripe, round and satisfying, full of lemon curd, pear, almond and vanilla, all on a rich swath of velvet. The moderate finish lacks just a bit of intensity. Drink now.–B.S. • $24 • (12/31/1999) • **89**

Grüner Veltliner Qualitätswein Trocken Kamptal Kammerner Heiligenstein MW 1998: Very fresh, with piercing scents of spring blossoms, apple and citrus, this white is light, lively and smooth in texture, with a citrus and mineral finish. Drink now.–B.S. • $16 • (9/15/1999) • **85**

Riesling Qualitätswein Trocken Kamptal Zöbinger Gaisberg 1998: Power and personality. Lean, firm and intense, this exudes subtle peach, apricot and plenty of stony notes on a medium framework, with a hint of alcohol at the finish. Best from 2001 through 2005.–B.S. • $19 • (12/31/1999) • **87**

Riesling Qualitätswein Trocken Kamptal Zöbinger Gaisberg Alte Reben 1998: Truly fascinating. Cardamom, passion fruit, lime, cilantro—all are here, in addition to other exotic tastes in this expressive, densely textured white. Extremely harmonious and well defined, finishing with a panoply of flavors. Brilliant effort. Drink now through 2005.–B.S. • $31 • (12/31/1999) • **90**

HIRTZBERGER, FRANZ

Grauburgunder Smaragd Trocken Wachau Pluris 1998: Reminiscent of a top Pinot Gris from Alsace's Zind-Humbrecht, offering violet, smoke, quince and pear aromas and flavors on a firm, full-bodied structure. Beautiful definition and balance. Drink now through 2003.–B.S. • $32 • (4/30/2000) • **90**

Grüner Veltliner Federspiel Trocken Wachau Spitzer Rotes Tor 1998: What an exotic wine, offering smoke, tropical fruit and citrus aromas and flavors married to a fat, glossy texture. Well balanced by moderate acidity and a touch of bitterness on the finish, which is long and satisfying. Tasted twice, with consistent notes. Drink now through 2002.–B.S. • $23 • (8/31/1999) • **88**

Grüner Veltliner Smaragd Trocken Wachau Spitzer Honivogl 1998: A sultry, smoky Grüner, luscious and creamy up front, with the underlying acidity revealing itself on the finish. Peach, vanilla and a white pepper note are some of the flavors in this complex, intense Austrian white. Drink now through 2010.–B.S. • $40 • (3/31/2000) HR • **94**

Grüner Veltliner Smaragd Trocken Wachau Spitzer Honivogl 1997: Concentrated aromas of banana and almond are the hallmarks of this intense, focused white. Young and unevolved, with bright underlying acidity, this has the richness and structure to develop over time. Drink now through 2005.–B.S. • $45 • (12/31/1998) • **89**

Grüner Veltliner Smaragd Trocken Wachau Spitzer Honivogl 1996 • $35 • (2/28/1998) • **87**

Grüner Veltliner Smaragd Trocken Wachau Spitzer Rotes Tor 1998: Starts off with a fat, viscous texture and aromas and flavors of vanilla custard, white flowers and thyme, all on a big, weighty frame. A little awkward right now, so give it time to come together. Best from 2002 through 2008.–B.S. • $32 • (4/30/2000) • **90**

Grüner Veltliner Smaragd Trocken Wachau Spitzer Rotes Tor 1996 • $26 • (2/28/1998) • **86**

Riesling Smaragd Trocken Wachau Spitzer Hochrain 1998: Ripe and expressive, showing citrus, smoke, mineral and spice flavors mingling with the broad structure and grainy finish. Fine aftertaste of quince and apricot. Drink now through 2004.–B.S. • $45 • (12/31/1999) • **88**

Riesling Smaragd Trocken Wachau Spitzer Hochrain 1997: Exotic aromas (botrytis?) of banana, lanolin and passion fruit are brought to earth by an intense mineral element. Packed with character, it coats the palate and is supported by a solid structure of acidity. Best from 2002 through 2010.–B.S. • $50 • (1/31/1999) • **91**

Riesling Smaragd Trocken Wachau Spitzer Singerriedel 1998: Huge Riesling, completely pumped up with apricot, grapefruit, peach pit, baking bread and licorice aromas and flavors. Broad, voluminous and in your face; botrytis gives an exotic, flamboyant touch. Great finish, too. Drink now through 2007.–B.S. • $55 • (4/30/2000) • **92**

Riesling Smaragd Trocken Wachau Spitzer Singerriedel 1997: A fabulous wine; from a top site and a brilliant expression of Austrian Riesling. Delivers cardamom, Indian spice and mineral intensity backed by ripe quince and apricot flavors, dense texture and sleek, racy structure. Best from 2002 through 2010.–B.S. • $68 • (1/31/1999) HR • **95**

Riesling Smaragd Trocken Wachau Spitzer Singerriedel 1996 • $50 • (2/28/1998) • **91**

Weissburgunder Smaragd Trocken Wachau Steinporz 1998: Amazing intensity and range of flavors in this complex, zingy white. Very ripe, it exhibits floral, pineapple, lemon, mineral and smoke, worn elegantly by the vibrant structure. Medium-bodied, concentrated and long on the aftertaste. Drink now through 2005.–B.S. • $35 • (4/30/2000) • **90**

HOCHRIEGL

Brut Reserve Austria NV • $20 • (12/15/1996) • **85**

HOLLER, J. & E.

Blaufränkisch Ruster Eiswein Neusiedlersee-Hügelland Elfenhof 1997: A delicate eiswein, showing rose, black currant and thyme. A vibrant structure keeps it lively, and there's an aftertaste of figs and smoke. Drink now through 2003.–B.S. • $44 • (4/30/2000) • **88**

Ruster Ausbruch Neusiedlersee-Hügelland Elfenhof Cuvée 1994: This is maturing, seems drier and has racy acidity. It's compact though, offering modest citrus and honey flavors, finishing with a bitter note. Not imported into the U.S. Drink now.–B.S. • $NA • (1/01/2000) • **87**

Ruster Eiswein Neusiedlersee-Hügelland Elfenhof 1997: Vibrant and focused, yet the flavors are a bit one-dimensional, despite good concentration. Finishes with a slight bitter element. Drink now through 2002.–B.S. • $44/500 ml. • (4/30/2000) • **87**

Weissburgunder Ruster Trockenbeerenauslese Neusiedlersee-Hügelland Elfenhof 1991: Absolutely gorgeous. Almost orange in color, with complex aromas and flavors of orange peel, honey, caramel, apricot and spice, all concentrated and married to a racy framework. Beautifully integrated and displayed, ending in a cascading finish. Not imported into the U.S. Drink now through 2004.–B.S. • $NA/500 ml. • (1/01/2000) • **93**

Weissburgunder-Chardonnay Ruster Trockenbeerenauslese Neusiedlersee-Hügelland Elfenhof 1995: Extremely concentrated, thick and sweet, this is monolithic, exhibiting caramel, honey, orange peel and grilled nuts on a

Key: SS—Spectator Selection. CS—Cellar Selection. HR—Highly Recommended. $NA—Price not available. (BT)—Barrel tasting. (A)—Auction Price.
For a key to the tasters' initials, see "How to Use These Listings."
Dates in parentheses represent the issues in which the ratings were published.

AUSTRIA

vibrant and dense structure that assaults the palate. Still needs time. Not imported into the U.S. Best from 2001 through 2006.–B.S. • $NA/500 ml. • (1/01/2000) • **90**

HOPLER

Blaufränkisch Qualitätswein Trocken Mittelburgenland Barrique 1997: Starts off very fruity, like a Beaujolais, with cherry and a slightly candied aroma, then turns quite firm and lean. Good fruit though. Drink now through 2002.–B.S. • $16 • (4/30/2000) • **86**

Eiswein Neusiedlersee 1998: A lively tartness adds structure and interest, driving the lime, apricot and caramel notes through to the lingering finish. Good concentration, with nice harmony. Drink now through 2003.–B.S. • $35/375 ml. • (4/30/2000) • **90**

Gewürztraminer Qualitätswein Trocken Neusiedlersee-Hügelland 1997: Soft and floral, here's a corpulent white, shy in its rose petal and litchi flavors, with a refreshing bitterness at the end. Drink now.–B.S. • $14 • (4/30/2000) • **82**

Grüner Veltliner Kabinett Trocken Neusiedlersee-Hügelland 1997: Already showing some marzipan and roasted corn aromas and flavors, this lively white starts off rich and firms up on the finish, with a citrus peel and herb aftertaste. Drink now through 2002.–B.S. • $10 • (12/31/1998) • **85**

Grüner Veltliner Qualitätswein Burgenland 1996 • $9 • (2/28/1998) • **85**

Pinot Blanc Kabinett Trocken Neusiedlersee 1997: Fresh and bright, this light-bodied, dry, rich white is marked by grass and almond character and a hint of beeswax. It finishes on a refreshing lemony note. Drink now.–B.S. • $11 • (2/28/1999) • **84**

Pinot Blanc Qualitätswein Trocken Neusiedlersee-Hügelland 1998: Rich and round, showing almond, beeswax and a hint of cherry, this white's firm structure emerges on the finish, with a fillip of bitterness. Drink now.–B.S. • $11 • (12/31/1999) • **85**

Pinot Blanc Qualitätswein Trocken Neusiedlersee-Hügelland 1997: A crisp, citrusy style of Pinot Blanc, with almond nuances. Straightforward and light, it's ready to enjoy. Drink now.–B.S. • $11 • (9/15/1999) • **82**

Pinot Blanc Trockenbeerenauslese Neusiedlersee 1995 • $25/375 ml. • (2/28/1998) HR • **93**

Pinot Blanc-Welschriesling Trockenbeerenauslese Neusiedlersee 1998: Complex and aromatic, with a violet note on top, offset by caramel and citrus nuances. Elegant, with bright acidity and just a hint of bitterness creeping in on the finish. Drink now through 2002.–B.S. • $30/375 ml. • (4/30/2000) • **88**

Pinot Gris Qualitätswein Burgenland 1996 • $11 • (2/28/1998) • **84**

Pinot Noir Qualitätswein Burgenland 1995 • $13 • (2/28/1998) • **83**

Pinot Noir Qualitätswein Trocken Neusiedlersee 1994 • $10 • (1/31/1997) • **73**

Pinot Noir Qualitätswein Trocken Neusiedlersee-Hügelland 1997: Smelling and tasting of red berries and currants, this light Pinot Noir shows a tart edge despite its silky texture. Drink now.–B.S. • $15 • (4/30/2000) • **83**

Pinot Noir Qualitätswein Trocken Neusiedlersee-Hügelland 1996: Silky-smooth and seductive, with raspberry and strawberry notes that persist through the good finish. A succulent character adds to the appeal. Drink now.–B.S. • $12 • (12/31/1998) • **84**

Riesling Kabinett Trocken Neusiedlersee Urgesteins 1997: An herbal-scented, lean style that lacks depth, leaving the earth, thyme and mineral thin and hard on the finish.–B.S. • $11 • (2/28/1999) • **78**

Welschriesling Eiswein Neusiedlersee 1997: Extremely pure and delicate, this ice wine is somewhat low in acidity but not cloying, sporting peach, pear and lime aromas and flavors. Clean, refreshing finish. Drink now through 2002.–B.S. • $35/375 ml. • (2/28/1999) • **89**

Zweigelt Qualitätswein Trocken Neusiedlersee Alesio 1994 • $11 • (1/31/1997) • **82**

INFUHR, KARL

Brut Austria Inführ Gold NV: There's richness and concentration here, with fig, lemon and honey flavors, a hint of sweetness, a lingering finish. Drink now.–B.S. • $15 • (4/30/2000) • **84**

Extra Brut Chardonnay-Pinot Noir Austria NV: A delicate, subtle sparkler, very dry, with apple and floral notes accented by mineral and a firm structure. The mouthwatering finish makes it a perfect apéritif. Drink now.–B.S. • $15 • (12/31/1998) • **86**

Extra Brut Chardonnay-Pinot Noir Austria NV: Dry and austere, with a touch of berry flavor, finishing more like beer than sparkling wine.–B.S. • $15 • (4/30/2000) • **78**

JAMEK, JOSEF

Grüner Veltliner Federspiel Wachau Ried Achleiten 1998: Plenty of mineral, spice and lentil notes highlight this restrained, elegant Austrian white. Its austere personality, moderate intensity and verve will make it a good partner at the table. Tasted twice, with consistent notes. Drink now through 2003.–B.S. • $19 • (8/31/1999) • **87**

Grüner Veltliner Smaragd Trocken Wachau Ried Achleiten 1998: A study in contrasts. Haunting, delicate aromas and flavors of spring blossoms and flowers are married to a bold, full-throttle body and structure. Has finesse and elegance, with fine potential for aging. Less well-defined on the finish. Best from 2001 through 2007.–B.S. • $40 • (4/30/2000) • **89**

Grüner Veltliner Smaragd Trocken Wachau Ried Achleiten 1997: Packed with pear and quince aromas and flavors, this Austrian white shows remarkable density and balance and an impressively rich midpalate. It finishes with serious acidity and a hint of alcohol, but is still an outstanding package. Not imported into the U.S. Drink now through 2005.–B.S. • $40 • (12/31/1998) HR • **90**

Riesling Smaragd Trocken Wachau Freiheit 1998: Tight and lean, showing more structure than fruit today, though the texture is creamy and it's densely packed, vibrant and well-defined. Give it time to integrate. Best from 2002 through 2010.–B.S. • $45 • (4/30/2000) • **91**

Weissburgunder Smaragd Wachau Ried Hochrain 1997: Very ripe, this medium-bodied, richly textured white bursts with peach, spring flower and almond character. It feels airy and delicate on the palate, with moderate intensity followed by a steely finish. Not imported into the U.S. Drink now through 2002.–B.S. • $NA • (1/01/1999) • **86**

JURIS

Ausbruch Neusiedlersee Georg Stiegelmar Imperialis 1996: This dessert wine is packed with apricot, honey and ginger, turning very honeyed on the finish. Starts off rich and concentrated, becoming elegant on the long, smooth aftertaste that hints at smoke. Not imported into the U.S. Drink now through 2004.–B.S. • $NA • (1/01/1999) • **89**

Pinot Noir Qualitätswein Neusiedlersee 1996: Resinous, spicy notes augment the cherry flavors in this moderately structured, silky red. Tannins are a little astringent on the finish. Drink now.–B.S. • $30 • (12/31/1998) • **83**

Pinot Noir Qualitätswein Neusiedlersee 1995 • $21 • (2/28/1998) • **85**

Qualitätswein Neusiedlersee St.-Georg Red 1996: Concentrated, with cherry jam and earth flavors, balancing acidity and a moderate aftertaste, but there's a little extra heat (alcohol) on the finish. Drink now.–B.S. • $NA • (12/31/1998) • **84**

Qualitätswein Neusiedlersee St.-Georg Red 1995 • $18 • (2/28/1998) • **84**

Saint Laurent Qualitätswein Neusiedlersee 1996: Solid, showing good concentration and cherry flavors, but lacks a bit of focus. Finishes with modest tannins. Drink now.–B.S. • $NA • (12/31/1998) • **82**

Saint Laurent Qualitätswein Neusiedlersee 1995 • $21 • (2/28/1998) • **85**

Trockenbeerenauslese Neusiedlersee Georg Stiegelmar 1995: Exciting stuff. Intense apricot, crème brûlée and orange notes foreshadow the ultrasweet nectar that follows. So intense, there's a petrol note that combines with an unctuous texture, completely concealing the crisp acidity. Very clean and focused on the finish. What a difference a year makes. Not imported into the U.S. Drink now through 2010.–B.S. • $NA/375 ml. • (1/01/1999) • **93**

KAISERGARTEN

Beerenauslese Neusiedlersee Seewinkler Impressionen 1997: Interesting aromas of shiso leaf and rhubarb highlight this medium-sweet BA. A delicate style, with honey notes emerging on the subtle finish. Not imported into the U.S. Drink now through 2001.–B.S. • $NA/375 ml. • (1/01/1999) • **84**

Blauer Zweigelt Qualitätswein Trocken Neusiedlersee Kaiser Symphonie 1997: This rich, round red shows up-front cherry flavors, with balancing acidity and firm tannins on the finish. The lasting impression is one of sweet fruit. Drink now.–B.S. • $9 • (12/31/1998) • **82**

Bouvier Trockenbeerenauslese Neusiedlersee Seewinkler Impressionen DNP 1997: Loads of tangy grapefruit and orange notes lead into honey and a hint of truffle on the palate in this fresh, lively version. Sweet, but not overly so, and the acidity should help it age. Not imported into the U.S. Drink through 2008.–B.S. • $NA/375 ml. • (1/01/1999) • **90**

KATTUS, JOHANN

Rheinriesling Kabinett Trocken Wien Nussberger Höhenweg 1997: Austere, displaying almond and stone aromas and flavors, with enough richness and

AUSTRIA

concentration to balance the firm acidity. Best with food. Drink now through 2001.–B.S. • $12 • (2/28/1999) • **83**

KNOLL

Grüner Veltliner Beerenauslese Wachau Loibner 1998: Fascinating. Distinctive piquancy and stoniness augment the honey and apricot character in this velvety BA. Balanced on the soft side, with enough structure to carry the flavors to a lingering conclusion. The finish is almost dry. Drink now through 2003.–B.S. • $56/500 ml. • (4/30/2000) • **93**

Grüner Veltliner Smaragd Trocken Wachau Ried Loibenberg 1998: Suave and broad-shouldered, yet the flavors are austere, holding back right now. A good structure bodes well for the future, and the aftertaste of peach, honey and vanilla expresses the ripeness. Best from 2001 through 2006.–B.S. • $37 • (4/30/2000) • **90**

Grüner Veltliner Smaragd Trocken Wachau Ried Loibenberg 1997: Very ripe, with exotic overtones of honey, vanilla custard and apricot, but it seems top-heavy right now, although there's plenty of acidity to support the flavors and rich body. Needs time to integrate. Drink through 2006.–B.S. • $30 • (12/31/1998) • **89**

Grüner Veltliner Smaragd Wachau Ried Loibenberg 1996 • $28 • (2/28/1998) • **87**

Riesling Beerenauslese Wachau Ried Pfaffenberg Steiner Süss 1995 • $38/500 ml. • (12/15/1996) • **90**

Riesling Smaragd Trocken Wachau Dürnsteiner Ried Schütt 1998: Haunting aromas of roses and violets give way to violets and cherry candy on the palate. The richness midpalate firms up nicely on the finish. Drink through 2004.–B.S. • $45 • (12/31/1999) • **89**

Riesling Smaragd Trocken Wachau Dürnsteiner Ried Schütt 1997: Rich and juicy, this is full of apricot and mineral aromas and flavors, beautifully displayed on a solid but balanced frame. Citrus notes linger on the finish. Drink through 2005.–B.S. • $50 • (2/28/1999) • **90**

Riesling Smaragd Trocken Wachau Ried Loibenberg 1998: More severe in style and not very expressive today, this firmly structured '98 nonetheless gains intensity in the mouth, with a fine and endless finish of apricot and grapefruit. Best from 2001 through 2005.–B.S. • $42 • (12/31/1999) • **89**

Riesling Smaragd Trocken Wachau Ried Loibenberg 1997: Tropical fruit and an herbal accent mark this expansive yet transparent Riesling. Lovely flavor concentration is seemingly packed into an airy framework, subtly integrating the acidity and mineral element. Drink through 2005.–B.S. • $45 • (1/31/1999) • **91**

Riesling Smaragd Wachau Dürnsteiner Ried Schütt 1996 • $56 • (2/28/1998) • **89**

KOLLWENTZ

Chardonnay Qualitätswein Trocken Neusiedlersee-Hügelland Tatschler 1997: An international style, offering nutmeg and vanilla from new oak but not much fruit. Broad, the structure comes from the oak as much as the acidity. Drink now.–B.S. • $40 • (12/31/1999) • **83**

Chardonnay-Welschriesling Trockenbeerenauslese Neusiedlersee-Hügelland 1996: Lean and racy, yet sweetness and concentration are here, too. The vibrant structure provides a great vehicle for the caramel, spice and cooked apple flavors, all well integrated and ending with a complex aftertaste. Drink now through 2003.–B.S. • $85/375 ml. • (4/30/2000) • **89**

Qualitätswein Trocken Neusiedlersee-Hügelland Eichkogel 1997: Stunning red. Pure and focused, displaying beautiful integration of raspberry, blackberry, cedar and vanilla with velvety texture and dense structure. Tightly wound, with an aftertaste of fresh berries and chocolate. Drink now through 2003.–B.S. • $28 • (4/30/2000) • **90**

Qualitätswein Trocken Neusiedlersee-Hügelland Steinzeiler Red 1997: Wonderful purity and freshness mark this cassis- and spice-laden young red. Grace notes of vanilla from new oak round out the flavor profile. Exhibits both elegance and solid structure. Long finish. Drink now through 2003.–B.S. • $44 • (4/30/2000) • **90**

KRACHER

Beerenauslese Neusiedlersee 1995 • $NA/375 ml. • (2/28/1998) • **90**

Key: SS—Spectator Selection. CS—Cellar Selection. HR—Highly Recommended. $NA—Price not available. (BT)—Barrel tasting. (A)—Auction Price. For a key to the tasters' initials, see "How to Use These Listings." **Dates in parentheses represent the issues in which the ratings were published.**

Beerenauslese Neusiedlersee Nouvelle Vague 1993 • $75/375 ml. • (12/15/1996) • **92**

Beerenauslese Neusiedlersee Weinlaubenhof Grande Cuvée 1997: A lean, vibrant BA, whose firm acidity drives the apricot and orange flavors, balancing the moderate richness. It has straightforward, attractive appeal and a modest finish. Drink now through 2004.–B.S. • $26/375 ml. • (2/28/1999) • **87**

Beerenauslese Neusiedlersee Weinlaubenhof Grande Cuvée 1995 • $90/375 ml. • (2/28/1998) • **91**

Beerenauslese Neusiedlersee Weinlaubenhof Grande Cuvée 1994 • $53/375 ml. • (12/15/1996) • **87**

Beerenauslese Neusiedlersee Weinlaubenhof Grande Cuvée 1991 • $53/375 ml. • (2/28/1997) • **89**

Bouvier Beerenauslese Neusiedlersee Nouvelle Vague No. 2 1997: Intriguing. A hint of truffle augments the white chocolate, honey, apricot and orange notes in this thick, concentrated BA. Wonderful balance and interplay of flavors across the palate, ending in a vibrant, long finish. Drink now through 2005.–B.S. • $47/375 ml. • (5/31/2000) • **91**

Bouvier-Muscat Trockenbeerenauslese Neusiedlersee Zwischen den Seen 1996: A TBA in a bright, slimmer style, evoking raisins and mixed spices in a grapey, easy-drinking manner. Finishes on an almond note. Drink now through 2003.–B.S. • $NA/375 ml. • (2/28/1999) • **87**

Chardonnay Trockenbeerenauslese Neusiedlersee Nouvelle Vague No. 8 1996: Beautiful wine. Gorgeous aromas of warm spice, orange, butterscotch and apricot. This flavorful, supersweet white has a firm structure if not quite the richness to round out all the edges. Drink now through 2007.–B.S. • $95/375 ml. • (2/28/1999) • **93**

Chardonnay Trockenbeerenauslese Neusiedlersee Nouvelle Vague No. 13 1995 • $100/375 ml • (2/28/1998) • **98**

Chardonnay Trockenbeerenauslese Neusiedlersee Nouvelle Vague 1994 • $75/375 ml. • (12/15/1996) • **93**

Chardonnay-Welschriesling Trockenbeerenauslese Neusiedlersee Nouvelle Vague No. 4 1996: An elegant TBA, full of apricot, smoke and spice character underscored by a racy acidity that maintains the flavor intensity through the long finish, where hints of orange peel emerge. Drink now through 2007.–B.S. • $NA/375 ml. • (2/28/1999) • **90**

Chardonnay-Welschriesling Trockenbeerenauslese Neusiedlersee Nouvelle Vague No. 7 1995 • $90/375 ml. • (2/28/1998) HR • **97**

Muscat Ottonel Trockenbeerenauslese Neusiedlersee Zwischen den Seen No. 5 1995 • $90/375 ml • (2/28/1998) • **93**

Muscat Ottonel Trockenbeerenauslese Neusiedlersee Zwischen den Seen No. 11 1995 • $95/375 ml • (2/28/1998) • **93**

Muscat Trockenbeerenauslese Neusiedlersee Zwischen den Seen No. 6 1996: Elegant and refined for Muscat, this TBA offers a hint of roses before the cinnamon, clove and cardamom mix takes over, all in a fresh, grapey style. Drink now through 2002.–B.S. • $83/375 ml. • (2/28/1999) • **87**

Qualitätswein Trocken Neusiedlersee Days of Wine and Roses 1998: Attractive for its floral and peach aromas and flavors, this white shows plenty of vibrant acidity and the overall presentation is balanced. The peach notes linger on the finish. Drink now.–B.S. • $15 • (9/15/1999) • **86**

Scheurebe Beerenauslese Neusiedlersee 1994 • $23/375 ml. • (12/15/1996) • **84**

Scheurebe Beerenauslese Neusiedlersee Zwischen den Seen 1994 • $43/375 ml. • (12/15/1996) • **90**

Scheurebe Beerenauslese Neusiedlersee Zwischen den Seen 1993 • $53/375 ml. • (12/15/1996) • **89**

Scheurebe Beerenauslese Neusiedlersee Zwischen den Seen 1991 • $43/375 ml. • (12/15/1996) • **90**

Scheurebe Trockenbeerenauslese Neusiedlersee Zwischen den Seen No. 3 1996: Almost amber in color, with the telltale grapefruit of Scheurebe and a lean, intense profile marked by searing acidity. Only moderately sweet, but its acidity should match well with lighter desserts. Drink now through 2005.–B.S. • $80/375 ml. • (2/28/1999) • **88**

Scheurebe Trockenbeerenauslese Neusiedlersee Zwischen den Seen No. 3 1995 • $72/375 ml • (2/28/1998) • **92**

Scheurebe Trockenbeerenauslese Neusiedlersee Zwischen den Seen No. 4 1995 • $90/375 ml • (2/28/1998) • **94**

Scheurebe Trockenbeerenauslese Neusiedlersee Zwischen den Seen No. 6 1995 • $75/375 ml. • (2/28/1998) • **88**

Scheurebe Trockenbeerenauslese Neusiedlersee Zwischen den Seen No. 14 1995 • $100/375 ml. • (2/28/1998) • **91**

Traminer Beerenauslese Neusiedlersee Nouvelle Vague No. 1 1996: Delicious. Vanilla and butterscotch from new oak vie with apricot, grapefruit and honey in this rich, sweet dessert white that's kept lively and interesting thanks to its zingy acidity. Drink now through 2006.–B.S. • $70/375 ml. • (2/28/1999) • **89**

Traminer Trockenbeerenauslese Neusiedlersee Nouvelle Vague No. 8 1995 • $90/375 ml. • (2/28/1998) • **91**

Trockenbeerenauslese Neusiedlersee Grand Cuvée No. 7 1996: Sweet and rich, with smoky, cooked apple flavors and zippy acidity, but it's all disjointed at this stage, with a moderate finish. May come together with time. Drink through 2006.–B.S. • $95/375 ml. • (2/28/1999) • **86**

Welschriesling Beerenauslese Neusiedlersee Zwischen den Seen 1994 • $75/375 ml. • (12/15/1996) • **88**

Welschriesling Trockenbeerenauslese Neusiedlersee Zwischen den Seen No. 9 1996: Incredible intensity here, with peach and apricot character and nuances of pine forest, all on a rich, thick texture. This exhibits power and harmony balanced by a vibrant structure. Long, peachy aftertaste. Drink now through 2007.–B.S. • $83/375 ml. • (2/28/1999) • **91**

Welschriesling Trockenbeerenauslese Neusiedlersee Zwischen den Seen No. 1 1995 • $65/375 ml. • (2/28/1998) • **91**

Welschriesling Trockenbeerenauslese Neusiedlersee Zwischen den Seen No. 2 1995 • $75/375 ml. • (2/28/1998) • **96**

Welschriesling Trockenbeerenauslese Neusiedlersee Zwischen den Seen No. 15 1995: Wow. Thick and mouthcoating, here's a superrich dessert-style wine that shows weight but never gets heavy or cloying. The flavors, ranging from candied orange peel and apricot to vanilla and crème brûlée, linger gracefully on the clean finish. Better than previously reviewed. Drink now through 2005.–B.S. • $110/375 ml. • (2/28/1999) • **93**

Zweigelt Rosé Trockenbeerenauslese Neusiedlersee Nouvelle Vague No. 10 1995 • $90/375 ml. • (2/28/1998) • **93**

Zweigelt Trockenbeerenauslese Neusiedlersee Nouvelle Vague No. 5 1996: A big, thick, honey- and apricot-flavored sweet wine that doesn't show a lot of nuance or pizzazz but is pleasant, with a caramel note that lingers on the finish. Drink now through 2002.–B.S. • $90/375 ml. • (2/28/1999) • **87**

KRAFT

Blauer Burgunder Beerenauslese Neusiedlersee-Hügelland 1995 • $NA/500 ml. • (2/28/1998) • **77**

Chardonnay Ruster Ausbruch Neusiedlersee-Hügelland 1995 • $NA/500 ml. • (2/28/1998) • **90**

KRUTZLER

Blaufränkisch Qualitätswein Trocken Südburgenland Bründlgfangen 1997: Promotes raspberry and currant flavors, with hints of chocolate and black pepper. Lively acidity and light, firm tannins support the fruit. A Chianti substitute. Drink now through 2001.–B.S. • $15 • (4/30/2000) • **85**

Blaufränkisch Qualitätswein Trocken Südburgenland Weinberg 1997: Here's an elegant mouthful of freshly crushed raspberries, cherries and blackberries on a framework of vibrant acidity and ripe tannins. Fine concentration and an excellent finish. Drink now through 2003.–B.S. • $20 • (4/30/2000) • **89**

Qualitätswein Trocken Südburgenland Alter Weingarten 1997: Aromatic, full of violets and cassis, this dark red is concentrated, with gracefulness and harmony that belies its firm structure. Delicious now for the succulent blackberry fruit and mineral accent. Blaufränkisch and Zweigelt. Drink now through 2003.–B.S. • $40 • (4/30/2000) • **89**

Qualitätswein Trocken Südburgenland Perwolff Red 1997: Serious stuff. Ripe, concentrated black fruits augmented by vanilla, coffee and a whisky note mark this intense, inky wine. The structure is medium-bodied, with lively acidity and firm tannins. Good length, too. Best from 2001 through 2004.–B.S. • $50 • (4/30/2000) • **91**

LANG

Chardonnay Ausbruch Neusiedlersee 1995 • $NA/375 ml. • (2/28/1998) • **87**

Chardonnay Trockenbeerenauslese Neusiedlersee 1995 • $NA/375 ml. • (2/28/1998) • **89**

Pinot Noir Trockenbeerenauslese Neusiedlersee 1995 • $NA/375 ml. • (2/28/1998) • **80**

Sämling 88 Trockenbeerenauslese Neusiedlersee 1995: Smelling and tasting like an apricot compote with a sprig of mint, this dessert wine's intense sweetness and rich texture are balanced by mouthwatering acidity. Not particularly complex, but well integrated. Not imported into the U.S. Drink now through 2004.–B.S. • $NA/375 ml. • (1/01/1999) • **89**

Sämling 88 Trockenbeerenauslese Neusiedlersee 1994 • $NA/375 ml • (2/28/1998) • **95**

Welschriesling Trockenbeerenauslese Neusiedlersee 1995 • $NA/375 ml. • (2/28/1998) • **91**

LANG, ERNST

Ruländer Neusiedlersee Lieblich 1997: With a hard-candy flavor augmented by cinnamon and ginger, this will appeal to some; however, it lacks the flesh and pure fruit of the variety. Drink now.–B.S. • $10 • (9/15/1999) • **81**

LEHRNER, PAUL

Blaufränkisch Qualitätswein Trocken Mittelburgenland Reserve 1997: Very pure and focused blackberry and cherry flavors. There's an almost mineral saltiness and good acidity on a lean texture, followed by a lingering finish. Drink now.–B.S. • $16 • (4/30/2000) • **88**

Blaufränkisch Qualitätswein Trocken Mittelburgenland Rosé Horitschoner 1998: Strawberries and a slight herbal accent mark this delightful dry rosé. A vibrant structure keeps the flavors focused and interesting. Drink now.–B.S. • $17 • (9/15/1999) • **84**

LENZ MOSER

Beerenauslese Neusiedlersee Prestige 1995 • $NA/350 ml. • (2/28/1998) • **88**

Grüner Veltliner Qualitätswein Austria Prestige Mailberg 1996 • $9 • (2/28/1998) • **82**

Grüner Veltliner Qualitätswein Trocken Kremstal Selection 1997: Offers a lovely combination of citrus, mineral and vegetable aromas and flavors. Focused and elegant, thanks to lively acidity. Not imported into the U.S. Drink now through 2003.–B.S. • $NA • (12/31/1998) • **84**

Servús Austria White 1997: Almond and herb blossoms, like chamomile and verbena, are accented by a hint of peach in this compact white. Finishes slightly bitter. Not imported into the U.S.–B.S. • $NA • (1/01/1999) • **79**

Trockenbeerenauslese Neusiedlersee Prestige 1995 • $NA/375 ml. • (2/28/1998) • **89**

LOIBEN, DINSTLGUT

Grüner Veltliner Auslese Lieblich Wachau Loibner Loibenberg L 1998: Viscous and full-bodied, with ripe flavors of apricot, grapefruit and tobacco, all balanced toward the soft side. Not imported into the U.S. Drink now through 2005.–B.S. • $NA • (1/01/2000) • **88**

Grüner Veltliner Qualitätswein Halbtrocken Wachau Loibner Loibenberg L 1997: Lovely expression of flavors—all passion fruit and kiwi augmented by mineral—and a grounding earthy note are married to a firm structure. Harmonious, with a lingering finish that echoes the tropical fruit nuances. Drink now through 2004.–B.S. • $24 • (12/31/1998) • **90**

Grüner Veltliner Qualitätswein Trocken Kremstal Kremser Pfaffenberg 1997: Delicate, showing richness rather than power and intensity, with mineral flavors and a lingering finish. Drink now through 2001.–B.S. • $13 • (12/31/1998) • **85**

Grüner Veltliner Qualitätswein Trocken Wachau Loibner Loibenberg 1998: Harmonious and deceptive, this offers pretty floral aromas backed by apricot and herbal flavors yet there's an intensity and latent power that builds to a complex, long finish. Not imported into the U.S. Drink now through 2003.–B.S. • $NA • (1/01/1999) • **89**

Grüner Veltliner Qualitätswein Trocken Wachau Loibner Schütt 1998: A delicious Grüner, delivering lentil, grapefruit and peach aromas and flavors that intensify on the palate, supported by lively acidity and good concentration. Drink now.–B.S. • $14 • (8/31/1999) • **87**

Grüner Veltliner Qualitätswein Wachau Loibner Loibenberg 1996 • $11 • (2/28/1998) • **86**

Grüner Veltliner Qualitätswein Wachau Loibner Schütt 1996 • $10 • (2/28/1998) • **83**

Riesling Qualitätswein Kremstal Kremser Pfaffenberg 1996 • $13 • (2/28/1998) • **84**

Riesling Qualitätswein Lieblich Wachau Loibner Loibenberg L 1997: A distinct sweetness marks this white whose profile alternates between ripe apple, honey notes and petrol, nutty elements (very Alsace-like). Balanced and appealing, it's forward, with a moderate finish. Not imported into the U.S. Drink now through 2002.–B.S. • $NA • (1/01/1999) • **88**

Riesling Qualitätswein Trocken Wachau Loibner Loibenberg 1997: More power than seduction here. Very rich, this medium-bodied white delivers pear and herb aromas and flavors on a densely textured, firm structure, with a mineral note lingering on the finish. Drink through 2005.–B.S. • $18 • (2/28/1999) • **90**

Riesling Spätlese Lieblich Wachau Loibner Loibenberg L 1998: Light in aroma and body, showing marzipan notes and a tight focus, with flavors that tail off on the finish. Not imported into the U.S. Drink now through 2002.–B.S. • $NA • (1/01/2000) • **86**

LOIMER

Chardonnay Qualitätswein Trocken Kamptal Langenloiser 1997: Good balance between the spicy oak and pear flavors, yet the overall impression is rigid and tough on the finish. May be better with food. Drink now.–B.S. • $31 • (12/31/1999) • **82**

Grüner Veltliner Qualitätswein Halbtrocken Kamptal Langenloiser Spiegel Alte Reben 1997: Extremely ripe, with new oak nuances of coconut, butter and nutmeg, this exotic, off-dry white is balanced and delicious. May be best as an aperitif. Drink now through 2002.–B.S. • $37 • (2/28/1999) • **87**

Grüner Veltliner Qualitätswein Kamptal Federleichter 1998: Ripe, lush and mouthcoating, this Grüner Veltliner leans toward peach, with lentil and herb flavors too. Fine balancing acidity is hidden by the sheer exuberance of the flavor and texture, ending crisply. Tasted twice, with consistent notes. Drink now.–B.S. • $14 • (8/31/1999) • **85**

Grüner Veltliner Qualitätswein Trocken Kamptal Langenloiser Spiegel 1998: Easygoing, broad and winey, with peach, apple and tobacco flavors of moderate length. Drink now through 2001.–B.S. • $20 • (12/31/1999) • **87**

Grüner Veltliner Qualitätswein Trocken Kamptal Langenloiser Spiegel 1997: Ripe, full and fleshy, this crowd-pleasing white bursts with apple, mineral and a hint of celery. Vibrant acidity keeps everything in focus right through to the apricot finish. Drink now through 2002.–B.S. • $20 • (12/31/1998) • **89**

Grüner Veltliner Qualitätswein Trocken Kamptal Langenloiser Spiegel 1996 • $16 • (2/28/1998) • **83**

Grüner Veltliner Qualitätswein Trocken Kamptal Langenloiser Spiegel Alte Reben 1998: A statement. Obvious new oak, and expensive, judging by the creamy vanilla and butterscotch flavors and grainy texture it imparts, while the grapefruit and apricot notes remain submerged for now. The oak lingers on the finish. Drink now through 2001.–B.S. • $31 • (12/31/1999) • **89**

Riesling Qualitätswein Kamptal Langenloiser Steinmassl 1998: Ripe and juicy with grapefruit, orange and honey aromas and flavors, this '98 Riesling is forward and rich, yet maintains a crispness on the finish for a refreshing aftertaste. Drink now through 2002.–B.S. • $33 • (12/31/1999) • **88**

Riesling Qualitätswein Kamptal Langenloiser Steinmassl 1997: A seamless white, exhibiting tropical fruit nuances underscored by minerally, nutty elements, concentrated flavors, lively acidity and a refreshing finish. Drink now through 2004.–B.S. • $32 • (2/28/1999) • **89**

Riesling Qualitätswein Kamptal Langenloiser Steinmassl 1996 • $24 • (2/28/1998) • **87**

Riesling Qualitätswein Trocken Kamptal Langenloiser Schenkenbichl 1998: Loads of apricot, passion fruit and orange aromas and flavors mark this lean, structured white. Shuts down on the finish today; perhaps needs a bit of time to open. Best from 2001 through 2003.–B.S. • $17 • (12/31/1999) • **85**

Riesling Qualitätswein Trocken Kamptal Langenloiser Seeberg 1998: Distinctive for its minty element, along with apricot and grapefruit backed by a juicy acidity that plays off the creamy texture. Round and satisfying. Drink now through 2004.–B.S. • $20 • (4/30/2000) • **89**

MALAT

Blauer Burgunder Qualitätswein Trocken Kremstal 1996: An effusively fruity red, with a hint of carbon dioxide lifting the cherry and berry aromas. Supple and juicy, it all comes together in a tasty, easy-drinking style. Not imported into the U.S. Drink now.–B.S. • $NA • (12/31/1998) • **82**

Chardonnay Trockenbeerenauslese Kremstal 1995 • $NA/375 ml. • (2/28/1998) • **97**

Grüner Veltliner Qualitätswein Trocken Kremstal Dreigärten 1998: Incredible aromas of violets, apricots and tropical nuances turn to red berries on the palate. Remains elegant and full of finesse, just tailing off a little on the finish. Not imported into the U.S. Drink now through 2001.–B.S. • $NA • (1/01/1999) • **88**

Riesling Qualitätswein Kremstal Silberbühel Reserve 1997: Packs in a lot of aromas and flavors—from apple and citrus to almond and mineral—all on a sleek frame. It's rich, densely textured and finishes on the firm side, with a long aftertaste. Not imported into the U.S. Drink now through 2004.–B.S. • $NA • (1/01/1999) • **89**

Riesling Qualitätswein Trocken Wachau Silberbühel 1998: A little bortytis lends a forward, tropical fruit character to this firm, minerally white that shows intensity and focus. Great flavors, if not a lot of terroir. Not imported into the U.S. Drink now through 2003.–B.S. • $NA • (1/01/2000) • **88**

Riesling Trockenbeerenauslese Kremstal 1998: Wow! Supersweet, ultraconcentrated and buzzing with bright acidity, this is immovable today. The sweetness covers the apricot, honey and orange flavors, while the acidity leaves a mouthwatering impression on the finish. Shows great promise. Not imported into the U.S. Best from 2002 through 2010.–B.S. • $NA/375 ml. • (1/01/2000) • **95**

Sauvignon Blanc Qualitätswein Kremstal 1996 • $NA • (2/28/1998) • **81**

Sauvignon Blanc Trockenbeerenauslese Kremstal 1996: A good effort in a difficult vintage. Deeply colored, with stewed rhubarb and apricot flavors and tart character, yet without the richness to balance all the components. A smoky note lingers on the finish. Not imported into the U.S. Drink through 2004.–B.S. • $70/375 ml. • (1/01/1999) • **86**

MALTESER RITTERORDEN

Cabernet Sauvignon-Merlot Weinviertel Kommende Mailberg 1994 • $20 • (2/28/1998) • **84**

Grüner Veltliner Qualitätswein Weinviertel Hundschupfen 1996 • $10 • (2/28/1998) • **78**

MANTLERHOF

Grüner Veltliner Kabinett Kremstal Speigel 1996 • $16 • (2/28/1998) • **81**

Riesling Qualitätswein Trocken Kremstal 1996 • $18 • (2/28/1998) • **84**

Riesling Qualitätswein Trocken Kremstal Tiefenthal 1998: Ripe, with aromas and flavors of forest floor, vanilla and tropical fruit. Rich, yet backed by a lively framework, finishing on a grapefruit note. Drink now through 2004.–B.S. • $26 • (4/30/2000) • **87**

Riesling Qualitätswein Trocken Kremstal Tiefenthal 1997: A fresh, graceful Riesling, with lovely floral, peach and mineral shadings, its richness balanced by juicy acidity and a subtle finish. Drink now through 2002.–B.S. • $19 • (2/28/1999) • **89**

Riesling Qualitätswein Trocken Kremstal Wieland 1997: Focused aromas of lime and mineral are augmented by peach and almond on the palate. It's so dense and rich, the vibrant acidity is covered, yet the balance is fine and its future promising. Drink now through 2004.–B.S. • $20 • (2/28/1999) • **88**

Riesling Qualitätswein Trocken Kremstal Zehetnerin 1998: This Riesling exhibits floral, tropical fruit and grapefruit, all balanced and vibrantly structured, with a mouthwatering finish. Drink now through 2004.–B.S. • $19 • (4/30/2000) • **86**

Roter Veltliner Beerenauslese Kremstal 1995 • $34/500 ml • (2/28/1998) • **88**

Roter Veltliner Qualitätswein Trocken Kremstal Reisenthal Selection 1997: Presents a mix of earth, nut and citrus aromas and flavors on a richly textured framework, followed by a firm finish. Drink now.–B.S. • $17 • (2/28/1999) • **83**

MARKOWITSCH

Grüner Veltliner Qualitätswein Carnuntum Ried Schanzäcker 1996 • $9 • (2/28/1998) • **85**

Grüner Veltliner Qualitätswein Trocken Carnuntum Alte Reben 1998: Bright and snappy, showing grapefruit, grass and mineral notes, all balanced, with a medium body and crisp texture. Drink now.–B.S. • $18 • (12/31/1999) • **85**

Grüner Veltliner Qualitätswein Trocken Carnuntum Alte Reben 1997: A fresh white, full of grapefruit with a touch of grass, almost Sauvignon-like, but it has more delicacy and finesse, showing subtle length. Appealing. Drink now.–B.S. • $16 • (2/28/1999) • **85**

Qualitätswein Trocken Carnuntum Redmont 1997: Cherry, vanilla and dill mingle in this medium-bodied red. Firmly structured, it's lean but intense, with a good finish. Drink now through 2001.–B.S. • $18 • (12/31/1998) • **83**

Qualitätswein Trocken Carnuntum Rosenberg 1997: A rich, concentrated red, full of berry flavors and sweet oak, yet there's a hint of herbaceousness and an astringency to the tannins suggesting a slight underripeness. Zweigelt, Cabernet Sauvignon and Blaufränkisch. Drink now through 2001.–B.S. • $35 • (4/30/2000) • **87**

Sauvignon Blanc Qualitätswein Trocken Carnuntum 1998: Very fresh and crisp, with ripe melon and a hint of grapefruit. Well balanced, with a lingering melon taste. Drink now.–B.S. • $20 • (4/30/2000) • **89**

Sauvignon Blanc Qualitätswein Trocken Carnuntum 1997: A delicate, balanced white, offering grapefruit and gooseberry aromas and flavors on an elegant and vivid structure. Drink now through 2001.–B.S. • $17 • (2/28/1999) • **84**

Key: SS—Spectator Selection. CS—Cellar Selection. HR—Highly Recommended. $NA—Price not available. (BT)—Barrel tasting. Ⓐ—Auction Price.
For a key to the tasters' initials, see "How to Use These Listings."
Dates in parentheses represent the issues in which the ratings were published.

MAYER, FRANZ

Chardonnay Qualitätswein Trocken Wien Ried Nussberg 1998: Creamy and rich, yet with a firm structure beneath the almond, dough and citrus notes. The finish is crisp. Drink now through 2001.–B.S. • $17 • (12/31/1999) • **84**

Chardonnay Qualitätswein Trocken Wien Ried Nussberg 1997: Round and broad, showing melon and pear aromas and flavors and a light structure for early consumption. A hint of bitterness graces the finish. Drink now.–B.S. • $16 • (12/31/1998) • **83**

Grüner Veltliner Kabinett Wien Grinzinger Schenkenberg 1996 • $9 • (2/28/1998) • **83**

Kabinett Wien White Nussberger Symphony 1996 • $10 • (2/28/1998) • **83**

Rheinriesling Kabinett Wien Vienna Classic 1996 • $11 • (2/28/1998) • **83**

Rheinriesling Qualitätswein Trocken Wien Nussberger Ried Preussen Vienna Classic 1998: Ripe and crisply textured, this Riesling offers straightforward peach and citrus flavors followed by a modest finish. Drink now.–B.S. • $18 • (12/31/1999) • **84**

Rheinriesling Qualitätswein Trocken Wien Nussberger Ried Preussen Vienna Classic 1997: A spice monster, dry and steely, its apple and almond notes remaining firm and compact right through the moderate finish. Drink now through 2002.–B.S. • $18 • (2/28/1999) • **87**

Weissburgunder Beerenauslese Wien Ried Reisenberg-Grinzing 1996: More like a supercharged Pinot Blanc than a BA, this white is medium-sweet, with a delicate profile and racy acidity. Its peach and citrus notes are tasty, but it lacks depth and intensity. Drink now through 2003.–B.S. • $21/500 ml. • (2/28/1999) • **86**

MICHLITS-STADLMANN

Cabernet Sauvignon Qualitätswein Trocken Neusiedlersee 1997: There's a feral, saddle-leather element here, yet it adds to the whole, bringing an extra dimension to the cherry and green olive notes. Smooth, with good underlying acidity and fine tannins. Drink now.–B.S. • $17 • (4/30/2000) • **88**

Pinot Blanc Qualitätswein Extra Trocken Neusiedlersee 1998: Although fresh and peachy, there's a whiff of sulfur here. Rich and round on the palate, this offers peach flavor and an earthy, nutty note typical of the variety. Drink now.–B.S. • $13 • (9/15/1999) • **83**

Traminer Ausbruch Neusiedlersee 1995 • $25/375 ml. • (2/28/1998) • **88**

Weissburgunder Trockenbeerenauslese Neusiedlersee 1995 • $38/375 ml. • (2/28/1998) • **79**

Welschriesling Spätlese Neusiedlersee 1998: Attractive, this white smells mature and tastes sweet, like honey and apples. Reminiscent of a soft Chenin Blanc. Drink now.–B.S. • $14 • (4/30/2000) • **84**

Welschriesling Trockenbeerenauslese Neusiedlersee 1995: A little barnyard smell blew off to reveal a fresh, pure, elegant white, sweet yet offset by juicy acidity and apricot and honey flavors. Hints of orange linger on the finish. Drink now through 2004.–B.S. • $37/375 ml. • (2/28/1999) • **88**

Zweigelt Qualitätswein Extra Trocken Neusiedlersee Falstaff Prämiert 1993 • $15 • (2/28/1997) • **84**

Zweigelt Qualitätswein Trocken Neusiedlersee 1997: Flavors of sweet oak, bell pepper and dill don't quite mesh in this lean, dry red.–B.S. • $13 • (4/30/2000) • **80**

MOORHOF

Weissburgunder Beerenauslese Neusiedlersee-Hügelland Barrique 1998: A pretty dessert white, full of spice, vanilla, pear and honey, all kept lively by the bright acidity and delicate structure. Echoes lemon tart on the long finish. Not imported into the U.S. Drink now through 2003.–B.S. • $NA/375 ml. • (1/01/2000) • **89**

MORANDELL

Blaufränkisch Qualitätswein Trocken Mittelburgenland Private Cuvée 1997: Spicy and smoky, this red has black cherry, meat and tobacco flavors on a balanced, vibrant framework, with firm, ripe tannins and a lingering finish. Drink now through 2003.–B.S. • $15 • (4/30/2000) • **86**

MUNZENRIEDER

Beerenauslese Burgenland 1998: Bold, thick and sweet, delivering a gush of apricot, honey and a hint of orange peel in an uncomplicated manner. Soft in structure, it finishes a bit short. Bouvier. Not imported into the U.S. Drink now.–B.S. • $NA/375 ml. • (1/01/2000) • **88**

Bouvier Trockenbeerenauslese Burgenland 1997: An ethereal TBA. It starts off bold and concentrated, full of apricot, orange, honey and spice notes that just seem to melt away, leaving the essence of its flavors behind. A tangy, mouthwatering finish completes the package. Not imported into the U.S. Drink now through 2003.–B.S. • $NA/375 ml. • (1/01/2000) • **91**

Bouvier Trockenbeerenauslese Neusiedlersee 1996: Rich and moderately concentrated, not intensely wound, yet shows nice smoke and crème brûlée character. It's developing quickly and the finish is slightly hot. Not imported to the U.S. Drink now through 2004.–B.S. • $NA/375 ml. • (1/01/1999) • **88**

Bouvier Trockenbeerenauslese Neusiedlersee 1995 • $NA/375 ml. • (2/28/1998) • **95**

Bouvier Trockenbeerenauslese Neusiedlersee 1994 • $NA/375 ml. • (2/28/1998) • **90**

Chardonnay Trockenbeerenauslese Burgenland 1998: An intense, smoky aroma of bacon fat gives this sweetie distinction. Apricot and orange peel round out the flavor spectrum. Fine underlying acidity keeps it all lively, finishing on a light smoky note. Not imported into the U.S. Drink now through 2004.–B.S. • $NA/375 ml. • (1/01/2000) • **91**

Grüner Veltliner Eiswein Burgenland 1997: A well-defined eiswein, offering concentrated pear, quince and honey flavors entwined with a bright beam of acidity. Excellent length of flavor on the finish. Drink now through 2004.–B.S. • $25/375 ml. • (4/30/2000) • **90**

Qualitätswein Trocken Burgenland Cuveè Neubruch 1997: Fat and glossy, showing blackberry and plum as well as a lashing of new oak, then the dusty tannins emerge on the finish. Ends in a vanilla aftertaste. Not imported into the U.S. Drink now.–B.S. • $NA • (1/01/2000) • **85**

Qualitätswein Trocken Burgenland Illmitzer Weg 1997: New oak is the dominant feature, covering the cherry and berry flavors. Tastes soft and easy, though there's moderate concentration. Not imported into the U.S. Drink now.–B.S. • $NA • (1/01/2000) • **85**

Ruländer Trockenbeerenauslese Neusiedlersee 1996: A hedonistic style, very rich and sweet, with good underlying acidity and the honey character of botrytis to accent the crème brûlée and smoke notes. Long, crisp smoke and butterscotch finish. Not imported to the U.S. Drink now through 2006.–B.S. • $NA • (1/01/1999) • **91**

Sämling 88 Trockenbeerenauslese Neusiedlersee 1995 • $NA/375 ml. • (2/28/1998) • **92**

Sämling 88 Trockenbeerenauslese Neusiedlersee 1991 • $NA/375 ml • (2/28/1998) • **89**

Welschriesling Trockenbeerenauslese Neusiedlersee 1995 • $NA/375 ml. • (2/28/1998) • **95**

NEKOWITSCH

Neusiedlersee Strohwein Schilfwein Tradition 1995 • $45/375 ml. • (2/28/1998) • **87**

Sämling 88 Beerenauslese Neusiedlersee 1997: An aggressive, almost soapy aroma introduces this sweet white, yet it has more pine and grapefruit on the palate. Moderately firm in structure, it ends with a touch of bitterness. Not imported into the U.S. Drink now through 2002.–B.S. • $NA/375 ml. • (1/01/2000) • **86**

Strohwein Neusiedlersee Schilfwein The Red One 1997: A distinctive smoked meat component dominates this moderately rich, modestly cherry-flavored red dessert wine. Finishes with astringency. Not for everyone. Not imported into the U.S. Drink now through 2003.–B.S. • $NA • (1/01/2000) • **84**

Strohwein Neusiedlersee Schilfwein Tradition 1997: A beautiful golden color and flavors of apricot, honey, orange peel and crème brûlée highlight this Austrian specialty. Rich and sweet, finely balanced and long on the finish, where a roasted nut element emerges. Not imported into the U.S. Drink now through 2005.–B.S. • $NA • (1/01/2000) • **91**

NIGL

Grüner Veltliner Beerenauslese Kremstal 1995 • $31/375 ml. • (2/28/1998) • **87**

Grüner Veltliner Qualitätswein Kremstal Alte Reben 1996 • $18 • (2/28/1998) • **87**

Grüner Veltliner Qualitätswein Kremstal Senftenberger Piri 1996 • $25 • (2/28/1998) • **89**

Grüner Veltliner Qualitätswein Trocken Kremstal Alte Reben 1998: Beautifully proportioned, this is ripe, elegant and vibrant, displaying peach, apple and citrus, all focused and persistent. Subtle aftertaste of peach and herbs lingers. Drink now.–B.S. • $30 • (12/31/1999) • **89**

Grüner Veltliner Qualitätswein Trocken Kremstal Kremser Freiheit 1998: Almost like a Riesling in its floral aromas and delicate structure (granite soils?), this Grüner displays citrus blossom, peach and mineral flavors, finesse and intensity right through to the long finish. Drink now through 2002.–B.S. • $20 • (8/31/1999) • **90**

Grüner Veltliner Qualitätswein Trocken Kremstal Privat Senftenberger Piri 1998: Delicious peach and apricot notes, yet it maintains the herbal, grapefruit elements that define this varietal. The whole is held together with some bracing acidity and persistent flavor. Drink now through 2002.–B.S. • $36 • (12/31/1999) • **89**

Grüner Veltliner Qualitätswein Trocken Kremstal Senftenberger Piri 1997: This delicious white combines peach and tobacco notes with a creamy, leesy character and an unctuous texture. The resonating finish unfolds on the palate layer by layer. Herbal aftertaste. Best from 2001 through 2006.–B.S. • $30 • (12/31/1998) • **90**

Riesling Qualitätswein Trocken Kremstal Kremser Kremsleiten 1998: Intense, with plenty of zippy acidity and body, but the white peach and mineral notes are tightly wound. Slightly grainy texture on the finish. Drink now through 2003.–B.S. • $36 • (12/31/1999) • **88**

Riesling Qualitätswein Trocken Kremstal Privat Senftenberger Piri 1998: A powerhouse, solidly structured and broad in approach, redolent of quince, peach, mineral and citrus notes, all displayed on a finely grained texture. Excellent length. Tasted twice, with consistent notes. Drink now through 2005.–B.S. • $50 • (12/31/1999) • **90**

Riesling Qualitätswein Trocken Kremstal Senftenberger Hochäcker 1998: This grows on you. Rich and openly knit, supported by bracing acidity and medium body, exhibiting earth, spice and apple flavors, focused and lingering on the finish. Drink now through 2003.–B.S. • $43 • (12/31/1999) • **88**

Riesling Qualitätswein Trocken Kremstal Senftenberger Piri 1997: Intriguing. Begins on the austere side, with stone and spice components, then explodes wth peach and spring flowers on the palate, allied to a delicate yet strong framework underscored by lively acidity. Drink now through 2004.–B.S. • $42 • (2/28/1999) • **90**

Riesling Qualitätswein Trocken Kremstal Urgesteins Kremser Kremsleiten 1996 • $25 • (2/28/1998) • **91**

Riesling Qualitätswein Trocken Kremstal Urgesteins Senftenberger Ried Hochäcker 1997: Rich texture and dense flavors of apple, almond and stone belie the firm, balancing acidity that sweeps the palate clean and resonates on the long finish. Tremendous extract and clarity simultaneously. Drink now through 2005.–B.S. • $36 • (2/28/1999) • **92**

Riesling Qualitätswein Trocken Kremstal Urgesteins Senftenberger Ried Hochäcker 1996 • $29 • (2/28/1998) • **90**

NIKOLAIHOF

Grüner Veltliner Federspiel Wachau Im Weingebirge 1998: A whiff of sulfur initially, yet there's a focused floral and apple-flavored white underneath, with a softness midpalate, firming up on the finish. Shows class and grace, with a little less density than the best in this category. Drink now.–B.S. • $28 • (8/31/1999) • **88**

Grüner Veltliner Federspiel Wachau Im Weingebirge 1997: Sleek, young and unevolved, barely hinting at peach and citrus flavors, but the density and mineral character are undeniable, all supported by acidity that's well integrated. Subtle, lingering aftertaste. Not imported into the U.S. Drink through 2006.–B.S. • $NA • (12/31/1998) • **89**

Grüner Veltliner Federspiel Wachau Im Weingebirge 1996 • $23 • (2/28/1998) • **85**

Riesling Smaragd Wachau Vom Stein 1997: An extremely ripe, tropical style. Exhibits passion fruit and apricot character in the beginning, then the firm, minerally structure takes over, leaving a steely, dry character on the finish. Give it time to integrate. Drink through 2006.–B.S. • $40 • (1/31/1999) • **93**

Riesling Spätlese Wachau Steiner Hund 1997: Exotic aromas of quince and honey, and the honey and a milky note continue on the palate. Very suave and smooth, with enough acidity for balance and a density of flavors that carries through the finish. Drink through 2005.–B.S. • $44 • (2/28/1999) • **90**

NITTNAUS

Blaufränkisch Eiswein Neusiedlersee 1998: Intriguing. Delivers the strawberry, watermelon and spice aromas and flavors of a Provence rosé, with a touch of sweetness. Light and lively, with a fillip of bitterness on the finish. Drink now.–B.S. • $20/375 ml. • (4/30/2000) • **87**

Key: SS—Spectator Selection. CS—Cellar Selection. HR—Highly Recommended. $NA—Price not available. (BT)—Barrel tasting. (A)—Auction Price.
For a key to the tasters' initials, see "How to Use These Listings."
Dates in parentheses represent the issues in which the ratings were published.

Chardonnay Qualitätswein Trocken Neusiedlersee Classic 1998: Fresh and appealing, this white has ripe pear and floral notes augmented by a hint of new oak, leaving the whole package delicate and lively. Drink now.–B.S. • $14 • (12/31/1999) • **87**

Eiswein Neusiedlersee 1998: Vivacious and exotic, showing apricot compote, candied citrus and honey, yet more like a BA than an eiswein, it lacks the tart acidity that provides the tension. Lovely flavors though. Drink now through 2003.–B.S. • $20/375 ml. • (4/30/2000) • **86**

Eiswein Neusiedlersee Premium 1998: No shortage of richness and concentration here, yet lacks the tension between sweetness and acidity typical of eiswein. Round, attractive flavors of apricot and honey combine with a moderate structure. Drink now through 2003.–B.S. • $23/375 ml. • (4/30/2000) • **89**

Qualitätswein Trocken Neusiedlersee Vigor Albus 1997: If you prefer new oak, this is for you. Nutmeg, vanilla and butterscotch take center stage, with apple and citrus in the supporting cast. Starts off rich, turns crisp at the end; mainly oak. Chardonnay and Weissburgunder. Drink now through 2001.–B.S. • $17 • (12/31/1999) • **84**

OPITZ, WILLI

Bouvier Trockenbeerenauslese Neusiedlersee 1995 • $85/375 ml. • (2/28/1998) • **87**

Gewürztraminer Trockenbeerenauslese Neusiedlersee 1995 • $95/375 ml. • (2/28/1998) • **95**

Neusiedlersee Weisser Schilfmandl 1995 • $75/375 ml. • (2/28/1998) • **79**

Neusiedlersee Weisser Schilfmandl 1994 • $75/375 ml. • (10/31/1997) • **86**

Pinot Gris Trockenbeerenauslese Neusiedlersee 1997: A pure apricot character marks this young, grapey TBA, which shows medium richness, good intensity and a nice balance between its components. Vibrant and juicy, but without the botrytis concentration. Drink now through 2005.–B.S. • $90/375 ml. • (2/28/1999) • **88**

Pinot Gris Trockenbeerenauslese Neusiedlersee 1995 • $90/375 ml. • (2/28/1998) • **91**

Trockenbeerenauslese Neusiedlersee Goldackerl 1997: Intense apricot, honey and botrytis components from the get-go, yet retains a sense of harmony. The racy acidity keeps the sweetness in check in this young, vibrant TBA. Delicate honey finish. This needs time. Drink through 2010.–B.S. • $85/375 ml. • (2/28/1999) • **90**

Trockenbeerenauslese Neusiedlersee Opitz One 1997: Pinkish-amber in color, this "red" TBA smells and tastes of red berries with a good dose of vanilla from new oak treatment. Light-bodied, subtle and bright, it may be best enjoyed by itself. Drink now through 2002.–B.S. • $80/375 ml. • (2/28/1999) • **88**

Trockenbeerenauslese Neusiedlersee Opitz One 1995 • $80/375 ml. • (2/28/1998) • **88**

Welschriesling-Scheurebe Trockenbeerenauslese Neusiedlersee Goldackerl 1995 • $85 • (2/28/1998) • **89**

PFAFFL

Chardonnay Qualitätswein Trocken Weinviertel Exklusiv 1998: Harmonious and complex, this white integrates the vanilla and smoke notes from new oak with licorice and fig flavors that culminate in a long finish. Seductive texture and solid structure. Drink now.–B.S. • $15 • (12/31/1999) • **89**

Chardonnay Qualitätswein Trocken Weinviertel Exklusiv 1997: Bright and lively, with a nice mix of apple, citrus, nutmeg and clove allied to a rich texture. The oak kicks in on the finish, leaving an aftertaste of butterscotch. Drink now.–B.S. • $17 • (12/31/1998) • **85**

Chardonnay Qualitätswein Weinviertel Exklusiv 1996 • $13 • (2/28/1998) • **79**

Grüner Veltliner Kabinett Trocken Weinviertel Haidviertel 1997: Offers peach and apple, tightly wound and a bit severe, but the concentration and intensity of flavor bode well for the future. Best from 2001 through 2006.–B.S. • $15 • (12/31/1998) • **88**

Grüner Veltliner Qualitätswein Trocken Weinviertel Haidviertel 1998: Offers plenty of peach aroma and flavor, along with white pepper and an herbal component. Solidly structured, with a crisp, mineral finish. Drink now through 2001.–B.S. • $11 • (8/31/1999) • **84**

Grüner Veltliner Qualitätswein Trocken Weinviertel Hundsleiten-Sandtal 1998: Not bone-dry, yet there's plenty of acidity for balance in this lean, focused Grüner, along with lentil and grapefruit. Finishes quite dry. Drink now through 2001.–B.S. • $14 • (12/31/1999) • **83**

Grüner Veltliner Qualitätswein Trocken Weinviertel Hundsleiten-Sandtal 1997: Shows a lot of the lentil, tobacco and celery side of Grüner Veltliner, with an austerity more typical of '96. Nonetheless, this has a rich midpalate and a slightly hot finish. Drink through 2004.–B.S. • $14 • (12/31/1998) • **86**

Qualitätswein Trocken Weinviertel Excellent Red 1997: Attractive black currant and leaf notes are reminiscent of Cabernet Franc in this lean, densely textured red. Juicy acidity bodes well for the table. Zweigelt and Cabernet Sauvignon. Drink now through 2001.–B.S. • $21 • (4/30/2000) • **87**

Riesling Qualitätswein Lieblich Weinviertel Terrassen Sonnleiten 1997: Peach, mineral and honey are the main themes in this off-dry, rich white, elegant and delicate, with a subtle profile. Moderate length. Drink now through 2002.–B.S. • $17 • (2/28/1999) • **87**

Riesling Qualitätswein Trocken Weinviertel Terrassen Sonnleiten 1998: Ample in size, and plump, with ripe peach, apple and tobacco aromas and flavors, good concentration and an underlying vibrancy that comes through on the finish. Tasted twice, with consistent notes. Drink now through 2002.–B.S. • $15 • (4/30/2000) • **87**

Sauvignon Blanc Qualitätswein Trocken Weinviertel 1998: Plenty of fresh melon, cut hay and citrus in this richly textured Sauvignon Blanc. Nice piquant finish. Drink now.–B.S. • $15 • (4/30/2000) • **87**

Sauvignon Blanc Qualitätswein Weinviertel 1996 • $18 • (2/28/1998) • **83**

Sauvignon Blanc Spätlese Trocken Weinviertel 1997: Atypical. Definitely has new oak, with bacon fat and vanilla notes, and maybe botrytis judging by the exotic litchi and passion fruit flavors. Distinctive, rich and structured. For adventuresome drinkers. Try now through 2001.–B.S. • $17 • (2/28/1999) • **87**

Zweigelt-Cabernet Sauvignon Weinviertel Excellent 1995 • $17 • (2/28/1998) • **82**

PICHLER, F.X.

Grüner Veltliner Smaragd Trocken Wachau Dürnsteiner Kellerberg 1998: A hint of banana in the aroma foreshadows this firmly structured, unevolved white. Almost in a state of suspended animation, it hints at the vanilla, peach and smoky fruit flavors to come. Best from 2002 through 2010.–B.S. • $60 • (4/30/2000) • **92**

Grüner Veltliner Smaragd Trocken Wachau Loibner Berg 1998: Amazing aromas of lily, rose, apricot and honey define this precocious, exotic Grüner. There's enough acidity for balance, and the body helps out. Fine length. Drink now through 2007.–B.S. • $50 • (4/30/2000) • **91**

Grüner Veltliner Smaragd Trocken Wachau M 1998: Stunning for its dense, creamy texture and ripe flavors of vanilla custard, peach and lentil. If you could fault it, it's high in alcohol, which provides structure and a touch of coarseness on the finish. Great aftertaste, though. Drink now through 2005.–B.S. • $70 • (4/30/2000) • **90**

Grüner Veltliner Smaragd Wachau Dürnsteiner Kellerberg 1996 • $40 • (2/28/1998) • **88**

Riesling Qualitätswein Trocken Wachau Unendlich 1998: A stunning Riesling. Floral scented and wonderfully exotic, with rosewater, cardamom and green tea components, quite racy and compact, with a dense, sinewy structure and a lingering finish. Drink now through 2007.–B.S. • $80 • (4/30/2000) • **93**

Riesling Smaragd Trocken Wachau Dürnsteiner Kellerberg 1998: Incredibly harmonious, with well-expressed flavors of banana, violet, apricot, grapefruit and bitter almond allied to a thick texture and crunchy acidity. This monolithic Austrian white is merely hinting at what's to come; your patience will be rewarded. Best from 2002 through 2010.–B.S. • $70 • (3/31/2000) CS • **93**

Riesling Smaragd Trocken Wachau Dürnsteiner Kellerberg 1996 • $50 • (2/28/1998) • **86**

Riesling Smaragd Trocken Wachau Loibner Steinertal 1998: So intense are the flavors that a strong licorice element comes through, along with apricot and vanilla. Monolithic right now, with good underlying acidity and broad shoulders. Give it time. Best from 2001 through 2005.–B.S. • $50 • (12/31/1999) • **91**

PICHLER, RUDOLF

Grüner Veltliner Smaragd Trocken Wachau Wösendorfer Hochrain 1998: Bold and in your face, bursting with peach, white flowers and grapefruit peel. Complex and thick, with a stiff underlying structure and heat on the finish. Beautifully displayed on a rich and creamy texture. Tasted twice, with consistent notes. Drink now through 2007.–B.S. • $45 • (4/30/2000) • **92**

Grüner Veltliner Smaragd Trocken Wachau Wösendorfer Hochrain 1997: Ripe, this has dense flavors and texture, with an herbal touch that accents the apple and grapefruit notes. It's a live wire, with bracing acidity and a stony element. Be patient. Best from 2001 through 2007.–B.S. • $30 • (2/28/1999) • **90**

Grüner Veltliner Smaragd Trocken Wachau Wösendorfer Kollmütz 1998: Crisp and reined in, yet very tightly wound and dense. A bit awkward right now, but there's ripe peach and tobacco at the core and a very serious structure. A little less flamboyant for the vintage and very well made. Tasted twice, with consistent notes. Best from 2002 through 2010.–B.S. • $40 • (4/30/2000) • **91**

Grüner Veltliner Smaragd Wachau Wösendorfer Hochrain 1996 • $34 • (2/28/1998) • **88**

Riesling Smaragd Trocken Wachau Weissenkirchner Achleiten 1998: Big and bold, yet not that expressive right now, this powerhouse white is all knees and elbows, requiring time to integrate and strut its stuff. Difficult to taste today. Best after 2001.–B.S. • $50 • (12/31/1999) • **89**

Riesling Smaragd Trocken Wachau Wösendorfer Kirchweg 1998: A match of purity and power. Pure apricot, passion fruit and grapefruit wrap around a rock-solid core that explodes on the palate, driving the fruit to a wonderful conclusion of refreshing mineral notes. Well done. Drink now through 2005.–B.S. • $50 • (12/31/1999) • **90**

Riesling Smaragd Trocken Wachau Wösendorfer Kirchweg 1997: Forward, ripe and ethereal, with a lemon-lime flavor accenting the quince, peach and mineral in this seamless, brilliant package. The fruit and vibrant structure blend beautifully with the supple texture. Stunning. Tasted twice, with consistent notes. Drink now through 2005.–B.S. • $40 • (2/28/1999) • **91**

Weissburgunder Smaragd Trocken Wachau Wösendorfer 1998: Racy and finely etched, this high-pitched white walks a tightrope between ripe quince and tropical nuances and a firm, minerally structure. Fine intensity. Drink now through 2002.–B.S. • $32 • (12/31/1999) • **87**

POCKL

Admiral Qualitätswein Trocken Neusiedlersee 1994 • $32 • (2/28/1997) • **84**

Pinot Noir Qualitätswein Neusiedlersee 1995 • $34 • (2/28/1998) • **85**

Qualitätswein Neusiedlersee Rosso E Nero Red 1994 • $30 • (2/28/1998) • **86**

Zweigelt Qualitätswein Trocken Neusiedlersee Classsique 1995 • $14 • (2/28/1997) • **76**

POLZ, ERICH & WALTER

Grauburgunder Qualitätswein Südsteiermark Grassnitzberg 1996 • $15 • (2/28/1998) • **80**

Grauburgunder Qualitätswein Trocken Südsteiermark Grassnitzberg 1997: Richly textured, bright and redolent of pear and quince, this medium-bodied white is pleasant and easy to drink. Drink now.–B.S. • $19 • (2/28/1999) • **84**

Morillon Qualitätswein Trocken Südsteiermark Hochgrassnitzberg 1997: Aromas and flavors of white flowers, vanilla custard and peach are the main themes in this soft, flavorful white, whose finish lingers pleasantly. Not imported into the U.S. Drink now.–B.S. • $NA • (12/31/1998) • **85**

Riesling-Sauvignon Blanc Qualitätswein Südsteiermark Steirischer Spiegel 1998: This unusual blend offers a crisp, refreshing character, with floral, peach, earth and grass flavors that grow on you. Drink now.–B.S. • $18 • (9/15/1999) • **82**

Sauvignon Blanc Qualitätswein Südsteiermark Hochgrassnitzberg 1996 • $31 • (2/28/1998) • **86**

Sauvignon Blanc Qualitätswein Trocken Südsteiermark Hochgrassnitzberg 1997: Full of gooseberry, herb and mineral flavors, this Sauvignon Blanc tastes like a scaled-down New Zealand version, with vibrant acidity and a flinty, smoky finish. Drink now.–B.S. • $23 • (2/28/1999) • **87**

Weissburgunder Qualitätswein Trocken Südsteiermark Grassnitzberg 1997: The flavor of pear is augmented by vanilla and clove from new oak in this generously textured white. It's pleasant for quaffing on its own, but has enough acidity for light dishes. Drink now.–B.S. • $15 • (2/28/1999) • **82**

PRAGER

Grüner Veltliner Auslese Halbtrocken Wachau Weissenkirchner Achleiten 1998: Bold and rich, here's a broad, honey-, apricot- and passion fruit-flavored white that's exotic, but balanced toward the upfront fruit component. Lingering tropical fruit aftertaste. Drink now through 2001.–B.S. • $50 • (12/31/1999) • **88**

Grüner Veltliner Qualitätswein Trocken Wachau Selection 1997: Fabulous. Ripe, exotic and expressive, yet the tobacco, apricot and vanilla bean aromas and flavors never exceed the backbone of acidity, which lends definition and clarity. Rich in texture, complex, with a never-ending aftertaste of dried apricot. Drink now through 2005.–B.S. • $40 • (12/31/1998) • **92**

Grüner Veltliner Smaragd Trocken Wachau Weissenkirchner Achleiten 1996 • $29 • (2/28/1998) • **90**

PRAGER

Riesling Auslese Halbtrocken Wachau Weissenkirchner Klaus 1998: Packed with Indian spices, apricot and citrus, this white makes no bones about its sweetness, which is matched by vibrant acidity, though it's moderately concentrated dissipates slightly on the finish. Drink now through 2005.–B.S. • $60 • (12/31/1999) • **90**

Riesling Federspiel Wachau Weissenkirchner Steinriegl 1998: Austere in its flavor profile, this white nonetheless displays a racy structure, good concentration and integration. Needs some time for the floral and apricot flavors to come to the fore. Try through 2001.–B.S. • $27 • (9/15/1999) • **88**

Riesling Federspiel Wachau Weissenkirchner Steinriegl 1996 • $24 • (2/28/1998) • **89**

Riesling Qualitätswein Halbtrocken Wachau Selection 1997: Rich, lush and spicy, with intense spice, peach and mineral flavors buoyed on a lively, mouthwatering acidity. Just off-dry, with an impressive beginning, yet tails off slightly at the end. Drink now through 2002.–B.S. • $45 • (2/28/1999) • **89**

Riesling Smaragd Trocken Wachau Dürnsteiner Kaiserberg 1998: Plenty of superripe, botrytized character, from the passion fruit, apricot and orange-tinged aromas and flavors to the thickness and slight coarseness on the finish. Feels low in acidity (although it has just over 8 grams per liter), with a nice spiciness peeking through on the finish. Drink now through 2004.–B.S. • $45 • (12/31/1999) • **91**

Riesling Smaragd Trocken Wachau Weissenkirchner Achleiten 1998: Perfumed, offering notes of violet, forest floor, apricot and citrus, round and velvety, then turns lean and crisp as the structural combination of acidity and alcohol shows on the finish. Best from 2001 through 2006.–B.S. • $50 • (4/30/2000) • **89**

Riesling Smaragd Trocken Wachau Weissenkirchner Achleiten 1996 • $35 • (2/28/1998) • **91**

Riesling Smaragd Trocken Wachau Weissenkirchner Klaus 1998: Fat, round and lush, this '98 Riesling is more about weight and texture than aromas and flavors today. Still, it shows apricot, vanilla custard and a slight cheesiness, fine supporting acidity and a long finish. Best from 2001 through 2005.–B.S. • $50 • (12/31/1999) • **90**

Riesling Smaragd Trocken Wachau Weissenkirchner Klaus 1997: A vin de terroir. Expressive of its site, this has an austerity to the stone and spice character, along with a seductive peachy element and a rich yet ethereal presence on the palate. An intense, individualistic and contemplative wine, with a long finish. Drink now through 2006.–B.S. • $40 • (1/31/1999) • **92**

Riesling Smaragd Trocken Wachau Weissenkirchner Klaus 1996 • $35 • (2/28/1998) • **89**

Riesling Smaragd Trocken Wachau Weissenkirchner Steinriegl 1998: Smelling and tasting like Indian spices, orange marmalade, smoke and mineral, this '98 is completely beguiling, in a forward, slightly top-heavy style. Impressive. Drink now through 2005.–B.S. • $45 • (4/30/2000) • **91**

Riesling Smaragd Trocken Wachau Weissenkirchner Steinriegl 1996 • $35 • (2/28/1998) • **89**

Smaragd Trocken Wachau Feinburgunder 1996 • $31 • (2/28/1998) • **85**

PRIELER

Blaufränkisch Qualitätswein Trocken Neusiedlersee-Hügelland 1997: A smoky vanilla note accents the cherry and ink aromas and flavors in this ripe, sensuous red. It turns firm, with stiff tannins, but it's balanced and lively. Not imported into the U.S. Drink now through 2003.–B.S. • $NA • (1/01/2000) • **90**

Pinot Blanc Qualitätswein Neusiedlersee 1997: A rich white, with citrus, earth and mineral character and creamy texture yet sufficient acidity to keep it all lively. Finishes on a flinty, citrusy note. Drink now.–B.S. • $23 • (9/15/1999) • **84**

RADETZKY

Bouvier Trockenbeerenauslese Neusiedlersee 1995: Lively and intense, but the tangerine, smoke and mushroom notes are wed to a slightly astringent, coarse texture. Maybe better with food, but doesn't seem to be going anywhere. Not imported to the U.S. Drink now.–B.S. • $NA • (1/01/1999) • **87**

Bouvier Trockenbeerenauslese Neusiedlersee Barrique 1998: Very sweet, round and straightforward in its apricot and crème brûlée flavors, this shows good balance and an additional note of caramel on the finish. Not imported into the U.S. Drink now through 2002.–B.S. • $NA/375 ml. • (1/01/2000) • **88**

Grüner Veltliner Qualitätswein Trocken Weinviertel 1998: There is some attractive fruit here, but overall it's marred by a rotten egg (sulfur) smell and flat taste. Tasted twice, with consistent notes. Not imported into the U.S.–B.S. • $NA • (1/01/1999) • **68**

Pinot Gris Neusiedlersee Ice Wine 1992: An aroma of roses and Gewürztraminer-like litchi and spice flavors are all wrapped in a pretty package with lively acidity, until the alcohol kicks up on the finish, leaving heat on the back of the palate. Not imported into the U.S. Drink now through 2002.–B.S. • $NA • (1/01/1999) • **86**

REBENHOF

Morillon Qualitätswein Trocken Südsteiermark Witscheiner Herrenberg 1997: Soft and inviting, offering a nice balance between the peachy flavors and spicy oak notes, all buoyed by a well-integrated acidity. Mouthwatering finish. Drink now.–B.S. • $19 • (12/31/1998) • **86**

Sauvignon Blanc Qualitätswein Trocken Südsteiermark Witscheiner Herrenberg 1997: A straightforward white, with modest herb and citrus flavors. Drink now.–B.S. • $32 • (2/28/1999) • **81**

Weissburgunder Qualitätswein Trocken Südsteiermark Steirischer 1997: A soprano of a white, high-toned, with lanolin and herbal notes and a hint of lemon adding complexity and firmness. Try with food. Drink now through 2001.–B.S. • $13 • (12/31/1999) • **83**

REINISCH, JOHANNESHOF

Cabernet Sauvignon Qualitätswein Trocken Thermenregion Reserve 1994 • $29 • (6/15/1997) • **84**

Chardonnay Qualitätswein Trocken Thermenregion Reserve 1997: Overtly oaky, this focused white could use a touch more apple and lemon to balance the clove and vanilla. Not imported into the U.S. Drink now through 2001.–B.S. • $NA • (1/01/1999) • **82**

Chardonnay Qualitätswein Trocken Thermenregion Reserve 1996 • $22 • (2/28/1998) • **82**

Chardonnay Trockenbeerenauslese Thermenregion 1996: A sweet, intense wine that displays citrus, spice and exotic elements as well as an earthy, sweaty element. It has a firm, tangy backbone, but exudes power over finesse, finishing on the coarse side. Drink now through 2001.–B.S. • $NA/375 ml. • (2/28/1999) • **87**

Chardonnay Trockenbeerenauslese Thermenregion 1995 • $60/375 ml. • (6/15/1997) • **94**

Eiswein Thermenregion 1996: Begins nicely, with good intensity, but herbal and bitter flavors don't get resolved, resulting in a wine that's off balance. Drink now through 2002.–B.S. • $46/375 ml. • (2/28/1999) • **82**

Pinot Blanc Qualitätswein Trocken Thermenregion 1996 • $11 • (2/28/1998) • **79**

Pinot Noir Qualitätswein Trocken Thermenregion Reserve 1997: All silk, and sporting the berry, vanilla and earth notes characteristic of Pinot Noir. There's firm structure and good concentration, ending with a touch of astringency. Not imported into the U.S. Drink now through 2001.–B.S. • $NA • (1/01/2000) • **86**

Pinot Noir Qualitätswein Trocken Thermenregion Reserve 1996: This softly structured Pinot Noir offers beet root, cherry and a light salty taste. Finishes on the coarse side.–B.S. • $18 • (12/31/1998) • **79**

Pinot Noir Qualitätswein Trocken Thermenregion Reserve 1994 • $17 • (2/28/1998) • **86**

Qualitätswein Trocken Thermenregion Dialog 1997: A rich white, moderate in acidity, with an attractive flinty, stony character similar to Chablis, and vanilla notes from gentle oak shading. Morillon, Weissburgunder and Sauvignon Blanc. Drink now.–B.S. • $NA • (12/31/1998) • **86**

Riesling Auslese Thermenregion 1998: Round and generous, showing straightforward passion fruit and grapefruit notes in an elegant way, ending with a lingering finish. Good aperitif. Not imported into the U.S. Drink now through 2003.–B.S. • $NA/375 ml. • (1/01/2000) • **87**

Saint Laurent Qualitätswein Trocken Thermenregion Reserve 1997: Ripe, juicy blackberry is the main theme here, accented by vanilla and clove. Firm tannins and bright acidity complete the package. Not imported into the U.S. Drink now through 2001.–B.S. • $NA • (1/01/2000) • **84**

Saint Laurent Qualitätswein Trocken Thermenregion Reserve 1996: Stewed tomato is the main theme, supported by firm acidity and tannins. A little disjointed.–B.S. • $18 • (12/31/1998) • **79**

Saint Laurent Qualitätswein Trocken Thermenregion Reserve 1995 • $23 • (2/28/1998) • **82**

Saint Laurent Qualitätswein Trocken Thermenregion Reserve 1994 • $19 • (6/15/1997) • **81**

Key: SS—Spectator Selection. CS—Cellar Selection. HR—Highly Recommended. $NA—Price not available. (BT)—Barrel tasting. Ⓐ—Auction Price.
For a key to the tasters' initials, see "How to Use These Listings."
Dates in parentheses represent the issues in which the ratings were published.

Zweigelt Qualitätswein Trocken Thermenregion 1997: Soft and fruity, slightly astringent, with cherry flavors and a woody note. Tasted twice, with consistent notes. Not imported into the U.S. Drink now.–B.S. • $NA • (1/01/2000) • **80**

Zweigelt Qualitätswein Trocken Thermenregion 1996 • $12 • (2/28/1998) • **85**

Zweigelt Qualitätswein Trocken Thermenregion 1995 • $12 • (6/15/1997) • **83**

ROSENHOF

Bouvier Trockenbeerenauslese Neusiedlersee 1995 • $NA/375 ml. • (2/28/1998) • **90**

Chardonnay Trockenbeerenauslese Neusiedlersee Barrique 1995 • $NA/375 ml • (2/28/1998) • **93**

Muscat Ottonel Beerenauslese Neusiedlersee 1995 • $NA/375 ml. • (2/28/1998) • **90**

SALOMON-WEINGUT UNDHOF, ERICH

Grüner Veltliner Qualitätswein Trocken Kremstal Hochterrassen 1998: Straightforward in its appeal, this white offers herbal flavors and a little apple nuance. Tasted twice, with consistent notes. Drink now.–B.S. • $14 • (9/15/1999) • **80**

Grüner Veltliner Qualitätswein Trocken Kremstal Undhof Wieden Reserve 1998: Broad-shouldered and very ripe, exhibiting passion fruit, apricot and cardamom, moderate structure and some high alcohol, but it wears it well. Fine intensity and perfume. Drink now.–B.S. • $23 • (12/31/1999) • **90**

Grüner Veltliner Qualitätswein Trocken Kremstal Undhof Wieden Reserve 1997: Vibrant and racy, this lean, compact Grüner has apple and bean flavors and an austerity that says '96 rather than '97. The finish is almost tart and begs for food. Drink through 2006.–B.S. • $16 • (12/31/1998) • **87**

Riesling Qualitätswein Trocken Kremstal Kremser Kögl 1998: Starts off with passion fruit, mandarin orange and mineral tones, supported by a firm structure, ending with a slight coarseness. May just need some time to integrate. Drink now through 2002.–B.S. • $28 • (12/31/1999) • **87**

Riesling Qualitätswein Trocken Kremstal Kremser Kögl Reserve 1997: Focused and elegant, showing pear and apple aromas and flavors, yet lacks the density and concentration of the best Rieslings. Still, a delicious white. Drink through 2004.–B.S. • $40 • (2/28/1999) • **87**

Riesling Qualitätswein Trocken Kremstal Pfaffenberg 1998: Austere in style, this white hints at tropical fruit, staying more in the citrus and mineral spectrum of flavors, with keen focus and intensity. Drink now through 2003.–B.S. • $28 • (12/31/1999) • **86**

Riesling Qualitätswein Trocken Kremstal Steiner Pfaffenberg 1997: Restrained and firm in character. Displays apple, citrus and mineral flavors, richness and concentration at midpalate, followed by a crisp, almost chalky finish and an almond aftertaste. Drink through 2005.–B.S. • $19 • (2/28/1999) • **89**

Riesling Qualitätswein Trocken Kremstal Steiner Pfaffenberg 1996 • $18 • (2/28/1998) • **90**

SATTLERHOF

Chardonnay Qualitätswein Trocken Südsteiermark 1996 • $13 • (2/28/1998) • **82**

Morillon Qualitätswein Trocken Südsteiermark Pfarrweingarten 1997: A modern Chardonnay, with plenty of oak character and apple and lemon flavors. Firmly structured and rich, with an aftertaste of spice. Drink now.–B.S. • $25 • (12/31/1999) • **85**

Sauvignon Blanc Qualitätswein Trocken Südsteiermark 1996 • $17 • (2/28/1998) • **84**

Sauvignon Blanc Qualitätswein Trocken Südsteiermark Kranachberg 1998: Reminiscent of New Zealand Sauvignon, offering ripe melon, passion fruit and citrus in a lively and juicy presentation. Finishes on a firm note. Drink now.–B.S. • $25 • (4/30/2000) • **87**

Sauvignon Blanc Qualitätswein Trocken Südsteiermark Kranachberg 1997: Delicious Sauvignon Blanc, packed with gooseberry, grass and mineral flavors and crisp underlying acidity. It has richness, but it's balanced toward the lean, mineral side. Drink now.–B.S. • $18 • (2/28/1999) • **87**

SCHLUMBERGER

Brut Blanc de Blancs Wien NV • $12 • (2/28/1998) • **80**

Brut Wien NV: A rich, creamy-textured sparkling wine showing lemon custard and a hint of herb, though it finishes on the earthy side. Drink now.–B.S. • $14 • (12/31/1998) • **83**

Brut Wien Cuvée Klimt NV: Lean and focused, showing earthy and yeasty aromas and flavors. Straightforward, with a modest finish. Try as an aperitif. Drink now.–B.S. • $14 • (4/30/2000) • **82**

Brut Wien Cuvée Klimt Der Kuss NV • $NA • (2/28/1998) • **81**

Brut Wien Cuvée Klimt Judith I NV • $NA • (2/28/1998) • **77**

Cabernet-Merlot Thermenregion Privat-Keller 1993 • $NA • (2/28/1998) • **86**

Cabernet-Merlot Thermenregion Vöslauer Goldeck 1994 • $NA • (2/28/1998) • **83**

SCHROCK, HEIDI

Furmint Qualitätswein Halbtrocken Neusiedlersee-Hügelland 1998: Fat, with an almost viscous mouthfeel, this white offers full body and breadth, with modest almond and citrus peel flavors. Drink now.–B.S. • $20 • (4/30/2000) • **84**

Furmint Qualitätswein Halbtrocken Neusiedlersee-Hügelland 1997: Its distinct white pepper character is interesting, but a marzipan component and lack of concentration leave this flat and dull.–B.S. • $18 • (2/28/1999) • **77**

Grauburgunder Qualitätswein Trocken Neusiedlersee-Hügelland 1998: Intriguing flavors of candied almond, vanilla bean and a hint of citrus preserves highlight this medium-bodied, well-defined white. Not the typical flavors for this varietal, but well made. Drink now through 2001.–B.S. • $20 • (4/30/2000) • **86**

Muscat Qualitätswein Trocken Neusiedlersee-Hügelland 1998: Dry and spicy, this medium-bodied white has typical varietal aromas and flavors, ending with a hint of bitter grapefruit. A good match for asparagus. Drink now.–B.S. • $20 • (4/30/2000) • **85**

Muscat Qualitätswein Trocken Neusiedlersee-Hügelland 1996 • $18 • (2/28/1998) • **79**

Ruster Ausbruch Neusiedlersee-Hügelland 1995 • $40/500 ml. • (2/28/1998) • **86**

Ruster Ausbruch Neusiedlersee-Hugelland 1993 • $41/375 ml. • (12/15/1996) • **86**

Ruster Ausbruch Neusiedlersee-Hügelland Ruster Fumé 1995 • $45/500 ml. • (2/28/1998) • **83**

Weissburgunder Qualitätswein Trocken Neusiedlersee-Hügelland 1998: Textbook Pinot Blanc, offering apple, lemon and nut flavors allied to a juicy texture. Excellent as an aperitif or with light poultry dishes. Drink now.–B.S. • $19 • (12/31/1999) • **85**

Weissburgunder Qualitätswein Trocken Neusiedlersee-Hügelland 1996 • $20 • (2/28/1998) • **83**

Weissburgunder Qualitätswein Trocken Neusiedlersee-Hügelland Gemerk 1997: A broad, medium-bodied white, displaying lanolin and earth notes, lemony acidity and a slightly bitter and alcoholic finish.–B.S. • $15 • (2/28/1999) • **78**

Welschriesling Auslese Neusiedlersee-Hügelland Vogelsang 1996 • $20 • (2/28/1998) • **86**

Zweigelt Qualitätswein Trocken Neusiedlersee-Hügelland 1998: A juicy, exuberant red, whose smoky black cherry notes are round and satisfying. Firms up on the finish. Try with simple roasted or grilled meats. Drink now.–B.S. • $19 • (4/30/2000) • **83**

SEPP MOSER

Blauer Burgunder Qualitätswein Kremstal Riede Gebling 1995 • $17 • (2/28/1998) • **80**

Blauer Zweigelt Qualitätswein Burgenland Riede Hedwighof 1995 • $17 • (2/28/1998) • **81**

Blauer Zweigelt Qualitätswein Trocken Neusiedlersee Reserve 1997: Ambitious but awkward. Candied vanilla and butterscotch, perhaps from oak treatment, mar the fruit. Moderately concentrated. Tasted twice, with consistent notes.–B.S. • $30 • (4/30/2000) • **78**

Chardonnay Trockenbeerenauslese Neusiedlersee 1998: A dessert Chardonnay with piquancy and snap. Thick and honeyed, yet the complex apricot, honey and spice flavors show lovely balance and harmony. Good, lingering finish, too. Drink now through 2002.–B.S. • $37/375 ml. • (4/30/2000) • **90**

Grüner Veltliner Qualitätswein Trocken Kremstal Breiter Rain 1998: Ripe, tropical notes show the exotic side of this varietal, offset by a firm structure and citrus flavor. Should develop nicely, although it has immediate appeal. Drink now through 2001.–B.S. • $32 • (12/31/1999) • **87**

Grüner Veltliner Qualitätswein Trocken Kremstal Breiter Rain 1997: Complex aromas and flavors of beeswax, honey and grain suffuse into a medium-bodied, powerful white that finishes on the coarse side, with an aftertaste of shiso leaf. Drink through 2004.–B.S. • $30 • (12/31/1998) • **86**

SEPP MOSER

Riesling Qualitätswein Trocken Kremstal Gebling Select 1998: Simply delicious. Not as flamboyant as others in this tasting, but concentrated and creamy in texture, showing flavors of vanilla custard, violets and lime. Drink now through 2003.–B.S. • $32 • (12/31/1999) • **88**

Riesling Qualitätswein Trocken Kremstal Gebling Select 1997: Delicious. Round and inviting, offering apple, verbena and mineral aromas and flavors, full body and a firm, crisp finish with a hint of Japanese shiso leaf as an aftertaste. Drink now through 2004.–B.S. • $30 • (2/28/1999) • **88**

Riesling Trockenbeerenauslese Kremstal 1998: Focused, concentrated and firmly structured, this TBA hardly seems sweet at all. Packed with apricot, honey and lime aromas and flavors that don't budge, following right through to the long finish. Drink now through 2006.–B.S. • $70/375 ml. • (4/30/2000) • **92**

Sauvignon Blanc Qualitätswein Kremstal Riede Kremser Gebling 1997: A strong herbal, grassy component is accented by gooseberry in this severe white. Finishes slightly bitter. Drink now.–B.S. • $36 • (2/28/1999) • **80**

SETZER

Grüner Veltliner Landwein Weinviertel Alte Reben 1997: New oak lends a sheen to this white, but at this stage the overall style lacks integration despite the fat, thick texture. Not imported into the U.S. Drink now through 2002.–B.S. • $NA • (12/31/1998) • **82**

Grüner Veltliner Qualitätswein Trocken Weinviertel Ried Eichholz 1997: Attractive for its floral and talc aromas and flavors, this elegant, light-bodied white has moderate intensity followed by a light finish. Not imported into the U.S. Drink now.–B.S. • $NA • (12/31/1998) • **84**

Grüner Veltliner Qualitätswein Weinviertel Ried Eichholz 1996 • $NA • (2/28/1998) • **85**

SIEGENDORF, KLOSTERKELLER

Qualitätswein Trocken Neusiedlersee-Hügelland Rot 97 1997: Soft and supple, showing leafy black currant aromas and flavors. Overall a bit diffuse, lacking focus on the finish. Cabernet Sauvignon and Blaufränkisch. Drink now.–B.S. • $9 • (4/30/2000) • **82**

Weissburgunder Kabinett Neusiedlersee 1998: Austere and linear, with a hint of cat's pee to the grassy flavor, ending crisply.–B.S. • $9 • (12/31/1999) • **79**

Weissburgunder Kabinett Neusiedlersee 1996 • $NA • (2/28/1998) • **82**

SKOFF, WALTER

Morillon Qualitätswein Trocken Südsteiermark 1998: An unadorned treatment of Chardonnay, showing apple, quince and lemon flavors supported by a juicy structure and minerally finish. Not imported into the U.S. Drink now.–B.S. • $NA • (1/01/1999) • **86**

Muskateller Qualitätswein Trocken Südsteiermark 1998: A lively burst of floral and grape flavors renders this medium-bodied white fresh and attractive. Perfect for summer picnics. Not imported into the U.S. Drink now.–B.S. • $NA • (9/15/1999) • **84**

Sauvignon Blanc Qualitätswein Trocken Südsteiermark 1998: A ripe, powerful white, integrating melon, grass and grapefruit notes with a rich texture and a solid backbone of acidity. Not overtly oaky, yet there's an attractive smoky, toasty component. Not imported into the U.S. Drink now through 2001.–B.S. • $NA • (1/01/2000) • **88**

Weissburgunder Qualitätswein Trocken Südsteiermark 1998: Compact and unevolved, the aromas and flavors are a touch blunt today, with fine structure, smooth texture and good density of flavor. Clean and refreshing finish. Not imported into the U.S. Drink now through 2001.–B.S. • $NA • (1/01/1999) • **84**

SONNHOF

Grüner Veltliner Qualitätswein Trocken Kamptal Grüve L+T 1998: An herbal, almost minty note heralds this clean, pretty white, its flavors tailing off toward the finish as the crisp structure emerges. Drink now through 2001.–B.S. • $12 • (12/31/1999) • **82**

Grüner Veltliner Qualitätswein Trocken Kamptal Langenloiser Steinhaus 1998: On the austere side despite its open-knit structure, and showing high alcohol, especially on the finish. Modest peach and herb flavors. May just need time to settle down. Drink now through 2001.–B.S. • $15 • (12/31/1999) • **84**

Grüner Veltliner Qualitätswein Trocken Kamptal Langenloiser Alte Reben 1998: Compact and dense, there's more intensity and solid structure here than in most '98s. Peach, mineral and tobacco notes hold sway, with weight that shows on the finish. Drink now through 2003.–B.S. • $27 • (12/31/1999) • **89**

Grüner Veltliner Qualitätswein Trocken Kamptal Langenloiser Steinhaus 1997: Seamlessly combines the ripe, peachy character and opulent texture of the vintage with a steely austerity that soars across the palate, culminating in a long, minerally finish. Drink through 2006.–B.S. • $15 • (12/31/1998) • **88**

Grüner Veltliner Qualitätswein Trocken Kamptal Loiserberg 1997: Round and voluptuous, with a mouthfilling texture, flavors of peach and clover honey and an appealing grassy note, this is a forward, exuberant white, with a slightly astringent finish and a tobacco aftertaste. Drink now.–B.S. • $19 • (12/31/1998) • **87**

Grüner Veltliner Qualitätswein Trocken Kamptal Loiserberg 1996 • $16 • (2/28/1998) • **88**

Pinot Blanc Qualitätswein Trocken Kamptal 1996 • $16 • (2/28/1998) • **88**

Riesling Qualitätswein Trocken Kamptal Urgestein Zöbinger Heiligenstein 1998: Strong botrytis component here, along with white pepper, peach and a luscious texture, finishing crisply, with a lingering aftertaste. Drink now through 2003.–B.S. • $23 • (12/31/1999) • **89**

Riesling Qualitätswein Trocken Kamptal Urgestein Zöbinger Heiligenstein 1997: A gorgeous, ethereal wine that glides across the palate after aromas of spring flowers, peaches and tropical fruit. Very forward yet deftly balanced, finishing firm with juicy acidity. Drink now through 2004.–B.S. • $22 • (2/28/1999) • **91**

Riesling Qualitätswein Trocken Kamptal Urgestein Zöbinger Heiligenstein 1996 • $19 • (2/28/1998) • **83**

STIFTUNG FURST LIECHTENSTEIN

Grüner Veltliner Qualitätswein Weinviertel Schloss Wilfersdorf 1998: A modestly flavored white, showing light peach and apricot notes on a crisp, lean structure.–B.S. • $13 • (8/31/1999) • **79**

Merlot Qualitätswein Weinviertel Anberola Clos Domaine 1995: Muddled, with a browning color and weedy, oaky notes, this doesn't come together, leaving an impression of stewed, underripe fruit and oak that sits apart.–B.S. • $27 • (2/28/1999) • **72**

Qualitätswein Trocken Weinviertel Anberola Red 1997: High-toned raspberry and herbal notes grace this bright, firm red. On the lean side, with some astringent tannins at the end. Good, lingering berry aftertaste. Not imported into the U.S. Drink now through 2001.–B.S. • $NA • (1/01/2000) • **82**

Qualitätswein Trocken Weinviertel Selektion Karlsberg Profundo Red 1997: Dark and rich, this is imbued with blackberry, plum and vanilla flavors, very glossy in texture and supported by medium tannins. A chocolate note lingers on the finish. Not imported into the U.S. Drink now through 2002.–B.S. • $NA • (1/01/2000) • **86**

Rheinriesling Spätlese Weinviertel Clos Domaine 1997: An elegant style, dry, with richness and weight, pear and lemon-custard flavors and a refreshing finish. Drink now through 2001.–B.S. • $18 • (2/28/1999) • **84**

Riesling-Sylvaner Spätlese Weinviertel Clos Domaine 1997: A soft, rich white, perfect as an aperitif with its peachy notes, juicy texture and crisp finish. Drink now.–B.S. • $18 • (2/28/1999) • **85**

Zweigelt Qualitätswein Trocken Weinviertel Clos Domaine 1997: A bit rustic, showing good concentration of blackberry flavors and a barnyard note. Well structured, with a lingering finish. Won't appeal to everyone. Drink now.–B.S. • $15 • (4/30/2000) • **84**

TEMENT, E. & M.

Morillon Beerenauslese Südsteiermark Puro Zieregg 1996: This is a bold, take-no-prisoners type of sweet wine, in your face from the first whiff to the resonant finish. Superrich, yet the apricot, honey and smoky maple flavors are offset by tangy acidity, keeping it lively, with a sense of grace. Not imported into the U.S. Drink now through 2006.–B.S. • $NA/375 ml. • (1/01/1999) • **91**

Morillon Qualitätswein Trocken Südsteiermark Zieregg 1997: For fans of oak, here's a midweight, vibrant white overflowing with butter, vanilla and nutmeg. Fig flavors and a rich texture act as foils. Appealing, in an overt style. Not imported into the U.S. Drink now.–B.S. • $NA • (1/01/1999) • **86**

Roter Traminer Qualitätswein Trocken Südsteiermark 1997: Distinctly perfumed and floral, with a rich texture and fine balance, here's a lovely

Key: SS—Spectator Selection. CS—Cellar Selection. HR—Highly Recommended. $NA—Price not available. (BT)—Barrel tasting. Ⓐ—Auction Price. For a key to the tasters' initials, see "How to Use These Listings."
Dates in parentheses represent the issues in which the ratings were published.

sipping wine, almost too delicate for food. The flavors linger nicely. Drink now.–B.S. • $NA • (12/31/1998) • **86**

Sauvignon Blanc Auslese Südsteiermark Zieregg 1996: Not all that sweet, with fine Sauvignon character, notes of gooseberry and peach and vibrant acidity that refreshes on the finish, though the flavors dissipate quickly. Good apéritif. Not imported into the U.S. Drink now through 2001.–B.S. • $NA/375 ml. • (1/01/1999) • **86**

Sauvignon Blanc Qualitätswein Trocken Südsteiermark 1996 • $20 • (2/28/1998) • **80**

Sauvignon Blanc Qualitätswein Trocken Südsteiermark Grassnitzberg 1998: A lean, firmly-structured white, yet with no shortage of apple, pear and spice accents, all densely textured and persistent through the long finish. Drink now through 2001.–B.S. • $31 • (4/30/2000) • **87**

Sauvignon Blanc Qualitätswein Trocken Südsteiermark Grassnitzberg 1997: Ripe, almost tropical-smelling, this exuberant Sauvignon Blanc, full of passion fruit, apricot and melon, shows richness and enough acidity for harmony. Not imported into the U.S. Drink now.–B.S. • $NA • (1/01/1999) • **85**

Sauvignon Blanc Qualitätswein Trocken Südsteiermark Steirische Klassik 1998: Leans toward the grassy, citrusy side of this varietal's taste profile, with a peach accent. Very firm and dry, however, lending itself more to drinking with food than on its own. Drink now through 2001.–B.S. • $25 • (4/30/2000) • **83**

Sauvignon Blanc Qualitätswein Trocken Südsteiermark Zieregg 1998: Rich and creamy, with ripe melon and pear flavors that take on a nutmeg and vanilla component from new oak treatment. A touch of bitterness emerges on the finish. Drink now.–B.S. • $50 • (4/30/2000) • **84**

Sauvignon Blanc Qualitätswein Trocken Südsteiermark Zieregg 1997: Shows characteristic grass and citrus aromas and flavors, yet they lack the focus and clarity to make this sing, despite the bright acid structure. Not imported into the U.S. Drink now.–B.S. • $NA • (2/28/1999) • **83**

Sauvignon Blanc Qualitätswein Trocken Südsteiermark Zieregg 1996 • $34 • (2/28/1998) • **85**

TERRA GALOS

Furmint Beerenauslese Neusiedlersee 1995 • $NA/500 ml. • (2/28/1998) • **87**

Müller-Thurgau Trockenbeerenauslese Neusiedlersee-Hügelland 1995 • $NA/375 ml. • (2/28/1998) • **90**

Pinot Noir Trockenbeerenauslese Neusiedlersee-Hügelland 1995 • $NA/375 ml. • (2/28/1998) • **87**

Sämling 88 Beerenauslese Neusiedlersee 1998: Racy and spicy in a Muscat-like way, with notes of rose, honey and apricot. Light and moderately sweet, this is better as an aperitif. Not imported into the U.S. Drink now through 2002.–B.S. • $NA/375 ml. • (1/01/2000) • **87**

Traminer Beerenauslese Neusiedlersee 1998: Vibrant, elegant and spicy, this delights the palate with its rose and unabashed grapey flavors. Not particularly complex or multidimensional, yet balanced and appealing. Not imported into the U.S. Drink now through 2002.–B.S. • $NA/375 ml. • (1/01/2000) • **88**

Trockenbeerenauslese Neusiedlersee-Hügelland Aurum 1996: Intense, ice-winelike aromas of apricot, honey and spice commingle in this rich, sweet TBA. The apricot, orange and honey flavors persist, while the richness is deftly balanced by a refreshing acidity. Not imported into the U.S. Drink now through 2004.–B.S. • $NA/375 ml. • (1/01/1999) • **88**

Weissburgunder Spätlese Neusiedlersee 1997: Rich, broad and medium-bodied, with lively acidity, but the peach and mineral flavors are a bit blunt and it finishes curtly. Not imported into the U.S. Drink now.–B.S. • $NA • (1/01/1999) • **83**

THIEL, RICHARD

Pinot-Chardonnay Qualitätswein Trocken Thermenregion 1998: There's spiciness to this, with moderate richness and concentration to the apple and citrus flavors, finishing with bitter almond. Not imported into the U.S. Drink now.–B.S. • $NA • (1/01/1999) • **83**

Riesling Kabinett Trocken Thermenregion Gumpoldskirchner 1998: A dry, bracing white offering moderate peach and citrus flavors augmented by a spicy component. Finishes a bit lean, but food should take care of that. Drink now through 2002.–B.S. • $20 • (12/31/1999) • **84**

Riesling Qualitätswein Thermenregion 1996 • $16 • (2/28/1998) • **88**

Riesling Qualitätswein Trocken Thermenregion Gumpoldskirchner Das Beste Vom 1998: Dry and spicy, offering straightforward grapefruit, white peach and apple notes on a firm, lean structure. Drink now through 2001.–B.S. • $24 • (4/30/2000) • **84**

Riesling Qualitätswein Trocken Thermenregion Gumpoldskirchner Das Beste Vom 1997: This young white expresses peach and mineral aromas and flavors, with a hint of chamomile or verbena at the finish. Richly textured and round, with just enough acidity to keep it lively. Drink now through 2003.–B.S. • $21 • (2/28/1999) • **87**

Riesling Qualitätswein Trocken Thermenregion Gumpoldskirchner Das Beste Vom 1996 • $20 • (2/28/1998) • **88**

Rotgipfler Auslese Lieblich Thermenregion Gumpoldskirchner 1998: Not too sweet, showing loads of vanilla and honey with plenty of structure, and a fillip of bitterness on the mouthwatering finish. Drink now through 2002.–B.S. • $24 • (4/30/2000) • **86**

Rotgipfler Spätlese Lieblich Thermenregion Gumpoldskirchner 1998: Broad and rich, yet there's an underpinning of acidity that keeps it lively, driving the subtle peach and lemon notes to a modest finish. Not imported into the U.S. Drink now.–B.S. • $NA • (1/01/2000) • **84**

Rotgipfler Spätlese Lieblich Thermenregion Gumpoldskirchner 1997: Peaches, honey and residual sweetness add up to an attractive white that has enough acidity for balance but whose round, soft style makes it a nice aperitif. Drink now.–B.S. • $20 • (2/28/1999) • **83**

Zierfandler Qualitätswein Thermenregion Gumpoldskirchner Classic Cuvée 1996 • $20 • (2/28/1998) • **83**

Zierfandler Qualitätswein Trocken Thermenregion Gumpoldskirchner Classic Cuvée 1998: Lovely floral and spice aromas and flavors are the hallmarks of this elegant, focused white. Richness midpalate gives way to a crisp, mouthwatering finish. Drink now.–B.S. • $20 • (4/30/2000) • **87**

Zierfandler-Rotgipfler Beerenauslese Thermenregion Gumpoldskirchner 1996: A transparent, off-dry, citrus-flavored offering marked more by its zippy acidity. Very light, finishing with soy and marzipan elements. Not imported into the U.S. Drink now.–B.S. • $NA/375 ml. • (1/01/1999) • **82**

Zierfandler-Rotgipfler Trockenbeerenauslese Thermenregion Gumpoldskirchner 1995 • $NA/375 ml. • (2/28/1998) • **90**

TRIEBAUMER, ERNST

Blaufränkisch Qualitätswein Neusiedlersee Ried Oberer Wald 1995 • $22 • (2/28/1998) • **85**

Blaufränkisch Qualitätswein Neusiedlersee-Hügelland Rust Aus Den Rieden 1996: This dark-colored red expresses black cherry aromas and flavors, with hints of spice, medium tannins and bright acidity. Finishes on a firm, crisp note. Drink now.–B.S. • $31 • (12/31/1998) • **84**

Blaufränkisch Qualitätswein Trocken Neusiedlersee-Hügelland Ried Gmark 1998: This is a heady, purple-tinged red, bursting with black cherry and spice aromas and flavors on a firm, lean structure. Drink now through 2002.–B.S. • $20 • (4/30/2000) • **84**

Blaufränkisch Qualitätswein Trocken Neusiedlersee-Hügelland Ried Marienthal 1997: Serious red. New oak lends an extra dimension to the black cherry and raspberry notes in this complex Blaufränkisch. Medium-bodied, it's concentrated and firmly structured, showing depth and length. Drink now through 2003.–B.S. • $55 • (4/30/2000) • **90**

Chardonnay Qualitätswein Trocken Neusiedlersee-Hügelland Rust Ried Pandkräftn 1997: A ripe, vibrant style of Chardonnay, exhibiting apple, pear and fig aromas and flavors mixed with a juicy texture. Finishes on a citrus note. Drink now.–B.S. • $19 • (2/28/1999) • **83**

Ruster Beerenauslese Neusiedlersee 1996: Intense, tropical character of coconut, pineapple, apricot and honey, supported by vibrant acidity. Balanced and light on its feet yet rich and persistent, it finishes on a tangy note, with orange accents. A blend of Welschriesling, Morillon and Weissburgunder. Not imported into the U.S. Drink now through 2004.–B.S. • $NA/375 ml. • (2/28/1999) • **90**

Sauvignon Blanc Ruster Ausbruch Neusiedlersee-Hügelland 1998: Thick, concentrated and intensely sweet, exhibiting orange marmalade and passion fruit aromas and flavors on a full-bodied framework. Impressive, if just a little cloying, slightly coarse on the finish. Drink now through 2005.–B.S. • $55/375 ml. • (4/30/2000) • **90**

Sauvignon Blanc Ruster Ausbruch Neusiedlersee-Hügelland 1995 • $39 • (2/28/1998) • **90**

Traminer Ausbruch Neusiedlersee-Hügelland Ried Mitterkräften 1995 • $35/375 ml. • (2/28/1998) • **88**

UMATHUM

Gelber-Roter Traminer Qualitätswein Trocken Neusiedlersee 1998: Rich and round, offering floral and apricot with accents of vanilla and butter. Very appealing, if a bit lacking in zip. Drink now.–B.S. • $14 • (4/30/2000) • **83**

Gelber-Roter Traminer Qualitätswein Trocken Neusiedlersee 1997: Delicate aromas and flavors of rose and litchi make this an attractive, easy-drinking white. Balanced on the soft side, with a hint of citrus peel on the finish. Drink now.–B.S. • $17 • (12/31/1998) • **83**

Pinot Noir Qualitätswein Neusiedlersee Junger Berg 1995 • $15 • (2/28/1998) • **83**

Pinot Noir Qualitätswein Trocken Neusiedlersee Blauburgunder 1994 • $20 • (2/28/1997) • **78**

Pinot Noir Qualitätswein Trocken Neusiedlersee Junger Berg 1997: Slightly gamy aromas lead to plum and licorice flavors, while the texture is chewy. Appealing; just lacks a little follow-through. Drink now.–B.S. • $22 • (4/30/2000) • **82**

Qualitätswein Trocken Neusiedlersee Frauenkirchner Ried Hallebühl Red 1997: Deeply colored, this is ambitious and unevolved, offering freshly crushed blackberries, milk chocolate and vanilla on a lush, ripe framework. Enough definition and tannins to keep it lively, yet it's enjoyable now. Drink now through 2002.–B.S. • $45 • (4/30/2000) • **90**

Qualitätswein Trocken Neusiedlersee Ried Hallebühl Red 1992 • $37 • (2/28/1997) • **81**

Riesling Qualitätswein Halbtrocken Neusiedlersee Urgesteins Hackelsberg 1996 • $15 • (2/28/1998) • **86**

Riesling Qualitätswein Neusiedlersee Urgesteins Hackelsberg 1997: A soft, gentle white that shows flavors of peach, talc and sweet corn. Has a medium body, good concentration and finishes on an almond note. Drink now.–B.S. • $17 • (2/28/1999) • **85**

Saint Laurent Qualitätswein Trocken Neusiedlersee Frauenkirchner Vom Stein 1996: This serious red displays leather and animal aromas and flavors in addition to black currant and blackberry. Full-bodied and solidly structured, it benefits from new oak, adding a vanilla element on the finish. Drink now through 2001.–B.S. • $28 • (12/31/1998) • **87**

Saint Laurent Qualitätswein Trocken Neusiedlersee Frauenkirchner Vom Stein 1993 • $38 • (2/28/1997) • **74**

Saint Laurent Qualitätswein Trocken Neusiedlersee Reserve 1997: Oozing with blackberries and ink, here's a suave, concentrated red whose freshly crushed raspberry and blackberry flavors hold court to the lingering finish. Drink now.–B.S. • $15 • (4/30/2000) • **87**

Scheurebe Trockenbeerenauslese Neusiedlersee 1995: A distinctive grassy, herbal note combines with lemon in this racy, almost tart TBA. Compact and tightly wound, it's medium-sweet, with a lingering aftertaste. Drink through 2005.–B.S. • $40/375 ml. • (2/28/1999) • **88**

Zweigelt Qualitätswein Neusiedlersee 1996 • $10 • (2/28/1998) • **84**

Zweigelt Qualitätswein Trocken Neusiedlersee 1998: A solid, medium-bodied Austrian red laced with blackberry flavors and a hint of bittersweet chocolate. Well-integrated, with ripe tannins and a lingering finish. Drink now through 2001.–B.S. • $13 • (4/30/2000) • **86**

Zweigelt Qualitätswein Trocken Neusiedlersee 1997: Fresh and fruity, in a Beaujolais style that's soft and easygoing, with flavors of black cherry and plum. Finishes with mouthwatering acidity. Drink now.–B.S. • $11 • (12/31/1998) • **83**

Zweigelt Qualitätswein Trocken Neusiedlersee 1995 • $17 • (2/28/1997) • **77**

Zweigelt Qualitätswein Trocken Neusiedlersee Reserve 1997: A modern, deeply colored version, with deft balance between the black cherry flavors and the corset of tannins. Elegant overall, it packs a lot of flavor, ending on a sweet fruit note. Drink now through 2001.–B.S. • $22 • (4/30/2000) • **88**

VELICH

Ausbruch Neusiedlersee 1991 • $NA/375 ml. • (2/28/1998) • **85**

Beerenauslese Neusiedlersee Seewinkel 1995 • $NA/375 ml. • (2/28/1998) • **87**

Muscat Ottonel Beerenauslese Neusiedlersee 1995 • $NA/375 ml. • (2/28/1998) • **90**

Welschriesling Trockenbeerenauslese Neusiedlersee 1995 • $NA/375 ml. • (2/28/1998) • **93**

Welschriesling Trockenbeerenauslese Neusiedlersee 1991 • $NA/375 ml. • (2/28/1998) • **86**

WALZER, EWALD

Grüner Veltliner Qualitätswein Halbtrocken Kremstal Kremser Gebling 1996 • $15 • (2/28/1998) • **82**

Key: SS—Spectator Selection. CS—Cellar Selection. HR—Highly Recommended. $NA—Price not available. (BT)—Barrel tasting. Ⓐ—Auction Price.
For a key to the tasters' initials, see "How to Use These Listings."
Dates in parentheses represent the issues in which the ratings were published.

WIENINGER

Blauburgunder Qualitätswein Trocken Wien Select 1997: Elegant and lively, this Pinot Noir has density to back its core of cherry and licorice flavors. Well balanced and long, it draws you back for more. Drink now through 2002.–B.S. • $32 • (4/30/2000) • **85**

Chardonnay Kabinett Wien 1996 • $15 • (2/28/1998) • **86**

Chardonnay Qualitätswein Trocken Wien Classic 1998: Austere in style, this firmly structured Chardonnay offers ripe apple, citrus and mineral elements, followed by a moderate, stony finish. Drink now through 2001.–B.S. • $16 • (12/31/1999) • **83**

Chardonnay Qualitätswein Trocken Wien Classic 1997: A light-bodied, lively Chardonnay, with modest flavors of apple and earth and a brief finish.–B.S. • $18 • (12/31/1998) • **79**

Chardonnay Qualitätswein Trocken Wien Select 1998: Offers some attractive, apple, peach, toast and vanilla aromas and flavors, married to a rich texture. Just a note of bitter grapefruit emerges on the finish, along with toasty oak. Drink now.–B.S. • $25 • (12/31/1999) • **85**

Chardonnay Qualitätswein Wien Select 1996 • $22 • (2/28/1998) • **84**

Grüner Veltliner Qualitätswein Trocken Wien Herrenholz 1998: Austere, with almond and herb flavors, this has medium weight and structure without a lot of flavor intensity. Picks up a nectarine note on the finish. Drink now.–B.S. • $16 • (12/31/1999) • **82**

Grüner Veltliner Qualitätswein Trocken Wien Herrenholz 1997: A hint of burnt match on the nose, but the palate reveals lentil, earth and herb notes. Medium-bodied and high in alcohol, which gives it a slightly coarse finish. Drink now through 2002.–B.S. • $16 • (2/28/1999) • **82**

Grüner Veltliner Qualitätswein Trocken Wien Leicht & Trocken 1998: Gorgeous Grüner. From the complex peach, lanolin and tobacco aromas to the crisp, minerally finish, this has good structure and balance and an immediate appeal. Drink now.–B.S. • $15 • (8/31/1999) • **88**

Grüner Veltliner Qualitätswein Wien Herrenholz 1996 • $17 • (2/28/1998) • **77**

Riesling Qualitätswein Trocken Wien Rieden Cuvée 1998: A gorgeous wine, ripe, with peach, apricot and citrus flavors all woven into a smooth texture and tensile structure. The finish picks up mineral notes. Drink now through 2004.–B.S. • $16 • (12/31/1999) • **89**

Riesling Qualitätswein Trocken Wien Rieden Cuvée 1997: A beautifully defined Riesling displaying floral, lime and tropical fruit aromas and flavors, a medium to full body, vivid structure and a mouthwatering finish. Drink through 2005.–B.S. • $16 • (2/28/1999) • **90**

Riesling Qualitätswein Trocken Wien Select 1998: Exotic, offering tropical fruit, apricot and honey aromas and flavors up front, rich and round, followed by a wave of refreshing acidity that cleanses the palate and keeps the flavors pumping. Drink now through 2004.–B.S. • $30 • (12/31/1999) • **89**

Riesling Qualitätswein Wien Select 1996 • $15 • (2/28/1998) • **86**

WINKLER-HERMADEN

Blauer Zweigelt Qualitätswein Trocken Südoststeiermark 1994 • $12 • (1/31/1997) • **78**

Blauer Zweigelt Qualitätswein Trocken Südoststeiermark Olivin 1995: Medium-bodied, concentrated and well balanced. Very fresh, with ripe cherry flavors that carry through on the aftertaste. Well done. Delicious now through 2001.–B.S. • $22 • (12/31/1998) • **86**

Grauburgunder Qualitätswein Trocken Südoststeiermark Kapfensteiner Kogel 1997: Lackluster, with only modest peach and spice notes.–B.S. • $20 • (2/28/1999) • **78**

Qualitätswein Trocken Südoststeiermark Caphenstein Steirische Klassik 1998: Floral and citrus aromas yield to a round, easygoing palate showing apple flavors that lack a bit of focus. Drink now.–B.S. • $12 • (9/15/1999) • **80**

Traminer Qualitätswein Trocken Südoststeiermark Kapfenstein Ried Kirchleiten 1997: The color is a lurid yellow, but this white displays plenty of spice, rose and grapefruit aromas and flavors, a rich texture and a soft structure. Butter and vanilla accents linger on the finish. Drink now.–B.S. • $20 • (12/31/1998) • **84**

WINZER KREMS

Chardonnay Kabinett Trocken Kremstal Kremser Kellermeister Privat 1998: Like peaches and cream, this unadorned Chardonnay is thick and rich, gaining structure from a touch of bitter citrus peel at the finish. Drink now.–B.S. • $13 • (4/30/2000) • **85**

Chardonnay Kabinett Trocken Kremstal Kremser Kellermeister Privat 1997: Rich and round, this up-front style shows pear and gooseberry aromas and flavors. Crisp finish. Not imported into the U.S. Drink now.–B.S. • $NA • (12/31/1998) • **82**

Grüner Veltliner Kabinett Trocken Kremstal Kremser Goldberg Kellermeister Privat 1998: Intense and minerally, this white displays grapefruit peel, bitter almond and peach flavors backed by acidity that borders on tartness. Needs food with herbs or root vegetables. Drink now through 2001.–B.S. • $10 • (12/31/1999) • **85**

Grüner Veltliner Kabinett Trocken Kremstal Kremser Goldberg Kellermeister Privat 1997: An austere style. Ripe yet restrained in its expression of grapefruit, mineral and tobacco and backed by firm acidity, it has the structure for food. Not imported into the U.S. Drink through 2005.–B.S. • $NA • (12/31/1998) • **86**

Grüner Veltliner Kabinett Trocken Kremstal Kremser Goldberg Kellermeister Privat 1996 • $NA • (2/28/1998) • **84**

Grüner Veltliner Kabinett Trocken Kremstal Kremser Sandgrube 1998: Broad and a bit blunt, exhibiting cut apple and almond flavors, moderate concentration and ending on a bitter grapefruit note.–B.S. • $8 • (12/31/1999) • **79**

Grüner Veltliner Kabinett Trocken Kremstal Kremser Sandgrube 1996 • $NA • (2/28/1998) • **84**

Rheinriesling Kabinett Kremstal Kremser Pfaffenberg Hauerinnung Krems-Stein 1997: Dry and steely, with an intensity and nervosité that keep the nutty, minerally character lively and persistent. A little severe, it should improve with time or food. Not imported into the U.S. Best from 2001 through 2006.–B.S. • $NA • (1/01/1999) • **87**

Riesling Kabinett Trocken Kremstal Kremser Kremsleiten Kellermeister Privat 1998: Taut like a drum, this white resonates with peach and orange on a racy, focused framework. Try with seafood or lemon chicken. Best from 2001 through 2004.–B.S. • $14 • (12/31/1999) • **85**

Riesling Kabinett Trocken Kremstal Kremser Kremsleiten Kellermeister Privat 1996 • $NA • (2/28/1998) • **88**

Saint Laurent Qualitätswein Trocken Kremstal Kremser Kellermeister Privat 1997: Oodles of blackberry and spice along with vibrant acidity and firm tannins add up to a very pleasurable young red. Should develop well over the next few years. Not imported into the U.S. Drink now through 2001.–B.S. • $14 • (12/31/1998) • **85**

Zweigelt Qualitätswein Trocken Kremstal Kremser Kellermeister Privat 1997: Plenty of structure here, both acidity and tannin, but the cherry and chocolate flavors lack focus, tasting stewed. Tasted twice, with consistent notes.–B.S. • $12 • (4/30/2000) • **79**

Zweigelt Qualitätswein Trocken Kremstal Kremser Kellermeister Privat 1995: There are clove and tobacco elements in the aroma, but the cherry and spice flavors are dilute and the finish is curt and tannic. Not imported into the U.S.–B.S. • $NA • (12/31/1998) • **77**

WINZERHAUS

Blauer Zweigelt Qualitätswein Weinviertel 1996 • $8 • (2/28/1998) • **82**

Pinot Blanc Beerenauslese Neusiedlersee 1995 • $NA/375 ml. • (2/28/1998) • **88**

WOHLMUTH

Chardonnay Qualitätswein Trocken Südsteiermark Summus 1998: Light on its feet, this Chardonnay packs a lot of apple, almond and nutmeg flavors into its elegant, vibrant frame. Drink now.–B.S. • $14 • (12/31/1999) • **84**

Pinot Gris Qualitätswein Trocken Südsteiermark Summus 1998: Textbook Pinot Gris, offering smoky, nutty aromas and flavors, with a hint of violets, all displayed on a broad, rich framework. Firms up on the finish. Drink now through 2001.–B.S. • $13 • (4/30/2000) • **88**

Sauvignon Blanc Qualitätswein Trocken Südsteiermark Summus 1998: New oak lends a spicy character and rounds out the structure of this medium-bodied, focused white. Apple and freshly cut grass complete the mix. Drink now.–B.S. • $17 • (4/30/2000) • **85**

ZULL

Chardonnay Qualitätswein Trocken Weinviertel Schrattenthal Ödfeld 1997: A pure style of Chardonnay, displaying apple and pear aromas and flavors, a rich texture and a lingering finish. Everything is balanced by crisp acidity. Drink now.–B.S. • $16 • (12/31/1998) • **85**

Grüner Veltliner Qualitätswein Trocken Weinviertel Schrattenthal Ödfeld 1998: Ripe and round, offering peach and melon, with an underlying tobacco note. Hints of bitterness and citrus lift the finish. Drink now.–B.S. • $15 • (12/31/1999) • **84**

Grüner Veltliner Qualitätswein Trocken Weinviertel Schrattenthal Ödfeld 1997: Reticent aromas, yet very ripe and integrated on the palate, with notes of passion fruit, orange and apricot, an unctuous midpalate texture and lively acidity that refreshes on the long finish. Drink through 2005.–B.S. • $13 • (12/31/1998) • **88**

Pinot Blanc Qualitätswein Trocken Weinviertel Schrattenthal Karollen 1998: Ripe and generous up front, with pear, quince and a hint of vanilla all underscored by a lemony acidity that carries the flavors through the finish. Not imported into the U.S. Drink now.–B.S. • $NA • (1/01/1999) • **86**

Qualitätswein Trocken Weinviertel Schrattenthal Cuvée Exclusive 1997: Very herbal, showing dill and green olive, though attractive for its concentration, elegant structure and focus. Not imported into the U.S. Drink now.–B.S. • $NA • (1/01/2000) • **84**

Riesling Qualitätswein Trocken Weinviertel Schrattenthal Innere Bergen 1998: Bursting with violet, quince and hints of tropical fruit. A juicy Riesling, well balanced and with moderate depth of flavor, finishing on a firm citrus note. Drink now.–B.S. • $14 • (9/15/1999) • **87**

Welschriesling-Müller Thurgau Beerenauslese Weinviertel 1998: Ripe and assertive, this moderately sweet white has dried apricot and candied citrus peel notes. Softly structured, it finishes on the short side, with a slight bitterness. Not imported into the U.S. Drink now.–B.S. • $NA/375 ml. • (1/01/2000) • **86**

Zweigelt Qualitätswein Trocken Weinviertel Schrattenthal 1998: Light-bodied, with refreshing acidity and a chewy texture, this focused red offers wild berry and spice notes. A pleasant astringency at the end should match well with food. Drink now through 2001.–B.S. • $15 • (4/30/2000) • **84**

Zweigelt Qualitätswein Trocken Weinviertel Schrattenthal 1997: A simple red whose flavors are a bit muddled, like stewed plums. The finish is crisp and short.–B.S. • $14 • (12/31/1998) • **78**

Chile

Stretching more than 2500 miles from its northern border in the Atacama Desert to Tierra del Fuego in the south, Chile has been called a paradise for the production of fine wine. Because Chile has never been touched by phylloxera, it is one of the few places on earth where vinifera vines can be planted on their own roots, without the necessity of being grafted onto phylloxera-resistant American rootstock. Clean, abundant water from the Andes makes irrigation reliable, and grapevines thrive in Chile's naturally fertile, light soil. A little over a decade ago, an international market thirsty for inexpensive varietal wines discovered Chile's favorable natural conditions and low production costs. Fueled by massive infusions of foreign capital, the country's wineries set out to supply bargain-priced Cabernet Sauvignon, Merlot, Chardonnay and Sauvignon Blanc. With so many good bottlings in the under-$10 range, almost overnight Chile became the third-largest wine exporter to the United States.

Having achieved notable success at the good-value end of the price scale, Chile has now set out on the next, and highly ambitious, phase of its modern evolution. The country's leading wineries are determined to unlock the potential that lies buried within Chile's top *terroirs*. Their goal is the production of concentrated, age-worthy wines that can challenge the world's best, and to achieve it, they are using every tool in the winemaker's arsenal: joint ventures with prestigious wineries in Europe, Australia and California, massive renovations of aging wineries and construction of new, state-of-the-art facilities, and an unprecedented focus on vineyard management. With every wave of new releases, the benefits of modernization and foreign investment in Chile's vineyards are increasingly apparent.

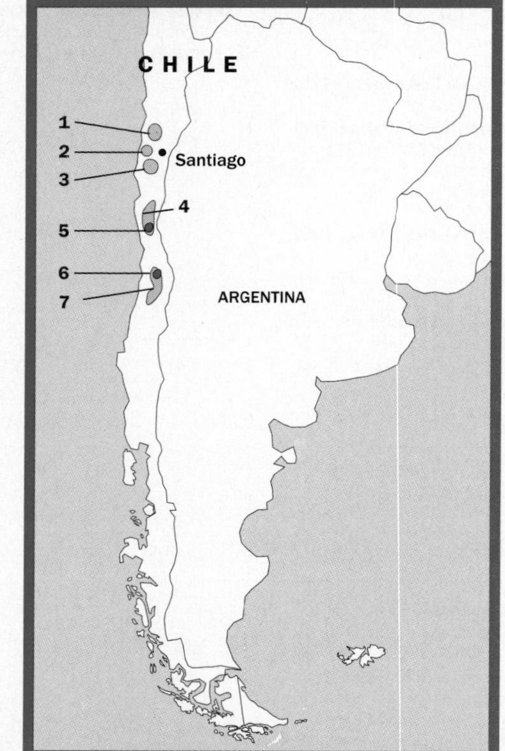

1. Aconcagua
2. Casablanca
3. Maipo
4. Rapel
5. Colchagua
6. Curicó
7. Maule

At the high end of the price scale, the results have been truly spectacular. Red wines based on the country's traditional strength, the Bordeaux varieties of Cabernet Sauvignon and Merlot (and including Carmenère, a variety imported from Bordeaux in the 19th century and now virtually extinct in its native land), have led the way.

A pathbreaking joint venture between Chile's venerable Concha y Toro winery and Bordeaux's first growth Château Mouton-Rothschild has provided a huge boost to Chile's image and prestige. The wine, called Viña Almaviva Puente Alto Maipo (the 1997 scored 91 points on *Wine Spectator's* 100-point scale) has established a new benchmark in quality—and, at $70, price. Casa Lapostolle's Merlot-based Clos Apalta Rapel Valley 1997 (91, $40)—a single-vineyard Bordeaux blend crafted by Pomerol-based international consultant Michel Rolland, provides another masterly example, as does the Seña Aconcagua Valley 1996 (92, $50), a polished Cabernet blend produced by a joint venture between the historic Errazuriz winery in Chile's Aconcagua Valley and the Robert Mondavi Winery in California.

But not all of Chile's modernization efforts have been expended on pleasing the elites. Other efforts have focused on offering wines with clean, fresh, fruit-driven personalities at moderate prices, with consistent quality. The wines from Dallas Conté (a joint venture between Australia's Mildara Blass and Chile's Viña Santa Carolina) and from Viña Calina (backed by California's Kendall-Jackson) are examples of this trend. Indigenous Chilean winemakers have also vastly improved and upgraded their offerings. Chile's star winemaker, Ignacio Recabarren, has contributed Trio, a line of well-priced varietals made by Concha y Toro, and is also responsible for the excellent wines from Viña Santa Carolina. Carmen winemaker Alvaro Espinoza has produced excellent wines from the once-forgotten Carmenère, to much acclaim. These and other wines prove that quality and value remain a Chilean preoccupation.

Mark Vaughan

Plowing at Cousiño Macul in the Maipo Valley.

CHILEAN WINE REGIONS

Chilean viticulture dates back to the 1850s, when a wave of French immigrants settled in the Santiago region, bringing with them native French grape types, such as Cabernet Sauvignon, Malbec, Merlot, Sémillon and Sauvignon Blanc. The French winemaking tradition remains strong here. Chilean wines tend more toward the elegant, European style than they do toward the heavier, more concentrated style found in much of the rest of the New World. However, regional variations are becoming increasingly significant as the Chilean wine industry expands.

Located in the northern part of Chile's central valley, a narrow, 300-mile long valley set between the Andes and a coastal range of mountains to the west, is the Maipo Valley. Starting just below Santiago and extending 25 miles south to the town of Buin, the Maipo is the heart of the Chilean wine industry. The red wines from vineyards closer to Santiago, such as Cousiño-Macul, have a distinctly earthy taste that is reminiscent of a red Graves. Farther south in the Central Valley, a number of newer sub-regions are being quickly developed. These include Lontue, Colchagua, Curicó and Rancagua. Many producers blend wines from a number of these regions, with the object of producing well-balanced reds and whites that combine the flavors of several regions. The top whites are from the Casablanca Valley, as its cool climate is well-suited for white wine grapes.

MAJOR CHILEAN GRAPE VARIETIES

Much like California wines, Chilean wines are marketed primarily by varietal labeling (for instance, "Chardonnay") rather than by regional appellations such as "Maipo Valley". The most important grape types remain the traditional red and white Bordeaux varieties, with Chardonnay receiving more and more attention.

Cabernet Sauvignon is widely planted. Many Cabernets display the cedary nuances and gentle herbal notes of a red Bordeaux. In place of the old rauli barrels of the past, many winemakers are using combinations of French and American oak to season the wine, adding an appealing vanilla note to the Cabernet varietal character. Because Chilean Cabernet Sauvignon is sufficiently soft and round, it has rarely needed the softening effect of Merlot to achieve a balanced wine. As a result, until recently, Chile had not produced much Merlot, which was thought of primarily as a blending grape. However, with Merlot's rise as a popular varietal in its own right throughout the world, Chilean Merlot production has become more significant. Chilean Merlots are of a high quality, displaying soft, luscious fruit and a nice Graves-like *goût de terroir*. Much Chilean "Merlot" is in fact Carmenère, which until recently had not been recognized as a separate variety. It is similar to true Merlot, with perhaps a bit more power.

Most Chilean wineries also produce decent, sometimes delicious white wines. Sauvignon Blanc remains the most consistent of the white varieties. Most is now cold-fermented in stainless steel vats, yielding wines that are fresh and ready to be drunk upon release. A more serious style, made in the manner of a white Graves using barrel fermentation, is also beginning to appear at a somewhat higher price. Viña Caliterra's Sauvignon Blanc Valle Central and the Montes Sauvignon Blanc Curicó Valley Fumé Blanc have both proved excellent.

Chardonnay is also becoming important, largely because of the almost insatiable international demand for this popular varietal. Generally warm conditions in many regions have meant that Chilean Chardonnays often lack crispness and definition. Several producers are experimenting with barrel fermentation, lees stirring and more careful selection of grapes in an effort to produce Chardonnays with more character. Concha y Toro Chardonnay Casablanca Valley Amelia Private Reserve ($18) and the Dallas Conté Chardonnay Casablanca Valley Reserve ($17) are among the leaders.

With a reputation built on value, and a new strategy aimed at achieving ever higher quality, Chile is on a trajectory toward world-class status.

ALAMEDA

Cabernet Sauvignon Colchagua Valley La Serenata Vineyard Vintner's Selection 1996: Yet another good-drinking value from Chile, this one offering jammy, forward flavors of black currant and violet. Soft in texture and well balanced, it's an attractive mouthful of red wine. Drink now.–B.S. • $6 • (10/15/1998) • **84**

Cabernet Sauvignon Maipo Valley 1994 • $5 • (2/28/1997) • **82**

Cabernet Sauvignon Maipo Valley 1988 • $6 • (6/15/1992) • **84**

Cabernet Sauvignon Maipo Valley Santa Maria Vineyard 1993 • $7 • (2/29/1996) • **81**

Cabernet Sauvignon Maipo Valley Vintner's Selection 1995 • $5 • (2/28/1997) • **83**

Cabernet Sauvignon Maipo Valley Vintner's Selection 1993 • $5 • (2/29/1996) • **85**

Cabernet Sauvignon Maipo Valley Vintner's Selection 1992 • $5 • (4/30/1995) • **85**

Cabernet Sauvignon Valle Central Santa Maria Vineyard Vintner's Selection 1997: Leans toward the herbal, bell pepper side of Cabernet character, with firm tannins and a smooth texture. It's fresh and balanced, with sweet raisin flavors that emerge on the finish. Drink now.–T.M. • $6 • (3/31/1999) • **81**

Cabernet Sauvignon-Merlot Valle Central 1997: This straightforward red offers clean cherry and berry flavors, with light herbal and vanilla accents and just enough tannin for grip. Drink now.–T.M. • $7/1.5 liter • (4/30/1999) • **81**

Chardonnay Maipo Valley Santa Maria Vineyard 1997: Clean and fresh, this sturdy Chilean white offers a pleasant blend of sweet vanilla and ripe apple and melon flavors, with just enough acidity to keep it lively. Hard to beat at this price. Drink now.–T.M. • $6 • (9/15/1998) • **84**

Chardonnay-Sauvignon Blanc Valle Central 1997: Clean and fresh, this shows modest flavors of apple, lime and vanilla. It doesn't taste much like either grape in the blend, but it's easy to drink. Try now.–T.M. • $7/1.5 liter • (4/30/1999) • **80**

Merlot Maipo Valley Santa Maria Vineyard 1995 • $6 • (2/28/1997) • **83**

Merlot Maipo Valley Santa Maria Vineyard 1994 • $6 • (4/30/1997) • **84**

Merlot Maipo Valley Santa Maria Vineyard 1993 • $6 • (2/29/1996) • **86**

Merlot Maipo Valley Santa Maria Vineyard 1992 • $6 • (6/15/1995) • **84**

Merlot Maipo Valley Santa Maria Vineyard Vintner's Selection 1997: This soft red offers appealing flavors of cedar and dried cherry, sweet and smooth on the palate, with light tannins. An easy-quaffing wine. Drink now.–T.M. • $6 • (3/31/1999) • **82**

Merlot Maule Valley La Vereda Vineyard Vintner's Selection 1996: Focused, with pleasant plum flavors and chocolate notes. Smooth and ripe, with leathery accents on the finish.–K.M. • $6 • (9/15/1998) • **83**

Sauvignon Blanc Lontué Valley La Gardinia Vineyard Vintner's Selection 1997: Full-bodied yet tart, this pungent white offers assertive, slightly clumsy herb, litchi and smoke aromas and flavors. Makes a lively aperitif. Drink now.–T.M. • $6 • (9/15/1998) • **83**

ALFASI

Cabernet Sauvignon Valle del Maule 1997: Simple and sweet, this supple red has jammy strawberry flavors with soft tannins. Tastes more like candy than wine. Kosher.–T.M. • $7 • (9/15/1999) • **76**

Cabernet Sauvignon Valle del Maule Reserve 1997: This round, supple red offers sweet vanilla and chocolate flavors from oak, with straightforward notes of cherries and plums. Just enough structure for food. Kosher. Drink now.–T.M. • $10 • (9/15/1999) • **80**

Merlot Valle del Maule 1997: A simple, cherry- and leather-flavored red, light in body and structure. Kosher.–B.S. • $7 • (9/15/1999) • **79**

Merlot Valle del Maule Reserve 1997: There's a nice smoky note here, but ultimately it's light and short on fruit and depth. Kosher.–B.S. • $10 • (9/15/1999) • **78**

ALMAVIVA, VINA

Puente Alto Maipo 1997: With Bordeaux-like aromatics of cedar, cigar smoke and cassis, this expansive but stylish Cabernet loads up the currant, plum, toast, sanguine and mineral flavors before the fine-grained and well-integrated tannins carry in the finish. A benchmark for the region. Drink now through 2003.–T.M. • $30 Ⓐ • (3/31/2000) HR • **91**

Puente Alto Maipo 1996: This massive red has more concentration than most Chilean reds, yet it's still polished and balanced, with ripe plum and cassis flavors accompanied by plenty of toasty, coffee notes from the heavy dose of new oak. It's more powerful than showy now, with a brooding depth that bodes well for the future. Best after 2001.–T.M. • $30 Ⓐ • (3/31/1999) • **91**

ANTU MAPU

Cabernet Sauvignon Maule Valley Reserva 1997: Supple and light, this red offers simple flavors of sweet berries and milk chocolate. An easy quaff without much substance.–T.M. • $8 • (9/15/1999) • **78**

Chardonnay Maule Valley Reserva 1998: Juicy and clean. This big-boned white shows apple and melon flavors, with a dollop of vanilla oak and crisp acidity. Balanced and refreshing. Drink now.–T.M. • $8 • (10/31/1999) • **84**

Merlot Maule Valley Reserva 1998: This supple red offers subdued cherry and herb flavors, with soft tannins and a short, clean finish. A small wine with good proportions. Drink now.–T.M. • $8 • (10/31/1999) • **81**

Sauvignon Blanc Maule Valley Reserva 1998: Light and crisp, this white is neutral in character, with lemony, light herbal flavors. Refreshing but simple. Drink now.–T.M. • $8 • (10/31/1999) • **80**

ARRIGORRIAGA

Cabernet Sauvignon San Fernando 1996 • $12 • (6/30/1997) • **84**

BALDUZZI

Cabernet Sauvignon Maule Valley Reserva 1996: Earthy, gamy flavors and firm tannins give this red a rustic edge, but ripe black cherry notes emerge on the finish and suggest this wine will be better with air and food. Drink now through 2002.–T.M. • $9 • (9/15/1999) • **82**

Chardonnay Maule Valley 1998: Cider and cooked apple flavors are straightforward and rather dull, and the sweet oak overwhelms the light acidity and leaves a slightly cloying finish.–T.M. • $8 • (10/31/1999) • **78**

Sauvignon Blanc Maule Valley Reserva 1997: This light, fresh white offers light apple and pear flavors, with floral and spicy notes that are appealing, though not varietally correct. A nice aperitif. Drink now.–T.M. • $8 • (10/31/1999) • **83**

BAREFOOT

Chardonnay Maule Valley NV: This round white offers pleasant apple and vanilla flavors, but an earthy note undercuts the pleasure. Drink now.–T.M. • $5 • (9/15/1998) • **78**

BEL ARBOR

Cabernet Sauvignon Valle Central Vintner's Selection 1996 • $6 • (10/31/1997) • **83**

Cabernet Sauvignon Valle Central Vintner's Selection 1995 • $6 • (2/28/1997) • **85**

Chardonnay Valle Central Vintner's Selection 1997: Simple refreshment. Thin, with light grapefruit and apple aromas, watery flavors. Drink now. • $6 • (9/15/1998) • **77**

BLACK HORSE CELLARS (VALDIVIESO)

Brut Chile NV: Quite earthy, with a little marmalade and honey too, all on a texture that starts out smooth, turns a bit coarse by the finish.–B.S. • $11 • (3/31/2000) • **79**

Cabernet Sauvignon Lontué Valley 1997: A lean, astringent red dominated by rhubarb flavors. Not much fun. –K.M. • $9 • (3/31/2000) • **73**

Chardonnay Lontué Valley 1999: Clean and fresh, with ripe apple and pear flavors that turn a bit soft and blunt in the end. Drink now.–T.M. • $9 • (3/31/2000) • **80**

Merlot Lontué Valley 1998: Tastes over-the-hill despite its youth, with murky, stewy flavors. –K.M. • $9 • (3/31/2000) • **73**

Sauvignon Blanc Lontué Valley 1998: Aromas and flavors of candied, lemony Lifesavers are all this simple, barely vinous white has to offer. –K.M. • $9 • (3/31/2000) • **76**

Key: SS—Spectator Selection. CS—Cellar Selection. HR—Highly Recommended. $NA—Price not available. (BT)—Barrel tasting. Ⓐ—Auction Price. For a key to the tasters' initials, see "How to Use These Listings." **Dates in parentheses represent the issues in which the ratings were published.**

BOUCHON, VINEDOS J.

Cabernet Sauvignon Maule Valley Chicureo Reserva 1996: Round and supple, this fruity red tastes of plums, strawberries and milk chocolate. Has just enough structure to match with food. Drink now.–T.M. • $9 • (9/15/1999) • **80**

Cabernet Sauvignon Maule Valley Las Mercedes 1995: A bit thin, with decent dried cherry and plum flavors and an herbal note on the finish.–K.M. • $11 • (10/15/1998) • **79**

Cabernet Sauvignon Maule Valley Las Mercedes Reserva 1996: Shows good balance and definition, with black cherry, mint and herbal flavors, firm tannins and a polished texture. A good match for lighter dishes. Drink now through 2001.–T.M. • $9 • (3/31/1999) • **83**

Chardonnay Maule Valley Chicureo 1998: Distinctive mineral and mango flavors give this white individuality. Muscular and clean, with a nice balance of oak and acidity, it brings you back for another sip. Drink now.–T.M. • $8 • (10/31/1999) • **85**

Chardonnay Maule Valley Las Mercedes 1998: This light white offers lemon, green apple and light vanilla flavors that linger nicely. It's no blockbuster, but has some intensity. Drink now.–T.M. • $9 • (4/30/1999) • **83**

Chardonnay Maule Valley Las Mercedes 1997: Decent tropical and pear flavors could mesh better. Ends on a lean, tart note.–K.M. • $10 • (9/30/1998) • **78**

Merlot Maule Valley Chicureo 1997: There are some berry and menthol notes in this lightweight, slightly raisiny Merlot. Drink now.–T.M. • $10 • (3/31/2000) • **81**

Merlot Maule Valley Chicureo 1996: Quite flavorful, satisfying and supple. This has oodles of blackberry and cherry flavors on a smooth texture, with light tannins and very good balance. Drink now. • $12 • (9/15/1998) • **86**

Merlot Maule Valley Las Mercedes 1996: This light, soft red shows a mix of sweet and bitter flavors, with herbal and cola notes. Has very light tannins and little concentration.–T.M. • $9 • (3/31/1999) • **77**

Sauvignon Blanc Maule Valley Chicureo 1998: This soft white lacks varietal character, but the peach and floral notes are appealing, if light. Stays crisp through the short finish. Drink now.–T.M. • $8 • (10/31/1999) • **81**

Sauvignon Blanc Maule Valley Las Mercedes 1998: Light and crisp, offering snappy gooseberry and grassy flavors with sharp, citrusy acidity. It's simple but clean and shows varietal character. Drink now.–T.M. • $9 • (3/31/1999) • **82**

Sauvignon Blanc Maule Valley Las Mercedes 1997 • $8 • (5/31/1998) • **79**

BRUNO, DOMAINE PAUL

Cabernet Sauvignon Maipo Valley 1994 • $15 • (6/30/1996) • **74**

CABALLERO DE CHILE

Cabernet Sauvignon Valle Central Reserva 1995 • $7 • (3/31/1998) • **82**

CABALLERO DE SANTIAGO

Cabernet Sauvignon Colchagua Valley 1997: Very floral, showing violet along with chocolate malt, cherry and black currant. Moderate concentration and depth, finishing short. Drink now.–B.S. • $6 • (10/15/1998) • **83**

CALINA

Cabernet Sauvignon Valle Central 1998: A supple red, with sweet spice and red fruit flavors. Espresso and dark chocolate notes chime in on the finish. Drink now through 2002.–K.M. • $11 • (3/31/2000) • **85**

Cabernet Sauvignon Valle Central 1995 • $8 • (6/30/1997) • **87**

Cabernet Sauvignon Valle del Rapel 1997: A character of chocolate-covered violets with dashes of black currant marks this well-made Chilean red. The rich, supple texture and an intensity on the palate are followed by a long finish. Drink now.–B.S. • $9 • (10/15/1998) • **87**

Chardonnay Valle de Casablanca 1997: More subtle than most Chilean Chards, this offers refined toasty and vanilla oak accents and ripe apple and light mineral flavors in a harmonious package. Clean and refreshing. Drink now.–T.M. • $9 • (9/15/1998) • **85**

Chardonnay Valle del Itata 1998: This buttery white has a rich texture, but the flavors are simple, with smoke, vanilla and pear notes and little acidity. Drink now.–T.M. • $9 • (10/31/1999) • **80**

Chardonnay Valle del Itata 1997: A solid, basic Chardonnay, with modest pear and peach flavors, light spicy accents and a smooth texture. Drink now. • $9 • (9/15/1998) • **82**

Merlot Valle del Maule 1998: A bit rustic in style, yet there's concentrated cherry flavor and an almost-chewy texture. Drink now.–B.S. • $11 • (9/15/1999) • **83**

CALINA, VINA

Cabernet Franc Chile 1994 • $20 • (2/29/1996) • **84**

Cabernet Sauvignon Chile 1993 • $20 • (2/29/1996) • **84**

Cabernet Sauvignon Chile Selección de las Lomas 1996: This polished red offers vivid fruit flavors of cherry and berry, with smoky, toasty accents, crisp acidity and firm, balanced tannins. Not a big wine, but clean and focused. Drink now through 2002.–T.M. • $17 • (10/31/1999) • **85**

Cabernet Sauvignon Chile Selección de las Lomas 1994 • $20 • (6/30/1997) • **88**

Cabernet Sauvignon Colchagua Vicuña Vineyard Selección de las Lomas 1996: Ripe and round. Sweet cherry and cola flavors are rich and soft, with just enough tannin for grip. Distinctive in character, but becomes a bit tiring after a glass or two. Drink now through 2002.–T.M. • $24 • (9/15/1999) • **83**

Carmenère Valle del Maipo Santa Emiliana Vineyard 1997: This inky red has the color and texture of black velvet, delivering plum, coffee and licorice flavors over round tannins that finish soft and sweet. Not complex, but pleasantly lush. Drink now through 2002.–T.M. • $20 • (10/31/1999) • **84**

Chardonnay Chile Selección de las Lomas 1997: This fleshy white offers ripe fruit, sweet oak and lemony acidity. Balanced and quite rich, it's straightforward, but has enough substance to match with bold foods. Drink now.–T.M. • $15 • (10/31/1999) • **85**

Merlot Chile 1994 • $20 • (2/29/1996) • **83**

Merlot Chile Selección de las Lomas 1997: Dark in color, with sweet Port-like notes of prune and molasses, but it manages to stay focused on the palate, with raspberry and chocolate notes leading to a chewy, full-bodied finish. Drink now.–T.M. • $17 • (3/31/2000) • **85**

Merlot Chile Selección de las Lomas 1996: Smooth, appealing and broad-textured, an easy Merlot to enjoy. Generous, ripe fruit flavors are accented by cedar and vanilla. Drink now. • $20 • (10/15/1998) • **85**

Merlot Chile Selección de las Lomas 1995 • $20 • (6/30/1997) • **85**

CALITERRA, VINA

Cabernet Sauvignon Maipo Valley 1994 • $8 • (2/28/1997) • **83**

Cabernet Sauvignon Maipo Valley 1992 • $7 • (5/31/1994) • **82**

Cabernet Sauvignon Maipo Valley 1991 • $6 • (4/30/1993) • **83**

Cabernet Sauvignon Maipo Valley 1990 • $6 • (3/15/1993) • **84**

Cabernet Sauvignon Maipo Valley 1989 • $6 • (6/15/1992) • **87**

Cabernet Sauvignon Maipo Valley 1988 • $6 • (10/15/1991) • **79**

Cabernet Sauvignon Maipo Valley Reserva 1997: Charry bacon fat aromas are strong, echoing on the palate. Some depth of fruit, but lacking a bit of definition and focus. Drink now.–K.M. • $12 • (3/31/2000) • **83**

Cabernet Sauvignon Maipo Valley Reserva 1994 • $11 • (2/28/1997) • **85**

Cabernet Sauvignon Maipo Valley Reserva 1988 • $9 • (12/15/1992) • **86**

Cabernet Sauvignon Valle Central 1998: Black olive and dark cherry flavors dominate this medium-bodied red. Ends on a slightly stewed note. Drink now.–K.M. • $8 • (3/31/2000) • **81**

Cabernet Sauvignon Valle Central 1996: Pleasant and minty, with sweet cherry and plum flavors mixed in. A medium-bodied Cabernet that's smooth, with a ripe finish. Drink now.–K.M. • $8 • (10/15/1998) • **84**

Cabernet Sauvignon Valle Central 1995 • $8 • (10/31/1997) • **84**

Cabernet Sauvignon Valle Central Reserva 1995 • $12 • (10/31/1997) • **87**

Chardonnay Casablanca Valley Reserva 1998: Full-bodied and polished, this oaky white offers flavors of toast, vanilla, apple and melon. Balanced and ripe, it has the muscle to stand up to food. Drink now.–T.M. • $12 • (3/31/2000) • **85**

Chardonnay Valle Central 1999: Ripe, a bit blowsy, and sweet on the finish; this generous white offers tropical fruit and vanilla flavors, round but soft. Drink now.–T.M. • $8 • (3/31/2000) • **83**

Chardonnay Valle Central 1997: Vanilla and toast notes dominate the light apple flavor in this clean but simple white. It has a crisp core of lemony acidity. Drink now.–T.M. • $8 • (9/15/1998) • **81**

Merlot Curicó Valley 1995 • $8 • (2/28/1997) • **84**

Merlot Valle Central 1998: Herbal aromas give way to a simple, light-bodied Merlot with some basic grape and plum notes. Drink now.–T.M. • $8 • (3/31/2000) • **82**

Merlot Valle Central 1996 • $8 • (10/31/1997) • **85**

Sauvignon Blanc Valle Central 1997: Firm and toasty, this is quite full-bodied, with clean, ripe flavors of apple and toast and enough acidity for balance. A good match for poultry. Drink now.–T.M. • $8 • (3/31/2000) • **86**

CANEPA

Cabernet Sauvignon Curicó Magnificum 1995: This juicy, vivid red shows blackberry and currant flavors that are intense yet delicate, with floral and vanilla accents and light but firm tannins. What it lacks in concentration it makes up for in exuberance. Tasted twice, with consistent notes. Drink now through 2002.–T.M. • $60 • (4/30/1999) • **86**
Cabernet Sauvignon Curicó Magnificum 1990 • $19 • (5/31/1995) • **86**
Cabernet Sauvignon Curicó Valley Private Reserve 1996: Light and lean, this red shows light cherry and vegetal flavors, with slightly dry tannins that keep the finish short.–T.M. • $13 • (4/30/1999) • **78**
Cabernet Sauvignon Curicó Valley Private Reserve 1995: Something wrong here. There's good sweet fruit, but an acetone note and overt dryness suggest a flawed wine. Tasted twice, with consistent notes.–T.M. • $13 • (3/31/1999) • **64**
Cabernet Sauvignon Maipo Valley 1995 • $7 • (6/30/1997) • **76**
Cabernet Sauvignon Maipo Valley 1994 • $7 • (6/30/1995) • **82**
Cabernet Sauvignon Maipo Valley 1993 • $6 • (4/30/1995) • **79**
Cabernet Sauvignon Maipo Valley 1991 • $6 • (4/30/1993) • **82**
Cabernet Sauvignon Maipo Valley 1990 • $6 • (6/15/1992) • **81**
Cabernet Sauvignon Maipo Valley Finisimo Estate Reserve 1990 • $NA • (6/30/1996) • **83**
Cabernet Sauvignon Maipo Valley Private Reserve 1994 • $10 • (4/30/1997) • **83**
Cabernet Sauvignon Maipo Valley Private Reserve 1993 • $10 • (2/28/1997) • **85**
Cabernet Sauvignon Maipo Valley Private Reserve 1992 • $8 • (4/30/1995) • **88**
Cabernet Sauvignon Maipo Valley Reserva 1988 • $7 • (6/15/1990) • **84**
Cabernet Sauvignon Rapel 1998: Supple and fruity, this red shows bright raspberry and strawberry flavors, with light vanilla accents, over soft tannins. A sunny, easy-drinking wine, with just enough stuffing for lighter dishes. Drink now.–T.M. • $9 • (4/30/1999) • **83**
Cabernet Sauvignon Rapel 1997: Mingles light floral, sweet cherry and earthy flavors. It's soft on the palate, finishing with light tannins.–T.M. • $9 • (3/31/1999) • **78**
Cabernet Sauvignon-Malbec Curicó 1997: A lively mix of cherry, cranberry, herb and smoke flavors gives this red distinctive character. The balance is good, and the tannins are firm but well integrated. A nice match for food. Drink now through 2003.–T.M. • $9 • (2/28/1999) • **86**
Cabernet Sauvignon-Malbec Curicó 1996 • $6 • (2/28/1997) • **77**
Cabernet Sauvignon-Malbec Curicó 1994 • $5 • (10/31/1995) • **85**
Cabernet Sauvignon-Malbec Curicó 1993 • $5 • (5/31/1995) • **84**
Cabernet Sauvignon-Malbec Maule 1998: This supple wine offers light cherry and berry flavors, fresh and clean, with light tannins and a short finish. An easy-quaffing red. Drink now.–T.M. • $9 • (4/30/1999) • **81**
Chardonnay Rancagua 1997: This full-bodied white is packed with toasty oak flavors supported by an intriguing mineral note that lingers on the finish. The apple and melon flavors are subtle, but the wine draws you back for another sip. Drink now.–T.M. • $9 • (2/28/1999) • **84**
Chardonnay Rancagua Private Reserve 1997: Tastes of butterscotch and almonds, with an underlying tart acidity that seems artificial and can't quite pull the flavors together.–T.M. • $13 • (2/28/1999) • **77**
Merlot Curicó 1996 • $7 • (4/30/1997) • **83**
Merlot Curicó 1994 • $6 • (6/15/1995) • **81**
Merlot Maipo Valley 1990 • $6 • (6/15/1992) • **84**
Merlot Maipo Valley 1988 • $6 • (6/30/1990) • **79**
Merlot Rapel 1998: Light and fresh. Cherry, berry and herbal flavors are simple but clean and focused in this balanced red. It has light tannins and a short finish. Drink now.–T.M. • $9 • (4/30/1999) • **83**
Merlot Rapel 1997: This light, simple red shows sweet vanilla and light berry flavors, soft and clean on the palate. Short finish. Drink now.–T.M. • $9 • (3/31/1999) • **80**
Merlot San Fernando Private Reserve 1996: This fruity red has a sweet appeal, is lively and accessible, with cherry flavors, light vanilla accents, bright acidity and light, firm tannins. Drink now.–T.M. • $13 • (4/30/1999) • **82**
Merlot San Fernando Private Reserve 1995: Has some expressive oak and ripe fruit, but the acidity seems raw and volatile and the flavors turn chemical and candied. Not recommended. Tasted twice, with consistent notes.–T.M. • $13 • (4/30/1999) • **62**
Sauvignon Blanc Cachapoal 1998: This lean white emphasizes the grassy, herbal side of the variety, well focused and firm but carried to an extreme that leaves it tart and tinny on the finish. For fans of Loire Valley Sauvignon Blanc. Drink now.–T.M. • $8 • (5/15/1999) • **82**
Sauvignon Blanc Cachapoal 1997: Earthy and herbal flavors mark this dull white. Lacks fruit and freshness.–T.M. • $8 • (4/30/1999) • **77**

Key: SS—Spectator Selection. CS—Cellar Selection. HR—Highly Recommended. $NA—Price not available. (BT)—Barrel tasting. (A)—Auction Price.
For a key to the tasters' initials, see "How to Use These Listings."
Dates in parentheses represent the issues in which the ratings were published.

CARMEN

Cabernet Sauvignon Maipo Valley 1993 • $6 • (6/30/1996) • **78**
Cabernet Sauvignon Maipo Valley 1990 • $6 • (5/31/1994) • **70**
Cabernet Sauvignon Maipo Valley Alto Jahuel 1990 • $6 • (7/15/1993) • **82**
Cabernet Sauvignon Maipo Valley Alto Jahuel Reserve 1989 • $8 • (7/15/1993) • **81**
Cabernet Sauvignon Maipo Valley Barrel Select Gold Reserve 1993 • $18 • (1/31/1995) • **86**
Cabernet Sauvignon Maipo Valley Gold Reserve 1995: Alluring black cherry and toast aromas follow through on the palate in this sophisticated, international-style red. With a nice marriage of fresh fruit and complexity, it's lively, balanced and has plenty of structure for food. Drink now through 2002.–T.M. • $24 • (9/15/1998) • **90**
Cabernet Sauvignon Maipo Valley Gold Reserve 1993 • $25 • (2/28/1997) • **86**
Cabernet Sauvignon Maipo Valley Reserve 1997: This chewy red shows flavors of currants and licorice, but leans toward the herbal, earthy side of the Cabernet spectrum, with muscular tannins and a smoky, slightly bitter finish. Drink now through 2002.–T.M. • $17 • (4/30/1999) • **83**
Cabernet Sauvignon Maipo Valley Reserve 1996: More serious in style than many Chilean Cabs, this has deep color, oaky complexity, abundant fruit flavor and firm texture framed by moderate tannins. Drink now. • $14 • (9/15/1998) • **88**
Cabernet Sauvignon Maipo Valley Reserve 1995 • $13 • (6/30/1997) • **88**
Cabernet Sauvignon Maipo Valley Reserve 1994 • $10 • (1/01/1997) • **87**
Cabernet Sauvignon Maipo Valley Reserve 1992 • $10 • (6/30/1996) • **78**
Cabernet Sauvignon Maipo Valley Reserve 1991 • $9 • (1/31/1995) • **80**
Cabernet Sauvignon Maipo Valley Reserve 1990 • $8 • (5/31/1994) • **72**
Cabernet Sauvignon Rapel Valley 1992 • $6 • (4/30/1995) • **87**
Cabernet Sauvignon Valle Central 1996: A good, light style of Cabernet, with pleasant but simple fruit flavors and light tannins. Drink now. • $8 • (9/15/1998) • **82**
Cabernet Sauvignon Valle Central 1994 • $8 • (1/01/1997) • **83**
Chardonnay Casablanca Valley Wine Maker's Reserve 1997: Ripe and thick. This ambitious white offers vanilla, toast and melon flavors, full-bodied but lacking acidity for balance. It's clean, yet a bit heavy-handed. Drink now.–T.M. • $17 • (5/15/1999) • **81**
Chardonnay Maipo Valley Reserve 1997: Lush yet tender, offering an alluring combination of ripe fruit and delicacy, with notes of melon, vanilla and citrus. Its distinctive spiciness and plushness bring you back for another sip. Drink now.–T.M. • $17 • (5/15/1999) • **87**
Chardonnay Valle Central 1998: Straightforward and clean. Vanilla and buttery oak flavors dominate this broad, somewhat flat-textured white. Ripe apple and light lemony accents keep the finish lively. Drink now.–T.M. • $8 • (5/15/1999) • **84**
Chardonnay Valle Central 1997: A good, serviceable Chardonnay, with clean, light citrus and pear flavors, medium body and a soft texture. Drink now. • $8 • (9/15/1998) • **82**
Grand Vidure-Cabernet Sauvignon Maipo Valley Reserve 1997: This generous red offers a mix of sweet oak and ripe fruit, with flavors of chocolate, plum, smoke and herbs. It's plump on the palate, with a core of firm tannins. Try with grilled, well-marbled meats. Grand Vidure is a synonym for Carmenère. Drink now through 2003.–T.M. • $13 • (4/30/1999) • **86**
Grand Vidure-Cabernet Sauvignon Maipo Valley Reserve 1996: Deliciously fruity in flavor and invitingly soft in texture, this blend has ripe raspberry and currant flavors, light tannins and a lingering, fruity finish. Drink now. • $15 • (9/15/1998) • **85**
Grand Vidure-Cabernet Sauvignon Maipo Valley Reserve 1995 • $13 • (2/28/1997) • **86**
Grand Vidure-Cabernet Sauvignon Maipo Valley Reserve 1994 • $12 • (2/28/1997) • **85**
Merlot Maipo Valley Alto Jahuel 1990 • $6 • (1/31/1994) • **80**
Merlot Maipo Valley Reserve 1993 • $9 • (1/31/1995) • **85**
Merlot Maule Valley 1994 • $6 • (5/31/1996) • **82**
Merlot Maule Valley 1993 • $6 • (6/15/1995) • **83**
Merlot Maule Valley Reserve 1994 • $10 • (5/31/1996) • **80**
Merlot Rapel Valley 1992 • $6 • (5/31/1994) • **82**
Merlot Rapel Valley Reserve 1997: A lush and ripe Chilean red, offering deep plum, licorice and chocolate flavors, yet remaining lively on the palate, with polished tannins and a clean, fresh finish. It's focused and

concentrated enough to improve with age. Drink now through 2007.–T.M. • $14 • (4/30/1999) HR • **89**

Merlot Rapel Valley Reserve 1996: Nicely balanced and complex in flavor. Touches of cinnamon and cedar flavor distinguish this moderately concentrated Merlot and linger on the finish. Just tannic enough. Drink now. • $15 • (9/30/1998) • **87**

Merlot Rapel Valley Reserve 1995 • $13 • (2/28/1997) HR • **89**

Merlot Rapel Valley Reserve 1993 • $9 • (5/15/1995) • **88**

Merlot Valle Central 1997: Assertive yet blunt, this chunky red shows jammy plum and smoke flavors over muscular tannins. It's rich but clumsy; may smooth out with food. Drink now through 2002.–T.M. • $8 • (4/30/1999) • **82**

Merlot Valle Central 1996: Frankly fruity and straightforward, this is a good, basic Merlot, with ample raspberry and cherry flavors and earthy accents. Light in texture. Drink now. • $8 • (9/15/1998) • **81**

Merlot Valle Central 1995 • $8 • (2/28/1997) • **85**

Petite Sirah Maipo Valley Reserve 1997: Lively blackberry and smoke character is expressive and inviting in this exuberant red. It's firm, with a heavy dose of oak that may be too much for some, but it has lots of stuffing, and the juicy fruit stays bright and clean. Drink now through 2003.–T.M. • $18 • (4/30/1999) • **88**

Petite Sirah Maipo Valley Reserve 1995 • $13 • (6/30/1997) • **87**

Petite Sirah Maipo Valley Reserve 1995: Ripe and plummy, but with a good dose of drying tannins. A little overwrought, though. Not for the faint of heart. Drink now.–K.M. • $14 • (10/15/1998) • **82**

Pinot Noir Maipo Valley Reserve 1997: Perhaps Chile's best Pinot Noir to date. Full of lively black cherry and plum flavors, with notes of spice and toast that stay true to the varietal character. Light tannins and balanced acidity round out this modest but well-proportioned package. Drink now through 2002.–T.M. • $17 • (5/15/1999) • **85**

Sauvignon Blanc Casablanca Valley Reserve 1997 • $15 • (5/31/1998) • **86**

Sauvignon Blanc Maipo Valley Reserve 1998: A marriage of vibrant acidity and ripe fruit flavors gives this wine personality and punch. It's quite round, with generous notes of melon, pineapple and herbs, but remains crisp and refreshing. Drink now.–T.M. • $13 • (5/15/1999) • **86**

Sauvignon Blanc Valle Central 1997 • $8 • (5/31/1998) • **83**

Sémillon Late Harvest Maipo Valley Reserve 1996: Ripe and honeyed, with nice concentration and plenty of ripe pear and peach flavors. Nutmeg and cinnamon notes linger on the finish. Drink now.–K.M. • $8/375 ml. • (10/15/1998) • **86**

Syrah Maipo Valley Reserve 1997: This plush red shows richly textured flavors of smoke, game, chocolate and prune. It's generous without exuberance; the firm structure suggests it would show best with food. Drink now through 2002.–T.M. • $18 • (4/30/1999) • **85**

Wine Maker's Reserve Maipo Valley 1997: Lush yet vibrant. This rich red is chock-full of ripe plum and currant flavors, accented with dark chocolate notes from oak, with a velvety texture wrapped around firm, ripe tannins. A blend of Cabernet Sauvignon, Carmenère, Petite Sirah and Merlot. Drink now through 2004.–T.M. • $18 • (4/30/1999) • **88**

CARTA VIEJA

Cabernet Sauvignon Maule Valley 1999: Juicy, with flavors of plum and black pepper. Chocolate and spice notes linger on the finish. Drink now.–K.M. • $6 • (3/31/2000) • **82**

Cabernet Sauvignon Maule Valley 1997: Simple but lively. This light red offers cherry, raspberry and light herbal flavors, with gentle tannins and a clean finish. Juicy acidity keeps it quaffable. Drink now.–T.M. • $6 • (4/30/1999) • **82**

Cabernet Sauvignon Maule Valley 1995 • $5 • (6/30/1997) • **80**

Cabernet Sauvignon Maule Valley 1994 • $5 • (2/28/1997) • **83**

Cabernet Sauvignon Maule Valley 1993 • $5 • (4/30/1995) • **82**

Cabernet Sauvignon Maule Valley 1991 • $5 • (5/31/1994) • **76**

Cabernet Sauvignon Maule Valley 1990 • $5 • (2/28/1993) • **81**

Cabernet Sauvignon Maule Valley Antiqua Selection 1988 • $8 • (4/30/1993) • **76**

Cabernet Sauvignon Maule Valley Reserve 1996: Grapey and straightforward, this lightweight Cab provides a simple yet enjoyable drink. Like a Beaujolais Nouveau with guts. This was the best of three samples, with considerable bottle variation. Drink now.–K.M. • $10 • (3/31/2000) • **81**

Chardonnay Maule Valley 1999: Smelling of tinned fruit cocktail, this light-bodied, simple Chardonnay finishes on a cloying note.–K.M. • $6 • (3/31/2000) • **78**

Chardonnay Maule Valley 1998: Very crisp and quite lean, this lively white offers green apple and citrus flavors, bracing and clean on the finish. It's not complex, but will make a vibrant complement to lighter dishes. Drink now.–T.M. • $6 • (5/15/1999) • **83**

Chardonnay Maule Valley Reserve 1997: On the flinty side, with light flavors that peter out in the face of cloying oak and spritz. Tasted twice, with consistent notes.–K.M. • $10 • (3/31/2000) • **77**

Merlot Maule Valley 1999: Simple and fruity, with grapey, banana aromas and flavors, this is a decent quaffer.–T.M. • $6 • (3/31/2000) • **79**

Merlot Maule Valley 1998: Good balance and structure provide this Chilean red with an appealing combination of muscle and freshness, with ripe berry flavors, light smoke and herb notes rounding out the package. Drink now through 2002.–T.M. • $6 • (5/15/1999) • **86**

Merlot Maule Valley 1996 • $5 • (6/30/1997) • **80**

Merlot Maule Valley 1993 • $5 • (6/15/1995) • **80**

Merlot Maule Valley 1991 • $5 • (2/28/1993) • **81**

Merlot Maule Valley Reserve 1996: Lean in scope, with herbal notes, stewy, muddled fruit and a tough finish. This was the better of two samples.–T.M. • $10 • (3/31/2000) • **77**

Sauvignon Blanc Maule Valley 1998: Enticing aromas of figs and heather give way to more neutral flavors of citrus and light herbs in this bracingly crisp white. Makes up in verve what it lacks in complexity. Drink now.–T.M. • $6 • (5/15/1999) • **84**

CASA DONOSO

Cabernet Sauvignon Maule Valley 1996: Straightforward and fruity, with decent plum and herbal flavors. Drink now.–K.M. • $10 • (10/15/1998) • **79**

Cabernet Sauvignon Maule Valley 1993 • $10 • (4/30/1997) • **88**

Chardonnay Maule Valley 1997: Pear and apple flavors dominate this simple wine, which shows a touch of sweetness. Drink now.–K.M. • $10 • (9/30/1998) • **82**

Merlot Maule Valley 1997: A Merlot of a different color. Extremely deep-hued, flavorful and rich in texture, almost like an Aussie Shiraz. Has light tannins and seductive layers of blackberry, herb and chocolate that linger on the finish. Drink now. • $10 • (9/15/1998) • **87**

Merlot Maule Valley 1996 • $10 • (4/30/1997) • **86**

CASA JULIA

Merlot San Fernando Valley 1996: An interesting Merlot, with an array of herb, berry and cedar flavors and a firm texture. Drink now. • $10 • (10/15/1998) • **83**

Merlot San Fernando Valley 1995 • $8 • (2/28/1997) • **79**

Sauvignon Blanc Lontué Valley 1997: Apple and melon flavors are ripe and balanced, if a bit muted, in this round, clean white. It's soft yet fresh. Drink now.–T.M. • $10 • (9/15/1998) • **80**

CASA LAPOSTOLLE

Cabernet Sauvignon Colchagua 1994 • $9 • (6/30/1996) • **87**

Cabernet Sauvignon Rapel Valley 1998: A solid red, with appealing berry and mineral flavors. Medium-bodied, with jammy and spicy notes on the finish. Good for pizza. Drink now.–K.M. • $10 • (3/31/2000) • **84**

Cabernet Sauvignon Rapel Valley 1997: Round and ripe, this lush red from Chile offers satisfying drinking for the price, with mouthfilling blackberry, toast and light herbal flavors, chewy tannins and a clean finish. Makes an impact, but stays supple and polished. Tasted twice, with consistent notes. Drink now through 2004.–T.M. • $11 • (5/15/1999) • **88**

Cabernet Sauvignon Rapel Valley 1995 • $10 • (5/31/1997) • **85**

Cabernet Sauvignon Rapel Valley Cuvée Alexandre 1998: A full-bodied and expressive red, with plenty of berry, red plum and chocolate-spice flavors. There are nice mineral and cedar notes mixed in, with fine tannins on the finish. Drink now through 2002.–K.M. • $18 • (3/31/2000) • **87**

Cabernet Sauvignon Rapel Valley Cuvée Alexandre 1997: This ambitious red shows plenty of concentration, its ripe flavors of blackberry and dried plum overlaid with coffee and toasty oak nuances and supported by muscular tannins. It seems a bit overdone now, oaky and alcoholic on the finish, but should harmonize with time. Tasted twice, with consistent notes. Best from 2001 through 2009.–T.M. • $18 • (4/30/1999) • **88**

Cabernet Sauvignon Rapel Valley Cuvée Alexandre 1996: This elegant and stylish Cabernet has a good balance of plum, mineral and milk chocolate flavors. Ripe and smooth, with notes of cardamom on the finish. Drink now.–K.M. • $18 • (10/15/1998) • **87**

Cabernet Sauvignon Rapel Valley Cuvée Alexandre 1995 • $15 • (6/30/1997) • **89**

Chardonnay Casablanca Valley 1997: Compared to the safe international-style typical of Chilean whites, this Chard goes for the gusto. It's thick-textured, heavy with oak, very ripe and delivers plenty of fruit and alcohol. Seems a bit clumsy now, but it has stuffing and may come around. Much better than previously reviewed. Drink through 2002.–T.M. • $11 • (5/15/1999) • **86**

Chardonnay Casablanca Valley Cuvée Alexandre 1997: Lavish use of oak has given this silky, full-bodied white plenty of toast, vanilla and cream flavors, but it shows only hints of melon and banana beneath the oak. Ambitious, but a bit unbalanced, it's a treat for those who love woody Chard. Tasted twice, with consistent notes. Drink now.–T.M. • $18 • (5/15/1999) • **85**

Chardonnay Rapel Valley 1998: Ambitious, with ripe orange and pineapple flavors and a round, creamy texture. Fruit-driven in style, but without much finesse in the end. Drink now.–T.M. • $10 • (3/31/2000) • **83**

Clos Apalta Rapel Valley 1997: This showstopper has all the bells and whistles: deep color, lavish oak, concentrated ripe fruit, power and harmony in a polished package. The boysenberry, chocolate and licorice flavors are voluptuous and velvety; the wine has elegance to match its power. It's hard to find Chile in its character, but easy to take pleasure in the result. 95 percent Merlot with 5 percent Cabernet Sauvignon. Drink now through 2007.–T.M. • $40 • (10/31/1999) • **91**

Merlot Colchagua Selection 1994 • $9 • (5/15/1995) • **87**

Merlot Rapel Valley 1996: A solid, well-made Merlot that shows ripe cherry, herb and raspberry flavors, firm tannins and a tight, dense texture. A bit more structured than most Chilean Merlots; may need time. Try through 2000. • $11 • (9/15/1998) • **84**

Merlot Rapel Valley 1995 • $10 • (4/30/1997) • **83**

Merlot Rapel Valley Cuvée Alexandre 1998: Glimpses of smoke and cassis give way to a thick, dense and extracted Merlot with ripe currant and boysenberry flavors. It's all harnessed by a tannic shell that's ripe and well-sculpted and needs a little time to unwind. Best after 2000.–T.M. • $25 • (3/31/2000) • **88**

Merlot Rapel Valley Cuvée Alexandre 1997: Great ripeness and concentration give this powerful Chilean red depth and persistence. It offers explosive cassis and blackberry flavors, with ripe, muscular tannins and plenty of toasty oak grace notes. It has some jagged edges now, but should bloom with some time in the bottle. Drink through 2010–T.M. • $18 • (4/30/1999) SS • **90**

Merlot Rapel Valley Cuvée Alexandre 1996: This well-integrated Chilean red boasts rich flavors and a good backbone of fine tannins. It's thick and plush, with loads of dark plum, blackberry, currant and dark chocolate flavors that linger on the finish. Delicious now, but with enough stuffing to age well, too. Drink through 2001.–K.M. • $18 • (10/15/1998) HR • **89**

Merlot Rapel Valley Cuvée Alexandre 1995 • $15 • (4/30/1997) • **90**

Merlot Rapel Valley Cuvée Alexandre 1994 • $15 • (6/30/1996) HR • **90**

Sauvignon Blanc Rapel Valley 1999: This rather disjointed white offers opulent aromas of toast and tropical fruit, but it turns hot and thin on the palate, with little varietal character. Tasted twice, with consistent notes.–T.M. • $8 • (3/31/2000) • **77**

Sauvignon Blanc Rapel Valley 1998: This round white offers ripe flavors of apples and melons, with spicy notes that hint at cinnamon and clove. Not a typical Sauvignon Blanc, lively enough to bring you back for another sip. Drink now.–T.M. • $8 • (5/15/1999) • **82**

Sauvignon Blanc Rapel Valley 1997: Ripe apple and herb flavors and accents of vanilla give this white a gentle appeal. It has just enough acidity for food. Drink now.–T.M. • $8 • (9/15/1998) • **83**

CASA PORTA

Cabernet Sauvignon Cachapoal Valley 1996 • $7 • (10/31/1997) • **79**

Chardonnay Valle Central 1997: Lean and slightly earthy, this dull white shows little fruit or finesse. Tasted twice, with consistent notes. Drink now.–T.M. • $6 • (9/15/1998) • **74**

Sauvignon Blanc Rapel Valley 1997 • $6 • (5/31/1998) • **82**

CASTILLO DEL RIO

Merlot Chile 1995 • $6 • (6/30/1997) • **84**

Merlot-Cabernet Sauvignon Chile 1995 • $6 • (6/30/1997) • **77**

CHATEAU LA JOYA

Cabernet Sauvignon Colchagua Valley 1997: Black cherry, licorice and light herbal notes are harmonious and clean in this round, solid red. It's modest, but the balance and structure are finely tuned and made for food. Drink now through 2004.–T.M. • $9 • (4/30/1999) • **86**

Cabernet Sauvignon Colchagua Valley 1996: An honest, solid Cabernet that's true to type and not gussied up with oak. It has concentrated herb and currant flavors, firm tannins and a lingering finish. Drink now. • $8 • (9/15/1998) • **87**

Cabernet Sauvignon Colchagua Valley Gran Reserva 1997: This muscular red is a bit raw now, with ripe blackberry and licorice flavors and plenty of firm yet integrated tannins. The oak is present but well integrated, and the wine promises improvement in the bottle. Drink through 2008–T.M. • $12 • (4/30/1999) • **88**

Cabernet Sauvignon Colchagua Valley Gran Reserva 1996: Fans of oak will love the sweet vanilla and chocolate character that dominates this flashy red. It also shows bright berry and cherry flavors, and firm tannins suggest it can age. Drink through 2005.–T.M. • $12 • (4/30/1999) • **85**

Cabernet Sauvignon Colchagua Valley Gran Reserva 1994: A hearty, tannic Cabernet, with intriguing flavors of cedar, spice and currant. Fully mature. Drink now. • $11 • (9/15/1998) • **84**

Chardonnay Colchagua Valley 1997: Straightforward and soft, this simple white shows melon and cooked apple flavors that turn a bit dull on the finish.–T.M. • $9 • (4/30/1999) • **77**

Chardonnay Colchagua Valley Gran Reserva 1997: This oaky white tastes mostly of smoke and herbs, with some melon and cooked apple accents. It's broad in texture, but lacks snap.–T.M. • $12 • (4/30/1999) • **79**

Merlot Colchagua Valley 1997: This chunky red is dominated by firm, slightly tough tannins, with light flavors of cherry, cola and herbs.–T.M. • $9 • (3/31/1999) • **79**

Merlot Colchagua Valley 1996: A smooth, spicy-tasting Merlot, with complex flavors of cinnamon, plum and cherry. Well balanced and not too tannic. Drink now. • $8 • (9/15/1998) • **86**

Merlot Colchagua Valley Gran Reserva 1997: Shows vivid cherry and cola flavors, bright acidity and firm tannins, but lacks harmony. May come together with time. Best after 2000.–T.M. • $12 • (3/31/1999) • **82**

Merlot Colchagua Valley Gran Reserva 1996: Delicious, from the deep purple color and smoky black raspberry aromas to the lush, velvety texture and black cherry notes. Concentrated, yet maintains a sense of elegance through the long, vanilla-tinged finish. Tasted twice, with consistent notes. Drink now.–B.S. • $11 • (10/15/1998) • **88**

Sauvignon Blanc Colchagua Valley 1997: Despite its good concentration and bracing acidity, this assertive white shows little fruit flavor, leaning toward the herbal, grassy side of the spectrum. Better with food than as an aperitif. Drink now.–T.M. • $9 • (3/31/1999) • **81**

CHATEAU LOS BOLDOS

Cabernet Sauvignon Requinoa 1995 • $6 • (4/30/1997) • **83**

Cabernet Sauvignon Requinoa 1991 • $8 • (6/15/1995) • **75**

Cabernet Sauvignon Requinoa CLB Reserve 1998: Tobacco and bell pepper aromas show restraint before the clean, fresh, medium-bodied cherry and plum character takes over. A good little Cab. Drink now.–K.M. • $16 • (3/31/2000) • **84**

Cabernet Sauvignon Requinoa CLB Reserve 1996: This firm red shows smoky, meaty flavors and muscular tannins that make an impact on the palate, turn into berry and floral notes on the lingering finish. Reminiscent of a good minor Graves from Bordeaux. Drink now through 2001.–T.M. • $20 • (3/31/1999) • **83**

Cabernet Sauvignon Requinoa Grand Cru 1996: Shows an interesting mix of mint, bell pepper, prune and chocolate notes on a medium-bodied, clean and fresh frame. Soft, ripe tannins complete the picture. Drink now.–T.M. • $38 • (3/31/2000) • **86**

Chardonnay Requinoa CLB Reserve 1998: This silky white shows grapefruit and vanilla flavors that keep the wine balanced and lively. Simple but satisfying. Drink now.–T.M. • $14 • (3/31/2000) • **83**

Chardonnay Requinoa Vieilles Vignes 1998: Fruity and refreshing. This crisp white offers bright flavors of apple, melon and light vanilla, with enough body to stand up to lighter fish and poultry dishes. Drink now.–T.M. • $10 • (2/28/1999) • **84**

Merlot Requinoa CLB Reserve 1998: Ebullient raspberry and blackberry aromas and flavors are allied to a clean, light-bodied frame. There's also a faint note of the grape's typical herbal side, which adds interest. Nicely done. Drink now.–T.M. • $16 • (3/31/2000) • **84**

Merlot Requinoa CLB Reserve 1996: This straightforward red shows good balance and firm structure, but the flavors are modest, with hints of cherry, cedar and herbs, and the finish is slightly dry. Best with food. Drink now through 2001.–T.M. • $20 • (3/31/1999) • **82**

Sauvignon Blanc Requinoa CLB Reserve 1999: Rich yet refreshing. This silky white is full-bodied in texture, yet crisp and citrusy in character. Can stand up to poultry and heavier fish. Drink now.–T.M. • $12 • (3/31/2000) • **84**

Key: SS—Spectator Selection. CS—Cellar Selection. HR—Highly Recommended. $NA—Price not available. (BT)—Barrel tasting. Ⓐ—Auction Price.
For a key to the tasters' initials, see "How to Use These Listings."
Dates in parentheses represent the issues in which the ratings were published.

Sauvignon Blanc Requinoa Vieilles Vignes 1998: This crisp white makes an impact on the palate, bright and tart, then blossoms with ripe flavors of fig and apple. Clean and fresh, with enough weight for food. Drink now.–T.M. • $10 • (3/31/1999) • **84**

COASTAL CELLARS

Cabernet Sauvignon Valle Central 1996: Quite cinnamon-tasting, with brown sugar and sweet notes, too. A smooth wine, if a bit overripe. Drink now.–K.M. • $NA • (10/15/1998) • **80**

CONCHA Y TORO

Cabernet Sauvignon Maipo Valley 1989 • $6 • (4/30/1993) • **81**

Cabernet Sauvignon Maipo Valley Casillero del Diablo 1998: Has some good Cabernet varietal character, with currant and bayleaf flavors and minty notes on the finish. Drink now.–K.M. • $10 • (3/31/2000) • **83**

Cabernet Sauvignon Maipo Valley Casillero del Diablo 1996: This good-value Chilean red shows harmonious ripe plum and coffee-scented oak character, with notes of mint, licorice and herb. The tannins are firm but don't get in the way, and a long, dark finish promises some further development. Drink now through 2004.–T.M. • $10 • (12/15/1998) • **88**

Cabernet Sauvignon Maipo Valley Casillero del Diablo 1995 • $10 • (5/31/1997) • **86**

Cabernet Sauvignon Maipo Valley Casillero del Diablo 1992 • $8 • (4/30/1995) • **82**

Cabernet Sauvignon Maipo Valley Casillero del Diablo Pirque Vineyard Special Reserve 1991 • $9 • (5/31/1994) • **81**

Cabernet Sauvignon Maipo Valley Casillero del Diablo Pirque Vineyard Special Reserve 1988 • $9 • (12/15/1992) • **81**

Cabernet Sauvignon Maipo Valley Marqués de Casa Concha Puente Alto Vineyard 1996: This thick, supple wine shows good concentration, with palate-coating blueberry, toast, earthy and herbal flavors. Balanced and clean, and may open up with further aging. Drink now through 2003.–T.M. • $14 • (1/31/1999) • **85**

Cabernet Sauvignon Maipo Valley Marqués de Casa Concha Puente Alto Vineyard 1995: Ripe, with leathery, plummy flavors, some bittersweet chocolate notes on the finish. Drink now.–K.M. • $14 • (10/15/1998) • **80**

Cabernet Sauvignon Maipo Valley Marqués de Casa Concha Puente Alto Vineyard 1994 • $13 • (5/31/1997) • **86**

Cabernet Sauvignon Maipo Valley Marqués de Casa Concha Puente Alto Vineyard 1991 • $10 • (1/01/1995) • **82**

Cabernet Sauvignon Maipo Valley Marqués de Casa Concha Puente Alto Vineyard 1989 • $11 • (6/30/1996) • **76**

Cabernet Sauvignon Maipo Valley Marqués de Casa Concha Puente Alto Vineyard 1988 • $11 • (4/30/1993) • **73**

Cabernet Sauvignon Maipo Valley Puente Alto Vineyard Don Melchor Private Reserve 1996: Rich and dark. Ripe flavors of plum, prune, coffee and eucalyptus swirl through this dense, velvety Chilean red. The tannins are firm but not overbearing, and the wine finishes clean and long. It speaks of both the varietal and the *terroir* in a seamless package. Drink now through 2010.–T.M. • $27 • (10/31/1999) SS • **90**

Cabernet Sauvignon Maipo Valley Puente Alto Vineyard Don Melchor Private Reserve 1995: This rich red has a voluptuous texture, round and velvety, with very firm tannins underneath flavors of plum, prune, coffee and tobacco. It needs food to unwind, but shows distinctive character. Drink through 2005–T.M. • $24 • (9/15/1998) • **88**

Cabernet Sauvignon Maipo Valley Puente Alto Vineyard Don Melchor Private Reserve 1994 • $23 • (5/31/1997) HR • **90**

Cabernet Sauvignon Maipo Valley Puente Alto Vineyard Don Melchor Private Reserve 1993 • $16 • (6/30/1996) CS • **91**

Cabernet Sauvignon Maipo Valley Puente Alto Vineyard Don Melchor Private Reserve 1991 • $13 • (4/30/1995) • **87**

Cabernet Sauvignon Maipo Valley Puente Alto Vineyard Don Melchor Private Reserve 1990 • $13 • (4/15/1994) • **84**

Cabernet Sauvignon Maipo Valley Puente Alto Vineyard Don Melchor Private Reserve 1989 • $14 • (7/15/1993) • **78**

Cabernet Sauvignon Maipo Valley Puente Alto Vineyard Don Melchor Private Reserve 1988 • $15 • (4/30/1993) • **74**

Cabernet Sauvignon Maipo Valley Puente Alto Vineyard Don Melchor Private Reserve 1987 • $13 • (6/30/1990) • **85**

Cabernet Sauvignon Maipo Valley Trio 1996: This very firm red shows the smoky, eucalyptus character typical of many Maipo Cabs, with very firm tannins and good concentration. It doesn't offer a lot of fruit, but should match with smoked and grilled meats. Drink now through 2002.–T.M. • $9 • (3/31/1999) • **85**

Cabernet Sauvignon Maipo Valley Trio 1995 • $9 • (11/30/1997) • **84**

Cabernet Sauvignon Maipo Valley Trio 1994 • $8 • (6/30/1996) • **84**

Cabernet Sauvignon Valle Central Sunrise 1998: This light-bodied red shows the cassis and currant notes typical of Cabernet allied to a fresh, readily accessible frame. Drink now.–K.M. • $7 • (3/31/2000) • **83**

Cabernet Sauvignon Valle Central Sunrise 1997: A good, solid red with plummy flavors, chocolaty notes and firm tannins. Drink now.–K.M. • $7 • (10/15/1998) • **83**

Cabernet Sauvignon-Merlot Rapel 1990 • $5 • (4/30/1993) • **78**

Cabernet Sauvignon-Merlot Rapel 1988 • $5 • (7/31/1992) • **79**

Cabernet Sauvignon-Merlot Valle Central 1997: Ripe-tasting, with some good dark plum, chocolate and leather flavors. Has an appetizing gamy note on the finish. Smooth, ready to drink.–K.M. • $8/1.5 liter • (10/15/1998) • **82**

Chardonnay Casablanca Valley Amelia Private Reserve 1997: Flamboyant in style, with deep, lush, smoky notes weaving through the ripe pear and tropical fruit flavors. The finish is well oaked, and fans of this style will appreciate it. Drink now.–T.M. • $18 • (3/31/2000) • **87**

Chardonnay Casablanca Valley Casillero del Diablo 1998: Bold baked apple and warm piecrust aromas introduce this very ripe, almost late-harvest-style white. Lush and tropical, but odd and overdone. Tasted twice, with consistent notes.–K.M. • $10 • (3/31/2000) • **76**

Chardonnay Casablanca Valley Casillero del Diablo 1997: Nice intensity of flavor, with ripe pear, apple and citrus notes and a crisp finish. Vibrant and juicy. Drink now.–K.M. • $10 • (9/30/1998) • **83**

Chardonnay Casablanca Valley Trio 1998: Ripe and broad on the nose, with fairly lush and pretty apple and pear flavors that are delineated nicely on the finish, thanks to ripe acidity. A solid little Chard. Drink now.–T.M. • $9 • (3/31/2000) • **85**

Chardonnay Casablanca Valley Trio 1997: This vibrant white shows assertive tropical fruit, ginger and nutmeg flavors, with fresh acidity and toasty oak. A bit flamboyant, it will make a nice match with fusion fish dishes. Drink now through 2001.–T.M. • $9 • (4/30/1999) • **86**

Chardonnay Maipo Valley Marqués de Casa Concha Santa Isabel de Pirque Vineyard 1997: This assertive white offers a rich, waxy texture, strong oaky notes of toast and coffee and ripe flavors of melon and pineapple. Bold and full-bodied, it prefers power to refinement. Drink now.–T.M. • $14 • (1/31/1999) • **85**

Chardonnay Valle Central 1997 • $8/1.5 liter • (5/15/1998) • **84**

Chardonnay Valle Central Sunrise 1998: Shows some zip to go along with the typical pear and vanilla profile. Light-bodied but lively, with moderate length on the finish. Drink now.–T.M. • $7 • (3/31/2000) • **84**

Chardonnay Valle Central Sunrise 1997: Round and ample, this white offers sweet vanilla, ripe apple and melon and light smoke flavors, with good acidity and depth. Good with grilled chicken. Drink now.–T.M. • $7 • (9/15/1998) • **84**

Merlot Peumo Valley Trio 1998: There's a nice density to this red, with pepper and plum flavors and tobaccolike notes. Nice and juicy, with espresso notes on the finish. Drink now.–K.M. • $9 • (3/31/2000) • **84**

Merlot Peumo Valley Trio 1997: Ripe and jammy, this thick, soft red offers sweet plum and chocolate flavors, with just enough tannin and acidity to keep the balance. Drink now.–T.M. • $9 • (3/31/1999) • **83**

Merlot Peumo Valley Trio 1996 • $9 • (11/15/1997) • **85**

Merlot Peumo Valley Trio 1995 • $8 • (6/30/1996) • **85**

Merlot Rapel Valley 1990 • $6 • (4/30/1993) • **83**

Merlot Rapel Valley Casillero del Diablo 1998: A plush, well-sculpted Merlot from a reputable and value-conscious Chilean winery, this, features fairly intense flavors of red plum and currant and well-integrated dark spice notes that linger on the finish. Drink now through 2002.–K.M. • $10 • (3/31/2000) • **86**

Merlot Rapel Valley Casillero del Diablo 1997: This wine has nice density and concentration, with plenty of rich cherry, plum and chocolate flavors. Firm and drinkable, now through 2000.–K.M. • $10 • (10/15/1998) • **84**

Merlot Rapel Valley Casillero del Diablo 1996 • $10 • (6/30/1997) • **86**

Merlot Rapel Valley Casillero del Diablo Peumo Vineyard 1994 • $8 • (5/15/1995) • **85**

Merlot Rapel Valley Marqués de Casa Concha 1997: Supple and fairly powerful, with concentrated dark plum and cherry flavors and plenty of dark spice notes. Light pepper and herbal notes linger appealingly on the finish. Drink now.–K.M. • $14 • (3/31/2000) • **85**

Merlot Rapel Valley Marqués de Casa Concha Peumo Vineyard 1996: Round and fruity, this soft, generous red offers black cherry and grapey flavors with accents of toast and earth. Tannins are well integrated, and the fruit flavors linger on the finish. Drink now through 2002.–T.M. • $14 • (1/31/1999) • **84**

Merlot Rapel Valley Marqués de Casa Concha Peumo Vineyard 1995: This wine has a firm core of cherry and red plum flavors and a nice dose of tannins. Flavorful, showing a touch of elegance, with appealing herbal and chocolaty notes on the finish. Drink now.–K.M. • $14 • (10/15/1998) • **85**

Merlot Rapel Valley Marqués de Casa Concha Peumo Vineyard 1994 • $13 • (6/30/1997) • **89**

Merlot Rapel Valley Marqués de Casa Concha Peumo Vineyard 1993 • $10 • (5/15/1995) • **89**

Merlot Rapel Valley Marqués de Casa Concha Peumo Vineyard 1992 • $10 • (5/31/1994) • **85**

Merlot Rapel Valley Marqués de Casa Concha Peumo Vineyard 1990 • $11 • (4/30/1993) • **76**

Merlot Rapel Valley Marqués de Casa Concha Peumo Vineyard 1989 • $10 • (5/15/1992) • **85**

Merlot Valle Central 1997 • $8/1.5 liter • (5/15/1998) • **83**

Merlot Valle Central Sunrise 1998: A good expression of Merlot, with a nice acidity and suppleness. Has pretty flavors of dark cherry and plum, with savory herbal notes on the finish. Drink now.–K.M. • $7 • (3/31/2000) • **85**

Merlot Valle Central Sunrise 1997: Straightforward, sturdy red, with deep color and rather light cherry and herb flavors. Moderately tannic. Drink now. • $7 • (10/15/1998) • **81**

Pinot Noir Valle Central Sunrise 1997: Spicy and berry aromas are intriguing, but the palate is grapey and simple, with aggressive tannins and a short finish.–T.M. • $8 • (1/31/1999) • **77**

Sauvignon Blanc Curicó Valley Casillero del Diablo 1997: An angular Sauvignon, with decent pineapple, herb and spice flavors. Drink now.–K.M. • $10 • (10/15/1998) • **80**

Sauvignon Blanc Valle Central Casillero del Diablo 1998: Simple pink grapefruit flavors run through this moderately endowed white. It has acidity and stays balanced, making for a decent aperitif. Drink now.–K.M. • $10 • (3/31/2000) • **80**

CONO SUR

Cabernet Sauvignon 1993 • $6 • (4/30/1995) • **82**
Cabernet Sauvignon Selection Reserve 1992 • $10 • (4/30/1995) • **85**
Pinot Noir 1994 • $7 • (4/15/1995) • **80**
Pinot Noir Selection Reserve 1994 • $10 • (4/15/1995) • **81**

COUSINO-MACUL

Cabernet Sauvignon Maipo Valley 1995 • $6 • (6/30/1997) • **80**
Cabernet Sauvignon Maipo Valley 1991 • $7 • (5/31/1994) • **79**
Cabernet Sauvignon Maipo Valley 1990 • $8 • (4/30/1993) • **75**
Cabernet Sauvignon Maipo Valley 1988 • $8 • (5/15/1992) • **81**

Cabernet Sauvignon Valle del Maipo Antiguas Reservas 1996: A rubbery character dominates this red, which also has modest plum flavors. Finishes on a stemmy note.–K.M. • $15 • (3/31/2000) • **75**

Cabernet Sauvignon Valle del Maipo Antiguas Reservas 1995: This smooth red offers ripe plum and toasty flavors, with a strong eucalyptus note. Tannins are well integrated, and the finish lingers with cedar and earth accents. Drink now.–T.M. • $12 • (1/31/1999) • **83**

Cabernet Sauvignon Maipo Valley Antiguas Reservas 1994: Evolved toward the vegetal and dried-fruit side, and the tannins are dry on the finish. Tasted twice, with consistent notes.–T.M. • $10 • (9/15/1998) • **76**

Cabernet Sauvignon Maipo Valley Antiguas Reservas 1993 • $9 • (6/30/1997) • **80**

Cabernet Sauvignon Maipo Valley Antiguas Reservas 1990 • $9 • (6/15/1995) • **82**

Cabernet Sauvignon Maipo Valley Antiguas Reservas 1989 • $12 • (5/31/1994) • **80**

Cabernet Sauvignon Maipo Valley Antiguas Reservas 1988 • $11 • (4/30/1993) • **74**

Cabernet Sauvignon Maipo Valley Antiguas Reservas 1987 • $10 • (6/15/1992) • **82**

Cabernet Sauvignon Maipo Valley Antiguas Reservas 1986 • $10 • (5/31/1992) • **83**

Cabernet Sauvignon Maipo Valley Antiguas Reservas 1985 • $11 • (10/15/1991) • **81**

Chardonnay Valle del Maipo 1998: Lean in its fruit profile, offering just a glimpse of baked apple. Finishes lean and rustic.–T.M. • $12 • (3/31/2000) • **78**

Key: SS—Spectator Selection. CS—Cellar Selection. HR—Highly Recommended. $NA—Price not available. (BT)—Barrel tasting. (A)—Auction Price.
For a key to the tasters' initials, see "How to Use These Listings."
Dates in parentheses represent the issues in which the ratings were published.

Finis Terrae Maipo Valley 1996: Smells and tastes of mint and bacon, with some dilute plummy flavors as well, followed by muddled cola notes on the finish.–K.M. • $30 • (3/31/2000) • **76**

Finis Terrae Maipo Valley 1995: This polished red offers harmonious flavors of black cherry, tobacco, licorice and herbs, with well-integrated tannins and toasty oak, good balance and a lingering finish. Not a show-off wine, but it draws you back for another sip. Drink now through 2003.–T.M. • $30 • (1/31/1999) • **87**

Finis Terrae Maipo Valley 1994: Eucalyptus and charred oak aromas and flavors dominate this ripe red; tannins are firm and a bit dry. Tasted twice, with consistent notes.–T.M. • $30 • (9/15/1998) • **78**

Finis Terrae Maipo Valley 1993 • $30 • (6/30/1997) • **87**
Finis Terrae Maipo Valley 1992 • $25 • (6/30/1996) • **83**

Merlot Valle del Maipo Limited Release 1997: A nice supple core of red plum and peppery flavors are held down by a cloying minty note.–K.M. • $15 • (3/31/2000) • **79**

Merlot Valle del Maipo Limited Release 1996: Aromas of flat root beer and rubber give way to an astringent, muddled red that finishes on a slightly stemmy note.–K.M. • $15 • (3/31/2000) • **74**

Merlot Valle del Maipo Limited Release 1995: This smooth, maturing red from Chile offers subdued but complex flavors of cherry and cedar, herbs and spices, with well-integrated tannins and an impressive finish. Doesn't bowl you over, but rewards with harmony and character. The reasonable price is the clincher. Drink now.–T.M. • $12 • (1/31/1999) • **86**

Merlot Maipo Valley Limited Release 1994 • $14 • (6/30/1997) • **81**
Merlot Maipo Valley Limited Release 1991 • $11 • (6/15/1995) • **78**
Merlot Maipo Valley Limited Release 1990 • $11 • (5/31/1994) • **83**
Merlot Maipo Valley Limited Release 1989 • $11 • (5/31/1992) • **85**
Merlot Maipo Valley Limited Release 1988 • $11 • (5/31/1992) • **84**

CRANE LAKE

Cabernet Sauvignon Colchagua Valley 1992 • $5 • (4/30/1995) • **86**
Merlot Colchagua Valley 1992 • $5 • (6/15/1995) • **84**

CREMASCHI FURLOTTI

Cabernet Sauvignon Maule Valley 1995 • $8 • (10/31/1997) • **81**

DALLAS CONTE

Cabernet Sauvignon Colchagua Valley 1997: A voluptuous red, with ripe fruit and lavish oak. The rich flavors—ranging from plum to prune and chocolate to coffee—are supported by firm, ripe tannins and echo on the long, minty finish. From a new joint venture between Australia's Mildara Blass and Chile's Viña Santa Carolina. Drink now through 2003.–T.M. • $10 • (9/15/1999) • **88**

Chardonnay Casablanca Valley Reserve 1998: Vivid aromas and flavors of pineapple, lime and hazelnut are distinctive and appealing in this expressive white. It's one of Chile's few whites that truly reflects the terroir of its origin. Drink now.–T.M. • $17 • (10/31/1999) • **87**

Chardonnay Colchagua Valley 1998: Strong vanilla aromas follow through on the palate to be joined by crisp citrus and mineral notes, creating a vibrant, balanced white that will make a lively match with fusion-style dishes—as well as earn kudos for its quality/price ratio. Drink now.–T.M. • $10 • (10/31/1999) • **85**

Merlot Colchagua Valley 1997: A serious red, from the deep-garnet color and roasted vanilla aromas to the concentrated black cherry and plum flavors. Bright, focused and showing good depth and intensity right through to the long finish. Drink now.–B.S. • $10 • (9/15/1999) • **88**

DONA SOL

Cabernet Sauvignon Colchagua Valley 1992 • $6 • (4/30/1995) • **85**
Merlot Colchagua Valley 1992 • $6 • (6/15/1995) • **77**

ECHEVERRIA

Cabernet Sauvignon Molina 1998: A rustic and brawny red, with interesting black olive, tobacco and herb flavors. Tannic, with good concentration and peppery notes on the finish. Drink now through 2001.–K.M. • $9 • (1/01/1999) • **84**

Cabernet Sauvignon Molina 1996 • $7 • (6/30/1997) • **84**
Cabernet Sauvignon Molina 1995 • $7 • (6/30/1997) • **85**

Cabernet Sauvignon Molina Family Reserve 1996: Mature aromas and flavors of cedar, leather, currant and smoke mingle in this elegant Cab. Finishes with firm but fine-grained tannins. Drink now.–B.S. • $25 • (5/31/2000) • **86**

Cabernet Sauvignon Molina Reserva 1996: Nicely concentrated fruit flavors and accents of sweet oak make this medium-bodied Cabernet quite appealing. Well balanced by firm acidity and tannins. Drink now. • $11 • (9/15/1998) • **86**

Cabernet Sauvignon Molina Reserva 1995 • $9 • (6/30/1997) • **88**

Cabernet Sauvignon Molina Reserva 1994 • $9 • (2/28/1997) • **84**

Chardonnay Molina Reserva 1997: Straightforward, offering light apple, earth and toast flavors, harmonious but a bit dull. Clean, but lacks intensity.–T.M. • $10 • (1/31/1999) • **78**

Chardonnay Molina Unwooded 1998: A quaffable white, with apple, light herbal and vanilla flavors, bright, crisp and simple. Has enough weight to match with richer fish dishes but is refreshing enough to enjoy on its own. Drink now.–T.M. • $8 • (1/31/1999) • **83**

Merlot Molina Reserva 1997: Ambitious, with coffee and toast aromas overlaying the lively raspberry and blackberry flavors. The firm, moderate-length finish should do well with food. Drink now.–B.S. • $12 • (5/31/2000) • **86**

Sauvignon Blanc Molina 1998: A round, soft white that verges on flabby, with pear and herbal flavors, ripe but without much focus.–T.M. • $8 • (2/28/1999) • **78**

EDWARDS, LUIS FELIPE

Cabernet Sauvignon Chile Pupilla 1995 • $7 • (4/30/1997) • **86**

Cabernet Sauvignon Colchagua 1997: Modest dried cherry flavors turn a bit thin on the finish.–K.M. • $9 • (3/31/2000) • **79**

Cabernet Sauvignon Colchagua 1996: This ripe red has an earthy, rustic character, with prune and tobacco flavors over tough tannins. Has enough concentration to match food, but lacks polish. Drink now through 2002.–T.M. • $9 • (4/30/1999) • **82**

Cabernet Sauvignon Colchagua 1994 • $8 • (6/30/1997) • **79**

Cabernet Sauvignon Colchagua Doña Bernarda Colección Privada 1997: Nice up-front flavors of cherry and spice, with herbal notes on the finish. Drink now.–K.M. • $25 • (3/31/2000) • **83**

Cabernet Sauvignon Colchagua Pupilla 1998: Earthy barnyard aromas give way to herbal and earthy flavors hemmed in by hard tannins. Light cherry flavor is buried.–T.M. • $8 • (4/30/1999) • **74**

Cabernet Sauvignon Colchagua Reserva 1997: A rustic red, with espresso and dark plum flavors that turn a tad stewy on the finish.–K.M. • $13 • (3/31/2000) • **78**

Cabernet Sauvignon Colchagua Reserva 1996: This polished red shows good balance and extraction, with ripe plum, toast and tobacco flavors, firm but ripe tannins and a long, clean finish. A nice mix of plush texture and firm backbone. Drink now through 2004.–T.M. • $13 • (4/30/1999) • **87**

Cabernet Sauvignon Colchagua Reserva 1994 • $12 • (6/30/1997) • **79**

Carmenère Colchagua 1997: Aromas of toast and chocolate follow through on the palate in this round, ripe red. Black cherry and plum notes add iveliness, and there's just enough tannin for grip. Drink now through 2002.–T.M. • $11 • (4/30/1999) • **84**

Chardonnay Colchagua 1999: Banana and apple flavors mark this round, soft white. Finishes weakly.–K.M. • $9 • (3/31/2000) • **78**

Chardonnay Colchagua 1997: This crisp white is clean but neutral, with light apple and herbal flavors and a short finish.–T.M. • $9 • (4/30/1999) • **79**

Merlot Colchagua 1998: Nice raspberry aromas and soft, warm, plummy fruit flavors are fresh and clean. A dash of chewy tannin keeps it interesting. Drink now.–T.M. • $10 • (3/31/2000) • **83**

ERRAZURIZ

Cabernet Sauvignon Aconcagua Valley Don Maximiano Estate Reserva 1997: Rich and firm. This ripe red is powerful yet harmonious, with ripe flavors of plums and cassis accented by toasty oak and notes of mint and licorice. Has balance and good structure and should bloom with age. Drink now through 2006.–T.M. • $16 • (9/15/1999) • **88**

Cabernet Sauvignon Aconcagua Valley Don Maximiano Estate Reserva 1996: A big and brawny Cabernet, with ripe character and a sprawling structure. Filled with dark plum, dried cherry and leather flavors, and some powerful tannins. Finishes on notes of bittersweet chocolate. Drink through 2002–K.M. • $15 • (10/15/1998) • **87**

Cabernet Sauvignon Aconcagua Valley Don Maximiano Estate Reserva 1995 • $15 • (2/28/1998) • **84**

Cabernet Sauvignon Aconcagua Valley Don Maximiano Estate Reserva 1994 • $15 • (10/31/1997) • **89**

Cabernet Sauvignon Aconcagua Valley Don Maximiano Estate Reserva 1993 • $12 • (10/31/1995) • **87**

Cabernet Sauvignon Aconcagua Valley Don Maximiano Estate Reserva 1991 • $9 • (4/15/1994) • **82**

Cabernet Sauvignon Aconcagua Valley Don Maximiano Estate Reserva 1990 • $9 • (4/30/1993) • **88**

Cabernet Sauvignon Aconcagua Valley Don Maximiano Estate Reserva 1989 • $10 • (6/15/1992) • **87**

Cabernet Sauvignon Aconcagua Valley Don Maximiano Estate Reserva 1988 • $9 • (6/15/1992) • **85**

Cabernet Sauvignon Aconcagua Valley Don Maximiano Founder's Reserve 1993 • $25 • (4/30/1997) • **88**

Cabernet Sauvignon Aconcagua Valley Don Maximiano Special Reserve 1989 • $9 • (4/30/1993) • **83**

Cabernet Sauvignon Aconcagua Valley El Ceibo Estate 1998: A modest red, with charry, meaty flavors. Bell pepper notes on the finish.–K.M. • $10 • (3/31/2000) • **78**

Cabernet Sauvignon Aconcagua Valley El Ceibo Estate 1997: This well-structured red offers black cherry, earth and game flavors, with plenty of tannin to match with grilled meats. Straightforward but harmonious. Drink now through 2002.–T.M. • $10 • (9/15/1999) • **84**

Cabernet Sauvignon Aconcagua Valley El Ceibo Estate 1996 • $9 • (10/31/1997) • **86**

Cabernet Sauvignon Aconcagua Valley Reserva 1993 • $15 • (6/30/1997) • **78**

Cabernet Sauvignon Curicó Valley El Descanso Estate 1995 • $9 • (4/30/1997) • **87**

Chardonnay Casablanca Valley La Escultura Estate 1998: Exuberant aromas of tropical fruit and toasted almond are distinctive and alluring. The citrus and vanilla flavors are less complex and interesting, though still bright and crisp. A nice aperitif. Drink now.–T.M. • $10 • (10/31/1999) • **84**

Chardonnay Casablanca Valley La Escultura Estate 1997 • $9 • (3/31/1998) • **82**

Chardonnay Casablanca Valley La Escultura Estate Reserva 1997: A nice, round Chardonnay, with appealing pear, ripe apple and spice notes and a good, clean finish. An oaky but not overdone style. Drink now.–K.M. • $15 • (9/30/1998) • **86**

Chardonnay Casablanca Valley Wild Ferment 1998: Broad and nutty on the nose, with rich flavors of pear, apple, toast and vanilla. Creamy and lush on the finish. Nice job. Drink now.–K.M. • $20 • (3/31/2000) • **86**

Chardonnay Casablanca Valley Wild Ferment 1997: There's plenty of pretty oak and sweet vanilla and creamy flavors, backed by ripe, soft apple and melon and enough acidity to keep it balanced. Drink now.–T.M. • $19 • (9/15/1998) • **85**

Don Maximiano Founder's Reserve Aconcagua Valley 1997: Ripe, with bold mint and cassis aromas, this medium-bodied red has some extracted prune and chocolate notes before turning a bit chewy on the finish. Needs food. Tasted twice, with consistent notes. Drink now.–T.M. • $25 • (3/31/2000) • **84**

Don Maximiano Founder's Reserve Aconcagua Valley 1996: A wine that shows both power and sophistication, this balanced red from Chile combines ripe, chewy fruit, toasty oak and polished texture. The plum, cassis, licorice and toast flavors are bright and well defined; the structure is firm but not overbearing. A blend: 85 percent Cabernet Sauvignon, 15 percent Cabernet Franc. Drink through 2005–T.M. • $25 • (9/15/1998) SS • **90**

Don Maximiano Founder's Reserve Aconcagua Valley 1995: Ripe and polished, this velvety red shows cassis, coffee and light herb flavors. It's chewy and generous, with a sweet finish, but it's more muscular than complex. Tasted twice, with consistent notes. A blend: 95 percent Cabernet Sauvignon, 5 percent Cabernet Franc. Drink now.–T.M. • $25 • (9/15/1998) • **86**

Don Maximiano Founder's Reserve Aconcagua Valley 1994 • $25 • (10/31/1997) • **89**

Merlot Aconcagua Valley Don Maximiano Estate Reserva 1998: A charry note on the nose leads into a dark, plummy, coffee-flavored but light-bodied Merlot that manages to stay lively on the finish. Drink now.–K.M. • $20 • (3/31/2000) • **82**

Merlot Aconcagua Valley Don Maximiano Estate Reserva 1997: Seems quite ripe, with plum, coffee and tobacco notes, yet also a hint of herbs. Starts out softly, then turns tough and astringent on the finish. May improve with time. Try through 2001.–B.S. • $20 • (9/15/1999) • **83**

Merlot Aconcagua Valley Reserva 1996 • $19 • (10/31/1997) • **89**

Merlot Aconcagua Valley Reserva 1995 • $19 • (4/30/1997) • **88**

Merlot Curicó Valley El Descanso Estate 1998: Earthy and charred, with bitter flavors, this is also bretty and fizzy. Tasted twice, with consistent notes.–T.M. • $10 • (10/31/1999) • **68**

Merlot Curicó Valley El Descanso Estate 1997: Quite leathery-tasting, with dried cherry and plum flavors.–K.M. • $9 • (9/30/1998) • **79**

Merlot Curicó Valley El Descanso Estate 1996 • $9 • (4/30/1997) • **82**

CHILE

ERRAZURIZ

Merlot Maule Valley 1994 • $8 • (6/30/1996) • **75**
Merlot Maule Valley 1992 • $8 • (3/31/1993) • **85**
Merlot Maule Valley 1991 • $8 • (12/15/1992) • **83**
Pinot Noir Casablanca Valley La Escultura Reserva 1997: Shows cola and earth flavors, with a thin, stemmy finish. Tasted twice, with consistent notes.–T.M. • $20 • (10/31/1999) • **75**
Sauvignon Blanc Casablanca Valley La Escultura Estate 1998: Supple and crisp. Light citrus and mineral flavors are subdued but pleasant in this clean white, and the refreshing acidity makes it a lively match for lighter dishes. Drink now.–T.M. • $15 • (10/31/1999) • **85**
Sauvignon Blanc Casablanca Valley La Escultura Estate 1997 • $8 • (5/31/1998) • **84**
Sauvignon Blanc Late Harvest Casablanca Valley 1998: Has impressive sweetness and viscosity, but the candied orange and apricot flavors are shrill and short.–T.M. • $11/375 ml. • (3/31/2000) • **78**
Sauvignon Blanc Late Harvest Casablanca Valley 1997: Fairly light, with sweet peach flavors and an herbal note. Drink now.–K.M. • $7/375 ml. • (10/15/1998) • **80**
Sauvignon Blanc Late Harvest Casablanca Valley 1996 • $7/375 ml. • (10/31/1997) • **88**
Sauvignon Blanc Late Harvest Casablanca Valley 1995 • $7/375 ml. • (4/30/1997) • **87**
Syrah Aconcagua Valley Don Maximiano Estate Reserva 1998: Shows typical espresso and roasted meat aromas before giving way to a spicy black cherry-filled palate that is lively and well defined by ripe, juicy acidity. Nicely done. Drink now through 2001.–K.M. • $20 • (3/31/2000) • **86**
Syrah Aconcagua Valley Don Maximiano Estate Reserva 1997: This firm red offers the ripe plum and bacon flavors characteristic of the variety, with toasty, oaky accents and mouthfilling tannins. Powerful, if a bit clumsy. Drink now through 2004.–T.M. • $20 • (10/31/1999) • **85**
Syrah Aconcagua Valley Don Maximiano Estate Reserva 1996: A luscious, ripe, exotic style of Chilean wine, with rich fruit flavors and spicy, oaky accents of cedar, cinnamon and vanilla. Full-bodied but not too tannic. Drink now through 2001. • $19 • (10/15/1998) • **88**

FOXRIDGE

Cabernet Sauvignon Valle Central 1996: Good plum and berry flavors, but a bit stewy-tasting. Drink now.–K.M. • $10 • (10/15/1998) • **82**

FURLOTTI

Cabernet Sauvignon Maule Valley 1997: This hefty red from Chile is ripe and concentrated, displaying peppery plum and cigar-box flavors. It has some power and finesse, and should respond well to short-term aging. Hard to beat it at this price and score. Drink through 2001–K.M. • $7 • (10/15/1998) • **85**
Chardonnay Maule Valley 1998: Toasty oak flavors add interest to this light, crisp white, adding depth to its modest apple and pear flavors without overwhelming the wine, while a core of acidity keeps it vibrant. Drink now.–T.M. • $7 • (4/30/1999) • **84**
Chardonnay Maule Valley 1997: Crisp and clean, this angular white offers well-defined apple, herb and smoke flavors, with a firm backbone of acidity. Drink now.–T.M. • $7 • (9/15/1998) • **83**

GARZAS, LAS

Cabernet Sauvignon Colchagua Valley 1990 • $7 • (4/30/1993) • **80**
Cabernet Sauvignon Colchagua Valley Proprietor Reserve 1990 • $7 • (5/31/1994) • **77**

GRACIA, VINA

Cabernet Sauvignon Cachapoal Conversado Reserva 1993 • $10 • (5/31/1997) • **85**
Cabernet Sauvignon Maipo Celebrado 1997: Awkward and stemmy, with sweet cherry flavors. Turns harsh on the finish.–K.M. • $9 • (10/15/1998) • **73**
Cabernet Sauvignon Maipo Celebrado 1995 • $8 • (6/30/1997) • **83**

Key: SS—Spectator Selection. CS—Cellar Selection. HR—Highly Recommended. $NA—Price not available. (BT)—Barrel tasting. (A)—Auction Price.
For a key to the tasters' initials, see "How to Use These Listings."
Dates in parentheses represent the issues in which the ratings were published.

Chardonnay Cachapoal Valley Reposado 1997: A good, crisp style, with nice apple and citrus flavors and spicy notes on the finish. Serve well chilled. Drink now.–K.M. • $9 • (9/30/1998) • **83**
Merlot Maipo Valley Curioso 1997: A bit stewy and stemmy, with rhubarb overtones. Tasted twice, with consistent notes. Past its prime.–K.M. • $9 • (10/15/1998) • **71**
Merlot Maipo Valley Curioso 1996 • $8 • (10/31/1997) • **85**

ITATA, AGRICOLA Y VITIVINICOLA

Cabernet Sauvignon Valle del Itata Condor Reserva 1997: A touch murky on the nose, with some dark plum, rhubarb and coffee notes. There's a slight spritz, and the finish turns a bit dry.–K.M. • $11 • (3/31/2000) • **77**
Cabernet Sauvignon Valle del Itata Condor Reserva 1996: This red mingles plummy, earthy and herbal flavors with coffee accents and enough underlying tannins to help it stand up to food. Not a fruit bomb, but it grows on you. Drink now through 2004.–T.M. • $11 • (4/30/1999) • **84**
Chardonnay Valle del Itata Condor 1997: A softer style, dominated by ripe pear and apple flavors, with a clean, minerally finish. Drink now.–K.M. • $10 • (10/15/1998) • **84**
Chardonnay Valle del Itata Condor Barrel Fermented 1998: Something wrong here. Thoroughly dilute, with the aroma of corkiness but not the astringency. Tasted twice, with consistent notes.–K.M. • $11 • (3/31/2000) • **55**

LAROSE, VINA DE

Cabernet Sauvignon Cachapoal Las Casas del Toqui 1995 • $10 • (6/30/1996) • **84**
Cabernet Sauvignon Totihue-Cachapoal Valley Las Casas del Toqui 1997: Crisp and herbal. This light, rather dry red shows modest cherry and berry flavors, with herbal and light earthy notes. It's clean, but a bit simple for food. Drink now.–T.M. • $6 • (1/01/1999) • **82**
Cabernet Sauvignon Totihue-Cachapoal Valley Las Casas del Toqui Réserve 1997: This refreshing red offers cherry, mint, vanilla and light herbal flavors, balanced and clean. A well-made wine that will complement lighter meat dishes. Drink now.–T.M. • $8 • (1/01/1999) • **86**
Cabernet Sauvignon Totihue-Cachapoal Valley Las Casas del Toqui Réserve 1995 • $9 • (10/31/1997) • **85**
Cabernet Sauvignon Totihue-Cachapoal Valley Las Casas del Toqui Réserve Prestige 1997: This herbal-scented red offers light cherry, mineral and cedar notes, with light, firm tannins and balanced acidity. It's modest, but would make a fine match for lighter dishes. Drink now.–T.M. • $12 • (1/01/1999) • **83**
Cabernet Sauvignon Totihue-Cachapoal Valley Las Casas del Toqui Réserve Prestige 1995 • $12 • (10/31/1997) • **87**
Chardonnay Totihue-Cachapoal Valley Las Casas del Toqui 1998: A strong herbal streak gives this a flavor profile more typical of Sauvignon Blanc, but it has the full body and toasty oak characteristic of Chardonnay. Drink now.–T.M. • $6 • (1/01/1999) • **80**
Chardonnay Totihue-Cachapoal Valley Las Casas del Toqui Grande Réserve 1997: Ripe tropical fruit flavors of papaya and coconut are backed by sweet vanilla and almond notes in this somewhat blowsy and almost sweet white, but it's seductive nonetheless. Drink now.–T.M. • $9 • (1/01/1999) • **85**
Sémillon Totihue-Cachapoal Valley Las Casas del Toqui 1998: Flavors of peaches and almonds give this white distinctive personality. It's clean and crisp, and makes a refreshing aperitif. Drink now.–T.M. • $5 • (1/01/1999) • **83**

LURTON, J. & F.

Cabernet Sauvignon Chile Gran Araucano 1997: Thick, rich and fairly ripe, with a beautiful aroma of coffee and plum that follows through on the palate. Concentrated, with a lot of upfront polish and plenty of spicy notes. Chocolaty notes linger appealingly on the broad, plush finish. Drink now through 2002.–K.M. • $24 • (3/31/2000) • **88**
Cabernet Sauvignon Lontue Valley Araucano 1998: A bit awkward, with dried cherry and berry flavors. Rhubarb notes on the finish.–K.M. • $6 • (3/31/2000) • **79**
Chardonnay Chile Gran Araucano 1997: Shows toast and almond on the nose, with tasty ripe pear, green apple and lime flavors. Drink now.–T.M. • $18 • (3/31/2000) • **85**
Chardonnay Lontué Valley Araucano 1998: Smells and tastes of canned pineapple juice before turning cloying on the finish.–T.M. • $6 • (3/31/2000) • **76**

Merlot Chile Araucano 1998: Chunky and tasty, with red plum and berry flavors and peppery notes on the firm finish. Drink now.–K.M. • $6 • (3/31/2000) • **83**
Merlot Lontué Valley 1995 • $7 • (10/31/1997) • **84**

MAISON DU LAC

Cabernet Sauvignon Maipo Valley 1994 • $6 • (2/28/1997) • **83**
Cabernet Sauvignon Maipo Valley 1989 • $5 • (7/15/1993) • **82**
Cabernet Sauvignon Maipo Valley Reserve 1995: Minty aromas and flavors are the hallmarks of this medium-bodied Cabernet, along with plenty of dark plum, chocolate and cherry flavor. Quite tasty. Drink now.–K.M. • $11 • (10/15/1998) • **84**
Cabernet Sauvignon Maipo Valley Special Selection 1997: Light and a bit lifted-tasting, with simple sweet cherry and spicy flavors.–K.M. • $7 • (3/31/2000) • **79**
Cabernet Sauvignon Maipo Valley Special Selection 1995: Herbal, eucalyptus and raisin flavors mingle in this firm, slightly dry red. It's ripe but a bit dull. Drink now.–T.M. • $7 • (9/15/1998) • **81**
Merlot Maipo Valley 1995: A good, simple Merlot, with just enough body, appealing for its smooth tannins and modest herb and fruit flavors. Drink now. • $8 • (9/30/1998) • **82**
Merlot Maipo Valley 1994 • $8 • (2/28/1997) • **84**
Merlot Maipo Valley 1992 • $7 • (2/28/1997) • **74**
Merlot Maipo Valley 1990 • $7 • (1/31/1994) • **81**
Merlot Maipo Valley Reserve 1996: A stylish and ripe-tasting red, with black cherry and black currant flavors, good smoky notes, plenty of stuffing and a spicy finish. Drink now.–K.M. • $13 • (12/15/1998) • **86**
Merlot Maipo Valley Special Selection 1997: Muddled and a bit cloying, with sweet cherry and spice notes dominating.–K.M. • $8 • (3/31/2000) • **77**

MAR, VINA DEL

Cabernet Sauvignon Curicó Selección Especial 35 1988 • $6 • (6/15/1991) • **81**
Cabernet Sauvignon Lontué 1988 • $6 • (6/15/1992) • **79**
Cabernet Sauvignon Maipo Valley 1992 • $7 • (4/30/1995) • **78**
Cabernet Sauvignon Maipo Valley 1990 • $6 • (5/31/1994) • **82**
Cabernet Sauvignon Maipo Valley Reserve 1988 • $9 • (6/15/1995) • **77**
Cabernet Sauvignon Maipo Valley Reserve 1987 • $10 • (5/31/1994) • **83**
Merlot Curicó Selección Especial 12 1989 • $6 • (6/15/1991) • **80**
Merlot Curicó Selección Especial 12 1988 • $6 • (9/15/1990) • **82**
Merlot Lontué 1990 • $6 • (6/15/1992) • **83**
Merlot Lontué 1988 • $6 • (7/31/1989) • **80**
Merlot Maipo Valley 1992 • $7 • (6/15/1995) • **77**
Merlot Maipo Valley 1991 • $6 • (5/31/1994) • **82**
Merlot Maipo Valley Reserve 1989 • $9 • (5/15/1992) • **78**

MARTINO, DE

Cabernet Sauvignon Maipo Valley 1995 • $9 • (11/30/1997) • **84**
Cabernet Sauvignon Maipo Valley Prima Reserve 1995 • $12 • (10/31/1997) • **87**
Cabernet Sauvignon Maipo Valley Prima Reserve 1994 • $5 • (2/29/1996) • **84**
Cabernet Sauvignon Maipo Valley Prima Reserve 1993 • $8 • (2/29/1996) • **87**
Cabernet Sauvignon Maipo Valley Reserva de Familia 1996: Muscular and intense, this rich Chilean red offers ripe cassis, mineral, licorice and light herb flavors that build on the palate, backed by firm, chewy tannins, but with balance and harmony. The long finish is spicy and refreshing. Tasted twice, with consistent notes. Drink through 2008–T.M. • $30 • (9/15/1998) HR • **91**
Cabernet Sauvignon Maipo Valley Santa Ines Vineyard 1991 • $6 • (4/30/1995) • **77**
Cabernet Sauvignon Maipo Valley Santa Ines Vineyard 1990 • $5 • (3/15/1993) • **85**
Carmenère Maipo Valley 1996 • $9 • (10/31/1997) • **83**
Carmenère Maipo Valley Prima Reserve 1996 • $12 • (10/31/1997) • **85**
Chardonnay Casablanca Valley Reserva de Familia 1997: Ripe, rich and concentrated, with loads of ripe pear, apple and butter flavors. A bit obvious with its blowsy style, but filled with gusto. Finishes with notes of caramel and cinnamon. Tasted twice, with consistent notes. Drink now.–K.M. • $30 • (10/15/1998) • **85**
Malbec Maipo Valley 1996 • $9 • (10/31/1997) • **84**
Malbec Maipo Valley Prima Reserve 1996 • $12 • (10/31/1997) • **86**
Merlot Maipo Valley 1996 • $9 • (10/31/1997) • **83**
Merlot Maipo Valley Prima Reserve 1994 • $6 • (2/29/1996) • **82**
Merlot Maipo Valley Santa Ines Vineyard 1993 • $7 • (6/15/1995) • **80**

MILLAHUE

Cabernet Sauvignon San Fernando 1997: Very ripe in style, with stemmy and rhubarblike flavors that don't add much.–K.M. • $8 • (10/15/1998) • **77**
Cabernet Sauvignon San Fernando Gran Reserva 1997: Bright berry and cherry flavors are pretty, and vanilla accents sweeten the pot in this juicy, vibrant red. It tastes a bit like candy, but draws you back for another sip. Drink now through 2002.–T.M. • $11 • (4/30/1999) • **84**
Cabernet Sauvignon San Fernando Gran Reserva 1995: A focused, fruit-driven Cabernet, with plenty of juicy cherry and currant flavors backed by firm acidity and moderate tannins. Tasty and uncomplicated. Drink now. • $11 • (9/15/1998) • **85**
Chardonnay San Fernando 1997: Begins with citrus and apple flavors, but they peter out quickly into an earthy finish.–K.M. • $8 • (9/30/1998) • **77**
Merlot San Fernando 1998: Simple and smooth, this soft red offers light cherry and licorice flavors, with a velvety texture and almost no tannins.–T.M. • $8 • (3/31/1999) • **79**
Merlot San Fernando 1997: Loaded with fruit, but very undeveloped, like a barrel sample. Has jammy, doughy, yeasty flavors and moderate tannins. Drink now. • $8 • (9/15/1998) • **78**

MONTES

Cabernet Sauvignon Curicó Valley 1997: Cola and black cherry flavors are juicy and sweet in this ripe, clean red. Accents of herb and smoke add interest. Has just enough structure for food. Drink now.–T.M. • $10 • (10/31/1999) • **84**
Cabernet Sauvignon Curicó Valley 1996: This lively red shows crisp berry and herbal flavors, vibrant and clean, with light, firm tannins and a minty finish. Try slightly chilled. Drink now.–T.M. • $10 • (2/28/1999) • **83**
Cabernet Sauvignon Curicó Valley 1995: There's a slight resinous quality to this red, accenting the juicy cherry, mint and herb flavors. Moderate concentration and structure. Drink now.–B.S. • $10 • (10/15/1998) • **82**
Cabernet Sauvignon Curicó Valley 1994 • $10 • (2/28/1998) • **79**
Cabernet Sauvignon Curicó Valley 1993 • $8 • (4/30/1997) • **84**
Cabernet Sauvignon Curicó Valley 1992 • $8 • (6/30/1996) • **84**
Cabernet Sauvignon Curicó Valley 1991 • $8 • (2/29/1996) • **88**
Cabernet Sauvignon Curicó Valley 1990 • $8 • (4/30/1995) • **78**
Cabernet Sauvignon Curicó Valley 1989 • $8 • (5/31/1994) • **80**
Cabernet Sauvignon Curicó Valley La Finca Estate 1995 • $9 • (4/30/1997) • **84**
Cabernet Sauvignon Curicó Valley Montes Alpha 1997: This ripe, rich red marries concentrated flavors with voluptuous texture. It delivers plum, prune, dark chocolate and cola flavors, with ripe, full tannins and a clean, sweet finish. Drink now through 2004.–T.M. • $18 • (10/31/1999) SS • **88**
Cabernet Sauvignon Curicó Valley Montes Alpha 1996: An expressive red of sweet cherry and blackberry flavors with accents of chocolate and toast. The tannins are light but firm; the acidity, crisp; the balance, impeccable. A vivid wine that brings you back for another sip. Drink now through 2003.–T.M. • $17 • (2/28/1999) • **88**
Cabernet Sauvignon Curicó Valley Montes Alpha 1995: Plummy and pleasantly tart, with a nice balance and a clean finish of cherry and spice. Drink now.–K.M. • $17 • (10/15/1998) • **84**
Cabernet Sauvignon Curicó Valley Montes Alpha 1994 • $17 • (3/31/1998) • **87**
Cabernet Sauvignon Curicó Valley Montes Alpha 1993 • $15 • (4/30/1997) • **89**
Cabernet Sauvignon Curicó Valley Montes Alpha 1992 • $14 • (6/30/1996) • **78**
Cabernet Sauvignon Curicó Valley Montes Alpha 1991 • $14 • (6/15/1995) • **87**
Cabernet Sauvignon Curicó Valley Montes Alpha 1990 • $14 • (4/30/1995) • **84**
Cabernet Sauvignon Curicó Valley Montes Alpha 1989 • $12 • (2/28/1994) • **78**
Cabernet Sauvignon Curicó Valley Montes Alpha Private Selection 1988 • $14 • (5/15/1992) • **87**
Cabernet Sauvignon Curicó Valley Villa Montes 1993 • $7 • (2/29/1996) • **82**
Cabernet Sauvignon Curicó Valley Villa Montes 1992 • $6 • (4/30/1995) • **83**
Cabernet Sauvignon Curicó Valley Villa Montes 1991 • $6 • (2/28/1994) • **79**
Cabernet Sauvignon Curicó Valley Villa Montes 1990 • $6 • (2/28/1993) • **84**
Cabernet Sauvignon Curicó Valley Villa Montes 1989 • $6 • (6/15/1992) • **84**
Cabernet Sauvignon Curicó Valley Villa Montes 1988 • $5 • (2/15/1990) • **73**
Cabernet Sauvignon Curicó Valley Villa Montes Special Selection 1987 • $12 • (9/15/1990) • **84**
Chardonnay Curicó Valley 1998: Round and ripe, this bold white offers mouthfilling flavors of melon, toast and coffee. A real treat for fans of oaky-style Chardonnay. Drink now.–T.M. • $11 • (5/15/1999) • **85**
Chardonnay Curicó Valley Montes Alpha Special Cuvée 1998: Deep golden in color, with late-harvestlike aromas and flavors of orange peel, caramel and golden raisin taking this over the top before breaking down on the dilute finish. Tasted three times, with consistent notes.–K.M. • $20 • (3/31/2000) • **77**

MONTES

Chardonnay Curicó Valley Montes Alpha Special Cuvée 1997: Deep color and concentrated, creamy flavors make this wine seductive and rich. Smooth and complex, with pear and tropical notes and mineral flavors that linger on the finish. Should integrate further with short-term aging, be best from 1999 through 2002. From Chile. Tasted twice, with consistent notes.–K.M. • $17 • (9/30/1998) HR • **89**

Gewüztraminer-Riesling Valle de Curicó Late Harvest 1996: Cross Gewürz with old Sherry and you might come up with this brassy, nutty dessert wine that turns a bit dull on the finish.–T.M. • $16/375 ml. • (10/31/1999) • **78**

Malbec Colchagua Valley 1998: Bursting with berry aromas and flavors, with a dash of mint, this has a chewy texture, good concentration and length and a firm finish with an ironlike aftertaste. Drink now through 2001.–B.S. • $10 • (9/15/1999) • **86**

Malbec Colchagua Valley 1997: A layer of buttery oak flavor tends to hide the fresh berry character in this otherwise young and exuberant red. Still tempting, though. Drink now. • $10 • (9/30/1998) • **81**

Malbec Colchagua Valley 1996 • $8 • (6/30/1997) • **87**

Malbec Colchagua Valley 1995 • $8 • (6/30/1996) • **86**

Malbec Curicó Valley 1996: Ample fruit flavors are held in by a firm, slightly tannic texture in this tight but agreeable and well-balanced red. Improves as you sip, and has a lingering finish. Drink now. • $10 • (9/30/1998) • **84**

Merlot Curicó Valley 1991 • $8 • (1/31/1994) • **82**

Merlot Curicó Valley 1990 • $8 • (4/30/1993) • **83**

Merlot Curicó Valley Montes Alpha Special Reserve Aged in French Oak 1994 • $14 • (6/30/1995) • **86**

Merlot Curicó Valley Montes Alpha 1997: Dark and brooding, displaying pure blackberry and cassis aromas and flavors with good complexity, concentration and structure. Long and satisfying finish, with a smoky aftertaste. Drink now through 2001.–B.S. • $18 • (9/15/1999) • **88**

Merlot Curicó Valley Montes Alpha 1996: An elegant Merlot that's pleasantly ripe, with nice cherry and berry flavors and plenty of spice to boot. Smooth and enjoyable. Drink now.–K.M. • $17 • (9/15/1998) • **87**

Merlot Curicó Valley Montes Alpha 1995 • $15 • (5/31/1997) • **89**

Merlot Curicó Valley Special Cuvée 1998: Ripe plum and black cherry flavors gain complexity from smoke, licorice and light herbal accents in this lush, round red. A nice combination of stuffing and freshness. Drink now through 2002.–T.M. • $11 • (5/15/1999) • **85**

Merlot Curicó Valley Special Cuvée 1997: A smooth, ripe and polished red hailing from Chile, with up-front plum and blackberry flavors, and pleasing clove notes that chime in on the finish. Represents good value in today's Merlot market and it's drinkable tonight.–K.M. • $10 • (9/15/1998) • **86**

Merlot Curicó Valley Special Cuvée 1996 • $9 • (10/31/1997) • **83**

Merlot Curicó Valley Special Cuvée 1995 • $8 • (4/30/1997) • **85**

Merlot Curicó Valley Special Cuvée 1994 • $8 • (5/31/1996) • **85**

Merlot Curicó Valley Special Cuvée 1993 • $8 • (12/31/1995) • **86**

Merlot Curicó Valley Special Cuvée 1992 • $8 • (5/31/1994) • **83**

Merlot Curicó Valley Villa Montes 1995 • $7 • (5/31/1996) • **85**

Merlot Curicó Valley Villa Montes 1994 • $8 • (2/29/1996) • **83**

Merlot Curicó Valley Villa Montes 1993 • $7 • (6/15/1995) • **83**

Merlot Curicó Valley Villa Montes 1991 • $7 • (1/31/1994) • **80**

Merlot Curicó Valley Villa Montes 1989 • $7 • (9/15/1990) • **79**

Montes Alpha M Colchagua 1997: A beautiful marriage of refinement and concentration, this firm, polished red shows currant, tobacco and cedar flavors that are balanced and deep and linger on the finish. Eucalyptus and herb notes add interest and harmony to this elegant wine. Tasted twice, with consistent notes. Drink now through 2006.–T.M. • $60 • (10/31/1999) • **91**

Montes Alpha M Colchagua 1996: This elegant red has a polished, international style, with firm but unaggressive tannins and ripe fruit. The flavors are cherry, cedar and eucalyptus, balanced and fine. Cabernet Sauvignon, Merlot and Cabernet Franc. Drink now through 2002.–T.M. • $54 • (9/15/1998) • **89**

Sauvignon Blanc Curicó Valley Fumé Blanc 1998: Apple and citrus flavors are crisp and expressive in this focused Chilean white, underscored by steely acidity and a pleasant earthy note. A clean, bold wine for assertive dishes. Drink now.–T.M. • $9 • (10/31/1999) • **86**

Sauvignon Blanc Curicó Valley Fumé Blanc 1997 • $9 • (5/31/1998) • **84**

Key: SS—Spectator Selection. CS—Cellar Selection. HR—Highly Recommended. $NA—Price not available. (BT)—Barrel tasting. Ⓐ—Auction Price. For a key to the tasters' initials, see "How to Use These Listings."
Dates in parentheses represent the issues in which the ratings were published.

MONTGRAS

Cabernet Sauvignon Colchagua Valley 1997: Firm and lean, this austere red offers light cherry, herbal and tobacco flavors on a light but tannic frame. Drink now through 2001.–T.M. • $8 • (4/30/1999) • **82**

Cabernet Sauvignon Colchagua Valley 1996 • $8 • (10/31/1997) • **86**

Cabernet Sauvignon Colchagua Valley 1995 • $8 • (10/31/1997) • **78**

Cabernet Sauvignon Colchagua Valley 1994 • $8 • (2/28/1997) • **78**

Cabernet Sauvignon Colchagua Valley Ninquén 1996: Dark and brooding. This red is rich with coffee, earth, plum, prune and chocolate flavors, tight and firm on the palate. Yet despite its austerity, it shows balance and a clean, refreshing finish. A distinctive wine, with a solid future ahead of it. Drink now through 2002.–T.M. • $16 • (4/30/1999) • **89**

Cabernet Sauvignon Colchagua Valley Reserva 1997: Ripe cherry and sweet vanilla flavors give this plush red from Chile an immediate appeal. It's round and balanced, with firm tannins under the baby fat, and has enough depth to improve in the bottle. A lot of wine for the price. Drink now through 2005.–T.M. • $11 • (4/30/1999) • **88**

Cabernet Sauvignon Colchagua Valley Reserva 1996: A lean yet complex Cabernet, with herb, plum and tomato flavors that mingle on the lingering finish. Smooth in texture, moderately tannic. Drink now. • $11 • (9/15/1998) • **84**

Cabernet Sauvignon Colchagua Valley Reserva 1995 • $11 • (6/30/1997) • **84**

Carmenère Colchagua Valley Reserva 1997: This soft, sweet red is thick with ripe cherry and grape flavors, but tastes as much like fruit juice as wine. An easy quaff, or good in punch.–T.M. • $11 • (4/30/1999) • **78**

Chardonnay Colchagua Valley 1997: A light but well-balanced Chardonnay, with crisp, appley flavors and a refreshing texture. Drink now. • $8 • (9/15/1998) • **83**

Chardonnay Colchagua Valley Ninquén 1997: Appealing smoky and toasty notes show a deft use of oak, and there's enough apple, melon and pear flavor for balance. It's crisp and clean, yet has a nice creaminess that lingers. Drink now.–T.M. • $16 • (4/30/1999) • **85**

Chardonnay Colchagua Valley Reserva 1997: Modest floral aromas and flavors dominate this simple wine.–K.M. • $11 • (9/30/1998) • **76**

Merlot Colchagua Valley 1997: A nice, chewy Merlot, showing good red cherry and berry flavors and spicy notes. A good match for pasta. Drink now.–K.M. • $8 • (9/15/1998) • **84**

Merlot Colchagua Valley 1996 • $8 • (10/31/1997) • **84**

Merlot Colchagua Valley 1995 • $8 • (2/28/1997) • **84**

Merlot Colchagua Valley Ninquén Barrel Select 1996: Light and lively. A balanced red , with vivid flavors of cherry, cedar and herbs over lean tannins. Though a bit austere for an aperitif, it will match nicely with lighter foods. Drink now through 2002.–T.M. • $16 • (3/31/1999) • **83**

Merlot Colchagua Valley Reserva 1997: Harmonious, with flavors that build on the palate. The kirsch, licorice and herbal notes are rich and well defined, and it has the structure to pair with food. Drink now through 2003.–T.M. • $11 • (3/31/1999) • **86**

Merlot Colchagua Valley Reserva 1996: Rustic, with leathery aromas, earthy flavors and a core of cherry. Still, it's solid, hearty and full-bodied. • $11 • (10/15/1998) • **79**

MOONSHINE VINEYARD

Merlot Rancagua Valley 1994 • $12 • (6/30/1997) • **85**

MORANDE, VINA

Cabernet Sauvignon Central Valley Pionero 1998: Soft and simple. This fleshy red offers ripe cherry and light vanilla flavors, with soft tannins and a clean finish. A lively wine for quaffing now.–T.M. • $7 • (5/15/1999) • **82**

Cabernet Sauvignon Valle Central Pionero 1997: A little soft around the edges but enjoyable, with plum and berry flavors. New line from Pablo Morandé, former Concha y Toro winemaker. Drink now.–K.M. • $7 • (10/15/1998) • **81**

Chardonnay Central Valley Pionero 1998: Straightforward and clean, this white shows good structure but rather austere flavors of light apple and minerals. It's balanced and crisp; may bloom with food. Drink now.–T.M. • $7 • (5/15/1999) • **83**

Chardonnay Valle Central Pionero 1997: Pear and apple flavors dominate this straightforward and quaffable Chardonnay. Drink now.–K.M. • $7 • (9/30/1998) • **82**

Merlot Central Valley Pionero 1998: Bitter chocolate and black cherry flavors are bright and well defined in this round, fruity red. It has a rich texture that remains firm and clean, and bright acidity keeps it lively. Drink now through 2001.–T.M. • $8 • (4/30/1999) • **84**

Merlot Valle Central Pionero 1997: A vibrant Merlot, with red cherry and ripe plum flavors and a nice tobacco note. Smooth and balanced, with appealing spicy accents on the finish. Drink now.–K.M. • $8 • (9/15/1998) • **84**
Sauvignon Blanc Central Valley Pionero 1998: Rich but heavy, this rather dull white shows ripe apple, herbaceous and light earthy flavors. A bit cloying on the finish.–T.M. • $6 • (5/15/1999) • **77**
Sauvignon Blanc Valle Central Pionero 1997 • $6 • (5/31/1998) • **82**

MORNING STAR

Cabernet Sauvignon Rapel Valley 1995 • $8 • (6/30/1997) • **84**
Cabernet Sauvignon Rapel Valley Reserve 1996: A good, hearty red wine, with concentrated currant and cherry flavors and a firm, moderately tannic texture. Drink now. • $8 • (9/15/1998) • **84**
Merlot Rapel Valley 1996: This wine shows a stewy flavor, with modest cherry and herb notes.–K.M. • $6 • (9/15/1998) • **77**
Merlot Rapel Valley 1995 • $8 • (6/30/1997) • **81**

PARTAGER

Cabernet Sauvignon Maule Valley 1995 • $10/1.5 liter • (2/28/1997) • **75**

PIDUCO CREEK

Cabernet Sauvignon Maule Valley 1998: Light and simple, this bright red shows berry, cranberry and light herbal flavors, with light tannins and a hint of spritz.–T.M. • $7 • (5/15/1999) • **78**
Cabernet Sauvignon Maule Valley 1997: A bit over the top with its overwhelming leathery flavor and an odd rubbery note that lingers. Tasted twice, with consistent notes.–K.M. • $7 • (10/15/1998) • **72**
Cabernet Sauvignon Maule Valley 1995 • $7 • (6/30/1997) • **83**
Chardonnay Maule Valley 1998: A mix of crisp green apple and soft vanilla flavors gives this wine balance and liveliness. Clean and straightforward. Drink now.–T.M. • $7 • (5/15/1999) • **81**
Chardonnay Maule Valley 1997: A basic, simple white with little Chardonnay character, a slightly sweet style and a very soft texture. Drink now. • $7 • (9/15/1998) • **76**
Merlot Maule Valley 1998: Bright berry flavors with light herb and smoke accents give this red a lively, accessible character. It has light tannins and a crisp, simple finish. Drink now.–T.M. • $7 • (5/15/1999) • **83**
Merlot Maule Valley 1997: Seductive and appealing. Ripe raspberry aromas and flavors combine with a lush, lightly tannic texture to make this charming and hard to resist. • $7 • (9/15/1998) • **85**
Merlot Maule Valley 1996 • $7 • (6/30/1997) • **79**
Sauvignon Blanc Maule Valley 1998: Crisp and neutral, this straightforward white has little varietal character and turns a bit earthy on the finish.–T.M. • $7 • (5/15/1999) • **77**
Sauvignon Blanc Maule Valley 1997: Not much excitement in this simple white with light apple flavors.–B.S. • $7 • (10/15/1998) • **75**

PLAYA, LA

Cabernet Sauvignon Maipo Valley 1992 • $6 • (6/30/1996) • **61**
Cabernet Sauvignon Maipo Valley 1989 • $6 • (5/31/1994) • **77**
Cabernet Sauvignon Maipo Valley 1988 • $5 • (4/30/1993) • **81**
Cabernet Sauvignon Maipo Valley Estate Reserve 1994: This Cabernet has nice texture, with good cherry and spice flavors that linger on the finish. Drink now.–K.M. • $9 • (10/15/1998) • **83**
Cabernet Sauvignon Maipo Valley Estate Reserve 1992 • $10 • (4/30/1997) • **84**
Cabernet Sauvignon Maipo Valley Estate Reserve 1990 • $8 • (6/15/1995) • **72**
Cabernet Sauvignon Maipo Valley Estate Reserve 1988 • $8 • (5/31/1994) • **81**
Merlot Maipo Valley 1994 • $6 • (4/30/1997) • **84**
Merlot Maipo Valley 1990 • $6 • (5/31/1994) • **86**
Merlot Maipo Valley 1988 • $5 • (4/30/1993) • **81**
Merlot Maipo Valley Estate Reserve 1995: A rich and polished Merlot that has inviting spicy aromas and a silky texture. This wine layers on the chocolate, plum and spice flavors. Ripe and round, with coffee and cassis notes on the finish. Drink now.–K.M. • $10 • (10/15/1998) • **87**
Merlot Maipo Valley Estate Reserve 1994 • $12 • (4/30/1997) • **88**

PORTA, VINA

Cabernet Sauvignon Cachapoal Valley 1996 • $9 • (10/31/1997) • **82**
Cabernet Sauvignon Valle del Cachapoal 1994 • $9 • (6/30/1996) • **83**
Cabernet Sauvignon Valle del Cachapoal 1993 • $9 • (12/31/1995) • **84**
Cabernet Sauvignon Valle del Cachapoal 1992 • $9 • (4/30/1995) • **87**
Cabernet Sauvignon Valle del Cachapoal 1991 • $9 • (5/31/1994) • **79**
Cabernet Sauvignon Valle del Cachapoal Reserva 1992 • $11 • (4/30/1995) • **88**
Chardonnay Valle del Cachapoal 1998: Racy and firm, with pretty toast and smoke character to back the refined citrus and melon notes. Relatively light-bodied, but has a core of crisp acidity that will match well with food. Drink now.–T.M. • $9 • (1/31/1999) • **84**
Chardonnay Cachapoal Valley 1997: A ripe, forward style, with appealing pear, tropical fruit and apple flavors and a smoky note. Drink now.–K.M. • $9 • (9/30/1998) • **83**
Merlot Cachapoal Valley 1997: Juicy and fresh, with plenty of berry and cherry flavor and a nice ripe note on the finish. Drink now.–K.M. • $9 • (9/15/1998) • **83**
Merlot Valle del Cachapoal Reserva 1997: Straightforward, with aromas and flavors of black cherries, toast and herbs, moderate tannins and good balance. Refreshing, and its slight bitterness should match well with food. Drink now through 2001.–T.M. • $12 • (1/31/1999) • **83**
Pinot Noir Valle del Cachapoal 1997: Light, clean and simple. Shows cherry and spice flavors over light, slightly bitter tannins. Has some varietal character but little personality.–T.M. • $12 • (1/31/1999) • **79**

PORTAL DEL ALTO

Cabernet Sauvignon Maipo Valley 1995: A wonderfully fruity and pure Cabernet, with delicious currant, cherry and raspberry flavors that last from the first whiff to the finish. Light in tannins but nicely balanced. Drink now. • $7 • (9/15/1998) • **86**
Cabernet Sauvignon Maipo Valley 1992 • $4 • (5/31/1994) • **77**
Cabernet Sauvignon Maipo Valley 1990 • $4 • (3/15/1993) • **84**
Cabernet Sauvignon Maipo Valley Gran Reserva 1993: A very solid, well-balanced and fresh-tasting wine, with lively cherry and cranberry flavors, firm tannins and a clean finish. Has modest flavors but great texture and structure. Drink now through 2001. • $9 • (9/15/1998) • **86**
Cabernet Sauvignon Maipo Valley Gran Reserva 1989 • $4 • (4/30/1993) • **72**
Cabernet Sauvignon Maipo Valley Reserva 1995: Easy to enjoy. Smooth-textured and a bit understated, but it has ample fruit flavors, integrated tannins and a soft finish. Drink now. • $9 • (9/15/1998) • **84**
Cabernet Sauvignon Valle Central 1998: Soft and smooth, this light red offers clean, simple cherry and herbal flavors, with light tannins. An easy-sipping party wine. Drink now.–T.M. • $6 • (4/30/1999) • **81**
Chardonnay Valle Central 1998: Here's a white wine for vodka lovers: It has almost no color, odor or flavor. But it's crisp and clean.–T.M. • $6 • (4/30/1999) • **78**
Chardonnay Valle Central 1997: Plenty of pear flavor in this smooth-textured wine. A pleasant creaminess gives it added dimension. For fans of a ripe style of Chardonnay. Nice, clean finish. Drink now.–K.M. • $7 • (9/30/1998) • **85**
Chardonnay Valle Central Reservado 1997: Vanilla and candied apple flavors are sweet and simple in this soft white. It makes an easy-quaffing aperitif, but begins to cloy on the second glass.–T.M. • $9 • (4/30/1999) • **78**
Merlot Maipo Valley 1992 • $4 • (5/31/1994) • **78**
Merlot Maipo Valley 1990 • $4 • (4/30/1993) • **77**
Merlot Valle Central 1998: This light, soft red has a Beaujolais Nouveau-like structure, with simple cherry flavors and hints of the gaminess that often result from carbonic maceration. Quaff it.–T.M. • $6 • (3/31/1999) • **78**
Merlot Valle Central 1997: Some richness, but assertive leathery notes are mixed in with the plum and berry flavors. Drink now.–K.M. • $7 • (9/15/1998) • **79**
Merlot Valle Central Reserva 1997: Straightforward, juicy and firm, with bright cherry flavors and hints of vanilla and spice. A fruit-driven style that has just enough grip for food. Drink now.–T.M. • $9 • (3/31/1999) • **83**
Sauvignon Blanc Maipo Valley 1997 • $7 • (5/31/1998) • **81**

PROSPERITY

Merlot Colchagua Valley 1995 • $7 • (2/28/1997) • **83**

QUEBRADA DE MACUL, VINA

Cabernet Sauvignon Macul Domus Aurea 1996: Ripe and rich, this muscular red is packed with bright flavors of blackberry and cassis, adding firm but not heavy tannins and enough acidity to keep it lively. It's firm, fresh and focused, and should improve with age. Tasted twice, with consistent notes. Drink now through 2004.–T.M. • $30 • (5/15/1999) • **90**

RABAT, DOMAINE

Cabernet Sauvignon Colchagua Valley Apalta Vineyard Reserva 1990 • $8 • (4/30/1995) • **85**
Cabernet Sauvignon Maipo Valley 1991 • $5 • (4/30/1995) • **72**
Merlot Colchagua Valley Apalta Vineyard Reserva 1992 • $8 • (6/15/1995) • **86**

RACO, CAVAS DEL

Cabernet Sauvignon Alto Maipo 1990 • $10 • (6/30/1996) • **71**
Cabernet Sauvignon Maipo Valley 1994 • $8 • (6/30/1997) • **80**
Sparkling Maipo Valley L'Héritage NV • $9 • (5/15/1997) • **79**

RIVER FALLS

Cabernet Sauvignon Colchagua 1995 • $7 • (2/28/1997) • **82**
Merlot Colchagua 1994 • $6 • (12/31/1995) • **83**
Merlot Maule 1995 • $7 • (2/28/1997) • **84**

ROSA, VINA LA

Cabernet Sauvignon Rapel La Palma 1997: A lively mix of black cherry and herbal flavors gives this red distinctive personality. The tannins are soft, and a pleasant minty note lingers on the finish. Drink now through 2002.–T.M. • $8 • (2/28/1999) • **84**

Cabernet Sauvignon Rapel La Palma Reserve 1997: Firm and tannic, this austere red shows cherry flavors, herbal and coffee notes. It has good concentration and should blossom given some time. Drink through 2005–T.M. • $11 • (2/28/1999) • **85**

Chardonnay Rapel La Palma 1997: Creamy, vanilla aromas give way to crisp flavors of apple and herbs in this round white. Balanced and lively. Drink now.–T.M. • $8 • (2/28/1999) • **83**

Chardonnay Rapel La Palma Gran Reserva 1997: This full-bodied white has plenty of ripe melon, butter, honey and vanilla flavor, and just enough acidity for balance. Shows firm structure and a lingering, toasty finish. Drink now.–T.M. • $14 • (2/28/1999) • **84**

Chardonnay Rapel La Palma Reserve 1997: This solid white offers muted flavors of hazelnuts, vanilla and herbs, with hints of melon and citrus that linger on the finish. A bit austere on its own, it should blossom with food. Drink now.–T.M. • $11 • (2/28/1999) • **83**

Merlot Rapel La Palma 1997: This soft red offers dark flavors of black cherry, coffee and licorice and takes its structure more from acidity than tannin. Will match with lighter, smoky foods. Drink now.–T.M. • $8 • (3/31/1999) • **81**

Merlot Rapel La Palma Gran Reserva 1997: Rich and ripe yet balanced, this fruit-driven red shows plenty of plum and cherry flavors, with sweet vanilla and coffee-oak notes and nicely integrated tannins. Drink now through 2002.–T.M. • $14 • (3/31/1999) • **85**

Merlot Rapel La Palma Reserve 1997: Round and velvety, with ripe flavors of plum and black cherry, notes of sweet chocolate and coffee-oak. Soft tannins have just enough grip to keep it from cloying. Drink now through 2002.–T.M. • $11 • (3/31/1999) • **84**

Merlot-Cabernet Sauvignon Rapel La Palma Gran Reserva 1997: This light red shows simple berry flavors with hints of herbs, balanced but straightforward. It turns a bit dry on the finish.–T.M. • $14 • (4/30/1999) • **79**

SAINT MORILLON

Cabernet Sauvignon Lontué 1995 • $7 • (3/31/1998) • **82**
Cabernet Sauvignon Lontué 1993 • $7 • (6/30/1997) • **83**
Cabernet Sauvignon Lontué 1992 • $5 • (4/30/1995) • **76**
Cabernet Sauvignon Maipo 1990 • $7 • (5/31/1994) • **85**
Chardonnay Lontué 1997 • $7 • (3/31/1998) • **77**
Merlot Lontué 1996: Leathery aromas and astringent flavors mark this unhappy wine. Not recommended. Tasted twice, with consistent notes.–K.M. • $7 • (10/15/1998) • **69**
Merlot Lontué 1995 • $7 • (6/30/1997) • **68**
Sauvignon Blanc Lontué 1997 • $7 • (5/31/1998) • **78**

Key: SS—Spectator Selection. CS—Cellar Selection. HR—Highly Recommended. SNA—Price not available. (BT)—Barrel tasting. (A)—Auction Price.
For a key to the tasters' initials, see "How to Use These Listings."
Dates in parentheses represent the issues in which the ratings were published.

SAN CARLOS

Cabernet Sauvignon Colchagua Valley 1995 • $7 • (6/30/1997) • **77**
Cabernet Sauvignon Colchagua Valley 1994 • $6 • (6/30/1997) • **83**
Cabernet Sauvignon Colchagua Valley 1991 • $7 • (10/31/1995) • **77**
Malbec Colchagua Valley 1996 • $7 • (6/30/1997) • **86**
Malbec Colchagua Valley Oak Aged 1994 • $6 • (2/29/1996) • **86**
Merlot Colchagua Valley 1996 • $6 • (5/31/1997) • **83**
Merlot Colchagua Valley 1994 • $6 • (12/31/1995) • **85**

SAN FRANCISCO DE MOSTAZAL

Cabernet Sauvignon Cachapoal Valley Viño de Eyzaguirre Reserva Especial 1995: A Cabernet with punch. Plenty of good currant, red plum and berry flavor. Medium-bodied, with notes of orange peel and spice on the finish. Drink now.–K.M. • $8 • (10/15/1998) • **84**

SAN JOSE DE SANTIAGO

Cabernet Sauvignon Colchagua Valley 1990 • $5 • (5/15/1992) • **85**
Cabernet Sauvignon Maule 1993 • $7 • (6/30/1996) • **79**

SAN-OBAREL

Cabernet Sauvignon Colchagua Valley Grand Reserve 1994: There's a nice solid core of ripe plum and dark cherry to this balanced, easy-drinking Cabernet. Spicy and chocolaty notes mark the finish. Drink now.–K.M. • $10 • (10/15/1998) • **85**

Merlot Maipo Valley Grand Reserve 1996: A no-nonsense, well-balanced Merlot, with concentrated herb and cherry flavors, a firm texture and a lingering finish. Drink now. • $10 • (10/15/1998) • **84**

SAN PEDRO, VINA

Cabernet Sauvignon Lontué Castillo de Molina Reserva 1998: Good intensity and focus here, with pleasant currant, berry and dark plum flavors. Firm structure, with a slightly herbal finish. Drink now.–K.M. • $10 • (3/31/2000) • **84**

Cabernet Sauvignon Lontué Castillo de Molina Reserva 1997: Rich and ripe, offering jammy flavors of black cherry and blackberry, with chocolate and coffee accents, while a streak of acidity keeps it lively. Tannins are firm but not aggressive; the wine is balanced and should complement food. Drink now through 2004.–T.M. • $10 • (2/28/1999) • **87**

Cabernet Sauvignon Lontué Gato Negro 1999: A simple Cabernet with modest plum and berry flavors, some charry notes on the finish.–K.M. • $5 • (3/31/2000) • **79**

Cabernet Sauvignon Lontué Gato Negro 1998: Offers plenty of straightforward cherry and berry flavor, with notes of sweet vanilla and just enough tannin for grip. Juicy and quaffable. Drink now through 2002.–T.M. • $5 • (4/30/1999) • **84**

Cabernet Sauvignon Lontué Gato Negro 1997: Nice and smooth, with good berry flavors, and a leathery note that lingers on the finish. Drink now through 2001.–K.M. • $6 • (10/15/1998) • **83**

Cabernet Sauvignon Lontué Gato Negro 1993 • $5 • (4/30/1995) • **75**
Cabernet Sauvignon Lontué Gato Negro 1989 • $5 • (6/15/1992) • **75**

Cabernet Sauvignon Lontué Valley 35 Sur 1998: Sweet raspberry and vanilla flavors shine though this soft yet thick and tannic red. It's a bit sweet and jammy, but has enough acidity to stay lively and fresh. Drink now through 2003.–T.M. • $8 • (4/30/1999) • **83**

Cabernet Sauvignon Lontué Valley 35 Sur 1996: Shows decent berry flavors, but there's an overwhelming leathery note that skews the balance.–K.M. • $8 • (10/15/1998) • **76**

Cabernet Sauvignon-Merlot Lontué Gato Negro 1999: Quite grapey, with just enough tannin to keep it serious. Clean and pure-tasting, with well-focused berry and red plum flavors that linger appealingly on the finish. Drink now.–K.M. • $5 • (3/31/2000) • **84**

Cabo de Hornos Special Reserve Lontué Valley 1996: Bordeaux-like, with cedary aromas and flavors of cherry and spice. Shows good length and a backbone of acidity as well. Nicely sculpted, with notes of cardamom and coffee on the finish. Drink now.–K.M. • $50 • (3/31/2000) • **86**

Cabo de Hornos Special Reserve Lontué Valley 1995: Sweet hedonism. This plush red has lavish toast and chocolaty oak flavors that envelop ripe plum and blackberry. Has just enough tannin for grip and enough acidity to keep it lively. A big wine that's more Californian than Chilean in style. Tasted twice, with consistent notes. Drink through 2005–T.M. • $30 • (2/28/1999) • **88**

Chardonnay Lontué Castillo de Molina Reserva 1998: Light-bodied, with simple pear and vanilla flavors. More sweet oak than fruit on the finish. Drink now.–T.M. • $10 • (3/31/2000) • **80**

Chardonnay Lontué Castillo de Molina Reserva 1997: Ripe yet balanced, this firm white offers hazelnut, apple and melon flavors with crisp underlying acidity. A good match for fish and light poultry dishes. Tasted twice, with consistent notes. Drink now.–T.M. • $10 • (2/28/1999) • **83**

Chardonnay Lontué Valley 35 Sur 1999: Honeysuckle and pear aromas introduce a white that sports a round texture and an obvious, though integrated, oaky finish. Just enough acidity to keep it lively. Drink now.–T.M. • $8 • (3/31/2000) • **82**

Chardonnay Lontué Valley 35 Sur 1998: Lots of oak. Sweet vanilla and buttery flavors dominate this fresh, clean white; the light apple and melon flavors get lost in the wood. Drink now.–T.M. • $8 • (5/15/1999) • **82**

Chardonnay Lontué Valley 35 Sur 1997: Starts off fruity, with apple and citrus flavors, but falls a bit flat in the end. Drink now.–K.M. • $8 • (9/30/1998) • **78**

Chardonnay Lontué Valley Gato Blanco 1998: This restrained white is round and firm; its subtle vanilla and melon flavors emerge slowly across the palate then linger on the finish. A good match for medium-weight dishes, and refreshing as well. Drink now.–T.M. • $5 • (5/15/1999) • **84**

Merlot Lontué 1989 • $7 • (5/31/1992) • **89**

Merlot Lontué 1988 • $5 • (12/31/1990) • **84**

Merlot Lontué Castillo de Molina Reserva 1998: Toasty vanilla and coffee aromas announce this attempt at a modern-style Merlot. Polished, with supple spice, espresso and chocolate notes, finishing with a round, ripe mouthfeel. Tasted twice, with consistent notes. Drink now through 2001.–T.M. • $10 • (3/31/2000) • **88**

Merlot Lontué Castillo de Molina Reserva 1996 • $NA • (1/01/1998) • **87**

Merlot Lontué Gato Negro 1999: An herbal note dominates this straightforward red, with currant and red berry flavors. Slightly spritzy on the finish. Drink now.–K.M. • $5 • (3/31/2000) • **80**

Merlot Lontué Gato Negro 1998: Soft and smooth. Simple cherry and berry flavors are clean and fresh in this straightforward red. It has light tannins and good balance. Drink now.–T.M. • $5 • (4/30/1999) • **83**

Merlot Lontué Gato Negro 1997: Smooth and round, with berry and cherry flavors. A good quaffer. Drink now.–K.M. • $6 • (9/30/1998) • **82**

Merlot Lontué Valley 35 Sur 1999: This Chilean red has good berry and currant flavors, with herbal notes. Finishes on an overtly smoky note. Drink now.–K.M. • $8 • (3/31/2000) • **83**

Merlot Lontué Valley 35 Sur 1998: This light, clean red offers cherry and herbal flavors, with light, soft tannins. A pleasing bitter note on the finish gives it the grip to match with lighter dishes. Drink now.–T.M. • $8 • (4/30/1999) • **82**

Merlot Lontué Valley 35 Sur 1996: Tastes mature, showing flavors of herbs and bittersweet chocolate.–K.M. • $8 • (10/15/1998) • **78**

Pinot Noir Lontué Castillo de Molina Reserva 1998: A simple Pinot, with a pleasant tealike aroma and sweet cherry and spice flavors. Drink now.–K.M. • $10 • (3/31/2000) • **80**

Sauvignon Blanc Lontué Valley 35 Sur 1999: An atypical Sauvignon Blanc with soft pear notes, this is a fat, soft white that lacks the usual zing. Drink now.–K.M. • $8 • (3/31/2000) • **81**

Sauvignon Blanc Lontué Valley 35 Sur 1998: This creamy-textured white has more presence and personality than most Chilean Sauvignon Blancs. It's ripe and round, sporting melon, vanilla and light herbal flavors that are expressive yet balanced, with enough crisp acidity to complement food. Drink now.–T.M. • $8 • (5/15/1999) • **86**

Sauvignon Blanc Lontué Valley 35 Sur 1997: One the herbal side but balanced, with pea, spice and tropical fruit flavors. Has a touch of richness as well, and a smooth finish. Drink now.–K.M. • $8 • (10/15/1998) • **83**

Sauvignon Blanc Lontué Valley Gato Blanco 1998: This crisp white offers light flavors of apples and herbs, with enough acidity to match with lighter dishes. Its rather neutral character is more refreshing than memorable. Drink now.–T.M. • $5 • (5/15/1999) • **82**

SANTA ALICIA

Cabernet Sauvignon Maipo Los Maitenes Vineyard Gran Reserva 1994: A ripe wine, with plum and berry flavors, and earthy notes in the middle. Drink now.–K.M. • $12 • (10/15/1998) • **82**

Cabernet Sauvignon Maipo Valley 1990 • $6 • (10/31/1995) • **82**

Cabernet Sauvignon Maipo Valley Reserve 1994: Herbal, with attenuating flavors on a light-bodied structure.–B.S. • $8 • (10/15/1998) • **78**

Cabernet Sauvignon Maipo Valley Reserve 1992 • $8 • (2/28/1997) • **78**

Cabernet Sauvignon Maipo Valley Reserve 1990 • $8 • (10/31/1995) • **83**

Merlot Maipo El Pimiento Vineyard Gran Reserva 1995: A simple style, with light fruit flavors and firm tannins. • $12 • (10/15/1998) • **78**

Merlot Maipo Valley 1992 • $6 • (12/31/1995) • **79**

Merlot Maipo Valley Limited Production 1993 • $6 • (4/30/1997) • **80**

Merlot Maipo Valley Reserve 1995: A light red, with fresh cherry flavors and a slight tannic bite, like a decent Chianti. • $8 • (10/15/1998) • **79**

Merlot Maipo Valley Reserve 1992 • $8 • (12/31/1995) • **88**

Merlot-Cabernet Sauvignon Curicó Valley Vintage Select 1992 • $5 • (10/31/1995) • **76**

SANTA AMELIA

Cabernet Sauvignon Colchagua 1995 • $7 • (2/28/1997) • **79**

Cabernet Sauvignon Colchagua 1994 • $6 • (10/31/1995) • **88**

Cabernet Sauvignon Maule Valley Reserve Selection 1997: This clean, lively red offers black cherry flavors framed by light cedar and herbal notes.Has enough tannin to match with moderate-weight dishes, but remains fresh and accessible. Drink now through 2002.–T.M. • $8 • (5/15/1999) • **85**

Chardonnay Maule Valley Reserve Selection 1998: This exuberant white combines sweet vanilla with tart lemon flavors; it's case of opposites attracting to make a lively, quaffable wine. Perfect for parties, less suitable for food. Drink now.–T.M. • $8 • (5/15/1999) • **83**

Merlot Colchagua 1995 • $7 • (2/28/1997) • **86**

Merlot Colchagua 1994 • $6 • (12/31/1995) • **86**

Merlot Maule Valley Reserve Selection 1998: Focused and balanced, this lively red from Chile offers bright cherry and cedar flavors with light, firm tannins and crisp acidity. Though no blockbuster, it has the character and complexity to match well with medium-weight dishes, and gives change from your $10 bill. Drink now through 2002.–T.M. • $8 • (5/15/1999) • **86**

SANTA ANA DE CURICO

Cabernet Sauvignon Colchagua Valley Santiago 1541 1995 • $5 • (6/30/1997) • **84**

Merlot Colchagua Valley Santiago 1541 1995 • $6 • (6/30/1997) • **84**

SANTA CAROLINA, VINA

Cabernet Sauvignon Maipo Valley Los Toros Vineyard Special Reserve 1988 • $8 • (4/30/1993) • **83**

Cabernet Sauvignon Maipo Valley Reserva 1997: This lively Chilean Cabernet offers expressive flavors of ripe fruit and toasty oak, with black cherry, plum, chocolate and vanilla. Soft, almost jammy in texture, it has just enough tannin and acidity to keep the balance. Drink now through 2002.–T.M. • $8 • (4/30/1999) • **86**

Cabernet Sauvignon Maipo Valley Reserva 1996: Nice and ripe-tasting, this red from Chile has delicious dark plum, ripe cherry and spicy flavors, hints of leather and chocolate that linger on the finish. A smooth and well-balanced wine that hits all the right notes and is easy on the budget, too. Tasted twice with consistent notes. Drink now.–K.M. • $9 • (10/15/1998) • **86**

Cabernet Sauvignon Maipo Valley Reserva 1995 • $7 • (5/31/1997) • **85**

Cabernet Sauvignon Maipo Valley Santa Rosa Vineyard Cinco Estrellas Gran Reserva 1987 • $14 • (2/28/1994) • **84**

Cabernet Sauvignon Maipo Valley Santa Rosa Vineyard Reserva 1990 • $8 • (5/31/1995) • **84**

Cabernet Sauvignon-Merlot Colchagua Valley 1995 • $8/1.5 liter • (6/30/1997) • **82**

Chardonnay Maipo Valley Reserva 1998: Lush tropical flavors of mango and papaya stay lively in this big, fresh Chilean white, thanks to a core of lime-scented acidity. It's exotic yet refreshing, making it a good match with fusion-type foods, and the asking price surely can't be quibbled over. Drink now.–T.M. • $8 • (5/15/1999) • **86**

Chardonnay Maipo Valley Reserva 1997: This ambitious white is full-bodied, aggressively oaked and very ripe. Shows toast, vanilla, melon, apple pie and lemon-lime flavors, powerful but slightly lacking in harmony.–T.M. • $9 • (9/15/1998) • **84**

Merlot Maipo Valley Santa Rosa Vineyard 1993 • $6 • (5/15/1995) • **86**

Merlot Maipo Valley Santa Rosa Vineyard 1989 • $6 • (3/31/1993) • **82**

Merlot Maipo Valley Santa Rosa Vineyard Reserva 1991 • $8 • (4/15/1994) • **84**

Merlot Maipo Valley Santa Rosa Vineyard Reserva 1990 • $8 • (4/30/1993) • **82**

Merlot Maipo Valley Santa Rosa Vineyard Reserva 1989 • $8 • (4/30/1993) • **82**

Merlot Maipo Valley Santa Rosa Vineyard Reserva Especial 1989 • $8 • (6/15/1992) • **83**

Merlot Maule Valley Reserva 1997: Brickish notes and dark plum and dark cherry flavors make this a warm and inviting red. Smooth and round, with roasted coffee notes that linger appealingly on the finish. Drink now.–K.M. • $8 • (1/01/1999) • **86**

Merlot Maule Valley Reserva 1995 • $7 • (6/30/1997) • **82**

SANTA CAROLINA, VINA

Merlot San Fernando Valley Cinco Estrellas Gran Reserva 1993 • $10 • (5/15/1995) • **86**
Merlot San Fernando Valley Reserva 1993 • $8 • (6/15/1995) • **81**
Merlot-Cabernet Sauvignon Colchagua Valley 1995 • $8/1.5 liter • (5/31/1997) • **83**
Merlot-Cabernet Sauvignon San Fernando Valley 1993 • $6 • (5/15/1995) • **85**
Pinot Noir Maipo Valley Santa Rosa Vineyard Reserva 1994 • $8 • (6/15/1995) • **77**

SANTA EMA

Cabernet Sauvignon Maipo Valley 1997: This crisp, fruity red offers bright black cherry, cola and vanilla flavors. A bit sweet with oak, with moderate tannins and a fruity finish, it has enough grip for food. Drink now through 2002.–T.M. • $9 • (10/31/1999) • **84**
Cabernet Sauvignon Maipo Valley 1996: Ripe, with a round texture and decent plum, berry and cherry flavors. Chocolate and mint notes on the finish. Drink now.–K.M. • $8 • (10/15/1998) • **82**
Cabernet Sauvignon Maipo Valley 1995: This red is broad but shallow, with ripe plum and coffee flavors and firm tannins that skip along the palate and finish short. Best with food. Tasted twice, with consistent notes.–T.M. • $7 • (9/15/1998) • **84**
Cabernet Sauvignon Maipo Valley 1994 • $7 • (2/28/1997) • **79**
Cabernet Sauvignon Maipo Valley Reserve 1996: This lean red offers cherry, herb and smoke flavors, with slightly dry tannins and crisp acidity. Firm and clean, it should marry well with food. Drink now through 2003.–T.M. • $14 • (10/31/1999) • **84**
Cabernet Sauvignon Maipo Valley Reserve 1995: Quite a minty mouthful, with nice plum and berry flavors to boot. Nicely balanced, with a good, firm structure and a drying note on the finish. Drink now.–K.M. • $12 • (10/15/1998) • **83**
Cabernet Sauvignon Maipo Valley Reserve 1994: A hearty-flavored red wine that's nicely mature. A bit tannic in texture, with ripe plum and tomato flavors. Tasted twice, with consistent notes. Drink now. • $11 • (9/15/1998) • **83**
Cabernet Sauvignon Maipo Valley Super Premium 1992 • $9 • (2/28/1997) • **82**
Cabernet Sauvignon-Merlot Maipo Valley Barrel Select 1997: This light red offers cherry, light herb and sweet vanilla flavors. Balanced but simple, with very light tannins and a short, clean finish. Drink now.–T.M. • $10 • (10/31/1999) • **82**
Cabernet Sauvignon-Merlot Maipo Valley Barrel Select 1996: A balanced and nicely concentrated red, with ripe cherry, dark plum and cassis flavors. Ripe and round, with appealing notes of brick and coffee. Finishes with spice and chocolate accents. Drink now.–K.M. • $9 • (10/15/1998) • **86**
Cabernet Sauvignon-Merlot Maipo Valley Barrel Select 1995: Decent berry, cherry and spice flavors, but with a stewy note. A bit muddled in the end. A blend: 60 percent Cabernet Sauvignon, 40 percent Merlot.–K.M. • $8 • (10/15/1998) • **79**
Chardonnay Maipo Valley 1998: Pleasing flavors of melon and vanilla mingle in this soft yet refreshing white. Has good balance and some depth, with sweet vanilla notes that linger on the finish. Drink now.–T.M. • $8 • (5/15/1999) • **84**
Chardonnay Maipo Valley 1997 • $7 • (5/31/1998) • **80**
Chardonnay Maipo Valley Reserve 1998: Sweet vanilla and cream flavors from oak dominate this round white, backed by light lemony notes. It's simple and sweet, though the acidity keeps it clean. Drink now.–T.M. • $14 • (10/31/1999) • **83**
Chardonnay Maipo Valley Reserve 1997: Lush and spicy, this ripe, rich Chardonnay has plenty of vanilla, toast, apple and melon character. A bit blowsy for food, but packs plenty of flavor. Drink now.–T.M. • $11 • (5/15/1999) • **84**
Merlot Maipo Valley 1997: Offering good Merlot character, full of raspberry, spice and cherry wrapped in a soft, bright structure, this red says "drink me." –B.S. • $9 • (9/15/1999) • **86**
Merlot Maipo Valley 1996: An interesting and lively style, with sweet cherry, spice and cigar-box flavors, finishing on a cinnamon note. Drink now.–K.M. • $8 • (10/15/1998) • **84**
Merlot Maipo Valley 1995: Smooth texture and mature fruit flavors make this a mellow Merlot that's easy to enjoy. Drink now. • $7 • (9/30/1998) • **81**
Merlot Maipo Valley 1994 • $7 • (2/28/1997) • **83**

Key: SS—Spectator Selection. CS—Cellar Selection. HR—Highly Recommended. $NA—Price not available. (BT)—Barrel tasting. Ⓐ—Auction Price. For a key to the tasters' initials, see "How to Use These Listings." **Dates in parentheses represent the issues in which the ratings were published.**

Merlot Maipo Valley Reserve 1997: Strong oaky vanilla and cola flavors dominate the light, sweet, simple cherry notes in this supple wine and give it a candied character. Pleasant but rather simple.–T.M. • $14 • (10/31/1999) • **79**
Merlot Maipo Valley Reserve 1996: An up-front, blowsy style, with sweet, spicy flavors and a core of dark plum and red cherry. Finishes on a cinnamon accent. Drink now.–K.M. • $12 • (10/15/1998) • **84**
Merlot Maipo Valley Reserve 1995: Drinkable but odd. Tastes like cherry candy and Danish pastry—not exactly what I look for in Merlot. Drink now. • $11 • (9/30/1998) • **74**
Merlot Maipo Valley Super Premium 1994 • $9 • (4/30/1997) • **83**
Merlot-Cabernet Franc-Cabernet Sauvignon Rapel Valley Catalina 1994: Still youthful, this harmonious red marries ripe fruit and firm tannins, with nicely defined and still-fresh plum, cherry and berry flavors. Its refreshing flavors and firm texture make it a good match with lighter meat dishes. Drink now through 2001.–T.M. • $25 • (4/30/1999) • **86**
Sauvignon Blanc Maipo Valley 1997: The herbal and earthy flavors are tart and a bit musty in this rustic white. Light-bodied and short. Drink now.–T.M. • $7 • (9/15/1998) • **74**

SANTA INES, VINA

Cabernet Sauvignon Maipo Valley Legado de Armida Reserva 1997: A murky red, with stewed and tarry flavors and a rubbery note on the finish. Tasted twice, with consistent notes.–K.M. • $6 • (3/31/2000) • **74**
Carmenère Maipo Valley Legado de Armida Reserva 1998: Hearty beef and stewed tomato aromas and flavors and a finish tinged with chewy cassis and currant make this perfect for barbecue fare. Drink now.–K.M. • $6 • (3/31/2000) • **83**
Chardonnay Maipo Valley Legado de Armida Reserva 1999: Nutty on the nose, with fleshy pear and apple flavors that are quickly overwhelmed by oak. A bit tiring on the heavy-handed finish. Drink now.–T.M. • $6 • (3/31/2000) • **81**
Merlot Maipo Valley Legado de Armida Reserva 1998: A rustic red, with rough-hewn flavors of dark plum and caramelized onion. Finishes on a rubbery note. 16 percent Cabernet Sauvignon.–K.M. • $6 • (3/31/2000) • **79**
Sauvignon-Sémillon-Chardonnay Maipo Valley Late Harvest 1997: Maturing now, this shows honey, brown sugar and candied apple flavors; it's sweet and viscous, but rather heavy. Drink now.–T.M. • $5/375 ml. • (3/31/2000) • **81**

SANTA LAURA

Cabernet Sauvignon Colchagua Valley Laura Hartwig 1997: A juicy and vibrant red, with nicely articulated red plum, berry and cherry flavors. Lively spice elements on the finish. Drink now through 2002.–K.M. • $13 • (3/31/2000) • **85**
Cabernet Sauvignon Colchagua Valley Laura Hartwig 1996: This refreshing red is firm, even a bit tart, with well-defined black cherry, licorice and herb flavors over ripe tannins. Balanced and clean, it's expressive and harmonious. A fine match with food. Drink now through 2003.–T.M. • $13 • (12/15/1998) • **88**
Cabernet Sauvignon Colchagua Valley Laura Hartwig 1995: Pleasant, with currant, ripe plum, cherry and spice flavors. There's a touch of sweetness, which isn't overbearing, and coffee and dark chocolate on the finish. Drink now.–K.M. • $13 • (10/15/1998) • **84**
Chardonnay Colchagua Valley Laura Hartwig 1998: Good acidity keeps this white lively, while distinctive orange blossom and smoke flavors give it character. Not a big wine, but persistent and appealing. Drink now.–T.M. • $13 • (3/31/2000) • **85**
Chardonnay Colchagua Valley Laura Hartwig 1997: This harmonious white shows an elegant balance of crisp apple and light toasty oak, with lively acidity and a clean, lingering finish. Subtle but firm, it's a good match for food. Drink now.–T.M. • $13 • (12/15/1998) • **84**

SANTA MARVISTA

Cabernet Sauvignon Central Valley Reserva 1998: Roasted, olive aromas give way to a firm, black cherry Cabernet that gets a bit outmuscled by firm, toasty flavors on the finish. Drink now.–B.S. • $6 • (5/31/2000) • **83**
Cabernet Sauvignon Central Valley Reserva 1997: Boysenberry and kirsch flavors are exotic and appealing, but they turn a bit candied and firm tannins shut down the finish. It has character but lacks harmony. Drink now through 2002.–T.M. • $7 • (4/30/1999) • **80**
Cabernet Sauvignon Colchagua 1996: A medium-bodied, almost chewy red dominated by herbal aromas and flavors, with only modest fruit.–B.S. • $6 • (10/15/1998) • **77**
Cabernet Sauvignon Rapel 1995 • $7 • (6/30/1997) • **82**

Chardonnay Casablanca 1997: Good, ripe pear and apple flavors turn flabby on the finish. Drink now.–K.M. • $6 • (9/30/1998) • **79**

Chardonnay Central Valley Reserva 1998: Rich, with butter, vanilla and butterscotch flavors, this makes a sweet impression, just counterbalanced by lemony acidity and flavors of pineapple and mango. Best for fans of oak. Drink now.–T.M. • $7 • (5/15/1999) • **83**

Merlot Central Valley Reserva 1999: Straightforward, with plum and chocolate flavors on a soft, accessible frame. Drink now.–B.S. • $6 • (5/31/2000) • **82**

Merlot Central Valley Reserva 1998: The jammy berry flavor is appealing in this thick, soft red, but it's a bit candied, and a sharp underlying acidity throws it off-balance.–T.M. • $7 • (4/30/1999) • **76**

Merlot Maipo 1997: Pleasant Merlot, somewhat light-bodied, with ripe, grapey, berrylike flavors and a soft texture. Drink now. • $6 • (10/15/1998) • **82**

Merlot Rapel 1996 • $7 • (5/31/1997) • **84**

SANTA MONICA, VINA

Cabernet Sauvignon Rancagua 1994 • $8 • (6/30/1997) • **80**

Cabernet Sauvignon Rancagua 1993 • $7 • (6/30/1996) • **77**

Cabernet Sauvignon Rancagua 1992 • $7 • (6/30/1996) • **77**

Cabernet Sauvignon Rancagua 1991 • $6 • (4/30/1995) • **77**

Cabernet Sauvignon Rancagua 1989 • $5 • (10/15/1991) • **85**

Cabernet Sauvignon Rancagua 1988 • $6 • (3/15/1990) • **86**

Cabernet Sauvignon Rancagua Tierra de Sol Reserva 1993: Aromas and flavors of iodine and varnish are all this lean, unhappy wine has to offer. Not recommended. Tasted twice, with consistent notes.–K.M. • $14 • (3/31/2000) • **67**

Cabernet Sauvignon Rancagua Tierra de Sol Reserva 1990 • $12 • (4/30/1995) • **81**

Cabernet Sauvignon Rapel Valley 1996: Showing cola and sundried tomato notes, this middling Cab provides a modicum of cherry flavor. Dilute finish.–K.M. • $8 • (3/31/2000) • **75**

Chardonnay Rapel Valley 1997: Earthy aromas, faint pear flavors and a dilute finish don't add up to much.–T.M. • $8 • (3/31/2000) • **74**

Merlot Rancagua 1996: Fresh raspberry and strawberry flavors and good balance make this light red inviting. Drink now. • $12 • (9/30/1998) • **84**

Merlot Rancagua 1994 • $7 • (6/30/1996) • **73**

Merlot Rancagua 1993 • $6 • (6/15/1995) • **79**

Merlot Rancagua 1992 • $6 • (1/31/1994) • **79**

Merlot Rapel Valley 1997: Has murky rhubarb and cooked strawberry aromas and a short, dry finish.–T.M. • $8 • (3/31/2000) • **75**

SANTA RITA

Cabernet Sauvignon Maipo Valley 120 1996: A firm-textured, medium-bodied red, with the smoky accents typical of Maipo backed up by light cherry and plum flavors. Drink now. • $8 • (9/15/1998) • **84**

Cabernet Sauvignon Maipo Valley 120 1990 • $6 • (5/31/1994) • **83**

Cabernet Sauvignon Maipo Valley 120 1989 • $7 • (2/15/1993) • **85**

Cabernet Sauvignon Maipo Valley 120 1988 • $6 • (5/31/1992) • **86**

Cabernet Sauvignon Maipo Valley 120 1987 • $11 • (6/15/1990) • **78**

Cabernet Sauvignon Maipo Valley Casa Real 1997: Dark, with a brooding nose that offers glimpses of cedar, coffee and smoke. The dense chocolate- and cassis-laden palate is harnessed by ripe, round tannins and snappy acidity. Winey and extracted, this should develop finesse with short-term cellaring. Best from 2001 through 2003.–K.M. • $40 • (3/31/2000) • **90**

Cabernet Sauvignon Maipo Valley Casa Real 1995: Rich and full-bodied, with plenty of cherry, leather, tobacco and plum flavors. Ripe, balanced and seductive, with fine tannins, an appealing herbal component and dark chocolate on the lingering finish. Drink now.–K.M. • $26 • (10/15/1998) • **89**

Cabernet Sauvignon Maipo Valley Casa Real 1994 • $25 • (6/30/1997) • **86**

Cabernet Sauvignon Maipo Valley Casa Real 1993 • $25 • (6/30/1996) • **88**

Cabernet Sauvignon Maipo Valley Casa Real 1989 • $NA • (6/15/1992) • **81**

Cabernet Sauvignon Maipo Valley Medalla Real 1994 • $13 • (6/30/1997) • **84**

Cabernet Sauvignon Maipo Valley Medalla Real 1993 • $13 • (6/30/1996) • **85**

Cabernet Sauvignon Maipo Valley Medalla Real 1992 • $12 • (4/30/1995) • **87**

Cabernet Sauvignon Maipo Valley Medalla Real 1990 • $11 • (4/15/1994) • **87**

Cabernet Sauvignon Maipo Valley Medalla Real 1989 • $12 • (2/15/1993) HR • **89**

Cabernet Sauvignon Maipo Valley Medalla Real 1988 • $11 • (5/15/1992) • **88**

Cabernet Sauvignon Maipo Valley Medalla Real 1987 • $12 • (6/15/1991) • **82**

Cabernet Sauvignon Maipo Valley Medalla Real Special Reserve 1997: A French-roastlike red, with toasty flavors and espressolike notes. Highly extracted, but could have more finesse. Minty notes on the finish. For fans of flamboyant oaky flavors. Drink now.–K.M. • $15 • (3/31/2000) • **86**

Cabernet Sauvignon Maipo Valley Medalla Real Special Reserve 1996: Focused intensity. This polished wine is powerful yet graceful, with ripe, firm tannins supporting expressive flavors of black cherry, blackberry and eucalyptus framed with toasty notes from new oak. Though accessible now, its balance and depth suggest it will bloom with time. Drink through 2008.–T.M. • $14 • (4/30/1999) • **89**

Cabernet Sauvignon Maipo Valley Medalla Real Special Reserve 1995: Pleasant and juicy, with ripe plum, berry and spice flavors. Smooth and easy to drink, with chocolaty notes on the finish. Drink now.–K.M. • $14 • (10/15/1998) • **85**

Cabernet Sauvignon Maipo Valley Reserva 1998: This medium-bodied red has a minty aroma that follows through to the palate, where it's joined by currant and red plum flavors. Drink now through 2002.–K.M. • $12 • (3/31/2000) • **83**

Cabernet Sauvignon Maipo Valley Reserva 1997: Delicate and lively. Light-bodied yet firm, this red offers pretty floral and berry character with an underpinning of sweet vanilla oak. It's graceful enough for an aperitif yet can stand up to food. Drink now through 2002.–T.M. • $12 • (4/30/1999) • **84**

Cabernet Sauvignon Maipo Valley Reserva 1996: A solid, straightforward Cabernet with lots of nice berry flavors and spice notes. Drink now.–K.M. • $12 • (10/15/1998) • **81**

Cabernet Sauvignon Maipo Valley Reserva 1994 • $10 • (4/30/1997) • **86**

Cabernet Sauvignon Maipo Valley Reserva 1993 • $10 • (6/30/1996) • **85**

Cabernet Sauvignon Maipo Valley Reserva 1992 • $9 • (4/30/1995) • **81**

Cabernet Sauvignon Maipo Valley Reserva 1990 • $9 • (4/15/1994) • **85**

Cabernet Sauvignon Maipo Valley Reserva 1989 • $10 • (4/30/1993) • **83**

Cabernet Sauvignon Maipo Valley Reserva 1988 • $9 • (6/15/1992) • **86**

Cabernet Sauvignon Maipo Valley Reserva 1987 • $12 • (9/15/1990) • **85**

Cabernet Sauvignon Rapel Valley 120 1998: A straightforward red, with good cherry and spice flavors. Herbal notes on the finish. Drink now.–K.M. • $8 • (3/31/2000) • **82**

Cabernet Sauvignon Rapel Valley 120 1997: Black cherry and tobacco flavors are clean and well defined in this supple red. It has just enough tannin to stand up to food, and the fruit lingers on the finish. Drink now through 2002.–T.M. • $8 • (4/30/1999) • **83**

Cabernet Sauvignon Rapel Valley 120 1995: A pleasant and satisfying Chilean Cabernet, with a sweet cherry-berry flavor profile. It's medium-bodied, with tasty spice notes chiming in on the finish. Reasonably priced and ready for drinking.–K.M. • $8 • (10/15/1998) • **85**

Cabernet Sauvignon Rapel Valley 120 1994 • $6 • (6/30/1996) • **79**

Cabernet Sauvignon Rapel Valley 120 1992 • $7 • (4/30/1995) • **85**

Carmenère Maipo Valley Reserva 1997: Cedar and shiso leaf aromas are overt in this medium-bodied red, showing lively black cherry and plum and finishing on a tobacco note. Needs hearty food, but a nice change of pace. Drink now.–K.M. • $12 • (3/31/2000) • **84**

Chardonnay Casablanca Valley Medalla Real 1997: Aromas of vanilla and banana give way to butter and melon flavors in this round, easy-drinking white. Lemony acidity keeps it lively. Best as an aperitif. Drink now.–T.M. • $14 • (9/15/1998) • **83**

Chardonnay Casablanca Valley Medalla Real Special Reserve 1997: Shows some of the tropical fruit character typical of Casablanca, but in an oaky, rather muted style, with vanilla, mango and lemon flavors. It's balanced, and the spicy fruit lingers on the finish. Drink now.–T.M. • $14 • (5/15/1999) • **85**

Chardonnay Lontué Valley 120 1997: Juicy and straightforward, with apple and citrus flavors and an appealing mineral note on the finish, this very good Chardonnay is a prime example of the quality-value tandem Chile is known for. Ready to drink. 42,000 cases imported.–K.M. • $8 • (9/30/1998) • **86**

Chardonnay Maipo Valley Reserva 1998: Pear and apple aromas and flavors pick up a hint of nutmeg in this white, with just enough acidity to keep it honest. Drink now.–K.M. • $12 • (3/31/2000) • **81**

Chardonnay Maipo Valley Reserva 1997: This big white shows good concentration, toasty and smoky oak flavors and ripe apple and pineapple character, with enough acidity for balance. Drink now.–T.M. • $12 • (9/15/1998) • **85**

Merlot Lontué Valley 120 1998: Smoke, herbal and plum aromas lead into a light-bodied, graceful Merlot that sports crushed raspberry followed by easy tannins on the finish. Drink now.–T.M. • $8 • (3/31/2000) • **83**

Merlot Lontué Valley 120 1997: Eucalyptus and tobacco flavors give this wine a distinctive personality but dominate the light cherry flavors. Firm tannins allow it to stand up to grilled meats. Drink through 2003–T.M. • $8 • (4/30/1999) • **84**

Merlot Lontué Valley 120 1996: Straightforward, with light, simple herb and raspberry flavors and a soft texture. Drink now. • $8 • (9/30/1998) • **79**

Merlot Maipo Valley 120 1990 • $7 • (4/30/1993) • **78**

Merlot Maipo Valley 120 1989 • $7 • (6/15/1991) • **80**

■ ■ ■ ■

SANTA RITA

Merlot Maipo Valley Reserva 1998: Decent plum flavors are quickly overwhelmed by an assertive bell pepper flavor. Drink now.–K.M. • $13 • (3/31/2000) • **81**

Merlot Maipo Valley Reserva 1997: Polished and smooth, this well-integrated red balances black cherry, blackberry, tobacco and light herbal flavors. It has harmony and finesse. Drink now through 2003.–T.M. • $12 • (4/30/1999) • **86**

Merlot Maipo Valley Reserva 1996: A full-bodied, serious style, with the overt smoky character typical of Maipo reds, backed up by ripe, concentrated fruit. Well balanced but idiosyncratic. Drink now through 2001. • $13 • (10/15/1998) • **84**

Merlot Maule Valley 120 1994 • $6 • (6/30/1996) • **79**

Merlot Maule Valley 120 1992 • $7 • (6/15/1995) • **82**

Merlot Rapel Valley 120 1991 • $6 • (5/31/1994) • **81**

Petite Sirah-Merlot Central Valley 1996: Decent plum, herb and tea, but this comes off a bit disjointed in the end.–K.M. • $10 • (10/15/1998) • **79**

Sauvignon Blanc Lontué Valley 120 1999: Light and fresh, this shows typical grapefruit character, but comes off a bit short and coarse in the end.–K.M. • $8 • (3/31/2000) • **79**

Sauvignon Blanc Lontué Valley 120 1998: Round yet crisp, showing good structural balance without offering much fruit character; light apple and herb notes fade quickly on the clean, short finish. Drink now.–T.M. • $8 • (5/15/1999) • **81**

Sauvignon Blanc Lontué Valley 120 1997 • $8 • (5/31/1998) • **84**

Sauvignon Blanc Maipo Valley 120 NV • $5 • (7/15/1987) • **77**

Sauvignon Blanc Maule Valley Reserva 1999: Shows some life, with vibrant lemon zest and grass aromas and flavors. Remains crisp, fresh, even a little racy on the finish. Drink now.–K.M. • $12 • (3/31/2000) • **84**

Sauvignon Blanc Maule Valley Reserva 1998: This light, crisp white offers a mix of light peach and herbal flavors that are modest but refreshing, with an enticing liveliness. A fine aperitif. Drink now.–T.M. • $11 • (5/15/1999) • **84**

Sauvignon Blanc Maule Valley Reserva 1997: Apple, herb and light earth flavors mingle in this clean, well-balanced white. It's fresh and straightforward. Drink now.–T.M. • $11 • (9/15/1998) • **80**

Sémillon Maipo Valley Late Harvest 1996: Balanced, with peach flavors and a touch of citrus. Finishes on a honeyed note. Drink now.–K.M. • $9/375 ml. • (10/15/1998) • **82**

SEGU OLLE, VINA

Cabernet Sauvignon Maule Valley Doña Consuelo 1997: Soft and smooth, with appealing dark plum and spicy flavors, some chocolate notes on the finish. Drink now.–K.M. • $7 • (10/15/1998) • **83**

Cabernet Sauvignon Maule Valley Doña Consuelo 1995 • $6 • (6/30/1997) • **81**

Cabernet Sauvignon Maule Valley Doña Consuelo 1994 • $6 • (6/30/1996) • **75**

Cabernet Sauvignon Maule Valley Doña Consuelo 1992 • $6 • (4/30/1995) • **77**

Cabernet Sauvignon Maule Valley Doña Consuelo Reserve 1996: Chocolaty, with stemmy and tea-like notes as well. Quite a mix of flavors; not for the faint of heart. Drink now.–K.M. • $10 • (10/15/1998) • **82**

Cabernet Sauvignon Maule Valley Doña Consuelo Reserve 1994 • $8 • (4/30/1997) • **86**

Cabernet Sauvignon Maule Valley Doña Consuelo Reserve 1993 • $8 • (6/15/1996) • **83**

Cabernet Sauvignon Maule Valley Doña Consuelo Reserve 1992 • $8 • (6/30/1996) • **84**

Cabernet Sauvignon Maule Valley Doña Consuelo Reserve 1991 • $14 • (6/30/1996) • **76**

Cabernet Sauvignon-Merlot Maule Valley 1996: A good everyday quaff that reminds us of Zinfandel, with its bright raspberry flavors, light tannins and forward personality. Drink now. • $8/1.5 liter • (9/15/1998) • **82**

Cabernet Sauvignon-Merlot Maule Valley 1995 • $7/1.5 liter • (6/30/1997) • **81**

Chardonnay Maule Valley Doña Consuelo 1997: Decent, with mineral and lime overtones and an herbal finish. A little rough around the edges. Drink now.–K.M. • $7 • (10/15/1998) • **80**

Chardonnay-Sauvignon Blanc Maule Valley 1997: Tastes tired and slightly bitter, with only modest citrus and apple flavors.–K.M. • $8/1.5 liter • (9/30/1998) • **73**

Merlot Maule Valley Doña Consuelo 1997: A fresh-tasting, thick-textured young Merlot, with firm tannins and satisfying black cherry and raspberry flavors. Drink now. • $7 • (10/15/1998) • **83**

Key: SS—Spectator Selection. CS—Cellar Selection. HR—Highly Recommended. $NA—Price not available. (BT)—Barrel tasting. Ⓐ—Auction Price. For a key to the tasters' initials, see "How to Use These Listings."
Dates in parentheses represent the issues in which the ratings were published.

Merlot Maule Valley Doña Consuelo 1995 • $6 • (5/31/1996) • **81**

Merlot Maule Valley Doña Consuelo 1994 • $6 • (6/15/1995) • **78**

SENA

Aconcagua Valley 1996: Impressive marriage of polish and grip. This firm red shows mouthfilling fruit, with notes of cassis, blackberry and plum, backed by vanilla and toasty oak notes, brightened by clean, fresh acidity and given a firm backbone of ripe, clean tannins. Accessible now, but will improve. Drink through 2010.–T.M. • $35 Ⓐ • (5/15/1999) • **92**

Aconcagua Valley 1995: This powerful red is ripe and tannic, with dark, thick flavors of coffee, black olive and prune. It's very thick now, but the finish shows better focus, suggesting the wine will be more harmonious with time. Tasted twice, with consistent notes. A blend of Cabernet Sauvignon, Merlot and Carmenère. From a new joint venture between California's Robert Mondavi and Chile's Errazuriz. Drink through 2005–T.M. • $43 Ⓐ • (9/15/1998) • **88**

SOUTH VALLEY

Cabernet Sauvignon Chile 1989 • $9 • (10/31/1997) • **81**

Cabernet Sauvignon Rancagua 1989 • $9 • (2/28/1994) • **83**

Cabernet Sauvignon Rancagua 1989 • $NA • (1/01/1995) • **81**

STONELAKE

Cabernet Sauvignon Lontué 1995 • $13 • (2/28/1998) • **86**

Cabernet Sauvignon Lontué 1994 • $12 • (2/28/1997) • **85**

Cabernet Sauvignon Lontué 1993 • $13 • (6/30/1996) • **85**

Merlot Lontué 1996: Spicy, cedary, seductive oak character accents the ripe fruit in this polished, attractive Merlot. A firm but smooth texture and a lingering finish make it memorable. Drink now. • $14 • (10/15/1998) • **87**

Merlot Lontué 1995 • $12 • (2/28/1997) • **87**

Merlot Lontué 1994 • $13 • (5/31/1996) • **84**

Pinot Noir Lontué La Primavera Vineyard 1996 • $14 • (2/28/1998) • **84**

Pinot Noir Lontué La Primavera Vineyard 1995 • $13 • (6/30/1997) • **85**

Pinot Noir Lontué La Primavera Vineyard 1994 • $14 • (6/30/1996) • **85**

STONY HOLLOW

Cabernet Sauvignon Rapel 1998: This light-bodied Cab verges on muddled, but there's enough prune and chocolate to keep it drinkable.–B.S. • $6 • (5/31/2000) • **79**

Cabernet Sauvignon Rapel 1997: Dried cherry and raisin flavors mark this ripe red, yet it retains a fresh profile, with firm tannins that turn slightly tough on the finish. Should soften nicely with grilled meats. Drink through 2002.–T.M. • $6 • (4/30/1999) • **82**

Cabernet Sauvignon Rapel 1996: Overripe, with sweet cherry and ripe plum flavors, cinnamon notes on the finish. Drink now.–K.M. • $7 • (10/15/1998) • **79**

Cabernet Sauvignon Rapel 1995 • $6 • (6/30/1997) • **78**

Cabernet Sauvignon San Fernando 1988 • $6 • (6/15/1992) • **84**

Chardonnay Aconcagua 1997: Herbal and sweet pea aromas and a tart texture. Not much fun.–K.M. • $7 • (9/30/1998) • **70**

Chardonnay Rapel 1998: Look at all this fruity white offers for so few dollars—a nice mix of lush, spicy flavors and crisp, light texture, with rich notes of toast, cinnamon, butter and apricot, a bit sweet, but with a nice core of lemony acidity to keep the balance. Drink now.–T.M. • $6 • (5/15/1999) • **86**

Chardonnay Rapel 1997: Refreshing and clean, with appealing apple, mineral and spice flavors. Has a nice touch of elegance, and would be a good stand-in for a simple village-level Chablis. The better of this Chilean winery's two '97 Chardonnays, and affordably priced. (The appellation appears only on the back label.) Drink now.–K.M. • $7 • (9/30/1998) • **84**

Merlot Aconcagua 1997: A firm style of Merlot, with cherry, berry and spice flavors and rhubarblike notes on the finish. Drink now.–K.M. • $7 • (9/15/1998) • **81**

Merlot Rapel 1998: This light red leans toward the herbal side of its varietal character, with notes of mint and berries. It has light tannins and a clean, slightly bitter finish. Drink now.–T.M. • $6 • (4/30/1999) • **82**

Merlot Rapel 1996 • $6 • (6/30/1997) • **79**

TARAPACA, VINA

Cabernet Sauvignon Maipo Valley 1997: Modest in all the right ways. Nicely polished, round on the palate, with subdued flavors of plum and cedar, this red is so harmonious it seems simple, except that it keeps bringing you back for another sip. Drink now through 2002.–T.M. • $7 • (4/30/1999) • **83**

Cabernet Sauvignon Maipo Valley Reserva 1997: Straightforward, with plum and spice flavors. Herbal notes on the finish. Drink now.–K.M. • $10 • (3/31/2000) • **80**
Cabernet Sauvignon Maipo Valley Reserva 1996: Graceful. This supple red offers clean, modest flavors of black cherry and tobacco, balanced and accessible. The fruit lingers on the refreshing finish. Drink now.–T.M. • $10 • (4/30/1999) • **83**
Cabernet Sauvignon Maipo Valley Reserva 1994: A firm-textured, well-preserved Cabernet, with complex aromas and tart cherry and currant flavors, spicy accents and a lingering finish. Drink now. • $10 • (9/15/1998) • **85**
Cabernet Sauvignon Maipo Valley Reserva 1993 • $10 • (5/31/1997) • **88**
Cabernet Sauvignon Valle Central 1996 • $7 • (11/30/1997) • **85**
Chardonnay Maipo Valley 1999: Shows a simple canned pear juice aroma and flavor, finishing on the sweet side. This was the best of three samples, with considerable bottle variation.–K.M. • $7 • (3/31/2000) • **79**
Chardonnay Maipo Valley 1998: Plenty of vanilla-scented oak gives this wine noticeable sweetness and a creamy texture, while apple and melon flavors keep it fresh and lively. Drink now.–T.M. • $7 • (4/30/1999) • **84**
Chardonnay Maipo Valley 1997 • $7 • (3/31/1998) • **82**
Chardonnay Maipo Valley Reserva 1997: A ripe style, with a creamy texture and pear and tropical fruit flavors. Spicy, minerally notes linger on the finish. Drink now.–K.M. • $10 • (9/30/1998) • **85**
Merlot Maipo Valley 1997: Herbal and tobacco notes mingle with the light cherry flavor in this balanced, straightforward red. It has firm tannins and a clean, short finish. Drink now.–T.M. • $7 • (4/30/1999) • **82**
Merlot Maipo Valley 1996: An acceptable, basic red. Has light plummy, smoky, earthy flavors and moderate tannins. Drink now. • $7 • (9/15/1998) • **79**
Merlot Maipo Valley 1995 • $7 • (5/31/1997) • **84**
Merlot Maipo Valley Reserva 1997: Polished and rich, (not to mention affordable) describe this Chilean red, its bright, deep flavors of plum, chocolate and mint giving concentration and length. It's well structured, with firm tannins and good balance. 25,000 cases imported. Drink now through 2003.–T.M. • $10 • (4/30/1999) • **87**
Sauvignon Blanc Maipo Valley 1999: Grassy notes give way to hints of citrus in this light-bodied, moderately crisp quaffer. Drink now.–K.M. • $7 • (3/31/2000) • **81**
Sauvignon Blanc Maipo Valley 1998: Clean and well structured, this firm white combines crisp acidity with a plump texture. The flavors are modest but round, with light notes of melon and vanilla. Drink now.–T.M. • $7 • (5/15/1999) • **83**
Sauvignon Blanc Maipo Valley La Isla Vineyard 1999: Lemon curd, herb and pear notes are evident in this Sauvignon that leans towards the round, soft side rather than the vibrant spectrum. Good, but no zip. Drink now.–K.M. • $12 • (3/31/2000) • **82**
Sauvignon Blanc Maipo Valley La Isla Vineyard 1998: This round, toasty white tastes more of oak than of fruit, showing light apple and honey flavors under smoke and vanilla notes. An ambitious wine, with distinctive personality but not much varietal character. Drink through 2001.–T.M. • $12 • (3/31/1999) • **82**
Sauvignon Blanc Valle Central 1997 • $7 • (5/31/1998) • **84**
Zavala Maipo Valley 1997: Ambitious, with lots of extracted dark plum and blackberry, but this full-bodied red is diminished in the end by an overtly smoky note and a slightly tough finish. Tasted twice, with consistent notes. Cabernet Sauvignon, Merlot and Syrah. Best after 2000.–K.M. • $25 • (3/31/2000) • **83**
Zavala Maipo Valley 1996: Elegant, if a bit lean, this Cab blend offers ripe black cherry and plum flavors with strong notes of cedar and eucalyptus. Has good intensity, with firm tannins and a clean, fruity finish. A bit disjointed now, but should come around. Cabernet Sauvignon, Merlot and Syrah. Drink through 2005.–T.M. • $25 • (5/15/1999) • **89**

TERRA ANDINA, VINA

Cabernet Sauvignon Valle Central 1997: Tea and brown-sugar flavors dominate this tired red, which finishes on a stemmy note.–K.M. • $8 • (3/31/2000) • **73**
Cabernet Sauvignon Valle Central 1995 • $7 • (6/30/1997) • **84**
Cabernet Sauvignon Valle del Cachapoal Alto Reserva 1997: A stewy aroma and pruny flavors are the calling cards of this red.–K.M. • $15 • (3/31/2000) • **77**
Cabernet-Merlot Central Valley 1998: Roasted red plum flavors dominate this fairly lean red. Drink now.–K.M. • $8 • (3/31/2000) • **80**
Chardonnay Valle Central 1998: Toasty vanilla aromas give way to a flinty-style Chardonnay, with crisp Granny Smith apple and lime notes and a medium-length, pear-tinged finish. Tasted twice, with consistent notes. Drink now.–K.M. • $8 • (3/31/2000) • **83**
Chardonnay Valle de Casablanca Alto Reserva 1998: Nice, round pear and baked apple flavors stay the course in this medium-bodied white that will appeal to fans of the oaky style. Drink now.–K.M. • $13 • (3/31/2000) • **83**
Merlot Valle Central 1997: Lean and herbal-tasting, with modest plum and berry flavors that turn dry on the finish.–K.M. • $9 • (3/31/2000) • **75**
Sémillon Valle Central 1998: Chive and green pepper aromas are odd. Shows the grape's usual weight and waxy texture but none of its fruit. Finishes neutral and dilute.–K.M. • $8 • (3/31/2000) • **77**

TERRA NOBLE, VINEDOS

Merlot San Clemente-Maule 1997: Appealing, almost sweet fruit flavors are wrapped in a thick texture of tannins in this rough-and-ready Merlot. Drying finish. • $7 • (10/15/1998) • **78**
Sauvignon Blanc San Clemente-Maule 1997: Assertive herbal and vegetal notes overwhelm the citrus-accented fruit. Shows some varietal character; might bloom with food.–T.M. • $6 • (9/15/1998) • **78**

TERRA NOVA

Cabernet Sauvignon Maipo Valley 1995: A firm and straightforward Cabernet, with red cherry and spice notes.–K.M. • $8 • (10/15/1998) • **79**
Cabernet Sauvignon Maipo Valley 1993 • $10 • (2/28/1997) • **76**
Chardonnay Maipo Valley 1997: This lush white offers vanilla and tropical fruit flavors that remain clean and harmonious as they linger on the finish. Drink now.–T.M. • $8 • (9/15/1998) • **84**
Merlot Maipo Valley 1996: Simple and stewy-tasting, with plum and rhubarb flavors.–K.M. • $8 • (10/15/1998) • **76**
Merlot Maipo Valley 1994 • $10 • (2/28/1997) • **80**
Sauvignon Blanc Maipo Valley 1997: Straightforward, with hints of apple and smoke. Fine as an aperitif or as a base for punches.–T.M. • $8 • (9/15/1998) • **78**

TERRA ROSA

Cabernet Sauvignon Valle Central 1998: Made in a ripe style, with currant and plum flavors, some herbal notes of bayleaf. Firm on the finish. Drink now.–K.M. • $10 • (3/31/2000) • **82**
Cabernet Sauvignon Valle Central 1997: Sappy and resinous tasting, with only modest cherry flavors. Finishes dry.–K.M. • $10 • (1/01/2000) • **75**
Cabernet Sauvignon Valle Central 1996: Vanilla and cedar nuances accent the black currant aromas and flavors, with tannins for support. This is bright and focused, and the flavors linger.–B.S. • $10 • (10/15/1998) • **84**
Cabernet Sauvignon Central Valley 1995 • $10 • (10/31/1997) • **80**

TOLVA, DOMAINE

Cabernet Sauvignon Maule Valley 1991 • $5 • (5/31/1994) • **82**
Cabernet Sauvignon Maule Valley 1989 • $5 • (12/15/1992) • **74**
Merlot Maule Valley 1992 • $5 • (5/31/1994) • **83**

TORREON DE PAREDES

Cabernet Sauvignon Rengo 1997: Ripe and jammy. Flavors of stewed cherries and dark chocolate are vivid but clumsy in this rustic red. Best with hearty foods. Drink now through 2002.–T.M. • $9 • (9/15/1999) • **81**
Cabernet Sauvignon Rengo Reserve 1991: Light and simple, with sweet cherry and rhubarb flavors. Maturing fast, though. Drink soon.–K.M. • $12 • (10/15/1998) • **76**
Chardonnay Rengo 1998: Simple and rather earthy, this lean white shows green apple and herb flavors. A rustic style.–T.M. • $8 • (10/31/1999) • **78**
Sauvignon Blanc Rengo 1997 • $10 • (5/31/1998) • **81**

TORRES, MIGUEL

Cabernet Sauvignon Curicó 1996: A satisfying, straightforward Cab, with plenty of currant and black cherry flavor, firm tannins and medium body. Drink now. • $9 • (9/15/1998) • **85**
Cabernet Sauvignon Curicó 1992 • $7 • (6/15/1995) • **78**
Cabernet Sauvignon Curicó 1991 • $7 • (5/31/1994) • **78**
Cabernet Sauvignon Curicó 1990 • $7 • (6/15/1992) • **85**
Cabernet Sauvignon Curicó 1989 • $7 • (6/15/1991) • **82**
Cabernet Sauvignon Curicó 1988 • $5 • (9/15/1990) • **87**
Cabernet Sauvignon Curicó District Manso de Velasco Reserva 1995 • $14 • (10/31/1997) • **88**

TORRES, MIGUEL

Cabernet Sauvignon Curicó District Manso de Velasco Reserva 1994 • $15 • (4/30/1997) • **84**
Cabernet Sauvignon Curicó Manso de Velasco Reserve 1993 • $16 • (10/31/1995) • **84**
Cabernet Sauvignon Curicó Manso de Velasco Reserve 1990 • $15 • (5/31/1995) • **84**
Cabernet Sauvignon Curicó Manso de Velasco Reserve 1989 • $15 • (6/15/1995) • **83**
Chardonnay Curicó District 1997: Pretty vanilla and toast flavors testify to a deft use of oak in this polished white, but the apple and herb flavors are a bit muted. Drink now.–T.M. • $9 • (9/15/1998) • **82**
Cordillera 1998: Nice smoky aromas and bright notes of cassis, plum and spicy black cherry are enveloped in a plush, caressing mouthfeel. Modern in approach, this polished wine shows a harmonious finish and should win many friends. Cariñena, Syrah and Merlot. Drink now through 2001.–K.M. • $22 • (3/31/2000) • **87**
Sauvignon Blanc Curicó District 1997 • $7 • (10/31/1997) • **83**

TRAVERSO, SERGIO

Cabernet Sauvignon Colchagua 1992 • $7 • (6/15/1995) • **76**
Cabernet Sauvignon Colchagua 1990 • $7 • (12/15/1992) • **79**
Cabernet Sauvignon Rapel Reserva 1994 • $7 • (2/28/1997) • **81**
Merlot Colchagua 1992 • $7 • (6/30/1996) • **77**
Merlot Colchagua 1990 • $7 • (12/15/1992) • **83**
Merlot Rapel Reserva 1994 • $8 • (4/30/1997) • **83**

UNDURRAGA

Bodega de Familia Maipo Valley 1996: This sturdy red is balanced and fresh. Plum and coffee flavors gain weight from the muscular structure and carry through to the clean finish, with notes of herbs and cedar. A good match for rich dishes accented with herbs. Drink now through 2005.–T.M. • $23 • (4/30/1999) • **87**
Cabernet Sauvignon Colchagua Valley 1996 • $7 • (3/31/1998) • **78**
Cabernet Sauvignon Colchagua Valley 1995 • $7 • (2/28/1997) • **84**
Cabernet Sauvignon Maipo Valley 1992 • $7 • (4/30/1995) • **84**
Cabernet Sauvignon Maipo Valley 1991 • $5 • (5/31/1994) • **77**
Cabernet Sauvignon Maipo Valley 1990 • $6 • (7/15/1993) • **79**
Cabernet Sauvignon Maipo Valley 1989 • $6 • (6/15/1992) • **74**
Cabernet Sauvignon Maipo Valley 1988 • $5 • (9/15/1990) • **83**
Cabernet Sauvignon Maipo Valley Reserva 1995: What's not to like? Very harmonious Cabernet. It's nicely balanced, well-rounded in texture, showing ample currant and cherry flavors and spicy oak accents. Drink now. • $12 • (9/15/1998) • **86**
Cabernet Sauvignon Maipo Valley Reserva 1994 • $9 • (2/28/1997) • **87**
Cabernet Sauvignon Maipo Valley Reserve Selection 1991 • $9 • (5/31/1995) • **88**
Cabernet Sauvignon Maipo Valley Reserve Selection 1989 • $8 • (5/31/1994) • **82**
Cabernet Sauvignon Maipo Valley Reserve Selection 1988 • $9 • (4/30/1993) • **81**
Chardonnay Colchagua Valley 1997: This lively mélange of apple, melon, toast and smoke flavors is more vibrant than harmonious, but crisp acidity keeps it refreshing and the flavors keep you coming back for more. Drink now.–T.M. • $8 • (9/15/1998) • **84**
Chardonnay Maipo Valley 1998: This firm white has good body and very crisp acidity, making it a solid accompaniment to food. Flavors are a bit austere, with citrus and light earthy notes. Drink now.–T.M. • $8 • (2/28/1999) • **82**
Merlot Colchagua Valley 1995 • $7 • (2/28/1997) • **82**
Merlot Maipo Valley 1993 • $7 • (1/01/1995) • **82**
Merlot Maipo Valley 1992 • $6 • (4/30/1993) • **76**
Pinot Noir Maipo Valley 1998: This light, soft red is no substitute for Burgundy, but it offers some attractive cherry and spicy flavors to go with its light herbal notes.–T.M. • $10 • (3/31/1999) • **79**
Pinot Noir Maipo Valley 1997: Fresh, straightforward and fruity, with good cherry and berry flavors. Drink now.–K.M. • $9 • (10/15/1998) • **82**
Pinot Noir Maipo Valley 1995 • $8 • (6/30/1997) • **83**
Pinot Noir Maipo Valley 1992 • $8 • (4/15/1995) • **78**

Key: SS—Spectator Selection. CS—Cellar Selection. HR—Highly Recommended. $NA—Price not available. (BT)—Barrel tasting. Ⓐ—Auction Price.
For a key to the tasters' initials, see "How to Use These Listings."
Dates in parentheses represent the issues in which the ratings were published.

Sauvignon Blanc Lontué Valley 1998: Tart and tangy. This light-bodied white offers grapefruit and herbal flavors, very crisp and clean but rather simple. A refreshing aperitif. Drink now.–T.M. • $7 • (4/30/1999) • **80**
Sauvignon Blanc Lontué Valley 1997 • $8 • (5/31/1998) • **85**

VASCOS, LOS

Cabernet Sauvignon Colchagua 1998: A good, medium-bodied red on the firm side. Bell pepper notes hold sway, with some plummy flavors that linger on the finish. Drink now.–K.M. • $10 • (3/31/2000) • **83**
Cabernet Sauvignon Colchagua 1996: Aromas of toast and coffee give way to a firmly textured wine with dark coffee, prune and mineral flavors. It's balanced but austere, though it might open with food. Drink now through 2002.–T.M. • $8 • (12/15/1998) • **84**
Cabernet Sauvignon Colchagua 1995 • $7 • (6/30/1997) • **80**
Cabernet Sauvignon Colchagua 1993 • $7 • (4/30/1995) • **85**
Cabernet Sauvignon Colchagua 1992 • $7 • (5/31/1994) • **83**
Cabernet Sauvignon Colchagua 1991 • $9 • (4/15/1994) • **82**
Cabernet Sauvignon Colchagua 1990 • $7 • (5/31/1992) • **88**
Cabernet Sauvignon Colchagua 1989 • $7 • (6/15/1992) • **83**
Cabernet Sauvignon Colchagua 1988 • $7 • (6/15/1991) • **82**
Cabernet Sauvignon Colchagua Reserve 1997: A solid, fruity Cabernet with nice flavors of plum and berry and some sweetly spicy notes on the finish. Drink now.–K.M. • $15 • (3/31/2000) • **85**
Cabernet Sauvignon Colchagua Reserve 1995: Solid, with berry and plum flavors and a good backbone. Herbal notes linger appealingly on the finish. Drink now.–K.M. • $13 • (10/15/1998) • **83**
Cabernet Sauvignon Colchagua Reserve 1994 • $12 • (6/30/1997) • **82**
Cabernet Sauvignon Colchagua Reserve 1993 • $10 • (2/28/1997) • **83**
Cabernet Sauvignon Colchagua Reserve 1992 • $12 • (4/30/1995) • **84**
Cabernet Sauvignon Colchagua Reserve 1991 • $12 • (5/31/1994) • **83**
Cabernet Sauvignon Colchagua Reserve 1990 • $12 • (5/31/1994) • **81**
Cabernet Sauvignon Colchagua Reserve 1989 • $11 • (6/15/1992) • **84**
Le Dix Colchagua 1997: Soft and medium-bodied, with plum and chocolate flavors. Good tobacco and cedar notes on the finish. Tasted twice, with consistent notes. Debut release, being co-released with the '96 vintage. Drink now.–K.M. • $40 • (3/31/2000) • **84**
Le Dix Colchagua 1996: Medium-bodied, with pleasant plum, cedar and dark cherry flavors and some tobacco notes. Smooth, clean finish. Debut release, being co-released with the '97 vintage. Tasted twice, with consistent notes. Drink now.–T.M. • $40 • (3/31/2000) • **83**

VERAMONTE

Cabernet Sauvignon Alto de Casablanca 1998: High-toned, with red currant and olive flavors and nice mineral and dust elements. Herbal notes linger on the finish. Drink now with food.–K.M. • $10 • (3/31/2000) • **83**
Cabernet Sauvignon Alto de Casablanca 1997: Dark in color, lush in texture and with lots of toasty, chocolate-scented oak, this polished Cabernet from Chile offers a lot for these few dollars. Light fruit flavors show hints of plum and black cherry that linger on the finish. Drink now through 2002.–T.M. • $10 • (12/15/1998) • **85**
Cabernet Sauvignon Curicó Valley 1995 • $10 • (2/28/1997) • **86**
Cabernet Sauvignon Valle Central 1996: Quite delicious, with balanced flavors of plum, herb, currant and cherry. Solid and balanced, with some nice spice notes. A good dinner wine. Drink now.–K.M. • $10 • (10/15/1998) • **84**
Chardonnay Alto de Casablanca 1998: Nice floral and apple notes run through this light-bodied yet clean and varietally correct Chardonnay. A decent aperitif. Drink now.–T.M. • $10 • (3/31/2000) • **83**
Chardonnay Alto de Casablanca 1997: Tropical aromas and flavors are lush and lively in this vivid white, though the very toasty oak tends to dominate the palate. Bold and expressive, it's made in a California style. Drink now.–T.M. • $10 • (12/15/1998) • **84**
Chardonnay Casablanca Valley 1997: An oaky, fat style that goes for obvious spicy and buttery flavors, but could use more fruit and acidity to back it up. Drink now. • $10 • (9/15/1998) • **78**
Merlot Alto de Casablanca 1998: Overt dill and pickle juice aromas give way to a very herbal-tasting Merlot that has only hints of the grape's fruitier side. Finishes tart. Tasted twice, with consistent notes.–K.M. • $10 • (3/31/2000) • **77**
Merlot Alto de Casablanca 1997: Herbal and vegetal notes dominate this firm red, with cherry and toast more as accents than main themes. Broad and a bit flat in texture. Drink now through 2001.–T.M. • $10 • (3/31/1999) • **81**
Merlot Casablanca Valley Primus 1996: A showy, voluptuous Merlot, from the effusive oak aromas of cedar and vanilla to the concentrated cherry and

mint flavors to the lingering finish. A deep color and firm but lush texture add to its appeal. Drink now through 2001. • $15 • (9/30/1998) • **88**

Merlot Casablanca Valley Primus 1995 • $15 • (6/30/1997) • **85**

Merlot Valle Central 1996: Very ripe, with prune, leather and herb notes. Airy and lively, with a lingering, smoky finish. Tasted twice, with consistent notes. Drink now.–B.S. • $10 • (10/15/1998) • **82**

Primus Alto de Casablanca 1997: Overt bell pepper and malted milk aromas clash with a tart, cranberry note in this unharmonious red. Tasted twice, with consistent notes. 100 percent Carmenère.–T.M. • $15 • (3/31/2000) • **75**

Sauvignon Blanc Alto de Casablanca 1998: Lush yet lively. Vibrant flavors of grapefruit, papaya and herbs give this white a racy character, yet it's soft on the palate. A nice aperitif. Drink now.–T.M. • $10 • (3/31/2000) • **84**

VILLA RICA

Cabernet Sauvignon Colchagua Valley La Nobleza 1994 • $10 • (2/28/1997) • **78**

VILLARD

Cabernet Sauvignon Colchagua 1994: Going over the hill, with cedary, spicy aromas, a smooth, soft texture and stewed fruit flavors backed by slightly drying tannins. • $10 • (9/15/1998) • **77**

Cabernet Sauvignon Rancagua 1992 • $8 • (4/30/1995) • **81**

Cabernet Sauvignon Rancagua 1991 • $8 • (5/31/1994) • **76**

Merlot Cachapoal 1992 • $8 • (6/15/1995) • **87**

VINTERRA

Cabernet Sauvignon Maipo-Napa Valleys NV • $7 • (2/15/1990) • **86**

Chardonnay Maipo-Napa Valleys NV • $7 • (3/31/1990) • **84**

VISTAMAR

Cabernet Sauvignon Central Valley Vistasur 1997: A good, meaty-tasting Cabernet with ripe plum, spice and cherry flavors, and an appealing herbal edge on the finish. Smooth and supple. Drink now.–K.M. • $10 • (10/15/1998) • **84**

Cabernet Sauvignon Maipo Valley Niebla 1997: A firm and flavorful Cabernet with plum and cherry flavors, a good dose of tannin on the finish. Medium-bodied, with some herbal notes. Drink now.–K.M. • $14 • (10/15/1998) • **83**

Chardonnay Casablanca Valley Niebla 1997: A straightforward, entry-level Chardonnay, with decent spice and apple flavors. Drink now.–K.M. • $14 • (9/30/1998) • **81**

Chardonnay Central Valley Vistasur 1997: A bit rough around the edges, but still enjoyable, with lime, green apple and mineral flavors. Give it some time in the glass to develop. Drink now.–K.M. • $10 • (9/30/1998) • **84**

Merlot Maipo Valley Niebla 1997: A forward style, with juicy and jammy flavors and an herbal note as well. Drink now.–K.M. • $14 • (10/15/1998) • **82**

Merlot Valle Central Vistasur 1997: Crisp and stylish, with well-defined cherry and berry flavors and a touch of cinnamon. Drink now.–K.M. • $10 • (10/15/1998) • **84**

Sauvignon Blanc Casablanca Valley Niebla 1997: A thickish Sauvignon, with powerful grassy and herbal flavors and some onion notes.–K.M. • $14 • (9/30/1998) • **77**

Sauvignon Blanc Valle Central Vistasur 1997: Crisp and clean, this light-bodied white offers straightforward herb, citrus and light smoke flavors. It's fresh and refreshing, if a bit light for food. Drink now.–T.M. • $10 • (9/15/1998) • **83**

VIU MANENT

Cabernet Sauvignon Colchagua Valley 1997: Silky red, with a core of sweet cherry and accents of mint, licorice and dark chocolate, crisp and juicy with firm tannins. Balanced and well defined. Drink now through 2003.–T.M. • $8 • (9/15/1999) • **85**

Cabernet Sauvignon Colchagua Valley 1996: A pure, intense, exotic flavor of black currants makes this unoaky style of Cabernet compelling. It's smooth in texture, delicious to drink now and has a lingering finish. • $8 • (9/15/1998) • **88**

Cabernet Sauvignon Colchagua Valley Proprietor's Reserve 1992 • $9 • (5/31/1997) • **87**

Cabernet Sauvignon Colchagua Valley Proprietor's Reserve 1991 • $6 • (10/31/1995) • **85**

Cabernet Sauvignon Colchagua Valley Reserve 1997: This intense, elegant red shows an alluring combination of toasty oak and ripe fruit, with expressive and harmonious flavors of plums, licorice, chocolate and mint. It's firm, balanced and long. Drink now through 2005.–T.M. • $12 • (9/15/1999) HR • **89**

Cabernet Sauvignon Colchagua Valley Reserve 1996: This rich, highly extracted red shows very ripe flavors of plum and prune braced by lavish oak, adding notes of chocolate and coffee. Crisp acidity keeps it in balance, but it will appeal most to fans of the blockbuster style. Drink now through 2002.–T.M. • $9 • (10/31/1999) • **84**

Cabernet Sauvignon Colchagua Valley Reserve 1995: Smooth and soft, with sweet cherry, spice and ripe plum flavors. Not much backbone, but still enjoyable. Drink now.–K.M. • $12 • (10/15/1998) • **81**

Cabernet Sauvignon Colchagua Valley Reserve 1993 • $8 • (5/31/1997) • **86**

Cabernet Sauvignon Colchagua Valley San Carlos 1997: Starts off with some bright currant and berry flavors, but they fade quickly on the finish.–K.M. • $9 • (3/31/2000) • **78**

Cabernet Sauvignon Colchagua Valley San Carlos Oak Aged Reserva 1996: An oddball red, with stemmy aromas and flavors of kirsch and beets.–K.M. • $12 • (3/31/2000) • **74**

Chardonnay Colchagua Valley 1998: Straightforward and simple, this white is rather neutral in character, except for a dull earthy note.–T.M. • $8 • (10/31/1999) • **77**

Chardonnay Colchagua Valley 1997: Assertive oaky notes dominate this thick-textured white. Apple and herb notes are present as well. Drink now.–T.M. • $8 • (9/15/1998) • **80**

Chardonnay Colchagua Valley Reserve 1997: Soft and blowsy. This fleshy white offers cooked apple and toast flavors, without much vibrancy or definition. Gentle and a bit sweet, but already fading.–T.M. • $12 • (10/31/1999) • **79**

Chardonnay Colchagua Valley San Carlos 1997: Honeyed (oxidized?) on the nose, offering overt toast and vanilla flavors that are dull and tiring.–T.M. • $9 • (3/31/2000) • **78**

Chardonnay Colchagua Valley San Carlos Oak Aged Reserva 1997: Creamy and round-textured, with toast, cinnamon, pear and hazelnut flavors. Well-integrated oak lends weight to the lengthy finish. Tasted twice, with consistent notes. Drink now.–K.M. • $11 • (3/31/2000) • **85**

Fumé Blanc Colchagua Valley Reserve 1997: A rough-hewn but flavorful wine, medium-bodied, with plenty of buttery and spicy flavor. Drink now.–K.M. • $10 • (9/30/1998) • **81**

Malbec Colchagua Valley 1998: Beautifully displayed black cherry, cassis and mint mark this firmly structured, densely flavored red. Vibrant and balanced, with a lingering finish. Drink now through 2001.–B.S. • $8 • (9/15/1999) • **87**

Malbec Colchagua Valley 1997: In the mood for a drink-me-now red value? Chile has that, too. This one's fresh and delicious, young and vibrant, packed with ripe cherry and blackberry flavors that linger on the finish. Firmly tannic and well balanced. Enjoy now. • $8 • (9/30/1998) • **86**

Malbec Colchagua Valley 1995 • $8 • (6/30/1997) • **85**

Malbec Colchagua Valley Reserve 1998: This firm, bright red delivers ripe plum flavors that gain interest from the gamy notes typical of the variety. Shows good structure and balance in a clean, fruity style. Drink now through 2003.–T.M. • $12 • (10/31/1999) • **85**

Malbec Colchagua Valley Reserve 1997: Slick and polished, this thick-textured Malbec offers plum and licorice notes, bright acidity and a solid framework of tannins. Fine depth and length. Drink now through 2001.–B.S. • $10 • (9/15/1999) • **87**

Malbec Colchagua Valley Reserve 1996: This effusive, elegant wine has a lovely mint aroma and plum, currant and sweet cherry flavors. Finishes with chocolaty notes. Tasted twice, with consistent notes. Drink now.–K.M. • $12 • (10/15/1998) • **88**

Malbec Colchagua Valley San Carlos 1997: A decent mix of berry, cherry and plum flavors, finishing on a slightly spicy note. A good wine for pizza. Drink now.–K.M. • $9 • (3/31/2000) • **83**

Malbec Colchagua Valley San Carlos Oak Aged Reserva 1997: Lively, with good flavors of blackberry and dark cherry and a fair amount of stuffing. Short finish. Drink now.–K.M. • $12 • (3/31/2000) • **83**

Merlot Colchagua Valley 1998: Lovely fresh cherry aromas and flavors along with concentration and a soft yet supportive framework add up to an appealing red. Drink now.–B.S. • $8 • (9/15/1999) • **85**

Merlot Colchagua Valley 1997: Robust and flavorful, this has a fresh blast of ripe cherry and berry flavor and a firm, tannic texture. Not complex, but solid. Drink now. • $8 • (10/15/1998) • **84**

Merlot Colchagua Valley Reserve 1998: Deep-colored and exotically scented courtesy of some oak treatment, this red offers black cherry, spice and chocolate flavors, good intensity and fine tannins to back it all up. Good length, too. Drink now.–B.S. • $12 • (9/15/1999) • **87**

Merlot Colchagua Valley San Carlos 1997: A good straightforward Merlot, with plum and bell pepper flavors and coffee notes on the finish. Smooth. Drink now.–K.M. • $9 • (3/31/2000) • **83**

VIU MANENT

Sauvignon Blanc Colchagua Valley 1998: This very crisp white leans toward the herbal, cat's-pee side of the varietal, with underlying apple flavors and a hint of spritz on the palate. An assertive wine that needs food for balance. Drink now.–T.M. • $8 • (10/31/1999) • **82**

Sauvignon Blanc Colchagua Valley 1997: Crisp and clean, this round white shows apple, herb and mint flavors that refresh the palate, yet can stand up to food. Drink now.–T.M. • $8 • (9/15/1998) • **84**

Sauvignon Blanc Colchagua Valley Reserve 1998: Quite rich for a Chilean Sauvignon Blanc, this is balanced and shows restrained flavors of pear, apple and herb. The clean, juicy finish brings you back for another sip. Drink now.–T.M. • $11 • (10/31/1999) • **85**

Sémillon Colchagua Valley 1998: An intriguing herbal gooseberry note gets washed out on the palate in this medium-bodied white. Dilute finish.–B.S. • $8 • (1/01/1999) • **79**

WALNUT CREST

Cabernet Sauvignon Rapel Valley 1999: Shows the bell pepper and tobacco leaf side of Cabernet, but still has enough fresh black cherry to keep it interesting. Drink now.–B.S. • $6 • (5/31/2000) • **82**

Cabernet Sauvignon Rapel Valley 1997: This soft-textured Cabernet from Chile has plenty of up-front appeal, with rich, dense, forward flavors of black currant and plum, and a price tag that makes it a good choice when the occasion calls for multiple bottles. Drink now.–B.S. • $6 • (10/15/1998) • **84**

Cabernet Sauvignon Rapel Valley 1995 • $6 • (6/30/1997) • **84**

Cabernet Sauvignon Rapel Valley Estate Selection 1996: Lean and firm, with dried plum and cherry flavors.–K.M. • $9 • (10/15/1998) • **77**

Cabernet Sauvignon Rapel Valley Estate Selection 1995: Hearty red wine, but a bit rough in texture and rangy in flavor. Has firm tannins and herbal, plummy flavors that are already maturing. Drink now. • $10 • (9/15/1998) • **82**

Chardonnay Rapel Valley 1997: This goes for a rich style, from the buttery aromas to the earthy flavors and smooth texture. A good attempt. A good value. Drink now. • $6 • (9/15/1998) • **82**

Merlot Maipo Valley Estate Selection 1996: A rugged style that features firm tannins, full body and rather raw fruit and herb flavors. Drink now. • $10 • (9/30/1998) • **77**

Merlot Rapel Valley 1999: This quaffable Merlot sports bell pepper, plum and tobacco notes. Finishes on a slightly charry note. Drink now.–B.S. • $6 • (5/31/2000) • **82**

Merlot Rapel Valley 1997: A fresh, very fruity Merlot, with lots of cherry and raspberry character, light tannins and a smooth texture. Drink now. • $7 • (9/15/1998) • **84**

Merlot Rapel Valley 1996 • $7 • (5/31/1997) • **87**

Merlot Rapel Valley 1993 • $5 • (5/15/1995) • **86**

Merlot Rapel Valley 1992 • $5 • (5/31/1994) • **79**

Merlot Rapel Valley 1990 • $5 • (4/30/1993) • **84**

Merlot Rapel Valley 1989 • $5 • (5/15/1992) • **83**

Key: SS—Spectator Selection. CS—Cellar Selection. HR—Highly Recommended. $NA—Price not available. (BT)—Barrel tasting. (A)—Auction Price.
For a key to the tasters' initials, see "How to Use These Listings."
Dates in parentheses represent the issues in which the ratings were published.

France

Although France is not the world's largest wine producer, it makes more great wine than any other country, and remains the standard by which all others are judged. Bordeaux, Burgundy, the Rhône and Champagne all testify to the historic reputation of French wine. Yet, France is not merely about tradition. With California, it is at the cutting edge of enology (the science of winemaking), and shows no slackening in its commitment to remain the world standard.

At the same time, France has seen a serious erosion in its position as a supplier of wine to the masses. Many countries have shown the ability to produce inexpensive Cabernet Sauvignon, Merlot, Chardonnay and other consumer mainstays that are as good as, if not better than, their French equivalents at the same price. The French have taken up the challenge as a matter of national pride, which should lead to more and better French wines at affordable prices in the coming years. Overall, the future holds many delights for lovers of French wine.

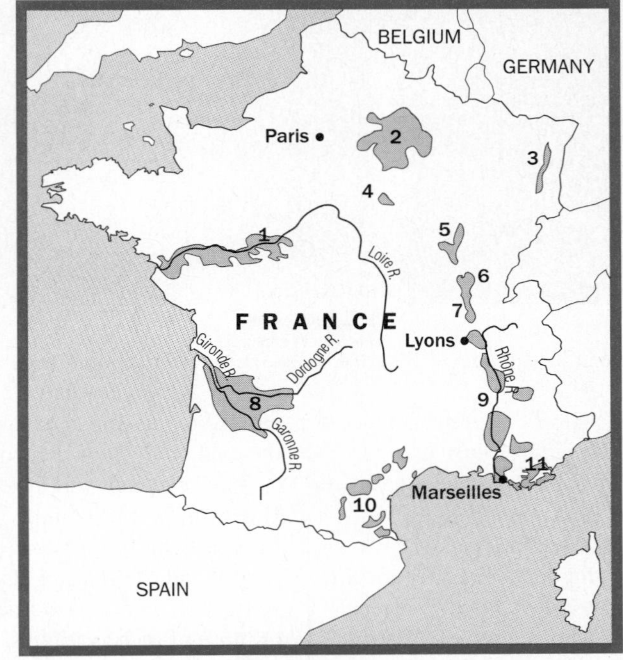

1. Loire
2. Champagne
3. Alsace
4. Chablis
5. Côte d'Or
6. Mâcon
7. Beaujolais
8. Bordeaux
9. Rhône
10. Languedoc-Roussillion (d'Oc)
11. Provence

THE FRENCH APPELLATION SYSTEM

Established in the 1930s, the *Appellation (d'Origine) Controllée* laws (AC) are key to understanding French wines. Widely misperceived as a guarantee of quality, the AC laws are in fact a guarantee of authenticity. In other words, they ensure that the wine in the bottle actually comes from the place stated on its label, and adheres to a set of winemaking regulations (regarding permissible grape types, vine training and pruning methods, and minimum alcoholic strength) for that place. This system embodies the core philosophy of French winemaking: that soils are unique and that the character and quality of wine flows from the precise interplay of soil, climate and grape varieties, an idea known as *"terroir."* In its purest form, the winemaker's sole duty is to guide the confluence of these elements into the bottle, exerting his own influence only to enhance the expression of what nature has provided.

There are roughly 275 recognized AC wine types, ranging from large regional appellations, such as "Bordeaux AC," which covers tens of thousands of acres, to mini-appellations, such as "Château Grillet" or "Romanée-Conti," which cover a single vineyard. Most ACs fall somewhere in the middle. Generally, the more specific the AC, the better the quality of the soil and the wine that derives from it. Thus, to take Bordeaux as an example, at the top of the AC hierarchy are the specific communes, such as Pauillac, St.-Julien, Margaux and Pomerol. At the base of the AC pyramid are the basic Bordeaux wines, which can come from anywhere in the region. In between are intermediate levels such as Médoc and Haut-Médoc. As one moves up the pyramid, specifications as to yields per acre, alcohol content, and other factors grow increasingly tighter. Other important regions—including Burgundy, the Rhône, and the Loire—have similar gradations of specificity and quality within their respective appellations.

Since regions with lower rankings can petition the government for admission to full AC status if the quality of their wines improves, the AC system spurs sub-par regions to invest in better winemaking facilities and to improve viticultural practices. An intermediate category called VDQS *(vins delimités de qualité supérieure)* was initiated in 1949 to recognize regions of special merit that had not quite achieved the quality and consistency expected of a wine in the AC category. The VDQS category has now largely disappeared as many of its original members, such as Corbières, Minervois, Cahors, Côtes de Provence, and Côtes du Ventoux, have been elevated to full AC status.

Fred Seidman

Champagne barrels with bellows system at Dom Perignon.

Today much innovation is taking place in a category created in 1973 called *vin de pays* (VDP). Over a hundred defined areas have the right to use this term on their labels, of which the best known include Vin de Pays d'Oc, Vin de Pays de l'Hérault, Vin de Pays de l'Aude, Vin de Pays du Jardin de la France, and Vin de Pays des Côtes du Gascogne. More than 75 percent of the VDPs are from the vast Midi region on France's Mediterranean coast, which in the past had been devoted almost solely to bulk wine production.

Although VDP wines are associated with geographic place names, regional character has become secondary. Instead, the VDPs are now the major source of France's budget-priced varietal wines; the name of the grape, e.g., Chardonnay, Sauvignon Blanc, Cabernet or Merlot is the main feature on the label. (French law requires that varietally labeled wines must contain 100% of the named grape, whereas in California, for example, up to 25% of "other" varieties may be blended in without any indication on the label.) The VDPs have attracted much foreign and domestic investment, with firms such as Robert Mondavi, Baron de Rothschild (Mouton), Louis Latour, Fortant de France and Beringer turning out sound, commercial wines at competitive prices. These offerings allow consumers to enjoy good French wines without the need to master the often complex *appellation controllée* system.

FRENCH WINE REGIONS

Bordeaux

Bordeaux accounts for 20 to 25 percent of all AC production, the most of any region. Indeed, at more than sixty million cases, Bordeaux's annual production also accounts for about 10 percent of all French wine production, a considerable percentage given the overall high quality and international reputation that Bordeaux has achieved. Almost 250,000 acres of vineyards are entitled to the Bordeaux appellation, and 80 percent of the total production is devoted to red wines.

The key grape of Bordeaux is Cabernet Sauvignon. However, Merlot is more widely planted, and accounts for nearly half of all acreage. Cabernet Franc, Petit Verdot and Malbec are also important red grapes in Bordeaux, and most Bordeaux wines are blends of two or more of these varieties.

The most widely planted white grape variety is Sémillon, followed closely by Sauvignon Blanc. Muscadelle, Colombard and Ugni Blanc account for most of the remaining white production. Like the reds, most white Bordeaux is a blend of two or more varieties.

The Médoc is historically the most important Bordeaux appellation. Cabernet Sauvignon is dominant here, accounting for the sturdy structure and long aging potential of classic Médoc clarets. Four major communes of the Médoc have achieved worldwide reputations. These are Margaux, St.-Julien, Pauillac and St.-Estephe. Each has its own distinctive style. Margaux is known for its delicate bouquet and aristocratic svelteness; St.-Julien may be the best balanced, combining Margaux finesse with the classic characteristics of its neighbor Pauillac, known for its masculine cedar and cigar box aromas and powerful structure. St.-Estephe, with the heaviest soil, produces the sturdiest claret.

In 1855, the top 60 or so châteaux of the Médoc were classified into five levels, from first to fifth growth. The first growths, called the *premiers crus,* are perhaps the most famous wine names in the world: Lafite-Rothschild, Margaux, Latour, Mouton-Rothschild (originally a second growth, but promoted in 1973) and Haut-Brion. (The last is actually in the Graves region, but was too prominent to be ignored.) In recent years the quality of several lower classified growths has improved to the point where they now challenge the first growths. These so-called super-seconds include Leoville Las-Cases, Pichon-Longueville-Lalande, Ducru-Beaucaillou, Cos d'Estournal, Palmer (actually a third growth), Montrose and La Mission Haut-Brion (a first growth in Graves). Just below the classified growths are the many excellent *crus bourgeois,* several of which (Château Gloria, and Château Chasse-Spleen, for instance) would almost certainly be ranked with the classified growths in the unlikely event of a reclassification.

Because it is close to the port of Bordeaux, the Médoc dominated the Bordeaux wine trade for centuries. However, St.-Emilion and Pomerol, on the so-called right bank of the Dordogne River, have achieved their rightful places alongside the great wines of the Médoc. Pomerol is dominated by Merlot. Its most famous estate, Château Petrus, now sells its wines for more than any Médoc *premier cru.* Pomerol estates tend to be tiny, and demand for their best wines vastly outstrips supply. Other top Pomerol properties include Trotanoy, L'Evangile, La Conseillante, Lafleur, Vieux-Château-Certan, Certan de May, Clinet, Latour-à-Pomerol, Gazin and the microscopic Le Pin.

St.-Emilion is a larger region than Pomerol, and the quality of its estates is more variable. While Merlot is still the most important grape, it is often blended with significant quantities of Cabernet Franc and, less often, Cabernet Sauvignon. Unlike Pomerol, which has never had a classification, St.-Emilion was first classified in 1954, and had subsequent reclassifications in 1985 and 1995. Its two top wines, Cheval-Blanc and Ausone, are considered on a par with the Médoc first growths. Just below them are a dozen or so other fine estates that would rank with the better second and third growths of the Médoc. These include Figeac, Canon, Pavie, Magdelaine, Angélus and Clos Fourtet.

The Graves region, which surrounds the town of Pessac, a suburb of the city of Bordeaux, is unusual in that its reputation rests equally on the quality of its reds and whites. Many top estates, such as Haut-Brion, La Mission-Haut-Brion, Domaine de Chevalier, Fieuzal and Olivier produce exquisite whites from a blend of Sémillon and Sauvignon Blanc. Reds here rely more heavily on Merlot than do the wines of the Médoc, located just to the north of Graves. As a result, a red Graves tends to mature more quickly than a typical Médoc, though it shares the Médoc's robust structure.

Just south of the Graves, the regions of Sauternes and Barsac produce one of the world's great sweet dessert wines, mostly from Sémillon, but with some Sauvignon Blanc used at certain estates. Like the great German late harvest wines, the key to great Sauternes is the development of noble rot *(botrytis cinerea),* which gradually draws water out of the grape, shriveling it and greatly concentrating the flavors of the grape. Among the wines of Sauternes, Château d'Yquem has no equal. However, great Sauternes are also made at Château Rieussec, Climens, Guiraud, Rayne-Vigneau, Suduiraut and others.

Burgundy

The heart of Burgundy is the Côte d'Or, which at 20,000 acres, is less than a tenth the size of Bordeaux. The northern half of the Côte d'Or, the Côte de Nuits, specializes in red Burgundy, which is almost always exclusively from the Pinot Noir grape. The southern half of the Côte d'Or, the Côte de Beaune, produces both red Burgundy and white Burgundy, which is almost always made from Chardonnay, though other grape varieties, such as Pinot Blanc, are permitted. The extraordinary quality of great Burgundy, combined with its relatively small output, makes it highly sought-after by collectors of great wine.

The appellation system of Burgundy is not as complicated as it may seem at first. At the top of the Burgundy hierarchy are the *grand cru* vineyards. The best known of these include Le Chambertin, Le Musigny, Romanée-Conti, Richebourg, La Tâche and Clos de Vougeot for red wines; Le Montrachet, Chevalier-Montrachet, Bâtard-Montrachet and Corton-Charlemagne for white wines. Classified below the *grands crus* are the *premier crus.* Though more numerous than the *grands crus,* and usually less expensive, several *premiers crus* produce wines that are virtually on par with *grands crus.* Some of the best-known *premier crus* in the Côte de Nuits include Gevrey-Chambertin le Cazetiers, Chambolle-Musigny

Les Amoureuses, Chambolle-Musigny Les Charmes and Vosne-Romanée Les Suchots. In the Côte de Beaune, *premiers crus* include Beaune Clos des Mouches, (white and red), Beaune Les Greves (red), Pommard Les Epenots (red), Volnay Clos des Ducs (red), Meursault Charmes (white), Puligny-Montrachet Les Combettes (white) and Puligny-Montrachet Les Pucelles (white).

Many *grands crus* have had their names appended to the nearby villages. Thus, the villages of Gevrey-Chambertin, Chambolle-Musigny, Vosne-Romanee, Puligny-Montrachet and Aloxe-Corton all produce wines under their names. While often quite good, these "village" wines rarely have the depth and dimension of the *grands crus* or the *premiers crus,* which come from the most favored sites.

Another point that should be emphasized is that most great Burgundy vineyards have multiple owners (Clos de Vougeot, for example, has nearly 80), and the range in quality between the best and the worst producers is enormous. The best way for consumers to assure themselves of a quality product is to consult a reliable wine publication (such as *Wine Spectator*) for ratings of individual producers' wines.

An important emerging region of Burgundy is the Côte Chalonnaise, which is developing a reputation for reasonably priced reds and whites that come close in style and quality to the wines of the Côte d'Or. The four major appellations of the Chalonnaise are Mercurey, Givry, Rully and Montagny. The first two are noted for their red wines, most of which are made exclusively from the Pinot Noir grape. Both are more similar to the soft, fruity style of the Côte de Beaune than to the denser, earthier reds of the Côte de Nuits. While Mercurey is larger and better known than Givry, the latter boasts several exceptionally fine vineyards—Cellier-aux-Moines and Domaine Thénard among them—which gives it the stronger following among connoisseurs.

While Rully also makes good reds, both it and Montagny are better known for their whites, which are made from Chardonnay. Both are a distinct cut above the white wines of the Mâcon (also made from Chardonnay), and offer much of the taste of Côte de Beaune whites at fair prices. Classic, labor-intensive Burgundian techniques, such as barrel fermentation and lees stirring, are becoming more common in Rully and Montagny, further improving the flavor profiles of these wines. The best producers in the Chalonnaise include Rodet, Joblot, and Faiveley.

South of the Côte d'Or lie the highly productive regions of Beaujolais and Mâcon. Red Beaujolais is made from the vigorously fruity Gamay grape. The Mâcon wines are made largely from Chardonnay. (Pouilly-Fuissé is also made from Chardonnay in the Mâcon area, but it has achieved a status more akin to whites from the Côte d'Or.) While not in a class with the great wines of the Côte d'Or, Beaujolais and the Mâcon are an excellent source of affordable everyday wines. Of particular distinction are the ten *crus* of Beaujolais, which offer some complexity and concentration. The most prominent are Moulin-à-Vent, Fleurie, and Morgon. Many wine lovers find the debut of Beaujolais Nouveau, a grapey wine that is released the third Thursday of each November, a reason for special celebration.

The Rhône

Though often lumped together, the northern and southern regions of the Rhône are best viewed separately. The northern Rhône has a continental climate, with moderate summers. The southern Rhône is primarily Mediterranean, with much hotter summers. The wines of the north are firmly structured and tannic. The warmth of the south produces wines that are higher in alcohol, with a riper, softer edge. Vintages differ as well. For example, 1996 barely qualified as good in the south, while in the north it was outstanding.

The major appellations of the north are Côte Rôtie, Hermitage, Crozes-Hermitage, St.-Joseph and Cornas for the reds; Condrieu for the whites. Hermitage, Crozes-Hermitage and St.-Joseph also make whites, primarily from Marsanne; Condrieu uses Viognier. All northern reds rely on the Syrah grape.

Châteauneuf-du-Pape, located in the southern Rhône, is without doubt the most famous appellation of the entire Rhône; other southern appellations include Gigondas and the somewhat more rustic Vacqueyras. The south also produces 80 percent of the region's Côtes-du-Rhône. Though inexpensive, Côtes-du-Rhône can be very good, in styles ranging from grapey Beaujolais types to serious wines that could almost pass for Châteauneuf-du-Pape. In the south, the major grape varieties include Grenache, Mourvèdre, Cinsault, Syrah and Cournoise. In recent years however, Grenache has been de-emphasized in favor of the more complex Mourvèdre and Syrah. White grapes are less important in the south than in the north, but small cuvées of superb white Châteauneuf-du-Pape are produced from Roussanne and Marsanne.

Mas de Gourgonnier Provence.

Fred Seidman

Other French Regions

The Loire is known for its crisp white wines. The best dry whites of the Loire are Sancerre and Pouilly-Fumé. Both are made from the Sauvignon Blanc grape, which produces an especially crisp, flinty style of wine quite unlike examples from Bordeaux and California. Also well-known is Muscadet, made from the Melon de Bourgogne grape. Muscadet is made to be drunk when it is young and vigorous; those labeled *sur lie* (meaning aged on yeasty sediment) are generally richer in style. The Chenin Blanc grape also produces a number of distinctive Loire wines. The best known is Vouvray, which can range from bone dry to quite sweet, depending on the style chosen by the producer.

Red Loire is a relative rarity, but a few interesting types are made. These include Chinon rouge, made from Cabernet Franc, and Sancerre rouge, made from Pinot Noir.

Alsace lies on the French-German border and utilizes the major German varietals, including Riesling, Gewürztraminer and Sylvaner. Unlike German wines, which tend to be off-dry or sweet, most Alsatian wines are dry. However, in especially ripe years, the region produces late harvest wines called *vendage tardive,* some of which can be sweet, and *sélections de grains nobles,* which are always sweet.

Champagne

Champagne is widely imitated around the world, but true Champagne can only come from the Champagne region of France. It must be made by the *méthode champenoise,* in which a second fermentation takes place in the bottle. Most Champagne is made from a blend of Pinot Noir, Pinot Meunier and Chardonnay; when only the last is used, the Champagne is called a *blanc de blancs.* Most Champagne is also a blend of different vintages, which helps ensure a consistently reliable product. In exceptional years, however, many houses produce a vintage-dated Champagne. Vintage Champagne is usually more distinctive and commands a higher price than non-vintage. Most houses also produce a luxurious—and expensive—prestige cuvée (formerly called the *tète de cuvée*). Dom Perignon is the best known, but it is rare to find a prestige cuvée that does not deliver a magnificent drinking experience.

ABARBANEL

Cabernet Sauvignon Vin de Pays d'Oc 1998: Firm and fruity, with bright plum and red cherry flavors, some herbal touches and coffee notes on the finish. Kosher.–K.M. • $10 • (8/31/1999) • **84**

Cabernet Sauvignon Vin de Pays d'Oc 1997: There's a menthol aroma to this wine, with currant and geranium flavors. Awkward, with a slightly bitter finish. Kosher.–K.M. • $10 • (2/28/1999) • **76**

Cabernet Sauvignon Vin de Pays d'Oc 1996 • $9 • (12/15/1997) • **65**

Cabernet Sauvignon Vin de Pays d'Oc Premium Barrel Reserve 1997: An exaggerated style, with syrupy, cloying sweet cherry flavors and overly charry notes on the finish. Kosher. Tasted twice, with consistent notes.–K.M. • $17 • (8/31/1999) • **71**

Cabernet Sauvignon Vin de Pays de Cassan 1994 • $8 • (12/15/1996) • **77**

Chardonnay Vin de Pays d'Oc 1996 • $10 • (9/30/1997) • **72**

Grenache Vin de Pays d'Oc French Blush 1996 • $9 • (9/30/1997) • **76**

Merlot Vin de Pays d'Oc 1998: A straightforward red with cherry and red plum flavors. Medium-bodied, with touches of wild herbs and juniper on the finish. Kosher. Drink now.–K.M. • $10 • (9/15/1999) • **82**

Merlot Vin de Pays d'Oc 1997: A straightforward, balanced red from the south of France, with cherry and green olive flavors, leathery notes on the finish. Kosher. Drink now.–K.M. • $10 • (2/28/1999) • **83**

Merlot Vin de Pays d'Oc 1996 • $9 • (11/15/1997) • **72**

Merlot Vin de Pays d'Oc 1995 • $8 • (12/15/1996) • **81**

Merlot Vin de Pays d'Oc Premium Barrel Reserve 1997: This odd red has some candied cherry and plum flavors, as well as a chalky texture. Sweet spicy notes on the finish. Kosher. Drink now.–K.M. • $17 • (9/15/1999) • **80**

Syrah Vin de Pays d'Oc 1997: This red has flavors of red plum and leather, with a roasted quality mixed in. Spicy and floral elements linger on the finish, with a stewy note. Kosher. Drink now through 2004.–K.M. • $10 • (2/28/1999) • **82**

ABBAYE DE THOLOMIES

Minervois Réserve 1996: Quite focused, dense and tightly wound, with cherry, dried plum and mineral flavors. Shows great balance, finishing with appealing game and leather notes. Drink through 2005.–K.M. • $14 • (2/28/1999) • **88**

Minervois Réserve 1993 • $11 • (6/30/1997) • **85**

ABBAYE DE VALMAGNE

Coteaux du Languedoc 1994 • $11 • (5/15/1997) • **85**

Coteaux du Languedoc 1991 • $10 • (3/15/1994) • **87**

Coteaux du Languedoc 1989 • $10 • (10/31/1992) • **72**

Coteaux du Languedoc 1988 • $12 • (8/31/1991) • **80**

ABBE DE BREYAC, L'

Côtes du Marmandais 1997: Red cherry and pepper notes dominate this light, thin wine that turns weedy on the finish.–K.M. • $7 • (7/31/1999) • **78**

ABBOTS

Cabardès Cirrus 1998: Has a nice pepper character, with red plum and brickish notes that linger on the finish joined by leathery elements. Drink now.–K.M. • $NA • (1/01/2000) • **83**

Shiraz Minervois Cumulus 1998: Smooth and supple, with nicely concentrated red plum, cherry and leather flavors. Ends on notes of cardamom and black pepper. Drink now.–K.M. • $NA • (1/01/2000) • **84**

ABEILLE DE FIEUZAL

Pessac-Léognan 1996: A very aromatic wine with blackberry, smoke and cherry. Full-bodied, with firm, polished tannins and a berry, black cherry aftertaste. Well-crafted claret. Second label of Château de Fieuzal. Best after 2002.–J.S. • $15 • (1/31/1999) • **86**

Pessac-Léognan 1995 • $15 • (1/31/1998) • **86**

Key: SS—Spectator Selection. CS—Cellar Selection. HR—Highly Recommended. $NA—Price not available. (BT)—Barrel tasting. Ⓐ—Auction Price.
For a key to the tasters' initials, see "How to Use These Listings."
Dates in parentheses represent the issues in which the ratings were published.

Pessac-Léognan White 1996: Extremely attractive aromas of cream, honey and apples follow through to a medium-bodied palate with firm acidity and an oaky finish. Needs a bit more fruit. Drink now.–J.S. • $NA • (1/01/1999) • **85**

ABELE, HENRI

Brut Champagne NV: Plenty of Pinot character in this crisp, finely knit Champagne. Aromas and flavors of red berry mingle with dough and honey, but the finish doesn't live up to the intro. Drink now.–B.S. • $25 • (11/30/1999) • **87**

ADAM, J.-B.

Alsace Gentil 1998: Bright, floral and spicy, with pear notes, this is an appealing white. Light and frisky, it's perfect as an aperitif. Drink now.–B.S. • $11 • (6/15/2000) • **83**

Alsace Grand Cru Kaefferkopf Traditionnelle 1996 • $20 • (11/15/1997) • **88**

Gewürztraminer Alsace Kaefferkopf Cuvée Jean-Baptiste Réserve Particulière 1998: Ample and lush, with a hint of sweetness emphasizing the honey, tropical fruit and citrus flavors, all seamless followed by a moderate finish. Drink now.–B.S. • $20 • (6/15/2000) • **85**

Gewürztraminer Alsace Réserve 1996 • $16 • (9/30/1997) • **87**

Gewürztraminer Alsace Sélection de Grains Nobles 1997: Plenty of structure, with nice honey flavor. Broad, sweet and lush. Drink now.–B.S. • $50/500 ml. • (6/15/2000) • **85**

Gewürztraminer Alsace Sélection de Grains Nobles 1989 • $52 • (9/30/1994) • **93**

Gewürztraminer Alsace Vendanges Tardives 1997: An opulent VT, dripping with honey, rosewater and pear, it cuts a thick swath across the palate. A grapefruit note and supporting acidity keep the finish firm. Drink now through 2001.–B.S. • $30 • (6/15/2000) • **87**

Muscat Alsace Réserve 1998: No mistaking this varietal, with its pungent floral, spice and grape flavors, all displayed on a vivid, juicy frame. A delicious Muscat. Drink now.–B.S. • $12 • (6/15/2000) • **86**

Pinot Blanc Alsace Réserve 1998: A touch of residual sugar rounds out this soft, apple- and peach-flavored white. Loses oomph on the finish, but tasty. Drink now.–B.S. • $11 • (6/15/2000) • **84**

Pinot Blanc Alsace Réserve 1996 • $11 • (9/30/1997) • **79**

Pinot Gris Alsace Réserve 1996 • $15 • (9/30/1997) • **85**

Pinot Noir Alsace Cuvée Jean-Baptiste 1995 • $18 • (11/15/1997) • **84**

Riesling Alsace Kaefferkopf Cuvée Jean-Baptiste 1997: Broad, round and medium-bodied, with subtle almond, apple and a hint of petrol. A touch chunky, but not bad. Drink now.–B.S. • $18 • (6/15/2000) • **85**

Riesling Alsace Réserve 1998: Begins on an appley note, with a touch of sweetness balancing the firm backbone. Moderately intense, with richness and a modest finish. Drink now through 2001.–B.S. • $13 • (6/15/2000) • **82**

Tokay Pinot Gris Alsace Cuvée Jean-Baptiste 1997: Rich and minerally in character, offering quince and peach aromas and flavors, medium body and good concentration. The flavors persist through the finish. Drink now.–B.S. • $18 • (6/15/2000) • **86**

Tokay Pinot Gris Alsace Letzenberg Cuvée Jean-Baptiste 1998: Rich and round, with a lush texture and a touch of sweetness that brings out the apricot, smoke and mineral flavors. Very attractive and delicious now. Drink now.–B.S. • $16 • (6/15/2000) • **87**

Tokay Pinot Gris Alsace Réserve 1998: Crisp, this white delivers apple and lemon flavors on a rich, broad texture midpalate, ends on a nutty, smoky note. Drink now.–B.S. • $14 • (6/15/2000) • **84**

Tokay Pinot Gris Alsace Sélection de Grains Nobles 1994 • $60/500 ml. • (10/15/1996) • **91**

Tokay Pinot Gris Alsace Sélection de Grains Nobles 1990 • $52 • (9/30/1994) • **89**

Tokay Pinot Gris Alsace Vendanges Tardives 1997: Simply delicious, this broad, honeyed white delivers plenty of violet and apricot flavors up front, trailing off a little on the finish. Try with foie gras. Drink now through 2001.–B.S. • $30 • (6/15/2000) • **88**

AGASSAC, CHATEAU D'

Haut-Médoc 1998: Aromas of cooked cherries with hints of tar. Medium- to full-bodied, with medium tannins and finish. Slightly hollow midpalate.–J.S. • $NA • (5/31/1999) (BT) • **85-89**

Haut-Médoc 1997: Fresh aromas of cherries and plums. Medium to light in body, with medium tannins and a slightly lean finish. Drink now.–J.S. • $NA • (1/31/2000) • **85**

Haut-Médoc 1996: Pretty currant and earth aromas and flavors mark this wine. It's medium-bodied, with firm tannins and a fruity, fresh aftertaste. Slightly one-dimensional, but well made. Best after 2001.–J.S. • $NA • (1/31/1999) • **86**

Haut-Médoc 1995: Rich wild berry and tobacco aromas. Medium- to full-bodied, with velvety tannins and a long, caressing finish. Built for aging. A bit rustic but interesting. Best from 2005 through 2010.–J.S. • $NA • (9/15/1998) • **87**

Haut-Médoc 1989 • $20 • (3/15/1992) • **88**

AIGLON, MAISON L'

Chardonnay Vin de Pays d'Oc Grand Reserve 1996: Straightforward, with apple, citrus and spice notes. Buttery flavors linger on the finish. Drink now.–K.M. • $NA • (12/31/1998) • **82**

St.-Chinian Grand Reserve 1995 • $NA • (1/01/1998) • **79**

St.-Chinian Grand Reserve 1994 • $7 • (6/15/1997) • **86**

St.-Chinian Grand Réserve 1993 • $8 • (7/31/1996) • **85**

St.-Chinian Grand Réserve 1990 • $6 • (7/15/1992) • **83**

AIGUELIERE, DOMAINE L'

Coteaux du Languedoc Grenat 1997: There are some sweet cherry flavors in this wine, but it comes off tasting thin and volatile in the end. Tasted twice, with consistent notes.–K.M. • $16 • (2/29/2000) • **76**

Coteaux du Languedoc Grenat 1995 • $15 • (3/31/1998) • **83**

Coteaux du Languedoc Montpeyroux 1997: A mix of sweet cherry and ripe plum flavors, with some meaty notes and a tongue-rasping acidity. Drink now.–K.M. • $18 • (4/30/2000) • **82**

Coteaux du Languedoc Montpeyroux 1996: Thin, with dried cherry and rhubarb flavors. Tasted twice, with consistent notes.–K.M. • $16 • (2/29/2000) • **76**

Coteaux du Languedoc Montpeyroux 1995 • $17 • (12/15/1997) • **84**

Coteaux du Languedoc Montpeyroux 1991 • $12 • (3/15/1994) • **86**

Coteaux du Languedoc Montpeyroux 1989 • $11 • (4/15/1993) • **77**

Coteaux du Languedoc Montpeyroux Côte Dorée 1997: Sweet cherry and red plum flavors dominate this red. Searing acidity, with espresso notes on the finish. Drink now.–K.M. • $38 • (4/30/2000) • **82**

Coteaux du Languedoc Montpeyroux Côte Dorée 1996: A firm, concentrated and full-bodied red with a meaty, bacony aroma and loads of plum, dark cherry and beefy flavors. Powerful, focused and seductive, with leathery notes that linger on the finish and enough stuffing to last. Drink through 2004.–K.M. • $35 • (11/15/1998) • **90**

Coteaux du Languedoc Montpeyroux Côte Dorée 1993 • $38 • (3/31/1998) • **89**

Coteaux du Languedoc Montpeyroux Côte Dorée 1991 • $NA • (3/15/1994) • **89**

Coteaux du Languedoc Montpeyroux Côte Rousse 1997: Sweet and spicy components are the hallmarks of this structured and intense wine, with some plum, chocolate and meat flavors. Spicy notes linger on the finish. Drink now through 2004.–K.M. • $38 • (4/30/2000) • **86**

Coteaux du Languedoc Montpeyroux Côte Rousse 1996: Rich and refined, with good, gamy aromas and plenty of ripe plum and dark cherry flavors, also some currant and peppery notes. A sophisticated red that has plenty of character and finesse. Drink through 2005.–K.M. • $35 • (11/15/1998) • **90**

Coteaux du Languedoc Montpeyroux Côte Rousse 1991 • $NA • (3/15/1994) • **87**

Coteaux du Languedoc Montpeyroux Tradition 1997: This has some meaty flavors along with decent red cherry, plum, spice and hot stone components. Tart on the finish, with some currant notes. Drink now.–K.M. • $22 • (4/30/2000) • **84**

Coteaux du Languedoc Montpeyroux Tradition 1996: Tired and thin, with caramelized and stewy flavors. Not much fun. Tasted twice, with consistent notes.–K.M. • $21 • (2/29/2000) • **74**

Coteaux du Languedoc Montpeyroux Tradition 1995 • $20 • (12/15/1997) • **82**

Vin de Pays du Mont Baudile Grenat 1998: A full-bodied and fairly tart red with decadent flavors of dark plum, tobacco box and bacon. The tartness will need some time to integrate with the fruit flavors. Drink through 2002.–K.M. • $15 • (4/30/2000) • **83**

AIGUILHE, CHATEAU D'

Côtes de Castillon 1999: Amazingly dark ruby, with intense mineral, berry and raspberry aromas. Medium-bodied, with racy tannins and a medium finish. A bit hollow midpalate, but very good.–J.S. • $NA • (1/01/2000) (BT) • **85-89**

Côtes de Castillon 1998: A bit lean and not giving much right now. Medium-bodied, with firm tannins and a mineral and berry aftertaste.–J.S. • $NA • (5/31/1999) (BT) • **85-89**

AILE D'ARGENT

Bordeaux 1997: Rather subdued but enjoyable. Sliced apple, vanilla and hints of melon follow through to the palate. Medium-bodied, with good acidity and a mineral and fruit finish. A bit more intensity would make it outstanding. Drink now.–J.S. • $35 • (9/30/1999) • **88**

AIRES HAUTES, DOMAINE DES

Chardonnay Vin de Pays d'Oc 1998: Vinous, with modest apple and citrusy flavors. Dull finish.–K.M. • $10 • (12/31/1999) • **78**

Sauvignon Vin de Pays d'Oc 1998: A straightforward white with herbal and vanilla flavors and an oniony element, which lingers on the finish. Drink now.–K.M. • $10 • (12/31/1999) • **82**

Sauvignon Vin de Pays d'Oc 1997: A medium-bodied Sauvignon, with plenty of woody and spicy flavors but not much finesse. Herbal notes intensify on the finish.–K.M. • $10 • (12/31/1998) • **79**

ALARY, DOMAINE

Côtes du Rhône 1997: Light and a bit green, with some modest fruit. Crisp finish.–P.M. • $11 • (11/15/1999) • **77**

Côtes du Rhône 1996: Diluted, this is watery, herbal and somewhat astringent.–P.M. • $11 • (11/15/1998) • **70**

Côtes du Rhône Non-Filtré 1996: Tastes more of grape leaves than of grapes. Light in color, of modest ripeness.–P.M. • $11 • (11/15/1998) • **74**

Côtes du Rhône-Villages Cairanne 1997: A bit diluted, with a cedary herbal flavor. Short finish.–P.M. • $14 • (11/15/1999) • **77**

Côtes du Rhône-Villages Cairanne 1995 • $13 • (10/15/1997) • **80**

Côtes du Rhône-Villages Cairanne La Font d'Estévenas 1997: Tart, green, herbal; a tough red that dries on the finish.–P.M. • $22 • (11/15/1999) • **73**

Côtes du Rhône-Villages Cairanne La Font d'Estévenas 1996: Very, very nice '96, full of personality. Good concentration, from the meaty, smoked bacon, charcoal, notes to the black currant, black cherry and spicy plum. Full-bodied and fresh, with well-integrated tannins. A bit hard on the finish, but still tempting. Drink now through 2001.–P.M. • $14 • (11/15/1998) • **89**

Côtes du Rhône-Villages Cairanne La Font d'Estévenas 1995 • $14 • (10/15/1997) • **85**

Côtes du Rhône-Villages Cairanne Réserve du Vigneron 1997: Soft, this supple red is easy to drink, with its pretty spice, cherry and smoke aromas and flavors. Nice peppery finish. Drink now.–P.M. • $20 • (11/15/1999) • **84**

Côtes du Rhône-Villages Cairanne Réserve du Vigneron 1996: Delicate and elegant, with lovely floral, toasted bread, blackberry and raspberry flavors, good ripeness and well-integrated tannins. A pleasure for its pure fruit character and balance. Drink now through 2003.–P.M. • $17 • (11/15/1998) • **86**

Côtes du Rhône-Villages Cairanne Réserve du Vigneron 1995 • $18 • (10/15/1997) • **85**

Côtes du Rhône-Villages White Cairanne La Font d'Estévenas 1997: Fresh but a little simple, with modest ripeness, tasting crisp and a bit herbal.–P.M. • $19 • (11/15/1999) • **78**

Côtes du Rhône-Villages White Cairanne La Font d'Estévenas 1996: Very tasty, like a lemon popsicle, showing clean notes of lemon, pear and freshly cut grass. Well made, light- to medium-bodied, it's superfresh and crisp on the finish. Drink now.–P.M. • $14 • (11/15/1998) • **84**

ALBRECHT, LUCIEN

Auxerrois Alsace Cuvée "A"de Albrecht 1996: Exotic smelling, like a mélange of tropical fruits, turning to honey on the palate. There's richness, but it never gets heavy—the '96 acidity keeping everything lively and attractive. Good length, with a smoky aftertaste. Drink now.–B.S. • $18 • (3/31/1999) • **87**

Gewürztraminer Alsace 1998: Round, bright and smelling of roses and grapefruit, with a pleasant bitterness and medium body, yet it lacks concentration and depth and finishes short. Drink now.–B.S. • $13 • (10/31/1999) • **80**

Gewürztraminer Alsace 1996 • $15 • (11/15/1997) • **82**

Gewürztraminer Alsace Bollenberg 1997: Flavors of nuts, orange and smoke highlight this round, almost oily-textured wine. Balanced on the soft side, showing a bit of heat on the finish. Attractive floral aftertaste. Drink now.–B.S. • $16 • (9/30/1999) • **86**

ALBRECHT, LUCIEN

Gewürztraminer Alsace Grand Cru Pfingstberg Cuvée "A"de Albrecht 1996: Seems a bit evolved, displaying white pepper and canned pear flavors along with an underlying gingersnap note. Lacks the concentration and complexity of a *grand cru.* Drink now.–B.S. • $58 • (4/30/1999) • **83**

Gewürztraminer Alsace Sélection de Grains Nobles 1989 • $NA • (11/15/1990) • **93**

Gewürztraminer Alsace Vendange Tardive 1996: Very exotic and ripe, and showing a slight cheesy note due to its youth, but there's plenty of concentrated pear flavor along with a silky texture and solid framework. The high alcohol upsets the balance a little. Drink now through 2004.–B.S. • $50 • (4/30/1999) • **89**

Pinot Blanc Alsace 1998: A wrestling match between the earthy flavors and the ripe peach notes make this succulent Pinot Blanc hard to warm up to.–B.S. • $9 • (6/15/2000) • **79**

Pinot Blanc Alsace 1997: Odd. Ripe aromas of guava burst from the glass, then, on the palate, there's a combination of earth and tropical fruit in a lean, structured style. Finishes on a canned fruit-cocktail note.–B.S. • $9 • (3/31/1999) • **78**

Pinot Blanc Alsace 1996 • $16 • (9/15/1997) • **83**

Pinot Gris Alsace Grand Cru Pfingstberg Cuvée "A"de Albrecht 1996: Tastes concocted, with an overt earthy streak. No fun at all. Tasted twice, with consistent notes.–B.S. • $58 • (10/31/1999) • **72**

Riesling Alsace 1998: Very ripe, showing peach and a touch of earthiness, along with a fat, glossy texture and lowish acidity. A bit shy on the finish. Drink now.–B.S. • $10 • (10/15/1999) • **84**

Riesling Alsace Grand Cru Pfingstberg 1996: A bit ripe and over the top, despite the acidity of the vintage. it lacks harmony, grace and focus.–B.S. • $24 • (10/15/1999) • **79**

Riesling Alsace Grand Cru Pfingstberg Cuvée "A"de Albrecht 1996: Extremely ripe, bursting with apricot, quince and tropical notes (botrytis?) yet also vegetal, and it seems clumsy at this stage, like an awkward adolescent. Drink through 2005.–B.S. • $58 • (9/15/1999) • **88**

Riesling Alsace Pfingstberg Sélection de Grains Nobles 1989 • $NA • (11/15/1990) • **87**

Tokay Pinot Gris Alsace 1997: Very ripe and assertive aromas of guava and decadent fruit turn to smoke and mineral flavors, while the texture is almost oily. Fat and leaning toward heaviness, but retains balance thanks to acidity and a twinge of bitterness on the finish. Drink now.–B.S. • $11 • (4/30/1999) • **86**

Tokay Pinot Gris Alsace Sélection de Grains Nobles 1994 • $75 • (10/15/1997) • **90**

ALESME-BECKER, CHATEAU MARQUIS-D'

Margaux 1998: A wine of pleasant currant and raspberry character. Medium-bodied, with medium, slightly rough tannins and a short finish.–J.S. • $NA • (5/31/1999) (BT) • **85-89**

Margaux 1995: Violets and perfume on the nose. Medium-bodied, with fine tannins and a fresh and fruity aftertaste. Tannins sneak up on the finish. Needs time. Drink through 2005–J.S. • $NA • (9/15/1998) • **87**

Margaux 1985 • $19 • (6/30/1988) • **84**

Margaux 1983 • $15 • (12/31/1986) • **84**

ALLAINES, FRANCOIS D'

Chassagne-Montrachet Les Champsgains 1996: The tension between the wood and the clean acidity is almost unbearable to the human palate, but it tastes good, thanks to the creamy, malic, ripe midpalate character. The finish is gorgeous, with the wood fading in the background to leave space for ripe fruit. Not imported into the U.S. Best from 2003 through 2010.–P.M. • $NA • (9/30/1999) • **94**

Mâcon La Roche Vineuse 1996 • $NA • (5/31/1998) • **92**

Santenay White 1997: A heavy wine that tastes like a big California high-alcohol white. Thick and rich, with caramel, honey and ripe midpalate character. Not imported into the U.S. Drink now through 2010.–P.M. • $NA • (9/30/1999) • **87**

Key: SS—Spectator Selection. CS—Cellar Selection. HR—Highly Recommended. $NA—Price not available. (BT)—Barrel tasting. (A)—Auction Price.
For a key to the tasters' initials, see "How to Use These Listings."
Dates in parentheses represent the issues in which the ratings were published.

ALLEES DE CANTEMERLE, LES

Haut-Médoc 1996: Light-bodied and watery, with some fruit on the finish. Smells like a weedy pond. A second label of Château Cantemerle.–J.S. • $NA • (2/28/1999) • **70**

ALLEMAND, THIERRY

Cornas 1991 • $25 • (5/31/1994) • **84**

Cornas Chaillot 1997: Much fruit, little terroir. Good extraction in this medium-bodied, dark-colored red brings out clean, fresh and lively blackberry, wild raspberry, leather, grilled meat, spice and black pepper notes. Supple and a bit watery, kicking in with mouthpuckering acidity on the finish. Drink now through 2003.–P.M. • $45 • (11/30/1999) • **86**

Cornas Chaillot 1996: A tannic, chewy, concentrated Cornas, distinctively earthy, with lovely floral, blueberry, cassis, smoked bacon and wet earth character. Monolithic now, though the ripe tannins might render it approachable with red meats. Best after 2005.–P.M. • $30 • (11/15/1998) • **94**

Cornas Chaillot 1995: Beauty and power in a single package. This ink-colored red shows ripe plum and cassis flavors, with notes of bacon, smoke, mineral and licorice. Full-bodied, with muscular tannins, yet it remains clean and fresh, propelled by the ripe, deep fruit. Tempting now, but much better with time. Drink through 2010.–T.M. • $29 • (11/15/1998) • **95**

Cornas Chaillot 1991 • $27 • (5/31/1994) • **86**

Cornas Reynard 1996: Quite earthy-smelling, but it tastes delicious. Medium-bodied, it tastes young, ripe and sweet, showing a velvety texture of well-integrated, smooth tannins, and spice, mocha and blackberry flavors. Balanced and intense on the succulent, long finish. Drink now through 2007.–P.M. • $33 • (11/15/1998) • **92**

Cornas Reynard 1995: This massive Northern Rhône red arrives with full, muscular tannins, but they can't hide the ripe, concentrated flavors of plum, cassis and wild berry. Game and black pepper accents keep the wine firmly grounded in the region, despite its New World polish, and its density promises pleasures to come. Best after 2000.–T.M. • $32 • (11/15/1998) CS • **96**

ALLIET, PHILIPPE

Chinon Coteau de Noiré 1996: This red has the deep color and ripe, earthy aromas of a wine from the south, but its brisk tannins and herbaceous accents are classic Loire. Lush yet firm, ripe yet crisp, it promises a long development. Drink through 2005.–T.M. • $21 • (6/30/1999) • **89**

Chinon Vieilles Vignes 1995 • $16 • (6/15/1998) HR • **91**

ALLOUCHERY-PERSEVAL

Brut Champagne Réserve NV • $27 • (11/15/1997) • **88**

Brut Champagne Tradition NV: A good all-around Champagne with enough lively fruit flavors to fill out the smooth but crisp texture and linger a bit on the finish. Drink now. • $23 • (12/31/1998) • **85**

ALQUIER, GILBERT

Faugères 1997: A solid red, with good red plum, pepper and spice flavors and appealing leathery notes on the finish. A good effort for the vintage. Drink now.–K.M. • $13 • (2/29/2000) • **83**

Faugères 1996: Like a fine *cru* Beaujolais, with intensely focused and concentrated flavors of red plum, currant and spice that explode across the palate with a fresh, tough, firm juiciness. Shows leather character, with berry notes that linger on the finish. Drink through 2003.–K.M. • $13 • (11/30/1998) • **89**

Faugères 1995 • $14 • (8/31/1997) • **86**

Faugères 1991 • $9 • (3/15/1994) • **87**

Faugères 1990 • $9 • (3/15/1994) • **84**

Faugères La Maison Jaune Réserve 1996: A massive red that has the stuffing to age beautifully. Packed with flavors of brick, dried cherry, dark plum, lavender and cardamom, with hints of anise and leather. Despite its power and complexity, it has a supple finish full of dark chocolate. Best from 2001 through 2006.–K.M. • $14 • (2/28/1999) • **91**

Faugères La Maison Jaune Réserve 1995 • $13 • (3/31/1998) • **86**

Faugères Les Bastides d'Alquier Réserve 1996: A plush-tasting red, with ripe plum and cherry flavors and a leather aroma. Nicely concentrated and smooth, with bittersweet chocolate and coffee notes on the finish. Drink now.–K.M. • $18 • (11/30/1998) • **87**

Faugères Les Bastides d'Alquier Réserve 1995 • $17 • (12/15/1997) HR • **91**

Faugères Les Bastides d'Alquier Réserve 1991 • $15 • (3/15/1994) • **87**

Faugères Les Bastides d'Alquier Réserve 1990 • $NA • (3/15/1994) • **87**
Faugères Rosé 1997: Simple melony character dominates this rosé, which ends on a slightly sweet note.–K.M. • $11 • (10/31/1998) • **78**

AMADIEU, PIERRE

Côtes du Rhône Roulepierre 1995 • $6 • (2/28/1997) • **84**
Gigondas Romane-Machotte 1995 • $18 • (10/15/1997) • **80**

AMBROISE, BERTRAND

Bourgogne Hautes-Côtes de Nuits White 1997: Fabulous. This delicious '97 white Burgundy has a seductive combination of vanilla bean, mineral, toasted coconut and tropical flavors. A supersilky package supported by good acidity on the ultracreamy, exquisite finish. Brilliant winemaking. Drink now through 2003.–P.M. • $25 • (5/31/1999) • **92**
Bourgogne White 1997: Fruity and light-bodied, with crisp citrus notes and a buttery, ripe character.–P.M. • $18 • (5/31/1999) • **79**
Bourgogne White 1996 • $18 • (5/31/1998) • **79**
Chassagne-Montrachet La Maltroie 1997: Fairly lush and ripe, medium-bodied and flavorful, showing honey, pear and spice, with obvious wood tannins. Should come together with cellaring. Drink through 2005.–P.M. • $60 • (5/31/1999) • **87**
Clos de Vougeot 1996: Ultrarich and thick, a plummy style of '96 red Burgundy, extremely dark in color, very oaky and overdone. Tastes of kirsch, blackberry and cassis concentrate; lacks finesse on the finish. Might rate higher at its peak. Best from 2005.–P.M. • $85 • (9/30/1998) • **90**
Clos de Vougeot 1995 • $90 • (11/15/1997) • **91**
Clos de Vougeot 1994 • $75 • (11/15/1996) • **93**
Clos de Vougeot 1993 • $90 • (11/15/1995) • **96**
Corton-Charlemagne 1997: A bit odd at first, with a menthol, apple pie and wet earth character. Shows some rich fruit in the end, but don't expect it up front. A big wine. Better than previously reviewed. Best from 2004 through 2009.–P.M. • $125 • (9/30/1999) • **92**
Corton-Charlemagne 1996: Very woody, smelling of plywood, but there is fatness to this toasted, smoky, floral-scented wine. Full-bodied, with excellent intensity of mineral, pear, toasted bread character. Not so pleasant or balanced now, but should improve with cellaring. Best from 2010.–P.M. • $NA • (8/31/1998) • **90**
Corton Le Rognet 1997: A solid '97 Pinot Noir, offering nice crisp fruit in an oaky package, with cold red berry flavor. Medium-bodied, quite tannic and chewy on the finish. Best from 2002 through 2010.–P.M. • $80 • (1/01/2000) • **86**
Corton Le Rognet 1995 • $80 • (11/15/1997) • **90**
Corton Le Rognet 1994 • $60 • (11/15/1996) • **90**
Corton Le Rognet 1993 • $75 • (11/15/1995) CS • **97**
Corton Le Rognet 1992 • $55 • (12/15/1994) • **89**
Corton Le Rognet 1991 • $49 • (1/31/1994) • **85**
Corton Le Rognet 1990 • $60 • (12/15/1992) • **94**
Corton Le Rognet 1989 • $45 • (1/31/1992) • **93**
Corton Le Rognet 1988 • $43 • (11/30/1990) • **92**
Corton Le Rognet 1987 • $38 • (3/31/1990) • **90**
Côte de Nuits-Villages 1995 • $20 • (11/15/1997) • **85**
Côte de Nuits-Villages 1994 • $20 • (11/15/1996) • **80**
Côte de Nuits-Villages 1992 • $19 • (12/15/1994) • **79**
Côte de Nuits-Villages 1987 • $15 • (2/28/1990) • **82**
Ladoix White Les Gréchons 1997: Very woody and dry, showing decent citrus intensity, but the oak makes this a toasted, hot wine.–P.M. • $30 • (5/31/1999) • **75**
Ladoix White Les Gréchons 1996 • $25 • (5/31/1998) • **84**
Nuits-St.-Georges 1997: Ripe, with an acidic undertone. Distinctive for its animal, grilled meat and wet fur aromas, but this rustic side also gives it personality. Rich on the palate, with marvelous ripe red berry and blackberry character. Has length and can age. Drink now through 2007.–P.M. • $40 • (1/01/2000) • **88**
Nuits-St.-Georges 1995 • $33 • (11/15/1997) • **86**
Nuits-St.-Georges 1994 • $30 • (11/15/1996) • **79**
Nuits-St.-Georges 1993 • $40 • (11/15/1995) • **86**
Nuits-St.-Georges 1992 • $NA • (12/15/1994) • **77**
Nuits-St.-Georges 1991 • $28 • (1/31/1994) • **83**
Nuits-St.-Georges 1990 • $38 • (12/15/1992) • **89**
Nuits-St.-Georges 1989 • $30 • (1/31/1992) • **90**
Nuits-St.-Georges Cuvée Vieilles Vignes 1996: Superlative Nuits. Marries lovely, smoky, toasted wood accents with excellent concentration of red- and blackberry character; also has an interesting note of petrol from the oak. Thick but fresh, it oozes supple, ripe character despite all the tannins that wrap around the palate. Long, balanced finish. Drink now through 2008.–P.M. • $40 • (9/30/1998) HR • **92**
Nuits-St.-Georges Cuvée Vieilles Vignes 1994 • $35 • (11/15/1996) • **79**
Nuits-St.-Georges En Rue de Chaux 1997: Ultradark and dense, this big, rich and full-bodied Pinot Noir has a surprisingly tannic backbone and a firm grip that won't let go. Powers to a long finish. Has plenty of fruit, so expect this ager to improve with cellaring. Best from 2005 through 2010.–P.M. • $55 • (1/01/2000) • **93**
Nuits-St.-Georges En Rue de Chaux 1996: Very dark in color, beautifully aromatic, full-bodied and highly extracted, with loads of new oak, game, vanilla, black currant, raspberry, violet and blackberry flavors below the tough wood tannins. Time in the cellar is needed to tame this savage. Best from 2007 through 2015.–P.M. • $48 • (5/15/1999) • **89**
Nuits-St.-Georges En Rue de Chaux 1995 • $48 • (11/15/1997) • **87**
Nuits-St.-Georges En Rue de Chaux 1994 • $40 • (11/15/1996) • **87**
Nuits-St.-Georges En Rue de Chaux 1992 • $38 • (12/15/1994) • **85**
Nuits-St.-Georges En Rue de Chaux 1991 • $36 • (1/31/1994) • **86**
Nuits-St.-Georges En Rue de Chaux 1990 • $48 • (12/15/1992) • **90**
Nuits-St.-Georges En Rue de Chaux 1989 • $38 • (1/31/1992) • **91**
Nuits-St.-Georges En Rue de Chaux 1988 • $40 • (5/15/1991) • **93**
Nuits-St.-Georges Les Vaucrains 1997: This fabulous '97 is a stunning effort in this vintage. This full-bodied, deep and dark-colored red Burgundy is round and supple, showing well-integrated tannins, but also loads of ripe fruit combined with spice and wet earth. Best from 2002 through 2012.–P.M. • $60 • (1/01/2000) • **93**
Nuits-St.-Georges Les Vaucrains 1996: Huge, brooding, powerful wine. Dark in color, sporting exotic toasty oak aromas, blackberry flavors and monolithic structure, searing intensity and creamy, mouthcoating tannins. Brilliant '96 red. Best from 2005 through 2012.–B.S. • $60 • (9/30/1998) • **93**
Nuits-St.-Georges Les Vaucrains 1995 • $58 • (11/15/1997) • **90**
Nuits-St.-Georges Les Vaucrains 1994 • $45 • (11/15/1996) • **83**
Nuits-St.-Georges Les Vaucrains 1993 • $65 • (11/15/1995) • **90**
Nuits-St.-Georges Les Vaucrains 1992 • $44 • (12/15/1994) • **78**
Nuits-St.-Georges Les Vaucrains 1991 • $39 • (1/31/1994) • **85**
Nuits-St.-Georges Les Vaucrains 1990 • $45 • (12/15/1992) • **90**
Nuits-St.-Georges Les Vaucrains 1989 • $38 • (1/31/1992) • **94**
Pommard Les Saussilles 1996: Truly exciting Pommard whose blackberry flavor is cloaked in spicy new oak that takes on a coffee tone toward the finish. Deep, dense, rich and ripe, it has magnitude and power and a fatness that persists right through the tannic finish. Bravo. Best from 2003 through 2010.–B.S. • $45 • (9/30/1998) • **92**
St.-Romain 1997: Very toasty, tasting of caramel and toffee, with a good polish of mineral, butter and cream, but it turns a bit tart on the finish. Drink now through 2001.–P.M. • $28 • (5/31/1999) • **80**
St.-Romain 1996 • $25 • (5/31/1998) • **83**
St.-Romain 1995 • $18 • (8/31/1997) • **80**
Volnay Santenots Hospices de Beaune Cuvée Jehan de Massol 1996: Deep and powerful, showing plenty of floral and spice notes, but the cherry flavors are augmented by mineral and iodine, racy acidity and concentration. Excellent finish, where the mineral character lingers. Drink through 2004. –B.S. • $90 • (9/30/1998) • **90**
Vosne-Romanée 1994 • $32 • (11/15/1996) • **77**
Vosne-Romanée Aux Damaudes 1995 • $38 • (11/15/1997) • **85**
Vosne-Romanée Aux Damaudes 1993 • $45 • (11/15/1995) • **88**
Vougeot Les Crâs 1997: What it lacks in focus in makes up in power and flavor gumption, with grilled meat, mucho toasted oak, vanilla, mocha, spice and nice red berry character. This full-bodied wine has personality, albeit not much class. Best from 2002 through 2007.–P.M. • $64 • (1/01/2000) • **90**
Vougeot Les Crâs 1996: Huge aromas of grilled meats and smoky roasted fruit. Rich in texture and concentrated, before the massive structure shuts everything down. Tons of sweet fruit on the finish. Best from 2002 through 2008.–B.S. • $60 • (9/30/1998) • **93**

AMEILLAUD, DOMAINE DE L'

Côtes du Rhône 1998: Clean, fresh, fruity, with black pepper, blackberry and spice, its midpalate grip makes it a bit chewy on the finish, but it has personality and balance. Not imported into the U.S. Drink now.–P.M. • $NA • (1/01/1999) • **83**
Côtes du Rhône-Villages Cairanne 1998: Flavorful, spicy, a wonderful little Rhône red packed with black fruit and black pepper. A balanced, medium-bodied, intense wine that takes off on the explosive palate. Drink now through 2001.–P.M. • $11 • (11/15/1999) • **89**
Vin de Pays de Vaucluse 1998: Medium in body, with exuberant, compacted fruit—blueberry, cassis, plum—and a fresh-textured character. Crisp finish. Drink now.–P.M. • $8 • (11/15/1999) • **82**

AMIOT, GUY

Bourgogne Aligoté 1995 • $15 • (8/31/1997) • **85**

Bourgogne White 1997: A bit diluted, with cardboard aromas, decent Chardonnay character and modest lemon notes. Drink now through 2003.–P.M. • $24 • (9/30/1999) • **83**

Bourgogne White 1995 • $18 • (8/31/1997) • **80**

Chassagne-Montrachet 1997: A straightforward Chardonnay that tastes of high yields and dilution.–P.M. • $44 • (9/30/1999) • **75**

Chassagne-Montrachet 1995 • $30 • (5/31/1997) • **77**

Chassagne-Montrachet Clos St.-Jean 1997: Thick, with a rustic, stinky, paint varnish character. Finishes short and bitter.–P.M. • $62 • (9/30/1999) • **73**

Chassagne-Montrachet Clos St.-Jean 1995 • $40 • (8/31/1997) • **92**

Chassagne-Montrachet Les Caillerets 1997: A bit simple, tasting a bit resinous, with a paint varnish character that seems like pine sap. Fairly rich in the mouth, but turns sour on the finish.–P.M. • $62 • (9/30/1999) • **70**

Chassagne-Montrachet Les Caillerets 1995 • $40 • (5/31/1997) • **80**

Chassagne-Montrachet Les Champgains 1997: Very thick, almost too ripe, this tastes a bit over-the-top. Shows caramel and dried fig. A bit heavy on the finish. Drink now through 2010.–P.M. • $58 • (9/30/1999) • **88**

Chassagne-Montrachet Les Champgains 1995 • $40 • (5/31/1997) • **79**

Chassagne-Montrachet Les Macherelles 1997: A bit rustic, showing a lot of extract, giving it density and concentration. Tastes a bit rustic now, but it's built to become a smooth, silky white with age. Best from 2002 through 2010.–P.M. • $49 • (9/30/1999) • **88**

Chassagne-Montrachet Les Macherelles 1995 • $37 • (5/31/1997) • **87**

Chassagne-Montrachet Les Vergers 1997: A bit obvious and overripe. Butterscotch, butter and honey mix with acidity in this full-bodied, somewhat awkward white. Good fatness, but a bit astringent on the finish. Drink now through 2003.–P.M. • $62 • (9/30/1999) • **84**

Chassagne-Montrachet Les Vergers 1996: Rich and full-bodied, but packed with fresh acidity, this is a well-made package. Subtly oaked and focused on crisp, clean and pure fruit and silky-smooth texture from the minerally terroir. Long, intense finish. Best from 2003 through 2010.–P.M. • $54 • (5/31/1999) • **94**

Chassagne-Montrachet Les Vergers 1995 • $42 • (5/31/1997) • **78**

Montrachet 1997: There's beautiful thick texture in this ripe white. Very concentrated and lovingly honeyed, with loads of character. Superripe, deftly toasted and beautifully harmonious. Drink now through 2005.–P.M. • $348 • (9/30/1999) • **91**

Montrachet 1995 • $250 • (5/31/1997) • **85**

Puligny-Montrachet Les Demoiselles 1997: Lovely, thick and rich, with good concentration. The finish has an extra dimension of anise, fennel and hazelnut, along with pear, cooked apple and dried fig. Drink now through 2007.–B.S. • $104 • (9/30/1999) • **94**

Puligny-Montrachet Les Demoiselles 1996: Intriguing style. Very distinctive, displaying vivid toast and mineral aromas, yet fresh, packed with intense flavors of smoke, mineral, pear and citrus combined with a thick texture. It remains firm and lively right through the long, long finish. Impressive. Best from 2001 through 2008.–P.M. • $98 • (5/31/1999) • **95**

Puligny-Montrachet Les Demoiselles 1995 • $45 • (5/31/1997) • **83**

St.-Aubin En Remilly 1997: Rather concentrated, dense and well defined, with nettle, vanilla and a lot of acidity. Long on the finish, although dominated by oak right now. Best from 2001 through 2008.–B.S. • $44 • (9/30/1999) • **92**

St.-Aubin En Remilly 1995 • $25 • (5/31/1997) • **78**

AMIOT, PIERRE

Clos de la Roche 1997: Light and weedy. Tastes dry and unpleasant.–P.M. • $59 • (9/30/1999) • **72**

Clos de la Roche 1988 • $75 • (3/15/1991) • **86**

Clos de la Roche 1987 • $49 • (12/15/1989) • **86**

Clos de la Roche 1982 • $28 • (6/16/1985) SS • **93**

Clos St.-Denis 1997: A touch herbal but appealing, showing excellent fat on the midpalate, with toast, smoke, olive and raspberry flavors. Drink now through 2001.–P.M. • $59 • (9/30/1999) • **85**

Gevrey-Chambertin Les Combottes 1997: Light in color and kind of sweet, this has succulent flavors that seem smooth, but it turns a bit herbal on the finish.–P.M. • $39 • (9/30/1999) • **75**

Gevrey-Chambertin Les Combottes 1988 • $64 • (3/15/1991) • **89**

Gevrey-Chambertin Les Combottes 1987 • $42 • (12/15/1989) • **88**

Morey-St.-Denis Aux Charmes 1982 • $18 • (7/01/1985) • **88**

Morey-St.-Denis Les Millandes 1997: Slightly stemmy, it tastes herbal and astringent.–P.M. • $35 • (9/30/1999) • **72**

Morey-St.-Denis Les Ruchots 1997: A sweet-tasting wine, with licorice and raspberry. Fairly light in body, with a chewy finish.–P.M. • $35 • (9/30/1999) • **79**

Morey-St.-Denis Les Ruchots 1988 • $57 • (2/28/1991) • **80**

AMIRAL DE BEYCHEVELLE

St.-Julien 1996: Berry, tobacco and mushroom aromas follow through to the palate. Medium-bodied, with velvety tannins and a medium finish. A bit one-dimensional and earthy. Second label of Château Beychevelle. Best after 2000.–J.S. • $NA • (1/31/1999) • **81**

St.-Julien 1995 • $13 • (1/31/1998) • **80**

AMOURIERS, DOMAINE DES

Corbières Vieilles Vignes 1991 • $8 • (3/15/1994) • **82**

Côtes du Rhône 1994 • $9 • (10/15/1997) • **80**

Vacqueyras 1995 • $9 • (10/15/1997) • **84**

Vin de Pays de Vaucluse 1996 • $7 • (10/15/1997) • **79**

ANDRE, PIERRE

Aloxe-Corton 1993 • $35 • (11/15/1995) • **72**

Beaune Clos des Avaux 1994 • $23 • (11/15/1996) • **79**

Chassagne-Montrachet Red Chanvennes 1993 • $25 • (11/15/1995) • **73**

Châteauneuf-du-Pape 1990 • $21 • (4/15/1993) • **77**

Châteauneuf-du-Pape 1988 • $23 • (3/31/1991) • **84**

Clos Vougeot 1993 • $70 • (11/15/1995) • **77**

Corton 1994 • $75 • (11/15/1996) • **72**

Corton Hautes Mourottes 1992 • $36 • (12/15/1994) • **74**

Corton Le Clos du Roi 1985 • $45 • (7/15/1988) • **88**

Corton Pougets 1996: Pretty Pinot, quite ripe, showing some plum, blackberry, vanilla, wet earth and spice complexity. Supple tannin structure, with fresh, vibrant acidity that follows through on the lingering, intense finish. Made from Pierre André's own vineyards, this is one of the domaine's best wines in years. Drink now through 2003.–P.M. • $42 • (9/30/1998) • **89**

Corton Pougets 1993 • $48 • (11/15/1995) • **84**

Corton Pougets 1985 • $45 • (7/15/1988) • **90**

Gevrey-Chambertin Champlain 1994 • $29 • (11/15/1996) • **82**

Gevrey-Chambertin Champlain 1993 • $21 • (11/15/1995) • **82**

Gevrey-Chambertin Champlain 1992 • $21 • (12/15/1994) • **82**

Ladoix Clos des Chagnots 1993 • $20 • (11/15/1995) • **79**

Meursault 1996: A bit overdone. Butter, butterscotch and loads of mocha are counterbalanced by ripe fruit on the palate. The heavy toasted wood application brings about an intense, burning character on the finish, but the fruit is clean and pure. Best from 2006 through 2012.–P.M. • $25 • (5/31/1999) • **85**

Nuits-St.-Georges 1993 • $30 • (11/15/1995) • **76**

Pommard 1996: Quite elegant Pommard, pure and nicely silky, but a bit one-dimensional. It's sweet-tasting, with some cherry, raspberry and strawberry. Not very oaky. A bit hot on the finish, with the musty hint you sometimes get in filtered wines. Drink now through 2010.–P.M. • $36 • (9/30/1998) • **84**

Pommard Premier Cru 1993 • $38 • (11/15/1995) • **80**

Santenay Domaine du Prieuré Ste.-Agathe 1993 • $18 • (11/15/1995) • **79**

Savigny-lès-Beaune Aux Guettes 1993 • $25 • (11/15/1995) • **82**

Savigny-lès-Beaune Aux Guettes 1985 • $20 • (7/31/1988) • **85**

Savigny-lès-Beaune Clos des Guettes 1996: Full-bodied wine, with some ripe fruit but, unfortunately, it has a slight herbal aroma as well, and turns a bit metallic on the crisp finish.–P.M. • $25 • (9/30/1998) • **80**

Volnay 1994 • $30 • (11/15/1996) • **76**

Vosne-Romanée Les Suchots 1996: Very ripe version, showing kirsch and plum, gentle structure and friendly personality. Expresses the charm of the vintage. Drink through 2003.–B.S. • $33 • (9/30/1998) • **85**

Key: SS—Spectator Selection. CS—Cellar Selection. HR—Highly Recommended. $NA—Price not available. (BT)—Barrel tasting. Ⓐ—Auction Price.
For a key to the tasters' initials, see "How to Use These Listings."
Dates in parentheses represent the issues in which the ratings were published.

ANDREAS, CHATEAU

St.-Emilion 1998: Floral and berry character throughout this young wine. Medium-bodied, with fine tannins and a medium finish.–J.S. • $NA • (5/31/1999) (BT) • **85-89**

ANDRON-BLANQUET, CHATEAU

St.-Estèphe 1995 • $20 • (1/31/1998) • **87**
St.-Estèphe 1994 • $18 • (1/31/1997) • **83**
St.-Estèphe 1993 • $18 • (1/31/1996) • **79**
St.-Estèphe 1990 • $18 • (3/31/1993) • **88**

ANGELIQUE DE MONBOUSQUET, CHATEAU

St.-Emilion 1995 • $23 • (1/31/1998) • **76**

ANGELUS, CHATEAU

St.-Emilion 1999: Gorgeous aromas of minerals, violets and berries. Medium-bodied, with well-integrated tannins and a long finish. Very well done considering the hail damage here.–J.S. • $NA • (1/01/2000) (BT) • **85-89**
St.-Emilion 1998: Ripe and spicy. Full-bodied and silky, with plenty of ripe fruit and polished tannins on the finish. Very close to classic. Big, modern wine.–J.S. • $NA • (5/31/1999) (BT) • **90-94**
St.-Emilion 1997: A big and luscious wine for the vintage, this outstanding Bordeaux delivers loads of plum, berry and pomegranate character on the nose. It's full-bodied, with lots of velvety tannins and a long, long finish. Best after 2000.–J.S. • $75 • (1/31/2000) CS • **90**
St.-Emilion 1996: Promises more in its color and nose than it gives on the palate, but a very, very good glass of wine nonetheless. Full-bodied, with silky tannins and lots of berry and chocolate character. Just a slight lack of fruit in the center-palate keeps it from outstanding. Best after 2000.–J.S. • $70 Ⓐ • (1/31/1999) • **89**
St.-Emilion 1995 • $101 Ⓐ • (1/31/1998) • **94**
St.-Emilion 1994 • $56 Ⓐ • (1/31/1997) HR • **92**
St.-Emilion 1993 • $52 Ⓐ • (1/31/1996) • **90**
St.-Emilion 1992 • $41 Ⓐ • (5/15/1996) • **89**
St.-Emilion 1991 • $32 • (3/31/1994) • **80**
St.-Emilion 1990 • $170 Ⓐ • (3/31/1993) • **93**
St.-Emilion 1989: A young, very modern and sleek '89. Inky color. Wonderful aromas of spices, blackberries, cinnamon and vanilla. Full-bodied, with loads of silky tannins and a long, berry-cherry aftertaste. Just how I remember it.—1989 Bordeaux horizontal. Best after 2005.–J.S. • $138 Ⓐ • (5/31/1999) • **94**
St.-Emilion 1988: I have always loved this wine. It's just so flashy and showy, with everything up front. Incredibly rich and fruity, with chocolate and spice undertones. Full-bodied and extremely well concentrated, with big, velvety tannins and a long aftertaste of fruit and chocolaty vanilla.—1988 Bordeaux horizontal. Best after 2003.–J.S. • $80 Ⓐ • (11/30/1998) • **94**
St.-Emilion 1987 • $27 • (5/15/1990) • **85**
St.-Emilion 1986 • $58 Ⓐ • (6/30/1989) • **94**
St.-Emilion 1985 • $56 Ⓐ • (10/15/1994) • **89**
St.-Emilion 1983 • $53 Ⓐ • (10/15/1994) • **83**
St.-Emilion 1982: A weak period for this estate. Medium-garnet in color, with a ruby center. Pretty floral, berry and dried cherry aromas. Medium-bodied, with tobacco and fruit flavors, medium tannins and a slightly short finish. (1982 Bordeaux horizontal tasting). Drink now.–J.S. • $60 Ⓐ • (11/30/1998) • **87**
St.-Emilion 1981 • $30 Ⓐ • (10/15/1994) • **84**
St.-Emilion 1979 • $30 • (10/15/1989) • **82**
St.-Emilion 1947 • $NA • (5/31/1997) • **85**

ANGERVILLE, MARQUIS D'

Volnay Champans 1996: A little unforgiving in aroma and flavor today, this red nonetheless has lovely velvety texture, bright acidity and depth. I'd give it the benefit of the doubt. Best from 2002 through 2008.–B.S. • $60 • (1/01/2000) • **87**
Volnay Champans 1993 • $29 • (5/15/1996) • **90**
Volnay Champans 1992 • $25 • (5/15/1995) • **84**
Volnay Champans 1953 • $NA • (12/31/1994) • **92**
Volnay Clos des Ducs 1996: No holds barred in this traditional red Burgundy. From the spicy oak and leather aromas and sous-bois, tealike flavors to the stiff, tannic structure this shows personality, but needs some time. Best from 2001 through 2005.–B.S. • $90 • (1/01/2000) • **87**
Volnay Clos des Ducs 1992 • $32 • (5/15/1995) • **87**
Volnay Clos des Ducs 1988 • $47 • (10/31/1993) • **88**
Volnay Clos des Ducs 1985 • $35 • (3/15/1988) • **80**
Volnay Les Caillerets 1992 • $30 • (5/15/1995) • **87**
Volnay Premier Cru 1995: A wine that grows on you. Not much show-and-tell on the nose, but the palate is filled with lovely, rich, ripe fruit, and the massive tannins are superfine. Beautiful, *terroir*-driven, soil-comes-first kind of gravelly, medium-bodied Burgundy. Drink now through 2005.–P.M. • $25 • (8/31/1998) • **89**
Volnay Premier Cru 1993 • $30 • (5/15/1996) • **92**
Volnay Taillepieds 1995: Racy and elegant, showing violet, black currant and cherry flavors blanketed for now by oak and lively acidity. Vibrant, sauvage, medium-bodied, with tough tannins, but not as ripe and rich as you might hope. Drink through 2005.–P.M. • $35 • (8/31/1998) • **89**
Volnay Taillepieds 1992 • $27 • (5/15/1995) • **86**

ANGLUDET, CHATEAU D'

Margaux 1998: Rather odd, slightly burnt and herbal in character. Some decent fruit concentration, but short and aggressive on the finish.–J.S. • $NA • (5/31/1999) (BT) • **75-79**
Margaux 1997: Shows bright plum, berry and spice aromas. Medium-bodied, with fine tannins and a light finish. Drink now.–J.S. • $18 • (1/31/2000) • **85**
Margaux 1996: Not a big wine, but a delicious drinkable style that shows good finesse. Aromas of berries and spices follow through to the palate. Medium-bodied, with medium tannins and a fruity, spicy aftertaste. Drink now through 2001.–J.S. • $18 • (1/31/1999) • **85**
Margaux 1995 • $30 Ⓐ • (1/31/1998) • **88**
Margaux 1994 • $27 • (1/31/1997) • **84**
Margaux 1993 • $30 • (1/31/1996) • **80**
Margaux 1990 • $48 Ⓐ • (3/31/1993) • **86**
Margaux 1989: Ready to drink. Medium-ruby color and enticing aromas of blackberries and tobacco. Medium-bodied, with milk chocolate and coffee flavors and soft texture. (1989 Bordeaux horizontal tasting).–J.S. • $49 Ⓐ • (5/31/1999) • **87**
Margaux 1988: Not holding up well, with rather earthy and sweaty saddle character on the nose. Medium-bodied, with fine tannins and a ripe fruit finish. Hurry.—(1988 Bordeaux horizontal tasting).–J.S. • $38 Ⓐ • (11/30/1998) • **80**
Margaux 1987 • $12 • (5/15/1990) • **78**
Margaux 1986 • $38 Ⓐ • (6/15/1989) • **91**
Margaux 1985 • $36 Ⓐ • (4/15/1988) • **90**
Margaux 1983 • $44 Ⓐ • (10/15/1986) • **93**
Margaux 1982 • $53 Ⓐ • (8/31/1992) • **91**
Margaux 1961 • $28 • (4/30/1996) • **84**

ANNEREAUX, CHATEAU DES

Lalande-de-Pomerol 1996: Nice silky texture to this red, but it's slightly weedy under the berry and cherry aromas and flavors. Medium body, fruity finish. Drink now.–J.S. • $16 • (2/28/1999) • **81**

ANNICHE, CHATEAU

Premières Côtes de Bordeaux 1982: Not much here. Medium-garnet color, with a gold edge. Medium-bodied and very light. (1982 Bordeaux horizontal tasting).–J.S. • $NA • (11/30/1998) • **78**

ANSELME, PERE

Châteauneuf-du-Pape 1989 • $16 • (3/31/1994) • **83**
Châteauneuf-du-Pape 1986 • $14 • (10/15/1991) • **84**
Châteauneuf-du-Pape 1985 • $14 • (10/15/1991) • **86**
Châteauneuf-du-Pape 1983 • $13 • (10/15/1991) • **89**
Châteauneuf-du-Pape 1981 • $25 • (10/15/1991) • **88**
Châteauneuf-du-Pape Clos Bimard 1989 • $NA • (10/15/1991) • **84**
Châteauneuf-du-Pape Cuvée Prestige Clos Bimard 1988 • $20 • (10/15/1991) • **88**
Châteauneuf-du-Pape La Fiole 1990 • $17 • (4/15/1993) • **85**
Châteauneuf-du-Pape La Fiole 1984 • $12 • (10/31/1987) • **88**
Châteauneuf-du-Pape La Fiole du Pape NV • $14 • (9/30/1989) • **86**
Châteauneuf-du-Pape La Fiole du Pape Uno Bono Fiolo NV • $13 • (1/31/1988) • **82**
Châteauneuf-du-Pape La Fiole Grand Cuvée 1984 • $13 • (10/31/1987) • **74**
Côtes du Rhône-Villages 1994 • $14 • (10/15/1997) • **85**
Côtes du Rhône-Villages Seguret 1990 • $9 • (4/15/1993) • **83**

ANSELME, PERE

Côtes du Ventoux 1991 • $7 • (6/15/1993) • **84**
Gigondas 1989 • $14 • (4/15/1993) • **78**
Merlot Vin de Pays des Côteaux d'Enserune NV • $6 • (7/15/1989) • **78**

ANTECH

Brut Blanquette de Limoux Tête de Cuvée NV: A good, solid bubbly that combines fresh, doughy aromas with citrus flavors and a creamy texture. Drink now. • $13 • (10/15/1999) • **84**

ANTONIN, AUGUSTE

Côte de Brouilly 1997: Deeply colored, this smells slightly lifted and tastes like kirsch and cassis. Saturated in fruit, it's firm, tight and alcoholic on the finish, yet shows good concentration, substance and character. Drink now through 2002.–B.S. • $15 • (10/15/1999) • **84**
Côte de Brouilly 1995 • $17 • (4/30/1997) • **86**

APOLLINE, CHATEAU L'

St.-Emilion 1997: A good, well-focused red with berry and cherry character, medium body and fine tannins. Drink now through 2002.–J.S. • $NA • (1/31/2000) • **85**

AQUERIA, CHATEAU D'

Lirac 1997: Light and a bit unripe, this simple red offers modest fruit and a short finish.–P.M. • $11 • (12/15/1999) • **75**
Lirac 1996: Delicate, fairly sweet-tasting and ripe, with raspberry, plum, smoke, toasty oak and currant notes of medium intensity. Medium-bodied, with well-integrated tannins that make it accessible now. Drink now.–P.M. • $10 • (11/15/1998) • **83**
Lirac White 1996: Good structure and acidity, with a lime note, but it also has a slight cooked apple flavor. A decent, medium-bodied white to drink with fish or chicken. Drink now.–P.M. • $12 • (11/15/1998) • **80**
Tavel 1998: A crisp rosé, tasting of orange marmalade, plums and cherries. Tart finish.–P.M. • $15 • (11/15/1999) • **78**
Tavel 1997: A straightforward and slightly tough rosé, but it has raspberry and strawberry character, with an attractive sweetness on the finish. Drink now.–P.M. • $15 • (11/15/1998) • **80**
Tavel 1996 • $15 • (10/15/1997) • **85**

ARCAUTE, J.M.

Merlot Bordeaux 1995 • $8 • (1/31/1998) • **81**
Merlot Bordeaux 1994 • $8 • (7/31/1996) • **81**

ARCHAMBAULT, PIERRE

Sancerre Domaine de la Perrière 1996 • $16 • (5/31/1998) • **85**

ARCHE, CHATEAU D'

Haut-Médoc 1997: Strange aromas of green apple and grape. Light-bodied, with a watery finish.–J.S. • $20 • (1/01/2000) • **79**
Haut-Médoc 1996: A bit lean but with some good fruit character. Aromas of mineral and blackberry follow through to the palate. Medium-bodied, with firm and slightly dry tannins, a mineral and fruit aftertaste.–J.S. • $15 • (1/31/1999) • **83**
Haut-Médoc 1995 • $15 • (1/31/1998) • **86**

ARCHE, CHATEAU D'

Sauternes 1997: Full-bodied, very sweet, thick and rich, with wonderful lemon, pineapple, honey and spice character. This is holding back, so give it time. Best after 2001.–J.S. • $33 • (1/31/2000) • **91**
Sauternes 1990 • $31 • (4/15/1995) • **93**
Sauternes 1989 • $26 • (4/15/1995) • **91**
Sauternes 1988 • $25 • (4/15/1995) • **88**
Sauternes 1987 • $32 • (6/15/1990) • **85**
Sauternes 1986 • $23 • (4/15/1995) • **93**
Sauternes 1983 • $23 • (1/31/1988) • **93**

ARCINS, CHATEAU D'

Haut-Médoc 1996: Offering berry and mahogany aromas and flavors, this is medium- to light-bodied, with light tannins and a light finish.–J.S. • $NA • (2/28/1999) • **79**
Haut-Médoc 1995 • $12 • (1/31/1998) • **88**

ARFEULIERE, DOMAINE DE L'

Mâcon-Uchizy Les Maranches 1996 • $10 • (5/31/1998) • **73**
Mâcon-Uchizy Les Maranches 1995 • $13 • (5/31/1997) • **84**

ARJOLLE, DOMAINE DE L'

Cabernet Sauvignon Vin de Pays des Côtes de Thongue 1995 • $16 • (6/15/1998) • **84**
Sauvignon Blanc Vin de Pays des Côtes de Thongue 1996 • $9 • (5/15/1998) • **78**
Syrah Vin de Pays des Côtes de Thongue 1995 • $11 • (1/01/1998) • **85**
Vin de Pays des Côtes de Thongue Cuvée de l'Arjolle 1995: Full-bodied, very tannic and rustic in texture and fruity in flavor, this deep-colored, smoky and gamy-tasting red needs equally robust food. A blend: 70 percent Cabernet Sauvignon, 30 percent Merlot. Drink now. • $11 • (8/31/1998) • **84**

ARLOT, DOMAINE DE L'

Côte de Nuits-Villages Clos du Châpeau 1989 • $24 • (1/31/1992) • **83**
Côte de Nuits-Villages Clos du Châpeau 1988 • $21 • (3/31/1991) • **80**
Nuits-St.-Georges 1993 • $21 Ⓐ • (5/15/1996) • **88**
Nuits-St.-Georges 1990 • $33 • (12/15/1992) • **79**
Nuits-St.-Georges Clos de l'Arlot 1997: An old-fashioned red Burgundy, light-colored and light- to medium-bodied, with wet forest underbrush, wild mushroom, plum and cherry aromas. Decent sweetness, but rather dry on the finish, with tough tannins. • $51 • (1/01/2000) • **77**
Nuits-St.-Georges Clos de l'Arlot 1995: Maturing fast, browning on the edges and tasting of cinnamon and brown sugar. Silky on the palate like an old wine, but turns bitter on the finish.–P.M. • $30 • (8/31/1998) • **78**
Nuits-St.-Georges Clos de l'Arlot 1993 • $34 • (5/15/1996) • **89**
Nuits-St.-Georges Clos de l'Arlot 1990 • $58 Ⓐ • (12/15/1992) • **78**
Nuits-St.-Georges Clos de l'Arlot 1989 • $48 • (1/31/1992) • **78**
Nuits-St.-Georges Clos de l'Arlot 1988 • $43 • (3/31/1991) • **87**
Nuits-St.-Georges Clos des Forêts St.-Georges 1997: Seductive Pinot Noir perfumes, offering red- and blackberry notes along with a smoky, grilled meat, plummy character. Definitely tannic but the tannins are well-integrated all the way to the chewy, ripe-tasting finish. Drink now through 2004.–P.M. • $56 • (1/01/2000) • **87**
Nuits-St.-Georges Clos des Forêts St.-Georges 1996: Wonderful, sweet-tasting fruit, with black cherry, blackberry, mineral, spice and smoke layers that roll around the palate like pebbles in the waves, repeatedly delivering seductive flavors. Drink now through 2005.–P.M. • $48 • (7/31/1999) • **90**
Nuits-St.-Georges Clos des Forêts St.-Georges 1995: An international style, tasting like a good California Pinot, with mocha, spice and flavors like sugar-glazed orange peel covered with chocolate. A bit one-dimensional. Drink now.–P.M. • $37 • (8/31/1998) • **83**
Nuits-St.-Georges Clos des Forêts St.-Georges 1993 • $43 Ⓐ • (5/15/1996) • **92**
Nuits-St.-Georges Clos des Forêts St.-Georges 1990 • $59 Ⓐ • (12/15/1992) • **87**
Nuits-St.-Georges Clos des Forêts St.-Georges 1989 • $55 • (1/31/1992) • **90**
Nuits-St.-Georges Clos des Forêts St.-Georges 1988 • $46 Ⓐ • (3/31/1991) • **85**
Nuits-St.-Georges Clos des Forêts St.-Georges 1987 • $43 • (3/31/1990) • **83**
Nuits-St.-Georges Clos des Forêts St.-Georges Cuvée Jeunes Vignes 1997: Elegant and floral red Burgundy, offering a lovely, sweet-tasting midpalate character. Tastes of black cherry, some toasted oak, plum and mineral. Balanced in a delicate way on the lingering finish. Wonderful. Drink now through 2005. • $34 • (1/01/2000) • **88**
Romanée St.-Vivant 1995: Silky beauty. A creamlike, full-bodied red that takes you by surprise. Starts out reserved, with some vanilla and cinnamon notes, but on the palate it ambushes the senses, delivering rich, ripe, opulent texture laced with smooth tannins and plenty of red- and blackberry flavor. Drink now through 2005.–P.M. • $90 • (8/31/1998) • **93**
Vosne-Romanée Les Suchots 1997: Ripe and medium-bodied, but it has a mature profile already, with wet earth, wet underbrush and mushroom

Key: SS—Spectator Selection. CS—Cellar Selection. HR—Highly Recommended. $NA—Price not available. (BT)—Barrel tasting. Ⓐ—Auction Price.
For a key to the tasters' initials, see "How to Use These Listings."
Dates in parentheses represent the issues in which the ratings were published.

FRANCE

notes and drying tannins. Still, the black fruit is delicious. Drink now through 2005. • $56 • (1/01/2000) • **84**

Vosne-Romanée Les Suchots 1996: Rather lean style, a bit astringent, delivering some faint cherry and herb notes.–P.M. • $56 • (7/31/1999) • **78**

ARMAILHAC, CHATEAU D'

Pauillac 1999: Lovely plum, berry and chocolate character. Full-bodied, with full velvety tannins and a long, fruity finish. Amazing quality for the vintage.–J.S. • $NA • (1/01/2000) (BT) • **90-94**

Pauillac 1998: Shows some lovely currant, berry character but the palate is slightly diluted. Medium- to light-bodied, with fine tannins and a light finish. A bit disappointing really, but may improve.–J.S. • $NA • (5/31/1999) (BT) • **80-84**

Pauillac 1997: A fresh and perfumed wine with plum and berry character and a hint of currants. Medium-bodied, with velvety tannins and a medium finish. Drink now.–J.S. • $21 • (1/31/2000) • **87**

Pauillac 1996: A good, sleek '96. Attractive aromas of raspberry and dried cherry. Medium-bodied, with firm tannins and a silky texture. Medium finish with a chalky, berry aftertaste. Best after 2000.–J.S. • $31 Ⓐ • (1/31/1999) • **87**

Pauillac 1995 • $25 Ⓐ • (1/31/1998) • **92**

Pauillac 1994 • $27 • (1/31/1997) • **86**

Pauillac 1993 • $25 • (1/31/1996) • **89**

Pauillac 1992 • $20 • (4/15/1995) • **80**

Pauillac 1991 • $20 • (3/31/1994) • **85**

Pauillac 1990 • $25 • (3/31/1993) • **89**

Pauillac 1989: A burly, tannic wine. Dark ruby-colored. Plenty of cherry, bark and mint aromas. Full-bodied, with chewy tannins and a long, minty, cherry aftertaste. Diamond in the rough. Needs time to mellow.—1989 Bordeaux horizontal. Best after 2004.–J.S. • $63 Ⓐ • (5/31/1999) • **92**

ARMAND, COMTE

Pommard Clos des Epeneaux 1997: Thick, ripe and full-bodied, with a round texture. Offers nice black fruit and interesting petrol and tar notes, but a slight herbal character creeps in, especially on the nose. Has just enough tannic chewiness to extend the long finish. Drink now through 2010.–P.M. • $61 • (1/01/2000) • **87**

Pommard Clos des Epeneaux 1996: A deep wine—one where you have to put your nose far into the glass to capture the subtleties. The black fruit, game, mineral and currant notes fill the palate, proving how dense and thick this '96 red Burgundy is. A brilliant Pommard. Best from 2006 through 2020.–P.M. • $102 Ⓐ • (9/30/1999) HR • **97**

Pommard Clos des Epeneaux 1995: Serious red, offering sweet-tasting ripe fruit on the midpalate, lovely mineral, lead-penci and earth complexity and deft oak treatment. Firm texture, with hard but ripe tannins, it's tempting now but should improve with cellaring. Best from 2002 through 2007.–P.M. • $60 • (8/31/1998) • **91**

Pommard Clos des Epeneaux 1993 • $40 Ⓐ • (5/15/1996) • **85**

Pommard Clos des Epeneaux 1990 • $50 Ⓐ • (12/15/1992) • **93**

Pommard Clos des Epeneaux 1989 • $50 • (11/30/1992) • **82**

Pommard Clos des Epeneaux 1988 • $52 Ⓐ • (2/28/1991) • **90**

Pommard Clos des Epeneaux 1987 • $41 • (8/31/1990) • **81**

Pommard Clos des Epeneaux 1985 • $89 Ⓐ • (3/15/1988) • **91**

ARMES DE BRANDEAU, CHATEAU LES

Côtes de Castillon 1997: Like watered-down fruit juice. Strawberry aromas. Light body and a diluted finish.–J.S. • $10 • (2/28/1999) • **71**

Côtes de Castillon 1995 • $10 • (1/01/1998) • **79**

ARNAULD, CHATEAU

Haut-Médoc 1998: A bit diluted with some pleasant berry, plum character. Medium-bodied, with firm tannins and a watery finish.–J.S. • $NA • (5/31/1999) (BT) • **80-84**

Haut-Médoc 1996: Rather simple, but well done. Some intriguing berry and mineral character. Medium-bodied, with silky tannins and a light, fruity aftertaste. Drink now.–J.S. • $20 • (1/31/1999) • **85**

Haut-Médoc 1995 • $20 • (1/31/1998) • **85**

Haut-Médoc 1993 • $17 • (1/31/1996) • **81**

Haut-Médoc 1992 • $11 • (4/15/1995) • **78**

Haut-Médoc 1991 • $11 • (3/31/1994) • **77**

Haut-Médoc 1990 • $19 • (3/31/1993) • **86**

Haut-Médoc 1989: A bit rustic but very ripe, slight raisin and earth character on both nose and palate. Full-bodied and round, with soft texture and ripe fruit, but slightly simple in character. (1989 Bordeaux horizontal tasting). Drink now.–J.S. • $NA • (5/31/1999) • **84**

Haut-Médoc 1988 • $15 • (4/30/1991) • **84**

Haut-Médoc 1987 • $13 • (11/30/1989) • **79**

Haut-Médoc 1986 • $18 • (11/30/1989) • **82**

Haut-Médoc 1985 • $15 • (2/15/1988) • **82**

Haut-Médoc 1982 • $17 • (11/30/1989) • **71**

ARNOUX, ROBERT

Bourgogne 1997: Good quality for a Bourgogne rouge, but shows a slightly stemmy character along with sweet berry notes. Turns a bit dry on the finish, but still a very satisfying Pinot. Drink now through 2007.–P.M. • $NA • (1/01/2000) • **85**

Bourgogne 1994 • $16 • (11/15/1996) • **80**

Bourgogne 1993 • $18 • (5/15/1996) • **85**

Clos de Vougeot 1997: Firm and tannic. Full-bodied and a bit earthy, a fruity and flavorful Pinot Noir that offers black cherry, wild berry, mineral and wet earth. Kicks in with a tannic backbone as the spice, mocha and coffee notes from the oak treatment take over on the chewy finish. Best from 2005 through 1010.–P.M. • $NA • (1/01/2000) • **90**

Clos de Vougeot 1996: Earthy blackberry aromas and flavors are enveloped in a huge structure in this bold, brawny red. Serious tannins here, along with richness and intensity. Major-league finish. Best from 2004 through 2012.–B.S. • $90 • (9/30/1998) • **90**

Clos de Vougeot 1994 • $75 • (11/15/1996) • **81**

Clos de Vougeot 1993 • $80 • (11/15/1995) • **91**

Clos de Vougeot 1991 • $60 • (8/31/1994) • **86**

Clos de Vougeot 1988 • $70 • (3/15/1991) • **78**

Echézeaux 1997: Rather light and delicate, even a bit diluted, with rough tannins. Lacks a bit of ripeness, although it shows red and black fruit. Tannic finish. Drink now through 2002.–P.M. • $110 • (1/01/2000) • **80**

Echézeaux 1996: Broad, ripe and opulent displaying black cherry, spice and earth, all rich and fleshy, lively and expressive, finishing with silky tannins and sweet fruit. Best from 2001 through 2006.–B.S. • $66 Ⓐ • (9/30/1998) • **91**

Echézeaux 1994 • $73 • (11/15/1996) • **89**

Echézeaux 1993 • $80 • (11/15/1995) • **89**

Echézeaux 1991 • $72 • (5/31/1995) • **87**

Nuits-St.-Georges 1991 • $30 • (5/31/1995) • **86**

Nuits-St.-Georges Les Corvées Pagets 1997: A well-made Pinot, ripe and silky, with fine fruit, balanced oak and wet earth complexity. Lacks perhaps some intensity to rate higher, but there's a chalky, minerally character that is subtly appealing. Drink now through 2010.–P.M. • $NA • (1/01/2000) • **90**

Nuits-St.-Georges Les Corvées Pagets 1996: Sappy, spicy fruit, along with smoke tones and a mineral note, yet it lacks the flesh to fill out its Schwarzenegger-like structure. Best from 2001.–B.S. • $60 • (9/30/1998) • **84**

Nuits-St.-Georges Les Corvées Pagets 1994 • $50 • (11/15/1996) • **83**

Nuits-St.-Georges Les Corvées Pagets 1993 • $55 • (11/15/1995) • **81**

Nuits-St.-Georges Les Corvées Pagets 1991 • $55 • (5/31/1995) • **88**

Nuits-St.-Georges Les Poisets 1997: Delicious. Rich and full-bodied Pinot with a lovely mouthfeel, all suppleness and ripeness—and for a '97, unusually firm tannins. Sweet red berry, smoke and toasted bread character. Drink now through 2005.–P.M. • $NA • (1/01/2000) • **90**

Nuits-St.-Georges Les Poisets 1996: Fresh and zesty, a red that bursts with cassis bush, green olive, cranberry and dried herb character. Fairly lean, but it has good acidity perking up the finish. Drink now.–P.M. • $55 • (9/30/1998) • **82**

Nuits-St.-Georges Les Poisets 1994 • $44 • (11/15/1996) • **84**

Nuits-St.-Georges Les Poisets 1993 • $50 • (11/15/1995) • **81**

Nuits-St.-Georges Les Poisets 1991 • $55 • (5/31/1995) • **87**

Nuits-St.-Georges Les Procès 1997: Soft and supple, but without much depth, this '97 red Burgundy has redeeming ripe fruit mixed with a stemmy character. Turns crisp on the finish. Drink now.–P.M. • $NA • (1/01/2000) • **80**

Nuits-St.-Georges Les Procès 1996: More terroir than fruit. This is fresh, intense and minerally, with iron and blood elements, blackberry notes and a persistence of flavor and concentration. Ends with big, ripe tannins. Best from 2002 through 2008.–B.S. • $56 • (9/30/1998) • **88**

Romanée St.-Vivant 1997: This silky, flavorful, thick red Burgundy is soft and lush, showing lovely, deep red berry and blackberry character, with toast and smoke. Good ripeness through the natural-tasting finish. Drink now through 2005.–P.M. • $NA • (1/01/2000) • **88**

ARNOUX, ROBERT

Romanée St.-Vivant 1996: Seductive black cherry, plum, spice and earth combine with richness and depth to deliver immense pleasure, supported by vibrant acidity and firm tannins. The finish is long and satisfying. Best from 2001 through 2005.–B.S. • $364 Ⓐ • (9/30/1998) • **92**
Romanée St.-Vivant 1994 • $160 • (11/15/1996) • **92**
Romanée St.-Vivant 1993 • $NA • (11/15/1995) • **93**
Romanée St.-Vivant 1991 • $210 • (5/31/1995) • **92**
Romanée St.-Vivant 1988 • $250 • (11/15/1990) • **91**
Vosne-Romanée 1997: Fresh and elegant. Medium-bodied, it offers a range of well-focused, sweet-tasting, ripe fruit flavors backed by deftly dosed oak. Not a blockbuster, but what's there is attractive. Drink now through 2003.–P.M. • $NA • (1/01/2000) • **86**
Vosne-Romanée 1996: Offers decent fruit and an elegant frame, but lacks a bit of opulence, tasting a bit crisp and tart, with cherry, olives and dried herb notes. Short finish.–P.M. • $45 • (9/30/1998) • **82**
Vosne-Romanée 1992 • $38 • (5/15/1995) • **84**
Vosne-Romanée Aux Reignots 1997: Supple and ripe, medium-bodied and pleasant, with red fruit, toasted oak and petrol notes. Lacks a bit of depth, but fun to drink on release. Drink now through 2003.–P.M. • $NA • (1/01/2000) • **83**
Vosne-Romanée Aux Reignots 1996: Good red fruit here, ripe cherries and berries, in a silky, refined style with moderate tannins. Elegant and well integrated at this stage. Drink through 2004.–B.S. • $55 • (9/30/1998) • **89**
Vosne-Romanée Aux Reignots 1994 • $60 • (11/15/1996) • **84**
Vosne-Romanée Hautes Maizières 1997: Fairly ripe but also slightly stemmy, this medium-bodied wine seems a bit rootless and unanchored in a specific site, but it has licorice, red berry and blackberry notes. A bit rustic on the finish. Best from 2002 through 2005.–P.M. • $NA • (1/01/2000) • **83**
Vosne-Romanée Hautes Maizières 1996: Very reticent on the nose, yet the palate offers concentrated black cherry flavor in a sophisticated style, with firm ripe tannins, lively acidity and a lingering finish. Drink through 2005.–B.S. • $50 • (9/30/1998) • **87**
Vosne-Romanée Hautes Maizières 1994 • $40 • (11/15/1996) • **82**
Vosne-Romanée Hautes Maizières 1993 • $50 • (11/15/1995) • **78**
Vosne-Romanée Hautes Maizières 1991 • $40 • (5/31/1995) • **86**
Vosne-Romanée Les Chaumes 1997: There's ripe fruit in this subtle and underhanded red. Aromatically shy, it's only on the palate that you get the sense of wet earth and mineral character. Medium-bodied, with a lingering finish. Needs time. Best from 2002 through 2007.–P.M. • $NA • (1/01/2000) • **88**
Vosne-Romanée Les Chaumes 1996: Elegant and suave, with a supple mouthfeel. Tastes a bit astringent, but also delivers some red- and blackberry notes. The color is near to brick-red, suggesting it's best to drink soon. Slightly dry on the finish.–P.M. • $60 • (9/30/1998) • **81**
Vosne-Romanée Les Chaumes 1994 • $52 • (11/15/1996) • **82**
Vosne-Romanée Les Chaumes 1993 • $55 • (11/15/1995) • **88**
Vosne-Romanée Les Chaumes 1991 • $50 • (5/31/1995) • **89**
Vosne-Romanée Les Chaumes 1988 • $45 • (2/28/1991) • **80**
Vosne-Romanée Les Suchots 1997: Beautifully crafted. Clean and pure, thick and rich, a full-bodied '97 red Burgundy that tastes sweet, harmonious, supple and velvety, but turns on the fireworks on the intense finish. Hopefully a slight vegetal aroma will go away with age. Best from 2001 through 2007.–P.M. • $120 • (1/01/2000) • **90**
Vosne-Romanée Les Suchots 1996: A touch earthy, with ripe plummy flavor and a hint of griottes beneath. Excellent acidity and richness, finishing with supple yet firm tannins. Drink through 2004.–B.S. • $100 • (9/30/1998) • **90**
Vosne-Romanée Les Suchots 1994 • $75 • (11/15/1996) • **79**
Vosne-Romanée Les Suchots 1993 • $72 Ⓐ • (11/15/1995) • **87**
Vosne-Romanée Les Suchots 1991 • $70 • (5/31/1995) • **88**
Vosne-Romanée Les Suchots 1988 • $60 • (2/28/1991) • **86**
Vosne-Romanée Les Suchots 1985 • $52 • (7/31/1988) • **90**

ARNOUX PERE & FILS

Bourgogne 1996: Fruity and fresh, this is well-made. Fairly compacted, with intense red- and blackberry and black cherry character. Balanced, pleasant finish.–P.M. • $12 • (9/30/1998) • **86**
Chorey-lès-Beaune Confrelin 1994 • $NA • (11/15/1996) • **75**
Hautes-Côtes de Beaune 1996: A bit earthy, but has some lush texture, with a vanilla, spice and delicate raspberry character. Juicy finish. Drink now.–P.M. • $15 • (9/30/1998) • **82**

Key: SS—Spectator Selection. CS—Cellar Selection. HR—Highly Recommended. $NA—Price not available. (BT)—Barrel tasting. Ⓐ—Auction Price.
For a key to the tasters' initials, see "How to Use These Listings."
Dates in parentheses represent the issues in which the ratings were published.

Savigny-lès-Beaune 1994 • $NA • (11/15/1996) • **78**

ARRETXEA, DOMAINE

Irouléguy Cuvée Haitza 1997: An intense and pure-tasting red from southwest France, with a firm backbone of acidity and a muscular structure supported by cassis, dark plum, red cherry and currant flavors, with notes of tobacco box and wet earth. There's also good peppery elements throughout, from the aroma to the finish. Tannat and Cabernet Sauvignon. Best from 2001 through 2006.–K.M. • $22 • (4/30/2000) • **89**

ARROSEE, CHATEAU L'

St.-Emilion 1997: A very good wine with pretty tobacco, cherry and plum character. Medium-bodied, with chewy tannins and a fresh finish. Best after 2000.–J.S. • $49 • (1/31/2000) • **87**
St.-Emilion 1989 • $46 Ⓐ • (4/30/1992) HR • **93**
St.-Emilion 1988: I have tasted this numerous times over the last year and I always scored it very good to outstanding, but this bottle seems a little tired. There is an amber hue to the ruby color, with cedar and berry aromas and flavors and a slightly short finish. (1988 Bordeaux horizontal tasting). Drink now.–J.S. • $38 Ⓐ • (11/30/1998) • **83**
St.-Emilion 1987 • $28 • (5/15/1990) • **82**
St.-Emilion 1986 • $70 Ⓐ • (2/15/1989) • **87**
St.-Emilion 1985 • $89 Ⓐ • (2/29/1988) • **85**
St.-Emilion 1983 • $36 Ⓐ • (5/16/1986) • **87**
St.-Emilion 1982: You've got to like this juicy 1982. Seriously young color, with chocolate, cherry, berry and earth character. Medium-bodied, with a silky, fine finish. Caressing. (1982 Bordeaux horizontal tasting). Drink now.–J.S.
• $84 Ⓐ • (11/30/1998) • **90**

ARTIGUE DE SENEJAC

Haut-Médoc 1995 • $11 • (4/30/1997) • **83**

ARUMS DE LAGRANGE, LES

Bordeaux White 1998: An excellent young white, with lots of lemon meringue. Medium- to full-bodied, with a coconut character and a long, flavorful finish. Drink now through 2004.–J.S. • $25 • (2/29/2000) • **90**
Bordeaux White 1997: This solid white Bordeaux is a new wine from Lagrange, with lots of pear, vanilla and apple character. Medium-bodied, with a light chalkiness and a fresh, light coconut finish. Drink now.–J.S. • $25 • (9/30/1999) • **87**

ASPES, DOMAINE DES

Chardonnay-Viognier Vin de Pays d'Oc 1997: Firm, with green peach and tea flavors. Ends on notes of lemon and lime. Drink now.–K.M. • $13 • (12/15/1998) • **81**
Merlot Vin de Pays d'Oc 1997: Inviting fruit flavors and a juicy texture make this Merlot appealing, though it turns lean on the finish. Moderately tannic. Drink now. • $9 • (10/31/1998) • **83**
Viognier Vin de Pays d'Oc 1997: Smooth and fairly supple, with ripe peach flavors and onion notes. A bit heavy-handed, but still enjoyable. Drink now.–K.M. • $15 • (12/15/1998) • **80**

AUBAC, LOUIS D'

Anjou La Berverie 1996: Extremely ripe, with Bing cherry aromas and flavors rather than the typical black currant and leaf notes. Nonetheless, it shows concentration and a lush texture, with light tannins for support. Drink now.–B.S. • $12 • (10/31/1998) • **85**
Muscadet de Sèvre et Maine Château de la Bourdinière 1996: Mature in color, aroma and flavor, yet the beeswax, honey and apple flavors are appealing and backed up by a sharp acidity that keeps the elements together nicely. Drink now.–B.S. • $12 • (11/15/1998) • **85**
Vin de Pays du Jardin de la France Musquet 1996: Young-tasting, with green apple and pear flavors. Not particularly complex, but serviceable. Drink now. • $12 • (9/15/1998) • **80**

AUBERT, DOMAINE MAX

Châteauneuf-du-Pape La Nonciature 1995 • $20 • (10/15/1997) • **80**

Châteauneuf-du-Pape La Nonciature 1994 • $20 • (10/15/1995) • **82**

Châteauneuf-du-Pape White Domaine de la Présidente 1997: Tart, even astringent, rather lean, with modest fruit and spice complexity.–P.M. • $21 • (11/15/1998) • **74**

Châteauneuf-du-Pape White La Nonciature 1997: Just wonderful. Tastes like a barrel sample (it was bottled only a few months after the harvest). Superripe yet refined and elegant, it shows wonderful balance of fruit, acidity and what appears to be oak. Rich and thick, succulent and juicy, this full-bodied Southern Rhône white caresses the palate with fat, oily texture as you enjoy the mandarin orange, peach, apricot, pear and pie flavors. Drink now through 2005.–P.M. • $35 • (9/30/1998) • **92**

Châteauneuf-du-Pape White La Nonciature 1996 • $20 • (10/15/1997) • **87**

Châteauneuf-du-Pape White La Nonciature Grande Réserve 1998: Rich and ripe, with a midpalate fatness that's attractive. Chewy and full-bodied, with pear tart, honey and spice character. Lingering finish. Drink now through 2010.–P.M. • $30 • (6/30/2000) • **89**

Châteauneuf-du-Pape White La Nonciature Grande Réserve 1996: Traditional, with white peach, floral, quince tart, walnut oil and butter notes. Rather round, but it has a burnt butter and rustic finish that turns tough. Best from 2002 through 2010.–P.M. • $30 • (12/15/1999) • **84**

Côtes du Rhône Château de Galliffet 1996: Medium bodied, with plum, fig and milk chocolate character. Slightly unbalanced and drying finish.–P.M. • $23 • (11/15/1998) • **74**

Côtes du Rhône Château de Galliffet 1995 • $23 • (10/15/1997) • **85**

Côtes du Rhône Château de Galliffet 1994 • $18 • (10/15/1997) • **85**

Côtes du Rhône Domaine de la Présidente 1998: Balanced and seductive. Medium-bodied, showing caressing tannins and medium intensity of black fruit, vanilla and spice. Well made but not too concentrated. Drink now through 2003.–P.M. • $12 • (12/15/1999) • **85**

Côtes du Rhône Domaine de la Présidente 1997: Light in color, body and flavors, it tastes oxidized and shows a rustic character, with drying tannins.–P.M. • $12 • (11/15/1998) • **71**

Côtes du Rhône Domaine de la Présidente 1995 • $9 • (10/15/1996) • **85**

Côtes du Rhône Domaine de la Presidente 1994 • $10 • (11/15/1995) • **79**

Côtes du Rhône Domaine de la Présidente Blanc de Blancs 1997: A bit rustic, with burnt vanilla, truffle, soy and mushroom character. Medium-bodied, it's fat midpalate but turns a bit tough on the finish. Drink now through 2001.–P.M. • $12 • (12/15/1999) • **80**

Côtes du Rhône Domaine de la Présidente Cuvée Simon Alexandre 1994: Seems to have peaked, with its drying mouthfeel, forest underbrush character and short finish.–P.M. • $15 • (11/15/1998) • **72**

Côtes du Rhône Rosé Domaine de la Présidente 1998: Cardboard aromas and flavors suggest overindulgence in the yields. Not much here.–P.M. • $12 • (12/15/1999) • **74**

Côtes du Rhône White Château de Galliffet 1998: A bit cooked apple, showing a floral, apricot and peachlike character. Soft, round and quite rich, it's not bad, as it kicks in with freshness. Drink now through 2001.–P.M. • $25 • (12/15/1999) • **81**

Côtes du Rhône White Domaine de la Présidente Blanc de Blancs 1996 • $14 • (10/15/1997) • **83**

Côtes du Rhône-Villages Cairanne 1996: Fairly ripe, with an underpinning of crisp acidity, this has attractive earth, dried Provençal herbs, currant and black cherry flavors. Tannins are a bit chewy, but the finish is long. Try with meats. Drink now.–P.M. • $10 • (11/15/1998) • **82**

Côtes du Rhône-Villages Cairanne Domaine de la Présidente 1996: Light-bodied and light-colored, this straightforward red turns a bit bitter, dries a bit on the finish.–P.M. • $10 • (11/15/1998) • **76**

Côtes du Rhône-Villages Cairanne Domaine de la Présidente 1995 • $10 • (10/15/1997) • **70**

Côtes du Rhône-Villages Cairanne Domaine de la Présidente 1994 • $12 • (11/15/1995) • **83**

Côtes du Rhône-Villages Cairanne Domaine de la Présidente Goutillonnage 1995 • $16 • (10/15/1997) • **84**

Côtes du Rhône-Villages Cairanne Domaine de la Présidente Goutillonnage 1994 • $14 • (9/30/1995) • **86**

Côtes du Rhône-Villages Cairanne Les Partides 1997: Round in texture, but lacking fruit intensity, offering some cherry, cedar and wet earth, with a short, chewy finish.–P.M. • $10 • (11/15/1999) • **77**

AUBIERS, CHATEAU LES

Premières Côtes de Blaye 1996: Simple berry and earth character. Light- to medium-bodied, with light tannins and a medium finish. Drink now.–J.S. • $10 • (7/31/1999) • **81**

AUBUISIERES, DOMAINE DES

Vouvray Le Marigny 1997: Light and appley, this simple white mingles lightly sweet and tart flavors that are refreshing but short. Best as an aperitif. Drink now.–T.M. • $15 • (2/28/1999) • **81**

Vouvray Moelleux Le Marigny 1993 • $14 • (12/15/1995) • **87**

Vouvray Moelleux Les Girardières 2ème Trie 1996 • $22 Ⓐ • (5/31/1998) • **83**

AUGEY

Bordeaux 1997: Watery, with clean berry aromas but not much else.–J.S. • $6 • (2/28/1999) • **78**

Bordeaux 1996: Mint and other herbs mingle in this light, insipid red.–B.S. • $7 • (10/15/1998) • **74**

Bordeaux 1993 • $7 • (12/15/1995) • **80**

Bordeaux 1991 • $6 • (11/15/1994) • **79**

Bordeaux 1989 • $7 • (11/30/1992) • **78**

Bordeaux White 1997: Traditional white Bordeaux, with lemon and wax and a hint of honey. Medium-bodied. Slightly diluted finish. Drink now.–J.S. • $6 • (2/28/1999) • **81**

Merlot Bordeaux 1997: Verges on rosé. Light-bodied, with light tannins and a watery finish.–J.S. • $6 • (2/28/1999) • **72**

AUJOUX, JEAN-MARC

Beaujolais 1996 • $6 • (9/15/1997) • **76**

Beaujolais-Villages 1996 • $8 • (9/15/1997) • **84**

Beaujolais-Villages Limited Edition 1993 • $7 • (6/30/1994) • **79**

Beaujolais-Villages Limited Edition 1992 • $7 • (6/30/1994) • **79**

Brouilly 1996 • $11 • (7/31/1997) • **85**

Brouilly 1994 • $8 • (6/15/1995) • **84**

Brouilly Domaine François Chevalier 1996 • $14 • (9/15/1997) • **84**

Brouilly Limited Edition 1993 • $8 • (6/30/1994) • **80**

Brouilly Limited Edition 1992 • $8 • (6/30/1994) • **80**

Chiroubles 1994 • $9 • (7/31/1995) • **79**

Chiroubles Limited Edition 1993 • $9 • (6/30/1994) • **84**

Chiroubles Limited Edition 1992 • $9 • (6/30/1994) • **87**

Fleurie 1994 • $10 • (6/15/1995) • **85**

Fleurie Limited Edition 1993 • $10 • (6/30/1994) • **84**

Fleurie Limited Edition 1992 • $10 • (6/30/1994) • **82**

Juliénas 1996 • $11 • (9/15/1997) • **85**

Juliénas 1994 • $9 • (7/31/1995) • **82**

Juliénas Château de la Prat 1996 • $14 • (8/31/1997) • **88**

Juliénas Limited Edition 1993 • $9 • (6/30/1994) • **83**

Juliénas Limited Edition 1992 • $9 • (6/30/1994) • **84**

Morgon 1996 • $11 • (9/15/1997) • **84**

Morgon 1994 • $8 • (7/31/1995) • **83**

Morgon Côte de Py Domaine Charles Jenny 1996 • $14 • (9/15/1997) • **80**

Morgon Limited Edition 1993 • $8 • (6/30/1994) • **86**

Moulin-à-Vent 1996 • $12 • (9/15/1997) • **84**

Moulin-à-Vent 1994 • $10 • (7/31/1995) • **83**

Moulin-à-Vent Limited Edition 1993 • $10 • (6/30/1994) • **86**

St.-Amour 1994 • $10 • (7/31/1995) • **81**

St.-Amour Limited Edition 1993 • $10 • (6/30/1994) • **82**

AUPILHAC, DOMAINE D'

Coteaux du Languedoc Montpeyroux 1997: A pure and lively French red, filled with luscious berry, currant and red plum flavors and hints of anise. It's balanced and elegant, with crisp acidity, plenty of concentration and alluring aromas of game and spice. A nice chocolaty note chimes in on the finish. Drink now through 2002.–K.M. • $10 Ⓐ • (12/31/1999) HR • **90**

Coteaux du Languedoc Montpeyroux 1996: Starts off with nice berry aromas and flavors but closes down quickly. Concentrated, but may need time to smooth out. Drink through 2001–K.M. • $16 • (10/31/1998) • **82**

Coteaux du Languedoc Montpeyroux 1992 • $9 • (3/15/1994) • **87**

Vin de Pays du Mont Baudile Le Carignan 1996: Red plum and berry flavors dominate this straightforward red. There's some nice depth to the flavors. Drink now through 2001.–K.M. • $12 • (8/31/1998) • **83**

Vin de Pays du Mont Baudile Le Carignan 1992 • $8 • (3/15/1994) • **88**

Vin de Pays du Mont Baudile White 1996: A full-bodied and slightly mature-tasting white, with an inviting orange-peel aroma, honeyed flavors and herbal notes. Robust and flavorful. Drink now.–K.M. • $13 • (11/15/1998) • **86**

AURY, DOMAINE D'

Merlot Vin de Pays des Coteaux des Fenouillèdes 1997: Decent concentration, with good dried cherry and spice flavors and leathery notes. A medium-bodied red that finishes with appealing herbal notes. Drink now.–K.M. • $8 • (12/15/1998) • **82**

Vin de Pays des Coteaux des Fenouillèdes Lou Garrigue 1997: Firm and a bit tart, with dried cherry and herb flavors. Finishes on a slightly astringent note.–K.M. • $8 • (11/30/1998) • **77**

AUSONE, CHATEAU

St.-Emilion 1999: Solid for the vintage. Plenty of mineral, berry and cherry aromas. Full-bodied, with fine tannins and a very long and fruity finish. Very fine.–J.S. • $NA • (1/01/2000) (BT) • **90-94**

St.-Emilion 1998: A silky and well-constructed '98, with chocolate, cherry and spice character. Full-bodied, with elegant, refined tannins and a long finish.–J.S. • $NA • (5/31/1999) (BT) • **90-94**

St.-Emilion 1997: Pure fruit on the nose, with violet, berry and raspberry aromas. Medium-bodied, with silky tannins and a long, polished finish. Super well done for the vintage. Drink now through 2005.–J.S. • $203 • (1/31/2000) • **90**

St.-Emilion 1996: Impressive dark color, with blackberry and dark-chocolate aromas. Medium- to full-bodied, with firm yet silky tannins and a chocolate, toasted-oak aftertaste. Another ace from Ausone. Proves great *terroir* produces the best wines in less-than-great years. Best after 2002.–J.S. • $156 Ⓐ • (1/31/1999) • **90**

St.-Emilion 1995 • $149 Ⓐ • (1/31/1998) HR • **95**

St.-Emilion 1993 • $76 Ⓐ • (1/31/1996) • **88**

St.-Emilion 1990 • $167 Ⓐ • (3/31/1993) • **94**

St.-Emilion 1989: Fine Ausone. Fresh and understated. Subtle aromas of flowers, berries and spices. Medium- to full-bodied, with fine tannins and a silky-textured finish. Give it time to open up.—1989 Bordeaux horizontal. Best after 2006.–J.S. • $125 Ⓐ • (5/31/1999) • **93**

St.-Emilion 1988: Made when the château supposedly produced exciting wines, this is rather simple, with berry and tobacco character, full body and velvety tannins. Austere and slightly dry on the finish.—1988 Bordeaux horizontal. Drink now.–J.S. • $89 Ⓐ • (11/30/1998) • **85**

St.-Emilion 1986 • $110 Ⓐ • (10/15/1994) • **89**

St.-Emilion 1985 • $92 Ⓐ • (10/15/1994) • **92**

St.-Emilion 1983 • $118 Ⓐ • (10/15/1994) • **90**

St.-Emilion 1982: A real beauty. Dark ruby color, with a garnet hue. Very fresh fruit with floral, berry and perfume character. Full-bodied, with superfine tannins and long, sweet fruit. (1982 Bordeaux horizontal tasting). Drink now.–J.S. • $237 Ⓐ • (11/30/1998) • **93**

St.-Emilion 1981 • $95 • (10/15/1994) • **88**

St.-Emilion 1980 • $30 • (11/30/1987) • **86**

St.-Emilion 1979 • $91 Ⓐ • (10/15/1989) • **92**

St.-Emilion 1978 • $101 Ⓐ • (11/30/1987) • **93**

St.-Emilion 1977 • $29 • (11/30/1987) • **83**

St.-Emilion 1976 • $105 • (11/30/1987) • **89**

St.-Emilion 1974 • $28 • (11/30/1987) • **76**

St.-Emilion 1973 • $45 • (11/30/1987) • **77**

St.-Emilion 1972 • $30 • (11/30/1987) • **75**

St.-Emilion 1971 • $90 • (11/30/1987) • **83**

St.-Emilion 1970 • $88 Ⓐ • (5/15/1993) • **89**

St.-Emilion 1969 • $NA • (11/30/1987) • **76**

St.-Emilion 1967 • $65 • (11/30/1987) • **79**

St.-Emilion 1966 • $82 Ⓐ • (11/30/1987) • **85**

St.-Emilion 1964 • $146 Ⓐ • (11/30/1987) • **78**

St.-Emilion 1962 • $65 Ⓐ • (11/30/1987) • **85**

St.-Emilion 1961 • $296 Ⓐ • (4/30/1996) • **89**

St.-Emilion 1959 • $300 • (10/15/1990) • **79**

St.-Emilion 1958 • $95 • (11/30/1987) • **79**

St.-Emilion 1957 • $250 • (11/30/1987) • **74**

St.-Emilion 1956 • $175 • (11/30/1987) • **86**

St.-Emilion 1955 • $288 Ⓐ • (11/30/1987) • **91**

St.-Emilion 1954 • $180 • (11/30/1987) • **87**

St.-Emilion 1953 • $240 • (11/30/1987) • **78**

Key: SS—Spectator Selection. CS—Cellar Selection. HR—Highly Recommended. $NA—Price not available. (BT)—Barrel tasting. Ⓐ—Auction Price.
For a key to the tasters' initials, see "How to Use These Listings."
Dates in parentheses represent the issues in which the ratings were published.

St.-Emilion 1952 • $107 Ⓐ • (11/30/1987) • **85**

St.-Emilion 1950 • $220 • (11/30/1987) • **78**

St.-Emilion 1949 • $350 • (11/30/1987) • **91**

St.-Emilion 1947 • $370 Ⓐ • (5/31/1997) • **84**

St.-Emilion 1945 • $662 Ⓐ • (3/16/1986) • **75**

St.-Emilion 1943 • $NA • (11/30/1987) • **84**

St.-Emilion 1942 • $250 • (11/30/1987) • **81**

St.-Emilion 1937 • $NA • (11/30/1987) • **83**

St.-Emilion 1936 • $300 • (11/30/1987) • **82**

St.-Emilion 1929 • $201 Ⓐ • (11/30/1987) • **83**

St.-Emilion 1928 • $640 • (11/30/1987) • **83**

St.-Emilion 1926 • $680 • (11/30/1987) • **82**

St.-Emilion 1925 • $175 • (11/30/1987) • **75**

St.-Emilion 1924 • $250 • (11/30/1987) • **95**

St.-Emilion 1923 • $200 • (11/30/1987) • **76**

St.-Emilion 1921 • $1,150 • (11/30/1987) • **94**

St.-Emilion 1918 • $850 • (11/30/1987) • **87**

St.-Emilion 1916 • $460 Ⓐ • (11/30/1987) • **86**

St.-Emilion 1914 • $380 • (11/30/1987) • **79**

St.-Emilion 1913 • $380 • (11/30/1987) • **81**

St.-Emilion 1912 • $230 Ⓐ • (11/30/1987) • **79**

St.-Emilion 1905 • $600 • (11/30/1987) • **82**

St.-Emilion 1902 • $300 • (11/30/1987) • **83**

St.-Emilion 1900 • $3,887 Ⓐ • (11/30/1987) • **78**

St.-Emilion 1899 • $1,250 • (11/30/1987) • **77**

St.-Emilion 1894 • $800 • (11/30/1987) • **85**

St.-Emilion 1879 • $700 • (11/30/1987) • **93**

St.-Emilion 1877 • $2,250 • (11/30/1987) • **92**

AUTARD, DOMAINE PAUL

Châteauneuf-du-Pape 1996: Vibrant and fresh, but a bit herbal and metallic. Light in color and body and short on the finish.–P.M. • $18 • (9/30/1998) • **70**

Châteauneuf-du-Pape 1993 • $17 • (10/15/1995) • **84**

Châteauneuf-du-Pape Cuvée de la Côte Ronde 1996: Showed nice red berry flavors, then turned not so clean in contact with air. Drying on the finish.–P.M. • $40 • (9/30/1998) • **72**

Côtes du Rhône 1995 • $9 • (2/28/1997) • **79**

Côtes du Rhône 1994 • $8 • (11/15/1995) • **80**

AUVENAY, DOMAINE D'

Auxey-Duresses 1989 • $42 • (1/31/1992) • **88**

Auxey-Duresses White 1997: Unique, beautifully balanced and thick in texture, this terroir-driven, full-bodied white is superbly woven with wet earth, matchstick and flint notes. Terrific lime and lemon flavors mingle on the honeyed finish. Drink now through 2017.–P.M. • $76 • (9/30/1999) • **95**

Auxey-Duresses White 1996: Incredibly intense but also very odd, with matchstick, acidic, cat-pee and buttery notes blending with lemon, herb and grassy flavors, all of which explode like a reduced sauce on the finish. Not so harmonious. An acquired taste; if you have it, go for it. From Lalou Bize-Leroy. Best from 2005.–P.M. • $60 • (8/31/1998) • **74**

Auxey-Duresses White 1995 • $56 • (8/31/1997) • **91**

Auxey-Duresses White Les Boutonniers 1997: Amazing. This almost tannic white is so powerful and pungent, it's hard to know what sensory planet you're on. Use a compass to bring your bearing back to the purity of the Burgundian soil, and enjoy the matchstick, earth and fruit components. Best from 2005 through 2025.–P.M. • $76 • (9/30/1999) • **95**

Auxey-Duresses White Les Boutonniers 1996: There are thousands of "easy" wines to drink in the world, but be forewarned—this isn't one of them. As hard, tough, acidic and oddball as they come, this low-yield Auxey from the distinguished winemaker Lalou Bize-Leroy is a shockingly lemony, limy, earthy oddity. Stick with it, and learn to appreciate the soil and mineral character. A wine that could rate from 70 to 90 on our 100-point scale. Drink through 2005.–P.M. • $60 • (8/31/1998) • **90**

Auxey-Duresses White Les Clous 1997: Thick and crisp, this is lively on the taste buds, offering restraint along with ripe body. Good, firm structure, tingling with a citrusy, green character on the smoky finish. Drink through 2007.–P.M. • $76 • (9/30/1999) • **91**

Auxey-Duresses White Les Clous 1996: Great concentration on the palate, but also an odd-smelling, herbaceous, burnt butter character that's unappealing; fortunately, the first impression gives way to a ripe, concentrated fruit character with a minerally undertow. Still, it's difficult to appreciate. From Lalou Bize-Leroy. Best from 2007.–P.M. • $60 • (8/31/1998) • **88**

Bonnes Mares 1997: An extremely silky, medium-bodied '97 red. Not many aromas and flavors now, but delicate and balanced, with supple tannins. Drink now through 2007.–P.M. • $661 • (9/30/1999) • **89**

Bonnes Mares 1996: Loads of spice, also excellent depth and concentration, with green olive and smoke accents to the cassis and black cherry. There's sweetness and fatness midpalate, and the finish is extremely long, showing firm, muscular tannins. Best from 2005 through 2010.–B.S. • $260 Ⓐ • (9/30/1998) • **95**

Bonnes Mares 1995 • $550 • (11/15/1997) • **93**

Bonnes Mares 1994 • $459 • (9/30/1997) • **93**

Bourgogne Aligoté Sous Chatelet 1997: The rich, ripe fruit that coats the palate is rather exceptional. Still, the intensity rips your taste buds apart. Best from 2001 through 2010.–P.M. • $31 • (9/30/1999) • **89**

Chevalier-Montrachet 1997: A very clean and beautifully polished white Burgundy, playing deftly among the slightly spicy oak, ripe fruit and lemon background. Balanced and almost delicate. Drink now through 2007.–P.M. • $686 • (9/30/1999) • **90**

Chevalier-Montrachet 1995 • $492 • (8/31/1997) HR • **99**

Criots-Bâtard-Montrachet 1997: Dominated by oak. There's decent fruit (such as lemon) here but it's overtaken by the hot, tarry charcoal character. Still, it has a long, fresh, crisp, mouthpuckering finish. Drink now through 2003.–P.M. • $661 • (9/30/1999) • **85**

Criots-Bâtard-Montrachet 1996: One of the world's rarest wines, it's exotic and unique-tasting; expect controversy at the table if you serve it. Where to begin? Full-bodied, very rich, cascading with ripe, tropical fig, sugar-glazed lemon, orange and honey, along with toasted coconut, spice, mocha, matchstick and wet earth (and, some might argue, paint varnish). Overall it's thick, complex, earthy. This is the ripest white Burgundy I've tasted in the '96 vintage. It was aged in a half-barrel, which explains the heavy wood. Give it time, if you're lucky enough to have a bottle. Best from 2005.–P.M. • $425 • (8/31/1998) • **98**

Criots-Bâtard-Montrachet 1995 • $498 • (8/31/1997) • **98**

Mazis-Chambertin 1997: Pretty red berry mixes with wet earth in this medium-bodied, crisp red. It doesn't take off for now on the finish, but cellar medium-term and see what happens. Best from 2002 through 2005.–P.M. • $686 • (9/30/1999) • **84**

Mazis-Chambertin 1996: Thick, ripe and deceptively seductive, this beautiful wine mingles deftly made oak accents with wet earth, clean black fruit and mineral-laden character. Full-bodied, it's impressive for its balance, silky tannins and long finish. Best after 2005.–P.M. • $660 • (9/30/1998) • **94**

Mazis-Chambertin 1994 • $459 • (9/30/1997) • **93**

Meursault 1996: A racy, classy wine of good concentration. Starts out closed and ungenerous, but in contact with air it gained volume and opulence, delivering a ripe, thick texture with pear, pineapple, lemon, rose petal, peach and grassy-minerally notes. Of medium body, with a finish of good finesse. Best from 2005.–P.M. • $98 • (8/31/1998) • **90**

Meursault Chaumes des Perrières 1997: Greatness in a glass, this monumental '97 white goes to the very heart of Burgundy's terroir. Full-bodied and rich in texture, with caramel, mocha and honey. Plenty of red berry, citrus, pear tart, green apple and grass character makes this a must for collectors. Best from 2002 through 2017.–P.M. • $108 • (9/30/1999) • **97**

Meursault Les Gouttes d'Or 1997: Hard to judge, but it shows an interesting matchstick character, with an impressive, superripe, old-vine kind of mouthfeel as it wraps tightly around the palate. Citrus blossom, honey, and smoky notes come in on the long, racy, vibrant finish. Drink now through 2010.–P.M. • $220 • (9/30/1999) • **93**

Meursault Les Gouttes d'Or 1996: Very distinctive, with a dried herbs, green olive, piney, new oak, paint varnish character. OK, it's a bit weird, but there is sweet fruit and good concentration. Medium-bodied, it's chewy, with lots of dry extract, making it seem tough on the lingering finish. Either a terrible wine (for the strange aromas) or an outstanding one (for its midpalate concentration). A relatively recent label from Bize-Leroy, who swears that her '96 whites need decades to come around. Try from 2010.–P.M. • $185 • (8/31/1998) • **92**

Meursault Les Narvaux 1997: This has an intriguing olive, smoke and matchstick character. Tastes really ripe at first, with exotic tropical fruit and freshly cut grass. Turns very acidic in a mouthpuckering way. Best from 2002 through 2010.–P.M. • $117 • (9/30/1999) • **87**

Meursault Les Narvaux 1996: A provocateur of a wine. None among the '96 Meursaults, from village to *premier cru*, equals the sheer intensity and plain pain-in-the-palate rage shown by this savage, uncivilized, mad wine; summarizing in its rough, unedited form the character of the vintage—that is, loads of acidity, lean body, firm structure, little opulence and even less charm. A critic's nightmare, this is the sort of wine that leaves no choice but rate it "not recommended" or "outstanding". I give it the benefit of the doubt since it comes from Lalou Bize-Leroy, who has a track record for making cellar-worthy wines. Best after 2010?–P.M. • $189 • (8/31/1998) • **93**

Meursault Les Narvaux 1995 • $155 • (8/31/1997) • **97**

Meursault Pré de Manche 1997: This beautiful wine hides nothing and gives a lot of pleasure, from the open malic, dough (leesy, yeasty), citrus, honey and toasted oak character to the wonderful, ripe, rich texture on the palate and the amazingly lemony finish. Great intensity. Drink now through 2010.–P.M. • $108 • (9/30/1999) • **93**

Puligny-Montrachet Les Folatières 1997: This offers the ultimate "white Burgundy treatment"—amazing, smoky, in-your-face toasted oak, full body, rich texture and a cascade of hazelnut, mineral and honey. Everything hangs together with delicious balance on the long finish. Drink now through 2010.–P.M. • $202 • (9/30/1999) • **95**

Puligny-Montrachet Les Folatières 1996: Very oaky and acidic, but also very ripe, with tropical pear, honey, hazelnut, pistachio and toasted bread complexity. Full-throttle international-style, very woody. Thick and tough at once. Best from 2010.–P.M. • $170 • (8/31/1998) • **80**

Puligny-Montrachet Les Folatières 1995 • $133 • (8/31/1997) • **98**

AUVIGUE, ANDRE

Pouilly-Fuissé Solutré 1997: Ripe and rather rich, offering pear, honey and spice, a velvety midpalate and just-so toasted oak. Drink now through 2002.–P.M. • $18 • (5/31/1999) • **88**

Pouilly-Fuissé Solutré 1996 • $18 • (5/31/1998) • **89**

Pouilly-Fuissé Solutré 1995 • $18 • (5/31/1997) • **81**

AUVIGUE & REVEL

Mâcon-Fuissé Le Moulin du Pont Vendanges Manuelles 1997: Straightforward little Mâcon, showing a chewy, "tannic," slightly herbal character that makes it taste a bit green on finish.–P.M. • $14 • (5/31/1999) • **76**

Mâcon-Fuissé Vendanges Manuelles 1996 • $15 • (8/31/1997) • **86**

Mâcon-Villages Vendanges Manuelles 1996 • $15 • (8/31/1997) • **75**

Pouilly-Fuissé Les Chailloux 1997: A bit tart, this light-bodied Pouilly tastes ungenerous, offering some green apple and lemon notes but a short finish.–P.M. • $12 • (5/31/1999) • **77**

Pouilly-Fuissé Les Crays 1997: Showing some pretty honey, toasted bread and mineral character, this fills the palate generously, kicking in with red-hot intensity on the finish. But lo and behold, it works. Drink now through 2005.–P.M. • $22 • (5/31/1999) • **90**

Pouilly-Fuissé Vieilles Vignes 1997: Elegant, stressing fresh lemon over opulent oak treatment, there's a refreshing quality to this zingy, succulent yet ripe Pouilly. Drink now through 2002.–P.M. • $25 • (5/31/1999) • **86**

St.-Véran 1995 • $13 • (5/31/1997) • **87**

St.-Véran Les Chênes 1997: Intriguing style, clean, crisp and polished on the midpalate, with wonderful lemon, cream, butter, dried apricot aromas and flavors. Too bad the finish is a bit tough, but this St.-Véran should match nicely with fish. Drink now through 2001.–P.M. • $15 • (5/31/1999) • **87**

AUZIAS, DOMAINE

Vin de Pays de la Cité de Carcassonne 1998: Simple, with red plum flavors and a slightly chalky finish. Drink now.–K.M. • $NA • (1/01/2000) • **80**

AVERY

Richebourg 1947 • $NA • (5/31/1997) • **88**

AVRIL, PASCAL & CATHERINE

Chinon Champ du Pin 1995: Light, herbal and lacking in concentration, this has only modest fruit.–B.S. • $16 • (10/31/1998) • **77**

Chinon Champ du Pin Vieilles Vignes 1997: Round and fruity. This fleshy red shows very ripe plum and candied flavors, with round tannins and a chocolate-scented finish. Lush and soft. Drink now through 2001.–T.M. • $18 • (6/30/1999) • **86**

Touraine Red 1995 • $12 • (6/15/1998) • **84**

AYALA

Brut Champagne NV • $33 • (11/15/1996) • **87**

Brut Rosé Champagne NV • $40 • (11/15/1996) • **85**

AYDIE, CHATEAU D'

Madiran 1993 • $17 • (6/15/1997) • **85**
Madiran 1991 • $14 • (6/30/1994) • **87**

BACHELET, DENIS

Charmes-Chambertin 1990 • $53 • (12/15/1992) • **94**
Charmes-Chambertin Vieilles Vignes 1986 • $43 • (7/15/1989) • **87**
Côte de Nuits-Villages 1990 • $18 • (12/15/1992) • **84**
Gevrey-Chambertin Les Corbeaux Vieilles Vignes 1996: Plenty of animal character. The berry, game and mineral notes are well displayed on a bright structure, without the concentration and density of some. Drink now through 2003.–B.S. • $60 • (1/01/2000) • **90**
Gevrey-Chambertin Les Corbeaux Vieilles Vignes 1986 • $30 • (7/15/1989) • **83**
Gevrey-Chambertin Vieilles Vignes 1996: Mind-blowing red Burgundy. Complex and harmonious, unfolding its aromas and flavors of pure raspberry cassis, cherry ansd exotic spices. It retains an sense of grace, too, ending with a fantail of flavors. Drink now through 2009.–B.S. • $40 • (1/01/2000) • **93**
Gevrey-Chambertin Vieilles Vignes 1995 • $38 Ⓐ • (1/31/1998) • **91**
Gevrey-Chambertin Vieilles Vignes 1990 • $43 • (12/15/1992) • **91**
Gevrey-Chambertin Vieilles Vignes 1986 • $24 • (7/15/1989) • **88**

BAHANS HAUT-BRION, CHATEAU

Pessac-Léognan 1999: Sweet ripe fruit, with vanilla and berry and lively aromas. Medium- to full-bodied, with velvety tannins and a fresh finish. A bit short.–J.S. • $NA • (1/01/2000) (BT) • **85-89**
Pessac-Léognan 1998: One of the great values of the vintage considering the superb quality. Just a notch below the great Haut-Brion. Of course, it is the second wine. Powerful, rich and velvety, with layers of chocolate, cherry and berry character. Full-bodied. Goes on and on.–J.S. • $NA • (5/31/1999) (BT) • **90-94**
Pessac-Léognan 1996: Got to like the ripe berry character, well enveloped with toasted oak. Full-bodied and soft, with a round texture and a ripe berry and vanilla aftertaste. Slightly diluted at the end. Best after 2000.–J.S. • $27 Ⓐ • (1/31/1999) • **86**
Pessac-Léognan 1989 • $76 Ⓐ • (3/15/1992) • **90**
Pessac-Léognan 1986 • $22 • (9/15/1989) • **86**

BAILLAT, DOMAINE

Corbières 1995 • $8 • (4/30/1998) • **84**

BAILLY, FRANCK & JEAN-FRANCOIS

Sancerre Cuvée Chavignol 1996 • $17 • (5/31/1998) • **88**

BAILLY-REVERDY, B.

Sancerre Chavignol 1997: This rustic white leans toward the earthy side, with only hints of the bright citrus and mineral flavors of Sancerre at its best. Has enough body and acidity to match with food, however. Drink now.–T.M. • $18 • (6/30/1999) • **80**

BALESTARD, CHATEAU

Bordeaux 1998: Lovely crushed berry aromas with hints of vanilla and spice. Full-bodied, round and soft, with delicious ripe fruit and velvety tannins. Slightly short finish. Still, unreal for a simple Bordeaux.–J.S. • $NA • (5/31/1999) (BT) • **85-89**

BALESTARD-LA-TONNELLE, CHATEAU

St.-Emilion 1997: A delicious red with berry, tobacco and chocolate character. Medium-bodied, with light to medium, soft tannins and a fruity finish. Drink now.–J.S. • $43 • (1/31/2000) • **85**

Key: SS—Spectator Selection. CS—Cellar Selection. HR—Highly Recommended. $NA—Price not available. (BT)—Barrel tasting. Ⓐ—Auction Price.
For a key to the tasters' initials, see "How to Use These Listings."
Dates in parentheses represent the issues in which the ratings were published.

St.-Emilion 1996: Aromas of crushed berries and earth. Medium-bodied, with velvety tannins and good fruit midpalate, but lacks a bit of ripe intensity. Very good wine from this estate considering the vintage. Best after 2000.–J.S. • $45 • (1/31/1999) • **86**
St.-Emilion 1989 • $28 • (3/15/1992) • **85**
St.-Emilion 1988 • $25 • (4/30/1991) • **91**
St.-Emilion 1982: Seriously good. Dark ruby in color. Very ripe, with berry, licorice, roses and wet earth. Full-bodied and ever so sexy, with chocolate, berry and cherry flavors. Long, long, sweet fruit finish. A truly superb wine. (1982 Bordeaux horizontal tasting). Drink through 2006.–J.S. • $NA • (11/30/1998) • **92**

BALESTE, CHATEAU

Buzet 1994: Shows decent red cherry, leather and spice flavors, but they fade a bit on the finish. Drink now.–K.M. • $10 • (5/31/1999) • **80**

BALLAND, JEAN-PAUL

Sancerre 1997: Round in texture and delicate in flavor, this white shows floral, spice and light citrus flavors. The flavors are clean and the finish is crisp and lingering. Drink now.–T.M. • $20 • (10/31/1999) • **86**
Sancerre 1996: Shows the vibrance and intensity of the vintage, along with gooseberry and grass flavors, all richly textured and lingering on the finish.–B.S. • $20 • (10/31/1998) • **86**

BALLAN-LARQUETTE, CHATEAU

Bordeaux 1998: Pleasant currant and raspberry aromas follow through to a medium-bodied palate, with light tannins and a fresh finish. Drink now.–J.S. • $11 • (6/15/2000) • **82**

BALLENA

Cabernet Sauvignon Vin de Pays d'Oc 1995 • $7 • (7/31/1997) • **83**
Chardonnay Vin de Pays d'Oc 1996 • $7 • (6/30/1997) • **82**
Merlot Vin de Pays d'Oc 1995 • $7 • (7/31/1997) • **84**

BALLOT-MILLOT & FILS, R.

Chassagne-Montrachet Morgeot 1998: An odd white, with a neutral, somewhat cardboardy aroma, it turns rather thick-textured at midpalate (suggesting some concentration) but finishes sour.–P.M. • $55 • (5/31/2000) • **76**
Chassagne-Montrachet Morgeot 1997: Odd nail polish notes turn this into an astringent, woody tough customer.–P.M. • $52 • (9/30/1999) • **72**
Meursault 1997: Soft and woody, with butter and butterscotch aromas and flavors. A bit oxidized, with a flabby finish.–P.M. • $34 • (9/30/1999) • **77**
Meursault 1995 • $35 • (5/31/1997) • **90**
Meursault Bouchères 1997: Rather light, with butterscotch, popcorn and grilled corn character. Shows a slight green, herbal note on the toasted finish. Drink now through 2002.–P.M. • $52 • (9/30/1999) • **80**
Meursault Bouchères 1996 • $48 • (5/31/1998) • **84**
Meursault Charmes 1998: A tightly wound, rather tart Meursault, with dried herbs and some mineral notes. The intensity is there, but this is a tough white, tasting rather lean and a bit green now. A sharp edge on the finish might round itself out with time. Best from 2002 through 2005.–P.M. • $58 • (5/31/2000) • **85**
Meursault Charmes 1997: Supple in texture and medium-bodied, with dried herb, earth, citrus and green apple character on the vibrant, crisp finish. Drink now through 2005.–P.M. • $54 • (9/30/1999) • **83**
Meursault Genevrières 1997: Very full on the palate with lavish butter, vanilla, spice and citrus notes. Impressively built in a smooth way, ending with a wisp that lacks a bit of concentration. Drink now through 2005.–P.M. • $54 • (9/30/1999) • **88**
Meursault Genevrières 1996 • $54 • (5/31/1998) • **85**
Meursault Genevrières 1995 • $50 • (5/31/1997) • **91**
Meursault Les Criots 1998: Distinctive and anything but boring. Full-bodied, with a substantial midpalate. The aromas are a bit stinky, but the action is on the palate, where this wine offers a rich diversity of flavors, an exquisite silkiness, clean fruit and impressive concentration. Good length, too, with a mineral, wet earth component. Drink now through 2010.–P.M. • $43 • (5/31/2000) • **93**
Meursault Les Criots 1997: A bit green, with cardboard character suggesting a dilution. Turns tart on the finish.–P.M. • $37 • (9/30/1999) • **73**
Meursault Les Narvaux 1997: Luxuriously ripe and opulent, thick-textured and seductive, this is a big, lavishly oaked wine. It's a mouthful, with a

FRANCE

showy finish; perhaps time will let the fruit and earth resurface. Drink now through 2005.–P.M. • $39 • (9/30/1999) • **82**

Meursault Les Narvaux 1996 • $39 • (5/31/1998) • **82**

Meursault Les Narvaux 1995 • $40 • (5/31/1997) • **87**

Meursault Perrières 1997: Green, vegetal and light, with a tart character.–P.M. • $54 • (9/30/1999) • **72**

BALMONT, JEAN

Cabernet Sauvignon Vin de Pays d'Oc 1995 • $7 • (12/15/1996) • **84**

Chardonnay Vin de Pays du Jardin de la France 1997: Ripe aromas of peaches and flowers are followed by citrus and mineral flavors, all interwoven with moderate concentration and a lingering finish. Drink now.–B.S. • $6 • (11/15/1998) • **82**

Chardonnay-Sauvignon Blanc Vin de Pays du Jardin de la France 1997: Decent lemon, lime and spice flavors here, but it's a bit coarse overall. Drink now.–K.M. • $6 • (9/15/1998) • **78**

Merlot Vin de Pays d'Oc 1995 • $7 • (12/15/1996) • **76**

Merlot-Cabernet Sauvignon Vin de Pays d'Oc 1995 • $7 • (12/15/1996) • **81**

Sauvignon Blanc Vin de Pays du Jardin de la France 1997: A crisp, citrus-tasting white that has some power, and finesse. Nice flavors of grapefruit and lemon, with a mouthwatering finish. Drink now.–K.M. • $6 • (9/15/1998) • **86**

Syrah Rosé Vin de Pays d'Oc 1997: Has a sweaty character that is quite overpowering. Very funky for a rosé.–K.M. • $6 • (8/31/1998) • **73**

BANNERET, DOMAINE DU

Châteauneuf-du-Pape 1994: Offers mocha and licorice, some candied strawberry and cherry. Supple tannins at midpalate turn a bit astringent on the herbal finish.–P.M. • $NA • (11/15/1998) • **71**

BARA, PAUL

Brut Champagne 1990: Smooth and expansive, blending ripe apple and butter flavors with nutty, smoky accents. Full-bodied and assertive in style. Drink now through 2004. • $45 • (9/15/1999) • **89**

Brut Champagne Réserve NV: Dry and firm in texture, this has solid citrus and apple flavors, firm acidity and a clean finish. Drink now. • $34 • (10/15/1999) • **86**

Brut Rosé Champagne NV: Almost like a bubbling Pinot Noir, this has plenty of fresh cherry flavors, great balance and a lively finish. Quite dry and really good in this style. Drink now through 2001. • $39 • (10/15/1999) • **89**

BARAT, MICHEL

Chablis 1998: Grassy in style, like a Sauvignon Blanc, showing lovely fruit (apple, pear, melon, citrus), with a matchstick and wet earth character. Balanced and delicious. Drink now through 2001.–P.M. • $16 • (5/15/2000) • **85**

Chablis 1997: Very steely, tight as a clenched fist, bursting with vibrant lemon and apple flavors, offering a touch of palate-soothing honey character. Try with shellfish or bistro goodies. Drink now.–P.M. • $16 • (5/31/1999) • **88**

Chablis 1996 • $12 • (8/31/1997) • **85**

Chablis 1995 • $15 • (8/31/1996) • **87**

Chablis Côte de Léchet 1998: Quite intense, with mineral, green apple and dried herb character. Medium-bodied, it kicks in with a chewiness on the finish. Needs time for all that intensity to harmonize. Best from 2002 through 2006.–P.M. • $20 • (5/15/2000) • **88**

Chablis Côte de Léchet 1997: Smooth but kicking with lemony acidity, this is as tight as a clenched fist, delivering layers of mineral, sea salt, wet earth and fruit concentration. Beautifully pure, clean finish. Cellar. Best from 2002 through 2010.–P.M. • $19 • (5/31/1999) • **90**

Chablis Côte de Léchet 1996 • $15 • (5/31/1998) • **94**

Chablis Côte de Lechet 1995 • $15 • (6/15/1997) • **89**

Chablis Les Fourneaux 1998: Tightly structured, tough, acidic, chewy and dry, but you've got to admire its intensity. Surprising firmness for a '98. Not for the faint of heart, this medium-bodied white calls for serious cellaring before the mineral will take over and soften it. Best from 2003 through 2010.–P.M. • $20 • (5/15/2000) • **87**

Chablis Les Fourneaux 1997: Lovely, with a buttery, minerally, wet earth personality, a firm, even chewy mouthfeel, but delivering nice lemon-spiked intensity on the long finish. Drink through 2005.–P.M. • $19 • (5/31/1999) • **89**

Chablis Les Fourneaux 1996: Super Chablis—ripe and sweet-tasting yet elegant, packed with earth, mineral, spice, lime, honey and tropical fruit. Beware the herbal, matchstick, earthy, flinty note—it may not be for everyone. Still, it's full-bodied, silky-textured and racy. Drink now through 2005.–P.M. • $18 • (8/31/1998) • **94**

Chablis Mont de Milieu 1998: Very clean and quite powerful. Subtle on the nose, it suggests mineral and *terroir,* then offers a full-bodied mouthfeel, with a slight oak character. Lots of fresh citrus and pear on the ultrapure finish. Best from 2003 through 2008.–P.M. • $20 • (5/15/2000) • **91**

Chablis Mont de Milieu 1997: Delicious. Typical '97 Chablis, offering mineral, sea salt, lemon, tropical complexity in a charming, medium-bodied package that retains enough vibrancy to stay lively on the lingering finish. Drink now through 2003.–P.M. • $19 • (5/31/1999) • **89**

Chablis Mont de Milieu 1996 • $15 • (5/31/1998) • **94**

Chablis Mont de Milieu 1995 • $15 • (6/15/1997) • **86**

Chablis Vaillons 1998: Good mineral and a smooth texture. Medium-bodied and rather easy to appreciate now, as its pleasant ripe fruit character seduces. Drink now through 2003.–P.M. • $20 • (5/15/2000) • **85**

Chablis Vaillons 1997: Steely. Good firm structure gives this medium-bodied Chablis plenty of personality; there's dried herb and green apple flavors and, on the finish, a chewy, slightly astringent character. Drink now through 2003.–P.M. • $19 • (5/31/1999) • **83**

Chablis Vaillons 1996 • $15 • (5/31/1998) • **93**

Chablis Vaillons 1995 • $15 • (6/15/1997) • **87**

BARET, CHATEAU

Pessac-Léognan 1998: Silky and racy young '98. Perhaps not as concentrated as some, but shows a medium body and good core of ripe fruit.–J.S. • $NA • (5/31/1999) (BT) • **85-89**

Pessac-Léognan 1997: Lovely raspberry, cherry and mineral. Medium-bodied, with fine tannins and a fresh finish. Slightly one-dimensional. Drink now.–J.S. • $NA • (1/31/2000) • **83**

Pessac-Léognan 1996: Aromas of tea, berry and tobacco. Medium-bodied, with medium tannins and a light finish. Needs more fruit concentration. Best after 2000.–J.S. • $19 • (1/31/1999) • **80**

Pessac-Léognan 1995 • $18 • (1/31/1998) • **86**

Pessac-Léognan 1992 • $12 • (4/15/1995) • **73**

Pessac-Léognan 1991 • $12 • (3/31/1994) • **81**

Pessac-Léognan 1989: A bit rustic but packed with fruit. Dark ruby-red in color, offering ripe blackberry and hints of tobacco on the nose. Full-bodied and very ripe, with a raisin, tobacco and cedar character for the palate. Long, chewy finish. Not quite as outstanding as I remember. (1989 Bordeaux horizontal tasting). Best after 2000.–J.S. • $NA • (5/31/1999) • **88**

Pessac-Léognan White 1998: Wonderful aromas of apple, honey and vanilla. Medium-bodied, with good fruit and a delicious aftertaste. Drink now through 2003.–J.S. • $NA • (2/29/2000) • **88**

Pessac-Léognan White 1996: Clean and fresh. Aromas and flavors of freshly sliced lemons with a hint of minerals. Medium-bodied, with fresh acidity and a light finish. Drink now.–J.S. • $NA • (1/01/1999) • **84**

BARGE, GILLES

Côte-Rôtie 1991 • $NA • (5/31/1994) • **83**

Côte-Rôtie 1990 • $NA • (5/31/1994) • **86**

Côte-Rôtie 1989 • $30 • (4/15/1993) • **83**

Côte-Rôtie Côte Brune 1996: Supple and ripe, with a minty, minerally, floral, meaty, cassis complexity, this medium-bodied red is well made, fanning out with sweet tannins on the intense finish. Best from 2003.–P.M. • $30 • (11/15/1998) • **87**

Côte-Rôtie Cuvée du Plessy 1996: Slighty diluted, tart and lean, with drying tannins and modest fruit.–P.M. • $35 • (11/15/1998) • **78**

Côte-Rôtie Cuvée du Plessy 1995: Fairly light in aroma, with some smooth tannins, it's pleasant for drinking now, with some mocha, plum and red berry character.–P.M. • $30 • (11/15/1998) • **81**

BARMES BUECHER

Chasselas Alsace Vieilles Vignes 1996: Very ripe, even tropical notes of guava here, as well as a grapey frankness and a hint of earth. It's fat and broad on the palate, with a cleansing citrus finish. Drink now.–B.S. • $12 • (3/31/1999) • **83**

Gewürztraminer Alsace Rosenberg 1997: Big-boned and broad yet seems hollow, with only modest quince and marzipan notes.–B.S. • $18 • (6/15/2000) • **79**

FRANCE

FRANCE

BARMES BUECHER

Gewürztraminer Alsace Rosenberg 1996: There's an ethereal quality to this (and perhaps some dissolved carbon dioxide), with flavors of biscuit, marzipan and orange marmalade. Powerful and evocative, it finishes a little coarse due to the high alcohol. Drink now through 2002.–B.S. • $15 • (4/30/1999) • **87**

Gewürztraminer Alsace Wintzenheim 1996: The main flavors are litchi and honey, and it's packing some heat—as in alcohol. Though rich, attractive and clean in flavor, the alcohol level begins to dominate midpalate and the finish is hot. Drink now.–B.S. • $24 • (4/30/1999) • **82**

Pinot Blanc Alsace Rosenberg 1997: Broad and lush, showing the richness of the '97 vintage. The quince, peach and smoke notes are deliciously draped over a soft, slightly sweet yet balanced structure. Drink now.–B.S. • $14 • (6/15/2000) • **87**

Pinot Blanc Alsace Rosenberg 1996: Clean and zippy, this white offers lemon and quince flavors with a rich texture that's backed by screaming acidity. Ultimately, it may be too high in acid for perfect balance, but I'd give it the benefit of the doubt. Try with food. Drink through 2005.–B.S. • $13 • (3/31/1999) • **86**

Pinot Blanc-Auxerrois Alsace 1996: Reserved and firm, showing a lot of lemon and apple flavors, well balanced and smooth, with just a hint of bitterness at the end. A good partner for chicken or light seafood. Drink now through 2002.–B.S. • $12 • (3/31/1999) • **85**

Pinot Noir Alsace Vieilles Vignes 1996: Browning and mature, with modest berry and spice and a slight spritz.–B.S. • $33 • (1/01/2000) • **78**

Riesling Alsace Rosenberg 1997: Excellent delineation and structure drives the almond, spice and mineral notes in this reserved, forceful Riesling. The almond flavor lingers on the finish. Drink now through 2003.–B.S. • $15 • (5/31/2000) • **86**

Riesling Alsace Rosenberg 1996: Shows ripe apple, quince and red berry flavors, but the overall impression is tart, from the teeth rattling acidity. May be in an awkward stage. Best from 2002 through 2010.–B.S. • $15 • (3/31/1999) • **83**

Sylvaner Alsace Rosenberg Vieilles Vignes 1997: Sleek and lemony, showing density and a structure that could pair well with food. Drink now.–B.S. • $11 • (6/15/2000) • **82**

Sylvaner Alsace Rosenberg Vieilles Vignes 1996: Out of sync. Smells a bit odd, like decaying fruit, while the palate smacks of new oak, which doesn't mesh well with the apple and herb flavors. Finishes on the tart side.–B.S. • $13 • (3/31/1999) • **76**

Tokay Pinot Gris Alsace Rosenberg Vieilles Vignes 1996: An atypical style. New oak adds a marked vanilla component and a bitter edge that currently overwhelms the peach and grapefruit flavors, but the firm acidity may allow the elements to integrate in time. Not for everyone. Drink through 2005.–B.S. • $20 • (4/30/1999) • **84**

BARONNE, CHATEAU LA

Corbières Montagne d'Alaric 1997: This straightforward red has mineral and dried plum flavors, with tobacco box and chocolate notes on the finish. Drink now.–K.M. • $7 • (11/15/1999) • **82**

Corbières Montagne d'Alaric 1991 • $10 • (3/15/1994) • **81**

Corbières Montagne d'Alaric 1990 • $10 • (3/15/1994) • **83**

BARRABAQUE, CHATEAU

Canon-Fronsac 1997: Solid wine for a 1997. Canon-Fronsac does it well here. Good dark color, with lots of ripe berry and cherry character on the nose. Full-bodied, with lots of fruit and a firm backbone of tannins. Best after 2000.–J.S. • $NA • (1/31/2000) • **88**

BARRAL, LEON

Faugères 1997: Well rounded, with interesting flavors of mineral, earth and even herbs de Provence. Delicious, lovely notes of cardamom and chocolate on the finish. Smooth and ready to drink. Drink now.–K.M. • $13 • (4/30/2000) • **85**

Faugères 1994 • $10 • (6/15/1998) • **86**

Key: SS—Spectator Selection. CS—Cellar Selection. HR—Highly Recommended. $NA—Price not available. (BT)—Barrel tasting. Ⓐ—Auction Price.
For a key to the tasters' initials, see "How to Use These Listings."
Dates in parentheses represent the issues in which the ratings were published.

BARRAUD, DANIEL

Mâcon 1996 • $16 • (5/31/1998) • **82**

Pouilly-Fuissé Cuvée Vieilles Vignes 1997: Polished and subtle, promoting more fruit than oak. Medium-bodied and succulent, leaving a fresh, clean but sweet-tasting finish. A wine you won't tire of drinking.–P.M. • $30 • (5/31/1999) • **88**

Pouilly-Fuissé Cuvée Vieilles Vignes 1996 • $30 • (5/31/1998) • **81**

Pouilly-Fuissé La Roche 1997: Vibrant, lively, succulent, the sort of medium-bodied, minerally Pouilly that delivers enough creaminess along with the citrus and ripe fruit to hit all the right spots. Smoky, balanced finish. Drink now through 2003.–P.M. • $27 • (5/31/1999) • **89**

Pouilly-Fuissé La Roche 1996 • $26 • (5/31/1998) • **83**

Pouilly-Fuissé La Verchère 1997: Starts out in a fresh, lemony style then moves on to ripe fruit laced with honey and cream, but it turns a bit green and astringent on the finish. Drink now through 2001.–P.M. • $25 • (5/31/1999) • **84**

Pouilly-Fuissé La Verchère 1996 • $25 • (5/31/1998) • **90**

St.-Véran En Crêches 1996 • $17 • (5/31/1998) • **81**

BARREYRES, CHATEAU

Haut-Médoc 1995 • $12 • (1/31/1998) • **88**

BARROT, DOMAINE LUCIEN

Châteauneuf-du-Pape 1994 • $21 • (9/15/1997) • **88**
Châteauneuf-du-Pape 1989 • $20 • (10/15/1991) • **88**
Châteauneuf-du-Pape 1988 • $18 • (10/15/1991) • **87**
Châteauneuf-du-Pape 1986 • $18 • (10/15/1991) • **89**
Châteauneuf-du-Pape 1981 • $16 • (9/30/1987) • **87**

BARTET, G.

Gevrey-Chambertin Clos St.-Jacques 1995 • $71 • (11/15/1997) • **87**
Gevrey-Chambertin Clos St.-Jacques 1994 • $NA • (11/15/1996) • **86**

BARTHOD, GHISLAINE

Bourgogne 1990 • $23 • (12/15/1992) • **83**
Bourgogne 1988 • $20 • (3/31/1991) • **82**
Chambolle-Musigny 1990 • $25 • (12/15/1992) • **87**
Chambolle-Musigny 1988 • $50 • (3/15/1991) • **88**
Chambolle-Musigny Aux Beaux Bruns 1994 • $NA • (11/15/1996) • **81**
Chambolle-Musigny Aux Beaux Bruns 1990 • $50 • (12/15/1992) • **93**
Chambolle-Musigny Aux Beaux Bruns 1988 • $34 Ⓐ • (2/28/1991) • **83**
Chambolle-Musigny Les Charmes 1994 • $NA • (11/15/1996) • **85**
Chambolle-Musigny Les Charmes 1990 • $50 • (12/15/1992) • **90**
Chambolle-Musigny Les Cras 1990 • $50 • (12/15/1992) • **87**
Chambolle-Musigny Les Cras 1988 • $36 Ⓐ • (2/28/1991) • **87**
Chambolle-Musigny Les Véroilles 1990 • $50 • (12/15/1992) • **90**
Chambolle-Musigny Les Véroilles 1988 • $45 • (2/28/1991) • **81**

BARTON & GUESTIER

Beaujolais St.-Louis 1995 • $7 • (9/15/1996) • **82**
Beaujolais St.-Louis 1994 • $7 • (10/31/1995) • **82**
Beaujolais St.-Louis 1993 • $7 • (6/30/1994) • **82**
Beaujolais-Villages 1995 • $9 • (9/15/1996) • **82**
Beaujolais-Villages 1993 • $7 • (6/15/1995) • **72**
Beaujolais-Villages 1988 • $9 • (5/31/1989) • **77**
Beaujolais-Villages St.-Louis 1988 • $8 • (5/31/1989) • **75**
Bordeaux Fondation 1725 1990 • $9 • (3/15/1993) • **82**
Bordeaux Fondation 1725 1989 • $9 • (7/31/1991) • **75**
Brouilly 1988 • $11 • (5/31/1989) • **82**
Cabernet Sauvignon Bordeaux 1990 • $6 • (11/30/1992) • **78**
Cabernet Sauvignon Bordeaux 1988 • $6 • (2/15/1990) • **73**
Cabernet Sauvignon Vin de Pays d'Oc 1996 • $7 • (10/31/1997) • **80**
Cabernet Sauvignon Vin de Pays d'Oc 1995 • $8 • (7/31/1997) • **80**
Cabernet Sauvignon Vin de Pays d'Oc 1994 • $6 • (10/31/1995) • **80**

Chardonnay Vin de Pays d'Oc 1998: On the light side, with only modest ripe apple flavors and white pepper notes on the finish.–K.M. • $7 • (4/30/2000) • **78**

Chardonnay Vin de Pays d'Oc 1996 • $7 • (10/31/1997) • **78**
Châteauneuf-du-Pape 1992 • $17 • (11/15/1995) • **79**

Châteauneuf-du-Pape 1990 • $16 • (10/31/1993) • **71**
Châteauneuf-du-Pape 1983 • $11 • (9/30/1987) • **74**
Châteauneuf-du-Pape Tradition 1998: Beautiful ripeness in this full-bodied and tannic red, delivering vanilla, plum and mineral character. Not as generous and opulent as some '98 Châteauneufs, but with time it should deliver plenty of drinking pleasure. Best from 2004 through 2010.–P.M. • $20 • (6/30/2000) SS • **89**
Côtes du Rhône 1990 • $7 • (11/15/1993) • **80**
Côtes du Rhône 1989 • $6 • (4/15/1993) • **75**
Gevrey-Chambertin 1985 • $21 • (4/30/1988) • **89**
Margaux 1985 • $12 • (4/30/1988) • **75**
Merlot Bordeaux 1990 • $6 • (11/30/1992) • **82**
Merlot Bordeaux 1988 • $6 • (2/15/1990) • **84**
Merlot Bordeaux Founder's Collection 1998: A pleasant, grapey red, with mint and berry. Medium-bodied, with fine tannins and a light finish. Drink now.–J.S. • $10 • (6/15/2000) • **82**
Merlot Bordeaux Founder's Collection 1995 • $10 • (8/31/1997) • **81**
Merlot Vin de Pays d'Oc 1996 • $7 • (11/15/1997) • **85**
Merlot Vin de Pays d'Oc 1995 • $8 • (12/15/1996) • **82**
Merlot Vin de Pays d'Oc 1994 • $6 • (10/31/1995) • **82**
Merlot Vin de Pays d'Oc 1993 • $6 • (2/28/1995) • **81**
Moulin-à-Vent 1988 • $13 • (5/31/1989) • **84**
Pommard 1985 • $21 • (11/30/1987) • **81**
St.-Emilion Roi Chevalier 1997: Light and fruity, with wet earth and berry character. Light- to medium-bodied, with a fresh finish. Drink now.–J.S. • $14 • (6/15/2000) • **80**
St.-Julien 1985 • $13 • (2/15/1988) • **83**
Sauternes 1985 • $12 • (5/31/1988) • **75**
Sauternes Tradition 1997: A light Sauternes, with fresh fruit in a lightly sweet style. Medium-bodied, with good acidity and a tangy orange peel and lemon aftertaste. Drink now.–J.S. • $24 • (1/01/2000) • **86**
Sauvignon Blanc Bordeaux Founder's Collection 1998: Pleasant and well made, with cream aromas. Medium-bodied, with pear, lemon and a hint of lime. Fresh finish. Drink now.–J.S. • $10 • (6/15/2000) • **85**
Syrah Vin de Pays d'Oc 1995 • $7 • (10/31/1997) • **78**
Vouvray Tradition 1998: Candied lime and green apple flavors run through this simple, off-dry Vouvray. Soft finish. Drink now.–K.M. • $9 • (5/15/2000) • **81**

BASQUE, CHATEAU DU

St.-Emilion 1995 • $20 • (1/31/1998) • **79**

BASTIDE BLANCHE, LA

Bandol 1995: Firm and youthful despite its age, with lovely peppery aromas and luscious flavors of red cherry, vanilla, nutmeg and cinnamon. A focused red with plenty of punch, some leathery, meaty qualities as well. Needs a little more time. Drink through 2004.–K.M. • $17 • (11/15/1998) • **88**
Bandol Cuvée Fontanieu 1995: An appealingly savage wine, with a generous meaty aroma and flavors of bouillon, dried plum and pepper. Balanced and generous, and maturing nicely; the fine tannins give good backbone. Finishes with notes of coffee and bittersweet chocolate. Drink now through 2002.–K.M. • $24 • (11/15/1998) • **90**
Bandol Longue Garde 1996: Big and brawny, with plenty of meaty flavors. This wine lets you know it means business via its berry and dried cherry elements and gamy aroma. Some dark chocolate notes on the finish, though it's showing some maturity as well. Drink now through 2005.–K.M. • $20 • (12/31/1999) • **89**
Bandol Longue Garde 1993 • $20 • (3/31/1998) • **81**
Bandol Rosé 1997: A bit muddled, with dried cherry and berry flavors, a hint of onion on the finish.–K.M. • $13 • (11/15/1998) • **78**
Bandol Vieilles Vignes 1994 • $18 • (3/31/1998) • **74**

BASTIDE DAUZAC, LA

Margaux 1996: A bit rustic, but with good concentration of berry and mineral on the nose and palate. Medium-bodied, with chewy tannins and a medium finish. Second label of Château Dauzac. Best after 2001.–J.S. • $NA • (1/31/1999) • **86**
Margaux 1995 • $20 • (1/31/1998) • **84**
Margaux 1994 • $18 • (1/31/1997) • **79**
Margaux 1991 • $11 • (3/31/1994) • **80**

BASTIDE DE SIRAN, LA

Margaux 1996: A pleasant yet firmly structured red, with mineral and cool blackberry aromas and flavors. Medium-bodied. Best after 2000.–J.S. • $NA • (1/31/1999) • **83**
Margaux 1995 • $15 • (1/31/1998) • **87**

BASTOR-LAMONTAGNE, CHATEAU

Sauternes 1997: Pleasant Sauternes for current drinking. Pretty apple, honey and vanilla aromas. Medium-bodied, medium sweet, with good acidity and a long finish. Delicious. Drink now.–J.S. • $NA • (5/15/2000) • **87**
Sauternes 1990 • $25 • (4/15/1995) • **92**
Sauternes 1989 • $33 • (4/15/1995) • **88**
Sauternes 1988 • $21 • (4/15/1995) • **80**
Sauternes 1987 • $17 • (6/15/1990) • **67**
Sauternes 1986 • $NA • (4/15/1995) • **88**
Sauternes 1985 • $20 • (5/31/1988) • **82**
Sauternes 1983 • $23 • (1/31/1988) • **82**

BATACCHI, PHILIPPE

Clos de la Roche 1991 • $54 • (1/31/1994) • **86**
Clos de la Roche 1990 • $59 • (12/15/1992) • **93**
Côte de Nuits-Villages 1990 • $20 • (12/15/1992) • **88**
Fixin 1990 • $23 • (12/15/1992) • **87**
Gevrey-Chambertin Les Evosselles 1991 • $30 • (1/31/1994) • **79**
Gevrey-Chambertin Les Evosselles 1990 • $32 • (12/15/1992) • **91**
Gevrey-Chambertin Les Jeunes Rois 1991 • $30 • (1/31/1994) • **85**
Gevrey-Chambertin Les Jeunes Rois 1990 • $38 • (12/15/1992) • **90**
Morey-St.-Denis Premier Cru 1991 • $27 • (1/31/1994) • **79**
Morey-St.-Denis Premier Cru 1990 • $44 • (12/15/1992) • **93**

BATAILLEY, CHATEAU

Pauillac 1999: Pretty, with aromas of tar, berry and smoke. Medium- to full-bodied, with chewy tannins and a long finish.–J.S. • $NA • (1/01/2000) (BT) • **85-89**
Pauillac 1998: Plum and berry aromas with a hint of dried sage. Medium-bodied, with medium tannins and a light, slightly diluted finish.–J.S. • $NA • (5/31/1999) (BT) • **80-84**
Pauillac 1997: Rather herbal, with a stewed fruit character. Medium-bodied, with firm tannins and a slightly dry finish. Hard to get excited about.–J.S. • $NA • (1/31/2000) • **79**
Pauillac 1996: Wonderful aromas, but it falls a bit short on the palate. Plenty of currant and lead-pencil character. Medium-bodied, with polished tannins and a slightly hollow center-palate. Best after 2001.–J.S. • $22 • (1/31/1999) • **86**
Pauillac 1995 • $25 Ⓐ • (1/31/1998) • **89**
Pauillac 1992 • $19 • (4/15/1995) • **80**
Pauillac 1991 • $19 • (3/31/1994) • **83**
Pauillac 1989: A delicious '89. Ruby-colored center and a brick-red edge. Lovely ripe fruit, with hints of mushroom and earth aromas. Medium-bodied and round, sporting a lovely velvety texture.—1989 Bordeaux horizontal. Try now through 2004.–J.S. • $40 Ⓐ • (5/31/1999) • **87**
Pauillac 1988 • $38 Ⓐ • (4/30/1991) • **90**
Pauillac 1982: Thick and delicious. Dark ruby color, with a hint of garnet. Bright cherry and tobacco aromas have a hint of spice. Full-bodied and very concentrated, with big, velvety tannins and a long, sweet fruit finish.—1982 Bordeaux horizontal. Drink now.–J.S. • $43 Ⓐ • (11/30/1998) • **89**
Pauillac 1970 • $30 Ⓐ • (5/15/1993) • **88**
Pauillac 1961 • $67 Ⓐ • (4/30/1996) • **84**
Pauillac 1945 • $200 • (11/30/1995) • **78**

BATARD, SERGE

Muscadet-Côtes de Grandlieu Sur Lie Domaine Les Hautes Noëlles 1998: Clean and fresh, this light, crisp white tastes like mineral water, with hints of citrus and green apple. A bit of effervescence adds to its charm. Drink now.–T.M. • $10 • (6/30/1999) • **82**
Muscadet-Côtes de Grandlieu Sur Lie Domaine les Hautes Noëlles 1996 • $9 • (5/31/1998) • **83**

BATISTE PERTOIS

Brut Blanc de Blancs Champagne Cuvée de Réserve NV • $36 • (11/30/1995) • **86**

Brut Blanc de Blancs Champagne Cuvée de Réserve Premier Cru NV • $33 • (12/31/1992) • **80**

BAUBIAC, DOMAINE DE

Coteaux du Languedoc 1995 • $12 • (3/31/1998) • **83**

Merlot Vin de Pays d'Oc 1996 • $12 • (3/31/1998) • **74**

BAUCHET PERE & FILS

Brut Champagne Sélection NV • $NA • (12/15/1996) • **83**

BAUDRY, DOMAINE BERNARD

Chinon Les Granges 1996 • $14 • (2/28/1998) • **87**

Chinon Les Granges 1995 • $14 • (5/15/1997) • **89**

BAUDRY, JEAN & CHRISTOPHE

Chinon Domaine de la Perrière Vieilles Vignes 1996: Concentrated and intense, the black currant aromas and flavors hold sway in this lean, firmly structured red. Beginning to show some tobacco notes, with a lingering aftertaste of cassis. Tannins on the finish need duck or lamb. Drink now through 2002.–B.S. • $15 • (10/31/1998) • **90**

BAUER SELECTION

Chardonnay Vin de Pays d'Oc 1998: Cloyingly sweet to start, with a cardboardy finish. Kosher.–K.M. • $8 • (10/15/1999) • **73**

Chenin Vin de Pays du Jardin de la France 1998: Bright and fruity, this juicy white offers apple and peach flavors, with lively acidity and a clean finish. An easy, refreshing quaff. Kosher. Drink now.–T.M. • $10 • (10/31/1999) • **85**

Rosé d'Anjou 1998: This simple, off-dry rosé offers light cherry and berry flavors, with noticeable sweetness that turns a bit cloying on the finish. Kosher.–T.M. • $9 • (10/15/1999) • **78**

BAUGET-JOUETTE

Brut Blanc de Blancs Champagne 1993: A posh style of bubbly. Has a soft but lively texture and layers of flavor, from fresh dough aromas to bright lemon and vanilla accents. Drink now through 2001. • $49 • (11/15/1999) • **90**

Brut Blanc de Blancs Champagne 1990 • $52 • (11/30/1996) • **91**

Brut Champagne NV: Straightforward flavors of honey and pear with a hint of toast wrap around the rich, soft texture, finishing on the short side. Drink now.–B.S. • $35 • (11/30/1999) • **84**

Brut Champagne Cuvée Jouette NV: Smooth and subdued, this modestly flavorful Champagne has the requisite apple and citrus notes, accents of toast and mushroom and a soft, inviting effervescence. Drink now. • $56 • (12/31/1998) • **86**

Brut Champagne Grande Réserve NV: Plenty of honey, almond and baking bread notes highlight this medium-bodied, rich bubbly. Balanced on the soft side, with a fine, lingering finish. Drink now.–B.S. • $40 • (11/30/1999) • **87**

Brut Rosé Champagne NV • $33 • (12/15/1995) • **89**

BAUMARD, DOMAINE DES

Anjou Logis de la Giraudière 1997: Light and soft. Cherry, berry and herb flavors are round but diluted in this easy-drinking red. Clean and fresh, it lacks the structure to age.–T.M. • $9 • (6/30/1999) • **79**

Anjou Logis de la Giraudière 1995 • $8 • (6/15/1997) • **83**

Coteaux du Layon 1997: This late-harvest white shows the delicacy of the vintage, but has the intensity that comes from a good site and careful winemaking. Lean but silky, with orange and honey flavors that ride a clean wave of acidity through a long, spicy finish. Drink now through 2007.–T.M. • $20 • (6/30/1999) • **90**

Côteaux du Layon 1990 • $20 • (3/31/1992) • **87**

Coteaux du Layon Carte d'Or NV • $12 • (5/31/1998) • **83**

Coteaux du Layon Clos Ste.-Catherine 1997: This powerful white marries concentration and verve. It's very sweet, with flavors of dried pineapple, raisin and honey, but a lively streak of acidity keeps it fresh and clean. Delicious now, better later. Drink through 2010.–T.M. • $35 • (6/30/1999) • **93**

Coteaux du Layon Clos Ste.-Catherine 1996 • $25 • (5/31/1998) • **90**

Coteaux du Layon Clos Ste.-Catherine 1995 • $22 • (5/15/1997) • **92**

Coteaux du Layon Cuvée le Paon 1995 • $20 • (5/15/1997) • **89**

Crémant de Loire 1996: An exuberant mousse carries light flavors of green apple and citrus in this lively, straightforward sparkler. Though not complex, it's fresh and clean. A good base for punches. Drink now.–T.M. • $16 • (6/30/1999) • **82**

Quarts de Chaume 1997: Rich and soft. A puzzling, almost musty aroma gives way to more lush and appealing flavors of vanilla, spice, candied lemon, marzipan and honey. Very sweet, with a velvety texture and just enough underlying acidity to keep it lively. Hard to resist—but not up to the level of the great '95/'96 duo and a big price jump, too. Tasted twice, with consistent notes. Drink now through 2005.–T.M. • $65 • (6/30/1999) • **91**

Quarts de Chaume 1996 • $35 • (5/31/1998) CS • **95**

Quarts de Chaume 1995 • $29 Ⓐ • (5/15/1997) CS • **98**

Quarts de Chaume 1993 • $27 • (12/15/1995) • **88**

Quarts de Chaume 1990 • $45 • (3/31/1992) • **89**

Savennières 1997: Fresh and vibrant. Well-defined flavors of peach, almond and light vanilla are harmonious and balanced in this firm white. Has the liveliness and stuffing to match well with richer fish dishes. Drink now through 2002.–T.M. • $17 • (6/30/1999) • **85**

Savennières 1996 • $17 • (5/31/1998) • **89**

Savennières Clos du Papillon 1997: This light white offers peach and almond flavors characteristic of the region, but somewhat diluted. Balanced but thin. Drink now.–T.M. • $20 • (6/30/1999) • **80**

Savennières Clos du Papillon 1996 • $20 • (5/31/1998) • **87**

Savennières Trie Spéciale 1997: Subtle aromas of honey and spice follow through onto the soft, generous palate, but this white remains dry and refreshing, with bright acidity matching up with apple, pear and almond flavors. Not big, but alluring. Drink now through 2002.–T.M. • $30 • (6/30/1999) • **86**

BAUME, DOMAINE DE LA

Cabernet Sauvignon France 1995 • $6 • (6/15/1998) • **79**

Cabernet Sauvignon Vin de Pays d'Oc 1997: This is a well-balanced and focused wine, with vibrant red currant and red cherry flavors. Drink now with food.–K.M. • $7 • (2/28/1999) • **83**

Chardonnay France 1996 • $6 • (6/15/1998) • **83**

Chardonnay Vin de Pays d'Oc 1997: A soft and supple Chardonnay, with ripe apple flavors and some spicy notes. Flavors linger on the finish. Drink now.–K.M. • $7 • (2/28/1999) • **82**

Merlot France 1995 • $6 • (6/15/1998) • **78**

Merlot Vin de Pays d'Oc 1997: Young and straightforward, with decent cherry and plum flavors that soften on the finish.–K.M. • $7 • (2/28/1999) • **79**

Sauvignon Blanc France 1998: Almost neutral-tasting, with slightly herbal and waxy flavors and a flabby finish.–K.M. • $8 • (10/15/1999) • **76**

Sauvignon Blanc Vin de Pays d'Oc 1997: Light and fresh, this simple white shows crisp acidity, with citrus and light herbal flavors. A pleasant aperitif. Drink now.–T.M. • $7 • (2/28/1999) • **80**

Syrah France 1996: Packed full of berry, red plum and cherry flavors, with a good zip of acidity and leathery notes. Smooth and nicely concentrated, with a pleasing mouthfeel. Drink now.–K.M. • $6 • (8/31/1998) • **84**

Syrah Vin de Pays d'Oc 1997: Quite young, with grapey character. Medium body and balance, with red cherry flavors that linger on the finish. Drink now.–K.M. • $7 • (2/28/1999) • **83**

Vin de Pays d'Oc Cuvée Propriétaire 1994 • $8 • (7/31/1996) • **78**

BAUR, FRANCOIS

Pinot Blanc Alsace Herrenweg 1998: Fresh, offering citrus, nut and peach aromas and flavors, a rich texture and a slightly tart finish. Drink now.–B.S. • $13 • (10/31/1999) • **83**

Riesling Alsace Grand Cru Brand 1997: A bit heavy-handed, the earth, licorice and almond notes are a tad rustic and coarse for Riesling, however it has an underlying mineral note that lingers and a firm structure. May just need time. Best from 2001 through 2005.–B.S. • $17 • (10/31/1999) • **84**

Key: SS—Spectator Selection. CS—Cellar Selection. HR—Highly Recommended. $NA—Price not available. (BT)—Barrel tasting. Ⓐ—Auction Price.
For a key to the tasters' initials, see "How to Use These Listings."
Dates in parentheses represent the issues in which the ratings were published.

FRANCE

Tokay Pinot Gris Alsace Herrenweg 1998: Noticably sweet, this is full of apricot, honey and lemon offsetting the rich, open texture. Turns a bit hot (alcohol) on the finish, though. Drink now.–B.S. • $19 • (10/31/1999) • **82**

BEATES, DOMAINE DES

Coteaux d'Aix-en-Provence Les Matines 1998: Rich and meaty, with an aroma to match. Medium-bodied, with plum, leather and spice flavors that linger on the finish. A hearty red full of finesse that bursts with lively aromas and flavors. From M. Chapoutier's new Provence domaine. Drink now through 2003.–K.M. • $12 • (6/15/2000) • **87**

Coteaux d'Aix-en-Provence Terra d'Or 1997: Rich and full-bodied, with plenty of dark plum and dark cherry flavors and chocolaty, spicy notes. Supple and alluring, with a ripe aroma. Flavors linger on the long finish. Quite impressive for the appellation. Tasted twice, with consistent notes. Cabernet Sauvignon and Syrah. Drink now through 2003.–K.M. • $72 • (6/15/2000) • **89**

BEAUCASTEL, CHATEAU DE

Châteauneuf-du-Pape 1997: A clever effort for '97. Dark and fruit-driven, this fresh, compacted Châteauneuf delivers blackberry, toasted oak, plum and game. The tannins are well integrated in the ways of modern winemaking. Drink now through 2005.–P.M. • $18 Ⓐ • (12/15/1999) • **88**

Châteauneuf-du-Pape 1996: Fresh and fruity, with smooth tannins, this delivers nice cassis, blackberry and cherry notes. Good acidity leads to a mouthpuckering, racy finish. Drink now through 2003.–P.M. • $20 Ⓐ • (11/15/1998) • **85**

Châteauneuf-du-Pape 1995: This rich red still shows the backward intensity of youth, with a dark color and initially reductive aromas. But be patient—behind the firm tannins there's a core of ripe, rich plum, with notes of game, herb and mineral that promise complexity with age. Best after 2000.–T.M. • $41 Ⓐ • (11/15/1998) • **92**

Châteauneuf-du-Pape 1994 • $33 Ⓐ • (2/28/1997) • **87**
Châteauneuf-du-Pape 1993 • $34 Ⓐ • (11/15/1996) • **86**
Châteauneuf-du-Pape 1992 • $31 • (11/30/1994) • **85**
Châteauneuf-du-Pape 1991 • $25 • (3/31/1994) HR • **89**
Châteauneuf-du-Pape 1990 • $87 Ⓐ • (3/15/1993) HR • **92**
Châteauneuf-du-Pape 1989 • $98 Ⓐ • (10/15/1991) CS • **97**
Châteauneuf-du-Pape 1988 • $47 Ⓐ • (10/15/1991) • **90**
Châteauneuf-du-Pape 1987 • $17 • (9/30/1989) • **86**
Châteauneuf-du-Pape 1986 • $49 Ⓐ • (10/15/1991) • **91**
Châteauneuf-du-Pape 1985 • $64 Ⓐ • (10/15/1991) • **91**
Châteauneuf-du-Pape 1984 • $22 • (11/30/1989) • **89**
Châteauneuf-du-Pape 1983 • $59 Ⓐ • (10/15/1991) • **90**
Châteauneuf-du-Pape 1982 • $40 Ⓐ • (11/30/1989) • **92**
Châteauneuf-du-Pape 1981 • $70 Ⓐ • (10/15/1991) • **96**
Châteauneuf-du-Pape 1980 • $67 Ⓐ • (11/30/1989) • **83**

Châteauneuf-du-Pape Hommage à Jacques Perrin Grande Cuvée 1995: Inky dark in color, rich and ripe, this clean Southern Rhône red has superbly refined tannins, flavors of roasted nuts, spices, plum, black olive, cassis and fig. Opulent and classy, with the silky texture of a Châteauneuf and plenty of fruit. Drink now through 2008.–P.M. • $237 Ⓐ • (11/15/1998) HR • **95**

Châteauneuf-du-Pape White 1998: Medium-bodied but rather flavorful, with wonderful ripe fruit, showing pear, citrus, honey and quince in a fat package. A lemony finish keeps things fresh. Drink now through 2002.–P.M. • $44 • (12/15/1999) • **87**

Châteauneuf-du-Pape White 1997: This classy, distinctive white shows wonderful personality and fantastic balance. The smooth mouthfeel has a tight grip that explodes with cedar, spice, tropical, iodine, lemon and mineral notes, all swirling around beautifully. An ager for sure, but tempting now because of its full body. The ripe flavors linger on the bitter almondlike finish. Tasted twice, with consistent notes. Drink now through 2010.–P.M. • $40 • (11/15/1998) • **95**

Côtes du Rhône Coudoulet de Beaucastel 1997: A decent red, very clean and "polite," but without much complexity, showing black fruit. Lacks a bit of depth, and turns surprisingly tannic on the finish.–P.M. • $21 • (12/15/1999) • **79**

Côtes du Rhône Coudoulet de Beaucastel 1996: Excellent vibrant-yet-ripe berry flavors bring this light- to medium-bodied red to life. Delicious from start to finish, delivering sweet-tasting tannins and clean flavors. Succulent finish. Drink now.–P.M. • $20 • (11/15/1998) • **85**

Côtes du Rhône Coudoulet de Beaucastel 1987 • $12 • (12/15/1989) • **76**
Côtes du Rhône Coudoulet de Beaucastel 1986 • $15 • (9/30/1988) • **84**
Côtes du Rhône Coudoulet de Beaucastel 1985 • $12 • (4/30/1988) • **85**

Côtes du Rhône White Coudoulet de Beaucastel 1998: Rather balanced and very clean, with good fruit and acidity, this shows nice focus, with lemon, pear and apple notes bursting forth. Drink now through 2001.–P.M. • $21 • (12/15/1999) • **84**

Côtes du Rhône White Coudoulet de Beaucastel 1997: A flavorful, medium-bodied white, showing lovely peach, apricot and melon character. Good acidity keeps it lively on the surprisingly elegant finish. Drink now.–P.M. • $22 • (11/15/1998) • **86**

Roussanne Châteauneuf-du-Pape Vieilles Vignes 1998: A powerful yet very ripe white, showing very toasted oak treatment, with smoke, toasted coconut, honey and chocolate complexity. But it works because there's enough rich fruit to support the wood shock treatment. A wine with a track record for aging. Best from 2005 through 2010.–P.M. • $110 • (12/15/1999) • **93**

Roussanne Châteauneuf-du-Pape Vieilles Vignes 1997: With aromas of a late-harvest white but fermented dry, it's thick, rich and silky—almost in the lineage of a ripe Condrieu. Floral, peach, apricot and macadamia nut character combines with oozing honey on the delicious, lingering finish. Tasted twice, with consistent notes. Drink now through 2005.–P.M. • $100 • (9/30/1999) • **96**

BEAUDET, PAUL

Mâcon-Berzé-le-Ville Château de Berzé 1995 • $NA • (8/31/1996) • **76**
Mâcon-Viré 1995 • $12 • (5/31/1997) • **85**

Pouilly-Fuissé Domaine des Trois Tilleuls 1997: Clean and pure, with lemon and honey character, a medium body. Rather firm, but displaying good class and some lovely honey, pear and tropical fruit on the finish. Drink now.–P.M. • $21 • (5/31/1999) • **87**

St.-Véran Domaine du Poète 1997: Decent-to-good ripeness brings out pear, apple and a hint of pineapple, but don't expect much complexity in this fresh, straightforward, light-bodied St.-Véran. Drink now.–P.M. • $14 • (5/31/1999) • **80**

St.-Véran Domaine du Poète 1996 • $14 • (5/31/1998) • **85**

BEAUFORT, HERBERT

Brut Blanc de Blancs Champagne Cuvée du Mélomane NV: A good, solid bottle of bubbly, with clean citrus aromas and flavors, good acidity and a refreshing finish. Drink now. • $33 • (12/31/1998) • **84**

Brut Champagne Carte d'Or NV: A lush, inviting Champagne, with a smooth texture and appealing flavors of butter, pear and vanilla. Layered, complex and soothing to drink. Drink now. • $34 • (12/31/1998) • **89**

Brut Rosé Champagne Pinot Noir NV: A vivid reddish color and bright, straightforward fruit flavors make this a Beaujolais of Champagnes. Refreshing, flavorful and easy to quaff. Drink now. • $36 • (11/30/1998) • **81**

BEAULIEU, CHATEAU

Pomerol 1996: Delivers plenty of berry and chocolate aromas and flavors. Medium- to light-bodied, with firm tannins and a short finish. Rather simple. Drink now.–J.S. • $NA • (1/31/1999) • **83**

BEAUMONT, CHATEAU

Haut-Médoc 1998: A bit lean really, but there are some well-crafted tannins in this wine. Medium-bodied, with cherry-berry character. Light finish.–J.S. • $NA • (5/31/1999) (BT) • **80-84**

Haut-Médoc 1997: Some good berry and cherry character to this. Medium- to light-bodied, with velvety tannins and a fresh finish. Drink now.–J.S. • $11 • (1/31/2000) • **81**

Haut-Médoc 1996: A pretty, balanced '96, with ripe berry character and fine tannins. Medium-bodied and harmonious, with a fine, silky texture. Best after 2000.–J.S. • $18 • (1/31/1999) • **87**

Haut-Médoc 1995 • $21 Ⓐ • (1/31/1998) • **88**
Haut-Médoc 1994 • $15 Ⓐ • (1/31/1997) • **82**
Haut-Médoc 1993 • $13 • (1/31/1996) • **79**
Haut-Médoc 1992 • $11 • (4/15/1995) • **76**
Haut-Médoc 1991 • $11 • (3/31/1994) • **77**
Haut-Médoc 1990 • $13 • (3/31/1993) • **80**
Haut-Médoc 1989 • $27 Ⓐ • (3/15/1992) • **82**
Haut-Médoc 1988 • $20 Ⓐ • (7/15/1991) • **82**
Haut-Médoc 1986 • $30 Ⓐ • (6/30/1989) • **84**
Haut-Médoc 1985 • $14 • (4/30/1988) • **74**
Haut-Médoc 1982 • $26 Ⓐ • (8/31/1992) • **87**

BEAUMONT, DOMAINE DES

Morey-St.-Denis 1996: Pure and clean, very fruity, somewhat herbal but also showing nice cherry, currant and toasted spice notes. The high acidity and fine tannins make for an elegant, light-bodied Pinot, if not a very complex one. Drink now through 2002.–P.M. • $45 • (2/28/1999) • **85**

BEAUMONT DES CRAYERES

Brut Champagne Cuvée de Prestige NV: Full-flavored and assertive. Fresh grapefruit and herb flavors are rounded by creamy accents. Drink now. • $33 • (10/31/1999) • **87**

Brut Champagne Cuvée de Prestige 1994: Lean in style and modest in flavor, this is nicely soft and soothing in texture. Quite dry and light on the finish. Drink now. • $40 • (12/31/1998) • **83**

Brut Champagne Cuvée de Réserve NV: An intriguing, austere style of Champagne that stands out from the crowd. Has a a tangy texture and vivid citrus and mineral flavors that refresh the palate and linger on the finish. Drink now. • $32 • (12/31/1998) • **89**

Brut Champagne Grande Prestige 1994: Good effort from a weak vintage. Has nice complexity of fruit and richness of texture, with a lingering finish. Drink now. • $36 • (11/15/1999) • **87**

Brut Champagne Grande Réserve NV: Cloying, candied ginger and a slight oxidized note combine with the coarse texture in this light, simple Champagne. Tasted twice, with consistent notes.–B.S. • $30 • (11/30/1999) • **76**

Brut Champagne Nostalgie 1991: An attractive layer of mature flavors marks this otherwise lean and dry Champagne. It should not be aged; enjoy it now for its nutty, mushroomy flavors and smooth texture. • $44 • (12/31/1998) • **85**

Brut Champagne Nostalgie 1990: A grand, full-bodied 1990 layered with toasty, nutty, honeylike flavors. Very dry, this is supple in texture, with a lingering finish. Great now, but has plenty of life ahead. Drink now through 2005. • $55 • (11/15/1999) • **92**

Brut Champagne Nuit d'Or Cuvée 2000 1990: Full-bodied, flavorful and quite dry, this is a serious Champagne for the dinner table. Has ripe fruit and mellow mushroom nuances that linger on the finish. Drink now through 2002. • $54 • (11/15/1999) • **91**

Brut Rosé Champagne Fleur de Rosé 1995: Full, rich and creamy, this rosé packs in plenty of cherry, dough and lanolin flavors allied to a firm structure. Young and intense, this could benefit from a little aging on the cork. Drink now through 2002.–B.S. • $36 • (11/30/1999) • **89**

Brut Rosé Champagne Privilège NV: Pink in color, this elegant, fresh, rather subtle rosé blends light, bright cherry aromas and flavors with a firm texture. Drink now. • $36 • (11/30/1998) • **87**

BEAUREGARD, CHATEAU

Pomerol 1999: Medium-bodied, with pretty mineral, cherry and smoke aromas and flavors, fine tannins and a fruity finish. Well done.–J.S. • $NA • (1/01/2000) (BT) • **85-89**

Pomerol 1998: Very ripe aromas of blackberries and spices, with a hint of black olive. Full-bodied and very, very chewy, with a solid core of fruit and tannins. Long, long finish. Almost classic.–J.S. • $NA • (5/31/1999) (BT) • **90-94**

Pomerol 1997: A bit closed, but very good. Lovely berry, tobacco, mineral aromas. Medium-bodied, with firm tannins and a medium finish. Best after 2000.–J.S. • $45 • (1/31/2000) • **87**

Pomerol 1996: A pleasant wine, if a bit too much oak for the vintage. Pleasing aromas of blackberries with hints of toasted oak. Medium-bodied, with berry flavors and a big shot of vanilla oak in the aftertaste. Drink now.–J.S. • $NA • (1/31/1999) • **86**

Pomerol 1995 • $50 • (1/31/1998) • **91**

Pomerol 1994 • $26 • (1/31/1997) • **89**

Pomerol 1993 • $26 • (1/31/1996) • **87**

Pomerol 1989: A silky and elegant '89 displaying plenty of finesse and character. Full-bodied yet fine, with black olive, chocolate and fruit. Lovely sweet fruit on the finish. (1989 Bordeaux horizontal tasting). Drink now through 2005.–J.S. • $NA • (5/31/1999) • **90**

Pomerol 1988 • $36 • (7/31/1991) HR • **90**

Key: SS—Spectator Selection. CS—Cellar Selection. HR—Highly Recommended. $NA—Price not available. (BT)—Barrel tasting. Ⓐ—Auction Price.
For a key to the tasters' initials, see "How to Use These Listings."
Dates in parentheses represent the issues in which the ratings were published.

Pomerol 1986 • $24 • (6/15/1989) • **87**

Pomerol 1982 • $NA • (8/31/1992) • **87**

BEAUSEJOUR, CHATEAU

Montagne-St.-Emilion Clos l'Eglise 1995: A bit light, but shows some delicious berry, cherry and vanilla aromas and flavors. Medium- to light-bodied, with a delicate finish. Drink now.–J.S. • $NA • (9/15/1998) • **80**

BEAU-SEJOUR BECOT, CHATEAU

St.-Emilion 1997: Outstanding. Aromas of plums, berries, cherries and ripe fruit. Medium- to full-bodied, with a solid backbone of tannins and a long, long finish. Very well done for the vintage. Best after 2000.–J.S. • $40 • (1/31/2000) • **90**

St.-Emilion 1996: An extremely well-done '96. Lovely combination of crushed berries and exotic spices. Medium-bodied, with a pretty balance of fruit and tannins. Best after 2000.–J.S. • $48 • (1/31/1999) • **88**

St.-Emilion 1995: Blackberry and cinnamon aromas introduce this gorgeous young wine. Full-bodied and velvety-textured, with plenty of fruit and spice flavors and a long, caressing finish. Best from 2002 through 2007.–J.S. • $35 • (9/15/1998) • **92**

St.-Emilion 1993 • $25 • (1/31/1996) • **86**

St.-Emilion 1988 • $37 Ⓐ • (6/30/1991) • **87**

St.-Emilion 1986 • $22 • (7/31/1989) • **79**

St.-Emilion 1982: A very dark-colored and youthful red, with floral and ripe fruit aromas and hints of earth. Full-bodied and very chewy, yet fruity and sweet, with well-integrated tannins and a lovely finish. (1982 Bordeaux horizontal tasting). Drink now.–J.S. • $NA • (11/30/1998) • **92**

BEAUSEJOUR DUFFAU-LAGAROSSE, CHATEAU

St.-Emilion 1999: Plenty of tobacco, mineral and berry character in this young wine. Medium-bodied, with a good core of ripe fruit and tannins and a medium finish.–J.S. • $NA • (1/01/2000) (BT) • **988**

St.-Emilion 1996: Really well done for the vintage. Complex aromas of berries, tobacco and grilled meats. Medium-bodied, with chewy tannins and a long, succulent finish. Best after 2000.–J.S. • $70 • (1/31/1999) • **88**

St.-Emilion 1995 • $48 Ⓐ • (1/31/1998) • **89**

St.-Emilion 1994 • $23 Ⓐ • (1/31/1997) • **86**

St.-Emilion 1993 • $30 • (1/31/1996) • **87**

St.-Emilion 1992 • $33 • (4/15/1995) • **80**

St.-Emilion 1990 • $350 Ⓐ • (3/31/1993) • **95**

St.-Emilion 1989: Loads of smoky, meaty and berry aromas and flavors in this wine. Full-bodied, with lots of berry, tobacco character and a medium-chewy finish that's slightly papery.—(1989 Bordeaux horizontal tasting). Drink now.–J.S. • $56 Ⓐ • (5/31/1999) • **89**

St.-Emilion 1988: Always a really good bottle of claret, this is slightly better than I remember, with lots of concentrated fruit and chocolate character on the nose and palate. Full-bodied, with velvety tannins and a long finish. (1988 Bordeaux horizontal tasting). Best after 2002.–J.S. • $NA • (11/30/1998) • **90**

St.-Emilion 1986 • $34 • (6/30/1989) • **91**

St.-Emilion 1982: Amazingly dark ruby in color, with a slightly red edge. Complex aromas of berry, dried cherry, mineral and spice. Full-bodied and tannic, yet well integrated and very youthful. Still backward. (1982 Bordeaux horizontal tasting). Best after 2000.–J.S. • $NA • (11/30/1998) • **93**

St.-Emilion 1947 • $240 Ⓐ • (5/31/1997) • **88**

BEAU-SITE, CHATEAU

St.-Estèphe 1998: Slightly one-dimensional, but has some good black currant and earth character. Medium-bodied, with medium tannins. Slightly diluted.–J.S. • $NA • (5/31/1999) (BT) • **80-84**

St.-Estèphe 1997: Pretty berry and cherry character. Light-bodied, with fresh acidity and a light, fruity finish. Drink now through 2003.–J.S. • $18 • (1/31/2000) • **83**

St.-Estèphe 1996: A good level of blackberry and cherry aromas, with hints of spices. Medium-bodied, with earth and bark flavors and undertones of black fruits. Velvety tannins. Drink now.–J.S. • $13 • (1/31/1999) • **86**

St.-Estèphe 1995 • $24 • (1/31/1998) • **86**

St.-Estèphe 1992 • $14 • (4/15/1995) • **76**

St.-Estèphe 1991 • $13 • (3/31/1994) • **78**

St.-Estèphe 1990 • $23 • (3/31/1993) • **90**

St.-Estèphe 1989: A beautiful and elegant '89, with a dark-ruby color and loads of raspberry and cherry aromas that turn to licorice and mint.

Medium- to full-bodied, very chewy and plenty of fine tannins. Will still improve with age.—(1989 Bordeaux horizontal tasting). Drink now through 2008.–J.S. • $NA • (5/31/1999) • **90**

St.-Estèphe 1987 • $12 • (11/30/1989) • **81**
St.-Estèphe 1986 • $18 • (11/30/1989) • **86**
St.-Estèphe 1982 • $18 • (8/31/1992) • **86**
St.-Estèphe 1970 • $36 • (5/15/1993) • **82**

BEAU-SOLEIL, CHATEAU

Pomerol 1998: Some berry and cherry character, but rather lean and short for the vintage.–J.S. • $NA • (5/31/1999) (BT) • **80-84**

Pomerol 1997: Pretty plum and milk chocolate aromas here. Medium-bodied, with silky tannins and a short, slightly diluted finish. Drink now.–J.S. • $50 • (1/31/2000) • **84**

Pomerol 1996: An impressive Right Bank red. Dark ruby-colored, with lots of blackberry and cherry with wet-earth character. Full-bodied and chewy, with a long, fruity, oaky aftertaste. Best after 2001.–J.S. • $28 • (1/31/1999) • **88**

Pomerol 1995 • $28 • (1/31/1998) • **84**

BEAU-VALLON, CHATEAU DU

St.-Emilion 1990 • $14 • (8/31/1995) • **83**
St.-Emilion 1987 • $10 • (5/15/1990) • **81**
St.-Emilion 1986 • $10 • (9/30/1989) • **84**

BEGUDE, DOMAINE DE LA

Bandol 1996: A medium-bodied red with a smooth texture and flavors of dried cherry and leather. Some berry tones on the finish. Drink now.–K.M. • $16 • (12/31/1999) • **84**

BEL AIR, CHATEAU

Côtes de Castillon 1993 • $17 • (4/30/1997) • **81**

BEL AIR, CHATEAU

Haut-Médoc 1994 • $14 • (12/31/1997) • **87**
Haut-Médoc 1988 • $15 • (4/30/1991) • **85**

BELAIR, CHATEAU

St.-Emilion 1996: Shows some pretty aromas of blackberries and dark chocolate. Medium-bodied, with fine tannins and a light finish. Slightly diluted midpalate, but pleasant Drink now.–J.S. • $NA • (1/31/1999) • **84**

St.-Emilion 1993 • $16 Ⓐ • (1/31/1996) • **81**

St.-Emilion 1990 • $33 • (3/31/1993) • **90**

St.-Emilion 1989: A fresh and deliciously young '89, with berry and milk chocolate aromas and flavors. Full-bodied, adding fine tannins and a caressing finish. Beautiful. Very fine. (1989 Bordeaux horizontal tasting). Best after 2004.–J.S. • $NA • (5/31/1999) • **90**

St.-Emilion 1986 • $30 Ⓐ • (3/31/1990) • **82**

St.-Emilion 1982: Not as outstanding as I remember, but delicious, subtle and elegant. Good ruby color. Medium-bodied, with medium, silky tannins, a floral, berry and fresh earth character and a fruity, chocolate and berry aftertaste. (1982 Bordeaux horizontal tasting). Drink now.–J.S. • $44 Ⓐ • (11/30/1998) • **89**

St.-Emilion 1970 • $49 • (5/15/1993) • **88**

St.-Emilion 1961 • $68/1.5 liter • (4/30/1996) • **87**

BEL AIR PERPONCHER, CHATEAU

Bordeaux Cuvée Passion 1996: Clean and fruity, with vanilla and strawberry aromas and flavors. Medium-bodied, with light tannins and a fresh aftertaste. Drink now.–J.S. • $11 • (1/31/1999) • **80**

Bordeaux Supèrieur Grande Cuvée 1997: Pleasant, with aromas of coffee, chocolate and berry. Medium-bodied, with velvety tannins and a medium finish. Drink now.–J.S. • $16 • (6/15/2000) • **85**

Bordeaux White Cuvée Passion 1996: Lots of fruit in this wine, but a little raw. Full-bodied, with honey, lemon, apple and coconut flavors, firm acidity and a fresh finish. Drink through 2002–J.S. • $NA • (1/01/1999) • **85**

Entre-Deux-Mers 1999: A steely, clean white, with apple, honey and pear aromas and flavors. Medium-bodied, with fresh acidity and a long finish. Drink now.–J.S. • $8 • (1/01/2000) • **85**

BEL EVEQUE, CHATEAU

Corbières 1995 • $10 • (4/30/1998) • **82**
Corbières 1991 • $12 • (2/28/1995) • **82**

BELGRAVE, CHATEAU

Haut-Médoc 1998: Aromas of cocoa and blueberry follow through to a compacted, medium-bodied palate with velvety tannins and a medium finish. Very good sample.–J.S. • $NA • (5/31/1999) (BT) • **85-89**

Haut-Médoc 1997: Very pleasant red, with plum and berry character and a light mineral undertone. Medium-bodied, with firm tannins and a fruity finish. Drink now.–J.S. • $NA • (1/31/2000) • **86**

Haut-Médoc 1996: Very well-made fifth-growth. Dark-colored, with lots of ripe berry, vanilla, spice and cinnamon. Medium- to full-bodied, with silky tannins and a fresh aftertaste of fruit and spice. Best after 2001.–J.S. • $25 • (1/31/1999) • **88**

Haut-Médoc 1995 • $25 • (1/31/1998) • **85**
Haut-Médoc 1994 • $20 • (1/31/1997) • **84**
Haut-Médoc 1993 • $20 • (1/31/1996) • **81**
Haut-Médoc 1991 • $14 • (3/31/1994) • **80**

Haut-Médoc 1989: Finely crafted red. Dark-ruby color. Very fresh berry and cherry aromas. Medium-bodied, with fine tannins and a mint, tobacco and cassis aftertaste. (1989 Bordeaux horizontal tasting). Drink now.–J.S. • $NA • (5/31/1999) • **89**

Haut-Médoc 1988 • $28 • (7/31/1991) • **79**
Haut-Médoc 1986 • $16 • (3/31/1990) • **81**

Haut-Médoc 1982: Dark ruby in color, with a brick edge. Slightly musty, with ripe fruit and mushroom aromas. Medium-bodied and dry, and starting to fall apart. (1982 Bordeaux horizontal tasting).–J.S. • $NA • (11/30/1998) • **74**

BELINGARD, CHATEAU

Côtes de Bergerac 1994 • $9 • (5/31/1997) • **82**
Monbazillac 1994 • $16 • (5/31/1997) • **83**

BELLAND, JEAN-CLAUDE

Santenay 1995 • $16 Ⓐ • (11/15/1997) • **82**

BELLAND, ROGER

Chassagne-Montrachet Morgeot-Clos Pitois 1997: Full-bodied, this is thick and ripe, with a firm, lemony personality. The fruit flavors taste concentrated and long. The oak is smartly subtle. Has the potential to improve with age. Drink now through 2007.–P.M. • $50 • (9/30/1999) • **93**

Chassagne-Montrachet Morgeot-Clos Pitois 1996 • $50 • (5/31/1998) • **85**

Criots-Bâtard-Montrachet 1997: Ultrasmooth and velvety, full-bodied and ripe, caressing the palate with caramel, pear, pie crust and toasted oak notes that float to a soft landing. Drink now through 2007.–P.M. • $105 • (9/30/1999) • **92**

Criots-Bâtard-Montrachet 1996 • $90 • (5/31/1998) • **95**

Puligny-Montrachet Les Champs-Gains 1997: Beautiful. As full-bodied and silky as they get yet balanced, with a clean, pure, lemony vanilla bean character and decently toasted oak, this coats the palate with caressing, mineral-inspired waves. Drink now through 2005.–P.M. • $53 • (9/30/1999) • **91**

BELLE PERE & FILS

Crozes-Hermitage 1990 • $20 • (2/28/1993) HR • **90**

Crozes-Hermitage Cuvée Louis Belle 1997: Difficult to judge this split-personality, medium-bodied red. Starts round and supple, with fine fruit, mineral, black cherry and vanilla-chocolate character, then turns hard on the finish. Might soften with time. Best from 2001 through 2005.–P.M. • $18 • (12/15/1999) • **87**

Crozes-Hermitage Cuvée Louis Belle 1995 • $22 • (10/15/1997) • **85**

Crozes-Hermitage Les Pierrelles 1997: A thick and dense Crozes, showing mineral, earth and oatmeal, it has a chewy character, but there is also ripe fruit for balance. A *terroir* wine. Drink now through 2004.–P.M. • $24 • (12/15/1999) • **88**

Crozes-Hermitage Les Pierrelles 1995 • $18 • (10/15/1997) • **79**

BELLE PERE & FILS

Crozes-Hermitage Les Pierrelles 1991 • $17 • (5/31/1994) • **84**
Crozes-Hermitage White 1997: A white with modest complexity. Medium-bodied and dry, with almond, wet earth and pear flavors, but also a slight cardboard character.–P.M. • $18 • (12/15/1999) • **79**
Hermitage 1991 • $40 • (5/31/1994) • **90**
Hermitage 1990 • $46 • (4/15/1993) • **93**

BELLEGARDE, CHATEAU

Margaux 1997: A light red, with some berry character, but diluted.–J.S. • $23 • (1/31/2000) • **79**
Margaux 1996: Pretty aromas of mushroom, cherry and berry. Medium-bodied, with firm tannins. Slightly hollow midpalate. Not a big, powerful wine, it's reserved and racy. Second label of Château Siran. Best after 2000.–J.S. • $22 • (1/31/1999) • **86**

BELLEGRAVE, CHATEAU

Pomerol 1998: Lovely, silky young wine with plenty of blackberry and smoke character. Full-bodied and balanced, with velvety tannins. Delicious.–J.S. • $NA • (5/31/1999) (BT) • **90-94**
Pomerol 1994 • $38 • (4/30/1997) • **84**

BELLEVUE-FIGEAC, CHATEAU

St.-Emilion 1998: Rather diluted and slightly herbaceous. Medium- to light-bodied, with light tannins and a short finish. Rain affected.–J.S. • $NA • (5/31/1999) (BT) • **75-79**
St.-Emilion 1997: Has some pleasant berry character, but a bit thin. Medium-bodied, with medium tannins and a short finish. Drink now.–J.S. • $NA • (1/31/2000) • **84**
St.-Emilion 1996: Light ruby-colored, with delicate blackberry aromas, hints of herb. Light-bodied, with light tannins and a short finish. Tasted twice, with consistent notes.–J.S. • $NA • (2/28/1999) • **78**
St.-Emilion 1993 • $28 • (1/31/1996) • **79**

BELLEVUE LAFFONT, CHATEAU

Listrac 1997: Rather earthy, with a slightly funky aroma. Light-bodied. Light finish. Tasted twice, with consistent notes.–J.S. • $NA • (1/31/2000) • **76**

BEL-ORME-TRONQUOY-DE-LALANDE, CHATEAU

Haut-Médoc 1998: Some decent fruit here, but rather simple and short on the palate. Medium body. Light finish. Austere tannins.–J.S. • $NA • (5/31/1999) (BT) • **80-84**
Haut-Médoc 1997: A lovely, soft wine with berry, plum and cherry character. Medium-bodied. Light on the finish. Drink now.–J.S. • $NA • (1/31/2000) • **86**
Haut-Médoc 1996: A fresh and lively little red, with currant and floral aromas and flavors. Medium-bodied, with silky tannins, but a slight dilution on the finish. Drink now.–J.S. • $22 • (1/31/1999) • **83**
Haut-Médoc 1982: Slightly high in acidity, but has a good, youthful color, with a ruby center and an amber edge. Rather milky, with chocolate and berry aromas, and slightly acidic. Full-bodied and velvety, but short on the finish. (1982 Bordeaux horizontal tasting). Drink now.–J.S. • $NA • (11/30/1998) • **84**
Haut-Médoc 1995 • $20 • (1/31/1998) • **86**
Haut-Médoc 1994 • $NA • (1/31/1997) • **83**

BELVEZEL, DOMAINE DU

Vin de Pays des Côteaux de l'Ardèche 1995 • $9 • (10/15/1996) • **83**

BENAZETH, DOMAINE

Minervois 1994: Tough and still tannic, with plum and berry flavors and an earthy streak. Hard to say if it will come around.–K.M. • $8 • (8/31/1998) • **79**

Key: SS—Spectator Selection. CS—Cellar Selection. HR—Highly Recommended. $NA—Price not available. (BT)—Barrel tasting. Ⓐ—Auction Price. For a key to the tasters' initials, see "How to Use These Listings."
Dates in parentheses represent the issues in which the ratings were published.

Vin de Pays de l'Aude 1995: Not for the faint of palate. An extremely flavorful, challenging red, packed with fruit flavors and accented by wild game and earth notes that lend complexity. Full-bodied. Tannic, with a lingering, earthy finish. Drink now. • $10 • (7/31/1998) • **88**

BERAT, J. & JACQUES

Brut Champagne NV: Very crisp and lively, displaying citrus and apple notes, and a hint of candied fruit, on a smooth texture. Good follow-through on the citrus note. Drink now through 2001.–B.S. • $27 • (2/29/2000) • **87**

BERERD & FILS, JEAN

Beaujolais-Villages Le Perréon Domaine de la Madone 1997: Soft and quaffable, with black cherry character and moderate concentration and length. Drink now.–B.S. • $11 • (10/15/1999) • **82**
Beaujolais-Villages Le Perréon Domaine de la Madone 1996: Earth notes give distinctive pleasure, but overwhelm the modest cherry.–T.M. • $11 • (8/31/1998) • **77**

BERGAT, CHATEAU

St.-Emilion 1999: Dark ruby, with violet, berry and cherry aromas. Medium- to full-bodied, with well-integrated tannins and a medium finish. Very fine.–J.S. • $NA • (1/01/2000) (BT) • **85-89**
St.-Emilion 1998: Plenty of chocolate and berry character in this round and delicious young wine. Medium-bodied, with fine tannins and a fresh finish. Almost outstanding.–J.S. • $NA • (5/31/1999) (BT) • **85-89**
St.-Emilion 1997: Decent berry and plum character, but slightly weedy. Medium- to light-bodied, with light tannins. Drink now.–J.S. • $NA • (1/31/2000) • **80**
St.-Emilion 1996: Berry and dark chocolate aromas follow through to the palate, with a hint of white pepper. Medium-bodied, with firm tannins and a light finish. Simple. Drink now.–J.S. • $25 • (1/31/1999) • **82**
St.-Emilion 1995 • $25 • (1/31/1998) • **87**
St.-Emilion 1991 • $13 • (3/31/1994) • **80**
St.-Emilion 1990 • $19 • (3/31/1993) • **86**
St.-Emilion 1989: Rather mature color of brick-red. Wonderful aromas of strawberries, plums and berries. Medium-bodied, with soft tannins and a fresh and fruity aftertaste. (1989 Bordeaux horizontal tasting). Drink now.–J.S. • $NA • (5/31/1999) • **87**

BERGERIE, DOMAINE DE LA

Anjou White Les Pierres Girard 1996 • $11 • (6/30/1998) • **78**
Coteaux du Layon 1996: This elegant white is only moderately sweet, but offers intriguing flavors of quince, orange peel and cinnamon, with vivid acidity and a long, clean finish. Try it with richer fish and poultry dishes. Drink now through 2003.–T.M. • $14 • (6/30/1999) • **89**
Coteaux du Layon Cuvée Fragrance 1996: A beauty. This sensuous white is delicate yet assertive, with intense flavors of ripe apple, pineapple and spice. Quite sweet yet never heavy or dull. Impressive yet refreshing, with great balance. Drink now through 2010.–T.M. • $28/500 ml. • (6/30/1999) • **91**
Coteaux du Layon Cuvée Fragrance 1995 • $26/500 ml. • (6/15/1998) • **88**
Coteaux du Layon Le Clos de la Bergerie 1995 • $13 • (6/15/1998) • **89**
Quarts de Chaume 1997: Silky-smooth, this unctuous, sweet white offers rich flavors of banana, honey and spice. Well integrated and clean, balanced and quite intense, it should improve with age. Drink now through 2008.–T.M. • $38/500 ml. • (6/30/1999) • **90**
Quarts de Chaume 1995 • $31/500 ml. • (6/15/1998) • **92**

BERLIQUET, CHATEAU

St.-Emilion 1998: Dark in color, with pretty violet and blackberry aromas. Full-bodied and velvety, with lovely ripe fruit and a medium finish. Delicious sweet fruit aftertaste.–J.S. • $NA • (5/31/1999) (BT) • **90-94**
St.-Emilion 1983 • $12 • (12/31/1986) • **90**

BERNADOTTE, CHATEAU

Haut-Médoc 1997: Rather lean, with some berry and cherry character. Light-bodied, with light tannins and a short finish.–J.S. • $14 • (1/31/2000) • **78**
Haut-Médoc 1998: Good berry character, but with a slight tarry, metallic undertone. Full- to medium-bodied, with a good center palate and velvety tannins, a medium finish.–J.S. • $NA • (5/31/1999) (BT) • **80-84**

Haut-Médoc 1996: Pretty aromas of plums and porcini mushrooms. Medium-bodied, with a spicy pepperiness on the palate. Medium tannins, but slightly hollow at midpalate. Best after 2000.–J.S. • $16 • (1/31/1999) • **83**

BERNARD, JEAN

St.-Véran Château de Leynes Vieilles Vignes 1996 • $13 • (5/31/1998) • **83**
St.-Véran Château de Leynes Vieilles Vignes 1995 • $NA • (8/31/1996) • **83**

BERNARD, LOUIS

Châteauneuf-du-Pape 1998: Very clean and beautiful. Full-bodied, with exotic cassis and red berry character, plus smoke, mocha, chocolate and toasted oak. Modern in style, intense and flavorful, loaded with ripe tannins. Best from 2004 through 2015.–P.M. • $28 • (6/30/2000) • **92**

BERNARD, MICHEL

Châteauneuf-du-Pape 1995 • $19 • (10/15/1997) • **85**
Châteauneuf-du-Pape La Réserve des Pontifes 1997: On the light side, showing red berry character but not much *terroir* complexity. Drink now through 2001.–P.M. • $33 • (8/31/1999) • **80**
Châteauneuf-du-Pape La Réserve des Pontifes 1996: Hedonistic. A big, full-bodied, balanced and silky red. Dark in color, it has loads of extracted fruit and fine tannins. Layered with subtle, spicy oak notes, fresh red berry and blackberry flavors and smacking acidity. The combination gives great harmony to the intense finish. Best after 2000.–P.M. • $36 • (9/30/1998) • **92**
Côtes du Rhône 1996 • $7 • (10/15/1997) • **84**
Côtes du Rhône Domaine des Estrémières 1997: Nice black cherry, vanilla and mocha character—but of just modest intensity—with pronounced acidity on a finish accented by supple tannins. Drink now.–P.M. • $9 • (11/15/1999) • **80**
Côtes du Rhône Domaine des Masses Réserve 1997: Starts out nicely, with dried herbs and red berry flavors mingling in a light-bodied, juicy package, but a bit herbal on the finish.–P.M. • $9 • (11/15/1998) • **77**
Côtes du Rhône Domaine St.-Laurent 1998: A bit simple, showing a cardboard character and a drying feel. Not much here. Disappointing quality for this vintage.–P.M. • $9 • (12/15/1999) • **72**
Côtes du Rhône La Réserve des Pontifes 1998: Straightforward, with licorice, blueberry and plum, it shows good flavors but tastes a bit superficial.–P.M. • $8 • (11/15/1999) • **79**
Côtes du Rhône La Réserve des Pontifes 1997: A meaty generic Rhône, with bacon, spice and currant character. Medium to full in body, a bit heavy, but it has a certain opulence on the supple, harmonious finish. Drink now.–P.M. • $7 • (11/15/1998) • **81**
Côtes du Rhône-Villages 1997: Quite oaky, but also refined with all those fine tannins. Has depth and complexity, showing cassis, spicy oak, and black cherry accents. Medium to full in body, well-balanced, though quite crisp now on the lingering finish. Drink through 2001.–P.M. • $8 • (11/15/1998) • **86**
Côtes du Rhône-Villages 1996 • $8 • (10/15/1997) • **85**
Côtes du Rhône-Villages Domaine Plantevin 1998: Middle-of-the-road, consumer-friendly, with spicy black fruit character. Has refined tannins, and the intensity makes for a decent finish of medium complexity. Drink now.–P.M. • $9 • (11/15/1999) • **84**
Côtes du Rhône-Villages La Réserve des Pontifes 1998: Smooth and supple, but where's the complexity? Easy to drink, with red berry and anise notes, it turns a bit chewy on the finish.–P.M. • $8 • (11/15/1999) • **79**
Gigondas La Réserve des Pontifes 1997: Smooth but a bit simple, with licorice, plum and leather notes. Medium-bodied, with tannins that turn dry and chewy on the finish.–P.M. • $13 • (11/15/1998) • **78**
Hermitage 1996: Elegant and aromatic, this exotic wine bursts with currant, violet, black pepper and loads of spices. Pure, clean and vibrant in texture, of medium to full body, very black in color, it's rather hard with firm tannins. Hopefully time will soften it. Drink through 2005.–P.M. • $24 • (9/15/1998) • **84**
Lirac Domaine La Rocalière Elevé en Fûts de Chêne 1997: Delivers lovely flavors and good fruit. Compacted, loaded with pure and clean blackberry, plum, and toasted mocha. Medium-bodied, the tannins are a bit rough, but it should go well with food. Drink now through 2005.–P.M. • $12 • (11/15/1998) • **84**
Lirac La Réserve des Pontifes 1998: Round and dense, thick with ripe black fruit, showing wet earth character. Rustic but with well-integrated tannins, here's a very flavorful, good-quality house wine. Drink now through 2004.–P.M. • $11 • (12/15/1999) • **86**
Lirac La Réserve des Pontifes 1997: Smooth, but a bit alcoholic, tasting of plum, blackberry and cherry. Slightly astringent finish.–P.M. • $10 • (11/15/1998) • **79**

BERNARD, PAUL

Fleurie 1995 • $18 • (6/30/1997) • **80**
Fleurie 1990 • $13 • (10/31/1991) • **87**
Fleurie Clos des Grands Fers 1995: This distinctive red offers concentrated flavors of plum, coffee and tobacco, with firm tannins and good balance, though it has lost the exuberant fruit of youth. Should match well with grilled foods. Drink now.–T.M. • $22 • (8/31/1998) • **86**

BERNEAU, C.

Pouilly-Fumé Les Japeloups 1996: Neutral in aroma and flavor, this is vinous but doesn't have much character.–B.S. • $12 • (10/31/1998) • **76**
Sancerre Domaine de l'Orme 1996: Ripe yet firm, this big-boned white offers melon, apple and light earthy flavors, acidity that's gentle yet balanced and a spicy, vanilla-scented finish. Drink now.–T.M. • $12 • (9/15/1998) • **85**

BERROD, RENE

Beaujolais-Villages Les Roches du Vivier 1997: A sturdy red with black cherry and plum flavors, this shows good ripeness and structure, with enough tannin to match with grilled meats.–T.M. • $10 • (8/31/1998) • **82**
Fleurie Les Roches du Vivier 1997: Sturdy structure, with firm tannins, but the fruit flavors are simple and a bit dull. Better with food.–T.M. • $14 • (8/31/1998) • **79**
Moulin-à-Vent Les Roches du Vivier 1997: Earthy flavors and a bit of spritziness throw this off-kilter; despite some ripe black cherry flavors beneath. Drink now.–T.M. • $14 • (8/31/1998) • **78**

BERTAGNA

Bourgogne Les Croix Blanches 1996: Beautiful, pure Pinot Noir aromas of cherry and spice are so terrific they make your mouth water. Turns a bit crisp on the palate, as expected from a '96, and delivers wet earth and red berry notes. Drink now through 2001.–P.M. • $18 • (1/01/1999) • **86**
Chambertin 1997: Ripe, smooth and rich, this '97 Gevrey offers smoke, black cherry and herb aromas and flavors. Has a touch more gras than most, lending a fullness to the finish to match the fine tannins. Best from 2001 through 2005.–B.S. • $128 • (9/30/1999) • **87**
Chambertin 1996: Serious '96 red Burgundy, showing an impressive backbone of firm tannins and good intensity of red- and blackberry character, chocolate, spice and other oak-infused accents. Rather opulent, this attention-grabber ends with a long, juicy finish. Best from 2003 through 2010.–P.M. • $67 • (2/28/1999) • **94**
Chambertin 1991 • $NA • (1/31/1994) • **85**
Chambolle-Musigny Les Plantes 1996: Smooth and polished, tasting of vanilla cream, butter, cherry and toasted bread, this is a supple red with a seductive finish. Clever winemaking dominates the *terroir* a bit, but it's enjoyable nevertheless. Drink now through 2002.–P.M. • $34 • (2/28/1999) • **85**
Chambolle-Musigny Les Plantes 1994 • $51 • (11/15/1996) • **85**
Clos de Vougeot 1997: Rich and ripe, with plenty of flavorful plum, currant and blackberry character. Sweet, smooth and intense, with velvety tannins. Hard to resist this charmer. Drink now through 2007.–P.M. • $117 • (9/30/1999) • **89**
Clos de Vougeot 1996: A reserved, firm, medium-bodied red, but it has a lot of fruit stuffing to keep your attention. An ager, it displays some *terroir* in its wet earth and mineral notes, giving it good personality. Best from 2002 through 2006.–P.M. • $89 • (2/28/1999) • **90**
Clos de Vougeot 1994 • $90 • (11/15/1996) • **85**
Clos de Vougeot 1993 • $90 • (5/15/1996) • **88**
Clos de Vougeot 1991 • $NA • (1/31/1994) • **77**
Clos St.-Denis 1997: Very oaky, tasting of fancy new wood, which blankets the fruit. But it's decent midpalate, with ripe fruit and a smoky finish. Drink now through 2001.–P.M. • $99 • (9/30/1999) • **88**
Clos St.-Denis 1996: Sensational '96—deep, rich and ripe, a wine that plumbs the depths of terroir, fruit, oak. Full-bodied yet very elegant, this has wonderful balance, sweet-tasting red berry flavors and a spicy, wet earth-tasting finish. Drink now through 2010.–P.M. • $77 • (2/28/1999) • **91**
Clos St.-Denis 1994 • $70 • (11/15/1996) • **77**
Clos St.-Denis 1993 • $71 • (5/15/1996) • **90**

BERTAGNA

Corton Les Grandes Lolières 1997: Soft but pretty, with a smoky, toasty, plummy layer. Turns a bit hot on the finish, but at least this '97 Pinot has gumption. Drink now through 2002.–P.M. • $94 • (9/30/1999) • **86**

Corton-Charlemagne 1996: Ripe and full-bodied, with a bit too much new oak for the amount of fruit, but has nice citrus, pineapple, herbal, mineral and stony character. Hopefully time will tame the wood. Best after 2005.–P.M. • $73 • (8/31/1998) • **81**

Hautes-Côtes de Nuits Les Dames Huguettes Vieilles Vignes 1997: Light in body and color, with a lean structure and modest fruit.–P.M. • $22 • (9/30/1999) • **73**

Nuits-St.-Georges Les Murgers 1996: A wonderful wine in a subtle, reserved style, offering good blackberry and cherry character with a nice portion of wet earth, mineral notes and some rugged tannins. Best from 2003 through 2007.–P.M. • $60 • (2/28/1999) • **89**

Nuits-St.-Georges Les Murgers 1990 • $NA • (12/15/1992) • **89**

Nuits-St.-Georges Les Murgers 1985 • $41 • (2/28/1989) • **85**

Vosne-Romanée Les Beaux Monts 1996: Well made and racy, showing beautifully ripe, sweet-tasting fruit. Not opulent, but it's a deeply satisfying, medium-bodied Pinot with a long, exciting finish. Best from 2002 through 2008.–P.M. • $62 • (2/28/1999) • **89**

Vosne-Romanée Les Beaux Monts Bas 1985 • $35 • (10/15/1988) • **82**

Vougeot Clos de la Perrière 1997: Very oaky in character, offering concentration and intensity on a firm, tannic frame that supports the cherry, mineral and spice flavors. Needs a little time for the elements to integrate. Drink through 2007.–B.S. • $67 • (9/30/1999) • **86**

Vougeot Clos de la Perrière 1996: A pleasant, sweet-tasting Pinot with some wet earth, cherry, blackberry notes. Displays good focus and a firm tannic structure, delivering smoky, toasted oak character. Well made and satisfying. Drink now through 2008.–P.M. • $60 • (2/28/1999) • **89**

Vougeot Clos de la Perrière 1994 • $56 • (11/15/1996) • **79**

Vougeot Clos de la Perrière 1993 • $58 • (5/15/1996) • **86**

Vougeot Clos de la Perrière 1991 • $NA • (1/31/1994) • **78**

Vougeot Clos de la Perrière 1990 • $NA • (12/15/1992) • **85**

Vougeot Clos de la Perrière 1985 • $40 • (4/15/1989) • **87**

Vougeot Les Crâs 1985 • $30 • (3/31/1988) • **85**

Vougeot White 1996: A racy wine that takes you aback with its great fruit intensity, sharp acidity and crisp mineral quality, but it has a thick, fat texture that keeps all this stuff tied together. Just forget it in the cellar for a while. Best from 2001 through 2006.–P.M. • $55 • (1/01/1999) • **94**

BERTHET-RAYNE, DOMAINE

Côtes du Rhône-Villages Cairanne 1995 • $9 • (2/28/1997) • **86**

Côtes du Rhône-Villages Cairanne Castel Mireio Vieilli en Fûts de Chêne Neufs 1996: Thick and opulent, with lots of toast, mocha and new-oakish accents playing nicely against the generous plum, currant and smoke flavors. Full-bodied, with supple, ripe tannins. A beauty. Drink through 2005.–P.M. • $9 • (11/15/1998) • **87**

Côtes du Rhône-Villages White Cairanne Castel Mireio Vieilli en Fûts de Chêne Neufs 1997: A wonderful white, with personality. Shows pineapple, butter, spice and toasty oak accents, all supported by good citrusy acidity. Medium-bodied, it's enchanting as it rockets to a long finish. Unique and worth the hunt.–P.M. • $NA • (11/15/1998) • **88**

BERTOLLA, ALFRED GINO

Moulin-à-Vent Domaine du Granit 1995 • $17 • (9/15/1997) • **86**

Moulin-à-Vent Domaine du Granit 1994 • $14 • (9/15/1996) • **83**

Moulin-à-Vent Domaine du Granit Cuvée Vieilles Vignes Réserve 1996 • $21 • (5/31/1998) • **89**

BERTRAND, DOMAINE GEORGES

Corbières Domaine Ste.-Paule 1994 • $12 • (5/31/1997) • **84**

BERTRAND, MAURICE

Montagny Les Coeres 1995 • $NA • (5/31/1997) • **79**

Montagny Premier Cru 1995 • $NA • (5/31/1997) • **85**

Key: SS—Spectator Selection. CS—Cellar Selection. HR—Highly Recommended. $NA—Price not available. (BT)—Barrel tasting. Ⓐ—Auction Price. For a key to the tasters' initials, see "How to Use These Listings."
Dates in parentheses represent the issues in which the ratings were published.

BERTRAND-BERGE, DOMAINE

Fitou Cuvée Ancestrale 1997: A warm, brickish-tasting red, with nice, ripe red plum and leather flavors and good acidity. Medium-bodied, youthful and lip-smacking, with peppery notes on the finish. Drink now.–K.M. • $14 • (11/15/1999) • **86**

Fitou Cuvée Ancestrale 1996: On the light side, with pepper and red plum flavors. Flavors linger on the finish, with a slight bittersweet note. A blend of Carignane, Grenache and Syrah. Drink now.–K.M. • $10 • (1/31/1999) • **81**

BESSANE, CHATEAU LA

Margaux 1997: Offers plenty of berry character and a hint of spice. Medium-bodied, with light tannins and a fresh but slightly dry finish. Drink now.–J.S. • $NA • (1/31/2000) • **84**

BESSERAT DE BELLEFON

Brut Champagne 1990: Seamless and seductive, this is inviting, generous and mellow in flavor but lively in texture. Packed with bright fruit, lifted by firm acidity and layered with subtle flavor nuances that last on the finish. Drink now through 2005. • $37 • (11/15/1999) • **94**

Brut Champagne Cuvée des Moines NV: Fascinating aromas and flavors of red berry augment the toast and citrus flavors in this firm, stylish sparkling wine. Shows a good combination of elegance and power. Drink now through 2001.–B.S. • $32 • (11/30/1999) • **89**

Brut Champagne Grande Tradition NV: A lively, assertive and sinewy bubbly, with honeysuckle, vanilla and toasted brioche notes on a medium body. Good length and bracing finish. Drink now through 2001.–B.S. • $30 • (11/30/1999) • **88**

Brut Rosé Champagne Cuvée des Moines NV: An appealing and focused rosé, like Pinot Noir with bubbles, with a subtle yet firm structure to carry the flavors to a lingering conclusion. Drink now.–B.S. • $34 • (11/30/1999) • **87**

BEYCHEVELLE, CHATEAU

St.-Julien 1999: Pretty dried cherry and spice aromas. Medium-bodied, with fine tannins and a clean, fresh finish.–J.S. • $NA • (1/01/2000) (BT) • **85-89**

St.-Julien 1998: Pleasant ripe fruit for the vintage, but slightly one-dimensional. Medium-bodied, with medium tannins and a light finish.–J.S. • $NA • (5/31/1999) (BT) • **85-89**

St.-Julien 1997: Fresh and fruity wine with mineral and cherry character. Medium-bodied, with silky tannins. Drink now.–J.S. • $30 • (1/31/2000) • **85**

St.-Julien 1996: Shows wet earth, tobacco and fruit character on the nose and palate. Medium-bodied, with velvety tannins and a dark-chocolate aftertaste. A bit more fruit concentration in the center-palate would be nice. Best after 2000.–J.S. • $30 Ⓐ • (1/31/1999) • **87**

St.-Julien 1995 • $33 Ⓐ • (1/31/1998) • **89**

St.-Julien 1994 • $22 Ⓐ • (1/31/1997) • **81**

St.-Julien 1993 • $26 Ⓐ • (1/31/1996) • **80**

St.-Julien 1992 • $23 • (4/15/1995) • **82**

St.-Julien 1991 • $25 • (3/31/1994) • **85**

St.-Julien 1990 • $75 Ⓐ • (3/31/1993) • **87**

St.-Julien 1989: Blockbuster for Beychevelle. Slightly rustic, but featuring loads of chocolate and berry and hints of flowers. Full-bodied, with minty, floral and cherry flavors and a velvety texture. Loads of mouthpuckering tannins. Needs time. (1989 Bordeaux horizontal tasting). Best after 2008.–J.S. • $74 Ⓐ • (5/31/1999) • **93**

St.-Julien 1988: One of the best bottles from Beychevelle in a long time. Full-bodied, with silky tannins and aromas of raspberry and mint with a hint of violet. Lead pencil and fruit appear on the long aftertaste. (1988 Bordeaux horizontal tasting). Best after 2000.–J.S. • $47 Ⓐ • (11/30/1998) • **90**

St.-Julien 1987 • $29 • (5/15/1990) • **79**

St.-Julien 1986 • $66 Ⓐ • (5/31/1989) • **93**

St.-Julien 1985 • $58 Ⓐ • (10/15/1994) • **91**

St.-Julien 1984 • $24 • (5/15/1987) • **78**

St.-Julien 1983 • $51 Ⓐ • (10/15/1994) • **85**

St.-Julien 1982: Get ready to pull the cork. Dark ruby-garnet in color, with plenty of roses and ripe fruit on the nose. Medium- to full-bodied, with lots of silky tannins. Almost dry on the finish, but finely textured. (1982 Bordeaux horizontal tasting). Drink now.–J.S. • $88 Ⓐ • (11/30/1998) • **88**

St.-Julien 1981 • $37 Ⓐ • (10/15/1994) • **81**

St.-Julien 1979 • $37 Ⓐ • (10/15/1989) • **92**

St.-Julien 1978 • $42 Ⓐ • (12/31/1989) • **86**
St.-Julien 1971 • $28 Ⓐ • (12/31/1989) • **85**
St.-Julien 1970 • $42 Ⓐ • (5/15/1993) • **90**
St.-Julien 1967 • $32 Ⓐ • (12/31/1989) • **83**
St.-Julien 1962 • $NA • (11/30/1987) • **95**
St.-Julien 1961 • $121 Ⓐ • (4/30/1996) • **89**
St.-Julien 1959 • $97 Ⓐ • (10/15/1990) • **80**
St.-Julien 1948 • $175 • (12/31/1989) • **92**
St.-Julien 1947 • $NA • (5/31/1997) • **83**
St.-Julien 1945 • $380 • (11/30/1995) • **82**
St.-Julien 1929 • $233 Ⓐ • (12/31/1989) • **95**

BEYER, LEON

Alsace La Cuvée 1998: Distinctive, yet the strong pine or petrol note in this elegant white may not appeal to everyone. Drink now.–B.S. • $12 • (6/15/2000) • **82**
Gewürztraminer Alsace 1998: Shows floral and spice notes, but more grapefruit. Soft and forward, it finishes with characteristic bitterness. Drink now.–B.S. • $19 • (10/31/1999) • **83**
Gewürztraminer Alsace 1997: Ripe and diffuse around the edges, offering grapefruit, passion fruit and vanilla aromas and flavors with moderate concentration.–B.S. • $16 • (10/31/1999) • **79**
Gewürztraminer Alsace 1996: Ripe and floral, with juicy acidity, but runs out of gas quickly, lacking depth and intensity of flavor. Drink now.–B.S. • $16 • (9/15/1998) • **80**
Gewürztraminer Alsace Sélection de Grains Nobles 1989 • $60 • (9/15/1995) • **88**
Pinot Blanc Alsace 1998: Rich, yet with fine supporting acidity, this white offers grapefruit and mineral notes, firming up on the finish. Very good intensity. Drink now through 2001.–B.S. • $14 • (9/30/1999) • **86**
Riesling Alsace 1998: Young, full of ripe peach and mineral, this is bone-dry, firmly structured and medium-bodied. Will pair nicely with simple poultry or pork dishes. Drink through 2002.–B.S. • $17 • (9/15/1999) • **87**
Riesling Alsace 1997: Austere, complex and concentrated, this densely textured Riesling offers petrol, apple and honey flavors, relying on a slight bitterness for structure, rather than firm acidity. Drink now through 2002.–B.S. • $15 • (8/31/1999) • **85**
Riesling Alsace 1996: Here's an austere, dry, pine- and mineral-scented white showing concentration and extract on the palate. Beeswax, mineral and spice are dominant, persisting through the finish. Best with food. Drink now through 2002.–B.S. • $15 • (9/15/1998) • **88**
Riesling Alsace Les Écaillers 1998: Gorgeous, with ripe peach and floral aromas that jump from the glass. Concentrated, vibrant and ever changing in the mouth, this has personality and class, with a lovely, creamy vanilla aftertaste. Drink now through 2005.–B.S. • $35 • (5/31/2000) • **90**
Riesling Alsace Sélection de Grains Nobles 1989 • $NA • (11/15/1990) • **80**
Tokay Pinot Gris Alsace 1998: Lovely aromas of smoke and violets lead into a firm, dry, mineral- and citrus-flavored white. Bordering on austere at the finish, this needs food. Drink now through 2002.–B.S. • $17 • (6/15/2000) • **87**
Tokay Pinot Gris Alsace 1996: Different flavor profile in this thickly textured Pinot Gris, with some herbaceous elements, white pepper and tobacco, and modest concentration.–B.S. • $16 • (9/15/1998) • **83**
Tokay Pinot Gris Alsace Réserve 1998: Distincitve, exhibiting licorice, tarragon, vanilla and quince aromas and flavors, moderate richness and a lively structure. Broad-shouldered and persistent on the finish. Drink now through 2002.–B.S. • $35 • (6/15/2000) • **88**
Tokay Pinot Gris Alsace Sélection de Grains Nobles 1989 • $35 • (9/15/1995) • **86**

BIBIAN, DOMAINE

Madiran 1995 • $11 • (5/15/1998) • **87**
Madiran Cuvée de Prestige 1993 • $14 • (5/15/1998) • **89**

BICHOT, ALBERT

Aloxe-Corton 1995 • $20 • (11/15/1997) • **74**
Aloxe-Corton 1983 • $18 • (11/30/1986) • **68**
Beaune 1988 • $15 • (8/31/1990) • **82**
Beaune Champs Pimont 1994 • $21 • (11/15/1996) • **85**
Beaune Hospices de Beaune Cuvée Guigone-de-Salins 1989 • $68 • (1/31/1992) • **83**
Beaune Les Bressandes 1986 • $24 • (7/31/1988) • **80**
Beaune Les Teurons 1992 • $NA • (12/15/1994) • **77**
Bourgogne 1996: Crisp, with lively cherry and red berry notes. A touch herbal, but a very decent red wine. Drink now.–P.M. • $12 • (9/30/1998) • **81**
Bourgogne 1993 • $12 • (11/15/1995) • **82**
Bourgogne Château de Montpatey 1989 • $10 • (6/15/1992) • **85**
Bourgogne Croix St.-Louis 1996: Fairly crisp, and a bit spritzy on the palate, this has decent berry character but turns dry and herbal on the finish.–P.M. • $12 • (9/30/1998) • **76**
Bourgogne Croix St.-Louis 1995 • $12 • (11/15/1997) • **76**
Bourgogne Croix St.-Louis 1989 • $9 • (6/15/1992) • **83**
Bourgogne White Croix St.-Louis 1996 • $10 • (5/31/1998) • **84**
Chablis 1997: Polished, with a hint of wood, tasting of butter, popcorn, spice and pear tart. Has decent complexity, and a lemon-spiked flavor gives it a clean finish. Drink now.–P.M. • $17 • (5/31/1999) • **85**
Chablis 1996 • $22 • (5/31/1998) • **88**
Chablis 1995 • $NA • (8/31/1996) • **82**
Chablis Côte de Léchet 1997: A tightly built Côte de Lechet, packed with vibrant pure fruit and excellent acidity that makes it taste more like a '96. A well-made, impressive, medium-bodied white. Cellar. Best from 2002 through 2008.–P.M. • $25 • (5/31/1999) • **89**
Chambolle-Musigny 1997: Smells horsey despite cherry notes underneath. Tastes bitter, leaving an astringent sensation on the palate.–B.S. • $24 • (9/30/1999) • **72**
Chambolle-Musigny 1995 • $27 • (11/15/1997) • **72**
Chassagne-Montrachet Red 1997: A bit unfocused, showing a woody, grapey, dry character. Short finish.–P.M. • $16 • (9/30/1999) • **72**
Chassagne-Montrachet Red 1995 • $25 • (11/15/1997) • **72**
Chassagne-Montrachet Red Morgeot 1992 • $NA • (12/15/1994) • **77**
Châteauneuf-du-Pape 1988 • $13 • (9/30/1990) • **84**
Châteauneuf-du-Pape 1987 • $10 • (3/15/1990) • **82**
Châteauneuf-du-Pape 1985 • $12 • (11/15/1987) • **86**
Corton 1995 • $43 • (11/15/1997) • **79**
Corton Hospices de Beaune Cuvée Docteur-Peste 1989 • $100 • (1/31/1992) • **88**
Côte de Beaune-Villages 1993 • $15 • (11/15/1995) • **74**
Côte de Nuits-Villages 1993 • $15 • (11/15/1995) • **77**
Côtes de Duras 1989 • $6 • (3/31/1992) • **81**
Côtes du Rhône Château d'Orsan 1989 • $7 • (6/15/1992) • **74**
Gevrey-Chambertin 1995 • $26 • (11/15/1997) • **72**
Gevrey-Chambertin 1993 • $30 • (11/15/1995) • **81**
Latricières-Chambertin 1995 • $51 • (11/15/1997) • **70**
Mâcon-Villages 1997: Musty tasting, with a cardboard flavor and a very bitter, astringent finish.–P.M. • $13 • (5/31/1999) • **70**
Monthélie Hospices de Beaune Cuvée Lebelin 1985 • $52 • (10/15/1987) • **86**
Nuits-St.-Georges 1995 • $26 • (11/15/1997) • **77**
Nuits-St.-Georges Aux Boudots Hospices de Nuits Cuvée Mesn 1986 • $36 • (3/31/1990) • **77**
Nuits-St.-Georges Les Maladières Hospices de Nuits 1986 • $33 • (2/28/1989) • **75**
Nuits-St.-Georges Les Maladières Hospices de Nuits Cuvée Grangier 1986 • $30 • (3/31/1990) • **80**
Nuits-St.-Georges Les Vignerondes Hospices de Nuits Cuvée 1986 • $40 • (2/28/1989) • **85**
Pommard 1993 • $26 • (11/15/1995) • **78**
Pommard 1988 • $25 • (8/31/1990) • **87**
Pommard 1986 • $20 • (9/15/1989) • **79**
Pommard 1983 • $19 • (9/15/1986) • **83**
Pommard Clos Micault 1996: If Pommard can be delicate, this is the wine. Floral and berry aromas and flavors mingle with earth and smoke in this lively, straightforward red that shows grip on the finish. Drink through 2003.–B.S. • $39 • (9/30/1998) • **85**
Pommard Hospices de Beaune Cuvée Cyrot-Chaudron 1989 • $70 • (1/31/1992) • **86**
Pommard Hospices de Beaune Cuvée Cyrot-Chaudron 1985 • $60 • (10/31/1988) • **91**
Pouilly-Fuissé 1996 • $NA • (5/31/1998) • **79**
Rully 1996 • $13 • (5/31/1998) • **83**
St.-Véran 1996 • $NA • (5/31/1998) • **80**
Santenay 1986 • $12 • (10/15/1989) • **78**
Santenay Clos Bellefond 1997: Crisp and a bit rustic, but with succulent red fruit and a rich midpalate. The firm tannins and cassis bush character make for a slightly harsh finish. Drink now through 2004.–P.M. • $13 • (9/30/1999) • **82**
Savigny-lès-Beaune 1995 • $18 • (11/15/1997) • **80**
Savigny-lès-Beaune 1986 • $10 • (10/15/1989) • **81**
Savigny-lès-Beaune Hospices de Beaune Cuvée Fouquerand 1988 • $39 • (1/31/1992) • **78**
Vin Rouge NV • $3 • (8/31/1989) • **75**

BICHOT, ALBERT

Volnay 1988 • $25 • (8/31/1990) • **84**
Volnay 1986 • $25 • (7/31/1988) • **84**
Volnay 1983 • $18 • (9/15/1986) • **68**
Volnay Champans 1997: Aromas of cherry, wild berry and herb continue in the mouth. Forward and accessible, soft and pleasant, without a lot of depth or structure.–B.S. • $23 • (9/30/1999) • **78**
Volnay Clos des Chênes 1992 • $NA • (12/15/1994) • **81**
Volnay Cuvée Blondeau Hospices de Beaune 1988 • $60 • (6/15/1992) • **87**
Volnay Hospices de Beaune Cuvée Blondeau 1985 • $53 • (4/30/1989) • **88**
Volnay Hospices de Beaune Cuvée Blondeau 1982 • $26 • (8/01/1984) SS • **92**
Volnay Premier Cru 1993 • $25 • (11/15/1995) • **83**
Volnay-Santenots 1986 • $22 • (10/31/1989) • **77**
Vosne-Romanée Aux Malconsorts 1994 • $41 • (11/15/1996) • **80**
Vosne-Romanée Les Beaux Monts 1988 • $34 • (7/15/1990) • **87**

BIENFAISANCE, CHATEAU LA

St.-Emilion 1993 • $20 • (4/30/1997) • **84**

BILLARD-GONNET

Pommard Les Chaponnières 1995 • $45 • (11/15/1997) • **85**
Pommard Les Charmots 1995 • $45 • (11/15/1997) • **77**
Pommard Les Pezerolles 1995 • $45 • (11/15/1997) • **85**
Pommard Rugiens 1995 • $54 • (11/15/1997) • **82**

BILLAUD-SIMON

Chablis 1998: This medium-bodied, medium-intense Chardonnay has smoky, flinty, ripe fruit character. Drink now.–P.M. • $18 • (5/15/2000) • **80**
Chablis 1997: On the crisp, grassy side, and a bit dry, this unyielding, steely, clean Chablis should match nicely with brasserie foods. Drink now.–P.M. • $19 • (5/31/1999) • **84**
Chablis 1996 • $NA • (8/31/1997) • **87**
Chablis 1995 • $NA • (8/31/1996) • **85**
Chablis Blanchots Vieille Vigne 1998: Well crafted. Lively, vibrant fruit bursts in this tightly structured, firm Chardonnay. Medium-bodied, with pear, honey, grass and lime notes that combine to form a long finish. Best from 2002 through 2008.–P.M. • $60 • (5/15/2000) • **88**
Chablis Blanchots Vieille Vigne 1997: Stupendous '97 Chablis *cru*, clean and pure, without any obvious oak but with plenty of supple mineral character in a firm but balanced, full-bodied package. For fans of idiosyncratic, tight-fisted Chardonnay. Best from 2005 through 2015.–P.M. • $56 • (5/31/1999) • **94**
Chablis Blanchots Vieille Vigne 1996 • $60 • (5/31/1998) • **92**
Chablis Blanchots Vieille Vigne 1995 • $56 • (6/15/1997) • **89**
Chablis Fourchaume 1998: Clean, pure and ripe. Nothing complex or intense, but the honey, lemon and apple tart character folds nicely into this medium-bodied white. Harmonious—but for now, chewy—finish. Drink through 2003.–P.M. • $34 • (5/15/2000) • **87**
Chablis Fourchaume 1997: Clean, buttery and lemony, presented in a medium-intense, very supple package. Ready to enjoy, it lacks a bit of panache and seems soft on the slightly astringent finish. Drink now through 2002.–P.M. • $30 • (5/31/1999) • **82**
Chablis Fourchaume 1996 • $26 • (5/31/1998) • **90**
Chablis Fourchaume 1995 • $24 • (6/15/1997) • **83**
Chablis Les Clos 1998: Impressive. Nothing heavy in this full-bodied white. Clean and razor-sharp, with firm structure, holding back more than it gives and showing a racy class as it focuses on pure fruit and a minerally, chalky component. Nice citrusy finish. Drink now through 2007.–P.M. • $50 • (5/15/2000) • **93**
Chablis Les Clos 1997: Ripe, lush style of Les Clos, but also a bit oaky, showing toasted spice, apple pie and honey flavors that burn a bit on the heavy, astringent finish. Surprisingly forward for this vineyard. Drink now through 2007.–P.M. • $48 • (5/31/1999) • **83**
Chablis Les Clos 1996 • $NA • (5/31/1998) • **94**
Chablis Les Preuses 1998: There is a light touch to this fresh little Chardonnay, with good fruit salad character. Deceptive intensity is picked up on the finish, with pear, toast and smoke. Drink now through 2003.–P.M. • $45 • (5/15/2000) • **85**
Chablis Les Preuses 1997: Clean and pure, superminerally, supercitrusy, with enough ripe, honey-laced fruit to bridge it all, this races around the palate like Michael Schumacher on a Formula One circuit, bringing excitement to the event. Best from 2003 through 2010.–P.M. • $45 • (5/31/1999) • **94**
Chablis Les Preuses 1995 • $36 • (6/15/1997) • **88**
Chablis Mont de Milieu 1998: Easy, very pleasant and balanced. Nothing complicated, but is there fruit! Clean, pure, vibrant and lively from start to finish. Medium-bodied, this is a joy to drink now if you like orange rind, lime, spice and a hedonistic glass. Drink now through 2003.–P.M. • $28 • (5/15/2000) • **86**
Chablis Mont de Milieu 1997: Clean, pure and vibrant, this is all fruit and no obvious oak, making for a focused, medium-bodied Chardonnay laced with a veil of pear, mineral and honey. Drink now through 2003.–P.M. • $29 • (5/31/1999) • **88**
Chablis Mont de Milieu 1996 • $24 • (5/31/1998) • **91**
Chablis Mont de Milieu 1995 • $21 • (6/15/1997) • **89**
Chablis Mont de Milieu Vieille Vigne 1998: Beautifully clean and pure. Bursts with floral and ripe fruit aromas laced with honey, lime and dried herb. Mouthpuckeringly vibrant and medium-bodied, with lots of intensity on the zesty finish. Needs cellaring to show it all. Best from 2003 through 2010.–P.M. • $34 • (5/15/2000) • **90**
Chablis Mont de Milieu Vieille Vigne 1997: Rich and ripe, with a distinct spiced oak character, this full-bodied Mont de Milieu has more opulence than many '97s, with pear, toasted bread and melon complexity plus a bite on the finish that suggests short-term cellaring. Drink through 2007.–P.M. • $32 • (5/31/1999) • **88**
Chablis Mont de Milieu Vieille Vigne 1996 • $27 • (5/31/1998) • **91**
Chablis Mont de Milieu Vieille Vigne 1995 • $25 • (6/15/1997) • **89**
Chablis Montée de Tonnerre 1998: Well made in a crisp, fresh style of Chablis. Medium-bodied, it displays mineral, ripe pear and vanilla bean all unhindered from wood, so you get a pure, clean focus of fruit and vibrant wet earth. Drink now through 2004.–P.M. • $28 • (5/15/2000) • **87**
Chablis Montée de Tonnerre 1997: Good mineral quality in this medium-bodied, medium-ripe Chablis, delivering a firm mouthfeel that needs time to soften and show its layers of pear, spice, green apple and earth. Best from 2002 through 2007.–P.M. • $29 • (5/31/1999) • **87**
Chablis Montée de Tonnerre 1996 • $24 • (5/31/1998) • **93**
Chablis Montée de Tonnerre 1995 • $24 • (6/15/1997) • **87**
Chablis Tête d'Or 1998: Clean and pure, balanced and delicious, with a creamy midpalate. Medium-bodied, offering chalk, wet earth, pear and green apple notes. Crisp, chewy finish. Drink now through 2001.–P.M. • $22 • (5/15/2000) • **83**
Chablis Tête d'Or 1997: A bit oaky, with a cedar, mocha, spicy and slightly bitter character; lacks elegance and seems heavy-handed.–P.M. • $23 • (5/31/1999) • **75**
Chablis Tête d'Or 1996: Although just a village Chablis, with its smooth midpalate, this medium-bodied wine matches the quality of a ripe *premier cru*. Its pronounced acidity suggests it needs some cellaring to soften and to integrate the herbal, pear, spicy, minerally accents. Best from 2003.–P.M. • $20 • (8/31/1998) • **90**
Chablis Vaillons 1998: Pleasant and harmonious. The finesse is seductive. Medium-bodied, with smoky, minerally, chalky, ripe fruit notes. The chewy finish suggests cellaring. Best from 2002 through 2008.–P.M. • $27 • (5/15/2000) • **86**
Chablis Vaillons 1997: Lovely full-bodied and supple *premier cru*, so likable with its tropical, honey, lemon flavors and relatively silky yet fresh and succulent finish. Drink now through 2002.–P.M. • $27 • (5/31/1999) • **87**
Chablis Vaillons 1996 • $22 • (5/31/1998) • **86**
Chablis Vaillons 1995 • $21 • (6/15/1997) • **85**
Chablis Vaudésir 1998: Light- to medium-bodied, this delicate Chablis has a lively texture of zesty citrus. Lovely honey character carries through to the crisp, minerally, chalky, chewy finish. Drink now through 2004.–P.M. • $42 • (5/15/2000) • **85**
Chablis Vaudésir 1997: Smooth and ripe, with an elegant grip of mineral, salty nuts, green apple notes, this medium-bodied Vaudésir should age gracefully, in an elegant food-friendly style. Best from 2003 through 2007.–P.M. • $45 • (5/31/1999) • **88**
Chablis Vaudésir 1996 • $40 • (5/31/1998) • **89**
Chablis Vaudésir 1995 • $36 • (6/15/1997) • **90**

BILLECART-SALMON

Brut Champagne NV • $28 • (12/31/1991) • **86**

Key: SS—Spectator Selection. CS—Cellar Selection. HR—Highly Recommended. $NA—Price not available. (BT)—Barrel tasting. Ⓐ—Auction Price.
For a key to the tasters' initials, see "How to Use These Listings."
Dates in parentheses represent the issues in which the ratings were published.

FRANCE

BILLION, FRANCOIS

Brut Champagne Cuvée de Réserve NV: A light yet lively and appealing brut, with a smooth texture. Balanced on the soft side, with fresh lemon and apple flavors and a clean finish. Drink now. • $30 • (12/31/1998) • **88**

Brut Rosé Champagne NV: Wow. This deep salmon-hued rosé is expansive and sophisticated, with gorgeous, complex aromas, full-bodied flavors of plum, toast and ginger, a rich texture and a long, lingering finish. Drink now. • $35 • (12/15/1998) • **92**

BILLIOT, HENRI

Brut Champagne 1992: Tasty but tired already, with an unusually dark, brassy color and nutty flavors. Tasted twice, with consistent notes. • $36 • (12/31/1998) • **72**

Brut Champagne 1990 • $39 • (11/30/1997) • **90**

Brut Champagne Cuvée Laetitia NV • $54 • (11/30/1997) • **88**

Brut Champagne Réserve NV: Not a cookie-cutter Champagne. Deep and brassy in color, rich in fruit flavor, almost thick in texture, slightly sweet in balance. Drink now. • $42 • (9/15/1999) • **88**

BIRE, CHATEAU

Bordeaux Supérieur 1996: Aromas of grape skins and seeds. Medium-bodied, slightly cloying on the palate, with a grapey, leafy character. Acidic and rather unpleasant. Tasted twice, with consistent notes.–J.S. • $NA • (2/28/1999) • **68**

BISTON, CHATEAU

Moulis 1996: Slightly simple, but with some interesting fruit character. Good aromas of cherry and blackberry. Medium-bodied, with a smoky, earthy, berry character and chewy tannins. Drink now.–J.S. • $NA • (1/31/1999) • **86**

BISTON-BRILLETTE, CHATEAU

Moulis 1998: Pretty floral wine with silky tannins, medium body and a light finish.–J.S. • $NA • (5/31/1999) (BT) • **80-84**

Moulis 1997: This has good body but it's slightly austere. Medium-bodied, with a polished, velvety texture and a medium, dry finish. Best after 2001.–J.S. • $NA • (1/31/2000) • **82**

Moulis 1996: Well made for its berry and mineral aromas and flavors, medium body and medium tannins, but has a slightly short finish, a slightly hollow midpalate. Drink now.–J.S. • $NA • (1/31/1999) • **84**

Moulis 1995: Impressive effort. Wonderful spicy, berry, cedar and fruit character. Full-bodied, with velvety tannins and a long, spicy, fruit finish. Delicious now, better with time. Best from 2001 through 2005.–J.S. • $NA • (9/15/1998) • **90**

BITOUZET, PIERRE

Aloxe-Corton Les Valozières 1994 • $29 • (11/15/1996) • **81**
Aloxe-Corton Les Valozières 1990 • $NA • (12/15/1992) • **88**
Aloxe-Corton Les Valozières 1989 • $28 • (11/30/1992) • **82**
Aloxe-Corton Les Valozières 1986 • $19 • (8/31/1990) • **78**
Bourgogne White 1995 • $NA • (8/31/1997) • **74**
Corton-Charlemagne 1995 • $NA • (5/31/1997) • **75**
Pommard La Platière 1994 • $33 • (11/15/1996) • **81**
Pommard La Platière 1993 • $40 • (11/15/1995) • **84**
Savigny-lès-Beaune 1994 • $24 • (11/15/1996) • **76**
Savigny-lès-Beaune 1993 • $25 • (11/15/1995) • **83**
Savigny-lès-Beaune Les Lavières 1994 • $27 • (11/15/1996) • **85**
Savigny-lès-Beaune Les Lavières 1993 • $30 • (11/15/1995) • **76**
Savigny-lès-Beaune Les Lavières 1990 • $NA • (12/15/1992) • **88**
Savigny-lès-Beaune Les Lavières 1986 • $15 • (3/31/1990) • **87**
Savigny-lès-Beaune Les Lavières 1985 • $19 • (3/15/1988) • **67**
Savigny-lès-Beaune White Les Goudelettes 1995 • $NA • (8/31/1997) • **86**
Savigny-lès-Beaune White Les Talmettes 1995 • $NA • (8/31/1997) • **88**

BITOUZET-PRIEUR

Meursault 1997: Green and stemmy in aroma, rather thick-textured on the palate, it doesn't taste very ripe, just big and broad, without focus. Turns chewy, with floral, green apple, butter notes on the finish. Drink now through 2003.–P.M. • $NA • (1/01/1999) • **80**

Meursault Charmes 1997: Beautiful. All in finesse, with lovely toast, lemon, pear and dough accents. Medium-bodied and balanced, it begs for another sip. Drink now through 2003.–P.M. • $54 • (9/30/1999) • **89**

Meursault Clos du Cromin 1997: A pleasant Meursault that lacks a bit of midpalate interest, but coats the palate with pretty butter, pear and passion fruit notes. Silky in texture, with crisp flavors on the soft finish. Drink now through 2005.–P.M. • $38 • (9/30/1999) • **84**

Meursault Les Corbins 1997: Rich and sweet-tasting, smelling of new wood staves and oak perfumes, this yellowish wine is full-bodied and a bit over-the-top.–P.M. • $35 • (9/30/1999) • **78**

Meursault Perrières 1997: Lots of finesse in this elegant white Burgundy, delivering medium-intense oaky notes and ripe pear, citrus and marzipan character. Clean and silky, it's a pleasure to drink, now through 2005. –P.M. • $54 • (9/30/1999) • **90**

Meursault Santenots 1997: Gorgeous, thick, yellowish in color and elegant, this full-bodied Meursault struts its earthy personality. Velvety in texture, with a subtle intensity of softly toasted oak, tropical, pear and charcoal flavors. Lingering Cuban cigar smoke on the finish. Drink now through 2007.–P.M. • $37 • (9/30/1999) • **93**

Volnay Clos des Chênes 1987 • $36 • (12/31/1990) • **80**
Volnay Pitures 1985 • $36 • (7/31/1988) • **91**

BIZE & FILS, SIMON

Aloxe-Corton Le Suchot 1997: Old-fashioned red Burgundy, with chestnut and old-wood sort of aromas. Light in color, drying on the palate. Tart finish.–P.M. • $38 • (1/01/2000) • **77**

Aloxe-Corton Le Suchot 1993 • $24 • (5/15/1996) • **90**
Aloxe-Corton Le Suchot 1991 • $28 • (1/31/1994) • **77**
Bourgogne Les Perrières 1990 • $17 • (12/15/1992) • **87**
Bourgogne White Les Perrières 1996 • $NA • (1/01/1998) • **83**

Latricières-Chambertin 1997: This old-fashioned Pinot is light in color and body and mature for its age, with mushroom, wet forest underbrush. Tastes dry and stripped. The sort of red Burgundy that gives Burgundy a bad reputation. • $161 • (1/01/2000) • **76**

Savigny-lès-Beaune 1990 • $20 • (12/15/1992) • **85**

Savigny-lès-Beaune Aux Fournaux 1997: Decent red berry notes, with a stemmy aroma. Modest ripeness, with licorice and raspberry, but this medium-bodied Pinot turns dry on the unhappy finish. • $42 • (1/01/2000) • **77**

Savigny-lès-Beaune Aux Fournaux 1996: Shows ripe cherry and plum notes along with richness and a supple texture before the firm tannins emerge on the finish. Good underlying power and expression of *terroir*. Drink through 2005.–B.S. • $40 • (9/30/1998) • **87**

Savigny-lès-Beaune Aux Fournaux 1993 • $25 • (5/15/1996) • **82**
Savigny-lès-Beaune Aux Fournaux 1992 • $NA • (6/15/1995) • **78**
Savigny-lès-Beaune Aux Fournaux 1991 • $25 • (1/31/1994) • **60**
Savigny-lès-Beaune Aux Fournaux 1990 • $28 • (12/15/1992) • **89**

Savigny-lès-Beaune Aux Grands Liards 1996: A pretty red, whose floral and red berry aromas and spicy flavors are displayed with elegance and finesse. Appealing now for its delicacy, but there's good structure and depth, with a lingering finish. Drink through 2005.–B.S. • $34 • (9/30/1998) • **88**

Savigny-lès-Beaune Aux Grands Liards 1993 • $19 • (5/15/1996) • **84**
Savigny-lès-Beaune Aux Grands Liards 1992 • $20 • (6/15/1995) • **78**
Savigny-lès-Beaune Aux Grands Liards 1991 • $21 • (1/31/1994) • **75**
Savigny-lès-Beaune Aux Grands Liards 1990 • $22 • (12/15/1992) • **87**
Savigny-lès-Beaune Aux Guettes 1991 • $30 • (1/31/1994) • **67**
Savigny-lès-Beaune Aux Guettes 1990 • $33 • (12/15/1992) • **86**
Savigny-lès-Beaune Aux Vergelesses 1992 • $24 • (5/15/1995) • **84**
Savigny-lès-Beaune Aux Vergelesses 1991 • $28 • (1/31/1994) • **80**
Savigny-lès-Beaune Aux Vergelesses 1990 • $48 Ⓐ • (12/15/1992) • **90**
Savigny-lès-Beaune Aux Vergelesses 1989 • $27 • (1/31/1992) • **87**

Savigny-lès-Beaune Les Bourgeots 1997: Mature, light and slightly oxidized, this is old-fashioned Burgundy, with wet forest underbrush and mushroom character. Dries on the palate. Old before its time. • $32 • (1/01/2000) • **74**

Savigny-lès-Beaune Les Bourgeots 1996: Spicy cherry flavors are accented by vanilla and a touch of earth in this moderately structured Pinot Noir that shows good concentration and length. Drink through 2005.–B.S. • $29 • (9/30/1998) • **85**

Savigny-lès-Beaune Les Bourgeots 1991 • $20 • (1/31/1994) • **72**
Savigny-lès-Beaune Les Bourgeots 1989 • $19 • (1/31/1992) • **85**
Savigny-lès-Beaune Les Marconnets 1993 • $25 • (5/15/1996) • **86**
Savigny-lès-Beaune Les Marconnets 1992 • $24 • (6/15/1995) • **82**
Savigny-lès-Beaune Les Marconnets 1991 • $30 • (1/31/1994) • **80**
Savigny-lès-Beaune Les Marconnets 1990 • $33 • (12/15/1992) • **90**

BLACHON, ROGER

St.-Joseph 1997: Pleasant and approachable, this supple, medium-bodied red has distinct toasted oak, spice, mocha and blackberry, kicking in with a good dose of acidity on the balanced finish. Drink now through 2001.–P.M. • $18 • (10/31/1999) • **87**

St.-Joseph 1993 • $17 • (11/15/1995) • **84**

St.-Joseph 1990 • $15 • (4/15/1993) • **84**

BLAGUEURS, DOMAINE DES

Syrah Vin de Pays d'Oc Sirrah 1998: From the south of France comes this delicious red at a great price, with lovely flavors of cherry, mineral and pepper. Well concentrated and attractive in color, with plenty of meaty, chocolaty flavors too. From Bonny Doon's Randall Grahm. Drink now through 2002.–K.M. • $10 • (4/30/2000) • **86**

Syrah Vin de Pays d'Oc Sirrah 1997: A hearty red, with ripe flavors of plum and cherry, along with leather and smoke notes. Spicy-chocolaty touches on the finish. Drink now.–K.M. • $9 • (9/15/1999) • **84**

Syrah Vin de Pays de l'Ardèche 1997: A well-focused red, with good plum, mineral and cherry flavors and meat notes. Nice concentration and depth of flavor, with an appealing herbal note on the finish.–K.M. • $NA • (12/31/1998) • **87**

Syrah Vin de Pays du Gard 1996: Quite focused, with berry flavors and leather and game notes. Firm and concentrated, with a nice crispness and power. Drink now.–K.M. • $13 • (7/31/1998) • **85**

BLAIN-GAGNARD

Bâtard-Montrachet 1997: Impressive acidity and focus for a '97, showing ripe fruit, lemon and honey and intense but well-integrated toast notes. Needs aging. Best from 2003 through 2010.–P.M. • $120 • (5/31/1999) • **91**

Bâtard-Montrachet 1996 • $110 • (5/31/1998) CS • **97**

Chassagne-Montrachet Caillerets 1997: A good attempt at making a round, flavorful white, with decent fruit and acidity. Turns a bit heavy and chewy on the midpalate, with a slight chestnut flavor on the rustic finish.–P.M. • $47 • (5/31/1999) • **79**

Chassagne-Montrachet Caillerets 1996: Thick and ripe, with lots of malic-milky-yogurt character, this is quite oaky in a toasted way, but tropical, citrus and apple flavors keep the balance. Opulent on the finish, it swirls its velvety liquid around the palate. Better than previously reviewed. Best after 2005.–P.M. • $45 • (8/31/1998) • **90**

Chassagne-Montrachet Caillerets 1995 • $42 Ⓐ • (5/31/1997) • **91**

Chassagne-Montrachet Clos St.-Jean 1997: Lemony character makes this refreshingly crisp—mouthpuckeringly so among the fat white Burgundies of '97. Offers some nice honey, green apple, toasted bread notes. Lingering firm finish. Better than previously reviewed. Drink now through 2005.–P.M. • $47 • (9/30/1999) • **87**

Chassagne-Montrachet Clos St.-Jean 1996 • $39 Ⓐ • (5/31/1998) • **88**

Chassagne-Montrachet La Boudriotte 1997: Beautiful, both lemony and honeyed, showing balance and a crisp side; this medium-bodied Chassagne has the stuffing to age. Ripe fruit, deftly toasted aromas, but cellar to let it meld. Better than previously reviewed. Best from 2002 through 2007.–P.M. • $47 • (9/30/1999) • **87**

Chassagne-Montrachet La Boudriotte 1996: Beautifully crafted '96, sparkling with lime, honey and dried herb, even grassy, flavors. Medium-bodied, with a crisp framework, some nicely integrated toasted oak and a plush finish that could use some time to show it all. Better than previously reviewed. Best after 2005.–P.M. • $45 • (8/31/1998) • **88**

Chassagne-Montrachet La Boudriotte 1995 • $45 • (8/31/1997) • **93**

Chassagne-Montrachet Morgeot 1997: Clean and tightly focused, with a core of fancy oak, toasted spice, smoke, some pear, grilled pineapple and lemon, there is plenty going on in this medium-bodied Chardonnay, and with good intensity. A bit tart on the finish. Better than previously reviewed. Drink now through 2003.–P.M. • $38 Ⓐ • (9/30/1999) • **86**

Chassagne-Montrachet Morgeot 1996 • $36 Ⓐ • (5/31/1998) • **91**

Criots-Bâtard-Montrachet 1997: A full-bodied wine with an attitude. This '97 performs high-wire acts on the palate. Pure and understated, focused on delivering clean, ripe fruit in a tightly wound package—something difficult to do in this soft vintage—it delivers mineral, green apple, fresh herb and honey notes on the long finish. An ager for patient aficionados only. Best from 2010 through 2030.–P.M. • $120 • (5/31/1999) • **96**

Criots-Bâtard-Montrachet 1996 • $110 • (5/31/1998) • **95**

BLANCHET, FRANCIS

Pouilly-Fumé Cuvée Silex Très Vieilles Vignes 1997: Good acidity keeps this lively, while flavors of mango, almond and white chocolate give it an exotic touch. Not a typical Sauvignon Blanc, but it has complexity and character. Drink now.–T.M. • $35 • (2/28/1999) • **86**

Pouilly-Fumé Cuvée Silex Très Vieilles Vignes 1996 • $30 • (2/28/1998) • **88**

Pouilly-Fumé Vieilles Vignes 1996: This has a sense of ripe peach and nectarine, yet it still maintains an herbal, minerally component, remaining fresh and juicy through the finish. Drink now.–B.S. • $16 • (10/31/1998) • **84**

BLANCK, PAUL

Gewürztraminer Alsace 1998: The aromas are the best feature of this white. Though fresh and young, it is delicately flavored and finishes weak.–B.S. • $17 • (10/31/1999) • **78**

Gewürztraminer Alsace 1996: Smells and tastes yeasty and beery. Something's wrong here. Not recommended. Tasted three times, with consistent notes.–B.S. • $18 • (9/15/1998) • **65**

Gewürztraminer Alsace Altenbourg 1997: Vivid in its aromas and flavors, which range from grapefruit and rose to passion fruit and papaya, this has intensity and persistence of flavor right through to the finish. Drink now through 2002.–B.S. • $20 • (10/31/1999) • **88**

Gewürztraminer Alsace Altenbourg 1996 • $22 • (4/30/1998) • **86**

Pinot Auxerrois Alsace Vieilles Vignes 1996 • $15 • (3/31/1998) • **87**

Pinot Blanc Alsace 1997: Seductive, smoky and well delineated, washing effortlessly across the palate. The smoke, pear, nut and spice flavors are concentrated and come to a crisp conclusion, lingering momentarily on the aftertaste. Drink now.–B.S. • $12 • (9/30/1999) • **88**

Pinot Blanc Alsace 1996: Very floral in character, adding delicacy to the firm structure, peach and mineral flavors. Elegant and concentrated, with moderate length on the finish. Drink through 1999.–B.S. • $14 • (8/31/1998) • **85**

Pinot Noir Alsace 1997: Intriguing black cherry and spice aromas followed by game, plum and cherry flavors. Ripe, balanced and well structured, though it lightens up on the finish. Drink now through 2001.–B.S. • $15 • (10/15/1999) • **84**

Riesling Alsace 1998: Floral, peach and fruit cocktail flavors highlight this young Riesling. Soft and round, it's balanced and straightforward, finishing a little short. Drink now through 2001.–B.S. • $17 • (10/15/1999) • **82**

Riesling Alsace 1996: Hard and unyielding, this seems very ripe, with apricot, lime and passion fruit, searing acidity underneath and intensity of flavor right through to the explosive finish. Best from 2001 through 2007.–B.S. • $18 • (9/15/1998) • **90**

Riesling Alsace Grand Cru Furstentum 1996: An exotic, almost overripe fruit component in aroma, while the palate exhibits a lean, minerally feel. Sleek and focused, finishing with a subtle, yet persistent aftertaste of smoke and apricot. Drink now through 2006.–B.S. • $24 • (10/15/1999) • **91**

Riesling Alsace Grand Cru Furstentum Vieilles Vignes 1996: Ripe peach, honey and mineral notes are allied to a firm structure and rich texture, adding extra dimension to this amazing French white, yet it remains elegant and balanced. A very long, smoky finish is the capper. Drink through 2007.–B.S. • $30 • (10/15/1999) HR • **92**

Riesling Alsace Grand Cru Schlossberg 1996: Ripe and racy, this offers plenty of passion fruit, quince and mineral aromas and flavors. Balanced, concentrated and harmonious, this is delicious now, yet will age gracefully. Drink now through 2005.–B.S. • $26 • (10/15/1999) • **90**

Riesling Alsace Rosenbourg 1996: Gorgeous aromas of lime and talc, a mouthful of ripe appley flavors and searing acidity give this white loads of personality. It wraps up on an almond note. Drink now through 2006.–B.S. • $21 • (8/31/1998) • **89**

Tokay Pinot Gris Alsace 1998: This white displays the apricot and smoke typical of Pinot Gris, but seems one-dimensional and finishes short. Drink now.–B.S. • $17 • (10/31/1999) • **82**

Tokay Pinot Gris Alsace 1996 • $18 • (3/31/1998) • **85**

Tokay Pinot Gris Alsace Patergarten 1997: Smoky notes overlay the peach and mineral aromas and flavors in this lush white that delivers the power without the amplitude of flavor. Tasted twice, with consistent notes. Drink now through 2002.–B.S. • $20 • (10/31/1999) • **84**

Key: SS—Spectator Selection. CS—Cellar Selection. HR—Highly Recommended. $NA—Price not available. (BT)—Barrel tasting. Ⓐ—Auction Price.
For a key to the tasters' initials, see "How to Use These Listings."
Dates in parentheses represent the issues in which the ratings were published.

FRANCE

BLANQUEFORT, DOMAINE DE

Côtes de Provence 1998: Both samples provided were corky.–K.M. • $13 • (1/01/2000) • **55**

Côtes de Provence Rosé 1998: Both samples provided were corky.–T.M. • $10 • (3/31/2000) • **55**

Côtes de Provence Rosé 1997: Firm and flavorful, with dried cherry and melon flavors, some aniselike notes. A balanced and refreshing rosé, with a touch of richness on the finish. Drink now.–K.M. • $13 • (11/15/1998) • **85**

BLASON D' ISSAN

Margaux 1996: Plenty of mineral and spice character to this, with a hint of berry. Medium-bodied, with well-integrated tannins and a fresh fruit aftertaste. Delicious. Second label of Château d'Issan. Drink now.–J.S. • $NA • (1/31/1999) • **86**

Margaux 1995 • $12 • (1/31/1998) • **85**

BLEND STORMING

Vin de Table Français 1995: A smooth, softly fruity red, with little tannin and no harsh edges. Enjoy now. • $8 • (8/31/1998) • **83**

BOCARD, GUY

Bourgogne Aligoté 1997: This medium-bodied white tastes fresh, with good crispness and a round texture. Green apples make for a zingy finish. Drink now.–P.M. • $15 • (9/30/1999) • **82**

Bourgogne Aligoté 1996 • $15 • (5/31/1998) • **81**

Bourgogne White 1997: Shows decent fruit, but it's a bit odd, with flinty, earthy flavors.–P.M. • $17 • (9/30/1999) • **79**

Bourgogne White 1996 • $18 • (5/31/1998) • **78**

Bourgogne White 1995 • $17 • (8/31/1997) • **72**

Meursault Charmes 1997: Quite oaky, with butter, butterscotch and grilled aromas and medium-intense green apple and pear character. A nice, toasty, smoky finish, but not much opulent fruit. Drink now through 2002.–P.M. • $50 • (5/31/1999) • **84**

Meursault Charmes 1996 • $50 • (5/31/1998) • **75**

Meursault Charmes 1995 • $NA • (8/31/1997) • **92**

Meursault Genevrières 1997: Very woody for the fruit, showing an intense, burning, toasty sensation, with a tough, chewy, hot finish.–P.M. • $50 • (5/31/1999) • **77**

Meursault Les Grands Charrons 1997: Nice ripe fruit in this medium-bodied '97 caresses the palate, providing pear, apple pie, cream, vanilla bean and spice complexity and a long, generous, elegant finish. Drink now through 2003.–P.M. • $40 • (5/31/1999) • **89**

Meursault Les Grands Charrons 1996: Good mineral notes, but it seems a bit green and herbal. Medium-bodied, with sweet, ripe fruit; the round, silky, Meursault-like mouthfeel came forth after decanting. Cellar it. Best from 2005.–P.M. • $30 • (8/31/1998) • **89**

Meursault Les Narvaux 1997: Clean, pure and deep yet reserved on the nose, this thick, luxurious Chardonnay stays focused, delivering a velvety, full-bodied character with sexy raciness and sparkling the palate with pear, tropical, wet earth and toasted oak. Drink now through 2005.–P.M. • $40 • (9/30/1999) • **93**

Meursault Les Narvaux 1996: A vibrant, juicy style of Meursault. Lovely, showing herbal, grassy, dried herbs, minty and violetlike notes. Intense and concentrated, with supple texture; balanced and full-bodied, with ripe fruit. Best from 2005.–P.M. • $40 • (8/31/1998) • **88**

Meursault Les Narvaux 1995 • $NA • (5/31/1997) • **70**

Meursault Limozin 1997: A floral, sweet perfume aroma from the oak dominates ths medium-bodied, fairly ripe '97. Tropical, pear and lemon flavors do a good balancing job. Supple, succulent finish. Drink now through 2002.–P.M. • $40 • (5/31/1999) • **86**

Meursault Limozin 1996 • $38 • (5/31/1998) • **79**

Meursault Limozin 1995 • $NA • (5/31/1997) • **90**

Meursault Sous la Velle 1996: Wonderful village wine. Great personality, with some mineral, grassy and herbal notes complementing the honey, pear and toasted oak. Full-bodied, supervibrant on the lively finish, cellar this. Best from 2000.–P.M. • $30 • (8/31/1998) • **90**

Meursault Vieilles Vignes 1997: A light and pleasant little Chardonnay, showing little depth but with green apple and pear. Drink now.–P.M. • $45 • (9/30/1999) • **82**

BOILEAU, ETIENNE

Chablis 1997: As charming as village Chablis gets. This isn't a complex wine, just a tight, fruity, minerally Chardonnay that's pure and vibrant on a steely finish coated with honey. Drink now.–P.M. • $17 • (5/31/1999) • **87**

Chablis 1996 • $16 • (8/31/1997) • **84**

Chablis Mont de Milieu 1997: Soft yet lively, medium-bodied, delivering ripe tropical, pear and melon notes combined with spice and smoke complexity, with a superharmonious finish that goes on and on. Drink now through 2004.–P.M. • $25 • (5/31/1999) • **89**

Chablis Mont de Milieu 1995 • $22 • (6/15/1997) • **79**

Chablis Montée de Tonnerre 1997: Clean, spicy style, a Chablis that has seen some oak seemingly, this mingles green apple, cream and butter notes with a slightly astringent finish. Drink through 2005.–P.M. • $25 • (5/31/1999) • **80**

Chablis Montée de Tonnerre 1996 • $25 • (5/31/1998) • **92**

Chablis Montée de Tonnerre 1995 • $25 • (6/15/1997) • **80**

Chablis Montmains 1997: Rather opulent, but still showing a hard, slightly metallic undertone of citrusy acidity; this has minerally intensity and tastes more like a '96. Should be ready in a few years. Best from 2002 through 2006.–P.M. • $24 • (5/31/1999) • **85**

Chablis Montmains 1995 • $25 • (6/15/1997) • **89**

Chablis Vaillons 1997: Quaffable and juicy, this Chablis lacks some complexity but delivers succulent fruit of good ripeness. Drink now.–P.M. • $25 • (5/31/1999) • **83**

Chablis Vaillons 1996 • $25 • (5/31/1998) • **85**

Chablis Vaillons 1995 • $25 • (6/15/1997) • **78**

Chablis Vaugiraut 1995 • $23 • (6/15/1997) • **75**

Petit Chablis 1996 • $14 • (8/31/1997) • **78**

BOILLOT, HENRI

Bourgogne 1985 • $13 • (12/31/1988) • **76**

Bourgogne White 1997: Lime and wood combine to create a hard, tough, ungenerous '97, with an astringent finish.–P.M. • $NA • (5/31/1999) • **77**

Chevalier-Montrachet 1997: Medium-bodied, it tastes of citrus yet only hints at ripe fruit, and you wish for more depth and focus. Shows toasted oak and spice accents. Drink now through 2002.–P.M. • $255 • (9/30/1999) • **84**

Meursault 1997: Round, attractive and medium-bodied, with nice lemon, green apple and herb notes and a clean finish. Drink now through 2002.–P.M. • $NA • (5/31/1999) • **85**

Meursault Les Charmes 1997: Tastes more of wood than fruit. Medium-bodied, with a dry mouthfeel and a chewy, chalky finish.–P.M. • $NA • (5/31/1999) • **77**

Meursault Les Perrières 1997: Medium-bodied, with obvious oak notes but little ripe fruit, turning a bit drying on the finish.–P.M. • $NA • (5/31/1999) • **79**

BOILLOT, JEAN

Beaune Clos du Roi 1996: Seductive cherry aromas and flavors are augmented by vanilla and butterscotch in this lovely *premier cru*. Real richness and concentration with balancing acidity and tannins make for a delicious presentation. Drink through 2005.–B.S. • $48 • (9/30/1998) • **90**

Beaune Clos du Roi 1995 • $44 • (11/15/1997) • **86**

Beaune Clos du Roi 1994 • $41 • (11/15/1996) • **80**

Beaune Clos du Roi 1992 • $29 • (12/15/1994) • **79**

Beaune Clos du Roi 1991 • $32 • (1/31/1994) • **81**

Beaune Les Epenottes 1996: Ripe and rich, a full-bodied Beaune with a lot of juicy acidity, some nice oak accents and thick midpalate concentration. Tastes like a nonfiltered wine. Has herbal, cassis bush and blackberry character and a long, pure finish. Drink now through 2003.–P.M. • $48 • (9/30/1998) • **88**

Beaune Les Epenottes 1994 • $41 • (11/15/1996) • **80**

Beaune Les Epenottes 1992 • $29 • (12/15/1994) • **80**

Beaune Les Epenottes 1991 • $32 • (1/31/1994) • **83**

Beaune Les Epenottes 1995 • $44 • (11/15/1997) • **78**

Meursault Les Genevrières 1997: Clean if a bit neutral, offering pear, vanilla bean and wet earth character. The focused, minerally finish has just a slight astringency. Cellar short-term. Drink now through 2005.–P.M. • $83 • (5/31/1999) • **85**

Nuits-St.-Georges Les Cailles 1996: Lovely purity of fruit, with blackberries and spice, gentle oak and an elegant harmony; all the elements are in proportion. Just a bit hot on the finish. Drink through 2004.–B.S. • $66 • (9/30/1998) • **89**

Nuits-St.-Georges Les Cailles 1995 • $58 • (11/15/1997) • **83**

Nuits-St.-Georges Les Cailles 1994 • $51 • (11/15/1996) • **80**

Nuits-St.-Georges Les Cailles 1992 • $38 • (12/15/1994) • **77**

FRANCE

■ ■ ■ ■

BOILLOT, JEAN

Nuits-St.-Georges Les Cailles 1991 • $48 • (1/31/1994) • **81**

Puligny-Montrachet 1997: Good mineral, ripe fruit and honey combine prettily in this clean, pure white. Full-bodied, it's fresh and nicely underoaked to bring uncomplicated drinking pleasure from start to finish. Drink now through 2002.–P.M. • $50 • (5/31/1999) • **88**

Puligny-Montrachet Clos de la Mouchère 1997: Starts out okay, with a minerally note, but turns a bit overripe as pear-spirit and cooked fruit flavors take over. The astringent, drying finish is unpleasantly tart.–P.M. • $73 • (5/31/1999) • **71**

Puligny-Montrachet Les Perrières 1997: Full-bodied, stressing lovely mineral and vanilla bean notes wrapped around sweet-tasting, ripe tropical and pear flavors. The *terroir* takes center stage in this harmonious, focused beauty. Best from 2003 through 2007.–P.M. • $73 • (5/31/1999) • **91**

Puligny-Montrachet Les Pucelles 1997: Minerally and chalky, this bone-dry, firm white nicely displays the *terroir* of Puligny and hints at honey, lemon and tropical flavors on the balanced finish. Cellar for more suppleness. Best from 2002 through 2005.–P.M. • $83 • (5/31/1999) • **90**

Savigny-lès-Beaune Les Lavières 1997: Hints at cherry on the nose, then turns diffuse, compact and tannic, showing only modest cherry compote.–B.S. • $40 • (9/30/1999) • **78**

Savigny-lès-Beaune Les Lavières 1992 • $27 • (12/15/1994) • **82**

Savigny-lès-Beaune Les Lavières 1991 • $30 • (1/31/1994) • **84**

Savigny-lès-Beaune White Les Vergelesses 1997: Quite oaky, with spice and butter turning up first, this full-bodied Chardonnay includes lovely ripe fruit that fights the spice-toast concoction. The finish tastes of toasted coconut. Drink through 2005.–P.M. • $42 • (5/31/1999) • **85**

Volnay En Chevret 1992 • $34 • (12/15/1994) • **80**

Volnay En Chevret 1991 • $40 • (1/31/1994) • **83**

Volnay Les Caillerets 1996: A crowd-pleaser, just lovely, with supple tannins, marvelous cherry, blueberry, wild raspberry and spice character, and not too much oak (just enough to round off the corners). Full-bodied, with creamy texture despite the high fresh acidity. Refined finish. Best After 2005.–P.M. • $66 • (9/30/1998) • **91**

Volnay Les Caillerets 1995 • $59 • (11/15/1997) • **86**

Volnay Les Caillerets 1994 • $51 • (11/15/1996) • **80**

Volnay Les Caillerets 1992 • $36 • (12/15/1994) • **83**

Volnay Les Caillerets 1991 • $44 • (1/31/1994) • **86**

Volnay Les Chevrets 1997: Cherry and anise aromas and flavors highlight this light, straightforward red, whose tannins are firm on the finish. Drink now through 2002.–B.S. • $62 • (9/30/1999) • **81**

Volnay Les Chevrets 1996: Wonderful Volnay, very fruity. Not so deep and complex, but shows lovely cherry, earth, blueberry and cassis notes. Smooth tannins, but the good, citrus-tasting acidity gives a vibrant finish. Best After 2005.–P.M. • $66 • (9/30/1998) • **88**

Volnay Les Chevrets 1995 • $54 • (11/15/1997) • **78**

Volnay Les Chevrets 1994 • $49 • (11/15/1996) • **74**

Volnay Les Fremiets 1997: Light and a bit stemmy, but fruity and juicy, with soft tannins. Shows raspberry, strawberry and wild berry notes on the finish. Drink now through 2001.–P.M. • $68 • (9/30/1999) • **84**

Volnay Les Fremiets 1996: Lovely wine. Supple and ripe, with a firm tannin structure. Offers cedar and spicy oak but also some nice red- and blackberry character. Full-bodied, with a silky midpalate and a fresh, zesty finish. Best After 2005.–P.M. • $66 • (9/30/1998) • **89**

Volnay Les Frémiets 1995 • $54 • (11/15/1997) • **83**

Volnay Les Frémiets 1994 • $49 • (11/15/1996) • **80**

Volnay Les Frémiets 1992 • $34 • (12/15/1994) • **79**

Volnay Les Frémiets 1991 • $40 • (1/31/1994) • **84**

BOILLOT, JEAN-MARC

Bâtard-Montrachet 1998: Amazing mouthfeel to this ultrarich and supersilky white Burgundy. Full-bodied, it displays loads of personality, with floral, dried apricot, perfume, late-harvestlike notes, and the texture is to die for as this balanced beauty curls around the palate and ends with honeyed opulence. Drink now through 2015.–P.M. • $195 • (5/31/2000) CS • **97**

Bâtard-Montrachet 1996 • $83 Ⓐ • (5/31/1998) • **85**

Bâtard-Montrachet 1995 • $131 • (5/31/1997) • **93**

Beaune Montrevenots 1997: Ripe and rich, showing good intensity of fruit, with firm tannins. Full-bodied, with plum and fig flavors kicking in on the lingering, slightly cooked finish. Drink now through 2002.–P.M. • $40 • (9/30/1999) • **86**

Beaune Montrevenots 1996: Cassis and black cherry aromas and mineral flavors are accented by spice, and there's a silkiness of texture despite firm tannins, bright acidity and backward character. Best from 2004 through 2010.–B.S. • $36 • (9/30/1998) • **90**

Beaune Montrevenots 1995 • $33 • (1/31/1998) • **83**

Beaune Montrevenots 1994 • $27 • (11/15/1996) • **90**

Beaune Montrevenots 1993 • $30 • (11/15/1995) • **85**

Beaune Montrevenots 1992 • $29 • (12/15/1994) • **85**

Beaune Montrevenots 1991 • $30 • (1/31/1994) • **88**

Beaune Montrevenots 1990 • $39 • (12/15/1992) • **92**

Beaune Montrevenots 1988 • $37 • (5/15/1991) • **88**

Beaune White Montrevenots 1998: Marvelous. Supple and ripe-tasting—a delicious, medium-bodied white that begs to be consumed. Some mint, dried herb and honey complexity, but it's the harmony on the silky finish that's so seductive. Drink now through 2002.–P.M. • $54 • (5/31/2000) • **88**

Bourgogne 1997: A ripe and jammy Pinot Noir, showing lovely, smooth tannins and raspberry, black cherry and toasted mocha. Turns just a bit heavy on the finish, but a good-quality Bourgogne Rouge. Drink now.–P.M. • $20 • (9/30/1999) • **83**

Bourgogne 1996: Pretty Bourgogne, ripe and lush, with blackberry notes and a smoky, tarry, matchstick character. Medium-bodied and flavorful. Drink now through 2002.–P.M. • $19 • (9/30/1998) • **84**

Bourgogne 1994 • $16 • (11/15/1996) • **80**

Bourgogne 1993 • $17 • (11/15/1995) • **86**

Bourgogne 1990 • $19 • (12/15/1992) • **88**

Corton-Charlemagne 1997: Superthick and full-bodied, with nice pear, lemon and green apple vibrancy. Harmonious finish, with a subtle toastiness. Drink now through 2010.–P.M. • $93 • (5/31/1999) • **88**

Givry White 1997: Quite lovely, sweet-tasting and ripe, showing honey, pear, delicious fruit and nicely dosed oak. Opulent and silky, with a medium-intense finish. Drink now through 2001.–P.M. • $24 • (9/30/1999) • **89**

Givry White 1996 • $21 • (5/31/1998) • **86**

Givry White Clos de la Brûlée 1998: Very interesting. Shows wet earth, matchstick, it's even a bit stinky, but so what? There is *terroir* concentration here plus honey and pear flavors, making it a captivating medium-bodied wine. Drink now through 2002.–P.M. • $28 • (5/31/2000) • **87**

Meursault 1997: Round and easy to drink, showing delicate pear and citrus flavors on a rather light frame. Short, slightly drying finish.–P.M. • $44 • (5/31/1999) • **79**

Meursault 1996 • $39 • (5/31/1998) • **93**

Montagny Le Vieux Château 1998: Lovely. Intense, full-bodied white Burgundy offering delicious dried herb, honey and smoke aromas. The good acidity and vibrant mouthfeel are balanced by the ripe fruit. Talented winemaking makes the best of this *terroir*. Not imported into the U.S. Drink now through 2003.–P.M. • $NA • (5/31/2000) • **88**

Montagny Premier Cru 1997: Very buttery and butterscotchy, possibly showing a bit of volatile acidity, this medium-bodied white tastes crisp, with a tart finish. Drink now through 2003.–P.M. • $23 • (5/31/1999) • **84**

Montagny Premier Cru 1996 • $20 • (5/31/1998) • **91**

Pommard Jarollières 1997: This beautiful *terroir* wine draws its strength from wet earth, wet stone and mineral components. Turns chalky and chewy on the palate, with focused red and black fruit. Not smooth, but a medium-bodied Pinot with personality. Best from 2002 through 2007.–P.M. • $70 • (1/01/2000) • **89**

Pommard Jarollières 1996: Marked by ripe fruit, plummy even, along with earth and hints of rose. Starts off richly, before stiff tannins take over, but it's chewy and has good acidity to balance. Needs some time to integrate. Not as good as when tasted from barrel. Best from 2001 through 2006.–B.S. • $60 • (9/30/1998) • **88**

Pommard Jarollières 1994 • $44 • (11/15/1996) • **85**

Pommard Jarolières 1993 • $50 • (11/15/1995) • **90**

Pommard Jarolières 1992 • $50 • (12/15/1994) • **89**

Pommard Jarolières 1991 • $46 • (1/31/1994) • **87**

Pommard Jarolières 1990 • $68 Ⓐ • (12/15/1992) • **94**

Pommard Les Saussilles 1991 • $NA • (1/31/1994) • **85**

Pommard Les Saussilles 1990 • $48 • (12/15/1992) • **92**

Pommard Les Saussilles 1988 • $47 • (5/15/1991) • **77**

Pommard Rugiens 1997: Minerally in character, with elegant cherry and spice and a sinewy texture. Not a blockbuster, but has good length. Drink now through 2003.–B.S. • $104 • (9/30/1999) • **87**

Pommard Rugiens 1996: Gorgeous. Exotic and very ripe, this opulent Pinot Noir is packed with just about everything—acidity, intriguing flavors of plum, ginger, Asian spices, blueberry and wild raspberry, and lots of

Key: SS—Spectator Selection. CS—Cellar Selection. HR—Highly Recommended. $NA—Price not available. (BT)—Barrel tasting. Ⓐ—Auction Price.
For a key to the tasters' initials, see "How to Use These Listings."
Dates in parentheses represent the issues in which the ratings were published.

FRANCE

smooth, ripe tannins. Full-bodied, this is an exciting wine. Best after 2003.–P.M. • $93 • (9/30/1998) • **93**

Pommard Rugiens 1994 • $68 • (11/15/1996) • **86**

Puligny-Montrachet 1998: Delicious in a simple way. A very pleasant wine that shows a vanilla, chewy, minerally character and ripe fruit. Drink now through 2006.–P.M. • $56 • (5/31/2000) • **89**

Puligny-Montrachet 1997: Great quality for a village wine. Round and polished, with a malic-lactic and butterscotch character backed by lime, lemon, green pineapple and other juicy flavors. Drink now through 2017.–P.M. • $31 Ⓐ • (5/31/1999) • **90**

Puligny-Montrachet 1996 • $42 • (5/31/1998) • **89**

Puligny-Montrachet 1995 • $41 • (8/31/1997) • **92**

Puligny-Montrachet Champ-Canet 1998: A mellow white Burgundy, with distinctive lactic, butter, milk and dried-fruit character. Medium-bodied, with a soft midpalate. Nice fruit and spice on the medium-intense, ripe-tasting finish. Drink now through 2004.–P.M. • $83 • (5/31/2000) • **87**

Puligny-Montrachet Champ-Canet 1997: Very pretty, showing clean flavors, with pear, lemon, honey, spice and butter notes and a butterscotch aroma that verges on volatile acidity. A supple, soft package made for enjoying on release, with a delicious honey and lime finish. Drink now through 2002.–P.M. • $73 • (5/31/1999) • **89**

Puligny-Montrachet Champ-Canet 1996 • $62 • (5/31/1998) • **88**

Puligny-Montrachet Champ-Canet 1995 • $58 • (8/31/1997) • **95**

Puligny-Montrachet La Garenne 1997: An atypical white Burgundy, this exotic, superrich '97 borders on late harvest, delivering dried apricot, peach, lime and butterscotch. Volatile acidity notes prevent it from receiving an outstanding score.–P.M. • $46 Ⓐ • (5/31/1999) • **89**

Puligny-Montrachet La Truffière 1998: A lactic aroma defines this wine, but it's very sweet and ripe, rating high on the pleasure scale. Shows beautiful dried apricot, peach and honey aromas and flavors, while a chewy, minerally finish reveals good *terroir*. Drink now through 2010.–P.M. • $93 • (5/31/2000) • **91**

Puligny-Montrachet La Truffière 1997: Buttery aromas verge on butterscotch and volatile acidity, with a core of lemon, quince jam and mango. A pleasant, medium-bodied, supple '97, with attractive lime and honey intensity. Drink now.–P.M. • $83 • (5/31/1999) • **86**

Puligny-Montrachet La Truffière 1996 • $72 • (5/31/1998) • **96**

Puligny-Montrachet La Truffière 1995 • $74 • (5/31/1997) • **95**

Puligny-Montrachet Les Combettes 1998: The Yquem of the white (and dry) Burgundy world. What a delicious wine. Amazingly rich, ripe and exotic with its dried fruit character, this bowls you over with silky texture and honey, honeysuckle, peach and dried apricot character. An amazing achievement in '98. Drink now through 2015.–P.M. • $93 • (5/31/2000) • **94**

Puligny-Montrachet Les Combettes 1997: Starts out with pronounced butter and butterscotch aromas that verge on white wine vinegar (volatile acidity?), but there's nice pear, pineapple, honey and, especially, fresh and vibrant citrus flavors on the palate. Clean, delicious, long finish. Drink now through 2002.–P.M. • $83 • (5/31/1999) • **84**

Puligny-Montrachet Les Combettes 1996 • $72 • (5/31/1998) • **94**

Puligny-Montrachet Les Combettes 1995 • $75 • (8/31/1997) • **94**

Puligny-Montrachet Les Folatières 1996 • $56 • (5/31/1998) • **93**

Puligny-Montrachet Les Pucelles 1997: A buttery, butterscotch, malic-lactic character dominates this full-bodied, round, supervelvety white Burgundy. Beautiful, but a bit soft in the acidity department. Drink now through 2003.–P.M. • $73 • (5/31/1999) • **92**

Puligny-Montrachet Les Pucelles 1996 • $62 • (5/31/1998) • **94**

Puligny-Montrachet Les Referts 1998: Seductive. Clean and pure white, very lovely. Offering vanilla, lactic and milky sort of flavors, backed by spice and honey, here is a wine to adore on release. Drink now through 2005.–P.M. • $83 • (5/31/2000) • **88**

Puligny-Montrachet Les Referts 1997: Buttery, with distinct butterscotch, caramel and earth notes, this soft, low-acidity wine tastes of cooked pears and lacks depth. Drink now through 2007.–P.M. • $53 Ⓐ • (5/31/1999) • **80**

Puligny-Montrachet Les Referts 1996 • $62 • (5/31/1998) • **95**

Puligny-Montrachet Les Referts 1995 • $58 • (5/31/1997) • **92**

Rully Grésigny 1998: Delicious. Ripe and honeyed, with dried herb, minty subtlety. Medium-bodied, it remains fresh and attractive on the vibrant finish. Drink now through 2002.–P.M. • $31 • (5/31/2000) • **85**

Rully Grésigny 1996 • $21 • (5/31/1998) • **90**

Rully La Pucelle 1998: Balanced and delicious. Ripe and rich, layered with toasted oak, honey, lime and vanilla sorbetlike flavors, this is delightfully agile on the palate, delivering a bang of flavors on the finish—and what an intense finish it is. Drink now through 2005.–P.M. • $31 • (5/31/2000) • **89**

Rully La Pucelle 1997: Very ripe, showing almost late-harvest character, with dried apricot, butter, honey, lemon and cooked pear notes. A nice aperitif. Drink now through 2002.–P.M. • $24 • (5/31/1999) • **86**

Volnay 1997: With herb and cherry on the nose, this red begins well enough, then disappears midpalate before ending on an up note. Firm and lively in a delicate sense. Drink now through 2002.–B.S. • $40 • (9/30/1999) • **83**

Volnay 1996: A thick and supple wine, offering ripe and fruity tannins, this is full of sappy cherry, cassis and currant character. Quite tough on the finish now, it has enough fruit to outlast the tannic, high-acidity structure. Rather ripe finish. Not as good as when tasted from barrel. Best After 2003.–P.M. • $36 • (9/30/1998) • **88**

Volnay 1995 • $32 • (1/31/1998) • **83**

Volnay 1994 • $27 • (11/15/1996) • **80**

Volnay 1993 • $30 • (11/15/1995) • **93**

Volnay 1992 • $29 • (12/15/1994) • **83**

Volnay 1991 • $NA • (1/31/1994) • **80**

Volnay 1990 • $40 • (12/15/1992) • **92**

Volnay Carelle sous la Chapelle 1997: A soft Pinot, with modest fruit definition, showing cherry and raspberry along with wet earth. Smooth tannic structure, but a bit short on the finish.–P.M. • $60 • (9/30/1999) • **79**

Volnay Carelle sous la Chapelle 1996: Serious *vin de garde*. Gorgeous fruit character. Full of ripe cherries, with a fleshy, beefy quality, lively acidity and mouthpuckering tannins. Only the drying tannins on the finish prevent it from rating higher. Best after 2003.–B.S. • $53 • (9/30/1998) • **89**

Volnay Carelle Sous La Chapelle 1995 • $11 Ⓐ • (1/31/1998) • **59**

Volnay Carelle Sous La Chapelle 1994 • $39 • (11/15/1996) • **88**

Volnay Carelle Sous La Chapelle 1993 • $11 Ⓐ • (11/15/1995) • **89**

Volnay Carelle Sous La Chapelle 1992 • $42 • (12/15/1994) • **88**

Volnay Le Ronceret 1991 • $NA • (1/31/1994) • **86**

Volnay Pitures 1997: Decent cherry, raspberry and wet earth fold into a slightly citrusy-tasting finish. Drink now.–P.M. • $60 • (9/30/1999) • **82**

Volnay Pitures 1996: Fragrant with violets and spice and a whiff of acetone, this falls short on the palate, very quickly turning dry and astringent. Could be an off-bottle. Best from 2002.–B.S. • $53 • (9/30/1998) • **79**

Volnay Pitures 1995 • $47 • (1/31/1998) • **84**

Volnay Pitures 1994 • $39 • (11/15/1996) • **86**

Volnay Pitures 1993 • $42 • (11/15/1995) • **92**

Volnay Pitures 1992 • $NA • (12/15/1994) • **85**

Volnay Pitures 1991 • $37 • (1/31/1994) • **80**

Volnay Pitures 1990 • $55 • (12/15/1992) • **94**

BOILLOT, LUCIEN

Bourgogne 1990 • $14 • (12/15/1992) • **86**

Gevrey-Chambertin Cherbaudes 1994 • $38 • (11/15/1996) • **71**

Gevrey-Chambertin Cherbaudes 1993 • $40 • (11/15/1995) • **88**

Gevrey-Chambertin Cherbaudes 1991 • $34 • (1/31/1994) • **82**

Gevrey-Chambertin Cherbaudes 1990 • $35 • (12/15/1992) • **85**

Gevrey-Chambertin Cherbaudes 1987 • $25 • (5/31/1990) • **85**

Gevrey-Chambertin Les Corbeaux 1994 • $35 • (11/15/1996) • **82**

Gevrey-Chambertin Les Corbeaux 1993 • $40 • (11/15/1995) • **87**

Gevrey-Chambertin Les Corbeaux 1990 • $33 • (12/15/1992) • **88**

Nuits-St.-Georges Les Pruliers 1994 • $38 • (11/15/1996) • **87**

Nuits-St.-Georges Les Pruliers 1993 • $40 • (11/15/1995) • **85**

Nuits-St.-Georges Les Pruliers 1991 • $36 • (1/31/1994) • **83**

Nuits-St.-Georges Les Pruliers 1987 • $25 • (7/15/1990) • **88**

Pommard Les Croix Noires 1991 • $30 • (1/31/1994) • **75**

Pommard Les Fremiers 1994 • $35 • (11/15/1996) • **85**

Pommard Les Fremiers 1993 • $38 • (11/15/1995) • **91**

Volnay Les Angles 1994 • $34 • (11/15/1996) • **81**

Volnay Les Angles 1991 • $30 • (1/31/1994) • **80**

Volnay Les Angles 1990 • $32 • (12/15/1992) • **87**

Volnay Les Angles 1985 • $33 • (7/15/1988) • **86**

Volnay Les Brouillards 1993 • $37 • (11/15/1995) • **87**

Volnay Les Brouillards 1991 • $28 • (1/31/1994) • **81**

Volnay Les Brouillards 1990 • $32 • (12/15/1992) • **90**

Volnay Les Caillerets 1994 • $35 • (11/15/1996) • **79**

Volnay Les Caillerets 1993 • $38 • (11/15/1995) • **91**

BOIS DE LA GARDE, CHATEAU DU

Côtes du Rhône 1996: This light, red shows cherry, licorice and tobacco flavors, with light, slightly dry tannins and a clean, short finish.–T.M. • $9 • (11/15/1998) • **77**

Côtes du Rhône 1995 • $9 • (5/15/1998) • **78**

Côtes du Rhône 1989 • $8 • (5/31/1991) • **83**

Côtes du Rhône 1988 • $7 • (10/31/1990) • **82**

BOIS DE LA SALLE, CAVE DU

Beaujolais-Villages Marquis du Bois 1997: Fresh and firm, displaying hints of coffee, plum and leather, this red is medium-bodied and beginning to show maturity. A good match for roast chicken, baked ham or charcuterie. Drink now.–B.S. • $10 • (10/15/1999) • **85**

BOIS-MARTIN, CHATEAU

Pessac-Léognan 1997: A wine with lovely perfumes of violet and flowers. Medium-bodied, with medium tannins and a simple, fruity finish. A new château from Sarte. Drink now.–J.S. • $NA • (1/31/2000) • **85**

BOISSAN, DOMAINE DE

Côtes du Rhône 1995 • $NA • (10/15/1997) • **70**
Côtes du Rhône Clos de Fontvive Réserve 1994 • $NA • (10/15/1997) • **74**
Côtes du Ventoux Le Montsegur Cuvée Speciale 1995 • $NA • (10/15/1997) • **83**
Gigondas Vieilles Vignes 1995 • $NA • (10/15/1997) • **75**
Vacqueyras 1995 • $NA • (10/15/1997) • **76**

BOISSET

Cabernet Sauvignon Vin de Pays d'Oc Méditerranée 1998: Pleasant and soft, with appealing ripe cherry and peppery flavors. A good pizza or burger wine. Drink now.–K.M. • $7 • (4/30/2000) • **84**
Chardonnay Vin de Pays d'Oc Méditerranée 1998: Soft, with faint pear and apple flavors. Barely vinous.–K.M. • $7 • (4/30/2000) • **77**
Merlot Vin de Pays d'Oc 1998: Fresh and juicy, with good berry and grapey flavors, some peppery notes on the finish. Drink now.–K.M. • $7 • (4/30/2000) • **83**
Syrah Vin de Pays d'Oc Méditerranée 1998: The good earthy aroma is a nice introduction to this medium-bodied and approachable Syrah with an attractive mix of meat and red fruit flavors. Leathery notes chime in on the finish. Drink now through 2001.–K.M. • $7 • (4/30/2000) • **84**

BOISSET, JEAN-CLAUDE

Beaujolais 1993 • $6 • (6/30/1994) • **76**
Beaujolais 1988 • $7 • (11/15/1990) • **77**
Beaujolais-Villages 1993 • $7 • (6/30/1994) • **83**
Beaujolais-Villages 1988 • $8 • (11/15/1990) • **76**
Bourgogne 1993 • $NA • (11/15/1995) • **74**
Bourgogne 1992 • $9 • (11/30/1994) • **82**
Bourgogne Charles de France 1993 • $NA • (11/15/1995) • **75**
Bourgogne Conférie des Chevaliers du Tastevin 1989 • $7 • (6/15/1992) • **76**
Bourgogne Tastevinage 1988 • $11 • (8/31/1991) • **72**
Brouilly 1993 • $9 • (6/30/1994) • **77**
Cabernet Sauvignon Vin de Pays d'Oc 1996 • $7 • (12/15/1997) • **79**
Cabernet Sauvignon Vin de Pays d'Oc 1994 • $6 • (10/31/1995) • **85**
Chardonnay Vin de Pays d'Oc 1997: Decent, with green apple flavors and a citrus note, though a touch bitter on the finish.–K.M. • $8 • (5/31/1999) • **79**
Chardonnay Vin de Pays d'Oc 1996 • $7 • (12/15/1997) • **82**
Charmes-Chambertin 1993 • $56 • (11/15/1995) • **77**
Chassagne-Montrachet Red 1993 • $18 • (11/15/1995) • **82**
Châteauneuf-du-Pape 1986 • $12 • (11/30/1988) • **80**
Clos de Vougeot 1993 • $46 • (11/15/1995) • **79**
Côte de Nuits-Villages 1983 • $13 • (2/01/1986) • **78**
Côtes du Rhône 1992 • $6 • (11/30/1994) • **78**
Côtes du Rhône 1990 • $9 • (7/31/1992) • **84**
Côtes du Ventoux 1988 • $4 • (10/15/1990) • **75**
Gevrey-Chambertin 1993 • $16 • (11/15/1995) • **76**
Gevrey-Chambertin 1991 • $NA • (1/31/1994) • **82**
Gevrey-Chambertin 1990 • $17 • (1/01/1994) • **82**
Merlot Vin de Pays d'Oc 1996 • $7 • (12/15/1997) • **84**
Merlot Vin de Pays d'Oc 1994 • $6 • (10/31/1995) • **75**
Morgon 1993 • $9 • (6/30/1994) • **80**
Nuits-St.-Georges 1985 • $25 • (4/30/1988) • **79**

Key: SS—Spectator Selection. CS—Cellar Selection. HR—Highly Recommended. $NA—Price not available. (BT)—Barrel tasting. Ⓐ—Auction Price.
For a key to the tasters' initials, see "How to Use These Listings."
Dates in parentheses represent the issues in which the ratings were published.

Pommard 1985 • $28 • (4/30/1988) • **78**
Pommard Les Rugiens 1985 • $33 • (3/15/1988) • **76**
Rully Red 1992 • $9 • (1/01/1994) • **76**
Sauvignon Blanc Vin de Pays d'Oc 1996 • $7 • (12/31/1997) • **82**
Savigny-lès-Beaune 1993 • $12 • (11/15/1995) • **82**
Syrah Vin de Pays d'Oc 1996 • $7 • (12/15/1997) • **79**
Syrah Vin de Pays d'Oc 1994 • $6 • (10/31/1995) • **80**
Syrah Vin de Pays d'Oc 1993 • $6 • (2/28/1995) • **77**
Viognier Vin de Pays d'Oc 1996 • $9 • (12/15/1997) • **78**
Volnay Clos des Chênes 1985 • $28 • (4/15/1988) • **86**

BOISSON, JEAN-PIERRE

Châteauneuf-du-Pape Domaine du Père Caboche 1998: Here's a goodie from '98—an extracted, compacted fruit bomb, with silky tannins and a round, rich, full mouthfeel. Modern winemaking approach focuses more on fruit than *terroir*, but the smoothness is impressive. Drink now through 2005.–P.M. • $18 • (12/15/1999) HR • **90**
Châteauneuf-du-Pape Domaine du Père Caboche 1997: Diluted, and its tannins are drying. Modest strawberry flavors try to come through.–P.M. • $15 • (11/15/1998) • **70**
Châteauneuf-du-Pape Domaine du Père Caboche 1994 • $15 • (12/15/1996) • **78**
Châteauneuf-du-Pape Domaine du Père Caboche 1989 • $20 • (10/15/1991) • **84**
Châteauneuf-du-Pape Domaine du Père Caboche 1988 • $20 • (10/15/1991) • **87**
Châteauneuf-du-Pape Domaine du Père Caboche 1986 • $20 • (10/15/1991) • **81**
Châteauneuf-du-Pape Domaine du Père Caboche 1985 • $20 • (10/15/1991) • **85**
Châteauneuf-du-Pape Domaine du Père Caboche 1983 • $18 • (10/15/1991) • **77**
Châteauneuf-du-Pape Domaine du Père Caboche 1981 • $30 • (10/15/1991) • **87**
Châteauneuf-du-Pape Elisabeth Chambellan Vieilles Vignes 1998: An early indication of the potential of '98. There's depth and ripeness in this medium-bodied Châteauneuf. With its amazingly silky tannins, it comes through as easy and accessible, but the stuffing is there. Long, balanced finish. Drink now through 2010.–P.M. • $23 • (12/15/1999) • **90**
Châteauneuf-du-Pape Elisabeth Chambellan Vieilles Vignes 1997: Light in color and body, with a pronounced herb and bell pepper character.–P.M. • $20 • (11/15/1998) • **72**
Châteauneuf-du-Pape Elisabeth Chambellan Vieilles Vignes 1994 • $20 • (12/15/1996) • **83**
Châteauneuf-du-Pape White Domaine du Père Caboche 1998: Traditional, woody and a bit earthy, showing modest fruit in a rustic package. A bit drying on the finish and lacking in fatness.–P.M. • $19 • (12/15/1999) • **79**
Châteauneuf-du-Pape White Domaine du Père Caboche 1997: Smooth and full-bodied, packing in the dried herbs, subtle honey and blanched almond, growing more powerful as it unfolds its muscular frame to a long, minerally, silky-smooth finish. Well made. Drink now through 2005.–P.M. • $17 • (11/15/1998) • **89**

BOLLINGER

Brut Champagne Grande Année 1990: A sense of opulence marks this highly concentrated, creamy-textured 1990 Champagne, with its ripe, generous fruit flavors complementing the toasty, honeyed nuances acquired from aging on the lees. Lingering finish. Drink now through 2004. • $70 • (9/15/1999) HR • **95**
Brut Champagne Special Cuvée NV: A mellow gold-amber color and ripe, generous peach, honey and fig flavors indicate this French bubbly is wonderfully mature. Ample and enjoyable, it shows great balance and a long finish. Drink now. • $29 Ⓐ • (9/15/1999) SS • **90**

BONALGUE, CHATEAU

Pomerol 1998: Plenty of chocolaty berry character in this young wine. Medium- to full-bodied, with chewy tannins and a medium finish. Almost outstanding.–J.S. • $NA • (5/31/1999) (BT) • **85-89**
Pomerol 1997: Metallic, with some fruit, but very light.–J.S. • $NA • (1/31/2000) • **76**
Pomerol 1996: Slightly rustic but very good, with good dark color, fruit and fresh herb character. Medium-bodied, with velvety tannins and a berry, tobacco aftertaste. Best after 2000.–J.S. • $NA • (1/31/1999) • **85**
Pomerol 1994 • $28 • (12/15/1995) • **80**
Pomerol 1993 • $27 • (12/15/1995) • **86**

BONDIEU, CHATEAU LE

Côtes de Bergerac Cuvée Gabriel 1995: Rich and well rounded, with loads of character. Red plum, cassis and currant flavors, with subtle spicy notes wrapped inside. Finishes on notes of tobacco, cedar and coffee. An intense and distinctive red. Drink now.–K.M. • $10 • (12/31/1998) • **87**

Montravel 1998: An assertive and vibrant style, with plenty of herb and grass flavors and a good shot of lemon-lime. Good structure and length. Drink now.–K.M. • $9 • (11/15/1999) • **83**

BONGRAN, DOMAINE DE LA

Mâcon-Clessé Quintaine Cuvée Tradition 1996 • $25 • (5/31/1998) • **90**

Mâcon-Clessé Quintaine Cuvée Tradition 1995 • $25 • (5/31/1998) • **94**

Mâcon-Clessé Quintaine Cuvée Tradition Sélection E.J. Thévenet 1997: Good combination of fruit, spice, citrus, butter and honey; there's much going on in this medium-bodied white, including a firm grip on the finish. Worth cellaring short-term. From Jean Thévenet. Drink now through 2001.–P.M. • $28 • (5/31/1999) • **89**

BONHOMME, ANDRE

Mâcon-Viré 1997: Elegant, racy, balanced Mâcon, delivering nice intensity of fruit, some traditional notes of wet earth and wet hay, ending on a finish of pear and pineapple. Drink now through 2001.–P.M. • $17 • (5/31/1999) • **88**

BONNAIRE

Brut Blanc de Blancs Champagne Cramant NV: Crisp and vibrant, with bright apple and lemon flavors, fresh acidity and a zingy finish. Refreshing to drink now, but could age a bit, too. Drink through 2001. • $34 • (10/31/1999) • **90**

Brut Blanc de Blancs Champagne Cramant 1993: Round, balanced and a bit one-dimensional, this appley sparkling wine nevertheless has good concentration and length. Drink now.–B.S. • $NA • (11/30/1999) • **88**

Brut Blanc de Blancs Champagne Cramant 1990: A big, plush style of Champagne, with earthy, ripe and fruity flavors and a soft texture. Mineral accents and a lingering finish make it distinctive. Drink now. • $45 • (12/31/1998) • **90**

Brut Blanc de Blancs Champagne Premier Cru NV • $40 • (12/31/1994) • **90**

BONNAT, CHATEAU LE

Graves 1996: Rather weedy and light, with some plum character, but a light body and slightly dry tannins detract from the overall quality.–J.S. • $NA • (2/28/1999) • **79**

Graves 1989 • $18 • (4/30/1992) • **81**

Graves 1988 • $18 • (12/31/1990) • **87**

Graves 1987 • $12 • (4/15/1990) • **83**

Graves White 1996: Clean and fresh, with freshly cut melon and grass aromas and flavors. Medium-bodied, with well-integrated acidity and a fresh finish. A bit one-dimensional, but well made. Drink now.–J.S. • $NA • (1/01/1999) • **85**

BONNEAU, HENRI

Châteauneuf-du-Pape 1991: Extremely earthy, with tough tannins and almost no fruit, this has spent far too long in wood. Should have been bottled and drunk years ago. Past its prime.–T.M. • $33 • (11/15/1998) • **74**

Châteauneuf-du-Pape Cuvée Marie Beurrier 1992: A delicious, "hunt-it-down" Châteauneuf. Get this one and enjoy a mouthful of meat, plum, mineral and wet earth flavors, all anchored in the pebbly *terroir* of the appellation. Superb, natural winemaking here, and a terrific effort in a poor vintage for Châteauneuf. Drink now through 2005.–P.M. • $40 • (2/28/1999) • **93**

Châteauneuf-du-Pape Cuvée Marie Beurrier 1991: Mature aromas of tea, sandalwood and spice give way to a firmly structured palate, followed by astringent tannins. A bit like chewing on a stick. Past its prime.–T.M. • $147 Ⓐ • (11/15/1998) • **75**

Châteauneuf-du-Pape Cuvée Marie Beurrier 1989 • $81 Ⓐ • (1/01/1998) • **94**

Châteauneuf-du-Pape Cuvée Marie Beurrier 1988 • $125 Ⓐ • (1/01/1998) • **94**

Châteauneuf-du-Pape Réserve des Célestins 1992: Browning now, this maturing red shows gamy and earthy aromas, hard tannins and herbal, earthy flavors. Past its prime.–T.M. • $80 • (11/15/1998) • **77**

Châteauneuf-du-Pape Réserve des Celestins 1986 • $250 Ⓐ • (5/31/1989) • **82**

BONNEAU DU MARTRAY

Corton 1997: Nice flavors for a '97, with vibrant red berry and spicy oak character. Full-bodied, with a slightly crisp finish. Drink now through 2002.–P.M. • $62 • (9/30/1999) • **85**

Corton 1996: Lovely freshness, richness and harmony. The blackberry flavors, spicy oak, bright acidity and ripe tannins only need time to integrate in this flavorful, mouthwatering red. Good, subtle length on the finish. Drink through 2006.–B.S. • $55 Ⓐ • (9/30/1998) • **90**

Corton 1995 • $54 Ⓐ • (11/15/1997) • **87**

Corton 1994 • $55 • (11/15/1996) • **89**

Corton 1993 • $45 • (11/15/1995) • **88**

Corton 1985 • $62 • (10/15/1988) • **91**

Corton-Charlemagne 1997: Very lovely in a soft, vanilla-tasting way, showing pretty Chardonnay aromas of green apple, pear, honey and pie tart. Tasted twice, with consistent notes. Drink now through 2002.–P.M. • $100 • (9/30/1999) • **86**

Corton-Charlemagne 1996: A prototypical '96. Racy, full-bodied, intensely stony and citrusy, it offers ripe yet delicate aromas and flavors of pear, pineapple, wet stone, mineral and toasted oak. Delicious as it swirls in the palate, then kicks in with vengence on the citrus-smacking finish. The best part: not overdone in the oak department. Best after 2005.–P.M. • $109 Ⓐ • (8/31/1998) • **95**

Corton-Charlemagne 1995 • $75 Ⓐ • (8/31/1997) • **93**

BONNET, CHATEAU | BORDEAUX

Bordeaux 1996: Impressive ripeness from this appellation, with plenty of plum and berry character and a hint of leafiness. Full-bodied, very chewy, with loads of tannins. Long, racy finish. Slightly one-dimensional but well structured. Best after 2002.–J.S. • $8 • (1/31/1999) • **85**

Bordeaux 1995 • $8 • (1/31/1998) • **87**

Bordeaux 1994 • $8 • (7/31/1996) • **83**

Bordeaux 1989 • $9 • (7/15/1992) • **79**

Bordeaux 1988 • $8 • (4/30/1991) • **77**

Bordeaux Réserve 1997: Aromas of plums and green olives follow through to a medium-bodied palate with silky tannins. Sweet fruit finish. Drink now.–J.S. • $10 • (1/31/2000) • **85**

Bordeaux Réserve 1994 • $11 • (1/31/1997) • **80**

Bordeaux Réserve 1993 • $10 • (1/31/1996) • **82**

Bordeaux Réserve 1992 • $8 • (4/15/1995) • **78**

Bordeaux Réserve 1991 • $10 • (3/31/1994) • **77**

Bordeaux Réserve 1990 • $NA • (3/31/1993) • **82**

Bordeaux Réserve 1988 • $11 • (7/15/1991) • **78**

Bordeaux Réserve Vieilli en Fûts de Chêne 1989: Still holding on with little trouble. Color is medium-brick-red surrounding a ruby center. Aromas of spices and dried cherries. Medium-bodied, with fine tannins and a leather, tobacco aftertaste. (1989 Bordeaux horizontal tasting). Drink now.–J.S. • $NA • (5/31/1999) • **85**

Entre-Deux-Mers 1998: Aromas of grapefruit and melon follow through to a medium-bodied palate, with medium acidity and a fruity finish. Very good quality for the money. Drink now.–J.S. • $9 • (2/29/2000) • **86**

Entre-Deux-Mers Vinifié en Fûts de Chêne 1996: Very clean Sauvignon character here. Good mineral, grass and lemon aromas and flavors. Medium-bodied, with fresh acidity and a zingy finish with a celery aftertaste. Drink now.–J.S. • $8 • (3/31/1999) • **86**

BONNET, CHATEAU | LANGUEDOC

Minervois 1997: Quite lush and lively, with flavors of cherry, currant and allspice and good concentration. Builds to a finish redolent of blueberries and chocolaty notes. Drink through 2004.–K.M. • $7 • (2/28/1999) • **87**

Minervois 1995 • $7 • (3/31/1998) • **84**

BONNET, F.

Brut Champagne Comte L. de Ferande NV: Like a well-aged vintage Champagne, this offers complex aromas, ample toasty, figgy flavors and a lingering, mellow finish. A smooth, inviting texture wraps it up. Drink now through 2001. • $18 • (10/31/1999) • **91**

Brut Rosé Champagne Comte L. de Ferande NV: Brassy in color, displaying plenty of character, with toast, berry and a hint of truffle. Expansive and creamy on the palate, it ends with a refreshing astringency and a lingering aftertaste of red berries. Drink now.–B.S. • $16 • (11/30/1999) • **89**

BONNIGAL, M.

Sauvignon Blanc Touraine Domaine La Prévôté 1997: Lovely, ripe aromas of gooseberry and peach, augmented by a flinty note on the palate. Soft and round, this has more up-front appeal than finish. Drink now.–B.S. • $9 • (11/15/1998) • **83**

BON-PASTEUR, CHATEAU LE

Pomerol 1999: Black as ink. Aromas of ripe plums and berries. Medium- to full-bodied, with velvety tannins and a long finish. Serious effort from owner Michel Rolland.–J.S. • $NA • (1/01/2000) (BT) • **85-89**
Pomerol 1998: Dark-colored, with intense spice, berry and mineral. Full-bodied and very tannic, with loads of bright berry and earth character.–J.S. • $NA • (5/31/1999) (BT) • **90-94**
Pomerol 1997: Very pretty blackberry, mineral and licorice aromas. Medium-bodied, with velvety tannins and a long, fruity finish. Best after 2000.–J.S. • $43 • (1/31/2000) • **87**
Pomerol 1996: Aromas of cherries, mushrooms and some oak. Medium-bodied, with slightly drying tannins but some pretty berry and toasted oak on the finish. A bit lean, but very good; not as good, however, as the barrel sample. Drink now.–J.S. • $36 • (1/31/1999) • **85**
Pomerol 1995 • $38 Ⓐ • (1/31/1998) • **90**
Pomerol 1994 • $31 Ⓐ • (1/31/1997) • **85**
Pomerol 1993 • $32 • (1/31/1996) • **87**
Pomerol 1992 • $21 • (4/15/1995) • **81**
Pomerol 1990 • $60 Ⓐ • (3/31/1993) • **93**
Pomerol 1989: Earthy and decadent. Dark ruby-garnet. Aromas of black olives, berries and meat. Full-bodied, chewy, with lots of tannins and a sweet fruit and earth aftertaste. Slightly dry tannins. (1989 Bordeaux horizontal tasting). Best after 2000.–J.S. • $NA • (5/31/1999) • **88**
Pomerol 1988 • $40 Ⓐ • (2/28/1991) • **85**
Pomerol 1987 • $22 • (5/15/1990) • **81**
Pomerol 1986 • $45 Ⓐ • (6/15/1989) • **92**
Pomerol 1985 • $42 Ⓐ • (5/15/1988) • **92**
Pomerol 1984 • $13 • (6/15/1987) • **86**
Pomerol 1983 • $33 Ⓐ • (6/16/1986) • **86**
Pomerol 1982: This slightly bad bottle tastes much fresher than it looks. Fresh blueberries have a hint of bark and fresh mushroom. Medium-bodied, with velvety tannins and a ripe fruit and chocolate aftertaste.—1982 Bordeaux horizontal. Drink now.–J.S. • $235 Ⓐ • (11/30/1998) • **88**
Pomerol 1979 • $NA • (10/15/1989) • **91**

BORD, CHATEAU DE

Côtes du Rhône-Villages Laudun 1996: Light in body and color, this delicate red offers modest strawberry and raspberry notes. Crisp, slightly herbal, finish.–P.M. • $12 • (11/15/1998) • **73**
Côtes du Rhône-Villages Laudun 1995 • $10 • (10/15/1997) • **79**
Côtes du Rhône-Villages Laudun 1994 • $10 • (10/15/1997) • **81**
Côtes du Rhône-Villages White Laudun 1996 • $10 • (10/15/1997) • **79**

BORGEOT

Bourgogne 1996: Juicy and fresh, with some lively raspberry and cherry flavors. Drink now.–P.M. • $14 • (9/30/1998) • **83**
Bourgogne White 1996 • $15 • (5/31/1998) • **80**
Chassagne-Montrachet 1997: Lovely. This pure, ripe Chassagne melts on the palate thanks to its round, silky texture. Full-bodied, with superlative fruit concentration, it enchants with dried herb, honey, pear, quince jam and apricot flavors, delivering a wonderfully harmonious, succulent, slightly toasty finish. Drink now through 2005.–P.M. • $32 • (5/31/1999) • **92**
Chassagne-Montrachet Morgeot 1998: Beautiful *terroir* here. For aficionados of midpalate concentration, where this wine turns silky-smooth and minerally. Subtle and elegant, it's aromatically shy, but it tastes compacted and shows vanilla bean, pear, some deft smoke and toast notes. A well-made ager. Drink through 2010.–P.M. • $43 • (5/31/2000) • **93**

Key: SS—Spectator Selection. CS—Cellar Selection. HR—Highly Recommended. $NA—Price not available. (BT)—Barrel tasting. Ⓐ—Auction Price.
For a key to the tasters' initials, see "How to Use These Listings."
Dates in parentheses represent the issues in which the ratings were published.

Chassagne-Montrachet Morgeot 1997: Lively and lovely, very fresh and slightly spritzy, displaying layers of honey, pear, vanilla and pineapple concentration in a full-bodied, supple, exciting and delicious Chassagne. Drink now through 2003.–P.M. • $43 • (5/31/1999) • **93**
Chassagne-Montrachet Red Clos St.-Jean 1996: Deep in color and marked by vanilla tones from new oak, it's a modern style with polished cherry and cassis flavors, good concentration, silky texture and fine tannins. Drink now through 2002.–B.S. • $40 • (9/30/1998) • **87**
Puligny-Montrachet Les Charmes 1998: Deliciously fresh, clean and balanced. Offers plenty of ripe fruit presented in a limelike package. Medium-bodied, with some pear, freshly cut grass, dried herbs and chalky character. Without pretentions, it's a pleasure to drink, now through 2002.–P.M. • $50 • (5/31/2000) • **87**
Puligny-Montrachet Vieilles Vignes 1998: Great quality for a village wine. Thick and rather fat, with a smooth midpalate, this is all cream, pear tart and honey. Full-bodied, it lacks a bit of firm structure, but with all that spice, toasted oak and lemon, it's a wonderful white Burgundy. Tasted twice, with consistent notes. Drink now through 2008.–P.M. • $40 • (5/31/2000) • **92**
Santenay Les Beauregards 1996: Plenty of spicy, smoky new oak greets the senses, but it's light on fruit, showing more herbal character followed by too much dry tannin on the finish. Drink now.–B.S. • $23 • (9/30/1998) • **78**
Santenay Les Gravières 1996: Kirsch, wet earth and a stemmy note mark this tough, tannic red. Doubtful that the modest fruit will outlive the tannins. Drink through 2002.–B.S. • $23 • (9/30/1998) • **77**
Santenay Vieilles Vignes 1996: Supple and fruity, but lacking a bit in depth and character. Still it's a nice everyday wine—sweet-tasting, with cedar, black cherry and wild berry character. Drink now.–P.M. • $20 • (9/30/1998) • **83**
Santenay White Les Gravières 1997: Talk about *goût de terroir.* Not very refined aromas—earthy, smoky, flinty, salty—but there's a nice ripe, oily texture, with amazingly clean fruit. Buy! Drink now through 2003.–P.M. • $29 • (5/31/1999) • **93**
Santenay White Les Gravières 1996 • $26 • (5/31/1998) • **93**

BORIE DE MAUREL, DOMAINE

Minervois Cuvée Sylla 1995 • $18 • (3/31/1998) • **90**
Syrah Minervois 1998: A lip-smacking, youthful Syrah, with lively flavors of dark plum, leather and pepper. Mineral and roasted coffee notes on the finish. Drink now.–K.M. • $9 • (12/31/1999) • **85**
Syrah Minervois 1996 • $9 • (5/31/1998) • **85**

BORIE LA VITARELE

St.-Chinian 1995 • $10 • (5/31/1998) • **90**

BOSCQ, CHATEAU LE

St.-Estèphe 1998: Slightly raisiny, with a burnt character. Full-bodied and velvety, with a medium finish. Needs a bit more ripe fruit on the center palate.–J.S. • $NA • (5/31/1999) (BT) • **80-84**
St.-Estèphe 1997: Seriously good for the vintage. Blackberry and tobacco aromas with a hint of mint. Medium-bodied, with velvety tannins and a medium, fruity aftertaste. Slightly one-dimensional but it's good, clean fruit.–J.S. • $NA • (1/31/2000) • **87**
St.-Estèphe 1996: A very good, flavorful '96, with berries and milk chocolate on the nose and palate. Medium-bodied, with medium tannins and a vanilla and fruit aftertaste. Best after 2000.–J.S. • $15 • (1/31/1999) • **87**
St.-Estèphe 1995 • $20 • (1/31/1998) • **88**

BOSQUET DES PAPES

Châteauneuf-du-Pape 1998: Lovely. Typical Châteauneuf character, with roasted, toasted and grilled notes in a supple envelope. Full of ripe plum and sweet but firm tannins. Full-bodied and deeply satisfying, tasting authentic on the lingering finish. Drink now through 2015.–P.M. • $27 • (6/30/2000) HR • **94**
Châteauneuf-du-Pape 1997: Light and easy, a straightforward, cherry-flavored red, with forest underbrush and mushrooms. Drying tannins.–P.M. • $23 • (12/15/1999) • **75**
Châteauneuf-du-Pape 1996: A polished and refined Châteauneuf, with wet earth, game, leather, plum and roasted nut character. Full-bodied, with refined tannins and a ripe, rich texture. Delicious now, but the massive tannins could use time. Drink through 2008.–P.M. • $25 • (11/15/1998) • **90**
Châteauneuf-du-Pape 1995 • $25 • (10/15/1997) • **80**

Châteauneuf-du-Pape 1994 • $25 • (10/15/1997) • **90**
Châteauneuf-du-Pape 1989 • $18 • (10/15/1991) • **85**
Châteauneuf-du-Pape 1988 • $18 • (10/15/1991) • **83**
Châteauneuf-du-Pape 1986 • $18 • (10/15/1991) • **90**
Châteauneuf-du-Pape 1985 • $18 • (10/15/1991) • **86**
Châteauneuf-du-Pape 1984 • $17 • (11/15/1987) • **91**
Châteauneuf-du-Pape 1983 • $NA • (10/15/1991) • **86**
Châteauneuf-du-Pape 1981 • $NA • (10/15/1991) • **93**
Châteauneuf-du-Pape Cuvée Chantemerle 1995 • $40 • (10/15/1997) • **87**
Châteauneuf-du-Pape Cuvée Chantemerle 1994 • $40 • (10/15/1997) • **83**
Châteauneuf-du-Pape White 1998: Strikes a nice balance between richness and freshness. Offers pretty floral notes and layers of fruit flavors, but also a chestnut wood character. Drink now through 2010.–P.M. • $27 • (6/30/2000) • **88**
Châteauneuf-du-Pape White 1997: With cardboard aromas and flavors, this white is slightly oxidized in its appley character and turns a bit dry on the finish.–P.M. • $23 • (12/15/1999) • **79**
Grenache Châteauneuf-du-Pape 1998: Unique. Starts out with rustic aromas, but shows superb authority midpalate, where it produces great ripe but firm minerally tannins. A smoky, chocolaty, plummy wet earth character leads to a sense of *terroir*. A bit rustic again on the finish, but with immense concentration and uncompromising purity. Best from 2005 through 2030.–P.M. • $32 • (6/30/2000) • **97**

BOSSIS, LAURENT

Muscadet de Sèvre et Maine Sur Lie Château de la Cantrie 1996: A racy and exuberant Loire white at an attractive price, showing loads of citrus, apple and mineral, with spine-tingling acidity that powers the persistent flavors to a lingering finish. A racehorse of a Muscadet that needs to be harnessed by food.–B.S. • $8 • (11/15/1998) • **88**

BOTT-GEYL

Gewürztraminer Alsace Beblenheim 1996: Redolent of quince and pear, this Gewürztraminer is juicy and vibrant in a straightforward, easygoing way. Drink now.–B.S. • $19 • (4/30/1999) • **84**
Gewürztraminer Alsace Grand Cru Furstentum 1996: This Gewürztraminer is dry, sinewy and packed with ripe passion fruit and grapefruit character, but what sets it apart are the racy acidity, balance and harmony missing in so many other '96s. Drink through 2006.–B.S. • $33 • (4/30/1999) • **92**
Gewürztraminer Alsace Grand Cru Sonnenglanz Vieilles Vignes 1996: Ginger and cardamom accents add interest to the ripe quince and grapefruit character in this rich yet structured Gewürztraminer. It's fresh and pure, very concentrated, with a lovely, succulent finish. Drink now through 2003.–B.S. • $33 • (4/30/1999) • **91**
Muscat Alsace Riquewihr 1996: Ripe and round, offering tropical fruit character, richness and citrusy acidity lurking underneath, and a smoky accent. Well structured and focused. Drink now through 2001.–B.S. • $16 • (3/31/1999) • **87**
Pinot Blanc Alsace Beblenheim 1996: Very rich and textured, with underlying acidity, along with maturing flavors of quince, lemon and honey typical of the vintage. Still tight and firm, this needs time to show its stuff. Drink now through 2002.–B.S. • $12 • (3/31/1999) • **86**
Riesling Alsace Burgreben 1996: Lovely apple and floral aromas and flavors, all finely etched into a vibrant, racy structure. Though it's rich and ripe, the acidity dominates now. Be patient. Best from 2002 through 2010.–B.S. • $17 • (3/31/1999) • **88**
Riesling Alsace Grafenreben 1996: Ripe yet austere, this white shows apple and almond aromas and flavors in a firm yet rich structure. The bright acidity will provide longevity and match well with food. Drink through 2007.–B.S. • $20 • (3/31/1999) • **86**
Riesling Alsace Grand Cru Mandelberg 1996: Focused, crisp and elegant, this '96 Riesling shows hints of apricot along with apple and citrus flavors. Fills out nicely midpalate before finishing dry and firm. Drink through 2006.–B.S. • $27 • (3/31/1999) • **88**
Riesling Alsace Grand Cru Schoenenbourg 1996: A touch of sweetness gives this white's peach and smoke flavors a juiciness and balances the racy acidity nicely. It's forward and appealing, with a dry, crisp finish. Drink now through 2004.–B.S. • $30 • (3/31/1999) • **87**
Sylvaner Alsace Beblenheim 1996: Extremely ripe flavors of passion fruit on a sleek framework. Richly textured yet very firmly structured, this is an interesting, well-made Sylvaner. Drink now.–B.S. • $12 • (3/31/1999) • **86**
Tokay Pinot Gris Alsace Beblenheim 1996: Plenty of ripe quince, passion fruit and smoke, along with a fat, glossy texture and surprisingly good acidity that carries the flavors through to a grapefruitlike finish. Drink now through 2004.–B.S. • $19 • (4/30/1999) • **87**
Tokay Pinot Gris Alsace Grand Cru Sonnenglanz 1996: Soft, with obvious sweetness, this is lush and appealing, with a caramel and toffee edge to the baked apple, nutmeg and marmalade flavors, but it misses both the structure of the vintage and the dimensions of the best wines in this category. Drink now through 2002.–B.S. • $33 • (4/30/1999) • **88**

BOUACHON, HENRY

Châteauneuf-du-Pape La Tiare du Pape 1994 • $15 • (11/15/1996) • **84**
Côtes du Rhône Chabrière 1994 • $8 • (10/15/1996) • **82**
Côtes du Rhône-Villages Bellecombes 1994 • $9 • (10/15/1996) • **84**
Crozes-Hermitage La Maurelle 1994 • $11 • (12/15/1996) • **74**

BOUCHARD, PASCAL

Chablis 1997: Straightforward, with modest fruit, but it's clean and zesty albeit a bit green on the finish. P. Bouchard's Chablis are is also distributed under the Tremblay-Bouchard label.–P.M. • $27 • (5/31/1999) • **78**
Chablis 1996 • $21 • (8/31/1997) • **86**
Chablis 1995 • $NA • (8/31/1996) • **78**
Chablis Blanchot 1997: Minerally concentration is superb in this full-bodied, racy yet ripe and oaky beauty, delivering layers of pear, tropical and smoky subtleties that burst like little geysers on the palate, infusing the senses. Best from 2005 through 2015.–P.M. • $60 • (5/31/1999) • **93**
Chablis Blanchot 1996 • $44 • (5/31/1998) • **91**
Chablis Blanchot 1995 • $37 • (6/15/1997) • **83**
Chablis Fourchaume 1996 • $29 • (5/31/1998) • **83**
Chablis Fourchaume 1995 • $NA • (8/31/1996) • **84**
Chablis Fourchaume Vieilles Vignes Grande Réserve 1997: Opulent, ripe and well made, offering loads of character, with clean and pure pear tart, tropical, lemon and honey elements. A bit astringent on the finish, but should improve with cellaring. Drink now through 2007.–P.M. • $52 • (5/31/1999) • **85**
Chablis Les Clos 1997: Tight and firm, spiced up with toast, piecrust, lemon and ripe fruit flavors, this is a showy, international style Chablis that's a bit hot and astringent on the finish. Best from 2005 through 2015.–P.M. • $60 • (5/31/1999) • **88**
Chablis Les Clos 1996 • $44 • (5/31/1998) • **90**
Chablis Mont de Milieu 1996 • $29 • (5/31/1998) • **86**
Chablis Mont de Milieu 1995 • $23 • (6/15/1997) • **65**
Chablis Mont de Milieu Vieilles Vignes Grande Réserve 1997: Pure and vibrant, but also nicely endowed with ripe fruit, and the lemon, gooseberry, floral, rose petal complexity gives it a nice touch. Well made, but worth cellaring a bit. Drink through 2005.–P.M. • $52 • (5/31/1999) • **90**
Chablis Montmains 1996 • $29 • (5/31/1998) • **88**
Chablis Montmains 1995 • $23 • (6/15/1997) • **73**
Chablis Montmains Vieilles Vignes Grande Réserve 1997: A bit easy, with butter and only a decent concentration of fruit, it turns somewhat bitter on the short finish.–P.M. • $52 • (5/31/1999) • **78**
Chablis Vaudésir 1997: Vibrant yet quite opulent, this is a beautiful wine—packed with earthy compexity, mineral, seaweed, nuts and dried herbs. Give it time to smooth out. Best from 2003 through 2008.–P.M. • $60 • (5/31/1999) • **89**
Chablis Vaudésir 1996 • $44 • (5/31/1998) • **93**
Chablis Vieilles Vignes Grande Réserve 1997: Super quality for a straight Chablis. Lovely in every respect, delivering a rich terroir-driven character with honey, mineral, cedar and spice complexity that almost vaults it to the *premier cru* level. Drink now through 2002.–P.M. • $30 • (5/31/1999) • **90**
Petit Chablis 1996 • $20 • (8/31/1997) • **81**

BOUCHARD, PHILIPPE

Corton-Charlemagne 1997: Malic-lactic and buttersotch notes dominate the aromas, but it's fabulous, round, ripe and sweet-tasting, with layers of toasted oak, pure pineapple, lemon, honey and mineral. Harmonious, juicy finish. Drink now through 2010.–P.M. • $68 • (5/31/1999) • **92**
Mâcon-Villages 1997: Woody, with a distinct old-barrel, wet cardboard character. Astringent finish.–P.M. • $9 • (5/31/1999) • **70**
Meursault 1997: Buttery and very oaky, this heavyhanded Meursault has only modest fruit.–P.M. • $40 • (5/31/1999) • **76**
Pouilly-Fuissé 1997: Superripe but a bit dull, this tastes a bit of cooked pears, even more so on the finish where it tastes of pear spirit.–P.M. • $20 • (5/31/1999) • **73**

BOUCHARD, PHILIPPE

Puligny-Montrachet 1997: A bit heavy in the wood department, showing mocha, spice and cedar before releasing fruit notes. Astringent, hot finish.–P.M. • $42 • (5/31/1999) • **79**

BOUCHARD, ROMAIN

Côtes du Rhône-Villages Valréas 1995: Lean style, with some dried herbs and cassis bush flavors, but also enough raspberry and black currant to make it interesting. Of light to medium body, it sparkles with juicy life on the finish. Food should soften this vibrant wine. Drink now.–P.M. • $12 • (11/15/1998) • **82**

BOUCHARD-AINE & FILS

Beaujolais-Villages La Vigneronne 1995 • $12 • (4/30/1997) • **84**
Bourgogne White Le Chardonnay de Chardonnay 1995 • $15 • (1/31/1998) • **76**
Bourgogne White Les Vendangeurs 1995 • $14 • (1/31/1997) • **83**
Chambertin-Clos de Bèze 1959 • $NA • (8/31/1990) • **84**
Chambertin-Clos de Bèze Domaine Marion 1989 • $NA • (1/31/1992) • **88**
Echézeaux 1996: Masculine and severe. This dense, massive red has black raspberry and floral aromas and flavors, moderate acidity and is saturated with thick, ripe tannins. Best from 2002 through 2008.–B.S. • $80 • (9/30/1998) • **92**
Gevrey-Chambertin 1996: Lovely wine, pure and clean, with fresh red- and blackberry character, supple tannins and good depth in the earth and mineral department. Has grip on the finish, but its balance and acidity suggest it should improve with age. Best from 2003.–P.M. • $32 • (9/30/1998) • **88**
Mâcon Dry Réserve 1995 • $12 • (1/31/1997) • **78**
Merlot Vin de Pays de l'Aude NV • $5 • (6/30/1990) • **72**
Meursault 1995 • $31 • (2/28/1997) • **84**
Pommard 1996: Pungent mineral, forest floor and smoke accents complement cherry flavors. Tough now, with modest concentration but not the density of flavor to carry the tannins long-term. Best from 2001.–B.S. • $32 • (9/30/1998) • **84**
Pouilly-Fuissé Dry Réserve 1995 • $26 • (1/31/1997) • **82**
Puligny-Montrachet 1995 • $36 • (2/28/1997) • **84**

BOUCHARD PERE & FILS

Aloxe-Corton 1992 • $30 • (12/15/1994) • **82**
Aloxe-Corton 1991 • $30 • (1/31/1994) • **84**
Aloxe-Corton 1990 • $30 • (12/15/1992) • **88**
Aloxe-Corton 1989 • $36 • (1/31/1992) • **87**
Auxey-Duresses White 1996 • $22 • (5/31/1998) • **87**
Bâtard-Montrachet 1996: Well balanced and showing great, silky finesse. Vibrant and fruity, with an earthy, wet soil, mineral-laden quality that is very appealing. Medium-bodied, ripe and lush, with tropical, honey and pear flavors. Seductive, slightly toasted finish. Drink through 2005.–P.M. • $150 • (8/31/1998) • **91**
Beaujolais Nouveau 1999: Firm and juicy, this shows as much structure as fruit, with notes of black cherry and plum. Less generous on its own; better with food. Drink now.–T.M. • $9 • (1/01/2000) • **82**
Beaujolais-Villages Le Chamville 1997: A peppery nose is followed by moderately intense earth and cherry flavors with hints of dried herbs. It's lean, finishes on the astringent side.–B.S. • $12 • (10/15/1999) • **79**
Beaujolais-Villages Le Chamville 1996: Floral and sandalwood notes add interest to this harmonious red; the cherry flavors are fresh and the wine shows a good balance of acid and tannins. Drink now.–T.M. • $12 • (8/31/1998) • **84**
Beaujolais-Villages Le Chamville 1993 • $10 • (6/30/1994) • **79**
Beaune Grèves Vigne de l'Enfant Jésus 1997: A big, soft, round wine, with slightly cooked plum and fig flavors. Forward in appeal and a bit cooked on the finish. Drink now through 2002.–B.S. • $88 • (9/30/1999) • **81**
Beaune Grèves Vigne de l'Enfant Jésus 1996: Spicy berry flavors and good balance mark this straightforward, satisfying red. Drink now through 2001.–B.S. • $45 Ⓐ • (9/30/1998) • **82**
Beaune Grèves Vigne de l'Enfant Jésus 1995 • $63 • (11/15/1997) • **86**
Beaune Grèves Vigne de l'Enfant Jésus 1994 • $49 • (11/15/1996) • **85**
Beaune Grèves Vigne de l'Enfant Jésus 1993 • $50 • (11/15/1995) • **82**

Key: SS—Spectator Selection. CS—Cellar Selection. HR—Highly Recommended. $NA—Price not available. (BT)—Barrel tasting. Ⓐ—Auction Price.
For a key to the tasters' initials, see "How to Use These Listings."
Dates in parentheses represent the issues in which the ratings were published.

Beaune Grèves Vigne de l'Enfant Jésus 1992 • $40 • (10/31/1994) • **86**
Beaune Grèves Vigne de l'Enfant Jésus 1991 • $48 • (2/28/1995) • **88**
Beaune Grèves Vigne de l'Enfant Jésus 1990 • $37 Ⓐ • (2/28/1995) • **88**
Beaune Grèves Vigne de l'Enfant Jésus 1989 • $38 Ⓐ • (2/28/1995) • **91**
Beaune Grèves Vigne de l'Enfant Jésus 1988 • $59 • (2/28/1995) • **85**
Beaune Grèves Vigne de l'Enfant Jésus 1987 • $38 • (2/28/1995) • **86**
Beaune Grèves Vigne de l'Enfant Jésus 1986 • $47 • (2/28/1995) • **79**
Beaune Grèves Vigne de l'Enfant Jésus 1985 • $61 • (2/28/1995) • **89**
Beaune Grèves Vigne de l'Enfant Jésus 1983 • $34 • (2/28/1995) • **82**
Beaune Le Clos de la Mousse 1997: Penetrating kirsch and earth aromas are augmented by a licorice note in this sinewy, tannic '97 red. Lovely fruit. Drink now through 2003.–B.S. • $40 • (9/30/1999) • **85**
Beaune Le Clos de la Mousse 1996: Herbaceous and tough, not one of the vintage's more pleasurable offerings.–B.S. • $37 • (9/30/1998) • **78**
Beaune Le Clos de la Mousse 1995 • $33 • (11/15/1997) • **82**
Beaune Le Clos de la Mousse 1994 • $28 • (11/15/1996) • **79**
Beaune Le Clos de la Mousse 1993 • $28 • (11/15/1995) • **85**
Beaune Le Clos de la Mousse 1992 • $25 • (12/15/1994) • **81**
Beaune Le Clos de la Mousse 1991 • $28 • (1/31/1994) • **79**
Beaune Le Clos de la Mousse 1986 • $33 • (7/31/1988) • **78**
Beaune Les Marconnets 1994 • $29 • (11/15/1996) • **79**
Beaune Les Marconnets 1992 • $27 • (12/15/1994) • **79**
Beaune Les Marconnets 1991 • $30 • (1/31/1994) • **74**
Beaune Les Marconnets 1990 • $28 • (12/15/1992) • **93**
Beaune Les Marconnets 1989 • $39 • (1/31/1992) • **90**
Beaune Les Marconnets 1986 • $24 • (7/31/1988) • **83**
Beaune Les Marconnets 1985 • $35 • (1/31/1989) • **89**
Beaune Les Teurons 1993 • $28 • (11/15/1995) • **86**
Beaune Les Teurons 1991 • $29 • (1/31/1994) • **80**
Beaune Les Teurons 1990 • $30 • (12/15/1992) • **84**
Beaune Les Teurons 1986 • $32 • (7/31/1988) • **81**
Beaune Les Teurons 1985 • $35 • (1/31/1989) • **85**
Beaune Les Teurons 1983 • $21 • (9/15/1986) • **71**
Beaune White Clos St.-Landry 1997: At first whiff this is very clean, but while it's fairly round, there's a slight astringent note creeping up along the pear and green apple character in this medium-bodied white.–P.M. • $63 • (5/31/1999) • **77**
Beaune White Clos St.-Landry 1996 • $50 • (5/31/1998) • **90**
Beaune White Clos St.-Landry 1995 • $50 • (8/31/1997) • **89**
Beaune White Premier Cru 1996 • $38 • (5/31/1998) • **92**
Beaune White Premier Cru 1995 • $38 • (8/31/1997) • **92**
Bonnes Mares 1997: This lovely '97 offers a round and ripe mouthfeel, with balanced intensity and focused flavors of red berry and blackberry. The clean, lingering, natural-tasting finish makes it stand out in this heavy vintage. Drink now through 2005.–P.M. • $131 • (9/30/1999) • **90**
Bonnes Mares 1996: Very tough, impenetrable at this early stage, showing an unusually hard edge for a '96. But as uncompromising as it is, you have to admire the *terroir*. Tastes of mineral, earth, iron, smoked bacon, coats the palate with rich but extremely firm tannins. Should be a beauty with age; will perhaps rate much higher at its peak. Serious winemaking at work. Best after 2010.–P.M. • $99 • (9/30/1998) • **90**
Bonnes Mares 1995 • $89 • (11/15/1997) • **92**
Bourgogne La Vignée 1992 • $NA • (12/15/1994) • **70**
Bourgogne White 1996 • $12 • (5/31/1998) • **80**
Chambertin 1994 • $100 • (11/15/1996) • **76**
Chambertin 1990 • $NA • (12/15/1992) • **88**
Chambertin 1986 • $78 • (7/31/1988) • **81**
Chambertin-Clos de Bèze 1996: Superb '96. Firm, oriented more to earth than to fruit, showing layers of mineral and iron, with some hard tannins that will need time to soften. Of medium body, it has good intensity of *terroir* along with the blackberry flavors. Best after 2005.–P.M. • $142 • (9/30/1998) • **92**
Chambertin-Clos de Bèze 1989 • $92 • (1/31/1992) • **92**
Chambertin-Clos de Bèze 1988 • $82 • (4/30/1991) • **89**
Chambolle-Musigny 1997: Tastes a bit oaky, with dry wood tannins dominating the texture. An extracted style, with cherry and blackberry notes and a tough, chewy finish.–P.M. • $55 • (9/30/1999) • **78**
Chambolle-Musigny 1996: A bit green and herbal, of medium body, this tastes fairly round but turns astringent on the finish. Drink now.–P.M. • $42 • (9/30/1998) • **76**
Chambolle-Musigny 1994 • $35 • (11/15/1996) • **74**
Chambolle-Musigny 1993 • $36 • (11/15/1995) • **88**
Chambolle-Musigny 1992 • $32 • (12/15/1994) • **79**
Chambolle-Musigny 1990 • $NA • (12/15/1992) • **86**
Chambolle-Musigny 1986 • $29 • (7/31/1988) • **73**
Chassagne-Montrachet 1996 • $39 • (5/31/1998) • **90**
Chassagne-Montrachet Red 1993 • $25 • (11/15/1995) • **87**

Chassagne-Montrachet Red 1990 • $21 • (12/15/1992) • **80**
Chassagne-Montrachet Red 1988 • $22 • (4/30/1991) • **85**
Châteauneuf-du-Pape 1990 • $16 • (4/15/1993) • **83**
Châteauneuf-du-Pape 1985 • $11 • (9/30/1987) • **82**
Chevalier-Montrachet 1996 • $88 Ⓐ • (5/31/1998) • **96**
Chevalier-Montrachet 1995 • $150 • (8/31/1997) • **87**
Chevalier-Montrachet La Cabotte 1997: Defines elegance and subtlety, but lacks a bit of power and freshness. Shows floral, pear, honey, vanilla bean and citrus notes and natural-tasting acidity. Best from 2003 through 2007.–P.M. • $350 • (9/30/1999) • **89**
Clos de la Roche 1989 • $NA • (1/31/1992) • **89**
Clos Vougeot 1996: Built like a rock, but with the deep fruit to balance. Clean, pure and well made, this full-bodied red presents a firm backbone of tannins and cold fruit for now, suggesting it's built for the long term. Magnificent red- and blackberry flavors zoom across the palate, delivering mineral-laden and earth-oriented spicy notes that will need time to integrate with the tough, woodsy finish. As big as it is, this wine doesn't tire the palate.–P.M. • $88 • (9/30/1998) • **96**
Clos Vougeot 1995 • $80 • (11/15/1997) • **88**
Clos Vougeot 1959 • $NA • (8/31/1990) • **85**
Corton-Charlemagne 1997: A bit earthy, with racy lemon pie, passion fruit and toast notes. Elegant and medium-bodied, with a focused finish. Drink now through 2003.–P.M. • $130 • (9/30/1999) • **89**
Corton-Charlemagne 1996 • $110 • (5/31/1998) • **95**
Corton-Charlemagne 1995 • $110 • (8/31/1997) • **90**
Corton Le Corton 1997: A very nice red, showing a ripe purity of black fruit, a smooth texture, supple tannins and a lingering finish. Drink now through 2007.–P.M. • $88 • (9/30/1999) • **88**
Corton Le Corton 1996: Ripe and juicy, of medium body, this delivers layers of red berry and spice flavors. A good dose of fine-textured tannins gives structure. Lovely delicate fruit, but not very complex. Not as good as when tasted from barrel. Best after 2003.–P.M. • $51 Ⓐ • (9/30/1998) • **85**
Corton Le Corton 1995 • $63 • (11/15/1997) • **85**
Corton Le Corton 1992 • $38 • (10/31/1994) • **88**
Corton Le Corton 1991 • $46 • (1/31/1994) • **77**
Corton Le Corton 1990 • $50 • (12/15/1992) • **91**
Corton Le Corton 1989 • $79 • (1/31/1992) • **92**
Corton Le Corton 1988 • $77 • (3/31/1991) • **91**
Corton Le Corton 1986 • $47 • (7/31/1988) • **85**
Corton Le Corton 1983 • $37 • (9/15/1986) • **83**
Côte de Beaune-Villages 1982 • $19 • (5/16/1984) SS • **88**
Côte de Beaune-Villages Clos des Topes Bizot 1983 • $22 • (9/15/1986) • **82**
Côte de Nuits-Villages 1990 • $NA • (12/15/1992) • **78**
Côtes du Rhône 1989 • $9 • (7/15/1991) • **82**
Côtes du Rhône Le Chamville 1993 • $10 • (11/15/1995) • **78**
Echézeaux 1997: An advanced, quickly maturing Pinot, with mushroom, mocha and toast notes. A bit dry on the finish.–P.M. • $106 • (9/30/1999) • **76**
Echézeaux 1991 • $54 • (1/31/1994) • **89**
Echézeaux 1990 • $42 • (10/31/1992) • **89**
Echézeaux 1989 • $62 • (1/31/1992) • **88**
Gevrey-Chambertin 1997: There's modest fruit in this rather lean, tart-tasting Pinot.–P.M. • $38 • (9/30/1999) • **75**
Gevrey-Chambertin 1993 • $29 • (11/15/1995) • **86**
Gevrey-Chambertin 1992 • $27 • (12/15/1994) • **79**
Gevrey-Chambertin 1982 • $18 • (6/16/1984) • **80**
Gevrey-Chambertin Les Cazetiers 1996: Wonderful, showing explosive, pure and exciting aromas. Medium-bodied, it tastes of fantastic terroir, with wet earth, mineral, toast and clean red berry character. Long, smoky, crisp finish could use some cellaring. Best from 2005 through 2012.–P.M. • $75 • (5/15/1999) • **92**
La Romanée Château de Vosne-Romanée 1996: Monolithic and rock-solid at this stage, packed with dense black fruit flavors and earth notes wrapped in a thick coating of tannins that need time to integrate. The sweet fruit wins out in the end. Best from 2005 through 2012.–P.M. • $180 Ⓐ • (9/30/1998) • **90**
La Romanée Château de Vosne-Romanée 1995 • $210 • (11/15/1997) HR • **95**
La Romanée Château de Vosne-Romanée 1994 • $160 • (11/15/1996) • **94**
La Romanée Château de Vosne-Romanée 1993 • $82 Ⓐ • (11/15/1995) • **90**
La Romanée Château de Vosne-Romanée 1992 • $118 • (12/15/1994) • **85**
La Romanée Château de Vosne-Romanée 1986 • $200 • (7/31/1988) • **91**
Mâcon-Villages Le Chamville 1996 • $13 • (8/31/1997) • **73**
Meursault 1997: Tough and chewy, offering nice tropical, lemon and honey notes, but the oak dominates on the drying finish. Drink now through 2003.–P.M. • $45 • (5/31/1999) • **83**
Meursault 1996 • $35 • (5/31/1998) • **90**
Meursault Genevrières 1997: Very pretty, clean, ripe and balanced, showing lovely pear, tropical, toast and spice flavors that cascade to a generous, smooth and absolutely delicious finish. Drink now through 2005.–P.M. • $88 • (5/31/1999) • **91**
Meursault Genevrières 1996: Very impressive. Subtle, with the aromas cleverly disguised for now, it really kicks into high gear on the palate, showing amazingly silky, creamlike texture. Full-bodied, with loads of lemon, pear and vanilla-flavored mineral character, this is an exciting wine that's tempting now, will be better with cellaring. Best from 2003.–P.M. • $66 • (8/31/1998) • **93**
Meursault Genevrières 1995 • $66 • (5/31/1997) • **91**
Meursault Perrières 1997: Round and soft, medium-bodied and showing lemon, toasted oak, green apple character, padding the taste buds with some fatness but not much depth. Better than previously reviewed. Drink now through 2005.–P.M. • $90 • (9/30/1999) • **81**
Monthélie Clos Les Champs Fulliot 1996: Red currants and herbaceous flavors mark this lean '96. The tough tannins dominate the modest concentration and leave the finish dry. Best from 2000.–B.S. • $30 • (9/30/1998) • **78**
Montrachet 1996: Very supple and smooth, velvety and even a bit soft, with ripe, lush fruit texture, pear, honey, and melon. Balanced and seductive for trying upon release, there is enough vibrant acidity for improvement in the cellar. Rated higher as a barrel sample; seemed more impressive, muscular and firm. Tasted twice, with consistent notes. Drink now through 2005.–P.M. • $320 • (8/31/1998) • **90**
Montrachet 1995 • $320 • (8/31/1997) • **92**
Nuits-St.-Georges 1983 • $21 • (9/15/1986) • **68**
Nuits-St.-Georges Domaine du Clos St.-Marc 1997: Very ripe aromas and flavors of chocolate and plum, with roundness, moderate concentration and firm but not aggressive tannins. Drink now through 2002.–B.S. • $67 • (9/30/1999) • **88**
Nuits-St.-Georges Domaine du Clos St.-Marc 1996: Elegant, with good concentration and flesh, slightly herbaceous aromas and flavors, ending with dry tannins. Best from 2002.–B.S. • $55 • (9/30/1998) • **86**
Nuits-St.-Georges Domaine du Clos St.-Marc 1995 • $53 • (11/15/1997) • **72**
Nuits-St.-Georges Domaine du Clos St.-Marc 1994 • $40 • (11/15/1996) • **79**
Nuits-St.-Georges Domaine du Clos St.-Marc 1993 • $47 • (11/15/1995) • **82**
Nuits-St.-Georges Domaine du Clos St.-Marc 1992 • $43 • (12/15/1994) • **73**
Nuits-St.-Georges Domaine du Clos St.-Marc 1991 • $45 • (1/31/1994) • **75**
Nuits-St.-Georges Domaine du Clos St.-Marc 1989 • $59 • (1/31/1992) • **89**
Nuits-St.-Georges Domaine du Clos St.-Marc 1985 • $53 • (2/28/1989) • **87**
Nuits-St.-Georges Domaine du Clos St.-Marc 1983 • $33 • (9/15/1986) • **74**
Nuits-St.-Georges La Richemone 1989 • $NA • (1/31/1992) • **89**
Nuits-St.-Georges Les Argillières 1990 • $31 • (12/15/1992) • **86**
Nuits-St.-Georges Les Cailles 1997: Round and supple, with a core of bark, cherry, and toasted oak. Quite intense and slightly hot, but sleek on the finish. Drink now through 2002.–P.M. • $67 • (9/30/1999) • **87**
Nuits-St.-Georges Les Cailles 1959 • $90 • (8/31/1990) • **87**
Pommard 1994 • $27 • (11/15/1996) • **75**
Pommard 1992 • $35 • (12/15/1994) • **79**
Pommard 1988 • $37 • (4/30/1991) HR • **90**
Pommard 1983 • $23 • (9/15/1986) • **74**
Pommard Clos du Pavillon 1989 • $NA • (1/31/1992) • **92**
Pommard Premier Cru 1996: Fresh and pure, a vibrant wine that cleanses the palate thanks to good acidity and laser-sharp red- and blackberry and wet earth flavors. Of medium body, it's succulent on the zesty finish. Best After 2003.–P.M. • $48 • (9/30/1998) • **88**
Pommard Premier Cru 1990 • $39 • (12/15/1992) • **94**
Pommard Premier Cru 1988 • $53 • (3/31/1991) • **89**
Pommard Premier Cru 1986 • $41 • (7/31/1988) • **87**
Pouilly-Fuissé 1995 • $22 • (5/31/1997) • **86**
Puligny-Montrachet 1996 • $39 • (5/31/1998) • **89**
Puligny-Montrachet Les Chalumeaux 1996 • $50 • (5/31/1998) • **91**
Puligny-Montrachet Les Folatières 1996 • $55 • (5/31/1998) • **90**
Puligny-Montrachet Les Folatières 1995 • $55 • (5/31/1997) • **82**
Puligny-Montrachet Les Pucelles 1997: Starts out seductive, with ripe fruit coating the palate, but it turns a bit overripe and cooked. A medium-bodied wine to drink right away, chilled.–P.M. • $93 • (9/30/1999) • **85**
Puligny-Montrachet Les Pucelles 1996 • $68 • (5/31/1998) • **92**
Puligny-Montrachet Les Pucelles 1995 • $68 • (5/31/1997) • **72**
Rully 1996 • $17 • (5/31/1998) • **84**
Savigny-lès-Beaune 1989 • $29 • (1/31/1992) • **82**
Savigny-lès-Beaune Les Lavières 1990 • $NA • (12/15/1992) • **82**
Savigny-lès-Beaune Les Lavières 1988 • $29 • (4/30/1991) • **83**
Savigny-lès-Beaune Les Lavières 1986 • $25 • (7/31/1988) • **78**
Volnay 1992 • $NA • (12/15/1994) • **79**
Volnay Caillerets Ancienne Cuvée Carnot 1997: A rather crisp wine of medium ripeness, turning tough and showing modest cherry notes.–P.M. • $55 • (9/30/1999) • **78**

BOUCHARD PERE & FILS

Volnay Caillerets Ancienne Cuvée Carnot 1995 • $44 • (11/15/1997) • **85**
Volnay Caillerets Ancienne Cuvée Carnot 1994 • $37 • (11/15/1996) • **78**
Volnay Caillerets Ancienne Cuvée Carnot 1993 • $37 • (11/15/1995) • **83**
Volnay Caillerets Ancienne Cuvée Carnot 1992 • $29 • (10/31/1994) • **85**
Volnay Caillerets Ancienne Cuvée Carnot 1991 • $37 • (1/31/1994) • **85**
Volnay Caillerets Ancienne Cuvée Carnot 1990 • $37 • (12/15/1992) • **90**
Volnay Caillerets Ancienne Cuvée Carnot 1989 • $52 • (2/29/1992) CS • **94**
Volnay Caillerets Ancienne Cuvée Carnot 1986 • $34 • (7/31/1988) • **83**
Volnay Frémiets Clos de la Rougeotte 1994 • $35 • (11/15/1996) • **79**
Volnay Frémiets Clos de la Rougeotte 1993 • $35 • (11/15/1995) • **84**
Volnay Frémiets Clos de la Rougeotte 1992 • $38 • (12/15/1994) • **82**
Volnay Frémiets Clos de la Rougeotte 1990 • $NA • (12/15/1992) • **86**
Volnay Frémiets Clos de la Rougeotte 1985 • $35 • (1/31/1989) • **88**
Volnay Taille Pieds 1992 • $32 • (12/15/1994) • **82**
Volnay Taille Pieds 1991 • $34 • (1/31/1994) • **78**
Volnay Taille Pieds 1990 • $50 • (12/15/1992) • **92**
Volnay Taille Pieds 1989 • $48 • (1/31/1992) • **88**
Volnay Taille Pieds 1988 • $47 • (3/31/1991) • **87**
Vosne-Romanée Aux Raignots 1994 • $48 • (11/15/1996) • **85**
Vosne-Romanée Aux Raignots 1993 • $51 • (11/15/1995) • **88**
Vosne-Romanée Aux Raignots 1992 • $40 • (10/31/1994) • **89**
Vosne-Romanée Aux Raignots 1991 • $51 • (1/31/1994) • **80**
Vosne-Romanée Aux Raignots 1990 • $53 • (12/15/1992) • **85**
Vosne-Romanée Aux Raignots 1989 • $55 • (1/31/1992) • **93**
Vosne-Romanée Aux Raignots 1986 • $50 • (7/31/1988) • **89**
Vosne-Romanée Aux Raignots 1985 • $51 • (2/28/1989) • **90**
Vosne-Romanée Aux Raignots Château de Vosne-Romanée 1996: Sleek, yet packed with ripe flavors, delivering a hedonistic, silky mouthfeel. The floral, spice, cassis and blackberry aromas and flavors fly off in all directions, then come together with tender but massive tannins and good acidity on the long finish.–P.M. • $73 • (9/30/1998) • **89**

BOUCHE PERE & FILS

Brut Blanc de Blancs Champagne NV: Ripe in flavor, soft in texture, with light fresh fruit accents and a clean finish. Drink now. • $36 • (10/31/1999) • **87**
Brut Champagne Cuvée 2000 NV: Round and well balanced by bright acidity, this has plenty of citrus and apple flavors without a lot of depth or complexity. Drink now.–B.S. • $80 • (11/30/1999) • **86**
Brut Champagne Cuvée Réservée NV • $20 • (1/31/1992) • **87**
Brut Champagne Grande Réserve 1990: A lot more than bubbles. This is smooth, mellow, full-bodied and packed with flavors of ripe pear and toasted almond that linger on the finish. Drink now through 2002. • $60 • (11/15/1999) • **93**

BOUCHOT, DOMAINE DU

Pouilly-Fumé 1997: Light, simple and clean, this white shows the herb and citrus character of the region. Will match well with lighter dishes. Drink now.–T.M. • $14 • (6/30/1999) • **83**

BOUGRIER, JEAN-CLAUDE

Vouvray 1997: Aromas of flowers and herbs segue into honey flavors in this rich, broad white, whose slight sweetness is deftly balanced by lively acidity. Subtle and lingering.–B.S. • $9 • (11/15/1998) • **85**
Vouvray 1996 • $9 • (5/31/1998) • **85**

BOUREE PERE & FILS

Beaune Les Epenotes 1989 • $30 • (1/31/1992) • **91**
Beaune Les Epenotes 1987 • $35 • (6/15/1990) • **88**
Bonnes Mares 1985 • $85 • (5/31/1988) • **91**
Bourgogne 1988 • $15 • (3/31/1992) • **73**
Chambertin 1990 • $85 • (12/15/1992) • **84**
Chambertin 1987 • $100 • (5/31/1990) • **90**
Chambertin 1985 • $113 • (5/31/1988) • **92**
Chambolle-Musigny 1987 • $44 • (6/15/1990) • **82**
Chambolle-Musigny Les Charmes 1987 • $56 • (6/15/1990) • **82**
Charmes-Chambertin 1994 • $NA • (11/15/1996) • **70**
Charmes-Chambertin 1988 • $75 • (3/31/1991) • **89**
Charmes-Chambertin 1987 • $66 • (5/31/1990) • **87**
Charmes-Chambertin 1985 • $68 • (5/31/1988) • **88**
Clos de la Roche 1990 • $70 • (12/15/1992) • **90**
Clos de la Roche 1989 • $65 • (1/31/1992) • **94**
Clos de la Roche 1988 • $85 • (3/31/1991) • **91**
Clos de la Roche 1987 • $86 • (6/15/1990) • **85**
Côte de Nuits-Villages 1994 • $NA • (11/15/1996) • **77**
Gevrey-Chambertin 1989 • $35 • (1/31/1992) • **85**
Gevrey-Chambertin La Justice 1988 • $30 Ⓐ • (3/31/1992) • **78**
Gevrey-Chambertin La Justice 1985 • $65 Ⓐ • (5/31/1988) • **85**
Gevrey-Chambertin Le Clos St.-Jacques 1990 • $60 • (12/15/1992) • **90**
Gevrey-Chambertin Le Clos St.-Jacques 1987 • $56 • (5/31/1990) • **86**
Gevrey-Chambertin Les Cazetiers 1994 • $NA • (11/15/1996) • **80**
Gevrey-Chambertin Les Cazetiers 1987 • $66 • (5/31/1990) • **80**
Gevrey-Chambertin Les Cazetiers 1985 • $67 • (5/31/1988) • **91**
Latricières-Chambertin 1959 • $NA • (8/31/1990) • **98**
Morey-St.-Denis 1987 • $35 • (5/15/1990) • **74**
Nuits-St.-Georges Les Vaucrains 1985 • $68 • (5/31/1988) • **93**
Santenay Les Gravières 1985 • $30 • (5/31/1988) • **88**
Vosne-Romanée 1987 • $44 • (7/15/1990) • **68**

BOURGEOIS, HENRI

Pouilly-Fumé 1998: Flavors of gooseberry, smoke and citrus mix well in this medium-bodied white. Green apple and spice notes chime in on the finish. Drink now.–K.M. • $10 • (5/15/2000) • **84**
Pouilly-Fumé 1996 • $15 • (2/28/1998) • **89**
Pouilly-Fumé La Demoiselle de Bourgeois 1997: Has richness and depth, with round flavors of pear and melon. Dry on the palate but not tart, restrained yet balanced, this muscular wine will match well with fish and poultry. Drink now through 2003.–T.M. • $19 • (6/30/1999) • **86**
Quincy Clos des Victoires 1998: Fairly assertive, with lively flavors of green apple and green plum. Almond notes on the finish. Drink now.–K.M. • $12 • (5/15/2000) • **83**
Sancerre Etienne Henri 1996: Alluring toast and vanilla flavors suggest oak aging on this ripe, vibrant white and give it almost a California profile. It has plenty of lemon and melon flavors to keep it lively, and will match with light dishes. Drink now through 2002.–T.M. • $28 • (6/30/1999) • **91**
Sancerre Grande Réserve 1997: Both complex and refreshing, with delicate aromas of herbs, mineral and apples, and bright fruit on the palate. Fairly light-bodied. Would work as an aperitif and with lighter dishes. Drink now.–T.M. • $14 • (9/15/1998) • **86**
Sancerre Grande Réserve 1996 • $15 • (5/31/1998) • **86**
Sancerre La Bourgeoise 1996: Atypical but intriguing. A new-wave wine with class, this rich white marries round, sweet vanilla and toast flavors from new oak with ripe peach and pear. Has enough acidity to keep it lively, with a lovely spicy note on the finish. Drink now through 2003.–T.M. • $19 • (6/30/1999) • **90**
Sancerre La Bourgeoise 1990 • $15 • (12/15/1995) • **83**
Sancerre Le MD de Bourgeois 1997: Soft and round for a Sancerre, this white offers ripe flavors of pear and melon, with a light citrusy acidity that keeps it lively enough for food. Hints of herb emerge on the finish. Drink now.–T.M. • $18 • (6/30/1999) • **84**
Sancerre Le MD de Bourgeois 1996: Ripe and bold, this full-bodied white mingles pear and even pineapple flavors with lemon-lime acidity and light herb notes to offer power and vibrancy. Still firm and fresh. Drink now through 2002.–T.M. • $18 • (6/30/1999) • **89**
Sancerre Les Baronnes 1998: Pungent, vibrant and mouthwatering, this lively white opens with textbook aromas of gooseberry and new hay. Follows with intense mineral, citrus and herb flavors and a racy structure. A great shellfish wine. Drink now through 2001.–T.M. • $14 • (6/30/1999) • **89**
Sancerre Les Baronnes 1997: This firm white isn't giving much, and it's dominated by tart green apple and grapefruit flavors. But the thick texture and hints of herb and mineral may fill out with time. Drink through 2003.–T.M. • $14 • (6/30/1999) • **83**
Sancerre Red La Bourgeoise 1995 • $22 • (5/31/1998) • **84**
Sancerre Red La Bourgeoise 1990 • $22 • (5/31/1998) • **82**
Sancerre Red Les Baronnes 1997: This light, soft red offers pretty, round spice and berry flavors but without harsh tannins. Good match for fish dishes. Drink now through 2002.–T.M. • $14 • (6/30/1999) • **82**
Sancerre Rosé Les Bonnes Bouches 1996 • $20 • (5/31/1998) • **80**

Key: SS—Spectator Selection. CS—Cellar Selection. HR—Highly Recommended. $NA—Price not available. (BT)—Barrel tasting. Ⓐ—Auction Price. For a key to the tasters' initials, see "How to Use These Listings."
Dates in parentheses represent the issues in which the ratings were published.

BOURGEON, PAUL

Mâcon-Villages 1996 • $11 • (5/31/1998) • **86**
Mâcon-Villages 1995 • $NA • (8/31/1996) • **71**

BOURGEON, RENE

Bourgogne Côte Chalonnaise Les Pourrières 1996: Fresh and crisp, with cassis bush, dried herbs and wet earth character, this remains a tough customer, with dry tannins despite its fruity side.–P.M. • $NA • (9/30/1998) • **79**
Bourgogne Les Pourrières 1995 • $14 • (11/15/1997) • **78**
Givry 1996: Very nice. Ripe yet elegant, offering pure red berry flavors in a firm, medium-bodied package with spice, toasted bread and a plummy blackberry complexity. Needs time. Best from 2005 through 2012.–P.M. • $NA • (5/15/1999) • **90**
Givry 1995 • $18 • (11/15/1997) • **82**
Givry La Baraude 1995 • $20 • (11/15/1997) • **78**
Givry White Clos de la Brûlée 1996 • $NA • (5/31/1998) • **75**
Givry White Clos de la Brûlée 1995 • $NA • (5/31/1997) • **88**

BOURGNEUF, CHATEAU

Pomerol 1999: Well done. Black color. Intense aromas of black licorice, coffee and dried herbs. Full-bodied, with velety tannins and a long, chewy finish. Tiny bit of hollowness.–J.S. • $NA • (1/01/2000) (BT) • **85-89**
Pomerol 1998: Mouthpuckering young wine. Black-colored, with intense crushed grape and wet earth character. Full-bodied, very chewy, with masses of tannins and fruit. One of the best ever from this estate.–J.S. • $NA • (5/31/1999) (BT) • **90-94**
Pomerol 1997: Very herbal, with cut grass tones and slightly aggressive tannins. Medium-bodied. Unripe.–J.S. • $35 • (1/31/2000) • **79**
Pomerol 1996: Some pretty tobacco, cherry and toasted oak character, but there's an intense herbal grassiness beneath. Medium-bodied, with good texture and a funky finish. Drink now.–J.S. • $30 • (1/31/1999) • **81**
Pomerol 1995 • $30 • (1/31/1998) • **92**
Pomerol 1994 • $20 • (1/31/1997) • **82**
Pomerol 1993 • $23 • (1/31/1996) • **81**
Pomerol 1990 • $33 Ⓐ • (3/31/1993) • **94**
Pomerol 1989: An ultrarich wine here. Dark-ruby color. Essence of ripe plums, coffee and chocolate. Full-bodied, lots of tannins, yet round and chewy with loads of ripe fruit character. A big mouthful of decadent fruit. (1989 Bordeaux horizontal tasting). Drink now through 2008.–J.S. • $44 Ⓐ • (5/31/1999) • **90**
Pomerol 1988 • $19 • (6/30/1991) • **90**
Pomerol 1985 • $28 • (11/30/1988) • **86**
Pomerol 1982: Ruby-garnet in color, with grilled meat and truffle aromas. Medium-bodied and velvety, with berry and tobacco flavors and a light finish. Slightly diluted. (1982 Bordeaux horizontal tasting).–J.S. • $NA • (11/30/1998) • **83**

BOUSCASSE, CHATEAU

Madiran 1996: Full of character and quite drinkable now, with red plum and game flavors and a great backbone of acidity. Appealing herbal notes build on the finish. Smooth and concentrated. Drink now through 2004.–K.M. • $15 • (10/31/1999) • **87**
Madiran 1995 • $15 • (9/30/1997) • **89**
Madiran Vieilles Vignes 1996: A brooding and rich red, with bright fruit flavors of plum, cranberry and cherry and some notes of game and leather. Has a good dose of well-rounded tannins and plenty of acidity. Herb and tobacco notes linger appealingly on the finish. Drink through 2006.–K.M. • $30 • (10/31/1999) • **89**
Madiran Vieilles Vignes 1995 • $25 • (9/30/1997) • **91**
Madiran Vieilles Vignes 1994 • $26 • (9/30/1997) • **87**
Madiran Vieilles Vignes 1990 • $22 • (1/01/1997) • **92**
Madiran Vieilles Vignes 1989 • $26 • (1/01/1997) • **88**
Pacherenc du Vic-Bilh Le Calendrier des Pacherencs Doux 1995 • $19/500 ml. • (9/30/1997) • **84**

BOUSCAUT, CHATEAU

Pessac-Léognan 1998: Harmonious and balanced, medium-bodied, with pretty fruit and a fine tannin structure.–J.S. • $NA • (5/31/1999) (BT) • **85-89**
Pessac-Léognan 1997: Shows good berry, tobacco character, with a medium body, medium tannins and a slightly dry finish. Drink now.–J.S. • $15 • (1/31/2000) • **84**
Pessac-Léognan 1996: Pretty plum, chocolate and vanilla aromas. Medium-bodied, with some tannins, but slightly lean and short on the finish. Best after 2000.–J.S. • $19 • (1/31/1999) • **82**
Pessac-Léognan 1995 • $22 • (1/31/1998) • **86**
Pessac-Léognan 1993 • $25 • (1/31/1996) • **82**
Pessac-Léognan 1990 • $18 • (3/31/1993) • **88**
Pessac-Léognan 1989: A rich and slightly earthy wine, but wonderfully fruity. Dark ruby-red color and blackberry, dark chocolate and earth. Medium- to full-bodied, with chewy tannins and a slightly rustic yet caressing finish. (1989 Bordeaux horizontal tasting). Best after 2002.–J.S. • $NA • (5/31/1999) • **89**
Pessac-Léognan 1988 • $14 Ⓐ • (4/30/1991) • **87**
Graves 1985 • $15 • (12/31/1988) • **90**
Graves 1982: Ripe but short, with plenty of fresh berry and tobacco aromas. Medium-bodied and silky, but slightly alcoholic on the finish. (1982 Bordeaux horizontal tasting).–J.S. • $NA • (11/30/1998) • **85**
Graves 1981 • $12 • (5/01/1984) • **86**
Graves 1970 • $27 • (5/15/1993) • **85**
Graves 1961 • $NA • (4/30/1996) • **85**
Pessac-Léognan White 1998: Medium-bodied, with good fruit and pear drop, lemon and mineral character. Light finish. Drink now.–J.S. • $25 • (2/29/2000) • **85**
Pessac-Léognan White 1997: A lively and fresh white, with lots of mineral and flint character. Medium-bodied, with firm acidity and a zingy aftertaste. Drink now.–J.S. • $30 • (9/30/1999) • **88**
Pessac-Léognan White 1996: Some good grapefruit and apple character, with firm acidity, but a little hard at the moment. Medium-bodied and fresh. Give it a bit more age. Drink through 2003.–J.S. • $23 • (3/31/1999) • **86**

FRANCE

BOUSQUET, CHATEAU DU

Côtes de Bourg 1995 • $9 • (1/31/1998) • **85**

BOUSSAGOL, DOMAINE

St.-Chinian 1995 • $15 • (5/31/1998) • **83**

BOUVERIE, LA

Cabernet Sauvignon Vin de Pays d'Oc Maison Nicolas Réserve 1995 • $7 • (5/15/1997) • **78**
Cabernet Sauvignon Vin de Pays d'Oc Maison Nicolas Réserve 1994 • $7 • (7/31/1996) • **82**
Cabernet Sauvignon Vin de Pays d'Oc Maison Nicolas Réserve 1993 • $6 • (10/31/1995) • **78**
Chardonnay Vin de Pays d'Oc Maison Nicolas Réserve 1996 • $7 • (9/15/1997) • **83**
Costières de Nîmes 1995 • $7 • (12/15/1996) • **78**
Costières de Nîmes 1994 • $6 • (11/15/1995) • **82**
Costières de Nîmes 1989 • $6 • (7/15/1991) • **79**
Merlot Vin de Pays d'Oc Cuvée Spéciale 1996: Something wrong here. Bizarre aromas and flavors of Worcestershire sauce make this unpalatable. Not recommended. Tasted twice, with consistent notes.–K.M. • $7 • (2/28/1999) • **58**
Merlot Vin de Pays d'Oc Cuvée Spéciale 1995 • $7 • (4/30/1998) • **82**
Merlot Vin de Pays d'Oc Cuvée Spéciale 1994 • $8 • (12/15/1996) • **85**
Merlot Vin de Pays d'Oc Cuvée Spéciale 1993 • $7 • (10/31/1995) • **84**
Merlot Vin de Pays d'Oc Maison Nicolas Réserve 1997: An herbal style of Merlot, with bell pepper and red cherry flavors. Slightly astringent on the finish.–K.M. • $6 • (2/28/1999) • **81**
Merlot Vin de Pays d'Oc Maison Nicolas Réserve 1996 • $7 • (11/15/1997) • **80**
Merlot Vin de Pays d'Oc Maison Nicolas Réserve 1995 • $7 • (5/15/1997) • **83**
Merlot Vin de Pays d'Oc Maison Nicolas Réserve 1994 • $6 • (1/31/1997) • **53**
Merlot Vin de Pays d'Oc Maison Nicolas Réserve 1993 • $6 • (10/31/1995) • **84**
Syrah Vin de Pays d'Oc Maison Nicolas Réserve 1998: A boring red, with a light, simple grapey flavor that is more like Beaujolais than Syrah.–K.M. • $7 • (7/31/1999) • **77**

BOUVET

Brut Rosé Saumur NV • $13 • (5/15/1997) • **82**
Brut Saumur Signature NV • $12 • (5/15/1997) • **85**

BOUVIER, RENE

Bourgogne White 1998: Offers some pear and candy aromas. Medium-bodied, with a smoky aftertaste.–P.M. • $16 • (5/31/2000) • **79**

Marsannay White Le Clos 1998: A "little" Chardonnay that's balanced, with some decent ripe fruit, but it turns a bit tart on the slightly bitter finish. Still, it's a clean, medium-bodied white with a touch of honey. Drink now through 2001.–P.M. • $25 • (5/31/2000) • **83**

Marsannay White Vieilles Vignes 1998: Odd wine. Full-bodied, but a bit lacking in midpalate concentration. Has ripe fruit, but also a strange varnishlike aroma. Dried herbs and honey on the finish.–P.M. • $22 • (5/31/2000) • **79**

BOUZEREAU & FILS, MICHEL

Bourgogne White 1997: This has decent fruit, but it's chewy, and there's a hint of cardboard character on the tough finish.–P.M. • $15 • (5/31/1999) • **77**

Bourgogne White 1996 • $NA • (5/31/1998) • **88**

Meursault Genevrières 1998: Impressive ripeness in this '98. This rich Meursault emits floral aromas reminiscent of Viognier, then lays it thick on the palate, with loads of dried fruit and honey character. Seductive, opulent finish. Drink now through 2005.–P.M. • $55 • (5/31/2000) • **89**

Meursault Genevrières 1997: Wonderful effort in the '97. Ripe honey, lemon, tropical and pear flavors allow for a lush, sweet-tasting, round mouthfeel. Long, clean finish. Drink now through 2005.–P.M. • $55 • (5/31/1999) • **90**

Meursault Genevrières 1996 • $NA • (5/31/1998) • **93**

Meursault Le Limozin 1997: A golden-colored, Viognier-tasting Chardonnay, this ripe, medium-bodied '97 offers peach, apricot and pineapple flavors and a ripe, almost off-dry character on the delicious finish. Drink now through 2005.–P.M. • $40 • (5/31/1999) • **87**

Meursault Le Limozin 1996 • $NA • (5/31/1998) • **90**

Meursault Le Limozin 1995 • $NA • (5/31/1997) • **87**

Meursault Les Charmes-Dessus 1998: A ripe '98 Meursault. Flavorful and intense, with pineapple, spice and smoke complexity. Medium-bodied and delicious, round and fleshy, it delivers a long, sweet-tasting finish. Drink now through 2005.–P.M. • $55 • (5/31/2000) • **88**

Meursault Les Charmes-Dessus 1997: Smooth and round, this lightweight Meursault flirts with pretty flavors of pear, quince and pineapple in a balanced package of medium intensity. Drink now through 2002.–P.M. • $55 • (5/31/1999) • **84**

Meursault Les Charmes-Dessus 1996 • $NA • (5/31/1998) • **90**

Meursault Les Charmes-Dessus 1995 • $50 • (5/31/1997) • **92**

Meursault Les Grands Charrons 1998: A bit rustic, with an appley character. Ripe, delivering some butter, spice, dried herb and honey. Chewy, chalky finish. Drink now through 2003.–P.M. • $40 • (5/31/2000) • **85**

Meursault Les Grands Charrons 1997: Fairly ripe, with decent butter, pear, floral and tropical notes and a supple texture. Medium-bodied and medium-intense, this young Meursault can be drunk on release. Drink now through 2002.–P.M. • $35 • (5/31/1999) • **82**

Meursault Les Grands Charrons 1996 • $36 • (5/31/1998) • **91**

Meursault Les Grands Charrons 1995 • $40 • (5/31/1997) • **91**

Meursault Les Tessons 1998: Ripe and full-bodied. Citrus, dried apricot and honey blend in this spicy Meursault to produce a lingering, rich, sweet-tasting and silky white. Drink now through 2002.–P.M. • $45 • (5/31/2000) • **87**

Meursault Les Tessons 1997: Medium-bodied, nicely structured and fairly ripe, with tropical, pear and dried herb notes, this round, supple yet lively Meursault sweeps to a succulent finish. Drink now through 2004.–P.M. • $40 • (5/31/1999) • **89**

Meursault Les Tessons 1996 • $NA • (5/31/1998) • **80**

Meursault Les Tessons 1995 • $NA • (5/31/1997) • **88**

Puligny-Montrachet Les Champs Gains 1997: Ripe and thick, of medium fruit intensity, showing modest lemon and green apple notes. Short finish. Drink now through 2007.–P.M. • $45 • (5/31/1999) • **81**

Puligny-Montrachet Les Champs Gains 1996 • $55 • (5/31/1998) • **91**

Puligny-Montrachet Les Champs Gains 1995 • $50 • (5/31/1997) • **95**

Key: SS—Spectator Selection. CS—Cellar Selection. HR—Highly Recommended. $NA—Price not available. (BT)—Barrel tasting. Ⓐ—Auction Price. For a key to the tasters' initials, see "How to Use These Listings." **Dates in parentheses represent the issues in which the ratings were published.**

BOXLER, ALBERT

Alsace Edelzwicker 1996: A mouthful of soft, ripe, floral and apricot, very appealing and upfront in its flavors. Drink now.–B.S. • $13 • (10/15/1999) • **83**

Gewürztraminer Alsace Grand Cru Brand 1997: Thick and opulent, offering honey, white pepper and litchi up front, its structure takes over on the back half of the palate, for a slightly coarse ending. Drink now.–B.S. • $43/500 ml. • (6/15/2000) • **84**

Sylvaner Alsace 1996: Mature, this exhibits attractive pear, apricot and earth notes, a crisp underlying structure and modest finish. Drink now.–B.S. • $13 • (10/15/1999) • **85**

Tokay Pinot Gris Alsace Grand Cru Sommerberg 1997: Bold and in-your-face, this slightly sweet, opulent Pinot Gris shows honey, apricot and spice, floral notes up front, with a powerful structure and harmony too. Drink now.–B.S. • $53 • (6/15/2000) • **90**

BOYD-CANTENAC, CHATEAU

Margaux 1998: Wonderful aromas of spices, cherries and plums. Full-bodied, with a lovely core of ripe fruit, round tannins and a long finish. Amazing sample for the vintage.–J.S. • $NA • (5/31/1999) (BT) • **85-89**

Margaux 1997: Very late-harvest in style. Dark color, with intense aromas of licorice, berries and raisins. Full-bodied and very raisiny, with a tobacco, coffee aftertaste. Slightly hollow midpalate and overdone, but interesting.–J.S. • $33 • (1/31/2000) • **85**

Margaux 1996: More like a Rioja than a Bordeaux, but pleasant. Dark-colored, with ripe fruit, but really oaky and round. Medium-bodied. Drink now.–J.S. • $30 • (1/31/1999) • **84**

Margaux 1995: Raspberry sauce on nose and palate, with hints of milk chocolate. Medium- to full-bodied, with velvety tannins and a long, fruity finish. Impressive for this producer. Delicious red. Drink now through 2005.–J.S. • $NA • (9/15/1998) • **90**

Margaux 1985 • $28 Ⓐ • (4/15/1988) • **90**

Margaux 1982: Always a sleeper from Margaux. Dark ruby in color, with an inky center. Full-bodied, very tannic and mouthpuckering, with loads of blackberry and earth aromas. Will improve with age. (1982 Bordeaux horizontal tasting). Drink now through 2006.–J.S. • $45 Ⓐ • (11/30/1998) • **91**

Margaux 1983 • $36 Ⓐ • (4/16/1986) • **86**

Margaux 1961 • $55 Ⓐ • (4/30/1996) • **84**

BRAC DE LA PERRIERE

Beaujolais Château des Péthières 1998: A straightforward, juicy red offering cherry and earth aromas and flavors that remain lively and focused. Finishes a little short. Drink now.–B.S. • $14 • (10/15/1999) • **82**

Beaujolais-Villages Domaine de la Brasse 1998: Fresh and bright, full of cherry and currant flavors, this red is medium-bodied and has good structure, the latter lending a crispness to the finish. Drink now.–B.S. • $11 • (10/15/1999) • **83**

Beaujolais-Villages Domaine de la Brasse 1997: Cherry and earth are the dominant themes in this light-bodied, simple Beaujolais, whose soft structure makes for easy drinking. Drink now.–B.S. • $8 • (10/31/1998) • **81**

Beaujolais-Villages Domaine de la Brasse 1996 • $9 • (9/15/1997) • **83**

Beaujolais-Villages Domaine de la Brasse 1995 • $NA • (8/31/1996) • **84**

Brouilly Château du Pavé 1998: Light cherry flavors and a hint of spice mark this red, whose structure lends a tartness that firms up on the finish. Drink now.–B.S. • $13 • (10/15/1999) • **81**

Chiroubles Domaine des Gatilles 1998: An initial sulfur odor dissipates, giving way to sweet cherry in this round, easy-drinking red. It's attractive, if without a lot of character. Drink now.–B.S. • $14 • (10/15/1999) • **82**

Chiroubles Domaine des Gatilles 1996 • $13 • (9/15/1997) • **86**

Juliénas Les Bucherats 1998: Broad, displaying concentrated black cherry and earth notes allied to firm acidity and supporting tannins. Traditional in style. Drink now through 2002.–B.S. • $14 • (10/15/1999) • **84**

Juliénas Les Bucherats 1997: A straightforward cru Beaujolais, offering cherry and earth character, modest concentration and soft structure. Drink now.–B.S. • $12 • (11/15/1998) • **82**

Juliénas Les Bucherats 1996 • $12 • (9/15/1997) • **79**

Juliénas Les Bucherats 1995 • $9 • (9/15/1996) • **74**

Moulin-à-Vent Les Brigands 1998: Light for the appellation, this shows only a modicum of cherry flavor and turns astringent on the finish.–B.S. • $15 • (10/15/1999) • **78**

Moulin-à-Vent Les Brigands 1997: Lovely aromas of black cherry and chocolate, but the palate is a letdown, offering dilute flavors and not much depth or structure.–B.S. • $14 • (10/31/1998) • **83**

Moulin-à-Vent Les Brigands 1996 • $16 • (9/15/1997) • **82**
Moulin-à-Vent Les Brigands 1994 • $16 • (9/15/1996) • **85**

BRANAIRE-DUCRU, CHATEAU

St.-Julien 1999: Lots of plum and grape aromas follow through to a medium-bodied palate, with medium firm tannins and a fresh finish.–J.S. • $NA • (1/01/2000) (BT) • **85-89**
St.-Julien 1998: Lots of mint and berries on the nose. Medium- to full-bodied, with a good core of fruit and a velvet-textured finish. Well made.–J.S. • $NA • (5/31/1999) (BT) • **85-89**
St.-Julien 1997: I like the berry and violet character in this wine. Medium-bodied, with firm tannins and a fresh finish. Drink now through 2004.–J.S. • $34 • (1/31/2000) • **86**
St.-Julien 1996: Gorgeous aromas of raspberry and perfume. Medium-bodied, with firm tannins and a fresh and fruity aftertaste. Silky and fine. Best after 2003.–J.S. • $22 Ⓐ • (1/31/1999) • **89**
St.-Julien 1995: Very pretty aromas of currants and cinnamon. Medium- to full-bodied, with fine tannins and a silky, caressing texture. Hard to resist now. Tasted better from barrel but a fine wine indeed. Tasted numerous times. Best from 2001 through 2006.–J.S. • $31Ⓐ • (9/15/1998) • **89**
St.-Julien 1994 • $31 Ⓐ • (1/31/1997) • **87**
St.-Julien 1993 • $25 • (1/31/1996) • **85**
St.-Julien 1991 • $22 • (3/31/1994) • **80**
St.-Julien 1990 • $51 Ⓐ • (3/31/1993) • **90**
St.-Julien 1989: Harmonious, balanced and very fresh '89. Color is medium-dark ruby, with lovely fresh floral and raspberry aromas. Medium- to full-bodied, well-integrated tannins and a fruity, minty aftertaste. (1989 Bordeaux horizontal tasting). Best after 2001.–J.S. • $59 Ⓐ • (5/31/1999) • **90**
St.-Julien 1988: Medium-bodied, this has rather intense green tobacco aromas, with hints of redwood and fruit, slightly high acidity and an austere finish. (1988 Bordeaux horizontal tasting). Drink now.–J.S. • $NA • (11/30/1998) • **84**
St.-Julien 1985 • $31 Ⓐ • (6/30/1988) • **89**
St.-Julien 1983 • $36 Ⓐ • (3/01/1986) • **88**
St.-Julien 1982: A big, traditional-style red. Ruby-garnet in color, with chestnut, berry and truffle aromas. Full-bodied and very concentrated, with velvety tannins and lots of mushroom and earth flavors. Slightly dry. (1982 Bordeaux horizontal tasting). Drink now.–J.S. • $62 Ⓐ • (11/30/1998) • **88**
St.-Julien 1961 • $80 Ⓐ • (4/30/1996) • **80**
St.-Julien 1959 • $98 Ⓐ • (10/15/1990) • **86**

BRANE, LE BARON DE

Margaux 1996: Some dilution in this second label from Château Brane-Cantenac, but it shows interesting berry and tar aromas and flavors. Medium-bodied, with firm tannins. Drink now.–J.S. • $NA • (1/31/1999) • **81**
Margaux 1994 • $NA • (6/30/1995) • **70**
Margaux 1989 • $NA • (3/15/1992) • **89**

BRANE-CANTENAC, CHATEAU

Margaux 1999: Balanced and harmonious, with aromas of spice, berry and tobacco. Medium-bodied, with fine tannins and a delicate finish.–J.S. • $NA • (1/01/2000) (BT) • **85-89**
Margaux 1998: Austere really, with some berry, herbal character but hard to get excited about. Medium body. Medium fruit finish. Just 80 points.–J.S. • $NA • (5/31/1999) (BT) • **80-84**
Margaux 1996: Plenty of tobacco, spice, cedar and fruit. Full-bodied, with extremely polished tannins and a lengthy aftertaste of plum and chocolate. One of the best wines I have ever tasted from Brane. Best after 2001.–J.S. • $40 • (1/31/1999) • **90**
Margaux 1995: Firm and straightforward, with plenty of berry and chocolate aromas and flavors, medium tannins and a fresh and fruity finish. Drink through 2005.–J.S. • $31 Ⓐ • (9/15/1998) • **87**
Margaux 1994 • $32 • (1/31/1997) • **81**
Margaux 1993 • $25 • (1/31/1996) • **85**
Margaux 1991 • $24 • (3/31/1994) • **80**
Margaux 1990 • $30 • (3/31/1993) • **91**
Margaux 1989: A big, brutish wine with lots of everything. Rich aromas of cooked strawberries, earth and tobacco. Full-bodied and chewy, providing masses of tannins, yet it's smooth with ripe fruit and lots of character on the finish. Give it time. (1989 Bordeaux horizontal tasting).–J.S. • $39 Ⓐ • (5/31/1999) • **94**
Margaux 1988: A bit strange, with green, stemmy aromas and flavors. Medium-bodied, with lots of astringent tannins and a tart, light fruit finish. Not a success story. (1988 Bordeaux horizontal tasting).–J.S. • $26 Ⓐ • (11/30/1998) • **78**
Margaux 1986 • $36 Ⓐ • (6/15/1989) • **87**
Margaux 1985 • $40 Ⓐ • (6/30/1988) • **89**
Margaux 1983 • $40 Ⓐ • (4/16/1986) • **94**
Margaux 1982: This shows wonderful finesse. Brick red in color, with a garnet edge. Lovely perfumed aromas of blackberry and chocolate, with a hint of raisin. Medium-bodied, with velvety tannins and a long, sweet fruit finish. Drink now or hold. (1982 Bordeaux horizontal tasting).–J.S. • $55 Ⓐ • (11/30/1998) • **90**
Margaux 1979 • $23 Ⓐ • (10/15/1989) • **80**
Margaux 1961 • $71 Ⓐ • (4/30/1996) • **84**
Margaux 1947 • $NA • (5/31/1997) • **88**
Margaux 1945 • $NA • (3/16/1986) • **87**

BRANGER, CLAUDE

Muscadet de Sèvre et Maine Sur Lie Domaine de la Haute-Févrie L'Excellence Vieilles Vignes 1996 • $13 • (6/30/1998) • **83**

BREDIF, MARC

Chinon 1997: Expressive and harmonious, this vivid red offers alluring aromas of cherries, cinnamon and smoke that follow through on the firm yet lively palate. It's balanced, and quite long on the finish. Drink now through 2002.–T.M. • $16 • (9/15/1999) • **87**
Chinon 1996 • $16 • (6/15/1998) • **87**
Chinon 1995 • $16 • (6/15/1997) • **88**
Chinon 1993 • $12 • (12/15/1995) • **85**
Chinon 1992 • $12 • (10/31/1994) • **84**
Vouvray 1998: Round and refreshing, showing good typicity, with lime, almond and chalk notes, nice acidity and a pretty medium-weight frame. Drink now.–B.S. • $12 • (6/15/2000) • **85**
Vouvray 1997: Balanced and fresh, this offers straightforward apple and light peach flavors, with good acidity and a touch of sweetness. Clean and straightforward. Drink now.–T.M. • $15 • (10/31/1999) • **84**
Vouvray Moelleux Nectar 1989 • $25/375 ml. • (4/30/1996) • **90**

BREGEON, ANDRE-MICHEL

Muscadet de Sèvre et Maine Sur Lie 1996 • $12 • (5/31/1998) • **81**

BRETON, CATHERINE & PIERRE

Bourgueil Grand Mont 1996: Deep in color and lush in texture, this exuberant wine offers crushed fruit and floral notes. Well defined, balanced and lively, it's drinkable now but can age too. Drink now through 2004.–T.M. • $17 • (2/28/1999) • **87**
Bourgueil Les Galichets 1993 • $15 • (5/15/1996) • **84**
Bourgueil Les Galichets 1992 • $14 • (10/31/1994) • **75**

BRETON, GUY

Morgon Vieilles Vignes 1998: Spicy aromas give way to soft fruit flavors of plum and cherry, with light tannins and gentle acidity. A pleasant quaff. Drink now.–T.M. • $18 • (3/31/2000) • **84**
Morgon Vieilles Vignes 1997: Rich and plush, this red is almost jammy, with soft, thick grape flavors and round, soft tannins. Has more fruit than structure, but is appealing now. Drink now.–T.M. • $20 • (12/31/1998) • **85**
Morgon Vieilles Vignes 1996: This ripe red shows an unusual mix of sweet berry and game flavors that stretch the traditional character of Gamay. Silky and deep on the palate. Rich enough to accompany strong meat dishes. Not typical, but impressive. Drink now through 2001.–T.M. • $20 • (7/31/1998) • **87**
Morgon Vieilles Vignes 1994 • $19 • (9/15/1996) • **88**

BREUIL, CHATEAU DU

Haut-Médoc 1997: A light and fruity red with cherry and mineral character. Has fine tannins and a short finish. Drink now.–J.S. • $NA • (1/31/2000) • **80**
Haut-Médoc 1996: Pretty, although simple, with dried cherry and berry aromas and flavors. Medium-bodied, with medium tannins and a fruity finish. Drink now.–J.S. • $NA • (1/31/1999) • **82**

Haut-Médoc 1995: Rather light for the vintage, with clean berry and cherry flavors, light tannins and a clean finish. Drink now.–J.S. • $15 • (9/15/1998) • **76**
Haut-Médoc 1992 • $NA • (4/15/1995) • **80**
Haut-Médoc 1989: This needs drinking. Medium-brick-red color. Aromas of plums, coffee and tobacco. Full-bodied and extremely ripe, with medium tannins and a slightly hot and dry finish. (1989 Bordeaux horizontal tasting).–J.S. • $NA • (5/31/1999) • **82**

BRICOUT

Brut Champagne Carte d'Or Prestige NV • $30 • (12/31/1991) • **83**
Brut Champagne Carte Noire Réserve NV • $30 • (12/31/1991) HR • **90**
Brut Champagne Cuvée Arthur Bricout NV • $62 • (12/31/1993) • **86**
Brut Champagne Cuvée Prestige 1991 • $26 • (4/30/1998) SS • **91**

BRILLETTE, CHATEAU

Moulis 1998: Soft and pleasing wine for the vintage. Lovely aromas of crushed berries and currants. Medium- to full-bodied, velvety, with pleasant tannins and a medium finish. Very good for this estate.–J.S. • $NA • (5/31/1999) (BT) • **85-89**
Moulis 1997: A light-bodied wine with decent fruit and plum character. Short finish. Drink now.–J.S. • $NA • (1/31/2000) • **81**
Moulis 1995 • $17 • (1/31/1998) • **84**
Moulis 1990 • $18 • (3/31/1993) • **87**
Moulis 1989: A bit rustic and overly tannic but impressively concentrated. Dark brick-red in color. Very ripe fruit on the nose, verging on raisins. Full-bodied and soft, with loads of chewy tannins. Slightly drying on the finish. (1989 Bordeaux horizontal tasting). Drink now.–J.S. • $NA • (5/31/1999) • **86**
Moulis 1988 • $15 • (8/31/1991) • **81**
Moulis 1987 • $15 • (11/30/1989) • **72**
Moulis 1986 • $14 • (6/30/1989) • **78**
Moulis 1982 • $19 • (11/30/1989) • **85**
Moulis Comte du Périer de Larsan 1996: Hard not to drink this pretty wine now. Delicious aromas of blackberry, spices and grilled meats. Medium-bodied, with fine tannins and a fresh, fruity, spicy aftertaste. Best after 2000.–J.S. • $NA • (1/31/1999) • **88**

BRISEBARRE, PHILIPPE

Vouvray Sec 1997: This silky white is rather restrained on the palate, but it's balanced and well structured, with pear, apple and mineral flavors that finish clean and crisp. Subtle but rewarding. Drink now through 2001.–T.M. • $11 • (10/31/1999) • **86**
Vouvray Sec 1996 • $12 • (6/30/1998) • **79**

BROCARD, JEAN-MARC

Bourgogne White Jurassique 1998: Just lovely. Ripe and crisp, with added earthy, pungent, "reduced," yeasty-leesy character. Medium-bodied and slightly spritzy, it's fresh and sweet-tasting, ending with honey, melon and pear flavors. Drink now through 2008.–P.M. • $16 • (5/15/2000) • **86**
Bourgogne White Kimmeridgien 1998: Interesting *terroir* here, with matchsticklike, pungent, earthy, yeasty aromas and flavors. Medium-bodied, with a silky texture, it's a smoky and ripe white, seducing with its harmony. Amazing quality for a Bourgogne. Tasted twice, with consistent notes. Drink now through 2005.–P.M. • $16 • (5/15/2000) SS • **89**
Bourgogne White Oxfordien 1998: Delicate, with good mineral aromas. Crisp but flavorful, offering salt, wet earth and lemon notes. Light- to medium-bodied, with a lively finish. Drink now through 2002.–P.M. • $16 • (5/15/2000) • **86**
Bourgogne White Portlandien 1998: Grassy, floral and very ripe, this is just delicious. Medium-bodied, showing a sweet-tasting fruit that is seductive. Harmonious finish. Drink now through 2003.–P.M. • $16 • (5/15/2000) • **89**
Bourgogne White sur Jurassique 1997: Clean, straight and pure, with a vibrant core of lemon, mineral and green apple. It has weight on the midpalate and good concentration, giving wonderful balance to this focused Chardonnay. Drink now through 2002.–P.M. • $16 • (5/31/1999) • **87**
Bourgogne White sur Jurassique 1995 • $13 • (6/15/1997) • **89**
Bourgogne White sur Kimmeridgien 1997: Attractive. This medium-bodied, well-made Chardonnay pops with crisp lemon and pear and clean personality accented by a minerally touch. The vibrancy carries to a long, mouth-puckering, steely finish. Try with seafood. Drink now through 2002.–P.M. • $18 • (5/31/1999) • **84**
Bourgogne White sur Kimmeridjien 1996 • $15 • (8/31/1997) • **91**
Bourgogne White sur Kimmeridjien 1995 • $14 • (6/15/1997) • **88**
Bourgogne White sur Portlandien 1997: Pure, clean, firm and steely, showing citrus and chalk character. Medium-bodied, this should be great with a seafood platter. Drink now through 2002.–P.M. • $17 • (5/31/1999) • **82**
Bourgogne White sur Portlandien 1996 • $8 • (5/31/1998) • **88**
Chablis 1996: Rather exotic, with a floral character and notes of freshly cut grass, along with pear, green apple and buttered-croissant. Good acidity holds this medium-bodied, vibrant and pure Chablis together. Best from 2005.–P.M. • $16 • (8/31/1998) • **89**
Chablis Beauregard 1998: Delicious in a grassy, floral, fruity style. Medium-bodied, tasting like lime juice, this is fresh and crisp, delivering intensity of flavor on the finish. Drink now.–P.M. • $27 • (5/15/2000) • **85**
Chablis Beauregard 1997: Good intensity in this idiosyncratic, *terroir*-driven, medium-bodied Beauregard *premier cru.* It's supple and ripe, delivering wet earth, salt, lemon and a touch of sweet honey, with a lingering finish. Drink now through 2003.–P.M. • $26 • (5/31/1999) • **90**
Chablis Beauregard 1996 • $25 • (5/31/1998) • **95**
Chablis Beauregard 1995 • $23 • (6/15/1997) • **89**
Chablis Beauroy 1998: A bit earthy, but with lots of fresh fruit folded into a slightly smoky, oaky, spicy framework. Medium-bodied and thick on the palate, tasting natural and promising for the future, with lime, gooseberry, dough and green apple character. Drink now through 2005.–P.M. • $27 • (5/15/2000) • **87**
Chablis Blanchot 1997: This rather pungent Chablis shows butter, green apple and wet earth character. A rustic Chardonnay that turns firm, chewy and a bit astringent on the finish. Drink now through 2003.–P.M. • $47 • (9/30/1999) • **84**
Chablis Bougros 1998: Lively, pungent and unique. Medium-bodied, it has a crisp mouthfeel but also good intensity, with loads of interesting grassy, citrusy, floral character. Explodes on the finish, so give it time. Best from 2002 through 2008.–P.M. • $47 • (5/15/2000) • **87**
Chablis Bougros 1997: Lovely Bougros, opulent and thick yet full of zest, offering layers of dried fruit, ripe pear and honey. Full-bodied, seductive, with a clear focus on mineral notes on the attractive, long finish. Drink now through 2010.–P.M. • $47 • (5/31/1999) • **93**
Chablis Bougros 1996 • $45 • (5/31/1998) • **93**
Chablis Bougros 1995 • $43 • (6/15/1997) • **91**
Chablis Côtes de Jouan 1998: Elegant and polished. Medium in body and intensity, it fans out with lovely wet earth, mineral, matchstick and grass notes. Good citrus character kicks in on the lingering finish. Drink now through 2002.–P.M. • $27 • (5/15/2000) • **86**
Chablis Côtes de Jouan 1997: Big, but with a dried herb, salt and iodine core supported by honey and green apple notes. Drink now through 2005.–P.M. • $26 • (9/30/1999) • **84**
Chablis Cuvée Boissoneuse 1998: Flavorful and zesty, with vibrant grasslike green apple character folded into some mineral and chalk notes. Medium-bodied, it's quite crisp on the finish, but should hold up nicely to seafood dishes. Drink now through 2005.–P.M. • $18 • (5/15/2000) • **86**
Chablis Cuvée Chichée 1998: Distinctive—a wine that stands apart. Pungent, with matchstick, flint and earth character, displaying concentration. Full-bodied and thick midpalate, it sails to a lovely finish. Drink now through 2001.–P.M. • $18 • (5/15/2000) • **86**
Chablis Cuvée Malantes 1998: Thick and ripe for a village wine, Medium-bodied, with a butter, wood, spice and grilled meat character that works because of the good fruit. Drink now through 2002.–P.M. • $18 • (5/15/2000) • **84**
Chablis Fourchaume 1997: Clean and pure, this is a tight, vibrant wine, but lovely as you get plenty of lemon, mineral, mandarin orange and pineapple flavors whetting your taste buds all the way to the crisp, lingering end. Best from 2002 through 2010.–P.M. • $26 • (5/31/1999) • **90**
Chablis Fourchaume 1996 • $25 • (5/31/1998) • **93**
Chablis Les Clos 1997: Gorgeous. Buttery, thick, ripe yet also elegant, delivering a firm core of lemon, quince and apple. The minerally, smooth, round palate is terrific—this melts in the mouth like a soufflé. Hedonists should buy it. Best from 2003 through 2010.–P.M. • $47 • (5/31/1999) • **95**
Chablis Les Clos 1996 • $45 • (5/31/1998) • **93**
Chablis Montée de Tonnerre 1995 • $23 • (6/15/1997) • **86**

Key: SS—Spectator Selection. CS—Cellar Selection. HR—Highly Recommended. $NA—Price not available. (BT)—Barrel tasting. Ⓐ—Auction Price.
For a key to the tasters' initials, see "How to Use These Listings."
Dates in parentheses represent the issues in which the ratings were published.

Chablis Montmain 1998: A real matchsticklike, earthy, leesy, yeasty savage. Medium-bodied, it shows great fruit—ripe and sweet—and displays idiosyncratic Chablis character. Drink now through 2008.–P.M. • $27 • (5/15/2000) • **88**

Chablis Montmain 1997: A beauty. Clean and pure but, above all, extravagantly opulent and ripe, seducing with full-bodied, silky texture and layers of tropical, lemon tart, mandarin orange, spice, butter and cream flavors. Racy finish. Drink now through 2005.–P.M. • $26 • (5/31/1999) • **92**

Chablis Montmain 1996 • $23 • (5/31/1998) • **87**

Chablis Montmain 1995 • $23 • (6/15/1997) • **89**

Chablis Vaillons 1998: Quite lovely and intense. Full-bodied, with toasted, smoky, honeyed character and a silky mouthfeel. The wood is well integrated in the ripe fruit. Fresh lime notes on the lingering finish. Best from 2002 through 2008.–P.M. • $29 • (5/15/2000) • **90**

Chablis Valmur 1998: This ripe, medium- to full-bodied white bursts with mineral, wet earth and flint character. Supple, pleasant and flavorful, it's a delight to drink, with a fresh, lingering finish. Drink now through 2002.–P.M. • $47 • (5/15/2000) • **86**

Chablis Vaucoupin 1998: Elegant and supple. Medium-bodied, with a clean, pure lemon, salt cracker, green apple and mineral character. A medium-intense, focused Chardonnay. Drink now through 2002.–P.M. • $27 • (5/15/2000) • **85**

Chablis Vaucoupin 1997: Amazing Chablis. Thick, rich and ripe, with a lovely mouthfeel, nice honey, pear, wet earth and mineral character and a subtle, silky finish that is just ravishing. Bravo. Drink now through 2007.–P.M. • $26 • (9/30/1999) HR • **93**

Chablis Vaugiraut 1998: A bit earthy, but with wonderful intensity. Medium-bodied, with white pepper, mineral, matchstick, pineapple and honey character. Delicious through and through. Drink now through 2003.–P.M. • $27 • (5/15/2000) • **89**

Chablis Vaugiraut 1997: A thick, ripe '97 Chablis dripping with rich fruit, honey and lightly toasted, lemony flavors. Hard not to fall madly in love with this balanced wine. Drink now through 2005.–P.M. • $26 • (9/30/1999) • **94**

Chablis Vieilles Vignes 1998: Fun and refreshing, like a lemon tart. Fresh and slightly spritzy, with earth and honey notes. Light- to medium-bodied, sparkling with limelike flavors and a crisp, delicious finish. Drink now through 2001.–P.M. • $23 • (5/15/2000) • **84**

Chablis Vieilles Vignes 1997: Clean and refined, showing a nice, vibrant midpalate delivering citrus and green apple flavors, with a pure finish. Drink now.–P.M. • $24 • (5/31/1999) • **85**

Chablis Vieilles Vignes Domaine Ste.-Claire 1996 • $21 • (8/31/1997) • **91**

Petit Chablis 1996 • $18 • (8/31/1997) • **90**

Petit Chablis Domaine Ste.-Claire 1997: A full-bodied '97 Chablis, offering a salt, iodine and mineral character, with lime and green apple. Firms up on the finish. Drink now.–P.M. • $17 • (9/30/1999) • **84**

Sauvignon de St.-Bris 1998: This light-feathered white tastes of lime and grass notes, delivering a tart mouthfeel that should fit nicely with all sorts of food. Not complex. Drink now through 2001.–P.M. • $12 • (5/15/2000) • **80**

Sauvignon de St.-Bris Domaine Ste.-Claire 1997: Clean and zesty, fresh and lively, offering decent honey, spice and green apple character. Steely finish. Drink now.–P.M. • $12 • (5/31/1999) • **81**

Sauvignon de St.-Bris Domaine Ste.-Claire 1995 • $12 • (6/15/1997) • **86**

BROUSSE, CHATEAU DE

Côtes de Castillon 1996: Clean but very diluted, with strawberry and earth aromas and flavors, a light body and a fresh finish.–J.S. • $NA • (2/28/1999) • **78**

BROUSTET, CHATEAU

Barsac 1998: Pretty young wine, with a thick mouthfeel and lots of honey, melon, spice character. Full-bodied and fine, with a lively finish.–J.S. • $NA • (1/01/1999) (BT) • **90-94**

Barsac 1997: A big, spicy, dried style of Sauternes, with lovely aromas of lemon and apricot. Medium-bodied and medium sweet, with a spice, honey and cinnamon character and a long finish. Drink now.–J.S. • $NA • (1/31/2000) • **87**

Barsac 1990 • $23 • (4/15/1995) • **83**

Barsac 1988 • $19/375 ml. • (3/31/1991) • **83**

BROWN, CHATEAU

Pessac-Léognan 1998: Wonderfully perfumed with chocolate, floral and berry character thoughout. Full-bodied, with velvety tannins and a long, long finish. Very good for this estate. Almost outstanding.–J.S. • $NA • (5/31/1999) (BT) • **85-89**

Pessac-Léognan 1997: Lovely blackberry, cherry and toasted oak. Medium-bodied, with medium, velvety tannins and a fruity finish. Needs a bit more fruit concentration. Drink now.–J.S. • $NA • (1/31/2000) • **84**

Pessac-Léognan 1996: A lean but well-crafted red. Light aromas of plums and tobacco, with a hint of mineral. Medium-bodied, with good fruit flavors, firm tannins and a slightly short finish. Best after 2000.–J.S. • $20 • (1/31/1999) • **84**

Pessac-Léognan 1995 • $18 • (1/31/1998) • **88**

Pessac-Léognan 1994 • $15 • (1/31/1997) • **84**

Pessac-Léognan White 1998: A ripe white, with delicious pineapple, pear and honey character. Medium-bodied, with good fruit, but slightly short. Drink now.–J.S. • $NA • (2/29/2000) • **85**

Pessac-Léognan White 1997: A straightforward and very good Bordeaux white, with lots of grassy character and lively acidity. Medium-bodied, with a fresh finish. Drink now.–J.S. • $18 • (9/30/1999) • **86**

Pessac-Léognan White 1996: Showing some maturity now but delicious. Aromas of appleskin, honey, maple syrup and wood. Medium- to full-bodied, with a round texture and fresh acidity on the simple finish. Drink now.–J.S. • $17 • (6/30/1999) • **87**

BROYER, BERNARD

Chénas Cuvée Vieilles Vignes 1996: Soft and jammy, this smooth red offers candied cherry and plum flavors, very light tannins.–T.M. • $18 • (8/31/1998) • **79**

Juliénas 1996: Firm, polished texture, with flavors of black cherry, smoke and herbs. Turns a bit dry on the finish. Drink now.–T.M. • $16 • (8/31/1998) • **83**

BRUGNON, M.

Brut Champagne NV: Inviting, well-balanced and well-rounded; generous fruit flavors and a soft but lively texture make a fine combination. Drink now. • $20 • (10/31/1999) • **88**

Brut Champagne Sélection NV: A rich texture and abundant flavors make this very appealing. Has lively but mellow pear and apple flavors, spicy accents, and a honeyed quality on the finish. Drink now through 2001. • $25 • (10/31/1999) • **90**

BRUN, JEAN-PAUL

Beaujolais Domaine des Terres Dorées 1992 • $9 • (6/15/1994) • **85**

Beaujolais Nouveau Domaine des Terres Dorées Cuvée à l'Ancienne 1999: This clumsy red lacks the usual fruity appeal of a Nouveau, with stewed and herbal flavors.–T.M. • $8 • (1/01/2000) • **77**

Beaujolais Domaine des Terres Dorées Cuvée à l'Ancienne 1996 • $10 • (9/15/1997) • **79**

Beaujolais Domaine des Terres Dorées Cuvée à l'Ancienne 1995 • $12 • (9/15/1996) • **82**

Beaujolais Domaine des Terres Dorées Cuvée à l'Ancienne 1993 • $12 • (6/15/1995) • **77**

Beaujolais Domaine des Terres Dorées Cuvée Tradition 1993 • $10 • (7/31/1995) • **77**

Chardonnay Beaujolais Domaine des Terres Dorées 1996 • $11 • (9/15/1997) • **82**

BRUNET, PATRICK

Fleurie Domaine de Robert 1993 • $15 • (9/15/1996) • **77**

Fleurie Domaine de Robert 1992 • $16 • (1/31/1995) • **87**

Morgon Domaine de Robert 1992 • $14 • (1/31/1995) • **86**

BRUSSET, DOMAINE

Côtes du Rhône Laurent Brusset 1998: Well made, with attractive aromas and flavors of cherry, earth and spice. A decent little wine for daily consumption, it won't break the weekly wine budget, and offers good tannic grip to hold up against flavorful meals. Drink now through 2003.–P.M. • $10 • (12/15/1999) • **85**

Côtes du Rhône-Villages Cairanne 1996: If you like mocha-chocolate candy, try this. Fairly thick and rustic, with a good, round mouthfeel. Has tobacco and currant but also an herbal, citrusy element. Medium-bodied, fresh. Try with meals. Drink through 2001.–P.M. • $10 • (11/15/1998) • **81**

Côtes du Rhône-Villages Cairanne 1995 • $11 • (10/15/1997) • **84**

BRUSSET, DOMAINE

Côtes du Rhône-Villages Cairanne Côteaux des Travers 1997: Well made. Deep-colored, medium-bodied red that shows refined, ripe tannins and bursts with cassis, blackberry and cigar-box character. Excellent acidity and good intensity on the lingering finish. Drink now through 2003.–P.M. • $13 • (11/15/1998) • **90**
Côtes du Rhône-Villages Cairanne Côteaux des Travers 1990 • $11 • (4/15/1993) • **71**
Côtes du Rhône-Villages Cairanne Côteaux des Travers 1988 • $8 • (12/15/1990) • **86**
Gigondas Le Grand Montmirail 1998: Perfect. This Rhône red is amazing for its clean, pure fruit, silky tannins and balance of natural alcohol and acidity. One sip will convince you of its greatness. It slips down the throat like the most velvety drink possible, yet there's enough grip to hold it together for the future. Drink now through 2010.–P.M. • $20 • (12/15/1999) HR • **94**
Gigondas Le Grand Montmirail 1997: This gorgeous, big wine is extracted, with compacted, clean red berry and blackberry character. Offers depth and a wet earth and mineral complexity that anchors it in Gigondas despite its modern treatment. Best after 2000.–P.M. • $22 • (10/31/1999) • **89**
Gigondas Les Hauts de Montmirail 1997: This international-style red is heavily extracted and deep-colored, stressing blackberry, cassis, toast and violet notes. Pretty and velvety beneath the tough tannins. Best after 2002.–P.M. • $30 • (10/31/1999) • **88**
Gigondas Les Hauts de Montmirail 1996: Outstanding. Yes, it's oaky, but this exciting Southern Rhône red is also packed with freshly crushed black currant, black cherry, cranberry and blueberry flavors that burst from the glass. Thick, dense and seamless in its smooth texture, it's inky black in color, full in body and layered with violet, spice and mocha notes. The finish is silky-smooth. Drink through 2007.–P.M. • $32 • (10/15/1998) HR • **93**
Gigondas Les Hauts de Montmirail 1994 • $24 • (10/15/1997) • **90**
Gigondas Les Hauts de Montmirail 1991 • $18 • (3/31/1994) • **87**
Gigondas Les Hauts de Montmirail 1990 • $28 • (4/15/1993) • **89**
Gigondas Les Hauts de Montmirail 1989 • $22 • (11/15/1991) HR • **91**
Gigondas Les Hauts de Montmirail 1988 • $17 • (9/30/1990) • **90**

BRUT DE LAFAURIE

Bordeaux White 1996: Rather strange aromas of cut wood and geraniums, with some fruit. Medium-bodied and slightly cloying, with a woody, earthy aftertaste. Barely acceptable. Dry wine from the Sauternes estate of Lafaurie-Peyraguey.–J.S. • $NA • (1/01/1999) • **72**

BUCY, MAISON JOSEPH DE

Mâcon-Clessé 1996 • $10 • (5/31/1998) • **77**

BUFFET, FRANCOIS

Pommard Les Rugiens 1985 • $40 • (10/15/1988) • **88**
Volnay Champans 1995 • $30 • (11/15/1997) • **89**
Volnay Champans 1985 • $35 • (10/15/1988) • **91**
Volnay Clos de la Rougeotte 1995 • $30 • (11/15/1997) • **84**

BUNAN, DOMAINES

Bandol Château La Rouvière 1995 • $NA • (5/31/1998) • **83**
Bandol Château La Rouvière 1989 • $19 • (3/31/1995) • **83**
Bandol Mas de la Rouvière 1997: Medium-bodied, with a gamy aroma and good dried cherry, red plum and leather flavors. Brick, chocolate and mineral notes linger on the finish. Drink now through 2002.–K.M. • $15 • (5/15/2000) • **87**
Bandol Mas de la Rouvière 1995 • $14 • (5/31/1998) • **85**
Bandol Mas de la Rouvière 1990 • $15 • (3/31/1995) • **87**
Bandol Mas de la Rouvière 1982 • $NA • (8/31/1986) • **73**
Bandol Mas de la Rouvière 1979 • $NA • (8/31/1986) • **80**
Bandol Rosé Château la Rouvière 1998: Good cherry and berry flavors make this an appealing and fairly lively rosé. Spicy, smoky notes linger on the finish. Drink now.–K.M. • $20 • (5/15/2000) • **86**
Bandol Rosé Château La Rouvière 1996 • $14 • (5/31/1998) • **84**

Key: SS—Spectator Selection. CS—Cellar Selection. HR—Highly Recommended. $NA—Price not available. (BT)—Barrel tasting. Ⓐ—Auction Price.
For a key to the tasters' initials, see "How to Use These Listings."
Dates in parentheses represent the issues in which the ratings were published.

Bandol Rosé Mas de la Rouvière 1998: There's a nice white pepper aroma to this rosé, followed by dried cherry flavors that end on a slightly smoky note. Drink now.–K.M. • $13 • (5/15/2000) • **84**
Bandol White Château la Rouvière 1998: A good, hearty white, with honey notes and green peach flavors. Drink now.–K.M. • $20 • (5/15/2000) • **83**
Bandol White Mas de la Rouvière 1998: Nutty aromas and flavors dominate this fairly smooth though rough-hewn white. Drink now.–K.M. • $14 • (5/15/2000) • **80**
Bandol White Mas de la Rouvière 1996 • $14 • (5/31/1998) • **83**

BURGAUD, BERNARD

Côte-Rôtie 1997: The inky-black color and big mouthfeel translate into a full-bodied red with a solid tannic structure, a good acidity level, some fine red and black fruit character and a firm, chewy, even hard finish. Drink now through 2003.–P.M. • $29 • (9/15/1999) • **87**
Côte-Rôtie 1996: Like biting into raspberry-filled dark chocolate. A wine of finesse, and despite the obvious presence of oak, this impressively racy and elegant Syrah delivers layers of mocha, spice and red berry in a balanced, full-bodied package. Fresh, lively texture balanced by ripe tannins. Needs time. Best from 2003 through 2010.–P.M. • $40 • (9/15/1998) • **92**
Côte-Rôtie 1995 • $38 • (10/15/1997) • **92**
Côte-Rôtie 1994 • $38 • (10/15/1997) • **90**
Côte-Rôtie 1992 • $30 • (12/15/1996) • **89**
Côte-Rôtie 1991 • $36 • (5/31/1994) • **87**
Côte-Rôtie 1990 • $37 • (4/15/1993) • **91**
Côte-Rôtie 1989 • $32 • (1/31/1992) • **84**
Côte-Rôtie 1988 • $40 • (3/31/1991) • **87**
Côte-Rôtie 1987 • $29 • (2/28/1990) • **85**
Côte-Rôtie 1986 • $31 • (1/31/1989) • **93**
Côte-Rôtie 1984 • $22 • (10/15/1987) • **90**
Côte-Rôtie 1983 • $15 Ⓐ • (5/01/1986) • **92**

BURGUET, ALAIN

Bourgogne 1992 • $15 • (12/15/1994) • **82**
Bourgogne 1990 • $18 • (12/15/1992) • **84**
Gevrey-Chambertin 1992 • $26 • (12/15/1994) • **80**
Gevrey-Chambertin 1991 • $30 • (1/31/1994) • **83**
Gevrey-Chambertin 1990 • $NA • (12/15/1992) • **89**
Gevrey-Chambertin Les Champeaux 1995: Quite distinctive, with a unique blood, iodine, salt, raw meat quality, before the sweet fruit kicks in with vibrant acidity. This well-balanced, medium-bodied character-filled wine isn't for everyone, but the courageous will be rewarded. Best from 2002 through 2010.–P.M. • $55 • (8/31/1998) • **90**
Gevrey-Chambertin Vieilles Vignes 1996: A strong eucalyptus note in the aroma, followed by rich, well-defined cherry and berry flavors bordered by spice. Seems a little lean and crisp, backed by some firm tannins. Best from 2001 through 2005.–B.S. • $45 • (1/01/2000) • **87**
Gevrey-Chambertin Vieilles Vignes 1995: Old-style Burgundy at its best. Not a charmer, this is a connoisseur's wine, filled with distinctive iron, mineral, wet earth and game character. Delivers lots of ripe fruit, even if it's hidden in a tough, iron-fisted package that isn't for everyone. Best from 2003 through 2008.–P.M. • $40 • (8/31/1998) • **90**
Gevrey-Chambertin Vieilles Vignes 1991 • $39 • (1/31/1994) • **75**
Gevrey-Chambertin Vieilles Vignes 1990 • $51 Ⓐ • (12/15/1992) • **90**
Gevrey-Chambertin Vieilles Vignes 1988 • $36 Ⓐ • (12/31/1990) • **88**
Gevrey-Chambertin Vieilles Vignes 1986 • $33 • (7/15/1989) • **84**

BURN, ERNEST

Gewürztraminer Alsace Grand Cru Goldert Clos St.-Imer 1996: Thickly textured and polished, this offers weight and amplitude, but the flavor is one-dimensional and it lacks concentration, ending on a coarse note. Disappointing for the appellation. Drink now.–B.S. • $27 • (4/30/1999) • **82**
Gewürztraminer Alsace Grand Cru Goldert Clos St.-Imer La Chapelle 1997: Rich, broad and open, this Gewürz has a modicum of honey and litchi yet, ultimately, the alcohol emerges on the finish. Drink now.–B.S. • $35 • (6/15/2000) • **83**
Gewürztraminer Alsace Grand Cru Goldert Clos St.-Imer Sélection de Grains Nobles 1994: Golden amber and very sweet, with concentrated caramel and a slightly burnt note married to a firm structure. Seems to have plenty of life ahead. Drink now through 2005.–B.S. • $80/375 ml. • (6/15/2000) • **88**
Muscat Alsace Grand Cru Goldert Clos St.-Imer 1996: A subtle, reserved *grand cru* that delivers flavors of white pepper, honey and vanilla in a lean,

FRANCE

concentrated style. Good length and intensity. Drink through 2004.–B.S. • $25 • (3/31/1999) • **86**

Pinot Blanc Alsace 1997: Showing a lot of lees (dead yeast sediment) contact, hence the creamy texture, along with flavors of apple, peach and lemon. Has just enough acidity to keep it lively, finishing slightly hot. Drink now through 2001.–B.S. • $18 • (3/31/1999) • **85**

Riesling Alsace 1996: Rich and reserved, this Riesling displays apple and mineral flavors and an innate power. Medium-bodied, it finishes on a crisp, citrusy note. Drink through 2004.–B.S. • $15 • (9/15/1998) • **88**

Riesling Alsace Grand Cru Goldert Clos St.-Imer 1996: Dry, stony and spicy, this Riesling is elegant, firmly structured and exhibits moderate richness. Peach flavors midpalate persist through the finish. Drink now through 2005.–B.S. • $25 • (3/31/1999) • **84**

Riesling Alsace Grand Cru Goldert Clos St.-Imer La Chapelle 1997: Bursting with apricot aromas and flavors joined by a dash of grapefruit and orange, this is smooth, forward and open, with enough bite on the finish to keep it lively. Drink now through 2003.–B.S. • $33 • (5/31/2000) • **89**

Riesling Alsace Grand Cru Goldert Clos St.-Imer La Chapelle 1996: Incredible ripeness. Soft, lush and apricotlike, yet the flavors resonate on the palate, with a juicy texture that's deceiving given the level of ripeness. There's a mineral note and a purity, ending gracefully. Drink now through 2005.–B.S. • $30 • (9/15/1998) • **91**

Tokay Pinot Gris Alsace Grand Cru Goldert Clos St.-Imer La Chapelle 1997: Thick and almost chewy, exuding vanilla, licorice and honey aromas and flavors married to a big, loosely knit structure. Drink now through 2001.–B.S. • $33 • (6/15/2000) • **87**

Tokay Pinot Gris Alsace Grand Cru Goldert Clos St.-Imer La Chapelle 1996: A vibrant white that seems more precocious than powerful. This has intensity of flavor, richness and fine acidity to support the nectarine, smoke and honey notes in this young Pinot Gris. Drink now through 2001.–B.S. • $30 • (9/15/1998) • **88**

BURRIER, JACQUES

Pouilly-Fuissé Château de Beauregard 1997: Elegant and restrained on the nose, a minerally Pouilly with ripe fruit and some pronounced toasted oak character. Medium-bodied. Drink now.–P.M. • $28 • (5/31/1999) • **85**

Pouilly-Fuissé Château de Beauregard 1996 • $21 • (5/31/1998) • **91**

Pouilly-Fuissé Château de Beauregard 1995 • $21 • (5/31/1997) • **81**

Pouilly-Fuissé Château de Beauregard Cuvée Prestige 1996 • $21 • (5/31/1998) • **92**

Pouilly-Fuissé Château de Beauregard Les Chataigners Cuvée de Vieilles Vignes 1997: Polished, with distinct toasted oak accents playing against just as pronounced butterscotch, pear tart and spice flavors. A bit tough on the finish. Drink through 2004.–P.M. • $35 • (5/31/1999) • **85**

St.-Véran Les Perriers 1996 • $14 • (5/31/1998) • **83**

BY, CHATEAU DE

Médoc 1996: Not very exciting, and slightly unripe and herbal despite some berry and cherry character. Medium-bodied, with medium, slightly dry tannins.–J.S. • $NA • (2/28/1999) • **79**

BZIKOT PERE & FILS

Bourgogne White 1997: Medium-bodied, with pear and lemon, it turns very tart and tough on the finish.–P.M. • $17 • (5/31/1999) • **78**

Puligny-Montrachet 1997: Cooked fruit turns to oxidized flavors in this rustic, astringent, tart white.–P.M. • $36 • (5/31/1999) • **70**

Puligny-Montrachet 1996: Soft, supple and smooth, with spicy oak, pear and melon and prosciuttolike flavors, this is a '96 that's accessible upon release; of medium body and medium intensity, it offers a velvety finish without great complexity. Drink now through 2002.–P.M. • $31 • (8/31/1998) • **84**

Puligny-Montrachet Les Folatières 1997: An unbalanced Chardonnay showing spicy oak character and cooked fruit notes, this tastes of burnt butter on the astringent, heavyhanded finish.–P.M. • $53 • (5/31/1999) • **75**

Puligny-Montrachet Les Folatières 1996: Beautiful fruit and gorgeous mineral character drive this full-bodied wine. Shows some pronounced smoky, toasted oak spiciness, but also a stony, pebblelike, mineral-laden quality that gives smoothness and personality. Best from 2005.–P.M. • $40 • (8/31/1998) • **92**

CABANES, DIDIER

Coteaux du Languedoc Domaine des Tourelles 1998: A good, light- to medium-bodied quaffer, with nice cherry and juniper flavors that carry through to the finish. Drink now.–K.M. • $10 • (6/15/2000) • **84**

CABANNE, CHATEAU LA

Pomerol 1997: Fresh currant and berry aromas with a hint of mineral. Medium-bodied, with medium tannins and a short finish. Needs a bit more. Best after 2000.–J.S. • $34 • (1/31/2000) • **84**

Pomerol 1996: Not a big wine, but delivers some attractive berry, chocolate and cherry character. Medium-bodied, with light tannins and a berry, chocolate and tobacco aftertaste Drink now.–J.S. • $NA • (1/31/1999) • **85**

Pomerol 1995: Fresh berry, tobacco and game everywhere. Full-bodied, with full, velvety tannins and a long, caressing finish. Real wine. Best from 2001 through 2005.–J.S. • $NA • (9/15/1998) • **90**

Pomerol 1991 • $15 • (3/31/1994) • **73**

Pomerol 1990 • $27 • (3/31/1993) • **87**

Pomerol 1989: A bit funky and dry, but there's plenty of berries, chocolate and meat in this wine. Full-bodied and very soft, with lots of ripe fruit character.—1989 Bordeaux horizontal. Drink now.–J.S. • $NA • (5/31/1999) • **88**

Pomerol 1982 • $23 • (8/31/1992) • **84**

CABASSE, DOMAINE DE

Côtes du Rhône-Villages Rosé Seguret Le Marie Antoinette 1998: A well-made rosé, easy and crisp—just what you expect. Fresh, with lime and peach flavors and a tart but not sour finish, because there's always honey to go along. Drink now through 2001.–P.M. • $15 • (12/15/1999) • **84**

Côtes du Rhône-Villages Rosé Seguret Le Marie Antoinette 1996 • $14 • (10/15/1997) • **80**

Côtes du Rhône-Villages Séguret 1995: Refined and fresh, a fairly easy wine with fine tannins and nice black currant, even citrus, character. Medium in body, lingering and juicy, with a clean finish. Drink now.–P.M. • $13 • (11/15/1998) • **85**

Côtes du Rhône-Villages Séguret Cuvée de la Casa Bassa 1997: A very tannic red, which gives it interest and structure, but the tannins seem to overwhelm the fruit, leaving a drying finish.–P.M. • $25 • (12/15/1999) • **77**

Côtes du Rhône-Villages Séguret Cuvée de la Casa Bassa 1996: Nice balance to this dark-colored, lively red, showing good, flavorful character with a distinctive cherry and pepper aroma. Fresh finish. Drink now.–P.M. • $24 • (11/15/1999) • **82**

Côtes du Rhône-Villages Séguret Cuvée de la Casa Bassa 1995: Fairly opulent and soft, showing spice, mocha and freshly ground coffee notes, this medium-bodied, oak-aged red also offers plum, tobacco and currant. Slightly short finish.–P.M. • $23 • (11/15/1998) • **85**

Côtes du Rhône-Villages Séguret Cuvée Garnacho 1997: Good tannin structure supports the black cherry and dry herb notes. Rather good ripeness, as shown on the fat midpalate. Drink now through 2001.–P.M. • $20 • (12/15/1999) • **81**

Côtes du Rhône-Villages Séguret Cuvée Garnacho 1996: Flavorful but a bit rustic and one-dimensional, delivering black pepper and black cherry notes and crisp tannins in a clean package. Drink now.–P.M. • $18 • (11/15/1999) • **80**

Côtes du Rhône-Villages Séguret Cuvée Garnacho 1995: Very soft and supple, with some mocha and spice along with the plum and cherry, this medium-bodied red is pleasurable and harmonious. Drink now.–P.M. • $17 • (11/15/1998) • **83**

Côtes du Rhône-Villages White Séguret 1998: Rustic, dry and a bit oxidized, with just a bit of honey to save the day.–P.M. • $15 • (12/15/1999) • **78**

Gigondas 1997: A cowboy, "hey man" Rhône Ranger wine. This muscular, firm, tannic red shows a tough grip, delivering *terroir* and earth along with good ripeness of fruit, terrific concentration and good balance. Expect a chewy finish that should match your steak. Drink now through 2005.–P.M. • $28 • (12/15/1999) • **89**

CABLANC, CHATEAU

Bordeaux 1996: Has light but good berry and currant flavors. Light- to medium-bodied, with a light finish. Drink now.–J.S. • $9 • (7/31/1999) • **80**

CABRIAC, CHATEAU DE

Corbières 1992 • $9 • (3/15/1994) • **87**

Corbières Cuvée Marquise de Puivert 1995 • $10 • (12/15/1997) • **85**

CABRIERES, CHATEAU

Châteauneuf-du-Pape 1998: A silky '98 Rhône red, so full in the mouth, so ripe and balanced. Fresh while delivering richness, it doesn't taste alcoholic or hot, just clean and pure, with a velvety mouthfeel from start to finish. Drink now through 2010.–P.M. • $25 • (12/15/1999) SS • **90**
Châteauneuf-du-Pape 1997: Light-colored and a bit diluted, with cherry and strawberry flavors, a light body and a chewy finish.–P.M. • $26 • (8/31/1999) • **77**
Châteauneuf-du-Pape Prestige Tête de Cru 1998: Classy. Like sipping cream, it's so silky. Ripe but not overdone, delivering mineral, sweet black fruit and red berry, with a toasted, smoky grilled fowl character. Harmonious finish. Drink now through 2010.–P.M. • $42 • (6/30/2000) • **94**

CABRIERES, DOMAINE DE

Châteauneuf-du-Pape 1996: Ripe and rich, with a robust backbone of flavor and tannin. Shows cedar, chocolate and cigar-box flavors and an herbal black olive note on the somewhat drying finish. A bit disjointed now, best from 2000.–P.M. • $23 • (9/30/1998) • **84**
Châteauneuf-du-Pape 1995 • $23 • (9/15/1997) • **84**
Châteauneuf-du-Pape 1994 • $23 • (12/15/1996) • **85**
Châteauneuf-du-Pape 1988 • $17 • (11/30/1990) • **82**
Châteauneuf-du-Pape Prestige Tête de Cru 1995: Made for aficionados of the contemporary style, with a milk chocolate character, very creamy and extremely supple tannins. Hankers for a bit more complex *terroir* or length. Drink now through 2005.–P.M. • $35 • (11/15/1998) • **86**
Châteauneuf-du-Pape White 1997: Quite aromatic, with peach, apricot and pear. Of medium body, it turns a bit hot on the midpalate, showing some caramel and butter character. Drink now.–P.M. • $20 • (9/30/1998) • **80**

CADEAUX

Brut Blanc de Blancs France Royal Crown Cuvée Privée NV • $10 • (12/31/1997) • **85**

CADET-BON, CHATEAU

St.-Emilion 1998: Some pretty berry and cherry character, with well-knit tannins. Medium-bodied, medium finish.–J.S. • $NA • (5/31/1999) (BT) • **85-89**
St.-Emilion 1997: Bright berry and currant aromas and flavors. Medium-bodied, with firm tannins, almost austere. Best after 2000.–J.S. • $NA • (1/31/2000) • **86**
St.-Emilion 1996: Pleasant and soft, with chocolate and berry aromas and flavors, medium to light body and a delicate finish. Drink now.–J.S. • $29 • (1/31/1999) • **85**
St.-Emilion 1995 • $28 • (1/31/1998) • **87**
St.-Emilion 1994 • $NA • (1/31/1997) • **82**

CADET DE LARMANDE, LE

St.-Emilion 1996: Pretty plum and berry aromas. Medium-bodied, with fine tannins and a light, fruity afertaste. Second label of Château Larmande. Drink now.–J.S. • $NA • (1/31/1999) • **81**

CADET-PIOLA, CHATEAU

St.-Emilion 1998: Impressive concentration for the vintage, but slightly one-dimensional. Full-bodied, with velvety tannins and a slightly hollow midpalate.–J.S. • $NA • (5/31/1999) (BT) • **85-89**
St.-Emilion 1997: Bright berry and cherry character, with a hint of spice. Medium-bodied, with medium, firm tannins and a fresh fruit aftertaste. Drink now through 2004.–J.S. • $NA • (1/31/2000) • **85**
St.-Emilion 1996: A Right Bank wine with lovely chocolate and berry aromas and flavors. Medium-bodied, with firm tannins, but a rather short, diluted finish. Drink now.–J.S. • $NA • (1/31/1999) • **84**
St.-Emilion 1988 • $20 • (7/15/1991) • **89**
St.-Emilion 1982: Big yet balanced. Dark ruby in color, with a slight amber tint. Dried cherry, rose petal and vanilla. Full-bodied and very ripe, with velvety tannins and a long, intense berry and green tobacco aftertaste. Drink now or hold. (1982 Bordeaux horizontal tasting).–J.S. • $NA • (11/30/1998) • **91**

CADY, DOMAINE

Coteaux du Layon St.-Aubin Les Varennes 1995 • $20 • (5/31/1998) • **90**

CAILBOURDIN, DOMAINE A.

Pouilly-Fumé Cuvée de Boisfleury 1996 • $15 • (5/31/1998) • **88**
Pouilly-Fumé Les Cris 1998: Clean herbal and apple flavors are quite rich in this crisp white. Has the body and balance for food. Drink now.–T.M. • $15 • (3/31/2000) • **85**
Pouilly-Fumé Les Cris 1997: Subtle but well focused, this firm white shows clean, brisk flavors of citrus and mineral, with typical herbal and grassy notes. Has good concentration, and the flavors linger on the finish. Drink now through 2002.–T.M. • $17 • (6/30/1999) • **88**
Pouilly-Fumé Les Cris 1996 • $17 • (5/31/1998) • **83**

CAILLOT

Bâtard-Montrachet 1997: Pungent and earthy but fresh and elegant, with a good citrusy backbone, this delivers dried herbs, mineral, chalky character. Medium-bodied, it's a bit rough on the finish. Best from 2002 through 2005.–P.M. • $195 • (5/31/2000) • **87**
Bâtard-Montrachet 1996: A pure grand white Burgundy that's fantastic. Rich and full-bodied, with tropical, ripe pear, lemon and honey notes and toast flavors, this full-bodied, fruit-driven, bright white is balanced and deeply satisfying. Drink now through 2016.–P.M. • $115 Ⓐ • (5/31/1999) • **99**
Bâtard-Montrachet 1995 • $92 • (8/31/1997) • **95**
Beaune Avaux 1997: Nicely ripe and balanced. Medium-bodied, with a good dose of tannins and flavorful red- and black berry character. Rather linear—nothing big or rich here—but what's there makes a pretty little Pinot Noir. Drink now through 2003.–P.M. • $NA • (1/01/2000) • **86**
Beaune Avaux 1996: Ripe enough but a bit odd, with a blood, lead pencil, game, mushroom character in a very high acidity, citrus-spiked package with a mouthpuckering finish.–P.M. • $26 • (5/15/1999) • **78**
Bourgogne 1996: Elegant style, but already showing an underbrush, tea leaf character that makes it taste mature, or complex depending on your perspective. The finish is a bit astringent.–P.M. • $16 • (5/15/1999) • **79**
Bourgogne 1995 • $13 • (11/15/1997) • **81**
Bourgogne White Les Herbeux 1997: Intriguing, but great quality for a simple Bourgogne Blanc. Not especially lovable, with its firm, wet stone, mineral and gunpowder character, but it attaches itself to your palate with all the might of a powerful wine. Drink now through 2005.–P.M. • $15 • (1/01/2000) • **90**
Bourgogne White Les Herbeux 1995 • $16 • (8/31/1997) • **89**
Meursault Clos du Cromin 1997: Superb. Very ripe and full-bodied, with intense tropical, citrus and honey character. Tingles with nervous, fresh tension on the palate, exploding with vibrant fruit flavors from start to long toasted finish. Drink now through 2010.–P.M. • $39 • (1/01/2000) • **93**
Meursault Clos du Cromin 1996: A bit earthy yet polished, this displays minerally raciness and shows green apple, pear and lemon in a sublimely focused, intense, crisp package. the long finish is unhindered by heavy-handed oak. Best from 2006 through 2016.–P.M. • $30 • (5/31/1999) • **94**
Meursault Clos du Cromin 1995 • $32 • (8/31/1997) • **89**
Meursault La Barre Dessus Clos Marguerite 1997: Rich and full-bodied, this ripe white has loads of personality, showing dosed oak and much citrus. Smells and tastes a bit spritzy and earthy, with good fruit and an intense finish. Drink now through 2007.–P.M. • $36 • (1/01/2000) • **87**
Meursault La Barre Dessus Clos Marguerite 1996: Full-bodied yet incredibly elegant. So refined it smells of little but a vague mineraliness, and it's the same story on the palate—a great concentration of *terroir*, cream, compact tropical fruit and stone—with good acidity and subtle toastiness. Best from 2006 through 2015.–P.M. • $32 • (5/31/1999) • **96**
Meursault La Barre Dessus Clos Marguerite 1995 • $32 • (8/31/1997) • **92**
Meursault Le Limozin 1997: More fruit than mineral, but it's an intense, full-bodied white. Classy on the reserved nose, with the ripe fruit and crisp citrus flavors kicking in on the sweet-tasting finish. Drink now through 2007.–P.M. • $39 • (1/01/2000) • **89**
Meursault Le Limozin 1996: Elegant, with good ripe fruit balancing the acidity, offering lime, pear, mineral and honey in a lush and intensely flavored package. Has an oily aftertaste but also overwhelmingly tart toasted oak. Best from 2002 through 2012.–P.M. • $38 • (5/31/1999) • **89**
Meursault Le Limozin 1995 • $32 • (8/31/1997) • **94**

Key: SS—Spectator Selection. CS—Cellar Selection. HR—Highly Recommended. $NA—Price not available. (BT)—Barrel tasting. Ⓐ—Auction Price.
For a key to the tasters' initials, see "How to Use These Listings."
Dates in parentheses represent the issues in which the ratings were published.

FRANCE

Meursault Les Tessons 1997: Rich, ripe and deliciously hedonistic, it marries lemon, honey and pineapple in a full-bodied package. Vibrates with intensity on the palate to a long, zesty finish. Drink now through 2010.–P.M. • $39 • (1/01/2000) • **90**

Meursault Les Tessons 1996: From rising Meursault star Caillot comes a sensational village wine that rivals some producers' *grands crus*. Oily and silky in texture and full-bodied, with beautiful concentration of pure, clean, vibrant fruit, subtle toasted oak accents, a mineral character and honey and tropical notes on the polished, seamless finish. Drink now through 2016.–P.M. • $34 • (5/31/1999) • **95**

Meursault Les Tessons 1995 • $31 • (8/31/1997) • **90**

Monthélie 1997: An elegant Pinot but with surprising personality for a '97 red Burgundy. Ripe fruit mingles with impressive concentration of earth. A chewy *terroir* drives the wine along the palate, giving a sense of focus. Drink now through 2007.–P.M. • $NA • (1/01/2000) • **88**

Monthélie 1996: A bit tough, with an iron, blood, mineral component, turning earthy and tart on the finish.–P.M. • $19 • (5/15/1999) • **75**

Monthélie 1995 • $17 • (11/15/1997) • **76**

Pommard 1997: Impressive winemaking. Pure and ripe, this '97 offers subtle red and black fruit, wonderful midpalate sweetness, medium body and a *goût de terroir* in its wet earth, mineral and chalk character. Long, balanced, delicious finish. Drink now through 2007.–P.M. • $NA • (1/01/2000) • **93**

Pommard 1996: Petrol and smoky oak in the mouth are disturbing. Tasted twice, with consistent notes.–P.M. • $32 • (9/30/1999) • **65**

Pommard 1995 • $27 • (11/15/1997) • **77**

Pommard 1987 • $35 • (9/15/1989) • **79**

Pommard Epenots 1995 • $30 • (11/15/1997) • **79**

Pommard Epenots 1997: Has an interesting petrol-like aroma that's not for everyone. Medium-bodied and thick-textured, with crisp flavors and smooth tannins. Medium-intense toast combines with berry and plum. Drink now through 2003.–P.M. • $NA • (1/01/2000) • **84**

Pommard Epenots 1996: Rustic, with wood giving off odd smoke and petrol aromas. Tasted twice, with consistent notes.–P.M. • $42 • (9/30/1999) • **65**

Pommard Epenots 1995 • $30 • (11/15/1997) • **79**

Puligny-Montrachet Les Folatières 1997: Only in Burgundy. This is a gorgeous wine exploding with idiosyncratic *goût de terroir*. Subtle and complex dried herb, butter, wet stone and ripe fruit notes kick up a tornado that persists on the deftly oaked finish. Drink now through 2010.–P.M. • $60 • (5/31/2000) • **93**

Puligny-Montrachet Les Folatières 1996: Lovely, medium-bodied and fairly crisp, showing cream, lemon and toasty oak, with superb ripe, tropical flavors on the seductive, refined finish. Best from 2002 through 2008.–P.M. • $53 • (5/31/1999) • **94**

Puligny-Montrachet Les Folatières 1995 • $45 • (8/31/1997) • **93**

Puligny-Montrachet Les Pucelles 1997: Rich, ripe and very intense in a fresh, lively, vibrant sense. Full-bodied and packed with tropical and citrus character, this amazingly powerful and seductive white Burgundy has a mineral, wet earth and smoke personality. Drink now through 2010.–P.M. • $80 • (1/01/2000) • **94**

Puligny-Montrachet Les Pucelles 1995 • $68 • (8/31/1997) • **90**

Santenay White 1997: Thick, ripe, rich and oozing tropical, honey and mineral character, with the feel of extra virgin oil. Seamless, with great citrus intensity to cleanse the palate on the finish. Incredible quality for a Santenay. A sexy white from a young, "artsy" Meursault producer. Drink now through 2007.–P.M. • $20 • (1/01/2000) • **92**

Santenay White 1996: An earthy, crisp, lemony, sharp, tart white, with a rustic finish.–P.M. • $20 • (5/31/1999) • **76**

Santenay White 1995 • $18 • (8/31/1997) • **88**

Volnay Clos des Chênes 1997: A balanced '97. This medium-bodied red Burgundy has pretty toast, spice, chocolate, raspberry and black cherry complexity, with a supple texture and a pleasantly chewy tannin structure. Drink now through 2003.–P.M. • $NA • (1/01/2000) • **88**

Volnay Clos des Chênes 1996: Odd. Smells muted and tastes a bit dusty and strange, with a drying palate. Tasted twice, with consistent notes.–P.M. • $37 • (9/30/1999) • **73**

Volnay Clos des Chênes 1995 • $27 • (11/15/1997) • **86**

CAILLOU, CHATEAU

Barsac 1998: Plenty of apple and pear aromas and flavors. Medium-bodied, with spicy apple flavors. Zingy acidity.–J.S. • $NA • (1/01/1999) (BT) • **85-89**

Barsac 1991 • $NA • (4/15/1995) • **83**

Barsac 1990 • $NA • (4/15/1995) • **92**

Barsac 1989 • $40 • (4/15/1995) • **87**

Barsac 1988 • $39 • (4/15/1995) • **84**

Barsac 1987 • $32 • (6/15/1990) • **85**

Barsac 1983 • $22 • (1/31/1988) • **76**

Barsac Private Cuvée 1986 • $NA • (4/15/1995) • **92**

Barsac Private Cuvée 1983 • $NA • (4/15/1995) • **89**

Sauternes 1997: Young, with loads of apple pie, honey and butterscotch character. Full-bodied and very sweet, with a long, long finish. Drink now.–J.S. • $NA • (1/31/2000) • **90**

CAILLOU BLANC DU CHATEAU TALBOT

Bordeaux 1998: A clean, fresh, medium-bodied white, with lemon rind and mineral character and a zingy finish. Drink now.–J.S. • $24 • (2/29/2000) • **87**

Bordeaux 1997: Pretty aromas of sliced peach and apple. Full-bodied and mouthfilling, but slightly hard on the finish. Drink now.–J.S. • $27 • (9/30/1999) • **87**

Bordeaux 1996: Promises more on the nose than the palate gives at the moment, but seriously good. Wonderfully exotic aromas of pineapple, passion fruit and melon, with hints of vanilla. Medium-bodied, with lots of toasted oak flavors and a creamy, fruit aftertaste. Needs more time to develop. Drink through 2004.–J.S. • $24 • (3/31/1999) • **88**

CAILLOUX, LES

Châteauneuf-du-Pape 1995: This round, soft red shows ripe flavors of cherry, raisin, herb and spice, with firm tannins and a clean finish. It's expressive and shows good typicity, but lacks depth. Drink now through 2002.–T.M. • $23 • (11/15/1998) • **86**

Châteauneuf-du-Pape 1990 • $24 • (4/15/1993) • **88**

Châteauneuf-du-Pape 1989 • • (10/15/1991) • **93**

Châteauneuf-du-Pape 1988 • $18 • (10/15/1991) • **88**

Châteauneuf-du-Pape 1986 • $18 • (10/15/1991) • **79**

Châteauneuf-du-Pape 1985 • $16 • (10/15/1991) • **82**

Châteauneuf-du-Pape 1983 • $55 • (10/15/1991) • **88**

Châteauneuf-du-Pape 1981 • $30 • (10/15/1991) • **76**

Châteauneuf-du-Pape Cuvée Centenaire 1995: Subtle yet complex aromas are rich and intriguing, and the flavors carry through on the palate, with notes of spice, ripe cherry and raisin, cedar and wild herb. Well defined, showing good intensity in a classic regional style. Drink now through 2005.–T.M. • $80 • (11/15/1998) • **91**

Châteauneuf-du-Pape Cuvée Centenaire 1990 • $45 • (4/15/1993) • **93**

Châteauneuf-du-Pape Sélection Reflets 1986 • $18 • (5/31/1989) • **89**

CAIRANNE, CAVE DE

Côtes du Rhône-Villages Cairanne Grande Réserve 1995: Light in color, body, texture and flavor, this tastes herbal, with a shadow of fruit.–P.M. • $NA • (11/15/1998) • **72**

Côtes du Rhône-Villages Cairanne Temptation 1996: Strongly herbal, turning dry on the finish.–P.M. • $12 • (11/15/1998) • **73**

Côtes du Rhône-Villages Cairanne Terre de Cuvée 1995: Light- to medium-bodied, showing maturing flavors, with spice and mocha accents to the plummy and rough finish.–P.M. • $10 • (11/15/1998) • **79**

Côtes du Rhône-Villages Cuvée Antique 1995: Delicious little red, bursting with floral, plum, cassis, wild raspberry character. Medium-bodied with sweet tannins, it's balanced and pretty without being "serious." A succulent wine for everyday meals. Drink now through 2003.–P.M. • $15 • (11/15/1998) • **88**

CALADROY, CHATEAU DE

Côtes du Roussillon Rosé 1998: An assertive rosé, with wild berry and cherry flavors, and some gamey notes. Spicy flavors linger on the finish. Drink now.–K.M. • $14 • (2/29/2000) • **84**

Côtes du Roussillon-Villages Les Grenats 1998: Violet and cassis flavors dominate this fairly powerful red, also loaded with red plum and roasted espresso notes. A firm backbone of focused tannins adds to its appeal. Dark and bittersweet chocolate notes linger on the finish. Drink now through 2003.–K.M. • $20 • (2/29/2000) • **88**

Côtes du Roussillon-Villages Les Schistes 1998: A rich, medium-bodied red, with a nice array of flavors: boysenberry, licorice and dark plum. Well-rounded and supple, with chocolaty and spicy notes on the finish. Drink now through 2002.–K.M. • $15 • (2/29/2000) • **86**

CALCE, CHATEAU DE

Côtes du Roussillon 1996: A ripe, round and almost effusive wine, with pretty flavors of plum, currant, spice and pepper. Medium-bodied and well balanced, this is an easy-to-like red that will go down easily. Drink now through 2001.–K.M. • $8 • (4/30/1999) • **86**

CALISSANNE, CHATEAU

Coteaux d'Aix-en-Provence Clos Victoire 1995 • $30 • (3/31/1998) • **83**
Coteaux d'Aix-en-Provence Clos Victoire 1994 • $28 • (10/15/1996) • **90**
Coteaux d'Aix-en-Provence Cuvée du Château 1995 • $10 • (3/31/1998) • **85**
Coteaux d'Aix-en-Provence Cuvée du Château 1994 • $10 • (2/28/1998) • **85**
Coteaux d'Aix-en-Provence Cuvée Prestige 1995 • $15 • (2/28/1998) • **85**
Coteaux d'Aix-en-Provence Cuvée Prestige 1994 • $16 • (10/15/1996) • **87**
Coteaux d'Aix-en-Provence Cuvée Prestige 1990 • $15 • (6/15/1993) • **79**
Coteaux d'Aix-en-Provence Cuvée Prestige 1988 • $12 • (8/31/1991) • **78**
Coteaux d'Aix-en-Provence Rosé Cuvée du Château 1996 • $10 • (12/31/1997) • **84**
Coteaux d'Aix-en-Provence White Clos Victoire 1996 • $30 • (3/31/1998) • **80**
Coteaux d'Aix-en-Provence White Cuvée Prestige 1996 • $15 • (3/31/1998) • **75**

CALON-SEGUR, CHATEAU

St.-Estèphe 1999: Balanced and delicious, with plenty of spicy berry and cherry character. Medium body, medium tannins, a fresh finish.–J.S. • $NA • (1/01/2000) (BT) • **85-89**
St.-Estèphe 1997: Rather light for Calon but very aromatic, with cherry, spice aromas and a light, fruity finish. Drink now.–J.S. • $25 • (1/31/2000) • **83**
St.-Estèphe 1996: Aromas of blackberry, currant, strawberry, tar and mint. Medium- to full-bodied, with a polished and caressing texture. Not as good as the great '95, but excellent. This chewy yet closed wine needs years to come around. Best after 2003.–J.S. • $47 Ⓐ • (1/31/1999) • **90**
St.-Estèphe 1995 • $53 Ⓐ • (1/31/1998) SS • **96**
St.-Estèphe 1993 • $25 • (1/31/1996) • **84**
St.-Estèphe 1991 • $21 • (3/31/1994) • **82**
St.-Estèphe 1989: An enormous, bruising, highly extracted wine. Dark brick-red color. Plummy, earthy aromas and hints of aniseed and game. Full-bodied, incredibly ripe, with raisin, tobacco and earth on the slightly dry and overextracted finish. Overdone? I overrated this when it was young. (1989 Bordeaux horizontal tasting). Best after 2004.–J.S. • $60 Ⓐ • (5/31/1999) • **87**
St.-Estèphe 1988 • $54 Ⓐ • (7/15/1991) • **85**
St.-Estèphe 1986 • $46 Ⓐ • (5/31/1989) • **86**
St.-Estèphe 1985 • $52 Ⓐ • (5/31/1988) • **88**
St.-Estèphe 1983 • $66 Ⓐ • (10/31/1986) • **83**
St.-Estèphe 1982: Not the most complex wine, but rich and youthful. Dark ruby in color, with a garnet edge. Medium- to full-bodied, with velvety tannins, cherry and wet earth aromas and a fruity, crisp finish. (1982 Bordeaux horizontal tasting). Drink now.–J.S. • $92 Ⓐ • (11/30/1998) • **87**
St.-Estèphe 1970 • $43 Ⓐ • (5/15/1993) • **83**
St.-Estèphe 1962 • $57 Ⓐ • (11/30/1987) • **70**
St.-Estèphe 1961 • $118 Ⓐ • (4/30/1996) • **86**
St.-Estèphe 1959 • $116 Ⓐ • (10/15/1990) • **82**
St.-Estèphe 1947 • $415 Ⓐ • (7/31/1997) • **84**
St.-Estèphe 1945 • $226 Ⓐ • (11/30/1995) • **90**

CALOT, DOMAINE

Morgon Cuvée Unique Vieilles Vignes Réserve 1996: Far from typical for Beaujolais, this intense red offers loads of sweet, concentrated fruit, like a cherry liqueur, with a thick texture and firm underlying tannins. Impressive if not quite harmonious. A North Berkeley Wine Company barrel selection. Drink through 2001.–T.M. • $19 • (7/31/1998) • **88**

CAMENSAC, CHATEAU DE

Haut-Médoc 1998: Perfumed and captivating, with mineral, berry, currant and spice aromas. Medium-bodied, with well-knit tannins and a silky, caressing texture. Well made.–J.S. • $NA • (5/31/1999) (BT) • **85-89**
Haut-Médoc 1997: Berry and cherry character, with a slight stewed fruit undertone. Medium-bodied, with medium tannins and a light finish.–J.S. • $22 • (1/31/2000) • **83**
Haut-Médoc 1996: A very round and enjoyable '96. Pretty aromas of berry and porcini continue onto a medium-bodied palate, with velvety tannins and a fruity aftertaste. Best after 2001.–J.S. • $21 • (1/31/1999) • **89**
Haut-Médoc 1995: Best Camensac ever. Rich aromas of blackberries and chocolate. Full-bodied, with sweet, ripe fruit flavors, loads of velvety tannins and a long finish. An absolutely delicious wine for now, for later. Drink through 2010.–J.S. • $28 • (9/15/1998) • **90**
Haut-Médoc 1989 • $16 • (3/15/1992) • **86**
Haut-Médoc 1986 • $14 • (6/30/1989) • **83**
Haut-Médoc 1982: Fading fast. Chestnut and mushroom. Medium-bodied, with chestnut and mushroom but not much berry character. (1982 Bordeaux horizontal tasting).–J.S. • $NA • (11/30/1998) • **78**
Haut-Médoc 1979 • $22 • (10/15/1989) • **82**

CAMPEROS, CHATEAU

Sauternes 1995 • $27 • (11/30/1997) • **78**

CAMUS-BRUCHON, LUCIEN

Savigny-lès-Beaune Aux Grands Liards Vieilles Vignes 1997: A bit dull and lacking in focus, with a light yet chewy texture and cooked fruit character. Dry tannins on the finish.–B.S. • $29 • (9/30/1999) • **79**
Savigny-lès-Beaune Lavières 1997: Tastes very natural, with nice fruit and a bit of fatness midpalate. Racy and smooth, with wet earth and *terroir* character, silky tannins and lovely wild berry and raspberry notes. Delicious. Drink now through 2003.–P.M. • $29 • (9/30/1999) • **87**
Savigny-lès-Beaune Narbantons 1997: Full-bodied and fresh, delivering crisp character but also focused red and black fruit aromas and flavors. A bit hot on the finish, but it's a big wine. Drink now through 2004.–P.M. • $29 • (9/30/1999) • **85**
Savigny-lès-Beaune Vieilles Vignes 1997: Slightly cooked and on the soft side, though it's modestly concentrated, with plum flavors. Tough tannins on the finish. Drink now through 2002.–B.S. • $27 • (9/30/1999) • **80**

CANET, CHATEAU

Minervois Cuvée Elevée en Futs Grande Réserve 1988 • $6 • (5/31/1990) • **69**
Minervois Les Evangiles 1995: Plummy, with sweet cherry flavors and spicy notes on the finish. A ready-to-drink style that's medium-bodied and balanced. Drink now.–K.M. • $17 • (10/31/1998) • **85**

CANET VALETTE

St.-Chinian 1995 • $10 • (1/01/1998) • **88**

CANON, CHATEAU

Canon-Fronsac 1990 • $18 • (3/31/1993) • **85**
Canon-Fronsac 1989 • $28 Ⓐ • (3/15/1992) • **82**

CANON, CHATEAU

St.-Emilion 1999: Surprisingly good for Canon after the hail in early September. Plenty of tobacco, berry and milk chocolate character. Medium-bodied, with fine tannins and a fresh finish.–J.S. • $NA • (1/01/2000) (BT) • **85-89**
St.-Emilion 1998: Elegant, but a bit disappointing for this estate. Medium-bodied. Slightly unripe and hard.–J.S. • $NA • (5/31/1999) (BT) • **80-84**
St.-Emilion 1997: Some decent berry, tobacco character, but rather lean. Medium to light in body, with firm tannins. Drink through 2003–J.S. • $NA • (1/31/2000) • **85**
St.-Emilion 1996: Some good berry and tobacco character but slightly herbal. Medium-bodied, with fine tannins, but a diluted center-palate. Rather light for Canon. Drink now.–J.S. • $28 Ⓐ • (1/31/1999) • **83**
St.-Emilion 1995 • $28 Ⓐ • (1/31/1998) • **86**
St.-Emilion 1993 • $28 Ⓐ • (1/31/1996) • **85**
St.-Emilion 1992 • $20 Ⓐ • (4/15/1995) • **76**
St.-Emilion 1990 • $56 Ⓐ • (3/31/1993) • **91**
St.-Emilion 1989: Starts up slowly on the palate, then builds to lovely, sweet fruit flavors. Dark-ruby color. Dusty, smoky, gamy and berry aromas open to a full-bodied palate with loads of ripe fruit and chocolate and a long,

Key: SS—Spectator Selection. CS—Cellar Selection. HR—Highly Recommended. $NA—Price not available. (BT)—Barrel tasting. Ⓐ—Auction Price. For a key to the tasters' initials, see "How to Use These Listings." **Dates in parentheses represent the issues in which the ratings were published.**

sweet aftertaste. A beauty. (1989 Bordeaux horizontal tasting). Drink now through 2006.–J.S. • $62 Ⓐ • (5/31/1999) • **90**

St.-Emilion 1988: The '88 Canon I tasted a few years ago received 88 points, but this bottle seems on its way down. Amber and ruby in color, this has berry and cedar aromas and flavors. Medium-bodied, with fine tannins and a short, slightly dry finish. (1988 Bordeaux horizontal tasting). Drink now.–J.S. • $47 Ⓐ • (11/30/1998) • **81**

St.-Emilion 1987 • $30 • (4/30/1995) • **86**
St.-Emilion 1986 • $57 Ⓐ • (4/30/1995) • **90**
St.-Emilion 1985 • $72 Ⓐ • (4/30/1995) • **91**
St.-Emilion 1983 • $54 Ⓐ • (4/30/1995) • **84**

St.-Emilion 1982: This has always been one of the great wines of the vintage and one of the greatest ever produced at this estate. Seriously dark ruby in color, with blackberry, earth and fresh floral aromas. Full-bodied, with full silky tannins and thick, ripe fruit. Still needs time. (1982 Bordeaux horizontal tasting). Best after 2000.–J.S. • $132 Ⓐ • (11/30/1998) • **96**

St.-Emilion 1981 • $29 Ⓐ • (10/15/1994) • **89**
St.-Emilion 1980 • $19 • (4/30/1995) • **79**
St.-Emilion 1979 • $25 Ⓐ • (4/30/1995) • **90**
St.-Emilion 1978 • $38 Ⓐ • (4/30/1995) • **91**
St.-Emilion 1977 • $18 • (4/30/1995) • **74**
St.-Emilion 1976 • $33 Ⓐ • (4/30/1995) • **81**
St.-Emilion 1975 • $33 Ⓐ • (4/30/1995) • **86**
St.-Emilion 1974 • $20 • (4/30/1995) • **62**
St.-Emilion 1973 • $20 • (4/30/1995) • **72**
St.-Emilion 1972 • $20 • (4/30/1995) • **79**
St.-Emilion 1971 • $45 • (4/30/1995) • **85**
St.-Emilion 1970 • $52 Ⓐ • (4/30/1995) • **88**
St.-Emilion 1969 • $25 • (4/30/1995) • **74**
St.-Emilion 1967 • $65 • (4/30/1995) • **83**
St.-Emilion 1966 • $150 • (4/30/1995) • **84**
St.-Emilion 1964 • $92 Ⓐ • (4/30/1995) • **90**
St.-Emilion 1962 • $175 • (4/30/1995) • **91**
St.-Emilion 1961 • $108 Ⓐ • (4/30/1995) • **95**
St.-Emilion 1960 • $75 • (4/30/1995) • **79**
St.-Emilion 1959 • $200 • (4/30/1995) • **86**
St.-Emilion 1958 • $80 • (4/30/1995) • **89**
St.-Emilion 1957 • $75 • (4/30/1995) • **82**
St.-Emilion 1955 • $110 • (4/30/1995) • **90**
St.-Emilion 1953 • $125 • (4/30/1995) • **91**
St.-Emilion 1952 • $95 • (4/30/1995) • **79**
St.-Emilion 1950 • $190 • (4/30/1995) • **76**
St.-Emilion 1949 • $375 • (4/30/1995) • **92**
St.-Emilion 1948 • $375 • (4/30/1995) • **90**
St.-Emilion 1947 • $191 Ⓐ • (4/30/1995) • **93**
St.-Emilion English Bottling 1947 • $NA • (4/30/1995) • **90**
St.-Emilion 1945 • $475 • (4/30/1995) • **84**
St.-Emilion 1943 • $125 • (4/30/1995) • **86**
St.-Emilion 1942 • $200 • (4/30/1995) • **80**
St.-Emilion 1937 • $150 • (4/30/1995) • **81**
St.-Emilion 1934 • $175 • (4/30/1995) • **50**
St.-Emilion 1933 • $160 • (4/30/1995) • **77**
St.-Emilion 1929 • $250 • (4/30/1995) • **89**
St.-Emilion 1928 • $300 • (4/30/1995) • **87**
St.-Emilion 1926 • $225 • (4/30/1995) • **79**
St.-Emilion 1923 • $175 • (4/30/1995) • **90**
St.-Emilion 1920 • $200 • (4/30/1995) • **86**
St.-Emilion 1916 • $175 • (4/30/1995) • **79**

CANON-DE-BREM, CHATEAU

Canon-Fronsac 1998: Crushed raspberries and earth in this one. Medium-bodied, compacted, with fine tannins and a fruity finish.–J.S. • $NA • (5/31/1999) (BT) • **85-89**

Canon-Fronsac 1997: An attractive wine with mineral, berry and dark chocolate character. Medium-bodied, with fine tannins and a fresh finish. Drink now.–J.S. • $NA • (1/31/2000) • **85**

Canon-Fronsac 1996: Lovely aromas of ripe berries and chocolate. Medium-bodied and velvety, with a long chocolate and light berry aftertaste. Slightly short but fruity. Very good for this estate considering the vintage. Drink now through 2002.–J.S. • $13 • (1/31/1999) • **86**

Canon-Fronsac 1995 • $18 • (1/31/1998) • **86**
Canon-Fronsac 1994 • $17 • (1/31/1997) • **74**
Canon-Fronsac 1993 • $14 • (1/31/1996) • **80**
Canon-Fronsac 1992 • $13 • (4/15/1995) • **75**
Canon-Fronsac 1990 • $17 • (3/31/1993) • **89**
Canon-Fronsac 1989 • $23 • (3/15/1992) • **84**
Canon-Fronsac 1986 • $15 • (3/31/1990) • **86**
Canon-Fronsac 1982 • $NA • (8/31/1992) • **91**

CANON-LA GAFFELIERE, CHATEAU

St.-Emilion 1999: Extremely well done for the vintage. Very ripe, with chocolate, berry and coffee aromas. Full-bodied, with lots of velvety tannins and a long finish.–J.S. • $NA • (1/01/2000) (BT) • **90-94**

St.-Emilion 1998: Plenty of mineral, berry and dried cherry character. Medium-bodied, with fine tannins and a medium finish. A bit disappointing.–J.S. • $NA • (5/31/1999) (BT) • **85-89**

St.-Emilion 1997: Lovely perfumes of tobacco, cedar, berry and earth. Medium-bodied, with firm tannins and a slightly short finish. Drink now through 2003.–J.S. • $38 Ⓐ • (1/31/2000) • **87**

St.-Emilion 1996: One of the best St.-Emilions going this vintage. Lovely aromas of crushed berries, flowers and a touch of oak. Medium-bodied, with velvety tannins and a long, fruity finish. Has a really good core of fruit. Best after 2000.–J.S. • $31 Ⓐ • (1/31/1999) • **89**

St.-Emilion 1995 • $49 Ⓐ • (1/31/1998) • **95**
St.-Emilion 1994 • $27 Ⓐ • (1/31/1997) • **89**
St.-Emilion 1993 • $30 • (1/31/1996) HR • **92**
St.-Emilion 1992 • $20 • (4/15/1995) • **82**
St.-Emilion 1990 • $75 Ⓐ • (3/15/1993) HR • **95**

St.-Emilion 1989: Silky and elegant. Perfumes of blackberry and cassis follow to a medium-bodied palate with fine tannins and a sweet fruit finish. Very fine indeed. (1989 Bordeaux horizontal tasting). Best after 2000.–J.S. • $42 Ⓐ • (5/31/1999) • **89**

St.-Emilion 1988: Much better than I expected, as the estate was not making the top-quality wines then that it does today. Full-bodied, with loads of velvety tannins, ripe fruit character and a long aftertaste of spice, violet and fruit. (1988 Bordeaux horizontal tasting). Best after 2000.–J.S. • $48 Ⓐ • (11/30/1998) • **90**

St.-Emilion 1986 • $21 • (6/30/1989) • **91**

CANON-MOUEIX, CHATEAU

Canon-Fronsac 1998: Wonderful nose of raspberry jam. Full-bodied and chewy, yet soft and round. One of the sleepers of the vintage.–J.S. • $NA • (5/31/1999) (BT) • **90-94**

Canon-Fronsac 1997: Good perfumed berry and cherry character. Medium-bodied, with light tannins and a light, fruity finish. Drink now.–J.S. • $20 • (1/31/2000) • **81**

Canon-Fronsac 1996: Pretty cherry and berry aromas, with hints of herbs. Medium-bodied texture, but slightly herbal and diluted at midpalate.–J.S. • $13 Ⓐ • (1/31/1999) • **83**

Canon-Fronsac 1995 • $21 • (1/31/1998) • **87**
Canon-Fronsac 1994 • $21 • (1/31/1997) • **80**
Canon-Fronsac 1993 • $18 • (1/31/1996) • **81**
Canon-Fronsac 1992 • $14 • (4/15/1995) • **78**
Canon-Fronsac 1990 • $15 • (3/31/1993) • **84**

Canon-Fronsac 1989: A ripe and soft '89 with milk chocolate, berry and coffee aromas and flavors. Full-bodied, adding rustic tannins and a touch of bitterness on the finish. (1989 Bordeaux horizontal tasting). Drink now.–J.S. • $NA • (5/31/1999) • **86**

CANTELOUP, CHATEAU

Médoc 1995 • $10 • (1/31/1998) • **78**

CANTELYS, CHATEAU

Pessac-Léognan 1997: Rather forward red, with some plum and tobacco character. Medium- to light-bodied, with soft tannins and a light finish. Drink now.–J.S. • $35 • (1/31/2000) • **81**

Pessac-Léognan 1996: A flavorful little wine with berry, tobacco and cherry character. Medium-bodied, with velvety tannins and a slightly diluted mid-palate. Simple really. Drink now.–J.S. • $30 • (1/31/1999) • **82**

Pessac-Léognan 1995 • $30 • (1/31/1998) • **88**

Pessac-Léognan White 1998: Quite soft for a 1998 white Bordeaux, with lemon, honey and vanilla character galore. Medium-bodied, with a very fruity finish. Drink now.–J.S. • $30 • (2/29/2000) • **87**

FRANCE

CANTELYS, CHATEAU

Pessac-Léognan White 1997: Oaky and ripe throughout. Medium-bodied, with apple, pineapple and vanilla flavors, but slightly diluted on the finish. Drink now.–J.S. • $35 • (9/30/1999) • **87**
Pessac-Léognan White 1996: Big and rich Pessac with lots of character. Wonderful aromas of vanilla, pineapple and almonds. Full-bodied and powerful, with lots of toasted oak but plenty of tropical fruit to back it up. Needs food. Drink now through 2005.–J.S. • $30 • (3/31/1999) • **89**

CANTEMERLE, CHATEAU

Haut-Médoc 1999: Attractive plum and berry character. Medium-bodied, with fine tannins and a fresh, fruity aftertaste.–J.S. • $NA • (1/01/2000) (BT) • **85-89**
Haut-Médoc 1998: Crushed berries with a leafy undertone. Full-bodied and chewy, with a medium finish. Needs a tiny bit more ripe fruit at midpalate to score outstanding.–J.S. • $NA • (5/31/1999) (BT) • **85-89**
Haut-Médoc 1997: Very attractive tobacco, cherry and dried herb aromas. Medium-bodied, slightly harsh, with an herbal finish. Drink now.–J.S. • $20 • (1/31/2000) • **83**
Haut-Médoc 1996: The best Cantemerle in years, beautiful and rich, with a wonderful core of fruit. Pretty plum and berry aromas, with hints of tobacco and chocolate, lead to a full-bodied wine with loads of chocolate and berry character. Long, long aftertaste. Best after 2005.–J.S. • $21 Ⓐ • (1/31/1999) HR • **91**
Haut-Médoc 1995: Ready to pull the cork, with simple berry and chocolate flavors, medium body and medium tannins, but should improve with some age. Drink now.–J.S. • $21 Ⓐ • (9/15/1998) • **82**
Haut-Médoc 1991 • $22 • (3/31/1994) • **80**
Haut-Médoc 1990 • $33 Ⓐ • (3/31/1993) • **81**
Haut-Médoc 1989: Huge wine. Best Cantemerle ever? Dark ruby-colored. Intense aromas of ripe fruit and game. Full-bodied and compacted, with masses of tannins and fruit, yet still closed and not giving much on the palate. Give this brute time. (1989 Bordeaux horizontal tasting). Best after 2004.–J.S. • $58 Ⓐ • (5/31/1999) • **95**
Haut-Médoc 1988 • $34 Ⓐ • (3/15/1991) • **85**
Haut-Médoc 1987 • $21 • (5/15/1990) • **87**
Haut-Médoc 1986 • $40 Ⓐ • (6/30/1989) • **89**
Haut-Médoc 1984 • $17 • (6/15/1987) • **85**
Haut-Médoc 1982: Not as good as I remember, but pretty and delicious. Medium-ruby in color, with chocolate and ripe berry aromas. Medium-bodied, with medium, velvety tannins and a medium, smooth finish. (1982 Bordeaux horizontal tasting). Drink now.–J.S. • $46 Ⓐ • (11/30/1998) • **86**
Haut-Médoc 1981 • $23 Ⓐ • (5/01/1984) • **70**
Haut-Médoc 1979 • $NA • (10/15/1989) • **78**
Haut-Médoc 1970 • $44 Ⓐ • (5/15/1993) • **88**
Haut-Médoc 1962 • $NA • (11/30/1987) • **90**
Haut-Médoc 1961 • $116 Ⓐ • (4/30/1996) • **84**
Haut-Médoc 1945 • $NA • (3/16/1986) • **92**

CANTENAC-BROWN, CHATEAU

Margaux 1999: Lots of plumskin and spice character. Medium body. Medium tannins. Delicious spicy finish.–J.S. • $NA • (1/01/2000) (BT) • **85-89**
Margaux 1998: Lovely mint, berry and currant character. Medium-bodied, with polished tannins. Slightly hollow midpalate, but well done.–J.S. • $NA • (5/31/1999) (BT) • **85-89**
Margaux 1997: A bit lean, but has some good polished tannins and a berry, earthy character. Drink now.–J.S. • $24 • (1/31/2000) • **82**
Margaux 1996: Some good berry and tobacco character, but slightly lean in fruit concentration in the center-palate. Medium-bodied, with medium tannins and a short finish. Drink now.–J.S. • $31 • (1/31/1999) • **85**
Margaux 1995 • $28 Ⓐ • (1/31/1998) • **88**
Margaux 1994 • $29 • (1/31/1997) • **85**
Margaux 1993 • $23 • (1/31/1996) • **85**
Margaux 1992 • $20 • (4/15/1995) • **84**
Margaux 1991 • $23 • (3/31/1994) • **82**
Margaux 1990 • $38 Ⓐ • (3/31/1993) • **92**
Margaux 1989: A balanced, elegant wine. Dark ruby-colored at the center and a red edge. Lovely aromas of raspberries, spices and cherries follow through to a full-bodied palate with supersilky tannins and a long, caressing finish. (1989 Bordeaux horizontal tasting). Drink now through 2008.–J.S. • $32 Ⓐ • (5/31/1999) • **89**
Margaux 1988: Really a funky bottle. Mint, pepper and berry aromas greet you, but they turn to an ugly green, leeky character. Medium-bodied, with austere tannins. (1988 Bordeaux horizontal tasting).–J.S. • $NA • (11/30/1998) • **78**
Margaux 1987 • $18 • (2/15/1990) • **78**
Margaux 1984 • $19 • (5/15/1987) • **85**
Margaux 1982 • $37 Ⓐ • (5/01/1985) • **91**
Margaux 1981 • $12 • (3/01/1985) • **91**
Margaux 1970 • $19 Ⓐ • (5/15/1993) • **83**
Margaux 1961 • $65 Ⓐ • (4/30/1996) • **82**
Margaux 1959 • $NA • (10/15/1990) • **89**
Margaux 1945 • $NA • (3/16/1986) • **75**

CANTIN, CHATEAU DE

St.-Emilion 1997: A bit lean, with berry, cherry and herbs. Medium- to light-bodied, with light tannins. Light finish.–J.S. • $NA • (1/31/2000) • **80**

CANUET, CHATEAU

Margaux 1997: Lovely, fresh wine with plum, berry and raspberry character. Medium-bodied, with a solid, silky-tannin structure and a long, fruity finish.–J.S. • $NA • (1/31/2000) • **86**
Margaux 1996: Not a blockbuster, but a warm and elegant claret that's a joy to taste. Good dark color, with dark chocolate and cherry aromas. Full-bodied and very velvety, with lovely ripe fruit and fine tannins. Second label of Château Cantenac-Brown. Best after 2000.–J.S. • $NA • (1/31/1999) • **88**
Margaux 1995 • $20 • (1/31/1998) • **90**
Margaux 1994 • $18 • (1/31/1997) • **80**
Margaux 1993 • $13 • (1/31/1996) • **74**
Margaux 1992 • $12 • (4/15/1995) • **74**
Margaux 1991 • $12 • (3/31/1994) • **69**
Margaux 1990 • $17 • (3/31/1993) • **89**
Margaux 1989 • $18 • (3/15/1992) • **82**
Margaux 1987 • $13 • (5/15/1990) • **74**
Margaux 1986 • $15 • (11/30/1989) • **88**

CANYON CREST

Chardonnay Vin de Pays d'Oc 1997: Vinous, but lackluster in the end. Simple green apple flavors dominate.–K.M. • $8 • (12/31/1998) • **75**
Merlot Vin de Pays d'Oc 1997: Candylike flavors that seem sweet contrast with a lean, tannic texture in this light red. A bit awkward overall.–P.M. • $8 • (11/15/1998) • **74**
Pinot Noir Vin de Pays de l'Ile de Beauté 1997: Fizzy and volatile, with a prickly, weedy finish. Tasted twice, with consistent notes.–K.M. • $8 • (12/31/1998) • **65**

CAP DE FAUGERES, CHATEAU

Côtes de Castillon 1999: Medium-bodied, with subtle berry, cherry and plum aromas and flavors. Medium tannins, with a light finish.–J.S. • $NA • (1/01/2000) (BT) • **85-89**
Côtes de Castillon 1998: Complex aromas of violets, dark chocolate and olives. Medium-bodied, with fine tannins and a good core of fruit. A bit more fruit concentration would make it outstanding.–J.S. • $NA • (5/31/1999) (BT) • **85-89**
Côtes de Castillon 1997: A bit lean, but shows some pretty plum and chocolate aromas and flavors. Medium-bodied, with light tannins and a fresh finish. Drink now.–J.S. • $13 • (1/31/2000) • **84**
Côtes de Castillon 1996: Slightly simple, but has good chunky fruit. Dark ruby in color, with chocolate and blackberry aromas. Medium- to full-bodied, with chewy tannins and a chocolaty aftertaste. Drink through 2003–J.S. • $NA • (2/28/1999) • **85**

CAP DE HAUT, CHATEAU

Haut-Médoc 1995 • $NA • (1/01/1997) • **88**

CAP-DE-HAUT MAUCAILLOU, CHATEAU

Moulis 1996: Some decent fruit but slightly herbal, with a grassy, diluted character. Medium-bodied, with medium tannins and a light finish.–J.S. • $NA • (2/28/1999) • **79**

Key: SS—Spectator Selection. CS—Cellar Selection. HR—Highly Recommended. $NA—Price not available. (BT)—Barrel tasting. Ⓐ—Auction Price. For a key to the tasters' initials, see "How to Use These Listings." **Dates in parentheses represent the issues in which the ratings were published.**

CAP DE MOURLIN, CHATEAU

St.-Emilion 1996: Interesting aromas, plenty of chocolate and plum, but lacks a bit in the palate. Medium- to light-bodied, with firm tannins and a short finish. Drink now.–J.S. • $NA • (1/31/1999) • **82**
St.-Emilion 1989 • $23 • (3/15/1992) • **87**
St.-Emilion 1988 • $20 • (4/30/1991) • **84**
St.-Emilion 1986 • $18 • (6/30/1989) • **87**
St.-Emilion 1982: An elegant and delicious '82. Medium-red in color, with a garnet hue. Milk chocolate, floral and fruit. Medium-bodied, with very fine tannins and a long, sweet fruit aftertaste. (1982 Bordeaux horizontal tasting). Drink now.–J.S. • $NA • (11/30/1998) • **89**

CAPBERN-GASQUETON, CHATEAU

St.-Estèphe 1996: Slightly grassy on the nose, with hints of berry and bush. Medium-bodied, with a bit of vegetal character and a medium finish. Doesn't seem to be going anywhere.–J.S. • $NA • (2/28/1999) • **78**
St.-Estèphe 1995: Straightforward, with violet and cherry aromas and flavors, medium body and well-integrated tannins. Drink now through 2002.–J.S. • $NA • (9/15/1998) • **85**
St.-Estèphe 1991 • $13 • (3/31/1994) • **74**
St.-Estèphe 1989 • $27 • (3/15/1992) • **84**
St.-Estèphe 1986 • $20 • (11/30/1989) • **76**
St.-Estèphe 1985 • $23 • (8/31/1988) • **85**
St.-Estèphe 1982: Still holding on. Medium brick-red color, with a ruby center and a garnet rim. Medium-bodied, with firm tannins, light meat and fruit aromas and slightly high acidity. (1982 Bordeaux horizontal tasting). Drink now.–J.S. • $23 Ⓐ • (11/30/1998) • **82**

CAPELLE, DOMAINE DE LA

Muscat de Mireval 1997: No mistaking the grape, floral and spice aromas and flavors here, though a hint of coffee adds complexity. Sweet, round and easy to like, with a touch of bitterness on the finish. Drink now.–B.S. • $19 • (1/01/2000) • **87**

CAPENDU, CHATEAU

Cabernet Vin de Pays d'Oc 1998: Smooth and fairly rich, with nice flavors of dark plum, red cherry and spice. Finishes with some ripe fruit and pepper. Drink now.–K.M. • $12 • (12/31/1999) • **85**
Cabernet Vin de Pays d'Oc 1996 • $12 • (4/30/1998) • **82**
Chardonnay Vin de Pays d'Oc 1998: Zippy, with well-defined lemon-lime flavors and a spicy component. An interesting and refreshing Chardonnay. Drink now.–K.M. • $12 • (12/31/1999) • **85**
Chardonnay Vin de Pays d'Oc 1997: Hits you with its big, ripe flavors of butter, pear and almond. Nutmeg and vanilla notes linger on the finish. Not much finesse, but plenty of chutzpah. Try with poultry dishes. Drink now.–K.M. • $12 • (12/31/1998) • **85**
Corbières Cuvée Elevée en Futs Grande Réserve 1988 • $6 • (5/31/1990) • **77**
Corbières L'Excellence 1995: A supple and luscious red with flavors of cherry, spice and ripe plum, finishing with chocolaty notes. Fine-grained tannins give some depth without being overpowering. Drink now through 2003.–K.M. • $9 • (8/31/1998) • **86**
Merlot Vin de Pays d'Oc 1998: Concentrated flavors of dark plum and cherry are a bit overwhelmed by charry elements. Dries out on the finish. Drink now.–K.M. • $12 • (12/31/1999) • **82**
Merlot Vin de Pays d'Oc 1996 • $12 • (3/31/1998) • **83**

CAPITAIN-GAGNEROT

Aloxe-Corton Les Moutottes 1996: Bordering on acetone in aroma and flavor, this is a simple, dilute wine.–B.S. • $35 • (9/30/1998) • **77**
Corton 1996: Solid and a bit on the rustic side, showing slightly herbaceous aromas and flavors and tough tannins, despite good concentration. Best from 2001 through 2006.–B.S. • $44 • (9/30/1998) • **83**
Ladoix La Micaude 1996: On the ripe side, showing beet root aromas and flavors, but not much richness or concentration to offset the firm tannins.–B.S. • $24 • (9/30/1998) • **78**

CAPITOUL, CHATEAU DE

Coteaux du Languedoc La Clape 1998: A smoky, leathery aroma with flavors to match makes this a pure and fairly intense red that's quite approachable now despite its sinewy muscularity. Red plum flavors persist, with roasted and coffeelike flavors on the finish. Drink now.–K.M. • $13 • (6/15/2000) • **87**
Coteaux du Languedoc La Clape Les Lavandines 1998: Supple and harmonious, this medium-bodied red delivers well-rounded flavors of plum, ripe cherry and currant, with leathery and brickish notes on the finish. Drink now through 2003.–K.M. • $8 • (6/15/2000) • **84**

CARBONNIERES, DOMAINE DES

Côtes du Rhône-Villages Séguret 1996 • $10 • (10/15/1997) • **76**
Gigondas 1996 • $15 • (10/15/1997) • **85**

CARBONNIEUX, CHATEAU

Pessac-Léognan 1999: Light and fruity, with attractive berry and cherry character, light tannins and a fresh finish.–J.S. • $NA • (1/01/2000) (BT) • **80-84**
Pessac-Léognan 1998: A polished, well-crafted young wine. Medium-bodied, with medium tannins and a caressing texture.–J.S. • $NA • (5/31/1999) (BT) • **85-89**
Pessac-Léognan 1997: Bright and fruity, with an herb and berry character, light to medium body and a fresh finish. Drink now.–J.S. • $NA • (1/31/2000) • **84**
Pessac-Léognan 1996: A typical '96, with cool fruit and mineral aromas and flavors, medium body and a sleek and racy tannin structure. Very good effort for a red from Carbonnieux. Best after 2000.–J.S. • $25 • (1/31/1999) • **87**
Pessac-Léognan 1995 • $20 • (1/31/1998) • **89**
Pessac-Léognan 1994 • $29 • (1/31/1997) • **80**
Pessac-Léognan 1993 • $23 • (1/31/1996) • **82**
Pessac-Léognan 1992 • $17 • (4/15/1995) • **84**
Pessac-Léognan 1991 • $17 • (3/31/1994) • **78**
Pessac-Léognan 1990 • $20 • (3/31/1993) • **87**
Pessac-Léognan 1989: Balanced and light. Medium-red. Aromas of flowers and cherries. Medium-bodied, with fine tannins and a light finish. (1989 Bordeaux horizontal tasting). Drink now.–J.S. • $26 Ⓐ • (5/31/1999) • **85**
Pessac-Léognan 1988 • $22 Ⓐ • (2/28/1991) • **86**
Pessac-Léognan 1987 • $15 • (5/15/1990) • **80**
Pessac-Léognan 1986 • $18 • (9/15/1989) • **87**
Graves 1985 • $26 Ⓐ • (11/30/1988) • **87**
Graves 1982 • $33 Ⓐ • (8/31/1992) • **83**
Graves 1970 • $33 • (5/15/1993) • **84**
Graves 1961 • $53 Ⓐ • (4/30/1996) • **86**
Pessac-Léognan White 1998: This château is as good as gold for white Bordeaux. Lovely and subtle aromas and flavors of lemon, lime and mineral. Medium- to full-bodied, with good acidity and a fresh finish. Drink now through 2004.–J.S. • $21 • (2/29/2000) • **90**
Pessac-Léognan White 1997: Wonderful creamy apple, honey and pineapple character. Medium- to full-bodied, with fresh acidity and a long, delicious finish. A joy to taste. Almost outstanding. Drink now.–J.S. • $28 • (9/30/1999) • **89**
Pessac-Léognan White 1996: A pretty and delicious young white Bordeaux, emanating fresh apple, lemon and vanilla aromas that follow through to the very creamy palate. It's medium-bodied, medium in acidity and fresh on the finish. Drink now.–J.S. • $20 Ⓐ • (3/31/1999) SS • **89**

CARDONNE, CHATEAU LA

Médoc 1998: Cool and racy '98, with berry, currant and mineral aromas and flavors. Medium-bodied, with fine tannins and a light finish.–J.S. • $NA • (5/31/1999) (BT) • **85-89**
Médoc 1997: Some decadent fruit here, with coffee and tobacco undertones. Medium- to light-bodied, with a light, fresh finish. Drink now.–J.S. • $15 • (1/31/2000) • **81**
Médoc 1996: A firm '96, with a lean structure but some pretty berry and fresh earth aromas and flavors. Medium finish. Best after 2003.–J.S. • $12 • (1/31/1999) • **87**
Médoc 1995 • $18 • (1/31/1998) • **90**
Médoc 1994 • $16 • (11/30/1997) • **89**
Médoc 1986 • $10 • (2/15/1990) • **84**
Médoc 1985 • $12 • (12/31/1988) • **83**
Médoc 1983 • $13 • (10/15/1986) • **79**
Médoc 1982 • $17 Ⓐ • (8/31/1992) • **86**

CARDONNET, CHATEAU

Bordeaux 1994 • $8 • (4/30/1997) • **79**

CARDUS, CHATEAU

Médoc 1998: Some good black currant and leafy character in this wine. Medium-bodied, with decent tannins and a slightly diluted finish.–J.S. • $NA • (5/31/1999) (BT) • **80-84**

Médoc 1997: Rather watery, with some berry, cherry character. Short finish.–J.S. • $NA • (1/31/2000) • **79**

Médoc 1996: Some berry and frozen blackberry character, but an underlying metallic quality detracts. Medium-bodied, with firm tannins.–J.S. • $14 • (1/31/1999) • **78**

Médoc 1995 • $12 • (1/31/1998) • **85**

CARIGNAN, CHATEAU

Premières Côtes de Bordeaux Cuvée Prima 1997: Very herbal, with a cut grass and fruit character. Too much for me.–J.S. • $NA • (1/31/2000) • **78**

CARILLON, CHATEAU DU

Fronsac 1994 • $10 • (6/30/1997) • **83**

CARILLON, LOUIS

Bienvenues-Bâtard-Montrachet 1996: Fabulous from start to finish, this is ultrasmooth and packed with brilliant, ripe fruit that's so concentrated it easily balances the toasted oak. Bright acidity combines to build the sort of luxuriant, silky, thick, seductive and flavorful white Burgundy the aficionados dream of. Best from 2006 through 2026.–P.M. • $125 • (5/31/1999) • **98**

Puligny-Montrachet 1998: Wonderful quality for a village wine. Creamy in texture and seductive, it's a full-bodied Chardonnay that offers focused mineral, vanilla bean, pear tart, lemon and some spicy character. Best from 2002 through 2008.–P.M. • $54 • (5/31/2000) • **90**

Puligny-Montrachet 1997: Subdued on the nose, medium-bodied and medium-intense, showing clean fruit, crisp citrus and hints of dried herb on the slightly tart finish. Drink now.–P.M. • $49 • (9/30/1999) • **86**

Puligny-Montrachet 1996: Clean and pure, but with a grassy note, this full-bodied white is honeyed, ripe and elegant but a bit aggressive on the finish. Best from 2003 through 2008.–P.M. • $32 Ⓐ • (5/31/1999) • **88**

Puligny-Montrachet 1995 • $40 • (5/31/1997) • **92**

Puligny-Montrachet Les Champs Canet 1997: Good crispness in this medium-bodied, clean, pure and unyielding white, with lemony, succulent pineapple and green apple skin character. Don't expect a fat wine, just a sharp jolt that must be applauded in a '97. Drink now through 2001.–P.M. • $69 • (9/30/1999) • **88**

Puligny-Montrachet Les Champs Canet 1996: Rich and full-bodied, but also has an herbal, high-acidity backbone. A pure, clean wine that has a lot of potential for improving in the cellar, as it already hints at a velvety, creamlike texture. Best after 2005.–P.M. • $77 Ⓐ • (8/31/1998) • **90**

Puligny-Montrachet Les Champs Canet 1995 • $57 • (8/31/1997) • **93**

Puligny-Montrachet Les Perrières 1997: A unique white that delivers rich, thick, concentrated fruit. Smooth, round and compacted, providing peach, pear and honey. Lovely. Drink now through 2005.–P.M. • $64 • (9/30/1999) • **93**

Puligny-Montrachet Les Perrières 1996: As Burgundian as they come, with loads of personality. Earthy but also ripe, with pear, melon, honey, truffle, tropical flavors, this full-bodied wine has a lot going for it. Comes across as a bit rustic now, but has fresh, vibrant, nervous acidity that overwhelms the otherwise fat, opulent texture beneath. Given time, it should be just beautiful. Decanted for 18 hours, it didn't oxidize but gained marvelous silky texture. Best after 2008.–P.M. • $64 • (8/31/1998) • **95**

Puligny-Montrachet Les Perrières 1995 • $53 • (8/31/1997) • **92**

CARLES, CHATEAU DE

Fronsac 1995: One of the sleepers of the vintage, this young red Bordeaux is not only outstanding, it's quite a bargain. Massive, yet balanced, it's dark-colored, with complex aromas of blackberries, tobacco, earth and flowers, and full-bodied, with loads of tannin and ripe fruit.–J.S. • $15 • (8/31/1998) HR • **90**

Fronsac 1993 • $10 • (1/31/1996) • **81**

Key: SS—Spectator Selection. CS—Cellar Selection. HR—Highly Recommended. $NA—Price not available. (BT)—Barrel tasting. Ⓐ—Auction Price. For a key to the tasters' initials, see "How to Use These Listings."
Dates in parentheses represent the issues in which the ratings were published.

CARMES-HAUT-BRION, CHATEAU LES

Pessac-Léognan 1998: Has a good core of berry and cherry, medium tannins and a medium finish. Nicely made. Could move up a notch next year.–J.S. • $NA • (5/31/1999) (BT) • **85-89**

Pessac-Léognan 1997: Lovely berry, plum and dark chocolate aromas follow through to a medium-bodied palate with light tannins. Short finish. Drink now.–J.S. • $28 • (1/31/2000) • **81**

Pessac-Léognan 1996: Plum and vanilla aromas unfold to a medium-bodied but slightly diluted palate. Light tannins, fresh finish. Another weak red from Pessac-Léognan.–J.S. • $29 Ⓐ • (1/31/1999) • **79**

Pessac-Léognan 1995: Violet, floral and tobacco aromas. Full-bodied and tannic, with berry and tobacco character and an underlying barnyard tone. Needs time to come together. A bit rustic. Best from 2001 through 2006.–J.S. • $40 • (9/15/1998) • **87**

Pessac-Léognan 1961 • $50 • (4/30/1996) • **86**

CARONNE-STE.-GEMME, CHATEAU

Haut-Médoc 1998: Offers a good backbone of ripe tannins, but lacks a bit of flesh. Medium-bodied, with full tannins and a medium finish. Good, but not up to the quality of the 1996.–J.S. • $NA • (5/31/1999) (BT) • **85-89**

Haut-Médoc 1997: Some good fruit in this delicious red, with plum and berry character. Light tannins. Drink now.–J.S. • $NA • (1/31/2000) • **82**

Haut-Médoc 1996: Delicious—medium- to full-bodied, with velvety tannins and a chocolate, berry, tobacco aftertaste—it's hard not to drink now, it's so balanced. This outstanding red is one of the big surprises of the vintage and among its best buys; this estate is a rising star in the Médoc. Best after 2001.–J.S. • $22 • (1/31/1999) HR • **90**

Haut-Médoc 1995 • $20 • (1/31/1998) • **89**

CARRUADES DE LAFITE ROTHSCHILD

Pauillac 1999: A beauty. Aromas of tobacco, cherry and chocolate. Medium body. Medium fine tannins. Very long, and for a second wine, very, very good.–J.S. • $NA • (1/01/2000) (BT) • **85-89**

Pauillac 1998: A bit green for my taste, with green tobacco and cherry character. Medium-bodied, with fine tanins and a light finish.–J.S. • $NA • (5/31/1999) (BT) • **80-84**

Pauillac 1997: A very grapey red with berry, cherry character. Full- to medium-bodied, with velvety tannins and a long, caressing finish. A bit hollow. Second wine of Lafite. Best after 2000.–J.S. • $30 • (1/31/2000) • **86**

Pauillac 1996: An aromatic yet compact wine, dark and rich with floral, berry and mineral aromas. Medium-bodied, with firm tannins and a silky-textured finish. Best after 2000.–J.S. • $34 • (1/31/1999) • **87**

Pauillac 1995 • $39 Ⓐ • (1/31/1998) • **90**

Pauillac 1994 • $38 Ⓐ • (1/31/1997) • **86**

Pauillac 1993 • $27 Ⓐ • (1/31/1996) • **83**

Pauillac 1992 • $17 • (4/15/1995) • **84**

Pauillac 1989 • $41 Ⓐ • (3/15/1992) • **89**

Pauillac 1988: Pretty, with floral, cedar and berry character and fine tannins. Medium-bodied, it's fresh and soothing to taste. (1988 Bordeaux horizontal tasting). Drink now.–J.S. • $27 Ⓐ • (11/30/1998) • **88**

Pauillac 1983 • $14 • (10/31/1986) • **88**

Pauillac 1982: Promises more on the nose than it gives on the palate. Medium-ruby color, with a garnet edge. Fresh blackberry and mineral aromas. Medium-bodied, with firm tannins and a light finish. (1982 Bordeaux horizontal tasting). Drink now.–J.S. • $NA • (11/30/1998) • **84**

Pauillac 1961 • $45 • (4/30/1996) • **90**

Pauillac 1959 • $NA • (10/15/1990) • **84**

CARTILLON, CHATEAU DU

Haut-Médoc 1997: Very diluted, with some berry and tobacco character but light on the finish.–J.S. • $NA • (1/31/2000) • **77**

Haut-Médoc 1996: Very light and weedy, with light body, light tannins and a stewed-tomato finish. Shows how much rain really fell that year.–J.S. • $15 • (1/31/1999) • **74**

Haut-Médoc 1995 • $15 • (1/31/1998) • **78**

Haut-Médoc 1994 • $NA • (1/31/1997) • **77**

Haut-Médoc 1993 • $12 • (1/31/1996) • **76**

Haut-Médoc 1991 • $10 • (3/31/1994) • **74**

CASANOVA, LA

Muscat de Rivesaltes 1995 • $16 • (12/31/1997) • **88**

CASENOVE, DOMAINE DE LA

Côtes du Roussillon 1996: Simple, juicy and full of fresh raspberry and spice flavors. A nice party wine. Drink now.–K.M. • $14 • (11/30/1998) • **82**
Côtes du Roussillon 1995 • $11 • (9/30/1997) • **84**
Côtes du Roussillon Cuvée François Jaubert 1995 • $24 • (9/30/1997) • **86**
Côtes du Roussillon Cuvée François Jaubert 1993 • $22 • (1/31/1997) • **89**
Côtes du Roussillon La Garrigue 1994 • $10 • (9/30/1997) • **82**
Côtes du Roussillon La Garrigue 1993 • $10 • (1/31/1997) • **83**

CASSAGNE-HAUT-CANON, CHATEAU

Canon-Fronsac La Truffiäre 1997: A wine with pleasant plum, berry and cedar character. Medium-bodied, with firm tannins, a medium finish. Drink through 2003.–J.S. • $NA • (1/31/2000) • **86**

CASTAGNIER, GUY

Bonnes Mares 1990 • $NA • (12/15/1992) • **94**
Bonnes Mares 1989 • $67 • (1/31/1992) • **91**
Bonnes Mares 1988 • $67 • (7/15/1991) • **87**
Bonnes Mares 1986 • $50 • (4/15/1989) • **91**
Chambolle-Musigny 1990 • $NA • (12/15/1992) • **87**
Chambolle-Musigny 1989 • $39 • (1/31/1992) • **88**
Chambolle-Musigny 1986 • $31 • (7/15/1989) • **84**
Charmes-Chambertin 1996: A crisp, fruity, extremely high-acid Pinot, showing blueberry and cherry notes. Chewy finish. Drink now through 2002.–P.M. • $99 • (7/31/1999) • **85**
Charmes-Chambertin 1990 • $NA • (12/15/1992) • **89**
Charmes-Chambertin 1989 • $62 • (1/31/1992) • **90**
Clos de la Roche 1996: What the '96 vintage is all about. Lots of freshness underpins this flavorful, medium-bodied Pinot, with plenty of cassis, black cherry, smoke and spice notes zipping around the palate to a vibrant yet supple finish. Drink now through 2005.–P.M. • $99 • (7/31/1999) • **91**
Clos de la Roche 1990 • $NA • (12/15/1992) • **90**
Clos de la Roche 1989 • $62 • (1/31/1992) • **90**
Clos de la Roche 1988 • $63 • (7/15/1991) • **91**
Clos de la Roche 1986 • $43 • (7/15/1989) • **75**
Clos de Vougeot 1990 • $NA • (12/15/1992) • **87**
Clos de Vougeot 1989 • $64 • (1/31/1992) • **85**
Clos de Vougeot 1988 • $65 • (8/31/1991) • **86**
Clos St.-Denis 1990 • $NA • (12/15/1992) • **93**
Clos St.-Denis 1989 • $62 • (1/31/1992) • **91**
Clos St.-Denis 1988 • $63 • (7/15/1991) • **89**
Clos St.-Denis 1986 • $43 • (7/15/1989) • **84**
Gevrey-Chambertin 1996: Very aromatic, but with a lot of acidity that makes it mouthpuckering. Shows lovely blueberry, wild raspberry and loads of cassis (and some green stem) character. Tough, crisp finish. Drink now through 2005.–P.M. • $36 • (7/31/1999) • **88**
Gevrey-Chambertin 1990 • $NA • (12/15/1992) • **87**
Latricières-Chambertin 1990 • $NA • (12/15/1992) • **89**
Latricières-Chambertin 1989 • $62 • (1/31/1992) • **93**
Latricières-Chambertin 1988 • $63 • (7/15/1991) • **93**
Mazy-Chambertin 1990 • $NA • (12/15/1992) • **94**
Mazy-Chambertin 1989 • $62 • (1/31/1992) • **93**
Mazy-Chambertin 1988 • $63 • (7/15/1991) • **91**
Morey-St.-Denis 1990 • $NA • (12/15/1992) • **85**
Morey-St.-Denis 1989 • $NA • (1/31/1992) • **86**
Morey-St.-Denis 1986 • $28 • (7/15/1989) • **66**

CASTAING, CHATEAU

Côtes de Bourg 1996: Straightforward and fresh, with berry aromas and flavors. Medium-bodied, with firm tannins and a berry aftertaste. Drink now through 2003.–J.S. • $12 • (2/28/1999) • **82**

CASTEL MONTPLAISIR

Cahors 1997: A juicy red with plum, berry and red cherry flavors. Shows good balance of acidity as well, and a lively finish. Drink now through 2001.–K.M. • $11 • (10/15/1999) • **84**

CASTELNAU, DOMAINE

Chardonnay Vin de Pays d'Oc 1998: A straightforward Chardonnay, with green apple, lemon and spice flavors. Gingerlike notes on the finish. Drink now.–K.M. • $NA • (1/01/2000) • **82**

CASTELNAU DE SUDUIRAUT

Sauternes 1995 • $30 • (4/30/1998) • **86**

CASTELOT, CHATEAU LE

St.-Emilion 1995 • $27 • (1/31/1998) • **77**

CATHARE, COMTE

Cabernet Sauvignon Vin de Pays d'Oc Domaine de Combebelle Prestige 1995: A well-oaked style, thick and fairly concentrated, with plummy flavors, as well as some meaty aromas and flavors which give a decadent edge. Quite tannic on the finish. Drink through 2002.–K.M. • $18 • (11/15/1998) • **87**
Chardonnay Vin de Pays d'Oc 1996: This tart white has plenty of acidity but not much fruit flavor. Tastes a bit brassy and earthy.–T.M. • $9 • (12/15/1998) • **76**
Minervois Château Maris 1995: Quite meaty-tasting, with a bacon quality and dried cherry and brown sugar flavors. Ends on a stewy note.–K.M. • $10 • (11/30/1998) • **79**
Minervois Château Maris Prestige 1995: Mature flavors and aromas are fairly thick and smooth. Ripe plum and coffee flavors dominate, with some burnt caramel notes on the finish. Drink now.–K.M. • $14 • (11/30/1998) • **81**
St.-Chinian Château de Combebelle 1995: A good straightforward red, with plum and cherry flavors and nice herb touches. Finishes with notes of clove and leather.–K.M. • $10 • (11/30/1998) • **85**
St.-Chinian Château de Combebelle 1994 • $10 • (5/31/1998) • **84**
St.-Chinian Château de Combebelle Prestige 1995: Rich, smoky and voluptuous, with concentrated red plum, ripe cherry and leather flavors, an intriguing aroma of raspberry and bacon and a long finish, with notes of cardamom. Full-bodied, with a touch of elegance that's tempting now but should gain with age. Drink through 2003.–K.M. • $14 • (11/30/1998) • **89**

CATHERINE DE ST.-JUERY

Coteaux du Languedoc 1993 • $9 • (3/31/1995) • **84**
Coteaux du Languedoc 1992 • $8 • (3/15/1994) • **87**
Coteaux du Languedoc 1991 • $8 • (6/15/1993) • **80**
Coteaux du Languedoc 1990 • $8 • (10/31/1992) • **85**
Syrah Coteaux du Languedoc 1995 • $9 • (3/31/1998) • **86**

CATON, DOMAINE

Cabernet Sauvignon Vin de Pays de l'Hérault 1995 • $6 • (12/15/1996) • **76**
Cabernet Sauvignon Vin de Pays des Côtes de Thongue 1993 • $7 • (12/15/1996) • **84**
Chardonnay Vin de Pays des Côtes de Thongue 1997: Not much here. Dull, earthy character.–K.M. • $5 • (9/30/1998) • **71**
Chardonnay Vin de Pays des Côtes de Thongue Vieille Vigne 1997: Like an exaggerated, buttery style? This is your wine. Also has ripe pear flavors, and some burnt caramel notes on the finish. Drink now.–K.M. • $7 • (10/15/1999) • **81**
Merlot Vin de Pays de l'Hérault 1995 • $6 • (12/15/1996) • **77**

CATTIER

Brut Champagne NV • $29 • (11/30/1995) • **88**
Brut Champagne 1990: A frank fruitiness and slightly sweet character make this Champagne charming. It's easy to drink and enjoy for its ripe apple and grapefruit notes and smooth texture. Drink now. • $50 • (12/31/1998) • **87**
Brut Champagne Antique NV: Lots of fruit flavors and a slight sweetness make this easy to enjoy. Has fresh apple and citrus notes and a soft, creamy texture. Drink now. • $38 • (10/31/1999) • **87**
Brut Champagne Chigny-Les-Roses Premier Cru NV • $30 • (12/31/1991) • **92**
Brut Champagne Clos du Moulin NV • $60 • (12/31/1993) • **85**
Brut Rosé Champagne NV: Bright in fruit flavor, vivacious in style and light salmon in color, this blends strawberry, vanilla and ginger notes on a rich

texture that's nicely balanced with acidity. Drink now. • $46 • (11/30/1998) • **88**

CAUMONT, DOMAINE DE

Merlot Vin de Pays d'Oc 1996: Bright, clean fruit and herb flavors shine through in this soft-textured, easy-drinking wine. Drink now. • $9 • (10/31/1998) • **84**

CAUSE, DOMAINE DE

Cahors Notre Dame des Champs 1996: A layer of toasty oak and a core of bright cherry flavor are fresh and appealing in this vibrant red, but it has tart acidity, and the tannins are quite firm, even austere; the wine needs food to unwind. Drink through 2004.–T.M. • $17 • (12/15/1998) • **86**

CAZANOVE, CHARLES DE

Brut Champagne NV • $28 • (12/31/1991) • **84**
Brut Champagne 1990 • $30 • (11/30/1997) • **92**
Brut Champagne Azur NV: Light in style and balanced toward the soft side, this is a fresh-tasting bubbly, with subtle fig and vanilla accents and good fruit flavors. Drink now. • $25 • (12/31/1998) • **86**
Brut Champagne Classique NV: A sturdy Champagne with toasty-doughy aromas, strong apple flavors, firm acidity and a full texture. Much better than last year. Drink now. • $28 • (10/15/1999) • **86**
Brut Champagne Grande Réserve An 2000 NV: A solid Champagne that joins ripe fruit flavors with a lively texture. Drink now. • $NA • (10/31/1999) • **87**
Brut Champagne Magenta NV • $25 • (11/15/1997) • **75**
Brut Champagne Millésimé 1992: A classic style of Champagne with the fabled fresh-baked bread aromas, vibrant fruit flavors and creamy texture. Quite dry and well balanced. Even better than last year. Drink now through 2001. • $37 • (10/15/1999) • **91**
Brut Champagne Ruban Azur NV • $32 • (12/31/1991) • **87**
Brut Rosé Champagne NV: For fans of restraint, this is a dry rosé with a light copper color, toasty-earthy aromas and subtle fruit flavors. Drink now. • $37 • (10/15/1999) • **87**
Demi-Sec Champagne NV: Quite sweet and enjoyable. Lots of fruit, crisp acidity and a cushy texture make this easy to quaff. Drink now. • $25 • (12/31/1998) • **86**

CAZENEUVE, CHATEAU DE

Coteaux du Languedoc Pic St.-Loup 1996: Powerful and intriguing, with loads of ripe plum, black cherry and pepper flavors mixed with leather notes. Builds to a peppery-gamy finish, with bittersweet chocolate notes. Concentrated and delicious, with fine tannins and textbook Syrah flavors. Drink through 2005.–K.M. • $12 • (1/31/1999) • **90**
Coteaux du Languedoc Pic St.-Loup Grande Cuvée 1996: Rich and well balanced, with beautiful cassis and cherry flavors and mineral notes. The lovely smoked quality, not overdone, is offset nicely by the gorgeous fruit. Finishes with white pepper and cardamom notes. Drink now through 2004.–K.M. • $20 • (1/31/1999) • **89**
Coteaux du Languedoc Pic St.-Loup Le Roc des Mates 1997: A luscious red that's intense and concentrated, with nicely articulated flavors of spice, red plum, leather and red currant. Firm, with plenty of acidity, a good tannic structure and a lingering finish of coffee, chocolate and spice. Drink now through 2002.–K.M. • $20 • (11/15/1999) • **87**
Coteaux du Languedoc Pic St.-Loup Les Calcaires 1997: This has nice red plum, berry and leather flavors, with firm tobacco box and herb notes. Nicely sculpted, with a spicy finish. Drink now through 2003.–K.M. • $15 • (11/15/1999) • **84**
Coteaux du Languedoc Pic St.-Loup Les Terres Rouges 1998: Vibrant and racy, with a firm core of cherry, red currant and leather flavors. Almost Beaujolais-like, with spice and pepper on the finish. Drink now.–K.M. • $11 • (11/15/1999) • **85**
Coteaux du Languedoc Rosé Pic St.-Loup 1996: This rosé has backbone, with dried cherry and berry flavors and a slightly herbal note on the finish. Drink now.–K.M. • $10 • (12/31/1998) • **83**

Key: SS—Spectator Selection. CS—Cellar Selection. HR—Highly Recommended. $NA—Price not available. (BT)—Barrel tasting. Ⓐ—Auction Price.
For a key to the tasters' initials, see "How to Use These Listings."
Dates in parentheses represent the issues in which the ratings were published.

CAZES, DOMAINE

Muscat de Rivesaltes 1995 • $12 • (8/31/1997) • **84**
Rivesaltes 1989 • $12 • (8/31/1997) • **80**
Rivesaltes Ambré 1988 • $10 • (8/31/1997) • **83**
Vin de Pays des Côtes Catalanes Le Credo 1994 • $12 • (9/30/1997) • **87**

CEDRE, CHATEAU DU

Cahors 1989 • $11 • (10/31/1992) • **82**
Cahors 1988 • $10 • (8/31/1991) • **83**
Cahors 1987 • $11 • (8/31/1991) • **81**
Cahors Le Cèdre 1996: An impressive and explosive red, with an alluring blueberry aroma and deeply concentrated flavors of cassis, red raspberry and cedar. A gripping and well-focused acidity adds to its richness. Still youthful and lively, this will need some time balance the considerable tannins. Made from 100 percent Malbec. Best from 2001 through 2015.–K.M. • $60 • (10/31/1999) • **91**
Cahors Le Prestige 1988 • $14 • (8/31/1991) • **84**
Cahors Le Prestige 1987 • $14 • (3/15/1990) • **75**

CELESTIN BLONDEAU

Pouilly-Fumé Les Rabichottes 1997: This supple white is clean and fresh, with simple apple flavors and light spice and mineral accents. Balanced and quaffable, though without much varietal character. Drink now.–T.M. • $13 • (6/30/1999) • **81**
Sancerre Cuvée des Moulins Bâles 1997: Herb and mineral aromas and flavors are crisp and clean in this tart white. It's quite lean, but remains focused through the citrusy finish. Drink now through 2001.–T.M. • $13 • (6/30/1999) • **83**

CELLIER DES BARONNIES

Côtes du Lubéron 1993 • $NA • (11/15/1995) • **81**
Vacqueyras 1990 • $NA • (9/30/1995) • **87**

CELLIER DES VESTIGES ROMAINS

Costières de Nîmes 1998: Appealing cherry and spice flavors are overwhelmed by assertive stemmy notes, which intensify on the drying finish.–K.M. • $5 • (4/30/2000) • **78**
Costières de Nîmes Rosé 1998: A pleasant rosé, with dried cherry and smoke flavors. Berrylike notes on the finish. Drink now.–K.M. • $5 • (4/30/2000) • **82**
Costières de Nîmes White 1998: A soft and spicy white, with herbal, lemony and doughy flavors. White peppery notes on the finish. Drink now.–K.M. • $5 • (4/30/2000) • **83**

CERTAN DE MAY, CHATEAU

Pomerol 1999: Some decent berry, cherry character, but rather light. Medium to light body. Short finish. Disappointing. Tasted twice, with consistent notes.–J.S. • $NA • (1/01/2000) (BT) • **75-79**
Pomerol 1998: Subtle aromas of blackberries and spices lead to a full-bodied and very, very tannic wine that sneaks up on you and grabs you. Almost classic.–J.S. • $NA • (5/31/1999) (BT) • **90-94**
Pomerol 1997: Good solid red. Aromas of plums, berries and black olives. Medium-bodied, with firm tannins and a fruity finish. Not as good as in barrel, but very good for the vintage. Best after 2000.–J.S. • $110 • (1/31/2000) • **87**
Pomerol 1996: Some attractive berry and dried-herb aromas follow through on the palate. Medium-bodied, with fine tannins and a light finish. Slightly austere; lost some of the pretty fruit it had from barrel. Not Certan de May's normally stellar quality, but blame the vintage. Drink now.–J.S. • $115 Ⓐ • (1/31/1999) • **85**
Pomerol 1995: Juicy, burly red. Fascinating aromas of ripe fruit, game and earth. Full-bodied, very velvety, with a long, rich aftertaste. Not giving away what it really has, but what classic potential. Best from 2003 through 2013.–J.S. • $76 Ⓐ • (9/15/1998) • **96**
Pomerol 1994 • $43 Ⓐ • (1/31/1997) • **90**
Pomerol 1990 • $83 Ⓐ • (10/15/1994) • **91**
Pomerol 1989: Old style, but attractive. Color is deep red, with a brick edge. Intense aromas of milk chocolate, berry and tobacco. Full-bodied and rather earthy, showing funky cedar and redwood flavors. Dry finish. Will it

come around? Not sure. (1989 Bordeaux horizontal tasting). Best after 2002.–J.S. • $56 Ⓐ • (5/31/1999) • **89**

Pomerol 1988: Aromas of tobacco, berry and flowers follow through on the palate. Medium-bodied, with firm tannins. More on the nose than the palate, but should improve with age. (1988 Bordeaux horizontal tasting). Best after 2000.–J.S. • $83 Ⓐ • (11/30/1998) • **89**

Pomerol 1986 • $91 Ⓐ • (9/15/1989) • **93**

Pomerol 1985 • $87 Ⓐ • (10/15/1994) • **90**

Pomerol 1983 • $54 Ⓐ • (10/15/1994) • **96**

Pomerol 1982: Rather closed. Very dark ruby color, with a slight amber edge. Intense blackberry, earth and chocolate aromas. Full-bodied and chewy, with lots of berry and dark chocolate flavors. Full and velvety yet slightly hard, astringent tannins. Still needs time. (1982 Bordeaux horizontal tasting). Best after 2000.–J.S. • $262 Ⓐ • (11/30/1998) • **93**

Pomerol 1981 • $57 Ⓐ • (10/15/1994) • **95**

Pomerol 1979 • $45 Ⓐ • (10/15/1989) • **90**

CERTAN-GIRAUD, CHATEAU

Pomerol 1995: Decadent character of berries and earth, with hints of barnyard. Medium body, with medium tannins and a soft texture. Drink now or hold.–J.S. • $43 • (9/15/1998) • **85**

Pomerol 1988 • $23 • (2/28/1991) • **89**

Pomerol 1986 • $22 • (6/30/1989) • **86**

Pomerol 1985 • $45 • (4/30/1988) • **85**

Pomerol 1982 • $31 Ⓐ • (5/15/1989) • **90**

Pomerol 1961 • $59 • (4/30/1996) • **87**

CHABLIS, CAVE DE

Chablis La Porte d'Or 1995 • $16 • (6/15/1997) • **78**

CHABLISIENNE, LA

Chablis 1998: An intriguing Chablis that wins you over, offering good fruit, earth and chalk notes. Light- to medium-bodied, with a crisp finish. Drink now through 2002.–P.M. • $19 • (5/15/2000) • **84**

Chablis 1996 • $20 • (8/31/1997) • **85**

Chablis Beauroy 1998: Balanced, showing a lovely combination of spice, smoke and toast, with a fat texture and rich (almost late-harvest) fruit. Full-bodied, this is an excellent effort for '98. Drink now through 2008.–P.M. • $27 • (5/15/2000) • **88**

Chablis Beauroy 1996: Compacted, minerally, muscular Chablis, showing firm structure, lovely vanilla bean, tropical and pear flavors. Full-bodied. Best to hold long-term before uncorking to get the full range of its qualities, such as a supple texture. Best from 2007.–P.M. • $42 • (8/31/1998) • **93**

Chablis Beauroy 1995 • $25 • (6/15/1997) • **86**

Chablis Blanchot 1998: Smooth, even silky, but with a pronounced butterscotch character. Full-bodied and rather intense, with toast, smoky wood, burnt honey and ripe pear. Very spicy on the finish. Needs time. Best from 2003 through 2010.–P.M. • $47 • (5/15/2000) • **89**

Chablis Blanchot 1997: Wonderfully silky in texture, this full-bodied Chablis is oaky but offers plenty of sweet-tasting ripe fruit, honey and toast notes, and ends with a supple, balanced and impressively clean finish. Drink now through 2007.–P.M. • $50 • (5/31/1999) • **94**

Chablis Blanchot 1996 • $42 • (5/31/1998) • **79**

Chablis Blanchot 1995 • $25 • (6/15/1997) • **89**

Chablis Bougros 1998: Polished and ripe-tasting, with honey, ripe pear and apricot. Medium-bodied, with a toasted spice character that gives the wine a lingering, smoky finish. Drink now through 2008.–P.M. • $47 • (5/15/2000) • **88**

Chablis Bougros 1997: A grand white Burgundy, full-bodied, balanced between the ripe fruit, spicy complexity, wet earth and distinctively toasted oak notes. Beautifully silky in the midpalate, it has pleasure written all over it. Drink now through 2009.–P.M. • $47 • (5/31/1999) • **93**

Chablis Bougros 1996 • $42 • (5/31/1998) • **94**

Chablis Bougros 1995 • $25 • (6/15/1997) • **87**

Chablis Côte de Léchet 1998: A bit woody, with cedar, toast and smoke notes. Medium-bodied, offering ripe fruit that struggles to balance the oak. Time will tell the outcome. Best from 2003 through 2008.–P.M. • $27 • (5/15/2000) • **84**

Chablis Côte de Léchet 1997: Brilliant Chardonnay—simultaneously ripe, with tropical and pear flavors, and tightly knitted into a ball of citrus and mineral. Medium-bodied, it dissolves into harmony on the finish. Drink now through 2005.–P.M. • $47 • (5/31/1999) • **91**

Chablis Côte de Léchet 1996 • $25 • (5/31/1998) • **87**

Chablis Côte de Léchet 1995 • $25 • (6/15/1997) • **86**

Chablis Fourchaume 1998: Ripe and delicious. Round and medium-bodied, with tropical, pear and fig aromas and flavors. Not terribly intense and a touch diluted, but balanced on the finish. Drink now through 2002.–P.M. • $27 • (5/15/2000) • **84**

Chablis Fourchaume 1996 • $27 • (5/31/1998) • **94**

Chablis Fourchaume 1995 • $25 • (6/15/1997) • **89**

Chablis Fourchaumes Les Vaulorents 1995 • $25 • (6/15/1997) • **89**

Chablis Grenouilles 1998: A silky, ripe Chablis. Buttery, smoky and spicy, it's surprisingly full-bodied for a '98. The oily texture is deeply satisfying, with ripe fruit character and a lingering, intense finish. An excellent effort for the vintage. Drink now through 2005.–P.M. • $50 • (5/15/2000) • **90**

Chablis Grenouilles 1997: Very clean, very pure, very honeyed, this balanced, medium-bodied Chablis is both ripe and citrusy, offering a good, firm structure and a vibrant, minerally finish. Best from 2003 through 2010.–P.M. • $50 • (5/31/1999) • **89**

Chablis Grenouilles Château Grenouilles 1997: An international style of Chardonnay. Heavily toasted, offering a smoky, intense, full-bodied mouthfeel, it blends honey, pear, lemon and hazelnut notes. Lacks the subtle charm of a top '97 Chablis. Best from 2001 through 2005.–P.M. • $50 • (9/30/1999) • **87**

Chablis Grenouilles Château Grenouilles 1995 • $NA • (6/15/1997) • **90**

Chablis Les Clos 1998: Polished and refined, with beautiful focus. Medium-bodied and not overly intense, but it fans out with beautiful complexity, from the ripe pear to the smoke, spice and honey character. Drink now through 2004.–P.M. • $50 • (5/15/2000) • **88**

Chablis Les Clos 1997: An oaky, smoky and toasted style of Les Clos, but it's not overdone as it glides over the palate with clean, full-bodied appeal, offering piecrust, bread dough, pear and, above all, smooth mineral character. For fans of woody Chablis. Best from 2005 through 2015.–P.M. • $47 • (5/31/1999) • **93**

Chablis Les Clos 1996 • $58 • (5/31/1998) • **88**

Chablis Les Lys 1998: Oak dominates this full-bodied Chablis, but the oily texture and ripe fruit go a long way to make this pleasant. Still, the perfumy, floral notes are not for everyone. Drink now through 2003.–P.M. • $27 • (5/15/2000) • **82**

Chablis Les Lys 1997: Rather oaky, but fairly lush, medium-bodied, it displays a cooked apple, slightly oxidized character along with pear and lemon notes. Chewy, drying finish.–P.M. • $40 • (5/31/1999) • **79**

Chablis Les Preuses 1997: Rich and thick, not as deep and intensely fruity as some '97 Chablis, but likable for its smooth character and wet earth, dried herb and green apple flavors. Drink now through 2005.–P.M. • $40 • (9/30/1999) • **86**

Chablis Les Vaulorents 1998: Delicious and well made, showing a crisp, fresh fruit complexity and a smooth, minerally texture midpalate. Ripe flavors of fig and melon are backed by spice. Full-bodied, with an intriguing smoky finish. Drink now through 2008.–P.M. • $30 • (5/15/2000) • **88**

Chablis Mont de Milieu 1998: Beautifully made, well oaked and ripe-tasting. A serious Chardonnay, with toasted wood integrated with the pear, tropical and mineral character. Full-bodied, with a long, smoky, lemony finish. Drink now through 2008.–P.M. • $30 • (5/15/2000) • **91**

Chablis Mont de Milieu 1996 • $27 • (5/31/1998) • **88**

Chablis Mont de Milieu 1995 • $30 • (6/15/1997) • **90**

Chablis Montée de Tonnerre 1998: Tender, with a smooth, polished texture and lovely buttery, pearlike, even tropical flavors. Medium-bodied, balanced, seductive and just plain delicious, with enough fresh lemon zest to carry through to the finish. Drink now through 2001.–P.M. • $30 • (5/15/2000) • **86**

Chablis Montée de Tonnerre 1996 • $27 • (5/31/1998) • **94**

Chablis Montée de Tonnerre 1995 • $25 • (6/15/1997) • **85**

Chablis Montmain 1998: Good intensity in this flavorful '98, with matchstick, flint and chalk character. Medium- to full-bodied, with ripe fruit and a lingering, smoky, harmonious finish. Drink now through 2006.–P.M. • $27 • (5/15/2000) • **88**

Chablis Montmain 1996 • $25 • (5/31/1998) • **93**

Chablis Montmain 1995 • $25 • (6/15/1997) • **88**

Chablis Premier Cru 1998: Supple and lovely, balanced and medium-bodied, with a soft core of apple, pear, smoke and flint. Charming, with an intensity to the finish. Drink now through 2004.–P.M. • $25 • (5/15/2000) • **85**

Chablis Premier Cru 1996 • $25 • (5/31/1998) • **79**

Chablis Premier Cru Vieilles Vignes 1998: Attractive. Good balance, with a mineral, chalk, wet stone and vanilla bean character leaning toward terroir. Medium-bodied, with green apple, pear and cakelike flavors emerging on the lingering finish. Best from 2001 through 2005.–P.M. • $27 • (5/15/2000) • **88**

Chablis Premier Cru Vieilles Vignes 1996 • $25 • (5/31/1998) • **93**

Chablis Premier Cru Vieilles Vignes 1995 • $23 • (6/15/1997) • **89**

CHABLISIENNE, LA

Chablis Vaillon 1998: Wonderful balance, with lovely fruit backed by mineral, chalk and flint. Medium-bodied, with a wet stone character midpalate. A wine of finesse that delivers lots of fresh flavors. Drink now through 2008.–P.M. • $27 • (5/15/2000) • **89**
Chablis Vaillon 1996 • $25 • (5/31/1998) • **93**
Chablis Vaillon 1995 • $25 • (6/15/1997) • **86**
Chablis Valmur 1996 • $42 • (5/31/1998) • **94**
Chablis Valmur 1995 • $30 • (6/15/1997) • **89**
Chablis Vaudésir 1998: Supple and pleasant, buttery and creamy, offering a clean midpalate, with pear tart flavor. Light- to medium-bodied, falling a bit short on the slightly diluted finish. Drink now through 2001.–P.M. • $50 • (5/15/2000) • **80**
Chablis Vaudésir 1997: Stylish, compact *grand cru*, still firm and restrained, offering hints of ripe character (tropical, orange, fig) along with classy mineral, lime and toasted bread notes. Needs time. Best from 2003 through 2008.–P.M. • $47 • (5/31/1999) • **88**
Chablis Vaudésir 1996 • $42 • (5/31/1998) • **76**
Chablis Vaudésir 1995 • $30 • (6/15/1997) • **86**

CHABOT, PATRICK

Pouilly-Fuissé 1996 • $15 • (1/31/1998) • **74**

CHAINIER, DOMAINE

Chinon Moulin des Sablons 1996: Raspberry compote greets the nose, while pure raspberry and cassis flavors keep pumping through on the palate. Lean, firm and packed with flavor, with a fine finish. Enjoy now for its pure fruit or cellar until it softens. Drink now through 2001.–B.S. • $11 • (10/31/1998) • **88**
Chinon Moulin des Sablons Vieilles Vignes 1995 • $13 • (5/15/1997) • **87**
Sauvignon Touraine Château de Pocé 1996 • $10 • (6/15/1997) • **83**
Vouvray Moelleux Clos de Nouys Vendange par Tries 1996: This white shows impressive sweetness and distinctive character, with flavors of cream, custard and banana, but tastes a bit disjointed, lacking concentration. May show better with time in the bottle. Best after 2000.–T.M. • $15 • (6/30/1999) • **84**
Vouvray Moelleux Meloterie 1996: An earthy, mineral component is the overriding element in this white, with a firm underlying structure that gives a hard, unyielding impression. Sweet-and-tart now, may improve with time. Drink through 2005.–B.S. • $11 • (11/15/1998) • **85**
Vouvray Moelleux Meloterie 1995 • $12 • (6/15/1997) • **87**

CHAINTRE, CAVE DE

Mâcon-Chaintré 1995 • $NA • (8/31/1996) • **74**
Mâcon-Fuissé 1995 • $NA • (8/31/1996) • **79**
St.-Véran 1995 • $NA • (8/31/1996) • **74**

CHAIZE, CHATEAU DE LA

Brouilly 1996: Bright cherry aromas and flavors are elegantly presented in this light-bodied red, whose acidity should match well with light meals. Drink now.–B.S. • $16 • (11/15/1998) • **84**
Brouilly 1995 • $13 • (9/15/1996) • **85**
Brouilly 1993 • $10 • (7/31/1995) • **81**
Brouilly 1992 • $10 • (6/30/1994) • **75**

CHAMBERT-MARBUZET, CHATEAU

St.-Estèphe 1997: A lot of new wood and lacking a bit in fruit. Medium-bodied, with dry tannins and a short finish. Drink now.–J.S. • $NA • (1/31/2000) • **81**
St.-Estèphe 1996: Shows some pleasant ripe berry character on the nose and palate, but remains diluted, with a short finish.–J.S. • $NA • (2/28/1999) • **79**
St.-Estèphe 1995 • $30 • (1/31/1998) • **84**
St.-Estèphe 1994 • $25 • (1/31/1997) • **84**
St.-Estèphe 1993 • $25 • (1/31/1996) • **79**
St.-Estèphe 1992 • $15 • (4/15/1995) • **76**
St.-Estèphe 1991 • $14 • (3/31/1994) • **83**
St.-Estèphe 1990 • $25 • (3/31/1993) • **86**
St.-Estèphe 1987 • $18 • (11/30/1989) • **79**
St.-Estèphe 1986 • $29 • (11/30/1989) • **89**
St.-Estèphe 1985 • $32 • (6/30/1988) • **87**
St.-Estèphe 1983 • $15 • (9/30/1986) • **77**
St.-Estèphe 1982 • $30 • (11/30/1989) • **88**

CHAMBRUN, CHATEAU DE

Lalande-de-Pomerol 1999: Attractive floral, berry and mineral aromas. Medium-bodied, with fine tannins, but falls short and hollow on the finish.–J.S. • $NA • (1/01/2000) (BT) • **80-84**
Lalande-de-Pomerol 1998: Fabulous ripe berry, violet and cherry aromas and flavors. Full-bodied, with loads of fruit and a velvety tannin structure. Delicious ripe fruit on the long finish.–J.S. • $NA • (5/31/1999) (BT) • **90-94**

CHAMFORT, BERNARD

Côtes du Rhône Cuvée de Rochedouble 1995 • $5 • (2/28/1997) • **84**

CHAMIREY, CHATEAU DE

Mercurey 1997: Very ripe and lush, showing a distinct, intense licorice and black cherry character, but balsamic vinegar distracts. Too bad, because there's decent grip. Drink now through 2004.–P.M. • $23 • (9/30/1999) • **82**
Mercurey 1991 • $NA • (1/31/1994) • **81**
Mercurey White 1997: A Mercurey that tastes like a little Montrachet. With its beautiful blend of tropical and toasty aromas, this full-bodied white is generous and silky, coating every taste bud with its luscious, thick-as-oil liquid. Remarkable concentration of refined flavors—dried apricot, honey, lemon and mango. Drink now.–P.M. • $17 • (5/31/1999) SS • **94**
Mercurey White 1995 • $18 • (8/31/1997) • **92**

CHAMPAGNON, JEAN-PAUL

Fleurie Les Rôches 1996: Black cherry and game flavors mingle nicely in this firm red. Very fresh, almost tart acidity and noticeable tannins. Should go well with grilled meats.–T.M. • $13 • (8/31/1998) • **84**

CHAMPALOU

Vouvray 1998: Ripe apple and melon flavors are sweet and juicy in this broad white, with enough acidity to remain crisp and refreshing. Drink now.–T.M. • $15 • (2/29/2000) • **84**
Vouvray 1997: Apple and apple cider flavors are round and simple in this soft, slightly sweet white. More drinkable than memorable. Try now.–T.M. • $14 • (2/28/1999) • **81**
Vouvray 1996: An austere style that's dry and minerally, with an underlying tartness. Could use a little more flesh, but has good intensity. Drink now through 2002.–B.S. • $14 • (11/15/1998) • **84**
Vouvray Cuvée Moelleuse 1997: Shows elegance and finesse. Botrytis flavors of spice, vanilla and crème brûlée are sweet and appealing, and although it's a bit soft to match with food, its creamy texture makes it lovely with or as dessert. Drink now through 2002.–T.M. • $24 • (2/28/1999) • **87**
Vouvray Cuvée Moelleuse 1996: The sweetness, which has plenty of tart acidity, frames the crème brûlée, honey and apple skin flavors. Finishes on a chalky, minerally note. A little awkward now. Drink through 2006.–B.S. • $23 • (11/15/1998) • **87**
Vouvray Cuvée Moelleuse 1994 • $20 • (5/15/1996) • **83**
Vouvray Trie de Vendange 1997: Sweet and vibrant, this thick, rich white offers deep flavors of orange, vanilla, honey and spice, with enough underlying acidity to stay vivid and refreshing. Harmonious and long. Drink now through 2005.–T.M. • $32/500 ml. • (2/28/1999) • **91**
Vouvray Trie de Vendange Cuvée CC 1997: Very sweet yet very subtle, this harmonious white is packed with honey, dried pineapple and sweet peach flavors that weave their way across the palate, then linger on the finish. Delicious now, but will age well. Drink now through 2005.–T.M. • $24/500 ml. • (10/31/1999) • **90**

CHAMPAULT, DOMAINE

Sancerre 1996 • $15 • (5/31/1998) • **78**

Key: SS—Spectator Selection. CS—Cellar Selection. HR—Highly Recommended. $NA—Price not available. (BT)—Barrel tasting. Ⓐ—Auction Price. For a key to the tasters' initials, see "How to Use These Listings." **Dates in parentheses represent the issues in which the ratings were published.**

CHAMPS CLOS, LES

Sancerre 1997: Keen and crisp, this refreshing white offers well-defined flavors of citrus and minerals, with light herbal notes. Fresh and clean on the finish. Drink now.–T.M. • $14 • (9/15/1998) • **85**
Sancerre 1996 • $14 • (3/31/1998) • **88**
Sancerre Red 1996: Muddled flavors don't add up to much in this light red, which finishes slightly bitter.–B.S. • $15 • (11/15/1998) • **78**
Sancerre Rosé 1997: This very crisp, pale rosé shows light cherry and spice flavors and a pleasant, silky texture. A hint of spice emerges on the finish. Drink now.–T.M. • $15 • (8/31/1998) • **81**

CHANRION, NICOLE

Côte de Brouilly Domaine de la Voûte des Crozes 1998: Very soft notes of cherry and spice are simple and lack crispness in this light red.–T.M. • $14 • (3/31/2000) • **78**
Côte de Brouilly Domaine de la Voûte des Crozes 1997: Quite chocolaty, with cherry flavors that are lean and firmly structured and a racy character missing in many '97s, but it could use more concentration.–B.S. • $14 • (10/31/1998) • **84**
Côte de Brouilly Domaine de la Voûte des Crozes 1996 • $14 • (6/15/1998) • **87**

CHANSON PERE & FILS

Beaune Clos des Fèves 1997: A focused red Burgundy, with a good combination of toast, smoke and spice and chewy berry character. Medium-bodied, with a satisfying finish. Drink now through 2003.–P.M. • $49 • (1/01/2000) • **85**
Beaune Clos des Fèves 1988 • $35 • (8/31/1990) • **84**
Beaune Clos des Fèves 1987 • $23 • (7/31/1989) • **85**
Beaune Clos des Fèves 1985 • $25 • (1/31/1989) • **92**
Beaune Clos des Marconnets 1997: Starts out soft and a little diffuse, with moderately concentrated cherry, vanilla and spice, then turns quite tannic and austere on the finish. Best after 2001.–B.S. • $38 • (9/30/1999) • **81**
Beaune Clos des Marconnets 1986 • $20 • (5/31/1989) • **81**
Beaune Clos des Mouches 1997: A rich, lively '97, full of cherry and spice on a slightly coarse texture, with moderate concentration and intensity. Firm tannins on the finish. Drink now through 2003.–B.S. • $40 • (9/30/1999) • **83**
Beaune White Clos des Mouches 1997: Balanced, delivering pear, smoke and spice notes, this white coats your palate with flavors, offering a crisp but nice finish. Drink now through 2002.–P.M. • $55 • (5/31/1999) • **83**
Corton 1986 • $30 • (4/30/1989) • **90**
Gevrey-Chambertin 1997: Herbal, lean and off-putting.–B.S. • $36 • (9/30/1999) • **70**
Givry 1988 • $13 • (12/31/1990) • **78**
Mâcon-Villages 1997: Deliciously polished, medium-bodied but tasting fat, firm and structured, with smoky, minerally, flinty character and clean fruit, ending on a harmonious, stony finish. Drink now through 2002.–P.M. • $11 • (5/31/1999) • **88**
Mercurey Red 1997: Light- to medium-bodied, with herb and raspberry compote flavors, ending crisply.–B.S. • $18 • (9/30/1999) • **76**
Meursault 1997: A crisp, herbal style of Meursault, showing modest fruit. Astringent finish.–P.M. • $40 • (5/31/1999) • **75**
Montagny Premier Cru 1997: Clean and fairly ripe, with nice tropical, lemon, dried herb and toasted oak complexity. Slightly chewy, hot and drying on the finish. Drink now through 2006.–P.M. • $16 • (5/31/1999) • **84**
Pernand-Vergelesses Les Vergelesses 1997: Chewy cherry and strawberry on a light framework. Slightly astringent and dusty.–B.S. • $28 • (9/30/1999) • **79**
Pernand-Vergelesses Les Vergelesses 1988 • $24 • (8/31/1990) • **85**
Pernand-Vergelesses White 1997: Very ripe, with wood playing a good supporting role to the phenomenally fresh, vibrant fruit and lively acidity of this medium-bodied, seductive Chardonnay. Drink now through 2002.–P.M. • $24 • (5/31/1999) • **87**
Pommard 1997: Stemmy and vegetal.–P.M. • $42 • (9/30/1999) • **76**
Pouilly-Fuissé 1997: Showy, buttered up with butterscotch, popcorn, coconut and pear character, this full-bodied wine has polish from start to finish, ending with a toasted, smoky finish that's not overdone. Drink now through 2002.–P.M. • $22 • (5/31/1999) • **88**
Puligny-Montrachet 1997: Oxidized, with rustic, old barrel and bitter character.–P.M. • $45 • (5/31/1999) • **70**
St.-Véran 1997: Good mouthfeel, coating the palate with mineral, wet earth, dried herbs, green apple character. Light-bodied, it turns a bit bitter on the finish.–P.M. • $12 • (5/31/1999) • **82**
Savigny-lès-Beaune Dominode 1997: Smooth and ripe, with raspberries and cherries galore, showing a velvety structure but a somewhat oatmeal- and flourlike finish. Drink now.–P.M. • $30 • (9/30/1999) • **84**
Vosne-Romanée Les Suchots 1988 • $55 • (9/30/1990) • **87**

CHANTE-ALOUETTE, CHATEAU

St.-Emilion 1997: A light red with some berry and earth character. Medium- to light-bodied, with light tannins. Sweet fruit finish.–J.S. • $NA • (1/31/2000) • **83**
St.-Emilion 1996: Fresh floral and berry aromas and flavors. Medium-bodied, with light tannins and fresh fruit, but a rather diluted finish. Drink now.–J.S. • $30 • (1/31/1999) • **81**
St.-Emilion 1995 • $28 • (1/31/1998) • **87**

CHANTEFLEUR

Cabernet Sauvignon Vin de Pays d'Oc 1997: A mix of plum and vegetal flavors, accessible but rather simple.–T.M. • $6 • (12/15/1998) • **77**
Cabernet Sauvignon Vin de Pays d'Oc 1995 • $8 • (12/15/1996) • **79**
Cabernet Sauvignon Vin de Pays d'Oc 1994 • $5 • (10/31/1995) • **78**
Cabernet Sauvignon Vin de Pays d'Oc 1993 • $5 • (2/28/1995) • **81**
Cabernet Sauvignon Vin de Pays de l'Ardèche 1991 • $5 • (6/15/1993) • **81**
Cabernet Sauvignon Vin de Pays de l'Ardèche 1988 • $6 • (5/31/1990) • **80**
Chardonnay Vin de Pays d'Oc 1997: Simple, with flavors of fruit cocktail and a slightly bitter finish. Tasted twice, with consistent notes.–B.S. • $6 • (12/15/1998) • **74**
Merlot Vin de Pays d'Oc 1997: Smells and tastes weedy and vegetal, and lacks concentration. Tasted twice, with consistent notes.–B.S. • $6 • (12/15/1998) • **73**
Merlot Vin de Pays d'Oc 1995 • $8 • (12/15/1996) • **82**
Merlot Vin de Pays d'Oc 1994 • $5 • (10/31/1995) • **76**
Merlot Vin de Pays d'Oc 1993 • $5 • (2/28/1995) • **82**
Merlot Vin de Pays d'Oc 1992 • $5 • (3/15/1994) • **80**
Merlot Vin de Pays d'Oc 1991 • $5 • (3/15/1993) • **81**
Merlot Vin de Pays d'Oc 1988 • $6 • (5/31/1990) • **75**
Syrah Vin de Pays d'Oc 1993 • $5 • (2/28/1995) • **80**

CHANTEGRIVE, CHATEAU DE

Graves 1998: Some good fruit, but a bit herbal and unripe. Medium-bodied, with slightly astringent tannins. Short finish.–J.S. • $NA • (5/31/1999) (BT) • **80-84**
Graves 1997: A medium-bodied wine, with tobacco, mineral and berry character. Fresh finish. A bit lean. Best after 2000.–J.S. • $18 • (1/31/2000) • **85**
Graves 1996: Dark-colored, with an abundance of tobacco, berry and cherry character. Medium-bodied, with milk chocolate, berry and tobacco on the aftertaste. Velvety tannin structure for the vintage. Very good effort from this estate. Best after 2001.–J.S. • $14 • (1/31/1999) • **88**
Graves 1995: Intense raspberry aromas, medium-bodied, with silky tannins, but very woody and slightly dry. Wait and see if the fruit can take the wood? Drink through 2005–J.S. • $15 • (9/15/1998) • **84**
Graves 1991 • $11 • (3/31/1994) • **72**
Graves 1990 • $14 • (3/31/1993) • **87**
Graves 1989 • $20 • (3/15/1992) • **88**
Graves 1982 • $20 • (8/31/1992) • **88**
Graves Cuvée Edouard 1990 • $16 • (3/31/1993) • **88**
Graves Cuvée Edouard 1989: Hard to put this one down. Intense aromas of licorice, raisin, mint and berries. Medium- to full-bodied, with lots of spicy, berry and cherry flavors and a long, succulent finish. A delicious wine. (1989 Bordeaux horizontal tasting). Drink now through 2006.–J.S. • $NA • (5/31/1999) • **90**
Graves White 1998: Clean and fresh, with lemon and apple character. Medium-bodied, with good acidity and a sliced apple aftertaste. Drink now.–J.S. • $14 • (2/29/2000) • **85**
Graves White Cuvée Caroline 1998: A pretty white, with melon, apple, vanilla and honey character. Medium-bodied, with lots of fruit and a fresh finish. Drink now through 2003.–J.S. • $23 • (2/29/2000) • **88**
Graves White Cuvée Caroline 1997: If you like Sauvignon, you'll like this. Very intense aromas of fennel and fruit, with hints of oak. Medium- to full-bodied, with lovely Sauvignon character and a medium finish. Drink now.–J.S. • $20 • (9/30/1999) • **87**
Graves White Cuvée Caroline 1996: Emits interesting aromas of lemon curd, beeswax and fruit. Medium-bodied, with lots of almond, vanilla-oak character and a short finish. A bit too much wood for my taste. Drink now.–J.S. • $20 • (3/31/1999) • **85**

FRANCE

CHANTELEUSERIE, DOMAINE DE LA

Bourgueil Cuvée Alouettes 1997: Quite lush for the Loire, this rich red offers plum, black cherry, chocolate and cedar notes, with ripe tannins and just enough acidity for balance. Generous and fresh. Drink through 2003.–T.M. • $11 • (2/28/1999) • **86**

Bourgueil Cuvée Alouettes 1996 • $11 • (2/28/1998) • **85**

Bourgueil Cuvée Beauvais 1997: Herbal and earthy flavors dominate this lean, somewhat astringent red. It offers cherry flavor but needs food to soften and come into balance. Tasted twice, with consistent notes.–T.M. • $15 • (6/30/1999) • **76**

Bourgueil Cuvée Beauvais 1996: Black currant and a hint of tobacco are the main themes in this crisply structured red. Of medium weight and concentration, turning a little shy on the finish. Drink now.–B.S. • $13 • (11/15/1998) • **84**

Bourgueil Vieilles Vignes 1997: This soft, supple red offers bright cherry flavors deepened by tobacco and herbal notes and braced by light tannins. Not an ager, but pleasant drinking. Drink now.–T.M. • $12 • (10/15/1999) • **83**

CHANTE-PERDRIX, DOMAINE

Châteauneuf-du-Pape 1993 • $17 • (12/15/1996) • **76**

Châteauneuf-du-Pape 1990 • $20 • (4/15/1993) • **79**

Châteauneuf-du-Pape 1989 • $20 • (8/31/1992) • **82**

Châteauneuf-du-Pape 1988 • $17 • (5/31/1991) • **82**

CHAPELLE DE LA MISSION-HAUT-BRION, LA

Pessac-Léognan 1999: Delicious wine. Aromas of berries, cherries and tobacco. Medium body, with medium tannins and a medium finish.–J.S. • $NA • (1/01/2000) (BT) • **85-89**

Pessac-Léognan 1998: A lovely, harmonious and young '98, with cherry and tobacco character. Medium-bodied, with fine tannins and a medium finish.–J.S. • $NA • (5/31/1999) (BT) • **85-89**

Pessac-Léognan 1996: Slightly diluted, this has some berry and tomato character but it lets you down a bit on the palate. Medium-bodied, with round tannins, a light finish. Second label of Château La Mission-Haut-Brion. Drink now.–J.S. • $29 • (1/31/1999) • **84**

CHAPOUTIER, M.

Châteauneuf-du-Pape Barbe Rac 1997: Light in color, stemmy and diluted.–P.M. • $119 • (6/30/2000) • **73**

Châteauneuf-du-Pape Barbe Rac 1995 • $63 Ⓐ • (10/15/1997) • **88**

Châteauneuf-du-Pape Barbe Rac 1994 • $40 Ⓐ • (10/15/1997) • **86**

Châteauneuf-du-Pape Barbe Rac 1992 • $77 • (10/15/1995) • **84**

Châteauneuf-du-Pape La Bernardine 1998: Impressive. Ripe, rich and full-bodied, showing silky texture, with lots of plum, red berry and blackberry character. Also digging for the earth, with a nice minerally, chalky personality that comes through on the long, tightly structured finish. Best from 2003 through 2012.–P.M. • $31 • (6/30/2000) • **92**

Châteauneuf-du-Pape La Bernardine 1994 • $26 • (12/15/1996) • **82**

Châteauneuf-du-Pape La Bernardine 1992 • $26 • (11/15/1995) • **77**

Châteauneuf-du-Pape La Bernardine 1990 • $40 Ⓐ • (8/31/1992) SS • **90**

Châteauneuf-du-Pape La Bernardine 1989 • $20 • (8/31/1991) • **84**

Châteauneuf-du-Pape La Bernardine 1988 • $17 • (12/31/1991) • **81**

Châteauneuf-du-Pape La Bernardine 1985 • $25 • (3/15/1990) • **89**

Châteauneuf-du-Pape La Bernardine 1983 • $15 • (9/30/1987) • **89**

Châteauneuf-du-Pape White La Bernardine 1998: Rather opulent in texture, but tastes a bit heavy and traditional, with a chestnut character and wood tannins that dominate the fruit. Dries a bit on the finish.–P.M. • $31 • (6/30/2000) • **79**

Châteauneuf-du-Pape White La Bernardine 1996 • $29 • (10/15/1997) • **85**

Condrieu 1998: Ripe and rich, this '98 Condrieu offers comfy floral, bark and apricot notes, but not a very intense experience. A rather subtle, medium-bodied white. Drink now through 2002.–P.M. • $75 • (12/15/1999) • **84**

Key: SS—Spectator Selection. CS—Cellar Selection. HR—Highly Recommended. $NA—Price not available. (BT)—Barrel tasting. Ⓐ—Auction Price. For a key to the tasters' initials, see "How to Use These Listings." **Dates in parentheses represent the issues in which the ratings were published.**

Condrieu 1997: Fat and ultrathick, lacking a bit of aromatic focus but showing smoke, honey, caramel, mocha and tropical character. A bit soft on the low-acidity finish. Drink now through 2001.–P.M. • $74 • (9/15/1999) • **85**

Condrieu 1996 • $61 • (5/15/1998) • **83**

Cornas 1997: This medium-bodied red tastes a bit diluted, with the aromas just stagnating in the glass.–P.M. • $44 • (8/31/1999) • **77**

Cornas 1996: Quite lovely, with cassis bush and a touch of earthiness. Has great elegance, good ripeness and wonderful balance. Medium in body, satisfying. Drink now through 2003.–P.M. • $34 • (11/15/1998) • **86**

Cornas 1995 • $32 • (10/15/1997) • **89**

Cornas 1991 • $32 • (5/31/1994) • **86**

Cornas 1990 • $32 • (5/31/1994) • **58**

Côte-Rôtie 1997: Wonderful harmony. Rich and full on the palate, showing smooth tannin structure. Lovely balance, with the clean blackberry, mint, vanilla and black pepper paving the way to a velvety finish. Drink now through 2003.–P.M. • $77 • (9/15/1999) • **88**

Côte-Rôtie 1996: Straightforward, with some cherry and raspberry, a bit on the simple side, but it sure is smooth and supple. Pretty. Drink now through 2003.–P.M. • $64 • (11/15/1998) • **80**

Côte-Rôtie 1995 • $56 • (10/15/1997) • **76**

Côte-Rôtie 1992 • $35 • (5/31/1994) • **83**

Côte-Rôtie 1991 • $37 • (10/31/1993) • **85**

Côte-Rôtie 1990 • $41 • (5/31/1994) • **80**

Côte-Rôtie 1989 • $30 • (7/31/1991) • **86**

Côte-Rôtie 1988 • $27 • (11/15/1991) • **84**

Côte-Rôtie Brune et Blonde 1992 • $48 • (12/31/1995) • **87**

Côte-Rôtie Brune et Blonde 1990 • $35 • (11/15/1992) • **90**

Côte-Rôtie La Mordorée 1996: Quite oaky, but very suave and smooth despite the massive tannins, which are ripe. Lots of blackberry, mocha and toasted bread character. Full-bodied and well made. Best from 2003 through 2010.–P.M. • $84 Ⓐ • (11/15/1998) • **91**

Côte-Rôtie La Mordorée 1995 • $109 Ⓐ • (10/15/1997) • **90**

Côte-Rôtie La Mordorée 1992 • $93 • (10/15/1995) • **83**

Côte-Rôtie La Mordorée 1991 • $87 • (5/31/1994) • **86**

Côte-Rôtie La Mordorée 1990 • $169 Ⓐ • (5/31/1994) • **91**

Côtes du Rhône Belleruche 1997: Very ripe and sweet-tasting, this likable, full-bodied red delivers plum, prune, raisin and currant notes in a silky package. A bit hot on the finish, but very nicely done. Should complement grilled meats. Drink now through 2002.–P.M. • $10 • (11/15/1998) • **88**

Côtes du Rhône Belleruche 1994 • $10 • (12/31/1995) • **82**

Côtes du Rhône Belleruche 1993 • $10 • (11/15/1995) • **83**

Côtes du Rhône Belleruche 1990 • $11 • (11/30/1992) • **77**

Côtes du Rhône Belleruche 1989 • $13 • (6/15/1992) • **82**

Côtes du Rhône Belleruche 1986 • $12 • (12/15/1989) • **87**

Côtes du Rhône Rosé Belleruche 1996 • $10 • (10/15/1997) • **79**

Côtes du Rhône-Villages Rasteau 1990 • $14 • (4/15/1993) • **79**

Côtes du Rhône White Belleruche 1997: Medium-bodied, with a honey, pear tart and melon character, this is delicious if not complex. Shows a supple finish, yet with good, lemon-flavored length. Perfect as an aperitif or with simple fare. Drink now.–P.M. • $10 • (11/15/1998) • **85**

Côtes du Rhône White Belleruche 1996 • $10 • (10/15/1997) • **82**

Côtes du Ventoux La Ciboise 1993 • $9 • (11/15/1995) • **76**

Côtes du Ventoux La Ciboise 1990 • $8 • (4/15/1993) • **76**

Crozes-Hermitage Les Meysonniers 1997: Refined tannins impress in this wonderful, silky mouthfeel, with clean black cherry, smoke, olive and pepper character. Juicy, medium-intense finish. Drink now through 2002.–P.M. • $24 • (10/31/1999) • **88**

Crozes-Hermitage Les Meysonniers 1996: An elegant and racy style of Crozes, showing a mineral, stone dust, violet and well-defined cassis character that makes for a seductive combination. The sort of red you won't get tired of. Medium-bodied, with a lively, succulent finish. 1,700 cases imported. Drink now through 2005.–P.M. • $19 • (10/15/1998) • **90**

Crozes-Hermitage Les Meysonniers 1995 • $20 • (10/15/1997) • **80**

Crozes-Hermitage Les Meysonniers 1994 • $20 • (2/28/1997) • **84**

Crozes-Hermitage Les Meysonniers 1993 • $22 • (12/31/1995) • **85**

Crozes-Hermitage Les Meysonniers 1992 • $20 • (10/15/1995) • **84**

Crozes-Hermitage Les Meysonniers 1991 • $17 • (5/31/1994) • **80**

Crozes-Hermitage Les Varonniers 1996: Fairly complex, in an international, new-oakish style. Quite generous, showing ripe berry and plum flavors accented by mocha, spice and toasty oak. Medium- to full-bodied, with sweet tannins that soften the edges a bit. Balanced finish, but a green character does peek through at the end. Drink through 2003.–P.M. • $68 • (10/15/1998) • **85**

Crozes-Hermitage Les Varonniers 1995 • $60 • (10/15/1997) • **88**

Crozes-Hermitage Les Varonniers 1994 • $55 • (10/15/1997) • **92**

Crozes-Hermitage Petite Ruche 1998: Light and easy, with black pepper and raspberry flavors. A bit simple, but it's pleasant to guzzle down slightly chilled.–P.M. • $NA • (12/15/1999) • **79**
Crozes-Hermitage Petite Ruche 1997: Lively, showing black pepper, anise, blackberry and green olive paste. A hint herbaceous on the crisp finish. Drink now through 2003.–P.M. • $20 • (10/31/1999) • **80**
Crozes-Hermitage Petite Ruche 1996: Chewy, with decent red berry flavor, but shy on ripeness. Of light to medium body, crisp on the short finish.–P.M. • $16 • (10/15/1998) • **77**
Crozes-Hermitage Petite Ruche 1991 • $18 • (5/31/1994) • **86**
Crozes-Hermitage White Les Meysonniers 1997: This clean and vibrant white has cream, candle waxlike, melon and almond notes. Smooth and balanced, it kicks in with fresh acidity on the finish. Drink now.–P.M. • $23 • (11/15/1998) • **85**
Crozes-Hermitage White Les Meysonniers 1996: Shows flavors of caramel, cotton candy and cooked apple. Lacks finesse, tastes oxidized. Tasted twice, with consistent notes.–P.M. • $23 • (11/15/1998) • **76**
Crozes-Hermitage White Petite Ruche 1998: A straightforward and modest white, showing a clean streak, with green apple and flowers and a tight, tart, dry finish. Drink now.–P.M. • $NA • (12/15/1999) • **80**
Crozes-Hermitage White Petite Ruche 1997: A bit green and diluted, without much power beyond almond and green apple notes. Disappointing.–P.M. • $NA • (11/15/1998) • **79**
Ermitage L'Ermite 1996: A blockbuster red wine, delivering heavyweight power with amazing finesse. Thick, ripe, rich and superextracted, it's inky-dark, full-bodied, tastes of the earth, cassis and blackberry, mocha and spice, ink, iron, mineral and blood, with a massive amount of full, ripe and sweet tannins. A monumental effort from the Northern Rhône. Best from 2005 through 2020.–P.M. • $190 • (11/15/1998) HR • **98**
Ermitage Le Méal 1996: Near-perfect balance brings appeal to this sumptuous, silky red. Think of crushed black olives mixed with spicy virgin olive oil, add cassis, mocha, spice and toasted bread. Think of a texture so suave and opulent as to bring a smile on your face and the glass to your lips again and again. Get the picture? Drink now through 2010.–P.M. • $170 • (11/15/1998) • **95**
Ermitage Le Pavillon NV • $60 • (1/31/1989) • **88**
Ermitage Le Pavillon 1996: What a silky wine. Lush and ripe, with elegance, it coats the palate with the finest, most velvety tannins, providing loads of pleasure with its mocha, plum, wild berry, grilled meat flavors. Full-bodied, with excellent intensity on the smooth, lingering finish. Delicious. Drink now through 2008.–P.M. • $170 • (11/15/1998) • **94**
Ermitage Le Pavillon 1995 • $195 Ⓐ • (10/15/1997) • **94**
Ermitage Le Pavillon 1994 • $91 Ⓐ • (4/30/1997) • **90**
Ermitage Le Pavillon 1992 • $94 Ⓐ • (10/15/1995) • **87**
Ermitage Le Pavillon 1991 • $195 Ⓐ • (5/31/1994) • **87**
Ermitage Le Pavillon 1990 • $229 Ⓐ • (12/15/1993) • **85**
Ermitage White de l'Orée 1996: Absolutely divine from start to finish. Shows subtle power and wonderful concentration. Reserved on the nose, silky in texture and thick on the palate, this wine is ripe with exotic flavors—melon, cream, beeswax, honey, dried herb, wet earth and smoked lard—and has an ultrasmooth finish. Drink now through 2005.–P.M. • $100 Ⓐ • (11/15/1998) • **94**
Gigondas 1995 • $22 • (10/15/1997) • **90**
Gigondas 1994 • $22 • (2/28/1997) • **87**
Hermitage Chante-Alouette 1996: A distinctive, powerful Hermitage—not for the fainthearted. Rich and thick, it coats the palate with fruit, spice and an earthy character. Turns a bit bitter on the finish, but it delivers the goods. Full-bodied. Drink now through 2005.–P.M. • $57 • (11/15/1998) • **88**
Hermitage La Sizeranne 1997: A supple, medium-bodied red of medium concentration, delivering some spice and black fruit character, with a kick of crisp acidity on the juicy finish. Drink now through 2002.–P.M. • $83 • (9/15/1999) • **86**
Hermitage La Sizeranne 1996: Wonderful minerally red, with ripe fruit flavors backed by subtle toasted oak, grilled meat, black pepper, cassis and mint. Deploys ripe, sweet, palate-coating tannins. Full-bodied, its earthy, rocky notes are lovely on the balanced finish. Drink now through 2010.–P.M. • $25 Ⓐ • (11/15/1998) • **95**
Hermitage La Sizeranne 1995 • $41 Ⓐ • (10/15/1997) • **84**
Hermitage La Sizeranne 1994 • $42 • (4/30/1997) • **90**
Hermitage La Sizeranne 1992 • $45 • (11/15/1995) • **87**
Hermitage La Sizeranne 1991 • $42 • (5/31/1994) • **86**
Hermitage La Sizeranne 1989 • $46 Ⓐ • (8/31/1991) • **89**
Hermitage La Sizeranne 1988 • $25 • (12/31/1991) • **85**
Hermitage La Sizeranne 1983 • $19 • (5/01/1986) • **83**
Hermitage La Sizeranne 1981 • $10 • (11/01/1984) • **88**
Hermitage La Sizeranne Grande Cuvée NV • $14 • (5/01/1986) • **83**
Hermitage Monier de la Sizeranne 1990 • $58 Ⓐ • (8/31/1992) • **91**
Hermitage White Chante-Alouette 1997: Nice richness to this white, but it tastes clumsy and heavy as the cooked fruit character kicks in on the hot finish.–P.M. • $77 • (9/15/1999) • **78**
Muscat de Beaumes-de-Venise 1996 • $17/375 ml. • (10/15/1997) • **84**
Muscat de Beaumes-de-Venise 1995 • $25 • (2/28/1997) • **85**
Muscat de Beaumes-de-Venise 1993 • $13 • (10/15/1995) • **86**
Muscat de Rivesaltes NV • $NA • (10/15/1997) • **85**
St.-Joseph Deschants 1997: A straightforward, medium-bodied red, with anise and red berry character. Drink now.–P.M. • $31 • (10/31/1999) • **80**
St.-Joseph Deschants 1996: Supple and ripe, with cassis, raspberry and wet earth, this medium-bodied red is quite attractive, a fun wine to enjoy with simple fare. Drink now through 2003.–P.M. • $26 • (11/15/1998) • **87**
St.-Joseph Deschants 1995 • $23 • (10/15/1997) • **87**
St.-Joseph Deschants 1994 • $22 • (11/30/1996) • **87**
St.-Joseph Deschants 1992 • $20 • (5/31/1994) • **88**
St.-Joseph Deschants 1991 • $20 • (5/31/1994) • **79**
St.-Joseph Deschants 1990 • $20 • (4/15/1993) • **83**
St.-Joseph Les Granits 1996: Showy, in super-woody style that dominates the fruit, at least for now. Underneath are some pretty black cherry, raspberry and wet earth notes. Tough finish. Drink through 2005.–P.M. • $NA • (11/15/1998) • **87**
St.-Joseph Les Granits 1995 • $56 • (10/15/1997) • **89**
St.-Joseph White Deschants 1997: Neutral smelling, but good-tasting, with great texture. Silky-smooth, full-bodied and opulent, dishing up the creamy, buttery, honeyed and pearlike flavors in good amounts. Balanced to a T. Drink now.–P.M. • $NA • (11/15/1998) • **88**
St.-Joseph White Deschants 1996 • $23 • (10/15/1997) • **83**
St.-Joseph White Les Granits 1996: A bit herbal despite the ripe fruit. Lacks a bit of harmony, turning tart on the bitter finish.–P.M. • $76 • (11/15/1998) • **78**
Tavel Beaurevoir 1996 • $19 • (5/15/1998) • **85**

CHARBAUT & FILS, A.

Brut Blanc de Blancs Champagne NV • $35 • (12/31/1994) • **80**
Brut Blanc de Blancs Champagne 1990: An intriguing array of toasty, smoky, spicy accents blend with solid fruit flavors and fine bubbles in this enticing Champagne. Drink now through 2001. • $45 • (12/31/1998) • **88**
Brut Champagne NV: A distinctive, traditional style of Champagne, with enticing accents of walnut and honey that add complexity to the vibrant fruit flavors and firm, elegant mousse. Drink now. • $27 • (12/15/1998) • **90**
Brut Champagne André Charbaut NV • $35 • (11/30/1993) • **77**
Brut Champagne Cuvée de Réserve NV • $35 • (12/31/1991) • **90**
Brut Champagne Extra Quality NV • $30 • (12/31/1991) • **86**
Brut Champagne Gold Label NV • $28 • (12/31/1994) • **82**
Brut Rosé Champagne NV • $35 • (10/31/1996) • **89**
Demi-Sec Champagne Sélection NV • $35 • (12/31/1994) • **86**

CHARBONNIERE, DOMAINE DE LA

Châteauneuf-du-Pape Cuvée Mourre des Perdrix 1996: Very ripe, soft-textured, with smooth tannins; a deliciously velvety palate, but lacking a bit of flavor intensity. Drink now through 2001.–P.M. • $26 • (8/31/1999) • **85**
Châteauneuf-du-Pape Cuvée Mourre des Perdrix 1995 • $NA • (10/15/1997) • **77**
Châteauneuf-du-Pape Cuvée Vieilles Vignes 1995 • $20 • (10/15/1997) • **75**

CHARLEMAGNE, GUY

Brut Blanc de Blancs Champagne Cuvée Charlemagne 1992: A wild earthy character dominates this crisp, dry wine from the aromas to the finish. The earthy, toasty flavor profile (which is spare on fruit components) makes it distinctive, but it's not for everyone. Drink now through 2001. • $39 • (12/31/1998) • **86**
Brut Blanc de Blancs Champagne Mesnillésime 1995: Full-bodied, quite flavorful but not heavy, with lively acidity backing ripe fruit and toasted nut nuances. Drink now through 2005. • $60 • (11/15/1999) • **89**
Brut Blanc de Blancs Champagne Réserve NV: Crisp and full of fruit flavor, this is high on quality and easy to enjoy. Buttery, toasty accents remind you it's made from Chardonnay. Drink now. • $39 • (10/31/1999) • **89**
Extra Brut Blanc de Blancs Champagne NV: A pure, clean, tantalizing Champagne. Really bright and refreshing in personality, backed with solid fruit flavors and crisp acidity. Drink now. • $30 • (12/31/1998) • **89**
Extra Brut Champagne NV: Crisp and focused, this sparkling wine displays a dough aroma, apple and lemon flavors, moderate concentration and a lingering finish. Drink now.–B.S. • $30 • (11/30/1999) • **86**

CHARLOPIN-PARIZOT, PHILIPPE

Bourgogne 1995 • $14 • (11/15/1997) • **85**
Bourgogne Cuvée Prestige 1997: Thick and minerally, this very pleasant Pinot has character, black fruit and an impressively persistent finish for a Bourgogne Rouge. Drink now through 2001.–P.M. • $16 • (9/30/1999) • **85**
Bourgogne Cuvée Prestige 1994 • $13 • (11/15/1996) • **80**
Bourgogne Tête de Cuvée 1996: Balanced and pretty, a supple red Burgundy with a light, red berry character, licorice and floral notes. Drink now.–P.M. • $19 • (9/30/1998) • **83**
Chambertin 1996: Interesting mocha, vanilla, spice character. Lots of wood, with a slight dryness on the finish, yet it has a fatness in the palate, with some blackberry and black cherry notes, and the richness is delicious. Still needs time as the finish remains a bit tough for now. Much better than previously reviewed. Best from 2006 through 2016.–P.M. • $105 • (9/30/1999) • **92**
Chambertin 1995 • $95 • (11/15/1997) • **95**
Chambertin 1994 • $92 • (11/15/1996) • **93**
Chambertin 1990 • $90 • (8/31/1992) • **94**
Chambertin 1989 • $35 • (11/15/1991) • **91**
Chambolle-Musigny 1996: On the simple side, this tastes a bit diluted and straightforward, with some oak and modest fruit. Drink now.–P.M. • $38 • (9/30/1998) • **78**
Chambolle-Musigny 1995 • $37 • (11/15/1997) • **84**
Chambolle-Musigny 1994 • $36 • (11/15/1996) • **84**
Charmes-Chambertin 1997: Unique yet natural-tasting, with a mineral, lead pencil and blackberry character. Excellent intensity picks up on the sleek finish. Amazing quality for a '97, digging profoundly into the roots of its *terroir* to pull out magic. Full-bodied, its tannins are all velvet. Drink now through 2015.–P.M. • $92 • (9/30/1999) • **95**
Charmes-Chambertin 1996: Clean and pure, with some licorice, black cherry, spice and floral notes. More elegant than powerful, quite plummy, lingering on the finish. The very toasted wood tannins are a bit chewy on the finish. Much better than previously reviewed. Best from 2006 through 2016.–P.M. • $92 • (9/30/1999) • **91**
Charmes-Chambertin 1995 • $87 • (11/15/1997) • **96**
Charmes-Chambertin 1994 • $79 • (11/15/1996) • **91**
Charmes-Chambertin 1993 • $94 • (5/15/1996) • **94**
Charmes-Chambertin 1990 • $70 • (8/31/1992) • **92**
Clos St.-Denis 1997: Ripe and rich, with raisin, dried fruit, petrol and almost oxidized character, as well as a touch of mocha, chocolate and spice. Soft finish. California style. Drink now through 2001.–P.M. • $82 • (9/30/1999) • **83**
Clos St.-Denis 1996: A monster with the sensibility of a child, this huge wine has come around beautifully since it was tasted last year shortly after bottling. Black and ultrathick, voluptuous and unctuous, delivering loads of mocha, spice and wet earth along with cassis, blackberry and black cherry. The sort of wine a Burgundy-lover dreams about. Much better than previously reviewed. Best from 2006 through 2026.–P.M. • $92 • (9/30/1999) • **97**
Clos St.-Denis 1995 • $80 • (11/15/1997) • **93**
Clos St.-Denis 1994 • $79 • (11/15/1996) • **95**
Clos St.-Denis 1993 • $94 • (5/15/1996) • **90**
Clos St.-Denis 1990 • $76 • (8/31/1992) • **89**
Echézeaux 1997: Well made. Medium-bodied, it keeps a clear focus as the toasted oak and black fruit integrate on the palate. The finish remains firm and fresh. Best from 2002 through 2007.–P.M. • $92 • (9/30/1999) • **89**
Fixin 1996: Ripe and plummy, with licorice galore, this is a supple red that lacks finesse but delivers lots of flavors and balanced tannins. Drink now.–P.M. • $21 • (9/30/1998) • **84**
Fixin 1995 • $NA • (11/15/1997) • **88**
Fixin 1994 • $22 • (11/15/1996) • **81**
Gevrey-Chambertin Cuvée Vieilles Vignes 1997: The aromas and flavors seem ripe, evoking plum and cassis, although maybe they're a bit diffuse on the palate, with light tannins. The whole package turns crisp on the finish, competing with the fruit. Drink through 2003.–B.S. • $39 • (9/30/1999) • **83**
Gevrey-Chambertin Cuvée Vieilles Vignes 1996: Wonderful balance. Lovely wine, full of finesse despite its thick, ripe texture, showing plum, cream, wet earth, mocha character. Full-bodied, silky and flavorful, with an elegant yet deeply satisfying, long and spicy finish. Best After 2003.–P.M. • $38 • (9/30/1998) • **90**
Gevrey-Chambertin Cuvée Vieilles Vignes 1995 • $37 • (11/15/1997) • **90**
Gevrey-Chambertin Cuvée Vieilles Vignes 1994 • $35 • (11/15/1996) • **85**
Gevrey-Chambertin Cuvée Vieilles Vignes 1993 • $NA • (5/15/1996) • **88**
Gevrey-Chambertin Cuvée Vieilles Vignes 1990 • $40 • (4/30/1992) • **90**
Gevrey-Chambertin Cuvée Vieilles Vignes 1989 • $75 • (11/15/1991) • **88**
Gevrey-Chambertin Cuvée Vieilles Vignes 1988 • $31 • (12/31/1990) • **79**
Gevrey-Chambertin La Justice 1996: Very ripe '96, with plum, kirschlike and black cherry aromas and flavors. Full-bodied and a bit hot, it has a nice underpinning of silky tannins, wet earth and acidity to hold it together. Best after 2003.–P.M. • $34 • (9/30/1998) • **85**
Gevrey-Chambertin La Justice 1995 • $NA • (11/15/1997) • **86**
Gevrey-Chambertin La Justice 1994 • $33 • (11/15/1996) • **81**
Marsannay 1994 • $20 • (11/15/1996) • **79**
Marsannay En Montchenevoy 1996: Very ripe, with floral overtones, raspberry notes and a tannic structure without the depth of fruit to match. Best from 2002 through 2006.–B.S. • $24 • (9/30/1998) • **81**
Marsannay En Montchenevoy 1995 • $20 • (11/15/1997) • **87**
Marsannay En Montchenovoy 1990 • $19 • (4/30/1992) • **84**
Mazis-Chambertin 1996: Fairly burly but with a lot of character, this delivers earth, mineral, plum and ripe blackberry flavors, some roasted chestnut, vanilla and toasted bread accents from oak. Full-bodied, with a silky texture until a wall of firm tannins hits on the finish, suggesting cellaring. Best after 2003.–P.M. • $92 • (9/30/1998) • **89**
Morey-St.-Denis 1996: Bursting with ripe licorice and cherry flavors, but also big-time tannins. Best After 2001.–B.S. • $34 • (9/30/1998) • **84**
Morey-St.-Denis 1995 • $32 • (11/15/1997) • **91**
Morey-St.-Denis 1994 • $31 • (11/15/1996) • **78**
Vosne-Romanée 1996: Unctuous and thick, tasting ripe, with a distinctive oaky-petrol, spicy, black cherry character. Full-bodied, it lacks a bit of class, but will perhaps improve with cellaring. Best after 2003.–P.M. • $38 • (9/30/1998) • **83**
Vosne-Romanée 1995 • $37 • (11/15/1997) • **90**
Vosne-Romanée 1994 • $37 • (11/15/1996) • **84**

CHARMAIL, CHATEAU

Haut-Médoc 1997: Very good for this château. Serious dark color, with blackberry, lead pencil and berry aromas. Full-bodied, with a solid core of fruit but a slightly dry finish. Best after 2002.–J.S. • $22 • (1/31/2000) • **88**
Haut-Médoc 1994 • $14 • (2/28/1998) • **78**

CHARME, MAISON

Cabernet Sauvignon Vin de Pays de l'Hérault 1993 • $5 • (7/31/1996) • **81**
Merlot Vin de Pays de l'Hérault 1993 • $5 • (12/15/1996) • **67**

CHARME LABORY, LE

St.-Estèphe 1995 • $12 • (1/31/1998) • **87**

CHARMES DE KIRWAN, LES

Margaux 1996: Dark-colored, with an impressive concentration of plum, black currant and berry. Full-bodied, chunky, with velvety tannins and a ripe fruit aftertaste. Slightly one-dimensional and rustic, but well made. Second label of Château Kirwan.–J.S. • $NA • (1/31/1999) • **87**
Margaux 1995 • $18 • (1/31/1998) • **88**

CHARMES DE LIVERSAN, LES

Haut-Médoc 1995 • $10 • (1/31/1998) • **81**

CHARMES-GODARD, CHATEAU LES

Côtes de Francs 1995 • $18 • (1/31/1998) • **88**
Côtes de Francs 1989: This is a big, monolithic wine, but you have to appreciate the concentration, especially for the appellation. Good dark-ruby color. Intense aromas of dark chocolate and prunes. Full-bodied, very chewy, with rustic tannins and superripe fruit flavors. Will improve with age. (1989 Bordeaux horizontal tasting). Drink through 2005.–J.S. • $NA • (5/31/1999) • **87**
Côtes de Francs White 1998: A bit closed right now, but with very good honey, apple and citrus character. Medium- to full-bodied, with fresh acidity and a medium finish. Drink now through 2003.–J.S. • $NA • (2/29/2000) • **88**
Côtes de Francs White 1997: Big and rich for this appellation, with loads of mango and honey character. Full-bodied, oily and opulent. A bit more acidity

Key: SS—Spectator Selection. CS—Cellar Selection. HR—Highly Recommended. $NA—Price not available. (BT)—Barrel tasting. Ⓐ—Auction Price.
For a key to the tasters' initials, see "How to Use These Listings."
Dates in parentheses represent the issues in which the ratings were published.

would make it outstanding. Not imported into the U.S. Drink now.–J.S. • $NA • (9/30/1999) • **88**

CHARRIERE, CHATEAU DE LA

Santenay White Sous La Roche 1998: Ripe and buttery style, with vanilla, pear and spice notes. Full-bodied, this is a rather fat-tasting white that's pleasant to drink on release. Turns fresh and citrusy on the finish. Drink now through 2002.–P.M. • $26 • (5/31/2000) • **86**

CHARRON, CHATEAU

Premières Côtes de Blaye 1995: Lots of berry and chestnut character. Medium-bodied, with round tannins and a light finish. A bit simple, really. Drink now.–J.S. • $NA • (9/15/1998) • **83**

CHARTOGNE-TAILLET

Brut Champagne Cuvée Fiacre Taillet NV: Fine flavor concentration and a slightly mature aroma give substance to this well-balanced, full-bodied brut. Drink now. • $69 • (9/15/1999) • **90**

Brut Champagne Cuvée Ste.-Anne NV: A mouth-filling texture and slightly sweet fruit flavors make this soft and easygoing in style. Drink now. • $40 • (10/15/1999) • **85**

CHARTRON, JEAN

Beaune Hospices de Beaune Cuvée Cyrot-Chaudron 1988 • $40 • (2/15/1991) • **88**

Bourgogne Clos de la Combe 1990 • $11 • (3/31/1992) • **85**

Bourgogne White Clos de la Combe 1996 • $10 • (5/31/1998) • **84**

Chevalier-Montrachet Clos des Chevaliers 1998: Well made and refined. Medium-bodied and rather silky, fresh and subtle, with smoke, chalk, wet earth notes, ripe fruit and a vibrant backbone of citrus character. Has the stuffing to improve with age. Drink now through 2010.–P.M. • $235 • (5/31/2000) • **90**

Chevalier-Montrachet Clos des Chevaliers 1997: Supple and delicious on release. Medium-bodied and pleasant for its marzipan, honey, tropical and spice notes. A slightly burning finish reveals its low acidity. Drink now through 2002.–P.M. • $220 • (5/31/1999) • **87**

Chevalier-Montrachet Clos des Chevaliers 1996 • $170 • (5/31/1998) • **97**

Puligny-Montrachet Clos de la Pucelle 1998: Elegant as well as rich, with a minerally, chalky, lemony character. Impressive for its focus and broad flavors. Turns chewy on the finish, with dried herbs, toasted oak and a slightly grassy character. Drink now through 2008.–P.M. • $80 • (5/31/2000) • **89**

Puligny-Montrachet Clos de la Pucelle 1997: Elegant, medium-bodied and medium-intense, with a pure mineral, wet chalk and pear character. Very pleasant and harmonious; perfect for drinking young. Drink now through 2007.–P.M. • $70 • (5/31/1999) • **92**

Puligny-Montrachet Clos de la Pucelle 1996 • $60 • (5/31/1998) • **83**

Puligny-Montrachet Clos du Cailleret 1998: Lovely from start to finish. Silky and seductive, with honey, ripe pear and tropical flavors, all presented in a restrained package that stresses elegance. Medium-bodied, the mineral, wet soil notes sing on the creamy, lemony finish. Drink now through 2008.–P.M. • $85 • (5/31/2000) • **92**

Puligny-Montrachet Clos du Cailleret 1997: Full-bodied and showing an opulent texture, with delicious intensity. Delivers a ripe, intense mouthfeel, with a surprising lineup of fresh herb, pineapple, lemon and honey. Drink now through 2007.–P.M. • $72 • (5/31/1999) • **92**

Puligny-Montrachet Clos du Cailleret 1996 • $60 • (5/31/1998) • **90**

Puligny-Montrachet Les Folatières 1998: Lovely white Burgundy. Medium-bodied, offering a chalky, minerally, soily, wet stone character along with the ripe fruit and honey. Fresh and deliciously vibrant on the citrusy finish. Should improve with cellaring. Best from 2002 through 2008.–P.M. • $80 • (5/31/2000) • **88**

Puligny-Montrachet Les Folatières 1997: Well made. Ripe fruit brings forth mandarin, fresh fig and tropical notes. Nice oak accents add spicy complexity to this flinty white. Drink now through 2002.–P.M. • $65 • (5/31/1999) • **89**

Puligny-Montrachet Les Folatières 1996 • $55 • (5/31/1998) • **88**

St.-Aubin Les Murgers des Dents de Chien 1998: Gorgeous mineral, wet stone, matchstick, smoke aromas combine with lime, honey and ripe fruit. Intriguing and aromatically complex, although the slightly astringent finish lacks a bit of refinement. Drink now through 2005.–P.M. • $35 • (5/31/2000) • **87**

St.-Aubin Les Murgers des Dents de Chien 1997: A bit green but lively, with plenty of herbal intensity and a honeyed touch. Slightly bitter on the juicy, clean finish. Drink now through 2002.–P.M. • $32 • (5/31/1999) • **83**

CHARTRON LA FLEUR

Bordeaux 1996: A bit diluted, with berry, blackberry and tomato aromas and flavors. Medium- to light-bodied, with light tannins, a fresh finish.–J.S. • $NA • (2/28/1999) • **78**

CHARTRON & TREBUCHET

Auxey-Duresses White 1997: Wonderful. The subtle and enticing toasted oak and spicy aromas and flavors play joyfully with the piecrust, apple, lemon, cream and vanilla bean character in this smooth-tasting white. Drink now through 2001.–P.M. • $NA • (1/01/1999) • **90**

Bâtard-Montrachet 1998: Focused and racy; takes off on the palate to finish powerfully. Much going on in this refined medium-bodied white with its lemon, spice, toast and mineral character. Drink now through 2010.–P.M. • $175 • (5/31/2000) • **92**

Bâtard-Montrachet 1997: Ultraripe, almost late harvest due to the tropical and apricot flavors, but in contact with air it develops a slight hard, cedary, spiritlike, hot note on the finish.–P.M. • $175 • (5/31/1999) • **79**

Bienvenues-Bâtard-Montrachet 1998: Cream-textured white Burgundy that grows on you. The woody notes dominate now in this medium-bodied Chardonnay of good mineral character, with lovely ripe fruit and a subtle finish of toasted bread and spice. First Bienvenues from this producer. Best from 2002 through 2008.–P.M. • $200 • (5/31/2000) • **89**

Bourgogne White 1997: Clean and crisp, this medium-bodied, rather pleasant white Burgundy is fairly ripe and lush on the midpalate. Drink now.–P.M. • $13 • (5/31/1999) • **80**

Bourgogne White Cuvée Jean Chartron Vieilles Vignes 1998: Fresh and lively but not very sophisticated, this medium-bodied white offers some grass, dried herb, green apple character. Chewy finish. Drink now through 2003.–P.M. • $18 • (5/31/2000) • **86**

Bourgogne White Cuvée Jean Chartron Vieilles Vignes 1997: Clean aromas are followed by butter, pear and bread dough notes. Not bad, but it seems a bit diluted and stripped. Lacks balance.–P.M. • $15 • (5/31/1999) • **77**

Bourgogne White Cuvée Jean Chartron Vieilles Vignes 1995 • $15 • (5/31/1998) • **84**

Chablis Domaine Goublot 1998: A bit astringent, but also showing a Chablis-like mineral, sea salt character. Light- to medium-bodied, with a chewy, citrusy finish that's very crisp at this stage. Drink now through 2003.–P.M. • $17 • (5/15/2000) • **80**

Chassagne-Montrachet 1997: Medium-bodied, with pear, quince and butter notes. A bit soft and burning on the finish.–P.M. • $60 • (5/31/1999) • **79**

Chassagne-Montrachet 1996 • $40 • (5/31/1998) • **86**

Chassagne-Montrachet Morgeot 1998: Wonderful, rich but firm white Burgundy. Has lovely mineral, ripe fruit character, a rich midpalate-feel, balanced oak accents and a lingering finish with fresh fruit. Best from 2001 through 2008.–P.M. • $70 • (5/31/2000) • **90**

Chassagne-Montrachet Morgeot 1997: Decent ripe fruit peeks through in this medium-bodied, medium-intense white, with a touch of honey and pear. Short finish. Drink now.–P.M. • $60 • (5/31/1999) • **80**

Corton-Charlemagne 1998: Very oaky now, and it tastes better than it smells with a distinctive perfumy, roselike aroma from the wood, but it offers lovely texture and ripe fruit as well, with a fresh underpinning of lime and honey character that gives this medium-bodied Chardonnay length. Best from 2003 through 2008.–P.M. • $105 • (5/31/2000) • **87**

Corton-Charlemagne 1997: Clean, with attractive mineral, butter, cream, pear and lemon character, this medium-intense white is beautifully balanced, coating the palate with harmony. Supple, subtly toasted, lemony finish. Drink now through 2007.–P.M. • $80 • (5/31/1999) • **91**

Côte de Beaune-Villages 1988 • $16 • (2/28/1991) • **79**

Criots-Bâtard-Montrachet 1997: Well made. Good ripe fruit combines with spice, mocha and heavy oak flavors. Very intense and even burning mouthfeel, but the rich pear, tropical, chocolate and lemon character bursts like a volcano on an opulent finish that leaves your palate scorched...and tired. Drink now through 2027.–P.M. • $NA • (5/31/1999) • **86**

Mâcon-Villages 1997: Nice intensity in this clean, crisp Chardonnay, which shows some mineral, tart citrus and straightforward wet hay character. Drink now.–P.M. • $11 • (5/31/1999) • **80**

Mâcon-Villages 1995 • $NA • (8/31/1996) • **75**

Mercurey White 1996 • $20 • (5/31/1998) • **84**

FRANCE

CHARTRON & TREBUCHET

Meursault 1998: A somewhat tough style, with a crisp edge, but it also delivers decent Chardonnay fruit and some smoky, toasted aromas. Drink now through 2004.–P.M. • $55 • (5/31/2000) • **80**

Meursault 1997: Smooth and a bit light, showing modest fruit concentration, with a touch of green apple and dried herb character.–P.M. • $48 • (5/31/1999) • **79**

Meursault 1996 • $35 • (5/31/1998) • **87**

Meursault Les Charmes 1998: Rich and ripe, with a distinct backbone of fancy wood. Enough fruit to balance it all, with a chalky, chewy, wet soil character that suggests good *terroir*. Full-bodied, it coats the palate. Elegant finish, with just a slight heat from the toasted oak. Best from 2002 through 2010.–P.M. • $75 • (5/31/2000) • **90**

Meursault Les Charmes 1997: An elegant, medium-bodied Meursault—not very ripe, but clean, with wet earth, mineral, spice and toast character. Drink now through 2002.–P.M. • $70 • (5/31/1999) • **83**

Montagny Les Grandes Vignes 1997: At first sip there's a lot to be attracted to in this medium-bodied white, such as butter, cream and pear, but it turns hot and drying on the finish.–P.M. • $18 • (5/31/1999) • **78**

Montagny Les Grandes Vignes 1996 • $17 • (5/31/1998) • **85**

Montrachet 1998: An ager that tastes wonderful (and better than it smells). Starts out very oaky, with sandalwood, rose water and floral aromas, but the palate offers dense Chardonnay character, with ripe fruit and a silky texture. Beautifully structured, as demonstrated by the racy, minerally finish. Best from 2003 through 2010.–P.M. • $300 • (5/31/2000) • **92**

Montrachet 1996 • $240 • (5/31/1998) • **85**

Pernand-Vergelesses White 1997: A bit of wood adds a buttery, toasty layer but interferes a bit with the pure expression of the fruit. Turns chewy on the midpalate before showing lovely lemony freshness on the finish. Drink now through 2002.–P.M. • $27 • (5/31/1999) • **86**

Pommard Les Epenots 1988 • $45 • (2/28/1991) • **87**

Pouilly-Fuissé Domaine de la Chapelle 1997: A rich, ripe and oaky Pouilly. The toasted wood battles it out with the lovely tropical fruit in this full-bodied white. There's a lot going here. Best after 2000.–P.M. • $27 • (5/31/1999) • **87**

Pouilly-Fuissé Domaine de la Chapelle 1996 • $20 • (5/31/1998) • **84**

Puligny-Montrachet 1997: Nicely earthy, honeyed, silky, grassy—there's lots for a white Burg aficionado to like here—but its round mouthfeel lacks a bit of depth despite a lemony flavored finish. Not as good as previously reviewed. Drink now through 2005.–P.M. • $47 • (9/30/1999) • **88**

Puligny-Montrachet 1996 • $45 • (5/31/1998) • **87**

Puligny-Montrachet Les Referts 1998: Structured and firm, with elegant ripe fruit and a citrusy undertow that holds it together. A bit too woody to score outstanding but perhaps time will balance it out as this full-bodied, silky Chardonnay blends mineral, vanilla bean and pearlike flavors. Best from 2003 through 2010.–P.M. • $75 • (5/31/2000) • **89**

Puligny-Montrachet Les Referts 1997: Supple and minerally, offering good pear and tropical notes, with a pleasant, ripe-tasting finish. Drink now through 2002.–P.M. • $55 • (5/31/1999) • **87**

Rully La Chaume 1997: Soft and a bit oaky, showing good midpalate fruitiness and lemon vibrancy, but it turns slightly drying and chewy on the finish. Drink now.–P.M. • $25 • (5/31/1999) • **81**

Rully La Chaume 1996 • $19 • (5/31/1998) • **85**

St.-Aubin La Chatenière 1997: Lovely, with ripe pear, banana and tropical notes. Smooth and medium-bodied, with a succulent and balanced finish. Drink now through 2003.–P.M. • $30 • (5/31/1999) • **88**

St.-Aubin La Chatenière 1996 • $25 • (5/31/1998) • **90**

St.-Romain 1997: A bit woody and bitter. Buttery, medium-bodied, dry and disjointed.–P.M. • $28 • (5/31/1999) • **74**

St.-Véran Château de Chasselas 1997: Crisp but well-structured, with apple, wet hay, honey, dried herbs, this is a good white that turns just a bit bitter and rustic on the finish. Drink now.–P.M. • $NA • (5/31/1999) • **80**

St.-Véran Château de Chasselas 1996 • $14 • (5/31/1998) • **85**

Santenay White 1997: Quite oaky, with heavily toasted coffee and coconut character. Despite the clean lemon pie, citrus and tropical intensity, this showy, medium-bodied white turns slightly astringent on the finish. Drink through 2005.–P.M. • $29 • (5/31/1999) • **82**

Santenay White 1996 • $25 • (5/31/1998) • **77**

Savigny-lès-Beaune White 1997: Very nice. Buttery and earthy, wth beautiful ripe pear and tropical flavors, this smooth white lacks just a bit of fresh acidity on the finish. Try as an aperitif. Drink now.–P.M. • $31 • (5/31/1999) • **85**

Key: SS—Spectator Selection. CS—Cellar Selection. HR—Highly Recommended. $NA—Price not available. (BT)—Barrel tasting. Ⓐ—Auction Price.
For a key to the tasters' initials, see "How to Use These Listings."
Dates in parentheses represent the issues in which the ratings were published.

CHARVIN, GERARD

Châteauneuf-du-Pape 1997: Fruity, with a mellow mouthfeel that tastes of licorice, plum and black fruit, but lacking in depth and real rich ripeness. Medium-bodied, it's fun to drink now, as the tannins are approachable. Try through 2003.–P.M. • $25 • (12/15/1999) • **85**

Châteauneuf-du-Pape 1996: Exotic and appealing. Elegant and refined, yet ripe and flavorful, this balanced Châteauneuf delivers good acidity along with the roasted game, dry prune, black cherry, wild mushroom and dark chocolate flavors. Ripe and sweet-tasting, with silky tannins. Drink now through 2005.–P.M. • $28 • (11/15/1998) • **90**

Côtes du Rhône 1997: Tart and a bit herbal, with a crisp, diluted character. Green finish.–P.M. • $13 • (11/15/1999) • **72**

Côtes du Rhône 1996: Has personality, with currant, toasted oak and crushed black pepper character. Medium-bodied, quite chewy on the finish, which is a challenge to appreciate now.–P.M. • $12 • (11/15/1998) • **80**

CHASSE, MARQUIS DE

Bordeaux 1990 • $7 • (3/15/1993) • **82**
Bordeaux Reserve 1994 • $8 • (4/30/1997) • **76**
Bordeaux Reserve 1993 • $8 • (12/15/1995) • **83**
Merlot-Cabernet Sauvignon Bordeaux Reserve 1995 • $8 • (1/31/1998) • **79**
Sauvignon Blanc-Sémillon Bordeaux Reserve 1996 • $7 • (2/28/1998) • **79**

CHASSE-SPLEEN, CHATEAU

Bordeaux White 1998: Very odd. Slightly candied, with pear drop and honey character. Tasted twice, with consistent notes.–J.S. • $NA • (2/29/2000) • **78**

Moulis 1999: Medium-bodied, with pleasant berry and plum character and medium tannins, but slightly hollow midpalate.–J.S. • $NA • (1/01/2000) (BT) • **80-84**

Moulis 1998: A pretty, balanced wine with blackberry, mineral and toasted oak character. Medium- to full-bodied, with well-integrated tannins and a chocolate aftertaste. Almost outstanding.–J.S. • $NA • (5/31/1999) (BT) • **85-89**

Moulis 1997: Elegant and fruity, with currant, berry and violet character. Medium-bodied, with light tannins and a fresh finish. Drink now.–J.S. • $21 • (1/31/2000) • **84**

Moulis 1996: Chasse-Spleen did seriously well here. This impressive '96 is darkly colored, with mineral, berry and licorice aromas, a medium body, racy tannins and an interesting licorice, boysenberry and cherry aftertaste. Best after 2000.–J.S. • $56 Ⓐ • (1/31/1999) HR • **90**

Moulis 1995 • $26 Ⓐ • (1/31/1998) • **90**
Moulis 1994 • $18 Ⓐ • (1/31/1997) • **85**
Moulis 1993 • $17 Ⓐ • (1/31/1996) • **88**
Moulis 1992 • $21 • (4/15/1995) • **80**
Moulis 1991 • $21 • (3/31/1994) • **84**
Moulis 1990 • $44 Ⓐ • (3/31/1993) • **90**

Moulis 1989: Big and chewy Chasse-Spleen. Impressive. Dark ruby-colored, with cocoa, coffee and chocolate aromas covered by ripe fruit. Full-bodied and very rich, showing lots of chewy tannins and a long, roasted coffee and berry aftertaste.—1989 Bordeaux horizontal. Best after 2004.–J.S. • $48 Ⓐ • (5/31/1999) • **91**

Moulis 1988: An '88 *cru bourgeois* on the decline. Pretty leaf, berry and earth aromas and flavors, but the palate is slightly dry, with austere tannins and medium fruit concentration.—1988 Bordeaux horizontal. Drink now.–J.S. • $33 Ⓐ • (11/30/1998) • **82**

Moulis 1987 • $15 • (11/30/1989) • **82**
Moulis 1986 • $38 Ⓐ • (11/30/1989) • **90**
Moulis 1985 • $48 Ⓐ • (5/15/1988) • **86**
Moulis 1984 • $15 • (6/15/1987) • **74**
Moulis 1983 • $37 Ⓐ • (10/15/1994) • **90**

Moulis 1982: Holding on. Bright ruby color, with a brick-red edge. Chocolate and berry aromas, with hints of tobacco. Medium-bodied, with ripe fruit and tobacco character, but rather dry on the finish. (1982 Bordeaux horizontal tasting). Drink now.–J.S. • $47 Ⓐ • (11/30/1998) • **86**

Moulis 1981 • $32 Ⓐ • (10/15/1994) • **88**
Moulis 1970 • $61 • (5/15/1993) • **84**
Moulis 1961 • $52 • (4/30/1996) • **82**

CHASTAN, CLAUDE

Châteauneuf-du-Pape Domaine de St.-Siffrein 1993 • $16 • (2/28/1997) • **85**

CHATELAIN, JEAN-CLAUDE

Pouilly-Fumé 1996 • $17 • (5/31/1998) • **89**
Pouilly-Fumé Domaine de St.-Laurent-l'Abbaye 1996 • $17 • (5/31/1998) • **89**
Pouilly-Fumé Pilou 1996 • $50/500 ml. • (5/31/1998) • **92**

CHATONET

Chardonnay Vin de Pays d'Oc 1997: A medium-bodied Chardonnay, with decent concentration and good baked-apple and spice flavors. Drink now.–K.M. • $8 • (11/15/1998) • **83**
Merlot Vin de Pays d'Oc 1997: A straightforward red marked by fresh cherry and herb flavors. Just tannic enough, but still fine for everyday drinking. Drink now.–P.M. • $7 • (11/15/1998) • **83**

CHAUSSE, CHATEAU DE

Côtes de Provence 1996: Thin, peppery and herbal, with stewy notes on the finish.–K.M. • $7 • (10/15/1999) • **76**
Côtes de Provence Rosé 1998: This pale pink wine is pretty and refreshing, but very light in body and flavor, with hints of berry and herb and a short, crisp finish. Drink now.–T.M. • $7 • (10/15/1999) • **82**
Côtes de Provence White 1998: Dull and coarse, with an earthy aroma and woody flavors.–K.M. • $7 • (10/15/1999) • **73**

CHAUVENET, F.

Auxey-Duresses Le Val 1989 • $NA • (1/31/1992) • **79**
Beaune 1993 • $24 • (11/15/1995) • **70**
Beaune Hospices de Beaune Rosseau-Deslandes 1980 • $36 • (6/16/1986) • **91**
Beaune Le Clos des Mouches 1986 • $27 • (12/31/1988) • **82**
Beaune Les Grèves 1993 • $29 • (11/15/1995) • **80**
Beaune Les Grèves 1990 • $35 • (12/15/1992) • **89**
Beaune Les Grèves 1989 • $30 • (1/31/1992) • **91**
Beaune Les Grèves 1986 • $25 • (12/31/1988) • **79**
Beaune Les Teurons 1985 • $23 • (7/31/1987) • **88**
Bourgogne 1990 • $NA • (12/15/1992) • **80**
Bourgogne Château Marguerite de Bourgogne 1993 • $14 • (11/15/1995) • **80**
Bourgogne Château Marguerite de Bourgogne 1985 • $10 • (6/30/1988) • **80**
Cabernet Sauvignon Vin de Pays d'Oc 1994 • $9 • (10/31/1995) • **84**
Chambolle-Musigny 1993 • $37 • (11/15/1995) • **78**
Chambolle-Musigny 1990 • $45 • (12/15/1992) • **85**
Chambolle-Musigny Les Charmes 1982 • $33 • (4/30/1987) • **83**
Charmes-Chambertin 1993 • $78 • (11/15/1995) • **86**
Charmes-Chambertin 1986 • $65 • (7/31/1988) • **90**
Charmes-Chambertin 1985 • $72 • (7/31/1987) • **97**
Charmes-Chambertin 1983 • $24 • (9/15/1986) • **88**
Clos de la Roche 1990 • $76 • (12/15/1992) • **87**
Clos de Vougeot 1990 • $69 • (12/15/1992) • **92**
Clos de Vougeot 1989 • $60 • (1/31/1992) • **90**
Clos de Vougeot 1986 • $57 • (12/31/1988) • **79**
Clos St.-Denis 1990 • $65 • (12/15/1992) • **95**
Clos St.-Denis 1989 • $60 • (1/31/1992) • **87**
Clos St.-Denis 1986 • $50 • (2/28/1989) • **90**
Clos St.-Denis 1985 • $67 • (7/31/1987) • **94**
Corton 1993 • $54 • (11/15/1995) • **78**
Corton 1990 • $60 • (12/15/1992) • **94**
Corton 1989 • $50 • (1/31/1992) • **93**
Corton 1986 • $50 • (7/31/1988) • **87**
Corton 1985 • $53 • (7/31/1987) • **96**
Corton Hospices de Beaune Docteur-Peste 1985 • $133 • (7/15/1988) • **97**
Côte de Beaune-Villages 1985 • $16 • (7/31/1987) • **84**
Echézeaux 1990 • $62 • (12/15/1992) • **91**
Echézeaux 1989 • $56 • (1/31/1992) • **92**
Echézeaux 1985 • $79 Ⓐ • (7/31/1987) • **89**
Gevrey-Chambertin Charreux 1985 • $33 • (10/15/1987) • **88**
Gevrey-Chambertin Estournelles St.-Jacques 1990 • $56 • (12/15/1992) • **89**
Gevrey-Chambertin Estournelles St.-Jacques 1989 • $40 • (1/31/1992) • **91**
Gevrey-Chambertin Estournelles St.-Jacques 1986 • $35 • (7/31/1988) • **89**
Gevrey-Chambertin Lavaut St.-Jacques 1991 • $NA • (1/31/1994) • **79**
Gevrey-Chambertin Lavaut St.-Jacques 1990 • $56 • (12/15/1992) • **90**
Gevrey-Chambertin Lavaut St.-Jacques 1989 • $45 • (1/31/1992) • **88**
Gevrey-Chambertin Lavaut St.-Jacques 1986 • $35 • (7/31/1988) • **86**
Gevrey-Chambertin Le Clos St.-Jacques 1989 • $45 • (1/31/1992) • **89**
Gevrey-Chambertin Le Clos St.-Jacques 1986 • $35 • (7/31/1988) • **85**
Mazis-Chambertin 1983 • $27 • (6/30/1987) • **72**
Merlot Vin de Pays d'Oc 1994 • $9 • (10/31/1995) • **78**
Monthélie 1990 • $21 • (12/15/1992) • **84**
Monthélie Les Champs Fulliot 1990 • $NA • (12/15/1992) • **87**
Monthélie Les Champs Fulliot 1989 • $20 • (1/31/1992) • **81**
Nuits-St.-Georges 1994 • $30 • (11/15/1996) • **83**
Nuits-St.-Georges 1993 • $40 • (11/15/1995) • **78**
Nuits-St.-Georges 1991 • $NA • (1/31/1994) • **81**
Nuits-St.-Georges Aux Chaignots 1990 • $53 • (12/15/1992) • **83**
Nuits-St.-Georges Aux Chaignots 1989 • $45 • (1/31/1992) • **91**
Nuits-St.-Georges Aux Chaignots 1986 • $40 • (7/31/1988) • **87**
Nuits-St.-Georges Les Perrières 1985 • $48 • (7/31/1987) • **80**
Nuits-St.-Georges Les Plâteaux 1985 • $34 • (7/31/1987) • **84**
Nuits-St.-Georges Les Plâteaux 1982 • $16 • (1/01/1985) • **78**
Nuits-St.-Georges Les Pruliers 1990 • $52 • (12/15/1992) • **90**
Nuits-St.-Georges Les Pruliers 1989 • $45 • (1/31/1992) • **88**
Pommard 1990 • $45 • (12/15/1992) • **86**
Pommard Hospices de Beaune Cuvée Dames-de-la-Cha 1982 • $36 • (2/01/1985) CS • **91**
Pommard Les Chanlins 1990 • $59 • (12/15/1992) • **87**
Pommard Les Chanlins 1989 • $45 • (1/31/1992) • **86**
Pommard Les Chanlins 1986 • $40 • (7/31/1988) • **90**
Pommard Les Epenots 1989 • $45 • (1/31/1992) • **94**
Pommard Les Epenots 1985 • $48 • (7/31/1987) • **95**
Puligny-Montrachet Red 1985 • $16 • (6/15/1987) • **81**
Santenay 1985 • $18 • (7/31/1987) • **84**
Syrah Vin de Pays d'Oc 1994 • $9 • (10/31/1995) • **74**
Volnay Clos de Chênes 1990 • $58 • (12/15/1992) • **86**
Volnay Clos de Chênes 1989 • $40 • (1/31/1992) • **90**
Volnay Premier Cru 1989 • $36 • (1/31/1992) • **88**
Vosne-Romanée Les Suchots 1985 • $34 Ⓐ • (7/31/1987) • **92**

CHAUVENET, JEAN

Nuits-St.-Georges Aux Bousselots 1994 • $44 • (11/15/1996) • **87**
Nuits-St.-Georges Aux Bousselots 1985 • $49 • (5/31/1988) • **88**
Nuits-St.-Georges Les Vaucrains 1994 • $44 • (11/15/1996) • **87**

CHAUVENET-CHOPIN

Chambolle-Musigny 1994 • $40 • (11/15/1996) • **83**
Côte de Nuits-Villages 1994 • $25 • (11/15/1996) • **77**
Nuits-St.-Georges 1996: Subdued and slightly simple, with modest strawberry and cherry flavors. While rather round and smooth in the midpalate, it turns somewhat herbal on the firm finish.–P.M. • $48 • (9/30/1998) • **80**
Nuits-St.-Georges Aux Argillas 1996: Yummy Nuits, with delicious licorice, plum and blackberry flavors along with a distinctive petrol note. Sweet, ripe and full-bodied, it kicks in with a delicately toasted oak accent on the finish. Lovely from start to finish. Drink now through 2005.–P.M. • $55 • (9/30/1998) • **88**
Nuits-St.-Georges Aux Argillas 1995 • $54 • (11/15/1997) • **84**
Nuits-St.-Georges Aux Argillas 1994 • $48 • (11/15/1996) • **81**
Nuits-St.-Georges Les Murgers 1996: Fairly oaky, with vanilla, mocha, herbal character, some red- and blackberry flavors. Medium-bodied, with good acidity, it's firm and very juicy. Succulent finish. Drink now.–P.M. • $55 • (9/30/1998) • **84**
Nuits-St.-Georges Les Murgers 1995 • $54 • (11/15/1997) • **89**
Nuits-St.-Georges Les Murgers 1994 • $48 • (11/15/1996) • **84**
Nuits-St.-Georges Vieilles Vignes 1994 • $40 • (11/15/1996) • **82**

CHAVE, BERNARD

Crozes-Hermitage 1997: Odd and herbaceous, but not bad in concentration. Shows bell pepper and black fruit character, with lovely ripeness underneath and sweet-fruit richness. Tasted twice, with consistent notes.–P.M. • $17 • (10/31/1999) • **73**
Crozes-Hermitage 1996: Earthy in style, with a leathery aroma, floral and red berry notes, this medium-bodied Crozes has enough ripe character and supple tannins to make it attractive and distinctive. Best from 2003.–P.M. • $17 • (11/15/1998) • **85**
Crozes-Hermitage 1994 • $18 • (10/15/1997) • **84**
Crozes-Hermitage 1991 • $45 • (6/15/1993) • **85**
Crozes-Hermitage 1988 • $14 • (2/15/1991) • **78**
Crozes-Hermitage 1985 • $12 • (11/30/1988) • **86**

CHAVE, BERNARD

Crozes-Hermitage Tête de Cuvée 1997: A ripe mouthfeel, with supple, full-bodied texture, but the aromas veer distinctively toward herb, matchstick, mint and bell pepper, and the finish turns tart.–P.M. • $20 • (10/31/1999) • **77**

Crozes-Hermitage White 1998: Simple and straightforward, with modest fruit, showing cardboard and almond character.–P.M. • $18 • (12/15/1999) • **75**

Crozes-Hermitage White 1997: Odd and unclean, with wet cardboard and tart pineapple flavors. Tasted twice, with consistent notes.–P.M. • $17 • (8/31/1999) • **60**

Crozes-Hermitage White Domaine de la Burge 1996: Distinctively earthy, but despite some odd aromas, it has a delicious mouthfeel and delivers rich flavors, fresh acidity, lots of honey and ripe pear notes. Its great finish makes up for the negatives. Tasted twice, with consistent notes.–P.M. • $18 • (11/15/1998) • **84**

Hermitage 1997: Very earthy, even swampy, with herbal and stewed artichoke notes leading to a tart finish. Tasted twice, with consistent notes.–P.M. • $39 • (9/15/1999) • **60**

Hermitage 1996: Earthy aromas introduce a wine of sweet fruit, supple texture and ripe tannins, its fabulous blackberry, grilled meat, smoked ham and currant flavors fanning out to a long and balanced finish. Should be a match made in heaven with barbecued lamb chops. Drink now through 2005.–P.M. • $39 • (11/15/1998) • **94**

Hermitage 1994 • $44 • (9/15/1997) • **85**

Hermitage 1990 • $45 • (4/15/1993) • **87**

Hermitage 1989 • $40 • (12/31/1991) • **91**

Hermitage 1986 • $32 • (11/30/1988) • **86**

CHAVE, JEAN-LOUIS

Ermitage Cathelin 1995: A unique wine that floats like a cloud on the palate but tastes of a garden in full bloom, of freshly plowed earth, of a stable of horses and worn leather saddles. Extraordinary marriage between fresh acidity and full-bodied, voluptuous texture, this is the sort of wine you'll never tire of drinking and one that should age for more than a decade. Silky finish with grilled meat, animal-like accents. Have I said enough? It's just brilliant. Drink now through 2015.–P.M. • $455 Ⓐ • (9/15/1998) • **98**

Hermitage 1996: Complex while firm and crisp in style, this Rhône red is a well-rounded package, cascading with pretty game, smoke and toasted notes, showing supple tannins and a succulent, clean and intense finish. Drink now through 2003.–P.M. • $57 Ⓐ • (9/15/1999) CS • **93**

Hermitage 1995: Deep and complex, with currant, Provençal herbs, green olive and mineral-laden character, this full-bodied red from France's Northern Rhône region is smooth, ripe and round until the very finish, which is now quite chewy and tannic. Should blossom with cellaring. Best from 2003 through 2007.–P.M. • $97 Ⓐ • (9/15/1998) HR • **90**

Hermitage 1994 • $60 Ⓐ • (4/30/1997) CS • **94**

Hermitage 1992 • $50 • (10/15/1995) • **88**

Hermitage 1991 • $86 Ⓐ • (5/31/1994) • **85**

Hermitage 1990 • $198 Ⓐ • (5/31/1994) CS • **96**

Hermitage 1987 • $51 Ⓐ • (6/30/1990) • **89**

Hermitage 1984 • $29 • (8/31/1987) • **89**

Hermitage 1980 • $40 • (5/01/1986) • **83**

Hermitage White 1996: An ultrathick, oily white, showing great intensity of fruit, staying clean, balanced, even racy despite the illusion of off-dryness; seduces with honey, kiwi, lime and almond character. Drink now through 2002.–P.M. • $90 • (8/31/1999) • **90**

St.-Joseph 1996: Gamy, peppery aromas give way to fresh, ripe flavors of blackberry and plum, with notes of violet and vanilla. Moderate tannins and crisp acidity give good definition and freshness. Drink now through 2003.–T.M. • $25 • (11/15/1998) • **88**

St.-Joseph 1994 • $25 • (11/30/1996) • **89**

St.-Joseph 1992 • $NA • (5/31/1994) • **76**

St.-Joseph Offerus 1996: This mouthfilling red is packed with pure flavors of raspberry and blackberry, nicely framed by ripe tannins. Stylish and even elegant, though not overly muscular, with appealing vividness and purity. Drink now through 2002.–T.M. • $25 • (11/15/1998) • **88**

St.-Joseph Offerus 1995: Firm and tight, this ripe red shows good concentration, with well-defined flavors of plum, chocolate and mint. Clean and vivid, it should develop more flavor complexity with age. Drink through 2004.–T.M. • $22 • (11/15/1998) • **89**

Key: SS—Spectator Selection. CS—Cellar Selection. HR—Highly Recommended. $NA—Price not available. (BT)—Barrel tasting. Ⓐ—Auction Price.
For a key to the tasters' initials, see "How to Use These Listings."
Dates in parentheses represent the issues in which the ratings were published.

CHAVY, GERARD

Puligny-Montrachet 1997: Clean, medium-bodied and medium-intense, with green apple, lemon and pear flavors and a chewy, chalky texture on the finish. Best from 2002 through 2007.–P.M. • $42 • (5/31/1999) • **84**

Puligny-Montrachet 1996: A real winner for a village wine. Lush, thick, fat and full-bodied, it stays fresh and elegant thanks to excellent ctirus-spiked acidity, and offers complexity with its notes of wet earth and stone dust. Fantastic ripe flavors of pear, melon, pineapple, and supple, creamlike texture that coats the palate and is marvelously seductive. Oak is subtle on the velvety finish.–P.M. • $45 • (8/31/1998) • **90**

Puligny-Montrachet 1995 • $29 • (5/31/1997) HR • **93**

Puligny-Montrachet Les Clavoillons 1997: Wonderful, fresh, clean citrus intensity storms the palate, delivering masses of pure fruit, honey and fresh herbs. Lovely spice and toast notes add complexity on the lingering, balanced finish. Drink now through 2005.–P.M. • $49 • (5/31/1999) • **90**

Puligny-Montrachet Les Clavoillons 1995 • $35 • (5/31/1997) • **93**

Puligny-Montrachet Les Folatières 1998: Rich and ripe, if a bit rustic. Has a chewy side, with a citrus edge. Good fruit, just not very velvety. Drink now through 2003.–P.M. • $48 • (5/31/2000) • **83**

Puligny-Montrachet Les Folatières 1997: This well-made '97 is a bit earthy and herbal, but packed with lively, vibrant and ripe tropical, lime and honey flavors. There's excellent, exciting acidity in this medium-bodied, pure and clean white Burgundy. Drink now through 2005.–P.M. • $49 • (5/31/1999) • **91**

Puligny-Montrachet Les Folatières 1996 • $40 • (5/31/1998) • **88**

Puligny-Montrachet Les Folatières 1995 • $35 • (5/31/1997) • **91**

Puligny-Montrachet Les Perrières 1998: Amazing. A beautifully ripe, rich and thick white Burgundy, silky and concentrated. It's hard to imagine getting closer to the earth than this; tastes of peach and dried apricot, with wet earth on the finish. Best from 2003 through 2015.–P.M. • $48 • (5/31/2000) • **92**

Puligny-Montrachet Les Perrières 1997: Earthy, herbal and medium-bodied, showing tart fruit and an astringent finish.–P.M. • $49 • (5/31/1999) • **72**

Puligny-Montrachet Les Perrières 1996 • $40 • (5/31/1998) • **92**

Puligny-Montrachet Les Perrières 1995 • $35 • (5/31/1997) • **93**

CHAVY, PHILIPPE

Bourgogne White 1998: Surprisingly rich for a '98 regional Bourgogne. Tropical-scented, with pineapple flavors, you get plenty of wine for your buck here. Tastes of ripe fruit combined with vibrant citrusy character, all wrapped in a blanket of vanilla- and butter-tasting oak. Drink now through 2003.–P.M. • $20 • (5/31/2000) • **87**

Meursault-Blagny Sous le Dos d'Ane 1998: A tart, medium-bodied Meursault showing mineral, green apple and dried herb character, but it's tough and a bit lean on the finish. Best from 2002 through 2005.–P.M. • $51 • (5/31/2000) • **83**

Meursault-Blagny Sous le Dos d'Ane 1997: A bit green, with cold fruit and herb and green apple skin flavors. Medium-bodied, with a light finish.–P.M. • $49 • (5/31/1999) • **76**

Puligny-Montrachet Les Corvées des Vignes 1998: A tough white Burgundy with an oaky edge plus some grassy, herbal notes. Redeems itself with a thick texture, but still rather crisp and lean on the finish. Drink now through 2003.–P.M. • $41 • (5/31/2000) • **81**

Puligny-Montrachet Les Corvées des Vignes 1997: Ultrarich and full-bodied, it's still a refined, polished biggie of a Chardonnay, with palate-coating, sexy pear, apricot, lemon, cream and honey flavors. The powerful finish has slightly too much toastiness. Best from 2004 through 2017.–P.M. • $40 • (5/31/1999) • **93**

Puligny-Montrachet Les Corvées des Vignes 1996: Supple but straightforward Chardonnay, showing some nice vanilla, mineral, ripe apple and pear character. Lacks a bit of *terroir* character. Medium-bodied. Drink now through 2002.–P.M. • $37 • (8/31/1998) • **85**

Puligny-Montrachet Les Corvée des Vignes 1995 • $35 • (5/31/1997) • **78**

Puligny-Montrachet Les Folatières 1998: Powerful, but more so on the finish than at midpalate. Shows a full body, ripe flavors, nice toasted hazelnut, some fine wet stone and honey notes. Drink now through 2010.–P.M. • $57 • (5/31/2000) • **91**

Puligny-Montrachet Les Folatières 1997: Gold-colored, very ripe and full-bodied, but a bit soft. Clean, it massages the palate with seductive caresses, showing fresh fig, tropical and honey character. Turns slightly drying on the finish. Drink now through 2003.–P.M. • $56 • (5/31/1999) • **80**

CHAVY-CHOUET, CLAUDE & HUBERT

Meursault Les Casse-Têtes Vieille Vigne 1997: Modest fruit in this medium-bodied white that offers green apple, butter and spice. Crisp finish. Drink now through 2002.–P.M. • $45 • (5/31/1999) • **80**

Meursault Les Casse-Têtes Vieille Vigne 1996 • $45 • (5/31/1998) • **84**

Puligny-Montrachet Hameau de Blagny Vieille Vigne 1997: Clean and fresh, showing a balance of good acidity, delicious fruit and deft use of oak. A very agreeable, supple and fruity Chardonnay. Drink now.–P.M. • $60 • (5/31/1999) • **88**

Puligny-Montrachet Hameau de Blagny Vieille Vigne 1996 • $60 • (5/31/1998) • **90**

Puligny-Montrachet Les Chalumaux 1997: Supple, with pear, banana and a slight cooked apple, oxidized character, it turns heavy and flabby on the astringent, hot, spiritlike finish.–P.M. • $60 • (5/31/1999) • **77**

Puligny-Montrachet Les Enseignères 1996 • $45 • (5/31/1998) • **92**

Puligny-Montrachet Les Enseignères Vieille Vigne 1997: Impressively firm and fresh as well as opulent, here's a delicious, well-made '97 that delivers delicious intensity and length, with lemon, vanilla and cream on the finish. Drink now through 2002.–P.M. • $45 • (5/31/1999) • **90**

CHAZELLES, DOMAINE DES

Mâcon-Viré 1997: Something's wrong here. Tastes like cider, with a bitter, cooked green apple character. Not recommended. Tasted twice, with consistent notes.–P.M. • $14 • (5/31/1999) • **68**

Mâcon-Viré 1996 • $15 • (5/31/1998) • **84**

CHENADE, CHATEAU LA

Lalande-de-Pomerol 1996: Plenty of chocolate, berry and dried-herb character in this wine. Medium-bodied with velvety tannins and a chocolate, berry aftertaste. Well done. A blend from the owner of Château L'Eglise Clinet. Drink now.–J.S. • $NA • (1/31/1999) • **85**

Lalande-de-Pomerol 1995: A bit short, with medium-bodied berry and earth character and medium, dry tannins. Needs more fresh fruit. Drink now.–J.S. • $NA • (9/15/1998) • **83**

CHENE, DOMAINE DU

Condrieu 1997: Big, thick, rich, ripe—an ultra-oily wine. Has some flavor character, with floral, tropical and smoky notes. Balanced, but medium-long on the finish. Drink now through 2001.–P.M. • $30 • (8/31/1999) • **88**

St.-Joseph 1997: Uncomplicated, but stressing crisp black pepper aromas. Fresh, zesty and medium-bodied, with spice, mocha, coffee, game and blackberry notes that mingle on the flavorful finish. Tasted twice, with consistent notes. Drink now through 2001.–P.M. • $18 • (10/31/1999) • **85**

St.-Joseph 1996: Well made. Clean, succulent, vibrant and medium-bodied, it tastes crisp from grapey red berry notes, but it feels round thanks to smooth texture and supple tannins. Lovely black pepper flavors. Drink now through 2002.–P.M. • $18 • (10/31/1999) • **86**

St.-Joseph 1992 • $20 • (5/31/1994) • **72**

St.-Joseph Anaïs 1996: Delicious. Very dark in color, medium-bodied, with a supple, almost silky midpalate despite the juicy acidity. Lovely game, leather, black pepper, mocha and toast character. Best after 2000.–P.M. • $21 • (10/31/1999) • **88**

St.-Joseph Anaïs 1992 • $20 • (5/31/1994) • **79**

St.-Joseph Anaïs 1991 • $20 • (5/31/1994) • **82**

St.-Joseph Anaïs 1989 • $20 • (5/31/1994) • **82**

St.-Joseph White 1997: Clean and succulently ripe, here's an impressive, off-dry St.-Joseph with good freshness and delicious pineapple, pear, peach and honey character. Medium-bodied. A delight to drink for its balance, but expect a slightly rustic finish. Drink now.–P.M. • $18 • (8/31/1999) • **85**

St.-Joseph White 1996: A bit appley and slightly oxidized, offering some floral, tart character.–P.M. • $18 • (8/31/1999) • **75**

CHEREAU-CARRE

Chardonnay Vin de Pays du Jardin de la France 1997: Accents of butter and vanilla add to the apple and peach notes in this attractive, soft-textured white. Tails off a little on the finish. Drink now.–B.S. • $10 • (11/15/1998) • **83**

Muscadet de Sèvre et Maine Les Vergers 1996 • $9 • (2/28/1998) • **84**

Muscadet de Sèvre et Maine Sur Lie Château de Chasseloir Cuvée des Ceps Centenaires 1996 • $14 • (5/31/1998) • **83**

Muscadet de Sèvre et Maine Sur Lie Château de la Gravelle 1997: Light, with good apple and mineral notes, a smooth texture and a lemony bite on the lingering finish. Drink now.–B.S. • $10 • (11/15/1998) • **82**

Muscadet de Sèvre et Maine Sur Lie Château de la Gravelle 1996 • $11 • (2/28/1998) • **85**

Muscadet de Sèvre et Maine Sur Lie Château du Coing de St.-Fiacre 1997: Earth and mineral scents give way to apple and lemon flavors in this lean and lively white. Balanced, with the mineral note returning on the finish. Drink now.–B.S. • $11 • (11/15/1998) • **84**

Muscadet de Sèvre et Maine Sur Lie Château du Coing de St.-Fiacre 1996 • $11 • (2/28/1998) • **84**

Muscadet de Sèvre et Maine Sur Lie Château du Coing de St.-Fiacre Comte de St.-Hubert 1996 • $14 • (5/31/1998) • **87**

Muscadet de Sèvre et Maine Sur Lie Château l'Oiselinière de la Ramée 1996 • $11 • (5/31/1998) • **84**

Muscadet de Sèvre et Maine Sur Lie Grand Fief de la Cormeraie 1996 • $13 • (5/31/1998) • **85**

Muscadet de Sèvre et Maine Sur Lie Les Greniers du Moulin 1996 • $10 • (5/31/1998) • **84**

Muscadet de Sèvre et Maine Sur Lie Réserve Numérotée 1996 • $12 • (5/31/1998) • **84**

Muscadet Primeur Château du Coing de St.-Fiacre 1996 • $11 • (6/15/1997) • **83**

Saumur-Champigny Domaine des Elettes 1996 • $16 • (5/31/1998) • **87**

Sauvignon Blanc Touraine Fief de la Houssière 1996 • $10 • (5/31/1998) • **78**

CHEREAU-GUNTHER, V.

Muscadet de Sèvre et Maine Les Vergers 1998: Clean and focused. Crisp aromas of lime, mineral and almond follow through on the palate in this lively, well-balanced white. It's a bit tart, but that just makes it a better match for oysters. Drink now.–T.M. • $7 • (6/15/1999) • **85**

Muscadet de Sèvre et Maine Les Vergers 1997: This clean, round white shows good body and crisp acidity, but the flavors are fairly neutral. A modest accompaniment to lighter dishes. Drink now.–T.M. • $7 • (6/15/1999) • **82**

Muscadet de Sèvre et Maine Sur Lie Château du Coing de St.-Fiacre Comte de St.-Hubert 1997: This big-boned, mineral-scented white makes an austere first impression, but rounder, riper flavors of pear and apple emerge on the palate and linger through the finish. Clean, firm and balanced. Drink now.–T.M. • $14 • (6/15/1999) • **87**

Muscadet de Sèvre et Maine Sur Lie Le Commandeur 1997: Ripe apple and light herb flavors have a slight earthy edge in this firm white. An old-fashioned style with traditional appeal. Drink now.–T.M. • $9 • (6/15/1999) • **80**

Muscadet de Sèvre et Maine Sur Lie Les Greniers du Moulin 1997: Almond, apple and a light soapy note combine in this round white. The acidity is crisp, but the flavors lack focus and vibrancy.–T.M. • $8 • (6/15/1999) • **77**

CHEREAU PERE & FILS, B.

Anjou Château de Pimpéan 1995 • $9 • (6/15/1997) • **80**

Saumur-Champigny Domaine des Elettes 1997: Polished and supple. Red berry and light licorice and herbal notes run through this focused red, with light but firm tannins and a clean, fruity finish. Drink now.–T.M. • $13 • (5/31/1999) • **84**

St.-Nicolas de Bourgueil Domaine de la Rodaie 1996 • $16 • (6/15/1998) • **84**

St.-Nicolas de Bourgueil Domaine de la Rodaie 1995 • $17 • (6/15/1997) • **83**

Vin de Pays du Jardin de la France Le Florès NV • $7 • (6/15/1997) • **83**

CHERRIER & FILS, PIERRE

Sancerre Domaine de la Rossignole Cuvée Vieilles Vignes 1996 • $15 • (3/31/1998) • **87**

CHERVIN, DOMAINE DE

Mâcon-Burgy 1998: Lacks a bit of depth, but it's ripe in style with a slight late-harvest (*sur-maturité*) character of tropical dried fruit and caramel. Nice aperitif wine that's medium-bodied, with a round mouthfeel. Drink now through 2002.–P.M. • $14 • (5/31/2000) • **86**

CHEVAL-BLANC, CHATEAU

St.-Emilion 1999: Splendidly subtle with plum, chocolate and berry character throughout. Full-bodied, with round and caressing tannins and a long finish. A beauty.–J.S. • $NA • (1/01/2000) (BT) • **90-94**

CHEVAL-BLANC, CHATEAU

St.-Emilion 1998: Exhibits amazing ripeness and power, yet great finesse at the same time. Full-bodied, with massive silky tannins and a long, long, fruity finish. Really superb—the greatest young Cheval-Blanc I have ever tasted.–J.S. • $NA • (5/31/1999) (BT) • **95-99**

St.-Emilion 1997: Lovely aromas of ripe fruit, coffee and toasted oak. Medium- to full-bodied, with a good backbone of tannin and a medium finish. A bit austere. Too much wood? Give this a little time. Best after 2000.–J.S. • $158 • (1/31/2000) • **87**

St.-Emilion 1996: A very fine '96, but what else would you expect from Cheval-Blanc? Medium- to full-bodied, with a good deep-ruby color, this has aromas of freshly crushed blackberry, fine tannins and a silky, fresh aftertaste. Best after 2001.–J.S. • $156 Ⓐ • (6/30/1999) • **90**

St.-Emilion 1995 • $167 Ⓐ • (1/31/1998) • **94**

St.-Emilion 1994 • $80 Ⓐ • (1/31/1997) • **91**

St.-Emilion 1993 • $80 Ⓐ • (1/31/1996) CS • **90**

St.-Emilion 1992 • $65 • (4/15/1995) • **80**

St.-Emilion 1990: This shows a richer, rounder profile than most Cheval vintages, with very ripe plum, chocolate and cedar flavors and a plush texture. Accessible now, but better after 2002. (Cheval-Blanc vertical tasting, as are all notes below.).–T.M. • $387 Ⓐ • (3/31/1999) • **94**

St.-Emilion 1989: This has never been a great Cheval-Blanc but it has always been a beautiful glass of wine. Aromas of tobacco, earth and ripe fruit. It's clean and very ripe, with berry, tobacco and chocolate flavors. Medium- to full-bodied, velvety, long finish. Needs a bit more concentration to score classic. (1989 Bordeaux horizontal tasting). Drink now through 2008.–J.S. • $160 Ⓐ • (5/31/1999) • **92**

St.-Emilion 1988: An outstanding Cheval-Blanc, often forgotten by fans of this château. Layers of ripe fruit show highlights of chocolate and earth. Full-bodied, with full, velvety tannins and a chunky texture. (1988 Bordeaux horizontal tasting). Best after 2001.–J.S. • $124 Ⓐ • (11/30/1998) • **92**

St.-Emilion 1987 • $72 Ⓐ • (2/15/1991) • **82**

St.-Emilion 1986 • $163 Ⓐ • (2/15/1991) • **93**

St.-Emilion 1985: Beginning to show maturity. Spice and cedar aromas give way to a silky texture and flavors of tobacco and roasted fruits. Drink or hold.–T.M. • $216 Ⓐ • (3/31/1999) • **92**

St.-Emilion 1984 • $69 • (2/15/1991) • **78**

St.-Emilion 1983: A giant of a wine. The complex aromas and thickly textured flavors range from plum and raisin to coffee, minerals and mint. Not so elegant as a typical Cheval; more in the mold of the powerful '47 and legendary '21. Drink or hold.–T.M. • $230 Ⓐ • (3/31/1999) • **96**

St.-Emilion 1982: Ripe and balanced. Dark garnet in color, with an amber rim. Medium- to full-bodied, with berry, tobacco and leather aromas, velvety tannins and plenty of tobacco, berry and cedar flavors. Wonderful, but not as great a wine as it's purported to be. The '83 is better. (1982 Bordeaux horizontal tasting). Best after 2001.–J.S. • $521 Ⓐ • (11/30/1998) • **93**

St.-Emilion 1981: Maturing now, but still vibrant, this offers berry, cedar and tobacco aromas and flavors, a bit lean but with good intensity. Drink now through 2009.–T.M. • $112 Ⓐ • (3/31/1999) • **90**

St.-Emilion 1980: Though fading now, this light, silky red still shows some fresh cherry flavor, along with raisin, cedar and brown sugar notes. Drink now.–T.M. • $70 Ⓐ • (3/31/1999) • **84**

St.-Emilion 1979: The group disagreed on this light, mature wine; I found it lean and dry, with light raisin and dusty notes. Drink up.–T.M. • $100 Ⓐ • (3/31/1999) • **77**

St.-Emilion 1978: Bold and tough. Aromas of roasted cocoa, earth and iron give way to tobacco and earthy flavors over firm tannins. It's fully mature, but still has character. Drink now through 2003.–T.M. • $135 Ⓐ • (3/31/1999) • **84**

St.-Emilion 1977: Light and dry, with some simple berry and floral notes. Drink up.–T.M. • $43 • (3/31/1999) • **74**

St.-Emilion 1976: Fleshy yet still tannic, this mature red offers ripe, sweet cherry and raisin flavors with coffee and tobacco accents. Drink now through 2002.–T.M. • $96 Ⓐ • (3/31/1999) • **82**

St.-Emilion 1975: Though many '75s never shed their tannins, this shows good balance, with thick-textured cherry, raisin and cedar flavors and a long, spicy finish. Drink now through 2004.–T.M. • $148 Ⓐ • (3/31/1999) • **88**

St.-Emilion 1974: This brown, barnyardy swill shows, by its contrast, just how miraculous it is that fine wine can improve over decades in the bottle.–T.M. • $NA • (3/31/1999) • **57**

St.-Emilion 1973 • $60 • (2/15/1991) • **83**

Key: SS—Spectator Selection. CS—Cellar Selection. HR—Highly Recommended. $NA—Price not available. (BT)—Barrel tasting. Ⓐ—Auction Price.
For a key to the tasters' initials, see "How to Use These Listings."
Dates in parentheses represent the issues in which the ratings were published.

St.-Emilion 1972 • $40 • (2/15/1991) • **82**

St.-Emilion 1971 • $109 Ⓐ • (2/15/1991) • **89**

St.-Emilion 1970: This vintage shows notable bottle variation at Cheval; we had a good one, fragrant with plum, floral and spice aromas, round and velvety on the palate, balanced and long. Drink now through 2006.–T.M. • $148 Ⓐ • (3/31/1999) • **91**

St.-Emilion 1969 • $62 Ⓐ • (2/15/1991) • **75**

St.-Emilion 1967: Light and silky, this mingles well-defined cedar, spice and earthy flavors that turn a bit dry on the finish. Drink now.–T.M. • $92 Ⓐ • (3/31/1999) • **84**

St.-Emilion 1966: Meaty and solid. Ripe flavors of raisin, cherry and cedar are integrated and chunky in this firm wine. Not elegant, but still lively. Drink now through 2004.–T.M. • $184 Ⓐ • (3/31/1999) • **87**

St.-Emilion 1964: At its best, Cheval challenges Château Latour for wine of the vintage in 1964. This bottle was delicious, fragrant and deep, with floral, spicy, berry and chocolate flavors, complex and long. Drink now.–T.M. • $434 Ⓐ • (3/31/1999) • **92**

St.-Emilion 1962 • $116 Ⓐ • (2/15/1991) • **85**

St.-Emilion 1961: We had two bottles of this vintage. One, recently recorked in California, was rich but clumsy, with an odd earthy/tart contrast; Serena Sutcliffe, who was leading the tasting, suspected adulteration. The other bottle was fantastic, a beautiful expression of this rich, ripe vintage, velvety with plum, prune and meaty flavors, balanced and long. It can hold for another decade.–T.M. • $528 Ⓐ • (3/31/1999) • **96**

St.-Emilion 1960 • $NA • (2/15/1991) • **81**

St.-Emilion 1959: This bottle was also recorked in California. It was elegant but light, with silky cedar and raisin flavors and a spicy finish. Drink now.–T.M. • $399 Ⓐ • (3/31/1999) • **87**

St.-Emilion 1958: Surprising success from an unheralded vintage. This thick, meaty wine is a bit dry but still has character, with raisin and coffee flavors. Drink now.–T.M. • $195 Ⓐ • (3/31/1999) • **83**

St.-Emilion 1955: Once outstanding, now fading, but still velvety and lively, it offers sweet raisin and spice flavors with a mineral-accented finish. Drink now.–T.M. • $290 Ⓐ • (3/31/1999) • **86**

St.-Emilion 1953: Elegant, balanced and long. This silky red still offers cherry and berry flavors, with cedar and spicy accents and just enough grip to keep it lively. Drink now through 2003.–T.M. • $358 Ⓐ • (3/31/1999) • **92**

St.-Emilion 1952: Arguably the wine of the vintage, and still outstanding. Silky in texture, yet with firm tannins, it offers cedar, tobacco and raisin flavors, mature and harmonious. Drink now.–T.M. • $161 Ⓐ • (3/31/1999) • **90**

St.-Emilion 1951 • $150 • (2/15/1991) • **76**

St.-Emilion 1950 • $280 • (2/15/1991) • **89**

St.-Emilion 1949: Fully mature and glorious. Lovely aromas of berries and spice lead to intense flavors of dried fruit, cedar and tobacco, balanced, vivid and long. Shows great elegance and class.–T.M. • $924 Ⓐ • (3/31/1999) • **97**

St.-Emilion 1948 • $527 Ⓐ • (2/15/1991) • **97**

St.-Emilion 1947 • $1,993 Ⓐ • (2/15/1991) • **85**

St.-Emilion 1946 • $470 • (2/15/1991) • **87**

St.-Emilion 1945: A high level of volatile acidity put some tasters off, but had the effect of lifting and intensifying the raspberry, raisin and spicy flavors. The tannins are soft and the finish long. Drink now.–T.M. • $712 Ⓐ • (3/31/1999) • **87**

St.-Emilion 1943 • $316 Ⓐ • (2/15/1991) • **85**

St.-Emilion 1941 • $175 • (2/15/1991) • **71**

St.-Emilion 1940 • $520 • (2/15/1991) • **83**

St.-Emilion 1938 • $150 • (2/15/1991) • **75**

St.-Emilion 1937: Most of the tasters did not find this bottle an accurate representation of this wine, which is generally considered one of the best of the vintage. It was fading here, with earthy and barnyard flavors and perhaps a hint of corkiness.–T.M. • $129 Ⓐ • (3/31/1999) • **71**

St.-Emilion 1936 • $280 • (2/15/1991) • **81**

St.-Emilion 1934: Reaching the end of its road. Berry, strawberry and floral notes are lively, lifted a bit by volatile acidity, silky and soft. Drink up.–T.M. • $252 Ⓐ • (3/31/1999) • **81**

St.-Emilion 1933 • $270 • (2/15/1991) • **88**

St.-Emilion 1931 • $230 • (2/15/1991) • **72**

St.-Emilion 1930 • $280 • (2/15/1991) • **82**

St.-Emilion 1929: Harmonious and balanced. This ethereal, complex wine shows lovely sweet, spicy and cedar aromas and flavors, with dried fruit and mushroom notes, still lively and long on the finish. Drink now.–T.M. • $959 Ⓐ • (3/31/1999) • **92**

St.-Emilion 1928 • $570 Ⓐ • (2/15/1991) • **92**

St.-Emilion 1926: Often good, but this bottle, recorked at the château, was dull, earthy, and very dry on the finish.–T.M. • $565 Ⓐ • (3/31/1999) • **70**

St.-Emilion 1924 • $431 Ⓐ • (2/15/1991) • **69**

St.-Emilion 1923 • $200 • (2/15/1991) • **65**
St.-Emilion 1919 • $500 • (2/15/1991) • **70**
St.-Emilion 1917 • $500 • (2/15/1991) • **70**
St.-Emilion 1916 • $300 • (2/15/1991) • **71**
St.-Emilion 1915 • $500 • (2/15/1991) • **72**
St.-Emilion 1908 • $500 • (2/15/1991) • **71**
St.-Emilion 1905 • $600 • (2/15/1991) • **70**
St.-Emilion 1899 • $1,250 • (2/15/1991) • **90**

CHEVAL NOIR

St.-Emilion 1997: Fresh berry and cherry character. Medium-bodied, with light tannins and a fruity finish. Drink now.–J.S. • $17 • (6/15/2000) • **81**

CHEVAL QUANCARD

Entre-Deux-Mers Cuvée Clémence Élevé en Fût de Chêne 1997: Fresh and fruity, with lots of character. Pretty aromas of lemons, pears and vanilla. Medium-bodied, with fine acidity and a lively, fruity aftertaste. Built like a good Chardonnay. Drink now.–J.S. • $10 • (2/28/1999) • **87**

CHEVALIER, DOMAINE DE

Pessac-Léognan 1999: A bit light for DC. Aromas of berry and orange peel, with a touch of mineral. Medium-bodied, with delicate tannins and a fresh, fruity finish.–J.S. • $NA • (1/01/2000) (BT) • **85-89**
Pessac-Léognan 1998: A well-crafted wine, classy and refined in style, with firm yet fine tannins, medium to full body and a medium fruity finish. Silky texture.–J.S. • $NA • (5/31/1999) (BT) • **90-94**
Pessac-Léognan 1997: Wonderfully aromatic, with beautiful plum and toasted oak character on the nose. Medium-bodied, with velvety tannins and a medium, fruity finish. Drink now through 2002.–J.S. • $31 • (1/31/2000) • **88**
Pessac-Léognan 1996: Ripe berry aromas, with hints of smoke and earth. Medium-bodied, with firm, sleek tannins, pretty raspberry and mineral flavors and a medium finish. Tight and closed. Best after 2001.–J.S. • $37 Ⓐ • (1/31/1999) • **86**
Pessac-Léognan 1995 • $22 Ⓐ • (1/31/1998) • **87**
Pessac-Léognan 1994 • $45 • (1/31/1997) • **85**
Pessac-Léognan 1993 • $45 Ⓐ • (1/31/1996) • **84**
Pessac-Léognan 1992 • $24 Ⓐ • (4/15/1995) • **80**
Pessac-Léognan 1991 • $30 • (3/31/1994) • **86**
Pessac-Léognan 1990 • $59 Ⓐ • (3/31/1993) • **92**
Pessac-Léognan 1989: A smooth, sculpted giant. Dark-ruby color. Wonderful aromas of fruit, roasted meat and fresh mushrooms. Full-bodied and very thick, with soft, velvety tannins and a long, long finish of sweet, ripe fruit. Beautiful now, but wait.—1989 Bordeaux horizontal. Best after 2005.–J.S. • $55 Ⓐ • (5/31/1999) • **96**
Pessac-Léognan 1988: Medium-bodied, with soft tannins, tobacco and earth character and ripe fruit throughout. Not as good as I expected, though it seems ready to drink. (1988 Bordeaux horizontal tasting).–J.S. • $44 Ⓐ • (11/30/1998) • **86**
Pessac-Léognan 1986 • $49 Ⓐ • (6/15/1989) • **89**
Graves 1985 • $54 Ⓐ • (10/15/1994) • **91**
Graves 1984 • $25 • (8/31/1987) • **90**
Graves 1983 • $53 Ⓐ • (10/15/1994) • **91**
Graves 1982: Slightly rustic, but with a good concentration of ripe fruit. Brick-red color, with a ruby center. Medium- to full-bodied, with ripe berry and tobacco aromas, rather coarse yet velvety tannins and a slightly funky aftertaste. (1982 Bordeaux horizontal tasting). Drink now.–J.S. • $47 Ⓐ • (11/30/1998) • **86**
Graves 1981 • $35 Ⓐ • (10/15/1994) • **94**
Graves 1979 • $44 • (10/15/1989) • **87**
Graves 1961 • $352 Ⓐ/1.5 liter • (4/30/1996) • **90**
Graves 1959 • $100 • (10/15/1990) • **97**
Graves 1945 • $200 • (11/30/1995) • **74**
Pessac-Léognan White 1997: A red wine masquerading as a white. Tight and powerful, with lots of fruit, though it's giving very little at the moment. Full-bodied, with firm acidity and a long mineral and apple finish. Give it time. Best after 2000.–J.S. • $90 • (9/30/1999) • **91**
Pessac-Léognan White 1996: A tightly knit Bordeaux white, built for aging. Full-bodied and powerful, its intense aromas of mineral, apple, spice and honey are followed in the mouth by a compact and rich fruit structure and lively acidity. This estate is always tops. Needs some cellar time. Best from 2001 through 2006.–J.S. • $46 Ⓐ • (3/31/1999) CS • **92**

CHEVALIERE, DOMAINE LA

Cabernet Sauvignon Vin de Pays d'Oc Chevalière Réserve 1996: Tastes a bit over the hill, with a gamy aroma and flavors of dried plum. Tasted twice, with consistent notes.–K.M. • $10 • (2/28/1999) • **73**
Chardonnay Vin de Pays d'Oc Chevalière Réserve 1998: A soft and subtle wine, with pleasant flavors of ripe pear, ripe apple and vanilla. Spicy notes linger appealingly on the finish. Drink now.–K.M. • $10 • (4/30/2000) • **84**
Chardonnay Vin de Pays d'Oc Chevalière Réserve 1997: Nice and juicy, with good flavors of apple and pear and some buttery-spicy notes mixed in. Drink now.–K.M. • $10 • (1/01/1999) • **83**
Chardonnay Vin de Pays d'Oc Réserve 1996 • $10 • (10/31/1997) • **84**
Merlot Vin de Pays d'Oc Chevalière Réserve 1998: Focused and flavorful, with red plum and cassis flavors, as well as black olive and smoke notes. This has a good backbone of acidity; peppery notes linger on the finish. Drink now through 2002.–K.M. • $10 • (2/29/2000) • **85**
Merlot Vin de Pays d'Oc Chevalière Réserve 1997: Stewy flavors and aromas dominate this lackluster red. Tasted twice, with consistent notes.–K.M. • $10 • (2/28/1999) • **72**
Red Vin de Pays d'Oc Première Cuvée 1995 • $13 • (4/30/1998) • **88**
Sauvignon Blanc Vin de Pays d'Oc Chevalière Réserve 1996: Decent citrus and green apple flavors and some herbal notes in this full-bodied white, but it comes off a bit disjointed in the end. Drink now.–K.M. • $10 • (1/01/1999) • **80**
Syrah Vin de Pays d'Oc Chevalière Réserve 1998: A good, focused Syrah, with pretty plum, dark cherry and cassis flavors and some appealing game notes. A delicious introduction to the Syrah grape. Drink now.–K.M. • $10 • (2/29/2000) • **86**
Syrah Vin de Pays d'Oc Chevalière Réserve 1997: Decent but light, with tea and cherry flavors. Ends on a charry note. Drink now.–K.M. • $10 • (2/28/1999) • **81**
Syrah Vin de Pays d'Oc Chevalière Réserve 1996: Lively, with delicious berry, plum and leather flavors. A good, quaffable red from the south of France. Drink now.–K.M. • $10 • (8/31/1998) • **84**
Syrah Vin de Pays d'Oc Réserve 1996 • $10 • (10/31/1997) • **85**
Viognier Vin de Pays d'Oc Réserve 1996 • $13 • (10/31/1997) • **75**

CHEVILLON, ROBERT

Bourgogne 1989 • $16 • (1/31/1992) • **77**
Nuits-St.-Georges 1992 • $NA • (12/15/1994) • **75**
Nuits-St.-Georges 1989 • $36 • (1/31/1992) • **89**
Nuits-St.-Georges 1986 • $37 • (12/15/1989) • **74**
Nuits-St.-Georges 1985 • $40 • (4/30/1988) • **85**
Nuits-St.-Georges Les Bousselots 1996: In this glass: what the hype on '96 red Burgundy is all about. This wine is inky-black in color, fat in texture, showing clean but ripe flavors of blackberry, spice and a touch of oak-infused mocha. A great follow-up to the classic '95 from this unheralded *premier cru* vineyard. Should live for a decade. Drink now through 2010.–P.M. • $40 • (7/31/1999) HR • **95**
Nuits-St.-Georges Les Bousselots 1995: Red Burgundy at its best. This superb *premier cru* tastes like a grand cru thanks to its deep floral, violet-scented and plummy aromas, thick, rich and ripe mouthfeel of red- and blackberry flavors, and supple, silky finish. Needs time for the oak to integrate. Drink through 2010.–P.M. • $35 • (8/31/1998) HR • **95**
Nuits-St.-Georges Les Bousselots 1992 • $NA • (12/15/1994) • **84**
Nuits-St.-Georges Les Cailles 1996: Sensational. Bursting with complexity, it's like fireworks on the palate. Beautifully toasty, with smoke, tar, vanilla, plum, black cherry, and the texture is like velvet despite the massive tannin structure. Best from 2002 through 2006.–P.M. • $60 • (7/31/1999) • **92**
Nuits-St.-Georges Les Cailles 1992 • $NA • (12/15/1994) • **84**
Nuits-St.-Georges Les Cailles 1991 • $48 • (1/31/1994) • **87**
Nuits-St.-Georges Les Chaignots 1996: Sleek as a thoroughbred, the tannins are beautifully integrated with great minerally intensity, chalk, toast, spice and black cherry notes, and it has serious *terroir* etched all over it. Best from 2001 through 2005.–P.M. • $58 Ⓐ • (7/31/1999) • **94**
Nuits-St.-Georges Les Chaignots 1995: Totally *terroir*-driven, this medium-bodied red is very reserved and elegant at first, then draws forth its seductive, mineral-laden character, along with sandalwood, floral and plum notes that will seduce any Burgundy-lover. A little tough now, so be patient. Best from 2005 through 2010.–P.M. • $35 • (8/31/1998) • **92**
Nuits-St.-Georges Les Chaignots 1992 • $NA • (12/15/1994) • **70**
Nuits-St.-Georges Les Chaignots 1991 • $38 • (1/31/1994) • **84**
Nuits-St.-Georges Les Perrières 1996: Jazzy, and pure as a mountain spring, it sings with wet earth, spice, blackberry and mineral and unusual elements

FRANCE

like blood and iron—its *terroir* does the talking, its succulent long finish, the walking. Best from 2001 through 2005.–P.M. • $40 • (7/31/1999) • **92**

Nuits-St.-Georges Les Perrières 1992 • $NA • (12/15/1994) • **73**

Nuits-St.-Georges Les Pruliers 1996: Starting out with lots of black cherry and cassis, it's clean and pure, but turns a bit tough on the very tannic finish. May need some time to fill out. Best from 2001 through 2005.–P.M. • $40 • (7/31/1999) • **88**

Nuits-St.-Georges Les Pruliers 1995: Wonderfully distinctive, with terrific mineral character, but also some tough tannins and lots of acidity. Medium-bodied, it tastes a bit dry on the intense finish. Slightly disjointed, it could use some cellaring. Drink through 2005.–P.M. • $35 • (8/31/1998) • **86**

Nuits-St.-Georges Les Pruliers 1992 • $NA • (12/15/1994) • **84**

Nuits-St.-Georges Les Roncières 1995: Very reserved aromatically, this medium-bodied red doesn't deliver much on the palate either, but has nice plum, cherry, and blackberry character. Needs time for the tough tannins to come around. Drink through 2005.–P.M. • $35 • (8/31/1998) • **88**

Nuits-St.-Georges Les St.-Georges 1992 • $NA • (12/15/1994) • **78**

Nuits-St.-Georges Les St.-Georges 1991 • $39 • (2/28/1995) • **91**

Nuits-St.-Georges Les St.-Georges 1990 • $115 Ⓐ • (2/28/1995) • **92**

Nuits-St.-Georges Les St.-Georges 1989 • $53 • (2/28/1995) • **86**

Nuits-St.-Georges Les St.-Georges 1988 • $59 • (2/28/1995) • **90**

Nuits-St.-Georges Les St.-Georges 1987 • $43 • (2/28/1995) • **88**

Nuits-St.-Georges Les St.-Georges 1986 • $55 • (2/28/1995) • **82**

Nuits-St.-Georges Les St.-Georges 1985 • $75 • (2/28/1995) • **89**

Nuits-St.-Georges Les St.-Georges 1983 • $NA • (2/28/1995) • **84**

Nuits-St.-Georges Les Vaucrains 1992 • $NA • (12/15/1994) • **80**

Nuits-St.-Georges Les Vaucrains 1991 • $39 • (8/31/1994) • **91**

Nuits-St.-Georges Les Vaucrains 1989 • $65 • (1/31/1992) • **89**

Nuits-St.-Georges Roncière 1992 • $NA • (12/15/1994) • **78**

Nuits-St.-Georges Roncière 1991 • $34 • (8/31/1994) • **91**

CHEYSSON, DOMAINE

Chiroubles 1997: Nice cherry flavor here, with ripe notes of leather and spice, some herbal notes, too. Medium- to light-bodied. Drink now.–K.M. • $11 • (10/15/1999) • **84**

CHEZE, CHATEAU LA

Premières Côtes de Bordeaux 1997: Fresh and fruity, with strawberry character and a hint of grass. Light- to medium-bodied, with slightly green tannins and a short finish. Tough to get excited about.–J.S. • $13 • (7/31/1999) • **79**

CHEZE, DOMAINE

St.-Joseph 1991 • $NA • (11/15/1995) • **78**

St.-Joseph Cuvée des Anges 1996: Woody, international-style that's well made. Full-bodied, with plenty of violet, spice and mocha along with lovely currant and raspberry flavors, a round mouthfeel. Drink through 2002.–P.M. • $25 • (11/15/1998) • **86**

St.-Joseph Cuvée des Anges 1995 • $23 • (10/15/1997) • **89**

St.-Joseph Cuvée Prestige de Caroline 1995 • $17 • (10/15/1997) • **87**

St.-Joseph Cuvée Prestige de Caroline 1994 • $23 • (11/30/1996) • **82**

St.-Joseph Cuvée Prestige de Caroline 1992 • $18 • (5/31/1994) • **76**

St.-Joseph Cuvée Prestige de Caroline 1991 • $18 • (5/31/1994) • **81**

St.-Joseph Cuvée Ro-Rée 1996: Ultrasweet, superripe, thick and delicious, this medium- to full-bodied, versatile red is balanced, delivering raspberry, black cherry and a touch of earth. Delicate yet concentrated, it's a charmer. Drink now through 2002.–P.M. • $15 • (11/15/1998) • **91**

St.-Joseph Cuvée Ro-Rée 1995 • $13 • (10/15/1997) • **81**

CHIDAINE, FRANÇOIS

Montlouis Brut Methode Traditionnelle NV • $14 • (5/15/1997) • **85**

Touraine Collection 1996 • $10 • (5/31/1998) • **78**

Key: SS—Spectator Selection. CS—Cellar Selection. HR—Highly Recommended. $NA—Price not available. (BT)—Barrel tasting. Ⓐ—Auction Price. For a key to the tasters' initials, see "How to Use These Listings." **Dates in parentheses represent the issues in which the ratings were published.**

CHIGNARD, MICHEL

Fleurie Les Moriers 1997: Purple in color, this smells and tastes like freshly crushed blackberries. Fairly elegant, with a hint of jamminess tailing off on the finish. Drink now.–B.S. • $18 • (10/31/1998) • **85**

Fleurie Les Moriers 1995 • $20 • (9/15/1997) • **83**

CHIQUET, GASTON

Brut Blanc de Blancs Champagne NV: Fine fruit flavor and a soft, plush texture make this satisfying. Has a rather sweet balance and a lingering finish. Drink now. • $45 • (10/15/1999) • **87**

Brut Champagne 1991: An overtly buttery Champagne that's extreme in style and rich in texture. Ripe apple, vanilla and butterscotch notes get your attention. Drink now. • $36 • (12/31/1998) • **83**

Brut Champagne Carte Verte Tradition NV: Generous and mature. Buttery, custardlike flavors and a soft texture make this easygoing in style. Drink now. • $40 • (9/15/1999) • **88**

Brut Champagne Special Club 1990 • $39 • (11/30/1997) • **92**

Brut Champagne Tradition NV • $31 • (11/30/1997) • **86**

CHIROULET, DOMAINE

Vin de Pays des Côtes de Gascogne Grande Reserve 1997: A lip-smacking and well-defined red from southwestern France, with delicious flavors of red plum, herb and spice that linger on the finish. Smooth. Drink now.–K.M. • $20 • (10/31/1999) • **86**

Vin de Pays des Côtes de Gascogne Grande Reserve 1996: Smooth, ripe and nicely concentrated, with delicious flavors of ripe plum and currant and leathery notes on the finish. This well-balanced red is a deft mixture of maturing fruit flavors and softening tannins, with a nice touch of wildness. Drink now through 2001.–K.M. • $20 • (12/31/1998) • **87**

CHOBLET, LUC & ANDREE-MARIE

Muscadet-Côtes de Grandlieu Sur Lie Clos de la Sénaigerie 1996 • $10 • (5/31/1998) • **86**

CHOFFLET-VALDENAIRE

Givry 1997: Brimming with authenticity and clarity. A '97 Burgundy with real personality, showing a concentration of pure, clean, ripe black fruit. Loaded with supple tannins, it delivers a firm texture and a focused finish. Drink now through 2005.–P.M. • $16 • (9/30/1999) • **86**

Givry 1995 • $15 • (11/15/1997) • **83**

Givry 1993 • $20 • (5/15/1996) • **86**

Givry 1992 • $15 • (6/15/1995) • **82**

Givry Clos de Choue 1997: Very ripe and full of fresh fruit, delivering a lively, natural-tasting freshness on the juicy, succulent (but a bit rustic) finish that beckons for another sip. Might develop with time. Try through 2005.–P.M. • $22 • (9/30/1999) • **88**

Givry Clos de Choue 1995 • $18 • (11/15/1997) • **85**

Givry Clos Jus 1997: Beautiful grip. Supple and ripe, full-bodied and of medium intensity, this is clean, pure and flavorful (raspberry, black cherry and plum). Very nice finish, all silk yet with *terroir* (wet earth). Drink now through 2005.–P.M. • $25 • (9/30/1999) • **87**

Givry Clos Jus 1995 • $18 • (11/15/1997) • **86**

CHON & FILS, GILBERT

Muscadet de Sèvre et Maine Sur Lie Domaine de la Jousselinière 1996: A sinewy, firmly structured white, displaying apple and lemon aromas and flavors, with a laserlike focus and crisp finish. Begs for a plate of oysters.–B.S. • $10 • (11/15/1998) • **86**

CHOPIN-GROFFIER

Chambolle-Musigny 1989 • $32 • (1/31/1992) • **90**

Clos Vougeot 1995 • $92 • (11/15/1997) • **92**

Clos Vougeot 1994 • $80 • (11/15/1996) • **86**

Clos Vougeot 1993 • $85 • (11/15/1995) • **88**

Clos Vougeot 1992 • $80 • (12/15/1994) • **85**

Clos Vougeot 1991 • $62 • (1/31/1994) • **85**

Clos Vougeot 1990 • $70 • (12/15/1992) • **94**

Clos Vougeot 1989 • $72 • (1/31/1992) • **94**

Clos Vougeot 1988 • $70 • (5/15/1991) • **87**
Côte de Nuits-Villages 1994 • $22 • (11/15/1996) • **80**
Côte de Nuits-Villages 1993 • $22 • (11/15/1995) • **83**
Côte de Nuits-Villages 1992 • $18 • (12/15/1994) • **82**
Nuits-St.-Georges 1994 • $35 • (11/15/1996) • **84**
Nuits-St.-Georges 1993 • $45 • (11/15/1995) • **79**
Nuits-St.-Georges 1991 • $33 • (1/31/1994) • **83**
Nuits-St.-Georges 1990 • $37 Ⓐ • (12/15/1992) • **89**
Nuits-St.-Georges 1989 • $32 • (1/31/1992) • **91**
Nuits-St.-Georges Aux Chaignots 1995 • $56 • (11/15/1997) • **88**
Nuits-St.-Georges Aux Chaignots 1994 • $50 • (11/15/1996) • **85**
Nuits-St.-Georges Aux Chaignots 1993 • $60 • (11/15/1995) • **82**
Nuits-St.-Georges Aux Chaignots 1992 • $45 • (12/15/1994) • **84**
Nuits-St.-Georges Aux Chaignots 1991 • $40 • (1/31/1994) • **86**
Nuits-St.-Georges Aux Chaignots 1990 • $40 • (12/15/1992) • **91**
Nuits-St.-Georges Aux Chaignots 1989 • $40 • (1/31/1992) • **93**
Vougeot 1994 • $35 • (11/15/1996) • **70**
Vougeot 1992 • $35 • (12/15/1994) • **84**
Vougeot 1991 • $NA • (1/31/1994) • **79**
Vougeot 1990 • $44 • (12/15/1992) • **93**
Vougeot 1988 • $32 • (5/15/1991) • **92**

CHRISTOPHE

Merlot Vin de Pays d'Oc 1996 • $NA • (1/01/1998) • **82**

CIEL, LE

Chardonnay Vin de Pays d'Oc 1996: Crisp, with green apple, citrus and mineral flavors and buttery notes on the finish. Drink now, with food.–K.M. • $9 • (11/15/1998) • **84**
Merlot Rosé Vin de Pays d'Oc 1997: A straightforward rosé with flavors of dried cherry and melon, nice spicy notes on the finish. Drink now.–K.M. • $7 • (11/15/1998) • **83**
Merlot Vin de Pays d'Oc 1996: A soft red, with dried cherry flavors and a chalky finish.–K.M. • $9 • (12/15/1998) • **74**
Minervois Le Vin Qui Tue 1996: A good, meaty red, with solid plum and cherry flavors. Balanced and accessible, with a lingering finish of clove and pepper. Drink now through 2002.–K.M. • $9 • (10/31/1998) • **86**

CINQUIN, PAUL

Régnié Domaine des Braves 1994 • $10 • (9/15/1996) • **84**

CISSAC, CHATEAU

Haut-Médoc 1998: Currant bush and green tobacco aromas. Medium-bodied, with medium tannins and a short finish. Tough little wine right now.–J.S. • $NA • (5/31/1999) (BT) • **85-89**
Haut-Médoc 1997: Pleasing soft wine with chocolate and berry character, medium body and a light finish. A bit diluted. Drink now.–J.S. • $NA • (1/31/2000) • **81**
Haut-Médoc 1996: Slightly tough '96, with a good amount of ripe fruit character but a slightly diluted finish. Still, a good glass of wine. Drink now through 2001.–J.S. • $NA • (1/31/1999) • **81**
Haut-Médoc 1995: Good violet and blackberry aromas. Full-bodied and very rich with slightly hard, austere tannins. Needs time. Old-style, burly wine. Best from 2003 through 2008.–J.S. • $NA • (9/15/1998) • **86**
Haut-Médoc 1992 • $14 • (4/15/1995) • **81**
Haut-Médoc 1991 • $14 • (3/31/1994) • **76**
Haut-Médoc 1990 • $35 Ⓐ • (3/31/1993) • **88**
Haut-Médoc 1989: Extremely well-crafted red that caresses your palate. Blackberry and cherry aromas, bark and earth character. Medium-bodied, with fine tannins and a long, silky texture on the finish. A beauty. (1989 Bordeaux horizontal tasting). Drink now through 2010.–J.S. • $26 Ⓐ • (5/31/1999) • **90**
Haut-Médoc 1987 • $14 • (11/30/1989) • **81**
Haut-Médoc 1986 • $23 Ⓐ • (11/30/1989) • **79**
Haut-Médoc 1985 • $36 Ⓐ • (7/31/1988) • **79**
Haut-Médoc 1982: Rather hard and unyielding. Floral and berry aromas, not much on the palate. (1982 Bordeaux horizontal tasting). Drink now.–J.S. • $37 Ⓐ • (11/30/1998) • **81**
Haut-Médoc 1961 • $36 • (4/30/1996) • **88**

CITADELLE, DOMAINE DE LA

Cabernet Sauvignon Vin de Pays de Vaucluse 1997: Pleasing for its supple and dense texture, but there is a slight herb and bell pepper character that distracts from the plum and cassis flavors. The sweet tannins fold into this full-bodied wine, but end a bit dry. Drink now through 2004.–P.M. • $5 • (12/15/1999) • **84**
Cabernet Sauvignon Vin de Pays de Vaucluse 1995: Fresh and delicate, with rose petal, licorice and ripe plum, it unfolds gently its complex, subtle, supple character, bringing out floral, red berry flavors that are just deliciously balanced with the acidity and tannins. Drink now through 2002.–P.M. • $9 • (11/15/1999) • **87**
Côtes du Lubéron 1996: Light and tart, even astringent, with a bitter aftertaste.–P.M. • $NA • (1/01/1999) • **71**
Côtes du Lubéron Cuvée Le Châtaignier 1998: Fresh in a grapey, nouveau style, showing anise, cherry and raspberry aromas and flavors, this sings with lovely ripe and succulent character. Perfect to have around the house for the next year. Drink now.–P.M. • $10 • (11/15/1999) • **85**
Côtes du Lubéron Rosé 1998: A clean and fresh rosé, showing finesse and good acidity. There is a bite to the finish, but ultimately you want to drink this light-bodied wine for its cherries, raspberries and chewy tannins. Drink now.–P.M. • $11 • (11/15/1999) • **84**
Côtes du Lubéron White 1998: Good effort. Zesty and fresh, with intense aromas in a fairly simple package of lime, green apple and odd flinty notes. Clean, stony, minerally, unyielding style. Drink now through 2002.–P.M. • $NA • (1/01/1999) • **87**
Côtes du Lubéron White Cuvée Le Châtaignier 1998: Straightforward, with a tart, bitter, astringent note.–P.M. • $NA • (1/01/1999) • **70**
Vin de Pays de Vaucluse Rosé Cuvée Souleïado 1998: Light and lean, meager and lacking vibrant fruit.–P.M. • $NA • (1/01/1999) • **77**
Viognier Vin de Pays de Vaucluse 1998: Light style, with a supple, sweet-tasting character showing some pineapple, lemon and pear. A bit diluted, but balanced in its style. Drink now.–P.M. • $NA • (1/01/1999) • **80**
Viognier Vin de Pays de Vaucluse 1997: A bit light, this simple white has some crisp lemon and green apple character. Tart finish.–P.M. • $NA • (1/01/1999) • **79**

CITRAN, CHATEAU

Haut-Médoc 1998: Marked intensity of currant, mint and spices on the nose. Full-bodied, with a compacted fruit and tannin structure and a silky finish. Serious sample.–J.S. • $NA • (5/31/1999) (BT) • **85-89**
Haut-Médoc 1997: Attractive berry, cherry and coffee aromas follow through to a medium-bodied palate with good fruit. Light finish. Drink now through 2004.–J.S. • $NA • (1/31/2000) • **86**
Haut-Médoc 1996: An enjoyable wine, without pretension. Berry character, and dried-herb undertone. Medium-bodied, with velvety tannins and a pleasant, fruity aftertaste. Drink now.–J.S. • $22 • (1/31/1999) • **86**
Haut-Médoc 1995 • $20 • (1/31/1998) • **87**
Haut-Médoc 1994 • $17 Ⓐ • (1/31/1997) • **82**
Haut-Médoc 1993 • $20 • (1/31/1996) • **80**
Haut-Médoc 1991 • $13 • (3/31/1994) • **84**
Haut-Médoc 1990 • $20 • (3/31/1993) • **86**
Haut-Médoc 1989: A gorgeous, seductive wine now, and should improve with age. Aromas of roses, berries and cherries. Full-bodied, round in texture, with lots of tobacco, cherry and vanilla flavors. Long, caressing finish.—1989 Bordeaux horizontal. Drink through 2008.–J.S. • $24 Ⓐ • (5/31/1999) • **90**
Haut-Médoc 1988 • $22 Ⓐ • (4/30/1991) • **91**
Haut-Médoc 1983 • $23 Ⓐ • (4/01/1986) • **82**
Haut-Médoc 1982 • $12 • (4/01/1985) • **78**
Haut-Médoc 1961 • $22 • (4/30/1996) • **77**

CLAIR, BRUNO

Aloxe-Corton 1997: Ripe, lush and smooth, with a very soft core of fruit, delivering plum and black cherry character. Short finish. Drink now through 2004.–P.M. • $38 • (9/30/1999) • **83**
Chambertin-Clos de Bèze 1997: Delicate cherry and herb flavors on a firm, compact structure. A bit pinched and light for the appellation. Drink now through 2002.–B.S. • $149 • (9/30/1999) • **81**
Chambertin-Clos de Bèze 1996: A bit herbal and tough, but shows decent red berry character too. Of medium body, it's drying slightly on the finish. Drink now through 2005.–P.M. • $140 • (9/30/1998) • **84**
Chambertin-Clos de Bèze 1995 • $100 • (11/15/1997) • **88**
Chambertin-Clos de Bèze 1994 • $97 • (11/15/1996) • **86**

CLAIR, BRUNO

Chambertin-Clos de Bèze 1991 • $78 • (1/31/1994) • **91**
Chambertin-Clos de Bèze 1990 • $70 • (12/15/1992) • **93**
Chambolle-Musigny Les Véroilles 1997: Light and aromatically shy, this slightly diluted red Burgundy shows modest red berry aromas and flavors, with a hint of herb.–P.M. • $48 • (9/30/1999) • **79**
Chambolle-Musigny Les Véroilles 1996: Pure and clean, with cherry, cassis and blackberry character but also an herbal note. Of medium body, it's fairly lean and a bit tough, at least now, on the finish. May improve with cellaring. Drink now through 2007.–P.M. • $46 • (9/30/1998) • **85**
Chambolle-Musigny Les Véroilles 1995 • $33 • (11/15/1997) • **87**
Chambolle-Musigny Les Véroilles 1994 • $35 • (11/15/1996) • **80**
Corton-Charlemagne 1997: Pretty, with clean apple, pineapple and pear. Medium in body and intensity. Drink now through 2003.–P.M. • $98 • (9/30/1999) • **87**
Corton-Charlemagne 1995 • $89 • (8/31/1997) • **87**
Gevrey-Chambertin 1997: Cherry is married to an elegant, lithe framework. Lean and balanced, with moderate concentration and a firm, lingering finish. Best from 2001 through 2005.–B.S. • $51 • (9/30/1999) • **83**
Gevrey-Chambertin 1996: Intriguing aromas of cherries and vanilla oak set this apart. Light-bodied and fresh, with astringent tannins. Lacks integration now, but the fruit is delicious. Best from 2001 through 2006.–B.S. • $56 • (9/30/1998) • **86**
Gevrey-Chambertin 1993 • $47 • (5/15/1996) • **86**
Gevrey-Chambertin Cazetiers 1997: A bit stemmy, with mushroom and herb character. A light Pinot.–P.M. • $101 • (9/30/1999) • **78**
Gevrey-Chambertin Cazetiers 1996: Lovely wine that gained in contact with air, suggesting it will improve with cellaring. Medium-bodied and medium-intense, with lots of clean, pure cherry and cassis character. Not overoaked by any means, emphasizing the fruit. Best after 2003.–P.M. • $96 • (9/30/1998) • **89**
Gevrey-Chambertin Cazetiers 1995 • $66 • (11/15/1997) • **82**
Gevrey-Chambertin Cazetiers 1994 • $74 • (11/15/1996) • **85**
Gevrey-Chambertin Cazetiers 1991 • $53 • (1/31/1994) • **87**
Gevrey-Chambertin Cazetiers 1990 • $55 • (12/15/1992) • **89**
Gevrey-Chambertin Cazetiers 1989 • $61 • (1/31/1992) • **89**
Gevrey-Chambertin Clos du Fonteny 1997: Cherry and a touch of herb in this lean, tough '97 Gevrey offer more structure than pleasure. Difficult to ascertain whether it will flesh out.–B.S. • $78 • (9/30/1999) • **79**
Gevrey-Chambertin Clos du Fonteny 1996: Pretty, medium-bodied, with tannins and flavors that coat the palate unobstructed by unwarranted wood. Moderately intense. A pleasure to drink upon release, through 2003.–P.M. • $73 • (9/30/1998) • **85**
Gevrey-Chambertin Clos du Fonteny 1995 • $54 • (11/15/1997) • **86**
Gevrey-Chambertin Clos du Fonteny 1994 • $54 • (11/15/1996) • **80**
Gevrey-Chambertin Clos du Fonteny 1992 • $50 • (6/15/1995) • **83**
Gevrey-Chambertin Clos du Fonteny 1991 • $42 • (1/31/1994) • **86**
Gevrey-Chambertin Clos du Fonteny 1990 • $45 • (12/15/1992) • **92**
Gevrey-Chambertin Petite Chapelle 1997: On the lean side, showing herb and cherry aromas and flavors. Lightly tannic structure—dilute for the appellation and vintage.–B.S. • $73 • (9/30/1999) • **79**
Gevrey-Chambertin Petite Chapelle 1996: Lush and supple, of medium body, with light tannins, good red berry character and a smooth finish, it lacks some structure and depth, but makes for a pretty Pinot upon release, with fresh acidity on the finish. Drink now through 2002.–P.M. • $70 • (9/30/1998) • **85**
Gevrey-Chambertin Premier Cru 1997: Herbaceous, thin, weedy and anemic.–B.S. • $58 • (9/30/1999) • **76**
Gevrey-Chambertin Premier Cru 1994 • $41 • (11/15/1996) • **78**
Marsannay 1997: Crisp, with lemon tart, raspberry and strawberry character. Earthy notes dominate the finish of this fairly light wine.–P.M. • $24 • (9/30/1999) • **78**
Marsannay 1996: A nice little Pinot to drink tonight. Light and pretty, with cherry, strawberry and raspberry flavors and a round mouthfeel.–P.M. • $23 • (9/30/1998) • **83**
Marsannay 1994 • $20 • (11/15/1996) • **80**
Marsannay 1992 • $19 • (6/15/1995) • **83**
Marsannay 1988 • $16 • (11/15/1991) • **80**
Marsannay Les Grasses Têtes 1997: Ripe and plummy, a little over-the-top in aromas and flavors, this lacks midpalate texture and ends on a tough, astringent note.–B.S. • $29 • (9/30/1999) • **78**

Key: SS—Spectator Selection. CS—Cellar Selection. HR—Highly Recommended. $NA—Price not available. (BT)—Barrel tasting. Ⓐ—Auction Price.
For a key to the tasters' initials, see "How to Use These Listings."
Dates in parentheses represent the issues in which the ratings were published.

Marsannay Les Grasses Têtes 1996: Straightforward, with an herbal, asparagus and bell pepper character. Modest ripe fruit. Astringent finish.–P.M. • $27 • (9/30/1998) • **77**
Marsannay Les Grasses Têtes 1995 • $21 • (11/15/1997) • **82**
Marsannay Les Grasses Têtes 1994 • $24 • (11/15/1996) • **80**
Marsannay Les Grasses Têtes 1993 • $25 • (5/15/1996) • **86**
Marsannay Les Grasses Têtes 1990 • $28 • (12/15/1992) • **80**
Marsannay Les Longeroies 1997: Rich, succulent and spicy, this '97 red shows black cherry, earth and forest aromas and flavors allied to a firm, rustic structure. Best from 2001 through 2005.–B.S. • $29 • (9/30/1999) • **82**
Marsannay Les Longeroies 1995 • $21 • (11/15/1997) • **86**
Marsannay Les Longeroies 1994 • $24 • (11/15/1996) • **81**
Marsannay Les Longeroies 1992 • $23 • (5/15/1995) • **85**
Marsannay Les Longeroies 1990 • $18 • (12/15/1992) • **83**
Marsannay Les Longeroies 1989 • $18 • (1/31/1992) • **87**
Marsannay Les Vaudenelles 1997: A touch herbal, like freshly cut grass, with strawberry and chocolate, offering modest fruit and finishing on the astringent side.–B.S. • $29 • (9/30/1999) • **79**
Marsannay Les Vaudenelles 1996: Wonderfully pure, sappy fruit in this large-scale, honest red of straightforward appeal, with black cherry aromas and flavors and a slightly rustic finish. Drink through 2004.–B.S. • $26 • (9/30/1998) • **86**
Marsannay Les Vaudenelles 1995 • $20 • (11/15/1997) • **89**
Marsannay Les Vaudenelles 1994 • $22 • (11/15/1996) • **78**
Marsannay Les Vaudenelles 1993 • $22 • (5/15/1996) • **85**
Marsannay Les Vaudenelles 1992 • $21 • (6/15/1995) • **81**
Marsannay Les Vaudenelles 1989 • $18 • (1/31/1992) • **81**
Marsannay White 1997: A pure, crisp, light-bodied white that's lovely. Drink now.–P.M. • $29 • (5/31/1999) • **86**
Marsannay White 1996 • $29 • (5/31/1998) • **88**
Marsannay White 1995 • $21 • (5/31/1997) • **85**
Morey-St.-Denis 1985 • $20 • (5/15/1988) • **73**
Morey-St.-Denis En la Rue de Vergy 1997: Herbal and tannic, full of crispness yet no richness. Finishes on a tart, astringent note.–B.S. • $49 • (9/30/1999) • **78**
Morey-St.-Denis En la Rue de Vergy 1996: Beautiful spicy berry flavor to this; not too oaky, just a mouthful of clean, fresh Pinot Noir fruit. Silky and elegant with flavors of violets and red berries. Drink through 2003.–B.S. • $47 • (9/30/1998) • **85**
Morey-St.-Denis En la Rue de Vergy 1995 • $34 • (11/15/1997) • **86**
Morey-St.-Denis En la Rue de Vergy 1994 • $35 • (11/15/1996) • **78**
Morey-St.-Denis En la Rue de Vergy 1991 • $33 • (1/31/1994) • **86**
Morey-St.-Denis En la Rue de Vergy 1990 • $29 Ⓐ • (12/15/1992) • **90**
Morey-St.-Denis En la Rue de Vergy 1989 • $36 • (1/31/1992) • **90**
Morey-St.-Denis White En la Rue de Vergy 1997: A wondrous, balanced and extremely polished white, this shows a master at work as the clean, lemon-spiked acidity intersects the ripe tropical, pear and quince fruit. Sweet, toasted oak fuels the long finish. Drink now through 2005.–P.M. • $47 • (5/31/1999) • **92**
Morey-St.-Denis White En la Rue de Vergy 1996 • $55 • (5/31/1998) • **85**
Morey-St.-Denis White En la Rue de Vergy 1995 • $49 • (5/31/1997) • **91**
Savigny-lès-Beaune La Dominode 1997: Shows focus and definition, offering moderately concentrated cherry and earth notes and good midpalate depth, with astringent tannins on the finish. Drink through 2005.–B.S. • $57 • (9/30/1999) • **87**
Savigny-lès-Beaune La Dominode 1996: Ripe and thick, this shows lovely intensity of cassis, blueberry and black currant. Of medium body, pure and clean, with a mineral, iron and blood-orange character at midpalate and some lovely sweetness on the finish. Best from 2003.–P.M. • $56 • (9/30/1998) • **90**
Savigny-lès-Beaune La Dominode 1995 • $40 • (11/15/1997) • **91**
Savigny-lès-Beaune La Dominode 1994 • $40 • (11/15/1996) • **83**
Savigny-lès-Beaune La Dominode 1991 • $32 • (1/31/1994) • **86**
Savigny-lès-Beaune La Dominode 1990 • $28 Ⓐ • (12/15/1992) • **92**
Savigny-lès-Beaune La Dominode 1989 • $34 • (1/31/1992) • **89**
Savigny-lès-Beaune La Dominode 1985 • $24 • (3/15/1988) • **80**
Vosne-Romanée Les Champs Perdrix 1997: Tomato and herb aromas and flavors ally to a light structure and soft texture before drying tannins emerge on the finish.–B.S. • $57 • (9/30/1999) • **78**
Vosne-Romanée Les Champs Perdrix 1996: Pure Pinot. Enticing, spicy berry flavors in this straightforward yet lively and satisfying red. Starts out silky, with medium tannins for support. Drink through 2004.–B.S. • $55 • (9/30/1998) • **87**
Vosne-Romanée Les Champs Perdrix 1995 • $38 • (11/15/1997) • **75**
Vosne-Romanée Les Champs Perdrix 1994 • $41 • (11/15/1996) • **79**
Vosne-Romanée Les Champs Perdrix 1991 • $28 • (1/31/1994) • **81**
Vosne-Romanée Les Champs Perdrix 1989 • $30 • (1/31/1992) • **91**

CLAIR, FRANCOISE & DENIS

Puligny-Montrachet La Garenne 1997: Very appealing, thick-textured and showy, it reveals a drying, acidic character, with apricot and pineapple flavors and sweet, rose-scented wood. The astringent finish is dominated by wood tannins.–P.M. • $NA • (5/31/1999) • **79**

St.-Aubin Les Frionnes 1998: Appealing for its midpalate concentration of sweet-tasting fruit. Aromatically shy, this full-bodied white picks up honey and ripe pear, has a creamy texture. Nice lingering finish. Drink now through 2003.–P.M. • $28 • (5/31/2000) • **87**

St.-Aubin Les Frionnes 1997: Firm in style yet balanced, with green apple, wet earth, lemon and mushroom character. Medium-bodied, it's a bit chewy and drying on the finish. Drink now through 2002.–P.M. • $27 • (5/31/1999) • **82**

St.-Aubin Les Murgers des Dents de Chien 1998: Oaky, with modest fruit, the toasty notes dominate as this wine lacks enough ripe-tasting character.–P.M. • $30 • (5/31/2000) • **79**

St.-Aubin Les Murgers des Dents de Chien 1997: Cooked applesauce notes are the motif of this medium-bodied, slightly oxidative white, with a lemony, buttery character on the finish.–P.M. • $27 • (5/31/1999) • **77**

St.-Aubin Les Murgers des Dents de Chien 1995 • $28 • (5/31/1997) • **87**

Santenay Clos de Tavannes 1990 • $29 • (2/15/1993) • **83**

Santenay La Comme 1990 • $26 • (2/15/1993) • **81**

Santenay La Comme 1988 • $25 • (6/15/1992) • **85**

Santenay White 1998: Yellow in color and medium in body, it's a bit shy in aroma, delivering some modest fruit character. Slightly dry on the finish.–P.M. • $26 • (5/31/2000) • **79**

CLAIREFONT, CHATEAU DE

Margaux 1993 • $15 • (1/31/1996) • **79**

CLAIRFONT, DOMAINE DE

Vin de Pays de Vaucluse 1995 • $8 • (12/15/1996) • **80**

Vin de Pays de Vaucluse 1994 • $8 • (12/15/1996) • **74**

Vin de Pays de Vaucluse 1991 • $6 • (10/31/1992) • **82**

CLAPE, A.

Cornas 1997: *Terroir*-driven in its polish and concentration, this clean Rhône-grown Syrah tastes smooth, while a mineral component suggests the good *terroir* at play on the superb finish. It's a bit woody for now, but this is a ripe red, just needing time. Best from 2002 through 2007.–P.M. • $42 • (12/15/1999) CS • **92**

Cornas 1996: Impressively complex, mingling wonderful fruit and spice accents with black pepper, tar, cassis and olive. Dark and brooding, this full-bodied Northern Rhône red is amazingly ripe, sweet-tasting, seductive—just plain delicious. So balanced, it's tempting now, but it will keep for years. Drink through 2015.–P.M. • $35 • (10/15/1998) CS • **96**

Cornas 1995 • $36 • (10/15/1997) • **91**

Cornas 1991 • $24 • (5/31/1994) • **87**

Cornas 1990 • $26 • (4/15/1993) • **87**

Cornas 1986 • $22 • (1/31/1989) • **88**

Cornas 1984 • $13 • (8/31/1987) • **78**

Cornas Renaissance 1997: A nice Syrah, but on the light side. Still, shows polish, with deft oak, blackberry and smoke notes. A mineral concentration on the finish suggests fine terroir. From Clape's younger Cornas vines. Best from 2002 through 2010.–P.M. • $25 • (12/15/1999) • **88**

Côtes du Rhône Cuvée Spéciale 1996: Gorgeous and hedonistic, with ripe berries all over the palate. Smoke and floral notes suggest very smart handling of oak and grapes. Full-bodied and dense, it's the impeccable red berry and blackberry flavors that shine through in the end. Cellar. Made from declassified Cornas. Best from 2002 through 2010.–P.M. • $19 • (12/15/1999) • **90**

St.-Péray 1997: A nice little white, with a full, round texture, and a milky, spicy, buttery character that's fairly neutral. Silky mouthfeel and finish are attractive. Drink now.–P.M. • $18 • (11/15/1998) • **81**

St.-Péray 1996 • $18 • (10/15/1997) • **84**

Vin de Table Français Le Vin des Amis 1998: Smooth but a bit simple, with red berry and tough tannin character. Chewy, herbal finish.–P.M. • $15 • (12/15/1999) • **77**

CLARKE, CHATEAU

Listrac 1997: A wine with decent blackberry and mushroom aromas. Medium-bodied, with plummy, fruity character and a light finish. Best after 2000.–J.S. • $NA • (1/31/2000) • **84**

Listrac 1996: Some good berry and chocolate character in this medium-bodied wine. It doesn't try to be too much, and shows pleasant, friendly tannins and a fruity finish. Drink now.–J.S. • $NA • (1/31/1999) • **85**

Listrac 1995 • $26 • (10/15/1997) • **86**

Listrac 1992 • $18 • (7/31/1996) • **81**

Listrac 1991 • $14 • (3/31/1994) • **83**

Listrac 1990 • $18 • (3/31/1993) • **83**

Listrac 1989: A big, rich and delicious wine. Dark ruby-colored, and interesting aromas of blackberry and orange peel. Full-bodied and chewy, with round tannins and a dark chocolate and cherry aftertaste.—1989 Bordeaux horizontal. Drink now through 2008.–J.S. • $NA • (5/31/1999) • **90**

Listrac 1988 • $24 Ⓐ • (4/30/1991) • **81**

Listrac 1986 • $17 • (11/15/1989) HR • **90**

CLAVEL, DOMAINE

Coteaux du Languedoc La Copa Santa 1997: Smooth and supple, with red plum, mineral and brickish flavors on a broad frame. Has a pepper aroma and a lingering finish of chocolate and mocha. A seductive, well-balanced wine. Drink now through 2002.–K.M. • $20 • (9/30/1999) • **88**

Coteaux du Languedoc La Copa Santa 1996: Quite a mouthful. Dense and incredibly concentrated, with layers of complex yet well-defined flavors of bacon, dark chocolate, ripe plum and raspberry, finishing with mineral and coffeelike notes. Rather plush despite its power, but this French red will need time in the cellar to integrate even further. Best from 2002 through 2008.–K.M. • $20 • (2/28/1999) HR • **92**

Coteaux du Languedoc La Copa Santa 1995 • $15 • (2/28/1998) • **91**

Coteaux du Languedoc La Méjanelle 7ème Printemps des Comédiens 1991 • $8 • (3/15/1994) • **86**

Coteaux du Languedoc Terroir de la Méjanelle Les Garrigues 1997: A vibrant and luscious red, with loads of red plum, red cherry, leather and some spice flavors. Also has a firm backbone of acidity and a long finish dominated by pepper and mineral notes. Drink through 2003.–K.M. • $10 • (9/30/1999) • **87**

Coteaux du Languedoc Terroir de la Méjanelle Les Garrigues 1996: Muscular, with plenty of cherry, game and ripe plum flavors that go on and on through the finish. Well proportioned, well balanced, fresh and lively. Spicy notes linger on the aftertaste. Drink through 2005–K.M. • $10 • (2/28/1999) • **89**

Coteaux du Languedoc Terroir de la Méjanelle Les Garrigues 1995 • $10 • (3/31/1998) • **89**

Coteaux du Languedoc Terroir de la Méjanelle Mas de Clavel 1998: A solid and inviting red, with well-defined flavors of plum, red cherry, leather, sage and wild herb. Balanced and firm, with a clean finish. Carignane. Drink now.–K.M. • $9 • (11/15/1999) • **84**

Coteaux du Languedoc Terroir de la Méjanelle Mas de Clavel Vieilles Vignes 1996: Medium-bodied, with decent dried plum and cherry flavors and blueberry notes on the finish. Tasted twice, with consistent notes. Drink now.–K.M. • $9 • (2/28/1999) • **82**

Coteaux du Languedoc Terroir de la Méjanelle Mas de Clavel Vieilles Vignes 1995 • $7 • (2/28/1998) • **88**

CLEMENT, BERNARD & PIERRE

Sauvignon Blanc Vin de Pays du Jardin de la France 1996 • $NA • (6/30/1998) • **84**

CLEMENT PICHON, CHATEAU

Haut-Médoc 1997: A bit light. Tastes more like a light Burgundy with its strawberry and tea character.–J.S. • $16 • (1/31/2000) • **79**

Haut-Médoc 1996: Impressively concentrated with plum and earthy character, if a bit rustic and fat in style. Full-bodied, with velvety tannins and a medium finish. Much better than when tasted from barrel. Best after 2000.–J.S. • $NA • (1/31/1999) • **87**

Haut-Médoc 1995 • $15 • (1/31/1998) • **86**

Haut-Médoc 1994 • $15 • (1/31/1997) • **71**

Haut-Médoc 1993 • $15 • (1/31/1996) • **80**

Haut-Médoc 1991 • $12 • (3/31/1994) • **68**

Haut-Médoc 1988 • $15 • (8/31/1991) • **78**

Haut-Médoc 1987 • $14 • (11/30/1989) • **73**

CLEMENT PICHON, CHATEAU

Haut-Médoc 1986 • $11 • (11/30/1989) • **85**

CLERC, LAURENT

Puligny-Montrachet Les Charmes 1996 • $42 • (5/31/1998) • **82**
Puligny-Montrachet Les Charmes 1995 • $NA • (8/31/1997) • **71**
Puligny-Montrachet Les Folatières 1995 • $45 • (5/31/1997) HR • **94**

CLERC & FILS, HENRI

Bâtard-Montrachet 1996: Odd, sweetish perfumes reminiscent of green tea or Earl Grey seem out of place; definitely an acquired taste. Dry wood on the finish. Drink now through 2003.–P.M. • $110 • (8/31/1998) • **73**
Bâtard-Montrachet 1995 • $100 • (5/31/1997) • **76**
Beaune Chaume Gaufriot 1996: Supple and nicely oaked, but slightly one-dimensional in structure, with vanilla, plum and black cherry flavors. A bit watery at midpalate. Drink now.–P.M. • $25 • (9/30/1998) • **78**
Beaune Chaume Gaufriot 1995 • $27 • (11/15/1997) • **70**
Beaune Chaume Gaufriot 1985 • $29 • (11/15/1988) • **81**
Beaune White Chaume Gaufriot 1996 • $24 • (5/31/1998) • **79**
Beaune White Chaume Gaufriot 1995 • $35 • (8/31/1997) • **77**
Bienvenues-Bâtard-Montrachet 1996: Strange new-oakish, paint-varnish perfumes destroy this otherwise ripe and supple wine. Terrible *élevage* (barrel aging) here. Full-bodied, overdone. Best from 2003.–P.M. • $100 • (8/31/1998) • **70**
Bienvenues-Bâtard-Montrachet 1995 • $95 • (5/31/1997) • **73**
Blagny Sous le Dos d'Ane 1996: Clean and pure red berry character, with a linear, high acidity, this medium-bodied red offers ripe tannins, with clever toasted oak and good fruit. Best from 2002 through 2007.–P.M. • $NA • (5/15/1999) • **87**
Blagny Sous le Dos d'Ane 1995 • $NA • (11/15/1997) • **73**
Bourgogne White Les Riaux 1995 • $12 • (8/31/1997) • **87**
Chevalier-Montrachet 1996 • $120 • (5/31/1998) • **92**
Chevalier-Montrachet 1995 • $110 • (5/31/1997) • **93**
Clos de Vougeot 1996: Beautiful *terroir*-driven red Burgundy. A bit herbal, which lowers the score slightly, but it shows great intensity on the mid-palate and delivers layers of complex spice, earth and mineral along with the usual red- and blackberry character. Not overly oaky, it has a long finish.–P.M. • $60 • (9/30/1998) • **89**
Clos de Vougeot 1995 • $NA • (11/15/1997) • **86**
Echézeaux 1996: A rich mouthful of plum and earth, broad and opulent before the sinewy tannins close it down. Best from 2002.–B.S. • $50 • (9/30/1998) • **86**
Meursault-Blagny Sous le Dos d'Ane 1995 • $50 • (8/31/1997) • **90**
Puligny-Montrachet 1996 • $36 • (5/31/1998) • **74**
Puligny-Montrachet 1995 • $35 • (5/31/1997) • **80**
Puligny-Montrachet Les Champs Gains 1996 • $48 • (5/31/1998) • **80**
Puligny-Montrachet Les Champs Gains 1995 • $45 • (5/31/1997) • **82**
Puligny-Montrachet Les Combettes 1996 • $48 • (5/31/1998) • **79**
Puligny-Montrachet Les Folatières 1996: Woody, perfumed, unbalanced, the sort of white Burgundy that depresses you because it has ripe fruit but is totally messed up by the winemaker. Drink now.–P.M. • $50 • (8/31/1998) • **72**
Puligny-Montrachet Les Folatières 1995 • $38 • (8/31/1997) • **87**
Puligny-Montrachet Red 1996: A sturdy, broad-shouldered red with stiff tannins and earthy cherry notes, chewy texture and a licorice-tinged finish. For fans of a more traditional style. Best from 2000.–B.S. • $30 • (9/30/1998) • **83**
Santenay Les Potets 1996: Lovely, balanced red Burgundy, showing tender tannins that just melt in the mouth. This medium-bodied wine holds together through good acidity and sappy fruit, making it lively on the lingering finish. Drink now through 2003.–P.M. • $22 • (9/30/1998) • **85**
Santenay Les Potets 1995 • $NA • (11/15/1997) • **78**

CLERC MILON, CHATEAU

Pauillac 1999: A pretty, aromatic red with floral, currant and licorice character. Medium body. Medium fine tannins. Long finish.–J.S. • $NA • (1/01/2000) (BT) • **85-89**

Key: SS—Spectator Selection. CS—Cellar Selection. HR—Highly Recommended. $NA—Price not available. (BT)—Barrel tasting. Ⓐ—Auction Price. For a key to the tasters' initials, see "How to Use These Listings." **Dates in parentheses represent the issues in which the ratings were published.**

Pauillac 1998: Mineral, berry and mint character on the nose grabs your attention. Full-bodied and very tannic, yet the tannins are refined and polished. Long finish. Clerc is the business in such a hard vintage; shows better now than Mouton.–J.S. • $NA • (5/31/1999) (BT) • **90-94**
Pauillac 1997: Very aromatic red. Interesting aromas of ripe berry and spices. Medium-bodied, with firm tannins and a slightly short finish. Best after 2000.–J.S. • $28 • (1/31/2000) • **88**
Pauillac 1996: Shows pretty floral and berry aromas and flavors. Medium-bodied, with firm tannins and a fruity, mineral aftertaste. A very good Clerc, but rather lean for this fine estate. Best after 2001.–J.S. • $31 • (1/31/1999) • **88**
Pauillac 1995 • $46 Ⓐ • (1/31/1998) SS • **95**
Pauillac 1994 • $22 Ⓐ • (1/31/1997) • **89**
Pauillac 1993 • $24 • (1/31/1996) • **89**
Pauillac 1992 • $22 • (4/15/1995) • **88**
Pauillac 1991 • $22 • (3/31/1994) • **85**
Pauillac 1990 • $60 Ⓐ • (3/31/1993) • **94**
Pauillac 1989: Big, young, chewy wine. Good dark-ruby color. Black cherry, green tobacco and mint aromas. Full-bodied and tannic, yet there's lovely mint and cherry character. Still tight and closed. Needs time to show what it's got. (1989 Bordeaux horizontal tasting). Best after 2002.–J.S. • $62 Ⓐ • (5/31/1999) • **96**
Pauillac 1988 • $42 Ⓐ • (4/30/1991) SS • **94**
Pauillac 1986 • $57 Ⓐ • (5/31/1989) • **97**
Pauillac 1985 • $67 Ⓐ • (5/15/1988) • **91**
Pauillac 1984 • $16 Ⓐ • (6/15/1987) • **78**
Pauillac 1983 • $35 Ⓐ • (10/15/1994) • **87**
Pauillac 1982: Fading a bit, but delicious. Dark ruby-garnet color. Wild raspberry and blackberry, with a hint of cedar. Medium-bodied, with medium, slightly drying tannins and a tobacco and berry finish. (1982 Bordeaux horizontal tasting). Drink now.–J.S. • $46 Ⓐ • (11/30/1998) • **86**
Pauillac 1981 • $27 • (10/15/1994) • **88**
Pauillac 1961 • $NA • (4/30/1996) • **76**

CLIMENS, CHATEAU

Barsac 1997: Masses going on in this glass. Superconcentrated, with aromas of honey, flowers, lemon curd and spice. Full-bodied and very thick, with lots of sweet fruit and a long, spicy finish. A beauty. Best after 2002.–J.S. • $70 • (1/31/2000) • **94**
Barsac 1996: A very young and very fine sticky wine, with intense botrytis spice aromas and hints of lemon rind and mineral. Full-bodied and medium sweet, with lively acidity and a long, sweet fruit and almond cake finish. Best after 2003.–J.S. • $75 • (1/01/2000) • **90**
Barsac 1991 • $NA • (4/15/1995) • **86**
Barsac 1990 • $61 Ⓐ • (4/15/1995) • **93**
Barsac 1989 • $56 Ⓐ • (4/15/1995) • **93**
Barsac 1988 • $71 Ⓐ • (4/15/1995) • **91**
Barsac 1986 • $73 Ⓐ • (4/15/1995) • **94**
Barsac 1983 • $64 Ⓐ • (1/31/1988) CS • **95**
Barsac 1947 • $572 Ⓐ • (5/31/1997) • **89**

CLINET, CHATEAU

Pomerol 1999: Intense aromas of smoke, meat, roasted coffee and ripe fruit. Medium- to full-bodied, with a solid core of velvety tannins and a long, fruity finish.–J.S. • $NA • (1/01/2000) (BT) • **85-89**
Pomerol 1998: Loads of coffee, toasted oak and berry aromas. Full-bodied and chewy, with chocolate and berry on the aftertaste, which needs a bit more ripe fruit. May move up a notch next year.–J.S. • $NA • (5/31/1999) (BT) • **85-89**
Pomerol 1997: Beautiful Clinet. Very pretty berry and spice aromas. Medium-bodied, with toast, cinnamon and berry character. Medium finish. Slightly hollow center palate. Best from 2001 through 2005.–J.S. • $71 • (1/31/2000) • **89**
Pomerol 1996: Black-colored, with masses of vanilla and coffee aromas. Medium-bodied, with some fruit (needs more center-palate) but very oaky and slightly dry on the finish. Drink now.–J.S. • $98 Ⓐ • (1/31/1999) • **85**
Pomerol 1995 • $124 Ⓐ • (1/31/1998) • **95**
Pomerol 1994 • $64 Ⓐ • (1/31/1997) HR • **93**
Pomerol 1993 • $49 Ⓐ • (1/31/1996) • **90**
Pomerol 1992 • $31 Ⓐ • (4/15/1995) • **85**
Pomerol 1991 • $32 • (3/31/1994) • **85**
Pomerol 1989: Starts well on the palate but slows down. Lovely aromas of cherry and dark chocolate and hints of earth and vanilla. Full-bodied and velvety, with medium fruit and a medium finish. Slightly one-dimensional.

Give it time. (1989 Bordeaux horizontal tasting). Best after 2003.–J.S. • $260 Ⓐ • (5/31/1999) • **89**

Pomerol 1988: Rather Port-like, with an impressive concentration of ripe fruit on the nose and palate. Full-bodied, with loads of chocolate and berry flavors and long, long velvety tannins on the finish. (1988 Bordeaux horizontal tasting). Best after 2002.–J.S. • $76 • (11/30/1998) • **93**

Pomerol 1986 • $66 Ⓐ • (9/15/1989) • **78**

Pomerol 1985 • $47 Ⓐ • (4/30/1988) • **91**

Pomerol 1982 • $61 Ⓐ • (5/15/1989) • **78**

Pomerol 1970 • $39 • (5/15/1993) • **84**

Pomerol 1961 • $33 • (4/30/1996) • **88**

CLOS BEAUREGARD

Pomerol 1993 • $20 • (7/31/1996) • **84**

CLOS CANON

St.-Emilion 1996: Lots of new wood here. Medium- to light-bodied, with some berry and cherry character, but slightly dry and woody on the finish. Drink now.–J.S. • $NA • (1/31/1999) • **80**

CLOS CHAUMONT

Premières Côtes de Bordeaux 1995 • $18 • (1/31/1998) • **87**

CLOS DAVIAUD, LE

Montagne-St.-Emilion 1996: A decent red but slightly rustic. Medium-bodied, with light tannins and a fruity, earthy aftertaste. Lacks concentration of fruit.–J.S. • $16 • (2/28/1999) • **79**

CLOS DE BERNOUX

Beaujolais-Villages Domaine de la Chapelle de Vatre 1997: Austere, with bitter notes, lean cherry flavors. A hint of spritz.–T.M. • $9 • (8/31/1998) • **76**

Brouilly 1995: This distinctive red offers very ripe kirsch, coffee and raisin flavors, with firm tannins and a thick palate unusual for the appellation. Drink now.–T.M. • $12 • (8/31/1998) • **82**

Fleurie Domaine du Grand Garant 1997: This simple red offers straightforward cherry and berry flavors, with light tannins and a candied note. Clean finish. Drink now.–T.M. • $13 • (8/31/1998) • **80**

Mâcon-Villages 1997 • $9 • (1/01/1998) • **82**

Morgon Côte du Py 1996: Still quite firm, this red offers plum, cedar and light earth flavors over hard tannins and sharp acidity. Should soften and bloom with food.–T.M. • $12 • (8/31/1998) • **83**

CLOS DE LA ROILETTE

Fleurie 1998: Bright and focused, this '98 Fleurie offers violet, cherry and a hint of earth in an elegant presentation. Juicy in texture, it ends on a firm note. Drink through 2001.–B.S. • $15 • (10/15/1999) • **84**

Fleurie 1997: Sharply focused berry and smoke flavors are lean and elegant in this fresh, firm red. Has the seductive quaffability of good Beaujolais, with a little added stuffing for interest. Try with rich fish dishes. Drink now.–T.M. • $15 • (5/15/1999) • **87**

Fleurie 1995 • $15 • (7/31/1997) • **86**

Fleurie Cuvée Tardive 1997: This expressive red leans towards the earthy, gamy side of Gamay, but it's ripe and rich and has enough berry and plum to balance, along with impressive structure and a long finish. A fine example of the traditional style. Drink now through 2003.–T.M. • $16 • (10/15/1999) • **87**

Fleurie Cuvée Tardive 1996: This rich red offers good concentration, with deep plum and black cherry flavors, round, ripe tannins and lively acidity. A solid Fleurie, with depth. Tasted twice, with consistent notes.–T.M. • $20 • (8/31/1998) • **87**

Fleurie Cuvée Tardive 1995 • $20 • (7/31/1997) • **88**

CLOS DE LA VIEILLE EGLISE

Pomerol 1997: Clean, with silky tannins and a fresh finish. Mint and berry aftertaste. Drink now.–J.S. • $42 • (6/15/2000) • **83**

CLOS DE L'ESCANDIL

Minervois 1995: Smooth and pleasant, with good concentration of plum, dark cherry and game flavors. Has a nice mature quality, with just a touch of earthiness, finishing with coffee and spice elements. Drink now.–K.M. • $18 • (12/31/1999) • **84**

Minervois 1994 • $16 • (3/31/1998) • **88**

CLOS DE L'ORATOIRE

St.-Emilion 1999: Intense aromas of chocolate, berry, licorice and spice. Medium- to full-bodied, with soft tannins and a syruplike consistency. Interesting, though it fades a bit on the finish.–J.S. • $NA • (1/01/2000) (BT) • **85-89**

St.-Emilion 1998: A firm '98, with lots of polished, cool tannins that are tightly knit, and a steely berry character. Medium- to full-bodied, with a long finish.–J.S. • $NA • (5/31/1999) (BT) • **90-94**

St.-Emilion 1997: Captivating blackberry, mineral and dark chocolate character. Medium- to full-bodied, with velvety tannins and a fruity finish. Lovely. Drink now through 2005.–J.S. • $28 • (1/31/2000) • **89**

St.-Emilion 1996: Clever winemaking here. Dark in color, with vanilla, berry and cream aromas. Medium-bodied, with fine tannins and a toasted oak and berry aftertaste. One wishes only for a bit more fruit center-palate. Best after 2000.–J.S. • $24 • (1/31/1999) • **87**

St.-Emilion 1995 • $30 • (1/31/1998) • **90**

St.-Emilion 1994 • $29 • (1/31/1997) • **90**

St.-Emilion 1993 • $25 • (1/31/1996) • **88**

St.-Emilion 1992 • $19 • (4/15/1995) • **81**

St.-Emilion 1990 • $28 • (3/31/1993) • **94**

St.-Emilion 1982 • $NA • (5/15/1989) • **78**

CLOS DE PAULILLES, LES

Banyuls 1996: A sweet red, with pretty flavors of orange, chocolate and spice and ripe plum notes. A good introduction to this unique fortified wine from France. Drink now through 2002.–K.M. • $15/375 ml. • (12/31/1998) • **85**

Banyuls 1995 • $13/375 ml. • (6/30/1997) • **85**

Banyuls 1989 • $17 • (12/15/1994) • **72**

Collioure 1996: Bright and lively, with juicy flavors of cherry and nutmeg and an almost floral aroma. Inviting and balanced, with spicy notes that linger on the finish. Drink now.–K.M. • $23 • (11/30/1998) • **83**

Collioure 1989 • $20 • (12/15/1994) • **80**

Collioure Rosé 1997: Juicy and fresh, with a fruity aroma and intense raspberry and dark cherry flavors. Delicious and easy to like. Drink now.–K.M. • $14 • (12/31/1998) • **85**

CLOS DE RAMAGE

Haut-Médoc 1996: Not a big wine but shows very good fruit character. Interesting aromas of berries and porcini mushrooms. Medium-bodied, with fine tannins and a succulent, fruit aftertaste. Drink now.–J.S. • $NA • (1/31/1999) • **86**

CLOS DE SARPE

St.-Emilion 1982: Big and youthful, yet still a little rough. Dark-colored, almost inky. Full-bodied, very concentrated, with tobacco, dried cherry, mineral and berry flavors and a long, velvety, tannic finish. (1982 Bordeaux horizontal tasting). Best after 2000.–J.S. • $NA • (11/30/1998) • **90**

CLOS DE VILLEMAJOU

Corbières 1994 • $8 • (4/30/1998) • **85**

Corbières 1988 • $6 • (4/30/1990) • **78**

CLOS DES JACOBINS

St.-Emilion 1998: Plenty of finesse, with fine tannins and a medium body of ripe fruit. Long, silky finish. Would rate outstanding with a bit more fruit in the midpalate.–J.S. • $NA • (5/31/1999) (BT) • **85-89**

St.-Emilion 1997: Some good fruit but slightly diluted, with soft tannins and a fruity finish. Drink now.–J.S. • $35 • (1/31/2000) • **81**

St.-Emilion 1996: A pretty St.-Emilion with aromas and flavors of berries and bark. Medium-bodied, with medium tannins and a rather short finish.

FRANCE

Lacks fruit at midpalate. Not quite as good as I remember from barrel. Drink now.–J.S. • $27 • (1/31/1999) • **87**

St.-Emilion 1995 • $30 • (1/31/1998) • **90**
St.-Emilion 1994 • $30 • (1/31/1997) • **87**
St.-Emilion 1993 • $25 • (1/31/1996) • **85**
St.-Emilion 1991 • $20 • (3/31/1994) • **77**
St.-Emilion 1990 • $35 • (3/31/1993) • **77**
St.-Emilion 1989: Very impressive for this estate, offering lovely earth, tobacco and ripe fruit character. Full-bodied, with firm tannins and a superrich, chewy finish.—1989 Bordeaux horizontal. Drink now.–J.S. • $34 Ⓐ • (5/31/1999) • **90**
St.-Emilion 1988 • $33 Ⓐ • (4/15/1991) HR • **90**
St.-Emilion 1987 • $24 • (5/15/1990) • **73**
St.-Emilion 1986 • $34 • (6/30/1989) • **94**
St.-Emilion 1985 • $22 Ⓐ • (9/30/1988) • **89**
St.-Emilion 1984 • $20 • (5/15/1987) • **83**
St.-Emilion 1982: I have always enjoyed this racy red, with its youthful ruby color. Very fresh, with berry, mineral and dried tobacco. Full-bodied, with intense chocolate and berry, firm tannins and a long, silky finish. (1982 Bordeaux horizontal tasting). Drink now.–J.S. • $NA • (11/30/1998) • **91**
St.-Emilion 1981 • $16 • (6/01/1984) • **81**

CLOS DES PAPES

Châteauneuf-du-Pape 1997: A bit advanced for a young wine, with mature notes of game, mushroom and toasted, cooked plum. Slightly tough finish.–P.M. • $29 • (8/31/1999) • **79**
Châteauneuf-du-Pape 1996: Ripe flavors of black cherry and blackberry give this wine a lively character, and the firm structure supports the fruit without overwhelming it. Notes of herb and tobacco emerge on the finish. Tasted twice, with consistent notes. Drink now through 2003.–T.M. • $26 • (11/15/1998) • **87**
Châteauneuf-du-Pape 1995: This unique, aromatic *terroir* wine shows plenty of earth, mineral, lead pencil, leather, plum and currant complexity, all presented in a fairly opulent package. Ripe but firm tannins and a long finish. Drink through 2005.–P.M. • $25 • (9/30/1998) • **88**
Châteauneuf-du-Pape 1990 • $30 • (4/15/1993) • **85**
Châteauneuf-du-Pape 1989 • $20 • (10/15/1991) • **86**
Châteauneuf-du-Pape 1988 • $19 • (10/15/1991) • **86**
Châteauneuf-du-Pape 1986 • $18 • (10/15/1991) • **74**
Châteauneuf-du-Pape 1985 • $NA • (10/15/1991) • **89**
Châteauneuf-du-Pape 1983 • $NA • (10/15/1991) • **88**
Châteauneuf-du-Pape 1981 • $30 • (10/15/1991) • **87**

CLOS DU CHENE, LE

Cahors 1994 • $9 • (1/31/1997) • **84**

CLOS DU CLOCHER

Pomerol 1998: Very subtle, very elegant. Lovely aromas of licorice and spice. Full- to medium-bodied, with superfine tannins, building on the finish. Fine Pomerol.–J.S. • $NA • (5/31/1999) (BT) • **90-94**
Pomerol 1997: Attractive plum and berry character, but a bit austere. Medium-bodied, with medium tannins, a lean finish. Tad too much wood? Drink now.–J.S. • $NA • (1/31/2000) • **84**
Pomerol 1996: Berry and dried herbs on the nose. Medium- to light-bodied, with berry, tobacco flavors and a light, fruity aftertaste. Drink now.–J.S. • $NA • (1/31/1999) • **82**
Pomerol 1994 • $29 • (12/15/1995) • **84**
Pomerol 1993 • $28 • (12/15/1995) • **86**
Pomerol 1985 • $20 • (2/29/1988) • **88**
Pomerol 1982 • $33 • (5/15/1989) • **83**

CLOS DU MARQUIS

St.-Julien 1996: Thoroughly well-crafted red. Aromas of berries and asphalt with hints of mint. Medium-bodied, with a complement of polished, silky tannins and a long, caressing finish. Second label of Château Léoville Las Cases. Drink through 2005.–J.S. • $27 Ⓐ • (1/01/1999) • **90**
St.-Julien 1995: The essence of wild strawberries and blackberries on the nose. Medium-bodied, with medium tannins and a silky finish. Elegant beauty. Drink through 2005.–J.S. • $27 Ⓐ • (9/15/1998) • **90**
St.-Julien 1988 • $31 Ⓐ • (10/31/1991) • **80**
St.-Julien 1987 • $12 • (5/15/1990) • **79**
St.-Julien 1986 • $53 Ⓐ • (9/15/1989) • **84**
St.-Julien 1985 • $40 Ⓐ • (9/30/1988) • **84**
St.-Julien 1982: Ripe and delicious, with loads of fruit. Dark ruby in color, with a hint of garnet. Full-bodied and balanced, with velvety, smooth tannins, lovely cherry, berry and floral aromas and a long, ripe fruit finish. (1982 Bordeaux horizontal tasting). Drink now.–J.S. • $NA • (11/30/1998) • **89**

CLOS DU MONT-OLIVET

Châteauneuf-du-Pape 1990 • $53 Ⓐ • (4/15/1993) • **83**
Châteauneuf-du-Pape 1989 • $29 • (10/15/1991) • **85**
Châteauneuf-du-Pape 1988 • $19 • (10/15/1991) • **88**
Châteauneuf-du-Pape 1986 • $17 • (10/15/1991) • **87**
Châteauneuf-du-Pape 1985 • $31 Ⓐ • (10/15/1991) • **92**
Châteauneuf-du-Pape 1983 • $28 • (10/15/1991) • **86**
Châteauneuf-du-Pape 1982 • $12 • (3/16/1986) • **91**
Châteauneuf-du-Pape 1981 • $30 • (10/15/1991) • **87**

CLOS DU PAVILLON, DOMAINE DU

Aloxe-Corton Clos des Maréchaudes 1997: Very soft and a bit unfocused, showing red berry character and chewy tannins.–P.M. • $28 • (9/30/1999) • **79**
Aloxe-Corton Clos des Maréchaudes 1996: Aromatic and spicy, this displays currant and cherry aromas and flavors, modest depth and stiff tannins. Balanced on the alcoholic side. A monopole of Domaine du Pavillon. Best from 2000.–B.S. • $42 • (9/30/1998) • **84**
Aloxe-Corton Les Fournières 1995 • $34 • (11/15/1997) • **79**
Beaune Les Epenottes 1995 • $24 • (11/15/1997) • **80**
Corton Clos des Maréchaudes 1996: Fruity and crisp, with medium-intense red berry flavors and fairly rough tannins. Short finish.–P.M. • $70 • (5/15/1999) • **76**
Pommard 1997: Very ripe, with plum and cherry notes. Medium-bodied, with soft tannins. Drink now through 2002.–P.M. • $26 • (9/30/1999) • **83**
Pommard 1996: This full-bodied Pommard stands out for its zesty berry character. Delicate, it also shows good length and intensity of flavor. Supple tannins blend nicely with the fresh-tasting acidity, and there's wet earth, blackberry, raspberry, blueberry and cranberry notes. Long, pure finish. Best After 2003.–P.M. • $36 • (9/30/1998) • **87**
Pommard 1995 • $32 • (11/15/1997) • **80**
Pommard 1994 • $36 • (11/15/1996) • **75**

CLOS FOURTET

St.-Emilion 1999: Wonderful aromas of mineral, berry and plum. Medium-bodied, with silky tannins, but falls slightly short on the finish.–J.S. • $NA • (1/01/2000) (BT) • **85-89**
St.-Emilion 1998: Wonderful ripe fruit in this wine, with masses of berry, cherry and tobacco character. Full-bodied and tannic. Massive. Almost classic.–J.S. • $NA • (5/31/1999) (BT) • **90-94**
St.-Emilion 1997: Pretty blackberry and cherry aromas. Medium-bodied, with a solid core of fruit and silky tannins. Clos Fourtet did well here. Lovely now. Best after 2001.–J.S. • $65 • (1/31/2000) • **88**
St.-Emilion 1996: Lovely aromas of berries, chocolate and currants. Medium-bodied, with velvety tannins and a medium, fruity aftertaste. Not as good as from barrel, but delicious all the same. Best after 2000.–J.S. • $31 Ⓐ • (1/31/1999) • **87**
St.-Emilion 1995 • $24 Ⓐ • (1/31/1998) • **90**
St.-Emilion 1994 • $35 • (1/31/1997) • **86**
St.-Emilion 1993 • $33 Ⓐ • (1/31/1996) • **82**
St.-Emilion 1992 • $17 • (4/15/1995) • **78**
St.-Emilion 1990 • $43 Ⓐ • (3/31/1993) • **90**
St.-Emilion 1989: Very refined. Lovely perfumed wine of floral, berry and strawberry aromas. Full-bodied, with velvety tannins and a long, silky aftertaste. Why wait? (1989 Bordeaux horizontal tasting). Best after 2004.–J.S. • $62 Ⓐ • (5/31/1999) • **90**
St.-Emilion 1988 • $27 • (10/31/1991) • **86**
St.-Emilion 1986 • $41 • (6/30/1989) • **80**

Key: SS—Spectator Selection. CS—Cellar Selection. HR—Highly Recommended. $NA—Price not available. (BT)—Barrel tasting. Ⓐ—Auction Price.
For a key to the tasters' initials, see "How to Use These Listings."
Dates in parentheses represent the issues in which the ratings were published.

St.-Emilion 1982: Medium-red in color, with a garnet hue. Cherry, fresh mushroom and leaves on the nose. Medium-bodied. Very earthy, slightly funky and overripe. (1982 Bordeaux horizontal tasting).–J.S. • $NA • (11/30/1998) • **84**
St.-Emilion 1961 • $45 • (4/30/1996) • **84**

CLOS FRANTIN, DOMAINE DU

Chambertin 1989 • $73 • (1/31/1992) • **88**
Chambertin 1986 • $63 • (2/28/1989) • **90**
Clos de Vougeot 1996: Very good, even if the style is a bit forced, with candied cherry aromas and flavors and firm tannic support but not the richness and concentration to balance. Best from 2001 through 2006.–B.S. • $65 • (9/30/1998) • **88**
Clos de Vougeot 1995 • $55 • (11/15/1997) • **84**
Clos de Vougeot 1994 • $50 • (11/15/1996) • **73**
Clos de Vougeot 1992 • $NA • (12/15/1994) • **77**
Clos de Vougeot 1989 • $56 • (1/31/1992) • **91**
Clos de Vougeot 1987 • $56 • (7/15/1990) • **85**
Clos de Vougeot 1986 • $37 • (11/30/1988) • **87**
Corton 1990 • $53 • (11/30/1992) • **81**
Corton 1989 • $58 • (1/31/1992) • **86**
Echézeaux 1996: Supple wine, so fat it's approachable upon release. Offers a round, smooth tannin structure, ripe fruit and excellent complexity of toasted oak, wet earth, plum and red- and blackberry notes. Turns silky on the finish. Drink now through 2005.–P.M. • $63 • (9/30/1998) • **88**
Echézeaux 1995 • $55 • (11/15/1997) • **80**
Echézeaux 1994 • $50 • (11/15/1996) • **81**
Echézeaux 1993 • $NA • (11/15/1995) • **85**
Echézeaux 1992 • $NA • (12/15/1994) • **87**
Echézeaux 1990 • $42 • (11/30/1992) • **88**
Echézeaux 1989 • $45 • (1/31/1992) • **93**
Echézeaux 1986 • $30 • (11/30/1988) • **90**
Echézeaux 1985 • $37 • (9/15/1987) • **96**
Gevrey-Chambertin 1996: Decent fruit in this medium-bodied Pinot, showing cherry, strawberry and earth character. Turns dry and a bit hot on the finish.–P.M. • $36 • (9/30/1998) • **79**
Gevrey-Chambertin 1995 • $30 • (11/15/1997) • **79**
Gevrey-Chambertin 1992 • $NA • (12/15/1994) • **78**
Gevrey-Chambertin 1990 • $28 • (11/30/1992) • **84**
Gevrey-Chambertin 1989 • $29 • (1/31/1992) • **84**
Gevrey-Chambertin 1988 • $37 • (7/15/1990) • **87**
Gevrey-Chambertin 1987 • $20 • (3/31/1990) • **82**
Grands Echézeaux 1997: Plum jam aromas and flavors dissipate rapidly, giving way to light tannins and a vanilla aftertaste. Not much depth, but pleasant. Drink now through 2001.–B.S. • $66 • (9/30/1999) • **80**
Grands Echézeaux 1995 • $65 • (11/15/1997) • **78**
Grands Echézeaux 1994 • $60 • (11/15/1996) • **79**
Grands Echézeaux 1993 • $60 • (11/15/1995) • **88**
Grands Echézeaux 1989 • $56 • (1/31/1992) • **90**
Grands Echézeaux 1987 • $56 • (7/15/1990) • **86**
Grands Echézeaux 1986 • $60 • (2/28/1989) • **87**
Nuits-St.-Georges 1990 • $29 • (11/30/1992) • **81**
Nuits-St.-Georges 1989 • $29 • (2/29/1992) • **91**
Nuits-St.-Georges 1986 • $20 • (11/15/1988) • **82**
Nuits-St.-Georges 1983 • $18 • (2/01/1986) • **83**
Richebourg 1989 • $117 • (1/31/1992) • **95**
Richebourg 1986 • $100 • (8/31/1989) • **88**
Vosne-Romanée 1996: Some delicate fruit in this medium-bodied, ripe-tasting wine. Supple tannic structure and all its raspberry, black cherry and blackberry flavors make it pretty upon release. Drink now through 2003.–P.M. • $38 • (9/30/1998) • **85**
Vosne-Romanée 1990 • $28 • (11/30/1992) • **78**
Vosne-Romanée 1989 • $30 • (1/31/1992) • **89**
Vosne-Romanée 1986 • $19 • (12/31/1988) • **80**
Vosne-Romanée 1985 • $29 • (10/15/1987) • **91**
Vosne-Romanée Les Malconsorts 1997: Odd on the nose and a bit spirity, this '97 red is devoid of fruit, turning dry and astringent on the finish.–B.S. • $38 • (9/30/1999) • **78**
Vosne-Romanée Les Malconsorts 1995 • $43 • (11/15/1997) • **75**
Vosne-Romanée Les Malconsorts 1993 • $50 • (11/15/1995) • **87**
Vosne-Romanée Les Malconsorts 1992 • $NA • (12/15/1994) • **79**
Vosne-Romanée Les Malconsorts 1990 • $37 • (11/30/1992) • **86**
Vosne-Romanée Les Malconsorts 1987 • $30 • (7/15/1990) • **88**
Vosne-Romanée Les Malconsorts 1986 • $35 • (10/31/1988) • **79**
Vosne-Romanée Les Malconsorts 1985 • $55 • (9/30/1987) • **95**

CLOS HAUT-PEYRAGUEY, CHATEAU

Sauternes 1998: Very clean and fresh, with lemon peel and honey aromas and flavors. Medium-bodied, medium sweet, with a medium finish.–J.S. • $NA • (1/01/1999) (BT) • **85-89**
Sauternes 1997: Lovely aromas of vanilla, cream and almond, with a hint of tropical fruit. Full-bodied and very sweet, yet ripe and balanced, with a lovely, ripe fruit aftertaste. Best after 2001.–J.S. • $NA • (1/31/2000) • **91**
Sauternes 1990 • $NA • (4/15/1995) • **90**
Sauternes 1989 • $30 • (4/15/1995) • **86**
Sauternes 1988 • $26 • (4/15/1995) • **88**
Sauternes 1987 • $21 • (6/15/1990) • **83**
Sauternes 1986 • $23 • (4/15/1995) • **89**

CLOS L'ABEILLEY

Sauternes 1990 • $NA • (4/15/1995) • **84**

CLOS LA COUTALE

Cahors 1996: Lean and austere, this red has a core of pretty cherry flavor and hints of herbs and minerals that add complexity. It's clean and fresh but a bit hard, and needs food for balance. Drink now through 2002.–T.M. • $13 • (12/15/1998) • **83**
Cahors 1995 • $13 • (5/15/1998) • **88**

CLOS LA FLEUR FIGEAC

St.-Emilion 1994 • $18 • (10/15/1997) • **86**

CLOS LARCIS

St.-Emilion 1995 • $15 • (1/31/1998) • **82**
St.-Emilion 1994 • $14 • (1/31/1997) • **84**
St.-Emilion 1993 • $14 • (1/31/1996) • **79**
St.-Emilion 1992 • $12 • (4/15/1995) • **83**
St.-Emilion 1991 • $12 • (3/31/1994) • **78**
St.-Emilion 1990 • $25 • (3/31/1993) • **85**
St.-Emilion 1989: Very good and pleasant '89 St.-Emilion, with chocolate, berry and cherry character throughout. Medium-bodied, adding subtle tannins and a fresh finish. (1989 Bordeaux horizontal tasting). Drink now.–J.S. • $NA • (5/31/1999) • **88**

CLOS L'EGLISE

Côtes de Castillon 1999: Starts with a bang but the light finish is short. Medium-bodied, with lots of plum and violet aromas and fine tannins.–J.S. • $NA • (1/01/2000) (BT) • **80-84**

CLOS L'EGLISE

Pomerol 1998: Big and chewy, with masses of tannins and ripe fruit. Full-bodied, with a long, long finish.–J.S. • $NA • (5/31/1999) (BT) • **90-94**
Pomerol 1997: Plenty of coffee, tobacco and cherry character. Medium-bodied, with medium tannins and a fresh finish. Hollow center palate. Slightly overdone. Drink now through 2002.–J.S. • $64 • (1/31/2000) • **85**
Pomerol 1995 • $30 • (1/31/1998) • **91**
Pomerol 1994 • $25 • (1/31/1997) • **85**
Pomerol 1993 • $25 • (1/31/1996) • **85**
Pomerol 1988 • $26 • (6/30/1991) • **83**
Pomerol 1986 • $33 • (2/15/1990) • **86**
Pomerol 1982 • $29 • (5/15/1989) • **88**
Pomerol 1947 • $NA • (5/31/1997) • **88**
Pomerol 1945 • $230 • (11/30/1995) • **84**

CLOS MARSALETTE

Pessac-Léognan 1998: A bit simple, but shows good mineral and berry character. Medium-bodied, with fine tannins. Medium finish.–J.S. • $NA • (5/31/1999) (BT) • **85-89**

CLOS MARSALETTE

Pessac-Léognan 1996: A bit rustic, but some good fruit character. Aromas of blackberry and cèpe mushroom. Medium-bodied, with medium tannins and a wet earth and berry aftertaste. Slightly diluted. Drink now.–J.S. • $22 • (1/31/1999) • **82**

Pessac-Léognan 1995 • $20 • (1/31/1998) • **88**

Pessac-Léognan 1994 • $18 • (1/31/1997) • **85**

Pessac-Léognan 1993 • $NA • (1/31/1996) • **84**

Pessac-Léognan White 1996: Slightly clumsy. Lovely aromas of clove, honey, vanilla and lemon but the medium-bodied palate with medium acidity and attractive toasted oak is slightly out of sync with the nose. Drink now.–J.S. • $NA • (1/01/1999) • **85**

CLOS NOIR

Clos de la Roche 1992 • $NA • (12/15/1994) • **86**

Côte de Nuits-Villages Préau 1994 • $NA • (11/15/1996) • **74**

Côte de Nuits-Villages Préau 1992 • $NA • (12/15/1994) • **79**

Fixin 1994 • $NA • (11/15/1996) • **77**

Gevrey-Chambertin Les Jeunes Rois 1992 • $NA • (12/15/1994) • **84**

Morey-St.-Denis 1992 • $NA • (12/15/1994) • **85**

CLOS PLINCE

Pomerol 1998: Subtle aromas of mineral, berry and oak. Medium-bodied, with full tannins and a mouthpuckering finish. Needs a bit more fruit to score outstanding.–J.S. • $NA • (5/31/1999) (BT) • **85-89**

Pomerol 1997: Slightly light, but some good berry, tobacco character. Medium- to light-bodied, with light tannins and a fresh finish. Drink now.–J.S. • $NA • (1/31/2000) • **83**

CLOS RENE

Pomerol 1998: Compacted and tight young wine, with floral, berry and cherry character. Medium- to full-bodied, with well-knit tannins and a long finish.–J.S. • $NA • (5/31/1999) (BT) • **90-94**

Pomerol 1997: A ready red with lovely chocolate and berry aromas and flavors. Medium-bodied, with soft tannins and a fresh and fruity finish. Drink now through 2003.–J.S. • $34 • (1/31/2000) • **85**

Pomerol 1996: Attractive chocolate, berry character, a light body and a fresh finish. Needs a bit more fruit, but it's not overdone. Drink now.–J.S. • $NA • (1/31/1999) • **84**

Pomerol 1995: Soft and velvety, with lots of black olive and tobacco character. Medium- to full-bodied, with medium tannins and finish. Drink now or hold.–J.S. • $20 Ⓐ • (9/15/1998) • **87**

Pomerol 1988 • $24 • (4/30/1991) • **88**

Pomerol 1985 • $17 • (3/15/1988) • **92**

Pomerol 1982 • $40 Ⓐ • (5/15/1989) • **87**

Pomerol 1959 • $50 • (10/15/1990) • **88**

Pomerol 1945 • $175 • (11/30/1995) • **88**

CLOS ST.-MARTIN

St.-Emilion 1999: Serious concentration of fruit and velvety tannins for the vintage, with a large dose of new wood. Full-bodied, velvety and long in the mouth. Beautiful.–J.S. • $NA • (1/01/2000) (BT) • **90-94**

St.-Emilion 1998: Lovely blackberry aromas with hints of licorice. Full-bodied, thick and rich, with masses of fruit and tannins. Port-like. Really impressive. Watch this tiny estate in the future.–J.S. • $NA • (5/31/1999) (BT) • **90-94**

St.-Emilion 1997: A wine with wonderful smoky, berry, meaty aromas. Medium-bodied, with lovely sweet fruit and a medium finish. Delicious. Drink now through 2004.–J.S. • $NA • (1/31/2000) • **88**

St.-Emilion 1996: Really grapey, with mineral and mint aromas. Medium-bodied, with firm tannins and a slightly hollow midpalate; well crafted, but slightly diluted. Drink now.–J.S. • $NA • (1/31/1999) • **85**

Key: SS—Spectator Selection. CS—Cellar Selection. HR—Highly Recommended. $NA—Price not available. (BT)—Barrel tasting. Ⓐ—Auction Price.
For a key to the tasters' initials, see "How to Use These Listings."
Dates in parentheses represent the issues in which the ratings were published.

CLOSEL, DOMAINE DU

Savennières Clos du Papillon Cuvée Spéciale 1996: This beautifully balanced white is clean, pure, refreshing and deep, with fresh flavors of apple, peach and melon that linger on the finish and bring you back for another sip. Drink now through 2005.–T.M. • $19 • (2/29/2000) • **90**

CLOSERIE DE CAMENSAC, LA

Haut-Médoc 1996: Pretty berry, tobacco and meat aromas. Medium- to full-bodied, with polished tannins and a berry-flavored, though slightly diluted, finish. Best after 2000.–J.S. • $NA • (1/31/1999) • **84**

CLOSERIE DE MALESCASSE, LA

Haut-Médoc 1996: A grapey wine with floral aromas and flavors. Medium-bodied, with firm tannins but a slightly short finish. Needs more ripe fruit. Second label of Château Malescasse. Best after 2000.–J.S. • $NA • (1/31/1999) • **80**

CLOTTE, CHATEAU LA

St.-Emilion 1998: A berry, floral, leafy character marks this young red. Medium-bodied, with medium tannins and a short finish.–J.S. • $NA • (5/31/1999) (BT) • **80-84**

St.-Emilion 1996: Some blackberry and earthy character, but really diluted on the palate. Light-bodied, with a watery aftertaste.–J.S. • $NA • (2/28/1999) • **77**

St.-Emilion 1995: Delicate and delicious St.-Emilion. Some good blackberry and earth with hints of sand. Medium-bodied, with medium to light tannins and a medium finish. Drink now through 2005.–J.S. • $NA • (9/15/1998) • **86**

St.-Emilion 1985 • $27 • (5/15/1988) • **87**

St.-Emilion 1959 • $NA • (10/15/1990) • **86**

CLUSEL ROCH

Côte-Rôtie 1996: A Middle-of-the-road Northern Rhône, with light fruit, black pepper and smoke character. A bit watery and herbaceous on the finish.–P.M. • $30 • (9/15/1999) • **77**

Côte-Rôtie 1995: Beautiful right after you pour it, but turns a bit dry and herbal in contact with air. Offers wild berry, blackberry and wet earth notes, but lacks length. Best after 2002.–P.M. • $33 • (9/15/1998) • **80**

Côte-Rôtie 1994 • $32 • (10/15/1997) • **89**

Côte-Rôtie 1993 • $32 • (4/30/1997) • **88**

Côte-Rôtie 1991 • $40 • (5/31/1994) • **85**

Côte-Rôtie Les Grandes Places 1994 • $NA • (10/15/1997) • **89**

Côte-Rôtie Les Grandes Places 1991 • $50 • (5/31/1994) • **90**

Côte-Rôtie Les Grandes Places 1990 • $50 • (5/31/1994) • **91**

COCHE-DURY, J.-F.

Bourgogne White 1997: Very good, but a bit easy and straightforward, showing clean vanilla, pear tart, flour and green apple character. A bit tight on the almost tannic finish. Best from 2003 through 2017.–P.M. • $34 • (9/30/1999) • **88**

Corton-Charlemagne 1997: A beautifully put together white Burgundy. Rich and silky, with pear, butter and toasted coconut flavors. Wonderful intensity and grip on the clean finish. Drink now through 2007.–P.M. • $205 • (9/30/1999) • **92**

Corton-Charlemagne 1996: The cult wine per excellence hits another home run. Ripe but racy, with a lush, opulent and fat mouthfeel. Very attractive thanks to its richness, this vibrates on the palate as it powers its way to a toasty, ripe, velvety finish that will need years to show it all. Best from 2006 through 2026.–P.M. • $1,342 Ⓐ • (5/31/1999) • **99**

Corton-Charlemagne 1995 • $175 • (5/31/1998) • **98**

Meursault 1997: A bit square and angular, showing medium intensity on a slightly toasted frame. Could use a bit more ripe fruit, but it's clean. Drink now through 2005.–P.M. • $98 Ⓐ • (9/30/1999) • **85**

Meursault 1996: Very showy and intensely oaky, with lemon and honey notes. Medium-bodied, turning a bit astringent as the wood tannins burn on the palate. Best from 2004 through 2010.–P.M. • $68 • (5/31/1999) • **87**

Meursault Caillerets 1996: Quite oaky, but with a rich, ripe, sexy body—there's plenty to chew on. Ripe, tropical and lemony, with loads of oaky spice and a chewy, sweet-tasting finish. Best from 2004 through 2008.–P.M. • $92 • (5/31/1999) • **93**

Meursault Les Perrières 1996: A fantastic, traditional white Burgundy, with a slightly earthy note, fresh lemon and marvelous pear, tropical and honey. Smartly oaked, delivering remarkable finesse on the silky, super-minerally, thick-as-cream finish. Best from 2006 through 2016.–P.M. • $138 • (5/31/1999) • **98**

Meursault Les Perrières 1995 • $130 • (5/31/1998) • **97**

Meursault Les Rougeots 1997: Very attractive oak treatment, showing toasted, spicy notes. Silky on the midpalate, but lacking in ripe fruit that would give it the balance of an outstanding wine. Green finish. Drink now through 2003.–P.M. • $85 • (9/30/1999) • **87**

Meursault Les Rougeots 1996: Smoky, toasted, malic-lactic notes play elegantly in this rich, flavorful, buttery beauty. Full-bodied, with delicious roasted hazelnut, pear, lemon and cream and a sublime, supple, clean finish. Drink now through 2010.–P.M. • $158 Ⓐ • (5/31/1999) • **95**

Meursault Les Rougeots 1995 • $165 Ⓐ • (5/31/1998) • **93**

Meursault Red 1987 • $30 • (2/28/1990) • **80**

Puligny-Montrachet Les Enseignères 1997: A muscular, superclean, sleek, ripe and racy white, showing great mineral complexity. Cellar this *vin de meditation* ("meditation wine") and then taste the silky beauty that should emerge from the low yields. Best after 2005.–P.M. • $82 • (9/30/1999) • **95**

Puligny-Montrachet Les Enseignères 1996: This big wine tastes of malic-lactic, butter, pear and apple pie flavors, but it's quite oaky and chewy. Wonderfully thick on the midpalate, with a lovely lemony acidity, it has a clean, long, beautifully fruit-intensive finish. Best from 2006 through 2026.–P.M. • $82 • (5/31/1999) • **95**

COL DES VENTS

Corbières 1995 • $8 • (4/30/1998) • **77**

COLBOIS, DANIEL

Chablis 1995 • $20 • (6/15/1997) • **84**

COLIN, MARC

Bâtard-Montrachet 1998: Subtle white Burgundy. Medium-bodied and not particularly intense, but it shows good balance of toasted bread, spice and fairly ripe fruit, with a succulent lemony character as well. All comes together smartly on the rather refined finish. Drink now through 2003.–P.M. • $150 • (5/31/2000) • **87**

Bâtard-Montrachet 1996 • $130 • (5/31/1998) • **97**

Chassagne-Montrachet 1997: Pear aromas and flavors are okay, but this light-bodied white is a bit hollow on the distinctly toasted midpalate.–P.M. • $45 • (5/31/1999) • **79**

Chassagne-Montrachet Les Caillerets 1998: Well made. Distinctive in its butterscotch, vanilla and butter character, it impresses with its full body and good concentration of mineral and fruit at midpalate. Balanced and supple on the delicious finish. Drink now through 2010.–P.M. • $50 • (5/31/2000) • **89**

Chassagne-Montrachet Les Caillerets 1997: Butterscotch and popcornlike flavors accent this crisp, medium-bodied, vibrant Chassagne. Delivers green apple, chalk and lemon notes and a tart finish. Drink now through 2002.–P.M. • $55 • (5/31/1999) • **82**

Chassagne-Montrachet Les Caillerets 1996 • $50 • (5/31/1998) • **91**

Chassagne-Montrachet Les Champs-Gains 1998: Fruit and balanced oak dosage along with a fresh, vibrant midpalate make for a succulent, medium-bodied white Burgundy. Not overly complex, but it should improve with short-term cellaring. Drink now through 2005.–P.M. • $45 • (5/31/2000) • **84**

Chassagne-Montrachet Les Champs-Gains 1997: Delightful, showing pear, tropical and toasted walnut notes, with a ripe mouthfeel and an elegant, lingering finish. Drink now through 2003.–P.M. • $50 • (5/31/1999) • **87**

Chassagne-Montrachet Les Champs-Gains 1996: A bit odd, with a slightly musty aroma, turning dry on the palate. Tasted twice, with consistent notes.–P.M. • $50 • (8/31/1998) • **65**

Chassagne-Montrachet Les Champs-Gains 1995 • $50 • (5/31/1997) • **93**

Chassagne-Montrachet Les Encégnières 1998: Rather neutral Chardonnay for now, built in a crisp and citrusy style, revealing slowly its mineral, ripe fruit character. Give it a bit of time in the cellar and it should open up. Best from 2002 through 2006.–P.M. • $40 • (5/31/2000) • **84**

Chassagne-Montrachet Les Encégnières 1996: Gorgeous, ripe, full-bodied, balanced white Burgundy. Has an earthy, *terroir* character and supple, creamlike texture, all of which make for a supervelvety, superseductive experience. Burgundy at its most typical. Tasted twice, with consistent notes. Drink now through 2010.–P.M. • $45 • (8/31/1998) • **92**

Chassagne-Montrachet Les Vide-Bourses 1998: Loads of personality. Full-bodied with ripe and rich fruit, it offers wet earth, wood smoke and mineral notes; you name it, it has what it takes to hold the attention of one's senses. The deft oak treatment and intriguing soil components make for a treat. Best from 2002 through 2008.–P.M. • $55 • (5/31/2000) • **90**

Chassagne-Montrachet Les Vide-Bourses 1997: This beautiful, full-bodied Chassagne is smooth and ripe, showing a dried herb, olive and eucalyptus complexity, with a generous mouthfeel and lovely, opulent harmony. Smoky, clean, pure finish. Drink now through 2002.–P.M. • $55 • (5/31/1999) • **90**

Chassagne-Montrachet Les Vide-Bourses 1996 • $45 • (5/31/1998) • **80**

Montrachet 1998: Thick, dense, rich, ripe—but also elegant and fresh. Silky and full-bodied, with wet earth, honey, subtle toasted oak notes and plenty of fruit complexity, this wine finishes long and manages to remain elegant. Another great one from the Montrachet master. Drink now through 2010.–P.M. • $325 • (5/31/2000) • **95**

Montrachet 1997: Montrachet master Marc Colin scores again with this supersilky, rich, fat, opulent '97 white Burgundy. It's refined, powering away with very pretty fruit, mineral and acidity, showing pineapple, pear, honey and subtle toasty, spicy oak notes. Drink now through 2012.–P.M. • $325 • (5/31/1999) • **96**

Montrachet 1996 • $250 • (5/31/1998) • **99**

Montrachet 1995 • $273 Ⓐ • (5/31/1997) • **98**

Puligny-Montrachet Le Trézin 1998: Impressive structure and ripeness in this woody wine. Clean, pure and elegant, full-bodied and rich, it delivers a lasting impression on the palate, with much fruit, wet stone, mineral character. Balanced finish. Best from 2005 through 2010.–P.M. • $45 • (5/31/2000) • **94**

Puligny-Montrachet Le Trézin 1997: Showy, with lots of toast and spicy oak aromas and flavors, but it's balanced thanks to a good center packed with lemon and classy fruit. Full-bodied, opulent and long on the finish. Best from 2002 through 2010.–P.M. • $45 • (5/31/1999) • **89**

Puligny-Montrachet Le Trézin 1996 • $40 • (5/31/1998) • **87**

Puligny-Montrachet Les Garennes 1998: Beautiful white Burgundy. Aromatically expressive, with subtle smoke, toasted bread, grilled meat, and honey notes that follow through on an impeccably balanced midpalate. Rich and concentrated but not heavy, this full-bodied white sings on the vibrant finish. Drink now through 2010.–P.M. • $60 • (5/31/2000) • **93**

Puligny-Montrachet Les Garennes 1997: Well made. Earthy but ripe, with sweet-tasting honeyed fruit and some flinty, smoky, minerally complexity. This can only be white Burgundy, and a very interesting one to boot, with a long finish. Much better than previously reviewed. Drink now through 2007.–P.M. • $55 • (9/30/1999) • **93**

Puligny-Montrachet Les Garennes 1996 • $50 • (5/31/1998) • **90**

Puligny-Montrachet Les Garennes 1995 • $50 • (5/31/1997) • **91**

St.-Aubin En Montceau 1998: Complex and stunning. Stands out with all that smoke, matchstick, fire wood and charcoal character. Of medium to full body, offering a succulent mouthful of ripe, fresh fruit and a flavor like honey on toasted bread. Great balance. Worth the hunt. Drink now through 2007.–P.M. • $33 • (5/31/2000) • **92**

St.-Aubin En Remilly 1998: A *terroir* wine, this offers intriguing wet earth, stone, matchstick, smoke and some earthy notes. It's full in body and rich in texture, with honey, pear, melon, and the smooth and graceful finish is satisfying. Drink now through 2005.–P.M. • $33 • (5/31/2000) HR • **92**

St.-Aubin En Remilly 1997: Fairly ripe, with pear, mineral, smoke and dried herb complexity unfolding beautifully, this medium-bodied, intense '97 holds its balanced course through a long-lasting finish. Drink now through 2005.–P.M. • $35 • (5/31/1999) • **90**

St.-Aubin En Remilly 1996 • $35 • (5/31/1998) • **90**

St.-Aubin En Remilly 1995 • $34 • (5/31/1997) • **87**

St.-Aubin La Chatenière 1998: Delightful. Thick yet refined, with a smooth texture, full body, rich fruit and spicy, smoky, minerally components that are the icing on the cake. Drink now through 2005.–P.M. • $33 • (5/31/2000) • **91**

St.-Aubin La Chatenière 1997: Ripe, sweet-tasting, medium-bodied and silky, this unfolds its charming pear, tropical, honey and quince jam complexity to a seductive, harmonious and delightful finish. Drink through 2005.–P.M. • $35 • (5/31/1999) • **91**

St.-Aubin La Chatenière 1996 • $35 • (5/31/1998) • **90**

St.-Aubin La Chatenière 1995 • $33 • (5/31/1997) • **89**

St.-Aubin Le Charmois 1998: Wonderful, with ripe fruit, smoky aromas. Full-bodied, anchored in the soil, with mineral and matchstick. Also offers also intense tropical and toasted coconut notes. Should last in the cellar for a few years. Drink now through 2007.–P.M. • $33 • (5/31/2000) • **92**

St.-Aubin Le Charmois 1997: Clean as a whistle, showing crafty wine making, this polished St.-Aubin is clean and pure. Buttery, with subtle toast, green apple, lemon, honey and pear notes. Drink now through 2002.–P.M. • $35 • (5/31/1999) • **90**

COLIN, MARC

St.-Aubin Le Charmois 1996 • $35 • (5/31/1998) • **93**
St.-Aubin Le Charmois 1995 • $32 • (5/31/1997) • **80**
St.-Aubin Le Pitangeret 1998: Beautiful and complex. Elegant and racy, with delicious ripe fruit along with wet stone, smoke, matchstick and mineral character. Balanced finish. Drink now through 2005.–P.M. • $33 • (5/31/2000) • **89**
St.-Aubin Les Combes 1998: Fabulous. Minerally, with dried herbs and matchstick complexity, wet earth aromas. Full-bodied, it exudes honey and ripe fruit and attractive scents of basil and rosemary. The texture is creamy-smooth. Drink now through 2005.–P.M. • $33 • (5/31/2000) • **92**
St.-Aubin Les Combes 1997: Of medium intensity, with butterscotch and mocha notes from the oak, it kicks in with lovely, clean and pure fruit that tastes ripe and delicious on the succulent finish. Drink now through 2002.–P.M. • $35 • (5/31/1999) • **86**
St.-Aubin Les Combes 1996 • $35 • (5/31/1998) • **93**
St.-Aubin Les Combes 1995 • $33 • (5/31/1997) • **89**
St.-Aubin Les Cortons 1998: Lovely wine, graceful, not big, but showing complex smoke, mineral, quince, even tropical character. The fruit is ripe and attractive and the finish pleasant if not intense. Drink now through 2003.–P.M. • $33 • (5/31/2000) • **88**
St.-Aubin Les Cortons 1997: Very buttery in style, showing lots of toastiness. Fat, vibrant and packed with ripe fruit, this is a short, serious, silky, full-bodied and age-worthy St.-Aubin. Drink through 2005.–P.M. • $35 • (5/31/1999) • **92**
St.-Aubin Les Cortons 1996 • $35 • (5/31/1998) • **90**

COLIN, PIERRE

Bâtard-Montrachet 1995 • $NA • (5/31/1997) • **86**

COLIN-DELEGER, MICHEL

Bâtard-Montrachet 1997: Unique, it tastes ripe but also of *terroir*, unfolding its flint, mineral, petrol, apricot, mango and just-so toasted oak flavors to a rich but classy finish. Worth the splurge. Drink now through 2007.–P.M. • $142 • (9/30/1999) • **94**
Bâtard-Montrachet 1996: Defines purity, pleasure and raciness in a Chardonnay. Hedonistic, supersupple *grand cru* of extraordinary smoothness. Full-bodied, rich, ripe and seductive, with distinctive malic, milky, yogurt, leesy and caramel flavors along with its lovely ripe pear and tropical character, this melts like thick cream in the mouth, engulfing the midpalate on the way to the long, delicious, slightly smoky, toasty finish. (And, amazingly, the oak plays only a subtle, supporting role to the fruit.) Decant if you plan to enjoy it young. Drink now through 2010.–P.M. • $100 • (8/31/1998) • **99**
Chassagne-Montrachet 1998: Unctuous '98, with good complexity of toasted nuts, dried fruit, bread dough, pear and melon. Elegant and juicy, this medium-bodied white lasts on the finish. Drink now through 2005.–P.M. • $42 • (5/31/2000) • **87**
Chassagne-Montrachet 1996: Thick and ripe, this a lush wine with a subtle, supple midpalate, offering mineral, vanilla, butter and pear flavors. Full-bodied, silky, delicious upon release. Drink now through 2005.–P.M. • $32 • (8/31/1998) • **89**
Chassagne-Montrachet En Remilly 1997: A unique *terroir*-driven wine that develops in the glass, showing layers of wet earth, mineral and flint concentration. A bit earthy, but who cares? It coats the palate with real Chardonnay flavors. Drink now through 2002.–P.M. • $58 • (9/30/1999) • **90**
Chassagne-Montrachet En Remilly 1996: Stands out for its buttery, butterscotch, caramel aromas and flavors. Full-bodied, lacks a bit of finesse. Milky, vanilla notes follow through on the finish. Drink now through 2003.–P.M. • $42 • (8/31/1998) • **84**
Chassagne-Montrachet En Remilly 1995 • $50 • (5/31/1997) • **94**
Chassagne-Montrachet La Maltroie 1998: Classy white Burgundy. Very reserved on the nose, it hides its potential for now. Delivers some fruit, dried herbs, mineral and a touch of honey in an elegant package. Rather subtle finish. Best from 2002 through 2006.–P.M. • $54 • (5/31/2000) • **88**
Chassagne-Montrachet La Maltroie 1997: This beautiful, concentrated, *terroir*-driven white Burgundy is lathered with layers of fat and richness, mineral and an intriguing complexity that surprises your palate. Full-bodied in a subtle way, this is a winner. Drink now through 2007.–P.M. • $56 • (9/30/1999) • **94**
Chassagne-Montrachet La Maltroie 1996: Buttery and butterscotchy, it has a lactic, milky taste that may not please everyone. Full-bodied, fairly opulent and supple. A bit showy and overdone, but seductive upon release. Drink now through 2003.–P.M. • $40 • (8/31/1998) • **86**
Chassagne-Montrachet La Maltroie 1995 • $47 • (5/31/1997) • **86**
Chassagne-Montrachet Les Chaumées 1998: Overripe fruit defines this round, fat white Burgundy. Tastes a bit like cooked pears or apples, but the mouthfeel is agreeable and there is a nice chalky component on the finish. Drink now.–P.M. • $54 • (5/31/2000) • **80**
Chassagne-Montrachet Les Chaumées 1996: Thick and ripe, a buttery style, but despite the oak treatment it remains elegant, offering lots of clean and pure citrus, fruit and mineral character. Has a smooth finish that lingers. Best after 2005.–P.M. • $40 • (8/31/1998) • **89**
Chassagne-Montrachet Les Chaumées 1995 • $44 Ⓐ • (5/31/1997) • **93**
Chassagne-Montrachet Les Chenevottes 1998: Aromatically reserved but showing a fatness on the palate, with some ripe fruit flavors sneaking in on the finish. Still, this medium-bodied white lacks complexity and length. Drink now through 2003.–P.M. • $54 • (5/31/2000) • **82**
Chassagne-Montrachet Les Chenevottes 1997: Supple and easy to like, with butter, cream, flint, earth, smoke and gunpowder character that makes this distinctive. Voluptuous on the palate, with a fabulous ripeness that veers clear of heaviness. Silky finish. Drink now through 2005.–P.M. • $58 • (9/30/1999) • **91**
Chassagne-Montrachet Les Chenevottes 1996: Supple white, medium in intensity and concentration but with nice ripe fruit. Shows attractive malic, milky, pear pie, apple character. Medium-bodied, with an elegant, nicely toasted finish. Enjoy upon release. Drink now.–P.M. • $46 Ⓐ • (8/31/1998) • **88**
Chassagne-Montrachet Les Chenevottes 1995 • $50 • (5/31/1997) • **91**
Chassagne-Montrachet Les Vergers 1998: Unique in its smoky, *terroir*-scented aromas. Beautifully constructed, this is what white Burgundy is all about. Delivers rich texture, supple mouthfeel, ripe fruit mingled with honey and a matchstick note on the silky finish. Drink now through 2010.–P.M. • $59 • (5/31/2000) • **93**
Chassagne-Montrachet Les Vergers 1997: Superthick and oozing with opulent texture, this full-bodied white is balanced, with lemon, vanilla, cream, pear and tropical notes. Just don't cellar it long. Drink now through 2002.–P.M. • $62 • (9/30/1999) • **88**
Chassagne-Montrachet Les Vergers 1996: Medium-bodied and minerally, clean and pure, offering a supersoft texture backed by some decent fruit, toasted oak and lemon character. Balanced and pretty, the smoky, toasted bread finish is silky. You wish for a bit more concentration. Best after 2005.–P.M. • $52 Ⓐ • (8/31/1998) • **86**
Chassagne-Montrachet Les Vergers 1995 • $42 Ⓐ • (8/31/1997) • **91**
Chassagne-Montrachet Morgeot 1997: A flinty, *terroir* wine, with a gunpowder note and plenty of personality. Unctuous and classy, showing interesting dried herb character and power on the finish. Drink now through 2005.–P.M. • $56 • (9/30/1999) • **91**
Chassagne-Montrachet Morgeot 1996: One of the vintage's great values. Classy, racy and refined, a *premier cru* that packs in mineral, ripe fruit and acidity without a collision with new oak. This is truly white Burgundy on the grandest scale as it melts in the mouth like vanilla sauce, waltzing around until you're ready to yield all critical faculties. Do whatever you can to get this seamless beauty. Best from 2005 through 2010.–P.M. • $67 Ⓐ • (8/31/1998) • **95**
Chassagne-Montrachet Morgeot 1995 • $50 • (8/31/1997) • **90**
Chevalier-Montrachet 1998: Ripe and seductive. Full-bodied white Burgundy, with dried apricot and honey in an almost late-harvest style; but it's ultimately a dry wine, and delivers layers of complex mineral and chalky character, along with a toasted finish. Drink now through 2010.–P.M. • $166 • (5/31/2000) • **93**
Chevalier-Montrachet 1997: A unique *terroir* wine. With flint, mineral, smoke and gunpowder, there's an earthy quality to this thick yet elegant and racy Chardonnay. Ripe and sleek without being heavy, it guides its apricot, melon, garlic and white truffle flavors to a harmonious finish. Bravo! Drink now through 2010.–P.M. • $160 • (9/30/1999) • **96**
Chevalier-Montrachet 1996: Pure, clean, full-bodied white, reflecting sophisticated winemaking that brings together lovely lime, honey and toasted oak notes in a supple, rich and exciting wine. Toasted, supple finish. Drink now through 2011.–P.M. • $115 • (8/31/1998) • **93**
Puligny-Montrachet La Truffière 1998: Young and fresh, with a core of ripe fruit. Medium-bodied, with dried herbs, subtle oak accents and some honey, it delivers a silky, creamy-textured midpalate before turning succulently vibrant and lime-tasting on the finish. Drink now through 2005.–P.M. • $82 • (5/31/2000) • **89**

Key: SS—Spectator Selection. CS—Cellar Selection. HR—Highly Recommended. $NA—Price not available. (BT)—Barrel tasting. Ⓐ—Auction Price.
For a key to the tasters' initials, see "How to Use These Listings."
Dates in parentheses represent the issues in which the ratings were published.

Puligny-Montrachet La Truffière 1997: Earthy yet clean, this full-bodied, rich and ripe Chardonnay offers earth, citrus, honey and mineral character within balanced boundaries. You wish for more vibrant fruit. Drink now through 2005.–P.M. • $82 • (9/30/1999) • **88**
Puligny-Montrachet La Truffière 1996: Clean and pure '96 white, exploding with beautiful spice, honey and lemon flavors in a firm package that's not too oaky. Full-bodied, the texture is supple and smooth despite all the citrusy acidity. Wonderful oak-infused milky, lactic, matchstick, smoky character on the long, succulent finish. Delicious now, better after cellaring. Best after 2003.–P.M. • $58 • (8/31/1998) • **93**
Puligny-Montrachet La Truffière 1995 • $58 Ⓐ • (5/31/1997) • **92**
Puligny-Montrachet Les Demoiselles 1998: Delicious and balanced. Interesting midpalate concentration boosts this full-bodied Chardonnay to an impressive height. Dried herbs, black olive and loads of honey make for a seductive drink. Drink now through 2003.–P.M. • $120 • (5/31/2000) • **91**
Puligny-Montrachet Les Demoiselles 1997: A wild white Burgundy that mixes earth and grass with opulent ultraripeness, it wins the day with concentrated fruit, silky texture and layers of complex flinty, smoky and minerally personality. For adventuresome aficionados. Drink now through 2007.–P.M. • $120 • (9/30/1999) • **93**
Puligny-Montrachet Les Demoiselles 1996: Serious *premier cru*. Very concentrated and intense, also very oaky, fat and lush, with opulent texture. Delivers plenty of spice, burnt pizza dough, caramelized pear, crème brûlée flavors, but also fresh lime, apple and pear notes. Full-bodied, palate-searing; needs years to calm down. Best after 2005.–P.M. • $100 • (8/31/1998) • **96**
St.-Aubin En Charmois 1998: Beautifully smooth, ripe and sweet-tasting. Medium-bodied, it adds a layer of complexity via a wet stone, mineral and smoky-matchstick character before turning oh-so subtle on the elegant finish. Drink now through 2007.–P.M. • $34 • (5/31/2000) • **92**
St.-Aubin En Charmois 1997: This beautiful '97 is thick and ripe, with peach, pear and honey at the core, kicking in with lemon. Turns toasty and a bit chalky on the finish. Drink now through 2002.–P.M. • $34 • (9/30/1999) • **88**
St.-Aubin En Charmois 1996: This medium-bodied white is supple and smooth, with delicate pear, melon, prosciutto, wet stone and mineral character supported by some toasted oak accents. Drink now through 2005.–P.M. • $32 • (8/31/1998) • **86**
St.-Aubin Les Combes 1998: Lovely in an elegant way. Balanced, of light to medium body, with refined pear, bread dough, wet stone complexity. Drink now through 2005.–P.M. • $34 • (5/31/2000) • **88**
St.-Aubin Les Combes 1997: Thick and ripe, with an earthy character but also a voluptuous mouthfeel, showing honey, toasted spice and pear flavors. Good concentration, and it tastes natural. Drink now through 2005.–P.M. • $34 • (9/30/1999) • **88**
St.-Aubin Les Combes 1996: Lovely, supple white, of medium body, with wonderful silky texture. Shows some intensity of lime, toasted oak, pear and green apple. Well made and smooth, yet intense on the finish. The sort of wine you want to have a case of to taste through the years. Best after 2005.–P.M. • $27 • (8/31/1998) • **90**

COLLET, JEAN

Chablis 1995 • $15 • (6/15/1997) • **80**
Chablis Mont de Milieu 1995 • $35 • (6/15/1997) • **85**
Chablis Montée de Tonnerre 1995 • $35 • (6/15/1997) • **87**
Chablis Montmains 1995 • $25 • (6/15/1997) • **78**
Chablis Vaillons 1997: Some buttery, toasted character creeps into the fruit of this medium-bodied white, which tastes a bit hot and not all that harmonious.–P.M. • $35 • (5/31/1999) • **79**
Chablis Vaillons 1995 • $25 • (6/15/1997) • **85**
Chablis Valmur 1995 • $45 • (6/15/1997) • **79**

COLLONGE, DOMAINE DE LA

Pouilly-Fuissé 1997: A star. Thick yet racy, this opulent, clean, mineral-packed, full-bodied wine brims with charisma from the ripe fruit to the toasted spices and slightly honeyed accents. Just a touch astringent on the aftertaste, but should smooth out in the cellar. Drink now through 2005.–P.M. • $15 • (5/31/1999) • **90**
Pouilly-Fuissé 1996 • $15 • (5/31/1998) • **78**

COLOMBIER D'ARSAC

Haut-Médoc 1996: Has berry and cherry but it's rather herbal, with a cut grass character. Medium-bodied, with aggressive tannins and a green fruit finish. Hard to get excited about. From Château d'Arsac.–J.S. • $20 • (7/31/1999) • **78**

COLOMBIER DE CHATEAU BROWN, LE

Pessac-Léognan 1996: Attractive aromas of spice and plums. Medium-bodied, with firm tannins and a medium finish. Rather simple. Second label of Château Brown. Drink now.–J.S. • $NA • (1/31/1999) • **80**
Pessac-Léognan 1995 • $15 • (1/31/1998) • **78**
Pessac-Léognan White 1996: A tight, well-made white with apple, vanilla aromas and flavors. Medium-bodied, with firm acidity and a short finish. Needs a bit more age. Drink through 2003–J.S. • $NA • (1/01/1999) • **85**

COLOMBIER, DOMAINE DU

Crozes-Hermitage 1997: Quite attractive if you don't mind a slight herbal character. Floral and raspberry notes mix nicely in this medium-bodied red, with supple tannins. Drink now.–P.M. • $17 • (12/15/1999) • **81**
Crozes-Hermitage 1996: Distinctive, showing wonderful green olive, dried herb, smoke and stone dust aromas. Medium-bodied, it delivers ripe berry character but also some tough tannins on a slightly tough finish. Should go well with food. Drink now through 2002.–P.M. • $16 • (10/15/1998) • **84**
Crozes-Hermitage 1995 • $12 • (10/15/1997) • **88**
Crozes-Hermitage 1992 • $12 • (5/31/1994) • **76**
Crozes-Hermitage Cuvée Gaby 1997: A bit earthy, this medium-bodied Crozes shows plenty of chocolate, red berry, black cherry, spice, black pepper and wet earth notes. Made in a commercial style, but should go nicely with grilled red meat. Best from 2001 through 2005.–P.M. • $20 • (12/15/1999) • **85**
Crozes-Hermitage Cuvée Gaby 1996: Shows personality, but a bit herbal. Medium-bodied, with a fresh, red berry character, a lively and crisp texture and nice flavors of black olive, thyme and Provençal herb. Narrows to a lean yet smoky finish, but should cut through a fat steak. Drink now.–P.M. • $22 • (10/15/1998) • **80**
Crozes-Hermitage Cuvée Gaby 1995 • $18 • (10/15/1997) • **75**
Crozes-Hermitage Cuvée Gaby 1992 • $15 • (5/31/1994) • **80**
Crozes-Hermitage White 1998: Interesting thanks to the minerally, silky midpalate that suggests serious work in the vineyards. Delicious flavors of sea salt, shrimp make this a natural with seafood. Drink now.–P.M. • $17 • (12/15/1999) • **84**
Crozes-Hermitage White 1997: So fresh and zesty, it tastes like a barrel sample. The floral, almond, peach, lime, quince, gooseberry and mineral notes are seductive, and the body is rich, creamy yet clean, pure and vibrant. The long, sweet- and ripe-tasting finish is accented by a bitter almond note. Drink now.–P.M. • $16 • (10/15/1998) • **90**
Crozes-Hermitage White 1996 • $12 • (10/15/1997) • **87**
Hermitage 1997: Cassis and blackberry dominate in this rich, ripe and lovely wine. Medium-bodied, it's intensely fruit-driven (rather than *terroir*-driven) and it delivers lovely spice, black pepper, smoke, bacon and game notes on the lingering finish. Drink now through 2005.–P.M. • $65 • (11/30/1999) • **88**
Hermitage 1996: A great, sexy wine that inspires one to write a poem instead of just another tasting note. So sweet and ripe, yet with fresh underlying acidity to anchor it, delivering layers of complex fruit and spicy oak in a seamless, full-bodied whole. Firm but seductive finish makes it tempting now. Drink through 2010.–P.M. • $55 • (9/15/1998) • **95**
Hermitage 1995 • $54 • (10/15/1997) • **88**
Hermitage 1991 • $28 • (5/31/1994) • **83**

COLOMBO, JEAN-LUC

Châteauneuf-du-Pape Les Bartavelles 1998: Focused and ripe, this interesting red has plenty of flavors, from berry to citrus to wet earth. Medium-bodied, it turns a bit crisp on the finish. Best from 2003 through 2010.–P.M. • $35 • (6/30/2000) • **87**
Châteauneuf-du-Pape Les Bartavelles 1997: Very light and a bit diluted, this is a straightforward, simple red to be drunk chilled at a picnic.–P.M. • $40 • (12/15/1999) • **78**
Châteauneuf-du-Pape Les Bartavelles 1995: Racy, firm, elegant and polished, this medium-bodied red is built for the cellar. Balanced, with exotic violet, rose petal, raspberry, tropical and anise flavors. Fine quality to the still-chewy tannins; ripe on the seductive finish. Best from 2002 through 2007.–P.M. • $40 • (9/30/1998) • **90**
Cornas Cuvée X 1994 • $NA • (10/15/1997) • **90**
Cornas La Louvée 1997: A dark-colored, medium-bodied red, with blackberry, grilled, black pepper, smoke and floral flavors. Smooth and accessible,

FRANCE

with limited depth and length. Juicy, acid-tasting finish. Drink now through 2003.–P.M. • $60 • (11/30/1999) • **83**

Cornas La Louvée 1994 • $51 • (10/15/1997) • **89**

Cornas Les Méjeans 1997: Soft and simple, with a slight herbal character making its unwelcome presence known among the cassis and wild berry notes. Tart, drying finish.–P.M. • $50 • (11/30/1999) • **75**

Cornas Les Méjeans 1995: Astringent and herbaceous, this is full-bodied and dark-colored, but the flavors struggle to come together.–P.M. • $50 • (10/15/1998) • **77**

Cornas Les Ruchets 1997: A natural-tasting Cornas, with a flotsam of solids that suggests little if any filtering. Tastes of the earth and lovely black fruit, including cassis, with a touch of toasted wood. Elegant finish. Drink now through 2005.–P.M. • $55 • (11/30/1999) • **88**

Cornas Les Ruchets 1996: Elegant but a bit crisp, showing some red- and blackberry character, slightly short on the finish. Drink now through 2005.–P.M. • $45 • (11/15/1998) • **84**

Cornas Les Ruchets 1993 • $39 • (10/15/1996) • **87**

Cornas Les Ruchets 1991 • $35 • (5/31/1994) • **82**

Cornas Les Ruchets 1989 • $45 • (11/15/1991) • **89**

Cornas Les Ruchets 1988 • $45 • (10/15/1991) • **87**

Cornas Les Ruchets 1987 • $45 • (11/15/1991) • **75**

Cornas Terres Brûlées 1997: Light and diluted, an easy wine with simple red berry flavors.–P.M. • $50 • (11/30/1999) • **75**

Cornas Terres Brûlées 1993 • $30 • (10/15/1996) • **87**

Cornas Terres Brûlées 1992 • $30 • (10/15/1995) • **89**

Côtes du Rhône 1993 • $13 • (9/30/1995) • **86**

Côtes du Rhône Les Abeilles 1997: A good house wine. Nice ripeness but not much complexity in this light- to medium-bodied red. Kicks in with intense fruit on the palate, and the rustic tannin structure suggests it'll stand up to many dishes. Drink now through 2003.–P.M. • $10 • (12/15/1999) • **80**

Côtes du Rhône Les Forots 1998: A wine with a rustic character, showing figs, dates, toasted oak and dried herbs, with lovely plum and black fruit notes. Has personality and richness. A good house wine. Drink now through 2002.–P.M. • $15 • (12/15/1999) • **85**

Côtes du Rhône Les Forots 1997: Delicate, light- to-medium-bodied, bursting with floral, plum and red berry character, this wine is vibrant and pure, with a smooth tannin texture and lots of attractive, ripe flavors to coat the palate. Seductive finish. Drink now.–P.M. • $12 • (11/15/1998) • **89**

Côtes du Rhône Les Forots 1996 • $18 • (9/15/1997) • **86**

Côtes du Rhône White Les Figuières 1998: The sort of wine you wish to have around when friends drop by. A delicious, unpretentious little wine that's balanced and wonderful to drink young. Not deep or rich, but elegant, subtle and very floral. Drink now through 2001.–P.M. • $15 • (12/15/1999) • **86**

Crozes-Hermitage 1998: Red berry flavors are attractive in this medium-bodied red, but expect a rather straightforward drink that wimps out on the midpalate.–P.M. • $17 • (12/15/1999) • **79**

Crozes-Hermitage 1995 • $18 • (10/15/1997) • **84**

Hermitage Le Rouet 1996: A crisp, fruit-driven wine, packed with freshly crushed red berry character. A bit light on the palate, turning tart on the finish. Where is the opulent texture expected from Hermitage? Drink now through 2002.–P.M. • $55 • (11/30/1999) • **80**

Hermitage White Le Rouet 1996: Silky and opulent, a full-bodied white with subtle fruit and oak character. Hard to pinpoint what it tastes like—wet hay, almond and celery root, perhaps. But the texture is nice. Drink now.–P.M. • $65 • (11/30/1999) • **85**

St.-Joseph 1997: A rather crisp and lean red, with cherry and toasted oak character. Light- to medium-bodied, it turns a bit tough and rustic on the finish.–P.M. • $20 • (12/15/1999) • **79**

St.-Joseph 1996: Simple, a bit green and herbaceous, this medium-bodied red shows ripe cassis and good acidity. Try chilled with salads and cheeses.–P.M. • $20 • (11/15/1998) • **79**

St.-Joseph 1994 • $17 • (11/30/1996) • **85**

St.-Joseph Les Lauves 1994 • $23 • (10/15/1997) • **86**

Syrah Côtes du Rhône 1994 • $13 • (10/15/1996) HR • **88**

Syrah Côtes du Rhône 1993 • $18 • (9/30/1995) • **86**

Syrah Vin de Pays des Collines Rhodaniennes La Serine Pointue 1997: Polished and deliciously vibrant, this pure red sparkles with cassis, blueberry, violet, chocolate truffle and spices. Well made, round and balanced despite a veiled citrusy character that keeps it fresh. Long and chewy on the finish. Drink now.–P.M. • $12 • (11/15/1998) • **85**

Syrah Vin de Table Français Les Collines de Laure 1996 • $16 • (9/30/1997) • **82**

Syrah Vin de Table Français Les Collines de Laure 1993 • $18 • (12/31/1995) • **76**

COLOUR VOLANT

Cabernet Sauvignon Vin de Pays d'Oc 1995 • $9 • (8/31/1997) • **81**

Cabernet Sauvignon Vin de Pays des Coteaux de l'Ardèche 1996: Balanced and straightforward, with nice plum and herb flavors and an appealing texture. Drink now.–K.M. • $7 • (11/15/1998) • **82**

Chardonnay Vin de Pays de l'Aude 1996: Tart, with buttery aromas and pineapple flavors.–K.M. • $7 • (11/15/1998) • **78**

Merlot Vin de Pays d'Oc 1995 • $9 • (8/31/1997) • **81**

Merlot Vin de Pays des Coteaux de l'Ardèche 1996: Smooth and engaging. Medium-bodied, with attractive cedar, mint and plum flavors and a firmly tannic texture. Drink now. • $7 • (9/30/1998) • **83**

Sauvignon Blanc Vin de Pays d'Oc 1996: Earthy, herbal flavors are the main theme in this simple, crisp white.–B.S. • $7 • (10/15/1998) • **79**

Syrah Vin de Pays des Coteaux de l'Ardèche 1996: Lean and simple, with light plum and herb flavors and a tart, tannic texture. Drink now. • $7 • (10/15/1998) • **77**

COMBIER, DOMAINE

Crozes-Hermitage 1997: Ripe and round, with sweet flavors, yet the aromas are green, allowing an olive, somewhat herbaceous aroma to mingle with a lovely cassis flavor. Drink now through 2002.–P.M. • $25 • (10/31/1999) • **81**

Crozes-Hermitage 1996: This harmonious, ripe, sweet-tasting Crozes shows a lovely cassis, blueberry, spice, black olive, mineral-laden stone dust and spice character. Of medium body, it's elegant and beautiful, with sweet tannins and a tasty, balanced finish. Drink now through 2003.–P.M. • $22 • (10/15/1998) • **89**

Crozes-Hermitage 1995 • $18 • (10/15/1997) • **78**

Crozes-Hermitage 1994 • $20 • (11/30/1996) • **83**

Crozes-Hermitage 1992 • $14 • (10/15/1994) • **85**

Crozes-Hermitage 1991 • $17 • (5/31/1994) • **86**

Crozes-Hermitage Clos des Grives 1997: Pleasant with all that fancy oak rounding out the corners, here's a medium-bodied, medium-intense Syrah accented by anise, blackberry, earth and spicy black pepper character. Drink now through 2003.–P.M. • $40 • (10/31/1999) • **86**

Crozes-Hermitage Clos des Grives 1996: This international style of Crozes is balanced and smooth, with a licorice, spearmint, currant, plumlike character. Full-bodied, this red delivers harmony in a zesty, fresh package. Intense finish. Tastes of smoky new oak now, and should improve with cellaring. Drink through 2005–P.M. • $40 • (10/15/1998) • **90**

Crozes-Hermitage Clos des Grives 1995 • $35 • (10/15/1997) • **88**

Crozes-Hermitage Clos des Grives 1994 • $35 • (11/30/1996) • **91**

Crozes-Hermitage Clos des Grives 1992 • $20 • (10/15/1994) • **87**

Crozes-Hermitage Clos des Grives 1991 • $25 • (5/31/1994) • **84**

Crozes-Hermitage Clos des Grives 1990 • $20 • (4/15/1993) • **92**

Crozes-Hermitage White 1997: Exciting, cascading with pure, clean, deep, complex aromas and flavors. Packed with fruit, spice and wet earth flavors, it amounts to a silky wine with lots of character. Drink now through 2003.–P.M. • $22 • (11/15/1998) • **91**

Crozes-Hermitage White 1996 • $20 • (10/15/1997) • **85**

COMMANDERIE, CHATEAU LA | POMEROL

Pomerol 1991 • $15 • (3/31/1994) • **72**

COMMANDERIE, CHATEAU LA | ST. EMILION

St.-Emilion 1998: A pretty berry, floral wine, with fine tannins and a caressing texture.–J.S. • $NA • (5/31/1999) (BT) • **85-89**

St.-Emilion 1997: A bit light, but some good berry, plum character. Drink now.–J.S. • $NA • (1/31/2000) • **81**

St.-Emilion 1996: Some decent berry and mineral aromas, with a hint of dried herbs. Medium- to light-bodied, with some berry flavors that are rather light and diluted. Drink now.–J.S. • $17 • (1/31/1999) • **80**

St.-Emilion 1994 • $18 • (1/31/1997) • **83**

St.-Emilion 1993 • $15 • (1/31/1996) • **83**

St.-Emilion 1989: A lovely, silky St.-Emilion showing plenty of chocolate and tobacco character. Full-bodied, with a cherry, dried herb aftertaste.

Key: SS—Spectator Selection. CS—Cellar Selection. HR—Highly Recommended. $NA—Price not available. (BT)—Barrel tasting. (A)—Auction Price.
For a key to the tasters' initials, see "How to Use These Listings."
Dates in parentheses represent the issues in which the ratings were published.

Seductive mouthfeel. (1989 Bordeaux horizontal tasting). Drink through 2003.–J.S. • $NA • (5/31/1999) • **90**
St.-Emilion 1988 • $17 Ⓐ • (10/31/1991) • **79**
St.-Emilion 1983 • $11 • (1/01/1986) • **79**

COMMANDERIE, CHATEAU LA | St. Estèphe

St.-Estèphe 1997: Cherry and currant character follow through to a medium-bodied palate, with light tannins and a diluted finish. Drink now.–J.S. • $20 • (1/31/2000) • **81**

COMMANDERIE DE LA BARGEMONE

Coteaux d'Aix-en-Provence 1995: Lively and fruity, with sweet cherry and spice flavors. A straightforward, medium-bodied red. Drink now.–K.M. • $10 • (8/31/1998) • **81**
Coteaux d'Aix-en-Provence Cuvée Tournebride 1995: Offers modest cherry and red plum flavors, with a leathery note in the middle.–K.M. • $13 • (8/31/1998) • **79**

CONFRERIE DES VIGNERONS DE OISLY & THESEE

Sauvignon Touraine Les Gourmets 1998: Flavors of apple and spice and a grassy aroma dominate this medium-bodied white. A good quaff. Drink now.–K.M. • $7 • (5/15/2000) • **84**
Touraine Prestige de la Vallée des Rois 1997: The grass and apple flavors are simple, yet there's a bit more crunch than other 1997s, along with a richly textured midpalate. Drink now.–B.S. • $7 • (11/15/1998) • **83**

CONFURON, JEAN-JACQUES

Bourgogne Aligoté 1997: A very buttery, butterscotchy wine, with a hard, acidic, metallic, unfriendly taste.–P.M. • $NA • (1/01/1999) • **75**
Chambolle-Musigny 1997: An elegant style of red Burgundy, showing a touch of dilution as the herb and strawberry notes come out, but it's juicy.–P.M. • $52 • (9/30/1999) • **79**
Chambolle-Musigny 1996: Well made. A full-bodied, still-shy '96 that's aromatically reserved, but wait until you taste it. This red reveals a burst of cassis, plum, violet, rose petal, mocha and toasty, smoky, gamy complexity—all ripe-tasting on the supple, never-ending finish. Best from 2003 through 2015.–P.M. • $48 • (5/15/1999) • **93**
Chambolle-Musigny 1994 • $35 • (11/15/1996) • **82**
Chambolle-Musigny 1989 • $35 • (11/30/1992) • **81**
Chambolle-Musigny Premier Cru 1995 • $62 • (11/15/1997) • **84**
Chambolle-Musigny Premier Cru 1994 • $50 • (11/15/1996) • **90**
Chambolle-Musigny Premier Cru 1993 • $60 • (11/15/1995) HR • **94**
Chambolle-Musigny Premier Cru 1991 • $37 • (1/31/1994) • **86**
Clos Vougeot 1997: Very perfumed and spicy, even exotic, showing sandalwood, black olive and cherry underscored by firm tannins and lively acidity. Sleek and refined, with a density that bodes well for the future. Best from 2001 through 2007.–B.S. • $135 • (9/30/1999) • **93**
Clos Vougeot 1996: Succulent and very fruity, full-bodied and blending good doses of toasted oak, sweet tannins and pure wild berry and cassis character. Supple yet vibrant, its finish is so velvety. Tempting now. Best from 2003 through 2012.–P.M. • $125 • (5/15/1999) • **94**
Clos Vougeot 1994 • $80 • (11/15/1996) • **90**
Clos Vougeot 1993 • $85 • (11/15/1995) • **90**
Clos Vougeot 1991 • $60 • (1/31/1994) • **85**
Côte de Nuits-Villages Les Vignottes 1997: There's a slightly cooked jam character to this medium-bodied, gamy, overripe Pinot. Turns hard and crisp on the disjointed finish.–P.M. • $27 • (9/30/1999) • **79**
Côte de Nuits-Villages Les Vignottes 1996: Medium-bodied, fruity in style, delivering a crisp mouthfeel with black cherry, plum and lemon notes. A bit dilute. Drink now through 2002.–P.M. • $24 • (5/15/1999) • **80**
Côte de Nuits-Villages Les Vignottes 1994 • $22 • (11/15/1996) • **81**
Côte de Nuits-Villages Les Vignottes 1989 • $16 • (11/30/1992) • **84**
Nuits-St.-Georges Aux Boudots 1997: Raspberry, smoke, spice and a little animal element introduce this pretty, elegant '97 red Burgundy. Balanced in a charming, light-bodied way. Drink now through 2002.–B.S. • $80 • (9/30/1999) • **86**
Nuits-St.-Georges Aux Boudots 1996: Full-bodied, balanced, palate-coating, this silky yet vibrant wine is brimming with cassis, black cherry, toast and mineral complexity. Refined tannins make for an opulent, stylish finish. Best from 2003 through 2012.–P.M. • $70 • (5/15/1999) • **95**
Nuits-St.-Georges Aux Boudots 1995 • $62 • (11/15/1997) • **85**
Nuits-St.-Georges Aux Boudots 1989 • $32 • (11/30/1992) • **81**
Nuits-St.-Georges Les Chaboeufs 1997: On the cooked side, like cherry or raspberry jam, this red begins softly, then turns hot and dry on the finish. Drink now through 2001.–B.S. • $68 • (9/30/1999) • **82**
Nuits-St.-Georges Les Chaboeufs 1996: A bit tannic and sharp, with some mineral, crisp acidity, fresh berry character along with firm tannins and a tart finish.–P.M. • $60 • (5/15/1999) • **79**
Nuits-St.-Georges Les Chaboeufs 1995 • $56 • (11/15/1997) • **83**
Nuits-St.-Georges Les Chaboeufs 1994 • $45 • (11/15/1996) • **88**
Nuits-St.-Georges Les Chaboeufs 1993 • $60 • (11/15/1995) • **89**
Nuits-St.-Georges Les Chaboeufs 1989 • $32 • (11/30/1992) • **83**
Nuits-St.-Georges Les Fleurières 1996: Fresh and succulent, medium-bodied and medium-ripe, showing some decent red berry character, toasted flavors and dried herb, cassis bush notes. Crisp finish. Best from 2001 through 2005.–P.M. • $45 • (5/15/1999) • **82**
Nuits-St.-Georges Les Fleurières 1989 • $26 • (11/30/1992) • **69**
Nuits-St.-Georges Les Fleurières LD 1993 • $45 • (11/15/1995) • **90**
Romanée St.-Vivant 1997: Smooth and round, showing warm fruit in a soft package, with plum and black cherry character. Rather short finish. Drink now through 2001.–P.M. • $170 • (9/30/1999) • **85**
Romanée St.-Vivant 1996: Fabulous. Clean, pure but also full-bodied, showing great elegance, delivering mineral, cassis, plum and smoky, toasted oak along with fresh acidity. Mesmerizes the senses with its ripe, velvety touch. Best from 2004 through 2010.–P.M. • $155 • (5/15/1999) • **95**
Romanée St.-Vivant 1994 • $120 • (11/15/1996) • **91**
Romanée St.-Vivant 1993 • $150 • (11/15/1995) • **89**
Romanée St.-Vivant 1989 • $113 • (10/31/1992) • **90**
Vosne-Romanée Les Beaux Monts 1996: Distinctive, with game, cassis, smoke and grilled meat aromas and flavors in a succulent, medium-bodied package. Seductive, sweet tannins along with a savage character make this memorable. Best from 2003 through 2010.–P.M. • $70 • (5/15/1999) • **91**
Vosne-Romanée Les Beaux Monts 1995 • $70 • (11/15/1997) • **90**
Vosne-Romanée Les Beaux Monts 1993 • $63 • (11/15/1995) • **94**

CONFURON-COTETIDOT, J.

Bourgogne 1996: Tart and difficult, a bit green, tasting of vegetables, black cherry and iron. Tough finish.–P.M. • $22 • (5/15/1999) • **70**
Chambolle-Musigny 1997: A charred oak component dominates the delicate fruit in this tannic, dry red.–B.S. • $55 • (9/30/1999) • **78**
Chambolle-Musigny 1996: Fruit, oak, *terroir* fill your sensorial cup in this full-bodied, rich but elegant red Burgundy, where the cassis, mocha-toasted oak and plum combination fire exciting flavor waves that roll to a long finish. Best from 2002 through 2010.–P.M. • $50 • (5/15/1999) • **93**
Chambolle-Musigny 1993 • $NA • (5/15/1996) • **88**
Chambolle-Musigny 1992 • $38 • (12/15/1994) • **83**
Chambolle-Musigny 1991 • $41 • (1/31/1994) • **74**
Chambolle-Musigny 1989 • $32 • (11/30/1992) • **89**
Charmes-Chambertin 1996: Brilliant. Rich, velvety, fruity, thick and beautifully complete. Medium-bodied, it plums the depths of the Burgundian soil, offering dark fruit like plum, cherry and blackberry, plus toasted oak, spice, mocha—and it stays fresh and elegant despite its massive, ultraripe character. Best from 2003 through 2015.–P.M. • $94 • (5/15/1999) • **97**
Clos de Vougeot 1996: A bit herbal, with cassis bush and green notes, a tightly wound, minerally character, turning astringent on the finish.–P.M. • $100 • (5/15/1999) • **79**
Clos de Vougeot 1993 • $NA • (5/15/1996) • **89**
Clos de Vougeot 1991 • $65 • (1/31/1994) • **86**
Clos de Vougeot 1989 • $60 • (9/15/1992) HR • **91**
Echézeaux 1993 • $NA • (5/15/1996) • **81**
Echézeaux 1991 • $65 • (1/31/1994) • **79**
Echézeaux 1990 • $65 • (12/15/1992) • **91**
Echézeaux 1989 • $52 • (10/31/1992) • **83**
Gevrey-Chambertin 1996: Lovely vanilla, milkshake and cassis aromas make this a superpleasurable, medium-bodied red, with some nice cassis notes and lively, ripe tannins on the balanced finish. Best from 2002 through 2010.–P.M. • $52 • (5/15/1999) • **90**
Gevrey-Chambertin 1993 • $NA • (5/15/1996) • **94**
Gevrey-Chambertin Lavaut St.-Jacques 1996: A wine that gives fruit precedence. Fabulous cassis, plum and wild strawberry explode in this full-bodied Burgundy, while fresh acidity lines its velvety texture. Seduces from first whiff to long finish. Best from 2003 through 2015.–P.M. • $61 • (5/15/1999) • **95**
Gevrey-Chambertin Lavaut St.-Jacques 1995 • $70 • (11/15/1997) • **85**
Gevrey-Chambertin Petite Chapelle 1997: Full of sandalwood and spice notes, with cherry and a lean, trim flavor profile, showing more oak than

fruit at this stage. Crisp, astringent finish. Best from 2001 through 2005.–B.S. • $64 • (9/30/1999) • **83**

Gevrey-Chambertin Petite Chapelle 1996: Exotically plummy, even minty, packed with raspberry and cassis, this full-bodied, ripe '96 has good structure, smacking acidity and nice balance; just lacks a bit of class. Drink now through 2007.–P.M. • $61 • (5/15/1999) • **87**

Mazis-Chambertin 1996: Bursts with exotic, ripe fruit—plum, crushed wild raspberries, blueberries—and wonderfully oak-tinged, spicy, lightly smoky grilled meat notes, giving this full-bodied jewel a silky mouthfeel and deeply satisfying finish. Best from 2003 through 2010.–P.M. • $100 • (5/15/1999) • **94**

Nuits-St.-Georges 1997: Wonderful texture and exotic aromas. Stands out with its spice, smoke, olive paste and cooked raspberry jam character. Seems a bit advanced already, but picks up intensity on the slightly crisp, cassis-packed finish. Drink now through 2004.–P.M. • $55 • (9/30/1999) • **88**

Nuits-St.-Georges 1996: Mind-boggling village wine. Very open and flavorful, loaded with cassis, plum and gamy, toasty, smoky flavors, with supersupple tannins. A rich, ripe red Burgundy that pushes the envelope. Best from 2005 through 2015.–P.M. • $52 • (5/15/1999) • **94**

Nuits-St.-Georges 1995 • $50 • (11/15/1997) • **89**

Nuits-St.-Georges 1993 • $NA • (5/15/1996) • **89**

Nuits-St.-Georges 1992 • $38 • (12/15/1994) • **84**

Nuits-St.-Georges Premier Cru 1997: Light and stemmy, very green and tasting of tomato.–P.M. • $70 • (9/30/1999) • **72**

Nuits-St.-Georges Premier Cru 1993 • $NA • (5/15/1996) • **89**

Nuits-St.-Georges Premier Cru 1991 • $47 • (1/31/1994) • **77**

Nuits-St.-Georges Premier Cru 1990 • $28 • (12/15/1992) • **91**

Vosne-Romanée 1997: Olives and dried herbs mix with the red berry, floral, smoke and game character in this smooth wine, backed by a crisp core of lemony acidity. Best from 2002 through 2005.–P.M. • $54 • (9/30/1999) • **87**

Vosne-Romanée 1996: Incredible quality for a village wine. Big and tough, but beautifully ripe and flavorful, full-bodied and exotic, with plum, rose petal, mineral, toast, smoke, cassis character. Tannins are ripe, but the firm finish suggests cellaring. Best from 2010 through 2020.–P.M. • $51 • (5/15/1999) • **93**

Vosne-Romanée 1995 • $48 • (11/15/1997) • **87**

Vosne-Romanée 1993 • $NA • (5/15/1996) • **80**

Vosne-Romanée 1992 • $34 • (12/15/1994) • **78**

Vosne-Romanée 1990 • $30 • (12/15/1992) • **84**

Vosne-Romanée 1989 • $27 • (10/31/1992) • **89**

Vosne-Romanée Les Suchots 1996: Pure, clean and refined; the subtle dose of toasted oak allows the rich, ripe red berry flavors and mineral, wet earth notes to star in this medium-bodied, classy, *terroir*-anchored Pinot. Chewy tannins on the finish, so cellar. Best from 2003 through 2010.–P.M. • $66 • (5/15/1999) • **93**

Vosne-Romanée Les Suchots 1995 • $60 • (11/15/1997) • **85**

Vosne-Romanée Les Suchots 1993 • $NA • (5/15/1996) • **84**

Vosne-Romanée Les Suchots 1991 • $NA • (1/31/1994) • **81**

Vosne-Romanée Les Suchots 1990 • $44 • (12/15/1992) • **83**

CONNETABLE DE TALBOT

St.-Julien 1996: A ripe, round red with tobacco and berry aromas and flavors. Medium-bodied, with medium, silky tannins and a fruity, rich aftertaste. Very good. Second label of Château Talbot. Best after 2000.–J.S. • $35 • (1/31/1999) • **87**

St.-Julien 1995 • $18 • (1/31/1998) • **84**

CONSEILLANTE, CHATEAU LA

Pomerol 1999: Delicious, with plum, cherry, raspberry and milk chocolate character. Medium-bodied, with soft tannins and a silky texture.–J.S. • $NA • (1/01/2000) (BT) • **88**

Pomerol 1998: An elegant wine, with sweet fruit and well-integrated, fine tannins. Long, sweet fruit finish. Simply outstanding, with ripe and beautiful fruit; could use a bit more fruit concentration but what's there is impressive.–J.S. • $NA • (5/31/1999) (BT) • **85-89**

Pomerol 1997: A delicious and balanced Pomerol, with tobacco, berry and meaty aromas and flavors. Medium-bodied, with soft tannins and a fruity finish. Drink now through 2004.–J.S. • $140 • (1/31/2000) • **88**

Key: SS—Spectator Selection. CS—Cellar Selection. HR—Highly Recommended. $NA—Price not available. (BT)—Barrel tasting. Ⓐ—Auction Price. For a key to the tasters' initials, see "How to Use These Listings."
Dates in parentheses represent the issues in which the ratings were published.

Pomerol 1996: Has pretty berry and cherry character with hints of chocolate, a medium body with polished tannins and a chocolate aftertaste. Not overdone, and it's harmonious, though it isn't a great Conseillante. Drink now.–J.S. • $63 Ⓐ • (1/31/1999) • **87**

Pomerol 1995 • $64 Ⓐ • (1/31/1998) • **94**

Pomerol 1992 • $35 • (4/15/1995) • **77**

Pomerol 1990 • $170 Ⓐ • (3/31/1993) • **94**

Pomerol 1989: An outstanding wine of subtle spice, cherry and herb aromas and flavors. Full-bodied, with ripe fruit and soft tannins. Long, chocolate and spice aftertaste. (1989 Bordeaux horizontal tasting). Drink through 2006.–J.S. • $167 Ⓐ • (5/31/1999) • **90**

Pomerol 1988: Delicious and soft, with chocolate, berry and cherry aromas. Full-bodied, with round tannins and a long, succulent finish. Can improve with age, but why wait? (1988 Bordeaux horizontal tasting). Drink now. –J.S. • $60 Ⓐ • (11/30/1998) • **90**

Pomerol 1987 • $35 • (5/15/1990) • **86**

Pomerol 1986 • $62 Ⓐ • (6/15/1989) • **93**

Pomerol 1985 • $134 Ⓐ • (2/29/1988) • **93**

Pomerol 1984 • $26 • (3/31/1987) • **93**

Pomerol 1983 • $73 Ⓐ • (11/15/1986) • **84**

Pomerol 1982: Big and rich. Dark brick-red color, with a ruby center. Very ripe fruit on the nose, with raisin, dark chocolate and earth. Lots of tobacco and cherry flavors and velvety, slightly coarse tannins. (1982 Bordeaux horizontal tasting). Best after 2000.–J.S. • $164 Ⓐ • (11/30/1998) • **92**

Pomerol 1981 • $64 Ⓐ • (10/15/1994) • **88**

Pomerol 1970 • $104 Ⓐ • (5/15/1993) • **94**

Pomerol 1962 • $55 • (11/30/1987) • **60**

Pomerol 1961 • $248 Ⓐ • (4/30/1996) • **87**

Pomerol 1959 • $150 • (10/15/1990) • **88**

Pomerol 1947 • $240 Ⓐ • (5/31/1997) • **87**

Pomerol 1945 • $650 • (11/30/1995) • **88**

CORBILLIERES, DOMAINE DES

Cabernet Touraine Angeline 1997: Pleasant and grapey, with red plum, currant and pepper notes. Drink now.–K.M. • $11 • (5/15/2000) • **83**

CORBIN-MICHOTTE, CHATEAU

St.-Emilion 1988 • $15 • (7/15/1991) • **72**

St.-Emilion 1982: Not the most complex wine, but a beauty. Medium-ruby in color, with an amber edge. Very floral aromas, with hints of wood, truffle and ripe fruit. Medium-bodied, with velvety tannins and a long, sweet fruit and vanilla aftertaste. (1982 Bordeaux horizontal tasting). Drink now.–J.S. • $NA • (11/30/1998) • **88**

St.-Emilion 1961 • $NA • (4/30/1996) • **86**

CORDEILLAN-BAGES, CHATEAU

Pauillac 1996: Pretty aromas of currants and vanilla. Medium-bodied, with round and well-integrated tannins and a fruity aftertaste. Slightly one-dimensional, but well done. Best after 2000.–J.S. • $NA • (1/31/1999) • **87**

Pauillac 1995: A wonderful Pauillac. Dark-colored, with a superripe berry and currant nose. Full-bodied, quite velvety, with lovely fruit and a long, tannic finish. Needs time. Best from 2004 through 2010.–J.S. • $NA • (9/15/1998) • **91**

Pauillac 1994 • $20 • (1/31/1997) • **88**

Pauillac 1992 • $18 • (4/15/1995) • **85**

Pauillac 1991 • $16 • (3/31/1994) • **83**

Pauillac 1990 • $33 • (3/31/1993) • **95**

Pauillac 1989: Super Pauillac. Racy, powerful and built for aging. This is a baby Lynch-Bages. Inky color. Wonderful fresh aromas of mint, raspberry and cherry. Full-bodied, with steely tannins and a long finish of berries and cassis. (1989 Bordeaux horizontal tasting). Best after 2008.–J.S. • $NA • (5/31/1999) • **95**

CORDIER PERE & FILS

Mâcon Blanc 1997: Butter and butterscotch precede lemon, toasted oak and slightly bitter wood tannins, but it's full and round in the mouth. Drink now.–P.M. • $16 • (5/31/1999) • **84**

Mâcon Blanc-Villages 1995 • $12 • (5/31/1997) • **84**

Mâcon-Fuissé 1997: Ripe, full-bodied Mâcon made in a buttery style, offering lovely tropical, pear tart, spice and slightly toasted bread notes. Drink now through 2002.–P.M. • $20 • (5/31/1999) • **86**

Mâcon-Fuissé 1996 • $12 • (5/31/1998) • **83**

Pouilly-Fuissé 1997: Delicious, showing a tight, firm core of acidity and good intensity that burns a bit from smoke and toast, all underscored by ripe fruit. A bit angular on the finish. Best after 2000.–P.M. • $36 • (5/31/1999) • **86**
Pouilly-Fuissé Au Metertière 1997: Serious juice. Classy, with all the elegance of a black circus panther jumping through loops, this delivers a lemon, toasted hazelnut and honey ensemble that floats to a long, simmering, balanced, oak-accented finish. Tempting now. Best after 2001.–P.M. • $38 • (5/31/1999) • **92**
Pouilly-Fuissé Au Metertière 1996 • $32 • (5/31/1998) • **90**
Pouilly-Fuissé Champs-Murgers 1997: Well made, rich and ripe, attractively combining coconut, pear, honey and tropical flavors in a deftly oaked, creamy package. Medium-bodied, there's plenty of lemon-spiked succulence to bring it to a balanced finale. Drink now through 2004.–P.M. • $33 • (5/31/1999) • **90**
Pouilly-Fuissé Juliette la Grande 1997: Opulent and rich, exploding with floral, yeasty-leesy, butterscotch aromas, this full-bodied white envelops the palate with sweet-tasting fruit, spice, lemon and honey flavors. Balanced finish. Drink now through 2005.–P.M. • $65 • (5/31/1999) • **90**
Pouilly-Fuissé Les Vignes Blanches 1997: Open and inviting, with plenty of ripe fruit character, this delights for its smoke, pear, lemon, fruit tart and burnt bread crust aromas and flavors. Intensely toasty on the finish, which turns a bit tart. Best after 2000.–P.M. • $38 • (5/31/1999) • **87**
Pouilly-Fuissé Les Vignes Blanches 1996 • $20 Ⓐ • (5/31/1998) • **88**
Pouilly-Fuissé Les Vignes Blanches 1995 • $33 • (5/31/1997) • **76**
Pouilly-Fuissé Lot No. 1 1995 • $25 • (5/31/1997) • **77**
Pouilly-Fuissé Lot No. 2 1995 • $25 • (5/31/1997) • **92**
Pouilly-Fuissé Lot No. 3 1995 • $25 • (5/31/1997) • **89**
Pouilly-Fuissé Vieilles Vignes 1997: Ripe and fairly rich, with an interesting milky-malic, leesy accent atop the honey and lemon flavors. Full-bodied and well made, ending on a very toasted oak note. Tempting now. Best after 2001.–P.M. • $38 • (5/31/1999) • **90**
Pouilly-Fuissé Vieilles Vignes 1996 • $29 • (5/31/1998) • **94**
Pouilly-Fuissé Vieilles Vignes 1995 • $35 • (5/31/1997) • **78**
Pouilly-Fuissé Vieilles Vignes 2ème Tri Sélection 1996 • $63 • (5/31/1998) • **86**
Pouilly-Fuissé Vieilles Vignes Grapillage 1996 • $63 • (5/31/1998) • **88**
Pouilly-Loché 1997: Showy, ripe and oaky, offering plenty of lemon, green apple, melon and pear, along with toasted, grilled flavors and a long, full finish that's very toasty but laced with palate-cleansing citrus. Drink now through 2002.–P.M. • $25 • (5/31/1999) • **87**
St.-Véran Clos à la Côte 1997: A cellar-worthy, oaky St-Véran, showy and ambitious. Toasted, honeyed style, medium-bodied and fairly rich, turning intense on the lingering, smoky, floral-scented finish. Drink now through 2001.–P.M. • $30 • (5/31/1999) • **87**
St.-Véran Clos à la Côte 1996 • $21 • (5/31/1998) • **88**

CORIANCON, DOMAINE DU

Côtes du Rhône-Villages Vinsobres 1996: Mature flavors in a light- to medium body. Tannins are a bit dry.–P.M. • $10 • (11/15/1998) • **73**
Côtes du Rhône-Villages Vinsobres 1995: Crisp, with cassis bush and wild raspberries under dried herb and grass flavors. Of medium body, it's fresh, but rather hard.–P.M. • $10 • (11/15/1998) • **79**
Côtes du Rhône-Villages Vinsobres Cuvée Claude Vallot 1994: Attractive, with raspberry, spice, plum and cherry character, round tannins and good acidity. Fresh, light- to medium-bodied. Try with grilled sausage or cheeses. Drink now.–P.M. • $13 • (11/15/1998) • **81**

CORMEIL-FIGEAC, CHATEAU

St.-Emilion 1996: Some good fruit concentration for the vintage, with blackberry and dark chocolate aromas and flavors, but slightly hollow midpalate. Medium- to light-bodied, with fine tannins and a light, fruity aftertaste. Drink now.–J.S. • $30 • (1/31/1999) • **84**
St.-Emilion 1988 • $20 • (4/30/1991) • **85**
St.-Emilion 1986 • $12 • (6/30/1989) • **75**

CORNEAU, PAUL

Pouilly-Fumé Tradition 1996 • $15 • (5/31/1998) • **88**

CORNU, EDMOND

Aloxe-Corton 1995 • $29 • (11/15/1997) • **75**
Aloxe-Corton 1994 • $26 • (11/15/1996) • **77**
Aloxe-Corton 1991 • $24 • (1/31/1994) • **78**
Aloxe-Corton Les Moutottes 1997: Round and full-bodied, showing ripe fruit with a touch of oatmeal, vanilla and spice. Modestly long finish. Drink now through 2002.–P.M. • $40 • (9/30/1999) • **86**
Aloxe-Corton Les Moutottes 1996: Pretty '96 red Burgundy, showing supple texture, lovely blackberry character, good fresh acidity, but it's a bit herbal with a slightly burning aftertaste.–P.M. • $43 • (9/30/1998) • **83**
Aloxe-Corton Les Moutottes 1991 • $33 • (1/31/1994) • **85**
Aloxe-Corton Les Moutottes 1987 • $35 • (12/31/1990) • **83**
Aloxe-Corton Les Valozières 1997: A chocolaty depth augments the black cherry and vanilla aromas and flavors in this medium-bodied '97 red. Seems focused, with stiff tannins as the lasting impression. Best from 2002 through 2007.–B.S. • $41 • (9/30/1999) • **87**
Aloxe-Corton Les Valozieres 1996: Very fresh, with modest berry flavors, but overall it's light and airy, without much concentration. Subtle vanilla on the finish. Best from 2000.–B.S. • $43 • (9/30/1998) • **84**
Aloxe-Corton Les Valozières 1995 • $40 • (11/15/1997) • **87**
Aloxe-Corton Vieille Vigne 1997: Diffuse around the edges and hollow, this is tough and tannic, offering only a modicum of fruit.–B.S. • $31 • (9/30/1999) • **78**
Aloxe-Corton Vieille Vigne 1996: Smells a bit herbal, yet there's good richness and an almost chewy texture to this fleshy red. The finish is coarse. Best from 1999.–B.S. • $30 • (9/30/1998) • **84**
Bourgogne 1997: Green, herbal and astringent, with a tart, unripe finish.–P.M. • $15 • (9/30/1999) • **72**
Bourgogne 1996: Well made. Fairly smooth, with vanilla, raspberry and cherry notes, succulent fruit on the finish. Drink now.–P.M. • $17 • (9/30/1998) • **85**
Bourgogne 1995 • $15 • (11/15/1997) • **71**
Bourgogne 1990 • $15 • (12/15/1992) • **85**
Chorey-lès-Beaune Les Bons Ores 1997: Cherry and licorice hold sway in this light, slightly diffuse '97 red. Stiff tannins. A bit short on the finish.–B.S. • $20 • (9/30/1999) • **79**
Chorey-lès-Beaune Les Bons Ores 1996: Tar and licorice flavors pervade this beefy, slightly rustic red whose firm tannins should soften with food. Best from 2000.–B.S. • $23 • (9/30/1998) • **80**
Chorey-lès-Beaune Les Bons Ores 1995 • $19 • (11/15/1997) • **75**
Chorey-lès-Beaune Les Bons Ores 1994 • $22 • (11/15/1996) • **73**
Chorey-lès-Beaune Les Bons Ores 1993 • $20 • (11/15/1995) • **81**
Chorey-lès-Beaune Les Bons Ores 1992 • $17 • (12/15/1994) • **85**
Chorey-lès-Beaune White 1998: Round and ripe, with butter, butterscotch, caramel character. Lacks a bit of finesse, but at least here's a '98 with enough stuffing to chew on. Drink now through 2002.–P.M. • $22 • (5/31/2000) • **84**
Corton Bressandes 1997: Round but lacking flavors on the midpalate. Short finish.–P.M. • $60 • (9/30/1999) • **78**
Corton Bressandes 1996: Silky-smooth, a lovely wine of great finesse, it melts on the palate like syrup. A touch herbal, with cassis bush, currant and earth character. Marvelously silky tannins make this a "pick me" wine upon release, but the intense, almost hot finish could use some cellaring. Best After 2003.–P.M. • $60 • (9/30/1998) • **89**
Corton Bressandes 1995 • $60 • (11/15/1997) • **83**
Corton Bressandes 1994 • $55 • (11/15/1996) • **83**
Corton Les Bressandes 1993 • $57 • (11/15/1995) • **87**
Corton Les Bressandes 1992 • $43 • (12/15/1994) • **81**
Corton Les Bressandes 1991 • $48 • (1/31/1994) • **88**
Corton Les Bressandes 1990 • $60 • (12/15/1992) • **89**
Corton Les Bressandes 1987 • $53 • (12/31/1990) • **90**
Ladoix 1994 • $24 • (11/15/1996) • **79**
Ladoix 1993 • $22 • (11/15/1995) • **82**
Ladoix 1992 • $18 • (12/15/1994) • **80**
Ladoix 1991 • $18 • (1/31/1994) • **81**
Ladoix 1987 • $18 • (2/28/1991) • **78**
Ladoix Bois Roussot 1996: Round and structured, yet the fruit character is on the herbaceous, vegetal side. Best from 1999.–B.S. • $26 • (9/30/1998) • **79**
Ladoix La Corvée 1997: There's cherry in this rich '97 red, with good midpalate concentration, then it turns tough. May come around. Drink now through 2002.–B.S. • $28 • (9/30/1999) • **82**
Ladoix La Corvée 1992 • $25 • (12/15/1994) • **84**
Ladoix La Corvée 1991 • $24 • (1/31/1994) • **79**
Ladoix Les Carrières 1997: Not a lot of aroma, but there's a chewy, spicy element on the palate, with modest density, before turning tart and tannic.–B.S. • $26 • (9/30/1999) • **78**
Ladoix Les Carrières 1996: A soft, forward style that has racy acidity and plummy flavors without a lot of concentration or depth, and a touch of alcohol. Drink through 2002.–B.S. • $26 • (9/30/1998) • **81**
Ladoix Les Carrières 1995 • $25 • (11/15/1997) • **75**
Ladoix Les Carrières 1994 • $26 • (11/15/1996) • **80**
Ladoix Les Carrières 1993 • $27 • (11/15/1995) • **89**

CORNU, EDMOND

Ladoix Les Carrières 1992 • $22 • (12/15/1994) • **78**
Ladoix Les Corvées 1996: Slightly stemmy, with black cherry, pepper and concentrated fruit flavors, bright acidity and medium tannins. Drink through 2003.–B.S. • $30 • (9/30/1998) • **81**
Ladoix Les Corvées 1995 • $28 • (11/15/1997) • **74**
Ladoix Vieille Vigne 1997: A bit herbal, but it has a soft core of tannins, with decent red fruit and smoky, toasted notes. Chewy finish. Drink now through 2002.–P.M. • $23 • (1/01/2000) • **83**
Ladoix Vieille Vigne 1995 • $20 • (11/15/1997) • **80**
Savigny-lès-Beaune 1997: A bit diluted, with light strawberry flavors.–P.M. • $22 • (9/30/1999) • **75**
Savigny-lès-Beaune 1996: Barnyardy in aroma, fairly thick, with good red berry character, but it ends so sharply it's difficult to judge now. Best After 2003.–P.M. • $23 • (9/30/1998) • **75**
Savigny-lès-Beaune 1995 • $20 • (11/15/1997) • **76**
Savigny-lès-Beaune 1994 • $22 • (11/15/1996) • **74**
Savigny-lès-Beaune 1993 • $22 • (11/15/1995) • **85**
Savigny-lès-Beaune 1992 • $18 • (12/15/1994) • **81**

CORON PERE & FILS

Aloxe-Corton 1996: Smells a bit rubbery, though it has some flesh, with tangy cherry and spice flavors. Finishes with light tannins, turning dry. Drink now through 2001.–B.S. • $23 • (9/30/1998) • **80**
Beaune 1996: Restrained and elegant, unveiling its charm slowly. Medium-bodied, with a firm but balanced personality, there is decent *terroir* and fruit here, albeit not much complexity. Best from 2003 through 2007.–P.M. • $23 • (5/15/1999) • **86**
Beaune 1995 • $25 • (11/15/1997) • **85**
Beaune Clos des Mouches 1996: Has an odd resinous note that the modest fruit struggles to breach, without success. Dry finish. Not recommended. Tasted twice, with consistent notes.–B.S. • $37 • (9/30/1998) • **61**
Beaune Clos des Mouches 1995 • $43 • (11/15/1997) • **85**
Beaune Les Aigrots Domaine du Château de Bligny 1996: Light and fresh. A juicy little Pinot, showing exuberant pure fruit aromas, with crisp acidity and some chocolate, vanilla, cherry and mocha flavors. Clean, balanced finish. Fine now, but could improve with short-term cellaring. Drink through 2005.–P.M. • $30 • (5/15/1999) • **85**
Bonnes Mares 1996: Not showing much on the fruit front, this delivers some mineral, wet earth, game and cherry character, then kicks in with alarmingly dry tannins on the finish.–P.M. • $NA • (2/28/1999) • **79**
Bourgogne White 1996 • $13 • (1/01/1998) • **84**
Chablis Fourchaume 1996 • $21 • (1/01/1998) • **65**
Chambolle-Musigny 1996: A very pretty '96, showing floral, spice and red berry character and an elegant structure, though there's a hint of dry tannins on the finish. Drink now through 2001.–B.S. • $34 • (9/30/1998) • **84**
Chassagne-Montrachet 1995 • $33 • (1/31/1998) • **84**
Clos de la Roche 1996: Lovely, fresh, berry-accented red Burgundy, packed with violet, rose petal, blueberry and blackberry notes, but also loads of acidity. Doesn't offer quite the harmony of some other '96s, but it's still very good. Drink now through 2005.–P.M. • $NA • (2/28/1999) • **88**
Clos de Vougeot 1996: Lovely Clos Vougeot. Not a blockbuster, but the black cherry and spice notes build on the palate, supported by subtle power and firm tannins. Well balanced, young and well integrated. Best from 2001 through 2006.–B.S. • $56 • (9/30/1998) • **89**
Clos de Vougeot 1995 • $63 • (11/15/1997) • **90**
Corton Les Paulands 1996: A fairly tough customer, with lots of cheesy, licorice and cherry notes. Some decent fruit, but also old chestnut aromas as if from tired oak barrels. Lacks a bit of harmony. Drink through 2004.–P.M. • $NA • (2/28/1999) • **83**
Echézeaux Domaine du Château de Bligny 1996: The floral and cherry aromas and flavors are submerged, yet there is good concentration of fruit and structure in this young Pinot, with a just slightly dry and bitter finish. Drink through 2005.–B.S. • $56 • (9/30/1998) • **86**
Gevrey-Chambertin 1996: This has a touch of candied cherry, along with a sauvage, animal element and dense texture, but comes off as foursquare and rigid at this stage. Well balanced, though, so may just need time. Best after 2000.–B.S. • $30 • (9/30/1998) • **86**
Gevrey-Chambertin Lavaut St.-Jacques 1995 • $53 • (11/15/1997) • **77**

Key: SS—Spectator Selection. CS—Cellar Selection. HR—Highly Recommended. $NA—Price not available. (BT)—Barrel tasting. Ⓐ—Auction Price.
For a key to the tasters' initials, see "How to Use These Listings."
Dates in parentheses represent the issues in which the ratings were published.

Gevrey-Chambertin Les Champeaux 1996: An elegant red, full of black cherry and violet character, yet it doesn't unfold on the palate and ultimately promises more than it delivers. May come together with time. Drink through 2005.–B.S. • $44 • (9/30/1998) • **86**
Juliénas Domaine de la Cure Meyrie 1996: A solid, structured and slightly rustic style that displays plum and black currant as well as high acidity. May still have something in reserve.–B.S. • $12 • (10/31/1998) • **84**
Mâcon-Loché Château de Loché 1996 • $11 • (1/01/1998) • **81**
Mâcon-Loché Château de Loché 1995 • $14 • (10/15/1997) • **84**
Meursault 1996: A bit odd, but very interesting. Full-blown Burgundian treatment here, with lots of doughlike and butterscotch aromas, full body and fat texture, a surprisingly tart finish. Drink now through 2002.–P.M. • $29 • (2/28/1999) • **87**
Meursault 1995 • $31 • (1/31/1998) • **78**
Montagny 1996 • $16 • (1/01/1998) • **84**
Moulin-à-Vent Domaine de la Roche 1996: Elegant and racy, typical of the 1996 vintage, with good, concentrated black cherry and vanilla aromas and flavors that unfold across the palate and firm, supporting tannins. Drink now.–B.S. • $13 • (10/31/1998) • **87**
Moulin-à-Vent Domaine de la Roche 1995 • $13 • (4/30/1997) • **87**
Nuits-St.-Georges 1996: Good, concentrated fruit in this blackberry- and mineral-laden '96. Dense and almost chewy, yet the tannins are fine and the lasting impression is more earth and iron than fruit. Best from 2001 through 2008.–B.S. • $30 • (9/30/1998) • **86**
Nuits-St.-Georges 1995 • $33 • (10/15/1997) • **83**
Nuits-St.-Georges Les Cailles 1996: A *terroir*-driven red that shows more earth and mineral than fruit, with juicy acidity and a real presence on the palate. There's depth and concentration, and a licorice note lingers on the finish. Drink through 2005.–B.S. • $43 • (9/30/1998) • **88**
Nuits-St.-Georges Les Cailles 1995 • $52 • (11/15/1997) • **86**
Nuits-St.-Georges Les Pruliers Domaine du Château de Bligny 1996: Tannic and a bit tough, offering wet earth, mineral, leather and game notes, but not much supple charm. Still, it has *terroir* character and the clean structure and pure flavors to stand some cellaring. Best from 2003 through 2008.–P.M. • $40 • (5/15/1999) • **86**
Pommard La Chanière Domaine du Château de Bligny 1996: Plenty of bright cherry notes here, along with vibrant acidity and a touch of mineral. Stylish for Pommard, but it also has firm tannins. A bit dry on the finish. Best from 2001 through 2006.–B.S. • $40 • (9/30/1998) • **84**
Pommard Les Epenots 1995 • $54 • (11/15/1997) • **87**
Pouilly-Fuissé 1995 • $24 • (10/15/1997) • **79**
Pouilly-Fuissé Domaine S. Mornand 1996 • $18 • (1/01/1998) • **83**
Pouilly-Vinzelles Château de Loché 1995 • $19 • (10/15/1997) • **84**
Santenay 1996: A light-bodied, simple red, with spicy, tangy red fruit character, finishing short. Drink now.–B.S. • $17 • (9/30/1998) • **78**
Santenay 1995 • $22 • (11/15/1997) • **77**
St.-Véran Domaine de Montagny 1996 • $12 • (1/01/1998) • **83**
St.-Véran Domaine de Montagny 1995 • $19 • (10/15/1997) • **83**
Volnay 1996: Aromas of raspberry, strawberry and cherry along with vibrant acidity give this light-bodied Pinot a pretty, elegant profile. Drink now.–B.S. • $26 • (9/30/1998) • **81**
Vosne-Romanée Domaine du Château de Bligny 1996: Wet earth and camphor aromas followed by dirty flavors. Not recommended. Tasted twice, with consistent notes.–B.S. • $30 • (9/30/1998) • **56**
Vosne-Romanée Les Suchots 1996: Delicious, with concentrated, spicy cherry and vanilla notes and juicy acidity, all on a supple texture. Charming and forward, this is a crowd-pleaser. Drink now through 2002.–B.S. • $42 • (9/30/1998) • **87**
Vosne-Romanée Les Suchots 1995 • $54 • (11/15/1997) • **88**

CORSIN

Mâcon-Villages 1997: Fresh and pure, zipping along with gooseberry, lime, honey and pear flavors, all in a balanced, delicious, unpretentious package. Enjoy. Drink now.–P.M. • $15 • (5/31/1999) • **86**
Mâcon-Villages 1996 • $13 • (8/31/1997) • **91**
Mâcon-Villages 1995 • $NA • (8/31/1996) • **88**
Pouilly-Fuissé 1997: Ripe, generous and just delicious, with honey, lemon, toasted walnut notes—but mostly it delivers lovely fruit in a seductive texture, like cream on the midpalate. Slightly bitter wet hay and grilled bread character creeps in on the otherwise balanced finish. Drink now through 2002.–P.M. • $25 • (5/31/1999) • **89**
Pouilly-Fuissé 1996 • $23 • (5/31/1998) • **92**
Pouilly-Fuissé 1995 • $20 • (5/31/1997) • **87**

St.-Véran 1997: Smooth and supple, with some nice honey, spice and chocolate notes. Medium-bodied, it's a delight to drink now.–P.M. • $19 • (5/31/1999) • **86**
St.-Véran 1996 • $16 • (5/31/1998) • **88**
St.-Véran 1995 • $15 • (5/31/1997) • **84**
St.-Véran Tirage Précoce 1997: Ripe, honeyed pear and tropical flavors give this soft-edged, medium-bodied Chardonnay immediate appeal. Drink now.–P.M. • $16 • (5/31/1999) • **84**
St.-Véran Tirage Précoce 1996 • $15 • (5/31/1998) • **86**
St.-Véran Tirage Précoce 1995 • $NA • (8/31/1996) • **88**

CORTON ANDRE, CHATEAU

Corton 1994 • $NA • (11/15/1996) • **68**

COS-D'ESTOURNEL, CHATEAU

St.-Estèphe 1999: Attractive. Aromas of Indian spices, berries and meat. Medium-bodied, with good velvety tannins and a medium finish. Slightly hollow center palate.–J.S. • $NA • (1/01/2000) (BT) • **85-89**
St.-Estèphe 1998: Pretty young wine with spices and berries throughout. Medium-bodied, with medium tannins and a silky finish. Slightly hollow midpalate. Not up to Cos' usual stellar quality, but very good.–J.S. • $NA • (5/31/1999) (BT) • **85-89**
St.-Estèphe 1997: Serious concentration of fruit in this wine, with plenty of chocolate and berry character and a hint of dried herbs on the nose. Full- to medium-bodied, with plenty of fruit and a velvety texture. Best from 2001 through 2006.–J.S. • $68 • (1/31/2000) • **89**
St.-Estèphe 1996: A classy and impressive young Bordeaux from an appellation that stepped up in '96. Dark-colored, with plenty of currant and spice aromas, the wine is full-bodied, with very velvety tannins and all-spice, berry and currant flavors. Long, long finish. One of the wines of the vintage, it's a beauty. Best after 2005.–J.S. • $70 Ⓐ • (1/31/1999) CS • **95**
St.-Estèphe 1995 • $83 Ⓐ • (1/31/1998) • **93**
St.-Estèphe 1994 • $50 Ⓐ • (1/31/1997) HR • **91**
St.-Estèphe 1993 • $43 Ⓐ • (1/31/1996) • **88**
St.-Estèphe 1992 • $24 Ⓐ • (4/15/1995) • **87**
St.-Estèphe 1991 • $31 • (3/31/1994) • **88**
St.-Estèphe 1990 • $108 Ⓐ • (3/31/1993) • **90**
St.-Estèphe 1989: A huge, seamless wine of fabulous elegance. Deep, dark-ruby color. Intense aromas of blackberries, spices, mushrooms and bark. Full-bodied and extremely silky, with a long, long finish. Seductive as hell. (1989 Bordeaux horizontal tasting). Best after 2002.–J.S. • $83 Ⓐ • (5/31/1999) • **95**
St.-Estèphe 1988: This powerhouse is rather traditional and decadent compared to the modern-day wines from Cos. Ink-colored and full-bodied, with ripe fruit aromas, velvety tannins and intense berry and spice flavors. (1988 Bordeaux horizontal tasting). Best after 2002.–J.S. • $70 Ⓐ • (11/30/1998) • **95**
St.-Estèphe 1987 • $53 Ⓐ • (5/15/1990) • **81**
St.-Estèphe 1986 • $117 Ⓐ • (5/31/1989) • **93**
St.-Estèphe 1985 • $102 Ⓐ • (9/15/1996) • **93**
St.-Estèphe 1984 • $29 • (3/31/1987) • **93**
St.-Estèphe 1983 • $60 Ⓐ • (10/15/1994) • **91**
St.-Estèphe 1982: Built for aging. Very dark ruby in color, with a garnet rim. Dried flower and berry aromas. Full-bodied and very solid, with masses of fruit and tannins. Still has plenty of time to go. (1982 Bordeaux horizontal tasting). Best after 2000.–J.S. • $151 Ⓐ • (11/30/1998) • **95**
St.-Estèphe 1981 • $53 Ⓐ • (10/15/1994) • **87**
St.-Estèphe 1980 • $41 Ⓐ • (5/15/1990) • **83**
St.-Estèphe 1979 • $50 Ⓐ • (10/15/1989) • **87**
St.-Estèphe 1978 • $58 Ⓐ • (5/15/1990) • **93**
St.-Estèphe 1977 • $30 • (5/15/1990) • **85**
St.-Estèphe 1976 • $48 Ⓐ • (5/15/1990) • **84**
St.-Estèphe 1975 • $47 Ⓐ • (5/15/1990) • **88**
St.-Estèphe 1973 • $31 • (5/15/1990) • **82**
St.-Estèphe 1971 • $48 • (5/15/1990) • **91**
St.-Estèphe 1970 • $66 Ⓐ • (5/15/1990) • **89**
St.-Estèphe 1969 • $27 Ⓐ • (5/15/1990) • **58**
St.-Estèphe 1967 • $NA • (5/15/1990) • **82**
St.-Estèphe 1966 • $71 Ⓐ • (5/15/1990) • **74**
St.-Estèphe 1964 • $65 • (5/15/1990) • **84**
St.-Estèphe 1962 • $NA • (11/30/1987) • **85**
St.-Estèphe 1961 • $174 Ⓐ • (4/30/1996) • **89**
St.-Estèphe 1960 • $85 • (5/15/1990) • **79**
St.-Estèphe 1959 • $230 • (10/15/1990) • **90**
St.-Estèphe 1958 • $95 • (5/15/1990) • **89**
St.-Estèphe 1956 • $60 • (5/15/1990) • **79**
St.-Estèphe 1955 • $167 Ⓐ • (5/15/1990) • **90**
St.-Estèphe 1954 • $80 • (5/15/1990) • **81**
St.-Estèphe 1953 • $146 Ⓐ • (5/15/1990) • **91**
St.-Estèphe 1952 • $90 • (5/15/1990) • **95**
St.-Estèphe 1950 • $100 • (5/15/1990) • **86**
St.-Estèphe 1949 • $218 Ⓐ • (5/15/1990) • **80**
St.-Estèphe 1947 • $330 • (5/15/1990) • **91**
St.-Estèphe 1945 • $382 Ⓐ • (5/15/1990) • **77**
St.-Estèphe 1943 • $220 • (5/15/1990) • **85**
St.-Estèphe 1942 • $110 • (5/15/1990) • **78**
St.-Estèphe 1934 • $232 Ⓐ • (5/15/1990) • **88**
St.-Estèphe 1929 • $124 Ⓐ • (5/15/1990) • **92**
St.-Estèphe 1928 • $698 Ⓐ • (5/15/1990) • **90**
St.-Estèphe 1926 • $300 • (5/15/1990) • **77**
St.-Estèphe 1924 • $200 Ⓐ • (5/15/1990) • **82**
St.-Estèphe 1920 • $350 • (5/15/1990) • **93**
St.-Estèphe 1917 • $250 • (5/15/1990) • **73**
St.-Estèphe 1899 • $1,248 Ⓐ • (5/15/1990) • **87**
St.-Estèphe 1898 • $500 • (5/15/1990) • **72**
St.-Estèphe 1870 • $1,250 • (5/15/1990) • **90**
St.-Estèphe 1869 • $1,250 • (5/15/1990) • **82**

COS-LABORY, CHATEAU

St.-Estèphe 1999: Gorgeous floral, currant and mineral aromas. Medium- to full-bodied, with lots of fruit and a very good finish. Very good effort by this estate.–J.S. • $NA • (1/01/2000) (BT) • **85-89**
St.-Estèphe 1998: Well crafted, with pretty, polished tannins, but it needs more fruit concentration to score outstanding. Medium-bodied, with berry, currant character.–J.S. • $NA • (5/31/1999) (BT) • **85-89**
St.-Estèphe 1997: A bit lean, but some good berry and currant character. Medium-bodied, with medium tannins and a short finish. Drink now.–J.S. • $23 • (1/31/2000) • **85**
St.-Estèphe 1996: Good dark color, with lots of currant, floral and vanilla aromas. Medium-bodied, with fine tannins and a long, racy finish. A sleek and well-crafted red. Best after 2003.–J.S. • $22 • (1/31/1999) • **88**
St.-Estèphe 1995 • $20 Ⓐ • (1/31/1998) • **88**
St.-Estèphe 1994 • $14 Ⓐ • (1/31/1997) • **86**
St.-Estèphe 1993 • $20 • (1/31/1996) • **80**
St.-Estèphe 1992 • $20 • (4/15/1995) • **85**
St.-Estèphe 1991 • $20 • (3/31/1994) • **83**
St.-Estèphe 1990 • $40 Ⓐ • (3/31/1993) • **94**
St.-Estèphe 1989: Big and tannic red. Best Cos-Labory ever made. Dark-ruby in color. Mint, chocolate and berry aromas. Full-bodied and very tannic, with a mouthpuckering, velvety texture. Still needs time. (1989 Bordeaux horizontal tasting). Try after 2005.–J.S. • $NA • (5/31/1999) • **91**
St.-Estèphe 1988 • $20 • (4/30/1991) • **85**
St.-Estèphe 1985 • $16 • (4/30/1988) • **87**
St.-Estèphe 1984 • $12 • (6/15/1987) • **73**
St.-Estèphe 1982 • $25 Ⓐ • (8/31/1992) • **86**
St.-Estèphe 1961 • $NA • (4/30/1996) • **75**

COSTE, DOMAINE DE LA

Coteaux du Languedoc St.-Christol 1991 • $8 • (3/15/1994) • **85**
Coteaux du Languedoc St.-Christol Cuvée Sélectionnée 1993 • $7 • (3/31/1995) • **82**
Coteaux du Languedoc St.-Christol Cuvée Sélectionnée 1991 • $8 • (12/15/1994) • **85**
Syrah Coteaux du Languedoc 1994 • $10 • (6/30/1997) • **79**
Syrah Coteaux du Languedoc 1993 • $10 • (1/31/1997) • **87**

COSTE-CAUMARTIN

Beaune Les Chouacheux 1995 • $36 • (11/15/1997) • **74**
Bourgogne 1995 • $13 • (11/15/1997) • **75**
Bourgogne 1994 • $15 • (11/15/1996) • **72**
Bourgogne 1993 • $18 • (11/15/1995) • **83**
Bourgogne 1990 • $16 • (12/15/1992) • **88**
Bourgogne 1989 • $15 • (1/31/1992) • **87**
Pommard 1995 • $28 • (11/15/1997) • **77**
Pommard 1994 • $25 • (11/15/1996) • **80**
Pommard 1993 • $37 • (11/15/1995) • **80**
Pommard 1991 • $30 • (1/31/1994) • **79**

COSTE-CAUMARTIN

Pommard 1990 • $28 • (12/15/1992) • **94**
Pommard 1987 • $21 • (11/15/1990) • **76**
Pommard Les Boucherottes 1995 • $36 • (11/15/1997) • **83**
Pommard Les Boucherottes 1994 • $35 • (11/15/1996) • **82**
Pommard Les Boucherottes 1993 • $42 • (11/15/1995) • **90**
Pommard Les Boucherottes 1992 • $35 • (12/15/1994) • **87**
Pommard Les Boucherottes 1991 • $38 • (1/31/1994) • **83**
Pommard Les Boucherottes 1990 • $37 • (12/15/1992) • **95**
Pommard Les Boucherottes 1989 • $38 • (1/31/1992) • **92**
Pommard Les Fremiers 1995 • $36 • (11/15/1997) • **77**
Pommard Les Fremiers 1994 • $30 • (11/15/1996) • **73**
Pommard Les Fremiers 1993 • $NA • (5/15/1996) • **88**
Pommard Les Fremiers 1992 • $31 • (12/15/1994) • **81**
Pommard Les Fremiers 1991 • $33 • (1/31/1994) • **85**
Pommard Les Fremiers 1990 • $32 • (12/15/1992) • **94**
Pommard Les Fremiers 1989 • $35 • (1/31/1992) • **92**
Pommard Les Fremiers 1987 • $26 • (11/15/1990) • **79**
Pommard Les Vignots 1992 • $26 • (12/15/1994) • **78**

COSTIERES DE POMEROLS, LES

Picpoul de Pinet Coteaux du Languedoc Domaine St.-Peyre 1997: Crisp and lively, with pretty flavors of green plum, pepper and honeydew melon, this wine has a nice backbone of acidity and a good clean finish. Drink now.–K.M. • $8 • (4/30/1999) • **84**

Picpoul de Pinet Coteaux du Languedoc Hugues Beaulieu 1996 • $7 • (4/30/1998) • **83**

COTAT, FRANCOIS

Sancerre La Grande Côte 1997: Lovely aromas of newly mown hay give way to a rich texture and ripe flavors of herb, pear and citrus. This white is both concentrated and crisp, muscular and balanced. Though not showy, it is classic in flavor and structured to age. Drink now through 2004.–T.M. • $30 • (11/15/1999) • **91**

Sancerre Les Culs de Beaujeu 1997: This muscular white shows straight-ahead flavors of pear, melon and herb that are well integrated but unadorned. Balanced and clean, it seems to show sheer concentration more than complexity or verve. Good with food. Drink now through 2002.–T.M. • $27 • (11/15/1999) • **86**

Sancerre Les Monts Damnés 1997: This big-boned wine is rich with powerful aromas and flavors of toast and coffee that frame ripe pear and herb notes. Atypical, but it remains fresh and distinctive enough to bring you back for another sip. Drink now through 2002.–T.M. • $25 • (11/15/1999) • **87**

Sancerre Les Monts Damnés Cuvée Spéciale 1997: This white is rich and viscous, with toasty, spicy accents to the ripe pear and melon flavors. It has the texture of a late-harvest wine, and there's a hint of sweetness on the palate; clearly not your typical Sancerre, it nonetheless is a tour de force. Drink now through 2003.–T.M. • $30 • (11/15/1999) • **90**

Sancerre Rosé 1997: This rosé offers juicy, herb-scented flavors of strawberry and cherry, with grip and good length on the finish. Dry and well balanced, it should match well with food. Drink now.–T.M. • $22 • (11/15/1999) • **86**

Vin de Table Français La Grande Côte 1998: Alluring toast and almond notes lead into a frankly sweet and exotic but well-integrated white, with plump, juicy flavors of lime, straw, honeysuckle and lanolin that push through on the mouthwatering finish. Not what you expect from Sancerre, but downright delicious. Drink now through 2002.–B.S. • $17 • (6/15/2000) • **91**

Vin de Table Français Les Culs de Beaujeu 1998: Beeswax, white peach, chamomile and hay aromas and flavors run through this remarkably dense and rich white. Maintains a gorgeous, round and suave mouthfeel all the way through to the lengthy, mineral-tinged finish. Drink now through 2002.–B.S. • $15 • (6/15/2000) HR • **92**

Vin de Table Français Les Monts Damnés 1998: Ripe and lush, with lime and pear flavors that verge on sweet but are kept honest by distinctive grass and chive notes that chime in on the authoritative finish. Needs a little time to knit together. Drink now through 2002.–B.S. • $15 • (6/15/2000) • **88**

Key: SS—Spectator Selection. CS—Cellar Selection. HR—Highly Recommended. $NA—Price not available. (BT)—Barrel tasting. Ⓐ—Auction Price. For a key to the tasters' initials, see "How to Use These Listings." **Dates in parentheses represent the issues in which the ratings were published.**

COTAT, PAUL

Sancerre La Grande Côte 1996: Atypical but appealing. This rich white shows classic citrus and herbal aromas, then turns lush and slightly sweet on the palate, where firm underlying acidity keeps it balanced and refreshing. Not the usual match with shellfish, but an interesting, distinctive white. Drink now through 2002.–T.M. • $37 • (2/28/1999) • **89**

Sancerre Les Culs de Beaujeu Cuvée Spéciale 1996: Don't confuse this with a typical Sancerre. It does offer the classic pear, mineral and grass flavors, but in a late-harvest style. Thick on the palate, with underlying honey and vanilla. A seductive wine best to drink on its own. Drink now through 2002.–T.M. • $28 • (6/30/1999) • **89**

Sancerre Les Monts Damnés 1996: A heavy earth aroma blows off somewhat to reveal light herbal notes that take over and follow through on the palate, where crisp, lemony acidity gives backbone and a refreshing finish. It's both delicate and rich, though not for everyone. Drink now.–T.M. • $27 • (2/28/1999) • **83**

Sancerre Red 1989 • $21 • (9/30/1992) • **79**

COTE DE BALEAU, CHATEAU

St.-Emilion 1997: Beautiful wine. Intriguing plum and chocolate aromas follow through to a medium-bodied palate, with velvety tannins and a long finish. Well done. Drink now through 2004.–J.S. • $NA • (1/31/2000) • **87**

COTE MONTPEZAT, CHATEAU

Côtes de Castillon 1994 • $15 • (6/30/1997) • **86**
Côtes de Castillon 1993 • $NA • (1/31/1996) • **83**

COTEAUX DES TRAVERS, DOMAINE DES

Côtes du Rhône-Villages Cairanne 1996: Smells of barnyard and tastes like, well ... not recommended. Tasted twice, with consistent notes.–P.M. • $14 • (11/15/1998) • **50**

Côtes du Rhône-Villages Rasteau 1996: Green flavors compete with modest red berry ones in this unripe, light-bodied red.–P.M. • $14 • (11/15/1998) • **71**

COTES DE ROL, CHATEAU

St.-Emilion 1997: A light and pleasant red with tobacco, cherry character, light tannins and a fresh finish. Drink now.–J.S. • $NA • (1/31/2000) • **81**

St.-Emilion 1995 • $15 • (1/31/1998) • **80**

COTTAT, PATIENT

Sancerre Vieilles Vignes 1997: This white's buttery aromas are unusual for Sancerre, but on the palate the wine comes into focus, with crisp, herb-scented, lively citrus and mineral flavors. Not a powerhouse, but balanced for food. Drink now.–T.M. • $24 • (11/15/1999) • **87**

COTTON, PATRICK

Brouilly Cuvée Clos Cadard 1996: Harsh smoky and earthy aromas—and the core of black cherry isn't enough to offset them. Rustic.–T.M. • $18 • (8/31/1998) • **76**

COUCHEROY, CHATEAU

Pessac-Léognan 1996: Some decent fruit, but rather weedy and herbal too, with dry tannins. Medium- to light-bodied, with a light fruit finish. Hard to like.–J.S. • $NA • (2/28/1999) • **79**

Pessac-Léognan 1995 • $18 • (1/31/1998) • **85**
Pessac-Léognan 1993 • $11 • (1/31/1996) • **84**

Pessac-Léognan White 1996: Not an overly serious wine, but delicious. Fresh, with lemon, apple and grassy character on nose and palate. Medium-bodied, with a clean aftertaste. Drink now.–J.S. • $11 • (3/31/1999) • **85**

COUDERT, FERNAND

Fleurie Clos de la Roilette 1994 • $16 • (9/15/1996) • **84**
Fleurie Clos de la Roilette 1993 • $17 • (6/15/1995) • **81**
Fleurie Clos de la Roilette 1992 • $15 • (6/15/1994) • **88**
Fleurie Clos de la Roilette 1991 • $13 • (7/31/1992) • **85**

COUEDIC, PAUL DU

Mercurey 1995 • $18 • (11/15/1997) • **71**
Mercurey Les Veleys 1995 • $20 • (11/15/1997) • **85**

COUFRAN, CHATEAU

Haut-Médoc 1998: A pleasant core of Merlot fruit in this young wine. Medium-bodied, with medium tannins and a sweet fruit finish. Well done for the vintage.–J.S. • $NA • (5/31/1999) (BT) • **85-89**
Haut-Médoc 1997: Very raisiny aromas and hints of chocolate. Medium-bodied, with a good core of fruit but slightly raised acidity. Drink now.–J.S. • $23 • (1/31/2000) • **83**
Haut-Médoc 1996: Plenty of blackberry, blueberry and tanned leather on the nose. Medium-bodied, with firm tannins and a chewy texture. Fruity and spicy aftertaste. Slightly hollow midpalate. Best after 2000.–J.S. • $30 • (1/31/1999) • **86**
Haut-Médoc 1995 • $25 • (1/31/1998) • **87**
Haut-Médoc 1994 • $20 • (1/31/1997) • **85**
Haut-Médoc 1992 • $12 • (4/15/1995) • **81**
Haut-Médoc 1991 • $12 • (3/31/1994) • **78**
Haut-Médoc 1990 • $17 • (3/31/1993) • **88**
Haut-Médoc 1989: A generous wine for drinking now. Lots of ripe fruit, such as prunes and red berries, on the nose. Full-bodied, with chewy tannins and a caressing, velvety texture. Ripe and delicious yet slightly dry on the finish. (1989 Bordeaux horizontal tasting).–J.S. • $NA • (5/31/1999) • **89**
Haut-Médoc 1988 • $15 • (4/30/1991) • **84**
Haut-Médoc 1987 • $12 • (11/30/1989) • **81**
Haut-Médoc 1986 • $13 • (11/30/1989) • **82**
Haut-Médoc 1985 • $11 • (6/30/1988) • **85**
Haut-Médoc 1982 • $21 Ⓐ • (8/31/1992) • **85**

COUHINS-LURTON, CHATEAU

Pessac-Léognan 1996: Quite a thick white, with chalk, apple and mineral aromas and flavors. Full-bodied, with medium acidity and an apple aftertaste. A bit rustic really. Drink now.–J.S. • $NA • (1/01/1999) • **83**
Pessac-Léognan White 1998: Classy. Wonderful freshness to this white, with a floral, lemon and stream character. Full-bodied and reserved, with fresh fruit and a long, zingy finish. Best after 2000.–J.S. • $28 • (2/29/2000) • **90**

COUILLAUD, LES FRERES

Chardonnay Vin de Pays du Jardin de la France Domaine La Morinière 1996 • $7 • (5/31/1998) • **81**
Chardonnay Vin de Pays du Jardin de la France Domaine Trois Frères 1997: Vanilla and butter dominate the light apple flavors in this soft white. Smooth and polished, it lacks the vivacity to match food well.–T.M. • $9 • (6/30/1999) • **78**
Muscadet de Sèvre et Maine Sur Lie Château La Morinière 1996 • $8 • (5/31/1998) • **85**
Muscadet de Sèvre et Maine Sur Lie Domaine La Morinière 1996 • $8 • (5/31/1998) • **80**
Muscadet de Sèvre et Maine Sur Lie Domaine Trois Frères 1997: Shows an appealing delicacy for Muscadet, with floral and light citrus aromas and flavors, yet it has enough body to match well with light fish such as sole and flounder. Drink now.–T.M. • $10 • (6/30/1999) • **84**
Vin de Pays du Jardin de la France Chardet Cuvée Prestige Couillaud 1996 • $8 • (5/31/1998) • **79**

COULON & FILS, PAUL

Châteauneuf-du-Pape Boisrenard 1998: Clean, ripe and balanced. Full-bodied, with cassis, blackberry, spice and mocha. Modern in style, quite extracted and vibrant in its ruby color and lively flavors. Tannins clamp down on the finish, so cellar. Best from 2005 through 2015.–P.M. • $48 • (6/30/2000) • **90**
Châteauneuf-du-Pape Boisrenard 1997: Well made, supple and balanced, offering a delicious array of earth, spice, plum, and smoke; medium-bodied, its strong, ripe-tasting character continues on the lovely, minerally finish. Impressive '97. Drink now through 2007.–P.M. • $55 • (8/31/1999) • **90**
Châteauneuf-du-Pape Boisrenard 1996: Exotic, fresh and clean, with lovely currant, violet, rose petal, blackberry, roasted coffee and wood-inspired spice notes that waltz on the palate and seduce the nose. Full-bodied and fairly dense, it offers good intensity and a velvety mouthfeel thanks to the fine-tannin texture. Pure, racy finish. Could use some cellaring. Best from 2002 through 2006.–P.M. • $48 • (9/30/1998) • **92**
Châteauneuf-du-Pape Boisrenard 1995 • $45 • (10/15/1997) • **92**
Châteauneuf-du-Pape Boisrenard 1994 • $45 • (10/15/1997) • **89**
Châteauneuf-du-Pape Domaine de Beaurenard 1998: Attractive. Sweet-tasting and ripe, sophisticated in its smooth, round and silky mouthfeel, delivering loads of fruit and wet earth. Drink now through 2015.–P.M. • $25 • (6/30/2000) HR • **93**
Châteauneuf-du-Pape Domaine de Beaurenard 1997: Chewy and firm, delivering good black fruit, solid tannin and a smoky character. Showing good, ripe concentration, it's a deliciously balanced red in a medium-bodied, medium-intense package. Drink through 2005.–P.M. • $25 • (8/31/1999) • **89**
Châteauneuf-du-Pape Domaine de Beaurenard 1996 • $24 • (10/15/1997) • **83**
Châteauneuf-du-Pape Domaine de Beaurenard 1995 • $24 • (10/15/1997) • **87**
Châteauneuf-du-Pape Domaine de Beaurenard 1994 • $23 • (11/15/1996) • **86**
Châteauneuf-du-Pape Domaine de Beaurenard 1991 • $19 • (6/15/1993) • **82**
Châteauneuf-du-Pape Domaine de Beaurenard 1990 • $19 • (11/15/1992) HR • **90**
Châteauneuf-du-Pape Domaine de Beaurenard 1989 • $21 • (10/15/1991) • **86**
Châteauneuf-du-Pape Domaine de Beaurenard 1988 • $20 • (10/15/1991) • **89**
Châteauneuf-du-Pape Domaine de Beaurenard 1986 • $24 • (10/15/1991) • **88**
Châteauneuf-du-Pape Domaine de Beaurenard 1985 • $20 • (10/15/1991) • **87**
Châteauneuf-du-Pape Domaine de Beaurenard 1983 • $20 • (10/15/1991) • **87**
Châteauneuf-du-Pape Domaine de Beaurenard 1981 • $20 • (10/15/1991) • **88**
Châteauneuf-du-Pape White Domaine de Beaurenard 1998: Clean and fresh, with a smoky intensity and floral, wet hay and hazelnut notes. Full-bodied and a bit hot on the finish. Drink now through 2002.–P.M. • $28 • (9/30/1999) • **85**
Châteauneuf-du-Pape White Domaine de Beaurenard 1997: Nice and fairly sweet, clean and crisp, with lemon pie, pear and apple notes. Of medium body, it tastes somewhat bitter on the finish, but has good ripeness. Drink now.–P.M. • $25 • (9/30/1998) • **85**
Châteauneuf-du-Pape White Domaine de Beaurenard 1996 • $24 • (10/15/1997) • **87**
Côtes du Rhône Domaine de Beaurenard 1997: Has some grip of fruit and spice, delivering a certain ripeness on the palate, turning chewy and a bit herbal on the smoky finish.–P.M. • $10 • (11/15/1999) • **79**
Côtes du Rhône Domaine de Beaurenard 1996 • $10 • (10/15/1997) • **75**
Côtes du Rhône Domaine de Beaurenard 1994 • $10 • (10/15/1996) • **79**
Côtes du Rhône Domaine de Beaurenard 1991 • $10 • (6/15/1993) • **83**
Côtes du Rhône Domaine de Beaurenard 1990 • $10 • (4/15/1993) • **78**
Côtes du Rhône Domaine de Beaurenard 1989 • $10 • (11/15/1992) • **78**
Côtes du Rhône Rosé Domaine de Beaurenard 1998: If there were such a thing as *terroir* in pink wines, this would qualify. A rosé in a pale rose shade, it has a tough and tannic edge to it, definitely offering lots of character for the buck. The tightness opens up on the lingering, ripe finish. Drink now.–P.M. • $10 • (11/15/1999) • **87**
Côtes du Rhône Rosé Domaine de Beaurenard 1997: Pretty, clean and pure, with a sense of elegance, this medium-bodied rosé offers cherry and raspberry of decent intensity. Well made, if shy on *terroir*. Drink now.–P.M. • $10 • (11/15/1998) • **85**
Côtes du Rhône Rosé Domaine de Beaurenard 1996 • $10 • (10/15/1997) • **79**
Côtes du Rhône-Villages Rasteau Domaine de Beaurenard 1997: Pleasant and easy to drink, with supple tannins and decent intensity of black fruit and gamy, toasty notes. Drink now.–P.M. • $14 • (11/15/1999) • **81**
Côtes du Rhône-Villages Rasteau Domaine de Beaurenard 1996 • $17 • (10/15/1997) • **73**
Côtes du Rhône-Villages Rasteau Domaine de Beaurenard 1996: Elegant and flavorful, with supple, well-integrated tannins and spice, mocha, currant and raspberry flavors. Medium- to full-bodied, it's quite woody now but has enough fruit to achieve balance with some cellaring. Drink now.–P.M. • $15 • (11/15/1998) • **85**

COULY-DUTHEIL

Chinon Clos de l'Echo 1995: Cherry, sage and tobacco are the main themes in this moderately structured red, with juicy acidity and dry tannins on the finish. Drink now.–B.S. • $22 • (10/31/1998) • **84**
Chinon Clos de l'Echo 1989 • $NA • (10/31/1994) • **88**
Chinon Domaine de Versailles 1981 • $13 • (3/15/1987) • **86**
Chinon Domaine René Couly 1993 • $12 • (10/31/1994) • **84**
Chinon La Diligence 1993 • $NA • (10/31/1994) • **87**
Chinon Les Gravières d'Amador Abbé de Turpenay 1997: Cherry and black currant aromas are followed by a silky, rich, almost chewy texture, with up-front cherry and berry flavors, moderate acidity. Drink now.–B.S. • $13 • (10/31/1998) • **85**

COULY-DUTHEIL

Chinon Les Gravières d'Amador Abbé de Turpenay 1993 • $11 • (10/31/1994) • **86**

Chinon Les Gravières d'Amador Abbé de Turpenay 1986 • $10 • (4/30/1988) • **72**

Chinon Rosé Domaine René Couly 1993 • $NA • (10/31/1994) • **83**

Chinon White Les Chanteaux 1996: Austere, with good concentration of green apple and chamomile and a framework of sharp acidity. Drink now.–B.S. • $13 • (11/15/1998) • **82**

Saumur-Champigny La Vigneronne 1985 • $10 • (2/15/1987) • **87**

COUR PAVILLON, LA

Bordeaux 1994 • $10 • (4/30/1997) • **77**

COURANCONNE, CHATEAU LA

Côtes du Rhône-Villages White Seguret 1996 • $14 • (10/15/1997) • **82**

COURBIS, DOMAINE

Cornas Champelrose 1997: Well made in an oaky style. Loads of mocha, coffee, vanilla and smoke notes dominate this full-bodied Syrah, but there's lovely intensity and good concentration, and the acidity is decently integrated. Drink now.–P.M. • $17 • (8/31/1999) • **88**

Cornas Champelrose 1996: Lovely, smooth, round and fruity, this medium-bodied Cornas shows pretty red- and blackberry, cherry, grilled meat and wet earth flavors, plus a barnyardy note. Not so complex perhaps, but the tannins are ripe and velvety, so who will complain? Harmonious finish. Drink now through 2005.–P.M. • $21 • (11/15/1998) • **90**

Cornas Champelrose 1995 • $29 • (10/15/1997) • **88**

Cornas La Sabarotte 1997: A showy Syrah, beautifully packed with toasted oak, spice and roasted coffee flavors, accented by some black fruit that zooms on the finish. Full-bodied, showing nice integration of tannins, acidity, fruit and oak. Drink now through 2001.–P.M. • $23 • (8/31/1999) • **89**

Cornas La Sabarotte 1996: A modern, international style of Cornas with lots of toasty, spicy, mocha-flavored oak accents, this Northern Rhône red also delivers plenty of lovely cassis, wild berry, wet earth and tarlike character and a supple, silky texture. Long, succulent finish. Wonderful. Drink now through 2010.–P.M. • $26 • (10/15/1998) HR • **95**

Cornas La Sabarotte 1995 • $29 • (10/15/1997) • **93**

Cornas La Sabarotte 1994 • $28 • (12/15/1996) • **88**

Cornas Les Eygats 1997: A huge, inky-black, warm-weather Cornas. Full-bodied, with impressive blackberry, currant, game, leather and toasted spices. Complex and above all thick-textured, with ripe tannins. On the finish it stays crisp and tastes a bit hot. Best after 2002.–P.M. • $35 • (12/15/1999) • **90**

St.-Joseph 1997: Rather full in body, with ripe fruit character, it delivers anise, blackberry and vanilla notes in a round package. Best after 2000.–P.M. • $12 • (10/31/1999) • **86**

St.-Joseph 1995 • $19 • (10/15/1997) • **80**

St.-Joseph Domaine des Royes 1995 • $NA • (10/15/1997) • **88**

St.-Joseph Domaine des Royes 1994 • $20 • (11/30/1996) • **87**

St.-Joseph Domaine des Royes 1991 • $NA • (5/31/1994) • **78**

St.-Joseph Les Royes 1997: A pumped-up wine that's so oaky it hints at a petrol aroma. Full-bodied and ripe, very extracted in style, with loads of toasted oak and mocha plus black fruit, a slight bitter character and chewy tannins. A bit overdone. Drink now through 2002.–P.M. • $16 • (10/31/1999) • **81**

St.-Joseph Les Royes 1996: Marvelous wine, bursting with cassis, blackberry, floral and toasted oak, showing harmony, excellent acidity and a ripe core of tannins. Medium- to full-bodied, slightly earthy, it's sophisticated, long and pure, with fresh and vibrant fruit. Drink now through 2005.–P.M. • $15 • (11/15/1998) • **93**

St.-Joseph White 1998: A rather lean and acid-crisp sort of white, showing a fresh lemon and pear skin character.–P.M. • $13 • (12/15/1999) • **79**

St.-Joseph White 1997: Crisp and a bit tart, this medium-bodied white almond, cedar and apple aromas and flavors. A decent wine to match all sorts of foods. Drink now.–P.M. • $21 • (11/15/1998) • **80**

Key: SS—Spectator Selection. CS—Cellar Selection. HR—Highly Recommended. $NA—Price not available. (BT)—Barrel tasting. Ⓐ—Auction Price. For a key to the tasters' initials, see "How to Use These Listings." **Dates in parentheses represent the issues in which the ratings were published.**

St.-Joseph White 1996: Nice and clean, with good acidity, showing green apple, pear and floral notes. Of medium body, with lime and lemon on the finish. Drink now through 2005.–P.M. • $16 • (11/15/1998) • **85**

COURCEL, DOMAINE DE

Pommard Grand Clos des Epenots 1997: A stewed character marks the aroma in this austere '97 that offers plum, earth and an iron component supported by moderate tannins. Drink now through 2002.–B.S. • $54 • (9/30/1999) • **85**

Pommard Clos des Epenots 1996: Traditional style, a bit rustic, with the chestnut-oak notes putting a somewhat astringent feel atop the decently ripe plum and blackberry flavors. Tough finish. Best from 2002 through 2007.–P.M. • $48 • (5/15/1999) • **84**

Pommard Grand Clos des Epenots 1993 • $33 • (11/15/1995) • **88**

Pommard Grand Clos des Epenots 1985 • $53 Ⓐ • (4/30/1988) • **89**

Pommard Les Rugiens 1997: A crowd-pleaser. Nicely oaked, this '97 Pommard features soft, round, ripe plum and vanilla notes and a good dose of tannins underneath. Drink now through 2004.–B.S. • $56 • (9/30/1999) • **87**

Pommard Les Rugiens 1996: A bit tart, with an advanced mushroom, forest underbrush character. Has some ripe fruit and chewy tannins.–P.M. • $42 Ⓐ • (5/15/1999) • **79**

Pommard Les Rugiens 1993 • $42 Ⓐ • (11/15/1995) • **90**

Pommard Les Rugiens 1985 • $40 • (4/30/1988) • **92**

COURLAT, CHATEAU DU

Lussac-St.-Emilion 1982: Pleasant and elegant. Medium-red in color, with an amber edge. Chocolate and cherry aromas and flavors, fine tannins and a medium silky finish. (1982 Bordeaux horizontal tasting). Drink now.–J.S. • $NA • (11/30/1998) • **86**

COURONNE, CHATEAU LA

St.-Emilion 1996: Light and diluted, with some berry and tobacco character but also a rather watery finish. Hard to get excited about.–J.S. • $22 • (1/31/1999) • **76**

St.-Emilion 1995 • $15 • (1/31/1998) • **78**

St.-Emilion 1993 • $16 • (7/31/1996) • **82**

St.-Emilion 1992 • $16 • (7/31/1996) • **75**

COURONNEAU, CHATEAU

Bordeaux Supérieur 1996: Rather odd, with stewed tomato and basil notes. Watery finish. Yikes.–J.S. • $10 • (2/28/1999) • **76**

COUROULU, DOMAINE LE

Vacqueyras 1996: Clean and fresh, this straightforward Rhône red shows nice red berry and pepper character. Harmonious finish. Drink now.–P.M. • $12 • (10/31/1999) • **81**

Vacqueyras 1995 • $13 • (10/15/1997) • **87**

Vacqueyras 1993 • $12 • (2/28/1997) • **81**

Vacqueyras 1992 • $10 • (10/31/1995) • **86**

Vacqueyras 1990 • $10 • (4/15/1993) • **83**

COURSODON, PIERRE

St.-Joseph 1997: This has a nice round mouthfeel at first, but it turns rather tart as the cassis bush, olive and herb flavors kick in on the chewy, bitter finish.–P.M. • $21 • (10/31/1999) • **79**

St.-Joseph 1996: Dense and ripe, showing succulent raspberry, wet earth, cedar and spice. Medium- to full-bodied, with supple, sweet tannins. Just a hint of herbal-like cassis bush distracts. Drink now through 2002.–P.M. • $17 • (11/15/1998) • **86**

St.-Joseph 1995 • $17 • (10/15/1997) • **81**

St.-Joseph 1994 • $16 • (10/15/1997) • **89**

St.-Joseph 1992 • $NA • (5/31/1994) • **78**

St.-Joseph 1991 • $NA • (5/31/1994) • **85**

St.-Joseph L'Olivaie 1997: Violet and cassis coexist in this cleverly oaked international-style red, offering lots of toast, smoke and coffee aromas and flavors, with some raspberry and cherry character in the background. Not imported into the U.S. Drink now through 2003.–P.M. • $NA • (1/01/1999) • **85**

St.-Joseph L'Olivaie 1996: Shows decent black cherry and wet earth character, but also some herbaceous notes. Medium-bodied, tart on the finish.–P.M. • $18 • (11/15/1998) • **79**

St.-Joseph L'Olivaie 1995 • $18 • (10/15/1997) • **85**

St.-Joseph La Sensonne 1997: Inky-black, heavily extracted, bursting with fancy oak-infused violet, cassis, blackberry and smoke aromas, it's revved up to impress you—and succeeds. Delicious finish. Not imported into the U.S. Drink through 2003.–P.M. • $NA • (1/01/1999) • **88**

St.-Joseph Le Paradis St.-Pierre 1997: Rather thick-textured and tasting like freshly ground black peppercorns, here's a mouthfilling St.-Joseph, with wet earth, dark chocolate and clean black cherry. A bit crisp on the aftertaste, but it shows length and personality. Not imported into the U.S. Drink now through 2002.–P.M. • $NA • (12/15/1999) • **88**

St.-Joseph Le Paradis St.-Pierre 1996: Fairly ripe, showing wild raspberry and black cherry flavors, plus citrus-spiked acidity and a thin blanket of toasted oak. A bit herbal on the chewy finish. Drink now through 2001.–P.M. • $NA • (11/15/1998) • **82**

St.-Joseph White 1998: Crisp and lean, showing mineral and a very clean structure, this should go well with foods but doesn't have much complexity. Still, it's well made. Not imported into the U.S. Drink now.–P.M. • $NA • (1/01/1999) • **84**

St.-Joseph White 1997: Fresh and lively, full-bodied and smooth despite the good acidity, with pleasant floral, honeydew, melon and honey aromas and flavors. Balanced and lovely, super-supple on the finish. Drink now.–P.M. • $17 • (11/15/1998) • **89**

St.-Joseph White 1996 • $17 • (10/15/1997) • **85**

St.-Joseph White Le Paradis St.-Pierre 1996 • $NA • (10/15/1997) • **88**

COURTAULT, JEAN-CLAUDE

Chablis 1996 • $NA • (8/31/1997) • **92**

Chablis Montmain Domaine de la Tour 1996 • $NA • (5/31/1998) • **87**

Petit Chablis 1996 • $NA • (8/31/1997) • **86**

COURTEILLAC, DOMAINE DE

Bordeaux Supérieur 1995 • $18 • (1/31/1998) • **90**

Bordeaux Supérieur 1994 • $15 • (1/31/1997) • **84**

Bordeaux Supérieur 1993 • $NA • (1/31/1996) • **79**

COURTY, ARLETTE & VIRGINIE

Chablis 1996: After decanting, this wine turned smooth and silky, suggesting it should be cellared. The buttery, butterscotch, creamlike, malic character may not be for everyone, but it certainly leaves an impression—the wine is very supple and pleasant on the finish. Best from 2005.–P.M. • $NA • (8/31/1998) • **87**

COUSPAUDE, CHATEAU LA

St.-Emilion 1997: Seductive young wine. Pretty plum and berry character with a hint of mushroom. Medium-bodied, with lovely, polished tannins and a long, caressing finish. Drink now through 2004.–J.S. • $39 • (1/31/2000) • **89**

St.-Emilion 1996: Enticing aromas of crushed berries, blackberries and toasted oak. Medium-bodied, with pretty fruit flavors and silky tannins. Intense toasted coconut finish is a bit too woody. Lacks some midpalate fruit. Drink now through 2003.–J.S. • $27 Ⓐ • (1/31/1999) • **85**

COUSSERGUES, DOMAINE DE

Chardonnay Vin de Pays d'Oc 1996 • $8 • (4/30/1998) • **82**

Merlot Vin de Pays d'Oc 1996 • $8 • (4/30/1998) • **79**

Sauvignon Blanc Vin de Pays d'Oc 1996 • $8 • (4/30/1998) • **78**

Syrah Vin de Pays d'Oc 1996 • $8 • (1/01/1998) • **78**

COUSTOLLE, CHATEAU

Canon-Fronsac 1982: Slightly overdone and dry. Very good, dark brick-red color, with an amber edge. Full-bodied and somewhat tough, with raisin and tobacco flavors, black cherry and redwood aromas and a slightly dry finish. (1982 Bordeaux horizontal tasting). Drink now.–J.S. • $NA • (11/30/1998) • **84**

COUTET, CHATEAU | BARSAC

Barsac 1998: Plenty of honey, lemon and lime in this young wine. Medium-bodied, medium sweet, with a spicy finish. Rather short really. Slightly disappointing for this estate.–J.S. • $NA • (1/01/1999) (BT) • **85-89**

Barsac 1997: Pretty and fresh, with lemon, honey, meringue and pineapple character. Medium-bodied and medium sweet, with a long, fresh finish. Best after 2001.–J.S. • $53 • (1/31/2000) • **90**

Barsac 1992 • $NA • (4/15/1995) • **81**

Barsac 1991 • $NA • (4/15/1995) • **80**

Barsac 1990 • $46 Ⓐ • (4/15/1995) • **89**

Barsac 1989 • $40 Ⓐ • (4/15/1995) • **90**

Barsac 1988 • $47 Ⓐ • (4/15/1995) • **91**

Barsac 1987 • $27 • (6/15/1990) • **80**

Barsac 1983 • $32 Ⓐ • (4/15/1995) • **83**

Barsac 1982: Golden-colored, with coconut and tropical fruit aromas. Full-bodied and medium sweet, with very ripe fruit, apricot skin flavor and a light finish. A bit hot. (1982 Bordeaux horizontal tasting). Drink now.–J.S. • $NA • (11/30/1998) • **86**

Barsac 1947 • $108 Ⓐ • (5/31/1997) • **83**

Barsac Cuvée Madame 1989 • $250 Ⓐ • (4/15/1995) • **90**

Barsac Cuvée Madame 1988 • $175 • (4/15/1995) • **91**

COUTET, CHATEAU | FRONSAC

Fronsac 1997: A light '97, with pepper, tobacco and cherry character. Fruity finish. Drink now.–J.S. • $NA • (1/31/2000) • **80**

COUTOUX, MICHEL

Chassagne-Montrachet La Maltroie 1997: A super white. Seductive, with reined-in toast, smoke and mint aromas and lovely honey, lemon, orange and hazelnut flavors. Round and rich, well balanced toward the soft side. Drink now through 2003.–P.M. • $59 • (2/28/1999) • **91**

Chassagne-Montrachet Les Chenevottes 1997: Beautiful balance marks this harmonious, seductive white. It's fat and rich without being heavy, coats the palate with honey, smoke and lots of fruit, and you don't notice the oak, just the silky texture. Sensational. Drink now through 2005.–P.M. • $58 • (2/28/1999) • **92**

Chassagne-Montrachet Morgeot 1997: Complex and attractive, this delivers lime and mineral flavors and smoky, toasted complexity; delicious Chassagne character—lemon, herbs, green olive—mixes with some honey and hazelnut on the finish. Fat texture, but medium-intense finish. Drink now through 2003.–P.M. • $59 • (2/28/1999) • **89**

COUVENT DES JACOBINS

St.-Emilion 1989 • $28 • (4/30/1992) • **89**

St.-Emilion 1988 • $28 • (3/31/1991) • **81**

St.-Emilion 1985 • $27 • (3/31/1988) • **84**

St.-Emilion 1983 • $27 • (3/16/1986) • **95**

St.-Emilion 1982: This beautiful red is a sleeper of the vintage. Dark ruby in color, with a hint of garnet. Full-bodied and velvety, with lovely ripe berry, spice and tobacco aromas and flavors. Long, long aftertaste. Delicious. (1982 Bordeaux horizontal tasting). Drink now.–J.S. • $NA • (11/30/1998) • **92**

COYEUX, DOMAINE DES

Muscat de Beaumes-de-Venise 1993 • $20 • (10/15/1996) • **83**

Muscat de Beaumes-de-Venise 1992 • $20 • (11/15/1995) • **84**

CRABITEY, CHATEAU

Graves White 1997: A fresh and lively white. Aromas of lemon and banana follow through to the palate. Medium-bodied, with crisp acidity and a medium finish. Drink now.–J.S. • $13 • (7/31/1999) • **85**

CRISTIA, DOMAINE DE

Châteauneuf-du-Pape 1998: A show-off wine that's totally woody. Hard tannins dominate. Tastes like plywood, at least now. The oak just takes over; will the fruit emerge later? Not imported into the U.S.–P.M. • $NA • (1/01/2000) • **79**

CROCHET, LUCIEN

Sancerre 1998: Subtle pear and quince flavors run through this medium-bodied and lively white. Picks up perky grass notes on the finish. Drink now.–B.S. • $17 • (6/15/2000) • **84**

Sancerre Cuvée Prestige 1997: There's a suave smoky note weaving deftly around ripe pear, lemon custard and vanilla bean flavors in this rich Sancerre. Has a caressing mouthfeel throughout, though the toasty oak overwhelms a bit in the end. Drink now.–B.S. • $45 • (6/15/2000) • **88**

Sancerre La Croix du Roy 1998: Showing faint lime and pear aromas and flavors, this Sancerre turns nearly sweet before finishing short. Lacks zip. Drink now.–B.S. • $17 • (6/15/2000) • **82**

Sancerre Le Chêne 1998: Subtle lime and pear flavors fade a bit before firm acidity wins out on the finish. Drink now.–B.S. • $21 • (6/15/2000) • **84**

Sancerre Le Chêne 1997: Nice aromas of lime, herbs and wet stones give way to lean and tart citrus flavors. Clean, but needs food.–T.M. • $19 • (9/15/1999) • **78**

Sancerre Le Chêne 1996: Lovely aromas of ripe quince and melon, and the flavors have shadings of citrus and grass with a mineral note encroaching on the finish. Brightly displayed and focused. Drink now.–B.S. • $20 • (10/31/1998) • **88**

Sancerre Red La Croix du Roy 1995: Aromas and flavors of cherry, spice and game exhibit good Pinot Noir character. There's an intensity and a concentration on the palate missing in many red Sancerres. Lingering finish. Drink now.–B.S. • $23 • (11/15/1998) • **85**

Sancerre Red La Croix du Roy 1994 • $23 • (6/15/1997) • **83**

CROCK, CHATEAU LE

St.-Estèphe 1998: Has some berry, cherry character, but it's rather light and slightly diluted.–J.S. • $NA • (5/31/1999) (BT) • **75-79**

St.-Estèphe 1997: A bit lean, but with some pretty berry and currant character. Medium-bodied, with firm tannins and a light, fruity finish. Drink now through 2005.–J.S. • $16 • (1/31/2000) • **85**

St.-Estèphe 1995 • $16 • (1/31/1998) • **87**

St.-Estèphe 1987 • $16 • (11/30/1989) • **79**

St.-Estèphe 1986 • $21 • (11/30/1989) • **92**

St.-Estèphe 1985 • $18 • (2/15/1988) • **79**

St.-Estèphe 1982 • $20 • (11/30/1989) • **80**

CROIX, CHATEAU LA

Pomerol 1996: Berry and herbal aromas follow through to the palate. Medium-bodied, with velvety tannins and a light herbal aftertaste. Rather simple. Drink now.–J.S. • $NA • (1/31/1999) • **82**

Pomerol 1988 • $19 • (7/31/1991) • **82**

Pomerol 1985 • $25 • (5/15/1988) • **93**

Pomerol 1983 • $14 • (11/30/1986) • **84**

Pomerol 1982 • $30 • (5/15/1989) • **89**

Pomerol 1981 • $14 • (5/01/1989) • **72**

CROIX-BEAUCAILLOU, LA

St.-Julien 1995: Straightforward red with berry, tobacco and cherry aromas and flavors. Medium-bodied, with medium tannins and a fruity finish. Second label of Château Ducru-Beaucaillou. Drink through 2005.–J.S. • $NA • (9/15/1998) • **87**

CROIX CANON, CHATEAU LA

Canon-Fronsac 1998: Pleasant and fruity, with berry, earth and chocolate. Medium-bodied, with fine tannins and a light finish. Slightly diluted.–J.S. • $NA • (5/31/1999) (BT) • **80-84**

Canon-Fronsac 1997: Pretty plum and milk chocolate character. Medium-bodied, with light tannins and a fresh finish. Drink now.–J.S. • $NA • (1/31/2000) • **85**

Canon-Fronsac 1996: Soft and easy to enjoy with chocolate and berry aromas and flavors. Medium- to light-bodied with light tannins but a silky texture. Needs more fruit concentration. Drink now.–J.S. • $22 • (1/31/1999) • **84**

Key: SS—Spectator Selection. CS—Cellar Selection. HR—Highly Recommended. $NA—Price not available. (BT)—Barrel tasting. (A)—Auction Price. For a key to the tasters' initials, see "How to Use These Listings."
Dates in parentheses represent the issues in which the ratings were published.

CROIX CARDINAL, CHATEAU LA

St.-Emilion 1996: Very grapey and youthful, with plum and boysenberry aromas. Medium-bodied, with well-integrated, light tannins and a fresh finish. Nicely crafted. Drink now.–J.S. • $NA • (9/30/1998) • **84**

CROIX-DE-GAY, CHATEAU LA

Pomerol 1999: Port-like aromas of berry, raspberry and dried plum. Medium-bodied, with well-integrated tannins and a short finish.–J.S. • $NA • (1/01/2000) (BT) • **85-89**

Pomerol 1998: A cool, minerally '98 with firm tannins and a solid core of fruit. Full-bodied. Long finish. Needs but a bit more ripe fruit character to score outstanding.–J.S. • $NA • (5/31/1999) (BT) • **85-89**

Pomerol 1997: Good berry and tobacco character. Medium- to light-bodied, fresh on the finish. Drink now.–J.S. • $22 • (1/31/2000) • **84**

Pomerol 1996: Some good berry and dried-cherry character. Medium-bodied, with light tannins and a short but fresh finish. Better than I remember. Drink now.–J.S. • $25 • (1/31/1999) • **82**

Pomerol 1995 • $25 • (1/31/1998) • **89**

Pomerol 1994 • $25 • (1/31/1997) • **87**

Pomerol 1993 • $20 • (1/31/1996) • **85**

Pomerol 1992 • $17 • (4/15/1995) • **82**

Pomerol 1991 • $17 • (3/31/1994) • **78**

Pomerol 1990 • $28 • (3/31/1993) • **94**

Pomerol 1989: Wonderfully perfumed '89, of strawberry, vanilla and cherry flavors. Medium-bodied, with soft tannins and a delicious fruity aftertaste. Lovely glass of wine. (1989 Bordeaux horizontal tasting).–J.S. • $NA • (5/31/1999) • **88**

Pomerol 1988 • $30 • (6/30/1991) • **89**

Pomerol 1985 • $33 • (3/15/1988) CS • **91**

Pomerol 1983 • $16 • (7/01/1986) CS • **94**

Pomerol 1982 • $17 • (5/15/1989) • **91**

Pomerol 1961 • $NA • (4/30/1996) • **82**

Pomerol 1945 • $NA • (3/16/1986) • **70**

CROIX DE LABRIE, CHATEAU

St.-Emilion 1996: Fine and delicious. Bubbling over with bright berry, tobacco and toasted oak. Medium-bodied, with firm tannins and a lovely silky texture. Long finish. Drink through 2005.–J.S. • $NA • (1/01/1999) • **87**

CROIX DE RAMBEAU, CHATEAU

Lussac-St.-Emilion 1997: Very diluted, with berry and tobacco character. Watery finish.–J.S. • $18 • (1/01/2000) • **77**

CROIX DES MOINES, CHATEAU LA

Lalande-de-Pomerol 1997: Light and fruity, with coconut and berry character, but diluted on the finish.–J.S. • $19 • (1/01/2000) • **78**

CROIX DU CASSE, CHATEAU LA

Pomerol 1998: Intense aromas of coffee and raisin. Full-bodied, with chewy tannins and a medium finish of dried herbs. Almost outstanding.–J.S. • $NA • (5/31/1999) (BT) • **85-89**

Pomerol 1997: Wonderful aromas of chocolate mousse and berries, with hints of spice. Medium- to full-bodied, with velvety tannins and a long, fruity finish. Well done. Drink through 2005.–J.S. • $39 • (1/31/2000) • **89**

Pomerol 1996: Dark-colored, with some berry and mineral aromas, a hint of mint. Medium-bodied, with polished tannins and a slightly diluted finish. Nice use of new wood, but nothing special overall. Best after 2000.–J.S. • $26 • (1/31/1999) • **81**

Pomerol 1995 • $23 • (1/31/1998) • **89**

Pomerol 1994 • $25 • (1/31/1997) • **89**

Pomerol 1993 • $24 • (1/31/1996) • **78**

Pomerol 1989: Rich and funky. Color is deep ruby-red. Intense aromas of dried berries and English Christmas pudding. Full-bodied and chunky, with chewy tannins which turn slightly dry and rustic on the finish. (1989 Bordeaux horizontal tasting). Drink now.–J.S. • $NA • (5/31/1999) • **87**

Pomerol 1988: Slightly cheesy in character, with an amber-edged ruby color. Medium-bodied, with medium, velvety tannins and a slightly dry finish. On the way down. (1988 Bordeaux horizontal tasting). Drink now.–J.S. • $NA • (11/30/1998) • **81**
Pomerol 1985 • $25 • (5/15/1988) • **82**
Pomerol 1982: Fading. Ruby-colored, with an intense garnet edge. Meaty and autumnal, with fruit aromas. Medium-bodied, soft and light, with earth and berry flavors, but very short. Slightly dry. (1982 Bordeaux horizontal tasting).–J.S. • $NA • (11/30/1998) • **79**

CROIX ST.-GEORGES, CHATEAU LA

Pomerol 1995 • $44 • (1/31/1998) • **87**

CROIZET-BAGES, CHATEAU

Pauillac 1999: Fresh and fruity but rather diluted, with light tannins and a plum and currant aftertaste.–J.S. • $NA • (1/01/2000) (BT) • **80-84**
Pauillac 1998: Impressive perfumes of currants and crushed raspberries. Full- to medium-bodied, with fine tannins and a long, silky finish. Well done.–J.S. • $NA • (5/31/1999) (BT) • **85-89**
Pauillac 1997: Thin and meager. Some decent plum flavors, but short.–J.S. • $NA • (1/31/2000) • **78**
Pauillac 1996: Some good fruit character, but slightly hollow on the palate, with light berry and tar aromas and flavors. Medium-bodied, with chewy tannins and a short finish.–J.S. • $20 Ⓐ • (1/31/1999) • **83**
Pauillac 1995 • $20 • (1/31/1998) • **86**
Pauillac 1994 • $25 • (1/31/1997) • **75**
Pauillac 1993 • $25 • (1/31/1996) • **74**
Pauillac 1988 • $28 • (8/31/1991) • **73**
Pauillac 1986 • $15 • (6/30/1989) • **78**
Pauillac 1982: Much better than I anticipated. Brilliant ruby-garnet color. Very fresh, with blackberry, dark chocolate and cherry. Full-bodied and concentrated, with plenty of fruit and velvety tannins. (1982 Bordeaux horizontal tasting). Drink now.–J.S. • $NA • (11/30/1998) • **89**
Pauillac 1962 • $60 • (11/30/1987) • **83**
Pauillac 1961 • $37 • (4/30/1996) • **85**

CROS, DOMAINE

Minervois 1995 • $7 • (5/31/1998) • **85**
Minervois Cuvée Tradition 1998: Nice density and balance of flavors, favoring currant and spice, with a ripe plum element. Dark chocolate notes on the finish. Drink now.–K.M. • $9 • (6/15/2000) • **85**
Minervois Cuvée Tradition 1997: Nice smooth, ripe texture to this medium-bodied red from the south of France, which is dominated by flavors of dark plum, black cherry and leather. Interesting tar and mineral notes on the finish. Drink now through 2001.–K.M. • $9 • (9/15/1999) • **84**
Minervois Les Aspres 1997: Distinctive and flavorful, with ripe, warm notes of red plum, black cherry, chocolate and spice backed by a firm core of acidity. Well concentrated and seductive, with coffee and mochalike notes that linger on the finish. A hearty red that still has plenty of finesse. Drink now through 2002.–K.M. • $14 • (9/15/1999) • **88**

CRUZEAU, CHATEAU DE

Pessac-Léognan 1998: An earthy, slightly herbal young wine, with medium body, medium tannins and a light finish. Water affected.–J.S. • $NA • (5/31/1999) (BT) • **75-79**
Pessac-Léognan 1997: Pleasant plum and dried cherry character, with medium body, light tannins, a fresh finish. Drink now.–J.S. • $18 • (1/31/2000) • **82**
Pessac-Léognan 1996: A simple '96, with clean berry and tobacco character on the nose and the same, slightly diluted, on the palate. Drink now.–J.S. • $14 • (1/31/1999) • **81**
Pessac-Léognan 1995 • $15 • (1/31/1998) • **90**
Pessac-Léognan 1994 • $14 • (1/31/1997) • **84**
Pessac-Léognan 1993 • $14 • (1/31/1996) • **83**
Pessac-Léognan 1992 • $12 • (4/15/1995) • **75**
Pessac-Léognan 1990 • $16 • (3/31/1993) • **91**
Pessac-Léognan 1989: Rather rustic but good. Aromas of berries and dried herbs verging on grassiness. Full-bodied, with firm tannins and a medium-spicy finish.—1989 Bordeaux horizontal. Drink now.–J.S. • $NA • (5/31/1999) • **85**
Pessac-Léognan 1988 • $14 • (2/28/1991) • **87**
Pessac-Léognan 1986 • $10 • (6/30/1989) • **87**
Graves 1982 • $20 • (8/31/1992) • **91**
Pessac-Léognan White 1998: A fresh and fruity white, with lemon and melon character and a hint of vanilla. Medium-bodied, with fresh acidity and a clean finish. Drink now.–J.S. • $15 • (2/29/2000) • **86**
Pessac-Léognan White 1996: Shows simple Sauvignon character of grass and flint on both nose and palate. Medium-bodied, with fresh acidity and a simple finish. A good, light white Bordeaux. Drink now.–J.S. • $14 • (3/31/1999) • **83**

CUCKOO HILL

Chardonnay Vin de Pays d'Oc 1996 • $7 • (4/30/1998) • **80**
Merlot Vin de Pays d'Oc 1996 • $6 • (3/31/1998) • **81**
Viognier Vin de Pays d'Oc 1996 • $10 • (4/30/1998) • **72**

CUILLERON, YVES

Condrieu Ayguets 1997: Ah, the exotic flavors of a truly botrytized wine. Like a German TBA, this Rhône white is a zingy, full-bodied beauty bursting with clean raw honey, dried apricot, fig, spice, vanilla and grilled pineapple character, thick and hedonistic on the finish. A dessert on its own. Drink now through 2010.–P.M. • $60 • (9/15/1999) HR • **98**
Condrieu La Côte 1996 • $43 • (10/15/1997) • **90**
Condrieu La Petite Côte 1998: Quite dry, with lime-lemon aromas and flavors, it has structure but lacks a bit of fat and opulence. A hard white wine, it still has plenty of dried and fresh herb character, and no one could fault its balance. Drink now through 2003.–P.M. • $50 • (12/15/1999) • **86**
Condrieu La Petite Côte 1997: Ultrarich and oily-thick, the mouthfeel is impressive, but where's the structure? A bit of an obese wine, it's Jell-O, no muscle. But the honey, concentrated pineapple and smoky, off-dry flavors make you do a double take. Drink now through 2001.–P.M. • $42 • (9/15/1999) • **87**
Condrieu Les Chaillets Vieilles Vignes 1998: A well-made white, offering delicious complexity but not the sort of depth that warrants an outstanding score. Shows deft oak treatment balanced by floral, butter and sea salt flavors mixed with honey. Turns smooth and seductive on the finish. Drink now through 2005.–P.M. • $62 • (12/15/1999) • **88**
Condrieu Les Chaillets Vieilles Vignes 1996 • $58 • (10/15/1997) • **93**
Condrieu Les Eguets Récoltes Tardives 1996 • $60/500 ml. • (10/15/1997) • **95**
Côte-Rôtie Coteau de Bassenon 1997: A rich and ripe Syrah, with violet-scented, toasted oak character kept on track by lovely and intense blueberry, blackberry and currant aromas and flavors. But tough wood tannins clamp down on the finish. Drink now through 2001.–P.M. • $40 • (9/15/1999) • **88**
Côte-Rôtie Coteau de Bassenon 1996: Wonderful combination of bright floral, red berry character and spicy, smoky, grilled meat and toasted oak notes. Distinctive and complex in aroma, it offers an elegant mouthfeel with a fairly crisp finish. Smells divine now, and should soften with cellaring. Drink through 2005.–P.M. • $35 • (9/15/1998) • **90**
Côte-Rôtie Coteau de Bassenon 1995 • $35 • (10/15/1997) • **86**
Côte-Rôtie Coteau de Bassenon 1994 • $35 • (11/30/1996) • **90**
St.-Joseph Cuvée de la Côte 1987 • $16 • (11/30/1990) • **80**
St.-Joseph Cuvée Prestige 1991 • $20 • (5/31/1994) • **82**
St.-Joseph L'Amarybelle Cuvée Prestige 1997: A bit herbaceous and tart, with a rather lean body, it struggles to deliver cherry and cedar notes on the crisp finish.–P.M. • $30 • (10/31/1999) • **78**
St.-Joseph L'Amarybelle Cuvée Prestige 1996: An awesome St.-Joseph. Deep-colored and ultrasweet, this supple-textured, harmonious red explodes with floral, wild raspberry and toasted oak aromas and flavors. Balanced. Drink now through 2002.–P.M. • $24 • (11/15/1998) • **92**
St.-Joseph L'Amarybelle Cuvée Prestige 1994 • $22 • (11/30/1996) • **86**
St.-Joseph Les Pierres Sèches 1997: Green, herbal and tough, with chewy, aggressive tannins. Tart finish.–P.M. • $24 • (10/31/1999) • **75**
St.-Joseph Les Pierres Sèches 1996: Clean, pure and vibrant. With lots of nice raspberry, black cherry, and mocha-spice-coffee flavors, this is a tough cookie that's firmly constructed. Medium-bodied, with tannins and sharp acidity galore. Best from 2001 through 2005.–P.M. • $NA • (11/15/1998) • **86**
St.-Joseph Les Serines 1997: An international style of St.-Joseph. Powerful and very dark, this full-bodied red smells and tastes exotic, with a marriage of leather, horse stable, violet and cassis notes. Round until the chewy finish. Drink now through 2001.–P.M. • $45 • (12/15/1999) • **87**
St.-Joseph Les Serines 1996: Impressive for its depth, complexity and length. Unbelievable St.-Joseph, in a new-oak, international style, with delicate floral, mocha, raspberry and spice flavors. Drink now through 2003.–P.M. • $35 • (11/15/1998) • **93**

CUILLERON, YVES

St.-Joseph White Coteau St.-Pierre 1998: Very yellow in color, very oaky in aroma, here's a wine hinting at richness—and sure enough it fills the palate with round, ripe fruit, honey and deftly oaked notes. Serious and complex, it's just delicious. Drink now through 2001.–P.M. • $30 • (12/15/1999) • **88**

St.-Joseph White Coteau St.-Pierre 1997: St.-Joseph given the royal oak-barrel treatment. Here's a big, butter-and-popcorn job, striving for Montrachet status, dripping with toasty, smoky, tropical, honeyed character—and surprisingly good acidity. Drink now.–P.M. • $25 • (9/15/1999) • **88**

St.-Joseph White Izeras 1996 • $21 • (10/15/1997) • **80**

St.-Joseph White Le Lombard Cuvée Prestige 1998: Fat and buttery, even creamy in mouthfeel, this borders on full-bodied. A slight hint of honey sets off the butter, butterscotch and floral character of this balanced and well-made St.-Joseph. Drink now through 2001.–P.M. • $28 • (12/15/1999) • **87**

St.-Joseph White Le Lombard Cuvée Prestige 1997: A big-bodied '97 St.-Joseph white that's fat and heavy because it's so ripe, with fig, raisin, butterscotch and caramel flavors. Off-dry finish. Drink now.–P.M. • $25 • (9/15/1999) • **84**

St.-Joseph White Le Lombard Cuvée Prestige 1996 • $24 • (10/15/1997) • **86**

St.-Joseph White Lyseras 1998: A good house wine. Nicely round, this medium-bodied white lacks a bit in complex aromas, but it still has pear, litchi and white peach character. Drink now through 2001.–P.M. • $24 • (12/15/1999) • **82**

St.-Joseph White Lyseras 1997: Like a little Condrieu. Rich and ripe, with a lovely, lush floral, white peach, almond, butter, macadamia nut and honey character of full-bodied complexity all the way to the seductive, late-harvest-like finish. Drink now.–P.M. • $22 • (9/15/1999) • **90**

CURE-BON, CHATEAU

St.-Emilion 1998: Some good sweet berry in this wine, with medium body and tannins and a fine finish. Slightly one-dimensional.–J.S. • $NA • (5/31/1999) (BT) • **85-89**

St.-Emilion 1997: Lovely aromas of green tobacco, fruit and meat. Medium- to full-bodied, with polished tannins and a long, flavorful finish. Delicious. Drink through 2004.–J.S. • $36 • (1/31/2000) • **88**

St.-Emilion 1996: Some alluring primary crushed grape and raspberry character. Medium-bodied, with firm tannins, but a slightly dry finish takes away from the overall quality. Drink now.–J.S. • $25 • (1/31/1999) • **83**

St.-Emilion 1995 • $26 • (1/31/1998) • **86**

CURE-BON-LA-MADELEINE, CHATEAU

St.-Emilion 1994 • $23 • (1/31/1997) • **84**

St.-Emilion 1982: A beautiful Merlot-based wine. Brick red color, with an amber edge. Medium-bodied and velvety, with fruit and green olive aromas and fine tannins. (1982 Bordeaux horizontal tasting). Drink now.–J.S. • $NA • (11/30/1998) • **90**

CYGNE BLANC DE FONREAUD, LE

Bordeaux 1996: Fine and subtle style of white Bordeaux. Plenty of lemon, mineral and apple aromas and flavors in this wine. Medium-bodied, with fresh acidity and a long, minerally, smoky, toasted oak finish. Drink now.–J.S. • $NA • (1/01/1999) • **87**

CYRANO

Chardonnay Vin de Pays 1997: A soft, buttery component dominates, though there are appley flavors as well. Finish is a bit rough.–K.M. • $8 • (8/31/1998) • **79**

CYROT-BUTHIAU

Pommard La Chanière 1997: Wet earth and iron combine with plum and cherry in this attractive, approachable red. On the light side, showing slight dilution midpalate. Drink now through 2001.–B.S. • $NA • (9/30/1999) • **81**

Key: SS—Spectator Selection. CS—Cellar Selection. HR—Highly Recommended. $NA—Price not available. (BT)—Barrel tasting. Ⓐ—Auction Price.
For a key to the tasters' initials, see "How to Use These Listings."
Dates in parentheses represent the issues in which the ratings were published.

Pommard La Chanière 1996: Ripe, offering fresh, vibrant red- and blackberry character, supple tannins and medium body, with a succulent acidity weaving around the lovely fruit and just enough toasty, smoky complexity. Best from 2002 through 2010.–P.M. • $NA • (1/01/1999) • **87**

Pommard Les Arvelets 1996: Fresh and fruity, mingling red berry, wet earth and subtle oak accents with delicious cherry, raspberry flavors, but don't expect much generosity here. Drink through 2005.–P.M. • $NA • (1/01/1999) • **82**

DAGUENEAU, DIDIER

Maudit 1990 • $50 • (9/30/1993) • **84**

Pouilly-Fumé En Chailloux 1997: Ripe and lively. This big-boned white makes an impact, with fig, pear, chalk and citrus flavors that linger on the finish. Balanced and clean, with plenty of acidity to match with food. Drink now through 2002.–T.M. • $28 Ⓐ • (9/15/1999) • **87**

Pouilly-Fumé En Chailloux 1996 • $26 • (5/31/1998) • **87**

Pouilly-Fumé Pur Sang 1997: Lively and balanced. Expressive flavors of herbs and minerals, ripe apples and pears give this white distinctive character while it remains typical of the region. A good match for rich foods, but not up to the usual level of this producer. Drink now through 2004.–T.M. • $28 Ⓐ • (9/15/1999) • **88**

Pouilly-Fumé Pur Sang 1996 • $35 • (2/28/1998) HR • **94**

Pouilly-Fumé Silex 1997: This concentrated white has real weight on the palate, with intense flavors of dried apple, marzipan, fig and coconut. The impact is impressive, but the high alcohol and almost-cooked flavors are a bit tiring. Somewhat disappointing for this usually outstanding producer. Drink now through 2002.–T.M. • $40 Ⓐ • (9/15/1999) • **86**

Pouilly-Fumé Silex 1996 • $50 • (2/28/1998) • **93**

DAGUENEAU, JEAN-CLAUDE

Pouilly-Fumé Comte de Berge 1997: Clean and well defined, this white tastes of citrus and herbs. It's a bit sharp and thin, but should balance out with food. Drink now.–T.M. • $12 • (3/31/2000) • **84**

DAGUENEAU, SERGE

Pouilly-Fumé Les Pentes 1997: This light, soft white offers sweet melon and vanilla flavors, but lacks the mineral firmness characteristic of the appellation. A bit cloying on the finish.–T.M. • $14 • (6/30/1999) • **79**

Pouilly-Fumé Les Pentes 1996: Ripe and seductive, showing apricot, smoke and flint aromas and flavors on a lively structure, yet the flavors tail off oh-so-slightly at the end. Drink now.–B.S. • $18 • (10/31/1998) • **85**

DALEM, CHATEAU

Fronsac 1998: Amazing ripe fruit and wild flowers on the nose. Full-bodied, with very well-integrated tannins and a long, long finish. Superb. Fronsacs are on a roll.–J.S. • $NA • (5/31/1999) (BT) • **90-94**

Fronsac 1997: Good berry and dried cherry character with a hint of cinnamon. Medium- to light-bodied. Drink now.–J.S. • $NA • (1/31/2000) • **85**

Fronsac 1996: Rather simple. Dried cherry and mineral aromas and flavors. Medium-bodied, with firm tannins and light fruit on the finish. Drink now.–J.S. • $NA • (1/31/1999) • **81**

Fronsac 1995: Very ripe and extracted; slightly overdone for me. Aromas of red fruits and cinnamon. Full-bodied, with full, soft tannins and a medium, flavorful finish. Slightly mouthpuckering now; best from 2003 through 2007.–J.S. • $NA • (9/15/1998) • **88**

Fronsac 1990 • $20 • (3/31/1993) • **86**

DAMASE, CHATEAU

Bordeaux Supérieur 1996: Simple, with some berry, cherry character and an herbal edge.–J.S. • $10 • (2/28/1999) • **78**

DAMOY, PIERRE

Chambertin 1997: Soft and delicious. Medium-bodied, with ripe tannins and a supple texture. The flavors veer toward cherry, toast, spice and raspberry. Holds together on the chewy, fresh finish. Drink now through 2003.–P.M. • $110 • (1/01/2000) • **87**

Chambertin 1994 • $70 • (11/15/1996) • **74**

Chambertin 1993 • $69 • (11/15/1995) • **91**

FRANCE

Chambertin-Clos de Bèze 1997: A bit simple, with raspberry and strawberry notes, turning tart and herbaceous on the finish.–P.M. • $120 • (1/01/2000) • **72**
Chambertin-Clos de Bèze 1994 • $87 Ⓐ • (11/15/1996) • **78**
Chambertin-Clos de Bèze 1993 • $84 Ⓐ • (11/15/1995) • **91**
Chapelle-Chambertin 1997: A medium-bodied, juicy red, with a clean, pure Pinot Noir aroma and nice raspberry, black cherry and wet earth. Good ripeness and supple tannins. Drink now through 2005.–P.M. • $110 • (1/01/2000) • **86**
Chapelle-Chambertin 1994 • $65 • (11/15/1996) • **80**
Chapelle-Chambertin 1993 • $63 Ⓐ • (11/15/1995) • **91**
Gevrey-Chambertin Clos Tamisot 1994 • $35 • (11/15/1996) • **70**
Gevrey-Chambertin Clos Tamisot LD 1993 • $30 • (11/15/1995) • **89**

DAMPIERRE, COMTE AUDOIN DE

Brut Blanc de Blancs Champagne NV: Generous aromas and flavors of butter, vanilla and pear give way to a lighter finish in this appealing blanc de blanc. Drink now. • $40 • (10/15/1999) • **87**
Brut Champagne Cuvée des Ambassadeurs NV: Nicely fruity in flavor, easygoing in texture and clean on the finish. Drink now. • $35 • (10/15/1999) • **87**
Brut Champagne Grande Année 1990: An abundant, buttery-flavored Champagne that's generous, soft and easy to enjoy. Has an appealing combination of butter, honey and apple notes that linger on the finish. Better than previously reviewed. Drink now. • $49 • (12/15/1998) • **90**
Brut Rosé Champagne Oeil de Perdrix 1995: Dry, crisp, almost austere in texture, but it has bright and lively fruit flavors that should mellow with time. Drink through 2005. • $50 • (10/15/1999) • **88**
Brut Rosé Champagne Oeil de Perdrix 1992: A light, fresh, strawberry and cherry character comes through in this deeply colored, smooth-textured Champagne. Richness of flavor and delicacy of texture combine in an appealing manner. Drink now. • $49 • (11/30/1998) • **88**
Brut Rosé Champagne Oeil de Perdrix 1990 • $49 • (4/30/1998) • **85**
Demi-Sec Champagne Goût Américain NV: Light, easy and sweet, fine in a dessert style. Has apple and citrus flavors, a soft texture and a sweet finish. Drink now. • $38 • (10/15/1999) • **85**

DASSAULT, CHATEAU

St.-Emilion 1996: Simple plum and fruit aromas and flavors, with a light to medium body, medium tannins and a short finish. Drink now.–J.S. • $NA • (1/31/1999) • **81**
St.-Emilion 1995: Ripe berry, coffee and chocolate character throughout. Full-bodied and tannic, with a velvety finish. Very concentrated. Needs time. Best from 2003 through 2008.–J.S. • $NA • (9/15/1998) • **90**
St.-Emilion 1988 • $17 • (7/15/1991) • **83**
St.-Emilion 1982 • $20 • (5/15/1989) • **90**

DAUBREE, LUCETTE & MARTIN

Côte-Rôtie 1997: *Terroir*-driven from all that lead pencil, mineral and blackberry concentration. Medium-bodied, with a firmer tannin structure than most '97s, it turns elegant, with a smoky complexity. Time should smooth out the tannins. Tempting now, but better to cellar short-term. Try through 2005.–P.M. • $35 • (11/30/1999) • **89**

DAUPHINE, CHATEAU DE LA

Fronsac 1998: Plenty of crushed berries and earth. Medium- to full-bodied, with velvety tannins and a light finish. Slight dilution at the end, yet very good.–J.S. • $NA • (5/31/1999) (BT) • **85-89**
Fronsac 1997: Some pretty ripe fruit to this young claret. Medium-bodied, with medium, firm tannins and a minerally, fruity finish. Slightly one-dimensional. Drink now.–J.S. • $21 • (1/31/2000) • **84**
Fronsac 1996: Clean floral and berry aromas. Medium- to light-bodied, with some pleasant cherry flavors but a very light finish. Drink now.–J.S. • $20 • (1/31/1999) • **81**
Fronsac 1995 • $20 • (1/31/1998) • **89**
Fronsac 1994 • $20 • (1/31/1997) • **79**
Fronsac 1993 • $22 • (1/31/1996) • **82**
Fronsac 1992 • $17 • (4/15/1995) • **75**
Fronsac 1990 • $17 • (3/31/1993) • **81**
Fronsac 1989: This is light and fruity, sporting a slight herbal edge. Medium-bodied, with medium tannins and a light, earthy, raisin finish. (1989 Bordeaux horizontal tasting). Drink now.–J.S. • $NA • (5/31/1999) • **83**
Fronsac 1985 • $20 • (9/30/1988) • **84**

DAUVISSAT, JEAN

Chablis 1996 • $18 • (5/31/1998) • **92**
Chablis Les Preuses 1997: Unctuous and ultraopulent, this grand white Burgundy is packed to the hilt with mineral, flint and wet earth personality and loads of fruit. Firms up on the lemony finish. Drink now through 2007.–P.M. • $55 • (9/30/1999) • **93**
Chablis Les Preuses 1996 • $45 • (5/31/1998) • **87**
Chablis Les Preuses 1995 • $45 • (6/15/1997) • **86**
Chablis Montmains 1997: Pure fruit and pure *terroir* emerge in this honeyed, ripe, full-bodied and well-made '97 Chablis. A pleasure to drink, it seduces with its balance, showing subtle toasty oak notes on the vibrant finish. Drink now through 2007.–P.M. • $30 • (9/30/1999) • **92**
Chablis Montmains 1996: Ripe and lush, a sweet-tasting Chablis with tropical, pear, honey character. Deliciously smooth and full-bodied, it delivers a burst of flavor that renders it tempting upon release. Drink now through 2005.–P.M. • $28 • (8/31/1998) • **91**
Chablis Montmains 1995 • $NA • (6/15/1997) • **87**
Chablis Séchet 1997: A bit earthy, with a salt, iodine and dried herb character. Smooth on the midpalate, with a purity of fruit that makes this medium-bodied wine attractive. Drink now through 2007.–P.M. • $30 • (9/30/1999) • **88**
Chablis Séchet 1996 • $23 • (5/31/1998) • **92**
Chablis Séchet 1995 • $23 • (6/15/1997) • **89**
Chablis Vaillons 1997: Unctuous in texture, with ripe fruit but also a crisp dried herb character that lends a slight tartness to the finish. Drink now through 2005.–P.M. • $30 • (9/30/1999) • **86**
Chablis Vaillons 1996 • $25 • (5/31/1998) • **94**
Chablis Vaillons 1995 • $24 • (6/15/1997) • **84**
Chablis Vaillons Vieilles Vignes 1997: Clean and attractive, with flavorful floral, pear and toast notes. Full-bodied, with a crisp edge to the honey that peeks through on the finish. Drink now through 2002.–P.M. • $45 • (9/30/1999) • **88**
Chablis Vaillons Vieilles Vignes 1996 • $30 • (5/31/1998) • **87**
Chablis Vaillons Vieilles Vignes 1995 • $30 • (6/15/1997) • **89**

DAUVISSAT, RENE & VINCENT

Chablis 1998: Clever winemaking. Unusual for its grilled meat and smoke combined with floral, perfume and petrol notes. Full-bodied, very smooth and supple. Drink now through 2002.–P.M. • $28 • (5/15/2000) • **85**
Chablis 1997: Fairly easy and soft, lacking some intensity but offering a cushion of decent fruit.–P.M. • $26 • (5/31/1999) • **79**
Chablis 1996: Pure, crystalline Chablis, with honey, lemon, bread dough character. Fairly crisp, medium-bodied, made complex by its toasted, smoky, spicy notes. Long finish suggests cellaring. Best from 2005.–P.M. • $26 • (8/31/1998) • **88**
Chablis La Forest 1998: With its oak shadings, this medium-bodied Chablis delivers spice, mocha, smoke and pear tart character on a polished and supple texture. A bit flat on the finish, though. Drink now through 2002.–P.M. • $38 • (5/15/2000) • **82**
Chablis La Forest 1997: Pure as a mountain spring, well made and medium-bodied, this wonderfully balanced Les Forêts *premier cru* delivers a minerally, supple mouthfeel, good fruit and good intensity. Tempting now, but worth cellaring. Best from 2001 through 2005.–P.M. • $35 • (5/31/1999) • **89**
Chablis La Forest 1996: For fans of ultraminerally Chablis. This full-bodied beauty reveals almost nothing on the nose except a sense of class and anticipation, but does strut its stuff on the midpalate, activating its mineral, ripe fruit, slightly spicy notes, rewally turning on the power on the vibrant, long and smoky finish. Best from 2005.–P.M. • $35 • (8/31/1998) • **93**
Chablis La Forest 1995 • $26 Ⓐ • (6/15/1997) • **87**
Chablis Les Clos 1998: Well made, polished, flavorful and balanced. Nothing big, opulent or very intense, but it's a class act, with butter, pear and hazelnut notes. Medium-bodied, with a racy finish. Drink now through 2003.–P.M. • $64 • (5/15/2000) • **87**
Chablis Les Clos 1997: Racy, classy and as pure as crystal, this medium-bodied but uncompromising, idiosyncratic Chablis is so tightly wound now it's like a lemon and mineral ball on the palate, as hard as pebbles, without even a hint of obvious oak. A great accomplishment in the '97 vintage, this is for patient, serious collectors of the Les Clos vineyard. Best from 2007 through 2020.–P.M. • $61 • (5/31/1999) CS • **95**
Chablis Les Clos 1996: Thick and unctuous, sailing harmoniously over the palate, leaving behind a silky trail of mineral, smoky, matchstick and flinty character. A real *vin de terroir*, although it's still tough on the finish. Best from 2010.–P.M. • $61 • (8/31/1998) • **95**

DAUVISSAT, RENE & VINCENT

Chablis Les Preuses 1998: Unusually big and burly, full-bodied and rich for a '98 Chablis. Buttery flavors take the vanguard in this round, fat, pleasant Chardonnay, which offers grilled meat, bacon and toast flavors. Give it time. Best from 2003 through 2008.–P.M. • $64 • (5/15/2000) • **89**

Chablis Les Preuses 1997: Pure, clean, vibrant, thick and ripe, offering rich fruit, plenty of minerally vanilla bean character to soothe the midpalate, zesty citrus and a mouthpuckering finish. Cellar. Best from 2005 through 2010.–P.M. • $61 • (5/31/1999) • **92**

Chablis Les Preuses 1996: Polished, with a buttery, butterscotch and caramel character, this full-bodied Chablis delivers plenty of spicy, mocha and bread dough accents backed by fresh citrus notes. Dries a bit on the finish. Best from 2005.–P.M. • $61 • (8/31/1998) • **84**

Chablis Séchet 1998: Fat in style for a '98 Chablis, with attractive opulence. Has rather shy floral, pear and melon notes, with an easygoing, honey-laced finish. Drink now through 2002.–P.M. • $38 • (5/15/2000) • **83**

Chablis Séchet 1997: Nice harmony to this medium-bodied, minerally and ripe *premier cru*, with its vanilla bean, pear and green apple combination. Balanced finish. Drink now through 2002.–P.M. • $35 • (5/31/1999) • **88**

Chablis Séchet 1996: For lovers of uncompromisingly steely, minerally Chablis. Beautifully intense, concentrated, compacted and clean, it tastes of the earth and of roasted chestnut, ripe pear, melon, cured ham and, above all, of iodine, mineral and vanilla bean. Stands out for its straight-as-an-arrow style, bursting with hard acidity that will need years to soften. Best from 2007.–P.M. • $35 • (8/31/1998) • **93**

Chablis Séchet 1995 • $32 • (6/15/1997) • **90**

Chablis Vaillons 1998: Very perfumy, floral and exotic. The richness of the ripe, almost late-harvest fruit is impressive. Full-bodied and surprisingly opulent for a '98 Chablis, with a lingering finish. Drink now through 2005.–P.M. • $38 • (5/15/2000) • **88**

Chablis Vaillons 1997: Polished, and perhaps appealing to an international audience for the distinct oak character attached to the lemon, green apple, butter and spice flavors. Good intensity, but a quite woody finish. Drink now through 2002.–P.M. • $35 • (5/31/1999) • **81**

Chablis Vaillons 1996: Complex, full-bodied, storms around the palate with a whirlwind of honey, mineral, wet earth, pear and green apple flavors. Very intense, with loads of acidity—will probably always be steely, but likely to rate higher at its peak. Best from 2005.–P.M. • $35 • (8/31/1998) • **87**

Chablis Vaillons 1995 • $32 • (6/15/1997) • **87**

Petit Chablis 1996: A thick, unctuous '96 Chablis of wonderful mineral, vanilla bean, chalk and lemon-honey character. Full-bodied. There is no distracting wood, only a lot of crisp character. The finish remained tough even after hours of airing. Best from 2005.–P.M. • $23 • (8/31/1998) • **88**

DAUZAC, CHATEAU

Margaux 1999: Subtle and well crafted, with firm tannins that are silky and fine. Medium-bodied, with a long finish.–J.S. • $NA • (1/01/2000) (BT) • **85-89**

Margaux 1998: A pretty, harmonious wine with blackberry, currant and spice aromas and flavors. Medium-bodied, with medium tannins and a light finish. Starts off great, but comes to a halt on the finish.–J.S. • $NA • (5/31/1999) (BT) • **85-89**

Margaux 1997: Lovely smoky red, with cherry and chocolate aromas and flavors. Medium-bodied. Medium, slightly austere tannins. Best after 2000.–J.S. • $NA • (1/31/2000) • **87**

Margaux 1996: A polished, well-made wine with lovely tannins, and berry and dark chocolate aromas and flavors. Medium- to full-bodied. Slightly hollow midpalate but still very good. Best after 2000.–J.S. • $26 • (1/31/1999) • **88**

Margaux 1995 • $22 Ⓐ • (1/31/1998) • **92**

Margaux 1994 • $26 • (1/31/1997) • **88**

Margaux 1993 • $24 • (1/31/1996) • **86**

Margaux 1992 • $17 • (4/15/1995) • **84**

Margaux 1990 • $23 • (3/31/1993) • **85**

Margaux 1989: Not as big as I remember, but delicious. An aromatic '89 of rose petal, berry character. Medium-bodied, with medium-chewy tannins and a medium finish. A pretty '89 for current drinking. (1989 Bordeaux horizontal tasting). Drink now.–J.S. • $NA • (5/31/1999) • **87**

Margaux 1988 • $20 • (6/30/1991) HR • **90**

Margaux 1985 • $21 • (9/30/1988) • **87**

Key: SS—Spectator Selection. CS—Cellar Selection. HR—Highly Recommended. $NA—Price not available. (BT)—Barrel tasting. Ⓐ—Auction Price.
For a key to the tasters' initials, see "How to Use These Listings."
Dates in parentheses represent the issues in which the ratings were published.

Margaux 1982: A slightly tough red. Dark ruby-garnet in color, with an amber edge. Cherry, black mushroom and earth aromas. Medium- to full-bodied, with very hard tannins and a slightly astringent finish. Wait and see. (1982 Bordeaux horizontal tasting). Best after 2000.–J.S. • $NA • (11/30/1998) • **86**

DAUZAN LA VERGNE, CHATEAU

Haut-Montravel 1994 • $11/500 ml. • (8/31/1997) • **83**

DAVENAY, CHATEAU DE

Bourgogne 1994 • $13 • (11/15/1996) • **82**

Hautes-Côtes de Beaune 1994 • $18 • (11/15/1996) • **80**

DECELLE, CHATEAU LA

Coteaux du Tricastin 1997: Crisp, even tart, gamy and very odd, showing a wet grass character.–P.M. • $8 • (12/15/1999) • **70**

Coteaux du Tricastin 1989 • $7 • (7/15/1991) • **82**

Coteaux du Tricastin Rosé 1998: This diluted, acidic wine is more like water.–P.M. • $9 • (12/15/1999) • **72**

Côtes du Rhône 1997: Light in body and color, there's only modest fruit in this straightforward red.–P.M. • $10 • (12/15/1999) • **72**

Côtes du Rhône-Villages Valreas 1997: A bit green and herbal, this rustic, medium-bodied wine shows astringency.–P.M. • $14 • (12/15/1999) • **77**

DEFAIX, BERNARD

Chablis 1996 • $13 • (8/31/1997) • **84**

Chablis Côte de Léchet 1997: Off the beaten path. This very smooth, polished white shows good weight on the palate, but it delivers a slight mustiness along with the intense lemon, mineral, vanilla bean, spice complexity. Astringent finish.–P.M. • $28 • (5/31/1999) • **79**

Chablis Côte de Léchet 1996 • $26 • (5/31/1998) • **89**

Chablis Côte de Léchet Vieilles Vignes 1997: Slightly oaky, this intense wine bursts with toasted bread, spicy grilled pineapple and lemon flavors that obscure a bit the *terroir* of Chablis. Slightly overdone, as the finish turns astringent. Best from 2002 through 2006.–P.M. • $33 • (5/31/1999) • **82**

Chablis Vaillons 1997: Strange, with a bitter varnish and astringent burnt butter character.–P.M. • $28 • (5/31/1999) • **70**

Chablis Vaillons 1996 • $26 • (5/31/1998) • **84**

Chablis Vieilles Vignes 1997: Buttery, but also strangely cardboardy, this is terribly bitter. Where's the fruit?–P.M. • $20 • (5/31/1999) • **72**

Chablis Vieilles Vignes 1996: Impressive at first, it turns increasingly butterscotchy, buttery and caramel-like in contact with the air. Full-bodied, with some pear and honey, it's ready for consumption. Slightly bitter on the finish.–P.M. • $20 • (8/31/1998) • **80**

DEHOURS

Brut Champagne Confidentielle NV • $33 • (12/15/1996) • **88**

Brut Champagne Grande Réserve NV • $30 • (12/15/1996) • **75**

Brut Rosé Champagne NV • $33 • (12/15/1996) • **84**

Demi-Sec Champagne NV • $30 • (12/31/1991) • **84**

DEISS, MARCEL

Gewürztraminer Alsace Bergheim 1997: Gorgeous Gewürz. Smoky, mineral-ly and exotic, you could just sniff this all day. Ripe, vibrant and silky, it's complex, concentrated and well-integrated, with a lingering aftertaste of honey. Drink now through 2001.–B.S. • $30 • (6/15/2000) • **89**

Gewürztraminer Alsace Bergheim 1996: Very concentrated, evocative aromas of orange marmalade, brioche and exotic fruits turn to grapefruit, ripe quince and a hint of spearmint on the palate. Expressive, dense and silky-smooth, with a deft underlying structure that keeps everything vibrant. Drink now through 2004.–B.S. • $28 • (4/30/1999) • **92**

Gewürztraminer Alsace Grand Cru Altenberg de Bergheim Sélection de Grains Nobles 1995: Like a breath of fresh air, this SGN offers clean aromas and flavors of citrus sorbet, with a mint leaf for accent. Lush and intense, the acidity is firm, and the wine ends up a touch hot. Fine length. Drink now through 2007.–B.S. • $55 • (4/30/1999) • **90**

Gewürztraminer Alsace Grand Cru Altenberg de Bergheim Sélection de Grains Nobles 1994 • $79 • (10/15/1997) • **90**

Gewürztraminer Alsace St.-Hippolyte 1996: Rose petal, litchi, lanolin and vanilla intermingle in this minerally, restrained white. Quite dry, with a vivid intensity and a lingering finish. Drink now through 2002.–B.S. • $25 • (10/31/1999) • **89**

Riesling Alsace Grand Cru Schoenenbourg Sélection de Grains Nobles 1994: An intriguing mix of polished wood, lanolin, honey and pine, all rendered in an elegant fashion. Not a blockbuster, yet it's medium sweet, focused and persistent. Drink now through 2005.–B.S. • $NA • (1/01/2000) • **89**

Pinot Gris Alsace Beblenheim 1997: Beautiful expression of site and grape. Bold and full-bodied, this '97 Pinot Gris shows distinctive character with its licorice, quince, smoke and mineral nuances, all displayed on a broad, dense profile. Fine length. Drink now through 2001.–B.S. • $25 • (6/15/2000) • **90**

Pinot Gris Alsace Bergheim 1996: What an exotic range of flavors. Ripe and forward, with a touch of residual sugar, this hedonistic Pinot Gris smacks of caramel, ripe mango, orange peel, honey and maple syrup. Just as it seems soft, a soupçon of acidity adds life, extending the finish. Drink now through 2004.–B.S. • $29 • (4/30/1999) • **91**

Pinot Noir Alsace Burlenberg Vieille Vigne 1996: Wow. Very ripe and extracted, this has a feral, smoky, spicy character, with clove, sage and blackberry exhibited on a muscular, full-bodied structure with a firm backbone. Silky, intense and concentrated in flavor, but its distinctive, gamy personality might not appeal to everyone. Drink now through 2002.–B.S. • $40 • (3/31/1999) • **88**

Pinot Noir Alsace Burlenberg Vieille Vigne 1995: A beguiling Pinot Noir relying on spice and smoke aromas and flavors more than fruit, though there's a raspberry compote element as well as licorice notes. Its silky texture is supported by a firm acidic backbone and moderate tannins. Fine length. Drink now through 2004.–B.S. • $40 • (3/31/1999) • **87**

Riesling Alsace Burg 1996: A huge '96 Riesling, displaying ripe quince, pear and mineral aromas and flavors, with a hint of sweetness up front. Firm acidity provides a framework for the rich fruit and it finishes dry. Young and unevolved, this needs time for its component parts to integrate. Best from 2002 through 2010.–B.S. • $35 • (9/30/1999) • **91**

Riesling Alsace Engelgarten 1997: Intriguing and complex, showing pine, smoke, apple and honey flavors wrapped in a lush texture (read residual sugar), all backed by moderate acidity. More up front than on the finish. Drink now through 2002.–B.S. • $25 • (6/15/2000) • **88**

Riesling Alsace Grand Cru Altenberg de Bergheim Vendanges Tardives 1996: Incredibly fresh, ripe and enticing, this Riesling VT shows plenty of honey, vanilla custard and apricot flavors, all on a firm, vibrant structure. It shows a touch of alcohol on the finish, pulling it just slightly out of balance though. Drink now through 2006.–B.S. • $55 • (9/30/1999) • **88**

Riesling Alsace Grand Cru Schoenenbourg Sélection de Grains Nobles 1994: An intriguing mix of polished wood, lanolin, honey and pine, all rendered in an elegant fashion. Not a blockbuster, yet it's medium sweet, focused and persistent. Drink now through 2005.–B.S. • $NA • (1/01/2000) • **89**

DELABY-GENOT, MARIE

Pommard Château Génot-Boulanger 1995 • $27 • (1/31/1998) • **79**

DELAMOTTE

Brut Blanc de Blancs Champagne NV • $31 • (11/15/1996) • **88**

Brut Blanc de Blancs Champagne 1992: Like a Chardonnay with bubbles. Ripe and forward, this displays coconut and pineapple nuances in addition to spice and vanilla, all on a lively framework. Drink now.–B.S. • $60 • (11/30/1999) • **89**

Brut Blanc de Blancs Champagne 1990: Just gorgeous. Mouthfilling and wonderfully flavorful but not overpowering, it blends abundant ripe fruit flavors with a subtle mousse and weaves great complexity with an elegant restraint. Like a classic Meursault that sparkles. Drink now through 2003. • $50 • (12/31/1998) HR • **95**

Brut Champagne NV: Quite mature in character, this brut has nutty, earthy aromas and flavors, a soft mousse and a rather simple finish. Drink now. • $32 • (12/31/1998) • **82**

Brut Rosé Champagne NV • $38 • (12/31/1991) • **88**

DELAPORTE, DOMAINE VINCENT

Sancerre 1996 • $23 • (3/31/1998) • **90**

Sancerre Cuvée Maxime Les Galifards 1996 • $35 • (5/31/1998) • **90**

Sancerre Cuvée Maxime Vieilles Vignes 1998: Smoke and almond notes linger nicely throughout, while the plump, ripe citrus flavors take over in this full-bodied Sancerre. Just needs a little time to come together on the finish. Drink now through 2001.–B.S. • $36 • (6/15/2000) • **88**

Sancerre Cuvée Maxime Vieilles Vignes 1997: Has dull herbal flavors and aromas, with spicy, buttery notes on the finish. Tasted twice, with consistent notes.–K.M. • $36 • (5/15/2000) • **77**

DELARCHE PERE & FILS, MARIUS

Corton Les Renardes 1990 • $49 • (6/15/1993) • **87**

Corton-Charlemagne 1995 • $NA • (5/31/1997) • **96**

Pernand-Vergelesses 1995 • $NA • (8/31/1997) • **82**

Pernand-Vergelesses 1989 • $15/375 ml. • (4/30/1991) • **82**

Pernand-Vergelesses Ile des Vergelesses 1990 • $28 • (6/15/1993) • **87**

Pernand-Vergelesses Ile des Vergelesses 1985 • $23 • (10/15/1988) • **89**

Pernand-Vergelesses Les Vergelesses 1990 • $25 • (6/15/1993) • **84**

DELAS

Châteauneuf-du-Pape 1985 • $17 • (10/31/1987) • **91**

Châteauneuf-du-Pape 1983 • $18 • (10/15/1991) • **72**

Châteauneuf-du-Pape Cuvée de Haute Pierre 1989 • $16 • (10/15/1991) • **90**

Châteauneuf-du-Pape Cuvée de Haute Pierre 1988 • $17 • (10/15/1991) • **86**

Châteauneuf-du-Pape Cuvée de Haute Pierre 1986 • $20 • (10/15/1991) • **86**

Châteauneuf-du-Pape Cuvée de Haute Pierre 1985 • $20 • (10/15/1991) • **86**

Châteauneuf-du-Pape Les Calcerniers 1997: Ripe and silky, tasting a bit mature, with a very plummy, fresh mushroom and forest underbrush aroma. Medium-bodied, it turns a bit crisp and tart on the palate. Drink now through 2003.–P.M. • $28 • (6/30/2000) • **80**

Châteauneuf-du-Pape Les Calcerniers 1996: Lovely from start to finish and quite exotic, with violet, rose petal, Oriental spice, wild raspberry and deftly toasted oak accents mingling in a medium-bodied package of firm but well-integrated tannins. Drink through 2005.–P.M. • $19 • (9/30/1998) • **88**

Châteauneuf-du-Pape Les Calcerniers 1995 • $19 • (10/15/1997) • **86**

Châteauneuf-du-Pape Les Calcerniers 1993 • $20 • (11/15/1995) • **84**

Condrieu Clos Boucher 1997: Rich and thick, this full-bodied white lacks focus. Tastes of burnt toasted wood. Hot finish.–P.M. • $36 Ⓐ • (12/15/1999) • **76**

Condrieu Clos Boucher 1996: Lush and smooth, full-bodied, showing oak, cedar and toast, but the decent fruit is buried under the wood at this stage. Best from 2000.–P.M. • $50 • (11/15/1998) • **84**

Condrieu La Galopine 1998: Soft and pleasant, with a buttery popcorn character. A bit burning from the toasted wood, which dominates the tough finish. Not imported into the U.S.–P.M. • $NA • (1/01/1999) • **80**

Cornas Chante-Perdrix 1991 • $28 • (5/31/1994) • **86**

Cornas Chante-Perdrix 1990 • $28 • (9/30/1993) • **88**

Côte-Rôtie La Landonne 1997: Marvelous, rich and dense, with the typical Syrah smells of leather, black pepper and earthy horse stable. Fine tannin structure makes this a pleasurable, full-bodied red on release. Smooth, blackberry-scented finish. Not imported into the U.S. Drink through 2005.–P.M. • $NA • (11/30/1999) • **90**

Côte-Rôtie Seigneur de Maugiron 1997: A dark, very pretty '97, with delicious, ripe black fruit supported by black pepper, spice and subtle earth notes. Medium-bodied, balanced and smooth, it makes for a delicious drink on release. Not imported into the U.S. Drink now through 2003.–P.M. • $NA • (11/30/1999) • **88**

Côte-Rôtie Seigneur de Maugiron 1996: Gorgeous. Elegant and polished, this racy, sexy, medium-bodied Syrah blossoms with floral, citrus, currant, spice, white truffle and mocha flavors that come together laser-sharply on the clean, pure and long finish. Quite acidic, but the tannins are supple. Drink now through 2010.–P.M. • $35 • (9/15/1998) • **91**

Côte-Rôtie Seigneur de Maugiron 1995 • $35 • (10/15/1997) • **85**

Côte-Rôtie Seigneur de Maugiron 1994 • $35 • (10/15/1997) • **78**

Côte-Rôtie Seigneur de Maugiron 1991 • $36 • (5/31/1994) • **81**

Côte-Rôtie Seigneur de Maugiron 1990 • $30 • (11/30/1996) • **89**

Côtes du Rhône St.-Esprit 1997: Rather rustic, kicking in with sweet-tasting currant, black cherry, and spicy black pepper flavors. Medium-bodied, with firm tannins and a chewy, intense finish; try it with bistro dishes. Drink now.–P.M. • $8 • (11/15/1998) • **81**

Côtes du Rhône St.-Esprit 1996 • $8 • (10/15/1997) • **85**

Côtes du Rhône St.-Esprit 1995 • $8 • (9/15/1997) • **85**

Côtes du Rhône St.-Esprit 1994 • $9 • (12/15/1996) • **81**

Côtes du Rhône St.-Esprit 1993 • $9 • (11/15/1995) • **83**

Côtes du Rhône St.-Esprit 1988 • $7 • (12/15/1990) • **84**

Côtes du Rhône White St.-Esprit 1998: Very soft, dull and alcoholic. A bit oxidized and turning sour.–P.M. • $9 • (12/15/1999) • **74**

Côtes du Rhône White St.-Esprit 1997: A flat wine that tastes oxidized, turning dry on the palate.–P.M. • $8 • (11/15/1998) • **70**

Côtes du Ventoux Escarlate 1998: Good fruit but also a bit of herbal character, with midpalate dryness. Not imported into the U.S.–P.M. • $NA • (1/01/1999) • **78**

Côtes du Ventoux Val Muzols 1996: Well made. Fruity, flavorful and medium-bodied, with a silky mouthfeel, this shows wonderful character. Unpretentious but deliciously versatile, with currant, leather, grilled meat and crushed black pepper notes. Drink now.–P.M. • $7 • (11/15/1998) • **86**

Côtes du Ventoux Val Muzols 1995 • $7 • (9/15/1997) • **84**

Côtes du Ventoux Val Muzols 1994 • $7 • (10/15/1996) • **85**

Côtes du Ventoux Val Muzols 1993 • $8 • (11/15/1995) • **76**

Crozes-Hermitage Les Launes 1997: Crisp but showing floral, lemon, raspberry, black pepper and leather character. Toasted oak surfaces on the lean, slightly acidic finish. Drink now through 2001.–P.M. • $15 • (12/15/1999) • **80**

Crozes-Hermitage Les Launes 1996: Exotic and simply delicious, bursting with an unusual combination of raspberry, violet, rose petals, mocha, cassis and dried Provençal herbs. Ripe tannins add to the pleasure of drinking this suave, medium-bodied red, which has a succulent licorice note on the lingering finish. Drink now through 2007.–P.M. • $13 • (10/15/1998) • **89**

Crozes-Hermitage Les Launes 1995 • $13 • (10/15/1997) • **85**

Crozes-Hermitage Les Launes 1994 • $13 • (10/15/1997) • **91**

Crozes-Hermitage Les Launes 1992 • $14 • (11/30/1996) • **78**

Crozes-Hermitage Les Launes 1990 • $12 • (10/15/1995) • **89**

Crozes-Hermitage White Les Launes 1997: Wonderful harmony and balance in this supple, silky, rich, full-bodied white. Offers subtle aromas and flavors of wet earth, white pepper, spice, banana, melon and almond. Nicely ripe on the attractive finish. Drink now.–P.M. • $13 • (11/15/1998) • **88**

Crozes-Hermitage White Les Launes 1996: A bit of paint varnish and some strange perfumes dominate the nose. Fairly dry and inelegant.–P.M. • $13 • (11/15/1998) • **76**

Gigondas Les Reinages Vieilles Vignes 1997: Fruity, with licorice and cherry aromas. Lightish and showing a smooth polish, but not much grip to keep you interested.–P.M. • $20 • (12/15/1999) • **79**

Gigondas Les Reinages Vieilles Vignes 1996: Thick and chewy in a supple way, this is a wonderful, full-bodied and generous wine, although very oaky. Offers wet earth, cassis, blackberry, plum and mineral-laden character, good acidity and a long, toasty finish. Best from 2002 through 2007.–P.M. • $16 • (10/15/1998) • **89**

Hermitage 1996: A gutsy wine that gets a lift toward the heavens from its pure, silky currant and cassis notes. Packed with earth, wet foxlike tones, leather, grilled meat character. This full-bodied, firm yet elegant wine is not so much seductive as it is impressive for packing so much personality and muscle into one package. The toasted oak finish tastes of sweet fruit, and you can tell this is an ager. Best from 2005 through 2010.–P.M. • $35 • (9/15/1998) • **91**

Hermitage Cuvée Marquise de la Tourette 1997: A supple red that verges on opulence, as it delivers a rich texture and delicious blackberry, smoked bacon and black pepper flavors that suggest ripe grapes. Chewy tannins give backbone to this medium-bodied Hermitage. Not imported into the U.S. Drink now through 2004.–P.M. • $NA • (1/01/1999) • **87**

Hermitage Cuvée Marquise de la Tourette 1996: Judging by how it improved when aired, this wine will benefit from aging—the tannins soften and the flavors burst with floral, blueberry and cherry notes. Elegant, even delicate, with a touch of smoke on the finish. Drink through 2005.–P.M. • $35 • (11/15/1998) • **88**

Hermitage Cuvée Marquise de la Tourette 1995 • $35 • (10/15/1997) • **79**

Hermitage Cuvée Marquise de la Tourette 1994 • $35 • (10/15/1997) • **80**

Hermitage Cuvée Marquise de la Tourette 1991 • $35 • (5/31/1994) • **84**

Hermitage Cuvée Marquise de la Tourette 1990 • $30 • (11/30/1996) • **91**

Hermitage Les Bessards 1997: Very oaky and international in style, but at least it's an opulent '97. Rich and dense, offering a silky mouthfeel and refined tannins. The fruit is sweet and deeply satisfying, and the blackberry and cassis fold nicely into the mocha and vanilla. The finish is a bit acidic. Not imported into the U.S. Drink now through 2010.–P.M. • $NA • (11/30/1999) • **92**

Hermitage Les Bessards 1996: Impressive wine for its dark color, full body and complex aromas that range from pure, clean cassis and blackberry to some lightly toasted bread, animal and leather notes. Quite elegant despite its robust build. Could use some cellaring to flesh out. Best from 2003 through 2006.–P.M. • $65 • (9/15/1998) • **87**

Hermitage Les Bessards 1995 • $65 • (10/15/1997) • **82**

Hermitage Les Bessards 1994 • $65 • (9/15/1997) • **90**

Key: SS—Spectator Selection. CS—Cellar Selection. HR—Highly Recommended. $NA—Price not available. (BT)—Barrel tasting. Ⓐ—Auction Price. For a key to the tasters' initials, see "How to Use These Listings."
Dates in parentheses represent the issues in which the ratings were published.

Hermitage Les Bessards 1990 • $75 • (10/15/1995) • **89**

Hermitage White Cuvée Marquise de la Tourette 1998: The wood stands out first, but then there is smoothness and richness that bring its silken blanket to patch up the bad spots. Where is the fruit? Not imported into the U.S. Drink now.–P.M. • $NA • (1/01/1999) • **80**

Hermitage White Cuvée Marquise de la Tourette 1997: Shows some fat, with a butter, toasted oak and creamlike character. Medium-bodied, turning a bit short on the finish.–P.M. • $29 Ⓐ • (11/30/1999) • **79**

Hermitage White Cuvée Marquise de la Tourette 1996: Rich, ripe and buttery, with lots of butterscotch and caramelized pear flavors, this toasty, full-bodied wine turns a bit bitter on the finish. Drink now through 2005.–P.M. • $29 • (11/15/1998) • **81**

Merlot Vin de Pays d'Oc 1995 • $7 • (11/15/1997) • **78**

Merlot Vin de Pays d'Oc 1994 • $7 • (12/15/1996) • **74**

Merlot Vin de Pays d'Oc 1993 • $9 • (7/31/1995) • **83**

St.-Joseph 1996: Quite crisp, this medium-bodied red is dark in color, firm in texture and packed with vibrant, juicy and succulent berry flavors. Makes for fun drinking now, but can stand some cellaring. Drink now through 2005.–P.M. • $18 • (11/15/1998) • **85**

St.-Joseph Cuvée François de Tournon 1997: A gutsy red. Starts out smooth, rich and ripe on the palate, delivering charm and sweet tannins, with black pepper, blackberry and truffle chocolate flavors. It ends on the tough, slightly acidic side, but give it a year or so in the cellar. Not imported into the U.S. Drink through 2003–P.M. • $NA • (1/01/1999) • **87**

St.-Joseph Cuvée François de Tournon 1996: Lean but juicy, showing decent cedar, pepper, cherry and blackberry notes. Turns fairly ripe on the finish. Should gain roundness with food. Drink now through 2001.–P.M. • $18 • (11/15/1998) • **83**

St.-Joseph Cuvée François de Tournon 1994 • $18 • (10/15/1997) • **87**

St.-Joseph Cuvée Francois de Tournon 1991 • $NA • (5/31/1994) • **79**

St.-Joseph Ste.-Epine 1994 • $25 • (10/15/1997) • **84**

Tavel La Comballe 1998: A bit bitter and herbal. A vegetal style of rosé.–P.M. • $15 • (12/15/1999) • **70**

DELBECK

Brut Champagne 1990: Distinctive for its heady aromas, full body and mellow flavors. Has an attractive earthy character, smooth effervescence and a lingering finish. Drink now through 2003. • $60 • (11/15/1999) • **90**

Brut Champagne Bouzy NV: Brassy in color and showing mature elements of nuts and a Sherry-like note, this dryish, firm Champagne with a slightly astringent finish won't appeal to everyone, yet it has personality and length of flavor. Drink now.–B.S. • $56 • (11/30/1999) • **88**

Brut Champagne Cramant NV: Mature in style, exuding ginger, walnut and antique wood aromas and flavors that balance deftly with the glycerinlike texture and firm backbone. Fine complexity and persistence of flavor, ending on refreshing notes of lemon and walnut. Drink now.–B.S. • $56 • (11/30/1999) • **91**

Brut Champagne Heritage NV: A focused beam of ripe apple, pear and toast for accent allied to a compact, solid structure, with moderate depth and intensity. Terrific as an apéritif. Drink now.–B.S. • $40 • (11/30/1999) • **88**

Brut Rosé Champagne Heritage NV: Compact and concentrated, offering dough, cherry and citrus flavors on a rich texture. Medium-bodied, with a good, crisp finish. Drink now.–B.S. • $49 • (11/30/1999) • **87**

DELESVAUX, PHILIPPE

Anjou 1996 • $11 • (5/31/1998) • **86**

Anjou-Villages 1997: This soft red is youthful yet generous, with simple but appealing grape and plum flavors and slightly bitter tannins. A nice quaff with simple foods. Drink now.–T.M. • $12 • (6/30/1999) • **81**

Coteaux du Layon Carbonifera 1997: Offering good concentration, this white is almost oily on the palate and very sweet, with honey, spice, apricot and dried pineapple flavors. Very intense—it has an earthy, nearly overripe barnyard quality—but it certainly has the stuffing to improve with age. Best after 2002.–T.M. • $75/500 ml. • (6/30/1999) • **92**

Coteaux du Layon Sélection de Grains Nobles 1997: This intense white combines richness and delicacy. The honey, earth, pineapple and spice flavors are not quite harmonious yet, but it has distinctive character and impressive concentration. Better with development. Best after 2002.–T.M. • $40/500 ml. • (6/30/1999) • **91**

Coteaux du Layon Sélection de Grains Nobles 1996 • $38/500 ml. • (5/31/1998) • **92**

Coteaux du Layon Sélection de Grains Nobles 1995 • $35/500 ml. • (5/15/1997) HR • **94**

DELETANG, DOMAINE

Montlouis Demi-Sec Les Batisses 1996 • $17 • (5/31/1998) • **86**
Montlouis Les Batisses 1996 • $15 • (5/31/1998) • **86**
Montlouis Moelleux 1996: There's an appealing citrus component along with peach and honey in this clean, lightly sweet white whose flavors intensify in the mouth, culminating in a chalky, minerally finish. Elegant and focused. Drink now through 2006.–B.S. • $24 • (11/15/1998) • **90**
Montlouis Moelleux Grande Réserve Tris 1996: Beautiful aromas of peaches, apricots, honey and flowers are elegant on the palate. The vibrant acidity balances the sweetness, giving an impression of being off-dry. Minerally finish. Drink now through 2004.–B.S. • $35 • (11/15/1998) • **89**
Sauvignon Blanc Touraine 1996 • $9 • (5/31/1998) • **76**

DELIAS, CHATEAU DU

Pomerol 1982: A simple, caressing red. Brick red in color, with light leaf, berry and earth aromas. Medium-bodied and soft, with light milk chocolate and berry flavors. Silky texture. (1982 Bordeaux horizontal tasting). Drink now.–J.S. • $NA • (11/30/1998) • **83**

DELMAS, Y. & D.

Cabernet Sauvignon Vin de Pays de l'Aude La Noble 1996 • $6 • (5/15/1998) • **75**
Chardonnay Vin de Pays de l'Aude La Noble 1996 • $6 • (4/30/1998) • **83**
Merlot Vin de Pays de l'Aude La Noble 1996 • $7 • (5/31/1998) • **77**
Sauvignon Blanc Vin de Pays de l'Aude La Noble 1996 • $6 • (5/15/1998) • **75**

DELORME, ANDRE

Montagny Domaine de la Renarde 1996: A bit green and grassy, not unlike a Sauvignon Blanc, showing vanilla, whipped cream and pear-pie character. Medium-bodied. Drink now.–P.M. • $NA • (8/31/1998) • **75**

DEMESSEY

Bourgogne White 1997: Crisp, even a bit tart, with a tough, vegetal side, but it's very vibrant.–P.M. • $NA • (1/01/1999) • **79**
Bourgogne White 1996 • $14 • (5/31/1998) • **75**
Bourgogne White 1995 • $14 • (8/31/1997) • **72**
Bourgogne White Cuvée Spéciale 1997: Tastes of butterscotch and mocha in an overdone, oaky way. Round on the palate, though the finish turns a bit astringent.–P.M. • $17 • (5/31/1999) • **76**
Bourgogne White Cuvée Spéciale 1996 • $17 • (5/31/1998) • **77**
Bourgogne White Premier Tri Elevé en Fûts de Chêne 1995 • $15 • (8/31/1997) • **79**
Chassagne-Montrachet Morgeot 1997: Buttery and round on the palate, with a popcorn note, it delivers a slight wet plywood flavor on the dull finish.–P.M. • $48 • (5/31/1999) • **75**
Chassagne-Montrachet Morgeot 1995 • $39 • (5/31/1997) • **90**
Meursault 1997: Ripe-tasting, this round, thick Meursault coats the palate with delightful fruit, honey and spice. Displays a fun floral note on the smooth finish. Drink now through 2005.–P.M. • $39 • (5/31/1999) • **88**
Meursault 1995 • $32 • (5/31/1997) • **72**
Montagny Les Resses 1997: Dull and diluted, with cardboard, wet paper and earth character. Turns astringent.–P.M. • $18 • (5/31/1999) • **70**
Montagny Les Resses 1996: Distinctive, with loads of butterscotch, toasted oak and whipped cream flavors that would seem overdone except that a limelike citrus character brings this medium-bodied wine into balance. Lovely mineral character on the intense finish. Best after 2000.–P.M. • $18 • (8/31/1998) • **86**
Montagny Les Resses 1995 • $18 • (8/31/1997) • **77**
Pernand-Vergelesses White Sous le Bois de Noël et Belles Filles 1996 • $19 • (5/31/1998) • **90**
Pouilly-Fuissé 1997: Tight and crisp, with mouthpuckering lemon, pear and apricot jam flavors spread on a steely frame. Best after 2000.–P.M. • $23 • (5/31/1999) • **84**
Pouilly-Fuissé 1996 • $23 • (5/31/1998) • **83**
Puligny-Montrachet Le Cailleret 1996: Wonderful. Packed with wet earth, wet stone, pebble, mineral character, along with pear, tropical, vanilla bean notes. Full-bodied and opulent, yet well-anchored in the Burgundian soil. A grand wine that grows on you, to a smoky, subtle finish. Delicious. Drink now through 2010.–P.M. • $42 • (8/31/1998) • **93**
Puligny-Montrachet Le Cailleret 1995 • $49 • (8/31/1997) • **77**
Puligny-Montrachet Les Pucelles 1996: Fat and thick, the butterscotch, caramel and butter tones dominate in this lush, soft, full-bodied white. Kicks in with good acidity on the crisp finish. A bit disjointed. Drink now through 2002.–P.M. • $45 • (8/31/1998) • **81**
Puligny-Montrachet Les Pucelles 1995 • $47 • (5/31/1997) • **79**
Puligny-Montrachet Les Referts 1997: Odd, perfumed, floral and woody aromas mask the pure fruit that may lurk in this wine. Crisp, drying finish.–P.M. • $NA • (1/01/1999) • **75**
Rully 1997: Distinctive, with a flinty, smoky, tropical character, this medium-bodied Chardonnay delivers pear notes on the finish. Drink now.–P.M. • $18 • (5/31/1999) • **84**
St.-Aubin Les Frionnes 1996 • $25 • (5/31/1998) • **84**
St.-Véran 1997: Nice ripe fruit delivers pleasure in this honeyed, medium-bodied Chardonnay, accented by some tropical notes and an attractively subtle toastiness on the finish.–P.M. • $19 • (5/31/1999) • **84**
St.-Véran 1996: A bit bitter and odd, showing slight dilution and a cardboard note, delivering only modest fruit. Serve chilled. Drink now.–P.M. • $18 • (8/31/1998) • **73**
St.-Véran 1995 • $14 • (5/31/1997) • **79**

DESAUNAY-BISSEY, BRUNO

Echézeaux 1996: Deftly oaked, with seductive, ripe red berry and black fruit flavors, it has more opulence than most '96s, with fine tannins, pronounced acidity and a lingering, spicy, vanilla- and mocha-scented end. Drink now through 2005.–P.M. • $60 • (7/31/1999) • **89**
Vosne-Romanée Les Beaumonts 1996: A bit earthy but also showing nice ripe fruit and high acidity, with crisp, succulent cherry and blackberry character. Medium-bodied, it takes off on the intense finish. Drink now through 2001.–P.M. • $50 • (7/31/1999) • **89**

DESCHAMPS, MARC

Pouilly-Fumé Cuvée des Porcheronnes 1997: Bright, juicy lemon and grapefruit notes run through this lively white, picking up grass and smoke notes on the finish. Drink now.–B.S. • $18 • (6/15/2000) • **85**
Pouilly-Fumé Les Champs de Cri 1997: Solid, with nice density, this has a smoky aroma overlaying the ripe and intense lemon peel, stone and almond notes. Pure and vibrant. Drink now.–B.S. • $21 • (6/15/2000) • **88**
Pouilly-Fumé Les Vignes de Berge 1997: Showing a textbook mix of smoke, lemon, straw and earth, this medium-weight white stays clean, focused and bright throughout. Drink now.–B.S. • $18 • (6/15/2000) • **87**
Pouilly-sur-Loire Vieilles Vignes 1997: A slightly earthy aroma gives way to a light-bodied and crisp Chasselas, with straightforward hay and lemon flavors that stay juicy on the finish. Drink now.–B.S. • $10 • (6/15/2000) • **83**

DESCHAUX, LUCIEN

Beaujolais Le Vieux Presbytère 1995: Light-bodied, seems to be losing its grip; pleasant light spicy cherry flavors fade quickly on the finish. Drink now.–T.M. • $7 • (8/31/1998) • **77**
Beaujolais Le Vieux Presbytère 1994 • $8 • (9/15/1996) • **79**
Beaujolais-Villages Le Vieux Presbytère 1995: Light, with a pleasantly silky texture, but the soft cherry flavor is fading.–T.M. • $8 • (8/31/1998) • **78**
Beaujolais-Villages Le Vieux Presbytère 1994 • $10 • (9/15/1996) • **84**
Cabernet Sauvignon Vin de Pays d'Oc 1996 • $6 • (12/15/1997) • **82**
Cabernet Sauvignon Vin de Pays d'Oc 1994 • $8/1 liter • (12/15/1996) • **78**
Chardonnay Vin de Pays d'Oc 1996 • $6 • (12/15/1997) • **81**
Châteauneuf-du-Pape Le Vieux Abbé 1994 • $14 • (12/15/1996) • **80**
Châteauneuf-du-Pape Le Vieux Abbé 1992 • $14 • (10/15/1994) • **83**
Châteauneuf-du-Pape Le Vieux Abbé 1990 • $13 • (11/15/1992) • **86**
Côtes du Rhône 1995 • $8 • (5/15/1998) • **84**
Côtes du Rhône 1994 • $9 • (10/15/1996) • **81**
Côtes du Rhône Le Vieux Presbytère 1991 • $8 • (10/15/1994) • **83**
Haut-Médoc 1995 • $9 • (1/31/1998) • **81**
Merlot Vin de Pays d'Oc 1996 • $6 • (12/15/1997) • **81**
Merlot Vin de Pays d'Oc 1995 • $8/1 liter • (12/15/1996) • **78**
Pouilly-Fuissé La Cuvée du Maître 1995 • $16 • (1/31/1998) • **70**
Rosé d'Anjou 1992 • $8 • (11/15/1994) • **77**
Syrah Vin de Pays d'Oc 1996 • $6 • (12/15/1997) • **83**

DESCOMBES, ANTOINE

Beaujolais-Villages 1996: Gamy and smoky tones dominate the fruit in this firm wine, but it has some concentration and black cherry notes emerge on the finish. Best with food. Drink now.–T.M. • $7 • (8/31/1998) • **82**

DESHENRYS, DOMAINE

Chardonnay Vin de Pays des Côtes de Thongue 1996 • $10 • (5/31/1997) • **79**
Coteaux du Languedoc 1994 • $11 • (5/15/1997) • **84**
Merlot Vin de Pays des Côtes de Thongue 1995 • $10 • (5/15/1997) • **85**
Tradition Red Vin de Pays des Côtes de Thongue 1995 • $10 • (5/15/1997) • **87**

DESLINES, DOMAINE

St.-Chinian Tonneaux 1998: A good medium-bodied red, with pleasant flavors of red plum and white pepper. Spicy notes on the finish. Drink now.–P.M. • $13 • (6/15/2000) • **84**

DESMEURE, DOMAINE

Crozes-Hermitage Domaine des Remizières Cuvée Christophe 1997: Blackish in color, this heavily extracted red has compacted fruit, with mint, herb, spice and blackberry notes. Tannins are a bit chewy and tough on the somewhat astringent finish. Drink now through 2001.–P.M. • $19 • (10/31/1999) • **83**
Crozes-Hermitage Domaine des Remizières Cuvée Christophe 1996: Overlook the earthy aromas (which dissipate with air) and you're in for a treat, as this medium-bodied Crozes offers plenty of lovely wet earth, red- and blackberry notes, and ripe, sweet tannins. Balanced finish. Drink now through 2005.–P.M. • $23 • (11/15/1998) • **88**
Crozes-Hermitage Domaine des Remizières 1991 • $26 • (5/31/1994) • **83**
Crozes-Hermitage White Domaine des Remizières Cuvée Christophe 1997: Fancy oak helps create butterscotch and very toasty notes that mingle with honey and pear to produce a smoky, international-style, slightly hot white Crozes. Drink now.–P.M. • $17 • (9/15/1999) • **83**
Crozes-Hermitage White Domaine des Remizières Cuvée Christophe 1996: Balanced and delicious, this silky, full-bodied white shows pear and melon notes, with distinct butter, toast, mocha and spice character. Drink now.–P.M. • $20 • (11/15/1998) • **85**
Hermitage Domaine des Remizières 1997: Well made and delicious. Lovely violet and cassis zoom along in this bright, succulent and balanced red of medium body and supple tannins. Drink now through 2003.–P.M. • $31 • (9/15/1999) • **87**
Hermitage Domaine des Remizières Cuvée Emilie 1996: A well-made '96. Ripe and opulent, packed with intense currant and blackberry flavors, grilled meat and black pepper notes, a slight earth and leather character and velvety tannins. Finishes with vibrating intensity. Drink now through 2008.–P.M. • $38 • (11/15/1998) • **92**
Hermitage White Domaine des Remizières 1997: A big white showing a solid oak structure, but it's fresh, with a rich, full mouthfeel and intense aromas of pineapple, mango, banana, lime. Just on the dry side of off-dry. Drink now through 2005.–P.M. • $30 • (9/15/1999) • **90**
Hermitage White Domaine des Remizières Cuvée Emilie 1996: A straightforward white, shy on fruit, a bit dry on the finish.–P.M. • $38 • (11/15/1998) • **77**

DESMIRAIL, CHATEAU

Margaux 1994 • $23 • (1/31/1997) • **83**
Margaux 1993 • $23 • (1/31/1996) • **83**
Margaux 1991 • $16 • (3/31/1994) • **78**
Margaux 1990 • $27 • (3/31/1993) • **91**
Margaux 1989 • $27 • (3/15/1992) • **86**
Margaux 1986 • $22 • (6/30/1989) • **90**
Margaux 1982: Medium brick-red color, with a ruby center. Medium-bodied and silky, with chocolate, berry and cedar aromas and lovely autumnal flavors. (1982 Bordeaux horizontal horizontal). Drink now.–J.S. • $NA • (11/30/1998) • **86**

DESPRES, THIERRY

Monbazillac Grande Maison Cuvée Madame 1996: A delicious dessert wine that's lively and full-flavored. This has a good acidity, with delicious flavors of baked apple and crème brûlée, that intensify on the finish. Drink now through 2004.–K.M. • $53/375 ml. • (1/01/2000) • **89**

Key: SS—Spectator Selection. CS—Cellar Selection. HR—Highly Recommended. $NA—Price not available. (BT)—Barrel tasting. Ⓐ—Auction Price.
For a key to the tasters' initials, see "How to Use These Listings."
Dates in parentheses represent the issues in which the ratings were published.

Monbazillac Grande Maison Cuvée Monsieur 1996: Made in a softer style, this dessert wine has a good acidity and appealing flavors of apple, spice and a touch of honey. Smokey notes chime in the on the finish. Drink now through 2003.–K.M. • $16/500 ml. • (1/01/2000) • **87**

DESVIGNES, LOUIS-CLAUDE

Morgon Côte du Py 1993 • $16 • (7/31/1995) • **83**
Morgon Javernières 1997: Lacks focus and concentration, giving only a modest cherry character.–B.S. • $18 • (10/15/1999) • **79**
Morgon Javernières 1995 • $17 • (9/15/1997) • **86**
Morgon Javernières 1993 • $17 • (7/31/1995) • **79**

DEURRE, DOMAINE DE

Côtes du Rhône 1996: A bit weird, with earthy, herbal aromas and only modest ripe fruit. Light-bodied, with a bitter finish.–P.M. • $6 • (11/15/1998) • **74**
Côtes du Rhône 1995 • $10 • (10/15/1996) • **83**
Côtes du Rhône-Villages St.-Maurice 1996: Offers modest wild strawberry, cherry, raspberry, but the overall feel is lean, with a tart finish. Food should help tame it.–P.M. • $9 • (11/15/1998) • **77**
Côtes du Rhône-Villages Vinsobres 1996: Fresh, vibrant, with a core of cassis bush, dried herbs, citrus and black cherry notes. Crisp in texture, intense and pure, but not harmonious. Food should help. Drink now.–P.M. • $9 • (11/15/1998) • **81**
Côtes du Rhône-Villages Vinsobres 1992 • $13 • (12/15/1996) • **80**
Côtes du Rhône-Villages Vinsobres 1989 • $10 • (8/31/1992) • **84**

DEUTZ

Brut Blanc de Blancs Champagne 1993: Smooth and delicious. An enticing combination of subtle fruit flavor, supple texture and lingering aftertaste make this appealing. Enjoyable now, but should develop even more flavor with time. Drink through 2001. • $65 • (12/31/1998) • **89**
Brut Blanc de Blancs Champagne 1990 • $45 • (11/30/1995) • **89**
Brut Blanc de Noirs Champagne Cuvée Marie-Damarisse NV • $25 • (12/31/1994) • **87**
Brut Champagne NV • $25 • (12/31/1991) • **82**
Brut Champagne 1993: Nice mouthful of Champagne. Rather full-bodied and full-flavored, with generous citrus and apple tones and a soothing texture. Drink now through 2001. • $48 • (10/15/1999) • **89**
Brut Champagne 1990 • $35 • (12/31/1997) • **89**
Brut Champagne Classic NV: Generous, mature flavors make this brut substantive. Full-bodied, ripe and complex, with a plush texture and lingering finish. Drink now. • $38 • (9/15/1999) • **89**
Brut Champagne Cuvée Lallier Gold Lack NV • $33 • (12/31/1990) • **80**
Brut Champagne Cuvée Porsche NV • $35 • (12/31/1994) • **86**
Brut Champagne Cuvée William Deutz 1990: Broad and brassy at first sip, this dry, full-bodied bubbly has a blast of buttery flavor and an expansive texture. Turns lean and smoky on the finish. Drink now. • $85 • (12/31/1998) • **87**
Brut Rosé Champagne 1993: Quite flavorful and smooth in texture, a complete, satisfying rosé. Has toasty aromas, bright cherry flavors, spicy accents and a clean, zingy finish. Drink now through 2001. • $52 • (10/15/1999) • **90**
Brut Rosé Champagne 1990: Vivid but subtle fruit flavors, bracing acidity and a firm texture point to an elegant wine. Crisp and delightful now, it should be even better with age. Drink now through 2003. • $40 • (11/30/1998) • **90**
Brut Rosé Champagne Cuvée Marie-Damarisse NV • $29 • (12/31/1997) • **84**

DEUX ROCHES, DOMAINE DES

Mâcon-Davayé 1996 • $14 • (8/31/1997) • **89**
Mâcon-Villages 1995 • $NA • (8/31/1996) • **87**
St.-Véran 1995 • $NA • (8/31/1996) • **86**
St.-Véran Les Terres Noires 1995 • $NA • (8/31/1996) • **88**
St.-Véran Vieilles Vignes 1995 • $24 • (5/31/1997) • **85**

DEVISE DE LILIAN, LA

St.-Estèphe 1996: Fruit and leather aromas follow through on the palate. Medium-bodied, with medium tannins, but a slightly watery finish.–J.S. • $NA • (2/28/1999) • **79**
St.-Estèphe 1995 • $15 • (1/31/1998) • **84**

DEYDIER & FILS, DOMAINE JEAN

Châteauneuf-du-Pape Les Clefs d'Or 1997: Attractive and polished, lacking a bit of depth but showing vanilla, wet earth, red berry and plum flavors. Only decent ripeness to balance the firm tannins. Hold short-term for a smoother drink. Best from 2001 through 2004.–P.M. • $NA • (12/15/1999) • **80**
Châteauneuf-du-Pape Les Clefs d'Or 1995: Supple as can be, this medium-bodied red shows finesse, with sweet-tasting black cherry, prune, leather, game, roasted peanut and black truffle flavors and silky, ripe tannins. Good acidity on the finish. Drink now through 2005.–P.M. • $20 • (11/15/1998) • **88**
Châteauneuf-du-Pape Les Clefs d'Or 1994 • $25 • (12/15/1996) • **82**
Châteauneuf-du-Pape Les Clefs d'Or 1993 • $20 • (11/15/1995) • **82**
Châteauneuf-du-Pape Les Clefs d'Or 1983 • $16 • (10/31/1987) • **78**
Côtes du Rhône Les Clefs d'Or 1995 • $13 • (12/15/1996) • **71**
Côtes du Rhône Les Clefs d'Or 1993 • $13 • (9/30/1995) • **85**
Côtes du Rhône Les Clefs d'Or 1990 • $12 • (4/15/1993) • **82**

DICONNE, JEAN-PIERRE

Auxey-Duresses White 1997: A bit earthy. A flinty wet earth personality emerges in this balanced, thick Chardonnay. Crisp, lemony, slightly bitter and rustic finish. Drink now through 2002.–P.M. • $22 • (9/30/1999) • **84**
Auxey-Duresses White 1996: A bit herbal and green, this medium-bodied white shows decent earth, wet stone and green apple character, but turns slightly astringent on the finish.–P.M. • $NA • (8/31/1998) • **71**
Auxey-Duresses White 1995 • $NA • (8/31/1997) • **86**
Meursault Clos des Luchets 1997: A bit earthy, with a round mouthfeel but not much fruit intensity. An accessible Meursault on release that will make for pleasant, if unchallenging, drinking. Drink now through 2001.–P.M. • $33 • (9/30/1999) • **80**
Meursault Clos des Luchets 1996: Racy and elegant, showing a subtle grass, herb, honey, mineral and pear character. Not overly oaked, this medium-bodied white is quite intense, turns chewy on the long finish. Best after 2005.–P.M. • $NA • (8/31/1998) • **86**
Meursault Clos des Luchets 1995 • $NA • (5/31/1997) • **90**
Meursault Les Narvaux 1996: Attractive, subtle wine. Medium-bodied, with plenty of vanilla, lemon, grass, honey, pear and toasted oak, this delights with its intensity of flavors, ripe character and chewy, chalky finish; only lacks the finesse to rate outstanding. Drink now through 2005.–P.M. • $NA • (8/31/1998) • **87**

DIEBOLT-VALLOIS

Brut Blanc de Blancs Champagne 1995: Focused and vibrant, this young vintage Champagne revolves around citrus, bread dough and apple flavors, allied to a firm, ripe framework. Drink now through 2004.–B.S. • $43 • (2/29/2000) • **89**

DIOCHON

Moulin-à-Vent Cuvée Vieilles Vignes 1997: Plum and cassis flavors are ripe and clean in this round red. Tannins are firm but unobtrusive, and there's enough acidity to match with food. A rich, fruity wine with more charm than complexity. Drink now.–T.M. • $18 • (12/31/1998) • **85**
Moulin-à-Vent Cuvée Vieilles Vignes 1996: Earthy and lean, with more vegetal and herbal notes than fruit, and the tannins are dry. Past its prime.–T.M. • $17 • (8/31/1998) • **76**
Moulin-à-Vent Cuvée Vieilles Vignes 1995 • $16 • (7/31/1997) • **89**
Moulin-à-Vent Cuvée Vieilles Vignes 1994 • $19 • (9/15/1996) • **85**

DIRLER

Gewürztraminer Alsace Grand Cru Saering 1996 • $28 • (3/31/1998) • **88**
Pinot d'Alsace Alsace 1996 • $16 • (3/31/1998) • **83**
Riesling Alsace Grand Cru Saering 1996: Virtually crackles with crisp acidity, along with smoky, stony accents. Firmly structured, dry and tightly wound, the fruit evokes apple and lime. Be patient and you'll be rewarded. Serious Riesling. Best from 2001 through 2007.–B.S. • $25 • (10/31/1999) • **91**
Sylvaner Alsace Cuvée Vieilles Vignes 1996 • $14 • (3/31/1998) • **84**

DISTINCTION

Cabernet Sauvignon Vin de Pays d'Oc 1998: Plummy flavors and herbal notes makes this a good, fruity Cabernet. Drink now.–K.M. • $8 • (8/31/1999) • **83**
Merlot Vin de Pays d'Oc 1997: Roasted aromas and flavors dominate this red, which also has dark plum and black cherry flavors. Notes of coffee grounds and chocolate on the finish. Drink now.–K.M. • $8 • (9/15/1999) • **80**

DOISY-DAENE, CHATEAU

Barsac 1998: Shows a lovely balance of spicy apple and apricot character. Full-bodied and sweet, with a long, spicy finish.–J.S. • $NA • (1/01/1999) (BT) • **90-94**
Barsac 1997: A Sauternes with lovely caramel and pineapple character. Full-bodied and medium sweet, with a long, flavorful finish. Best after 2001.–J.S. • $37 • (1/31/2000) • **91**
Barsac 1991 • $NA • (4/15/1995) • **85**
Barsac 1988 • $55 Ⓐ • (4/15/1995) • **87**
Barsac 1986 • $35 • (4/15/1995) • **89**
Barsac 1985 • $24 • (5/31/1988) • **73**
Barsac 1983 • $44 Ⓐ • (1/31/1988) • **73**

DOISY-DUBROCA, CHATEAU

Barsac 1998: A wine with lots of finesse and fresh fruit, offering apple, pinapple and honey character. Medium-bodied and medium sweet.–J.S. • $NA • (1/01/1999) (BT) • **85-89**
Barsac 1997: Wonderful finesse in this white, with spice, honey and vanilla character. Full-bodied, with lively acidity and a long, long finish. Super. Best after 2001.–J.S. • $NA • (1/31/2000) • **91**

DOISY-VEDRINES, CHATEAU

Barsac 1998: Plenty of fresh fruit, with lemon and cream character. Medium-bodied, medium sweet, with a fresh finish.–J.S. • $NA • (1/01/1999) (BT) • **85-89**
Barsac 1997: Lots of spice, honey, apricot and dried fruit character. Full-bodied and very sweet, with a long, spicy vanilla aftertaste. A lively young thing. Best after 2002.–J.S. • $32 • (1/31/2000) • **93**
Barsac 1992 • $NA • (4/15/1995) • **79**
Barsac 1990 • $28 Ⓐ • (4/15/1995) • **88**
Barsac 1989 • $50 • (4/15/1995) • **91**
Barsac 1988 • $32 • (4/15/1995) • **93**
Barsac 1986 • $52 • (12/31/1989) • **86**

DOMANIALES, LES

Châteauneuf-du-Pape Elevé en Barriques 1997: Fruity (red berry) and medium-bodied, but quite tannic. Dries a bit on the end, with leather and smoke notes. Time might smooth it out, but the wine lacks a bit of real ripeness. Drink soon with a hunk of meat. From Michel Bernard. Drink now through 2002.–P.M. • $35 • (1/01/1999) • **82**
Châteauneuf-du-Pape Elevé en Fûts de Chêne 1996: A nice négociant wine, with violet, smoky-oakish character. Medium- to full-bodied, it starts out very smooth, but turns a bit dry on the finish. From Michel Bernard. Drink now through 2005.–P.M. • $20 • (9/30/1998) • **87**
Côtes du Lubéron Domaine des Vaudois Réserve 1998: A bit rustic, but it has personality. Medium-bodied. Good fruit and supple tannins are set against a rather firm, chewy wet earth character. From Michel Bernard. Drink now through 2003.–P.M. • $7 • (1/01/1999) • **83**
Côtes du Rhône 1998: Offers nice black fruit that tastes ripe and lush, with a fresh, succulent, peppery character. From Michel Bernard. Drink now.–P.M. • $7 • (11/15/1999) • **84**
Côtes du Rhône 1997: Pretty fruit and soft texture make this appealing now. Of light to medium body, it shows nice aromas and flavors of cherry, cedar, tobacco-box and currant. From Michel Bernard.–P.M. • $7 • (11/15/1998) • **83**
Côtes du Rhône 1993 • $6 • (12/31/1995) • **68**
Côtes du Rhône Le Fort des Papes 1998: A big, oaky, dark red, delivering a supersmooth mouthfeel of ultraripe and very sweet tannins, plenty of sandlewood and black fruit aromas and a chewy but balanced finish. Should improve with short-term cellaring as the wood integrates with the fruit. From Michel Bernard. Drink through 2004.–P.M. • $11 • (1/01/1999) • **86**
Hermitage Beaudefond 1994: Smoky, gamy aromas and flavors are backed by full, firm tannins and good concentration in this muscular red, with ripe plum and prune flavors and notes of sandalwood and tobacco. A fine example of the traditional style. From Michel Bernard. Drink now through 2007.–T.M. • $25 • (11/15/1998) • **89**
Lirac Domaine des Muretins Elevé en Barriques 1998: A warm-weather, hot-vintage sort of wine. Very plummy and even showing prunelike

FRANCE

aromas, along with nice blackberry flavors, this is ultradense, massively tannic but ripe and balanced, stressing fruit above all. From Michel Bernard. Drink through 2005.–P.M. • $15 • (12/15/1999) • **88**

DOMEQUE, CHATEAU LA

Corbières 1994: A robust and seductive red loaded with dark plum and chocolate flavors. Cola and spice notes chime in on the finish, giving the wine a mature quality. Drink now.–K.M. • $14 • (10/31/1998) • **85**

DOMINIQUE, CHATEAU LA

St.-Emilion 1999: Has a slightly burnt fruit quality, but very ripe and fruity. Full-bodied and chewy, with lots of tannins and a long finish. Slightly hollow midpalate.–J.S. • $NA • (1/01/2000) (BT) • **85-89**

St.-Emilion 1998: A round yet compacted young wine, with plenty of berry and chocolate aromas and flavors. Medium- to full-bodied, with lovely tannins and a long finish. Delicious.–J.S. • $NA • (5/31/1999) (BT) • **90-94**

St.-Emilion 1997: A fresh and pure red with mineral, cherry and violet character. Medium- to full-bodied, with a solid core of velvety tannins and a long mineral aftertaste. Serious wine. Drink now through 2002.–J.S. • $41 • (1/31/2000) • **89**

St.-Emilion 1996: Interesting aromas of roasted chestnuts and berries. Medium-bodied, with soft tannins and a roasted oak and berry aftertaste. Would be better with more fruit at midpalate, but still well done. Drink now.–J.S. • $24 Ⓐ • (1/31/1999) • **86**

St.-Emilion 1995 • $37 Ⓐ • (1/31/1998) • **89**

St.-Emilion 1994 • $31 Ⓐ • (1/31/1997) • **87**

St.-Emilion 1993 • $30 • (1/31/1996) • **87**

St.-Emilion 1992 • $18 • (4/15/1995) • **83**

St.-Emilion 1991 • $18 • (3/31/1994) • **80**

St.-Emilion 1990 • $57 Ⓐ • (3/31/1993) • **88**

St.-Emilion 1989: Absolutely delicious. Dark ruby-red color. Fresh blackberry, black truffle and cherry character; tastes like Sachertorte, with chocolate and cherries, velvety tannins and a long finish. (1989 Bordeaux horizontal tasting). Drink now through 2010.–J.S. • $71 Ⓐ • (5/31/1999) • **91**

St.-Emilion 1988 • $25 • (6/30/1991) • **86**

St.-Emilion 1986 • $39 Ⓐ • (6/30/1989) • **95**

St.-Emilion 1985 • $33 Ⓐ • (3/31/1988) • **83**

St.-Emilion 1983 • $40 Ⓐ • (5/16/1986) • **88**

St.-Emilion 1982: I never thought much of this wine, but it's a voluptous red. Black ink in color, with a garnet edge. Blackberry, black truffle and ripe fruit. Full-bodied, with full integrated tannins and a long, silky finish. Big yet harmonious. (1982 Bordeaux horizontal tasting). Drink now.–J.S. • $NA • (11/30/1998) • **92**

St.-Emilion 1979 • $27 • (10/15/1989) • **81**

St.-Emilion 1961 • $NA • (4/30/1996) • **85**

DONJON, CHATEAU DU

Merlot Vin de Pays d'Oc 1995 • $7 • (5/31/1998) • **82**

Minervois Cuvée Prestige 1994 • $11 • (5/31/1998) • **84**

Minervois Cuvée Tradition 1995 • $8 • (5/31/1998) • **79**

DOPFF AU MOULIN

Brut Crémant d'Alsace Cuvée Bartholdi 1997: Delicate, this offers citrus and a touch of earth on a sprightly, focused frame. A good aperitif. Drink now.–B.S. • $18 • (6/15/2000) • **84**

Brut Crémant d'Alsace Cuvée Julien NV: A straightforward sparkler, offering lemon and apple notes on a light, crisp frame. Drink now.–B.S. • $14 • (6/15/2000) • **81**

Gewürztraminer Alsace 1999: Simple and vinous, without a lot of varietal character or concentration.–B.S. • $15 • (6/15/2000) • **77**

Gewürztraminer Alsace 1998: Deeply colored, exotic and plush, boasting apricot and litchi flavors, soft texture and a grapefruit note on the finish. Drink now.–B.S. • $15 • (6/15/2000) • **83**

Key: SS—Spectator Selection. CS—Cellar Selection. HR—Highly Recommended. $NA—Price not available. (BT)—Barrel tasting. Ⓐ—Auction Price.
For a key to the tasters' initials, see "How to Use These Listings."
Dates in parentheses represent the issues in which the ratings were published.

Gewürztraminer Alsace 1997: Spice and grapefruit hold court, with a barely perceptible hint of roses in this rich, full-bodied white that finishes with a twist of citrus peel.–B.S. • $15 • (9/15/1998) • **86**

Gewürztraminer Alsace Domaines de Riquewihr Vendange Tardive 1997: Shy on the nose, this moderately sweet VT tastes one-dimensional right now, with honey notes allied to a powerful structure. Try with Muenster cheese. Best from 2001 through 2004.–B.S. • $44 • (6/15/2000) • **88**

Gewürztraminer Alsace Grand Cru Brand Domaines de Riquewihr 1998: Plump, with a medium to full body, this white exhibits honey, citrus and vanilla integrated in a smooth manner. The flavors linger on the finish, with an aftertaste of apricot. Drink now.–B.S. • $24 • (6/15/2000) • **87**

Gewürztraminer Alsace Sélection de Grains Nobles 1989 • $NA • (11/15/1990) • **94**

Pinot Blanc Alsace 1999: A textbook Pinot Blanc, showing lemon and apple flavors and a crisp framework, with good richness and balance. Clean and vibrant, it's perfect as an aperitif or with light foods. Drink now.–B.S. • $10 • (6/15/2000) • **86**

Pinot Blanc Alsace 1997: On the tart side, with mineral and grass notes and a mouthpuckering, lemony finish. Needs food. Drink now.–B.S. • $10 • (9/15/1998) • **80**

Pinot Blanc Alsace Domaines de Riquewihr 1998: Lean and racy, this white offers lemon and earth notes, moderate concentration and a crisp finish. Drink now.–B.S. • $12 • (6/15/2000) • **83**

Riesling Alsace 1999: On the tart side, with apple, lemon and earth flavors. Focused, yet light in flavor and weight. Drink now.–B.S. • $13 • (6/15/2000) • **82**

Riesling Alsace 1998: A good, simple Riesling that offers modest varietal character in a direct, easy-drinking style. Drink now.–B.S. • $13 • (5/31/2000) • **83**

Riesling Alsace 1997: A crowd pleaser. Very ripe for Riesling, with floral, citrus and vanilla custard aromas and flavors. Broad on the palate, rich and weighty. Balanced on the soft side. Drink now.–B.S. • $13 • (9/15/1998) • **86**

Riesling Alsace Domaines de Riquewihr 1996: Aromatic, with appealing white peach, apple, mineral and spice followed by moderately intense flavors, all on a lithe, compact frame. Long, delicate finish. Drink now through 2003.–B.S. • $17 • (6/15/2000) • **89**

Riesling Alsace Grand Cru Schoenenbourg Domaines de Riquewihr 1996: Awkward and imposing today, showing breadth and richness up front, with one-dimensional flavors and a searing acidity that takes over on the back end. Difficult to assess. Best from 2001 through 2005.–B.S. • $24 • (6/15/2000) • **87**

Riesling Alsace Sélection de Grains Nobles 1989 • $NA • (11/15/1990) • **95**

Tokay Pinot Gris Alsace Réserve 1999: Fresh and lively, offering moderate apple and almond flavors on a lightweight frame. Appealing and direct. Drink now.–B.S. • $15 • (6/15/2000) • **84**

Tokay Pinot Gris Alsace Réserve 1998: This has a candied character, like tinned peaches or pears. Simple and short.–B.S. • $15 • (6/15/2000) • **79**

Tokay Pinot Gris Alsace Sélection de Grains Nobles 1989 • $NA • (11/15/1990) • **87**

DOPFF & IRION

Alsace Crustacés 1998: Crisp and lean, offering lemon and almond aromas and flavors followed by a firm finish. Drink now.–B.S. • $9 • (9/15/1999) • **82**

Alsace Crustacés 1997: Shows mild almond and kerosene flavors and moderate richness, then finishes short. Drink now.–B.S. • $10 • (9/15/1998) • **78**

Gewürztraminer Alsace 1998: Delicate peach and nectarine aromas and flavors are juxtaposed with a rich, round, soft texture. A little too soft and lacking depth. Drink now.–B.S. • $17 • (10/31/1999) • **81**

Gewürztraminer Alsace 1997: Though deep in color, this is dilute, with modest flavors of litchi and grapefruit. Drink now.–B.S. • $17 • (9/15/1998) • **78**

Gewürztraminer Alsace 1996 • $17 • (9/30/1997) • **74**

Gewürztraminer Alsace Grand Cru Sporen 1998: Definitely on the spicy side, offering East Indian garam masala aromas, a moderately firm structure and oily texture, tailing off on the finish. Drink now.–B.S. • $27 • (6/15/2000) • **84**

Gewürztraminer Alsace Grand Cru Sporen 1997: Piercing scents of ripe apple and rose petal, but unfortunately this goes nowhere on the palate, tasting of high yields that dissipates quickly.–B.S. • $30 • (10/31/1999) • **76**

Gewürztraminer Alsace Grand Cru Vorbourg 1998: Subtle power and a see-through structure frame the rose and litchi flavors in this wine. Could use a little more concentration, though it wears the alcohol well. Drink now.–B.S. • $29 • (6/15/2000) • **86**

Gewürztraminer Alsace Les Sorcières 1998: Velvety smooth and round, here's a delightful white whose apricot, litchi and grapefruit flavors and open-knit structure make for enjoyable sipping. Drink now.–B.S. • $19 • (6/15/2000) • **84**

Gewürztraminer Alsace Les Sorcières 1997: Very ripe, displaying red berry notes along with grapefruit peel and spice. The overall impression is soft and short, however.–B.S. • $22 • (10/31/1999) • **79**

Gewürztraminer Alsace Les Sorcières 1996: A simple, serviceable white with meek aromas and flavors of apple and spice. Drink now.–B.S. • $22 • (9/15/1998) • **78**

Gewürztraminer Alsace Sélection de Grains Nobles 1994 • $99 • (11/15/1997) • **89**

Gewürztraminer Alsace Vendanges Tardives 1997: Airy yet dense at the same time, this focused late-harvest white shows pear, apricot, honey and floral notes, all elegantly wrought. Beautiful purity of fruit. Drink now through 2004.–B.S. • $41 • (6/15/2000) • **90**

Gewürztraminer Alsace Vendanges Tardives 1996: Sweet, redolent of honey, apricot and coconut, yet with an underlying earthiness. Well structured and balanced, it should age well, but the aggressive earthy note is disturbing. This was the better of two bottles, with significant bottle variation. Drink now through 2003.–B.S. • $60 • (10/31/1999) • **81**

Muscat Alsace Les Amandiers 1998: A dry, slightly austere style, the type that matches the local white asparagus in season. Vibrant and floral. Drink now.–B.S. • $15 • (6/15/2000) • **85**

Muscat Alsace Les Amandiers 1997: A dry, spicy Muscat, redolent of roses and grapefruit. Medium-bodied, with a hint of citrus peel on the finish. Try with light summer dishes or as an aperitif. Drink now.–B.S. • $20 • (9/15/1998) • **84**

Muscat Alsace Les Amandiers 1996 • $18 • (9/30/1997) • **84**

Pinot Blanc Alsace 1998: Fresh, round and appealing, this white delivers peach, apple and floral notes, all on a rich, medium-bodied framework. A bit short on the finish. Drink now.–B.S. • $11 • (9/15/1999) • **83**

Pinot Blanc Alsace 1997: Subtle and appealing. The aromas are shy, but the palate shows richness, with citrus, apple and almond flavors that combine with lively acidity.–B.S. • $11 • (9/15/1998) • **84**

Pinot Blanc Alsace 1996 • $11 • (9/15/1997) • **82**

Pinot Noir Alsace 1997: Light, with candied cherry and leather notes.–B.S. • $17 • (10/15/1999) • **79**

Pinot Noir Alsace Les Tonnelles 1998: Meager in flavor and structure.–B.S. • $19 • (1/01/2000) • **75**

Pinot Noir Alsace Les Tonnelles 1997: Straightforward and evoking cherry and spice, this is ripe and pleasant. Drink now.–B.S. • $22 • (10/15/1999) • **82**

Riesling Alsace 1998: A full-bodied, spicy Riesling, fresh and grapey, with smooth, straightforward appeal and a soft structure. Fine summer sipper. Drink now.–B.S. • $13 • (8/31/1999) • **85**

Riesling Alsace 1997: Delicate lime and mineral aromas and flavors mingle in this bright, reserved Riesling. Drink now.–B.S. • $14 • (9/15/1998) • **84**

Riesling Alsace 1996 • $14 • (9/30/1997) • **83**

Riesling Alsace Grand Cru Schoenenbourg 1998: Apple and quince notes forge an alliance with the sensuous texture and moderate intensity in this medium-bodied white, picking up a lemon nuance on the finish. Drink now through 2002.–B.S. • $29 • (6/15/2000) • **86**

Riesling Alsace Grand Cru Schoenenbourg 1997: Very floral and perfumed, exhibiting apricot and exotic spice aromas and flavors, this is a well-delineated, intense white with a firm, palate-tingling finish. Drink now through 2003.–B.S. • $30 • (8/31/1999) • **88**

Riesling Alsace Grand Cru Vorbourg 1998: Floral, like rose or tuberose, this grand cru exhibits delicate apple and lemon flavors, all displayed on a subtle yet supporting structure. Moderate finish. Drink now through 2003.–B.S. • $30 • (6/15/2000) • **87**

Riesling Alsace Les Murailles 1997: Has density and balance, though it lacks expression in its apple and almond flavors. Muted today, but may just need time. Drink now through 2001.–B.S. • $20 • (6/15/2000) • **84**

Riesling Alsace Les Murailles 1996: Tight, compact and vibrant, showing concentrated flavors of almond, honey and mineral, all fresh as a walk through the forest after a gentle rain. Try now with light seafood or poultry dishes, or give it time to soften. Drink now through 2006.–B.S. • $19 • (8/31/1999) • **88**

Riesling Alsace Vendanges Tardives 1997: An assertive, moderately sweet VT, delivering honey and earth notes. Starts rich, turning more elegant and firm by the finish. Drink now through 2002.–B.S. • $39 • (6/15/2000) • **87**

Sylvaner Alsace 1997: A rather neutral white, this has lemon and earth notes, bright acidity and a good finish. Drink now.–B.S. • $10 • (9/15/1998) • **81**

Sylvaner Alsace 1996 • $11 • (9/15/1997) • **79**

Tokay Pinot Gris Alsace 1998: This shows good focus and depth, offering apricot, honey and citrus notes allied to a rich texture. Just a hint of sweetness. Drink now.–B.S. • $15 • (10/31/1999) • **84**

Tokay Pinot Gris Alsace 1997: Shows richness, a little sweetness and baked apple, but not a lot of definition due to low acidity. Drink now.–B.S. • $16 • (9/15/1998) • **78**

Tokay Pinot Gris Alsace 1996 • $16 • (9/30/1997) • **79**

Tokay Pinot Gris Alsace Grand Cru Vorbourg 1998: Elegance and harmony are the themes in this medium-bodied, vibrant Pinot Gris. The floral, apple and pear flavors unfold nicely, ending in a long finish. Well put-together. Drink now through 2001.–B.S. • $31 • (6/15/2000) • **87**

Tokay Pinot Gris Alsace Les Maquisards 1998: On the lean side, with modest apple, lemon and smoke notes. Drink now.–B.S. • $22 • (6/15/2000) • **82**

Tokay Pinot Gris Alsace Les Maquisards 1997: Smells and tastes like canned pear-juice. Soft and insipid. A second bottle was corky.–B.S. • $21 • (10/31/1999) • **74**

Tokay Pinot Gris Alsace Les Maquisards 1996: Lovely white, rich and balanced, full of flowers and peaches on a soft, easygoing framework that begs for drinking. Bit short on the finish. Drink now.–B.S. • $22 • (9/15/1998) • **84**

DOUDET, DOMAINE

Aloxe-Corton 1994 • $19 • (11/15/1996) • **81**

Beaune Cent-Vignes 1996: A large-scale red, offering slightly herbaceous cherry aromas and flavors of modest concentration before the firm tannins take over. Too much tannin for balance. Best after 2001.–B.S. • $28 • (9/30/1998) • **81**

Savigny-lès-Beaune 1993 • $18 • (11/15/1995) • **80**

DOUDET-NAUDIN

Aloxe-Corton Les Boutières 1996: A big, beefy, rustic style of '96 red Burgundy that has good cherry flavors, chewy tannins and moderate length. Best after 2003.–B.S. • $26 • (9/30/1998) • **84**

Beaune Clos du Roy 1996: Fairly lush and ripe, this medium-bodied red delivers some pretty plum, toasted oak and spice character. Nice and thick, it has quite a mouthfeel but still turns a bit dry and herbal on the finish.–P.M. • $28 • (9/30/1998) • **80**

Beaune Clos du Roi 1994 • $18 • (11/15/1996) • **83**

Corton Maréchaudes Vieille Vigne 1996: Lovely Pinot Noir, of medium body, with a grip of good acidity, fruit and tannin. Offers pretty red berry flavors, some earth and spice. The lingering finish needs time to soften. Best after 2003.–P.M. • $45 • (9/30/1998) • **85**

Corton Les Maréchaudes Vieilles Vignes 1994 • $60 • (11/15/1996) • **91**

Fixin 1996: Light-bodied and very herbal, this tastes diluted and unripe. Astringent finish.–P.M. • $16 • (9/30/1998) • **73**

Nuits-St.-Georges Les Cailles 1996: Smooth, with lovely balance between the chewy, ripe fruit and toasted, smoky, gamy notes, fresh acidity and sweet tannins. Supple texture, full body and flavorful finish. Cellar. Best from 2005 through 2012.–P.M. • $NA • (1/01/1999) • **93**

Nuits-St.-Georges Les Cailles 1994 • $39 • (11/15/1996) • **79**

Pernand-Vergelesses Les Fichots 1996: Supple and fruity, this straightforward, medium-bodied red kicks in with good intensity, showing wet earth, black cherry and blood-orange character. Drink now through 2003.–P.M. • $20 • (9/30/1998) • **82**

Pommard Les Rugiens 1996: A burly, cherry- and herb-flavored red with good flesh and persistence. A wall of tannins makes the finish severe, but nonetheless, there's a good wine beneath. Best from 2001 through 2005.–B.S. • $39 • (9/30/1998) • **83**

Pouilly-Fuissé 1997: Very reduced (that is, it tastes like an ice box or a bit earthy); this might go away with time, and the mineral, honey and lemon character also evident in this medium-bodied Pouilly come to the fore. Cellaring should be rewarded. Best from 2002 through 2010.–P.M. • $NA • (5/31/1999) • **89**

St.-Véran Domaine de Malatray 1997: Tastes a bit watery and stripped, with modest fruit and a cardboardy note throughout.–P.M. • $NA • (5/31/1999) • **72**

Savigny-lès-Beaune 1996: Full-bodied, rich and ripe Savigny, showing some tender tannins, a thick mouthfeel and loads of blackberry flavor along with nice hints of iron-laced, minerally wet earth. Fresh and fairly crisp finish. Will turn supple with age. Best after 2005.–P.M. • $16 • (9/30/1998) • **88**

Savigny-lès-Beaune Aux Guettes Vieilles Vignes 1994 • $24 • (11/15/1996) • **88**

Volnay Les Brouillards 1996: Light in color, texture and character, tasting of strawberry and modest cherry. Drink now.–P.M. • $29 • (9/30/1998) • **74**

Vosne-Romanée Les Suchots 1996: Ripe, plummy and jammy, with vanilla overtones, this is a good mouthful of red wine that finishes on the dry and austere side. Best after 2000.–B.S. • $45 • (9/30/1998) • **85**

Vosne-Romanée Les Suchots 1993 • $36 • (11/15/1995) • **76**

DOURTHE, PIERRE

Bordeaux Numéro 1 1995 • $9 • (1/31/1998) • **86**
Bordeaux Numéro 1 1993 • $9 • (1/31/1996) • **83**
Bordeaux Numéro 1 1990 • $9 • (5/15/1994) • **88**
Bordeaux White Numéro 1 1997: Always a good glass of white Bordeaux. Plenty of grassy and mineral character, with crisp, clean acidity and a long, refreshing aftertaste. Drink now.–J.S. • $9 • (3/31/1999) • **85**
Bordeaux White Numéro 1 1996: Impressive for a Bordeaux blend. Rich aromas of toasted oak, apple, lemon and pineapple follow through to a full- to medium-bodied palate and a rich aftertaste. Drink now.–J.S. • $9 • (3/31/1999) • **86**

DOYENNE, CHATEAU LE

Premières Côtes de Bordeaux 1997: Some berry and cherry character in this medium- to light-bodied red. Fresh finish. Drink now.–J.S. • $15 • (1/31/2000) • **81**
Premières Côtes de Bordeaux 1995 • $14 • (1/31/1998) • **86**

DOZON, DOMAINE

Chinon Clos du Saut au Loup 1995 • $13 • (6/15/1997) • **83**
Chinon Clos du Saut au Loup Cuvée Alexandre 1991 • $15 • (10/31/1994) • **75**

DRACY, CHATEAU DE

Bourgogne 1996: Nice, fairly ripe, with some red berry, wet earth character, but the finish is herbal and dry. From Albert Bichot.–P.M. • $13 • (9/30/1998) • **76**
Bourgogne 1995 • $12 • (11/15/1997) • **71**
Bourgogne 1989 • $9 • (6/15/1992) • **82**
Bourgogne 1988 • $8 • (2/28/1990) • **68**
Bourgogne Baron de Charette 1997: Herbal and a bit astringent, with a lean finish.–P.M. • $9 • (9/30/1999) • **73**
Bourgogne White 1996 • $11 • (5/31/1998) • **82**
Monthélie 1993 • $NA • (11/15/1995) • **84**
Monthélie Baron de Charette 1995 • $18 • (11/15/1997) • **77**
Pommard Baron de Charette 1995 • $25 • (11/15/1997) • **84**

DRAPPIER

Brut Blanc de Blancs Champagne Cuvée Signature NV: A lush-textured, easy-to-enjoy Champagne with broad, ripe fruit flavors and a slight sweetness. Drink now. • $44 • (10/15/1999) • **86**
Brut Champagne Carte Blanche NV: A delicious glass of bubbly with opulent California-style fruit flavors, lively balance, velvety texture and a lingering finish. Drink now. • $33 • (10/15/1999) • **90**
Brut Champagne Carte d'Or NV: Subtle, elegant and subdued, but the flavors grow as you sip. A refined texture and complex spice, fruit and honey flavors make it special. • $37 • (10/15/1999) • **89**
Brut Champagne Carte d'Or 1995: A soft, posh style of Champagne, with a light and fruity character. Drink now. • $48 • (10/15/1999) • **85**
Brut Champagne Carte d'Or 1991: A brightly flavored and smooth-textured Champagne that is quite good for the vintage. It has solid grapefruit and apple flavors and a soothing effervescence. • $46 • (12/31/1998) • **86**
Brut Champagne Carte d'Or 1990 • $45 • (12/31/1997) • **91**
Brut Champagne Cuvée du Millénaire 2000 1995: Complex flavors and a great jazzy texture make this a seriously lively wine. Nuances of toasted almond, honey and grapefruit are harmonious and linger on the finish. Drink now through 2005. • $70 • (10/15/1999) • **92**
Brut Champagne Cuvée du Millénaire 2000 Eclipse 1993: Full-bodied and mature in character, this has plenty of fruit flavor accented by spices and honey. Drink now through 2001. • $70 • (10/15/1999) • **88**
Brut Champagne Cuvée Maurice Chevalier NV • $45 • (11/30/1992) • **87**
Brut Champagne Général de Gaulle Collection 1992: Restrained but well balanced, this citrusy brut is almost austere in flavor, but refreshing and smooth in texture. Drink now. • $49 • (10/15/1999) • **88**

Key: SS—Spectator Selection. CS—Cellar Selection. HR—Highly Recommended. $NA—Price not available. (BT)—Barrel tasting. Ⓐ—Auction Price. For a key to the tasters' initials, see "How to Use These Listings." **Dates in parentheses represent the issues in which the ratings were published.**

Brut Champagne Grande Sendrée 1990: Easy to enjoy for its straightforward fruit flavors and slightly sweet balance. Tastes simpler than when reviewed last year. Drink now through 2001. • $84 • (10/15/1999) • **86**
Brut Rosé Champagne Grande Sendrée 1990: Floral aromas, soft texture and ripe cherry flavors mark this easygoing rosé. Made in a broad style. Drink now. • $99 • (10/15/1999) • **86**
Brut Rosé Champagne Val des Demoiselles NV: This lively, generous rosé has ample fresh fruit flavors and a deep coral color backed by good acidity and a clean finish. Drink now. • $44 • (10/15/1999) • **88**
Demi-Sec Champagne NV • $34 • (11/30/1992) • **90**

DROIN, JEAN-PAUL

Chablis Grenouille 1998: Oaky, it stands out with its butterscotch, marzipan, spice and green apple notes. Round midpalate, with a crisp finish. Best after 2001.–P.M. • $55 • (5/15/2000) • **84**
Chablis Grenouille 1997: Balanced, with some toasty, smoky, flinty notes along with the honey and ripe pear character. Lush, soft, very charming. Drink now.–P.M. • $50 • (5/31/1999) • **87**
Chablis Grenouille 1996 • $45 • (5/31/1998) • **85**
Chablis Les Clos 1998: Way too oaky. Cedar, chewy wood tannins and toasted, smoky character overtake the fruit. Slightly astringent on the finish.–P.M. • $50 • (5/15/2000) • **78**
Chablis Les Clos 1997: Terrific balance in this un-Chablisian Chablis. Lovely, with oak and lush fruit mingling nicely. Medium-bodied, the intensity, with pear, lemon and toasted oak, builds to a long finish. Drink now through 2005.–P.M. • $45 • (5/31/1999) • **90**
Chablis Les Clos 1996 • $40 • (5/31/1998) • **96**
Chablis Montée de Tonnerre 1998: Lemon and honey mingle in this intense, mouthpuckeringly crisp white that delivers fatness midpalate and on the finish. Medium-bodied and brilliant, with oak deftly integrated into the ripe fruit. Minerally *terroir* lifts its veil on the long finish. Well crafted. Drink now through 2010.–P.M. • $30 • (5/15/2000) HR • **93**
Chablis Montée de Tonnerre 1997: Beautifully balanced, with a core of ripe, tropical and pear character offset by mineral and citrus notes in a clean, pure and elegant package that trails off with a delicious, sweet-tasting finish. Best from 2003 through 2010.–P.M. • $NA • (5/31/1999) • **94**
Chablis Montée de Tonnerre 1996 • $18 • (8/31/1997) • **94**
Chablis Montmains 1998: A bit woody, with green tannins. Medium-bodied, it tastes of pine and cedar, but offers good fruit and flinty mineral character. Best after 2002.–P.M. • $30 • (5/15/2000) • **80**
Chablis Montmains 1997: Rather ripe, with tropical, honey and pear tart character, this medium-bodied charmer makes for delicious drinking. Drink now through 2003.–P.M. • $25 • (5/31/1999) • **86**
Chablis Montmains 1996 • $23 • (5/31/1998) • **94**
Chablis Tête de Cuvée 1998: Oak is well integrated in this medium-bodied Chablis, which shows butterscotch, marzipan, ripe pear and cream notes. Turns crisp and even astringent on the finish.–P.M. • $20 • (5/15/2000) • **78**
Chablis Tête de Cuvée 1997: Excessive wood taste harms this wine.–P.M. • $NA • (5/31/1999) • **71**
Chablis Vaillons 1998: Distinctive. Smoky, pungent and earthy, with a salty wood fire aroma. Medium-bodied and delicate yet well made, it's round and balanced on the lively finish. Drink now through 2002.–P.M. • $30 • (5/15/2000) • **85**
Chablis Vaillons 1997: An easy, charming wine that shows some cooked apple, pear, piecrust character. Soft and round, slightly bitter on the finish. Drink now.–P.M. • $25 • (5/31/1999) • **80**
Chablis Vaillons 1996 • $23 • (5/31/1998) • **94**
Chablis Vaillons 1995 • $NA • (8/31/1996) • **84**
Chablis Valmur 1998: Elegant, with good fruit and fresh acidity. The woody, spicy, cedary character will hopefully fold into the wine with cellaring; for now it seems tough and disjointed but fruity.–P.M. • $50 • (5/15/2000) • **78**
Chablis Valmur 1997: Nice balance, but the low acidity makes this a drink-soon, as the wood and fruit plays out into a slightly burning finish. Drink now.–P.M. • $45 • (5/31/1999) • **84**
Chablis Valmur 1996 • $40 • (5/31/1998) • **95**
Chablis Vaudésir 1998: Supple and pleasant, with a soft core of apple, pear pie, chocolate sauce and toast character. Medium- to full-bodied, it shows lovely concentration of ripe fruit. The harmonious, smoky finish is quite complex. Drink now through 2010.–P.M. • $47 • (5/15/2000) • **90**
Chablis Vaudésir 1997: Smooth, even soft, the ripe fruit, floral and spice notes make for an appealing if not overly complex package for current drinking pleasure. Drink now.–P.M. • $42 • (5/31/1999) • **86**
Chablis Vaudésir 1996 • $40 • (5/31/1998) • **95**

FRANCE

Chablis Vosgros 1998: An odd style, with a butter and bee wax character. Medium-bodied, it tastes of mineral, with a chalky texture and a smoky finish. Drink now through 2002.–P.M. • $30 • (5/15/2000) • **80**

Chablis Vosgros 1997: Smells like a honey jar and tastes like a buttered toast spread with honey. This is vivid and medium-bodied, packed with fresh herbs, lemon and mineral notes. Needs time. Best from 2003 through 2008.–P.M. • $25 • (5/31/1999) • **88**

Chablis Vosgros 1996 • $23 • (5/31/1998) • **94**

DROUET, PAUL

Brut Champagne Alain Ducasse Special Reserve NV: A classy, traditional Champagne with toasty, spicy aromas, plenty of fruit flavor and a deliciously tangy texture. Drink now through 2001. • $35 • (10/31/1999) • **91**

DROUHIN, JOSEPH

Aloxe-Corton 1991 • $25 • (1/31/1994) • **85**

Aloxe-Corton 1990 • $33 • (12/15/1992) • **88**

Aloxe-Corton 1989 • $27 • (1/31/1992) • **89**

Aloxe-Corton 1986 • $25 • (4/30/1989) • **83**

Aloxe-Corton 1985 • $23 • (11/15/1987) • **90**

Auxey-Duresses White 1998: Nice little Chardonnay with some honey, pear and spice. Light to medium in body, it lacks a bit of length, but it's clean. Drink now through 2001.–P.M. • $28 • (5/31/2000) • **83**

Bâtard-Montrachet 1998: Aromatically reserved, but what gorgeous ripe and sweet fruit. Medium-bodied, with a silky feel midpalate, it offers a symphony of flavors (quince, tropical, toasted oak, butter, lime and cream) that seduce. Fresh and vibrant finish. Best from 2002 through 2008.–P.M. • $227 • (5/31/2000) • **89**

Bâtard-Montrachet 1997: Pleasant but a bit soft, with decent mineral and ripe fruit character, but it lacks vibrant concentration on the palate. Drink now.–P.M. • $220 • (5/31/1999) • **88**

Bâtard-Montrachet 1996: Elegant and sleek, full-bodied, with very ripe fruit, this is a balanced beauty, but don't expect a showy, big white. Instead, its subtle pear, lemon, orange, freshly cut grass, mineral and honey notes grow on you like a slow-burning fuse. The seductive, supple finish is smartly toasted just-so for ultimate balance. Classic Drouhin winemaking style. Drink now through 2010.–P.M. • $150 • (8/31/1998) • **95**

Beaujolais Nouveau 1999: Supple and crisp, this light red shows cherry and light herbal flavors, a bit lean and tart on the finish. Drink now.–T.M. • $9 • (1/01/2000) • **81**

Beaune Clos des Mouches 1998: Wonderful. Exotically scented from all that wet stone, mineral, matchstick character, this medium-bodied, graceful, creamy-textured white Burgundy offers ripe fruit and a slight floral aroma. Balanced on the finish, but it needs time to smooth the hard edges. Best from 2001 through 2005.–P.M. • $79 • (5/31/2000) • **90**

Beaune Clos des Mouches 1997: Lovely Pinot Noir aromas—black cherry, raspberry, blackberry—emerge from the glass. Medium-bodied and nicely ripe, with a firm tannic backbone and a clean, fresh character. Delicious length thanks to the chewy but ripe tannins. Drink now through 2005.–P.M. • $50 • (1/01/2000) • **88**

Beaune Clos des Mouches 1996: Balanced and lush, this is truly pretty, and stands out in the Beaune appellation for its lovely harmony. Ripe and round, with red- and blackberry character. Has a grip of wet earth and *terroir* on the palate, but the finish is a tad short. Drink now through 2001.–P.M. • $69 Ⓐ • (9/30/1998) • **87**

Beaune Clos des Mouches 1995 • $35 Ⓐ • (1/31/1998) • **88**

Beaune Clos des Mouches 1993 • $56 Ⓐ • (11/15/1995) • **86**

Beaune Clos des Mouches 1992 • $33 • (12/15/1994) • **84**

Beaune Clos des Mouches 1991 • $37 • (1/31/1994) • **86**

Beaune Clos des Mouches 1990 • $52 • (12/15/1992) • **93**

Beaune Clos des Mouches 1989 • $77 Ⓐ • (2/29/1992) • **92**

Beaune Clos des Mouches 1988 • $48 Ⓐ • (2/15/1991) • **88**

Beaune Clos des Mouches 1987 • $47 • (6/15/1990) • **83**

Beaune Grèves 1997: Ah, so balanced. Clean, pure and medium-bodied, with a velvety texture and supple tannins, this '97 remains straight and firm, showing freshness and well-handled fruit. Lively in a natural way. Drink now through 2007.–P.M. • $37 • (9/30/1999) • **88**

Beaune Grèves 1995 • $35 • (11/15/1997) • **84**

Beaune Grèves 1994 • $33 • (11/15/1996) • **79**

Beaune Grèves 1992 • $25 • (12/15/1994) • **80**

Beaune Grèves 1991 • $28 • (1/31/1994) • **82**

Beaune Grèves 1989 • $47 • (1/31/1992) • **88**

Beaune Grèves 1959 • $NA • (8/31/1990) • **80**

Beaune Hospices de Beaune Cuvée Maurice Drouhin 1990 • $NA • (12/15/1992) • **88**

Beaune White Clos des Mouches 1997: This is a big white Burgundy, with lots of pear, tropical, vanilla bean, smoke and toast notes. There is great balance here as the lemony acidity holds its own against the oak and ripe fruit. Can age. Drink now through 2005.–P.M. • $80 • (5/31/1999) • **90**

Beaune White Clos des Mouches 1996 • $78 • (5/31/1998) • **90**

Beaune White Clos des Mouches 1995 • $70 • (8/31/1997) • **90**

Bonnes Mares 1996: Teases you by mixing up the signals—it's both opulent and racy. Wonderful berry, earth and oak characters blend beautifully on the palate; still, this medium-bodied wine remains a bit crisp on the finish now. Needs some cellaring; best after 2003.–P.M. • $118 • (9/30/1998) • **90**

Bonnes Mares 1995 • $61 Ⓐ • (11/15/1997) • **87**

Bonnes Mares 1993 • $100 • (11/15/1995) • **88**

Bonnes Mares 1992 • $64 • (12/15/1994) • **86**

Bonnes Mares 1991 • $76 • (1/31/1994) • **89**

Bonnes Mares 1990 • $111 Ⓐ • (12/15/1992) • **93**

Bonnes Mares 1989 • $NA • (1/31/1992) • **93**

Bourgogne Laforêt 1989 • $9 • (4/30/1991) • **85**

Bourgogne Laforêt 1988 • $10 • (3/31/1991) • **84**

Bourgogne White Laforet 1998: Nice honey, ripe pear aftertaste in this little Chardonnay. Medium-bodied, it lacks a bit of midpalate intensity, but a good everyday sort of white. Drink now through 2001.–P.M. • $15 • (5/31/2000) • **80**

Brouilly 1998: Bursting with black cherry, spice and a hint of bittersweet chocolate, this red is concentrated and vibrant, offering a succulent texture and a lingering finish. Drink now through 2001.–B.S. • $16 • (10/15/1999) • **87**

Brouilly 1997: Black cherry and herbal flavors are balanced and clean. Sufficient grip to complement food. Drink now.–T.M. • $16 • (8/31/1998) • **82**

Brouilly 1996 • $15 • (9/15/1997) • **83**

Brouilly 1995 • $16 • (8/31/1996) • **86**

Brouilly 1994 • $13 • (6/15/1995) • **82**

Brouilly 1993 • $12 • (6/30/1994) • **86**

Chablis 1998: Crisp and even steely, with a grassy bite, this light- to medium-bodied white displays green apple and honey on the zingy, lingering finish. Should go well with food. Drink now through 2001.–P.M. • $18 • (5/15/2000) • **83**

Chablis 1997: With a buttery, lemony character, this is green, dry and more ungenerous than many village Chablis.–P.M. • $18 • (5/31/1999) • **79**

Chablis 1996 • $19 • (8/31/1997) • **87**

Chablis Domaine de Vaudon 1996 • $20 • (5/31/1998) • **93**

Chablis Les Clos 1997: True to type. A *terroir*-driven Chablis—all iodine, sea salt, salt crackers, wet earth and mineral—but with loads of ripe fruit to support its odd personality. The opulent, silky mouthfeel is out of this world. Drink now through 2007.–P.M. • $51 • (9/30/1999) • **93**

Chablis Les Clos 1996 • $50 • (5/31/1998) • **98**

Chablis Montmains 1998: Fruity in style, delivering mineral, chalk, lemon and wet earth character in moderate doses. Medium-bodied, with a decent finish. Drink now through 2002.–P.M. • $29 • (5/15/2000) • **82**

Chablis Premier Cru 1997: Clean, crisp style, with a steely core of green apple, but also showing good maturity to balance the acidity. A light-bodied little white that's a bit tart on the finish. Try with seafood. Drink now.–P.M. • $28 • (5/31/1999) • **82**

Chablis Premier Cru 1996 • $25 • (8/31/1997) SS • **90**

Chablis Sécher 1998: Very lively and expressive, with floral aromas and good fruit. Medium-bodied, with a chalky, minerally finish. Drink now through 2004.–P.M. • $29 • (5/15/2000) • **86**

Chablis Vaudésir 1998: An international style of Chardonnay. Very woody, with loads of butterscotch, marzipan and caramel character. Well made, with good apple tart. Fat, opulent body on the finish. With time this oaky, full-bodied white should do well. Drink now through 2008.–P.M. • $50 • (5/15/2000) • **87**

Chablis Vaudésir 1997: Really ripe and sweet-tasting, with tropical, toasted bread, lemon, piecrust complexity, and full-bodied, showing a firm core of acidity that vibrates on the lingering finish. Best from 2003 through 2008.–P.M. • $49 • (5/31/1999) • **90**

Chablis Vaudésir 1996 • $48 • (5/31/1998) • **89**

Chambertin 1997: Black cherry, licorice and herb aromas and flavors are supported by a chewy, moderately intense structure. Finishes with firm, solid but not overbearing tannins. Drink now through 2002.–B.S. • $141 • (9/30/1999) • **84**

Chambertin 1996: Juicy and racy, showing good intensity of smoke, toasted oak, spice and clean red berry notes. Medium-bodied, it's firm, even hard for now, and the tannins and acidity need time to smooth. Best from 2005 through 2010.–P.M. • $100 • (5/15/1999) • **88**

Chambertin 1995 • $100 • (11/15/1997) • **86**

FRANCE

DROUHIN, JOSEPH

Chambertin 1994 • $94 • (11/15/1996) • **91**
Chambertin 1993 • $119 • (11/15/1995) • **91**
Chambertin 1992 • $74 • (12/15/1994) • **79**
Chambertin 1991 • $84 • (1/31/1994) • **86**
Chambertin 1990 • $107 Ⓐ • (12/15/1992) • **91**
Chambertin 1989 • $114 • (1/31/1992) • **90**
Chambertin 1988 • $77 Ⓐ • (2/15/1991) • **94**
Chambertin 1986 • $80 • (2/28/1989) • **90**
Chambertin 1985 • $127 Ⓐ • (11/15/1987) • **95**
Chambolle-Musigny 1996: Beautiful sappy fruit. Red cherries and raspberries with floral accents saturate the palate, while the lively acidity and firm tannins keep everything in check. Sweet fruit finish. Drink through 2005.–B.S. • $41 • (9/30/1998) • **82**
Chambolle-Musigny 1995 • $34 • (11/15/1997) • **89**
Chambolle-Musigny 1992 • $25 • (12/15/1994) • **82**
Chambolle-Musigny 1991 • $29 • (1/31/1994) • **75**
Chambolle-Musigny 1990 • $36 • (12/15/1992) • **87**
Chambolle-Musigny 1989 • $41 • (1/31/1992) • **91**
Chambolle-Musigny 1986 • $27 • (7/31/1988) • **88**
Chambolle-Musigny 1985 • $33 • (11/15/1987) • **93**
Chambolle-Musigny Les Amoureuses 1995 • $85 • (11/15/1997) • **79**
Chambolle-Musigny Les Amoureuses 1994 • $67 • (11/15/1996) • **84**
Chambolle-Musigny Les Amoureuses 1992 • $55 • (12/15/1994) • **85**
Chambolle-Musigny Les Amoureuses 1991 • $67 • (1/31/1994) • **77**
Chambolle-Musigny Les Amoureuses 1990 • $68 Ⓐ • (12/15/1992) • **93**
Chambolle-Musigny Les Amoureuses 1988 • $38 Ⓐ • (12/31/1990) • **87**
Chambolle-Musigny Les Amoureuses 1955 • $230 • (8/31/1990) • **65**
Chambolle-Musigny Les Baudes 1991 • $39 • (1/31/1994) • **86**
Chambolle-Musigny Les Baudes 1989 • $52 • (1/31/1992) • **89**
Chambolle-Musigny Les Feusselottes 1989 • $55 • (1/31/1992) • **92**
Chambolle-Musigny Les Hauts Doix 1990 • $53 • (12/15/1992) • **88**
Chambolle-Musigny Les Sentiers 1989 • $55 • (1/31/1992) • **92**
Chambolle-Musigny Premier Cru 1993 • $45 • (11/15/1995) • **87**
Chambolle-Musigny Premier Cru 1991 • $33 • (1/31/1994) • **83**
Chambolle-Musigny Premier Cru 1989 • $50 • (1/31/1992) • **89**
Charmes-Chambertin 1995 • $85 • (11/15/1997) • **90**
Charmes-Chambertin 1994 • $71 • (11/15/1996) • **87**
Charmes-Chambertin 1993 • $84 • (11/15/1995) • **85**
Charmes-Chambertin 1991 • $59 • (1/31/1994) • **87**
Charmes-Chambertin 1990 • $126 Ⓐ • (12/15/1992) • **96**
Charmes-Chambertin 1989 • $67 Ⓐ • (1/31/1992) • **92**
Charmes-Chambertin 1988 • $56 Ⓐ • (11/15/1990) • **93**
Charmes-Chambertin 1986 • $38 Ⓐ • (2/28/1989) CS • **91**
Charmes-Chambertin 1985 • $60 • (11/15/1987) • **89**
Chassagne-Montrachet 1998: A bit too oaky, but it's fairly ripe, with a nice lemony backbone. Medium-bodied, pleasant and easy to appreciate. Delivers some toasted oak, mocha and spice notes on the finish. Drink now through 2003.–P.M. • $52 • (5/31/2000) • **83**
Chassagne-Montrachet 1995 • $46 • (5/31/1997) • **76**
Chassagne-Montrachet Marquis de Laguiche 1998: Rather oaky, but underneath is ripe, sweet-tasting fruit in an elegant, medium-bodied, silky package. Turns smoky and oaky on the subtle finish. Should improve with short-term cellaring. Drink now through 2006.–P.M. • $78 • (5/31/2000) • **85**
Chassagne-Montrachet Marquis de Laguiche 1997: Round and agreeable, lacking a bit of fresh zest but delivering decent pear notes. A bit short on the finish. Drink now.–P.M. • $76 • (5/31/1999) • **80**
Chassagne-Montrachet Marquis de Laguiche 1995 • $65 • (8/31/1997) • **90**
Chassagne-Montrachet Red 1990 • $22 • (12/15/1992) • **84**
Chassagne-Montrachet Red 1989 • $23 • (1/31/1992) • **87**
Chassagne-Montrachet Red Morgeot 1991 • $20 • (1/31/1994) • **82**
Chiroubles 1998: Like crunching into a fresh black cherry. This red is pretty, offering floral nuances, with enough substance and structure to provide depth and intensity. Fine, lingering finish. Drink now.–B.S. • $13 • (10/15/1999) • **86**
Chiroubles 1996 • $16 • (9/15/1997) • **85**
Chiroubles 1995 • $17 • (8/31/1996) • **86**
Chiroubles 1993 • $12 • (6/30/1994) • **83**
Chorey-lès-Beaune 1995 • $19 • (11/15/1997) • **79**
Chorey-lès-Beaune 1993 • $20 • (11/15/1995) • **83**
Chorey-lès-Beaune 1992 • $16 • (12/15/1994) • **83**

Key: SS—Spectator Selection. CS—Cellar Selection. HR—Highly Recommended. $NA—Price not available. (BT)—Barrel tasting. Ⓐ—Auction Price.
For a key to the tasters' initials, see "How to Use These Listings."
Dates in parentheses represent the issues in which the ratings were published.

Clos de la Roche 1991 • $49 • (1/31/1994) • **85**
Clos de la Roche 1990 • $69 • (12/15/1992) • **89**
Clos de la Roche 1989 • $77 • (1/31/1992) • **88**
Clos de la Roche 1988 • $73 • (2/15/1991) • **93**
Clos de la Roche 1986 • $53 • (7/15/1989) • **83**
Clos de la Roche 1985 • $60 • (11/15/1987) • **97**
Clos de Vougeot 1997: A lean, structured red, evoking earth, iron and cherry aromas and flavors. Moderately intense, dissipating a little on the finish. Definitely needs time. Best from 2001 through 2006.–B.S. • $89 • (9/30/1999) • **87**
Clos de Vougeot 1996: Rich, firmly structured and spicy. A very reserved style that shows good density and concentration right through to the spicy berry aftertaste. Best from 2003 through 2010.–B.S. • $85 • (9/30/1998) • **90**
Clos de Vougeot 1995 • $70 • (11/15/1997) • **83**
Clos de Vougeot 1992 • $44 • (12/15/1994) • **85**
Clos de Vougeot 1991 • $62 • (1/31/1994) • **86**
Clos de Vougeot 1990 • $71 • (12/15/1992) • **91**
Clos de Vougeot 1989 • $88 • (1/31/1992) • **89**
Clos de Vougeot 1988 • $85 • (2/15/1991) • **90**
Clos de Vougeot 1986 • $55 • (4/15/1989) • **86**
Clos de Vougeot 1985 • $92 Ⓐ • (11/15/1987) • **94**
Clos St.-Denis 1995 • $75 • (1/31/1998) • **87**
Clos St.-Denis 1989 • $76 • (1/31/1992) • **91**
Corton 1991 • $42 • (1/31/1994) • **84**
Corton 1990 • $58 • (12/15/1992) • **88**
Corton 1985 • $48 • (11/15/1987) • **92**
Corton Les Bressandes 1993 • $70 • (11/15/1995) • **93**
Corton Les Bressandes 1988 • $60 • (11/15/1990) • **92**
Corton Les Bressandes 1986 • $45 • (4/30/1989) • **90**
Corton-Charlemagne 1997: A fairly angular white, with lemon and green apple, showing a mineral and cedar character that seems tough on the chewy, slightly drying finish. Lacks ripe fruit.–P.M. • $85 • (5/31/1999) • **79**
Corton-Charlemagne 1996 • $92 • (5/31/1998) • **92**
Côte de Beaune 1994 • $23 • (11/15/1996) • **76**
Côte de Beaune 1992 • $18 • (12/15/1994) • **81**
Côte de Beaune-Villages 1986 • $13 • (6/15/1989) • **78**
Côte de Beaune-Villages 1985 • $14 • (11/15/1987) • **85**
Côte de Nuits-Villages 1995 • $22 • (11/15/1997) • **82**
Côte de Nuits-Villages 1994 • $22 • (11/15/1996) • **78**
Côte de Nuits-Villages 1990 • $20 • (12/15/1992) • **82**
Côte de Nuits-Villages 1985 • $19 • (11/15/1987) • **86**
Echézeaux 1994 • $58 • (11/15/1996) • **76**
Echézeaux 1991 • $49 • (1/31/1994) • **87**
Echézeaux 1990 • $60 Ⓐ • (12/15/1992) • **91**
Echézeaux 1988 • $60 • (11/15/1990) HR • **93**
Echézeaux 1986 • $60 • (7/31/1988) • **92**
Fleurie 1997: This round red offers fresh plum and black cherry flavors, with light tannins and soft acidity. Soft and clean. Drink now.–T.M. • $19 • (8/31/1998) • **83**
Fleurie 1996 • $18 • (9/15/1997) • **81**
Fleurie 1995 • $19 • (9/15/1996) • **84**
Fleurie 1994 • $13 • (6/15/1995) • **84**
Gevrey-Chambertin 1996: Tough customer. Shows decent red berry character, but the tannins in this medium-bodied red are a bit dry. Will they soften? Perhaps. Best after 2002.–P.M. • $42 • (9/30/1998) • **81**
Gevrey-Chambertin 1995 • $35 • (11/15/1997) • **70**
Gevrey-Chambertin 1992 • $24 • (12/15/1994) • **84**
Gevrey-Chambertin 1991 • $25 • (1/31/1994) • **81**
Gevrey-Chambertin 1990 • $36 • (12/15/1992) • **88**
Gevrey-Chambertin 1986 • $27 • (2/28/1989) • **83**
Gevrey-Chambertin 1985 • $33 • (11/15/1987) • **91**
Gevrey-Chambertin Champeaux 1991 • $37 • (1/31/1994) • **80**
Gevrey-Chambertin Champeaux 1990 • $70 • (12/15/1992) • **91**
Gevrey-Chambertin Lavaut St.-Jacques 1989 • $70 • (1/31/1992) • **86**
Gevrey-Chambertin Les Cazetiers 1989 • $70 • (1/31/1992) • **91**
Grands Echézeaux 1997: A soft, medium-bodied Pinot. It lacks a bit of fresh fruit character, but shows cherry, oatmeal and croissantlike flavors. Drink now.–P.M. • $143 • (9/30/1999) • **82**
Grands Echézeaux 1996: Lovely, charming Pinot, all floral and raspberry in character, with mocha and toasted bread notes adding interest. Medium-bodied and quite crisp; a little cellaring is in order. Best after 2003.–P.M. • $135 • (9/30/1998) • **87**
Grands Echézeaux 1994 • $92 • (11/15/1996) • **82**
Grands Echézeaux 1992 • $74 • (12/15/1994) • **80**
Grands Echézeaux 1991 • $85 • (2/28/1995) • **93**
Grands Echézeaux 1990 • $100 • (2/28/1995) • **91**

Grands Echézeaux 1989 • $101 Ⓐ • (2/28/1995) • **90**
Grands Echézeaux 1988 • $85 • (2/28/1995) • **88**
Grands Echézeaux 1987 • $40 • (2/28/1995) • **90**
Grands Echézeaux 1986 • $55 • (2/28/1995) • **84**
Grands Echézeaux 1985 • $83 Ⓐ • (2/28/1995) • **86**
Grands Echézeaux 1983 • $NA • (2/28/1995) • **79**
Griotte-Chambertin 1996: Good ripe fruit balances the firm tannins in this medium-bodied, flavorful red. Lacks some volume, but has nice licorice and ripe red- and blackberry flavors and turns pretty on the finish. Drink now through 2001.–P.M. • $105 • (9/30/1998) • **86**
Griotte-Chambertin 1995 • $95 • (11/15/1997) • **90**
Griotte-Chambertin 1994 • $73 • (11/15/1996) • **78**
Griotte-Chambertin 1991 • $63 • (1/31/1994) • **88**
Griotte-Chambertin 1990 • $84 • (12/15/1992) • **94**
Griotte-Chambertin 1989 • $90 • (1/31/1992) • **91**
Griotte-Chambertin 1988 • $81 • (11/15/1990) • **91**
Griotte-Chambertin 1986 • $81 • (7/31/1988) • **92**
Griotte-Chambertin 1985 • $68 • (11/15/1987) • **95**
Juliénas 1997: Chocolate and toasty accents set this wine apart (and suggest oak-aging) and marry nicely with ripe plum and cherry flavors. Atypical but appealing.–T.M. • $15 • (8/31/1998) • **85**
Juliénas 1996 • $14 • (8/31/1997) • **83**
Juliénas 1995 • $15 • (9/15/1996) • **85**
Juliénas 1994 • $13 • (7/31/1995) • **85**
Juliénas 1993 • $12 • (6/30/1994) HR • **88**
Ladoix 1993 • $20 • (11/15/1995) • **81**
Ladoix 1991 • $17 • (1/31/1994) • **83**
Latricières-Chambertin 1991 • $59 • (1/31/1994) • **85**
Latricières-Chambertin 1988 • $72 • (2/15/1991) • **87**
Mâcon-Villages 1997: Clean, steely even, this offers pure fruit in a medium-bodied package showing nice lemon, mineral, flint and pear notes. Try with shellfish. Drink now.–P.M. • $12 • (5/31/1999) • **84**
Mâcon-Villages 1995 • $NA • (8/31/1996) • **85**
Maranges 1994 • $20 • (11/15/1996) • **77**
Maranges Premier Cru 1993 • $20 • (11/15/1995) • **84**
Maranges Premier Cru 1990 • $19 • (12/15/1992) • **83**
Maranges Premier Cru 1989 • $20 • (1/31/1992) • **85**
Mazis-Chambertin 1989 • $86 • (1/31/1992) • **92**
Meursault 1998: Good concentration in this Meursault brings out a chalky, minerally character as subtext to the good fruit, grassy aroma and honeyed character. Medium-bodied, it should smooth out with age. Best from 2002 through 2005.–P.M. • $48 • (5/31/2000) • **87**
Meursault 1997: A medium-bodied, toasty Meursault, with herb and green apple character on a crisp finish. Drink now through 2002.–P.M. • $41 • (5/31/1999) • **80**
Meursault 1995 • $42 • (5/31/1997) • **87**
Meursault Charmes 1998: Very woody style; the oak dominates the fruit, at least for now. Medium-bodied, with green apple and toasted bread aromas, it has an interesting wet earth, silky component that suggests a good play on *terroir*. Best from 2002 through 2008.–P.M. • $NA • (5/31/2000) • **88**
Meursault Perrières 1998: Powerful and well-crafted. Pure and clean, with dried herbs, honey and amazingly ripe yet elegant fruit. Most impressive is the beautiful, silky texture that coats the palate in this full-bodied white Burgundy. Very long, chewy finish. Best from 2002 through 2006.–P.M. • $81 • (5/31/2000) • **94**
Meursault Perrières 1997: A standard Chardonnay, but it's fairly silky on the palate, delivering medium-intense fruit and a delicate finish. Drink now through 2002.–P.M. • $68 • (5/31/1999) • **83**
Meursault Perrières 1995 • $60 • (5/31/1997) • **94**
Montagny 1997: A straightforward, slightly acidic and hard white, with mineral and butter notes and redeeming ripe fruit throughout. Drink now.–P.M. • $18 • (5/31/1999) • **80**
Montagny 1995 • $22 • (5/31/1997) • **88**
Monthélie 1991 • $17 • (1/31/1994) • **78**
Montrachet Marquis de Laguiche 1995 • $282 Ⓐ • (8/31/1997) • **93**
Morey-St.-Denis 1993 • $NA • (11/15/1995) • **81**
Morey-St.-Denis 1990 • $33 • (12/15/1992) • **88**
Morey-St.-Denis Clos Sorbè 1993 • $43 • (11/15/1995) • **87**
Morey-St.-Denis Clos Sorbè 1989 • $45 • (1/31/1992) • **86**
Morey-St.-Denis Monts Luisants 1988 • $38 • (2/28/1991) • **92**
Morgon 1997: Bright and fruity, this vibrant red offers straightforward black cherry flavor backed by crisp acidity and light tannins. A pleasant quaffer. Drink now.–T.M. • $15 • (8/31/1998) • **82**
Morgon 1996 • $15 • (9/15/1997) • **84**
Morgon 1995 • $16 • (9/15/1996) • **86**
Morgon 1993 • $12 • (6/30/1994) • **86**
Moulin-à-Vent 1998: Moderate black cherry character, about as tannic as Beaujolais gets. This is drinkable now, best with light summer fare, yet has the structure to age for a year or two. Best through 2002.–B.S. • $15 • (10/15/1999) • **84**
Moulin-à-Vent 1997: Ripe and meaty, with black cherry and plum flavors, this shows good concentration for the vintage and true appellation-character. A rich, fruity accompaniment to food.–T.M. • $18 • (8/31/1998) • **87**
Moulin-à-Vent 1996 • $17 • (9/15/1997) • **86**
Moulin-à-Vent 1995 • $18 • (9/15/1996) • **87**
Moulin-à-Vent 1994 • $16 • (7/31/1995) • **84**
Moulin-à-Vent 1993 • $13 • (6/30/1994) • **85**
Musigny 1997: Pretty aromas of black cherry, vanilla and toasty oak are followed by rich, round, suave blackberry and spice flavors. Charming and enjoyable now. Drink now through 2002.–B.S. • $177 • (9/30/1999) • **88**
Musigny 1996: Rich and elegant, with raspberry flavors and a sinewy structure dominated by dry tannins. Best after 2005.–B.S. • $160 • (9/30/1998) • **88**
Musigny 1995 • $110 • (1/31/1998) • **90**
Musigny 1994 • $100 • (11/15/1996) • **82**
Musigny 1993 • $130 • (11/15/1995) • **88**
Musigny 1991 • $98 • (1/31/1994) • **88**
Musigny 1990 • $129 • (12/15/1992) • **95**
Nuits-St.-Georges 1996: A delicate Nuits, with decent red berry flavors. Of medium body, it turns a bit dry on the slightly herbal finish.–P.M. • $41 • (9/30/1998) • **79**
Nuits-St.-Georges 1995 • $35 • (11/15/1997) • **86**
Nuits-St.-Georges 1986 • $25 • (4/30/1989) • **86**
Nuits-St.-Georges 1985 • $29 • (11/15/1987) • **92**
Nuits-St.-Georges Aux Boudots 1990 • $57 • (12/15/1992) • **88**
Nuits-St.-Georges Aux Boudots 1989 • $70 • (1/31/1992) • **80**
Nuits-St.-Georges Proces 1997: A bit stemmy and green, with a cheesy character.–P.M. • $50 • (9/30/1999) • **78**
Nuits-St.-Georges Roncière 1986 • $38 • (4/30/1989) • **85**
Nuits-St.-Georges Roncière 1985 • $38 • (11/15/1987) • **93**
Pernand-Vergelesses 1990 • $21 • (12/15/1992) • **87**
Pernand-Vergelesses 1985 • $17 • (11/15/1987) • **91**
Pernand-Vergelesses White 1998: Big on the butterscotch and English caramel character, this stands out. Showing some fresh flavors, but veers toward heavy on the chewy finish. Drink now through 2005.–P.M. • $28 • (5/31/2000) • **83**
Pommard 1995 • $35 • (11/15/1997) • **84**
Pommard 1992 • $25 • (12/15/1994) • **83**
Pommard 1991 • $27 • (1/31/1994) • **84**
Pommard 1990 • $36 • (12/15/1992) • **82**
Pommard 1989 • $43 • (1/31/1992) • **85**
Pommard 1986 • $27 • (4/30/1989) • **87**
Pommard 1985 • $33 • (11/15/1987) • **93**
Pommard 1981 • $28 • (9/01/1984) • **83**
Pommard Les Epenots 1993 • $35 • (11/15/1995) • **85**
Pommard Les Epenots 1991 • $36 • (1/31/1994) • **83**
Pommard Les Epenots 1990 • $43 Ⓐ • (12/15/1992) • **91**
Pommard Les Epenots 1989 • $56 • (1/31/1992) • **89**
Pommard Les Epenots 1986 • $40 • (7/31/1988) • **83**
Pommard Les Epenots 1985 • $64 Ⓐ • (11/15/1987) • **95**
Pommard Les Rugiens 1989 • $56 • (1/31/1992) • **87**
Pouilly-Fuissé 1996 • $15 • (5/31/1998) • **86**
Puligny-Montrachet 1998: Easygoing Chardonnay. Displays lemon, some honey and dried herbs, with toasted oak and spice on the chewy finish. A bit diluted at midpalate. Drink now through 2002.–P.M. • $54 • (5/31/2000) • **80**
Puligny-Montrachet 1997: A straightforward Chardonnay, offering lemon, green apple, butter and toasted spice character on a slightly chewy and crisp finish. Drink now through 2004.–P.M. • $47 • (5/31/1999) • **82**
Puligny-Montrachet 1995 • $47 • (8/31/1997) • **87**
Puligny-Montrachet Clos de la Garenne 1996 • $65 • (5/31/1998) • **92**
Puligny-Montrachet Folatières 1998: Straightforward Chardonnay, with a lean body and crisp flavors; lemon and lime seem to be the dominating flavors. A bit dry on the finish.–P.M. • $77 • (5/31/2000) • **79**
Puligny-Montrachet Folatières 1997: Minerally, with clean pear aromas, presented in a soft, medium-bodied package that's deftly oaked for maximum subtlety and fruit pleasure. Drink now through 2001.–P.M. • $72 • (5/31/1999) • **85**
Puligny-Montrachet Les Folatières 1996 • $65 • (5/31/1998) • **87**
Puligny-Montrachet Les Folatières 1995 • $62 • (8/31/1997) • **82**
Romanée St.-Vivant 1996: Reserved, with a spicy black cherry character and richness that remain one-dimensional. Well structured and balanced, but finishes a little short. Best after 2000.–B.S. • $160 • (9/30/1998) • **86**
Romanée St.-Vivant 1992 • $80 • (12/15/1994) • **89**

DROUHIN, JOSEPH

Romanée St.-Vivant 1991 • $90 • (1/31/1994) • **86**
Romanée St.-Vivant 1989 • $94 • (1/31/1992) • **92**
Rully 1998: Well made, ripe and attractive. Honeyed, with pear, chalk and floral notes. Balanced, medium-bodied, good acidity. It makes the mouth water, and it's delicious on the fruity finish. Drink now through 2001.–P.M. • $23 • (5/31/2000) • **85**
Rully 1997: Sheer pleasure sings in this drink-me-now white. Ripe, clean and medium-bodied, with superattractive pear, tropical and lemon notes and a long, succulent finish. Drink now through 2001.–P.M. • $20 • (5/31/1999) • **90**
Rully 1996 • $21 • (5/31/1998) • **86**
Rully 1995 • $22 • (8/31/1997) • **87**
St.-Amour 1998: A light style, with cherry and cranberry flavors and a fairly smooth finish with persistent spice notes. Drink now.–K.M. • $16 • (10/15/1999) • **84**
St.-Amour 1997: Light-bodied, simple, with cherry, berry, and herbal flavors. Bit dry on the finish.–T.M. • $19 • (8/31/1998) • **79**
St.-Amour 1996 • $18 • (9/15/1997) • **85**
St.-Amour 1995 • $19 • (8/31/1996) • **86**
St.-Aubin 1998: Not showy, but a medium-bodied Chardonnay that grows on you. Subdued in aroma, it's nicely textured, with some concentration of ripe fruit at midpalate, showing apple, lemon and mineral notes. Drink now through 2005.–P.M. • $26 • (5/31/2000) • **86**
St.-Aubin 1996 • $32 • (5/31/1998) • **86**
St.-Aubin 1995 • $31 • (5/31/1997) • **80**
St.-Romain 1998: Clean white, with attractive ripe tropical and pear flavors. Medium-bodied, the intensity creeps up on the slightly smoky and minerally finish. Drink now through 2002.–P.M. • $26 • (5/31/2000) • **85**
St.-Romain 1997: Crisp, with lemon peel, green apple and toasted oak flavors presented in a firm but succulent and balanced package, giving this medium-bodied white good freshness on the slightly drying finish. Drink now through 2002.–P.M. • $24 • (5/31/1999) • **84**
St.-Véran 1996 • $13 • (5/31/1998) • **86**
St.-Véran 1995 • $23 • (5/31/1997) • **80**
Santenay 1995 • $22 • (11/15/1997) • **82**
Santenay 1990 • $22 • (12/15/1992) • **83**
Santenay 1989 • $44 • (1/31/1992) • **87**
Santenay 1985 • $17 • (11/15/1987) • **88**
Santenay Beaurepaire 1991 • $17 • (1/31/1994) • **81**
Savigny-lès-Beaune 1995 • $23 • (11/15/1997) • **73**
Savigny-lès-Beaune 1994 • $22 • (11/15/1996) • **80**
Savigny-lès-Beaune 1993 • $25 • (11/15/1995) • **80**
Savigny-lès-Beaune 1992 • $16 • (12/15/1994) • **80**
Savigny-lès-Beaune 1991 • $18 • (1/31/1994) • **83**
Savigny-lès-Beaune 1990 • $22 • (12/15/1992) • **84**
Savigny-lès-Beaune 1989 • $23 • (1/31/1992) • **87**
Savigny-lès-Beaune 1985 • $25 • (11/15/1987) SS • **91**
Savigny-lès-Beaune 1981 • $16 • (9/01/1984) • **79**
Volnay 1995 • $29 • (1/31/1998) • **82**
Volnay 1991 • $26 • (1/31/1994) • **81**
Volnay 1990 • $33 • (12/15/1992) • **90**
Volnay 1985 • $29 • (11/15/1987) • **88**
Volnay Chevret 1997: Very light but attractive Pinot aromas emerge, with cherry and spice character. A bit short. Drink now.–P.M. • $40 • (9/30/1999) • **80**
Volnay Chevret 1996: Light-bodied, with light color and light texture, tastes herbal and astringent.–P.M. • $36 • (9/30/1998) • **74**
Volnay Chevret 1994 • $32 • (11/15/1996) • **77**
Volnay Chevret 1993 • $38 • (11/15/1995) • **88**
Volnay Chevret 1992 • $21 • (12/15/1994) • **81**
Volnay Chevret 1989 • $50 • (1/31/1992) • **90**
Volnay Clos des Chênes 1997: An easy, smooth Pinot Noir, with ripe fruit. Black cherry character kicks in on the finish. Drink now through 2001.–P.M. • $45 • (9/30/1999) • **82**
Volnay Clos des Chênes 1995 • $37 • (11/15/1997) • **84**
Volnay Clos des Chênes 1991 • $32 • (1/31/1994) • **81**
Volnay Clos des Chênes 1990 • $42 • (12/15/1992) • **93**
Volnay Clos des Chênes 1989 • $50 • (1/31/1992) • **91**
Volnay Clos des Chênes 1988 • $45 • (2/15/1991) • **85**
Volnay Clos des Chênes 1987 • $30 • (6/15/1990) • **85**
Volnay Clos des Chênes 1986 • $31 • (4/30/1989) • **80**

Key: SS—Spectator Selection. CS—Cellar Selection. HR—Highly Recommended. $NA—Price not available. (BT)—Barrel tasting. Ⓐ—Auction Price.
For a key to the tasters' initials, see "How to Use These Listings."
Dates in parentheses represent the issues in which the ratings were published.

Vosne-Romanée 1993 • $38 • (11/15/1995) • **82**
Vosne-Romanée Les Beaux Monts 1989 • $70 • (1/31/1992) • **91**
Vosne-Romanée Les Beaux Monts 1988 • $56 • (3/31/1991) • **80**
Vosne-Romanée Les Beaux Monts 1985 • $77 Ⓐ • (11/15/1987) • **93**
Vosne-Romanée Les Petits Monts 1997: Has a slight vinegar aroma, but it's crisp and fresh on the palate, with nice toasted oak, spice and mocha. Medium-bodied, it turns chewy and tart on the finish.–P.M. • $70 • (1/01/2000) • **77**
Vosne-Romanée Les Petits Monts 1994 • $52 • (11/15/1996) • **77**
Vosne-Romanée Les Petits Monts 1990 • $NA • (12/15/1992) • **90**
Vosne-Romanée Les Suchots 1990 • $58 • (12/15/1992) • **86**
Vosne-Romanée Les Suchots 1989 • $70 • (1/31/1992) • **89**
Vosne-Romanée Les Suchots 1988 • $57 • (2/28/1991) • **90**
Vosne-Romanée Les Suchots 1985 • $42 • (11/15/1987) • **94**

DROUHIN-LAROZE

Bonnes Mares 1997: Showing an earthy character, this '97 red offers supple plum, game and roasted flavors in a loosely knit, gently tannic style. Drink now through 2003.–B.S. • $99 • (9/30/1999) • **85**
Bonnes Mares 1996: Clean and pure, with crisp acidity and medium ripeness. Enticing rose petal character runs through this charmer, with pretty cassis, blueberry and light smoky accents. Not fat or lush, but give it some time to soften. Best after 2003.–P.M. • $90 • (9/30/1998) • **87**
Bonnes Mares 1995 • $56 • (11/15/1997) • **77**
Bonnes Mares 1993 • $62 • (11/15/1995) • **78**
Bonnes Mares 1992 • $50 • (12/15/1994) • **77**
Bonnes Mares 1988 • $81 • (12/31/1990) • **93**
Bonnes Mares 1987 • $38 • (3/31/1990) • **89**
Chambertin-Clos de Bèze 1997: Sweet-tasting and traditional. The strawberry, cherry and spice notes are okay, but it turns a bit astringent on the finish.–P.M. • $99 • (9/30/1999) • **79**
Chambertin-Clos de Bèze 1996: Gorgeous mouthful of Pinot. From the mixture of blackberry, spice and vanilla to the lingering aftertaste, this is a harmonious, balanced red, concentrated and smooth, with the right amounts of acidity and tannins for support. Best from 2001 through 2006.–B.S. • $93 • (9/30/1998) • **93**
Chambertin-Clos de Bèze 1995 • $58 • (11/15/1997) • **88**
Chambertin-Clos de Bèze 1994 • $49 • (11/15/1996) • **77**
Chambertin-Clos de Bèze 1993 • $68 • (11/15/1995) • **81**
Chambertin-Clos de Bèze 1992 • $60 • (12/15/1994) • **78**
Chambertin-Clos de Bèze 1988 • $88 • (12/31/1990) • **92**
Chambertin-Clos de Bèze 1987 • $40 • (3/31/1990) • **90**
Chambertin-Clos de Bèze 1985 • $110 • (10/15/1988) • **92**
Chambolle-Musigny Premier Cru 1994 • $35 • (11/15/1996) • **79**
Chapelle-Chambertin 1994 • $49 • (11/15/1996) • **72**
Chapelle-Chambertin 1992 • $45 • (12/15/1994) • **84**
Chapelle-Chambertin 1988 • $68 • (12/31/1990) • **88**
Clos de Vougeot 1997: A well-made '97. Medium-bodied, showing distinct vanilla, mocha and toasted oak, but also fine-grained Pinot fruit, ripe tannins and a somewhat crisp finish. Tasted twice, with consistent notes. Drink now through 2005.–P.M. • $NA • (1/01/2000) • **87**
Clos de Vougeot 1996: Ripe, spicy red cherry and mineral flavors in this elegant, delicately structured wine. Racy, with pure fruit intensity and a lacy finish. Drink through 2004.–B.S. • $85 • (9/30/1998) • **90**
Clos de Vougeot 1995 • $56 • (11/15/1997) • **88**
Clos de Vougeot 1994 • $46 • (11/15/1996) • **82**
Clos de Vougeot 1993 • $62 • (11/15/1995) • **89**
Clos de Vougeot 1992 • $50 • (12/15/1994) • **78**
Clos de Vougeot 1988 • $81 • (12/31/1990) • **89**
Clos de Vougeot 1987 • $38 • (3/31/1990) • **79**
Clos de Vougeot 1985 • $60 • (10/15/1988) • **88**
Gevrey-Chambertin 1996: A bit diluted, tasting slightly watery, with some cherry and raspberry character. Somewhat drying on the finish.–P.M. • $40 • (9/30/1998) • **79**
Gevrey-Chambertin 1994 • $36 • (11/15/1996) • **73**
Gevrey-Chambertin Clos Prieur 1988 • $44 • (12/31/1990) • **88**
Gevrey-Chambertin Lavaut St.-Jacques 1993 • $38 • (11/15/1995) • **77**
Gevrey-Chambertin Lavaut St.-Jacques 1988 • $44 • (12/31/1990) • **80**
Gevrey-Chambertin Premier Cru 1996: Seductive, like a raspberry dessert. Shows lovely fruit, silky texture and good concentration before the stiff tannins take over. Lingering aftertaste of raspberries. Best from 2002 through 2008.–B.S. • $50 • (9/30/1998) • **89**
Latricières-Chambertin 1997: This simple Pinot tastes as if it is quickly maturing, showing mushroom and forest underbrush aromas. Light-bodied

FRANCE

and light brick in color, with a slightly astringent finish.–P.M. • $89 • (9/30/1999) • **77**

Latricières-Chambertin 1996: Pure, intense aromas and flavors of griottes—the wild cherries of the region—and raspberries. Very pretty, elegant and lithe on the palate, with a firm underlying structure. Best from 2001 through 2006.–B.S. • $80 • (9/30/1998) • **89**

Latricières-Chambertin 1994 • $49 • (11/15/1996) • **81**

Latricières-Chambertin 1993 • $52 • (11/15/1995) • **80**

Latricières-Chambertin 1992 • $45 • (12/15/1994) • **77**

Latricières-Chambertin 1988 • $68 • (12/31/1990) • **91**

Latricières-Chambertin 1987 • $36 • (3/31/1990) • **88**

Mazis-Chambertin 1985 • $47 • (10/15/1988) • **90**

Musigny 1996: Beautiful, ripe, lush and opulent, with loads of firm but ripe tannins, lots of clean and pure fruit. Full-bodied, it sparkles with cassis, blackberry and wild raspberry flavors. Some toasted, smoky oak notes add complexity, and a bit of heat, on the finish. A seductive package. Best after 2005.–P.M. • $260 • (9/30/1998) • **92**

DRUET, PIERRE-JACQUES

Bourgueil Cuvée Beauvais 1996: Firm and crisp, with cherry, berry, herb and light chocolate flavors. Appealing, but without much depth. Finishes with lean, drying tannins. Drink now through 2001.–T.M. • $19 • (2/28/1999) • **82**

Bourgueil Fiefs de Louys 1996: This firm red shows muscular tannins and concentration. The flavors range from cherry to chocolate, with accents of earth and herb. Drink now through 2003.–T.M. • $27 • (2/28/1999) • **84**

Bourgueil Les Cent Boissellées 1996 • $16 • (6/15/1998) • **83**

Bourgueil Les Cent Boissellées 1995 • $14 • (5/15/1997) • **88**

Bourgueil Rosé 1997: Cherry and cinnamon flavors are bold, if a bit clumsy, in this round rosé. Has plenty of weight for food, and the slightly sweet flavors linger on the finish. Drink now.–T.M. • $14 • (1/01/2000) • **85**

Chinon Clos de Danzay 1996: Sinewy and dense, exhibiting cassis and raspberry notes, a firm structure and an intensity of flavors that engage the palate through the long, tobaccolike finish. Drink now through 2001.–B.S. • $19 • (10/31/1998) • **87**

DUBOEUF, GEORGES

Beaujolais Blanc Flower Label 1998: Ripe, round aromas of apples and butter give way to a lean, crisp palate of grapefruit and herbs. The end result is a bit disjointed, but still refreshing.–T.M. • $10 • (10/15/1999) • **79**

Beaujolais Château de Buffavent 1997: Well-defined black cherry and smoky flavors give this red good varietal character. Well balanced, with moderate tannins; a nice match for charcuterie and pâté. Drink now.–T.M. • $6 • (8/31/1998) • **83**

Beaujolais Château de Buffavent 1996 • $8 • (9/15/1997) • **81**

Beaujolais Flower Label 1997: Pretty good stuffing for a simple Beaujolais; it's grapey and plush, with pretty cherry notes on the soft finish. Drink now.–T.M. • $7 • (8/31/1998) • **83**

Beaujolais Flower Label 1994 • $7 • (6/15/1995) • **81**

Beaujolais Nouveau 1999: Quite firm, this red shows good structure for a Nouveau, but the cherry, berry and herbal flavors seem a bit muted. Better with food. Drink now.–T.M. • $9 • (1/01/2000) • **83**

Beaujolais-Villages Château de la Grande Grange 1994 • $8 • (6/15/1995) • **82**

Beaujolais-Villages Château de la Grande Grange 1993 • $8 • (6/30/1994) • **73**

Beaujolais-Villages Château de Varennes 1998: There's some depth to this firmly structured Beaujolais-Villages, packing black cherry and raspberry notes into an elegant frame. Flavors linger on the finish. Drink now.–B.S. • $11 • (10/15/1999) • **85**

Beaujolais-Villages Château de Varennes 1997: Slightly tannic and tart, lacks generosity, but the berry and strawberry flavors are fresh and well defined. Try with lighter dishes. Drink now.–T.M. • $8 • (8/31/1998) • **79**

Beaujolais-Villages Château de Varennes 1996 • $9 • (8/31/1997) • **83**

Beaujolais-Villages Château de Varennes 1995 • $8 • (9/15/1996) • **84**

Beaujolais-Villages Château de Varennes 1994 • $8 • (6/15/1995) • **86**

Beaujolais-Villages Château des Vierres 1998: Aromas and flavors hint at kirsch, with grace notes of earth and herbs. It's soft, yet lively enough to carry the fruit, with light tannins showing on the finish. Drink now.–B.S. • $10 • (10/15/1999) • **83**

Beaujolais-Villages Château des Vierres 1997: This straightforward red offers well-defined black cherry and smoky flavors, but it's a bit hollow, turning lean on the finish. May flesh out with food. Drink now.–T.M. • $8 • (8/31/1998) • **81**

Beaujolais-Villages Château des Vierres 1996 • $9 • (8/31/1997) • **84**

Beaujolais-Villages Château des Vierres 1995 • $8 • (9/15/1996) • **84**

Beaujolais-Villages Château des Vierres 1994 • $8 • (6/15/1995) • **83**

Beaujolais-Villages Domaine du Granit Bleu 1996 • $9 • (8/31/1997) • **84**

Beaujolais-Villages Domaine du Granit Bleu 1995 • $8 • (8/31/1996) • **85**

Beaujolais-Villages Domaine du Granit Bleu 1994 • $8 • (6/15/1995) • **84**

Beaujolais-Villages Flower Label 1998: Smelling like cherries and flowers, turning more to cherry candy on the palate, this charming, easygoing red falls short on the finish. Drink now.–B.S. • $12 • (10/15/1999) • **83**

Beaujolais-Villages Flower Label 1997: There's good concentration of black cherry and plum in this round French red, and a nice balance of firm tannins. Smoke and herb notes add depth. A fine match for grilled meats.–T.M. • $7 • (8/31/1998) • **85**

Beaujolais-Villages Flower Label 1996 • $9 • (8/31/1997) • **84**

Beaujolais-Villages Flower Label 1995 • $8 • (9/15/1996) • **83**

Beaujolais-Villages Flower Label 1994 • $7 • (6/15/1995) • **87**

Brouilly Château de Nervers 1997: A few sharp edges, but the cherry flavors are lively and the tannins have definition and grip. Will show more generosity with food. Drink now.–T.M. • $10 • (8/31/1998) • **82**

Brouilly Château de Nervers 1996 • $11 • (7/31/1997) • **86**

Brouilly Château de Nervers 1995 • $10 • (8/31/1996) • **87**

Brouilly Château de Nervers 1994 • $10 • (6/15/1995) • **85**

Brouilly Château de Pierreux 1996 • $11 • (8/31/1997) • **84**

Brouilly Château de Pierreux 1994 • $10 • (6/15/1995) • **88**

Brouilly Château de Pierreux 1993 • $9 • (6/30/1994) • **79**

Brouilly Château de Pierreux Comte de Toulgoët 1995 • $10 • (8/31/1996) • **87**

Brouilly Domaine de Combillaty 1997: A good middle-of-the-road Beaujolais, showing soft cherry flavors without real definition and focus, followed by a firm finish. Drink now.–B.S. • $10 • (10/31/1998) • **83**

Brouilly Domaine de Combillaty 1996 • $11 • (7/31/1997) • **85**

Brouilly Flower Label 1995 • $10 • (8/31/1996) • **86**

Brouilly Flower Label 1994 • $10 • (6/15/1995) • **86**

Brouilly Grand Cuvée Flower Label 1997: Ripe flavors of black cherry and chocolate give some generosity, and it's balanced too, with just enough tannin for grip. A nice quaff. Drink now.–T.M. • $10 • (8/31/1998) • **83**

Brouilly Grand Cuvée Flower Label 1996 • $11 • (7/31/1997) • **86**

Brouilly Grande Cuvée Flower Label 1998: Light-bodied, fruity and gulpable, this Brouilly is attractive for its fresh cherry notes yet remains lively and crisp on the finish. Drink now.–B.S. • $13 • (10/15/1999) • **82**

Chardonnay Vin de Pays d'Oc Flower Label 1996 • $11/1.5 liter • (5/15/1998) • **83**

Chénas Domaine des Darroux 1998: A light red wine with pleasant flavors of cherry, currant and spice. It also has a slight spritziness. Drink now.–K.M. • $11 • (10/15/1999) • **83**

Chénas Domaine des Darroux 1997: Berry and grape flavors are bright and juicy in this appealing red. It's light for Chénas, but balanced and quaffable. Drink now.–T.M. • $10 • (8/31/1998) • **83**

Chénas Domaine des Darroux 1996 • $10 • (7/31/1997) • **86**

Chénas Domaine des Darroux 1995 • $9 • (9/15/1996) • **88**

Chénas Domaine des Darroux 1994 • $9 • (7/31/1995) • **79**

Chénas Flower Label 1996 • $10 • (7/31/1997) • **86**

Chénas Flower Label 1994 • $9 • (6/15/1995) • **85**

Chiroubles Château de Javernand 1998: The cherry and earth aromas and flavors have snap in this firm, pretty Chiroubles. Compact, with moderate concentration, finishing a little short. Drink now.–B.S. • $12 • (10/15/1999) • **84**

Chiroubles Château de Javernand 1997: Soft, pretty, offering ripe flavors of cherries and chocolate, tender and fresh on the palate. Lush but lacks structure. Drink now.–T.M. • $10 • (8/31/1998) • **82**

Chiroubles Château de Javernand 1995 • $10 • (8/31/1996) • **85**

Chiroubles Château de Javernand 1994 • $10 • (6/15/1995) • **85**

Chiroubles Domaine Desmures 1997: An exuberant red, with juicy cherry and strawberry aromas and flavors, good concentration and a touch of spice on the finish. Drink now.–B.S. • $11 • (10/31/1998) • **86**

Chiroubles Domaine Desmures 1996 • $10 • (7/31/1997) • **85**

Chiroubles Domaine Desmures 1994 • $10 • (6/15/1995) • **84**

Chiroubles Flower Label 1998: A whiff of banana is followed by cherry flavors in this soft, quaffable Chiroubles. Forward and mouthfilling, without the depth and length of the appellation's best. Drink now.–B.S. • $12 • (10/15/1999) • **83**

Chiroubles Flower Label 1997: Light and fruity, this has the vivacity typical of the appellation, with ripe flavors of cherries and strawberries. It's tender and fresh, a lovely aperitif. Drink now.–T.M. • $9 • (8/31/1998) • **84**

Chiroubles Flower Label 1996 • $10 • (7/31/1997) • **85**

Chiroubles Flower Label 1995 • $10 • (9/15/1996) • **83**

Chiroubles Flower Label 1994 • $9 • (6/15/1995) • **79**

Côte de Brouilly Domaine de la Feuillée 1997: This ripe, aromatic red is distinctive in character, with notes of violets, kirsch and chocolate. Balanced, and shows good intensity for the vintage. Drink now.–T.M. • $10 • (8/31/1998) • **86**

FRANCE

Côte de Brouilly Domaine de la Feuillée 1995 • $10 • (8/31/1996) • **85**
Côte de Brouilly Flower Label 1998: True to its *terroir*, here's a structured red, showing cherry and chocolate flavors, a firm underpinning of acidity and light tannins. Drink now through 2001.–B.S. • $13 • (10/15/1999) • **83**
Côte de Brouilly Flower Label 1997: Grapey and fresh, this round, soft wine offers straightforward fruit and light herbal flavors, with modest tannins. Drink now.–T.M. • $11 • (8/31/1998) • **83**
Côte de Brouilly Flower Label 1996 • $11 • (8/31/1997) • **84**
Côte de Brouilly Flower Label 1995 • $9 • (9/15/1996) • **84**
Côte de Brouilly Flower Label 1994 • $9 • (6/15/1995) • **80**
Côte-Rôtie Domaine de la Rousse 1991 • $NA • (5/31/1994) • **87**
Côte-Rôtie Domaine de la Rousse 1989 • $24 • (2/28/1993) • **82**
Côte-Rôtie Domaine de la Rousse 1988 • $18 • (7/31/1991) • **87**
Côtes du Rhône 1994 • $9 • (12/15/1996) • **83**
Côtes du Rhône 1992 • $5 • (11/15/1993) • **80**
Côtes du Rhône Domaine Agnès 1995 • $11 • (12/15/1996) • **82**
Côtes du Rhône Domaine des Aires Vieilles 1994 • $7 • (6/15/1995) • **78**
Côtes du Rhône Domaine des Aires Vieilles 1992 • $6 • (4/30/1994) • **82**
Côtes du Rhône Domaine des Moulins 1995 • $11 • (12/15/1996) • **84**
Côtes du Rhône Domaine des Moulins 1994 • $7 • (11/15/1995) • **81**
Côtes du Ventoux 1994 • $6 • (6/15/1995) • **80**
Fleurie Château de Grand Pre 1997: Bright acidity gives this light red a lively character; soft tannins make it drinkable now. Berry and cherry flavors are pleasant but light. Drink now.–T.M. • $13 • (8/31/1998) • **83**
Fleurie Château de Grand Pre 1993 • $10 • (6/30/1994) • **86**
Fleurie Château des Bachelards 1998: This fruity red offers plenty of black cherry and dark plum flavors, with hints of tobacco and smoke. It's round, yet has enough firm tannin to stand up to hearty food. Drink now through 2001.–T.M. • $15 • (10/15/1999) • **86**
Fleurie Château des Bachelards 1997: Alluring violet and plum aromas. Soft and silky on the palate, with fresh plum, cherry and banana flavors. A nice aperitif. Drink now.–T.M. • $13 • (8/31/1998) • **84**
Fleurie Château des Bachelards 1996 • $13 • (7/31/1997) • **88**
Fleurie Château des Déduits 1997: A pleasant combination of bright acidity and soft texture gives this round, fruity red immediate appeal. The straightforward cherry and berry flavors are fresh and clean. Drink now.–T.M. • $13 • (8/31/1998) • **84**
Fleurie Château des Déduits 1996 • $13 • (8/31/1997) • **84**
Fleurie Château des Déduits 1995 • $11 • (8/31/1996) • **86**
Fleurie Château des Déduits 1994 • $12 • (6/15/1995) • **87**
Fleurie Domaine des Quatre Vents 1998: A seductive red, packed with ripe flavors of raspberries and cherries, this has the smoky and meaty notes characteristic of ripe Gamay, and polishes them off with toasty oak notes. Alluring and harmonious. Drink now through 2001.–T.M. • $15 • (10/15/1999) • **88**
Fleurie Domaine des Quatre Vents 1997: Bright plum and black cherry flavors are clean and fresh, framed by pleasant tannins, in this well-focused red. Drink now.–T.M. • $13 • (8/31/1998) • **85**
Fleurie Domaine des Quatre Vents 1996 • $13 • (7/31/1997) • **85**
Fleurie Flower Label 1998: Generous yet supple, this fruity red offers ripe flavors of plums and black cherries with alluring overtones of smoke and game. The tannins are firm but light, the balance good. Drink now.–T.M. • $15 • (10/15/1999) • **87**
Fleurie Flower Label 1997: Nicely balanced, this vibrant red offers ripe plum and black cherry flavors, refreshing acidity and tannins firm enough to marry well with food. It's fresh and clean. 5,000 cases imported.–T.M. • $12 • (8/31/1998) • **87**
Fleurie Flower Label 1996 • $13 • (7/31/1997) • **86**
Fleurie Flower Label 1995 • $11 • (8/31/1996) • **86**
Fleurie Flower Label 1994 • $11 • (6/15/1995) • **89**
Gamay Vin de Pays de l'Ardèche Nouveau 1999: If it weren't for the exuberant, grapey fruit, this wine would hardly seem like Nouveau, as its concentration and structure are bigger and deeper than normal. Lovely fruit and good balance. Drink now.–T.M. • $5 • (1/01/2000) • **86**
Juliénas Domaine de la Seigneurie de Juliénas 1997: Fruity, clean and straightforward, with ripe cherry and plum flavors and moderate tannins. Balanced and refreshing. Drink now.–T.M. • $10 • (8/31/1998) • **84**
Juliénas Domaine de la Seigneurie de Juliénas 1995 • $10 • (9/15/1996) • **86**
Juliénas Domaine de la Seigneurie de Juliénas 1993 • $9 • (6/30/1994) • **80**

Key: SS—Spectator Selection. CS—Cellar Selection. HR—Highly Recommended. $NA—Price not available. (BT)—Barrel tasting. Ⓐ—Auction Price.
For a key to the tasters' initials, see "How to Use These Listings."
Dates in parentheses represent the issues in which the ratings were published.

Juliénas Flower Label 1998: Vivid, bursting with cherry. It's balanced toward the tart side, a bit short, yet fresh and ideal for summer picnics, slightly chilled. Drink now.–B.S. • $13 • (10/15/1999) • **83**
Juliénas Flower Label 1997: A solid red, showing deep color, muscular structure and rich flavors of ripe plums, game and smoke. It's balanced and should develop well in the bottle. Drink now.–T.M. • $9 • (8/31/1998) • **87**
Juliénas Flower Label 1996 • $10 • (7/31/1997) • **86**
Juliénas Flower Label 1995 • $9 • (9/15/1996) • **85**
Juliénas Flower Label 1994 • $9 • (6/15/1995) • **84**
Mâcon-Villages Domaine Lenoir 1996 • $9 • (8/31/1997) • **82**
Mâcon-Villages Domaine les Chenevières 1996 • $9 • (8/31/1997) • **82**
Mâcon-Villages Flower Label 1997: Clean, with some butter notes mingling with a touches of spice and honey, here's a medium-bodied Mâcon with personality and plenty of charm. Drink now.–P.M. • $8 • (5/31/1999) • **87**
Mâcon-Villages Flower Label 1996 • $8 • (8/31/1997) • **81**
Mâcon-Villages Flower Label 1995 • $8 • (8/31/1996) • **83**
Merlot Vin de Pays d'Oc Domaine de Bordeneuve 1997: A fresh, simple red with grapey flavors and leathery accents. • $7 • (8/31/1998) • **79**
Merlot Vin de Pays d'Oc Domaine de Bordeneuve 1994 • $7 • (7/31/1995) • **84**
Merlot Vin de Pays d'Oc Domaine de Bordeneuve 1993 • $6 • (9/15/1994) • **83**
Merlot Vin de Pays d'Oc Domaine St.-Louis 1997: Extremely young-tasting, but very fruity and exuberant, with simple, grapey flavors and slightly yeasty accents. • $7 • (8/31/1998) • **79**
Merlot Vin de Pays d'Oc Domaine St.-Louis 1996 • $7 • (8/31/1997) • **82**
Merlot Vin de Pays d'Oc Domaine St.-Pierre 1997: Fresh, grapey flavors, a deep color and a smooth, soft texture make this appealing. Tannins are light, but the jammy fruit flavor is substantial. Drink now. • $7 • (8/31/1998) • **84**
Merlot Vin de Pays d'Oc Flower Label 1998: Tastes young, fruity and light, with effusive grapey flavors and banana-bubblegum notes.–K.M. • $7 • (7/31/1999) • **79**
Merlot Vin de Pays d'Oc Flower Label 1997: Like fresh grape soda-pop. A simple, fruity, very young red wine in the style of Beaujolais Nouveau. Drink now. • $6 • (8/31/1998) • **81**
Merlot Vin de Pays d'Oc Flower Label 1996 • $7 • (8/31/1997) • **79**
Merlot Vin de Pays d'Oc Flower Label 1995 • $7 • (12/15/1996) • **85**
Merlot Vin de Pays d'Oc Flower Label 1994 • $7 • (7/31/1995) • **83**
Morgon Domaine Bellevue 1998: Lean, with a vinegary aroma and prickly acidity that doesn't quite integrate with the whole, despite good concentration.–B.S. • $13 • (10/15/1999) • **77**
Morgon Domaine Bellevue 1997: Both rich and fresh, this deeply colored red offers exuberant fruit flavors of plums and cherries with hints of spice and toast. Ripe and clean, a balanced expression of the Gamay grape.–T.M. • $10 • (8/31/1998) • **85**
Morgon Domaine Bellevue 1996 • $10 • (9/15/1997) • **89**
Morgon Domaine Bellevue 1994 • $10 • (6/30/1995) • **88**
Morgon Flower Label 1998: A hint of banana and high-toned cherry appear in this lush, soft-textured red. Turns a bit crisp and firm on the palate, yet has an overall appeal. Drink now through 2001.–B.S. • $13 • (10/15/1999) • **83**
Morgon Flower Label 1997: This red is round and tender, with a soft texture and lively flavors of black cherries and plums. Light tannins give it enough grip for food. Drink now.–T.M. • $9 • (8/31/1998) • **84**
Morgon Flower Label 1996 • $10 • (8/31/1997) • **83**
Morgon Flower Label 1995 • $9 • (9/15/1996) • **85**
Morgon Flower Label 1994 • $9 • (6/30/1995) • **87**
Morgon Jean Descombes 1998: Saturated cherry, chocolate and cassis notes weave throughout this medium-bodied, firmly structured Morgon that has density and a lingering finish. Drink now through 2001.–B.S. • $13 • (10/15/1999) • **84**
Morgon Jean Descombes 1997: This slightly candied red shows hints of spritz and reduced flavors, but has a core of ripe fruit and vibrant acidity. Drink now.–T.M. • $10 • (8/31/1998) • **82**
Morgon Jean Descombes 1996 • $11 • (9/15/1997) • **85**
Morgon Jean Descombes 1995 • $10 • (9/15/1996) HR • **88**
Morgon Jean Descombes 1994 • $11 • (6/30/1995) • **88**
Moulin-à-Vent Aged in Oak 1998: Plenty of vanilla and coffee aromas greet the nose in this purple-hued Moulin-à-Vent. There's plum and black cherry underneath, in a suave and smooth package. Drink now through 2002.–B.S. • $15 • (10/15/1999) • **87**
Moulin-à-Vent Aged in Oak 1997: New oak flavors of toast and chocolate add sweetness and complexity to this firm red, but tend to dominate the rather light cherry flavors. Drink now.–T.M. • $13 • (8/31/1998) • **86**
Moulin-à-Vent Aged in Oak 1993 • $11 • (7/31/1995) • **85**
Moulin-à-Vent Aged in Oak 1991 • $11 • (6/30/1994) SS • **91**

Moulin-à-Vent Domaine de la Tour du Bief 1997: Marries power and subtlety, with ripe black cherry, tobacco and licorice flavors and a firm, polished texture. Has good balance. Drink now.–T.M. • $13 • (8/31/1998) • **87**
Moulin-à-Vent Domaine de la Tour du Bief 1996 • $13 • (9/15/1997) • **87**
Moulin-à-Vent Domaine de la Tour du Bief 1994 • $12 • (7/31/1995) • **86**
Moulin-à-Vent Domaine de la Tour du Bief 1993 • $10 • (6/30/1994) • **87**
Moulin-à-Vent Domaine des Rosiers 1997: This generous red offers ripe black cherry and plum flavors, with herbal and gamy accents. Round and soft, but lacks the structure to age. Drink now.–T.M. • $12 • (8/31/1998) • **83**
Moulin-à-Vent Domaine des Rosiers 1995 • $11 • (9/15/1996) • **87**
Moulin-à-Vent Domaine des Rosiers 1994 • $12 • (7/31/1995) • **87**
Moulin-à-Vent Domaine des Rosiers 1993 • $10 • (6/30/1994) • **89**
Moulin-à-Vent Flower Label 1998: Deeply colored, with cherry and violet notes and a hint of earth. Tight and unyielding today, with firm tannins and good underlying power and structure. Drink through 2003.–B.S. • $14 • (10/15/1999) • **84**
Moulin-à-Vent Flower Label 1997: Black cherry and gamy flavors are ripe yet focused in this firm, well-defined red. It's balanced, and has a pleasantly spicy finish.–T.M. • $13 • (8/31/1998) • **84**
Moulin-à-Vent Flower Label 1996 • $13 • (9/15/1997) • **85**
Moulin-à-Vent Flower Label 1994 • $11 • (7/31/1995) • **87**
Moulin-à-Vent Flower Label 1993 • $10 • (6/30/1994) • **86**
Moulin-à-Vent Windmill Label 1997: A rustic red, with lively acidity and slightly rough tannins framing its bright cherry and smoke flavors. The lively fruit brings you back for another sip. Drink now through 2001.–T.M. • $15 • (3/31/2000) • **87**
Pouilly-Fuissé Aged in Oak 1997: Lively, racy and full-bodied, this white Burgundy is packed with deftly created oak accents, showing a pronounced toasted character along with plenty of lemon notes, good fruit and impressive length on the finish. It's tempting now, but worth cellaring short-term. Drink through 2005.–P.M. • $17 • (5/31/1999) HR • **90**
Pouilly-Fuissé Aged in Oak 1996 • $20 • (5/31/1998) • **87**
Pouilly-Fuissé Domaine Béranger 1996 • $20 • (5/31/1998) • **88**
Pouilly-Fuissé Flower Label 1997: Woody but beautifully made, a full-bodied Pouilly with the buttery, floral, toasted oak notes folding into rich fruit, all nicely balanced. Cellar short-term for even more smoothness. Drink through 2004.–P.M. • $13 • (5/31/1999) • **87**
Pouilly-Fuissé Flower Label 1996 • $19 • (5/31/1998) • **87**
Pouilly-Fuissé Flower Label 1995 • $16 • (5/31/1997) • **78**
Régnié Château de Ponchon 1994 • $8 • (7/31/1995) • **82**
Régnié Château de Ponchon 1993 • $8 • (6/30/1994) • **82**
Régnié Domaine des Buyats 1997: A round red with ripe plum and black cherry flavors, generous and fresh, moderate tannins and a clean finish. Fine on its own or with food. Drink now.–T.M. • $10 • (8/31/1998) • **84**
Régnié Domaine des Buyats 1996 • $10 • (8/31/1997) • **84**
Régnié Domaine des Buyats 1994 • $9 • (7/31/1995) • **85**
Régnié Domaine des Buyats 1993 • $8 • (6/30/1994) • **82**
Régnié Domaine du Potet 1997: This firm red offers black cherry and light chocolate flavors, balanced and fresh, with modest tannins. Straightforward and clean. Drink now.–T.M. • $9 • (8/31/1998) • **83**
Régnié Domaine du Potet 1995 • $9 • (8/31/1996) • **87**
Régnié Domaine du Potet 1994 • $9 • (7/31/1995) • **86**
Régnié Flower Label 1998: Nice and juicy, with luscious flavors of black cherry, currant and spice. Medium-bodied, with licorice notes on the finish. Drink now.–K.M. • $11 • (10/15/1999) • **85**
Régnié Flower Label 1997: Firm and straightforward, with black cherry and light herbal flavors and modest tannins. Balanced but anonymous. Drink now.–T.M. • $8 • (8/31/1998) • **81**
Régnié Flower Label 1996 • $10 • (7/31/1997) • **85**
Régnié Flower Label 1995 • $8 • (8/31/1996) • **85**
Régnié Flower Label 1994 • $8 • (7/31/1995) • **83**
St.-Amour Domaine de la Pirolette 1998: Refreshing and lively, with effusive flavors of bright cherry, currant and spice. Medium-bodied, with a nice trace of orange peel on the finish. Drink now.–K.M. • $15 • (10/15/1999) • **85**
St.-Amour Domaine de la Pirolette 1997: Has a grapey exuberance that's simple but appealing, with black cherry and light spicy notes. Round and soft. Drink now.–T.M. • $13 • (8/31/1998) • **83**
St.-Amour Domaine de la Pirolette 1996 • $13 • (7/31/1997) • **86**
St.-Amour Domaine de la Pirolette 1995 • $11 • (8/31/1996) • **87**
St.-Amour Domaine de la Pirolette 1994 • $12 • (7/31/1995) • **85**
St.-Amour Flower Label 1998: Smooth and supple, with a nicely concentrated mix of cherry, red plum and some nutmeglike flavors. Appealingly ripe peppery notes chime in on the finish. Drink now.–K.M. • $15 • (10/15/1999) • **87**
St.-Amour Flower Label 1997: Displays good concentration of ripe, plummy fruit. The tannins have just enough grip for food; the wine turns a bit hot on the finish. Drink now.–T.M. • $12 • (8/31/1998) • **83**
St.-Amour Flower Label 1996 • $13 • (7/31/1997) • **85**
St.-Amour Flower Label 1995 • $11 • (9/15/1996) • **84**
St.-Amour Flower Label 1994 • $11 • (7/31/1995) • **84**
St.-Véran Domaine de la Bâtie 1996 • $10 • (8/31/1997) • **78**
St.-Véran Domaine de la Feuillarde 1995 • $NA • (8/31/1996) • **84**
St.-Véran Domaine St.-Martin 1995 • $NA • (8/31/1996) • **82**
St.-Véran Flower Label 1997: Fairly ripe, with some almond, apple, quince, earth and peach notes, yet this medium-bodied Chardonnay isn't particularly smooth. Its intensity perks up the taste buds though. Drink now.–P.M. • $9 • (5/31/1999) • **80**
St.-Véran Flower Label 1996 • $10 • (5/31/1998) • **82**
St.-Véran Flower Label 1995 • $9 • (8/31/1996) • **84**
Syrah Vin de Pays d'Oc Domaine St.-Louis 1992 • $7 • (3/15/1994) • **82**
Syrah Vin de Pays d'Oc Flower Label 1994 • $6 • (7/31/1995) • **82**
Syrah Vin de Pays d'Oc Flower Label 1992 • $5 • (3/15/1994) • **83**
Vin de Pays d'Oc Milenage 1998: Soft, with ripe and exuberant flavors of berry, plum and spice. Tannins build on the finish, adding character. Cabernet Sauvignon, Merlot and Syrah. Drink now.–K.M. • $9 • (10/31/1999) • **83**
Viognier Vin de Pays de l'Ardèche Or Blanc 1997: There's some power to this earthy white, with dried pear and pepper flavors and mineral notes on the finish. Drink now.–K.M. • $11 • (10/15/1999) • **83**

DUBOIS CHALLON, CHATEAU

Bordeaux White 1996: Impressive for a simple Bordeaux. Subtle aromas of apple, mango and vanilla. Medium-bodied, with coconut flavors and a tropical fruit aftertaste. Well done, but needs more fruit concentration to score outstanding. Drink now.–J.S. • $NA • (1/01/1999) • **87**

DUBREUIL-FONTAINE PERE & FILS, P.

Aloxe-Corton Les Vercots 1997: A light, stemmy and disappointing Pinot, with dilution and little character.–P.M. • $NA • (1/01/2000) • **70**
Aloxe-Corton Les Vercots 1996: A supple '96 red, showing a good amount of tannin but a soft texture. Medium-bodied, with some licorice notes and modest red berry character.–P.M. • $39 • (9/30/1998) • **85**
Aloxe-Corton Les Vercots 1995 • $38 • (11/15/1997) • **78**
Corton Bressandes 1997: Modest red berry in this simple '97 Pinot Noir. Light- to medium-bodied, with a slight dilution midpalate.–P.M. • $55 • (1/01/2000) • **78**
Corton Bressandes 1996: A subtle, delicate red whose cherry aromas and flavors persist on the palate. There's a harmony and balance that's very appealing, firm tannins too. Drink now.–B.S. • $60 • (9/30/1998) • **88**
Corton Bressandes 1995 • $57 • (11/15/1997) • **80**
Corton Bressandes 1993 • $NA • (5/15/1996) • **88**
Corton Bressandes 1992 • $57 • (12/15/1994) • **85**
Corton Bressandes 1991 • $50 • (1/31/1994) • **88**
Corton Bressandes 1990 • $59 • (12/15/1992) • **89**
Corton Bressandes 1985 • $50 • (1/31/1989) • **86**
Corton Bressandes 1982 • $24 • (10/16/1985) • **85**
Corton Clos du Roi 1997: A pleasantly fruity Pinot, with toasted oak notes. Medium-bodied, it offers only medium intensity and a slightly short finish.–P.M. • $NA • (1/01/2000) • **79**
Corton Clos du Roi 1996: A delicate wine evoking raspberries and cherries, showing good richness and concentration. Balanced toward elegance, with moderate tannins and a lingering finish. Drink through 2005.–B.S. • $62 • (9/30/1998) • **88**
Corton Clos du Roi 1993 • $NA • (5/15/1996) • **87**
Corton Clos du Roi 1992 • $60 • (12/15/1994) • **87**
Corton Clos du Roi 1991 • $52 • (1/31/1994) • **90**
Corton Clos du Roi 1990 • $61 • (12/15/1992) • **93**
Corton Clos du Roi 1989 • $63 • (1/31/1992) • **92**
Corton Clos du Roi 1987 • $34 • (12/31/1990) • **85**
Corton Clos du Roi 1985 • $49 • (7/15/1988) • **90**
Corton Clos du Roi 1982 • $25 • (9/16/1985) • **86**
Corton Les Perrières 1993 • $NA • (5/15/1996) • **88**
Corton-Charlemagne 1998: Lush and minty, a lovely, appealing white that is full-bodied and silky in texture, with a richness accented by dried fruit, ripe pear and apple. Drink now through 2006.–P.M. • $85 • (5/31/2000) • **90**
Corton-Charlemagne 1997: A bit earthy and herbal, with wet earth and green apple character, it tastes acidic and hard. Drying, cardboardy finish.–P.M. • $81 • (5/31/1999) • **74**
Corton-Charlemagne 1995 • $74 • (5/31/1997) • **98**
Pernand-Vergelesses 1994 • $20 • (11/15/1996) • **77**
Pernand-Vergelesses 1993 • $NA • (5/15/1996) • **85**

DUBREUIL-FONTAINE PERE & FILS, P.

Pernand-Vergelesses 1991 • $33 • (1/31/1994) • **82**
Pernand-Vergelesses Clos Berthet 1997: Green and stemmy, this is disappointing, tasting diluted and stripped of all flavors.–P.M. • $NA • (1/01/2000) • **70**
Pernand-Vergelesses Ile des Vergelesses 1997: Light in color and flavor, a light-bodied red with simple raspberry and strawberry flavors; but has a nice round feel in the palate before the crisp finish.–P.M. • $NA • (1/01/2000) • **77**
Pernand-Vergelesses Ile des Vergelesses 1996: Fairly simple and straightforward Pinot, showing decent red berry flavor and fresh acidity. Light to medium in body; serve chilled. Drink now.–P.M. • $39 • (9/30/1998) • **79**
Pernand-Vergelesses Ile des Vergelesses 1995 • $38 • (11/15/1997) • **79**
Pernand-Vergelesses Ile des Vergelesses 1993 • $NA • (5/15/1996) • **77**
Pernand-Vergelesses Ile des Vergelesses 1990 • $37 • (12/15/1992) • **88**
Pernand-Vergelesses Ile des Vergelesses 1989 • $40 • (1/31/1992) • **84**
Pernand-Vergelesses Ile des Vergelesses 1982 • $18 • (10/16/1985) • **78**
Pernand-Vergelesses White 1998: Crisp and tart, even a bit sour, with little ripe fruit.–P.M. • $25 • (5/31/2000) • **75**
Pernand-Vergelesses White Clos Berthet 1998: A Chardonnay with some pretty honey, pear, green apple flavors. Has a firm, vibrant, citrusy character. A bit sharp on the finish. Drink now through 2001.–P.M. • $34 • (5/31/2000) • **81**
Pernand-Vergelesses White Clos Berthet 1997: Clean, fresh, ripe and medium-bodied, this is like sucking on a lime-and-pear sorbet, with a dollop of honey and a piece of pineapple added. You can't ask for more pure pleasure in a "petit village" from Burgundy. Get cases of this stuff. Drink now.–P.M. • $39 • (5/31/1999) • **90**
Pernand-Vergelesses White Clos Berthet 1996 • $33 • (5/31/1998) • **85**
Pernand-Vergelesses White Clos Berthet 1995 • $33 • (8/31/1997) • **82**
Pommard Epenots 1996: Very fresh, vibrant and pure, with an elegant structure and an austere character, but lacks concentration and depth in the midpalate and finishes with some heat and tannins. Drink now.–B.S. • $55 • (9/30/1998) • **84**
Pommard Epenots 1995 • $55 • (11/15/1997) • **85**
Pommard Epenots 1990 • $59 • (12/15/1992) • **91**
Savigny-lès-Beaune Aux Vergelesses 1994 • $22 • (11/15/1996) • **74**
Savigny-lès-Beaune Aux Vergelesses 1993 • $NA • (5/15/1996) • **81**
Savigny-lès-Beaune Aux Vergelesses 1992 • $25 • (12/15/1994) • **81**
Savigny-lès-Beaune Aux Vergelesses 1991 • $22 • (1/31/1994) • **82**
Savigny-lès-Beaune Aux Vergelesses 1990 • $25 • (12/15/1992) • **81**
Savigny-lès-Beaune Aux Vergelesses 1985 • $24 • (1/31/1989) • **88**
Volnay Les Brouillards 1994 • $27 • (11/15/1996) • **78**

DUCLA, CHATEAU

Bordeaux 1996: Pretty Merlot aromas of olive and blackberry. Medium-bodied, with a good balance of medium tannins and a fruity aftertaste. Drink now. –J.S. • $NA • (9/30/1998) • **84**
Bordeaux 1988 • $7 • (8/31/1991) • **74**
Bordeaux Coeur de Cuvée 1995 • $9 • (10/15/1997) • **83**
Bordeaux Cuvée Extrème 1988 • $11 • (7/15/1992) • **83**
Entre-Deux-Mers Cœur de Cuvée 1996 • $8 • (9/30/1997) • **81**

DUCLUZEAU, CHATEAU

Listrac 1993 • $12 • (1/31/1996) • **77**
Listrac 1986 • $11 • (11/30/1989) • **83**
Listrac 1982 • $16 • (8/31/1992) • **81**

DUCOIN, CHARLES

Brut Champagne Carte Blanche NV • $20 • (12/31/1994) • **81**

DUCRU-BEAUCAILLOU, CHATEAU

St.-Julien 1999: Solid core of ripe fruit and tannins in this wine. Interesting aromas of spices, berries and cinnamon. Medium-bodied, with firm tannins and a medium finish.–J.S. • $NA • (1/01/2000) (BT) • **85-89**
St.-Julien 1998: A bit diluted, but has some good berry, currant and earth character. Medium-bodied, with medium tannins and a short finish.–J.S. • $NA • (5/31/1999) (BT) • **85-89**
St.-Julien 1997: Attractive perfumes of berries and cherries. Light- to medium-bodied, with fresh fruit and a short finish.–J.S. • $62 • (1/31/2000) • **85**
St.-Julien 1996: A thoroughly outstanding wine, sleek and racy with loads of character. Intense floral and blackberry aromas, with hints of mineral. Full-bodied, with supersilky tannins and a long, long finish. Give it time. Best after 2003.–J.S. • $92 Ⓐ • (1/31/1999) • **92**
St.-Julien 1995 • $102 Ⓐ • (1/31/1998) CS • **97**
St.-Julien 1994 • $43 Ⓐ • (1/31/1997) • **87**
St.-Julien 1993 • $37 Ⓐ • (1/31/1996) • **81**
St.-Julien 1992 • $28 • (4/15/1995) • **79**
St.-Julien 1991 • $31 • (3/31/1994) • **83**
St.-Julien 1990 • $70 Ⓐ • (3/31/1993) • **89**
St.-Julien 1989: Dark-ruby in color and a hint of brick red at the edge. Ripe fruit aromas of plums and raspberries. Full-bodied and very soft, with round tannins and a delicious chocolaty aftertaste. Slightly dry, papery finish. (1989 Bordeaux horizontal tasting). Drink now through 2005.–J.S. • $73 Ⓐ • (5/31/1999) • **89**
St.-Julien 1988 • $52 Ⓐ • (4/30/1991) • **92**
St.-Julien 1987 • $45 Ⓐ • (5/15/1990) • **86**
St.-Julien 1986 • $80 Ⓐ • (6/30/1989) • **91**
St.-Julien 1985 • $86 Ⓐ • (10/15/1994) • **90**
St.-Julien 1984 • $27 Ⓐ • (8/31/1987) • **87**
St.-Julien 1983 • $56 Ⓐ • (10/15/1994) • **87**
St.-Julien 1982: This Ducru '82 has always been a beauty. Dark ruby in color, with a slight amber edge. Very fresh and floral, with loads of berry and rose character. Medium-bodied, with a good balance of soft tannins and a caressing finish. (1982 Bordeaux horizontal tasting). Drink now.–J.S. • $136 Ⓐ • (11/30/1998) • **91**
St.-Julien 1981 • $54 Ⓐ • (10/15/1994) • **89**
St.-Julien 1980 • $23 • (5/01/1984) CS • **88**
St.-Julien 1979 • $51 Ⓐ • (10/15/1989) • **87**
St.-Julien 1978 • $73 Ⓐ • (10/15/1992) • **84**
St.-Julien 1977 • $NA • (10/15/1992) • **76**
St.-Julien 1976 • $41 Ⓐ • (10/15/1992) • **87**
St.-Julien 1974 • $NA • (10/15/1992) • **76**
St.-Julien 1973 • $NA • (10/15/1992) • **77**
St.-Julien 1971 • $18 Ⓐ • (10/15/1992) • **86**
St.-Julien 1970 • $79 • (5/15/1993) • **91**
St.-Julien 1962 • $49 • (11/30/1987) • **80**
St.-Julien 1961 • $233 • (4/30/1996) • **92**
St.-Julien 1959 • $158 Ⓐ • (10/15/1990) • **90**
St.-Julien 1958 • $100 • (10/15/1992) • **83**
St.-Julien 1957 • $85 • (10/15/1992) • **77**
St.-Julien 1955 • $133 Ⓐ • (10/15/1992) • **87**
St.-Julien 1953 • $240 • (10/15/1992) • **88**
St.-Julien 1952 • $160 • (10/15/1992) • **81**
St.-Julien 1949 • $220 • (10/15/1992) • **90**
St.-Julien 1945 • $500 • (11/30/1995) • **84**
St.-Julien 1934 • $190 • (10/15/1992) • **82**
St.-Julien 1929 • $166 • (10/15/1992) • **83**
St.-Julien 1928 • $388 Ⓐ • (10/15/1992) • **88**
St.-Julien 1924 • $197 Ⓐ • (10/15/1992) • **80**
St.-Julien 1898 • $450 • (10/15/1992) • **97**
St.-Julien 1887 • $450 • (10/15/1992) • **89**
St.-Julien 1867 • $950 • (10/15/1992) • **92**

DUFOULEUR PERE & FILS

Beaune Champs Pimont 1991 • $17 • (5/31/1995) • **84**
Bourgogne Cuvée Napoléon 1993 • $12 • (9/15/1996) • **81**
Fixin Clos du Chapitre 1993 • $24 • (9/15/1996) • **84**

DUGAT, CLAUDE

Charmes-Chambertin 1997: Has herb and black cherry aromas and flavors, moderate intensity and a rich texture. Firm tannins on the finish. Needs time to come together. Best from 2001 through 2005.–B.S. • $135 • (9/30/1999) • **89**
Charmes-Chambertin 1996: Literally drenched in black fruit flavors, with hints of vanilla and game, this is a round, chunky '96 bordering on chocolaty. Rich and satisfying, with a lingering, slightly hot finish. 40 cases imported. Drink through 2004.–B.S. • $553 Ⓐ • (9/30/1998) • **90**
Charmes-Chambertin 1995 • $460 Ⓐ • (11/15/1997) • **93**
Charmes-Chambertin 1994 • $75 • (11/15/1996) • **82**
Charmes-Chambertin 1993 • $480 Ⓐ • (11/15/1995) • **90**

Key: SS—Spectator Selection. CS—Cellar Selection. HR—Highly Recommended. $NA—Price not available. (BT)—Barrel tasting. Ⓐ—Auction Price.
For a key to the tasters' initials, see "How to Use These Listings."
Dates in parentheses represent the issues in which the ratings were published.

Gevrey-Chambertin 1997: Smooth and supple, this silky, modern-style '97 red Burgundy delivers ripe fruit, velvety tannins, a satisfying mouthfeel and a sense of opulence, with layers of game, blackberry and smoke complexity. Drink now through 2005.–P.M. • $60 • (9/30/1999) • **89**
Gevrey-Chambertin 1995 • $48 • (11/15/1997) • **88**
Gevrey-Chambertin 1994 • $40 • (11/15/1996) • **86**
Gevrey-Chambertin 1993 • $40 • (11/15/1995) • **90**
Gevrey-Chambertin Lavaux St.-Jacques 1997: The oak brings out chocolate, mocha and spice in this firm, chewy, crisp Pinot Noir. Mouthpuckering on the midpalate, with a lemony taste. The tannins kick in on the tough, herbal finish. Best from 2002 through 2007.–P.M. • $85 • (9/30/1999) • **84**
Gevrey-Chambertin Lavaux St.-Jacques 1996: Terrific '96 red Burgundy. Full-bodied and ripe yet not overdone, silky in texture yet with firm tannins, it packs in delicious flavors of blackberry, cassis, rose petal, wet earth and mineral. Oak plays a subtle tone in this symphony of a wine. Long finish. 45 cases imported. Best after 2005.–P.M. • $201 Ⓐ • (9/30/1998) • **94**
Gevrey-Chambertin Lavaux St.-Jacques 1995 • $134 Ⓐ • (11/15/1997) • **85**
Gevrey-Chambertin Lavaux St.-Jacques 1993 • $65 • (11/15/1995) • **92**
Gevrey-Chambertin Premier Cru 1997: Violets, cassis and kirsch mark this refined red, offering more substance midpalate and *terroir* than most in this category, along with a silky texture and bright acidity. Finishes on a firm, tannic note. Best from 2001 through 2005.–B.S. • $85 • (9/30/1999) • **91**
Gevrey-Chambertin Premier Cru 1996: Great saturation of fruit, tasting of blackberry, cassis and vanilla, all on a suave, supple texture punctuated by vibrant acidity and ripe tannins. Hints of chocolate and spices add complexity. Excellent finish. 44 cases imported. Best from 2005 through 2012.–B.S. • $80 • (9/30/1998) • **94**
Gevrey-Chambertin Premier Cru 1995 • $60 • (11/15/1997) • **87**
Gevrey-Chambertin Premier Cru 1994 • $52 • (11/15/1996) • **81**
Gevrey-Chambertin Premier Cru 1993 • $50 • (11/15/1995) • **91**
Griotte-Chambertin 1996: Young red Burgudy doesn't get much silkier than this. Full-bodied, it melts in the mouth, showing great refinement and class as it delivers soft flavor cushions of cassis, griottes and wild berries, some subtle toasted accents. A mineral, grilled meat subtext contributes to this great, velvety '96, with its gently intense finish. Tempting now. Best from 2003 through 2015.–P.M. • $911 Ⓐ • (5/15/1999) • **98**

DUGAT-PY, BERNARD

Gevrey-Chambertin Coeur de Roy Vieilles Vignes 1995 • $40 • (1/31/1998) HR • **95**
Gevrey-Chambertin Coeur de Roy Vieilles Vignes 1994 • $38 • (9/30/1997) • **81**
Gevrey-Chambertin Lavaux-St.-Jacques 1994 • $43 • (9/30/1997) • **87**
Gevrey-Chambertin Petite-Chapelle 1994 • $43 • (9/30/1997) • **92**
Gevrey-Chambertin Vieilles Vignes 1994 • $35 • (9/30/1997) • **77**

DUHART-MILON ROTHSCHILD, CHATEAU

Pauillac 1999: Pretty tobacco, smoke and chocolate character. Medium body. Fine tannins. Fresh finish.–J.S. • $NA • (1/01/2000) (BT) • **85-89**
Pauillac 1998: A very good amount of ripe fruit in this wine, with a complement of cedar and tobacco character. Full-bodied, with firm tannins that verge on being aggressive, but overall an attractive '98.–J.S. • $NA • (5/31/1999) (BT) • **85-89**
Pauillac 1997: Good fresh fruit character. Medium- to light-bodied, with fine tannins and a fruity finish. Drink through 2004.–J.S. • $22 Ⓐ • (1/31/2000) • **85**
Pauillac 1996: Dark-colored, with lovely aromas of licorice, berry and spice. Medium-bodied, with fine tannins and a spicy, fruity aftertaste. A bit tough on the finish, but well made. Drink now.–J.S. • $28 • (1/31/1999) • **89**
Pauillac 1995 • $26 Ⓐ • (1/31/1998) • **90**
Pauillac 1994 • $30 • (1/31/1997) • **88**
Pauillac 1993 • $20 Ⓐ • (1/31/1996) • **80**
Pauillac 1992 • $22 • (4/15/1995) • **76**
Pauillac 1990 • $42 Ⓐ • (10/15/1994) • **92**
Pauillac 1989: Big and rich for Duhart. Aromas of blackberry, cherry and wood. Full-bodied, with velvety tannins and a ripe fruit aftertaste. Needs time to mellow and open. (1989 Bordeaux horizontal tasting). Best after 2001.–J.S. • $42 Ⓐ • (5/31/1999) • **90**
Pauillac 1988 • $43 Ⓐ • (8/31/1991) • **88**
Pauillac 1987 • $22 • (5/15/1990) • **79**
Pauillac 1986 • $40 Ⓐ • (5/31/1989) • **90**
Pauillac 1985 • $27 • (10/15/1994) • **93**
Pauillac 1983 • $40 Ⓐ • (10/15/1994) • **89**
Pauillac 1982: Pretty. Brilliant ruby color, with a garnet hue. Medium- to full-bodied, with silky tannins, loads of ripe berry and floral aromas and a medium sweet fruit aftertaste. Slightly short finish. (1982 Bordeaux horizontal tasting). Drink now.–J.S. • $75 Ⓐ • (11/30/1998) • **87**
Pauillac 1981 • $26 • (10/15/1994) • **87**
Pauillac 1979 • $35 Ⓐ • (10/15/1989) • **86**

DUJAC

Bonnes Mares 1987 • $31 • (3/31/1990) • **91**
Bonnes Mares 1986 • $34 • (4/15/1989) • **85**
Chambolle-Musigny 1993 • $37 • (5/15/1996) • **86**
Chambolle-Musigny Les Gruenchers 1987 • $47 • (3/31/1990) • **93**
Chambolle-Musigny Les Gruenchers 1986 • $48 • (7/31/1988) • **76**
Chambolle-Musigny Les Gruenchers 1985 • $43 • (3/31/1988) • **74**
Charmes-Chambertin 1996: Very distinctive. Once you adapt to the truffle, *sous-bois* (wet forest floor), mature Pinot aromas and focus on the lovely, pure, ripe red berry flavors, there's plenty to enjoy in this medium-bodied, rather racy, traditional red Burgundy. Drink now through 2005.–P.M. • $110 • (7/31/1999) • **91**
Charmes-Chambertin 1995 • $75 • (1/31/1998) • **82**
Charmes-Chambertin 1991 • $71 • (1/31/1994) • **83**
Charmes-Chambertin 1990 • $126 Ⓐ • (12/15/1992) • **92**
Charmes-Chambertin 1989 • $72 • (1/31/1992) • **90**
Charmes-Chambertin 1988 • $60 • (3/31/1991) • **85**
Charmes-Chambertin 1986 • $50 • (7/31/1988) • **85**
Charmes-Chambertin 1985 • $144 Ⓐ • (3/15/1988) • **95**
Clos de la Roche 1991 • $77 • (1/31/1994) • **88**
Clos de la Roche 1990 • $164 Ⓐ • (12/15/1992) • **92**
Clos de la Roche 1989 • $127 Ⓐ • (1/31/1992) • **89**
Clos de la Roche 1988 • $118 Ⓐ • (3/31/1991) • **90**
Clos de la Roche 1987 • $53 • (3/31/1990) • **86**
Clos de la Roche 1986 • $57 Ⓐ • (7/31/1988) • **79**
Clos de la Roche 1985 • $228 Ⓐ • (3/15/1988) • **95**
Clos St.-Denis 1993 • $79 • (5/15/1996) • **91**
Clos St.-Denis 1992 • $66 • (5/15/1995) • **87**
Clos St.-Denis 1991 • $77 • (1/31/1994) • **86**
Clos St.-Denis 1990 • $172 Ⓐ • (12/15/1992) • **90**
Clos St.-Denis 1989 • $97 Ⓐ • (1/31/1992) • **91**
Clos St.-Denis 1987 • $58 • (3/31/1990) • **85**
Clos St.-Denis 1986 • $56 • (7/31/1988) • **89**
Clos St.-Denis 1985 • $187 Ⓐ • (3/15/1988) • **91**
Echézeaux 1991 • $81 • (1/31/1994) • **86**
Echézeaux 1990 • $88 • (12/15/1992) • **91**
Echézeaux 1988 • $70 • (3/31/1991) • **90**
Echézeaux 1987 • $56 • (5/15/1990) • **82**
Echézeaux 1986 • $52 • (4/30/1989) • **89**
Gevrey-Chambertin Aux Combottes 1995 • $70 • (1/31/1998) • **82**
Gevrey-Chambertin Aux Combottes 1993 • $65 • (5/15/1996) • **88**
Gevrey-Chambertin Aux Combottes 1991 • $63 • (1/31/1994) • **84**
Gevrey-Chambertin Aux Combottes 1990 • $92 Ⓐ • (12/15/1992) • **92**
Gevrey-Chambertin Aux Combottes 1989 • $65 • (1/31/1992) • **86**
Gevrey-Chambertin Aux Combottes 1988 • $54 • (3/31/1991) • **86**
Gevrey-Chambertin Aux Combottes 1987 • $42 • (5/31/1990) • **80**
Morey-St.-Denis 1996: Distinctive Pinot, showing a wet forest floor and mushroom character mingling with fresh red berry notes to create an intriguing smoke and spice complexity. Good concentration. Drink now through 2005.–P.M. • $37 Ⓐ • (7/31/1999) • **90**
Morey-St.-Denis 1995 • $39 Ⓐ • (1/31/1998) • **78**
Morey-St.-Denis 1993 • $37 • (5/15/1996) • **88**
Morey-St.-Denis 1992 • $31 • (5/15/1995) • **88**
Morey-St.-Denis 1991 • $38 • (1/31/1994) • **84**
Morey-St.-Denis 1990 • $41 • (12/15/1992) • **87**
Morey-St.-Denis 1989 • $40 • (1/31/1992) • **84**

DULONG

Cabernet Sauvignon Vin de Pays d'Oc 1997: A roasted aroma and an oddly sweet and charry bell pepper flavor don't add up to much.–K.M. • $7 • (7/31/1999) • **73**
Cabernet Sauvignon Vin de Pays d'Oc 1996 • $7 • (5/15/1998) • **78**
Cabernet Sauvignon Vin de Pays d'Oc 1995 • $7 • (12/15/1996) • **86**
Chardonnay Vin de Pays d'Oc 1997: A soft-tasting Chardonnay, with buttery notes and pearlike flavors. Neutral finish.–K.M. • $7 • (4/30/1999) • **78**
Chardonnay Vin de Pays d'Oc 1996 • $7 • (5/31/1998) • **78**
Merlot Vin de Pays d'Oc 1997: A softly earthy red, with plum and leather notes. Smooth, with a mature taste. Drink now.–K.M. • $7 • (6/30/1999) • **82**
Merlot Vin de Pays d'Oc 1996 • $7 • (5/15/1998) • **85**

Merlot Vin de Pays d'Oc 1995 • $7 • (12/15/1996) • **81**

DULUC, CHATEAU

St.-Julien 1996: Aromas of fruit and tobacco, with a hint of spice. Medium-bodied, with medium, velvety tannins and a medium finish. Well made. Second label of Château Branaire-Ducru. Best after 2000.–J.S. • $28 • (1/31/1999) • **85**
St.-Julien 1995: Pretty blackberry, tobacco aromas with a slightly herbal note. Medium-bodied, with medium tannins and a short finish. Second label of Château Branaire-Ducru. Drink through 2004.–J.S. • $35 • (9/15/1998) • **77**
St.-Julien 1994 • $NA • (1/31/1997) • **76**
St.-Julien 1991 • $14 • (3/31/1994) • **77**
St.-Julien 1989 • $NA • (3/15/1992) • **84**

DUMANGIN, JEAN

Brut Champagne NV • $30 • (10/31/1997) • **86**

DUMAS, LAURENT

Beaujolais-Villages 1992 • $10 • (6/30/1994) • **83**
Fleurie 1996 • $17 • (9/15/1997) • **85**
Fleurie 1995 • $17 • (1/01/1997) • **84**
Fleurie 1993 • $18 • (1/01/1997) • **74**
Fleurie 1992 • $16 • (6/30/1994) • **83**

DUMIEN-SERETTE

Cornas 1995: Very earthy, with leather, cassis, blackberry and grilled meat complexity. Medium-bodied and quite ripe-tasting, it's a bit rustic but offers fairly supple tannins and a nicely balanced finish. Drink now through 2003.–P.M. • $25 • (10/15/1998) • **84**
Cornas Cuvée Vieilles Vignes 1997: A bit diluted, but the flavors of blackberry, grilled meat, smoke and black pepper are decent. Turns a bit tough and green on the finish, with slightly unripe tannins.–P.M. • $NA • (11/30/1999) • **78**

DUPOND, PIERRE

Chardonnay Vin de Pays d'Oc 1997: Baked apple and spice flavors dominate this medium-bodied Chardonnay. Drink now.–K.M. • $8 • (11/15/1998) • **81**

DUPUIS, ANDRE

Mâcon-Villages 1995 • $NA • (8/31/1996) • **83**

DURAND, ERIC & JOEL

Cornas 1997: A bit tough, but full in body; offers some decent black fruit and toasty, spicy character, turning rather crisp in the midpalate and showing a firm grip on the finish. Drink now through 2001.–P.M. • $22 • (8/31/1999) • **84**
Cornas 1996: Fantastic intensity and concentration in this full-bodied, bold and rich wine, which packs in dried herb, green olive, black pepper, tar, currant and cassis character, then takes off like a rocket on the finish. Complex, harmonious, very distinctive and savage. A terrific wine that will age. Drink now through 2015.–P.M. • $25 • (10/15/1998) • **95**
Cornas 1995: With warm fruit and a touch of herb, this is overshadowed by the darker-colored '96 version. A bit dry on the midpalate and a bit short on the finish. Drink now through 2002.–P.M. • $25 • (10/15/1998) • **83**
St.-Joseph 1996: Earthy aromas introduce this ripe, rich and full-bodied wine, creamy as can be, with velvety, sweet tannins, milk chocolate and coffee bean notes, ripe red- and blackberry flavors and a long, balanced, smooth finish. Drink now through 2005.–P.M. • $20 • (11/15/1998) • **92**
St.-Joseph Les Coteaux 1997: Round in the mouth, with shy aromas and a silky midpalate, this medium-intense red has decent berry character, but lacks a bit of lively freshness to lift the aromas. Drink now through 2001.–P.M. • $28 • (10/31/1999) • **84**
St.-Joseph Les Coteaux 1996: Big, muscular, delicious. A bit rustic, but intense and sparkling with vibrancy, showing cassis bush, dried herbs, black olive and raspberry flavors. Medium- to full-bodied. Drinkable now with food. Drink through 2005.–P.M. • $20 • (11/15/1998) • **87**
St.-Joseph Les Coteaux 1995: Fresh and vibrant, with sweet raspberry and black cherry flavors, but a bit herbal on the hard finish.–P.M. • $20 • (11/15/1998) • **76**

DURAND, NOEL & JOEL

Cornas 1994 • $20 • (10/15/1997) • **91**
St.-Joseph Les Côteaux 1994 • $15 • (10/15/1997) • **93**

DURBAN, DOMAINE DE

Muscat de Beaumes-de-Venise 1993 • $18 • (10/31/1995) • **85**

DURDILLY, PIERRE & PAUL

Beaujolais Les Grandes Coasses 1998: Light and refreshing, this supple red offers bright cherry and light smoke flavors, with little tannin and perky acidity. Best chilled. Drink now.–T.M. • $11 • (11/15/1999) • **81**
Beaujolais Les Grandes Coasses 1996 • $10 • (6/30/1997) • **81**
Beaujolais Les Grandes Coasses 1990 • $7 • (9/30/1991) • **74**
Beaujolais Nouveau Les Grandes Coasses 1999: This generous red shows rich flavors of plum and chocolate, with broad, soft tannins and low acidity. A bit clumsy, but very ripe. Drink now.–T.M. • $8 • (1/01/2000) • **83**

DURFORT-VIVENS, CHATEAU

Margaux 1993 • $23 • (1/31/1996) • **84**
Margaux 1991 • $20 • (3/31/1994) • **83**
Margaux 1990 • $22 • (3/31/1993) • **88**
Margaux 1989 • $28 • (3/15/1992) • **92**
Margaux 1988 • $40 • (8/31/1991) • **73**
Margaux 1986 • $30 Ⓐ • (6/15/1989) • **90**
Margaux 1982: Elegant. Medium ruby-garnet color, with a light rim. Fresh berry, with a hint of cedar. Medium-bodied, with fine tannins and a fresh finish. (1982 Bordeaux horizontal tasting). Drink now.–J.S. • $29 Ⓐ • (11/30/1998) • **86**

DUVAL-LEROY

Brut Blanc de Blancs Champagne Chardonnay NV • $30 • (12/31/1991) • **88**
Brut Champagne NV • $NA • (12/31/1991) • **89**
Brut Champagne Elegance de Champagne NV: Generous fruit flavors and a broad, soothing texture make this easy to like and satisfying to drink. Well balanced, fresh-tasting and clean in character. Drink now. • $25 • (12/31/1998) • **87**
Brut Champagne Fleur de Champagne NV • $25 • (12/31/1991) • **87**

DUVAL-PRETROT

Brut Champagne Cuvée Edouard Prétrot 1994: A good, straightforward Champagne in a rather light style, offering crisp apple flavors, a soft, frothy mousse and a slightly sweet balance. • $40 • (12/31/1998) • **84**

ECARD, MAURICE

Savigny-lès-Beaune Aux Serpentières 1993 • $25 • (5/15/1996) • **93**
Savigny-lès-Beaune Aux Serpentières 1989 • $25 • (11/15/1991) • **88**
Savigny-lès-Beaune Aux Serpentières 1987 • $17 • (10/15/1989) • **80**
Savigny-lès-Beaune Les Jarrons 1997: Crisp and spicy, this red has character and a firm structure to carry the cherry, chocolate and vanilla flavors. Light-bodied, with a tart, tannic finish. Drink through 2004.–B.S. • $45 • (9/30/1999) • **84**
Savigny-lès-Beaune Les Narbantons 1997: Ripe and pure, with strawberry and cherry jam, this red borders on chocolate and has a soft, up-front appeal, though stiff tannins wait in the wings. Drink now through 2003.–B.S. • $45 • (9/30/1999) • **88**
Savigny-lès-Beaune Les Peuillets 1997: Pretty plum provides a satisfyingly ripe character, backed by a mint, floral and black cherry complexity. Supple and fruity, it's a good choice for early drinking. Drink now through 2003.–P.M. • $45 • (9/30/1999) • **88**
Savigny-lès-Beaune Les Peuillets 1989 • $25 • (11/15/1991) • **87**

Key: SS—Spectator Selection. CS—Cellar Selection. HR—Highly Recommended. $NA—Price not available. (BT)—Barrel tasting. Ⓐ—Auction Price.
For a key to the tasters' initials, see "How to Use These Listings."
Dates in parentheses represent the issues in which the ratings were published.

Savigny-lès-Beaune Les Serpentières 1997: Beautiful cherry flavors with touches of game, spice and vanilla mark this succulent, satisfying '97 red. Very forward and appealing. Chewy texture, with a lingering finish. Drink now through 2003.–B.S. • $45 • (9/30/1999) • **87**

ECU, DOMAINE DE L'

Muscadet de Sèvre et Maine Sur Lie 1997: A rather sharp, mineral edge gives this wine crisp focus, and there's just enough apple flavor to keep it generous. The balance seems a bit tenuous, though.–T.M. • $10 • (6/15/1999) • **78**

EGLISE, CHATEAU DU DOMAINE DE L'

Pomerol 1999: Lovely aromas of black licorice, berry and cherry. Medium-bodied, with fine tannins and a fresh fruit finish. Needs more fruit midpalate to be more than very good.–J.S. • $NA • (1/01/2000) (BT) • **85-89**

Pomerol 1998: Plenty of floral and crushed berry character. Medium- to full-bodied, with fine tannins and a medium finish. Very good indeed.–J.S. • $NA • (5/31/1999) (BT) • **85-89**

Pomerol 1997: A light and simple red with some plum character.–J.S. • $NA • (1/31/2000) • **79**

Pomerol 1996: Really watery, with some ripe berry and tobacco character, but the palate is just too diluted. Light-bodied, with medium tannins, a very short finish.–J.S. • $25 • (1/31/1999) • **76**

Pomerol 1995 • $21 • (1/31/1998) • **88**

Pomerol 1992 • $18 • (4/15/1995) • **80**

Pomerol 1991 • $18 • (3/31/1994) • **82**

Pomerol 1990 • $37 • (3/31/1993) • **87**

Pomerol 1989: Pretty, easy Pomerol. Good ruby-red color with a garnet edge. Medium-bodied, offering silky tannins and a fresh and easy aftertaste. Slightly diluted. (1989 Bordeaux horizontal tasting). Drink now.–J.S. • $NA • (5/31/1999) • **87**

Pomerol 1982: Not as good as I expected. Good, simple red, with autumnal flavors and berry, earth and cherry aromas. Brilliant ruby in color, with brick-red edges. Medium-bodied, with firm, slightly drying tannins and a chocolate and berry aftertaste. (1982 Bordeaux horizontal tasting). Drink now.–J.S. • $NA • (11/30/1998) • **84**

Pomerol 1961 • $NA • (4/30/1996) • **87**

EGLISE CLINET, CHATEAU L'

Pomerol 1999: Always outstanding. Wonderful floral and berry aromas follow through to medium- to full-bodied palate. Medium tannins. Long finish. Well-crafted.–J.S. • $NA • (1/01/2000) (BT) • **90-94**

Pomerol 1998: What can I say? Superb. This wine is concentrated, with a fabulous core of ripe berry, raspberry and earthy fruit, and full-bodied, with full, velvety tannins and a long, long finish. Greatest modern-age L'Eglise Clinet?–J.S. • $NA • (5/31/1999) (BT) • **95-99**

Pomerol 1997: Wine of the vintage in Bordeaux. Lovely dark ruby in color, emitting wonderful aromas of violets and berries with hints of raspberries. Full- to medium-bodied, with velvety tannins and a long, long, fruity finish. Really gorgeous. Best after 2002.–J.S. • $123 Ⓐ • (1/31/2000) CS • **91**

Pomerol 1996: A solid and steely Pomerol with impressive richness for the vintage. Plenty of blackberry and cherry aromas and flavors and a hint of earth. Full in body, with silky tannins and a caressing finish. (L'Eglise Clinet vertical tasting, as are all notes below from the 4/30/1999 issue). Best from 2001 through 2010.–J.S. • $98 Ⓐ • (4/30/1999) • **90**

Pomerol 1995: One of the greatest wines ever produced at this estate, but the bottle at this tasting was corked. Nonetheless, for the record, here is my note from a tasting in Bordeaux in early 1998: A big and decadent wine that beckons you to taste it. Fabulous. Opulent aromas of fruit, game and tobacco. Full-bodied and super-velvety, with a lengthy autumnal aftertaste. Best from 2002 through 2010.–J.S. • $150 Ⓐ • (4/30/1999) • **96**

Pomerol 1994: A very good glass of claret, if slightly one-dimensional and lacking elegance. Pretty aromas of earth, spice and raisins. Medium-bodied, with an earthy, fruity aftertaste. The alcohol shows a bit on the finish. Best after 2000.–J.S. • $57 Ⓐ • (4/30/1999) • **86**

Pomerol 1993: I have always been a fan of '93 Pomerols, and this is a good example of the vintage. It's sweet and silky, with lovely smoke and berry aromas and flavors. Medium-bodied, with fine tannins and a succulent aftertaste. Hard not to ask for another glass at the tasting. Drink now through 2006.–J.S. • $44 Ⓐ • (4/30/1999) • **90**

Pomerol 1992: Not a bad '92 but, like most of them, it's starting to break up a bit. Aromas of tobacco, berry and cherry follow through to the palate. Medium-bodied, with slightly hard tannins and a short, slightly dry finish. Drink now.–J.S. • $32 Ⓐ • (4/30/1999) • **84**

Pomerol 1991: Surprisingly fine for a '91 Pomerol. Pleasant aromas of ripe black cherry and green tobacco. Medium-bodied, with silky tannins and a fresh finish. Drink now.–J.S. • $NA • (4/30/1999) • **88**

Pomerol 1990: Wonderfully harmonious red with an abundance of blackberries, chocolate and spice on the nose and palate. Full-bodied, adding loads of velvety tannins and a long, fruity finish. Delicious now but will improve with age. Drink through 2015.–J.S. • $121 Ⓐ • (4/30/1999) • **94**

Pomerol 1989: Hedonistic and powerful, with masses of ripe fruit and exotic character. Aromas of violet, blackberry, cherry and grilled meat follow through to a full and velvety palate. Full-bodied, with very silky tannins and a long, long finish. Tons of tannins still, but balanced and well proportioned. A wine that can age for decades. Drink now through 2025.–J.S. • $93 Ⓐ • (4/30/1999) • **96**

Pomerol 1988: Slightly austere but it shows a lovely allspice and fruit character that draws you back to the glass. Medium- to full-bodied, with silky tannins and a long, racy finish. Drink now through 2008.–J.S. • $60 Ⓐ • (4/30/1999) • **89**

Pomerol 1987: A sleek and elegant wine, surprisingly delicious still, considering the weakness of the vintage. Medium-bodied, with fine tannins and a sweet fruit finish. Slightly annoying vegetal aftertaste. Drink now.–J.S. • $NA • (4/30/1999) • **86**

Pomerol 1986: Impressive concentration of fruit here, but slightly hard and foursquare. Intense aromas of berries and black olives. Very full-bodied and bruisingly tannic, a bit too tannic and hard to score outstanding. Drink now.–J.S. • $81 Ⓐ • (4/30/1999) • **89**

Pomerol 1985: Fabulous aromas of exotic fruits, chocolate, tobacco and earth. Full-bodied, with very velvety tannins and a long, rich fruit aftertaste. Could still use time to mellow, but it's a gorgeous glass of Pomerol. Drink through 2008–J.S. • $144 Ⓐ • (4/30/1999) • **94**

Pomerol 1983 • $19 • (3/16/1986) • **88**

Pomerol 1982 • $81 Ⓐ • (5/01/1985) • **92**

Pomerol 1961 • $30 • (4/30/1996) • **88**

Pomerol 1959: A gorgeous, mature wine with everything going for it. Aromas of cherry, mint, blackberry and flowers. Full-bodied and very ripe, featuring a raisiny undertone. Velvety and fruity on the finish, with an exotic aftertaste. Drink now.–J.S. • $NA/1.5 liter • (4/30/1999) • **97**

EGLY-OURIET

Brut Blanc de Noirs Champagne Cuvée Vieilles Vignes NV • $36 • (4/30/1998) • **80**

Brut Champagne Cuvée Spéciale NV • $40 • (4/30/1998) • **89**

Brut Champagne Tradition NV • $30 • (4/30/1998) • **89**

Brut Rosé Champagne NV • $35 • (4/30/1998) • **89**

Brut Rosé Champagne Grand Cru NV • $30 • (6/15/1993) • **87**

ELLNER, CHARLES

Brut Champagne 1990: Grand but not showy. Rich and generous in style, the bright fruit flavors blend with mellow, toasty, nutty nuances on a firm but smooth texture. Drink now through 2004. • $55 • (9/15/1999) • **89**

Brut Champagne Carte Blanche NV: Richly flavored and smooth-textured, this has ample pear, lemon and vanilla notes and a lingering finish. Drink now. • $24 • (9/15/1999) • **88**

Brut Champagne Carte d'Or NV: Rich and round, this smooth-textured brut has nicely mature aromas of honey and toasted almonds, backed by peach and citrus flavors. Lingering finish. Drink now. • $28 • (9/15/1999) • **89**

Brut Champagne Premier Cru Réserve NV: Engagingly rich. Layers of fruity, floral flavors on a smooth texture lead to a lingering finish. Drink now. • $36 • (9/15/1999) • **89**

Brut Champagne Réserve NV: A frank fruitiness and a soft texture make this easy to enjoy. Drink now. • $32 • (10/15/1999) • **85**

Brut Champagne Séduction 1993: Rich, mature flavors and an agreeably soft texture make this a pleasure to drink. Drink now. • $42 • (10/15/1999) • **89**

Brut Rosé Champagne NV: A big, assertive, dry rosé, with a deep amber color, ripe aromas, expansive flavors and firm acidity. Best with dinner, not before. Drink now through 2001. • $34 • (10/15/1999) • **89**

EMILIUS DE TRIMOULET

St.-Emilion 1996: A bit lean, but with good berry and nut aromas and flavors. Light- to medium-bodied, with firm tannins. Second wine of Château Trimoulet. Drink now.–J.S. • $27 • (7/31/1999) • **82**

ENCLOS, CHATEAU L'

Pomerol 1998: Has a good amount of cherry, berry and chocolate character, and is medium to full-bodied, with round tannins and a medium finish. Almost outstanding.–J.S. • $NA • (5/31/1999) (BT) • **85-89**

Pomerol 1997: Aromas of violets, berries, tobacco and spice. Medium-bodied, with light tannins and a fruity, herbal aftertaste. Drink now.–J.S. • $33 • (1/31/2000) • **83**

Pomerol 1996: Not overdone, and very pretty. Delicate berry and chocolate aromas. Medium-bodied, with silky tannins and a fresh finish. Silky and harmonious. Delicious. Drink now.–J.S. • $NA • (1/31/1999) • **87**

Pomerol 1995: Intense aromas of leather, berry and tobacco. Medium- to full-bodied, with velvety tannins and a delicious earthy aftertaste. Real wine. Best from 2001 through 2003.–J.S. • $40 • (9/15/1998) • **90**

Pomerol 1989 • $56 Ⓐ • (4/30/1992) • **82**

Pomerol 1988 • $20 • (3/15/1991) • **85**

Pomerol 1986 • $20 • (6/15/1989) • **92**

Pomerol 1984 • $20 • (3/31/1987) • **83**

Pomerol 1982: A well-made red. Good dark-ruby color, with a garnet edge. Fresh berry and cherry, with a hint of olive on the nose. Medium-bodied, with firm tannins and a youthful berry, dried cherry and dark chocolate finish. 1982 Bordeaux horizontal tasting). Drink now.–J.S. • $NA • (11/30/1998) • **88**

Pomerol 1945 • $529 Ⓐ • (3/16/1986) • **78**

ENCLOS DES ANGES, L'

Corbières 1995: Balanced and ready to drink, with red plum, berry and leather flavors. A good, hearty red for everyday drinking. Drink now through 2001.–K.M. • $10 • (8/31/1998) • **84**

Corbières White 1996: An assertive white, with aromas of hay and honey and interesting mineral flavors. Finishes on a lemony note. Drink now.–K.M. • $NA • (10/31/1998) • **83**

ENGEL

Gewürztraminer Alsace Réserve 1997: Nectarine, papaya and orange mark this slightly sweet, easygoing style, with balance relying as much on the touch of bitterness at the end as the mild acidity. Drink now.–B.S. • $10 • (10/31/1999) • **83**

Pinot Blanc Alsace Réserve 1998: Bright and juicy, this white offers peach and apple notes, with a hint of lemon. Rich in texture, everything is in proportion. Medium-bodied, with a refreshing finish. Drink now.–B.S. • $8 • (6/15/2000) • **85**

Pinot Blanc Alsace Réserve 1997: Rich, lush and noticeably sweet, this has appeal from the apple, honey and lemon notes, the latter creeping in at the end. Drink now.–B.S. • $8 • (10/15/1999) • **84**

Pinot Gris Alsace Réserve 1997: Very aromatic, offering red fruit, honey and a hint of chamomile on an open-knit framework that finishes quickly. Drink now.–B.S. • $10 • (10/31/1999) • **83**

Riesling Alsace Réserve 1997: A touch of sweetness marks this white, which lacks concentration and focus. Shows only a modicum of apple and peach flavors.–B.S. • $10 • (9/15/1999) • **78**

Tokay Pinot Gris Alsace Réserve 1998: Firm and elegant, offering floral aromas and citrus flavors backed by good acidity. Shows good concentration and a lingering finish. Drink now through 2001.–B.S. • $8 • (6/15/2000) • **85**

ENGEL, RENE

Clos Vougeot 1996: Lovely, well-made, medium-bodied Pinot, showing a sleek quality to the texture and ripe fruit aromatics. Tastes balanced, with pretty black cherry, spice, vanilla and blackberry character. Drink now through 2005.–P.M. • $72 Ⓐ • (7/31/1999) • **91**

Clos Vougeot 1995: Beautiful, in a *terroir*-driven traditional style. Reserved and deep on the nose, it kicks into high gear on the palate, offering layers of rich fruit and complex soil and earth character, with ripe flavors like plum as well as lovely mineral-laden notes. Medium-bodied. Drink through 2007.–P.M. • $67 • (8/31/1998) • **90**

Clos Vougeot 1992 • $NA • (12/15/1994) • **86**

Clos Vougeot 1989 • $66 • (11/15/1991) • **85**

Key: SS—Spectator Selection. CS—Cellar Selection. HR—Highly Recommended. $NA—Price not available. (BT)—Barrel tasting. Ⓐ—Auction Price.
For a key to the tasters' initials, see "How to Use These Listings."
Dates in parentheses represent the issues in which the ratings were published.

Clos Vougeot 1988 • $65 Ⓐ • (3/15/1991) • **91**

Clos Vougeot 1986 • $50 • (11/30/1988) • **81**

Clos Vougeot 1985 • $89 Ⓐ • (10/15/1987) • **85**

Clos Vougeot 1983 • $30 • (2/16/1986) • **80**

Echézeaux 1997: Maturing fast, with mushroom, wet forest floor and wet leaf aromas. Light- to medium-bodied, it turns crisp on the palate.–P.M. • $NA • (1/01/2000) • **72**

Echézeaux 1996: Intense and flavorful, medium-bodied and focused, with massive tannins balanced by ripe black fruit, there's plenty to admire here. But the tannins need time to smooth. Best from 2002 through 2005.–P.M. • $75 • (7/31/1999) • **90**

Echézeaux 1992 • $NA • (12/15/1994) • **83**

Echézeaux 1989 • $47 • (11/15/1991) • **89**

Echézeaux 1988 • $41 • (3/31/1991) • **92**

Echézeaux 1986 • $46 Ⓐ • (11/30/1988) • **78**

Echézeaux 1985 • $32 • (10/15/1987) • **90**

Grands Echézeaux 1997: An impressive, natural-tasting red, showing lots of ripe fruit married to toast, spice and intensity. Good, pure, clean freshness suggests precise winemaking from excellent raw material. Medium-bodied, with a long, lingering finish. Drink now through 2005.–P.M. • $NA • (1/01/2000) • **91**

Grands Echézeaux 1995: Sensational. Because of its dark color. Because of its seductive rose petal, violet, plummy aromas. Because of its nod to the earth, the soil, the mineral. Because, because, because.... Who will not love to drink this full-bodied red Burgundy? Well-made in a modern style, but not overly oaked. Very classy. Drink now through 2006.–P.M. • $73 • (8/31/1998) • **93**

Grands Echézeaux 1989 • $75 • (11/15/1991) • **90**

Grands Echézeaux 1986 • $50 • (11/30/1988) • **71**

Grands Echézeaux 1985 • $43 • (10/15/1987) • **86**

Vosne-Romanée 1997: Surprisingly intense and full of finesse, with rose petal aromas, this medium-bodied, sweet-tasting Pinot has interesting wet earth, iron, lead pencil, mineral and red and black fruit character. A chalky, chewy tannic backbone brings length to this red Burgundy. Needs time for the tannins to soften. Best from 2003 through 2010.–P.M. • $NA • (1/01/2000) • **90**

Vosne-Romanée 1992 • $NA • (12/15/1994) • **76**

Vosne-Romanée 1989 • $34 • (11/15/1991) • **85**

Vosne-Romanée 1988 • $30 • (7/15/1990) • **81**

Vosne-Romanée 1986 • $29 • (2/28/1989) • **75**

Vosne-Romanée 1985 • $24 • (10/15/1987) • **77**

Vosne-Romanée Les Brûlées 1997: Beautiful suppleness and gorgeous sweetness lie underneath the mineral and iron aromas. This *terroir* Pinot shows real grip in the flavor department but turns silky on the full-bodied palate. Elegant finish. Drink now through 2015.–P.M. • $NA • (1/01/2000) • **92**

Vosne-Romanée Les Brûlées 1996: Dark in color, succulently intense with pure, clean blackberry, violet and cassis notes, this tightens on the midpalate, with a crisp texture on the lingering finish. Drink now through 2004.–P.M. • $55 • (7/31/1999) • **90**

Vosne-Romanée Les Brûlees 1995: Racy and elegant, of medium body, with good red berry flavor, this is quite tannic and turns rather lean on the tough finish. Drink now through 2002.–P.M. • $35 • (8/31/1998) • **83**

Vosne-Romanée Les Brûlées 1989 • $35 • (11/15/1991) • **87**

Vosne-Romanée Les Brûlées 1988 • $45 • (2/28/1991) • **89**

Vosne-Romanée Les Brûlées 1986 • $32 • (10/31/1988) • **68**

Vosne-Romanée Les Brûlées 1985 • $28 • (10/15/1987) • **85**

Vosne-Romanée Les Brûlées 1983 • $22 • (3/16/1986) • **78**

ENTE, ARNAUD

Meursault 1997: Clean as a whistle, packed with gorgeous, ripe, rich, thick fruit. Set it aside and see it blossom as it deepens with age. Full-bodied and refined, hinting at honey, pear, apple tart and mirabelle plum. Best from 2002 through 2010.–P.M. • $42 • (9/30/1999) • **93**

Meursault La Goutte d'Or 1997: What a seducer of a wine. Intense but harmonious, this delicious white Burgundy tastes like a great pastry dessert, showing lemon, cream, pear, toasted oak and caramelized apple flavors, even while maintaining a racy acidity and mineral tones. Fat and long on the finish. Best from 2003 through 2012.–P.M. • $56 • (9/30/1999) HR • **94**

Puligny-Montrachet Les Referts 1997: Tastes floral and very ripe—even a bit too ripe for a Chardonnay—turning thick, with one-dimensional flavors that don't go very far, despite hints of pear and dried apricot. Drink now through 2005.–P.M. • $66 • (9/30/1999) • **86**

ENTRE NOUS

Vin de Pays d'Oc 1995 • $NA • (10/15/1997) • **81**

ENTREFAUX, DOMAINE DES

Crozes-Hermitage 1997: A straightforward red, with anise and black cherry flavors, offering spice, smoke and vanilla. Pleasant, smooth, slightly diluted and tart finish.–P.M. • $12 • (10/31/1999) • **79**

Crozes-Hermitage 1996: A lovely, delicate Crozes. Medium-bodied, showing floral, blackberry and cherry tomatolike flavors, with a subtle, grilled meat tone. Finishes a bit short, but it's delicious. Drink now through 2005.–P.M. • $10 • (11/15/1998) • **84**

EOLE, DOMAINE D'

Coteaux d'Aix-en-Provence Cuvée Tradition 1996: A fairly smooth red, with plum and berry notes and herbal flavors. Pepper notes linger on the finish. Drink now.–K.M. • $10 • (7/31/1999) • **82**

EPIRE, CHATEAU D'

Savennières Cuvée Spéciale 1997: This full-bodied white is almost oily in texture, with assertive peach and bitter almond flavors that linger on the finish. A big wine that builds its muscle without oak or sugar, it should age well. Drink now through 2005.–T.M. • $18 • (2/28/1999) • **87**

ERMITAGE, CHATEAU L'

Sauternes 1996: Delightful. Aromas of peaches, cream and spices follow through to a medium-bodied palate with medium sweetness and a round mouthfeel. Drink now.–J.S. • $24/375 ml. • (7/31/1999) • **87**

Sauternes 1995: Well-made little Sauternes. Delicate and spicy, with honey and almond aromas and flavors. Medium-bodied, medium sweet, with a clean, fresh aftertaste. Drink now through 2005.–J.S. • $24/375 ml. • (1/01/1999) • **86**

Sauternes 1994: Vivid honey, pear and cream, with hints of lemon, on the nose and palate. Medium-bodied, lightly sweet, with a creamy, lemony finish. Delicious aperitif-style Sauternes. Drink now.–J.S. • $NA/500 ml. • (1/01/1999) • **86**

Sauternes 1993: Golden, with a honey, grass, lemon and lime aroma. Medium-bodied, lightly sweet, with a slightly vegetal, honeyed finish. Hard to get too excited about. Drink now.–J.S. • $24/375 ml. • (1/01/1999) • **80**

Sauternes 1992: A ripe and delicious Sauternes in a lightly sweet style. Medium-bodied, with pineapple, honey and cream character and fresh acidity. Could complement fish or light meats in cream sauces. Drink now through 2004.–J.S. • $24/375 ml. • (1/01/1999) • **85**

ESMONIN, FREDERIC

Bourgogne Les Geneverières 1994 • $15 • (11/15/1996) • **79**
Gevrey-Chambertin Clos Prieur 1994 • $27 • (11/15/1996) • **77**
Gevrey-Chambertin Clos Prieur 1993 • $30 • (11/15/1995) • **86**

Gevrey-Chambertin Estournelles St.-Jacques 1997: This medium-bodied, rather crisp '97 red Burgundy has lovely, pure blackberry and black cherry aromas and flavors, with intriguing wet earth and spice. Best from 2002 through 2005.–P.M. • $38 • (9/30/1999) • **86**

Gevrey-Chambertin Estournelles St.-Jacques 1996: Light-bodied and straightforward, with some cherry and strawberry notes and light tannins.–P.M. • $30 • (9/30/1998) • **78**

Gevrey-Chambertin Estournelles St.-Jacques 1995 • $35 • (11/15/1997) • **76**
Gevrey-Chambertin Estournelles St.-Jacques 1993 • $40 • (11/15/1995) • **84**
Gevrey-Chambertin Estournelles St.-Jacques 1990 • $39 • (10/31/1992) • **84**
Gevrey-Chambertin Estournelles St.-Jacques 1989 • $42 • (3/31/1992) • **86**

Gevrey-Chambertin Lavaux St.-Jacques 1996: Elegant and polished, with pure, lovely blackberry, cassis and slightly smoky flavors, the fresh acidity mingles superbly with the ripe fruit and medium-toasted wood. A delicious, medium-bodied Pinot Noir. Drink now through 2003.–P.M. • $30 • (9/30/1998) • **87**

Gevrey-Chambertin Lavaux St.-Jacques 1990 • $39 • (10/31/1992) • **83**
Gevrey-Chambertin Lavaux St.-Jacques 1989 • $42 • (3/31/1992) • **88**
Gevrey-Chambertin Les Corbeaux 1990 • $39 • (10/31/1992) • **82**
Gevrey-Chambertin Les Corbeaux 1989 • $42 • (3/31/1992) • **88**
Griotte-Chambertin 1989 • $80 • (3/31/1992) • **92**
Mazis-Chambertin Hospices de Beaune Cuvée Madeleine Collignon 1995 • $85 • (11/15/1997) • **95**
Mazy-Chambertin 1990 • $71 • (10/31/1992) • **83**
Mazy-Chambertin 1989 • $80 • (3/31/1992) • **89**

Ruchottes-Chambertin 1996: Fresh berry character, with modest fruit and concentration. Drink now.–B.S. • $40 • (9/30/1998) • **84**

Ruchottes-Chambertin 1993 • $65 • (11/15/1995) • **90**
Ruchottes-Chambertin 1990 • $71 • (10/31/1992) • **86**
Ruchottes-Chambertin 1989 • $80 • (3/31/1992) • **91**

ESMONIN, MICHEL

Gevrey-Chambertin 1994 • $NA • (11/15/1996) • **80**
Gevrey-Chambertin 1993 • $29 • (11/15/1995) • **83**
Gevrey-Chambertin Estournelles St.-Jacques 1988 • $40 • (3/31/1991) • **84**
Gevrey-Chambertin Les Clos St.-Jacques 1994 • $NA • (11/15/1996) • **77**
Gevrey-Chambertin Les Clos St.-Jacques 1993 • $64 • (11/15/1995) • **89**
Gevrey-Chambertin Les Clos St.-Jacques 1987 • $44 • (3/31/1990) • **87**
Mazy-Chambertin 1991 • $48 • (8/31/1994) • **85**
Ruchottes-Chambertin 1991 • $48 • (8/31/1994) • **82**

ESPERANCE, CHATEAU L'

Bordeaux Supérieur 1994 • $10 • (6/30/1997) • **81**

ESPIERS, DOMAINE DES

Gigondas Cuvée Tradition 1996: A seductive red with loads of personality, bursting with black currant, wild raspberry, mocha, charcoal-grilled meat and blueberry aromas and flavors. Full-bodied, with sweet and ripe tannins and a fresh and vibrant finish. Drink now through 2005.–P.M. • $NA • (10/15/1998) • **89**

Gigondas Cuvée Tradition 1995: A wonderful, international-style Rhône. Seductive and bursting with oak-accented violet, blueberry, tar, currant, cassis, soya, coriander and other spices, all presented in a full-bodied, supple, velvety package that will delight you from start to finish. Delicious now, but could be cellared too. Drink now through 2005.–P.M. • $NA • (10/15/1998) • **92**

ESPIGOUETTE, DOMAINE DE L'

Côtes du Rhône Vieilles Vignes 1993 • $9 • (9/30/1995) • **88**
Côtes du Rhône-Villages Plan de Dieu 1993 • $10 • (11/15/1995) • **84**
Syrah Côtes du Rhône Vieilles Vignes 1993 • $10 • (11/15/1995) • **79**

ESPRIT DE CHEVALIER, L'

Pessac-Léognan 1997: A lovely, silky wine with medium body, plenty of chocolate, berry and mineral character and a long finish. Second label of Domaine de Chevalier. Drink now through 2002.–J.S. • $NA • (1/31/2000) • **86**

Pessac-Léognan 1996: Slightly one-dimensional, but shows good fruit concentration. Cool mineral and fruit aromas. Medium-bodied, with firm tannins and a fruity finish. Best after 2000.–J.S. • $NA • (1/31/1999) • **86**

Pessac-Léognan 1994 • $NA • (1/31/1997) • **80**

Pessac-Léognan White 1998: Medium-bodied, with lots of tightly wound fruit and a long finish. A well-made white that needs bottle age. Best after 2000. –J.S. • $NA • (2/29/2000) • **89**

Pessac-Léognan White 1997: A bit chalky and short, but with attractive lemon-lime and celery character throughout. Lively acidity. Drink now.–J.S. • $NA • (9/30/1999) • **83**

Pessac-Léognan White 1996: A bit obvious but well done. Medium-bodied, with lots of lemon, vanilla and appleskin character, lots of toasted coconut flavors and an apple finish. Drink now.–J.S. • $NA • (1/01/1999) • **86**

ESTERLIN

Brut Blanc de Blancs Champagne NV: A luxurious texture, mellow flavors and firm acidity give plenty of personality to this dry brut. A serious wine for the table. Drink now through 2001. • $32 • (10/15/1999) • **88**

Brut Champagne NV: Rich and mouthfilling, ripe and satisfying. What's not to like in this forward, fruity but nicely balanced Champagne? Drink now. • $30 • (10/15/1999) • **90**

Brut Champagne 1990: Dry style of vintage Champagne, with toasty aromas and a fine bead. Has vibrant fruit at the core and good balance. Drink now through 2005. • $42 • (10/15/1999) • **88**

FRANCE

Brut Champagne Elzevia 2000 NV: Quite dry and lean in style, with crisp, appetizing fruit flavors and firm acidity. Hints of toast and hazelnut add complexity. Drink now through 2001. • $55 • (10/15/1999) • **86**

Brut Rosé Champagne NV: A serious, dry rosé with lots of character and mature flavors. Has a copper-amber color, nutty aromas, dried cherry flavors and a lingering finish. Drink now. • $38 • (10/15/1999) • **89**

ESTEVE, J.C.

Faugères Nuance 1998: A hearty and nicely honed red, with lots of grip and character. Quite peppery and fruity, with nice berry and smoke elements and a firm finish. Would go well with roasted chicken. Drink now through 2002.–K.M. • $10 • (6/15/2000) • **87**

Faugères Tonneaux 1998: Nicely crafted, with plenty of fairly rich, ripe flavors—dark plum, cassis and blueberry—along with a good supporting array of spicy and smoky notes. Drink now.–K.M. • $16 • (6/15/2000) • **87**

ESTOURNEL, MAITRE-D'

Bordeaux 1995 • $12 • (1/31/1998) • **78**
Bordeaux 1990 • $10 • (11/30/1992) • **81**
Bordeaux 1989 • $10 • (11/30/1992) • **76**
Bordeaux 1988 • $10 • (11/30/1992) • **81**

ESTREMIERES, DOMAINE DES

Côtes du Rhône 1996 • $NA • (10/15/1997) • **87**

ETANG DES COLOMBES, CHATEAU

Corbières 1991 • $8 • (3/15/1994) • **80**

Corbières Bicentenaire Vieilles Vignes 1995: A smooth and supple red wine, showing good concentration of lively red cherry, berry and spice flavors that linger with coffee and bittersweet chocolate notes on the finish. Balanced and delicious. Drink now.–K.M. • $12 • (10/31/1998) • **87**

Corbières Bicentenaire Vieilles Vignes 1994 • $12 • (1/01/1998) • **79**
Corbières Bicentenaire Vieilles Vignes 1993 • $11 • (5/15/1997) • **85**
Corbières Bicentenaire Vieilles Vignes 1991 • $10 • (3/15/1994) • **80**
Corbières Bois des Dames 1993 • $19 • (6/15/1997) • **87**
Corbières Tradition 1993 • $9 • (5/15/1997) • **85**

ETANG DU MOULIN

Minervois Réserve 1996 • $8 • (5/31/1998) • **87**

ETXEGARAYA, DOMAINE

Irouléguy 1998: A crisp and pure-tasting red, with focused berry, cherry and herb flavors that blend seamlessly and carry through to the finish. Drink now.–K.M. • $15 • (6/15/2000) • **86**

EUZIERE, CHATEAU L'

Coteaux du Languedoc Pic St.-Loup 1998: Broad and brooding, with plenty of sinew, this has chewy meat, baker's chocolate and ripe plum flavors as well as brick, earth and leather notes. Good medium density, with flavors that are well integrated with the firm tannins. Tempting now. Best from 2001 through 2005.–K.M. • $10 • (6/15/2000) • **88**

EVANGILE, CHATEAU L'

Pomerol 1999: Gorgeous. Wonderfully smoky, with tobacco, cherry and berry aromas. Full-bodied. Medium velvety tannins and a long, long finish. Not the '98, but supergood.–J.S. • $NA • (1/01/2000) (BT) • **90-94**

Pomerol 1998: Big and chewy, yet refined and classy—perhaps the classiest young Evangile I have touched to my lips. Full-bodied, with full, velvety tannins but a racy and powerful finish that goes on and on.–J.S. • $NA • (5/31/1999) (BT) • **95-99**

Key: SS—Spectator Selection. CS—Cellar Selection. HR—Highly Recommended. $NA—Price not available. (BT)—Barrel tasting. Ⓐ—Auction Price.
For a key to the tasters' initials, see "How to Use These Listings."
Dates in parentheses represent the issues in which the ratings were published.

Pomerol 1997: Really delicious. Complex aromas of plums, tobacco and coffee. Medium to full in body, with soft, medium tannins. Just a bit short. Drink now through 2003.–J.S. • $108 • (1/31/2000) • **89**

Pomerol 1996: Lovely chocolate, berry and strawberry aromas. Medium-bodied, with sweet fruit and fine tannins. Long, fruity finish. Delicious to taste; not for long-term aging but you've got to love it. Best after 2000.–J.S. • $68 Ⓐ • (1/31/1999) • **89**

Pomerol 1995: Well structured yet elegant and refined. Complex aromas of violets, berries and spice. Full-bodied and very velvety, with a smoke, berry and cherry aftertaste. Best from 2004 through 2009.–J.S. • $104 Ⓐ • (9/15/1998) • **94**

Pomerol 1993 • $42 Ⓐ • (1/31/1996) • **87**
Pomerol 1990 • $146 Ⓐ • (3/31/1993) • **92**

Pomerol 1989: Finely crafted traditional wine. Intense aromas of blackberry, cherry and tobacco. Full-bodied, with lots of tobacco and ripe fruit and velvety tannins. (1989 Bordeaux horizontal tasting). Best after 2001.–J.S. • $112 Ⓐ • (5/31/1999) • **92**

Pomerol 1988: Rather dusty, with earthy aromas and flavors. Medium-bodied, with ripe fruit and velvety tannins, but dry on the finish. This has always been rather disappointing. (1988 Bordeaux horizontal tasting). Drink now.–J.S. • $51 Ⓐ • (11/30/1998) • **85**

Pomerol 1986 • $65 Ⓐ • (9/15/1989) • **88**
Pomerol 1985 • $127 Ⓐ • (2/29/1988) • **92**
Pomerol 1984 • $75 • (2/15/1987) • **79**
Pomerol 1983 • $84 Ⓐ • (10/15/1994) • **92**

Pomerol 1982: I have never had a great bottle of this wine. Ink-colored, with an amber edge. Has gorgeous floral, berry and raspberry aromas, but turns slightly papery. Full-bodied and rich despite its dry finish. (1982 Bordeaux horizontal tasting). Drink now.–J.S. • $223 Ⓐ • (11/30/1998) • **86**

Pomerol 1981 • $52 • (10/15/1994) • **82**
Pomerol 1961 • $1,170 Ⓐ • (4/30/1996) • **83**
Pomerol 1947 • $2,070 Ⓐ • (5/31/1997) • **87**
Pomerol 1945 • $NA • (11/30/1995) • **87**

FABRE CORDIER, DOMAINE

Côtes de Provence Rosé Château de la Clapière 1997: There's a nice zip and freshness to this rosé, with pleasant fruit and berry flavors and dried cherry notes on the finish. Drink now.–K.M. • $9 • (12/31/1998) • **85**

Côtes de Provence Rosé Cuvée Victoria 1997: Fruity and pleasant, with strawberry and dried cherry flavors. Finishes with a note of nutmeg and a touch of richness. Drink now.–K.M. • $7 • (12/31/1998) • **82**

Côtes de Provence Rosé Domaine de l'Aumerade Cuvée Marie Christine 1997: Clean, balanced and fresh, with rich raspberry and spice flavors. An appealing rosé, with plenty of stuffing. Drink now.–K.M. • $8 • (12/31/1998) • **83**

Côtes de Provence Rosé Imperial Pradel 1997: A bit coarse, with berry and dried cherry flavors and a slightly sweet, fruity finish.–K.M. • $8 • (12/31/1998) • **79**

FABRE GASPARETS, CHATEAU

Corbières 1995: Red cherry and plum flavors finish on a slightly stewy note.–K.M. • $11 • (10/31/1998) • **78**

FAIVELEY, J.

Beaune Champs Pimont 1989 • $34 • (1/31/1992) • **90**
Beaune Champs Pimont 1985 • $36 • (3/15/1988) • **86**
Bourgogne 1995 • $13 • (11/15/1997) • **85**
Bourgogne 1990 • $11 • (12/15/1992) • **85**
Bourgogne 1989 • $12 • (1/31/1992) • **84**
Chambertin-Clos de Bèze 1993 • $82 Ⓐ • (5/15/1996) • **91**
Chambertin-Clos de Bèze 1992 • $92 • (12/15/1994) • **78**
Chambertin-Clos de Bèze 1991 • $89 • (1/31/1994) • **78**
Chambertin-Clos de Bèze 1990 • $144 Ⓐ • (12/15/1992) • **93**
Chambertin-Clos de Bèze 1989 • $69 Ⓐ • (1/31/1992) • **90**
Chambertin-Clos de Bèze 1987 • $70 • (3/31/1990) • **83**
Chambertin-Clos de Bèze 1986 • $66 • (7/15/1989) • **88**
Chambertin-Clos de Bèze 1985 • $176 Ⓐ • (3/15/1988) • **96**
Chambolle-Musigny 1989 • $34 • (1/31/1992) • **85**
Chambolle-Musigny 1985 • $45 • (5/15/1988) • **89**
Chambolle-Musigny 1981 • $24 • (5/01/1986) • **88**
Chambolle-Musigny La Combe d'Orveau 1995 • $61 • (11/15/1997) • **89**
Chambolle-Musigny La Combe d'Orveau 1992 • $56 • (12/15/1994) • **77**
Chambolle-Musigny Les Fuées 1992 • $56 • (12/15/1994) • **81**
Chambolle-Musigny Les Fuées 1991 • $49 • (1/31/1994) • **83**

Chambolle-Musigny Les Fuées 1990 • $50 • (12/15/1992) • **89**
Charmes-Chambertin 1992 • $74 • (12/15/1994) • **83**
Charmes-Chambertin 1991 • $75 • (1/31/1994) • **92**
Clos de la Roche 1995 • $93 • (11/15/1997) • **90**
Clos de la Roche 1986 • $55 • (7/15/1989) • **82**
Clos de la Roche 1985 • $106 Ⓐ • (3/15/1988) • **78**
Clos de Vougeot 1992 • $92 Ⓐ • (12/15/1994) • **74**
Clos de Vougeot 1991 • $63 • (1/31/1994) • **86**
Clos de Vougeot 1990 • $82 • (12/15/1992) • **92**
Clos de Vougeot 1989 • $78 • (1/31/1992) • **85**
Corton Clos des Cortons 1995: Thick, rich and yet so elegant—this is gorgeous red Burgundy. Inky-black in color, concentrated, packing in fruit, fine tannins and acidity, it bursts with complexity, showing violet, plum, soya, currant, clove and spice character. Full-bodied, will improve with cellaring. Drink through 2010.–P.M. • $93 • (8/31/1998) CS • **94**
Corton Clos des Cortons 1992 • $62 • (12/15/1994) • **85**
Corton Clos des Cortons 1991 • $63 • (1/31/1994) • **83**
Corton Clos des Cortons 1990 • $133 Ⓐ • (12/15/1992) • **90**
Corton Clos des Cortons 1989 • $68 • (1/31/1992) • **91**
Corton Clos des Cortons 1988 • $70 Ⓐ • (3/31/1991) • **90**
Corton Clos des Cortons 1987 • $50 • (3/31/1990) • **92**
Corton Clos des Cortons 1985 • $100 • (3/15/1988) • **79**
Echézeaux 1993 • $56 • (5/15/1996) • **91**
Echézeaux 1991 • $68 • (1/31/1994) • **77**
Echézeaux 1990 • $82 • (12/15/1992) • **91**
Echézeaux 1989 • $68 • (1/31/1992) • **89**
Echézeaux 1987 • $53 • (3/31/1990) • **80**
Echézeaux 1985 • $86 Ⓐ • (3/31/1988) • **89**
Fixin 1989 • $21 • (1/31/1992) • **85**
Gevrey-Chambertin 1989 • $34 • (1/31/1992) • **87**
Gevrey-Chambertin 1985 • $38 • (4/15/1988) • **90**
Gevrey-Chambertin Combe au Moine 1989 • $47 • (1/31/1992) • **87**
Gevrey-Chambertin Les Cazetiers 1996: Only in Burgundy. Game, toasted bread, smoke and lots of cassis—talk about an exotic Pinot; medium-bodied and dark in color, with a chewy texture and lots of succulent, ripe fruit on the zesty finish. Drink now.–P.M. • $50 • (7/31/1999) • **89**
Gevrey-Chambertin Les Cazetiers 1992 • $NA • (12/15/1994) • **80**
Gevrey-Chambertin Les Cazetiers 1991 • $33 • (1/31/1994) • **79**
Gevrey-Chambertin Les Cazetiers 1990 • $49 • (12/15/1992) • **89**
Gevrey-Chambertin Les Cazetiers 1989 • $47 • (1/31/1992) • **89**
Gevrey-Chambertin Les Cazetiers 1988 • $57 • (3/31/1991) • **89**
Gevrey-Chambertin Les Cazetiers 1985 • $53 • (3/31/1988) • **92**
Gevrey-Chambertin Les Marchais 1992 • $NA • (12/15/1994) • **85**
Gevrey-Chambertin Les Marchais 1990 • $45 • (12/15/1992) • **92**
Latricières-Chambertin 1992 • $70 • (12/15/1994) • **81**
Latricières-Chambertin 1991 • $69 • (1/31/1994) • **87**
Latricières-Chambertin 1989 • $81 • (1/31/1992) • **89**
Latricières-Chambertin 1985 • $77 • (3/15/1988) • **88**
Mazis-Chambertin 1995 • $97 • (11/15/1997) • **94**
Mazis-Chambertin 1991 • $52 Ⓐ • (1/31/1994) • **85**
Mazis-Chambertin 1990 • $89 • (12/15/1992) • **91**
Mazis-Chambertin 1989 • $79 • (1/31/1992) • **95**
Mazis-Chambertin 1985 • $196 Ⓐ • (3/15/1988) • **92**
Mercurey Clos des Myglands 1995 • $23 • (11/15/1997) • **84**
Mercurey Clos du Roy 1997: Rich and ripe, with a distinctive earthy, gamy animal and wet fur character. Supple midpalate, medium-bodied and delicious, with a lingering, chewy and satisfying finish. Drink now through 2005.–P.M. • $NA • (1/01/2000) • **88**
Mercurey Clos du Roy 1993 • $25 • (5/15/1996) • **84**
Mercurey Clos du Roy 1988 • $22 • (3/31/1991) • **84**
Mercurey Clos du Roy 1985 • $23 • (4/30/1988) • **81**
Mercurey Domaine de la Croix Jacquelet 1988 • $18 • (3/31/1991) • **81**
Mercurey La Framboisière 1997: Odd, with a sweat and wet socks aroma. A bit dry. Disappointing.–P.M. • $NA • (1/01/2000) • **70**
Morey-St.-Denis Clos des Ormes 1990 • $NA • (12/15/1992) • **92**
Morey-St.-Denis Clos des Ormes 1989 • $44 • (1/31/1992) • **88**
Nuits-St.-Georges 1990 • $36 • (12/15/1992) • **85**
Nuits-St.-Georges 1989 • $33 • (1/31/1992) • **83**
Nuits-St.-Georges 1985 • $40 • (3/15/1988) • **90**
Nuits-St.-Georges Aux Chaignots 1992 • $NA • (12/15/1994) • **76**
Nuits-St.-Georges Aux Chaignots 1990 • $48 • (12/15/1992) • **90**
Nuits-St.-Georges Aux Lavières 1992 • $NA • (12/15/1994) • **78**
Nuits-St.-Georges Clos de la Marechale 1995: Distinctive, for fans of *terroir*. Forget opulence, forget charm, forget even pleasure, this is a tough customer, as solid as rock, with kirsh, mint and cherry pit character. The wall of tannins shuts everything down, but it has great Burgundian character, with clean, pure fruit. An ager that needs time to show its stuff. Best from 2005 through 2015.–P.M. • $43 • (8/31/1998) • **89**
Nuits-St.-Georges Clos de la Maréchale 1992 • $NA • (12/15/1994) • **80**
Nuits-St.-Georges Clos de la Maréchale 1991 • $33 • (1/31/1994) • **78**
Nuits-St.-Georges Clos de la Maréchale 1990 • $73 Ⓐ • (11/30/1992) HR • **90**
Nuits-St.-Georges Clos de la Maréchale 1989 • $42 • (1/31/1992) • **85**
Nuits-St.-Georges Clos de la Maréchale 1988 • $46 Ⓐ • (3/15/1991) • **76**
Nuits-St.-Georges Clos de la Maréchale 1985 • $51 • (3/15/1988) • **85**
Nuits-St.-Georges Clos de la Maréchale 1982 • $20 • (5/01/1986) • **84**
Nuits-St.-Georges Les Damodes 1992 • $NA • (12/15/1994) • **80**
Nuits-St.-Georges Les Damodes 1990 • $45 • (12/15/1992) • **91**
Nuits-St.-Georges Les Damodes 1989 • $45 • (1/31/1992) • **90**
Nuits-St.-Georges Les Damodes 1988 • $52 • (3/31/1991) • **85**
Nuits-St.-Georges Les St.-Georges 1996: Very distinctive style. Gamy, earthy and toasty, this Hollywood-in-Burgundy Pinot has nice black fruit and, oddly, geranium character, with a round mouthfeel and a crisp finish. You'll love it or you'll hate it. Drink now.–P.M. • $60 • (7/31/1999) • **87**
Nuits-St.-Georges Les St.-Georges 1992 • $62 • (12/15/1994) • **77**
Nuits-St.-Georges Les St.-Georges 1991 • $62 • (1/31/1994) • **79**
Nuits-St.-Georges Les St.-Georges 1989 • $54 • (1/31/1992) • **92**
Nuits-St.-Georges Porrets St.-Georges 1993 • $43 • (5/15/1996) • **90**
Nuits-St.-Georges Porrets St.-Georges 1992 • $NA • (12/15/1994) • **79**
Nuits-St.-Georges Porrets St.-Georges 1991 • $37 • (1/31/1994) • **76**
Nuits-St.-Georges Porrets St.-Georges 1990 • $45 • (12/15/1992) • **90**
Nuits-St.-Georges Porrets St.-Georges 1989 • $42 • (1/31/1992) • **84**
Nuits-St.-Georges Porrets St.-Georges 1985 • $47 • (3/15/1988) • **76**
Pommard Les Chaponnières 1990 • $65 • (12/15/1992) • **90**
Pommard Les Chaponnières 1989 • $50 • (1/31/1992) • **90**
Rully Red 1986 • $18 • (6/15/1989) • **83**
Vosne-Romanée 1989 • $35 • (1/31/1992) • **88**

FAIZEAU, CHATEAU

Montagne-St.-Emilion Sélection Vieilles Vignes 1998: Plenty of dried cherry and mineral character. Full-bodied and well-structured wine, with good fruit and a stony finish. Almost outstanding.–J.S. • $NA • (5/31/1999) (BT) • **85-89**
Montagne-St.-Emilion Sélection Vieilles Vignes 1996: A vividly fruity red with a light and natural structure. Lovely aromas of strawberry, raspberry and plum. Medium-bodied, with light tannins and a fresh, fruity finish. Drink now.–J.S. • $14 • (1/31/1999) • **85**
Montagne-St.-Emilion Sélection Vieilles Vignes 1995 • $18 • (1/31/1998) • **90**
Montagne-St.-Emilion Sélection Vieilles Vignes 1994 • $15 • (1/31/1997) • **86**
Montagne-St.-Emilion Sélection Vieilles Vignes 1993 • $15 • (1/31/1996) • **84**
Montagne-St.-Emilion Sélection Vieilles Vignes 1992 • $NA • (4/15/1995) • **78**
Montagne-St.-Emilion Sélection Vieilles Vignes 1991 • $12 • (3/31/1994) • **80**
Montagne-St.-Emilion Sélection Vieilles Vignes 1989: Superfresh and youthful. Wow for this estate. Dark ruby-colored, almost purple. Bubbling-over raspberry, cherry and milk chocolate aromas. Full-bodied, with a lovely, thick fruit and tannic structure. Loads of blackberry and dark chocolate on the palate. (1989 Bordeaux horizontal tasting). Best after 2002.–J.S. • $NA • (5/31/1999) • **90**
Montagne-St.-Emilion Vieilles Vignes 1997: Aromas of raspberries, cherries and berries follow through to medium-bodied palate with a solid core of fruit and silky tannins. Drink now through 2003.–J.S. • $12 • (1/31/2000) • **86**
Montagne-St.-Emilion Vieilles Vignes 1990 • $15 • (3/31/1993) • **89**

FARAUD, MICHEL

Gigondas Domaine du Cayron 1997: A bit rustic, with mushroom, forest undergrowth and game character and a chewy finish.–P.M. • $20 • (10/31/1999) • **79**
Gigondas Domaine du Cayron 1996: Soft and rich, with supple tannins and decent plum, roasted meat and toast flavors, but it's a bit unbalanced on the astringent finish.–P.M. • $19 • (11/15/1998) • **78**
Gigondas Domaine du Cayron 1994 • $17 • (1/01/1998) • **88**
Gigondas Domaine du Cayron 1988 • $14 • (10/15/1991) • **89**
Gigondas Domaine du Cayron 1985 • $16 • (11/30/1988) • **93**

FARGUES, CHATEAU DE

Sauternes 1990 • $86 Ⓐ • (1/31/1997) • **94**
Sauternes 1988 • $67 Ⓐ • (4/15/1995) • **88**

FAUGERES, CHATEAU

St.-Emilion 1998: Slightly overdone. Blackberry and tar aromas. Full-bodied, chewy, with velvety tannins and a finish that melts away on the palate. Needs a bit more on the finish.–J.S. • $NA • (5/31/1999) (BT) • **85-89**

St.-Emilion 1997: A wonderfully deep nose of crushed berries, violets and mushrooms. Medium- to full-bodied, with polished tannins and a long finish. Well done.–J.S. • $18 • (1/31/2000) • **88**

St.-Emilion 1996: An elegant and delicate '96, with some pleasant berry and cherry aromas and flavors. Medium- to light-bodied, with light tannins and a fresh finish. Drink now.–J.S. • $16 • (1/31/1999) • **85**

FAURIE, BERNARD

Hermitage 1994 • $40 • (1/01/1998) • **92**
Hermitage 1991 • $30 • (5/31/1994) • **88**
Hermitage 1990 • $30 • (5/31/1994) • **89**
Hermitage Meal 1995 • $60 • (1/01/1998) • **93**

FAURIE-DE-SOUCHARD, CHATEAU

St.-Emilion 1982: Outstanding. Good color, dark red with a ruby center. Chocolate, strawberry and fruit aromas. Full-bodied, with solid fruit and tannin structure. Like chocolate mousse. Long aftertaste. (1982 Bordeaux horizontal tasting). Drink now.–J.S. • $NA • (11/30/1998) • **90**

FAURY, PHILIPPE

Condrieu 1997: Good intensity emerges in this rich, thick, full-bodied and flavorful white. Packed with floral, peach, lime and wet stone complexity, it's off-dry and graced by a long-simmering finish. Drink now through 2001.–P.M. • $32 • (8/31/1999) • **93**

St.-Joseph 1997: A big-mouthed, thick-textured red, showing pretty black fruit, black pepper, distinctive mocha and vanilla. Shows good balance on the juicy, crisp finish. Drink now through 2002.–P.M. • $20 • (10/31/1999) • **87**

St.-Joseph White 1997: Rich, but made in a dry style. Very big and ripe, and slightly hot and alcoholic on the finish. Drink now.–P.M. • $20 • (8/31/1999) • **81**

St.-Joseph White 1996: Overly rustic and slightly corky, with a bitter aftertaste. Not recommended. Tasted twice, with consistent notes.–P.M. • $17 • (11/15/1998) • **69**

FAUTERIE, DOMAINE DE

Cornas 1995 • $23 • (10/15/1997) • **83**
Cornas 1994 • $24 • (12/15/1996) • **88**
Cornas 1993 • $23 • (12/15/1996) • **84**
Cornas 1991 • $NA • (5/31/1994) • **84**
St.-Joseph 1995 • $14 • (10/15/1997) • **83**
St.-Joseph 1994 • $17 • (12/15/1996) • **85**
St.-Joseph 1991 • $17 • (4/15/1993) • **82**
St.-Joseph 1990 • $13 • (8/31/1992) • **80**

FAUX FROG, LE

Chardonnay Vin de Pays d'Oc 1996 • $8 • (5/31/1998) • **77**
Merlot Vin de Pays d'Oc 1996 • $8 • (5/31/1998) • **80**

FAVRAY, CHATEAU DE

Pouilly-Fumé 1997: Light and clean. Lemon, lime and light grass flavors keep this focused and refreshing. A bit tart on its own, it would marry nicely with lighter fish dishes. Drink now.–T.M. • $23 • (6/30/1999) • **83**

Pouilly-Fumé 1996 • $20 • (5/31/1998) • **85**

FAVREAU, YANNICK

Pomerol 1993 • $NA • (2/29/1996) • **86**

Key: SS—Spectator Selection. CS—Cellar Selection. HR—Highly Recommended. $NA—Price not available. (BT)—Barrel tasting. (A)—Auction Price. For a key to the tasters' initials, see "How to Use These Listings."
Dates in parentheses represent the issues in which the ratings were published.

FENOUILLET, DOMAINE DE

Côtes du Rhône-Villages Beaumes-de-Venise 1995 • $13 • (10/15/1997) • **71**
Côtes du Rhône-Villages Beaumes-de-Venise 1994 • $13 • (10/15/1997) • **72**
Côtes du Ventoux 1995 • $10 • (10/15/1997) • **76**
Côtes du Ventoux White 1996 • $10 • (10/15/1997) • **81**
Muscat de Beaumes-de-Venise 1995 • $23 • (10/15/1996) • **86**
Muscat de Beaumes-de-Venise 1996 • $17 • (10/15/1997) • **83**

FERE, CHARLES DE

Brut Blanc de Blancs France Cuvée Jean-Louis NV: A firm-textured, lively sparkling wine with very modest fruit flavors. Drink now. • $9 • (10/15/1999) • **84**

Brut Blanc de Blancs France Réserve NV: This French sparkler from white grapes is smooth and subtle in style, displaying good richness and nice fruit flavors that linger on the finish. A fine value. Drink now. • $10 • (10/15/1999) • **85**

Brut Chardonnay France Tradition NV: Good enough to be from Champagne, and an excellent value, this is an elegant but flavorful bubbly that's fresh and clean in character. Drink now. • $12 • (10/15/1999) • **86**

FERME ST.-MARTIN, DOMAINE DE LA

Côtes du Rhône-Villages Beaumes de Venise Cuvée Princesse 1995 • $NA • (10/15/1997) • **70**

FERRAND, CHATEAU

Bordeaux 1995 • $7 • (4/30/1997) • **79**

FERRANDE, CHATEAU

Graves 1996: Rather light and watery, with some pleasant strawberry aromas and flavors. Medium- to light-bodied, with light tannins and a short finish.–J.S. • $15 • (1/31/1999) • **79**

Graves 1995 • $12 • (1/31/1998) • **90**

Graves 1989: Completely ready to drink. Color is medium-red and an amber edge. Tobacco, earth, ripe fruit character. Medium-bodied, with a silky finish. (1989 Bordeaux horizontal tasting).–J.S. • $NA • (5/31/1999) • **81**

Graves White 1997: A bit clumsy, with grass and lime character. Medium-bodied, with a light finish. Hard to get excited about. Drink now.–J.S. • $15 • (9/30/1999) • **80**

Graves White 1996: A modern and delicious wine. Lovely and subtle aromas of lemon, mango and apple, with a hint of oak. Full- to medium-bodied, harmonious, with fresh acidity yet a silky texture. Slightly simple finish. Drink now.–J.S. • $14 • (3/31/1999) • **86**

FERRATON, MICHEL

Crozes-Hermitage La Matinière 1997: Light and simple, light in color, showing a slight tartness, with modest fruit. Not imported into the U.S.–P.M. • $NA • (12/15/1999) • **76**

Crozes-Hermitage La Matinière 1995 • $18 • (10/15/1997) • **76**
Crozes-Hermitage La Matinière 1994 • $18 • (11/30/1996) • **87**
Crozes-Hermitage La Matinière 1990 • $16 • (4/15/1993) • **89**
Crozes-Hermitage La Matinière 1988 • $14 • (6/30/1990) • **85**

Crozes-Hermitage White La Matinière 1998: A straightforward white, with an empty middle, modest fruit and a dry finish. Not imported into the U.S.–P.M. • $NA • (12/15/1999) • **78**

Ermitage Le Méal 1998: Tastes a tad stemmy, but has good flavors, with decent fruit. Dark and medium-bodied, but the tannins are a bit dry. Not imported into the U.S. Drink now through 2005.–P.M. • $NA • (1/01/2000) • **80**

Ermitage Les Dionnières 1998: Has a firm structure, with massive but refined tannins. Offers red berry, grilled tomato, dried herb and wood accents. Lacks a bit of opulence and ripeness, turning a bit dry on the finish. Not imported into the U.S. Drink now through 2005.–P.M. • $NA • (1/01/2000) • **83**

Hermitage Les Miaux 1997: A '97 that shows real Syrah character. Dark and richly textured but of medium body, it offers loads of ripe fruit, tonic black pepper spiciness, wet earth, game and leather complexity. Smooth tannins and good fresh acidity on the balanced, long finish. Not imported into the U.S. Drink now through 2005.–P.M. • $NA • (11/30/1999) • **91**

Hermitage Les Miaux 1995: Herbal and gamy aromas and flavors give this chunky red a slightly rustic note and distract from the ripe plum and black-

FRANCE

berry flavors. It's rich, with good concentration in a thick, traditional style. Drink through 2005.–T.M. • $37 • (11/15/1998) • **87**

Hermitage Les Miaux 1994 • $38 • (11/30/1996) • **87**

Hermitage Les Miaux 1990 • $33 • (5/31/1994) • **86**

Hermitage White Les Miaux 1997: Medium in body and intensity, showing a drying character as the almond and wet hay mingle with a touch of honey and ripe pear. Not imported into the U.S. Drink now through 2002.–P.M. • $NA • (11/30/1999) • **85**

St.-Joseph La Source 1997: Straightforward, with cherry character. Medium-bodied in an angular style. Lacks a bit of ripe fruit. Tough finish. Not imported into the U.S.–P.M. • $NA • (12/15/1999) • **78**

St.-Joseph White La Source 1997: Clean and fruity, light to medium in body. A bit reserved aromatically, very smooth and nicely endowed with pear, white peach and flat-leaf parsley character that plays nicely into the sufficiently fresh finish. Not imported into the U.S. Drink now.–P.M. • $NA • (12/15/1999) • **81**

FERRAUD & FILS, PIERRE

Beaujolais-Villages 1996: This very ripe red shows good concentration for the appellation, and it's holding up well. Dried cherry, raisin and spice flavors are backed by ripe, firm tannins. Drink now.–T.M. • $12 • (8/31/1998) • **84**

Brouilly Domaine Rolland 1996: Quite rich for a Brouilly, this is firm and ripe, with cherry, licorice and light game flavors. It's balanced, with the structure to stand up to food. Drink now.–T.M. • $18 • (8/31/1998) • **84**

Brouilly Domaine Rolland 1992 • $12 • (6/30/1994) • **76**

Chénas Côte Remont 1996: Disjointed with candied fruit and earth flavors and bitter, dry tannins. May soften with food. Past its prime.–T.M. • $17 • (8/31/1998) • **74**

Chénas Côte Remont 1992 • $12 • (6/30/1994) • **83**

Chiroubles Domaine de La Chapelle des Bois 1996: This light, fresh red shows strawberry and spice flavors typical of Chiroubles, with just enough tannin for grip and a pleasantly spicy finish. Drink now.–T.M. • $17 • (8/31/1998) • **85**

Côte de Brouilly Domaine Rolland 1992 • $12 • (6/30/1994) • **80**

Fleurie Domaine du Clos des Garands 1996: Some concentration, but it's lean and sharp, with dried cherry and cranberry flavors and dry tannins. Drink now.–T.M. • $20 • (8/31/1998) • **77**

Fleurie Domaine du Clos des Garands 1992 • $14 • (6/30/1994) • **80**

Juliénas Château d'Envaux 1997: Cherry and herbal flavors are a bit diluted, but the wine is still fresh and lively. Best now, as an aperitif.–T.M. • $17 • (8/31/1998) • **80**

Mâcon-Fuissé 1996 • $9 • (8/31/1997) • **75**

Mâcon-Villages 1997: Sour and bitter, a tart wine with a grassy, herbal character. Short finish.–P.M. • $16 • (5/31/1999) • **70**

Mâcon-Villages 1996 • $9 • (8/31/1997) • **84**

Mâcon-Villages 1995 • $NA • (8/31/1996) • **80**

Morgon Domaine de l'Evêque 1997: Bright cherry flavors—leaning toward kirsch and pie—are vivid and ripe in this solid red, backed by firm tannins. Fresh, fruity and rich.–T.M. • $18 • (8/31/1998) • **86**

Morgon Domaine de l'Eveque 1988 • $16 • (5/31/1989) • **89**

Moulin-à-Vent Domaine des Héritiers Fontaine 1996: Ripe and firm, this round red offers plum and light chocolate flavors, with a thick, soft texture. It's pleasant. Drink now.–T.M. • $19 • (8/31/1998) • **82**

Pouilly-Fuissé La Chardonneraie 1997: Straightforward and fairly dull, with a slight cardboard aroma. Medium-bodied, offering only modest fruit and a crisp finish.–P.M. • $28 • (5/31/1999) • **74**

Pouilly-Fuissé La Chardonneraie 1995 • $16 • (5/31/1997) • **89**

Pouilly-Vinzelles 1997: Round in the mouth, with butterscotch, popcorn, toast nuances, showing polish on the lemon- and pear-flavored finish, with hints of honey and dried herbs. Drink now.–P.M. • $22 • (5/31/1999) • **84**

Régnié Cuvée Antoine Ferraud 1996: Still plenty of fresh cherry flavor in this firm red, and it's balanced and clean. It's not gaining with age, though. Drink now.–T.M. • $17 • (8/31/1998) • **83**

Régnié Cuvée Antoine Ferraud 1992 • $12 • (6/30/1994) • **75**

St.-Amour Château du Chapître 1992 • $12 • (6/30/1994) • **79**

St.-Véran 1997: Aromatically attractive, this smiling white presents subtle honey, floral, fruit character in a balanced, medium-bodied package. Tastes of ripe grapes. Drink now.–P.M. • $19 • (5/31/1999) • **84**

St-Véran 1995 • $NA • (8/31/1996) • **81**

FERRER RIBIERE, DOMAINE

Côtes du Roussillon 1996: Bright cherry and plum flavors are nicely focused in this fairly lively and intense red. Spicy notes chime on the finish, with chocolaty accents. Drink now through 2002.–K.M. • $10 • (11/30/1998) • **84**

Grenache Blanc Vin de Pays des Côtes Catalanes Empreinte du Temps 1996: A distinctive white, with floral aromas and flavors, and nice concentration. Balanced and firm, with a finish of capers and a hint of lime. Drink now.–K.M. • $13 • (11/15/1998) • **85**

FERRET, J.-A.

Pouilly-Fuissé Le Clos Cuvée Spéciale Tête de Cru 1997: Wonderfully ripe, rich and seductively thick without going over-the-top, this stays fresh, interesting and silky, with the wood reined in to allow the wet earth, pineapple and pie crust notes to coat the palate. Opulent finish. Drink now through 2003.–P.M. • $37 • (9/30/1999) • **92**

Pouilly-Fuissé Les Clos 1995 • $33 • (5/31/1998) • **89**

Pouilly-Fuissé Les Ménétrières Cuvée Spéciale Hors=Classe 1997: There's decent ripeness, and its medium body is satisfying. The butter, honey and green apple combination ends on a firm, vibrant finish. Drink now through 2005.–P.M. • $45 • (9/30/1999) • **86**

Pouilly-Fuissé Les Ménétrières 1995 • $41 • (5/31/1998) • **91**

Pouilly-Fuissé Les Moulins Cuvée Spéciale 1997: Oaked in a heavy-handed way, showing lots of toasted spice, floral and perfume character; a full-bodied package with an astringent aftertaste.–P.M. • $30 • (5/31/1999) • **74**

Pouilly-Fuissé Les Moulins 1996 • $25 • (5/31/1998) • **85**

Pouilly-Fuissé Les Perrières Cuvée Spéciale Tête de Cru 1997: Beautiful Chardonnay, ripe yet also fresh, delivering apricot, tropical and wet earth character. Full-bodied, it has a sense of elegance on the flavorful, medium-intense finish. Drink now through 2001.–P.M. • $37 • (9/30/1999) • **88**

Pouilly-Fuissé Les Perrières 1995 • $33 • (5/31/1998) • **82**

Pouilly-Fuissé Les Scélés Cuvée Spéciale 1997: Enchanting for its off-dry, full-bodied ripeness, it mingles harmoniously opulent texture, honey and well-integrated toasted oak, tropical and pear flavors in one of the most seductive Pouillys of the vintage. Bravissimo. Drink now through 2010.–P.M. • $29 • (5/31/1999) • **94**

Pouilly-Fuissé Les Scélés 1996 • $26 • (5/31/1998) • **91**

Pouilly-Fuissé Les Vernays 1997: Ripe and attractive, with honey, pear, melon and apricot aromas and flavors, this isn't an intense style of wine, but it should go over well as an aperitif or with light dishes. Drink now.–P.M. • $30 • (5/31/1999) • **84**

Pouilly-Fuissé Les Vernays 1996 • $26 • (5/31/1998) • **83**

Pouilly-Fuissé Tournant de Pouilly Cuvée Spéciale Cuvée Hors=Classe 1997: A crisp, unyielding, slightly greenish white, intense but in a herbal way, showing green apple flavors.–P.M. • $45 • (9/30/1999) • **77**

FERRIERE, CHATEAU

Margaux 1999: Well done. Dark ruby, with lots of dark cherry, coffee and tobacco character. Medium- to full-bodied, with well-integrated tannins but a slightly short finish.–J.S. • $NA • (1/01/2000) (BT) • **85-89**

Margaux 1998: Lots of tannin in this wine, but it's a bit austere. Medium-bodied. Berry, mineral character come through in the end, but a bit more fruit in the center palate would make it more impressive.–J.S. • $NA • (5/31/1999) (BT) • **85-89**

Margaux 1997: Gorgeous aromas of blackberries, cherries and Indian spices. Medium-bodied, with very polished tannins and a long, flavorful finish. A beauty for the vintage. Best after 2000.–J.S. • $21 • (1/31/2000) • **88**

Margaux 1996: Gorgeous to smell with its complex aromas of blackberries, raspberries and spices. Medium-bodied, with firm tannins and a medium, fruity aftertaste. Slightly diluted midpalate.–J.S. • $24 • (1/31/1999) • **87**

Margaux 1995 • $53 Ⓐ • (1/31/1998) • **94**

Margaux 1994 • $27 • (1/31/1997) • **85**

Margaux 1993 • $NA • (1/31/1996) • **87**

Margaux 1992 • $NA • (4/15/1995) • **81**

FERY-MEUNIER, MAISON

Corton-Charlemagne 1997: Very oaky. Plywood and sawdust from nose to finish. Too bad, because there's rich fruit.–P.M. • $NA • (9/30/1999) • **74**

Latricières-Chambertin 1997: Soft, with forest underbrush, truffle, tea leaf and strawberry character. Fairly elegant and smooth on the midpalate. Drink now through 2002.–P.M. • $NA • (9/30/1999) • **80**

Pernand-Vergelesses Premier Cru 1997: Fragrant, with a slightly cooked fruit character and moderate density. Turns tart and tannic on the finish.–B.S. • $NA • (9/30/1999) • **78**

Pommard 1997: A bit green, stemmy and diluted.–P.M. • $NA • (9/30/1999) • **75**

Pommard Les Epenots 1997: Very modern in style, heavily oaked and full of plum, vanilla and spice notes, with a smooth, rich texture and forward appeal. Almost lush, with light tannins. Drink through 2004.–B.S. • $NA • (9/30/1999) • **88**

Volnay 1997: Smells like cherry candy, followed by modest flavors of licorice and a slight mintiness. Simple and short.–B.S. • $NA • (9/30/1999) • **79**

FESLES, CHATEAU DE

Anjou Château de la Roulerie Les Maronis 1998: Plenty of ripe fruit in this firm, smooth red, with notes of plum, licorice and herbs. Firm tannins promise good development; the wine is clean and harmonious. Not imported into the U.S. Drink now through 2002.–T.M. • $NA • (1/01/1999) • **85**

Anjou Château de la Roulerie Les Maronis 1995 • $13 • (6/15/1997) • **85**

Anjou Vieilles Vignes 1998: This soft, round red offers light flavors of cherries and herbs, with light tannins. Has a nice roundness on the palate, but not much stuffing. Not imported into the U.S. Drink now.–T.M. • $NA • (1/01/1999) • **80**

Anjou Vieilles Vignes 1996 • $12 • (5/31/1998) • **83**

Anjou Vieilles Vignes 1995 • $13 • (6/15/1997) • **82**

Anjou White Château de la Roulerie Le Grand Clos 1997: Shows mineral, smoke, earth and almond notes on a round, soft but still lush frame. Try with pork or veal in a cream sauce. Not imported into the U.S. Drink now.–K.M. • $NA • (1/01/2000) • **85**

Bonnezeaux 1997: Concentration and balance mark this white, which is intense yet lively, sweet yet refreshing, with flavors of dried apple, vanilla, peach and honey that linger on the finish. Elegant and harmonious, it will continue to improve with age. Drink now through 2010.–T.M. • $60 • (6/30/1999) • **92**

Bonnezeaux Elisabeth H. 1997: (Auction wine). Made in a light, rather delicate style, this white offers good focus and balance, with clean, fresh flavors of apple, pear and vanilla. Sweet yet never cloying, with a long, refreshing finish that echoes lily and mango. Drink now through 2007.–T.M. • $NA/500 ml. • (6/30/1999) • **90**

Chardonnay Vin de Pays F de Fesles 1996 • $11 • (4/30/1998) • **74**

Coteaux du Layon-Chaume Château de la Roulerie 1992 • $25 • (6/15/1997) • **84**

Coteaux du Layon Château de la Roulerie Le Cerisier 1994 • $29 • (6/15/1997) • **82**

Coteaux du Layon-Chaume Château de la Roulerie Les Aunis 1997: Elegant and complex. This sweet white is rich and honeyed, with coconut and dried pineapple flavors, but it's also balanced, with citrus and spice notes that keep it interesting through the long finish. The lovely texture is dense yet suave. Not imported into the U.S. Drink now through 2005.–T.M. • $NA/500 ml. • (1/01/1999) • **91**

Rosé d'Anjou Le Jardin 1998: This exuberant quaffer offers an appealing mix of slightly sweet berry flavors and refreshing acidity. Not complex, but balanced, lively. Drink now.–T.M. • $8 • (6/30/1999) • **82**

FESSY, HENRY

Beaujolais-Villages Domaine de la Roche 1996: A more ambitious Beaujolais, with muscular tannins, ripe fruit flavors of plums and prunes and distinctive gamy, smoky accents. Doesn't fit the usual easy-drinking profile, but has real character.–T.M. • $7 • (8/31/1998) • **85**

Brouilly Cuvée du Plateau de Bel-Air 1996: A papery, light-bodied red, with slightly drying tannins. Some attractive spice and tobacco notes on the finish. Tasted twice, with consistent notes.–T.M. • $10 • (8/31/1998) • **73**

Mâcon-Villages 1997: Straightforward, offering a woodsy, tough character with modest fruit.–P.M. • $10 • (5/31/1999) • **79**

Mâcon-Villages St.-Maurice de Sathonnay 1996 • $9 • (2/28/1998) • **84**

Pouilly-Fuissé Cuvée Vigne Vierge 1997: Tastes a bit sickly of rose perfume and candies, but it's hard to fault the round, opulent mouthfeel of this ripe and oaky Pouilly.–P.M. • $24 • (5/31/1999) • **78**

Pouilly-Vinzelles Cuvée des Vergers Fleuris 1997: Emits odd smells of paint varnish, shows tart astringency on the finish.–P.M. • $18 • (5/31/1999) • **70**

St.-Véran 1997: Light and diluted, a simple, forgettable Chardonnay with modest fruit.–P.M. • $13 • (5/31/1999) • **74**

Vin de Pays de l'Ile de Beauté White Cuvée Moustache 1996: Slightly spicy aromas and flavors give this medium-bodied white a pleasant allure. Peachy flavors follow through from the midpalate to the finish. Made from Vermentino. Drink now.–K.M. • $6 • (12/31/1998) • **83**

FESSY, SYLVAIN

Fleurie La Roilette 1991 • $15 • (6/30/1994) • **82**

Morgon Cuvée André Gauthier 1991 • $15 • (6/30/1994) • **71**

Vosne-Romanée Maizières 1994 • $NA • (11/15/1996) • **83**

FEUILLATTE, NICOLAS

Brut Champagne Cuvée Palmes d'Or 1992: Delicious and easy drinking, with lots of complex flavor and a velvety mouthfeel. The pear, almond and vanilla notes have good depth, and the finish lingers. Drink now through 2001. • $110 • (10/15/1999) • **89**

Brut Champagne Cuvée Palmes d'Or 1990: A full-bodied Champagne that combines ripe fruit with a generous texture. Subtle vanilla and toast nuances linger on the finish. Drink now through 2001. • $110 • (12/31/1998) • **87**

Brut Champagne Premier Cru NV: A smooth, velvet-textured bubbly with ripe, focused flavors of pear and vanilla that linger on the finish. Drink now. • $30 • (10/15/1999) • **87**

Brut Champagne Premier Cru Cuvée Spéciale 1990: Bright, lively fruit aromas lead to more subtle flavors and an elegant texture in this wonderfully balanced '90. Drink now through 2003. • $55 • (9/15/1999) • **89**

Brut Champagne Premier Cru Réserve Particulière NV • $22 • (10/31/1996) SS • **89**

Brut Rosé Champagne NV • $27 • (11/30/1997) • **86**

Brut Rosé Champagne Premier Cru NV: Lots of fruit flavor in this dry, serious rosé. It has vibrant cherry notes accented by peach and cinnamon, and a lively, crisp texture. Drink now through 2001. • $35 • (10/15/1999) • **89**

Brut Rosé Champagne Premier Cru 1994: An appealing, refreshing rosé that is bright and lightly fruity in flavor, with a crisp, tangy texture. Drink now. • $30 • (11/30/1998) • **86**

FEVRE, WILLIAM

Chablis 1997: Clean on the nose, but perfumy on the palate, with some odd rosewater, bubble-gum stuff that makes it unpleasant.–P.M. • $15 • (5/31/1999) • **75**

Chablis 1996 • $NA • (8/31/1997) • **84**

Chablis 1995 • $NA • (8/31/1996) • **80**

Chablis Beauroy 1998: Racy and ripe. Medium-bodied, it powers its way forward, delivering layers of ripe fruit while remaining clean and fresh. Ends with citrus, honey and a mineral touch. Drink now through 2004.–P.M. • $37 • (5/15/2000) • **87**

Chablis Blanchot 1998: Distinctive butterscotch and caramel character masks the fruit a bit, but there's good balance overall. Full-bodied, with wonderful midpalate silkiness. Lacks the length to score outstanding. Not imported into the U.S. Drink now through 2005.–P.M. • $NA • (5/15/2000) • **88**

Chablis Bougros 1998: Appealingly fresh and ripe. Full-bodied, with a zesty personality, it delivers sweet-tasting fruit and salty crackerlike notes. Kicks in with firm acidity on a finish full of vitality. Drink now through 2004.–P.M. • $60 • (5/15/2000) • **87**

Chablis Côte de Léchet 1998: International-style Chablis that's smoky, toasty and oaky; balanced by some fairly ripe fruit, with spice, vanilla and butter. Has a smooth midpalate texture before turning chewy and slightly astringent on the woody-tasting finish. Drink now through 2005.–P.M. • $36 • (5/15/2000) • **85**

Chablis Fourchaume 1998: Ripe and rich. Tasty, zesty, vibrant and full-bodied, it's a bit tough in texture. Tastes slightly overoaked, showing citrus, honey and toast notes on the finish. Drink now through 2005.–P.M. • $45 • (5/15/2000) • **87**

Chablis Grenouilles 1998: Balanced and attractive. Slightly rustic but shows good ripe fruit. The sweetness on the palate is impressive in this medium-bodied, pure and clean Chablis. Turns a bit tough on the finish, but should smooth in time. Drink now through 2006.–P.M. • $73 • (5/15/2000) • **85**

Chablis Les Clos 1998: Tastes a bit disjointed now, with a slight rusticity, but it powers through the palate, delivering intense fruit flavors and mineral character. Full-bodied, it leaves a clean, pure path on the finish, proving it has concentration. Best from 2005 through 2012.–P.M. • $80 • (5/15/2000) • **91**

Chablis Les Clos 1997: Lean and crisp, showing so-so ripeness, there is decent fruit, spice and honey in this medium-bodied white, which should go well with shellfish. Drink now.–P.M. • $32 • (5/31/1999) • **84**

Chablis Les Clos 1996 • $34 • (5/31/1998) • **79**

Key: SS—Spectator Selection. CS—Cellar Selection. HR—Highly Recommended. $NA—Price not available. (BT)—Barrel tasting. (A)—Auction Price. For a key to the tasters' initials, see "How to Use These Listings." **Dates in parentheses represent the issues in which the ratings were published.**

FRANCE

Chablis Les Lys 1998: Frisky and breezy, made in a superfresh style. Medium-bodied, with good ripe fruit and an attractively supple mouthfeel. Turns chewy on the long finish. Not imported into the U.S. Drink now through 2004.–P.M. • $NA • (1/01/2000) • **86**

Chablis Les Preuses 1998: Full-bodied, oak-aged Chablis, showing mineral, wet stone and salty, shellfishlike aromas. Coats the palate and sails to a beautifully balanced finish. One negative: The fruit flavors are a bit muted. Drink now through 2007.–P.M. • $72 • (5/15/2000) • **87**

Chablis Mont de Milieu 1998: Zesty and lively, with nice vanilla, cream and pear flavors. Seems "little" but balloons to a bigger, fuller wine on the palate, finishing a bit heavy. Not imported into the U.S. Drink now through 2003.–P.M. • $NA • (1/01/2000) • **81**

Chablis Montée de Tonnerre 1998: Good but rather straightforward. A bit spritzy, with nice tropical, pear and grilled notes. A bit rustic on the finish. Drink now through 2001.–P.M. • $39 • (5/15/2000) • **81**

Chablis Montée de Tonnerre 1996 • $22 • (5/31/1998) • **92**

Chablis Montmains 1998: Distinctive buttery style, with a hint of butterscotch, folded into a smooth texture and nice citrusy backbone. Medium-bodied, with a vibrant finish. Drink now through 2004.–P.M. • $38 • (5/15/2000) • **86**

Chablis Vaillons 1998: Young, fresh and sweet-tasting. Medium- to full-bodied, this charmer has ripe pear, citrus and lots of honey. Delicious and uncomplicated, it's well worth the hunt. Not imported into the U.S. Drink now through 2003.–P.M. • $NA • (1/01/2000) • **87**

Chablis Vaillons 1997: A bit oaky, but with a lovely combination of lemon, fruit and spice. Good ripe fruit on the buttery, toasted and sweet-tasting finish. Drink now through 2006.–P.M. • $22 • (5/31/1999) • **85**

Chablis Valmur 1998: Class act. Beautiful *terroir* in this full-bodied, firm, structured and flavorful Chablis. Offers mineral, matchstick and smoke, moves on to ripe fruit, and finally delivers a deft dose of toastiness on the balanced finish. Tempting now, but will improve. Drink now through 2010.–P.M. • $69 • (5/15/2000) • **93**

Chablis Vaudésir 1998: A fresh wine with good ripe fruit. Medium-bodied, displaying some intensity as the pear, toasted bread, mineral notes kick in at midpalate and propel forward to a lingering finish. Drink now through 2005.–P.M. • $65 • (5/15/2000) • **88**

Chablis Vaudésir 1995 • $32 • (6/15/1997) • **86**

FEYTIT-CLINET, CHATEAU

Pomerol 1995: Why wait to drink this? Soft and easy, with chocolate, berry and cherry aromas and flavors, medium body and a delicate, silky finish. Drink now through 2003.–J.S. • $NA • (9/15/1998) • **85**

Pomerol 1985 • $30 • (4/30/1988) • **88**

Pomerol 1983 • $13 • (7/16/1986) • **70**

Pomerol 1982 • $15 • (3/16/1985) • **87**

FIEFS DE LAGRANGE, LES

St.-Julien 1996: A pretty wine. Interesting aromas of fruit and tea follow through to the palate. Medium-bodied, with fine tannins and a light, fruity aftertaste. Second label of St.-Julien's Château Lagrange. Drink now.–J.S. • $26 • (1/31/1999) • **84**

St.-Julien 1995 • $19 • (1/31/1998) • **88**

St.-Julien 1994 • $18 • (1/31/1997) • **81**

St.-Julien 1993 • $16 • (1/31/1996) • **85**

St.-Julien 1991 • $13 • (3/31/1994) • **79**

St.-Julien 1990 • $18 • (3/31/1993) • **88**

St.-Julien 1988 • $17 • (4/30/1991) • **92**

St.-Julien 1983 • $10 • (5/01/1986) • **85**

FIEUZAL, CHATEAU DE

Pessac-Léognan 1999: Fresh, floral aromas have hints of plum. Medium-bodied, with light tannins and a watery finish.–J.S. • $NA • (1/01/2000) (BT) • **75-79**

Pessac-Léognan 1998: Very tannic and mouthpuckering. Full-bodied and silky, with a fruity aftertaste. Needs a bit more fruit in the center palate to score outstanding.–J.S. • $NA • (5/31/1999) (BT) • **85-89**

Pessac-Léognan 1997: Lovely licorice, berry and cherry aromas. Medium-bodied, with fine tannins and a fruity finish. A pretty wine. Drink now through 2004.–J.S. • $32 • (1/31/2000) • **87**

Pessac-Léognan 1996: Tough, and tightly constructed. Plenty of crushed-berry character with hints of tobacco and mushroom. Medium-bodied, with firm tannins and a dark-chocolate aftertaste. Slightly dry on the finish from the masses of tannin. Best after 2002.–J.S. • $31 • (1/31/1999) • **88**

Pessac-Léognan 1995 • $35 Ⓐ • (1/31/1998) • **91**

Pessac-Léognan 1994 • $18 Ⓐ • (1/31/1997) • **87**

Pessac-Léognan 1993 • $25 • (1/31/1996) • **87**

Pessac-Léognan 1992 • $20 • (4/15/1995) • **82**

Pessac-Léognan 1991 • $14 • (3/31/1994) • **79**

Pessac-Léognan 1990 • $36 Ⓐ • (3/31/1993) • **92**

Pessac-Léognan 1989: Very earthy and barnyardy. Full-bodied, with soft tannins and a plummy, tomato aftertaste. A disappointment; this wine did not turn out as I had hoped. Tasted twice, with consistent notes. (1989 Bordeaux horizontal tasting). Drink now.–J.S. • $37 Ⓐ • (5/31/1999) • **84**

Pessac-Léognan 1988 • $29 Ⓐ • (4/30/1991) • **91**

Pessac-Léognan 1987 • $18 • (5/15/1990) • **81**

Pessac-Léognan 1986 • $35 Ⓐ • (6/30/1989) • **90**

Graves 1985 • $24 • (10/15/1994) • **90**

Graves 1983 • $25 • (10/15/1994) • **85**

Graves 1982: A very good yet rather one-dimensional wine. Dark brick-red in color, with a ruby center. Berry, stone and earth aromas. Medium- to full-bodied, with sharp tannins and a wet earth and tobacco aftertaste. (1982 Bordeaux horizontal tasting). Drink now.–J.S. • $NA • (11/30/1998) • **85**

Graves 1981 • $24 • (10/15/1994) • **88**

Graves 1979 • $NA • (10/15/1989) • **83**

Pessac-Léognan White 1998: A big and solid white, with lemon, lime, mineral and vanilla character. Full-bodied, with good acidity and a long, flavorful finish. Best after 2000.–J.S. • $33 • (2/29/2000) • **90**

Pessac-Léognan White 1996: Fun to smell, with intriguing aromas of lemon, lime, and honeysuckle, but offers less on the palate. Medium-bodied, with fresh acidity and a lemony, creamy aftertaste. Drink now.–J.S. • $31 Ⓐ • (3/31/1999) • **88**

Pessac-Léognan White 1995 • $30 • (4/30/1998) • **89**

FIGEAC, CHATEAU

St.-Emilion 1999: Rather rustic and overdone, with very roasted coffee, raisin and burnt fruit character. Medium-bodied, with medium tannins and a short finish. Almost metallic. Very odd. Tasted twice, with consistent notes.–J.S. • $NA • (1/01/2000) (BT) • **75-79**

St.-Emilion 1998: There's a superb, solid core of fruit in this wine. It's full-bodied yet refined, with a thick, velvety mouthfeel and a long, long finish. Wonderful texture.–J.S. • $NA • (5/31/1999) (BT) • **90-94**

St.-Emilion 1997: Delicious for early drinking. Loads of tobacco, perfume and plum character. Medium-bodied, with soft tannins and a long, ripe fruit finish. Drink now through 2003.–J.S. • $42 • (1/31/2000) • **88**

St.-Emilion 1996: A light '96, but offers some very pleasant berry and chocolate aromas and flavors. Medium- to light-bodied, with fresh fruit and a light finish. Best after 2000.–J.S. • $39 Ⓐ • (1/31/1999) • **85**

St.-Emilion 1995 • $57 Ⓐ • (1/31/1998) • **95**

St.-Emilion 1994 • $32 Ⓐ • (1/31/1997) • **88**

St.-Emilion 1993 • $21 Ⓐ • (1/31/1996) • **87**

St.-Emilion 1990 • $123 Ⓐ • (3/31/1993) • **92**

St.-Emilion 1989: A rich Figeac with lots of character. Chewy St.-Emilion, featuring green tobacco, dried cherry and fruit aromas. Full-bodied, with velvety tannins and a chocolate finish. (1989 Bordeaux horizontal tasting). –J.S. • $64 Ⓐ • (5/31/1999) • **91**

St.-Emilion 1988: This wine showed better when it was younger; today it's rather tart and lean. Nonetheless, it has pleasant berry and cherry character, with hints of leaves and chocolate. (1988 Bordeaux horizontal tasting). Drink now.–J.S. • $54 Ⓐ • (11/30/1998) • **84**

St.-Emilion 1987 • $35 • (10/31/1991) • **83**

St.-Emilion 1986 • $69 Ⓐ • (10/15/1994) • **84**

St.-Emilion 1985 • $67 Ⓐ • (10/15/1994) • **90**

St.-Emilion 1984 • $30 • (3/31/1987) • **83**

St.-Emilion 1983 • $58 Ⓐ • (10/15/1994) • **91**

St.-Emilion 1982: A big and velvety red. Dark garnet color, with a black center and an amber edge. Cherry, dark chocolate and earth. Full-bodied and very velvety, with tobacco, chocolate and berry flavors. Good tannin structure. (1982 Bordeaux horizontal tasting). Drink now.–J.S. • $132 Ⓐ • (11/30/1998) • **93**

St.-Emilion 1981 • $45 Ⓐ • (10/15/1994) • **87**

St.-Emilion 1980 • $30 • (5/01/1985) • **90**

St.-Emilion 1979 • $31 • (10/31/1991) • **88**

St.-Emilion 1978 • $34 • (10/31/1991) • **89**

St.-Emilion 1976 • $46 • (10/31/1991) • **87**

St.-Emilion 1975 • $22 Ⓐ • (10/31/1991) • **78**

St.-Emilion 1971 • $75 • (10/31/1991) • **84**

St.-Emilion 1970 • $NA • (10/31/1991) • **92**

St.-Emilion 1966 • $119 Ⓐ • (10/31/1991) • **85**

St.-Emilion 1964 • $204 Ⓐ • (10/31/1991) • **93**

St.-Emilion 1962 • $67 Ⓐ • (10/31/1991) • **85**
St.-Emilion 1961 • $204 Ⓐ • (4/30/1996) • **90**
St.-Emilion 1955 • $403 Ⓐ • (10/31/1991) • **96**
St.-Emilion 1953 • $178 Ⓐ • (10/31/1991) • **86**
St.-Emilion 1952 • $48 • (10/31/1991) • **85**
St.-Emilion 1950 • $220 • (10/31/1991) • **91**
St.-Emilion 1949 • $261 Ⓐ • (10/31/1991) • **99**
St.-Emilion 1947 • $661 Ⓐ • (7/31/1997) • **94**
St.-Emilion 1945 • $300 • (10/31/1991) • **96**
St.-Emilion 1943 • $150 • (10/31/1991) • **90**
St.-Emilion 1942 • $125 • (10/31/1991) • **85**
St.-Emilion 1939 • $125 • (10/31/1991) • **83**
St.-Emilion 1937 • $125 • (10/31/1991) • **69**
St.-Emilion 1934 • $160 • (10/31/1991) • **79**
St.-Emilion 1929 • $400 • (10/31/1991) • **98**
St.-Emilion 1926 • $300 • (10/31/1991) • **87**
St.-Emilion 1924 • $350/1.5 liter • (10/31/1991) • **88**
St.-Emilion 1911 • $400 • (10/31/1991) • **78**
St.-Emilion 1906 • $350/1.5 liter • (10/31/1991) • **78**
St.-Emilion 1905 • $430/1.5 liter • (10/31/1991) • **95**

FILHOT, CHATEAU

Sauternes 1998: Loads of spice, honey, syrup and apple aromas and flavors. Full-bodied, with a lovely balance and harmony.–J.S. • $NA • (1/01/1999) (BT) • **90-94**
Sauternes 1991 • $NA • (4/15/1995) • **80**
Sauternes 1990 • $29 • (4/15/1995) • **81**
Sauternes 1989 • $27 • (4/15/1995) • **85**
Sauternes 1988 • $26 Ⓐ • (4/15/1995) • **84**
Sauternes 1987 • $19 • (6/15/1990) • **68**
Sauternes 1986 • $36 Ⓐ • (12/31/1989) • **83**
Sauternes 1983 • $30 Ⓐ • (4/15/1995) • **87**
Sauternes 1980 • $11 • (5/01/1984) • **80**
Sauternes Crème de Tête 1990 • $NA • (4/15/1995) • **90**

FILIPPI, JEANNE PAULE

Chablis Champs Royaux 1996 • $17 • (5/31/1998) • **88**
Chablis Montée de Tonnerre 1996 • $25 • (5/31/1998) • **89**
Chablis Vaillons 1996 • $25 • (5/31/1998) • **89**

FILLIATREAU, L.

Saumur-Champigny La Grande Vignolle 1995 • $14 • (6/15/1997) • **85**
Saumur-Champigny La Grande Vignolle 1992 • $13 • (11/15/1994) • **84**

FINES ROCHES, CHATEAU DES

Châteauneuf-du-Pape 1996: Lots of spice and coffee, but slightly flat on the palate and simple in aroma. Full-bodied, but going nowhere.–P.M. • $22 • (9/30/1998) • **74**
Châteauneuf-du-Pape 1995 • $22 • (5/15/1998) • **88**
Châteauneuf-du-Pape 1994 • $20 • (11/15/1996) • **85**
Châteauneuf-du-Pape 1989 • $20 • (5/31/1992) • **81**
Châteauneuf-du-Pape 1986 • $14 • (9/30/1990) • **85**
Châteauneuf-du-Pape 1985 • $12 • (10/31/1987) • **80**
Châteauneuf-du-Pape 1984 • $12 • (9/30/1987) • **89**
Châteauneuf-du-Pape White 1996: Attractive, with an original combination of floral, lime, rose petal, toast and truffle aromas and flavors. Medium-bodied, fresh and very pure on the midpalate. Drink now.–P.M. • $22 • (9/30/1998) • **85**

FLAUGERGUES, CHATEAU DE

Coteaux du Languedoc La Méjanelle 1996: A hearty red, with plenty of muscle. Flavors of red plum, berry and pepper are backed up by fine tannins and leathery notes. Flavors linger on the finish. A firm style that will go well with roasted meats. Should gain with age. Drink now through 2002.–K.M. • $12 • (4/30/1999) • **87**
Coteaux du Languedoc La Méjanelle Cuvée Sélection 1996: Young and intense, delivering loads of flavor and plenty of character, this focused French red has a big core of red fruit flavors—plum, raspberry and currant—flanked by serious tannins and notes of leather and game. Finishes with pepper and cardamom accents; Syrah, Mourvèdre and Grenache. Best from 2001 through 2005.–K.M. • $9 • (4/30/1999) HR • **89**

FLEUR, CHATEAU LA

St.-Emilion 1998: Some pretty berry, chocolate character, with medium body and silky tannins, but slightly diluted on the finish.–J.S. • $NA • (5/31/1999) (BT) • **80-84**
St.-Emilion 1997: Some decent berry and mineral character. Medium-bodied, with medium tannins and a short finish. Drink now.–J.S. • $9 • (1/31/2000) • **84**
St.-Emilion 1995 • $18 • (1/31/1998) • **85**
St.-Emilion 1994 • $19 • (1/31/1997) • **82**
St.-Emilion 1993 • $17 • (1/31/1996) • **85**
St.-Emilion 1992 • $14 • (4/15/1995) • **77**
St.-Emilion 1990 • $22 • (3/31/1993) • **89**
St.-Emilion 1989 • $18 • (3/15/1992) • **84**
St.-Emilion 1986 • $14 • (2/15/1990) • **82**
St.-Emilion 1982: Gorgeous wine. Dark ruby-garnet color. Plenty of chocolate, berry and earth aromas. Rich, full-bodied, very velvety, with a long, ripe fruit and chocolate finish. (1982 Bordeaux horizontal tasting). Drink now.–J.S. • $NA • (11/30/1998) • **89**

FLEUR-CARDINALE, CHATEAU

St.-Emilion 1995 • $22 • (1/31/1998) • **87**
St.-Emilion 1994 • $20 • (1/31/1997) • **85**
St.-Emilion 1993 • $NA • (1/31/1996) • **84**

FLEUR DE BOUARD, LA

Lalande-de-Pomerol 1999: Beautiful plum, berry and orange peel aromas. Full-bodied, with lovely silky tannins and a medium finish. Very fine.–J.S. • $NA • (1/01/2000) (BT) • **988**

FLEUR DE GAY, CHATEAU LA

Pomerol 1999: Wonderful red licorice, berry and cherry character. Medium-bodied, with well-integrated tannins.–J.S. • $NA • (1/01/2000) (BT) • **988**
Pomerol 1998: Extremely plummy and soft, with lots of tannins and a round, caressing mouthfeel. Full-bodied. A slight cooked fruit character detracts in the end. May be better next year.–J.S. • $NA • (5/31/1999) (BT) • **85-89**
Pomerol 1997: A bit lean and disappointing, but some good berry, tobacco character. Medium- to light-bodied, with firm tannins, short finish. Drink now.–J.S. • $75 • (1/31/2000) • **82**
Pomerol 1996: Smoky, berry and tobacco aromas and flavors. Medium-bodied, with fine tannnins, but the diluted midpalate reduces the overall quality. Disappointing for this normally super wine. Drink now.–J.S. • $84 • (1/31/1999) • **83**
Pomerol 1995 • $67 Ⓐ • (1/31/1998) • **90**
Pomerol 1994 • $43 Ⓐ • (1/31/1997) • **88**
Pomerol 1993 • $34 Ⓐ • (1/31/1996) CS • **94**
Pomerol 1992 • $28 Ⓐ • (4/15/1995) • **85**
Pomerol 1991 • $37 Ⓐ • (3/31/1994) • **85**
Pomerol 1990 • $96 Ⓐ • (3/31/1993) • **95**
Pomerol 1989: A modern and enticingly young '89. Dark-ruby color. Bubbling-over blueberry, cherry and milk chocolate flavors. Full-bodied, with velvety tannins and a long and caressing finish. Very tannic. Needs time. (1989 Bordeaux horizontal tasting). Best after 2005.–J.S. • $116 Ⓐ • (5/31/1999) • **94**
Pomerol 1988: Massive, with loads of ripe fruit and polished tannins. Full-bodied, with exotic flavors of berry and raspberry highlighted by chocolate and vanilla. Still needs time to mellow, but it's a roller coaster of flavors across your palate. (1988 Bordeaux horizontal tasting). Best after 2005. –J.S. • $77 Ⓐ • (11/30/1998) • **97**
Pomerol 1986 • $94 Ⓐ • (10/31/1989) CS • **95**
Pomerol 1985 • $192 Ⓐ • (10/15/1994) • **92**
Pomerol 1983 • $50 Ⓐ • (10/15/1994) • **89**
Pomerol 1982 • $72 Ⓐ • (5/15/1989) • **88**

Key: SS—Spectator Selection. CS—Cellar Selection. HR—Highly Recommended. $NA—Price not available. (BT)—Barrel tasting. Ⓐ—Auction Price. For a key to the tasters' initials, see "How to Use These Listings." **Dates in parentheses represent the issues in which the ratings were published.**

FLEUR DU DOMAINE DES PINS, LA

Vin de Pays d'Oc Rosé 1997: Dried cherry and melon flavors dominate this modest rosé. Made from Grenache and Cinsault.–K.M. • $7 • (11/15/1998) • **77**

FLEUR GAZIN, CHATEAU LA

Pomerol 1999: Aromas of plums, ripe berries and tobacco follow through to a medium-bodied palate, with medium tannins and a light finish.–J.S. • $NA • (1/01/2000) (BT) • **85-89**

FLEUR LARTIGUE, CHATEAU

St.-Emilion 1995 • $20 • (1/31/1998) • **78**

FLEUR-PETRUS, CHATEAU LA

Pomerol 1999: Lots of pretty plum and wet earth character on the nose. Medium-bodied, with a good core of velvety tannins and a medium finish. A bit hollow at midpalate.–J.S. • $NA • (1/01/2000) (BT) • **85-89**

Pomerol 1998: Dark-colored, with floral, berry and stone character. Full-bodied, with wonderfully silky tannins and a long, long finish. Well-made young wine.–J.S. • $NA • (5/31/1999) (BT) • **90-94**

Pomerol 1997: A solid and well-made wine. Lovely blackberry, milk chocolate and cherry aromas. Medium-bodied, with chewy tannins and a long, fruity finish.–J.S. • $54 • (1/31/2000) • **89**

Pomerol 1996: Lovely chocolate and berry aromas, with hints of dried herbs. Medium-bodied, with well-integrated tannins and a long, silky aftertaste. Slightly diluted finish. Showed better from barrel. Drink now.–J.S. • $48 Ⓐ • (1/31/1999) • **86**

Pomerol 1995 • $69 Ⓐ • (1/31/1998) • **89**

Pomerol 1994 • $40 Ⓐ • (1/31/1997) • **88**

Pomerol 1993 • $29 Ⓐ • (1/31/1996) • **86**

Pomerol 1992 • $41 Ⓐ • (4/15/1995) • **84**

Pomerol 1990 • $98 Ⓐ • (3/31/1993) • **90**

Pomerol 1989: A juicy, succulent '89 offering lots of chocolate, black olive and plum character. Full-bodied, with velvety tannins and a long, caressing finish. Slightly one-dimensional but a joy to taste. (1989 Bordeaux horizontal tasting). Best after 2005.–J.S. • $90 Ⓐ • (5/31/1999) • **92**

Pomerol 1988: An outstanding beauty, with generous mineral, berry and earth aromas and flavors. Full-bodied, with round yet silky tannins and a long, caressing finish. (1988 Bordeaux horizontal tasting). Best after 2000.–J.S. • $56 Ⓐ • (11/30/1998) • **92**

Pomerol 1986 • $56 Ⓐ • (2/15/1990) CS • **93**

Pomerol 1985 • $50 • (10/15/1994) • **90**

Pomerol 1983 • $46 Ⓐ • (10/15/1994) • **86**

Pomerol 1982: A massive wine, traditional in style but amazing. Like a great '47. Inky in color, with an amber edge. Extremely ripe, with mineral, berry, cherry, meat and pepper. Big and burly, with full velvety tannins. Still needs time. (1982 Bordeaux horizontal tasting). Best after 2003.–J.S. • $152 Ⓐ • (11/30/1998) • **96**

Pomerol 1981 • $60 Ⓐ • (10/15/1994) • **86**

Pomerol 1961 • $432 Ⓐ • (4/30/1996) • **89**

Pomerol 1959 • $190 Ⓐ • (10/15/1990) • **92**

FLEUR-ST.-GEORGES, CHATEAU LA

Lalande-de-Pomerol 1997: A good, gentle Bordeaux, with light aromas of currant bush and green tobacco. Light- to medium-bodied, with fine tannins and a light, fruity aftertaste. Drink now.–J.S. • $30 • (7/31/1999) • **84**

Lalande-de-Pomerol 1995 • $20 • (1/31/1998) • **85**

Lalande-de-Pomerol 1994 • $18 • (1/31/1997) • **78**

Lalande-de-Pomerol 1990 • $NA • (3/31/1993) • **88**

FLEUROT, RENE

Montrachet 1995: Clean and pure, full-bodied, showing good concentration, with toasted oak, coconut, spice, and apple pie flavors. But new oak is still very present, along with a slight herbal element, and it turns bitter on the minty finish. Might turn racy and elegant around 2010.–P.M. • $NA • (8/31/1998) • **85**

FLEURY PERE & FILS

Brut Champagne NV: An elegant but flavorful brut, with silky texture and slightly sweet balance. Combines ripe apple and pear flavors with subtle vanilla and toast nuances. Drink now. • $45 • (9/15/1999) • **89**

Brut Champagne 1990: A grand Champagne that's bold in style and may need time to develop more nuances. Has very solid, focused fruit flavors of cherry and apple accented by hints of vanilla and almond that expand on the finish. Drink through 2004. • $38 • (12/15/1998) • **91**

Brut Champagne Fleur de l'Europe NV: A refreshing, fruity style, with lemon and green apple aromas, crisp citrus flavors and a light but smooth texture. • $53 • (9/15/1999) • **88**

Brut Rosé Champagne NV: Expansive flavors and a luxurious texture make this special. It's deep copper in color, with toasty-spicy aromas, mature fruit flavors and a lingering finish. Drink now through 2001. • $51 • (10/15/1999) • **90**

FOILLARD, JEAN

Morgon Côte du Py 1998: Appealing flavors of black cherry, cinnamon and smoke float through this light, slightly dry red. It has character, but lacks concentration. Drink now.–T.M. • $19 • (3/31/2000) • **85**

Morgon Côte du Py 1997: Rich and ripe, this well-structured red offers balance and depth. Though the fruit flavors are muted now, there's a core of plum and cherry that should emerge with time or food. Drink now through 2002.–T.M. • $23 • (12/31/1998) • **87**

Morgon Côte du Py 1995 • $23 • (9/15/1997) • **89**

Morgon Côte du Py 1994 • $19 • (9/15/1996) • **90**

FOLIE, DOMAINE DE LA

Rully Clos du Chaigne 1998: A delightful '98. Elegant yet ripe, with some smoke, mineral, ripe fruit character. Medium-bodied, it's attractively chalky on the vanilla-tasting finish. Drink now through 2002.–P.M. • $31 • (5/31/2000) • **85**

Rully Clos St.-Jacques 1998: Candied and a bit heavy, lacking the needed balance. The sweetness continues on the finish.–P.M. • $35 • (5/31/2000) • **73**

FOLLIN-ARBELET, FRANCK

Aloxe-Corton Clos du Chapitre 1995 • $NA • (11/15/1997) • **76**

Aloxe-Corton Les Vercots 1995 • $NA • (11/15/1997) • **70**

FOMBRAUGE, CHATEAU

St.-Emilion 1997: Likable meaty, spicy, berry character in this, but it's a bit lean, with firm tannins and a medium finish. Tasted twice, with consistent notes. Drink now through 2003.–J.S. • $26 • (1/31/2000) • **82**

St.-Emilion 1996: A real '96 St.-Emilion that isn't overdone. Aromas of game and berries. Medium-bodied, with chewy tannins and a simple, fruity finish. Drink now.–J.S. • $24 • (1/31/1999) • **86**

St.-Emilion 1995: Very ripe, verging on raisiny. Full-bodied, with full tannins and a long, slightly dry, tannic finish. Needs time to mellow. Impressive concentration. Slightly rustic. Best from 2003 through 2006.–J.S. • $28 • (9/15/1998) • **88**

St.-Emilion 1994 • $19 • (6/30/1997) • **84**

St.-Emilion 1990 • $20 • (2/28/1994) • **74**

St.-Emilion 1988 • $14 • (11/30/1992) • **85**

St.-Emilion 1986 • $19 • (6/30/1989) • **86**

St.-Emilion 1985 • $25 • (5/15/1988) • **87**

FONBADET, CHATEAU

Pauillac 1998: Very light and diluted, this has ripe fruit character and some tannins but it's disjointed.–J.S. • $NA • (5/31/1999) (BT) • **75-79**

Pauillac 1997: Shows some decent berry and strawberry character and a hint of earth. Drink now.–J.S. • $NA • (1/31/2000) • **81**

Pauillac 1996: Promises more on the nose than it gives on the palate, with subtle aromas of blackberries, plums and wet earth. Medium-bodied, with fine tannins but a slightly hollow palate. Best after 2000.–J.S. • $NA • (1/31/1999) • **83**

Pauillac 1995: Lots of ripe berry character with hints of mint. Full-bodied, velvety, with plenty of tannins and fruit. Slightly rustic but powerful. Needs time. Best from 2003 through 2008.–J.S. • $NA • (9/15/1998) • **89**

Pauillac 1988 • $16 • (8/31/1991) • **89**

■ ■ ■ ■

FONBADET, CHATEAU

Pauillac 1982 • $16 • (8/01/1985) • **86**

FONPLEGADE, CHATEAU

St.-Emilion 1997: Rather meager, with some berry and tobacco character. Light-bodied, light on the finish.–J.S. • $NA • (1/31/2000) • **79**
St.-Emilion 1996: Lots of cherry and berry character but in a delicate style. Light- to medium-bodied, with soft tannins and a light, fruity finish. Drink now.–J.S. • $26 • (1/31/1999) • **81**
St.-Emilion 1995 • $24 • (1/31/1998) • **88**
St.-Emilion 1992 • $16 • (4/15/1995) • **77**
St.-Emilion 1990 • $25 • (3/31/1993) • **90**
St.-Emilion 1988 • $18 • (6/30/1991) • **85**
St.-Emilion 1982 • $NA • (5/15/1989) • **77**
St.-Emilion 1961 • $NA • (4/30/1996) • **86**

FONREAUD, CHATEAU

Bordeaux White Le Cygne 1998: Lots of Sauvignon character in this white, with grapefruit and gooseberry. Medium-bodied, with good fruit and a long finish. Delicious. Drink now through 2004.–J.S. • $NA • (2/29/2000) • **86**
Bordeaux White Le Cygne 1997: Lovely apple, pear and lime character. Medium-bodied, with fresh acidity and a light grapefruit and tropical fruit aftertaste. Drink now.–J.S. • $NA • (9/30/1999) • **85**
Listrac 1998: A bit lean and simple. Medium-bodied, with slightly dry tannins and a medium finish.–J.S. • $NA • (5/31/1999) (BT) • **80-84**
Listrac 1997: Some decent berry and tobacco character, but slightly dry on the finish. A tad too much wood? Still, there's some good fruit. Drink now.–J.S. • $10 • (1/31/2000) • **81**
Listrac 1996: Some decent berry and grape character here, but it's somewhat lean and hard, with firm tannins and a hollow midpalate. Drink now.–J.S. • $NA • (1/31/1999) • **81**
Listrac 1995: A drink-me '95. Lovely floral and berry aromas. Medium-bodied, with fine tannins and a delicate fruit finish. Drink now.–J.S. • $NA • (9/15/1998) • **85**
Listrac 1992 • $15 • (4/15/1995) • **76**
Listrac 1990 • $16 • (3/31/1993) • **83**
Listrac 1988 • $15 • (4/30/1991) • **82**

FONROQUE, CHATEAU

St.-Emilion 1998: Black ink-colored, with intense blackberry and crushed grape character. Full-bodied, with lots of fruit and tannins, but just a hint of dilution on the finish.–J.S. • $NA • (5/31/1999) (BT) • **85-89**
St.-Emilion 1995: Subtle, well-crafted red. Aromas of raspberries with undertones of orange peel. Medium-bodied, with silky tannins and a caressing, fruity finish. Drink through 2004.–J.S. • $24 • (9/15/1998) • **88**
St.-Emilion 1993 • $19 • (1/31/1996) • **83**
St.-Emilion 1992 • $16 • (4/15/1995) • **78**
St.-Emilion 1990 • $28 • (3/31/1993) • **94**
St.-Emilion 1989 • $55 Ⓐ • (3/15/1992) • **88**
St.-Emilion 1982 • $24 Ⓐ • (8/31/1992) • **89**

FONSALADE

St.-Chinian 1995: Smooth and mature-tasting, with good flavors of cherry, smoke and spice. Medium-bodied and balanced, finishing with notes of brown sugar and tea. Drink now.–K.M. • $11 • (11/30/1998) • **84**

FONSALETTE, CHATEAU DE

Côtes du Rhône Réservé 1995: This chewy red offers vivid flavors of kirsch and chocolate, with impressive ripeness and concentration, but the aggressive tannins dominate the fruit, and the wine turns a bit rustic on the finish. Drink through 2001.–T.M. • $28 • (11/15/1998) • **84**
Côtes du Rhône Réservé 1994 • $25 • (10/15/1997) • **86**
Côtes du Rhône Réservé 1993 • $25 • (1/01/1998) • **88**
Côtes du Rhône Réservé 1992 • $30 • (9/30/1995) • **85**
Côtes du Rhône Réservé 1991 • $25 • (11/30/1994) • **87**

Key: SS—Spectator Selection. CS—Cellar Selection. HR—Highly Recommended. $NA—Price not available. (BT)—Barrel tasting. Ⓐ—Auction Price.
For a key to the tasters' initials, see "How to Use These Listings."
Dates in parentheses represent the issues in which the ratings were published.

Côtes du Rhône Réservé 1990: An extraordinary Côtes du Rhône from a superlative vintage. Rich, ripe, round, deeply satisfying and full-bodied, with supple tannins. Bursting with lovely, intense black currant and game notes. The elegant structure veers clear of heavy, raisiny or alcoholic tendencies. A class act. Drink now through 2010.–P.M. • $NA • (1/01/1999) • **94**
Côtes du Rhône Réservé 1989 • $20 • (11/30/1992) • **88**
Côtes du Rhône Réservé 1986: A lovely red, with a distinct minerally character accented by notes of plum, cherry and faded roses. Medium-bodied, with smooth tannins but an intense finish. Drink now through 2003.–P.M. • $NA • (1/01/1999) • **87**
Côtes du Rhône Réservé 1985 • $16 • (9/30/1988) • **87**
Côtes du Rhône White Réservé 1997: Fresh and lively, showing citrus, honey, fresh dill, sage and rosemary character. Medium-bodied and ripe-tasting, with a slight oak-smoke finish, it's a delight. Drink now through 2001.–P.M. • $36 • (12/15/1999) • **86**
Côtes du Rhône White Réservé 1996: This full-bodied yet crisp white shows alluring pear and honey aromas, with ripe flavors of pear and melon and a vivid streak of citrusy acidity. It has the weight and definition to match well with richer dishes. Drink now.–T.M. • $25 • (11/15/1998) • **85**
Syrah Côtes du Rhône Réservé 1997: Modern-styled, medium-bodied, smoky and oaky, with cassis and blackberry bursting forth in this stylish red. Turns a bit crisp and dryingly tannic on the finish. Nice fruit, but very angular. Will it soften? Best after 2002.–P.M. • $47 • (12/15/1999) • **83**
Syrah Côtes du Rhône Réservé 1995: Very fruity, with chocolate, toast, currant and cherry character. Firm and chewy tannins make for a slightly bitter finish now, but there is enough stuffing here to suggest it should smooth out with cellaring. Best from 2005 through 2010.–P.M. • $NA • (1/01/1999) • **88**
Syrah Côtes du Rhône Réservé 1994 • $35 • (1/01/1998) • **89**
Syrah Côtes du Rhône Réservé 1993 • $32 • (1/01/1998) • **88**
Syrah Côtes du Rhône Réservé 1990 • $25 • (4/15/1993) • **88**

FONT DE MICHELLE, DOMAINE

Châteauneuf-du-Pape 1997: Well made, offering some succulent red berry and black cherry character, lightly smoky notes. Medium-bodied, with a fresh finish. Drink through 2003.–P.M. • $22 • (8/31/1999) • **86**
Châteauneuf-du-Pape 1990 • $17 • (4/15/1993) • **82**
Châteauneuf-du-Pape 1989 • $18 • (10/15/1991) • **83**
Châteauneuf-du-Pape 1988 • $21 • (10/15/1991) • **86**
Châteauneuf-du-Pape 1986 • $20 • (10/15/1991) • **89**
Châteauneuf-du-Pape 1985 • $20 • (10/15/1991) • **84**
Châteauneuf-du-Pape 1983 • $25 • (10/15/1991) • **85**
Châteauneuf-du-Pape 1981 • $20 • (10/15/1991) • **88**
Châteauneuf-du-Pape Cuvée Etienne Gonnet 1998: Ultrasupple, it massages the palate with its ripe fruit flavors, soft tannins and rich texture. Full-bodied, it's so harmonious, with plum, red berry and blackberry character, a touch of mocha and grilled nuts from the oak. Long, smoky and intense finish. Drink now through 2015.–P.M. • $45 • (6/30/2000) • **93**
Châteauneuf-du-Pape Cuvée Etienne Gonnet 1997: A satisfying Châteauneuf. Round and supple, nicely toasted, with a silky, flavorful core of fruit, along with floral aromas, ripe tannins and a balanced, lingering finish. Drink now through 2002.–P.M. • $32 • (8/31/1999) • **88**
Châteauneuf-du-Pape Cuvée Etienne Gonnet 1996: Fat and dripping with velvety tannins, this thick-as-syrup-textured wine shows some decent fruit flavors. If it's smoothness you're after, buy it. Drink now through 2001.–P.M. • $29 • (8/31/1999) • **87**
Châteauneuf-du-Pape White 1999: Clean and flavorful, a fruity wine, with lime, peach and apricot character. Lacks gras, or fat, but it's medium-bodied, sparkling with life and a vibrant finish. Drink now through 2008.–P.M. • $32 • (6/30/2000) • **84**
Châteauneuf-du-Pape White 1998: Very round and full-bodied, with pear, floral and white pepper complexity and enough fresh character to keep it balanced. Good intensity drives the finish. Drink now through 2003.–P.M. • $24 • (9/30/1999) • **88**
Châteauneuf-du-Pape White Cuvée Etienne Gonnet 1997: Beautiful. Good intensity in this full-bodied white, displaying a midpalate grip of tropical, litchi, floral and subtly toasty character. Lingering, smoky finish. Best after 2002.–P.M. • $33 • (9/30/1999) • **88**
Côtes du Rhône 1998: Zesty, lively and vibrant. Expect black pepper, black cherry and spice to bounce around on the smooth-tannined palate, carpeting it with pleasure that persists on the balanced, peppery finish. Drink now through 2001.–P.M. • $24 • (11/15/1999) • **89**
Viognier Côtes du Rhône 1998: A balanced, wonderful little white, with lively citrus and green apple notes mixed with honey and pear flavors. A delicious everyday quaff. Drink now.–P.M. • $14 • (11/15/1999) • **87**

FONTAINE-GAGNARD

Bâtard-Montrachet 1997: Earthy, crisp and medium-bodied, with citrus and modest fruit, it turns very tart on the aggressively oak-toasted finish, which is dominated by green wood tannins.–P.M. • $165 • (5/31/1999) • **71**
Bâtard-Montrachet 1996 • $148 • (5/31/1998) • **91**
Bourgogne 1995 • $10 • (11/15/1997) • **70**
Bourgogne 1993 • $14 • (11/15/1995) • **88**
Chassagne-Montrachet 1997: Pear and mineral notes are on display, but this turns dry and earthy, with a reduced "icebox" note on the crisp, chewy aftertaste.–P.M. • $50 • (5/31/1999) • **78**
Chassagne-Montrachet 1996 • $51 • (5/31/1998) • **84**
Chassagne-Montrachet Clos St.-Jean Clos Les Murées 1997: Lively, grassy aromas start out this tart, acidic, tough wine. Offers green apple, dried herb and green olive character on the chewy, astringent finish.–P.M. • $64 • (5/31/1999) • **77**
Chassagne-Montrachet Clos St.-Jean Clos Les Murées 1996 • $60 • (5/31/1998) • **90**
Chassagne-Montrachet La Boudriotte 1997: Subdued on the nose but with good ripe fruit, this medium-bodied '97 delivers fresh pear and citrus quality of medium intensity. Drink now.–P.M. • $64 • (5/31/1999) • **85**
Chassagne-Montrachet La Boudriotte 1996 • $60 • (5/31/1998) • **84**
Chassagne-Montrachet La Grande Montagne 1997: This traditional, even rustic white has a woody, buttery taste, with astringent wood tannins and modest fruit. Slight oxidation turns the finish a bit heavy.–P.M. • $64 • (5/31/1999) • **77**
Chassagne-Montrachet La Maltroie 1997: Clean, medium-bodied and steely, with butter and coconut character, this bursts with crisp fruit and mineral intensity on the succulent finish. Drink now through 2002.–P.M. • $64 • (5/31/1999) • **83**
Chassagne-Montrachet La Maltroie 1996 • $60 • (5/31/1998) • **89**
Chassagne-Montrachet Les Caillerets 1997: Quite tart, with a tough, astringent mouthfeel. Medium-bodied, kicking off with lime, fresh herb and green apple notes, but it lacks a bit of ripeness. Drink now through 2002.–P.M. • $64 • (5/31/1999) • **82**
Chassagne-Montrachet Les Caillerets 1996 • $60 • (5/31/1998) • **90**
Chassagne-Montrachet Les Chenevottes 1997: Good fruit aromas are followed by a heavyhanded palate accented by astringent, herbal, toasted oak, burnt butter and wood tannins. Tough, bitter finish.–P.M. • $64 • (5/31/1999) • **78**
Chassagne-Montrachet Les Chenevottes 1996 • $60 • (5/31/1998) • **87**
Chassagne-Montrachet Les Vergers 1997: This clean, medium-bodied white is firm, chalky and tough, with green apple skins and a mouthpuckering acidity that overwhelms the finish. Drink now through 2003.–P.M. • $64 • (5/31/1999) • **80**
Chassagne-Montrachet Les Vergers 1996 • $60 • (5/31/1998) • **86**
Chassagne-Montrachet Morgeot 1997: A Chassagne built for the cellar. Very clean, pure and focused, it's a ball of mineral, with hints of pear, lemon and spice. Medium-bodied, with a gorgeous white marble-like personality. For those who like a reserved style. Drink through 2005.–P.M. • $64 • (5/31/1999) • **90**
Chassagne-Montrachet Morgeot 1996 • $60 • (5/31/1998) • **89**
Chassagne-Montrachet Red 1995 • $28 • (11/15/1997) • **73**
Chassagne-Montrachet Red 1993 • $23 • (11/15/1995) • **87**
Chassagne-Montrachet Red 1985 • $16 • (12/31/1988) • **85**
Chassagne-Montrachet Red Clos St.-Jean 1995 • $36 • (11/15/1997) • **85**
Chassagne-Montrachet Red Clos St.-Jean 1994 • $36 • (11/15/1996) • **78**
Chassagne-Montrachet Red Clos St.-Jean 1992 • $32 • (12/15/1994) • **85**
Chassagne-Montrachet Red Morgeot 1995 • $36 • (11/15/1997) • **87**
Chassagne-Montrachet Red Morgeot 1994 • $36 • (11/15/1996) • **79**
Chassagne-Montrachet Red Morgeot 1993 • $27 • (11/15/1995) • **89**
Criots-Bâtard-Montrachet 1997: A bit herbal and buttery—a combination that works with the added complexity of toasted oak, plum and tropical notes. Good flavor concentration on the opulent, fresh, balanced, long finish. Best from 2004 through 2007.–P.M. • $165 • (5/31/1999) • **90**
Criots-Bâtard-Montrachet 1996 • $148 • (5/31/1998) • **93**
Montrachet 1997: Heavy toasted oak treatment combines with citrus to compensate somewhat for a slight dilution. Drying, woody finish.–P.M. • $375 • (5/31/1999) • **79**
Montrachet 1996 • $335 • (5/31/1998) • **93**
Pommard Les Rugiens 1995 • $60 • (11/15/1997) • **87**
Pommard Les Rugiens 1994 • $56 • (11/15/1996) • **77**
Volnay Clos des Chênes 1995 • $60 • (11/15/1997) • **76**
Volnay Clos des Chênes 1994 • $56 • (11/15/1996) • **81**
Volnay Clos des Chênes 1993 • $43 • (11/15/1995) • **90**
Volnay Clos des Chênes 1992 • $48 • (12/15/1994) • **85**

FONTANELLES, DOMAINE DES

Merlot Vin de Pays d'Oc 1996: An assertive style, with cherry and herb flavors. Cleanly made and fairly bright, with spice and herb notes on the finish. Drink now.–K.M. • $NA • (12/31/1998) • **82**
Merlot Vin de Pays d'Oc 1995 • $7 • (11/15/1997) • **80**
Merlot Vin de Pays d'Oc 1993 • $7 • (7/31/1996) • **83**
Sauvignon Blanc Vin de Pays d'Oc 1996 • $8 • (5/31/1997) • **85**
Shiraz-Syrah Vin de Pays d'Oc 1995 • $8 • (12/15/1997) • **77**
Shiraz-Syrah Vin de Pays d'Oc 1993 • $7 • (7/31/1996) • **77**

FONTENAY, HENRY DE

Muscadet de Sèvre et Maine 1997: Fresh and round, this white has apple aromas and flavors and a rich texture. Finishes with lemony acidity and a hint of mineral.–B.S. • $6 • (11/15/1998) • **85**
Muscadet de Sèvre et Maine Sur Lie Les Roches Noires 1997: The apple, mineral and even peach flavors, with a hint of bitter grapefruit, are well concentrated and backed up by a rich texture and a lemony acidity that resonates on the finish. Drink now.–B.S. • $7 • (11/15/1998) • **84**
Pouilly-Fumé La Rogeray 1997: Green apple and peach notes are buoyed upon a rich texture underscored by moderately low acidity. Slightly one-dimensional, but satisfying. Drink now.–B.S. • $11 • (10/31/1998) • **84**
Sancerre Les Roysiers 1997: Vivid, this has an almost New Zealand-like intensity, with vibrant acidity, exaggerated herbal and grassy flavors and quite-full body. May be more food-friendly when it settles down. Drink now.–T.M. • $12 • (9/15/1998) • **87**
Vouvray 1997: Lovely richness, with honey, apple and lime notes, a moderate structure and a refreshing finish. A good introduction to the charms of Chenin Blanc. Drink now.–B.S. • $7 • (11/15/1998) • **86**

FONTENIL, CHATEAU

Fronsac 1998: Lovely sweet fruit in this young wine. Full-bodied, with velvety tannins and a long aftertaste of raspberry and other berries.–J.S. • $NA • (5/31/1999) (BT) • **90-94**
Fronsac 1997: Bright berry and cherry character, with jammy, cooked strawberry aromas. Medium-bodied, with light tannins and a fruity finish. Best after 2000.–J.S. • $18 • (1/31/2000) • **87**
Fronsac 1996: A likable wine that doesn't try to be more than it is. Pleasant blackberry and bramble-bush aromas. Medium-bodied, with silky tannins and a light, fruity finish. Drink now.–J.S. • $13 • (1/31/1999) • **86**
Fronsac 1995 • $15 • (1/31/1998) • **90**
Fronsac 1994 • $18 • (1/31/1997) • **84**
Fronsac 1993 • $12 • (1/31/1996) • **83**
Fronsac 1990 • $17 • (3/31/1993) • **91**
Fronsac 1989: An attractive and enjoyable '89. Very floral, with crushed berries on the nose and palate. Medium- to full-bodied, adding medium-silky tannins and a fresh, fruity finish.—1989 Bordeaux horizontal. Drink now through 2005.–J.S. • $NA • (5/31/1999) • **87**
Fronsac 1986 • $14 • (2/15/1990) • **76**
Fronsac 1985 • $14 • (9/30/1988) • **87**

FONTIS, CHATEAU

Médoc 1997: Pretty berry aromas and hints of mint. Medium-bodied, with firm tannins but a diluted finish. Drink now.–J.S. • $NA • (1/31/2000) • **81**

FONTSAINTE, DOMAINE DE

Corbières 1990 • $7 • (3/15/1994) • **82**
Corbières Gris de Gris 1997: Fresh and lively, though on the light side, with berry and cherry flavors and spicy notes on the finish. Drink now.–K.M. • $10 • (10/31/1998) • **82**
Corbières Réserve la Demoiselle 1994 • $10 • (6/15/1997) • **84**
Corbières Réserve la Demoiselle 1990 • $10 • (3/15/1994) • **85**

FOREAU

Vouvray Demi-Sec Domaine du Clos Naudin 1997: Beautifully balanced. This off-dry white offers harmonious flavors of cooked apple, burnt sugar and smoky vanilla. Intense without being heavy. Better than previously reviewed. Drink now through 2005.–T.M. • $29 • (1/01/2000) • **88**
Vouvray Demi-Sec Domaine du Clos Naudin 1996: The honey, vanilla, apple and floral flavors are focused and intense in this young unevolved white.

Concentrated and deep, with racy acidity, a creamy texture and a lengthy finish. Drink through 2010.–B.S. • $24 • (11/15/1998) • **91**

Vouvray Moelleux Domaine du Clos Naudin 1997: Though rather delicate on the palate, this white has rich, intense flavors of piecrust, baked apple, caramel and quince. It's quite sweet, but maintains a lively acidity and excellent balance. Delicious now, but will improve with age. Drink now through 2008.–T.M. • $45 • (6/30/1999) • **90**

Vouvray Moelleux Domaine du Clos Naudin 1996: A sweet Vouvray sporting honey, beeswax and citrus flavors and a soft texture, yet with enough acidity to avoid being cloying. Moderate length on the finish. Drink now through 2003.–B.S. • $39 • (11/15/1998) • **87**

Vouvray Moelleux Domaine du Clos Naudin 1995 • $38 • (5/15/1997) • **89**

Vouvray Moelleux Domaine du Clos Naudin 1990 • $33 • (6/30/1993) • **85**

Vouvray Moelleux Domaine du Clos Naudin 1989 • $34 • (4/30/1991) • **83**

Vouvray Moelleux Domaine du Clos Naudin Réserve 1995 • $60 • (5/15/1997) HR • **95**

Vouvray Moelleux Domaine du Clos Naudin Réserve 1989 • $54 • (3/31/1991) • **89**

Vouvray Sec 1998: Soft lime flavors run through this somewhat simple, just off-dry Vouvray. Drink now.–B.S. • $21 • (6/15/2000) • **81**

FOREST, MICHEL

Pouilly-Fuissé Les Crays 1997: Elegant, with a popcorn, butter, spice and pear tart character. Medium-bodied, it's pretty, but the wood tannins come through as a bit astringent, at least for now. Best after 2000.–P.M. • $30 • (5/31/1999) • **87**

FORET, CHATEAU LA

Sauternes 1991 • $14 • (8/31/1997) • **86**

FOREY PERE & FILS

Bourgogne 1993 • $12 • (11/15/1995) • **79**

Echézeaux 1996: This very honest expression of Pinot Noir is refined and elegant, showing great purity and force, digging its claws into the soil to extract iron and mineral notes that are balanced by raspberries and deft wood dosage. Best from 2003 through 2016.–P.M. • $70 • (9/30/1999) • **95**

Echézeaux 1994 • $60 • (11/15/1996) • **92**

Echézeaux 1993 • $45 • (11/15/1995) • **91**

Echézeaux 1990 • $65 • (12/15/1992) • **92**

Echézeaux 1989 • $NA • (1/31/1992) • **90**

Nuits-St. Georges 1994 • $28 • (11/15/1996) • **78**

Nuits-St.-Georges 1993 • $24 • (11/15/1995) • **82**

Nuits-St.-Georges Les Perrières 1994 • $36 • (11/15/1996) • **82**

Nuits-St.-Georges Les Perrières 1993 • $33 • (11/15/1995) • **85**

Nuits-St.-Georges Les Perrières 1990 • $40 • (12/15/1992) • **79**

Nuits-St.-Georges Les Perrières 1989 • $NA • (1/31/1992) • **89**

Nuits-St.-Georges Les St.-Georges 1994 • $40 • (11/15/1996) • **87**

Vosne-Romanée 1994 • $30 • (11/15/1996) • **84**

Vosne-Romanée 1993 • $26 • (11/15/1995) • **88**

Vosne-Romanée 1990 • $30 • (12/15/1992) • **85**

Vosne-Romanée 1989 • $NA • (1/31/1992) • **85**

Vosne-Romanée Les Gaudichots 1994 • $NA • (11/15/1996) • **85**

Vosne-Romanée Les Gaudichots LD 1993 • $45 • (11/15/1995) • **92**

FORGE, LA

Côtes du Lubéron 1989 • $7 • (11/15/1991) • **79**

Morey-St.-Denis Premier Cru 1994 • $NA • (11/15/1996) • **84**

FORT DE ROQUETAILLADE, CHATEAU

Graves White 1996: Lots of grass and mineral character in this clean, well-made white. Medium-bodied, with lively acidity and a light finish. Drink now.–J.S. • $NA • (1/01/1999) • **84**

Key: SS—Spectator Selection. CS—Cellar Selection. HR—Highly Recommended. $NA—Price not available. (BT)—Barrel tasting. (A)—Auction Price. For a key to the tasters' initials, see "How to Use These Listings."
Dates in parentheses represent the issues in which the ratings were published.

FORTANT DE FRANCE

Cabernet Sauvignon Vin de Pays d'Oc 1998: A medium-bodied red, with plum, berry and red cherry flavors, herbal notes on the finish. Drink now.–K.M. • $7 • (10/15/1999) • **82**

Cabernet Sauvignon Vin de Pays d'Oc 1994 • $7 • (7/31/1996) • **79**

Cabernet Sauvignon Vin de Pays d'Oc 1993 • $8 • (2/28/1995) • **83**

Cabernet Sauvignon Vin de Pays d'Oc 1990 • $7 • (3/15/1994) • **82**

Cabernet Sauvignon Vin de Pays d'Oc 1988 • $6 • (4/30/1991) • **70**

Cabernet Sauvignon Vin de Pays d'Oc Collection 1993 • $11 • (12/15/1996) • **78**

Cabernet Sauvignon Vin de Pays d'Oc Réserve 1996: Deep-colored, full-bodied and quite tannic, this red achieves a blockbuster style. The heady aromas of perfumed, smoky French oak and the concentrated black cherry flavors linger on the finish. Drink now through 2001. • $25 • (9/30/1998) • **87**

Chardonnay Vin de Pays d'Oc 1998: Modest, with buttery notes, green apple flavors and a slight aroma of lime.–K.M. • $7 • (10/15/1999) • **78**

Chardonnay Vin de Pays d'Oc Réserve 1996: A broad and muscular Chardonnay, with pear, butter and spice flavors that hang together nicely. Could use more focus, but still seductive. Drink now.–K.M. • $20 • (9/30/1998) • **85**

Merlot Vin de Pays d'Oc 1998: Plummy herbal flavors dominate this medium-bodied Merlot, which finishes on a chalky note. Drink now.–K.M. • $7 • (10/15/1999) • **81**

Merlot Vin de Pays d'Oc 1996 • $NA • (3/31/1998) • **77**

Merlot Vin de Pays d'Oc 1995 • $7 • (12/15/1996) • **86**

Merlot Vin de Pays d'Oc 1994 • $7 • (10/31/1995) • **83**

Merlot Vin de Pays d'Oc 1993 • $7 • (2/28/1995) • **79**

Merlot Vin de Pays d'Oc 1992 • $7 • (9/15/1994) • **82**

Merlot Vin de Pays d'Oc 1991 • $7 • (3/15/1994) • **81**

Merlot Vin de Pays d'Oc 1990 • $7 • (3/15/1994) • **83**

Merlot Vin de Pays d'Oc 1988 • $6 • (5/31/1991) • **70**

Merlot Vin de Pays d'Oc Collection 1993 • $11 • (12/15/1996) • **85**

Merlot Vin de Pays d'Oc Réserve 1996: Tightly wound, with appealing red cherry, plum and nutmeg flavors. Smooth and elegant, with a lingering finish. Drink through 2001.–K.M. • $25 • (9/30/1998) • **85**

Sauvignon Blanc Vin de Pays d'Oc 1998: Oniony and herbal-tasting, with just hint of citrus. Grassy notes on the finish.–K.M. • $7 • (10/15/1999) • **78**

Syrah Vin de Pays d'Oc 1998: Straightforward, with peppery and plummy flavors, and minerallike notes on the finish. Drink now.–K.M. • $7 • (10/15/1999) • **81**

Syrah Vin de Pays d'Oc 1991 • $7 • (3/15/1994) • **82**

FORTIA, CHATEAU

Châteauneuf-du-Pape 1997: Tastes and smells a bit unripe, with herb, green olive and cassis bush character. Tannins are tough. Drying finish.–P.M. • $24 • (6/30/2000) • **77**

Châteauneuf-du-Pape 1996: Light in body and color, tasting herbal, showing bell pepper aromas and drying tannins.–P.M. • $25 • (12/15/1999) • **74**

Châteauneuf-du-Pape 1995: Delicious, maturing already, with forest underbrush and mushroom notes and lovely plum, mineral, smoke and coffee bean flavors. Full-bodied and ripe, with smooth tannins and blood-orange notes on the finish. Approachable now, with red meat, but should improve. Drink now through 2008.–P.M. • $23 • (11/15/1998) • **88**

Châteauneuf-du-Pape 1994: Sweet-tasting and ripe, showing cassis, spice, plum, game and mocha. Supersupple tannins make it attractive now, although the raw power on the finish suggests it can last. Drink now through 2005.–P.M. • $21 • (11/15/1998) • **85**

Châteauneuf-du-Pape 1989 • $20 • (11/15/1996) • **86**

Châteauneuf-du-Pape 1988 • $22 • (6/15/1993) • **78**

Châteauneuf-du-Pape 1985 • $22 • (5/31/1992) • **81**

Châteauneuf-du-Pape 1983 • $14 • (12/31/1987) • **87**

Châteauneuf-du-Pape White 1998: Full-bodied and voluptuous, but it's woody in a rustic way and tastes of chestnut. Not much clean, focused fruit.–P.M. • $25 • (12/15/1999) • **78**

Châteauneuf-du-Pape White 1997: Smooth, with some decent melon, pink grapefruit, green apple character, turning crisp on the finish. Drink now.–P.M. • $23 • (11/15/1998) • **82**

FORTS DE LATOUR, LES

Pauillac 1999: Lots of plum, mineral and berry character. Medium- to full-bodied, with well-integrated tannins and a medium to long finish. Bloody good for a second wine.–J.S. • $NA • (1/01/2000) (BT) • **85-89**

Pauillac 1998: Solid second wine for Latour, although a bit elegant in style. Wonderful licorice and currant character. Medium-bodied, with ripe and fine tannins and a long, fruity finish. Tempting now.–J.S. • $NA • (5/31/1999) (BT) • **85-89**

Pauillac 1996: Very fine indeed. A perfumed wine with blackberry and mineral aromas and flavors. Medium-bodied, with firm tannins that are polished and fine. Long on the finish. Second label of Château Latour. Best after 2000.–J.S.• $41 Ⓐ • (1/31/1999) • **88**

Pauillac 1995 • $46 Ⓐ • (1/31/1998) • **91**

Pauillac 1994 • $30 Ⓐ • (1/31/1997) • **82**

Pauillac 1993 • $28 • (1/31/1996) • **83**

Pauillac 1992 • $22 • (4/15/1995) • **80**

Pauillac 1991 • $23 • (3/31/1994) • **78**

Pauillac 1990 • $89 Ⓐ • (3/31/1993) • **94**

Pauillac 1989 • $58 Ⓐ • (3/15/1992) • **91**

Pauillac 1985 • $48 Ⓐ • (8/31/1991) • **87**

Pauillac 1983 • $32 • (10/15/1990) • **85**

Pauillac 1982: What a wine. Dark ruby color, with a hint of garnet. Ripe berry, with a hint of raisin, licorice and spice. Full-bodied and very concentrated, with velvety tannins and a long, ripe fruit finish. Second label of Château Latour. (1982 Bordeaux horizontal tasting). Drink now.–J.S. • $NA • (11/30/1998) • **93**

Pauillac 1979 • $43 Ⓐ • (10/15/1989) • **87**

FORTUNE, DOMAINE

Beaujolais-Villages 1994 • $9 • (10/31/1995) • **84**

FOUASSIER PERE & FILS

Pouilly-Fumé Cuvée Jules 1996: Complex aromas and flavors, melon, peach, citrus and mineral notes, are balanced with bright acidity, moderate concentration. Finishes a bit short. Drink now.–B.S. • $15 • (10/31/1998) • **84**

Sancerre Clos Paradis 1996 • $22 • (6/15/1998) • **85**

Sancerre Les Chasseignes 1996: This traditional-style Sancerre has good structure and typical flavors of apples, herbs and light earthy notes. It's crisp, and has enough body to match with food. Drink now.–T.M. • $15 • (9/15/1998) • **85**

Sancerre Les Romains 1997: Sweet melon and vanilla flavors mingle with tart citrus and herb notes in this light white. The elements taken separately are appealing, but as a whole this lacks harmony and complexity. Drink now.–T.M. • $22 • (6/30/1999) • **82**

Sancerre Les Romains 1996 • $20 • (6/15/1998) • **87**

FOUGERAY, DOMAINE

Bonnes Mares 1991 • $NA • (1/31/1994) • **87**

Gevrey-Chambertin Les Leuvrées 1995 • $26 • (11/15/1997) • **73**

Marsannay St.-Jacques 1991 • $NA • (1/31/1994) • **77**

Vosne-Romanée Les Damodes 1996: Floral, fruity aromas draw you into this fresh, berry-flavored red, whose flesh and richness don't quite match the solid tannins. Drink through 2004.–B.S. • $29 • (9/30/1998) • **84**

FOUGERAY DE BEAUCLAIR

Bonnes Mares 1996: Magnificent. Ripe and sweet, full-bodied, thick and opulent, this dances with grace across the palate, delivering subtle kisses of flavor—spicy mocha, blackberry, rose petal and mineral. The finish is smooth and silky, yet it's not soft or dull because the acidity carries it to a long, fresh completion. Drink now through 2010.–P.M. • $82 • (9/30/1998) • **94**

Bonnes Mares 1995 • $85 • (11/15/1997) • **82**

Bonnes Mares 1994 • $90 • (11/15/1996) • **88**

Bourgogne L'Ormichal 1996: Medium-bodied, nice and juicy, with fresh red berry character. Drink now.–P.M. • $13 • (9/30/1998) • **81**

Chambolle-Musigny 1995 • $26 • (11/15/1997) • **80**

Côte de Nuits-Villages 1996: Impressive. Black fruit flavors, depth and a touch of earth marry with richness and a firm structure for a red that's balanced and enjoyable now, should be best from 2000 through 2005.–B.S. • $20 • (9/30/1998) • **87**

Côte de Nuits-Villages 1995 • $18 • (11/15/1997) • **80**

Fixin Clos Marion 1996: Pretty fruit. This medium-bodied red has lush texture and ripe red berry flavors. Lovely balance makes it seductive on the ripe finish. Nice work. Drink now through 2005.–P.M. • $26 • (9/30/1998) • **87**

Fixin Clos Marion 1995 • $27 • (11/15/1997) • **83**

Fixin Clos Marion 1994 • $27 • (11/15/1996) • **73**

Marsannay Le Dessus des Longeroies 1995 • $19 • (11/15/1997) • **74**

Marsannay Les Favières 1996: Quite round and sweet, with licorice, plum and black cherry character, turning a bit astringent on the finish.–P.M. • $19 • (9/30/1998) • **85**

Marsannay Les Favières 1995 • $19 • (11/15/1997) • **75**

Marsannay Les Grasses Têtes 1996: Light in color, body and flavor, this shows some strawberry, spice and vanilla notes and a supple, delicate finish. Drink now.–P.M. • $19 • (9/30/1998) • **81**

Marsannay Les Grasses Têtes 1995 • $19 • (11/15/1997) • **70**

Marsannay St.-Jacques 1996: Aromas of concentrated, spicy cherry and raspberry, bright flavors and rich texture mark this big-boned, burly red. What it lacks in finesse it makes up for in power. Best from 2002 through 2008.–B.S. • $25 • (9/30/1998) • **86**

Marsannay St.-Jacques 1995 • $26 • (11/15/1997) • **70**

Savigny-lès-Beaune Les Golardes 1995 • $20 • (11/15/1997) • **76**

Vosne-Romanée Les Damaudes 1995 • $28 • (11/15/1997) • **77**

FOURCAS-DUMONT, CHATEAU

Listrac 1997: A light and thoroughly drinkable red, with plum and green tobacco character. Light and fruity finish. Drink now.–J.S. • $NA • (1/31/2000) • **82**

FOURCAS-DUPRE, CHATEAU

Listrac 1998: Slightly herbal and metallic, with a medium body, medium tannins and an austere finish. Good but not exciting.–J.S. • $NA • (5/31/1999) (BT) • **80-84**

Listrac 1997: Some decent berry and herbal character. Light-bodied, with light tannins. Short finish. Drink now.–J.S. • $NA • (1/31/2000) • **80**

Listrac 1996: Dark-colored, with a good intensity of blackberry and mineral aromas. Medium-bodied, with well-integrated tannins and a plum and currant aftertaste. Best Fourcas-Dupré in years. Best after 2001.–J.S. • $NA • (1/31/1999) • **88**

Listrac 1995: Silky and reserved, with berry and blackberry aromas and flavors. Medium-bodied, with fine tannins and a caressing finish. Drink through 2005.–J.S. • $18 • (9/15/1998) • **86**

Listrac 1992 • $15 • (4/15/1995) • **79**

Listrac 1991 • $15 • (3/31/1994) • **74**

Listrac 1990 • $17 • (3/31/1993) • **82**

Listrac 1989 • $25 • (3/15/1992) • **86**

Listrac 1988 • $22 • (4/30/1991) • **83**

Listrac 1982: A funky and tired red, with mushroom, tobacco and slightly volatile character. Medium-bodied, with a sharp finish. Drink if you must. (1982 Bordeaux horizontal tasting).–J.S. • $NA • (11/30/1998) • **75**

FOURCAS-HOSTEN, CHATEAU

Listrac 1998: A bit raisiny, with hints of blackcherry and earth. Medium-bodied, with medium tannins and a hollow midpalate.–J.S. • $NA • (5/31/1999) (BT) • **80-84**

Listrac 1997: A pretty and delicious red with light berry and strawberry character. Fresh finish. Drink now.–J.S. • $NA • (1/31/2000) • **82**

Listrac 1996: A sleek and simple red with a good amount of plum character and very firm tannins. Medium-bodied. Chewy texture. Best after 2000.–J.S. • $NA • (1/31/1999) • **85**

Listrac 1994 • $19 • (10/15/1997) • **85**

Listrac 1992 • $15 • (4/15/1995) • **76**

Listrac 1991 • $15 • (3/31/1994) • **79**

Listrac 1990 • $20 • (3/31/1993) • **85**

Listrac 1989: A wine at its peak. Very ripe fruit, raisin and tobacco on the nose and palate. Medium- to full-bodied, with a tobacco, chestnut aftertaste. (1989 Bordeaux horizontal tasting). Drink now.–J.S. • $NA • (5/31/1999) • **87**

Listrac 1988 • $13 • (7/15/1991) • **82**

Listrac 1986 • $14 • (11/15/1989) • **79**

Listrac 1983 • $16 • (10/15/1986) • **83**

Listrac 1982 • $18 • (8/31/1992) • **90**

Listrac 1961 • $26 • (4/30/1996) • **81**

FOURNIER PERE & FILS

Pouilly-Fumé Les Caillottes 1996: This white puts its peach, melon and mineral notes in harmony, supported by juicy acidity and enough depth and intensity to carry the flavors to a lingering conclusion. Drink now.–B.S. • $16 • (10/31/1998) • **87**

FOURNIER PERE & FILS

Sancerre Grande Cuvée Vieilles Vignes 1997: Bright and zippy, with lemon zest and grapefruit flavors on a clean, vibrant, medium-bodied frame. Drink now.–B.S. • $18 • (6/15/2000) • **87**

Sancerre Grande Cuvée Vieilles Vignes 1996: A vivid white in an almost Californian style, with plenty of ripe apple, fig and melon flavors and less of the grassy, herbal notes of Sancerre. Has plenty of vibrant acidity, and should match well with food. Drink now.–T.M. • $19 • (9/15/1998) • **88**

Sancerre Les Belles Vignes 1996: Rich yet crisp, this full-bodied white shows citrus, apple and mineral flavors, clean and focused, that should soften with time. A fine match for food. Drink through 2002.–T.M. • $16 • (9/15/1998) • **87**

FRANC-JAUGUE-BLANC, CHATEAU

St.-Emilion 1995 • $20 • (1/31/1998) • **82**

FRANC LA ROSE, CHATEAU

St.-Emilion 1997: Pleasant berry and cherry character. Medium-bodied, with light tannins and a fresh finish. Drink now.–J.S. • $29 • (6/15/2000) • **82**

FRANC-MAYNE, CHATEAU

St.-Emilion 1999: Well done, with lovely plum, berry and cherry character. Full-bodied with super well-integrated tannins and a long, long finish. Outstanding.–J.S. • $NA • (1/01/2000) (BT) • **90-94**

St.-Emilion 1998: Firm and compacted, with berry, dried cherry and mineral character. Medium-bodied, with firm tannins and a compact fruit structure. Dry finish; too much wood?–J.S. • $NA • (5/31/1999) (BT) • **85-89**

St.-Emilion 1997: Delicious, caressing wine. Very pretty berry, cherry and milk chocolate aromas. Medium-bodied, with a solid core of ripe fruit and a long, velvety finish. Drink now through 2004.–J.S. • $33 • (1/31/2000) • **87**

St.-Emilion 1996: Very fresh berry and tobacco aromas in this young red. Medium-bodied, with firm yet silky tannins and a medium to light finish. Drink now.–J.S. • $27 • (1/31/1999) • **86**

St.-Emilion 1993 • $20 • (1/31/1996) • **81**

St.-Emilion 1992 • $17 • (4/15/1995) • **79**

St.-Emilion 1991 • $15 • (3/31/1994) • **82**

St.-Emilion 1990 • $23 • (3/31/1993) • **91**

St.-Emilion 1989: Really amazing for this estate. Inky, ruby color. Spices, blackberries, cherries and cinnamon. Full-bodied yet reserved, with fabulously refined structure. Persists beautifully on the palate. (1989 Bordeaux horizontal tasting). Best after 2004.–J.S. • $NA • (5/31/1999) • **94**

St.-Emilion 1988 • $41 Ⓐ • (7/15/1991) • **83**

FRANC-PERAT, CHATEAU

Bordeaux White 1998: Aromas of pear and grapefruit. Medium-bodied, with zingy acidity and a light celery finish. Drink now.–J.S. • $10 • (6/15/2000) • **84**

Premières Côtes de Bordeaux 1998 : Good, with mint and berry character, medium body and fine tannins. Best after 2001.–J.S. • $10 • (6/15/2000) • **84**

FRANCE, CHATEAU DE

Pessac-Léognan 1998: Perfumed, with cherry and licorice aromas and flavors. Medium- to full-bodied, with ripe fruit flavors and a lengthy ripe fruit aftertaste. Very well done. Almost outstanding.–J.S. • $NA • (5/31/1999) (BT) • **85-89**

Pessac-Léognan 1997: Intense aromas of black licorice and minerals. Medium-bodied, with firm tannins and a lean finish. A bit tough. Best after 2000.–J.S. • $NA • (1/31/2000) • **85**

Pessac-Léognan 1996: A fresh and lean '96, with currant and grape aromas and flavors. Medium-bodied, with firm tannins and a refreshing finish. Drink now.–J.S. • $NA • (1/31/1999) • **83**

Pessac-Léognan 1995: A delicious red. Pretty aromas of chocolate and berries. Medium-bodied, with soft, round tannins and a long, chocolaty, fruity aftertaste. Drink through 2005–J.S. • $NA • (9/15/1998) • **86**

Pessac-Léognan 1992 • $13 • (4/15/1995) • **76**

Pessac-Léognan 1991 • $13 • (3/31/1994) • **78**

Pessac-Léognan 1990 • $20 • (3/31/1993) • **85**

Pessac-Léognan 1989: A rather mature-looking wine, yet it's fresh on the palate. Brick-red, ruby-centered color. Plum and leather on the nose. Medium-bodied and round, with velvety tannins and a lovely milk chocolate, gamy character. (1989 Bordeaux horizontal tasting). Drink now.–J.S. • $NA • (5/31/1999) • **84**

Pessac-Léognan 1988 • $18 • (2/28/1991) SS • **92**

Graves 1982 • $NA • (8/31/1992) • **79**

Pessac-Léognan White 1998: This shows loads of fruit character, with a major dose of new wood. Yet it's solid and full-bodied, with a long finish. Best after 2001.–J.S. • $NA • (2/29/2000) • **90**

Pessac-Léognan White 1997: Serious winemaking delivers loads of spice, honey and ripe pineapple character, with a hint of grass. Full-bodied and very rich but slightly short on the finish. Not imported into the U.S. Drink now.–J.S. • $NA • (9/30/1999) • **88**

Pessac-Léognan White 1996: Aromas of very ripe apples and piecrust, with a hint of celery. Full-bodied, thick and oily, with a waxy character on the aftertaste. Rather tired already.–J.S. • $NA • (1/01/1999) • **79**

FRANCS, CHATEAU DE

Côtes de Francs 1996: Light and soft, with clean fruit character, but diluted on the finish. Too bad.–J.S. • $20 • (7/31/1999) • **78**

Côtes de Francs White 1997: A delicious white Bordeaux, with loads of ripe and tropical fruit character and lovely aromas of pineapple, pear and cream. Medium-bodied, with hints of fruit and vanilla on the finish. Drink now.–J.S. • $16 • (7/31/1999) • **87**

FRANK PHELAN

St.-Estèphe 1996: Pretty aromas of raspberries and mushrooms. Medium-bodied, with firm tannins and a long, fresh aftertaste. A bit lean, but beautifully aromatic. Second label of Château Phélan-Segur. Best after 2001.–J.S. • $NA • (1/31/1999) • **85**

St.-Estèphe 1995 • $14 • (1/31/1998) • **85**

FREYNELLE, CHATEAU LA

Bordeaux 1995 • $8 • (1/31/1998) • **86**

Bordeaux Clairet Rosé 1996 • $8 • (2/28/1998) • **84**

Bordeaux White 1996 • $8 • (2/28/1998) • **84**

FRICK, PIERRE

Sylvaner Alsace Bihl 1997: Ripe, yet retains the citrus and earth notes typical of the variety. Moderate acidity keeps it lively and crisp on the finish. Drink now.–B.S. • $14 • (10/15/1999) • **83**

FRONTON, CAVE DE

Côtes du Frontonnais Excellence du Comte de Négrit 1995: A thin red, with only vague plummy flavors and a stewy, almost sour finish.–K.M. • $10 • (11/15/1999) • **74**

FUISSE, CHATEAU

Pouilly-Fuissé 1997: Tart midpalate is packed with lemon and toasted bread notes and astringent wood tannins. Lacks a bit of charm, but has a steely finish.–P.M. • $34 • (5/31/1999) • **78**

Pouilly-Fuissé 1996 • $32 • (5/31/1998) • **88**

Pouilly-Fuissé 1995 • $16 • (5/31/1997) • **85**

Pouilly-Fuissé Le Clos 1997: Whoa. Exotic, full-bodied crowd-pleaser, nicely oaked, with some floral, peach and apricot notes reminiscent of Viognier, and a similarly opulent, Condrieu-like mouthfeel. Yet it has a restrained, polished finish, accented by honey and ripe fruit. Drink now through 2004.–P.M. • $37 • (5/31/1999) • **90**

Pouilly-Fuissé Le Clos 1995 • $37 • (5/31/1997) • **85**

Pouilly-Fuissé Les Brûlées 1997: Rich and ripe, with tropical, honey, toasted bread and spice notes, there's plenty to like in this generously thick Pouilly, just turns a bit hot on the finish. Drink through 2005.–P.M. • $37 • (5/31/1999) • **88**

Pouilly-Fuissé Les Brûlées 1995 • $37 • (5/31/1997) • **87**

Pouilly-Fuissé Les Combettes 1997: Shows some good ripeness, but it's a bit drying and crisp on the finish.–P.M. • $37 • (5/31/1999) • **79**

Key: SS—Spectator Selection. CS—Cellar Selection. HR—Highly Recommended. $NA—Price not available. (BT)—Barrel tasting. Ⓐ—Auction Price. For a key to the tasters' initials, see "How to Use These Listings."
Dates in parentheses represent the issues in which the ratings were published.

FRANCE

Pouilly-Fuissé Les Combettes 1996 • $37 • (5/31/1998) • **88**
Pouilly-Fuissé Vieilles Vignes 1997: Clean and flavorful, with ripe fruit, lemon and toasted oak adding a nice dimension; round on the midpalate, firing perhaps a bit too much wood intensity on the finish. Drink through 2004.–P.M. • $49 • (5/31/1999) • **86**
Pouilly-Fuissé Vieilles Vignes 1996 • $49 • (5/31/1998) • **91**
Pouilly-Fuissé Vieilles Vignes 1995 • $48 • (5/31/1997) • **91**
St.-Véran 1997: Tastes odd, with wet cardboard notes, and it's tart and lean.–P.M. • $17 • (5/31/1999) • **70**
St.-Véran 1995 • $15 • (5/31/1997) • **87**

GAFFELIERE, CHATEAU LA

St.-Emilion 1999: A lovely, silky 1999, with mineral, berry and currant character. Medium-bodied, with firm tannins.–J.S. • $NA • (1/01/2000) (BT) • **85-89**
St.-Emilion 1998: Wonderful aromas of toasted oak, berry and cherry. Full-bodied, with well-integrated tannins and a long, long finish. Very fine indeed.–J.S. • $NA • (5/31/1999) (BT) • **90-94**
St.-Emilion 1997: A delicate and fruity wine with some tobacco and mineral character. Light and fresh on the finish. Drink now.–J.S. • $35 Ⓐ • (1/31/2000) • **84**
St.-Emilion 1996: Fresh and vivacious, with chocolate, cherry and raspberry aromas and flavors. Medium-bodied, with fine tannins and a medium, fruity finish. Needs a bit more fruit concentration to be outstanding, but well done. Drink now.–J.S. • $18 Ⓐ • (1/31/1999) • **88**
St.-Emilion 1995 • $37 • (1/31/1998) • **89**
St.-Emilion 1988 • $33 Ⓐ • (4/30/1991) • **84**
St.-Emilion 1982: A big and alcoholic wine. Overdone but impressive. Dark brick-red color, with tobacco, milk chocolate and cedar aromas. Full-bodied, jammy and thick, with loads of berry and tobacco character and a long finish. Slightly hot. (1982 Bordeaux horizontal tasting). Drink now.–J.S. • $34 Ⓐ • (11/30/1998) • **89**
St.-Emilion 1979 • $34 • (10/15/1989) • **81**
St.-Emilion 1962 • $38 Ⓐ • (11/30/1987) • **88**
St.-Emilion 1961 • $72 Ⓐ • (4/30/1996) • **79**
St.-Emilion 1959 • $95 • (10/15/1990) • **82**
St.-Emilion 1947 • $432 Ⓐ • (5/31/1997) • **87**
St.-Emilion 1945 • $200 • (11/30/1995) • **85**

GAGNARD, JEAN-NOEL

Bâtard-Montrachet 1997: Crisp intensity explodes in this expressive, concentrated white Burgundy. Wonderful toasted oak is supported by grilled pineapple, pear pie, dough and curry notes. Focused, long finish. Drink now through 2005.–P.M. • $150 • (9/30/1999) • **94**
Bâtard-Montrachet 1996: Brilliant. Magical winemaking, fine *terroir* and an outstanding vintage combine to make this enormously successful white. Clean, pure, vibrant, with toasted oak, pine-tree sorbet, honey, lime and deep mineral flavors, this is a sensationally balanced wine that rises to the top of its vintage. Full-bodied, it vibrates with energy and toasted oak on the palate, staying animated for what seems like 60 seconds or more on the finish. Best after 2005.–P.M. • $220 Ⓐ • (8/31/1998) HR • **98**
Chassagne-Montrachet 1996: Lovely, supple, silky-smooth village wine, well built, palate-coating with its opulence. Offers vanilla bean, mineral-laden, pebble and wet stone character, with ripe fruit, honey and toasted oak, in good proportion. Delicious finish. Drink now through 2005.–P.M. • $23 • (8/31/1998) • **90**
Chassagne-Montrachet Clos de la Maltroye 1997: Easy and likable, this medium-bodied, smooth white has a toasted oak, fig, caramel, pear and slight petrol character. Drink now through 2001.–P.M. • $65 • (9/30/1999) • **87**
Chassagne-Montrachet Clos de la Maltroye 1996: Straightforward, with some dried herbs, grassy, buttery character. Of medium body, it lacks a bit of class. Steely finish dries a bit. Drink now through 2003.–P.M. • $NA • (8/31/1998) • **80**
Chassagne-Montrachet Clos de la Maltroye 1995 • $55 • (8/31/1997) • **96**
Chassagne-Montrachet Les Caillerets 1997: A bit tough, but there's good *terroir* in this flinty, gunpowderlike, minerally white Burgundy. Shows enough intensity to tease the palate all the way to a lingering finish. Needs time. Drink through 2005.–P.M. • $75 • (9/30/1999) • **88**
Chassagne-Montrachet Les Caillerets 1996: Wonderful balance in this full-bodied '96. Distinguished and racy, with clean, pure fruit, it also offers superconcentration of mineral, earth, wet stone, pebble and lime character. Just enough toasted bread, wood accents to add a bit of complexity. Supple finish packed with ripe fruit.–P.M. • $77 Ⓐ • (8/31/1998) • **93**
Chassagne-Montrachet Les Caillerets 1995 • $31 Ⓐ • (8/31/1997) • **93**
Chassagne-Montrachet Les Champs Gain 1997: Plenty goes on in this full-bodied, intense white Burgundy. It lacks real midpalate thickness, but it tickles the senses with caramel flan, coffee, intriguing toasted oak, smoke and pear pie character. Drink now through 2005.–P.M. • $65 • (9/30/1999) • **89**
Chassagne-Montrachet Les Champs Gain 1996: A bit rustic for a *premier cru*, with decent honey, fruit and wood, but it turns a bit dry and tough in the midpalate. Medium-bodied. Drink now.–P.M. • $NA • (8/31/1998) • **80**
Chassagne-Montrachet Les Champs Gain 1995 • $65 • (8/31/1997) • **86**
Chassagne-Montrachet Les Chenevottes 1997: Butterscotch and perfume, with toasted oak that makes it taste a bit odd and slightly astringent.–P.M. • $60 • (9/30/1999) • **79**
Chassagne-Montrachet Les Chenevottes 1996: Thick and opulent, this full-bodied, rich and ripe white manages to maintain a firm structure packed with intense acidity. Offers plenty of lime, pink grapefruit, melon and cream flavors. Not overly oaky, just a bit toast and smoky on the incredibly intense finish. Best from 2003.–P.M. • $NA • (8/31/1998) • **93**
Chassagne-Montrachet Les Chenevottes 1995 • $65 • (8/31/1997) • **93**
Chassagne-Montrachet Les Masures 1997: Has butterscotch character, with lemon, honey, lots of ripe fruit and a firm, tightly wound, acidic mouthfeel. Should turn out nice with age. Best from 2001 through 2005.–P.M. • $40 • (9/30/1999) • **90**
Chassagne-Montrachet Maltroie 1997: Fat and creamy, lacking a bit of clean focus. The flabbiness borders on burnt grease, with orange, pear and caramel thrown in. Toasty finish. Drink now through 2002.–P.M. • $60 • (9/30/1999) • **83**
Chassagne-Montrachet Morgeot 1997: Odd butter and butterscotch aromas and flavors—and volatile acidity?—make for a slightly bitter taste. Very tart. Maybe age will turn this ugly duckling into a swan.–P.M. • $43 Ⓐ • (9/30/1999) • **79**
Chassagne-Montrachet Morgeot 1996: A bit overoaked, with marzipan and toasted wood, it also delivers a thick mouthfeel of ripe flavors. Still, all that oak is a bit tiring. Full-bodied, it might improve in the cellar. Best from 2002.–P.M. • $26 • (8/31/1998) • **82**
Chassagne-Montrachet Morgeot 1995 • $55 • (5/31/1998) • **70**
Chassagne-Montrachet Premier Cru 1996: Subtle, but also quite oaky (you can tell from the malic, milky, yogurt taste). Creamlike in texture, full in body and very supple on the finish. Impressive. Very pretty upon release. Drink now through 2003.–P.M. • $45 • (8/31/1998) • **90**
Chassagne-Montrachet Red 1995 • $35 • (11/15/1997) • **70**
Chassagne-Montrachet Red 1994 • $23 • (11/15/1996) • **74**
Chassagne-Montrachet Red 1990 • $50 • (11/30/1992) • **84**
Chassagne-Montrachet Red Clos St.-Jean 1997: Pure, showing a round, minerally and ripe midpalate, with menthol, raspberry and cassis character. A tough customer now, but the clean focus bodes well for the future. Best from 2002 through 2006.–P.M. • $28 • (9/30/1999) • **85**
Chassagne-Montrachet Red Clos St.-Jean 1996: New oak adds vanilla and spice to the cherry character and suave texture of this light-bodied wine. A bit more concentration would help the balance, yet the tannins are soft. Drink now through 2003.–B.S. • $25 • (9/30/1998) • **86**
Chassagne-Montrachet Red Clos St.-Jean 1995 • $55 • (11/15/1997) • **74**
Chassagne-Montrachet Red Cuvée L'Estimée 1997: A bit light, with light color and a lean body, showing a stemmy, herbal character.–P.M. • $25 • (9/30/1999) • **73**
Chassagne-Montrachet Red Morgeot 1997: Smoky, minerally and *terroir*-driven, this has the seductive appeal on the palate of many a grand cru, with red and black fruit. Balanced, with a pure and clean finish, which is impressive considering the flabbiness of many '97s. Drink now through 2005.–P.M. • $28 • (9/30/1999) • **91**
Chassagne-Montrachet Red Morgeot 1996: Smoke and clove accents add dimension to the cherry flavors in this concentrated, slightly rustic red. It finishes on the astringent side, and needs time for the oak to integrate. Drink through 2004.–B.S. • $27 • (9/30/1998) • **85**
Chassagne-Montrachet Red Morgeot 1995 • $58 • (11/15/1997) • **81**
Chassagne-Montrachet Red Morgeot 1994 • $25 • (11/15/1996) • **79**
Chassagne-Montrachet Red Morgeot 1990 • $25 • (2/15/1993) • **86**
Chassagne-Montrachet Red Morgeot 1989 • $25 • (11/15/1991) • **87**
Chassagne-Montrachet Red Morgeot 1988 • $20 • (12/31/1990) • **86**
Chassagne-Montrachet Red Morgeot 1985 • $18 • (11/30/1987) • **79**
Santenay Clos de Tavannes 1997: Light and straightforward. A weak Pinot.–P.M. • $30 • (9/30/1999) • **79**
Santenay Clos de Tavannes 1996: Power and a mineral character augment the new oak and ripe fruit in this expressive Pinot Noir. Has a richness lacking in other wines from this appellation, with balance and length. Drink now through 2003.–B.S. • $NA • (9/30/1998) • **87**
Santenay Clos de Tavannes 1995 • $30 • (11/15/1997) • **83**
Santenay Clos de Tavannes 1994 • $27 • (11/15/1996) • **70**

GAGNARD, JEAN-NOEL

Santenay Clos de Tavannes 1990 • $16 • (11/30/1992) • **80**
Santenay Clos de Tavannes 1989 • $25 • (11/15/1991) • **85**
Santenay Clos de Tavannes 1988 • $25 • (11/15/1990) • **84**

GAGNARD-DELAGRANGE

Montrachet 1995: A wine in *sur-maturité*, or overripe, showing an appley, new-oakish side, with a violet, toasted coconut character that seems a bit overdone. But it's full-bodied, opulent, and rich, and you must admire the wonderful texture. Best after 2010.–P.M. • $NA • (8/31/1998) • **90**

GALET DES PAPES, DOMAINE DU

Châteauneuf-du-Pape 1996: Odd and rustic, this chewy and astringent-herbal wine turns hot on the finish.–P.M. • $25 • (9/30/1998) • **70**
Châteauneuf-du-Pape 1995 • $25 • (10/15/1997) • **85**
Châteauneuf-du-Pape 1993 • $23 • (12/15/1996) • **79**
Châteauneuf-du-Pape 1992 • $23 • (10/15/1995) • **82**
Châteauneuf-du-Pape 1989 • $21 • (8/31/1992) • **88**
Châteauneuf-du-Pape Tradition 1997: Diluted and a bit green, light in color and body, showing some black cherry, plum and roasted game notes on the slightly flat finish.–P.M. • $25 • (8/31/1999) • **79**
Châteauneuf-du-Pape Vieilles Vignes 1997: Light in color, body and aroma, it's a bit earthy and herbal, with a plummy note on the finish.–P.M. • $35 • (8/31/1999) • **77**
Châteauneuf-du-Pape Vieilles Vignes 1994 • $31 • (12/15/1996) • **78**
Châteauneuf-du-Pape Vieilles Vignes 1993 • $28 • (12/15/1996) • **82**
Châteauneuf-du-Pape Vieilles Vignes 1992 • $32 • (10/15/1995) • **81**
Châteauneuf-du-Pape Vieilles Vignes 1990 • $28 • (9/30/1993) • **76**
Châteauneuf-du-Pape White 1996 • $22 • (10/15/1997) • **86**

GALETS BLONDS, LES

Châteauneuf-du-Pape 1996: Light in body, color and flavor. Tastes modestly of strawberry and raspberry.–P.M. • $20 • (11/15/1998) • **74**

GALTIER, DOMAINE

Coteaux du Languedoc 1996: This pleasant country wine has appealing aromas of berry, plum and tea, with flavors to match. Hearty, with just the right amount of tannins and backbone, and a nice spicy note on the finish. Drink now.–K.M. • $11 • (10/31/1998) • **84**

GAMBIER, JEAN

Bourgueil Domaine del Galluches Cuvée Ronsard 1993 • $13 • (5/15/1996) • **88**

GANGLOFF, MATHILDE & YVES

Côte-Rôtie 1996: Beautifully put together, this blockbuster with finesse shows great complexity, depth and seduction. Bursting with black fruit, smoke and toasted oak notes and refined tannins. Medium-bodied, it's balanced from start to minerally finish. Best after 2002.–P.M. • $65 • (12/15/1999) • **90**
Côte-Rôtie La Barbarine 1996: A tough wine that rips your palate away, but it's thick—thicker than the lovely, more refined regular Gangloff Côte-Rôtie. Tasting as if it were heavily extracted, this has mucho wood and loads of expressive blackberry, cassis, violet, spice, black pepper and smoke complexity. The finish is coarse and very hot now, but should soften with age. Best from 2005 through 2010.–P.M. • $50 • (12/15/1999) • **90**
Côte-Rôtie La Barbarine 1995: Serious juice. This very intense, pungent, ripe, warm-vintage wine delivers powerful fruit aromas in a smooth and full-bodied package. Thick and dense, with plum, mineral and black pepper purity. A blockbuster that tastes of *terroir* and not of oak. Best from 2003 through 2015.–P.M. • $50 • (11/30/1999) • **93**

Key: SS—Spectator Selection. CS—Cellar Selection. HR—Highly Recommended. $NA—Price not available. (BT)—Barrel tasting. (A)—Auction Price.
For a key to the tasters' initials, see "How to Use These Listings."
Dates in parentheses represent the issues in which the ratings were published.

GARAUDET, PAUL

Bourgogne Aligoté 1997: Crisp and fruity, but with a buttery, creamlike character that's not totally clean and a drying finish.–P.M. • $NA • (1/01/1999) • **78**
Bourgogne White 1997: A bit astringent, with a green, herbal character. It's tough to warm up to this.–P.M. • $19 • (5/31/1999) • **75**
Bourgogne White 1996 • $15 • (5/31/1998) • **84**
Bourgogne White 1995 • $15 • (8/31/1997) • **72**
Meursault Vieille Vigne 1997: Of fairly good texture, with a lively midpalate, it turns a bit crisp on the finish, with its modestly ripe fruit, green apple and toasted oak tannins. Drink now through 2002.–P.M. • $40 • (5/31/1999) • **83**
Meursault Vieille Vigne 1996 • $32 • (5/31/1998) • **90**
Meursault Vieilles Vignes 1995 • $NA • (5/31/1997) • **85**
Monthélie White Les Champs Fulliot 1997: Crisp and fruity, offering a mineral note along with ripe pear. Turns a bit drying on the finish, with a wet paper character.–P.M. • $28 • (5/31/1999) • **78**
Monthélie White Les Champs Fulliot 1996 • $24 • (5/31/1998) • **85**
Monthélie White Les Champs Fulliot 1995 • $23 • (5/31/1997) • **91**
Puligny-Montrachet 1997: Fruity, with honey, green apple and tropical notes. Full-bodied and supple, with a wonderful intensity of pure and clean fresh herb, honey and spice flavors. A delicious '97 to drink on release. Drink now through 2001.–P.M. • $36 • (5/31/1999) • **88**
Puligny-Montrachet 1996 • $32 • (5/31/1998) • **89**
Puligny-Montrachet 1995 • $30 • (5/31/1997) • **79**

GARDE, CHATEAU LA

Pessac-Léognan 1998: Serves up violets, fresh berries and minerals. Full-bodied yet reserved, with fine tannins and a silky, long finish. Very fine. Almost outstanding.–J.S. • $NA • (5/31/1999) (BT) • **85-89**
Pessac-Léognan 1997: Some good berry and green tobacco character in this medium-bodied red. Firm tannins, but slightly short finish. Drink now.–J.S. • $15 • (1/31/2000) • **83**
Pessac-Léognan 1996: A good little wine, slightly simple, but delicious all the same. Pretty cherry and vanilla aromas. Medium-bodied, with medium, velvety tannins and a fresh finish. Drink now.–J.S. • $18 • (1/31/1999) • **85**
Pessac-Léognan 1995 • $15 • (1/31/1998) • **90**
Pessac-Léognan 1994 • $17 • (1/31/1997) • **87**
Pessac-Léognan Réserve de Château 1993 • $17 • (1/31/1996) • **83**
Pessac-Léognan Réserve de Château 1991 • $13 • (3/31/1994) • **78**
Pessac-Léognan White 1997: Very ripe, with pineapple and tropical character. Full-bodied, with good fruit, but the new wood dominates at the moment. Give it time. Best after 2000.–J.S. • $20 • (9/30/1999) • **88**
Pessac-Léognan White 1996: A balanced, easygoing glass of white, with apple and grass aromas and flavors, medium body and a fresh finish. Drink now.–J.S. • $NA • (1/01/1999) • **83**

GARDINE, CHATEAU DE LA

Châteauneuf-du-Pape 1997: Smooth and round, medium-bodied and balanced, this is no blockbuster, but there's a fatness on the palate that checks the firm tannins. Reasonable amount of fruit, wet earth and oak-scented vanilla and a lingering finish. Drink now through 2005.–P.M. • $30 • (12/15/1999) • **88**
Châteauneuf-du-Pape 1996: Polished and attractive in an accessible, medium-bodied style. Shows decent cherry and red berry, with a hint of wood smoke. The tannins clamp down on the slightly short finish. Drink now through 2003.–P.M. • $30 • (12/15/1999) • **82**
Châteauneuf-du-Pape 1995 • $31 • (10/15/1997) • **87**
Châteauneuf-du-Pape 1994 • $28 • (10/15/1997) • **75**
Châteauneuf-du-Pape 1990 • $24 • (9/30/1993) • **87**
Châteauneuf-du-Pape 1989 • $25 • (10/15/1991) • **95**
Châteauneuf-du-Pape 1988 • $33 • (10/15/1991) • **85**
Châteauneuf-du-Pape 1986 • $17 • (10/15/1991) • **90**
Châteauneuf-du-Pape 1985 • $15 • (12/31/1987) • **87**
Châteauneuf-du-Pape 1984 • $15 • (12/31/1987) • **78**
Châteauneuf-du-Pape 1983 • $25 • (10/15/1991) • **89**
Châteauneuf-du-Pape 1981 • $NA • (10/15/1991) • **86**
Châteauneuf-du-Pape Cuvée des Générations 1996: Fairly racy, but also shows vanilla, mocha, smoke and toasty accents. Dark-colored, extracted, with supple tannins and plenty of clean fruit and spice notes. For fans of slightly oaky, international-style Châteauneuf. Drink now through 2005.–P.M. • $80 • (11/15/1998) • **88**
Châteauneuf-du-Pape Cuvée des Générations 1995 • $78 • (10/15/1997) • **93**
Châteauneuf-du-Pape Cuvée des Générations 1994 • $60 • (10/15/1997) • **91**
Châteauneuf-du-Pape Cuvée des Générations 1990 • $38 • (9/30/1993) • **89**

Châteauneuf-du-Pape Cuvée des Générations 1989 • $38 • (2/28/1993) CS • **94**
Châteauneuf-du-Pape Cuvée des Générations 1985 • $NA • (10/15/1991) • **92**
Châteauneuf-du-Pape White 1996 • $35 • (10/15/1997) • **87**
Châteauneuf-du-Pape White Vieilles Vignes 1996: New-oakish style. Full-bodied, with shaved wood notes but also lots of fat, ripe, honeyed character, with pear, apple and roasted walnut. Good lemony acidity means it might come together nicely with age; for now it's quite toasty. Best from 2005.–P.M. • $46 • (11/15/1998) • **86**
Côtes du Rhône White 1996 • $12 • (10/15/1997) • **82**
Côtes du Rhône-Villages 1995 • $18 • (10/15/1997) • **81**
Côtes du Rhône-Villages 1990 • $15 • (9/30/1993) • **82**

GARENNE, DOMAINE DE LA

Mâcon-Azé 1995 • $12 • (5/31/1997) • **79**

GARON, JEAN-FRANCOIS & CARMEN

Côte-Rôtie 1997: Oaky and redolent of oak tannins, mocha and vanilla notes, this dark-colored Syrah is full on the palate, but the wood covers up the fruit, which hibernates. Will it wake up? Try through 2002.–P.M. • $35 • (9/15/1999) • **80**

GARREAU, CHATEAU

Côtes de Bourg 1997: Shows a good core of fruit for the vintage, with currant, berry and cherry character. Medium-bodied, with silky tannins. Rather short finish. Drink now through 2003.–J.S. • $20 • (1/31/2000) • **85**
Premières Côtes de Blaye 1997: Some berry and cherry character to this, but slightly stewed. Medium to light in body, with a light finish.–J.S. • $18 • (1/31/2000) • **79**

GARRICQ, CHATEAU LA

Moulis 1997: Very pretty smoke, berry and tobacco aromas. Medium-bodied, with pleasant fruit. Drink now.–J.S. • $NA • (1/31/2000) • **86**
Moulis 1996: Lots of solid berry, cherry and chocolate fruit on the palate. Medium-bodied, with lovely spice flavors and a medium fine tannic aftertaste. This is an estate to watch. Best after 2003.–J.S. • $NA • (6/30/1999) • **87**

GARRIGUES, LES

Côtes du Rhône 1996 • $NA • (10/15/1997) • **79**

GARTIEUX, DOMAINE DES

Pauillac 1996: Raspberry and wet earth aromas have a hint of cedar. Medium-bodied, with soft tannins and a vanilla and chocolate aftertaste. Drink now.–J.S. • $30 • (6/15/2000) • **84**
Pauillac 1995: Medium- to full-bodied, with lovely, bright berry, currant and raspberry, velvety tannins and a long berry and mint aftertaste. Very impressive, solidly built '95. Needs time. From the young vines of Pichon Lalande. Best from 2001 through 2007.–J.S. • $19 • (1/01/1999) • **88**

GASCOGNE, COMTE DE

Blanc de Blancs France NV • $9 • (5/31/1997) • **83**

GATINOIS

Brut Champagne Réserve NV: Quite dry and nicely mature in style, with appealing lemon and apple flavors and spicy nuances that linger on the finish. Drink now. • $28 • (10/31/1999) • **88**
Brut Rosé Champagne NV: Round and mellow, this rosé smells and tastes like strawberries and cherries, with a smooth texture and a touch of crisp apple on the finish. Drink now.–B.S. • $28 • (11/30/1999) • **85**

GAUBY, DOMAINE

Côtes du Roussillon 1991 • $8 • (3/15/1994) • **82**
Côtes du Roussillon Élevé en Fûts de Chêne 1996 • $15 • (5/31/1998) • **84**
Côtes du Roussillon Les Calcinaires 1997: A powerful, medium-bodied red wine, with flavors of black currant, berry, tar and coffee. Ends on a spicy, mochalike note. Tight now, but still approachable. Drink now through 2003.–K.M. • $14 • (1/31/1999) • **87**
Côtes du Roussillon-Villages Vieilles Vignes 1996: Nice up-front richness, with juicy cherry, plum and spice flavors. Finishes with appealing chocolaty notes. A good wine for grilled meats. Drink now.–K.M. • $21 • (11/30/1998) • **86**
Côtes du Roussillon-Villages Vieilles Vignes 1995 • $21 • (12/15/1997) • **88**
Côtes du Roussillon-Villages Vieilles Vignes 1991 • $9 • (3/15/1994) • **85**

GAUDET, JEAN-FRANCOIS

Morgon 1988 • $10 • (5/31/1989) • **87**
Régnié Domaine de la Grange-Barjot 1995 • $11 • (9/15/1997) • **80**
Régnié Domaine de la Grange-Barjot 1994 • $12 • (9/15/1996) • **76**
Régnié Domaine de la Grange-Barjot 1993 • $12 • (7/31/1995) • **84**

GAUDRY, DENIS

Pouilly-Fumé 1998: Fans of the grassy, herbal side of Sauvignon Blanc will enjoy this pungent white, with its assertive aromas and flavors and light, crisp character. Others may find it a bit sharp and unbalanced. Drink now.–T.M. • $20 • (11/15/1999) • **83**
Pouilly-Fumé 1996 • $19 • (2/28/1998) • **87**

GAUTHIER

Brut Champagne 1990: Focused and flavorful, this has the keen balance and lively fruit to age into an outstanding Champagne. Delicious now, but should gain even more complexity with time. Drink now through 2005. • $37 • (11/15/1999) • **92**
Brut Champagne Grande Reserve NV: Appealing flavors of honey, lanolin and vanilla are enhanced by the smooth, creamy texture, all supported by a Granny Smith acidity. Fine concentration and a refreshing finish complete the package. Drink now through 2001.–B.S. • $29 • (11/30/1999) • **90**
Brut Rosé Champagne Grande Reserve NV: Aromas of baking bread are augmented by an almond flavor in this soft, loose-knit rosé that finishes crisply, but short. Drink now.–B.S. • $32 • (11/30/1999) • **85**

GAUTHIER, PIERRE

Bourgueil Domaine du Bel Air Clos Sénéchal 1996: Offers smoky, spicy aromas and vanilla-tinged berry flavors. Finishes with astringent tannins. Ambitious, but too far on the oaky side. Drink now.–B.S. • $20 • (10/31/1998) • **82**
Bourgueil Domaine du Bel Air Les Caillots 1996: Pretty aromas and concentrated flavors of cassis, raspberry and vanilla, all elegantly displayed and beautifully integrated. Supple, dense and long. A fine expression of Cabernet Franc. Drink now through 2001.–B.S. • $12 • (10/31/1998) • **89**
Bourgueil Domaine du Bel Air Les Caillots 1995 • $12 • (5/15/1997) • **87**
Bourgueil Domaine du Bel Air Les Grandmonts 1995 • $21 • (6/15/1998) • **90**

GAUTIER, BENOIT

Vouvray 1996: Shows a mix of lemon, cooked apple and herb flavors, with a hint of spritz. Lively, but a bit unbalanced.–B.S. • $10 • (11/15/1998) • **77**
Vouvray Demi-Sec 1996 • $18 • (6/30/1998) • **82**
Vouvray Moelleux Clos la Lanterne 1996 • $18 • (6/15/1998) • **84**
Vouvray Sec Clos la Lanterne 1996 • $15 • (6/30/1998) • **82**

GAY, CHATEAU LE

Pomerol 1999: Pleasant wine, with plum, berry and cherry character. Medium body. Light finish.–J.S. • $NA • (1/01/2000) (BT) • **80-84**
Pomerol 1998: Floral and stony aromas come through. Medium- to full-bodied, with silky tannins and a medium finish. A compacted wine not giving much right now.–J.S. • $NA • (5/31/1999) (BT) • **90-94**
Pomerol 1997: Lovely plum, violet and berry character. Medium-bodied, with silky tannins and a medium, fruity finish. Pretty wine. Drink now.–J.S. • $NA • (1/31/2000) • **86**
Pomerol 1995: Racy Pomerol. Seductive aromas of blackberries, flowers and raspberries. Medium- to full-bodied, with integrated tannins and a medium finish. Needs time to mellow. Best from 2002 through 2007.–J.S. • $40 • (9/15/1998) • **90**
Pomerol 1993 • $29 • (1/31/1996) • **80**
Pomerol 1992 • $22 • (4/15/1995) • **73**
Pomerol 1990 • $46 Ⓐ • (3/31/1993) • **96**
Pomerol 1989: Tannic monster. Full-bodied, with masses of superripe fruit and mouthpuckering tannins. Port lovers like me love this stuff. Age it for decades

FRANCE

to come. (1989 Bordeaux horizontal tasting). Best after 2006.–J.S. • $75 Ⓐ • (5/31/1999) • **95**

Pomerol 1988: Never a very interesting bottle of Le Gay, this has a good dark ruby color, but is rather hard and slightly drying. Medium-bodied, with ripe fruit but austere tannins. (1988 Bordeaux horizontal tasting). Drink now.–J.S. • $45 Ⓐ • (11/30/1998) • **84**

Pomerol 1982: A Pomerol with delicious fruit and ripeness. Deep ruby-garnet color, with cherry, tobacco and green olive aromas. Medium- to full-bodied, with velvety tannins and a long dark chocolate and berry aftertaste. (1982 Bordeaux horizontal tasting). Drink now.–J.S. • $65 Ⓐ • (11/30/1998) • **89**

Pomerol 1961 • $88 Ⓐ • (4/30/1996) • **82**

GAZIN, CHATEAU

Pomerol 1999: Flashy. Dark ruby, with lots of coffee, berry and ripe fruit. Medium-bodied, with velvety tannins and a slightly short finish. Hollow midpalate.–J.S. • $NA • (1/01/2000) (BT) • **85-89**

Pomerol 1998: A well-made, modern-style '98. Amazing aromas of exotic spices, cherries and berries. Full-bodied and silky, with fine tannins and a toasted oak, berry aftertaste. Almost outstanding. Tasted three times, with consistent notes.–J.S. • $NA • (5/31/1999) (BT) • **85-89**

Pomerol 1997: Good berry and earth character, but a bit lean on the finish. Medium-bodied, with vanilla, chocolate and berry flavors. Slightly dry finish. Too much wood? Not as good as when tasted from barrel. Tasted twice, with consistent notes. Best after 2000.–J.S. • $NA • (1/31/2000) • **84**

Pomerol 1996: Lots of new wood, with hints of blackberry and cherry. Medium-bodied, with pretty berry flavors and lots of toasted vanilla oak on the finish. Tasted twice, with consistent notes. Best after 2000.–J.S. • $59 • (1/31/1999) • **86**

Pomerol 1995 • $45 • (1/31/1998) • **90**

Pomerol 1994 • $43 • (1/31/1997) • **90**

Pomerol 1993 • $30 • (1/31/1996) • **87**

Pomerol 1992 • $24 • (4/15/1995) • **78**

Pomerol 1991 • $24 • (3/31/1994) • **81**

Pomerol 1990 • $32 • (3/31/1993) • **88**

Pomerol 1989: This wine is going through a strange period. It shows impressive concentration of ripe fruit, with plenty of berry and chocolate character, and it's full-bodied, but the palate turns slightly papery and dry on the finish. Tasted three times, with consistent notes. (1989 Bordeaux horizontal tasting). Drink now.–J.S. • $NA • (5/31/1999) • **80**

Pomerol 1988: Beautiful aromas of milk chocolate, berry and coffee. Medium-bodied, with finely textured, well-integrated, medium tannins. (1988 Bordeaux horizontal tasting). Best after 2000.–J.S. • $NA • (11/30/1998) • **90**

Pomerol 1985 • $21 • (9/30/1988) • **90**

Pomerol 1982: A concentrated, delicious wine. Ruby-colored, with an amber hue. Plenty of chocolate, ripe fruit and seashells on the nose. Full-bodied and very ripe, with velvety tannins and lots of chocolate, berry and tobacco flavors. Long finish. (1982 Bordeaux horizontal tasting). Drink now.–J.S. • $NA • (11/30/1998) • **91**

Pomerol 1961 • $55 • (4/30/1996) • **84**

Pomerol 1945 • $220 • (11/30/1995) • **83**

GEANTET-PANSIOT

Bourgogne 1992 • $16 • (11/30/1994) • **85**

Charmes-Chambertin 1993 • $62 Ⓐ • (5/15/1996) • **90**

Gevrey-Chambertin Poissenot 1993 • $45 • (5/15/1996) • **90**

GENDRIER, MICHEL

Cheverny 1996 • $11 • (5/31/1998) • **82**

Cheverny Domaine des Huards 1997: Light and clean, this white is almost neutral in flavor, but hints of zesty acidity and light herbal notes keep it refreshing.–T.M. • $11 • (6/30/1999) • **79**

GENILLON, DOMAINE DE

Morgon Le Terrain Rouge 1994 • $10 • (10/31/1995) • **82**

Key: SS—Spectator Selection. CS—Cellar Selection. HR—Highly Recommended. $NA—Price not available. (BT)—Barrel tasting. Ⓐ—Auction Price. For a key to the tasters' initials, see "How to Use These Listings."
Dates in parentheses represent the issues in which the ratings were published.

GEOFFRAY, CL.

Côte de Brouilly Château Thivin 1998: This solid red is quite rich for a Beaujolais, with firm tannins and deep, rather austere flavors of plum, smoke and bitter almond. Needs food to show its best. Drink now through 2001.–T.M. • $16 • (11/15/1999) • **84**

Côte de Brouilly Château Thivin 1997: Some good stuffing here. The bright cherry flavor is fresh, if slightly candied, and there are earthy and piney notes that add complexity. It's big and bold, if not your typical Gamay. Drink now.–T.M. • $16 • (5/15/1999) • **85**

Côte de Brouilly Château Thivin 1995 • $17 • (7/31/1997) • **85**

Côte de Brouilly Château Thivin 1994 • $15 • (9/15/1996) • **82**

GEOFFROY, ALAIN

Chablis 1996 • $NA • (8/31/1997) • **87**

Chablis 1995 • $NA • (8/31/1996) • **84**

Chablis Beauroy 1998: Supple and generous, with medium-intense fruit, this medium-bodied Chablis turns smoky and lively on the finish. Drink now through 2002.–P.M. • $20 • (5/15/2000) • **85**

Chablis Beauroy 1996 • $20 • (5/31/1998) • **86**

Chablis Beauroy 1995 • $20 • (6/15/1997) • **88**

Chablis Domaine Le Verger Cuvée Vieilles Vignes 1998: This ripe-tasting, delicate-smelling, balanced, medium-bodied village wine is delicious on release. Offers honey, pear and apple, with a smoky undertone. The chewy, chalky finish is interesting. Drink now through 2001.–P.M. • $15 • (5/15/2000) • **84**

Chablis Domaine Le Verger Cuvée Vieilles Vignes 1996 • $NA • (8/31/1997) • **85**

Chablis Fourchaume 1997: Soft and a bit oxidized, with a spicy, tart, astringent finish. 12 cases imported.–P.M. • $NA • (1/01/1999) • **73**

Chablis Vau-Ligneau 1998: A well-done play on minerally *terroir* that gains momentum on the smoky palate. Don't expect much ripe fruit in this medium-bodied Chardonnay, but the voltage is displayed in a tingling intensity on the long finish. An ager. Best from 2003 through 2008.–P.M. • $20 • (5/15/2000) • **89**

Chablis Vau-Ligneau 1997: Pure, clean, vibrant, with a taste combining the salty sea and an orchard of apples. Medium-bodied, very balanced, open and charming, with low-acidity. 50 cases imported. Drink now through 2003.–P.M. • $30 • (5/31/1999) • **88**

Petit Chablis 1996 • $NA • (8/31/1997) • **86**

GEOFFROY, RENE

Brut Champagne Cuvée de Réserve NV: A subtle, elegant style of brut, with subdued fruit accented by earthy, toasty notes. Very smooth in texture. Seems to grow on the finish. Drink now. • $40 • (9/15/1999) • **89**

Brut Champagne Cuvée Prestige NV: A no-nonsense style, frankly fruity, nicely dry, with lean texture and a crisp finish. Drink now. • $55 • (10/15/1999) • **87**

Brut Champagne Cuvée Sélectionnée NV: A distinctive Champagne, with an unusual flavor profile. Has strong cherry character, firm but fine texture and a lingering, fruity finish. May need time to develop. Drink now through 2001. • $50 • (9/15/1999) • **88**

GERIN, JEAN-MICHEL

Condrieu Coteau de la Loye 1997: Wonderful, ripe but (since it's recently bottled) backward character, with loads of dry wood. Give it time to show its pineapple, honey and ripe pear. Very balanced, with fresh lime, oak complexity and a long finish.–P.M. • $38 • (10/15/1998) • **94**

Condrieu Vendange Suprême 1997: Thick, ripe and off-dry, offering some fat, oily character, vanilla and smoke notes, decent vibrancy. Drink now through 2001.–P.M. • $40 • (8/31/1999) • **87**

Côte-Rôtie 1991 • $NA • (5/31/1994) • **88**

Côte-Rôtie Champin Le Seigneur 1996: Gorgeous for its seductive floral, rose petal, grilled meat, plum and cassis notes. Medium-bodied and fairly firm, elegant and racy, with a juicy, somewhat crisp finish accented by toasted, spicy oak. A lovely, well-made and harmonious wine that's tempting upon release but should soften with cellaring. Drink now through 2005.–P.M. • $40 • (9/15/1998) • **91**

Côte-Rôtie Champin Le Seigneur 1995 • $40 • (10/15/1997) • **90**

Côte-Rôtie Champin Le Seigneur 1994 • $36 • (11/30/1996) • **88**

Côte-Rôtie Champin Le Seigneur 1993 • $33 • (11/30/1996) • **88**

Côte-Rôtie Champin Le Seigneur 1992 • $32 • (5/31/1994) • **88**

Côte-Rôtie Champin Le Seigneur 1991 • $27 • (5/31/1994) • **84**

FRANCE

Côte-Rôtie Champin-Junior 1995 • $36/500 ml. • (10/15/1997) • **85**
Côte-Rôtie Champin-Junior 1994 • $38 • (11/30/1996) • **90**
Côte-Rôtie La Landonne 1996: Big, muscular, oaky, compacted red with lots of acidity to keep it fresh but also lots of flesh on the frame to give it fatness. Full-bodied, it's a bit awkward now, showing little except a lemony, cassis bush, raspberry character and loads of spicy, toasted wood accents, but it should gain. Best from 2002 through 2007.–P.M. • $75 • (9/15/1998) • **88**
Côte-Rôtie Les Grandes Places 1996: Great Côte-Rôtie, woodier than most, but it marries beautifully the pronounced toasted oak flavors with clean, pure and fresh currant and floral notes. Complex wine, and elegant, with plenty of lemonlike acidity to guide it to a long, succulent, harmonious finish. Best from 2003 through 2006.–P.M. • $75 • (9/15/1998) • **93**
Côte-Rôtie Les Grandes Places 1995 • $69 • (10/15/1997) • **91**
Côte-Rôtie Les Grandes Places 1994 • $56 • (11/30/1996) • **92**
Côte-Rôtie Les Grandes Places 1993 • $46 • (11/30/1996) • **87**
Côte-Rôtie Les Grandes Places 1992 • $45 • (5/31/1994) • **86**
Côte-Rôtie Les Grandes Places 1991 • $45 • (5/31/1994) • **92**
Côtes du Rhône 1997: Smells like a clever woodmeister's wine, with beautiful smoky and toasty aromas marrying the red berry, blackberry, violet, rose petal and mocha notes. Of medium body, it's balanced on the smooth finish. Drink now.–P.M. • $15 • (11/15/1999) • **87**

GERMAIN, HENRI

Brut Champagne NV • $25 • (12/15/1995) • **89**
Brut Champagne 1990 • $39 • (12/31/1996) • **89**
Brut Champagne Président NV • $35 • (12/15/1995) • **87**
Brut Rosé Champagne Tête de Cuvée NV • $30 • (12/15/1996) • **87**
Brut Champagne 1990: A plush texture and light, creamy flavors make this Champagne hard to resist. It has bright, light notes of lemon, apple, toast and vanilla and a pillow-soft mouthfeel. More subtleties emerge on the long finish. Drink now. • $36 • (12/15/1998) • **93**
Brut Champagne Président Tête de Cuvée NV: You can practically sink your teeth into this substantial, full-bodied brut. Though it has a fine mousse, it's the butter, toast, apple and spice flavors that stand out from the aroma to the lingering finish. Drink now. • $40 • (12/15/1998) • **90**
Brut Champagne Tête de Cuvée NV: Extremely inviting and enjoyable, this brut has earthy, doughy aromas and a full, soft mousse. Modest, crisp citrus flavors are accented by honey. Lingering finish. Drink now. • $29 • (12/31/1998) • **88**

GERMAIN, JACQUES

Beaune Aux Cras 1992 • $NA • (12/15/1994) • **83**
Beaune Aux Cras 1991 • $33 • (1/31/1994) • **85**
Beaune Aux Cras 1990 • $46 • (12/15/1992) • **89**
Beaune Aux Cras 1989 • $48 • (1/31/1992) • **90**
Beaune Aux Cras Vieilles Vignes 1994 • $NA • (11/15/1996) • **85**
Beaune Les Boucherottes 1990 • $42 • (12/15/1992) • **89**
Beaune Les Cents Vignes 1990 • $46 • (12/15/1992) • **91**
Beaune Les Teurons 1992 • $NA • (12/15/1994) • **84**
Beaune Les Teurons 1991 • $33 • (1/31/1994) • **79**
Beaune Les Teurons 1990 • $48 • (12/15/1992) • **91**
Beaune Les Teurons 1989 • $50 • (1/31/1992) • **92**
Beaune Les Teurons 1988 • $42 • (2/15/1991) • **90**
Beaune Les Teurons 1986 • $33 • (7/31/1988) • **70**
Beaune Les Teurons Vieilles Vignes 1994 • $NA • (11/15/1996) • **80**
Beaune Les Vignes Franches 1994 • $NA • (11/15/1996) • **80**
Beaune Les Vignes Franches 1992 • $NA • (12/15/1994) • **78**
Beaune Les Vignes Franches 1991 • $30 • (1/31/1994) • **86**
Beaune Les Vignes Franches 1990 • $46 • (12/15/1992) • **91**
Beaune Les Vignes Franches 1989 • $45 • (1/31/1992) • **91**
Chorey-Côte de Beaune Château de Chorey-lès-Beaune 1990 • $24 • (12/15/1992) • **85**
Chorey-Côte de Beaune Château de Chorey-lès-Beaune 1989 • $24 • (1/31/1992) • **84**
Chorey-lès-Beaune Château de Chorey-lès-Beaune 1992 • $NA • (12/15/1994) • **76**
Chorey-lès-Beaune Château de Chorey-lès-Beaune 1991 • $20 • (1/31/1994) • **78**
Chorey-lès-Beaune Château de Chorey-lès-Beaune 1986 • $16 • (7/31/1989) • **80**

GERMAIN, THIERRY

Saumur-Champigny Domaine des Roches Neuves 1998: Light and soft in texture, slightly bitter on the palate, with green, stemmy notes alongside the cherry and light earth. Light tannins.–T.M. • $13 • (6/30/1999) • **77**
Saumur-Champigny Domaine des Roches Neuves Marginale 1996: Round and generous, this inky red offers chocolate, cola, black cherry and black olive flavors. Generous yet focused, it has firm underlying tannins and good balance. Drink now through 2002.–T.M. • $30 • (6/30/1999) • **86**
Saumur-Champigny Domaine des Roches Neuves Terres Chaudes 1997: Smoky and meaty aromas follow through onto the palate in this deeply colored red, with black cherry and tobacco notes and lively acidity. Shows good concentration for the vintage, but turns a bit dry on the finish. Drink now through 2002.–T.M. • $20 • (6/30/1999) • **84**
Saumur-Champigny La Marginale 1993 • $30 • (6/15/1997) • **81**
Saumur-Champigny Terres Chades Domaine des Roches Neuves 1992 • $13 • (1/01/1995) • **86**

GERMAIN, VIGNOBLES

Anjou Château de la Guimonière La Haie Fruitière 1998: Firm and flavorful, with a note of pure red currant. Medium-bodied, with an herbal, peppery finish. Drink now.–K.M. • $10 • (5/15/2000) • **85**
Anjou White La Guimonière 1997: Assertive nectarine and tangerine aromas herald this dry white, with a bracing mineral streak and mature notes of earth and marzipan. Finishes firm, with food-friendly acidity. Drink now.–K.M. • $15 • (5/15/2000) • **85**
Coteaux du Layon-Chaume Château de la Guimonière 1997: Rich yet elegant, this plush, sweet white offers spicy honey and vanilla flavors over clean, ripe notes of peach and apricot. Has a beautiful balance of crisp and sweet, with a long, spicy finish. Drink now through 2006.–T.M. • $40/500 ml. • (2/29/2000) • **90**

GIBALAUX, DOMAINE

Merlot Vin de Pays d'Oc 1996 • $7 • (3/31/1998) • **84**
Merlot Vin de Pays d'Oc 1995 • $8 • (8/31/1997) • **82**

GIBALAUX-BONNET, CHATEAU

Merlot Vin de Pays d'Oc 1998: Has an appealing core of red plum and red currant flavors, with nice minerally notes on the finish. Medium-bodied and smooth. Drink now.–K.M. • $7 • (10/31/1999) • **85**
Minervois 1998: Starts nice and fresh, with red plum and serious mineral flavors, but clamps down a bit on the finish. Drink now through 2002.–K.M. • $7 • (11/15/1999) • **84**

GIGAULT, CHATEAU

Premières Côtes de Blaye Cuvée Viva 1999: Black, with intense berry, blackberry and black licorice aromas. Medium-bodied, with fine tannins, but slightly hollow midpalate.–J.S. • $NA • (1/01/2000) (BT) • **85-89**
Premières Côtes de Blaye Cuvée Viva 1998: Very grapey and rich, with loads of black licorice. Full-bodied and velvety. Long, long finish. A tribute to this appellation and the vintage.–J.S. • $NA • (5/31/1999) (BT) • **90-94**

GIGOGNAN, CHATEAU

Châteauneuf-du-Pape Clos du Roi 1998: A firm Châteauneuf, with cold fruit at the core, tough and hard tannins, a slight herbal character and black cherry and citrus notes. Chewy, slightly drying finish. Best from 2001 through 2006.–P.M. • $24 • (1/01/2000) • **82**
Châteauneuf-du-Pape Clos du Roi 1997: Seductive, silky and unctuous, a medium-bodied Châteauneuf that tastes as if made in an oxidative, traditional style: a bit light in color, with brown sugar and licorice and signs of advanced maturity from forest underbrush and truffle notes. But it has lots of gras ("fat"). Lovely balance, with sweet, well-integrated tannins. Drink now through 2010.–P.M. • $27 • (12/15/1999) • **90**
Châteauneuf-du-Pape Clos du Roi 1995: Rustic, with attractive, strong smoke, leather, earth, prune, plum and fig flavors along with red berry and blackberry character. Medium-bodied, it tastes a bit hot, but has smooth tannins. Drink now through 2003.–P.M. • $30 • (9/30/1998) • **84**
Châteauneuf-du-Pape Vigne du Dauphin 1995: A bit funky, with vanilla bean, cream and strawberry flavors, this is a simple wine that's tough to warm up to.–P.M. • $26 • (11/15/1998) • **72**
Côtes du Rhône Rosé Vigne du Prieuré 1997: There is ripe fruit here, but it is also alcoholic. Nice honey and beeswax save the day. Still not very harmonious. Not imported into the U.S. Drink now through 2001.–P.M. • $NA • (1/01/1999) • **80**

Côtes du Rhône Vigne du Prieuré 1997: Light in body and color but fairly ripe and delicate, with some raspberry, cedar and plum notes.–P.M. • $13 • (11/15/1998) • **79**

Côtes du Rhône-Villages Bois des Moines 1997: Very earthy in style, quite mature, but showing a good ripe character. A chewy, interesting *terroir* keeps your taste buds alert, bringing you back for another sip of this medium-bodied red. Much better than previously reviewed. Drink now through 2003.–P.M. • $15 • (12/15/1999) • **87**

GILETTE, CHATEAU

Sauternes Doux 1947 • $NA • (5/31/1997) • **80**

GILLET, EMILIAN

Mâcon-Viré Quintaine 1997: A home run from one of the stars of the Mâconnais. Understated, lovely wine, delivering intense ripe fruit, honey and spice in a supple texture that shows a dagger of firm grip on the sweet-tasting yet lemony, long and fresh finish. From Jean Thévenet. Drink now through 2002.–P.M. • $23 • (5/31/1999) • **90**

GILOUX, ISABELLE & PATRICK

Beaujolais-Villages Clos de Creuse Noire 1995 • $10 • (9/15/1997) • **78**

GIMONNET & FILS, PIERRE

Brut Blanc de Blancs Champagne NV • $30 • (11/30/1997) • **86**

Brut Blanc de Blancs Champagne Fleuron 1993: Pleasant bubbly, with straightforward fruit flavors and a rather lean texture. Drink now. • $45 • (10/15/1999) • **86**

Brut Blanc de Blancs Champagne Fleuron 1990 • $40 • (11/30/1997) • **89**

Brut Blanc de Blancs Champagne Gastronome 1993: Elegant in style and beautifully balanced, this offers crisp fruit flavors and soft vanilla accents on a velvety texture. Drink now. • $29 • (12/31/1998) • **89**

Brut Blanc de Blancs Champagne Premier Cru Cuis NV: Buttery, slightly toasty Chardonnay flavors distinguish this smooth, rather full-bodied wine. Hints of pear and honey linger on the finish. Drink now. • $35 • (9/15/1999) • **88**

Brut Champagne Special Club 1992: Dry and tangy in style and powerfully citruslike in flavor, this is a full-bodied, bold Champagne that needs time to mellow. Drink through 2003. • $33 • (12/31/1998) • **88**

Brut Champagne Special Club 1990: Really solid and lively in character. Bright citrus and pineapple flavors blend with crisp acidity and a clean finish in this very good bubbly. Drink now. • $37 • (12/31/1998) • **87**

GIRARD, DOMAINE

Sancerre La Garenne 1998: Clean, ripe flavors of pear and apple have just enough acidity to keep them juicy and refreshing. A pleasant herbal note enlivens the finish. Drink now.–T.M. • $13 • (2/29/2000) • **86**

Sancerre La Garenne 1996: Clean, crisp acidity with focused flavors of grapefruit and flint give this wine good typicity, while round notes of melon and butter add depth and interest. A juicy white that will match well with food. Drink now.–T.M. • $16 • (12/31/1998) • **88**

GIRARDIN, ALETH

Beaune Clos des Mouches 1995 • $32 • (11/15/1997) • **78**
Beaune Clos des Mouches 1993 • $48 • (11/15/1995) • **90**
Beaune Clos des Mouches 1988 • $36 • (7/15/1991) • **71**
Pommard 1995 • $27 • (11/15/1997) • **85**
Pommard Charmots 1995 • $39 • (11/15/1997) • **82**
Pommard Charmots 1988 • $44 • (7/15/1991) • **87**
Pommard Epenots 1995 • $44 • (11/15/1997) • **87**
Pommard Rugiens 1995 • $44 • (11/15/1997) • **88**

Key: SS—Spectator Selection. CS—Cellar Selection. HR—Highly Recommended. $NA—Price not available. (BT)—Barrel tasting. Ⓐ—Auction Price.
For a key to the tasters' initials, see "How to Use These Listings."
Dates in parentheses represent the issues in which the ratings were published.

GIRARDIN, ARMAND

Pommard Les Charmots 1993 • $60 • (11/15/1995) • **91**
Pommard Les Epenots 1993 • $60 • (11/15/1995) • **90**

GIRARDIN, VINCENT

Bâtard-Montrachet 1998: Powerful white Burgundy, yet silky in texture. A beautiful, full-bodied, complex Chardonnay, layered with toast, pear, pineapple and other flavors. Terrific from start to finish—ripe, rich and sweet-tasting, but above all, balanced. Bravo. Drink now through 2010.–P.M. • $209 • (5/31/2000) • **93**

Bâtard-Montrachet 1997: Gorgeous. Thick, rich and ripe yet fresh, with lots of nice pineapple, lemon pie, lime, pear and quince flavors that vibrate to a fresh, lively and opulent finish. Best from 2005 through 2017.–P.M. • $173 • (5/31/1999) • **96**

Beaune Clos des Vignes Franches 1997: Ripe, cooked plum and black cherry compote on a round, soft framework, yet concentrated and long on the palate, finishing with a licorice chewiness. Drink now through 2003.–B.S. • $44 • (9/30/1999) • **85**

Beaune Clos des Vignes Franches 1996: Deeply colored, this modern-style red shows ripe red- and black cherry, a touch of vanilla and a freshness that carries through to the finish. Drink now through 2002.–B.S. • $39 • (9/30/1998) • **86**

Beaune Clos des Vignes Franches 1995 • $27 • (11/15/1997) • **86**
Beaune Clos des Vignes Franches 1994 • $31 • (11/15/1996) • **84**

Chassagne-Montrachet La Romanée 1997: Intensely flavored, with a grass, pear, tropical and green apple character and a minerally, supple midpalate. Medium-bodied, turning tough and crisp on the mouthpuckering finish. Drink through 2005.–P.M. • $80 • (5/31/1999) • **87**

Chassagne-Montrachet Le Cailleret 1998: Pleasant. Shows some pear, tropical, lemon character. Medium-bodied, it's succulent on the lemony, honeyed finish. Drink now through 2005.–P.M. • $70 • (5/31/2000) • **86**

Chassagne-Montrachet Le Cailleret 1997: This very nice '97 Chassagne has fresh lemon, honey, mandarin and quince character. Lively on the palate, medium-bodied and just delicious on the long, clean, vibrant, slightly toasty finish. Drink now through 2002.–P.M. • $62 • (5/31/1999) • **89**

Chassagne-Montrachet Le Cailleret 1996 • $51 • (5/31/1998) • **88**

Chassagne-Montrachet Morgeot Vieilles Vignes 1998: Pretty '98. Medium-bodied, it doesn't reveal many aromas for now, but it has a core of ripe fruit that tastes agreeably sweet, with some fresh citrus, dried herbs and nicely dosed toasted oak to bring it into balance on the finish. Drink now through 2003.–P.M. • $66 • (5/31/2000) • **86**

Chassagne-Montrachet Morgeot Vieilles Vignes 1997: Good, ripe, flavorful complexity shines in this golden-colored, medium-bodied, round and harmonious '97. Sparkles with clean lemon, honey and mineral notes on the lovely finish. Drink now through 2002.–P.M. • $60 • (5/31/1999) • **87**

Chassagne-Montrachet Morgeot Vieilles Vignes 1996 • $NA • (5/31/1998) • **93**

Chassagne-Montrachet Red Clos de la Boudriotte 1996: Pure expression of Pinot Noir. Red cherry and hints of spice combine with concentration and a raw-silk texture to provide immediate appeal. Drink now through 2003.–B.S. • $44 • (9/30/1998) • **87**

Chassagne-Montrachet Red Clos de la Boudriotte 1995 • $30 • (11/15/1997) • **90**

Chassagne-Montrachet Red Clos de la Boudriotte 1994 • $32 • (11/15/1996) • **79**

Chassagne-Montrachet Red Clos de la Boudriotte Vieilles Vignes 1997: Moderate intensity and concentration mark this round, approachable Chassagne. Sturdy tannins support the plum and vanilla notes. Drink now through 2003.–B.S. • $49 • (9/30/1999) • **85**

Chassagne-Montrachet Red Morgeot 1997: Nicely balanced in a rustic way. Shows a deep, sappy, grapey, freshly crushed red and black fruit character, with a firm structure of sweet tannins. Whets your palate for another sip. Drink now through 2006.–P.M. • $46 • (9/30/1999) • **88**

Chassagne-Montrachet Red Morgeot 1996: Smooth and approachable. A lovely red Burgundy, of medium body, with pure and clean red- and blackberry character. Delicious. Drink now through 2003.–P.M. • $41 • (9/30/1998) • **86**

Chassagne-Montrachet Red Morgeot 1995 • $27 • (11/15/1997) • **83**
Chassagne-Montrachet Red Morgeot 1994 • $30 • (11/15/1996) • **85**

Corton Clos du Roi 1997: Very ripe and plummy, with accents of vanilla and fig. Good concentration matches the licorice chewiness in the fat texture. Stiff tannins on the long finish. Needs time. Tasted twice, with consistent notes. Drink through 2005.–B.S. • $86 • (9/30/1999) • **89**

Corton Perrières 1997: Smoke, plum and truffle aromas and flavors mingle with the rich texture and stiff tannins, producing a powerful expression of

Pinot Noir. This has gras, concentration and length. Drink now through 2003.–B.S. • $76 • (9/30/1999) • **84**

Corton Perrières 1996: Well made, showing a lovely, ripe red berry character. Clean and pure, this full-bodied wine just needs time to shed its chewy, chalky, tannic side. Best after 2003.–P.M. • $69 • (9/30/1998) • **87**

Corton Perrières 1995 • $46 • (11/15/1997) • **85**

Corton Renardes Vieilles Vignes 1997: Clean, thick and rather fresh, with licorice, raspberry and cherry. Shows a soft midpalate but a decent finish. Drink now through 2003.–P.M. • $84 • (9/30/1999) • **88**

Corton-Charlemagne 1998: Clean and pure white, medium-bodied, showing a good tension of acidity and ripe fruit, though nothing very complex or deep. Enjoyable on release. Drink now through 2004.–P.M. • $111 • (5/31/2000) • **87**

Corton-Charlemagne 1997: Thick yet fresh—a refined white Burgundy with a dual personality. Beautifully crisp despite being ripe, showing a firm midpalate, with tropical, lemon, pear and green apple skin. Seamless, clean, pure finish. Drink now through 2006.–P.M. • $96 • (5/31/1999) • **95**

Corton-Charlemagne 1996 • $83 • (5/31/1998) • **94**

Maranges Clos des Loyères Vieilles Vignes 1996: Good concentration here, along with wild red berry flavors and an herbal note. Balanced toward the tannic side, but this wine should repay a little patience. Drink through 2005.–B.S. • $26 • (9/30/1998) • **85**

Maranges Clos des Loyères Vieilles Vignes 1995 • $20 • (11/15/1997) • **84**

Maranges Clos des Loyères Vieilles Vignes 1994 • $23 • (11/15/1996) • **86**

Meursault Les Charmes 1998: Pleasant and quite rich and ripe, bursting with honey, dried fruit character. Full-bodied, it powers its way to the finish, fueled by spice and crisp acidity. Drink now through 2002.–P.M. • $75 • (5/31/2000) • **88**

Meursault Les Charmes 1997: Vibrant and slightly spritzy on the palate, this shows dried herb, pear and green apple notes. Elegant and medium-bodied, with a medium-intense personality and a chewy, fresh, lemony finish. Drink now through 2003.–P.M. • $67 • (5/31/1999) • **85**

Meursault Les Narvaux 1998: Gorgeous. Powerful, full-bodied white Burgundy, bursting with intense yet refined smoke, toast and ripe fruit aromas. The flavors follow in a densely packed texture, and the seductive finish is exciting. Drink now through 2010.–P.M. • $52 • (5/31/2000) HR • **93**

Meursault Les Narvaux 1997: Lots of concentration and ripe fruit in this near-late harvest Meursault. Delicious and well made from start to finish, with the citrus, honey and passion fruit taking a brisk walk along the edge of the palate, zeroing in on the pleasure spots. Much better than previously reviewed. Drink now through 2005.–P.M. • $47 • (9/30/1999) • **92**

Meursault Les Narvaux 1996 • $42 • (5/31/1998) • **93**

Meursault Les Perrières 1997: Very grassy in style, almost like a Sauvignon Blanc. It bursts with freshly cut grass, crisp lemon rind, honey and toasted oak aromas. Clean and aggressive. Better than previously reviewed. Drink now through 2001.–P.M. • $75 • (9/30/1999) • **87**

Meursault Les Perrières 1996 • $65 • (5/31/1998) • **95**

Meursault Les Poruzots 1998: Beautiful white Burgundy. Refined aromas of wet earth, *terroir*, dried herbs; medium-bodied and not voluptuous, elegant and showing a wonderful array of aromas including honey, ripe pear and toasted bread notes on the finish. Not imported into the U.S. Best from 2001 through 2005.–P.M. • $NA • (5/31/2000) • **90**

Pommard Clos de Lambots Vieilles Vignes 1997: Gorgeous nose, showing wild berry, cherry and licorice notes, with a hint of corruption. Firm, intense and beautifully balanced on the palate, it's deceptive in its power and length. Drink through 2005.–B.S. • $51 • (9/30/1999) • **89**

Pommard Clos des Lambots Vieilles Vignes 1996: Rich and ripe, full-bodied, slightly earthy and beefy but loaded with fruit, acidity, wet earth and sweet tannins, this outstanding red Burgundy cascades with complexity, powering its way with intensity. Balanced and harmonious on the finish. Drink now through 2010.–P.M. • $46 • (9/30/1998) HR • **93**

Pommard Clos des Lambots 1994 • $35 • (11/15/1996) • **85**

Pommard Les Chanlins 1997: Rather thick, showing ripe black fruit and toast character, kicking in with a fresh mouthfeel on the persistent finish. Drink now through 2003.–P.M. • $66 • (9/30/1999) • **86**

Pommard Les Chanlins Vieilles Vignes 1996: Wonderfully ripe and sweet, this stays faithful to its appellation, delivering plenty of earth and mineral character along with lovely notes of cassis and plum. With supple tannins and laser-sharp flavors, this is a pure, clean, vibrant and full-bodied package. Drink now through 2006.–P.M. • $59 • (9/30/1998) • **93**

Pommard Les Chanlins Vieilles Vignes 1995 • $40 • (11/15/1997) • **90**

Pommard Les Chanlins Vieilles Vignes 1994 • $43 • (11/15/1996) • **92**

Pommard Les Chaponnières 1997: Very flavorful, with lovely ripe plum, floral and blackberry character that was extracted with care to create a lively yet supple, full-bodied and satisfying '97 Pommard. Drink now through 2005.–P.M. • $66 • (9/30/1999) • **91**

Pommard Les Grands Epenots Vieilles Vignes 1997: Cherry, plum and vanilla on the nose are underscored by an earthy, minerally richness and plum notes that show concentration. Lean and sinewy, with a protective sheath of tannins. Drink now through 2004.–B.S. • $76 • (9/30/1999) • **87**

Pommard Les Grands Epenots Vieilles Vignes 1996: Serious Pommard. Pure cherry, earth and spice character on a framework of bright acidity and firm tannins, with good depth of ripe fruit. Firm finish. Needs time to resolve the tannins. Best from 2001 through 2006.–B.S. • $70 • (9/30/1998) • **90**

Pommard Les Rugiens 1997: Lovely aromas and flavors of cherry, violet and iron and an animal note provide personality that's wed to a strong backbone of tannins and acidity, all presented in a seamless fashion. Best from 2001 through 2007.–B.S. • $89 • (9/30/1999) • **89**

Pommard Les Rugiens 1996: Great concentration. A reserved nose is followed by blackberry and vanilla in this backward, upright Pommard that's packed with fruit and has the structure to carry it all for many years. All the elements are there, it just needs time. Best from 2002 through 2007.–B.S. • $74 • (9/30/1998) • **90**

Pommard Les Rugiens Vieilles Vignes 1995 • $44 • (11/15/1997) • **88**

Pommard Les Vignots 1995 • $31 • (11/15/1997) • **86**

Puligny-Montrachet Les Charmes 1997: Complex in a firm, crisp way. Clean and polished, this slightly toasted, spicy, medium-bodied white has lively lemon, fresh herb, green apple, honey and pie crust notes. Drink now through 2007.–P.M. • $51 • (5/31/1999) • **90**

Puligny-Montrachet Les Enseignères 1998: Oozing rich, ripe fruit, this is an opulent Chardonnay. Vibrant and fresh from a good citrus-acidity backbone, this full-bodied white has loads of honey, fruit and personality. Drink now through 2010.–P.M. • $56 • (5/31/2000) • **90**

Puligny-Montrachet Les Perrières 1997: Flavorful but a bit earthy and crisp, with lime, green apple and tropical notes. Medium-bodied, its fresh quality makes it refreshingly mouthpuckering on the steely finish. Drink now through 2007.–P.M. • $75 • (5/31/1999) • **82**

Puligny-Montrachet Les Referts 1998: Decent Chardonnay beefed up with oak. Medium-bodied, with OK ripeness of fruit, but it tastes rather straightforward, with lime and green apple character. Short finish. Drink now.–P.M. • $83 • (5/31/2000) • **80**

Puligny-Montrachet Les Referts 1997: Well made, with clean, juicy fruit. A bit of herbal, grassy character gives it a vibrant, attractive core, but don't expect opulence—just honest, delicious Chardonnay flavors and a lingering finish. Drink now.–P.M. • $75 • (5/31/1999) • **88**

Puligny-Montrachet Les Referts 1996 • $NA • (5/31/1998) • **89**

Santenay Clos de la Confrérie 1994 • $25 • (11/15/1996) • **82**

Santenay La Maladière 1997: An exciting, lovely red. Very grapey and clean, packed with mineral, red and black fruit and firm yet sweet tannins that add length and character to the persistent, balanced, slightly toasted finish. Drink now through 2005.–P.M. • $36 • (9/30/1999) • **89**

Santenay La Maladière 1996: A solid '96, underscored by rich cherry and earth flavors, good concentration and stiff tannins for a rustic and satisfying finish. Drink through 2003.–B.S. • $33 • (9/30/1998) • **85**

Santenay La Maladière 1995 • $25 • (11/15/1997) • **83**

Santenay La Maladière 1994 • $27 • (11/15/1996) • **86**

Santenay Les Gravières 1994 • $27 • (11/15/1996) • **84**

Santenay Les Gravières Vieilles Vignes 1997: Appealingly ripe on the palate. Sweet tannins mingle with cassis and deftly toasted oak to produce a full-bodied and succulent red Burgundy. Turns a bit chewy, even slightly rustic, but has the sort of panache that's rare in a '97. Best from 2002 through 2006.–P.M. • $37 • (9/30/1999) • **87**

Santenay Les Gravières Vieilles Vignes 1996: Real class and depth, with tangy cherry and wet earth notes, freshness and concentration followed by fine, ripe tannins and a lingering finish. Well made. Drink through 2004.–B.S. • $34 • (9/30/1998) • **88**

Santenay White Clos du Beauregard 1998: A honeyed, medium-bodied Chardonnay, yellow in color, offering a crisp and fresh character along with some green apple, toasted oak notes. Not imported into the U.S. Drink now through 2002.–P.M. • $NA • (1/01/2000) • **84**

Santenay White Clos du Beauregard 1997: Interesting. Reserved on the nose, it kicks in with lively, ripe flavors of dried apricot and pineapple on the palate. Medium-bodied, with a crisp citrus finish that leaves a fresh, zesty impression. Drink now through 2003.–P.M. • $34 • (5/31/1999) • **90**

Santenay White Clos du Beauregard 1996 • $NA • (5/31/1998) • **87**

Santenay White Le Beaurepaire 1998: Yellow in color, rich in flavor, full in body, it's not subtle. But it has personality with its almost late-harvest quality, offering grilled pineapple, pear, toasted bread, dried fruit notes. Drink now through 2003.–P.M. • $40 • (5/31/2000) • **83**

Santenay White Le Beaurepaire 1997: A ripe but very intense white Burgundy, with mouthpuckering aromas. Tasting like a reduced pineapple and lime sauce, it's almost spritzy in the palate, where the vibrant, sweet-tasting fruit

comes through. Lovers of crystal-chiseled Chardonnays will worship this beauty. Drink now through 2003.–P.M. • $38 • (5/31/1999) • **92**
Santenay White Le Beaurepaire 1996 • $33 • (5/31/1998) • **88**
Santenay White Les Gravières 1996 • $33 • (5/31/1998) • **88**
Savigny-lès-Beaune White Les Vergelesses 1996 • $32 • (5/31/1998) • **87**
Savigny-lès-Beaune White Les Vermots-Dessus 1998: Wonderful. Elegant yet ripe, medium-bodied white that enchants from the first sniff to the last sip. Beautifully smoky, toasted and attractively scented, with menthol, tropical, honey character. Sweet-tasting finish. A winner. Drink now through 2003.–P.M. • $33 • (5/31/2000) • **91**
Savigny-lès-Beaune White Les Vermots-Dessus 1997: Pure and medium-bodied, this delivers vibrant, crisp lemon, tropical and spice notes, then kicks off on the palate, making it taste very exciting and clean. You'll beckon for another glass. Drink now through 2002.–P.M. • $32 • (5/31/1999) • **90**
Savigny-lès-Beaune White Les Vermots-Dessus 1996 • $28 • (5/31/1998) • **92**
Volnay Clos des Chênes 1997: Shows dried fruit—fig, raisin—with raspberry and grilled aromas and flavors. Smooth midpalate, kicking in with a citrusy touch on the finish. Drink now through 2001.–P.M. • $60 • (9/30/1999) • **84**
Volnay Clos des Chênes 1996: A taut, concentrated and jammy, mouthpuckeringly zesty and vibrant red, with a lot of citrus-spiked acidity. Of medium body, this drinks almost like an Italian Dolcetto. Lacks a bit of warm fruit, but has good natural sweetness. Drink now through 2005.–P.M. • $53 • (9/30/1998) • **85**
Volnay Clos des Chênes 1995 • $35 • (11/15/1997) • **92**
Volnay Les Champans 1997: Nice Pinot Noir aromas of black cherry and wild berry, with wet earth and a touch of spice. Medium-bodied, with attractive grip and good balance. Drink now through 2002.–P.M. • $55 • (9/30/1999) • **85**
Volnay Les Champans 1995 • $35 • (11/15/1997) • **85**
Volnay Les Santenots 1997: Fresh and zingy, with definite citrusy, mouthpuckering character. A medium-bodied Pinot that displays interesting mint, smoke, raspberry and wet earth grip on the chewy, somewhat astringent finish. Drink now through 2002.–P.M. • $55 • (9/30/1999) • **81**
Volnay Les Santenots 1996: Spicy cherries, bright acidity and a light tannic structure give this wine a delicacy and intensity that are appealing and frank. Good, lingering finish. Drink through 2004.–B.S. • $49 • (9/30/1998) • **87**
Volnay-Santenots 1995 • $35 • (11/15/1997) • **85**
Volnay-Santenots 1994 • $38 • (11/15/1996) • **82**

GISCOURS, CHATEAU

Margaux 1999: Lots of ripe plum, dark chocolate and berry on the nose. Medium-bodied, with fine tannins and a medium finish.–J.S. • $NA • (1/01/2000) (BT) • **85-89**
Margaux 1998: Alluring aromas of toasted oak, berry and chocolate. Medium- to full-bodied, with firm tannins and a short finish. Starts off very well but comes to a halt.–J.S. • $NA • (5/31/1999) (BT) • **85-89**
Margaux 1997: Pleasant and fruity, with a nice complement of new wood, but diluted on the finish. Drink now.–J.S. • $25 • (1/31/2000) • **83**
Margaux 1996: Aromas of black cherry and fresh mushroom. Medium-bodied, with some chocolate character, but a bit lean. Best after 2000.–J.S. • $31 • (1/31/1999) • **85**
Margaux 1995 • $34 Ⓐ • (1/31/1998) • **92**
Margaux 1993 • $24 • (1/31/1996) • **86**
Margaux 1991 • $24 • (3/31/1994) • **78**
Margaux 1990 • $38 Ⓐ • (3/31/1993) • **92**
Margaux 1989: Big and brutish. One of the best Giscours ever. Shows an abundance of spice, earth and ripe berry. Full-bodied. Lots of tannins. Finishes with loads of chocolate, raisin and cherry. (1989 Bordeaux horizontal tasting). Best after 2005.–J.S. • $43 Ⓐ • (5/31/1999) • **92**
Margaux 1988 • $35 Ⓐ • (4/30/1991) • **89**
Margaux 1986 • $36 Ⓐ • (6/15/1989) • **83**
Margaux 1985 • $41 Ⓐ • (9/30/1988) • **86**
Margaux 1983 • $42 Ⓐ • (5/01/1989) • **78**
Margaux 1982: Dark ruby-garnet in color, with tobacco, chocolate and berry aromas. Medium- to full-bodied, with velvety tannins and plenty of milk chocolate on the finish. Slightly dry. (1982 Bordeaux horizontal tasting). Drink now.–J.S. • $NA • (11/30/1998) • **87**
Margaux 1981 • $23 Ⓐ • (6/01/1984) • **82**
Margaux 1980 • $NA • (2/16/1984) • **80**

Key: SS—Spectator Selection. CS—Cellar Selection. HR—Highly Recommended. $NA—Price not available. (BT)—Barrel tasting. Ⓐ—Auction Price. For a key to the tasters' initials, see "How to Use These Listings."
Dates in parentheses represent the issues in which the ratings were published.

Margaux 1979 • $41 Ⓐ • (10/15/1989) • **87**
Margaux 1978 • $43 Ⓐ • (2/16/1984) • **87**
Margaux 1976 • $45 • (2/16/1984) • **83**
Margaux 1970 • $88 Ⓐ • (5/15/1993) • **86**
Margaux 1964 • $25 Ⓐ • (2/16/1984) • **89**
Margaux 1961 • $64 Ⓐ • (4/30/1996) • **80**

GISSELBRECHT, WILLY

Gewürztraminer Alsace Cuvée Guillaume 1997: Extremely ripe, showing pear, apricot and violet married to a soft framework that dissipates on the finish. Drink now.–B.S. • $17 • (6/15/2000) • **84**
Gewürztraminer Alsace Réserve 1998: Modest litchi and apricot flavors are diffuse, despite the lush texture. Finishes short. Drink now.–B.S. • $14 • (6/15/2000) • **80**
Riesling Alsace Grand Cru Frankstein 1996: This beautiful expression of Riesling exudes the ripeness of the '96 vintage in its quince, spice and passion fruit flavors, backed by a tender structure. A nice creaminess midpalate adds depth. Drink now through 2004.–B.S. • $18 • (6/15/2000) • **89**
Riesling Alsace Réserve 1998: Crisp and balanced, offering almond, pine forest and mineral aromas and flavors. Firm and steely, with a lemon finish. Drink now through 2003.–B.S. • $12 • (6/15/2000) • **83**
Tokay Pinot Gris Alsace 1998: Ripe fruit cocktail aromas and flavors are married to a bright structure. Picks up some almond and beeswax accents, with a firm, slightly austere finish. Drink now.–B.S. • $12 • (6/15/2000) • **83**
Tokay Pinot Gris Alsace Réserve Spéciale 1997: Rich and vibrant, this is full of forward apricot and quince flavors, turning firm; still tight on the finish. Drink now through 2001.–B.S. • $14 • (6/15/2000) • **84**

GLANA, CHATEAU DU

St.-Julien 1998: Hints of currant, strawberry and vanilla on the nose and palate. Medium-bodied, with chewy tannins and a velvety finish. Needs a bit more fruit on the midpalate.–J.S. • $NA • (5/31/1999) (BT) • **85-89**
St.-Julien 1997: Medium-bodied red, with a cherry, slightly herbal character, medium tannins and a fresh finish. Drink now through 2005.–J.S. • $NA • (1/31/2000) • **82**
St.-Julien 1996: A cool, multilingual wine, with complex aromas of berries, cumin, coffee and earth. Full-bodied, with full tannins, but balanced and silky. Long, refreshing finish. Would be outstanding with a bit more ripe fruit. Best after 2001.–J.S. • $30 Ⓐ • (1/31/1999) • **88**
St.-Julien 1995 • $15 • (1/31/1998) • **87**
St.-Julien 1994 • $15 • (1/31/1997) • **80**
St.-Julien 1990 • $20 • (3/31/1993) • **88**
St.-Julien 1989 • $NA • (3/15/1992) • **87**
St.-Julien 1987 • $NA • (11/30/1989) • **81**
St.-Julien 1986 • $17 • (11/30/1989) • **84**
St.-Julien 1982: Slightly out of balance. A bit overripe, with loads of berry, raisin and tobacco character. Full-bodied, with full tannins but a very hot, alcoholic finish. (1982 Bordeaux horizontal tasting). Drink now.–J.S. • $NA • (11/30/1998) • **85**

GLEON MONTANIE, CHATEAU

Corbières Cuvée Spéciale 1990 • $11 • (3/15/1994) • **87**
Corbières Cuvée Tradition 1990 • $9 • (3/15/1994) • **85**

GLORIA, CHATEAU

St.-Julien 1999: Some pleasant berry, cherry character. Medium to light body. Light finish.–J.S. • $NA • (1/01/2000) (BT) • **80-84**
St.-Julien 1998: Dark-colored, with an intense blackberry, cherry, green olive and mineral character on both nose and palate. Full-bodied and velvety, with loads of fruit and tannins. Slightly green on the finish.–J.S. • $NA • (5/31/1999) (BT) • **85-89**
St.-Julien 1997: A wine with pleasant berry and wet earth character. Medium-bodied, with silky tannins and a fresh fruit finish. Drink now through 2005.–J.S. • $24 • (1/31/2000) • **86**
St.-Julien 1996: Harmonious and balanced. Good dark color, with lovely berry and eucalyptus aromas and flavors. Medium-bodied, with well-integrated tannins and a long, silky and caressing finish. Not quite as good as I remember, but very good indeed. Best after 2000.–J.S. • $25 Ⓐ • (1/31/1999) • **88**
St.-Julien 1995 • $30 Ⓐ • (1/31/1998) • **90**
St.-Julien 1994 • $27 • (1/31/1997) • **84**
St.-Julien 1992 • $17 • (4/15/1995) • **84**
St.-Julien 1991 • $19 • (3/31/1994) • **77**

St.-Julien 1990 • $38 Ⓐ • (3/31/1993) • **89**

St.-Julien 1989: A wine soon arriving at its peak. Medium-ruby color. Wonderful aromas of strawberries and pie tart. Medium-bodied, with velvety tannins and a chocolate, berry aftertaste. (1989 Bordeaux horizontal tasting). Drink through 2006.–J.S. • $44 Ⓐ • (5/31/1999) • **89**

St.-Julien 1988 • $35 Ⓐ • (10/15/1992) • **88**

St.-Julien 1987 • $15 • (11/30/1989) • **84**

St.-Julien 1986 • $34 Ⓐ • (10/15/1992) • **89**

St.-Julien 1985 • $43 Ⓐ • (10/15/1992) • **90**

St.-Julien 1984 • $14 • (10/15/1992) • **79**

St.-Julien 1982: Big, warm and ripe. Medium ruby color. Fresh and fruity, with perfume, berry and raspberry aromas. Medium-bodied, with berry, cherry and chocolate flavors, medium tannins and a medium finish. (1982 Bordeaux horizontal tasting). Drink now.–J.S. • $NA • (11/30/1998) • **89**

St.-Julien 1983 • $24 • (10/15/1992) • **83**

St.-Julien 1981 • $18 • (10/15/1992) • **83**

St.-Julien 1979 • $NA • (10/15/1989) • **83**

St.-Julien 1978 • $27 Ⓐ • (10/15/1992) • **74**

St.-Julien 1976 • $24 • (10/15/1992) • **86**

St.-Julien 1975 • $32 Ⓐ • (10/15/1992) • **83**

St.-Julien 1971 • $39 • (10/15/1992) • **86**

St.-Julien 1970 • $29 Ⓐ • (10/15/1992) • **88**

St.-Julien 1967 • $28 • (10/15/1992) • **84**

St.-Julien 1966 • $47 Ⓐ • (10/15/1992) • **87**

St.-Julien 1964 • $50 • (10/15/1992) • **81**

St.-Julien 1962 • $55 • (10/15/1992) • **79**

St.-Julien 1961 • $84 Ⓐ • (4/30/1996) • **88**

St.-Julien 1960 • $NA • (10/15/1992) • **71**

St.-Julien 1948 • $NA • (10/15/1992) • **85**

GODEAU, CHATEAU

St.-Emilion 1994 • $20 • (4/30/1997) • **83**

GOERG, PAUL

Brut Blanc de Blancs Champagne NV • $27 • (11/30/1995) • **87**

Brut Champagne Cuvée du Centenaire NV • $50 • (11/30/1995) • **86**

Brut Champagne Tradition NV • $27 • (12/31/1995) • **82**

Brut Rosé Champagne NV • $32 • (12/15/1995) • **84**

GOISOT, GHISLAINE & JEAN-HUGUES

Bourgogne Aligoté Domaine du Corps de Garde 1997: The talented Goisot scores again with an impressive Aligoté. Pleasant and medium-bodied, with ripe pear, fresh herb and a buttery, toasted butterscotch character, it turns a bit soft on the finish. Drink now.–P.M. • $14 • (5/31/1999) • **86**

Bourgogne Aligoté Domaine du Corps de Garde 1996 • $14 • (5/31/1998) • **91**

Bourgogne Aligoté Domaine du Corps de Garde 1995 • $13 • (6/15/1997) • **79**

Bourgogne Côtes d'Auxerre Domaine du Corps de Garde 1996: Bell pepper and herbal notes dominate this sharp wine. Disappointing.–P.M. • $16 • (5/15/1999) • **73**

Bourgogne Côtes d'Auxerre Domaine du Corps de Garde 1995 • $15 • (6/15/1997) • **80**

Bourgogne Côtes d'Auxerre White 1998: Light but good, offering some ripe fruit and a slight bitter almond note that gives it some grip. Straightforward finish. Drink now.–P.M. • $15 • (5/15/2000) • **81**

Bourgogne Côtes d'Auxerre White 1997: Lovely, with citrus, wet earth and a touch of butter, pear, and honey. A balanced, attractive, medium-bodied white, with a round mouthfeel. Drink now through 2001.–P.M. • $15 • (5/31/1999) • **86**

Bourgogne Côtes d'Auxerre White Domaine du Corps de Garde 1998: Subtle and balanced. Interesting wet earth and wet stone notes here, along with some ripe fruit and a backbone of acidity. A full-bodied Chardonnay delivering character, with a milky, creamy aftertaste. Drink now through 2003.–P.M. • $19 • (5/15/2000) • **88**

Bourgogne Côtes d'Auxerre White Domaine du Corps de Garde 1997: Ripe, rich and fairly thick, with a honey, lemon, mineral and green apple combination folding gently into this soft, delicious, full-bodied, deftly spiced and oaked Chardonnay. Drink now through 2005.–P.M. • $17 • (5/31/1999) • **90**

Bourgogne Côtes d'Auxerre White Domaine du Corps de Garde 1996 • $17 • (5/31/1998) • **88**

Bourgogne Côtes d'Auxerre White Domaine du Corps de Garde 1995 • $15 • (6/15/1997) • **91**

Sauvignon de St.-Bris 1998: Superlative Sauvignon Blanc. Seductive sweet-pea, freshly cut grass and lovely gooseberry aromas and flavors. The balance and silky texture suggest excellent concentration of fruit, but it lacks a bit in acidity. Tasted twice, with consistent notes. Drink now through 2001.–P.M. • $14 • (5/15/2000) • **90**

Sauvignon de St.-Bris Domaine du Corps de Garde 1997: Clean, pure, ripe and crisp, with a buttery, mocha-tasting undertone, this medium-bodied white fills the palate with plenty of fruit. Good ripeness on the citrusy finish. Drink now.–P.M. • $14 • (5/31/1999) • **82**

Sauvignon de St.-Bris Domaine du Corps de Garde 1996 • $14 • (5/31/1998) • **92**

Sauvignon de St.-Bris Domaine du Corps de Garde 1995 • $14 • (6/15/1997) • **90**

Sauvignon de St.-Bris Domaine du Corps de Garde Gourmand Fié Gris 1998: A bit rustic but there's genuine concentration of fruit here. Balanced and cream-textured. Has an herbal, dried herb, grass and gooseberry character but also some ripe flavors—all of it blended with some chestnut-scented, tannic oak. Chewy finish. Drink now through 2003.–P.M. • $16 • (5/15/2000) • **86**

Sauvignon de St.-Bris Domaine du Corps de Garde Gourmand Fié Gris 1997: Light-bodied and delicate, this tastes ripe, with grass, dried herb and gooseberry notes. Medium-bodied, it's quite crisp and intense on the slightly tough finish. Drink now.–P.M. • $17 • (5/31/1999) • **82**

Sauvignon de St.-Bris Domaine du Corps de Garde Gourmand Fié Gris 1996 • $17 • (5/31/1998) • **85**

GOMBAUDE-GUILLOT, CHATEAU

Pomerol 1998: A pretty wine with floral, mineral character. Medium-bodied, with medium tannins and a medium finish. Nice.–J.S. • $NA • (5/31/1999) (BT) • **85-89**

Pomerol 1997: A light red, but with some pleasant strawberry and cherry character. Light- to medium-bodied. Light finish. Drink now.–J.S. • $NA • (1/31/2000) • **80**

Pomerol 1996: An enjoyable Pomerol. Pretty berry and cherry aromas, with hints of mineral. Medium-bodied, with fine tannins but a slightly watery palate. Drink now.–J.S. • $NA • (1/31/1999) • **84**

Pomerol 1995: Aromas of plums, tobacco and cherries follow through on the palate. Medium-bodied, with silky tannins and a slightly short, dry finish. Needs time to mellow. Best from 2001 through 2006.–J.S. • $NA • (9/15/1998) • **87**

GOMERIE, CHATEAU LA

St.-Emilion 1997: Lots of ripe fruit for the vintage, with plum, tobacco and toasted oak character. Medium-bodied, with soft tannins and a long finish. A tad too much wood, but a beautiful wine overall. Drink now through 2002.–J.S. • $73 • (1/31/2000) • **89**

St.-Emilion 1996: Offers a lot of blackberry and tar character, with a hint of earth. Medium-bodied, with velvety tannins and a smoky, dark chocolate and earth aftertaste. Slightly hollow finish. Best after 2000.–J.S. • $92 • (1/31/1999) • **87**

St.-Emilion 1995: Masses of everything in this one. A big, Right Bank red with loads of cherry, chocolate and blackberry aromas and flavors. Full-bodied, very ripe, with velvety tannins and a long finish. Needs time to open. Best from 2001 through 2006.–J.S. • $100 • (9/15/1998) • **93**

GONON, PIERRE

St.-Joseph 1997: A soft, unexciting, medium-bodied red, with mocha, vanilla and red berry notes. Drink now.–P.M. • $23 • (10/31/1999) • **80**

St.-Joseph 1996: Opens with great subtlety, then kicks in with superripe raspberry, wild berry and cassis flavors. Harmonious and seductive, slightly earthy, of medium body, it's a succulent, delicious St.-Joseph. Drink now through 2002.–P.M. • $23 • (11/15/1998) • **91**

St.-Joseph 1995 • $22 • (10/15/1997) • **85**

St.-Joseph 1994 • $22 • (10/15/1997) • **83**

St.-Joseph Les Oliviers 1996: Velvety as can be, with a buttery, fat texture, this oozes charm. Layered with pure tropical, lemon, mineral, wet earth and stone complexity—like a Puligny in a great vintage. Full-bodied and ripe, it turns in a long finish. Drink now through 2005.–P.M. • $25 • (11/15/1998) • **93**

St.-Joseph White Les Oliviers 1997: Smells and tastes a bit appley, like cooked fruit, and the oxidized flavors turn a bit dry and tough on the finish.–P.M. • $25 • (8/31/1999) • **78**

GOSSET

Brut Champagne Celebris 1990: Smooth and harmonious, this '90 seduces the palate with its ripe pear and fig notes and lush texture. A real joy to drink, all the way to the long, cherry-tinged aftertaste. Drink now through 2004.–B.S. • $115 • (2/29/2000) • **91**

Brut Champagne Excellence NV: On the dry side, this Champagne provides fresh lemon, mineral and honey aromas and flavors, very tightly wound, leaving a mouthwatering sensation. Drink now through 2002.–B.S. • $35 • (2/29/2000) • **88**

Brut Champagne Grand Millésime 1993: Crisp and lean, this will please fans of citrus and apple, in a style that's mouthwatering and austere on the finish. Ideal with canapés. Drink now through 2002.–B.S. • $70 • (2/29/2000) • **86**

Brut Champagne Grand Réserve NV: A broad sparkler, offering toast and butterscotch on a firm structure. It's concentrated, with honey and fig on the aftertaste, if a bit coarse. Drink now.–B.S. • $50 • (2/29/2000) • **88**

Brut Rosé Champagne Grand Rosé NV: Well-delineated, showing a firm structure upon which the cherry and berry flavors are displayed. Turns a bit lean on the finish, but should go well with food. Drink now through 2003.–B.S. • $50 • (2/29/2000) • **88**

Brut Rosé Champagne Grand Rosé 1990 • $59 • (12/31/1996) • **89**

GOUBARD, MICHEL

Bourgogne Côte Chalonnaise 1996: Modest plum, red- and blackberry character, ending with a sweet and somewhat hot finish.–P.M. • $14 • (9/30/1998) • **80**

Bourgogne Côte Chalonnaise Mont-Avril 1989 • $10 • (3/15/1993) • **77**

Bourgogne White 1996 • $12 • (5/31/1998) • **82**

GOUBERT, DOMAINE LES

Côtes du Rhône Cuvée de V 1996: Rustic, with thick, ripe, late-harvest character and an acidic finish.–P.M. • $19 • (11/15/1998) • **70**

Côtes du Rhône White Cuvée de V 1997: A medium-bodied white that has a tough finish and shows only modest fruit.–P.M. • $19 • (12/15/1999) • **79**

Côtes du Rhône-Villages Beaumes de Venise 1997: A bit herbal, with modest fruit. The drying finish makes this hard to enjoy.–P.M. • $16 • (12/15/1999) • **74**

Côtes du Rhône-Villages Sablet 1996: Of light to medium body, it touches on plum, raisin and currant, but also shows metallic herbal notes on the finish.–P.M. • $11 • (11/15/1998) • **77**

Côtes du Rhône-Villages Sablet Blanc de Blancs 1997: Pleasant, with a lively, fresh core of green apple, dried herb and vibrant citrus. Light-bodied.–P.M. • $15 • (12/15/1999) • **79**

Côtes du Rhône-Villages White Sablet Blanc de Blancs 1996: A hard-to-like white, lacking in definition and showing cedar, butter and perfumy character.–P.M. • $13 • (11/15/1998) • **77**

Gigondas 1997: A traditional Rhône with plenty of character. Earth, cow dung and wet foxlike aromas lead the way to a gamy, leathery, smoky, animal-like character. Tough and tannic, with a minerally, ironlike, drying finish. Just the stuff for wild boar steak or pheasant shot on your plantation. Drink now through 2010.–P.M. • $23 • (12/15/1999) • **88**

Gigondas 1994 • $17 • (10/15/1997) • **81**

Gigondas 1989 • $13 • (10/15/1994) • **87**

Gigondas 1986 • $13 • (3/15/1990) • **81**

Gigondas 1985 • $20 Ⓐ • (4/30/1988) • **89**

Gigondas Cuvée Florence 1994 • $20 • (10/15/1997) • **87**

Gigondas Cuvée Florence 1989 • $23 • (10/15/1994) • **87**

Gigondas Cuvée Florence 1986 • $23 Ⓐ • (4/30/1988) • **92**

GOUGES, HENRI

Nuits-St.-Georges 1997: Very sweet and ripe-tasting, with an intriguing lead pencil, plum and prune character. Full-bodied, with well-integrated tannins, it turns attractively chalky and chewy on the lingering finish. Drink now through 2007.–P.M. • $40 • (1/01/2000) • **91**

Nuits-St.-Georges 1995: Full-bodied, and has potential, but its down-up-down profile is questionable. Starts off earthy, then delivers rich texture on the midpalate—before the overly tannic, astringent finish.–P.M. • $35 • (8/31/1998) • **74**

Nuits-St.-Georges 1991 • $30 • (1/31/1994) • **83**

Nuits-St.-Georges 1990 • $42 Ⓐ • (12/15/1992) • **88**

Nuits-St.-Georges 1986 • $30 • (7/31/1988) • **84**

Nuits-St.-Georges Aux Chaignots 1986 • $40 • (7/31/1988) • **90**

Nuits-St.-Georges Clos des Porrets St.-Georges 1997: Full in body and flavor, with wonderful personality and amazing complexity. Wonderfully rich and ripe, tasting a bit earthy, with grilled meat, blackberry and wild berry notes, plus loads of smoke, mineral, mocha and coffee. Turns firm and "serious" on the long finish. Best from 2002 through 2007.–P.M. • $NA • (1/01/2000) • **93**

Nuits-St.-Georges Clos des Porrets St.-Georges 1991 • $40 • (1/31/1994) • **81**

Nuits-St.-Georges Clos des Porrets St.-Georges 1990 • $58 • (12/15/1992) • **92**

Nuits-St.-Georges Clos des Porrets St.-Georges 1989 • $45 • (1/31/1992) • **87**

Nuits-St.-Georges Les Chaignots 1997: A ripe '97, offering loads of tannins. Full-bodied, it's aromatically reserved, but on the palate it picks up velocity, with fruit, wet earth, stone dust and tannins. The long, beautiful finish won't quit—surprising for this vintage. An ager. Best from 2003 through 2010.–P.M. • $NA • (1/01/2000) • **91**

Nuits-St.-Georges Les Chênes Carteaux 1997: A beautiful, supervelvety Pinot Noir. Full-bodied, with a mind-boggling texture. Has subtle ripeness underneath, as the spice, wet earth, lead pencil, mineral and smoke complexity come together on the exquisite finish. Drink now through 2015.–P.M. • $52 • (1/01/2000) • **90**

Nuits-St.-Georges Les Pruliers 1996: Stunning. Massive and backward, this young '96 Pinot begins with seductive aromas of blackberries and vanilla and a sauvage element, then saturates the palate with its intense concentration of blackberry, black currant and smoky oak flavors before yielding to the stiff tannins. A great Nuits from a vintage where this commune excelled. Best from 2002 through 2010.–B.S. • $45 • (9/30/1998) • **94**

Nuits-St.-Georges Les Pruliers 1991 • $40 • (1/31/1994) • **81**

Nuits-St.-Georges Les Pruliers 1990 • $58 • (12/15/1992) • **90**

Nuits-St.-Georges Les Pruliers 1989 • $45 • (1/31/1992) • **86**

Nuits-St.-Georges Les St.- Georges 1997: Gorgeous, black-colored, full-bodied, rich and intense '97 Pinot. Amazing quality, really, with immense concentration for the vintage. It tastes of *terroir* as the wet earth bursts on the scene, and there is fabulous fruit. Best from 2003 through 2010.–P.M. • $71 • (1/01/2000) • **92**

Nuits-St.-Georges Les St.-Georges 1996: A stellar Nuits-St.-Georges. This gorgeous young red combines a deep, almost opaque color, roasted coffee and plum aromas and focused black cherry and plum flavors accented with spice and minerals. Impeccably balanced and long, this has a great future ahead. Best from 2002 through 2010.–B.S. • $53 Ⓐ • (9/30/1998) • **92**

Nuits-St.-Georges Les St.-Georges 1992 • $NA • (12/31/1994) • **86**

Nuits-St.-Georges Les St.-Georges 1991 • $46 • (12/31/1994) • **88**

Nuits-St.-Georges Les St.-Georges 1990 • $39 Ⓐ • (12/15/1992) • **92**

Nuits-St.-Georges Les St.-Georges 1989 • $49 • (1/31/1992) • **89**

Nuits-St.-Georges Les St.-Georges 1985 • $45 • (2/15/1988) • **68**

Nuits-St.-Georges Les Vaucrains 1991 • $44 • (1/31/1994) • **80**

Nuits-St.-Georges Les Vaucrains 1990 • $60 • (12/31/1994) • **88**

Nuits-St.-Georges Les Vaucrains 1989 • $49 • (12/31/1994) • **89**

GOULAINE, MARQUIS DE

Brut Vouvray NV: A slightly perfumed aroma and flavors of green apple and quince are joined by a nice backbone of acidity. A pleasant quaff. Drink now.–K.M. • $13 • (5/15/2000) • **84**

Cabernet Touraine 1996: Aromas of cassis, with plenty of forward berry and tobacco flavors that tail off slightly at the finish. Light-bodied, fresh and lively.–B.S. • $7 • (10/31/1998) • **84**

Chardonnay Vin de Pays du Jardin de la France 1998: Simple candied apple notes and an odd, sour, soapy note form this mixed-up white. Tasted twice, with consistent notes.–B.S. • $7 • (6/15/2000) • **76**

Chardonnay Vin de Pays du Jardin de la France 1996 • $11 • (5/31/1998) • **82**

Merlot Vin de Pays d'Oc 1998: A lively red, with black olive and cherry flavors and a definite herbal streak. Cranberry notes on the finish. Drink now.–K.M. • $7 • (4/30/2000) • **82**

Muscadet de Sèvre et Maine Sur Lie Château de Goulaine 1998: This Muscadet has bright peach, citrus and sea salt flavors, all kept lively with a refreshing spritz on the finish. Drink now.–K.M. • $9 • (5/15/2000) • **83**

Muscadet de Sèvre et Maine Sur Lie Cuvée du Millénaire 1998: Shows toast and melon before displaying its rich, round texture. Though atypical for the region, citrus and grapefruit flavors keep it interesting. Drink now.–K.M. • $11 • (5/15/2000) • **84**

Key: SS—Spectator Selection. CS—Cellar Selection. HR—Highly Recommended. $NA—Price not available. (BT)—Barrel tasting. Ⓐ—Auction Price.
For a key to the tasters' initials, see "How to Use These Listings."
Dates in parentheses represent the issues in which the ratings were published.

FRANCE

Sancerre 1998: Juicy, with an herb aroma and lingering citrus flavors. Finishes with onion notes. Drink now.–K.M. • $16 • (5/15/2000) • **82**
Sancerre 1996 • $17 • (3/31/1998) • **88**
Saumur-Champigny Domaine des Varinelles 1998: Light-bodied, with berry and light cherry flavors. Can serve slightly chilled. Drink now.–K.M. • $12 • (5/15/2000) • **81**
Sauvignon Blanc Vin de Pays du Jardin de la France 1998: Straightforward, with lemony and herbal flavors that turn tart on the finish.–K.M. • $7 • (5/15/2000) • **79**
Sauvignon Blanc Vin de Pays du Jardin de la France 1997: Rich and broad in texture, with straightforward apple and mineral flavors that dissipate quickly. Drink now.–B.S. • $7 • (11/15/1998) • **82**
Vouvray 1998: Soft, with tangerine and kiwi flavors and a lightly sweet, blowsy finish.–B.S. • $11 • (6/15/2000) • **79**
Vouvray 1996 • $11 • (5/31/1998) • **84**

GOUR DE CHAULE, DOMAINE DU

Gigondas 1993 • $18 • (10/15/1996) • **86**
Gigondas 1986 • $13 • (9/15/1990) • **90**

GOURGAZAUD, CHATEAU DE

Minervois 1994 • $9 • (12/15/1997) • **78**
Minervois 1991 • $8 • (12/15/1994) • **79**

GOURNIER, DOMAINE DE

Merlot Vin de Pays des Cévennes-Uzège 1998: A fresh, young, juicy Merlot in a Beaujolais-like style, with appealing plum and currant flavors. Lively, with peppery notes on the finish. Drink now.–K.M. • $7 • (10/15/1999) • **83**

GOUZOTTE D'OR, LA

Chablis 1996 • $18 • (5/31/1998) • **87**
Mâcon-Villages 1997: Deliciously ripe and vibrant, just wonderful '97, balanced, succulent and a great pleasure to drink as an aperitif or with a light dish. Buy a case. Drink now through 2001.–P.M. • $14 • (5/31/1999) • **89**
Mâcon-Villages 1996 • $14 • (5/31/1998) • **83**
Pouilly-Fuissé 1996 • $22 • (5/31/1998) • **76**
St.-Romain 1996 • $14 • (5/31/1998) • **88**
St.-Véran 1997: Lovely to drink, and sweet-tasting, but there's a slight dry note; still, the tropical and citrus notes roar back to reclaim the wine. Drink now.–P.M. • $16 • (5/31/1999) • **85**
St.-Véran 1996 • $15 • (5/31/1998) • **84**

GOYARD, ALBERT

Mâcon-Burgy 1998: A pretty raspberry aroma sets this medium-bodied, elegant Chardonnay apart. A bit diluted, but its citrus, haylike character gives it vibrancy. Drink now through 2001.–P.M. • $12 • (5/31/2000) • **81**

GRACIA, CHATEAU

St.-Emilion 1998: A bit one-dimensional but the fruit concentration is very good, with velvety tannins and a rather short finish.–J.S. • $NA • (5/31/1999) (BT) • **85-89**
St.-Emilion 1997: A spicy wine, with lots of good fruit, fine tannins and a flavorful finish. A wine to watch for. Drink now through 2004.–J.S. • $79 • (1/31/2000) • **86**

GRAILLOT, ALAIN

Crozes-Hermitage 1997: Exciting aromas of dried herb, olive, violet, cassis, blood orange and cinnamon. But it tastes acidic and the finish is tough. Drink now through 2003.–P.M. • $14 Ⓐ • (12/15/1999) • **83**
Crozes-Hermitage 1996: Syrah doesn't come much cleaner and purer than in this elegant Northern Rhône wine, offering black raspberry, mineral, smoke, licorice and tobacco character. The haunting aromas and alluring flavors seem to dance across the palate. It's no powerhouse, but the intensity is exceptional. Delicious now; different yet just as delicious with time. Drink through 2008.–T.M. • $17 • (11/15/1998) SS • **93**
Crozes-Hermitage 1995 • $15 • (10/15/1997) • **92**
Crozes-Hermitage 1994 • $15 • (11/30/1996) HR • **92**
Crozes-Hermitage 1993 • $15 • (10/15/1995) • **85**
Crozes-Hermitage 1992 • $14 Ⓐ • (5/31/1994) • **84**
Crozes-Hermitage 1991 • $15 • (5/31/1994) • **79**
Crozes-Hermitage 1990 • $17 • (4/15/1993) • **88**
Crozes-Hermitage 1989 • $14 • (3/31/1991) • **88**
Crozes-Hermitage La Guiraude 1996: Lovely *terroir* as the earth, leather and currant notes mingle to create something distinctive and seductive. Full in body, silky in texture, with an undertow of fresh acidity, this has terrific balance and glides to a long, subtle, cassis-flavored finish that is delicious. Best from 2002 through 2010.–P.M. • $25 • (10/15/1998) • **91**
Crozes-Hermitage La Guiraude 1995 • $20 • (10/15/1997) • **87**
Crozes-Hermitage La Guiraude 1994 • $20 • (11/30/1996) • **90**
Crozes-Hermitage La Guiraude 1992 • $18 • (5/31/1994) • **80**
Crozes-Hermitage La Guiraude 1991 • $18 • (5/31/1994) • **84**
Crozes-Hermitage White 1998: Very nice, keeping a brisk pace across the palate as the flavors dig down into the taste buds and roam wide and large on the flavor spectrum. Deliciously balanced. Drink now.–P.M. • $19 • (8/31/1999) • **88**
Crozes-Hermitage White 1996 • $15 • (10/15/1997) • **81**
Hermitage 1997: On the fruity, lightish side—lacking a bit of *terroir* despite the hint of something more from the dark color. Medium-bodied, displaying blackberry, black pepper and a crisp finish. Drink now through 2004.–P.M. • $53 • (11/30/1999) • **85**
Hermitage 1996: Alluring aromas of mineral and game give way to rich, almost jammy flavors of blackberry and cassis, kept vivid by crisp acidity and firm yet unobtrusive tannins. Good typicity despite the modern, fruit-driven style. Drink through 2008.–T.M. • $60 • (11/15/1998) • **92**
Hermitage 1995: Not very ripe in aroma, with some herbal and metallic accents, but on the midpalate it has mineral-laden concentration, with intriguing spice, chocolate and toasted oak accents. Tannins turn a bit chewy on the finish. Disappointing for this producer. Tasted twice, with consistent notes. Drink now through 2005.–P.M. • $53 • (9/15/1998) • **81**
Hermitage 1994 • $43 • (11/30/1996) • **90**
Hermitage 1990 • $45 • (5/31/1994) • **90**
St.-Joseph 1997: A gorgeous St.-Joseph. Full-bodied, inky black, subtle and showy at the same time as the senses try to recognize all the notes—violet, smoke, cassis and freshly plowed earth sprayed with cow dung. Refined, ripe tannins are just the icing. Drink now through 2003.–P.M. • $24 • (12/15/1999) • **89**
St.-Joseph 1996: Impressive. Big, muscular and slightly earthy, strutting its stuff, showing firm structure of acidity and ripe tannins, and wonderful concentration of black fruit and red berries. Harmonious, with a supple midpalate and a good dose of toasted oak on the finish. Drink now through 2005.–P.M. • $20 • (11/15/1998) • **92**
St.-Joseph 1995 • $19 • (10/15/1997) • **91**
St.-Joseph 1994 • $NA • (11/30/1996) • **87**
St.-Joseph 1993 • $17 • (11/15/1995) • **80**
St.-Joseph 1992 • $18 • (5/31/1994) • **80**
St.-Joseph 1991 • $18 • (5/31/1994) • **86**

GRAMENON, DOMAINE

Côtes du Rhône 1996: Fruity and fresh, with cherry, raspberry and cedar flavors. Too crisp and tart on the finish, but food should tame it a bit.–P.M. • $10 • (2/28/1999) • **79**
Côtes du Rhône La Sagesse 1995 • $15 • (1/01/1998) • **76**

GRAND CAUMONT, CHATEAU DU

Corbières 1990 • $10 • (3/15/1994) • **83**
Corbières Cuvée Spéciale 1995: A medium-bodied red, with ripe plum, berry and coffee flavors and gamy notes on the finish. Lacks a bit of freshness in the end.–K.M. • $12 • (11/30/1998) • **78**
Corbières Tentation 1995: Vibrant and focused, with firm cherry, berry and currant flavors and herb notes. Bright and appealing, this hearty red ends on notes of tobacco and olive. Drink now through 2001.–K.M. • $17 • (11/30/1998) • **86**

GRAND CHARIOT

Corbières 1990 • $NA • (3/15/1994) • **81**

GRAND CORBIN, CHATEAU

St.-Emilion 1999: Dark, with blackberry, cherry and raspberry aromas. Medium-bodied, with fine tannins and a medium finish. Well done. Drink now.–J.S. • $NA • (1/01/2000) • **85**

GRAND-CORBIN-DESPAGNE, CHATEAU

St.-Emilion 1961 • $14 • (4/30/1996) • **84**
St.-Emilion 1945 • $NA • (3/16/1986) • **70**

GRAND CRES, DOMAINE DU

Corbières 1990 • $10 • (6/15/1993) • **82**

GRAND-MAYNE, CHATEAU

St.-Emilion 1999: A lovely, grapey red, with lots of tobacco, plum and berry character. Medium-bodied, with medium tannins and a fresh finish.–J.S. • $NA • (1/01/2000) (BT) • **85-89**
St.-Emilion 1998: Loads of crushed berries in this. Full-bodied, with caressing, velvety tannins and a long, sweet fruit aftertaste. Really well done.–J.S. • $NA • (5/31/1999) (BT) • **90-94**
St.-Emilion 1997: Pretty plum and chocolate aromas and flavors. Medium-bodied, with fine tannins and a light, fruity aftertaste. Drink now through 2004.–J.S. • $44 • (1/31/2000) • **87**
St.-Emilion 1996: Decent chocolate and smoky vanilla aromas and flavors, but it lacks a core of fruit. Medium-bodied, with silky tannins but a diluted finish.–J.S. • $23 Ⓐ • (1/31/1999) • **77**
St.-Emilion 1995: In-your-face aromas of toasted oak, ripe berries and chocolate. Full-bodied, with loads of ripe fruit and a long, smoke and berry finish. Absolutely moreish. Best from 2002 through 2006.–J.S. • $29 Ⓐ • (9/15/1998) • **90**
St.-Emilion 1989: Big and chewy young wine featuring loads of fruit. It's like Port. Full-bodied, with masses of chocolate and berry character and a long finish. (1989 Bordeaux horizontal tasting). Best after 2005.–J.S. • $45 Ⓐ • (5/31/1999) • **92**
St.-Emilion 1988 • $20 • (4/30/1991) • **89**
St.-Emilion 1986 • $16 • (6/30/1989) • **87**
St.-Emilion 1982: A bit funky and old-style, but very good. Dark brick-red in color, with a ruby center. Medium-bodied, with dried cherry and floral aromas, silky tannins and ripe berry, cherry and fresh mushroom flavors. Long finish. (1982 Bordeaux horizontal tasting). Drink now.–J.S. • $NA • (11/30/1998) • **87**

GRAND MONTMIRAIL, DOMAINE DU

Gigondas Cuvée Vieilles Vignes 1993 • $15 • (10/15/1997) • **79**
Gigondas Cuvée Vieilles Vignes 1989 • $15 • (10/15/1996) • **82**

GRAND MOULAS, CHATEAU DU

Côtes du Rhône-Villages 1995 • $11 • (10/15/1997) • **75**

GRAND MOULIN, CHATEAU

Corbières 1994 • $16 • (4/30/1998) • **84**

GRAND-MOULINET, CHATEAU

Pomerol 1996: Attractive blackberry and mineral aromas. Medium-bodied, with some fruit and fine tannins, but a short and uninteresting finish. Drink now.–J.S. • $25 • (1/31/1999) • **82**
Pomerol 1995 • $20 • (1/31/1998) • **90**

GRAND-PONTET, CHATEAU

St.-Emilion 1997: Lovely raspberry and cherry character. Medium-bodied, with fine tannins and a fresh finish. Delicious. Drink now through 2003.–J.S. • $40 • (1/31/2000) • **86**
St.-Emilion 1996: Can't complain about this St.-Emilion. Very dark color, with mineral, berry and spice aromas. Medium-bodied, with a good core of berry and toasted oak character on the palate. Slightly dry on the finish, but still impressive. Best after 2000.–J.S. • $25 • (1/31/1999) • **87**
St.-Emilion 1995: Amazing quality for this estate. Bubbling over with blackberries, violets and cherries, adding hints of new wood. Full-bodied, concentrated, with loads of silky tannins and a long, long, flavorful finish. New World-style Bordeaux. Best from 2005 through 2015.–J.S. • $35 • (9/15/1998) • **91**
St.-Emilion 1993 • $22 • (1/31/1996) • **86**
St.-Emilion 1988 • $21 • (7/15/1991) • **86**

GRAND-PUY-DUCASSE, CHATEAU

Pauillac 1999: Lots of grape, tar and currant character. Medium-bodied, with well-integrated tannins and a long finish. Well done.–J.S. • $NA • (1/01/2000) (BT) • **85-89**
Pauillac 1998: A silky wine, but it's rather austere and dry, needing more fruit concentration. Medium-bodied. Short finish. May be slightly better next year.–J.S. • $NA • (5/31/1999) (BT) • **80-84**
Pauillac 1997: Good core of fruit in this wine. Medium-bodied, with some tobacco and cherry character. A bit tough, but should improve with age. Well done for the vintage. Best after 2001.–J.S. • $20 • (1/31/2000) • **87**
Pauillac 1996: A bit tough, but shows interesting yet reserved aromas and flavors of cherry and raspberry and mineral. Medium-bodied, with firm tannins and a short finish. Best after 2000.–J.S. • $18 • (1/31/1999) • **85**
Pauillac 1995: Straightforward '95, with currant and berry aromas and flavors, medium body and medium tannins. Fruity finish. Drink through 2003.–J.S. • $45 • (9/15/1998) • **85**
Pauillac 1989: A big, bruising '89. Seriously good for Grand-Puy-Ducasse. Superdark, inky color. Intense blackberry and cherry character and hints of black licorice. Full-bodied, very velvety, with loads of tannins and an earth, berry and dark chocolate aftertaste. (1989 Bordeaux horizontal tasting). Best after 2004.–J.S. • $39 Ⓐ • (5/31/1999) • **91**
Pauillac 1988 • $34 Ⓐ • (4/30/1991) • **89**
Pauillac 1986 • $31 Ⓐ • (6/30/1989) • **85**
Pauillac 1985 • $19 • (2/29/1988) • **90**
Pauillac 1982: Tasted from magnum. Dark ruby-garnet in color. Rich and slightly stinky, with earth, currant and tobacco aromas. Medium- to full-bodied, with well-integrated tannins and a pretty currant flavor. Slightly short on the finish. (1982 Bordeaux horizontal tasting). Drink now.–J.S. • $32 Ⓐ • (11/30/1998) • **87**
Pauillac 1961 • $43 • (4/30/1996) • **87**

GRAND-PUY-LACOSTE, CHATEAU

Pauillac 1999: Some good ripe fruit with medium body and medium tannins, but falls away on the finish a bit quickly.–J.S. • $NA • (1/01/2000) (BT) • **85-89**
Pauillac 1998: Interesting prune and earth aromas and flavors in this wine. Medium- to full-bodied, with velvety tannins and a medium finish. A bit rustic.–J.S. • $NA • (5/31/1999) (BT) • **85-89**
Pauillac 1997: Rather light, with berry and herbal character. Short finish. Not as good as I hoped for GPL.–J.S. • $39 • (1/31/2000) • **81**
Pauillac 1996: A seamless, pretty '96 claret. Extremely fruity aromas of plums and blackberries. Medium-bodied, with polished tannins and silky texture. Best after 2001.–J.S. • $56 Ⓐ • (1/31/1999) • **90**
Pauillac 1995 • $62 Ⓐ • (1/31/1998) • **92**
Pauillac 1994 • $28 Ⓐ • (1/31/1997) • **88**
Pauillac 1993 • $32 Ⓐ • (1/31/1996) • **85**
Pauillac 1992 • $24 • (4/15/1995) • **76**
Pauillac 1991 • $24 • (3/31/1994) • **82**
Pauillac 1990 • $84 Ⓐ • (3/31/1993) • **95**
Pauillac 1989: Big and muscular, with loads of fruit and tannins, this will age for as long as you like. Dark ruby color. Loads of blackberry, cherry and pepper. Full-bodied, adding lots of chewy tannins and a long aftertaste of cherry, black licorice and dark chocolate. (1989 Bordeaux horizontal tasting). Best after 2003.–J.S. • $52 Ⓐ • (5/31/1999) • **93**
Pauillac 1988: Always beautiful, this full-bodied '88 shows terrific fruit character and racy, silky tannins that are wonderfully knit together. Thoroughly satisfying. (1988 Bordeaux horizontal tasting). Best after 2001.–J.S. • $42 Ⓐ • (11/30/1998) • **91**
Pauillac 1987 • $18 • (5/15/1990) • **77**
Pauillac 1986 • $63 Ⓐ • (5/31/1989) • **88**
Pauillac 1985 • $57 Ⓐ • (10/15/1994) • **90**
Pauillac 1984 • $15 • (10/15/1987) • **83**
Pauillac 1983 • $49 Ⓐ • (10/15/1994) • **84**
Pauillac 1982: Not as impressive as it once was; nonetheless, a rich and caressing wine. Sweet berry flavor, with hints of tobacco and raisin.

Key: SS—Spectator Selection. CS—Cellar Selection. HR—Highly Recommended. $NA—Price not available. (BT)—Barrel tasting. Ⓐ—Auction Price. For a key to the tasters' initials, see "How to Use These Listings."
Dates in parentheses represent the issues in which the ratings were published.

Medium- to full-bodied, with velvety tannins and a caressing finish. (1982 Bordeaux horizontal tasting). Drink now.–J.S. • $108 Ⓐ • (11/30/1998) • **92**
Pauillac 1981 • $29 Ⓐ • (10/15/1994) • **88**
Pauillac 1979 • $40 Ⓐ • (10/15/1989) • **88**
Pauillac 1970 • $67 Ⓐ • (5/15/1993) • **90**
Pauillac 1961 • $100 Ⓐ • (4/30/1996) • **86**
Pauillac 1945 • $333 Ⓐ • (11/30/1995) • **86**

GRAND-ROMAINE, DOMAINE

Gigondas 1994 • $NA • (10/15/1997) • **82**
Gigondas 1990 • $13 • (4/15/1993) • **85**
Gigondas 1989 • $16 • (8/31/1991) • **87**
Gigondas Medaille d'Argent 1990 • $16 • (1/31/1992) • **85**
Gigondas Medaille d'Or 1990 • $16 • (1/31/1992) • **87**

GRAND TINEL, DOMAINE DU

Châteauneuf-du-Pape 1997: Super-duper. Fat, oozing with ripeness, delivering some cherry, plum, cedar and toast notes and kicking in with a certain tartness on the finish. Drink now through 2001.–P.M. • $17 • (8/31/1999) • **84**
Châteauneuf-du-Pape 1995: A gem of harmony, exotic flavors, ripe tannins and full mouthfeel. Impossible not to love this wine for its roasted game, leather, mineral, dark chocolate, currant and crème brûlée character and superfine texture. Drink now through 2008.–P.M. • $17 • (11/15/1998) • **90**
Châteauneuf-du-Pape 1989 • $15 • (10/15/1991) • **88**
Châteauneuf-du-Pape 1988 • $17 • (10/15/1991) • **87**
Châteauneuf-du-Pape 1986 • $20 • (10/15/1991) • **86**
Châteauneuf-du-Pape 1985 • $23 • (10/15/1991) • **75**
Châteauneuf-du-Pape 1983 • $25 • (10/15/1991) • **87**
Châteauneuf-du-Pape 1981 • $27 • (10/15/1991) • **89**
Côtes du Rhône 1995: Light-bodied and light-colored, this is maturely earthy in character, a bit astringent on the finish.–P.M. • $8 • (11/15/1998) • **78**

GRAND VILLAGE, CHATEAU

Bordeaux Supérieur 1997: Good berry character here, but a bit lean. Medium- to light-bodied, with a fresh finish. Drink now.–J.S. • $NA • (1/31/2000) • **83**
Bordeaux Supérieur 1996: A slightly simple but good young red. Silky tannins, with good ripe fruit. Medium-bodied, with a caressing texture. Could use a bit more fruit at center-palate, but still a nice glass of wine. Drink now.–J.S. • $NA • (1/31/1999) • **83**
Bordeaux Supérieur 1995 • $15 • (1/31/1998) • **88**

GRANDE CASSAGNE, CHATEAU

Syrah Costières de Nîmes 1997: Fresh and fruity, with berry, plum and briar flavors. Despite its youthfulness, this has a nice backbone, with ripe cherry notes on the finish. Drink now through 2001.–K.M. • $9 • (10/31/1998) • **85**

GRANDE GARDIOLE, CHATEAU DE LA

Châteauneuf-du-Pape 1996: This smooth, ripe red shows raspberry, game and herb flavors, with moderate, well-integrated tannins and fresh acidity. Good typicity in a lighter style. Drink now through 2002.–T.M. • $19 • (11/15/1998) • **87**

GRANDES MURAILLES, CHATEAU LES

St.-Emilion 1999: A pretty, balanced red with berry, cherry and licorice character. Medium body, fine tannins and a medium finish. Lacks a bit of fruit in the center palate.–J.S. • $NA • (1/01/2000) (BT) • **85-89**
St.-Emilion 1998: Lovely soft texture to this young wine, with cooked cherry and berry character. Medium to full body.–J.S. • $NA • (5/31/1999) (BT) • **85-89**
St.-Emilion 1997: Beautiful sweet fruit character, with chocolate and toasted oak undertones. Medium-bodied, with a soft texture and a long, fruity finish. Delicious. Drink now.–J.S. • $NA • (1/31/2000) • **86**

GRANDES VIGNES DU ROY, LES

Châteauneuf-du-Pape White 1998: This racy white is crisp in texture, with grass, citrus and pear character. Light-bodied and clean. Drink now.–P.M. • $24 • (9/30/1999) • **82**
Châteauneuf-du-Pape White 1997: Flavorful and aromatic, this clean, fruity white has white peach, white pepper, apricot and pear notes. Of medium body, it's ripe and sweet-tasting, though dry on the balanced finish. Distinctive. From Patrice Magni. Drink now.–P.M. • $NA • (9/30/1998) • **88**
Côtes du Rhône Les Vieilles Vignes 1998: Light-colored and light-bodied, a bit diluted, with cherry and strawberry notes.–P.M. • $12 • (11/15/1999) • **74**
Côtes du Rhône White Les Vieilles Vignes 1998: Very crisp, but still lovely for its clean, pure and vibrant green apple, honey, pear and lemon notes. Sufficient ripeness balances it. Drink now.–P.M. • $12 • (11/15/1999) • **85**

GRANDIN

Brut Vin de Table Français NV • $9 • (5/15/1997) • **84**
Brut Vin de Table Français Cuvée de Réserve NV • $10 • (5/15/1997) • **84**

GRANDS CLOCHERS, LES

Cabernet Sauvignon-Syrah Vin de Pays d'Oc 1995: Firm and focused, with fairly well-concentrated cherry and spice flavors. Medium-bodied and balanced. Finishes on a tart note. Drink now.–K.M. • $10 • (11/15/1998) • **84**

GRANDS DEVERS, DOMAINE DES

Côtes du Rhône-Villages Valreas 1996: Mature Rhône red, with gamy, animal and wet forest underbrush, black pepper notes. Tart finish. Not imported into the U.S.–P.M. • $NA • (1/01/1999) • **77**
Côtes du Rhône-Villages Valreas 1995: Supple and soft, a lovely wine offering nice spice, tobacco-box, black currant and plum flavors. Medium-bodied, balanced. Drink now.–P.M. • $11 • (11/15/1998) • **83**
Côtes du Rhône-Villages Valreas 1994 • $13 • (10/15/1997) • **72**
Syrah Côtes du Rhône 1996: A distinctive, slightly earthy, very plummy, interesting red, showing dark color, mineral, lead pencil and blackberry character, ripe and pure flavors that'll appeal to Rhône aficionados. Not imported into the U.S. Drink now through 2002.–P.M. • $NA • (1/01/1999) • **88**

GRANDS MARECHAUX, CHATEAU LES

Premières Côtes de Blaye 1999: Nice plum, berry and fruity character. Medium-bodied, with fine tannins and a medium finish. Lots of finesse.–J.S. • $NA • (1/01/2000) (BT) • **85-89**
Premières Côtes de Blaye 1998: Tastes like chocolate-covered raisins with a hint of vanilla. Medium- to full-bodied, with soft tannins and a medium finish. Slightly one-dimensional, but very good.–J.S. • $NA • (5/31/1999) (BT) • **85-89**
Premières Côtes de Blaye 1997: Good, simple red, with plum, berry and slightly stewed fruit. Medium-bodied, with velvety tannins and a slightly herbal finish. Drink now.–J.S. • $17 • (1/31/2000) • **85**

GRANGE CLINET, CHATEAU LA

Premières Côtes de Bordeaux 1996: Good berry and mineral aromas, but slightly diluted on the short finish. Medium-bodied, with medium tannins. Best after 2001.–J.S. • $9 • (1/31/1999) • **80**
Premières Côtes de Bordeaux 1995 • $8 • (1/31/1998) • **83**
Premières Côtes de Bordeaux 1993 • $8 • (12/15/1995) • **80**

GRANGE DE GRENET, CHATEAU LA

Bordeaux 1995 • $8 • (6/30/1997) • **85**

GRANGENEUVE, DOMAINE DE

Coteaux du Tricastin Cuvée de la Truffière 1995 • $15 • (10/15/1997) • **83**

GRANOUPIAC, DOMAINE DE

Coteaux du Languedoc 1998: Intense and powerful, brimming with ripe plum and dark cherry flavors that are framed by an appealing roasted element. Gains complexity with leather, brick and hot stone notes. The flavors linger on the long finish. Quite smooth and appealing now. Best from 2001 through 2004.–K.M. • $10 • (6/15/2000) • **90**
Coteaux du Languedoc Tonneaux 1998: Packs quite a punch, with intense cassis and dark plum flavors as well as coffee, brick and mineral components. Full-bodied and full-blown, with a good dose of tannins and a balanced backbone

FRANCE

of acidity. Meaty and chocolaty notes chime in on the long finish. Best from 2001 through 2004.–K.M. • $18 • (6/15/2000) • **90**

Merlot Vin de Pays d'Oc 1998: Flavors of dark plum and coffee have leathery and meaty notes. Finishes with a mix of herb and chocolate. Drink now.–K.M. • $10 • (6/15/2000) • **84**

GRAPILLON D'OR, DOMAINE DU

Gigondas 1997: Don't expect a silky palate massage, just a tough, sweaty workout that will leave your senses satisfied. Tough and sinewy, muscular and impressive in its firm tannin structure, there's plenty going on. Think campfire and grilled meat with this hardy, rustic, gamy, leathery red. Drink now through 2008.–P.M. • $20 • (12/15/1999) • **88**

Gigondas 1995: Supple and decadent, a smooth, round, silky and ripe Gigondas. Perfectly balanced, it might not deliver enormous complexity, but who cares? Enjoy the plums, currants, leather, game, dried prunes and Oriental spice character. Drink now through 2005.–P.M. • $19 • (11/15/1998) • **89**

GRAS, ALAIN

Auxey-Duresses 1996: Nice cherry and spice character carries through the midpalate, then full-bore tannins take over. Ends with lingering accents of cherry and vanilla. Drink through 2004.–B.S. • $23 • (9/30/1998) • **85**

Auxey-Duresses 1995 • $23 • (11/15/1997) • **85**

Auxey-Duresses 1993 • $20 • (11/15/1995) • **86**

Auxey-Duresses 1992 • $23 • (12/15/1994) • **85**

Auxey-Duresses 1990 • $29 • (12/15/1992) • **85**

Auxey-Duresses Vieilles Vignes 1997: Another winner for Côte de Beaune. Lively and succulent Pinot character—mineral, slightly toasted mocha and spice—takes you on an exciting ride, with smooth, velvety tannins, coming together on a sexy finish that's unbelievably juicy and pure for the '97 vintage. Drink now through 2006.–P.M. • $30 • (9/30/1999) • **92**

Meursault Les Tillets 1998: Soft, round, a bit heavy, with medium body. Some nice toasted bread and spice aromas. Decent, but not great fruit concentration. Drink now through 2002.–P.M. • $46 • (5/31/2000) • **82**

St.-Romain 1998: Wood dominates this medium-bodied Chardonnay for now, giving it a cardboard character and bitter finish. There is some nice fruit concentration too, though.–P.M. • $30 • (5/31/2000) • **79**

St.-Romain 1997: Exotic, and it works. Ripe, almost late harvest in the aromatic profile, with dried apricot, peach and passion fruit aromas and flavors. Slightly hot on the finish, but the flavors are yummy and there's enough freshness. Drink now.–P.M. • $31 • (9/30/1999) • **87**

St.-Romain 1996: Good intensity in this medium-bodied '96. Shows a taut marriage between herbal, honey, green lime and toasted oak flavors; they just explode on the palate, before settling down for a supple, balanced, albeit slightly herbaceous, finish. Drink now through 2005.–P.M. • $NA • (8/31/1998) • **86**

St.-Romain 1995 • $20 • (8/31/1997) • **81**

St.-Romain Red 1997: Has earthiness, a touch of licorice and a chewy texture. Rustic and frank. Drink now through 2003.–B.S. • $28 • (9/30/1999) • **84**

St.-Romain Red 1996: Depth and a concentrated, jammy fruit character make for a delicious wine, full of freshly crushed berries and with balanced structure for early enjoyment. A good introduction to red Burgundy. Drink now through 2001.–B.S. • $19 • (9/30/1998) • **86**

St.-Romain Red 1995 • $23 • (11/15/1997) • **84**

St.-Romain Red 1993 • $18 • (11/15/1995) • **84**

St.-Romain Red 1992 • $21 • (12/15/1994) • **78**

St.-Romain Red 1990 • $24 • (12/15/1992) • **86**

GRATIEN, ALFRED

Brut Champagne NV • $38 • (10/31/1996) • **90**

Brut Champagne 1990: A luxurious Champagne that's rich and smooth, with butter and lemon flavors, full body and a lingering finish. Drink now through 2002. • $100 • (11/15/1999) • **89**

Brut Champagne Classique NV: Fresh fruit flavors and lively acidity make this appetizing. Dry in style, bracing in texture, with complex spicy nuances that linger on the finish. Drink now through 2001. • $40 • (10/31/1999) • **90**

Key: SS—Spectator Selection. CS—Cellar Selection. HR—Highly Recommended. $NA—Price not available. (BT)—Barrel tasting. (A)—Auction Price. For a key to the tasters' initials, see "How to Use These Listings."
Dates in parentheses represent the issues in which the ratings were published.

Brut Champagne Cuvée Paradis NV: A soft, inviting Champagne with ample fruit flavors and an easy texture. Turns slightly sweet on the finish. Drink now. • $90 • (10/31/1999) • **86**

Brut Rosé Champagne Cuvée Paradis NV: Complex, rich and creamy, this rosé is subtle in its approach, exhibiting brioche, chocolate and berry notes that mesh beautifully with the velvety texture and vibrant underlying structure. Finishes with a long and subtle aftertaste of berries. Drink now.–B.S. • $90 • (11/30/1999) • **91**

GRATIEN & MEYER

Brut Saumur Cuvée Renaissance NV • $18 • (5/31/1998) • **83**

Brut Saumur Fleur de Lys NV • $14 • (5/31/1998) • **82**

Saumur Demi-Sec Noir de Noirs Cardinal NV • $14 • (6/30/1998) • **79**

GRAVE A POMEROL, CHATEAU LA

Pomerol 1999: Well done. Lovely sweet fruit to this wine, with hints of dried herbs and wet earth. Medium- to full-bodied, with velvety tannins and a long finish.–J.S. • $NA • (1/01/2000) (BT) • **85-89**

Pomerol 1998: A shy young wine, with lots of ripe fruit and compacted tannins. Full-bodied and balanced, with full tannins and a long, sweet fruit finish. Balanced.–J.S. • $NA • (5/31/1999) (BT) • **90-94**

Pomerol 1997: Delicious. Lovely aromas of dark tobacco, cedar and berries. Medium-bodied, with fine, polished tannins and a long, sweet fruit finish. Drink now through 2003.–J.S. • $23 • (1/31/2000) • **88**

Pomerol 1996: Good berry and tobacco character, but a bit lean. Medium-bodied, with firm tannins and a hollow midpalate. Disappointing for this estate. Best after 2000.–J.S. • $26 • (1/31/1999) • **84**

Pomerol 1995: Refined wine. Raspberry and perfumed character on the nose. Medium-bodied, with well-integrated tannins and a fruity aftertaste. Very well made. Drink through 2004.–J.S. • $38 • (9/15/1998) • **89**

Pomerol 1994 • $35 • (1/31/1997) • **88**

Pomerol 1993 • $28 • (1/31/1996) • **87**

Pomerol 1992 • $NA • (4/15/1995) • **80**

Pomerol 1990 • $28 • (3/31/1993) • **92**

Pomerol 1989: A fresh and elegant '89. Color is red with a garnet tint. Lovely ripe berry, tobacco and cherry aromas. Full-bodied, including soft tannins and a berry and plum aftertaste. Why wait to drink this? (1989 Bordeaux horizontal tasting). Try now through 2006.–J.S. • $NA • (5/31/1999) • **88**

Pomerol 1986 • $35 • (3/31/1990) • **89**

Pomerol 1982 • $NA • (8/31/1992) • **86**

Pomerol 1979 • $NA • (10/15/1989) • **90**

Pomerol 1970 • $NA • (5/15/1993) • **90**

GRAVE, CHATEAU DE LA

Bordeaux Supérieur 1988 • $8 • (7/15/1990) • **82**

Minervois 1990 • $8 • (3/15/1994) • **82**

GRAVEGEAL, DOMAINE

Coteaux du Languedoc Château Roumanieres Terres du Bout du Monde 1998: This has nice cherry and ripe plum flavors, with just a touch of saddle leather and mineral. Spice and milk chocolate notes on the finish. Drink now through 2002.–K.M. • $10 • (6/15/2000) • **85**

Vin de Pays d'Oc Terres du Bout du Monde 1998: A thick, almost rustic-tasting red, with a lively, spicy aroma and concentrated flavors of red plum and dark cherry. Tannins clamp down a bit on the finish, with bittersweet chocolate flavors. Best from 2001 through 2004.–K.M. • $8 • (6/15/2000) • **86**

GRAVIERES, CHATEAU DES

Graves 1996: Light-bodied, with decent strawberry and leaf character and light tannins. Sweet fruit finish.–J.S. • $15 • (7/31/1999) • **79**

Graves 1995: A simple '95 Bordeaux, with light dried cherry and raspberry. Medium bodied, with light tannins and a slightly green aftertaste. Drink now.–J.S. • $15 • (7/31/1999) • **80**

GREFFET, DOMAINE

St.-Véran 1995 • $14 • (5/31/1997) • **72**

GRESSIER-GRAND-POUJEAUX, CHATEAU

Moulis 1993 • $16 • (1/31/1996) • **85**

GREYSAC, CHATEAU

Bordeaux White 1998: A sturdy white, with lots of apple, melon and pineapple character. Medium- to full-bodied, with good acidity and a fresh finish. Best after 2000.–J.S. • $NA • (2/29/2000) • **88**

Bordeaux White 1996: Intense aromas of toasted oak with apple. Full-bodied, with loads of vanilla and coconut, but it's rather hard to find the fruit beneath. Interesting, but slightly overdone in the new wood department. Drink now.–J.S. • $NA • (1/01/1999) • **82**

Médoc 1998: Attractive blackberry and mint aromas and flavors. Medium-bodied, very balanced, with fine tannins and a silky finish. Not overdone—just right for its category.–J.S. • $NA • (5/31/1999) (BT) • **85-89**

Médoc 1997: I like the berry and mineral character in this '97 but it finishes rather short. Medium to light body. Drink now.–J.S. • $15 • (1/31/2000) • **83**

Médoc 1996: Light and slightly diluted, with tobacco and berry character but also an undertone of weediness. Medium- to light-bodied, with a light finish.–J.S. • $11 • (1/31/1999) • **79**

Médoc 1995: Plenty of cherry and light earth aromas. Medium-bodied, with silky tannins and a light finish. A bit simple really. Drink now.–J.S. • $15 • (9/15/1998) • **83**

Médoc 1994 • $15 • (11/30/1997) • **87**

Médoc 1990 • $12 • (3/31/1993) • **84**

Médoc 1989 • $12 • (3/15/1992) • **79**

Médoc 1988 • $15 • (4/30/1991) • **87**

Médoc 1986 • $10 • (11/30/1989) • **85**

Médoc 1982: Interesting, but falling short. Berry, tobacco aromas. Medium-bodied, medium tannins, good earthy flavors, but drying on the finish. (1982 Bordeaux horizontal tasting). Drink now.–J.S. • $NA • (11/30/1998) • **83**

GRIPPAT, J.L.

Hermitage White 1996: Reserved in aroma, yet a powerhouse on the palate, here's an earth-driven white, delivering mineral, butter, light spice and compacted fruit and acidity that take your palate for quite a ride. Drink now through 2005.–P.M. • $55 • (10/15/1999) • **94**

St.-Joseph 1997: Shows vanilla mixed with some mocha, herbs, roasted coffee and black cherry. It's supple on the palate, turning a bit chewy and smoky on the juicy, olive- and chocolate-tasting finish. Drink now through 2002.–P.M. • $19 • (10/15/1999) • **85**

St.-Joseph 1991 • $22 • (5/31/1994) • **78**

St.-Joseph Vignes de l'Hospice 1991 • $32 • (5/31/1994) • **83**

St.-Joseph Vignes de l'Hospice 1990 • $32 • (5/31/1994) • **85**

St.-Joseph White 1997: Ripe and round in texture, uncomplicated, offering butter, almond, cedar and a whiff that's odd and hard to describe—perhaps cardboard? Too bad because the oily, thick texture is great. A second bottle was oxidized.–P.M. • $19 • (10/15/1999) • **79**

GRIVAULT, ALBERT

Meursault 1997: Unripe-tasting fruit framed by dry wood makes for an astringent, crisp wine.–P.M. • $35 • (5/31/1999) • **73**

Meursault 1996: Stands out for its odd aromas in this group of clean '96s. Has some peanut, wet wool and butterscotch character, turns a bit dry on the finish. Tasted twice, with consistent notes. Drink now through 2003.–P.M. • $35 • (8/31/1998) • **76**

Meursault 1995 • $28 • (5/31/1997) • **88**

Meursault Clos des Perrières 1997: Odd aromas of stewed cabbage lead to a tart, astringent finish.–P.M. • $73 • (5/31/1999) • **70**

Meursault Clos des Perrières 1996 • $60 • (5/31/1998) • **92**

Meursault Clos des Perrières 1995 • $62 • (5/31/1997) • **90**

Meursault Les Perrières 1995 • $46 • (5/31/1997) • **90**

Meursault Perrières 1997: An odd earthy aroma leads to an herbal, astringent character.–P.M. • $41 Ⓐ • (5/31/1999) • **70**

Meursault Perrières 1996 • $48 Ⓐ • (5/31/1998) • **94**

GRIVIERE, CHATEAU

Médoc 1998: Lots of blackberry, currant and milk chocolate notes. Full-bodied and velvety, with a lovely core of ripe fruit. Medium finish. Well done for this estate.–J.S. • $NA • (5/31/1999) (BT) • **85-89**

Médoc 1997: A bit thin and short, but some decent berry character.–J.S. • $NA • (1/31/2000) • **79**

Médoc 1996: Inky in color, with intense aromas of allspice, berry and earth. Full-bodied, with plenty of fruit and velvety tannins, it's a round and delicious wine. Slightly rustic, but juicy. Best after 2000.–J.S. • $18 • (1/31/1999) • **86**

Médoc 1995 • $18 • (1/31/1998) • **88**

Médoc 1993 • $16 • (4/30/1997) • **73**

GRIVOT, JEAN

Chambolle-Musigny La Combe d'Orvaux 1987 • $47 • (6/15/1990) • **85**

Clos de Vougeot 1997: Clean and pure fruit, with easy raspberry and blackberry swirling around the palate. Medium-bodied, it firms up with chewy tannins on the finish. Best from 2002 through 2007.–P.M. • $63 • (9/30/1999) • **87**

Clos de Vougeot 1996: Massive, showing loads of red- and blackberry, cassis, wet earth and mineral-laden character. Firm tannins need time to soften, but this is serious, full-bodied red Burgundy, with layers of complexity. Best after 2005.–P.M. • $58 • (9/30/1998) • **91**

Clos de Vougeot 1995 • $60 • (11/15/1997) • **88**

Clos de Vougeot 1993 • $65 Ⓐ • (5/15/1996) CS • **92**

Clos de Vougeot 1988 • $70 • (4/30/1991) • **85**

Clos de Vougeot 1985 • $83 Ⓐ • (4/30/1988) • **81**

Echézeaux 1997: Black cherry and blackberry aromas and flavors turn a little monolithic on the palate, and there's a dry edge to this medium-bodied, dense red. Moderate finish. Drink now through 2001.–B.S. • $63 • (9/30/1999) • **85**

Echézeaux 1996: Lush and elegant, showing lovely blackberry character, with wet earth and mineral notes. Full-bodied, it turns on the power midpalate, then kicks in with firm tannins on the fruity, succulent and fresh finish. Needs time for the tannins to soften. Best after 2005.–P.M. • $47 • (9/30/1998) • **89**

Echézeaux 1995 • $60 • (11/15/1997) • **94**

Echézeaux 1994 • $50 • (9/30/1997) • **90**

Echézeaux 1993 • $45 • (5/15/1996) • **92**

Nuits-St.-Georges Aux Boudots 1995 • $45 • (11/15/1997) • **88**

Nuits-St.-Georges Aux Boudots 1993 • $32 • (5/15/1996) • **90**

Nuits-St.-Georges Aux Boudots 1990 • $96 Ⓐ • (12/15/1992) • **79**

Nuits-St.-Georges Aux Boudots 1989 • $NA • (1/31/1992) • **77**

Nuits-St.-Georges Aux Boudots 1988 • $54 • (4/30/1991) • **87**

Nuits-St.-Georges Les Boudots 1997: A big, round, black cherry–scented and –flavored '97 red, with vanilla overtones and moderate concentration. Firm and tannic, with a lingering finish. Best after 2001.–B.S. • $44 • (9/30/1999) • **86**

Nuits-St.-Georges Les Boudots 1996: Supercharged. Thick, ripe and delicious, with intensity and concentration; shows deep color, tight midpalate, wonderful acidity and a lovely combination of cassis, blackberry, spice and earth notes. Firm finish, with massive tannic structure. Impressive. Best after 2005.–P.M. • $47 • (9/30/1998) • **90**

Nuits-St.-Georges Les Charmois 1996: Decent concentration, but the aromas and flavors are on the herbal side and the tannins are a bit tough. Best after 2000.–B.S. • $30 • (9/30/1998) • **80**

Nuits-St.-Georges Les Charmois 1987 • $47 • (7/15/1990) • **81**

Nuits-St.-Georges Les Pruliers 1988 • $53 • (4/30/1991) • **89**

Nuits-St.-Georges Les Pruliers 1987 • $55 • (7/15/1990) • **71**

Nuits-St.-Georges Roncière 1987 • $55 • (7/15/1990) • **88**

Richebourg 1997: Round and soft, showing wet earth and a bit of tannic backbone, but a red of medium-intense fruit. Very supple on the pretty finish that picks up intensity on the aftertaste. Drink now through 2003.–P.M. • $170 • (9/30/1999) • **87**

Richebourg 1996: Majestic red Burgundy. Big, massive and racy, this full-bodied Pinot is loaded with pure, clean and sharp cassis, blackberry and raspberry character that marries nicely with subtly toasted and spicy oak accents. The tannins are tender, but the crisp, fresh acidity and zesty finish suggest cellaring this monster wine. Best after 2005.–P.M. • $215 Ⓐ • (9/30/1998) • **93**

Richebourg 1995 • $139 Ⓐ • (11/15/1997) • **90**

Richebourg 1994 • $160 • (9/30/1997) • **91**

Richebourg 1993 • $128 • (5/15/1996) • **96**

Richebourg 1990 • $129 Ⓐ • (12/15/1992) • **84**

Richebourg 1989 • $106 Ⓐ • (1/31/1992) • **93**

Vosne-Romanée 1996: Ripe, rich and fleshy, hedonistic in style, sporting plum flavors, juicy acidity and muscular tannins that dominate the finish. Best from 2001 through 2005.–B.S. • $28 Ⓐ • (9/30/1998) • **87**

Vosne-Romanée 1995 • $54 Ⓐ • (11/15/1997) • **80**

■ ■ ■ ■

GRIVOT, JEAN

Vosne-Romanée 1993 • $22 • (5/15/1996) • **88**
Vosne-Romanée 1990 • $NA • (12/15/1992) • **69**
Vosne-Romanée 1985 • $31 • (4/30/1988) • **87**
Vosne-Romanée Les Beaux Monts 1997: Beautiful balance. Bright ruby defines this woody-tasting red, but black pepper and spice and a ripe, voluptuous mouthfeel come through as it glides with grace to a fine, elegant finish. Best from 2002 through 2005.–P.M. • $45 • (9/30/1999) • **90**
Vosne-Romanée Les Beaux Monts 1996: The toasty, spicy oak complements the ripe plum and cassis in this flamboyant Vosne. It's lively, rich and concentrated, with plenty of stiff tannins that dominate in the end. Best from 2002 through 2007.–B.S. • $47 • (9/30/1998) • **90**
Vosne-Romanée Les Beaux Monts 1995 • $45 • (11/15/1997) • **89**
Vosne-Romanée Les Beaux Monts 1993 • $32 • (5/15/1996) HR • **94**
Vosne-Romanée Les Beaux Monts 1990 • $NA • (12/15/1992) • **76**
Vosne-Romanée Les Beaux Monts 1989 • $NA • (1/31/1992) • **75**
Vosne-Romanée Les Suchots 1993 • $NA • (5/15/1996) • **85**

GROFFIER, ROBERT

Bonnes Mares 1995 • $120 Ⓐ • (1/31/1998) • **96**
Bonnes Mares 1989 • $79 • (1/31/1992) • **81**
Bonnes Mares 1988 • $80 • (11/15/1990) • **90**
Bonnes Mares 1987 • $67 • (7/31/1989) • **89**
Bourgogne 1997: Light and juicy, this easy and rather simple red offers modest fruit and a tart, somewhat drying finish.–P.M. • $25 • (1/01/2000) • **74**
Bourgogne 1996: Lovely, round, ripe and lush regional Bourgogne, showing a sweet midpalate and silky tannins. Very pretty, albeit slightly hot on the finish. Drink now through 2001.–P.M. • $26 • (9/30/1998) • **85**
Bourgogne 1989 • $14 • (1/31/1992) • **78**
Chambertin-Clos de Bèze 1987 • $45 • (7/31/1989) • **88**
Chambolle-Musigny Les Amoureuses 1997: Seems quite mature, with a distinct gamy character and a round mouthfeel, but it's enjoyable for its medium-bodied, silky personality and plum and blackberry character. Delicious, sweet-tasting finish. Drink now through 2003.–P.M. • $72 Ⓐ • (1/01/2000) • **87**
Chambolle-Musigny Les Amoureuses 1996: Almost great, but a bit odd. Dark-colored, sweet-tasting, exotic, with lots of fruit and fine tannins on the midpalate, it all seemed to go well ... until the finish, which turns bitter from what seems overly toasted oak barrels. Disappointing for this producer. Best from 2002 through 2007.–P.M. • $134 Ⓐ • (2/28/1999) • **87**
Chambolle-Musigny Les Amoureuses 1995 • $75 • (1/31/1998) • **90**
Chambolle-Musigny Les Amoureuses 1988 • $66 • (11/15/1990) • **93**
Chambolle-Musigny Les Amoureuses 1987 • $51 • (8/31/1989) • **86**
Chambolle-Musigny Les Amoureuses 1986 • $50 • (2/28/1989) • **84**
Chambolle-Musigny Les Sentiers 1996: Lovely, with supple red- and blackberry character, also some plum and mineral complexity. Pure and clean, this medium-bodied wine shows class. Best from 2004.–P.M. • $69 • (9/30/1998) • **88**
Chambolle-Musigny Les Sentiers 1995 • $55 • (1/31/1998) HR • **95**
Chambolle-Musigny Les Sentiers 1988 • $45 • (11/15/1990) • **89**
Chambolle-Musigny Les Sentiers 1987 • $37 • (8/31/1989) • **87**
Chambolle-Musigny Les Sentiers 1986 • $36 • (2/28/1989) • **90**
Gevrey-Chambertin 1996: Traditional-style, with a blood, iron, mineral and slightly earthy character; *terroir* is privileged over oak in this medium-bodied, medium-fruity wine. Crisp finish. Best from 2003 through 2010.–P.M. • $50 • (5/15/1999) • **85**
Gevrey-Chambertin 1986 • $27 • (2/28/1989) • **85**

GROLLE, PERE LA

Beaujolais 1996 • $9 • (9/15/1997) • **78**
Beaujolais Rosé 1996 • $9 • (9/15/1997) • **82**

GROS, A.-F.

Chambolle-Musigny 1996: Wonderful from start to finish. A deep, seductive Pinot, packed with classy red- and blackberry character, smoky and floral overtones and refined tannins. The acidity gives this sweet-tasting, fresh wine a kick on the finish. Drink now through 2005.–P.M. • $27 Ⓐ • (2/28/1999) • **88**
Echézeaux 1995 • $83 Ⓐ • (11/15/1997) • **86**
Echézeaux 1994 • $55 • (11/15/1996) • **87**
Echézeaux 1993 • $84 • (11/15/1995) • **83**
Echézeaux 1992 • $106 • (12/15/1994) • **83**
Echézeaux 1991 • $70 • (1/31/1994) • **76**
Echézeaux 1990 • $90 • (12/15/1992) • **90**
Echézeaux 1988 • $84 • (2/15/1991) • **91**
Hautes-Côtes de Nuits 1996: Light in color and body and modest in flavor, showing already an aged mushroom, underbrush note along with some prune and licorice.–P.M. • $19 • (2/28/1999) • **77**
Hautes-Côtes de Nuits 1995 • $20 • (11/15/1997) • **70**
Hautes-Côtes de Nuits 1993 • $20 • (11/15/1995) • **75**
Hautes-Côtes de Nuits 1992 • $22 • (12/15/1994) • **81**
Hautes-Côtes de Nuits 1989 • $19 • (6/15/1992) • **78**
Hautes-Côtes de Nuits 1988 • $22 • (3/31/1991) • **80**
Richebourg 1992 • $NA • (12/15/1994) • **86**
Richebourg 1990 • $180 • (12/15/1992) • **94**
Richebourg 1989 • $130 • (1/31/1992) • **97**
Richebourg 1988 • $190 • (2/15/1991) • **97**
Savigny-lès-Beaune Clos des Guettes 1996: Fruity and pleasant, this straightforward Pinot has orange, wet earth and lots of licorice notes. Smooth and comfortable, it's a medium-bodied wine. Drink now.–P.M. • $40 • (2/28/1999) • **81**
Savigny-lès-Beaune Clos des Guettes 1995 • $38 • (11/15/1997) • **78**
Vosne-Romanée Aux Réas 1996: Clean and pure, a vibrant, lively, sexy and racy '96, delivering a lot of sweet-tasting red- and blackberry character, as well as a crisp, lemonlike note. Balanced and lovely, this wine should sing with foods in a few years. Best from 2002 through 2010.–P.M. • $54 • (2/28/1999) • **90**
Vosne-Romanée Aux Réas 1995 • $45 • (11/15/1997) • **84**
Vosne-Romanée Aux Réas 1994 • $40 • (11/15/1996) • **80**
Vosne-Romanée Aux Réas 1993 • $44 • (11/15/1995) • **87**
Vosne-Romanée Aux Réas 1992 • $47 • (12/15/1994) • **79**
Vosne-Romanée Aux Réas 1991 • $35 • (1/31/1994) • **83**
Vosne-Romanée Aux Réas 1990 • $40 • (12/15/1992) • **79**
Vosne-Romanée Aux Réas 1988 • $41 • (2/28/1991) • **71**
Vosne-Romanée Clos de la Fontaine 1996: Attractive for all its fresh Pinot Noir aromas—cherry as well as rose petal, currant and raspberry—and its supple and fine tannins make it accessible now. Drink now through 2005.–P.M. • $54 • (2/28/1999) • **87**
Vosne-Romanée Maizières 1996: An exotically flavored red Burgundy, offering violet, rose petal, blackberry, currant and ginger notes. Medium-bodied and fresh, it's an elegantly constructed Pinot that has good zip and length. Drink now through 2005.–P.M. • $54 • (2/28/1999) • **89**
Vosne-Romanée Maizières 1993 • $50 • (11/15/1995) • **87**

GROS, ANNE & FRANCOIS

Bourgogne 1997: Fresh aromas of wild berry and raspberry emerge in this well-made Bourgogne Rouge. Very pretty finish. Drink now.–P.M. • $22 • (9/30/1999) • **84**
Bourgogne 1996: Hard and unyielding, showing tough green tannins, with cedar, rust and iron notes. Herbaceous on the finish.–P.M. • $24 • (9/30/1998) • **73**
Bourgogne 1995 • $19 • (11/15/1997) • **83**
Bourgogne 1994 • $125 Ⓐ • (11/15/1996) • **80**
Bourgogne 1993 • $13 • (11/15/1995) • **81**
Bourgogne 1992 • $NA • (12/15/1994) • **80**
Bourgogne 1990 • $17 • (12/15/1992) • **84**
Chambolle-Musigny La Combe d'Orveau 1996: Full of blackberry and spice, this offers saturated, intense fruit character, racy acidity and solid tannins. The lasting impression is sweet, fresh and almost jammy. Best from 2001 through 2006.–B.S. • $50 • (9/30/1998) • **89**
Chambolle-Musigny La Combe d'Orveau 1995 • $38 • (11/15/1997) • **73**
Chambolle-Musigny La Combe d'Orveau 1993 • $29 • (11/15/1995) • **88**
Chambolle-Musigny La Combe d'Orveau 1992 • $NA • (12/15/1994) • **83**
Chambolle-Musigny La Combe d'Orveau 1990 • $40 • (12/15/1992) • **72**
Clos Vougeot Le Grand Maupertuis 1996: Concentrated, jammy fruit, just a bit herbal, with decent cassis and blackberry notes and impressive midpalate concentration. Medium-bodied, with clean, crisp character on the finish, it earns kudos for not being overoaked in this vintage.–P.M. • $90 • (9/30/1998) • **88**
Clos Vougeot Le Grand Maupertuis 1995 • $80 • (11/15/1997) • **92**
Clos Vougeot Le Grand Maupertuis 1994 • $59 • (11/15/1996) • **94**
Clos Vougeot Le Grand Maupertuis 1993 • $55 • (11/15/1995) • **95**
Clos Vougeot Le Grand Maupertuis 1992 • $NA • (12/15/1994) • **88**
Clos Vougeot Le Grand Maupertuis 1991 • $58 • (1/31/1994) • **82**
Clos Vougeot Le Grand Maupertuis 1990 • $75 • (12/15/1992) • **95**

Key: SS—Spectator Selection. CS—Cellar Selection. HR—Highly Recommended. $NA—Price not available. (BT)—Barrel tasting. Ⓐ—Auction Price.
For a key to the tasters' initials, see "How to Use These Listings."
Dates in parentheses represent the issues in which the ratings were published.

Clos Vougeot Le Grand Maupertuis 1989 • $NA • (1/31/1992) • **90**

Richebourg 1997: Clarity and pure Pinot fruit define the aromas in this Burgundy, while the cherry and spice flavors are matched with decent focus, density and length. Not a blockbuster, but attractive for the vintage. Drink now through 2002.–B.S. • $237 • (9/30/1999) • **88**

Richebourg 1996: Thick, ripe and supple, this is a beautiful, full-bodied, suave wine. Combines lots of acidity, fruit intensity and a velvety midpalate with a long, sweet finish. A green olive note verges on herbaceousness, but I love the terrific cardamom, blackberry and deftly toasted oak flavors. Extremely complex and seductive on the long finish. Drink now through 2010.–P.M. • $200 • (9/30/1998) • **92**

Richebourg 1995 • $170 • (11/15/1997) • **90**

Richebourg 1994 • $105 Ⓐ • (11/15/1996) • **90**

Richebourg 1993 • $100 • (11/15/1995) • **91**

Richebourg 1992 • $NA • (12/15/1994) • **86**

Richebourg 1991 • $100 • (1/31/1994) • **89**

Richebourg 1990 • $130 • (12/15/1992) • **97**

Vosne-Romanée 1993 • $40 • (11/15/1995) • **88**

Vosne-Romanée 1992 • $NA • (12/15/1994) • **82**

Vosne-Romanée 1991 • $32 • (1/31/1994) • **86**

Vosne-Romanée Les Barreaux 1997: Delicate and elegant in aroma, with a crisp midpalate that tastes lemony. Supple tannins turn soft, and there's an acidity-driven kick on the disjointed finish.–P.M. • $63 • (9/30/1999) • **79**

Vosne-Romanée Les Barreaux 1996: Pure, spicy red fruit character, along with juicy acidity and a fleshy, concentrated texture that finds good support from the firm tannins. Best from 2001 through 2005.–B.S. • $NA • (9/30/1998) • **88**

Vosne-Romanée Les Barreaux 1995 • $55 • (11/15/1997) • **93**

Vosne-Romanée Les Barreaux 1994 • $29 • (11/15/1996) • **85**

GROS, JEAN

Bourgogne 1990 • $16 • (12/15/1992) • **81**

Clos de Vougeot 1994 • $89 • (11/15/1996) • **82**

Clos de Vougeot 1992 • $NA • (12/15/1994) • **83**

Clos de Vougeot 1991 • $80 • (1/31/1994) • **81**

Nuits-St.-Georges 1994 • $NA • (11/15/1996) • **80**

Nuits-St.-Georges 1993 • $32 • (11/15/1995) • **79**

Nuits-St.-Georges 1991 • $NA • (1/31/1994) • **67**

Nuits-St.-Georges 1990 • $31 Ⓐ • (12/15/1992) • **85**

Nuits-St.-Georges 1989 • $39 • (1/31/1992) • **87**

Nuits-St.-Georges 1988 • $42 • (2/28/1991) • **81**

Nuits-St.-Georges 1985 • $36 • (7/31/1988) • **85**

Richebourg 1994 • $160 • (9/30/1997) • **77**

Richebourg 1993 • $160 • (11/15/1995) • **94**

Richebourg 1992 • $150 • (12/15/1994) • **88**

Richebourg 1991 • $149 • (1/31/1994) • **92**

Richebourg 1990 • $150 • (12/15/1992) • **94**

Richebourg 1989 • $180 • (1/31/1992) • **98**

Richebourg 1988 • $134 Ⓐ • (2/28/1991) • **98**

Richebourg 1987 • $177 Ⓐ • (3/31/1990) • **95**

Vosne-Romanée 1994 • $NA • (11/15/1996) • **81**

Vosne-Romanée 1993 • $35 • (11/15/1995) • **89**

Vosne-Romanée 1992 • $35 • (12/15/1994) • **78**

Vosne-Romanée 1989 • $39 • (1/31/1992) • **90**

Vosne-Romanée 1988 • $38 • (2/28/1991) • **90**

Vosne-Romanée 1987 • $32 • (4/30/1990) • **89**

Vosne-Romanée Clos des Réas 1994 • $63 • (11/15/1996) • **83**

Vosne-Romanée Clos des Réas 1993 • $60 • (11/15/1995) • **91**

Vosne-Romanée Clos des Réas 1991 • $53 • (1/31/1994) • **78**

Vosne-Romanée Clos des Réas 1990 • $48 • (12/15/1992) • **93**

Vosne-Romanée Clos des Réas 1989 • $70 • (1/31/1992) • **92**

Vosne-Romanée Clos des Réas 1988 • $59 Ⓐ • (2/28/1991) HR • **94**

Vosne-Romanée Clos des Réas 1987 • $60 Ⓐ • (4/30/1990) • **93**

Vosne-Romanée Clos des Réas 1986 • $75 Ⓐ • (2/28/1989) • **90**

Vosne-Romanée Clos des Réas 1985 • $134 Ⓐ • (7/31/1988) • **87**

GROS, MICHEL

Chambolle-Musigny 1996: Thick and ripe, complex, with lots of game, cassis, spice and smoke—all presented in an exciting, full-bodied, silky, sweet-tasting package. Chewy, fresh finish. Best from 2003 through 2012.–P.M. • $45 • (5/15/1999) • **91**

Chambolle-Musigny 1994 • $38 • (11/15/1996) • **83**

Chambolle-Musigny 1993 • $35 • (11/15/1995) • **91**

Clos Vougeot Le Grand Maupertuis 1997: Lots of oak, cranberry and balsamic vinegar character defines this fairly ripe, big, ruby-colored wine, with a crisp midpalate. Smoky, toasted and gamy, it has vivid flavors that may come together nicely. Best from 2003 through 2007.–P.M. • $116 • (9/30/1999) • **87**

Clos Vougeot Le Grand Maupertuis 1996: Intense and very concentrated, showing a supple, silky texture, a fresh burst of cassis character and an interesting smoky, gamy, earthy thread that makes this full-bodied '96 distinctive. Best from 2003 through 2012.–P.M. • $112 • (5/15/1999) • **91**

Côte de Nuits-Villages 1990 • $NA • (12/15/1992) • **85**

Hautes-Côtes de Nuits 1997: A ripe, smooth red, with cherry and herb components, soft tannins and a balanced but fresh, toasted finish. Drink now.–P.M. • $19 • (9/30/1999) • **84**

Hautes-Côtes de Nuits 1996: Nicely ripe and dark-colored, with some herbal and citrus as well as raspberry and black cherry notes, but it's very crisp on the mouthpuckering finish. Best from 2003 through 2010.–P.M. • $20 • (5/15/1999) • **82**

Hautes-Côtes de Nuits 1994 • $17 • (11/15/1996) • **74**

Hautes-Côtes de Nuits 1993 • $16 • (11/15/1995) • **82**

Hautes-Côtes de Nuits 1989 • $15 • (1/31/1992) • **82**

Hautes-Côtes de Nuits 1987 • $14 • (2/28/1990) • **78**

Nuits-St.-Georges 1996: Such purity, such gorgeous fruit offered by this village wine. Medium-bodied and quite refined, the laser-sharp red- and blackberry flavors taste ripe. Sweet tannins and toasted, smoky complexity on the seductive finish. Best from 2003 through 2008.–P.M. • $44 • (5/15/1999) • **93**

Nuits-St.-Georges Les Chaliots 1997: Good aromas of pure fruit, but it tastes awfully tart, crisp and acidic, lacking fatness on the midpalate and smoothness on the finish.–P.M. • $45 • (9/30/1999) • **79**

Nuits-St.-Georges Premier Cru 1997: This lush, broad Pinot pushes the limits, with a huge, fragrant nose of cassis, black cherry, chocolate and wet earth. Also has a firm backbone and flavors and concentration in reserve. Drink now through 2005.–B.S. • $NA • (1/01/2000) • **90**

Vosne-Romanée 1997: Very open and flowery, showing lovely aromas of rose petal, blackberry and violet. Smooth on the palate, with a lingering aftertaste. Drink now through 2002.–P.M. • $49 • (9/30/1999) • **90**

Vosne-Romanée 1996: Crisp, with cassis bush and dried herb character, but the medium-bodied, ripe and succulent flavors and sweet tannins caress the midpalate. Very tasty, very fresh. Drink now through 2006.–P.M. • $45 • (5/15/1999) • **89**

Vosne-Romanée 1991 • $36 • (1/31/1994) • **76**

Vosne-Romanée Aux Brûlées 1997: Very perfumed, reminiscent of black cherry, cassis and violet. Modestly structured, round, charming and accessible now. Drink now through 2003.–B.S. • $NA • (9/30/1999) • **88**

Vosne-Romanée Clos de la Fontaine 1993 • $NA • (5/15/1996) • **87**

Vosne-Romanée Clos des Réas 1997: Moderate intensity to the floral, cassis and spice aromas and flavors, along with elegance and finesse in this tender '97. Finishes with a dry feel, yet with a lingering aftertaste. Drink now through 2002.–B.S. • $82 • (9/30/1999) • **88**

GROS FRERE & SOEUR

Clos Vougeot Musigni 1997: Supple and ripe, a thick-textured red that turns surprisingly crisp on the palate. Toasted mocha and spice with black fruit make for a good panoply of aromas, but the chewy, slightly acidic finish disappoints. Drink now through 2003.–P.M. • $85 • (1/01/2000) • **82**

Clos Vougeot Musigni 1996: Showbiz Pinot. Pure, vibrant red- and blackberry aromas and flavors are supported by loads of grilled meat, along with a smoky, toasted complexity—there's no subtlety in this full-bodied Burgundy. Best from 2003 through 2010.–P.M. • $72 • (5/15/1999) • **90**

Clos Vougeot Musigni 1995: Decent fruit in this medium-bodied red Burgundy, showing cherry and cassis character. Fairly silky and smooth, it should be pretty through 2003.–P.M. • $55 • (8/31/1998) • **87**

Clos Vougeot Musigni 1994 • $63 • (11/15/1996) • **89**

Clos Vougeot Musigni 1992 • $NA • (12/15/1994) • **85**

Clos Vougeot Musigni 1991 • $75 • (1/31/1994) • **86**

Clos Vougeot Musigni 1990 • $72 • (12/15/1992) • **93**

Clos Vougeot Musigni 1989 • $60 • (1/31/1992) • **91**

Clos Vougeot Musigni 1988 • $43 Ⓐ • (3/31/1991) • **92**

Clos Vougeot Musigni 1985 • $102 • (3/31/1988) • **75**

Côte de Nuits-Villages 1990 • $18 • (12/15/1992) • **86**

Grands Echézeaux 1997: Fresh, crisp Pinot, with lively berry aromas, some cassis and juice flavors along with a smoky, toasty character. Medium-bodied, it's a pleasant red Burgundy that's easy to appreciate. Drink now through 2003.–P.M. • $135 • (1/01/2000) • **84**

GROS FRERE & SOEUR

Grands Echézeaux 1996: Supple and soft, like silk, with cranberry, cassis and wild strawberry notes, this ripe wine shows a lovely sweetness on the palate and a balanced finish laced with subtle oak and milk chocolate. 23 cases imported. Best from 2003 through 2012.–P.M. • $93 • (5/15/1999) • **89**
Grands Echézeaux 1994 • $83 • (11/15/1996) • **91**
Grands Echézeaux 1993 • $69 • (11/15/1995) • **93**
Grands Echézeaux 1992 • $NA • (12/15/1994) • **87**
Grands Echézeaux 1991 • $75 • (1/31/1994) • **85**
Grands Echézeaux 1990 • $85 • (12/15/1992) • **91**
Grands Echézeaux 1989 • $80 • (1/31/1992) • **92**
Grands Echézeaux 1985 • $75 • (3/31/1988) • **71**
Hautes-Côtes de Nuits 1997: Warm and generous on the palate, but surprisingly green and herbaceous in aroma. Medium-bodied, it turns chewy on the slightly dry finish.–P.M. • $NA • (1/01/2000) • **77**
Hautes-Côtes de Nuits 1996: Flavorful but also quite crisp, with cassis bush, black cherry and wild raspberry character and zingy acidity. Medium-bodied. Best from 2002 through 2007.–P.M. • $17 • (5/15/1999) • **81**
Hautes-Côtes de Nuits 1994 • $17 • (11/15/1996) • **80**
Hautes-Côtes de Nuits 1993 • $15 • (11/15/1995) • **80**
Hautes-Côtes de Nuits 1992 • $NA • (12/15/1994) • **79**
Hautes-Côtes de Nuits 1989 • $NA • (1/31/1992) • **82**
Hautes-Côtes de Nuits White 1997: Very ripe but oxidized, with cooked apple flavors and a tart finish.–P.M. • $21 • (5/31/1999) • **72**
Hautes-Côtes de Nuits White 1995 • $NA • (8/31/1997) • **81**
Richebourg 1997: A very nice Pinot Noir. Medium-bodied, with a crisp texture, firm tannins and fresh red berry and blackberry character. Clamps down on the slightly acidic finish. Best from 2002 through 2005.–P.M. • $210 • (1/01/2000) • **86**
Richebourg 1996: Exciting, invading the senses with the most seductive red- and blackberry and spiced-up toasted oak imaginable, this full-bodied, rich wine melts like cream, with the long draw of a fine cigar. Burgundy's Cohiba. 54 cases imported. Best from 2005 through 2015.–P.M. • $180 • (5/15/1999) • **95**
Richebourg 1995: Total harmony. This sensational red Burgundy is so silky, so well made you can only marvel at its brilliant crafting. Full-bodied, the deftly toasted oak is married to black cherry *(griottes)*, cassis, plum, wet earth and chalk character. Ripe, suave tannins on the delicious finish. Best from 2003.–P.M. • $130 • (8/31/1998) • **97**
Richebourg 1994 • $135 • (11/15/1996) • **93**
Richebourg 1993 • $110 • (11/15/1995) • **94**
Richebourg 1992 • $NA • (12/15/1994) • **86**
Richebourg 1991 • $100 • (1/31/1994) • **90**
Richebourg 1990 • $51 • (12/15/1992) • **96**
Richebourg 1989 • $81 • (1/31/1992) • **95**
Richebourg 1988 • $192 • (2/28/1991) • **91**
Vosne-Romanée 1997: Full and ripe, a smoothie of a red Burgundy, with licorice, black cherry and wild berry, offering medium-intense character. A bit short on the finish. Drink now through 2003.–P.M. • $47 • (1/01/2000) • **86**
Vosne-Romanée 1996: Clean and fresh Pinot, showing decent fruit, with a touch of black currant, vanilla and wet earth character. 85 cases imported. Best from 2003 through 2007.–P.M. • $36 • (5/15/1999) • **86**
Vosne-Romanée 1994 • $33 • (11/15/1996) • **81**
Vosne-Romanée 1993 • $35 • (11/15/1995) • **91**
Vosne-Romanée 1992 • $NA • (12/15/1994) • **80**
Vosne-Romanée 1991 • $35 • (1/31/1994) • **84**
Vosne-Romanée 1989 • $39 • (1/31/1992) • **91**
Vosne-Romanée 1988 • $46 • (3/31/1991) • **89**
Vosne-Romanée 1985 • $35 • (4/15/1988) • **70**

GROS NORE, DOMAINE DU

Bandol 1997: Crisp and focused, with intense raspberry and berry flavors and plenty of spice and earth notes. Has a lovely, fresh red fruit aroma, with hints of tobacco and mushroom on the finish. Best from 2001 through 2005.–K.M. • $23 • (12/31/1999) • **88**

GROSSOT, CORINNE & JEAN-PIERRE

Chablis 1998: Crisp, with citrus and pear character. Medium-bodied, with medium complexity. A bit simple. Drink now.–P.M. • $14 • (5/15/2000) • **80**
Chablis 1997: Lovely fig, honey and melon notes give plenty of pleasure in this clean, vibrant, well-made Chablis. Drink now.–P.M. • $16 • (5/31/1999) • **86**
Chablis 1996 • $18 • (8/31/1997) • **86**
Chablis 1995 • $16 • (10/15/1997) • **87**
Chablis Les Fourneaux 1998: There's sweet fruit in this medium-bodied Chablis. Turns a bit tough, with a chewy, minerally character. Drink now through 2004.–P.M. • $22 • (5/15/2000) • **84**
Chablis Les Fourneaux 1997: So clean, even refined, on the nose and palate, cascading ripe, sweet-tasting fruit combined with citrus and mineral notes. Medium-bodied, delicious on the lush finish. Drink now through 2005.–P.M. • $22 • (5/31/1999) • **90**
Chablis Les Fourneaux 1996 • $22 • (5/31/1998) • **90**
Chablis Les Fourneaux 1995 • $24 • (6/15/1997) • **88**
Chablis Vaucoupin 1998: A perfectly decent Chardonnay, with nice fruit and chalky, chewy character. Medium-bodied, clean and pure, but lacking a bit of lively complexity. Drink now through 2003.–P.M. • $25 • (5/15/2000) • **83**
Chablis Vaucoupin 1997: Clean, pure and fresh fruit mingles nicely with some mineral, salt, lemon notes. Medium-bodied, this juicy, intense package offers pleasure on a finish of pretty pear and honey. Drink now through 2004.–P.M. • $25 • (5/31/1999) • **89**
Chablis Vaucoupin 1996 • $25 • (5/31/1998) • **90**
Chablis Vaucoupin 1995 • $24 • (6/15/1997) • **90**

GROTHE, CAVES JEAN

Pouilly-Fumé Acacia 1996 • $15 • (5/31/1998) • **87**
Sancerre Acacia 1996 • $15 • (5/31/1998) • **90**

GROUPEMENT DE PRODUCTEURS DE PRISSE

Mâcon-Villages 1997: A bit musty, this odd-tasting white is tart and astringent.–P.M. • $11 • (5/31/1999) • **70**
Mâcon-Villages 1996 • $11 • (8/31/1997) • **85**
Mâcon-Villages 1995 • $NA • (8/31/1996) • **83**
St.-Véran 1995 • $NA • (8/31/1996) • **78**

GRUAUD-LAROSE, CHATEAU

St.-Julien 1999: Lovely violet, berry and raspberry aromas. Medium-bodied, with a very grapey, slight stemmy character and a light finish.–J.S. • $NA • (1/01/2000) (BT) • **85-89**
St.-Julien 1998: Loads of new oak on this wine, but plenty of ripe fruit also. Medium- to full-bodied, with a good core of fruit, and medium tannins on the finish. Almost outstanding.–J.S. • $NA • (5/31/1999) (BT) • **85-89**
St.-Julien 1997: A good, medium-bodied '97 with cherry and tobacco aromas and flavors, medium tannins and a balanced finish. Best after 2000.–J.S. • $37 Ⓐ • (1/31/2000) • **86**
St.-Julien 1996: Harmonious and pretty. Good color, with plenty of tobacco, berry and mushroom character, a hint of iodine. Full-bodied, with polished, silky tannins and a long aftertaste of tobacco, cedar and vanilla. Best after 2001.–J.S. • $34 Ⓐ • (1/31/1999) • **90**
St.-Julien 1995 • $40 Ⓐ • (1/31/1998) • **88**
St.-Julien 1994 • $33 Ⓐ • (1/31/1997) • **82**
St.-Julien 1993 • $25 Ⓐ • (1/31/1996) • **88**
St.-Julien 1992 • $25 • (4/15/1995) • **85**
St.-Julien 1991 • $25 • (3/31/1994) • **85**
St.-Julien 1990 • $70 Ⓐ • (3/31/1993) • **90**
St.-Julien 1989: Brilliant and youthful raspberry color. Subtle aromas of raspberries and spices. Full-bodied, with firm tannins and long, silky-textured, minty, berry finish. Not the longest-lived Gruaud, but who cares? Very fine.(1989 Bordeaux horizontal tasting). Drink now through 2010.–J.S. • $64 Ⓐ • (5/31/1999) • **91**
St.-Julien 1988: This tight and powerful red has lots of tannin and fruit concentration. Full-bodied, with lovely violet and berry aromas and flavors. Built for aging.(1989 Bordeaux horizontal tasting). Best after 2002 –J.S. • $77 Ⓐ • (11/30/1998) • **92**
St.-Julien 1987 • $26 • (5/15/1990) • **78**
St.-Julien 1986 • $84 Ⓐ • (5/31/1989) • **93**
St.-Julien 1985 • $64 Ⓐ • (10/15/1994) • **87**
St.-Julien 1984 • $21 Ⓐ • (5/15/1987) • **88**
St.-Julien 1983 • $64 Ⓐ • (10/15/1994) • **90**
St.-Julien 1982: One of the best wines ever made at this estate. Dense ruby color with a slight amber edge. Intense grape, berry and raspberry aromas. Full-bodied, with loads of velvety tannins and a long, ripe fruit and mineral

Key: SS—Spectator Selection. CS—Cellar Selection. HR—Highly Recommended. $NA—Price not available. (BT)—Barrel tasting. Ⓐ—Auction Price.
For a key to the tasters' initials, see "How to Use These Listings."
Dates in parentheses represent the issues in which the ratings were published.

aftertaste.(1989 Bordeaux horizontal tasting). Drink now.–J.S. • $129 Ⓐ • (11/30/1998) • **94**

St.-Julien 1981 • $53 Ⓐ • (10/15/1994) • **91**
St.-Julien 1980 • $29 Ⓐ • (2/28/1991) • **83**
St.-Julien 1979 • $45 Ⓐ • (10/15/1989) • **83**
St.-Julien 1978 • $66 Ⓐ • (2/28/1991) • **91**
St.-Julien 1977 • $331 • (2/28/1991) • **71**
St.-Julien 1976 • $NA • (2/28/1991) • **85**
St.-Julien 1975 • $58 Ⓐ • (2/28/1991) • **89**
St.-Julien 1974 • $281 • (2/28/1991) • **63**
St.-Julien 1973 • $221 • (2/28/1991) • **76**
St.-Julien 1971 • $19 Ⓐ • (2/28/1991) • **85**
St.-Julien 1970 • $45 Ⓐ • (5/15/1993) • **86**
St.-Julien 1969 • $NA • (2/28/1991) • **50**
St.-Julien 1968 • $NA • (2/28/1991) • **65**
St.-Julien 1967 • $331 • (2/28/1991) • **78**
St.-Julien 1966 • $66 Ⓐ • (2/28/1991) • **87**
St.-Julien 1964 • $46 Ⓐ • (2/28/1991) • **88**
St.-Julien 1962 • $79 Ⓐ • (11/30/1987) • **88**
St.-Julien 1961 • $292 Ⓐ • (4/30/1996) • **90**
St.-Julien 1959 • $259 Ⓐ • (2/28/1991) • **85**
St.-Julien 1957 • $65 • (2/28/1991) • **78**
St.-Julien 1955 • $150 • (2/28/1991) • **87**
St.-Julien 1953 • $195 • (2/28/1991) • **88**
St.-Julien 1952 • $157 • (2/28/1991) • **85**
St.-Julien 1950 • $145 • (2/28/1991) • **83**
St.-Julien 1949 • $500 Ⓐ • (2/28/1991) • **85**
St.-Julien 1947 • $NA • (7/31/1997) • **94**
St.-Julien 1945 • $845 Ⓐ • (11/30/1995) • **88**
St.-Julien 1943 • $NA • (2/28/1991) • **83**
St.-Julien 1937 • $150 • (2/28/1991) • **87**
St.-Julien 1934 • $150 • (2/28/1991) • **83**
St.-Julien 1929 • $550 • (2/28/1991) • **85**
St.-Julien 1928 • $679 Ⓐ • (2/28/1991) • **94**
St.-Julien 1926 • $194 Ⓐ • (2/28/1991) • **95**
St.-Julien 1924 • $250 • (2/28/1991) • **89**
St.-Julien 1921 • $383 Ⓐ • (2/28/1991) • **87**
St.-Julien 1920 • $300 • (2/28/1991) • **85**
St.-Julien 1918 • $489 Ⓐ • (2/28/1991) • **78**
St.-Julien 1907 • $255 • (2/28/1991) • **72**
St.-Julien 1906 • $300 • (2/28/1991) • **85**
St.-Julien 1899 • $600 • (2/28/1991) • **83**
St.-Julien 1893 • $500 • (2/28/1991) • **78**
St.-Julien 1887 • $400 • (2/28/1991) • **71**
St.-Julien 1878 • $500 • (2/28/1991) • **83**
St.-Julien 1870 • $1,098 Ⓐ • (2/28/1991) • **87**
St.-Julien 1865 • $1,800 • (2/28/1991) • **65**
St.-Julien 1844 • $NA • (2/28/1991) • **85**
St.-Julien 1834 • $NA • (2/28/1991) • **83**
St.-Julien 1819 • $NA • (2/28/1991) • **89**

GUERIN, RENE

Pouilly-Fuissé La Roche Vieilles Vignes 1996 • $23 • (5/31/1998) • **81**

GUERIN, THIERRY

Pouilly-Fuissé 1996 • $23 • (5/31/1998) • **65**
Pouilly-Fuissé La Roche 1996 • $24 • (5/31/1998) • **88**
Pouilly-Fuissé La Roche 1995 • $20 • (5/31/1997) • **87**
Pouilly-Fuissé Sélection Vieilles Vignes 1996 • $25 • (5/31/1998) • **70**
St.-Véran 1996 • $16 • (5/31/1998) • **77**
St.-Véran Clos des Pierres Brûlées 1995 • $16 • (5/31/1997) • **86**

GUERRIN, GILLES

Mâcon-Vergisson La Roche 1996: Pure and clean, medium-bodied, with a supple midpalate, this nicely oaked wine integrates the spicy, wood accents well with the fruit. Offers lime, honey, pear and wet hay in a balanced package with a smoky finish. Drink now through 2002.–P.M. • $13 • (8/31/1998) • **87**

Pouilly-Fuissé 1996: Crisp, with lots of citrus and acidity. Lacks a bit of ripe fruit and fleshy texture. Tart but fresh finish. Drink now.–P.M. • $15 • (8/31/1998) • **79**

Pouilly-Fuissé Vieilles Vignes 1996: Pleasant. Clean, fresh and fairly lush, its ripe pear, tropical and honey flavors and pleasant oak accents playing subtle props to the whole medium-bodied package. Of medium intensity, delicious all the same. Drink now.–P.M. • $17 • (8/31/1998) • **86**

St.-Véran 1997: Neutral, lean, a bit bitter, offering modest fruit.–P.M. • $13 • (5/31/1999) • **72**

St.-Véran 1996: Clean but a bit on the light side, exhibiting lemon, green apple and oak accents. Of medium intensity, with some wet hay character, it displays a slight dilution on the midpalate. Drink now through 2002.–P.M. • $13 • (8/31/1998) • **84**

St.-Véran Cuvée Prestige 1997: Tart, astringent, with mostly modest, unfocused fruit flavors, though some decent honey and pear notes creep in.–P.M. • $14 • (5/31/1999) • **76**

GUEYZE, CHATEAU DE

Buzet 1993: Medium-bodied, with cherry and red plum flavors, leather and anise notes on the finish. Drink now.–K.M. • $14 • (5/31/1999) • **82**

Buzet 1992: Simple, with some dried cherry, plum and leather flavors, and some spicy notes on the finish. Drink now.–K.M. • $14 • (1/01/1999) • **81**

Buzet 1991: Good, ripe flavors of dark plum and leather, even some bacon notes, make this a hearty red with a rustic touch. Coffee-like flavors linger on the finish. Drink now.–K.M. • $14 • (1/01/1999) • **84**

GUFFENS-HEYNEN

Mâcon-Pierreclos 1996: Wonderful *vin de terroir*. Full of finesse, this medium-bodied beauty has a polished midpalate of mineral, matchstick, flinty, chalky character, backed by a just-so amount of acidity. Marvelously balanced from start to smoky finish. Drink now through 2005.–P.M. • $NA • (8/31/1998) • **94**

Mâcon-Pierreclos Le Chavigne 1997: Honey, dried herbs, mint and heavily toasted oak notes emerge in this flavorful, medium-bodied white. Drink now through 2001.–P.M. • $25 • (9/30/1999) • **86**

Mâcon-Pierreclos Le Chavigne 1996: Sublime. Both rich and elegant, hedonistic and full-bodied, layered with supple flavors of honey and spice, lightly toasted accents, pear and honeysuckle notes. Melts in the mouth, twirling its generous ripe flavors around like a jolly carousel. Dovetails on the finish with superb finesse. Drink now through 2008.–P.M. • $25 • (8/31/1998) • **94**

Mâcon-Pierreclos Le Chavigne 1995 • $20 • (5/31/1997) • **91**
Mâcon-Pierreclos Red Le Chavigne Bois Neuf 1990 • $18 • (8/31/1992) • **82**
Pouilly-Fuissé 1995 • $34 • (5/31/1998) • **90**

Pouilly-Fuissé Clos des Petits-Croux 1997: Terrific white Burgundy. Wonderfully flavorful, marrying deftly toasted oak notes with ripe fruit and honey. Round, smooth, thick on the palate, with a silky, seductive texture and a long finish. Drink now through 2005.–P.M. • $NA • (9/30/1999) • **93**

Pouilly-Fuissé Premier Jus 1995: Smooth and lush, harmonious and complex, this lovely, rich yet elegant beauty is worth the hunt. Stunning for its balance of honey and oak accents, ripe fruit and acidity. Coats the palate with its opulent texture, then glides ethereally to a long, sweet-tasting, spicy, smoky and toasted finish. Much better than previously reviewed. Drink now through 2010.–P.M. • $40 • (8/31/1998) • **94**

Pouilly-Fuissé Vinians L'Année Louise 1996: Seductive, this medium-bodied wine springs to life on the palate, dancing around to the tune of lime, spice, ripe pear, toasted bread and smoky notes. Blends its ripe fruit, acidity and wood nicely. Should improve. Drink now through 2005.–P.M. • $NA • (8/31/1998) • **92**

GUIBON, CHATEAU

Bordeaux 1994 • $5 • (7/31/1996) • **78**
Bordeaux 1989 • $8 • (7/15/1992) • **75**

GUIGAL, E.

Châteauneuf-du-Pape 1996: Attractively ripe, with a distinct plum note and soft tannins. A bit hot, as expected in Châteauneuf, but it's rather full-bodied for a '96. Turns a bit chewy and tough on the finish. Drink now through 2006.–P.M. • $28 • (12/15/1999) • **85**

Châteauneuf-du-Pape 1995: Very aromatic, with a grilled meat, spice, freshly ground coffee bean, pepper and animal character that's quite exotic. Polished but delicate. Medium-bodied, with toasty, smoky notes on the finish. Drink now through 2005.–P.M. • $24 • (9/30/1998) • **85**

Châteauneuf-du-Pape 1994 • $22 • (10/15/1997) • **72**
Châteauneuf-du-Pape 1991 • $20 • (12/15/1996) • **83**
Châteauneuf-du-Pape 1990 • $20 • (3/15/1994) HR • **89**
Châteauneuf-du-Pape 1988 • $20 • (11/30/1990) HR • **90**

GUIGAL, E.

Châteauneuf-du-Pape 1986 • $19 • (3/15/1990) • **87**
Châteauneuf-du-Pape 1985 • $18 • (10/15/1988) • **87**
Châteauneuf-du-Pape 1983 • $29 • (11/30/1987) • **87**
Condrieu La Doriane 1998: Has an underlying fatness, showing power but also grace and loads of apricot, peach and floral notes as expected from a top-flight Viognier. The wood needs time to melt into the wine. Not easy now, but it should develop nicely with cellaring. Best from 2002 through 2007.–P.M. • $60 • (12/15/1999) • **89**
Condrieu La Doriane 1996 • $41 Ⓐ • (10/15/1997) • **92**
Côte-Rôtie Brune et Blonde de Guigal 1996: Intense fruit and sharp definition power this wine forward, but there isn't much dense, thick and "fat" texture. Still, a mineral, vanilla and cream character surfaces and gives it a bit of smoothness. Cellar short-term. Best from 2002 through 2008.–P.M. • $35 • (11/30/1999) • **87**
Côte-Rôtie Brune et Blonde de Guigal 1995: Full-bodied and balanced, focusing on mineral, plum, blackberry, game and leather, the complexity grows as all these flavors cascade to a long, elegant finish in this lovely Rhône red. Drink now through 2010.–P.M. • $35 • (11/30/1999) SS • **90**
Côte-Rôtie Brune et Blonde 1994: Beautiful wine, showing a wide range of aromas—mocha, spice, currant, cassis, toasted oak, bitter chocolate, even a touch of minty eucalyptus. Satisfying and well made, harmonious to the very end. Drink now through 2005.–P.M. • $32 • (9/15/1998) • **86**
Côte-Rôtie Brune et Blonde 1993 • $33 • (4/30/1997) HR • **91**
Côte-Rôtie Brune et Blonde 1992 • $33 • (11/30/1996) • **87**
Côte-Rôtie Brune et Blonde 1991 • $35 Ⓐ • (11/15/1995) • **88**
Côte-Rôtie Brune et Blonde 1990 • $40 Ⓐ • (11/15/1995) • **90**
Côte-Rôtie Brune et Blonde 1989 • $47 Ⓐ • (11/15/1995) • **88**
Côte-Rôtie Brune et Blonde 1988 • $48 Ⓐ • (11/15/1995) • **89**
Côte-Rôtie Brune et Blonde 1987 • $28 • (11/15/1995) • **84**
Côte-Rôtie Brune et Blonde 1986 • $30 • (11/15/1995) • **88**
Côte-Rôtie Brune et Blonde 1985 • $71 Ⓐ • (3/15/1990) • **91**
Côte-Rôtie Brune et Blonde 1984 • $22 Ⓐ • (11/15/1995) • **79**
Côte-Rôtie Brune et Blonde 1983 • $49 Ⓐ • (11/15/1995) • **90**
Côte-Rôtie Brune et Blonde 1982 • $35 • (11/15/1995) • **87**
Côte-Rôtie Brune et Blonde 1980 • $40 • (11/15/1995) • **81**
Côte-Rôtie Brune et Blonde 1979 • $52 Ⓐ • (11/15/1995) • **83**
Côte-Rôtie Brune et Blonde 1978 • $63 Ⓐ • (11/15/1995) • **84**
Côte-Rôtie Brune et Blonde 1976 • $49 • (11/15/1995) • **85**
Côte-Rôtie Brune et Blonde 1971 • $75 • (11/15/1995) • **72**
Côte-Rôtie Brune et Blonde 1969 • $100 • (11/15/1995) • **78**
Côte-Rôtie Brune et Blonde 1966 • $72 Ⓐ • (11/15/1995) • **83**
Côte-Rôtie Brune et Blonde 1964 • $100 • (11/15/1995) • **83**
Côte-Rôtie Brune et Blonde 1962 • $NA • (3/15/1990) • **89**
Côte-Rôtie Brune et Blonde 1961 • $100 • (11/15/1995) • **90**
Côte-Rôtie Brune et Blonde Hommage à Etienne Guigal 1989 • $NA • (11/15/1995) • **85**
Côte-Rôtie Brune et Blonde La Pommière 1990 • $NA • (11/15/1995) • **94**
Côte-Rôtie Château d'Ampuis 1995: Very seductive. A beautiful, full-bodied, full-throttle Syrah with much personality. Offers layers of earthy currant, animal, mineral and anise character. Lacks a bit in concentration to rate higher, but what's here is delicious. Medium-intense finish and supple tannins make it tempting upon release. Drink now through 2005.–P.M. • $95 • (9/15/1998) • **89**
Côte-Rôtie La Landonne 1995: A full-bodied Syrah in an international-style that's complex and seductive, layered with cinnamon, toasted oak, plum, game, smoke, mineral and black fruit flavors. Turns massively tannic on the finish. Balanced and elegant despite the obvious richness, it's tempting on release, but needs a bit of time to tame the tannins. Drink now through 2015.–P.M. • $98 Ⓐ • (11/30/1999) CS • **94**
Côte-Rôtie La Landonne 1994: International in style, with plenty of new oak flavors—from violet to spicy, toasted mocha. Beneath the wood blanket is a soft pillow of blackberry, cassis and black cherry. Makes a seductive package if you like wines so obviously oaky. The *terroir* seems to get lost in translation, though. Full-bodied, it needs time. Best from 2005 through 2010.–P.M. • $145 Ⓐ • (9/15/1998) • **90**
Côte-Rôtie La Landonne 1993 • $98 Ⓐ • (12/15/1997) • **87**
Côte-Rôtie La Landonne 1992 • $79 Ⓐ • (11/30/1996) • **85**
Côte-Rôtie La Landonne 1991 • $224 Ⓐ • (11/15/1995) • **95**
Côte-Rôtie La Landonne 1990 • $295 Ⓐ • (11/15/1995) • **97**
Côte-Rôtie La Landonne 1989 • $231 Ⓐ • (11/15/1995) • **94**
Côte-Rôtie La Landonne 1988 • $264 Ⓐ • (11/15/1995) • **94**
Côte-Rôtie La Landonne 1987 • $166 Ⓐ • (11/15/1995) • **89**
Côte-Rôtie La Landonne 1986 • $182 Ⓐ • (11/15/1995) • **91**
Côte-Rôtie La Landonne 1985 • $411 Ⓐ • (11/15/1995) • **100**
Côte-Rôtie La Landonne 1984 • $125 • (11/15/1995) • **78**
Côte-Rôtie La Landonne 1983 • $218 Ⓐ • (11/15/1995) • **92**
Côte-Rôtie La Landonne 1982 • $196 Ⓐ • (11/15/1995) • **88**
Côte-Rôtie La Landonne 1981 • $115 Ⓐ • (11/15/1995) • **86**
Côte-Rôtie La Landonne 1980 • $141 Ⓐ • (11/15/1995) • **84**
Côte-Rôtie La Landonne 1979 • $134 Ⓐ • (11/15/1995) • **88**
Côte-Rôtie La Landonne 1978 • $482 Ⓐ • (11/15/1995) • **89**
Côte-Rôtie La Mouline 1995: Inky black. Suave, elegant, stylish, with loads of raspberry and chocolate flavors, smoke, cinnamon, toast and nutmeg nuances giving way to a seamless, mineral-tinged finish. Alluring, sexy, voluptuous wine that is remarkably approachable now; but just wait. Best from 2002 through 2015.–P.M. • $216 Ⓐ • (1/01/2000) • **95**
Côte-Rôtie La Mouline 1994: Classy and sexy, thick and full-bodied red from the Northern Rhône, ripe and rich. Maintains a racy elegance and an un-oaky decorum that leave room for the terroir to show. Delivers deeply satisfying aromas and flavors that include wet earth, blackberry, toasted oak, spicy mocha, milled coffee notes and crushed black pepper, with a creamy yet intense finish that fans out with all the flavors. Brilliant now, it can only improve in the cellar given its impeccable balance. Best from 2003 through 2010.–P.M. • $150 • (9/15/1998) CS • **94**
Côte-Rôtie La Mouline 1993 • $83 Ⓐ • (12/15/1997) • **87**
Côte-Rôtie La Mouline 1992 • $564 Ⓐ • (11/30/1996) CS • **91**
Côte-Rôtie La Mouline 1991 • $266 Ⓐ • (11/15/1995) • **92**
Côte-Rôtie La Mouline 1990 • $306 Ⓐ • (11/15/1995) • **98**
Côte-Rôtie La Mouline 1989 • $255 Ⓐ • (11/15/1995) • **95**
Côte-Rôtie La Mouline 1988 • $340 Ⓐ • (11/15/1995) • **95**
Côte-Rôtie La Mouline 1987 • $156 Ⓐ • (11/15/1995) • **91**
Côte-Rôtie La Mouline 1986 • $200 • (11/15/1995) • **94**
Côte-Rôtie La Mouline 1985 • $368 Ⓐ • (11/15/1995) • **97**
Côte-Rôtie La Mouline 1984 • $140 • (11/15/1995) • **87**
Côte-Rôtie La Mouline 1983 • $266 Ⓐ • (11/15/1995) • **93**
Côte-Rôtie La Mouline 1982 • $210 • (11/15/1995) • **87**
Côte-Rôtie La Mouline 1981 • $112 Ⓐ • (11/15/1995) • **88**
Côte-Rôtie La Mouline 1980 • $123 Ⓐ • (11/15/1995) • **83**
Côte-Rôtie La Mouline 1979 • $146 Ⓐ • (11/15/1995) • **85**
Côte-Rôtie La Mouline 1978 • $513 Ⓐ • (3/15/1990) • **96**
Côte-Rôtie La Mouline 1977 • $225 • (11/15/1995) • **86**
Côte-Rôtie La Mouline 1976 • $400 • (11/15/1995) • **87**
Côte-Rôtie La Mouline 1975 • $NA • (3/15/1990) • **75**
Côte-Rôtie La Mouline 1974 • $250 • (11/15/1995) • **86**
Côte-Rôtie La Mouline 1973 • $240 • (11/15/1995) • **78**
Côte-Rôtie La Mouline 1972 • $NA • (11/15/1995) • **75**
Côte-Rôtie La Mouline 1971 • $350 • (11/15/1995) • **79**
Côte-Rôtie La Mouline 1970 • $300 • (11/15/1995) • **82**
Côte-Rôtie La Mouline 1969 • $700 • (11/15/1995) • **91**
Côte-Rôtie La Mouline 1968 • $300 • (11/15/1995) • **84**
Côte-Rôtie La Mouline 1967 • $400 • (11/15/1995) • **85**
Côte-Rôtie La Mouline 1966 • $443 Ⓐ • (11/15/1995) • **81**
Côte-Rôtie La Turque 1995: A gorgeous terroir wine that's superharmonious, with a lot going on. Very jammy and rich, showing deft oak dosage and lovely plum, blackberry marmalade, mineral and toast character. While tempting now, it should improve with age. Drink now through 2003.–P.M. • $264 Ⓐ • (11/30/1999) • **94**
Côte-Rôtie La Turque 1994: A masculine and muscular wine. Quite woody, an international style of Syrah that's appealing, seductive and polished, with supple, ripe tannins. The toasted oak dominates the fruit now, but this full-bodied red may well turn more harmonious with time as it has plenty of red and blackberry character to support all the wood. The finish is infused with lovely mocha, spice, toasted bread notes. Best from 2005 through 2010.–P.M. • $150 • (9/15/1998) • **90**
Côte-Rôtie La Turque 1993 • $120 • (12/15/1997) • **88**
Côte-Rôtie La Turque 1992 • $88 Ⓐ • (11/30/1996) • **89**
Côte-Rôtie La Turque 1991 • $328 Ⓐ • (11/15/1995) • **93**
Côte-Rôtie La Turque 1990 • $323 Ⓐ • (11/15/1995) • **95**
Côte-Rôtie La Turque 1989 • $256 Ⓐ • (11/15/1995) • **91**
Côte-Rôtie La Turque 1988 • $305 Ⓐ • (11/15/1995) • **92**
Côte-Rôtie La Turque 1987 • $182 Ⓐ • (11/15/1995) • **89**
Côte-Rôtie La Turque 1986 • $230 Ⓐ • (11/15/1995) • **92**
Côte-Rôtie La Turque 1985 • $487 Ⓐ • (11/15/1995) • **95**
Côtes du Rhône 1996: A simple red, its cherry and herb flavors are round and accessible, with light tannins and just enough acidity to keep it lively. Expected more from this producer.–T.M. • $9 • (9/15/1999) • **79**

Key: SS—Spectator Selection. CS—Cellar Selection. HR—Highly Recommended. $NA—Price not available. (BT)—Barrel tasting. Ⓐ—Auction Price. For a key to the tasters' initials, see "How to Use These Listings."
Dates in parentheses represent the issues in which the ratings were published.

Côtes du Rhône 1995: Ripe in a plummy, pruny, floral mode, with roasted peanut and soy character, this might go well with Asian foods. Medium-bodied, with well-integrated tannins, a tad hot on the finish. Drink now through 2003.–P.M. • $10 • (11/15/1998) • **85**
Côtes du Rhône 1994 • $10 • (10/15/1997) • **83**
Côtes du Rhône 1993 • $10 • (10/15/1996) • **85**
Côtes du Rhône 1992 • $11 • (11/15/1995) • **83**
Côtes du Rhône 1991 • $10 • (10/15/1994) • **85**
Côtes du Rhône 1990 • $10 • (4/15/1993) • **85**
Côtes du Rhône 1989 • $12 • (8/31/1992) • **85**
Côtes du Rhône 1988 • $12 • (7/15/1991) • **81**
Côtes du Rhône Rosé 1996 • $10 • (10/15/1997) • **81**
Côtes du Rhône White 1998: A bit on the drying side, with a slight cardboard character. Tough and sour on the finish.–P.M. • $10 • (12/15/1999) • **75**
Côtes du Rhône White 1996 • $10 • (10/15/1997) • **85**
Gigondas 1996: A red that's deceptively tannic and delivers black fruit and black pepper on the lingering finish. Has a smooth midpalate, and kicks in on the finish with enough panache to cut down a hunk of red meat. Drink now through 2002.–P.M. • $18 • (12/15/1999) • **84**
Gigondas 1995: Elegant but also quite rich, sweet, full-bodied and ripe in texture. It's delicious and worth the hunt, but don't expect a blockbuster; the aromas are subtle. The plum, vanilla, spice, chocolate, pepper, leather and raspberry flavors knit together harmoniously on the medium-intense finish. Drink now through 2002.–P.M. • $17 • (10/15/1998) • **87**
Gigondas 1994 • $15 • (4/30/1997) • **87**
Gigondas 1992 • $15 • (10/15/1996) • **79**
Gigondas 1991 • $16 • (11/15/1995) • **83**
Gigondas 1990 • $15 • (3/15/1994) • **84**
Gigondas 1988 • $15 • (3/31/1991) • **85**
Gigondas 1986 • $17 • (11/30/1990) • **87**
Gigondas 1985 • $17 • (9/30/1988) SS • **91**
Gigondas 1984 • $15 • (11/30/1987) • **86**
Gigondas 1983 • $18 • (7/31/1987) • **91**
Hermitage 1993 • $33 • (9/15/1997) • **87**
Hermitage 1992 • $33 • (11/30/1996) • **86**
Hermitage 1991 • $39 • (12/31/1995) • **84**
Hermitage 1990 • $99 Ⓐ • (5/31/1994) CS • **93**
Hermitage 1989 • $33 • (4/15/1993) CS • **91**
Hermitage 1988 • $34 • (12/31/1991) • **83**
Hermitage 1987 • $29 • (1/31/1991) • **86**
Hermitage 1986 • $34 • (2/28/1990) CS • **92**
Hermitage 1985 • $34 • (4/15/1989) CS • **92**
Hermitage 1983 • $45 Ⓐ • (4/30/1987) • **87**
Hermitage 1982 • $35 Ⓐ • (5/01/1986) • **91**
Hermitage 1980 • $50 • (9/01/1984) CS • **91**
Hermitage 1978 • $63 Ⓐ • (3/15/1990) • **91**
Hermitage 1976 • $36 Ⓐ • (3/15/1990) • **80**
Hermitage 1969 • $100 • (3/15/1990) • **84**
Hermitage 1966 • $100 • (3/15/1990) • **90**
Hermitage 1964 • $100 • (3/15/1990) • **93**
Tavel 1996 • $14 • (10/15/1997) • **77**

GUILLEMOT, PIERRE

Savigny-lès-Beaune Aux Serpentières 1994 • $NA • (11/15/1996) • **78**
Savigny-lès-Beaune Aux Serpentières 1990 • $24 • (12/15/1992) • **89**
Savigny-lès-Beaune Les Jarrons 1997: A bit lean for a '97. Turns tough and acidic on the palate, delivering raspberry and strawberry notes. Tasted twice, with consistent notes.–P.M. • $28 • (1/01/2000) • **78**
Savigny-lès-Beaune Les Jarrons 1994 • $NA • (11/15/1996) • **83**
Savigny-lès-Beaune Les Jarrons 1990 • $24 • (12/15/1992) • **83**
Savigny-lès-Beaune Serpentières 1997: Well made. Rather unique for a '97, as it has a tightly wound, firm core of fresh fruit that fans out with lovely blackberry, floral and black cherry character. A discovery for us. Drink now through 2003.–P.M. • $28 • (9/30/1999) • **88**
Savigny-lès-Beaune Serpentières 1996: Delicious, with ripe fruit and lush texture, though the tannins and acidity need a moment after pouring to calm down. Of medium body and intensity, it delivers decent black cherry, currant and cassis. Not supercomplex, but nice. Drink now through 2005.–P.M. • $26 • (9/30/1998) • **87**

GUILLON, JEAN-MICHEL

Gevrey-Chambertin Clos Prieur 1997: Pure, intense aromas of kirsch and spice continue in the mouth, where this red becomes tight and the fruit takes a backseat to the *terroir*, firm tannins and crisp acidity. Needs time to harmonize. Best from 2001 through 2005.–B.S. • $36 • (9/30/1999) • **91**
Gevrey-Chambertin La Petite Chapelle 1997: This pretty wine has lovely black currant, black cherry and wet earth aromas, intense flavors of black cherry and earth and a tender, fleeting structure. Moderate tannins and a lingering finish. Drink now through 2003.–B.S. • $43 • (9/30/1999) • **88**
Gevrey-Chambertin Les Champonnets 1997: Lovely ripe fruit coats the palate in this full-bodied '97, layered with blackberry, black cherry *griottes* and wet earth. Rather chewy, it kicks in with lively acidity on the *terroir*-driven finish. Best from 2002 through 2007.–P.M. • $36 • (9/30/1999) • **90**
Gevrey-Chambertin Vieilles Vignes 1997: A crisp, fresh, medium-bodied red tasting of zippy acidity, with red berry and herb notes. Cold, rather short finish. Drink now through 2005.–P.M. • $29 • (9/30/1999) • **81**
Morey-St.-Denis La Riotte 1997: Spicy, with moderate density and ripe tannins. Still unevolved, evoking black cherry, plum and licorice allied to a solid tannic structure. Best from 2001 through 2005.–B.S. • $32 • (9/30/1999) • **86**

GUILLOT, MAISON

Cabernet Sauvignon Vin de Pays d'Oc Sélection 1997: Light-bodied, with red plum flavors and stewy notes on the finish.–K.M. • $7 • (12/31/1998) • **77**
Chardonnay Vin de Pays d'Oc Sélection 1997: Focused, with decent flavors of ripe apple and green fig, but turns a bit coarse on the finish. Drink now.–K.M. • $7 • (12/31/1998) • **80**
Merlot Vin de Pays d'Oc Sélection 1997: Dried cherry and leather flavors dominate this lackluster red, which finishes on a overt leathery note.–K.M. • $7 • (12/31/1998) • **73**

GUILLOT-CLAUZEL, CHATEAU

Pomerol 1996: Grapey aromas, with notes of strawberry and cherry. Medium-bodied, with slightly austere tannins and a short finish. Too much wood. Drink now.–J.S. • $NA • (1/31/1999) • **81**
Pomerol 1995: Very plummy and perfumed. Full-bodied, with round, caressing tannins and a long, long, flavorful finish. A drink-me, got-to-have-it red. Drink through 2006–J.S. • $NA • (9/15/1998) • **90**
Pomerol 1994 • $NA • (1/31/1997) • **88**
Pomerol 1993 • $NA • (1/31/1996) • **88**

GUIMONIERE, CHATEAU DE LA

Anjou La Haie Fruitière 1998: Silky yet firm, this red shows good concentration, with black cherry, chocolate and smoke flavors. The tannins are ripe and well integrated, and the finish is clean. Drink now through 2002.–T.M. • $NA • (1/01/1999) • **85**
Anjou La Haie Fruitière 1995 • $15 • (6/15/1997) • **84**
Coteaux du Layon-Chaume 1992 • $30 • (6/15/1997) • **86**
Coteaux du Layon-Chaume Les Julines 1997: Racy and elegant. This clean, fresh white is not too sweet, with flavors of quince, pineapple and vanilla that linger on the finish and lively acidity that keeps it balanced and fresh. Not a huge wine, but built for the long run. Not imported into the U.S. Drink now through 2010.–T.M. • $NA/500 ml. • (1/01/1999) • **91**
Coteaux du Layon-Chaume Les Julines 1993 • $14 • (8/31/1997) • **91**

GUIRAUD, CHATEAU

Sauternes 1998: An oily and rich young wine, with apple, pear and spice. Full-bodied and round, with a sweet finish. Stays with you a long time.–J.S. • $NA • (1/01/1999) (BT) • **90-94**
Sauternes 1997: An elegant and racy Guiraud, with pretty aromas of pineapple, melon and spice. Full-bodied and medium sweet, with an intense, spicy botrytis finish. Needs time. Best from 2002 through 2006.–J.S. • $44 • (1/31/2000) • **93**
Sauternes 1992 • $NA • (4/15/1995) • **84**
Sauternes 1990 • $46 Ⓐ • (4/15/1995) • **96**
Sauternes 1989 • $36 Ⓐ • (4/15/1995) • **92**
Sauternes 1988 • $46 Ⓐ • (4/15/1995) • **87**
Sauternes 1987 • $NA • (6/15/1990) • **72**
Sauternes 1986 • $38 Ⓐ • (4/15/1995) • **93**
Sauternes 1983 • $34 Ⓐ • (4/15/1995) • **89**
Sauternes Le Dauphin 1987 • $11 • (12/31/1989) • **72**

GUIRAUD-CHEVAL-BLANC, CHATEAU

Côtes de Bourg 1994 • $8 • (4/30/1997) • **74**

Côtes de Bourg 1989 • $6 • (11/30/1992) • **77**

GUNES, CHATEAU DES

Haut-Médoc 1993 • $15 • (11/30/1997) • **78**

GURGUE, CHATEAU LA

Margaux 1998: A bit herbal and diluted. Medium- to light-bodied, with slightly dry tannins.–J.S. • $NA • (5/31/1999) (BT) • **75-79**
Margaux 1997: Good fruit character, with hints of coffee and vanilla. Medium-bodied. Light finish. Drink now.–J.S. • $NA • (1/31/2000) • **84**
Margaux 1996: Aromas of spice, coffee and currants. Medium-bodied, with velvety tannins and a spicy, smoky aftertaste. Needs a bit more fruit in the center-palate to be outstanding, but very good. Best after 2000.–J.S. • $22 • (1/31/1999) • **87**
Margaux 1995 • $25 • (1/31/1998) • **90**
Margaux 1994 • $21 • (1/31/1997) • **85**
Margaux 1993 • $21 • (1/31/1996) • **85**
Margaux 1991 • $17 • (3/31/1994) • **84**
Margaux 1990 • $27 • (3/31/1993) • **87**
Margaux 1989: This chewy wine still isn't showing all it has, but it's delicious nonetheless. Dark ruby-red in color, with green tobacco and berry aromas and flavors. Medium- to full-bodied, adding velvety tannins and a chocolate, berry aftertaste. (1989 Bordeaux horizontal tasting). Drink through 2006–J.S. • $20 Ⓐ • (5/31/1999) • **90**
Margaux 1988 • $34 • (4/30/1991) • **90**
Margaux 1987 • $13 • (5/15/1990) • **81**
Margaux 1986 • $22 • (11/30/1989) • **85**
Margaux 1985 • $19 • (2/15/1988) • **90**
Margaux 1983 • $10 • (1/01/1986) • **90**
Margaux 1982: Slightly one-dimensional, but still going strong. Medium ruby-garnet color. Light tobacco and cherry aromas. Medium-bodied, with medium tannins and finish. (1982 Bordeaux horizontal tasting). Drink now.–J.S. • $NA • (11/30/1998) • **83**

GUY, BERNARD

Côte-Rôtie 1992 • $30 • (11/15/1995) • **87**
Côte-Rôtie 1990 • $30 • (4/15/1993) • **80**
Côte-Rôtie 1987 • $25 • (8/31/1989) • **87**
Côte-Rôtie 1986 • $29 • (9/30/1988) • **89**

GUYON, ANTONIN

Aloxe-Corton Les Vercots 1996: Deep, dark and brooding, showing smoky, roasted and earthy character of plums and black cherries. Awkward, with dry tannins on the finish. Best after 2002.–B.S. • $35 • (9/30/1998) • **84**
Aloxe-Corton Les Vercots Domaine Hippolyte Thevenot 1997: Dark in color, showing a crisp intensity of cherries on the midpalate, but tasting a bit short. Best from 2002 through 2004.–P.M. • $38 • (9/30/1999) • **81**
Chambolle-Musigny 1997: Elegant, showing cherry and wet earth flavors combined with a light body and vibrant personality. Tannins are just a tad coarse on the finish, yet may soon smooth out. Drink through 2005–B.S. • $37 • (9/30/1999) • **84**
Chambolle-Musigny 1996: A bit herbal, with cherry and olive character. Medium-bodied, turns dry on the palate.–P.M. • $35 • (9/30/1998) • **79**
Corton Bressandes 1996: Good depth. Black cherry, berry and spicy oak weave through this rich, fleshy '96, right to the long finish. The acidity and tannins are well integrated. Drink through 2005–B.S. • $48 • (9/30/1998) • **88**
Corton Bressandes Domaine Hippolyte Thevenot 1997: Light-bodied, with modest concentration, this plum-flavored red features a smooth, round texture that turns dry and tannic on the finish. Drink now through 2003.–B.S. • $49 • (9/30/1999) • **81**
Corton Clos du Roy Domaine Hippolyte Thevenot 1997: Slightly muted aromas of cherry and vanilla match the rich, almost chewy texture in this straightforward '97 red. Moderate finish has firm tannins. Drink now through 2004.–B.S. • $NA • (9/30/1999) • **83**

Key: SS—Spectator Selection. CS—Cellar Selection. HR—Highly Recommended. $NA—Price not available. (BT)—Barrel tasting. Ⓐ—Auction Price.
For a key to the tasters' initials, see "How to Use These Listings."
Dates in parentheses represent the issues in which the ratings were published.

Corton-Charlemagne 1997: A bit tart, with cooked apple pie flavors and toast, spice and plywood notes. Soft and accessible until the harsh wood tannins turn the finish harsh and bitter.–P.M. • $90 • (5/31/1999) • **79**
Corton-Charlemagne 1996: Full-throttle Burgundian white. Loads of wood-flavored butterscotch aromas, honey, pear and apple notes; oozing with new oak. Ripe, and if tasting of oak sawdust for now, the bounty rich, thick, oily stuff hints it will improve in the cellar. (It finished its malolactic and had been in bottle 10 days only.) Best after 2005.–P.M. • $80 • (8/31/1998) • **89**
Corton-Charlemagne 1995 • $105 Ⓐ • (5/31/1997) • **96**
Gevrey-Chambertin 1997: Sweet strawberry and cherry flavors turn crisp and lemony on the palate. A bit astringent on the finish.–P.M. • $37 • (9/30/1999) • **78**
Gevrey-Chambertin 1996: A solid, chunky '96 that doesn't express much character, finishing on a tannic note.–B.S. • $34 • (9/30/1998) • **78**
Hautes-Côtes de Nuits Cuvée des Dames de Vergy 1996: Decent red Burgundy, with some herbal notes but also blackberry and cherry character. Of medium body, with supple texture.–P.M. • $15 • (9/30/1998) • **79**
Meursault Charmes-Dessus 1997: Oaky in style, a bit dry and herbal, with modest fruit, but showing a cedary, perfumey character on the somewhat astringent finish.–P.M. • $55 • (5/31/1999) • **78**
Meursault Charmes-Dessus 1996: Gorgeous wine that unfolds its secrets slowly. Full-bodied, it engulfs the palate with mouthcoating, silky texture flavored with pear, spice, toasted oak, honey, earth and vanilla notes. The balanced, chalky-chewy finish is fresh, complex, smoky and very long. Best after 2005.–P.M. • $50 • (8/31/1998) • **93**
Meursault Charmes-Dessus 1995 • $40 • (5/31/1997) • **89**
Pernand-Vergelesses White 1997: Tastes candied, with cardboard notes that hurt the decent lemon and tropical flavors.–P.M. • $40 • (5/31/1999) • **76**
Pernand-Vergelesses White 1996: Stony, almost tannic in structure, medium-bodied, and with good concentration. Wet earth, mineral, pear and citrusy grass character. Tough and chewy now, needs to soften up. Best after 2005.–P.M. • $28 • (8/31/1998) • **86**
Pernand-Vergelesses White 1995 • $25 • (8/31/1997) • **84**
Savigny-lès-Beaune 1996: Lively and vibrant, showing cassis, herb, metal and blueberry character. Crisp and tough, it's juicy and succulent on the finish but lacks refinement and opulence. Light-bodied. Drink now through 2003.–P.M. • $24 • (9/30/1998) • **80**
Volnay Clos des Chênes 1996: Stemmy and herbaceous, this is a tough customer. Might improve with time.–B.S. • $38 • (9/30/1998) • **77**

GUYON, DOMINIQUE

Pernand-Vergelesses Les Vergelesses 1996: With some harmony, this medium-bodied Pinot Noir offers nice red- and blackberry notes with oak and mineral accents, though it turns a bit tannic and chewy. Drink now through 2003.–P.M. • $27 • (9/30/1998) • **80**

HAAG, JEAN-MARIE

Gewürztraminer Alsace Grand Cru Zinnkoepflé Cuvée Marie 1997: This has attractive aromas and flavors of pineapple, coconut and honey, with a hint of citrus, yet it lacks structure, leaving an impression of heaviness without definition. Drink now.–B.S. • $30 • (10/31/1999) • **84**
Gewürztraminer Alsace Grand Cru Zinnkoepflé Cuvée Marie 1996: A ripe, tropical fruit-nuanced Gewürz that shows restraint as well as intense flavors. Pear, quince and spice notes are supported by good acidity, and the finish lingers gracefully. Drink now.–B.S. • $25 • (9/15/1998) • **88**
Gewürztraminer Alsace Vallée Noble 1998: Exuding the floral side of Gewürztraminer, this white offers a gentle rose, litchi and citrus profile, richly textured, balanced and lingering on the finish. Drink now.–B.S. • $17 • (6/15/2000) • **85**
Gewürztraminer Alsace Vallée Noble 1997: Good concentration to the floral, spice and citrus notes, which are wed to a broad, rich texture. Well balanced, with a lingering finish. Drink now.–B.S. • $20 • (10/31/1999) • **84**
Gewürztraminer Alsace Vallée Noble 1996: Very ripe, showing exotic aromas and flavors of passion fruit and litchi. Soft and round, slightly sweet, with modest acidity and a lingering, slightly hot finish. Drink now.–B.S. • $15 • (9/15/1998) • **82**
Pinot Blanc Alsace 1997: A straightforward, balanced white with pear and a hint of banana. Drink now.–B.S. • $12 • (9/15/1998) • **79**
Pinot Blanc Alsace Vallée Noble 1998: Juicy and focused, boasting apple and lemon flavors on a lightweight frame, with a touch of nuts on the finish. Drink now.–B.S. • $13 • (6/15/2000) • **84**
Pinot Gris Alsace Vallée Noble 1998: Delicate in aroma, with a scent of violet, this firm, lively white takes on an earthy note along with the lemon

and white peach. Lingering aftertaste. Drink now through 2001.–B.S. • $17 • (6/15/2000) • **84**

Pinot Gris Alsace Vallée Noble 1997: There's an attractive nutty, smoky quality here, along with good balance and length, finishing with a little heat and a grapefruit-peel note. Drink now.–B.S. • $14 • (9/15/1998) • **84**

Riesling Alsace Grand Cru Zinnkoepflé Cuvée Marion 1997: Doesn't cut it. Tastes and feels green and unripe, with flavors of green olive, green apple and earth.–B.S. • $25 • (6/15/2000) • **79**

Riesling Alsace Vallée Noble 1998: Like biting into a lemon. Has moderate weight and bracing acidity without the requisite depth of flavor to match, but pleasant. Drink now through 2001.–B.S. • $16 • (6/15/2000) • **83**

Riesling Alsace Vallée Noble 1997: Lovely mineral and quince elements are buoyed by snappy acidity and a creamy texture in this appealing white. Manages to balance ripeness and finesse. Drink now through 2002.–B.S. • $15 • (10/15/1999) • **87**

Tokay Pinot Gris Alsace Grand Cru Zinnkoepflé Cuvée Théo 1997: Lush, expansive and with just a hint of sweetness too, boasting apricot, pear and honey flavors kept interesting by a moderately firm backbone. Drink now through 2001.–B.S. • $45 • (6/15/2000) • **87**

HAMELIN, THIERRY

Chablis 1998: Easy-going, supple and pleasant. Medium-bodied, it shows vanilla ice cream, spice and pear character. Drink now through 2003.–P.M. • $17 • (5/15/2000) • **84**

Chablis 1997: Buttery notes lead into a soft, spiced-up wine, medium-bodied, with mineral, pear and piecrust flavors. Should be quite attractive on release. Drink now.–P.M. • $16 • (5/31/1999) • **84**

Chablis 1996 • $17 • (8/31/1997) • **90**

Chablis 1995 • $15 • (8/31/1996) • **85**

Chablis Beauroy 1998: A very pleasant, candylike Chardonnay. Supple, soft, delicious and medium-bodied, with pear, green apple and honey. Enjoyable thanks to a clean finish that keeps it together. Drink now through 2003.–P.M. • $19 • (5/15/2000) • **85**

Chablis Beauroy 1997: Lovely medium-bodied wine, offering nice salty, wet earth, honey and fruit complexity in a clean, unoaked package of pure Chardonnay character.–P.M. • $27 • (5/31/1999) • **86**

Chablis Beauroy 1995 • $21 • (6/15/1997) • **86**

Chablis Vau Ligneau 1998: A winner. A bit earthy, but also packed with ripe, sweet-tasting fruit. Complex and silky, showing herb, green olive, pear, honey and pungent earth character. In short, a real animal. Drink now through 2008.–P.M. • $22 • (5/15/2000) • **90**

Chablis Vau Ligneau 1997: Ripe style, showing honey, pear and spice, picking up lemon at the end. Medium-bodied. Drink now through 2002.–P.M. • $27 • (5/31/1999) • **86**

Chablis Vau Ligneau 1995 • $21 • (6/15/1997) • **88**

Chablis Vieilles Vignes 1997: Very pretty, showing a blend of ripe fruit and honey, this is a warm '97 that turns slightly hot on the finish. Drink now.–P.M. • $20 • (5/31/1999) • **80**

Chablis Vieilles Vignes 1996 • $22 • (5/31/1998) • **79**

Petit Chablis 1996 • $14 • (8/31/1997) • **90**

HANTEILLAN, CHATEAU

Haut-Médoc 1997: Light and fruity, although there's a slight stewed fruit component. Fresh finish. Drink now.–J.S. • $NA • (1/31/2000) • **81**

Haut-Médoc 1996: A simple claret, easy to drink. Some currant, tomato-skin and mushroom aromas and flavors. Medium-bodied, with medium tannins and a simple, fruity finish. Drink now through 2003.–J.S. • $NA • (1/31/1999) • **83**

Haut-Médoc 1995: Very plummy aromas. Medium body, with extremely ripe fruit and chewy tannins. Starting to close down. Needs time. Best from 2001 through 2005.–J.S. • $NA • (9/15/1998) • **85**

Haut-Médoc 1991 • $15 • (3/31/1994) • **75**

Haut-Médoc 1990 • $17 • (3/31/1993) • **81**

Haut-Médoc 1989 • $14 • (3/15/1992) • **77**

Haut-Médoc 1987 • $13 • (11/30/1989) • **75**

Haut-Médoc 1986 • $19 Ⓐ • (11/30/1989) • **81**

Haut-Médoc 1982 • $18 • (8/31/1992) • **86**

HAUT-BAGES-AVEROUS, CHATEAU

Pauillac 1996: A silky and pretty wine, with medium body, medium tannins and a fresh and fruity palate of raspberry and cherry. Second label of Château Lynch-Bages. Best after 2000.–J.S. • $27 • (1/31/1999) • **86**

Pauillac 1995 • $25 • (1/31/1998) • **89**

Pauillac 1994 • $25 • (1/31/1997) • **79**

Pauillac 1993 • $19 • (1/31/1996) • **79**

Pauillac 1992 • $17 • (4/15/1995) • **71**

Pauillac 1991 • $16 • (3/31/1994) • **79**

Pauillac 1990 • $22 • (3/31/1993) • **91**

Pauillac 1989 • $26 • (3/15/1992) • **90**

Pauillac 1988 • $20 • (4/30/1991) • **93**

Pauillac 1987 • $15 • (11/30/1989) • **85**

Pauillac 1986 • $21 • (11/30/1989) • **90**

Pauillac 1985 • $17 • (4/30/1988) • **82**

Pauillac 1982 • $39 Ⓐ • (8/31/1992) • **81**

Pauillac 1979 • $18 • (10/15/1989) • **84**

HAUT-BAGES-LIBERAL, CHATEAU

Pauillac 1999: Decent fruit but a bit diluted, with medium body, light tannins and a fresh finish.–J.S. • $NA • (1/01/2000) (BT) • **80-84**

Pauillac 1998: Beautiful aromas of blackberries, olives and cherries. Full-bodied and very round, with velvety tannins and a medium finish. Serious for this vintage. Almost outstanding.–J.S. • $NA • (5/31/1999) (BT) • **85-89**

Pauillac 1997: Bright berry and mineral character, with hints of new wood. Medium-bodied, with silky tannins and a fresh finish. A bit of bottle age will help. Best after 2000.–J.S. • $36 • (1/31/2000) • **87**

Pauillac 1996: A rather discreet style, with understated currant and berry aromas and flavors. Medium-bodied, with firm tannins and a silky, fruity aftertaste. Needs time to open a bit. Best after 2003.–J.S. • $17 Ⓐ • (1/31/1999) • **88**

Pauillac 1995 • $20 • (1/31/1998) • **90**

Pauillac 1994 • $18 Ⓐ • (1/31/1997) • **84**

Pauillac 1993 • $22 • (1/31/1996) • **84**

Pauillac 1992 • $17 • (4/15/1995) • **79**

Pauillac 1991 • $17 • (3/31/1994) • **84**

Pauillac 1990 • $47 Ⓐ • (6/15/1993) • **83**

Pauillac 1989: Always a beautiful wine. Ruby-colored at the center, with a red edge. Aromas of game, dark chocolate and ripe fruit open to a medium-bodied, soft palate, velvety tannins and a long, rich aftertaste. Lovely. (1989 Bordeaux horizontal tasting). Drink now through 2004.–J.S. • $32 Ⓐ • (5/31/1999) • **88**

Pauillac 1988 • $34 Ⓐ • (3/15/1991) • **88**

Pauillac 1986 • $40 Ⓐ • (5/31/1989) • **91**

Pauillac 1985 • $42 Ⓐ • (4/30/1988) • **88**

Pauillac 1982: Fading a bit, but delicious. Ruby center, with a garnet edge. Cherry and rose character, with a hint of earth. Full-bodied, with velvety tannins and a lovely, silky finish. Drink now or hold. (1982 Bordeaux horizontal tasting).–J.S. • $45 Ⓐ • (11/30/1998) • **88**

Pauillac 1959 • $55 • (10/15/1990) • **85**

HAUT-BAILLY, CHATEAU

Pessac-Léognan 1999: Light yet fresh, with pleasant mineral, berry and cherry. Light- to medium-bodied, it's rather short.–J.S. • $NA • (1/01/2000) (BT) • **80-84**

Pessac-Léognan 1998: A fine and balanced young wine with good fruit and ripe tannins. Full-bodied and structured. Seriously good.–J.S. • $NA • (5/31/1999) (BT) • **90-94**

Pessac-Léognan 1997: A bit meager for this estate, with some chocolate and black olive character. Medium-bodied, with medium tannins and a light finish. Drink now.–J.S. • $36 • (1/31/2000) • **82**

Pessac-Léognan 1996: Shows wonderful berry, tobacco and vanilla character, is full- to medium-bodied, with velvety tannins and a mineral, spice aftertaste. Next to Haut-Brion, this is the wine from Pessac. Best after 2002.–J.S. • $29 Ⓐ • (1/31/1999) • **90**

Pessac-Léognan 1995 • $32 Ⓐ • (1/31/1998) • **92**

Pessac-Léognan 1994 • $31 Ⓐ • (1/31/1997) • **90**

Pessac-Léognan 1993 • $20 Ⓐ • (1/31/1996) • **86**

Pessac-Léognan 1992 • $25 • (4/15/1995) • **87**

Pessac-Léognan 1990 • $45 Ⓐ • (3/31/1993) • **88**

Pessac-Léognan 1989: Gorgeous wine, so well crafted. Good dark-ruby color. Aromas of cherry, spice and cocoa. Full-bodied, firmly tannic and a long finish of fruit and tannins. Needs time to mellow. (1988 Bordeaux horizontal tasting). Best after 2005.–J.S. • $59 Ⓐ • (5/31/1999) • **92**

Pessac-Léognan 1988: Medium-bodied, with silky tannins, dried cherry and herb character and a succulent finish. Slightly disappointing since it is so ready to drink. (1988 Bordeaux horizontal tasting).–J.S. • $49 Ⓐ • (11/30/1998) • **88**

Pessac-Léognan 1986 • $38 Ⓐ • (6/15/1989) • **91**

Graves 1985 • $42 Ⓐ • (10/15/1994) • **91**

HAUT-BAILLY, CHATEAU

Graves 1984 • $19 • (6/15/1987) • **87**
Graves 1983 • $37 Ⓐ • (10/15/1994) • **91**
Graves 1982: Still there, but barely. Medium- to light brick-red color, with an amber edge. Autumnal, leafy and fruit aromas, similar flavors. Medium-bodied, but rather diluted on the finish. (1982 Bordeaux horizontal tasting).–J.S. • $45 Ⓐ • (11/30/1998) • **79**
Graves 1981 • $28 Ⓐ • (10/15/1994) • **87**
Graves 1979 • $35 • (10/15/1989) • **84**
Graves 1961 • $192 Ⓐ • (4/30/1996) • **88**
Graves 1947 • $165 Ⓐ • (5/31/1997) • **86**
Graves 1945 • $200 • (3/16/1986) • **94**

HAUT-BATAILLEY, CHATEAU

Pauillac 1999: Serious effort for the vintage. Lovely fruity wine, with a solid core of fruit and ultrafine tannins. All in finesse. Very well done.–J.S. • $NA • (1/01/2000) (BT) • **85-89**
Pauillac 1998: There's some decent mineral and berry character in this medium-bodied wine, but it's very short and hollow.–J.S. • $NA • (5/31/1999) (BT) • **80-84**
Pauillac 1997: A pretty, fruity red with good berry character and a hint of new wood. Medium-bodied, with soft tannins and a fruity finish. Drink now through 2004.–J.S. • $23 • (1/31/2000) • **87**
Pauillac 1996: A well-toned wine, with ripe fruit. Subtle aromas of black currant, tobacco and cherry. Medium- to full-bodied, with polished tannins and a long, silky-textured finish. Best after 2003.–J.S. • $30 • (1/31/1999) • **89**
Pauillac 1995 • $30 Ⓐ • (1/31/1998) • **90**
Pauillac 1994 • $30 • (1/31/1997) • **85**
Pauillac 1993 • $23 • (1/31/1996) • **84**
Pauillac 1992 • $17 • (4/15/1995) • **80**
Pauillac 1991 • $17 • (3/31/1994) • **79**
Pauillac 1990 • $43 Ⓐ • (3/31/1993) • **84**
Pauillac 1989: An elegant, well-crafted '89. Bubbling over with blackberry, cherry and bark. Full-bodied, very velvety, well-integrated tannins and a ripe berry aftertaste. (1989 Bordeaux horizontal tasting). Best after 2001.–J.S. • $40 Ⓐ • (5/31/1999) • **90**
Pauillac 1988: This has good fruit character but is slightly herbal and green. Medium- to full-bodied, with firm tannins and a medium finish. Better with age; best after 2000. (1989 Bordeaux horizontal tasting).–J.S. • $32 Ⓐ • (11/30/1998) • **87**
Pauillac 1987 • $23 Ⓐ • (5/15/1990) • **86**
Pauillac 1986 • $36 Ⓐ • (5/31/1989) • **85**
Pauillac 1985 • $39 Ⓐ • (11/30/1988) • **81**
Pauillac 1982: This is a racy, well-integrated wine; always an outstanding bottle. Dark ruby-colored with a garnet hue. Bubbling over with fresh berry, cherry and currant aromas. Full-bodied, with well-integrated tannins and a long silky finish. Slightly closed; drink now through 2010. (1989 Bordeaux horizontal tasting).–J.S. • $52 Ⓐ • (11/30/1998) • **91**
Pauillac 1979 • $28 • (10/15/1989) • **82**
Pauillac 1961 • $52 • (4/30/1996) • **87**

HAUT-BEAUSEJOUR, CHATEAU

St.-Estèphe 1998: Shows some impressive ripe fruit, but has a slight dilution in the midpalate and heat on the finish. A bit unbalanced.–J.S. • $NA • (5/31/1999) (BT) • **80-84**
St.-Estèphe 1997: Some good berry and cherry character, but rather diluted. Drink now.–J.S. • $NA • (1/31/2000) • **80**
St.-Estèphe 1996: Some plum and berry character, but too diluted to be anything more than average. Medium- to light-bodied, with firm tannins and a watery finish.–J.S. • $NA • (2/28/1999) • **78**
St.-Estèphe 1995: Lovely ripe berry and dried cherry aromas and flavors. Medium-bodied, with medium tannins, a short finish. Drink through 2004–J.S. • $25 • (9/15/1998) • **85**
St.-Estèphe 1994 • $15 • (1/01/1997) • **88**
St.-Estèphe 1993 • $15 • (7/31/1996) • **85**

Key: SS—Spectator Selection. CS—Cellar Selection. HR—Highly Recommended. $NA—Price not available. (BT)—Barrel tasting. Ⓐ—Auction Price. For a key to the tasters' initials, see "How to Use These Listings." **Dates in parentheses represent the issues in which the ratings were published.**

HAUT-BERGERON, CHATEAU

Sauternes 1992 • $NA • (4/15/1995) • **87**
Sauternes 1991 • $NA • (4/15/1995) • **83**
Sauternes 1990 • $NA • (4/15/1995) • **93**
Sauternes 1989 • $NA • (4/15/1995) • **90**
Sauternes 1988 • $NA • (4/15/1995) • **79**
Sauternes 1987 • $NA • (6/15/1990) • **81**
Sauternes 1986 • $NA • (4/15/1995) • **92**

HAUT-BERGEY, CHATEAU

Pessac-Léognan 1998: Pretty floral, berry and mineral aromas and flavors. Medium-bodied, with fine tannins and a medium finish.–J.S. • $NA • (5/31/1999) (BT) • **85-89**
Pessac-Léognan 1997: Pleasant aromas of plums and chocolate. Medium-bodied, with soft tannins and a fruity finish. Slightly diluted. Drink now.–J.S. • $16 • (1/31/2000) • **83**
Pessac-Léognan 1996: Some good berry and tobacco character, with a hint of earth, but slightly diluted and short on the finish. Just good in quality.–J.S. • $NA • (1/31/1999) • **80**
Pessac-Léognan 1995: Pretty wine, with berry and chocolate and hints of cedar on the nose and palate. Medium body. Medium, soft tannins. Drink now through 2003.–J.S. • $NA • (9/15/1998) • **87**
Pessac-Léognan 1994 • $NA • (1/31/1997) • **79**
Pessac-Léognan White 1998: A creamy white, with a lovely balance of apple, banana and melon character. Medium-bodied, with a medium finish. Drink now through 2003.–J.S. • $NA • (2/29/2000) • **88**
Pessac-Léognan White 1997: Promises more on the nose than it delivers on the palate. Fig, apple and peach aromas give way to a medium-bodied wine with fresh acidity and a medium finish. Drink now.–J.S. • $NA • (1/01/1999) • **87**
Pessac-Léognan White 1996: Lovely aromas of cream, melon, pastry shell. Full-bodied, with lots of almond and cream flavors, fresh acidity on the finish. A rich white with plenty of character. Impressive for this estate. Drink now.–J.S. • $NA • (3/31/1999) • **90**

HAUT-BERNAT, CHATEAU

Puisseguin-St.-Emilion Vieilli en Fûts de Chêne 1992 • $NA • (4/15/1995) • **79**

HAUT-BRIE-CAILLOU, CHATEAU

Médoc 1995 • $13 • (6/30/1997) • **82**

HAUT-BRION, CHATEAU

Pessac-Léognan 1999: Dark ruby in color, with masses of tobacco, chocolate, berry and violet character. Full-bodied, with lots of fruit and superconcentration of velvety tannins. Long, long finish. Almost classic.–J.S. • $NA • (1/01/2000) (BT) • **90-94**
Pessac-Léognan 1998: An incredibly rich and complex Haut-Brion which could potentially equal the legendary 1989. Aromas of crushed berries, tobacco, lead, cinnamon, spice and wet earth follow through to a gorgeously caressing palate with big, velvety tannins and a long, delicious aftertaste. A triumph for the vintage.–J.S. • $NA • (5/31/1999) (BT) • **95-99**
Pessac-Léognan 1997: A stunningly gorgeous red. Beautiful aromas of licorice, berries and flowers. Medium- to full-bodied, with silky tannins and a long, succulent finish. Very fine indeed. Drink now through 2004.–J.S. • $132 • (1/31/2000) • **90**
Pessac-Léognan 1996: Seductive Haut-Brion. Complex, with cinnamon, vanilla, cherry, berry and dried fruits on the nose and palate. Full-bodied, with velvety tannins and a polished, caressing texture. Best after 2003.–J.S. • $148 Ⓐ • (1/31/1999) • **91**
Pessac-Léognan 1995 • $167 Ⓐ • (1/31/1998) • **94**
Pessac-Léognan 1994 • $99 Ⓐ • (4/30/1997) • **94**
Pessac-Léognan 1993 • $85 Ⓐ • (4/30/1997) • **91**
Pessac-Léognan 1992 • $75 Ⓐ • (4/30/1997) • **88**
Pessac-Léognan 1991 • $65 • (4/30/1997) • **85**
Pessac-Léognan 1990 • $216 Ⓐ • (4/30/1997) • **96**
Pessac-Léognan 1989: This is unbelievable. Greatest Haut-Brion ever made. It's so evocative and multitlayered. Exotic aromas of fruit, leather, tobacco and earth and hints of spices. Full-bodied, with an amazing concentration of fruit and velvety tannins. The finish goes on for minutes. (1989 Bordeaux horizontal tasting). Best after 2010.–J.S. • $395 Ⓐ • (5/31/1999) • **100**

Pessac-Léognan 1988: The wine of the vintage and one of the greatest Haut-Brions ever made. Superpowerful and ripe, with masses of spice, mint and berry character. Full-bodied, with full yet polished tannins, this wine is a joy to taste and will be for decades. (1988 Bordeaux horizontal tasting). Best after 2003.–J.S. • $171 Ⓐ • (11/30/1998) • **98**
Pessac-Léognan 1987 • $75 Ⓐ • (4/30/1997) • **84**
Pessac-Léognan 1986 • $151 Ⓐ • (4/30/1997) • **90**
Graves 1985 • $154 Ⓐ • (4/30/1997) • **93**
Graves 1984 • $61 Ⓐ • (4/30/1997) • **81**
Graves 1983 • $114 Ⓐ • (4/30/1997) • **88**
Graves 1982: Gorgeous, autumnal wine. Medium dark-ruby in color, with an amber edge. Lovely aromas of tobacco and fresh mushrooms with undertones of ripe fruit. Full-bodied, with velvety tannins and a long, leafy, berry, earthy finish. (1982 Bordeaux horizontal tasting). Drink now.–J.S. • $274 Ⓐ • (11/30/1998) • **94**
Graves 1981 • $84 Ⓐ • (10/15/1994) • **82**
Graves 1980 • $48 Ⓐ • (4/30/1997) • **83**
Graves 1979 • $140 Ⓐ • (4/30/1997) • **88**
Graves 1978 • $119 Ⓐ • (4/30/1997) • **90**
Graves 1976 • $64 Ⓐ • (4/30/1997) • **81**
Graves 1975 • $121 Ⓐ • (4/30/1997) • **90**
Graves 1974 • $37 • (11/15/1991) • **74**
Graves 1971 • $86 Ⓐ • (4/30/1997) • **84**
Graves 1967 • $83 Ⓐ • (4/30/1997) • **86**
Graves 1966 • $142 Ⓐ • (4/30/1997) • **92**
Graves 1964 • $161 Ⓐ • (4/30/1997) • **85**
Graves 1962 • $120 Ⓐ • (4/30/1997) • **77**
Graves 1961 • $733 Ⓐ • (4/30/1997) • **96**
Graves 1959 • $677 Ⓐ • (4/30/1997) • **98**
Graves 1958 • $NA • (4/30/1997) • **79**
Graves 1957 • $125 Ⓐ • (4/30/1997) • **86**
Graves 1955 • $326 Ⓐ • (4/30/1997) • **90**
Graves 1953 • $383 Ⓐ • (4/30/1997) • **91**
Graves 1952 • $263 Ⓐ • (4/30/1997) • **50**
Graves 1950 • $204 • (4/30/1997) • **88**
Graves 1949 • $654 Ⓐ • (4/30/1997) • **78**
Graves 1948 • $NA • (4/30/1997) • **87**
Graves 1947 • $498 Ⓐ • (4/30/1997) • **92**
Graves 1945 • $1,117 Ⓐ • (4/30/1997) • **91**
Graves 1937 • $128 • (4/30/1997) • **83**
Graves 1934 • $252 • (4/30/1997) • **77**
Graves 1929 • $572 Ⓐ • (4/30/1997) • **97**
Graves 1928 • $699 Ⓐ • (4/30/1997) • **87**
Graves 1926 • $561 Ⓐ • (4/30/1997) • **89**
Graves 1924 • $321 Ⓐ • (4/30/1997) • **83**
Graves 1920 • $NA • (4/30/1997) • **72**
Pessac-Léognan White 1998: Offering complex aromas of apple, mango and vanilla that folow through to a full-bodied palate, with great fruit and a long, long finish, this delicious white Bordeaux is in a league of its own. Drink now through 2005.–J.S. • $178 • (2/29/2000) CS • **93**
Pessac-Léognan White 1997: Stunning aromas of pineapple, mango, vanilla and coconut. Full-bodied, with lots of fruit and toasted oak as well as zingy acidity. The finish is slightly short but loaded with flavor. Drink now.–J.S. • $107 Ⓐ • (9/30/1999) • **92**
Pessac-Léognan White 1996: Wonderful white Bordeaux. A wine with masses of almond, fresh apple and honey aromas and flavors and more opulent, baked apple and cream flavors flowing through. Full-bodied and very rich, with a long, lingering finish. Delicious now, but will improve. Drink now through 2004.–J.S. • $142 Ⓐ • (3/31/1999) CS • **91**

HAUT-CHAIGNEAU, CHATEAU

Lalande-de-Pomerol 1998: Pretty aromas of blackberries and cherries with hints of mint and new wood. Medium-bodied, with polished tannins and a medium finish. Needs more fruit in the center palate to score outstanding.–J.S. • $NA • (5/31/1999) (BT) • **85-89**
Lalande-de-Pomerol 1996: Pretty and silky, with berry, chocolate and vanilla character. Medium-bodied, with a caressing finish. Drink now through 2003.–J.S. • $NA • (1/01/1999) • **86**
Lalande-de-Pomerol Cuvée Prestige 1997: Fresh and fruity, with silky tannins and a clean finish. Medium-bodied, with a coconut aftertaste. Drink now.–J.S. • $NA • (1/01/2000) • **84**
Lalande-de-Pomerol Cuvée Prestige 1995: Promises more on the nose than the palate delivers at the moment, but very good. Vivid aromas of crushed blackberry and cherry follow through to a medium-bodied palate, with slightly coarse tannins and a medium finish. Give it time. Drink now.–J.S. • $NA • (1/01/1999) • **88**

HAUT CONDISSAS, CHATEAU

Médoc Prestige 1997: Very impressive for the vintage. Dark ruby color, with currant, berry and blackberry aromas. Medium- to full-bodied, with velvety, polished tannins and a long, fruity finish. Best after 2001.–J.S. • $NA • (1/31/2000) • **88**

HAUT-CORBIN, CHATEAU

St.-Emilion 1998: Thick and rich, with loads of ripe fruit and round tannins. Full-bodied, very long on the finish. Serious red.–J.S. • $NA • (5/31/1999) (BT) • **90-94**
St.-Emilion 1997: A very good wine with lovely finesse and silky tannins. Medium-bodied, with lots of chocolate, berry and tobacco character. Fresh finish. Drink now through 2004.–J.S. • $30 • (1/31/2000) • **88**
St.-Emilion 1996: Well done for the vintage. Attractive aromas of chocolate and berry follow through to the palate, with fine tannins and a medium finish. Could use but a bit more fruit concentration. Drink now.–J.S. • $21 • (1/31/1999) • **86**
St.-Emilion 1995: Lovely, silky wine with fine tannins and plenty of tobacco, earth and chocolate character. Medium to full in body. Best from 2003 through 2006.–J.S. • $30 • (9/15/1998) • **88**
St.-Emilion 1991 • $16 • (3/31/1994) • **76**
St.-Emilion 1990 • $23 • (3/31/1993) • **91**
St.-Emilion 1989: A triumph for this estate. Black-colored, with intense aromas of mint, licorice, berry and new wood. Full-bodied and very thick, offering loads of compacted fruit and silky tannins. Not yet showing half of what it has. (1989 Bordeaux horizontal tasting). Best after 2002.–J.S. • $NA • (5/31/1999) • **91**

HAUT CORMEY, CHATEAU

St.-Emilion 1996: A clean but diluted 1996, with berry and cherry flavors and a short finish.–J.S. • $20 • (7/31/1999) • **79**

HAUT DE LA BECADE, CHATEAU

Pauillac 1994 • $16 • (2/28/1998) • **84**

HAUT DES TERRES BLANCHES, DOMAINE DU

Châteauneuf-du-Pape 1995: This firm red shows typical spice and dried-fruit flavors, with notes of nutmeg and tobacco and muscular tannins. Solid, with the structure to match well with food, but not that expressive right now. Drink through 2003–T.M. • $20 • (11/15/1998) • **88**
Châteauneuf-du-Pape 1989 • $16 • (5/31/1992) • **84**
Châteauneuf-du-Pape 1988 • $16 • (7/15/1991) • **85**
Châteauneuf-du-Pape Réserve du Vatican 1983 • $12 • (9/30/1987) • **88**

HAUT-GARDERE, CHATEAU

Pessac-Léognan 1996: Pretty berry and mineral character follows through to the palate, but it's slightly reserved, with medium body and firm tannins. Some dilution. Needs time. Best after 2000.–J.S. • $17 • (1/31/1999) • **84**
Pessac-Léognan 1995 • $15 • (1/31/1998) • **89**
Pessac-Léognan 1986 • $11 • (9/30/1989) • **81**
Graves 1985 • $15 • (7/31/1988) • **77**
Pessac-Léognan White 1996: Plenty of toasted coconut and lemon. Medium-bodied, with fresh acidity and a long, fruity aftertaste. Slightly one-dimensional now, but should develop nicely with age. Drink through 2005–J.S. • $NA • (1/01/1999) • **88**

HAUT-LAGRANGE, CHATEAU

Pessac-Léognan 1998: A lovely, balanced wine, with fresh fruit and round, caressing tannins. Medium-bodied, with a sweet fruit aftertaste. Almost outstanding.–J.S. • $NA • (5/31/1999) (BT) • **85-89**
Pessac-Léognan 1997: Rather light and weedy, with some fruity berry character.–J.S. • $20 • (1/31/2000) • **79**
Pessac-Léognan 1996: A good red, with decent fruit and a firm backbone of tannin. Pleasant dried cherry and tobacco aromas and flavors. Medium-

bodied. Mild herb and berry aftertaste. Best after 2000.–J.S. • $20 • (1/31/1999) • **80**
Pessac-Léognan 1995 • $20 • (1/31/1998) • **90**
Pessac-Léognan 1994 • $NA • (1/31/1997) • **79**
Pessac-Léognan 1993 • $17 • (1/31/1996) • **81**
Pessac-Léognan 1992 • $14 • (4/15/1995) • **81**
Pessac-Léognan 1991 • $14 • (3/31/1994) • **83**
Pessac-Léognan White 1998: A fresh and fruity white, with pretty tropical fruit and lemon character. Medium-bodied, with fresh acidity and a long finish. Drink now through 2002.–J.S. • $22 • (2/29/2000) • **88**
Pessac-Léognan White 1997: A lovely, well-crafted white Bordeaux. Medium-bodied, with apple and peach aromas and creamy coconut flavors. Long, fruity finish. Drink now.–J.S. • $16 • (9/30/1999) • **89**
Pessac-Léognan White 1996: Plenty of grapefruit and vanilla aromas and flavors. Medium-bodied, with good acidity, but rather short and slightly diluted on the finish. Drink now.–J.S. • $20 • (3/31/1999) • **83**

HAUT-LARIVEAU, CHATEAU

Canon-Fronsac 1998: Some decent fruit here, but rather green and leafy too, with a short finish.–J.S. • $NA • (5/31/1999) (BT) • **75-79**
Canon-Fronsac 1996: Attractive berry and tobacco aromas and flavors. Medium-bodied. A slightly diluted midpalate, but the texture of the tannins is nice. Drink now.–J.S. • $20 • (1/31/1999) • **85**
Canon-Fronsac 1995 • $20 • (1/31/1998) • **89**
Fronsac 1997: Attractive mineral, berry, cherry, and tobacco aromas. Medium-bodied, with well-integrated tannins and a long, silky finish. A pretty wine. Best after 2000.–J.S. • $NA • (1/31/2000) • **87**

HAUT-LOGAT, CHATEAU

Haut-Médoc 1996: A light and enjoyable claret. Dried-cherry character, with hints of leather and tobacco. Medium- to light-bodied, with light tannins and a fresh, fruity finish. Drink now.–J.S. • $NA • (1/31/1999) • **83**

HAUT-MAILLET, CHATEAU

Pomerol 1997: Rather thin, with berry, weedy character. Medium- to light-bodied, with light tannins and a fruity finish. Drink now.–J.S. • $NA • (1/31/2000) • **81**
Pomerol 1996: Offers light berry and chocolate aromas and flavors. Light-bodied, with fine tannins and a dried-cherry aftertaste. Drink now.–J.S. • $NA • (1/31/1999) • **81**
Pomerol 1995: Wonderful aromas of blackberries and grilled meats. Medium-bodied, with silky tannins and a sleek finish. Refined wine but could use a bit more body. Drink through 2005–J.S. • $40 • (9/15/1998) • **87**
Pomerol 1990 • $25 • (3/31/1993) • **88**
Pomerol 1989: Rather light and weedy with some chocolate and berry character, but finishing slightly dry. Drink soon. (1989 Bordeaux horizontal tasting).–J.S. • $NA • (5/31/1999) • **82**

HAUT-MARBUZET, CHATEAU

St.-Estèphe 1999: Wonderful aromas of licorice, berries and currants. Full-bodied, with velvety tannins and a long finish. Slightly hollow center palate but very good.–J.S. • $NA • (1/01/2000) (BT) • **85-89**
St.-Estèphe 1998: Plenty of raspberry character in this, with hint of mint. Full-bodied, with silky tannins and a moderate core of sweet fruit. Almost outstanding.–J.S. • $NA • (5/31/1999) (BT) • **85-89**
St.-Estèphe 1997: A delicious red, with plum, berry and tobacco character. Medium-bodied, with soft tannins and a sweet fruit finish. Lovely. Drink now.–J.S. • $32 • (1/31/2000) • **88**
St.-Estèphe 1996: An exaggerated woody style but it shows impressively rich fruit. Enticing aromas of blackberry, cherry and vanilla. Full-bodied with velvety tannins and loads of ripe fruit and vanilla on the finish. Best after 2000.–J.S. • $28 • (1/31/1999) • **90**
St.-Estèphe 1995 • $35 • (1/31/1998) • **91**
St.-Estèphe 1994 • $35 • (1/31/1997) • **87**
St.-Estèphe 1993 • $33 • (1/31/1996) • **85**
St.-Estèphe 1992 • $17 • (4/15/1995) • **83**
St.-Estèphe 1991 • $16 • (3/31/1994) • **84**
St.-Estèphe 1990 • $62 Ⓐ • (3/31/1993) • **92**
St.-Estèphe 1989: Exaggerated style, but outstanding. Dark brick-red color; loads of vanilla, berry and mushroom character; hints of raisins. Full-bodied and fresh, with intensely ripe fruit and full yet round tannins. Long aftertaste of dried fruit and Christmas cake. (1989 Bordeaux horizontal tasting). Best after 2002.–J.S. • $45 Ⓐ • (5/31/1999) • **90**
St.-Estèphe 1988: This big, ripe, soft and flashy red has decadent aromas of ripe fruit, tobacco, cedar and smoke. Medium- to full-bodied, with soft tannins and a long, fruity finish. Will improve but delicious now. (1988 Bordeaux horizontal tasting). Drink through 2005–J.S. • $37 Ⓐ • (11/30/1998) • **90**
St.-Estèphe 1987 • $20 • (11/30/1989) • **82**
St.-Estèphe 1986 • $42 Ⓐ • (11/30/1989) • **92**
St.-Estèphe 1985 • $56 Ⓐ • (10/15/1994) • **88**
St.-Estèphe 1983 • $49 Ⓐ • (10/15/1994) • **90**
St.-Estèphe 1982: A beautiful, sexy red. Dark ruby with a slightly garnet hue. Lovely floral, berry and spice aromas. Full-bodied, with lovely silky tannins and a fruity, complex aftertaste. (1982 Bordeaux horizontal tasting). Drink now.–J.S. • $97 Ⓐ • (11/30/1998) • **94**
St.-Estèphe 1981 • $24 • (10/15/1994) • **90**
St.-Estèphe 1979 • $30 • (10/15/1989) • **85**
St.-Estèphe 1962 • $50 • (11/30/1987) • **70**
St.-Estèphe 1959 • $60 • (10/15/1990) • **83**

HAUT-MILON, CHATEAU

Pauillac 1997: A pleasant luncheon claret. Simple berry and chocolate aromas and flavors follow through to a medium-bodied palate, with soft tannins and a fruity finish. Drink now through 2001.–J.S. • $25 • (10/31/1999) • **82**

HAUT-PEZAT, CHATEAU

St.-Emilion 1997: Light- to medium-bodied, with sweet berry and currant character and light tannins. Fresh but slightly diluted finish. Drink now.–J.S. • $20 • (7/31/1999) • **80**
St.-Emilion 1996: Has decent berry and chocolate character, but it's rather diluted.–J.S. • $20 • (7/31/1999) • **76**

HAUT-PONTET, CHATEAU

St.-Emilion 1982: Youthful, ruby-colored, with berry, raspberry, wet earth aromas. Medium-bodied with well-integrated tannins and a racy, fresh finish. Delicious. (1982 Bordeaux horizontal tasting). Drink now.–J.S. • $NA • (11/30/1998) • **88**

HAUT-REDON, CHATEAU

Bordeaux 1994 • $9 • (12/15/1995) • **83**

HAUT SARPE, CHATEAU

St.-Emilion 1996: Obviously affected by the rain. Shows a slightly amber hue to the color, and a slightly weedy, herbal character to the fruit. Light-bodied, light finish. Drink now.–J.S. • $NA • (1/31/1999) • **80**
St.-Emilion 1995 • $37 • (1/31/1998) • **82**
St.-Emilion 1988 • $19 • (6/30/1991) • **83**
St.-Emilion 1982: Slightly subdued, but some beautiful fruit. Dark ruby-red, with a tiny amber edge. Floral and perfumed aromas. Medium-bodied, with silky, well-integrated tannins and a long, fruity finish. (1982 Bordeaux horizontal tasting). Drink now.–J.S. • $NA • (11/30/1998) • **87**
St.-Emilion 1979 • $11 • (4/01/1984) • **78**

HAUT SELVE, CHATEAU

Graves White 1997: Not a complex wine, but it has plenty of Sauvignon character. Medium-bodied, with pretty aromas of mineral, fruit and fennel and lots of grass and celery character. Medium finish. Not imported into the U.S. Drink now.–J.S. • $NA • (1/01/1999) • **86**
Graves White 1996: Really attractive cream, apple, almond and piecrust aromas and flavors, but a bit simple in the end. Medium-bodied, with medium acidity and a chalky, creamy, appley aftertaste. Drink now.–J.S. • $NA • (1/01/1999) • **84**

Key: SS—Spectator Selection. CS—Cellar Selection. HR—Highly Recommended. $NA—Price not available. (BT)—Barrel tasting. Ⓐ—Auction Price.
For a key to the tasters' initials, see "How to Use These Listings."
Dates in parentheses represent the issues in which the ratings were published.

HAUT-SURGET, CHATEAU

Lalande-de-Pomerol 1996: Likable chocolate and berry character to this wine. Medium- to light-bodied, with light, velvety tannins and a light, fruity finish. Drink now.–J.S. • $20 • (1/31/1999) • **84**
Lalande-de-Pomerol 1995 • $15 • (1/31/1998) • **87**

HAUT-VIGNEAU, CHATEAU

Pessac-Léognan 1998: Really watery, with some pleasant berry, cherry character but light and diluted.–J.S. • $NA • (5/31/1999) (BT) • **75-79**
Pessac-Léognan 1997: Plenty of plum and berry in this '97, with medium body, medium, silky tannins and a fruity finish. Drink now through 2002.–J.S. • $NA • (1/31/2000) • **87**
Pessac-Léognan 1996: More to the nose than to the palate, with alluring aromas of crushed currants and berries. Medium-bodied, with medium tannins and a slightly diluted finish. Drink now.–J.S. • $20 • (1/31/1999) • **84**
Pessac-Léognan 1995 • $18 • (1/31/1998) • **74**

HAUT VIGNOBLE DU PARC, CHATEAU

Haut-Médoc 1996: Subtle cassis and berry character throughout. Medium-bodied, with light tannins and a fruity aftertaste. Rather simple but delicious. Drink now.–J.S. • $NA • (1/01/1999) • **82**
Haut-Médoc 1995: A delicious claret with cassis and berry aromas and flavors and hints of tobacco. Medium-bodied, with medium tannins and a fruity finish. Drink now through 2004.–J.S. • $NA • (1/01/1999) • **85**

HAUTS-CONSEILLANTS, CHATEAU LES

Lalande-de-Pomerol 1996: Impressive aromas of raspberries and minerals. Medium-bodied, with firm tannins and a good core of chewy berry and chocolate. Better than a lot of St.-Emilions and Pomerols. Best after 2000.–J.S. • $NA • (1/31/1999) • **86**
Lalande-de-Pomerol 1993 • $19 • (12/15/1995) • **84**

HAUTS DE BERGEY, LES

Pessac-Léognan 1996: Weedy, with some fruit, but the stewed tomato and vegetable character is hard to get excited about. Medium- to light-bodied, with medium tannins and a diluted finish.–J.S. • $NA • (2/28/1999) • **75**

HAUTS DE PEZ, CHATEAU LES

St.-Estèphe 1996: A very pretty, balanced red with berry, currant and cherry aromas and flavors. Medium-bodied, with fine tannins and a silky finish. Slightly hollow midpalate, but delicious all the same. Second label of Château Tour de Pez. Drink now.–J.S. • $NA • (1/31/1999) • **85**

HAUTS DE PLAISANCE, CHATEAU LES

Bordeaux White Cuvée Alix 1996 • $17 • (9/30/1997) • **84**
Bordeaux White Cuvée Alix 1995 • $17 • (10/15/1997) • **79**
Premières Côtes de Bordeaux Alix 1995 • $NA • (1/01/1997) • **79**

HAUTS DE PONTET, LES

Pauillac 1996: A ripe and subtle red with finesse. Wonderful aromas of currants, berries and lead pencil. Full-bodied, with silky tannins and a long, fruity aftertaste. Second label of Château Pontet-Canet. Best after 2002.–J.S. • $NA • (1/31/1999) • **88**

HAUTS DE SMITH, LES

Pessac-Léognan 1996: Delicious and enjoyable. A lovely, aromatic red with allspice, cinnamon and berry aromas. Medium- to full-bodied, with chunky tannins and a flavorful, spicy aftertaste. Very good second label of Château Smith-Haut-Lafitte. Best after 2001.–J.S. • $NA • (1/31/1999) • **85**
Pessac-Léognan 1995 • $18 • (1/31/1998) • **85**
Pessac-Léognan 1994 • $16 • (1/31/1997) • **79**
Pessac-Léognan 1993 • $NA • (1/31/1996) • **79**
Pessac-Léognan White 1998: A pretty white, with apple, pineapple and vanilla character. Full-bodied, with good fruit and a long finish. Seriously good for a second wine. Drink now.–J.S. • $NA • (2/29/2000) • **88**
Pessac-Léognan White 1996: Complex aromas of apples, almonds, butterscotch and pineapple. Full-bodied, with lots of rich fruit and lively acidity with layers of vanilla character. Seriously good for a second label; comes from Château Smith-Haut-Lafitte. Drink now.–J.S. • $NA • (1/01/1999) • **88**

HAUVETTE, DOMAINE

Les Baux de Provence 1995: A lean, herbal red, with plum and cinnamon flavors, but not enough flesh to keep it interesting.–K.M. • $20 • (7/31/1999) • **79**

HEART OF DARKNESS

Madiran 1997: A nicely intense and angular red, with well-focused red plum, currant and herbal flavors and a minerally character. Tobacco box and herbal flavors linger on the finish. Decant, or let it air awhile. From Bonny Doon's Randall Grahm. Best from 2001 through 2006.–K.M. • $12 • (4/30/2000) • **87**
Madiran 1995: Ripe and well rounded, with a ton of lovely plum, cherry and berry flavors, and rich spicy notes on the long finish. Balanced and harmonious. Drink now through 2004.–K.M. • $13 • (8/31/1998) • **87**

HEBRART, MARC

Brut Champagne Special Club 1990 • $47 • (4/30/1998) • **90**

HEIDSIECK, CHARLES

Brut Blanc de Blancs Champagne NV • $33 • (12/31/1990) • **84**
Brut Champagne 1990: Sophisticated and distinctive. An unforgettable taste experience that blends all the enticing, toasty, aristocratic nuances of aged Champagne with vibrant fruit flavors, a velvety texture, fine-beaded effervescence and long, lingering finish. Tasted twice, with consistent notes, and much better than when tasted last year. Drink now through 2010. • $55 Ⓐ • (12/15/1998) HR • **97**
Brut Champagne Mis en Cave 1995 Réserve NV: Here's something special in a nonvintage brut. It has rich, mature flavors, a velvety-smooth texture supported by lively acidity, and a lingering finish. Tasted twice, with consistent notes. Drink now. • $45 • (10/15/1999) • **91**
Brut Champagne Mis en Cave 1993 Réserve NV: Has personality plus. A vivid toasty-nutty aroma and vibrant fruit flavors mark this full-bodied, plush-textured brut. Drink now through 2001. • $47 • (10/15/1999) • **90**
Brut Champagne Mis en Cave 1992 Réserve NV: Grand style. A full-bodied, assertive brut with enticing toasty-earthy aromas, a broad texture and a lingering finish. Drink now. • $49 • (10/15/1999) • **90**
Brut Champagne Réserve NV: Luxurious and inviting in style, this has toasty, vanillin aromas, compelling and complex fruit flavors, a creamy smooth texture and a lingering finish. Much better than when tasted last year. Drink now. • $34 • (12/31/1998) • **91**

HEIDSIECK MONOPOLE

Brut Champagne Blue Top NV: Subtle but satisfying, with modest flavors of peach and honey that linger on the finish. Smooth-textured, too. Drink now. • $30 • (10/15/1999) • **86**
Brut Champagne Diamant Blanc NV: Wow. An exuberant, generous, concentrated brut with a wide band of caramel, pear and spice flavors, great depth and a lingering finish. Its complexity and character compare to vintage Champagne. Drink now through 2001. • $50 • (9/15/1999) • **93**
Brut Champagne Dry Monopole NV • $31 • (12/31/1991) • **82**
Extra Dry Champagne NV • $38 • (11/30/1992) • **82**

HELENE, CHATEAU

Corbières Cuvée Hélène de Troie 1994 • $20 • (4/30/1998) • **80**
Corbières Cuvée Tradition 1990 • $7 • (3/15/1994) • **83**

HENRIET-BAZIN, D.

Brut Champagne NV: A well-rounded Champagne that's fully fruity and generous in flavor. Pleasantly soft in texture, but comes through with lively acidity on the finish. Drink now. • $25 • (12/31/1998) • **87**
Brut Champagne 1991: Fine, mature nutty and woodsy aromas and flavors lend dimension to the dough and apple notes in this powerful, intense

bubbly. Lean and tugging at the leash, it has the assertiveness to match with food. Drink now through 2001.–B.S. • $30 • (11/30/1999) • **90**

Brut Champagne 1990: Generous, full-flavored and plush in texture, this is easy to drink and enjoy. Ample notes of apple, cherry and butter mingle on a mouthfilling mousse and linger on the soft finish. Drink now. • $30 • (12/15/1998) • **90**

HENRIOT

Brut Blanc de Blancs Champagne NV: Suave but full-bodied, showing its Chardonnay character in the green-gold color, lush texture and ripe, integrated fruit flavors. Drink now. • $36 • (9/15/1999) • **89**

Brut Blanc de Blancs Champagne de Chardonnay NV • $34 • (12/31/1994) • **89**

Brut Champagne 1990: Understated Champagne, smooth and elegant in texture, tangy in flavor, with firm acidity and a subtle fruit character. Drink now through 2001. • $40 • (10/15/1999) • **87**

Brut Champagne Souverain NV: There's fine concentration in this focused, Burgundy-like brut, with tasty Chardonnay flavors and a bright, smooth texture. Drink now. • $33 • (9/15/1999) • **89**

HERITAGE DE CHATEAU LE BOSCQ

St.-Estèphe 1996: Pretty berry on the nose, but rather diluted on the palate. Still, it's medium-bodied, with fine tannins and a cherry aftertaste. Drink now.–J.S. • $NA • (1/31/1999) • **80**

HERITIER-GUYOT, L'

Chambolle-Musigny 1994 • $28 • (11/15/1996) • **73**
Chambolle-Musigny 1993 • $30 • (11/15/1995) • **74**
Chassagne-Montrachet 1995 • $33 • (8/31/1997) • **79**
Clos de Vougeot 1994 • $49 • (11/15/1996) • **79**
Clos de Vougeot 1993 • $35 • (11/15/1995) • **84**
Clos de Vougeot 1988 • $51 • (3/15/1993) • **76**
Corton Les Renardes 1993 • $60 • (11/15/1995) • **86**
Corton-Charlemagne 1995 • $50 • (8/31/1997) • **85**
Côte de Nuits-Villages 1993 • $15 • (11/15/1995) • **83**
Echézeaux 1994 • $47 • (11/15/1996) • **76**
Gevrey-Chambertin Les Cazetiers 1993 • $45 • (11/15/1995) • **84**
Mâcon-Villages 1996 • $12 • (5/31/1998) • **80**
Mâcon-Villages 1995 • $NA • (8/31/1996) • **83**
Meursault 1995 • $NA • (8/31/1997) • **77**
Puligny-Montrachet Les Chalumaux 1995 • $45 • (8/31/1997) • **78**
Santenay 1994 • $18 • (11/15/1996) • **70**
Vougeot Clos Blanc de Vougeot 1995 • $43 • (8/31/1997) • **88**
Vougeot Les Crâs 1994 • $42 • (11/15/1996) • **71**
Vougeot Les Crâs 1993 • $35 • (11/15/1995) • **77**

HERMITAGE, CHATEAU L'

St.-Emilion 1998: Loads of crushed berries in this wine. Medium- to full-bodied, with fine tannins and a polished, caressing finish. Needs a bit more fruit to balance the wood.–J.S. • $NA • (5/31/1999) (BT) • **85-89**

HERON

Merlot Vin de Pays d'Oc 1997: Medium-bodied, with good cherry, berry and currant flavors. Nice orange-spice element on the finish. Smooth and ready to drink. Drink now.–K.M. • $10 • (1/01/2000) • **84**

Merlot Vin de Pays d'Oc 1996: A substantial style of Merlot whose plummy, smoky flavors are supported by a firmly tannic texture. Drink now. • $10 • (10/31/1998) • **84**

Merlot Vin de Pays d'Oc 1995 • $9 • (11/15/1997) • **84**
Merlot Vin de Pays d'Oc 1994 • $9 • (7/31/1996) • **79**

HERZOG

Cabernet Sauvignon Vin de Pays d'Oc NV • $7 • (3/31/1991) • **88**
Cabernet Sauvignon Vin de Pays d'Oc 1996 • $7 • (12/15/1997) • **76**

Key: SS—Spectator Selection. CS—Cellar Selection. HR—Highly Recommended. $NA—Price not available. (BT)—Barrel tasting. (A)—Auction Price. For a key to the tasters' initials, see "How to Use These Listings."
Dates in parentheses represent the issues in which the ratings were published.

Chardonnay Vin de Pays du Jardin de la France 1996 • $7 • (5/31/1998) • **81**
Merlot Vin de Pays d'Oc NV • $7 • (3/31/1991) • **75**

Merlot Vin de Pays d'Oc 1997: Fairly light, with dried plum and cherry flavors and a gamy note on the finish. Kosher.–K.M. • $NA • (1/01/1999) • **78**

Merlot Vin de Pays d'Oc 1996 • $7 • (12/15/1997) • **82**

HORTUS, DOMAINE DE L'

Coteaux du Languedoc 1991 • $8 • (3/15/1994) • **83**

Coteaux du Languedoc Pic St.-Loup Bergerie de l'Hortus 1997: Has mineral and dried cherry flavors, with smoky notes on the finish.–K.M. • $10 • (1/31/2000) • **79**

Coteaux du Languedoc Pic St.-Loup Classique 1996: This luscious red starts off restrained but builds to a sumptuous finish. Beautifully articulated cherry, cassis, red plum and spice flavors, with just a touch of leather and pepper. Balanced and lively. Drink now.–K.M. • $9 • (1/31/1999) • **87**

Coteaux du Languedoc Pic St.-Loup Grande Cuvée 1996: A bit closed but quite seductive, with sumptuous flavors of red plum, cassis, berry and cherry. Finishes with notes of cardamom, pepper and dark chocolate. A well-crafted red that should develop well. Drink through 2004–K.M. • $16 • (1/31/1999) • **88**

Coteaux du Languedoc Pic St.-Loup Grande Cuvée 1995 • $16 • (3/31/1998) • **85**

Coteaux du Languedoc Pic St.-Loup Jeunes Vignes de l'Hortus 1996: A straightforward, fruity red, with cranberry and cherry flavors. Simple and quaffable. Drink now.–K.M. • $9 • (1/31/1999) • **82**

Vin de Pays du Val de Montferrand White Classique 1997: Intense herbal and oniony flavors dominate this assertive, fairly full-bodied white. Finishes on a spicy note. Serve with fish or poultry. Drink now.–K.M. • $10 • (12/31/1998) • **86**

HOSANNA, CHATEAU

Pomerol 1999: Pretty plum and mineral aromas follow through to a medium-bodied palate, with fine tannins and a fresh, fruity finish. Lots of finesse here. Formerly Certan-Giraud but now from the Moueix family.–J.S. • $NA • (1/01/2000) (BT) • **85-89**

HOURME, CHATEAU DE L'

Côtes de Francs 1996: A light red, with creamy, nutty berry character. Light-bodied, with a short finish. Hard to get excited about.–J.S. • $19 • (7/31/1999) • **78**

HUET, S.A.

Vouvray Cuvée Constance 1997: Extraordinarily rich. An amazing amount of botrytis gives this sweet white a powerful, spicy character, its masses of ripe fruit kept lively by electrifying acidity. So concentrated it tastes as though all the flesh has evaporated, leaving only the spirit behind. Will easily last your lifetime and mine. Best from 2005 through 2050.–T.M. • $100/500 ml. • (2/29/2000) CS • **100**

Vouvray Cuvée Constance 1995 • $60/500 ml. • (6/15/1997) • **93**

Vouvray Demi-Sec Clos du Bourg 1996: Honey and spice aromas give way to a luscious palate, with notes of honey, marzipan, orange and dried apricot. Noticeable sweetness is well balanced with acidity. Though rich, it's not really a dessert wine, and though it would accompany food well, it's probably best appreciated on its own. Delicious now, and should improve. Drink now through 2010.–T.M. • $26 • (12/31/1998) • **91**

Vouvray Moelleux 1ère Trie 1990 • $41 • (12/15/1995) • **92**

Vouvray Moelleux Clos du Bourg 1ère Trie 1997: Sweet yet quite elegant. Sugary flavors of dried apple and pineapple have depth and persistence, with notes of clove and candied orange peel that linger on the finish. Good intensity. Drink now through 2007.–T.M. • $60 • (2/29/2000) • **89**

Vouvray Moelleux Clos du Bourg 1ère Trie 1996: Impressive richness marks this full-bodied, powerful and expressive dessert white from the Loire, with spicy botrytis, honey, pineapple and melon flavors. It's certainly sweet, but good acidity keeps it lively. Fresh and appealing now, it has the stuffing to improve. Drink now through 2010.–T.M. • $50 • (12/31/1998) HR • **93**

Vouvray Moelleux Clos du Bourg 1ère Trie 1995 • $35 • (5/15/1997) CS • **94**

Vouvray Moelleux Le Mont 1ère Trie 1997: Rich, complex and long. This beauty sings with ripe fruit, honey and spice flavors. Sweet and pure, with just enough acidity to keep it lively and refreshing. Thick but not cloying, the harmony persists through a long finish. Archetypal Vouvray. Drink now through 2010.–T.M. • $60 • (2/29/2000) • **95**

Vouvray Moelleux Le Mont 1ère Trie 1996: This very rich, luscious white is almost waxy in texture, with sweet honey, pineapple and dried apricot flavors. It maintains a lively underlying acidity and is balanced enough to match well with many foods. A strong, clean wine. Drink now through 2010.–T.M. • $40 • (12/31/1998) • **90**

Vouvray Sec Clos du Bourg 1998: Broad and round. Apple, pear and smoke flavors are harmonious and fresh. The finish is dry and lingering, with apple and herb notes. Drink now.–T.M. • $20 • (2/29/2000) • **85**

Vouvray Sec Le Mont 1996: This off-dry white marries ripe fruit and appreciable sweetness with lively acidity. Apricot and light honey flavors are clean and balanced. Definitely crisp enough for food, and should gain complexity with age. Drink now through 2003.–T.M. • $20 • (12/31/1998) • **87**

HUGEL

Alsace Gentil 1998: Here's a tasty value fom a good producer in France's Alsace region. It's a firm, well-defined and spicy white, though it has a rich texture midpalate and straightforward citrus and peach flavors. Drink now.–B.S. • $10 • (10/31/1999) • **84**

Alsace Gentil 1997: A delicious white representing a traditional Alsace blend of four white grape varieties. Aromas of peaches and spring flowers abound, followed by a ripe quince flavor and a rich texture, all well balanced and lingering on the finish. A unique bottling at a low-risk price. Drink now.–B.S. • $9 • (9/15/1998) • **86**

Alsace Gentil 1996 • $10 • (11/15/1997) • **85**

Gewürztraminer Alsace Hommage à Jean Hugel 1997: Simply delicious, this is ripe and fat, evoking litchi, honey and butter flavors, soft as a pillow, but never heavy or cloying. It finishes with a fillip of bitterness, punctuating the whole presentation nicely. Drink now.–B.S. • $50 • (4/30/1999) • **88**

Gewürztraminer Alsace Hugel 1998: Very pretty, sporting rose and violet character in a light, airy presentation. Good persistence of flavors. Drink now.–B.S. • $18 • (6/15/2000) • **84**

Gewürztraminer Alsace Jubilée Réserve Personnelle 1997: Aromas of vanilla, smoke and Indian spices lead off, followed by litchi, mango and crème brûlée flavors, all integrated with a buttery texture. A wave of fresh acidity keeps it almost light on the long finish. Drink now through 2003.–B.S. • $29 • (4/30/1999) • **89**

Gewürztraminer Alsace Sélection de Grains Nobles 1997: Absolutely delicious. A combination of fresh flowers, litchi and honey takes on vanilla and coconut nuances in the mouth. It's seamless, concentrated and has a most intriguing airy texture that gives it a wonderful sense of harmony and grace. Should get even better with bottle age. Drink now through 2010.–B.S. • $140 • (4/30/1999) • **95**

Gewürztraminer Alsace Sélection de Grains Nobles 1989 • $124 • (11/15/1996) • **93**

Gewürztraminer Alsace Tradition Hugel 1997: Bold,and rich, full of grapefruit, white pepper and tropical fruit nuances, silky and concentrated, ending with a characteristic grapefruit peel note but also a touch of heat. Drink now through 2002.–B.S. • $22 • (4/30/1999) • **87**

Gewürztraminer Alsace Tradition Hugel 1996: Reserved for this variety, displaying good structure and concentration, moderate richness and dry, spicy flavors, with a hint of red grapefruit.–B.S. • $22 • (9/15/1998) • **86**

Gewürztraminer Alsace Vendange Tardive 1997: Fresh, clean and thickly textured, here's a honeyed VT without a lot of expression and character today. Perhaps it just needs time for the residual sugar to integrate. Drink through 2005–B.S. • $65 • (4/30/1999) • **88**

Muscat Alsace Tradition Hugel 1997: Very perfumed, brimming with tuberose and freesia that morph to white pepper on the palate, with a grapey freshness. All the elements are balanced and harmonious. Drink now.–B.S. • $17 • (3/31/1999) • **87**

Pinot Blanc Alsace Cuvée Les Amours 1997: A lovely, peach-inflected white, this Pinot Blanc has breadth and a purity more akin to '96 than to '97. That said, there's a richness and body characteristic of the latter vintage, with less structure. Drink now.–B.S. • $13 • (3/31/1999) • **88**

Pinot Blanc Alsace Cuvée Les Amours 1996: Apple and citrus are the main flavors, along with a waxy note, allied to zippy acidity and finishing like a crisp green apple.–B.S. • $12 • (9/15/1998) • **84**

Pinot Blanc Alsace Hugel Cuvée Les Amours 1998: Rich, with good underlying acidity to focus the apple and peach notes. Drink now.–B.S. • $12 • (6/15/2000) • **82**

Pinot Noir Alsace Jubilée Hugel 1997: Here's an elegant Pinot Noir that shows cherry, vanilla and earth, medium weight and moderate intensity, all on a solid framework. There's still some tannin to be resolved but overall it's well balanced. Drink now through 2003.–B.S. • $32 • (3/31/1999) • **87**

Pinot Noir Alsace Jubilée Réserve Personnelle 1995 • $35 • (11/15/1997) • **87**

Pinot Noir Alsace Jubilée Réserve Personnelle 1990 • $29 • (11/15/1994) • **81**

Riesling Alsace 1997: This offers the steely, dry side of Alsace Riesling, combining elegance and power with herbal, earthy flavors and a hint of peach. Rich in texture, but compact and austere on the finish. Drink through 2003–B.S. • $16 • (4/30/1999) • **84**

Riesling Alsace Hommage à Jean Hugel 1997: Brilliant focus and clarity. Noticeable sweetness is offset by fine acidity, while the apricot, passion fruit and mineral flavors drape themselves seductively over an elegant framework. So pure and clean it melts in the mouth, with seamless texture leading into a long, refined finish. Drink now through 2007.–B.S. • $50 • (4/30/1999) • **92**

Riesling Alsace Jubilée 1997: A waxy note and an appealing earthiness lead off, followed by flavors of apricot, chamomile and a hint of orange blossom in this bright, focused young white. Opulent in texture, with juicy acidity and a long finish. Drink now through 2008.–B.S. • $33 • (3/31/1999) • **91**

Riesling Alsace Tradition Hugel 1997: Reticent aromas of forest floor, minerals and quince segue into a broad, rich and spicy palate, intense, with just a hint of austerity in flavor rather than texture and body. Fine length and concentration. Drink through 2007–B.S. • $22 • (3/31/1999) • **89**

Riesling Alsace Vendange Tardive 1997: Lovely peach and apricot aromas and flavors are allied to medium sweetness in this rich-textured, late-harvest white. Very structured, this young Riesling has a promising future ahead. Best from 2002 through 2012.–B.S. • $70 • (3/31/1999) • **91**

Tokay Pinot Gris Alsace Hommage à Jean Hugel 1997: This delicious Pinot Gris combines apricot, smoke, nut and floral character with a rich texture and a vibrant structure. Concentrated and intense, with a powerful finish that ends on a tropical note. Drink now through 2003.–B.S. • $50 • (4/30/1999) • **90**

Tokay Pinot Gris Alsace Jubilée Réserve Personnelle 1997: Banana, lanolin and nut oil character sits a little heavily in the mouth, yet there's no shortage of flavor here. Corpulent and heady, it finishes with a slight bitterness and an aftertaste of walnut oil. Drink now through 2002.–B.S. • $32 • (4/30/1999) • **88**

Tokay Pinot Gris Alsace Sélection de Grains Nobles 1989 • $NA • (11/15/1990) • **94**

Tokay Pinot Gris Alsace Tradition Hugel 1997: Pure apricot aromas and flavors mark this lively, succulent white. Smooth, balanced and moderately concentrated, it ends with a hint of bitterness. Drink now through 2002.–B.S. • $23 • (10/31/1999) • **86**

Tokay Pinot Gris Alsace Vendange Tardive 1997: Lush and exotic, this offers banana, lanolin, vanilla, cherry and passion fruit, all married to a medium sweetness. A pronounced apricot note carries through to the finish. Young and assertive, it needs some time to settle down. Drink through 2005–B.S. • $63 • (4/30/1999) • **90**

Tokay Pinot Gris Alsace Vendange Tardive 1989 • $81 • (11/15/1996) • **92**

HUNOLD, BRUNO

Brut Crémant d'Alsace Cuvée du Paradis NV: Crisp and lively, this sparkler from Alsace has an appley character, turning rich in texture midpalate and finishing on a refreshing citrus note. Perfect as an aperitif. Drink now.–B.S. • $14 • (9/15/1998) • **86**

Brut Crémant d'Alsace Cuvée du Paradis NV: A pleasant surprise. Complex aromas of toast and mushroom lead into a rich, powerful sparkling wine with depth and length to the autumn wood, soy and honey flavors. Drink now.–B.S. • $15 • (6/15/2000) • **87**

Gewürztraminer Alsace 1998: Rich, almost oily in texture, yet this Gewürztraminer has a crispness, thanks in part to a touch of grapefruit peel that keeps the rosewater and spice flavors buoyant. Drink now.–B.S. • $14 • (6/15/2000) • **86**

Gewürztraminer Alsace 1997: Bright and lush, this rose- and litchi-flavored white shows moderate depth and intensity, followed by a spicy grapefruit peel finish. Drink now.–B.S. • $13 • (10/31/1999) • **85**

Gewürztraminer Alsace 1996: Assertive aromas are on the soapy side, smelling and tasting more of Muscat. The herbal, grapey elements may appeal to some. Good richness and balance. Drink now.–B.S. • $12 • (9/15/1998) • **79**

Gewürztraminer Alsace Grand Cru Vorbourg 1997: Straightforward, slightly sweet and tasting of pears and peaches in syrup, this is round and soft, with a coarse finish. Drink now.–B.S. • $18 • (6/15/2000) • **82**

Gewürztraminer Alsace Grand Cru Vorbourg 1996: Leans to the floral, tropical fruit end of the spectrum, offering a hint of mint before turning lean, with a bitter grapefruit-almond aftertaste. Drink now through 2001.–B.S. • $16 • (10/31/1999) • **82**

Pinot Blanc Alsace 1998: Tastes candied, like tinned pears. Dilute and unpleasant.–B.S. • $10 • (6/15/2000) • **74**

HUNOLD, BRUNO

Pinot Blanc Alsace 1997: Plenty of violet aroma and flavor and a touch of cooked apple in this soft, slightly sweet white, whose finish is slightly coarse. Drink now.–B.S. • $10 • (10/15/1999) • **81**

Pinot Blanc Alsace 1996: Good ripeness, with apricot flavors, smooth texture and vibrant acidity. Just a hint of bitterness on the finish. Drink now.–B.S. • $10 • (9/15/1998) • **82**

Pinot Gris Alsace 1998: Subtle and clean, with modest flavors of peach and apple on a rich, medium-bodied frame with citrusy acidity. Drink now.–B.S. • $13 • (6/15/2000) • **84**

Pinot Gris Alsace Grand Cru Vorbourg 1998: Floral in aroma, this white is round and full-bodied, with exuberant pear, quince and peach notes that expand on the finish. High in alcohol, ending just slightly coarse. Drink now through 2001.–B.S. • $18 • (6/15/2000) • **86**

Riesling Alsace 1998: Floral-scented, this zippy white turns earthy in the mouth, displaying substantial weight and richness but finishing short. Drink now.–B.S. • $12 • (6/15/2000) • **80**

Riesling Alsace 1997: Smells very ripe, with canned fruit-cocktail flavors that remain simple and short.–B.S. • $12 • (10/15/1999) • **74**

Riesling Alsace 1996: Appealing, with plenty of beeswax and honey and an evolved character that seems older than a '96. The acidity finishes tart. Drink through 2005–B.S. • $11 • (9/15/1998) • **84**

Tokay Pinot Gris Alsace 1998: A fat, round Pinot Gris, exuding smoke and stone accents to the nutty aromas and flavors. Well made in a solid style. Drink now.–B.S. • $13 • (10/31/1999) • **85**

Tokay Pinot Gris Alsace 1996: The clarity and focus in the smoke and peach aromas are right on target, but the palate has a lactic note that detracts from the overall balance and appeal. Drink now.–B.S. • $12 • (9/15/1998) • **82**

Tokay Pinot Gris Alsace Grand Cru Vorbourg 1997: Exotic, showing peach, apricot and spice aromas and flavors, a medium body and a coarseness to the texture. Ends with heat (alcohol). Drink now.–B.S. • $16 • (10/31/1999) • **83**

HUSTE, CHATEAU DE LA

Fronsac 1998: Subtle aromas of violets and raspberries with undertones of mint. Medium-bodied, with medium tannins and a fresh fruit aftertaste. Very good wine.–J.S. • $NA • (5/31/1999) (BT) • **85-89**

Fronsac 1997: An impressive Fronsac with pretty blackberry, dried herb and black olive aromas. Medium- to full-bodied, with silky tannins and a good core of fruit on the finish. Drink now.–J.S. • $NA • (1/31/2000) • **87**

HYOT BEAUSEJOUR, CHATEAU

Côtes de Castillon 1993 • $8 • (4/30/1997) • **76**

HYVERNIERE, CHATEAU DE L'

Muscadet de Sèvre et Maine Sur Lie Réserve 1998: Light and crisp, this white offers floral, citrus and light pear flavors. Clean but a bit dilute, it's simple yet refreshing.–T.M. • $NA • (6/30/1999) • **79**

ILE, DOMAINE DE L'

Côtes de Provence Rosé Porquerolles 1996 • $13 • (12/31/1997) • **85**

ISSAN, CHATEAU D'

Margaux 1999: Lovely grapey wine. Pretty plum, berry and currant aromas follow through to a medium-bodied palate with medium tannins. Fresh, fruity finish.–J.S. • $NA • (1/01/2000) (BT) • **85-89**

Margaux 1998: Good fruit concentration, but slightly herbal and austere. Medium-bodied and short.–J.S. • $NA • (5/31/1999) (BT) • **80-84**

Margaux 1997: Nice velvety texture, but I am not impressed with the herbal, cut grass character. Light finish. Drink now.–J.S. • $NA • (1/31/2000) • **81**

Margaux 1996: Plenty of blackberry, currant and cherry character. Medium- to full-bodied, with velvety tannins and a long, fruity aftertaste. A mellow and well-defined '96. One of the best Issans in ages. Best after 2000.–J.S. • $25 • (1/31/1999) • **90**

Margaux 1995 • $25 • (1/31/1998) • **89**

Margaux 1994 • $25 • (1/31/1997) • **83**

Margaux 1993 • $25 • (1/31/1996) • **83**

Margaux 1990 • $48 Ⓐ • (3/31/1993) • **86**

Margaux 1989 • $38 Ⓐ • (3/15/1992) • **84**

Margaux 1988: Harmonious and pretty, this '88 Issan shows attractive berry and tobacco character, medium body and soft, velvety tannins. Delicious to drink now. (1988 Bordeaux horizontal tasting).–J.S. • $32 Ⓐ • (11/30/1998) • **89**

Margaux 1987 • $20 • (5/15/1990) • **76**

Margaux 1986 • $38 Ⓐ • (6/15/1989) • **83**

Margaux 1985 • $38 Ⓐ • (4/15/1988) • **88**

Margaux 1984 • $19 • (3/31/1987) • **86**

Margaux 1983 • $41 Ⓐ • (4/16/1986) • **91**

Margaux 1982: Very ripe, almost too ripe. Dark ruby-garnet in color. Plenty of berry and chocolate aromas with a floral hint. Full-bodied, with very chewy tannins and a lot of alcohol. A little light on the finish. (1988 Bordeaux horizontal tasting). Drink now.–J.S. • $48 Ⓐ • (11/30/1998) • **87**

JABOULET AINE, PAUL

Châteauneuf-du-Pape 1983 • $10 • (10/15/1991) • **85**

Châteauneuf-du-Pape Les Cèdres 1995: Supple and sophisticated, with smooth tannins and a lush mouthfeel, but where's the beef? Medium-bodied, with more oak than fruit. Drink now through 2003.–P.M. • $30 • (9/30/1998) • **81**

Châteauneuf-du-Pape Les Cèdres 1994 • $25 • (11/15/1996) • **87**

Châteauneuf-du-Pape Les Cèdres 1990 • $26 Ⓐ • (8/31/1992) • **87**

Châteauneuf-du-Pape Les Cèdres 1989 • $23 • (10/15/1991) • **88**

Châteauneuf-du-Pape Les Cèdres 1988 • $23 • (10/15/1991) • **86**

Châteauneuf-du-Pape Les Cèdres 1986 • $NA • (10/15/1991) • **87**

Châteauneuf-du-Pape Les Cèdres 1985 • $93 Ⓐ • (10/15/1991) • **88**

Châteauneuf-du-Pape Les Cèdres 1981 • $NA • (10/15/1991) • **86**

Condrieu 1997: Rather lively flavors of lemon, citrus and mango. Crisp and clean, like tasting a sorbet, so don't expect much opulence, but it might serve well for cutting through creamy dishes. Drink now through 2003.–P.M. • $46 • (12/15/1999) • **84**

Cornas 1997: Rather light in the flavor and tannin departments, this red turns a bit herbal and tough on the finish.–P.M. • $43 • (11/30/1999) • **77**

Cornas 1996: A crafty, powerful, tannic but fruit-packed Cornas, showing wild berry, cassis, wet earth, olive, tar and pepper. Incredibly interesting even if it's not the smoothest wine, this is fruit galore in a full-bodied package. Lay it down and it should bloom. Best from 2005 through 2010.–P.M. • $38 • (10/15/1998) • **89**

Cornas 1995 • $33 • (10/15/1997) • **85**

Cornas 1990 • $29 • (11/30/1992) • **82**

Cornas Domaine de St.-Pierre 1997: A well-made, satisfying and richly flavored Cornas, showing lovely cinnamon, licorice, black cherry and blackberry jam flavors. The leather, smoke and spicy mocha notes are attractive on the smooth finish. Drink now through 2005.–P.M. • $70 • (11/30/1999) • **87**

Cornas Domaine de St.-Pierre 1996: Rather savage but full-bodied, with nice currant, cassis, plum, earth and mineral character. There is a slight herbal note, but the overall feel is that you have a lot of wine in your mouth, and it bursts with personality. Time should tame it. Best from 2003 through 2010.–P.M. • $52 • (10/15/1998) • **90**

Côte-Rôtie Les Jumelles 1997: An intense, medium-bodied red with ripe tannins. The spice, black pepper and cassis bush aromas burst forth in waves, kicking the taste buds around and leaving a lasting impression. Drink now through 2004.–P.M. • $70 • (11/30/1999) • **87**

Côte-Rôtie Les Jumelles 1995 • $27 Ⓐ • (10/15/1997) • **88**

Côte-Rôtie Les Jumelles 1991 • $35 • (5/31/1994) • **86**

Côte-Rôtie Les Jumelles 1989 • $38 • (2/28/1993) • **81**

Côte-Rôtie Les Jumelles 1985 • $31 Ⓐ • (9/30/1988) • **93**

Côtes du Rhône Parallèle 45 1998: Shows the potential of the '98 vintage in Southern Rhône. Hedonistic and dense, with smoke, red berry, mocha and black chocolate, this medium-bodied, medium intense, nicely oaked red makes for delightful drinking. A great value. Drink now through 2003.–P.M. • $10 • (12/15/1999) • **86**

Côtes du Rhône Parallèle 45 1997: This generous red offers plenty of sweet cherry character, with moderate tannins and hints of wild rosemary and sage. Balanced. Drink now.–T.M. • $9 • (9/15/1999) • **83**

Côtes du Rhône Parallèle 45 1996 • $10 • (5/15/1998) • **87**

Côtes du Rhône Parallèle 45 1995 • $9 • (12/15/1996) • **86**

Côtes du Rhône Parallèle 45 1994 • $8 • (11/15/1996) • **84**

Côtes du Rhône Parallèle 45 1993 • $9 • (11/30/1994) • **83**

Côtes du Rhône Parallèle 45 1992 • $9 • (4/30/1994) • **83**

Côtes du Rhône Parallèle 45 1990 • $9 • (8/31/1992) • **88**

Key: SS—Spectator Selection. CS—Cellar Selection. HR—Highly Recommended. $NA—Price not available. (BT)—Barrel tasting. Ⓐ—Auction Price.
For a key to the tasters' initials, see "How to Use These Listings."
Dates in parentheses represent the issues in which the ratings were published.

Côtes du Rhône Parallèle 45 1988 • $7 • (12/15/1989) • **84**
Côtes du Rhône-Villages 1995 • $15 • (11/15/1996) • **86**
Côtes du Ventoux 1993 • $7 • (9/30/1995) • **85**
Côtes du Ventoux 1990 • $18 • (4/15/1993) • **82**
Crozes-Hermitage 2000 Famille Jaboulet 1996: A ripe, slightly raisiny style, this Crozes is impressive for its dense texture. Flavorful and tannic but lacks subtlety, showing smoke, blackberry, earth and game notes. Full-bodied, with acidity that seems a bit sharp on the chewy finish. Best after 2001.–P.M. • $100 • (12/15/1999) • **85**
Crozes-Hermitage Domaine de Thalabert 1997: A light-colored tinge and forest underbrush character suggest that this is maturing fast, and it tastes a bit drying on the finish. Brown sugar and licorice flavors. Lacks freshness.–P.M. • $11 Ⓐ • (12/15/1999) • **74**
Crozes-Hermitage Domaine de Thalabert 1996: An impressive and rich Crozes that verges on raisiny but manages to stay on an even, balanced keel, with ripe, lush tannins, clean and pure blackberry flavors, mocha and spice notes and a tender, silky mouthfeel accented by fresh lemony acidity on the pretty finish. Drink now through 2003.–P.M. • $28 Ⓐ • (10/15/1998) • **88**
Crozes-Hermitage Domaine de Thalabert 1995 • $18 Ⓐ • (1/01/1998) • **90**
Crozes-Hermitage Domaine de Thalabert 1994 • $16 Ⓐ • (12/15/1996) • **90**
Crozes-Hermitage Domaine de Thalabert 1992 • $22 • (10/15/1995) • **85**
Crozes-Hermitage Domaine de Thalabert 1991 • $16 • (5/31/1994) • **88**
Crozes-Hermitage Domaine de Thalabert 1989 • $25 Ⓐ • (7/15/1991) • **90**
Crozes-Hermitage Domaine de Thalabert 1988 • $15 • (10/15/1990) • **83**
Crozes-Hermitage Domaine de Thalabert 1987 • $10 • (3/31/1990) • **83**
Crozes-Hermitage Domaine de Thalabert 1986 • $16 • (9/30/1988) • **88**
Crozes-Hermitage Domaine de Thalabert 1985 • $22 • (9/30/1988) • **85**
Crozes-Hermitage Domaine Raymond Roure 1997: Light and diluted, tasting of strawberry and herbs, it turns sour on the lean finish.–P.M. • $34 • (12/15/1999) • **73**
Crozes-Hermitage Domaine Raymond Roure 1996: Distinctive for its slightly raisiny note, but full-bodied and sweet-tasting, ripe and lush, with round tannins. What this full-bodied Crozes lacks in elegance it makes up in pleasure, with plenty of lively cranberry, blueberry and currant character and a smoky finish. Drink now through 2002.–P.M. • $28 • (10/15/1998) • **88**
Crozes-Hermitage Les Jalets 1997: Light and diluted, with a sour flavor and a tart finish.–P.M. • $14 • (12/15/1999) • **71**
Crozes-Hermitage Les Jalets 1996: The aromas and flavors are ripe in this '96 Crozes, with lovely red berry notes but also a distinctive raisiny and plummy character. Full-bodied, with sweet tannins and a supple midpalate that turns quite crisp on the chewy finish. Needs time. Drink through 2005–P.M. • $13 • (10/15/1998) • **85**
Crozes-Hermitage Les Jalets 1995 • $14 • (10/15/1997) • **84**
Crozes-Hermitage Les Jalets 1994 • $14 • (11/30/1996) HR • **91**
Crozes-Hermitage Les Jalets 1992 • $14 • (10/15/1995) • **84**
Crozes-Hermitage Les Jalets 1990 • $14 • (3/31/1994) HR • **88**
Crozes-Hermitage White Mule Blanche 1997: Butter and butterscotch from the oak treatment have pumped up this white, giving it fat and roundness. Underneath are honey and ripe fruit, and the drying finish should suit food. Drink now through 2001.–P.M. • $22 • (12/15/1999) • **81**
Gigondas 1989 • $20 Ⓐ • (7/15/1991) • **84**
Gigondas Pierre Aiguille 1995: Medium-bodied, it offers a hint of ripe red berry character, but it smells and tastes neutral, with a whiff of oak, and turns bitter on the finish.–P.M. • $18 • (10/15/1998) • **74**
Hermitage La Chapelle 1997: Hedonistic and quite delicious but very ripe, with stewed fruit that makes it a bit heavy. Pepper, spice and mocha notes bring it all to a long and exciting finish—but it doesn't have the cellar potential you expect from better vintages of La Chapelle. Drink now through 2005.–P.M. • $74 Ⓐ • (12/15/1999) • **89**
Hermitage La Chapelle 1996: Much more expressive on the nose than the '97—and darker and thicker—adding to the evidence that '96 is a better vintage in the northern Rhône. Delivers a round, clean, pure mouthfeel of vibrant, focused red berry and blackberry flavors. Superb balance, as it walks a tightrope among the relatively high acidity, ripe tannins and delicious fruit. Worth cellaring. (La Chapelle vertical tasting). Best from 2003 through 2015.–P.M. • $57 Ⓐ • (12/15/1999) • **94**
Hermitage La Chapelle 1991: After a hot summer followed by rain at harvest, this "miracle" vintage produced many gorgeous northern Rhône Syrahs. Balanced, racy, elegant, fresh and sweet-tasting, with smooth tannins. Aromas of leather, roasted nuts, plum and wood smoke bring a complexity that seduces. Medium-bodied and in the lineage of '96. (La Chapelle vertical tasting). Drink now through 2015.–P.M. • $NA • (12/15/1999) • **94**
Hermitage La Chapelle 1990: As expected from this ideal vintage, this '90 is sensational. Inky in color and solidly anchored in its terroir, it springs to life with a symphony of flavors, from mineral to wet earth and blackberry. Marvelous balance among fruit, acidity and smooth tannins. Delicious now, but can hold.(La Chapelle vertical tasting). Drink now through 2025.–P.M. • $223 Ⓐ • (12/15/1999) • **97**
Hermitage La Chapelle 1989: A torrid summer with little rain and good weather during the harvest led to a Chapelle of immense potential. Burly and not as seamless as the '90, with layers of this wine's typical plum, mineral and blackberry notes. While monolithic like a granite block, all the pieces should come together as it ages.(La Chapelle vertical tasting). Best from 2005 through 2030.–P.M. • $135 Ⓐ • (12/15/1999) • **96**
Hermitage La Chapelle 1988: The hot summer with some rain in '88 made thick, full-bodied reds. This is no exception. Still young and closed, with tough and chewy tannins, with the *terroir* expressing a mineral, lead pencil and iron-tasting quality. Layered with Hermitage character. Connoisseurs will appreciate it now; others might cellar. (La Chapelle vertical tasting). Best from 2005 through 2020.–P.M. • $55 Ⓐ • (12/15/1999) • **94**
Hermitage La Chapelle 1985: A pleasant, expressive Hermitage, showing a ripe character, with lovely plum, blackberry, lead pencil and leather notes. The tannins are well integrated but still firm. Long finish. (La Chapelle vertical tasting). Drink now through 2007.–P.M. • $71 Ⓐ • (12/15/1999) • **91**
Hermitage La Chapelle 1983: Fantastic quality makes your palate spin with joy. Warm July and August with timely rains were a recipe for greatness, and this is a *vin de garde*. Seamless and silky, but also with a firm backbone of mineral, wet earth, plum, blackberry and leather notes. An old-fashioned red with a long finish. (La Chapelle vertical tasting). Drink now through 2020.–P.M. • $90 Ⓐ • (12/15/1999) • **98**
Hermitage La Chapelle 1982: From a vintage that wasn't memorable in northern Rhône. Drought conditions in the summer may explain the tough, rustic tannins. It's hard to cozy up to this red, but it shows characteristic mineral, leather and black fruit. May soften with time. (La Chapelle vertical tasting). Drink now through 2005.–P.M. • $60 Ⓐ • (12/15/1999) • **82**
Hermitage La Chapelle 1979: After a dry summer, the harvest was interrupted by rain, and this Chapelle shows its age, with plummy wet forest floor, wet leaf and autumn character. Medium-bodied, it's lovely until hard tannins surface on the slightly astringent finish. (La Chapelle vertical tasting). Drink now through 2005.–P.M. • $59 Ⓐ • (12/15/1999) • **87**
Hermitage La Chapelle 1978: A famous vintage for Hermitage. Greatness in a glass of wine. A deeply colored, thick yet elegant blockbuster, this 21-year-old red shows no sign of getting old. Instead, it has reached that seamless level of balance—ripe fruit, clean acidity, smooth tannins. So sit back for a vinous ride through exciting mineral, plum, blackberry, cassis, horse stable and roasted nut loops. (La Chapelle vertical tasting). Drink now through 2020.–P.M. • $438 Ⓐ • (12/15/1999) • **99**
Hermitage La Chapelle 1976: A drought year with a large crop left critics cool—to the dismay of the Jaboulets. An attractive Hermitage, but the fruit isn't as deep as in other vintages. Offering smoke, blackberry and cherry character, it's ready to drink, although the tannins are slightly tough. Dries a bit on the finish. (La Chapelle vertical tasting). Drink now through 2005.–P.M. • $NA • (12/15/1999) • **83**
Hermitage La Chapelle 1975: Tasted from magnum. Terrible weather—it rained for two days before the harvest—led to rot. But severe elimination of poor grapes led to this full-bodied Chapelle. Delivers plum, mineral, blackberry, smoke and roasted game character in a satisfying package. A somewhat crisp finish gives away the difficult vintage. (La Chapelle vertical tasting). Drink now through 2010.–P.M. • $NA • (12/15/1999) • **88**
Hermitage La Chapelle 1972: Rain at the end of the harvest set the stage for a mediocre vintage. A bit light for La Chapelle, but delicate and elegant, with black truffle, horse stable and cherry character. Turns astringent on the mouthpuckeringly chewy finish. (La Chapelle vertical tasting). Drink now through 2005.–P.M. • $200 Ⓐ • (12/15/1999) • **81**
Hermitage La Chapelle 1971: Tasted from magnum. From a vintage that the Jaboulets believe was underrated. More elegant than ripe, this red is still clean and fresh. Shows a bitter chocolate, plum and smoke intensity that kicks into high gear on the lingering, minerally, chalky, firm, chewy finish. For lovers of *terroir* character. (La Chapelle vertical tasting). Drink now through 2010.–P.M. • $NA • (12/15/1999) • **89**
Hermitage La Chapelle 1970: Supposedly just an easy, "commercial" vintage, this is still going strong. This dark, brooding, thick, very impressive 29-year-old wine shows an old-fashioned chestnut character but also ripe fruit, mineral and firm but well-integrated tannins. A wine that holds together very well. (La Chapelle vertical tasting). Drink now through 2015.–P.M. • $143 Ⓐ • (12/15/1999) • **93**
Hermitage La Chapelle 1969: Intense but a bit tough, with a pronounced mushroom, wet earth, forest underbrush, "old wine" character. Turns astringent on the mouthpuckering finish, but still pretty exotic, with plum and mineral below the surface. (La Chapelle vertical tasting). Drink now through 2002.–P.M. • $142 Ⓐ • (12/15/1999) • **80**

JABOULET AINE, PAUL

Hermitage La Chapelle 1967: Offers ripe plum but tastes a bit light, with salt water, fish stock, mushroom and chestnut character. Intensity on the drying finish. (La Chapelle vertical tasting).–P.M. • $NA • (12/15/1999) • **79**

Hermitage La Chapelle 1966: From a great vintage, with two months of fine weather that lasted through the harvest. Full-bodied, balanced and still lively, with richly flavored plum, blackberry, leather and smoke notes. Very expressive on the nose, it's more acidic and expressive than the '64, which is softer and riper. (La Chapelle vertical tasting). Drink now through 2010.–P.M. • $NA • (12/15/1999) • **94**

Hermitage La Chapelle 1964: A warm summer led to supple, low-acidity wines. This Chapelle reflects the vintage—smooth, silky and full-bodied. Less expressive than the '66, but tastes rounder and richer. Melts on the palate as it delivers white chocolate, spice, fresh plum and freshly roasted coffee bean. Seems younger than you'd expect from a 35-year-old wine. (La Chapelle vertical tasting). Drink now through 2005.–P.M. • $383 Ⓐ • (12/15/1999) • **94**

Hermitage La Chapelle 1962: Shows good intensity and concentration, but turns a bit dry on the palate, with chewy tannins on the finish. The final impression is that of a rustic Hermitage with chestnut, dark chocolate and plum. (La Chapelle vertical tasting).–P.M. • $NA • (12/15/1999) • **77**

Hermitage La Chapelle 1961: Always 100 points, still 100 points. From a vintage with a minuscule crop and great summer weather through the end of the harvest. Dark at the core, it lightens at the edge to the color of prune juice. Full-bodied, it lays thick on the palate, with loads of ripe berry, plum, mineral and game layers. Intense and harmonious. Should hold for years. (La Chapelle vertical tasting). Drink now through 2025.–P.M. • $2,378 Ⓐ • (12/15/1999) • **100**

Hermitage La Chapelle 1959: At age 40, this is holding up beautifully despite a large crop. What impresses is the sweet fruit layered thick on the midpalate, delivering plum, vanilla, brown sugar, smoke and leather notes. The tannins melt, and the finale is still fresh and balanced. A delight to taste. (La Chapelle vertical tasting). Drink now through 2005.–P.M. • $1,263 Ⓐ • (12/15/1999) • **94**

Hermitage La Chapelle 1953: From a very good vintage with a rather small crop, this Chapelle is stupendous. Rich, thick, dense, full-bodied and silky, it offers wonderful complexity, gorgeous balance and loads of everything you may wish from Jaboulet's flagship red: plum, mineral, truffle, smoke, chocolate, vanilla and grilled meat. Tastes elegant compared to the blockbuster '49. (La Chapelle vertical tasting). Drink now through 2010.–P.M. • $NA • (12/15/1999) • **97**

Hermitage La Chapelle 1949: This is 50 years old but still young and in perfect condition. Much riper than the '53, it's full-bodied and loaded with *terroir* and concentrated plum, mineral, blackberry and chestnut. Balanced and sweet-tasting, with firm but ripe tannins and a long finish. (La Chapelle vertical tasting). Drink now through 2030.–P.M. • $NA • (12/15/1999) • **99**

Hermitage Le Pied de la Côte 1995 • $33 • (10/15/1997) • **90**

Hermitage Le Pied de la Côte 1991 • $30 • (10/15/1995) • **90**

Hermitage White Le Chevalier de Sterimberg 1997: Very tight, lean and crisp in a mouthpuckering way. The acidity overwhelms.–P.M. • $40 Ⓐ • (11/30/1999) • **75**

Hermitage White Le Chevalier de Sterimberg 1996: Very ripe, with cooked apple flavors mingling with the otherwise interesting cedar, cigar, apple tart and tropical notes. A bit rustic, but it's showy and certainly notable for its wonderful, thick, ripe and smooth texture and character. Has grip on the finish, and needs time. Drink through 2005–P.M. • $40 • (9/15/1998) • **89**

Muscat de Beaumes-de-Venise 1995 • $22 • (12/15/1996) • **86**

Muscat de Beaumes-de-Venise 1993 • $22 • (10/15/1995) • **90**

Muscat de Beaumes-de-Venise 1990 • $22 • (4/15/1993) • **86**

St.-Joseph Le Grand Pompée 1997: Refined tannin structure laces this medium-bodied St.-Joseph. Tastes a bit diluted, though the black cherry and blackberry flavors come through nicely. A good guzzler. Drink now through 2003.–P.M. • $20 • (12/15/1999) • **85**

St.-Joseph Le Grand Pompée 1996: Pretty, with a distinctive crushed black pepper, blackberry character. Medium- to light-bodied, juicy but fairly straightforward on the rather short finish. Drink now through 2001.–P.M. • $21 • (11/15/1998) • **80**

St.-Joseph Le Grand Pompée 1994 • $21 • (11/30/1996) • **91**

St.-Joseph Le Grand Pompée 1992 • $15 • (5/31/1994) • **84**

St.-Joseph Le Grand Pompée 1985 • $12 • (10/15/1988) • **86**

St.-Joseph White Le Grand Pompée 1997: A mouthfilling white, unctuous and ripe, with a lovely, silky texture and fairly subtle aromas of fruit, spice and honey. Shows some power on the slightly toasted finish. Drink now.–P.M. • $21 • (11/15/1998) • **84**

Vacqueyras 1995 • $16 • (12/15/1996) • **86**

Vacqueyras 1990 • $14 • (9/30/1995) • **90**

JACQUART

Brut Blanc de Blancs Champagne Mosaïque 1992: Powerful and flavorful, like a fine white Burgundy with bubbles, this would be best at the dinner table. Vivid lemon, apple and butter flavors are accented by fig and vanilla, a rich texture and full body. Drink now. • $38 • (12/31/1998) • **90**

Brut Champagne Millésimé 1990: Something special. Intense, toasty aromas and ripe flavors match the richness of texture in this luscious, full-bodied wine. Layers of pear, almond, vanilla and mineral linger on the finish. Drink now through 2004. • $45 • (9/15/1999) • **92**

Brut Champagne Mosaïque NV: Generous, fruity and slightly soft in style, with hints of vanilla and spices to keep it interesting. Drink now. • $32 • (10/15/1999) • **86**

Brut Champagne Mosaïque Millésimé 1992: Nicely mature and well balanced. Has toasty-spicy aromas, solid fruit flavors and a generous texture. Drink now through 2001. • $39 • (10/15/1999) • **89**

Brut Champagne Tradition NV: Lots of fresh fruit flavor and an agreeably soft texture make this a bright, easygoing Champagne. Drink now. • $28 • (12/31/1998) • **84**

Brut Rosé Champagne Mosaïque NV: Smooth and well made, light copper in color, with lean cherry and spice flavors and firm acidity. Drink now. • $35 • (10/15/1999) • **87**

Demi-Sec Champagne NV: A serious, substantive wine despite its sweetness. Has toasty aromas, fine fruit flavors and a lingering finish. Drink now. • $30 • (10/15/1999) • **89**

JACQUESON, H. & P.

Rully La Pucelle 1996 • $20 • (5/31/1998) • **90**

JACQUESSON

Brut Blanc de Blancs Champagne NV • $27 • (12/31/1994) • **85**

Brut Blanc de Blancs Champagne 1990 • $35 • (12/31/1997) • **86**

Brut Champagne Perfection NV: Fresh and straightforward, with appealing vanilla and citrus flavors, bright acidity and a clean finish. Drink now through 2001. • $31 • (10/31/1999) • **86**

Brut Rosé Champagne Perfection NV: Good depth to the cherry and earth notes in this sparkling rosé, along with moderate structure and bright acidity. Decent length of flavor on the finish. Drink now.–B.S. • $34 • (11/30/1999) • **87**

JADOT, LOUIS

Auxey-Duresses Red 1997: Elegant and racy, deep in color, with blackberry, mineral and toast notes. Shows a sleek texture and a lingering, tarry finish that turns attractively chewy from the massive tannins. Drink now through 2002.–P.M. • $26 • (9/30/1999) • **88**

Bâtard-Montrachet 1997: Broad and a bit unfocused, with an easy, drink-me-now quality that lacks vibrancy. Medium-bodied, showing decent fruit and toasty accents, but it holds its own in contact with air; hours after being uncorked the wine hadn't moved—indeed, more finesse kept emerging. Drink now through 2002.–P.M. • $202 • (9/30/1999) • **90**

Bâtard-Montrachet 1996: Round, ripe and fairly opulent, this is a silky-as-they-come sort of wine. Lacks a bit of intensity and finesse, showing plenty of butter, ripe pear, lime and earth flavors. Full-bodied, with a malic-herbal tone on the finish. Best from 2002.–P.M. • $169 • (8/31/1998) • **88**

Beaujolais 1998: On the light side yet fresh and clean, this cherry-flavored, soft-textured red is ideal for summer. Serve slightly chilled. Drink now.–B.S. • $10 • (10/15/1999) • **80**

Beaujolais 1997: Light and lively, with simple but refreshing strawberry, tart cherry and banana notes. Drink lightly chilled as an aperitif. Drink now.–T.M. • $8 • (8/31/1998) • **78**

Beaujolais Jadot 1993 • $9 • (1/01/1995) • **77**

Beaujolais Jadot 1990 • $9 • (9/30/1991) • **85**

Beaujolais Jadot 1989 • $6 • (11/15/1990) • **79**

Beaujolais-Villages 1998: Silky and medium-bodied, this red offers sappy cherry and wet earth flavors, with vibrant acidity on the finish. Drink now.–B.S. • $11 • (10/15/1999) • **84**

Key: SS—Spectator Selection. CS—Cellar Selection. HR—Highly Recommended. $NA—Price not available. (BT)—Barrel tasting. Ⓐ—Auction Price.
For a key to the tasters' initials, see "How to Use These Listings."
Dates in parentheses represent the issues in which the ratings were published.

Beaujolais-Villages 1997: Gamy and slightly earthy flavors give personality to this slightly rustic red, but mute the cherry and berry. Firm enough to stand up to food. Drink now.–T.M. • $9 • (8/31/1998) • **80**
Beaujolais-Villages 1996 • $9 • (8/31/1997) • **83**
Beaujolais-Villages 1995 • $10 • (9/15/1996) • **81**
Beaujolais-Villages 1994 • $10 • (6/15/1995) • **84**
Beaujolais-Villages 1992 • $10 • (6/30/1994) • **78**
Beaujolais-Villages 1991 • $9 • (7/31/1992) • **80**
Beaujolais-Villages Blanc Château des Jacques Grand Clos de Loyse 1998: Balanced and clean. This firm white offers creamy apple and crisp lemon flavors that are focused and refreshing. A hint of spritz adds life. Drink now.–T.M. • $12 • (10/15/1999) • **83**
Beaune Boucherottes 1997: Beautiful. Except for a bit of charred petrol on the nose, this is a lovely, seductive, fruit-driven and focused Pinot Noir. Shows great ripeness without being heavy, as seen on the clean finish. Drink now through 2004.–P.M. • $34 • (9/30/1999) • **89**
Beaune Chouacheux 1996: Fairly rich, showing a very firm, tannic structure, this muscular '96 has the stuffing—with mineral, toasted oak and ripe fruit—to hold up to those tannins. Excellent finish, fresh and long. Best from 2004 through 2012.–P.M. • $28 • (5/15/1999) • **89**
Beaune Clos des Couchereaux 1996: Beautiful ripe fruit—cassis, plum, black cherry—massages the palate, coming together with firm tannins and succulent acidity on the long, minerally finish. Best from 2003 through 2012.–P.M. • $28 • (5/15/1999) • **92**
Beaune Clos des Couchereaux 1994 • $22 • (11/15/1996) • **82**
Beaune Clos des Couchereaux 1993 • $25 • (11/15/1995) • **87**
Beaune Clos des Couchereaux 1992 • $19 • (12/15/1994) • **81**
Beaune Clos des Couchereaux 1991 • $17 • (1/31/1994) • **78**
Beaune Clos des Couchereaux 1988 • $35 • (3/31/1991) • **90**
Beaune Clos des Couchereaux 1985 • $34 • (3/15/1988) • **91**
Beaune Clos des Ursules 1997: Wonderful harmony. Shows a tight, firm backbone but with plenty of succulent ripe fruit to give this medium-bodied, focused Pinot balance. Clean, long, intense and pure finish, but needs time. Best from 2002 through 2008.–P.M. • $44 • (9/30/1999) • **90**
Beaune Clos des Ursules 1996: Pretty red, with some licorice, raspberries and cherries. A bit simple. Tastes somewhat pasty on the finish, as if it lacks a bit of acidity. Slightly better than previously reviewed. Drink now through 2004.–P.M. • $38 • (9/30/1999) • **87**
Beaune Clos des Ursules 1995 • $35 • (11/15/1997) • **88**
Beaune Clos des Ursules 1994 • $31 • (11/15/1996) • **88**
Beaune Clos des Ursules 1993 • $35 • (11/15/1995) • **88**
Beaune Clos des Ursules 1992 • $29 • (12/15/1994) • **85**
Beaune Clos des Ursules 1991 • $23 • (1/31/1994) • **75**
Beaune Clos des Ursules 1990 • $63 Ⓐ • (12/15/1992) • **91**
Beaune Clos des Ursules 1989 • $43 • (2/29/1992) • **91**
Beaune Clos des Ursules 1988 • $44 Ⓐ • (3/31/1991) • **91**
Beaune Clos des Ursules 1987 • $30 • (6/15/1990) • **81**
Beaune Clos des Ursules 1986 • $33 • (3/15/1989) • **88**
Beaune Clos des Ursules 1985 • $30 • (3/15/1988) SS • **95**
Beaune Clos des Ursules 1983 • $NA • (3/15/1989) • **93**
Beaune Clos des Ursules 1980 • $26 • (3/15/1989) • **83**
Beaune Clos des Ursules 1978 • $47 • (3/15/1989) • **89**
Beaune Clos des Ursules 1976 • $NA • (3/15/1989) • **85**
Beaune Clos des Ursules 1973 • $40 • (3/15/1989) • **86**
Beaune Clos des Ursules 1971 • $70 • (3/15/1989) • **78**
Beaune Clos des Ursules 1969 • $120 • (3/15/1989) • **90**
Beaune Clos des Ursules 1966 • $NA • (3/15/1989) • **90**
Beaune Clos des Ursules 1964 • $90 • (3/15/1989) • **86**
Beaune Clos des Ursules 1962 • $90 • (3/15/1989) • **79**
Beaune Clos des Ursules 1961 • $125 • (3/15/1989) • **88**
Beaune Clos des Ursules 1959 • $160 • (3/15/1989) • **98**
Beaune Clos des Ursules 1957 • $110 • (3/15/1989) • **89**
Beaune Clos des Ursules 1954 • $75 • (3/15/1989) • **81**
Beaune Clos des Ursules 1952 • $100 • (3/15/1989) • **87**
Beaune Clos des Ursules 1949 • $175 • (3/15/1989) • **86**
Beaune Clos des Ursules 1947 • $175 • (3/15/1989) • **95**
Beaune Clos des Ursules 1945 • $250 • (3/15/1989) • **84**
Beaune Clos des Ursules 1937 • $175 • (3/15/1989) • **92**
Beaune Clos des Ursules 1933 • $200 • (3/15/1989) • **80**
Beaune Clos des Ursules 1928 • $200 • (3/15/1989) • **97**
Beaune Clos des Ursules 1926 • $200 • (3/15/1989) • **88**
Beaune Clos des Ursules 1923 • $175 • (3/15/1989) • **78**
Beaune Clos des Ursules 1919 • $300 • (3/15/1989) • **90**
Beaune Clos des Ursules 1915 • $400 • (3/15/1989) • **95**
Beaune Clos des Ursules 1911 • $300 • (3/15/1989) • **81**
Beaune Clos des Ursules 1906 • $NA • (3/15/1989) • **92**
Beaune Clos des Ursules 1904 • $NA • (3/15/1989) • **88**
Beaune Clos des Ursules 1895 • $NA • (3/15/1989) • **80**
Beaune Clos des Ursules 1887 • $NA • (3/15/1989) • **90**
Beaune Hospices de Beaune Cuvée Dames-Hospitalier 1985 • $85 • (3/15/1988) • **90**
Beaune Hospices de Beaune Cuvée Nicolas-Rolin 1985 • $85 • (3/15/1988) • **92**
Beaune Les Avaux 1990 • $28 • (12/15/1992) • **87**
Beaune Les Boucherottes 1996: A floral, very pretty red, full of raspberry, cassis and vanilla-scented oak. Smooth on the palate, but it lacks the complex *terroir* often found in '96s. A bit chewy on the finish, so cellar short-term. Best from 2002 through 2005.–P.M. • $28 • (9/30/1999) • **89**
Beaune Les Boucherottes 1989 • $38 • (1/31/1992) • **90**
Beaune Les Boucherottes 1988 • $33 • (3/31/1991) • **92**
Beaune Les Boucherottes 1985 • $30 • (3/15/1988) • **91**
Beaune Les Bressandes 1986 • $28 • (5/31/1989) • **90**
Beaune Les Bressandes 1985 • $35 • (3/15/1988) • **87**
Beaune Les Chouacheux 1986 • $24 • (5/31/1989) • **85**
Beaune Les Chouacheux 1985 • $30 • (3/15/1988) • **91**
Beaune Les Teurons 1991 • $NA • (1/31/1994) • **76**
Beaune Premier Cru 1991 • $19 • (1/01/1994) • **84**
Beaune Premier Cru 1988 • $26 • (6/15/1993) • **83**
Beaune Premier Cru 1987 • $28 • (9/15/1992) • **81**
Beaune White Grèves 1996: An impressively well-made, supple white, ready to drink, with butter, vanilla, pear, wet earth, mineral and toasted oak complexity well-integrated in an elegant package. Smooth but fairly light finish. Drink now through 2005.–P.M. • $55 • (8/31/1998) • **88**
Beaune White Grèves 1995 • $40 • (8/31/1997) • **83**
Bonnes Mares 1996: A seductive Pinot from start to finish. Ultrarich, full-bodied, plummy style of Burgundy, with a touch of petrol along with the pure wild berry, cassis and toasted oak notes and a velvety mouthfeel that coats the palate. Best from 2003 through 2010.–P.M. • $96 • (5/15/1999) • **93**
Bonnes Mares 1995 • $90 • (11/15/1997) • **83**
Bonnes Mares 1994 • $61 • (11/15/1996) • **89**
Bonnes Mares 1991 • $51 • (1/31/1994) • **87**
Bonnes Mares 1990 • $152 Ⓐ • (12/15/1992) • **91**
Bonnes Mares 1988 • $38 Ⓐ • (3/15/1991) • **88**
Bonnes Mares 1987 • $52 • (6/15/1990) • **91**
Bonnes Mares 1986 • $58 Ⓐ • (4/15/1989) • **89**
Bonnes Mares 1985 • $126 Ⓐ • (3/15/1988) • **95**
Bourgogne 1995 • $14 • (11/15/1997) • **81**
Bourgogne 1994 • $12 • (11/15/1996) • **79**
Bourgogne 1992 • $11 • (11/30/1994) • **83**
Bourgogne 1990 • $12 • (12/15/1992) • **77**
Bourgogne 1989 • $12 • (6/15/1993) • **76**
Bourgogne 1985 • $11 • (4/30/1988) • **78**
Bourgogne White 1996 • $14 • (10/15/1997) • **77**
Brouilly 1996 • $14 • (9/15/1997) • **86**
Brouilly 1995 • $16 • (8/31/1996) • **84**
Brouilly 1993 • $10 • (7/31/1995) • **78**
Brouilly 1992 • $12 • (6/30/1994) • **79**
Brouilly Domaine du Monnet 1998: A touch barnyardy, with a soft texture and diffuse cherry and licorice flavors, ending on the astringent side.–B.S. • $12 • (10/15/1999) • **79**
Chambertin-Clos de Bèze 1997: Very plummy style, with licorice and easy fruit, though it lacks midpalate concentration. Full-bodied, with soft tannins and toasty, smoky flavors on the finish. Drink now through 2006.–P.M. • $138 • (9/30/1999) • **89**
Chambertin-Clos de Bèze 1996: Simply fantastic. As thick, silky and round as they come in '96, this is a mouthful of wine that's fruit- and *terroir*-driven, full-bodied, ripe yet elegant. Has firm texture, plenty of black fruit flavors and a deftly smoked, toasted oak character that keeps pumping out its sweet wood, grilled meat complexity. The finish just won't stop. A monumental effort for the vintage. Best after 2008.–P.M. • $105 Ⓐ • (9/30/1998) • **96**
Chambertin-Clos de Bèze 1995 • $96 Ⓐ • (11/15/1997) CS • **92**
Chambertin-Clos de Bèze 1994 • $72 • (11/15/1996) • **91**
Chambertin-Clos de Bèze 1993 • $50 Ⓐ • (11/15/1995) • **90**
Chambertin-Clos de Bèze 1992 • $70 • (12/15/1994) • **86**
Chambertin-Clos de Bèze 1991 • $60 • (2/28/1995) • **91**
Chambertin-Clos de Bèze 1990 • $164 Ⓐ • (2/28/1995) • **92**
Chambertin-Clos de Bèze 1989 • $86 Ⓐ • (2/28/1995) • **88**
Chambertin-Clos de Bèze 1988 • $90 • (2/28/1995) • **88**
Chambertin-Clos de Bèze 1987 • $68 • (2/28/1995) • **88**
Chambertin-Clos de Bèze 1986 • $63 • (2/28/1995) • **85**
Chambertin-Clos de Bèze 1985 • $120 Ⓐ • (2/28/1995) • **88**
Chambertin-Clos de Bèze 1983 • $NA • (2/28/1995) • **83**
Chambolle-Musigny 1993 • $28 • (11/15/1995) • **84**

JADOT, LOUIS

Chambolle-Musigny 1992 • $26 • (12/15/1994) • **77**
Chambolle-Musigny 1991 • $22 • (1/31/1994) • **84**
Chambolle-Musigny 1990 • $46 Ⓐ • (12/15/1992) • **91**
Chambolle-Musigny 1986 • $30 • (7/15/1989) • **78**
Chambolle-Musigny 1985 • $33 • (5/15/1988) • **91**
Chambolle-Musigny Les Baudes 1997: A supple and gentle '97, with smooth tannins, a round mouthfeel and medium-intense currant and floral notes. Drink now through 2003.–P.M. • $61 • (9/30/1999) • **87**
Chambolle-Musigny Les Baudes 1994 • $35 • (11/15/1996) • **89**
Chambolle-Musigny Les Feusselottes 1996: Gorgeous. Full-bodied, ripe and sweet-tasting—but fresh and pure—it blossoms with cassis, black cherry, mineral character. Supple texture, smooth tannins and smoky, toasty flavors on the balanced, succulent finish. Best from 2003 through 2010.–P.M. • $54 • (5/15/1999) • **93**
Chambolle-Musigny Les Feusselottes 1991 • $31 • (1/31/1994) • **83**
Chambolle-Musigny Les Fuées 1996: Extraordinary. Dark-colored, focused on pure, ripe and rich fruit that's still shy on the nose but opens up on the palate, delivering lovely red- and blackberry, subtle toasted and violet-scented oak and distinct mineral complexity. Still a bit rough, so cellar. Best from 2005 through 2013.–P.M. • $54 • (5/15/1999) • **93**
Chapelle-Chambertin 1994 • $56 • (9/30/1997) • **92**
Chapelle-Chambertin 1988 • $75 • (3/15/1991) • **93**
Chapelle-Chambertin 1985 • $54 • (3/15/1988) • **90**
Charmes-Chambertin 1997: Cherry and herb aromas are followed by sap, cherry and spice flavors, all on a moderately tannic structure. Turns crisp and firm on the finish. Drink through 2004–B.S. • $95 • (9/30/1999) • **83**
Chassagne-Montrachet 1997: Ripe and honeyed, this medium-bodied, crisp white has attractive caramel, marzipan and lemon notes. Tart finish. Drink now through 2003.–P.M. • $45 • (9/30/1999) • **86**
Chassagne-Montrachet 1995 • $35 • (8/31/1997) • **84**
Chassagne-Montrachet Morgeot Clos de la Chapelle Duc de Magenta 1996: Smooth and lush, this hedonistic white offers a full-bodied mouthfeel, plenty of ripe fruit and some hazelnut and toasted oak. Lacks only a bit of concentration and purity of flavor to rate higher. Drink now through 2003.–P.M. • $55 • (8/31/1998) • **87**
Chassagne-Montrachet Morgeot Clos de la Chapelle Duc de Magenta 1995 • $40 • (8/31/1997) • **80**
Chassagne-Montrachet Red Morgeot Clos de la Chapelle Duc de Magenta 1997: Smells a bit "lifted" (from balsamic vinegar or volatile acidity) on the nose, but on the palate it's round, tasting of cedar, plum and chestnut. Turns tannic on the finish. Tasted twice, with consistent notes.–P.M. • $40 • (1/01/2000) • **79**
Chassagne-Montrachet Red Morgeot Clos de la Chapelle Duc de Magenta 1988 • $20 • (3/31/1991) • **85**
Chassagne-Montrachet Red Morgeot Clos de la Chapelle Duc de Magenta 1986 • $18 • (10/31/1989) • **77**
Chassagne-Montrachet Red Morgeot Clos de la Chapelle Duc de Magenta 1985 • $19 • (4/15/1988) • **83**
Chevalier-Montrachet Les Demoiselles 1997: Beautiful. Ripe and plentiful, showing a core of crisp acidity and ripe fruit (apricot, pear, green apple, spice and honey). A full-bodied wine of depth and freshness. Drink now through 2007.–P.M. • $225 • (9/30/1999) • **90**
Chevalier-Montrachet Les Demoiselles 1995 • $192 Ⓐ • (8/31/1997) • **92**
Clos St.-Denis 1994 • $55 • (11/15/1996) • **91**
Clos St.-Denis 1993 • $62 • (11/15/1995) • **82**
Clos St.-Denis 1992 • $58 • (12/15/1994) • **80**
Clos St.-Denis Domaine André Gagey 1996: Classy. Dark-colored, ripe yet elegant, full-bodied and chewy, with blackberry, spice and toast notes, this wine races to a long, delicious finish that pumps out the pure flavors in exciting little waves. Tempting now, but worth cellaring. Best from 2005 through 2012.–P.M. • $85 • (5/15/1999) • **93**
Clos Vougeot 1997: Lush, generous and rich, with a solid tannic backbone and loads of toasted, smoky wood. But plenty of ripe fruit keeps this full-bodied red Burgundy balanced through the thick, chewy, petrol-tasting finish. Drink now.–P.M. • $81 • (1/01/2000) • **88**
Clos Vougeot 1996: Dark in color and subtle in aroma, this ripe, full-bodied treasure displays terrific elegance as it lets go, from a firmly tannic structure, a series of blackberry, toasted oak, mineral and spice flavors. Solid, compacted finish, with some drying tannins; requires cellaring. Best from 2005 through 2015.–P.M. • $82 Ⓐ • (5/15/1999) • **90**

Key: SS—Spectator Selection. CS—Cellar Selection. HR—Highly Recommended. $NA—Price not available. (BT)—Barrel tasting. Ⓐ—Auction Price.
For a key to the tasters' initials, see "How to Use These Listings."
Dates in parentheses represent the issues in which the ratings were published.

Clos Vougeot 1995 • $43 Ⓐ • (11/15/1997) • **84**
Clos Vougeot 1994 • $42 • (11/15/1996) • **90**
Clos Vougeot 1993 • $NA • (11/15/1995) • **92**
Clos Vougeot 1992 • $42 • (12/15/1994) • **80**
Clos Vougeot 1991 • $37 • (1/31/1994) • **77**
Clos Vougeot 1990 • $109 Ⓐ • (12/15/1992) • **91**
Clos Vougeot 1989 • $81 Ⓐ • (1/31/1992) • **87**
Clos Vougeot 1988 • $53 Ⓐ • (11/15/1991) • **73**
Clos Vougeot 1986 • $50 • (4/15/1989) • **87**
Clos Vougeot 1985 • $85 • (3/31/1988) • **82**
Corton Les Pougets 1996: Seamless texture in this powerful but refined red Burgundy, with its gorgeous blackberry, cranberry, blueberry and smoky-toasty complexity. Full-bodied, long and intense, everything fits together. Much better than previously reviewed. Drink now through 2010.–P.M. • $61 • (9/30/1999) • **94**
Corton Les Pougets 1995 • $54 • (11/15/1997) • **85**
Corton Les Pougets 1994 • $40 • (11/15/1996) • **86**
Corton Les Pougets 1993 • $46 • (11/15/1995) • **92**
Corton Les Pougets 1992 • $40 • (12/15/1994) • **83**
Corton Les Pougets 1991 • $34 • (1/31/1994) • **86**
Corton Les Pougets 1990 • $60 Ⓐ • (12/15/1992) • **90**
Corton Les Pougets 1989 • $64 • (1/31/1992) • **93**
Corton Les Pougets 1988 • $61 • (3/31/1991) • **93**
Corton Les Pougets 1987 • $41 • (6/15/1990) • **87**
Corton Les Pougets 1986 • $42 • (4/30/1989) • **86**
Corton Les Pougets 1985 • $52 • (3/15/1988) • **89**
Corton White Vergennes 1997: Shy in the aroma department, this medium-intense, medium-bodied white offers a silky, round, fat mouthfeel that ends on a flinty, minerally, pear-flavored note. Drink now through 2003.–P.M. • $107 • (9/30/1999) • **87**
Corton-Charlemagne 1996: One of Jadot's greatest whites ever. Very impressive for its pure, clean and racy clarity of mineral flavors (as expected from a great Corton-Charlemagne). Powerful yet delicate, it has some heavy oak but is also full-bodied and marvelously balanced for long-aging. Greets you with violet and butter aromas from the new wood, then performs acrobatics with lots of chalky, wet stone, tropical and ripe fruit flavors. Refined finish is accessible now. 2000.–P.M. • $100 • (8/31/1998) • **95**
Corton-Charlemagne 1995 • $91 Ⓐ • (8/31/1997) • **94**
Côte de Beaune-Villages 1996: Lively red berry and blueberry flavors, with a nicely spicy, toasted character, crisp acidity and fresh finish. Light-bodied. Drink now through 2003.–P.M. • $16 • (5/15/1999) • **83**
Côte de Beaune-Villages 1994 • $16 • (1/01/1997) • **77**
Côte de Beaune-Villages 1990 • $15 • (12/15/1992) • **87**
Côte de Beaune-Villages 1989 • $19 • (8/31/1992) • **84**
Côte de Beaune-Villages 1986 • $15 • (6/15/1989) • **78**
Côte de Beaune-Villages 1985 • $17 • (4/15/1988) • **79**
Criots-Bâtard-Montrachet 1995 • $135 • (8/31/1997) • **93**
Echézeaux 1996: Oaky Pinot, with lots of mocha and vanilla, but the ripe fruit and cigar-tobacco complexity draw you in on the finish. Plenty of tannins, but it's round all the same. Pretty long finish. Much better than previously reviewed. Drink now through 2006.–P.M. • $96 • (9/30/1999) • **90**
Echézeaux 1995 • $90 • (11/15/1997) • **85**
Fixin 1993 • $18 • (11/15/1995) • **87**
Fixin 1990 • $15 • (12/15/1992) • **85**
Fixin 1989 • $21 • (1/31/1992) • **88**
Fleurie 1996 • $14 • (9/15/1997) • **84**
Fleurie 1994 • $13 • (10/31/1995) • **85**
Fleurie 1993 • $11 • (7/31/1995) • **81**
Fleurie 1992 • $13 • (6/15/1994) • **84**
Fleurie 1987 • $11 • (7/15/1988) • **79**
Fleurie Château de Poncié 1998: This rustic red has earthy and herbal aromas and flavors, with dry tannins. There's some underlying ripe fruit; this wine will show better with food. Drink now.–T.M. • $16 • (10/15/1999) • **83**
Gevrey-Chambertin 1996: Clean and minerally, with a wet earth, stone and cassis character that reveals a somewhat cool *terroir*. Firm, angular texture for now, so cellar. Best from 2005 through 2012.–P.M. • $56 Ⓐ • (5/15/1999) • **88**
Gevrey-Chambertin 1995 • $30 • (11/15/1997) • **85**
Gevrey-Chambertin 1986 • $25 • (7/15/1989) • **77**
Gevrey-Chambertin Clos St.-Jacques 1996: A firm style, with clean and pure Pinot character, this is medium-bodied, with chewy tannins but flavorful black cherry and cassis notes accented by subtle oak. Best from 2003 through 2010.–P.M. • $56 Ⓐ • (5/15/1999) • **88**
Gevrey-Chambertin Clos St.-Jacques 1995 • $60 • (11/15/1997) • **86**
Gevrey-Chambertin Clos St.-Jacques 1994 • $44 • (11/15/1996) • **86**
Gevrey-Chambertin Clos St.-Jacques 1992 • $44 • (12/15/1994) • **88**

FRANCE

Gevrey-Chambertin Clos St.-Jacques 1991 • $38 • (1/31/1994) • **80**
Gevrey-Chambertin Clos St.-Jacques 1990 • $100 Ⓐ • (12/15/1992) • **90**
Gevrey-Chambertin Clos St.-Jacques 1989 • $65 • (1/31/1992) • **90**
Gevrey-Chambertin Clos St.-Jacques 1988 • $52 • (3/15/1991) • **88**
Gevrey-Chambertin Clos St.-Jacques 1986 • $44 • (7/15/1989) • **84**
Gevrey-Chambertin Clos St.-Jacques 1985 • $45 • (3/31/1988) • **94**
Gevrey-Chambertin Estournelles St.-Jacques 1994 • $39 • (11/15/1996) • **78**
Gevrey-Chambertin Estournelles St.-Jacques 1993 • $48 • (11/15/1995) • **89**
Gevrey-Chambertin Estournelles St.-Jacques 1988 • $50 • (3/15/1991) • **91**
Gevrey-Chambertin Estournelles St.-Jacques 1986 • $40 • (7/15/1989) • **87**
Gevrey-Chambertin Estournelles St.-Jacques 1985 • $41 • (3/31/1988) • **86**
Griotte-Chambertin 1990 • $70 • (12/15/1992) • **91**
Griotte-Chambertin 1988 • $75 • (3/15/1991) • **94**
Griotte-Chambertin 1987 • $50 • (7/15/1990) • **80**
Mâcon Blanc-Villages Château des Jacques 1997: Buttery and overly oaky, with little fruit to keep up; astringent wood tannins on the bitter finish.–P.M. • $12 • (5/31/1999) • **71**
Mâcon Blanc-Villages Château des Jacques 1996 • $12 • (5/31/1998) • **82**
Mâcon-Lugny Les Petites Pierres 1996 • $13 • (5/31/1998) • **82**
Mâcon-Villages 1996 • $12 • (10/15/1997) • **78**
Mâcon-Villages Domaine de la Grange Magnien 1995 • $NA • (8/31/1996) • **77**
Marsannay Red 1997: Ripe and chocolaty, then the rough tannins take over. Where's the fruit?–B.S. • $21 • (9/30/1999) • **77**
Marsannay Red 1994 • $15 • (11/15/1996) • **76**
Marsannay Red 1986 • $11 • (6/15/1989) • **77**
Marsannay White 1997: Tastes a bit hard, as the ripe fruit just isn't there to balance the heavy oak. There is green apple, though it ends abruptly. Tasted twice, with consistent notes. Drink now through 2002.–P.M. • $21 • (9/30/1999) • **80**
Mazis-Chambertin 1990 • $70 • (12/15/1992) • **90**
Mazis-Chambertin 1987 • $50 • (5/31/1990) • **92**
Meursault Charmes 1997: A masterful '97. Stylish, well-made Meursault, delivering a beautifully soothing midpalate, packed with ripe fruit, mineral and vanilla spices and a silky texture. Excellent natural acidity makes its entrance humbly on the lingering finish. Drink now through 2007.–P.M. • $65 • (9/30/1999) • **92**
Meursault Perrières 1996: A classic '96 white Burgundy, deeply anchored in the soil, with lots of mineral and not that much oak. It's layers of oily, creamlike texture bespeak good concentration, with some smoke, toasted bread, ripe fruit and wet stone character. Beautifully made, it hangs in there on the long, supple finish. Tempting now, but should last for years. Best from 2005.–P.M. • $55 • (8/31/1998) HR • **96**
Meursault Perrières 1995 • $51 • (8/31/1997) • **88**
Monthélie 1990 • $18 • (12/15/1992) • **86**
Monthélie 1989 • $21 • (1/31/1992) • **87**
Montrachet 1995: Fantastic Montrachet that grabs you and doesn't let go. Built in the Jadot style, uncompromisingly closed and tough. Deep and firmly structured, packed with wonderful character and layered with sensational flavors. The long finish completes the experience. Best from 2010.–P.M. • $268 Ⓐ • (8/31/1998) • **95**
Morgon 1996 • $14 • (9/15/1997) • **85**
Morgon 1995 • $15 • (9/15/1996) • **84**
Morgon 1992 • $12 • (6/15/1994) • **86**
Morgon 1990 • $12 • (9/30/1991) • **83**
Morgon Château de Bellevue 1998: Begins lush and round, then turns crisp and almost tart. Light-bodied, showing cherry flavors followed by a firm finish. Drink through 2002–B.S. • $12 • (10/15/1999) • **81**
Moulin-à-Vent 1996 • $16 • (9/15/1997) • **86**
Moulin-à-Vent 1995 • $18 • (9/15/1996) • **84**
Moulin-à-Vent 1994 • $14 • (9/15/1996) • **86**
Moulin-à-Vent 1993 • $11 • (7/31/1995) • **82**
Moulin-à-Vent 1992 • $13 • (6/15/1994) • **87**
Moulin-à-Vent 1990 • $15 • (9/30/1991) • **79**
Moulin-à-Vent 1987 • $11 • (7/15/1988) • **83**
Moulin-à-Vent Château des Jacques 1998: This starts off with impressive aromas of kirsch, violets and spice, then turns tight and firm on the palate, giving up virtually nothing except crisp acidity and stiff tannins. Comes back on the finish with lingering cherry, so give this the benefit of the doubt. Drink through 2004–B.S. • $19 • (10/15/1999) • **89**
Moulin-à-Vent Château des Jacques 1997: This vivid red shows good concentration and intensity, with ripe plum, menthol and smoky flavors that linger on the finish. Firm and balanced. Drink now.–T.M. • $18 • (8/31/1998) • **88**
Moulin-à-Vent Château des Jacques 1996 • $19 • (5/31/1998) HR • **90**
Moulin-à-Vent Château des Jacques 1994 • $18 • (4/30/1997) • **84**
Moulin-à-Vent Château des Jacques Clos de Champ de Cour 1996 • $NA • (1/01/1998) • **86**
Moulin-à-Vent Château des Jacques Clos des Thorins 1996 • $NA • (1/01/1998) • **88**
Moulin-à-Vent Château des Jacques Clos du Grand Carquelin 1996 • $NA • (1/01/1998) • **89**
Moulin-à-Vent Château des Jacques Clos la Roche 1996 • $NA • (1/01/1998) • **88**
Moulin-à-Vent Château des Jacques Réserve des Vieilles Vignes 1985 • $10 • (3/15/1988) • **81**
Musigny Le Musigny 1986 • $70 • (4/15/1989) • **77**
Musigny Le Musigny 1985 • $74 • (3/31/1988) • **88**
Nuits-St.-Georges 1985 • $43 Ⓐ • (4/15/1988) • **91**
Nuits-St.-Georges Les Boudots 1996: Superbly balanced—from the ripe red berries, velvety tannins and creamy texture—it kicks into high gear with a toast, spice, mocha and mineral character. Deeply satisfying and smooth. Best from 2003 through 2010.–P.M. • $54 • (5/15/1999) • **93**
Nuits-St.-Georges Aux Boudots 1991 • $26 • (1/31/1994) • **84**
Nuits-St.-Georges Aux Boudots 1988 • $49 • (2/28/1991) • **88**
Nuits-St.-Georges Aux Boudots 1986 • $38 • (4/30/1989) • **85**
Nuits-St.-Georges Aux Boudots 1985 • $42 • (3/15/1988) • **75**
Nuits-St.-Georges Clos des Corvées 1994 • $31 • (11/15/1996) • **76**
Nuits-St.-Georges Clos des Corvées 1992 • $28 • (12/15/1994) • **80**
Nuits-St.-Georges Clos des Corvées 1990 • $36 • (12/15/1992) • **85**
Nuits-St.-Georges Clos des Corvées 1989 • $56 • (1/31/1992) • **85**
Nuits-St.-Georges Clos des Corvées 1988 • $49 • (2/28/1991) • **89**
Nuits-St.-Georges Clos des Corvées 1987 • $35 • (4/30/1990) • **84**
Nuits-St.-Georges Clos des Corvées 1986 • $37 • (4/30/1989) • **83**
Nuits-St.-Georges Clos des Corvées 1985 • $43 Ⓐ • (3/15/1988) • **96**
Pernand-Vergelesses 1985 • $18 • (4/15/1988) • **85**
Pernand-Vergelesses Clos de la Croix de Pierre 1995 • $24 • (11/15/1997) • **81**
Pernand-Vergelesses Clos de la Croix de Pierre 1994 • $20 • (11/15/1996) • **79**
Pernand-Vergelesses Clos de la Croix de Pierre 1993 • $19 • (11/15/1995) • **84**
Pernand-Vergelesses Clos de la Croix de Pierre 1992 • $18 • (12/15/1994) • **84**
Pernand-Vergelesses Clos de la Croix de Pierre 1991 • $15 • (1/31/1994) • **83**
Pernand-Vergelesses Clos de la Croix de Pierre 1990 • $18 • (12/15/1992) • **88**
Pernand-Vergelesses Clos de la Croix de Pierre 1989 • $21 • (1/31/1992) • **86**
Pernand-Vergelesses Clos de la Croix de Pierre 1988 • $17 • (3/31/1991) • **86**
Pernand-Vergelesses Clos de la Croix de Pierre 1987 • $15 • (11/15/1990) • **79**
Pernand-Vergelesses Clos de la Croix de Pierre 1986 • $17 • (7/31/1989) • **85**
Pernand-Vergelesses Clos de la Croix de Pierre 1985 • $18 • (4/15/1988) • **83**
Pernand-Vergelesses White 1995 • $21 • (8/31/1997) • **85**
Pommard 1996: Brimming with ripe, fresh, spicy red- and blackberry character, exploding with flavor intensity, this dark-colored, vibrant, medium-bodied '96 red Burgundy also packs in toasty mocha and wet earth complexity and stays balanced on the finish. Best from 2003 through 2010.–P.M. • $33 • (5/15/1999) SS • **92**
Pommard 1995 • $30 • (11/15/1997) • **80**
Pommard 1988 • $36 • (3/31/1991) • **83**
Pommard Clos des Poutures 1994 • $30 • (11/15/1996) • **81**
Pommard Les Arvelets 1990 • $42 • (12/15/1992) • **90**
Pommard Les Chaponnières 1985 • $39 • (3/15/1988) • **91**
Pommard Les Grands Epenots 1989 • $50 • (1/31/1992) • **88**
Pommard Les Grands Epenots 1988 • $38 • (3/31/1991) • **86**
Pouilly-Fuissé 1996 • $21 • (10/15/1997) • **81**
Pouilly-Fuissé Cuvée Réserve Spéciale 1996 • $32 • (5/31/1998) • **82**
Pouilly-Fuissé Cuvée Réserve Spéciale 1995 • $32 • (5/31/1997) • **79**
Pouilly-Fuissé Mont de Pouilly 1997: Good complexity in this full-bodied, ripe and rich white. Supple and fairly oaky style, it needs some cellaring to weave the toasted bread, crème brûlée edges into the nice lemon, pear and honey flavors. Best after 2001.–P.M. • $20 • (5/31/1999) • **87**
Puligny-Montrachet 1996: Very pure, clean and balanced, oozing with thick, ripe, lush texture. Full-bodied, with lovely mineral, vanilla bean and pebble character accented by just-right oaky notes and wonderfully sweet-tasting, ripe pear, tropical and melon notes. Butter flavors add complexity to the smooth finish. Drink now through 2005.–P.M. • $38 • (8/31/1998) • **91**
Puligny-Montrachet 1995 • $35 • (8/31/1997) • **79**
Puligny-Montrachet Clos de la Garenne Duc de Magenta 1997: Ripe and silky, a full-bodied white Burgundy that shows lots of power but also finesse, balancing the pronounced toasted oak with intense mango, grilled pineapple, pie crust and pear flavors. The persistent length is impressive. Drink through 2007–P.M. • $69 • (9/30/1999) • **93**
Puligny-Montrachet Clos de la Garenne Duc de Magenta 1996: Impressively balanced. Lovely, fruit-driven, full-bodied, with a silky texture and supple ripe pear, honey, medium-oaky character. A delicious wine that wraps

around the taste buds and delivers a seductive, creamlike, smoky, toasted finish. Drink now through 2005.–P.M. • $60 • (8/31/1998) • **93**

Puligny-Montrachet Clos de la Garenne Duc de Magenta 1995 • $91 Ⓐ • (8/31/1997) • **94**

Puligny-Montrachet Les Folatières 1997: Good balance, with smoke, flint, pie crust, pear, honey and lemon intensity. This medium-bodied white Burgundy rocks and rolls around the palate, with subtle complexity. Drink through 2005–P.M. • $69 • (9/30/1999) • **90**

Puligny-Montrachet Les Folatières 1995 • $51 • (8/31/1997) • **92**

Régnié 1994 • $12 • (10/31/1995) • **78**

Régnié 1993 • $9 • (7/31/1995) • **78**

Régnié 1992 • $10 • (12/15/1993) • **82**

Régnié 1992 • $11 • (6/30/1994) • **79**

Romanée St.-Vivant 1993 • $135 • (11/15/1995) • **88**

Ruchottes-Chambertin 1996: Subtle yet rich and full-bodied, ultraripe but elegant, this is masterfully crafted. Minerally and plummy, with a cassis undertone, and round with ripe tannins that carry to a long, vibrant, toasty and succulent finish. Best from 2003 through 2010.–P.M. • $96 • (5/15/1999) • **95**

Ruchottes-Chambertin 1988 • $75 • (3/15/1991) • **91**

St.-Aubin 1995 • $21 • (8/31/1997) • **90**

St.-Véran Domaine Chapelle aux Loups 1997: Lean, tart style—a straightforward, light-bodied white that's clean and juicy and lacks complexity, but its steely, slightly green character gives it a food-friendly personality. Drink now.–P.M. • $13 • (5/31/1999) • **80**

St.-Véran Domaine de Curis 1995 • $NA • (8/31/1996) • **80**

Santenay Clos de Malte 1997: Soft around the edges, offering red fruit compote, slightly evolved flavors and stiff tannins. Drink now through 2002.–B.S. • $25 • (9/30/1999) • **80**

Santenay Clos de Malte 1996: Impressive quality for a Santenay. Clean, pure, full-bodied, with ripe blackberry and wild raspberry flavors, wonderful *terroir* and mineral character, this has breeding and class written all over it. Firm structure, with crisp acidity. Good aging potential. Best from 2003 through 2010.–P.M. • $22 • (5/15/1999) • **93**

Santenay Clos de Malte 1993 • $16 • (11/15/1995) • **85**

Santenay Clos de Malte 1990 • $18 • (12/15/1992) • **87**

Santenay White Clos de Malte 1997: On the hedonism scale, it's hard to beat this ripe, rich, full-bodied and opulent white, with its seductive toast, smoke, lemon, butter, cream, pear and marzipan aromas and flavors. Drink now through 2002.–P.M. • $27 • (9/30/1999) • **87**

Santenay White Clos de Malte 1996: Well made. So balanced, it tastes supple and round despite massive citrus-spiked acidity. Medium-bodied, with lovely mineral, vanilla bean, wet earth and supple, toasted oak character. A complex wine that ends as it started—with smooth texture. Best from 2005.–P.M. • $24 • (8/31/1998) • **89**

Santenay White Clos de Malte 1995 • $22 • (8/31/1997) • **87**

Savigny-lès-Beaune Aux Guettes 1996: Swirls around the palate with impeccably focused currant, blackberry, violet, toasted flavors. Focused and racy, with a rather intense, medium-bodied midpalate and a clean, juicy and persistent finish. Much better than previously reviewed. Drink now through 2015.–P.M. • $25 • (9/30/1999) • **90**

Savigny-lès-Beaune La Dominode 1995 • $24 • (11/15/1997) • **79**

Savigny-lès-Beaune La Dominode 1992 • $16 • (12/15/1994) • **82**

Savigny-lès-Beaune La Dominode 1990 • $23 • (12/15/1992) • **88**

Savigny-lès-Beaune Les Dominodes 1996: Ripe and fruity, with black cherry, licorice and mocha flavors, showing a mouthpuckering acidity, with a juicy, fresh finish. Best from 2002 through 2006.–P.M. • $25 • (5/15/1999) • **86**

Savigny-lès-Beaune Les Vergelesses 1997: This beautiful '97 red Burgundy delivers tar and petrol aromas but also a rich, ripe, supple yet very clean and pure mouthfeel. Displays gorgeous integration of plum, blackberry and toast notes, with a racy and totally natural-tasting finish. Reflects brilliant winemaking in this vintage. Drink now through 2005.–P.M. • $28 • (9/30/1999) HR • **91**

Savigny-lès-Beaune White 1997: A beautiful, ripe and balanced white Burgundy, offering a lovely combination of toasted spice, honey, vanilla cookies and a wonderful mouthfeel with clean, ripe fruit. Drink now through 2001.–P.M. • $28 • (9/30/1999) • **87**

Savigny-lès-Beaune White Clos des Guettes 1996: Lovely, with good balance of wood, fruit and acidity. Fairly delicate, medium-bodied, it shows nice mineral, stone, pear and earth notes, and only a subtle toasted oak accent. Distinguished finish. Drink now through 2005.–P.M. • $24 • (8/31/1998) • **88**

Volnay 1990 • $28 • (12/15/1992) • **87**

Volnay Clos de la Barre 1997: A round and rich wine, with thickly ripe tannins that coat the palate. Intense and full-bodied, with mineral, smoke, dried raisin and blackberry flavors. A big wine that has length due to a firm tannin backbone. Needs cellaring. Best from 2005 through 2010.–P.M. • $44 • (9/30/1999) • **91**

Volnay Clos de la Barre 1996: Beautiful. Full-bodied and generous, with layers of cassis, black cherry, blackberry, smoke and toast in a fresh, pure package that's not overly oaked. Chewy tannins and a vibrant finish suggest cellaring. Best from 2003 through 2010.–P.M. • $37 • (5/15/1999) • **91**

Volnay-Santenots 1992 • $26 • (12/15/1994) • **83**

Vosne-Romanée 1996: Raspberries and licorice make for a nice, easy and fresh red, but it's quite compact in its tannin structure, with a tough finish. Best from 2004 through 2010.–P.M. • $33 • (5/15/1999) • **86**

Vosne-Romanée 1991 • $21 • (1/31/1994) • **83**

Vosne-Romanée 1990 • $30 • (12/15/1992) • **92**

Vosne-Romanée 1989 • $40 • (1/31/1992) • **89**

Vosne-Romanée 1985 • $33 • (3/31/1988) • **86**

Vosne-Romanée Les Beaumonts 1997: A soft texture and smooth tannins are the hallmarks of this slightly unfocused red, with modest red fruit. Drink now through 2003.–P.M. • $65 • (9/30/1999) • **83**

Vosne-Romanée Les Suchots 1996: An exceptional '96, lively, fresh, pure, showing seductive red berry, mineral and spice flavors presented in a rich, silky, full-bodied package. Elegant finish. Best from 2003 through 2015.–P.M. • $57 • (5/15/1999) • **93**

Vosne-Romanée Les Suchots 1993 • $46 • (11/15/1995) • **88**

Vosne-Romanée Les Suchots 1991 • $34 • (1/31/1994) • **81**

Vosne-Romanée Les Suchots 1990 • $49 • (12/15/1992) • **88**

JAFFELIN

Aloxe-Corton 1993 • $20 • (11/15/1995) • **74**

Aloxe-Corton 1992 • $19 • (12/15/1994) • **81**

Aloxe-Corton 1989 • $27 • (1/31/1992) • **89**

Auxey-Duresses Red 1993 • $12 • (11/15/1995) • **74**

Auxey-Duresses Red 1991 • $12 • (1/31/1994) • **79**

Auxey-Duresses Red 1990 • $16 • (12/15/1992) • **84**

Auxey-Duresses Red 1989 • $16 • (1/31/1992) • **85**

Beaujolais Nouveau 1999: This shows good structure for a Nouveau, with ripe plum and blackberry flavors and enough grip to match with lighter foods. Drink now.–T.M. • $9 • (1/01/2000) • **84**

Beaujolais-Villages Domaine de Riberolles 1994 • $8 • (6/15/1995) • **76**

Beaujolais-Villages Domaine de Riberolles 1993 • $7 • (6/30/1994) • **84**

Beaune Champs Pimont 1993 • $19 • (11/15/1995) • **73**

Beaune Champs Pimont 1992 • $22 • (12/15/1994) • **82**

Beaune Champs Pimont 1991 • $22 • (1/31/1994) • **85**

Beaune Champs Pimont 1990 • $25 • (12/15/1992) • **90**

Beaune Hospices de Beaune Cuvée Clos des Avaux 1986 • $65 • (12/31/1988) • **85**

Beaune Les Bressandes 1990 • $27 • (12/15/1992) • **87**

Beaune Les Bressandes 1989 • $28 • (1/31/1992) • **85**

Beaune Les Champimonts 1989 • $27 • (1/31/1992) • **89**

Bourgogne du Chapitre 1993 • $10 • (11/15/1995) • **78**

Bourgogne du Châpitre 1990 • $11 • (12/15/1992) • **82**

Bourgogne du Châpitre 1989 • $10 • (1/31/1992) • **83**

Bourgogne du Châpitre 1986 • $18 • (12/31/1988) • **77**

Brouilly 1994 • $12 • (7/31/1995) • **78**

Brouilly 1993 • $12 • (6/30/1994) • **77**

Brouilly 1992 • $11 • (6/30/1994) • **72**

Chambertin Le Chambertin 1986 • $65 • (12/31/1988) • **89**

Chambertin Le Chambertin 1983 • $48 • (4/16/1986) • **93**

Chambolle-Musigny 1993 • $24 • (11/15/1995) • **78**

Chambolle-Musigny 1989 • $28 • (1/31/1992) • **89**

Chambolle-Musigny 1988 • $32 • (12/31/1990) • **88**

Chambolle-Musigny 1983 • $21 • (3/16/1986) • **81**

Charmes-Chambertin 1990 • $55 • (12/15/1992) • **92**

Charmes-Chambertin 1989 • $66 • (1/31/1992) • **87**

Charmes-Chambertin 1986 • $45 • (12/31/1988) • **77**

Chassagne-Montrachet Red 1992 • $16 • (12/15/1994) • **83**

Chassagne-Montrachet Red 1990 • $16 • (12/15/1992) • **85**

Chassagne-Montrachet Red 1989 • $18 • (1/31/1992) • **86**

Chorey-Côte de Beaune 1989 • $13 • (1/31/1992) • **75**

Clos de Vougeot 1990 • $55 • (12/15/1992) • **86**

Clos de Vougeot 1989 • $60 • (1/31/1992) • **89**

Key: SS—Spectator Selection. CS—Cellar Selection. HR—Highly Recommended. $NA—Price not available. (BT)—Barrel tasting. Ⓐ—Auction Price.
For a key to the tasters' initials, see "How to Use These Listings."
Dates in parentheses represent the issues in which the ratings were published.

Clos de Vougeot 1986 • $45 • (12/31/1988) • **77**
Clos de Vougeot 1985 • $49 • (6/15/1988) • **96**
Clos St.-Denis 1989 • $53 • (1/31/1992) • **94**
Corton 1989 • $54 • (1/31/1992) • **91**
Corton 1986 • $45 • (12/31/1988) • **87**
Corton 1983 • $45 • (4/01/1986) CS • **91**
Côte de Beaune-Villages 1989 • $14 • (1/31/1992) • **82**
Côte de Nuits-Villages 1989 • $15 • (1/31/1992) • **84**
Echézeaux 1989 • $60 • (1/31/1992) • **91**
Echézeaux 1986 • $45 • (12/31/1988) • **86**
Echézeaux 1983 • $30 • (5/01/1986) • **90**
Fixin 1993 • $17 • (11/15/1995) • **76**
Fixin 1989 • $18 • (1/31/1992) • **85**
Fleurie 1993 • $15 • (6/30/1994) • **81**
Gevrey-Chambertin 1992 • $24 • (12/15/1994) • **82**
Gevrey-Chambertin 1989 • $30 • (1/31/1992) • **88**
Gevrey-Chambertin 1988 • $25 • (8/31/1991) • **88**
Gevrey-Chambertin 1986 • $49 • (2/28/1989) • **85**
Gevrey-Chambertin 1983 • $17 • (10/01/1985) • **77**
Gevrey-Chambertin Lavaut St.-Jacques 1990 • $42 • (12/15/1992) • **91**
Gevrey-Chambertin Lavaut St.-Jacques 1989 • $40 • (1/31/1992) • **81**
Hautes-Côtes de Beaune 1993 • $12 • (11/15/1995) • **79**
Hautes-Côtes de Beaune 1992 • $13 • (12/15/1994) • **80**
Ladoix Côte de Beaune 1989 • $13 • (1/31/1992) • **85**
Monthélie 1991 • $13 • (1/31/1994) • **85**
Monthélie 1990 • $17 • (12/15/1992) • **88**
Monthélie 1989 • $19 • (1/31/1992) • **87**
Monthélie 1986 • $15 • (6/15/1989) • **79**
Morey-St.-Denis Les Ruchots 1989 • $30 • (1/31/1992) • **86**
Morgon 1994 • $11 • (7/31/1995) • **81**
Morgon 1993 • $12 • (6/30/1994) • **88**
Nuits-St.-Georges 1993 • $25 • (11/15/1995) • **74**
Nuits-St.-Georges 1992 • $25 • (12/15/1994) • **79**
Nuits-St.-Georges 1989 • $27 • (1/31/1992) • **83**
Nuits-St.-Georges 1986 • $28 • (2/28/1989) • **80**
Nuits-St.-Georges 1983 • $19 • (9/15/1986) • **72**
Nuits-St.-Georges Les Damodes 1989 • $36 • (1/31/1992) • **90**
Pernand-Vergelesses 1993 • $14 • (11/15/1995) • **82**
Pernand-Vergelesses 1991 • $13 • (1/31/1994) • **80**
Pernand-Vergelesses 1990 • $16 • (12/15/1992) • **85**
Pernand-Vergelesses 1989 • $19 • (1/31/1992) • **86**
Pommard 1991 • $20 • (1/31/1994) • **83**
Pommard 1990 • $30 • (12/15/1992) • **89**
Pommard 1989 • $33 • (1/31/1992) • **85**
Pommard 1986 • $26 • (4/30/1989) • **79**
Pommard 1985 • $38 • (3/15/1988) • **89**
Pommard 1983 • $19 • (9/15/1986) • **81**
Romanée St.-Vivant 1990 • $75 • (12/15/1992) • **93**
Romanée St.-Vivant 1989 • $80 • (1/31/1992) • **91**
Rully Red 1986 • $13 • (6/15/1989) • **77**
St.-Aubin 1989 • $14 • (1/31/1992) • **84**
Santenay 1990 • $16 • (12/15/1992) • **85**
Santenay 1989 • $17 • (1/31/1992) • **85**
Santenay Clos Rousseau 1993 • $17 • (11/15/1995) • **84**
Santenay La Maladière 1990 • $19 • (12/15/1992) • **84**
Santenay La Maladière 1989 • $20 • (1/31/1992) • **82**
Santenay La Maladière 1988 • $21 • (8/31/1991) • **84**
Santenay La Maladière 1985 • $22 • (3/15/1988) • **84**
Savigny-lès-Beaune 1989 • $18 • (1/31/1992) • **85**
Volnay 1993 • $24 • (11/15/1995) • **86**
Volnay 1992 • $20 • (12/15/1994) • **79**
Volnay 1991 • $20 • (1/31/1994) • **81**
Volnay 1990 • $24 • (12/15/1992) • **85**
Volnay 1989 • $29 • (1/31/1992) • **89**
Volnay 1988 • $30 • (8/31/1991) • **88**
Volnay 1986 • $27 • (4/30/1989) • **86**
Volnay 1985 • $30 • (3/15/1988) • **88**
Volnay 1983 • $17 • (10/16/1985) • **92**
Vosne-Romanée 1989 • $29 • (1/31/1992) • **86**
Vosne-Romanée 1986 • $30 • (2/28/1989) • **79**

JAMELLES, LES

Cabernet Sauvignon Vin de Pays d'Oc 1998: Light- to medium-bodied, with good plum and cherry flavors. A tobacco note carries through to the finish. Drink now.–K.M. • $7 • (5/15/2000) • **82**
Cabernet Sauvignon Vin de Pays d'Oc 1996: Good Cabernet flavors of plum and cherry, with a nice herbal touch. There's a meaty aroma, and it has cinnamon on the finish. Drink now.–K.M. • $8 • (11/15/1998) • **84**
Cabernet Sauvignon Vin de Pays d'Oc 1994 • $7 • (10/31/1995) • **84**
Cabernet Sauvignon Vin de Pays d'Oc 1993 • $7 • (2/28/1995) • **82**
Chardonnay Vin de Pays d'Oc 1998: A workmanlike Chardonnay from the south of France, with baked apple and spice aromas and flavors. Drink now.–K.M. • $7 • (5/15/2000) • **82**
Chardonnay Vin de Pays d'Oc 1997: Looking for a nice French white at a reasonable price? How about this focused Chardonnay offering concentrated ripe apple, pear and spice flavors, unveiling minerally notes that linger on the finish. Drink now.–K.M. • $8 • (11/15/1998) • **85**
Cinsault Rosé Vin de Pays d'Oc 1998: Has decent berry and cherry character, finishing on a watermelon note. Drink now.–K.M. • $7 • (5/15/2000) • **82**
Cinsault Rosé Vin de Pays d'Oc 1997: Crisp and fruity, with good cherry and berry flavors and a clean finish. Drink now.–K.M. • $7 • (11/15/1998) • **81**
Merlot Vin de Pays d'Oc 1998: Fresh and lively, with plenty of red plum and berry flavors and a modestly chewy texture. A good quaffer. Drink now.–K.M. • $7 • (5/15/2000) • **84**
Merlot Vin de Pays d'Oc 1996: Simple in flavor and light in texture, this is a lean but drinkable red. Drink now. • $8 • (10/31/1998) • **76**
Merlot Vin de Pays d'Oc 1995 • $7 • (12/15/1996) • **85**
Merlot Vin de Pays d'Oc 1994 • $7 • (10/31/1995) • **82**
Merlot Vin de Pays d'Oc 1993 • $7 • (2/28/1995) • **77**
Merlot Vin de Pays d'Oc 1991 • $7 • (7/31/1993) • **84**
Mourvèdre Vin de Pays d'Oc 1993 • $7 • (10/31/1995) • **75**
Syrah Vin de Pays d'Oc 1997: Decent cherry flavors are muted by a stewy quality.–K.M. • $7 • (5/15/2000) • **77**
Syrah Vin de Pays d'Oc 1996: Has a beefy aroma and plenty of mineral and iodinelike flavors. Firm, with a slightly tart finish. Needs time to smooth out. Drink through 2001–K.M. • $8 • (11/15/1998) • **83**
Syrah Vin de Pays d'Oc 1994 • $7 • (10/31/1995) • **84**
Syrah Vin de Pays d'Oc 1992 • $7 • (7/31/1995) • **80**
Syrah Vin de Pays d'Oc 1991 • $7 • (3/31/1994) • **84**

JAMET, JEAN-PAUL & JEAN-LUC

Côte-Rôtie 1996: Stunning, this dark-colored, savage wine is unique in its aromatic profile, with black olive paste, blackberry, cassis, mineral, stone dust, rose and violet character, all presented in a full-bodied, ripe and lush package. Tempting upon release, but has enough excellent acidity to hold for years. Drink now through 2008.–P.M. • $40 • (11/15/1998) • **94**
Côte-Rôtie 1994 • $36 • (10/15/1997) • **91**
Côte-Rôtie 1991 • $39 • (5/31/1994) • **90**
Côte-Rôtie 1990 • $39 • (5/31/1994) • **92**
Côte-Rôtie 1988 • $49 • (6/15/1993) • **78**

JANASSE, DOMAINE DE LA

Châteauneuf-du-Pape 1997: Light and herbal, with some tough tannins, modest black cherry flavor and a chewy finish.–P.M. • $30 • (8/31/1999) • **78**
Châteauneuf-du-Pape 1995 • $30 • (10/15/1997) • **87**
Châteauneuf-du-Pape Chaupin 1997: Gorgeous, showing a superb, full-bodied, ripe silkiness. Medium-intense, but what's there makes for a balanced buffet of smoke, mineral, cassis, black pepper and toasty notes. Lovely finish. Drink now through 2005.–P.M. • $35 • (8/31/1999) • **90**
Châteauneuf-du-Pape Chaupin 1995 • $22 • (10/15/1997) • **88**
Châteauneuf-du-Pape Chaupin 1994 • $20 • (2/28/1997) • **84**
Châteauneuf-du-Pape Vieilles Vignes 1997: Somewhat tough and lean in style, but there's good focus on the fruit and the tannins and acidity give it a boost on the finish. Drink now through 2002.–P.M. • $40 • (8/31/1999) • **81**
Châteauneuf-du-Pape Vieilles Vignes 1996: A fresh and intense *terroir* wine. Medium-bodied, traditional-style, delivering plenty of roasted game, toasted peanut, mineral, jalapeño pepper and gazpacho aromas and flavors. Despite the round tannins, it needs time to soften. Best from 2003 through 2008.–P.M. • $22 • (11/15/1998) • **89**
Châteauneuf-du-Pape Vieilles Vignes 1994 • $40 • (10/15/1997) • **89**
Châteauneuf-du-Pape White 1998: Beautifully ripe. Clean and fresh, but also very round, supple and fat, showing a lovely, hedonistic mouthfeel, with butter, cream, honey and ripe fruit. Balanced finish. Drink now through 2008.–P.M. • $30 • (12/15/1999) • **89**
Châteauneuf-du-Pape White 1996 • $28 • (10/15/1997) • **84**
Châteauneuf-du-Pape White Cuvée Spéciale 1996 • $40 • (10/15/1997) • **83**
Châteauneuf-du-Pape White Prestige 1997: Fat on the midpalate, with quince and white apricot character, this white delivers a natural sweetness that's appealing. Best from 2001 through 2005.–P.M. • $35 • (12/15/1999) • **85**

FRANCE

JANASSE, DOMAINE DE LA

Côtes du Rhône 1998: Ripe and full-bodied, a serious Rhône red with a supple texture. Dark, with intense plum, blood orange, cacao and smoke. Supple tannins, but the finish has an interesting chewiness. Drink through 2004–P.M. • $12 • (12/15/1999) • **87**

Côtes du Rhône 1997: Light and diluted, tasting a bit oaky, with modest fruit.–P.M. • $12 • (11/15/1999) • **74**

Côtes du Rhône 1996: Pretty. Shows nice oak-inspired floral, spice and grilled bread character. Light-bodied, the finely tuned wood accents take the edge of the tannins to make this supple. Drink now.–P.M. • $10 • (11/15/1998) • **82**

Côtes du Rhône 1995 • $10 • (10/15/1997) • **80**

Côtes du Rhône Les Garrigues 1997: A red that has personality—a rustic one. But there's fruit, earth, herbs and spice; the complexity deepens on the palate to culminate in a multilayered, harmonious finish. Tannins are, well, rustic. Drink now through 2003.–P.M. • $20 • (11/15/1999) • **88**

Côtes du Rhône Les Garrigues 1996 • $20 • (10/15/1997) • **83**

Côtes du Rhône Les Garrigues 1995 • $20 • (10/15/1997) • **86**

Côtes du Rhône Les Garrigues 1994 • $NA • (10/15/1997) • **80**

Côtes du Rhône Rosé 1998: With good cherry and raspberry flavors, showing decent acidity, this medium-bodied rosé is holding together quite nicely. Shows a certain finesse. Drink now.–P.M. • $12 • (12/15/1999) • **86**

Côtes du Rhône-Villages 1997: Some nice toasted oak, floral, mocha and blackberry notes offer an interesting, ripe-tasting flavor spectrum, along with a freshly balanced finish that lingers. Drink now.–P.M. • $15 • (11/15/1999) • **82**

JANIN, PAUL

Beaujolais-Villages Domaine des Vignes des Jumeaux 1994 • $10 • (9/15/1996) • **84**

Beaujolais-Villages Domaine des Vignes des Jumeaux 1992 • $9 • (6/30/1994) • **80**

Moulin-à-Vent 1985 • $13 • (10/31/1987) • **85**

Moulin-à-Vent Domaine des Vignes du Tremblay 1993 • $10 • (9/15/1997) • **78**

Moulin-à-Vent Domaine des Vignes du Tremblay 1991 • $16 • (1/31/1995) • **89**

JANODET, JACKY

Beaujolais-Villages Domaine Les Fines Graves 1996: Black cherry flavors have good depth in this round yet firm red, and pleasant spicy notes emerge on the finish. Balanced and clean. Drink now.–T.M. • $15 • (8/31/1998) • **83**

Chénas Domaine Les Fines Graves 1996: This chewy red has good structure, with firm tannins and some concentration, but the plum flavors are dominated by earthy and herbal notes. Drink now.–T.M. • $12 • (8/31/1998) • **81**

Morgon 1991 • $12 • (6/15/1994) HR • **90**

Moulin-à-Vent 1991 • $13 • (6/15/1994) • **84**

Moulin-à-Vent Domaine Les Fines Graves 1997: Ripe and lush, offering cherry and plum, but lacks freshness and structure, ending on an earthy, diffuse note. Drink now.–B.S. • $18 • (10/15/1999) • **82**

Moulin-à-Vent Domaine Les Fines Graves 1996 • $15 • (5/31/1998) • **85**

Moulin-à-Vent Domaine les Fines Graves 1994 • $14 • (9/15/1996) • **83**

Moulin-à-Vent Domaine les Fines Graves 1992 • $17 • (7/31/1995) • **74**

JASMIN, ROBERT

Côte-Rôtie 1996: Clean, pure and fruit-driven, showing lovely cherry, wild berry and some earthy complexity. Medium-bodied, and while much better than a previously reviewed sample, it still turns slightly tough and a bit green on the finish. Drink now.–P.M. • $35 • (11/15/1998) • **85**

Côte-Rôtie 1995 • $35 • (10/15/1997) • **82**

Côte-Rôtie 1994 • $32 • (10/15/1997) • **79**

Côte-Rôtie 1992 • $42 • (5/31/1994) • **84**

Côte-Rôtie 1991 • $43 • (5/31/1994) • **82**

Côte-Rôtie 1990 • $45 • (5/31/1994) • **86**

Côte-Rôtie 1988 • $32 • (12/31/1990) • **89**

Côte-Rôtie 1987 • $30 • (6/30/1990) • **90**

Key: SS—Spectator Selection. CS—Cellar Selection. HR—Highly Recommended. $NA—Price not available. (BT)—Barrel tasting. Ⓐ—Auction Price. For a key to the tasters' initials, see "How to Use These Listings."
Dates in parentheses represent the issues in which the ratings were published.

JAU, CHATEAU DE

Côtes du Roussillon 1988 • $6 • (8/31/1991) • **75**

Côtes du Roussillon White 1997: Dried herbal and oniony flavors dominate this nicely balanced white wine that's reminiscent of Sauvignon Blanc.–K.M. • $11 • (11/15/1998) • **82**

Côtes du Roussillon White 1996 • $10 • (9/30/1997) • **82**

Côtes du Roussillon-Villages 1997: Juicy-tasting yet a bit light, this red has bright plum and berry flavors, with spicy notes on the finish. Drink now.–K.M. • $11 • (11/30/1998) • **82**

Côtes du Roussillon-Villages 1995 • $10 • (9/30/1997) • **85**

Muscat de Rivesaltes 1995 • $11/375 ml. • (5/31/1997) • **90**

Vin de Pays d'Oc Red Le Jaja de Jau Black Label 1997: Very light, with flavors reminiscent of strawberry soda. Syrah and Grenache.–K.M. • $7 • (12/15/1998) • **73**

Vin de Pays d'Oc Red Le Jaja de Jau Black Label 1996 • $7 • (10/31/1997) • **80**

Vin de Pays d'Oc Red Le Jaja de Jau Blue Label 1997: Juicy, with strawberry, cherry and even bananalike notes. Cabernet Sauvignon and Merlot. Drink now.–K.M. • $7 • (12/15/1998) • **81**

Vin de Pays d'Oc Red Le Jaja de Jau Blue Label 1996 • $7 • (12/15/1997) • **83**

Vin de Pays d'Oc Red Le Jaja de Jau Blue Label 1996 • $7 • (12/15/1997) • **83**

Vin de Pays d'Oc White Le Jaja de Jau Green Label 1997: An awkward white with a distinctive herbal edge and little fruit flavor to back it up. Vermentino and Roussanne.–K.M. • $7 • (11/15/1998) • **75**

Vin de Pays d'Oc White Le Jaja de Jau Green Label 1996 • $7 • (10/31/1997) • **80**

Vin de Pays d'Oc Rosé Le Jaja de Jau Purple Label 1996 • $7 • (9/15/1997) • **82**

Vin de Pays des Côtes Catalanes Le Jaja de Jau 1993 • $7 • (9/15/1994) • **83**

JAUME, DOMAINE

Côtes du Rhône Cuvée des Côtes 1995: A bit earthy, with decent red- and blackberry flavors, plum, cedar and mushroom tones. Tannins are a bit rough on the slightly hot finish.–P.M. • $12 • (11/15/1998) • **79**

Côtes du Rhône Vini Sober 1995: Fairly light, a bit oxidized, with some mushroom shadings to the modest plum and red berry flavors.–P.M. • $10 • (11/15/1998) • **77**

JAUMIER, DENIS

Quincy 1996: Smells mature, showing a marzipan aroma followed by cooked apple and almond flavors. The acidity is high and very prominent on the finish. Drink now.–B.S. • $13 • (11/15/1998) • **82**

JAVILLIER, PATRICK

Bourgogne White Cuvée des Forgets 1998: Ripe but rather elegant. Medium-bodied, it displays lemon tart, honey, butterscotch, ripe pear character and a slight malic, yogurt flavor. Silky at midpalate. Tasted twice, with consistent notes. Drink now through 2004.–P.M. • $23 • (5/31/2000) • **87**

Bourgogne White Cuvée des Forgets 1995 • $20 • (8/31/1997) • **87**

Bourgogne White Cuvée des Forgets Cuvée Spéciale 1997: Fairly lush and sweet, this medium-bodied, drink-me-now white has lovely pineapple, honey and lemon. Drink now.–P.M. • $23 • (9/30/1999) • **85**

Bourgogne White Cuvée des Forgets Cuvée Spéciale 1996: Very crisp, medium-bodied and fresh, with straightforward lemon and fresh herbs. The chewy, acidic finish begs for a bit more ripeness. Drink now through 2005.–P.M. • $22 • (5/31/1999) • **80**

Bourgogne White Cuvée Oligocène 1995 • $24 • (8/31/1997) • **80**

Bourgogne White Cuvée Oligocène Cuvée Spéciale 1997: A serious wine from the Bourgogne Blanc appellation. Crisp but hinting at smoke, toast, honey and passion fruit, this is a nice little white to drink on release. Succulent finish. Drink now.–P.M. • $30 • (9/30/1999) • **84**

Bourgogne White Cuvée Oligocène Cuvée Spéciale 1996: Very minerally, with a slight cooked apple note, this is full-bodied and ripe, lacking a bit of class but delivering clean, vibrant citrus flavors. Best from 2004 through 2010.–P.M. • $28 • (5/31/1999) • **87**

Meursault 1995 • $35 • (8/31/1997) • **86**

Meursault Au Murger de Monthélie 1995 • $45 • (8/31/1997) • **86**

Meursault Clos du Cromin 1998: Delicate Meursault, offering some smoky, pearlike notes. Light-bodied, not so intense, but pleasant. Drink now through 2002.–P.M. • $45 • (5/31/2000) • **85**

Meursault Clos du Cromin 1996: This refined, full-bodied white delivers caressing texture from the mineral concentration, yet it's crisp and lemony, showing just a touch of rusticity on the otherwise attractive finish. Best from 2006 through 2020.–P.M. • $44 • (5/31/1999) • **93**

FRANCE

Meursault Clos du Cromin Cuvée Spéciale Mise Tardive 1995 • $40 • (8/31/1997) • **91**

Meursault Cuvée Tête de Murger 1998: Pleasant and elegant Meursault. Balanced in its light-style way, offering deftly dosed toasted oak, some pear and honey. Drink now through 2002.–P.M. • $70 • (5/31/2000) • **88**

Meursault Cuvée Tête de Murger 1996: Beautiful. Imposing, intense and concentrated, this heavyweight white Burgundy hits one punch after another—lemon, honey, mocha, toast, butter—in a movement of sheer harmony. The finish is clean, fresh and long—and refined. Drink now through 2010.–P.M. • $70 • (5/31/1999) • **95**

Meursault Les Casse-Têtes 1995 • $45 • (8/31/1997) • **75**

Meursault Les Charmes 1995 • $50 • (8/31/1997) • **90**

Meursault Les Clous 1998: Rather thick-textured Meursault, with a floral aroma, chalky, minerally character and good fruit. Has a creamy midpalate and some fresh fruit that takes on power at the finish. Drink now through 2004.–P.M. • $48 • (5/31/2000) • **88**

Meursault Les Clous 1996: Medium-bodied and crisp, with green apple and floral flavors. Tight mineral structure is accented by very toasty notes. Should improve and soften with age. Best from 2004 through 2010.–P.M. • $47 • (5/31/1999) • **87**

Meursault Les Gillets Mise Tardive 1996: A bit crisp, lacking the generous flavors expected in a fine '96. Shows herb, toasted oak, butter and green apple, with a drying character.–P.M. • $44 • (5/31/1999) • **78**

Meursault Les Narvaux 1996: Heavyhanded, with an overoaked, lemony, appley character that's no fun to drink because it's so astringent and hot.–P.M. • $48 • (5/31/1999) • **73**

Meursault Les Narvaux 1995 • $NA • (5/31/1997) • **90**

Meursault Les Narvaux Cuvée Spéciale 1997: Big and blowsy, lacking finesse and turning tart on the finish. There's little substance to this oaky wine and its shallow, tart interior.–P.M. • $53 • (9/30/1999) • **75**

Meursault Les Tillets 1995 • $39 • (8/31/1997) • **89**

Meursault Les Tillets Cuvée Spéciale 1997: Racy and ripe, showing a range of flavors—pear tart, toasted oak, dough, spice, vanilla, lemon and mineral—all presented in an attractive, medium-bodied, succulent package. Drink now through 2003.–P.M. • $45 • (9/30/1999) • **87**

Puligny-Montrachet Les Levrons 1998: Very ripe and full-bodied. Shows dried apricot, floral, honeysuckle character. Fun to taste, it lacks a bit of terroir character (and midpalate concentration), but delivers a nice finish with toasted oak notes. Drink now through 2006.–P.M. • $65 • (5/31/2000) • **88**

Puligny-Montrachet Les Levrons 1996: A full-throttle white Burgundy, this delivers heavyweight punches of very toasted, spicy, buttery, mocha-flavored oak, all enveloped by ripe fruit. Full-bodied and opulent, but it's a bit appley and burning on the finish. Best from 2005 through 2010.–P.M. • $48 • (5/31/1999) • **85**

Puligny-Montrachet Les Levrons 1995: Thick and exotic, megaripe and superopulent, this borders on late-harvest with its exotic peach, floral, honeysuckle, ripe pear and pielike flavors. Remains anchored in the soil with a chalky, minerally, chewy character, and has more fruit than oak on the fresh, lemony, minute-long finish. Drink now through 2005.–P.M. • $45 • (8/31/1998) • **90**

Savigny-lès-Beaune White Les Montchenevoy 1997: Clean and pure, round on the palate, with a core of racy, lime-tasting acidity throughout. Kicks with spicy, toasted, buttery intensity. No taste buds will be asleep after this wake-up call. Drink through 2005–P.M. • $35 • (9/30/1999) • **86**

Savigny-lès-Beaune White Les Montchenevoy 1996: Clean and firm, with a minerally grip in front of spicy oak, lemon, butter, mocha and green apple. Vibrant and medium-bodied, with a crisp finish. Best from 2003 through 2010.–P.M. • $32 • (5/31/1999) • **86**

Savigny-lès-Beaune White Les Montchenevoy 1995 • $25 • (8/31/1997) • **87**

JAYER-GILLES

Bourgogne Aligoté 1997: Straightforward, with green apple, grilled pineapple and toasted oak notes. A pleasure to drink, but lacks a bit of class. Drink now.–P.M. • $16 • (5/31/1999) • **84**

Bourgogne Aligoté 1996 • $14 • (5/31/1998) • **80**

Côte de Nuits-Villages 1997: This firm, virile '97 has smoke, clove and bacon fat aromas, with cherry in the background. A bit tough and tannic at this stage, with plenty of fruit and concentration underneath. Best from 2001 through 2006.–B.S. • $48 • (9/30/1999) • **87**

Côte de Nuits-Villages 1996: Real class and depth. Seductive, smoky blackberry aromas segue into a rich, fleshy, spicy red with tangy acidity and ripe tannins that persist through the long finish. Best from 2002 through 2008.–B.S. • $45 • (9/30/1998) • **92**

Echézeaux du Dessus 1997: A beautiful '97, showing cassis, game and blackberry character, presented in a supple package that delivers excellent intensity for the vintage. Flavors linger on the finish. Drink now through 2007.–P.M. • $155 • (9/30/1999) • **90**

Echézeaux du Dessus 1996: Monumental. Explosive beefy aromas give way to a roasted, smoky palate of coffee, blackberry and cassis. Super-refined and elegant on the finish, with masses of tannins and laserlike intensity. This is simply a stunning wine, the kind that inspires passion for Burgundy. Best from 2005 through 2015.–B.S. • $140 • (9/30/1998) • **99**

Hautes-Côtes de Beaune 1997: Rich and unctuous, with distinctive toasted and grilled notes backing up the fresh raspberry and cherry flavors that engulf this rather firm and crisp red. Best from 2002 through 2006.–P.M. • $35 • (9/30/1999) • **86**

Hautes-Côtes de Beaune 1996: Well made. A pretty wine, showing lush, attractive texture, with cassis, game and earth character. This is toasted, smoky and intense, and needs time to show it all. Best After 2003.–P.M. • $33 • (9/30/1998) • **87**

Hautes-Côtes de Beaune White 1997: This supple '97 shows a subtle combination of butter, pear and perfumey wood. Turns a bit hot on the finish.–P.M. • $30 • (5/31/1999) • **79**

Hautes-Côtes de Beaune White 1996 • $24 • (5/31/1998) • **79**

Hautes-Côtes de Nuits 1997: Smoke, herb and plum aromas and flavors are interwoven with the supple texture and fine yet firm tannins. Lingering aftertaste. Drink now through 2003.–B.S. • $35 • (9/30/1999) • **83**

Hautes-Côtes de Nuits 1996: Supertoasted, gamy and ripe red Burgundy, well made, lush and silky, thick and full-bodied, with notes of cassis and smoky grilled meat. A lovely, intense wine with a balanced finish. Drink now through 2005.–P.M. • $33 • (9/30/1998) • **89**

Hautes-Côtes de Nuits White 1997: Beautifully smooth, clean and ripe, showing a lovely harmony that seduces the palate; spice, cloves, honey, pear tart, there is a lot going on, and it's very fresh and pure on the balanced finish. Much better than previously reviewed. Drink now through 2010.–P.M. • $30 • (9/30/1999) • **90**

Hautes-Côtes de Nuits White 1996 • $24 • (5/31/1998) • **85**

Nuits-St.-Georges Les Damodes 1997: Lavishly oaked, showing spice, smoke, game and cooked black cherry, yet there's good concentration underneath and fine structure, acidity and tannin. Excellent length and harmony on the finish. Best from 2001 through 2006.–B.S. • $90 • (9/30/1999) • **89**

Nuits-St.-Georges Les Damodes 1996: Incredibly sexy. Beaucoup de petrol here, with smoky, toasty oak, spice, black cherry and mineral notes all wrapped in a muscular structure. Excellent concentration and a long finish of sweet fruit and ripe tannins. Best from 2001 through 2006.–B.S. • $85 • (9/30/1998) • **91**

Nuits-St.-Georges Les Hauts Poirets 1997: Game and cassis mingle beautifully in this exotic wine, but don't expect much intensity, just a caress of soft tannins, red berry flavors and sufficient acidity. Drink now through 2003.–P.M. • $80 • (9/30/1999) • **87**

Nuits-St.-Georges Les Hauts Poirets 1996: Incredible intensity from start to finish. Petrol, blackberry and mocha highlight this racy, sauvage Nuits. Great concentration and persistence of flavor on the palate. Best from 2003 through 2010.–B.S. • $75 • (9/30/1998) • **92**

JAYER-GILLES, ROBERT

Bourgogne Aligoté 1995 • $14 • (8/31/1997) • **74**
Côte de Nuits-Villages 1995 • $40 • (11/15/1997) • **88**
Côte de Nuits-Villages 1994 • $30 • (11/15/1996) • **80**
Côte de Nuits-Villages 1993 • $36 • (11/15/1995) • **90**
Côte de Nuits-Villages 1992 • $28 • (12/15/1994) • **82**
Côte de Nuits-Villages 1991 • $29 • (1/31/1994) • **82**
Côte de Nuits-Villages 1990 • $34 • (12/15/1992) • **90**
Echézeaux 1994 • $115 • (11/15/1996) • **93**
Echézeaux 1992 • $110 • (12/15/1994) • **89**
Echézeaux 1989 • $101 • (1/31/1992) • **94**
Echézeaux du Dessus 1995 • $150 • (11/15/1997) • **95**
Echézeaux du Dessus 1993 • $135 • (11/15/1995) • **95**
Echézeaux du Dessus 1991 • $85 • (1/31/1994) • **91**
Echézeaux du Dessus 1990 • $100 • (12/15/1992) • **97**
Hautes-Côtes de Beaune 1995 • $30 • (11/15/1997) • **87**
Hautes-Côtes de Beaune 1994 • $25 • (11/15/1996) • **82**
Hautes-Côtes de Beaune 1993 • $22 • (11/15/1995) • **90**
Hautes-Côtes de Beaune 1990 • $24 • (12/15/1992) • **80**
Hautes-Côtes de Beaune 1989 • $24 • (1/31/1992) • **84**
Hautes-Côtes de Beaune 1988 • $26 • (5/15/1991) • **88**
Hautes-Côtes de Beaune White 1995 • $27 • (8/31/1997) • **70**
Hautes-Côtes de Nuits 1995 • $30 • (11/15/1997) • **84**
Hautes-Côtes de Nuits 1994 • $25 • (11/15/1996) • **82**
Hautes-Côtes de Nuits 1993 • $22 • (5/15/1996) • **88**

JAYER-GILLES, ROBERT

Hautes-Côtes de Nuits 1992 • $23 • (12/15/1994) • **82**
Hautes-Côtes de Nuits 1989 • $24 • (1/31/1992) • **86**
Hautes-Côtes de Nuits White 1995 • $27 • (8/31/1997) • **85**
Nuits-St.-Georges Les Damodes 1994 • $70 • (11/15/1996) • **90**
Nuits-St.-Georges Les Damodes 1993 • $85 • (11/15/1995) • **92**
Nuits-St.-Georges Les Damodes 1992 • $70 • (12/15/1994) • **85**
Nuits-St.-Georges Les Damodes 1991 • $55 • (1/31/1994) • **88**
Nuits-St.-Georges Les Hauts Poirets 1995 • $85 • (11/15/1997) • **92**
Nuits-St.-Georges Les Hauts Poirets 1994 • $65 • (11/15/1996) • **87**
Nuits-St.-Georges Les Poirets 1993 • $70 • (11/15/1995) • **93**
Nuits-St.-Georges Les Poirets 1992 • $58 • (12/15/1994) • **84**
Nuits-St.-Georges Les Poirets 1991 • $48 • (1/31/1994) • **86**
Nuits-St.-Georges Les Poirets 1990 • $48 • (12/15/1992) • **97**

JEAN, PIERRE

Bordeaux Supérieur 1989 • $9 • (7/15/1992) • **79**
Bordeaux Supérieur 1988 • $8 • (7/31/1991) • **75**
Cabernet Sauvignon Vin de Pays de l'Aude 1996: Thin-tasting, with light cherry flavors and a dry finish.–K.M. • $6 • (7/31/1999) • **74**
Merlot Vin de Pays de l'Aude 1997: Simple, with only modest cherry flavors and drying tannins on the finish.–K.M. • $6 • (7/31/1999) • **74**
St.-Emilion 1988 • $10 • (6/30/1991) • **85**

JEAN DE GOTH, CHATEAU

Graves White 1996: Straightforward Bordeaux white. Subtle aromas of apple and honeydew, with hints of oak. Medium-bodied, with lemon and lime flavors and a light, crisp aftertaste. Slight hint of oxidation on the finish. Drink now.–J.S. • $NA • (1/01/1999) • **81**

JENARD

Cabernet Sauvignon Vin de Pays d'Oc 1994 • $7 • (12/15/1996) • **81**
Merlot Vin de Pays d'Oc 1994 • $7 • (12/15/1996) • **83**

JOBARD, CHARLES & REMI

Meursault Le Porusot-Dessus 1995 • $45 • (5/31/1997) • **94**
Meursault Les Charmes 1995 • $50 • (8/31/1997) • **84**
Meursault Les Chevalières 1995 • $35 • (5/31/1997) • **90**
Meursault Les Genevrières 1995 • $47 • (5/31/1997) • **93**
Meursault Sous la Velle 1995 • $33 • (5/31/1997) • **90**

JOBARD, FRANCOIS

Bourgogne White 1996: Dry, ungenerous, herbal and astringent.–P.M. • $26 • (5/31/1999) • **74**
Meursault Charmes 1996: Concentrated and fat, showing honey and nut aromas and flavors. The richness and breadth are underscored by vibrant acidity that carries the flavors to a lingering finish. Drink now through 2004.–B.S. • $72 • (5/31/1999) • **87**
Meursault En la Barre 1997: Pungent petrollike and earthy aromas might be tolerable if the decent midpalate concentration weren't overrun by wood. Tasted twice, with consistent notes.–P.M. • $44 • (5/31/2000) • **79**
Meursault En la Barre 1995: A great Meursault village wine. Seamless in its opulent, lush, thick and fat texture, it is decadently flavored with ripe peach, pear, honey and spice. Offers earth, truffle, matchstick, flint and mineral complexity that's a downright aphrodisiac. Drink now through 2020.–P.M. • $45 • (8/31/1998) • **93**
Meursault Genevrières 1997: Once past the funny earth and matchstick aromas, you're in for a treat of a wine: rich, thick, dense, concentrated, with ripe peaches and, above all, a superseductive and silky texture. The *terroir* rears its distinctive head on the finish. But be warned: the nose on this wine is an "acquired taste." Drink now through 2002.–P.M. • $72 • (5/31/2000) • **90**
Meursault Genevrières 1996: Smells honeyed and nutty, with a broad, chamomile tea element emerging on the palate. Round, solid and firmly structured, delivering a mineral edge that remains on the finish. Drink through 2006–B.S. • $60 Ⓐ • (5/31/1999) • **90**
Meursault Genevrières 1995: Amazing. Uncompromisingly taut, with a firm backbone of toasted oak, impeccably pure, ripe fruit and bursting acidity, this is anything but a "soft" '95 white Burgundy. In fact, it's tough as hell. But it has supple, thick, opulent texture, and offers loads of pleasure once you get the hang o' this *terroir*-driven white Burgundy. Best after 2008. –P.M. • $76 Ⓐ • (8/31/1998) • **96**
Meursault Poruzot 1997: Beautiful Meursault. Smells a bit pungent (matchstick, earthy) but tastes wonderful. Full-bodied, it has density on the palate, delivering a chalky, chewy texture but also good vibrant acidity and some concentrated fruit character. Lingering finish. Needs time. Best from 2002 through 2010.–P.M. • $66 • (5/31/2000) • **90**
Meursault Poruzot 1996: This really blossoms in the glass. Tasting more of minerals than fruit, and densely textured, offering nuances of honey and apple, allied to firm acidity and good length. Drink now through 2005. –B.S. • $65 • (5/31/1999) • **89**
Meursault Poruzot 1995: One of the most intense '95 Meursaults reviewed. Bursts on the palate like a volcano in eruption—boom! boom! boom!—delivering hot spicy notes here, burnt butter there, toasted bread, ripe pear, honey and mineral flavors over there. Lacks finesse, but what character! Cellar first. Best after 2010.–P.M. • $65 • (8/31/1998) • **95**
Meursault-Blagny 1996: Smells and tastes nutty, with breadth of flavor, yet firm and the fruit is submerged beneath the structure. Drink now.–B.S. • $NA • (5/31/1999) • **83**
Puligny-Montrachet Le Trézin 1996: This has vibrant, rich and honeyed aromas, but an underlying tartness creeps in midpalate to the finish, leaving it one-dimensional and simple. Finishes short. Drink through 2004–B.S. • $NA • (5/31/1999) • **81**

JOBARD, REMI

Bourgogne White 1997: Attractive. Good lemon, honey and pear flavors stay clean from start to finish to deliver a beautiful Bourgogne-category white that's round and satisfying. Drink now.–P.M. • $28 • (5/31/1999) • **84**
Bourgogne White 1996 • $20 • (5/31/1998) • **90**
Meursault En Luraule 1997: Interesting ripe aromas, with floral, apricot and tropical character. Medium-intense and medium-bodied, with a mineral touch on the appealingly sweet-tasting finish. Drink now through 2002.–P.M. • $48 • (5/31/1999) • **85**
Meursault En Luraule 1996 • $37 • (5/31/1998) • **89**
Meursault Le Poruzot-Dessus 1997: Clean and flavorful, offering butter, lemon, honey and butterscotch flavors. Medium-bodied, it tastes ripe and delicious on the juicy, succulent, toasty finish. Drink now through 2005.–P.M. • $68 • (5/31/1999) • **87**
Meursault Le Poruzot-Dessus 1996 • $52 • (5/31/1998) • **90**
Meursault Les Charmes 1997: Round and thick-textured, with floral, butter, apricot and peach flavors, tasting like an exotic, full-bodied Viognier. Long, satisfying finish. Drink now through 2005.–P.M. • $68 • (5/31/1999) • **87**
Meursault Les Charmes 1996: A great '96. Thick, rich and ripe, exotically flavored with honey, floral, peach, cinnamon, toasted oak, spice and buttery notes, all presented in a lush, opulent package that verges on late harvest. Of full body, it caresses the palate with its smooth texture. Best from 2005.–P.M. • $59 • (8/31/1998) • **95**
Meursault Les Chevalières 1997: Light-bodied, with modest butter and fruit flavors and a round, agreeable finish. Drink now.–P.M. • $48 • (5/31/1999) • **82**
Meursault Les Chevalières 1996: Deceptively good village Meursault. A thick, ripe and full-bodied wine that starts out showing lots of butter, butterscotch, toasted oak, earth and pear notes, fanning out with oily texture before taking off like a rocket on the long, mouth-smacking finish with a fresh burst of intense lemon-lime flavors. Tasted twice, with consistent notes. Best from 2005.–P.M. • $40 • (8/31/1998) • **91**
Meursault Les Genevrières 1997: Flavorful, clean and focused on lime, spice and elegant texture, this medium-bodied, attractive, genteel Chardonnay lacks the energy of an outstanding performance. Should improve with short-term cellaring. Drink through 2005–P.M. • $70 • (9/30/1999) • **88**
Meursault Les Genevrières 1996 • $55 • (5/31/1998) • **93**
Meursault Sous la Velle 1997: A bit butterscotchy, with floral and green apple aromas, it's crisp, firm, even hard on the finish. Drink now through 2002.–P.M. • $38 • (5/31/1999) • **80**
Meursault Sous La Velle 1996 • $35 • (5/31/1998) • **91**

JOBLOT

Givry Clos de la Servoisine 1994 • $NA • (11/15/1996) • **85**
Givry Clos de la Servoisine 1989 • $25 • (1/31/1992) • **88**

Key: SS—Spectator Selection. CS—Cellar Selection. HR—Highly Recommended. $NA—Price not available. (BT)—Barrel tasting. Ⓐ—Auction Price.
For a key to the tasters' initials, see "How to Use These Listings."
Dates in parentheses represent the issues in which the ratings were published.

Givry Clos du Cellier-aux-Moines 1994 • $NA • (11/15/1996) • **82**
Givry Clos du Cellier-aux-Moines 1989 • $31 Ⓐ • (1/31/1992) • **90**
Givry Clos du Cellier-aux-Moines 1988 • $19 • (12/31/1990) • **84**

JOGUET, CHARLES

Chinon Clos de la Cure 1998: Light- to medium-bodied, with appealing cherry and red plum flavors. Finishes with herbal accents. Drink now. –K.M. • $17 • (5/15/2000) • **86**
Chinon Clos de la Cure 1997: Light and supple, this straightforward red offers simple cherry and berry flavors with hints of herbs, and refreshing acidity. An easy quaff. Drink now.–T.M. • $18 • (10/15/1999) • **82**
Chinon Clos de la Cure 1996 • $17 • (6/15/1998) • **83**
Chinon Clos de la Cure 1995 • $17 • (5/15/1997) • **90**
Chinon Clos de la Dioterie 1997: This suave red offers bright cherry and light herb flavors. Balanced, clean and refreshing, it finishes with a pleasant cinnamon and spice note. Drink now.–T.M. • $27 • (11/15/1999) • **84**
Chinon Clos de la Dioterie 1996: A nice balance of crisp berry and more lush notes of chocolate and game give this wine a distinctive personality. It's soft and clean on the palate, with a perfumed, lingering finish. Drink now through 2003.–T.M. • $24 Ⓐ • (5/31/1999) • **88**
Chinon Clos de la Dioterie Vieilles Vignes 1995 • $27 • (8/31/1997) • **90**
Chinon Clos de la Dioterie Vieilles Vignes 1993 • $26 • (12/15/1995) • **82**
Chinon Clos de la Dioterie Vieilles Vignes 1992 • $25 • (10/31/1994) • **88**
Chinon Clos de la Dioterie Vieilles Vignes 1986 • $21 • (12/31/1988) • **89**
Chinon Clos du Chêne Vert 1997: This expressive red offers punchy flavors of plum, cherry, licorice and earth, backed by firm tannins and notes of toast and smoke. It has a distinctive character and enough concentration to age. Drink now through 2004.–T.M. • $28 • (11/15/1999) • **87**
Chinon Clos du Chêne Vert 1995 • $28 • (8/31/1997) • **88**
Chinon Clos du Chêne Vert 1993 • $24 • (12/15/1995) • **88**
Chinon Cuvée Terroir 1997: This light red offers cherry, cinnamon and herb flavors, soft tannins and a clean, fresh finish. Soft on the palate, it's a nice match for richer fish dishes. Drink now.–T.M. • $14 • (2/28/1999) • **82**
Chinon Cuvée Terroir 1996 • $14 • (2/28/1998) • **87**
Chinon Jeunes Vignes 1997: Cherry, berry and leaf flavors are light but vivid in this supple red, with silky tannins and soft acidity. An easy quaffer that could benefit from light chilling. Drink now.–T.M. • $16 • (11/15/1999) • **82**
Chinon Jeunes Vignes 1996 • $15 • (6/15/1998) • **87**
Chinon Jeunes Vignes 1995 • $19 • (8/31/1997) • **84**
Chinon Les Varennes du Grand Clos 1997: Well knit and quite concentrated, this vibrant red offers ripe plum, cherry and spice flavors, with good balance and firm tannins. Not a blockbuster, but it really shows off its *terroir* and should be great with food. Drink now through 2002.–T.M. • $23 • (11/15/1999) • **88**
Chinon Les Varennes du Grand Clos 1996: Good concentration and distinctive personality mark this dense red. It offers an intriguing mix of black cherry, chocolate, game and smoke flavors, with a lush texture and firm tannins. Will gain with time. Drink now through 2007.–T.M. • $22 • (5/31/1999) • **88**
Chinon Les Varennes du Grand Clos 1995 • $20 • (6/15/1997) • **90**
Chinon Les Varennes du Grand Clos 1993 • $24 • (12/15/1995) • **85**
Chinon Les Varennes du Grand Clos 1986 • $15 • (4/30/1988) • **82**
Chinon Rosé 1998: Clean and crisp, this rosé has real stuffing, with a bit of tannin on the finish and serious flavors of cherries and earth, yet it remains light and lively. Meant for food. Drink now.–T.M. • $14 • (10/15/1999) • **84**
Chinon Rosé 1996 • $14 • (6/15/1998) • **82**

JOLIESSE

Merlot Vin de Pays d'Oc Reserve 1995 • $NA • (4/30/1997) • **80**

JOLIETTE, DOMAINE

Côtes du Roussillon-Villages Cuvée Romain Mercier 1995 • $7 • (5/31/1998) • **83**

JOLIVET, PASCAL

Menetou-Salon Château de Maupas 1998: Appealing smoky and herbal elements define this white and linger on the finish. Focused and flavorful. Drink now.–K.M. • $16 • (5/15/2000) • **85**
Pouilly-Fumé 1998: Alluring aromas of lime, fig and smoke mark this supple, clean white, along with light citrus and pear flavors. Shows admirable purity and balance. Drink now.–T.M. • $19 • (3/31/2000) • **87**
Pouilly-Fumé 1997: This round, rather soft white offers flavors of melon, pear and cooked apple, with light herb notes and a hint of sweetness that turns a bit cloying on the finish. Tasted twice, with consistent notes. Drink now.–T.M. • $16 • (6/30/1999) • **80**
Pouilly-Fumé 1996: This complex, concentrated and superbly balanced Loire white entices with an almost red berry aroma, followed by flavors of peach, apple, melon and mineral. Juicy acidity lends support and keeps the flavors pumping through the lingering finish. Drink now.–B.S. • $17 • (10/31/1998) SS • **90**
Pouilly-Fumé La Grande Cuvée 1996: This muscular white offers ripe flavors of melon and apple, with notes of herb and almond. Not a show-off, but a well-made, traditional wine that achieves power without oak and verve without tart acidity. Will match with a wide variety of foods. Drink now through 2003.–T.M. • $45 • (6/30/1999) • **90**
Pouilly-Fumé La Loge Aux Moines Vieilles Vignes 1997: Round but soft, offering apple, pear and smoke flavors, gentle on the palate but without much backbone. Tasted twice, with consistent notes. Drink now.–T.M. • $21 • (9/15/1999) • **80**
Sancerre 1998: A good, quaffable white, with an herb aroma and citrus flavors. Smoky notes linger on the finish. Drink now.–K.M. • $19 • (5/15/2000) • **84**
Sancerre 1997: Light and clean, this fresh white shows the mineral, citrus and herb flavors characteristic of the appellation, but in a subdued, light-bodied style. Balanced and refreshing. Drink now.–T.M. • $16 • (6/30/1999) • **85**
Sancerre 1996 • $17 • (3/31/1998) • **90**
Sancerre Château du Nozay 1998: Focused and defined. This big white has a delicious purity, with clean flavors of pear, mineral and anise that expand on the long finish. So harmonious it almost seems simple, with virtues emerging on the second glass or with food. Drink now through 2003.–T.M. • $21 • (2/29/2000) • **90**
Sancerre Château du Nozay 1997: Light and clean, with more apple- and pear-scented aromas and flavors, lacking the herbaceousness you expect from Sancerre. Tasted twice, with consistent notes. Drink now.–T.M. • $23 • (6/30/1999) • **82**
Sancerre Château du Nozay 1996 • $21 • (6/15/1998) • **88**
Sancerre Clos du Roy 1997: This firm white offers a good balance of pear and apple flavors, with citrusy acidity and light herbal notes. Not rich or deep, but it finishes clean and refreshing. Tasted twice, with consistent notes. Drink now.–T.M. • $22 • (6/30/1999) • **82**
Sancerre La Grande Cuvée 1996: This distinctive white is thick on the palate, with coconut and vanilla notes framing the herb and pineapple flavors. There's enough acidity to keep it balanced, and the finish is clean and long. Drink now.–T.M. • $45 • (10/31/1999) • **88**
Sancerre Red La Grande Cuvée 1996: This Pinot Noir–based red offers typical black cherry and spice notes, with an herbal edge characteristic of the appellation. Quite rich and ripe, with good color and firm yet light tannins. Drink now through 2002.–T.M. • $45 • (6/30/1999) • **87**

JOLY, N.

Savennières Becherelle 1997: This white offers aromas of caramel and smoke, delivering flavors of mineral, cooked apple and honey. Though it promises sweetness, it remains quite dry on the palate, with a very crisp finish. A bit awkward now, it should improve with age. Drink through 2010.–T.M. • $26 • (2/29/2000) • **89**
Savennières Becherelle 1996: Honey and vanilla components envelop the apple and mineral notes in this concentrated, racy white. It shows depth and breadth on the palate and needs time to integrate the vibrant acidity. Drink through 2006–B.S. • $25 • (11/15/1998) • **88**
Savennières-Coulée de Serrant Clos de la Coulée de Serrant 1997: Distinctive. Golden in color, with a range of flavors (earth, chamomile, wax, baked apple, anisette and ginger) that are pure, piercing and vibrant. Lengthy, with bass notes on the finish, this should gain even more charm with cellaring. Drink now through 2007.–B.S. • $63 • (6/15/2000) • **92**
Savennières-Coulée de Serrant Clos de la Coulée de Serrant 1996: This rich white has the golden color and viscous texture of a sweet wine, yet it's very dry. The complex flavors suggest honey, melon and spice, but as if the sugar were somehow removed. Concentrated, balanced and impressive, it should age well. Drink now through 2008.–T.M. • $62 • (2/29/2000) • **91**
Savennières-Coulée de Serrant Moelleux Clos de la Coulée de Serrant 1995: A chameleon. Full of honey, apple, beeswax and dried fruit and flower character, this begins slightly sweet, then turns dry while the flavors change to peach and mineral. There's extract and depth, and it shows promise for years to come. Drink now through 2007.–B.S. • $75 • (11/15/1998) • **90**
Savennières-Roche aux Moines Clos de la Bergerie 1996: Rich yet very dry, even austere, this powerful white offers intense flavors of coffee, toast, dried fruit and mineral. An almost searing acidity makes it difficult to drink now, but it has the stuffing to improve in the bottle. Best after 2002.–T.M. • $32 • (2/29/2000) • **91**

JOLYS, CHATEAU

Jurançon 1997: Lemon curd and milklike flavors dominate this simple white, which finishes with a touch of vanilla.–K.M. • $10 • (10/15/1999) • **79**

Jurançon 1996 • $13 • (4/30/1998) • **85**

Jurançon Vendanges Tardives 1996: Incredible truffle aromas leaps from the glass, yet the flavors in this dessert wine are redolent of honey, almond and orange peel. Sweet and exotic, with a crisp structure that keeps it balanced. A tad rustic. Drink now through 2003.–B.S. • $37 • (1/01/2000) • **88**

JONQUEYRES, CHATEAU

Bordeaux Supérieur 1995 • $12 • (1/31/1998) • **85**

Bordeaux Supérieur 1994 • $NA • (7/31/1996) • **84**

Bordeaux Supérieur 1992 • $10 • (8/31/1995) • **81**

Bordeaux Supérieur Cuvée Vieilles Vignes 1988 • $12 • (3/31/1991) • **65**

JONQUEYRES, LES COMTES DE

Bordeaux White Cuvée Alpha 1998: A very clean wine, with lemon meringue aromas and flavors. Medium-bodied, with clean acidity and a fresh finish. Drink now.–J.S. • $11 • (2/29/2000) • **86**

Bordeaux White Cuvée Alpha 1996: A rather dull and ponderous white. Aromas of lemon curd and cream, yet rather fat and rustic on the palate, with a short finish. Drink now.–J.S. • $12 • (3/31/1999) • **80**

JONQUIERES, CHATEAU DE

Corbières 1996: A balanced and smooth red wine, with red cherry and spice flavors and a nice smoky edge on the finish. Drink now.–K.M. • $9 • (10/31/1998) • **83**

Corbières 1991 • $7 • (3/15/1994) • **81**

JONQUIERES, DOMAINE DES

Côtes du Rhône 1995 • $NA • (10/15/1997) • **81**

JOSMEYER

Alsace LisaBelle 1997: Litchi and spice aromas lead off, turning to grapefruit flavors in this rich yet firm Gewürztraminer blend. Good character, but gets meager on the finish. The aromas are its best feature at this stage. Drink now through 2003.–B.S. • $10 • (5/15/1999) • **86**

Gewürztraminer Alsace 1998: On the sweet side and tasting like pears, with a dash of allspice. Rich, round and softly structured. Drink now.–B.S. • $20 • (6/15/2000) • **83**

Gewürztraminer Alsace 1996: Pungent aromas of smoked meat along with litchi and spices mark this rich, exuberant Gewürz. Satisfying, but finishes a little short. Drink now.–B.S. • $20 • (9/15/1998) • **83**

Gewürztraminer Alsace Cuvée des Folastries 1997: Quite dark in color, yet with haunting aromas of roses, litchi and Indian spices. Very young, unevolved and structured, with a lean, vibrant intensity usually associated with Riesling. Drink through 2005–B.S. • $26 • (5/15/1999) • **89**

Gewürztraminer Alsace Sélection de Grains Nobles 1990: Complex and satisfying. Amazingly pure and smoky, this 10-year-old SGN exhibits flavors of rose, caramel and horehound candy. Never heavy, the vibrant structure keeps the flavors coursing through the long aftertaste. Drink now through 2005.–B.S. • $84/375 ml. • (6/15/2000) • **92**

Gewürztraminer Alsace Sélection de Grains Nobles 1989 • $NA • (11/15/1990) • **85**

Pinot Auxerrois Alsace H Vieilles Vignes 1997: Rich and tasty, showing stone, peach and straw notes, but it lacks structure, tasting diffuse and flabby. Drink now.–B.S. • $31 • (6/15/2000) • **81**

Pinot Blanc Alsace 1996: Reserved and a little austere, showing firm acidity, delicate floral and peach aromas and flavors, and a mineral note on the finish. May need a little more time to open. Drink through 2003–B.S. • $12 • (8/31/1998) • **84**

Key: SS—Spectator Selection. CS—Cellar Selection. HR—Highly Recommended. $NA—Price not available. (BT)—Barrel tasting. Ⓐ—Auction Price. For a key to the tasters' initials, see "How to Use These Listings." **Dates in parentheses represent the issues in which the ratings were published.**

Pinot Gris Alsace 1998: A good, straightforward style of Pinot Gris that displays moderate richness and balance to support the peach and smoke flavors. Drink now.–B.S. • $NA • (6/15/2000) • **84**

Pinot Noir Alsace Cuvée Réservée 1996: Very pure aromas and flavors of cherries are augmented by spice in this velvety, sinewy red. Could use more flesh and concentration to balance the structure, finishing on a slightly hot note. Drink now through 2001.–B.S. • $25 • (5/15/1999) • **83**

Riesling Alsace 1997: Wonderful purity of aroma and flavor, with quince and almond, and more like a '96 with its zippy backbone, this compact Riesling fleshes out midpalate and ends on citrus and apple notes. A fine dinner companion. Drink now through 2005.–B.S. • $18 • (5/15/1999) • **86**

Riesling Alsace 1996: A floral, herbal style of Riesling, its violet and thyme notes mingling with vibrant acidity on a lean, elegant framework. Apple and mineral echo on the finish. Drink now through 2005.–B.S. • $17 • (8/31/1998) • **86**

Riesling Alsace Grand Cru Hengst 1997: Ripe and succulent, this '97 Riesling bursts with peach, apple, mineral and even honeysuckle, showing beautiful harmony and expression while remaining graceful and delicate. Great finish has a mineral aftertaste. Only available in magnum in the US. Drink now through 2005.–B.S. • $127/1.5 liter • (6/15/2000) • **90**

Riesling Alsace Le Kottabe 1997: Rich, medium- to full-bodied and tending toward peach and almond notes, this all the while maintains an aloofness accentuated by a steely structure. Not as opulent right now as some '97s, so give it some time. Drink through 2004–B.S. • $22 • (5/15/1999) • **84**

Tokay Pinot Gris Alsace 1996: On the austere side, with lively acidity but not the density and concentration to match. May be better with food.–B.S. • $20 • (9/15/1998) • **80**

Tokay Pinot Gris Alsace Hengst Sélection de Grains Nobles 1989 • $NA • (11/15/1990) • **86**

Tokay Pinot Gris Alsace Le Fromenteau 1997: Smells nutty, like peanut oil, then takes on a smokiness allied to a creamy texture. A little dissolved carbon dioxide is muting the flavors today, but the balance is good and there's concentration. Drink through 2004–B.S. • $27 • (5/15/1999) • **86**

Tokay Pinot Gris Alsace Le Fromenteau 1996: Compact and tight, with bright acidity, but only modest peach and smoke notes and a bitter accent on the finish.–B.S. • $26 • (9/15/1998) • **81**

JOUARD, GABRIEL

Chassagne-Montrachet Les Baudines 1998: Distinctive, with smoked bacon, wood fire, mineral and wet earth complexity. Aromatically reserved, this medium-bodied, silky-textured white gains intensity on the finish; still, lacks a bit of ripe fruit to rate higher. Drink now through 2005.–P.M. • $38 • (5/31/2000) • **86**

JOUBERT, C. & M.

Juliénas 1996 • $10 • (5/31/1998) • **84**

JOUGLA, DOMAINE DES

St.-Chinian 1996: Mature-tasting, with dried cherry and red plum flavors then a nice touch of savory herb and a bit of cinnamon on the finish. Drink now.–K.M. • $9 • (8/31/1999) • **83**

St.-Chinian 1995 • $9 • (12/15/1997) • **84**

St.-Chinian 1990 • $9 • (3/15/1994) • **84**

St.-Chinian Cuvée Classique 1997: A brickish and soft-tasting red, with a gamy aroma and flavors of dried plum. Drink now.–K.M. • $9 • (12/31/1999) • **82**

JUILLOT, EMILE

Mercurey La Cailloute 1994 • $NA • (11/15/1996) • **80**

Mercurey Les Combins 1995 • $NA • (11/15/1997) • **88**

Mercurey Les Combins 1994 • $NA • (11/15/1996) • **85**

Mercurey Les Croichots 1995 • $NA • (11/15/1997) • **85**

Mercurey White 1998: Wonderful. Ripe and sweet-tasting, with tropical, citrus and dried herb complexity. Full-bodied, this white has length, flavor, and balance and energy on the finish. Drink now through 2002.–P.M. • $20 • (5/31/2000) • **87**

Mercurey White La Cailloute 1998: Clean, pure Chardonnay, with green apple, a crisp midpalate and a citrusy aroma. Lacks opulence, but this light-bodied white should go well with meals. Drink now through 2002.–P.M. • $27 • (5/31/2000) • **83**

JUILLOT, MICHEL

Bourgogne White 1998: Smoky and chewy. A bit rustic, but it has character, with good fruit concentration and a touch of honey. Odd but distinctive, it will grow on some, not others. Not imported into the U.S. Best from 2001 through 2004.–P.M. • $NA • (1/01/2000) • **85**
Bourgogne White 1997: Diluted and stripped, with a wet carboard note. Tart finish.–P.M. • $16 • (5/31/1999) • **73**
Bourgogne White 1995 • $12 • (8/31/1997) • **74**
Corton Perrières 1994 • $48 • (11/15/1996) • **80**
Corton Perrières 1988 • $54 • (8/31/1992) • **75**
Corton-Charlemagne 1998: Full-bodied, with butter and pear tart, but there is a lack of focus and depth, and some odd paint varnish character. Surfs on the surface of serious flavors. Drink now through 2005.–P.M. • $140 • (5/31/2000) • **84**
Corton-Charlemagne 1997: Elegant and polished, with modest fruit, lemon, butter and spice. Medium-bodied, with a short, slightly drying finish. Drink through 2004.–P.M. • $95 • (5/31/1999) • **81**
Corton-Charlemagne 1996 • $72 Ⓐ • (5/31/1998) • **94**
Corton-Charlemagne 1995 • $95 • (5/31/1997) • **88**
Côte Chalonnaise 1990 • $13 • (10/31/1992) • **80**
Mercurey 1997: Elegant, yet perhaps a little cooked and advanced in its aromas and flavors of raspberry and cherry jam. Supple up front, turning a bit hot and astringent.–B.S. • $NA • (9/30/1999) • **79**
Mercurey 1994 • $26 • (11/15/1996) • **75**
Mercurey 1989 • $21 • (8/31/1992) • **75**
Mercurey Clos des Barraults 1995 • $30 • (11/15/1997) • **80**
Mercurey Clos Tonnerre 1994 • $25 • (11/15/1996) • **77**
Mercurey Clos Tonnerre 1989 • $24 • (8/31/1992) • **85**
Mercurey Les Champs Martins 1997: Intense and concentrated, with a tough, medium-bodied personality that brings it character; stands out in the '97 vintage for delivering a grip of lingering fruit flavors that taste clean, plus a mineral edge that gives the finish some interest. Drink now through 2006.–P.M. • $NA • (9/30/1999) • **87**
Mercurey Les Champs Martins 1989 • $24 • (8/31/1992) • **84**
Mercurey White 1998: Odd, wood character (cardboard aromas?) is followed by a tough, harsh taste.–P.M. • $23 • (5/31/2000) • **74**
Mercurey White 1997: A ripe, medium-bodied white, with nice pear and lemon intensity. Veers toward a chewy, slightly drying character on the finish. Drink now.–P.M. • $24 • (5/31/1999) • **80**
Mercurey White 1995 • $19 • (8/31/1997) • **79**
Mercurey White Clos des Barraults 1998: Very oaky. The wood dominates the fruit in this medium-bodied, citrusy and crisp Chardonnay.–P.M. • $38 • (5/31/2000) • **78**
Mercurey White Clos des Barraults 1997: The wood blankets this medium-bodied white right now, but underneath is a core of firm fruit, loads of citrus and a solid concentration of flavors. A vibrant, serious wine that's a fine achievement in this low-acidity vintage, but cellar so it can smooth out. Best from 2003 through 2007.–P.M. • $30 • (5/31/1999) • **89**
Mercurey White Clos des Barraults 1996 • $30 • (5/31/1998) • **79**
Mercurey White Les Champs Martins 1998: Quite woody, it delivers some concentrated citrus character along with the intense toasted oak, and some honey. Medium-bodied, with a lingering toasty finish. Give it time. Drink now through 2002.–P.M. • $40 • (5/31/2000) • **85**
Mercurey White Les Champs Martins 1997: This impressive, full-bodied white is clean, crisp and racy, showing mineral, lemon and superelegant, ripe tropical flavors. Turns creamy on the vibrant finish. Drink now through 2003.–P.M. • $30 • (5/31/1999) • **90**
Mercurey White Les Champs Martins 1996 • $30 • (5/31/1998) • **89**

JUNOT, RENE

Vin de Table Français Red NV • $5/1.5 liter • (5/15/1998) • **84**

JURAT, CHATEAU LE

St.-Emilion 1998: Velvety and chewy, with plenty of fruit and tannin. Full-bodied. Slightly hollow in the center palate.–J.S. • $NA • (5/31/1999) (BT) • **85-89**
St.-Emilion 1997: A bit austere, with berry, green tobacco character. Medium-bodied, with medium, slightly rustic tannins. Medium finish. Drink now.–J.S. • $23 • (1/31/2000) • **83**
St.-Emilion 1996: Nice fresh berry and mineral aromas continue on the palate. Medium- to light-bodied, with firm tannins and a simple, fruity aftertaste. A little short and hard. Tasted twice, with consistent notes.–J.S. • $15 • (1/31/1999) • **79**
St.-Emilion 1995: Balanced red, with cherry and berry aromas and flavors and hints of chocolate. Medium body, medium tannins. Drink now or hold.–J.S. • $NA • (9/15/1998) • **86**
St.-Emilion 1994 • $18 • (1/31/1997) • **87**
St.-Emilion 1991 • $14 • (3/31/1994) • **76**

JUSTICES, CHATEAU LES

Sauternes 1991 • $NA • (4/15/1995) • **81**
Sauternes 1990 • $NA • (4/15/1995) • **87**
Sauternes 1989 • $23 • (4/15/1995) • **91**
Sauternes 1988 • $38 • (4/15/1995) • **86**
Sauternes 1987 • $24 • (6/15/1990) • **75**
Sauternes 1986 • $20 • (4/15/1995) • **79**
Sauternes 1983 • $18 • (4/15/1995) • **65**

KIENTZHEIM-KAYSERBERG

Gewürztraminer Alsace 1997: Ripe, soft and thickly textured, this straightforward, ginger and litchi-flavored white finishes short.–B.S. • $13 • (10/31/1999) • **78**
Tokay Pinot Gris Alsace 1997: Sweet, with candied-fruit flavors of apricot and orange that dissipate quickly. Lacks structure and depth. Drink now.–B.S. • $13 • (10/31/1999) • **81**

KIENTZLER, ANDRE

Gewürztraminer Alsace 1997: Ripe and rich, showing floral, apricot and vanilla notes along with good acidity and a hint of astringency on the finish. Could use a bit more concentration to fill out the aftertaste. Drink now.–B.S. • $13 • (10/31/1999) • **84**
Gewürztraminer Alsace Vendange Tardive 1997: Fat and lushly textured, with straightforward honey and pear notes buoyed by acidity and a slight bitterness, lingering modestly on the finish. Drink now through 2002.–B.S. • $42 • (6/15/2000) • **87**
Riesling Alsace 1998: On the austere side, this white delivers green apple, almond and lemon flavors on a lean, firm body. Good concentration and density, ending on a slightly tart note. Drink now through 2004.–B.S. • $18 • (5/31/2000) • **84**
Riesling Alsace Grand Cru Geisberg 1997: Subtle and harmonious, full of ripe stone and fruit aromas and flavors, all displayed on a silky texture and a firm structure. Should develop well. Drink now through 2004.–B.S. • $32 • (6/15/2000) • **87**
Riesling Alsace Grand Cru Osterberg 1997: Fans of fruit beware: This is packed with dense mineral aromas and flavors on a lean frame. A pronounced acidity sits apart today, suggesting that this needs time. Best from 2001 through 2004.–B.S. • $26 • (6/15/2000) • **86**
Tokay Pinot Gris Alsace Grand Cru Kirchberg de Ribeauville 1997: Restrained, balanced and delicately wrought, offering pear, apricot and mineral notes on a silken texture that keeps on keeping on. Very intense and concentrated, with an appealing smoky note. Drink now through 2004.–B.S. • $31 • (6/15/2000) • **89**

KIRWAN, CHATEAU

Margaux 1999: This estate continues to be a big surprise in the Medoc. Beautiful plum, cherry and currant aromas. Medium- to full-bodied, with a good core of silky tannins and a fruity aftertaste.–J.S. • $NA • (1/01/2000) (BT) • **988**
Margaux 1998: Lots of new wood here, with good berry and cassis aromas and flavors. Medium-bodied, with some velvety tannins and a medium finish.–J.S. • $NA • (5/31/1999) (BT) • **85-89**
Margaux 1997: Lovely ripe berry and cherry character, with hints of mineral and toasted oak. Medium-bodied, with velvety tannins and a fresh fruit aftertaste. Kirwan is doing it right. Best from 2001 through 2005.–J.S. • $40 • (1/31/2000) • **88**
Margaux 1996: Gorgeous blackberry, smoke and raspberry aromas. Full-bodied, with chewy tannins and a chocolate, berry and cherry aftertaste. An exceptionally well-made and well-presented wine for the vintage; Kirwan is getting better and better.–J.S. • $26 • (1/31/1999) • **90**
Margaux 1995 • $28 Ⓐ • (1/31/1998) • **93**
Margaux 1994 • $21 Ⓐ • (1/31/1997) • **85**
Margaux 1993 • $18 Ⓐ • (1/31/1996) • **86**
Margaux 1992 • $22 • (4/15/1995) • **78**
Margaux 1990 • $28 • (3/31/1993) • **90**

Margaux 1989: Drying up a bit now but an impressive amount of extract. Medium-dark ruby-red, with raisin, tobacco and earth aromas. Full-bodied, offering loads of tannins and a chewy, slightly dry finish. (1989 Bordeaux horizontal tasting). Drink now.–J.S. • $40 • (5/31/1999) • **86**

Margaux 1988 • $28 • (4/30/1991) • **87**

Margaux 1986 • $25 • (6/30/1989) • **82**

Margaux 1985 • $27 • (2/15/1989) • **90**

Margaux 1983 • $43 Ⓐ • (7/16/1986) • **86**

Margaux 1982: Not a huge Margaux, but delicious all the same. Medium-ruby, with a garnet edge. Fresh berry aromas have a touch of earth. Medium-bodied, with well-integrated tannins and a long, silky finish. (1982 Bordeaux horizontal tasting). Drink now.–J.S. • $38 Ⓐ • (11/30/1998) • **88**

Margaux 1945 • $175 • (11/30/1995) • **82**

KLIPFEL, EUGENE

Brut Blanc de Blancs Crémant d'Alsace NV: Brisk, lively and refreshing, with honey, apple and citrus notes that develop a creaminess midpalate. A nice alternative to Champagne. Drink now.–B.S. • $18 • (6/15/2000) • **85**

Gewürztraminer Alsace 1997: On the exotic side, with tropical fruit, rose, vanilla and a hint of anise, this white offers breadth and density on a rich, full-bodied frame. Lingering aftertaste. Drink now.–B.S. • $16 • (6/15/2000) • **85**

Gewürztraminer Alsace Freiberg 1996: Mature, this Gewürztraminer delivers ripe apricot, rose petal and a touch of spice in an elegant fashion, backed by moderate acidity. Drink now.–B.S. • $20 • (6/15/2000) • **85**

Riesling Alsace 1998: Shows the finesse and delicacy of Riesling, but the flavors are just too earthy. Tasted twice, with consistent notes.–B.S. • $11 • (6/15/2000) • **78**

Tokay Pinot Gris Alsace Grand Cru Kirchberg 1997: Concentrated and powerful, this '97 Pinot Gris' peach and quince flavors ride a thickly textured swath, with just enough acidity to keep it balanced and clean on the finish. Drink now.–B.S. • $19 • (6/15/2000) • **87**

KLUG

Cabernet Sauvignon-Merlot Vin de Pays d'Oc Selection des Grands Chais 1994 • $7 • (12/31/1995) • **78**

Cabernet Sauvignon-Merlot Vin de Pays d'Oc Selection des Grands Chais 1993 • $7 • (7/31/1995) • **79**

Merlot Vin de Pays d'Oc Selection des Grands Chais 1994 • $7 • (12/31/1995) • **75**

KOEHLY & FILS, CHARLES

Auxerrois Alsace Vieilles Vignes 1996: Aromas of white flowers with attractive peach flavors, all in a thickly textured, soft framework. The finish is a bit dull. Drink now.–B.S. • $12 • (9/15/1998) • **83**

Gewürztraminer Alsace St.-Hippolyte 1997: Shows noticeable sweetness, along with grapefruit peel notes and a hint of earthiness. Drink now.–B.S. • $14 • (10/31/1999) • **83**

Pinot Blanc Alsace 1997: The flavors border on earthiness, while the structure is loosely knit and soft.–B.S. • $12 • (10/15/1999) • **79**

Pinot Gris Alsace St.-Hippolyte 1997: This has a slight metallic note in addition to peach and citrus flavors. Ripe and balanced on the soft side, with an underlying earthiness. Drink now.–B.S. • $15 • (10/31/1999) • **81**

KREYDENWEISS, MARC

Alsace L'âme de la Terre Clos du Val d'Eleon 1997: Almond, citrus and a hint of earthiness are the themes in this well defined, concentrated white. A firm structure and depth add to its appeal. Drink now.–B.S. • $24 • (9/15/1999) • **86**

Gewürztraminer Alsace Kritt 1997: Noticeably sweet and one-dimensional in its honey flavor, this seems dilute and simple.–B.S. • $23 • (10/31/1999) • **77**

Gewürztraminer Alsace Kritt 1996: Decent balance here, but the flavors are light, and the overall impression lacks focus. Drink now.–B.S. • $23 • (9/15/1998) • **77**

Key: SS—Spectator Selection. CS—Cellar Selection. HR—Highly Recommended. $NA—Price not available. (BT)—Barrel tasting. Ⓐ—Auction Price.
For a key to the tasters' initials, see "How to Use These Listings."
Dates in parentheses represent the issues in which the ratings were published.

Klevner Alsace Kritt 1997: Ripe and even a tad sweet, displaying vanilla custard, honey and lemon flavors. Moderately concentrated and intense, this is better as an aperitif than with food. Drink now.–B.S. • $25 • (9/15/1999) • **85**

Klevner Alsace Kritt 1996: Extremely ripe, smelling of tropical fruit and honey followed by passion fruit and litchi flavors. There's a hint of sweetness, yet it's balanced and finishes cleanly if a bit short. Drink now.–B.S. • $21 • (8/31/1998) • **83**

Pinot Blanc Alsace Kritt 1997: A modern style. Fat and rich, with butter, honey and vanilla character, along with a touch of bitterness combining with the acidity for structure. Atypical for the variety, yet it works. Drink now.–B.S. • $18 • (9/15/1999) • **87**

Pinot Blanc Alsace Kritt 1996: A tender '96, showing baked apple and honey nuances, good acidity and some lingering citrus elements. Drink now.–B.S. • $18 • (8/31/1998) • **84**

Pinot Gris Alsace Grand Cru Moenchberg 1997: Rich and round, this shows moderate violet and honey concentration. On the delicate side, with lowish acidity and a bit of heat on the finish. Drink now through 2001.–B.S. • $32 • (10/31/1999) • **86**

Pinot Gris Alsace Grand Cru Moenchberg 1996: Very dry, exhibiting lovely smoke and mineral aromas followed by apple and nut flavors and a big structure, with a finish bordering on hot. Try with roast pork or grilled sausage. Drink now through 2002.–B.S. • $32 • (9/15/1998) • **86**

Pinot Gris Alsace Lerchenberg 1997: This has plenty of clover honey flavor, yet it's essentially a one-note song.–B.S. • $23 • (10/31/1999) • **79**

Pinot Gris Alsace Lerchenberg 1996: A subtle, elegant Pinot Gris, showing citrus and apple notes, with tart acidity and lean texture. Lacks the ripeness and concentration of the best '96s. Drink now.–B.S. • $23 • (9/15/1998) • **82**

Riesling Alsace Andlau 1997: Shows the almond and apple side of Riesling, combined with a soft, round structure. Could use a tad more concentration. Drink now.–B.S. • $21 • (8/31/1999) • **82**

Riesling Alsace Andlau 1996: A firm, vibrant Riesling showing almond, peach and citrus notes, moderate richness and a lingering finish. Drink now through 2003.–B.S. • $19 • (8/31/1998) • **84**

Riesling Alsace Grand Cru Kastelberg 1997: Exotic, displaying almond, apple and spice, and a touch of sweetness that emphasizes the rich, round structure. The acidity shows on the finish, so give it time to integrate. Try through 2003.–B.S. • $49 • (8/31/1999) • **87**

Riesling Alsace Grand Cru Kastelberg 1996: Broad and waxy, showing peach and lees character (new oak?) with some firm underlying acidity and light tannins on the finish. Drink now through 2005.–B.S. • $39 • (8/31/1998) • **88**

Riesling Alsace Grand Cru Wiebelsberg 1997: Peach, spice and mineral aromas and flavors have a honeyed, brown sugar element around the edges, adding to the richness of texture in this firm, dry white. Moderate finish shows a touch of heat. Drink now through 2004.–B.S. • $30 • (8/31/1999) • **87**

Riesling Alsace Grand Cru Wiebelsberg 1996: Ripe, round and fleshy, the lime edge and apple flavors kept lively by well-integrated acidity. Some vanilla on the finish adds dimension. Well done. Drink now through 2004.–B.S. • $28 • (8/31/1998) • **90**

Tokay Pinot Gris Alsace Grand Cru Moenchberg Sélection de Grains Nobles 1989 • $NA • (11/15/1990) • **90**

KRUG

Brut Champagne Grande Cuvée NV: A mature, subtly flavored brut that invites you in with mellow aromas and flavors, coats the mouth with a rich effervescence and keeps your interest through the tangy aftertaste. Drink now. • $73 Ⓐ • (12/31/1998) • **88**

Brut Rosé Champagne NV • $150 • (12/31/1997) • **95**

KUENTZ-BAS

Gewürztraminer Alsace Cuvée Tradition 1998: This shows typical rose and litchi notes on a transparent framework, easy-drinking and elegant, with a hint of coarseness on the finish. Drink now.–B.S. • $17 • (6/15/2000) • **83**

Gewürztraminer Alsace Cuvée Tradition 1996: Weak and insipid, this is a poor example of Gewürztraminer.–B.S. • $16 • (4/30/1999) • **74**

Gewürztraminer Alsace Grand Cru Eichberg 1997: Corpulent and broad in its honey, apricot and orange notes, this open, inviting white shows more up front than on the finish. Drink now.–B.S. • $30 • (6/15/2000) • **83**

Pinot Blanc Alsace 1998: A lean, intense and racy style of Pinot Blanc that tastes like lemon custard, with an underlying citrus peel bitterness emerging on the finish. Needs food. Drink now.–B.S. • $13 • (6/15/2000) • **84**

Pinot Blanc Alsace 1997: Hints at banana and flowers, showing richness in the mouth before turning crisp. Modest finish. Drink now.–B.S. • $12 • (10/15/1999) • **81**

Pinot Blanc Alsace 1996: There's ripeness, guava with a lemon accent, in this racy '96 white. Has a dense, rich texture and concentrated flavors, all in a clear, focused profile. Drink now through 2003.–B.S. • $11 • (3/31/1999) • **87**

Riesling Alsace Cuvée Tradition 1998: Very pretty Riesling, showing rose, apple, citrus and mineral aromas and flavors in a delicate, firm presentation which ends with a mouthwatering tang. Drink now through 2003.–B.S. • $13 • (5/31/2000) HR • **88**

Riesling Alsace Cuvée Tradition 1997: Has the ripeness and richness of the '97 vintage, along with a hint of residual sugar, but the apricot flavors lack intensity and focus and seem flat, perhaps due to some carbon dioxide.–B.S. • $14 • (9/15/1999) • **79**

Riesling Alsace Grand Cru Pfersigberg 1997: Rich and mouthfilling, exhibiting forest floor, almond, apple and mineral tones, all underscored by a vibrant acidity. The refreshing finish makes it particularly suitable with food. Drink now through 2003.–B.S. • $25 • (5/31/2000) • **88**

Tokay Pinot Gris Alsace Cuvée Jeremy Sélection de Grains Nobles 1989 • $NA • (11/15/1990) • **90**

Tokay Pinot Gris Alsace Réserve Personnelle 1997: Round and juicy in texture, with honeysuckle and apricot flavors. Fresh, with lively acidity and medium body, it ends on a mineral note. Drink now through 2001.–B.S. • $20 • (6/15/2000) • **87**

Tokay Pinot Gris Alsace Réserve Personnelle 1996: Lacking the broad aromas and flavors that Pinot Gris typically achieved in '96. The overall impression is pleasant and racy, but pinched and balanced toward acidity. Drink now.–B.S. • $19 • (9/15/1998) • **82**

L DE LA LOUVIERE

Pessac-Léognan 1996: A tough '96. Aromas of crushed grapes and earth. Medium-bodied and slightly earthy, with a light finish and dry tannins. Hard to get excited about. Second label of Château La Louvière.–J.S. • $NA • (2/28/1999) • **78**

Pessac-Léognan 1995 • $15 • (1/31/1998) • **82**

Pessac-Léognan 1994 • $15 • (1/31/1997) • **84**

Pessac-Léognan 1993 • $15 • (1/31/1996) • **80**

Pessac-Léognan White 1998: Good grapefruit, lemon and mineral aromas. Medium- to full-bodied, with ripe pineapple and honey character and a medium vanilla aftertaste. Drink now through 2003.–J.S. • $14 • (2/29/2000) • **87**

Pessac-Léognan White 1996: Aromas of grapefruit, almond and hazelnuts follow through to a medium-bodied palate with fresh acidity and a simple finish. Second label of Château La Louvière. Drink now.–J.S. • $20 • (3/31/1999) • **83**

LABAT, CHATEAU

Haut-Médoc 1995 • $22 • (1/31/1998) • **87**

LABEGORCE, CHATEAU

Margaux 1998: Some mineral and berry character, with a hint of dried herbs. Medium-bodied, with some firm tannins and a light finish.–J.S. • $NA • (5/31/1999) (BT) • **80-84**

Margaux 1997: A light '97, with good ripe fruit character but rather diluted on the palate. Drink now.–J.S. • $21 Ⓐ • (1/31/2000) • **80**

Margaux 1996: Not a big-boned wine, but delicious nonetheless. Attractive blackberry, cherry and earth aromas and flavors. Medium-bodied, with well-integrated tannins and a pretty fruity aftertaste. Best after 2000.–J.S. • $NA • (1/31/1999) • **87**

Margaux 1991 • $14 • (3/31/1994) • **74**

Margaux 1990 • $20 • (3/31/1993) • **82**

Margaux 1989: A fresh and delicious '89. Medium-dark ruby in color. Aromas of flowers, berries and cassis. Medium-bodied, with fine tannins and a delicious, fresh fruit aftertaste. (1989 Bordeaux horizontal tasting). Drink now.–J.S. • $NA • (5/31/1999) • **87**

Margaux 1987 • $13 • (3/31/1991) • **77**

Margaux 1986 • $15 • (2/15/1990) • **86**

Margaux 1982: Medium brick-red, with an amber edge. Cedar and tobacco aromas with hints of fruit. Medium-bodied, with soft tannins, a slightly diluted finish. Fading fast. (1982 Bordeaux horizontal tasting). Drink now.–J.S. • $NA • (11/30/1998) • **80**

LABEGORCE-ZEDE, CHATEAU

Margaux 1999: Attractive and pleasant wine, with mineral and berry aromas. Medium-bodied, with fine tannis and a delicate finish.–J.S. • $NA • (1/01/2000) (BT) • **85-89**

Margaux 1997: Dark in color, with attractive berry, licorice and spice aromas. Medium-bodied, with light tannins and a fresh finish. A bit light. Drink now.–J.S. • $27 Ⓐ • (1/31/2000) • **83**

Margaux 1995 • $33 Ⓐ • (1/31/1998) • **89**

Margaux 1992 • $14 • (4/15/1995) • **79**

Margaux 1991 • $14 • (3/31/1994) • **84**

Margaux 1990 • $36 Ⓐ • (3/31/1993) • **89**

Margaux 1989 • $34 Ⓐ • (3/15/1992) • **86**

Margaux 1988 • $27 Ⓐ • (4/30/1991) • **83**

Margaux 1987 • $16 • (11/30/1989) • **84**

Margaux 1986 • $22 • (11/30/1989) • **91**

Margaux 1985 • $24 Ⓐ • (2/29/1988) • **84**

Margaux 1983 • $39 Ⓐ • (10/15/1986) • **88**

Margaux 1982 • $30 Ⓐ • (11/30/1989) • **87**

LABET, PIERRE

Beaune Aux Coucherias 1993 • $26 • (11/15/1995) • **73**

Beaune Aux Coucherias 1992 • $26 • (12/15/1994) • **80**

Beaune Aux Coucherias 1991 • $32 • (1/31/1994) • **66**

Beaune Aux Coucherias 1990 • $35 • (12/15/1992) • **88**

Beaune Clos des Monsnières 1997: Mineral, olive and cooked cherry aromas and flavors mark this moderately concentrated, light- to medium-bodied red, whose tannins grip the finish. Drink now through 2004.–B.S. • $36 • (9/30/1999) • **84**

Beaune Clos des Monsnières 1996: Deeply colored, full of cassis, black cherry and a purity that's refreshing. Rich and concentrated, with some stiff tannins to resolve, vibrant acidity and a long, vanilla and cassis aftertaste. Drink through 2005–B.S. • $28 • (9/30/1998) • **88**

Beaune Clos des Monsnières 1995 • $34 • (11/15/1997) • **83**

Beaune Clos des Monsnières 1994 • $29 • (11/15/1996) • **70**

Beaune Clos du Dessus des Marconnets 1997: Perfume, floral and sandalwood aromas accented by olive and orange peel highlight this pretty '97 red. Elegant yet concentrated, with persistent flavors of fig, plum and smoky oak. Drink now through 2005.–B.S. • $36 • (9/30/1999) • **85**

Beaune Clos du Dessus des Marconnets 1996: Very ripe and plummy. A sweet-tasting wine, with round, supple tannins. Medium-bodied, with a minty, petrol, herbal character. Turns a bit dry on the finish. Drink now through 2003.–P.M. • $28 • (9/30/1998) • **81**

Beaune Coucherias 1997: Open and forward, tasting of plum, prune and blood orange. Very ripe in style, full-bodied and a bit cooked, with dried fig on the rustic finish. Drink now through 2005.–P.M. • $40 • (9/30/1999) • **80**

Beaune Coucherias 1996: Starts out with licorice notes and chewy texture combined with good concentration, but succumbs to dry, astringent tannins on the finish. Difficult to assess.–B.S. • $31 • (9/30/1998) • **82**

Beaune Coucherias 1995 • $37 • (11/15/1997) • **75**

Beaune Les Chouacheux 1994 • $35 • (11/15/1996) • **73**

Beaune Les Monsnières 1993 • $20 • (11/15/1995) • **87**

Beaune Les Monsnières 1991 • $25 • (1/31/1994) • **70**

Beaune Les Monsnières 1990 • $30 • (12/15/1992) • **89**

Beaune White Clos des Monsnières 1997: A very nice '97, showing tropical, green apple and pear aromas, with a touch of butter and toasted oak. Medium-bodied and gently balanced. Drink now through 2001.–P.M. • $39 • (5/31/1999) • **85**

Beaune White Clos des Monsnières 1996 • $33 • (5/31/1998) • **90**

Bourgogne 1997: Bright in color, medium-bodied and tasting surprisingly cool-fruited for a '97, it turns hard and tough on the crisp finish.–P.M. • $19 • (9/30/1999) • **75**

Bourgogne 1996: A bit tough, with a hot taste, this red delivers some decent fruit but also an oddly smoky finish, which turns dry.–P.M. • $14 • (9/30/1998) • **75**

Bourgogne 1995 • $10 • (11/15/1997) • **78**

Bourgogne 1994 • $21 • (11/15/1996) • **77**

Bourgogne 1993 • $14 • (11/15/1995) • **84**

Savigny-lès-Beaune White Vergelesses 1997: Ripe and thick in texture, soft and cuddly on the palate, with pear, pineapple, almond and marzipan flavors. Turns slightly astringent on the finish, probably from the soft acidity. Makes a good aperitif. Drink now.–P.M. • $44 • (5/31/1999) • **85**

LABOURE-ROI

Beaujolais-Villages 1995 • $9 • (9/15/1997) • **78**
Bonnes Mares 1990 • $56 • (6/15/1993) • **78**
Bonnes Mares 1989 • $55 • (8/31/1992) • **92**
Bourgogne 1993 • $9 • (11/15/1995) • **80**
Bourgogne 1991 • $8 • (6/15/1993) • **83**
Bourgogne 1989 • $8 • (8/31/1992) • **83**
Bourgogne 1988 • $12 • (3/31/1991) • **83**
Bourgogne White Domaine René Manuel 1997: Very ripe in style, showing butterscotch, paint varnish and wood character. Over-the-top.–P.M. • $12 • (9/30/1999) • **78**
Chablis 1997: Very, very spicy and pumped up in the wood department, with a candied, overly-toasty intensity that's eye-catching but not very Chablis-like.–P.M. • $NA • (9/30/1999) • **79**
Chablis Fourchaume 1997: Oak notes burst from the glass with minty aromas, paving the way to even more obvious wood flavors; it all seems overdone, despite the lemon and ripe fruit.–P.M. • $24 • (5/31/1999) • **79**
Chablis Premier Cru 1997: Vibrant, crisp, light-bodied Chablis, offering some melon, green apple and pear flavors, it kicks in with good acidity on the finish. Drink now.–P.M. • $NA • (9/30/1999) • **83**
Chablis Vaillons 1997: Very oaky for a Chablis, but well-done; full-bodied, with lemon, toasted bread, spice, and tropical flavors on the palate and harmonious finish. Drink now through 2005.–P.M. • $NA • (9/30/1999) • **89**
Chambertin 1989 • $55 • (8/31/1992) • **88**
Chambertin-Clos de Bèze 1989 • $60 • (8/31/1992) • **84**
Chambolle-Musigny 1991 • $30 • (1/31/1995) • **85**
Chambolle-Musigny 1990 • $20 • (6/15/1993) • **84**
Chambolle-Musigny 1988 • $35 • (2/28/1991) • **86**
Chambolle-Musigny Domaine Cottin 1990 • $22 • (6/15/1993) • **83**
Chambolle-Musigny Domaine Cottin 1989 • $30 • (3/31/1992) • **76**
Charmes-Chambertin 1993 • $59 • (11/15/1995) • **86**
Charmes-Chambertin 1990 • $45 • (6/15/1993) • **85**
Chassagne-Montrachet 1997: Showing cedary, toasty notes, this medium-bodied white is a bit dilute and turns slightly hot on the finish.–P.M. • $40 • (5/31/1999) • **77**
Clos de Vougeot 1993 • $57 • (11/15/1995) • **80**
Clos de Vougeot 1990 • $44 • (6/15/1993) • **83**
Côtes du Rhône Domaine des Pervanches 1992 • $8 • (11/15/1995) • **83**
Crozes-Hermitage 1991 • $10 • (6/15/1993) • **86**
Echézeaux 1993 • $54 • (11/15/1995) • **89**
Echézeaux 1990 • $36 • (6/15/1993) • **80**
Gevrey-Chambertin 1993 • $22 • (11/15/1995) • **87**
Gevrey-Chambertin 1991 • $22 • (1/31/1995) • **85**
Gevrey-Chambertin 1990 • $20 • (6/15/1993) • **83**
Gevrey-Chambertin 1988 • $35 • (12/31/1990) • **81**
Gevrey-Chambertin Bel-Air Domaine Claudine Deschamps 1985 • $28 • (3/31/1988) • **87**
Mâcon Blanc-Villages 1997: Woody style where the minty, floral scents of the oak box the fruit into a corner. Astringent, dry-tasting finish.–P.M. • $10 • (5/31/1999) • **71**
Mazis-Chambertin 1990 • $29 • (6/15/1993) • **79**
Meursault 1997: Very oaky, tasting of astringent wood tannins and burnt rubber. Tart finish.–P.M. • $40 • (5/31/1999) • **73**
Meursault Clos de la Baronne Domaine René Manuel 1997: Nicely oaked but not a lot of ripe fruit underneath, so the aromas and flavors seem a bit short, despite an attempt by this medium-bodied Chardonnay to bring in green apple and honey on the finish. Drink now through 2005.–P.M. • $39 • (9/30/1999) • **85**
Meursault Clos des Bouches Chères Domaine René Manuel 1997: An interesting, almost late harvest Meursault, dripping with wax and spice character. The opulent, whipped cream package fills the palate, then bursts with citrus, butter, honey and toasted oak. Great effort from the improving Labouré-Roi. Drink now through 2005.–P.M. • $39 • (9/30/1999) • **90**
Meursault Le Porusot Domaine René Manuel 1997: Polished and flavorful, ripe and buttery. A nice effort from négociant Labouré-Roi, with pear, mineral and spice richness that coats the palate. Full-bodied, long, supple finish. Drink now through 2005.–P.M. • $55 • (5/31/1999) • **89**
Meursault Red Clos de la Baronne Domaine René Manuel 1993 • $22 • (11/15/1995) • **83**
Meursault Red Clos de la Baronne Domaine René Manuel 1988 • $18 • (3/31/1991) • **79**
Montagny 1997: Beautiful ripe fruit and classy toasted oak combine to create a polished, sophisticated, clean medium-bodied white, with a core of tropical and hazelnut flavors, crisp acidity and a creamy texture. Drink now through 2005.–P.M. • $16 • (5/31/1999) • **89**
Nuits-St.-Georges 1993 • $27 • (11/15/1995) • **75**
Nuits-St.-Georges 1991 • $28 • (1/31/1995) • **86**
Nuits-St.-Georges 1990 • $20 • (6/15/1993) • **86**
Pommard 1993 • $24 • (11/15/1995) • **84**
Pommard 1991 • $24 • (1/31/1995) • **85**
Pommard 1990 • $20 • (6/15/1993) • **85**
Pommard Les Bertins 1993 • $29 • (11/15/1995) • **86**
Pommard Les Bertins 1985 • $29 • (3/15/1988) • **79**
Pouilly-Fuissé 1997: Ambitious winemaking, with loads of toasted oak playing first fiddle to the apple, pear, lemon and honey notes. It's well made though, and could pass for a Puligny-Montrachet in this low-acid vintage. Drink now through 2002.–P.M. • $19 • (5/31/1999) • **87**
Richebourg 1990 • $71 • (6/15/1993) • **84**
St.-Véran 1997: Nice ripe fruit introduces this well-made, balanced, medium-bodied Chardonnay, with a toasty, spicy, lemony finish. Drink now.–P.M. • $13 • (5/31/1999) • **84**
Vosne-Romanée 1991 • $23 • (1/31/1995) • **83**

LABRY, A. & B.

Auxey-Duresses Red 1995 • $17 • (11/15/1997) • **84**
Auxey-Duresses Red 1992 • $16 • (5/15/1995) • **87**

LACHESNAYE, CHATEAU

Haut-Médoc 1998: A bit lean and diluted, with some berry, cherry character but light on the finish.–J.S. • $NA • (5/31/1999) (BT) • **75-79**
Haut-Médoc 1997: Light, with some berry and tobacco character.–J.S. • $NA • (1/31/2000) • **79**
Haut-Médoc 1996: Good intensity of blackberry and tar. Medium- to full-bodied, with fine tannins and a fruity aftertaste. Slightly diluted center-palate, but delicious. Best after 2000.–J.S. • $NA • (1/31/1999) • **85**
Haut-Médoc 1995: A wine with bright fruit and well-focused, fine tannins. Medium- to full-bodied, very silky, with a medium, fruity finish. Closing up. Best from 2002 through 2008.–J.S. • $NA • (9/15/1998) • **87**
Haut-Médoc 1992 • $18 • (4/15/1995) • **70**
Haut-Médoc 1990 • $17 • (3/31/1993) • **88**
Haut-Médoc 1989: A fine, rich wine shortly to reach its peak. Ruby-colored center and a red edge. Aromas of cassis bush and mint. Full-bodied, with very fine tannins and a lovely freshness, yet there's a meaty, autumnal aftertaste. (1989 Bordeaux horizontal tasting). Drink through 2010–J.S. • $NA • (5/31/1999) • **88**

LACHETEAU

Vouvray 1997: Firm and dry. Apple and almond flavors are light but clean in this straightforward white. Balanced, with the body to match simple dishes. Drink now.–T.M. • $9 • (6/30/1999) • **80**
Vouvray 1996 • $12 • (6/30/1998) • **79**

LACLAVERIE, CHATEAU

Côtes de Francs 1989: Medium-ruby color. Plenty of floral, blackberry and cherry aromas. Full-bodied, with loads of alcohol and round, soft-textured tannins. Slightly one-dimensional but still fresh and balanced. (1989 Bordeaux horizontal tasting) Drink now through 2005.–J.S. • $NA • (5/31/1999) • **87**

LACOMBE-NOAILLAC, CHATEAU

Médoc 1997: Some plum and rhubarb character. Light-bodied, light finish.–J.S. • $NA • (1/31/2000) • **79**
Médoc 1996: Some ripe fruit nuances on the nose, but also slightly earthy, with a chestnut character. Medium-bodied, with soft tannins and a funky, leathery aftertaste. Hard to like. Tasted twice, with consistent notes.–J.S. • $15 • (1/31/1999) • **76**
Médoc 1995 • $15 • (1/31/1998) • **79**
Médoc 1994 • $15 • (1/31/1997) • **79**

Key: SS—Spectator Selection. CS—Cellar Selection. HR—Highly Recommended. $NA—Price not available. (BT)—Barrel tasting. Ⓐ—Auction Price. For a key to the tasters' initials, see "How to Use These Listings."
Dates in parentheses represent the issues in which the ratings were published.

FRANCE

LACOSTE-BORIE

Pauillac 1993 • $19 • (1/31/1996) • **75**
Pauillac 1990 • $42 Ⓐ • (3/31/1993) • **87**
Pauillac 1989 • $15 • (3/15/1992) • **89**
Pauillac 1988 • $19 • (4/30/1991) • **89**
Pauillac 1986 • $15 • (6/30/1989) • **84**

LADOUCETTE, DE

Pouilly-Fumé 1998: Medium in weight, this sports simple lemon zest flavors to go with a faint smoky note. Drink now.–B.S. • $24 • (6/15/2000) • **84**
Pouilly-Fumé 1997: This clean, focused white offers assertive citrus and mineral flavors, with intriguing accents of vanilla and spice. Racy and intense, it will make a fine match with a wide variety of fish dishes. Drink now through 2002.–T.M. • $28 • (6/30/1999) • **87**
Pouilly-Fumé 1996: Shows the gunflint and spicy herb notes typical of the appellation in top vintages. Full-bodied yet crisp and clean, it has plenty of ripe apple and even tropical flavors. A fine food wine. Drink now through 2003.–T.M. • $29 • (6/30/1999) • **89**
Pouilly-Fumé Baron de L 1996: Green apple, pear and herb flavors are focused and clean in this muscular white. Clean, tight and tart. Drink through 2003–T.M. • $65 • (6/30/1999) • **87**
Sancerre Comte Lafond 1998: Nice mineral-tinged nose, with pretty pear and lemon zest flavors that bounce along on lively acidity. Finishes with nice cut. Drink now.–B.S. • $25 • (6/15/2000) • **86**
Sancerre Comte Lafond 1997: This gentle, balanced white is quite subdued for Sancerre, but its core of mineral-scented citrus flavors gives it life and enough grip to match with food. Drink now through 2002.–T.M. • $25 • (6/30/1999) • **85**
Sancerre Comte Lafond 1996 • $28 • (6/15/1998) • **87**

LAFARGE, MICHEL

Beaune Grèves 1995: A bit rustic, with good *terroir* and earth components backed by burly tannins, a chewy texture, plum and cherry flavors. Lacks a bit of ripe fruit. Best from 2001 through 2003.–P.M. • $55 • (8/31/1998) • **84**
Bourgogne 1992 • $20 • (12/15/1994) • **72**
Bourgogne 1990 • $18 • (12/15/1992) • **82**
Bourgogne 1989 • $19 • (1/31/1992) • **85**
Volnay 1995: Light in color and dull on the palate, with some anise, mint and herbal notes. Medium-bodied, with modest fruit. Drink now.–P.M. • $36 • (8/31/1998) • **80**
Volnay 1992 • $35 • (12/15/1994) • **80**
Volnay 1991 • $38 • (1/31/1994) • **77**
Volnay 1990 • $43 • (12/15/1992) • **90**
Volnay 1989 • $41 • (1/31/1992) • **88**
Volnay Clos des Chênes 1995: Tastes like a big-ticket red Burgundy. Very reserved on the nose, it turns up the harmonious volume on the silky palate, which displays layers of cassis and cassis bush, plum and black cherry. Good concentration, if a bit tough and slightly herbal on the finish. Best from 2003.–P.M. • $103 • (8/31/1998) • **92**
Volnay Clos des Chênes 1994 • $70 • (9/30/1997) • **92**
Volnay Clos des Chênes 1993 • $94 • (5/15/1996) • **88**
Volnay Clos des Chênes 1992 • $65 • (12/15/1994) • **85**
Volnay Clos des Chênes 1991 • $62 • (2/28/1995) • **92**
Volnay Clos des Chênes 1990 • $115 Ⓐ • (2/28/1995) • **94**
Volnay Clos des Chênes 1989 • $67 • (2/28/1995) • **93**
Volnay Clos des Chênes 1988 • $72 • (2/28/1995) • **89**
Volnay Clos des Chênes 1987 • $52 • (2/28/1995) • **88**
Volnay Clos des Chênes 1986 • $39 • (2/28/1995) • **87**
Volnay Clos des Chênes 1985 • $75 • (2/28/1995) • **89**
Volnay Clos des Chênes 1983 • $NA • (2/28/1995) • **82**
Volnay Clos du Château des Ducs 1995: Smells a bit herbal, but is fairly lush on the midpalate. Turns green and dry on the finish. Drink now through 2005.–P.M. • $93 • (8/31/1998) • **80**
Volnay Clos du Château des Ducs 1994 • $70 • (9/30/1997) • **87**
Volnay Clos du Château des Ducs 1993 • $65 • (11/15/1995) • **93**
Volnay Clos du Château des Ducs 1992 • $65 • (12/15/1994) • **83**
Volnay Clos du Château des Ducs 1991 • $62 • (1/31/1994) • **86**
Volnay Clos du Château des Ducs 1990 • $75 • (12/15/1992) • **95**
Volnay Clos du Château des Ducs 1989 • $67 • (1/31/1992) • **94**
Volnay Clos du Château des Ducs 1988 • $65 • (7/15/1991) • **90**
Volnay Premier Cru 1988 • $44 • (7/15/1991) • **87**
Volnay Vendanges Sélectionnées 1995: Polished, with licorice, earth, game and plum notes. A clean, medium-bodied red, lacking a bit of depth but easy to enjoy. Drink now.–P.M. • $40 • (8/31/1998) • **84**
Volnay Vendanges Sélectionnées 1992 • $40 • (12/15/1994) • **81**
Volnay Vendanges Sélectionnées 1991 • $40 • (1/31/1994) • **82**

LAFAURIE-PEYRAGUEY, CHATEAU

Sauternes 1998: Delicate young Sauternes, with lovely apple, pear and spice character. Medium- to full-bodied, with good concentration and a sweet, spicy finish.–J.S. • $NA • (1/01/1999) (BT) • **90-94**
Sauternes 1997: Medium-bodied and sweet, with pretty apple skin, vanilla and grappa aromas and a vanilla and honey aftertaste. Perhaps not as exciting as usual, but very good indeed. Drink now through 2005.–J.S. • $48 • (1/31/2000) • **89**
Sauternes 1995 • $30 • (4/30/1998) • **87**
Sauternes 1992 • $NA • (4/15/1995) • **86**
Sauternes 1991 • $NA • (4/15/1995) • **80**
Sauternes 1990 • $43 Ⓐ • (4/15/1995) • **90**
Sauternes 1989 • $47 Ⓐ • (4/15/1995) • **94**
Sauternes 1988 • $61 Ⓐ • (4/15/1995) • **89**
Sauternes 1987 • $27 • (6/15/1990) • **87**
Sauternes 1986 • $54 Ⓐ • (12/31/1989) • **86**
Sauternes 1985 • $32 • (9/30/1988) • **92**
Sauternes 1983 • $48 Ⓐ • (1/31/1988) • **91**

LAFERRERE, HUBERT

Mâcon 1996 • $17 • (5/31/1998) • **81**
Mâcon-Chardonnay Hand Picked 1995 • $19 • (5/31/1997) • **80**

LAFFOURCADE

Anjou-Villages Château Perray Jouannet 1996: This lively red offers a lush texture, bright flavors of black cherry, coffee and leaf, and just enough tannin for balance and food. Not complex, but solid and focused. Drink now through 2001.–T.M. • $13 • (2/28/1999) • **84**
Bonnezeaux Château Perray Jouannet Les Menus Clos 1996: Sweet and clean, this shows more overripe flavors than botrytis ones, with raisin, dark chocolate and toast, well defined, but firm rather than generous. May soften with time. Drink now through 2003.–T.M. • $30 • (2/28/1999) • **87**
Coteaux du Layon Château Perray Jouannet 1997: Plush yet focused, this round, soft white offers ripe apple, vanilla and creamy flavors, with good sweetness and a spicy finish. Not that powerful but tight and clean, and should bloom with time. Drink now through 2005.–T.M. • $16 • (2/28/1999) • **88**
Quarts de Chaume Château de L'Echarderie Sélection Vieilles Vignes 1996: Simple and light, this offers apple, light spice and citrus flavors. It's fresh and clean, but hardly representative of the possibilities of this prestigious appellation. Drink now.–T.M. • $45 • (2/28/1999) • **83**
Savennières 1997: Firm, with good balance and structure. The flavors, a bit muted now, hint at melon, pineapple, toast. Should develop well. Drink now through 2003.–T.M. • $16 • (2/28/1999) • **85**
Savennières Clos la Royauté 1996: Big and muscular, but the deep gold color and rather Sherry-like flavors are already mature, and there's little fruit.–T.M. • $19 • (2/28/1999) • **79**
Savennières Demi-Sec 1996: This broad, firm white is slightly sweet, with peach, ginger and caramel flavors and enough underlying acidity to keep it balanced. Unusual and appealing. Drink now through 2005.–T.M. • $17 • (2/28/1999) • **87**

LAFITE ROTHSCHILD, CHATEAU

Pauillac 1999: Super aromas of currants, berries and tobacco, with hints of cedar and vanilla. Full-bodied yet very balanced, with plenty of superfine tannins and a long, long finish. Wine of the vintage for the Médoc? Certainly very close.–J.S. • $NA • (1/01/2000) (BT) • **90-94**
Pauillac 1998: A warm and seductive '98, enticing for its blackberry, cherry and tobacco aromas. Full-bodied, with fine yet rich tannins and a long aftertaste. Needs a bit more on the center palate to score higher; wait and see.–J.S. • $NA • (5/31/1999) (BT) • **90-94**
Pauillac 1997: Wonderfully complex on the nose, with licorice, spice, berry and tobacco character. Medium-bodied, with fine tannins and a delicious finish. Drink now through 2005.–J.S. • $137 • (1/31/2000) • **90**
Pauillac 1996: Impressively dark in color, with mineral, mint and black currant aromas that hint also of spices and cedar. Full-bodied, with very firm tannins and a silky texture, this top Bordeaux goes on and on on the

LAFITE ROTHSCHILD, CHATEAU

palate. One of the most solid Lafites in recent history. Best after 2002.–J.S. • $218 Ⓐ • (1/31/1999) CS • **96**

Pauillac 1995 • $189 Ⓐ • (1/31/1998) CS • **97**
Pauillac 1994 • $88 Ⓐ • (1/31/1997) CS • **93**
Pauillac 1993 • $80 Ⓐ • (1/31/1996) • **86**
Pauillac 1992 • $87 Ⓐ • (4/15/1995) • **89**
Pauillac 1991 • $69 Ⓐ • (3/31/1994) • **85**
Pauillac 1990 • $207 Ⓐ • (3/31/1993) CS • **97**

Pauillac 1989: Rich and balanced Lafite. Dark ruby-red color. Very ripe and earthy, its aromas verging on raisin with hints of cedar and tobacco which follow through on the palate. Full-bodied and silky, adding a long, flavorful aftertaste. Give it time. (1989 Bordeaux horizontal tasting) . Best after 2004.–J.S. • $164 Ⓐ • (5/31/1999) • **94**

Pauillac 1988: Slightly disappointing for Lafite, this has medium body, fine tannins and pretty aromas and flavors of tobacco, cedar and fruit. Though lacking in fruit and tannin concentration, it's elegant and supple, giving plenty of pleasure. (1989 Bordeaux horizontal tasting). Drink now.–J.S. • $147 Ⓐ • (11/30/1998) • **90**

Pauillac 1987 • $NA • (11/30/1991) • **88**
Pauillac 1986 • $225 Ⓐ • (3/31/1989) • **96**
Pauillac 1985 • $159 Ⓐ • (9/15/1996) • **90**
Pauillac 1984 • $NA • (11/30/1991) • **87**
Pauillac 1983 • $132 Ⓐ • (10/15/1994) • **91**

Pauillac 1982: Superb red. Starts slowly and then comes through big-time on the palate. Balanced and harmonious. Brilliant ruby color, with a garnet hue. Currant character, with a hint of cedar. Medium- to full-bodied, with silky tannins and a sweet fruit finish. (1989 Bordeaux horizontal tasting) Drink now.–J.S. • $NA • (11/30/1998) • **95**

Pauillac 1981 • $108 Ⓐ • (10/15/1994) • **88**
Pauillac 1980 • $61 Ⓐ • (11/30/1991) • **86**
Pauillac 1979 • $102 Ⓐ • (10/15/1989) • **92**
Pauillac 1978 • $120 Ⓐ • (11/30/1991) • **94**
Pauillac 1977 • $72 Ⓐ • (11/30/1991) • **87**
Pauillac 1976 • $164 Ⓐ • (3/31/1989) • **92**
Pauillac 1974 • $62 Ⓐ • (11/30/1991) • **89**
Pauillac 1973 • $63 Ⓐ • (11/30/1991) • **87**
Pauillac 1972 • $NA • (11/30/1991) • **82**
Pauillac 1971 • $76 Ⓐ • (11/30/1991) • **87**
Pauillac 1970 • $119 Ⓐ • (11/30/1991) • **92**
Pauillac 1969 • $59 Ⓐ • (11/30/1991) • **80**
Pauillac 1967 • $50 Ⓐ • (11/30/1991) • **80**
Pauillac 1966 • $141 Ⓐ • (11/30/1991) • **84**
Pauillac 1965 • $45 • (11/30/1991) • **73**
Pauillac 1964 • $91 Ⓐ • (11/30/1991) • **87**
Pauillac 1962 • $147 Ⓐ • (11/30/1991) • **93**
Pauillac 1961 • $713/1.5 liter • (4/30/1996) • **94**
Pauillac 1959 • $823 Ⓐ • (11/30/1991) • **94**
Pauillac 1959 • $NA/1.5 liter • (11/30/1991) • **98**
Pauillac 1958 • $NA • (11/30/1991) • **77**
Pauillac 1957 • $158 Ⓐ • (11/30/1991) • **87**
Pauillac 1956 • $NA • (11/30/1991) • **85**
Pauillac 1955 • $279 Ⓐ • (11/30/1991) • **94**
Pauillac 1954 • $NA • (11/30/1991) • **82**
Pauillac 1953 • $586 Ⓐ • (11/30/1991) • **94**
Pauillac 1953 • $NA/1.5 liter • (11/30/1991) • **96**
Pauillac 1952 • $176 Ⓐ • (11/30/1991) • **90**
Pauillac 1951 • $148 Ⓐ • (11/30/1991) • **78**
Pauillac 1950 • $276 Ⓐ • (11/30/1991) • **91**
Pauillac 1949 • $613 Ⓐ • (11/30/1991) • **87**
Pauillac 1949 • $NA/1.5 liter • (11/30/1991) • **90**
Pauillac 1947 • $378 Ⓐ • (5/31/1997) • **92**
Pauillac 1946 • $242 Ⓐ • (11/30/1991) • **79**
Pauillac 1945 • $763 Ⓐ • (11/30/1995) • **90**
Pauillac 1943 • $320 • (11/30/1991) • **87**
Pauillac 1943 • $NA/1.5 liter • (11/30/1991) • **85**
Pauillac 1942 • $138 Ⓐ • (11/30/1991) • **80**
Pauillac 1940 • $700 • (11/30/1991) • **85**
Pauillac 1939 • $320 • (12/15/1988) • **78**
Pauillac 1938 • $307 Ⓐ • (11/30/1991) • **83**
Pauillac 1937 • $218 Ⓐ • (11/30/1991) • **81**
Pauillac 1934 • $420 • (11/30/1991) • **90**
Pauillac 1933 • $200 • (11/30/1991) • **80**
Pauillac 1931 • $550 • (11/30/1991) • **77**
Pauillac 1929 • $805 Ⓐ • (11/30/1991) • **87**
Pauillac 1929 • $NA/1.5 liter • (11/30/1991) • **88**
Pauillac 1928 • $820 Ⓐ • (12/15/1988) • **83**
Pauillac 1926 • $380 Ⓐ • (11/30/1991) • **89**
Pauillac 1925 • $NA • (12/15/1988) • **74**
Pauillac 1924 • $345 Ⓐ • (11/30/1991) • **88**
Pauillac 1923 • $195 Ⓐ • (11/30/1991) • **75**
Pauillac 1921 • $500 • (12/15/1988) • **77**
Pauillac 1920 • $1,104 Ⓐ • (11/30/1991) • **94**
Pauillac 1919 • $NA • (11/30/1991) • **76**
Pauillac 1918 • $863 Ⓐ • (11/30/1991) • **80**
Pauillac 1917 • $500 • (11/30/1991) • **75**
Pauillac 1916 • $446 Ⓐ • (11/30/1991) • **71**
Pauillac 1916 • $NA/1.5 liter • (11/30/1991) • **89**
Pauillac 1914 • $219 Ⓐ • (12/15/1988) • **75**
Pauillac 1913 • $500 • (11/30/1991) • **82**
Pauillac 1912 • $NA • (12/15/1988) • **76**
Pauillac 1911 • $NA • (11/30/1991) • **83**
Pauillac 1910 • $NA • (12/15/1988) • **77**
Pauillac 1909 • $500 • (11/30/1991) • **73**
Pauillac 1908 • $600/1.5 liter • (11/30/1991) • **86**
Pauillac 1907 • $NA • (12/15/1988) • **79**
Pauillac 1906 • $350 • (11/30/1991) • **90**
Pauillac 1905 • $762 Ⓐ • (11/30/1991) • **88**
Pauillac 1904 • $660 • (11/30/1991) • **84**
Pauillac 1902 • $750 Ⓐ • (11/30/1991) • **80**
Pauillac 1901 • $700 • (11/30/1991) • **74**
Pauillac 1900 • $3,792 Ⓐ • (11/30/1991) • **79**
Pauillac 1900 • $NA/1.5 liter • (11/30/1991) • **70**
Pauillac 1899 • $4,695 Ⓐ • (12/15/1988) • **78**
Pauillac 1898 • $1,725 Ⓐ • (12/15/1988) • **79**
Pauillac 1897 • $1,400 • (12/15/1988) • **81**
Pauillac 1896 • $800 • (12/15/1988) • **79**
Pauillac 1895 • $1,604 Ⓐ • (12/15/1988) • **89**
Pauillac 1894 • $1,500 • (11/30/1991) • **71**
Pauillac 1893 • $679 Ⓐ • (12/15/1988) • **84**
Pauillac 1892 • $1,300 • (11/30/1991) • **72**
Pauillac 1891 • $NA • (11/30/1991) • **70**
Pauillac 1890 • $1,368 Ⓐ • (12/15/1988) • **83**
Pauillac 1889 • $950 • (12/15/1988) • **85**
Pauillac 1888 • $550 • (12/15/1988) • **82**
Pauillac 1886 • $NA • (12/15/1988) • **88**
Pauillac 1882 • $800 • (12/15/1988) • **82**
Pauillac 1881 • $NA • (12/15/1988) • **85**
Pauillac 1880 • $1,500 • (12/15/1988) • **82**
Pauillac 1879 • $2,800 • (12/15/1988) • **83**
Pauillac 1878 • $1,840 Ⓐ • (12/15/1988) • **83**
Pauillac 1877 • $2,500 • (12/15/1988) • **88**
Pauillac 1876 • $1,750 • (12/15/1988) • **84**
Pauillac 1875 • $NA • (12/15/1988) • **91**
Pauillac 1875 • $NA/1.5 liter • (12/15/1988) • **97**
Pauillac 1874 • $1,680 Ⓐ • (12/15/1988) • **84**
Pauillac 1870 • $5,491 Ⓐ • (11/30/1991) • **92**
Pauillac 1869 • $3,500 • (11/30/1991) • **87**
Pauillac 1868 • $3,500 • (11/30/1991) • **91**
Pauillac 1865 • $5,874 Ⓐ • (12/15/1988) • **84**
Pauillac 1864 • $3,680 Ⓐ • (12/15/1988) • **84**
Pauillac 1858 • $4,000 • (12/15/1988) • **96**
Pauillac 1848 • $8,500 • (12/15/1988) • **92**
Pauillac 1846 • $7,541 Ⓐ • (12/15/1988) • **83**
Pauillac 1844 • $6,500 • (12/15/1988) • **84**
Pauillac 1832 • $8,485 Ⓐ • (11/30/1991) • **78**
Pauillac 1806 • $25,000 • (12/15/1988) • **83**

LAFITTE, CHARLES

Brut Champagne Tête de Cuvée NV: Flavorful and different. Has a deep, brassy color, smoky aromas and mature flavors of honey, pear and smoke. Drink now. • $45 • (10/15/1999) • **84**

Key: SS—Spectator Selection. CS—Cellar Selection. HR—Highly Recommended. $NA—Price not available. (BT)—Barrel tasting. Ⓐ—Auction Price.
For a key to the tasters' initials, see "How to Use These Listings."
Dates in parentheses represent the issues in which the ratings were published.

LAFLEUR, CHATEAU

Pomerol 1999: Black color. Powerful aromas of very ripe plums, berries and minerals. Full-bodied, with ripe tannins that build on the palate. Long, long finish. Almost classic quality. No. 2 wine of the vintage.–J.S. • $NA • (1/01/2000) (BT) • **90-94**

Pomerol 1998: Multidimensional nose of fruit, earth, stones and spices. Full-bodied. Starts off slowly on the palate than wham—the tannins hit. Builds and builds on the palate, has a long, long finish. This is a very well-structured young wine.–J.S. • $NA • (5/31/1999) (BT) • **95-99**

Pomerol 1997: A solid wine. Good dried cherry and berry aromas follow through to a medium-bodied palate, with light tannins and a fruity finish. Perhaps not as impressive as in barrel. Tasted twice, with consistent notes. Best from 2001 through 2005.–J.S. • $191 • (1/31/2000) • **89**

Pomerol 1996: Not a blockbuster Lafleur, but harmonious and pleasure-giving. Black chocolate and berry aromas and flavors continue to a medium-bodied palate, with fine tannins and a fruity, caressing finish. Not quite as exciting in bottle as from barrel, but still a beauty. Best after 2000.–J.S. • $130 • (1/31/1999) • **89**

Pomerol 1995: A '95 that exploded in the glass in contact with air. Solid and masculine, with dark chocolate and bitter mocha notes, there's big intensity here. While the tannins are burly for now, the aromas keep coming—rose petal, violet and currant backed by creamy, vanilla bean character. Elegant finish. (Château Lafleur vertical tasting, as are all notes below dated 1/31/2000). Best from 2005 through 2015.–P.M. • $262 Ⓐ • (1/31/2000) • **98**

Pomerol 1993: Wonderful—dark and brooding—with plenty of currant and mint character. Super balance, with ripe tannins and a sense of elegance. Excellent quality for this vintage. Drink now through 2010.–P.M. • $90 Ⓐ • (1/31/2000) • **91**

Pomerol 1992 • $83 Ⓐ • (4/15/1995) • **88**

Pomerol 1990 • $508 Ⓐ • (5/15/1994) • **95**

Pomerol 1989: Typically muscular Lafleur. Very dark-ruby color. Cherry, blackberry and dark chocolate aromas. Full-bodied and powerful, with loads of tannins and chunky fruit. Closed, not giving away much right now; give it time. (1989 Bordeaux horizontal tasting). Best after 2008.–J.S. • $342 Ⓐ • (5/31/1999) • **97**

Pomerol 1988: A bit tight, not giving much. Still dark-colored, with chocolate, berry and mineral character on the nose and palate. Full-bodied, with a balance of silky tannins. (1989 Bordeaux horizontal tasting). Best after 2001.–J.S. • $201 Ⓐ • (11/30/1998) • **90**

Pomerol 1988: Super wine that delivers great concentration. Terroir bursts through in this wine, as it tastes of soil and mineral, blackberry and concentrated fruit. Clean, classy and full-bodied, this '88 beat out the '86 and '85 in a blind flight. Drink now through 2010.–P.M. • $201 Ⓐ • (1/31/2000) • **98**

Pomerol 1986: A marvelous Lafleur, full-bodied, with supple tannins, offering lovely mineral, earth and black fruit character. Smooth and ripe from start to finish. Drink now through 2020.–P.M. • $243 Ⓐ • (1/31/2000) • **95**

Pomerol 1985: Very soft and elegantly styled, delivering floral, chocolate, earth, mineral, cranberry and currant notes. Drink now through 2005.–P.M. • $332 Ⓐ • (1/31/2000) • **90**

Pomerol 1984: Drying and a bit flat, with a tart finish.–P.M. • $82 Ⓐ • (1/31/2000) • **73**

Pomerol 1983 • $252 Ⓐ • (10/15/1994) • **91**

Pomerol 1982: This is a massive, Port-like wine with stunning potential. I have always underrated its greatness. They just don't make great Bordeaux like this anymore, or very seldom. Plenty of sweet berry, tobacco and olive aromas. Big and chewy, with masses of fruit and velvety tannins. Sweet fruit finish. (1982 Bordeaux horizontal tasting). Best after 2000.–J.S. • $727 Ⓐ • (11/30/1998) • **99**

Pomerol 1981: Shows a pretty balance between fairly ripe fruit and soft tannins. While showing some dilution, it keeps growing in the glass. Drink now through 2001.–P.M. • $96 Ⓐ • (1/31/2000) • **87**

Pomerol 1980: Nice red berry and olive character and displays good intensity. The structure is tight and the tannins firm, but it lacks a bit of ripeness. Drink now through 2005.–P.M. • $NA • (1/31/2000) • **80**

Pomerol 1979: Very tannic still, but with lots of fruit. Smells of crushed black olives. Medium-bodied, it tastes sweet and ripe, but is a bit lean on the palate. Drink now through 2010.–P.M. • $543 Ⓐ • (1/31/2000) • **87**

Pomerol 1978: Layered and complex, with loads of cassis and blackberry flavors and classic-tasting Lafleur terroir coming through in the mineral, lead pencil, wet earth character. A bit tougher than the '70. Best from 2002 through 2010.–P.M. • $192 Ⓐ • (1/31/2000) • **92**

Pomerol 1977: From a difficult vintage, this is a remarkable '77, offering good ripeness and fruit—plum, black cherry—and some olive, minerally lead-pencil complexity. Turns a bit hard on the finish. Drink now through 2002.–P.M. • $NA • (1/31/2000) • **83**

Pomerol 1976: Lacks a bit of complexity, but fairly round in the mouth, with cassis and raspberry notes. Kicks in with some tartness on the finish.–P.M. • $67 Ⓐ • (1/31/2000) • **78**

Pomerol 1975: Promising wine that's a bit burly now. Closed on the nose, but showing lots of ripe fruit. A bit tough, but this masculine wine makes an impressive mouthfeel. Best after 2005.–P.M. • $717 Ⓐ • (1/31/2000) • **85**

Pomerol 1974: A wine that's peaked. A bit dusty on the nose, lean and dry on the palate, with a bitter finish.–P.M. • $NA • (1/31/2000) • **73**

Pomerol 1973: Pleasant, with some cherry and cedar notes, but a bit dry, lean and short. Drink now.–P.M. • $NA • (1/31/2000) • **81**

Pomerol 1971: Some good fruit here, with cherry and raspberry aromas and flavors, but expect a rather lean wine—certainly less opulent than the '70—with tannins that seem a bit dry. Drink now through 2005.–P.M. • $NA • (1/31/2000) • **86**

Pomerol 1970: Harmonious, supple and very generous, full-bodied, with ripe tannins; perfect to enjoy now but it should last, it's almost black in color and explodes with cassis and green olive aromas and flavors. Drink now through 2010.–P.M. • $364 Ⓐ • (1/31/2000) • **96**

Pomerol 1966 • $538 Ⓐ • (5/15/1994) • **85**

Pomerol 1964 • $300 • (5/15/1994) • **87**

Pomerol 1962 • $423 Ⓐ • (5/15/1994) • **86**

Pomerol 1961: Tasted from magnum. Very harmonious on the nose, but it's tannic on the palate, where it shows a cedary, tough side. The fruit has faded a bit on the palate, but the black fruit aromas are wonderful. Drink now through 2005.–P.M. • $3,086 Ⓐ • (1/31/2000) • **82**

Pomerol 1959 • $119 Ⓐ • (5/15/1994) • **87**

Pomerol 1955: Smooth and silky, very ripe and lovely, with cassis, sweet oak and vanilla bean character, a balanced finish. Drink now through 2010.–P.M. • $408 Ⓐ • (1/31/2000) • **90**

Pomerol 1953 • $650 • (5/15/1994) • **85**

Pomerol 1952: Good year in Pomerol, but poor bottle. Lean, cedary, dry, even a bit musty.–P.M. • $NA • (1/31/2000) • **74**

Pomerol English Bottling 1952 • $375 • (5/15/1994) • **79**

Pomerol 1950: Tasted from magnum. Superdeep, with pronounced vanilla character from the oak, this is a thick wine, with totally smooth tannins and lovely cassis, black cherry and mocha. Grew more and more complex in the glass. Drink now through 2020.–P.M. • $NA • (1/31/2000) • **98**

Pomerol 1949: Tasted from magnum. Beautiful, exotic, marvelous, still dark in color. A Lafleur you can sniff forever, with aromatic layers of olives, cedar, plum and cigar smoke. Tastes great, offering mineral, lead pencil character. Delicious. Drink now through 2010.–P.M. • $NA • (1/31/2000) • **95**

Pomerol 1948: Tasted from magnum. Very deep, even closed on the nose, it tastes like a great blend of 1949 (95 points) and 1950 (98). A pure wine that's thicker than the '49, it's superintense, kicking and screaming with life, making it almost painful to drink. Cellar. Best after 2010.–P.M. • $11,500 • (1/31/2000) • **97**

Pomerol 1947: An amazing drinking experience, this Lafleur shadowboxes with your senses, hitting one pleasure spot after another. Clean and racy, yet very ripe, rich and with the full body of syrup, tasting of raspberry and chocolate yogurt. This is exotic, with beautifully silky tannins, and mocha and spice notes on the finish. Drink now through 2015.–P.M. • $1,762 • (1/31/2000) • **100**

Pomerol 1945: Tasted from magnum. The fruit is definitely fading in this bottle; tastes woody and cedary, a disappointing '45. Drink now.–P.M. • $NA • (1/31/2000) • **80**

LAFLEUR-GAZIN, CHATEAU

Pomerol 1998: Lovely cherry and chocolate character in a medium-bodied, medium-tannined package. Slightly diluted finish.–J.S. • $NA • (5/31/1999) (BT) • **80-84**

Pomerol 1997: A light red with some berry character and a very light finish.–J.S. • $NA • (1/31/2000) • **79**

Pomerol 1996: Interesting blackberry and tobacco aromas and flavors. Medium-bodied, with light tannins and a fruity aftertaste. Drink now.–J.S. • $NA • (1/31/1999) • **84**

Pomerol 1995 • $30 • (1/31/1998) • **90**

Pomerol 1994 • $25 • (1/31/1997) • **83**

Pomerol 1993 • $24 • (1/31/1996) • **85**

Pomerol 1990 • $30 • (3/31/1993) • **90**

Pomerol 1989: Pretty, balanced Pomerol. Good deep-ruby color. Lovely aromas of flowers and raspberries. Medium-bodied, with silky tannins and a fresh, fruity aftertaste. (1989 Bordeaux horizontal tasting). Best after 2000.–J.S. • $NA • (5/31/1999) • **88**

Pomerol 1982: Very impressive for this château. Cherry, floral and raspberry aromas and flavors. Medium- to full-bodied, with well-integrated tannins and a long, long finish. A refined and elegant wine with great length. (1989 Bordeaux horizontal tasting). Drink now.–J.S. • $NA • (11/30/1998) • **90**

Pomerol 1945 • $300 • (11/30/1995) • **80**

LAFON, DOMAINE DES COMTES

Meursault 1997: Elegant and ripe. A subtle, vanilla-scented and wonderfully textured white, full in body and silky, with green apple, citrus, toasted hazelnut, honey and a chewy, chalky character. Drink now through 2005.–P.M. • $60 • (5/31/2000) • **88**

Meursault 1996: Pure, rich, thick fruit expresses itself with the subtle support of toasted oak. Balanced acidity guides the tropical, lemon and mineral notes to a gracious, firm finish. Drink through 2010–P.M. • $86 Ⓐ • (5/31/1999) • **94**

Meursault 1995 • $134 Ⓐ • (5/31/1998) • **93**

Meursault Charmes 1997: Gorgeous white Burgundy. Full-bodied, silky, with a real spicy mocha-coffee and macadamia nut complexity. There is so much to love in this seductive, honeyed Chardonnay. A crowd-pleaser from start to finish. Drink now through 2010.–P.M. • $100 • (5/31/2000) • **93**

Meursault Charmes 1996: Elegant and racy, this superminerally, silky white shows lovely ripe fruit and impeccable balance. Full-bodied, it coats every inch of the palate with creamy texture and pumps out the clean vanilla, mineral and wet stone flavors on the deftly toasted finish. Best from 2006 through 2026.–P.M. • $249 Ⓐ • (5/31/1999) • **95**

Meursault Charmes 1995 • $80 • (5/31/1998) • **97**

Meursault Clos de la Barre 1997: A Chardonnay with personality. Clean and pure, with honey, earth, lemon and dried herb character; a taste of soil as well. Medium-bodied, the caramel, mocha, spice and toasted oak notes kick in on the chewy, chalky finish. Best from 2002 through 2008.–P.M. • $70 • (5/31/2000) • **88**

Meursault Clos de la Barre 1996: Fresh and lemony, with pear, mineral and honey character. Vibrant and clean on the midpalate but drying on the finish.–P.M. • $134 Ⓐ • (5/31/1999) • **78**

Meursault Clos de la Barre 1995 • $77 Ⓐ • (5/31/1998) • **94**

Meursault Désirée 1997: Interesting and distinctive *goût de terroir.* Aromatically sharp, offering dried herbs and pungent wet earth components. Medium-bodied and citrusy, it has a fairly supple midpalate, displaying good concentration of fruit. Gains silkiness on the intense long finish. Needs time. Best from 2003 through 2010.–P.M. • $70 • (5/31/2000) • **90**

Meursault Désirée 1996: Beautiful, with a clean and silky texture that caresses the palate. A lot goes on in this attractive, full-bodied gem, with lemon, mineral, honey and toasted oak flavors pulled together in a superhandsome, velvety finish. Bravo! Best from 2006 through 2016.–P.M. • $163 Ⓐ • (5/31/1999) • **95**

Meursault Désirée 1995 • $NA • (5/31/1998) • **93**

Meursault Genevrières 1997: Beautiful. Clean and densely textured, it delivers elegant flavors and a balanced mouthfeel; full-bodied, with refined fruit backed by honey, spice and a medium-long finish. Drink now through 2005.–P.M. • $100 • (5/31/2000) • **90**

Meursault Genevrières 1996: Unreal. This gorgeous, refined, seductive, full-bodied white Burgundy is packed with sensational, smooth texture. Soft as silk and loaded to the rafters with deliciously ripe fruit, surrounded by the sort of vanilla-infused, toasty, smoky oak accents that taste sweet. The balance is astounding. Drink now through 2026.–P.M. • $80 • (5/31/1999) • **99**

Meursault Goutte d'Or 1995 • $153 Ⓐ • (5/31/1998) • **89**

Meursault Perrières 1997: Rich and ripe, a thick Meursault that's beautifully balanced between the lightly toasted oak, honey-coated fruit and coffee and mocha complexity. Full-bodied, it lingers on the finish, seducing the senses. Drink now through 2010.–P.M. • $110 • (5/31/2000) • **93**

Meursault Perrières 1996: Elegant and classy, focused and beautifully oaked, this brims with pear, tropical and grilled game. The rich, velvety, minerally mouthfeel is inspiring as it swirls around the palate like a powerful tornado bursting with sweet, ripe flavors. Best from 2006 through 2016.–P.M. • $80 • (5/31/1999) • **96**

Meursault Perrières 1995 • $307 Ⓐ • (5/31/1998) • **95**

Key: SS—Spectator Selection. CS—Cellar Selection. HR—Highly Recommended. $NA—Price not available. (BT)—Barrel tasting. Ⓐ—Auction Price.
For a key to the tasters' initials, see "How to Use These Listings."
Dates in parentheses represent the issues in which the ratings were published.

Monthélie Les Duresses 1997: A juicy wine, with a supple mid-palate, but it stresses more straightforward flavors (strawberry), and offers a herbal touch. It's a tad simple. Drink now through 2003.–P.M. • $35 • (1/01/2000) • **82**

Monthélie Les Duresses 1996: A slightly herbal, tough and astringent red, showing cold black cherry flavors in a firm, chewy package. Time should soften it a bit.–P.M. • $35 • (5/15/1999) • **79**

Monthélie Les Duresses 1995: Interesting. Packed with wet earth, mineral and firm tannins, this is a rather tough wine, but the concentration of ripe fruit makes up for the burly, muscular frame. Good length. Best after 2005.–P.M. • $31 • (8/31/1998) • **89**

Monthélie Les Duresses 1992 • $25 • (5/31/1995) • **84**

Montrachet 1997: Subtle and silky. Full in body and yellow in color, it delivers lovely spice, crème brûlée, caramel, honey, ripe pear, toasted bread and even tropical notes. Very complex, superbalanced on the finish. Crafty winemaking. Drink now through 2010.–P.M. • $500 • (5/31/2000) • **94**

Montrachet 1996: Amazing fruit and power. Ripe and thick, with lots of lemon and toasted oak—a Chardonnay given the full Burgundian treatment. There's a chewy, chalky, buttery, intensely tropical side to this full-bodied wine. Needs years to show it all. Best from 2010 through 2020.–P.M. • $300 • (5/31/1999) • **98**

Montrachet 1995 • $400 • (5/31/1998) • **98**

Puligny-Montrachet Champ-Gain 1997: Pungent, earthy, rich and concentrated, this is for Burgundy aficionados who don't mind a bit of idiosyncrasy in their wine. Draws its personality from the *terroir* (smoke, horse manure, matchstick, you name it) while seducing with silky texture, honey, lemon and ripe fruit and an interminable finish. Best from 2002 through 2008.–P.M. • $90 • (5/31/2000) • **93**

Puligny-Montrachet Champ-Gain 1996: A fresh style of '96, with a lemony, floral, buttery, cooked applesauce character and lots of acidity. Some herbal notes emerge on the finish. Best from 2006 through 2012.–P.M. • $80 • (5/31/1999) • **82**

Puligny-Montrachet Champ-Gain 1995 • $NA • (5/31/1998) • **93**

Volnay 1992 • $NA • (12/15/1994) • **85**

Volnay Champans 1997: Soft, full-bodied and dark purple, with ripe tannins that fold easily into the structure. Has lovely fresh red and black fruit aromas, but lacks just a bit of depth and complexity to rate higher. Drink now through 2007. • $NA • (1/01/2000) • **87**

Volnay Champans 1996: Supple and showing lovely, pure fruit, brimming with black cherry, wild raspberry character. Medium-bodied, medium-intense; easy to appreciate on release. Drink now through 2004.–P.M. • $65 • (5/15/1999) • **87**

Volnay Champans 1995: Suave wine that is subtle and reserved on the nose now, but shows a fine, silky midpalate, with deft mocha and vanilla accents and lovely ripe cassis and currant flavors. Full-bodied, the lush, fine-textured finish is seductive. Best after 2003.–P.M. • $60 • (8/31/1998) • **89**

Volnay Champans 1994 • $55 • (9/30/1997) • **83**

Volnay Champans 1993 • $NA • (5/15/1996) • **85**

Volnay Champans 1991 • $54 • (1/31/1994) • **83**

Volnay Clos des Chênes 1996: Cold fruit in this angular, nicely fruity and fairly ripe but tannic wine, medium-bodied and a bit tough. Hard finish. Best from 2003 through 2010.–P.M. • $65 • (5/15/1999) • **83**

Volnay Clos des Chênes 1995: Burly Pinot Noir, at least now, with firm tannins. Has a slight herbal character, but also some ripe fruit and good midpalate concentration. Full-bodied, with black cherry, cassis, mocha and smoke flavors. Tough finish. Best after 2005.–P.M. • $60 • (8/31/1998) • **88**

Volnay Clos des Chênes 1994 • $55 • (9/30/1997) • **90**

Volnay Clos des Chênes 1993 • $NA • (5/15/1996) • **88**

Volnay-Santenots du Milieu 1997: Full -bodied and dark, with a rich, dense and chalky mouthfeel that hints at top-grade *terroir*. Its length and depth tantalize the senses, with loads of fruit and mineral character. Lafon's best Volnay-Santenots du-Milieu since 1990. Best from 2003 through 2015. • $65 • (1/01/2000) • **95**

Volnay-Santenots du Milieu 1996: Supple and well made, round and juicy, showing some fresh red berry with hints of mocha and toasted bread, this is delightful, clean and pure, with a grip of firm tannins on the classy finish. Drink now through 2005.–P.M. • $53 Ⓐ • (5/15/1999) • **89**

Volnay-Santenots du Milieu 1994 • $55 • (9/30/1997) • **92**

Volnay-Santenots du Milieu 1993 • $55 Ⓐ • (5/15/1996) • **93**

Volnay-Santenots du Milieu 1992 • $NA • (1/01/1994) • **90**

Volnay-Santenots du Milieu 1991 • $54 • (1/31/1994) • **84**

LAFON-ROCHET, CHATEAU

St.-Estèphe 1999: Chewy for a '99, with velvety tannins and a good concentation of ripe fruit. Rather short finish.–J.S. • $NA • (1/01/2000) (BT) • **85-89**

St.-Estèphe 1998: A velvety young wine, with a good core of ripe fruit, a medium body and medium tannins.–J.S. • $NA • (5/31/1999) (BT) • **85-89**
St.-Estèphe 1997: Good spicy vanilla and mineral aromas. Medium-bodied, with fine tannins and a fruity finish. Drink now through 2004.–J.S. • $23 • (1/31/2000) • **87**
St.-Estèphe 1996: Dark-colored, with floral, spice and dark-fruit character; the mineral and spice flavors follow through on the palate. Medium- to full-bodied, with silky tannins and a caressing texture. A refined and balanced Lafon-Rochet. Best after 2001.–J.S. • $30 • (1/31/1999) • **90**
St.-Estèphe 1995 • $34 Ⓐ • (1/31/1998) • **93**
St.-Estèphe 1994 • $30 • (1/31/1997) • **88**
St.-Estèphe 1993 • $57 Ⓐ • (1/31/1996) • **88**
St.-Estèphe 1992 • $18 • (4/15/1995) • **84**
St.-Estèphe 1991 • $18 • (3/31/1994) • **78**
St.-Estèphe 1990 • $28 • (3/31/1993) • **89**
St.-Estèphe 1989: A big, very ripe, overdone wine—but a delicious one. Seriously good dark-ruby color. Lots of raspberry and prune character on the nose. Full-bodied, with flavors verging on dried raisin, and toast and jam character on the aftertaste. (1989 Bordeaux horizontal tasting). Best after 2000.–J.S. • $42 Ⓐ • (5/31/1999) • **90**
St.-Estèphe 1982 • $36 Ⓐ • (8/31/1992) • **90**
St.-Estèphe 1970 • $36 Ⓐ • (5/15/1993) • **80**
St.-Estèphe 1945 • $100 • (3/16/1986) • **75**

LAFOND, DOMAINE

Côtes du Rhône 1997: Ripe and fairly rich, with plum, black cherry, licorice, dried fig. Medium-bodied, satisfying, but with chewy tannins on the slightly hot finish. Drink now.–P.M. • $9 • (11/15/1998) • **80**
Côtes du Rhône White 1998: Fresh but straightforward, with some interesting wet hay, lime and salt notes accenting the dominant pear and green apple character. Drink now.–P.M. • $9 • (11/15/1999) • **84**
Côtes du Rhône White 1997: Clean, ripe and quite crisp, but also showing fat, earth, and an overall *terroir* character. Interesting, with a chewy core of melon, cured ham, mineral and appleskin. Drink now.–P.M. • $9 • (11/15/1998) • **86**
Tavel 1998: A bit earthy but also tasting of clean fruit, it's a medium-bodied rosé that's balanced and smooth, yet has kick on the finish. Drink now.–P.M. • $10 • (11/15/1999) • **84**
Tavel 1997: Fairly lean, with little fruit.–P.M. • $11 • (11/15/1998) • **74**

LAFONT MENAUT, CHATEAU

Pessac-Léognan 1998: Lacks a bit in the mouth, with medium body, medium tannins and a slightly diluted midpalate.–J.S. • $NA • (5/31/1999) (BT) • **80-84**
Pessac-Léognan 1997: Attractive berry and cherry character to this, with a hint of dried herbs. Medium-bodied, with medium tannins and a short finish. Drink now.–J.S. • $NA • (1/31/2000) • **82**
Pessac-Léognan 1996: A simple, slightly rustic wine. Aromas of earth and cherries, with a hint of leather, follow through to a medium-bodied palate with medium tannins and a short finish.–J.S. • $NA • (2/28/1999) • **79**
Pessac-Léognan White 1998: A lively and fresh wine, with grapefruit and lemon character. Medium-bodied, with a fresh finish. Drink now.–J.S. • $NA • (2/29/2000) • **85**
Pessac-Léognan White 1997: A subtle, very good Bordeaux blanc, with cream, apple, honey and hints of tropical fruit on the nose and palate. Medium- to full-bodied, with lovely acidity and a medium finish. Drink now.–J.S. • $NA • (1/01/1999) • **87**
Pessac-Léognan White 1996: A typical and delicious Bordeaux blanc. Enticing aromas of minerals, honey, apple and piecrust follow through to the palate. Medium- to full-bodied, with well-integrated acidity and a rich aftertaste. Drink now through 2004.–J.S. • $NA • (1/01/1999) • **87**

LAGRANGE, CHATEAU | POMEROL

Pomerol 1999: Some decent fruit but a bit diluted, with berry, wet earth and cherry character. Lean.–J.S. • $NA • (1/01/2000) (BT) • **80-84**
Pomerol 1998: An elegant and fine young wine. Cherry and dark chocolate character with a hint of raspberry. Medium-bodied, with firm tannins and a subtle, velvety finish. Almost outstanding.–J.S. • $NA • (5/31/1999) (BT) • **85-89**
Pomerol 1994 • $35 • (1/31/1997) • **86**
Pomerol 1993 • $29 • (1/31/1996) • **83**
Pomerol 1992 • $24 • (4/15/1995) • **75**
Pomerol 1990 • $81 Ⓐ • (3/31/1993) • **95**
Pomerol 1989 • $54 Ⓐ • (3/15/1992) • **87**
Pomerol 1982: Delicious Pomerol. Dark ruby, with a garnet edge. Tobacco, cherry and berry aromas. Full-bodied, very velvety, with chocolate, berry and cherry flavors and a long, long aftertaste. All in finesse. (1989 Bordeaux horizontal tasting). Drink now.–J.S. • $38 Ⓐ • (11/30/1998) • **91**

LAGRANGE, CHATEAU | ST. JULIEN

St.-Julien 1999: A wine with good berry, blackberry aromas. Medium-bodied, with good tannins but a rather short finish.–J.S. • $NA • (1/01/2000) (BT) • **85-89**
St.-Julien 1998: A thick and chewy Médoc, with plenty of currant and berry character and velvety tannins. Full-bodied, with a caressing texture. Well done.–J.S. • $NA • (5/31/1999) (BT) • **90-94**
St.-Julien 1997: Pretty licorice and currant aromas. Medium-bodied, with silky tannins and a medium finish. Well-crafted. Drink now through 2004.–J.S. • $31 • (1/31/2000) • **88**
St.-Julien 1996: Enticing aromas of cinnamon and ripe fruit. Medium- to full-bodied, with ripe fruit flavors and a good fruit core. Medium tannins. St.-Julien's Lagrange seldom goes wrong, and this is certainly outstanding for the vintage. Best after 2002.–J.S. • $37 • (1/31/1999) • **90**
St.-Julien 1995 • $34 Ⓐ • (1/31/1998) • **91**
St.-Julien 1994 • $23 Ⓐ • (1/31/1997) • **88**
St.-Julien 1993 • $24 Ⓐ • (1/31/1996) • **89**
St.-Julien 1992 • $20 • (4/15/1995) • **87**
St.-Julien 1991 • $24 • (3/31/1994) • **86**
St.-Julien 1990 • $58 Ⓐ • (3/31/1993) SS • **95**
St.-Julien 1989: A youthful and tannic St.-Julien. Medium-dark ruby color. Fresh berry and cherry aromas, very perfumed. Full-bodied, with chewy tannins and a medium berry, chocolate and roasted coffee aftertaste. Needs more time to develop. (1989 Bordeaux horizontal tasting). Best after 2005.–J.S. • $44 Ⓐ • (5/31/1999) • **94**
St.-Julien 1988: The best value of the vintage and classic in quality. Dark-colored, with layers of violet, berry and currant on the nose and palate. Full-bodied, with loads of tannins and fruit and a finish that goes on and on. (1989 Bordeaux horizontal tasting). Best after 2003.–J.S. • $40 Ⓐ • (11/30/1998) • **96**
St.-Julien 1986 • $50 Ⓐ • (2/15/1990) • **86**
St.-Julien 1985 • $54 Ⓐ • (10/15/1994) • **91**
St.-Julien 1983 • $33 Ⓐ • (10/15/1994) • **88**
St.-Julien 1982: One of the sleepers of the vintage. Traditional and rich. Dark ruby-colored, with a slight garnet rim. Masses of berry, chocolate and raspberry character. Full-bodied and very tannic, packed with fruit. Lengthy finish. A youthful and concentrated wine; a relatively good value. (1989 Bordeaux horizontal tasting). –J.S. • $40 Ⓐ • (11/30/1998) • **94**
St.-Julien 1981 • $19 Ⓐ • (10/15/1994) • **85**
St.-Julien 1961 • $48 Ⓐ • (4/30/1996) • **86**

LAGREZETTE, CHATEAU

Cahors 1997: Packs quite a wallop. Masses of dark fruit flavors are dominated by plum, cherry and even a bit of boysenberry. Intense and lively despite the loads of fruit, with nice notes of cedar and spice. Tempting now, but best to see how it develops. Best from 2001 through 2006.–K.M. • $20 • (6/15/2000) • **89**
Cahors 1996: Powerful and brooding, with layers of rich plum, dark cherry and tobacco leaf and some minty notes. There's plenty of tannins as well, and bittersweet chocolate on the finish. Will benefit from short-term cellaring. Drink through 2004–K.M. • $20 • (10/15/1999) • **88**
Cahors 1994 • $19 • (8/31/1997) • **87**
Cahors 1993 • $19 • (1/31/1997) • **87**
Cahors 1992 • $12 • (3/31/1995) • **86**
Cahors 1990 • $10 • (9/15/1994) • **83**
Cahors 1990 • $12 • (6/15/1993) • **79**
Cahors 1989 • $10 • (9/15/1994) • **88**
Cahors Chevaliers Lagrezette 1994 • $13 • (5/15/1998) • **84**
Cahors Chevaliers Lagrezette 1992 • $14 • (2/28/1997) • **79**
Cahors Cuvée Dame Honneur 1994 • $21 • (5/15/1998) • **88**
Cahors Moulin Lagrezette 1995 • $11 • (5/15/1998) • **85**

LAGUNE, CHATEAU LA

Haut-Médoc 1997: Very aromatic, with berry, currant and vanilla aromas. Medium-bodied, with a lovely core of fruit and silky tannins. Delicious. Drink now through 2004.–J.S. • $19 Ⓐ • (1/31/2000) • **88**
Haut-Médoc 1996: Pretty aromas of berry and vanilla, with a hint of mineral. Medium-bodied, with chewy tannins but a slight herbal edge to the after-

taste. A bit one-dimensional for La Lagune, but still a good bottle. Best after 2000.–J.S. • $30 Ⓐ • (1/31/1999) • **85**

Haut-Médoc 1995: Slightly one-dimensional, with good blackberry aromas and flavors, medium body and medium tannins. Drink now through 2002.–J.S. • $28 Ⓐ • (9/15/1998) • **85**

Haut-Médoc 1990 • $54 Ⓐ • (10/15/1994) • **95**

Haut-Médoc 1989: An extremely friendly '89. Good dark-ruby color. Seductive aromas of berries, flowers and vanilla. Medium- to full-bodied, with velvety tannins and a berry, coconut and milk chocolate aftertaste. (1989 Bordeaux horizontal tasting). Best after 2003.–J.S. • $49 Ⓐ • (5/31/1999) • **90**

Haut-Médoc 1988: This may have been overrated previously. Rather herbal and funky, with bark and chestnut character. Medium-bodied, with medium tannins and a fruity, slightly austere finish. (1989 Bordeaux horizontal tasting). Drink now.–J.S. • $42 Ⓐ • (11/30/1998) • **84**

Haut-Médoc 1987 • $20 • (5/15/1990) • **89**

Haut-Médoc 1986 • $56 Ⓐ • (6/30/1989) • **89**

Haut-Médoc 1985 • $48 Ⓐ • (10/15/1994) • **89**

Haut-Médoc 1984 • $13 • (3/31/1987) • **86**

Haut-Médoc 1983 • $43 Ⓐ • (10/15/1994) • **91**

Haut-Médoc 1982: Very dark garnet-red, with an inky center. Ripe berry and tobacco aromas. Medium- to full-bodied, with tobacco, raspberry and light toasted oak flavors. Silky finish. Outstanding, if not quite as impressive as I anticipated. (1989 Bordeaux horizontal tasting). Drink now.–J.S. • $78 Ⓐ • (11/30/1998) • **90**

Haut-Médoc 1981 • $33 Ⓐ • (10/15/1994) • **91**

Haut-Médoc 1979 • $35 Ⓐ • (10/15/1989) • **86**

Haut-Médoc 1970 • $52 Ⓐ • (5/15/1993) • **87**

Haut-Médoc 1962 • $NA • (11/30/1987) • **80**

Haut-Médoc 1961 • $92 Ⓐ • (4/30/1996) • **88**

Haut-Médoc 1945 • $200 • (3/16/1986) • **87**

LAHERTE FRERES

Brut Champagne Tradition NV: Bright, fresh fruit flavors liven up this well-balanced bubbly. Accents of vanilla and cream emerge on the nose and last through the finish. Drink now through 2001. • $28 • (10/31/1999) • **88**

Brut Rosé Champagne NV: Austere in the flavor department, showing more dough and cereal nuances along with a rich, grainy texture. Not an obvious wine, but satisfying and long on flavor. Drink now.–B.S. • $30 • (11/30/1999) • **88**

LAISSUS, CHATEAU

Côte de Brouilly Vieilles Vignes 1994 • $13 • (9/15/1996) • **84**

LALANDE DE GRAVELONGUE, CHATEAU

Médoc 1996: Odd aromas of stewed tomatoes and petrol. Medium-bodied, with light tannins and a diluted finish. Hard to like.–J.S. • $NA • (1/01/1999) • **75**

LALANDE, DOMAINE DE

Mâcon-Chaintré 1997: Crisp but fruity, showing a freshly cut grass note that's reminiscent of Sauvignon Blanc. A bit herbal on the finish.–P.M. • $15 • (5/31/1999) • **79**

Mâcon-Chaintré 1995 • $NA • (5/31/1997) • **80**

Pouilly-Fuissé 1997: Very pretty Pouilly. Medium-bodied and deftly balanced, not overoaked but singing with pure fruit, some honeysuckle and smoke flavors on the seductive finish. Drink now through 2001.–P.M. • $24 • (5/31/1999) • **88**

Pouilly-Fuissé Clos Reyssié 1997: Rich, ripe and very attractive, offering plenty of butter, cream, lemon, tropical, spice complexity. A medium-bodied Pouilly that oozes with character, but turns a bit hot on the finish. Should cool down by 2001.–P.M. • $25 • (5/31/1999) • **88**

Pouilly-Fuissé Clos Reyssié 1996 • $25 • (5/31/1998) • **87**

Pouilly-Fuissé Clos Reyssié 1995 • $NA • (5/31/1997) • **86**

Key: SS—Spectator Selection. CS—Cellar Selection. HR—Highly Recommended. $NA—Price not available. (BT)—Barrel tasting. Ⓐ—Auction Price.
For a key to the tasters' initials, see "How to Use These Listings."
Dates in parentheses represent the issues in which the ratings were published.

St.-Véran 1997: Deliciously ripe, delivering more tropical, honey, and pear flavors than most '97 St-Vérans. The supple, sweet-tasting mouthfeel makes this full-bodied beauty a winner. Drink now.–P.M. • $16 • (5/31/1999) • **87**

LALANDE-BORIE, CHATEAU

St.-Julien 1995: Plenty of blackberry and cherry aromas and flavors. Medium-bodied, with fine, silky tannins and fruity finish. Slightly one-dimensional, still delicious. Drink through 2004–J.S. • $NA • (9/15/1998) • **87**

St.-Julien 1993 • $18 • (1/31/1996) • **85**

St.-Julien 1991 • $14 • (3/31/1994) • **77**

St.-Julien 1990 • $19 • (3/31/1993) • **90**

St.-Julien 1989: A fresh, easy-to-enjoy '89. Good ruby color, and raspberry, cherry and slightly bushy aromas. Medium-bodied, with tomato, berry, cherry flavors. Simple finish. (1989 Bordeaux horizontal tasting). Drink now.–J.S. • $NA • (5/31/1999) • **88**

St.-Julien 1988 • $48 Ⓐ • (4/30/1991) • **87**

St.-Julien 1987 • $15 • (11/30/1989) • **81**

St.-Julien 1986 • $21 Ⓐ • (11/30/1989) • **91**

St.-Julien 1982 • $38 Ⓐ • (8/31/1992) • **91**

LALEURE-PIOT

Aloxe-Corton 1996: Rustic, of medium body, it tastes a bit overdone, with plum and black cherry character. Dries on the alcoholic finish. Drink now through 2005.–P.M. • $34 • (9/30/1998) • **78**

Bourgogne Passe-tout-grains 1993 • $15 • (11/15/1995) • **84**

Chorey-lès-Beaune Les Champs Longs 1996: Raspberry and strawberry flavors show good concentration and harmony with the elegant structure and light tannic finish. Drink through 2003–B.S. • $24 • (9/30/1998) • **84**

Chorey-lès-Beaune Les Champs Longs 1995 • $22 • (11/15/1997) • **74**

Chorey-lès-Beaune Les Champs Longs 1993 • $17 • (11/15/1995) • **87**

Corton Bressandes 1997: Soft and easy, showing pretty licorice, smoke and blackberry notes. Clamps down on the finish—a good sign, as it brings unexpected length and taste to this medium-bodied Pinot. Drink now through 2003.–P.M. • $77 • (1/01/2000) • **85**

Corton Bressandes 1996: Impressively balanced. Rich and intense, packed with earth, cedar and lovely, compacted red- and blackberry character. The tannins are a bit stiff, so cellar. Best After 2003.–P.M. • $68 • (9/30/1998) • **89**

Corton Bressandes 1995 • $62 • (11/15/1997) • **87**

Corton Bressandes 1994 • $66 • (11/15/1996) • **82**

Corton Bressandes 1993 • $51 • (11/15/1995) • **91**

Corton Bressandes 1990 • $NA • (12/15/1992) • **90**

Corton Le Rognet 1997: A bit cheesy, displaying herb and cherry notes, with a slightly hollow midpalate and an astringent finish.–B.S. • $NA • (9/30/1999) • **77**

Corton Le Rognet 1996: Beguiling scents of wild blackberries lead to modest flavors of same, with good concentration. Finishes with firm tannins and a touch of heat. Drink through 2006–B.S. • $64 • (9/30/1998) • **87**

Corton Le Rognet 1995 • $59 • (11/15/1997) • **87**

Corton Le Rognet 1994 • $NA • (11/15/1996) • **85**

Corton Le Rognet 1993 • $47 • (11/15/1995) • **89**

Corton-Charlemagne 1997: Round and rich, but very elegant, showing sublime silkiness of texture while remaining firm in structure. Tropical, wet earth, mineral, apricot, pineapple and subtle oak accents lead to a superintense, amazingly long-lasting, ripe finish. Best from 2007 through 2017.–P.M. • $109 • (5/31/1999) • **94**

Corton-Charlemagne 1996 • $96 • (5/31/1998) • **93**

Côte de Nuits-Villages 1990 • $NA • (12/15/1992) • **65**

Côte de Nuits-Villages Les Bellevues 1997: On the light side in terms of flavors, it has a sharp, crisp texture backed by some firm, even drying tannins. Light to medium in body, with a hard, chewy finish.–P.M. • $28 • (1/01/2000) • **77**

Côte de Nuits-Villages Les Bellevues 1996: Fairly thick wine, but it's dominated by herbal character. Turns a bit astringent on the finish. Drink now.–P.M. • $25 • (9/30/1998) • **79**

Côte de Nuits-Villages Les Bellevues 1995 • $22 • (1/31/1998) • **86**

Pernand-Vergelesses 1997: Light and diluted, tasting watery and hard.–P.M. • $39 • (9/30/1999) • **77**

Pernand-Vergelesses 1996: Herbaceous and rustic. Hard to find the charm of the '96 vintage in this wine. Best from 2000.–B.S. • $28 • (9/30/1998) • **78**

Pernand-Vergelesses 1995 • $25 • (11/15/1997) • **74**

Pernand-Vergelesses Ile des Vergelesses 1997: Full-bodied and packed with seductive fruit, showing a welcome intensity on the finish for a '97.

Delivers length, wet soil and a rustic authenticity, with massive but ripe tannins. Drink now through 2007.–P.M. • $51 • (9/30/1999) • **87**

Pernand-Vergelesses Ile des Vergelesses 1996: Beautiful '96 Pernand. Displays concentrated blackberry aromas and flavors accented by new oak, and mouthsearing tannins that are balanced by racy acidity and sweet, ripe fruit. Well done. Drink through 2005–B.S. • $45 • (9/30/1998) • **88**

Pernand-Vergelesses Ile des Vergelesses 1995 • $40 • (11/15/1997) • **84**

Pernand-Vergelesses Ile des Vergelesses 1994 • $NA • (11/15/1996) • **79**

Pernand-Vergelesses Ile des Vergelesses 1993 • $33 • (11/15/1995) • **85**

Pernand-Vergelesses Ile des Vergelesses 1990 • $NA • (12/15/1992) • **90**

Pernand-Vergelesses Les Vergelesses 1997: A bit disjointed. Has a core of medium-intense red fruit. Light- to medium-bodied, with a toasted, charred character that turns chewy on the tannic finish.–P.M. • $30 • (1/01/2000) • **77**

Pernand-Vergelesses Les Vergelesses 1996: Firm, structured and unyielding, with a modicum of cassis and herbs. Best from 2000.–B.S. • $35 • (9/30/1998) • **83**

Pernand-Vergelesses Les Vergelesses 1995 • $31 • (11/15/1997) • **86**

Pernand-Vergelesses Les Vergelesses 1994 • $43 • (11/15/1996) • **79**

Pernand-Vergelesses Les Vergelesses 1993 • $24 • (11/15/1995) • **84**

Pernand-Vergelesses Les Vergelesses 1992 • $27 • (12/15/1994) • **83**

Pernand-Vergelesses Les Vergelesses 1990 • $NA • (12/15/1992) • **89**

Pernand-Vergelesses Premier Cru 1993 • $22 • (11/15/1995) • **84**

Pernand-Vergelesses White 1997: Ripe and sweet-tasting, with a flint, smoke and wet earth personality that brings complexity to the fabulous fruit. Balanced thanks to clean acidity, with a long finish. Drink now through 2001.–P.M. • $30 • (5/31/1999) • **89**

Pernand-Vergelesses White 1996 • $27 • (5/31/1998) • **89**

Pernand-Vergelesses White Premier Cru 1997: Supple and ripe, with lime, honey and pear flavors, this clean, delightful Chardonnay shows good acidity. Balanced on the lingering finish. Drink now through 2001.–P.M. • $39 • (5/31/1999) • **87**

Pernand-Vergelesses White Premier Cru 1996 • $35 • (5/31/1998) • **79**

Savigny-lès-Beaune Les Vergelesses 1997: Tough and astringent, this smells and tastes stemmy, with modest fruit and charm.–B.S. • $39 • (9/30/1999) • **77**

Savigny-lès-Beaune Les Vergelesses 1996: Full-bodied and brimming with fresh red berry flavors accented by peppery spices and toasted oak notes, unfolding its texture of fine tannins and complex flavors with grace, ending in a long, smoky finish. Best from 2003 through 2007.–P.M. • $32 • (5/15/1999) • **89**

Savigny-lès-Beaune Aux Vergelesses 1993 • $25 • (11/15/1995) • **86**

LALLEMENT, JEAN

Brut Champagne NV: Not your average non-vintage brut. This is deep-colored, very aromatic, dry and quite mature in flavor. It combines toasty, nutty aromas with honey and pear flavors on a plush texture. Great, lingering finish, too. Drink now through 2001. • $44 • (10/31/1999) • **89**

Brut Champagne Cuvée Réserve NV: The brioche and walnut nuances are intriguing, offering more mature character than most NV Champagnes. There's a firm underlying structure and intensity to the flavors, which carry through to the long finish. Drink now through 2001.–B.S. • $55 • (11/30/1999) • **90**

LAMARCHE, CHATEAU

Bordeaux Supérieur Lutet 1995: Aromatic, with blackberry and vanilla character that follows through on the palate. Medium- to light-bodied, with good flavors, but doesn't leave much on the finish. Drink now.–J.S. • $NA • (9/15/1998) • **81**

LAMARCHE, FRANCOIS

Clos de Vougeot 1995 • $64 • (11/15/1997) • **88**

Clos de Vougeot 1987 • $55 • (9/30/1990) • **86**

Clos de Vougeot 1985 • $48 • (10/15/1988) • **90**

Echézeaux 1995 • $61 • (11/15/1997) • **89**

Echézeaux 1987 • $48 • (9/30/1990) • **87**

Grands Echézeaux 1997: This charming, accessible '97 red has pure cherry and almost kirsch and chocolate aromas and flavors. Good volume, yet soft around the edges, with a modest finish. Drink now through 2002.–B.S. • $155 • (9/30/1999) • **85**

La Grande Rue 1995 • $98 • (11/15/1997) • **90**

La Grande Rue 1987 • $68 • (9/30/1990) • **91**

La Grande Rue 1985 • $60 • (10/15/1988) • **89**

Vosne-Romanée Les Suchots 1985 • $36 • (10/15/1988) • **91**

Vosne-Romanée Malconsorts 1997: Herbal and minty flavors are allied in this light, almost neutral red.–B.S. • $80 • (9/30/1999) • **77**

Vosne-Romanée Malconsorts 1995 • $56 • (11/15/1997) • **83**

Vosne-Romanée Malconsorts 1985 • $44 • (10/15/1988) • **84**

LAMARQUE, CHATEAU DE

Haut-Médoc 1998: Some pleasant berry, cherry character. Medium- to light-bodied, with fine tannins and a simple finish.–J.S. • $NA • (5/31/1999) (BT) • **80-84**

Haut-Médoc 1997: A light, fresh red with berry, plum and earth character. Drink now.–J.S. • $NA • (1/31/2000) • **80**

Haut-Médoc 1996: Good dark color, with plenty of tobacco and dark chocolate character on the nose. Medium-bodied, with soft tannins and a medium finish. A pretty wine, but needs a bit more on the center-palate to score higher. Best after 2000.–J.S. • $NA • (1/31/1999) • **86**

Haut-Médoc 1992 • $13 • (4/15/1995) • **74**

Haut-Médoc 1991 • $13 • (3/31/1994) • **80**

Haut-Médoc 1990 • $18 • (3/31/1993) • **86**

Haut-Médoc 1989 • $26 • (3/15/1992) • **89**

Haut-Médoc 1988 • $20 • (4/30/1991) • **86**

Haut-Médoc 1987 • $10 • (11/30/1989) • **74**

Haut-Médoc 1986 • $18 • (11/30/1989) • **75**

Haut-Médoc 1982 • $18 • (8/31/1992) • **82**

LAMARTINE, CHATEAU

Bordeaux Supérieur 1991 • $10 • (3/31/1994) • **78**

Bordeaux Supérieur 1990 • $NA • (3/31/1993) • **79**

Cahors Cuvée Particulière 1994: Crisp and tannic, with plum and cherry flavors and an earthy finish.–K.M. • $15 • (8/31/1998) • **81**

LAMARTINE, MAISON DE

Beaujolais-Villages 1993 • $10 • (1/31/1995) • **71**

Moulin-à-Vent 1993 • $15 • (1/31/1995) • **83**

Régnié 1996: Appealing flavors of cherry and spice mark this mature-tasting, medium-bodied red. Finishes with of cardamom and cinnamon. Drink now.–K.M. • $15 • (10/15/1999) • **83**

LAMBERTINS, DOMAINE DES

Vacqueyras 1997: Dark-colored and flavorful, showing good concentration and clean, pure fruit, with blackberry, black cherry and wet earth notes and a firm finish accented by plum. Drink now through 2002.–P.M. • $11 • (10/31/1999) • **85**

Vacqueyras 1996: Smooth-textured and spicy, with licorice, pepper, dried herbs, plum, bitter black-chocolate and red berry character. Medium-bodied, balanced and appealing. Drink now.–P.M. • $10 • (11/15/1998) • **84**

LAMBLIN & FILS

Bourgogne Aligoté 1997: Plenty to enjoy. Vivid, clean and crisp, with lively yet ripe honey, melon, pear and crisp apple flavors. A bit spritzy. Drink now.–P.M. • $6 • (5/31/1999) • **83**

Bourgogne White 1995 • $9 • (1/31/1997) • **80**

Chablis 1997: Straightforward, slightly stripped, providing little interest and only modest fruit.–P.M. • $9 • (5/31/1999) • **78**

Chablis 1996: A bit malic-lactic, clearly oaky, with pronounced butterscotch, butter, pie tart flavors as well as some cooked apple notes that are fresh but inelegant. Polished mineraliness, but rustic fruit. Drink now through 2010.–P.M. • $9 • (5/31/1999) • **84**

Chablis Fourchaume 1997: Supple, even a bit soft, offering medium intensity along with some spice, cedar and what seem like woody flavors. But the tart finish.–P.M. • $13 • (5/31/1999) • **78**

Chablis Fourchaume 1996 • $NA • (8/31/1997) • **92**

Chablis Vaillon 1996: Beautiful, clean fruit here, with buttery overtones, but above all, it's so pure, with delightful full body, smooth texture and plenty of earthy mineral flavors on the finish. Drink now through 2010.–P.M. • $12 • (5/31/1999) • **93**

LAMBRAYS, DOMAINE DES

Clos des Lambrays 1995: A rather lean, tough red Burgundy, lacking a bit of ripeness, but showing some cherry, dried herbs, green olive and tea leaf character. Slightly astringent finish. Drink now.–P.M. • $50 • (8/31/1998) • **83**

Clos des Lambrays 1993 • $50 • (5/15/1996) • **89**

LAMOTHE-GUIGNARD, CHATEAU

Sauternes 1998: Shows loads of spice, honey and fruit character. Full-bodied and very sweet, with a reserved finish yet suggests great potential.–J.S. • $NA • (1/01/1999) (BT) • **90-94**

Sauternes 1997: A Sauternes with plenty of ripe pineapple and vanilla character. Medium-bodied and medium sweet, with a long honey and cream aftertaste. Drink now.–J.S. • $35 • (1/31/2000) • **87**

Sauternes 1992 • $NA • (4/15/1995) • **78**

Sauternes 1990 • $30 • (4/15/1995) • **92**

Sauternes 1989 • $25 • (4/15/1995) • **88**

Sauternes 1988 • $28 Ⓐ • (4/15/1995) • **87**

Sauternes 1987 • $23 • (6/15/1990) • **77**

Sauternes 1986 • $30 • (4/15/1995) • **92**

Sauternes 1983 • $NA • (4/15/1995) • **92**

LAMY, HENRY

St.-Aubin En Remilly 1995 • $22 • (5/31/1997) • **90**

LAMY, HUBERT

Chassagne-Montrachet 1995 • $NA • (5/31/1997) • **88**

Chassagne-Montrachet Les Macherelles 1998: Lively aromas in this satisfying, medium-bodied white Burgundy. Lots of different fruit notes—from kiwi to pear and melon—a good backbone of vibrant acidity and a supple texture combine to make this a wonderful '98. Not imported into the U.S. Drink now through 2005.–P.M. • $NA • (5/31/2000) • **89**

Chassagne-Montrachet Les Macherelles 1997: A pretty little Chardonnay, with medium-intense pear, quince and toasted oak. Medium-bodied, it's a bit soft and short on the finish. Drink now.–P.M. • $40 • (5/31/1999) • **85**

Chassagne-Montrachet Les Macherelles 1996 • $38 • (5/31/1998) • **92**

Criots-Bâtard-Montrachet 1995 • $NA • (5/31/1997) • **84**

St.-Aubin Clos de la Chatenière 1998: Doesn't smell much, but the juicy, succulent and ripe mouthfeel, where the clean fruit sings beautifully, makes this wine stand out. Has gorgeous lemon-honey-tropical character. Long and elegant finish. Best from 2002 through 2008.–P.M. • $32 • (5/31/2000) • **90**

St.-Aubin Clos de la Chatenière 1997: A supple, ripe and seductive St.-Aubin, with lovely pear and tropical aromas. This full-bodied charmer is a delight to drink now, with a lemony, honeyed finish. Drink now through 2005.–P.M. • $25 • (5/31/1999) • **90**

St.-Aubin Clos de la Chatenière 1996 • $22 • (5/31/1998) • **92**

St.-Aubin Clos de la Chatenière 1995 • $22 • (5/31/1997) • **74**

St.-Aubin En Remilly 1998: Wonderous ripeness on the palate here. A bit oaky on the nose, but the real story is the honey, orange-peel jam, quince, tropical flavors that seduce the palate—and come as a real surprise in this '98 vintage. Clean and succulent, with a backbone of citrus on the lingering finish. Not imported into the U.S. Drink now through 2008.–P.M. • $NA • (5/31/2000) • **92**

St.-Aubin En Remilly 1997: Clean, pure and lively, with a wet earth, lemon, toasted oak and green apple intensity. A very satisfying, medium-bodied white that's well made and a joy to drink. Drink now through 2003.–P.M. • $24 • (5/31/1999) • **87**

St.-Aubin En Remilly 1996 • $22 • (5/31/1998) • **92**

St.-Aubin La Princée 1996 • $16 • (5/31/1998) • **83**

St.-Aubin La Princée 1995 • $17 • (5/31/1997) • **83**

St.-Aubin Les Cortons 1998: Straightforward Chardonnay with some decent fruit, just not enough of it to balance the toasted oak, which dominates. Tasted twice, with consistent notes. Not imported into the U.S.–P.M. • $NA • (1/01/2000) • **79**

St.-Aubin Les Cortons 1997: Ripe and deftly toasted, with mocha, spice and green apple accented by a hint of honey, but it turns a bit chewy, chalky and drying on the finish. Drink now through 2002.–P.M. • $24 • (5/31/1999) • **83**

St.-Aubin Les Cortons 1996 • $22 • (5/31/1998) • **87**

St.-Aubin Les Cortons 1995 • $22 • (5/31/1997) • **87**

St.-Aubin Les Frionnes 1998: Elegant yet flavorful. Delivers subtle mineral, vanilla and ripe fruit character in a supple and fresh, medium-bodied package. Satisfying finish, without excessive complexity. Drink now through 2002.–P.M. • $28 • (5/31/2000) • **88**

St.-Aubin Les Frionnes 1997: A steely, middle-of-the-road white Burgundy, with a tart character filled with dried herbs and lemon.–P.M. • $20 • (5/31/1999) • **78**

St.-Aubin Les Frionnes 1996 • $20 • (5/31/1998) • **91**

St.-Aubin Les Murgers des Dents de Chien 1998: Certain richness here, and it tastes ripe, with honey, pear, melon. Full-bodied, with some smoky, toasted bread and citrus character adding further complexity. Opened up in the glass, so should improve with short-term cellaring. Not imported into the U.S. Drink now through 2005.–P.M. • $NA • (1/01/2000) • **87**

St.-Aubin Les Murgers des Dents de Chien 1997: This polished St.-Aubin is full-bodied, clean and delicious in a soft way, deftly balancing the oak, fruit and acidity, with fresh herbs, pineapple and pear in medium quantities. Drink now through 2005.–P.M. • $30 • (5/31/1999) • **88**

St.-Aubin Les Murgers des Dents de Chien 1996 • $28 • (5/31/1998) • **92**

St.-Aubin Les Murgers des Dents de Chien 1995 • $NA • (5/31/1997) • **88**

LAMY-PILLOT

Chassagne-Montrachet Clos St.-Jean 1996: Two bottles were corked.–P.M. • $NA • (8/31/1998) • **60**

Chassagne-Montrachet La Grande Montagne 1996: First bottle was thick and ripe, showing some lovely fruit, except for a slight corkiness. Second bottle was corked.–P.M. • $NA • (8/31/1998) • **60**

Chassagne-Montrachet Les Pimonts 1996: First bottle tasted odd—swampy and unappealing. Second bottle was funky and earthy. Not recommended.–P.M. • $NA • (8/31/1998) • **60**

St.-Aubin Red Les Castets 1996: Strange, with earthy, stablelike aromas and a tart, steely finish.–P.M. • $23 • (5/15/1999) • **70**

LANCELOT-ROYER, P.

Brut Blanc de Blancs Champagne Cuvée des Chevaliers NV: Lovely, mature notes of nut and beeswax add depth and complexity to the honey and citrus. On the dry side, this exhibits a firm structure and beautiful harmony. The finish makes you want more. Drink now.–B.S. • $38 • (11/30/1999) • **89**

LANCON PERE & FILS

Châteauneuf-du-Pape Domaine de la Solitude 1994 • $20 • (11/15/1996) • **87**

Châteauneuf-du-Pape Domaine de la Solitude 1992 • $22 • (11/15/1995) • **79**

Châteauneuf-du-Pape Domaine de la Solitude 1990 • $27 • (4/15/1993) • **89**

Châteauneuf-du-Pape Domaine de la Solitude 1989 • $19 • (5/31/1992) • **86**

Châteauneuf-du-Pape White Domaine de la Solitude 1997: Rich and ripe, with honey, pear, lemon tart and toasty oak, but also a slightly oxidative cooked apple character. Turns crisp and a bit hot on the finish.–P.M. • $NA • (11/15/1998) • **79**

Côtes du Rhône Domaine de la Solitude 1997: Soft and supple at first, this straightforward red offers plum and cherry, turns a bit hot on the brown sugar-flavored finish.–P.M. • $NA • (11/15/1998) • **76**

Côtes du Rhône Domaine de la Solitude 1995 • $9 • (10/15/1996) • **80**

Côtes du Rhône Domaine de la Solitude 1993 • $12 • (11/15/1995) • **84**

LANCYRE, CHATEAU DE

Coteaux du Languedoc Pic St.-Loup Grande Cuvée 1995 • $22 • (5/31/1998) • **87**

Coteaux du Languedoc Pic St.-Loup Vieilles Vignes 1995 • $12 • (5/31/1998) • **80**

Coteaux du Languedoc White La Rouvière 1996 • $15 • (6/15/1998) • **87**

LANDE, DOMAINE DE LA

Bourgueil Cuvée Prestige 1993 • $17 • (5/15/1997) • **88**

Key: SS—Spectator Selection. CS—Cellar Selection. HR—Highly Recommended. $NA—Price not available. (BT)—Barrel tasting. Ⓐ—Auction Price. For a key to the tasters' initials, see "How to Use These Listings."
Dates in parentheses represent the issues in which the ratings were published.

LANDIRAS, CHATEAU DE

Graves 1995 • $15 • (1/31/1998) • **80**

LANDRAT-GUYOLLOT, DOMAINE

Pouilly-Fumé La Rambarde 1996 • $19 • (6/15/1998) • **86**

LANESSAN, CHATEAU

Haut-Médoc 1998: A rather cold wine, with mineral and cherry character. Medium-bodied, with firm tannins and a medium finish.–J.S. • $NA • (5/31/1999) (BT) • **80-84**

Haut-Médoc 1997: Pleasant berry and cherry character in this medium-bodied, velvety wine. Slightly diluted on the finish. Drink now.–J.S. • $13 • (1/31/2000) • **81**

Haut-Médoc 1996: A pretty nose of currants and blackberries. Medium-bodied, with firm tannins and plenty of fruit, but a slightly short finish. A very good wine from Lanessan. Best after 2000.–J.S. • $NA • (1/31/1999) • **87**

Haut-Médoc 1995: Attractive blackberry aromas. Medium-bodied, with fine tannins and a silky, long finish. Slightly one-dimensional but delicious.–J.S. • $14 Ⓐ • (9/15/1998) • **86**

Haut-Médoc 1992 • $15 • (4/15/1995) • **73**

Haut-Médoc 1990 • $18 • (3/31/1993) • **86**

Haut-Médoc 1989: Slightly rustic, but a big wine. Young and well structured. Good dark-ruby color. Blackberry, cherry and floral aromas. Full-bodied, with chewy tannins and a ripe berry, tobacco aftertaste.(1982 Bordeaux horizontal tasting). Best after 2001.–J.S. • $NA • (5/31/1999) • **90**

Haut-Médoc 1988 • $20 • (7/31/1991) • **80**

Haut-Médoc 1985 • $16 • (4/30/1988) • **87**

Haut-Médoc 1982: Still holding on. Medium brick-red, with an amber edge. Some decent tobacco, mushroom flavors but slightly funky, with velvety dry tannins. (1982 Bordeaux horizontal tasting). Drink now.–J.S. • $32 Ⓐ • (11/30/1998) • **80**

LANGLOIS-CHATEAU

Chinon Château de Rivière 1995 • $13 • (6/15/1997) • **84**

Chinon Château de Rivière 1992 • $11 • (10/31/1994) • **77**

Crémant de Loire NV: This sparkler is quite full-bodied but rather austere, with muted flavors of toast and pear held taut by crisp acidity. Has the weight to stand up to food. Drink now.–T.M. • $12 • (6/30/1999) • **80**

Crémant de Loire Quadrille Cuvée 2000 NV: This soft, blowsy sparkler has mature flavors of cooked apple, piecrust and spice, with a soft, lazy mousse and low acidity.–T.M. • $NA • (6/30/1999) • **78**

Sancerre Château de Fontaine-Audon 1997: Crisp and vibrant, this lean wine shows herbal and mineral flavors and citrusy acidity. A bit tart on its own, but should marry nicely with lighter foods.–T.M. • $18 • (9/15/1998) • **83**

Saumur 1993 • $11 • (5/15/1996) • **84**

Saumur Vieilles Vignes 1996: Round and gentle, this generous red marries ripe plum and black cherry flavors with notes of cola and herb. It has firm tannins, but lingers gently on the finish. Bright and fresh. Drink now through 2002.–T.M. • $10 • (6/30/1999) • **85**

Saumur White Vieilles Vignes 1997: Intriguing notes of spice and honey give this wine depth and allure. Though it's light and a bit dilute on the palate, it has enough going on to reward the attentive drinker. Try now.–T.M. • $10 • (6/30/1999) • **83**

Saumur-Champigny Château de Varrains 1997: This round, soft red offers appealing chocolate and cola flavors, but the fruit is muted, with hints of cherry and plum. It has light tannins, and is better suited to fish than meat. Drink now through 2002.–T.M. • $18 • (6/30/1999) • **81**

LANGOA BARTON, CHATEAU

St.-Julien 1999: A very serious effort, with pretty raspberry, cherry and mint aromas. Medium- to full-bodied, with firm tannins and a medium finish.–J.S. • $NA • (1/01/2000) (BT) • **85-89**

St.-Julien 1998: A solid and delicious '98. Plenty of currant and mint character. Medium- to full-bodied, with a velvety texture and a long finish. Almost outstanding.–J.S. • $NA • (5/31/1999) (BT) • **85-89**

St.-Julien 1997: Rather tough, but there's good berry and currant character. Medium-bodied, with silky tannins and a light, slightly dry finish. Best after 2000.–J.S. • $31 • (1/31/2000) • **85**

St.-Julien 1996: Harmonious and pretty. Beautiful dried cherry and blackberry aromas, with a hint of bark. Medium-bodied, with velvety tannins and a smoky berry aftertaste. Delicious. Best after 2000.–J.S. • $35 • (1/31/1999) • **90**

St.-Julien 1995 • $36 Ⓐ • (1/31/1998) • **93**

St.-Julien 1994 • $22 Ⓐ • (1/31/1997) • **88**

St.-Julien 1993 • $23 Ⓐ • (1/31/1996) • **86**

St.-Julien 1991 • $18 • (3/31/1994) • **77**

St.-Julien 1990 • $27 • (3/31/1993) • **91**

St.-Julien 1989: One of the best Langoas ever made. Aromas of blackberries, dark chocolate and plums. Full-bodied and very velvety, with a gorgeously caressing texture. Long, long finish. A joy to taste. (1989 Bordeaux horizontal tasting). Try after 2002.–J.S. • $41 Ⓐ • (5/31/1999) • **92**

St.-Julien 1988: A slightly austere St.-Julien, with berry, mint and vanilla aromas and flavors. Full-bodied, with firm tannins and a medium finish. (1989 Bordeaux horizontal tasting). Drink now.–J.S. • $40 Ⓐ • (11/30/1998) • **88**

St.-Julien 1985 • $54 Ⓐ • (6/15/1988) • **91**

St.-Julien 1982 • $45 Ⓐ • (8/31/1992) • **91**

St.-Julien 1970 • $50 • (5/15/1993) • **85**

St.-Julien 1945 • $300 • (11/30/1995) • **86**

LANGOUX, MARCEL

Pouilly-Fumé 1998: Grassy and mineral flavors are characteristic and well defined in this focused white. A bit lean and tart, it would be refreshing as an aperitif or with raw shellfish. Drink now through 2001.–T.M. • $15 • (6/30/1999) • **84**

LANSON

Brut Blanc de Blancs Champagne 1994: Nicely mature aromas and lean, earthy apple flavors make this good in an austere style. Drink now. • $90 • (11/15/1999) • **85**

Brut Champagne Black Label NV: Suave and richly textured, This sparkling wine sports baked apple, citrus and dough on a vivid framework. It remains smooth until the crisp finish kicks in. Drink now through 2001.–B.S. • $35 • (11/30/1999) • **88**

Brut Champagne Gold Label 1993: Vibrant and mouthfilling, this is packed with lively citrus flavors yet nicely rounded out with vanilla accents and a smooth finish. Drink now through 2001. • $50 • (11/15/1999) • **89**

Brut Champagne Gold Label 1990: Generous in flavor and lively in balance, this is an attractive, complete Champagne. Bright fruit flavors make a fine combination with firm acidity and a rich mousse. Drink now through 2001. • $32 • (12/31/1998) • **89**

Brut Rosé Champagne NV: The dough and apple flavors combine with a creaminess in this soft, easygoing rosé. A nice crispness on the finish keeps everything in perspective. Drink now.–B.S. • $NA • (11/30/1999) • **86**

Extra Dry Champagne Ivory Label NV: Like a lemon meringue pie in a bottle, this well-made bubbly is appealing, zingy in flavor and sweet enough to satisfy. Drink now. • $20 • (12/31/1998) • **88**

LANSON, J.C. & C.

Morgon Domaine de Leyre-Loup 1997: The level of brettanomyces, a spoilage yeast that manifests itself here as a horsey aroma and dry, barnyard flavors, is unacceptable in this red. Tasted twice, with consistent notes.–B.S. • $15 • (10/15/1999) • **68**

LANTAGE, COMTE DE

Brut Blanc de Blancs Champagne 1995: Combines depth of flavor with an elegant texture. Really appealing for its toasty aromas, tropical fruit flavors and vibrant mousse. Drink now through 2002. • $40 • (10/15/1999) • **90**

Brut Blanc de Blancs Champagne 1990: Very vibrant and promising. This intensely flavored, dry style of Champagne needs time to show its best stuff. Marked by a vivid green-gold color, extremely toasty-earthy aromas and forceful butter and lemon flavors. Drink through 2005 • $35 • (12/31/1998) • **92**

Brut Blanc de Blancs Champagne 2000 1990: Tempting toasty, earthy aromas in a bold, distinctive wine. Plush texture, with rich fig and nut flavors that linger on the finish. Drink now through 2010. • $80 • (10/15/1999) • **92**

Brut Champagne Cuvée de Réserve NV: This extroverted Champagne is rich in texture, flavorful and mature in style. Intriguing toasty, nutty, almost honeyed flavors give it depth, and the luscious mousse and firm acidity give it length on the finish. Drink now. • $30 • (12/31/1998) • **92**

LANTAGE, COMTE DE

Brut Rosé Champagne NV: A traditional style of rosé, with a light salmon color, slightly earthy aromas and light cherry and spice flavors. The overall effect is soft and subtle. Drink now. • $33 • (12/31/1998) • **86**

LAPELLETRIE, CHATEAU

St.-Emilion 1996: A bit lean but clean. Light- to medium-bodied, with raspberry character, light tannins and a fresh finish. A good luncheon wine. Drink now.–J.S. • $26 • (7/31/1999) • **80**
St.-Emilion 1990 • $19 • (2/28/1994) • **79**
St.-Emilion 1989 • $19 • (7/15/1992) • **82**

LAPIERRE, M.

Morgon 1997: Smoky, meaty aromas give way to clean fruit flavors of black cherry and plum, but the wine is rather dilute and soft on the palate. Drink now.–T.M. • $24 • (3/31/2000) • **83**
Morgon 1995 • $22 • (8/31/1997) • **87**
Morgon 1994 • $18 • (9/15/1996) • **84**

LAPLACE, DOMAINE FLEURY

Madiran 1994 • $10 • (6/30/1997) • **82**

LAPLACE, DOMAINE FREDERIC

Madiran 1994 • $12 • (6/15/1997) • **85**

LAPORTE, DOMAINE

Sancerre Domaine du Rochoy 1998: Soft, with lime and green apple flavors, this simple Sancerre lacks the zip or definition of the better examples.–B.S. • $14 • (6/15/2000) • **78**
Sancerre Domaine du Rochoy 1996 • $20 • (6/30/1998) • **86**

LARCIS-DUCASSE, CHATEAU

St.-Emilion 1999: A pleasant, fruity wine with chocolate, tobacco and plum character. Medium to light body. Light tannins. Fresh finish.–J.S. • $NA • (1/01/2000) (BT) • **80-84**
St.-Emilion 1998: A focused wine with pretty berry, cherry and mineral character. Medium-bodied, with medium tannins and a fresh finish.–J.S. • $NA • (5/31/1999) (BT) • **85-89**
St.-Emilion 1997: A bit weedy and diluted, but some decent berry and milk chocolate character. Medium to light in body.–J.S. • $NA • (1/31/2000) • **80**
St.-Emilion 1996: Better than I remember. Pretty aromas of blackberry, cherry and raspberry. Medium-bodied, with velvety tannins and sweet fruit, though a diluted midpalate detracts. Best after 2001.–J.S. • $20 • (1/31/1999) • **86**
St.-Emilion 1995 • $20 • (1/31/1998) • **88**
St.-Emilion 1994 • $NA • (1/31/1997) • **80**
St.-Emilion 1991 • $16 • (3/31/1994) • **74**
St.-Emilion 1990 • $37 Ⓐ • (3/31/1993) • **90**
St.-Emilion 1989: This wine continues to mellow. Dark-ruby in color, with strawberry, blackberry aromas. Medium- to full-bodied, adding silky tannins and a long, truffle and berry aftertaste. A beauty. (1989 Bordeaux horizontal tasting). Best after 2002.–J.S. • $NA • (5/31/1999) • **91**
St.-Emilion 1988 • $20 • (4/30/1991) • **82**
St.-Emilion 1982: Tasted from half-bottle. Dark, youthful ruby color, with a slightly amber edge. Very ripe and sweet fruit, with mineral, raspberry aromas. Medium-bodied, with a soft finish. (1989 Bordeaux horizontal tasting).Drink now.–J.S. • $NA/375 ml. • (11/30/1998) • **87**

LARMANDE, CHATEAU

St.-Emilion 1999: Has decent blackberry and licorice character, but rather light for the estate, with light tannins and a short finish.–J.S. • $NA • (1/01/2000) (BT) • **80-84**

Key: SS—Spectator Selection. CS—Cellar Selection. HR—Highly Recommended. $NA—Price not available. (BT)—Barrel tasting. Ⓐ—Auction Price. For a key to the tasters' initials, see "How to Use These Listings."
Dates in parentheses represent the issues in which the ratings were published.

St.-Emilion 1998: A bit hollow but well-crafted, with vanilla notes, polished tannins and berry character. Medium-bodied, with a tannic finish.–J.S. • $NA • (5/31/1999) (BT) • **85-89**
St.-Emilion 1997: Subtle and polished red. Plenty of violet and berry character. Medium-bodied, with silky tannins and a medium finish. Best after 2000.–J.S. • $32 • (1/31/2000) • **87**
St.-Emilion 1996: A wine with some pretensions, this has berry, chocolate and bark aromas and flavors but is slightly diluted on the palate. Medium-bodied, with polished tannins and a short finish. Drink now.–J.S. • $21 Ⓐ • (1/31/1999) • **85**
St.-Emilion 1995 • $31 Ⓐ • (1/31/1998) • **93**
St.-Emilion 1994 • $35 • (1/31/1997) • **88**
St.-Emilion 1993 • $24 • (1/31/1996) • **87**
St.-Emilion 1992 • $20 • (4/15/1995) • **84**
St.-Emilion 1990 • $57 Ⓐ • (3/31/1993) • **94**
St.-Emilion 1989: Wonderful. This is a concentrated, earthy red with lots going on. Deep dark-ruby color. Fresh aromas of blackberries, dried herbs and spices. Full-bodied and chewy, with lots of rustic tannins and a long, tobacco aftertaste. (1989 Bordeaux horizontal tasting). Best from 2001 through 2008.–J.S. • $42 Ⓐ • (5/31/1999) • **93**
St.-Emilion 1988 • $33 Ⓐ • (4/30/1991) • **86**
St.-Emilion 1986 • $33 Ⓐ • (6/30/1989) • **91**
St.-Emilion 1985 • $36 Ⓐ • (10/15/1994) • **89**
St.-Emilion 1983 • $34 Ⓐ • (10/15/1994) • **88**
St.-Emilion 1982: Medium-red, with a garnet hue. Aromas of dried cherry, with perfume and a hint of earth. Full-bodied, very firm, with well-integrated, silky tannins and a long, ripe fruit aftertaste. Much better than I remember. (1989 Bordeaux horizontal tasting). Best after 2000.–J.S. • $35 Ⓐ • (11/30/1998) • **92**
St.-Emilion 1981 • $35 Ⓐ • (10/15/1994) • **89**

LARMANDIER-BERNIER

Brut Blanc de Blancs Champagne NV: Fairly ripe and mature in flavor, yet lean on the finish. Pear and peach notes are accented by honey and almond. Drink now. • $40 • (10/15/1999) • **85**
Brut Blanc de Blancs Champagne Special Club 1994: A full texture and mature but austere fruit flavors make this one to uncork soon. Drink now. • $30 • (10/15/1999) • **85**
Brut Blanc de Blancs Champagne Special Club 1992 • $40 • (11/30/1997) • **86**
Brut Champagne Tradition NV • $25 • (10/31/1997) • **87**
Extra Brut Blanc de Blancs Champagne Vieilles Vignes de Cramant NV: Bracing and dry, yet flavorful; a fine antidote to the many simple, sweet Champagnes. Has plenty of pear and citrus flavors, subtle earthy-toasty nuances, great balance and a velvety texture. Drink now through 2001. • $50 • (10/15/1999) • **90**

LAROCHE, DOMAINE

Chablis 1995 • $NA • (8/31/1996) • **83**
Chablis Beauroys 1998: There's beautiful fruit in this medium-bodied Chardonnay, which sings with clearly focused, chiseled aromas and flavors that range from mineral, smoke and flint to spice, flowers, fig and apple tart. Not imported into the U.S. Drink now through 2004.–P.M. • $NA • (1/01/2000) • **88**
Chablis Blanchots 1997: All silk and opulence, with a lovely, honeyed pear and toasted oak character. Hard not to be seduced by this full-bodied, pure, elegant, charming Chablis. Drink now through 2007.–P.M. • $85 • (9/30/1999) • **93**
Chablis Blanchots 1996: A model of ripe, sweet-tasting fruit enveloped in fresh, citrusy acidity. Of medium body, this is a sleek wine, beautifully balanced, exploding with ripe pear, quince, orange and dried herbs. Very little oak disturbs the clean lines and great finesse of this aerodynamic, nonfiltered Chablis grand cru. Drink now through 2010.–P.M. • $73 • (8/31/1998) • **96**
Chablis Blanchots 1995 • $32 • (6/15/1997) • **89**
Chablis Bougerots 1997: Lush and smooth-textured, with honey, wet earth and a real *terroir* quality about it. Deliciously balanced, full-bodied, you want to hug this wine. Lingering finish. Not imported into the U.S. Drink now through 2005.–P.M. • $NA • (9/30/1999) • **90**
Chablis Fourchaumes 1996 • $40 • (5/31/1998) • **94**
Chablis Fourchaumes 1995 • $32 • (6/15/1997) • **85**
Chablis Fourchaumes Vieilles Vignes 1998: Lovely, floral and peachlike, almost Viognier in its flavor profile. Light- to medium-bodied, it screams with life, displaying lime, orange rind and slight toast notes. Delicious finish. Drink now through 2005.–P.M. • $50 • (5/15/2000) • **88**

FRANCE

Chablis Fourchaumes Vieilles Vignes 1997: A well-made crowd-pleaser. Lovely, with deft balance between wood, honey, lime, bread dough, piecrust and spice, but above all, this full-bodied Chablis tastes creamy and ripe, beckoning you to take another sip. Drink now through 2005.–P.M. • $50 • (5/31/1999) • **91**

Chablis Les Clos 1997: Very clean and wonderfully balanced, with a timeless charm and a focus on ripe fruit, *terroir*, honey, smoke and toasted oak notes. So harmonious you want to drink it now, but this full-bodied white Burgundy will improve in the cellar. Drink now through 2010.–P.M. • $102 • (9/30/1999) • **95**

Chablis Les Clos 1996 • $85 • (5/31/1998) CS • **99**

Chablis Montmains 1998: A lovely, minerally Chablis, with a vanilla bean and cream aroma, a tightly structured mouthfeel and enough acidity to keep it on an even keel. Medium-bodied, it will improve with time. Not imported into the U.S. Drink now through 2005.–P.M. • $NA • (1/01/2000) • **88**

Chablis Réserve de l'Obédience 1997: Fantastic. Clean as a whistle, full-bodied and silky, layered with pear, mineral, granite, stone and lemon flavors that come across as both powerful and subtle. Pretty neat. Best from 2003 through 2010.–P.M. • $152 • (9/30/1999) • **93**

Chablis Réserve de l'Obédience 1996 • $110 • (5/31/1998) • **98**

Chablis St.-Martin 1998: A complex, gorgeous village wine, with a flinty, minerally style. Medium-bodied and supple midpalate, with a wonderful smoke and matchstick character and a long, balanced finish. Drink now through 2002.–P.M. • $25 • (5/15/2000) • **87**

Chablis St.-Martin 1997: Clean and steely, lean but pure, with fresh pear, apple and even tropical notes, ending with a hint of mineral. Drink now.–P.M. • $25 • (5/31/1999) • **84**

Chablis St.-Martin 1996 • $23 • (5/31/1998) • **88**

Chablis St.-Martin 1995 • $19 • (8/31/1996) • **86**

Chablis St.-Martin Vieilles Vignes 1998: Intriguing, with smoke, flint, matchstick, sea salt and wet earth character. Medium-bodied, balanced, ripe, well made and packed with fruit, it has a long, sweet-tasting yet steely finish. Not imported into the U.S. Drink now through 2002.–P.M. • $NA • (1/01/2000) • **88**

Chablis St.-Martin Vieilles Vignes 1995 • $NA • (8/31/1996) • **87**

Chablis Vaillons 1996: Class act. Deep and complex, the for-now shy aromas titillate with their great promise while the wine, still closed, delivers a marvelously rich, thick mouthfeel and cascades with a multitude of flavors to a long, smooth but vibrant finish. Cellar. 275 cases imported. Best after 2005.–P.M. • $40 • (8/31/1998) • **94**

Chablis Vaillons 1995 • $30 • (6/15/1997) • **89**

Chablis Vaillons Vieilles Vignes 1998: Ripe, tasting sweet and lovely, with pear, apple tart, smoke, toasted oak and spice character. Supple and delicious on the palate, it flows to a long finish. Drink now through 2005.–P.M. • $45 • (5/15/2000) • **88**

Chablis Vaillons Vieilles Vignes 1997: What a delightful Vaillons. Packed with the purest, cleanest, most seductive sweet-tasting fruit—pineapple, mango, ripe pear—and a layer of cream and spices, this full-bodied '97 just melts on the palate while retaining plenty of freshness on the finish. Drink now through 2005.–P.M. • $45 • (5/31/1999) • **93**

Chablis Vaudevey 1998: An elegant '98 Chablis with a silky mouthfeel, it has moderate fruit intensity but also nice complexity of salt crackers, mineral and lime. Medium-bodied and a touch diluted, with a mineral side to the finish. Drink now through 2002.–P.M. • $40 • (5/15/2000) • **85**

Chablis Vaudevey 1997: Honeyed and ripe fruit, combined with good intensity of acidity make for a distinctive, medium-bodied Chablis, with a lingering, crisp, even steely finish. Needs cellaring. Drink through 2004–P.M. • $40 • (5/31/1999) • **88**

Chablis Vaudevey 1996: Beautiful. Unctuous, generous, thick and ripe, it displays much finesse and terrific fruit—pear, melon, pineapple—while also delivering some morsels of earth and mineral. Harmonious and balanced, with a lingering, succulent finish. If you drink now, decant. Best after 2005.–P.M. • $40 • (8/31/1998) • **93**

Chablis Vaudevey 1995 • $NA • (6/15/1997) • **84**

Nuits-St.-Georges 1988 • $28 • (11/15/1990) • **87**

Petit Chablis 1995: Ripe, round and honeyed, this white is so lush it's almost thick midpalate. Attractive flavors of green plum, nettles and minerals linger on the finish. Terrific for the appellation. Drink now through 2003.–B.S. • $14 • (1/01/2000) • **89**

LAROSE-TRINTAUDON, CHATEAU

Haut-Médoc 1998: A cool and aromatic wine. Medium- to full-bodied, with well-integrated tannins, but rather short and diluted in the midpalate.–J.S. • $NA • (5/31/1999) (BT) • **80-84**

Haut-Médoc 1996: Good dark color, but doesn't give much on the nose, which hints at fruit and paper. Medium-bodied, with firm tannins and a short finish with some berry. Tasted twice, with consistent notes. Drink now.–J.S. • $11 • (1/31/1999) • **84**

Haut-Médoc 1995 • $24 Ⓐ • (1/31/1998) • **84**

Haut-Médoc 1994 • $18 • (1/31/1997) • **84**

Haut-Médoc 1990 • $12 • (3/31/1993) • **75**

Haut-Médoc 1989: A slightly rustic red, and ready to drink. Medium-ruby color, with leaf, mushroom and berry aromas. Medium-bodied, highly extracted, showing lots of dry tannins and a medium finish. (1989 Bordeaux horizontal tasting).–J.S. • $NA • (5/31/1999) • **85**

Haut-Médoc 1988 • $9 • (4/30/1991) • **84**

Haut-Médoc 1986 • $10 • (11/30/1989) • **78**

Haut-Médoc 1983 • $13 • (10/15/1986) • **73**

Haut-Médoc 1982 • $16 • (11/30/1989) • **79**

Haut-Médoc 1979 • $15 • (10/15/1989) • **76**

LAROZE, CHATEAU

St.-Emilion 1999: A lovely, spicy wine, with berry, tobacco, cherry and chocolate aromas. Medium-bodied, with medium tannins and a fresh finish.–J.S. • $NA • (1/01/2000) • **85-89**

St.-Emilion 1982: An elegant, pretty red. Deep ruby-garnet in color, with pretty floral, berry and leafy aromas. Medium-bodied, with medium, velvety tannins and a long, sweet fruit finish. (1989 Bordeaux horizontal tasting) Drink now.–J.S. • $28 Ⓐ • (11/30/1998) • **88**

LARRIVET, DOMAINE DE

Pessac-Léognan 1996: Violet and berry aromas, with a hint of minerals. Medium-bodied, a bit lean, but silky and fine on the palate with a dark chocolate aftertaste. Second label of Château Larrivet-Haut-Brion. Best after 2000.–J.S. • $NA • (1/31/1999) • **86**

Pessac-Léognan 1995 • $20 • (1/31/1998) • **89**

Pessac-Léognan White 1996: A big and rich white for current drinking pleasure. Attractive aromas of apple, honey and vanilla follow through to the palate. Full-bodied, rather fat and oily, with a round texture and a medium, woody aftertaste. Second label of Château Larrivet-Haut-Brion. Drink now.–J.S. • $25 • (3/31/1999) • **86**

LARRIVET-HAUT-BRION, CHATEAU

Pessac-Léognan 1999: Well done. Dark ruby, with lovely aromas of plum, dark chocolate and berry. Medium- to full-bodied, with velvety tannins and a long finish.–J.S. • $NA • (1/01/2000) (BT) • **85-89**

Pessac-Léognan 1998: Subtle blackberry and licorice aromas and flavors. Medium- to full-bodied, with firm tannins and a long, silky finish. A lovely wine.–J.S. • $NA • (5/31/1999) (BT) • **90-94**

Pessac-Léognan 1997: Good color for the vintage, with plum and toasted oak aromas. Medium-bodied, with silky tannins and a fresh fruit finish. Slightly hollow center palate. Drink now.–J.S. • $25 • (1/31/2000) • **85**

Pessac-Léognan 1996: Loads of smoke, grilled meat and toasted oak on the nose, with ripe fruit beneath. Medium-bodied, with velvety tannins. Slightly dry. Needs a bit more fruit for the new and heavily toasted oak. Drink now.–J.S. • $22 • (1/31/1999) • **84**

Pessac-Léognan 1995 • $20 • (1/31/1998) • **86**

Pessac-Léognan 1994 • $20 • (1/31/1997) • **88**

Pessac-Léognan 1993 • $19 • (1/31/1996) • **86**

Pessac-Léognan 1992 • $15 • (4/15/1995) • **79**

Pessac-Léognan 1989: Promises more on the nose than it gives on the palate, with lots of smoky, cocoa, berry and tobacco aromas. Full-bodied; slightly dry tannins on the finish. (1989 Bordeaux horizontal tasting). Drink now.–J.S. • $24 Ⓐ • (5/31/1999) • **86**

Pessac-Léognan 1988 • $20 Ⓐ • (4/30/1991) • **94**

Pessac-Léognan 1986 • $25 Ⓐ • (6/15/1989) • **82**

Pessac-Léognan White 1998: Has a lot of wood and banana character, but slightly short on fruit. Medium-bodied, with a woody finish. Drink now.–J.S. • $25 • (2/29/2000) • **84**

Pessac-Léognan White 1997: Subtle aromas of apple, cream and pie crust follow through to a medium-bodied palate, with fresh fruit and a light finish. Drink now.–J.S. • $25 • (9/30/1999) • **86**

Pessac-Léognan White 1996: An interesting white with vanilla, lemon and almond aromas and flavors. Medium-bodied, with lots of fruit and a fruity, apple aftertaste. Dig it now. Drink now.–J.S. • $45 • (3/31/1999) • **88**

LARUE

Puligny-Montrachet Les Garennes 1996: Full-throttle white Burgundy that's magnificent. Well made, full-bodied, ripe, rich with hazelnut, honey, butter, popcorn, butterscotch and ripe pear character. Lush and opulent texture, with just-so toasted oak that doesn't overwhelm the fruit. Excellent fresh acidity. Impressive winemaking from a grower in St.-Aubin. Drink now through 2005.–P.M. • $NA • (8/31/1998) • **95**

St.-Aubin En Remilly 1996: Quite pretty, with butter, toasted oak and some clean citrus and apple pie character. Of medium body, with a delicate, harmonious finish. Nothing big or fancy—a good drink upon release. Drink now through 2003.–P.M. • $NA • (8/31/1998) • **86**

St.-Aubin Les Cortons 1996: Lots of new oak. Clean and crisp, with citrus, green apple and lightly smoky aromas and flavors, it's full-bodied but subtle, and deceptively attractive on the pure, balanced, round finish. Drink now through 2003.–P.M. • $NA • (8/31/1998) • **85**

St.-Aubin Murgers des Dent de Chien 1996: Very new-oakish, New Worldish. Lovely, thick and rich, with a voluptuous mouthfeel, showing butter, pear tart, spice, toasted bread, melon, white chocolate character. Subtle, it cascades to a delicate, round, supple finish. Drink now through 2005.–P.M. • $NA • (8/31/1998) • **86**

LASCAUX, CHATEAU DE

Coteaux du Languedoc 1998: Supple, with good up-front flavors of berry, cherry and spice. Leathery notes on the finish. Drink now.–K.M. • $10 • (6/15/2000) • **86**

Coteaux du Languedoc 1997: Already a bit mature-tasting, with modest red cherry and red plum flavors. Dried leathery notes on the finish.–K.M. • $9 • (2/29/2000) • **79**

Coteaux du Languedoc 1996: A distinct leather flavor is matched by plum and berry notes. Good, though a little hollow in the middle.–K.M. • $12 • (8/31/1998) • **82**

Coteaux du Languedoc 1994 • $10 • (6/30/1997) • **78**

Coteaux du Languedoc 1991 • $9 • (3/15/1994) • **84**

Coteaux du Languedoc 1990 • $9 • (3/15/1994) • **85**

Coteaux du Languedoc Pic St.-Loup Les Nobles Pierres 1997: Sweet cherry aromas and flavors are followed by some stemmy notes on the finish.–K.M. • $12 • (2/29/2000) • **79**

Coteaux du Languedoc Pic St.-Loup Les Nobles Pierres 1995: Dark and chewy, with plenty of plum, berry and cherry flavors and firm acidity. Balanced and smooth, with a lingering spicy finish. Tempting now, but should improve with cellaring to 2000.–K.M. • $14 • (10/31/1998) • **87**

Coteaux du Languedoc Pic St.-Loup Les Nobles Pierres 1994: A lovely red with interesting floral flavors mixed in with the plum and cherry. Balanced, with spicy and leathery notes on the finish. Drink now.–K.M. • $15 • (8/31/1998) • **85**

Coteaux du Languedoc White 1996: A firm white, with good flavors of herbs, apples and onions. Finishes on citrusy notes.–K.M. • $11 • (11/15/1998) • **84**

Coteaux du Languedoc White Les Pierres d'Argent 1998: Rich and thick-tasting, with a nice dollop of buttery and figgy flavors. Spicy flavors on the finish. Drink now.–K.M. • $15 • (2/29/2000) • **85**

Coteaux du Languedoc White Les Pierres d'Argent 1997: Spicy aromas and flavors dominate this ripe and exaggerated white. Tropical and appley flavors turn just a tad sharp on the finish. Drink now.–K.M. • $13 • (3/31/2000) • **82**

Coteaux du Languedoc White Les Pierres d'Argent 1996: Rich and flavorful, with ripe apple, honey and spice flavors that linger on the finish with a nice citrusy edge. Drink now.–K.M. • $14 • (11/15/1998) • **86**

LASCOMBES, CHATEAU

Margaux 1996: Pretty aromas of plum and raspberry unfold in this medium-bodied, fine-tannined red. Fresh and silky, but slightly tart on the finish. Drink through 2003–J.S. • $32 • (1/31/1999) • **85**

Margaux 1995 • $25 Ⓐ • (1/31/1998) • **92**

Margaux 1994 • $30 • (1/31/1997) • **88**

Margaux 1993 • $26 • (1/31/1996) • **80**

Key: SS—Spectator Selection. CS—Cellar Selection. HR—Highly Recommended. $NA—Price not available. (BT)—Barrel tasting. Ⓐ—Auction Price. For a key to the tasters' initials, see "How to Use These Listings."
Dates in parentheses represent the issues in which the ratings were published.

Margaux 1990 • $50 Ⓐ • (3/31/1993) • **86**

Margaux 1989: At its peak now. Lots of dried cherry and ripe berry aromas. Full-bodied and round textured, with a tobacco, cedar and leather aftertaste. (1989 Bordeaux horizontal tasting). Drink now.–J.S. • $39 Ⓐ • (5/31/1999) • **87**

Margaux 1988 • $41 Ⓐ • (8/31/1991) • **82**

Margaux 1983 • $32 • (2/15/1988) • **84**

Margaux 1982: A bit tough, but good fruit. Dark ruby-colored, with an amber edge. Pretty blackberry and fresh fruit aromas, with a hint of earth. Medium- to full-bodied, with well-integrated tannins and a mineral, chalk finish. (1982 Bordeaux horizontal tasting). Drink now.–J.S. • $46 Ⓐ • (11/30/1998) • **88**

Margaux 1981 • $33 Ⓐ • (5/16/1985) • **85**

Margaux 1979 • $28 Ⓐ • (10/15/1989) • **84**

Margaux 1961 • $55 Ⓐ • (4/30/1996) • **86**

LASCOURS, CHATEAU DE

Coteaux du Languedoc Pic St.-Loup 1995: Smooth and fairly supple, with ripe plum, spice and cherry flavors. Finishes with currant notes. Plenty of stuffing in this easy-drinking wine. A blend of Syrah and Grenache. Drink now.–K.M. • $11 • (10/31/1998) • **86**

Merlot Vin de Pays d'Oc 1997: An enjoyable Merlot, with pleasant plum and cherry flavors, a rather firm, tannic texture and a lean finish. Drink now. • $9 • (10/31/1998) • **82**

LASSALLE, J.

Brut Champagne NV: Intriguing and richly flavored. Toasty, spicy aromas lead to ripe pear and toasted almond notes that linger on the finish. Luxurious in texture, too. Drink now. • $26 • (9/15/1999) • **90**

Brut Champagne Cuvée Angéline 1990: Bold and rich in style, buttery in aroma and flavor. Ripe pear and lemon notes are accented by smoke and toast. Drink now through 2002. • $49 • (10/15/1999) • **88**

Brut Champagne Impérial Préférence NV: Quite mature for a nonvintage bottling, but it's really delicious. Has a deep gold color, toasty, nutty aromas and full, mellow flavors that linger on the finish. Drink now. • $32 • (10/15/1999) • **91**

Brut Champagne Special Club Premier Cru 1992 • $50 • (11/30/1997) • **86**

Brut Rosé Champagne Réserve NV: Mature in style, with a deep copper color, expansive buttery aromas and broad spicy flavors. Drink now. • $36 • (10/15/1999) • **87**

Brut Rosé Champagne Réserve des Grandes Années NV • $40 • (11/30/1997) • **91**

LASSERRE DU HAUT, DOMAINE

Merlot-Tannat Vin de Pays des Côtes de Gascogne 1996 • $7 • (3/31/1998) • **79**

LASSIME, MARQUISE DE

Cabernet Sauvignon Vin de Pays des Côtes de Gascogne 1996 • $6 • (12/15/1997) • **78**

Cabernet Sauvignon Vin de Pays des Côtes de Gascogne 1995 • $6 • (7/31/1996) • **80**

Merlot Vin de Pays des Côtes de Gascogne 1996 • $6 • (11/15/1997) • **84**

Merlot Vin de Pays des Côtes de Gascogne 1995 • $6 • (7/31/1996) • **80**

Merlot Vin de Pays des Côtes de Gascogne 1991 • $5 • (10/31/1992) • **76**

Vin de Pays des Côtes de Gascogne White Réserve 1996 • $6 • (9/30/1997) • **78**

LASTOURS, CHATEAU

Gaillac 1996: Tastes a bit over the hill despite its relative youth, with stew and dried cherry flavors. Past its prime.–K.M. • $9 • (12/31/1998) • **73**

Gaillac 1995 • $8 • (4/30/1998) • **78**

LATHAM, CHATEAU

Corbières 1995 • $6 • (6/30/1997) • **79**

Corbières Les Hauts de Mandourelle 1993 • $6 • (7/31/1996) • **77**

LATOUR, CHATEAU

Pauillac 1999: One of the wines of the vintage. Wonderful mineral, berry, currant, violet and toasted oak. Full-bodied, with superfine, silky tannins.

Very fine indeed. Wonderful texture; goes on and on.–J.S. • $NA • (1/01/2000) (BT) • **90-94**

Pauillac 1998: A harmonious Latour which shows refinement for the vintage. Loads of crushed black cherries and currants on the nose and the palate. Full-bodied, with very well-integrated tannins and a long, long finish. This will improve in the barrel—just watch.–J.S. • $NA • (5/31/1999) (BT) • **90-94**

Pauillac 1997: A lovely red but a bit light for Latour. Sweet berry, cherry and currant aromas. Medium-bodied, with firm tannins and a medium finish. Drink now through 2005.–J.S. • $135 • (1/31/2000) • **88**

Pauillac 1996: This muscular Latour is deep and dark-colored, its ripe berry oozing from the glass with undertones of vanilla and minerals. Full-bodied, and incredibly chewy, with masses of tannins and a long, long fruity finish. This is how they built clarets in the great years of the 1960s and 1950s. Best after 2005.–J.S. • $203 Ⓐ • (1/31/1999) CS • **97**

Pauillac 1995 • $215 Ⓐ • (1/31/1998) CS • **94**

Pauillac 1994 • $110 Ⓐ • (12/15/1997) • **90**

Pauillac 1993 • $91 Ⓐ • (12/15/1997) • **89**

Pauillac 1992 • $84 Ⓐ • (12/15/1997) • **83**

Pauillac 1991 • $85 Ⓐ • (12/15/1997) • **88**

Pauillac 1990 • $408 Ⓐ • (3/15/1993) • **100**

Pauillac 1989: A monster wine of huge structure. Superdark-ruby color. Intense aromas of plums, berries and spices with highlights of cinnamon. Full-bodied, massive, adding loads of chewy tannins. Mouthpuckering young thing. (1989 Bordeaux horizontal tasting). Best after 2005.–J.S. • $167 Ⓐ • (5/31/1999) • **97**

Pauillac 1988: Though this has always been an outstanding '88, I never thought it was classic quality—but this wine proves otherwise. Ink-colored, with an impressive concentration of mineral, currant and berry flavors. Full-bodied, with huge, velvety tannins and a long, caressing finish. (1988 Bordeaux horizontal tasting). Best after 2005.–J.S. • $128 Ⓐ • (11/30/1998) • **96**

Pauillac 1987 • $84 Ⓐ • (12/15/1997) • **84**

Pauillac 1986 • $146 Ⓐ• (12/15/1997) • **96**

Pauillac 1985 • $152 Ⓐ • (12/15/1997) • **95**

Pauillac 1984 • $79 Ⓐ • (3/31/1987) • **92**

Pauillac 1983 • $112 Ⓐ • (12/15/1997) • **88**

Pauillac 1982: Blockbuster. Grossly underrated for years, this is a classic Latour. Dark ruby-garnet colored. Loads of berry, mint and tobacco aromas. Full-bodied, very concentrated, with masses of tannins. A big wine. Needs time; best after 2000. (1988 Bordeaux horizontal tasting).–J.S. • $NA • (11/30/1998) • **97**

Pauillac 1981 • $96 Ⓐ • (12/15/1997) • **89**

Pauillac 1979 • $92 Ⓐ • (12/15/1997) • **89**

Pauillac 1978 • $165 Ⓐ • (12/15/1997) • **88**

Pauillac 1976 • $87 Ⓐ • (12/15/1997) • **87**

Pauillac 1975 • $153 Ⓐ • (12/15/1997) • **91**

Pauillac 1971 • $117 Ⓐ • (12/15/1997) • **82**

Pauillac 1970 • $347 Ⓐ • (12/15/1997) • **90**

Pauillac 1967 • $NA• (12/15/1997) • **87**

Pauillac 1966 • $305 Ⓐ • (12/15/1997) • **95**

Pauillac 1965 • $56 Ⓐ • (3/31/1990) • **74**

Pauillac 1964 • $226 Ⓐ • (12/15/1997) • **88**

Pauillac 1963 • $NA• (3/31/1990) • **77**

Pauillac 1962 • $72 Ⓐ • (12/15/1997) • **91**

Pauillac 1961 • $1,302 Ⓐ • (12/15/1997) • **99**

Pauillac 1960 • $172 Ⓐ • (12/15/1997) • **89**

Pauillac 1959 • $817 Ⓐ • (12/15/1997) • **89**

Pauillac 1958 • $NA • (3/31/1990) • **81**

Pauillac 1957 • $150 Ⓐ • (12/15/1997) • **81**

Pauillac 1955 • $400 Ⓐ • (12/15/1997) • **92**

Pauillac 1953 • $NA• (12/15/1997) • **90**

Pauillac 1952 • $274 Ⓐ • (12/15/1997) • **88**

Pauillac 1950 • $460 Ⓐ • (3/31/1990) • **79**

Pauillac 1949 • $1,200 Ⓐ • (12/15/1997) • **94**

Pauillac 1948 • $448 Ⓐ • (12/15/1997) • **85**

Pauillac 1947 • $424 Ⓐ • (12/15/1997) • **84**

Pauillac 1944 • $775 Ⓐ • (3/31/1990) • **70**

Pauillac 1937 • $349 Ⓐ • (3/31/1990) • **89**

Pauillac 1936 • $1,035 Ⓐ • (3/31/1990) • **75**

Pauillac 1934 • $623 Ⓐ • (12/15/1997) • **92**

Pauillac 1929 • $1,801 Ⓐ • (12/15/1997) • **50**

Pauillac 1928 • $NA• (12/15/1997) • **90**

Pauillac 1926 • $546 Ⓐ • (12/15/1997) • **83**

Pauillac 1924 • $1,163 Ⓐ • (3/31/1990) • **91**

Pauillac 1918 • $798 Ⓐ • (12/15/1997) • **91**

Pauillac 1908 • $1,064 Ⓐ • (12/15/1997) • **89**

Pauillac 1900 • $4,515 Ⓐ • (3/31/1990) • **90**

Pauillac 1899 • $6,248 Ⓐ • (12/15/1997) • **90**

Pauillac 1892 • $NA • (12/15/1997) • **92**

Pauillac 1875 • $NA • (3/31/1990) • **77**

Pauillac 1874 • $NA • (3/31/1990) • **97**

Pauillac 1870 • $2,066 Ⓐ • (3/31/1990) • **94**

Pauillac 1865 • $NA/1.5 liter • (3/31/1990) • **94**

Pauillac 1847 • $NA/1.5 liter • (3/31/1990) • **93**

LATOUR, LOUIS

Aloxe-Corton 1992 • $19 • (12/15/1994) • **80**

Aloxe-Corton 1955 • $NA • (8/31/1990) • **85**

Aloxe-Corton Domaine Latour 1995 • $26 • (11/15/1997) • **77**

Aloxe-Corton Domaine Latour 1993 • $21 • (11/15/1995) • **82**

Aloxe-Corton Domaine Latour 1991 • $18 • (1/31/1994) • **82**

Aloxe-Corton Domaine Latour 1990 • $22 • (12/15/1992) • **84**

Aloxe-Corton Domaine Latour 1989 • $24 • (1/31/1992) • **84**

Aloxe-Corton Les Chaillots 1995 • $32 • (11/15/1997) • **75**

Aloxe-Corton Les Chaillots 1985 • $37 • (4/15/1988) • **76**

Auxey-Duresses White 1995 • $19 • (8/31/1997) • **88**

Bâtard-Montrachet 1995 • $157 • (8/31/1997) • **95**

Beaune Domaine Latour 1995 • $28 • (11/15/1997) • **75**

Beaune Domaine Latour 1993 • $22 • (11/15/1995) • **80**

Beaune Domaine Latour 1991 • $17 • (1/31/1994) • **77**

Beaune Domaine Latour 1990 • $21 • (12/15/1992) • **87**

Beaune Domaine Latour 1989 • $22 • (1/31/1992) • **91**

Beaune Les Vignes Franches 1993 • $26 • (11/15/1995) • **80**

Beaune Les Vignes Franches 1992 • $20 • (12/15/1994) • **76**

Beaune Les Vignes Franches 1985 • $31 • (3/15/1988) • **90**

Bonnes Mares 1989 • $60 • (1/31/1992) • **93**

Bourgogne 1992 • $10 • (12/15/1994) • **74**

Bourgogne 1990 • $10 • (12/15/1992) • **79**

Bourgogne Cuvée Latour 1990 • $11 • (12/15/1992) • **86**

Bourgogne Cuvée Latour 1989 • $NA • (1/31/1992) • **80**

Chablis 1995 • $NA • (8/31/1996) • **85**

Chablis Beauroy 1996 • $27 • (5/31/1998) • **89**

Chablis Fourchaume 1997: Round and well made, of medium intensity and medium body, this white delivers plenty of wet earth, cedar and, yes, some astringency on the finish. Drink through 2005–P.M. • $NA • (5/31/1999) • **83**

Chablis Fourchaume 1996 • $30 • (5/31/1998) • **77**

Chablis Montmains 1997: Hard now but with a lush texture, offering ripe fruit and matchstick and earth aromas. Medium-bodied, with a chewy, tough finish. Best from 2001 through 2005.–P.M. • $NA • (1/01/2000) • **86**

Chablis Montmains 1996 • $28 • (5/31/1998) • **85**

Chablis Montmains 1995 • $NA • (8/31/1996) • **86**

Chambertin 1993 • $102 • (11/15/1995) • **84**

Chambertin Cuvée Hèritiers Latour 1989 • $90 • (1/31/1992) • **78**

Chambertin Cuvée Hèritiers Latour 1985 • $76 • (3/15/1988) • **95**

Charmes-Chambertin 1985 • $50 • (3/15/1988) • **85**

Chassagne-Montrachet 1995 • $38 • (5/31/1997) • **88**

Chassagne-Montrachet Morgeot 1995 • $43 • (8/31/1997) • **90**

Chevalier-Montrachet Les Demoiselles 1995 • $186 • (8/31/1997) • **98**

Clos de la Roche 1996: A bit earthy and crisp, deploying some decent red berry, mineral and toasted oak flavors. Short finish.–P.M. • $88 • (5/15/1999) • **79**

Clos Vougeot 1995 • $74 • (11/15/1997) • **71**

Corton-Charlemagne 1997: Really attractive, with showy spice, clove, smoke, pear and tart pie character. Full-bodied and flamboyant, but it lacks the midpalate richness and concentration to be outstanding. Drink now through 2004.–P.M. • $110 • (9/30/1999) • **89**

Corton-Charlemagne 1996: Clean and elegant, this is refined on the nose, with a stone, spice, mocha, chocolate and cream character. Quite woodsy on the palate, turning chewy and a bit rough, but with plenty of tropical and other ripe flavors. Drink through 2006.–P.M. • $112 Ⓐ • (5/31/1999) • **91**

Corton-Charlemagne 1995 • $91 Ⓐ • (8/31/1997) CS • **93**

Corton Château Corton Grancey 1996: Light-bodied Pinot, showing a purity of pretty berry flavor that's sweet-tasting on the midpalate. Well made in a subtle style. Should gain depth with age. Best from 2001 through 2005.–P.M. • $60 • (5/15/1999) • **87**

Corton Château Corton Grancey 1995 • $49 • (11/15/1997) • **78**

Corton Château Corton Grancey 1993 • $43 • (11/15/1995) • **88**

Corton Château Corton Grancey 1992 • $NA • (12/15/1994) • **80**

Corton Château Corton Grancey 1990 • $43 • (12/15/1992) • **89**

Corton Château Corton Grancey 1989 • $48 • (1/31/1992) • **89**

Corton Château Corton Grancey 1985 • $46 • (3/15/1988) • **89**

■ ■ ■ ■

LATOUR, LOUIS

Corton Château Corton Grancey 1959 • $NA • (8/31/1990) • **89**
Corton Château Corton Grancey 1953 • $NA • (8/31/1990) • **91**
Corton Château Corton Grancey 1947 • $NA • (8/31/1990) • **85**
Corton Clos de la Vigne au Saint 1985 • $43 • (3/15/1988) • **89**
Corton Domaine Latour 1991 • $29 • (1/31/1994) • **84**
Corton Domaine Latour 1990 • $35 • (12/15/1992) • **70**
Corton Domaine Latour 1985 • $38 • (3/15/1988) • **90**
Côte de Beaune-Villages 1990 • $16 • (12/15/1992) • **78**
Côte de Nuits-Villages 1995 • $15 • (11/15/1997) • **70**
Echézeaux 1985 • $49 • (3/15/1988) • **87**
Gevrey-Chambertin 1995 • $34 • (11/15/1997) • **75**
Gevrey-Chambertin 1992 • $27 • (12/15/1994) • **84**
Gevrey-Chambertin 1990 • $32 • (12/15/1992) • **78**
Gevrey-Chambertin 1989 • $35 • (1/31/1992) • **87**
Gevrey-Chambertin 1985 • $36 • (10/15/1988) • **77**
Gevrey-Chambertin Premier Cru 1996: A bit reserved aromatically, showing a firm grip of wet earth, but also a slight herbal edge. Still, there's good fruit and oak complexity in this medium-bodied '96. Drink now through 2003.–P.M. • $64 • (5/15/1999) • **83**
Mercurey 1995 • $18 • (11/15/1997) • **72**
Meursault 1995 • $30 • (5/31/1997) • **90**
Meursault Les Charmes 1995 • $52 • (8/31/1997) • **90**
Meursault Les Gouttes d'Or 1995 • $49 • (8/31/1997) • **90**
Meursault-Blagny Château de Blagny 1995 • $42 • (5/31/1997) • **90**
Montagny La Grande Roche 1995 • $14 • (5/31/1997) • **85**
Montrachet 1997: Starts better than it ends. Sour, with candied apple.–P.M. • $390 • (9/30/1999) • **75**
Montrachet 1996: Amazingly velvety in texture and full-bodied, offering ripe pear, butter and lively lemon pie flavors, kicking in with chewy, minerally intensity on the long finish. Tempting now, but cellar. Would have rated higher but for a slight off, cardboardy flavor (from filtration?) in the aftertaste. Best from 2002 through 2010.–P.M. • $218 Ⓐ • (5/31/1999) • **90**
Montrachet 1995: Opulent, rich, full-bodied and balanced, very pleasant, subtle, seductive, charming and soft. Loaded with fruit, toasted oak, and spice, and the wood is already well integrated. Drink now through 2010.–P.M. • $213 Ⓐ • (8/31/1998) • **94**
Nuits-St.-Georges 1996: A bit green and herbal, with drying tannins and a short, astringent finish.–P.M. • $218 Ⓐ • (5/15/1999) • **75**
Nuits-St.-Georges 1993 • $31 • (11/15/1995) • **78**
Nuits-St.-Georges 1991 • $28 • (1/31/1994) • **84**
Nuits-St.-Georges Clos des Argillières 1996: Pure raspberry and blackberry aromas burst from the glass. The wine is medium-bodied, offering a lively, fresh character on the palate, with subtle smoky-mocha flavors. Smooth tannins but crisp acidity on the clean, fruity finish. Should soften and deepen with age. Best from 2003 through 2007.–P.M. • $55 • (5/15/1999) • **87**
Pernand-Vergelesses White 1995 • $21 • (8/31/1997) • **85**
Pommard 1995 • $32 • (11/15/1997) • **82**
Pommard 1993 • $28 • (11/15/1995) • **82**
Pommard Epenots 1996: Light-bodied and a bit green, this smells earthy and tastes of tea leaf, ripe red berries and mushrooms. A bit mature on the somewhat astringent finish.–P.M. • $55 • (5/15/1999) • **77**
Pommard Les Epenots 1992 • $32 • (12/15/1994) • **83**
Pommard Les Epenots 1991 • $32 • (2/28/1995) • **85**
Pommard Les Epenots 1990 • $37 • (2/28/1995) • **88**
Pommard Les Epenots 1989 • $38 • (2/28/1995) • **85**
Pommard Les Epenots 1988 • $38 • (2/28/1995) • **81**
Pommard Les Epenots 1987 • $30 • (2/28/1995) • **81**
Pommard Les Epenots 1986 • $NA • (2/28/1995) • **82**
Pommard Les Epenots 1985 • $46 • (2/28/1995) • **88**
Pommard Les Epenots 1983 • $NA • (2/28/1995) • **84**
Pouilly-Fuissé 1995 • $15 • (5/31/1998) • **85**
Puligny-Montrachet 1995 • $39 • (8/31/1997) • **79**
Puligny-Montrachet La Garenne 1995 • $49 • (8/31/1997) • **90**
Puligny-Montrachet Les Folatières 1995 • $56 • (8/31/1997) • **92**
Romanée St.-Vivant Les Quatre Journaux 1996: Ripe yet refined, with licorice, smoke, toast and sweet-tasting red berry character. Medium-bodied, wonderfully balanced, with a long, peppery, deeply satisfying finish. Much better than the '95. Drink now through 2007.–P.M. • $175 • (5/15/1999) • **92**
Romanée St.-Vivant Les Quatre Journaux 1995 • $160 • (11/15/1997) • **74**
Romanée St.-Vivant Les Quatre Journaux 1993 • $NA • (5/15/1996) • **89**

Key: SS—Spectator Selection. CS—Cellar Selection. HR—Highly Recommended. $NA—Price not available. (BT)—Barrel tasting. Ⓐ—Auction Price. For a key to the tasters' initials, see "How to Use These Listings."
Dates in parentheses represent the issues in which the ratings were published.

Romanée St.-Vivant Les Quatre Journaux 1992 • $120 • (12/15/1994) • **81**
Romanée St.-Vivant Les Quatre Journaux 1990 • $139 • (12/15/1992) • **89**
Romanée St.-Vivant Les Quatre Journaux 1989 • $140 • (1/31/1992) • **93**
Romanée St.-Vivant Les Quatre Journaux 1985 • $99 • (3/15/1988) • **98**
Romanée St.-Vivant Les Quatre Journaux 1953 • $NA • (8/31/1990) • **94**
St.-Véran 1995 • $12 • (5/31/1997) • **79**
Santenay 1989 • $NA • (1/31/1992) • **80**
Savigny-lès-Beaune 1992 • $13 • (12/15/1994) • **78**
Savigny-lès-Beaune 1991 • $13 • (1/31/1994) • **79**
Savigny-lès-Beaune 1989 • $NA • (1/31/1992) • **84**
Vosne-Romanée Les Beaux Monts 1985 • $36 • (3/15/1988) • **86**
Vosne-Romanée Les Suchots 1996: Beautiful for its ripe, rich fruit and velvety tannins, this full-bodied red Burgundy caresses the palate with its toast, mineral, smoke, game, cassis flavors, and exits with a graceful bow. Best from 2003 through 2010.–P.M. • $58 • (5/15/1999) • **93**

LATOUR A POMEROL, CHATEAU

Graves 1982: Not very exciting, but shows some ripe flavors. Medium ruby-garnet color. Stone, cherry and tobacco aromas. Medium-bodied, with medium tannins and a slightly diluted finish.—1982 Bordeaux horizontal. Drink now.–J.S. • $NA • (11/30/1998) • **85**
Pomerol 1999: A young wine with very pleasant mineral, berry and cherry character. Medium body. Medium finish.–J.S. • $NA • (1/01/2000) (BT) • **85-89**
Pomerol 1998: Shows serious complexity, with cherry, vanilla, spice and earth character. Full-bodied, compacted, with full, chewy tannins and a long finish. Best Latour à Pomerol in a decade.–J.S. • $NA • (5/31/1999) (BT) • **90-94**
Pomerol 1997: A wine with lovely ripe fruit and smooth texture. Medium-bodied, with plenty of plum and cherry character. Fresh finish. Drink now through 2002.–J.S. • $NA • (1/31/2000) • **88**
Pomerol 1996: The tannins are polished, but the palate is slightly diluted, with berry and cherry flavors and a light chocolate and berry aftertaste. Disppointing for this estate. Drink now.–J.S. • $46 Ⓐ • (1/31/1999) • **82**
Pomerol 1995 • $56 Ⓐ • (1/31/1998) • **89**
Pomerol 1994 • $33 Ⓐ • (1/31/1997) • **89**
Pomerol 1993 • $39 Ⓐ • (1/31/1996) • **81**
Pomerol 1992 • $24 Ⓐ • (4/15/1995) • **80**
Pomerol 1990 • $74 Ⓐ • (10/15/1994) • **90**
Pomerol 1989: A traditional wine of autumnal aromas of leaves, game and fruit. Medium- to full-bodied, with velvety tannins and a big, chewy finish. Needs time. (1989 Bordeaux horizontal tasting). Best after 2004.–J.S. • $74 Ⓐ • (5/31/1999) • **90**
Pomerol 1988 • $49 Ⓐ • (10/15/1994) • **90**
Pomerol 1986 • $49 Ⓐ • (10/15/1994) • **86**
Pomerol 1985 • $68 Ⓐ • (5/15/1994) • **90**
Pomerol 1983 • $63 Ⓐ • (10/15/1994) • **92**
Pomerol 1982: A solid '82 Pomerol with good richness. Good deep-ruby, garnet color. Black olive, cherry, ripe fruit nose. Medium-bodied, with velvety tannins and a fresh fruit, tobacco and meat finish. Not as great as I remember, but an outstanding bottle all the same. (1989 Bordeaux horizontal tasting). Drink now.–J.S. • $161 Ⓐ • (11/30/1998) • **90**
Pomerol 1981 • $50 • (10/15/1994) • **88**
Pomerol 1979 • $37 Ⓐ • (5/15/1994) • **85**
Pomerol 1976 • $75 • (5/15/1994) • **87**
Pomerol 1975 • $56 Ⓐ • (5/15/1994) • **80**
Pomerol 1971 • $115 Ⓐ • (5/15/1994) • **82**
Pomerol 1970 • $119 Ⓐ • (5/15/1994) • **91**
Pomerol 1959 • $280 Ⓐ • (10/15/1990) • **90**
Pomerol 1966 • $129 Ⓐ • (5/15/1994) • **79**
Pomerol 1964 • $134 Ⓐ • (5/15/1994) • **82**
Pomerol 1962 • $200 • (5/15/1994) • **86**
Pomerol 1961 • $3530/1.5 liter • (4/30/1996) • **94**
Pomerol 1955 • $278 Ⓐ • (5/15/1994) • **82**
Pomerol 1953 • $350 • (5/15/1994) • **88**
Pomerol 1952 • $300 • (5/15/1994) • **85**
Pomerol 1949 • $1500 • (5/15/1994) • **72**
Pomerol 1947 • $3288 Ⓐ • (5/31/1997) • **91**
Pomerol 1945 • $1500 • (5/15/1994) • **74**

LATOUR-GIRAUD

Bourgogne Aligoté 1997: Tastes acidic and tart, with some sweetness underneath. Odd.–P.M. • $NA • (1/01/1999) • **76**

Bourgogne White 1997: Candied, dilute, green and awful.–P.M. • $15 • (9/30/1999) • **70**

Meursault Bouchères 1997: Shows power, delivering earthy, ripe fruit and a length on the finish that holds your attention. Full-bodied, with dried herb, pine honey, rosemary and lightly toasted accents. Drink now through 2005.–P.M. • $40 • (9/30/1999) • **88**

Meursault Bouchères 1996: Very supple, even soft 1996, with a creamy, palate-caressing texture. Rich, ripe and impressively opulent premier cru with lemon, honey, pear, citrus and tropical flavors—and no distracting new oak. Creamlike finish. Drink now through 2006.–P.M. • $35 • (8/31/1998) • **91**

Meursault Charmes 1997: Rich, ripe and very attractive. Full-bodied, it shows clean purity of fruit and good texture and length, with mineral, green apple, pear and a touch of honey. Drink now through 2004.–P.M. • $48 • (9/30/1999) • **90**

Meursault Charmes 1996: Subtle as can be, yet very firm and almost tannic, this grew into a very minerally, supple and complex wine after contact with air, suggesting cellaring will coax its full potential. Clean and pure, medium- to full-bodied, very subtle now in aroma, with mineral, pear, chalky and spicy notes. The finish is distinctive, chewy, bulky and very flavorful. Best from 2005.–P.M. • $42 • (8/31/1998) • **93**

Meursault Clos du Cromin 1997: Nicely concentrated, the fruit, dried herbs, flint and gun powder character wraps around the palate, giving some welcome terroir intensity and opulence to this intriguing, full-bodied Meursault. Drink now through 2007.–P.M. • $NA • (1/01/1999) • **90**

Meursault Clos du Cromin 1996: Lovely, full-bodied wine, packed with honey, vanilla, lime and earth character. Pure, clean and vibrant, this seduces with its multiple facets, deftly toasted oak accents and balanced finish. Needs time to smooth out and show its potential. Best from 2005.–P.M. • $30 • (8/31/1998) • **90**

Meursault Cuvée Charles Maxime 1997: A bit woody and earthy. Medium-bodied and rather round in texture, it turns a bit acidic on the finish, leaving a metallic taste.–P.M. • $40 • (9/30/1999) • **77**

Meursault Cuvée Charles Maxime 1996: Superbly made village Meursault, showing lush, opulent, complex texture that massages the palate. Very minerally, as expected from a top '96, as well as firm and chewy, with earth, herb, pear and a touch of honey and oak on the long, chalky finish. Needs time but it's worth waiting for. Best from 2005.–P.M. • $32 • (8/31/1998) • **90**

Meursault Genevrières 1997: This big, ripe white Burgundy tramples the palate with showy toasted oak. Fat and rich, with "Meursault" stamped across the taste buds. Fresh, lemony finish. Drink now through 2005. –P.M. • $50 • (9/30/1999) • **88**

Meursault Genevrières 1996: Gorgeous premier cru, clean, clear, deep and complex, with lots of fruit. You can tell from the subtle nose that it's classic white Burgundy. Full-bodied, lush and opulent, it's round, supple and silky, with ripe fruit, good acidity, subtle toasted oak. It all comes together on the long finish. Tempting upon release, but worth cellaring a few years. Drink now through 2010.–P.M. • $42 • (8/31/1998) • **97**

Meursault Genevrières 1995 • $NA • (8/31/1997) • **97**

Meursault Le Limozin 1997: Supple, even soft, this golden-colored Chardonnay offers a spike of fresh lemon, a bit of caramel, honey and marzipan character. Its broad flavors fan out a bit inelegantly on the finish. Drink now through 2003.–P.M. • $NA • (1/01/1999) • **82**

Meursault Le Limozin 1996: Beautiful Meursault. Clean and pure, a complex, full-bodied wine that offers ripe fruit, good acidity and buttery, butterscotch flavors. The finish is seductively balanced and very long. Best from 2005.–P.M. • $31 • (8/31/1998) • **88**

Meursault Le Limozin 1995 • $NA • (8/31/1997) • **70**

Meursault Les Narvaux 1997: Clean and focused, with nice ripe fruit and toasted accents. A bit too oaky, it turns slightly tart on the lemony finish. Drink now through 2003.–P.M. • $40 • (9/30/1999) • **82**

Meursault Les Narvaux 1996: Lovely wine, smooth and ripe, with butter, pear, pielike and some subtle toasted oak aromas and flavors. Full-bodied, you can taste an attractive malic-milky-lemon-honey combination that's very Meursault. Good length on the finish. Best after 2004.–P.M. • $32 • (8/31/1998) • **88**

Meursault Perrières 1997: A bit tart, but it has concentration midpalate, with floral, quince and a velvet touch that turns a bit rustic on the finish. Best from 2005 through 2010.–P.M. • $50 • (9/30/1999) • **87**

Meursault Perrières 1996: Classy and sleek, this elegant, subtle wine shows pure and vibrant fruit, and a superb minerally concentration in the midpalate that gives round texture. Medium-bodied, it rockets to life with a lemony, chalky, chewy finish. Best from 2005.–P.M. • $45 • (8/31/1998) • **95**

Meursault Perrières 1995 • $NA • (5/31/1997) • **93**

Meursault Poruzots 1997: Clean and pure, this acid-titillating, full-bodied white keeps your taste buds excited. Thick, it reveals itself in layer upon layer of smoke, honey and pear tart flavors. Best from 2003 through 2017.–P.M. • $45 • (9/30/1999) • **91**

Meursault Poruzots 1996: Full-bodied, but not very elegant. Quite earthy, with a tart character. Turns dry and astringent on the finish. Drink now through 2005.–P.M. • $40 • (8/31/1998) • **80**

Meursault Poruzots 1995 • $NA • (5/31/1997) • **88**

Pommard Refène Cuvée Sélectionnée 1997: A smooth, appealing Pommard whose plum flavors are accented with earth and mineral from the *terroir*. Ripe and forward, with moderate tannins and length. Drink now through 2003.–B.S. • $46 • (9/30/1999) • **84**

Puligny-Montrachet Champs Canet 1997: A wonderful, full-bodied, thick wine. Deep and complex, with plenty of toasted oak but also flavorful ripe fruit that swirls around the palate. The finish persists into the horizon. Drink now through 2003.–P.M. • $55 • (9/30/1999) • **94**

Puligny-Montrachet Champs Canet 1996: Clean and pure premier cru, medium-bodied, with plenty of fruit, acidity and a reasonable dose of toasted oak along with the attractive mineral, wet stone character. Juicy, mouthpuckering, steely and crisp finish. Drink now through 2005.–P.M. • $42 • (8/31/1998) • **83**

Puligny-Montrachet Champs Canet 1995 • $40 • (5/31/1997) • **83**

Volnay Clos des Chênes 1997: Mint, herb, smoke and a hint of chocolate are the main themes in this firm, rustic style. The flavors are dilute midpalate, the finish firm and dry. Drink now through 2002.–B.S. • $46 • (9/30/1999) • **80**

Pessac-Léognan 1998: Wonderful aromas of blackberries, olives and spices. Full-bodied and velvety, with a long, fruity aftertaste. Solid core of fruit. Just a tad dry on the finish. Almost outstanding.–J.S. • $NA • (5/31/1999) (BT) • **85-89**

Pessac-Léognan 1997: Intense aromas of plum skin and dark chocolate. Medium-bodied, with a solid core of fruit, firm tannins and a fresh finish. A bit tight right now. Best after 2000.–J.S. • $NA • (1/31/2000) • **87**

Pessac-Léognan 1996: Some decent blackberry, currant and dried herb notes. Medium- to light-bodied, with good tannins, but slightly rustic on the finish. Drink now.–J.S. • $30 • (1/31/1999) • **80**

Pessac-Léognan 1995: Refined and beautiful '95. Wonderful ripe plum aromas follow through onto the palate. Medium-bodied, with fine tannins and a fresh fruity aftertaste with hints of wood. Best from 2001 through 2006.–J.S. • $30 • (9/15/1998) • **90**

Pessac-Léognan 1993 • $18 • (1/31/1996) • **83**

Pessac-Léognan 1992 • $15 • (4/15/1995) • **83**

Pessac-Léognan 1991 • $15 • (3/31/1994) • **78**

Pessac-Léognan 1990 • $25 • (3/31/1993) • **91**

LATOUR MARTILLAC, CHATEAU

Pessac-Léognan 1989: Plenty of berry, chocolate and tobacco character. Full-bodied, with firm tannins and a fresh, fruity finish. A bit one-dimensional but very good nonetheless.—1989 Bordeaux horizontal. Best after 2004.–J.S. • $NA • (5/31/1999) • **89**

Pessac-Léognan 1988 • $24 • (2/28/1991) • **88**

Pessac-Léognan 1986 • $15 • (2/15/1990) • **90**

Graves 1985 • $19 • (8/31/1988) • **87**

Graves 1982: Not very exciting, but shows some ripe flavors. Medium ruby-garnet color. Stone, cherry and tobacco aromas. Medium-bodied, with medium tannins and a slightly diluted finish. (1982 Bordeaux horizontal tasting). Drink now.–J.S. • $NA • (11/30/1998) • **85**

Pessac-Léognan White 1997: A solid white Bordeaux, with lots of pear, vanilla and apple character. Medium-bodied, with a light chalkiness and a fresh, light coconut finish. Drink now.–J.S. • $30 • (9/30/1999) • **87**

Pessac-Léognan White 1996: Very clean and rich, with almond, apple, butterscotch and honey aromas and flavors. Medium-bodied, with well-integrated acidity and a flavorful finish. Delicious. Drink now.–J.S. • $NA • (1/01/1999) • **89**

LAUNAY, CHATEAU

Entre-Deux-Mers 1998: Rather dull, with pear and marzipan character and a light finish.–J.S. • $9 • (7/31/1999) • **78**

LAUNAY, PAUL DE

Mercurey White Domaine du Meix Foulot 1997: Very ripe in aroma, with dried apricot and tropical notes, yet it turns out ungenerous and slightly drying on the palate.–P.M. • $21 • (5/31/1999) • **79**

Mercurey White Premier Cru Domaine du Meix Foulot 1997: A ripe but dry style, showing dried apricot, tropical and honey aromas, but turning

FRANCE

surprisingly ungenerous on the palate and astringent on the finish.–P.M. • $27 • (5/31/1999) • **79**

LAURENT, DOMINIQUE

Beaune Les Grèves 1997: This gorgeous '97 shows toasted mocha, plum, black cherry and smoky tar notes, all coming together in this sleek yet rich wine. Impressive balance, sweet tannins and a long, clean finish. Drink now through 2005.–P.M. • $40 • (9/30/1999) • **91**

Beaune Les Grèves 1996: Beautifully open and smiling Pinot, sweet- and ripe-tasting, with fabulous cassis, plum, blackberry character—even a minty undertone for added complexity. Full-bodied, the toasted oak integrates nicely into the vibrant, exuberant but tannic finish. Best from 2005 through 2012.–P.M. • $80 • (5/15/1999) • **91**

Beaune Premier Cru 1994 • $38 • (9/30/1997) • **85**

Beaune Premier Cru Hospices de Beaune 1997: Most impressive. Big, pure, focused, and racy; a dark-colored, full-bodied ager that smells and tastes oaky in the mold of an international styled red, but the clean, clear and vibrant red berry character is pure Burgundy. Long, simmering, chewy finish. Give the tannins, flavors time. Best from 2003 through 2012.–P.M. • $NA • (1/01/2000) • **93**

Beaune Premier Cru Vieilles Vignes 1993 • $NA • (5/15/1996) • **86**

Bonnes Mares 1997: Amazing quality for '97 red Burgundy. Extremely dark, very rich and thick-textured, it tastes authentic, showing a fresh underpinning of blackberry and red berry flavors. It waltzes around the palate with great energy, delivering layers of mocha, spice, plum and smoke. An ager. Drink now through 2010.–P.M. • $270 • (1/01/2000) • **93**

Bonnes Mares 1996: Smells a bit of balsamic vinegar (volatile acidity?), but overall the ripe plum, cassis and toasted oak combination takes over. Rich, thick mouthfeel, with massive tannins, makes for an impressive finish. Best from 2002 through 2010.–P.M. • $210 • (5/15/1999) • **88**

Bonnes Mares 1995: Wonderful, sophisticated, unfiltered and unfined red Burgundy, showing a combination of ripe fruit and subtle oak in a full-bodied package. Fresh and lively, with layers of spice, cassis and black cherry. We wished for a bit more fat on the burly finish just after it was uncorked, but once in contact with air it went off the charts. Best after 2005.–P.M. • $79 • (8/31/1998) • **93**

Bonnes Mares 1994 • $160 • (9/30/1997) • **96**

Bonnes Mares 1992 • $NA • (12/15/1994) • **90**

Bourgogne Cuvée No. 1 1996: All velvet and pleasure, loaded with ripe fruit, red- and blackberry character, ending with firm tannin structure and vibrant acidity. Best from 2003 through 2012.–P.M. • $28 • (5/15/1999) • **91**

Bourgogne Cuvée No. 1 1994 • $18 • (9/30/1997) • **89**

Chambertin 1996: Sleek and racy. Beautiful *terroir* emerges in this thick, pure, minerally, ripe red. A compacted Pinot, built with power and massive tannins that are well integrated and sweet. Excellent length. Best from 2006 through 2016.–P.M. • $134 • (9/30/1999) • **94**

Chambertin 1995: Thick and ripe, this full-bodied red Burgundy displays good depth. Wonderful fresh acidity weaves through the raw-silk texture. Terrific concentration of fruit (cassis, plum, currant), accented by heavily oak-infused spice and mocha, ending with firm tannins. Huge wine, monolithic; could ultimately rate higher, difficult to judge now. Best after 2003.–P.M. • $77 • (8/31/1998) • **94**

Chambertin-Clos de Bèze 1997: A multifaceted, complex and impressive Pinot Noir. Vanilla and mocha aromas are the first impressions in this deep and full-bodied wine, followed by a velvety mouthfeel, with clean and pure red berry and blackberry notes and a citrusy undertow. Sweet tannins on the succulent finish. Drink now through 2010. • $270 • (1/01/2000) • **95**

Chambertin-Clos de Bèze 1996: Lush, thick yet very clean, this full-bodied '96 offers supersmooth, ripe tannins, delicious red berry, toast, smoke, mocha, grilled meat complexity, and a sweet-tasting, harmonious finish. Drink now through 2008.–P.M. • $272 • (5/15/1999) • **95**

Chambertin-Clos de Bèze 1995: Red Burgundy with lots of character. Impressively thick and ripe, full-bodied, with layers of plum, cooked prune, blackberry, black cherry and an iron-mineral character that's wonderful. Supple tannins. Should drink nicely served with game. Drink now through 2007.–P.M. • $79 • (8/31/1998) • **91**

Chambertin-Clos de Bèze 1994 • $53 Ⓐ • (9/30/1997) • **93**

Chambertin-Clos de Bèze 1992 • $125 • (12/15/1994) • **91**

Key: SS—Spectator Selection. CS—Cellar Selection. HR—Highly Recommended. $NA—Price not available. (BT)—Barrel tasting. Ⓐ—Auction Price.
For a key to the tasters' initials, see "How to Use These Listings."
Dates in parentheses represent the issues in which the ratings were published.

Chambolle-Musigny Les Charmes 1996: Wonderful class in this ripe, full-bodied, silky treasure, with waves of vibrant, mouthpuckering black cherry, black currant and blackberry, and just enough spicy, toasted oak accents. The full, sweet tannins are super on the long, gentle finish. Tempting now. Best from 2003 through 2015.–P.M. • $100 • (5/15/1999) • **96**

Chambolle-Musigny Les Sentiers 1994 • $95 • (9/30/1997) • **94**

Charmes-Chambertin 1997: Beautiful from start to finish. Warm and full-bodied, velvety and focused, showing a myriad of flavors (cassis, blackberry, wild raspberry), with subtle mocha and spice. Remains clean, pure and long to the very end. Drink now through 2010. • $120 • (1/01/2000) • **94**

Charmes-Chambertin 1992 • $62 • (12/15/1994) • **87**

Clos de la Roche 1997: What you dream red Burgundy to be. A superstar that's as velvety as Pinot Noir gets. Dark and thick-textured yet full of complex, rich, fresh flavors, from blackberry and wild raspberry to mocha, spice and mineral notes. Drink now through 2015. • $123 • (1/01/2000) • **95**

Clos Vougeot 1997: Exuberant and full-bodied, with beautiful wet earth, crushed blackberry, mocha and spice. Wonderful midpalate ripeness folds into the slightly tough finish. Best from 2002 through 2007. • $190 • (1/01/2000) • **90**

Clos Vougeot 1996: Supersupple and as opulent as Pinot gets. There's mega-plum, lemon-spiked acidity, cassis and black cherry character, remaining lively and vibrant on the palate, with a minerally note. Turns a bit tannic on the finish. Best from 2003 through 2010.–P.M. • $200 • (5/15/1999) • **91**

Clos Vougeot 1993 • $NA • (5/15/1996) • **94**

Corton 1997: Simply mind-boggling. Dense yet racy, this full-bodied, classy red delivers sweet tannins, with ripe black and red fruit, earthy terroir and a supple, thick and rich texture. Big yet fresh, it walks an exquisite tightrope. Best from 2003 through 2012. • $123 • (1/01/2000) • **95**

Corton Hospices de Beaune Cuvée Charlotte Dumay 1995: A bit odd, with resin and varnish notes. But it's dark in color, full in body and generous, showing a plummy, raisiny, slightly herbal character. Best after 2005.–P.M. • $NA • (8/31/1998) • **80**

Echézeaux 1997: Big and fat, delivering an opulent mouthfeel. Thickly textured, with a butter, vanilla, mocha and blackberry character. Full-bodied and very supple, with ripe flavors. The tannins melt in the mouth on the chewy finish. Drink now through 2005. • $150 • (1/01/2000) • **93**

Echézeaux 1994 • $75 • (9/30/1997) • **97**

Fixin Clos de la Perrière 1997: Maturing fast, with mushroom, forest underbrush, licorice and brown sugar notes. Light- to medium-bodied, with a tart, drying finish.–P.M. • $88 • (1/01/2000) • **70**

Gevrey-Chambertin Clos St.-Jacques 1996: Thick and ultraextracted, supertoasty, smoky, even with a slight hint of petrol, but it's deliciously rich, full-bodied and ripe, with supple, smooth tannins, cassis, grilled meat notes. Long, showy finish. Best from 2003 through 2015.–P.M. • $52 Ⓐ • (5/15/1999) • **94**

Gevrey-Chambertin Lavaux St.-Jacques 1994 • $80 • (9/30/1997) • **93**

Gevrey-Chambertin Les Combottes 1996: Pungent and earthy, there's nothing subtle here, only loads of fruit, ripe tannins, cassis and black cherry character. Very sweet, full-bodied, gamy and spicy, it unfolds a spectacular, seductive complexity. Best from 2002 through 2010.–P.M. • $80 • (5/15/1999) • **93**

Gevrey-Chambertin Vieilles Vignes 1997: Thick and ripe, with a lovely mocha, toasted oak, spice and chocolate character backing up the black cherry flavors. Well made, as the fruit balances out the wood; cellaring will help smooth the massive tannins. Best from 2002 through 2007.–P.M. • $30 • (9/30/1999) • **88**

Gevrey-Chambertin Vieilles Vignes 1993 • $NA • (5/15/1996) • **95**

Grands Echézeaux 1997: A fantastic Pinot Noir. Thick and dense yet fresh and elegant, aromatically shy now, but delivering mocha, spice, blackberry, black cherry, wet earth and mineral layers, with a supersupple texture. Smooth and attractive on the lingering, chewy finish. Great achievement in '97. Best from 2005 through 2015. • $270 • (1/01/2000) • **96**

Grands Echézeaux 1994 • $125 • (9/30/1997) • **90**

Mazis-Chambertin 1997: Gorgeous. Tough as nails now, it's tightly built in a firm style, with beautiful freshly crushed red berry and blackberry and ripe tannins. Full-bodied, it tastes fresh and citrusy. Deftly dosed oak is almost imperceptible. Clean, pure and even a bit crisp on the finish. Best from 2002 through 2010. • $150 • (1/01/2000) • **96**

Mazis-Chambertin 1996: Very rich, fat, extracted style. A full-bodied, full-throttle red Burgundy, inky-black in color, with a cover of toasted oak atop some ripe red berry and plum flavors. Very firm, tannic finish. Cellar. Best from 2005 through 2012.–P.M. • $160 • (5/15/1999) • **90**

Mazis-Chambertin 1995: Very impressive. Thick and unctuous, this huge, powerful, unfiltered and unfined Pinot Noir will need a decade or more, although it already shows deep concentration of plum, spice, mocha red- and blackberry character. Clearly oaky, but who cares? There is so much pure fruit, and the tannins are amazingly ripe and velvety. Brilliant winemaking. Best after 2008.–P.M. • $144 Ⓐ • (8/31/1998) • **98**

Mazis-Chambertin 1993 • $120 Ⓐ • (5/15/1996) • **98**

Mercurey Les Saumons 1997: A serious Pinot. Impressive richness and silkiness define this spicy, full-bodied, intense and concentrated red Burgundy. Milk, cassis, black cherry and mineral notes swirl around the palate to an excitingly long and balanced finish. Great effort for '97. Best from 2002 through 2007.–P.M. • $30 • (9/30/1999) • **93**

Musigny 1996: A monument. Starts out with a monolithic, hard-to-penetrate aroma of wood from all that oak, but there is so much pure, ripe, sweet fruit that all the parts just seem to balance. A seamless, huge red Burgundy built for the pleasure in the next millennium. Best from 2006 through 2036.–P.M. • $136 • (9/30/1999) • **97**

Nuits-St.-Georges 1996: Thick, rich, fat—an opulent style that delivers loads of ripe, sweet-tasting, red- and blackberry flavors but also a nearly overwhelming amount of toasted oak. The finish has accents of balsamic vinegar (volatile acidity?) and a crisp mouthfeel. Best from 2003 through 2008.–P.M. • $65 • (5/15/1999) • **84**

Nuits-St.-Georges La Richemone 1997: A surprising '97. Very dark, compacted and extracted, it offers an impressive focus of pure blackberry and red berry flavors dominated by cassis. Very firm on the palate, but it lacks a bit of class. Tastes a bit oaky, yet still satisfying. Best from 2002 through 2010. • $110 • (1/01/2000) • **88**

Nuits-St.-Georges La Richemone 1994 • $75 • (9/30/1997) • **92**

Nuits-St.-Georges Les Cailles 1996: Ripe and succulent, fresh and balanced, displaying full body, full, sweet tannins, a lovely silky texture and gorgeous berry flavors, all accented by some mineral and toast notes. Drink now through 2012.–P.M. • $78 • (5/15/1999) • **94**

Nuits-St.-Georges Les Vaucrains 1995: From 80-year-old vines comes this impressively dark-colored, compacted red. Shows ripe fruit flavors—plum, black cherry and cassis—and an almost Cabernet Sauvignon-like texture; lacks a bit of silkiness on the midpalate. The stiff tannins and slightly herbal and dry finish keep it from scoring outstanding, but it could rate higher after a few years in the cellar. Best after 2003.–P.M. • $58 Ⓐ • (8/31/1998) • **88**

Nuits-St.-Georges Les Vaucrains 1993 • $NA • (5/15/1996) • **89**

Pommard Epenots 1994 • $95 • (9/30/1997) • **94**

Pommard Epenots 1993 • $85 • (5/15/1996) • **93**

Pommard Vieilles Vignes 1993 • $48 • (5/15/1996) • **93**

Ruchottes-Chambertin 1997: A supercharged Pinot Noir. Ultrarich and ultra-thick (and ultra-oaked), it's difficult to believe that this inky black red, with its compact midpalate, is from '97. Has a firm structure, ripe tannins, cigar leaf notes and rigorous earth and black fruit. Built for the future, as it offers little charm now. Best from 2007 through 2020. • $166 • (1/01/2000) • **94**

Ruchottes-Chambertin 1993 • $117 • (5/15/1996) • **96**

Savigny-lès-Beaune 1997: A bit tannic, but delivering decent fruit and mineral flavors. Has a tough structure, with chewy, hard tannins, but this is one of the rare '97s that will benefit from cellaring. Best from 2002 through 2005.–P.M. • $24 • (9/30/1999) • **87**

Savigny-lès-Beaune 1996: Very good quality for a village Savigny-lès-Beaune. Both modern and traditional, a bit earthy, with truffle, forest, smoke and extraordinary cassis, wild berry and plum flavors that waltz around on the palate to an enchanting tune. Best from 2003 through 2012.–P.M. • $49 • (5/15/1999) • **89**

Volnay 1993 • $NA • (5/15/1996) • **86**

Vosne-Romanée 1997: Rather thick and appealingly smooth, with toast, black cherry and licorice notes, this full-bodied crowd pleaser is delicious in a soft, natural-tasting way. Drink now through 2003.–P.M. • $30 • (9/30/1999) • **89**

Vosne-Romanée 1994 • $46 • (9/30/1997) • **79**

Vosne-Romanée 1993 • $NA • (5/15/1996) • **86**

Vosne-Romanée Les Chaumes 1997: Fantastic harmony in this full-bodied red Burgundy. Starts out so velvety, it's dark for a '97, offering gorgeous integration of toasted wood and clean, pure, ripe berry character. Racy on the winning, subtle yet long finish. Best from 2002 through 2007.–P.M. • $91 • (1/01/2000) • **90**

Vosne-Romanée Les Suchots 1997: A monumental achievement in the '97 vintage. Made from well-situated 60-year-old vines, it tastes like the legendary red Burgundies of yesteryear. With explosive aromas and a velvety texture, this full-bodied beauty unfolds its pure and seductive blackberry aromas and flavors, with mocha, spice, smoke and earth notes. Tempting now, but can only improve. Drink now through 2015. • $87 • (1/01/2000) • **95**

LAURENT, JEAN

Brut Blanc de Blancs Champagne NV • $27 • (4/30/1998) • **88**

Brut Blanc de Noirs Champagne NV • $25 • (4/30/1998) • **88**

Brut Rosé Champagne NV • $29 • (4/30/1998) • **90**

LAURENT-PERRIER

Brut Champagne L.P. NV: This bright and flavorful brut combines vibrant apple and mellow vanilla notes on a firm texture of acidity and fine bubbles. The tangy fruit character lingers nicely on the finish. Drink now through 2001. • $28 • (12/31/1998) • **88**

Brut Champagne Cuvée La Lumière du Millénaire 1990: For the adventurous. Bold, full bodied and assertive from the toasty-earthy aromas to the broad texture and nutty, buttery flavors that linger on the finish. Drink now through 2005. • $200 • (10/15/1999) • **93**

Brut Champagne Cuvée Ultra Brut Cuvée Sans Dosage NV • $41 • (11/30/1995) • **90**

Brut Champagne Grand Siècle 1990: Suave in texture and earthy in flavor, this is a serious, traditional style of vintage Champagne. Has a subdued core of fruit flavor, with a sense of restraint and ample accents of yeasty complexity. Drink now through 2002. • $125 • (12/31/1998) • **90**

Brut Rosé Champagne NV: A very good, solid rosé Champagne that's well balanced and tangy in texture, with light cherry and citrus flavors that linger on the finish. Drink now. • $39 • (11/30/1998) • **86**

Extra Dry Champagne NV • $30 • (10/31/1993) • **89**

LAURETTE, CHATEAU

Madiran 1995: Thick and brooding, with distinctive flavors of plum, tea leaf and even a touch of menthol and iron. Powerful, concentrated and still quite tannic, with an aroma of saddle leather. Best after 2000.–K.M. • $16 • (11/30/1998) • **89**

LAUZE, COMTE DE

Châteauneuf-du-Pape 1996: Herbal juice. Dry and astringent, tasting of bell peppers and unripe olives, this light-colored red turns short on the finish.–P.M. • $18 • (9/30/1998) • **75**

Châteauneuf-du-Pape 1993 • $NA • (12/15/1996) • **80**

Châteauneuf-du-Pape White 1997: Fairly lean, with a cardboard character, crisp lemon notes, a tart finish.–P.M. • $18 • (9/30/1998) • **71**

LAVABRE, CHATEAU

Coteaux du Languedoc Pic St.-Loup 1995 • $13 • (2/28/1998) HR • **92**

LAVILLE HAUT BRION, CHATEAU

Pessac-Léognan White 1998: Slightly oxidized, with marzipan and lemon character. Medium-bodied, with a light finish. Tasted twice, with consistent notes. Drink now.–J.S. • $89 • (2/29/2000) • **83**

Pessac-Léognan White 1997: A bit disappointing for this producer. Plenty of lemon and lime character, but rather hard and subdued on the palate. Medium-bodied, with good acidity, but rather light on the finish. May be better with time? Drink now through 2005.–J.S. • $115 • (9/30/1999) • **88**

Pessac-Léognan White 1996: A mouthful for a white. Very woody, with toasted oak and vanilla aromas and hints of fruit, but it's concentrated. Full-bodied, with lemon and apple flavors and a fresh coconut aftertaste. Needs time to develop. Drink through 2004.–J.S. • $125 • (3/31/1999) • **90**

LEBEGUE & CO., J

Merlot Vin de Pays d'Oc 1995 • $6 • (8/31/1997) • **84**

LECHENEAUT

Chambolle-Musigny 1996: Crisp and fruity, with a slight herbal edge. Of medium body, it turns a bit hard on the finish. Very acidic. Drink now through 2003.–P.M. • $48 • (9/30/1998) • **76**

Chambolle-Musigny 1995 • $40 • (11/15/1997) • **88**

Chambolle-Musigny 1993 • $48 • (11/15/1995) • **88**

Chambolle-Musigny Premier Cru 1997: A compact '97, featuring cherry, earth and mineral allied to a firm structure that relies on acidity as much as tannin. A bit crisp on the finish. Drink through 2004.–B.S. • $72 • (9/30/1999) • **86**

Chambolle-Musigny Premier Cru 1996: Ripe and yummy, a thick-textured, opulent style of '96 red Burgundy, caressing the palate with its smooth tannins, full flavors of red- and blackberry, and well-integrated toasted oak.

Supple from start to finish, it's approachable upon release. Drink now through 2005.–P.M. • $65 • (9/30/1998) • **91**

Chambolle-Musigny Premier Cru 1995 • $60 • (11/15/1997) • **96**
Chambolle-Musigny Premier Cru 1994 • $50 • (11/15/1996) • **83**
Chambolle-Musigny Premier Cru 1993 • $68 • (11/15/1995) • **93**
Clos de la Roche 1996: Big and fleshy, full of ripe black fruits, spice and sweet oak. Somewhat burly in structure, with intensity and length, it delivers a mouthful of pleasure. Best from 2002 through 2008.–B.S. • $249 Ⓐ • (9/30/1998) • **91**
Clos de la Roche 1995 • $177 Ⓐ • (11/15/1997) • **89**
Clos de la Roche 1993 • $90 • (11/15/1995) • **91**
Clos de la Roche 1992 • $70 • (12/15/1994) • **88**
Morey-St.-Denis 1997: Plenty of new oak greets the nose, followed by spice, cedar and tobacco flavors. Firm, tannic and unyielding, with a crisp finish. Best from 2001 through 2004.–B.S. • $52 • (9/30/1999) • **84**
Morey-St.-Denis 1996: Character of forest undergrowth and wood smoke on an autumn day. Ripe blackberry and vanilla flavors turn to rough, astringent tannins, leaving one to question the balance. Best from 2003.–B.S. • $48 • (9/30/1998) • **82**
Nuits-St.-Georges 1992 • $26 • (12/15/1994) • **78**
Nuits-St.-Georges Les Cailles 1997: Soft and round, with light tannins and red berry notes, turning slightly herbal on the crisp finish. Drink now through 2002.–P.M. • $72 • (9/30/1999) • **84**
Nuits-St.-Georges Les Cailles 1996: Beautiful Nuits, with good fresh acidity blended nicely into the spicy oak and red- and blackberry character. Lots of cassis, toasted bread and mineral notes. Medium-bodied and well made. Long, toasted finish. Best After 2003.–P.M. • $82 Ⓐ • (9/30/1998) • **90**
Nuits-St.-Georges Les Cailles 1995 • $60 • (11/15/1997) • **86**
Nuits-St.-Georges Les Cailles 1994 • $55 • (11/15/1996) • **82**
Nuits-St.-Georges Les Cailles 1992 • $39 • (12/15/1994) • **82**
Nuits-St.-Georges Les Damodes 1997: A little herbal, with a resinous oak element. Stiff, drying tannins surround the cherry and vanilla flavors. A bit awkward; may come together with time. Best after 2001.–B.S. • $72 • (9/30/1999) • **86**
Nuits-St.-Georges Les Damodes 1996: A modern-style red showing loads of exotic, spicy oak backed by cherry and blackberry aromas and flavors, sappy concentration and a lingering finish. Best from 2001 through 2006.–B.S. • $65 • (9/30/1998) • **89**
Nuits-St.-Georges Les Damodes 1995 • $53 • (11/15/1997) • **85**
Nuits-St.-Georges Les Damodes 1994 • $45 • (11/15/1996) • **79**
Nuits-St.-Georges Les Damodes 1993 • $68 • (11/15/1995) • **93**
Nuits-St.-Georges Les Damodes 1992 • $35 • (12/15/1994) • **83**
Nuits-St.-Georges Premier Cru 1993 • $60 • (11/15/1995) • **90**
Vosne-Romanée 1997: Violet, mint and cassis are the hallmarks of this modest, elegant '97 red. Lacks a little focus, with a lingering finish. Drink now through 2002.–B.S. • $55 • (9/30/1999) • **81**

LECHERE

Brut Blanc de Blancs Champagne 1990: Gets your attention with a vivid green-gold color, assertive toasty-earthy aromas and a soft, full texture. Moderate apple and vanilla flavors fill in the middle. Drink now. • $40 • (12/31/1998) • **88**
Brut Champagne Orient Express Cuvée Spéciale NV: Quite inviting. A seamless combination of fresh, bright fruit flavors and velvety texture makes this Champagne hard to resist. Drink now. • $65 • (12/31/1998) • **87**
Brut Rosé Champagne NV: Fresh, light and charming, light pink in color, this nicely balanced, plush-textured rosé has crisp cherry flavors and a lingering finish. Easy to enjoy. Drink now. • $35 • (11/30/1998) • **85**

LECLERC, PHILIPPE

Bourgogne Les Bons Bâtons 1994 • $NA • (11/15/1996) • **80**
Bourgogne Les Bons Bâtons 1992 • $18 • (12/15/1994) • **80**
Bourgogne Les Bons Bâtons 1988 • $22 • (8/31/1991) • **64**
Chambolle-Musigny Les Babillères 1994 • $NA • (11/15/1996) • **70**
Chambolle-Musigny Les Babillères 1992 • $45 • (12/15/1994) • **79**
Gevrey-Chambertin 1994 • $NA • (11/15/1996) • **72**
Gevrey-Chambertin 1984 • $26 • (7/15/1987) • **90**
Gevrey-Chambertin Champaux 1994 • $NA • (11/15/1996) • **74**
Gevrey-Chambertin Champeaux 1991 • $65 • (1/31/1994) • **84**
Gevrey-Chambertin Champeaux 1990 • $50 • (12/15/1992) • **91**
Gevrey-Chambertin Champeaux 1985 • $55 • (10/31/1988) • **79**
Gevrey-Chambertin Combe au Moine 1994 • $NA • (11/15/1996) • **68**
Gevrey-Chambertin Combe au Moine 1992 • $72 • (12/15/1994) • **82**
Gevrey-Chambertin Combe au Moine 1991 • $83 • (1/31/1994) • **73**
Gevrey-Chambertin Combe au Moine 1990 • $73 Ⓐ • (12/15/1992) • **92**
Gevrey-Chambertin Combe au Moine 1988 • $68 Ⓐ • (7/15/1991) • **82**
Gevrey-Chambertin Combe au Moine 1987 • $68 • (5/31/1990) • **76**
Gevrey-Chambertin Combe au Moine 1985 • $86 Ⓐ • (10/15/1988) • **92**
Gevrey-Chambertin Combe au Moine 1984 • $42 • (8/31/1987) • **82**
Gevrey-Chambertin Cuvée Vieilles Vignes 1994 • $NA • (11/15/1996) • **73**
Gevrey-Chambertin En Champs 1992 • $42 • (12/15/1994) • **84**
Gevrey-Chambertin En Champs 1991 • $40 • (1/31/1994) • **80**
Gevrey-Chambertin La Platière 1992 • $39 • (12/15/1994) • **76**
Gevrey-Chambertin La Platière 1991 • $43 • (1/31/1994) • **72**
Gevrey-Chambertin La Platière 1990 • $35 • (12/15/1992) • **90**
Gevrey-Chambertin La Platière 1989 • $44 • (10/31/1992) • **81**
Gevrey-Chambertin La Platière 1988 • $40 • (7/15/1991) • **74**
Gevrey-Chambertin La Platière 1987 • $35 • (5/31/1990) • **81**
Gevrey-Chambertin La Platière 1985 • $38 • (10/15/1988) • **90**
Gevrey-Chambertin Les Cazetiers 1994 • $NA • (11/15/1996) • **73**
Gevrey-Chambertin Les Cazetiers 1992 • $68 • (12/15/1994) • **73**
Gevrey-Chambertin Les Cazetiers 1991 • $75 • (1/31/1994) • **79**
Gevrey-Chambertin Les Cazetiers 1990 • $65 • (12/15/1992) • **85**
Gevrey-Chambertin Les Cazetiers 1988 • $69 Ⓐ • (7/15/1991) • **82**
Gevrey-Chambertin Les Cazetiers 1987 • $63 • (5/31/1990) • **85**
Gevrey-Chambertin Les Cazetiers 1985 • $127 Ⓐ • (10/15/1988) • **89**
Gevrey-Chambertin Les Cazetiers 1984 • $38 • (8/31/1987) • **83**

LECLERC-BRIANT

Brut Blanc de Blancs Champagne NV • $29 • (12/31/1997) • **83**
Brut Champagne Cuvée de Réserve NV • $24 • (10/31/1997) • **84**
Brut Champagne Cuvée du Solstice 2000 1990: Lively, vivid style separates this from the crowd. Bright, concentrated citrus flavors and firm acidity power this focused, intense Champagne. No hurry to pop it open. Drink through 2007. • $180 • (9/15/1999) • **91**
Brut Champagne Le Clos des Champions NV • $36 • (10/31/1997) • **82**
Brut Champagne Les Chèvres Pierreuses NV • $36 • (12/31/1997) • **72**
Brut Champagne Les Crayères NV • $36 • (10/31/1997) • **84**
Extra Brut Champagne NV: Vibrant, fruity and focused, this has crystal-clear flavors, a nearly dry balance and a clean finish. Drink now through 2001. • $24 • (10/15/1999) • **90**

LEFLAIVE, DOMAINE

Bâtard-Montrachet 1997: Beautiful harmony from start to finish. Layers of attractive smoke, honey and ripe fruit are kept in focus as the seduction wraps around the palate. Not a big wine, but subtle. Drink now through 2007.–P.M. • $265 • (9/30/1999) • **93**
Bâtard-Montrachet 1996: Pumped up and oaky at this stage, showing smoky, toasty, seductive aromas. The fabulous fruit is buried by the oak but still has a wonderful, silky, almost creamy mouthfeel. Shows a mineral character midpalate, with ripe fruit and smoky, grilled and toasty notes. Best from 2006 through 2016.–P.M. • $258 Ⓐ • (5/31/1999) • **93**
Bienvenues-Bâtard-Montrachet 1997: Interesting *terroir* character, with a matchstick, smoke and wet earth character. Very tight and crisp, but it has sensational ripeness that brings balance to this treasure. Long, tart aftertaste. Best from 2002 through 2017.–P.M. • $255 • (9/30/1999) • **93**
Bienvenues-Bâtard-Montrachet 1996: Fat and rich, this is a charmer. It struggles to maintain decorum because of the ripe, almost tropical fruit and oak, then shows its vibrant, lemony acidity and mineral concentration on the long finish. Best from 2005 through 2013.–P.M. • $148 Ⓐ • (5/31/1999) • **91**
Bienvenues-Bâtard-Montrachet 1995: Incredible blockbuster that comes in the silkiest package you can imagine. The sort of wine that will make you do a little dance on the table in sheer joy of having gotten to taste such treasure. Unctuous yet racy, it is seamless from start to finish, so opulent it balloons on the palate with thick, ripe fruit and minerally, pebbly flavors. Tempting now, but the fresh finish means it will last. Drink now through 2010.–P.M. • $153 Ⓐ • (8/31/1998) • **98**
Bourgogne White 1995: Amazing quality for a simple Bourgogne. Clean and pure, with a pronounced mineral, wet stone, pie tart clarity. Quite seamless. Full-bodied. Wraps its flavors around the palate, then rockets to a long, superbly balanced, lemony, slightly toasted finish. Brilliant winemaking. Drink now through 2010.–P.M. • $36 • (8/31/1998) • **92**

Key: SS—Spectator Selection. CS—Cellar Selection. HR—Highly Recommended. $NA—Price not available. (BT)—Barrel tasting. Ⓐ—Auction Price.
For a key to the tasters' initials, see "How to Use These Listings."
Dates in parentheses represent the issues in which the ratings were published.

Chevalier-Montrachet 1997: Flamboyant in its massive, smoky, toasted, rich style, it hits you with grand cru kind of power, delivering lovely pear, honey and—yes—grilled oak on the finish. Drink now through 2007.–P.M. • $330 • (9/30/1999) • **92**

Chevalier-Montrachet 1996: The rich, powerful, ultratoasty oak dominates the incredibly minerally character of the terroir right now. Buttery and voluptous, showing beautiful pebble, stone and vanilla bean, with a slightly bitter, aggressive oak-induced flavor. A departure from the subtle style of the 100-point 1995. Tasted twice, with consistent notes. Best from 2006 through 2010.–P.M. • $191 Ⓐ • (5/31/1999) • **90**

Chevalier-Montrachet 1995: Wine of the vintage. Ultra-refined and sweet-tasting, elegant and amazingly seamless, this '95 white Burgundy has the texture of extra-virgin olive oil, and a decadent charm. Supple and smooth, full in body and medium in concentration, it shows wonderful vanilla, pear, bread dough flavors and a superthick midpalate. Melts in the mouth; so subtle its long, refined finish comes as a surprise. Drink now through 2010.–P.M. • $174 Ⓐ • (8/31/1998) HR • **100**

Puligny-Montrachet 1997: This very nice white Burgundy, rather thick yet clean and fresh, shows multidimensional layers of subtle and medium-toasted oak, with concentrated fruit and a silky finish backed by decent acidity. Drink now through 2005.–P.M. • $82 • (9/30/1999) • **89**

Puligny-Montrachet 1996: Very toasty, though beautiful mineral, cream, lemon and vanilla bean flavors emerge from underneath the wood. Intense, drawing like a flavorful Havanna with all that fancily toasted wood, but ultimately this full-bodied beauty covers the palate in a soothing and cooling silk sheet. Best from 2006 through 2026.–P.M. • $56 • (5/31/1999) • **93**

Puligny-Montrachet 1995: Fat and rich, also quite oaky, with spice, mocha, lemon, honey and toasted bread aromas and flavors. While lovely, it lacks a bit of serious soul/*terroir* and the intensity to rate outstanding. Drink now through 2003.–P.M. • $58 • (8/31/1998) • **88**

Puligny-Montrachet Clavoillon 1997: Clean and polished, showing a mineral side with a thick concentration of fruit and wet earth. Turns a bit chewy on the finish, but overall there is elegance. Drink now through 2007.–P.M. • $114 • (9/30/1999) • **92**

Puligny-Montrachet Clavoillon 1996: An elegant, racy, full-bodied white of great purity. Minerally and subtly toasted, displaying stone, lemon, ripe fruit, honey and fireworks of grilled flavors. Long finish. Best from 2004 through 2010.–P.M. • $86 Ⓐ • (5/31/1999) • **90**

Puligny-Montrachet Clavoillon 1995: Class act that stuns the senses. Rigorously structured, showing only subtle aromas of mineral and earth, this pushes the limits with one of the most fantastic mouthfeels that can be imagined in a Chardonnay. Clean, pure vanilla, ripe fruit and especially chalk and mineral notes make it seductively decadent. Supervelvety, with the texture of cream, you can only admire this white Burgundy. Drink now through 2010.–P.M. • $82 • (8/31/1998) • **96**

Puligny-Montrachet Les Combettes 1996: Amazing. Distinctive malic-lactic aromas open up this beautiful, full-bodied, vibrant, incredibly concentrated and intense white. Keeps your palate company for five minutes after sipping it—it's that long. Lemon, toasted oak, cream and mineral are all in perfect harmony. Classic Leflaive. Best from 2006 through 2026.–P.M. • $159 Ⓐ • (5/31/1999) • **97**

Puligny-Montrachet Les Folatières 1997: A beautiful white, with a lot of nice oak that delivers vanilla, smoke and pear. Full-bodied, it hardens a bit from the wood tannins on the finish, but it's well made. Best from 2001 through 2010.–P.M. • $150 • (9/30/1999) • **90**

Puligny-Montrachet Les Folatières 1996: The clean, marblelike structure holds this ripe but classy monument together. Magnificently focused, brimming with mineral intensity and worldly complexity. Cleverly built, with medium-toasty oak notes, a tightly wound lemon and pink grapefruit juiciness and cigar-box aromas. Long finish. Best from 2006 through 2020.–P.M. • $100 • (5/31/1999) • **95**

Puligny-Montrachet Les Folatières 1995: Incredible '95 from Domaine Leflaive, amazingly intense and concentrated, thick in texture, with decadent vanilla, mineral, pear, bread dough and just-so spicy oak. Seduces the palate with its fat, full-bodied opulence. Truly seamless, without a hitch from start to extra-long finish, filling the palate with layers of silkiness. Drink now through 2010.–P.M. • $46 Ⓐ • (8/31/1998) • **97**

Puligny-Montrachet Les Pucelles 1997: A bit angular, but there is a lot of fat underneath, with apple tart, honey, lemon, spice and vanilla bean character. Cellar and you should be rewarded. Best from 2005 through 2017.–P.M. • $170 • (9/30/1999) • **91**

Puligny-Montrachet Les Pucelles 1996: Aggressively oaked, with pumped-up toast notes, but underneath lies fabulously balanced *terroir*. The mineral and stone character is something to behold, packed with classy fruit, velvety texture and pear, cream and vanilla bean flavors. Huge, smoky finish. Best from 2006 through 2026.–P.M. • $125 Ⓐ • (5/31/1999) • **95**

Puligny-Montrachet Les Pucelles 1995: Lovely, offering a supersupple, extra-thick, elegant midpalate, delivering little flavor shocks of vanilla bean, mineral, spice, pear and pie tart. Seamless in texture, but a slight paint varnish note holds it back. The finish is fresh, with limelike acidity that renders it long and racy. Best after 2005.–P.M. • $67 Ⓐ • (8/31/1998) • **91**

LEFLAIVE FRERES, OLIVIER

Bâtard-Montrachet 1997: A bit heavy, with fig and dried fruit character. The aromas seem to stagnate under an oaky cover while the citrusy acidity kicks in on the palate, making for an awkward, slightly drying wine. Drink now.–P.M. • $175 • (9/30/1999) • **84**

Bâtard-Montrachet 1996: A bit tough, showing crisp fruit and astringent character. Drying, slightly musty finish. Tasted twice, with consistent notes.–P.M. • $125 • (5/31/1999) • **79**

Bâtard-Montrachet 1995 • $130 • (8/31/1997) • **89**

Bonnes Mares 1987 • $50 • (9/30/1990) • **88**

Bourgogne 1996: A bit herbal and hot, with dry tannins, this isn't very appealing.–P.M. • $13 • (9/30/1998) • **72**

Bourgogne 1992 • $9 • (11/30/1994) • **82**

Bourgogne Aligoté 1996 • $15 • (5/31/1998) • **77**

Bourgogne Aligoté 1995 • $16 • (8/31/1997) • **72**

Bourgogne White 1996 • $11 • (5/31/1998) • **80**

Bourgogne White Les Sétilles 1998: Delicate and elegant, here's a medium-bodied white Burgundy that has a matchstick, smoky character on a rather lean, citrusy framework. Drink now through 2002.–P.M. • $17 • (5/31/2000) • **83**

Bourgogne White Les Sétilles 1997: A bit too much obvious oak here, with lemon and butter. Turns a bit tough and astringent on the soft finish.–P.M. • $16 • (5/31/1999) • **76**

Bourgogne White Les Sétilles 1996 • $17 • (5/31/1998) • **81**

Bourgogne White Les Sétilles 1995 • $13 • (8/31/1997) • **70**

Charmes-Chambertin 1989 • $60 • (1/31/1992) • **88**

Charmes-Chambertin 1986 • $50 • (7/31/1988) • **88**

Chassagne-Montrachet 1997: Some nice lemon notes rev up the palate, followed by medium-ripe fruit. Medium-bodied, with a tartness to the finish. Drink now through 2002.–P.M. • $50 • (9/30/1999) • **84**

Chassagne-Montrachet 1996: Pretty wine, showing finesse and elegance, medium intensity and concentration. Medium-bodied, displaying honey, hazelnut, pear and melon notes. Enjoy upon release.–P.M. • $42 • (8/31/1998) • **86**

Chassagne-Montrachet 1995 • $41 • (8/31/1997) • **87**

Chassagne-Montrachet Abbaye de Morgeot 1997: Full-bodied and ripe, kicking in with caramelized pear tart, toasted oak and rich fruit flavors. A lemony note keeps an even keel on the lingering, chewy, sweet finish. Drink now through 2003.–P.M. • $69 • (9/30/1999) • **88**

Chassagne-Montrachet Les Caillerets 1997: Crisp and acidic, showing some lemony, honeyed character; a bit lightweight, but that makes it pleasant. Lively finish, flavorful. Drink now through 2005.–P.M. • $NA • (1/01/1999) • **88**

Chassagne-Montrachet Les Chaumées 1997: There is something straightforward here. Honeyed and easy, more varietal than *terroir*, it shows lemon and green apple. Drink now through 2003.–P.M. • $62 • (9/30/1999) • **81**

Chassagne-Montrachet Les Vergers 1996: Clean and pure, a vibrant wine with little fat but a nice mineral-laden, wet stone quality. Linear and firm, it has much acidity but also ripe fruit, and the overall feel of this medium-bodied white is one of balance. Drink now through 2005.–P.M. • $48 • (8/31/1998) • **89**

Chassagne-Montrachet Red 1997: A bit rustic, but it tastes succulent, turning a bit firm and crisp, with cool red berry character. A juicy wine. Drink now through 2002.–P.M. • $NA • (9/30/1999) • **81**

Chassagne-Montrachet Red 1996: Intriguingly rustic and polished at the same time, with wet earth, stone, chalk but also some vanilla and cherry character. Of medium body, with smooth tannins and a succulent finish. Drink now through 2002.–P.M. • $27 • (9/30/1998) • **84**

Chassagne-Montrachet Red 1992 • $NA • (12/15/1994) • **77**

Chassagne-Montrachet Red 1991 • $15 • (1/31/1994) • **84**

Chassagne-Montrachet Red 1990 • $17 • (12/15/1992) • **85**

Chassagne-Montrachet Red 1986 • $26 • (2/29/1988) • **89**

Chassagne-Montrachet Red 1985 • $32 • (10/31/1988) • **83**

Chassagne-Montrachet Red Morgeot 1995 • $52 • (8/31/1997) • **90**

Chassagne-Montrachet Red Morgeot 1993 • $34 • (11/15/1995) • **79**

Clos de la Roche 1989 • $63 • (3/15/1993) • **82**

Clos St.-Denis 1989 • $56 • (1/31/1992) • **93**

Corton Les Bressandes 1986 • $45 • (7/31/1988) • **88**

Corton-Charlemagne 1997: An aromatically shy '97, offering only modest flavors that never seem to take off. Drink now through 2002.–P.M. • $37 Ⓐ • (9/30/1999) • **82**

FRANCE

LEFLAIVE FRERES, OLIVIER

Corton-Charlemagne 1996: Balanced but oaky for now, with delicious ripe fruit, but give it time to develop its mineral, pineapple, pear and mango facets. Full-bodied, this will bring tremendous pleasure. Best from 2002 through 2007.–P.M. • $61 Ⓐ • (5/31/1999) • **94**

Côte de Beaune-Villages 1996: Only modest concentration to match the herbal character. Dry, astringent finish.–B.S. • $24 • (9/30/1998) • **77**

Criots-Bâtard-Montrachet 1997: A clean, racy, flavorful wine, showing citrus, passion fruit, honey and lemon tart character without obtrusive oak. Medium-bodied, with a subtle length that builds and builds and a zesty finish. Drink now through 2005.–P.M. • $175 • (9/30/1999) • **90**

Criots-Bâtard-Montrachet 1996: Disappointing for a grand cru, this vibrant '96 has mineral, lemon and green apple that give it a firm backbone. Balanced and well made to age, it lacks the ripe, lush fruit to rate outstanding. Best from 2006 through 2010.–P.M. • $129 • (5/31/1999) • **86**

Criots-Bâtard-Montrachet 1995 • $125 • (8/31/1997) • **92**

Mercurey White 1996 • $23 • (5/31/1998) • **86**

Mercurey White 1995 • $16 • (8/31/1997) • **90**

Meursault 1997: Fresh, zingy and of medium body and intensity, it's round and also juicy, showing a succulent flavor. Short, crisp finish. Drink now.–P.M. • $49 • (9/30/1999) • **80**

Meursault 1996: For now, it's very firm, even tough. Full-bodied, with lots of mineral character; nicely balanced with pear, vanilla bean, wet stone and toasted oak. After it was decanted for hours, the citruslike acidity turned into an opulent mouthfeel. Give it time. Best after 2005.–P.M. • $42 • (8/31/1998) • **90**

Meursault 1995 • $41 • (8/31/1997) • **90**

Meursault Charmes 1997: This full-bodied Chardonnay is balanced, with clean and flavorful tropical, wet earth and toast accents Delivers plenty of satisfaction, but don't expect great power or complexity. Fresh finish. Drink now through 2005.–P.M. • $67 • (9/30/1999) • **86**

Meursault Charmes 1996: Extremely well made Meursault, showing super-concentration of mineral, spice and wet stone character. Hard-as-nails now, it will need 10 to 15 years to loosen all that lime, grapefruit acidity and deliver its soil and terroir complexity to the fullest. Long finish. Best after 2008.–P.M. • $56 • (8/31/1998) • **93**

Meursault Charmes 1995 • $62 • (8/31/1997) • **91**

Meursault Les Narvaux 1997: Fairly ripe, tasting of sweet fruit, with an attractive suppleness supported by toasted oak accents. Lemony finish. Drink now through 2002.–P.M. • $55 • (9/30/1999) • **81**

Meursault Les Narvaux 1997: Muscular, firm, tough Meursault, full-bodied and showing good concentration of tropical pear, earth and mineral character. Explodes with juicy, lemony acidity. Has the stuffing to turn silky smooth if cellared for a decade or so—after it stood decanted for 12 hours, it grew to a round and velvety beauty with a seductive, creamlike finish. Best after 2008.–P.M. $55 • (8/31/1998) • **93**

Meursault Les Perrières 1996: What seduction in this silky, velvety wine. At least that's what you can expect if it's cellared for a decade or decanted for some hours before serving. At first it's hard and acidic, but then reveals layers of pure, clean mineral, wet stone and pebble and wonderful concentration of fruit. Full-bodied, it's deftly toasted to allow the classy soil flavors center stage. Best after 2010.–P.M. • $65 • (8/31/1998) • **95**

Meursault Les Perrières 1995 • $58 • (8/31/1997) • **88**

Meursault Les Tillets 1997: A bit earthy, even smelling of raw wet earth, there's a roundness and depth to this, delivering good concentration of mineral and fruit character. Finesse and balance are the keynotes of this full-bodied, thick-textured Meursault. Drink now through 2007.–P.M. • $NA • (1/01/1999) • **91**

Montagny Les Bonneveaux 1996 • $22 • (5/31/1998) • **84**

Monthélie 1991 • $19 • (1/31/1994) • **80**

Monthélie Premier Cru 1990 • $19 • (12/15/1992) • **82**

Montrachet 1996: Something's wrong. Very dry, tough and astringent, mouthpuckering in texture, with lime and herb notes. Smells a bit odd, almost corked. Tasted twice, with consistent notes.–P.M. • $325 • (5/31/1999) • **68**

Montrachet 1995 • $270 • (8/31/1997) • **92**

Morey-St.-Denis 1989 • $30 • (1/31/1992) • **87**

Pommard 1996: A supple Pommard, but with good terroir, showing mineral, iron, blood and beef character along with some smoky, toasted chestnut and grilled meat complexity. Full-bodied, it firms up on the slightly hot finish. Drink now through 2004.–P.M. • $45 • (9/30/1998) • **85**

Pommard 1993 • $32 • (11/15/1995) • **84**

Key: SS—Spectator Selection. CS—Cellar Selection. HR—Highly Recommended. $NA—Price not available. (BT)—Barrel tasting. Ⓐ—Auction Price.
For a key to the tasters' initials, see "How to Use These Listings."
Dates in parentheses represent the issues in which the ratings were published.

Pommard 1992 • $NA • (12/15/1994) • **84**

Pommard 1990 • $30 • (12/15/1992) • **92**

Pommard 1989 • $32 • (1/31/1992) • **84**

Pommard Charmots 1997: A well-made '97, showing good color, smooth texture and nice plum and black cherry character. Round and accessible on release. Drink now through 2002.–P.M. • $55 • (9/30/1999) • **86**

Pommard Charmots 1996: Tasting of ripe cherries, this firm, solid and tannic Pommard is a bit tough and not extremely ripe, but it has personality. Full-bodied, with a chewy mouthfeel. Best after 2003.–P.M. • $55 • (9/30/1998) • **82**

Pommard Les Epenots 1993 • $46 • (11/15/1995) • **82**

Pommard Les Epenots 1990 • $35 • (12/15/1992) • **90**

Pommard Les Epenots 1989 • $40 • (1/31/1992) • **88**

Pommard Rugiens 1997: Spicy cherry and mineral aromas and flavors show moderate concentration in this elegant red. Drink now through 2002.–B.S. • $60 • (9/30/1999) • **80**

Pommard Rugiens 1996: Firm and structured, with tough tannins, it's fairly rustic, with an earthy, red berry character. Given time, it should turn supple. Best after 2003.–P.M. • $60 • (9/30/1998) • **83**

Pommard Les Rugiens 1993 • $48 • (11/15/1995) • **86**

Pommard Les Rugiens 1992 • $NA • (12/15/1994) • **84**

Pommard Les Rugiens 1991 • $37 • (1/31/1994) • **77**

Pommard Les Rugiens 1990 • $35 • (12/15/1992) • **91**

Puligny-Montrachet 1997: Strangely for a low-acid vintage, the citrusy acidity is the first thing that hits you, dominating fruit and subtle notes. Tart finish. Drink now through 2003.–P.M. • $53 • (9/30/1999) • **80**

Puligny-Montrachet 1996: This medium-bodied white is almost painfully acidic on the palate, bursting with lime and cilantro, showing firm texture. But classic minerally character lies beneath, with ripe fruit. Tasted twice, with consistent notes. Best after 2003.–P.M. • $42 • (8/31/1998) • **80**

Puligny-Montrachet 1995 • $41 • (8/31/1997) • **85**

Puligny-Montrachet Champ Canet 1997: A bit earthy and tough, drying a bit on the finish, it offers apple, earth and lemon character. Tart finish.–P.M. • $68 • (9/30/1999) • **79**

Puligny-Montrachet Champ Canet 1996: Sleek and racy Puligny, showing a decent combination of mineral, fruit and oak. Very chalky and a bit rustic, with some vanilla bean, pear and melon character. Of medium body, the finish is quite ripe-tasting. Best after 2003.–P.M. • $52 • (8/31/1998) • **88**

Puligny-Montrachet Champ Canet 1995 • $52 • (8/31/1997) • **87**

Puligny-Montrachet Champ Gain 1997: Some ripe fruit gives a honeyed character, with limelike acidity kicking in to provide a fresh, somewhat smoky and flinty finish in this medium-bodied white. Drink now through 2007.–P.M. • $68 • (9/30/1999) • **89**

Puligny-Montrachet Champ Gain 1996: Tight and firm, with a slightly musty nose and dry, chalky character in the midpalate. Offering some mineral and lots of citrus, this comes across as uncompromisingly tough. A bit drying on the finish. Best after 2005.–P.M. • $52 • (8/31/1998) • **83**

Puligny-Montrachet Champ Gain 1996: Polished, minerally and oaky in style, with a firm but opulent full-bodied personality. Turns hard on the palate as it's tightly wound around nicely ripe pear, tropical, honey and citrus flavors. Much better than previously reviewed. Best from 2004 through 2010.–P.M. • $52 • (5/31/1999) • **93**

Puligny-Montrachet Champ Gain 1995 • $52 • (8/31/1997) • **91**

Puligny-Montrachet Les Folatières 1998: A Chardonnay with a crisp, oaky edge. Chewy and a bit tough, in a green way.–P.M. • $82 • (5/31/2000) • **79**

Puligny-Montrachet Les Folatières 1997: Lively and vibrant, this crisp wine perks up the taste buds with citrus and toast notes in a racy, medium-bodied package. Tart, slightly hot finish. Drink now through 2005.–P.M. • $80 • (9/30/1999) • **85**

Puligny-Montrachet Les Folatières 1996: A beautiful, full-bodied '96, packed with ripe pineapple, mandarin and pear that are nicely supported by well-dosed spicy oak accents. Balanced and yummy to the long finish. Best from 2003 through 2010.–P.M. • $62 • (5/31/1999) • **90**

Puligny-Montrachet Les Folatières 1995 • $62 • (8/31/1997) • **90**

Puligny-Montrachet Les Pucelles 1997: Intense in a pure, lemony, zesty way, it jumps with concentrated fruit flavors, balancing the ripe fig, date and pineapple notes nicely with the deft toasted oak. Drink now through 2007.–P.M. • $80 • (9/30/1999) • **90**

Rully Premier Cru 1996 • $23 • (5/31/1998) • **84**

Rully Red 1990 • $20 • (11/30/1992) • **80**

St.-Aubin En Remilly 1998: Flavorful. Filled with citrus, dried herbs, green apple character. Medium-bodied, it's smooth at midpalate but turns quite crisp on the finish. Might improve with short-term cellaring. Best from 2001 through 2005.–P.M. • $30 • (5/31/2000) • **85**

St.-Aubin En Remilly 1997: Clean, ripe and juicy, offering dried herb, butter and lactic-malic character in a supple, medium-bodied, flavorful package.

Delicious and very well made, with a medium-intense pure-fruit finish. Drink now through 2003.–P.M. • $30 • (5/31/1999) • **87**
St.-Aubin En Remilly 1996 • $29 • (5/31/1998) • **88**
St.-Aubin En Remilly 1995 • $26 • (5/31/1997) • **87**
St.-Aubin La Chatenière 1997: Packed with clean and delicious vibrancy, this delivers a polished, fruity, delightful impression. Light- to medium-bodied, it's fresh, with floral, pear, honey and green apple notes. Drink now through 2002.–P.M. • $30 • (5/31/1999) • **86**
St.-Aubin Le Charmois 1997: This beautifully made, pure and ripe St.-Aubin is grassy and intensely herbal but very fruity, with pear and honey coming into the complex picture. Zingy, minerally finish. Drink now through 2002.–P.M. • $30 • (5/31/1999) • **89**
Santenay 1993 • $20 • (11/15/1995) • **79**
Santenay 1986 • $17 • (7/31/1988) • **81**
Santenay Les Gravières 1990 • $17 • (12/15/1992) • **85**
Santenay White 1997: Crisp and fruity, brimming with lime, mineral, green apple and pineapple, it starts out great but turns a bit drying on the finish. Drink now through 2005.–P.M. • $NA • (1/01/1999) • **86**
Volnay 1996: On the light side, and the cherry and herb notes lack concentration, though the structure is not overwhelming.–B.S. • $38 • (9/30/1998) • **79**
Volnay Champans 1997: Herbaceous and light, offering only a modicum of fruit. Finishes short.–B.S. • $50 • (9/30/1999) • **75**
Volnay Clos de la Barre 1992 • $NA • (12/15/1994) • **81**
Volnay Clos de la Barre 1991 • $36 • (1/31/1994) • **84**
Volnay Clos de la Barre 1990 • $36 • (12/15/1992) • **92**
Volnay Clos de la Barre 1989 • $38 • (1/31/1992) • **92**
Volnay Clos de la Barre 1987 • $27 • (8/31/1990) • **78**
Volnay Clos de la Barre 1986 • $28 • (7/31/1988) • **89**
Volnay Clos des Angles 1997: Both samples provided were corky.–P.M. $42 • (1/01/2000) • **55**
Volnay Clos des Angles 1996: There's a barnyard element to the otherwise spicy cherry aromas and flavors, as well as stiff tannins and a slightly drying finish. Best after 2000.–B.S. • $55 • (9/30/1998) • **82**
Volnay Frémiets 1993 • $42 • (11/15/1995) • **93**
Volnay Frémiets 1991 • $33 • (1/31/1994) • **82**
Volnay Frémiets 1990 • $35 • (12/15/1992) • **92**

LEGER-PLUMET, BERNARD

Pouilly-Fuissé Clos du Chalet Pouilly 1997: Simple Chardonnay, and a bit dull, with modest fruit and a strange wet cardboard note.–P.M. • $18 • (5/31/1999) • **72**
St.-Véran 1996 • $10 • (5/31/1998) • **81**
St.-Véran Les Cornillauds 1997: Nice lemon-butter-honey combo yields to a slightly astringent, herbal-wet hay character. Deftly oaked, fairly rich-textured. All the pieces should come together with time. Best after 2000.–P.M. • $10 • (5/31/1999) • **85**

LEGLAND, BERNARD

Chablis 1996 • $NA • (8/31/1997) • **82**
Chablis Montmains 1996 • $24 • (5/31/1998) • **91**
Chablis Montmains 1995 • $22 • (6/15/1997) • **88**
Petit Chablis 1996 • $NA • (8/31/1997) • **74**

LEJEUNE

Bourgogne 1997: Simple and crisp, with strawberry and cherry notes, turning a bit herbal on the finish.–P.M. • $NA • (1/01/2000) • **76**
Bourgogne 1994 • $NA • (11/15/1996) • **74**
Bourgogne 1993 • $14 • (11/15/1995) • **76**
Bourgogne 1990 • $18 • (12/15/1992) • **85**
Bourgogne Passe-Tout-Grains 1994 • $NA • (11/15/1996) • **78**
Bourgogne Passe-Tout-Grains 1993 • $13 • (11/15/1995) • **80**
Pommard 1997: Light and a bit simple, showing a herbal side that turns tough and hard on the finish.–P.M. • $NA • (1/01/2000) • **74**
Pommard 1994 • $NA • (11/15/1996) • **75**
Pommard 1993 • $NA • (5/15/1996) • **84**
Pommard Les Argillières 1997: Disappointing. Light in color and a bit stemmy, it tastes dry and green and lacks ripeness. The sort of Pinot that gives Burgundy a bad reputation.–P.M. • $NA • (1/01/2000) • **72**
Pommard Les Argillières 1994 • $NA • (11/15/1996) • **72**
Pommard Les Argillières 1993 • $36 • (11/15/1995) • **88**
Pommard Les Argillières 1991 • $36 • (1/31/1994) • **77**
Pommard Les Argillières 1990 • $40 • (12/15/1992) • **88**
Pommard Les Poutures 1997: Light and a bit stemmy, this disappointing Pinot lacks ripe flavors, turning a bit green and dry on the finish.–P.M. • $NA • (1/01/2000) • **75**
Pommard Les Poutures 1994 • $NA • (11/15/1996) • **70**
Pommard Les Poutures 1993 • $31 • (11/15/1995) • **85**
Pommard Les Poutures 1991 • $32 • (1/31/1994) • **75**
Pommard Les Rugiens 1994 • $NA • (11/15/1996) • **81**
Pommard Les Rugiens 1993 • $65 • (11/15/1995) • **83**
Pommard Les Rugiens 1991 • $52 • (1/31/1994) • **79**
Pommard Les Rugiens 1990 • $49 • (12/15/1992) • **92**

LENOBLE, A.R.

Brut Blanc de Blancs Champagne NV: Full-flavored, crisp and lively. Fresh citrus and apple flavors are matched with firm acidity in this well-rounded Champagne. Drink now through 2001. • $28 • (10/31/1999) • **88**
Brut Champagne 1990: Bold in style and full-bodied, this has a deep-gold color and assertive butterscotch flavors. It's light on fruit flavor, however, and it turns a bit lean on the finish. Drink now. • $38 • (12/31/1998) • **83**
Brut Champagne Gentilhomme 1990: An unusually vivid, even racy style of Champagne, with a Riesling-like personality. Has dramatic, slightly sweet grapefruit and floral flavors, fresh acidity and a lingering finish. Drink now. • $53 • (12/15/1998) • **90**
Brut Champagne Réserve NV: An easygoing, frankly fruity brut with a soft texture and a rather sweet finish. Drink now. • $25 • (10/31/1999) • **85**
Brut Rosé Champagne NV: Attractive in a very easygoing way, with strawberry and cherry flavors that are just a bit yeasty. Rich in texture, with a firm finish. Drink now.–B.S. • $30 • (11/30/1999) • **84**

LEONARD DE ST.-AUBIN

Beaujolais-Villages 1997: Corrupt cherry and sandalwood aromas and flavors mark this style of Beaujolais, which resembles Pinot Noir more than Gamay. Silky and firm, finishing on the dry side. Drink through 2000.–B.S. • $9 • (10/15/1999) • **83**
Beaujolais-Villages 1995 • $9 • (8/31/1996) • **85**
Chambolle-Musigny 1993 • $30 • (5/15/1996) • **84**
Gevrey-Chambertin 1993 • $26 • (5/15/1996) • **84**
Meursault 1995 • $26 • (6/30/1997) • **77**
Nuits-St.-Georges 1993 • $26 • (5/15/1996) • **78**
Nuits-St.-Georges 1985 • $25 • (11/30/1987) • **71**
Pommard 1995 • $28 • (6/30/1997) • **77**
Pommard 1993 • $27 • (5/15/1996) • **85**
Puligny-Montrachet 1995 • $28 • (6/30/1997) • **78**
Volnay 1993 • $26 • (5/15/1996) • **89**

LEOVILLE BARTON, CHATEAU

St.-Julien 1999: Plenty of mineral, tar and berry aroma. Medium-bodied, with well-integrated tannins, good fruit and a medium finish.–J.S. • $NA • (1/01/2000) (BT) • **85-89**
St.-Julien 1998: Lovely aromas to this, with currants and raspberries galore. Full- to medium-bodied, with a good core of fruit in the midpalate, fine tannins and a medium finish. Scores finesse and class for the Médoc in '98.–J.S. • $NA • (5/31/1999) (BT) • **90-94**
St.-Julien 1997: Good berry, mineral character, with a hint of chocolate. Medium-bodied, with fine tannins and a fresh finish. Drink now.–J.S. • $39 • (1/31/2000) • **88**
St.-Julien 1996: A well-structured, racy red. Lovely, fresh aromas of raspberries, cream and currants. Medium- to full-bodied, with well-integrated tannins which are firm yet silky. One of the more reasonably priced top '96s. Best after 2000.–J.S. • $48 Ⓐ • (1/31/1999) • **90**
St.-Julien 1995 • $52 Ⓐ • (1/31/1998) • **93**
St.-Julien 1994 • $40 Ⓐ • (1/31/1997) SS • **90**
St.-Julien 1993 • $33 Ⓐ • (1/31/1996) • **88**
St.-Julien 1991 • $23 • (3/31/1994) • **84**
St.-Julien 1990 • $79 Ⓐ • (3/31/1993) • **93**
St.-Julien 1989: A delicious, well-structured Bordeaux, with plenty of ripe fruit, beautiful berry, green tobacco and cherry character. Full-bodied, adding velvety tannins and a long, caressing finish. (1989 Bordeaux horizontal tasting). Best after 2002.–J.S. • $65 Ⓐ • (5/31/1999) • **92**
St.-Julien 1988: A little more austere than when it was young, with green tobacco and cherry aromas. Full-bodied, with firm tannins and a fresh finish. (1988 Bordeaux horizontal tasting). Drink now.–J.S. • $54 Ⓐ • (11/30/1998) • **87**
St.-Julien 1987 • $30 Ⓐ • (5/15/1990) • **80**
St.-Julien 1986 • $63 Ⓐ • (5/31/1989) • **90**

FRANCE

LEOVILLE BARTON, CHATEAU

St.-Julien 1985 • $70 Ⓐ • (10/15/1994) • **90**
St.-Julien 1983 • $54 Ⓐ • (10/15/1994) • **90**
St.-Julien 1982: At its peak. Medium-dark ruby, with an amber edge. Cherry, coffee and cedar aromas. Medium-bodied, with sweet berry flavors and caressing, velvety tannins. Delicious, but slightly disappointing for this château. (1982 Bordeaux horizontal tasting). Drink now.–J.S. • $90 Ⓐ • (11/30/1998) • **88**
St.-Julien 1981 • $31 • (10/15/1994) • **88**
St.-Julien 1962 • $80 • (11/30/1987) • **70**
St.-Julien 1961 • $173 Ⓐ • (4/30/1996) • **87**
St.-Julien 1959 • $125 • (10/15/1990) • **85**
St.-Julien 1945 • $340 • (3/16/1986) • **73**

LEOVILLE LAS CASES, CHATEAU

St.-Julien 1996: A racy, silky red. Intense aromas of blackberries and raspberries. Full- to medium-bodied, with a lovely concentration of fine tannins and a long, long finish. Not as good as the '95. Best after 2002.–J.S. • $143 Ⓐ • (1/01/1999) • **92**
St.-Julien 1995: Slowly builds on your palate, then delivers fabulous character and structure. Extremely well-crafted young red. Complex aromas of violets, berries, cinnamon and currants. Full-bodied, with extremely well-integrated tannins and a long, long finish. Best from 2003 through 2013.–J.S. • $109 Ⓐ • (9/15/1998) • **95**
St.-Julien 1992 • $41 Ⓐ • (2/29/1996) • **84**
St.-Julien 1991 • $39 Ⓐ • (2/29/1996) • **89**
St.-Julien 1990 • $154 Ⓐ • (10/15/1994) • **93**
St.-Julien 1989: A Las Cases that's rather rustic. Very fresh aromas of dried cherries, blackberries and wet earth. Full-bodied, with extremely well-integrated, silky tannins and a fresh blackberry and mint aftertaste. Slightly dry and funky on the finish. Try it a bit later. (1989 Bordeaux horizontal tasting). Best after 2003.–J.S. • $107 Ⓐ • (5/31/1999) • **90**
St.-Julien 1988: An outstanding Las Cases, though completely forgotten by many people. Full-bodied, with velvety tannins and lovely tobacco, violet and berry aromas and flavors. Extremely fruity finish. (1988 Bordeaux horizontal tasting). Best after 2000.–J.S. • $76 Ⓐ • (11/30/1998) • **92**
St.-Julien 1987 • $NA • (2/15/1990) • **84**
St.-Julien 1986 • $76 Ⓐ • (2/15/1990) • **96**
St.-Julien 1985 • $143 Ⓐ • (10/15/1994) • **94**
St.-Julien 1984 • $37 Ⓐ • (2/15/1990) • **82**
St.-Julien 1983 • $70 Ⓐ • (10/15/1994) • **87**
St.-Julien 1982: A racy, classy, silky wine. Inky-ruby color. Black cherry, mineral and wet earth aromas. Medium-bodied, with very silky tannins and a long, superfine finish. Has always been excellent.—1982 Bordeaux horizontal. Best after 2000.–J.S. • $231 Ⓐ • (11/30/1998) • **95**
St.-Julien 1981 • $50 Ⓐ • (10/15/1994) • **88**
St.-Julien 1980 • $28 Ⓐ /1.5 liter • (2/15/1990) • **84**
St.-Julien 1979 • $50 Ⓐ • (2/15/1990) • **90**
St.-Julien 1978 • $83 Ⓐ • (2/15/1990) • **94**
St.-Julien 1977 • $20 • (2/15/1992) • **78**
St.-Julien 1976 • $38 Ⓐ • (2/15/1992) • **83**
St.-Julien 1975 • $78 Ⓐ • (2/15/1992) • **88**
St.-Julien 1971 • $66 • (4/01/1986) • **76**
St.-Julien 1970 • $51 Ⓐ • (2/15/1990) • **89**
St.-Julien 1966 • $95 Ⓐ • (2/15/1992) • **86**
St.-Julien 1964 • $47 Ⓐ • (2/15/1992) • **88**
St.-Julien 1962 • $94 Ⓐ • (11/30/1987) • **85**
St.-Julien 1961 • $195 Ⓐ • (4/30/1996) • **85**
St.-Julien 1959 • $201 Ⓐ • (10/15/1990) • **96**
St.-Julien 1955 • $146 Ⓐ • (2/15/1992) • **81**
St.-Julien 1953 • $225 • (2/15/1992) • **87**
St.-Julien 1952 • $132 Ⓐ • (2/15/1992) • **73**
St.-Julien 1950 • $165 • (2/15/1992) • **73**
St.-Julien 1949 • $200 • (2/15/1992) • **89**
St.-Julien 1947 • $NA • (2/15/1992) • **86**
St.-Julien 1945 • $600 • (11/30/1995) • **89**
St.-Julien 1928 • $450 • (2/15/1992) • **90**

Key: SS—Spectator Selection. CS—Cellar Selection. HR—Highly Recommended. $NA—Price not available. (BT)—Barrel tasting. Ⓐ—Auction Price.
For a key to the tasters' initials, see "How to Use These Listings."
Dates in parentheses represent the issues in which the ratings were published.

LEOVILLE POYFERRE, CHATEAU

St.-Julien 1999: Lots of licorice, spice and currant aromas. Medium- to full-bodied, with silky tannins and a medium finish. Slightly diluted midpalate, but attractive.–J.S. • $NA • (1/01/2000) (BT) • **85-89**
St.-Julien 1998: A young wine with good mineral, berry and spice character, but it's slightly hard, with aggressive tannins. Medium body. Medium berry and green leaf aftertaste.–J.S. • $NA • (5/31/1999) (BT) • **85-89**
St.-Julien 1997: A sexy wine for the vintage, with lovely cherry, berry and vanilla character. Medium-bodied, with silky tannins and a medium finish. Best after 2000.–J.S. • $25 Ⓐ • (1/31/2000) • **89**
St.-Julien 1996: Delivers on the nose, with intense aromas of spices, blackberry and dark chocolate. Full-bodied, with silky tannins and a medium finish. Slightly hollow midpalate. Best after 2002.–J.S. • $52 Ⓐ • (1/31/1999) • **88**
St.-Julien 1995 • $46 Ⓐ • (1/31/1998) • **93**
St.-Julien 1991 • $16 Ⓐ • (3/31/1994) • **81**
St.-Julien 1990 • $84 Ⓐ • (3/31/1993) • **92**
St.-Julien 1989: Slightly one-dimensional, but outstanding. Dark ruby-colored center, verging on purple. Superripe aromas of cassis, berry and mint. Full-bodied, very sleek, with fine tannins and a long, long, caressing finish. (1989 Bordeaux horizontal tasting). Best after 2000.–J.S. • $47 Ⓐ • (5/31/1999) • **90**
St.-Julien 1988: A slightly green '88, with tobacco and fruit underneath. Full-bodied, with slightly tough tannins and a medium finish. (1988 Bordeaux horizontal tasting). Drink now.–J.S. • $NA • (11/30/1998) • **86**
St.-Julien 1987 • $24 • (5/15/1990) • **86**
St.-Julien 1986 • $53 Ⓐ • (5/31/1989) • **86**
St.-Julien 1985 • $49 Ⓐ • (4/30/1988) • **92**
St.-Julien 1984 • $25 • (10/15/1987) • **85**
St.-Julien 1983 • $60 Ⓐ • (3/01/1986) • **83**
St.-Julien 1982: A gorgeous wine, and still holding back. A beautiful, perfumed red, with cherry, floral aromas. Full-bodied, very velvety, with a lot of fruit and a lovely structure. Will improve. (1982 Bordeaux horizontal tasting). Drink now through 2010.–J.S. • $85 Ⓐ • (11/30/1998) • **91**
St.-Julien 1981 • $28 Ⓐ • (6/01/1984) • **88**
St.-Julien 1970 • $36 Ⓐ • (5/15/1993) • **85**
St.-Julien 1961 • $117 Ⓐ • (4/30/1996) • **85**
St.-Julien 1945 • $342 Ⓐ • (3/16/1986) • **80**

LEQUIN-COLIN, RENE

Bâtard-Montrachet 1997: Full-bodied, with pear-spirit character and cream notes. Lacks a bit of intense fruit. Drink now through 2007.–P.M. • $140 • (5/31/1999) • **85**
Bourgogne 1997: Unpleasant. Light-bodied, dry and sour.–P.M. • $15 • (9/30/1999) • **70**
Chassagne-Montrachet Les Caillerets 1997: Decent lemon and apple aromas and flavors are on display in this clean, little Chardonnay. Drink now.–P.M. • $42 • (5/31/1999) • **80**
Chassagne-Montrachet Les Charrières 1997: Flat, stripped and lean, this tastes diluted and overfiltered, with a wet paper note.–P.M. • $35 • (5/31/1999) • **70**
Chassagne-Montrachet Les Vergets 1997: Grassy, showing a touch of green apple. Light-bodied, with a slight dilution.–P.M. • $42 • (5/31/1999) • **79**
Chassagne-Montrachet Morgeot 1997: Oxidized, with a woody, cardboardy, drying flavor and a bitter finish.–P.M. • $42 • (5/31/1999) • **70**
Chassagne-Montrachet Red Morgeot 1997: Reduced and earthy at the moment, but underneath these aromas lurks decent fruit, although the finish tastes a bit rustic and dry. Drink now through 2005.–P.M. • $30 • (9/30/1999) • **80**
Corton-Charlemagne 1997: Fairly ripe but a bit herbal and soft, showing an earthy side, this distinctive white offers a minerally midpalate and decent fruit, but has a bitter finish.–P.M. • $80 • (5/31/1999) • **79**
Corton-Charlemagne 1996: Full-bodied and opulent, with an earthy side, it displays mineral, citrus and spice character. A bit tough on the finish, but there's enough stuffing to balance this '96. Drink now through 2006.–P.M. • $75 • (5/31/1999) • **86**
Pommard Les Noizons 1997: Light, stemmy, watery and diluted.–P.M. • $36 • (9/30/1999) • **76**
Santenay La Comme 1997: Light and stemmy, turning sour on the palate.–P.M. • $25 • (9/30/1999) • **70**
Santenay Les Charmes 1997: Light and diluted, with a green, herbal character.–P.M. • $22 • (9/30/1999) • **72**
Santenay Old Vine Reserve 1997: Has light red fruit aromas and flavors. A bit tannic and crisp on the finish.–P.M. • $22 • (9/30/1999) • **79**
Santenay Passetemps 1997: Tart, green, astringent and short.–P.M. • $25 • (9/30/1999) • **70**

Santenay White Les Hâtes 1997: A tough, oaky, minerally and firm white, this offers a powerful midpalate, with a gripping core of lemon and other citrus notes, little generosity and a rather drying finish.–P.M. • $22 • (5/31/1999) • **74**

LEROY

Auxey-Duresses Les Clous 1988 • $52 • (5/15/1991) • **85**
Bourgogne 1990 • $23 Ⓐ • (12/15/1992) • **86**
Bourgogne 1989 • $18 • (1/31/1992) • **85**
Bourgogne d'Auvenay 1988 • $15 • (4/30/1991) • **87**
Bourgogne d'Auvenay 1985 • $12 • (3/31/1988) • **73**
Chambertin 1985 • $500 Ⓐ • (12/15/1996) • **93**
Chambertin 1978 • $183 • (12/15/1996) • **70**
Chambertin 1969 • $311 • (12/15/1996) • **98**
Chambertin 1961 • $220 • (12/15/1996) • **94**
Chambertin 1959 • $403 • (12/15/1996) • **95**
Chambertin 1955 • $690 Ⓐ • (12/15/1996) • **88**
Chambertin 1949 • $1,533 • (12/15/1996) • **94**
Chambertin-Clos de Bèze 1959 • $98 • (12/15/1996) • **84**
Chambertin-Clos de Bèze 1955 • $94 • (12/15/1996) • **86**
Chapelle-Chambertin 1964 • $118 • (12/15/1996) • **90**
Gevrey-Chambertin Les Cazetiers 1971 • $NA • (12/15/1996) • **89**
Gevrey-Chambertin Les Cazetiers 1969 • $180 • (12/15/1996) • **87**
Gevrey-Chambertin Les Cazetiers 1962 • $135 Ⓐ • (12/15/1996) • **87**
Gevrey-Chambertin Les Cazetiers 1961 • $NA • (12/15/1996) • **92**
Grands Echézeaux 1945 • $1,045 • (12/15/1996) • **87**
Mazis-Chambertin 1985 • $719 Ⓐ • (12/15/1996) • **91**
Mazis-Chambertin 1978 • $200 • (12/15/1996) • **83**
Mazis-Chambertin 1971 • $431 • (12/15/1996) • **86**
Mazis-Chambertin 1964 • $275 • (12/15/1996) • **95**
Mazis-Chambertin 1959 • $385 • (12/15/1996) • **94**
Mazis-Chambertin 1955 • $450 • (12/15/1996) • **95**
Mazis-Chambertin Hospices de Beaune Cuvée Madeleine Collignon 1985 • $495 • (12/15/1996) • **91**
Musigny 1985 • $537 Ⓐ • (12/15/1996) • **87**
Musigny 1969 • $183 • (12/15/1996) • **88**
Musigny 1966 • $575 Ⓐ • (12/15/1996) • **87**
Musigny 1961 • $498 • (12/15/1996) • **83**
Musigny 1949 • $990 • (12/15/1996) • **98**
Nuits-St.-Georges 1945 • $NA • (12/15/1996) • **75**
Nuits-St.-Georges La Richemone 1989 • $NA • (12/15/1996) • **85**
Nuits-St.-Georges La Richemone 1938 • $NA • (12/15/1996) • **75**
Pommard Grands Epenots 1964 • $92 • (12/15/1996) • **84**
Pommard Trois Follots 1990 • $863 Ⓐ • (12/15/1992) • **95**
Richebourg 1949 • $690 Ⓐ • (12/15/1996) • **89**
Vosne-Romanée 1969 • $60 • (12/15/1996) • **80**

LEROY, DOMAINE

Chambertin 1996: Massive. Blackberry flavors are coated in oak now, with great richness and vibrancy and a firm, elegant texture. The intensity of flavor, persistence and length are outstanding. Best from 2001 through 2006.–B.S. • $660 • (9/30/1998) • **93**
Chambertin 1994 • $448 • (11/15/1996) • **86**
Chambertin 1993 • $500 • (12/15/1996) • **98**
Chambertin 1992 • $266 • (12/15/1994) • **88**
Chambertin 1991 • $311 • (12/15/1996) • **94**
Chambertin 1990 • $481 • (12/15/1996) • **96**
Chambertin 1989 • $310 • (12/15/1996) • **91**
Chambertin 1988 • $480 • (12/15/1996) • **88**
Chambolle-Musigny Les Charmes 1997: Very perfumed—redolent of sandalwood, violet, blackberry and vanilla—before shutting down on the firm, structured palate. Density and substance counter the firm tannins, while the finish is long and mouthcoating. Best from 2001 through 2006.–B.S. • $282 • (9/30/1999) • **90**
Chambolle-Musigny Les Charmes 1996: Suave and smoky, elegant yet with a lush, fat structure. Offers intense fruit and lovely acidity, with black cherry, smoke and earth flavors that keep pumping on the long finish. Drink through 2005.–B.S. • $255 • (9/30/1998) • **90**
Chambolle-Musigny Les Charmes 1994 • $165 • (11/15/1996) • **89**
Chambolle-Musigny Les Charmes 1993 • $200 • (11/15/1995) • **90**
Chambolle-Musigny Les Charmes 1992 • $NA • (1/01/1994) • **79**
Chambolle-Musigny Les Fremières 1997: A huge nose of sandalwood, vanilla, olive and plum marks this medium-bodied, silky '97 red Burgundy. Concentrated and long, with lingering tannins. Drink now through 2004.–B.S. • $166 • (9/30/1999) • **87**
Chambolle-Musigny Les Fremières 1996: Rich, smoky green olive aromas lead to black cherry, roasted meat and spice flavors in this dense, impenetrable red. The concentration, tannins and mouthwatering acidity are followed by a sweet fruit finish. Everything is there, give it time. Best from 2005 through 2015.–B.S. • $165 • (9/30/1998) • **94**
Chambolle-Musigny Les Fremières 1994 • $80 • (11/15/1996) • **88**
Chambolle-Musigny Les Fremières 1993 • $125 • (11/15/1995) • **88**
Chambolle-Musigny Les Fremières 1992 • $NA • (1/01/1994) • **83**
Chambolle-Musigny Les Fremières 1991 • $74 • (1/31/1994) • **87**
Chambolle-Musigny Les Fremières 1990 • $79 • (12/15/1992) • **94**
Chambolle-Musigny Les Fremières 1989 • $80 • (1/31/1992) • **94**
Clos de la Roche 1997: Fine tannins support the black cherry, plum and olive flavors in this dense, full-bodied, round '97 red Burgundy. Long aftertaste. Drink now through 2002.–B.S. • $610 • (9/30/1999) • **93**
Clos de la Roche 1996: Huge wine. Aromas and flavors of smoke, earth and green olives are quickly surpassed by tough tannins and a coarse, rustic feel. Best from 2003 through 2008.–B.S. • $610 • (9/30/1998) • **87**
Clos de la Roche 1994 • $286 • (11/15/1996) • **86**
Clos de la Roche 1993 • $325 • (12/15/1996) • **94**
Clos de la Roche 1992 • $196 • (5/15/1995) • **84**
Clos de la Roche 1991 • $124 • (12/15/1996) • **90**
Clos de la Roche 1990 • $413 • (12/15/1996) • **94**
Clos de la Roche 1989 • $147 • (12/15/1996) • **85**
Clos de Vougeot 1997: Much spice and smoky oak, violet, dried herb, olive and currant rise from the glass of this silky, full-bodied red Burgundy. Broad and expansive, delivering lots of gras at midpalate and flavors that fan out on the hedonistic finish. Should improve in the cellar. Best from 2002 through 2007.–P.M. • $434 • (9/30/1999) CS • **93**
Clos de Vougeot 1996: Loads of sweet, vanilla oak wrap around the palate before yielding to a firm structure in this rich, juicy red. Good richness, if not the intensity of the best. Best from 2001 through 2006.–B.S. • $263 Ⓐ • (9/30/1998) • **92**
Clos de Vougeot 1994 • $97 Ⓐ • (11/15/1996) • **88**
Clos de Vougeot 1993 • $250 • (11/15/1995) • **96**
Clos de Vougeot 1992 • $100 • (12/15/1994) • **90**
Clos de Vougeot 1991 • $181 • (1/31/1994) • **90**
Clos de Vougeot 1990 • $290 Ⓐ • (12/15/1992) • **97**
Clos de Vougeot 1989 • $193 • (1/31/1992) • **95**
Clos de Vougeot 1988 • $260 • (4/30/1991) • **89**
Corton Renardes 1997: Modern, very extracted and ripe. Smells like cherry compote, with flavors that are quite exotic, almost Rhône-like. Full-bodied and full of character, with good concentration, intensity and length. Tasted twice, with consistent notes. Drink now through 2003.–B.S. • $307 • (9/30/1999) • **89**
Corton Renardes 1996: Very polished and fresh, with smoky, almost bacon-like aromas and cherry flavors. Moderately concentrated, with firm tannins and a suave texture. Great length and harmony. Drink through 2006–B.S. • $305 • (9/30/1998) • **91**
Corton Renardes 1995 • $250 • (11/15/1997) • **90**
Corton Renardes 1994 • $145 • (11/15/1996) • **90**
Corton Renardes 1993 • $185 • (11/15/1995) • **92**
Corton Renardes 1992 • $83 • (12/15/1994) • **91**
Corton Renardes 1991 • $100 • (1/31/1994) • **90**
Corton Renardes 1990 • $111 • (12/15/1992) • **92**
Corton Renardes 1989 • $117 • (1/31/1992) • **95**
Corton-Charlemagne 1995: Full in body, rich in texture, with ripe fruit, it comes across as a bit rustic, with a chewy, oaky character. Offers butter, chestnut and fig, but also an unpure paint varnish quality. Best from 2005.–P.M. • $275 • (8/31/1998) • **80**
Gevrey-Chambertin Les Combottes 1997: Tastes a bit like burnt fruit, but the texture is a bit lemony and crisp. Shows juicy red berry character.–P.M. • $257 • (9/30/1999) • **79**
Gevrey-Chambertin Les Combottes 1996: Smoky green olive and forest undergrowth aromas and flavors in this forward, attractive red. Not a blockbuster, nor densely concentrated, yet there's a persistence of flavor and a fatness that lasts. Drink through 2005.–B.S. • $255 • (9/30/1998) • **89**
Gevrey-Chambertin Les Combottes 1995 • $NA • (11/15/1997) • **90**
Gevrey-Chambertin Les Combottes 1994 • $145 • (11/15/1996) • **86**
Gevrey-Chambertin Les Combottes 1993 • $220 • (11/15/1995) • **89**
Gevrey-Chambertin Les Combottes 1992 • $83 • (12/15/1994) • **86**
Gevrey-Chambertin Les Combottes 1991 • $100 • (1/31/1994) • **88**
Gevrey-Chambertin Les Combottes 1990 • $111 • (12/15/1992) • **92**
Gevrey-Chambertin Les Combottes 1989 • $127 Ⓐ • (1/31/1992) • **93**

LEROY, DOMAINE

Latricières-Chambertin 1997: Vanilla and oak character overlay the tender, licorice-tinged, black cherry aromas and flavors. An elegant Gevrey, yet firmly structured, ending on a tannic, sweet fruit note. Drink through 2004.–B.S. • $610 • (9/30/1999) • **85**
Latricières-Chambertin 1996: The epitome of delicacy. Very smoky, earthy and spicy, showing fresh acidity and fatness matched to an elegant structure and refined tannins. Excellent length. Drink through 2004.–B.S. • $610 • (9/30/1998) • **94**
Latricières-Chambertin 1995 • $600 • (11/15/1997) • **91**
Latricières-Chambertin 1994 • $286 • (11/15/1996) • **90**
Latricières-Chambertin 1993 • $325 • (12/15/1996) • **95**
Latricières-Chambertin 1992 • $155 • (12/15/1994) • **86**
Latricières-Chambertin 1991 • $181 • (1/31/1994) • **89**
Latricières-Chambertin 1990 • $336 Ⓐ • (12/15/1996) • **93**
Latricières-Chambertin 1989 • $250 • (1/31/1992) • **93**
Musigny 1996: Superb '96 red. Ripe and extroverted, showing spicy oak, cassis and black cherry aromas and flavors, depth and richness and a suave finish. Harmonious structure to support the fruit and richness. Great wine. Best from 2002 through 2008.–B.S. • $660 • (9/30/1998) • **95**
Musigny 1994 • $448 • (11/15/1996) • **85**
Musigny 1993 • $500 • (12/15/1996) • **98**
Musigny 1992 • $NA • (12/15/1994) • **89**
Musigny 1991 • $439 • (12/15/1996) • **94**
Musigny 1990 • $1,073 • (12/15/1996) • **98**
Musigny 1989 • $225 • (12/15/1996) • **91**
Musigny 1988 • $480 • (12/15/1996) • **88**
Nuits-St.-Georges 1994 • $95 • (11/15/1996) • **88**
Nuits-St.-Georges 1993 • $110 • (11/15/1995) • **89**
Nuits-St.-Georges Au Bas de Combe 1997: A touch of cooked fruit, but appealing and generous in its smoky, spicy plum flavors. There's a fine underlying structure through the long, long finish. Best from 2001 through 2007.–B.S. • $115 • (9/30/1999) • **90**
Nuits-St.-Georges Au Bas de Combe 1996: Not the concentration of the best Nuits, but very appealing with its smoke, petrol, green olive character, sinewy structure, vibrant acidity and impressively long finish. Best from 2002 through 2008.–B.S. • $115 • (9/30/1998) • **89**
Nuits-St.-Georges Au Bas de Combe 1992 • $63 • (6/15/1995) • **82**
Nuits-St.-Georges Au Bas de Combe 1991 • $58 • (1/31/1994) • **90**
Nuits-St.-Georges Au Bas de Combe 1990 • $58 • (12/15/1992) • **88**
Nuits-St.-Georges Aux Allots 1997: Plum and black cherry compote are highlighted by spice and smoke, followed by a rich, dense texture, mid-palate concentration and a sturdy framework. A nice sense of terroir and a tannic finish leave the palate tingling. Best from 2001 through 2006.–B.S. • $115 • (9/30/1999) • **88**
Nuits-St.-Georges Aux Allots 1996: Green olive and cherry notes combine with a smoky mineral note and vanilla quality. The sweet fruit and oak need time to integrate with the grainy tannins. Best from 2001 through 2006.–B.S. • $115 • (9/30/1998) • **87**
Nuits-St.-Georges Aux Allots 1994 • $80 • (11/15/1996) • **83**
Nuits-St.-Georges Aux Allots 1992 • $55 • (12/15/1994) • **87**
Nuits-St.-Georges Aux Allots 1991 • $64 • (1/31/1994) • **85**
Nuits-St.-Georges Aux Allots 1990 • $67 • (12/15/1992) • **95**
Nuits-St.-Georges Aux Allots 1989 • $75 • (1/31/1992) • **92**
Nuits-St.-Georges Aux Allots 1988 • $54 Ⓐ • (4/30/1991) • **89**
Nuits-St.-Georges Aux Boudots 1997: Very floral and fragrant, redolent of sandalwood and olive, along with cherry flavor, intensity and concentration. Elegant, wrapped in a cloak of firm tannins. Drink through 2005.–B.S. • $257 • (9/30/1999) • **91**
Nuits-St.-Georges Aux Boudots 1996: Green olive, blackberry and vanilla are the dominant aromas and flavors in this lithe, sinewy wine. There's stuffing and concentration for the firm tannins, and the finish lingers. Best from 2001 through 2006.–B.S. • $261 Ⓐ • (9/30/1998) • **93**
Nuits-St.-Georges Aux Boudots 1995 • $178 Ⓐ • (11/15/1997) • **93**
Nuits-St.-Georges Aux Boudots 1993 • $185 • (11/15/1995) • **91**
Nuits-St.-Georges Aux Boudots 1992 • $79 • (12/15/1994) • **90**
Nuits-St.-Georges Aux Boudots 1991 • $93 • (1/31/1994) • **83**
Nuits-St.-Georges Aux Boudots 1990 • $108 • (12/15/1992) • **94**
Nuits-St.-Georges Aux Boudots 1989 • $117 • (1/31/1992) • **95**
Nuits-St.-Georges Aux Boudots 1988 • $230 • (4/30/1991) • **93**

Key: SS—Spectator Selection. CS—Cellar Selection. HR—Highly Recommended. $NA—Price not available. (BT)—Barrel tasting. Ⓐ—Auction Price.
For a key to the tasters' initials, see "How to Use These Listings."
Dates in parentheses represent the issues in which the ratings were published.

Nuits-St.-Georges Aux Lavières 1996: Lovely red, both delicate and ripe, sporting a supple texture and plenty of rose petal, wild berry, smoked bacon, cherry and raspberry character. Of medium body, with an elegant finish. Drink now through 2005.–P.M. • $115 • (9/30/1998) • **89**
Nuits-St.-Georges Aux Lavières 1994 • $80 • (11/15/1996) • **78**
Nuits-St.-Georges Aux Lavières 1992 • $63 • (5/15/1995) • **87**
Nuits-St.-Georges Aux Lavières 1991 • $59 • (1/31/1994) • **83**
Nuits-St.-Georges Aux Lavières 1990 • $59 • (12/15/1992) • **94**
Nuits-St.-Georges Aux Lavières 1989 • $75 • (1/31/1992) • **89**
Nuits-St.-Georges Aux Lavières 1988 • $84 • (4/30/1991) • **82**
Nuits-St.-Georges Aux Vignerondes 1997: Very ripe but showing lovely terroir, with wet earth, smoke, grilled and olive complexity. Medium-bodied, it seduces the palate and leaves a trail of aromas and flavors. Drink now through 2005.–P.M. • $257 • (9/30/1999) • **89**
Nuits-St.-Georges Aux Vignerondes 1996: Great *terroir* here. Forest undergrowth, soil and mineral character is supported by a monolithic structure, vanilla oak and intensity of flavor. The quality comes through in the length. Best from 2002 through 2008.–B.S. • $255 • (9/30/1998) • **90**
Nuits-St.-Georges Aux Vignerondes 1994 • $145 • (11/15/1996) • **82**
Nuits-St.-Georges Aux Vignerondes 1993 • $185 • (11/15/1995) • **95**
Nuits-St.-Georges Aux Vignerondes 1992 • $79 • (12/15/1994) • **85**
Nuits-St.-Georges Aux Vignerondes 1991 • $93 • (1/31/1994) • **87**
Nuits-St.-Georges Aux Vignerondes 1990 • $100 • (12/15/1992) • **95**
Nuits-St.-Georges Aux Vignerondes 1989 • $117 • (1/31/1992) • **92**
Pommard Les Vignots 1997: A thick red, with chestnut, floral and spice notes and a soft core of warm fruit (plum and black cherry). With such supple tannins, you can enjoy this mouthful of a Pommard on release, or keep it since has a great length. Drink now through 2007.–P.M. • $115 • (9/30/1999) • **90**
Pommard Les Vignots 1996: Sweet-smelling, with licorice, black cherry and spice that persist, and innate power and concentration despite the massive tannins and dry finish. Excellent. Best from 2000.–B.S. • $94 Ⓐ • (9/30/1998) • **88**
Pommard Les Vignots 1995 • $110 • (11/15/1997) • **92**
Pommard Les Vignots 1994 • $80 • (11/15/1996) • **87**
Pommard Les Vignots 1993 • $94 • (11/15/1995) • **92**
Pommard Les Vignots 1992 • $57 • (12/15/1994) • **85**
Pommard Les Vignots 1991 • $70 • (1/31/1994) • **89**
Pommard Les Vignots 1990 • $74 • (12/15/1992) • **97**
Pommard Les Vignots 1989 • $75 • (1/31/1992) • **96**
Pommard Les Vignots 1988 • $84 • (4/30/1991) • **88**
Richebourg 1997: Fragrant, with exotic spices like sandalwood, cinnamon and cardamom, this elegant red feels thick, with density on the midpalate and tannins sneaking in on the finish. Excellent aftertaste of strawberry and spice. Drink now through 2002.–B.S. • $610 • (9/30/1999) • **93**
Richebourg 1996: Exotic, smoky green olive character on the nose, followed by a rich, lush, opulent wine exhibiting great density of black raspberry and cassis and a finely delineated structure. It's richness and ripe fruit hide the mouthsearing intensity. Fabulous. Best from 2005 through 2010.–B.S. • $610 • (9/30/1998) • **95**
Richebourg 1995 • $540 Ⓐ • (11/15/1997) • **95**
Richebourg 1994 • $367 • (11/15/1996) • **90**
Richebourg 1993 • $500 • (12/15/1996) • **95**
Richebourg 1992 • $210 • (12/15/1994) • **91**
Richebourg 1991 • $220 • (12/15/1996) • **94**
Richebourg 1990 • $299 • (12/15/1992) • **98**
Richebourg 1990 • $472 Ⓐ • (12/15/1996) • **96**
Richebourg 1989 • $288 Ⓐ • (12/15/1996) • **85**
Richebourg 1988 • $345 • (12/15/1996) • **87**
Romanée St.-Vivant 1997: Gamy and quite fat, showing fine blackberry and rose petal aromas, it kicks into high gear as the acidity and lemony taste bring vibrancy. Medium-bodied, with a spicy, chocolaty finish. Drink now through 2002.–P.M. • $610 • (9/30/1999) • **92**
Romanée St.-Vivant 1996: Really exotic and intense, with spicy oak, concentrated blackberry, cassis and earth flavors, this is an exciting, multidimensional '96. Ultrafine tannins and racy acidity provide structure for the flavors, which keep pumping on a finish that goes on forever. Best from 2002 through 2008.–B.S. • $610 • (9/30/1998) • **98**
Romanée St.-Vivant 1995 • $600 • (11/15/1997) CS • **98**
Romanée St.-Vivant 1994 • $475 • (9/30/1997) • **93**
Romanée St.-Vivant 1993 • $500 • (12/15/1996) • **99**
Romanée St.-Vivant 1992 • $210 • (12/15/1994) • **91**
Romanée St.-Vivant 1991 • $219 • (12/15/1996) • **95**
Romanée St.-Vivant 1990 • $405 • (12/15/1996) • **92**
Romanée St.-Vivant 1989 • $197 • (12/15/1996) • **89**
Romanée St.-Vivant 1988 • $431 • (12/15/1996) • **88**

Savigny-lès-Beaune Les Narbantons 1997: Stunning quality for '97. Beautifully balanced and intense, packed with plum and blackberry. The rich mouthfeel is bursting with focus and length. Hunt down and enjoy this full-bodied treasure. Drink now through 2007.–P.M. • $85 • (9/30/1999) • **90**

Savigny-lès-Beaune Les Narbantons 1996: A lot is happening in this marvelous wine. Strange and different, this is earth at its barest, so naked you can taste the soil, the mineral, the stone, the petrol, the iron. No fruit juice here, this is a jewel that's thick and ripe, yet elegant and racy, with some fascinating oak and spicy aromas attached to the *terroir* coattails. Delivers layers of mocha, spice, plum and red- and blackberry character. Drink now through 2020.–P.M. • $85 • (9/30/1998) • **94**

Savigny-lès-Beaune Les Narbantons 1995 • $80 • (11/15/1997) • **85**

Savigny-lès-Beaune Les Narbantons 1994 • $56 • (11/15/1996) • **81**

Savigny-lès-Beaune Les Narbantons 1993 • $70 • (11/15/1995) • **89**

Savigny-lès-Beaune Les Narbantons 1992 • $40 • (12/15/1994) • **85**

Savigny-lès-Beaune Les Narbantons 1991 • $44 • (1/31/1994) • **89**

Savigny-lès-Beaune Les Narbantons 1990 • $48 • (12/15/1992) • **92**

Savigny-lès-Beaune Les Narbantons 1989 • $65 • (1/31/1992) • **91**

Volnay-Santenots 1997: This deeply colored Volnay carries a big wood stick, as the oak blankets the blackberry fruit now. Medium-bodied, it has grip and character, with wild berry, olive paste, citrus, grape and spicy vanilla notes thrown in. Best from 2001 through 2005.–P.M. • $181 • (9/30/1999) • **87**

Volnay-Santenots 1996: Brilliant wine. Elegant, with violet, raspberry and vanilla aromas and flavors that dance across the palate, along with sappy fruit, intensity of flavor and firm but ripe tannins. Textbook Volnay. Drink now through 2002.–B.S. • $180 • (9/30/1998) • **93**

Volnay-Santenots 1994 • $92 • (11/15/1996) • **85**

Volnay-Santenots 1993 • $185 • (11/15/1995) • **96**

Volnay-Santenots 1992 • $NA • (1/01/1994) • **83**

Vosne-Romanée Aux Genaivrières 1997: Exotic, spicy aromas followed by cherry, forest floor and olive flavors mark this tender yet persistent red Burgundy. Moderately concentrated, with good focus, fine tannins and the softness of the vintage. Drink now through 2003.–B.S. • $115 • (9/30/1999) • **89**

Vosne-Romanée Aux Genaivrières 1996: A crowd-pleaser. Racy yet seductive, with lots of plum, green olive, wet earth and cassis flavors. Fat and ripe, it displays a firm tannic structure and lots of fresh acidity on the lingering finish. Drink now through 2010.–P.M. • $115 • (9/30/1998) • **90**

Vosne-Romanée Aux Genaivrières 1994 • $80 • (11/15/1996) • **84**

Vosne-Romanée Aux Genaivrières 1992 • $61 • (5/15/1995) • **84**

Vosne-Romanée Aux Genaivrières 1991 • $57 • (1/31/1994) • **90**

Vosne-Romanée Aux Genaivrières 1990 • $61 • (12/15/1992) • **95**

Vosne-Romanée Aux Genaivrières 1989 • $75 • (1/31/1992) • **91**

Vosne-Romanée Aux Réas 1990 • $58 • (12/15/1992) • **97**

Vosne-Romanée Les Beaux Monts 1997: Fine concentration and sweet fruit mark this successful '97 red Burgundy. Flavors of black cherry, olive and spice, midpalate fat and a solid structure lead to a long, persistent finish. Well done for the vintage. Drink now through 2005.–B.S. • $257 • (9/30/1999) • **92**

Vosne-Romanée Les Beaux Monts 1996: Magnificent. Opulent and decadent, thick and ripe, yet remains very elegant and racy. A bit savage, with plenty of wild berry, dried herbs and currant aromas and flavors married to the deftly toasted oak accents. Balanced, full-bodied, with a long, silky finish. Best After 2003.–P.M. • $328 Ⓐ • (9/30/1998) • **92**

Vosne-Romanée Les Beaux Monts 1995 • $250 • (11/15/1997) • **92**

Vosne-Romanée Les Beaux Monts 1994 • $145 • (11/15/1996) • **87**

Vosne-Romanée Les Beaux Monts 1993 • $185 • (11/15/1995) • **94**

Vosne-Romanée Les Beaux Monts 1992 • $73 Ⓐ • (12/15/1994) • **85**

Vosne-Romanée Les Beaux Monts 1991 • $100 • (1/31/1994) HR • **91**

Vosne-Romanée Les Beaux Monts 1990 • $112 • (12/15/1992) HR • **95**

Vosne-Romanée Les Beaux Monts 1989 • $165 Ⓐ • (1/31/1992) • **92**

Vosne-Romanée Les Beaux Monts 1988 • $103 Ⓐ • (4/30/1991) • **93**

Vosne-Romanée Les Brûlées 1997: Plenty of new oak lends an exotic spice quality, accenting the olive and cherry. Elegantly wrought and subtle in its structure and length, with persistent flavors and good midpalate concentration. Drink now through 2004.–B.S. • $257 • (9/30/1999) • **90**

Vosne-Romanée Les Brûlées 1996: Ripe Pinot in a rich, plummy style. Delicious, thick and hedonistic, with supple tannins and pretty mocha and spice oak accents to the cherry and blackberry character. A bit tannic and slightly hot on the finish, but give it time. Best from 2003.–P.M. • $255 • (9/30/1998) • **89**

Vosne-Romanée Les Brûlées 1994 • $145 • (11/15/1996) • **89**

Vosne-Romanée Les Brûlées 1993 • $185 • (11/15/1995) • **93**

Vosne-Romanée Les Brûlées 1992 • $83 • (12/15/1994) • **85**

Vosne-Romanée Les Brûlées 1989 • $117 • (1/31/1992) • **94**

LESCURE, CHANTAL

Beaune Les Chouacheux 1997: A little amorphous, with spice and chocolate notes, lacking slightly in concentration. Remains light and dry on the finish. Drink now through 2002.–B.S. • $35 • (9/30/1999) • **82**

Beaune Les Chouacheux 1996: Smells and tastes like caramel or crème brûlée, with an herbaceous undercurrent and modest concentration. Tough finish. Best from 2000.–B.S. • $29 • (9/30/1998) • **79**

Beaune Les Chouacheux 1995 • $32 • (1/31/1998) • **85**

Beaune Les Chouacheux 1989 • $19 • (8/31/1992) • **88**

Bourgogne Les Sorbins 1997: This straightforward, smooth Pinot has cherry and licorice.–P.M. • $19 • (9/30/1999) • **78**

Bourgogne Les Taupes Maison Dieu 1997: Herb juice. Tart and astringent.–P.M. • $19 • (9/30/1999) • **71**

Chambolle-Musigny Les Mombies 1997: A slim, elegant '97 red, displaying more earth and mineral than fruit. Tough on the finish.–B.S. • $42 • (9/30/1999) • **77**

Chambolle-Musigny Les Mombies 1996: Tight and racy, a firm, lean kind of wine that has intensity. Masculine and chewy, it has depth of fruit on the finish and a sinewy framework. Best from 2002 through 2008.–B.S. • $34 • (9/30/1998) • **87**

Chambolle-Musigny Les Mombies 1995 • $37 • (1/31/1998) • **79**

Clos de Vougeot 1997: Light in color but medium-intense, with spice, red berry, herb and olive character. A bit stemmy in aroma but otherwise elegant, with a lingering finish. Drink now through 2005.–P.M. • $85 • (9/30/1999) • **84**

Clos de Vougeot 1996: Fragrant aromas of violets and red berries in this light-bodied, elegant Clos Vougeot. The silky texture stiffly tannic, with a lingering berry note. Best from 2001 through 2006.–B.S. • $66 • (9/30/1998) • **84**

Clos de Vougeot 1995 • $72 • (1/31/1998) • **71**

Clos de Vougeot 1990 • $44 • (6/15/1993) • **76**

Clos de Vougeot 1989 • $45 • (8/31/1992) • **82**

Côte de Beaune La Grande Châtelaine 1997: Volatile and stewed, with slightly attractive flavors, but overall unappealing.–B.S. • $23 • (9/30/1999) • **74**

Côte de Beaune La Grande Châtelaine 1995 • $23 • (1/31/1998) • **85**

Côte de Beaune Le Clos des Topes Bizot 1996: Crisp cassis bush and wild raspberry character is the hallmark of this medium-bodied red; but it turns slightly herbal and firm on the palate, with tough tannins.–P.M. • $24 • (9/30/1998) • **80**

Côte de Beaune Le Clos des Topes Bizot Vieilles Vignes 1997: A bit cooked and forward, with metallic-tasting acidity.–P.M. • $23 • (9/30/1999) • **72**

Nuits-St.-Georges Les Damodes 1997: A stewed tomato character and an anemic palate don't add up to much.–B.S. • $44 • (9/30/1999) • **76**

Nuits-St.-Georges Les Damodes 1996: Seems simple, candied and forced. Offers pretty strawberry and vanilla aromas and flavors, elegant and straightforward, with modest concentration and length. Drink through 2003–B.S. • $35 • (9/30/1998) • **83**

Nuits-St.-Georges Les Damodes 1995 • $38 • (1/31/1998) • **78**

Nuits-St.-Georges Les Damodes 1990 • $25 • (6/15/1993) • **80**

Pommard Les Bertins 1995 • $46 • (1/31/1998) • **85**

Pommard Les Bertins 1990 • $22 • (6/15/1993) • **76**

Pommard Les Bertins 1989 • $25 • (8/31/1992) • **87**

Pommard Les Bertins 1988 • $40 • (11/30/1990) • **88**

Pommard Les Chanlins 1997: Odd, with a slight petrol and burnt rubber aroma.–P.M. • $42 • (9/30/1999) • **73**

Pommard Les Tavannes 1997: Vanilla and chocolate notes swirl around in this medium-bodied red Burgundy. Turns a bit chunky and dry on the finish. Drink now through 2002.–P.M. • $42 • (9/30/1999) • **80**

Pommard Les Vaumuriens 1997: An earthy richness marks this fresh, spicy red, with black cherry. Very suave and moderately structured, it remains smooth until the tannins take over on the finish. Drink now through 2002.–B.S. • $42 • (9/30/1999) • **84**

Pommard Les Vaumuriens 1996: Kirsch and wet earth are the dominant themes, supported by very stiff tannins. Lacks the polish and finesse of the top wines, but has plenty of personality. Tough finish. Best from 2001.–B.S. • $NA • (9/30/1998) • **85**

Pommard Les Vaumuriens 1995 • $36 • (1/31/1998) • **85**

Pommard Les Vignots 1997: Oaky and ripe, displaying caramel and vanilla aromas and flavors, with stewed fruit. Simple and a bit diffuse. Drink now through 2002.–B.S. • $42 • (9/30/1999) • **80**

Volnay 1996: Shows some almond and cherry along with a lean, stemmy character, and finishes tough and astringent. Drink through 2004.–B.S. • $NA • (9/30/1998) • **77**

FRANCE

LESCURE, CHANTAL

Vosne-Romanée Les Suchots 1997: This soft, round red has a simple appeal, with black olive, herb and plum notes and a vanilla aftertaste.–B.S. • $64 • (9/30/1999) • **79**

Vosne-Romanée Les Suchots 1996: Light in color and body, but fairly flamboyant, fleshy and ripe, showing some lovely oak, vanilla and spice along with plum and cherry. Turns a bit hot on the finish. Drink now.–P.M. • $52 • (9/30/1998) • **85**

Vosne-Romanée Les Suchots 1995 • $49 • (1/31/1998) • **75**

Vosne-Romanée Les Suchots 1990 • $26 • (6/15/1993) • **81**

Vosne-Romanée Les Suchots 1989 • $25 • (8/31/1992) • **89**

LESTAGE, CHATEAU

Listrac 1998: Some pleasant berry and mineral character. Medium-bodied, with medium tannins and a short finish. Slight herbal quality.–J.S. • $NA • (5/31/1999) (BT) • **80-84**

Listrac 1996: Some pretty plum, bark and earthy character on the nose and palate, but rather light and diluted. Not much to it, really.–J.S. • $NA • (2/28/1999) • **78**

Listrac 1990 • $18 • (3/31/1993) • **88**

Listrac 1988 • $20 • (8/31/1991) • **82**

LESTAGE-SIMON, CHATEAU

Haut-Médoc 1997: Very light, although it shows some good berry, strawberry and tobacco character. Drink now.–J.S. • $24 • (1/31/2000) • **80**

Haut-Médoc 1987 • $13 • (11/30/1989) • **74**

Haut-Médoc 1986 • $13 • (11/30/1989) • **85**

Haut-Médoc 1982 • $15 • (11/30/1989) • **84**

LEVET, B.

Côte-Rôtie La Chavaroche 1992 • $30 • (11/30/1996) • **77**

LEVRAUDIERE, CHATEAU DE LA

Muscadet de Sèvre et Maine Sur Lie 1996: Stony aromas and flavors are accented by lemon and apple, yet the overall impression is a little hard, lacking the flesh for balance. Needs food.–B.S. • $7 • (11/15/1998) • **83**

LIAISON, LA

Chardonnay Vin de Pays d'Oc 1996 • $10 • (10/31/1997) • **86**

Merlot Vin de Pays d'Oc 1995 • $10 • (11/15/1997) • **83**

Viognier-Chardonnay Vin de Pays d'Oc 1996 • $11 • (10/31/1997) • **82**

LICHINE, ALEXIS

Bordeaux Premier de Lichine 1993 • $6 • (8/31/1995) • **77**

Cabernet Sauvignon Vin de Pays d'Oc 1993 • $6 • (7/31/1995) • **80**

Merlot Vin de Pays d'Oc 1993 • $6 • (7/31/1995) • **78**

LIEUJEAN, CHATEAU

Haut-Médoc 1997: Really watery, with some fruit but just too light.–J.S. • $NA • (1/31/2000) • **75**

LIGNIER, GEORGES

Bonnes Mares 1987 • $75 • (3/31/1990) • **92**

Chambolle-Musigny 1987 • $32 • (6/15/1990) • **77**

Clos de la Roche 1996: Starts off very nicely, with coffee, smoke, plum, truffle aromas, but it seems to be maturing at a surprisingly quick pace (it fell apart somewhat in the glass), and it lacks a bit of vibrancy on the finish. A gamble. Drink now through 2002.–P.M. • $50 • (7/31/1999) • **85**

Clos de la Roche 1987 • $55 • (3/31/1990) • **90**

Clos de la Roche 1985 • $127 Ⓐ • (3/15/1988) • **85**

Clos St.-Denis 1996: Tastes somewhat mature. Starts out with prune and plum notes, followed by a bit of forest underbrush. Dry on the finish. Drink now through 2002.–P.M. • $40 • (7/31/1999) • **81**

Clos St.-Denis 1987 • $49 • (5/15/1990) • **89**

Clos St.-Denis 1985 • $54 • (3/15/1988) • **91**

Gevrey-Chambertin 1987 • $29 • (5/31/1990) • **84**

Gevrey-Chambertin Aux Combottes 1987 • $34 • (5/31/1990) • **87**

Morey-St.-Denis 1987 • $25 • (5/15/1990) • **82**

Morey-St.-Denis 1985 • $23 • (3/15/1988) • **82**

Morey-St.-Denis Clos des Ormes 1996: A bit herbal, with a slightly stemmy, gamy, spicy character.–P.M. • $27 • (7/31/1999) • **76**

Morey-St.-Denis Clos des Ormes 1987 • $32 • (5/15/1990) • **88**

Morey-St.-Denis Clos des Ormes 1985 • $28 • (3/15/1988) • **86**

LIGNIER, HUBERT

Chambolle-Musigny 1997: Soft in texture but with crisp flavors. Medium-bodied, with fresh red berry character. Smells and tastes pure and clean, offering a focused aromatic panoply of raspberry and blackberry, with a deftly oaked finish. Drink now through 2003.–P.M. • $45 • (1/01/2000) • **85**

Chambolle-Musigny Les Baudes 1997: The aromas display "lifted" notes (a balsamic vinegar aroma that might come from volatile acidity). The texture is crisp and acidic, making the wine disjointed. Too bad, because it has sweet-tasting berry character.–P.M. • $90 • (1/01/2000) • **76**

Clos de la Roche 1997: Extraordinary quality for the vintage. Rich, ripe and ultrasmooth, with clean aromas of pure red berry and blackberry backed by oak-infused vanilla, spice and smoke. Dark and full-bodied, with a long finish that unfolds deliciously as the flavors linger. Drink now through 2007.–P.M. • $150 • (1/01/2000) • **93**

Clos de la Roche 1994 • $95 • (11/15/1996) • **87**

Clos de la Roche 1990 • $90 • (12/15/1992) • **92**

Gevrey-Chambertin 1997: A beautiful red Burgundy that seemingly has it all. Dark, with ripe fruit and a firm but balanced structure. Full-bodied, it coats the palate with its focused red berry and blackberry flavors. Grilled meat and spice add complexity to the fresh, long, smooth finish. Best from 2002 through 2010.–P.M. • $45 • (1/01/2000) • **92**

Gevrey-Chambertin 1994 • $NA • (11/15/1996) • **83**

Morey-St.-Denis 1997: Supple, rich and ripe, but with a beautiful, firm structure. Full-bodied, this is for fans of *terroir*. Hard to believe it's from '97 with its wet earth and mineral intensity. Drink now through 2005.–P.M. • $NA • (1/01/2000) • **92**

Morey-St.-Denis 1994 • $38 • (11/15/1996) • **73**

Morey-St.-Denis 1990 • $36 • (12/15/1992) • **86**

Morey-St.-Denis Les Chaffots 1997: A charmer. Very supple and quite attractive, with licorice and red berry character. Not much depth in this medium-bodied, succulent red, but the velvety texture is pleasant. Drink now through 2005.–P.M. • $63 • (1/01/2000) • **87**

Morey-St.-Denis Premier Cru 1990 • $36 • (12/15/1992) • **88**

Morey-St.-Denis Premier Cru Vieilles Vignes 1997: A focused, ripe and smooth Pinot Noir, with blackberry and black cherry notes, lovely toasty grilled meat flavors and smooth tannins in a medium-bodied package. Lacks just a bit of intensity to score higher. Drink now through 2005.–P.M. • $78 • (1/01/2000) • **89**

Morey-St.-Denis Premier Cru Vieilles Vignes 1994 • $50 • (11/15/1996) • **89**

LILIAN LADOUYS, CHATEAU

St.-Estèphe 1998: Pretty aromas of crushed berries. Medium-bodied, with some firm tannins and a slightly green finish.–J.S. • $NA • (5/31/1999) (BT) • **85-89**

St.-Estèphe 1997: A bit subdued, but shows an attractive berry, cherry character, medium body and a fresh finish. Drink now.–J.S. • $NA • (1/31/2000) • **83**

St.-Estèphe 1996: Not a big wine, but extremely enjoyable with good finesse. Wonderfully perfumed raspberry, cherry and mineral on the nose. Medium-bodied, with silky tannins and a fresh, fruity aftertaste. Best after 2000.–J.S. • $16 Ⓐ • (1/31/1999) • **88**

St.-Estèphe 1995 • $18 • (1/31/1998) • **85**

St.-Estèphe 1994 • $15 • (1/31/1997) • **81**

St.-Estèphe 1993 • $NA • (1/31/1996) • **82**

LION BEAULIEU, CHATEAU

Bordeaux 1996: Rather light in color, with an earthy, plummy, weedy aroma. Medium-bodied, with some fruit, but somewhat diluted on the finish.–J.S. • $NA • (2/28/1999) • **76**

Key: SS—Spectator Selection. CS—Cellar Selection. HR—Highly Recommended. $NA—Price not available. (BT)—Barrel tasting. Ⓐ—Auction Price. For a key to the tasters' initials, see "How to Use These Listings." **Dates in parentheses represent the issues in which the ratings were published.**

LIONNET, JEAN

Cornas 1987 • $23 • (3/31/1990) • **90**
Cornas 1986 • $23 • (1/31/1989) • **87**
Cornas Domaine de Rochepertuis 1994 • $NA • (1/01/1998) • **86**
Cornas Domaine de Rochepertuis 1993 • $NA • (1/01/1998) • **85**
Cornas Domaine de Rochepertuis 1992 • $12 • (10/15/1996) • **83**
Cornas Domaine de Rochepertuis 1991 • $23 • (5/31/1994) • **80**
Cornas Domaine de Rochepertuis 1990 • $23 • (5/31/1994) • **89**
Cornas Domaine de Rochepertuis 1988 • $28 • (1/31/1991) • **83**
Syrah Côtes du Rhône 1992 • $15 • (10/15/1994) • **83**
Syrah Côtes du Rhône 1990 • $16 • (8/31/1992) • **88**
Syrah Côtes du Rhône 1986 • $10 • (9/30/1988) • **79**

LIOT, CHATEAU

Barsac 1993 • $NA • (4/15/1995) • **82**
Barsac 1990 • $23 • (4/15/1995) • **81**
Barsac 1989 • $29 • (4/15/1995) • **84**
Barsac 1988 • $50 • (4/15/1995) • **86**
Barsac 1986 • $22 • (12/31/1989) • **87**
Barsac 1985 • $9 • (5/31/1988) • **84**

LIVERSAN, CHATEAU

Haut-Médoc 1997: A bit lean, but decent berry and mineral character. Light-bodied, with light tannins, a fresh finish. Drink now.–J.S. • $NA • (1/31/2000) • **81**
Haut-Médoc 1996: A rather chunky, monolithic wine, but it shows good concentration for the vintage. Lovely aromas of blackberry, chocolate and minerals. Full-bodied, with lots of berry, minty flavors and a hint of smoke. Best after 2003.–J.S. • $15 • (1/31/1999) • **85**
Haut-Médoc 1995 • $15 • (1/31/1998) • **85**
Haut-Médoc 1994 • $15 • (1/31/1997) • **76**
Haut-Médoc 1993 • $15 • (1/31/1996) • **85**
Haut-Médoc 1990 • $19 • (3/31/1993) • **89**
Haut-Médoc 1989: Beautiful and delicious young wine. Dark ruby-colored. Extremely ripe blackberry, plum and raisin aromas and hints of mint and dried spices. Full-bodied and very firm, with lots of ripe fruit and a solid, silky tannic structure.—1989 Bordeaux horizontal. Best after 2000.–J.S. • $NA • (5/31/1999) • **90**
Haut-Médoc 1988 • $14 • (7/31/1991) • **87**
Haut-Médoc 1985 • $21 Ⓐ • (4/30/1988) • **90**
Haut-Médoc 1982 • $24 • (8/31/1992) • **85**
Haut-Médoc 1961 • $29 • (4/30/1996) • **84**

LOEW, DOMAINE

Auxerrois Alsace Botrytis 1998: Round and lushly textured, this '98 starts slightly sweet and finishes on the dry side, with flavors of apple, pear, beeswax and mineral. Not imported into the U.S. Drink now.–B.S. • $NA • (1/01/2000) • **86**
Riesling Alsace Bruderbach Clos des Frères 1998: Round and balanced, showing apple and lemon and a hint of sweetness to soften the acidity. A good quaffer. Not imported into the U.S. Drink now.–B.S. • $NA • (1/01/2000) • **83**
Riesling Alsace Muschelkalck 1998: Pretty, floral notes introduce this dry, lively Riesling, with apple and lemon flavors lingering on the firm structure and delicate finish. Not imported into the U.S. Drink now through 2003.–B.S. • $NA • (1/01/2000) • **83**
Tokay Pinot Gris Alsace Cormier 1998: Firmly structured, carrying the apple, almond and smoke aromas and flavors to a satisfying finish. Elegant and balanced, it ends on a citrus note. Not imported into the U.S. Drink now.–B.S. • $NA/500 ml. • (1/01/2000) • **85**
Tokay Pinot Gris Alsace Elixir de Cormier 1998: Soft, round and almost opulent, yet this seems one-dimensional today, with some residual sugar masking the pear flavor; good underlying acidity, though. Not imported into the U.S. Drink now through 2001.–B.S. • $NA/500 ml. • (1/01/2000) • **84**

LOISEAU, YVES

Chinon Domaine du Colombier Clos de la Roche Bobreau 1996: Earth and a touch of licorice accent the black currant flavors in this masculine '96. Solid and unyielding now, but shows concentration and depth along with a lengthy finish. Drink through 2001.–B.S. • $16 • (10/31/1998) • **87**
Chinon Domaine du Colombier Cuvée de la Roche Bobreau 1997: An appealing mix of ripe black cherry and leafy, herbal flavors gives this red wine typical Loire character, with a polished texture and firm, balanced tannins. Light but well focused. Drink now through 2001.–T.M. • $20 • (6/30/1999) • **85**
Chinon Domaine du Colombier Cuvée Vieilles Vignes 1997: Still young and a bit raw, this red shows promise, with sawdust aromas and ripe flavors of cherry and plum. Has firm tannins and a polished texture. Drink through 2003.–T.M. • $14 • (6/30/1999) • **85**
Chinon Domaine du Colombier Cuvée Vieilles Vignes 1996: Rich and round, full of berry and cherry flavors that are shut down by the firm structure. Lacks the depth and concentration of the best in this appellation. Drink now.–B.S. • $13 • (10/31/1998) • **84**
Chinon Rosé Domaine du Colombier 1996: This pale rosé offers light flavors of cherry and herb. Clean and soft on the palate, with enough acidity to keep it fresh. Simple but harmonious. Drink now.–T.M. • $13 • (8/31/1998) • **82**
Chinon White Domaine du Colombier Clos du Centenaire 1997: Alluring floral and herbal accents give this white wine distinctive character, and ripe pear and apple flavors give it depth. It's not flashy, but it draws you back for another sip. Drink now through 2001.–T.M. • $14 • (6/30/1999) • **85**
Chinon White Domaine du Colombier Clos du Centenaire 1996: A green, grassy component turns to almond midpalate, while the rich texture is washed away by tangy acidity. Herbal notes echo on the finish. Drink now.–B.S. • $13 • (11/15/1998) • **84**

LONG-DEPAQUIT, A.

Chablis 1998: Clean and crisp in style, this steely Chablis has green apple and citrus character on a light-bodied frame. Drink now through 2001.–P.M. • $18 • (5/15/2000) • **80**
Chablis 1997: A bit neutral, showing some tannic character, this is a bit aggressive but turns ripe on the finish. Drink now.–P.M. • $19 • (5/31/1999) • **85**
Chablis 1996: Just delicious. A ripe, tropical-tasting Chablis that seems as if it still has some residual sugar, but who cares? It shows a lush, opulent texture and lovely honey and ripe pear mingled with hard, citrus-spiked acidity. Full-bodied, with a most seductive finish. Much better than previously reviewed. Drink now through 2007.–P.M. • $17 • (8/31/1998) • **92**
Chablis 1995 • $17 • (8/31/1996) • **86**
Chablis Blanchot 1997: Clean as a whistle, medium-bodied, with zesty grassy, honeyed, lemony notes, this challenges the taste buds, but the vibrant intensity combined with creamy texture leave a good impression. Best from 2003 through 2010.–P.M. • $48 • (5/31/1999) • **90**
Chablis Blanchot 1996: Beautiful harmony marks this medium- to-full-bodied white, with its lovely pear, honeysuckle, melon, honey and mineral character. Impressively ripe on the midpalate, and the finish tasted supple after the wine stood decanted. Best after 2005.–P.M. • $36 • (8/31/1998) • **92**
Chablis Les Beugnons 1998: This interesting combination of mineral and ripe fruit tastes of gooseberry, freshly cut grass, ripe pear, chalk and wet stone. Medium-bodied and rather complex, with a supple mouthfeel backed by fresh acidity. Drink now through 2003.–P.M. • $33 • (5/15/2000) • **84**
Chablis Les Beugnons 1997: A firm and rather tart style, showing a salty, minerally character and a tough midpalate that yields slowly to a hint of creaminess. For aficionados of uncompromisingly steely Chablis. Drink now through 2005.–P.M. • $29 • (5/31/1999) • **84**
Chablis Les Beugnons 1996 • $25 • (5/31/1998) • **90**
Chablis Les Clos 1997: Clean and pure, a crisp style of Les Clos, not giving much now but with plenty of lemon, grapefruit, melon and wet earth. Medium-bodied, it should come around with age. Best from 2005 through 2015.–P.M. • $53 • (5/31/1999) • **89**
Chablis Les Clos 1996: Stunning. This compacted, firm, muscular, full-bodied Chablis is simply majestic, oozing with ripe, sweet-tasting fruit, mineral and wet earth character and delivering serious tropical concentration. The beauty of it all is that the wine is clean, pure, fresh and vibrant, with no hint of heaviness or distracting oak. Tempting now, but will improve in the cellar. Best from 2005.–P.M. • $37 • (8/31/1998) • **95**
Chablis Les Lys 1998: Supple and graceful. Shows lovely fruit and mineral concentration at midpalate. Full-bodied, the texture is palate-coating and silky and the flavors fold into the balanced finish. Tempting now, but should only improve. Drink now through 2010.–P.M. • $NA • (5/15/2000) • **90**
Chablis Les Lys 1997: Wonderful, clean and pure, but also showing idiosyncratic salty, minerally, earthy notes that mingle with green apple, lemon and pineapple flavors on a superharmonious and juicy finish. Drink now through 2005.–P.M. • $34 • (5/31/1999) • **91**
Chablis Les Lys 1996 • $25 • (5/31/1998) • **89**

LONG-DEPAQUIT, A.

Chablis Les Preuses 1997: Woody and heavy-handed, lacking elegance and tasting of sweet perfume.–P.M. • $49 • (5/31/1999) • **75**

Chablis Les Preuses 1996 • $35 • (5/31/1998) • **95**

Chablis Moutonne 1997: Superpure, without any obvious oak interfering with the lemon, butter, vanilla bean and mineral flavors, this full-bodied, elegant Chablis presses all the right buttons. Very silky finish. (By the way, aged in stainless steel only.) Best from 2005 through 2012.–P.M. • $56 • (5/31/1999) • **94**

Chablis Moutonne 1996: Superbalanced grand cru. Give it time in the cellar (or decant) and it will turn silky smooth, delivering ripe pear, cherry (yes, cherry), smoky, minerally character. Opulent in the midpalate, with wonderful honey notes, the acidity calms down nicely when the wine is aerated. Best from 2005.–P.M. • $50 • (8/31/1998) • **94**

Chablis Moutonne 1995 • $36 • (6/15/1997) • **89**

Chablis Vaillons 1998: A typical '98 Chablis—fairly easy, not too much structure, with decent ripe fruit and a pleasant finish. Drink now through 2003.–P.M. • $34 • (5/15/2000) • **86**

Chablis Vaillons 1997: Absolutely gorgeous. Ripe, yet focused on the minerally soil of Chablis, this is creamy and refreshingly fruity, with masses of tropical, apricot, fig and pear character, with cream to boot on the buttery, caressing finish. Great winemaking. Drink through 2006.–P.M. • $30 • (5/31/1999) • **93**

Chablis Vaillons 1996 • $25 • (5/31/1998) • **92**

Chablis Vaillons 1995 • $22 • (6/15/1997) • **73**

Chablis Vaucopin 1998: Polished, with delicate floral, smoky, flinty notes. Rather complex aromatically, but a bit diluted on the palate. Still, it's good to drink, medium-bodied and accessible. Drink now through 2001.–P.M. • $33 • (5/15/2000) • **82**

Chablis Vaucopin 1997: A classy Vaucoupin—all ripe fruit, with lemon, honey, mineral notes. Drink now through 2003.–P.M. • $29 • (5/31/1999) • **88**

Chablis Vaucopin 1996 • $25 • (5/31/1998) • **88**

Chablis Vaucopin 1995 • $21 • (6/15/1997) • **85**

Chablis Vaudésir 1997: Fairly thick in texture, this harmonious, seductive grand cru makes delightful drinking with its marzipan, ripe pear, honeyed, lemony finesse and its concentration of mineral notes on the long, balanced finish. Best from 2003 through 2009.–P.M. • $48 • (5/31/1999) • **90**

Chablis Vaudésir 1995 • $29 • (6/15/1997) • **85**

LONGUA, CHATEAU LA

Fronsac 1997: Some decent berry and green tobacco character. Medium- to light-bodied, with light tannins and a fresh finish. Drink now.–J.S. • $NA • (1/31/2000) • **82**

LORENTZ, GUSTAVE

Tokay Pinot Gris Alsace Sélection de Grains Nobles 1989 • $NA • (11/15/1990) • **86**

LORIEUX, ALAIN

Chinon 1995 • $12 • (6/15/1997) • **86**

LORNET, FREDERIC

Arbois Ploussard 1996 • $13 • (4/30/1998) • **82**

Arbois Vin de Paille 1994 • $50/375 ml. • (4/30/1998) • **75**

Brut Rosé Arbois NV • $17 • (5/15/1998) • **82**

Pinot Noir Arbois 1996 • $15 • (4/30/1998) • **78**

LOUBIERE, CHATEAU LA

Pomerol 1997: A delicate, clean and fruity claret. Medium-bodied, with light tannins and a fresh but rather diluted finish. Good Pomerol character. Drink now.–J.S. • $27 • (7/31/1999) • **83**

Pomerol 1983 • $15 • (6/16/1986) • **77**

Key: SS—Spectator Selection. CS—Cellar Selection. HR—Highly Recommended. $NA—Price not available. (BT)—Barrel tasting. Ⓐ—Auction Price. For a key to the tasters' initials, see "How to Use These Listings."
Dates in parentheses represent the issues in which the ratings were published.

LOUDENNE, CHATEAU

Bordeaux White 1998: Medium-bodied, with lovely lemon and honey character and a fresh finish. Drink now.–J.S. • $11 • (2/29/2000) • **85**

Bordeaux White 1997: Medium-bodied, with pleasant apple and lime aromas, fresh acidity and a light, fruity finish. Drink now.–J.S. • $15 • (9/30/1999) • **84**

Bordeaux White 1996: A good, clean white with apple and butterscotch aromas and flavors, a medium body and a light, fresh fruit aftertaste. Drink now.–J.S. • $11 • (3/31/1999) • **84**

Médoc 1998: Lovely fruit in this wine, with a grapey, mineral character throughout. Medium-bodied, with firm tannins and a fruity finish. Slight dilution, but very good for this château.–J.S. • $NA • (5/31/1999) (BT) • **85-89**

Médoc 1997: Shows pretty berry, plum and cedar aromas and flavors, a medium body and a light finish. Drink now through 2004.–J.S. • $15 • (1/31/2000) • **85**

Médoc 1996: Very good depth of fruit for the vintage, although slightly one-dimensional. Dark purple in color, with intense aromas of blackberry and grape. Full-bodied and thick, with a velvety tannin structure. Serious effort by Loudenne. Best after 2000.–J.S. • $19 • (1/31/1999) • **87**

Médoc 1995: Bright blackberry and plum aromas and flavors with caressing, ripe tannins. Medium body. Ripe fruit aftertaste. Not a long-ager, but delicious. Drink now.–J.S. • $18 • (9/15/1998) • **85**

Médoc 1992 • $15 • (4/15/1995) • **73**

Médoc 1991 • $12 • (3/31/1994) • **80**

Médoc 1990 • $17 • (3/31/1993) • **87**

Médoc 1989 • $13 • (3/15/1992) • **81**

Médoc 1988 • $10 • (8/31/1991) • **82**

Médoc 1987 • $10 • (11/30/1989) • **75**

Médoc 1986 • $12 • (11/30/1989) • **74**

Médoc 1985 • $14 • (11/30/1988) • **75**

Médoc 1982 • $NA • (8/31/1992) • **88**

Médoc 1981 • $11 • (9/01/1984) • **84**

LOUVIERE, CHATEAU LA

Pessac-Léognan 1999: Chewy, with aromas of herb and very ripe fruit, almost burnt. Medium-bodied, with velvety tannins and a medium finish.–J.S. • $NA • (1/01/2000) (BT) • **85-89**

Pessac-Léognan 1998: Some decent berry and cherry aromas and flavors here, with a hint of greenness. Medium-bodied, with medium tannins and a short finish.–J.S. • $NA • (5/31/1999) (BT) • **80-84**

Pessac-Léognan 1997: A delicious red with plum, berry and mineral character. Medium- to light-bodied, with light tannins and a fresh finish. Drink now.–J.S. • $24 • (1/31/2000) • **85**

Pessac-Léognan 1996: Fresh and clean, with a lovely berry and mineral character. Medium-bodied, with fine tannins and a chocolate and berry aftertaste. Delicious, but not built for long aging. Drink now.–J.S. • $14 Ⓐ • (1/31/1999) • **86**

Pessac-Léognan 1995 • $25 • (1/31/1998) • **87**

Pessac-Léognan 1994 • $36 Ⓐ • (1/31/1997) • **83**

Pessac-Léognan 1993 • $23 • (1/31/1996) • **85**

Pessac-Léognan 1992 • $20 • (4/15/1995) • **80**

Pessac-Léognan 1991 • $20 • (3/31/1994) • **79**

Pessac-Léognan 1990 • $216 Ⓐ • (3/31/1993) • **94**

Pessac-Léognan 1989: This has always been a bit tough, and I'm afraid it's not going to mellow. Still, there's an impressive ripeness. Plenty of olive, berry, tobacco and earth character. Medium- to full-bodied, with chewy tannins and a medium, slightly dry finish. (1989 Bordeaux horizontal tasting). Drink now.–J.S. • $NA • (5/31/1999) • **86**

Pessac-Léognan 1988: Always seriously good and reasonably priced, this red has plenty of chocolate, berry and spice aromas and flavors. Medium- to full-bodied, with velvety tannins and a long, ripe fruit finish. (1988 Bordeaux horizontal tasting). Drink now.–J.S. • $29 Ⓐ • (11/30/1998) • **90**

Pessac-Léognan 1986 • $30 • (6/15/1989) • **91**

Graves 1985 • $16 • (6/30/1988) • **87**

Graves 1983 • $16 • (11/30/1986) • **78**

Graves 1982: Brick red, with light chocolate and fruit aromas. Medium-bodied, with earth, berry, tobacco flavors and a fresh yet slightly dry finish. A simple, mature Graves that tasted a lot better five years ago. (1982 Bordeaux horizontal tasting). Drink now.–J.S. • $NA • (11/30/1998) • **83**

Pessac-Léognan White 1998: Good honey and lemon character, with good acidity. A bit simple yet very fresh. Drink now.–J.S. • $20 • (2/29/2000) • **88**

Pessac-Léognan White 1996: A very clean and fresh '96 white Bordeaux—although slightly simple, with not quite the normal richness for this estate.

Medium-bodied, with lemon rind and green apple aromas and flavors and a light, crisp finish. May improve with a bit of age. Drink through 2004–J.S. • $16 Ⓐ • (3/31/1999) • **86**

LOYER BASTIE, DOMAINE

Cabernet Sauvignon Vin de Pays d'Oc 1997: Herbal-tasting, with drying tannins and dried plum flavors.–K.M. • $7 • (2/29/2000) • **78**
Sauvignon Vin de Pays d'Oc 1998: Smoky-tasting, with some appealing almond and citrus flavors, though a little soft in the middle. Drink now.–K.M. • $7 • (4/30/2000) • **80**

LUDEMAN-LA-COTE, CHATEAU

Graves 1995 • $14 • (11/30/1997) • **84**

LUDON-POMIES-AGASSAC, CHATEAU

Haut-Médoc 1997: Light, simple and weedy.–J.S. • $NA • (1/31/2000) • **78**
Haut-Médoc 1996: Disjointed, with a slightly herbal and metallic character and a dilution on the finish. Medium- to light-bodied. Not much there. Second label of Château La Lagune.–J.S. • $NA • (2/28/1999) • **77**

LUGNY, CAVE DE

Mâcon-Chardonnay Chardonnay de Chardonnay Vieilles Vignes 1995 • $NA • (8/31/1996) • **81**
Mâcon-Chardonnay Pierres Blanches 1997: Odd, with a cardboard aroma, a dry finish and unattractive green, herbal, bitter tastes.–P.M. • $8 • (5/31/1999) • **70**
Mâcon-Lugny Les Charmes 1997: Earthy and tart, a bit herbal, with an asparagus taste and a bitter finish.–P.M. • $9 • (5/31/1999) • **72**
Mâcon-Lugny Les Charmes 1996 • $12 • (8/31/1997) • **80**
Mâcon-Lugny Les Charmes 1995 • $NA • (8/31/1996) • **74**
Mâcon-Villages Pierres Blanches 1996 • $11 • (8/31/1997) • **80**
Mâcon-Villages Pierres Blanches 1995 • $11 • (8/31/1996) • **70**

LUMPP, FRANCOIS

Givry White Petit Marole 1995 • $20 • (5/31/1997) • **88**

LUPE-CHOLET

Aloxe-Corton 1985 • $18 • (3/15/1988) • **84**
Beaune Les Avaux 1986 • $NA • (7/31/1988) • **89**
Bourgogne Clos de la Roche 1986 • $10 • (7/31/1988) • **78**
Bourgogne Clos de Lupé 1997: Herbal and lean, with modest fruit and a tart finish.–P.M. • $15 • (9/30/1999) • **73**
Bourgogne Comte de Lupé 1993 • $12 • (11/15/1995) • **73**
Bourgogne Comte de Lupé 1992 • $NA • (12/15/1994) • **77**
Bourgogne Comte de Lupé 1989 • $8 • (1/31/1992) • **86**
Bourgogne Comte de Lupé 1988 • $9 • (2/28/1990) • **83**
Bourgogne Comte de Lupé 1985 • $15 • (3/31/1988) • **79**
Chablis 1998: Fresh and fruity. Light- to medium-bodied, it delivers plenty of lime, green apple and kiwi flavors, with mineral character. Lacks a bit of complexity, but refreshing. Drink now through 2003.–P.M. • $17 • (5/15/2000) • **84**
Chablis Blanchot Château de Viviers 1997: Silky smooth on the midpalate but packed with vibrant acidity, this a beautiful, balanced, full-bodied Chablis, delivering mineral, herb, lemon and melon character. Best from 2003 through 2008.–P.M. • $48 • (9/30/1999) • **90**
Chablis Blanchot Château de Viviers 1996 • $44 • (5/31/1998) • **93**
Chablis Château de Viviers 1998: Rather supple, with delicious fruit, this is easy to appreciate. Medium-bodied, with little depth or complexity, it delivers chewy character on the finish. Drink now through 2003.–P.M. • $19 • (5/15/2000) • **85**
Chablis Château de Viviers 1997: Fairly neutral but clean, this lean Chablis has a straight-as-an-arrow personality. Ripe, with lemon and apple notes on the steely finish. Drink now.–P.M. • $20 • (9/30/1999) • **87**
Chablis Château de Viviers 1996 • $18 • (5/31/1998) • **92**
Chablis Château de Viviers 1995 • $NA • (8/31/1996) • **80**
Chablis Vaillons Château de Viviers 1998: This full-bodied '98 has lovely balance despite a slight dilution midpalate. Charming and seductive, offering layers of ripe fruit and an oily texture rarely found in this vintage. Tastes of pineapple, pear pie and wet earth. The creamy finish is laced with lime juice. Drink now through 2004.–P.M. • $35 • (5/15/2000) • **88**
Chablis Vaillons Château de Viviers 1997: Pure and superlovely. Ripe, fruity and well made, this clean Chablis has polish and elegance, as the apple, tropical, spice and wet earth keep coming on the lingering finish. Drink now through 2005.–P.M. • $34 • (9/30/1999) • **91**
Chablis Vaillons Château de Viviers 1996 • $26 • (5/31/1998) • **93**
Chablis Vaucoupin Château de Viviers 1998: Pretty in a round, supple, easy way. Medium-bodied, with toasted, smoky, cedary character, offering lime, ripe pear and tobacco box notes. Chewy finish has astringent wood tannins. Drink now through 2003.–P.M. • $34 • (5/15/2000) • **84**
Chablis Vaucoupin Château de Viviers 1997: Up-front supple, ripe fruit and honey notes make this medium-bodied charmer a "pick-me-up" candidate. Nothing showy, just sweet-tasting harmony from start to finish. Drink now through 2002.–P.M. • $32 • (9/30/1999) • **89**
Chablis Vaucoupin Château de Viviers 1996 • $25 • (5/31/1998) • **92**
Chambolle-Musigny 1992 • $NA • (12/15/1994) • **83**
Chambolle-Musigny 1986 • $20 • (7/31/1988) • **81**
Chassagne-Montrachet Red Morgeot 1997: Diluted, with meager fruit, a weedy character and a dry finish.–P.M. • $33 • (9/30/1999) • **76**
Côte de Nuits-Villages 1997: Cherry and herb aromas and flavors combine with a mineral and iron component, moderate concentration and a solid structure.–B.S. • $22 • (9/30/1999) • **78**
Côte de Nuits-Villages 1992 • $NA • (12/15/1994) • **79**
Echézeaux 1997: A bit gamy, with a matured mushroom and forest underbrush character. Tannins melt like butter, giving way to a soft finish.–P.M. • $80 • (9/30/1999) • **77**
Gevrey-Chambertin 1997: Herbal and unripe, not only in aromas and flavors but in tannins.–B.S. • $36 • (9/30/1999) • **76**
Gevrey-Chambertin 1994 • $17 • (11/15/1996) • **74**
Hautes-Côtes de Beaune 1987 • $10 • (4/15/1990) • **78**
Maranges 1997: Rustic, evoking dried cherry, plum and earth, with a modest intensity that carries through to the finish. Firm tannins uphold the mix. Drink now through 2003.–B.S. • $20 • (9/30/1999) • **82**
Nuits-St.-Georges Château Gris 1997: Already a bit mature but pleasant, with a warm-weather, ripe fruit (prune, plum) character. Soft and easy on the finish. Drink now through 2002.–P.M. • $60 • (1/01/2000) • **83**
Nuits-St.-Georges Château Gris 1992 • $NA • (12/15/1994) • **78**
Nuits-St.-Georges Château Gris 1987 • $38 • (3/31/1990) • **84**
Nuits-St.-Georges Château Gris 1986 • $33 • (7/31/1988) • **86**
Nuits-St.-Georges Château Gris 1985 • $39 • (2/15/1988) • **88**
Nuits-St.-Georges Château Gris 1983 • $24 • (6/16/1986) • **77**
Nuits-St.-Georges Château Gris Premier Cru 1994 • $25 • (11/15/1996) • **72**
Nuits-St.-Georges Château Gris Premier Cru 1993 • $35 • (11/15/1995) • **82**
Nuits-St.-Georges Les Vignerondes Hospices de Nuits 1986 • $NA • (7/31/1988) • **91**
Pommard Les Boucherottes 1983 • $19 • (6/16/1986) • **86**
Santenay Clos Rousseau 1997: Tastes fairly ripe, with mineral and wet earth notes leading the way to a refreshingly firm backbone of tannin. Turns rustic on the finish. Drink now through 2006.–P.M. • $24 • (9/30/1999) • **80**
Savigny-lès-Beaune Aux Serpentières 1994 • $16 • (11/15/1996) • **80**
Savigny-lès-Beaune Aux Serpentières 1985 • $17 • (3/15/1988) • **83**
Volnay 1986 • $NA • (7/31/1988) • **91**

LUQUET, ROGER

Mâcon Clos de Condemine 1997: Odd. This tart, lean white seems a bit hot despite all the simplistic citrus flavors. Short finish.–P.M. • $NA • (5/31/1999) • **71**
Mâcon Clos de Condemine 1996 • $11 • (5/31/1998) • **86**
Mâcon Clos de Condemine 1995 • $NA • (8/31/1996) • **73**
Mâcon-Villages Les Mulots 1997: Strange and a bit diluted, displaying tart, earthy, spicy, tea leaf notes that lack charm. Short, slightly hot finish.–P.M. • $NA • (5/31/1999) • **71**
Pouilly-Fuissé 1996 • $19 • (5/31/1998) • **80**
Pouilly-Fuissé Vieilles Vignes 1997: Tart style, showing a bitter component, along with some odd wet cardboard, cedar, herbal and stemmy notes.–P.M. • $NA • (5/31/1999) • **73**
St.-Véran 1996 • $12 • (5/31/1998) • **83**
St.-Véran 1995 • $NA • (8/31/1996) • **82**
St.-Véran Vieilles Vignes 1997: Crisp St-Véran, combining wet hay, cedar and crisp apple notes in a tight, light-bodied and rather ungenerous package.–P.M. • $NA • (5/31/1999) • **78**

LURTON, J. & F.

Merlot Bordeaux 1996 • $7 • (11/30/1997) • **78**
Merlot Bordeaux 1995 • $8 • (10/15/1997) • **79**
Sauvignon Blanc Bordeaux 1996 • $7 • (11/15/1997) • **83**
Cabernet Sauvignon-Merlot Vin de Pays d'Oc Villa Garros 1996: A firm and mature-tasting red, with good dried cherry and roasted pepper flavors, currant notes on the finish. Drink now.–K.M. • $13 • (2/29/2000) • **84**
Chardonnay Vin de Pays d'Oc 1996 • $7 • (9/15/1997) • **81**
Chardonnay Vin de Pays d'Oc Domaine des Salices Réserve 1996: Very mature, with floral aromas and waxy flavors that fall limp on the nearly acidless finish.–K.M. • $10 • (4/30/2000) • **76**
Chardonnay Vin de Pays d'Oc Les Salices Elevé en fûts de chêne 1998: Has a lot of toasty and spicy flavors, with ripe pear notes and a short finish. Drink now.–K.M. • $8 • (4/30/2000) • **82**
Chardonnay-Terret Vin de Pays d'Oc Les Bateaux 1998: Soft pear and baked apple flavors end on a slightly spicy note in this somewhat dilute white. Drink now.–K.M. • $6 • (4/30/2000) • **80**
Corbières Château Merville 1997: Nicely concentrated, with a good combination of savory herb, dried cherry and mineral flavors. Brickish and leathery notes linger on the finish. Drink now.–K.M. • $12 • (1/31/2000) • **86**
Grenache Vin de Pays d'Oc Domaine de Bachellery 1995 • $6 • (10/31/1997) • **86**
Merlot Vin de Pays d'Oc 1996 • $7 • (11/15/1997) • **83**
Merlot Vin de Pays d'Oc Domaine des Salices 1996: Flavorful, mellow, rich and satisfying. Cedar and cinnamon accents lend complexity to the warm cherry and plum flavors. Medium-bodied, light in tannin. Drink now. • $7 • (7/31/1998) • **86**
Merlot Vin de Pays d'Oc Les Bateaux 1998: A good quaffer, with lively red plum, berry and pepper flavors, which linger on the finish, with some tobaccolike notes. Delicious. Drink now.–K.M. • $6 • (2/29/2000) • **84**
Merlot Vin de Pays d'Oc Les Salices Vieilli en fûts de chêne 1997: Simple, with some berry and rhubarb flavors, and some stewed spice notes on the finish.–K.M. • $8 • (2/29/2000) • **79**
Minervois Château La Plaine St.-Pierre 1997: Focused and plummy, with plenty of minerally notes and dried herb flavors on the finish. A clean, vibrant red. Drink now.–K.M. • $10 • (1/31/2000) • **85**
Pinot Noir Vin de Pays d'Oc Domaine d'Antugnac 1996 • $8 • (10/31/1997) • **79**
Pinot Noir Vin de Pays d'Oc Les Salices Vieilli en fûts de chêne 1998: Dried cherry and smoky flavors dominate this medium-bodied red. Drink now.–.M. • $8 • (2/29/2000) • **81**
Pinot Noir Vin de Pays d'Oc Les Salices Vieilli en fûts de chêne 1997: A bit stemmy and weedy tasting, with only modest dried cherry flavors.–K.M. • $8 • (3/31/2000) • **78**
Sauvignon Blanc Vin de Pays d'Oc Domaine des Salices 1996 • $7 • (11/15/1997) • **80**
Sauvignon Blanc Vin de Pays d'Oc Les Fumées Blanches 1998: Ripe, with some interesting licorice, melon and spice flavors, which linger on the finish. Drink now.–K.M. • $7 • (4/30/2000) • **83**
Sauvignon Blanc Vin de Pays d'Oc Les Fumées Blanches 1996 • $6 • (12/31/1997) • **85**
Sauvignon Blanc Vin de Pays d'Oc Les Salices Elevé en fûts de chêne 1998: Crisp and fairly juicy, with green apple and citrus flavors, and a touch of gooseberry as well. Refreshing. Drink now.–K.M. • $8 • (4/30/2000) • **82**
Syrah Vin de Pays d'Oc des Rives de l'Argent Double 1995 • $10 • (12/15/1997) • **73**
Syrah Vin de Pays d'Oc Domaine de Serame 1995 • $7 • (12/15/1997) • **84**
Syrah Vin de Pays d'Oc Domaine des Salices 1996: A luscious and well-concentrated red, with a beautifully ripe, red fruit aroma and rich flavors of plum, berry and raspberry. There's plenty of stuffing as well, and a nice lively acidity. Finishes with notes of chocolate and spice. Drink now through 2002.–K.M. • $7 • (7/31/1998) • **87**
Syrah Vin de Pays d'Oc Domaine des Salices Réserve 1997: This has modest dried cherry flavors and minerally notes. Turns tough on the finish.–K.M. • $10 • (1/31/2000) • **79**
Syrah Vin de Pays d'Oc Domaine des Salices Vieilli en fûts de chêne 1997: A straightforward red, with plum and cherry flavors and leathery notes on the finish. Drink now.–K.M. • $8 • (1/31/2000) • **82**
Syrah Vin de Pays d'Oc Les Bateaux 1998: A delicious and sinewy Syrah, with loads of red plum, berry and red cherry flavors overlaid with beautifully articulated game and leather notes. There's plenty of backbone and flavor. Drink now.–K.M. • $6 • (2/29/2000) • **87**
Vin de Pays d'Oc Domaine de Bachellery 1994 • $6 • (12/15/1997) • **87**
Viognier Vin de Pays d'Oc Domaine des Salices 1996 • $10 • (10/31/1997) • **84**

LUSSEAU, CHATEAU

St.-Emilion 1997: A light-bodied red with berry and vanilla character. Short, slightly weedy finish.–J.S. • $NA • (1/31/2000) • **79**
St.-Emilion 1995 • $24 • (1/31/1998) • **86**

LYNCH, MICHEL

Bordeaux 1993 • $10 • (1/31/1996) • **76**
Bordeaux 1988 • $8 • (10/31/1991) • **76**
Cabernet Sauvignon Bordeaux 1997: Light-bodied, with straightforward cherry aromas and flavors followed by a modest finish. Drink now.–B.S. • $9 • (10/15/1998) • **80**
Merlot Bordeaux 1996: Good depth of fruit, with black cherry, spice and cedar aromas followed by rich, mouthfilling cherry flavors. Falls off a little on the finish, though, and the light tannins are slightly astringent. Tasted twice, with consistent notes.–B.S. • $9 • (10/15/1998) • **81**
Merlot Bordeaux 1995 • $9 • (10/15/1997) • **83**
Sauvignon Blanc Bordeaux 1997: A soft, easy-drinking white, with just a hint of grapefruit and grass flavors. Tasted twice, with consistent notes.–B.S. • $9 • (10/15/1998) • **79**
Sauvignon Blanc Bordeaux 1996 • $9 • (9/30/1997) • **89**

LYNCH-BAGES, BLANC DE

Bordeaux 1998: A bit odd for a Lynch white, with mineral and apple character, but slightly subdued. Medium-bodied, with a fresh finish. Tasted twice, with consistent notes. Drink now.–J.S. • $38 • (2/29/2000) • **85-89**
Bordeaux 1997: A dry white, with lovely honey, apple and light cedar character. Medium- to full-bodied, with flavors that build on the slightly hollow center palate. Long finish of lime and honey. Drink now.–J.S. • $35 • (9/30/1999) • **88**

LYNCH-BAGES, CHATEAU

Pauillac 1999: A fresh and aromatic '99 with floral, cherry and currant. Medium-bodied, with fine tannins and a medium-long silky finish. Very pretty.–J.S. • $NA • (1/01/2000) (BT) • **85-89**
Pauillac 1998: Crushed black currants in this wine. Full-bodied, with chewy tannins and a long finish. Solid '98 for Médoc. Surprisingly well done given the difficulty of the vintage. Almost outstanding.–J.S. • $NA • (5/31/1999) (BT) • **85-89**
Pauillac 1997: Pretty plum and raspberry aromas in this young Lynch. Medium- to light-bodied, with fine tannins and a fresh finish. Drink now through 2004.–J.S. • $50 • (1/31/2000) • **87**
Pauillac 1996: Deep, dark ruby with intense aromas of mint, berries and currants. Full-bodied, with velvety tannins and a delicious ripe fruit and lead-pencil aftertaste. Very fine indeed. Typically outstanding for Lynch-Bages. Best after 2005.–J.S. • $52 Ⓐ • (1/31/1999) • **92**
Pauillac 1995 • $54 Ⓐ • (1/31/1998) • **94**
Pauillac 1994 • $34 Ⓐ • (1/31/1997) • **89**
Pauillac 1993 • $31 Ⓐ • (1/31/1996) • **87**
Pauillac 1992 • $28 Ⓐ • (4/15/1995) • **81**
Pauillac 1991 • $25 • (3/31/1994) • **86**
Pauillac 1990 • $109 Ⓐ • (3/31/1993) • **94**
Pauillac 1989: Perhaps the greatest Lynch-Bages ever produced. Dark-ruby in color, offering plenty of blackberry, mint and spice aromas and flavors. Full-bodied, with masses of velvety tannins and a superlong, fruity finish. Yet it's only giving half of what it's got; give it time.—1989 Bordeaux horizontal. Best after 2007.–J.S. • $132 Ⓐ • (5/31/1999) • **98**
Pauillac 1988: A marvelous bottle of Lynch—better than the 1990 and just a notch below the 1989 in quality. Wondrous aromas of mint, berry and black currant follow through to the palate. Full-bodied, with supervelvety tannins and a long, long finish. Beautiful.—1988 Bordeaux horizontal. Best after 2003.–J.S. • $76 Ⓐ • (11/30/1998) • **97**
Pauillac 1987 • $47 Ⓐ • (2/15/1990) • **86**
Pauillac 1986 • $101 Ⓐ • (10/31/1989) • **94**
Pauillac 1985 • $120 Ⓐ • (10/15/1994) • **97**
Pauillac 1984 • $27 • (10/31/1989) • **87**
Pauillac 1983 • $68 Ⓐ • (10/15/1994) • **90**

Key: SS—Spectator Selection. CS—Cellar Selection. HR—Highly Recommended. $NA—Price not available. (BT)—Barrel tasting. Ⓐ—Auction Price.
For a key to the tasters' initials, see "How to Use These Listings."
Dates in parentheses represent the issues in which the ratings were published.

FRANCE

Pauillac 1982: Extremely youthful ruby color, with a hint of garnet. Berry, currant and mint character, with an earth note. Full-bodied, extremely concentrated yet sweet and fruity, with fine tannins and a long, long finish. Inspirational; never considered classic by many people but it's very great indeed. (1982 Bordeaux horizontal tasting). Best after 2004.—J.S. • $138 Ⓐ • (11/30/1998) • **96**
Pauillac 1981 • $58 Ⓐ • (10/15/1994) • **90**
Pauillac 1980 • $29 Ⓐ • (10/31/1989) • **88**
Pauillac 1979 • $51 Ⓐ • (10/15/1989) • **91**
Pauillac 1978 • $52 Ⓐ • (10/31/1989) • **92**
Pauillac 1977 • $25 • (10/31/1989) • **78**
Pauillac 1976 • $47 Ⓐ • (10/31/1989) • **70**
Pauillac 1975 • $54 Ⓐ • (10/31/1989) • **90**
Pauillac 1973 • $NA • (10/31/1989) • **82**
Pauillac 1970 • $141 Ⓐ • (10/31/1989) • **90**
Pauillac 1967 • $NA • (10/31/1989) • **79**
Pauillac 1966 • $94 Ⓐ • (10/31/1989) • **90**
Pauillac 1964 • $42 Ⓐ • (10/31/1989) • **76**
Pauillac 1961 • $260 Ⓐ • (4/30/1996) • **88**
Pauillac 1960 • $55 • (10/31/1989) • **76**
Pauillac 1959 • $161 Ⓐ • (10/15/1990) • **95**
Pauillac 1958 • $60 • (10/31/1989) • **79**
Pauillac 1957 • $115 Ⓐ • (10/31/1989) • **88**
Pauillac 1955 • $250 • (10/31/1989) • **92**
Pauillac 1954 • $75 • (10/31/1989) • **74**
Pauillac 1953 • $NA • (10/31/1989) • **77**
Pauillac 1952 • $140 • (10/31/1989) • **83**
Pauillac 1949 • $175 • (10/31/1989) • **84**
Pauillac 1947 • $350 • (10/31/1989) • **90**
Pauillac 1945 • $500 • (11/30/1995) • **85**
Pauillac Danish Bottled 1945 • $250 • (10/31/1989) • **80**

LYNCH-MOUSSAS, CHATEAU

Pauillac 1998: Good berry, chocolate and toasted oak character. Medium-bodied, slightly hollow at the center, but with ripe tannins. Plenty of sweet fruit.–J.S. • $NA • (5/31/1999) (BT) • **85-89**
Pauillac 1997: Well done for this estate. Blackberry, mineral and cherry aromas follow through to a medium-bodied palate, with silky tannins and a lovely fruit finish. Drink now through 2005.–J.S. • $18 • (1/31/2000) • **86**
Pauillac 1995 • $22 • (1/31/1998) • **87**
Pauillac 1991 • $16 • (3/31/1994) • **73**
Pauillac 1990 • $20 • (3/31/1993) • **87**
Pauillac 1989: Pretty, and enjoyable now. Good dark-ruby color. Plum and berry aromas have cassis and floral undertones. Medium- to full-bodied, with soft tannins and a long, fresh and fruity finish. (1989 Bordeaux horizontal tasting).–J.S. • $NA • (5/31/1999) • **89**
Pauillac 1988 • $25 • (8/31/1991) • **85**
Pauillac 1986 • $18 • (6/30/1989) • **86**
Pauillac 1982 • $24 Ⓐ • (8/31/1992) • **81**
Pauillac 1961 • $21 • (4/30/1996) • **84**
Pauillac 1959 • $115 • (10/15/1990) • **86**

LYONNAT, CHATEAU

Lussac-St.-Emilion 1995 • $15 • (1/01/1998) • **81**

MACHARD DE GRAMONT

Aloxe-Corton Les Morais 1985 • $34 • (7/15/1988) • **80**
Beaune Aux Coucherias 1993 • $28 • (9/15/1996) • **84**
Beaune Les Chouacheux 1993 • $28 • (9/15/1996) • **85**
Beaune Les Chouacheux 1985 • $34 • (5/31/1988) • **89**
Beaune Les Epenotes 1993 • $28 • (9/15/1996) • **82**
Bourgogne Domaine de la Vierge Romaine 1985 • $13 • (6/30/1988) • **81**
Chorey-lès-Beaune Les Beaumonts 1993 • $18 • (9/15/1996) • **79**
Chorey-lès-Beaune Les Beaumonts 1985 • $22 • (7/31/1988) • **84**
Nuits-St.-Georges Aux Allots 1987 • $30 • (7/15/1990) • **82**
Nuits-St.-Georges Aux Allots 1985 • $35 • (5/31/1988) • **86**
Nuits-St.-Georges en la Perrière Noblot 1985 • $41 • (5/31/1988) • **89**
Nuits-St.-Georges Les Damodes 1990 • $48 • (5/31/1995) • **89**
Nuits-St.-Georges Les Hauts Poirets 1993 • $34 • (9/15/1996) • **89**
Nuits-St.-Georges Les Hauts Pruliers 1993 • $34 • (9/15/1996) • **87**
Nuits-St.-Georges Les Poirets 1985 • $41 • (6/15/1988) • **84**
Nuits-St.-Georges Les Pruliers 1988 • $37 • (7/15/1991) • **88**
Nuits-St.-Georges Les Pruliers 1987 • $32 • (4/30/1990) • **85**
Nuits-St.-Georges Les Pruliers 1986 • $22 • (12/15/1989) • **77**
Nuits-St.-Georges Les Pruliers 1985 • $36 • (2/15/1988) • **90**
Nuits-St.-Georges Les Vallerots 1985 • $47 • (5/31/1988) • **78**
Pommard Clos Blanc 1993 • $40 • (9/15/1996) • **85**
Savigny-lès-Beaune Aux Guettes 1993 • $25 • (9/15/1996) • **82**
Savigny-lès-Beaune Aux Guettes 1985 • $25 • (7/31/1988) • **89**
Vosne-Romanée Les Réas 1988 • $32 • (7/15/1991) • **89**

MADELEINE, DOMAINE DE LA

Carignane Vin de Pays de l'Hérault 1998: A lively, medium-bodied red from the south of France, loaded with red plum and blackberry flavors, with a touch of leather on the finish. Drink now.–K.M. • $11 • (8/31/1999) • **86**
Pinot Noir Vin de Pays d'Oc 1998: A basic Pinot Noir, medium-bodied, moderately fruity and just slightly tannic. • $11 • (8/31/1999) • **78**
Vin de Pays d'Oc Cuvée M.C. 1998: Supple and juicy, with berry, currant and cherry flavors. Reminiscent of Beaujolais, this red goes down easy. Drink now.–K.M. • $8 • (8/31/1999) • **84**

MAGDELAINE, CHATEAU

St.-Emilion 1999: Subtle, fine wine. Floral, berry and cherry aromas. Medium-bodied, with well-integrated tannins and a medium finish.–J.S. • $NA • (1/01/2000) (BT) • **988**
St.-Emilion 1998: Wonderful aromas of blackberries and earth, with serious intensity. Full-bodied and velvety, with a lovely, caressing texture and a long finish. Very fine indeed.–J.S. • $NA • (5/31/1999) (BT) • **90-94**
St.-Emilion 1997: Lovely plum and berry aromas. Medium-bodied, with polished tannins and a slightly diluted finish. Drink now through 2001.–J.S. • $NA • (1/31/2000) • **85**
St.-Emilion 1996: Raspberry and strawberry on the nose and palate. Medium- to light-bodied, with a slightly diluted midpalate and a light, silky finish. Drink now.–J.S. • $37 Ⓐ • (1/31/1999) • **85**
St.-Emilion 1995 • $43 Ⓐ • (1/31/1998) • **91**
St.-Emilion 1994 • $25 Ⓐ • (1/31/1997) • **90**
St.-Emilion 1993 • $36 • (1/31/1996) • **85**
St.-Emilion 1992 • $32 • (4/15/1995) • **80**
St.-Emilion 1990 • $144 Ⓐ • (3/31/1993) • **90**
St.-Emilion 1989: Gorgeous, joyful wine. Dark-ruby color. Beautiful aromas of strawberries, raspberries and spices. Full-bodied and very velvety, with lovely texture and a long, berry-vanilla aftertaste. (1989 Bordeaux horizontal tasting). Best after 2004.–J.S. • $65 Ⓐ • (5/31/1999) • **91**
St.-Emilion 1988: Medium-bodied, with pretty tobacco, spice and berry aromas and flavors, fine tannins and a caressing texture on the finish. Ready to drink. (1988 Bordeaux horizontal tasting).–J.S. • $42 Ⓐ • (11/30/1998) • **87**
St.-Emilion 1986 • $29 Ⓐ • (2/15/1990) • **94**
St.-Emilion 1982: This has always been a gorgeous, sexy wine. Dark ruby-colored, with a slight garnet rim. Full-bodied, with loads of sweet fruit flavors and a lovely, long aftertaste of fresh fruit, floral, earth character. (1982 Bordeaux horizontal tasting). Drink now.–J.S. • $87 Ⓐ • (11/30/1998) • **96**
St.-Emilion 1979 • $30 Ⓐ • (10/15/1989) • **89**
St.-Emilion 1970 • $80 Ⓐ • (5/15/1993) • **92**
St.-Emilion 1961 • $368 Ⓐ • (4/30/1996) • **90**
St.-Emilion 1959 • $150 • (10/15/1990) • **89**
St.-Emilion 1947 • $NA • (5/31/1997) • **87**
St.-Emilion 1945 • $250 • (11/30/1995) • **76**

MAGE, DOMAINE DU

Merlot-Tannat Vin de Pays des Côtes de Gascogne 1997: This medium-bodied red is vibrant and nicely fruity, with focused flavors of red plum, cherry and currant, and a nice herbal. Perfect for hearty food, with well-defined acidity. Drink now.–K.M. • $7 • (12/31/1998) • **87**
Merlot-Tannat Vin de Pays des Côtes de Gascogne 1996 • $7 • (11/15/1997) • **83**
Ugni Blanc-Colombard Vin de Pays des Côtes de Gascogne 1997: An earthy aroma combined with flavors of apple, orange peel and herb gives this wine punch. Turns slightly tart on the finish, with a distinctive oniony note. Drink now.–K.M. • $7 • (12/31/1998) • **84**
Ugni Blanc-Colombard Vin de Pays des Côtes de Gascogne 1996 • $7 • (10/31/1997) • **85**

MAGNOL, CHATEAU

Haut-Médoc 1997: Light and fruity but rather diluted, with berry and mint character.–J.S. • $24 • (6/15/2000) • **79**
Haut-Médoc 1993 • $19 • (4/30/1997) • **84**

MAILLARD PERE & FILS

Aloxe-Corton 1997: Light-bodied, showing herb and cherry notes that dissipate quickly.–B.S. • $33 • (9/30/1999) • **78**

Aloxe-Corton 1996: There are sappy cherry and earth aromas and flavors, and even a gamy note in this round, fleshy '96, with modest tannins and a slightly hot finish. Straightforward and enjoyable. Drink now through 2004.–B.S. • $30 • (9/30/1998) • **86**

Aloxe-Corton Les Grandes Lolières 1996: Harmonious Pinot. Smells like cherries, forest undergrowth and spices, turning to freshly crushed berries on the palate, with a texture of silk. Balanced, with ripe tannins. Delightful. Drink through 2004.–B.S. • $34 • (9/30/1998) • **88**

Beaune 1997: Quite crisp and a bit herbal, but underneath is a pure, ripe velvet-fruit. Appealing balance and a long, delicious finish. Drink now through 2003.–P.M. • $27 • (9/30/1999) • **85**

Beaune 1996: Refined Pinot Noir. Good *terroir*, with nice ripe berry character to give it opulence. Medium-bodied, sweet-tasting, with lovely plum and subtle oak accents, harmonious finish. Drink now through 2005.–P.M. • $23 • (9/30/1998) • **87**

Chorey-lès-Beaune 1996: Deep red fruit flavors and spice, along with a vanilla note that's totally seductive, make this delicious to drink now. Has soft, ripe tannins and a lingering finish. Drink now through 2002.–B.S. • $20 • (9/30/1998) • **87**

Chorey-lès-Beaune White 1997: Just terrific. A flinty, smoky, earthy, full-bodied wine that revels in *goût de terroir*. Seductive to taste, with a silky texture and clean, polished, minerally flavors. Drink now through 2005.–P.M. • $22 • (5/31/1999) • **93**

Corton-Charlemagne 1995 • $50 • (5/31/1997) • **87**

Corton Renardes 1997: Rich and ripe, showing a supple midpalate and pretty plum and black fruit flavors. Full-bodied, it tastes a bit heavy on the slightly hot finish. Drink now through 2003.–P.M. • $56 • (9/30/1999) • **84**

Corton Renardes 1996: Gorgeous fruit. Black raspberries, cherries and spice comingle in this elegant, silky '96. Everything is there in the right proportions, including ripe, fine tannins and a lingering finish. Very forward and accessible. Drink through 2006–B.S. • $55 • (9/30/1998) • **90**

Corton White 1998: Opulent and soft, thick-textured, offering a honey, tropical and chalky character. Very lovely wine, with some subtle toasted oak notes on the finish. Pleasant on release, but will improve with cellaring. Best from 2003 through 2008.–P.M. • $63 • (5/31/2000) • **90**

Corton White 1997: A certain polish exists in this medium-bodied white, with toasted oak, mineral and butter notes of medium intensity. A bit tart on the finish. Drink now through 2003.–P.M. • $63 • (5/31/1999) • **80**

Corton White 1996: Wonderful at first, but turns a bit rustic after a few hours contact with air. Thick, ripe and rich, it has grand cru etched all over it thanks to a distinctive, earthy, mineral-laden, silky smooth, oily style. Full-bodied and elegant, it's deeply satisfying as it allows the fruit and earth (not fancy oak) to hold center stage. Seductive finish. Tempting upon release, but cellar short-term. Drink now through 2005.–P.M. • $50 • (8/31/1998) • **90**

Pommard La Chanière 1997: This elegant, structured Pommard has aromas of cherry, earth and herb. Drink now.–B.S. • $34 • (9/30/1999) • **84**

Savigny-lès-Beaune 1997: This chewy, licorice- and cherry-flavored red is a bit hollow, yet attractive and ready to enjoy. Drink now through 2001.–B.S. • $23 • (9/30/1999) • **80**

Savigny-lès-Beaune 1996: Clean, crisp and pure, showing some wet earth, cassis and red berry character. Of medium body, it turns quite supple with some aeration. Zesty and fresh; serve at room temperature. Drink now through 2003.–P.M. • $23 • (9/30/1998) • **85**

MAINE GAZIN, CHATEAU

Premières Côtes de Blaye Livenne 1995: Very plummy character. Medium-bodied, with medium, velvety tannins and a silky, fruity finish. Delicious now, even better with time. Drink through 2003.–J.S. • $NA • (9/15/1998) • **88**

Key: SS—Spectator Selection. CS—Cellar Selection. HR—Highly Recommended. $NA—Price not available. (BT)—Barrel tasting. (A)—Auction Price.
For a key to the tasters' initials, see "How to Use These Listings."
Dates in parentheses represent the issues in which the ratings were published.

MALAGAR, CHATEAU

Bordeaux White 1998: A solid white, with apple, pineapple skin and light vanilla character. Medium-bodied, with firm acidity and a fruity finish. Drink now.–J.S. • $NA • (2/29/2000) • **86**
Premières Côtes de Bordeaux 1997: Very light and weedy. Light body. Light fruit.–J.S. • $NA • (1/31/2000) • **78**
Premières Côtes de Bordeaux 1994 • $14 • (1/31/1997) • **70**
Premières Côtes de Bordeaux 1992 • $NA • (4/15/1995) • **78**

MALAIRE, CHATEAU

Médoc 1998: A bit diluted, with some berry and herb character. Medium- to light-bodied, with a slightly metallic finish. It may be better next year.–J.S. • $NA • (5/31/1999) (BT) • **75-79**
Médoc 1997: This is light and herbal, with a very light finish.–J.S. • $NA • (1/31/2000) • **78**
Médoc 1996: A rather mean and diluted wine with herbal and metallic character. Medium-bodied, with medium tannins and a rather watery finish. Hard to like.–J.S. • $17 • (1/31/1999) • **74**
Médoc 1995 • $15 • (1/31/1998) • **79**
Médoc 1993 • $13 • (4/30/1997) • **83**

MALANDES, DOMAINE DES

Chablis 1998: Delicate and pleasant, even exotic, offering a tropical, floral, dried apricot character as if it's very ripe. Expressive and medium-bodied, with a crisp finish. Drink now through 2001.–P.M. • $12 • (5/15/2000) • **85**
Chablis 1997: Clean but a bit lean, better on the nose than on the palate, which is dry and astringent.–P.M. • $14 • (5/31/1999) • **78**
Chablis 1996 • $NA • (8/31/1997) • **86**
Chablis Côte de Léchet 1998: Rather ripe for a '98 Chablis. Medium-bodied and supple, with ripe fruit, honey, spice and chalk character. Complex smoky notes on the lingering finish. Drink now through 2002.–P.M. • $17 • (5/15/2000) • **86**
Chablis Côte de Léchet 1997: Straightforward, tart, showing great intensity but also a slight cardboardy character. Bitter finish, with green apple skin as the dominant character.–P.M. • $25 • (5/31/1999) • **75**
Chablis Côte de Léchet 1996 • $17 • (5/31/1998) • **94**
Chablis Côte de Léchet 1995 • $20 • (6/15/1997) • **85**
Chablis Les Clos 1996: Wet earth and tropical green apple notes combine in this full-bodied wine to produce a fruity, ripe package with a good velvety feel and distinctive personality. Best from 2002 through 2005.–P.M. • $39 • (5/31/1999) • **88**
Chablis Montmain Vieilles Vignes 1997: Surprisingly tough and uncompromising for a '97, this tastes young and reduced (like ice-box aromas), but it has good minerally concentration on the palate and a creamy finish that slowly reveals the wine's impressive underlying ripeness. Cellar. Best from 2003 through 2010.–P.M. • $27 • (5/31/1999) • **88**
Chablis Vaudésir 1998: Ripe-tasting, showing good fruit and floral, cooked pear and apple aromas. Not complex, with smoke and butter. A bit hot on the finish. Drink now through 2003.–P.M. • $33 • (5/15/2000) • **83**
Chablis Vaudevey 1997: Straightforward, in a flinty style, expect little generosity here as its apple and lemon notes dominate this crisp, light-bodied Chablis. Drink now.–P.M. • $25 • (5/31/1999) • **81**
Petit Chablis 1996 • $NA • (8/31/1997) • **87**

MALARTIC-LAGRAVIERE, CHATEAU

Pessac-Léognan 1999: Fine and polished, with plenty of berry, cherry and plum character. Medium-bodied, with very fine tannins and a long finish. Balanced. Almost outstanding.–J.S. • $NA • (1/01/2000) (BT) • **85-89**
Pessac-Léognan 1998: A firm wine, with a good backbone of tannins. Medium-bodied, with berry and green tobacco flavors and a medium finish. Needs a bit more ripe fruit to score outstanding.–J.S. • $NA • (5/31/1999) (BT) • **85-89**
Pessac-Léognan 1997: Very good for the vintage. Deep ruby color. Fabulous aromas of berries, spices and tobacco. Full-bodied, with well-defined, soft and succulent tannins and a medium finish. Bit hollow at center palate.–J.S. • $50 • (1/31/2000) • **88**
Pessac-Léognan 1996: Dark in color, with a pretty, ripe berry, raspberry and mineral aroma. Medium- to full-bodied, with well-integrated, silky tannins and a fruity, fresh aftertaste. One of the best wines of its appellation; a serious effort from this overlooked estate. Best after 2001.–J.S. • $21 • (1/31/1999) • **89**

FRANCE

Pessac-Léognan 1995 • $25 • (1/31/1998) • **88**

Pessac-Léognan 1994 • $25 • (1/31/1997) • **81**

Pessac-Léognan 1993 • $25 • (1/31/1996) • **83**

Pessac-Léognan 1989: A beautifully autumnal wine of game, earth and berry aromas and flavors. Full-bodied, with soft tannins, it caresses the palate and gives plenty of ripe fruit on the finish. I like it. (1989 Bordeaux horizontal tasting). Best after 2002.–J.S. • $NA • (5/31/1999) • **90**

Pessac-Léognan 1988 • $32 • (7/15/1991) • **84**

Pessac-Léognan 1986 • $18 • (6/15/1989) • **90**

Pessac-Léognan White 1998: Clean and fresh, with apple, lemon and vanilla aromas and flavors. Medium-bodied, with good acidity and a fruity finish. Drink now.–J.S. • $28 • (2/29/2000) • **87**

Pessac-Léognan White 1997: A complex white, with apple, pear, vanilla and mineral character. Medium- to full-bodied, with good acidity and a chalky apple finish. Slightly rustic on the finish. Not imported into the U.S. Drink now through 2005.–J.S. • $NA • (1/01/1999) • **87**

Pessac-Léognan White 1996: Very well made. Aromas of apple, lemon, passion fruit and vanilla follow through on the palate. Medium- to full-bodied, with fresh acidity and a lively, focused aftertaste. Slightly diluted midpalate. Not imported into the U.S. Drink now.–J.S. • $NA • (1/01/1999) • **87**

Graves 1982: Tasted from magnum. A delicious, drink-me wine. Dark red, with an amber edge. Ripe fruit aromas, with truffle, meat and earth. Full-bodied, with soft, velvety tannins and a berry, tobacco aftertaste.—1982 Bordeaux horizontal. Drink now.–J.S. • $NA/1.5 liter • (11/30/1998) • **86**

MALESAN

Bordeaux Élevé en Fûts de Chêne 1998: A decent Merlot-based red, with green olive, dried herb and berry aromas and flavors. Slightly austere finish. Drink now.–J.S. • $9 • (6/30/2000) • **81**

Bordeaux Fierté de Malesan 1998: Lovely, rich aromas of chocolate, berry and plum follow through to a medium- to full-bodied palate, with velvety tannins and a soft, caressing finish. Best after 2000.–J.S. • $10 • (6/30/2000) • **87**

Bordeaux Les Vieilles Vignes 1998: Well made, with plenty of vanilla, plum and cherry aromas. Medium-bodied, with soft, creamy tannins and a medium berry and vanilla aftertaste. Best after 2002.–J.S. • $12 • (6/30/2000) • **86**

Bordeaux Réserve de la Famille Malesan 1998: Has subtle complexity, with plum, mineral and berry character. Medium-bodied, with firm tannins and a somewhat short finish. Best after 2001.–J.S. • $14 • (6/30/2000) • **85**

Bordeaux White Élevé en Fûts de Chêne 1998: A fresh and creamy Sauvignon, with lovely pear and apple aromas and flavors and a clean finish. Drink now.–J.S. • $9 • (6/30/2000) • **85**

MALESCASSE, CHATEAU

Haut-Médoc 1999: Good, ripe tannins and pretty berry and cherry character. Medium body, tannins and finish.–J.S. • $NA • (1/01/2000) (BT) • **85-89**

Haut-Médoc 1998: This wine shows some good berry character, with hints of earth. Medium-bodied, with medium tannins and a light finish.–J.S. • $NA • (5/31/1999) (BT) • **80-84**

Haut-Médoc 1997: A rather light red, with a pleasant fruit character and a light and refreshing finish. Drink now.–J.S. • $23 • (1/31/2000) • **82**

Haut-Médoc 1996: A tightly knit wine with perfumed nose and a firm yet fruity palate. Medium-bodied, with good berry and currant flavors. Give it time to open. Best after 2001.–J.S. • $15 • (1/31/1999) • **88**

Haut-Médoc 1995: Interesting aromas of berries, spices and green tobacco follow through onto the palate. Medium- to light-bodied, with light tannins, a slightly grassy finish.–J.S. • $13 • (9/15/1998) • **79**

Haut-Médoc 1994 • $23 • (1/31/1997) • **85**

Haut-Médoc 1993 • $17 • (1/31/1996) • **83**

Haut-Médoc 1991 • $13 • (3/31/1994) • **78**

Haut-Médoc 1989 • $13 • (3/15/1992) • **84**

Haut-Médoc 1982 • $18 • (11/30/1989) • **82**

MALESCOT-ST.-EXUPERY, CHATEAU

Margaux 1998: A wine with a good, velvety mouthfeel and spice, berry and chocolate flavors. Medium- to full-bodied, with a light finish.–J.S. • $NA • (5/31/1999) (BT) • **85-89**

Margaux 1996: A chunky and delicious '96 of very good fruit concentration, albeit slightly one-dimensional. Plenty of blackberry and rose character. Medium-bodied, with velvety tannins and a fresh fruit aftertaste. Best after 2000.–J.S. • $60 • (1/31/1999) • **89**

Margaux 1995 • $46 Ⓐ • (1/31/1998) • **91**

Margaux 1994 • $26 Ⓐ • (1/31/1997) • **86**

Margaux 1990 • $24 • (2/28/1994) • **87**

Margaux 1989 • $27 • (3/15/1992) • **87**

Margaux 1988: I have always liked this wine. Powerful for a Margaux, with intense ripe berry, vanilla and mineral aromas that follow through to the palate. Full-bodied, with big, velvety tannins and a long, long aftertaste. Impressive for this estate. (1988 Bordeaux horizontal tasting). Best after 2002.–J.S. • $NA • (11/30/1998) • **90**

Margaux 1986 • $29 • (6/15/1989) • **88**

Margaux 1985 • $32 Ⓐ • (9/30/1988) • **87**

Margaux 1983 • $28 Ⓐ • (9/30/1986) • **82**

Margaux 1982: Rich and thick, with lots of flavor. Dark ruby-garnet in color, with an amber edge. Very ripe berry and chocolate aromas. Full-bodied and very chewy, with a lot of tannin and a long, tobacco, berry aftertaste. (1982 Bordeaux horizontal tasting). Drink now.–J.S. • $31 Ⓐ • (11/30/1998) • **89**

Margaux 1981 • $13 • (5/01/1989) • **87**

Margaux 1961 • $180 • (4/30/1996) • **85**

Margaux 1959 • $150 • (10/15/1990) • **87**

Margaux 1945 • $200 • (11/30/1995) • **79**

MALESTROIT, COMTE DE

Muscadet de Sèvre et Maine Sur Lie Château La Noë 1997: Intriguing waxy chamomile notes remain intense to the finish. Lean in texture, with lemon and mineral accents that linger. Drink now.–B.S. • $8 • (11/15/1998) • **83**

MALIGNY, CHATEAU DE

Chablis 1997: Clean, pure and nicely ripe, with a grass, mineral, honey and pear character, this is a balanced, medium-bodied Chardonnay of surprising acid-intensity. Drink now through 2002.–P.M. • $18 • (5/31/1999) • **86**

Chablis 1996 • $18 • (8/31/1997) • **85**

Chablis Fourchaume 1997: Both ripe and elegant, showing a butter, lemon, spice, tropical character. Very supple despite the firm core of acidity, this just coats the palate with waves of complex flavors. Chewy, earthy finish. Drink now through 2005.–P.M. • $24 • (5/31/1999) • **90**

Chablis Fourchaume 1996 • $25 • (8/31/1997) • **93**

Chablis Fourchaume 1995 • $22 • (6/15/1997) • **85**

Chablis L'Homme Mort 1997: Ripe and yet stylish; an intense '97 offering good fruit and mineral character. Medium-bodied, with dried herbs, honey, quince and lemon on the chewy finish. Needs time. Drink through 2005–P.M. • $24 • (5/31/1999) • **88**

Chablis L'Homme Mort 1995 • $22 • (6/15/1997) • **86**

Chablis Montée de Tonnerre 1995 • $22 • (6/15/1997) • **85**

Chablis Montmain 1995 • $22 • (6/15/1997) • **70**

Chablis Vau de Vey 1996 • $25 • (5/31/1998) • **89**

Chablis Vau de Vey 1995 • $22 • (6/15/1997) • **77**

Chablis Vieilles Vignes 1997: A bit odd, with some earth, asparagus, bell pepper and herbal notes, not so ripe.–P.M. • $20 • (5/31/1999) • **75**

Petit Chablis 1996 • $NA • (8/31/1997) • **83**

MALLE, CHATEAU DE

Sauternes 1998: A fresh and fruity '98 Sauternes, with medium body, medium sweetness and a spicy, dusty finish. Almost outstanding.–J.S. • $NA • (1/01/1999) (BT) • **85-89**

Sauternes 1997: Absolutely wonderful, with honey, vanilla and apple aromas that follow through to a full-bodied palate. Very good acidity and a long, flavorful finish. Best after 2001.–J.S. • $29 • (1/31/2000) • **91**

Sauternes 1991 • $NA • (4/15/1995) • **85**

Sauternes 1990 • $30 • (4/15/1995) • **95**

Sauternes 1989 • $28 • (4/15/1995) • **88**

Sauternes 1988 • $23 • (4/15/1995) • **88**

Sauternes 1987 • $15 • (6/15/1990) • **81**

Sauternes 1986 • $43 • (4/15/1995) • **94**

Sauternes 1981 • $13 • (8/31/1986) • **84**

MALLEPRAT, CHATEAU DE

Pessac-Léognan White 1998: Rather strange, with a very herbal grapefruit skin character that's a bit hard to like.–J.S. • $NA • (2/29/2000) • **79**

MALLERET, CHATEAU DE

Haut-Médoc 1996: A bit overly herbal and earthy, but with fine tannins and sweet fruit on the finish. Drink now.–J.S. • $19 • (7/31/1999) • **80**

MALLERET, CHATEAU DE

Haut-Médoc 1995: Medium-bodied, with wonderful blackberry, raspberry and wet earth character and velvety tannins. Delicious berry and cherry aftertaste. Very good indeed.–J.S. • $19 • (1/01/1999) • **87**
Haut-Médoc 1991 • $13 • (3/31/1994) • **79**
Haut-Médoc 1989 • $NA • (3/15/1992) • **90**

MALMAISON, CHATEAU

Moulis 1997: Light and fruity, with some earthiness. Silky tannins. Slightly diluted finish. Drink now.–J.S. • $NA • (1/31/2000) • **83**
Moulis 1991 • $14 • (3/31/1994) • **71**
Moulis 1990 • $19 • (3/31/1993) • **89**
Moulis 1989 • $16 • (3/15/1992) • **85**
Moulis Baronne Nadine de Rothschild 1996: Rather light and simple for the vintage, but with attractive aromas of dried cherries and flowers. Medium-bodied, with light tannins and a short finish.–J.S. • $NA • (2/28/1999) • **79**
Moulis Baronne Nadine de Rothschild 1995: Simple, light and fruity with some berry and tobacco character, light tannins and a fresh finish. Drink now.–J.S. • $NA • (9/15/1998) • **81**

MALTROYE, CHATEAU DE LA

Bâtard-Montrachet 1996 • $95 • (5/31/1998) • **75**
Chassagne-Montrachet Clos de la Maltroie 1996 • $40 • (5/31/1998) • **78**
Chassagne-Montrachet Grandes Ruchottes 1996 • $50 • (5/31/1998) • **92**
Chassagne-Montrachet Morgeot Vigne Blanche 1996 • $40 • (5/31/1998) • **73**
Chassagne-Montrachet Red Boudriottes 1985 • $17 • (10/15/1988) • **86**
Chassagne-Montrachet Red Clos St.-Jean 1985 • $19 • (10/15/1988) • **89**

MANCIAT, JEAN

Charnay-lès-Mâcon Franclieu 1997: Tart and a bit odd, with a sharp mouthfeel, some wet earth notes and lots of lemony character.–P.M. • $14 • (5/31/1999) • **78**
Mâcon 1996 • $12 • (5/31/1998) • **88**

MANDAGOT, CHATEAU

Coteaux du Languedoc Montpeyroux 1995 • $10 • (5/31/1998) • **77**

MANN, ALBERT

Pinot Auxerrois Alsace Vieilles Vignes 1996: Very ripe tropical fruit aromas and flavors highlight this rich, thick white, finishing with a juicy grapefruit accent. Drink now.–B.S. • $12 • (9/15/1998) • **84**
Riesling Alsace Altenbourg 1996: Ripe and almost fat for Riesling despite its delicate flavors of apple and mineral, yet the lively acidity is deceptive, keeping the flavors moving across the palate and refreshing the finish. Drink now through 2005.–B.S. • $15 • (8/31/1998) • **88**
Riesling Alsace Grand Cru Schlossberg 1997: Aromas of honey and ginger segue into tropical fruit and apricot in this lush Riesling that begins with a hint of residual sugar, ending up dry on the finish. Lovely underpinning of acidity. Drink now through 2003.–B.S. • $20 • (10/15/1999) • **89**
Riesling Alsace Grand Cru Schlossberg 1996: A combination of power and finesse. Apple, spice, mineral and wax aromas and flavors integrate beautifully with the sinewy structure and rich texture. Concentrated and intense, the flavors fade gracefully long after the wine is swallowed. Drink now through 2008.–B.S. • $18 • (8/31/1998) • **91**
Tokay Pinot Gris Alsace Grand Cru Furstentum 1996: A huge mouthful of ripe apricot, peach and mango, exotic and assertive, yet the rich texture and breadth are matched by vibrant acidity and a tangy, mouthwatering finish. A stony, smoky note adds complexity. Well done. Drink now through 2002.–B.S. • $20 • (9/15/1998) • **90**
Tokay Pinot Gris Alsace Grand Cru Hengst 1997: This has fine flavors of peach, honey and smoke, yet is compact on the palate, despite a better underlying structure than many '97 Pinot Gris. A touch coarse on the finish; may improve with time. Drink now through 2002.–B.S. • $20 • (10/31/1999) • **86**

Key: SS—Spectator Selection. CS—Cellar Selection. HR—Highly Recommended. $NA—Price not available. (BT)—Barrel tasting. Ⓐ—Auction Price. For a key to the tasters' initials, see "How to Use These Listings."
Dates in parentheses represent the issues in which the ratings were published.

Tokay Pinot Gris Alsace Vieilles Vignes 1997: Aromas of apricot, flowers and mineral follow through to the palate. Balanced, with moderate depth, it tails off on the finish. Drink now.–B.S. • $19 • (10/31/1999) • **84**
Tokay Pinot Gris Alsace Vieilles Vignes 1996: Smells like ripe quince and apricot, while the flavors add a dash of honey to the mix. Richly textured and full-bodied, with a grapefruit-peel note on the finish.–B.S. • $18 • (9/15/1998) • **85**

MANSENOBLE, CHATEAU

Corbières Réserve 1995: Over-the-hill, with brick and dried cherry flavors that dry out on the wispy finish.–K.M. • $8 • (11/15/1999) • **76**

MARBUZET, CHATEAU

St.-Estèphe 1998: Some berry and cherry character, but slightly unripe in the aftertaste. Medium-bodied, with medium tannins and a short finish.–J.S. • $NA • (5/31/1999) (BT) • **80-84**
St.-Estèphe 1997: Berry, cherry character with a hint of herbs. Medium- to light-bodied, with medium tannins and a slightly metallic finish. Drink now.–J.S. • $NA • (1/31/2000) • **80**
St.-Estèphe 1996: Impressive dark color and wonderful aromas of spices, berries and wet earth. Chunky and full-bodied, with loads of berry and tobacco on the palate and aftertaste. A tough yet darn-good young red. Best after 2003.–J.S. • $34 • (1/31/1999) • **89**
St.-Estèphe 1995 • $26 • (1/31/1998) • **85**
St.-Estèphe 1994 • $24 • (1/31/1997) • **80**
St.-Estèphe 1993 • $20 • (1/31/1996) • **78**
St.-Estèphe 1992 • $16 • (4/15/1995) • **78**
St.-Estèphe 1990 • $39 Ⓐ • (9/15/1993) • **86**
St.-Estèphe 1989 • $33 Ⓐ • (3/15/1992) • **89**
St.-Estèphe 1988 • $22 Ⓐ • (7/15/1991) SS • **92**
St.-Estèphe 1987 • $14 • (11/30/1989) • **80**
St.-Estèphe 1986 • $16 • (11/30/1989) • **86**
St.-Estèphe 1985 • $40 Ⓐ • (6/30/1988) • **87**
St.-Estèphe 1983 • $22 • (10/15/1986) • **91**
St.-Estèphe 1982: A pretty, delicious wine. Dark ruby, with an inky center and an amber rim. Fresh cherry, spice and berry aromas. Full-bodied, with medium, velvety tannins and a fruity aftertaste. (1982 Bordeaux horizontal tasting). Drink now.–J.S. • $NA • (11/30/1998) • **89**

MARCHAND, JEAN

Châteauneuf-du-Pape Clos des Pontifes 1994 • $NA • (12/15/1996) • **84**
Châteauneuf-du-Pape Clos des Pontifes 1993 • $26 • (11/15/1996) • **84**

MARCHERE

Cabernet Sauvignon Vin de Pays de l'Hérault 1996: A lean red, with dried cherry flavors and an astringent finish.–K.M. • $6 • (11/15/1998) • **76**
Chardonnay Vin de Pays des Côtes de Thongue 1997: Distinctive, with concentrated mineral and dried apple flavors and a smoky aroma. Racy, concentrated, balanced and pure-tasting. Drink now.–T.M. • $6 • (12/15/1998) • **86**
Merlot Vin de Pays de l'Hérault 1996: A light red, with modest tea and dried cherry flavors and herb notes.–K.M. • $6 • (11/30/1998) • **75**

MARCOUX, DOMAINE DE

Châteauneuf-du-Pape 1995: This lush red is ripe and sweet, with raspberry, candied cherry and chocolate flavors in a rich, tannic structure. Shows good extraction, but it's a bit rustic and lacks harmony. There's plenty of fruit, and it may round out with time. Drink through 2004–T.M. • $22 • (11/15/1998) • **87**
Châteauneuf-du-Pape 1990 • $57 Ⓐ • (8/31/1992) • **88**
Châteauneuf-du-Pape 1988 • $24 • (10/15/1991) • **82**
Châteauneuf-du-Pape 1986 • $20 • (10/15/1991) • **84**
Châteauneuf-du-Pape 1983 • $25 • (10/15/1991) • **87**
Châteauneuf-du-Pape 1981 • $30 • (10/15/1991) • **85**
Châteauneuf-du-Pape Vieilles Vignes 1995: Sweet, ripe, verging on candied nose of raspberry and blackberry. Polished entry shows modern-style fruit, but with pepper and herbal notes that are true to the appellation. Finish seems short and clumsy (overextracted?) and a touch hot. A lot going on, but a jumble right now. Best from 2001 through 2005.–P.M. • $61 Ⓐ • (1/01/2000) • **88**
Châteauneuf-du-Pape Vieilles Vignes 1989 • $178 Ⓐ • (10/15/1991) • **95**
Côtes du Rhône 1989 • $9 • (8/31/1992) • **82**

MARDON, DOMAINE

Quincy 1997: This white is firm and clean, but almond and herb flavors overshadow the light fruit notes. Light and lean. Drink now.–T.M. • $15 • (6/30/1999) • **81**

MARECHAL, CATHERINE & CLAUDE

Auxey-Duresses White Vieilles Vignes 1998: Nice and fresh, aromatically expressive, with honey, wet earth and lightly toasted bread notes. Medium-bodied and supple, it delivers a delicately seductive finish. Drink now through 2003.–P.M. • $29 • (5/31/2000) • **87**

MARGAINE, A.

Brut Blanc de Blancs Champagne Special Club 1992: A spunky, substantive Champagne, with lively acidity, focused fruit flavors and buttery vanilla accents. Has great balance and enough complexity to keep you coming back for another sip. Drink now through 2001. • $39 • (12/31/1998) • **89**

Brut Champagne NV: Light but bright flavors liven up this fresh, appealing brut. Has crisp apple and lemon notes with toasty, spicy accents that linger on the finish. Drink now through 2001. • $40 • (10/31/1999) • **89**

Demi-Sec Champagne NV: Appealing for its fresh fruit flavors and sweet balance. A nicely made Champagne. Drink now. • $43 • (10/31/1999) • **85**

MARGAUX, CHATEAU

Margaux 1999: Not powerful but very fine. Gorgeous and balanced red with lots of berry, spice and floral aromas and flavors. Full-bodied, with a solid core of ripe tannins and a long finish.–J.S. • $NA • (1/01/2000) (BT) • **90-94**

Margaux 1998: This is a Margaux wearing a suit of armor in tannins. Very tough for this premier estate, but of outstanding quality. Aromas of minerals, flowers, berries and cherries open to a full-bodied palate with powerful tannins and a mouthpuckering finish. Could use a bit more ripe fruit on the finish, but it's a serious wine.–J.S. • $NA • (5/31/1999) (BT) • **90-94**

Margaux 1997: All in finesse, with berry, currant and light vanilla character. Medium- to full-bodied, with silky tannins and a fresh finish. Lovely, long finish. Gorgeous core of fruit in this wine. Drink now through 2004.–J.S. • $101 Ⓐ • (1/31/2000) • **90**

Margaux 1996: Sleek and racy Margaux. Inky black in color, with intense aromas of wood-tinged blackberry, violet, cherry followed by mineral and berry flavors that unfold across the palate and go on and on. Full-bodied and powerful, with a compact fruit and tannin structure, it will be best after 2008.–J.S. • $257 Ⓐ • (1/31/1999) CS • **95**

Margaux 1995 • $279 Ⓐ • (1/31/1998) CS • **100**
Margaux 1994 • $112 Ⓐ • (1/31/1997) • **90**
Margaux 1993 • $101 Ⓐ • (1/31/1996) • **90**
Margaux 1992 • $91 Ⓐ • (4/15/1995) • **81**
Margaux 1991 • $94 Ⓐ • (3/31/1994) • **85**
Margaux 1990 • $396 Ⓐ • (3/31/1993) • **96**

Margaux 1989: This is a dormant volcano of a wine waiting to explode with fruit. Bubbling over with flowers, blackberries, cherries and chocolate. Full-bodied, very chewy, adding masses of tannins. Long dried cherry, berry aftertaste. Very closed; needs time. (1989 Bordeaux horizontal tasting). Best after 2009.–J.S. • $194 Ⓐ • (5/31/1999) • **99**

Margaux 1988: Still not giving all it has to offer, this shows wonderful aromas and flavors of currant, violet, tobacco and earth. Full-bodied and powerful, with a solid underpinning of firm yet silky tannins. A classic Margaux. (1988 Bordeaux horizontal tasting). Best after 2000.–J.S. • $148 Ⓐ • (11/30/1998) • **95**

Margaux 1987 • $96 Ⓐ • (5/15/1990) • **87**
Margaux 1986 • $242 Ⓐ • (6/15/1989) CS • **98**
Margaux 1985 • $202 Ⓐ • (10/15/1994) • **95**
Margaux 1984 • $78 Ⓐ • (2/28/1987) CS • **93**
Margaux 1983 • $258 Ⓐ • (10/15/1994) • **98**

Margaux 1982: Big and overripe. Dark ruby-colored, with an amber rim. Character of ripe blackberry, with a hint of earth. Full-bodied and very tannic, with a lot of fruit and more ripe fruit on the finish. (1982 Bordeaux horizontal tasting). Best after 2005.–J.S. • $393 Ⓐ • (11/30/1998) • **95**

Margaux 1981 • $134 Ⓐ • (10/15/1994) • **95**
Margaux 1980 • $84 Ⓐ • (5/01/1984) CS • **90**
Margaux 1979 • $146 Ⓐ • (12/15/1989) • **91**
Margaux 1978 • $149 Ⓐ • (12/15/1989) • **92**
Margaux 1977 • $NA • (7/15/1987) • **75**
Margaux 1976 • $68 Ⓐ • (7/15/1987) • **81**
Margaux 1975 • $76 Ⓐ • (7/15/1987) • **88**
Margaux 1970 • $91 Ⓐ • (7/15/1987) • **70**
Margaux 1971 • $50 Ⓐ • (7/15/1987) • **77**
Margaux 1967 • $38 Ⓐ • (7/15/1987) • **84**
Margaux 1966 • $108 Ⓐ • (7/15/1987) • **90**
Margaux 1964 • $62 Ⓐ • (7/15/1987) • **86**
Margaux 1962 • $240/1.5 liter • (12/15/1989) • **86**
Margaux 1961 • $1,015 Ⓐ • (4/30/1996) • **92**
Margaux 1959 • $470 Ⓐ • • (10/15/1990) • **93**
Margaux 1957 • $90 Ⓐ • (7/15/1987) • **90**
Margaux 1955 • $217 Ⓐ • (7/15/1987) • **79**
Margaux 1953 • $535 Ⓐ • (12/15/1989) • **84**
Margaux 1952 • $500/1.5 liter • (7/15/1987) • **85**
Margaux 1950 • $600/1.5 liter • (7/15/1987) • **89**
Margaux 1949 • $472 Ⓐ • (7/15/1987) • **95**
Margaux 1947 • $398 Ⓐ • (7/31/1997) • **89**
Margaux 1945 • $1,015 Ⓐ • (11/30/1995) • **90**
Margaux 1943 • $299 Ⓐ • (7/15/1987) • **78**
Margaux 1937 • $172 Ⓐ • (7/15/1987) • **82**
Margaux 1934 • $322 Ⓐ • (7/15/1987) • **88**
Margaux 1929 • $448 Ⓐ • (7/15/1987) • **83**
Margaux 1928 • $731 Ⓐ • (7/15/1987) • **84**
Margaux 1926 • $300 • (7/15/1987) • **77**
Margaux 1924 • $369 Ⓐ • (7/15/1987) • **73**
Margaux 1923 • $330 • (7/15/1987) • **81**
Margaux 1920 • $300 Ⓐ • (7/15/1987) • **79**
Margaux 1918 • $500 • (7/15/1987) • **80**
Margaux 1908 • $530 • (7/15/1987) • **85**
Margaux 1900 • $6,770 Ⓐ • (7/15/1987) • **93**
Margaux 1899 • $1,700 • (7/15/1987) • **94**
Margaux 1898 • $1,600 • (7/15/1987) • **75**
Margaux 1893 • $1,700 • (7/15/1987) • **95**
Margaux 1892 • $1,265 Ⓐ • (7/15/1987) • **80**
Margaux 1887 • $760 • (7/15/1987) • **81**
Margaux 1870 • $3,300 • (7/15/1987) • **89**
Margaux 1865 • $5,000 • (7/15/1987) • **97**
Margaux 1864 • $3,500 • (7/15/1987) • **98**
Margaux 1848 • $10,000 • (7/15/1987) • **95**
Margaux 1847 • $25,000/1.5 liter • (7/15/1987) • **96**
Margaux 1791 • $NA • (7/15/1987) • **97**
Margaux 1771 • $NA • (7/15/1987) • **99**

MARGON, DOMAINE DE

Chardonnay Vin de Pays des Côtes de Thongue Delphine de Margon 1996 • $11 • (4/30/1998) • **83**

MARIS, DOMAINE

Minervois Carte Noire 1995 • $9 • (2/28/1998) • **88**
Minervois Carte Noire 1990 • $9 • (3/15/1994) • **80**
Minervois J. Maris Cuvée Prestige 1990 • $9 • (3/15/1994) • **86**

MARJOSSE, CHATEAU

Bordeaux 1994 • $NA • (1/31/1997) • **77**
Bordeaux 1993 • $NA • (1/31/1996) • **80**
Bordeaux 1992 • $NA • (4/15/1995) • **75**

MAROSLAVAC-LEGER

Bourgogne White 1995 • $12 • (8/31/1997) • **70**

Bourgogne White La Combe 1998: Not an easy wine, but different. Distinctive, with some grass, matchstick and smoke character. Medium-bodied, it kicks in with honeyed sweetness and ripeness on the concentrated finish. Drink now through 2004.–P.M. • $15 • (5/31/2000) • **87**

Bourgogne White La Combe 1997: Floral and a bit woody, this seems slightly heavy, even oxidized, as the finish comes through as burning and astringent.–P.M. • $16 • (5/31/1999) • **72**

Bourgogne White La Combe 1996 • $17 • (5/31/1998) • **84**

Chassagne-Montrachet Les Voillenots 1998: What happened? Overfiltered? This wine tastes stripped of fruit and texture, turning crisp, with greenness on the finish.–P.M. • $39 • (5/31/2000) • **74**

Chassagne-Montrachet Les Voillenots 1997: There's modest fruit in this low-acidity white, with cedar and pear notes. A bit diluted on the finish, with a slight wet paper note.–P.M. • $40 • (5/31/1999) • **79**

■ ■ ■ ■

MAROSLAVAC-LEGER

Chassagne-Montrachet Les Voillenots 1996: Supple and fairly light-bodied, turning a bit diluted and tasting of wet cardboard. Tasted twice, with consistent notes. Drink now.–P.M. • $NA • (8/31/1998) • **71**

Chassagne-Montrachet Les Voillenots 1995 • $28 • (8/31/1997) • **75**

Meursault Les Murgers 1998: Delicate, with an attractive cookie dough aroma. Tastes of green apple, as it delivers a clean, if not very complex or deep, finish. Drink now through 2002.–P.M. • $39 • (5/31/2000) • **83**

Meursault Les Murgers 1997: Decent pear and toffee complexity surfaces in this medium-bodied, lightly toasted Meursault. Drink now through 2002.–P.M. • $40 • (5/31/1999) • **83**

Meursault Les Murgers 1996 • $36 • (5/31/1998) • **91**

Meursault Les Murgers 1995 • $28 • (8/31/1997) • **91**

Puligny-Montrachet Les Champs Gain 1997: Soft and slightly drying from lack of fresh acidity and intense fruit, it delivers modest pear and green apple. Short, spirit-tasting finish.–P.M. • $60 • (5/31/1999) • **72**

Puligny-Montrachet Les Champs Gain 1996 • $50 • (5/31/1998) • **89**

Puligny-Montrachet Les Combettes 1998: Thick on the palate, with a full-bodied texture, delivering pear, wet earth notes and good citrusy character on the finish, but it's a bit unfocused overall. Best from 2001 through 2004.–P.M. • $60 • (5/31/2000) • **83**

Puligny-Montrachet Les Combettes 1997: Balanced and medium-intense, with a supple texture and cooked pear and pineapple flavors. Lacks a bit of acidity and freshness on the short finish. Drink now.–P.M. • $60 • (5/31/1999) • **82**

Puligny-Montrachet Les Combettes 1996 • $50 • (5/31/1998) • **90**

Puligny-Montrachet Les Combettes 1995 • $40 • (8/31/1997) • **95**

Puligny-Montrachet Les Corvées des Vignes 1997: Clean, supple and well made, showing a nice core of lemon and pear with subtle oak. There's gentle winemaking behind this medium-bodied, flavorful, very enjoyable and balanced '97. Drink now through 2002.–P.M. • $40 • (5/31/1999) • **88**

Puligny-Montrachet Les Corvées des Vignes 1996 • $40 • (5/31/1998) • **85**

Puligny-Montrachet Les Corvées des Vignes 1995 • $30 • (8/31/1997) • **88**

Puligny-Montrachet Les Folatières 1998: Whoa! Earthy and frankly strange in aroma, but once you dig into this you find an amazingly thick, rich and ripe character. A dense '98 white that may not be for everyone, but makes my palate spin. Best from 2002 through 2010.–P.M. • $60 • (5/31/2000) • **90**

Puligny-Montrachet Les Folatières 1997: Smooth, round, opulent and full-bodied, with ripe pear, honey, lemon, mineral and toasted oak, it's flavorful but a bit inelegant. The finish is juicy and succulent. Drink now through 2003.–P.M. • $60 • (5/31/1999) • **87**

Puligny-Montrachet Les Folatières 1996 • $50 • (5/31/1998) • **93**

Puligny-Montrachet Les Folatières 1995 • $40 • (8/31/1997) • **93**

St.-Aubin Les Murgers des Dents de Chien 1998: Lean and tasting a bit unripe, with a crisp, slightly herbal character. Hard finish.–P.M. • $33 • (5/31/2000) • **78**

St.-Aubin Les Murgers des Dents de Chien 1997: Pearlike, with tropical notes, this supple and pleasant '97 is accessible on release as it stresses ripe fruit over oak. Drink now through 2002.–P.M. • $34 • (5/31/1999) • **88**

St.-Aubin Les Murgers des Dents de Chien 1996 • $34 • (5/31/1998) • **81**

MARSAU, CHATEAU

Côtes de Francs 1998: Bright berry aromas, with hints of dark chocolate. Full-bodied and velvety, with a lovely chewy structure. Slightly short finish.–J.S. • $NA • (5/31/1999) (BT) • **85-89**

Côtes de Francs 1997: Delicious red. Gorgeous aromas of blackberries, mint, tobacco and currants. Full-bodied, with velvety tannins and lots of beautiful fruit. Best after 2000.–J.S. • $NA • (1/31/2000) • **89**

Côtes de Francs 1996: Interesting berry and tanned-leather aromas. Medium-bodied, with chewy tannins and a medium finish. Could use more fruit on the midpalate. Drink now.–J.S. • $NA • (1/31/1999) • **84**

Côtes de Francs 1995 • $15 • (1/31/1998) • **88**

Côtes de Francs 1994 • $NA • (1/31/1997) • **75**

MARTIALIS, DOMAINE DE

St.-Emilion 1995 • $18 • (1/31/1998) • **72**

Key: SS—Spectator Selection. CS—Cellar Selection. HR—Highly Recommended. $NA—Price not available. (BT)—Barrel tasting. Ⓐ—Auction Price. For a key to the tasters' initials, see "How to Use These Listings." **Dates in parentheses represent the issues in which the ratings were published.**

MARTIN, JEAN-JACQUES

Beaujolais-Villages 1993 • $NA • (6/15/1995) • **80**

Beaujolais-Villages 1992 • $10 • (6/30/1994) • **83**

Juliénas 1993 • $14 • (7/31/1995) • **72**

Juliénas 1992 • $14 • (6/15/1994) • **85**

Pouilly-Fuissé Les Chevrières 1997: Mushrooms and wet earth make it taste oxidized, then it turns dry on the finish.–P.M. • $19 • (5/31/1999) • **74**

Pouilly-Fuissé Les Chevrières 1996 • $19 • (5/31/1998) • **85**

St.-Amour 1993 • $NA • (7/31/1995) • **80**

St.-Amour 1992 • $15 • (6/30/1994) • **78**

St.-Véran 1996 • $15 • (5/31/1998) • **78**

St.-Véran 1995 • $NA • (8/31/1996) • **86**

MARTIN, ROBERT

Mâcon-Villages Domaine de la Denante 1995 • $NA • (8/31/1996) • **85**

St.-Véran Domaine de la Denante 1997: Ripe and soft, an attractive, medium-bodied white with pear tart, cream and spice flavors. A thread of lovely honey balances the slightly astringent finish. Enjoy.–P.M. • $13 • (5/31/1999) • **84**

St.-Véran Domaine de la Denante 1995 • $NA • (8/31/1996) • **88**

MARTINE

Cabernet Sauvignon Vin de Pays d'Oc 1995: Harsh, with some plum flavors that turn astringent on the finish.–K.M. • $7 • (8/31/1998) • **71**

Chardonnay Vin de Pays de l'Ile de Beauté 1996 • $7 • (4/30/1998) • **78**

Merlot Vin de Pays d'Oc 1995 • $7 • (5/31/1998) • **74**

Sauvignon Blanc Vin de Pays d'Oc 1996 • $7 • (1/01/1998) • **84**

MARTINOLLES, DOMAINE DE

Chardonnay Vin de Pays de l'Aude 1996 • $9 • (10/31/1997) • **84**

MARZELLE, CHATEAU LA

St.-Emilion 1997: Pretty St.-Emilion. Vivid violet and berry aromas, with hints of dark chocolate. Medium- to full-bodied, with a solid core of fruit and silky tannins. Delicious finish. Drink now.–J.S. • $34 • (1/31/2000) • **87**

MAS BLANC, DOMAINE DU

Banyuls 1991 • $27 • (12/15/1994) • **78**

Collioure Cuvée Cosprons Levants 1991 • $21 • (12/15/1994) • **81**

MAS BRUGUIERE

Coteaux du Languedoc Pic St.-Loup 1997: Firm and flavorful, with beautiful raspberry and blueberry flavors and plenty of spice and leather. A balanced and lively red, with brickish notes on the finish. Drink now through 2002.–K.M. • $14 • (11/15/1999) • **87**

Coteaux du Languedoc Pic St.-Loup 1996: Decent cherry, ripe plum and pepper flavors in this straightforward red. Finishes on a beefy note. Drink now.–K.M. • $12 • (1/31/1999) • **80**

Coteaux du Languedoc Pic St.-Loup Élevé en fûts de chêne 1997: A high-toned and nicely chewy wine, with pretty cherry and spice flavors and a broad texture. Well defined and pure-tasting, with a bright finish of white pepper and a touch of leather. Drink now through 2002.–K.M. • $18 • (11/15/1999) • **87**

Coteaux du Languedoc Pic St.-Loup Élevé en fûts de chêne 1996: A good, lip-smacking red that's on the rustic side, but balanced and fairly powerful in its own right. Good, ripe cherry and plum flavors, with leathery notes. Finishes on a briery note. Drink now through 2001.–K.M. • $17 • (1/31/1999) • **87**

Coteaux du Languedoc Rosé Pic St.-Loup 1996: A rosé of power and distinction, with a minerally character that gives it added depth. Dried apple, cherry and berry flavors round out this seductive wine. Drink now.–K.M. • $10 • (12/31/1998) • **87**

MAS CHAMPART

Coteaux du Languedoc 1997: There are nice cherry and berry flavors in this wine, but it toughens up on the finish. Drink now.–K.M. • $15 • (1/31/2000) • **81**

Coteaux du Languedoc 1995 • $12 • (8/31/1997) • **87**

FRANCE

Coteaux du Languedoc 1991 • $9 • (3/15/1994) • **83**
Coteaux du Languedoc White 1997: Nice and fruity, with appley flavors and notes of spice and ripe pear. A touch of richness of the finish. A good quaff for a summer picnic. Drink now.–K.M. • $17 • (8/31/1999) • **86**
St.-Chinian 1997: Well focused and medium-bodied, with chewy flavors of red plum, berry and cherry, with peppery notes on the finish. Drink with food. Drink now through 2002.–K.M. • $14 • (4/30/2000) • **84**
St.-Chinian 1995 • $13 • (9/30/1997) • **83**
St.-Chinian 1991 • $9 • (3/15/1994) • **84**

MAS CREMAT, DOMAINE DU

Côtes du Roussillon 1995 • $12 • (12/15/1997) • **89**
Côtes du Roussillon 1991 • $10 • (3/15/1994) • **83**

MAS DE DAUMAS GASSAC

Vin de Pays de l'Hérault Haute Vallée du Gassac 1996: Firm and juicy, with good plum, berry and cherry flavors and some herbal and tobacco notes. A bit of a bite on the finish. This was the best of three samples tasted, with significant bottle variation.–K.M. • $13 Ⓐ • (11/15/1998) • **83**
Vin de Pays de l'Herault Haute Vallée du Gassac 1995 • $20 Ⓐ • (9/30/1997) • **84**
Vin de Pays de l'Herault Haute Vallée du Gassac 1994 • $14 Ⓐ • (1/31/1997) • **91**
Vin de Pays de l'Herault Haute Vallée du Gassac 1992 • $25 • (3/15/1994) HR • **90**
Vin de Pays de l'Herault Haute Vallée du Gassac 1991 • $8 Ⓐ • (3/15/1994) • **87**
Vin de Pays de l'Herault Haute Vallée du Gassac 1990 • $29 Ⓐ • (10/31/1992) • **87**
Vin de Pays de l'Herault Haute Vallée du Gassac 1989 • $35 Ⓐ • (3/15/1994) • **93**
Vin de Pays de l'Herault Haute Vallée du Gassac 1987 • $18 Ⓐ • (10/31/1989) • **85**
Vin de Pays de l'Herault Haute Vallée du Gassac 1986 • $25 • (12/15/1988) • **81**
Vin de Pays de l'Hérault White Haute Vallée du Gassac 1997: There are peachy flavors but little else in this blowsy white that finishes rough. Tasted twice, with consistent notes.–K.M. • $30 • (12/31/1998) • **73**

MAS DE GOURGONNIER

Coteaux d'Aix-en-Provence Les Baux de Provence 1990 • $11 • (3/15/1993) • **80**
Coteaux d'Aix-en-Provence Les Baux de Provence 1988 • $9 • (4/30/1991) • **79**
Les Baux de Provence 1995 • $9 • (2/28/1998) • **84**
Les Baux de Provence Réserve du Mas 1994 • $12 • (2/28/1998) • **87**

MAS DE LA DAME

Les Baux de Provence Cuvée Gourmande 1995 • $11 • (9/30/1997) • **87**
Les Baux de Provence Réserve du Mas 1995 • $14 • (9/30/1997) • **87**

MAS DES BRESSADES

Cabernet-Syrah Vin de Pays du Gard 1996: A warm and slightly rustic red with good red plum, berry and cherry flavors, some meaty components. Finishes on notes of bittersweet chocolate and spice. Drink now.–K.M. • $13 • (11/15/1998) • **85**
Cabernet-Syrah Vin de Pays du Gard 1990 • $13 • (4/15/1993) • **83**
Cabernet-Syrah France 1988 • $11 • (10/31/1990) • **81**
Syrah-Grenache Vin de Pays du Gard 1998: An easy-drinking red perfect for a barbecue. A bit on the light side but still zippy, with pretty plum, red cherry and currant flavors and some gamy notes. Finishes with pepper and spice. Drink now.–K.M. • $8 • (10/15/1999) • **85**

MAS DES CHIMERES

Coteaux du Languedoc 1994 • $12 • (3/31/1998) • **84**

MAS LLARO

Côtes du Roussillon Grande Réserve 1996: A medium-bodied red, with cherry and herb flavors that turn a bit stemmy on the finish.–K.M. • $10 • (11/30/1998) • **78**

MAS NEUF, CHATEAU

Costières de Nîmes 1996 • $8 • (4/30/1998) • **80**
Muscat de Mireval NV: Sweet and luscious, with peach, apricot and ripe apple character. An appealing dessert wine with plenty of flavor.–K.M. • $17 • (7/31/1998) • **85**

MAS STE.-BERTHE

Coteaux d'Aix-en-Provence Cuvée Louis David 1990 • $16 • (7/15/1992) • **81**
Coteaux d'Aix-en-Provence Cuvée Tradition 1993 • $11 • (1/31/1997) • **84**
Coteaux d'Aix-en-Provence Cuvée Tradition 1992 • $10 • (3/31/1995) • **80**

MAS VIALA

Vin de Pays de l'Hérault Cuvée T.S. 1998: A straightforward red, with blackberry flavors and tealike notes. Modest finish. Drink now.–K.M. • $12 • (8/31/1999) • **82**

MASSE

Brut Champagne NV: Features bright fruit flavors, a lively texture and a slightly sweet finish; weaves together fig, pear and toast accents on a backdrop of crisp acidity. Drink now through 2001. • $25 • (10/31/1999) • **88**

MASSON, MARIE-FRANCE

Côtes du Rhône-Villages Rasteau Cuvée Paul Emile 1997: An attractive, warm-vintage, low-acidity red, supple yet with exotic ripe plum, floral, smoke, wild berry and dried herb complexity. Chewy, slightly hot finish. Drink now through 2001.–P.M. • $14 • (11/15/1999) • **83**
Côtes du Rhône-Villages Rasteau Cuvée Paul Emile 1995: Complex and exotic. Pure, clean and aromatically explosive, this well-made, medium-bodied red packs in oak-accented floral, mocha, black olive, toasted spice, tar and cassis notes in a harmonious package with a long finish. Drink now through 2001.–P.M. • $14 • (11/15/1998) • **90**

MATHIEU, SERGE

Brut Blanc de Noirs Champagne Cuvée Tradition NV: Nicely dry, crisp and refreshing. A fruit-driven bubbly with focused citrus flavors and a clean, tangy finish. Drink now through 2001. • $32 • (10/15/1999) • **88**
Brut Champagne 1991 • $40 • (11/15/1997) • **85**
Brut Champagne 2000 NV: This dry brut has doughy, yeasty aromas and a tart, tight balance. Lean in character, but quite refreshing. Drink now. • $46 • (10/15/1999) • **86**
Brut Champagne Cuvée Prestige NV • $35 • (11/15/1997) • **82**
Brut Champagne Millésime 1990 • $39 • (12/15/1996) • **90**
Brut Champagne Tête de Cuvée Select NV • $40 • (11/15/1997) • **83**
Brut Rosé Champagne NV: Fresh and easy to drink, with light cherry and strawberry flavors and a soft texture. Drink now. • $38 • (10/15/1999) • **85**

MATIBAT, DOMAINE DE

Cabernet Sauvignon Vin de Pays d'Oc 1991 • $7 • (4/15/1993) • **72**
Côtes de Malepère 1994 • $7 • (4/30/1998) • **77**
Merlot Vin de Pays d'Oc 1995 • $6 • (5/31/1998) • **73**

MATROT, JOSEPH

Meursault 1996: The excellent minerally nose precedes a bitter, astringent, cooked and oxidized character on the palate.–P.M. • $32 • (5/31/1999) • **72**
Meursault 1995 • $32 • (8/31/1997) • **85**
Meursault Charmes 1996: A bit earthy, but showing clean bread dough and yeastlike aromas and flavors. Medium-bodied, with plenty of intensity and a crisp finish. Best from 2004 through 2007.–P.M. • $49 • (5/31/1999) • **86**
Meursault Charmes 1995 • $NA • (5/31/1997) • **90**
Meursault Les Chevalières 1995 • $30 • (8/31/1997) • **88**
Meursault-Blagny 1996: Very intense in a minerally way, this coats the palate and caresses the taste buds. The flavors are very distinct, showing a wet earth, herb and green apple personality. Has a track record for aging, so cellar. Best from 2005 through 2010.–P.M. • $46 • (5/31/1999) • **90**
Meursault-Blagny 1995 • $46 • (8/31/1997) • **93**
Puligny-Montrachet Les Chalumeaux 1995 • $44 • (5/31/1997) • **92**
Volnay-Santenots 1996: A bit lean, with a minerally component insufficiently supported by ripe fruit, leading to a slightly thin and unsatisfying finish.–P.M. • $NA • (5/15/1999) • **79**

MATROT, PIERRE

Meursault Perrières 1996: Great purity expresses itself in this full-bodied, elegant, refined white. Brims with mocha aromas and flavors accented by

lemon and a minerally, pebbly midpalate that gives it a silky texture. Drink now through 2010.–P.M. • $50 • (5/31/1999) • **93**
Puligny-Montrachet Les Combettes 1995 • $50 • (5/31/1997) • **90**

MAU, YVON

Bordeaux Officiel du Bicentenaire de la Revolution Francaise 1988 • $5 • (7/31/1989) • **77**
Bordeaux Yvecourt 1997: Simple and very grapey. Medium-bodied, with firm, rather dry tannins and a slightly hollow finish. Better after this year.–J.S. • $NA • (9/30/1998) • **78**
Cabernet Sauvignon Vin de Pays des Côtes de Gascogne 1996 • $6 • (12/15/1997) • **80**
Merlot Vin de Pays des Côtes de Gascogne 1996 • $6 • (11/15/1997) • **85**
Merlot Vin de Pays des Côtes de Gascogne 1994 • $6 • (7/31/1996) • **81**
Sauvignon Blanc Bordeaux 1996 • $6 • (9/30/1997) • **75**

MAUCAILLOU, CHATEAU

Moulis 1998: This has an herbal and rather burnt character to it. Medium-bodied, with rustic, slightly unripe tannins and a medium finish. Tough to like.–J.S. • $NA • (5/31/1999) (BT) • **75-79**
Moulis 1996: Slightly mature in color for a '96, but shows some pleasant berry and tobacco character on the nose and palate. Medium-bodied, with silky tannins and a short finish. Drink now.–J.S. • $17 • (1/31/1999) • **81**
Moulis 1992 • $14 • (4/15/1995) • **73**
Moulis 1988 • $24 Ⓐ • (7/31/1991) • **82**
Moulis 1985 • $18 • (8/31/1988) • **88**
Moulis 1983 • $16 • (3/15/1987) • **87**
Moulis 1982: Good, deep color of brick red, but rather funky, with chestnut and berry aromas. Medium-bodied and diluted, with unclean flavors. (1982 Bordeaux horizontal tasting).–J.S. • $NA • (11/30/1998) • **74**
Moulis 1981 • $14 • (10/01/1985) • **88**

MAUCOIL, CHATEAU

Châteauneuf-du-Pape 1998: A rather juicy and fruity Châteauneuf, showing good flavors but lacking a bit in complexity. Still offers silky tannins, with plum and black cherry. Crisp, chewy finish. Hopefully it will come together. Best from 2002 through 2010.–P.M. • $22 • (1/01/2000) • **83**
Châteauneuf-du-Pape Privilège 1998: Exotic, ripe and spicy, with cappuccino, mocha, toast and terrific red berry and blackberry character. Full-bodied, with silky and sweet tannins. Picks up intensity on the harmonious finish. Not imported into the U.S. Best from 2003 through 2015.–P.M. • $NA • (1/01/2000) • **88**
Châteauneuf-du-Pape Réserve Suzeraine 1994 • $20 • (2/28/1997) • **82**
Châteauneuf-du-Pape Réserve Suzeraine 1985 • $13 • (11/15/1987) • **86**

MAUME

Charmes-Chambertin 1988 • $60 • (7/15/1991) • **86**
Gevrey-Chambertin 1993 • $NA • (5/15/1996) • **90**
Gevrey-Chambertin 1987 • $25 • (3/31/1990) • **77**
Gevrey-Chambertin Champeaux 1996: A blast of pure raspberry greets the senses. This wine needs time to integrate the zippy acidity, firm tannins and bold, jammy raspberry and cassis. More on the elegant side, with loads of structure. Best from 2001 through 2006.–B.S. • $32 • (1/01/2000) • **89**
Gevrey-Chambertin En Pallud 1996: Packed with raspberry, cassis and licorice notes, with a gaminess adding complexity, this is all terroir and no wood. There's plenty of tannins and bracing acidity too. Give it some time. Best after 2001.–B.S. • $30 • (1/01/2000) • **91**
Gevrey-Chambertin En Pallud 1995: Tough and rather herbal now, showing some astringent character that needs time to soften. There are substantial wet earth, iron and mineral components to this medium-bodied red, with good terroir notes. Well made in the more traditional style of Burgundy. Drink through 2007.–P.M. • $25 • (8/31/1998) • **88**
Gevrey-Chambertin En Pallud 1994 • $28 • (11/15/1996) • **75**
Gevrey-Chambertin En Pallud 1987 • $36 • (3/31/1990) • **80**
Gevrey-Chambertin Lavaut St.-Jacques 1993 • $NA • (5/15/1996) • **86**

Key: SS—Spectator Selection. CS—Cellar Selection. HR—Highly Recommended. $NA—Price not available. (BT)—Barrel tasting. Ⓐ—Auction Price. For a key to the tasters' initials, see "How to Use These Listings."
Dates in parentheses represent the issues in which the ratings were published.

Gevrey-Chambertin Lavaut St.-Jacques 1991 • $40 • (8/31/1994) • **84**
Gevrey-Chambertin Premier Cru 1994 • $40 • (11/15/1996) • **82**
Gevrey-Chambertin Premier Cru 1991 • $28 • (8/31/1994) • **87**
Mazis-Chambertin 1996: On the edge, exhibiting coffee, Eastern spices, leather and game aromas and flavors, a broad structure and a grainy texture. Needs some time to come together. Best after 2001.–B.S. • $75 • (1/01/2000) • **88**
Mazis-Chambertin 1995: Impressive for its raw power, this wine is built for the long haul. Thick and distinctive, packed with ripe, seductive red- and blackberry flavors, but also loads of mineral, iron and iodine. The acidity is vibrant, the body is full, and it's built to last. Best from 2005 through 2010.–P.M. • $60 • (8/31/1998) • **93**
Mazis-Chambertin 1994 • $63 • (11/15/1996) • **88**
Mazis-Chambertin 1991 • $59 • (8/31/1994) • **82**
Mazis-Chambertin 1987 • $56 • (3/31/1990) • **74**

MAURIANE, LA

Puisseguin-St.-Emilion 1999: Wonderful violet, mineral and berry character. Medium-bodied, with well-integrated tannins and a long finish. Very well done.–J.S. • $NA • (1/01/2000) (BT) • **85-89**

MAVETTE, DOMAINE DE LA

Gigondas 1997: A fruity style of Gigondas, clean and pure, with a good grip of tannins and wet earth. Medium-bodied, a bit smoky, gamy and tough, but it has guts and personality, if little class. Cellaring should civilize it a bit. Best from 2002 through 2008.–P.M. • $17 • (12/15/1999) • **87**
Gigondas 1996: Mineral, smoke and tobacco box notes make for intriguing complexity. Medium-bodied and not overly fruity, just suggestive of cherry and plum, there is balance, although the finish has a slight bite of chewy tannins. Best after 2000.–P.M. • $17 • (12/15/1999) • **87**
Gigondas 1995 • $15 • (5/15/1998) • **84**

MAX, LOUIS

Chassagne-Montrachet Morgeot 1997: Burgundy's piña colada. Very rich and ripe but in a beautifully harmonious way, delivering toasted coconut, pineapple and baked apple flavors. Full-bodied and smooth, with toasted oak kicking in on the finish. Drink now through 2010.–P.M. • $75 • (9/30/1999) • **90**

MAYNE, CHATEAU DU

Sauternes 1995 • $NA • (4/30/1998) • **88**

MAZERIS, CHATEAU

Canon-Fronsac 1998: Earthy and ripe. Full-bodied, with firm tannins and a medium finish. Slightly one-dimensional, but delicious.–J.S. • $NA • (5/31/1999) (BT) • **85-89**
Canon-Fronsac 1996: Attractive strawberry aromas follow through to a fresh, light-bodied palate with firm tannins. Short finish. Drink now.–J.S. • $NA • (1/31/1999) • **80**
Canon-Fronsac 1995: Dark chocolate and earth aromas and flavors. Medium- to light-bodied, with light tannins and a dry finish. A bit rustic. Drink now.–J.S. • $18 • (9/15/1998) • **82**
Canon-Fronsac 1994 • $20 • (1/31/1997) • **75**
Canon-Fronsac 1993 • $19 • (1/31/1996) • **78**
Canon-Fronsac 1990 • $18 • (5/15/1994) • **80**

MAZERIS-BELLEVUE, CHATEAU

Canon-Fronsac 1997: A decent red, with berry, plum and tobacco character. Medium- to light-bodied, with light tannins. Drink now.–J.S. • $NA • (1/31/2000) • **80**
Canon-Fronsac 1990 • $15 • (3/31/1993) • **88**

MAZEYRES, CHATEAU

Pomerol 1998: Aromas of raspberries and currants. Medium-bodied, with round tannins and a lovely berry aftertaste.–J.S. • $NA • (5/31/1999) (BT) • **85-89**

Pomerol 1995: Green olive and berry aromas and flavors. Medium-bodied, with velvety tannins and a medium finish. Rich, traditional wine. Drink through 2004–J.S. • $NA • (9/15/1998) • **88**
Pomerol 1994 • $NA • (1/01/1998) • **86**
Pomerol 1993 • $NA • (1/01/1998) • **84**

MEDARD, FRANCOIS

Chinon Domaine des Closiers de St.-Hilaire Vieilles Vignes 1996: Licorice and toast notes run through this dark, alluring red, but its cherry and blackberry flavors are overshadowed by firm tannins. Ambitious, firm and spicy, but it may not have enough ripe fruit for balance in the long run. Drink now through 2002.–T.M. • $13 • (6/30/1999) • **85**

MEDITEO

Cabernet Sauvignon Vin de Pays d'Oc 1996 • $7 • (12/15/1997) • **84**
Chardonnay Vin de Pays d'Oc 1996 • $7 • (9/15/1997) • **85**
Merlot Vin de Pays d'Oc 1996 • $7 • (11/15/1997) • **85**
Syrah Vin de Pays d'Oc 1996 • $7 • (12/15/1997) • **86**

MEFFRE, GABRIEL

Chardonnay Vin de Pays d'Oc Thierry and Guy Fat Bastard 1998: A straightforward, medium-bodied Chardonnay from the south of France, with pear and citrus flavors, some buttery and spicy notes on the finish. Drink now.–K.M. • $12 • (1/01/1999) • **82**
Chardonnay Vin de Pays d'Oc Thierry and Guy Fat Bastard 1997: Fresh, lively and clean-tasting, with a good zip of acidity. Straightforward, showing apple and citrus flavors and spicy notes. Drink now.–K.M. • $12 • (9/30/1998) • **84**
Châteauneuf-du-Pape Laurus 1997: A soft '97 Châteauneuf, with some decent plum, red berry and smoke character. Velvety-textured and opulent, with a fat, lingering finish. Drink now through 2002.–P.M. • $36 • (8/31/1999) • **87**
Châteauneuf-du-Pape Laurus 1996: Supple, with modest fruit and earth notes. Medium-bodied, turning a bit sharp on the finish.–P.M. • $36 • (11/15/1998) • **79**
Coteaux du Languedoc Pic St.-Loup 1995: Berry and cherry flavors dominate this straightforward red. Drink now.–K.M. • $15 • (10/31/1998) • **81**
Côtes du Rhône La Chasse du Pape Réserve Barrique 1997: Straightforward but round, with some modest cherry, red berry and smoke notes. Drink now.–P.M. • $10 • (11/15/1999) • **80**
Côtes du Rhône-Villages Sablet Les Villages des Papes 1996: Smooth tannins in a straightforward red that's light-bodied with a drying finish. –P.M. • $12 • (11/15/1998) • **76**
Côtes du Rhône-Villages Séguret Château La Diffre 1996: Soft and lush, light-bodied, with plum, raisin, wet earth, black cherry character. A bit short on the finish. Drink now.–P.M. • $13 • (11/15/1998) • **80**
Gigondas Laurus 1997: A bit green and herbal, but a vanilla and spice veneer somewhat smooths this medium-bodied red.–P.M. • $24 • (10/31/1999) • **77**
Gigondas Laurus 1995: Ripe and smooth, this medium-bodied Gigondas has a distinctive red meat, salty crackers and dried fruit character that makes for a fun experience. Balanced finish. Drink now through 2005.–P.M. • $25 • (11/15/1998) • **87**
Lirac Laurus 1997: Light, simple and soft, with decent berry character.–P.M. • $17 • (12/15/1999) • **76**
Muscat de Beaumes-de-Venise Laurus 1997 • $28 • (1/01/1998) • **70**
Syrah Vin de Pays d'Oc Thierry and Guy Fat Bastard 1998: Straightforward, with dried cherry and spice flavors. Drying tannins on the finish. Drink now.–K.M. • $12 • (1/01/1999) • **82**
Vacqueyras Laurus 1997: Supple in texture, but of medium fruit intensity, showing red fruit character and a soft finish. Drink now.–P.M. • $21 • (10/31/1999) • **80**
Vin de Pays d'Oc Wild Goose White 1997: There's a slight honeyed taste to this medium-bodied white wine, which also has some figgy flavors. Herbal notes on the finish. Drink now.–K.M. • $8 • (11/15/1998) • **82**
Vin de Pays d'Oc Wild Pig Red 1997: Stemmy-tasting and dilute, turning a bit sour on the finish. A blend of Grenache, Syrah, Cinsault and Merlot. –K.M. • $8 • (12/15/1998) • **72**

MELLOT, ALPHONSE

Sancerre Domaine La Moussière 1996 • $18 • (5/31/1998) • **84**

MELLOT, JOSEPH

Pouilly-Fumé Le Troncsec 1996: Ripe, even tropical in aroma, this lively white has nectarine and citrus flavors, juicy acidity and good balance. Could be just a tad more concentrated and long. Drink now.–B.S. • $17 • (10/31/1998) • **84**
Sancerre La Chatellenie 1996: A finely etched white of delicacy and elegance, with light citrus, mineral and herb flavors well-balanced in a light body. Clean and refreshing. Drink now.–T.M. • $17 • (9/15/1998) • **87**

MEO-CAMUZET

Bourgogne 1990 • $20 • (6/15/1993) • **85**
Bourgogne 1989 • $23 • (11/15/1991) • **83**
Bourgogne Passe-tout-grains 1992 • $NA • (12/15/1994) • **83**
Bourgogne Passe-tout-grains 1990 • $17 • (3/31/1992) • **86**
Bourgogne Passe-tout-grains 1989 • $17 • (7/15/1991) • **84**
Clos de Vougeot 1997: Rich, round and supple, with vanilla and coffee augmenting the cherry flavors that persist through the medium finish. An attractive style. Drink now through 2003.–B.S. • $118 • (9/30/1999) • **87**
Clos de Vougeot 1996: Wow. Spicy blackberry aromas and flavors are matched by richness, power and a searing intensity as the vibrant acidity and tannins climax on the finish. Great length and focus. Best from 2002 through 2008.–P.M. • $98 • (9/30/1998) CS • **95**
Clos de Vougeot 1995 • $70 Ⓐ • (11/15/1997) • **92**
Clos de Vougeot 1994 • $50 Ⓐ • (11/15/1996) • **90**
Clos de Vougeot 1993 • $70 Ⓐ • (11/15/1995) • **88**
Clos de Vougeot 1992 • $57 • (12/15/1994) • **88**
Clos de Vougeot 1990 • $131 Ⓐ • (9/30/1993) • **84**
Clos de Vougeot 1989 • $91 • (11/15/1991) CS • **94**
Clos de Vougeot 1988 • $69 Ⓐ • (11/30/1990) • **92**
Clos de Vougeot 1986 • $55 • (11/30/1988) • **91**
Clos de Vougeot 1985 • $268 Ⓐ • (3/31/1988) • **93**
Corton 1997: Very oaky, with wood tannins blanketing the fruit. Full-bodied, it offers smoky, toasty, black character. Drink now through 2002.–P.M. • $125 • (9/30/1999) • **88**
Corton 1992 • $57 • (12/15/1995) • **91**
Corton 1989 • $76 • (11/15/1991) • **93**
Corton 1986 • $50 • (10/31/1988) • **89**
Corton Le Rognet 1995 • $70 • (11/15/1997) • **79**
Corton Le Rognet 1990 • $68 • (6/15/1993) • **89**
Nuits-St.-Georges 1997: Very ripe and sweet, with smoky character. Medium-bodied, it turns a bit tart on the finish, but there's freshness. Drink now through 2002.–P.M. • $58 • (9/30/1999) • **80**
Nuits-St.-Georges 1996: A pretty Nuits, all silk and finesse, exhibiting blackberry and spice. Seductive as it is, there's no shortage of firm tannins and lively acidity to support the fruit. Best from 2001 through 2006.–B.S. • $49 • (9/30/1998) • **90**
Nuits-St.-Georges 1992 • $33 • (12/15/1994) • **86**
Nuits-St.-Georges 1990 • $38 • (2/15/1993) • **88**
Nuits-St.-Georges 1989 • $52 • (11/15/1991) • **92**
Nuits-St.-Georges 1988 • $50 • (11/30/1990) • **91**
Nuits-St.-Georges 1987 • $42 • (12/15/1989) • **86**
Nuits-St.-Georges 1986 • $32 • (11/15/1988) • **90**
Nuits-St.-Georges Aux Boudots 1996: Subtle and spicy, this generously oaked wine is reserved on the nose, but quite round and fleshy on the palate; should gain harmony with time. Medium to full in body, with lots of mocha and vanilla on the finish. Best After 2005.–P.M. • $89 • (9/30/1998) • **92**
Nuits-St.-Georges Aux Boudots 1994 • $NA • (11/15/1996) • **88**
Nuits-St.-Georges Aux Boudots 1993 • $60 • (11/15/1995) • **90**
Nuits-St.-Georges Aux Boudots 1992 • $54 • (12/15/1994) • **85**
Nuits-St.-Georges Aux Boudots 1991 • $62 • (1/31/1994) • **84**
Nuits-St.-Georges Aux Boudots 1990 • $96 Ⓐ • (2/15/1993) • **91**
Nuits-St.-Georges Aux Boudots 1989 • $81 • (11/15/1991) • **90**
Nuits-St.-Georges Aux Boudots 1988 • $80 • (11/30/1990) • **92**
Nuits-St.-Georges Aux Boudots 1987 • $56 • (12/15/1989) • **88**
Nuits-St.-Georges Aux Boudots 1986 • $46 • (11/15/1988) • **92**
Nuits-St.-Georges Aux Murgers 1997: There's a lovely core of ripe cherry, wet earth and spice in this medium- to full-bodied Pinot. Firmly structured and lively, with a sense of grace. Best from 2001 through 2006.–B.S. • $96 • (9/30/1999) • **88**
Nuits-St.-Georges Aux Murgers 1996: Very pure, spicy, vibrant fruit marks this delicious '96 Nuits, with good concentration and intensity of flavor yet massive tannins. The fruit hangs in on the finish. Best from 2003 through 2010.–B.S. • $89 • (9/30/1998) • **91**
Nuits-St.-Georges Aux Murgers 1993 • $76 Ⓐ • (11/15/1995) • **93**

MEO-CAMUZET

Nuits-St.-Georges Aux Murgers 1992 • $54 • (12/15/1994) • **86**
Nuits-St.-Georges Aux Murgers 1991 • $62 • (1/31/1994) • **88**
Nuits-St.-Georges Aux Murgers 1990 • $68 • (2/15/1993) • **90**
Nuits-St.-Georges Aux Murgers 1989 • $81 • (11/15/1991) • **94**
Nuits-St.-Georges Aux Murgers 1988 • $80 • (11/30/1990) • **91**
Nuits-St.-Georges Aux Murgers 1987 • $56 • (12/15/1989) • **93**
Nuits-St.-Georges Aux Murgers 1986 • $48 • (11/15/1988) • **92**
Nuits-St.-Georges Aux Murgers 1985 • $73 • (4/15/1988) • **90**
Richebourg 1997: A slim, pretty red, offering blackberry, cherry and vanilla aromas and concentration. Drink now through 2001.–B.S. • $298 • (9/30/1999) • **85**
Richebourg 1996: Ripe and balanced, offering wet earth, mineral, smoke and red berry complexity, this is superbly intense on the finish, with a round, velvety mouthfeel. Grows on you as it kicks into high gear, rockets to a beautiful finish. This grand cru from Jean-Nicolas Méo tastes sweeter and more hedonistic than his minerally Clos de Vougeot, but both get the same classic rating. Best after 2007.–P.M. • $260 • (9/30/1998) • **95**
Richebourg 1995: Wonderful finesse and refinement define this aristocratic Pinot Noir. Not a showy blockbuster, it plays a delicate tune, delivering amazing, delightful aromas—rose petal, tar, plum—before moving into a sweet-tasting finale with ripe tannins. Best from 2005.–P.M. • $232 Ⓐ • (8/31/1998) • **95**
Richebourg 1993 • $175 • (11/15/1995) • **94**
Richebourg 1992 • $NA • (12/15/1994) • **91**
Richebourg 1990 • $445 Ⓐ • (6/15/1993) • **97**
Richebourg 1989 • $270 • (11/15/1991) • **97**
Richebourg 1988 • $210 Ⓐ • (11/30/1990) • **96**
Richebourg 1987 • $165 • (12/15/1989) • **96**
Richebourg 1986 • $160 • (10/31/1988) • **90**
Richebourg 1985 • $498 Ⓐ • (3/31/1988) • **97**
Vosne-Romanée 1994 • $30 • (11/15/1996) • **80**
Vosne-Romanée 1992 • $33 • (12/15/1994) • **80**
Vosne-Romanée 1990 • $36 • (2/15/1993) • **93**
Vosne-Romanée 1989 • $47 • (11/15/1991) • **91**
Vosne-Romanée 1988 • $50 • (12/31/1990) • **87**
Vosne-Romanée 1987 • $35 • (12/15/1989) • **90**
Vosne-Romanée 1986 • $30 • (10/31/1988) • **88**
Vosne-Romanée Aux Brûlées 1996: Opulent, pure and clean, with a pretty vanilla, mocha, spice backdrop to the lovely wet earth, red- and blackberry character. Full-bodied, with a firm structure of ripe tannins. Elegant, crisp and long finish. Best After 2005.–P.M. • $130 • (9/30/1998) • **92**
Vosne-Romanée Brûlées 1997: Moderate depth and concentration, with fine tannins and lively acidity to support the black cherry and earth notes. Drink now through 2002.–B.S. • $143 • (9/30/1999) • **85**
Vosne-Romanée Aux Brûlées 1995 • $70 • (11/15/1997) • **87**
Vosne-Romanée Aux Brûlées 1994 • $35 • (11/15/1996) • **89**
Vosne-Romanée Aux Brûlées 1993 • $75 • (11/15/1995) • **93**
Vosne-Romanée Aux Brûlées 1992 • $72 • (12/15/1994) • **85**
Vosne-Romanée Aux Brûlées 1991 • $73 • (1/31/1994) • **89**
Vosne-Romanée Aux Brûlées 1990 • $81 • (6/15/1993) • **93**
Vosne-Romanée Aux Brûlées 1989 • $91 • (11/15/1991) • **94**
Vosne-Romanée Aux Brûlées 1988 • $84 • (11/30/1990) • **89**
Vosne-Romanée Aux Brûlées 1987 • $63 • (12/15/1989) • **95**
Vosne-Romanée Cros Parantoux 1994 • $70 • (11/15/1996) • **87**
Vosne-Romanée Cros Parantoux 1992 • $73 • (12/15/1994) • **85**
Vosne-Romanée Cros Parantoux 1991 • $73 • (1/31/1994) • **88**
Vosne-Romanée Cros Parantoux 1990 • $179 Ⓐ • (6/15/1993) • **99**
Vosne-Romanée Cros Parantoux 1989 • $249 Ⓐ • (11/15/1991) • **95**
Vosne-Romanée Cros Parantoux 1988 • $84 • (11/30/1990) • **94**
Vosne-Romanée Cros Parantoux 1987 • $63 • (12/15/1989) • **95**
Vosne-Romanée Cros Parantoux 1986 • $144 Ⓐ • (7/31/1988) • **93**
Vosne-Romanée Chaumes 1997: A soft and easy '97 red, with a loosely knit structure and pretty cherry flavors. Round on the palate, with a moderate finish. Drink now through 2002.–B.S. • $88 • (9/30/1999) • **86**
Vosne-Romanée Les Chaumes 1996: A blockbuster '96. Huge, backward and unyielding, with masses of sweet fruit on the palate, racy acidity and ripe, dense tannins. Cassis and blackberry flavors emerge on the incredibly long finish. Immense wine. Best from 2004 through 2010.–B.S. • $78 • (9/30/1998) • **96**
Vosne-Romanée Les Chaumes 1994 • $60 Ⓐ • (11/15/1996) • **85**

Key: SS—Spectator Selection. CS—Cellar Selection. HR—Highly Recommended. $NA—Price not available. (BT)—Barrel tasting. Ⓐ—Auction Price. For a key to the tasters' initials, see "How to Use These Listings."
Dates in parentheses represent the issues in which the ratings were published.

Vosne-Romanée Les Chaumes 1993 • $50 Ⓐ • (11/15/1995) • **93**
Vosne-Romanée Les Chaumes 1992 • $43 • (12/15/1994) • **86**
Vosne-Romanée Les Chaumes 1990 • $116 Ⓐ • (2/15/1993) • **94**
Vosne-Romanée Les Chaumes 1989 • $62 • (1/31/1992) • **91**
Vosne-Romanée Les Chaumes 1986 • $38 • (12/31/1988) • **83**
Vosne-Romanée Les Chaumes 1985 • $80 • (3/31/1988) • **92**

MERCEY, DOMAINE DU CHATEAU DE

Hautes-Côtes de Beaune Vignes en Lyre 1997: The ripe cherry candy flavors are attractive yet simple in this medium-bodied red, offering licorice intensity and a firm structure. Drink now through 2004.–B.S. • $NA • (9/30/1999) • **83**

MERIC, DE

Brut Champagne NV • $30 • (10/31/1997) • **84**

MERISSAC, CHATEAU

St.-Emilion 1996: Has just enough berry and earth character to push it to a good rating. Light- to medium-bodied, with light tannins and a fruity finish. Second wine of Château Dassault. Drink now.–J.S. • $30 • (7/31/1999) • **80**

MERLE BLANC DE CHATEAU CLARKE, LE

Bordeaux 1998: Very well done, with melon, apple, pear and vanilla character. Medium- to full-bodied, with very good fruit and a creamy, fruity aftertaste. Drink now through 2003.–J.S. • $NA • (2/29/2000) • **89**

MERLIN-CHERRIER, DOMAINE

Sancerre 1996: A subtle wine that grows on you. Floral aromas are subdued, and on the palate this white is rather delicate, but there is good underlying acidity and the citrus, mineral and spice flavors build through the finish. Drink now through 2001.–T.M. • $17 • (6/30/1999) • **85**

MERODE, PRINCE FLORENT DE

Aloxe-Corton 1994 • $26 • (11/15/1996) • **78**
Aloxe-Corton 1987 • $30 • (2/28/1991) • **87**
Aloxe-Corton Premier Cru 1997: Ripe and a bit lacking in focus. The plum and fig flavors are supported by gripping tannins, ending with astringency.–B.S. • $37 • (9/30/1999) • **78**
Aloxe-Corton Premier Cru 1996: Shows pretty raspberry and cherry notes, moderate body and concentration that disappear midpalate. Finishes on the coarse side, with tannins and alcohol. Best from 2000.–B.S. • $34 • (9/30/1998) • **81**
Aloxe-Corton Premier Cru 1995 • $24 • (11/15/1997) • **74**
Aloxe-Corton Premier Cru 1990 • $37 • (12/15/1992) • **86**
Corton Clos du Roi 1997: A light-bodied red with simple but decent flavors. Tastes a bit of burnt wood, with a medium-intense cherry and raspberry character. Easy finish.–P.M. • $65 • (1/01/2000) • **77**
Corton Clos du Roi 1996: Delicate, even a bit on the light side, with some pretty raspberry and strawberry character. Shows nice fruit, lovely smooth tannins and a pretty, fresh finish. Delicious upon release.–P.M. • $56 • (9/30/1998) • **84**
Corton Clos du Roi 1995 • $38 • (11/15/1997) • **79**
Corton Le Clos du Roi 1994 • $42 • (11/15/1996) • **78**
Corton Le Clos du Roi 1993 • $44 • (11/15/1995) • **88**
Corton Le Clos du Roi 1992 • $42 • (12/15/1994) • **86**
Corton Le Clos du Roi 1990 • $38 • (12/15/1992) • **90**
Corton Le Clos du Roi 1987 • $44 • (3/31/1990) • **87**
Corton Le Clos du Roi 1986 • $49 • (8/31/1989) • **80**
Corton Les Bressandes 1997: A touch cooked, with light licorice and cherry flavors, a soft texture and a backbone of dry tannins. Drink now through 2002.–B.S. • $55 • (9/30/1999) • **80**
Corton Les Bressandes 1996: A solid red that exhibits cherries and spice without a lot of wood, but it's a bit one-dimensional and dissipates quickly on the finish. Drink through 2004.–B.S. • $50 • (9/30/1998) • **83**
Corton Les Bressandes 1994 • $36 • (11/15/1996) • **76**
Corton Les Bressandes 1993 • $37 • (11/15/1995) • **86**
Corton Les Bressandes 1992 • $35 • (12/15/1994) • **81**
Corton Les Bressandes 1990 • $58 Ⓐ • (12/15/1992) • **85**
Corton Les Bressandes 1989 • $56 • (11/30/1992) • **84**
Corton Les Bressandes 1987 • $45 • (3/31/1991) • **92**

FRANCE

Corton Les Bressandes 1986 • $38 • (8/31/1989) • **84**
Corton Les Bressandes 1985 • $52 • (2/15/1988) • **93**
Corton Les Maréchaudes 1997: Modest fruit and a diluted finish.–P.M. • $50 • (9/30/1999) • **73**
Corton Les Maréchaudes 1996: A light wine, showing some spice, oak and vanilla along with modest red berry character. A bit dry on the finish. Drink now.–P.M. • $50 • (9/30/1998) • **80**
Corton Les Maréchaudes 1995 • $34 • (11/15/1997) • **71**
Corton Les Maréchaudes 1994 • $32 • (11/15/1996) • **80**
Corton Les Maréchaudes 1993 • $32 • (11/15/1995) • **87**
Corton Les Maréchaudes 1992 • $32 • (12/15/1994) • **82**
Corton Les Maréchaudes 1990 • $58 Ⓐ • (12/15/1992) • **86**
Corton Les Maréchaudes 1987 • $36 • (8/31/1990) • **88**
Corton Les Maréchaudes 1986 • $33 • (8/31/1989) • **82**
Corton Les Maréchaudes 1985 • $49 • (3/15/1988) • **81**
Corton Les Renardes 1997: A diffuse nose of cherry turns a little pinched, offering only modest concentration and flavor. Tannic finish.–B.S. • $55 • (9/30/1999) • **79**
Corton Les Renardes 1996: Fruity wine, with light tannins, some succulent raspberry and cherry flavors. A bit diluted on the midpalate, it is still delicate and attractive. Enjoy upon release through 2003.–P.M. • $50 • (9/30/1998) • **84**
Corton Les Renardes 1994 • $36 • (11/15/1996) • **76**
Corton Les Renardes 1993 • $37 • (11/15/1995) • **85**
Corton Les Renardes 1992 • $35 • (12/15/1994) • **82**
Corton Les Renardes 1990 • $54 • (12/15/1992) • **94**
Corton Les Renardes 1987 • $36 • (3/31/1990) • **92**
Corton Les Renardes 1986 • $38 • (8/31/1989) • **76**
Ladoix Les Chaillots 1997: Easy in style, with herbal and diluted flavors.–P.M. • $23 • (9/30/1999) • **77**
Ladoix Les Chaillots 1996: Big wine all around. Displays loads of spicy black currant aromas and flavors, flesh and concentration, high acidity and stiff tannins. The balance and grip are there. Best from 2001 through 2005.–B.S. • $22 • (9/30/1998) • **86**
Ladoix Les Chaillots 1995 • $15 • (11/15/1997) • **75**
Ladoix Les Chaillots 1994 • $17 • (11/15/1996) • **74**
Ladoix Les Chaillots 1993 • $17 • (11/15/1995) • **90**
Ladoix Les Chaillots 1992 • $21 • (12/15/1994) • **76**
Ladoix Les Chaillots 1991 • $28 • (1/31/1994) • **81**
Ladoix Les Chaillots 1990 • $23 • (12/15/1992) • **88**
Ladoix Les Chaillots 1987 • $18 • (11/15/1990) • **77**
Ladoix Les Chaillots 1986 • $18 • (8/31/1989) • **74**
Pommard Clos de la Platière 1997: This earthy, minerally red is lean and light, offering cherry jam and plum flavors and a tannic structure. A bit rustic.–B.S. • $40 • (9/30/1999) • **79**
Pommard Clos de la Platière 1996: Delicious. This '96 Pommard offers cherry and mineral aromas and flavors, fine richness and depth that persist on the palate to the finish, where the tannins emerge, as does sweet fruit. Drink through 2006.–B.S. • $37 • (9/30/1998) • **89**
Pommard Clos de la Platière 1995 • $27 • (11/15/1997) • **74**
Pommard Clos de la Platière 1994 • $31 • (11/15/1996) • **74**
Pommard Clos de la Platière 1993 • $31 • (11/15/1995) • **88**
Pommard Clos de la Platière 1992 • $31 • (12/15/1994) • **79**
Pommard Clos de la Platière 1990 • $48 • (12/15/1992) • **90**
Pommard Clos de la Platière 1989 • $48 • (11/30/1992) • **86**
Pommard Clos de la Platière 1987 • $36 • (8/31/1990) • **76**
Pommard Clos de la Platière 1986 • $35 • (7/31/1989) • **86**
Pommard Clos de la Platière 1985 • $45 • (3/15/1988) • **94**
Pommard Clos de la Platière 1984 • $23 • (2/15/1988) • **71**

MERVILLE, CHATEAU

St.-Estèphe 1996: Intense berry and herbal aromas. Medium-bodied, with medium, silky tannins, but the slightly unripe character takes away from the overall quality. Drink now.–J.S. • $NA • (1/31/1999) • **81**

MESSEY, CHATEAU DE

Mâcon-Cruzilles Cuvée Spéciale 1996 • $14 • (8/31/1997) • **87**
Mâcon-Cruzilles Les Avoueries 1997: Decent tropical and pear character here, with crisp acidity. A sharp wine that should be OK with fish. From Demessey. Drink now through 2001.–P.M. • $14 • (5/31/1999) • **83**
Mâcon-Cruzilles Les Avoueries 1996 • $14 • (5/31/1998) • **82**
Mâcon-Cruzilles Les Avoueries 1995 • $13 • (5/31/1997) • **79**
Mâcon-Cruzilles Les Avoueries Oak Aged 1995 • $15 • (5/31/1997) • **79**

METAIREAU, LOUIS

Muscadet de Sèvre et Maine Sur Lie Carte Noire 1996: Fresh, with earth and apple notes that are straightforward and appealing. Finishes with a citrus component that lingers. Drink now.–B.S. • $14 • (11/15/1998) • **84**
Muscadet de Sèvre et Maine Sur Lie Cuvée One 1996: Ripe aromas and flavors border on peach, with plenty of lemon-lime and stone underneath. Lean and intense, with a vibrant acidity that leaves you smacking your lips. Try with oysters. Drink now.–B.S. • $20 • (11/15/1998) • **87**

METEORE, DOMAINE DU

Faugères Tonneaux 1998: Smooth and ripe, with rich flavors of dark plum, cassis and spice, fine tannins and a nice smoke/leather element. Flavors linger, with chocolate and cardamomlike notes on the finish. Drink now through 2002.–K.M. • $13 • (6/15/2000) • **89**

METRAS, YVON

Fleurie 1998: This rich red is atypical for a modern Beaujolais: It's highly extracted, with muscular tannins, and the flavors focus on the meaty, smoky end of the spectrum, with a core of ripe cherry that needs time to express itself. Drink now through 2004.–T.M. • $16 • (11/15/1999) • **86**
Fleurie 1997: This tender red has nicely delineated flavors of cherry, smoke and herb. Round on the palate, at once generous and firm enough for food. Harmonious and balanced, it's delicious now.–T.M. • $15 • (12/31/1998) • **87**

MEUNIER ST.-LOUIS, CHATEAU

Corbières 1991 • $NA • (3/15/1994) • **87**
Corbières White 1997: Balanced, with a good mixture of spice and fig and appealing grapefruit notes on the finish. Drink now.–K.M. • $9 • (10/31/1998) • **83**

MEYER-FONNE

Edelzwicker Alsace Katzenthal 1996 • $10/1 liter • (11/15/1997) • **83**
Extra Brut Crémant d'Alsace NV • $18 • (11/15/1997) • **86**
Gewürztraminer Alsace 1996: I'd swear I was drinking rose water. Aromatic in spades, but can't follow through on the palate, ending up light and short on the finish. Drink now.–B.S. • $16 • (9/15/1998) • **81**
Gewürztraminer Alsace Dorfburg Vieilles Vignes 1996: A crowd-pleaser. This pungent, apricot- and tropical fruit-scented version is full of flesh and richness, with an oily texture and good length.–B.S. • $20 • (9/15/1998) • **85**
Gewürztraminer Alsace Grand Cru Wineck-Schlossberg 1996: For fans of Gewürz. Full of exotic tropical fruits and roses, this is lush, round and balanced with excellent intensity of flavor and a long finish.–B.S. • $25 • (9/15/1998) • **90**
Gewürztraminer Alsace Grand Cru Wineck-Schlossberg Vendange Tardive 1994 • $33/500 ml. • (10/15/1996) • **88**
Gewürztraminer Alsace Réserve Particulière 1996 • $14 • (11/15/1997) • **88**
Muscat Alsace Katzenthal Tiré Sur Lie 1996: Rich and full of grapefruit and spice, full-bodied, yet with verve and a crisp, dry finish. Drink now.–B.S. • $15 • (9/15/1998) • **83**
Pinot Blanc Alsace Vieilles Vignes 1996 • $10 • (11/15/1997) • **87**
Pinot Noir Alsace 1994 • $14 • (10/15/1996) • **83**
Riesling Alsace Grand Cru Wineck-Schlossberg 1996: Wonderful clarity of fruit and terroir, yet this lacks the intensity and complexity of the best '96 Rieslings. Fine lime blossom, apple and mineral elements, racy acidity and a clean, lingering finish. Drink through 2006.–B.S. • $25 • (9/15/1998) • **89**
Riesling Alsace Kaefferkopf 1996: Delicious, combining vibrant acidity with ripe, stony apple and lime, all on an elegant structure with a smoky finish. Drink through 2004–B.S. • $24 • (9/15/1998) • **88**
Riesling Alsace Katzenthal 1996: Seductive. Smoke, quince and almond aromas and flavors hold court, held up by firm acidity, all ending on a mineral note. Needs time to unwind. Drink through 2003.–B.S. • $17 • (9/15/1998) • **89**
Riesling Alsace Réserve Particulière 1996 • $14 • (11/15/1997) • **90**
Tokay Pinot Gris Alsace Réserve Particulière 1996 • $15 • (11/15/1997) • **87**
Tokay Pinot Gris Alsace St.-Urbain Réserve 1996: Incredible ripeness here, late-harvest in style, displaying tropical fruit, flint, nectarine and mint character, a fat, juicy texture and good balance. It falls off slightly on the finish after such a lovely introduction, but delicious nonetheless. Drink now.–B.S. • $20 • (9/15/1998) • **90**

MEYNEY, CHATEAU

St.-Estèphe 1999: Very light for the vintage. Light- to medium-bodied, with light tannins and a fresh finish. Barely 80-84.–J.S. • $NA • (1/01/2000) (BT) • **80-84**
St.-Estèphe 1998: Interesting wine. Orange blossom and berry aromas. Full- to medium-bodied, with a solid core of fruit and a velvety texture. Almost outstanding.–J.S. • $NA • (5/31/1999) (BT) • **85-89**
St.-Estèphe 1997: This is really light and watery, with some plum character. What a shame for Meyney.–J.S. • $30 • (1/31/2000) • **78**
St.-Estèphe 1996: Rich aromas of spices, berries, meat and earth. Medium-bodied, with velvety tannins and a fruity aftertaste. Slightly hollow midpalate. Best after 2000.–J.S. • $24 • (1/31/1999) • **86**
St.-Estèphe 1995 • $33 Ⓐ • (1/31/1998) • **85**
St.-Estèphe 1994 • $21 • (1/31/1997) • **87**
St.-Estèphe 1993 • $17 • (1/31/1996) • **86**
St.-Estèphe 1992 • $15 • (4/15/1995) • **83**
St.-Estèphe 1991 • $15 • (3/31/1994) • **79**
St.-Estèphe 1990 • $20 • (3/31/1993) • **90**
St.-Estèphe 1989: One of the great buys of the vintage. Dark-colored, sporting loads of minty, berry and chocolate aromas and flavors. Full-bodied, with plenty of velvety tannins and a long, rich finish. Built for aging.(1989 Bordeaux horizontal tasting). Best after 2005.–J.S. • $46 Ⓐ • (5/31/1999) • **93**
St.-Estèphe 1987 • $14 • (5/15/1990) • **87**
St.-Estèphe 1986 • $46 Ⓐ • (11/30/1989) • **88**
St.-Estèphe 1984 • $11 • (5/15/1987) • **79**
St.-Estèphe 1982: A burly, chewy red, as usual. Dark ruby-garnet in color. Red licorice and ripe berry aromas. Full-bodied, with a lot of fruit and raisin character. Full tannins and a long finish. (1989 Bordeaux horizontal tasting). Best after 2000.–J.S. • $51 Ⓐ • (11/30/1998) • **90**
St.-Estèphe 1979 • $18 • (10/15/1989) • **87**
St.-Estèphe 1961 • $47 • (4/30/1996) • **83**

MEZIAT, PIERRE

Chiroubles Domaine Marquis des Pontheux Sélection Vieilles Vignes 1996: Angular in profile, with a strong backbone of acidity that carries the earthy cherry flavors across the palate. Good depth and intensity. Drink now.–B.S. • $16 • (10/31/1998) • **84**
Chiroubles Domaine Marquis des Pontheux Sélection Vieilles Vignes 1995 • $15 • (9/15/1997) • **77**

MIAUDOUX, CHATEAU

Bergerac 1995: A full-bodied, tannic, ripe-flavored red that seems to stress spicy oak over its black cherry and plum notes. Hearty and robust, and in need of a little more time. Drink through 2001. • $7 • (8/31/1998) • **84**
Saussignac Réserve 1994 • $11/500 ml. • (8/31/1997) • **84**

MICHAUD, ALAIN

Brouilly Cuvée Sélectionée 1995 • $14 • (9/15/1997) • **85**
Brouilly Cuvée Sélectionée 1994 • $15 • (9/15/1996) • **84**
Brouilly Prestige de Vieilles Vignes 1994 • $18 • (9/15/1996) • **88**
Brouilly Prestige de Vieilles Vignes 1993 • $17 • (6/15/1995) • **79**

MICHEL, ROBERT

Cornas Cuvée des Coteaux 1996: Green, herbal and metallic. Sour finish.–P.M. • $30 • (11/30/1999) • **70**
Cornas Cuvée des Coteaux 1995: Thick, rich and robust, a beautiful red under a thick blanket of slightly drying tannins, this is full-bodied and cellar-worthy, with deep red- and blackberry character, toasted oak, cedar and cigar-box complexity. A bit hot on the finish.–P.M. • $28 • (11/15/1998) • **88**
Cornas Cuvée des Coteaux 1994: Light in body, texture and color, fairly simple, with cherry and raspberry. Soft tannins.–P.M. • $25 • (11/15/1998) • **79**
Cornas Cuvée des Coteaux 1991 • $16 • (5/31/1994) • **89**
Cornas La Geynale 1996: A light, brick-colored, stemmy, green- and herbal-tasting red that turns tough on the finish.–P.M. • $37 • (11/30/1999) • **72**

Key: SS—Spectator Selection. CS—Cellar Selection. HR—Highly Recommended. $NA—Price not available. (BT)—Barrel tasting. Ⓐ—Auction Price.
For a key to the tasters' initials, see "How to Use These Listings."
Dates in parentheses represent the issues in which the ratings were published.

Cornas La Geynale 1991 • $20 • (5/31/1994) • **82**

MICHEL & FILS, LOUIS

Chablis 1998: Both samples provided were corky.–P.M. • $17 • (5/15/2000) • **55**
Chablis 1997: Nice village Chablis, showing a dusty-soily character that reveals mineral, some apple and a rather smooth mouthfeel despite the ultradry style. Drink now through 2001.–P.M. • $25 • (5/31/1999) • **85**
Chablis 1996: For a village Chablis this is wonderful, with plenty of wet earth, mineral, green apple, citrus and grass flavors, along with some suppleness. Almost matches the silky texture of a premier cru from Michel. Drink now through 2010.–P.M. • $25 • (8/31/1998) • **89**
Chablis 1995 • $NA • (8/31/1996) • **78**
Chablis Grenouilles 1998: Attractive. Pretty aromas of smoke, spice and chocolate combine with pear tart flavor in a supple, silky, medium-bodied wine of good length. Too bad about a slight midpalate dilution. Drink now through 2003.–P.M. • $40 • (5/15/2000) • **86**
Chablis Grenouilles 1997: Interesting. Definitely toasted from the oak, but very tight, firm and clean, showing remarkable depth of character and a delicious balance between the ripe fruit, smoky notes and citrus-mineral combo on the lingering, rich finish. Best from 2003 through 2010.–P.M. • $52 • (5/31/1999) • **92**
Chablis Grenouilles 1996 • $48 • (5/31/1998) • **88**
Chablis Grenouilles 1995 • $46 • (6/15/1997) • **91**
Chablis Les Clos 1998: Honeyed, buttery and smoky, this medium-bodied '98 tastes complex and ripe. Offers a sense of concentration, showing chalky, flinty, minerally character. Impressive length. Best from 2001 through 2008.–P.M. • $39 • (5/15/2000) • **90**
Chablis Les Clos 1997: Splendid. Rich, ripe, opulent, stressing fruit and more fruit, delivering delicious tropical, fig, sweet date, honey character and a lofty vanilla, mineral, wet earth complexity from the first whiff to the last sip of this silky liquid. Drink now through 2015.–P.M. • $51 • (5/31/1999) • **94**
Chablis Les Clos 1996 • $46 • (5/31/1998) • **94**
Chablis Montée de Tonnerre 1998: Steely and somewhat ungenerous, with muted wet earth and green apple flavors. Light-bodied, with crisp lemon and mineral character. Drink now through 2001.–P.M. • $24 • (5/15/2000) • **80**
Chablis Montée de Tonnerre 1997: Clean and crisp, a tightly wound wine that still has a distance to go before showing it all, with a firm core of citrus-spiked acidity, lemon-tart and mineral flavors and a mouthpuckering finish. Drink through 2005.–P.M. • $32 • (5/31/1999) • **86**
Chablis Montée de Tonnerre 1996 • $30 • (5/31/1998) • **93**
Chablis Montée de Tonnerre 1995 • $27 • (6/15/1997) • **89**
Chablis Montmain 1998: Fairly opulent and ripe, this seduces with its supple texture and clean flavors of apple, pear and butter. Medium-bodied, it kicks in with mineral, chalk and flint notes on the lingering finish. Best after 2001.–P.M. • $22 • (5/15/2000) • **86**
Chablis Montmain 1997: Crisp style here, but it packs plenty of minerally smoothness, lush ripe fruit and enough harmony to make it tempting on release—even though it has a vibrant, high-acidity finish that lingers long, strongly suggesting cellaring. Best from 2001 through 2005.–P.M. • $31 • (5/31/1999) • **90**
Chablis Montmain 1996: Ripe and rich, yet fresh and vibrant, this prototypical '96 Chablis offers full body, seductively supple texture (once past the zesty, limelike acidity), and loads of wet earth, honey, tropical and chalky flavors. Deeply satisfying for its balance.–P.M. • $31 • (8/31/1998) • **93**
Chablis Montmain 1995 • $26 • (6/15/1997) • **89**
Chablis Vaillons 1998: Crisp and steely in style, with lots of lemon, lime, grapefruit and green apple. Don't expect much fatness. Drink now through 2004.–P.M. • $22 • (5/15/2000) • **80**
Chablis Vaillons 1997: Intense stuff here, as it sweeps across the palate like a wild fire, delivering wet earth, ripe fruit, smoky and flinty flavors that are classic Chablis. Long finish. Drink now through 2007.–P.M. • $31 • (5/31/1999) • **90**
Chablis Vaillons 1996 • $29 • (5/31/1998) • **55**
Chablis Vaillons 1995 • $26 • (6/15/1997) • **87**
Chablis Vaudésir 1998: Ripe-tasting and sweetly delicious. Light- to medium-bodied, this is a pleasant, approachable, easygoing white, with pear, litchi and dried apricot. Drink now through 2003.–P.M. • $37 • (5/15/2000) • **87**
Chablis Vaudésir 1997: Exciting. In a ripe, buttery style, with pear and cakelike aromas, this full-bodied Chablis manages to stay elegant on the palate and true to its terroir, with complex mineral, salty, lime and dried herbs notes enveloping the balanced finish. Best from 2003 through 2008.–P.M. • $50 • (5/31/1999) • **90**

Chablis Vaudésir 1996 • $45 • (5/31/1998) • **84**
Chablis Vaudésir 1995 • $44 • (6/15/1997) • **89**

MICHEL FRERES

Brut Blanc de Blancs Crémant de Bourgogne 1995: A light-bodied bubbly with earthy aromas and lean fruit flavors. Drink now. • $16 • (10/15/1999) • **79**

Brut Rosé Crémant de Bourgogne 1997: Light, dry and extremely fruity; drink as an aperitif while it's fresh and lively. Drink now. • $16 • (10/15/1999) • **86**

MICHELE, ROBERT

Muscadet de Sèvre et Maine 1997: Round and soft, this generous white offers almond and apple flavors. Gentle and clean on the palate, it's still fresh but lacks verve. Drink now.–T.M. • $8 • (6/15/1999) • **81**

Vouvray 1997: Clean and fresh, this white offers straightforward apple flavors, with a nice balance of crisp acidity, slight sweetness and good body. Modest and well made. Drink now.–T.M. • $9 • (6/30/1999) • **82**

MICHELOT, G.

Meursault Les Grands Charrons 1995 • $40 • (5/31/1997) • **83**
Meursault Les Tillets 1995 • $45 • (5/31/1997) • **82**

MICHELOT-BUISSON

Bourgogne White 1995 • $18 • (8/31/1997) • **76**
Meursault Clos St.-Félix 1995 • $35 • (5/31/1997) • **79**
Meursault Genevrières 1995 • $65 • (5/31/1997) • **78**
Meursault Le Limozin 1995 • $40 • (5/31/1997) • **87**
Meursault Les Charmes 1995 • $65 • (5/31/1997) • **70**
Meursault Les Narvaux 1995 • $45 • (5/31/1997) • **87**
Meursault Les Perrières 1995 • $75 • (5/31/1997) • **88**
Meursault Sous la Velle 1995 • $33 • (5/31/1997) • **85**
Puligny-Montrachet 1995 • $NA • (8/31/1997) • **82**
Puligny-Montrachet La Garenne 1995 • $50 • (5/31/1997) • **86**

MILAN, JEAN

Brut Blanc de Blancs Champagne Carte Blanche NV: This posh style of Champagne invites you in, with bright fruit flavors and buttery, creamy accents that build on the palate and linger on the finish. The broad but light texture is hard to resist. Drink now. • $26 • (12/15/1998) • **92**

Brut Blanc de Blancs Champagne Spécial NV: Inviting and smooth, ripe enough in flavor and soft enough in texture to please most anyone. Drink now. • $42 • (10/15/1999) • **86**

Brut Blanc de Blancs Champagne Terres de Noël Sélection 1992: Very fresh, light and easygoing in style. Enticing for its almost-sweet flavors and soft, frothy texture. Drink now. • $60 • (10/15/1999) • **88**

MILLERIE, CHATEAU LA

Puisseguin-St.-Emilion 1997: More like a rosé than a red, with cherry and berry character and a light, diluted finish.–J.S. • $13 • (7/31/1999) • **78**

Puisseguin-St.-Emilion 1996: More like a rosé than a red. Light-bodied, with light vanilla and cherry flavors.–J.S. • $13 • (7/31/1999) • **77**

MILLET-DOUCET, DOMAINE

Sancerre 1996 • $19 • (6/15/1998) • **84**

MILLOT, BERNARD

Meursault La Goutte d'Or 1998: Wonderful. Intense smoke and toasted, spicy aromas explode from the glass. A full-bodied Meursault that delivers rich, dense texture and concentrated, compacted fruit and honey flavors. A silky package that lasts impressively on the finish. Drink now through 2010.–P.M. • $45 • (5/31/2000) • **92**

Meursault La Goutte d'Or 1997: Ripe and sweet-tasting, but also a bit oxidized and overly woody (in a dry way), the wine comes off as awkward.–P.M. • $42 • (9/30/1999) • **79**

Meursault Les Perrières 1997: Smooth and a bit dull, with a silky texture that suggests a fine appellation, but it doesn't come together.–P.M. • $NA • (1/01/1999) • **79**

Meursault Les Petits Charrons 1997: Nice Meursault experience. Ripe and supple, with some round texture, the fruit tastes sweet and full, accented by spicy mocha, chocolate and deftly oaked, vanilla-coated notes. Lacks intensity, so drink soon. Drink now through 2002.–P.M. • $NA • (1/01/1999) • **86**

Meursault Les Terres Blanches 1997: Thick in texture but odd in aroma, with a carboardy, filtered character.–P.M. • $38 • (9/30/1999) • **75**

Puligny-Montrachet 1998: Nice terroir-driven Chardonnay. Sweet-tasting and medium-bodied, with a chewy, minerally character and a finish that's balanced between citrus, honey and wet earth. Best from 2003 through 2010.–P.M. • $34 • (5/31/2000) • **90**

Puligny-Montrachet 1997: Very ripe, medium-bodied, with some cooked and dried fruit character, turning a bit dull on the finish.–P.M. • $33 • (9/30/1999) • **79**

MILLOT, JEAN-MARC

Clos de Vougeot 1997: A mature and light-colored Pinot, with mushroom and licorice notes. Tastes sweet but turns astringent on the finish.–P.M. • $100 • (9/30/1999) • **75**

Côte de Nuits-Villages 1997: Blackberry and spice flavors are allied to an elegant, tender structure, with ripe tannins and balancing acidity. Delicate for the appellation, with plenty of up-front appeal. Drink now through 2003.–B.S. • $29 • (9/30/1999) • **88**

Côte de Nuits-Villages 1996: Very pretty. Showing rose, lovely cassis and smoke character and bursting with fresh fruit and acidity, it's an elegant style, but it turns a bit dry on the finish. Drink now through 2003.–P.M. • $25 • (2/28/1999) • **84**

Echézeaux 1997: A good effort for the vintage. This lovely, smooth, round red Burgundy shows coffee, spice and black fruit, with a thickness of ripe fruit on the midpalate that provides length and complexity. Drink now through 2007.–P.M. • $90 • (9/30/1999) • **89**

Echézeaux 1996: Imagine a wine with the textural thickness of extra virgin olive oil and the raciness of freshly crushed blackberries, and you get a picture of this full-bodied, richly made, delicious and sweet-tasting Pinot with earth, chocolate and spice flavors. Drink now through 2010.–P.M. • $90 • (2/28/1999) • **93**

Echézeaux 1993 • $NA • (5/15/1996) • **86**

Savigny-lès-Beaune 1996: A crisp style, medium-bodied and fairly lean, it has decent cherry notes but turns a bit herbal on the finish.–P.M. • $30 • (2/28/1999) • **77**

Vosne-Romanée 1997: Vanilla and mocha aromas show nicely in this round, rather fat red Pinot Noir. Kicks in with cherry and raspberry notes on the finish. Drink now through 2002.–P.M. • $48 • (9/30/1999) • **81**

MINCHIN, ALBANE & BERTRAND

Menetou-Salon La Tour St.-Martin 1996: Ripe with quince and gooseberry character, bright acidity and intensity, all well balanced and refreshing. Citrus notes linger on the finish. Drink now.–B.S. • $14 • (11/15/1998) • **85**

MINET, REGIS

Pouilly-Fumé Vieilles Vignes 1998: Smooth and fairly supple, with green pear, smoke and citrus flavors that come together well on the long finish. Drink now.–K.M. • $15 • (5/15/2000) • **87**

Pouilly-Fumé Vieilles Vignes 1997: This lively white has vibrant acidity and the citrus and mineral flavors that go so well with food, but it also has a lush layer of ripe fruit, with notes of pear, melon and fig. The seamless combination is generous yet delicate, assertive yet crisp. Drink now through 2001.–T.M. • $18 • (12/31/1998) • **89**

Pouilly-Fumé Vieilles Vignes 1996 • $18 • (5/31/1998) • **88**

MIOLANE, CHRISTIAN

Beaujolais-Villages Cuvée des Chasseurs 1995 • $12 • (9/15/1997) • **84**

MIQUEL, DOMAINE

Merlot Vin de Pays d'Oc 1998: Straightforward, offering bright cherry and plum flavors with balanced acidity and tannin. A sturdy quaff that will match well with grilled meats. Drink now through 2001.–T.M. • $11 • (10/15/1999) • **84**

Syrah Vin de Pays d'Oc 1996: Quite aromatic, with intense and nicely concentrated red plum, currant and cherry flavors. Laserlike acidity on the herbal finish needs time to flesh out. Drink now.–K.M. • $11 • (12/31/1998) • **85**
Syrah Vin de Pays d'Oc 1995 • $12 • (10/31/1997) • **87**
Viognier Vin de Pays d'Oc 1998: Any assertive style, with herbal and green peach flavors. Finishes with some peppery notes. Drink now.–K.M. • $11 • (10/15/1999) • **82**
Viognier Vin de Pays d'Oc 1997: Clean and fresh-tasting. This is a nice, smooth white, with pleasant peach and cream flavors and spicy notes on the finish. Drink now.–K.M. • $11 • (12/15/1998) • **82**

MIREFLEURS, CHATEAU

Bordeaux Supérieur 1996: Watery and light, with some berry and herbal character on the nose and palate, but it's difficult to get excited about.–J.S. • $10 • (1/31/1999) • **78**
Bordeaux Supérieur 1995 • $8 • (1/31/1998) • **85**

MISSION-HAUT-BRION, CHATEAU LA

Pessac-Léognan 1999: Super aromas of crushed cherries, raspberries and minerals. Full-bodied, with a solid core of ripe and silky tannins and a long finish. Very pretty.–J.S. • $NA • (1/01/2000) (BT) • **90-94**
Pessac-Léognan 1998: Massive yet balanced '98, with lots of mineral, mint, wet earth, berry and cherry character. Full-bodied, with loads of round, velvety tannins and a long, long aftertaste.–J.S. • $NA • (5/31/1999) (BT) • **95-99**
Pessac-Léognan 1997: Outstanding mineral and licorice character on the nose, but rather austere and lean. Medium body. Needs time to develop. Best after 2002.–J.S. • $83 • (1/31/2000) • **87**
Pessac-Léognan 1996: A gentle, friendly wine for the vintage. Aromas of berries, tobacco and earth. Medium- to full-bodied, round, with soft tannins and a fruity aftertaste. Best after 2000.–J.S. • $97 • (1/31/1999) • **89**
Pessac-Léognan 1995 • $65 • (1/31/1998) • **93**
Pessac-Léognan 1993 • $60 • (1/31/1996) • **89**
Pessac-Léognan 1992 • $44 • (4/15/1995) • **84**
Pessac-Léognan 1991 • $45 • (3/31/1994) • **85**
Pessac-Léognan 1990 • $65 • (3/31/1993) • **95**
Pessac-Léognan 1989: A wine that literally reeks of the earth. Decadent and rich. Very dark ruby-red color. Complex aromas of berry, game, earth and chocolate. Full-bodied and incredibly extracted, with loads of tannins and a complement of earthy, berry, funky flavors. Long finish. (1989 Bordeaux horizontal tasting). Best after 2007.–J.S. • $NA • (5/31/1999) • **96**
Pessac-Léognan 1988: I don't remember the '88 La Mission as being so wonderfully opulent. It shows fabulous violet, berry and dried fruit aromas and flavors. Full-bodied, with big, velvety tannins and a long, ripe and delicious aftertaste. (1989 Bordeaux horizontal tasting). Best after 2002.–J.S. • $NA • (11/30/1998) • **96**
Pessac-Léognan 1987 • $41 • (11/15/1991) • **84**
Pessac-Léognan 1986 • $51 • (11/15/1991) • **97**
Graves 1985 • $111 Ⓐ • (10/15/1994) • **90**
Graves 1984 • $55 • (11/15/1991) • **85**
Graves 1983 • $83 Ⓐ • (10/15/1994) • **93**
Graves 1982: Slightly rustic, but firm and youthful. Dark ruby color. Beautiful aromas of berries and stones, with a hint of black truffles. Medium- to full-bodied, with silky tannins and a long, spicy-stony finish. (1982 Bordeaux horizontal tasting). Drink through 2010.–J.S. • $226 Ⓐ • (11/30/1998) • **94**
Graves 1981 • $76 Ⓐ • (11/15/1991) • **87**
Graves 1980 • $NA • (11/15/1991) • **86**
Graves 1979 • $74 Ⓐ • (11/15/1991) • **86**
Graves 1978 • $166 Ⓐ • (11/15/1991) • **94**
Graves 1975 • $390 Ⓐ • (11/15/1991) • **90**
Graves 1974 • $NA • (11/15/1991) • **87**
Graves 1973 • $52 • (11/15/1991) • **80**
Graves 1972 • $38 Ⓐ • (11/15/1991) • **77**
Graves 1971 • $86 Ⓐ • (11/15/1991) • **91**
Graves 1969 • $32 • (11/15/1991) • **84**
Graves 1967 • $58 Ⓐ • (11/15/1991) • **89**
Graves 1965 • $100 • (11/15/1991) • **76**
Graves 1963 • $100 • (11/15/1991) • **78**

Key: SS—Spectator Selection. CS—Cellar Selection. HR—Highly Recommended. $NA—Price not available. (BT)—Barrel tasting. Ⓐ—Auction Price.
For a key to the tasters' initials, see "How to Use These Listings."
Dates in parentheses represent the issues in which the ratings were published.

Graves 1961 • $982 Ⓐ • (4/30/1996) • **96**
Graves 1960 • $140 • (11/15/1991) • **84**
Graves 1959 • $839 Ⓐ • (11/15/1991) • **94**
Graves 1958 • $180 • (11/15/1991) • **83**
Graves 1957 • $165 • (11/15/1991) • **85**
Graves 1956 • $210 • (11/15/1991) • **87**
Graves 1954 • $375 • (11/15/1991) • **86**
Graves 1952 • $431 Ⓐ • (11/15/1991) • **98**
Graves 1950 • $350 • (11/15/1991) • **79**
Graves 1948 • $600 • (11/15/1991) • **98**
Graves 1946 • $700 • (11/15/1991) • **85**
Graves 1945 • $1,323 Ⓐ • (11/30/1995) • **96**
Graves 1944 • $350 • (11/15/1991) • **78**
Graves 1943 • $261 Ⓐ • (11/15/1991) • **88**
Graves 1942 • $275 • (11/15/1991) • **83**
Graves 1941 • $250 • (11/15/1991) • **81**
Graves 1940 • $330 • (11/15/1991) • **82**
Graves 1939 • $350 • (11/15/1991) • **87**
Graves 1938 • $190 • (11/15/1991) • **81**
Graves 1937 • $287 Ⓐ • (11/15/1991) • **88**
Graves 1935 • $575 • (11/15/1991) • **85**
Graves 1934 • $368 Ⓐ • (11/15/1991) • **86**
Graves 1933 • $475 • (11/15/1991) • **74**
Graves 1931 • $375 • (11/15/1991) • **70**
Graves 1924 • $550 • (11/15/1991) • **89**
Graves 1921 • $600 • (11/15/1991) • **85**
Graves 1919 • $600 • (11/15/1991) • **85**
Graves 1918 • $550 • (11/15/1991) • **83**
Graves 1916 • $350 • (11/15/1991) • **82**
Graves 1904 • $600 • (11/15/1991) • **85**
Graves 1899 • $850 • (11/15/1991) • **92**
Graves 1895 • $700 • (11/15/1991) • **99**
Graves 1888 • $1,000 • (11/15/1991) • **95**
Graves 1877 • $1,000 • (11/15/1991) • **93**

MISTRAL, CAVE DU

Chardonnay Vin de Pays de l'Herault Domaine La Grange Virginie 1996: A thin white whose main theme is canned pear flavor, accompanied by nutmeg.–B.S. • $11 • (12/15/1998) • **75**
Sauvignon Blanc Vin de Pays de l'Hérault Gallerie 1996 • $8 • (3/31/1998) • **83**
Viognier Vin de Pays de l'Hérault Gallerie 1996 • $10 • (12/15/1997) • **79**

MITTNACHT-KLACK

Gewürztraminer Alsace 1997: The floral aromas are promising, but they disappear quickly on the palate before finishing weakly. A second bottle was corky.–B.S. • $16 • (10/31/1999) • **75**
Muscat Alsace Kronenberg 1997: Smells floral, with grapey, spicy notes on the palate. Rich, round and dry, showing good balance and a crisp finish, this would make a pleasant aperitif. A second bottle was corky. Drink now.–B.S. • $20 • (10/31/1999) • **86**
Pinot Blanc Alsace Oberberg 1997: Vinous, but rather neutral in flavor. A second bottle was corky.–B.S. • $11 • (10/15/1999) • **75**
Riesling Alsace 1997: Balanced and intense, with stone and spice flavors rather than fruit right now. It's rich on the palate, finishing on a lemony note. A second bottle was corky. Drink now through 2002.–B.S. • $12 • (10/15/1999) • **84**
Riesling Alsace Grand Cru Schoenenbourg 1997: Rich and slightly sweet, this Riesling offers immediate appeal and moderate concentration, with flavors of peach, vanilla and mineral. The finish is on the dry side. Drink now through 2001.–B.S. • $30 • (10/15/1999) • **86**
Riesling Alsace Muhlforst 1997: Broad and honeyed, this Riesling trades elegance and finesse for richness and weight. Balanced to the soft side, with a slightly bitter finish. Drink now.–B.S. • $18 • (10/15/1999) • **84**
Tokay Pinot Gris Alsace 1997: Smells sweet and follows through with fruit cocktail flavors, a loosely knit texture and a weak finish.–B.S. • $16 • (10/31/1999) • **78**

MOC BARIL

Cabernet Rosé d'Anjou 1997 • $NA • (1/01/1998) • **79**

MOET & CHANDON

Brut Champagne Cuvée Dom Pérignon 1992: Mature flavors and a generous texture make this enjoyable now; has a good base of fruit flavors, with toasty, honeyed accents. Drink now. • $95 • (10/15/1999) • **87**
Brut Champagne Cuvée Dom Pérignon 1990: Fans of bold wine will love this Champagne. It's made in a full-bodied, assertive style that blends overt toasty, earthy aromas with bracing, dry fruit flavors and a robust but smooth texture. Drink now through 2003. • $110 • (12/15/1998) • **90**
Brut Champagne Impérial NV: With a mouthfilling mousse, ripe and concentrated fruit flavors and slight sweetness, this is easy to enjoy. Drink now. • $33 • (10/15/1999) • **87**
Brut Champagne Impérial 1992: Fine complexity and depth mark this assertive and flavorful Champagne. Layers of creamy, toasty, nutty flavors linger on the finish. Drink now through 2001. • $41 • (10/15/1999) • **88**
Brut Champagne Impérial 1990 • $40 • (12/31/1996) • **91**
Brut Champagne Impérial 2000 NV: Well-balanced and well-made. Bright and fresh in flavor, crisp but smooth in texture. Drink now. • $70/1.5 liter • (10/15/1999) • **87**
Brut Rosé Champagne NV: Traditional but exciting style of dry rosé, designed for dinner. Has a copper color, toasty aromas, firm texture and subtle fruit and spice flavors that linger on the finish. Drink now through 2001. • $35 • (10/15/1999) • **91**
Brut Rosé Champagne Impérial NV: A deep-copper rosé that really tastes like the Pinot Noir grapes that give it color. The subtle cherry, cinnamon and toast flavors are appealing and linger on the finish. Refined in texture. Drink now. • $40 • (12/31/1998) • **86**
Brut Rosé Champagne Impérial 1992: A grand, full-bodied rosé that's flavorful and mature. A deep amber color, toasty aromas and nutty-spicy flavors make it unique. Has a generous texture, too. Tasted twice, with consistent notes. Drink now through 2001. • $45 • (10/15/1999) • **87**
Brut Rosé Champagne Impérial 1990 • $47 • (12/15/1995) • **82**
Demi-Sec Champagne Nectar Impérial NV: A soft, sweet, dessert-style Champagne with easy flavors of pear, vanilla and almond that linger on the finish. Drink now. • $30 • (10/15/1999) • **87**
Extra Dry Champagne White Star NV • $29 • (10/31/1996) • **82**

MOILLARD

Aloxe-Corton 1996: Shows an herbaceous element, along with cherry aromas and flavors and a hint of vanilla. Easygoing, light-bodied and personable. Drink through 2004.–B.S. • $28 • (9/30/1998) • **83**
Aloxe-Corton Les Affouages 1989 • $NA • (1/31/1992) • **83**
Beaujolais Nouveau 1999: Round and soft, this generous red shows ripe cherry and plum flavors, more fleshy than structured. Drink slightly chilled. Drink now.–T.M. • $8 • (1/01/2000) • **83**
Beaujolais-Villages Domaine de Reyssiers 1996: Pretty cherry and spicy flavors in this lean red, but it's starting to dry out on the finish. May soften with food. Drink now.–T.M. • $9 • (8/31/1998) • **79**
Beaujolais-Villages Domaine de Reyssiers 1995 • $12 • (9/15/1997) • **74**
Beaune 1990 • $26 • (12/15/1992) • **87**
Beaune Hospices de Beaune Cuvée Clos des Avaux 1988 • $80 • (8/31/1991) • **88**
Bourgogne Passe-tout-grains Notre Dame des Ceps 1990 • $10 • (8/31/1991) • **75**
Brouilly Château Belliard 1990 • $13 • (9/15/1991) • **82**
Chambertin 1984 • $42 • (5/31/1987) • **76**
Chambertin-Clos de Bèze 1984 • $42 • (5/31/1987) • **80**
Chambertin-Clos de Bèze 1983 • $39 Ⓐ • (9/16/1985) CS • **93**
Chambolle-Musigny 1996: Offers sweet, plummy fruit flavors, is even overripe maybe. Lacks concentration midpalate, ends with dry tannins. Drink now through 2002.–B.S. • $33 • (9/30/1998) • **79**
Chambolle-Musigny 1984 • $15 • (11/30/1986) • **89**
Charmes-Chambertin 1996: Smooth, with modest red berry flavors and some drying tannins. Drink now.–P.M. • $62 • (9/30/1998) • **79**
Charmes-Chambertin 1990 • $35 • (12/31/1993) • **84**
Charmes-Chambertin 1985 • $55 • (5/31/1988) • **94**
Chassagne-Montrachet Red Morgeot 1985 • $15 • (5/31/1987) • **84**
Chénas Les Mélardières 1995 • $14 • (9/15/1997) • **80**
Chiroubles 1990 • $13 • (9/15/1991) • **84**
Chiroubles Domaine Plaforet 1994 • $15 • (9/15/1997) • **84**
Clos de Vougeot 1984 • $32 • (5/31/1987) • **90**
Clos de Vougeot 1983 • $45 • (10/16/1985) CS • **95**
Corton Clos des Vergennes 1990 • $53 • (12/15/1992) • **89**
Corton Clos des Vergennes 1989 • $40 • (1/31/1992) • **89**
Corton Clos des Vergennes 1985 • $36 • (5/31/1987) • **92**
Corton Clos des Vergennes 1983 • $19 • (10/01/1985) • **88**
Côte de Beaune-Villages 1995 • $15 • (11/15/1997) • **81**
Côte de Beaune-Villages 1994 • $20 • (11/15/1996) • **72**
Côte de Brouilly Château de la Perrière 1994 • $15 • (6/30/1997) • **78**
Côte de Brouilly Château de la Perrière 1989 • $15 • (6/30/1997) • **83**
Côte de Nuits-Villages 1996: Light and diluted, quite watery, tasting of strawberries and raspberries.–P.M. • $18 • (9/30/1998) • **73**
Côte de Nuits-Villages 1994 • $21 • (11/15/1996) • **73**
Côtes du Rhône Les Violettes 1996 • $9 • (9/15/1997) • **83**
Côtes du Rhône Les Violettes 1995 • $7 • (12/15/1996) • **83**
Côtes du Rhône Les Violettes 1991 • $7 • (8/31/1992) • **81**
Côtes du Rhône Les Violettes 1990 • $7 • (10/15/1991) • **82**
Côtes du Rhône Les Violettes 1989 • $8 • (5/31/1991) • **85**
Côtes du Rhône Les Violettes 1988 • $6 • (8/31/1989) • **84**
Echézeaux 1990 • $45 • (12/31/1993) • **81**
Echézeaux 1985 • $47 • (4/15/1988) • **94**
Echézeaux 1984 • $30 • (11/15/1986) SS • **96**
Fixin 1989 • $NA • (1/31/1992) • **88**
Fixin Clos d'Entre Deux Velles 1989 • $28 • (1/31/1992) • **86**
Fixin Clos d'Entre Deux Velles 1985 • $16 • (5/31/1987) • **79**
Fixin Clos d'Entre Deux Velles 1984 • $11 • (11/30/1986) • **78**
Fixin Clos de la Perrière 1990 • $30 • (12/15/1992) • **85**
Fixin Clos de la Perrière 1986 • $18 • (2/28/1989) • **85**
Fixin Clos de la Perrière 1983 • $12 • (10/16/1985) • **78**
Fixin Confrérie des Chevaliers du Tastevin 1988 • $19 • (8/31/1991) • **84**
Fleurie Château du Vivier 1990 • $17 • (9/15/1991) • **91**
Gevrey-Chambertin 1996: Floral and cherry aromas are lifted, and there's not much fruit.–B.S. • $29 • (9/30/1998) • **78**
Gevrey-Chambertin 1995 • $26 • (1/31/1998) • **88**
Gevrey-Chambertin 1994 • $34 • (11/15/1996) • **73**
Gevrey-Chambertin 1990 • $33 • (12/15/1992) • **85**
Gevrey-Chambertin 1987 • $20 • (3/31/1990) • **66**
Grands Echézeaux 1984 • $39 • (5/31/1987) • **90**
Hautes-Côtes de Beaune Les Alouettes 1994 • $17 • (11/15/1996) • **77**
Hautes-Côtes de Beaune Les Alouettes 1990 • $16 • (12/15/1992) • **79**
Hautes-Côtes de Beaune Les Alouettes 1989 • $17 • (1/31/1992) • **83**
Hautes-Côtes de Beaune Les Alouettes 1988 • $15 • (7/15/1991) • **83**
Hautes-Côtes de Nuits Les Hameaux 1986 • $11 • (12/31/1988) • **81**
Hautes-Côtes de Nuits Les Vignes Hautes 1989 • $NA • (1/31/1992) • **84**
Juliénas 1990 • $15 • (9/15/1997) • **77**
Juliénas Bois de la Salle 1990 • $13 • (9/15/1991) • **81**
Ladoix Côte de Beaune 1989 • $NA • (1/31/1992) • **85**
Maranges Les Clos Roussots 1994 • $23 • (11/15/1996) • **84**
Moillard Rouge NV • $5 • (5/31/1988) • **81**
Monthélie 1996: Vibrating with cherry and spice aromas and flavors, with just a hint of forest undergrowth, this has moderate concentration, a fleshiness and firm tannins on the finish. Drink through 2004.–B.S. • $17 • (9/30/1998) • **85**
Monthélie 1995 • $20 • (11/15/1997) • **79**
Morey-St.-Denis Monts Luisants 1995 • $26 • (11/15/1997) • **86**
Morey-St.-Denis Monts Luisants 1994 • $31 • (11/15/1996) • **74**
Morey-St.-Denis Monts Luisants 1991 • $30 • (3/15/1994) • **76**
Morey-St.-Denis Monts Luisants 1990 • $33 • (12/15/1992) • **90**
Morey-St.-Denis Monts Luisants 1989 • $28 • (1/31/1992) • **89**
Morey-St.-Denis Monts Luisants 1988 • $30 • (12/15/1990) HR • **91**
Morey-St.-Denis Monts Luisants 1985 • $21 • (5/31/1987) • **87**
Morgon Domaine du Crêt de Ruyère 1990 • $13 • (9/15/1991) • **86**
Morgon Tastevinage 1993 • $16 • (9/15/1997) • **75**
Moulin-à-Vent Château du Vivier 1990 • $16 • (9/30/1991) • **82**
Moulin-à-Vent Les Joies 1994 • $18 • (9/15/1997) • **84**
Musigny 1984 • $38 • (5/31/1987) • **92**
Nuits-St.-Georges Hospices de Nuits Cuvée Jacques Duret 1988 • $68 • (8/31/1991) • **89**
Pinot Noir Vin de Pays d'Oc Hugues le Juste 1994 • $9 • (1/01/1996) • **77**
Pinot Noir Vin de Pays d'Oc Pavillon St.-James 1994 • $9 • (7/31/1996) • **79**
Pommard Clos des Epeneaux 1985 • $45 • (6/30/1988) CS • **92**
Pommard Les Rugiens 1994 • $45 • (11/15/1996) • **82**
Pommard Les Rugiens 1990 • $50 • (12/15/1992) • **86**
Pommard Les Rugiens 1985 • $40 • (6/30/1988) • **85**
Pommard Murchaux 1994 • $38 • (11/15/1996) • **79**
Régnié Domaine de Reyssiers 1990 • $12 • (9/30/1991) • **66**
Romanée St.-Vivant 1984 • $42 • (5/31/1987) • **87**
Rully Red 1989 • $14 • (8/31/1991) • **82**
St.-Amour Domaine des Pins 1990 • $16 • (9/15/1991) • **86**
St.-Joseph 1988 • $15 • (8/31/1991) • **85**
Santenay 1994 • $25 • (11/15/1996) • **69**

MOILLARD

Syrah Vin de Pays d'Oc Hugues le Juste 1994 • $7 • (5/15/1996) • **79**
Syrah Vin de Pays d'Oc Pavillon St.-James 1995 • $7 • (10/31/1997) • **83**
Vacqueyras 1989 • $10 • (10/15/1991) • **77**
Volnay 1994 • $29 • (11/15/1996) • **81**
Volnay Clos des Chênes 1985 • $32 • (7/15/1988) • **89**
Volnay Clos des Chênes 1983 • $15 • (12/01/1985) • **75**

MOINGEON

Puligny-Montrachet 1997: Strange aromas of paint varnish, burnt butter and sweet wood. Medium-bodied, with a drying, astringent finish.–P.M. • $30 • (5/31/1999) • **70**
Puligny-Montrachet 1996: Tart, disjointed and astringent, veering toward the herbal category. Drink now.–P.M. • $27 • (8/31/1998) • **76**
Puligny-Montrachet La Garenne 1997: Astringent, woody notes undermine the fruit. Unbalanced, with a sweet rose perfume.–P.M. • $33 • (5/31/1999) • **70**
Puligny-Montrachet La Garenne 1996: Beautiful balance of searing acidity and voluptuous mouthfeel. Of medium to full body, it offers subtle mineral, apple pie, lime, cilantro and toasted oak accents. Superimpressive silky texture from start to seductive finish. Drink now through 2005.–P.M. • $30 • (8/31/1998) • **89**
St.-Aubin Les Frionnes 1997: Oxidized, with bitter, burning notes and malic-milky, appley aromas and flavors.–P.M. • $19 • (5/31/1999) • **70**
St.-Aubin Les Frionnes 1996: Tastes of vanilla-mocha. Oak-treated in a clever way, but it's quite tasty. Of medium body, ripe, and offers stone-dust, wet earth, mineral flavors, pie, spice, orange and chocolate notes. Smooth on the finish. Best from 2005.–P.M. • $18 • (8/31/1998) • **85**
St.-Aubin Sur Gamay 1997: Tastes "reduced"—like an icebox—and turns sour and astringent on the rustic, woody, cardboardy finish.–P.M. • $19 • (5/31/1999) • **70**
St.-Aubin Sur Gamay 1996: Distinctive style. Very malic, a taste that may not please everyone. Very tight and crisp at first, it turns velvety on the midpalate. Hard to predict how it will age. Drink now through 2002.–P.M. • $18 • (8/31/1998) • **84**
Savigny-lès-Beaune 1992 • $NA • (12/15/1994) • **80**
Vosne-Romanée Les Suchots 1992 • $NA • (12/15/1994) • **80**
Vougeot Les Crâs 1992 • $NA • (12/15/1994) • **77**

MOMMESSIN

Aloxe-Corton 1995 • $26 • (11/15/1997) • **89**
Aloxe-Corton 1994 • $29 • (11/15/1996) • **77**
Aloxe-Corton 1991 • $16 • (1/31/1994) • **80**
Aloxe-Corton 1990 • $20 • (12/15/1992) • **91**
Aloxe-Corton Les Valozières 1989 • $28 • (1/31/1992) • **88**
Auxey-Duresses 1989 • $13 • (1/31/1992) • **82**
Beaujolais-Villages 1997: This very good red shows a distinctive character for Beaujolais, with enticing aromas of framboise and toast, and a plush texture with firm underlying tannins. Ripe for the vintage and rich for the appellation. Drink now.–T.M. • $8 • (8/31/1998) • **86**
Beaujolais-Villages 1996 • $9 • (8/31/1997) • **84**
Beaujolais-Villages 1995 • $9 • (9/15/1996) • **84**
Beaujolais-Villages 1994 • $8 • (6/15/1995) • **83**
Beaujolais-Villages 1992 • $7 • (7/31/1995) • **79**
Beaujolais-Villages Château de Montmelas 1996 • $8 • (9/15/1997) • **79**
Beaujolais-Villages Château de Montmelas 1988 • $10 • (5/31/1989) • **78**
Beaujolais-Villages Château du Carra 1994 • $8 • (6/15/1995) • **83**
Beaune 1993 • $23 • (11/15/1995) • **85**
Beaune 1989 • $18 • (1/31/1992) • **90**
Beaune Les Cents Vignes 1995 • $26 • (11/15/1997) • **86**
Beaune Les Cents Vignes 1994 • $31 • (11/15/1996) • **83**
Beaune Les Cents Vignes 1993 • $30 • (11/15/1995) • **89**
Beaune Les Cents Vignes 1992 • $26 • (12/15/1994) • **83**
Beaune Les Cents Vignes 1990 • $20 • (12/15/1992) • **90**
Beaune Les Cents Vignes 1989 • $23 • (1/31/1992) • **86**
Beaune Premier Cru 1995 • $21 • (11/15/1997) • **80**
Bonnes Mares 1993 • $80 • (11/15/1995) • **89**
Bourgogne 1995 • $9 • (11/15/1997) • **74**
Bourgogne White 1995 • $12 • (8/31/1997) • **85**

Key: SS—Spectator Selection. CS—Cellar Selection. HR—Highly Recommended. $NA—Price not available. (BT)—Barrel tasting. Ⓐ—Auction Price.
For a key to the tasters' initials, see "How to Use These Listings."
Dates in parentheses represent the issues in which the ratings were published.

Brouilly 1997: Offers simple cherry flavors, light acidity and light tannins that turn dry on the finish.–T.M. • $12 • (8/31/1998) • **77**
Brouilly 1996 • $11 • (7/31/1997) • **86**
Brouilly 1995 • $14 • (9/15/1996) • **82**
Brouilly 1994 • $10 • (6/15/1995) • **82**
Brouilly Château de Briante 1997: Light, soft and simple, tasting as much like fruit juice as wine, with light sweetness.–T.M. • $13 • (8/31/1998) • **77**
Brouilly Château de Briante 1996 • $12 • (7/31/1997) • **86**
Brouilly Château de Briante 1995 • $14 • (9/15/1996) • **81**
Brouilly Château de Briante 1994 • $11 • (6/15/1995) • **82**
Brouilly Château de Briante 1988 • $12 • (5/31/1989) • **81**
Cabernet Sauvignon Vin de Pays d'Oc 1995: Hot-tasting, with menthol aromas and sweet cherry and herb flavors. Drink now.–K.M. • $7 • (11/15/1998) • **79**
Cabernet Sauvignon Vin de Pays d'Oc 1993 • $7 • (10/31/1995) • **82**
Chablis Fourchaume 1996 • $22 • (10/15/1997) • **83**
Chambolle-Musigny 1992 • $32 • (12/15/1994) • **77**
Chambolle-Musigny 1990 • $22 • (12/15/1992) • **86**
Chambolle-Musigny Premier Cru 1993 • $45 • (11/15/1995) • **88**
Chardonnay Vin de Pays d'Oc 1996: Clean-tasting, with herbal notes and good citrus flavors but not a lot of concentration. Drink now.–K.M. • $7 • (11/15/1998) • **80**
Charmes-Chambertin 1994 • $70 • (11/15/1996) • **83**
Charmes-Chambertin 1993 • $68 • (11/15/1995) • **85**
Charmes-Chambertin 1992 • $NA • (12/15/1994) • **82**
Charmes-Chambertin 1990 • $114 Ⓐ • (12/15/1992) • **96**
Charmes-Chambertin 1985 • $45 • (2/15/1988) • **83**
Châteauneuf-du-Pape 1995 • $17 • (10/15/1997) • **84**
Châteauneuf-du-Pape 1994 • $19 • (11/15/1996) • **88**
Châteauneuf-du-Pape Clos des Brusquières 1994 • $20 • (11/15/1996) • **85**
Châteauneuf-du-Pape Clos des Brusquières 1993 • $17 • (11/15/1995) • **80**
Chiroubles Château de Raosset 1988 • $12 • (5/31/1989) • **83**
Clos de Tart 1996: There's a roasted, smoky character to the blackberry and meaty aromas and flavors in this moderately concentrated red, and intensity and firm tannins leading up to the slightly hot finish. Drink through 2004.–B.S. • $86 Ⓐ • (9/30/1998) • **89**
Clos de Tart 1995 • $103 • (11/15/1997) • **89**
Clos de Tart 1994 • $99 • (11/15/1996) • **82**
Clos de Tart 1993 • $86 • (11/15/1995) • **84**
Clos de Tart 1992 • $99 • (12/15/1994) • **85**
Clos de Tart 1991 • $73 • (1/31/1994) • **87**
Clos de Tart 1990 • $110 Ⓐ • (12/15/1992) • **95**
Clos de Tart 1989 • $52 • (1/31/1992) • **92**
Clos de Tart 1985 • $137 Ⓐ • (2/15/1988) • **91**
Clos de Tart 1950 • $125 • (8/31/1990) • **78**
Corton 1985 • $46 Ⓐ • (2/15/1988) • **91**
Corton Les Grèves 1989 • $45 • (1/31/1992) • **91**
Côte de Beaune-Villages 1985 • $13 • (2/15/1988) • **85**
Côte de Nuits-Villages 1985 • $17 • (7/31/1988) • **85**
Côtes du Rhône 1997: Light in body and color, with modest fruit, astringent tannins and a diluted, drying finish.–P.M. • $7 • (11/15/1998) • **72**
Côtes du Rhône 1994 • $9 • (10/15/1996) • **77**
Côtes du Rhône Château de Domazan 1998: Pretty, with floral and cassis notes, it's intense and chewy, medium-bodied and showing some licorice. The finish is long, if a bit one-dimensional. Drink now through 2001.–P.M. • $10 • (11/15/1999) • **82**
Côtes du Rhône Château de Domazan 1997: Light in color, body and aroma, showing modest licorice, cherry and strawberry notes. Dry finish.–P.M. • $7 • (11/15/1998) • **71**
Côtes du Rhône Château de Domazan 1996 • $7 • (10/15/1997) • **77**
Côtes du Rhône Château de Domazan 1995 • $8 • (10/15/1996) • **84**
Côtes du Rhône Château de Domazan 1993 • $8 • (11/15/1995) • **78**
Côtes du Rhône-Villages Terroirs de Galet 1998: Pleasant but lacking in midpalate thickness. Medium-bodied, with ripe tannins and black cherry, dried herb, blackberry and black pepper flavors. Turns a bit chewy on the finish. Drink now through 2003.–P.M. • $10 • (12/15/1999) • **80**
Côtes du Ventoux 1996 • $7 • (10/15/1997) • **79**
Côtes du Ventoux 1994 • $NA • (10/15/1996) • **81**
Côtes du Ventoux 1993 • $7 • (11/15/1995) • **84**
Crozes-Hermitage 1996: Fresh and zesty, this light-bodied red delivers lime, cilantro, raspberry and cherry flavors. A bit unripe, with high acidity and a crisp finish. Drink now, chilled, with all sorts of foods, including cheesy pizza.–P.M. • $10 • (10/15/1998) • **80**
Crozes-Hermitage 1994 • $13 • (11/30/1996) • **83**
Crozes-Hermitage 1992 • $11 • (11/15/1995) • **79**
Echézeaux 1979 • $18 • (2/16/1986) • **86**
Fixin 1989 • $15 • (1/31/1992) • **87**

Fleurie 1997: This light, supple red offers berry and herbal flavors, simple and a bit diluted. Pleasant, but lacks stuffing. Drink now.–T.M. • $13 • (8/31/1998) • **79**
Fleurie 1996 • $14 • (8/31/1997) • **87**
Fleurie 1995 • $16 • (9/15/1996) • **82**
Fleurie 1994 • $12 • (6/15/1995) • **87**
Fleurie 1992 • $12 • (7/31/1995) • **85**
Fleurie 1988 • $14 • (5/31/1989) • **87**
Fleurie Clos de la Roilette 1995 • $17 • (9/15/1996) • **81**
Fleurie Clos de la Roilette 1994 • $12 • (6/15/1995) • **84**
Fleurie Domaine de la Presle 1996 • $15 • (8/31/1997) • **84**
Gamay Vin de Pays du Comté Tolosan 1996: Thin and slightly tart, with fading fruit. Past its prime.–B.S. • $6 • (12/15/1998) • **72**
Gevrey-Chambertin 1995 • $22 • (11/15/1997) • **78**
Gevrey-Chambertin 1991 • $22 • (1/31/1994) • **78**
Gevrey-Chambertin 1985 • $34 Ⓐ • (2/15/1988) • **90**
Gevrey-Chambertin Lavaut St.-Jacques 1990 • $45 • (12/15/1992) • **90**
Gevrey-Chambertin Lavaut St.-Jacques 1989 • $45 • (1/31/1992) • **85**
Gevrey-Chambertin Premier Cru 1995 • $35 • (11/15/1997) • **72**
Gevrey-Chambertin Premier Cru 1994 • $47 • (11/15/1996) • **83**
Gevrey-Chambertin Premier Cru 1993 • $45 • (11/15/1995) • **83**
Gevrey-Chambertin Premier Cru 1992 • $42 • (12/15/1994) • **81**
Gigondas 1995 • $12 • (10/15/1997) • **79**
Gigondas 1993 • $14 • (11/15/1995) • **87**
Gigondas Château de St.-André 1995: Odd, slightly stemmy and unclean, with an herbal, astringent character that turns bitter on the finish.–P.M. • $12 • (10/15/1998) • **70**
Gigondas Les Epices 1998: Light but pleasant, a nouveau-style red, with raspberry, strawberry and anise. Fun to drink, with attractive black pepper spiciness on the finish. Drink now.–P.M. • $20 • (10/31/1999) • **84**
Juliénas 1997: Cherry and berry flavors are fresh and well defined in this light-bodied red. Firm tannins turn a bit dry. Drink now.–T.M. • $12 • (8/31/1998) • **82**
Juliénas 1996 • $11 • (9/15/1997) • **86**
Juliénas Domaine de la Conseillère 1996 • $12 • (9/15/1997) • **86**
Juliénas Domaine de la Conseillère 1988 • $11 • (5/31/1989) • **81**
Mâcon-Villages 1997: Lemony and crisp, with a cedary character, this light-bodied Chardonnay is a bit tough, but clean.–P.M. • $12 • (5/31/1999) • **78**
Maranges 1989 • $13 • (1/31/1992) • **87**
Merlot Vin de Pays d'Oc 1996: Charred and muddled, this finishes on a slightly stemmy note. Not recommended. Tasted twice, with consistent notes.–K.M. • $7 • (12/31/1998) • **66**
Merlot Vin de Pays d'Oc 1994 • $7 • (12/15/1996) • **80**
Merlot Vin de Pays d'Oc 1993 • $7 • (10/31/1995) • **83**
Morey-St.-Denis La Forge 1996: Slightly candied and cheesy, with a rich texture, firm tannins and a hot finish. From Clos de Tart. Drink through 2004.–B.S. • $45 • (9/30/1998) • **83**
Morey-St.-Denis La Forge 1995 • $52 • (11/15/1997) • **87**
Morey-St.-Denis La Forge 1993 • $57 • (11/15/1995) • **81**
Morgon 1997: This light, simple red offers berry and cherry flavors, clean but with little depth or grip. Try now, chilled.–T.M. • $12 • (8/31/1998) • **79**
Morgon 1996 • $11 • (8/31/1997) • **88**
Morgon 1994 • $10 • (7/31/1995) • **84**
Morgon 1988 • $10 • (5/31/1989) • **86**
Morgon Domaine de Lathevalle 1997: This light red offers pleasant berry flavors, but has little concentration or structure. Soft and clean; best now, lightly chilled.–T.M. • $13 • (8/31/1998) • **78**
Morgon Domaine de Lathevalle 1996 • $12 • (8/31/1997) • **84**
Morgon Domaine de Lathevalle 1995 • $14 • (9/15/1996) • **83**
Morgon Domaine de Lathevalle 1994 • $10 • (7/31/1995) • **88**
Moulin-à-Vent 1997: Soft and generous, this fruity red offers cherry, plum and cassis flavors. It has enough structure for food, but not for aging. Drink now.–T.M. • $12 • (8/31/1998) • **83**
Moulin-à-Vent 1996 • $13 • (8/31/1997) • **87**
Moulin-à-Vent 1995 • $15 • (9/15/1996) • **84**
Moulin-à-Vent 1994 • $12 • (7/31/1995) • **85**
Moulin-à-Vent 1992 • $11 • (6/30/1995) • **88**
Moulin-à-Vent Domaine de Champ de Cour 1997: Ripe fruit flavors of black cherry and plum are round and soft in this generous red. Not powerful, but balanced and fresh. Drink now.–T.M. • $13 • (8/31/1998) • **84**
Moulin-à-Vent Domaine de Champ de Cour 1996 • $14 • (8/31/1997) • **89**
Moulin-à-Vent Domaine de Champ de Cour 1995 • $16 • (9/15/1996) • **87**
Moulin-à-Vent Domaine de Champ de Cour 1994 • $12 • (7/31/1995) • **89**
Moulin-à-Vent Domaine de Champ de Cour 1988 • $13 • (5/31/1989) • **91**
Nuits-St.-Georges 1996: Very herbal and somewhat disjointed, this light-bodied red is lean and tart.–P.M. • $29 • (9/30/1998) • **75**
Nuits-St.-Georges 1995 • $30 • (11/15/1997) • **85**
Nuits-St.-Georges Aux Boudots 1994 • $43 • (11/15/1996) • **80**
Nuits-St.-Georges Aux Chaignots 1993 • $57 • (11/15/1995) • **87**
Nuits-St.-Georges Aux Chaignots 1992 • $45 • (12/15/1994) • **82**
Nuits-St.-Georges Aux Chaignots 1990 • $29 • (12/15/1992) • **90**
Nuits-St.-Georges Les St.-Georges 1995 • $39 • (11/15/1997) • **81**
Nuits-St.-Georges Les Vaucrains 1989 • $45 • (1/31/1992) • **90**
Nuits-St.-Georges Premier Cru 1991 • $28 • (1/31/1994) • **83**
Pommard 1995 • $30 • (11/15/1997) • **83**
Pommard 1994 • $34 • (11/15/1996) • **79**
Pommard 1993 • $35 • (11/15/1995) • **84**
Pommard 1989 • $28 • (1/31/1992) • **88**
Pommard Premier Cru 1993 • $40 • (11/15/1995) • **76**
Pouilly-Fuissé 1997: Overdone, witha cooked apple character that seems a bit oxidated. Astringent finish confirms the first impression.–P.M. • $20 • (5/31/1999) • **71**
Pouilly-Fuissé 1996 • $15 • (10/15/1997) • **79**
Pouilly-Fuissé 1995 • $15 • (5/31/1998) • **70**
Santenay Clos Rousseau 1996: Fruity but also a bit rustic, with cedar, wood, herbal and black cherry character. Medium-bodied, it's a bit drying and astringent on the finish. Drink now.–P.M. • $19 • (9/30/1998) • **78**
Santenay Clos Rousseau 1995 • $22 • (11/15/1997) • **76**
Santenay Clos Rousseau 1994 • $25 • (11/15/1996) • **74**
Santenay Clos Rousseau 1993 • $26 • (11/15/1995) • **84**
Santenay Clos Rousseau 1992 • $23 • (12/15/1994) • **80**
Santenay Clos Rousseau 1990 • $14 • (12/15/1992) • **86**
Savigny-lès-Beaune 1995 • $15 • (11/15/1997) • **78**
Savigny-lès-Beaune 1994 • $20 • (11/15/1996) • **79**
Savigny-lès-Beaune 1993 • $21 • (11/15/1995) • **87**
Savigny-lès-Beaune 1992 • $19 • (12/15/1994) • **78**
Savigny-lès-Beaune 1991 • $16 • (1/31/1994) • **79**
Savigny-lès-Beaune 1990 • $14 • (12/15/1992) • **90**
Savigny-lès-Beaune 1985 • $17 • (7/31/1988) • **80**
St.-Amour 1996 • $14 • (8/31/1997) • **83**
St.-Amour Domaine de Monrève 1996 • $14 • (8/31/1997) • **84**
St.-Amour Domaine de Monreve 1988 • $12 • (5/31/1989) • **84**
St.-Aubin 1990 • $NA • (12/15/1992) • **77**
St.-Véran 1997: Tart, even bitter, light-bodied, with mouthpuckeringly acidity and modest fruit.–P.M. • $14 • (5/31/1999) • **74**
Syrah Vin de Pays d'Oc 1996: Light and soft. A modest red, with simple, fresh fruit flavors and little tannin. Drink now. • $7 • (10/15/1998) • **77**
Syrah Vin de Pays d'Oc 1993 • $7 • (10/31/1995) • **79**
Volnay 1985 • $80 • (3/15/1988) • **91**
Volnay Taillepieds 1995 • $28 • (11/15/1997) • **84**
Volnay Taillepieds 1994 • $33 • (11/15/1996) • **77**
Volnay Taillepieds 1993 • $40 • (11/15/1995) • **80**
Volnay Taillepieds 1992 • $29 • (12/15/1994) • **84**
Volnay Taillepieds 1991 • $23 • (1/31/1994) • **85**
Volnay Taillepieds 1990 • $23 • (12/15/1992) • **92**
Vosne-Romanée 1995 • $30 • (11/15/1997) • **86**
Vosne-Romanée 1993 • $40 • (11/15/1995) • **81**
Vosne-Romanée 1992 • $49 • (12/15/1994) • **80**
Vosne-Romanée Aux Brûlées 1989 • $38 • (1/31/1992) • **89**
Vosne-Romanée Les Suchots 1995 • $45 • (11/15/1997) • **88**
Vosne-Romanée Les Suchots 1994 • $49 • (11/15/1996) • **81**
Vosne-Romanée Les Suchots 1990 • $35 • (12/15/1992) • **91**
Vosne-Romanée Premier Cru 1993 • $46 • (11/15/1995) • **87**

MONARDIERE, DOMAINE LA

Côtes du Rhône Cuvée des Calades 1996 • $10 • (10/15/1997) • **80**
Côtes du Rhône Cuvée des Calades 1994 • $10 • (12/15/1996) • **78**
Vacqueyras 1994 • $15 • (12/15/1996) • **85**
Vacqueyras Réserve des 2 Monardes 1997: Straightforward and slightly earthy, with modest fruit.–P.M. • $16 • (10/31/1999) • **74**
Vacqueyras Réserve des 2 Monardes 1996: Ripe and attractive, with roasted peanut, plum, and black cherry flavors, this full-bodied red delivers full, lush tannins and plenty of character for pairing with spicy grilled meats. Drink now.–P.M. • $13 • (11/15/1998) • **85**
Vacqueyras Réserve des 2 Monardes 1995 • $13 • (10/15/1997) • **82**
Vacqueyras Vieilles Vignes 1995: Lovely, pure and clean, showing vibrant fruit but not very ripe tannins or flavors. Medium-bodied, with spice, cassis, blackberry and mocha notes on the lingering, fairly tough finish. Drink through 2005.–P.M. • $15 • (10/15/1998) • **86**
Vin de Pays de Vaucluse 1996 • $8 • (10/15/1997) • **84**

MONBADON, CHATEAU

Côtes de Castillon 1994 • $10 • (6/30/1997) • **83**

MONBOUSQUET, CHATEAU

St.-Emilion 1999: Well constructed, with good aromas of maple syrup, berry and cherry plus hints of mineral. Medium- to full-bodied, with velvety tannins, a solid core of fruit and a long finish.–J.S. • $NA • (1/01/2000) (BT) • **85-89**
St.-Emilion 1998: Plenty of fruit in this new-wave Bordeaux. Full-bodied and round, with velvety tannins and a long, caressing finish. A crowd-pleaser.–J.S. • $NA • (5/31/1999) (BT) • **90-94**
St.-Emilion 1997: Well-crafted for '97, with cherry, berry and spice character. Medium-bodied, with polished tannins and a fruity finish. Best after 2002.–J.S. • $38 • (1/31/2000) • **88**
St.-Emilion 1996: Very flashy for the vintage, although slightly hollow in the midpalate. Lovely aromas of spices, cinnamon and fruit. Medium-bodied, with silky tannins and a fruity, spicy aftertaste. Best after 2000.–J.S. • $43 Ⓐ • (1/31/1999) • **88**
St.-Emilion 1995 • $47 Ⓐ • (1/31/1998) • **92**
St.-Emilion 1993 • $23 • (1/31/1996) • **88**

MONBRISON, CHATEAU

Margaux 1998: Shows blackberry, tar and a hint of sage. Full-bodied, with a good core of fruit and velvety tannins, but short on the finish.–J.S. • $NA • (5/31/1999) (BT) • **85-89**
Margaux 1997: Rather lean, but some good currant and mineral character to it. Very light finish. Drink now.–J.S. • $NA • (1/31/2000) • **82**
Margaux 1996: Pleasant plum and berry aromas follow through on the palate. Medium-bodied, with firm tannins and a short finish. Rather tough. Best after 2000.–J.S. • $19 • (1/31/1999) • **84**
Margaux 1995 • $17 Ⓐ • (1/31/1998) • **87**
Margaux 1994 • $25 • (1/31/1997) • **79**
Margaux 1993 • $26 • (1/31/1996) • **75**
Margaux 1992 • $21 • (4/15/1995) • **77**
Margaux 1991 • $14 • (3/31/1994) • **81**
Margaux 1990 • $34 Ⓐ • (3/31/1993) • **91**
Margaux 1989: One of the best wines ever made here. Very fresh blackberry, mint and cassis bush character on the nose. Full-bodied and firm, with silky tannins and a medium berry aftertaste. (1989 Bordeaux horizontal tasting). Best after 2002.–J.S. • $35 Ⓐ • (5/31/1999) • **91**
Margaux 1988: A superb bottle from this underappreciated estate, which made superb wines during this period. Inky in color, with berry, grape and vanilla aromas and flavors. Full-bodied, with big, velvety tannins and a long, long finish. (1989 Bordeaux horizontal tasting). Best after 2001.–J.S. • $29 Ⓐ • (11/30/1998) • **90**
Margaux 1987 • $20 • (11/30/1989) • **86**
Margaux 1986 • $34 Ⓐ • (11/30/1989) • **92**
Margaux 1985 • $23 • (10/15/1994) • **90**
Margaux 1984 • $15 • (5/15/1987) • **78**
Margaux 1983 • $20 • (10/15/1994) • **86**
Margaux 1982 • $22 • (11/30/1989) • **90**
Margaux 1981 • $19 • (10/15/1994) • **82**

MONCUIT, PIERRE

Brut Blanc de Blancs Champagne Le Mesnil 1990: A sophisticated blend of light and bright with deep and mellow. A fresh, toasty, citrusy aroma leads to ripe, generous fruit accented with vanilla and fig. Long on complexity and on the finish. Drink now through 2005. • $40 • (11/15/1999) • **95**
Brut Blanc de Blancs Champagne Le Mesnil Cuvée de Réserve NV: Fine example of blanc de blancs. Has rich flavors of vanilla and pear and a velvety texture. Drink now through 2001. • $25 • (10/31/1999) • **90**

MONDOT

St.-Emilion 1995 • $25 • (1/31/1998) • **86**

Key: SS—Spectator Selection. CS—Cellar Selection. HR—Highly Recommended. $NA—Price not available. (BT)—Barrel tasting. Ⓐ—Auction Price.
For a key to the tasters' initials, see "How to Use These Listings."
Dates in parentheses represent the issues in which the ratings were published.

MONDOTTE, CHATEAU LA

St.-Emilion 1999: Superfine. La Mondotte is clearly a leader. Very dark ruby, with lovely ripe berry, floral and mineral aromas. Full-bodied, with a solid core of velvety tannins and a long, long finish. A beauty.–J.S. • $NA • (1/01/2000) (BT) • **90-94**
St.-Emilion 1997: Well-constructed wine and more harmonious than the 1996. Good dark color, with impressive aromas of spices, tobacco, coffee and toasted oak. Full-bodied and chewy, with lots of new wood on the palate. Give it time. Best after 2002.–J.S. • $273 • (1/31/2000) • **90**
St.-Emilion 1996: Shows pretty berry and wet earth character, medium to full body and firm tannins. It's an elegant young wine, but slightly woody and austere on the finish, needing a tad more fruit concentration in the midpalate to be outstanding, and not quite as good as when tasted from barrel. Still, an impressive debut wine from this estate after it was upgraded by the owner of Canon-La Gaffelière. Best after 2005.–J.S. • $429 • (1/01/1999) • **89**

MONGEARD-MUGNERET

Bourgogne 1994 • $14 • (11/15/1996) • **74**
Bourgogne 1993 • $16 • (11/15/1995) • **83**
Bourgogne 1992 • $14 • (12/15/1994) • **79**
Bourgogne 1989 • $10 • (1/31/1992) • **85**
Clos de Vougeot 1997: There are gorgeous aromas and flavors of black cherry, earth, game and mineral in this silky-smooth, intense '97 red, whose tannins firm up on the finish. Vanilla and cherry linger on the aftertaste. Drink now through 2005.–B.S. • $88 • (9/30/1999) • **88**
Clos de Vougeot 1994 • $61 • (11/15/1996) • **88**
Clos de Vougeot 1993 • $71 • (11/15/1995) • **93**
Clos de Vougeot 1992 • $61 • (12/15/1994) • **80**
Clos de Vougeot 1991 • $45 • (1/31/1994) • **83**
Clos de Vougeot 1989 • $77 • (1/31/1992) • **87**
Clos de Vougeot 1987 • $53 • (5/15/1990) • **81**
Clos de Vougeot 1986 • $56 • (7/31/1989) • **87**
Echézeaux 1995 • $47 • (11/15/1997) • **84**
Echézeaux 1993 • $50 • (11/15/1995) • **91**
Echézeaux 1992 • $44 • (12/15/1994) • **78**
Echézeaux Vieille Vigne 1997: Very soft, this light-colored Pinot tastes of cherry, olive and raspberry. Lingering aftertaste. Drink now.–P.M. • $71 • (9/30/1999) • **84**
Echézeaux Vieille Vigne 1996: An elegant '96 Pinot, concentrated and jammy, that displays smoky, spicy plum and cherry character and lively acidity. The tannins are well integrated and the smoke note persists on the finish. Drink through 2006.–B.S. • $60 • (9/30/1998) • **89**
Echézeaux Vieille Vigne 1993 • $60 • (11/15/1995) • **92**
Echézeaux Vieille Vigne 1991 • $43 • (1/31/1994) • **90**
Echézeaux Vieille Vigne 1989 • $59 • (1/31/1992) • **93**
Echézeaux Vieille Vigne 1988 • $83 Ⓐ • (2/15/1991) • **88**
Echézeaux Vieille Vigne 1987 • $41 Ⓐ • (5/15/1990) • **86**
Echézeaux Vieille Vigne 1986 • $44 • (8/31/1989) • **90**
Fixin 1997: Herbal, weedy and unpleasant.–B.S. • $25 • (9/30/1999) • **74**
Fixin 1995 • $20 • (11/15/1997) • **79**
Fixin 1994 • $20 • (11/15/1996) • **78**
Fixin 1992 • $20 • (12/15/1994) • **79**
Fixin 1991 • $18 • (1/31/1994) • **77**
Fixin 1990 • $26 • (3/15/1993) • **77**
Fixin 1989 • $25 • (1/31/1992) • **83**
Fixin 1986 • $19 • (10/15/1989) • **84**
Grands Echézeaux 1997: Seductive nose, offering cherry, spice and game. The flavors carry through, with moderate intensity, concentration and structure. The tannins are a bit drying on the finish, and there's volume for the vintage. Drink now through 2003.–B.S. • $112 • (9/30/1999) • **89**
Grands Echézeaux 1995 • $83 • (11/15/1997) • **89**
Grands Echézeaux 1994 • $73 • (11/15/1996) • **76**
Grands Echézeaux 1993 • $100 • (11/15/1995) • **87**
Grands Echézeaux 1992 • $75 • (12/15/1994) • **80**
Grands Echézeaux 1991 • $68 • (1/31/1994) HR • **91**
Grands Echézeaux 1989 • $95 • (1/31/1992) • **93**
Grands Echézeaux 1987 • $65 • (5/15/1990) • **85**
Grands Echézeaux 1986 • $73 • (8/31/1989) • **92**
Grands Echézeaux 1955 • $NA • (12/31/1994) • **82**
Grands Echézeaux 1953 • $NA • (12/31/1994) • **87**
Hautes-Côtes de Nuits 1994 • $15 • (11/15/1996) • **71**
Hautes-Côtes de Nuits 1993 • $17 • (11/15/1995) • **85**
Hautes-Côtes de Nuits 1992 • $15 • (12/15/1994) • **76**
Hautes-Côtes de Nuits 1989 • $16 • (1/31/1992) • **77**

Nuits-St.-Georges Aux Boudots 1989 • $49 • (1/31/1992) • **84**
Nuits-St.-Georges Aux Boudots 1987 • $32 • (4/30/1990) • **81**
Nuits-St.-Georges Aux Boudots 1984 • $23 • (2/15/1988) • **78**
Nuits-St.-Georges Les Boudots 1997: Seems less ripe, offering cherry, strawberry and herb in a compact presentation, with concentration and solid tannins on the finish. Drink now through 2002.–B.S. • $56 • (9/30/1999) • **85**
Richebourg 1997: Floral, black fruit and spice aromas are attractive, while a little stemmy flavor appears in this elegant red. A licorice chewiness midpalate and persistence of flavor add to its appeal. Drink now.–B.S. • $208 • (9/30/1999) • **93**
Richebourg 1994 • $138 • (11/15/1996) • **88**
Richebourg 1993 • $110 • (11/15/1995) • **88**
Richebourg 1992 • $134 • (12/15/1994) • **77**
Richebourg 1991 • $117 • (1/31/1994) • **88**
Richebourg 1989 • $126 Ⓐ • (1/31/1992) • **92**
Richebourg 1987 • $102 • (8/10/1990) • **90**
Richebourg 1985 • $123 • (3/15/1988) • **92**
Savigny-lès-Beaune 1994 • $20 • (11/15/1996) • **72**
Savigny-lès-Beaune 1993 • $22 • (11/15/1995) • **87**
Savigny-lès-Beaune Les Narbantons 1997: Stemmy and vegetal.–P.M. • $31 • (9/30/1999) • **73**
Savigny-lès-Beaune Les Narbantons 1995 • $23 • (11/15/1997) • **85**
Savigny-lès-Beaune Les Narbantons 1994 • $24 • (11/15/1996) • **80**
Savigny-lès-Beaune Les Narbantons 1993 • $26 • (11/15/1995) • **83**
Savigny-lès-Beaune Les Narbantons 1992 • $23 • (12/15/1994) • **80**
Savigny-lès-Beaune Les Narbantons 1991 • $21 • (1/31/1994) • **81**
Savigny-lès-Beaune Les Narbantons 1990 • $33 • (6/15/1993) • **80**
Savigny-lès-Beaune Les Narbantons 1989 • $28 • (1/31/1992) • **78**
Vosne-Romanée 1997: Cherry and herb are matched with a soft, open structure and a moderate finish.–B.S. • $39 • (9/30/1999) • **78**
Vosne-Romanée 1995 • $29 • (11/15/1997) • **87**
Vosne-Romanée 1992 • $29 • (12/15/1994) • **79**
Vosne-Romanée 1991 • $26 • (1/31/1994) • **84**
Vosne-Romanée 1989 • $34 • (1/31/1992) • **85**
Vosne-Romanée 1986 • $26 • (8/31/1989) • **79**
Vosne-Romanée Les Orveaux 1996: Toasty oak lends clove, nutmeg and bacon aromas to the rich cherry flavors in this velvety Pinot. Nice tension between the bright acidity and ripe tannins. Cherry notes prevail on the finish. Drink through 2005.–B.S. • $40 • (9/30/1998) • **88**
Vosne-Romanée Les Orveaux 1995 • $42 • (11/15/1997) • **74**
Vosne-Romanée Les Orveaux 1994 • $36 • (11/15/1996) • **78**
Vosne-Romanée Les Orveaux 1993 • $40 • (11/15/1995) • **82**
Vosne-Romanée Les Orveaux 1992 • $36 • (12/15/1994) • **78**
Vosne-Romanée Les Orveaux 1991 • $32 • (1/31/1994) • **82**
Vosne-Romanée Les Orveaux 1989 • $43 • (1/31/1992) • **94**
Vosne-Romanée Les Orveaux 1987 • $35 • (7/15/1990) • **62**
Vosne-Romanée Les Orveaux 1986 • $34 • (8/31/1989) • **82**
Vosne-Romanée Les Orveaux 1985 • $32 • (3/15/1988) • **82**
Vosne-Romanée Les Petits Monts 1987 • $35 • (4/30/1990) • **74**
Vosne-Romanée Les Suchots 1987 • $35 • (6/15/1990) • **82**
Vougeot Les Crâs 1989 • $NA • (1/31/1992) • **93**

MONLUC

Gros Manseng Côtes de Gascogne Le Vin de d'Artagnan 1997: Vivid in both color and flavor, this slightly sweet white evokes beeswax, sweet hay, spring blossoms and honey. Its rich texture is supported by a firm structure. Perfect partner for foie gras. Drink now through 2003.–B.S. • $8/375 ml. • (1/01/2000) • **89**
Tannat-Cabernet Côtes de Gascogne Le Vin de d'Artagnan 1997: Decent, with dried cherry and plum flavors that turn just a tad astringent on the finish.–K.M. • $7 • (1/01/1999) • **79**

MONMOUSSEAU, A.

Vouvray Château Gaudrelle 1997: Apple and pear flavors are ripe and round in this solid white, with lively acidity and a hint of spiciness on the finish. Good concentration for the vintage. Drink now through 2002.–T.M. • $15 • (6/30/1999) • **84**
Vouvray Clos le Vigneau 1997: Quite crisp for a Vouvray, this lean white shows apple and floral notes, with a hint of spice on the finish. Dry and clean. Drink now.–T.M. • $15 • (6/30/1999) • **81**

MONMOUSSEAU, J.M.

Cheverny 1997: This straightforward white shows traditional character, with notes of earth and spice adding depth to light pear and apple flavors. Soft on the palate.–T.M. • $9 • (6/30/1999) • **79**
Chinon 1997: A lively red, light yet focused and balanced. Offers clean cherry and strawberry flavors, with light notes of herb and spice and just-enough tannin for lighter dishes. Drink now through 2002.–T.M. • $14 • (6/30/1999) • **84**
Pouilly-Fumé 1997: Smooth and supple, this white is restrained but clean and refreshing, with light apple and citrus flavors and hints of herb on the finish. A modest match for food. Drink now.–T.M. • $14 • (6/30/1999) • **82**
St.-Nicolas-de-Bourgueil 1997: Light, fresh and simple. This grapey red shows soft, bright flavors of black cherry and berry, but a green, bitter note mars the pleasure.–T.M. • $12 • (6/30/1999) • **78**
Sancerre 1997: Soft and simple. This light white has appealing flavors of almond and pear, but lacks stuffing and vibrancy.–T.M. • $14 • (6/30/1999) • **77**
Touraine Les Granges 1997: Light and simple, this white is clean and soft, with hints of apple and pear and enough acidity to keep it fresh.–T.M. • $8 • (6/30/1999) • **79**
Vouvray Brut Blanc de Blancs NV: This gentle sparkler has an appealing foamy, pillowy mousse and light, clean flavors of lemon and meringue. Delicate but vivid, it's perfect for brunch or an afternoon on the porch. Drink now.–T.M. • $13 • (6/30/1999) • **84**
Vouvray Demi-Sec Blanc de Blancs 1997: Has a pleasant weight on the palate, a good balance of green apple acidity and light, fruity sweetness. The flavors are modest, with hints of apple and almond. May improve. Drink now through 2002.–T.M. • $10 • (6/30/1999) • **83**

MONNIER, RENE

Beaune Cent Vignes 1996: Sappy fruit and concentration, with a hint of herbal character to the vibrant cherry and earth. Straightforward, sturdy, with grainy texture and body that keeps it interesting. Drink through 2004.–B.S. • $30 • (9/30/1998) • **86**
Beaune Les Cents Vignes 1985 • $25 • (10/31/1987) • **89**
Beaune Toussaints 1996: Crisp and tart, of medium body, with some vibrant fruit, and a slightly herbal character to the cassis and raspberry. A bit one-dimensional and drying on the finish. Drink now through 2003.–P.M. • $30 • (9/30/1998) • **80**
Bourgogne White 1997: A bit too woody, it's crisp, showing green apple and a tart, cardboardy finish.–P.M. • $16 • (5/31/1999) • **72**
Maranges Clos de la Fussière 1996: Well constituted, showing earthy, cherry and spice notes with bright acidity, and a chewy texture that finishes on the rustic side. Drink through 2003.–B.S. • $16 • (9/30/1998) • **84**
Meursault Charmes 1998: Balanced, with a wet earth, matchstick intensity on the nose and palate. Still, it's light-bodied and lacks Meursault-like fatness. Roasted peanut aromas on the finish. Drink now through 2002.–P.M. • $60 • (5/31/2000) • **86**
Meursault Charmes 1997: Decent fruit gets wiped out by rustic barrel smells and a drying, astringent finish from the overbearing wood tannins.–P.M. • $60 • (5/31/1999) • **75**
Meursault Charmes 1996: A premier cru of great depth, with ripe fruit, smooth mineral character, subtle spice and oak. Full-bodied, it's so supple and smooth, you'll want to drink it upon release, but it's ageable. Drink now through 2007.–P.M. • $NA • (8/31/1998) • **93**
Meursault Charmes 1995 • $NA • (8/31/1997) • **81**
Meursault Le Limozin 1998: Supple yet crisp—a combination that brings a welcome tension in this medium-bodied Meursault, which delivers some intensity of fruit, spicy oak and mocha. Lingering, balanced finish. Drink now through 2002.–P.M. • $38 • (5/31/2000) • **87**
Meursault Le Limozin 1997: Not much fruit in this oaky, bitter white that smells of sweet perfume.–P.M. • $37 • (5/31/1999) • **74**
Meursault Le Limozin 1996: Full-bodied, ripe and packed with fruit flavors. Starts out with subtle aromas of great depth, then kicks in with lots of mineral, chalk, pear and honey character. Both silky and intensely citrusy on the finish. Drink now through 2010.–P.M. • $NA • (8/31/1998) • **91**
Meursault Les Chevalières 1998: Clean, silky and minerally Meursault. Pure fruit aromas are nicely backed by spicy toasted oak and honey notes. Medium-bodied, it kicks in with subtle sweetness on the lingering finish. Drink now through 2002.–P.M. • $38 • (5/31/2000) • **88**
Meursault Les Chevalières 1996: This full-bodied Meursault caresses the palate with wonderfully smooth texture, showering the palate with pear, mineral and spicy oak notes, as well as a bit of earthy character. Best after 2005.–P.M. • $NA • (8/31/1998) • **87**

FRANCE

MONNIER, RENE

Meursault Les Chevalières 1995 • $NA • (8/31/1997) • **90**
Pommard Les Vignots 1996: Quite delicious, showing good depth, with supple tannins, wet earth, licorice and sweet-tasting wild raspberry, blueberry, black cherry and currant notes. Medium-bodied, it lacks power at midpalate and seems just a bit hot on the finish. Drink now.–P.M. • $30 • (9/30/1998) • **84**
Pommard Les Vignots 1985 • $30 • (11/15/1988) • **89**
Pommard Les Vignots 1982 • $17 • (7/01/1985) • **81**
Puligny-Montrachet 1996: Steely and racy, a refined, medium-bodied white Burgundy, showing very nice mineral, vanilla bean notes but also ripe pear and melon character. Well made, with a supple texture, and some intriguingly complex matchstick, smoky flavors on the lingering finish. Best after 2005.–P.M. • $NA • (8/31/1998) • **90**
Puligny-Montrachet Les Folatières 1998: Subtle white. Packed with vanilla and wet stone character, it's a minerally sort of Chardonnay, showing a silky texture but still a firm backbone of acidity. Tough finish. Drink now through 2005.–P.M. • $60 • (5/31/2000) • **87**
Puligny-Montrachet Les Folatières 1997: This firm, chewy and medium-bodied white lacks a bit of generosity but delivers crisp, clean lemon, green apple and tropical flavors. Steely, tart finish. Drink now through 2004.–P.M. • $60 • (5/31/1999) • **80**
Puligny-Montrachet Les Folatières 1996: This premier cru is almost in the class of a grand cru. Gorgeous, thick and opulent, pure and ripe, presenting a most seductive, velvety texture along with plenty of complex flavors—spicy oak, malic, white chocolate, melon, ripe pear, honey. Has the palate-coating richness of extra-virgin olive oil. Best after 2005.–P.M. • $NA • (8/31/1998) • **94**
Volnay Clos des Chênes 1996: Traditional in style, with good concentration, smoky and mineral flavors accompanying the cherry, supported by a firm structure of acidity and tannin. Drink through 2004.–B.S. • $37 • (1/01/1999) • **85**

MONPERTUIS, DOMAINE DE

Châteauneuf-du-Pape 1995 • $23 • (10/15/1997) • **85**
Châteauneuf-du-Pape 1994 • $23 • (10/15/1997) • **76**
Châteauneuf-du-Pape 1993 • $23 • (11/15/1996) • **85**
Châteauneuf-du-Pape 1990 • $16 • (4/15/1993) • **83**
Châteauneuf-du-Pape 1987 • $14 • (6/30/1990) • **83**
Châteauneuf-du-Pape 1986 • $18 • (9/30/1989) • **73**
Châteauneuf-du-Pape Tradition 1994 • $35 • (10/15/1997) • **84**
Côtes du Rhône Vignoble de la Ramière 1996 • $12 • (10/15/1997) • **81**
Côtes du Rhône Vignoble de la Ramière 1995 • $12 • (10/15/1996) • **86**
Counoise Vin de Pays du Gard Vignoble de la Ramière 1995 • $9 • (10/15/1996) • **78**

MONT CLAIR

Chardonnay Vin de Pays d'Oc Cuvée Vieille Réserve 1996: A medium-bodied Chardonnay, with satisfying flavors of ripe apple and pear and a touch of butterscotch. Clean and well made, with a lingering finish. A good quaffer. Drink now.–K.M. • $NA • (12/31/1998) • **84**
Merlot Vin de Pays d'Oc Cuvée Vieille Réserve 1995: This has plum and cherry flavors, but it falls a bit flat, with a stewy note on the finish.–.M. • $NA • (12/31/1998) • **77**

MONT-REDON, CHATEAU

Châteauneuf-du-Pape 1997: Enticingly aromatic, with a classy blackberry, toast and floral aroma that suggests clever oak-aging, this red from France's Rhône Valley is very ripe and velvety on the palate and delivers a fresh character on the lively finish. Drink now through 2005.–P.M. • $30 • (8/31/1999) HR • **89**
Châteauneuf-du-Pape 1995: Well made. Lovely wine, showing a fresh edge of acidity, good plum, currant, cherry and roasted fowl flavors. Full-bodied, with impressive mineral, blood and iron qualities. The tannins are ripe, the finish intense. Drink now through 2008.–P.M. • $26 • (11/15/1998) • **89**
Châteauneuf-du-Pape 1994 • $24 • (10/15/1997) • **80**
Châteauneuf-du-Pape 1992 • $20 • (11/15/1996) • **85**
Châteauneuf-du-Pape 1990 • $23 • (9/30/1993) • **91**
Châteauneuf-du-Pape 1989 • $25 • (10/15/1991) • **91**
Châteauneuf-du-Pape 1988 • $22 • (10/15/1991) • **83**
Châteauneuf-du-Pape 1986 • $17 • (10/15/1991) • **85**
Châteauneuf-du-Pape 1985 • $25 • (10/15/1991) • **90**
Châteauneuf-du-Pape 1984 • $11 • (9/30/1987) • **92**
Châteauneuf-du-Pape 1983 • $25 • (10/15/1991) • **88**
Châteauneuf-du-Pape 1981 • $30 • (10/15/1991) • **90**
Châteauneuf-du-Pape White 1999: Intriguing and full-bodied, with clean and crisp fruit flavors, but also an opulent, fat mouthfeel. Floral undertone, with beeswax and lemon. Turns minerally on the finish, with a chalky character. Best from 2002 through 2008.–P.M. • $30 • (6/30/2000) • **89**
Châteauneuf-du-Pape White 1998: Clean and pure, traditional and really delicious, pumping out the intense flavors in a subtle but richer-than-you-think body. A bit herbal, with a slight olive undertone, it offers flint, matchstick and wet earth complexity. Drink now through 2003.–P.M. • $30 • (9/30/1999) • **92**
Châteauneuf-du-Pape White 1996 • $26 • (10/15/1997) • **88**
Côtes du Rhône 1997: Clean, juicy and succulent, with ripe fruit, this pretty wine offers cherry, currant, black pepper and plum. Balanced and ripe on the delicious finish. Drink now.–P.M. • $11 • (11/15/1998) • **85**
Côtes du Rhône 1995 • $11 • (9/15/1997) • **83**
Côtes du Rhône 1993 • $10 • (11/15/1995) • **78**
Côtes du Rhône 1992 • $9 • (10/15/1994) • **85**
Côtes du Rhône 1990 • $9 • (8/31/1992) • **78**
Côtes du Rhône White 1997: Fairly thick, this full-bodied wine displays attractive pineapple, pear and quince aromas and flavors. Balanced and lush, a lemon kick to the finish makes it taste fresh. Drink now through 2001.–P.M. • $11 • (11/15/1998) • **85**

MONT ROSE, DOMAINE

Merlot Vin de Pays d'Oc 1995 • $6 • (6/30/1997) • **83**

MONT ST.-MICHEL

Cabernet Sauvignon Vin de Pays d'Oc Unfiltered 1995 • $8 • (12/15/1996) • **82**
Merlot Vin de Pays d'Oc Unfiltered 1995 • $8 • (12/15/1996) • **85**

MONT-TANA

Merlot Vin de Pays d'Oc 1996 • $7 • (11/15/1997) • **80**
Sauvignon Blanc Vin de Pays d'Oc 1996 • $8 • (10/31/1997) • **84**

MONT TAUCH, LES PRODUCTEURS DU

Corbières 1991 • $7 • (3/15/1993) • **81**
Fitou 1990 • $8 • (4/15/1993) • **74**
Fitou Château de Ségure Réserve 1996: Medium-bodied and nicely focused, with dried cherry and red plum flavors and a nice mineral component on the finish. Smooth and ready to drink.–K.M. • $15 • (8/31/1999) • **85**
Fitou L'Exception 1998: A ripe red with touches of richness and lots of sweet and spicy notes backed up by black currant and dark cherry flavors. Still quite youthful, it's appealing now, but should smooth out with some age. Drink now through 2001.–K.M. • $20 • (8/31/1999) • **87**
Fitou Prestige 1997: Ripe and mature-tasting, with aromas of dark fruit and leather and flavors to match. There's some good muscle and tannins here, too. Hints of leather and spice linger on the finish. Drink now through 2001.–K.M. • $15 • (8/31/1999) • **84**
Fitou Prieuré du Château de Ségure Vieilles Vignes 1997: A medium-bodied red, with dried cherry, berry and plum flavors. A slight stewy note lingers on the finish. Drink now.–K.M. • $12 • (8/31/1999) • **83**
Merlot Vin de Pays du Torgan 1998: Ripe and smoky flavors and aromas mark this distinctive red. Attempts a serious style, with black cherry, plum and currant flavors, leather notes, nice concentration and backbone. A bit rustic in the end, but packs plenty of wallop, with a generous dose of tannin on the finish. Impressive for a co-op wine. Drink now through 2002.–K.M. • $20 • (9/15/1999) • **88**
Vin de Pays du Torgan Le Sanglier 1991 • $6 • (4/15/1993) • **83**

MONTAUDON

Brut Champagne NV: Exuberant in style, with lots of fresh citrus and butter flavors, good acidity and a rounded texture. Tasted twice, with consistent notes. Drink now. • $30 • (10/15/1999) • **88**

Key: SS—Spectator Selection. CS—Cellar Selection. HR—Highly Recommended. $NA—Price not available. (BT)—Barrel tasting. Ⓐ—Auction Price. For a key to the tasters' initials, see "How to Use These Listings."
Dates in parentheses represent the issues in which the ratings were published.

Brut Champagne 1995: Nicely balanced, full-flavored and velvety in texture. Complete and satisfying in character. Drink now through 2002. • $42 • (10/15/1999) • **87**

Brut Champagne Classe M NV: An attractive, full-bodied Champagne with toasty-earthy aromas, ripe fruit flavors and a generous texture. Enough substance to sink your teeth into. Drink now. • $48 • (10/15/1999) • **88**

Brut Chardonnay Champagne Premier Cru NV: An elegant, dry Champagne, on the light side, with bright citrus flavors and a creamy texture. Drink now. • $39 • (10/15/1999) • **89**

Brut Rosé Champagne Grande Rose NV: Ample fruit flavors and a soft texture make this deep-colored rosé easy to enjoy. A toasty aroma and cherry-like finish add to its interest. Drink now through 2001. • $35 • (10/15/1999) • **87**

MONTBAYON, DOMAINE DE

Côtes du Rhône-Villages Roaix 1996 • $NA • (10/15/1997) • **85**
Vacqueyras 1996 • $NA • (10/15/1997) • **87**
Vacqueyras 1995 • $NA • (10/15/1997) • **85**

MONTEILLET, DOMAINE DU

Condrieu 1997: Lovely balance bookends this rich but vibrant, full-bodied white, which shows honey, pineapple, matchstick and smoke complexity. Has character. Drink now through 2003.–P.M. • $38 • (8/31/1999) • **91**

Condrieu 1996: A sensational, full-bodied, rich but elegant white. Thick in texture, round and seductive, this world-class wine is balanced and exciting, with floral, peach, pineapple, orange marmalade and black cherry character. It's just a touch off-dry, so try as an aperitif or with foie gras or smoked salmon. Drink now through 2007.–P.M. • $NA • (11/15/1998) • **95**

St.-Joseph 1997: Delicious for its black pepper, game, earth, smoke and black fruit complexity, this medium-bodied red shows good concentration, a silky midpalate and a lingering, balanced finish. Drink now through 2002.–P.M. • $20 • (10/31/1999) • **88**

St.-Joseph Cuvée de Papy 1997: The aromas are prettier than the flavors. Smells of cassis, smoke, violet and horse stable. Medium-bodied and a bit hard and acidic on the palate, with tough tannins on the greenish finish. Drink now through 2002.–P.M. • $30 • (12/15/1999) • **80**

St.-Joseph Cuvée de Papy 1996: Multifaceted. Exotic, complex and satisfying earth, animal and grilled meat aromas combine seductively with black currant, pepper, white chocolate and vanilla bean notes. Massive but supple tannins, with a fresh underpinning of acidity and subtle oak accents. Drink now through 2015.–P.M. • $23 • (11/15/1998) • **93**

St.-Joseph Cuvée de Papy 1995: Classy, racy and elegant, with exotic floral, spice, coffee grind, vanilla, toasty oak, mocha, griottes and cassis character. Medium-bodied, with supple tannins, it's balanced to a T. Drink now through 2020.–P.M. • $23 • (11/15/1998) • **87**

St.-Joseph White 1997: Ripe and pretty, medium-bodied, with a so-so complexity as it offers almond and green pear and a rather short but clean finish. Drink now.–P.M. • $20 • (8/31/1999) • **82**

St.-Joseph White 1996: Straightforward, showing modest fruit and wet cardboard aromas, but fairly round on the palate. Tastes overly filtered.–P.M. • $20 • (11/15/1998) • **76**

MONTESQUIEU, DOMAINES H. DE

Bordeaux Baron de Montesquieu Le Secondat 1993 • $11 • (4/30/1997) • **79**
Bordeaux M de Montesquieu 1993 • $9 • (4/30/1997) • **78**

Bordeaux Réserve 1996: Very light, with delicate strawberry and vanilla character. More like a rosé than a red, but it's clean and refreshing.–J.S. • $11 • (7/31/1999) • **79**

Bordeaux White Réserve 1998: Here's a big and rich white Bordeaux at an unBordeaux-like price. It's medium- to full-bodied, boasting lots of toasted oak character, culminating in a delicous nutty, toasty, fruity aftertaste. Drink now.–J.S. • $11 • (7/31/1999) • **86**

Graves 1996: Clean and fruity, but rather light and diluted.–J.S. • $15 • (7/31/1999) • **78**

Graves Moelleux 1995: Rich but not overly sweet. Aromas of vanilla, pineapple and pear follow through to the medium-bodied palate. Fresh finish. Drink now.–J.S. • $15 • (7/31/1999) • **86**

Graves Supérieur Moelleux 1993 • $17/500 ml. • (4/30/1997) • **86**

Graves White 1996: A decent white Bordeaux, with pear and apple character. Medium-bodied, with a soft texture and a fruity finish. Drink now.–J.S. • $15 • (7/31/1999) • **80**

Merlot Bordeaux M de Montesquieu 1996: A light and watery '96, with very little fruit.–J.S. • $10 • (7/31/1999) • **74**

Sauvignon Blanc Bordeaux M de Montesquieu 1998: Lots of Sauvignon character in this young white. Light- to medium-bodied, with lovely fresh acidity and a long grapefruit and lime aftertaste. Drink now.–J.S. • $10 • (7/31/1999) • **84**

MONTFORT, CHATEAU DE

Vouvray 1996 • $10 • (5/31/1998) • **78**

MONTGRAND-MILON, CHATEAU

Pauillac 1997: A luncheon claret. The raspberry and mineral character dominates this medium-bodied, rather short young wine. Drink now.–J.S. • $45 • (7/31/1999) • **81**

MONTGUERET, CHATEAU DE

Rosé d'Anjou 1997: This simple rosé has little color and neutral flavors, with only a hint of sweetness to tickle the palate.–T.M. • $10 • (6/30/1999) • **78**
Rosé d'Anjou 1996 • $13 • (6/15/1998) • **79**

Saumur White 1997: Firm and crisp, this white offers apple and pear flavors, with notes of almond and herb. Tight and a bit tart, it should blossom with food. Drink now through 2001.–T.M. • $10 • (6/30/1999) • **83**
Saumur White 1996 • $13 • (6/30/1998) • **86**

MONTHELIE-DOUHAIRET

Bourgogne Aligoté 1996 • $17 • (5/31/1998) • **84**
Bourgogne Aligoté 1995 • $17 • (8/31/1997) • **70**
Meursault 1995 • $41 • (5/31/1997) • **86**
Meursault 1994 • $34 • (5/31/1996) • **84**

Meursault Les Cras 1998: Crisp style of Meursault. Tastes tart, a bit bitter. Unripe flavors on the finish.–P.M. • $39 • (5/31/2000) • **76**

Meursault Les Cras 1997: A rather nice little Chardonnay, with decent fruit and oak offered in a medium-bodied, medium-intense package. Fresh finish. Drink now through 2002.–P.M. • $39 • (5/31/1999) • **82**
Meursault Les Cras 1996 • $40 • (5/31/1998) • **77**

Meursault Les Santenots 1997: Not very ripe, with herbal notes. Light-bodied, showing only modest fruit intensity.–P.M. • $57 • (5/31/1999) • **79**
Meursault Les Santenots 1996 • $53 • (5/31/1998) • **93**
Meursault Les Santenots 1995 • $50 • (5/31/1997) • **89**

Meursault-Santenots 1998: Attractive. Ripe Meursault, with butter character and good fruit. Medium-bodied. Spicy oak adds complexity to the medium-intense finish. Drink now through 2002.–P.M. • $61 • (5/31/2000) • **86**

Monthélie 1997: Decent fruit; too bad it turns so mouthpuckeringly crisp. Drink now through 2003.–P.M. • $27 • (9/30/1999) • **80**
Monthélie 1994 • $26 • (11/15/1996) • **79**
Monthélie 1985 • $16 • (6/30/1988) • **81**

Monthélie Clos Le Meix Garnier 1997: A bit tart, with cold fruit character. Lacks seductive balance.–P.M. • $29 • (9/30/1999) • **72**

Monthélie Clos Le Meix Garnier 1996: Floral and spicy, with blackberry aromas and flavors too, an elegant structure and lovely presence on the palate. The tannins are very refined and the finish lingers. Drink now through 2002.–B.S. • $27 • (9/30/1998) • **88**
Monthélie Clos Le Meix Garnier 1995 • $30 • (11/15/1997) • **79**
Monthélie Clos Le Meix Garnier 1994 • $22 • (11/15/1996) • **79**
Monthélie Clos Le Meix Garnier 1992 • $23 • (10/31/1994) • **76**

Monthélie Le Meix Bataille 1997: Intriguingly minty, with a black cherry and blackberry character, supple tannins and a lively, grapey, succulent and natural-tasting finish. Medium-bodied, it's seductively balanced. Drink now through 2004.–P.M. • $34 • (9/30/1999) • **87**

Monthélie Le Meix Bataille 1996: Clean and pure. A lovely, round wine with terrific currant, black cherry and raspberry flavors. Deftly oaked, it has supple tannins that lead to a smooth finish. Drink now through 2001.–P.M. • $30 • (9/30/1998) • **88**
Monthélie Le Meix Bataille 1995 • $30 • (11/15/1997) • **84**
Monthélie Le Meix Bataille 1994 • $26 • (11/15/1996) • **82**

Monthélie Les Duressees 1997: Smooth and rich, ripe and thick but also very clean, pure and natural, this is '97 at its best, with refined tannins, full body and succulent acidity. Deeply satisfying. Drink now through 2005.–P.M. • $34 • (9/30/1999) • **91**

FRANCE

Monthélie Les Duresses 1996: Pure and clean fruit in this vibrant, ripe-tasting red Burgundy, with plenty of cassis, blueberry and wild berry, and a slight smoky character. Good acidity and a good amount of tannin suggest cellaring short-term. Drink now.–P.M. • $30 • (9/30/1998) • **87**

Monthélie Les Duresses 1995 • $27 • (11/15/1997) • **84**

Monthélie Les Duresses 1994 • $31 • (11/15/1996) • **77**

Monthélie White 1998: Balanced, in a straightforward, drink-now style. Attractive ripe fruit, honey and dried herbs. Medium-bodied. Good length. Drink now through 2001.–P.M. • $30 • (5/31/2000) • **86**

Monthélie White 1997: The wood covers up the fruit, dulling the flavors in this medium-bodied wine.–P.M. • $30 • (5/31/1999) • **79**

Monthélie White 1995 • $30 • (5/31/1997) • **86**

Monthélie White Les Duresses 1998: Flavorful '98, with a rather dense midpalate, offering some smoke, ripe fruit and honeyed character. Balanced, medium to full in body, you can chew on the thickness on the finish. Drink now through 2003.–P.M. • $38 • (5/31/2000) • **86**

Monthélie White Les Duresses 1997: A bit earthy, full-bodied and intense, with a distinctive flinty, smoky character, it shows good fruit, delicious honey and enough lemony acidity to make it a pretty drink on release. A bit hot on the finish. Drink now.–P.M. • $36 • (5/31/1999) • **87**

Monthélie White Les Duresses 1996 • $35 • (5/31/1998) • **85**

Monthélie White Les Duresses 1995 • $37 • (5/31/1997) • **88**

Pommard Les Chanlins 1997: Full of iron and mineral, this fresh Pinot offers cherry and earth in a compact, forthright way. Solidly structured and balanced, with firm yet ripe tannins. Drink now through 2005.–B.S. • $57 • (9/30/1999) • **87**

Pommard Les Chanlins 1996: Seductive. Round and sweet-tasting, supple from the ripe tannins, this is a delight with all that raspberry, black cherry and currant character. Delivers a spicy note on the slightly hot finish. Drink now through 2003.–P.M. • $54 • (9/30/1998) • **85**

Pommard Les Chanlins 1995 • $50 • (11/15/1997) • **84**

Pommard Les Fremiers 1997: Nice and round, showing ripe tannins and pretty blackberry, licorice and raspberry character. Medium-bodied, with a fresh finish. Drink now through 2004.–P.M. • $57 • (9/30/1999) • **86**

Pommard Les Fremiers 1996: Refined tannins and a supple structure make this lovely to drink over the next few years, as do delicious raspberry, cherry and currant flavors accented by a hint of smoke. Medium-bodied, it lacks a bit of power at midpalate. Sweet-tasting finish is seductive. Drink now through 2005.–P.M. • $54 • (9/30/1998) • **87**

Pommard Les Fremiers 1995 • $50 • (11/15/1997) • **80**

Pommard Les Fremiers 1994 • $42 • (11/15/1996) • **83**

Volnay En Champans 1997: Starts off with black cherry and smoke notes, then turns resinous, overshadowing the delicate fruit. Modest finish, but the strong oak note is troublesome at this stage.–B.S. • $47 • (9/30/1999) • **78**

Volnay En Champans 1996: Fairly tart, at least for now, but shows lovely cassis, blueberry, wild berry and plum character. Very sappy and crisp, it should flesh out with time as the tannins are ripe and sweet. Best after 2003.–P.M. • $43 • (9/30/1998) • **87**

Volnay En Champans 1995 • $40 • (11/15/1997) • **82**

Volnay En Champans 1994 • $35 • (11/15/1996) • **80**

Volnay En Champans 1993 • $44 • (11/15/1995) • **93**

Volnay En Champans 1992 • $38 • (10/31/1994) • **82**

Volnay En Champans 1985 • $25 • (7/15/1988) • **87**

MONTHIL, CHATEAU DU

Médoc 1996: Plummy and earthy, with a hint of dried herbs. Medium-bodied and peppery on the palate, with chewy tannins and a medium aftertaste. Slightly hollow midpalate. Best after 2000.–J.S. • $NA • (1/31/1999) • **84**

MONTMIRAIL, CHATEAU DE

Côtes du Rhône 1991 • $9 • (6/15/1993) • **78**

Gigondas Cuvée de Beauchamp 1990 • $13 • (4/15/1993) • **75**

Gigondas Cuvée de Beauchamp 1985 • $14 • (9/30/1988) • **78**

Gigondas Cuvée de Beauchamp 1983 • $11 • (11/30/1986) • **90**

Vacqueyras Cuvée de L'Ermite Red 1990 • $11 • (4/15/1993) • **82**

Key: SS—Spectator Selection. CS—Cellar Selection. HR—Highly Recommended. $NA—Price not available. (BT)—Barrel tasting. Ⓐ—Auction Price. For a key to the tasters' initials, see "How to Use These Listings."
Dates in parentheses represent the issues in which the ratings were published.

MONTNER, CHATEAU

Côtes du Roussillon-Villages 1998: Simple and grapey, with nice red plum and pepper flavors. Dusty notes on the finish. Drink now.–K.M. • $10 • (11/15/1999) • **81**

MONTPATEY, CHATEAU DE

Bourgogne White 1996 • $11 • (5/31/1998) • **77**

MONTPEZAT, DOMAINE DE

Cabernet-Syrah Vin de Pays d'Oc 1996: A ripe and oaky style, with dark plum, cherry and berry flavors and good dollops of spice and chocolate. Peppery notes chime in on the finish. Drink now through 2002.–K.M. • $13 • (11/15/1998) • **86**

MONTROSE, CHATEAU

St.-Estèphe 1999: Firm and linear, with racy tannins and good fruit. Medium-bodied, with chewy tannins and a spicy finish. A bit more fruit midpalate would be nice.–J.S. • $NA • (1/01/2000) (BT) • **85-89**

St.-Estèphe 1997: Very pretty red with berry, cherry character. Medium-bodied, with good fruit and a soft tannin structure. Well done and delicious. Drink now.–J.S. • $61 • (1/31/2000) • **88**

St.-Estèphe 1996: A classic St.-Estèphe with all the exotic character you expect from this appellation, along with a harmony, finesse and subtlety not seen in many '96s. Absolutely wonderful aromas of blackberries, anise seed, minerals and spices. Full-bodied, with layers of well-integrated, polished tannins and an intense spicy, fruity aftertaste. One of the best of the modern-day wines from Montrose. Try after 2004.–J.S. • $62 Ⓐ • (1/31/1999) CS • **95**

St.-Estèphe 1995 • $56 Ⓐ • (1/31/1998) • **88**

St.-Estèphe 1994 • $42 Ⓐ • (1/31/1997) • **84**

St.-Estèphe 1993 • $37 Ⓐ • (1/31/1996) • **90**

St.-Estèphe 1992 • $33 Ⓐ • (4/15/1995) • **86**

St.-Estèphe 1991 • $36 Ⓐ • (3/31/1994) • **85**

St.-Estèphe 1990 • $215 Ⓐ • (3/31/1993) • **94**

St.-Estèphe 1989: A big and chewy young thing. Dark ruby-colored, with powerful aromas of tobacco, spices and fruit. Full-bodied and very tannic. Leave this bottle alone for now.—1989 Bordeaux horizontal. Best after 2005.–J.S. • $92 Ⓐ • (5/31/1999) • **93**

St.-Estèphe 1988: Slightly angular and lean, this does have pretty spice, berry and cherry aromas and flavors. Full-bodied, with firm tannins and a medium finish.—1988 Bordeaux horizontal. Best after 2000.–J.S. • $46 Ⓐ • (11/30/1998) • **88**

St.-Estèphe 1987 • $17 • (2/15/1990) • **80**

St.-Estèphe 1986 • $68 Ⓐ • (5/15/1989) SS • **96**

St.-Estèphe 1985 • $51 Ⓐ • (10/15/1994) • **89**

St.-Estèphe 1984 • $24 • (3/31/1987) • **88**

St.-Estèphe 1983 • $44 Ⓐ • (10/15/1994) • **85**

St.-Estèphe 1982: Balanced and harmonious. Dark ruby-garnet. Fresh cherry and cinnamon aromas. Full-bodied and very fruity, with a good backbone of tannins and a long, spice, berry and cedar finish. Can age, but why wait?—1982 Bordeaux horizontal. Drink now.–J.S. • $87 Ⓐ • (11/30/1998) • **90**

St.-Estèphe 1981 • $41 Ⓐ • (10/15/1994) • **88**

St.-Estèphe 1979 • $36 Ⓐ • (10/15/1989) • **81**

St.-Estèphe 1970 • $106 Ⓐ • (5/15/1993) • **87**

St.-Estèphe 1962 • $67 Ⓐ • (11/30/1987) • **90**

St.-Estèphe 1961 • $269 Ⓐ • (4/30/1996) • **85**

St.-Estèphe 1959 • $140/1.5 liter • (10/15/1990) • **90**

St.-Estèphe 1947 • $603 Ⓐ • (5/31/1997) • **89**

St.-Estèphe 1945 • $417 Ⓐ • (11/30/1995) • **79**

MONTROSE, LA DAME DE

St.-Estèphe 1996: Very good fruit, but slightly simple. Medium-bodied and fruity, with berry and cherry character and an underlying earthiness. Velvety texture. Delicious. Second label of Château Montrose. Drink now.–J.S. • $29 • (1/31/1999) • **87**

St.-Estèphe 1995 • $30 • (1/31/1998) • **85**

St.-Estèphe 1994 • $30 • (1/31/1997) • **78**

MONTUS, CHATEAU

Madiran 1995 • $20 • (9/30/1997) • **86**

Madiran 1985 • $10 • (4/15/1989) • **79**
Madiran Cuvée Prestige 1995 • $38 • (9/30/1997) • **90**
Madiran Cuvée Prestige 1994 • $36 • (9/30/1997) • **85**
Madiran Cuvée Prestige 1990 • $35 • (1/01/1997) • **92**
Madiran Cuvée Prestige 1989 • $30 • (7/15/1992) • **85**
Madiran Elevée en Fûts de Chêne 1989 • $17 • (7/15/1992) • **77**

MONTVAC, DOMAINE DE

Vacqueyras 1995: A vivid and fresh red, with currant, blackberry and spice in a medium-bodied but fairly lean package. Enjoy the fruit now; this should develop chocolate, spice and tobacco complexity with a bit of cellaring. The finish is a bit short. Drink through 2001.–P.M. • $16 • (10/15/1998) • **80**
Vacqueyras 1993 • $12 • (2/28/1997) • **76**
Vacqueyras Cuvée Vincila 1993: Rich, ripe and plummy, with round tannins and a citrusy-lemony undertow, this medium-bodied wine has plenty of currant, leather, grilled meat, blueberry and spice character. Long, tannic finish is slightly dry. Drink through 2005–P.M. • $20 • (10/15/1998) • **80**

MONTVIEL, CHATEAU

Pomerol 1998: Full-bodied, round and chewy, with lots of tannins and ripe fruit. Long, big finish.–J.S. • $NA • (5/31/1999) (BT) • **90-94**
Pomerol 1997: Good blackberry and violet character. Medium body, soft tannins and a long, fruity finish. Drink now.–J.S. • $NA • (1/31/2000) • **85**
Pomerol 1996: Lovely smoky, berry and chocolate aromas and flavors through and through. Medium-bodied, with round tannins and a delicious berry aftertaste. Drink now.–J.S. • $NA • (1/31/1999) • **86**
Pomerol 1995: Autumnal aromas of earth, game and tobacco. Medium- to full-bodied, with velvety tannins and a medium finish. Needs time to open. Drink through 2006–J.S. • $35 • (9/15/1998) • **88**

MORDOREE, DOMAINE DE LA

Châteauneuf-du-Pape 1997: Lovely concentration in this pure, ripe, clean, dark-colored red, delivering little waves of balanced red berry and blackberry character, a velvety texture and layers of complex flavors folding seductively on the finish. Drink now through 2005.–P.M. • $45 • (8/31/1999) • **90**
Châteauneuf-du-Pape Cuvée de la Reine des Bois 1998: Thick, dense and immensely attractive. Harmonious from start to finish, with a distinct vanilla, sweet chocolate and spice character plus ripe black fruit, roasted game, grilled meat and smoke notes. Incredibly silky tannin structure. Melts like cream on the focused, clean finish. Drink now through 2015.–P.M. • $40 • (6/30/2000) HR • **95**
Châteauneuf-du-Pape Cuvée de la Reine des Bois 1996: Amazing quality for a '96. Like a top-class, opulent, thick and ripe Australian Shiraz. The tannins are sensational, velvety and supple, and this modern-style, new-oakish, hedonistic Rhône red explodes with spicy coffee, vanilla bean, smoked bacon and mocha notes, as well as blackberry and red berry flavors. Full-bodied, it walks a tightrope between power and finesse. Drink through 2010–P.M. • $50 • (9/30/1998) • **94**
Côtes du Rhône 1998: A '98 made in a compacted, chewy style, with good flavors of blackberry, green olives and wet earth. Medium-bodied, with ripe tannins and a lingering, juicy finish. Should go well with food. Drink now.–P.M. • $10 • (11/15/1999) • **84**
Côtes du Rhône 1992 • $8 • (11/30/1994) • **82**
Côtes du Rhône Rosé 1998: Light but juicy, showing some cherry, raspberry and citrus character. Overall impression: a bit dull and short.–P.M. • $10 • (11/15/1999) • **78**
Côtes du Rhône Rosé 1997: A rustic rosé that tastes of vanilla, cherries and popsicles. Medium-bodied, slightly diluted.–P.M. • $9 • (11/15/1998) • **77**
Côtes du Rhône White 1998: Medium-intense, built in a softer style, showing a civilized balance. Some crisp character peeks through the ripe, honeyed notes on the lingering finish. Drink now.–P.M. • $10 • (11/15/1999) • **84**
Côtes du Rhône White 1997: An appealing white that shows structure, with honey, lime and melon character. Medium-bodied, fresh and succulent, with a lingering finish.–P.M. • $9 • (11/15/1998) • **85**
Lirac 1996: Lively and fresh, with blueberry, citrus and black cherry notes. The tannins are a bit unripe in this medium-bodied red, but the acidity should play nicely against food. Drink now.–P.M. • $14 • (11/15/1998) • **80**
Lirac 1986 • $11 • (9/30/1988) • **88**
Lirac Cuvée de la Reine des Bois 1997: Pretty currant and plum coexist in this toasted, oaky, rather crisp red, with the flavors following on the decent finish. Drink now.–P.M. • $19 • (12/15/1999) • **83**
Lirac Cuvée de la Reine des Bois 1996: Elegant in style. Inky-purple in color, full-bodied, loaded with fresh, vibrant black and red fruit flavors. Tannins are massive, yet refined and sweet-tasting. Black pepper, red pepper, blackberry, toasty oak and spice notes keep it interesting. Best from 2001 through 2005.–P.M. • $18 • (11/15/1998) • **88**
Lirac White Cuvée de la Reine des Bois 1998: Charming, light but fresh, vibrant but ripe, with a lemony, intense, greenish character. Tastes pure and traditional, with wet earth, green olive, dried herb and pear notes. A style of Rhône that leaves an impression. Drink now.–P.M. • $15 • (12/15/1999) • **87**
Lirac White Cuvée de la Reine des Bois 1997: A structured white, with blanched almond, marzipan, citrus and dried herb flavors. Well made, quite chewy and mouthpuckeringly fresh. Not much fat, and a bit short. Drink now.–P.M. • $18 • (11/15/1998) • **80**
Tavel 1998: Balanced and lots of fun besides being delicious, this has a silky texture and ripe flavors, yet demonstrates a classy elegance. Sleek finish, with delectable cherry and raspberry notes folded into smooth tannins and fresh acidity. Drink now.–P.M. • $12 • (11/15/1999) • **86**

MOREAU, BERNARD

Chassagne-Montrachet 1998: Rather hard Chassagne, with pure and clean fruit. Medium-bodied, delivering crisp character and some lemon, green apple, toasted oak and honey. Should improve with short-term cellaring. Best from 2002 through 2006.–P.M. • $35 • (5/31/2000) • **85**
Chassagne-Montrachet 1997: Nice balance, with ripe apple, pear and citrus aromas and flavors on a medium-bodied frame. Good, fresh finish. Drink now.–P.M. • $35 • (5/31/1999) • **85**
Chassagne-Montrachet 1996 • $30 • (5/31/1998) • **87**
Chassagne-Montrachet 1995 • $30 • (8/31/1997) • **88**
Chassagne-Montrachet Grandes Ruchottes 1997: Nicely ripe and flavorful, with honey, tropical and pear character, here's a balanced, medium-bodied, lovely Chassagne with a deftly toasted, lingering, clean yet opulent finish. Drink now through 2003.–P.M. • $50 • (5/31/1999) • **89**
Chassagne-Montrachet Grandes Ruchottes 1996: Elegant and delicate, medium-bodied, medium-intense, showing some butter, pear and cream character. Clean and pure on the very supple palate, with a lovely, slightly lemony, minerally finish. Drink now through 2001.–P.M. • $40 • (8/31/1998) • **87**
Chassagne-Montrachet Grandes Ruchottes 1995 • $39 • (8/31/1997) • **89**
Chassagne-Montrachet La Maltroie 1998: Middle-of-the-road '98 white Burgundy. A bit lightish in character, offering some suppleness at midpalate before kicking in with citrus and herb notes on the astringent finish.–P.M. • $45 • (5/31/2000) • **79**
Chassagne-Montrachet La Maltroie 1997: A tart, lean, hard Chassagne, lacking harmonious ripeness and showing green apple and dried herb notes, with a hint of pretty pear character on the mouthpuckeringly sharp finish. Drink now through 2003.–P.M. • $42 • (5/31/1999) • **81**
Chassagne-Montrachet La Maltroie 1995 • $35 • (5/31/1997) • **84**
Chassagne-Montrachet Les Chenevottes 1998: Fairly rich and ripe and maintains elegance. Citrusy and honeyed, with pear tart and crusty bread character, and spice and crème brûlée flavors that add complexity. Full-bodied. A bit overly burnt toast-flavored on the finish. Drink now through 2007.–P.M. • $45 • (5/31/2000) • **88**
Chassagne-Montrachet Les Chenevottes 1997: Golden-colored and full-bodied, it tastes round, flavorful and rich, with delicious tropical, pear, quince and toast flavors that swirl seductively around the palate. Creamy texture leads to the clean, fresh finish. Drink now through 2003.–P.M. • $42 • (5/31/1999) • **91**
Chassagne-Montrachet Les Chenevottes 1996 • $38 • (5/31/1998) • **88**
Chassagne-Montrachet Les Chenevottes 1995 • $35 • (5/31/1997) • **90**
Chassagne-Montrachet Morgeot 1998: Well made. Not a *terroir*-driven wine, but it has more pure sweet-tasting fruit than most '98 white Burgundies. Complex, with spice, mocha, pear tart, honey, figs and vanilla. Clean and medium-bodied, with a fresh and elegant finish. Drink now through 2007.–P.M. • $45 • (5/31/2000) • **91**
Chassagne-Montrachet Morgeot 1997: Clean and medium-bodied, offering modest fruit with a buttery note. Minerally character on the short finish. Drink now.–P.M. • $42 • (5/31/1999) • **80**
Chassagne-Montrachet Morgeot 1996 • $38 • (5/31/1998) • **88**
Chassagne-Montrachet Morgeot 1995 • $35 • (5/31/1997) • **92**
Chassagne-Montrachet Red 1995: Light-bodied, delicate, showing some black cherry, with a slightly herbal character on the finish. Drink now.–P.M. • $20 • (8/31/1998) • **82**
Chassagne-Montrachet Red Morgeot La Cardeuse 1995: Very pretty, showing clean, fairly ripe red- and blackberry character, but also reflects nicely the soil of the vineyard site. Balanced and well structured, with good fresh acidity on the lingering finish. Drink now through 2002.–P.M. • $25 • (8/31/1998) • **86**

MOREAU, LOUIS

Chablis 1997: Unimpressive, with only modest aromas and flavors. Very lemony and tart.–P.M. • $16 • (9/30/1999) • **78**
Chablis 1996 • $17 • (8/31/1997) • **80**
Chablis 1995 • $NA • (8/31/1996) • **78**
Chablis Domaine de Bieville 1996 • $15 • (8/31/1997) • **83**
Chablis Domaine de Bieville 1995 • $NA • (8/31/1996) • **82**
Chablis Domaine du Cèdre Doré 1997: Vibrant, clean and balanced. A village Chablis with a lean frame that food should manage to tame. Drink now.–P.M. • $18 • (9/30/1999) • **80**
Chablis Les Fourneaux 1997: A smooth, honeyed, delicious, medium-bodied, "feminine" *premier cru*, this is clean and so attractive, with mineral and spice. Who can resist its charm on release? Drink now through 2003.–P.M. • $25 • (9/30/1999) • **90**
Chablis Les Fourneaux 1996 • $25 • (5/31/1998) • **87**
Chablis Les Fourneaux 1995 • $NA • (6/15/1997) • **86**
Chablis Premier Cru 1995 • $NA • (6/15/1997) • **85**
Chablis Vaulignot 1997: Elegant but also a bit tart, it's reserved on the nose and offers green apple, a salty character and a slight bitterness on the finish. Drink now.–P.M. • $23 • (9/30/1999) • **80**
Chablis Vaulignot 1996 • $22 • (5/31/1998) • **87**
Chablis Vaulignot 1995 • $NA • (6/15/1997) • **89**
Petit Chablis 1996 • $NA • (8/31/1997) • **84**

FRANCE

MOREAU & FILS, J.

Chablis 1998: Steely and crisp, with apple, bitter almond and citrus. Light- to medium-bodied, it's clean, kicking in with melon, wet earth and flint notes on the slightly astringent finish. Drink now through 2001.–P.M. • $15 • (5/15/2000) • **81**
Chablis 1997: Slightly spicy and buttery, with a vibrant core of green apple, this is a clean, perfectly decent little Chardonnay that whistles to a nice finish. Drink now.–P.M. • $18 • (5/31/1999) • **84**
Chablis 1996 • $NA • (8/31/1997) • **78**
Chablis 1995 • $15 • (8/31/1996) • **83**
Chablis Domaine de Biéville 1997: Lean and steely, a high-acidity Chablis, superclean and ungenerous, with green apple skin and lime flavors.–P.M. • $NA • (5/31/1999) • **79**
Chablis Les Clos 1998: Crisp in style but with good concentration as the honey and citrus flavors pick up velocity on the palate, with spice, toast and apple tart notes. Good minerally character on the full-bodied, zesty finish. Drink now through 2008.–P.M. • $40 • (5/15/2000) • **87**
Chablis Les Clos 1997: Incredibly fresh and vibrant in style, the character of this Chablis verges on green olive, dried herbs and freshly cut grass, but the flavors kick into classy gear on the palate, delivering a smooth mineral-lemon-pear combination on the elegant finish. Bravo. Best from 2003 through 2015.–P.M. • $52 • (5/31/1999) CS • **94**
Chablis Les Clos 1996 • $47 • (5/31/1998) • **98**
Chablis Vaillons 1998: Slightly oaky, but the wood is well integrated in this ripe-styled, oily-textured '98 Chablis. Medium- to full-bodied, with a butterscotch flavor and a slightly burning finish. Drink now through 2003.–P.M. • $28 • (5/15/2000) • **83**
Chablis Vaillons 1997: Well made, with good intensity of earth, mineral and fruit, this wine is full-bodied and balanced, with spice and what tastes like some oak, finely integrated and supple, ripe-tasting, and long on the finish. Drink now through 2005.–P.M. • $30 • (5/31/1999) • **91**
Chablis Vaillons 1996 • $25 • (5/31/1998) • **78**
Chablis Vaillons 1995 • $22 • (8/31/1996) • **88**
Chablis Vaillons Cuvée Préstige Guy Moreau 1995 • $27 • (6/15/1997) • **88**
Chablis Valmur 1997: Typical '97—clean, pure, slightly honeyed but ripe and lacking a bit of grip. It's delicious to drink, but the earlier the better. –P.M. • $NA • (5/31/1999) • **86**
Chablis Valmur 1996 • $46 • (5/31/1998) • **93**
Chablis Valmur 1995 • $43 • (6/15/1997) • **72**
Chablis Vaucoupin 1997: Very tight style, but full-bodied and concentrated. High acidity in this serious, minerally Chablis, with lemon, wet earth, salt, green apple flavors. Needs some cellaring. Drink through 2005–P.M. • $29 • (5/31/1999) • **87**

Key: SS—Spectator Selection. CS—Cellar Selection. HR—Highly Recommended. $NA—Price not available. (BT)—Barrel tasting. Ⓐ—Auction Price.
For a key to the tasters' initials, see "How to Use These Listings."
Dates in parentheses represent the issues in which the ratings were published.

Chablis Vaudésir 1996 • $45 • (5/31/1998) • **82**
Chablis Vaudésir 1995 • $43 • (6/15/1997) • **87**
Chardonnay Vin de Pays d'Oc 1997: Tart, with lemon and lime flavors and a simple finish.–K.M. • $8 • (9/30/1998) • **78**
Merlot Vin de Pays de Cassan 1992 • $6 • (2/28/1995) • **83**

MOREAU PERE & FILS, CHRISTIAN

Chablis 1998: Flinty in style, with good ripe fruit character. Delicate, with a good balance. A bit smoky on the finish. Debut release for this new label, which will start exporting to the U.S. with their '99 vintage. Drink now through 2001.–P.M. • $NA • (5/15/2000) • **85**

MOREY, BERNARD

Chassagne-Montrachet La Maltroie 1996 • $45 • (5/31/1998) • **88**
Chassagne-Montrachet Les Baudines 1997: Clean and full-bodied, with a mineral accent anchoring this in a fine terroir. Elegant and balanced, it's a pleasure to taste, with a lemon and toasty oak character on the finish. Drink now through 2002.–P.M. • $47 • (5/31/1999) • **88**
Chassagne-Montrachet Les Caillerets 1997: Toasty, ripe and delightful, offering a mouthful of full flavors and honey, pineapple, pear and smoke notes. Harmonious and clean, with a long, satisfying finish. Drink now through 2003.–P.M. • $52 • (5/31/1999) • **91**
Chassagne-Montrachet Les Caillerets 1996: Wonderful wine. Concentrated, ripe-tasting, packed with personality with all its earthy, herbal, mineral, minty, pear, citrusy character. Medium-bodied, it really makes a statement, especially on the smoky, toasted, matchsticklike finish. Best from 2003.–P.M. • $44 Ⓐ • (8/31/1998) • **90**
Chassagne-Montrachet Les Embrazées 1997: Decent ripe, sweet-tasting fruit peeks through in this medium-bodied, crisp Chardonnay. Clean and firmly structured, with a mineral and wet pebble finish. Drink now through 2002.–P.M. • $47 • (5/31/1999) • **83**
Chassagne-Montrachet Les Embrazées 1996: Extremely pure '96 Burgundy, showing a crisp herbal, citrus and green apple character with a smoky, matchsticklike aroma. Medium-bodied, it's quite smooth and thick midpalate. Fresh, mineral-laden finish could use some cellaring to soften. Best after 2005.–P.M. • $37 Ⓐ • (8/31/1998) • **92**
Chassagne-Montrachet Morgeot 1997: This lean, tough Chardonnay has a tart mouthfeel. Clean but also neutral, with modest green apple flavors.–P.M. • $47 • (5/31/1999) • **79**
Chassagne-Montrachet Morgeot 1996: Oozing thick, ripe texture and earthy, fruity, minerally, citrusy character, this is an impressive, full-bodied white Burgundy. You get your money's worth here, thanks to the silky, oily mouthfeel, wonderful sweet-tasting pear, melon, orange complexity, some wet earth and matchstick notes. Superlong, deftly smoked finish. Accessible upon release but will improve in the cellar. Best from 2005.–P.M. • $47 • (8/31/1998) • **93**
Chassagne-Montrachet Red 1990 • $28 • (6/15/1993) • **85**
Chassagne-Montrachet Red 1989 • $23 • (11/30/1992) • **81**
Chassagne-Montrachet Red 1987 • $20 • (10/31/1989) • **75**
Chassagne-Montrachet Vieille Vigne 1996: Clean, pure wine, bursting with vivid acidity, aromas and flavors. Tastes of freshly cut grass, green olives and green apples, also ripe pear, honey and pineapple. Add some earthy tones and you get a wine of character, if not very supple. Steely finish. Drink now through 2005.–P.M. • $40 • (8/31/1998) • **86**
Puligny-Montrachet La Truffière 1997: Well made, showing lovely mineral, wet stone and wet earth terroir notes, this full-bodied gem delivers lime, honey and tropical complexity on the firm but thick-textured finish. Drink now through 2007.–P.M. • $47 • (5/31/1999) • **92**
Puligny-Montrachet La Truffière 1996: An extraordinary achievement that places Bernard Morey firmly in the top ranks of white Burgundy specialists. A premier cru of wonderful concentration and finesse, this ripe Chardonnay walks a tightrope between its firm acidity, ripe flavors, well-integrated toasted oak, honey and spice notes. A marvel to contemplate, it has length, complexity, personality and purity. Bravo. Drink now through 2010.–P.M. • $69 • (8/31/1998) • **96**
St.-Aubin Les Charmois 1997: Decently ripe, medium-bodied and not very intense, with a supple core of pear, dried herb and green apple. Turns succulent on the balanced, accessible finish. Drink now through 2002.–P.M. • $32 • (5/31/1999) • **85**
St.-Aubin Les Charmois 1996: A beautiful but eccentric white, with earthy, plummy, minerally, tobacco leaf and smoke character. Good concentration of ripe fruit gives it a full-bodied feel, and the finish is a blanket of honey and tropical flavors. Give it time to shed the oak. Best after 2005.–P.M. • $33 • (8/31/1998) • **90**

Santenay Grand Clos Rousseau 1987 • $24 • (10/15/1989) • **87**

MOREY, MARC

Beaune Les Paules 1988 • $24 • (8/31/1990) • **85**
Beaune Les Paules 1985 • $15 • (12/31/1988) • **84**
Chassagne-Montrachet 1997: Buttery, honeyed and lemony, it's medium in body and vibrant in texture. Deftly oaked, fresh and fairly complex. Best from 2001 through 2007.–P.M. • $35 • (9/30/1999) • **88**
Chassagne-Montrachet 1996 • $32 • (5/31/1998) • **90**
Chassagne-Montrachet En Virondot 1997: Lovely opulence but also delicious focus, with smoke, toast, vanilla bean and ripe fruit flavors. Full-bodied, super-balanced, complex and layered with personality, with a lingering, lime-spiked finish. Best from 2001 through 2005.–P.M. • $48 • (9/30/1999) • **92**
Chassagne-Montrachet En Virondot 1996 • $44 • (5/31/1998) • **90**
Chassagne-Montrachet En Virondot 1995 • $45 • (5/31/1997) • **90**
Chassagne-Montrachet Les Caillerets 1997: Very tart, even a bit diluted, with a cardboard character. A disappointment from this producer.–P.M. • $60 • (9/30/1999) • **79**
Chassagne-Montrachet Les Caillerets 1995 • $72 Ⓐ • (8/31/1997) • **89**
Chassagne-Montrachet Les Chenevottes 1997: Subtle yet thick, rich and ripe, showing a delicacy of aromas and flavors, with vanilla bean, earth, lemon, honey and pear tart character. Full-bodied, it's beautifully balanced. Drink now through 2004.–P.M. • $48 • (9/30/1999) • **91**
Chassagne-Montrachet Les Chenevottes 1996 • $44 • (5/31/1998) • **91**
Chassagne-Montrachet Les Chenevottes 1995 • $42 • (8/31/1997) • **89**
Chassagne-Montrachet Les Vergers 1997: Fairly crisp, but with a good amount of toasted oak and fruit. Medium-bodied, the finish seems a bit hard now, but cellar; it should soften to a silky beauty. Best from 2001 through 2005.–P.M. • $53 • (9/30/1999) • **88**
Chassagne-Montrachet Les Vergers 1996 • $48 • (5/31/1998) • **93**
Chassagne-Montrachet Morgeot 1997: An intense, medium-bodied Chardonnay, showing wood but also plenty of lemon, honey and dried herb. Long finish. Drink now through 2002.–P.M. • $56 • (9/30/1999) • **89**
Chassagne-Montrachet Morgeot 1996 • $50 • (5/31/1998) • **91**
Chassagne-Montrachet Morgeot 1995 • $50 • (8/31/1997) • **89**
Puligny-Montrachet Les Pucelles 1995 • $45 • (5/31/1997) • **95**

MOREY, PIERRE

Bourgogne Aligoté 1997: A bit earthy and vegetal, not showing much charm, but with a crisp texture and finish.–P.M. • $18 • (9/30/1999) • **77**
Bourgogne White 1997: The wood is a bit too prevalent, with honey, lemon and green apple notes.–P.M. • $22 • (9/30/1999) • **78**
Meursault Les Tessons 1997: This has good fruit, a fat texture and a delicate, almost soft character, with medium-intense toast, pear and mineral flavors. Gains complexity in the glass, although the burning wood comes through on the finish. Drink now through 2003.–P.M. • $63 • (9/30/1999) • **87**

MOREY-BLANC

Meursault 1997: A rather crisp style of Meursault, with wood and sharp citrus notes. A young, medium-bodied white that tastes angular but with an intense finish. Drink now through 2003.–P.M. • $50 • (9/30/1999) • **83**

MOREY-COFFINET, MICHEL

Chassagne-Montrachet 1998: More wood than ripe fruit. Lacks a bit of balance, offering some sandalwood, sawdust, floral and green apple character. Turns somewhat lean on the finish. Drink now through 2002.–P.M. • $35 • (5/31/2000) • **80**
Chassagne-Montrachet 1997: Crisp and a bit green, this lean, firm, clean Chassagne shows an herb, green olive and cut grass character and little ripeness. Tart finish. Drink now.–P.M. • $35 • (5/31/1999) • **80**
Chassagne-Montrachet 1996 • $35 • (5/31/1998) • **89**
Chassagne-Montrachet 1995 • $32 • (8/31/1997) • **90**
Chassagne-Montrachet La Romanée 1998: Tastes exquisitely ripe and much better than it smells (very oaky), but give this medium-bodied white some time and it should come fully together. For now, it has toasted oak, pear, pineapple and lemon-jam notes. Supple texture. Best from 2002 through 2007.–P.M. • $50 • (5/31/2000) • **88**
Chassagne-Montrachet La Romanée 1997: A harmonious, round, supple, ripe wine. Golden-colored, with clean notes of pear, quince, pineapple and toast, it comes together beautifully on the long, opulent, fresh finish. Drink now through 2003.–P.M. • $50 • (5/31/1999) • **91**
Chassagne-Montrachet La Romanée 1996 • $47 • (5/31/1998) • **91**
Chassagne-Montrachet La Romanée 1995 • $45 • (8/31/1997) • **92**
Chassagne-Montrachet Les Caillerets 1998: Medium-bodied white in which the wood dominates the fruit, turning a bit astringent, with green apple, citrus character. Drink now through 2003.–P.M. • $49 • (5/31/2000) • **81**
Chassagne-Montrachet Les Caillerets 1997: Elegant and flavorful, with a spice, mocha, cedar and pearlike character, showing a supple, silky mid-palate and a citrusy, fresh finish. Drink now through 2001.–P.M. • $49 • (5/31/1999) • **87**
Chassagne-Montrachet Les Caillerets 1996 • $45 • (5/31/1998) • **82**

MORILLEAU, MICHEL

Chardonnay Vin de Pays du Jardin de la France Prieuré Royal St.-Laurent Réserve 1997: Clean and soft, this pretty white offers floral, citrus and apple flavors. Bright and focused, though without much depth, it shows varietal character and has enough acidity to match well with lighter dishes. Drink now.–T.M. • $8 • (6/30/1999) • **82**
Muscadet-Côtes de Grandlieu Sur Lie Prieuré Royal St.-Laurent 1998: Lemon zest, earth and green apple aromas and flavors run through this medium-weight Muscadet, finishing with a touch of white pepper. Drink now.–K.M. • $8 • (5/15/2000) • **82**
Muscadet-Côtes de Grandlieu Sur Lie Prieuré Royal St.-Laurent 1997: Mineral, floral and herb notes give this firm white more complexity than have most Muscadets. Not effusively fruity, but will match well with herb-accented dishes. Drink now.–T.M. • $9 • (6/30/1999) • **84**
Muscadet-Côtes de Grandlieu Sur Lie Prieuré Royal St.-Laurent 1996: A mouthful of apple, mineral and lemon that's fresh and vibrant, concentrated and rich, with a slightly bitter finish, a minerally aftertaste. Drink now.–B.S. • $7 • (11/15/1998) • **85**

MORIN, GERARD

Sancerre Vieilles Vignes 1996 • $15 • (5/31/1998) • **82**

MOROT, ALBERT

Beaune Bressandes 1995: Reserved and elegant, not a blockbuster, this medium-bodied wine has delicate flavors of *terroir*-driven earth, mineral, cherry, plum and spice, backed by modest oak accents. Smooth in texture, with a seductive finish. Drink now.–P.M. • $35 • (8/31/1998) • **88**
Beaune Bressandes 1990 • $38 • (12/15/1992) • **86**
Beaune Bressandes 1988 • $30 • (3/31/1991) • **87**
Beaune Cents-Vignes 1996: Smells delicate, with cherry notes, but on the palate it's chewy with black cherry flavors and some tough, astringent tannins. Not harmonious, for now.–P.M. • $34 • (7/31/1999) • **76**
Beaune Cents-Vignes 1995: A bit overripe, tough to cozy up to for its near-vinegar smells, cooked plum, and heavy-handed oak treatment.–P.M. • $35 • (8/31/1998) • **75**
Beaune Cents-Vignes 1991 • $28 • (1/31/1994) • **73**
Beaune Cents-Vignes 1988 • $30 • (4/30/1991) • **91**
Beaune Grèves 1988 • $32 • (7/15/1991) • **86**
Beaune Marconnets 1990 • $29 Ⓐ • (12/15/1992) • **84**
Beaune Teurons 1991 • $28 • (1/31/1994) • **78**
Beaune Teurons 1990 • $53 Ⓐ • (12/15/1992) • **85**
Beaune Teurons 1988 • $33 • (7/15/1991) • **80**
Beaune Toussaints 1996: Odd, obliterated by freshly cut wood, tasting tart with a spirit twist, finishing astringent. Too bad because the fruit may have been good.–P.M. • $34 • (7/31/1999) • **75**
Beaune Toussaints 1995: Rich and very ripe, with a round mouthfeel, but also plenty of tannins. A musty note tinges the plum, black cherry and dill. Drink through 2004–P.M. • $35 • (8/31/1998) • **81**
Beaune Toussaints 1991 • $28 • (1/31/1994) • **79**
Beaune Toussaints 1990 • $38 • (12/15/1992) • **84**
Savigny-lès-Beaune Aux Vergelesses La Bataillère 1991 • $26 • (1/31/1994) • **82**
Savigny-lès-Beaune Aux Vergelesses La Bataillère 1988 • $26 • (3/31/1991) • **86**

MORTET, DENIS

Bourgogne Les Charmes au Châtelain 1997: Smooth and rather delicate. Shows modest intensity but round tannins and a fresh finish, with black cherry, herb and subtle toasted oak.–P.M. • $24 • (9/30/1999) • **79**
Bourgogne Les Charmes au Châtelain 1996: Beautiful. Ripe, rich and packed with blackberry character, balanced with smooth tannins, deftly toasted aromas and pretty plum flavors. Drink now through 2002.–P.M. • $NA • (9/30/1998) • **88**

MORTET, DENIS

Bourgogne Les Charmes au Chatelain 1994 • $18 • (11/15/1996) • **83**
Bourgogne Les Charmes au Chatelain 1993 • $15 • (11/15/1995) • **88**
Bourgogne Les Charmes au Châtelain 1992 • $NA • (12/15/1994) • **83**
Chambertin 1997: Ripe black cherry and cassis aromas and flavors combine with finesse and harmony in this moderately intense '97 red. Balanced and fresh, it finishes crisply, with a long aftertaste of sweet, cassis-tinged fruit. Drink now through 2004.–B.S. • $144 • (9/30/1999) • **90**
Chambertin 1996: Very classy. Almost like blackberry jam it's so concentrated and focused, but a bit rigid at the moment. Great intensity of fruit, richness and supple tannins, finishing with pure fruit. Delicious. Best from 2001 through 2006.–B.S. • $125 • (9/30/1998) • **95**
Chambertin 1995 • $115 • (11/15/1997) • **93**
Chambertin 1994 • $90 • (11/15/1996) • **87**
Chambertin 1993 • $115 • (11/15/1995) • **94**
Chambertin 1992 • $NA • (12/15/1994) • **85**
Chambertin 1991 • $91 • (1/31/1994) • **86**
Chambolle-Musigny Aux Beaux Bruns 1997: Fantastic quality for the vintage. Supple as can be, but big, full and brooding, this deep, dark red Burgundy comes across as caressing and natural, with loads of plum, black currant, olive paste and mineral character. Explosive, long, harmonious finish. Drink now through 2007.–P.M. • $70 • (9/30/1999) HR • **94**
Chambolle-Musigny Aux Beaux Bruns 1996: Very ripe and fat '96, showing a lovely mocha, plum and cassis character. Supple and silky on the palate, this full-bodied red also delivers good acidity, leaving a trail of fresh fruit on the lingering finish. Tannins clamp down on the finish, so cellar. Try through 2007.–P.M. • $63 • (9/30/1998) • **91**
Chambolle-Musigny Aux Beaux Bruns 1995 • $59 • (11/15/1997) HR • **97**
Chambolle-Musigny Aux Beaux Bruns 1994 • $46 • (11/15/1996) • **90**
Chambolle-Musigny Aux Beaux Bruns 1993 • $43 • (11/15/1995) • **91**
Chambolle-Musigny Aux Beaux Bruns 1992 • $NA • (12/15/1994) • **84**
Chambolle-Musigny Aux Beaux Bruns 1991 • $46 • (1/31/1994) • **78**
Clos Vougeot 1997: Firmly packed with black fruit (plum and black cherry), this full-bodied, brooding red has well-integrated wood tannins, but the spicy oak, mocha and chocolate take over on the lingering finish. Best from 2003 through 2007.–P.M. • $99 • (9/30/1999) • **89**
Clos Vougeot 1996: Brilliant. The aromas reveal the great terroir and purity in this magnificent '96 red Burgundy; the huge mouthful of rich black fruit flavors and spice notes is also fabulous. Very harmonious but tight structure and rich midpalate give way to ripe, silky tannins. Best from 2004 through 2012.–B.S. • $87 • (9/30/1998) • **99**
Clos Vougeot 1995 • $81 • (11/15/1997) • **95**
Clos Vougeot 1994 • $63 • (11/15/1996) • **88**
Clos Vougeot 1993 • $80 • (11/15/1995) • **94**
Clos Vougeot 1992 • $NA • (12/15/1994) • **88**
Clos Vougeot 1991 • $63 • (1/31/1994) • **81**
Gevrey-Chambertin 1997: Clean and pure, showing wonderful intensity as the violet, red berry, smoke, toast and wet earth character follows through to a succulent, spicy finish. Best from 2002 through 2007.–P.M. • $48 • (9/30/1999) • **87**
Gevrey-Chambertin 1996: Fresh, smelling and tasting of crushed blackberries, spices and vanilla, this is terrific from start to finish. Understated power and elegant structure unfolds on the palate to a long finish. Best from 2001 through 2006.–B.S. • $42 • (9/30/1998) • **90**
Gevrey-Chambertin 1995 • $42 • (11/15/1997) • **91**
Gevrey-Chambertin 1994 • $33 • (11/15/1996) • **91**
Gevrey-Chambertin 1993 • $42 • (9/15/1996) • **90**
Gevrey-Chambertin 1992 • $NA • (12/15/1994) • **84**
Gevrey-Chambertin 1991 • $33 • (1/31/1994) • **78**
Gevrey-Chambertin Au Vellé 1997: This has black fruit, wet earth, vanilla and a rather citrusy and crisp character that makes for a chewy finish. Has the tannic power to age. Best from 2002 through 2007.–P.M. • $54 • (9/30/1999) • **85**
Gevrey-Chambertin Au Vellé 1996: Dark, with black cherries and plums covered with sweet oak, full of rich fruit and grainy in texture. Best after 2000.–B.S. • $48 • (9/30/1998) • **88**
Gevrey-Chambertin Au Vellé 1995 • $47 • (11/15/1997) • **92**
Gevrey-Chambertin Au Vellé 1994 • $37 • (11/15/1996) • **80**
Gevrey-Chambertin Au Vellé 1993 • $46 • (11/15/1995) • **88**
Gevrey-Chambertin Clos Prieur 1991 • $40 • (1/31/1994) • **85**

Key: SS—Spectator Selection. CS—Cellar Selection. HR—Highly Recommended. $NA—Price not available. (BT)—Barrel tasting. Ⓐ—Auction Price. For a key to the tasters' initials, see "How to Use These Listings."
Dates in parentheses represent the issues in which the ratings were published.

Gevrey-Chambertin Combe-du-Dessus 1997: A beautiful '97. This hedonistic and well-crafted Pinot Noir fills the palate with satisfying black cherry and plum. The underlying crispness is balanced by toasted, spicy oak notes. Focused and well built, with floral overtones. Best from 2002 through 2007.–P.M. • $54 • (9/30/1999) • **91**
Gevrey-Chambertin En Champs Vieille Vigne 1997: Deeply colored and bordering on cassis and violet in aromas and flavors, this is very pure and silky, with vanilla accents from the new oak. Still, it's elegant and tender for the appellation, showing balance, grace and refined tannins. Best from 2001 through 2005.–B.S. • $60 • (9/30/1999) • **89**
Gevrey-Chambertin En Champs Vieille Vigne 1996: Incredibly oaky, this inky-black, overly extracted wine is just a thick, burly bundle of spice, mocha and bitter chocolate now, but it has a lot of texture and concentration of fruit, so time will tell if it will come into balance. Ends on a hard, dry finish. Best after 2005.–P.M. • $53 • (9/30/1998) • **90**
Gevrey-Chambertin En Champs Vieille Vigne 1995 • $55 • (11/15/1997) • **93**
Gevrey-Chambertin En Champs Vieille Vigne 1993 • $50 • (11/15/1995) • **90**
Gevrey-Chambertin En Motrot 1997: Licorice and raspberry dominate this medium-bodied, succulent red Burgundy. A bit crisp on the finish. Best from 2001 through 2004.–P.M. • $54 • (9/30/1999) • **82**
Gevrey-Chambertin En Motrot 1996: Quite woody but also balanced, and the fruit sings through this lovely, medium-bodied, ethereal wine. Almost delicate in texture, but clearly well-built, it turns on the palate, juicing up with clean, clear, pure cassis, blackberry and black cherry flavors, some subtle oak accents.–P.M. • $48 • (9/30/1998) • **90**
Gevrey-Chambertin En Motrot 1995 • $47 • (11/15/1997) • **95**
Gevrey-Chambertin En Motrot 1994 • $37 • (11/15/1996) • **86**
Gevrey-Chambertin En Motrot 1993 • $46 • (11/15/1995) • **90**
Gevrey-Chambertin Lavaux St.-Jacques 1997: This succulent, tough and full-bodied '97 red Burgundy displays personality and character. It shows length—rare for the vintage—pumping out violet, smoke, game, blackberry and black cherry flavors on the firm, somewhat citrusy and crisp finish. Best from 2002 through 2005.–P.M. • $70 • (9/30/1999) • **89**
Gevrey-Chambertin Lavaux St.-Jacques 1996: Brooding '96, nearly black in color, full in body, rich in texture. Ripe yet pure and clean, delivering a distinguished personality on an aerodynamic framework. Nothing heavy here, just lovely fruit—blackberry and plum—along with silky tannins and a fresh finish. Let the heavy oak integrate. Best from 2005.–P.M. • $63 • (9/30/1998) • **91**
Gevrey-Chambertin Lavaux St.-Jacques 1995 • $59 • (11/15/1997) • **93**
Gevrey-Chambertin Lavaux St.-Jacques 1994 • $46 • (11/15/1996) • **84**
Gevrey-Chambertin Lavaux St.-Jacques 1993 • $58 • (11/15/1995) • **90**
Gevrey-Chambertin Les Champeaux 1997: This crisp, tight Gevrey '97 has plenty of vanilla oak, with black cherry, even kirsch, underneath. Lean and astringent on the finish. Best from 2001 through 2005.–B.S. • $70 • (9/30/1999) • **84**
Gevrey-Chambertin Les Champeaux 1996: Impressive. Very dark in color, showy in aroma and very oaky, this full-bodied wine bursts with superbly concentrated blackberry, cassis and black cherry flavors that blanket the palate with supple texture. Tannins are firm, but give it time for the ripe flavors to integrate the oak. Best After 2003.–P.M. • $62 Ⓐ • (9/30/1998) • **92**
Gevrey-Chambertin Les Champeaux 1995 • $59 • (11/15/1997) • **92**
Gevrey-Chambertin Les Champeaux 1994 • $46 • (11/15/1996) • **88**
Gevrey-Chambertin Les Champeaux 1993 • $58 • (11/15/1995) • **90**
Gevrey-Chambertin Les Champeaux 1992 • $NA • (12/15/1994) • **83**
Gevrey-Chambertin Les Champeaux 1991 • $46 • (1/31/1994) • **84**
Marsannay Les Longeroies 1997: Rich and ripe, but without the zooming fruit aromas you might expect. Round on the palate, it does show floral and spice character. Drink now through 2002.–P.M. • $35 • (9/30/1999) • **84**
Marsannay Les Longeroies 1996: Impressively dark in color, thick in body and flavorful. A seriously compacted wine, with lots of extract and hard, dry tannins. Shows some plum, black cherry and blackberry. Best from 2003.–P.M. • $30 • (9/30/1998) • **80**
Marsannay Les Longeroies 1994 • $24 • (11/15/1996) • **85**
Marsannay Les Longeroies 1993 • $30 • (11/15/1995) • **89**

MORTET, THIERRY

Bourgogne 1997: Very crisp, tart and bright in color, showing vibrant cherry and a mouthpuckering acidity on the finish. A bit unbalanced.–P.M. • $20 • (9/30/1999) • **77**
Bourgogne 1996: A bit green and herbal, this hard and tight wine has some decent ripe fruit character beneath. Drink now through 2002.–P.M. • $19 • (9/30/1998) • **79**
Bourgogne 1995 • $19 • (11/15/1997) • **80**
Bourgogne 1994 • $18 • (11/15/1996) • **79**

Bourgogne 1993 • $NA • (5/15/1996) • **84**
Chambolle-Musigny 1997: A very soft Pinot, offering modest aromas and flavors and just a hint of herbal character. Drink now.–P.M. • $40 • (9/30/1999) • **80**
Chambolle-Musigny 1996: Very seductive. Great purity of fruit, with raspberry, cherry and spice married to a rich, fleshy texture, all underlined by firm, ripe, elegant tannins. Drink through 2004–B.S. • $40 • (9/30/1998) • **89**
Chambolle-Musigny 1995 • $39 • (11/15/1997) • **79**
Chambolle-Musigny Les Beaux Bruns 1997: All three samples provided were corky.–P.M. • $40 • (1/01/2000) • **55**
Chambolle-Musigny Les Beaux Bruns 1996: Delicate, vibrant and delicious, showing red cherry aromas and flavors and a delicate structure. Enjoyable now through 2003.–B.S. • $65 • (9/30/1998) • **85**
Chambolle-Musigny Les Beaux Bruns 1995 • $62 • (11/15/1997) • **85**
Chambolle-Musigny Les Beaux Bruns 1994 • $47 • (11/15/1996) • **79**
Chambolle-Musigny Les Beaux Bruns 1993 • $58 • (5/15/1996) • **87**
Gevrey-Chambertin 1997: This has nice Pinot aromas, black cherry and raspberry character and wet earth and tea leaf notes. Trails off a bit on the finish. Best from 2002 through 2005.–P.M. • $37 • (9/30/1999) • **84**
Gevrey-Chambertin 1996: Fresh and vibrant, tasting of cherries and spice, this is light-bodied, delicately structured and pleasant. Best from 2000.–B.S. • $34 • (9/30/1998) • **84**
Gevrey-Chambertin 1995 • $39 • (11/15/1997) • **84**
Gevrey-Chambertin 1994 • $34 • (11/15/1996) • **74**
Gevrey-Chambertin 1993 • $42 • (9/15/1996) • **92**
Gevrey-Chambertin Clos Prieur 1997: An open, lush style, full of cassis, black cherry and plum notes. Moderate acidity, firm tannins and a crisp, citrusy finish. Is there enough fruit to outlast the structure? Drink now through 2003.–B.S. • $45 • (9/30/1999) • **81**
Gevrey-Chambertin Clos Prieur 1996: A solid, beefy '96 Gevrey, showing black cherry, spice and woodsy notes, moderate concentration and burly tannins. Best from 2002 through 2008.–B.S. • $50 • (9/30/1998) • **87**
Gevrey-Chambertin Clos Prieur 1995 • $48 • (11/15/1997) • **78**
Gevrey-Chambertin Clos Prieur 1994 • $40 • (11/15/1996) • **81**
Gevrey-Chambertin Clos Prieur 1993 • $50 • (5/15/1996) • **88**

MOSNIER, SYLVAIN

Chablis 1997: Decent ripeness laced with melon and honey and pure, lively citrus notes announce this harmonious, medium-bodied village Chablis. Delicious. Drink now.–P.M. • $16 • (5/31/1999) • **88**
Chablis 1996 • $17 • (5/31/1998) • **73**
Chablis Beauroy 1997: Clean as a whistle, light-bodied but with a ripe-fruit mouthfeel, showing some melon, grapefruit and mineral notes. Crisp but balanced finish. Drink now.–P.M. • $24 • (5/31/1999) • **84**
Chablis Beauroy 1996 • $24 • (5/31/1998) • **80**
Chablis Beauroy 1995 • $NA • (6/15/1997) • **86**
Chablis Côte de Léchet 1997: Lively, vibrant, zesty Chablis, showing good mineral character along with green apple, this is a tough customer for now but it delivers a superbly blunt message that's not for the faint of heart. Intense, chewy finish. An ager. Best from 2003 through 2007.–P.M. • $24 • (5/31/1999) • **90**
Chablis Côte de Lechet 1996 • $24 • (5/31/1998) • **87**
Chablis Côte de Léchet 1995 • $NA • (6/15/1997) • **87**
Chablis Vieilles Vignes 1997: Clean and fruity, with lemon, cream and pear notes, a minerally midpalate and good length. Sweet-tasting is finish accented by some grapefruit notes. Drink now.–P.M. • $19 • (5/31/1999) • **86**
Chablis Vieilles Vignes 1996 • $20 • (5/31/1998) • **79**

MOTTE, DOMAINE DE LA

Coteaux du Layon 1997: This white is quite sweet and fairly thick on the palate, but the flavors lean toward canned fruit, and it lacks the acidity for balance. Has a soft, fleshy charm but doesn't entice. Drink now.–T.M. • $12 • (6/30/1999) • **83**
Coteaux du Layon-Rochefort 1996 • $12 • (5/31/1998) • **87**

MOUCHET, CHATEAU DE

Montagne-St.-Emilion 1961 • $NA • (4/30/1996) • **87**

MOUEIX, CHRISTIAN

Merlot Bordeaux 1995 • $10 • (1/31/1998) • **83**
Merlot Bordeaux 1994 • $10 • (4/30/1997) • **80**
Merlot Bordeaux 1993 • $10 • (8/31/1995) • **79**
Merlot Bordeaux 1989 • $10 • (11/30/1992) • **83**
Merlot Bordeaux 1988 • $10 • (11/30/1992) • **76**

MOUEIX, JEAN-PIERRE

Merlot Bordeaux 1990 • $10 • (11/15/1994) • **82**
St.-Emilion 1995 • $16 • (1/31/1998) • **87**
St.-Emilion 1993 • $14 • (7/31/1996) • **79**
St.-Emilion 1989 • $14 • (6/15/1993) • **74**
St.-Emilion 1988 • $13 • (4/30/1992) • **82**

MOULIN, CHATEAU DU

Médoc 1996: A grapey, plummy, simple red. Medium-bodied, with light to medium tannins and a fruity finish. Drink now.–J.S. • $NA • (9/30/1998) • **81**

MOULIN, DOMAINE DU

Côtes du Rhône-Villages Vinsobres 1995 • $NA • (1/01/1998) • **81**
Côtes du Rhône-Villages White Vinsobres 1996 • $NA • (1/01/1998) • **85**

MOULIN DE DUHART

Pauillac 1996: Harmonious wine for the vintage. Intense aromas of blackberries and leather. Medium-bodied, with firm yet silky tannins and a smoky, berry aftertaste. A very good second label of Château Duhart-Milon Rothschild.–J.S. • $NA • (1/31/1999) • **86**
Pauillac 1995 • $18 • (1/31/1998) • **81**
Pauillac 1994 • $18 • (1/31/1997) • **78**
Pauillac 1993 • $16 • (1/31/1996) • **79**
Pauillac 1990 • $14 • (2/28/1994) • **75**
Pauillac 1989 • $20 • (12/31/1992) • **84**

MOULIN DE LA GARDETTE

Gigondas 1995 • $NA • (10/15/1997) • **88**
Gigondas 1994 • $NA • (10/15/1997) • **86**
Gigondas La Cuvée Classique 1996 • $18 • (1/01/1998) • **83**

MOULIN DE SARPE, CHATEAU

St.-Emilion 1996: Appealing sweet berry, cherry and chocolate aromas and flavors in this wine. Medium- to light-bodied, with silky tannins and a sweet fruit finish. Best after 2000.–J.S. • $NA • (1/31/1999) • **81**

MOULIN DE SERET, CHATEAU

Bordeaux 1996: Offers clean and fresh berry and floral aromas, but it's slightly watery on the palate, with light tannins and a fruity finish.–J.S. • $9 • (2/28/1999) • **79**

MOULIN DU CADET, CHATEAU

St.-Emilion 1993 • $NA • (1/31/1996) • **79**
St.-Emilion 1992 • $NA • (4/15/1995) • **70**
St.-Emilion 1990 • $NA • (3/31/1993) • **91**
St.-Emilion 1989 • $NA • (3/15/1992) • **86**

MOULIN DU PONT, LE

Mâcon-Fuissé Vendanges Manuelles 1995 • $NA • (8/31/1996) • **78**
St.-Véran Vendanges Manuelles 1995 • $NA • (8/31/1996) • **85**

MOULIN HAUT-LAROQUE, CHATEAU

Fronsac 1998: A lovely, polished Fronsac with velvety tannins and very good concentration of berry and cherry fruit. Medium- to full-bodied. Almost outstanding.–J.S. • $NA • (5/31/1999) (BT) • **85-89**
Fronsac 1997: A very good Fronsac. Delicious tobacco, berry and cherry aromas. Medium-bodied, with velvety tannins and a long, fruity finish. Drink through 2004–J.S. • $NA • (1/31/2000) • **88**
Fronsac 1990 • $14 • (3/31/1993) • **89**
Fronsac 1989: A modern, super well-crafted wine. Amazing Fronsac. Inky color. Intense aromas of spices and berries. Full-bodied, with silky tannins

and lots of ripe fruit. Well done. Give it time. (1989 Bordeaux horizontal tasting). Best after 2004.–J.S. • $NA • (5/31/1999) • **90**

Fronsac 1986 • $11 • (11/15/1989) • **78**

MOULIN PEY-LABRIE, CHATEAU

Canon-Fronsac 1998: Plenty of ripe fruit and tannins, with a medium body and a juicy, earthy character.–J.S. • $NA • (5/31/1999) (BT) • **85-89**

Canon-Fronsac 1997: Very good for Fronsac. Dark in color, with loads of tobacco, berry and cherry character on the nose. Slightly too herbal. Medium-bodied, with chewy tannins. Best after 2000.–J.S. • $NA • (1/31/2000) • **86**

Canon-Fronsac 1996: Delivers some berry character, but it's slightly hollow in the midpalate. Has medium, fine tannins and a fruity finish. Best after 2000.–J.S. • $18 • (1/31/1999) • **85**

Canon-Fronsac 1995 • $18 • (1/31/1998) • **90**

Canon-Fronsac 1990 • $16 • (3/31/1993) • **88**

Canon-Fronsac 1989: One of the great surprises of the vintage. Great color. Fabulously ripe cherry and blackberry flavors. Full-bodied, with loads of fresh fruit, firm tannins and a long, fruity aftertaste. (1989 Bordeaux horizontal tasting). Best after 2004.–J.S. • $NA • (5/31/1999) • **91**

MOULIN RICHE, CHATEAU

St.-Julien 1996: Displays cool berry and mineral character. Medium-bodied, with firm tannins that are slightly dry, yet some sweet fruit emerges on the finish. Second label of Château Léoville-Poyferré. Best after 2000.–J.S. • $24 • (1/31/1999) • **84**

St.-Julien 1995 • $25 • (1/31/1998) • **85**

St.-Julien 1987 • $18 • (11/30/1989) • **79**

St.-Julien 1986 • $20 • (11/30/1989) • **88**

St.-Julien 1985 • $20 • (6/15/1988) • **83**

St.-Julien 1982 • $22 • (11/30/1989) • **90**

MOULIN-ST.-GEORGES, CHATEAU

St.-Emilion 1999: Good core of ripe fruit, with chocolate and berry and fine, velvety tannins. Full- to medium-bodied, with a medium finish.–J.S. • $NA • (1/01/2000) (BT) • **85-89**

St.-Emilion 1998: Has plenty of fruit and finesse for the vintage. Full- to medium-bodied, with sweet fruit and fine tannins. Long finish.–J.S. • $NA • (5/31/1999) (BT) • **90-94**

St.-Emilion 1997: A polished red, with fine tannins and good fruit ranging from tobacco to cherries. Medium-bodied, light on the finish. Best after 2000.–J.S. • $23 • (1/31/2000) • **87**

St.-Emilion 1996: A bit one-dimensional, but you have to like the velvety texture. Impressively dark black color, with plenty of blackberry, tobacco and tar aromas. Medium-bodied and very soft. Nice now, but should improve with age. Best after 2001.–J.S. • $24 • (1/31/1999) • **87**

St.-Emilion 1995 • $24 • (1/31/1998) • **92**

St.-Emilion 1982: Tasted from half-bottle. Fresh, with a dark ruby color, an inky center. Dried cherry, berry and floral aromas and flavors. Medium-bodied, with well-integrated tannins and a long, flavorful finish. A pretty wine, if slightly hard. (1982 Bordeaux horizontal tasting). Drink now.–J.S. • $NA/375 ml. • (11/30/1998) • **87**

MOULIN-TACUSSEL, DOMAINE

Châteauneuf-du-Pape 1997: Straightforward black cherry and strawberry notes, drying tannins and a short finish.–P.M. • $22 • (12/15/1999) • **74**

Châteauneuf-du-Pape 1996: Fairly soft, with plum and raspberry character and some pronounced milk chocolate, mocha and toasty oak accents. Medium-bodied, with a lingering, fresh, sweet-tasting finish. Drink now.–P.M. • $19 • (9/30/1998) • **82**

Châteauneuf-du-Pape 1990 • $19 • (4/15/1993) • **88**

Key: SS—Spectator Selection. CS—Cellar Selection. HR—Highly Recommended. $NA—Price not available. (BT)—Barrel tasting. Ⓐ—Auction Price. For a key to the tasters' initials, see "How to Use These Listings." **Dates in parentheses represent the issues in which the ratings were published.**

MOULINES, DOMAINE DE

Viognier Vin de Pays de l'Hérault 1998: Fairly rich, with peachy aromas and flavors of melon, herbs and white pepper. Spice and butter notes linger on the finish. Drink now.–K.M. • $9 • (9/30/1999) • **85**

MOULINET, CHATEAU

Pomerol 1997: Rather lean, but some good fruit flavors, with berry, tobacco character, medium body and firm tannins. Light finish. Drink now.–J.S. • $NA • (1/31/2000) • **85**

Pomerol 1996: A delicate Pomerol with light but pretty fruit. Shows some vanilla and berry aromas. Medium- to light-bodied, with silky tannins and a light berry aftertaste. Drink now.–J.S. • $30 • (1/31/1999) • **85**

Pomerol 1992 • $16 • (4/15/1995) • **79**

Pomerol 1988 • $17 • (7/31/1991) • **88**

Pomerol 1982 • $10 • (5/15/1989) • **87**

MOULINIER, G.

St.-Chinian Cuvée des Sigillaires 1996 • $13 • (3/31/1998) • **87**

St.-Chinian Les Terrasses Grillées 1995 • $20 • (3/31/1998) • **89**

St.-Chinian Les Terrasses Grillées 1994 • $20 • (1/01/1998) • **88**

MOURGUE DU GRES, CHATEAU

Costières de Nîmes Terre d'Argence 1996 • $11 • (4/30/1998) • **84**

MOUSSET, LOUIS

Vin de Table Français Le P'tit Bistrot NV • $5 • (12/15/1997) • **75**

Vin de Table Français White Le P'tit Bistrot NV • $5 • (10/31/1997) • **65**

MOUSSOULENS, CHATEAU

Cabardès 1996: Herbal aromas and stewy flavors are the mark of this awkward and thin-tasting wine.–K.M. • $7 • (11/30/1998) • **74**

MOUTON, CHATEAU

Bordeaux Supérieur 1999: Delicate, fresh and fruity. Light- to medium-bodied, with fine tannins and a clean finish.–J.S. • $NA • (1/01/2000) (BT) • **80-84**

MOUTON-BARONNE-PHILIPPE, CHATEAU

Pauillac 1988 • $45 Ⓐ • (4/30/1991) • **90**

Pauillac 1986 • $37 Ⓐ • (5/31/1989) • **93**

Pauillac 1985 • $42 Ⓐ • (10/15/1994) • **91**

Pauillac 1983 • $17 • (10/15/1994) • **88**

Pauillac 1982 • $48 Ⓐ • (8/31/1992) • **88**

Pauillac 1981 • $34 Ⓐ • (10/15/1994) • **81**

Pauillac 1970 • $33 Ⓐ • (5/15/1993) • **86**

Pauillac 1961 • $116 Ⓐ • (4/30/1996) • **88**

MOUTON-CADET

Bordeaux 1997: Very light and watery, with some berry character. Clean, but not much to it really.–J.S. • $9 • (1/31/2000) • **75**

Bordeaux 1995 • $8 • (10/15/1997) • **82**

Bordeaux 1990 • $10 • (12/15/1994) • **84**

Bordeaux 1989 • $8 • (7/15/1992) • **84**

Bordeaux 1988 • $9 • (4/30/1991) • **81**

Bordeaux White 1997: A good white Bordeaux does not have to cost a fortune. This one has lots of Sauvignon character, with grass, celery and toasted oak. Medium- to full-bodied, with good acidity and plenty of fruit on the finish. Drink now.–J.S. • $9 • (9/30/1999) • **85**

Bordeaux White 1996 • $9 • (6/15/1998) • **83**

MOUTON-ROTHSCHILD, CHATEAU

Pauillac 1999: Outstanding Mouton. Some roasted, almost exotic fruit character. Full-bodied, with velvety tannins and a long, fruity finish.–J.S. • $NA • (1/01/2000) (BT) • **90-94**

Pauillac 1998: Mouton does it again in a tricky vintage for the Médoc. Black currant and mineral character. Full-bodied, with fine tannins and a silky finish. Lacks a bit of concentration in the midpalate, but has enough to rate outstanding.–J.S. • $NA • (5/31/1999) (BT) • **90-94**
Pauillac 1997: Very good Mouton, but not outstanding; lacks a bit of fruit in the center palate. Good dark ruby color, with lovely mineral, spice and currant aromas. Medium-bodied, with silky tannins and a light, fruity finish. Drink now through 2003.–J.S. • $129 • (1/31/2000) • **89**
Pauillac 1996: Gorgeous aromas of spices, berries, chocolate and raspberries introduce this pedigreed bottling. A glorious young wine that gets better and better as you taste it, it's full-bodied and incredibly silky, with super-integrated tannins and a long, long aftertaste. At its best after 2004.–J.S. • $170 Ⓐ • (1/31/1999) CS • **94**
Pauillac 1995 • $206 Ⓐ • (1/31/1998) CS • **96**
Pauillac 1994 • $92 Ⓐ • (1/31/1997) • **91**
Pauillac 1993 • $102 Ⓐ • (1/31/1996) • **90**
Pauillac 1992 • $101 Ⓐ • (4/15/1995) • **88**
Pauillac 1991 • $81 Ⓐ • (3/31/1994) HR • **89**
Pauillac 1990 • $163 Ⓐ • (3/31/1993) CS • **95**
Pauillac 1989: A monster Mouton that's incredibly closed and tight right now. Aromas of cassis, blackberries, plums and coffee with hints of licorice. Full-bodied and compacted, featuring very firm tannins and a long, long, silky texture on the finish. It's still a baby. If you have to drink it now, open it five or six hours before. (1989 Bordeaux horizontal tasting). Best after 2006.–J.S. • $196 Ⓐ • (5/31/1999) • **98**
Pauillac 1988: Though I don't consider this a perfect wine, it has always been classic in quality. It's rich and fruity, with loads of currant, tobacco, smoke and new wood on the nose and palate. Full-bodied, with silky tannins and an elegant finish. (1988 Bordeaux horizontal tasting). Best after 2000.–J.S. • $140 Ⓐ • (11/30/1998) • **94**
Pauillac 1987 • $89 Ⓐ • (5/15/1990) • **89**
Pauillac 1986 • $307 Ⓐ • (5/31/1989) CS • **98**
Pauillac 1985 • $180 Ⓐ • (10/15/1994) • **96**
Pauillac 1984 • $72 Ⓐ • (3/31/1987) • **92**
Pauillac 1983 • $118 • Ⓐ (10/15/1994) • **94**
Pauillac 1982: This has always been one of the wines of the vintage. Harmonious and beautifully structured. Brilliant ruby color, with a hint of garnet. A bounty of cherry, tobacco and cedar aromas and flavors. Full-bodied and tannic, with velvety texture and medium finish. (1982 Bordeaux horizontal tasting). Best after 2000.–J.S. • $432 Ⓐ • (11/30/1998) • **98**
Pauillac 1981 • $86 Ⓐ • (10/15/1994) • **91**
Pauillac 1979 • $87 Ⓐ • (10/15/1989) • **96**
Pauillac 1978 • $100 Ⓐ • (5/15/1991) • **92**
Pauillac 1976 • $70 Ⓐ • (6/16/1986) • **85**
Pauillac 1975 • $127 Ⓐ • (5/15/1991) • **89**
Pauillac 1973 • $89 Ⓐ • (6/16/1986) • **75**
Pauillac 1971 • $86 Ⓐ • (6/16/1986) • **78**
Pauillac 1970 • $139 Ⓐ • (5/15/1991) • **84**
Pauillac 1969 • $NA • (6/16/1986) • **78**
Pauillac 1967 • $85 Ⓐ • (6/16/1986) • **87**
Pauillac 1966 • $163 Ⓐ • (5/15/1991) • **88**
Pauillac 1964 • $92 Ⓐ • (6/16/1986) • **84**
Pauillac 1963 • $254 Ⓐ • (6/16/1986) • **77**
Pauillac 1962 • $239 Ⓐ • (11/30/1987) • **98**
Pauillac 1961 • $801 Ⓐ • (5/15/1991) • **90**
Pauillac 1961 • $NA/1.5 liter • (4/30/1996) • **92**
Pauillac 1960 • $236 Ⓐ • (6/16/1986) • **84**
Pauillac 1959 • $1,033 Ⓐ • (10/15/1990) • **99**
Pauillac 1957 • $171 Ⓐ • (6/16/1986) • **86**
Pauillac 1956 • $NA • (6/16/1986) • **85**
Pauillac 1955 • $456 Ⓐ • (5/15/1991) • **95**
Pauillac 1954 • $275 Ⓐ • (6/16/1986) • **81**
Pauillac 1953 • $750 Ⓐ • (5/15/1991) • **94**
Pauillac 1952 • $315 Ⓐ • (6/16/1986) • **90**
Pauillac 1951 • $203 Ⓐ • (6/16/1986) • **84**
Pauillac 1950 • $348 Ⓐ • (6/16/1986) • **83**
Pauillac 1949 • $993 Ⓐ • (5/15/1991) • **87**
Pauillac 1948 • $853 Ⓐ • (6/16/1986) • **87**
Pauillac 1947 • $1,236 Ⓐ • (5/31/1997) • **89**
Pauillac 1946 • $1,823 Ⓐ • (6/16/1986) • **77**
Pauillac 1945 • $3,270 Ⓐ • (11/30/1995) • **94**
Pauillac 1944 • $735 Ⓐ • (6/16/1986) • **86**
Pauillac 1943 • $240 Ⓐ • (6/16/1986) • **78**
Pauillac 1940 • $NA • (6/16/1986) • **77**
Pauillac 1938 • $NA• (6/16/1986) • **73**
Pauillac 1937 • $423 Ⓐ • (5/15/1991) • **91**
Pauillac 1934 • $278 Ⓐ • (5/15/1991) • **90**
Pauillac 1933 • $NA/375 ml. • (6/16/1986) • **78**
Pauillac 1929 • $794 Ⓐ • (5/15/1991) • **75**
Pauillac 1928 • $833 Ⓐ • (5/15/1991) • **89**
Pauillac 1921 • $633 Ⓐ • (5/15/1991) • **80**
Pauillac 1920 • $NA • (6/16/1986) • **75**
Pauillac 1919 • $NA • (5/15/1991) • **79**
Pauillac 1918 • $609 Ⓐ • (5/15/1991) • **83**
Pauillac 1910 • $NA • (5/15/1991) • **76**
Pauillac 1905 • $NA • (5/15/1991) • **88**
Pauillac 1900 • $3,729 Ⓐ • (5/15/1991) • **90**
Pauillac 1899 • $2,044 Ⓐ • (6/16/1986) • **82**
Pauillac 1881 • $NA • (6/16/1986) • **74**
Pauillac 1878 • $2,185 Ⓐ • (5/15/1991) • **99**
Pauillac 1874 • $1,724 Ⓐ • (5/15/1991) • **95**
Pauillac 1870 • $NA • (5/15/1991) • **87**

MUGNERET, GEORGES

Chambolle-Musigny Les Feusselottes 1992 • $NA • (12/15/1994) • **83**
Chambolle-Musigny Les Feusselottes 1989 • $47 • (4/30/1992) • **87**
Chambolle-Musigny Les Feusselottes 1988 • $54 • (11/15/1990) • **86**
Chambolle-Musigny Les Feusselottes 1987 • $41 • (10/15/1989) • **92**
Chambolle-Musigny Les Feusselottes 1986 • $45 • (11/15/1988) • **90**
Clos Vougeot 1994 • $NA • (11/15/1996) • **84**
Clos Vougeot 1991 • $90 • (1/31/1994) • **83**
Clos Vougeot 1990 • $89 • (12/15/1992) • **91**
Clos Vougeot 1988 • $90 • (11/15/1990) • **84**
Clos Vougeot 1987 • $68 • (10/15/1989) • **91**
Clos Vougeot 1986 • $73 • (11/30/1988) • **90**
Nuits-St.-Georges Aux Chaignots 1994 • $NA • (11/15/1996) • **70**
Nuits-St.-Georges Aux Chaignots 1993 • $NA • (5/15/1996) • **88**
Nuits-St.-Georges Aux Chaignots 1992 • $NA • (12/15/1994) • **79**
Nuits-St.-Georges Aux Chaignots 1991 • $50 • (1/31/1994) • **80**
Nuits-St.-Georges Aux Chaignots 1990 • $45 • (12/15/1992) • **88**
Nuits-St.-Georges Aux Chaignots 1989 • $43 • (4/30/1992) • **86**
Nuits-St.-Georges Aux Chaignots 1988 • $47 • (11/15/1990) • **80**
Nuits-St.-Georges Aux Chaignots 1987 • $41 • (10/15/1989) • **87**
Nuits-St.-Georges Aux Chaignots 1986 • $40 • (11/15/1988) • **89**
Nuits-St.-Georges Aux Chaignots 1984 • $26 • (3/15/1987) • **89**
Ruchottes-Chambertin 1994 • $65 • (12/31/1996) HR • **92**
Ruchottes-Chambertin 1992 • $NA • (12/15/1994) • **74**
Ruchottes-Chambertin 1990 • $78 • (12/15/1992) • **93**
Ruchottes-Chambertin 1989 • $66 • (4/30/1992) • **91**
Ruchottes-Chambertin 1988 • $69 • (11/15/1990) • **92**
Ruchottes-Chambertin 1987 • $44 • (10/15/1989) • **93**
Ruchottes-Chambertin 1986 • $45 • (11/15/1988) • **91**
Ruchottes-Chambertin 1985 • $150 • (2/15/1988) • **92**
Ruchottes-Chambertin 1984 • $34 • (3/15/1987) • **83**
Ruchottes-Chambertin 1982 • $26 • (9/01/1985) SS • **92**

MUGNERET-GIBOURG

Bourgogne 1994 • $NA • (11/15/1996) • **79**
Bourgogne 1992 • $NA • (12/15/1994) • **80**
Bourgogne 1990 • $18 • (12/15/1992) • **86**
Bourgogne 1989 • $17 • (6/15/1992) • **82**
Echézeaux 1994 • $NA • (11/15/1996) • **79**
Echézeaux 1992 • $NA • (12/15/1994) • **82**
Echézeaux 1991 • $68 • (1/31/1994) • **85**
Echézeaux 1990 • $66 • (12/15/1992) • **93**
Echézeaux 1989 • $62 • (4/30/1992) • **88**
Echézeaux 1988 • $70 • (11/15/1990) • **89**
Echézeaux 1987 • $50 • (10/15/1989) • **93**
Echézeaux 1986 • $55 • (11/30/1988) • **83**
Echézeaux 1985 • $57 • (2/29/1988) • **93**
Echézeaux 1984 • $32 • (3/15/1987) • **85**
Vosne-Romanée 1994 • $NA • (11/15/1996) • **78**
Vosne-Romanée 1993 • $NA • (5/15/1996) • **83**
Vosne-Romanée 1992 • $NA • (12/15/1994) • **79**
Vosne-Romanée 1991 • $40 • (1/31/1994) • **83**
Vosne-Romanée 1989 • $34 • (4/30/1992) • **81**
Vosne-Romanée 1988 • $34 • (12/31/1990) • **64**
Vosne-Romanée 1987 • $30 • (10/15/1989) • **90**
Vosne-Romanée 1986 • $33 • (12/31/1988) • **81**

MUGNERET-GIBOURG

Vosne-Romanée 1985 • $33 • (2/29/1988) • **85**

MUGNIER, JACQUES-FREDERIC

Bonnes Mares 1996: Traditional-style red Burgundy, authentic in a rustic way, pushing the terroir envelope, with wet earth, some stem, mineral, spice and red berry notes, and a tannic structure that could use some cellaring. Drink now through 2005.–P.M. • $81 Ⓐ • (7/31/1999) • **88**

Bonnes Mares 1995: Pleasant, with a core of sweet-tasting licorice, vanilla and cinnamon, showing chewy texture but decent ripeness too. Still, disappointing for the appellation. Drink now through 2003.–P.M. • $85 • (8/31/1998) • **85**

Bonnes Mares 1993 • $90 • (5/15/1996) • **92**

Chambolle-Musigny 1996: Very delicate, showing some pretty floral, rose petal, cherry, raspberry notes. Light- to medium-bodied, kicking in with fresh acidity on the lingering finish. Drink now through 2002.–P.M. • $35 • (7/31/1999) • **86**

Chambolle-Musigny 1993 • $53 Ⓐ • (5/15/1996) • **88**

Chambolle-Musigny 1989 • $41 • (1/31/1992) • **91**

Chambolle-Musigny 1988 • $48 • (5/15/1991) • **86**

Chambolle-Musigny Les Amoureuses 1996: Wonderful, both full and delicate, with a lot of lovely flavors wrapping around the taste buds. Concentrate on those wild berry, cherry, blackberry flavors, and enjoy their long ride. Drink now through 2002.–P.M. • $90 • (7/31/1999) • **90**

Chambolle-Musigny Les Amoureuses 1993 • $57 Ⓐ • (5/15/1996) • **85**

Chambolle-Musigny Les Amoureuses 1989 • $62 • (1/31/1992) • **90**

Chambolle-Musigny Les Amoureuses 1988 • $80 • (5/15/1991) • **86**

Chambolle-Musigny Les Fuées 1996: Full and muscular, quite powerful with all that black fruit character, showing round tannins and a chewy but attractive finish of mineral and wet earth. Drink through 2005–P.M. • $60 • (7/31/1999) • **89**

Chambolle-Musigny Les Fuées 1993 • $34 Ⓐ • (5/15/1996) • **89**

Chambolle-Musigny Les Fuées 1988 • $60 • (5/15/1991) • **89**

Musigny 1995: Interesting and quite aromatic, with cherry, cinnamon and licorice jumping out of the glass, then it moves into a superb, compact midpalate with good concentration. Complex finish of wet soil and tannins. Very good, but lacks the depth expected from this vineyard. Drink through 2005–P.M. • $78 Ⓐ • (8/31/1998) • **87**

Musigny 1989 • $125 • (1/31/1992) • **88**

MUMM, G.H.

Brut Blanc de Blancs Champagne Mumm de Cramant NV: A solid, straightforward Champagne, with lively citrus flavors, a crisp texture and a clean finish. Drink now. • $42 • (12/31/1998) • **87**

Brut Champagne Cordon Rouge NV: Generous fruit flavors and a rich texture give this bright, rather soft Champagne a forward personality. Smooth in texture, ripe in flavor and difficult to resist. Drink now. • $25 • (12/31/1998) • **88**

Brut Champagne Cordon Rouge Cuvée Limitée 1990: Rich and round textured with plenty of flavor and a melt-in-your-mouth quality. Has buttery aromas, fig and pear flavors and a rather soft balance. Drink now through 2002. • $56 • (10/15/1999) • **90**

Brut Rosé Champagne Cordon Rosé NV • $35 • (12/15/1995) • **88**

Extra Dry Champagne NV • $43 • (12/31/1991) • **84**

Extra Dry Champagne Carte Classique NV: Sweet, fresh and lively in character, this offers lots of grapefruit and crisp apple flavors, amply softened by a lush texture and a sugary finish. Drink now. • $23 • (12/31/1998) • **85**

Extra Dry Champagne Cordon Vert NV • $43 • (1/31/1992) • **86**

MURE

Gewürztraminer Alsace Côte de Rouffach 1997: The candied fruit flavors are obvious and show a hint of banana, with good balance and structure, but dissipate quickly on the finish. Drink now.–B.S. • $14 • (10/31/1999) • **82**

Gewürztraminer Alsace Grand Cru Vorbourg Clos St.-Landelin 1996: Elegance and restraint hold court, with rose, pear and honey flavors. Balanced more to the dry side, but shows only moderate depth and falls off on the finish. Drink now.–B.S. • $26 • (9/15/1998) • **86**

Key: SS—Spectator Selection. CS—Cellar Selection. HR—Highly Recommended. $NA—Price not available. (BT)—Barrel tasting. Ⓐ—Auction Price. For a key to the tasters' initials, see "How to Use These Listings." **Dates in parentheses represent the issues in which the ratings were published.**

Gewürztraminer Alsace Grand Cru Vorbourg Clos St.-Landelin Sélection de Grains Nobles 1989 • $56 • (9/15/1991) • **93**

Gewürztraminer Alsace Grand Cru Vorbourg Clos St.-Landelin Vendanges Tardives 1997: This is concentrated (perhaps from botrytis), offering honey, spice, citrus and mineral flavors. Intense, focused and moderately sweet, with a fat texture and a good finish. Drink now through 2002.–B.S. • $39 • (10/31/1999) • **88**

Gewürztraminer Alsace Schultzengass 1997: Elegant, almost delicate for Gewürztraminer, showing its floral side, with fine persistence of flavor, a vibrant structure and good length. Drink now through 2001.–B.S. • $19 • (10/31/1999) • **86**

Muscat Alsace Côte de Rouffach 1996: Good ripeness, verging on litchi, grapefruit and a hint of cardamom, all expressed in an elegant framework with bright acidity.–B.S. • $15 • (9/15/1998) • **85**

Muscat Alsace Grand Cru Vorbourg Clos St.-Landelin Sélection de Grains Nobles 1991 • $60 • (11/15/1994) • **88**

Muscat Alsace Grand Cru Vorbourg Clos St.-Landelin Vendanges Tardives 1997: Aromatic, grapey and noticeably sweet, this offers honey, spice and a roundness that carries through to the soft, light finish. Drink now.–B.S. • $41 • (10/15/1999) • **84**

Muscat Alsace Grand Cru Vorbourg Clos St.-Landelin Vendanges Tardives 1996: Bountiful tropical fruit nuances of banana, orange and spice settle down on the palate to more typical flavors of flowers, pine and raisins. Moderately sweet, with good acidity and length, this would be delicious over fresh fruit or with a fruit tart. Drink now through 2001.–B.S. • $50/500 ml. • (9/15/1998) • **87**

Pinot Noir Alsace Clos St.-Landelin 1997: On the chunky side, offering ripe, almost stewed aromas and flavors, with hints of licorice and tobacco. Lacks a bit of brightness and the silky texture of Pinot, but ambitious. Drink now through 2002.–B.S. • $22 • (10/15/1999) • **83**

Pinot Noir Alsace Clos St.-Landelin 1994 • $21 • (11/15/1996) • **81**

Pinot Noir Alsace Clos St. Landelin Viellie en Pièces de Chêne 1993 • $25 • (9/15/1995) • **84**

Pinot Noir Alsace Côte de Rouffach 1997: Flavorful, showing black cherry, spice and autumn leaves, this is lean and concentrated, yet lacks structure and elegance. Drink now through 2001.–B.S. • $13 • (10/15/1999) • **84**

Pinot Noir Alsace V 1997: Aromas of berry and spice lead into an elegant vibrancy on the palate. The flavors turn to pepper and leather, with some fine tannins on the finish. From the grand cru Vorbourg vineyard. Drink now through 2002.–B.S. • $15 • (10/15/1999) • **86**

Riesling Alsace Grand Cru Vorbourg Clos St.-Landelin 1997: Lean, focused and intense, offering incisive aromas and flavors of peach, apricot, mineral and citrus that leave the palate tingling. Long apricot aftertaste. Beautiful expression of Riesling. Drink now through 2007.–B.S. • $20 • (10/15/1999) • **91**

Riesling Alsace Grand Cru Vorbourg Clos St.-Landelin 1996: Melts in your mouth despite the laserlike acidity. Passion fruit, mineral and floral aromas and flavors give way to mouthwatering acidity and a finish on which the flavors have a featherlike touch. Drink through 2006–B.S. • $22 • (9/15/1998) • **92**

Riesling Alsace Grand Cru Vorbourg Clos St.-Landelin Sélection de Grains Nobles 1991 • $75 • (11/15/1994) • **85**

Riesling Alsace Grand Cru Vorbourg Clos St.-Landelin Sélection de Grains Nobles 1989 • $69 • (9/15/1991) • **87**

Riesling Alsace Grand Cru Vorbourg Clos St.-Landelin Vendanges Tardives 1997: Definitely sweet, sugar covers everything right now. Moderately concentrated and a bit awkward, showing high alcohol; this may balance out in time. Drink through 2005–B.S. • $42 • (10/15/1999) • **86**

Sylvaner Alsace Clos St.-Landelin Cuvée Oscar 1997: Unusual for Sylvaner, yet appealing. Very ripe, full of peach and honey flavors bolstered by a touch of sweetness and plush texture. Drink now.–B.S. • $15 • (10/15/1999) • **86**

Sylvaner Alsace Clos St.-Landelin Cuvée Oscar 1996: Very ripe, tropical fruit aromas and flavors grace this exuberant white that has the vibrant acidity of the 1996 vintage. Good length. Drink now.–B.S. • $15 • (9/15/1998) • **85**

Tokay Pinot Gris Alsace Grand Cru Vorbourg Clos St.-Landelin 1997: There's plenty of weight in this full-bodied, apricot-flavored white. Rich and creamy, yet offset by moderate acidity, it's well integrated, ending on a smoky note. Drink now through 2002.–B.S. • $28 • (10/31/1999) • **89**

Tokay Pinot Gris Alsace Grand Cru Vorbourg Clos St.-Landelin Sélection de Grains Nobles 1989 • $60 • (9/15/1991) • **85**

Tokay Pinot Gris Alsace Grand Cru Vorbourg Clos St.-Landelin Vendanges Tardives 1997: Ripe, honeyed and sweet, showing decent concentration allied to a rich texture, yet in the end it's rather one-dimensional, dissipating quickly. A touch hot on the aftertaste. Drink now.–B.S. • $37 • (10/31/1999) • **84**

Tokay Pinot Gris Alsace Lutzeltal 1997: Fat and plush, this Pinot Gris offers plenty of spice, honey and tropical fruit, showing decent acidity down the stretch, where it firms up. A touch coarse on the finish. Drink now through 2001.–B.S. • $19 • (10/31/1999) • **87**

MURETTES, DOMAINE DES

Minervois Clos de l'Olivier 1997: A beautifully defined and well-proportioned red, with plenty of rich, ripe plum and raspberry flavors. Pure and flavorful, with harmonious brick and leather notes. Drink now through 2001.–K.M. • $12 • (11/15/1999) • **88**

Minervois Clos de l'Olivier 1996: A broad-shouldered red from the south of France, this shows a balanced mix of red plum, cherry and leather/game flavors. Becomes focused and intense on the finish, where coffeelike notes linger. Drink now through 2004.–K.M. • $11 • (2/28/1999) • **87**

Minervois Clos de l'Olivier 1995 • $11 • (3/31/1998) • **87**

Minervois La Livinière Cuvée des Cimes 1997: A brooding red, with bittersweet chocolate and overripe plum flavors. Well concentrated, but it lacks finesse on the chewy finish. Drink now.–K.M. • $22 • (11/15/1999) • **83**

MURISALTIEN, LE MANOIR

Bourgogne White 1995 • $NA • (8/31/1997) • **73**

Mâcon-Cruzilles 1996 • $10 • (5/31/1998) • **85**

Mâcon-Fuissé 1996 • $12 • (5/31/1998) • **89**

Meursault 1997: Butter and butterscotch make strange bedfellows in this oddly perfumed '97. A bit of caramel, marzipan and oxidized quality. Tart finish.–P.M. • $NA • (1/01/1999) • **75**

Montagny Les Resses 1997: Strange—very ripe yet with a kick of tart acidity. Smells almost like pear spirit, turns a bit tough on the finish.–P.M. • $NA • (1/01/1999) • **78**

Pouilly-Fuissé 1996 • $18 • (5/31/1998) • **88**

Puligny-Montrachet Le Cailleret 1996: Very oaky style, showing a good vanilla bean, lime and mineral component, but the toasted wood dominates for now. Lacks a bit of finesse on the smoky, toasted finish. Best after 2003.–P.M. • $NA • (8/31/1998) • **82**

Puligny-Montrachet Les Pucelles 1996: Thick, rich and ripe, with loads of butter, butterscotch, toasted hazelnut and creamlike flavors. The texture is smooth, but with an underpinning of clean, crisp, lemony acidity. Oak is kept in check; still rather showy. Best after 2003.–P.M. • $NA • (8/31/1998) • **89**

Puligny-Montrachet Les Pucelles 1995 • $44 • (5/31/1997) • **84**

MUSSY

Beaune Les Epenottes 1997: Green and vegetal, light-bodied and tart. Tough on the finish.–P.M. • $40 • (1/01/2000) • **72**

Beaune Les Epenottes 1996: A bit herbal, diluted and crisp. Somewhat supple, but this medium-bodied red turns a bit dry on the finish.–P.M. • $28 • (9/30/1998) • **75**

Beaune Les Epenottes 1995 • $38 • (11/15/1997) • **73**

Beaune Les Epenottes 1994 • $38 • (11/15/1996) • **77**

Beaune Les Epenottes 1993 • $26 • (11/15/1995) • **78**

Beaune Les Epenottes 1992 • $32 • (12/15/1994) • **74**

Beaune Les Epenottes 1991 • $34 • (1/31/1994) • **88**

Beaune Les Epenottes 1986 • $28 • (5/31/1989) • **86**

Beaune Les Montrevenots 1995 • $38 • (11/15/1997) • **75**

Beaune Les Montrevenots 1994 • $38 • (11/15/1996) • **72**

Beaune Les Montrevenots 1993 • $26 • (11/15/1995) • **84**

Beaune Les Montrevenots 1992 • $32 • (12/15/1994) • **79**

Beaune Les Montrevenots 1991 • $34 • (1/31/1994) • **86**

Beaune Les Montrevenots 1990 • $45 • (12/15/1992) • **87**

Beaune Les Montrevenots 1986 • $28 • (5/31/1989) • **86**

Bourgogne 1996: A bit light in body and flavor, showing some cherry, green olive and smoky notes. Turns tough and hot on the finish.–P.M. • $13 • (9/30/1998) • **76**

Bourgogne 1994 • $18 • (11/15/1996) • **78**

Pommard 1997: A bit too much barnyard in this light, simple red. The finish is short.–B.S. • $50 • (9/30/1999) • **75**

Pommard 1996: Rich cherry and plum character combine with a mineral note in this beefy Pommard of medium structure and length. Drink through 2004–B.S. • $36 • (9/30/1998) • **84**

Pommard 1994 • $42 • (11/15/1996) • **75**

Pommard 1993 • $34 • (11/15/1995) • **82**

Pommard 1992 • $38 • (12/15/1994) • **84**

Pommard 1991 • $41 • (1/31/1994) • **81**

Pommard 1985 • $35 • (10/15/1988) • **86**

Pommard Epenots 1997: A little too much horse and barnyard character dominates the weak fruit.–B.S. • $NA • (9/30/1999) • **72**

Pommard Epenots 1996: Supple, with licorice, mocha and spice along with the plum and red berry character. Pretty wine, full-bodied and opulent, but it turns slightly hot on the finish. Drink now.–P.M. • $46 • (9/30/1998) • **83**

Pommard Les Epenots 1995 • $61 • (11/15/1997) • **74**

Pommard Les Epenots 1994 • $58 • (11/15/1996) • **80**

Pommard Les Epenots 1993 • $45 • (11/15/1995) • **79**

Pommard Les Epenots 1992 • $49 • (12/15/1994) • **82**

Pommard Les Epenots 1991 • $54 • (1/31/1994) • **80**

Pommard Les Epenots 1990 • $50 • (12/15/1992) • **86**

Pommard Pézerolles 1995 • $61 • (11/15/1997) • **74**

Pommard Premier Cru 1993 • $38 • (11/15/1995) • **79**

Pommard Premier Cru 1991 • $NA • (1/31/1994) • **83**

Pommard Premier Cru 1986 • $35 • (4/30/1989) • **86**

Pommard Saussilles 1997: This soft, anemic red has cooked plums and a lack of focus.–B.S. • $54 • (9/30/1999) • **74**

Pommard Saussilles 1996: Thick but slightly rustic, showing good concentration of plum, black cherry and wild raspberry blended with a bit of wet earth. Full-bodied, rich and ripe, it's well-anchored in the soil, with an iron, mineral and bloodlike taste that gives personality. Try with game. Best after 2005.–P.M. • $39 • (9/30/1998) • **88**

Pommard Saussilles 1995 • $52 • (11/15/1997) • **79**

Pommard Saussilles 1994 • $50 • (11/15/1996) • **80**

Volnay 1997: Light in color and body, it smells a bit stemmy, with straightforward strawberry and raspberry character. Tasty but slightly astringent.–P.M. • $41 • (9/30/1999) • **78**

Volnay 1996: A forthright style, with good concentration and an herbaceous edge to the red berry character, finishing tough and astringent. Drink through 2004–B.S. • $30 • (9/30/1998) • **79**

Volnay 1993 • $NA • (11/15/1995) • **79**

Volnay 1992 • $NA • (12/15/1994) • **77**

Volnay 1991 • $34 • (1/31/1994) • **86**

MUZARD & FILS, LUCIEN

Chassagne-Montrachet Red Vieilles Vignes 1996: This lovely, round, polished '96 is also quite firm and solid, showing sweet ripe cherry and wild berry character. Medium-bodied, it's delicious to drink now but has the stuffing to age a bit. Drink through 2002.–P.M. • $25 • (9/30/1998) • **86**

Côte de Beaune-Villages 1996: Smoky aromas precede cherry and herbal flavors and a structure with plenty of tannins, but it's somewhat lacking in richness and density. Drink through 2005–B.S. • $18 • (9/30/1998) • **83**

Pommard Les Cras 1996: Big, burly and structured with black cherry, vanilla and spice notes, length and intensity. Vibrant acidity and tannins provide the backbone for moderate aging. Delicious. Tasted twice, with consistent notes. Drink through 2004–P.M. • $38 • (9/30/1998) • **89**

Pommard Les Cras Vieilles Vignes 1995 • $20 • (11/15/1997) • **78**

Santenay Champs Claude Vieilles Vignes 1997: Wonderful. Medium-bodied, pure, clean and racy, with ripe fruit and supple tannins. Seductive on the palate, caressing the taste buds with a sexy, sweet appeal that is very rare for a '97 red Burgundy. Bravo! Drink now through 2005.–P.M. • $24 • (9/30/1999) • **91**

Santenay Champs Claude Vieilles Vignes 1996: A bit angular and dull, the oak dominates the fruit. Slightly drying finish. Drink now.–P.M. • $17 • (9/30/1998) • **75**

Santenay Clos Faubard 1997: This appealingly flavorful and balanced red shows gutsy wet earth and spicy mocha flavors. Ripe tannins but not much class. Drink now through 2003.–P.M. • $29 • (9/30/1999) • **87**

Santenay Clos Faubard 1996: A bit odd, with some flinty, smoky, earthy character, but also shows lovely, sappy red berry flavors. Medium-bodied, very ripe in terms of both fruit and tannin, even though the chewy finish-suggests it would improve with cellaring. Drink now through 2004.–P.M. • $22 • (9/30/1998) • **84**

Santenay Clos Tavannes 1997: Medium-bodied, it tastes a bit earthy, with wet earth and chewy tannins, but it shows a gutsy firmness on the finish that's refreshing in a '97. Drink now through 2002.–P.M. • $32 • (9/30/1999) • **84**

Santenay Clos Tavannes 1996: Aromas and flavors lean toward kirsch and beet root in this broad-shouldered, forward '96. Rustic and a bit raw now, it finishes slightly hot. Drink through 2002–B.S. • $22 • (9/30/1998) • **83**

Santenay Clos Tavannes 1995 • $20 • (11/15/1997) • **76**

Santenay Gravières 1997: Ripe and rich but also very clean, pure, focused and succulent, with sweet and smooth tannins. Sucks you in to discover mineral, wet earth and the area's terroir. Amazingly sexy, racy and seductive. Drink now through 2006.–P.M. • $29 • (9/30/1999) • **92**

MUZARD & FILS, LUCIEN

Santenay Gravières 1996: Starts off with cherry and a smoky, spicy note but quickly turns tannic and finishes dry and astringent. Drink through 2003.–B.S. • $22 • (9/30/1998) • **82**
Santenay Gravières 1995 • $20 • (11/15/1997) • **76**
Santenay Maladière 1997: A bit earthy and barnyardy, but it's thick and ripe. A bit rustic on the finish, but at least here's a '97 with a firm backbone. Drink now through 2005.–P.M. • $29 • (9/30/1999) • **83**
Santenay Maladière 1996: Mineral and smoke-tinged cherry aromas and flavors highlight this medium-bodied wine. The fruit, acidity and tannin are in balance and there's grip and length on the finish. Drink now through 2002.–B.S. • $22 • (9/30/1998) • **86**
Santenay Maladière 1995 • $20 • (11/15/1997) • **77**

MYRAT, CHATEAU DE

Barsac 1998: Lots of botrytis in this wine. Full-bodied and chewy, very sweet, with a long, spicy finish.–J.S. • $NA • (1/01/1999) (BT) • **90-94**
Barsac 1997: Wonderful purity of fruit, with lemon, pineapple and honey character. Full-bodied, with a sleek, racy texture and a long, sweet fruit aftertaste. Best after 2000.–J.S. • $NA • (1/31/2000) • **89**
Barsac 1991 • $NA • (4/15/1995) • **80**

NADDEF, PHILIPPE

Gevrey-Chambertin 1988 • $25 • (7/15/1991) • **80**
Gevrey-Chambertin 1987 • $19 • (3/31/1990) • **86**
Gevrey-Chambertin 1985 • $25 • (4/15/1988) • **94**
Gevrey-Chambertin Champeaux 1987 • $28 • (3/31/1990) • **90**
Gevrey-Chambertin Champeaux 1985 • $29 • (3/31/1988) • **80**
Gevrey-Chambertin Les Cazetiers 1987 • $35 • (3/31/1990) • **88**
Mazis-Chambertin 1988 • $60 • (7/15/1991) • **69**
Mazis-Chambertin 1987 • $50 • (3/31/1990) • **89**
Mazis-Chambertin Vieilles Vignes 1991 • $48 • (8/31/1994) • **89**

NAGES, CHATEAU DE

Costières de Nîmes Cuvée Joseph Torrès 1995 • $11 • (10/15/1997) • **84**
Costières de Nîmes Réserve du Château 1997: Fairly big and burly, with earthy, leathery, spicy and peppery character. Intense and rustic but very flavorful, this full-bodied red should benefit from cellaring. Drink through 2003–P.M. • $10 • (9/30/1998) • **82**
Costières de Nîmes Réserve du Château 1996 • $9 • (10/15/1997) • **82**
Costières de Nîmes Réserve du Château 1995 • $9 • (1/01/1998) • **79**
Costières de Nîmes White Réserve du Château 1998: Striving for some complexity, with a bit of spice, butter and caramel; not very subtle, but OK.–P.M. • $10 • (8/31/1999) • **79**
Costières de Nîmes White Réserve du Château 1996 • $9 • (10/15/1997) • **79**
Merlot Vin de Pays d'Oc 1995 • $8 • (5/31/1998) • **83**
Vin de Pays du Gard Les Cigales 1995: Rather rustic and mature in character, offering herb, plum and smoke flavors on a tannic texture. Drink now. • $6 • (8/31/1998) • **78**

NAIGEON-CHAUVEAU

Mâcon-Villages 1995 • $NA • (8/31/1996) • **79**
St.-Véran Les Monts 1995 • $NA • (8/31/1996) • **84**

NAIRAC, CHATEAU

Barsac 1992 • $NA • (4/15/1995) • **75**
Barsac 1991 • $NA • (4/15/1995) • **84**
Barsac 1990 • $31 • (4/15/1995) • **90**
Barsac 1989 • $38 • (4/15/1995) • **87**
Barsac 1988 • $34 Ⓐ • (4/15/1995) • **91**
Barsac 1987 • $31 • (6/15/1990) • **81**
Barsac 1986 • $31 • (12/31/1989) • **77**
Barsac 1983 • $33 • (4/15/1995) • **87**

Key: SS—Spectator Selection. CS—Cellar Selection. HR—Highly Recommended. $NA—Price not available. (BT)—Barrel tasting. Ⓐ—Auction Price.
For a key to the tasters' initials, see "How to Use These Listings."
Dates in parentheses represent the issues in which the ratings were published.

NATTER, HENRY

Sancerre Domaine de Montigny 1996 • $16 • (3/31/1998) • **87**
Sancerre Red Domaine de Montigny 1995 • $16 • (5/31/1998) • **83**
Sancerre Red Domaine de Montigny 1990 • $15 • (10/31/1994) • **84**

NAUDIN-FERRAND, HENRI

Côte de Nuits-Villages Le Clos de Magny 1997: Light and unpretentious, tasting of raspberry and strawberry, but showing a round mouthfeel with an almost delicate texture. Pretty licorice on the finish. Drink now through 2003.–P.M. • $19 • (1/01/2000) • **82**
Côte de Nuits-Villages Le Clos de Magny 1996: Delicate and pretty, showing attractive wild berry flavors, this sings on the palate with its sweet-tasting character, supple tannins and fresh, lemony acidity. Long, refined finish.–P.M. • $17 • (9/30/1998) • **86**
Côte de Nuits-Villages Le Clos de Magny 1995 • $16 • (11/15/1997) • **76**
Côte de Nuits-Villages Le Clos de Magny 1994 • $15 • (11/15/1996) • **84**
Côte de Nuits-Villages Vieilles Vignes 1997: Lovely cassis and black cherry elements mark this ripe, generous '97 Nuits. Forward and appealing, with balance and a lingering finish. Drink now through 2003.–B.S. • $23 • (9/30/1999) • **86**
Côte de Nuits-Villages Vieilles Vignes 1996: Big-boned, yet hollow and alcoholic, finishing with some stiff tannins. Best from 2000.–B.S. • $20 • (9/30/1998) • **77**
Côte de Nuits-Villages Vieilles Vignes 1995 • $18 • (11/15/1997) • **82**
Hautes-Côtes de Beaune 1996: Tart and crisp, with an herbal underpinning, this light-bodied wine delivers modest ripe flavors.–P.M. • $14 • (9/30/1998) • **76**
Hautes-Côtes de Beaune White 1997: Crisp, ripe and exciting, with butter, cream and butterscotch notes. The acidity is nicely integrated in the sweet fruit. Very intense, with a chewy finish. Drink now through 2005.–P.M. • $17 • (5/31/1999) • **87**
Hautes-Côtes de Beaune White 1996 • $14 • (5/31/1998) • **87**
Hautes-Côtes de Beaune White 1995 • $15 • (8/31/1997) • **84**
Hautes-Côtes de Nuits 1994 • $18 • (11/15/1996) • **71**
Hautes-Côtes de Nuits White 1997: Well made. A bit grassy, but full-bodied and polished, with ripe tropical, honey and fresh herb character. Bounces around the palate with nice intensity. Lingering, crisp finish. Drink now through 2003.–P.M. • $17 • (5/31/1999) • **88**
Hautes-Côtes de Nuits White 1996 • $14 • (5/31/1998) • **87**
Hautes-Côtes de Nuits White 1995 • $18 • (8/31/1997) • **86**

NAVARRE, T.

St.-Chinian Tonneaux 1998: Spice and cherry flavors dominate this up-front red, with sweet vanilla notes that turn just a bit astringent on the finish. Drink now.–K.M. • $16 • (6/15/2000) • **83**

NEGLY, CHATEAU DE LA

Coteaux du Languedoc Cuvée de la Côte 1998: Medium-bodied, with pepper and red fruit flavors and interesting leather notes. Hints of milk chocolate on the finish. An easy-to-drink red that will go well with grilled meats. Drink now through 2002.–K.M. • $10 • (11/15/1999) • **87**
Coteaux du Languedoc Cuvée de la Côte 1997: Young and fruity, with plenty of crushed black pepper and berry flavors and leather elements. Good concentration on the finish, with spicy notes. Drink now.–K.M. • $10 • (1/31/1999) • **85**
Coteaux du Languedoc Rosé Cuvée de la Brise Marine 1997: A good quaff, with a slightly sweet taste and strawberry flavors. Drink now.–K.M. • $10 • (12/31/1998) • **82**
Coteaux du Languedoc Rosé La Clape Les Embruns 1998: This pretty and flavorful rosé has plenty of structure and body, with delicious dried cherry and plum flavors and pepper and spice notes. Quite a quaff, but could be drunk with salmon or roast chicken. Drink now.–K.M. • $10 • (11/15/1999) • **87**
Coteaux du Languedoc White La Clape 1998: A lively and full-bodied white, with a nice, chewy texture and interesting flavors of quince and salted almond. Pepper and green peach notes linger on the finish. Would go well with fish or poultry. Drink now.–K.M. • $12 • (11/15/1999) • **85**
Syrah-Grenache Coteaux du Languedoc 1995 • $10 • (3/31/1998) • **87**

NENIN, CHATEAU

Pomerol 1990 • $51 Ⓐ • (3/31/1993) • **88**
Pomerol 1986 • $22 • (6/30/1989) • **84**

Pomerol 1982: Brick red, with a ruby center. Cedar, tobacco and light earth aromas. Medium-bodied, with some milk chocolate, berry character, but slightly drying on the finish. Fading quickly. (1982 Bordeaux horizontal tasting). Drink now.–J.S. • $40 Ⓐ • (11/30/1998) • **82**
Pomerol 1961 • $63 Ⓐ • (4/30/1996) • **91**
Pomerol 1959 • $100 • (10/15/1990) • **88**
Pomerol 1947 • $NA • (5/31/1997) • **85**
Pomerol 1945 • $250 • (11/30/1995) • **71**

NERTHE, CHATEAU LA

Châteauneuf-du-Pape 1997: A pleasant, new-oakish, international style of Rhône red, with chocolate, smoke, violet and toast character. Rather ripe and full, with nice blackberry on the lingering but firm finish. Cellar short-term. Better than when previously reviewed. Drink through 2003–P.M. • $35 • (12/15/1999) • **85**
Châteauneuf-du-Pape 1996: Supple and smooth, with a pleasantly silky mouthfeel and very round tannins, but only decent concentration of fruit, mainly cherry and plum. Drink now through 2002.–P.M. • $32 • (8/31/1999) • **85**
Châteauneuf-du-Pape 1995 • $26 Ⓐ • (10/15/1997) • **85**
Châteauneuf-du-Pape 1994 • $29 • (10/15/1997) • **89**
Châteauneuf-du-Pape 1993 • $25 • (11/15/1996) • **88**
Châteauneuf-du-Pape 1990 • $25 • (10/15/1994) • **89**
Châteauneuf-du-Pape 1989 • $25 • (10/15/1991) • **87**
Châteauneuf-du-Pape 1988 • $25 • (10/15/1991) • **88**
Châteauneuf-du-Pape 1986 • $18 • (10/15/1991) • **87**
Châteauneuf-du-Pape 1985 • $17 • (10/15/1991) • **86**
Châteauneuf-du-Pape 1983 • $25 • (10/15/1991) • **88**
Châteauneuf-du-Pape 1981 • $30 • (10/15/1991) • **94**
Châteauneuf-du-Pape Cuvée des Cadettes 1997: An impressive '97. A modern, international style of Rhône, here's a red with much fancy new oak, delivering wonderful toast, violet, cassis, roasted game and smoke character. Supple, ripe tannins turn this into a seductive, full-bodied, sweet-tasting winner that's very hard to resist. Drink now through 2007.–P.M. • $75 • (12/15/1999) • **91**
Châteauneuf-du-Pape Cuvée des Cadettes 1996: Likable for its balance, with some decent blackberry, cassis, plum and smoke notes. Unusually thick-textured for a '96, lacking a bit of flavor concentration. Drink now through 2002.–P.M. • $72 • (8/31/1999) • **88**
Châteauneuf-du-Pape Cuvée des Cadettes 1995: Full-bodied, ultrasmooth and refined, deeply colored, with plenty of black fruit character and showing a real grip of acidity, this is oh-so-seductive. Hard to fault; you could enjoy it upon release or into the next decade.–P.M. • $50 • (9/30/1998) HR • **93**
Châteauneuf-du-Pape Cuvée des Cadettes 1994 • $50 • (10/15/1997) • **92**
Châteauneuf-du-Pape Cuvée des Cadettes 1993 • $48 • (11/15/1996) • **88**
Châteauneuf-du-Pape Cuvée des Cadettes 1990 • $67 Ⓐ • (4/15/1993) • **89**
Châteauneuf-du-Pape Cuvée des Cadettes 1989 • $30 • (10/15/1991) • **88**
Châteauneuf-du-Pape Cuvée des Cadettes 1988 • $30 • (10/15/1991) • **89**
Châteauneuf-du-Pape White 1998: Big, round and thick, it lacks a bit of focus but kicks with citrusy life on the palate. Finishes with avocado, tropical fruit and wet hay. Drink now through 2002.–P.M. • $35 • (9/30/1999) • **86**
Châteauneuf-du-Pape White 1997: Thick and ripe, smooth and sweet-tasting, this has gras attached to its body. Harmonious, with a lovely combination of wet earth, bark, melon and honey, it shows terroir. Elegant on the lingering, fairly powerful finish. Drink now through 2005.–P.M. • $30 • (11/15/1998) • **89**
Châteauneuf-du-Pape White 1996 • $30 • (10/15/1997) • **91**
Châteauneuf-du-Pape White Clos de Beauvenir 1998: Beautiful. Balanced, supple and medium-bodied, with a rather lush mouthfeel and a sense of opulence. Offers good fruit and a tannic mineral character that's becoming. Medium-intense on the finish. Drink now through 2008.–P.M. • $55 • (6/30/2000) • **87**

NEVEU, ANDRE

Sancerre Le Grand Fricambault 1998: Traditional notes of earth mingle with grass and floral aromas and flavors. Round, almost plump finish. Drink now.–B.S. • $12 • (6/15/2000) • **83**

NEWMAN

Beaune Theurons 1996: Tight and clean, showing good terroir concentration with a minerally midpalate, and tasting of nice fruit, with a fairly smooth texture. Turns a bit hot on the finish. Drink now through 2002.–P.M. • $34 • (7/31/1999) • **87**
Bonnes Mares 1996: Pure and clean, elegant and medium-bodied Pinot Noir. Aromas burst from the glass, fanning out on the palate with black cherry, blackberry, raspberry flavors, little hindered by oak. Long, succulent finish. Drink now through 2005.–P.M. • $99 • (7/31/1999) • **90**
Latricières-Chambertin 1996: A little monument to the great '96 vintage. Reserved, even closed, this is all class, with some terrific mineral, *terroir*-driven character topped by blackberry and black cherry. Elegant, racy, bursting with acidity. Drink now through 2010.–P.M. • $95 • (7/31/1999) • **95**
Mazis-Chambertin 1996: Storms the palate like a "twister," with loads of crisp acidity and a stemmy, cassis bush character, but also offers fabulous blackberry and cassis aromas. Still, hard stuff on the finish. Best from 2000.–P.M. • $99 • (7/31/1999) • **88**

NICOLAS

Beaujolais-Villages 1989 • $8 • (11/15/1990) • **82**
Beaujolais-Villages Réserve 1995 • $9 • (4/30/1997) • **84**

NIELLON, MICHEL

Bâtard-Montrachet 1997: Wine of the vintage? There's nothing subtle about this full-bodied white Burgundy, with its grassy, earthy, primal personality. Built for the Burg aficionado, it has enough concentration to rip out your palate. Best from 2003 through 2010.–P.M. • $210 • (9/30/1999) • **98**
Chassagne-Montrachet 1997: A bit acidic, with tart and vegetal flavors. Tastes a bit grassy, like a Sauvignon Blanc.–P.M. • $36 Ⓐ • (9/30/1999) • **72**
Chassagne-Montrachet 1996: Solid white Burgundy with terrific balance. Shows apple, dried herb, grass, earth, also ripe and honeyed tones, mingling nicely with the toasted oak. Of medium body, with a lot of character thanks to the citrus, mineral and spice on the lingering, even chewy, finish. Best after 2000.–P.M. • $76 Ⓐ • (8/31/1998) • **89**
Chassagne-Montrachet Clos de la Maltroie 1997: There's good intensity in this '97 Chassagne, delivering crisp caramel and crème brûlée notes. Lush and thick, with a marzipan, slightly burning aftertaste. Drink now through 2001.–P.M. • $40 Ⓐ • (9/30/1999) • **88**
Chassagne-Montrachet Clos de la Maltroie 1996: Very Chassagne-like. Superherbal with grassy undertones, it has a great deal of silky, full-bodied structure at midpalate. Tastes like a blend of Chardonnay and Sauvignon Blanc, and delivers mouthpuckeringly intense flavors on the chewy finish. Personality-plus. Best after 2003.–P.M. • $91 Ⓐ • (8/31/1998) • **90**
Chassagne-Montrachet Clos de la Maltroie 1995 • $50 • (8/31/1997) • **90**
Chassagne-Montrachet Clos St.-Jean 1997: Half Burgundy, half New World. Sweet and medium-bodied, with a ripe pineapple, passion fruit, earth and flint character. Kicks with vibrancy on the lemony, crisp finish. Drink now through 2005.–P.M. • $43 Ⓐ • (9/30/1999) • **87**
Chassagne-Montrachet Clos St.-Jean 1996: Very Chassagne-like, with nice green olive, mint, basil, thyme complexity backed by a deft dose of toasted oak. Of medium body, exploding with intense fruit. Neither subtle nor very minerally, it's interesting and very long on the finish. Needs time. Best after 2003.–P.M. • $77 Ⓐ • (8/31/1998) • **90**
Chassagne-Montrachet Les Champgains 1997: Very strange, but that's why it's so intriguing. Talk about terroir—this sort of wine is impossible to copyright. Earthy, with a strange matchstick character, lemon and fruit aromas and a fat texture. Drink now through 2017.–P.M. • $65 • (9/30/1999) • **90**
Chassagne-Montrachet Les Champgains 1996: An intellectually demanding wine that has beautiful, firm structure and great flavors, but not all seductively smooth and attractive. Think of grassy, herbal, mineral, dried thyme and rosemary flavors and you get the picture. Would verge on rustic if not for a clean, pure, silky thread that should only grow with cellaring. Best after 2005.–P.M. • $60 • (8/31/1998) • **90**
Chassagne-Montrachet Les Champgains 1995 • $50 • (8/31/1997) • **95**
Chevalier-Montrachet 1997: Terrific fruit hides under very strange, sharply acidic, smoky notes. Full-bodied, with a silky midpalate suggesting impressive concentration of fruit, but it still makes for an awkward drinking experience. Drink through 2007–P.M. • $210 • (9/30/1999) • **87**
Chevalier-Montrachet 1996: Grassy and herbal in style, but there's ripe fruit and the wine is a pleasure to taste—full, vibrant and minerally—as long as you don't mind Sauvignon Blanc–like character in a grand cru white Burgundy. Best from 2004 through 2010.–P.M. • $220 • (5/31/1999) • **87**
Chevalier-Montrachet 1995 • $130 • (8/31/1997) • **95**

NOAILLAC, CHATEAU

Médoc 1998: This is herbal and diluted. Light body; light finish.–J.S. • $NA • (5/31/1999) (BT) • **75-79**

FRANCE

■ ■ ■ ■

NOAILLAC, CHATEAU

Médoc 1997: Light and delicate, with tobacco, cherry and vanilla aromas and flavors. Medium-bodied, with soft tannins and a light finish. Drink now through 2003.–J.S. • $NA • (1/31/2000) • **84**

Médoc 1996: Has a slightly stewed berry character and a muddled structure. Medium-bodied, with light tannins and a diluted finish. Hard to like.–J.S. • $NA • (2/28/1999) • **78**

NOBLE, DOMAINE LA

Merlot Vin de Pays de l'Aude 1991 • $7 • (6/15/1993) • **77**

Merlot Vin de Pays de l'Aude 1990 • $7 • (3/31/1992) • **73**

NOTRE-DAME DU QUATOURZE, CHATEAU

Coteaux du Languedoc 1996: Tart, with herbal and plummy flavors. Finishes on a stemmy note.–K.M. • $9 • (10/31/1998) • **75**

Coteaux du Languedoc 1995 • $9 • (1/01/1998) • **68**

NOUHEN, DANIEL

Mâcon-Chardonnay Domaine le Berceau du Chardonnay 1997: Showy oak, tart texture, straightforward flavors—not exactly a charming Chardonnay.–P.M. • $15 • (5/31/1999) • **78**

Mâcon-Chardonnay Domaine le Berceau du Chardonnay 1996: Fairly elegant on the midpalate, as it sports some mineral concentration, this medium-bodied Chardonnay offers pretty floral, pear, melon and toasted bread flavors. Drink now through 2003.–P.M. • $13 • (8/31/1998) • **88**

Mâcon-Chardonnay Domaine le Berceau du Chardonnay Les Beauvois 1997: Obviously oaky, showing lots of showy spice, caramel and floral-perfumey character, it's overdone and tires the palate.–P.M. • $15 • (5/31/1999) • **72**

Mâcon-Chardonnay Domaine le Berceau du Chardonnay Les Beauvois 1996: Oaky, showing malic, mocha and spice, but also a slight off-aroma reminiscent of plywood and paint varnish. Lacks harmony.–P.M. • $13 • (8/31/1998) • **73**

Mâcon-Chardonnay Domaine le Berceau du Chardonnay Vieilles Vignes 1997: Clearly oaky, a showy style of Mâcon, with some good fruit trying to keep pace with the wood. Round mouthfeel, but a burning character on the finish. Drink now through 2002.–P.M. • $17 • (5/31/1999) • **82**

Mâcon-Chardonnay Domaine le Berceau du Chardonnay Vieilles Vignes 1996: Rich and opulent for a Mâconnais white, with clean flavors of toasted oak, honey and ripe pear. Full-bodied, the silky texture makes it most appealing. Drink now.–P.M. • $16 • (8/31/1998) • **88**

NOUVEAU, CLAUDE

Maranges 1994 • $NA • (11/15/1996) • **73**

Maranges La Fussière 1994 • $NA • (11/15/1996) • **77**

Santenay Grand Clos Rousseau 1994 • $NA • (11/15/1996) • **74**

Santenay Les Charmes Dessus 1994 • $NA • (11/15/1996) • **71**

Santenay White 1995 • $NA • (8/31/1997) • **83**

NUMERO 2 DE LAFON-ROCHET, LE

St.-Estèphe 1996: Black-colored, with intense aromas of blackberry, currant and mint. Full-bodied, with well-integrated, silky tannins and a long, ripe fruit finish. Very impressive indeed, especially for a second label. From Château Lafon-Rochet.–J.S. • $25 • (1/31/1999) • **88**

OGEREAU, DOMAINE

Anjou 1997: This straightforward red is soft and fruity, with a pleasant round texture, light tannins and flavors of cherry, berry and spice. Well knit and balanced. Drink now.–T.M. • $12 • (6/30/1999) • **81**

Anjou-Villages 1996: Shows good concentration and color for the appellation, with firm tannins and dark flavors of plum, coffee and herb. Big enough to match well with food. Drink through 2001.–T.M. • $17 • (6/30/1999) • **83**

Anjou-Villages 1990 • $NA • (10/31/1994) • **85**

Coteaux du Layon-St.-Lambert Clos des Bonnes Blanches 1997: Apple pie in a glass. This rich, sweet white offers baked apple, piecrust, honey and cinnamon flavors that are thick yet never cloying, sweet yet still refreshing. A powerful wine best enjoyed on its own. Drink now through 2010.–T.M. • $50/500 ml. • (6/30/1999) • **93**

Coteaux du Layon-St.-Lambert Cuvée Prestige 1996: Luscious. Honey and orange flavors give this thick, viscous white a sweet appeal, while firm acidity keeps it fresh and brings you back for another sip. Balanced and long, a refreshing, focused wine that can match well with a main course or dessert. Drink now through 2010.–T.M. • $28 • (6/30/1999) • **92**

OGIER, MICHEL

Côte-Rôtie 1997: Lovely if you don't mind a slight herbal note along with the delicious black pepper, cherry, smoke and bacon flavors. Medium-bodied and smooth, it hits its stride on the balanced, accessible finish. Drink now through 2003.–P.M. • $46 • (11/30/1999) • **86**

Côte-Rôtie 1996: A beauty. Clean, exuberant, lush, packed with an exotic mixture of smoke, mint, mineral, blackberry, cassis and floral notes. Takes twists and turns on the palate that keep your attention. Full-bodied, with well-integrated tannins. Drink now through 2005.–P.M. • $38 • (11/15/1998) • **90**

Côte-Rôtie 1995: Some decent fruit here, but it tastes a bit on the green side, with cassis bush and herbal notes, and it turns somewhat dry and short on the finish. For the fruit to emerge, it probably needs simple foods like pizza or barbecue. Drink now through 2002.–P.M. • $38 • (9/15/1998) • **83**

Côte-Rôtie 1990 • $42 • (4/15/1993) • **88**

Côte-Rôtie 1988 • $38 • (11/15/1991) • **87**

Côte-Rôtie Cuvée Belle Hélène 1995: Started out great, but turned a bit dry after it had been in contact with air for over an hour. Inky black in color, ultrathick in body, one can taste the ripe, sweet fruit, including cassis, and the earthy, spicy flavors. Good, lingering finish. Drink now through 2015.–P.M. • $NA • (9/15/1998) • **88**

OLEK-MERY

Chinon Cuvée des Tireaux 1993 • $18 • (5/15/1996) • **87**

OLIVIER, CHATEAU

Pessac-Léognan 1999: A lovely, fruity wine, with milk chocolate, berry and cherry character. Medium-bodied and round, with soft tannins and a fresh finish.–J.S. • $NA • (1/01/2000) (BT) • **85-89**

Pessac-Léognan 1998: A cold and firm young wine, with mineral and spice character. Medium-bodied, with tight tannins and a medium finish.–J.S. • $NA • (5/31/1999) (BT) • **85-89**

Pessac-Léognan 1997: If you like cut grass, go for this; some decent fruit, but rather unripe.–J.S. • $21 • (1/31/2000) • **79**

Pessac-Léognan 1996: Offers good berry and tobacco character, but then turns rather lean and slightly hard on the palate. Medium-bodied. Tasted twice, with consistent notes. Best after 2000.–J.S. • $22 • (1/31/1999) • **85**

Pessac-Léognan 1995 • $25 • (1/31/1998) • **89**

Pessac-Léognan 1994 • $23 • (1/31/1997) • **84**

Pessac-Léognan 1993 • $23 • (1/31/1996) • **85**

Pessac-Léognan 1992 • $18 • (4/15/1995) • **83**

Pessac-Léognan 1990 • $19 • (3/31/1993) • **90**

Pessac-Léognan 1989: I overrated this when it was first released. It's sleek and delicious though. Good ruby color. Fresh aromas of flowers and raspberries. Medium-bodied, with firm tannins and a chocolate, blackberry aftertaste. (1989 Bordeaux horizontal tasting). Drink now through 2005.–J.S. • $34 Ⓐ • (5/31/1999) • **88**

Pessac-Léognan 1988 • $25 • (2/15/1991) HR • **91**

Graves 1985 • $20 • (2/15/1989) SS • **93**

Graves 1983 • $23 • (5/01/1989) • **92**

Graves 1982 • $21 • (8/31/1992) • **90**

Graves 1981 • $14 • (10/16/1985) • **86**

Pessac-Léognan White 1998: A very ripe white, with mango, honey and vanilla character. Full-bodied, with lots of flavor and a long finish. Will improve with age. Drink now through 2004.–J.S. • $23 • (2/29/2000) • **89**

Pessac-Léognan White 1997: Interesting, with grass, honey and pear aromas. Medium- to full-bodied, with lots of grass and hints of wood on the palate. Long finish. Drink now.–J.S. • $20 • (9/30/1999) • **88**

Pessac-Léognan White 1996: Good white here. Subtle and well made. Alluring aromas of stone, apple, almond and vanilla. Medium-bodied, with good acidity and a fruity, apple and vanilla aftertaste. Drink now.–J.S. • $19 • (3/31/1999) • **88**

ORATOIRE ST.-MARTIN, DOMAINE DE L'

Côtes du Rhône-Villages Cairanne Haut-Coustias 1993 • $16 • (12/15/1996) • **83**

Key: SS—Spectator Selection. CS—Cellar Selection. HR—Highly Recommended. $NA—Price not available. (BT)—Barrel tasting. Ⓐ—Auction Price. For a key to the tasters' initials, see "How to Use These Listings." **Dates in parentheses represent the issues in which the ratings were published.**

FRANCE

Côtes du Rhône-Villages Cairanne Réserve des Seigneurs 1998: Supple and packed with fruit, a medium-bodied red showing lots of ripe tannins. Lacks a bit of depth and density, but a pleasant house wine. Drink now through 2003.–P.M. • $16 • (12/15/1999) • **82**

Côtes du Rhône-Villages Cairanne Réserve des Seigneurs 1994 • $12 • (12/15/1996) • **78**

ORBIERS, DOMAINE DES

Volnay Clos des Chênes 1996: Beautiful wine, showing some nice wet earth, mineral and good solid fruit. Medium- to full-bodied, it has a firmer tannic structure than many '96 Volnays; packed with red- and blackberry character that follows through to the long, slightly hot finish. Drink now through 2005.–P.M. • $NA • (9/30/1998) • **89**

ORMES-DE-PEZ, CHATEAU LES

St.-Estèphe 1999: Plum and spice with cinnamon aromas. Medium-bodied, with pleasant tannins and a medium finish.–J.S. • $NA • (1/01/2000) (BT) • **85-89**

St.-Estèphe 1998: Aromas of currants and plum skins. Medium-bodied, with silky tannins and a fruity finish.–J.S. • $NA • (5/31/1999) (BT) • **85-89**

St.-Estèphe 1997: Delicious, with plum, spice and vanilla character. Medium-bodied, with silky tannins and a fresh fruit finish. Drink now through 2004.–J.S. • $23 Ⓐ • (1/31/2000) • **86**

St.-Estèphe 1996: Dark-colored, with good berry and mint aromas and hints of fresh tea leaves. Full-bodied and chewy, with serious concentration of ripe tannins and a medium finish. Needs but a bit more fruit intensity to be outstanding. Best after 2001.–J.S. • $25 • (1/31/1999) • **89**

St.-Estèphe 1994 • $25 • (1/31/1997) • **79**

St.-Estèphe 1993 • $19 • (1/31/1996) • **87**

St.-Estèphe 1992 • $17 • (4/15/1995) • **78**

St.-Estèphe 1991 • $15 • (3/31/1994) • **82**

St.-Estèphe 1990 • $33 Ⓐ • (3/31/1993) • **93**

St.-Estèphe 1989: Very, very closed, yet very, very impressive. Inky-colored. Gorgeous aromas of flowers, raspberries and black licorice. Medium- to full-bodied, yet reserved and very fine, with ultrasilky tannins and a long, long finish. (1989 Bordeaux horizontal tasting). Best after 2002.–J.S. • $42 Ⓐ • (5/31/1999) • **90**

St.-Estèphe 1988 • $21 • (4/30/1991) • **88**

St.-Estèphe 1987 • $15 • (5/15/1990) • **83**

St.-Estèphe 1986 • $36 Ⓐ • (11/30/1989) • **87**

St.-Estèphe 1985 • $30 Ⓐ • (4/30/1988) • **89**

St.-Estèphe 1983 • $17 • (10/15/1986) • **86**

St.-Estèphe 1982: Good wine, but drying out a bit. Dark ruby, with a garnet edge. Berry, green tobacco, game and cedar aromas. Medium-bodied and tannic, with a slightly sharp texture. (1982 Bordeaux horizontal tasting). Drink now.–J.S. • $42 Ⓐ • (11/30/1998) • **84**

St.-Estèphe 1961 • $55 • (4/30/1996) • **87**

ORMES-SORBET, CHATEAU LES

Médoc 1998: Cherry and raspberry character throughout. Medium-bodied, with medium tannins and a silky finish. Slightly hollow midpalate.–J.S. • $NA • (5/31/1999) (BT) • **85-89**

Médoc 1997: Fresh, with aromas of ripe berries and violets. Medium-bodied, with firm tannins and a short finish. Drink now.–J.S. • $NA • (1/31/2000) • **85**

Médoc 1988 • $20 • (4/30/1991) • **84**

ORSCHWIHR, CHATEAU D'

Gewürztraminer Alsace Hueben Steinbach 1996: Starts off well, with a pure expression of roses, litchi and lanolin, but the palate is light, and the finish is short.–B.S. • $20 • (9/15/1998) • **82**

ORVAL, L'

Merlot Vin de Pays d'Oc 1994 • $NA • (12/15/1996) • **86**

OSTERTAG

Gewürztraminer Alsace Epfig 1996 • $20 • (4/30/1998) • **86**

Muscat Alsace Fronholz 1996: A lovely dry Muscat exhibiting concentrated flavors of roses, thyme and grapefruit, balance and a crisp finish. Great as an aperitif. Drink now.–B.S. • $20 • (8/31/1998) • **86**

Pinot Blanc Alsace Barriques 1996: Smells and tastes a little cheesy, with bracing acidity and modest concentration.–B.S. • $14 • (10/15/1999) • **78**

Pinot Gris Alsace Barriques 1997: Atypical, this sports vanilla and spice accents from new oak, yet provides the necessary structure and flavor nuance to the apricot and honey. Interesting and tasty. Needs a bit of time for all the elements to integrate. Drink now through 2001.–B.S. • $24 • (10/31/1999) • **86**

Pinot Gris Alsace Barriques 1996: Not much character to go with the rich texture in this odd, introverted white, showing only a leesy note.–B.S. • $23 • (9/15/1998) • **78**

Pinot Gris Alsace Fronholz 1996: In a different style, this white reflects new oak shadings in its vanilla and freshly sawed wood character. Add ripe apricot and a fat presence on the palate, and the result is better balance and harmony. Drink through 2004–B.S. • $32 • (4/30/1999) • **87**

Pinot Gris Alsace Zellberg 1996: New oak lends a vanilla and carpentry-shop character to this lean, intense white. The wood dominates the quince and citrus notes at this stage, and it lacks the flesh and fruit to balance as it ages. Drink now through 2001.–B.S. • $36 • (4/30/1999) • **83**

Riesling Alsace Epfig 1998: Ripe and apricot-laced, round and appealing, yet with succulent acidity emerging on the finish, keeping everything focused and lively. Drink now through 2003.–B.S. • $16 • (5/31/2000) • **87**

Riesling Alsace Epfig 1997: Perfumed, offering floral, peach and mineral notes that take on a honeyed flavor in the mouth. Dry and rich, almost unctuous, with a texture that coats the palate. Ends with hints of citrus and mineral. Drink now through 2005.–B.S. • $20 • (3/31/1999) • **89**

Riesling Alsace Fronholz 1997: This '97 Riesling has fine weight and richness. Vibrant acidity carries the apple, peach, honeysuckle and mineral notes to a lingering conclusion. Drink now through 2002.–B.S. • $36 • (6/15/2000) • **87**

Riesling Alsace Fronholz 1996: Seems a bit advanced on the nose, giving accents of almond, mineral and citrus, while the palate is racy and austere. There's density and weight, and it's dry and long on the finish. Drink through 2005–B.S. • $25 • (10/31/1999) • **88**

Riesling Alsace Grand Cru Muenchberg 1997: Impeccably balanced, beautifully expressive and intensely wrought, exuding peach, apricot, smoke and mineral aromas and flavors on a firm, yet seamless structure. Haunting, ethereal finish. Drink now through 2005.–B.S. • $35 • (10/15/1999) • **92**

Riesling Alsace Grand Cru Muenchberg 1996: A reserved white, firm and tightly wound. Its aromas and flavors are closed in at this stage, yet there's a sense of harmony and length. An intriguing smoky note lingers on the finish. Best from 2001 through 2008.–B.S. • $32 • (3/31/1999) • **88**

Riesling Alsace Heissenberg 1997: A hint of residual sugar, and plenty of smoke, vanilla and peach notes make for a tasty white that's balanced, moderately deep and long. Drink through 2001.–B.S. • $28 • (10/15/1999) • **86**

Riesling Alsace Heissenberg 1996: Broad and ripe, offering quince, peach and flinty aromas and flavors, a round, rich mouthfeel and vibrant acidity. Firmly structured, with a lingering aftertaste of quince. Still youthful, needing time to integrate. Drink through 2007–B.S. • $26 • (3/31/1999) • **89**

OUPIA, CHATEAU D'

Minervois 1995 • $8 • (3/31/1998) • **81**

Minervois Les Barons 1996: A backward style, with flavors of coffee grounds and prune. Tough and stemmy on the finish.–K.M. • $11 • (11/15/1999) • **77**

PABIOT & FILS, JEAN

Pouilly-Fumé Domaine des Fines Caillottes 1996 • $17 • (5/31/1998) • **86**

PADERE, CHATEAU DE

Buzet 1996: Medium-bodied, with plum and dried cherry flavors. Smooth, with a nice minerally note on the finish. Drink now.–K.M. • $10 • (5/31/1999) • **83**

Buzet 1994 • $11 • (12/15/1997) • **85**

Buzet 1990 • $10 • (7/31/1996) • **83**

PAGODES DE COS, LES

St.-Estèphe 1996: Delivers plenty of spicy currant and berry character. Full-bodied, with well-integrated, silky tannins and a spicy, fruity aftertaste. Clever winemaking. Best second label of the vintage. From Château Cos d'Estournel. Try after 2002.–J.S. • $25 • (1/31/1999) • **89**

St.-Estèphe 1995 • $27 • (1/31/1998) • **87**

FRANCE

PAILLARD, BRUNO

Blanc de Blancs Champagne Crémant NV • $36 • (12/31/1990) • **85**
Brut Blanc de Blancs Champagne Réserve Privée NV: Not for everyone. Heady aromas of earth and smoke lead to mellow flavors of apple, lemon and cinnamon on a plush texture. Drink now through 2001. • $60 • (10/31/1999) • **86**
Brut Champagne Première Cuvée NV: Flavorful and bold in style, this has earthy, toasty aromas, a broad, rich texture and lemon-butter flavors that linger on the finish. Not just bubbly, but a real wine for the table. Drink now through 2001. • $35 • (10/31/1999) • **90**
Brut Rosé Champagne Première Cuvée NV: An attractive, substantive rosé in a winey style. Dry and full-bodied, with enough Pinot Noir character to keep your interest. Great balance and a luxurious mousse. Drink now. • $40 • (12/31/1998) • **89**

PAILLAS, CHATEAU

Cahors 1993 • $13 • (5/15/1997) • **85**
Cahors 1992 • $14 • (5/15/1997) • **79**

PALMER, CHATEAU

Margaux 1999: A harmonious Palmer. Lovely berry, cherry and tobacco aromas follow through to a medium- to full-bodied palate, with soft, silky tannins and a long finish.–J.S. • $NA • (1/01/2000) (BT) • **85-89**
Margaux 1998: Dark-colored, with fruit, violet and cherry aromas. Big tannin attack on the palate but medium-bodied, with a slightly austere finish. Burly and tannic, it needs a bit more ripe fruit to balance.–J.S. • $NA • (5/31/1999) (BT) • **85-89**
Margaux 1997: Classy wine. Lovely berry, plum and floral character. Medium-bodied, with silky tannins and a long, fruity finish. Love to drink this stuff. Drink now through 2006.–J.S. • $NA • (1/31/2000) • **90**
Margaux 1996: Dark-colored, and bubbling over with raspberry, black currant and spices. Full- to medium-bodied, with well-integrated, silky tannins and a spicy, fruity aftertaste. Palmer is always a joy to taste and the '96 is no exception. Best after 2002.–J.S. • $50 Ⓐ • (1/31/1999) • **91**
Margaux 1995 • $67 Ⓐ • (1/31/1998) • **94**
Margaux 1994 • $63 Ⓐ • (1/31/1997) • **89**
Margaux 1993 • $35 Ⓐ • (1/31/1996) • **88**
Margaux 1992 • $34 Ⓐ • (4/15/1995) • **80**
Margaux 1991 • $38 Ⓐ • (3/31/1994) • **87**
Margaux 1990 • $89 Ⓐ • (3/31/1993) • **91**
Margaux 1989: Muscular-style Palmer. Deep ruby color at the center, with a red edge. Shows lovely floral, berry and plum aromas and hints of earth. Full-bodied and chewy, with masses of tannins and a long, sweet and ripe berry aftertaste. Just peeking through the curtain. Great potential. (1989 Bordeaux horizontal tasting). Best from 2000.–J.S. • $131 Ⓐ • (5/31/1999) • **93**
Margaux 1988: Rather dry and austere, with some of the violet, berry and fruit character I expect in Palmer, but slightly hard and ungenerous on the palate. A big disappointment. (1988 Bordeaux horizontal tasting). Drink now.–J.S. • $68 Ⓐ • (11/30/1998) • **86**
Margaux 1987 • $46 Ⓐ • (5/15/1990) • **84**
Margaux 1986 • $119 Ⓐ • (6/15/1989) • **94**
Margaux 1985 • $86 Ⓐ • (10/15/1994) • **91**
Margaux 1984 • $39 Ⓐ • (10/15/1987) • **84**
Margaux 1983 • $159 Ⓐ • (10/15/1994) • **90**
Margaux 1982: A well-crafted red with beautiful structure. Dark ruby-garnet in color, with a lot of violet and earth aromas. Full-bodied, with loads of silky tannins and a long, sweet fruit finish. Has always been outstanding. (1982 Bordeaux horizontal tasting). Drink now.–J.S. • $95 Ⓐ • (11/30/1998) • **90**
Margaux 1981 • $55 Ⓐ • (10/15/1994) • **89**
Margaux 1980 • $41 Ⓐ • (5/01/1985) • **86**
Margaux 1979 • $131 Ⓐ • (10/15/1989) • **90**
Margaux 1978 • $87 Ⓐ • (5/01/1985) • **81**
Margaux 1970 • $189 Ⓐ • (5/15/1993) • **91**
Margaux 1962 • $80 • (11/30/1987) • **80**
Margaux 1961 • $NA/1.5 liter • (4/30/1996) • **93**
Margaux 1959 • $423 Ⓐ • (10/15/1990) • **98**
Margaux 1945 • $610 Ⓐ • (11/30/1995) • **91**

Key: SS—Spectator Selection. CS—Cellar Selection. HR—Highly Recommended. $NA—Price not available. (BT)—Barrel tasting. Ⓐ—Auction Price. For a key to the tasters' initials, see "How to Use These Listings." **Dates in parentheses represent the issues in which the ratings were published.**

PALMER & CO.

Brut Champagne NV • $29 • (11/15/1997) • **83**
Brut Rosé Champagne NV • $34 • (11/30/1997) • **90**

PALOUMEY, CHATEAU

Haut-Médoc 1997: Good core of berry and currant. Medium body, medium to light tannins. Fresh finish. Drink now.–J.S. • $NA • (1/31/2000) • **82**
Haut-Médoc 1994 • $15 • (4/30/1997) • **79**

PANNIER

Brut Champagne Cuvée Louis Eugène NV: Full-flavored and luxuriously dense in texture, with mature honey and nut nuances combined with a soft, smooth texture making this something special. Drink now. • $48 • (12/31/1998) • **89**
Brut Champagne Egérie 1990: This really packs in the flavor, yet remains light on its feet. A plush, mouthfilling mousse brings out rich, creamy, harmonious fruit and spice flavors that linger on the finish. Vibrant acidity keeps it balanced. Drink now through 2001. • $48 • (12/15/1998) • **92**
Brut Champagne Sélection NV: This soft powder puff of a Champagne gets your attention with assertive aromas and flavors of buttered popcorn, then turns light and frothy in texture. Appealing for its smoothness. Drink now. • $26 • (12/31/1998) • **86**
Brut Rosé Champagne Cuvée Louis Eugène NV: A bright reddish color and tangy but simple fruit flavors make this a good palate-cleanser. Short on the finish. • $45 • (11/30/1998) • **79**

PANNIER, REMY

Cabernet Franc Rosé Vin de Pays du Jardin de la France 1998: Berry flavors are bright and simple and backed by crisp acidity in this refreshing rosé. Drink now.–T.M. • $9 • (1/01/2000) • **83**
Cabernet Franc Rosé Vin de Pays du Jardin de la France 1997: Fresh and crisp, this pale, dry rosé has a vibrant texture and a vivid core of strawberry flavor. Enjoy it for the exuberance of youth. Drink now.–T.M. • $7 • (8/31/1998) • **83**
Cabernet Franc Rosé Vin de Pays du Jardin de la France 1996 • $6 • (12/15/1997) • **86**
Cabernet Sauvignon Vin de Pays d'Oc 1998: Medium-bodied and a bit dry around the edges, with red plum and herbal flavors, tobacco notes on the finish.–K.M. • $9 • (12/31/1999) • **79**
Cabernet Sauvignon Vin de Pays d'Oc 1997: A fresh, easygoing red, with light, simple fruit flavors and very little tannin. Drink now. • $7 • (8/31/1998) • **80**
Cabernet Sauvignon Vin de Pays d'Oc 1996 • $6 • (12/15/1997) • **78**
Chardonnay Vin de Pays d'Oc 1996 • $6 • (12/15/1997) • **77**
Chardonnay Vin de Pays du Jardin de la France 1998: A simple white, with clean pear and vanilla notes and a soft finish. Drink now.–K.M. • $8 • (5/15/2000) • **80**
Chardonnay Vin de Pays du Jardin de la France 1997: Has a butter component that's appealing, with some spicy flavors on the rather hot finish. Drink now.–K.M. • $7 • (9/15/1998) • **80**
Chardonnay Vin de Pays du Jardin de la France Terroirs de la Vallée 1997: Broad and soft, this white shows oaky flavors of butter and vanilla, with ripe apple notes and low acidity. A bit flabby for food; drink well chilled.–T.M. • $11 • (10/15/1999) • **79**
Merlot Vin de Pays d'Oc 1998: A modest red, with cherry and berry flavors. Sweet-spicy notes on the finish.–K.M. • $8 • (12/31/1999) • **76**
Merlot Vin de Pays d'Oc 1997: Light, smooth and appealing, with fresh strawberry and cherry flavors and very little tannin. Drink now. • $7 • (8/31/1998) • **83**
Merlot Vin de Pays d'Oc 1996 • $6 • (12/15/1997) • **78**
Muscadet de Sèvre et Maine 1998: Round for a Muscadet, with ripe lemon and lime flavors and a slightly oxidized, nutty finish. Drink now.–B.S. • $8 • (6/15/2000) • **81**
Sancerre 1998: Bold and broad. This ripe white offers pear and melon flavors and a creamy texture, with just a hint of the herbal notes typical of the region. Easy to like. Drink now.–T.M. • $14 • (2/29/2000) • **86**
Sancerre Domaine du Moulin Granger 1997: Grapefruit aromas and flavors hold sway in this soft, round, fresh-tasting Loire white. Moderate concentration and length.–B.S. • $12 • (10/31/1998) • **83**

Sauvignon Blanc Vin de Pays du Jardin de la France 1998: This refreshing white has good weight on the palate yet remains crisp, with light herbal notes and a pleasant citrus finish. Drink now.–T.M. • $9 • (3/31/2000) • **84**
Sauvignon Blanc Vin de Pays du Jardin de la France 1997: Fruity and pleasant, a straightforward white with a nice herbal touch and good elements of peach and pear. Drink now.–K.M. • $7 • (9/15/1998) • **84**
Vouvray 1998: This lively white tastes a bit like apple juice—crisp, fruity and refreshing. A quaffable aperitif. Drink now.–T.M. • $9 • (2/29/2000) • **82**
Vouvray Domaine de la Roche Vineuse 1997: On the lean side, showing modest apple and pear notes that turn tart on the finish.–B.S. • $8 • (11/15/1998) • **79**

PAPE, CHATEAU LE

Pessac-Léognan 1990 • $16 • (8/31/1995) • **83**

PAPE CLEMENT, CHATEAU

Pessac-Léognan 1999: Dried plum and berry with orange-peel character. Medium body. Medium tannins. Light finish. Slightly herbal.–J.S. • $NA • (1/01/2000) (BT) • **80-84**
Pessac-Léognan 1998: Pape got it right this year. Very grapey and chewy young wine, with full body, full tannins and a velvety finish.–J.S. • $NA • (5/31/1999) (BT) • **90-94**
Pessac-Léognan 1997: Plums and tobacco galore in this aromatic young wine. Medium-bodied, with velvety tannins and a fruit and tobacco aftertaste. Drink now through 2005.–J.S. • $41 • (1/31/2000) • **88**
Pessac-Léognan 1996: Aromas of plum, berry and earth, with a grilled meat and roasted oak character on the nose and palate. Rather decadent and slightly overdone. Full-bodied, with a velvety tannin structure. A bit funky on the finish.–J.S. • $39 Ⓐ • (1/31/1999) • **85**
Pessac-Léognan 1995 • $40 Ⓐ • (1/31/1998) • **92**
Pessac-Léognan 1994 • $25 Ⓐ • (1/31/1997) • **80**
Pessac-Léognan 1993 • $31 Ⓐ • (1/31/1996) • **84**
Pessac-Léognan 1992 • $26 • (4/15/1995) • **79**
Pessac-Léognan 1990 • $69 Ⓐ • (3/31/1993) • **92**
Pessac-Léognan 1989: Elegant and well made. Color is medium-dark ruby. Aromas of dried cherries and licorice. Full-bodied and well structured, with compacted velvety tannins and a long aftertaste of chocolate and fruit and hints of earth. (1989 Bordeaux horizontal tasting). Best after 2004. –J.S. • $42 Ⓐ • (5/31/1999) • **90**
Pessac-Léognan 1988: This is the first of a string of modern, well-made Papes, showing blackberry, mint and currant character throughout. Full-bodied, with silky, fine tannins. (1988 Bordeaux horizontal tasting). Best after 2000.–J.S. • $65 Ⓐ • (11/30/1998) • **90**
Pessac-Léognan 1987 • $24 • (5/15/1990) • **84**
Pessac-Léognan 1986 • $63 Ⓐ • (6/30/1989) • **92**
Graves 1982: At its peak. Dark brick-red, with an amber hue. Intense wet leaf and dust aromas, with hints of ripe fruit. Medium-bodied, with fine tannins and good berry, tobacco flavors. (1982 Bordeaux horizontal tasting). Drink now.–J.S. • $45 Ⓐ • (11/30/1998) • **88**
Graves 1979 • $20 • (10/15/1989) • **84**
Graves 1970 • $30 Ⓐ • (5/15/1993) • **84**
Graves 1962 • $120 • (11/30/1987) • **90**
Graves 1961 • $122 Ⓐ • (4/30/1996) • **88**
Graves 1959 • $NA /1.5 liter • (10/15/1990) • **80**
Pessac-Léognan White 1997: Reserved and subtle, with cream, lemon, banana, and tropical fruit. Medium- to full-bodied, with a wonderfully caressing texture and a long finish. Pape always makes serious whites. Drink now through 2008.–J.S. • $65 • (9/30/1999) • **90**

PAPES, CAVES DES

Cabernet Sauvignon Vin de Pays d'Oc Jenard 1996: Dried cherry flavors and pepper and leather notes on the finish.–K.M. • $8 • (11/15/1998) • **77**
Chardonnay Vin de Pays d'Oc Jenard 1997: This medium-bodied Chardonnay has pleasant pineapple and spice flavors with interesting honey and mineral notes mixed in. Drink now.–K.M. • $8 • (11/15/1998) • **84**
Châteauneuf-du-Pape Les Closiers 1998: Seductive because of the rich fruit and supple tannins, but also the fresh, clean and crisp character that cleanses the palate and gives this full-bodied, ripe red a sense of elegance and vibrancy. Has raisiny and plummy aromas, with roasted game, grilled lamb chops and cassis jam. Drink now through 2010.–P.M. • $24 • (6/30/2000) • **91**
Châteauneuf-du-Pape Les Closiers 1997: Very soft, with a delicate plum and roasted black cherry character that lingers on the focused finish. Drink now.–P.M. • $22 • (8/31/1999) • **84**
Châteauneuf-du-Pape Les Closiers 1996: Ripe, rich and supple, yet also a bit tough; the hot alcohol accompanies some plum, blackberry, lemon and banana flavors. Full-bodied.–P.M. • $20 • (9/30/1998) • **79**
Châteauneuf-du-Pape Les Closiers 1994 • $19 • (10/15/1997) • **86**
Châteauneuf-du-Pape Les Closiers 1993 • $17 • (4/30/1997) • **83**
Châteauneuf-du-Pape Les Closiers 1988 • $14 • (10/31/1993) • **83**
Châteauneuf-du-Pape White Les Closiers 1998: Lovely, balanced and quite intense, with lime and fresh fruit balancing the beeswax, spice and kiwi character. Medium-bodied, with nice acidity on the crisp finish. Drink now through 2008.–P.M. • $24 • (6/30/2000) • **86**
Côte-Rôtie La Serine 1996: Very light in color and tasting as much of water as of wine, it's terribly diluted, with a dry finish. Maturing fast.–P.M. • $39 • (11/30/1999) • **70**
Côtes du Rhône 1993 • $7 • (11/15/1995) • **83**
Côtes du Rhône 1990 • $6 • (10/31/1993) • **81**
Côtes du Rhône Domaine des Jonquiers 1993 • $8 • (10/15/1996) • **78**
Côtes du Rhône Domaine des Jonquiers 1990 • $7 • (4/30/1994) • **81**
Côtes du Rhône Elevé en Fûts de Chêne 1997: A simple and straightforward red, with licorice and red berry character. A good, light-bodied guzzler with interesting tannin structure.–P.M. • $9 • (12/15/1999) • **78**
Côtes du Rhône Elevé en Fûts de Chêne 1996: Odd, with mature aromas of forest underbrush, wet earth and green leaves. Light-bodied, dry on the finish.–P.M. • $9 • (11/15/1998) • **72**
Côtes du Rhône Héritage Elevé en Foudre de Chêne 1996: Straightforward, and quite mature. Light bodied, with soft, spicy, mocha character, it turns a bit astringent on the finish.–P.M. • $10 • (11/15/1998) • **75**
Côtes du Rhône Héritage Elevé en Foudre de Chêne 1995 • $11 • (10/15/1997) • **84**
Côtes du Rhône White 1998: A bit oxidized, tasting of cardboard. Sweet and appley, but not clean.–P.M. • $9 • (12/15/1999) • **70**
Côtes du Rhône White 1997: Delicate and flavorful, with a lime, grapefruit and melon character and fresh vibrancy. Turns round and supple on the second sip. A food wine. Drink now.–P.M. • $9 • (11/15/1998) • **84**
Côtes du Rhône White 1996 • $7 • (10/15/1997) • **85**
Côtes du Rhône White Héritage Blanc 1998: Fat and flabby, a bit overdone, with butter, cedar and lime character, turning tart on the finish.–P.M. • $9 • (11/15/1999) • **79**
Côtes du Ventoux Lavandin 1998: Cherries and strawberries offer solace in this otherwise angular and tough red.–P.M. • $8 • (12/15/1999) • **76**
Crozes-Hermitage Les Brunnelles 1997: Tart and a bit lean, this straightforward red has modest fruit and crisp tannins.–P.M. • $13 • (10/31/1999) • **76**
Crozes-Hermitage Les Brunnelles 1996: Intriguing, with dried and fresh herb, cassis bush and plum character. Toasty spice and oak and sweet-tasting plummy notes kick in on the slightly hot finish. Full-bodied, with supple tannins. Drink through 2005–P.M. • $12 • (10/15/1998) • **84**
Crozes-Hermitage Les Brunnelles 1990 • $11 • (2/28/1997) • **86**
Gigondas 1990 • $14 • (10/15/1996) • **88**
Gigondas 1988 • $13 • (10/31/1993) • **78**
Gigondas Oratorio 1996: Straightforward, with cherry, cedar and wet earth notes and a rather tough finish.–P.M. • $24 • (10/31/1999) • **79**
Gigondas Réserve des Fustiers 1997: A typical '97. Smooth and a bit simple, with a licorice and black fruit character. A fun, easy, accessible wine that is pleasant enough, but doesn't deliver much depth, terroir or complexity. Drink now through 2002.–P.M. • $17 • (12/15/1999) • **85**
Gigondas Réserve des Fustiers 1996: Ripe, rich and full-bodied, but overly oaky and extracted, showing a plummy, rustic character and tough texture.–P.M. • $14 • (10/15/1998) • **78**
Gigondas Réserve des Fustiers 1994 • $15 • (10/15/1997) • **79**
Hermitage Oratorio 1997: An oaky international style of Syrah, with smoky, toasty aromas, but the fruit is ripe and rich, although overall it lacks a bit of terroir complexity. Still, a medium-bodied, well-made '97. Drink now through 2003.–P.M. • $24 • (11/30/1999) • **86**
Merlot Vin de Pays d'Oc Jenard 1996: Good, accessible Merlot that has effusive herb and cherry aromas and modest flavors that linger on the finish. Smooth in texture. Drink now. • $8 • (10/31/1998) • **83**
St.-Joseph Les Chailles 1997: Green olive, herbal and rosemary notes dominate in this medium-bodied, lightly intense wine. Tough, chewy and rustic on the finish, where the tannins and acidity kick in.–P.M. • $18 • (12/15/1999) • **79**
Sauvignon Blanc Vin de Pays d'Oc Jenard 1996: Mineral and ripe apple flavors dominate.–K.M. • $8 • (10/15/1998) • **79**
Syrah Vin de Pays d'Oc Jenard 1996: Light, simple, acceptable red wine, with crisp cherry and raspberry flavors and moderate tannins. Drink now. • $8 • (10/15/1998) • **79**

FRANCE

PAQUET, JEAN-PAUL

Pouilly-Vinzelles Domaine de Fuissiacus 1997: Sparkling—literally. This slightly spritzy wine is fresh and lemony, with an earthy, herbal undertow that should be tamed with seafood or poultry dishes. Drink now.–P.M. • $15 • (5/31/1999) • **80**

PARAN-JUSTICE, CHATEAU

St.-Emilion 1995 • $20 • (1/31/1998) • **80**

PARAZA, CHATEAU DE

Minervois Cuvée Spéciale 1996 • $6 • (2/28/1998) • **83**

PARDE DE HAUT-BAILLY, LA

Pessac-Léognan 1996: A bit tough, but with some decent berry and spice aromas and flavors. Medium-bodied, with firm tannins and a light finish. Second label of Château Haut-Bailly. Drink now.–J.S. • $NA • (1/31/1999) • **80**

Pessac-Léognan 1995 • $15 • (1/31/1998) • **88**

PARENT

Beaune Les Epenottes 1996: Aromatically subtle, giving just some cherry and wet earth aromas, but it has a supple midpalate, fine tannic structure and an almost-delicate texture. A bit astringent on the racy finish. Drink now through 2002.–P.M. • $40 • (2/28/1999) • **84**

Beaune Les Epenottes 1995 • $38 • (11/15/1997) • **76**

Beaune Les Epenottes 1994 • $33 • (11/15/1996) • **80**

Beaune Les Epenottes 1993 • $57 • (11/15/1995) • **85**

Beaune Les Epenottes 1991 • $NA • (1/31/1994) • **69**

Beaune Les Epenottes 1990 • $NA • (12/15/1992) • **85**

Bourgogne 1996: Muted in aroma and flavor, a bit vegetal and herbal, with aggressive, green tannins.–P.M. • $18 • (1/01/1999) • **73**

Bourgogne 1995 • $18 • (11/15/1997) • **70**

Bourgogne 1994 • $17 • (11/15/1996) • **78**

Corton 1996: Fairly lean, but shows some wet earth, mineral, cedar, spice and cherry complexity. Of medium body, it's a bit tough on the finish. Needs cellaring. Best after 2002.–P.M. • $85 • (2/28/1999) • **82**

Corton Les Renardes 1994 • $57 • (11/15/1996) • **78**

Corton Les Renardes 1993 • $62 • (11/15/1995) • **90**

Corton Les Renardes 1992 • $76 • (12/15/1994) • **74**

Corton Les Renardes 1990 • $NA • (12/15/1992) • **83**

Corton White 1996: An ager. Restrained, elegant, racy, but with loads of mineral character and velvety texture taking over and caressing the palate before notching up the intensity on the long, long finish. Drink through 2005–P.M. • $100 • (2/28/1999) • **91**

Monthélie Les Champs Fulliot 1992 • $NA • (12/15/1994) • **81**

Monthélie Sur la Velle 1997: Cooked plum and berry notes and a hint of herb are tough and tannic.–B.S. • $25 • (9/30/1999) • **78**

Monthélie Sur la Velle 1996: Lovely wine, with fine-textured tannins, polished mouthfeel, some wild berry and black cherry aromas and flavors. A bit hot on the finish. Drink now.–P.M. • $23 • (9/30/1998) • **82**

Pommard 1982 • $18 • (11/01/1985) • **83**

Pommard La Croix Blanche 1996: Wonderful medium-bodied red Burgundy, very much in line with the '96 vintage. Fine tannins are its hallmark, with ripe but not showy fruit and smoky, cherry, wet earth, spice and licorice notes. Drink now through 2004.–P.M. • $48 • (2/28/1999) • **88**

Pommard La Croix Blanche 1995 • $45 • (11/15/1997) • **80**

Pommard Les Chanlins 1993 • $47 • (11/15/1995) • **78**

Pommard Les Chaponnières 1996: Straightforward, offering some polished texture, licorice and cherry notes, a fairly round midpalate, but the tannins turn a bit astringent on the finish. Drink now.–P.M. • $65 • (2/28/1999) • **81**

Pommard Les Chaponnières 1995 • $45 • (11/15/1997) • **83**

Pommard Les Chaponnières 1994 • $46 • (11/15/1996) • **80**

Pommard Les Chaponnières 1993 • $50 • (11/15/1995) • **86**

Pommard Les Chaponnières 1992 • $50 • (12/15/1994) • **80**

Pommard Les Chaponnières 1991 • $NA • (1/31/1994) • **82**

Key: SS—Spectator Selection. CS—Cellar Selection. HR—Highly Recommended. $NA—Price not available. (BT)—Barrel tasting. (A)—Auction Price.
For a key to the tasters' initials, see "How to Use These Listings."
Dates in parentheses represent the issues in which the ratings were published.

Pommard Les Chaponnières 1990 • $NA • (12/15/1992) • **81**

Pommard Les Epenots 1996: A fruity red Burgundy with some astringent character. Medium-bodied, the tannins start out feeling ripe, and the cherry, earth and spice are attractive, but the hard finish disappoints. Drink now through 2002.–P.M. • $70 • (2/28/1999) • **80**

Pommard Les Epenots 1994 • $51 • (11/15/1996) • **75**

Pommard Les Epenots 1993 • $57 • (11/15/1995) • **87**

Pommard Les Epenots 1992 • $70 • (12/15/1994) • **83**

Pommard Les Epenots 1991 • $NA • (1/31/1994) • **83**

Pommard Les Epenots 1990 • $NA • (12/15/1992) • **89**

Pommard Les Epenots 1959 • $NA • (8/31/1990) • **94**

Pommard Les Rugiens 1996: Very polished, this is a lovely, balanced Pinot Noir—a well-crafted red Burgundy with licorice, wet earth, cherry and a touch of spice all in a ripe but elegant package. Lacks a bit of intensity, but it's smooth. Drink now through 2002.–P.M. • $80 • (2/28/1999) • **85**

Pommard Les Rugiens 1992 • $NA • (12/15/1994) • **86**

Volnay Fremiets 1997: With a deeper color than most Volnays, this shows cassis, herbal and stemmy flavors and stiff tannins. Overall it's awkward at this stage, yet has good length, ending firm and dry. Drink through 2004–B.S. • $40 • (9/30/1999) • **81**

Volnay Fremiets 1996: Fairly round at first approach, this wine offers licorice, red berry and herbal notes. Shows nice fresh acidity, but is a bit shy on ripe concentration at midpalate. Medium-bodied, quite crisp on the finish. Drink now.–P.M. • $38 • (9/30/1998) • **83**

PARENT, A.

Pommard Les Rugiens 1997: Quite sleek, but it turns a bit herbal and hard on the finish. Still shows decent red berry character. Drink now.–P.M. • $40 • (9/30/1999) • **80**

Pommard Les Rugiens 1996: A sturdy red, full of earthy, herbaceous flavors, cherries and smoke. Good weight and intensity, just lacks a little ripeness. Drink through 2005–B.S. • $38 • (9/30/1998) • **82**

PASQUETTE, CHATEAU DE

St.-Emilion 1997: Light-bodied, with clean plum and strawberry character, light tannins and a fresh finish. Drink now.–J.S. • $NA • (1/31/2000) • **81**

PASTOU, PAUL & JEAN-MARC

Sancerre Les Boucaults 1997: Shows attractive aromas of flowers, peaches and a nutty quality before the grass and citrus typical of this variety enter on the palate. Ripe, rich and moderate in acidity, finishing crisply.–B.S. • $15 • (11/15/1998) • **86**

Sancerre Les Boucaults Vieilles Vignes 1998: Lemony and herbal flavors give this wine zip, with spicy notes on the finish. Drink now.–K.M. • $12 • (5/15/2000) • **83**

PASTOURELLE, DOMAINE DE LA

Coteaux du Languedoc 1996: Smooth, with pepper and cherry flavors. Starts and finishes on a leathery note. Drink now.–K.M. • $8 • (10/31/1998) • **81**

PATACHE, CHATEAU LA

Pomerol 1996: A light and simple claret, with cherry character throughout. Light-bodied, with a light finish. Drink now.–J.S. • $22 • (1/01/1999) • **80**

PATACHE D'AUX, CHATEAU

Médoc 1997: Pretty berry and tobacco character. Medium-bodied, with a good core of fruit and silky tannins. Delicious. Drink now through 2004.–J.S. • $NA • (1/31/2000) • **85**

Médoc 1996: Bright and aromatic, with berries, strawberries and cream on the nose and palate. Medium-bodied, with fine tannins and a fruity aftertaste. A bit lean in the end, but a pretty wine still. Best after 2000.–J.S. • $14 • (1/31/1999) • **87**

Médoc 1995 • $12 • (1/31/1998) • **83**

Médoc 1994 • $NA • (1/31/1997) • **80**

Médoc 1989: Slightly funky, but a pleasant, totally ready wine. Dark-ruby in color. Berry, tomato and chestnut aromas. Medium-bodied, with berry, earthy flavors and a velvety tannin structure.—1989 Bordeaux horizontal. Drink now.–J.S. • $NA • (5/31/1999) • **84**

Médoc 1988 • $21 (A) • (4/30/1991) • **80**

Médoc 1982: Dark ruby color, with a brick hue. Bright berry aromas, with a hint of earth. Medium-bodied, with berry, tobacco flavors and a slightly drying, tannic finish. Drink now or never.—1982 Bordeaux horizontal.–J.S. • $NA • (11/30/1998) • **84**

PATISSIER, G.

St.-Amour Vignoble Les Poulets 1994 • $13 • (10/31/1995) • **81**

PATISSIER, P.

Juliénas 1994 • $10 • (10/31/1995) • **88**

PATRIARCHE PERE & FILS

Hautes-Côtes de Nuits Cuvée Varache 1989 • $11 • (1/31/1992) • **81**
Mâcon-Villages Cuvée Pierre Bontemps 1995 • $11 • (5/31/1997) • **80**

PATRICK, BARON

Chablis Premier Cru 1995 • $32 • (6/15/1997) • **82**

PAUILLAC DE CHATEAU LATOUR

Pauillac 1999: Lovely berry and cherry character, with light to medium body. Fresh tannins and fruit.–J.S. • $NA • (1/01/2000) (BT) • **80-84**
Pauillac 1990 • $NA • (3/31/1993) • **89**

PAVELOT

Corton-Charlemagne 1997: An elegant, supple '97, showing a minerally, creamy texture, with hints of lemon, green apple and pear. Balanced, clean finish. Drink now through 2007.–P.M. • $85 • (5/31/1999) • **87**
Pernand-Vergelesses White 1997: This exuberant, clean, medium-bodied Chardonnay is sheer pleasure. Very fresh and fruity, balanced between the wet earth, tropical and lemon notes. Long, lively, vibrant, lemon-spiked finish. Enjoy! Drink now through 2001.–P.M. • $28 • (5/31/1999) • **90**

PAVELOT, JEAN-MARC

Pernand-Vergelesses Les Vergelesses 1991 • $NA • (1/31/1994) • **81**
Savigny-lès-Beaune 1993 • $22 • (11/15/1995) • **85**
Savigny-lès-Beaune 1992 • $NA • (12/15/1994) • **84**
Savigny-lès-Beaune 1991 • $20 • (1/31/1994) • **80**
Savigny-lès-Beaune 1990 • $22 • (12/15/1992) • **89**
Savigny-lès-Beaune 1986 • $18 • (10/15/1989) • **84**
Savigny-lès-Beaune Aux Gravains 1996: Spicy and bright, showing berry, currant and anise notes on a juicy texture backed by lively acidity, turning just a hint tough on the finish. Moderate length. Drink now through 2003.–B.S. • $30 • (1/01/2000) • **84**
Savigny-lès-Beaune Aux Gravains 1995: Rather big-boned and somewhat chunky for now, this medium- to-full-bodied Pinot offers good varietal character with black cherry, some plum and currant, but also cedar and oaky accents that seem a bit tough now. Drink through 2005–P.M. • $29 • (8/31/1998) • **87**
Savigny-lès-Beaune Aux Gravains 1994 • $20 • (11/15/1996) • **89**
Savigny-lès-Beaune Aux Gravains 1993 • $30 • (11/15/1995) • **89**
Savigny-lès-Beaune Aux Gravains 1992 • $NA • (12/15/1994) • **80**
Savigny-lès-Beaune Aux Gravains 1991 • $24 • (1/31/1994) • **81**
Savigny-lès-Beaune Aux Guettes 1996: Warm, rich and spicy, offering broad, meaty flavors of plum, cherry and licorice. Good length and aftertaste. Drink now through 2003.–B.S. • $33 • (1/01/2000) • **85**
Savigny-lès-Beaune Aux Guettes 1993 • $28 • (11/15/1995) • **90**
Savigny-lès-Beaune Aux Guettes 1992 • $NA • (12/15/1994) • **85**
Savigny-lès-Beaune Aux Guettes 1991 • $24 • (1/31/1994) • **86**
Savigny-lès-Beaune Aux Guettes 1990 • $33 • (12/15/1992) • **92**
Savigny-lès-Beaune Aux Guettes 1985 • $20 • (2/15/1988) • **89**
Savigny-lès-Beaune La Dominode 1995: Red Burgundy in a sophisticated, new-wave style, showing a nice touch of oak integrating the crisp, enticing tar, cassis, black cherry and plum. Concentrated midpalate and loads of refined tannins. Classy finish. Drink through 2005–P.M. • $30 • (8/31/1998) • **88**
Savigny-lès-Beaune La Dominode 1994 • $22 • (11/15/1996) • **80**
Savigny-lès-Beaune La Dominode 1993 • $28 • (11/15/1995) • **90**
Savigny-lès-Beaune La Dominode 1992 • $NA • (12/15/1994) • **86**
Savigny-lès-Beaune La Dominode 1991 • $27 • (1/31/1994) • **78**
Savigny-lès-Beaune Les Narbantons 1995: Full of finesse, delicate and flavorful, with clean, pure fruit that shows lovely ripeness on the midpalate. Violet, rose petal and tar aromas blend with plum, cherry and wet earth notes in a smooth-tannin package. Not a blockbuster, but pleasant on the lush finish. Drink now through 2003.–P.M. • $26 • (8/31/1998) • **89**
Savigny-lès-Beaune Les Narbantons 1994 • $18 • (11/15/1996) • **82**
Savigny-lès-Beaune Les Narbantons 1993 • $29 • (11/15/1995) • **87**
Savigny-lès-Beaune Les Narbantons 1992 • $NA • (12/15/1994) • **82**
Savigny-lès-Beaune Les Narbantons 1991 • $24 • (1/31/1994) • **84**

PAVIE, CHATEAU

St.-Emilion 1999: What a nose—superripe fruit with violet and crushed berry undertones. Full-bodied, with velvety tannins and a pretty finish.–J.S. • $NA • (1/01/2000) (BT) • **90-94**
St.-Emilion 1998: Raspberry and grape-skin aromas, with hints of minerals. Medium- to full-bodied, with silky tannins and a long, sweet fruit finish. Lacks some complexity, but almost outstanding.–J.S. • $NA • (5/31/1999) (BT) • **85-89**
St.-Emilion 1996: A light red for early drinking, with silky tannins and berry, tobacco aromas and flavors. Medium- to light-bodied. Disappointing from Pavie. Drink now.–J.S. • $93 Ⓐ • (1/31/1999) • **82**
St.-Emilion 1995 • $47 Ⓐ • (1/31/1998) • **88**
St.-Emilion 1994 • $29 Ⓐ • (1/31/1997) • **82**
St.-Emilion 1993 • $30 Ⓐ • (1/31/1996) • **88**
St.-Emilion 1992 • $30 • (4/15/1995) • **82**
St.-Emilion 1990 • $63 Ⓐ • (3/31/1993) • **94**
St.-Emilion 1989: All elegance and fine texture. Beautiful aromas of milk chocolate and ripe berries. Full- to medium-bodied, with silky tannins and a sweet fruit, chocolate aftertaste. Hard to resist now. (1989 Bordeaux horizontal tasting). Best after 2000.–J.S. • $51 Ⓐ • (5/31/1999) • **90**
St.-Emilion 1988: Very mature for its age, this has light aroma of leaves and fruit. Medium- to light-bodied, with medium tannins and a dry, astringent finish. A bit disappointing. (1988 Bordeaux horizontal tasting). Drink now.–J.S. • $41 Ⓐ • (11/30/1998) • **82**
St.-Emilion 1987 • $35 • (5/15/1990) • **82**
St.-Emilion 1986 • $54 Ⓐ • (6/30/1989) • **93**
St.-Emilion 1985 • $59 Ⓐ • (10/15/1994) • **91**
St.-Emilion 1983 • $44 Ⓐ • (10/15/1994) • **90**
St.-Emilion 1982: Youthful ruby color, with a garnet edge. Floral and perfumed, with a berry undertone on the nose. Medium-bodied, with fine tannins and a pretty, straightforward fruit aftertaste. A very good bottle but not the outstanding wine I have tasted in the past. (1982 Bordeaux horizontal tasting). Drink now.–J.S. • $103 Ⓐ • (11/30/1998) • **88**
St.-Emilion 1981 • $35 Ⓐ • (10/15/1994) • **89**
St.-Emilion 1979 • $45 Ⓐ • (10/15/1989) • **86**
St.-Emilion 1970 • $43 Ⓐ • (5/15/1993) • **89**
St.-Emilion 1961 • $131 Ⓐ • (4/30/1996) • **78**
St.-Emilion 1947 • $160 Ⓐ • (5/31/1997) • **86**

PAVIE-DECESSE, CHATEAU

St.-Emilion 1999: A serious wine, with lots of berry, cherry and milk chocolate character. Medium- to full-bodied, with soft, well-integrated tannins and a long, fruity finish.–J.S. • $NA • (1/01/2000) (BT) • **90-94**
St.-Emilion 1998: Impressive color and velvety, polished tannins, but needs more of a center palate to rate outstanding. Medium- to full-bodied. Where's the finish?–J.S. • $NA • (5/31/1999) (BT) • **85-89**
St.-Emilion 1997: Seriously good. Lots of blackberry, vanilla and tobacco character on the nose. Medium- to full-bodied, with velvety tannins and a long finish of polished texture. Finely crafted wine. Best after 2000.–J.S. • $65 • (1/31/2000) • **90**
St.-Emilion 1996: Diluted, like many other '96s. Some berry and tobacco character, with light body and delicate tannins. Disappointing for this estate. Drink now.–J.S. • $30 • (1/31/1999) • **80**
St.-Emilion 1995 • $28 • (1/31/1998) • **91**
St.-Emilion 1994 • $25 • (1/31/1997) • **80**
St.-Emilion 1993 • $24 • (1/31/1996) • **85**
St.-Emilion 1992 • $19 • (4/15/1995) • **84**
St.-Emilion 1990 • $22 • (3/31/1993) • **93**
St.-Emilion 1989: Lively and exciting. Black cherry, violet, dark chocolate character. Full-bodied, with firm silky tannins and a long, fresh and fruity aftertaste. (1989 Bordeaux horizontal tasting). Best after 2004.–J.S. • $NA • (5/31/1999) • **91**
St.-Emilion 1988 • $27 • (3/31/1991) HR • **94**

PAVIE-DECESSE, CHATEAU

St.-Emilion 1986 • $27 • (6/30/1989) • **93**
St.-Emilion 1985 • $22 • (10/15/1994) • **91**
St.-Emilion 1983 • $26 • (10/15/1994) • **91**
St.-Emilion 1982 • $30 • (8/31/1992) • **89**
St.-Emilion 1981 • $22 • (10/15/1994) • **88**
St.-Emilion 1961 • $74 Ⓐ • (4/30/1996) • **87**

PAVIE-MACQUIN, CHATEAU

St.-Emilion 1999: Very fine wine. Impressive aromas of minerals and raspberries follow through to a medium-bodied palate with good tannins and a medium finish.–J.S. • $NA • (1/01/2000) (BT) • **85-89**

St.-Emilion 1998: Serious use of wood, with lots of ripe fruit to boot. Full-bodied yet very balanced, with a complement of fine tannins and a long finish. Unique perfumed aromas in this wine.–J.S. • $NA • (5/31/1999) (BT) • **90-94**

St.-Emilion 1997: Lots of good, bright fruit in this young red, with plum, berry and cherry character. Medium-bodied and chewy, with a medium finish. Best after 2000.–J.S. • $53 • (1/31/2000) • **89**

St.-Emilion 1996: A thoroughly modern St.-Emilion. Dark-colored, with impressive mineral, berry and currant aromas. Medium-bodied and very grapey on the palate, with fine tannins but a slightly hollow midpalate. Tasted twice, with consistent notes. Best after 2000.–J.S. • $42 • (1/31/1999) • **88**

St.-Emilion 1995 • $32 Ⓐ • (1/31/1998) • **93**
St.-Emilion 1994 • $27 Ⓐ • (1/31/1997) • **90**
St.-Emilion 1993 • $18 • (1/31/1996) • **86**
St.-Emilion 1991 • $15 • (3/31/1994) • **78**

St.-Emilion 1989: Balanced, elegant wine. Blackberry, floral and berry aromas follow through to a medium- to full-bodied palate with fine tannins and a fruity, caressing finish. (1989 Bordeaux horizontal tasting). –J.S. • $50 Ⓐ • (5/31/1999) • **90**

PAVILLON, DOMAINE DU

Côte Roannaise 1998: This light, soft red offers bright grape flavors, with hints of herb and cola. It has little tannin, and could be enjoyed slightly chilled, à la Beaujolais.–T.M. • $10 • (6/30/1999) • **78**

PAVILLON BLANC DU CHATEAU MARGAUX

Bordeaux 1998: Has celery, apple and vanilla character, but lacks a bit of freshness. Medium-bodied, with good fruit, but a bit rustic. Drink now.–J.S. • $62 • (2/29/2000) • **84**

Bordeaux 1997: The best white from Château Margaux I have ever tasted. Full-bodied and creamy, with pears and peaches galore and a long, caressing finish. This is all finesse and class. Drink now through 2005.–J.S. • $65 • (9/30/1999) • **90**

Bordeaux 1996: A bit odd really. Aromas of apple, vanilla and light honey, with hints of pear and cellophane. Medium-bodied, with medium fruit and loads of wood on the finish. A bit too much? Hard to get excited about. Drink through 2002–J.S. • $70 • (3/31/1999) • **82**

PAVILLON DE LOUDENNE

Médoc 1996: Some decent berry and vanilla aromas and flavors here, but slightly diluted, with medium body and a short aftertaste. Hard to get excited about.–J.S. • $NA • (2/28/1999) • **77**

PAVILLON LA GRANGE

Margaux 1994 • $22 • (11/30/1997) • **86**

PAVILLON ROUGE DU CHATEAU MARGAUX

Margaux 1999: Delicious and aromatic, with floral, berry and cherry character. Medium body. Medium fine tannins, light finish.–J.S. • $NA • (1/01/2000) (BT) • **85-89**

Margaux 1998: Loads of berry, cherry and vanilla character. Full-bodied and very velvety, with big, chewy tannins on the finish. One heck of a second wine.–J.S. • $NA • (5/31/1999) (BT) • **90-94**

Margaux 1997: Some good berry and cherry character in this young red. Medium-bodied, with firm tannins and a light finish. A bit hollow. Second wine of Château Margaux. Drink now through 2004.–J.S. • $33 • (1/31/2000) • **86**

Margaux 1996: A wine of finesse. Dark-colored, with ripe berry and licorice aromas. Full-bodied, with silky tannins and a smoky, berry and vanilla aftertaste. Second label of Château Margaux. Best after 2001.–J.S. • $43 • (1/31/1999) • **87**

Margaux 1995 • $38 • (1/31/1998) • **91**
Margaux 1994 • $35 • (1/31/1997) • **80**
Margaux 1989 • $32 • (4/30/1992) • **87**
Margaux 1988 • $30 • (4/30/1991) • **88**
Margaux 1987 • $19 • (5/15/1990) • **79**
Margaux 1986 • $24 • (6/30/1989) • **84**
Margaux 1985 • $38 • (4/15/1988) SS • **93**
Margaux 1983 • $36 • (6/30/1987) • **80**

Margaux 1982: A warm, rich and cuddly wine. Wonderful. Dark ruby-garnet. Very fresh cherry, berry and mineral aromas. Full-bodied and rich, with velvety tannins and a long, sweet fruit finish. Drink now or hold. (1982 Bordeaux horizontal tasting).–J.S. • $NA • (11/30/1998) • **92**

Margaux 1981 • $21 • (7/15/1987) • **87**
Margaux 1980 • $20 • (7/15/1987) • **76**
Margaux 1979 • $NA • (7/15/1987) • **78**

PAYSAGE

Chardonnay Vin de Pays d'Oc Galet Vineyards 1996 • $9 • (8/31/1997) • **80**
Merlot Vin de Pays d'Oc Caillou Vineyards 1994 • $10 • (7/31/1996) • **84**
Merlot Vin de Pays d'Oc Caillou Vineyards 1993 • $10 • (3/31/1995) • **73**
Merlot Vin de Pays d'Oc Galet Vineyards 1996 • $9 • (8/31/1997) • **78**
Merlot Vin de Pays d'Oc Galet Vineyards 1994 • $9 • (7/31/1996) • **80**
Red Vin de Pays d'Oc Galet Vineyards 1993 • $10 • (10/31/1995) • **80**
Syrah Vin de Pays d'Oc Galet Vineyards 1994 • $9 • (7/31/1996) • **76**

PECH DE JAMMES, CHATEAU

Cahors 1989 • $9 • (9/30/1994) • **81**
Cahors 1988 • $10 • (9/30/1992) • **81**

PECH REDON, CHATEAU DE

Coteaux du Languedoc La Clape 1994 • $12 • (5/31/1997) • **84**
Coteaux du Languedoc La Clape 1991 • $10 • (3/15/1994) • **84**
Coteaux du Languedoc La Clape Cuvée Réservée 1995 • $10 • (5/15/1997) • **84**
Coteaux du Languedoc La Clape Cuvée Réservée 1991 • $10 • (3/15/1994) • **81**

PEDAUQUE, LA REINE

Corton Les Renardes 1993 • $50 • (11/15/1995) • **83**
Gevrey-Chambertin 1993 • $25 • (11/15/1995) • **79**
Nuits-St.-Georges 1993 • $25 • (11/15/1995) • **75**
Pommard 1993 • $30 • (11/15/1995) • **80**

PEGAU, DOMAINE DU

Châteauneuf-du-Pape Cuvée Réservée 1997: Round but light, with anise and toasted character, showing some spice and smoke on the medium-long finish. Drink now.–P.M. • $35 • (8/31/1999) • **80**

Châteauneuf-du-Pape Cuvée Réservée 1996: Sweet-tasting, almost like candy, except that it kicks in with nice wet earth, mineral, and gamy notes on the finish, where it turns a bit astringent. Drink now through 2005.–P.M. • $30 • (11/15/1998) • **86**

Châteauneuf-du-Pape Cuvée Réservée 1995: This round, generous red shows an international style, with plump, ripe flavors of plum and black cherry and firm tannins that support the fruit. Clean and balanced, with good definition. Drink now through 2007.–T.M. • $51 Ⓐ • (11/15/1998) • **89**

Châteauneuf-du-Pape Cuvée Réservée 1994 • $27 • (9/15/1997) • **88**
Châteauneuf-du-Pape Cuvée Réservée 1991 • $20 • (10/15/1995) • **89**
Châteauneuf-du-Pape Cuvée Réservée 1989 • $22 • (4/15/1993) • **85**
Châteauneuf-du-Pape Cuvée Réservée 1988 • $17 • (11/15/1991) • **88**

Key: SS—Spectator Selection. CS—Cellar Selection. HR—Highly Recommended. $NA—Price not available. (BT)—Barrel tasting. Ⓐ—Auction Price.
For a key to the tasters' initials, see "How to Use These Listings."
Dates in parentheses represent the issues in which the ratings were published.

PELAN

Côtes de Francs 1997: A delicious and very good '97, with pretty ripe fruit and toasted oak character. Medium-bodied and soft, with medium, velvety tannins and a fruity finish. Drink now through 2004.–J.S. • $24 • (1/31/2000) • **88**

PELAQUIE, DOMAINE

Côtes du Rhône 1997: Seems a bit mature, with floral, rose petal, smoke and anise notes. Rather crisp, with chewy tannins.–P.M. • $10 • (11/15/1999) • **78**
Côtes du Rhône-Villages Laudun 1997: A good little red showing mint, black fruit and delicious spicy notes on the lingering, slightly hot and chewy finish. Drink now.–P.M. • $12 • (11/15/1999) • **82**
Côtes du Rhône-Villages Laudun 1995 • $11 • (10/15/1997) • **74**
Côtes du Rhône-Villages White Laudun 1996 • $12 • (10/15/1997) • **89**
Lirac 1997: Supple and fun, with plum, black cherry and anise. Light-bodied, with modest complexity. Drink now.–P.M. • $13 • (12/15/1999) • **80**
Lirac 1995 • $11 • (10/15/1997) • **84**
Tavel 1996 • $13 • (10/15/1997) • **81**

PELISSIE, FRANCOIS

Cahors Croix du Mayne 1995: This lively, jammy red bursts with red plum and currant flavors, notes of tobacco and leather and a crisp finish. Appealing now, but still quite youthful. Drink through 2003–K.M. • $15 • (6/30/1999) • **86**

PELISSIERE, LA

Bergerac 1997: Powerful and well focused, with red plum, herb and currant flavors and a good dose of tannins on the finish. Pure and crisp, with plenty of stuffing, this wine needs some time to flesh out. Drink through 2003–K.M. • $8 • (12/31/1998) • **85**
Bergerac Sec 1997: This unsung region typically makes simple versions of Bordeaux wines (its neighbor), and this white is no exception. It's round on the palate, yet crisp, with light earthy and herbal flavors.–T.M. • $8 • (12/31/1998) • **78**

PELLE, DOMAINE HENRY

Menetou-Salon Morogues Clos des Blanchais 1996: This bright, crisp white offers vivid aromas and flavors of herb and lime, even hints of pineapple. Light-bodied, with very firm acidity, giving both delicacy and grip. Drink now.–T.M. • $17 • (2/28/1999) • **85**
Menetou-Salon Red Morogues 1994 • $15 • (12/15/1995) • **81**
Menetou-Salon Red Morogues 1987 • $11 • (7/15/1989) • **85**
Pouilly-Fumé 1996: This lively white shows the herb, grass and gooseberry flavors typical of Sauvignon Blanc from the Loire—harmonious from the aroma to the lingering finish. Crisp and clean, it draws you back for another sip. Drink now.–T.M. • $18 • (2/28/1999) • **88**
Sancerre Red La Croix au Garde 1994 • $18 • (12/15/1995) • **80**

PELLETIER & FILS, M.

Nuits-St.-Georges 1994 • $NA • (11/15/1996) • **82**
Nuits-St.-Georges Clos des Argillières 1994 • $NA • (11/15/1996) • **83**

PELOUX, DU

Châteauneuf-du-Pape 1986 • $12 • (4/15/1989) • **85**
Châteauneuf-du-Pape Domaine de Cristia 1997: On the light side, with approachable cherry character, this straightforward red offers a clean finish. Drink now.–P.M. • $24 • (8/31/1999) • **80**
Châteauneuf-du-Pape White Domaine de Cristia 1997: Overdone, with a woody, thick cedar, white plum, apple and butter character. A bit oxidized.–P.M. • $24 • (9/30/1999) • **77**
Côtes du Lubéron Les Bugadelles 1998: Light and fresh in a nouveau style, showing raspberry, cherry and spice. A good, fresh choice for a summer picnic. Drink now.–P.M. • $8 • (11/15/1999) • **81**
Côtes du Lubéron White Les Bugadelles 1998: A wine that grows on you. Crisp but clean, with a lot of lime, green apple and pear flavors. Good concentration on the lingering, sweet-tasting finish. Drink now through 2002.–P.M. • $8 • (11/15/1999) • **83**
Côtes du Rhône 1997: A crisp, straightforward red with some red berry and herbal character.–P.M. • $9 • (11/15/1999) • **76**
Côtes du Rhône White 1998: Something wrong here. Tart paint varnish, oxidized tones. Tasted twice, with consistent notes.–P.M. • $9 • (11/15/1999) • **60**
Crozes-Hermitage Domaine du Veau d'Or 1997: A straightforward red that tastes of fancy oak, but where is the fruit and the regional personality? Lightish and a bit diluted. Drying.–P.M. • $12 • (12/15/1999) • **76**
Grenache-Sauvignon Vin de Pays de Vaucluse Les Chanterelles 1998: A bit simple, with a slight dilution, tasting tart, with lime and green apple notes.–P.M. • $7 • (11/15/1999) • **79**
St.-Joseph 1997: Shows nice wild berry, black cherry, soy and ginger complexity in a medium-bodied envelope that turns smooth and balanced on the peppery finish. Drink now through 2002.–P.M. • $14 • (12/15/1999) • **86**
Syrah-Grenache Vin de Pays de Vaucluse Les Chanterelles 1998: A "nouveau-style" young Rhône, zesty and fresh. Fun to drink slightly chilled, it's an easy and well-made quaff, with pepper and red berry intensity on the juicy finish. Drink now.–P.M. • $7 • (11/15/1999) • **83**

PENA, CHATEAU DE

Côtes du Roussillon-Villages 1995 • $9 • (5/31/1998) • **85**
Muscat de Rivesaltes 1996 • $9/375 ml. • (4/30/1998) • **85**
Red Vin de Pays des Pyrénées-Orientales Cuvée de Peña 1996 • $6 • (4/30/1998) • **81**

PENNAUTIER, MARQUIS DE

Cabernet Sauvignon Vin de Pays d'Oc 1997: A bit diluted, with cherry and syrup flavors.–K.M. • $8 • (12/15/1998) • **76**
Chardonnay Vin de Pays d'Oc 1997: Already declining, this dull white shows nut, earth and dried fruit flavors. Past its prime.–T.M. • $8 • (12/15/1998) • **74**
Chardonnay Vin de Pays d'Oc 1996: A straightforward and simple Chardonnay, with decent apple and citrus flavors. Drink now.–K.M. • $8 • (9/30/1998) • **80**
Merlot Vin de Pays d'Oc 1997: Firm and flavorful, with good plum and berry notes and herbal and tobacco accents on the finish. Straightforward and satisfying. Drink now.–K.M. • $8 • (9/30/1998) • **83**
Syrah Vin de Pays d'Oc 1997: Only modest cherry flavors mark this very light red.–K.M. • $8 • (12/15/1998) • **74**
Syrah Vin de Pays d'Oc 1996: Lean and crisp, with light cherry flavors and herb accents. Very tannic. Drink now. • $8 • (10/15/1998) • **74**

PENSEES DE LAFLEUR

Pomerol 1999: A wine with good plum, tobacco and cherry character. Medium body. Medium velvety tannins. Delicate finish.–J.S. • $NA • (1/01/2000) (BT) • **85-89**
Pomerol 1998: A subtle, fine young wine, not giving much now but showing promise. Full-bodied and compacted, with well-integrated tannins and lovely ripe fruit. Slight dilution in the midpalate.–J.S. • $NA • (5/31/1999) (BT) • **85-89**
Pomerol 1997: Lovely wine. Bright berry, tobacco and wet earth aromas. Medium-bodied, with light tannins and a fruity, tobacco-flavored finish. Second wine of Lafleur. Drink now.–J.S. • $NA • (1/31/2000) • **86**
Pomerol 1996: Attractive berry and mineral aromas and flavors. Medium- to light-bodied, with light tannins and a fresh, fruity finish. Drink now. –J.S. • $100 • (1/31/1999) • **85**
Pomerol 1995 • $75 • (1/31/1998) • **93**
Pomerol 1987: In '87, Lafleur declassified their entire crop into Pensées, their second wine. Surprisingly good, with wet earth, currant and smoke notes in a modest package. Charming and offering decent ripeness. (Château Lafleur vertical tasting). Drink now through 2002.–P.M. • $NA • (1/31/2000) • **83**

PERDRIX, DOMAINE DES

Echézeaux 1997: A rich and ripe red, showing a soft core of tannins and fruit. Delivers blackberry and floral notes in a very pure, clean and vibrant style. Drink now through 2002.–P.M. • $90 • (9/30/1999) • **89**
Echézeaux 1996: Ultrathick and ultradark, full-bodied and very ripe, showing plum, oak, vanilla, toasted bread, mocha and currant accents. Not so classy, but it's a mouthful of a wine, with loads of firm tannins. From Bertrand Devillard. Best from 2005.–P.M. • $86 • (9/30/1998) • **82**
Nuits-St.-Georges 1997: This full-bodied, rich Pinot Noir has wonderfully ripe fruit. The slightly lifted nose—a hint of balsamic vinegar or volatile acidity—that seems to dissipate as you taste the purity of the wine. Drink now through 2007.–P.M. • $49 • (9/30/1999) • **87**
Nuits-St.-Georges Aux Perdrix 1997: Pretty black cherry and vanilla notes turn rich and broad on the palate, leaving an aftertaste of plum and vanilla.

FRANCE

Fine tannins and moderate acidity provide ample structure. Drink now through 2004.–B.S. • $60 • (9/30/1999) • **88**

Nuits-St.-Georges Aux Perdrix 1996: Modern red Burgundy. Ripe, concentrated cassis and blackberry aromas are a bit lifted, the flavors combine with sweet oak, the tannins are firm. Drink through 2005.–B.S. • $55 • (9/30/1998) • **84**

Vosne-Romanée 1997: Attractive aromas of black cherry, chocolate and spice promise more than the palate delivers. Medium-bodied and ready to enjoy, this has freshness and moderate intensity. Drink now through 2002.–B.S. • $50 • (9/30/1999) • **89**

PERE PAPE, DOMAINE DU

Châteauneuf-du-Pape La Crau de Ma Mère 1995: Hard and a bit rustic, but there are also hints of ripe red berry and blackberry underneath the blanket of tannins. Cellar. Best from 2002 through 2007.–P.M. • $NA • (9/30/1998) • **84**

PERLADE, MARQUIS DE

Brut Blanc de Blancs France NV: A simple sparkling wine with herb and apple flavors and a slightly coarse texture. Drink now. • $NA • (10/15/1999) • **78**

PERNOT, PAUL

Bâtard-Montrachet 1998: Full-bodied, with nutty character, showing an oily texture but a tough edge too, and plenty of hard citrus, earth character. Tightly wound right now, giving little away. Best from 2002 through 2010.–P.M. • $150 • (5/31/2000) • **88**

Beaune Les Teurons 1990 • $33 • (4/30/1992) • **90**

Beaune Les Teurons 1988 • $33 • (3/31/1991) • **86**

Bienvenues-Bâtard-Montrachet 1998: Straightforward, crisp style of white. A bit on the dry and tart side; lean and hard.–P.M. • $110 • (5/31/2000) • **78**

Blagny La Pièce sous le Bois 1990 • $33 • (4/30/1992) • **79**

Bourgogne White 1998: Rustic but clean. Shows a grassy, avocado character along with green apple. It's extremely crisp. Drink now through 2001.–P.M. • $15 • (5/31/2000) • **80**

Puligny-Montrachet 1998: A bit sharp, but vibrating with vivid aromas and flavors, from fresh grass to dried herbs and green apple. Lacks complexity, but should cut through saucy dishes. Drink now through 2003.–P.M. • $40 • (5/31/2000) • **83**

Puligny-Montrachet Les Folatières 1998: Soft in texture and a bit tough and green in character. Medium-bodied, with a malic, milky kind of taste folded into some heavily toasted oak notes. Lacks a bit of focus and ripe fruit. Drink now through 2004.–P.M. • $75 • (5/31/2000) • **84**

Puligny-Montrachet Les Pucelles 1998: Impressive. Elegant and medium-bodied, a subtle wine offering spice, mineral, vanilla bean, lemon, dried herbs in a fresh package of wonderful length. Not very intense, but delicious. Drink now through 2006.–P.M. • $85 • (5/31/2000) • **89**

PEROUSE, LA

Chardonnay-Viognier Vin de Pays d'Oc 1996: A straightforward white, offering some decent peach and appley flavors. Contains 81 percent Chardonnay, 19 percent Viognier.–K.M. • $8 • (8/31/1998) • **81**

Merlot Vin de Pays d'Oc 1995 • $8 • (12/15/1997) • **84**

Merlot Vin de Pays d'Oc 1994 • $8 • (7/31/1996) • **86**

Syrah-Cabernet Vin de Pays d'Oc 1996: A rough-hewn red, with plummy flavors and an herbal edge. A bit tough around the edges now, it needs some time to integrate. Best from 1999.–K.M. • $8 • (8/31/1998) • **83**

Vin de Pays d'Oc Cuvée Rouge 1995 • $8 • (12/15/1997) • **84**

Vin de Pays d'Oc Cuvée Rouge 1994 • $8 • (7/31/1996) • **82**

PERRACHON, PIERRE-YVES

Chénas Domaine de la Croix Marzelle 1994 • $13 • (9/15/1996) • **81**

Key: SS—Spectator Selection. CS—Cellar Selection. HR—Highly Recommended. $NA—Price not available. (BT)—Barrel tasting. Ⓐ—Auction Price.
For a key to the tasters' initials, see "How to Use These Listings."
Dates in parentheses represent the issues in which the ratings were published.

PERRAUD, MICHEL

Cornas Cuvée Sarah 1996: Crisp, even tart, of medium body, with cherry, floral and wet earth notes, tough tannins and a sharp finish.–P.M. • $28 • (11/15/1998) • **80**

PERRAUDIN, DOMAINE

Viognier Vin de Pays d'Oc 1996: Cidery-tasting, with notes of fruit cocktail.–K.M. • $14 • (12/15/1998) • **74**

PERRET, ANDRE

Condrieu Coteau de Chéry 1996: Thick and ripe, this unctuous Condrieu charms with its balance and amazing harmony. Laced with honey, almond, spice, pear, grilled pineapple, apricot tart and coconut milk, it remains elegant and dry to the long, powerful finish. Drink now through 2010.–P.M. • $45 • (11/15/1998) • **95**

St.-Joseph 1996: Smells and tastes of freshly crushed raspberries. Lovely wine, medium- to full-bodied, offering a seductive truffle, white pepper, chocolate character that fills the palate and flows to a long, succulent, complex finish. Drink now through 2003.–P.M. • $20 • (11/15/1998) • **90**

St.-Joseph Les Grisières 1996: Racy and refined, packed with delicious flavors—cassis, rose petal, blackberry, cilantro and black olive. Black in color, full in body but elegant in texture, the acidity brings it to a long and harmonious finish that bodes well for aging, although the tannins are supple now. Drink now through 2007.–P.M. • $24 • (11/15/1998) • **93**

St.-Joseph Les Grisières 1992 • $13 • (5/31/1994) • **77**

PERRIER, JOSEPH

Brut Blanc de Blancs Champagne Cuvée Royale NV • $37 • (12/31/1990) • **88**

Brut Champagne Cuvée Royale NV • $19 • (10/31/1997) • **85**

Brut Rosé Champagne Cuvée Royale NV • $45 • (11/30/1997) • **86**

PERRIER-JOUET

Brut Blanc de Blancs Champagne Fleur de Champagne Belle Epoque 1993: Bursting with flavor, this assertive, nicely maturing wine has vivid toasty-earthy aromas, ripe flavors and a rich mousse. Complex nuances of honey, toasted almond and spices linger on the finish. Drink now through 2002. • $150 • (10/15/1999) • **92**

Brut Champagne NV • $24 • (12/31/1994) • **83**

Brut Champagne Blason de France NV • $24 • (12/31/1996) • **81**

Brut Champagne Fleur de Champagne Belle Epoque 1995: There's depth and power here, along with a firm structure underlying the honey, vanilla and bread dough aromas and flavors. Seems to be on the dry side, but that may just be very high acidity. Fine length. Drink now through 2003.–B.S. • $117 • (2/29/2000) • **91**

Brut Champagne Fleur de Champagne Belle Epoque 1990: A grand, traditional Champagne in the best sense. Full-bodied, beautifully balanced and luxuriously smooth in texture, offering subtle, complex accents of toasted almond to complement the base of fine fruit flavor. Drink now through 2003. • $88 Ⓐ • (12/15/1998) • **94**

Brut Champagne Grand Brut NV: Great balance and a lingering finish mark this zesty, full-flavored brut as something special. Rich in fruit flavor, crisp in balance, with an underlying tangy quality that begs for another sip. Drink now. • $27 • (12/31/1998) • **89**

Brut Rosé Champagne Blason de France NV • $50 • (12/31/1996) • **84**

Extra Dry Champagne Cuvée Spéciale NV • $30 • (12/31/1992) • **84**

PERRIERE, DOMAINE DE LA

Coteaux du Languedoc Cuvée Prestige 1994 • $10 • (5/31/1998) • **80**

Merlot Vin de Pays d'Oc 1995 • $7 • (5/31/1998) • **84**

PERRIN, DOMAINES

Côtes du Rhône Réserve 1997: A juicy red in a "nouveau style," bursting with fresh and fruity raspberry and cherry aromas and flavors. Delicious served slightly chilled. Drink now.–P.M. • $11 • (11/15/1999) • **82**

Côtes du Rhône White Réserve 1998: Light but pleasant, showing a good tropical, lime and grassy freshness. Fun to drink thanks to its balance. Drink now.–P.M. • $11 • (11/15/1999) • **84**

Crozes-Hermitage 1997: Rich and ripe, a supple wine that shows earth, blackberry, leather, smoke and black pepper character. Balanced and just lovely to drink. Thick in texture, with smooth, sweet tannins. Drink now through 2003.–P.M. • $22 • (12/15/1999) • **89**

PERRIN, PIERRE

Gigondas 1995: Light in color and texture, very earthy and herbal. Bitter, short finish. Not recommended. Tasted twice, with consistent notes.–P.M. • $23 • (11/15/1998) • **65**

PERRIN RESERVE

Côtes du Rhône 1996 • $10 • (10/15/1997) • **85**
Côtes du Rhône 1995 • $10 • (10/15/1997) • **88**
Côtes du Rhône 1994 • $10 • (10/15/1996) • **86**
Côtes du Rhône White 1996 • $10 • (10/15/1997) • **83**

PERRON, CHATEAU DE

Madiran 1997: Suave, with plenty of dark plum, cassis and spice flavors that coat the tongue. Oak and spice dominate the finish. Drink now through 2004.–K.M. • $10 • (6/15/2000) • **87**
Madiran 1995: A powerful, full-bodied red with plum and cherry flavors and some pleasant herbal accents, joined by leathery and spicy notes on the long finish. Well concentrated. Though delicious, it's a bit heavy to drink now. Drink through 2005–K.M. • $12 • (8/31/1998) • **89**

PERROT-MINOT, HENRI

Chambolle-Musigny 1990 • $32 • (3/15/1994) • **82**
Chambolle-Musigny La Combe d'Orveau 1991 • $45 • (3/15/1994) • **74**
Charmes-Chambertin 1996: Beautiful from start to finish, bursting at the seams with clean and fresh berry flavors accented by toasted oak and spicy notes that give complexity. Refined tannins make it accessible young. Delicious, if not as impressive as when tasted from barrel. Drink now through 2005.–P.M. • $NA • (2/28/1999) • **89**
Charmes-Chambertin 1991 • $50 • (3/15/1994) • **85**
Morey-St.-Denis En la Rue de Vergy 1992 • $27 • (5/15/1995) HR • **89**
Morey-St.-Denis En la Rue de Vergy 1990 • $25 • (3/15/1994) • **87**
Morey-St.-Denis La Riotte 1990 • $40 • (12/31/1993) • **86**
Morey-St.-Denis La Riotte Premier Cru 1992 • $35 • (5/15/1995) • **86**

PESQUIER, DOMAINE DU

Côtes du Rhône 1991 • $10 • (6/15/1993) • **82**
Côtes du Rhône 1990 • $10 • (4/15/1993) • **83**
Côtes du Rhône Cuvée de la Principauté 1996: Light, simple but clean; a little red with black pepper and red berry character and a juicy finish.–P.M. • $10 • (11/15/1999) • **79**
Côtes du Rhône Cuvée de la Principauté 1995: Appealing and flavorful, with deep blackberry, cassis, plum and cherry character. Pure and vibrant, balanced if not complex. A medium-bodied, fun red. Drink now through 2001.–P.M. • $9 • (11/15/1998) • **84**
Gigondas 1996: Lovely aromas and beautiful plum, game, wet earth and smoky vine-wood character. Full-bodied, it kicks in with a slightly chewy tartness on the finish. Drink now through 2001.–P.M. • $19 • (10/31/1999) • **84**
Gigondas 1995: Beautiful, delivering a lovely lead-pencil, mineral, *terroir* character that mingles nicely with roasted nut, leather, cassis and blackberry flavors. Ripe but massive tannins on the finish need time to soften. Best from 2003.–P.M. • $16 • (11/15/1998) • **88**
Gigondas 1993 • $18 • (10/15/1996) • **82**
Gigondas 1990 • $15 • (4/15/1993) • **86**
Gigondas 1989 • $15 • (4/15/1993) • **83**
Vin de Pays de Vaucluse 1998: Ripe and juicy, made in a fresh and exuberant style, showing some plum, black cherry and smoke character. Has grip, with firm but ripe tannins on the finish. Drink now.–P.M. • $8 • (11/15/1999) • **84**

PETERS, PIERRE

Brut Blanc de Blancs Champagne 1995: Crisp and lively in character, but with underlying depth of flavor. Has firm citrus notes and a rather tight texture. Should improve with age, though already enjoyable. Drink now through 2005. • $60 • (10/15/1999) • **90**
Brut Blanc de Blancs Champagne Cuvée de Réserve NV: Generous, expansive and complex. Puts it all together with ripe fruit flavors, toasty, buttery nuances and a velvety texture. Drink now. • $20 • (9/15/1999) • **90**
Brut Blanc de Blancs Champagne Le Mesnil 1992: Full-bodied, rich and expansive in flavor. Tastes nicely mature already, with its array of apple, butter, cinnamon and nut flavors and lingering finish. Drink now. • $34 • (12/31/1998) • **88**
Brut Blanc de Blancs Champagne Le Mesnil 1991: Crisp and lean in style and straightforward in fruit flavor, this is well balanced but austere, making it good refreshment. Drink now. • $36 • (12/31/1998) • **84**
Brut Blanc de Blancs Champagne Millésime 1995: Rich, buttery flavors make this seem mature and complex at a young age. Toasty, nutty nuances blend with a backbone of citrus that keeps it lively. Drink now through 2001. • $53 • (10/15/1999) • **87**

PETIT-FIGEAC, CHATEAU

St.-Emilion 1993 • $22 • (1/31/1996) • **83**
St.-Emilion 1992 • $18 • (4/15/1995) • **80**
St.-Emilion 1990 • $24 • (3/31/1993) • **90**
St.-Emilion 1989: Slightly one-dimensional but shows lovely chocolate and berry character throughout. Medium- to full-bodied, with velvety tannins. (1989 Bordeaux horizontal tasting). Drink now.–J.S. • $NA • (5/31/1999) • **88**

PETIT MOUTON DE MOUTON-ROTHSCHILD, LE

Pauillac 1997: Aromatically lovely. Pretty cherry, berry and vanilla character. Medium-bodied, with silky tannins and a slightly diluted finish. Second wine of Mouton. Drink now.–J.S. • $55 • (1/31/2000) • **83**

PETIT-VILLAGE, CHATEAU

Pomerol 1999: Balanced red. Aromas of plumskin, berry and black licorice. Medium- to full-bodied, with silky tannins and a fresh and fruity finish.–J.S. • $NA • (1/01/2000) (BT) • **85-89**
Pomerol 1998: A cool and tannic wine, with steely structure and compacted fruit. Full-bodied and slightly hard, but shows potential for aging.–J.S. • $NA • (5/31/1999) (BT) • **90-94**
Pomerol 1997: Attractive aromas of fresh berries and mushrooms. Medium-bodied, with velvety tannins and a smoky, toasted oak aftertaste. Delicious. Drink now through 2004.–J.S. • $44 • (1/31/2000) • **88**
Pomerol 1996: Aromas of raspberries and dark chocolate follow through on the palate, but the wine is slightly dry, with firm tannins and a hollow midpalate. Not really up to par for P-V. Drink now.–J.S. • $46 • (1/31/1999) • **85**
Pomerol 1995 • $35 Ⓐ • (1/31/1998) • **88**
Pomerol 1994 • $16 Ⓐ • (1/31/1997) • **88**
Pomerol 1993 • $35 • (1/31/1996) • **86**
Pomerol 1992 • $34 • (4/15/1995) • **84**
Pomerol 1991 • $22 • (3/31/1994) • **75**
Pomerol 1990 • $83 Ⓐ • (3/31/1993) • **92**
Pomerol 1989: Loads of chocolate, berry and tobacco character here. Full-bodied, with firm, chewy tannins, a medium, ripe fruit aftertaste and a touch of coffee. (1989 Bordeaux horizontal tasting). Best after 2005.–J.S. • $67 Ⓐ • (5/31/1999) • **89**
Pomerol 1982: A pretty wine, with sweet, ripe fruit and fine caressing tannins but slightly short on the aftertaste. Medium-bodied, with chocolate, berry flavors. Tasted much better years ago. (1982 Bordeaux horizontal tasting). Drink now.–J.S. • $89 Ⓐ • (11/30/1998) • **86**
Pomerol 1959 • $NA • (10/15/1990) • **86**

PETITE EGLISE, LA

Pomerol 1996: You have to like the berry and chocolate character in this wine. Medium body, with firm tannins and a subtle chocolate and berry aftertaste. Drink now.–J.S. • $22 • (1/31/1999) • **86**
Pomerol 1995: Stunning red. Unbelievable value from Pomerol. Beautiful aromas of ripe berries, earth and bark. Medium- to full-bodied, with super-silky tannins and a long, long aftertaste. From the owner/winemaker of Château L'Eglise Clinet. Best from 2002 through 2007.–J.S. • $55 • (9/15/1998) • **93**
Pomerol 1986 • $15 • (9/15/1989) • **78**

PETITJEAN

Montrachet 1995: Has a supersilky texture but a sulphurlike aroma didn't blow off. Too bad because this seductive white offers lovely fruit and intriguing eucalyptus-minty, dried herb character. Difficult to say if it will improve with cellaring—try from 2005.–P.M. • $NA • (8/31/1998) • **85**

PETITS QUARTS, DOMAINE DES

Anjou White 1998: Bright, high-toned floral aromas give way to juicy apple and quince flavors, with mouthwatering acidity on the finish. Tasty little wine. Drink now.–B.S. • $8 • (6/15/2000) • **87**
Coteaux du Layon 1er Tri 1995 • $15 • (6/15/1997) • **87**

PETRUS, CHATEAU

Pomerol 1999: Good dark ruby color, with plum, grape and berry aromas. Medium-bodied, with good depth of velvety tannins and a long finish. Well done. Very fine.–J.S. • $NA • (1/01/2000) (BT) • **90-94**
Pomerol 1998: This has Renaissance beauty. Voluptuous yet reserved and guarded. Ink-colored. Magnificent aromas of perfume and crushed berries, with hints of earth. Full-bodied, with incredible tannins, yet round and velvety. Another 1989 in the making?–J.S. • $NA • (5/31/1999) (BT) • **95-99**
Pomerol 1997: Shows a solid core of fruit for the vintage. Gorgeous aromas of plums, licorice and toasted oak. Medium- to full-bodied, with silky tannins and a long, fruity finish. Best after 2000.–J.S. • $457 • (1/31/2000) • **90**
Pomerol 1996: A generous, friendly 1996. Dark-colored, with plenty of blueberry, blackberry and chocolate. Full-bodied, with velvety tannins and a fruity, caressing aftertaste. Best after 2003.–J.S. • $522 Ⓐ • (6/30/1999) • **90**
Pomerol 1995 • $751 Ⓐ • (1/31/1998) CS • **98**
Pomerol 1994 • $332 Ⓐ • (1/31/1997) CS • **93**
Pomerol 1993 • $311 Ⓐ • (1/31/1996) CS • **95**
Pomerol 1992 • $267 Ⓐ • (4/15/1995) • **88**
Pomerol 1990 • $1,014 Ⓐ • (3/31/1993) • **98**
Pomerol 1989: An absolute monster of a wine, yet it's agile and refined. This is the 1989. Dark inky color. Beautiful aromas of plums, berries, raspberries and a hint of spice. Full-bodied, with luscious wild berry character and mouth-caressing tannins. So concentrated. So perfect. What more is there to say? (1989 Bordeaux horizontal tasting). Best after 2010.–J.S. • $952 Ⓐ • (5/31/1999) • **100**
Pomerol 1988: Very fine Pétrus. Gorgeous aromas of violet and berry and hints of new oak. Full-bodied, with racy, silky tannins and a long, palate-caressing finish. (1988 Bordeaux horizontal tasting). Best after 2003.–J.S. • $385 Ⓐ • (11/30/1998) • **94**
Pomerol 1987 • $239 Ⓐ • (2/15/1991) • **85**
Pomerol 1986 • $373 Ⓐ • (2/15/1991) • **96**
Pomerol 1985 • $472 Ⓐ • (10/15/1994) • **93**
Pomerol 1984 • $270 Ⓐ • (2/15/1991) • **83**
Pomerol 1983 • $327 Ⓐ • (10/15/1994) • **93**
Pomerol 1982: Brilliant ruby-garnet color. Coffee, berry, dried leather aromas. Medium-bodied, with velvety tannins and ripe fruit and coffee flavors but slightly diluted on the finish. Not showing what it should. This wine is always a minefield; I have had superb bottles and weak ones like this one. Poor cork in this bottle. (1982 Bordeaux horizontal tasting). Drink now.–J.S. • $1298 Ⓐ • (11/30/1998) • **88**
Pomerol 1981 • $383 Ⓐ • (10/15/1994) • **89**
Pomerol 1980 • $254 Ⓐ • (2/15/1991) • **86**
Pomerol 1979 • $288 Ⓐ • (2/15/1991) • **90**
Pomerol 1978 • $306 Ⓐ • (2/15/1991) • **89**
Pomerol 1976 • $295 Ⓐ • (2/15/1991) • **86**
Pomerol 1975 • $609 Ⓐ • (2/15/1991) • **93**
Pomerol 1973 • $207 Ⓐ • (2/15/1991) • **78**
Pomerol 1971 • $716 Ⓐ • (2/15/1991) • **94**
Pomerol 1970 • $852 Ⓐ • (2/15/1991) • **92**
Pomerol 1968 • $460 Ⓐ • (2/15/1991) • **79**
Pomerol 1967 • $465 Ⓐ • (2/15/1991) • **87**
Pomerol 1966 • $561 Ⓐ • (2/15/1991) • **93**
Pomerol 1964 • $877 Ⓐ • (2/15/1991) • **94**
Pomerol 1962 • $835 Ⓐ • (2/15/1991) • **94**
Pomerol 1961 • $NA/1.5 liter • (4/30/1996) • **93**
Pomerol 1959 • $999 Ⓐ • (2/15/1991) • **96**
Pomerol 1958 • $NA • (2/15/1991) • **85**
Pomerol 1955 • $533 Ⓐ • (2/15/1991) • **91**
Pomerol 1953 • $686 Ⓐ • (2/15/1991) • **92**
Pomerol 1952 • $609 Ⓐ • (2/15/1991) • **89**
Pomerol 1950 • $2,328 Ⓐ • (2/15/1991) • **99**
Pomerol 1949 • $1,256 Ⓐ • (2/15/1991) • **98**
Pomerol 1948 • $1,355 Ⓐ • (2/15/1991) • **91**
Pomerol 1947 • $1,709 Ⓐ • (5/31/1997) • **89**
Pomerol 1945 • $3,637 Ⓐ • (11/30/1995) • **88**

PEUY-SAINCRIT, CHATEAU LE

Bordeaux Supérieur Montalon 1995: Intriguing aromas of vanilla, berry and chocolate. Medium- to full-bodied, with lots of soft, velvety tannins and a delicious aftertaste. Hard to resist now. Drink now through 2005.–J.S. • $NA • (9/15/1998) • **86**

PEYBONHOMME-LES-TOURS, CHATEAU

Premières Côtes de Blaye 1994 • $10 • (4/30/1997) • **83**

PEYCHAUD, CHATEAU

Côtes de Bourg 1995: Rather light, with a weedy, berry character. Fine tannins but finishes nowhere. Drink now.–J.S. • $NA • (9/15/1998) • **77**

PEYRADE, LA VICOMTE DE LA

Muscat de Frontignan NV • $10/500 ml. • (8/31/1997) • **88**

PEYREDOULLE, CHATEAU

Premières Côtes de Blaye Maine Criquau 1995: Plenty of blackberries with hints of pepper on the nose. Medium-bodied, with medium tannins and a slightly herbal aftertaste. Drink now through 2003.–J.S. • $NA • (9/15/1998) • **83**

PEYRE ROSE, DOMAINE

Coteaux du Languedoc Clos des Cistes 1995: Powerful, well focused and finely structured, with intense red fruit flavors and spicy, meaty notes. Clean and pure-tasting, with a delicate smoky aroma and an impressive core of cherry, currant and raspberry flavors that build through the finish. Approachable now, but should gain complexity with time in the cellar. Syrah and Grenache. Best from 2001 through 2005.–K.M. • $40 • (6/15/2000) HR • **93**
Coteaux du Languedoc Clos des Cistes 1994: This ripe and rich red fills your mouth with delicious red plum, dark cherry and meaty flavors, with aromas to match. A finely knit wine, with an appealing rustic streak, and enough gamy flavors to give plenty of character. Coffee notes linger on the finish. Drink through 2000–K.M. • $33 • (11/15/1998) • **91**
Coteaux du Languedoc Clos des Cistes 1993 • $27 • (2/28/1998) • **92**
Coteaux du Languedoc Clos Raphaël 1993 • $19 • (3/31/1998) • **84**
Syrah Coteaux du Languedoc Clos Léone 1995: A concentrated and broad-shouldered red, with meat, smoke and leather aromas and flavors plus ripe plum elements. Has plenty of stuffing, with a completely mouthcoating finish of roasted fruit and mochalike flavors. Syrah and Mourvèdre. Drink now through 2004.–K.M. • $40 • (6/15/2000) • **91**
Syrah Coteaux du Languedoc Clos Léone 1994: A big, deep wine with a rich meaty aroma and layers of ripe plum, dark cherry and bacony flavors. Has all the stuffing and the trimmings besides, from the thick texture to the sophisticated tannins and almost decadent flavors. An amazingly concentrated wine that's full of character. Drink through 2005–K.M. • $33 • (11/15/1998) • **93**
Syrah Coteaux du Languedoc Clos Léone 1993 • $26 • (10/31/1997) • **85**

PEYROS, CHATEAU

Madiran 1994 • $12 • (5/15/1998) • **79**
Madiran Le Couvent 1995: Like a cherry pie without the sugar, this powerful red brims with character and packs a wollop, with loads of red currant and red plum flavors and assertive tannins. Tobaccco and herb flavors linger on the finish. Balanced, but needs time. Drink through 2004–K.M. • $24 • (6/30/1999) • **88**

Key: SS—Spectator Selection. CS—Cellar Selection. HR—Highly Recommended. $NA—Price not available. (BT)—Barrel tasting. Ⓐ—Auction Price.
For a key to the tasters' initials, see "How to Use These Listings."
Dates in parentheses represent the issues in which the ratings were published.

PEYROU, CHATEAU

Côtes de Castillon 1995 • $10 • (1/31/1998) • **84**

PEZ, CHATEAU DE

St.-Estèphe 1998: There's a solid core of currant and green tobacco-flavored fruit in this '98. Medium-bodied, with firm tannins and a medium finish. –J.S. • $NA • (5/31/1999) (BT) • **85-89**
St.-Estèphe 1997: Attractive berry, cedar, tobacco character. Medium-bodied, with medium, fine tannins and a fruity, delicate finish. Drink now through 2003.–J.S. • $NA • (1/31/2000) • **85**
St.-Estèphe 1996: Grapey, with light hints of blackberry. Medium-bodied, with some berry flavors, but short and dry on the finish. Tasted twice, with consistent notes.–J.S. • $18 • (1/31/1999) • **80**
St.-Estèphe 1995: A beauty, with violet, berry and cherry aromas. Full-bodied yet reserved, with sleek, silky tannins. Really lovely. Best from 2001 through 2005.–J.S. • $24 • (9/15/1998) • **88**
St.-Estèphe 1994 • $15 • (1/01/1997) • **87**
St.-Estèphe 1990 • $40 Ⓐ • (3/31/1993) • **93**
St.-Estèphe 1989: A delicious and balanced wine for current drinking. Aromas of berry, vanilla and chocolate follow through to a medium-bodied palate with fine tannins and a caressing finish.—1989 Bordeaux horizontal.–J.S. • $27 Ⓐ • (5/31/1999) • **89**
St.-Estèphe 1988 • $19 • (6/15/1991) • **83**
St.-Estèphe 1986 • $24 Ⓐ • (6/30/1989) • **90**
St.-Estèphe 1985 • $29 Ⓐ • (6/30/1988) • **90**
St.-Estèphe 1982: Medium-ruby in color, with a garnet edge. Delicate berry and wet earth aromas. Medium-bodied, with slightly high acidity and a dry finish. I have had better bottles (1982 Bordeaux horizontal tasting). Drink now.–J.S. • $37 Ⓐ • (11/30/1998) • **84**
St.-Estèphe 1961 • $93 Ⓐ • (4/30/1996) • **85**

PHELAN-SEGUR, CHATEAU

St.-Estèphe 1999: Pretty violet, berry and cherry aromas. Medium-bodied, with firm tannins and a medium finish. Slight dilution at the end.–J.S. • $NA • (1/01/2000) (BT) • **85-89**
St.-Estèphe 1998: A bit lean, but shows some very good mineral and berry character. Medium-bodied, with firm tannins and a medium finish. Balanced wine for the vintage.–J.S. • $NA • (5/31/1999) (BT) • **85-89**
St.-Estèphe 1997: Delicious wine with good berry and chocolate character. Medium-bodied, with silky tannins and a light finish. Drink now.–J.S. • $16 Ⓐ • (1/31/2000) • **87**
St.-Estèphe 1996: This is not a blockbuster, but it is a delicious bottle. Beautiful chocolate and berry character. Medium-bodied, with a good core of fruit and velvety tannins. Medium finish. Best after 2001.–J.S. • $22 Ⓐ • (1/31/1999) • **88**
St.-Estèphe 1995 • $25 Ⓐ • (1/31/1998) • **88**
St.-Estèphe 1994 • $20 Ⓐ • (1/31/1997) • **86**
St.-Estèphe 1993 • $20 • (1/31/1996) • **84**
St.-Estèphe 1992 • $17 • (4/15/1995) • **85**
St.-Estèphe 1991 • $15 • (3/31/1994) • **85**
St.-Estèphe 1990 • $43 Ⓐ • (3/31/1993) • **91**
St.-Estèphe 1989: A very pretty red for current drinking. Ruby-colored center, and a brick-red edge. Plenty of berry and chocolate aromas. Medium-bodied, with fine, silky tannins and a long, ripe plum aftertaste. Delicious now but can hold for years.—1989 Bordeaux horizontal. Drink now through 2006.–J.S. • $36 Ⓐ • (5/31/1999) • **88**
St.-Estèphe 1988 • $26 Ⓐ • (7/15/1991) • **87**
St.-Estèphe 1987 • $16 • (11/30/1989) • **82**
St.-Estèphe 1986 • $20 • (11/30/1989) • **86**
St.-Estèphe 1982: Medium-ruby color, with a garnet edge. Cherry and fresh mushroom aromas. Medium-bodied, with silky tannins and a light, delicate finish. Peaked; drink now. (1982 Bordeaux horizontal tasting).–J.S. • $37 Ⓐ • (11/30/1998) • **87**
St.-Estèphe 1961 • $42 • (4/30/1996) • **84**

PHILIPPONNAT

Brut Champagne Grand Blanc 1991: Crisp and focused, typical of the '91 vintage, this offers some mature toast and nut aromas and flavors, citrusy acidity and a lingering finish. Drink now through 2002.–B.S. • $42 • (2/29/2000) • **88**
Brut Champagne Grand Blanc 1990: Full of flavor and cushy as a pillow in texture, this Champagne is welcoming to sip and easy to swallow. It features butter, vanilla and lemon flavors, a rich effervescence and a lingering finish. Drink now. • $49 • (12/31/1998) • **89**
Brut Champagne Le Reflet NV • $40 • (11/15/1997) • **89**
Brut Champagne Le Reflet du Millénaire NV: Initially forward, this Champagne shows nut and fruit confit aromas and flavors, round and rich on entry before turning crisp, with a firm finish. Drink now through 2002. –B.S. • $39 • (2/29/2000) • **88**
Brut Champagne Royale Réserve NV: A lean, dryish Champagne, tasting of marmalade and honey, with a lively texture and structure. Try as an aperitif. Drink now.–B.S. • $33 • (2/29/2000) • **86**
Brut Rosé Champagne Réserve NV: Soft and easy to drink, this mature, well-rounded Champagne has ripe fruit flavors and honeyed accents. Smooth in texture and slightly sweet on the finish. Drink now. • $36 • (12/31/1998) • **86**

PIA

Grenache Vin de Pays Catalan 1998: Juicy and fruity, with berry and ripe plum flavors, like a young Beaujolais. Good with barbecue. Drink now.–K.M. • $13 • (8/31/1999) • **84**

PIADA, CHATEAU

Barsac 1991 • $NA • (4/15/1995) • **86**
Barsac 1990 • $NA • (4/15/1995) • **93**
Barsac 1989 • $NA • (4/15/1995) • **91**
Barsac 1988 • $NA • (4/15/1995) • **87**
Barsac 1987 • $35 • (3/31/1991) • **86**
Barsac 1986 • $NA • (4/15/1995) • **83**
Barsac 1983 • $11 • (4/15/1995) • **84**

PIAUGIER, DOMAINE DE

Côtes du Rhône 1996: Light and straightforward, with some cedar, smoke, grilled meat, herbal and strawberry flavors. A bit dry on the finish.–P.M. • $10 • (11/15/1998) • **75**
Côtes du Rhône 1995 • $10 • (10/15/1997) • **77**
Côtes du Rhône-Villages Sablet 1997: Some spice, mocha and smoke mingle with black pepper and red berry notes in this medium-bodied, medium-ripe, pleasant Rhône. Drink now.–P.M. • $16 • (11/15/1999) • **82**
Côtes du Rhône-Villages Sablet Les Briguières 1994 • $16 • (10/15/1997) • **79**
Côtes du Rhône-Villages Sablet Montmartel 1997: Wonderful. A bit horsey and earthy, but it's round and almost full-bodied, delivering plum, black pepper and black fruit. An interesting tannic and authentic Southern Rhône taste is as appealing as Provençal, garlic-scented food. Drink now through 2002.–P.M. • $18 • (12/15/1999) • **86**
Côtes du Rhône-Villages Sablet Montmartel 1995: Herbal juice, diluted, metallic, difficult to like.–P.M. • $16 • (11/15/1998) • **70**
Côtes du Rhône-Villages Sablet Montmartel 1994 • $16 • (10/15/1997) • **83**
Côtes du Rhône-Villages Sablet Montmartel 1990 • $10 • (4/15/1993) • **84**
Côtes du Rhône-Villages Sablet Ténébi 1995: Rustic, this is tough to enjoy now, but it gained with 24 hours aeration, turning quite round and velvety, so perhaps there is hope.–P.M. • $16 • (11/15/1998) • **77**
Côtes du Rhône-Villages Sablet Ténébi 1994 • $17 • (10/15/1997) • **82**
Côtes du Rhône-Villages White Sablet 1998: Nice ripe fruit balanced by crisp acidity turns this wine into an interesting Provençal white, with beeswax, honey and pear notes. A bit acidic on the finish. Drink now through 2001.–P.M. • $18 • (12/15/1999) • **80**
Côtes du Rhône-Villages White Sablet 1997: Impressive for this appellation. Supple and fat, very rich and just on the dry side of off-dry, showing good balance and lovely floral, mint, pear, citrus character. Drink now through 2002.–P.M. • $16 • (11/15/1999) • **87**
Gigondas 1997: Light and fruity, offering cherry, plum and smoke, with a certain chewy texture. Drink now through 2001.–P.M. • $19 • (10/31/1999) • **80**
Gigondas 1996: Light in color, body and flavor, tasting of modest red berry and drying tannins.–P.M. • $19 • (11/15/1998) • **72**
Gigondas 1994 • $19 • (10/15/1997) • **76**
Gigondas 1990 • $15 • (4/15/1993) • **88**

PIBARNON, CHATEAU DE

Bandol 1996: Quite a mouthful. Concentrated, with nice power to it and deliciously focused flavors of red cherry, leather, ripe plum and cranberry. Peppery and chocolaty notes linger appealingly on the finish. Drink now through 2004.–K.M. • $19 • (10/31/1999) • **87**

FRANCE

PIBARNON, CHATEAU DE

Bandol 1995 • $25 • (5/31/1998) • **88**
Bandol 1994 • $24 • (6/30/1997) • **87**
Bandol 1990 • $23 • (4/15/1993) • **80**
Bandol 1987 • $17 • (3/15/1990) • **75**
Bandol 1985 • $17 • (10/15/1988) • **79**
Bandol 1984 • $NA • (8/31/1986) • **70**

PIBRAN, CHATEAU

Pauillac 1998: There's a pleasant texture to this young red, but it's slightly diluted in the midpalate. Medium-bodied, with a light finish.–J.S. • $NA • (5/31/1999) (BT) • **80-84**
Pauillac 1997: A bit weedy, with berry, herbal character. Light body.–J.S. • $23 • (1/31/2000) • **79**
Pauillac 1996: Starts off better than it ends. Dark-colored, with an impressive intensity of berry and licorice aromas and flavors. Medium- to full-bodied, with velvety tannins, but slightly short on the finish. Best after 2000.–J.S. • $22 • (1/31/1999) • **87**
Pauillac 1995 • $20 • (1/31/1998) • **88**
Pauillac 1994 • $19 • (1/31/1997) • **83**
Pauillac 1993 • $19 • (1/31/1996) • **78**
Pauillac 1992 • $15 • (4/15/1995) • **75**
Pauillac 1991 • $15 • (3/31/1994) • **82**
Pauillac 1990 • $25 • (3/31/1993) • **93**
Pauillac 1989: This is hard to believe, but it's real. Big, young wine. Dark inky color. Intense aromas of blackberry, smoke and meat. Full-bodied and powerful, with loads of velvety tannins and a wonderful intensity of blackberry flavor. (1989 Bordeaux horizontal. tasting). Best after 2004.–J.S.• $NA • (5/31/1999) • **92**
Pauillac 1987 • $16 • (11/30/1989) • **85**
Pauillac 1986 • $18 • (11/30/1989) • **88**
Pauillac 1982 • $18 • (11/30/1989) • **90**

PICARD, CHATEAU

St.-Estèphe 1997: Loads of vanilla and coconut character plus fruit. Medium-bodied, with soft tannins and a fruity finish. Drink now.–J.S. • $23 • (6/15/2000) • **85**

PICARD, MICHEL

Beaujolais-Villages 1996: A light red with cherry and berry flavors that have delicacy but lack depth. Crisp acidity keeps it lively; try chilled, with fish. Drink now.–T.M. • $11 • (8/31/1998) • **79**
Cabernet Sauvignon Vin de Pays d'Oc 1996 • $10 • (12/31/1997) • **83**
Chablis 1996 • $22 • (1/31/1998) • **85**
Chardonnay Vin de Pays d'Oc 1997: Opens with appealing pear and apple flavors, but they fade quickly on the coarse finish.–K.M. • $10 • (4/30/2000) • **79**
Chardonnay Vin de Pays d'Oc 1996 • $10 • (5/31/1998) • **82**
Châteauneuf-du-Pape 1998: A nouveau-styled Châteauneuf that doesn't really work. This young-tasting, fresh red tastes mostly of raspberries and cherries, delivering modest complexity. Tannic finish.–P.M. • $19 • (12/15/1999) • **78**
Châteauneuf-du-Pape 1997: Smooth, medium-bodied, it's pleasantly fruity but lacks a bit of intensity and length. Approachable now through 2000–P.M. • $23 • (8/31/1999) • **82**
Châteauneuf-du-Pape 1996 • $23 • (5/15/1998) • **87**
Côtes du Rhône 1997: Crisp style, with some red berry and a citrusy, broccolilike character. Chewy finish.–P.M. • $11 • (11/15/1999) • **79**
Côtes du Rhône 1996 • $11 • (5/15/1998) • **83**
Mâcon-Villages 1996 • $12 • (1/31/1998) • **83**
Merlot Vin de Pays d'Oc 1996 • $10 • (12/31/1997) • **82**
Pouilly-Fuissé 1996 • $24 • (1/31/1998) • **87**
Syrah Vin de Pays d'Oc 1997: A candied flavor and volatile acidity aroma dominate this lackluster red.–K.M. • $10 • (2/29/2000) • **73**
Syrah Vin de Pays d'Oc 1996 • $10 • (4/30/1998) • **86**

Key: SS—Spectator Selection. CS—Cellar Selection. HR—Highly Recommended. $NA—Price not available. (BT)—Barrel tasting. Ⓐ—Auction Price. For a key to the tasters' initials, see "How to Use These Listings." **Dates in parentheses represent the issues in which the ratings were published.**

Vouvray 1997: The slight sweetness in this white tries to mask the tinny, thin flavors of apple and pear. Not much substance, and the finish is a bit cloying.–T.M. • $12 • (10/31/1999) • **77**
Vouvray 1996 • $12 • (5/31/1998) • **83**

PICCININI, DOMAINE

Minervois 1997: There's good backbone here, with nice cherry and red plum flavors and leather notes, with herb notes on the finish. Not complex, but a good expression of the appellation. Drink through 2001–K.M. • $10 • (11/30/1998) • **84**
Minervois 1996 • $10 • (5/31/1998) • **87**
Minervois 1995 • $10 • (6/30/1997) • **78**
Minervois 1992 • $8 • (6/30/1994) • **75**
Minervois Clos l'Angély 1994 • $12 • (6/15/1997) • **84**

PICHON, CHRISTOPHE

Condrieu 1997: A dry style of Condrieu, showing nice structure, lemony, pebbly, honeyed, minerally character, a very oily, fat mouthfeel and a flinty note on the finish. Lacks a bit of vibrant length. Drink now through 2001.–P.M. • $30 • (8/31/1999) • **87**
Condrieu 1996: Refined, just lovely, with floral, blanched almond, matchstick, earth, fresh peach and apricot flavors, complex and elegant. Medium-bodied, very dry and superbly balanced, it coats the palate but turns a bit tart on the finish. Should go great with rich fish dishes. Drink now through 2001.–P.M. • $38 • (11/15/1998) • **90**
Condrieu Moelleux 1997: Delicious intensity to this Rhône Valley white, with its spice, vanilla, nut, honey, tropical and *terroir* character presented with great finesse. Frankly sweet but refined, it has grip and length that give it class. Drink now through 2005.–P.M. • $38 • (8/31/1999) HR • **95**

PICHON, PHILIPPE

Condrieu 1998: A dry-style Condrieu that's a bit rustic, offering wet hay, wet earth and apple skin. Not much opulence or charm, but it has guts and delivers mineral and *terroir* midpalate. A cold-fruit wine with a chewy finish. No known U.S. importer. Best from 2001 through 2007.–P.M. • $NA • (1/01/2000) • **85**
Condrieu 1997: Wonderfully ripe but balanced by crisp, racy acidity, with beautiful citrus, rhubarb, honey, vanilla, stone and mineral complexity. Great length; just explodes on the palate. No known U.S. importer. Drink now through 2003.–P.M. • $NA • (10/15/1999) • **92**
St.-Joseph 1988 • $22 • (11/15/1991) • **76**

PICHON-LONGUEVILLE-BARON, CHATEAU

Pauillac 1999: A medium-bodied red with lovely spicy cinnamon and ripe fruit character. Well-integrated tannins. Fresh finish.–J.S. • $NA • (1/01/2000) (BT) • **85-89**
Pauillac 1998: A very good wine for the vintage, with lots of firm, polished tannins and a good core of fruit. Medium- to full-bodied, with a silky finish. Almost outstanding.–J.S. • $NA • (5/31/1999) (BT) • **85-89**
Pauillac 1997: Good berry and mineral character, with medium body, fine tannins and a delicate finish. Drink now.–J.S. • $50 • (1/31/2000) • **87**
Pauillac 1996: Marvelous aromas of raspberry, coconut and mineral. Full-bodied, with superbly well-integrated yet powerful tannins. Chewy and fruity finish. Needs a lot of time to mellow. Much better than the barrel samples I tasted. Best Pichon-Baron since 1990. Best after 2006.–J.S. • $78 Ⓐ • (1/31/1999) • **92**
Pauillac 1995 • $98 Ⓐ • (1/31/1998) • **88**
Pauillac 1994 • $47 Ⓐ • (1/31/1997) • **86**
Pauillac 1993 • $36 Ⓐ • (1/31/1996) • **85**
Pauillac 1992 • $28 • (4/15/1995) • **84**
Pauillac 1991 • $27 • (3/31/1994) • **84**
Pauillac 1990 • $110 Ⓐ • (3/31/1993) • **94**
Pauillac 1989: Youthful and gorgeous. Hedonistic. Superyoung ruby, black color. Masses of ripe fruit. Blackberry, cassis and spices. Full-bodied and very soft, with round, caressing tannins and a deliciously fresh berry, plum aftertaste. Hard not to drink it now. (1989 Bordeaux horizontal tasting). Best after 2005.–J.S. • $118 Ⓐ • (5/31/1999) • **98**
Pauillac 1988: A classic new style of Pichon-Baron, with rich, thick, velvety tannins and complex berry, currant and mint character. Full-bodied, it's extremely balanced for showing such impressive power. A real beauty. (1988 Bordeaux horizontal tasting).–J.S. • $76 Ⓐ • (11/30/1998) • **95**
Pauillac 1987 • $25 • (10/15/1990) • **88**

Pauillac 1986 • $122 Ⓐ • (5/31/1989) • **97**
Pauillac 1985 • $101 Ⓐ • (10/15/1994) • **90**
Pauillac 1984 • $23 • (9/30/1988) • **78**
Pauillac 1983 • $110 Ⓐ • (10/15/1994) • **85**
Pauillac 1982: Big surprise. Dark ruby, with a garnet rim. Cassis, berry, tobacco, cherry. Incredibly complex. Full-bodied, incredibly velvety, with masses of fruit, currant, berry, tobacco. Never that highly rated but seriously good. Drink now or hold. (1982 Bordeaux horizontal tasting).–J.S. • $251 Ⓐ • (11/30/1998) • **94**
Pauillac 1981 • $33 • (10/15/1994) • **85**
Pauillac 1980 • $17 • (9/30/1988) • **79**
Pauillac 1979 • $72 Ⓐ • (10/15/1989) • **88**
Pauillac 1978 • $89 Ⓐ • (9/30/1988) • **80**
Pauillac 1977 • $13 • (9/30/1988) • **76**
Pauillac 1976 • $52 Ⓐ • (9/30/1988) • **73**
Pauillac 1975 • $78 Ⓐ • (9/30/1988) • **74**
Pauillac 1974 • $15 • (9/30/1988) • **78**
Pauillac 1973 • $27 • (9/30/1988) • **78**
Pauillac 1971 • $31 • (9/30/1988) • **71**
Pauillac 1970 • $85 Ⓐ • (9/30/1988) • **83**
Pauillac 1969 • $21 • (9/30/1988) • **78**
Pauillac 1967 • $43 Ⓐ • (9/30/1988) • **80**
Pauillac 1966 • $91 Ⓐ • (9/30/1988) • **80**
Pauillac 1964 • $46 Ⓐ • (9/30/1988) • **88**
Pauillac 1962 • $65 • (9/30/1988) • **88**
Pauillac 1961 • $155 Ⓐ • (4/30/1996) • **85**
Pauillac 1960 • $50 • (9/30/1988) • **81**
Pauillac 1959 • $322 Ⓐ • (10/15/1990) • **94**
Pauillac 1958 • $95 • (9/30/1988) • **79**
Pauillac 1957 • $53 Ⓐ • (9/30/1988) • **76**
Pauillac 1955 • $119 Ⓐ • (9/30/1988) • **81**
Pauillac 1954 • $95 • (9/30/1988) • **80**
Pauillac 1953 • $134 Ⓐ • (9/30/1988) • **80**
Pauillac 1952 • $63 Ⓐ • (9/30/1988) • **84**
Pauillac 1950 • $150 • (9/30/1988) • **83**
Pauillac 1949 • $175 • (9/30/1988) • **87**
Pauillac 1947 • $NA • (5/31/1997) • **78**
Pauillac 1945 • $400 • (11/30/1995) • **82**

PICHON-LONGUEVILLE-LALANDE, CHATEAU

Pauillac 1999: A beauty. Violet, mineral, berry and currant aromas. Medium- to full-bodied, with fine tannins and a lovely finish. Fine wine; much better than the '98.–J.S. • $NA • (1/01/2000) (BT) • **85-89**
Pauillac 1998: Not very exciting for this estate. Some interesting berry and herb aromas and flavors, but the palate is slightly hollow. Firm tannin structure.–J.S. • $NA • (5/31/1999) (BT) • **85-89**
Pauillac 1997: A pretty wine, even though it's rather light for this estate. Medium- to light-bodied, with berry, spice and toasted oak character. Soft finish. Drink now.–J.S. • $62 • (1/31/2000) • **85**
Pauillac 1996: Black color, with intense Cabernet aromas of blackberries and currants and hints of mint. Full-bodied and very firm, with silky tannins and a long, flavorful and caressing finish. A racy and well-structured Pichon-Lalande. Best after 2002.–J.S. • $119 • (1/31/1999) • **92**
Pauillac 1995 • $75 • (1/31/1998) CS • **96**
Pauillac 1994 • $NA • (11/15/1997) • **88**
Pauillac 1993 • $NA • (11/15/1997) • **80**
Pauillac 1992 • $NA • (11/15/1997) • **83**
Pauillac 1991 • $NA • (11/15/1997) • **86**
Pauillac 1990 • $NA • (11/15/1997) • **94**
Pauillac 1989: Voluptuous and velvety Pichon. Dark ruby color. Intense aromas of blackberries, fresh mushrooms and dried herbs. Full-bodied, with loads of ripe fruit and velvety tannins. A big, youthful wine that needs time to mellow. (1989 Bordeaux horizontal tasting).–J.S. • $NA • (5/31/1999) • **94**
Pauillac 1988: The more I taste this, the less I like it. It has strange aromas of funk and herbal, green fruit. Medium-bodied, with medium tannins and a fruity finish. (1988 Bordeaux horizontal tasting). –J.S. • $NA • (11/30/1998) • **78**
Pauillac 1987 • $44 Ⓐ • (11/15/1997) • **87**
Pauillac 1986 • $NA • (11/15/1997) • **97**
Pauillac 1985 • $NA • (11/15/1997) • **96**
Pauillac 1984 • $34 Ⓐ • (11/15/1997) • **88**
Pauillac 1983 • $NA • (11/15/1997) • **92**
Pauillac 1982: A voluptuous red. Very dark ruby-garnet. Aromas of currant, meat and berries. Full-bodied and velvety, with lovely ripe berry and earth and a long, ripe finish of caressing texture. This has always been a great wine. I marvel at it each time I taste it. (1982 Bordeaux horizontal tasting). Drink now.–J.S. • $NA • (11/30/1998) • **95**
Pauillac 1981 • $75 Ⓐ • (11/15/1997) • **89**
Pauillac 1980 • $43 Ⓐ • (11/15/1997) • **80**
Pauillac 1979 • $NA • (11/15/1997) • **93**
Pauillac 1978 • $NA • (11/15/1997) • **88**
Pauillac 1976 • $NA • (11/15/1997) • **87**
Pauillac 1975 • $NA • (11/15/1997) • **89**
Pauillac 1970 • $NA • (11/15/1997) • **94**
Pauillac 1964 • $NA • (11/15/1997) • **89**
Pauillac 1962 • $NA • (11/15/1997) • **78**
Pauillac 1961 • $NA • (11/15/1997) • **90**
Pauillac 1959 • $NA • (11/15/1997) • **92**
Pauillac 1957 • $NA • (11/15/1997) • **72**
Pauillac 1955 • $NA • (11/15/1997) • **86**
Pauillac 1953 • $NA • (11/15/1997) • **86**
Pauillac 1950 • $NA • (11/15/1997) • **83**
Pauillac 1949 • $192 Ⓐ • (11/15/1997) • **86**
Pauillac 1947 • $144 Ⓐ • (11/15/1997) • **91**
Pauillac 1945 • $532 Ⓐ • (11/15/1997) • **93**
Pauillac 1942 • $NA • (11/15/1997) • **82**
Pauillac 1940 • $225 Ⓐ • (11/15/1997) • **50**
Pauillac 1937 • $NA • (11/15/1997) • **81**
Pauillac 1928 • $NA • (11/15/1997) • **80**
Pauillac 1922 • $NA • (11/15/1997) • **80**
Pauillac 1920 • $NA • (11/15/1997) • **50**
Pauillac 1914 • $NA • (11/15/1997) • **82**

PICHOT, J.-C.

Vouvray Domaine Le Peu de la Moriette 1998: Candied apple aromas and flavors are sweet and sour, too crisp for dessert yet too cloying for food.–T.M. • $15 • (2/29/2000) • **78**
Vouvray Domaine Le Peu de la Moriette 1996 • $8 • (5/31/1998) • **86**
Vouvray Les Larmes de Bacchus 1996 • $30/375 ml. • (5/31/1998) • **92**
Vouvray Moelleux Domaine Le Peu de la Moriette 1996 • $19 • (5/31/1998) • **84**
Vouvray Moelleux Domaine Le Peu de la Moriette 1995 • $18 • (6/15/1996) • **75**
Vouvray Moelleux Domaine Le Peu de la Moriette Cuvée Exceptionelle 1989 • $19 • (6/15/1991) • **80**

PICO, GEORGES

Chablis Montmains Domaine de Bois d'Yver 1995 • $NA • (6/15/1997) • **86**

PICQ, GILBERT

Chablis 1998: Well made and complex. Intense, with pungent earth, matchstick, flint and smoke character. Medium-bodied and balanced, with a lingering finish. Drink now through 2001.–P.M. • $18 • (5/15/2000) • **85**
Chablis 1996 • $19 • (8/31/1997) • **89**
Chablis Vaucoupin 1998: Supple and ripe. Medium-bodied, with apple tart, pear, dough and smoke flavors and good complexity. Seductive on release. Drink now through 2005.–P.M. • $25 • (5/15/2000) • **86**
Chablis Vaucoupin 1996: Gained in contact with air—went from a fairly straightforward Chardonnay to one of ripe character, with pear, mineral and honey notes. Clean and vibrant, light to medium in body; grew supple as it warmed to room temperature. Best after 2005.–P.M. • $24 • (8/31/1998) • **87**
Chablis Vaucoupin 1995 • $17 • (6/15/1997) • **87**
Chablis Vosgros 1998: Nicely crafted, yet attractively down-to-earth. Medium-bodied, rather tough and linear in style, but the concentration of fruit and mineral gives it a fatness midpalate. An ager. Best after 2004.–P.M. • $25 • (5/15/2000) • **87**
Chablis Vosgros 1996 • $22 • (5/31/1998) • **90**
Chablis Vosgros 1995 • $17 • (6/15/1997) • **82**

PICQUE-CAILLOU, CHATEAU

Pessac-Léognan 1998: Shows lovely sweet fruit character, with plums and berries throughout. Medium-bodied, with fine tannins and a slightly hollow midpalate. May move up next year.–J.S. • $NA • (5/31/1999) (BT) • **85-89**
Pessac-Léognan 1997: Well done for the vintage. Lovely perfumes to this medium-bodied wine, with silky tannins and a fresh fruit finish. Best after 2000.–J.S. • $18 • (1/31/2000) • **85**
Pessac-Léognan 1996: Watery and light-bodied, with berry and tobacco character, fine tannins and a light finish. Drink now.–J.S. • $NA • (1/31/1999) • **80**

PICQUE-CAILLOU, CHATEAU

Pessac-Léognan 1995: A bit rough now but should mellow with age. Bright aromas of blackberries and wet earth with a stony undertone. Full- to medium-bodied, with plenty of tannins and a cassis, dried herb finish. Best from 2001 through 2005.–J.S. • $NA • (9/15/1998) • **87**
Pessac-Léognan 1993 • $25 • (4/30/1997) • **85**
Graves 1982 • $NA • (8/31/1992) • **78**
Pessac-Léognan White 1998: Medium-bodied, with delicious apple, banana and vanilla character and a fresh finish. Drink now.–J.S. • $NA • (2/29/2000) • **87**
Pessac-Léognan White 1997: Slightly candied, with watermelon and fruit cocktail character. Medium-bodied, chalky on the finish. Hard to get excited about.–J.S. • $NA • (9/30/1999) • **79**

PIERRE-BISE, CHATEAU

Coteaux du Layon-Beaulieu Clos de la Soucherie 1997: Tropical flavors of apricot, mango and coconut run through this dessert wine, picking up floral and smoky notes on the open-knit finish. Drink now through 2002.–K.M. • $22 • (5/15/2000) • **87**
Coteaux du Layon-Beaulieu L'Anclaie 1997: An open and inviting nose of clove, orange peel and crème brûlée leads to a plush, expansive palate. The long, juicy finish picks up pretty hints of green gunpowder tea. Drink now through 2002.–K.M. • $24/500 ml. • (5/15/2000) • **90**
Coteaux du Layon-Beaulieu L'Anclaie 1996: Ripe and sweet, this golden wine offers honey, spice and raisin flavors. It has good balance and distinctive character, but it's more expressive than deep. Drink now through 2003.–T.M. • $20/500 ml. • (2/28/1999) • **87**
Coteaux du Layon-Beaulieu Les Rouannières 1997: Focused and coiled like a spring, with a mineral streak keeping the orange peel, honeycomb and apricot flavors in check. Stays stylish through the lengthy finish. Should unwind a bit with short-term cellaring. Best from 2001 through 2004.–K.M. • $28/500 ml. • (5/15/2000) • **91**
Coteaux du Layon-Beaulieu Les Rouannières 1996: Sweet and velvety, this white offers an appealing mix of crème brûlée, vanilla, dried orange and tropical fruit flavors, balanced and fresh, that draw you back for another sip. Has good weight on the palate and good length on the finish. Drink now through 2008.–T.M. • $20/500 ml. • (2/28/1999) • **92**
Coteaux du Layon-Chaume 1996: This white has terrific weight on the palate, is unctuous yet muscular, with assertive flavors of honey, spice, dried fruit and smoke. It's quite sweet, yet finishes on a refreshing bitter note. Has the concentration to improve with time. Drink now through 2008.–T.M. • $18/500 ml. • (2/28/1999) • **92**
Coteaux du Layon-Chaume Le Verger 1997: Shows intense botrytized aromas of orange peel, spice and smoke, with rich, vibrant flavors of clove, nutmeg and honeycomb all kept taut by mouthwatering, live-wire acidity. Textbook for the appellation. Drink now through 2004.–K.M. • $26/500 ml. • (5/15/2000) • **92**
Coteaux du Layon-Rochefort Les Rayelles 1997: This dessert wine shows pretty dried pineapple, cinnamon and pie crust aromas and flavors on a comparatively soft, accessible frame. Lacks the vibrancy of the best examples of the region, but still delicious. Drink now.–K.M. • $23/500 ml. • (5/15/2000) • **88**
Coteaux du Layon-Rochefort Les Rayelles 1996: Sweet and lush, with open flavors of dried orange, vanilla, clove and honey, this is a supple crowd-pleaser with good balance and depth. The texture is silky and the finish is long. Drink now through 2005.–T.M. • $20/500 ml. • (2/28/1999) • **90**
Quarts de Chaume 1997: Gorgeous nectar. Lithe and high-toned, with floral notes atop the concentrated guava, white peach, honey and green tea flavors. Shows admirable finesse throughout despite its obvious density, as the ripe, well-integrated acidity carries it along. Drink now through 2005.–K.M. • $60/500 ml. • (5/15/2000) HR • **94**
Quarts de Chaume 1996: Thick and rich, this sacrifices elegance for power. It's quite sweet on the palate, with an unctuous texture and flavors of bitter almond, clove, honey and smoke. The finish is a bit hot. A big wine that may come around. Best after 2000.–T.M. • $28/500 ml. • (2/28/1999) • **88**

PIGNAN

Châteauneuf-du-Pape Réservé 1995: Offers attractive chocolate and raspberry character, with some toughness on the palate, but comes back with fresh, crisp acidity on the finish. Lacks the opulence and smoothness you'd expect from top '95 Châteauneufs. Drink now through 2002.–P.M. • $70 Ⓐ • (2/28/1999) • **86**
Châteauneuf-du-Pape Réservé 1994 • $30 • (1/01/1998) • **86**
Châteauneuf-du-Pape Réservé 1993 • $29 Ⓐ • (1/01/1998) • **79**
Châteauneuf-du-Pape Réservé 1992 • $25 • (1/01/1998) • **88**
Châteauneuf-du-Pape Réservé 1991 • $28 • (10/15/1994) • **83**
Châteauneuf-du-Pape Réservé 1989 • $27 • (8/31/1992) • **83**
Châteauneuf-du-Pape Réservé 1988 • $30 • (10/15/1991) • **82**
Châteauneuf-du-Pape Réservé 1986 • $29 • (10/15/1991) • **83**
Châteauneuf-du-Pape Réservé 1985 • $38 • (8/31/1987) SS • **95**
Châteauneuf-du-Pape Réservé 1983 • $38 • (10/15/1991) • **85**
Châteauneuf-du-Pape Réservé 1981 • $35 • (10/15/1991) • **94**
Châteauneuf-du-Pape Réservé 1980 • $30 • (10/15/1986) • **87**

PIGUET-GIRARDIN

Santenay La Comme 1994 • $23 • (11/15/1996) • **81**

PILLOT, FERNAND & LAURENT

Bourgogne Aligoté 1997: A bit earthy, but this very crisp white shows good ripeness, with tropical and pear notes. Slightly earthy and astringent on the finish.–P.M. • $NA • (5/31/1999) • **78**
Chassagne-Montrachet 1998: A hate-or-love white Burgundy that's pretty unique. It smells earthily pungent, with a sort of gluelike note, but it convinces on the palate with its thick yet elegant texture, its *terroir* flavor, full body and balanced finish. Give it time. Best from 2002 through 2010.–P.M. • $42 • (5/31/2000) • **90**
Chassagne-Montrachet Grandes Ruchottes 1998: Impressive quality for '98. The intensity of fruit and toasted oak along with a mineral quality start in the aroma and follow through on the thick-textured, balanced midpalate. Full-bodied, with length on the delicious, balanced finish. Drink now through 2006.–P.M. • $80 • (5/31/2000) • **90**
Chassagne-Montrachet Grandes Ruchottes 1997: Lovely balance between a honey, sweet fruit character and some lime and grass flavors. Smoky and toasted notes add complexity to this medium-bodied, balanced white Burgundy. Drink now through 2003.–P.M. • $65 • (2/28/1999) • **88**
Chassagne-Montrachet Les Vergers 1998: Rather lean and tough, but clean and pure with a mineral aroma, this elegant, medium-bodied white Burgundy lacks a bit of generous ripe fruit, but it has enough lime and grapefruit character to cozy up to many dishes. Drink now through 2005.–P.M. • $60 • (5/31/2000) • **83**
Chassagne-Montrachet Les Vergers 1997: Impressive. Focused and intense, full-bodied but not showy, this creamy and silky, yet still shy and undeveloped white offers plenty of wet earth, mineral and honey, and subtle oak. Fat mouthfeel, seductive finish. Drink now through 2007.–P.M. • $50 • (2/28/1999) • **93**
Chassagne-Montrachet Morgeot 1998: A home run. Complex, with *terroir*-driven mineral, smoke, matchstick, wet earth notes, it follows through with rich texture and a lively combination of ripe fruit and moderately toasted oak for a long, balanced finish. Drink now through 2007.–P.M. • $62 • (5/31/2000) • **92**
Chassagne-Montrachet Morgeot 1997: Wonderful white Burgundy, fat and ripe, yet also fresh and lively, offering typical Chassagne character—grassy, slightly herbal and almost green olivelike—along with honey, hazelnut, smoke and toasted bread complexity. Drink now through 2003.–P.M. • $54 • (2/28/1999) • **92**
Chassagne-Montrachet Red Morgeot 1996: Beautiful Pinot Noir aromas, with good depth, showing an intriguing earth, red berry, spice and cinnamon complexity. Medium-bodied, it has a lush midpalate, with fine texture, but turns slightly astringent on the finish. Drink now through 2003.–P.M. • $32 • (2/28/1999) • **87**
Chassagne-Montrachet Red Vieilles Vignes 1995 • $39 • (6/30/1997) • **80**
Chassagne-Montrachet Vide Bourse 1998: Surprisingly unctuous for a '98, and built a bit like a late-harvest Chardonnay. Rich and rather ripe, with a honey and toasted nut character, this is seductively round and smooth. Full-bodied, balanced on the flavorful finish. Drink now through 2003.–P.M. • $70 • (5/31/2000) • **87**
Pommard Rugiens 1996: Excellent *terroir* peeks through in this beautifully crafted, intense, firmly structured '96. Has it all—wet earth, cherry and smoke complexity, refined tannins, smooth texture, at least until the racy and ripe finish. Best from 2001 through 2007.–P.M. • $62 • (2/28/1999) • **90**
Puligny-Montrachet Noyers Brets 1998: Remarkably silky, concentrated—and idiosyncratic. There's an odd matchstick, wet earth aroma that's not for everyone, but once the taste buds get used to the uniqueness of this *terroir* wine it

Key: SS—Spectator Selection. CS—Cellar Selection. HR—Highly Recommended. $NA—Price not available. (BT)—Barrel tasting. Ⓐ—Auction Price.
For a key to the tasters' initials, see "How to Use These Listings."
Dates in parentheses represent the issues in which the ratings were published.

will seem a delightful treasure in the rough, amazingly long and tantalizingly seductive. Drink now through 2010.–P.M. • $53 • (5/31/2000) • **91**

Puligny-Montrachet Noyers Brets 1997: Earthy, with a minerally, smoky, flinty character, this may not be everyone's style, but the wine delivers focused, medium-intense fruit and a fresh finish. Drink now through 2003.–P.M. • $55 • (9/30/1999) • **87**

Volnay 1996: Some cherry and wet earth peek through some unfocused stewed, herbal notes that are unpleasant. Astringent finish, too.–P.M. • $30 • (2/28/1999) • **75**

Volnay 1995 • $39 • (6/30/1997) • **75**

PILLOT, JEAN

Chassagne-Montrachet 1998: Plays some soft notes of toasted oak and ripe fruit. Medium-bodied, with a supple midpalate; turns smoky on the finish. Drink now through 2003.–P.M. • $37 • (5/31/2000) • **84**

Chassagne-Montrachet 1997: A bit green and lean, showing a crisp midpalate, with a tight structure that lacks a bit of ripe fruit. Short finish.–P.M. • $39 • (5/31/1999) • **79**

Chassagne-Montrachet 1996: A full-bodied, rich and ripe '96 with lots of malic, milk chocolate and spice flavors, also some ripe fruit. Smooth, minerally and supple—until the firm, acidic finish kicks in, that is. Needs time. Best from 2002.–P.M. • $NA • (8/31/1998) • **88**

Chassagne-Montrachet 1995 • $28 • (5/31/1997) • **88**

Chassagne-Montrachet Les Caillerets 1998: Not a big wine, but what's there is elegant and anchored in the Burgundian soil. Offers mineral, smoke, dried herbs, honey and ripe fruit, with a nice sheet of toasted oak. Medium-bodied, its grace gains on the lingering finish. Drink now through 2005.–P.M. • $58 • (5/31/2000) • **89**

Chassagne-Montrachet Les Caillerets 1997: This medium-bodied Chardonnay has pear and spice notes, but it's a bit rustic, with a chestnut, chewy, tart mouthfeel.–P.M. • $55 • (5/31/1999) • **79**

Chassagne-Montrachet Les Caillerets 1996 • $50 • (5/31/1998) • **76**

Chassagne-Montrachet Les Champs-Gain 1996 • $38 • (5/31/1998) • **90**

Chassagne-Montrachet Les Champs-Gain 1995 • $35 • (5/31/1997) • **94**

Chassagne-Montrachet Les Chenevottes 1997: Fairly simple and one-dimensional, with modest lemon and green apple character and a chewy, chalky finish.–P.M. • $42 • (5/31/1999) • **77**

Chassagne-Montrachet Les Chenevottes 1996 • $35 • (5/31/1998) • **90**

Chassagne-Montrachet Les Chenevottes 1995 • $33 • (5/31/1997) • **92**

Chassagne-Montrachet Les Vergers 1996 • $38 • (5/31/1998) • **88**

Chassagne-Montrachet Morgeot 1998: Multifaceted '98 that needs time in the cellar to smooth out. Opens with a smoky, meaty, salami character, continues with pronounced toasted oak. Medium-bodied, a bit astringent on the finish, which offers some ripe fruit. Best from 2001 through 2006. –P.M. • $53 • (5/31/2000) • **87**

Chassagne-Montrachet Morgeot 1997: This tough, drying, lean white is cedary, even cardboardy. Where's the fruit?–P.M. • $45 • (5/31/1999) • **72**

Chassagne-Montrachet Morgeot 1996 • $40 • (5/31/1998) • **93**

Chassagne-Montrachet Morgeot 1995 • $38 • (5/31/1997) • **90**

Chevalier-Montrachet 1996 • $150 • (5/31/1998) • **94**

Puligny-Montrachet 1998: Thick and clean, but not very deep. Well made, full-bodied white Burgundy, offering some good acidity and a honeyed smoke and pearlike character. Supple, silky, medium-intense finish. Drink now through 2003.–P.M. • $40 • (5/31/2000) • **87**

Puligny-Montrachet 1997: Crisp and lemony, with tart green apple notes. An ungenerous style.–P.M. • $39 • (5/31/1999) • **76**

Puligny-Montrachet 1996 • $30 • (5/31/1998) • **85**

Puligny-Montrachet 1995 • $30 • (5/31/1997) • **90**

PILLOT, JEAN-MARC

Chassagne-Montrachet Les Vergers 1997: Medium-bodied, with fresh, citrus-spiked acidity, showing green apple, toast, spice and dried herb character. Clean finish. Drink now through 2002.–P.M. • $45 • (5/31/1999) • **87**

Puligny-Montrachet Les Caillerets 1997: *Terroir*-driven, showing wonderful mineral, vanilla bean, lemon and pear character. Lovely in a nonshowy, medium-bodied, clean way. A slight burning taste creeps through on the finish. Drink now through 2005.–P.M. • $NA • (5/31/1999) • **88**

Puligny-Montrachet Les Caillerets 1996 • $NA • (5/31/1998) • **86**

PILONNIERE, CHATEAU DE LA

Brouilly 1997: There's some decent cherry and plum flavor here, but a cardboard note and a dry, astringent finish raise questions. Tasted twice, with consistent notes.–B.S. • $14 • (10/15/1999) • **75**

PIN, CHATEAU LE

Pomerol 1999: A monster. Full-bodied, with loads of soft, ripe tannins and a finish that lasts for minutes. Perhaps as good, maybe even better, than the legendary '98. Clearly the wine of the vintage.–J.S. • $NA • (1/01/2000) (BT) • **95-99**

Pomerol 1998: Exotic and rich young wine, with wonderfully velvety texture and masses of fruit. Full-bodied and long, it really caresses the palate. The best young Le Pin I have ever tasted.–J.S. • $NA • (5/31/1999) (BT) • **95-99**

Pomerol 1997: Weird wine. Very herbal, with stewed berry and rhubarb character. Medium- to full-bodied, with big, velvety tannins but slightly cloying and green on the finish. Drink now.–J.S. • $312 Ⓐ • (1/31/2000) • **84**

Pomerol 1996: Aromas of blackberry and toasted oak follow through to the palate. Medium- to light-bodied, with chocolate and coffee flavors. A slightly diluted finish, although there's plenty of wood at the end. Overall, a bit too much wood for me. Not one of the great Le Pins, but enjoyable. Drink now through 2005.–J.S. • $1208 • (1/31/1999) • **86**

Pomerol 1995 • $582 Ⓐ • (1/31/1998) • **93**

Pomerol 1994 • $347 Ⓐ • (1/31/1997) CS • **95**

Pomerol 1993 • $317 Ⓐ • (1/31/1996) • **90**

Pomerol 1992 • $231 Ⓐ • (4/15/1995) • **74**

Pomerol 1990 • $962 Ⓐ • (3/31/1993) • **97**

Pomerol 1989: Love this rich, decadent style. Tons of coffee, tobacco, cherry and dried fruit on the palate. Full-bodied and very chewy, with a long, long finish containing plenty of ripe, sweet fruit. Slightly high acidity at the end. (1989 Bordeaux horizontal tasting). Best after 2005.–J.S. • $615 Ⓐ • (5/31/1999) • **92**

Pomerol 1988: A voluptuous Merlot, with ripe, wild and very intense fruit aromas and flavors. Full-bodied, with lots of new wood and a round, caressing texture. Can be aged, but really enjoyable now. (1988 Bordeaux horizontal tasting).–J.S. • $390 Ⓐ • (11/30/1998) • **92**

Pomerol 1986 • $602 Ⓐ • (6/15/1989) • **95**

Pomerol 1985 • $775 Ⓐ • (10/15/1994) • **98**

Pomerol 1983 • $800 Ⓐ • (10/15/1994) • **91**

Pomerol 1982: A sexy and exotic wine that starts off slowly but builds on the palate into something extraordinary. Loads of wild, ripe raspberry and milk chocolate aromas. Full-bodied, very velvety, with a long, long aftertaste. (1982 Bordeaux horizontal tasting). Drink now.–J.S. • $1,771 Ⓐ • (11/30/1998) • **97**

Pomerol 1981 • $339 Ⓐ • (10/15/1994) • **91**

Pomerol 1979 • $576 Ⓐ • (5/15/1994) • **90**

PIN BEAUSOLEIL, CHATEAU LE

Bordeaux Supérieur 1999: Serious stuff for Bordeaux Supérieur. Dark purple, with intense aromas of crushed berry, mineral and spice. Medium- to full-bodied, with a solid core of tannins and a medium finish. Chewy.–J.S. • $NA • (1/01/2000) (BT) • **85-89**

PINARD, VINCENT

Sancerre Cuvée Florès 1998: Intense and assertive, this lively white bursts with smoky gunflint and herbaceous flavors backed by very crisp acidity. Not easy on its own, but will energize a meal. Drink now through 2002.–T.M. • $16 • (2/29/2000) • **88**

Sancerre Cuvée Florès 1997: Round and quite ripe, with apple, melon and light earthy flavors and fairly soft acidity. Generous and made in a traditional style. Drink now.–T.M. • $16 • (9/15/1998) • **84**

Sancerre Harmonie 1996: This big, complex white marries crisp acidity, tropical fruit flavors and the vanilla, toasty notes of new oak. Though powerful, it lacks harmony now; should be delicious with a bit of bottle age. Drink through 2004–T.M. • $25 • (9/15/1998) • **90**

Sancerre Nuance 1996: There's an exotic, tropical note here, in addition to a hint of vanilla from new oak to augment the melon and citrus flavors. Round and smooth, with a mouthwatering finish that echoes vanilla.–B.S. • $20 • (10/31/1998) • **88**

Sancerre Red 1997: Light but firm. This red shows straightforward cherry and light spice flavors, but adds toast and vanilla notes that increase depth and sweetness. Drink now through 2002.–T.M. • $17 • (6/30/1999) • **84**

Sancerre Red 1996: Lovely fresh berry aromas are followed by delicate and succulent cherry and berry flavors, a vibrant structure and light yet firm tannins, all well balanced.–B.S. • $17 • (11/15/1998) • **84**

Sancerre Red 1995 • $18 • (6/15/1997) • **85**

PINDEFLEURS, CHATEAU

St.-Emilion 1982: Medium-red, garnet color. Strawberry and fresh mushroom character. Very peppery palate. Dry and lacking. Off-bottle?—1982 Bordeaux horizontal.–J.S. • $NA • (11/30/1998) • **75**

PINEY, CHATEAU

St.-Emilion 1995 • $20 • (1/31/1998) • **81**

PINS, CHATEAU LES

Côtes du Roussillon-Villages 1996: Lots of sweet oak notes in this medium-bodied red, though a bit overdone, with some red plum and berry flavors. Spicy notes linger on the finish. Drink now.–K.M. • $15 • (8/31/1999) • **81**

Côtes du Roussillon-Villages 1995 • $11 • (5/31/1998) • **87**

Muscat de Rivesaltes 1996: A distinctive, sweet wine that's concentrated and fairly rustic. An interesting mix, with flavors of custard, pear and white pepper and a dash of anise and bitter almond. Finishes on a rich note. Drink now through 2002.–K.M. • $10/375 ml. • (12/31/1998) • **87**

PINSON, LOUIS

Chablis 1998: Pretty. A fruity, medium-bodied white, with a ripe, smooth midpalate and a combination of green and dried apple. Turns freshly crisp on the finish, with wet hay overtones. Not imported into the U.S. Drink now through 2001.–P.M. • $NA • (1/01/2000) • **84**

Chablis 1997: Pretty flavorful, with pear and honey, and there is some nice lemon and toasted spice adding length and complexity to the finish. Drink now through 2001.–P.M. • $21 • (5/31/1999) • **88**

Chablis 1996 • $19 • (5/31/1998) • **85**

Chablis La Forêt 1998: Clean and pure, elegant and racy, this is a crisp style of Chablis. Light- to medium-bodied, showing decent green apple and citrus character. Drink now through 2002.–P.M. • $28 • (5/15/2000) • **81**

Chablis Les Clos 1997: Supple, opulent, forward style of Les Clos, delivering plenty of excellent citrus-spiked acidity, some toasted oak and a slight rustic, old barrel character. Drink now through 2007.–P.M. • $34 • (5/31/1999) • **85**

Chablis Les Clos 1996: Pumps out earth and *terroir*, more earth and *terroir*. Fantastic Chablis that could make an aficionado cry with pleasure. So ripe and subtle, full-bodied and ultrarefined, this sexy, hedonistic Chardonnay swirls around the palate with pear, butter, mineral, quince, fig and deftly toasted oak flavors. The silky smooth texture is the hallmark of a top *grand cru*, but the finish remains vibrant. Just be aware that the nose is a bit rustic, funky and earthy. Better than previously reviewed. Drink now through 2010.–P.M. • $35 • (8/31/1998) • **96**

Chablis Mont de Milieu 1998: Polished and elegant, it offers medium-intense fruit complexity, with mineral, smoke and lemon character. Medium-bodied and harmonious on the finish. Drink now through 2002.–P.M. • $28 • (5/15/2000) • **85**

Chablis Mont de Milieu 1997: The pure fruit is pleasant but a certain tough astringency creeps in on the finish in this firm, medium-bodied, minerally Mont de Milieu. Drink now through 2002.–P.M. • $24 • (5/31/1999) • **81**

Chablis Mont de Milieu 1996 • $22 • (5/31/1998) • **93**

Chablis Mont de Milieu 1995 • $23 • (6/15/1997) • **90**

Chablis Montmain 1998: Very woody in style, its perfumy, floral and spicy aromas cover up the fruit, at least for now. Medium-bodied, it lacks a bit of zesty crispness. Best from 2001 through 2005.–P.M. • $28 • (5/15/2000) • **83**

Chablis Montmain 1997: A bit odd, with popcorn and butterscotch notes pushing aside the fruit; full-bodied and ripe, it's slightly unbalanced, with an astringent finish.–P.M. • $23 • (5/31/1999) • **78**

PIPER-HEIDSIECK

Brut Champagne NV: A sunny, fruit-driven brut, with lively citrus and apple flavors and an expansive texture. Drink now. • $30 • (9/15/1999) • **88**

Brut Champagne 1990: Very dry, nicely austere, with plenty of life ahead. Toasty, mineral-like flavors and a bracingly crisp texture infuse this distinctive and elegant Champagne. Drink now through 2010. • $50 • (10/15/1999) • **92**

Brut Champagne Cuvée Brut NV • $25 • (12/31/1994) • **87**

Brut Rosé Champagne NV: A classy, traditional style of rosé, with a salmon color, complex flavors and rich, lingering finish. Drink now through 2001. • $40 • (10/15/1999) • **89**

Extra Dry Champagne NV: This lightly sweet bubbly goes down easy, with light, toasty aromas, fresh pear and citrus flavors, a smooth texture and a lingering finish. Drink now. • $28 • (12/31/1998) • **87**

Extra Dry Champagne Cuvée Year 2000 NV: Easy to like. This ripe and generous Champagne is quite fruity in flavor and rich in texture. Drink now. • $30 • (10/31/1999) • **87**

PIQUEMAL, DOMAINE

Côtes du Roussillon 1995 • $10 • (5/31/1998) • **87**

Côtes du Roussillon Elevé en Fûts de Chêne 1994 • $16 • (5/31/1998) • **89**

PIQUE-SEGUE, CHATEAU

Bergerac Rosé 1996 • $6 • (6/15/1998) • **73**

PIRET, JACKY

Beaujolais La Combe 1996: A round red with simple flavors of grape jelly and candied cherries. A bit dry on the finish.–T.M. • $8 • (8/31/1998) • **77**

PIRLET, LUC

Merlot Vin de Pays d'Oc Les Grandes Vallées 1995 • $10 • (5/15/1997) • **81**

PIRON, DOMINIQUE

Morgon Domaine des Grands Cras 1997: There's a ripeness to the sappy cherry and spice in this firmly structured red, with an urgency to the flavors and the backbone for aging. Drink through 2003–B.S. • $18 • (10/15/1999) • **83**

PITRAY, CHATEAU DE

Côtes de Castillon 1992 • $8 • (11/15/1994) • **80**

Côtes de Castillon 1990 • $9 • (3/15/1993) • **80**

Côtes de Castillon 1988 • $7 • (2/28/1991) • **83**

PIZAY, CHATEAU DE

Beaujolais 1997: This light, grapey red is soft and fruity, with light tannins and a hint of spritz. For the fans of Beaujolais Nouveau. Drink now.–T.M. • $9 • (8/31/1998) • **79**

Beaujolais 1995 • $9 • (9/15/1997) • **80**

Morgon 1997: This generous red marries roundness and firmness in a fresh, ripe wine that's clean and fruity. Nicely balanced, it should match well with lighter dishes. Drink now.–T.M. • $12 • (8/31/1998) • **82**

Morgon 1995 • $11 • (9/15/1997) • **85**

Régnié 1997: Light but plush, with ripe black cherry and toasty flavors that linger on the finish. Lively and fresh, and draws you back for another sip. Drink now.–T.M. • $11 • (8/31/1998) • **83**

Régnié 1995 • $11 • (9/15/1997) • **86**

PLAGNAC, CHATEAU

Médoc 1998: Some good currant and licorice character, but slightly diluted on the palate, with medium body, medium tannins and a light finish.–J.S. • $NA • (5/31/1999) (BT) • **80-84**

Médoc 1997: Pleasant and light, with plum and tobacco character, a light body and a fresh finish. Drink now.–J.S. • $14 • (1/31/2000) • **81**

Médoc 1996: Light and weedy, with a brown sugar and coffee character that is dilute and uninteresting.–J.S. • $11 • (1/31/1999) • **74**

Médoc 1995: Plummy, spicy and ready to drink. Medium- to light-bodied, with a light, fruity aftertaste. Drink now.–J.S. • $14 • (9/15/1998) • **80**

Médoc 1994 • $15 • (1/31/1997) • **70**

Médoc 1993 • $11 • (1/31/1996) • **70**

Médoc 1991 • $11 • (3/31/1994) • **78**

Médoc 1989 • $12 • (3/15/1992) • **88**

Médoc 1988 • $9 • (4/30/1991) • **79**

Key: SS—Spectator Selection. CS—Cellar Selection. HR—Highly Recommended. $NA—Price not available. (BT)—Barrel tasting. (A)—Auction Price.
For a key to the tasters' initials, see "How to Use These Listings."
Dates in parentheses represent the issues in which the ratings were published.

PLAIMONT, UNION DE PRODUCTEURS

Côtes de St.-Mont Les Vignes Retrouvées 1997: A bit awkward, with lemony flavors and some wax and almond notes.–K.M. • $9 • (10/15/1999) • **79**
Pacherenc du Vic-Bilh Collection 1996: A light- to medium-bodied dessert wine that's tangy and full of tangerine, grapefruit and unripe pear flavors. Balanced and ready to drink.–K.M. • $16 • (12/31/1998) • **86**
Vin de Pays des Côtes de Gascogne White Colombelle 1998: Shows a good crisp edge, with lime and fresh-cut grass flavors and a clean finish. A nice quaff. Drink now.–K.M. • $6 • (10/15/1999) • **83**
Vin de Pays des Côtes de Gascogne White Colombelle 1997: Nice tropical fruit flavors in this crisp white from southwest France, with spicy and citrusy notes mixed in as well.–K.M. • $6 • (8/31/1998) • **82**
Vin de Pays des Côtes de Gascogne White Colombelle 1996 • $6 • (8/31/1997) • **85**

PLANELS, CHATEAU DES

Minervois Cuvée Unique 1995 • $8 • (3/31/1998) • **84**

PLANTIERS DU HAUT-BRION, LES

Graves 1974 • $24 • (3/31/1989) • **80**
Pessac-Léognan White 1996: Rustic and funky, with lots of grassy Sauvignon character and an underlying earthiness. Medium-bodied. Woody, alcoholic finish.–J.S. • $NA • (1/01/1999) • **79**

PLINCE, CHATEAU

Pomerol 1998: A traditional and exciting wine. Very, very ripe aromas verging on raisins. Full-bodied and chewy, with earthy, funky and rich flavors. Port-like.–J.S. • $NA • (5/31/1999) (BT) • **90-94**
Pomerol 1997: Red with an amber edge. Medium- to light-bodied and slightly weedy. Tough to get excited about.–J.S. • $NA • (1/31/2000) • **79**
Pomerol 1996: Decent berry and cherry aromas and flavors, with hints of tobacco, but diluted on the palate. Medium to light in body with firm, slightly austere tannins. Drink now.–J.S. • $NA • (1/31/1999) • **80**
Pomerol 1995: Tobacco and cedar aromas open to a round and full-bodied palate with similar flavors. Very velvety texture. Needs some age. Drink through 2003–J.S. • $23 • (9/15/1998) • **86**
Pomerol 1993 • $24 • (1/31/1996) • **78**
Pomerol 1990 • $25 • (1/01/1994) • **82**
Pomerol 1982 • $NA • (5/15/1989) • **92**

PLUMET HERITIERS, HENRI

Pouilly-Fuissé Clos du Chalet Pouilly 1995 • $24 • (5/31/1997) • **85**
St.-Véran Les Cornillauds 1995 • $12 • (5/31/1997) • **74**

POCHON, DOMAINES

Crozes-Hermitage 1997: A bit herbal and astringent, but it's dark in color, medium-bodied, with anise, wood, red berry and grass flavors.–P.M. • $NA • (1/01/1999) • **78**
Crozes-Hermitage Château Curson 1997: Impressively silky tannins and a round texture. Full-bodied, with black cherry, smoke and herbs and a harmonious, medium-intense finish. Drink now through 2003.–P.M. • $NA • (1/01/1999) • **88**
Crozes-Hermitage Château Curson 1989 • $17 • (7/15/1991) • **89**
Crozes-Hermitage White Château Curson 1997: Medium-bodied, with a ripe, pineapple, apricot character. A soft, supple wine that is ready to drink. Serve chilled. Not imported into the U.S. Drink now.–P.M. • $NA • (1/01/1999) • **84**

POINTE, CHATEAU LA

Pomerol 1999: Slightly herbal, with berry and leaf aromas. Medium-bodied, with silky tannins. Slightly hollow midpalate.–J.S. • $NA • (1/01/2000) (BT) • **80-84**
Pomerol 1998: A friendly wine, with delicious ripe berry and tobacco character. Medium-bodied, with medium tannins and an aftertaste of mineral and berry.–J.S. • $NA • (5/31/1999) (BT) • **90-94**
Pomerol 1997: A delicate wine with very pretty plum and milk chocolate character. Medium-bodied, with soft tannins and a fresh, fruity finish. Drink now through 2003.–J.S. • $23 • (1/31/2000) • **87**
Pomerol 1996: Pretty aromas to this dark-colored red, showing mineral and berry character. Medium-bodied, with fine tannins, but lacking a midpalate. Best after 2000.–J.S. • $20 • (1/31/1999) • **85**
Pomerol 1995 • $24 Ⓐ • (1/31/1998) • **93**
Pomerol 1994 • $29 • (1/31/1997) SS • **90**
Pomerol 1992 • $19 • (4/15/1995) • **78**
Pomerol 1990 • $31 Ⓐ • (3/31/1993) • **86**
Pomerol 1989: A soft, delicious '89 that tastes like chocolate mousse. Good dark-ruby color and loads of milk chocolate, earth, berry and mushroom. Full-bodied and round, with soft, velvety tannins. Not as great as I remember, but outstanding. (1989 Bordeaux horizontal tasting). Drink now through 2005.–J.S. • $27 Ⓐ • (5/31/1999) • **91**
Pomerol 1988 • $35 • (7/31/1991) • **83**
Pomerol 1986 • $21 • (6/15/1989) • **90**
Pomerol 1982: Elegant, drink-me wine. Medium-red color, with a garnet edge. Soft and silky, with tobacco, cherry and autumnal character. (1982 Bordeaux horizontal tasting). Drink now.–J.S. • $31 Ⓐ • (11/30/1998) • **86**
Pomerol 1962 • $35 • (11/30/1987) • **80**
Pomerol 1961 • $39/1.5 liter • (4/30/1996) • **85**
Pomerol 1945 • $250 • (11/30/1995) • **80**

POIRON, HENRI

Muscadet de Sèvre et Maine Sur Lie Le Fief Giraud 1996: This crisp white offers a clean, firm texture, with herb and mineral flavors that make it a great match for shellfish. A bit austere on its own.–T.M. • $10 • (2/28/1999) • **80**

POL ROGER

Brut Champagne NV: A Champagne of substance. Ripe and generous, with sophisticated toasty aromas and good fruit concentration backed by vibrant acidity and a lingering finish. Drink now through 2001. • $30 • (10/15/1999) • **89**
Brut Champagne 1990: An attractive fruit character and appealing, round mouthfeel make this easy to enjoy. Very good quality. Drink now through 2001. • $48 Ⓐ • (10/15/1999) • **88**
Brut Champagne Réserve NV • $32 • (11/15/1991) • **87**
Brut Chardonnay Champagne 1990: Sophisticated, lively and flavorful. Has wonderful pastry shop aromas and vibrant fruit that lingers on the finish. Multidimensional and delicious. Drink now through 2005. • $61 Ⓐ • (10/15/1999) • **95**
Brut Rosé Champagne 1990: Great combination of abundant fruit flavors and elegant texture in a memorable rosé. Has an authentic copper color, bright cherry-berry aromas shaded by spices and toast, and a lingering finish. Drink now through 2005. • $65 • (10/15/1999) • **91**

POMAREDES, LES

Merlot Vin de Pays d'Oc 1996 • $6 • (5/31/1998) • **79**

POMEAUX, CHATEAU

Pomerol 1998: Plenty of sweet berry aromas here. Full-bodied and round, with ripe tannins and a sweet fruit aftertaste. Almost outstanding.–J.S. • $NA • (5/31/1999) (BT) • **85-89**

POMIES-AGASSAC, CHATEAU

Haut-Médoc 1996: A clean and well-presented red, but it lacks some concentration. Fresh and aromatic, with currant and berry character. Medium-bodied, with fine tannins and a light finish. Second label of Château d'Agassac. Drink now.–J.S. • $NA • (1/31/1999) • **85**

POMMARD, CHATEAU DE

Pommard 1997: Light and easy, this fruity red has soft tannins. Turns chunky on the vanilla-inspired finish.–P.M. • $NA • (9/30/1999) • **79**
Pommard 1996: Pretty, full of raspberry aromas and flavors, yet there's no shortage of structure, with firm tannins and lively acidity to complement the earthy note on the finish. Drink through 2004–B.S. • $45 • (9/30/1998) • **87**
Pommard 1994 • $40 • (11/15/1996) • **73**
Pommard 1993 • $36 • (11/15/1995) • **88**
Pommard 1992 • $NA • (12/15/1994) • **82**
Pommard 1991 • $40 • (1/31/1994) • **82**
Pommard 1990 • $60 • (12/15/1992) • **88**

POMMARD, CHATEAU DE

Pommard 1989 • $65 • (1/31/1992) • **86**
Pommard 1988 • $53 • (9/15/1992) • **87**
Pommard 1979 • $33 • (9/01/1985) • **88**

POMMERY

Brut Champagne 1992: Distinctive in style and generous for a lean vintage. Has assertive toasty, earthy aromas, ample fruit flavor and a mouthfilling mousse. Drink now. • $45 • (10/15/1999) • **87**
Brut Champagne 1991: A light, lean Champagne, with an austere but appealing character. Has earthy, mineral-like flavors, firm balance and a dry finish. Drink now. • $40 • (12/31/1998) • **84**
Brut Champagne Louise 1990: Nicely mature, with mellow aromas and flavors of baked apples, herbs and toasted almonds. Full and round in texture and long on the finish. Drink now through 2002. • $125 • (9/15/1999) • **90**
Brut Champagne Royal NV: Shows pronounced herb and citrus flavors, smooth but lean texture and a tangy finish. Drink now. • $24 • (10/15/1999) • **86**
Brut Champagne Royal Apanage NV: The concentration is impressive in this intense, aromatic, full-bodied Champagne, with its assertive doughy and toasty aromas leading into flavors of ripe fruit and spices that linger enticingly on the finish. Drink now. • $33 • (9/15/1999) SS • **91**
Brut Rosé Champagne NV: A very good, dry rosé with a light amber color, modest peach and apple flavors and firm acidity. Very refreshing. Drink now. • $36 • (10/15/1999) • **86**
Brut Rosé Champagne Louise 1990: This intense, full-bodied, dry and traditional rosé has come into it's own since last years' tasting. It's light amber in color, with doughy, figgy aromas and complex fruit and spice flavors that really linger on the finish. Drink now through 2005. • $120 • (10/15/1999) • **93**

POMMIER, DENIS

Chablis 1997: A bit buttery and spicy, showing a medium body, some lemon notes; a bit disjointed.–P.M. • $19 • (5/31/1999) • **79**
Chablis 1996 • $NA • (8/31/1997) • **80**
Chablis Beauroy 1997: Beautiful in a humble, nonshowy style, letting its ripe fruit, mineral character speak for itself, offering a harmonious, smooth whole that makes it tempting on release. Drink now through 2001.–P.M. • $26 • (5/31/1999) • **88**
Chablis Beauroy 1996 • $25 • (5/31/1998) • **87**
Chablis Côte de Léchet 1997: Ripe, a bit overdone, with apricot and cooked apple character, tasting almost like an off-dry Viognier.–P.M. • $26 • (5/31/1999) • **79**
Petit Chablis 1996 • $NA • (8/31/1997) • **80**

PONIATOWSKI, PRINCE

Vouvray Moelleux Aigle Blanc 1989 • $23 • (12/15/1995) • **79**
Vouvray Moelleux Aigle Blanc Vin de Tris 1990 • $38 • (12/15/1995) • **89**
Vouvray Moelleux Clos Baudoin 1989 • $50 • (12/15/1995) • **87**

PONNELLE, PIERRE

Beaune Les Grèves 1993 • $21 • (11/15/1995) • **82**
Bonnes Mares 1993 • $48 Ⓐ • (11/15/1995) • **76**
Bonnes Mares 1990 • $56 • (1/01/1994) • **86**
Chambolle-Musigny Les Argillières 1991 • $NA • (1/31/1994) • **79**
Clos de Vougeot 1993 • $57 • (11/15/1995) • **77**
Clos de Vougeot 1991 • $NA • (1/31/1994) • **72**
Clos de Vougeot 1990 • $48 • (1/01/1994) • **86**
Corton Le Clos du Roi 1993 • $43 • (11/15/1995) • **82**
Corton Le Clos du Roi 1990 • $36 • (12/31/1993) • **84**
Côte de Beaune Les Pierres Blanches 1992 • $11 • (12/15/1994) • **81**
Côte de Beaune Les Pierres Blanches 1987 • $14 • (3/31/1991) • **83**
Fixin Les Hervelets 1959 • $NA • (8/31/1990) • **94**
Mazoyères-Chambertin 1991 • $NA • (1/31/1994) • **82**
Musigny 1990 • $125 • (12/31/1993) • **71**

Key: SS—Spectator Selection. CS—Cellar Selection. HR—Highly Recommended. $NA—Price not available. (BT)—Barrel tasting. Ⓐ—Auction Price.
For a key to the tasters' initials, see "How to Use These Listings."
Dates in parentheses represent the issues in which the ratings were published.

PONSOT

Chambolle-Musigny Les Charmes 1997: A straightforward red, light in body and color, it tastes stripped of flavors, offering a short green and wood character.–P.M. • $80 • (1/01/2000) • **75**
Chambolle-Musigny Les Charmes 1996: Traditional and elegant, displaying sweet tannins, full body, opulent fruit and only subtle oak notes. Brings mineral, wet earth and the purest floral, wild berry and black currant aromas and flavors to center stage. Drink now through 2010.–P.M. • $85 • (5/15/1999) • **90**
Chambolle-Musigny Les Charmes 1988 • $58 • (4/30/1991) • **92**
Chambolle-Musigny Les Charmes 1985 • $80 Ⓐ • (6/15/1988) • **94**
Chapelle-Chambertin 1997: Supple, with good wet earth. Medium-bodied, it kicks in with surprising intensity of smoke and charcoal on the palate. Turns just a bit tough and hot on the rather sweet finish. Best from 2002 through 2010.–P.M. • $174 • (1/01/2000) • **86**
Chapelle-Chambertin 1996: Gorgeous. Ripe and refined Pinot fruit is the hallmark of this full-bodied, smooth-tannined seducer, with sirenlike currant, mineral, spice, mocha, smoke and game notes that would make many a Burgundy aficionado swoon. Best from 2003 through 2010.–P.M. • $150 • (5/15/1999) • **94**
Chapelle-Chambertin 1991 • $65 • (8/31/1994) • **80**
Clos de la Roche 1992 • $102 • (12/15/1994) • **88**
Clos de la Roche 1984 • $48 • (2/15/1988) • **73**
Clos de la Roche 1959 • $NA • (12/31/1994) • **94**
Clos de la Roche Cuvée William 1988 • $92 Ⓐ • (5/15/1991) • **89**
Clos de la Roche Vieilles Vignes 1997: Subtle and elegant, with real *goût de terroir*. Has odd aromas, but a mineral, steel, wet earth character that is accompanied by ripe fruit makes it stand out as very interesting. Long, sweet finish. Best from 2002 through 2007.–P.M. • $201 • (1/01/2000) • **88**
Clos de la Roche Vieilles Vignes 1996: Delicious, vibrant, pure blackberry and raspberry character blends nicely with smoky, toasted aromas. Elegant and medium-bodied, with smooth tannins, this a delightful, well-made '96. Long finish. Best from 2003 through 2012.–P.M. • $150 Ⓐ • (5/15/1999) • **90**
Clos de la Roche Vieilles Vignes 1990 • $280 Ⓐ • (3/15/1993) • **92**
Clos de la Roche Vieilles Vignes 1988 • $125 Ⓐ • (5/15/1991) • **88**
Clos de la Roche Vieilles Vignes 1985 • $529 Ⓐ • (6/15/1988) • **90**
Clos St.-Denis Vieilles Vignes 1996: Attractive, with good ripe fruit and distinctive dark chocolate, mocha and blackberry flavors. Medium-bodied, it has both crisp and smooth mouthfeel. Vibrant, balanced, lasting finish has a lovely toasted, grilled meat complexity. Best from 2003 through 2008.–P.M. • $175 • (5/15/1999) • **87**
Clos St.-Denis Vieilles Vignes 1988 • $113 Ⓐ • (7/15/1991) • **85**
Gevrey-Chambertin 1994 • $NA • (11/15/1996) • **83**
Gevrey-Chambertin Cuvée de l'Abeille 1997: An elegant and flavorful Pinot. Medium-bodied, with good, ripe red berry, deft oak complexity, and vanilla, spice and toast. Jammy-tasting finish. Drink now through 2005.–P.M. • $48 • (1/01/2000) • **87**
Gevrey-Chambertin Cuvée de l'Abeille 1991 • $30 • (8/31/1994) • **83**
Givry 1994 • $NA • (11/15/1996) • **73**
Griotte-Chambertin 1997: Ripe and smoky, this powers its way through the palate. Cascades with wet earth, spice, mocha, red berry flavors. Medium-bodied, it offers good elan on the firm, oaked finish. Best from 2002 through 2007.–P.M. • $174 • (1/01/2000) • **88**
Griotte-Chambertin 1996: Crisp and a bit green, showing a fresh, high-acidity component, with cherry notes on the tart finish. Disappointing from this producer. Drink now through 2003.–P.M. • $104 Ⓐ • (5/15/1999) • **80**
Griotte-Chambertin 1991 • $38 • (8/31/1994) • **83**
Griotte-Chambertin 1988 • $104 Ⓐ • (5/15/1991) • **89**
Hautes-Côtes de Beaune 1994 • $NA • (11/15/1996) • **80**
Hautes-Côtes de Nuits Dame Huguette 1994 • $NA • (11/15/1996) • **70**
Latricières-Chambertin 1988 • $85 Ⓐ • (5/15/1991) • **91**
Mercurey Clos l'Evêque 1994 • $NA • (11/15/1996) • **84**
Morey-St.-Denis 1990 • $68 • (3/15/1993) • **91**
Morey-St.-Denis Clos des Monts Luisants 1988 • $40 • (4/30/1991) • **85**
Morey-St.-Denis Cuvée des Alouettes 1996: Exuberant and pure floral, red- and blackberry aromas storm the senses as this ripe, full-bodied and stylish '96 deploys its charisma on a firm, tannic structure engineered to last. Best from 2005 through 2015.–P.M. • $33 Ⓐ • (5/15/1999) • **92**
Morey-St.-Denis White Clos des Monts Luisants 1997: Straightforward but fresh and lively. Crisp, lemony and light-bodied, with a bite of persistent acidity. Tastes a bit rustic, with caramel on the finish. Drink now through 2001.–P.M. • $79 • (1/01/2000) • **80**
Morey-St.-Denis White Clos des Monts Luisants 1996: Crisp and a bit appley, offering very fresh aromas, with a vibrant midpalate that sings with lime and

citrus flavors. Medium-bodied and long. Drink now through 2005.–P.M. • $62 • (5/31/1999) • **80**

Pommard 1994 • $NA • (11/15/1996) • **78**

Pommard Hospices de Beaune Cuvée Suzanne Chaudron 1994 • $NA • (11/15/1996) • **86**

PONSOT, CHRISTINE

Coteaux du Tricastin 1994 • $NA • (11/15/1995) • **79**
Coteaux du Tricastin 1993 • $NA • (11/15/1995) • **83**
Côtes du Rhône 1994 • $NA • (11/15/1995) • **81**
Côtes du Rhône-Villages 1994 • $NA • (11/15/1995) • **79**

PONTAC-LYNCH, CHATEAU

Margaux 1993 • $26 • (4/30/1997) • **79**

PONTET-CANET, CHATEAU

Pauillac 1998: Good amount of grape and tar character in this medium-bodied wine, but it's slightly diluted in the midpalate and on the finish. Will perhaps move up a notch next year. Tasted twice, with consistent notes.–J.S. • $NA • (5/31/1999) (BT) • **80-84**

Pauillac 1997: Some decent plum and berry character, with hints of herbs. Light-bodied, light finish. Slightly lighter than I remember. Drink now.–J.S. • $31 • (1/31/2000) • **83**

Pauillac 1996: A young red, with bright black licorice and berry aromas and hints of spice. Full-bodied, with firm tannins and compact fruit structure. Slightly closed on the finish, but impressive nonetheless. Best after 2002.–J.S. • $84 Ⓐ • (1/31/1999) • **90**

Pauillac 1995 • $39 Ⓐ • (1/31/1998) SS • **94**
Pauillac 1994 • $40 Ⓐ • (1/31/1997) • **88**
Pauillac 1993 • $22 Ⓐ • (1/31/1996) • **89**
Pauillac 1992 • $16 • (4/15/1995) • **82**
Pauillac 1991 • $16 • (3/31/1994) • **80**
Pauillac 1990 • $29 • (3/31/1993) • **82**

Pauillac 1989: A vibrant '89 with a wonderful fresh fruit character. Dark-ruby color. Very fresh aromas of blackberries and plums. Full-bodied and packed to the brim with fruit, adding fine yet slightly green tannins. Hard to resist now. (1989 Bordeaux horizontal tasting). Best after 2002.–J.S. • $45 Ⓐ • (5/31/1999) • **90**

Pauillac 1988: Hard to get excited about this confused wine, particularly since the nose has a slightly earthy and funky character. Nonetheless, it's full-bodied, with velvety tannins and a soft texture. Pleasant on the finish. (1988 Bordeaux horizontal tasting). Drink now.–J.S. • $36 Ⓐ • (11/30/1998) • **85**

Pauillac 1986 • $21 • (5/31/1989) • **89**

Pauillac 1982: Backward and structured, though a bit coarse. Brilliant, deep ruby color, with a hint of garnet on the edge. Currant, floral and berry aromas. Big and chewy, with plenty of fruit and tannins. (1982 Bordeaux horizontal tasting). Best after 2000–J.S. • $47 Ⓐ • (11/30/1998) • **90**

Pauillac 1961 • $85 Ⓐ • (4/30/1996) • **87**
Pauillac 1945 • $227 Ⓐ • (11/30/1995) • **79**

POTEL, NICOLAS

Bourgogne 1996: Exuberant red berry aromas fill the glass, the ripe, supple tannins charm the palate, and the balanced finish makes a convincing case for stocking up on this medium-bodied, medium-tannic '96. Drink now through 2006.–P.M. • $16 • (5/15/1999) • **89**

Santenay Beauregard 1996: Quite earthy, with a grilled meat, leather, red berry character. Juicy and vibrant at midpalate, it's smooth, but not as ripe-tasting and fruity as some. Fresh finish. Best from 2003 through 2010.–P.M. • $26 • (5/15/1999) • **85**

Volnay 1996: Slightly earthy, with some tartness attached to the otherwise decent cassis, plum and mineral notes. All-in-all quite ripe, but lacks a bit of balance on the tart finish.–P.M. • $33 • (5/15/1999) • **79**

POTENSAC, CHATEAU

Médoc 1996: Lots of ripe fruit, with intense aromas of blackberries and raspberries and layers of fruit flavors. Full-bodied, round and rich. Best after 2000.–J.S. • $21 Ⓐ • (1/01/1999) • **90**

Médoc 1995: Pretty aromas of blackberries, violets and spices. Medium- to full-bodied, with a lovely velvety-tannin structure and medium finish. Best from 2001 through 2008.–J.S. • $33 Ⓐ • (9/15/1998) • **88**

Médoc 1988 • $30 Ⓐ • (10/31/1991) • **80**
Médoc 1987 • $13 • (5/15/1990) • **72**
Médoc 1986 • $16 • (11/30/1989) • **86**

Médoc 1982: Slightly simple. Dark ruby-garnet color, with an inky center. Ripe berry, oyster and mushroom aromas. Medium-bodied and velvety in texture, with good fruit flavors and a medium finish. (1982 Bordeaux horizontal tasting). Drink now.–J.S. • $34 Ⓐ • (11/30/1998) • **85**

POTHIER-RIEUSSET

Beaune Les Boucherottes 1989 • $28 • (11/30/1992) • **88**
Beaune Les Boucherottes 1988 • $35 • (11/30/1990) • **88**
Beaune Les Boucherottes 1986 • $19 • (5/31/1989) • **88**
Bourgogne 1986 • $10 • (6/15/1989) • **79**
Pommard 1989 • $32 • (11/30/1992) • **82**
Pommard 1986 • $25 • (9/15/1989) • **76**
Pommard Clos de Verger 1989 • $44 • (11/30/1992) • **83**
Pommard Clos de Verger 1986 • $33 • (9/15/1989) • **87**
Pommard Les Epenots 1989 • $49 • (11/30/1992) • **82**
Pommard Les Rugiens 1989 • $49 • (11/30/1992) • **84**
Pommard Les Rugiens 1986 • $35 • (9/15/1989) • **72**
Volnay 1985 • $21 • (2/15/1988) • **93**

POUGET, CHATEAU

Margaux 1998: Grapey and fruity, with hints of mint. Medium-bodied, with medium tannins and a slightly hollow center. Good attack, but needs a finish.–J.S. • $NA • (5/31/1999) (BT) • **80-84**

Margaux 1997: Interesting mineral and berry character. Medium-bodied, with light tannins and a fresh finish. Drink now.–J.S. • $NA • (1/31/2000) • **85**

Margaux 1996: Very dark color, with wonderful berry, spice and cherry aromas that evolve nicely in the glass. Full-bodied, with full tannins and a lovely spice, vanilla and fruit aftertaste. A very good wine from an often overlooked château. Best after 2002.–J.S. • $30 • (1/31/1999) • **89**

Margaux 1990 • $22 • (3/31/1993) • **91**
Margaux 1983 • $11 • (2/15/1987) • **86**
Margaux 1970 • $NA • (5/15/1993) • **84**

POUJEAUX, CHATEAU

Moulis 1999: Plum, tobacco and coffee aromas follow through to a medium-bodied palate, with light, velvety tannins and a medium finish.–J.S. • $NA • (1/01/2000) (BT) • **85-89**

Moulis 1998: Lovely aromas of blackberries and chocolate. Medium- to full-bodied, with well-integrated tannins and a medium finish. Nice wine.–J.S. • $NA • (5/31/1999) (BT) • **85-89**

Moulis 1997: Beautiful aromas of berries, currants and cherries, with a hint of vanilla. Medium- to full-bodied, with delicious berry and cherry flavors. Long, long finish. Drink now through 2004.–J.S. • $22 • (1/31/2000) • **89**

Moulis 1996: Bubbling over with blackberry, cherry and spice, with a hint of coconut. Full-bodied and chewy, yet refined and well manicured. A silky texture that goes on and on. Big and tannic wine. A super effort from Poujeaux. Best after 2001.–J.S. • $22 • (1/31/1999) • **90**

Moulis 1995 • $18 Ⓐ • (1/31/1998) • **92**
Moulis 1994 • $27 Ⓐ • (1/31/1997) • **87**
Moulis 1992 • $15 • (4/15/1995) • **78**
Moulis 1991 • $15 • (3/31/1994) • **83**
Moulis 1990 • $38 Ⓐ • (3/31/1993) • **88**

Moulis 1989: Biggest Poujeaux I have ever tasted, except for the 1928. Dark-ruby in color, with wonderful berry, cherry and grapey aromas. Full-bodied, loads of tannins and tons of fruit. Still closed; needs time. (1989 Bordeaux horizontal tasting). Drink through 2008–J.S. • $35 Ⓐ • (5/31/1999) • **93**

Moulis 1988: Better than many wines with a more esteemed pedigree, this '88 Poujeaux shows complex aromas of berry, tobacco and spice, with a hint of mineral. Full-bodied, with fine tannins and a fruity finish. (1988 Bordeaux horizontal tasting). Best after 2001.–J.S. • $27 Ⓐ • (11/30/1998) • **90**

Moulis 1987 • $15 • (5/15/1990) • **74**
Moulis 1986 • $37 Ⓐ • (11/30/1989) • **88**
Moulis 1985 • $18 • (9/30/1988) • **87**
Moulis 1983 • $19 • (10/31/1986) • **79**

Moulis 1982: Good but simple red; usually better than this. Dark ruby color, with tobacco, berry and fresh fruit aromas. Medium-bodied and slightly one-dimensional, with dark chocolate and fruit character and a slightly dry finish.—1982 Bordeaux horizontal. Drink now.–J.S. • $38 Ⓐ • (11/30/1998) • **84**

POUJOL, DOMAINE DU

Coteaux du Languedoc 1996: Nicely concentrated and fairly fruity, with focused berry, cherry, currant and cranberry flavors. Finishes on a leathery note. Drink now.–K.M. • $12 • (10/31/1998) • **83**

Vin de Pays de l'Hérault 1997: Interesting for its assertive gamy aroma and flavor, which is followed up by a mix of dried cherry and sage notes. Medium-bodied and already mature-tasting, this is a walk on the wild side. Drink now.–K.M. • $10 • (1/31/2000) • **84**

Vin de Pays de l'Hérault 1996 • $10 • (12/15/1997) • **84**

POUMEY, CHATEAU

Pessac-Léognan 1995 • $15 • (1/31/1998) • **83**

POUPILLE

Côtes de Castillon 1999: Impressive berry, currant and cherry aromas follow through to a medium-bodied palate, with fine tannins and a short finish.–J.S. • $NA • (1/01/2000) (BT) • **85-89**

POURCIEUX, CHATEAU DE

Côtes de Provence Rosé 1998: A tad heavy-handed, with dried cherry flavors and herbal notes.–K.M. • $9 • (10/15/1999) • **79**

POUSSE D'OR, DOMAINE DE LA

Pommard Les Jarollières 1995 • $60 • (11/15/1997) • **88**
Pommard Les Jarollières 1994 • $62 • (11/15/1996) • **76**
Pommard Les Jarollières 1993 • $33 Ⓐ • (11/15/1995) • **85**
Pommard Les Jarollières 1992 • $57 • (12/15/1994) • **88**
Pommard Les Jarollières 1991 • $50 • (1/31/1994) • **80**
Pommard Les Jarollières 1988 • $57 • (8/31/1991) • **88**
Pommard Les Jarollières 1986 • $45 • (4/30/1989) • **70**
Pommard Les Jarollières 1985 • $39 • (3/15/1988) • **87**

Santenay Clos Tavannes 1997: Vegetal, herbal, diluted and short.–P.M. • $NA • (9/30/1999) • **70**

Santenay Clos Tavannes 1996: Bright-edged, aromatic, medium-bodied Pinot, pumping out the smoke, spice and black cherry aromas and flavors. High acidity and supple tannins make it attractive on release. Drink now.–P.M. • $25 • (7/31/1999) • **84**

Santenay Clos Tavannes 1994 • $30 • (11/15/1996) • **87**
Santenay Clos Tavannes 1993 • $40 • (11/15/1995) • **87**
Santenay Clos Tavannes 1991 • $26 • (1/31/1994) • **84**
Santenay Clos Tavannes 1989 • $29 • (1/31/1992) • **91**
Santenay Clos Tavannes 1988 • $28 • (8/31/1991) • **83**
Santenay Clos Tavannes 1986 • $27 • (6/15/1989) • **78**

Santenay Les Gravières 1997: Light-colored, tasting a bit stemmy and rustic, with a chewy, dry finish.–P.M. • $32 • (9/30/1999) • **79**

Santenay Les Gravières 1992 • $28 • (12/15/1994) • **81**

Volnay Clos d'Audignac 1997: Aromas of cherry, wet earth and a hint of herb introduce this delicate, elegant Volnay. Decent concentration of flavors and light structure balance the tender fruit. Drink now through 2002.–B.S. • $49 • (9/30/1999) • **82**

Volnay Clos d'Audignac 1989 • $45 • (1/31/1992) • **92**

Volnay Clos de la Bousse d'Or 1997: There's lovely balance in this elegant wine, with a good *gras* on the midpalate. The flavors come at you in nice waves. Worth hunting down for its hedonistic qualities. Drink now through 2003.–P.M. • $73 • (9/30/1999) • **85**

Volnay Clos de la Bousse d'Or 1996: A fresh '96 red Burgundy, showing some clean black cherry, spice, smoke character. Medium-bodied and rather structured, with a tannic bite on the lingering, vibrant, chewy finish. Drink now through 2002.–P.M. • $38 Ⓐ • (7/31/1999) • **86**

Volnay Clos de la Bousse d'Or 1995 • $65 • (11/15/1997) • **83**
Volnay Clos de la Bousse d'Or 1994 • $70 • (11/15/1996) • **75**
Volnay Clos de la Bousse d'Or 1993 • $47 Ⓐ • (11/15/1995) • **88**
Volnay Clos de la Bousse d'Or 1992 • $28 Ⓐ • (12/15/1994) • **86**
Volnay Clos de la Bousse d'Or 1991 • $55 • (1/31/1994) • **86**
Volnay Clos de la Bousse d'Or 1990 • $86 Ⓐ • (11/30/1992) CS • **93**
Volnay Clos de la Bousse d'Or 1989 • $60 • (1/31/1992) • **90**
Volnay Clos de la Bousse d'Or 1986 • $46 • (4/30/1989) • **75**
Volnay En Chevret 1994 • $NA • (11/15/1996) • **82**

Volnay Les Caillerets 1997: Rustic and light in color and body, tasting of sweet fruit, with woody underbrush and tea leaf, cherry and raspberry notes.–P.M. • $58 • (9/30/1999) • **78**

Volnay Les Caillerets 1995 • $52 • (11/15/1997) • **89**
Volnay Les Caillerets 1993 • $53 • (11/15/1995) • **85**
Volnay Les Caillerets 1992 • $49 • (12/15/1994) • **85**
Volnay Les Caillerets 1988 • $49 • (8/31/1991) • **85**
Volnay Les Caillerets 1985 • $35 • (3/15/1988) • **90**

Volnay Les Caillerets Clos des 60 Ouvrées 1997: Intriguing aromas of violet, cherry, earth, and smoke segue into cassis and violet flavors in this bright, elegant Volnay. Well structured, with fine intensity and a sense of *terroir*. Firm finish. Drink now through 2005.–B.S. • $63 • (9/30/1999) • **88**

Volnay Les Caillerets Clos des 60 Ouvrées 1996: Elegant. A medium-bodied, medium-intense package, showing ripe and clean berry character, with a spicy, smoky undertow. Lovely on release. Drink now through 2001.–P.M. • $34 Ⓐ • (7/31/1999) • **86**

Volnay Les Caillerets Clos des 60 Ouvrées 1995 • $55 • (11/15/1997) • **89**
Volnay Les Caillerets Clos des 60 Ouvrées 1993 • $60 • (11/15/1995) • **89**
Volnay Les Caillerets Clos des 60 Ouvrées 1992 • $53 • (12/15/1994) • **86**
Volnay Les Caillerets Clos des 60 Ouvrées 1990 • $86 Ⓐ • (12/15/1992) HR • **91**
Volnay Les Caillerets Clos des 60 Ouvrées 1987 • $29 • (6/15/1990) • **82**
Volnay Les Caillerets Clos des 60 Ouvrées 1986 • $41 • (4/30/1989) • **83**
Volnay Les Caillerets Clos des 60 Ouvrées 1985 • $39 • (3/15/1988) • **86**

POUSSIE, LA

Sancerre 1998: Restrained in style, this nonetheless has nice richness and delineation, with crisp, refreshing citrus, white peach and grass flavors. Drink now.–B.S. • $24 • (6/15/2000) • **85**

Sancerre 1997: This straightforward white is almost neutral in flavor, with firm acidity and hints of mineral and herb. Refreshing, but it doesn't bring much to the table.–T.M. • $25 • (6/30/1999) • **79**

Sancerre 1996 • $25 • (6/15/1998) • **87**

Sancerre Red 1996: Maturing, with charry barnyard aromas and earthy, slightly bitter flavors, firm tannins and a bitter finish.–T.M. • $27 • (6/30/1999) • **76**

Sancerre Red 1995 • $27 • (6/15/1997) • **85**

Sancerre Rosé 1997: Though pale, this rosé is round on the palate, with soft, neutral flavors that hint of berry and earth. Balanced, but with little varietal character.–T.M. • $27 • (6/30/1999) • **78**

Sancerre Rosé 1996 • $27 • (6/15/1998) • **83**

PRAT DE CEST, CHATEAU

Corbières 1998: A lip-smacking, effusively fruity young red, with red berry and plum flavors, notes of cassis on the finish. Drink now through 2001.–K.M. • $9 • (8/31/1999) • **84**

PRATS, BRUNO

Cabernet Sauvignon Bordeaux 1995 • $10 • (6/30/1997) • **84**

PRELUDE A GRAND-PUY-DUCASSE

Pauillac 1996: A well-crafted red, with berry and tobacco character. Medium-bodied, with medium tannins and a fresh finish. Needs more fruit on the midpalate. Best after 2000.–J.S. • $NA • (1/31/1999) • **86**

PREMEAUX, DOMAINE DU CHATEAU DE

Bourgogne 1996: Bitter and astringent, with a green, herbaceous character that's difficult to warm up to.–P.M. • $14 • (9/30/1998) • **72**

Nuits-St.-Georges 1996: Deliciously fruity, yet there's structure and concentration to go with the deep black cherry flavors. Begins with a silkiness, then the tannins take over, ripe and mouthcoating. Fine length. Best from 2002 through 2008.–B.S. • $28 • (9/30/1998) • **88**

Nuits-St.-Georges Clos des Argillières 1996: Fresh and fruity, with a mineral, blood, iron quality that makes it stand out. Supple on the midpalate, with delicate raspberry and cherry flavors, it kicks in with firm tannins on the finish. Best After 2005.–P.M. • $36 • (9/30/1998) • **87**

Key: SS—Spectator Selection. CS—Cellar Selection. HR—Highly Recommended. $NA—Price not available. (BT)—Barrel tasting. Ⓐ—Auction Price.
For a key to the tasters' initials, see "How to Use These Listings."
Dates in parentheses represent the issues in which the ratings were published.

PREMIUS

Bordeaux Élevè en Fût de Chêne 1996: Light and fruity, with lots of toasted oak, silky tannins and a fruity finish. Could use a little more fruit concentration. Drink now.–J.S. • $10 • (7/31/1999) • **80**

PRESIDENTE, DOMAINE DE LA

Merlot Vin de Pays d'Oc 1996 • $6 • (4/30/1998) • **84**
Mourvèdre Vin de Pays d'Oc 1994: Tastes ripe and overly mature, with brown sugar and raisin flavors and leathery notes. A bit over-the-hill.–K.M. • $7 • (8/31/1998) • **75**
Syrah Vin de Pays d'Oc 1995 • $7 • (1/01/1998) • **82**

PREUILLAC, CHATEAU

Médoc 1996: Bright berry and hints of earth and toasted oak appear throughout this medium-bodied, well-crafted '96. Drink now through 2003.–J.S. • $24 • (7/31/1999) • **86**

PREYS & FILS, JACKY

Touraine Cuvée de Fié Gris 1996: This firm white marries pungent grassy flavors with more austere mineral notes. Might settle down with strongly flavored foods.–T.M. • $10 • (6/30/1999) • **78**
Touraine Les Pillotières 1997: This pungent white shows the distinctive grassy, herbal character of Sauvignon Blanc, but it's a bit one-dimensional and turns tart on the finish.–T.M. • $9 • (6/30/1999) • **79**
Touraine Red Côte Cuvée Prestige 1989 • $9 • (1/31/1992) • **75**

PRIEUR, JACQUES

Beaune Champs Pimont 1997: A bit tart, but with juicy aromas and flavors. Turns unnaturally dry on the finish.–P.M. • $46 • (9/30/1999) • **77**
Beaune Champs Pimont 1996: Rather tart, medium-bodied, with a firm structure that leads to mineral, vanilla bean and stony notes as well as citrus, honey and herbal flavors that take over on the tough finish. Should go well with food. Best after 2005.–P.M. • $48 • (8/31/1998) • **83**
Beaune Clos de la Féguine 1996: Delicious fruit. Sappy, spicy red berries and a hint of vanilla in a fleshy, rich package surrounded by ripe, full tannins and a bit of alcohol at the end. Long, smoky aftertaste. Drink through 2006–B.S. • $50 • (9/30/1998) • **88**
Beaune Clos de la Féguine 1995 • $43 • (11/15/1997) • **77**
Beaune Clos de la Féguine 1994 • $33 • (11/15/1996) • **87**
Beaune Clos de la Féguine 1993 • $30 • (11/15/1995) • **88**
Beaune Grèves 1997: Hedonistic. Beautiful, clean, pure fruit in a velvety package shows lots of ripeness. A well-made '97, layered with smoke, toast, spice and lovely blackberry character. Balanced, long finish. Drink now through 2007.–P.M. • $50 • (1/01/2000) • **92**
Beaune Grèves 1997: Hedonistic. Beautiful, clean, pure fruit in a velvety package shows lots of ripeness. A well-made '97, layered with smoke, toast, spice and lovely blackberry character. Balanced, long finish. Drink now through 2007.–P.M. • $NA • (1/01/2000) • **92**
Beaune Grèves 1996: Showy and flamboyant, with wet earth, cedar, plum and black cherry character. Medium-bodied, this one has real personality. It also is fairly supple and ripe, showing sweet-tasting tannins. Drink now through 2005.–P.M. • $44 • (9/30/1998) • **85**
Beaune White Champs Pimont 1997: This pleasant white has a flinty, smoky, lemony character. Shows decent freshness and lingering toasty notes on the finish. Drink now.–P.M. • $56 • (9/30/1999) • **83**
Beaune White Clos de la Féguine 1997: Ultraripe and delicious, a bit reserved in aroma, but this has an opulent mouthfeel, with pronounced toasted oak mingling with (overripe?) pear, pineapple and smoke. Drink now through 2001.–P.M. • $56 • (9/30/1999) • **87**
Beaune White Clos de la Féguine 1996: Thick and ripe, with honey, pear, sweet corn and butter flavors, this opulent, full-bodied white is a delight to drink upon release. Kicks in with fresh, pure citrus flavors on the finish. Drink now through 2005.–P.M. • $54 • (8/31/1998) • **90**
Beaune White Clos de la Féguine 1995 • $45 • (8/31/1997) • **91**
Bourgogne White 1995 • $15 • (8/31/1997) • **88**
Chambertin 1996: Ripe, full-bodied wine with loads of personality. Has firm tannins and an earthy concentration that delivers a lot of tea leaf, tobacco, cigar-box, plum and black cherry character. Impressively long, flavorful finish. Best after 2003.–P.M. • $130 • (9/30/1998) • **90**
Chambertin 1995 • $112 • (11/15/1997) • **79**
Chambertin 1994 • $81 • (11/15/1996) • **76**
Chambertin 1993 • $90 • (5/15/1996) • **89**
Chevalier-Montrachet 1997: A thick wine with a beautiful mouthfeel, blending suave oak treatment with a silky texture and lovely ripe (somewhat late harvest–like) flavors of mango, passion fruit and dried apricot. Has enough clean, fresh acidity to anchor it safely in Burgundy's *terroir*. Drink now through 2005.–P.M. • $240 • (9/30/1999) • **92**
Chevalier-Montrachet 1996: Quite oaky in an overly perfumed way, this medium-bodied wine lacks the fruity opulence to rate higher. But its texture is supple, smooth and seductive. Best from 2003.–P.M. • $200 • (8/31/1998) • **83**
Chevalier-Montrachet 1995 • $175 • (8/31/1997) • **95**
Clos Vougeot 1996: Vibrant black cherry and wild raspberry notes are followed by some smoky oak accents in this full-bodied, rich, thick and intensely toasted wine. Ripe, refined tannins offer a mineral-laden, palate-coating sensation. Long finish. Best after 2005.–P.M. • $90 • (9/30/1998) • **90**
Clos Vougeot 1995 • $80 • (11/15/1997) • **83**
Clos Vougeot 1993 • $54 • (11/15/1995) • **92**
Clos Vougeot 1991 • $NA • (1/31/1994) • **85**
Corton Bressandes 1997: This fantastic '97 red Burgundy delivers exciting, pure, ripe and focused red berry and blackberry flavors, Silky midpalate, showing excellent balance among the tannins, acidity and fruit. All is in place in this sexy wine. Good length. Drink now through 2006.–P.M. • $112 • (9/30/1999) • **93**
Corton Bressandes 1996: Sensational. Ultrasmooth, with classy tannins that melt in the mouth. Immensely ripe yet elegant in structure, this full-bodied, royal '96 brims with cassis, wild berry, toasted spice, chocolate, wet earth and mineral nuances that unfold their charisma to a seductive finish. Best from 2003 through 2015.–P.M. • $120 • (5/15/1999) • **98**
Corton Bressandes 1995 • $92 • (11/15/1997) • **85**
Corton Bressandes 1994 • $70 • (11/15/1996) • **88**
Corton Bressandes 1993 • $70 • (11/15/1995) • **88**
Corton Bressandes 1992 • $NA • (12/15/1994) • **89**
Corton Bressandes 1991 • $NA • (1/31/1994) • **87**
Corton-Charlemagne 1997: Fantastic. A rare specimen in '97, this has the magic to hold your palate's attention while hitting a home run with its ripe fruit, natural acidity and well-dosed oak accents. Drink now through 2007.–P.M. • $120 • (9/30/1999) • **93**
Corton-Charlemagne 1996: Fat and ripe but also superoaky, the new wood flavor overwhelms everything right now, robbing the wine of freshness. Decanted however, it gains complexity, oozing rich honey and pear. Still, less impressive than when tasted from barrel. Best after 2005.–P.M. • $144 Ⓐ • (8/31/1998) • **88**
Corton-Charlemagne 1995 • $90 • (8/31/1997) • **90**
Echézeaux 1997: Shows promise, with lovely cherry and spice notes, good concentration, a balanced midpalate and moderate tannins on the finish. A sweet fruit character returns on the aftertaste. Drink now through 2003.–B.S. • $130 • (9/30/1999) • **86**
Echézeaux 1996: Gorgeous. Very dark in color and full in body, it's loaded with classy fruit and earth character and ripe tannins. Hard to ask for more in a Pinot Noir, as it layers the palate with plum, ripe black cherry, raspberry, mineral and some subtle mocha and coffee bean character. Tempting upon release, but should improve with cellaring. Best after 2003.–P.M. • $120 • (9/30/1998) • **93**
Meursault Clos de Mazeray 1997: Ripe and rich, with tropical, citrusy and floral notes, all presented in a full-bodied package. Lacks a bit of class and *terroir*, but shows megaintensity, with a slight late harvest, dried fruit finish that's exotic. Drink now through 2003.–P.M. • $50 • (9/30/1999) • **90**
Meursault Clos de Mazeray 1996: Fabulous Meursault, lush, opulent, ripe. Full-bodied, it coats the palate yet shows plenty of firm acidity. Imagine ripe pear, melon, vanilla bean and lots of pink grapefruit flavors. Long, intensely fruity, toasted finish. Drink now through 2005.–P.M. • $50 • (8/31/1998) • **92**
Meursault Clos de Mazeray 1995 • $42 • (8/31/1997) • **90**
Meursault Clos de Mazeray 1991 • $NA • (1/31/1994) • **80**
Meursault Perrières 1997: Very oaky; tastes almost like a late harvest wine. A bit simple, with the sawdust and plywood character dominating the light fruit. Drink now through 2003.–P.M. • $107 • (9/30/1999) • **83**
Meursault Perrières 1996: Well crafted, ultrasmooth and super-rich for a '96, this explodes with tropical, toasted hazelnut and pear flavors. Full-bodied, with lush texture, but maintains a good, zesty lemony character on the long finish. Needs time to shed that fancy wood. Best from 2005.–P.M. • $92 • (8/31/1998) • **90**
Meursault Perrières 1995 • $80 • (8/31/1997) • **96**
Meursault Red Clos de Mazeray 1993 • $30 • (11/15/1995) • **82**

■ ■ ■ ■

PRIEUR, JACQUES

Montrachet 1997: Powerful, a bulldozer of a white Burgundy that stays on your palate, this smells of wood, but on the palate unveils some melon, dried apricot, lemon, lime, smoke and ripe fruit notes. Tingling acidity mingles with the wet earth character of the Montrachet *terroir* to lend a long—and we mean long—finish. Drink now through 2027.–P.M. • $460 • (9/30/1999) CS • **97**

Montrachet 1996: Incredible depth of aroma and flavor, tantalizing with its potential after but one whiff of the complex spice, fruit and oak. As opulent as white Burgundy gets, it's round, thick and creamlike, full-bodied yet racy with acidity. Although very fat, it's firm and muscular, with solid aging potential. Exotically violet-scented (from the oak) on the incredibly balanced finish, which hangs in suspended animation for at least 60 seconds as your palate vibrates in the wake of swallowing this monster beauty. Best from 2005 through 2020.–P.M. • $240 Ⓐ • (8/31/1998) • **98**

Montrachet 1995 • $360 Ⓐ • (8/31/1997) HR • **99**

Musigny 1997: A gorgeous, full-bodied '97 red Burgundy, tasting natural and smooth yet digging into the soil in *terroir* overdrive, showing mineral, wet earth, blackberry, currant and ripe cherry. The supple tannin structure precedes great intensity on the long finish. Best from 2002 through 2007.–P.M. • $170 • (9/30/1999) • **93**

Musigny 1996: One of the greatest wines of the '96 red Burgundy vintage. Magnificent and multilayered, this full-bodied *grand cru* delivers mind-boggling complexity, marrying ripe plum, licorice and blackberry character with—and this is the beauty of it—masses of *terroir*-driven mineral, iron and wet earth. Delicious now, but has the stuffing to last. Best after 2005.–P.M. • $162 • (9/30/1998) CS • **96**

Musigny 1995 • $140 • (11/15/1997) • **87**

Musigny 1994 • $85 • (11/15/1996) • **82**

Musigny 1993 • $96 Ⓐ • (11/15/1995) • **94**

Musigny 1992 • $NA • (12/15/1994) • **85**

Musigny 1991 • $NA • (1/31/1994) • **89**

Puligny-Montrachet Les Combettes 1997: Attractive in a crisp way. Light yellow, very lively and fresh, showing honey, pear tart, pie crust, dough and deftly accented oak. Turns a bit hard and acidic on the zingy finish. Best from 2003 through 2010.–P.M. • $80 • (9/30/1999) • **87**

Puligny-Montrachet Les Combettes 1996: Graceful, full-bodied seducer. This *premier cru* engulfs the senses, packing the palate with fat, thick, cream-like flavors ranging from violet, rose petal, mineral, vanilla bean, pear, mocha and pineapple. Nicely balanced, and although the perfumed oak distracted a bit at first, it disappeared after 12 hours aeration. Best from 2005.–P.M. • $73 • (8/31/1998) • **95**

Puligny-Montrachet Les Combettes 1995 • $60 • (8/31/1997) • **97**

Volnay Champans 1997: Cherry, earth and tarragon aromas and flavors mark this firm, vibrant '97 red. With a bit more stuffing than most Volnays, it holds your interest to the moderately tannic finish, where a cherry note lingers. Drink now through 2003.–B.S. • $63 • (9/30/1999) • **86**

Volnay Champans 1996: Ripe and sweet-tasting, this harmonious Volnay is a pleasure to taste. Full-bodied, deliciously opulent, with good earth, mineral and spicy notes along with the cherry, cassis and plum. Drink now through 2005.–P.M. • $60 • (9/30/1998) • **91**

Volnay En Champans 1995 • $50 • (11/15/1997) • **89**

Volnay En Champans 1993 • $36 • (11/15/1995) • **88**

Volnay En Champans 1992 • $NA • (12/15/1994) • **85**

Volnay-Santenots 1997: A nice-smelling '97 red Burgundy, with raspberry, violet, blackberry and cherry. Balanced, offering a soft midpalate and smooth tannins, it beckons to be enjoyed young. Drink now through 2001.–P.M. • $63 • (9/30/1999) • **87**

Volnay-Santenots 1996: Impressively supple, with a lush, opulent mouthfeel. Shows some lovely cherry, wild berry and blueberry character, also some deft, oak-inspired mocha, spice and toasted bread notes. Full-bodied, it's smooth and rounded on the long finish. Best from 2003 through 2010.–P.M. • $58 • (9/30/1998) • **90**

Volnay-Santenots Clos des Santenots 1997: Ripe and spicy, offering black cherry, plum, vanilla and cinnamon aromas and flavors, with moderate intensity and structure. It has sufficient acidity and tannin to develop. Drink through 2004–B.S. • $74 • (9/30/1999) • **84**

Volnay-Santenots Clos des Santenots 1996: Marvelous Burgundy, full of sappy fruit and ripe, sweet concentration of cherry, cassis, plum and blueberry. Supple tannins, but the acidity gives it a kick on the palate. Full-bodied, this should hold for years although it's tempting upon release. Drink now through 2006.–P.M. • $64 • (9/30/1998) • **92**

Volnay-Santenots Clos des Santenots 1995 • $52 • (11/15/1997) • **73**

Volnay-Santenots Clos des Santenots 1993 • $37 • (11/15/1995) • **90**

Volnay-Santenots Clos des Santenots 1992 • $NA • (12/15/1994) • **85**

Volnay-Santenots Clos des Santenots 1991 • $NA • (1/31/1994) • **85**

PRIEUR-BRUNET

Bâtard-Montrachet 1997: Intense and subtle. The butter and butterscotch character dominates in this white, but the honey-lemon combination unfolds beautifully to a balanced, seductive, toasty and smoky finish. Drink through 2005–P.M. • $195 • (9/30/1999) • **92**

Bâtard-Montrachet 1996: A bit woody, and not very ripe, with some herbal and green apple character. Short, drying finish.–P.M. • $165 • (8/31/1998) • **77**

Beaune Clos du Roi 1991 • $34 • (1/31/1994) • **80**

Beaune Clos du Roi 1990 • $32 • (2/15/1993) • **86**

Beaune Clos du Roi 1988 • $30 • (12/31/1990) • **82**

Bourgogne White Cuvée Ste.- Jehanne de Chantal 1997: A bit earthy, swampy and salty.–P.M. • $17 • (9/30/1999) • **72**

Bourgogne White Cuvée Ste.-Jehanne de Chantal 1995 • $13 • (8/31/1997) • **83**

Chassagne-Montrachet Les Embazées 1997: This has butterscotch, butter and lots of oak, with a nice lemon-honey connection. Medium-bodied, with excellent, crisp sharpness on the finish. Drink now through 2005.–P.M. • $62 • (9/30/1999) • **86**

Chassagne-Montrachet Les Embazées 1996: Candylike in character, this straightforward Chardonnay lacks the structure expected from a Chassagne. Drink now.–P.M. • $55 • (8/31/1998) • **75**

Chassagne-Montrachet Les Embazées 1995 • $45 • (8/31/1997) • **80**

Chassagne-Montrachet Red Morgeot 1991 • $29 • (1/31/1994) • **82**

Chassagne-Montrachet Red Morgeot 1988 • $17 • (11/15/1990) • **83**

Meursault 1997: Rather closed on the nose, but with an opulent, silky mouthfeel, even though the flavors aren't totally clean. A bit musty.–P.M. • $45 • (9/30/1999) • **77**

Meursault 1996: Tough and close at first, revealing dried herb, grassy, honey and tropical flavors in good combination. Full-bodied, quite minerally, it turned lush and opulent in contact with air, so cellar. Best from 2005.–P.M. • $26 • (8/31/1998) • **89**

Meursault 1995 • $30 • (8/31/1997) • **89**

Meursault Charmes 1997: This fruity Chardonnay shows a full mouthfeel, with citrus, passion fruit and dough character. A bit chewy on the finish. Drink now through 2003.–P.M. • $56 • (9/30/1999) • **82**

Meursault Charmes 1996: Like many '96 Meursaults this was tough and firm at first, but turned into an opulent, ripe, seductive wine with the texture of olive oil after decanting. Magnificent for its very ripe, sweet fruit flavors—ranging from tropical pear and melon to toasted coconut and smoke. Long, thick finish. Best from 2005.–P.M. • $45 • (8/31/1998) • **94**

Meursault Charmes 1995 • $40 • (8/31/1997) • **89**

Meursault Chevalières 1997: Beautiful harmony and *terroir*. This thick, round, ripe, delectable Meursault cascades down the palate with its refined pear, mineral, smoke, citrus and wet earth notes. Drink now through 2005.–P.M. • $50 • (9/30/1999) • **91**

Meursault Chevalières 1996: Ripe and round, a voluptuous '96 that's a delight to taste. Full-bodied, it shows pineapple, ripe pear, cedar and spice, and a silky smooth texture that gives way to lots of crisp fruit flavors on the long, elegant finish. Best from 2005.–P.M. • $40 • (8/31/1998) • **92**

Meursault Chevalières 1995 • $36 • (8/31/1997) • **92**

Meursault Les Forges Dessus 1997: A bit tart and crisp, with green, dried herb and fresh herb notes, it's full in body, offering harsh toasted accents on the long, slightly burning finish. A bit overdone.–P.M. • $47 • (9/30/1999) • **77**

Meursault Les Forges Dessus 1995 • $35 • (1/01/1998) • **74**

Pommard La Platière 1991 • $40 • (1/31/1994) • **82**

Pommard La Platière 1990 • $40 • (2/15/1993) • **85**

Santenay La Comme 1991 • $21 • (1/31/1994) • **78**

Santenay La Maladière 1991 • $21 • (1/31/1994) • **80**

Santenay La Maladière 1990 • $23 • (2/15/1993) • **77**

Santenay La Maladière 1988 • $20 • (11/15/1990) • **80**

Santenay White Clos Rousseau 1997: Of medium ripeness, this tastes a bit herbal, with a crisp, lemony finish.–P.M. • $46 • (9/30/1999) • **79**

Santenay White Clos Rousseau 1996: Aromatically dull, simple and straightforward, light- to medium-bodied, with modest fruit. Tart on the finish. Drink now.–P.M. • $38 • (8/31/1998) • **75**

Santenay White Clos Rousseau 1995 • $33 • (8/31/1997) • **86**

Santenay White En Boichot 1997: Tastes a bit dull, with hard wood tannins and a harshness on the finish.–P.M. • $33 • (9/30/1999) • **78**

Key: SS—Spectator Selection. CS—Cellar Selection. HR—Highly Recommended. $NA—Price not available. (BT)—Barrel tasting. Ⓐ—Auction Price.
For a key to the tasters' initials, see "How to Use These Listings."
Dates in parentheses represent the issues in which the ratings were published.

Santenay White En Boichot 1996: A bit rustic, with a light nose that doesn't show much, but pretty seductive on the smooth palate, showing stony, mineral-laden character. Supple finish. Drink now through 2001.–P.M. • $20 • (8/31/1998) • **82**

Santenay White En Boichot 1995 • $24 • (8/31/1997) • **83**

Volnay-Santenots Clos des Santenots 1991 • $NA • (1/31/1994) • **83**

Volnay-Santenots Clos des Santenots 1990 • $35 • (2/15/1993) • **85**

Volnay-Santenots Clos des Santenots 1988 • $35 • (11/30/1990) • **85**

PRIEUR DE MEYNEY

St.-Estèphe 1996: Very light and watery, with some berry character, but it's just too diluted to be anything but average. Second label of Château Meyney.–J.S. • $NA • (2/28/1999) • **77**

PRIEUR & FILS, PAUL

Sancerre La Croix du Perthuis 1996 • $NA • (6/15/1998) • **85**

PRIEUR & FILS, PIERRE

Sancerre Domaine de St.-Pierre 1998: This firm, well-structured white offers grapefruit, herb and mineral flavors that show good intensity through the lively finish. Very crisp, it will match well with food. Drink now.–T.M. • $16 • (10/31/1999) • **86**

PRIEURE, CHATEAU DU

Brouilly 1997: This fleshy red is soft but delivers a mouthful of fresh fruit, with plum, cherry and berry flavors accented by light vanilla. It's gentle, balanced, and brings you back for another sip. Drink now.–T.M. • $15 • (5/15/1999) • **84**

Côtes du Rhône 1993 • $8 • (11/15/1995) • **82**

PRIEURE DE ST.-JEAN DE BEBIAN

Coteaux du Languedoc 1997: Something wrong here. There's a bizarre, overly smoky and bretty aroma and cooked, muddy flavors, then volatile acidity mars the finish. Tasted twice, with consistent notes.–K.M. • $30 • (12/31/1999) • **67**

Coteaux du Languedoc 1996: A wine with a touch of elegance and class. Lively berry, cherry and spice flavors are well integrated in this medium-bodied red. Beautifully sculpted, with restrained leathery notes. Vanilla and nutmeg linger on the finish. Drink now.–K.M. • $25 • (10/31/1998) • **89**

Coteaux du Languedoc 1995 • $34 Ⓐ • (10/31/1997) • **92**

Coteaux du Languedoc 1994 • $20 • (5/31/1997) • **86**

Coteaux du Languedoc 1993 • $20 • (1/01/1997) • **90**

Coteaux du Languedoc 1991 • $20 • (1/01/1997) • **89**

Coteaux du Languedoc 1989 • $23 • (6/30/1992) • **77**

Coteaux du Languedoc La Chapelle de Bébian 1995 • $15 • (2/28/1998) • **87**

Coteaux du Languedoc White 1996 • $37 • (2/28/1998) • **90**

PRIEURE-LICHINE, BLANC DU CHATEAU

Bordeaux 1998: A very good white, with apple, honey and vanilla character. Medium-bodied, with good fruit and a fresh finish. Drink now.–J.S. • $NA • (2/29/2000) • **86**

PRIEURE-LICHINE, CHATEAU

Margaux 1999: Pleasant, with berry and cherry character. Medium-bodied, with a light finish.–J.S. • $NA • (1/01/2000) (BT) • **80-84**

Margaux 1998: A bit lean, with some berry and tobacco character. Medium- to light-bodied. Short finish. Firm and slightly austere tannins.–J.S. • $NA • (5/31/1999) (BT) • **80-84**

Margaux 1997: Lovely aromas of berries and chocolate, with a hint of spice. Medium-bodied, with good fruit and a fresh finish. A bit short. Drink now.–J.S. • $28 • (1/31/2000) • **85**

Margaux 1996: Plum and strawberry aromas, with hints of stone. Medium-bodied, with firm tannins and a medium aftertaste. A bit lean, but fresh and clean. Best after 2001.–J.S. • $38 • (1/31/1999) • **85**

Margaux 1995 • $31 Ⓐ • (1/31/1998) • **90**

Margaux 1994 • $19 Ⓐ • (1/31/1997) • **88**

Margaux 1993 • $17 Ⓐ • (1/31/1996) • **81**

Margaux 1992 • $15 • (4/15/1995) • **82**

Margaux 1991 • $15 • (3/31/1994) • **84**

Margaux 1990 • $33 Ⓐ • (3/31/1993) • **86**

Margaux 1989: Ready for drinking and starting to dry out a bit from the big tannic structure. Medium-ruby color, dusty berry and tobacco aromas. Medium-bodied, with velvety tannins and a medium, slightly dry finish. (1989 Bordeaux horizontal tasting).–J.S. • $36 Ⓐ • (5/31/1999) • **86**

Margaux 1988 • $31 Ⓐ • (4/30/1991) • **90**

Margaux 1987 • $15 • (2/15/1990) • **78**

Margaux 1986 • $48 Ⓐ • (6/15/1989) • **92**

Margaux 1985 • $35 Ⓐ • (2/15/1988) • **82**

Margaux 1984 • $14 • (11/30/1986) • **80**

Margaux 1983 • $36 Ⓐ • (4/16/1986) • **96**

Margaux 1982: Rich and delicious. Dark ruby-garnet color, with an amber rim. Loads of crushed berry character, with hints of new wood. Full-bodied and very chewy, with masses of fruit and a long, long finish. Drink now or hold. (1982 Bordeaux horizontal tasting).–J.S. • $45 Ⓐ • (11/30/1998) • **89**

Margaux 1981 • $30 • (11/01/1984) • **86**

Margaux 1959 • $50/1.5 liter • (10/15/1990) • **80**

PRIEURE MALESAN, CHATEAU

Premières Côtes de Blaye 1999: Good fruit, with mineral, berry and dark chocolate character. Medium-bodied, light tannins and a light finish.–J.S. • $NA • (1/01/2000) (BT) • **80-84**

Premières Côtes de Blaye 1998: A well-made, modern Bordeaux. Dark ruby, with intense raspberry, cherry and mineral aromas. Full-bodied, with firm, sleek tannins and a long, lively finish. Best after 2002.–J.S. • $16 • (6/30/2000) • **88**

PRIEURE-ROCH

Bourgogne Grand Ordinaire 1991 • $16 • (6/15/1993) • **74**

Chambertin-Clos de Bèze 1997: This lovely red Burgundy tastes ripe, with black cherry and plum, but an earth component adds complexity. Moderately oaked, with a chewy and fresh character on the balanced, succulent finish. Drink now through 2005.–P.M. • $NA • (1/01/2000) • **88**

Clos de Vougeot 1990 • $65 • (6/15/1993) • **83**

Nuits-St.-Georges Clos des Corvées 1996: Mature-tasting, with game, oak, plum, black cherry and toast notes, but also a slight forest underbrush, mushroom character that turns a bit dry on the finish. Drink now through 2003.–P.M. • $50 • (7/31/1999) • **87**

Vosne-Romanée Clos Goillotte 1997: Already mature and going downhill. Smells like earth, but it turns surprisingly acidic and limey on the palate.–P.M. • $NA • (1/01/2000) • **70**

Vosne-Romanée Hautes Maizières 1990 • $50 • (6/15/1993) • **82**

Vosne-Romanée Les Clous 1990 • $30 • (6/15/1993) • **85**

Vosne-Romanée Les Suchots 1996: Very spicy, with pepper, toast, plum, mocha, and showing a crisp texture but enough minerally complexity to turn up the voltage on the finish. Best from 2001 through 2004.–P.M. • $70 • (7/31/1999) • **87**

PRIEURS DE LA COMMANDERIE, CHATEAU

Pomerol 1997: Good berry flavors, with hints of dried herbs. Medium-bodied, with firm tannins and a short finish. A bit lean.–J.S. • $NA • (1/31/2000) • **83**

Pomerol 1995 • $18 • (1/31/1998) • **81**

Pomerol 1985 • $27 • (9/30/1988) • **93**

Pomerol 1983 • $25 • (9/30/1986) • **79**

PRISSE, CAVE DE

Bourgogne Madame Costeau 1997: Not very complex, but pure and clean black fruit character, with a black pepper, roasted game aroma. Medium-bodied, with a fresh kick of acidity. Drink now.–P.M. • $NA • (1/01/1999) • **82**

Chardonnay Vin de Pays d'Oc Madame Costeau 1996 • $8 • (10/31/1997) • **72**

Mâcon-Prissé Madame Costeau 1997: Woody, with a tart, drying character. A straightforward Chardonnay with modest fruit.–P.M. • $10 • (5/31/1999) • **70**

Mâcon-Prissé Madame Costeau 1996 • $9 • (10/15/1997) • **82**

Merlot Vin de Pays d'Oc Madame Costeau 1996: Fresh and fruity, with nice plum and berry flavors and even hints of banana. Drink now.–K.M. • $8 • (9/30/1998) • **82**

Merlot Vin de Pays d'Oc Madame Costeau 1995 • $7 • (11/15/1997) • **81**

PROSPER-MAUFOUX

Aloxe-Corton 1982 • $27 • (6/15/1992) • **79**
Beaujolais Nouveau 1999: Fresh and fruity, this supple red offers black cherry and plum flavors with very light tannins. It's crisp and clean. Drink now.–T.M. • $9 • (1/01/2000) • **82**
Beaujolais-Villages 1995 • $9 • (9/15/1997) • **78**
Beaujolais-Villages 1994 • $10 • (6/15/1995) • **74**
Beaujolais-Villages 1993 • $9 • (7/31/1995) • **76**
Beaujolais-Villages 1992 • $9 • (6/30/1994) • **81**
Beaujolais-Villages 1991 • $9 • (7/31/1992) • **80**
Brouilly 1995 • $14 • (9/15/1997) • **82**
Brouilly 1994 • $12 • (6/15/1995) • **78**
Brouilly 1993 • $10 • (7/31/1995) • **77**
Brouilly 1992 • $11 • (6/30/1994) • **80**
Châteauneuf-du-Pape 1988 • $16 • (5/31/1992) • **81**
Côtes du Rhône 1990 • $8 • (6/15/1992) • **84**
Côtes du Rhône 1989 • $9 • (5/31/1991) • **84**
Côtes du Rhône 1988 • $7 • (6/30/1990) • **79**
Fleurie La Madone 1995 • $16 • (9/15/1997) • **84**
Moulin-à-Vent 1991 • $12 • (6/15/1994) • **86**
Muscat de Beaumes-de-Venise NV • $21 • (10/31/1993) • **84**
Pouilly-Fuissé 1995 • $20 • (5/31/1998) • **70**
St.-Amour 1992 • $12 • (6/15/1994) • **85**
St.-Véran 1996 • $12 • (5/31/1998) • **79**
Santenay Les Gravières 1985 • $17 • (10/15/1989) • **85**

PROTHEAU, MAURICE

Mercurey White Champmartins 1998: Straightforward Chardonnay, with green apple character and a tart finish.–P.M. • $22 • (5/31/2000) • **79**
Mercurey White Clos l'Evêque 1998: Smells fine, but tastes a bit odd. Has candied and perfumy aromas. Tough, astringent finish.–P.M. • $24 • (5/31/2000) • **74**
Mercurey White Les Ormeaux 1998: Nice ripeness to this vanilla-tasting, heavily oaked white. Full-bodied, it packs plenty of punch, delivering rich fruit character along with some spice and honey. Seductive finish. Drink now through 2003.–P.M. • $22 • (5/31/2000) • **87**
Rully La Chatalienne Domaine des Fromanges 1998: Asparagus and smoke in this odd wine; sour finish.–P.M. • $19 • (5/31/2000) • **70**
Rully Les Fromanges Domaine des Fromanges 1998: Exotic, with its floral, grassy style. Medium-bodied, it has a taste of ripeness (honey, pear) and good succulent character, but gets hard and crisp on the finish. Drink now.–P.M. • $19 • (5/31/2000) • **82**
Rully Les Fromanges Domaine des Fromanges 1995 • $14 • (6/30/1997) • **78**
Rully Red La Chatalienne Domaine des Fromanges 1990 • $14 • (6/15/1993) • **74**

PROTHEAU & FILS, F.

Mâcon-Villages Domaine de Montbellet 1998: A bit watery and diluted, with simple fruit flavors.–P.M. • $10 • (5/31/2000) • **75**

PROVIDENCE, CHATEAU LA

Pomerol 1998: Good velvety texture to this young wine, with berry character. Medium body. Medium finish.–J.S. • $NA • (5/31/1999) (BT) • **85-89**

PRUNIER, MICHEL

Auxey-Duresses 1996: Elegant, showing spicy currant and cherry flavors with firm tannins. Lacking a bit in flesh to balance the tannins, but bright and tasty. The finish is dry. Drink through 2002–B.S. • $22 • (9/30/1998) • **83**
Auxey-Duresses Clos du Val 1996: Herb and licorice aromas and flavors mark this red Burgundy of modest concentration and length. Drink now.–B.S. • $28 • (9/30/1998) • **82**
Auxey-Duresses Clos du Val 1995 • $40 • (11/15/1997) • **75**
Auxey-Duresses Clos du Val 1994 • $33 • (11/15/1996) • **79**
Auxey-Duresses Premier Cru 1995 • $36 • (11/15/1997) • **82**
Auxey-Duresses White 1997: A supple white, with a cooked pear, lemon, slightly herbal character. Medium-bodied and of medium ripeness. Drink now.–P.M. • $NA • (1/01/1999) • **84**
Auxey-Duresses White Vieilles Vignes 1997: A bit herbal, with a buttery, metallic character and a hot finish.–P.M. • $NA • (1/01/1999) • **76**
Auxey-Duresses White Vieilles Vignes 1996 • $22 • (5/31/1998) • **85**
Beaune Les Sizies 1994 • $35 • (11/15/1996) • **81**
Meursault Les Clous 1996 • $35 • (5/31/1998) • **89**
Volnay Caillerets 1995 • $49 • (11/15/1997) • **79**
Volnay Caillerets 1994 • $39 • (11/15/1996) • **74**

PRUNIER, PASCAL

Auxey-Duresses Les Duresses 1996: There's a lot of style and pretty cherry aromas and flavors to this wine, backed up by solid tannins and lively acidity. Moderate finish. Drink now through 2002.–B.S. • $21 • (9/30/1998) • **85**
Beaune Les Sizies 1996: Smoky, blackberry aromas and flavors are the highlights of this elegant '96 Beaune. Otherwise, there's a touch of cardboard, it lacks concentration and depth, has a hot finish. Best after 2000.–B.S. • $22 • (9/30/1998) • **79**
Monthélie 1996: Fragrant aromas of roses and violets contrast with the licorice and foresty flavors in this attractive, fleshy red. There's good density, and the structure is for early drinking. Drink through 2004–B.S. • $17 • (9/30/1998) • **86**
Monthélie Les Vignes Rondes 1996: An atypical Burgundy that tastes like a delicious Barolo. Polished and fine-textured, with tar, rose petal and smoky oak character. Medium-bodied, with refined tannins, you can sit and sniff this one with pleasure. Drink now through 2005.–P.M. • $20 • (9/30/1998) • **89**

PRUNIER, VINCENT

Auxey-Duresses Clos du Val 1987 • $25 • (11/15/1989) • **84**
Auxey-Duresses White 1996: Tight and fairly tart,with green, mouthpuckering citrus notes. Of medium body, needing more round ripeness on the crisp finish. Has good intensity though, and should cut through food just fine. Drink now through 2003.–P.M. • $NA • (8/31/1998) • **80**
Chassagne-Montrachet Red 1990 • $16 • (6/15/1993) • **77**
Puligny-Montrachet Les Garennes 1996: Well-made white Burgundy, with supple texture. Quite spicy, with chocolate, mocha and coffee, plus clean, pure fruit and good lemon notes. Of medium body, with a burst of life on the vibrant finish. Best after 2003.–P.M. • $NA • (8/31/1998) • **87**
St.-Aubin La Chalenière 1996: Ripe and full of finesse, of light to medium body, and singing with delicate pear, melon and lemon flavors. Quite crisp on the clean finish. Drink now through 2003.–P.M. • $NA • (8/31/1998) • **86**

PUECH COCUT, DOMAINE

Cabernet Sauvignon Vin de Pays d'Oc 1994 • $6 • (12/15/1997) • **76**
Chardonnay Vin de Pays d'Oc 1998: A bit green-tasting, with some nutty flavors. Finish clamps down hard.–K.M. • $7 • (10/15/1999) • **76**
Chardonnay Vin de Pays d'Oc 1996 • $6 • (9/30/1997) • **78**
Merlot Vin de Pays d'Oc 1996 • $6 • (11/15/1997) • **82**

PUECH-HAUT, CHATEAU

Coteaux du Languedoc St.-Drézéry 1995 • $10 • (3/31/1998) • **86**
Coteaux du Languedoc St.-Drézéry Le Rouge Epicurien 1996: Made in an obvious international style, this has a meaty, gamy aroma and thick, rich flavors of dark cherry, plum and berry. Intense, with plenty of savage character alongside the sweet oak flavors and lovely spice notes. Still youthful, this should develop in the years ahead. Drink through 2005–K.M. • $29 • (11/15/1999) • **89**
Coteaux du Languedoc White St.-Drézéry Le Blanc Epicurien 1997: A heavy-handed and extremely idiosyncratic white, this sports a high-toned floral aroma and mature flavors of apricot, honey and almond that give it a late-harvest quality. Loads of mineral and gravel notes carry to the finish. Viognier, Roussanne and Marsanne. Drink now through 2003.–K.M. • $29 • (11/15/1999) • **86**

PUGET, DOMAINE DU

Cabernet Sauvignon Vin de Pays de l'Aude 1995 • $7 • (12/15/1997) • **79**
Cabernet Sauvignon Vin de Pays de l'Aude 1991 • $6 • (6/30/1994) • **78**
Cabernet Sauvignon Vin de Pays de l'Aude 1989 • $5 • (9/30/1992) • **83**
Merlot Vin de Pays de l'Aude 1995 • $7 • (11/15/1997) • **81**
Merlot Vin de Pays de l'Aude 1994 • $7 • (7/31/1997) • **83**
Merlot Vin de Pays de l'Aude 1991 • $6 • (6/30/1994) • **73**

Key: SS—Spectator Selection. CS—Cellar Selection. HR—Highly Recommended. $NA—Price not available. (BT)—Barrel tasting. (A)—Auction Price.
For a key to the tasters' initials, see "How to Use These Listings."
Dates in parentheses represent the issues in which the ratings were published.

FRANCE

Merlot Vin de Pays de l'Aude 1990 • $6 • (6/15/1993) • **78**
Merlot Vin de Pays de l'Aude 1989 • $5 • (6/30/1992) • **77**
Merlot Vin de Pays de l'Aude 1988 • $4 • (6/30/1990) • **76**

PULIGNY-MONTRACHET, DOMAINE DU CHATEAU DE

Bourgogne White Clos du Château 1997: A bit simple but sweet-tasting, with nice pineapple juice, touching off lime, peach and apricot. Vibrant finish, but lacking a bit of structure. Drink now through 2002.–P.M. • $20 • (5/31/1999) • **80**
Bourgogne White Clos du Château 1996 • $16 • (5/31/1998) • **82**
Chassagne-Montrachet 1997: Very clean and steely in style, this tart Chassagne offers little opulent fruit, showing instead lemon and green apple notes, with a floral aroma. Drink now through 2002.–P.M. • $45 • (5/31/1999) • **82**
Chevalier-Montrachet 1997: A bit tart and drying on the aftertaste, with green apple notes and a short finish.–P.M. • $180 • (5/31/1999) • **74**
Chevalier-Montrachet 1996: Unctuous, opulent, thick-textured, full-bodied, this oozes class and ripe fruit. Tastes like a *grand cru* with its lush, fat midpalate, its wonderful pineapple, ripe pear and deftly toasted oak accents. Velvety finish with just enough lemon to make it exciting. Best after 2005.–P.M. • $175 • (8/31/1998) • **96**
Côte de Nuits-Villages 1990 • $21 • (8/31/1992) • **78**
Côte de Nuits-Villages 1988 • $17 • (3/31/1991) • **82**
Meursault 1997: Clean, buttery and medium-bodied, this is rather woody and offers modest ripe fruit on the drying finish.–P.M. • $40 • (5/31/1999) • **78**
Meursault 1996 • $26 • (5/31/1998) • **92**
Meursault Les Perrières 1997: Medium-bodied, with a crisp, modestly fruity character, this shows green apple, wet earth and lemon. Drying on the finish.–P.M. • $65 • (5/31/1999) • **79**
Meursault Les Perrières 1995 • $36 • (1/31/1998) • **93**
Meursault Les Poruzots 1997: Well made. Full-bodied, elegant and polished, delivering a round, minerally mouthfeel, with clean, vibrant fruit concentration, subtle toasty notes and good acidity on the finish. Drink now through 2002.–P.M. • $60 • (5/31/1999) • **88**
Meursault Les Poruzots 1995 • $42 • (1/31/1998) • **93**
Monthélie 1990 • $21 • (8/31/1992) • **84**
Monthélie 1988 • $16 • (11/15/1990) • **77**
Monthélie White 1997: Earthy, but with a certain richness from the lush tropical and fresh herb concentration. The intensity picked up after the wine was open for a couple of hours, but the finish is still a bit tart. Drink now.–P.M. • $30 • (5/31/1999) • **80**
Monthélie White 1996 • $22 • (5/31/1998) • **89**
Monthélie White 1995 • $20 • (1/31/1998) • **90**
Montrachet 1995: Beautifully creamy, ripe and seductive, with plenty of fruit, toasted coconut and banana aromas and flavors. Full-bodied, but not overdone, fairly elegant, with a finish that gains in intensity as the wine airs. Best after 2005.–P.M. • $NA • (8/31/1998) • **93**
Pommard 1990 • $40 • (8/31/1992) • **79**
Pommard 1988 • $34 • (8/31/1990) • **83**
Puligny-Montrachet 1997: This medium-bodied, attractively balanced '97 has a firm core of clean citrus, honey and green apple, with a display of nice mineral character, good acidity and an impressive, succulent length. Drink now through 2005.–P.M. • $45 • (5/31/1999) • **88**
Puligny-Montrachet 1995 • $32 • (8/31/1997) • **90**
Puligny-Montrachet La Garenne 1997: Ripe, with tropical, dried apricot, honey and lemon notes, it turns a bit hard on the finish. Drink now through 2003.–P.M. • $65 • (5/31/1999) • **84**
Puligny-Montrachet La Garenne 1996: Fantastic concentration of fruit in this full-bodied, rich and ripe 1996. Despite all the oak, it's subtle and reserved on the nose; only when you sip it do you realize its explosive power. Incredible silky, oily mouthfeel, with honey, lemon, ripe pear and pineapple flavors. Tempting upon release, better to cellar. Best from 2005 through 2020.–P.M. • $58 • (8/31/1998) • **95**
Puligny-Montrachet Les Chalumeaux 1997: Ripe, toasty and spicy in style. Medium-bodied, with mango, pineapple and lime character, but it turns strangely astringent on the palate and has a hard, drying and acidic finish that's disjointed.–P.M. • $60 • (5/31/1999) • **75**
Puligny-Montrachet Les Chalumeaux 1996: Wonderful, brimming with fruit, backed by not-too-much oak, this wine is balanced and palate-cleansing, beckoning you back for another sip. Lovely lemon, honey and butter aromas and flavors, seductive, opulent, well-balanced texture. Ah! A dreamlike wine with a dreamlike finish. Best after 2005.–P.M. • $56 • (8/31/1998) • **95**
Puligny-Montrachet Les Folatières 1997: The obvious oak—with butter, butterscotch and spice—adds a dimension to the honey, pear and lemon flavors. Medium-bodied, with an oak-dominated intensity on the finish. Drink now through 2002.–P.M. • $70 • (5/31/1999) • **84**
Puligny-Montrachet Les Folatières 1996: Clean and pure, lovely, full-bodied, opulent, ripe, with a velvety texture despite loads of exciting lime, pear and tropical character. Beckons to be drunk it's so balanced, but it will age. Best after 2005.–P.M. • $65 • (8/31/1998) • **95**
Puligny-Montrachet Les Folatières 1995 • $48 • (1/31/1998) • **90**
St.-Aubin En Remilly 1997: Gold-colored, thick, ripe and full-bodied, this blends a sweet-tasting, supple core—accented by pear, honey and toasted oak—with typical St.-Aubin flavors of citrus, wet earth and fresh herb. Long, chewy, satisfying finish. Drink now through 2005.–P.M. • $30 • (5/31/1999) • **91**
St.-Aubin En Remilly 1996: A bit dull, with butter and oak notes dominating the fruit. Medium-bodied, turns bitter.–P.M. • $26 • (8/31/1998) • **78**
St.-Aubin En Remilly 1995 • $25 • (5/31/1997) • **79**
St.-Aubin En Remilly 1990 • $25 • (8/31/1992) • **79**

PUY-BLANQUET, CHATEAU

St.-Emilion 1994 • $20 • (11/30/1997) • **84**
St.-Emilion 1993 • $15 • (1/31/1996) • **78**
St.-Emilion 1990 • $17 • (3/31/1993) • **87**
St.-Emilion 1989 • $14 • (3/15/1992) • **90**
St.-Emilion 1983 • $12 • (12/31/1986) • **76**
St.-Emilion 1982: Holding on. Darkish brick-red color. Leafy, earthy character, with a hint of ripe fruit. Medium-bodied, with tobacco and mushroom flavors, velvety tannins and a short finish. (1982 Bordeaux horizontal tasting). Drink now.–J.S. • $NA • (11/30/1998) • **86**

PUYGUERAUD, CHATEAU

Côtes de Francs 1999: A bit lean and racy, but with good berry, cherry and mineral character.–J.S. • $NA • (1/01/2000) (BT) • **80-84**
Côtes de Francs 1998: Very grapey, with hints of mineral and raspberry. Medium- to full-bodied, with loads of firm tannins. Medium finish. Juicy.–J.S. • $NA • (5/31/1999) (BT) • **85-89**
Côtes de Francs 1997: Well done—a very good quality red Bordeaux at a very affordable price. It shows good dark color, intense violet and berry aromas, and is medium- to full-bodied, with polished tannins and a long finish. Needs time. Best after 2000.–J.S. • $10 • (1/31/2000) • **88**
Côtes de Francs 1996: Lots of plum-skin and berry character on the nose. Medium-bodied, with firm tannins and a slightly tough and dry finish.–J.S. • $15 • (1/31/1999) • **85**
Côtes de Francs 1995 • $16 • (1/31/1998) • **87**
Côtes de Francs 1993 • $18 • (1/31/1996) • **80**
Côtes de Francs 1990 • $18 • (3/31/1993) • **81**
Côtes de Francs 1989: Chewy and rustic, yet still fresh and lively. Medium-ruby color. Bright cherry, berry aromas and hints of earth. Medium- to full-bodied, with full tannins and a slightly dry finish. (1989 Bordeaux horizontal tasting). Drink now through 2003.–J.S. • $NA • (5/31/1999) • **86**
Côtes de Francs 1986 • $12 • (6/15/1989) • **84**

QUANTIN, CHATEAU DE

Pessac-Léognan 1995 • $15 • (1/31/1998) • **78**
Pessac-Léognan White 1996: Rather simple, with freshly sliced apple and lemon character. Medium-bodied, with fresh acidity and a clean, crisp finish. Drink now.–J.S. • $NA • (1/01/1999) • **82**

QUINAULT, CHATEAU

St.-Emilion 1995 • $15 • (1/31/1998) • **80**
St.-Emilion L'Enclos 1999: A wine with harmony. Wonderful aromas of mineral, berry and raspberry. Medium- to full-bodied, with silky tannins and a fresh finish.–J.S. • $NA • (1/01/2000) (BT) • **85-89**
St.-Emilion L'Enclos 1998: Purple-colored, with intense aromas of blackberries and spices. Full-bodied, with a solid core of fruit and tannins. Quite chewy. Short finish.–J.S. • $NA • (5/31/1999) (BT) • **85-89**
St.-Emilion L'Enclos 1997: Beautiful aromas of plum, berry and toasted oak. Medium- to full-bodied, with a solid core of fruit and a long aftertaste of berry and chocolate. Very pleasing. Best after 2000.–J.S. • $24 • (1/31/2000) • **87**

RABASSE CHARAVIN, DOMAINE

Côtes du Rhône-Villages Cairanne 1997: Light, its modest strawberry and cherry flavors laced with an unclean oak element.–P.M. • $14 • (11/15/1998) • **72**

RABASSE CHARAVIN, DOMAINE

Côtes du Rhône-Villages Cairanne 1996 • $14 • (10/15/1997) • **73**
Côtes du Rhône-Villages Rasteau 1994 • $14 • (10/15/1997) • **70**

RABAUD-PROMIS, CHATEAU

Sauternes 1991 • $NA • (4/15/1995) • **82**
Sauternes 1990 • $NA • (4/15/1995) • **88**
Sauternes 1989 • $30 • (4/15/1995) • **86**
Sauternes 1988 • $52 Ⓐ • (4/15/1995) • **93**
Sauternes 1987 • $22 • (6/15/1990) • **83**
Sauternes 1986 • $31 Ⓐ • (4/15/1995) • **84**
Sauternes 1983 • $29 Ⓐ • (4/15/1995) • **91**
Sauternes 1947 • $NA • (5/31/1997) • **85**

RAFFAULT, OLGA

Chinon Les Picasses 1990 • $16 • (10/31/1994) • **77**
Chinon White Champ-Chenin 1997: Golden in color and rich in texture, this white offers apple, melon and earth flavors. A bit blunt but kept in balance by firm acidity. Good with poultry. Drink now.–T.M. • $16 • (2/29/2000) • **83**

RAISSAC, DOMAINE DE

Chardonnay Vin de Pays d'Oc 1998: Offers some green banana flavors and buttery notes which linger on the finish.–K.M. • $8 • (10/15/1999) • **77**

RAMAFORT, CHATEAU

Médoc 1998: Currant and cherry aromas ooze out of the glass. Full-bodied, compacted, with ripe fruit and velvety tannins. Long, caressing finish. A bit hard to believe, really—let's see it next year.–J.S. • $NA • (5/31/1999) (BT) • **85-89**
Médoc 1997: Attractive aromas of plums, berries and violets. Medium-bodied, with fine tannins and a medium, fruity finish. Drink now through 2004.–J.S. • $NA • (1/31/2000) • **87**
Médoc 1996: Impressive concentration, but earthy and rustic on the palate. Dark-colored, with intense berry, earth and spice aromas. Medium-bodied, with velvety tannins. Tarry and earthy on the aftertaste. Drink now.–J.S. • $20 • (1/31/1999) • **86**
Médoc 1995 • $18 • (1/31/1998) • **87**

RAMAGE LA BATISSE, CHATEAU

Haut-Médoc 1997: Pretty raspberry, violet and cherry character. Medium- to full-bodied, with a chewy texture and a medium, fruity aftertaste. Well done for this estate.–J.S. • $NA • (1/31/2000) • **88**
Haut-Médoc 1996: Clean and grapey, with mineral and cherry character. Medium-bodied, with firm tannins, but the midpalate is hollow. Best after 2000.–J.S. • $NA • (1/31/1999) • **84**
Haut-Médoc 1995: A bit herbal, with earth, berry and cherry aromas and flavors. Medium-bodied, with medium, velvety tannins and a firm finish. Best from 2003 through 2008.–J.S. • $NA • (9/15/1998) • **85**
Haut-Médoc 1990 • $18 • (3/31/1993) • **84**
Haut-Médoc 1989: Extremely well-crafted '89. Color is dark-ruby, with aromas of blackberry, mint and stones. Full-bodied and velvety, sporting lots of cherry, green tobacco and cedar on the palate. Impressive for this estate. Still needs time, but hard to resist now. (1989 Bordeaux horizontal tasting). Best after 2000.–J.S. • $NA • (5/31/1999) • **90**
Haut-Médoc 1987 • $12 • (11/30/1989) • **82**
Haut-Médoc 1986 • $14 • (11/30/1989) • **82**

RAME, CHATEAU LA

St.-Croix-du-Mont 1997: A very good sweet wine from a minor appellation. Aromas of spice, almond, coconut and ripe pineapple follow through to a medium- to full-bodied palate. Medium sweet, with a light, fruity aftertaste. Drink now.–J.S. • $25 • (1/01/2000) • **88**

Key: SS—Spectator Selection. CS—Cellar Selection. HR—Highly Recommended. $NA—Price not available. (BT)—Barrel tasting. Ⓐ—Auction Price. For a key to the tasters' initials, see "How to Use These Listings." **Dates in parentheses represent the issues in which the ratings were published.**

St.-Croix-du-Mont 1996: Dark yellow, with intense aromas of lemon curd and spice. Medium-bodied and medium sweet, with a pleasing allspice and honey aftertaste. Drink now.–J.S. • $24 • (1/01/2000) • **86**
St.-Croix-du-Mont 1993 • $11/500 ml. • (8/31/1997) • **85**

RAMONET

Bienvenues-Bâtard-Montrachet 1997: This pretty white has nice toast, smoke and pear tart character. Forward, with a touch of lime and honey kicking in on the long-fused finish. Drink now through 2002.–P.M. • $123 Ⓐ • (9/30/1999) • **88**
Bourgogne Aligoté 1995 • $20 • (8/31/1997) • **89**
Chassagne-Montrachet 1996: Racy, structured and very lively, here's a '96 full of apple and citrus flavors augmented by a smoky character from the new oak. Drink now through 2004.–B.S. • $30 • (5/31/1999) • **86**
Chassagne-Montrachet 1995 • $40 • (8/31/1997) • **93**
Chassagne-Montrachet Boudriotte 1997: Beautifully ripe, but very crisp and not totally together. The intensity and the sweet fruit zip to a long, persistent finish. Best from 2006 through 2010.–P.M. • $60 • (9/30/1999) • **89**
Chassagne-Montrachet Boudriotte 1996: Lovely aromas of honey, flowers and spice are followed by intense apple and stone flavors in this balanced, textured and firmly structured white. Long, lingering aftertaste of mineral and honey. Drink now through 2005.–B.S. • $48 Ⓐ • (5/31/1999) • **90**
Chassagne-Montrachet Boudriotte 1995 • $50 • (8/31/1997) • **93**
Chassagne-Montrachet Les Caillerets 1995 • $45 • (5/31/1997) • **95**
Chassagne-Montrachet Les Grandes Ruchottes 1995 • $70 • (8/31/1997) • **97**
Chassagne-Montrachet Les Vergers 1997: What great white Burgundy is all about. Concentrated, with loads of ripe, elegant fruit, showing a tightly wound honey and citrus character that holds it together and fights off the subtle oak flavors. Silky texture from start to finish. Great length. A beauty made in heaven. Drink now through 2007.–P.M. • $58 • (9/30/1999) • **95**
Chassagne-Montrachet Les Vergers 1996: Starts off with a smoky aroma. On the palate it's racy, lean and focused, with a tightly packed core of citrus, apple and mineral flavors. Beautiful balance and expressiveness. Drink now through 2005.–B.S. • $60 • (5/31/1999) • **91**
Chassagne-Montrachet Les Vergers 1995 • $50 • (5/31/1997) • **92**
Chassagne-Montrachet Morgeot 1997: A distinctive white, showing greenish, grassy, sharp aromas, but in the mouth it turns thicker than expected, with intense fruit for the vintage and a persistent finish. Drink now through 2005.–P.M. • $58 • (9/30/1999) • **89**
Chassagne-Montrachet Morgeot 1996: Tightly wound, with leesy, creamy, minerally aromas. Intense and concentrated, this white delivers mineral, citrus and white peach flavors, all on a lean and focused framework. Will improve with bottle age. Drink now through 2006.–B.S. • $67 Ⓐ • (5/31/1999) • **91**
Chassagne-Montrachet Red Clos St.-Jean 1997: There's lovely chewy, licorice-tinged fruit and a bit of cooked plum in this straightforward, enjoyable '97 red. Good structure underneath. Drink now through 2003.–B.S. • $37 • (9/30/1999) • **83**
Montrachet 1995: Lovely, full-bodied, very silky. Offers great power and toasted oak, spicy coconut, mint and dried herbal notes. Extraordinary mouthful of a wine, showing superconcentration, great length. Best after 2010.–P.M. • $486 Ⓐ • (8/31/1998) • **98**
Puligny-Montrachet Champ Canet 1995 • $70 • (8/31/1997) • **92**
St.-Aubin Les Charmois 1995 • $35 • (5/31/1997) • **87**

RAPET PERE & FILS

Aloxe-Corton 1995 • $32 • (11/15/1997) • **82**
Bourgogne en Bully 1988 • $19 • (3/31/1991) • **80**
Corton-Charlemagne 1998: A tough wine that may need some time to soften. Unusually rustic for a '98, this full-bodied white is expressive with its toasted hazelnut, clean citrus and crisp edge. Shows a chalky, minerally side on the finish. Drink now through 2005.–P.M. • $85 • (5/31/2000) • **88**
Corton-Charlemagne 1997: What is this New World–styled Chardonnay doing in Burgundy? Very oaky in a buttery, spicy way, it tastes astringent as the wood overwhelms the modest fruit. Drying finish.–P.M. • $85 • (5/31/1999) • **75**
Corton-Charlemagne 1996 • $79 • (5/31/1998) • **90**
Corton-Charlemagne 1995 • $NA • (5/31/1997) • **98**
Corton Pougets 1995 • $50 • (11/15/1997) • **78**
Pernand-Vergelesses 1988 • $31 • (2/28/1991) • **79**
Pernand-Vergelesses Ile des Vergelesses 1995 • $34 • (11/15/1997) • **78**
Pernand-Vergelesses White Premier Cru 1998: Round in texture and smoky in aroma, with ripe flavors. Full-bodied, its lovely fruit is sprinkled with dried herbs, honey and spice; tastes balanced, albeit not overly complex. Long on the finish. Drink now through 2003.–P.M. • $36 • (5/31/2000) • **87**

Pernand-Vergelesses White Premier Cru 1997: Fresh, zesty and vibrant from delicious, crisp acidity and delightful, sweet-tasting tropical, pear and green apple flavors, it displays just a bit of dryness on the palate but stays clean on the finish. Drink now through 2001.–P.M. • $36 • (5/31/1999) • **86**
Pernand-Vergelesses White Premier Cru 1996 • $28 • (5/31/1998) • **85**

RASPAIL-AY, DOMAINE

Gigondas 1995: Generous and ripe, showing plum and cherry jam flavors, this is a mouthful of a red that delivers cedar, earth and lemon notes on the finale. Full-bodied, fairly alcoholic and not too refined. Best after 2000.–P.M. • $20 • (10/15/1998) • **85**
Gigondas 1994 • $20 • (12/15/1996) • **81**
Gigondas 1993 • $20 • (11/15/1995) • **90**
Gigondas 1990 • $20 • (4/15/1993) • **80**
Gigondas 1989 • $19 • (4/15/1993) • **83**
Gigondas 1988 • $19 • (11/15/1991) • **79**
Gigondas 1986 • $15 • (1/31/1989) • **92**

RATEAU, JEAN-CLAUDE

Beaune Clos des Mariages 1988 • $25 • (1/31/1992) • **77**
Beaune Les Bressandes 1997: Spice, pepper and licorice accent the cherry aromas and flavors in this light-bodied, chewy '97. A touch cooked, with a round midpalate and stiff tannins on the finish. Best after 2001.–B.S. • $30 • (9/30/1999) • **82**
Beaune Les Bressandes 1996: Very gamy, toasted and a bit odd, with a petrol character and a dry, astringent finish. 75 cases imported.–P.M. • $28 • (5/15/1999) • **70**
Beaune Les Reversées 1997: A bit heavy-handed with the oak and a haylike aroma, but there's substance and cherry flavor underneath, along with a fresh and firm structure. Should come together with time. Best after 2001.–B.S. • $30 • (9/30/1999) • **83**
Beaune Les Reversées 1995 • $29 • (11/15/1997) • **79**
Beaune White Les Coucherias 1997: The oak is a bit too much for the fruit, with a smoke, toast, pie crust, honey and pear character. Tough finish. Drink now through 2002.–P.M. • $39 • (9/30/1999) • **82**

RAUSAN-SEGLA, CHATEAU

Margaux 1993 • $33 Ⓐ • (1/31/1996) • **87**
Margaux 1992 • $30 • (4/15/1995) • **86**
Margaux 1990 • $25 Ⓐ • (3/31/1993) • **87**
Margaux 1989: Wonderfully balanced and harmonious '89. Inky-ruby color, and a brick-red edge. Intense aromas of berries, spices and licorice. Full-bodied and velvety, with lovely ripe fruit and a long, caressing finish. (1989 Bordeaux horizontal tasting). Best after 2001.–J.S. • $72 Ⓐ • (5/31/1999) • **90**
Margaux 1988: Full-bodied, with a slightly austere, harsh earth and berry character. Hard to get excited about. (1988 Bordeaux horizontal tasting). Drink now.–J.S. • $71 Ⓐ • (11/30/1998) • **81**
Margaux 1986 • $84 Ⓐ • (9/15/1989) • **87**
Margaux 1985 • $57 Ⓐ • (5/31/1988) • **92**
Margaux 1982: A rich, plush wine. Shows blackberry and chocolate character, with a hint of cedar. Full-bodied and thick, yet very velvety, with lots of sweet fruit on the finish. (1982 Bordeaux horizontal tasting). Drink now.–J.S. • $48 Ⓐ • (11/30/1998) • **89**
Margaux 1981 • $16 • (5/01/1984) • **90**
Margaux 1979 • $NA • (10/15/1989) • **69**
Margaux 1970 • $36 Ⓐ • (5/15/1993) • **89**
Margaux 1961 • $91 Ⓐ • (4/30/1996) • **84**
Margaux 1947 • $NA • (5/31/1997) • **86**
Margaux 1945 • $NA • (3/16/1986) • **73**

RAUZAN-DESPAGNE, CHATEAU

Bordeaux 1998: A good, straightforward Bordeaux, with fresh raspberry and mint character. Medium-bodied, with fine tannins and a fruity finish. Drink now.–J.S. • $9 • (6/15/2000) • **84**
Bordeaux 1994 • $10 • (6/30/1997) • **83**
Bordeaux Cuvée Passion 1997: Pretty and balanced, with aromas of currant and tobacco. Medium-bodied, with silky tannins and a pleasant finish. Drink now.–J.S. • $12 • (6/15/2000) • **86**
Bordeaux Cuvée Passion 1996: Aromatic, with black cherry and mineral character. Medium- to light-bodied, with fine tannins and a light finish. Drink now through 2002.–J.S. • $NA • (1/31/1999) • **82**
Bordeaux White 1996: Refreshing melon, gooseberry and coconut aromas and flavors. Medium-bodied, with light fruit and a light finish. Clean, but slightly short. Drink now.–J.S. • $NA • (1/01/1999) • **82**
Bordeaux White Cuvée Passion 1999: Clean and grassy, with a steely lemon undertone. Medium-bodied, with superclean acidity and a long, zingy finish. Drink now.–J.S. • $12 • (6/15/2000) • **87**

RAUZAN-GASSIES, CHATEAU

Margaux 1998: Some pleasant fruit in this wine, with berry, currant and chocolate character. Medium- to full-bodied, with fine tannins and a medium finish.–J.S. • $NA • (5/31/1999) (BT) • **85-89**
Margaux 1997: A pleasant, light and fruity red with raspberry and cherry character. Drink now.–J.S. • $40 • (1/31/2000) • **83**
Margaux 1996: Lovely perfumed aromas of raspberries and flowers. Medium-bodied, with firm tannins and a fruity aftertaste. Not a major-league wine, but an admirable effort from this property. Best after 2000.–J.S. • $32 • (1/31/1999) • **86**
Margaux 1995 • $30 • (1/31/1998) • **91**
Margaux 1994 • $25 • (1/31/1997) • **77**
Margaux 1993 • $25 • (1/31/1996) • **77**
Margaux 1989: Rather dusty in character, but a very good, mature bottle of wine. Plenty of berry, allspice and chocolate aromas. Medium-bodied and round-textured, with tobacco, cherry and chestnut flavors. (1989 Bordeaux horizontal tasting). Drink now.–J.S. • $NA • (5/31/1999) • **85**
Margaux 1988 • $35 • (8/31/1991) • **85**
Margaux 1986 • $34 Ⓐ • (6/30/1989) • **88**
Margaux 1982: A delicious glass of red. Dark ruby-garnet color, with an amber edge. Berry and coffee aromas. Medium-bodied, with lovely, well-integrated, velvety tannins and a ripe fruit finish. (1982 Bordeaux horizontal tasting). Drink now.–J.S. • $NA • (11/30/1998) • **88**
Margaux 1961 • $275 Ⓐ • (4/30/1996) • **85**
Margaux 1959 • $81 Ⓐ • (10/15/1990) • **73**
Margaux 1945 • $300 • (3/16/1986) • **91**

RAUZAN-SEGLA, CHATEAU

Margaux 1999: Fine and solid, with attractive berry, chocolate and mineral aromas and flavors. Medium- to full-bodied, with fine tannins and a long cherry aftertaste.–J.S. • $NA • (1/01/2000) (BT) • **85-89**
Margaux 1998: Impressive concentration for the Médoc this vintage. Full-bodied and round, with velvety tannins and a chewy mouthfeel. Slightly hollow midpalate, but damn good. Almost outstanding.–J.S. • $NA • (5/31/1999) (BT) • **85-89**
Margaux 1997: A very pretty and aromatic wine, with spices, berries and violets. Medium-bodied with medium, fine tannins and a polished finish. Best after 2000.–J.S. • $48 • (1/31/2000) • **88**
Margaux 1996: Looks seriously good, with a dark color, and smells seriously good, with raspberry and vanilla character on the nose, but lacks some concentration on the palate. Medium- to full-bodied, adding firm and silky tannins. Lots of wood, but should mellow with age. Best after 2002.–J.S. • $40 Ⓐ • (1/31/1999) • **90**
Margaux 1995 • $48 Ⓐ • (1/31/1998) • **94**
Margaux 1994 • $42 Ⓐ • (1/31/1997) • **90**

RAVAILLE FRERES

Coteaux du Languedoc Ermitage du Pic St.-Loup 1997: Stewy and dried cherry flavors dominate this medium-bodied red.–K.M. • $9 • (2/29/2000) • **78**
Coteaux du Languedoc Ermitage du Pic St.-Loup 1995: This has a slightly herbal quality, with cherry and red plum flavors and lavender notes on the finish. Medium-bodied, with lively acidity. Drink now.–K.M. • $13 • (1/31/1999) • **85**
Coteaux du Languedoc Ermitage du Pic St.-Loup 1992 • $7 • (3/15/1994) • **83**
Coteaux du Languedoc Ermitage du Pic St.-Loup Cuvée Ste.-Agnès 1997: A light- to medium-bodied red with currant and anise flavors, finishing on some stemmy and peppery notes. Drink now.–K.M. • $13 • (2/29/2000) • **80**
Coteaux du Languedoc White Ermitage du Pic St.-Loup Cuvée Ste.-Agnès 1997: A thick-tasting white, with wild herb and anise character. Robust and distinctive; try if you're in the mood for something different. Drink now.–K.M. • $16 • (11/15/1998) • **85**

RAVENEAU, FRANCOIS

Chablis Blanchot 1997: A bit coarse right now, showing high alcohol in addition to wet stones, gunflint and a nutty, honey finish. Big and brooding, lacking the finesse (for now) of the best, yet still very impressive. Give it time. Best from 2001 through 2010.–B.S. • $70 • (5/15/2000) • **93**

Chablis Blanchot 1996: A complete wine. Beautiful combination of muscle and intensity, as the flint, apple and vanilla flavors unfold on a firm, lively strucure. Complex and satisfying on the long aftertaste. Best from 2001 through 2008.–B.S. • $80 • (1/01/2000) • **94**

Chablis Blanchot 1995: Rustic yet sophisticated, here's a real statement of true Chablis *terroir*. Offers lots of weight on the palate, with beeswax, mineral, pear and honey notes. Full-bodied, but clean as a whistle. An ager. Best from 2002 through 2010.–P.M. • $80 • (1/01/1999) • **92**

Chablis Butteaux 1997: Not offering much aroma today, but this delivers a mouthful of cream, lemon, honey and mineral; deep and concentrated, beautifully put together and very long on the finish. Great promise for the future. Best from 2001 through 2010.–B.S. • $45 • (5/15/2000) • **94**

Chablis Butteaux 1995: Impressive '95 Chablis, very broad and complex, offering honey, beeswax, spice and vanilla cream notes on a minerally frame. Pure and clean, it's an indestructible Chablis that will age gracefully. Drink through 2010–P.M. • $72 Ⓐ • (1/01/1999) • **92**

Chablis Forêt 1997: Gorgeous, rich and elegant, showing wet earth, subtle wood, mineral and citrus flavors. What counts is the texture—this creams the palate with an oily feel that is unforgettable. Drink now through 2010.–P.M. • $58 • (5/15/2000) • **92**

Chablis Montée de Tonnerre 1997: Unyielding on the nose, but oh so rich and creamy in the mouth, combining depth of honey, lemon, mineral and nuts with a bracing acidity. Seamless and incredibly long on the finish. Best from 2001 through 2010.–B.S. • $60 • (5/15/2000) • **95**

Chablis Montée de Tonnerre 1996: Great *terroir* here. Laser focus and breeding define this intense, precision white. The green fruit, mineral and apple flavors build on the palate to a long, long aftertaste. Best from 2001 through 2006.–B.S. • $60 • (1/01/2000) • **91**

Chablis Montée de Tonnerre 1995: Excellent winemaking. Beautiful, pure and ripe, with a firm structure, this full-bodied white offers lime, chalk, pear and green apple notes that glide to a lovely, crisp, fresh finish. Minimal obvious new oak allows the fruit and *terroir* to show through. Drink now through 2010.–P.M. • $65 • (8/31/1998) • **90**

Chablis Monts Mains 1997: The aromas hint at honey and mineral, and the palate delivers. Open and inviting, the honey notes are allied to a rich texture and racy acidity. Fine length, with a butterscotch aftertaste. Drink now through 2005.–B.S. • $45 • (5/15/2000) • **92**

Chablis Vaillons 1997: Honey, lemon and green bush fruits introduce this round, medium-weight white. Lovely concentration, yet this needs some time to integrate its vibrant underlying acidity. Best from 2001 through 2008.–B.S. • $45 • (5/15/2000) • **90**

Chablis Valmur 1997: Could be the wine of the '97 vintage in Chablis. A seamless work of art, simply mindboggling in its sheer balance. Medium- to full-bodied, it casts a curtain of silk on the palate. Lovely fruit, earth and mineral, too, but it's the texture that is truly unforgettable. Drink now through 2010.–P.M. • $95 • (5/15/2000) CS • **96**

Chablis Valmur 1996: A big, brooding style of Chardonnay, rounded out by a hint of new oak and a creamy texture. The lanolin, pear, honey and vanilla flavors integrate nicely with the powerful framework. Great finish. Best from 2001 through 2008.–B.S. • $80 • (1/01/2000) • **93**

Chablis Valmur 1995: A firmly structured Chardonnay, showing good mouthfeel and lime, green apple, wet earth and pear flavors. Not so fat in texture, it's of medium body and intensity, with lots of finesse. Juicy finish lacks a bit of concentration. Drink now through 2005.–P.M. • $144 Ⓐ • (8/31/1998) • **89**

RAVIER, OLIVIER

Beaujolais Domaine des Sables d'Or 1996: Soft, fruity, tastes a bit like a cherry hard candy—slightly sweet and slightly sour. A good base for a wine punch.–T.M. • $6 • (8/31/1998) • **78**

Beaujolais-Villages Domaine des Hayes 1996: This round red offers plush cherry and light plum flavors, with soft tannins and gentle acidity. Clean, fresh—a pleasant quaff. Drink now.–T.M. • $8 • (8/31/1998) • **82**

Brouilly Pisse-Vieille Domaine de la Grange Charton 1996 • $11 • (6/15/1998) • **84**

Chiroubles Château de Raousset 1996: Tight and firm upfront, with cherry and herbal flavors and firmer tannins than most Chiroubles. A bit muddy on the finish, though.–T.M. • $10 • (8/31/1998) • **82**

Key: SS—Spectator Selection. CS—Cellar Selection. HR—Highly Recommended. $NA—Price not available. (BT)—Barrel tasting. Ⓐ—Auction Price. For a key to the tasters' initials, see "How to Use These Listings." **Dates in parentheses represent the issues in which the ratings were published.**

Côte de Brouilly Domaine de la Pierre Bleue 1996 • $10 • (6/15/1998) • **84**

Fleurie La Madone 1996 • $12 • (6/15/1998) • **84**

Juliénas Château de la Bottière 1996 • $10 • (5/31/1998) • **86**

Morgon Côte du Puy 1996: Full-bodied and fleshy, yet with a firm backbone, this characteristic red offers ripe plum, meat, smoke and light herb flavors. Intense, yet still lively and approachable. Delicious with roasts and stews. Drink now through 2002.–T.M. • $10 • (7/31/1998) • **89**

Moulin-à-Vent Château de Chénas 1996 • $12 • (5/31/1998) • **84**

Régnié 1996: Enticing smoke and black cherry aromas give way to ripe, full flavors of cherries, plums and herbs in this dark, rich red. Shows good concentration and balance; a fine match for grilled meats.–T.M. • $8 • (8/31/1998) • **85**

Régnié Domaine de la Grange Charton 1996: Good concentration for Régnié, with firm tannins and bright acidity. The flavors range from black cherry to smoke to citrus. A bit austere, it will benefit from food. Drink now.–T.M. • $9 • (8/31/1998) • **83**

St.-Amour Domaine des Pins 1996: Quite rich and firm, with ripe black cherry and gamy notes, rustic earthy accents. A traditional style best with hearty food. Drink now.–T.M. • $12 • (8/31/1998) • **82**

RAYAS, CHATEAU

Châteauneuf-du-Pape Réservé 1997: A sinewy, uncompromising, traditional wine. Light in color and body, with a bitter mineralness that gives a certain fatness on the midpalate. The fruit is secondary—just modest cherry—but the iron and rust character is something else. Tannins are a bit tough and astringent on the finish. Best from 2005 through 2015.–P.M. • $91 • (12/15/1999) • **88**

Châteauneuf-du-Pape Réservé 1996: Excellent effort for this vintage, which was difficult in the Southern Rhône. A lush, ripe, lovely wine, packed with blackberry and cassis flavors. Full-bodied; a good candidate for the cellar. Best from 2005 through 2015. (Châteauneuf-du-Pape Réservé vertical tasting–and all Reserve notes below)–P.M. • $104 Ⓐ • (12/15/1999) • **88**

Châteauneuf-du-Pape Réservé 1995: Gorgeous and silky, this fabulous Rayas has plenty of power, with blackberry and cassis flavors and more fruit than mineral character. Just delicious. Drink now through 2015.–P.M. • $NA • (12/15/1999) • **91**

Châteauneuf-du-Pape Réservé 1994: A tough, intense wine packed with cedar and blackberry, this is all power and no finesse. Time will tell if it comes around—as some collectors believe it will—to deliver an outstanding package one day. Best from 2003 through 2015.–P.M. • $NA • (12/15/1999) • **88**

Châteauneuf-du-Pape Réservé 1993: Very drinkable, elegant and supple, this medium-bodied Rayas shows decent fruit, although it tastes slightly diluted. Drink now.–P.M. • $NA • (12/15/1999) • **84**

Châteauneuf-du-Pape Réservé 1992: Off bottle? Drying on the palate, bitter and astringent, this tastes as if it were corky, although it doesn't smell very corky—just a bit musty.–P.M. • $NA • (12/15/1999) • **70**

Châteauneuf-du-Pape Réservé 1990: A polished, rich and ripe red, this Rayas is just sensational, offering chocolate and spice and a minerally wet earth character. Tempting now, but worth cellaring. Even better than when reviewed upon release. Best from 2010 through 2020.–P.M. • $525 Ⓐ • (12/15/1999) • **94**

Châteauneuf-du-Pape Réservé 1989: Intense, big and packed with fruit. A bit tough and drying on the slightly alcoholic and hot finish. Needs time. Best from 2005 through 2015.–P.M. • $176 Ⓐ • (12/15/1999) • **86**

Châteauneuf-du-Pape Réservé 1988 • $173 Ⓐ • (10/15/1991) • **90**

Châteauneuf-du-Pape Réservé 1986 • $58 • (12/15/1989) • **88**

Châteauneuf-du-Pape Réservé 1985 • $41 • (7/31/1988) • **93**

Châteauneuf-du-Pape Réservé 1983: A wine that seems to be improving with age. Lovely, minerally, ripe and sweet-tasting, offering wet earth complexity and good intensity of flavors. Medium-bodied, it's long on the finish and balanced—a super Châteauneuf. Drink now through 2008.–P.M. • $150 Ⓐ • (12/15/1999) • **90**

Châteauneuf-du-Pape Réservé 1981: Superelegant, with polished tannins, this is as balanced as Châteauneuf gets. Almost delicate and of medium body, it shows lovely blackberry character along with a firm tannic grip on the finish. Drink now through 2010.–P.M. • $NA • (12/15/1999) • **90**

Châteauneuf-du-Pape Réservé 1979: The wine of the tasting. Ready to drink, ripe, rich and exotic, it has a minty note along with black currant. Medium-bodied, it's immensely supple and very balanced, with sweet-tasting fruit, offering the texture of a great Burgundy *grand cru* like Romanée-St.-Vivant. Most impressive. Drink now through 2005.–P.M. • $NA • (12/15/1999) • **95**

Châteauneuf-du-Pape Réservé 1978: A super-fruity, incredibly intense Rayas. Youthful, with black cherry and baked tomato notes, but it also offers a hard backbone of tough tannins, which still need time to come

FRANCE

around. Not up to the quality of the vintage—but perhaps not a representative bottle. Drink now through 2010.–P.M. • $NA • (12/15/1999) • **86**

Châteauneuf-du-Pape Réservé 1976: The drought conditions of this year are especially present in the dry, tough tannins, but this medium-bodied, somewhat lean '76 also shows nice earthy, dusty, soily character that's quite appealing. Too bad the fruit has faded a bit. Drink now through 2005.–P.M. • $NA • (12/15/1999) • **80**

Châteauneuf-du-Pape Réservé 1974: A nice, medium-bodied red, with a smooth texture and brown sugar, cinnamon and red berry notes. Drink now.–P.M. • $NA • (12/15/1999) • **84**

Châteauneuf-du-Pape Réservé 1973: Good intensity on the palate, but it's all a bit astringent and tough, as this Rayas lacks a bit of sweet character and round tannins. The fruit is fading, and the finish delivers some drying tannins.–P.M. • $NA • (12/15/1999) • **79**

Châteauneuf-du-Pape Réservé 1971: Evocative of faded roses, this delicious Châteauneuf offers a sweet-tasting display of plum mixed with distinct mineral notes. Supple tannins and good length on the finish. Very pretty and satisfying. Drink now through 2005.–P.M. • $NA • (12/15/1999) • **89**

Châteauneuf-du-Pape Réservé 1962: Fabulous balance takes your breath away. Rich, ripe and full-bodied yet very delicate, it has the silky texture of cream on the palate, and supple tannins just melt on the finish as you enjoy the cinnamon and black currant flavors. Has the harmony to hold for years. Drink now through 2010.–P.M. • $NA • (12/15/1999) • **91**

Châteauneuf-du-Pape Réservé 1961: Zesty and lively, this medium-bodied, wonderful Rayas has good acidity, as evidenced by a lemony note, but plenty of sweet-tasting plum and brown sugar flavors. Drink now through 2005.–P.M. • $NA • (12/15/1999) • **89**

Châteauneuf-du-Pape Réservé 1959: Disappointing. Slightly oxidized, or maderized, tasting a bit like Sherry, with cedar and chestnut aromas and a bitter, astringent texture.–P.M. • $NA • (12/15/1999) • **77**

Châteauneuf-du-Pape White Réservé 1997: Very deceptive. Shows excellent ripe fruit underneath the awkward traditional, rustic exterior. Buttery and toasty, but tasting a bit dry and tough on the palate, like old wood, it turns up the volume on the finish. Still, this is an acquired taste. Drink now.–P.M. • $78 • (12/15/1999) • **85**

Côtes du Rhône La Pialade 1994 • $16 • (12/15/1996) • **82**
Côtes du Rhône La Pialade 1991 • $14 • (11/30/1994) • **82**

RAYMOND-LAFON, CHATEAU

Sauternes 1991 • $NA • (4/15/1995) • **80**
Sauternes 1990 • $65 Ⓐ • (4/15/1995) • **90**
Sauternes 1989 • $45 Ⓐ • (4/15/1995) • **87**
Sauternes 1988 • $58 Ⓐ • (4/15/1995) • **91**
Sauternes 1987 • $58 • (4/15/1995) • **86**
Sauternes 1986 • $53 • (4/15/1995) • **87**
Sauternes 1983 • $46 Ⓐ • (1/31/1988) • **93**

RAYNE, CHATEAU DE

Bordeaux White 1996 • $6 • (2/28/1998) • **83**

RAYNE-VIGNEAU, CHATEAU DE

Sauternes 1998: Pretty young wine, with pear and vanilla character, medium body and medium sweetness.–J.S. • $NA • (1/01/1999) (BT) • **85-89**

Sauternes 1997: Has botrytis character and intense aromas of honey, spice, almond and dried apricot. Full-bodied and very sweet, with a long, thick finish. Best after 2004.–J.S. • $35 • (1/31/2000) • **93**

Sauternes 1992 • $NA • (4/15/1995) • **82**
Sauternes 1991 • $NA • (4/15/1995) • **85**
Sauternes 1990 • $30 • (4/15/1995) • **88**
Sauternes 1988 • $36 Ⓐ • (4/15/1995) • **90**
Sauternes 1987 • $25 • (6/15/1990) • **77**
Sauternes 1986 • $33 Ⓐ • (4/15/1995) • **91**
Sauternes 1983 • $31 Ⓐ • (1/31/1988) • **77**
Sauternes 1947 • $NA • (5/31/1997) • **81**

RAZ, CHATEAU LE

Bergerac Sec 1997: There are some nicely defined apple, herb and spice flavors in this medium-bodied white. Finishes on rich notes of fig and anise. Drink now.–K.M. • $8 • (11/15/1998) • **84**

REAL MARTIN, CHATEAU

Côtes de Provence 1996: Plenty to sink your teeth into here, with blood and iron flavors and plummy components. A good, mature, medium-bodied red with cardamom and tealike notes on the finish. Drink now.–K.M. • $14 • (4/30/2000) • **85**

Côtes de Provence 1990 • $15 • (7/31/1996) • **78**

Côtes de Provence White 1998: Smells of canned fruit, with modest peach flavors and almond notes on the finish. Tasted twice, with consistent notes.–K.M. • $12 • (5/15/2000) • **78**

RECOUGNE, CHATEAU

Bordeaux Supérieur 1995 • $10 • (1/01/1998) • **84**

RECTORIE, DOMAINE DE LA

Banyuls Cuvée Elisabeth NV • $24 • (5/15/1997) • **87**
Banyuls Cuvée Léon Parcé 1994 • $29 • (5/15/1997) • **85**
Banyuls Cuvée Parcé Frères 1995 • $20 • (5/15/1997) • **82**
Collioure Cuvée I 1990 • $34 • (10/31/1992) • **85**

REDDE, MICHEL

Pouilly-Fumé La Moynerie 1997: Pear and melon flavors are ripe and round in this rich white. It's clean and balanced, but lacks the refreshing acidity typical of the region. Drink now.–T.M. • $19 • (3/31/2000) • **84**

Pouilly-Fumé La Moynerie 1996: Lovely quince and pear character up front in this vibrant, balanced white, followed by a hint of mineral before waning slightly on the finish. Drink now.–B.S. • $19 • (11/15/1998) • **86**

Sancerre Les Tuilières 1997: This broad white is rich with pear and apple flavors. Shows maturity in its nutty and toasty accents, but lemony acidity keeps it lively. Try with fish in creamy sauces. Drink now.–T.M. • $20 • (2/29/2000) • **86**

Sancerre Les Tuilières 1996: Peach, smoke and mineral flavors are attractively displayed and intensely focused, with all the elements in proportion, ending in a succulent, mouthwatering finish.–B.S. • $20 • (11/15/1998) • **88**

REFLETS DU CHATEAU CISSAC

Haut-Médoc 1996: Decent currant and berry character on the nose and palate, but rather diluted, with medium body, firm tannins and a short finish. Drink now.–J.S. • $NA • (1/31/1999) • **80**

REIGNAC, CHATEAU DE

Bordeaux Supérieur Cuvée Prestige 1995 • $13 • (1/31/1998) • **85**

Bordeaux Supérieur Cuvée Spéciale 1997: Interesting aromas of ripe fruit, spices, ginger. Medium-bodied, with velvety tannins and a fruity vanilla aftertaste. Well done. Drink now through 2004.–J.S. • $NA • (1/31/2000) • **85**

Bordeaux Supérieur Cuvée Spéciale 1996 • $25 • (1/01/1998) • **78**

RELAIS DE PATACHE D'AUX, LE

Médoc 1995 • $14 • (1/31/1998) • **83**

REMAURY, DOMAINE

Cabernet Sauvignon Vin de Pays d'Oc 1998: Fairly ripe and juicy, with red plum, berry and currant flavors. Finishes with tobacco and herbal notes. Drink now.–K.M. • $10 • (12/31/1999) • **82**

Mourvèdre Vin de Pays d'Oc 1998: Lip-smacking and effusive, offering exuberant flavors and aromas of raspberry, blueberry and red cherry with some nice smoky and spicy notes mixed in. Peppery on the finish. Drink now through 2001.–K.M. • $10 • (12/31/1999) • **86**

REMEJEANNE, DOMAINE DE LA

Côtes du Rhône Les Arbousiers 1998: A pretty '98, showing silky tannins and a caressing texture, with lovely wet earth, chalk, dried herb, spice, floral and cassis complexity. Medium-bodied, with a smoky, lingering finish. Drink now through 2003.–P.M. • $12 • (12/15/1999) • **86**

Côtes du Rhône Les Arbousiers 1996 • $12 • (10/15/1997) • **85**
Côtes du Rhône Les Arbousiers 1995 • $11 • (9/15/1997) • **80**

■ ■ ■ ■

REMEJEANNE, DOMAINE DE LA

Côtes du Rhône Les Chevrefeuilles 1998: Lots of character in this medium-bodied red, bursting with earth, game, pepper, green olive and blackberry flavors. The tannins are ripe and fold nicely into the long, chewy finish. Try with garlicky Provençal food. Drink now through 2004.–P.M. • $10 • (12/15/1999) • **85**

Côtes du Rhône Les Chevrefeuilles 1997: Supple and balanced, showing clean, pure fruit in a smooth package, with lovely raspberry, black cherry, cassis, spice and plum. Medium-bodied, with a long, delicate finish. Drink now.–P.M. • $10 • (11/15/1998) • **84**

Côtes du Rhône Les Chevrefeuilles 1996 • $10 • (10/15/1997) • **84**

Côtes du Rhône Les Chevrefeuilles 1995 • $9 • (9/15/1997) • **85**

Côtes du Rhône Les Eglantiers 1997: Is it Rhône? Never mind; it's seriously international, supple and impressive. Very ripe yet elegant, showing subtle but fancy oak treatment that leads to violet, toast, grilled meat and blackberry flavors. Drink now through 2005.–P.M. • $25 • (12/15/1999) • **84**

Côtes du Rhône Les Eglantiers 1996: Some lovely currant, blackberry, spice and plum flavors make this charming. Medium-bodied but warm and generous, with an opulent, toasted oak finish that's harmonious. Drink now.–P.M. • $14 • (11/15/1998) • **86**

Côtes du Rhône Les Genevriers 1997: Beautifully made, suave and ripe, with silky tannins, delicious palate-coating, pure and clean red- and blackberry flavors. Medium-bodied, balanced. Harmonious from start to finish. Drink now through 2003.–P.M. • $15 • (11/15/1998) • **88**

Côtes du Rhône Les Genèvriers 1996 • $16 • (10/15/1997) • **85**

Côtes du Rhône Les Genèvriers 1994 • $14 • (9/15/1997) • **84**

Côtes du Rhône Rosé Les Arbousiers 1998: Impressive, clean and fruity, with a muscular structure and good balance. There is excellent ripe fruit without alcohol in this elegant and superflavorful rosé. Loads of "fat" gives this away as a seriously made effort. Drink now.–P.M. • $12 • (12/15/1999) • **85**

Côtes du Rhône-Villages Les Genevriers 1998: Full-bodied and rich, showing very decent, ripe black fruit, this tastes of vanilla, blackberry and loads of Provençal flavors. No question—this is a great little red, as the silky tannins just melt in your mouth. Drink now through 2003.–P.M. • $16 • (12/15/1999) • **88**

Côtes du Rhône White Les Arbousiers 1998: A crisp lemon, butter, wood and honey combo gives it a nervous tension to perk up your palate. A bit sharp on the midpalate, so serve it with lunch rather than dinner. Drink now through 2001.–P.M. • $12 • (12/15/1999) • **88**

Côtes du Rhône White Les Arbousiers 1997: Clean and straightforward, showing green apple, melon and lime. Crisp and a bit hot on the finish. Drink now.–P.M. • $10 • (11/15/1998) • **80**

Côtes du Rhône White Les Arbousiers 1996 • $11 • (10/15/1997) • **85**

Côtes du Rhône White Les Eglantiers 1997: An intriguing, exotic white, with mint, honey, almond and ricelike flavors. Crisp and fresh, showing depth and good structure. Well made. Drink now.–P.M. • $13 • (11/15/1998) • **87**

REMORIQUET, HENRI & GILLES

Nuits-St.-Georges Les Allots 1997: Lush and round, but quite elegant. Medium-bodied, with some cooked berry, jammy, smoked, and spice notes. Smooth texture, round in the palate, with firm tannins kicking in on the sweet-tasting end. Drink now through 2005.–P.M. • $32 • (1/01/2000) • **88**

Nuits-St.-Georges Les Allots 1996: This exotic '96 bursts with game, toast, smoke and cassis character. It's full-bodied, shows ripe tannins and supple texture, but displays a firm backbone that bodes well for the future. 75 cases imported.–P.M. • $34 • (5/15/1999) • **92**

Nuits-St.-Georges Les Bousselots 1997: Polished and flavorful, round and rich, with a bite of firm acidity, chewy tannins, good fruit (blackberry, black cherry) and toasted intensity. Still, this full-bodied Pinot is accessible now. Drink now through 2003.–P.M. • $40 • (1/01/2000) • **86**

Nuits-St.-Georges Les Bousselots 1996: Oh-so-supple, this creamy, oaky, full-bodied and showy '96 red fills every corner of the palate with toasty, smoky, grilled flavors, but engineers exciting black currant notes on the chewily tannic finish. What it lacks in elegance it makes up in power. 75 cases imported. Best from 2006 through 2020.–P.M. • $40 • (5/15/1999) • **95**

Nuits-St.-Georges Les Damodes 1997: A gorgeous '97. This heavyweight Pinot is profound from the first sniff to the last sip, layered with ripe berry, petrol-like and vanilla oak complexity. Full-bodied, with wet earth, mineral and iron-like notes, it finishes with a flourish of fireworks that keep popping on the long aftertaste. Drink now through 2005.–P.M. • $40 • (1/01/2000) • **93**

Nuits-St.-Georges Les Damodes 1996: Pure Pinot, mingling ripe black cherry, raspberry and plum with deftly toasted, spice and grilled flavors, all in a velvety yet fresh wine that sparks joy as you drink. 62 cases imported. Best from 2003 through 2010.–P.M. • $40 • (5/15/1999) • **92**

Nuits-St.-Georges Les St.-Georges 1996: Mineral-based, this unfolds its classy, deep, intense berry perfumes in a ripe, silky cocoon that rolls around the palate to maximum effect, without breaking its spellbinding harmony. 25 cases imported. Best from 2002 through 2020.–P.M. • $46 • (5/15/1999) • **96**

Nuits-St.-Georges Rue de Chaux 1985 • $22 • (7/31/1988) • **81**

RENARD, CHATEAU

Fronsac 1997: A delicate red, with good berry and tobacco character. Light-to medium-bodied, with a fine finish. Second wine of Château Renard Mondesir. Drink now.–J.S. • $13 • (7/31/1999) • **83**

Fronsac 1996: Light and weedy. Hard to get excited about.–J.S. • $14 • (7/31/1999) • **75**

RENARD MONDESIR, CHATEAU

Fronsac 1997: A light wine, with pleasant berry and tea character. Medium-to light-bodied, with light tannins and a fresh finish. Drink now.–J.S. • $NA • (1/31/2000) • **81**

RENAUDIE, CHATEAU LA

Bordeaux Supérieur 1995 • $NA • (1/01/1997) • **77**

RENJARDE, DOMAINE DE LA

Côtes du Rhône-Villages 1998: Good ripeness, sweet fruit and a firm tannin structure combine to provide a feeling of depth in this medium-bodied red from the Rhône. A good wine for medium-term aging, at a no-quibble price. Drink through 2004–P.M. • $9 • (12/15/1999) • **85**

Côtes du Rhône-Villages 1997: Light- to medium-bodied, with modest red berry character, cedar and oak accents. A quaffable wine, but already maturing. Try slightly chilled.–P.M. • $11 • (11/15/1998) • **78**

Côtes du Rhône-Villages 1996: Supple but also fairly neutral, with a cherry, spice, citrus character. Light-bodied, with an herbal finish.–P.M. • $11 • (11/15/1998) • **74**

Côtes du Rhône-Villages 1995: A simple, smooth and delicious, light-bodied little red, with raspberry, cherry, tar, spice rack and currant notes. Chill slightly. Drink now.–P.M. • $11 • (11/15/1998) • **80**

Côtes du Rhône-Villages 1991 • $10 • (4/30/1994) • **85**

Côtes du Rhône-Villages 1990 • $11 • (11/15/1992) • **87**

Côtes du Rhône-Villages Réserve 1998: Hedonistic. This silky-smooth red just melts on the palate. It's hard to find any fault in this gem, with ripe blackberry, smoke, spice and chocolate notes. Above all the sweet tannins and opulent texture win you over with their caressing feel. Drink now through 2004.–P.M. • $13 • (12/15/1999) • **92**

RENOIR, RENE

Cabernet Sauvignon Vin de Pays du Gard 1995 • $5 • (12/15/1996) • **83**

Côtes du Rhône 1995 • $7 • (10/15/1996) • **83**

Côtes du Ventoux 1995 • $6 • (10/15/1996) • **82**

Merlot Vin de Pays du Gard 1995 • $5 • (1/31/1997) • **83**

RENOU, RENE

Bonnezeaux Anne 1997: Fresh and balanced, this clean, late-harvest white offers an appealing mix of fresh apple, honey and dried apricot flavors that are sweet but still refreshing. This was the better of two bottles. Drink now through 2004.–T.M. • $55/500 ml. • (2/29/2000) • **87**

Bonnezeaux Cuvée Zénith 1997: This sweet white offers attractive flavors of caramel and dried apple that are clean and rather light on the palate. Soft and straightforward. Tasted three times, this was the best showing. Drink now through 2003.–T.M. • $80/500 ml. • (2/29/2000) • **85**

Bonnezeaux La Montagne 1997: This moderately sweet white offers a range of apple flavors—fresh, dried and cooked—backed by firm acidity to yield a balanced, pleasant wine. Drink now through 2003.–T.M. • $30/500 ml. • (2/29/2000) • **86**

Key: SS—Spectator Selection. CS—Cellar Selection. HR—Highly Recommended. $NA—Price not available. (BT)—Barrel tasting. Ⓐ—Auction Price.
For a key to the tasters' initials, see "How to Use These Listings."
Dates in parentheses represent the issues in which the ratings were published.

Bonnezeaux Les Melleresses 1997: This is Bonnezeaux? Dilute, with simple canned cider flavors and oxidized apple skin notes. Very disappointing. –K.M. • $38 • (5/15/2000) • **76**

Bonnezeaux Tri de Vendanges 1997: Cooked apple, honey and light spice notes are fairly sweet and clean in this straightforward white. Has richness but seems a bit light for the region. This was the better of two bottles. Drink now.–T.M. • $28 • (2/29/2000) • **84**

RESERVE DE LA COMTESSE

Pauillac 1996: Ripe and soft for the vintage, but slightly one-dimensional. Very dark color, showing violet, berry and currant aromas with a hint of minerals. Full-bodied, with chewy tannins and an aftertaste of berry and smoke. Very good Second label from Château Pichon-Lalande.–J.S. • $NA • (1/31/1999) • **88**

Pauillac 1995 • $25 • (1/31/1998) • **88**

Pauillac 1988 • $26 • (3/15/1991) • **88**

Pauillac 1987 • $18 • (5/15/1990) • **82**

Pauillac 1986 • $30 • (5/31/1989) • **90**

Pauillac 1983 • $21 • (3/01/1986) • **82**

Pauillac 1982: Rather hard, but good. Medium-ruby color, with a garnet hue. Tobacco, cherry and fruit aromas. Medium-bodied, with firm tannins and a tobacco and cedar aftertaste. (1982 Bordeaux horizontal tasting). Drink now.–J.S. • $NA • (11/30/1998) • **87**

RESERVE DE LEOVILLE BARTON, LA

St.-Julien 1996: Pretty aromas of dried cherries and flowers. Medium-bodied, with some berry flavor, but slightly short and diluted on the finish. A second label of Château Léoville Barton. Drink now through 2001.–J.S. • $NA • (1/31/1999) • **81**

St.-Julien 1995 • $22 • (1/31/1998) • **87**

RESERVE DU GENERAL

Margaux 1997: Well done for the vintage, with grape and berry aromas. Medium-bodied, with light, silky tannins and a fresh finish. Second wine of Palmer. Drink now.–J.S. • $45 • (6/15/2000) • **86**

Margaux 1996: Delicate berry and floral character shows clearly on the nose and palate, making this young, medium-bodied wine fresh and vibrant. Light to medium tannins. Best after 2000.–J.S. • $NA • (1/31/1999) • **85**

RESERVE J.-J. DE BETHMANN

Pessac-Léognan 1995 • $12 • (1/31/1998) • **79**

REVELETTE, CHATEAU

Coteaux d'Aix-en-Provence 1995 • $13 • (9/30/1997) • **84**

Coteaux d'Aix-en-Provence 1993 • $12 • (10/15/1996) • **83**

Coteaux d'Aix-en-Provence Le Grand Rouge 1993 • $20 • (10/15/1996) • **87**

Coteaux d'Aix-en-Provence Le Grand Rouge 1992 • $20 • (10/15/1996) • **78**

Coteaux d'Aix-en-Provence Rosé 1996 • $9 • (9/15/1997) • **82**

REVERDI, CHATEAU

Listrac 1982: Tasted from magnum. Medium-red, garnet color, with slightly funky berry and tobacco aromas. Medium-bodied, with berry and cherry flavors and a light, silky finish. (1982 Bordeaux horizontal tasting). Drink now.–J.S. • $NA/1.5 liter • (11/30/1998) • **85**

REVERDY, BERNARD

Sancerre 1996 • $20 • (6/15/1998) • **84**

REVERDY, HIPPOLYTE

Sancerre 1998: Crisp and herbaceous, this shows typical regional character, but it's a bit thin and green. Would match well with shellfish; a bit tart on its own. Drink now.–T.M. • $17 • (2/29/2000) • **83**

Sancerre 1997: Alluring aromas of smoke and citrus give way to clean, fresh flavors of citrus, herb and apple in this crisp yet round white. Well balanced and refreshing. Drink now.–T.M. • $22 • (12/31/1998) • **87**

Sancerre 1996 • $21 • (6/15/1998) • **90**

Sancerre Red 1996 • $NA • (5/31/1998) • **84**

REVERDY, JEAN

Sancerre La Reine Blanche 1997: This refreshing white offers a lively combination of citrus, mineral and almond flavors. Clean and well focused, yet delicate and soft on the palate. Not a blockbuster, but alluring. Drink now. –T.M. • $18 • (6/30/1999) • **86**

REY, DOMAINE DU

Vin de Pays des Côtes de Gascogne 1997: Light peachy aromas lead into straightfoward flavors of apple and onion. A bit rustic, but enjoyable. Drink now.–K.M. • $7 • (11/15/1998) • **81**

REYSSAC, CHATEAU LE

Bergerac Sec 1996 • $8 • (2/28/1998) • **83**

REZE, CHATEAU LA

Minervois 1996: Focused and flavorful, with bright cherry and red plum flavors. A medium-bodied red that's nicely balanced and would go well with roasted meat or poultry dishes. Kosher. Drink now.–K.M. • $NA • (1/01/1999) • **84**

Minervois White 1997: A simple wine, with a floral aroma and fruit-cocktail flavors. Made from Roussanne and Grenache Blanc. Kosher.–K.M. • $NA • (1/01/1999) • **76**

RICAUD, DOMAINE DE

Bordeaux White 1999: Delicious, with aromas of pear, honey and flowers. Medium-bodied, with fresh acidity and a long, clean finish. Drink now.–J.S. • $11 • (6/15/2000) • **86**

RICHARD, CHATEAU

Côtes de Bergerac 1994 • $12 • (9/30/1997) • **85**

RICHAUD, DOMAINE

Côtes du Rhône Les Garrigues 1997: A bit herbal, light-bodied, seems diluted. Dry finish.–P.M. • $10 • (11/15/1998) • **70**

Côtes du Rhône Les Garrigues 1996 • $10 • (10/15/1997) • **77**

Côtes du Rhône-Villages Cairanne 1997: Delightful. Fairly ripe Cairanne, with wild raspberries, mocha, spice. Tannins are supple and sweet. Drink now.–P.M. • $12 • (11/15/1998) • **85**

Côtes du Rhône-Villages Cairanne 1996 • $14 • (10/15/1997) • **86**

Côtes du Rhône-Villages Cairanne 1995 • $14 • (10/15/1997) • **86**

RICHEMONT

Cabernet Sauvignon Vin de Pays d'Oc Reserve 1995 • $7 • (4/30/1998) • **85**

Chardonnay Vin de Pays d'Oc Reserve 1996 • $7 • (3/31/1998) • **82**

Merlot Vin de Pays d'Oc 1993 • $6 • (10/31/1995) • **81**

Merlot Vin de Pays d'Oc Reserve 1995 • $7 • (3/31/1998) • **79**

Sauvignon Blanc Vin de Pays d'Oc Reserve 1996 • $7 • (3/31/1998) • **82**

Syrah Vin de Pays d'Oc 1993 • $6 • (10/31/1995) • **83**

Syrah Vin de Pays d'Oc Reserve 1995 • $7 • (4/30/1998) • **87**

RIEFLE & FILS, JOSEPH

Gewürztraminer Alsace Côte de Rouffach Bergweingarten de Pfaffenheim 1997: Seductive flavors of rose, litchi and fig are matched by richness and moderate intensity in this lush, big-boned white. A dry finish, with a touch of bitter grapefruit. Drink now.–B.S. • $22 • (10/31/1999) • **85**

Muscat Alsace 1997: The spice and grape notes lean toward the soapy side in this dry, richly textured white. Finishes a little short. Drink now.–B.S. • $17 • (10/31/1999) • **82**

Pinot Blanc Alsace 1997: Lemon, apple and nut flavors unfold gradually in this richly textured, seamless '97 Pinot Blanc. Very ripe and just off-dry, yet with good acidity and lingering flavors of citrus. Drink now.–B.S. • $14 • (9/30/1999) • **87**

Tokay Pinot Gris Alsace Côte de Rouffach 1997: A big, full-bodied white, rich and exhibiting some residual sugar, apricot and earth flavors. Round and powerful, but lacks definition and length. Drink now.–B.S. • $20 • (10/31/1999) • **83**

RIEFLE & FILS, JOSEPH

Tokay Pinot Gris Alsace Grand Cru Steinert 1996: The essence of quince and apricot, this is thick and mouthfilling, not too top-heavy, though soft in structure and a touch astringent on the finish. Drink now through 2001.–B.S. • $35 • (10/31/1999) • **86**

RIEUSSEC, CHATEAU

Sauternes 1998: Thick and rich, with a lovely balance of botrytis and spice character. Full-bodied and oily, with a long, sweet finish. Could be one of the wines of the vintage. Almost classic.–J.S. • $NA • (1/01/1999) (BT) • **90-94**
Sauternes 1993 • $NA • (4/15/1995) • **92**
Sauternes 1992 • $NA • (4/15/1995) • **85**
Sauternes 1991 • $NA • (4/15/1995) • **88**
Sauternes 1990 • $60 Ⓐ • (4/15/1995) • **92**
Sauternes 1989 • $52 Ⓐ • (4/15/1995) • **89**
Sauternes 1988 • $65 Ⓐ • (4/15/1995) • **91**
Sauternes 1987 • $25 Ⓐ • (6/15/1990) • **89**
Sauternes 1986 • $52 Ⓐ • (4/15/1995) • **89**
Sauternes 1985 • $36 Ⓐ • (5/31/1988) • **86**
Sauternes 1983 • $59 Ⓐ • (1/31/1988) • **94**
Sauternes 1981 • $14 • (12/01/1984) • **90**

RIJCKAERT

Hautes-Côtes de Beaune White Bois de Messé 1998: Decent fruit in this light-bodied Chardonnay, offering a touch of honey and sweet toasted oak on the finish. Drink now through 2001.–P.M. • $18 • (5/31/2000) • **83**

Hautes-Côtes de Nuits White Aux Herbeux 1998: Medium-bodied Chardonnay, clean but a bit on the lean side, with tart green apple, some nicely toasted aromas and a citrusy finish. Doesn't taste very ripe, but it's fresh. Drink now through 2002.–P.M. • $18 • (5/31/2000) • **80**

Mâcon-Bissy Les Crays vers Vaux Vieilles Vignes 1998: Heavily oaked—but nicely so—with mint, toasted bread and nutty notes combining with lemon and honey. Medium-bodied and vibrant, with a pleasant if uncomplicated finish. Drink now through 2003.–P.M. • $17 • (5/31/2000) • **83**

Mâcon-Montbellet En Pottes Vieilles Vignes 1998: Well made, and balanced between honey, ripe fruit and citrus. Medium-bodied, it lacks a bit of depth and expression, but what's there is attractive. Toasted oak and mineral character adds to the package. Drink now through 2005.–P.M. • $17 • (5/31/2000) • **85**

Maranges White En Borgy 1998: A crisp style. Offers decent fruit, but tastes a bit tart and woody; a chewy, medium-bodied white that seems overly oaky for the amount of ripe fruit. Drink now through 2002.–P.M. • $20 • (5/31/2000) • **80**

St.-Véran En Avonne Vieilles Vignes 1998: Firm but fairly rich. A medium-bodied wine with ripe fruit and a citrusy backbone that delivers a lingering finish of toasted bread, spice and dried apricot. Drink now through 2002.–P.M. • $18 • (5/31/2000) • **85**

Viré-Clessé L'Epinet 1998: Uncomplicated but fresh, with toasted oak, honey, ripe fruit. Full-bodied, it has a firm, citrusy midpalate that extends into a lingering finish that comes with an ambitious toasty note. Drink now through 2002.–P.M. • $17 • (5/31/2000) • **85**

Viré-Clessé Les Vercherres Vieilles Vignes 1998: Rather crisp and tart, with a good mineral, stony character, but you wish for more ripe fruit. Medium-bodied, with appleskin, toasted oak and dried herbs components, turning a bit astringent on the finish. Drink now through 2002.–P.M. • $18 • (5/31/2000) • **81**

RION, DANIEL

Bourgogne-Hautes Côtes de Nuits White Les Millottes 1998: Clean, with some honey and citrus. Medium-bodied, in a lean, pure style. Nothing complex, just a pretty little Chardonnay. Drink now through 2001.–P.M. • $15 • (5/31/2000) • **84**

Bourgogne White 1998: Quite delicious. With its ripe fruit, chalky subtext, smacking acidity and medium body, this is a delightful Chardonnay that's easy to enjoy. Nothing complex, but fun. Drink now through 2001.–P.M. • $14 • (5/31/2000) • **86**

Key: SS—Spectator Selection. CS—Cellar Selection. HR—Highly Recommended. $NA—Price not available. (BT)—Barrel tasting. Ⓐ—Auction Price.
For a key to the tasters' initials, see "How to Use These Listings."
Dates in parentheses represent the issues in which the ratings were published.

Chambolle-Musigny Les Beaux-Bruns 1997: This has pretty cherry and vanilla aromas and flavors, with a hint of mint and a resinous note in the background. Firm and well balanced, with good intensity of flavor and a lingering finish. Drink through 2004–B.S. • $39 • (9/30/1999) • **89**

Chambolle-Musigny Les Beaux-Bruns 1996: Vibrant, scintillating flavors of blackberry and plum, rich in texture and dense, finishing with grip and intensity. Long, ripe aftertaste. Best from 2001 through 2006.–B.S. • $48 • (9/30/1998) • **90**
Chambolle-Musigny Les Beaux-Bruns 1991 • $43 • (1/31/1994) • **76**
Chambolle-Musigny Les Beaux-Bruns 1989 • $45 • (1/31/1992) • **89**
Chambolle-Musigny Les Beaux-Bruns 1988 • $37 • (1/31/1991) • **87**
Chambolle-Musigny Les Beaux-Bruns 1986 • $21 Ⓐ • (4/15/1989) • **86**
Chambolle-Musigny Les Beaux-Bruns 1985 • $33 • (3/31/1988) • **88**

Chambolle-Musigny Les Charmes 1997: A mint and spice edge adds interest to the black cherry aroma and flavor in this rich, concentrated, supple red. A hint of astringency firms up the finish. Drink now through 2004.–B.S. • $62 • (9/30/1999) • **89**

Chambolle-Musigny Les Charmes 1996: Wonderful Chambolle. Clean and pure, showing marvelous, ripe rose petal, plum and currant character; a supersilky seducer delivering a thick mouthfeel in a racy package. Lush tannins make it accessible now, but it should hold for a few years. Drink now through 2005.–P.M. • $59 • (9/30/1998) • **91**
Chambolle-Musigny Les Charmes 1995 • $82 • (11/15/1997) • **87**
Chambolle-Musigny Les Charmes 1994 • $46 Ⓐ • (11/15/1996) • **88**
Chambolle-Musigny Les Charmes 1993 • $38 Ⓐ • (11/15/1995) • **92**
Chambolle-Musigny Les Charmes 1991 • $70 • (1/31/1994) • **84**
Clos Vougeot 1995 • $99 • (11/15/1997) • **91**
Clos Vougeot 1994 • $76 • (11/15/1996) • **92**
Clos Vougeot 1993 • $90 • (11/15/1995) HR • **97**
Clos Vougeot 1992 • $90 • (12/15/1994) • **89**
Clos Vougeot 1991 • $85 • (1/31/1994) • **87**
Clos Vougeot 1990 • $100 • (12/15/1992) • **97**
Clos Vougeot 1989 • $94 • (1/31/1992) • **92**
Clos Vougeot 1988 • $75 • (1/31/1991) • **92**
Clos Vougeot 1986 • $70 • (4/15/1989) • **90**
Côte de Nuits-Villages 1993 • $17 • (11/15/1995) • **87**
Côte de Nuits-Villages 1990 • $25 • (12/15/1992) • **85**
Côte de Nuits-Villages 1986 • $15 • (7/31/1988) • **81**
Nuits-St.-Georges 1986 • $31 • (4/30/1989) • **85**
Nuits-St.-Georges 1985 • $28 • (3/15/1988) • **85**

Nuits-St.-Georges Aux Vignerondes 1997: Terrific—what great red Burgundy should aspire to. A beam of pure blackberry, black currant and violet arrests the senses, and the concentrated, intense fruit flavors just won't quit. It's well structured and balanced, with a long, long finish. Drink now through 2005.–B.S. • $45 • (9/30/1999) HR • **93**

Nuits-St.-Georges Aux Vignerondes 1996: Lovely, fresh and vibrant Pinot, showing a good complexity of spice, petrol, chocolate, cherry, cassis and raspberry notes. Medium-bodied, it's pure and clean, with supple and ripe tannins, but it needs time to shed some of them. Best after 2003.–P.M. • $48 • (9/30/1998) • **89**
Nuits-St.-Georges Aux Vignerondes 1995 • $66 • (11/15/1997) • **86**
Nuits-St.-Georges Aux Vignerondes 1994 • $36 Ⓐ • (11/15/1996) • **87**
Nuits-St.-Georges Aux Vignerondes 1993 • $50 • (11/15/1995) • **94**
Nuits-St.-Georges Aux Vignerondes 1992 • $NA • (12/15/1994) • **84**
Nuits-St.-Georges Aux Vignerondes 1991 • $52 • (1/31/1994) • **84**
Nuits-St.-Georges Aux Vignerondes 1990 • $70 • (12/15/1992) • **92**
Nuits-St.-Georges Aux Vignerondes 1989 • $63 • (1/31/1992) • **93**
Nuits-St.-Georges Aux Vignerondes 1988 • $42 Ⓐ • (1/31/1991) • **92**
Nuits-St.-Georges Aux Vignerondes 1987 • $35 • (4/30/1990) • **95**
Nuits-St.-Georges Aux Vignerondes 1986 • $43 • (4/30/1989) • **88**
Nuits-St.-Georges Aux Vignerondes 1985 • $40 • (3/15/1988) • **91**

Nuits-St.-Georges Clos des Argillières 1997: The gorgeous nose is saturated with blackberry, spice and mineral. Fresh, with volume, density and firm tannic support. Long, minerally aftertaste. Drink through 2006–B.S. • $49 • (9/30/1999) • **89**

Nuits-St.-Georges Clos des Argillières 1996: Deliciously elegant, this sexy wine bursts with pretty floral, spice, mint, currant and black cherry notes. Of medium body, it melts on the palate, fanning out with its supple and ripe tannins to a long, intense finish. Drink now through 2005.–P.M. • $49 • (9/30/1998) • **90**
Nuits-St.-Georges Clos des Argillières 1995 • $66 • (11/15/1997) • **90**
Nuits-St.-Georges Clos des Argillières 1994 • $43 • (11/15/1996) • **85**
Nuits-St.-Georges Clos des Argillières 1993 • $50 • (11/15/1995) • **88**
Nuits-St.-Georges Clos des Argillières 1992 • $55 • (12/15/1994) • **85**
Nuits-St.-Georges Clos des Argillières 1991 • $52 • (1/31/1994) • **82**
Nuits-St.-Georges Clos des Argillières 1990 • $70 • (12/15/1992) • **93**

Nuits-St.-Georges Clos des Argillières 1989 • $63 • (1/31/1992) • **91**
Nuits-St.-Georges Clos des Argillières 1988 • $48 • (1/31/1991) HR • **91**
Nuits-St.-Georges Clos des Argillières 1987 • $36 • (4/30/1990) • **92**
Nuits-St.-Georges Clos des Argillières 1986 • $47 • (4/30/1989) • **90**
Nuits-St.-Georges Clos des Argillières 1985 • $75 • (3/15/1988) • **94**
Nuits-St.-Georges Les Grandes Vignes 1996: Full, rich and fleshy, with lively floral and spice accents to the lush red cherry character, this is completely seductive, combining ripe fruit with good intensity and a silky texture. Even the tannins are silky. Well done. Best from 2001 through 2006.–B.S. • $32 • (9/30/1998) • **92**
Nuits-St.-Georges Les Grandes Vignes 1995 • $44 • (11/15/1997) • **90**
Nuits-St.-Georges Les Grandes Vignes 1994 • $30 • (11/15/1996) • **80**
Nuits-St.-Georges Les Grandes Vignes 1993 • $32 • (11/15/1995) • **93**
Nuits-St.-Georges Les Grandes Vignes 1992 • $36 • (12/15/1994) • **81**
Nuits-St.-Georges Les Grandes Vignes 1990 • $42 • (12/15/1992) • **92**
Nuits-St.-Georges Les Grandes Vignes 1989 • $38 • (1/31/1992) • **88**
Nuits-St.-Georges Les Hauts Pruliers 1997: The "lifted" nose of balsamic vinegar is followed by a much better palate, where lovely berry character dominates through a wonderfully smoky, grilled finish. Drink now through 2005.–P.M. • $50 • (1/01/2000) • **82**
Nuits-St.-Georges Les Hauts Pruliers 1996: Deeply colored, plummy red Burgundy, very ripe, fleshy and round, with silky texture, soft, light tannins and a fruit-compote character. Best after 2000.–B.S. • $48 • (9/30/1998) • **87**
Nuits-St.-Georges Les Hauts Pruliers 1995 • $66 • (11/15/1997) • **86**
Nuits-St.-Georges Les Hauts Pruliers 1994 • $43 • (11/15/1996) • **85**
Nuits-St.-Georges Les Lavières 1997: A focused wine that bursts with rose petal, raspberry, fig and black cherry. There's a slight balsamic vinegar note to the aroma, but this medium-bodied Pinot has a smooth, plum-tasting finish. Drink now through 2002.–P.M. • $34 • (9/30/1999) • **87**
Nuits-St.-Georges Les Lavières 1996: Beautiful balance defines this jewel of a wine. Full-bodied yet racy, it displays a good backbone of acidity, lots of ripe tannins and lovely, seductive wild raspberry, floral, mint and toasted oak accents. Lingering, pretty finish. Drink now through 2005.–P.M. • $32 • (9/30/1998) • **91**
Nuits-St.-Georges Les Lavières 1991 • $35 • (1/31/1994) • **86**
Nuits-St.-Georges Les Lavières 1988 • $38 Ⓐ • (2/15/1991) HR • **93**
Nuits-St.-Georges Les Lavières 1987 • $21 • (4/30/1990) • **87**
Nuits-St.-Georges Les Pruliers 1993 • $50 • (11/15/1995) • **88**
Nuits-St.-Georges Les Pruliers 1991 • $54 • (1/31/1994) • **84**
Nuits-St.-Georges Les Pruliers 1990 • $70 • (12/15/1992) • **90**
Nuits-St.-Georges Les Pruliers 1989 • $63 • (1/31/1992) • **92**
Nuits-St.-Georges Les Pruliers 1988 • $54 • (1/31/1991) • **91**
Nuits-St.-Georges Les Pruliers 1987 • $35 • (4/30/1990) • **91**
Nuits-St.-Georges Les Pruliers 1986 • $45 • (4/30/1989) • **91**
Nuits-St.-Georges Les Pruliers 1985 • $43 • (3/15/1988) • **88**
Nuits-St.-Georges White Les Terres Blanches 1998: Straightforward Chardonnay. Has some ripe pear character, with floral, perfumelike notes. Crisp, chewy finish.–P.M. • $48 • (5/31/2000) • **77**
Vosne-Romanée 1996: Great village wine from talented winemaker Patrice Rion. Textbook Vosne-Romanée, exploding with rose petal, violet, blackberry and currant character. Voluptuous and sexy, its silky texture is simply marvelous, as it coats the palate and delivers layers of complex, pure fruit flavors in a seductive, ripe and elegant package. Best after 2003.–P.M. • $32 • (9/30/1998) • **91**
Vosne-Romanée 1995 • $44 • (11/15/1997) • **90**
Vosne-Romanée 1994 • $30 • (11/15/1996) • **81**
Vosne-Romanée 1993 • $32 • (11/15/1995) • **90**
Vosne-Romanée 1991 • $35 • (1/31/1994) • **83**
Vosne-Romanée 1990 • $42 • (12/15/1992) • **91**
Vosne-Romanée 1989 • $37 • (1/31/1992) • **89**
Vosne-Romanée 1987 • $15 Ⓐ • (4/30/1990) • **89**
Vosne-Romanée 1986 • $31 • (4/30/1989) • **87**
Vosne-Romanée 1985 • $28 • (2/29/1988) • **78**
Vosne-Romanée Les Beaux Monts 1997: Great elegance and lovely, pure rose petal, violet, raspberry and blackberry flavors burst with joyful excitement in this well-defined, supple, lovely, full-bodied '97. Lingering finish. Drink now through 2007.–P.M. • $49 • (9/30/1999) • **91**
Vosne-Romanée Les Beaux Monts 1996: One sniff and you know it's great. Beautifully displayed blackberry, kirsch, spice and mineral character, all very elegant and firmly yet delicately structured. Great length and refinement. Best from 2001 through 2006.–B.S. • $48 • (9/30/1998) • **92**
Vosne-Romanée Les Beaux Monts 1995 • $66 • (11/15/1997) • **92**
Vosne-Romanée Les Beaux Monts 1994 • $34 Ⓐ • (11/15/1996) • **87**
Vosne-Romanée Les Beaux Monts 1993 • $38 Ⓐ • (11/15/1995) • **92**
Vosne-Romanée Les Beaux Monts 1992 • $56 • (12/15/1994) • **86**
Vosne-Romanée Les Beaux Monts 1991 • $52 • (1/31/1994) • **84**
Vosne-Romanée Les Beaux Monts 1990 • $65 Ⓐ • (12/15/1992) • **92**
Vosne-Romanée Les Beaux Monts 1989 • $63 • (1/31/1992) • **90**
Vosne-Romanée Les Beaux Monts 1988 • $48 • (2/15/1991) • **92**
Vosne-Romanée Les Beaux Monts 1986 • $43 • (4/30/1989) • **91**
Vosne-Romanée Les Beaux Monts 1985 • $55 • (2/29/1988) • **95**
Vosne-Romanée Les Chaumes 1997: A pretty cherry- and spice-scented '97 red. Supple and tender in structure, light- to medium-bodied and forward in its appeal. Drink now through 2002.–B.S. • $45 • (9/30/1999) • **87**
Vosne-Romanée Les Chaumes 1996: Sensual red Burgundy. Its depth and class is immediately evident from the black cherry, cassis and sweet vanilla aromas. In the mouth, it caresses with silky texture and harmonious structure, culminating in a long, complex finish. Best from 2002 through 2008.–B.S. • $51 • (9/30/1998) • **92**
Vosne-Romanée Les Chaumes 1995 • $66 • (11/15/1997) • **87**
Vosne-Romanée Les Chaumes 1994 • $58 • (11/15/1996) • **86**
Vosne-Romanée Les Chaumes 1993 • $50• (11/15/1995) • **93**
Vosne-Romanée Les Chaumes 1992 • $58 • (12/15/1994) • **84**
Vosne-Romanée Les Chaumes 1991 • $54 • (2/28/1995) • **91**
Vosne-Romanée Les Chaumes 1990 • $70 • (2/28/1995) • **93**
Vosne-Romanée Les Chaumes 1989 • $63 • (2/28/1995) • **85**
Vosne-Romanée Les Chaumes 1988 • $54 • (2/28/1995) • **91**
Vosne-Romanée Les Chaumes 1987 • $35 • (2/28/1995) • **88**
Vosne-Romanée Les Chaumes 1986 • $54 • (2/28/1995) • **84**
Vosne-Romanée Les Chaumes 1985 • $NA • (2/28/1995) • **91**
Vosne-Romanée Les Chaumes 1983 • $36 • (2/28/1995) • **82**

RION, MICHELE & PATRICE

Bourgogne Les Bons Batons 1997: Delicate and appealing, showing rose petal, cherry and raspberry in a slightly toasted package. Juicy, balanced finish. Drink now through 2001.–P.M. • $NA • (9/30/1999) • **84**
Bourgogne Les Bons Bâtons 1996: Impressively black in color, thick in texture and ripe in character. Complex as Bourgognes go, showing plum, black cherry and a slight minty, herbal note. Drink now through 2002.–P.M. • $18 • (9/30/1998) • **87**
Bourgogne Les Bons Bâtons 1993 • $15 • (11/15/1995) • **88**
Chambolle-Musigny Les Cras 1997: This has more depth and intensity than most '97s, from the lovely black cherry, cassis, mint and coffee aromas and flavors to the rich midpalate and smooth texture. Fine, ripe tannins, good acidity and a long aftertaste complete the package. Drink now through 2006.–B.S. • $NA • (9/30/1999) • **93**
Chambolle-Musigny Les Cras 1996: Ripe and thick, this opulent Pinot Noir is a crowd-pleaser, with multiple layers of fruit, oak and acidity that bundle together in a suave, supple package, ending in a fresh and tannic finish tasting of cassis. Best after 2003.–P.M. • $48 • (9/30/1998) • **87**
Chambolle-Musigny Les Cras 1995 • $48 • (11/15/1997) • **92**
Chambolle-Musigny Les Cras 1993 • $38 • (11/15/1995) • **90**
Chambolle-Musigny Les Cras 1992 • $NA • (12/15/1994) • **78**

RIVEFORT DE FRANCE

Cabernet Sauvignon Vin de Pays d'Oc 1996: On the light side, with dried cherry and some plummy flavors, then stewy notes on the finish.–K.M. • $6 • (8/31/1999) • **78**
Chardonnay Vin de Pays d'Oc 1997: A straightforward white from the south of France, clean and refreshing, with nice pear and butter flavors. Drink now.–K.M. • $6 • (5/31/1999) • **82**
Merlot Vin de Pays d'Oc 1996: A fairly light red, with dried cherry and red plum flavors, and a cooked note on the finish.–K.M. • $6 • (8/31/1999) • **79**
Sauvignon Blanc Vin de Pays d'Oc 1997: A good, focused white with herbal and citrus flavors, some nice touches of spice on the finish. Drink now.–K.M. • $6 • (8/31/1999) • **84**
Syrah Vin de Pays d'Oc Limited Release 1997: Fairly light in texture, with some sweet-spicy flavors and smoky, leathery notes. A good quaffer for barbecue fare.–K.M. • $10 • (9/15/1999) • **83**
Viognier Vin de Pays d'Oc Limited Release 1997: A bit cidery-tasting, with flavors of apple and pear, spicy notes on the finish.–K.M. • $10 • (10/15/1999) • **77**

RIVIERE, CHATEAU DE LA

Fronsac 1997: Nice, simple and fruity, with fresh and easy structure and good fruit. Drink now.–J.S. • $NA • (1/31/2000) • **83**
Fronsac 1994 • $19 • (6/30/1997) • **84**

ROALLY, DOMAINE DE

Mâcon-Viré 1995 • $23 • (5/31/1997) • **93**

ROBERT, DOMAINE DE

Fleurie 1994 • $17 • (6/30/1997) • **81**
Morgon 1994 • $16 • (6/30/1997) • **83**

ROBIN, CHATEAU

Côtes de Castillon 1995 • $15 • (1/31/1998) • **89**
Côtes de Castillon 1994 • $NA • (1/31/1997) • **85**
Côtes de Castillon 1993 • $NA • (1/31/1996) • **79**

ROBIN, GILLES

Crozes-Hermitage Cuvée Albéric Bouvet 1997: This fantastic Crozes is thick but has lots of finesse. Lovely harmony defines this smooth, supple, sweet-tasting, delicious red, with ripe, succulent red berry and blackberry flavors and oaky notes. Full-bodied, with round tannins that make it accessible now, but it should hold. A newcomer in Crozes that's a discovery for us. Drink now through 2006.–P.M. • $19 • (12/15/1999) • **90**

ROBLIN & FILS, GEORGES

Sancerre Château de Maimbray 1996 • $18 • (3/31/1998) • **84**

ROC DE CAMBES, CHATEAU LE

Côtes de Bourg 1996: Good ruby color, with aromas of milk chocolate and hints of berry. Full-bodied and chewy, with lots of new wood, it's a bit dry on the finish. Will this come around? Not sure. Drink now.–J.S. • $29 • (6/30/1999) • **83**
Côtes de Bourg 1995: A fruit bomb. Loads of chocolate, raspberry and cherry character in a full-bodied and softly tannic package. The finish of fruit and vanilla oak character goes on and on. A beauty.–J.S. • $25 • (1/01/1999) • **91**

ROCHEMORIN, CHATEAU DE

Pessac-Léognan 1998: A cool and velvety young wine, with berry, vanilla and chocolate character. Medium-bodied, with a short, slightly dilute finish.–J.S. • $NA • (5/31/1999) (BT) • **80-84**
Pessac-Léognan 1997: Pretty blackberry and tobacco aromas with hints of cherries. Medium-bodied, with soft tannins and a fruity finish. Drink through 2004–J.S. • $NA • (1/31/2000) • **86**
Pessac-Léognan 1996: Diluted and weedy, with light body, herbal flavors and a tomato aftertaste.–J.S. • $16 • (1/31/1999) • **78**
Pessac-Léognan 1995 • $15 • (1/31/1998) • **81**
Pessac-Léognan 1994 • $14 • (1/31/1997) • **86**
Pessac-Léognan 1993 • $14 • (1/31/1996) • **84**
Pessac-Léognan 1992 • $13 • (4/15/1995) • **72**
Pessac-Léognan 1991 • $13 • (3/31/1994) • **72**
Pessac-Léognan 1990 • $12 • (3/31/1993) • **89**
Pessac-Léognan 1989: This is like Port. Traditional, concentrated wine. Very ripe and spicy black olive, raisin and tomato. Full-bodied, with velvety tannins and a hot fruit character. (1989 Bordeaux horizontal). Best after 2005.–J.S. • $NA • (5/31/1999) • **90**
Pessac-Léognan 1986 • $15 • (6/15/1989) • **84**
Graves 1985 • $14 • (6/15/1988) • **85**
Graves 1982 • $22 • (8/31/1992) • **90**
Pessac-Léognan White 1998: Attractive mineral, apple and lime aromas. Medium-bodied, with fresh acidity and a medium finish. Drink now.–J.S. • $NA • (2/29/2000) • **87**
Pessac-Léognan White 1996: Fresh and zingy Bordeaux white, with mineral and appleskin character. Medium-bodied, with clean, vivid acidity and a palate-cleansing finish. Drink now.–J.S. • $NA • (1/01/1999) • **85**

Key: SS—Spectator Selection. CS—Cellar Selection. HR—Highly Recommended. $NA—Price not available. (BT)—Barrel tasting. Ⓐ—Auction Price.
For a key to the tasters' initials, see "How to Use These Listings."
Dates in parentheses represent the issues in which the ratings were published.

ROCHER, DOMAINE

Côtes du Rhône 1997: A distinct, gamy wine that's earthy, with its regional authenticity intact. Good ripe fruit and lush tannins help on the medium-intense finish. Try with a gutsy dish. Drink now through 2003.–P.M. • $12 • (12/15/1999) • **85**
Côtes du Rhône Rosé 1998: Like smelling a horse stable. In the mouth, it's rich, ripe and sweet. Very bizarre.–P.M. • $12 • (12/15/1999) • **72**
Côtes du Rhône-Villages Cairanne 1997: Earthy, even dirty, with a bitter, tart character. Dry finish.–P.M. • $17 • (12/15/1999) • **72**
Côtes du Rhône-Villages Cairanne Monsieur Paul 1997: A very new-oakish sort of wine, redolent of smoke and fancy toasted wood, built for an international audience hooked on these aromas. Overdone, but it's ripe, lush and smooth at its core, with blackberry and floral notes that are almost Burgundian and Pinot-like. Drink now.–P.M. • $25 • (12/15/1999) • **80**

ROCHER BELLEVUE FIGEAC, CHATEAU

St.-Emilion 1998: A well-structured and toasty young wine. Full-bodied and chewy. Slightly one-dimensional, but big. Almost outstanding.–J.S. • $NA • (5/31/1999) (BT) • **85-89**
St.-Emilion 1996: Some berry, tobacco and meat character, but a slightly diluted palate with light-bodied, silky tannins and a fresh finish.–J.S. • $16 • (1/31/1999) • **82**
St.-Emilion 1994 • $17 • (1/31/1997) • **72**
St.-Emilion 1991 • $12 • (3/31/1994) • **73**
St.-Emilion 1990 • $17 • (3/31/1993) • **79**
St.-Emilion 1988 • $18 • (4/30/1991) • **87**

ROCHETTE, JOEL

Brouilly Pisse-Vieille 1997: Big, bold and redolent of kirsch and almond, this is structured and broad in its attack. Still some tannins on the finish, but some charcuterie should take care of that. Drink now.–B.S. • $10 • (10/15/1999) • **84**
Régnié Cuvée des Braves Vieilles Vignes 1997: Mature already, with red plum and dried cherry flavors, some stewy notes on the finish.–K.M. • $10 • (10/15/1999) • **79**

ROCHEVINE, DOMAINE

St.-Joseph 1994 • $17 • (10/15/1997) • **85**

RODET, ANTONIN

Beaujolais-Villages 1988 • $8 • (11/15/1990) • **75**
Beaune Cave Privée 1997: The aromas are lifted and evoke chlorine, with rose and cherry flavors that shut down quickly under the hard tannins.–B.S. • $48 • (9/30/1999) • **74**
Beaune Cave Privée 1994 • $NA • (11/15/1996) • **85**
Bourgogne Les Vignes Rouges 1996: Decent, ripe red- and blackberry flavor makes this medium-bodied Pinot a nice drink, but it's a bit hot on the finish.–P.M. • $18 • (9/30/1998) • **80**
Bourgogne Vieilles Vignes 1997: A delicious Bourgogne Rouge. Round, ripe and lovely, with vivid aromas of red berry, a clean structure and soft tannins. Drink now.–P.M. • $12 • (9/30/1999) • **84**
Chablis Côte de Léchet Cave Privée 1997: Superoaky. The wood covers the fruit in an astringent, unbalanced blanket.–P.M. • $36 • (9/30/1999) • **78**
Chambolle-Musigny 1993 • $30 • (11/15/1995) • **84**
Chambolle-Musigny Cave Privée 1997: A high-toned, slightly lifted aroma like balsamic vinegar distracts in this full-bodied '97. A bit dry on the finish, though it delivers red berry and blackberry flavors.–P.M. • $45 • (9/30/1999) • **79**
Chambolle-Musigny Cave Privée 1996: Extremely ripe and slightly raisiny, this lacks midpalate richness and finishes with firm, dry tannins. Best from 2002 through 2007.–B.S. • $40 • (9/30/1998) • **82**
Charmes-Chambertin Cave Privée 1997: Smells lifted on the nose, like balsamic vinegar, suggesting a volatile acidity problem. Tastes of cranberry and clamps down on the dry finish.–P.M. • $92 • (9/30/1999) • **73**
Charmes-Chambertin Cave Privée 1996: Ripe and supple, with mineral, blackberry flavors and gamy, toasty notes, this is a delight to taste with its fresh underpinning of bright fruit and acidity. Drink now through 2007.–P.M. • $80 • (5/15/1999) • **87**

Chassagne-Montrachet 1997: A slightly late harvest–style Chardonnay, with a dried apricot and peach character, it turns oddly acidic midpalate, with a metallic aftertaste. Unbalanced.–P.M. • $47 • (9/30/1999) • **79**

Chassagne-Montrachet 1996: Bland, slightly oxidized, this tastes of perfume and rose petals. Not very elegant and overdone on the oaky side.–P.M. • $40 • (8/31/1998) • **70**

Chassagne-Montrachet La Grande Montagne 1996: Wood, wood and more wood. This oaky, commercially driven wine tastes of sawdust, while the fruit struggles to get through.–P.M. • $53 • (8/31/1998) • **79**

Chassagne-Montrachet La Grande Montagne 1995 • $54 • (5/31/1997) • **90**

Clos de Vougeot Cave Privée 1997: Violet, cassis and cherry elements are volatile. Silky, with supple tannins. Drink now through 2003.–B.S. • $90 • (9/30/1999) • **83**

Clos de Vougeot Cave Privée 1996: Very ripe, very plummy, very dark in color, very full in body. Plenty of wine here, but it's a bit overdone, showing more fruit than *terroir*. Dries slightly on the finish. Best after 2005.–P.M. • $69 • (9/30/1998) • **85**

Clos de Vougeot Cave Privée 1995 • $65 • (1/31/1998) • **80**

Corton-Charlemagne 1995 • $75 • (5/31/1997) • **93**

Gevrey-Chambertin 1997: Crisp mouthfeel. Expect grapey, juicy red berry flavors, but it tastes a bit short on the finish.–P.M. • $38 • (9/30/1999) • **78**

Gevrey-Chambertin 1996: A dark, powerful '96, showing wild blackberry and spice character, concentrated and finely structured, with bright acidity and gentle tannins. Drink through 2004–B.S. • $44 • (9/30/1998) • **87**

Gevrey-Chambertin 1986 • $25 • (7/15/1990) • **86**

Gevrey-Chambertin Estournelles St.-Jacques 1995 • $50 • (11/15/1997) • **85**

Gevrey-Chambertin Estournelles St.-Jacques Cave Privée 1996: Apart from a slight aroma of balsamic vinegar (volatile acidity?), this is an attractively exotic red Burgundy, with black currant, lemon, raspberry and subtle toasted oak all presented in a full-bodied, ripe-tasting package. Crisp finish. Best from 2003 through 2012.–P.M. • $52 • (5/15/1999) • **87**

Gevrey-Chambertin Lavaut St.-Jacques 1982 • $35 • (6/30/1987) • **92**

Gevrey-Chambertin Les Cazetiers 1997: This has a big whiff of volatile acidity, with a tough, lean palate offering minor fruit.–B.S. • $48 • (9/30/1999) • **74**

Gevrey-Chambertin Les Cazetiers 1996: Packed with sweet vanilla oak, black cherry and licorice, this is broad-shouldered and masculine, yet manages to stay balanced and fresh, without a lot of concentration or depth. Best from 2002 through 2008.–B.S. • $52 • (9/30/1998) • **88**

Gevrey-Chambertin Les Cazetiers 1993 • $45 • (11/15/1995) • **84**

Mâcon-Villages 1997: Floral (jasmine?) and apricot notes give this light-bodied, picnic quaffer an interesting slant. Drink now.–P.M. • $10 • (5/31/1999) • **81**

Mâcon-Villages 1996 • $14 • (8/31/1997) • **87**

Mâcon-Villages 1995 • $NA • (8/31/1996) • **80**

Mazis-Chambertin 1994 • $NA • (11/15/1996) • **92**

Mazis-Chambertin Cave Privée 1997: A vibrant ruby hue belies the volatile acidity and oatmeal flavor in this sham of a red Burgundy. There's no substance midpalate, and it finishes crisp and lean.–B.S. • $110 • (9/30/1999) • **79**

Meursault 1997: This wonderful white Burgundy shows finesse and subtle aromas and flavors of sweet butter, jasmine, peach and pear. Reined-in oak, smoke and mineral accents tease you to a long and harmonious finish. Drink now through 2005.–P.M. • $44 • (9/30/1999) • **89**

Meursault Goutte d'Or Cave Privée 1997: Sweet butter notes introduce this supple wine. Very ripe, verging on late harvest, with some raisin and dried apricot accents. Medium-bodied and brown-yellow, it turns a bit astringent on the finish. Drink now through 2002.–P.M. • $65 • (9/30/1999) • **80**

Meursault Goutte d'Or Cave Privée 1995 • $54 • (5/31/1997) • **87**

Meursault Perrières 1996: A bit too soft, but it's seductive in an opulent, lush style, showing well-integrated ripe pear, honey and toasted oak flavors. Full-bodied, it generously coats the palate, but turns slightly woody on the finish despite all the fruit. Needs time. Best after 2005.–P.M. • $60 • (8/31/1998) • **88**

Meursault Perrières Cave Privée 1997: A very rich, pumped-up style of Meursault, with toasted coconut, butterscotch, sweet wood perfume and popcorn.–P.M. • $72 • (9/30/1999) • **79**

Meursault Perrières Cave Privée 1995 • $58 • (5/31/1997) • **89**

Nuits-St.-Georges Cave Privée 1997: A bit lifted on the nose, with a slight balsamic vinegar note that comes through on the palate. Has a lot of fresh aromas, but tastes crisp and a bit dry on the finish. Best from 2002 through 2005.–P.M. • $45 • (9/30/1999) • **80**

Nuits-St.-Georges Cave Privée 1996: Rich, full-bodied, opulent, with compacted blackberry character, toasted oak and massive tannins that are supple and ripe. Fresh, zingy, high-acidity finish is a bit tough. Best from 2005 through 2015.–P.M. • $40 • (5/15/1999) • **85**

Nuits-St.-Georges Les Porêts 1995 • $50 • (11/15/1997) • **70**

Nuits-St.-Georges Les Porêts 1994 • $59 • (11/15/1996) • **79**

Nuits-St.-Georges Les Porêts Cave Privée 1997: Tastes better than it smells. Medium-bodied, the balsamic vinegar aroma is disturbing, but on the palate it has a fresh quality. Tastes of freshly crushed raspberry, wild berry and cassis.–P.M. • $65 • (1/01/2000) • **78**

Nuits-St.-Georges Les St.-Georges 1996: Very supple and plummy, showing some excellent ripeness. Thick, full-bodied Nuits, it lacks a bit of class and clamps down on the finish, but it's a mouthful of a wine.–P.M. • $57 • (9/30/1998) • **85**

Nuits-St.-Georges Les St.-Georges 1995 • $55 • (11/15/1997) • **82**

Nuits-St.-Georges Roncière 1993 • $45 • (11/15/1995) • **88**

Pouilly-Fuissé 1997: Lean and a bit herbal, with modest ripeness around the steely core of green acidity. Hard to warm up to with its bitter finish.–P.M. • $18 • (5/31/1999) • **77**

Pouilly-Fuissé Cave Privée 1997: Tastes mature and almost oxidized. Oozing honey, it lacks elegance but provides loads of up-front fruit and immediate pleasure.–P.M. • $22 • (5/31/1999) • **79**

Puligny-Montrachet Hameau de Blagny Cave Privée 1997: Disappointing. Brown-yellow, smelling overripe, with an oxidized raisiny apple juice character.–P.M. • $63 • (9/30/1999) • **78**

Puligny-Montrachet Le Cailleret 1996: Oaky and disjointed, with strange perfumes of rose petal and violet, this wine is tart and dry.–P.M. • $80 • (8/31/1998) • **74**

Puligny-Montrachet Le Cailleret Cave Privée 1997: A bit oxidized, with cooked fruit and maderized aromas, turning bitter on the finish.–P.M. • $90 • (9/30/1999) • **70**

Savigny-lès-Beaune 1995 • $25 • (11/15/1997) • **86**

Savigny-lès-Beaune Cave Privée 1997: The lifted nose has a balsamic vinegar character.–P.M. • $30 • (9/30/1999) • **78**

Savigny-lès-Beaune Les Gravains 1996: Thick and full-bodied Savigny, this pure and lovely red is lush and smooth (once it warms up to room temperature or is decanted). Shows wonderful red- and blackberry character, then kicks in with firm acidity on the finish, but it stays the course with its clean fruit.–P.M. • $29 • (9/30/1998) • **86**

Volnay-Santenots 1993 • $35 • (11/15/1995) • **84**

Vosne-Romanée 1993 • $30 • (11/15/1995) • **86**

ROEDERER, LOUIS

Brut Blanc de Blancs Champagne 1993: This suave, elegant Champagne is bright and light in flavor, yet pleasingly supple and rich in texture. It weaves citrus notes with subtle vanilla accents that linger on the finish. Drink now. • $55 • (12/31/1998) • **88**

Brut Blanc de Blancs Champagne 1990 • $54 • (12/31/1997) • **91**

Brut Champagne 1990 • $42 Ⓐ • (11/15/1996) • **92**

Brut Champagne Brut Premier NV: A memorable, full-bodied brut with assertive, complex flavors and a lingering finish. Aromas of fresh bread and toasted walnut are backed up by crisp, full-bore fruit flavors. Drink now. • $42 • (9/15/1999) • **91**

Brut Champagne Cristal 1993: Fine example of the vintage, with clean fruit flavors, plenty of depth, great balance and a soothing array of fine bubbles. Drink now through 2001. • $147 Ⓐ • (10/15/1999) • **90**

Brut Champagne Cristal 1990: You won't soon forget this vivid and expressive Champagne. It packs in compound layers of citrus, vanilla, pear and nutmeg that harmonize and linger on the finish. Bright acidity makes it extra refreshing and layered. It has really opened up since last year. Tasted twice, with consistent notes. Drink through 2010 • $185 Ⓐ • (12/15/1998) • **94**

Brut Champagne Vintage 1993: Crisp and lively, with plenty of tangy fruit flavor to hold your interest. Has apple and citrus notes, firm acidity and a generous texture. Drink now through 2001. • $55 • (10/15/1999) • **89**

Brut Rosé Champagne 1993: A rich, full-bodied rosé, with a sense of elegance. Light amber in color, with enticing fruit and spice aromas, a plush texture and a lingering finish. Drink now. • $56 • (11/30/1998) • **89**

Brut Rosé Champagne 1991 • $48 • (11/30/1996) • **88**

Demi-Sec Champagne Carte Blanche NV: More complex than most sweet Champagnes. Has intriguing toasty, nutty flavors, a rich texture and a lingering finish. Drink now. • $42 • (10/15/1999) • **88**

ROGER, DOMINIQUE

Sancerre Red Domaine du Carrou 1996: Vibrant structure, but only modest cherry and earth flavors and a short finish.–B.S. • $16 • (11/15/1998) • **79**

FRANCE

ROL VALENTIN, CHATEAU

St.-Emilion 1999: Nice mineral, floral and berry aromas in this young wine. Medium-bodied, with well-integerated tannins and a fresh finish.–J.S. • $NA • (1/01/2000) • **85-89**

St.-Emilion 1998: Juicy, rich young wine, with a lovely velvety structure and a long, caressing finish. Loads of natural, ripe and gorgeous berry character. A beauty. An estate to watch.–J.S. • $NA • (5/31/1999) (BT) • **90-94**

St.-Emilion 1996: Good dark color, with berry and mint aromas. Medium-bodied, with silky, polished tannins and a medium finish, slightly dry. A bit too much wood for me. A tiny château on the move up. Best after 2000.–J.S. • $51 Ⓐ • (1/31/1999) • **86**

St.-Emilion 1995: Blackberry and cherry aromas and flavors, with a hint of raisin. Medium- to full-bodied, with medium tannins and a ripe finish. Slightly rustic, but very good richness. Best from 2001 through 2005.–J.S. • $55 Ⓐ • (9/15/1998) • **89**

ROLLAN DE BY, CHATEAU

Médoc 1998: Lovely character of currants and crushed berries. Medium-bodied, with a good core of fruit, but slightly short on the finish.–J.S. • $NA • (5/31/1999) (BT) • **85-89**

Médoc 1997: Super well-crafted for a *cru bourgeois*. Plum, raspberry, violet and a hint of vanilla on the nose. Medium-bodied, with velvety tannins and a fresh, long finish. Best after 2000.–J.S. • $NA • (1/31/2000) • **86**

ROLLET, CATHERINE & PASCAL

Mâcon-Solutré-Pouilly 1997: Very pretty, offering lovely ripe fruit in a clean package that blossoms on the buttery, floral, slightly honeyed and zesty finish. Drink now.–P.M. • $11 • (5/31/1999) • **84**

Mâcon-Solutré-Pouilly 1995 • $11 • (5/31/1997) • **86**

Pouilly-Fuissé Au Coeur du Cru 1996 • $18 • (5/31/1998) • **89**

Pouilly-Fuissé Domaine de la Chapelle 1997: Clean and zesty, with enough ripe fruit to make it attractive, although a bite on the firm finish makes for a tough, slightly astringent aftertaste, at least for now. Cellar short-term. Drink through 2003–P.M. • $18 • (5/31/1999) • **81**

Pouilly-Fuissé Domaine de la Chapelle 1995 • $18 • (5/31/1998) • **85**

Pouilly-Fuissé Domaine de la Chapelle Vieilles Vignes 1997: Racy, with some lovely lemon, honey and melon, this aristocratic Pouilly sparkles with life, showing refined mineral character. Takes a balanced walk between oak, spice and ripe fruit nuances. Has the firm, citrusy grip to improve in the cellar. Drink through 2005–P.M. • $21 • (5/31/1999) • **90**

Pouilly-Fuissé Domaine de la Chapelle Vieilles Vignes 1996 • $20 • (5/31/1998) • **87**

Pouilly-Fuissé Domaine de la Chapelle Vieilles Vignes 1995 • $20 • (5/31/1997) • **86**

ROMANEE-CONTI, DOMAINE DE LA

Echézeaux 1996: This beautifully round '96, made in a very spicy, oaky, tobaccolike style, shows subtle fruit along with menthol and vanilla. Long, persistent and clean finish. Tempting now, but to get the full experience, give it time. Drink now through 2007.–P.M. • $173 Ⓐ • (9/30/1999) • **91**

Echézeaux 1995: Beautiful wine, with a hint of exotic rose petal, violet and oak aromas. Full-bodied, silky, showing nice mocha, spice and blackberry character, more fruit than *terroir*. Deftly made. Ripe, suave finish. More delicate and lighter than DRC's Grands Echézeaux. Drink now through 2005.–P.M. • $124 Ⓐ • (8/31/1998) • **93**

Echézeaux 1994 • $94 Ⓐ • (9/30/1997) • **88**

Echézeaux 1993 • $259 Ⓐ • (5/15/1996) • **90**

Echézeaux 1992 • $52 • (5/15/1995) • **79**

Echézeaux 1991 • $95 • (8/31/1994) CS • **93**

Echézeaux 1990 • $269 Ⓐ • (12/31/1993) CS • **94**

Echézeaux 1989 • $114 • (10/31/1992) • **90**

Echézeaux 1988 • $150 Ⓐ • (4/30/1991) • **92**

Echézeaux 1987 • $132 Ⓐ • (9/30/1990) • **92**

Echézeaux 1986 • $115 Ⓐ • (8/31/1989) • **92**

Echézeaux 1985 • $255 Ⓐ • (2/29/1988) • **96**

Key: SS—Spectator Selection. CS—Cellar Selection. HR—Highly Recommended. $NA—Price not available. (BT)—Barrel tasting. Ⓐ—Auction Price.
For a key to the tasters' initials, see "How to Use These Listings."
Dates in parentheses represent the issues in which the ratings were published.

Echézeaux 1984 • $68 • (2/28/1987) • **90**

Echézeaux 1952 • $96 • (8/31/1990) • **97**

Grands Echézeaux 1996: Earthy and gamy yet thick and ripe, it explodes with blackberry, currant and sun-dried tomato character. Spicy, smoky finish. Drink now through 2010.–P.M. • $249 Ⓐ • (9/30/1999) • **94**

Grands Echézeaux 1995: Opulent, its fat yet elegant texture coats the palate. Appealing for all that sweet oak, it tastes of plum, black cherry and cassis, with mocha and freshly ground coffee beans added in. Full-bodied, supple-textured, with refined tannins. Tempting now, but cellar. Best after 2005. –P.M. • $167 Ⓐ • (8/31/1998) • **93**

Grands Echézeaux 1994 • $122 Ⓐ • (9/30/1997) • **89**

Grands Echézeaux 1993 • $225 Ⓐ • (5/15/1996) • **88**

Grands Echézeaux 1992 • $86 Ⓐ • (5/15/1995) • **84**

Grands Echézeaux 1991 • $175 Ⓐ • (8/31/1994) • **93**

Grands Echézeaux 1990 • $298 Ⓐ • (12/31/1993) CS • **94**

Grands Echézeaux 1989 • $192 Ⓐ • (10/31/1992) HR • **93**

Grands Echézeaux 1988 • $364 Ⓐ • (4/30/1991) • **92**

Grands Echézeaux 1987 • $165 Ⓐ • (9/30/1990) • **89**

Grands Echézeaux 1986 • $160 • (8/31/1989) • **94**

Grands Echézeaux 1985 • $367 Ⓐ • (2/29/1988) • **94**

Grands Echézeaux 1984 • $91 Ⓐ • (2/28/1987) • **88**

Grands Echézeaux 1942 • $230 • (8/31/1990) • **93**

La Tâche 1996: A powerful red Burgundy of legendary origin, this wine displays intense fruit and a silky, compacted midpalate. Fans of oak will like the vanilla and toast flavors that tie the knot with the raspberry and black cherry. The finish is superlong, but this is an ager. Best from 2006 through 2036.–P.M. • $480 Ⓐ • (9/30/1999) CS • **96**

La Tâche 1995: A sensational La Tâche that's as good as I remember upon release. Shows a suppleness in the tannins without compromising the compact mineral, wet earth and ironlike flavors that express this *grand cru's terroir*. Balanced, with lots of beautiful fruit, but above all it has pleasure and harmony etched all over it. (La Tâche vertical tasting–and all 9/30/1999 notes below).–P.M. • $349 Ⓐ • (9/30/1999) • **95**

La Tâche 1994 • $217 Ⓐ • (9/30/1997) • **85**

La Tâche 1993: Tastes young, like a barrel sample, with wonderful mineral notes. Medium-bodied, tough and edgy, with a huge amount of acidity and sensational wet earth, ironlike stuff. Quite lean, though, so don't expect opulence in the normal sense, but it's delicious. Best from 2005 through 2015.–P.M. • $338 Ⓐ • (9/30/1999) • **92**

La Tâche 1992 • $140 Ⓐ • (5/15/1995) • **84**

La Tâche 1991: Superlative and packed with great, ripe fruit, this is creamy on the midpalate, but a minerally edge kicks in that makes it look very tough. A really long, long finish, with an explosion of fruit that doesn't end. Brilliant, but don't expect much smoothness now, as it's built in a lean style. Best from 2007 through 2020.–P.M. • $293 Ⓐ • (9/30/1999) • **92**

La Tâche 1990: Tough, intense and as good now as when it was released—and still so young it has almost not moved. Loaded with intense red berry and blackberry, but the tannins are well integrated and ripe, the structure is firm and this is really just a baby La Tâche that should develop. For now it's quite tough, almost green and herbal. Best from 2010 through 2020. –P.M.• $706 Ⓐ • (9/30/1999) • **93**

La Tâche 1989: A crisp, hard wine that doesn't come close to the outstanding '89 reviewed upon release. Has unusually dry tannins for this year and surprising acidity for a wine from this low-acidity vintage. Seems disjointed, with a slight mustiness and metallic edge.–P.M. • $449 Ⓐ • (9/30/1999) • **79**

La Tâche 1988: Excellent, showing a minerally concentration that gives it a silky feel on the midpalate. Lots of great acidity makes it fresh and zesty. Medium-bodied, with lovely red berry flavor and firm, gripping tannins that provide a chewy finish. Expect a rather lean wine, not an opulent one. Best from 2005 through 2020.–P.M. • $356 Ⓐ • (9/30/1999) • **92**

La Tâche 1987: Drying, with some mineral, plum and cherry notes, and some decent grip on the palate and the finish. A flavorful package, though slightly dry. Drink now through 2003.–P.M. • $216 Ⓐ • (9/30/1999) • **80**

La Tâche 1986: Showing good fruit, nice concentration and a firm tannic structure, this has personality, grip and character. Medium- to full-bodied, it has great length but not much elegance. Cellar. Best from 2005 through 2010.–P.M. • $270 Ⓐ • (9/30/1999) • **87**

La Tâche 1985: Very disappointing, this seems over-the-hill, tasting cooked and burnt, with a dry, musty character. Terrible winemaking or bad storage? Just a shadow of the classic-rated '85 reviewed 11 years ago. –P.M. • $641 Ⓐ • (9/30/1999) • **68**

La Tâche 1984 • $388 Ⓐ • (2/28/1987) • **95**

La Tâche 1983: Simply awful. Smells and tastes of burnt rubber, sulfur and rot—it has serious flaws. Dry, lean and disgusting. DRC should be ashamed for having released this wine..–P.M. • $263 Ⓐ • (9/30/1999) • **50**

La Tâche 1982: Starts out supple and silky, showing a nice combination of acidity and fruit, then kicks in with a good, intense finish. Medium-bodied, it finishes a bit crisp and sharp. Drink now through 2010.–P.M. • $214 Ⓐ • (9/30/1999) • **88**

La Tâche 1980: Smooth and silky, this is fairly ripe but also shows brown sugar, cinnamon and mineral character. A bit burnt on the sweet-tasting, lingering finish. Drink now through 2005.–P.M. • $418 Ⓐ • (9/30/1999) • **83**

La Tâche 1979: Crisp in aromas and creamy on the palate, this turns a bit astringent on the finish. Medium-bodied, with a nice mineral hint, but the tartness dominates. Disappointing, short finish.–P.M. • $319 Ⓐ • (9/30/1999) • **76**

La Tâche 1978: Just amazing, just to die for, just everything. Full-bodied, this is the sort of wine you can never forget, with mineral, wet earth and truffle and loads of compact red berry and blackberry character. Silky, yet firm and structured, this tantalizes you with its ethereal yet masculine, gamy, woodsy, fruity complexity. Long, balanced finish. Drink now through 2020.–P.M. • $771 Ⓐ • (9/30/1999) • **99**

La Tâche 1976: Round, ripe and sweet-tasting, medium-bodied and balanced, this is a very good, mature red Burgundy, with brown sugar, cinnamon and black cherry flavors but not much minerally *terroir* quality. Drink now through 2005.–P.M. • $228 Ⓐ • (9/30/1999) • **85**

La Tâche 1972: Aromatically reserved, this has good acidity, showing lemon flavors, with modest spice, plum and black cherry character. Medium-bodied, it's dry and tart on the short finish..–P.M. • $265 Ⓐ • (9/30/1999) • **79**

La Tâche 1971: This is what the La Tâche cult is all about. Fantastic for its mineral, wet earth, bark and fruit character, it's downright primal in its gamy aromas and flavors. Exotic, but not in a floral way—think hunting lodge with slain wild boars and you get the picture. Full-bodied, masculine and firm, yet also silky. Eat with game.. Drink now through 2010.–P.M. • $701 Ⓐ • (9/30/1999) • **99**

La Tâche 1970: La Tâche's typical wet earth, mineral and ironlike flavors come through nicely in this full-bodied wine. While the tannins are fairly smooth, an underlying lemon-spiked, unresolved acidity makes a slightly mouthpuckering finish. Drink now through 2005.–P.M. • $162 Ⓐ • (9/30/1999) • **87**

La Tâche 1969: Still fruity and somewhat light-bodied, but it is fresh, with a lemony, zesty, vibrant core, showing good red berry flavor but not much *terroir* complexity. Turns a bit dry and hot on the slightly raw finish. Drink now through 2005.–P.M. • $553 Ⓐ • (9/30/1999) • **86**

La Tâche 1966: An outstanding La Tâche showing lovely mineral, brown sugar and wet earth intensity, it's packed with *terroir*. Balanced and smooth, with a creamy midpalate despite the tannic backbone. It walks a tightrope between seemingly contradictory poles, but it works. Long finish.–P.M. • $512 Ⓐ • (9/30/1999) • **94**

La Tâche 1964: Cedary and tasting of chestnut, mushroom and forest underbrush, this is a mature, over-the-hill, medium-bodied red Burgundy with a drying finish.–P.M. • $435 Ⓐ • (9/30/1999) • **75**

La Tâche 1962: Rich, thick, opulent and incredibly powerful. Big, burly and roomy, filling up your senses with all sorts of fantasies. A classic and musky red Burgundy, with white truffle, brown sugar, maple syrup and mineral notes. Huge, indestructible finish. Drink now through 2020.–P.M. s• $716 Ⓐ • (9/30/1999) • **98**

La Tâche 1961: Wonderful, balanced and silky, showing a muscular, youthful quality despite its age. Complex and full-bodied, with mineral, wet earth and compacted red berry character. The only reproach is that it comes across as a bit hot on the finish. Drink now through 2008.–P.M. • $356 Ⓐ • (9/30/1999) • **89**

La Tâche 1960: Like a Port, showing plum, brown sugar, spice and mushroom—and a bit oxidized. Strange; more dessert wine than red Burgundy, with nutty, maderized aromas.–P.M. • $NA • (9/30/1999) • **79**

La Tâche 1959: Lovely, with mineral, plum, wet earth and red berry character. Complex and supple, this tightly wound wine is both sweet and firm, holding up beautifully. Great stuff. The silky character mixes nicely with the still-rigorous tannins. Drink through 2010.–P.M. • $917 Ⓐ • (9/30/1999) • **93**

La Tâche 1957: Recorked by DRC in 1971. Lovely, ethereal and delicate, with good acidity holding it up. Medium-bodied, it has a mineral, wet earth and iron character, with spice and currant notes. The lingering finish—with floral and ginger—is just a bit tart. Drink now through 2005.–P.M. • $491 Ⓐ • (9/30/1999) • **86**

La Tâche 1955: Crisp and zesty, showing cedar, chanterelle, plum and cherry notes. A bit lean, very intense and slightly acidic, it ends a bit aggressively. Drink now through 2005.–P.M. • $657 Ⓐ • (9/30/1999) • **80**

La Tâche 1953: Odd, brown-yellow color of an aged Cognac, with orange, nut and lemon notes but not much mineral character. Tastes a bit madeirized.–P.M. • $479 Ⓐ • (9/30/1999) • **79**

La Tâche 1949: Mineral, earth, truffle, red berry—this has a lot of *terroir* and a fabulous streak of clean acidity. The texture is a bit lean, but there is wonderful sweetness to compensate and balance it all. Great elegance. Drink now through 2010.–P.M. • $NA • (9/30/1999) • **97**

La Tâche 1947: Out of this world and even better than when last reviewed. Orange-brown in color, incredibly minerally and soily in aromas, with wet earth notes, this is full-bodied, sweet-tasting, balanced, intense and fresh on the palate. Hard to ask for more from a red Burgundy that's more than half-a-century old. Drink now through 2015.–P.M. • $789 Ⓐ • (9/30/1999) • **97**

La Tâche 1945: Just lovely. Balanced and full of life, with great acidity keeping it on an even keel. Offers plenty of DRC's lovely floral, rose petal and exotic gingerlike notes. You just sink to your knees before this goddess of a *grand cru*. Ethereal and intense, it pumps out the flavors on the long finish. Drink now through 2010.–P.M. • $NA • (9/30/1999) • **97**

Montrachet 1995: A New World-styled Montrachet that's a bit overdone, with lots of caramel and butterscotch flavors. Very buttery and oaky, it's still appealing. While it lacks the tightness and firm structure expected from a grand Montrachet, the texture is silky. Drinkable now, but given DRC's reputation, it should be better with cellaring. Best after 2005.–P.M. • $907 Ⓐ • (8/31/1998) • **90**

Richebourg 1996: Full-bodied, showing gorgeous fruit, this is very intense. It holds your attention as it settles its foundations into the palate, tightening its grip with seductive cassis, blackberry, fresh acidity and terrific floral character. A tamed monster. Drink now through 2026.–P.M. • $319 Ⓐ • (9/30/1999) • **95**

Richebourg 1995: Fabulous red Burgundy—a true *vin de terroir*. The pure, crafty aromas jump out of the glass, titillating with rose petal, violet and tar notes. Fans out with the silkiest mouthfeel imaginable, delivering layers of wet earth, chalky stone, black currant and oak-infused spice. The tannins are amazingly classy, so it's enjoyable upon release, but clearly it should get even better in the cellar. Best from 2005 through 2015.–P.M. • $251 Ⓐ • (8/31/1998) CS • **98**

Richebourg 1994 • $147 Ⓐ • (9/30/1997) • **90**
Richebourg 1993 • $489 Ⓐ • (5/15/1996) • **90**
Richebourg 1992 • $103 Ⓐ • (5/15/1995) • **83**
Richebourg 1991 • $155 Ⓐ • (8/31/1994) • **80**
Richebourg 1990 • $454 Ⓐ • (12/31/1993) • **91**
Richebourg 1989 • $292 Ⓐ • (10/31/1992) • **90**
Richebourg 1988 • $258 Ⓐ • (4/30/1991) • **94**
Richebourg 1987 • $159 Ⓐ • (9/30/1990) • **93**
Richebourg 1986 • $186 Ⓐ • (8/31/1989) • **94**
Richebourg 1985 • $521 Ⓐ • (2/29/1988) • **100**
Richebourg 1984 • $102 • (2/28/1987) • **91**
Richebourg 1954 • $175 • (8/31/1990) • **88**

Romanée-Conti 1996: Incredible harmony to this pedigreed red Burgundy. Closed on the nose now, it unfolds layers of elegant yet superripe fruit, wrapping around the palate, coating every taste bud with the silky flavors. Full-bodied and not powerful, it's just lovely, with an aftertaste that seems to last for minutes. Best from 2006 through 2036.–P.M. • $1,754 Ⓐ • (9/30/1999) CS • **98**

Romanée-Conti 1995: Sensational, very serious. Clearly a *vin de garde*, this burly, cellar-worthy red lacks suppleness now, but has amazing depth and great midpalate concentration. Displays lovely rose petal, violet, tar aromas followed by plum, black cherry and cassis flavors. Loads of ripe tannins leads to a sweet-tasting finish that won't quit. The best Romanée-Conti in years. Best after 2010.–P.M. • $1,650 Ⓐ • (8/31/1998) • **98**

Romanée-Conti 1994 • $1,323 Ⓐ • (9/30/1997) • **84**
Romanée-Conti 1993 • $1,382 Ⓐ • (5/15/1996) CS • **94**
Romanée-Conti 1992 • $1,130 Ⓐ • (5/15/1995) • **85**
Romanée-Conti 1991 • $1,445 Ⓐ • (8/31/1994) • **93**
Romanée-Conti 1990 • $2,725 Ⓐ • (12/31/1993) CS • **93**
Romanée-Conti 1989 • $1,912 Ⓐ • (10/31/1992) • **97**
Romanée-Conti 1987 • $1,256 Ⓐ • (9/30/1990) • **89**
Romanée-Conti 1986 • $1,279 Ⓐ • (8/31/1989) • **95**
Romanée-Conti 1985 • $3,180 Ⓐ • (1/31/1990) • **99**
Romanée-Conti 1984 • $1,034 Ⓐ • (1/31/1990) • **94**
Romanée-Conti 1983 • $1,301 Ⓐ • (1/31/1990) • **78**
Romanée-Conti 1982 • $1,113 Ⓐ • (1/31/1990) • **85**
Romanée-Conti 1979 • $1,393 Ⓐ • (1/31/1990) • **90**
Romanée-Conti 1978 • $2,883 Ⓐ • (1/31/1990) • **95**
Romanée-Conti 1975 • $1,217 Ⓐ • (1/31/1990) • **82**
Romanée-Conti 1964 • $1,419 Ⓐ • (1/31/1990) • **98**
Romanée-Conti 1953 • $1,955 Ⓐ • (1/31/1990) • **93**
Romanée-Conti 1937 • $1,900 Ⓐ • (12/15/1988) • **94**

ROMANEE-CONTI, DOMAINE DE LA

Romanée St.-Vivant 1996: Gentle at first, offering rose petal aromas, it turns quite savage and tough on the palate, with loads of fruit cloaked in the very firm tannin structure. The acidity is there, and the length is terrific, but it needs time. Best from 2006 through 2026.–P.M. • $192 Ⓐ • (9/30/1999) • **95**
Romanée St.-Vivant 1995: Unctuous, showing delicious fruit and *terroir* character. Almost delicate, but also full-bodied, rich and ripe, with attractive rose petal, plum, black cherry and currant character. So ripe, it's almost hot on the finish, but still a lovely, velvety wine. Best after 2005.–P.M. • $169 Ⓐ • (8/31/1998) • **93**
Romanée St.-Vivant 1994 • $136 Ⓐ • (9/30/1997) • **80**
Romanée St.-Vivant 1993 • $173 Ⓐ • (5/15/1996) • **92**
Romanée St.-Vivant 1992 • $73 • (5/15/1995) • **74**
Romanée St.-Vivant 1991 • $133 Ⓐ • (8/31/1994) • **88**
Romanée St.-Vivant 1990 • $295 Ⓐ • (12/31/1993) • **90**
Romanée St.-Vivant 1989 • $253 Ⓐ • (10/31/1992) • **91**
Romanée St.-Vivant 1987 • $131 Ⓐ • (9/30/1990) • **89**
Romanée St.-Vivant 1986 • $195 • (8/31/1989) • **98**
Romanée St.-Vivant 1985 • $357 Ⓐ • (2/29/1988) • **88**
Romanée St.-Vivant 1984 • $96 Ⓐ • (2/28/1987) • **96**

ROMANIN, CHATEAU

Les Baux de Provence 1995: A good, chewy red, with cherry and tea flavors and herbal notes. This has a firm structure, with currant notes that linger on the finish. Drink now.–K.M. • $19 • (12/31/1998) • **84**
Les Baux de Provence 1990 • $17 • (2/15/1993) • **80**

ROMER DU HAYOT, CHATEAU

Sauternes 1997: Full-bodied, with lovely acidity, plenty of ripe fruit and lots of apple, pineapple and honey character. Medium sweet, with a fresh finish. A ripe and enticing wine. Drink now through 2004.–J.S. • $NA • (1/31/2000) • **88**
Sauternes 1988 • $22/375 ml. • (4/30/1991) • **72**
Sauternes 1986 • $22 • (12/31/1989) • **78**
Sauternes 1983 • $19 • (1/31/1988) • **72**
Sauternes 1982 • $13 • (10/16/1985) • **82**

RONCEE, DOMAINE DU

Chinon 1996: This firm, crisp red has focus and liveliness, with black cherry, smoke and herb flavors and an inky note more reminiscent of Syrah than Cabernet Franc. Fresh and clean. Drink now.–T.M. • $12 • (2/28/1999) • **83**
Chinon 1993 • $12 • (10/31/1994) • **84**
Chinon Clos des Marronniers 1996: Concentrated yet beautifully polished, this deep red is packed with ripe fruit flavors of plums and cherries, accented with licorice, smoke and light herb flavors. Marries subtlety and power in an elegant, harmonious package. Drink now through 2006.–T.M. • $17 • (9/15/1999) • **90**
Chinon Clos des Marronniers 1993 • $20 • (5/15/1997) • **88**

RONTETS, CHATEAU DES

Pouilly-Fuissé 1997: Very rich and ripe. A slight burning butter, caramelized pear tart and spice character surfaces, but it comes together on the full, flavorful finish. Drink now through 2002.–P.M. • $21 • (9/30/1999) • **87**
Pouilly-Fuissé Clos Varambon 1998: Elegant, fresh, and surprisingly firm and structured for a '98. Light to medium in body, it tastes of citrus and green apples, but also offers a ripe undertow that verges on honey. Vibrant finish. Drink now through 2002.–P.M. • $18 • (5/31/2000) • **84**
Pouilly-Fuissé Les Birbettes Cuvée Vieilles Vignes 1997: Thick and flavorful, with a lime, green apple and honey tightness that gives it length and freshness. Medium-bodied, it takes off on the finish as few '97 white Burgundies do. Drink now through 2005.–P.M. • $28 • (9/30/1999) • **90**
Pouilly-Fuissé Pierrefolle 1998: Soft and pleasant, showing good ripe fruit and a full mouthfeel, with some pear, bread dough and quince-jam notes. Supple and deliciously balanced finish. Drink now through 2002.–P.M. • $20 • (5/31/2000) • **87**

Key: SS—Spectator Selection. CS—Cellar Selection. HR—Highly Recommended. $NA—Price not available. (BT)—Barrel tasting. Ⓐ—Auction Price.
For a key to the tasters' initials, see "How to Use These Listings."
Dates in parentheses represent the issues in which the ratings were published.

Pouilly-Fuissé Pierrefolle 1997: Attractive, with good ripeness and flavor, layered with lemon, passion fruit and pie crust character. Full-bodied, with a juicy, pleasant finish. Drink now through 2001.–P.M. • $23 • (9/30/1999) • **87**

ROPITEAU FRERES

Bourgogne 1993 • $9 • (11/15/1995) • **79**
Chassagne-Montrachet Red 1993 • $17 • (11/15/1995) • **80**
Côte de Beaune-Villages 1993 • $13 • (11/15/1995) • **75**
Côte de Nuits-Villages 1993 • $14 • (11/15/1995) • **77**
Gevrey-Chambertin 1993 • $23 • (11/15/1995) • **79**
Hautes-Côtes de Nuits 1993 • $12 • (11/15/1995) • **72**
Meursault Red 1993 • $16 • (11/15/1995) • **78**
Pommard 1993 • $25 • (11/15/1995) • **80**
Santenay 1993 • $16 • (11/15/1995) • **85**
Volnay Clos des Chênes 1993 • $30 • (11/15/1995) • **75**
Vosne-Romanée 1993 • $26 • (11/15/1995) • **74**

ROQ DUR

Syrah Vin de Pays d'Oc 1995 • $9 • (1/01/1998) • **76**
Vin de Pays de la Vallée du Paradis Talairan 1995: A plain and simple red, with hardly any fruit flavor. Past its prime. • $6 • (8/31/1998) • **71**

ROQUE, CHATEAU DE LA

Bordeaux 1994 • $6 • (7/31/1996) • **80**

ROQUE, CHATEAU LA

Coteaux du Languedoc 1990 • $9 • (2/15/1993) • **75**
Coteaux du Languedoc Pic St.-Loup 1997: A full-bodied red, with roasted and muted red plum flavors. Meaty notes on the finish. Drink now.–K.M. • $10 • (4/30/2000) • **83**
Coteaux du Languedoc Pic St.-Loup 1996: A little rough around the edges but still quite impressive, with a high-toned acidity and well-defined flavors of dried cherry, red plum and leather. Finishes with an earthy note. Drink now through 2001.–K.M. • $10 • (11/15/1999) • **86**
Coteaux du Languedoc Pic St.-Loup 1995: Lush, with good concentration and meat and berry flavors that make this a solid red. Finishes on a spicy note. Medium-bodied, it's accessible now.–K.M. • $10 • (10/31/1998) • **85**
Coteaux du Languedoc Pic St.-Loup 1991 • $8 • (3/15/1994) • **82**
Coteaux du Languedoc Pic St.-Loup Cupa Numismae 1997: This medium-bodied red has flavors of red plum and spice draped over a firm frame of acidity and smooth tannins. Appealing leather and dried herb notes on the finish. Syrah and Mourvèdre. Drink now through 2001.–K.M. • $15 • (11/15/1999) • **84**
Coteaux du Languedoc Pic St.-Loup Cupa Numismae 1996: This ripe and well-rounded wine really packs in the gorgeous dark plum, cherry and spice flavors. Balanced and well defined, with a enticing coffeelike aroma. Spice and chocolate notes linger on the finish. Delicious and inviting. A blend of Syrah and Mourvèdre. Drink now through 2003.–K.M. • $14 • (10/31/1998) • **89**
Coteaux du Languedoc Pic St.-Loup Cupa Numismae 1995 • $15 • (5/31/1998) • **89**
Coteaux du Languedoc Pic St.-Loup Cupa Numismae 1990 • $10 • (3/15/1994) • **86**
Coteaux du Languedoc White Pic St.-Loup 1996 • $9 • (2/28/1998) • **86**
Coteaux du Languedoc White Pic St.-Loup Cuvée Clos des Bénédictins 1997: An oaky-tasting white, with plenty of butter and ripe apple flavor. Straightforward and satisfying, with a spicy note on the finish. Drink now.–K.M. • $13 • (11/15/1998) • **83**
Mourvèdre Coteaux du Languedoc Pic St.-Loup Cuvée Vieilles Vignes 1997: A truly savage red wine, with plenty of sinew. Its enticing meaty aroma leads to tightly wrapped and intense flavors, including notes of dried plum, cherry, dark hummus, mushroom, pepper and spice. Drink through 2005–K.M. • $11 • (11/15/1999) HR • **90**
Mourvèdre Coteaux du Languedoc Pic St.-Loup Cuvée Vieilles Vignes 1996: Intense and concentrated, with plum, berry, cherry and cassis flavors and a wild leathery note that gives some punch. Drink now.–K.M. • $11 • (10/31/1998) • **87**

ROQUE DE BY, CHATEAU LA

Médoc 1997: Too weedy and stewed to be anything more than average in quality.–J.S. • $NA • (1/31/2000) • **76**

Médoc 1996: Weedy and earthy on the nose, with hints of berry. Medium- to light-bodied, with light tannins and an herbal aftertaste. Hard to like. Second label of Château La Tour-de-By.–J.S. • $NA • (2/28/1999) • **78**

ROQUEBRUN, CAVE LES VINS DE

Coteaux du Languedoc White Château Roquebrun 1997: Lots of oaky flavors in this white, with some apple and spice notes. Turns a tad astringent on the finish. Drink now.–K.M. • $NA • (1/01/1999) • **81**

St.-Chinian 1996: A lean but balanced red, with dried cherry and currant flavors. Finishes on wild herb notes.–K.M. • $9 • (11/30/1998) • **79**

St.-Chinian Château Roquebrun 1995: Pure and quite polished, with red plum, berry and pepper flavors and a good balance of lively acidity. This is a focused and impressive red that's quite lovely, with rich spice notes on the finish. Medium-bodied, it still tastes youthful. Drink now through 2001.–K.M. • $NA • (1/01/1999) • **88**

St.-Chinian Cuvée Roches Noires 1994 • $11 • (6/30/1997) • **83**

St.-Chinian Cuvée Roches Noires 1991 • $10 • (3/15/1994) • **85**

St.-Chinian Domaine de Cabrio 1997: Smooth and medium-bodied, with a peppery character and berry and plum flavors. Balanced and ready to drink. Drink now.–K.M. • $NA • (1/01/1999) • **84**

St.-Chinian Domaine de la Serre 1997: A straightforward red, with red plum and leather flavors. Mature, with rhubarb and coffee notes on the finish. Drink now.–K.M. • $11 • (12/31/1999) • **82**

St.-Chinian Domaine de Layrolle 1997: A delicious and hearty red, with plenty of red plum and leather flavors and a silky texture. An appealing smoky note lingers on the finish. Drink now through 2001.–K.M. • $NA • (1/01/1999) • **86**

St.-Chinian Domaine du Bouscadel Roches Noires 1997: Ripe and plummy. A bit lumbering and rustic in the end, with brickish, gamy notes. Drink now.–K.M. • $11 • (12/31/1999) • **81**

St.-Chinian Prestige 1994 • $7 • (6/30/1997) • **81**

St.-Chinian Prestige 1991 • $9 • (3/15/1994) • **80**

St.-Chinian Sir de Roc Brun 1995: Smooth and mature, but almost over the hill, with appealing dark plum and leather flavors and dark chocolate notes. Spicy notes linger on the finish. Drink now.–K.M. • $NA • (1/01/1999) • **81**

St.-Chinian Tradition 1991 • $8 • (3/15/1994) • **82**

ROQUETAILLADE, CHATEAUFORT DE

Graves White 1996 • $11 • (2/28/1998) • **83**

ROQUETTE, DOMAINE DE LA | BORDEAUX

Pessac-Léognan 1995 • $NA • (1/31/1998) • **85**

ROQUETTE, DOMAINE DE LA | RHONE

Châteauneuf-du-Pape 1997: The plum and red berry notes are decent enough, although there's a touch of herbaceousness. Supple tannins on the medium-intense finish. Drink now.–P.M. • $22 • (8/31/1999) • **84**

Châteauneuf-du-Pape 1995 • $25 • (10/15/1997) • **89**

Châteauneuf-du-Pape 1993 • $20 • (11/15/1996) • **86**

Châteauneuf-du-Pape 1992 • $20 • (10/15/1995) • **85**

Châteauneuf-du-Pape 1990 • $15 • (6/15/1993) • **83**

Châteauneuf-du-Pape 1989 • $17 • (10/15/1991) • **86**

Châteauneuf-du-Pape 1988 • $17 • (10/15/1991) • **86**

Châteauneuf-du-Pape 1986 • $18 • (10/15/1991) • **85**

Châteauneuf-du-Pape 1985 • $13 • (7/31/1988) SS • **90**

Châteauneuf-du-Pape White 1997: Big and a bit oaky, with a slight wood-tannin astringency and a fat, buttery almond character. Lacks finesse. Not imported into the U.S. Drink now through 2002.–P.M. • $NA • (1/01/1999) • **82**

Châteauneuf-du-Pape White 1996 • $25 • (10/15/1997) • **79**

Vin de Pays de la Principauté d'Orange Le Pigeoulet 1996 • $10 • (10/15/1997)• **86**

ROQUEVIGNAN, DOMAINE DE

Côtes du Rhône 1994 • $10 • (10/15/1997) • **83**

Côtes du Rhône 1990 • $8 • (12/15/1996) • **77**

ROSE MONTVIEL, CHATEAU LA

Pomerol 1997: Some good berry, tobacco character, but rather light. Medium-to light-bodied, light on the finish. Drink now.–J.S. • $NA • (1/31/2000) • **81**

Pomerol 1996: Diluted, with some berry and herb character, but light and watery on the finish.–J.S. • $NA • (2/28/1999) • **78**

ROSSI, G.

Chénas En Guinchay 1994 • $9 • (10/31/1995) • **86**

ROSSIGNOL, MICHEL & MARC

Volnay 1995 • $22 • (1/31/1998) • **77**

Volnay Les Pitures 1995 • $33 • (1/31/1998) • **86**

ROSSIGNOL, PHILIPPE

Bourgogne 1997: Medium-bodied, with toasted oak, cherry and plum character. A bit heavy on the finish.–P.M. • $10 Ⓐ • (9/30/1999) • **78**

Bourgogne 1994 • $15 • (11/15/1996) • **75**

Côte de Nuits-Villages 1997: This rustic red is very ripe, offering plum and licorice notes allied to a firm, tannic structure. Ends on the dry side, with an aftertaste of tobacco. Best after 2002.–B.S. • $22 • (9/30/1999) • **82**

Côte de Nuits-Villages 1994 • $20 • (11/15/1996) • **79**

Côte de Nuits-Villages 1985 • $24 • (7/31/1988) • **89**

Fixin En Tabellion 1994 • $24 • (11/15/1996) • **81**

Fixin En Tabellion Cuvée Vieilles Vignes 1997: Not much depth, with light fruit flavors. Stemmy, green and tough.–P.M. • $25 • (9/30/1999) • **75**

Gevrey-Chambertin Cuvée Vieilles Vignes 1997: Animal elements combine with plum, licorice and a hint of coffee in this broad-shouldered, firm '97 red. A bit diffused now, but there's good balance and concentration, followed by modest length. Drink through 2004–B.S. • $32 • (9/30/1999) • **84**

Gevrey-Chambertin Cuvée Vieilles Vignes 1994 • $28 • (11/15/1996) • **85**

Gevrey-Chambertin Les Corbeaux 1993 • $NA • (5/15/1996) • **89**

Gevrey-Chambertin Les Corbeaux Cuvée Vieilles Vignes 1997: Shows pretty aromas, but it's a bit astringent in the mouth and rather straightforward. Not much stuffing, with black cherry and raspberry notes. Somewhat short finish.–P.M. • $42 • (9/30/1999) • **79**

Gevrey-Chambertin Les Corbeaux Cuvée Vieilles Vignes 1994 • $42 • (11/15/1996) • **83**

Gevrey-Chambertin Les Corbeaux Cuvée Vieilles Vignes 1993 • $NA • (5/15/1996) • **90**

ROSSIGNOL-CHANGARNIER

Beaune Les Theurons 1995: Pretty Pinot Noir, with lovely up-front cherry, spice, mocha, herbal notes. Firm on the palate, but layered with good richness and the concentration. Very pure wine built for short-term cellaring. Best after 2003.–P.M. • $NA • (8/31/1998) • **89**

ROSSIGNOL-FEVRIER

Bourgogne 1996: With odd, smoky, herbal, burnt-butter character, this is disjointed and dry.–P.M. • $12 • (9/30/1998) • **71**

Volnay 1996: Well-made. Pure, solid Pinot, showing cold fruit but clean flavors, medium-bodied with wet earth, black cherry notes and a firm, tannic structure. Lacks a bit of ripe charm. Not available in the U.S. Drink through 2006–P.M. • $NA • (1/01/1999) • **81**

Volnay 1988 • $32 • (3/31/1991) • **92**

Volnay Robardelle 1996: Clean, solid, pure, minerally, *terroir*-driven sort of Pinot Noir, well-made with delicious intensity of red berry and wet soil character, offering enough ripe fruit to balance the subtle, mocha-flavored, oak accents. Not available in the U.S. Best from 2003 through 2007.–P.M. • $NA • (1/01/1999) • **90**

ROSSIGNOL-TRAPET

Beaune Teurons 1995 • $30 • (11/15/1997) • **82**

Beaune Teurons 1994 • $NA • (11/15/1996) • **82**

Beaune Teurons 1993 • $33 • (11/15/1995) • **90**

Beaune Teurons 1992 • $30 • (12/15/1994) • **83**

Beaune Teurons 1991 • $27 • (1/31/1994) • **81**

Beaune Teurons 1990 • $46 • (12/15/1992) • **91**

FRANCE

ROSSIGNOL-TRAPET

Chambertin 1996: A brettanomycic monster. Blackberry and earth, silky texture and lively structure, with hints of vanilla and a dry finish. Worth cellaring it to see if the brett burns off?–B.S. • $86 • (9/30/1998) • **70**
Chambertin 1995 • $68 • (11/15/1997) • **90**
Chambertin 1994 • $NA • (11/15/1996) • **83**
Chambertin 1993 • $77 • (11/15/1995) • **90**
Chambertin 1992 • $NA • (12/15/1994) • **87**
Chambertin 1991 • $58 • (1/31/1994) • **87**
Chambertin 1990 • $106 • (12/15/1992) • **95**
Chapelle-Chambertin 1996: Sweet on the palate but earthy in aroma, turning tart and bitter on the finish.–P.M. • $70 • (5/15/1999) • **74**
Chapelle-Chambertin 1995 • $55 • (11/15/1997) • **75**
Chapelle-Chambertin 1994 • $NA • (11/15/1996) • **79**
Chapelle-Chambertin 1993 • $77 • (11/15/1995) • **87**
Chapelle-Chambertin 1992 • $56 • (12/15/1994) • **79**
Chapelle-Chambertin 1991 • $49 • (1/31/1994) CS • **94**
Chapelle-Chambertin 1990 • $83 • (12/15/1992) • **95**
Gevrey-Chambertin 1996: Medium-bodied, earthy, with cassis bush notes and a crisp, high-acidity character.–P.M. • $32 • (5/15/1999) • **78**
Gevrey-Chambertin 1995 • $25 • (11/15/1997) • **83**
Gevrey-Chambertin 1994 • $NA • (11/15/1996) • **77**
Gevrey-Chambertin 1993 • $28 • (11/15/1995) • **87**
Gevrey-Chambertin 1992 • $26 • (12/15/1994) • **79**
Gevrey-Chambertin 1991 • $23 • (1/31/1994) • **84**
Gevrey-Chambertin Petite Chapelle 1996: Unripe, with green, herbaceous character that turns bitter and astringent at the end.–B.S. • $70 • (9/30/1998) • **75**
Gevrey-Chambertin Petite Chapelle 1994 • $NA • (11/15/1996) • **77**
Gevrey-Chambertin Petite Chapelle 1993 • $43 • (11/15/1995) • **88**
Gevrey-Chambertin Petite Chapelle 1992 • $39 • (12/15/1994) • **82**
Gevrey-Chambertin Petite Chapelle 1991 • $33 • (1/31/1994) • **80**
Gevrey-Chambertin Petite Chapelle 1990 • $61 • (12/15/1992) • **90**
Latricières-Chambertin 1996: Herbal, smoky and light, there's a silkiness to the texture, but it doesn't capture the charm of the vintage. Best from 2000.–B.S. • $70 • (9/30/1998) • **79**
Latricières-Chambertin 1995 • $55 • (11/15/1997) • **86**
Latricières-Chambertin 1994 • $NA • (11/15/1996) • **77**
Latricières-Chambertin 1993 • $64 • (11/15/1995) • **92**
Latricières-Chambertin 1992 • $56 • (12/15/1994) • **86**
Latricières-Chambertin 1991 • $49 • (1/31/1994) • **90**
Latricières-Chambertin 1990 • $74 Ⓐ • (12/15/1992) • **97**

ROSTAING, R.

Côte-Rôtie 1996: This traditional-style red shows fine texture, with good balance and firm tannins, but the flavors are quite rustic, leaning toward gamy, earthy notes that dominate the black cherry; decanting before serving will help. Drink now through 2003.–T.M. • $38 • (9/15/1999) • **85**
Côte-Rôtie 1994 • $35 • (10/15/1997) • **83**
Côte-Rôtie 1990 • $31 • (5/31/1994) • **84**
Côte-Rôtie Côte Blonde 1996: Firm and dense yet elegant and reserved, this fine-grained, voluptuous red shows complex black cherry, plum, game and toasty flavors, balanced and harmonious. Delicious now, and has the stuffing to improve. Drink through 2010.–T.M. • $45 • (9/15/1999) • **91**
Côte-Rôtie Côte Blonde 1987 • $40 • (6/30/1990) • **86**
Côte-Rôtie La Landonne 1996: Elegant, even delicate, this silky red offers vivid cherry, herb and light game flavors, with fine tannins and lively acidity. Not a blockbuster, but has a subtle appeal that grows with every sip. Drink now through 2006.–T.M. • $53 Ⓐ • (9/15/1999) • **89**
Côte-Rôtie La Landonne 1995: Ripe and deep, this firm red offers plum, tar and smoke flavors over rich, chewy tannins. A smoky, slightly bitter note on the finish whets your palate for another sip. A nice marriage of typicity and polish. Closed now, but still balanced and lively. Drink through 2008–T.M. • $75 • (11/15/1998) • **91**
Côte-Rôtie La Landonne 1994 • $33 Ⓐ • (10/15/1997) • **87**
Côte-Rôtie La Viaillere 1995: This stylish red is firm yet elegant, with black cherry and blackberry flavors and notes of violet and spice. Fresh and clean, very modern in style, balanced and still tight. Give it time to unwind. Drink through 2006–T.M. • $57 • (11/15/1998) • **89**
Côte-Rôtie La Viaillere 1994 • $41 • (10/15/1997) • **85**

Key: SS—Spectator Selection. CS—Cellar Selection. HR—Highly Recommended. $NA—Price not available. (BT)—Barrel tasting. Ⓐ—Auction Price.
For a key to the tasters' initials, see "How to Use These Listings."
Dates in parentheses represent the issues in which the ratings were published.

ROTHSCHILD, BARON PHILIPPE DE

Cabernet Sauvignon Vin de Pays d'Oc 1994 • $10 • (12/31/1995) • **83**
Cabernet Sauvignon Vin de Pays d'Oc Cadet 1996 • $7 • (6/15/1998) • **82**
Cabernet Sauvignon Vin de Pays d'Oc Cadet 1995 • $7 • (8/31/1997) • **84**
Graves White 1997: Straightforward Graves, with apple, gooseberry and celery aromas. Medium-bodied, with grassy flavors and a light finish. Drink now.–J.S. • $12 • (9/30/1999) • **84**
Médoc 1995 • $12 • (6/15/1998) • **80**
Médoc 1989 • $11 • (11/15/1994) HR • **89**
Merlot Vin de Pays d'Oc 1994 • $10 • (12/31/1995) • **82**
Merlot Vin de Pays d'Oc Cadet 1996 • $7 • (5/31/1998) • **82**
Merlot Vin de Pays d'Oc Cadet 1995 • $7 • (8/31/1997) • **81**
Pauillac 1994 • $21 • (6/15/1998) • **85**
Pomerol 1995 • $23 • (6/15/1998) • **81**
Sauternes 1994 • $27 • (6/15/1998) • **74**
Sauternes 1991 • $25 • (11/15/1994) • **85**
St.-Emilion 1994 • $15 • (6/15/1998) • **80**
St.-Emilion 1985 • $11 • (9/30/1988) • **85**

ROTY, JOSEPH

Bourgogne Cuvée de Pressonier 1992 • $NA • (12/15/1994) • **80**
Charmes-Chambertin Cuvée de Très Vieilles Vignes 1992 • $135 • (12/15/1994) • **82**
Charmes-Chambertin Vieilles Vignes 1995: A fabulous red that will knock your socks off. Offering the best of both worlds, it mingles the modern-style oak treatment with the traditional grilled meat, toasted spice, smoked bacon, mineral and wet earth notes. Lush, powerhouse finish. Full-bodied, deep and complex, it needs time to show all it has. Best from 2005 through 2010.–P.M. • $170 • (8/31/1998) • **91**
Gevrey-Chambertin Brunelle 1996: Slightly more traditional in its approach, showing earth and mineral as much as pure fruit, along with some stiff tannins. Open in texture and backed by zippy acidity, this will benefit from food. Best from 2001 through 2004.–B.S. • $42 • (1/01/2000) • **88**
Gevrey-Chambertin Champs-Chenys 1996: Just a hint of herbaceousness, along with a spicy oak component, in this moderately structured, berry-tinged red. A little astrignent on the finish. Drink now through 2002.–B.S. • $38 • (1/01/2000) • **83**
Gevrey-Chambertin Champs-Chenys 1995: A tough customer that seems a bit rustic. Wild, with sauvage aromas of dried herbs and earth, and plenty of cherry, wild raspberry and cassis notes. High acidity kicks in on the finish, making it vibrant. Drink through 2007–P.M. • $38 Ⓐ • (8/31/1998) • **87**
Gevrey-Chambertin Champs-Chenys 1992 • $NA • (12/15/1994) • **84**
Gevrey-Chambertin Clos Prieur 1996: An Eastern bazaar meets Pinot Noir in this spicy, warm, inviting red Burgundy. Toys with licorice, but mainly raspberry and wild berries as it expands on the palate. Broad and almost chewy, with a long aftertaste. Drink now through 2003.–B.S. • $49 • (1/01/2000) • **89**
Gevrey-Chambertin Clos Prieur 1995: A highly individualistic red, this exotic, medium-bodied wine has plenty of everything, including iodine, blood and salt notes. Balanced, with ripe fruit, deep flavors and a superintense finish that should be opulent in a few years. Best from 2005 through 2010.–P.M. • $50 • (8/31/1998) • **89**
Gevrey-Chambertin Clos Prieur 1992 • $50 • (12/15/1994) • **83**
Gevrey-Chambertin Fontenys 1996: A solid, beefy red sporting earth, meat and plum aromas and flavors. Lacks the charm of the best, with some firm tannins and a burly personality. Best from 2001 through 2004.–B.S. • $34 Ⓐ • (1/01/2000) • **87**
Gevrey-Chambertin Fontenys 1992 • $72 • (12/15/1994) • **85**
Griotte-Chambertin 1992 • $200 • (12/15/1994) • **83**
Marsannay Les Ouzeloy 1992 • $NA • (12/15/1994) • **80**
Mazis-Chambertin 1992 • $200 • (12/15/1994) • **88**

ROUANET, DOMAINE

St.-Chinian Nuance 1998: Nicely concentrated, with plenty of smoke and leather notes and roasted and plummy flavors. A bit rustic in the end, but quite flavorful. Drink now through 2002.–K.M. • $9 • (6/15/2000) • **84**
St.-Chinian Tonneaux 1998: Dominated by sweet spice and cherry aromas and flavors, this puts up a showy front but turns a bit coarse on the finish. Drink now.–K.M. • $13 • (6/15/2000) • **82**

ROUGE & NOIR

Brut Blanc de Blancs France NV: A good, basic bottle of bubbly with modest apple flavors and a smooth effervescence. Drink now. • $13 • (10/15/1999) • **82**

ROUGET, CHATEAU

Pomerol 1998: Plenty of blackberry and smoke character on the nose and palate. Medium- to full-bodied, with silky tannins and a sweet fruit finish. All in finesse.–J.S. • $NA • (5/31/1999) (BT) • **90-94**
Pomerol 1997: Good plum and earth aromas, with hints of berries. Medium-bodied, with velvety tannins and soft texture. Drink now through 2004.–J.S. • $35 • (1/31/2000) • **85**
Pomerol 1996: Rustic, but good concentration for the vintage. Like frozen berries on the nose, with a hint of grape skins. Medium-bodied, with silky tannins and a black cherry aftertaste. Best after 2000.–J.S. • $NA • (1/31/1999) • **86**
Pomerol 1995: Subtle aromas of blackberries, plums and flowers open to a delicate palate with medium body, soft tanins and a light finish. Good now through 2003.–J.S. • $NA • (9/15/1998) • **83**
Pomerol 1982 • $28 • (5/15/1989) • **86**
Pomerol 1961 • $51 • (4/30/1996) • **85**
Pomerol 1947 • $267 Ⓐ • (5/31/1997) • **90**
Pomerol 1945 • $400 • (11/30/1995) • **87**

ROUGET, EMMANUEL

Echézeaux 1993 • $153 Ⓐ • (5/15/1996) • **95**
Echézeaux 1991 • $115 Ⓐ • (8/31/1994) • **89**
Echézeaux 1988 • $149 Ⓐ • (11/15/1990) • **96**
Echézeaux 1987 • $55 • (3/31/1990) • **88**
Echézeaux 1986 • $55 • (12/31/1988) • **87**
Nuits-St.-Georges 1996: There's an honesty in this pure, clean and authentic-tasting Pinot Noir. Mineral, blood-orange, blackberry character takes off unhindered by fancy oak; for aficionados of the real McCoy. Drink now through 2005.–P.M. • $67 Ⓐ • (7/31/1999) • **90**
Nuits-St.-Georges 1995 • $35 • (1/31/1998) • **88**
Nuits-St.-Georges 1993 • $NA • (5/15/1996) • **90**
Nuits-St.-Georges 1989 • $48 • (11/15/1991) • **86**
Nuits-St.-Georges 1987 • $32 • (3/31/1990) • **86**
Savigny-lès-Beaune 1993 • $NA • (5/15/1996) • **89**
Vosne-Romanée 1996: Ripe plum and cassis notes are augmented by coffee and spice in this silky-smooth red. All elegance and finesse as it glides across the palate, ending with an echo of freshly crushed berries. Drink now through 2004.–B.S. • $43 Ⓐ • (1/01/2000) • **89**
Vosne-Romanée 1995 • $35 • (1/31/1998) • **82**
Vosne-Romanée 1993 • $NA • (5/15/1996) • **83**
Vosne-Romanée 1989 • $48 • (11/15/1991) • **91**
Vosne-Romanée 1987 • $32 • (3/31/1990) • **91**
Vosne-Romanée Cros Parantoux 1993 • $184 Ⓐ • (5/15/1996) • **95**
Vosne-Romanée Cros Parantoux 1989 • $83 • (11/15/1991) • **94**
Vosne-Romanée Les Beaumonts 1996: Absolutely stunning. Deep, pure aromas of cassis, violets and vanilla are followed by rich flavors and silky texure. Everything is woven together by juicy acidity,with a cascade of berries on the finish. Best from 2001 through 2007.–B.S. • $101 Ⓐ • (1/01/2000) • **94**
Vosne-Romanée Les Beauxmonts 1993 • $55 • (5/15/1996) • **91**
Vosne-Romanée Les Beauxmonts 1986 • $40 • (12/31/1988) • **89**

ROULOT, GUY

Bourgogne White 1997: Clean, with green apple and slightly underripe pineapple, showing a crisp edge on the finish. Drink now.–P.M. • $22 • (9/30/1999) • **81**
Bourgogne White 1995 • $20 • (8/31/1997) • **90**
Meursault Les Charmes 1997: Richly textured, full-bodied and unctuous yet reserved on the nose, it coats the palate with honey, passion fruit, mineral and light toast character. What the Meursault legend (fat, silky Chardonnays) is all about. All sexy curves compared to Roulot's savage, machete-wielding Perrières, showing that Roulot is at the top of the *terroir* game. Drink now through 2007.–P.M. • $78 • (9/30/1999) • **93**
Meursault Les Charmes 1996: Lush and opulent, sweet and rich, with a lovely texture that coats the palate with its silky feel. Seductive upon release, with wonderful pear, melon, litchi, earth and pineapple flavors, nicely toasted oak accents; will hold in the cellar. Drink now through 2005.–P.M. • $75 • (8/31/1998) • **92**
Meursault Les Charmes 1995 • $80 • (8/31/1997) • **95**
Meursault Les Luchets 1997: Clean and pure, this medium-bodied, intense, focused Meursault flies with precision, delivering passion fruit, citrus, mineral and cream drops with lingering effect. Drink now through 2005.–P.M. • $47 • (9/30/1999) • **90**
Meursault Les Luchets 1996: Delicious for its balance and ripe smoothness. A beautiful, full-bodied Meursault that has loads of acidity buffered by pear, toasted oak and tropical flavors and an herbal accent. Smoky, toasted notes come through on the lingering finish. Best after 2005.–P.M. • $50 • (8/31/1998) • **92**
Meursault Les Luchets 1995 • $45 • (5/31/1997) • **93**
Meursault Les Meix Chavaux 1997: A sensitive soul had a hand in this refined Meursault. Finesse defines this elegant yet deeply satisfying Chardonnay. Reserved on the nose, it rolls to life on the palate, coating the taste buds with pear, citrus, mineral and light toast notes. Drink now through 2005.–P.M. • $47 • (9/30/1999) • **93**
Meursault Les Meix Chavaux 1996: Creamy, mineral character is wonderful. Impressively thick and lush for a '96, this full-bodied white delivers plenty of citrus, honey and pear aromas and flavors, along with a slight grassy note. Lovely elegance in the midpalate bodes well for cellaring as it should keep its racy structure for years. Best after 2005.–P.M. • $50 • (8/31/1998) • **92**
Meursault Les Meix Chavaux 1995 • $45 • (5/31/1997) • **90**
Meursault Les Tessons Clos de Mon Plaisir 1997: Green apple and pear show the way in this straightforward Chardonnay, with good acidity and a hint of honey. Tasted twice, with consistent notes. Drink now through 2002.–P.M. • $58 • (9/30/1999) • **84**
Meursault Les Tessons Clos de Mon Plaisir 1996: Simply fantastic. So ripe it tastes almost sweet. Mingles lovely earth, herbal-grassy, mineral and pear-honey notes for an ultraseductive, full-bodied Meursault. The texture is silky smooth, yet there's excellent concentration of fruit, deftly toasted oak and good acidity. Buy as much as you can afford or find. Tempting now thanks to its impeccable balance, but will age for a decade at least. Best after 2005.–P.M. • $55 • (8/31/1998) • **92**
Meursault Les Tessons Clos de Mon Plaisir 1995 • $50 • (5/31/1998) • **94**
Meursault Les Vireuils 1997: A beautifully balanced, clean and natural white Burgundy. Focused, with dried herbs and accents of honey, pear and light oak, it's megafull in body. Well-integrated acidity carries the wine like a surfboard on a breaking wave. Bravo! Drink now through 2007.–P.M. • $47 • (9/30/1999) • **90**
Meursault Les Vireuils 1995 • $45 • (5/31/1997) • **90**
Meursault Perrières 1997: This collectible '97 is well made and opulent, with good depth, but it has the sort of searing acidity more common in '96s. Full-bodied, with vibrant, integrated acidity, rich fruit concentration, mineral accents and a clean, long, explosively citrusy finish. Focused and elegant. Best from 2003 through 2007.–P.M. • $86 • (9/30/1999) • **94**
Meursault Perrières 1996: Classic Meursault. Excellent concentration in this full-bodied, supple yet vibrant, compacted *premier cru*. Wraps around the palate with grassy, honey, lime and mineral notes, tasting both intense and mellow. Best after 2005.–P.M. • $75 • (8/31/1998) • **95**
Meursault Perrières 1995 • $62 Ⓐ • (8/31/1997) • **95**

ROUMIER, CHRISTOPHE

Charmes-Chambertin 1992 • $55 • (12/15/1994) • **88**
Charmes-Chambertin 1990 • $105 • (12/15/1992) • **93**
Ruchottes-Chambertin 1992 • $58 • (12/15/1994) • **85**
Ruchottes-Chambertin 1991 • $58 • (1/31/1994) • **90**
Ruchottes-Chambertin 1990 • $80 • (12/15/1992) • **97**
Ruchottes-Chambertin 1989 • $70 • (1/31/1992) • **94**

ROUMIER, G.

Bonnes Mares 1996: A gorgeous red Burgundy, ripe yet firm, playing the field of Pinot Noir complexity. It has smoke, game, mineral and black fruit character, a thick texture and well-integrated tannins. Bravo. Drink now through 2006.–P.M. • $147 Ⓐ • (7/31/1999) CS • **93**
Bonnes Mares 1992 • $58 • (12/15/1994) • **82**
Bonnes Mares 1991 • $89 Ⓐ • (1/31/1994) • **91**
Bonnes Mares 1990 • $247 Ⓐ • (12/15/1992) • **96**
Bonnes Mares 1989 • $70 • (1/31/1992) • **93**
Chambolle-Musigny 1996: Shows blackberry, black cherry and spice notes, but some tartness on the finish makes it a tough Pinot. Drink now through 2002.–P.M. • $35 Ⓐ • (7/31/1999) • **84**

FRANCE

ROUMIER, G.

Chambolle-Musigny 1995: Attractive from start to finish. Not a big wine, but elegant, showing depth of aroma, with cherry, earth, cranberry, rose petal and some cassis notes. Medium-bodied, with elegant tannins on the seamless finish. Drink now through 2005.–P.M. • $30 • (8/31/1998) • **88**
Chambolle-Musigny 1992 • $24 • (12/15/1994) • **79**
Chambolle-Musigny 1991 • $22 • (1/31/1994) • **80**
Chambolle-Musigny 1990 • $28 • (12/15/1992) • **88**
Chambolle-Musigny 1989 • $38 • (1/31/1992) • **90**
Chambolle-Musigny 1988 • $30 • (7/15/1991) • **89**
Chambolle-Musigny 1985 • $26 • (2/15/1988) • **87**
Chambolle-Musigny Les Amoureuses 1992 • $48 • (12/15/1994) • **84**
Chambolle-Musigny Les Amoureuses 1991 • $48 • (1/31/1994) • **85**
Chambolle-Musigny Les Amoureuses 1990 • $55 • (12/15/1992) • **92**
Chambolle-Musigny Les Amoureuses 1989 • $62 • (1/31/1992) • **88**
Chambolle-Musigny Les Cras 1997: Grilled aromas and flavors dominate this wine, with its slightly earthy, smoky cassis character. Medium-bodied, it's hedonistic in its ripe texture. Turns nicely chewy on the long, toasted finish. Drink now through 2005.–P.M. • $60 • (1/01/2000) • **89**
Clos Vougeot 1992 • $48 • (12/15/1994) • **79**
Clos Vougeot 1991 • $45 • (1/31/1994) • **84**
Clos Vougeot 1990 • $65 • (12/15/1992) • **92**
Clos Vougeot 1989 • $62 • (1/31/1992) • **87**
Morey-St.-Denis Clos de la Bussière 1997: An attractive, rich red Burgundy that's savage. Rather dense and focused on wet earth and black fruit. Tastes ripe on the palate, with sweet, velvety tannins. Full-bodied, it's round and exquisite on the yummy finish. Drink now through 2007.–P.M. • $45 • (1/01/2000) • **91**
Morey-St.-Denis Clos de la Bussière 1996: Closed for now, but a marvel of fresh, vibrant red berry character. Has a slightly greenish ending, but it's still succulent and pleasant. Drink now through 2002.–P.M. • $42 • (7/31/1999) • **86**
Morey-St.-Denis Clos de la Bussière 1995: Effusive aromas of cherry, dried herbs and cassis, and though this medium-bodied wine doesn't have much depth, it seduces with its sappy, lovely, fresh red berry character. Drink now.–P.M. • $40 Ⓐ • (8/31/1998) • **86**
Morey-St.-Denis Clos de la Bussière 1992 • $24 • (12/15/1994) • **84**
Morey-St.-Denis Clos de la Bussière 1991 • $22 • (1/31/1994) • **85**
Morey-St.-Denis Clos de la Bussière 1990 • $53 • (12/15/1992) • **89**
Morey-St.-Denis Clos de la Bussière 1989 • $38 • (1/31/1992) • **85**
Morey-St.-Denis Clos de la Bussière 1988 • $30 • (7/15/1991) • **83**
Morey-St.-Denis Clos de la Bussière 1985 • $27 • (4/30/1988) • **92**
Musigny 1992 • $NA • (12/15/1994) • **90**
Musigny 1991 • $85 • (1/31/1994) • **78**
Musigny 1989 • $95 • (1/31/1992) • **96**

ROUMIER, LAURENT

Bonnes Mares 1997: Medium-bodied, with toasted oak, mocha, chocolate and spice, holding black currant in the background. A bit chewy and crisp on the finish. Drink now through 2003.–P.M. • $84 • (9/30/1999) • **83**
Chambolle-Musigny 1997: Light, stemmy and slightly diluted, with herb and strawberry notes.–P.M. • $70 • (9/30/1999) • **75**
Chambolle-Musigny 1996: Ripe and silky, showing flesh and body and a moderate structure. The flavors are in the raspberry-blackberry range, and the acidity is bright. Concentrated fruit on the finish. Best from 2001 through 2005.–B.S. • $35 • (9/30/1998) • **90**
Clos Vougeot 1997: Rather tough, at least in the '97 group, but it has a midpalate firmness, chewy tannins and plenty of stuffing. Medium-bodied, lush and rich, it digs into the wet earth, delivering a rather unique style for '97. Best from 2002 through 2007.–P.M. • $70 • (1/01/2000) • **88**
Clos Vougeot 1996: Tough and hard, with herbal, cassis and dry tannic character. Medium-bodied. Best from 2003.–P.M. • $67 • (9/30/1998) • **79**
Hautes-Côtes de Nuits 1997: A little cooked in character, it lacks focus, though there's moderate depth and firm tannins for support. Drink now through 2002.–B.S. • $18 • (9/30/1999) • **81**
Hautes-Côtes de Nuits 1996: Medium-bodied, with decent ripeness, smooth tannins and interesting matchstick, flinty, smoky character. Finish turns hot and disjointed.–P.M. • $19 • (9/30/1998) • **77**

Key: SS—Spectator Selection. CS—Cellar Selection. HR—Highly Recommended. $NA—Price not available. (BT)—Barrel tasting. Ⓐ—Auction Price.
For a key to the tasters' initials, see "How to Use These Listings."
Dates in parentheses represent the issues in which the ratings were published.

ROUMIEU, CHATEAU

Barsac 1995 • $NA • (4/30/1998) • **88**

ROUMIEU-LACOSTE, CHATEAU

Barsac 1990 • $33 Ⓐ • (4/15/1995) • **91**

ROUSSEAU, ARMAND

Chambertin 1997: Herbaceous cherry flavors underlie the spiciness of new oak in this medium-bodied, vanilla-accented Gevrey. There's chewy intensity and enough density to stand up to the firm structure. Best from 2002 through 2006.–B.S. • $99 Ⓐ • (9/30/1999) • **87**
Chambertin 1995 • $167 Ⓐ • (11/15/1997) HR • **96**
Chambertin 1994 • $78 Ⓐ • (9/30/1997) • **76**
Chambertin 1993 • $140 Ⓐ • (9/15/1996) • **95**
Chambertin 1992 • $NA • (12/15/1994) • **88**
Chambertin 1991 • $158 Ⓐ • (1/31/1994) • **91**
Chambertin 1990 • $269 Ⓐ • (12/15/1992) • **92**
Chambertin 1988 • $147 Ⓐ • (5/15/1991) • **93**
Chambertin 1985 • $100 • (3/15/1988) • **97**
Chambertin-Clos de Bèze 1997: Fine black cherry and earth Pinot aromas and flavors appear on a medium-bodied framework that's loose-knit and forward. Tasty, without the depth for long aging. Drink now through 2003.–B.S. • $98 Ⓐ • (9/30/1999) • **84**
Chambertin-Clos de Bèze 1996: Quite oaky at this stage, with a layer of sweet vanilla and butterscotch covering the fruit. The wood also lends some fine tannins, which integrate well on the finish. The aftertaste echoes sweetness. Best from 2001 through 2006.–B.S. • $173 Ⓐ • (9/30/1998) • **89**
Chambertin-Clos de Bèze 1993 • $1,823 Ⓐ • (9/15/1996) • **93**
Chambertin-Clos de Bèze 1992 • $NA • (12/15/1994) • **88**
Chambertin-Clos de Bèze 1991 • $139 Ⓐ • (1/31/1994) • **88**
Chambertin-Clos de Bèze 1990 • $196 Ⓐ • (12/15/1992) • **95**
Chambertin-Clos de Bèze 1989 • $127 Ⓐ • (1/31/1992) • **93**
Chambertin-Clos de Bèze 1988 • $188 • (5/15/1991) • **95**
Charmes-Chambertin 1994 • $75 • (9/30/1997) • **83**
Charmes-Chambertin 1985 • $156 Ⓐ • (10/15/1988) • **86**
Clos de la Roche 1992 • $NA • (12/15/1994) • **88**
Clos de la Roche 1991 • $75 • (1/31/1994) • **89**
Clos de la Roche 1990 • $182 Ⓐ • (12/15/1992) • **92**
Clos de la Roche 1988 • $75 • (5/15/1991) • **91**
Gevrey-Chambertin 1989 • $NA • (1/31/1992) • **88**
Gevrey-Chambertin Clos St.-Jacques 1996: Light and delicate, with pure raspberry, strawberry and cherry notes, and a smoky, grilled-meat character on the chewy, vanilla-scented finish. Drink now through 2003.–P.M. • $105 Ⓐ • (9/30/1998) • **85**
Gevrey-Chambertin Clos St.-Jacques 1995 • $136 Ⓐ • (11/15/1997) • **85**
Gevrey-Chambertin Clos St.-Jacques 1994 • $38 Ⓐ • (9/30/1997) • **79**
Gevrey-Chambertin Clos St.-Jacques 1993 • $107 Ⓐ • (9/15/1996) • **92**
Gevrey-Chambertin Clos St.-Jacques 1992 • $NA • (12/15/1994) • **78**
Gevrey-Chambertin Clos St.-Jacques 1991 • $75 • (1/31/1994) • **82**
Gevrey-Chambertin Clos St.-Jacques 1990 • $184 Ⓐ • (12/15/1992) • **90**
Gevrey-Chambertin Clos St.-Jacques 1989 • $95 • (1/31/1992) • **90**
Gevrey-Chambertin Clos St.-Jacques 1985 • $122 Ⓐ • (10/15/1988) • **92**
Mazy-Chambertin 1992 • $NA • (12/15/1994) • **82**
Mazy-Chambertin 1991 • $75 • (1/31/1994) • **90**
Mazy-Chambertin 1990 • $75 • (12/15/1992) • **93**
Mazy-Chambertin 1989 • $80 • (1/31/1992) • **90**
Mazy-Chambertin 1985 • $63 • (10/15/1988) • **85**
Ruchottes-Chambertin Clos des Ruchottes 1997: Tastes light and diluted, with a mushroom and tea leaf character and an astringent finish.–P.M. • $92 • (9/30/1999) • **78**
Ruchottes-Chambertin Clos des Ruchottes 1996: Nice, delicate red Burgundy, medium in body, showing pretty cherry, raspberry, vanilla, chocolate and green olive notes. Complex, but not very opulent. Drink now through 2003.–P.M. • $75 Ⓐ • (9/30/1998) • **87**
Ruchottes-Chambertin Clos des Ruchottes 1995 • $62 Ⓐ • (11/15/1997) • **91**
Ruchottes-Chambertin Clos des Ruchottes 1993 • $67 Ⓐ • (9/15/1996) • **93**
Ruchottes-Chambertin Clos des Ruchottes 1992 • $NA • (12/15/1994) • **84**
Ruchottes-Chambertin Clos des Ruchottes 1991 • $80 Ⓐ • (1/31/1994) • **89**
Ruchottes-Chambertin Clos des Ruchottes 1990 • $80 • (12/15/1992) • **96**
Ruchottes-Chambertin Clos des Ruchottes 1989 • $85 • (1/31/1992) • **90**

ROUSSELLE, CHATEAU LA

Fronsac 1997: Plenty of mineral, blackberry and cherry aromas. Medium-bodied, with a solid core of fruit, medium tannins and a light finish. Slightly one-dimensional. Drink now.–J.S. • $NA • (1/31/2000) • **84**
Fronsac 1990 • $NA • (3/31/1993) • **83**

ROUTAS, CHATEAU

Carignan Vin de Pays du Var Vieilles Vignes 1997: On the light side but bright-tasting, with currant and cherry flavors and a touch of spice and leather on the finish. Drink now.–K.M. • $12 • (11/30/1998) • **83**
Carignan Vin de Pays du Var Vieilles Vignes 1996 • $NA • (1/01/1998) • **83**
Chardonnay-Viognier Vin de Pays du Var Coquelicot 1997: Interesting for its butteriness, this shows nice, ripe pear flavors, finishing with honey notes. Drink now.–K.M. • $18 • (12/15/1998) • **80**
Chardonnay-Viognier Vin de Pays du Var Coquelicot 1996 • $15 • (3/31/1998) • **83**
Coteaux Varois 1993 • $7 • (11/30/1994) • **82**
Coteaux Varois 1992 • $7 • (6/30/1994) • **82**
Coteaux Varois Agrippa 1992 • $18 • (7/31/1996) • **83**
Coteaux Varois Cyrano 1994 • $18 • (7/31/1996) • **86**
Coteaux Varois Infernet 1995 • $11 • (1/01/1998) • **84**
Coteaux Varois Infernet 1994 • $10 • (7/31/1996) • **84**
Coteaux Varois Infernet 1993 • $11 • (3/31/1995) • **85**
Coteaux Varois Infernet 1992 • $8 • (6/30/1994) • **83**
Coteaux Varois Luc Sorin 1994 • $15 • (1/31/1997) • **87**
Coteaux Varois Luc Sorin 1993 • $15 • (3/31/1995) • **87**
Coteaux Varois Luc Sorin 1992 • $11 • (6/30/1994) • **87**
Coteaux Varois Mistral 1993 • $20 • (7/31/1996) • **88**
Coteaux Varois Rosé Rouvière 1998: A light and refreshing rosé, with dried cherry and berry flavors and a spicy aroma. Drink now.–K.M. • $9 • (10/15/1999) • **83**
Coteaux Varois Rosé Rouvière 1997: Offers pretty cherry and dried berry aromas, herbal notes on the finish. Drink now.–K.M. • $9 • (11/15/1998) • **82**
Coteaux Varois Rosé Rouvière 1996 • $9 • (12/15/1997) • **78**
Coteaux Varois White Pyramus 1996: An oaky style, with a decadent aroma and herbal and butter flavors. A bit overdone.–K.M. • $11 • (11/15/1998) • **79**
Grenache-Cabernet Sauvignon-Syrah Coteaux Varois Infernet 1996: This herbal-scented red shows ripe cherry and plum flavors with firm underlying tannins. Better with food. Drink now.–T.M. • $13 • (12/15/1998) • **83**
Red Vin de Pays du Var Traditionel 1995 • $9 • (1/01/1998) • **83**
Syrah Vin de Pays du Var Cyrano 1997: Fairly intense sweet cherry and spice flavors dominate this medium-bodied red, which ends on a note of cinnamon. Needs time to let the flavors integrate. Best from 2001 through 2004.–K.M. • $16 • (5/15/2000) • **86**
Syrah Vin de Pays du Var Cyrano 1996: A luscious, ready-to-drink red. Quite peppery, with loads of spice, cherry and plum notes, which linger with warm, brickish elements on the finish. Drink now.–K.M. • $15 • (1/01/2000) • **86**
Syrah-Cabernet Sauvignon Coteaux Varois Agrippa 1996: Quite tart, with plum and cherry flavors and cardamom notes on the finish. Drink now.–K.M. • $16 • (12/15/1998) • **80**
Syrah-Cabernet Sauvignon Coteaux Varois Agrippa 1995 • $17 • (12/15/1997) • **87**

ROUTIER, CHATEAU DE

Côtes de Malepère Cuvée Jean Lèzerat 1995 • $8 • (4/30/1998) • **84**

ROUX, ARMAND

Bordeaux Verdillac 1989 • $7 • (1/31/1992) • **71**
Bordeaux Verdillac 1988 • $6 • (7/15/1990) • **79**
Cabernet Sauvignon Vin de Pays d'Oc L'Epayrié 1995 • $8 • (12/15/1996) • **78**
Chardonnay Vin de Pays d'Oc L'Epayrié 1997: A straightforward white, with apple and fig flavors. Spicy notes on the finish. Drink now.–K.M. • $7 • (11/15/1998) • **80**
Coteaux du Languedoc Pic St.-Loup 1996: Loaded with sweet-spicy flavors, with a chocolaty note on the finish. Not a lot of complexity, but plenty of flavor. Drink now.–K.M. • $7 • (10/31/1998) • **84**
Coteaux du Languedoc Pic St.-Loup 1994 • $7 • (7/31/1996) • **85**
Côtes du Lubéron La Forge 1989 • $6 • (4/15/1993) • **80**
Côtes du Rhône La Berberine 1994 • $8 • (12/31/1995) • **83**
Côtes du Rhône La Berberine 1988 • $8 • (10/31/1990) • **81**
Echézeaux 1959 • $110 • (8/31/1990) • **94**
L'Epayrié Special Reserve France Red NV • $7 • (7/31/1996) • **74**
Merlot Vin de Pays d'Oc L'Epayrié 1995 • $8 • (12/15/1996) • **83**
Muscadet Sur Lie Domaine du Fief Guérin 1997: This smooth, round white has good weight on the palate, with fresh flavors of green apple and ripe pear. Tart and clean on the finish. Drink now.–T.M. • $10 • (6/30/1999) • **82**
Richebourg 1959 • $130 • (8/31/1990) • **91**
Rosé d'Anjou La Pucelle 1998: This off-dry rosé offers soft cherry flavors, but overall it tastes candied and a bit artificial.–T.M. • $8 • (6/30/1999) • **77**
Sauvignon Blanc Vin de Pays d'Oc L'Epayrié 1997: Vivid and crisp, this assertive white marries clean citrus and herb flavors with round notes of mango and coconut. Has an exotic character rare in French versions of this varietal. Drink now.–T.M. • $7 • (12/31/1998) • **87**
Syrah Vin de Pays d'Oc L'Epayrié 1997: Juicy and fairly fresh-tasting, with cherry and red plum flavors, some spicy and leather notes. Drink now.–K.M. • $7 • (11/15/1998) • **83**
Volnay Hospices de Beaune Général Muteau 1959 • $115 • (8/31/1990) • **91**

ROUX PERE & FILS

Bourgogne White 1995 • $9 • (8/31/1997) • **85**
Chassagne-Montrachet 1995 • $31 • (8/31/1997) • **85**
Chassagne-Montrachet Les Macherelles 1995 • $35 • (5/31/1997) • **93**
Chassagne-Montrachet Red Clos St.-Jean 1983 • $13 • (9/16/1985) • **86**
Meursault Clos des Porusots 1995 • $32 • (5/31/1997) • **90**
Puligny-Montrachet Les Enseignères 1995 • $38 • (5/31/1997) • **91**
Santenay 1985 • $21 • (10/31/1987) • **83**
St.-Aubin 1995 • $25 • (5/31/1997) • **79**
St.-Aubin La Chatenière 1995 • $29 • (5/31/1997) • **87**
Volnay En Champans 1988 • $35 • (3/31/1990) • **86**
Volnay En Champans 1985 • $25 • (3/15/1987) • **92**

ROUZE, JACQUES

Quincy 1996 • $14 • (6/30/1998) • **84**

ROY-THEVENIN, ALAIN

Montagny Les Burnins 1995 • $19 • (5/31/1997) • **88**
Montagny Premier Cru 1995 • $17 • (5/31/1997) • **87**

ROYLLAND, CHATEAU

St.-Emilion 1997: Very good for the vintage. Lovely aromas of berry, currant and chocolate carry through to a medium-bodied wine with fine tannins and a medium finish. Clean and fruity. Drink now through 2003.–J.S. • $19 • (7/31/1999) • **86**
St.-Emilion 1995 • $NA • (1/01/1997) • **86**

RUET

Brouilly Cuvée Spéciale 1993 • $15 • (6/15/1995) • **78**
Brouilly Vieilles Vignes 1996 • $15 • (6/15/1998) • **85**
Brouilly Vieilles Vignes 1994 • $16 • (9/15/1996) • **85**

RUINART

Brut Blanc de Blancs Champagne Dom Ruinart 1990: Compelling, delicious and distinctive. Very fresh, lively yet almost delicate, supported by vivid citrus flavors and zingy acidity, lending it depth and a lingering finish. Drink now through 2009. • $130 • (9/15/1999) • **94**
Brut Champagne R de Ruinart NV: Very dry and tangy in character, refreshing in a lean, citrusy style. Drink now. • $48 • (10/15/1999) • **87**
Brut Champagne R de Ruinart 1993: Bold and distinctive, featuring assertive toast and earth flavors, firm texture and a lingering finish. An adventurous bubbly with a lot more than fizz. Drink now through 2003. • $64 • (10/15/1999) • **88**
Brut Champagne R de Ruinart 1992: Sophisticated in flavor and elegant in texture, this is worth seeking out. Has a provocative toasty, spicy aroma, firm fruit flavors and a supple mouthfeel. Tasty now, but should improve. Drink now through 2002. • $64 • (12/15/1998) • **91**
Brut Champagne R de Ruinart 1990 • $46 • (7/31/1996) • **91**
Brut Rosé Champagne R de Ruinart NV: A deep color and light fruit flavors mark this easygoing, soft-textured, slightly sweet rosé. Drink now. • $83 • (10/15/1999) • **85**

RULLY, CHATEAU DE

Rully 1997: Buttery, perfumey oak gets in the way of the ripe, clean fruit. Vanilla, spice and a slight burning character prevent the finish from being balanced.–P.M. • $15 • (5/31/1999) • **77**
Rully 1995 • $18 • (8/31/1997) • **85**
Rully Red 1991 • $NA • (1/31/1994) • **83**

SABON & FILS, DOMAINE ROGER

Châteauneuf-du-Pape 1988 • $20 • (9/30/1990) • **88**
Châteauneuf-du-Pape Cuvée Prestige 1995: A touch of brett on the nose quickly gives way to clove and chocolate notes. Extremely dense and ripe, with powerful, heady fruit and a brooding, tannic, extracted core. Raw, but oozing with fruit and glycerin, this traditionally styled CdP seems almost primordial right now. Cellar to let this monster resolve itself. Best from 2003 through 2020.–P.M. • $30 • (1/01/2000) • **94**
Châteauneuf-du-Pape Cuvée Prestige 1988 • $23 • (9/30/1990) • **85**
Châteauneuf-du-Pape Cuvée Réserve 1988 • $20 • (9/30/1990) • **80**
Côtes du Rhône 1989 • $12 • (11/15/1991) • **70**
Côtes du Rhône 1988 • $11 • (10/31/1990) • **79**

SADE, MARQUIS DE

Brut Blanc de Blancs Champagne NV • $NA • (12/31/1994) • **87**
Brut Blanc de Blancs Champagne Grand Cru NV • $35 • (3/31/1992) • **85**
Brut Champagne NV • $25 • (12/31/1995) • **82**

SAIER

Clos des Lambrays 1990 • $70 Ⓐ • (3/15/1993) • **80**
Clos des Lambrays 1989 • $68 • (11/15/1991) • **85**
Clos des Lambrays 1988 • $75 • (3/31/1991) • **91**
Clos des Lambrays Domaine des Lambrays 1985 • $55 • (2/15/1988) • **78**
Mercurey Les Champs Martins 1988 • $17 • (8/31/1991) • **80**
Mercurey Les Champs Martins 1985 • $20 • (3/31/1988) • **83**
Mercurey Les Chenelots 1988 • $17 • (4/30/1991) • **67**

SAINCRIT, VINCENT

Bordeaux 1995: Slightly one-dimensional, but delicious and silky, with berry and vanilla aromas and flavors. Drink now through 2003.–J.S. • $NA • (9/15/1998) • **85**

ST.-AHON, CHATEAU

Haut-Médoc 1996: Rather unripe and metallic in character, with medium body and tannins, a light finish.–J.S. • $17 • (2/28/1999) • **77**
Haut-Médoc 1995: A slightly mature '95, with berry, bark and light earth character. Light- to medium-bodied, with firm tannins and a slightly diluted finish. Not bad. Drink now.–J.S. • $19 • (1/01/1999) • **80**

ST.-ANDRE-CORBIN, CHATEAU

St.-Georges-St.-Emilion 1998: Wonderful floral and fruit character in this subtle wine. Medium-bodied, with firm tannins and a medium finish.–J.S. • $NA • (5/31/1999) (BT) • **85-89**
St.-Georges-St.-Emilion 1996: Very diluted, with berry and light chocolate character, a light-bodied palate and a watery finish. At least it's clean and fresh.–J.S. • $NA • (2/28/1999) • **77**
St.-Georges-St.-Emilion 1995 • $14 • (1/31/1998) • **87**
St.-Georges-St.-Emilion 1994 • $12 • (1/31/1997) • **82**
St.-Georges-St.-Emilion 1993 • $15 • (1/31/1996) • **77**
St.-Georges-St.-Emilion 1990 • $15 • (3/31/1993) • **88**
St.-Georges-St.-Emilion 1989 • $15 • (4/30/1992) • **91**
St.-Georges-St.-Emilion 1986 • $22 • (3/31/1990) • **77**

Key: SS—Spectator Selection. CS—Cellar Selection. HR—Highly Recommended. $NA—Price not available. (BT)—Barrel tasting. Ⓐ—Auction Price.
For a key to the tasters' initials, see "How to Use These Listings."
Dates in parentheses represent the issues in which the ratings were published.

ST.-ANDRIEU, DOMAINE

Coteaux du Languedoc Montpeyroux La Seranne 1997: Fairly ripe and gamy, with ripe cherry and spice flavors and herbal notes. A bit muddled but tasty, with bricklike notes on the finish. Drink now.–K.M. • $15 • (2/28/1999) • **84**

STE.-ANNE, DOMAINE

Côtes du Rhône-Villages 1996: Lots of finesse here. Delicious, unpretentious, light-bodied, with lovely black cherry, cassis and spice character, along with a slight earthy whiff. Very fruity and smooth. Drink now.–P.M. • $13 • (11/15/1998) • **85**
Côtes du Rhône-Villages 1995 • $12 • (12/15/1996) • **81**
Côtes du Rhône-Villages Cuvée Notre Dame des Cellettes 1996: Shows good depth and concentration, with ripe plum and blackberry flavors and notes of chocolate and licorice. The tannins are firm but well integrated. Accessible now, but should develop well through 2002.–T.M. • $15 • (11/15/1998) • **87**
Côtes du Rhône-Villages Cuvée Notre Dame des Cellettes 1995 • $16 • (10/15/1997) • **84**
Côtes du Rhône-Villages Cuvée Notre Dame des Cellettes 1994 • $15 • (12/15/1996) • **83**
Côtes du Rhône-Villages St.-Gervais 1996: Round and ripe, this velvety red offers plum, tar and light herb flavors and soft tannins. Clean and straightforward, with good fruit and harmony. Drink now through 2001.–T.M. • $17 • (11/15/1998) • **86**
Côtes du Rhône-Villages St.-Gervais 1995 • $16 • (10/15/1997) • **87**
Côtes du Rhône-Villages St.-Gervais 1994 • $16 • (12/15/1996) • **87**
Syrah Côtes du Rhône 1994 • $19 • (10/15/1997) • **86**
Syrah Côtes du Rhône 1990 • $20 • (4/15/1993) • **82**

ST.-ANTONIN, DOMAINE

Faugères 1996 • $10 • (6/15/1998) • **87**

STE.-COLOMBE, CHATEAU

Côtes de Castillon 1999: A bit light but showing pretty plum and berry aromas and flavors. Light- to medium-bodied, with fine tannins and a fresh finish.–J.S. • $NA • (1/01/2000) (BT) • **80-84**

STE.-CROIX, CHATEAU

Coteaux du Languedoc Le Quatourze 1998: Firm and flavorful, with good red plum and berry flavors, some appealing herbal notes on the finish. Medium-bodied and quite youthful-tasting. Drink now through 2001.–K.M. • $8 • (8/31/1999) • **84**

ST.-CYRGUES, CHATEAU

Costières de Nîmes 1997: A mouthfilling red from the south of France with cherry, plum and berry flavors and plenty of leather notes. A walk on the wild side, but worth it. Drink through 2003–K.M. • $9 • (8/31/1998) • **84**
Costières de Nîmes Cuvée Amérique 1996: A blowsy style, with plenty of sweet cherry flavor and spicy notes. Drink now.–K.M. • $12 • (10/31/1998) • **82**
Costières de Nîmes White 1997: A bit resinous-tasting, with modest apple and citrus notes.–K.M. • $9 • (10/31/1998) • **77**
Costières de Nîmes White Cuvée Amérique 1997: Floral aromas and oaky flavors make this wine appealing, though not very subtle.–K.M. • $12 • (10/31/1998) • **79**

ST.-DESIRAT, CAVE DE

St.-Joseph 1992 • $14 • (11/15/1995) • **78**
Syrah Vin de Pays des Collines Rhodaniennes 1994 • $8 • (10/15/1997) • **83**
Syrah Vin de Pays des Collines Rhodaniennes 1993 • $8 • (7/31/1995) • **76**

ST.-EMILION, L'UNION DE PRODUCTEURS DE

St.-Emilion Cuvée Galius 1995 • $25 • (1/31/1998) • **84**

ST.-ESTEVE D'UCHAUX, CHATEAU

Côtes du Rhône 1989 • $9 • (11/15/1991) • **80**
Côtes du Rhône Grand Réserve 1989 • $12 • (11/15/1991) • **83**
Côtes du Rhône White 1998: Nice and smooth, a well-made, civilized white. Ripe and round, showing fresh acidity, with green apple, honey and roasted nuts. Impressive for this appellation. Drink now through 2002.–P.M. • $13 • (12/15/1999) • **87**
Côtes du Rhône-Villages 1997: A dilute, simple, light-bodied red, with a green finish.–P.M. • $13 • (11/15/1999) • **73**
Côtes du Rhône-Villages 1989 • $10 • (11/15/1991) • **84**
Viognier Côtes du Rhône Jeunes Vignes 1998: Fabulous and surprisingly unctuous for "young vines." Pure, clean and ripe, like a New Zealand Sauvignon Blanc, with gooseberry, freshly cut grass and sweet green pea flavors. Add the fatness on the palate and you have a white that's enchanting, at least for fanatics of this sort of wine. Buy by the case! Drink now through 2002.–P.M. • $15 • (12/15/1999) • **90**

ST.-ETIENNE, DOMAINE

Côtes du Rhône Les Albizzias 1997: Supple, ripe and easy to like, with a roasted game, cherry, mocha and spice character, this is pretty yummy. Drink now.–P.M. • $9 • (11/15/1999) • **83**
Côtes du Rhône-Villages Les Galets 1997: Shows personality and a rustic sort of concentration. Has "traditional Rhône" written all over it, with herb, green olive, smoke, game and pepper. A bit herbal on the fruity but chewy finish. Drink now through 2002.–P.M. • $11 • (11/15/1999) • **85**

STE.-EULALIE, CHATEAU

Minervois 1994 • $8 • (5/31/1998) • **77**
Minervois 1992 • $8 • (6/30/1994) • **78**
Minervois 1991 • $NA • (3/15/1994) • **85**
Minervois Cuvée Tradition 1996: Robust and focused, with appealing red plum and ripe cherry flavors and a nice bricklike note. Good concentration and firm acidity give this red plenty of backbone. Tobacco and currant flavors linger on the finish. Drink now through 2002.–K.M. • $10 • (11/30/1998) • **84**
Minervois Cuvée Tradition 1995 • $9 • (5/31/1998) • **85**
Minervois Elevé en Futs de Chêne 1996: Firm and intense, with concentrated flavors of red plum, cherry and currant and intriguing tobacco and wild game notes. Finishes long, with spice and leather flavors and a touch of maturity despite its youth. A tightly wound red that should blossom in the cellar. Drink through 2003–K.M. • $10 • (11/30/1998) • **87**

ST.-GALL, DE

Brut Blanc de Blancs Champagne NV: A serious style of brut that would be great at the dinner table. Distinctive aromas and flavors of grilled bread, lemon and apple have earthy accents. The texture is round and full, and the finish lingers. Drink now. • $43 • (12/15/1998) • **90**
Brut Blanc de Blancs Champagne 1990: Generous in flavor and mouthfilling in texture, this full-bodied Champagne offers bright fruit and buttery, toasty accents that kick in on the finish. Drink now through 2001. • $45 • (12/15/1998) • **91**
Brut Champagne NV • $25 • (12/31/1997) • **83**
Extra Dry Blanc de Blancs Champagne NV • $30 • (12/31/1997) • **86**

STE.-GEMME, CHATEAU DE

Haut-Médoc 1998: A bit light, but shows some good berry, tobacco character. Medium-bodied, with medium to light tannins and a short finish. Just good.–J.S. • $NA • (5/31/1999) (BT) • **80-84**
Haut-Médoc 1997: Pleasant berry, cherry and tobacco character, with a hint of herbs. Medium- to light-bodied. Light finish.–J.S. • $NA • (1/31/2000) • **79**
Haut-Médoc 1996: Diluted, with some decent plum and herb character. Light- to medium-bodied, with fine tannins and a light aftertaste.–J.S. • $NA • (2/28/1999) • **78**

ST.-GEORGES-COTE-PAVIE, CHATEAU

St.-Emilion 1982: Dark ruby color, with a brick-red hue. Ripe berry and cherry aromas, with hints of wet earth and tea. Full-bodied and very extracted, with lots of ripe fruit and intense berry, tobacco and olive flavors. (1982 Bordeaux horizontal tasting). Drink now.–J.S. • $NA • (11/30/1998) • **87**

ST.-GERMAIN, CHATEAU

Coteaux du Languedoc 1996: A thick red, with a good mix of dark plum, dried cherry, leather, spice and even mineral and anise flavors. Balanced and nicely sculpted, with bittersweet chocolate notes on the finish. Drink now.–K.M. • $11 • (2/28/1999) • **86**
Coteaux du Languedoc 1995 • $12 • (3/31/1998) • **91**

ST.-JACQUES, CHATEAU

Bordeaux Supérieur 1997: Slightly lean, but shows good tobacco and berry character. Medium-bodied, with firm tannins. Drink now.–J.S. • $NA • (1/31/2000) • **83**
Bordeaux Supérieur 1995 • $15 • (1/31/1998) • **83**
Bordeaux Supérieur 1993 • $13 • (6/30/1997) • **82**

ST.-JEAN, DOMAINE

Coteaux du Languedoc Tonneaux 1998: Rich and ripe, with loads of cassis, red plum and ripe cherry flavors and powerful smoke and mineral components. This complete package has alluring cardamom and chocolate elements and a good backbone of acidity. Impressive. Tempting now. Best from 2001 through 2005.–K.M. • $11 • (6/15/2000) • **91**

ST.-JEAN DE LA GINESTRE, DOMAINE

Corbières 1997: Muddled and pruny-tasting, with plum and red berry flavors. Tastes slightly green on the finish.–K.M. • $10 • (11/15/1999) • **79**
Corbières Élevé en fûts de chêne 1997: A solid red, with nice plum and berry flavors and tobacco and leather notes. Bittersweet chocolate chimes in on the finish. Drink now.–K.M. • $12 • (11/15/1999) • **84**

ST.-LAURENT, CHATEAU

Corbières Réserve Privée 1994 • $7 • (12/15/1997) • **84**
Corbiéres Réserve Privée 1991 • $7 • (6/15/1993) • **78**

ST.-LOUIS, DOMAINE DE

Cabernet Sauvignon Vin de Pays d'Oc 1998: A straightforward red, with plum, spice and currant flavors. Comes on nicely with tobacco and pepper notes on the finish. Drink now.–K.M. • $11 • (12/31/1999) • **83**
Chardonnay Vin de Pays d'Oc 1998: Canned fruit flavors and a cloying, slightly bitter finish don't add up to much fun.–K.M. • $11 • (12/31/1999) • **73**

ST.-LOUIS LA PERDRIX, CHATEAU

Costières de Nîmes 1997: Soft, with cola and tea flavors and dried berry notes on the finish. Drink now.–K.M. • $10 • (10/31/1998) • **80**
Costières de Nimes 1990 • $8 • (4/15/1993) • **83**
Costières de Nimes Cuvée Marianne 1989 • $11 • (2/28/1993) • **75**

ST.-LUC, DOMAINE

Coteaux du Tricastin 1996: Crisp and ungenerous, with modest berry character and some astringent tannins on the slightly herbal finish.–P.M. • $13 • (11/15/1999) • **74**
Côteaux du Tricastin 1993 • $8 • (12/31/1995) • **84**
Coteaux du Tricastin 1989 • $7 • (12/31/1991) • **83**
Coteaux du Tricastin 1988 • $11 • (8/31/1991) • **77**
Coteaux du Tricastin LC 1996: Flavorful but not very ripe, with violet, blackberry, toasted notes; a fruity-style Rhône with a succulent, mouthpuckering finish. Drink now through 2001.–P.M. • $18 • (11/15/1999) • **83**
Côtes du Rhône-Villages 1998: Sensual in its soft, silky texture, an elegant, clean and pure red. Medium-bodied and very focused on red and black fruit, delivering much pleasure and fabulous balance for this appellation. Buy by the case! Drink now through 2002.–P.M. • $15 • (12/15/1999) • **90**
Syrah Coteaux du Tricastin Elevé en Fût de Chêne 1993 • $14 • (12/31/1995) • **85**

STE.-MARIE, CHATEAU

Bordeaux Supérieur 1996: Aromas of ripe fruit, chocolate and tobacco follow through to a medium-bodied palate with velvety tannins in this gentle and delicous red that's fresh and delicate on the finish. Don't hesitate at this price. Drink now.–J.S. • $10 • (7/31/1999) • **85**

Entre-Deux-Mers 1998: Clean, fresh and simple. Medium-bodied, with a lemony, waxy character. Drink now.–J.S. • $10 • (7/31/1999) • **80**

ST.-MARTIN, DOMAINE

Bonnes Mares 1997: Dark in color and vibrant in character, it tastes mouthpuckeringly lemonlike, with a tart and drying finish.–P.M. • $76 • (9/30/1999) • **73**

Fixin Hervelets 1997: Ripe and flavorful, showing black fruit character in a full-bodied package that delivers decent intensity on the finish.–P.M. • $29 • (9/30/1999) • **86**

Marsannay Les Finottes 1997: Herbal and lean, tasting tart in a mouthpuckeringly limelike way on the short finish.–P.M. • $15 • (9/30/1999) • **71**

ST.-MARTIN DE LA GARRIGUE, CHATEAU

Coteaux du Languedoc Bronzinelle 1998: An impressive red from the south of France. Quite concentrated, with pure and intense flavors of cassis, raspberry, spice and dark chocolate. Has a nicely perfumed aroma and a distinctive delicacy and elegance. Fine tannins, with juniper and sagelike notes on the finish. Full-bodied and well balanced. Best from 2001 through 2004.–K.M. • $12 • (6/15/2000) • **92**

Coteaux du Languedoc Bronzinelle 1997: Plenty of mineral, iron and dried red fruit flavors in this red from the south of France. It's well focused and balanced, with a leathery aroma, some red brick notes on the finish. Drink now through 2002.–K.M. • $11 • (9/30/1999) • **85**

Coteaux du Languedoc Cuvée Tradition 1998: An intense and vibrant red, with loads of pretty red plum, cassis, red cherry and roasted flavors and plenty of appealing game and leather notes as well. Mocha flavors linger on the finish. Drink now through 2003.–K.M. • $9 • (2/29/2000) • **88**

Coteaux du Languedoc Cuvée Tradition 1997: Muscular and taut, with some serious leather aromas and flavors as well as dried cherry, pepper and mineral notes. Coffee and spice chime in on the long finish. Drink now through 2002.–K.M. • $9 • (9/30/1999) • **87**

Coteaux du Languedoc White 1998: Medium-bodied, with a nice subtle spiciness and good flavors of peach and apple. Finishes with a note of richness. Drink now.–K.M. • $13 • (12/31/1999) • **84**

ST.-MARTIN DE LA GARRIGUE, DOMAINE

Chardonnay Vin de Pays d'Oc 1997: Quite green and woody, with no discernible fruit flavors.–K.M. • $16 • (10/15/1999) • **75**

Coteaux du Languedoc White 1997: Well-rounded, with pretty peach and apricot flavors and appealing herbal notes on the finish. Concentrated and rich, with a nice honeyed quality. Drink now.–K.M. • $11 • (11/15/1998) • **84**

Vin de Pays d'Oc 1996: Fairly rich and concentrated, with inviting aromas of leather, plum and olive. The meaty flavors are backed up by dark plum and cherry notes. A touch balsamic and a bit tight, it should smooth out with time. Drink through 2005–K.M. • $16 • (11/30/1998) • **86**

Vin de Pays des Coteaux de Bessilles Bronzinelle 1995: Ripe, rich and round, with dark plum, leather and black cherry flavors. Finishes on notes of currant and spice. Has a rustic edge, but still quite smooth and enjoyable. Drink through 2002–K.M. • $11 • (11/30/1998) • **85**

Vin de Pays des Coteaux de Bessilles Cuvée Réservée 1997: Somewhat murky, with minerally and stewy flavors and a sharp finish.–K.M. • $10 • (11/15/1999) • **78**

Vin de Pays des Coteaux de Bessilles Cuvée Tradition 1996: A medium-bodied red, with exotic aromas and flavors of spice and leather and slightly stewing notes. Balanced and ready. Drink now.–K.M. • $8 • (11/30/1998) • **83**

ST.-MAURICE, CHATEAU

Côtes du Rhône 1995 • $8 • (10/15/1997) • **70**

Côtes du Rhône-Villages Laudun Cuvée Vicomte Guillaue de Joyeuse 1995 • $9 • (10/15/1997) • **81**

Key: SS—Spectator Selection. CS—Cellar Selection. HR—Highly Recommended. $NA—Price not available. (BT)—Barrel tasting. Ⓐ—Auction Price.
For a key to the tasters' initials, see "How to Use These Listings."
Dates in parentheses represent the issues in which the ratings were published.

ST.-MICHEL, CHATEAU

Lussac-St.-Emilion 1995 • $10 • (1/31/1998) • **79**

ST.-PIERRE, CHATEAU

St.-Julien 1999: Interesting aromas of ripe plums and spices. Medium-bodied, with some fine tannins. Good subtle finish.–J.S. • $NA • (1/01/2000) (BT) • **85-89**

St.-Julien 1998: Plenty of currant and mint character. Medium- to full-bodied, with very well-integrated tannins and a medium finish. Well crafted. Almost outstanding.–J.S. • $NA • (5/31/1999) (BT) • **85-89**

St.-Julien 1997: Aromatic, with currant, smoky wood and a plummy undertone. Medium-bodied, with a good core of fruit and a silky-textured finish. Drink now through 2005.–J.S. • $35 • (1/31/2000) • **87**

St.-Julien 1996: Burly, traditional claret. Great dark color and intense aromas of black cherry and berry with hints of mineral and spice. Full-bodied, with full tannins and a sweet berry aftertaste. Very chewy. Best after 2002.–J.S. • $35 • (1/31/1999) • **90**

St.-Julien 1995 • $25 • (1/31/1998) • **90**

St.-Julien 1994 • $19 Ⓐ • (1/31/1997) • **86**

St.-Julien 1993 • $22 • (1/31/1996) • **85**

St.-Julien 1992 • $18 • (4/15/1995) • **87**

St.-Julien 1991 • $17 • (3/31/1994) • **84**

St.-Julien 1990 • $26 • (3/31/1993) • **92**

St.-Julien 1989: Seductive and exciting. Good, dark-ruby color, with lovely ripe aromas of raspberries and mint. Full-bodied and very silky on the palate. Long aftertaste of dark chocolate and berries and a hint of mint. Beautiful now, but will continue to improve. (1989 Bordeaux horizontal tasting). Drink through 2008–J.S. • $35 Ⓐ • (5/31/1999) • **91**

St.-Julien 1988 • $37 Ⓐ • (10/15/1992) • **88**

St.-Julien 1987 • $17 • (10/15/1992) • **80**

St.-Julien 1986 • $30 Ⓐ • (10/15/1992) • **90**

St.-Julien 1985 • $39 Ⓐ • (10/15/1992) • **84**

St.-Julien 1984 • $12 • (10/15/1992) • **79**

St.-Julien 1983 • $NA • (10/15/1992) • **86**

St.-Julien 1982: A very ripe wine. Dark ruby-garnet color, with an inky center. Floral and berry character and a long, slightly raisiny finish. Drink now or hold. (1982 Bordeaux horizontal tasting).–J.S. • $43 Ⓐ • (11/30/1998) • **88**

St.-Julien 1981 • $NA • (10/15/1992) • **82**

St.-Julien 1979 • $24 • (10/15/1992) • **77**

St.-Julien 1978 • $28 • (10/15/1992) • **83**

St.-Julien 1975 • $20 • (10/15/1992) • **72**

St.-Julien 1970 • $45 • (10/15/1992) • **84**

St.-Julien 1969 • $15 • (10/15/1992) • **70**

St.-Julien 1962 • $55 • (10/15/1992) • **72**

St.-Julien 1961 • $95 • (10/15/1992) • **74**

St.-Julien 1959 • $90 • (10/15/1992) • **75**

ST.-ROBERT, CHATEAU

Graves 1996: A diluted and weedy '96, with light body, light tannins and a watery finish. Tough to like.–J.S. • $20 • (1/31/1999) • **74**

Graves Cuvée Poncet-Deville 1996: A wine with a diluted palate but some decent berry and tobacco character. Medium-bodied, with light, velvety tannins and a short finish.–J.S. • $30 • (1/31/1999) • **79**

Graves Cuvée Poncet-Deville 1995 • $25 • (1/31/1998) • **89**

STE.-ROSELINE, CHATEAU

Côtes de Provence 1995: A middle-of-the-road red, with dried cherry, cola and herb flavors that turn a tad astringent on the finish.–K.M. • $25 • (12/31/1998) • **78**

Côtes de Provence Blush 1997: This rosé has good berry and dried cherry flavors, with a touch of richness. Serve well-chilled. Drink now.–K.M. • $25 • (10/31/1998) • **84**

ST.-SULPICE, CHATEAU

Bordeaux 1994 • $9 • (10/15/1997) • **78**

Bordeaux 1988 • $8 • (8/31/1991) • **81**

ST.-YZANS, CHATEAU

Médoc 1995 • $NA • (1/01/1997) • **85**

SALES, CHATEAU DE

Pomerol 1997: Light and watery, with some tobacco, berry character.–J.S. • $20 • (1/31/2000) • **74**

Pomerol 1996: Berry aromas with a hint of herb follow through to a light- to medium-bodied palate, with firm tannins and a short finish. Needs more fruit. Drink now.–J.S. • $26 • (1/31/1999) • **82**

Pomerol 1995: Good blackberry and milk chocolate aromas and flavors, but lacks the structure of a top '95. Medium-bodied, with medium tannins, a light finish. Drink through 2003.–J.S. • $34 Ⓐ • (9/15/1998) • **87**

Pomerol 1986 • $25 Ⓐ • (6/30/1989) • **86**

Pomerol 1985 • $22 • (6/30/1988) • **87**

Pomerol 1982: Drying out. Ruby-colored, with an intense garnet edge. Some good chocolate and berry flavors, but it's firm and slightly dry in the mouth. (1982 Bordeaux horizontal tasting). Drink now.–J.S. • $38 Ⓐ • (11/30/1998) • **83**

SALIEGE, DOMAINE

Coteaux du Languedoc St.-Christol Cuvée Vieilles Vignes 1998: A strong herbal aroma announces this distinctive medium-bodied red that is dominated by currant, olive and hot stone flavors.–K.M. • $8 • (6/15/2000) • **79**

SALLE, DOMAINE DE LA

Beaune Champimonts 1995 • $NA • (11/15/1997) • **74**

SALVARD, DOMAINE DU

Cheverny 1998: This light, crisp white is a bit tart to enjoy by itself, but its keen citrus and herb flavors make it a refreshing accompaniment to light shellfish dishes. Drink now.–T.M. • $11 • (2/29/2000) • **84**

SALVAT, DOMAINE

Muscat de Rivesaltes 1995 • $17 • (5/31/1997) • **89**

Vin de Pays des Coteaux des Fenouillèdes Fenouill 1996: Peppery and quite grapey-tasting, this red from the south of France turns a bit thin on the finish.–K.M. • $10 • (4/30/1999) • **79**

Vin de Pays des Coteaux des Fenouillèdes Fenouill 1995 • $8 • (6/30/1997) • **81**

SAMBARDIER, JEAN-NOEL

Beaujolais-Villages Domaine Manoir du Carra 1997: An appealing red, ripe, redolent of sweet cherries, with a smooth texture and some richness. The finish is firm and mouthwatering. Drink now.–B.S. • $10 • (10/15/1999) • **84**

SAN CELIES, DOMAINE

Corbières 1996: Lively and full of character, from the meaty aromas to the ripe and pure currant, berry and cherry flavors. Finishes on notes of coffee and cassis, with an appealing gamy edge as well. Drink through 2003–K.M. • $8 • (10/31/1998) • **87**

SANCERRE, CHATEAU DE

Sancerre 1996: This crisp white shows typical Sancerre character, with flavors of apples, herbs and minerals, and vibrant citrusy acidity. Balanced and clean. Drink now.–T.M. • $15 • (9/15/1998) • **86**

SANCERRE, LA CAVE DE

Sancerre Séduction Vieilles Vignes 1997: Lemon and green apple acidity overwhelm the fruit in this rich yet very tart white. But it has the trademark grassiness, and it's crisp and clean. May soften with food. Drink now.–T.M. • $16 • (9/15/1998) • **84**

SANG DES CAILLOUX, DOMAINE LE

Vacqueyras 1997: Very plummy in character, with blackberry, toast and floral complexity. Medium-bodied, it's rather seductive and flavorful. Drink now.–P.M. • $15 • (10/31/1999) • **85**

Vacqueyras 1996: Fresh and clean, with good acidity, this shows lovely red and blackberry character plus some crisp texture that makes it lively. A medium-bodied, food-friendly wine. Drink now through 2001.–P.M. • $14 • (11/15/1998) • **85**

Vacqueyras 1993 • $13 • (9/30/1995) • **86**

Vacqueyras 1990 • $12 • (4/15/1993) • **83**

SANTA DUC, DOMAINE

Côtes du Rhône 1996: Beautiful, rich and ripe, full-bodied, packed with cassis, toasted bread, plum, clove, cinnamon and raisin, this is complex and satisfying, an opulent wine that stays balanced to the end. Drink now through 2005.–P.M. • $13 • (11/15/1998) • **88**

Côtes du Rhône 1990 • $11 • (4/15/1993) • **78**

Gigondas 1997: A straightforward red, with game, smoke and red fruit. Medium-bodied, with wet earth and a tight, chewy finish. Drink now.–P.M. • $22 • (10/31/1999) • **82**

Gigondas 1996: Silky and seductive, with game, leather, plum and saffron character, this full-bodied, smooth-textured red displays good ripeness to balance the tannic structure. Excellent quality for a '96. Best from 2000.–P.M. • $22 • (11/15/1998) • **88**

Gigondas 1990 • $21 • (4/15/1993) • **80**

Gigondas Prestige des Hautes Garrigues 1996: Distinctive mocha, vanilla, plum, and toast aromas and flavors. A rustic, medium-bodied red, with grip and a chewy finish. Drink now through 2002.–P.M. • $42 • (10/31/1999) • **82**

Gigondas Prestige des Hautes Garrigues 1995: Supple and balanced, showing finesse and elegance, with silky tannins coating the palate, and earth, toasted oak, roasted walnut, mineral, leather, fig and blackberry flavors unfolding to a gentle, nicely balanced finish. Drink now through 2005.–P.M. • $36 • (11/15/1998) • **89**

SANTE, BERNARD

Chénas 1994 • $15 • (6/30/1997) • **79**

Moulin-à-Vent 1994 • $18 • (4/30/1997) • **86**

SARGET DE GRUAUD-LAROSE

St.-Julien 1996: Pretty plum and spice character, with medium body, fine tannins and a fresh aftertaste. Slightly lean structure, but fresh and clean. Second label of Château Gruaud-Larose. Best after 2001.–J.S. • $25 • (1/31/1999) • **86**

St.-Julien 1995 • $24 • (1/31/1998) • **85**

SARRAU, ROBERT

Beaujolais-Villages 1996 • $8 • (9/15/1997) • **84**

Beaujolais-Villages 1995 • $8 • (4/30/1997) • **83**

Brouilly Clos Reissier 1995 • $10 • (4/30/1997) • **85**

Fleurie Domaine du Grand Garant 1996 • $13 • (9/15/1997) • **86**

Fleurie Grand Pré 1995 • $12 • (4/30/1997) • **84**

Juliénas Château des Capitans 1996 • $11 • (9/15/1997) • **84**

Juliénas Château des Capitans 1995 • $10 • (4/30/1997) • **88**

Mâcon-Fuissé 1995 • $10 • (2/28/1997) • **76**

Mâcon-Villages 1996 • $9 • (8/31/1997) • **76**

Merlot Vin de Pays d'Oc 1995 • $7 • (12/15/1996) • **79**

Morgon Domaine des Bouviers 1996 • $11 • (9/15/1997) • **83**

Moulin-à-Vent Domaine de la Tour du Bief 1995 • $12 • (4/30/1997) • **85**

Pouilly-Fuissé 1995 • $15 • (1/31/1997) • **78**

St.-Véran 1996 • $10 • (8/31/1997) • **78**

St.-Véran 1995 • $9 • (1/31/1997) • **72**

SARRY, DOMAINE DE

Sancerre 1998: This firm white is quite full-bodied for Sancerre, with mineral, pear and melon accented by notes of herb and wet stone. Appealing flavors of ripe pear and herb linger on the finish. Can match with poultry and white meats. Drink now through 2002.–T.M. • $20 • (6/30/1999) • **88**

Sancerre 1997 • $14 • (6/15/1998) • **82**

SARTRE, CHATEAU LE

Pessac-Léognan 1998: Some good ripe fruit in this wine, with silky tannins, but a slightly hollow midpalate.–J.S. • $NA • (5/31/1999) (BT) • **85-89**
Pessac-Léognan 1997: A pleasant red, with berry, tobacco character throughout. Medium- to light-bodied, with light tannins and a fresh fruit finish. Drink now.–J.S. • $NA • (1/31/2000) • **81**
Pessac-Léognan 1996: Light aromas of berries and mushrooms. Medium- to light-bodied, with firm tannins and a short and slightly diluted finish.–J.S. • $22 • (1/31/1999) • **79**
Pessac-Léognan 1995 • $22 • (1/31/1998) • **86**
Pessac-Léognan 1994 • $NA • (1/31/1997) • **74**
Pessac-Léognan 1993 • $18 • (1/31/1996) • **84**
Pessac-Léognan 1992 • $14 • (4/15/1995) • **79**
Pessac-Léognan 1991 • $14 • (3/31/1994) • **77**
Pessac-Léognan 1990 • $19 • (3/31/1993) • **87**
Pessac-Léognan White 1998: Delicious pineapple and mango character has vanilla undertones. Medium- to full-bodied, with good acidity and a fresh finish. Drink now.–J.S. • $NA • (2/29/2000) • **86**
Pessac-Léognan White 1997: Ripe and fruity, with a good combination of wood and tropical fruit character throughout. Medium-bodied, with a round mouthfeel and a medium fruity finish. Almost outstanding. Drink now.–J.S. • $15 • (9/30/1999) • **88**

SAUGERE, LYLIANE

Côte-Rôtie La Colline d'Argent 1991 • $27 • (5/31/1994) • **86**
Hermitage 1992 • $32 • (10/15/1995) • **86**
Hermitage 1991 • $32 • (10/15/1995) • **90**
Hermitage La Côte des Seigneurs 1990 • $26 • (4/15/1994) HR • **91**

SAUMAIZE-MICHELIN

Mâcon-Villages Les Sertaux 1997: Nice little Chardonnay, showing medium ripeness, decent fruit, butter, honey and spice, plus a crisp, citrusy finish with a hint of wet hay. Drink now.–P.M. • $17 • (5/31/1999) • **81**
Mâcon-Villages Les Sertaux 1996 • $NA • (8/31/1997) • **79**
Pouilly-Fuissé Clos sur la Roche 1997: Lovely for its ripe, honeyed character, and though it's hard to dig through a cover of toasted, smoky oak, the tropical fruit saves the day. Best after 2000.–P.M. • $37 • (5/31/1999) • **87**
Pouilly-Fuissé Clos sur la Roche 1996 • $23 • (5/31/1998) • **89**
Pouilly-Fuissé Clos sur la Roche 1995 • $28 • (5/31/1997) • **86**
Pouilly-Fuissé Les Ronchevats 1997: Super Pouilly, showing both restraint and power, delivering a lovely honey-lemon-spice-butter-tropical combination, with a harmonious finish. Tempting now. Best after 2002.–P.M. • $40 • (5/31/1999) • **92**
Pouilly-Fuissé Les Ronchevats 1995 • $29 • (5/31/1997) • **87**
Pouilly-Fuissé Vigne Blanche 1997: Quite attractive, with good lemon, ripe pear and melon flavors. Medium-bodied, it's a bit burning on the finish from toasted oak. Drink now.–P.M. • $23 • (5/31/1999) • **86**
Pouilly-Fuissé Vigne Blanche 1996 • $22 • (5/31/1998) • **89**
Pouilly-Fuissé Vigne Blanche 1995 • $23 • (5/31/1997) • **83**
St.-Véran Les Crèches 1997: Fresh and clean, offering lemon, honey and pear, it's firmly structured and delivers harmony, if not much complexity, on the finish. Drink now.–P.M. • $18 • (5/31/1999) • **83**
St.-Véran Les Crèches 1996 • $15 • (5/31/1998) • **78**
St.-Véran Les Vieilles Vignes 1997: Polished, despite its showy, catwalk strut. Opulently oaked, with plenty of butter, butterscotch, toasted nut and grilled meat notes accented by honey and pear, this is a rich, ripe, yellow-colored, full-bodied St-Véran that stands out in the crowd. Worth cellaring. Best after 2000.–P.M. • $22 • (5/31/1999) • **92**
St.-Véran Poncetys 1995 • $20 • (5/31/1998) • **94**

SAUTEREAU, DOMAINE

Sancerre Côtes de Reigny 1998: A textbook Sancerre. This clean white with a cutting edge has mineral, citrus and herb flavors that are fresh, lively and well integrated. A bit tart for drinking as an aperitif, but perfect for shellfish. Try now through 2002.–T.M. • $14 • (6/30/1999) • **88**

Key: SS—Spectator Selection. CS—Cellar Selection. HR—Highly Recommended. $NA—Price not available. (BT)—Barrel tasting. Ⓐ—Auction Price.
For a key to the tasters' initials, see "How to Use These Listings."
Dates in parentheses represent the issues in which the ratings were published.

Sancerre Côtes de Reigny 1996: Ripe apple and vanilla flavors give a generous character. Round and slightly soft on the palate, but has enough acidity to match with food. Drink now.–T.M. • $12 • (9/15/1998) • **84**
Sancerre Red Côtes de Reigny 1996: The cherry flavors take on some spice and earth accents, but leave one wanting more concentration and depth of flavor. Drink now.–B.S. • $14 • (11/15/1998) • **81**
Sancerre Red Côtes de Reigny 1995 • $15 • (6/15/1997) • **83**
Sancerre Rosé Côtes de Reigny 1998: This very pale rosé is aggressively tart on the palate, with puckering citrus flavors and a very crisp finish. Perhaps best in a punch.–T.M. • $14 • (6/30/1999) • **76**
Sancerre Rosé Côtes de Reigny 1996: Pleasant strawberry and cherry flavors in this salmon-colored rosé, which has lively acidity and just a hint of earth lingering on the finish. Drink now.–B.S. • $14 • (11/15/1998) • **83**

SAUVAGEONNE, CHATEAU LA

Coteaux du Languedoc Cuvée Prestige 1995 • $18 • (2/28/1998) • **86**

SAUVANES, DOMAINE GUY

Faugères Cuvée Sarah 1996: The essence of Syrah, with flavors of red plum, roasted black pepper, game and mineral introduced by intense aromas of violets, spice and leather. Despite this concentration, it remains lively and approachable, with a good backbone, approachable tannins and bittersweet chocolate notes on the finish. Stylish and seductive. Best from 2001 through 2006.–K.M. • $11 • (12/31/1999) • **90**
Faugères Cuvée Sarah 1995 • $8 • (3/31/1998) • **87**

SAUVESTRE, VINCENT

Chablis 1998: Fruity and succulent. With pear, sweet pea and mineral, this medium-bodied Chablis has a lot going for it. Ripe and satisfying, albeit not deep or complex, it's the prototypical fresh and balanced seafood-wine. Drink now through 2003.–P.M. • $NA • (1/01/2000) • **87**
Savigny-lès-Beaune White Les Goudelettes 1998: Tastes better than it smells. Almost full in body, this has wet earth, oak and caramelized pear character. Lacks finesse, but it's a mouthful of Chardonnay. Drink now through 2001.–P.M. • $NA • (1/01/2000) • **80**

SAUVION & FILS

Anjou 1997: Soft and easy to drink, yet there's subtle structure to support and express the cassis and berry aromas and flavors. Everything's balanced and charming, with a lingering berry and tobacco finish.–B.S. • $8 • (10/31/1998) • **86**
Anjou 1996 • $9 • (6/15/1998) • **81**
Anjou 1995 • $8 • (6/15/1997) • **79**
Cheverny 1997: Shows the earth and mineral side of Sauvignon Blanc. Distinctive, with floral notes and moderate concentration, but won't appeal to everyone. Drink now.–B.S. • $11 • (11/15/1998) • **82**
Cheverny Red 1997: Gorgeous aromas of freshly crushed raspberry and black currant in this light-bodied, smooth red. Finishes on a crisp, firm, leafy note. Drink now.–B.S. • $11 • (10/31/1998) • **85**
Chinon 1996 • $9 • (6/15/1998) • **78**
Chinon Les Roches Cachées 1995 • $9 • (6/15/1997) • **87**
Crémant de Loire NV: Apple, honey and toast flavors highlight this rich sparkling white that's balanced on the soft side, finishing on a refreshing citrus note. Drink now.–B.S. • $NA • (11/15/1998) • **83**
Menetou-Salon 1997: Flavors of peach, thyme and mineral are attractive, if a bit shy in depth for this appellation. Finishes on the tart side. Drink now.–B.S. • $9 • (11/15/1998) • **82**
Muscadet de Sèvre et Maine 1997: A creamy texture and flavors of vanilla and butter set this apart from most Muscadets. Clean and fresh, it lacks the stony crispness characteristic of the region. Drink now.–T.M. • $7 • (6/30/1999) • **81**
Muscadet de Sèvre et Maine 1996 • $7 • (6/30/1998) • **79**
Muscadet de Sèvre et Maine Sur Lie Château du Cléray 1997: Lively. The apple, earth and mineral flavors have a smoothness until the acidity washes the palate clean. Finishes a bit earthy. Drink now.–B.S. • $8 • (11/15/1998) • **82**
Muscadet de Sèvre et Maine Sur Lie La Landelle 1997: Distinctive herb, mineral and citrus aromas and flavors are concentrated and intense, combining with a firm backbone and lingering finish to create a delicious overall impression. Try with shellfish.–B.S. • $10 • (11/15/1998) • **87**
Muscadet de Sèvre et Maine Sur Lie La Nobleraie 1997: Citrus aromas and flavors, with lemon and a dash of grapefruit, are married to a soft structure and modest concentration. Drink now.–B.S. • $6 • (11/15/1998) • **81**

Pouilly-Fumé 1996: Sweaty, earthy, oniony aromas and a flat, earthy palate. Tasted twice, with consistent notes.–B.S. • $13 • (10/31/1998) • **61**

Pouilly-Fumé Les Ombelles 1997: Rich and round, displaying floral and peach flavors, modest concentration and a slightly bitter finish.–B.S. • $16 • (10/31/1998) • **83**

Reuilly 1997: Good varietal character. Apple and leafy green flavors predominate, and the acidity is moderate, balancing the rich texture. Finishes a bit short. Drink now.–B.S. • $9 • (11/15/1998) • **83**

St.-Nicolas-de-Bourgueil 1997: Rich cassis flavors border on plum in this fleshy, attractive Loire red. It's concentrated and expressive, with a spry yet firm structure and good length. Drink now.–B.S. • $9 • (11/15/1998) • **86**

Sancerre 1997: Earthy and vegetal notes are rustic and dull in this white. Tastes old before its time.–T.M. • $13 • (6/30/1999) • **75**

Sancerre 1996 • $13 • (6/15/1998) • **77**

Sancerre Les Fondettes 1997: Full-bodied, rich and concentrated. Ripe yet balanced, with melon, fig and lanolin flavors, but also has the herbal and mineral notes characteristic of Sancerre. Drink now through 2002.–T.M. • $16 • (9/15/1998) • **88**

Saumur-Champigny 1996 • $9 • (6/15/1998) • **85**

Saumur-Champigny Les Gravières du Roy 1997: There's a mineral element in addition to the mint and black currant aromas and flavors that are displayed on a soft structure for early consumption. Drink now.–B.S. • $10 • (10/31/1998) • **83**

Saumur-Champigny Les Gravières du Roy 1995 • $10 • (6/15/1997) • **88**

Vouvray 1997: Ripe and fruity, this off-dry Vouvray exhibits apple, honey and floral flavors, a rich texture and balancing acidity. Straightforward and pleasant. Drink now.–B.S. • $7 • (11/15/1998) • **84**

Vouvray 1996: Complex and firm, this vibrant white displays floral, honey and herb aromas and flavors, a smooth texture and a chalky, minerally finish that lingers. Drink through 2000.–B.S. • $8 • (11/15/1998) • **87**

SAUZET, ETIENNE

Bâtard-Montrachet 1997: Very ripe and almost late harvest in its aromatic profile, showing dried raisin, cooked fruit, violet and wood character. Full-bodied and a bit heavyhanded, lacking elegance. Best from 2001 through 2005.–P.M. • $109 Ⓐ • (9/30/1999) • **80**

Bâtard-Montrachet 1996: Ripe but also showing inelegant cooked fruit and paint varnish notes. Quite buttery, spicy and oaky, with a burning, astringent finish from the overwhelming toasted wood.–P.M. • $162 Ⓐ • (5/31/1999) • **79**

Bâtard-Montrachet 1995 • $266 Ⓐ • (8/31/1997) • **95**

Bienvenues-Bâtard-Montrachet 1997: Good intensity, with dried herb, spice, floral and new oakish aromas and flavors. Lacks a bit of integrated harmony but provides a full-throttle, full-bodied white Burgundy experience. Crisp finish. Best from 2002 through 2010.–P.M. • $225 • (9/30/1999) • **89**

Bienvenues-Bâtard-Montrachet 1995 • $185 • (8/31/1997) • **96**

Bourgogne White 1997: This medium-bodied Bourgogne Blanc has green apple, grilled pineapple and nut flavors. Toasty, crisp finish. Drink now.–P.M. • $34 • (9/30/1999) • **82**

Bourgogne White 1995 • $28 • (8/31/1997) • **88**

Chassagne-Montrachet 1997: Silky-smooth, this full-bodied white Burgundy displays a canvas of vanilla bean, cream, pear and burnt toast character. Chewy, smoky aftertaste. For amateurs of charred barrels. Drink now through 2005.–P.M. • $59 • (9/30/1999) • **85**

Chassagne-Montrachet 1995 • $53 • (8/31/1997) • **92**

Chevalier-Montrachet 1997: Ripe and oaky, showing marzipan, honey, toasted oak and pear tart character. Medium-bodied, with good intensity. Drink now through 2005.–P.M. • $272 • (9/30/1999) • **89**

Chevalier-Montrachet 1995 • $267 Ⓐ • (8/31/1997) • **98**

Montrachet 1996: Marvelously opulent in a refined style. Bursts with toasted oak, seems overdone and overly perfumed (rose petal, violet, sweetish notes), but this full-bodied white turns smooth and complex in contact with air, a good sign for its cellar-worthiness. Shows butter, butterscotch, pineapple, pear and lime. Don't touch for a long time. Best after 2010.–P.M. • $440 • (8/31/1998) • **94**

Montrachet 1995: A firm, tough and firmly textured '95 Montrachet. While steely, it's full-bodied and has plenty of fruit, even hints at a silky texture that should expand with age. Complex and layered, the wood seems more subtle in this bottle than in two bottles tasted last year. Kicks off like a rocket on the finish. Deeply satisfying, and you can taste the soil. Best after 2010.–P.M. • $440 • (8/31/1998) • **97**

Puligny-Montrachet 1997: A bit dull on the nose and acidic, it's tart on the palate, leaving you citrus-saturated.–P.M. • $62 • (9/30/1999) • **79**

Puligny-Montrachet 1996: Lovely and balanced, with good mineral, pear, apple and spice character. Of medium body, it shows some sweet, ripe fruit and good length. Best after 2005.–P.M. • $62 • (8/31/1998) • **87**

Puligny-Montrachet 1995 • $55 • (8/31/1997) • **92**

Puligny-Montrachet Champ Canet 1997: With more wood than ripe fruit, this is a tough customer. Tastes of new oak, with wood tannins galore, lemon and green apple and little velvety fatness to recommend it. Might improve with time. Best after 2002.–P.M. • $120 Ⓐ • (9/30/1999) • **82**

Puligny-Montrachet Champ Canet 1995 • $147 Ⓐ • (8/31/1997) • **93**

Puligny-Montrachet La Garenne 1997: Medium-bodied, showing honey and lemon. The mouthfeel is round but the finish turns crisp. Cellar short-term. Drink through 2003–P.M. • $38 Ⓐ • (9/30/1999) • **86**

Puligny-Montrachet La Garenne 1995 • $87 • (8/31/1997) • **93**

Puligny-Montrachet Les Combettes 1997: Broad on the palate but not deep. Flat and dull, offering a crisp citrusy character that leaves a drying impression on the finish. What happened?–P.M. • $54 Ⓐ • (9/30/1999) • **78**

Puligny-Montrachet Les Combettes 1996: Prototypical '96 with good mineral notes, lush texture and lots of acidity for a vibrant finish. Impressive concentration and thick midpalate bring out a velvety smoothness. The oak is overdone and strangely perfumey, giving an odd floral character that disappeared somewhat after the wine was aired for 12 hours. Don't touch for a long time. Best after 2007.–P.M. • $105 Ⓐ • (8/31/1998) • **90**

Puligny-Montrachet Les Combettes 1995 • $112 • (8/31/1997) • **94**

Puligny-Montrachet Les Folatières 1997: This crisp, medium-bodied wine shows finesse, with lemon, green apple tartness and medium toastiness. Drink through 2003.–P.M. • $41 Ⓐ • (9/30/1999) • **81**

Puligny-Montrachet Les Folatières 1996: What a pure, clean and fruity wine. Packed with flavor, this medium-bodied, minerally '96 offers plenty of character. Juicy and mouthpuckering now, it has the stuffing to age. Best after 2003.–P.M. • $45 Ⓐ • (8/31/1998) • **88**

Puligny-Montrachet Les Perrières 1997: This attractive, medium-bodied white Burgundy displays toast, passion fruit, earth and green apple quality. Nice ripeness and a succulent, crisp finish. Best from 2001 through 2005.–P.M. • $43 Ⓐ • (9/30/1999) • **88**

Puligny-Montrachet Les Perrières 1995 • $54 • (8/31/1997) • **94**

Puligny-Montrachet Les Referts 1997: Has a tightly wound midpalate, where mineral and a zoo of fruit flavors run wild, but it settles down to perform a good act on the crisp finish. Best from 2001 through 2007.–P.M. • $30 Ⓐ • (9/30/1999) • **89**

Puligny-Montrachet Les Referts 1995 • $67 Ⓐ • (8/31/1997) • **93**

SAVARY, FRANCINE & OLIVIER

Chablis 1998: Delicate and fruity, with banana, melon, pear and lime. Kicks in with an amazing citrusy feel on the finish, but balanced thanks to the ripe fruit. Drink now through 2002.–P.M. • $18 • (5/15/2000) • **84**

Chablis 1997: Very vibrant, lemony, and hinting at a tropical character, this is fairly complex but turns a bit dry on the finish. Drink now.–P.M. • $18 • (5/31/1999) • **83**

Chablis 1996 • $22 • (8/31/1997) • **90**

Chablis Fourchaume 1998: This '98 has nice, ripe, sweet-tasting flavors, with grass, honey, pie tart and chocolate character. Medium-bodied and balanced, with a chewy mineralness on the lingering finish. Drink now through 2003.–P.M. • $25 • (5/15/2000) • **84**

Chablis Sélection Vieilles Vignes 1998: Stands out with its oak treatment. Toast, vanilla and spice flavors play with pear, melon and apple. Light- to medium-bodied, with astringent wood tannins on the finish.–P.M. • $23 • (5/15/2000) • **79**

Chablis Sélection Vieilles Vignes 1996: Firm and well structured, but showing lovely silky texture once it opens up, this full-bodied Chablis starts out intensely citrusy but turns smoother in contact with air. Still, the finish is pretty zesty. Drink now through 2005.–P.M. • $25 • (8/31/1998) • **88**

SCARAMOUCHE

Cabernet Sauvignon Vin de Pays d'Oc 1997: Decent cherry and berry flavors, with herbal notes on the finish. Drink now.–K.M. • $9 • (11/15/1998) • **80**

Chardonnay Vin de Pays d'Oc 1997: Quite oaky-tasting, with a floral, minty aroma and good apple and fig flavors. There's also a nice mineral note, with a touch of richness on the finish. Drink now.–K.M. • $9 • (11/15/1998) • **84**

Chardonnay Vin de Pays d'Oc 1996 • $9 • (5/31/1998) • **79**

Merlot Vin de Pays d'Oc 1997: Medium-bodied, with modest dried cherry and tobacco-box aromas and flavors. Soft on the finish. Drink now.–K.M. • $9 • (12/15/1998) • **81**

Syrah Vin de Pays d'Oc 1997: A delicious, medium-bodied red, smooth and beguiling. Good Syrah flavors of cherry, meat and spice combine with a touch of elegance, linger on the finish. Drink now through 2001.–K.M. • $9 • (11/15/1998) • **85**

Syrah Vin de Pays d'Oc 1996 • $9 • (1/01/1998) • **82**

SCHAETZEL, MARTIN

Alsace Edelzwicker 1998: Simple and vinous, showing nutty, appley notes and a rich texture, but not much length.–B.S. • $10/1 liter • (10/15/1999) • **77**

Gewürztraminer Alsace Cuvée Réserve 1998: Pretty, understated and silken-textured, with pure flavors of roses, orange peel and passion fruit, elegantly wrought and buoyed by a juicy acidity. Just a tad coarse on the finish. Drink now.–B.S. • $15 • (9/30/1999) • **87**

Gewürztraminer Alsace Cuvée Réserve 1996: Gorgeous Gewürz. Varietal aromas of roses, litchi and grapefruit are augmented by a mineral note and power that can only be derived from site. Fine intensity and definition that need time to integrate. Drink through 2002–B.S. • $15 • (9/15/1998) • **88**

Muscat Alsace Cuvée Réserve 1998: Complex and dry, with lively flavors of flowers, spices and grapefruit displayed on a firm, balanced structure. Drink now through 2001.–B.S. • $14 • (10/15/1999) • **87**

Pinot Blanc Alsace Cuvée Réserve 1998: Lush, clean and uncomplicated, this is full of juicy apple, lemon and earth aromas and flavors. Balanced on the soft side, it's better as an aperitif. Drink now.–B.S. • $11 • (9/30/1999) • **85**

Pinot Blanc Alsace Cuvée Réserve 1996: Lovely ripeness, depth and concentration. The mouthwatering acidity keeps the peach and quince flavors pumping through this dry, richly layered Pinot Blanc. Finishes with mineral and smoke notes.–B.S. • $11 • (9/15/1998) • **88**

Riesling Alsace Cuvée Réserve 1998: Aromatic, featuring flowers, citrus and stone fruits supported by firm acidity, it has moderate intensity, ending on a tart earthy note. Tasted twice, with consistent notes. Drink through 2003–B.S. • $14 • (10/15/1999) • **84**

Riesling Alsace Cuvée Réserve 1996: Fans of fruit beware. This racy white reeks of flint and wet stone, and there's not an ounce of fat on this frame. The apple, citrus, almond and mineral flavors are all locked up, yet there's great density and extract and a long finish. Drink through 2007–B.S. • $13 • (9/15/1998) • **91**

Riesling Alsace Kaefferkopf Ammerschwihr 1998: Very ripe, almost tropical in character, with smoke, quince, pear and citrus notes that hang together beautifully thanks to the bright acidity and smooth texture. A mineral element lingers on the finish. Drink now through 2005.–B.S. • $18 • (9/15/1999) • **89**

Tokay Pinot Gris Alsace Cuvée Réserve 1998: There are citrus tones, along with noticeable residual sugar, yet the nut and grapefruit flavors remain focused, even lean on the finish. Could use a bit more concentration. Drink now through 2001.–B.S. • $15 • (10/31/1999) • **85**

Tokay Pinot Gris Alsace Cuvée Réserve 1996: Beautiful Pinot Gris. This has the focus and clarity of the '96 vintage, combining ripe, smoky quince and mineral character with juicy acidity and density. Lovely interplay on the palate, with a bright finish. Drink now.–B.S. • $15 • (9/15/1998) • **89**

Tokay Pinot Gris Alsace Sélection de Grains Nobles 1995: This SGN coats the palate with sweet, unctuous honey and crème brûlée flavors, remaining a bit chunky and one-dimensional in the end, with a slightly coarse finish. Drink now through 2002.–B.S. • $40/500 ml. • (9/15/1998) • **89**

SCHLERET, CHARLES

Gewürztraminer Alsace Herrenweg 1998: A thickly textured white whose aromas are shy, but the rose, litchi and grapefruit notes emerge on the palate. Moderate concentration and finish. Drink now.–B.S. • $19 • (6/15/2000) • **83**

Gewürztraminer Alsace Herrenweg Cuvée Réserve 1998: A textbook Gewürztraminer. Very aromatic, offering white pepper, rose and litchi married to a rich texture, with a vibrant structure that keeps it all focused. Long finish of anise and tobacco. Drink now.–B.S. • $24 • (6/15/2000) • **89**

Pinot Blanc Alsace Herrenweg 1998: Ripe, round and sweet, this lacks vibrancy and structure. The finish falls flat.–B.S. • $15 • (6/15/2000) • **78**

Sylvaner Alsace 1998: Tasty, with good balancing acidity that carries the floral and candied peach or pear flavors. Light and refreshing. Drink now.–B.S. • $12 • (6/15/2000) • **82**

Tokay Pinot Gris Alsace Herrenweg 1998: Effusive floral and tropical fruit aromas turn more conservative on the palate in this bright, juicy white. Moderate depth and finish. Drink now.–B.S. • $24 • (6/15/2000) • **84**

Key: SS—Spectator Selection. CS—Cellar Selection. HR—Highly Recommended. $NA—Price not available. (BT)—Barrel tasting. (A)—Auction Price.
For a key to the tasters' initials, see "How to Use These Listings."
Dates in parentheses represent the issues in which the ratings were published.

SCHLUMBERGER, DOMAINES

Alsace Schlumberger Réserve 1997: A light-bodied, floral- and spice-flavored white, fresh, round and easygoing. A blend of Pinot Blanc, Riesling and Gewürztraminer. Drink now.–B.S. • $15 • (10/31/1999) • **80**

Gewürztraminer Alsace Fleur 1997: Smells and tastes like there's botrytis and starts off like gangbusters, showing tropical fruit, spice and citrus, but it turns weak, with a disappointing finish. Drink now.–B.S. • $20 • (10/31/1999) • **83**

Gewürztraminer Alsace Grand Cru Kessler 1997: Rich and sweet, showing honey and crème brûlée notes along with tropical fruit on a lush frame. Modest concentration and a lingering finish. Drink now.–B.S. • $30 • (6/15/2000) • **85**

Gewürztraminer Alsace Sélection de Grains Nobles 1989 • $NA • (11/15/1990) • **79**

Pinot Blanc Alsace 1998: This grows on you. Not particularly expressive, yet delivers richness and an intriguing almond, apple and mineral combination that lingers on the finish. Drink now.–B.S. • $13 • (6/15/2000) • **85**

Pinot Blanc Alsace 1997: Apricot and nectarine flavors show the ripeness, and there's good acidity to match, but also some sweetness that carries through to the finish and leaves a slight heaviness. Drink now.–B.S. • $13 • (10/31/1999) • **83**

Pinot Blanc Alsace 1996: Smelling and tasting like a fruit punch, with tropical nuances, this Pinot Blanc is easygoing but lacks some acidity for structure. Drink now.–B.S. • $13 • (8/31/1998) • **83**

Pinot Gris Alsace Grand Cru Kitterlé 1997: Beautiful definition and harmony. Ripe, smooth and characteristically smoky, with apricot and mineral nuances and a bright structure that keeps it all focused. Good lingering finish. Drink now through 2003.–B.S. • $37 • (6/15/2000) • **89**

Pinot Gris Alsace Grand Cru Kitterlé 1996: A forward, rich-tasting white, offering apricot, mineral and tea aromas and flavors, an elegant profile and a lingering finish. Drink now through 2002.–B.S. • $37 • (10/31/1999) • **87**

Pinot Gris Alsace Les Princes Abbés 1997: Ample in weight and flavor, showing the ripeness of '97. Peach, smoke and herbal notes are highlighted on a firm, big-boned structure. Long smoky aftertaste. Drink now through 2001.–B.S. • $16 • (6/15/2000) • **86**

Pinot Gris Alsace Les Princes Abbés 1996: Nectarine and mandarin orange render this exotic. Almost like a fruit juice, but the sweetness is matched easily by bracing acidity, leaving a fresh mineral feel and taste. Slightly better than previously reviewed. Drink now through 2004.–B.S. • $20 • (9/15/1999) • **86**

Pinot Gris Alsace Vendange Tardive 1996: Full-bore wine. Ripe and smoky, a blanket of apricot- and orange-tinged aromas and flavors is interwoven with vivacious texture and lively acidity. Very harmonious and concentrated, it shows fine length of flavor and a promising future. Drink now through 2010.–B.S. • $65 • (4/30/1999) • **92**

SCHOFFIT

Gewürztraminer Alsace Grand Cru Rangen de Thann Clos St.-Théobold 1997: Evokes Asian spices and rose petal, settling into vanilla on the palate. Softly structured, never heavy, it hangs together nicely through the lingering finish. Drink now.–B.S. • $45 • (10/31/1999) • **88**

Gewürztraminer Alsace Harth Cuvée Caroline 1997: There's fine complexity in this smoke, honey, citrus and tropical fruit bomb. A touch of sweetness and full body are balanced by moderate acidity and citrus peel. One wishes only for a bit more length. Drink now through 2001.–B.S. • $24 • (10/31/1999) • **87**

Pinot Blanc-Auxerrois Alsace Cuvée Caroline 1997: Gorgeous Pinot Blanc. Aromatic, rich and complex, while maintaining a sense of elegance. Offers white peach, orange and mineral elements on a fat texture, yet stays balanced and bright, ending with a nutty taste. Drink now through 2001.–B.S. • $14 • (3/31/1999) • **88**

Riesling Alsace Grand Cru Rangen de Thann Clos St.-Théobold 1997: Intriguing and exotic. Overt aromas are almost herbaceous or like smoky green tea, then it turns to dried citrus and pineapple on the palate, with a rich texture and great length of flavor on the finish. Drink now through 2003.–B.S. • $45 • (10/31/1999) • **90**

Riesling Alsace Grand Cru Rangen de Thann Clos St.-Théobold 1996: Gorgeous aromas and flavors ranging from flowers to peaches and minerals. Seductive and beguiling, ample in body, with a spicy character and nerves of steel. The finish is long, with a haunting aftertaste of roses. Drink now through 2005.–B.S. • $42 • (9/15/1998) • **90**

Riesling Alsace Grand Cru Sommerberg 1997: A forward, up-front style, it starts out with rich, smoke- and mineral-laced quince and apricot notes.

Medium-bodied and lively, it fades on the finish. Drink now.–B.S. • $27 • (6/15/2000) • **87**

Riesling Alsace Harth Cuvée Prestige 1997: Hints of nectarine and candied lemon-peel mark the aromas, yet it's more almondy in flavor. This crisp white is moderately concentrated, with a mouthwatering finish. Drink now through 2002.–B.S. • $20 • (10/31/1999) • **85**

Riesling Alsace Harth Cuvée Prestige 1996: With pungent aromas of cut apple and some developed red berry and almond notes, this '96 Riesling has earthy, apple flavors and a broad, firmly structured profile. Needs time. Drink through 2008–B.S. • $20 • (3/31/1999) • **89**

Tokay Pinot Gris Alsace Cuvée Alexandre 1996: Has a subtle approach, with ripe peach and passion-fruit flavors building on the palate. Dry, spicy, powerful, with a tangy, citrus-peel note to balance the almost syrupy texture. Drink now.–B.S. • $27 • (9/15/1998) • **89**

Tokay Pinot Gris Alsace Cuvée Alexandre Vieilles Vignes 1997: Firmly in the sweet camp, this is almost vendange tardive in style. Very forward and luscious in its peach, honey and grapefruit-peel flavors, with a combination of acidity and bitterness for structure. Drink now through 2001.–B.S. • $19 • (10/31/1999) • **86**

Tokay Pinot Gris Alsace Cuvée Caroline 1996: A Pinot Gris with immediate appeal. It's ripe with pear and quince character, showing a hint of sweetness and a thick, rich texture. Good finish.–B.S. • $24 • (9/15/1998) • **85**

Tokay Pinot Gris Alsace Grand Cru Rangen de Thann Clos St.-Théobold 1997: A big, ripe, unctuous white, offering honey, orange and mineral flavors and a touch of sweetness, which may need to be integrated into the soft structure before the whole comes together. Drink now through 2002.–B.S. • $40 • (10/31/1999) • **87**

SCHRODER & SCHYLER & CO.

Bordeaux Signatures 1997: Pleasant and easy, with plum and berry character. Medium- to light-bodied, with light tannins and finish. Drink now.–J.S. • $15 • (1/31/2000) • **80**

Bordeaux Signatures 1996: Mature-looking color, with an amber hue. Strange aromas of bark, fruit and ginger. Medium-bodied, with light tannins and a short finish.–J.S. • $15 • (2/28/1999) • **79**

Bordeaux Signatures 1995 • $15 • (1/31/1998) • **82**

Bordeaux White Signatures 1998: Rather woody, but with good pineapple and honey character. Medium-bodied, with good acidity and a lively finish. Drink now.–J.S. • $12 • (2/29/2000) • **85**

Cabernet Sauvignon Vin de Pays d'Oc Elevé en Futs de Chêne 1995: Bright blackberry and floral aromas, with hints of ripe plum. Medium-bodied and very fruity, with big, chewy tannins. Slightly rough and dry on the finish; needs time to mellow. Drink through 2000–J.S. • $8 • (9/30/1998) • **82**

Chardonnay Vin de Pays d'Oc Vinifié en Futs de Chêne 1997: Well-crafted, with lemon, vanilla and apple aromas and flavors. Medium-bodied, with good acidity and a crisp, fruity finish. Drink now.–J.S. • $8 • (9/30/1998) • **85**

SECOND DE CARNET, LE

Haut-Médoc 1995 • $12 • (1/31/1998) • **71**

SEGLA

Margaux 1996: A very well-crafted and elegant '96. Extremely pretty spice and berry aromas with hints of mint. Medium-bodied, with well-integrated tannins and a fine, silky texture. Slightly hollow center-palate but impressive for a second label from Château Rauzan-Ségla. Best after 2001.–J.S. • $25 • (1/31/1999) • **88**

Margaux 1995 • $25 • (1/31/1998) • **89**

Margaux 1994 • $NA • (1/31/1997) • **82**

Margaux 1993 • $NA • (1/31/1996) • **83**

SEGRIES, CHATEAU DE

Côtes du Rhône 1998: A bit light in structure, with a light color and strawberry-cherry character. Dries a bit on the finish.–P.M. • $9 • (11/15/1999) • **74**

Lirac 1997: Deliciously ripe, with flavorful blackberry, plum and black pepper aromas and flavors. Brick in color at the edges and supple in texture, so drink on release.–P.M. • $11 • (12/15/1999) • **83**

SEGUIN, CHATEAU DE

Bordeaux Supérieur 1997: A very grapey red with lots of fruit and some dark chocolate character. Medium-bodied, with a solid core of tannins. Medium finish. Drink now.–J.S. • $14 • (1/31/2000) • **85**

Bordeaux Supérieur 1996: Decent claret. A little lean, with some nice blackberry and mineral character. Slightly dry and astringent finish. Drink now.–J.S. • $14 • (1/01/1999) • **82**

Bordeaux Supérieur Cuvee Prestige 1997: A bit lean, with some berry and mineral character. Medium-bodied, with firm tannins and a short finish. Too much wood. Drink now.–J.S. • $18 • (1/31/2000) • **84**

Bordeaux Supérieur Cuvée Prestige 1996: A straightforward claret with berry and plum character. Medium-bodied, with velvety tannins and a short finish. Drink now.–J.S. • $17 • (1/01/1999) • **85**

Bordeaux Supérieur Cuvée Prestige 1995: A pleasant and very drinkable claret. Pretty blackberry and cocoa aromas in this medium-bodied, lightly tannic wine. Drink now through 2002.–J.S. • $17 • (1/01/1999) • **84**

Bordeaux Supérieur Réserve du Château 1995: Elegant and well crafted. Plenty of blackberry and cherry character, with wet earth undertones. Medium-bodied, with fresh acidity, fine tannins and a long chocolaty aftertaste. Drink now through 2006.–J.S. • $NA • (1/01/1999) • **87**

Bordeaux White 1996: Promises more on the nose than it gives on the palate, but still delicious. Fresh and superclean, with cream, vanilla, pineapple and other tropical fruits. Medium-bodied, with a round and creamy texture and a delicious finish. Drink now.–J.S. • $11 • (3/31/1999) • **87**

Bordeaux White Cuvée Prestige 1998: Oxidized, with a candied character. Short finish. Not very impressive.–J.S. • $16 • (2/29/2000) • **78**

Bordeaux White Cuvée prestige 1997: Medium-bodied, with attractive lemon and cream character, a creamy texture and a citrusy finish. Delicious. Drink now.–J.S. • $15 • (9/30/1999) • **85**

SEGUIN, HERVE

Pouilly-Fumé 1998: Assertive earthy and herbal aromas mark this traditional white. It's concentrated, bracingly crisp and quite austere. Best with savory dishes. Drink now through 2002.–T.M. • $17 • (3/31/2000) • **86**

Pouilly-Fumé 1997: This rich white offers round, ripe flavors of apple, pear and melon. Rather soft on the palate, with notes of smoke and earth. Drink now.–T.M. • $14 • (12/31/1998) • **85**

SEIGNEURIE D'OLIVIER

Pessac-Léognan du Château Olivier 1996: Pretty currant and mineral aromas, with an undertone of tea. Medium- to full-bodied, with polished tannins and a smoky berry aftertaste. Slightly hollow midpalate. A lot of style for a second label. Best after 2001.–J.S. • $NA • (1/31/1999) • **85**

Pessac-Léognan White 1996: A pretty white. Subtle aromas and flavors of lemon, coconut and grass. Medium-bodied, with fresh acidity and a medium finish. Second label of Château Olivier. Drink now.–J.S. • $10 • (3/31/1999) • **86**

SEIGNEURIE DE GICON

Côtes du Rhône-Villages Chusclan 1995 • $NA • (10/15/1997) • **72**

Côtes du Rhône-Villages Rosé Chusclan 1996 • $NA • (10/15/1997) • **87**

SEIGNEURS DU PERIGORD

Bergerac 1997: A light red, with faint cherry notes and a weedy finish.–K.M. • $7 • (7/31/1999) • **79**

Bergerac 1996 • $7 • (9/30/1997) • **82**

Bergerac 1995 • $7 • (7/31/1996) • **80**

Bergerac White 1998: Light and simple, with some herbal and oniony flavors and a touch of green peach. Drink now.–K.M. • $7 • (10/15/1999) • **80**

Bergerac White 1996 • $7 • (9/30/1997) • **84**

Monbazillac 1995 • $15 • (10/31/1997) • **78**

SEIZE, CHATEAU DE

Bordeaux 1997: Strange aromas of wet wool and old socks. Green flavors.–J.S. • $10 • (1/01/2000) • **74**

SELTZ, ALBERT

Gewürztraminer Alsace Réserve 1997: Shows the ripeness of the 1997 vintage with aromas and flavors that border on minty, plus spicy accents and a touch of sweetness balanced by moderate acidity.–B.S. • $15 • (9/15/1998) • **85**

Pinot Auxerrois Alsace Sélection 1996: Bold and rich, full of nut and peach character, this has the breadth and weight of Auxerrois, yet shows enough acidity to keep it from plodding. The lemony finish is slightly bitter. Drink now.–B.S. • $18 • (9/15/1998) • **85**

Pinot Blanc Alsace Réserve 1998: A fresh, crisp style of Pinot Blanc, with richness midpalate and flavors of apple, pear and fruit blossom that linger on the finish. Drink now.–B.S. • $11 • (6/15/2000) • **83**

Pinot Blanc Alsace Réserve 1997: Big, rich and full-bodied, with subtle lemon custard and apple aromas that turn to peach and grapefruit flavors, this is a mouthful of Pinot Blanc that feels high in alcohol, yet has the bold flavors to match.–B.S. • $9 • (8/31/1998) • **85**

Riesling Alsace Brandluft 1996: Intense and unevolved, with ripe honey, mineral and spice notes submerged at this stage, yet there's density, verve and a rich finish—which shows promise for the future. Best from 2001 through 2005.–B.S. • $18 • (6/15/2000) • **88**

Sylvaner Alsace Io Sono Contento Vieilles Vignes 1998: Fresh and lively, offering straightforward lemon and apple notes, with a hint of nuts. Drink now.–B.S. • $18 • (6/15/2000) • **83**

Sylvaner de Mittelbergheim Alsace Zotz 1996: Plenty of character, showing apple, lemon and herbs, underlined by lively acidity. Slightly bitter finish. Drink now.–B.S. • $10 • (8/31/1998) • **82**

Tokay Pinot Gris Alsace Réserve Personnelle 1997: Apricot and orange notes prevail, richly textured and medium in weight. Some heat and bitterness emerge on the finish, disrupting the overall balance. Drink now through 2002.–B.S • $18 • (6/15/2000) • **83**

SENARD, DANIEL

Aloxe-Corton Les Valozières 1995 • $40 • (11/15/1997) • **77**
Aloxe-Corton Les Valozières 1991 • $38 • (1/31/1994) • **68**
Corton Clos des Meix 1995 • $64 • (11/15/1997) • **82**
Corton En Charlemagne 1995 • $72 • (11/15/1997) • **87**
Corton En Charlemagne 1994 • $61 • (11/15/1996) • **75**
Corton En Charlemagne 1992 • $52 • (12/15/1994) • **84**
Corton En Charlemagne 1991 • $65 • (1/31/1994) • **81**
Corton En Charlemagne 1990 • $NA • (12/15/1992) • **93**
Corton Le Clos du Roi 1995 • $75 • (11/15/1997) • **79**
Corton Le Clos du Roi 1994 • $63 • (11/15/1996) • **76**
Corton Le Clos du Roi 1992 • $52 • (12/15/1994) • **85**
Corton Le Clos du Roi 1991 • $65 • (1/31/1994) • **79**
Corton Le Clos du Roi 1990 • $55 • (12/15/1992) • **93**
Corton Les Bressandes 1995 • $75 • (11/15/1997) • **79**
Corton Les Bressandes 1994 • $63 • (11/15/1996) • **73**
Corton Les Bressandes 1991 • $65 • (1/31/1994) • **77**
Corton Les Bressandes 1990 • $NA • (12/15/1992) • **88**
Corton Les Meix 1992 • $38 • (12/15/1994) • **81**
Corton Les Meix 1990 • $NA • (12/15/1992) • **93**

SENECHAUX, DOMAINE DES

Châteauneuf-du-Pape 1998: This structured Châteauneuf is packed with ripe, sweet-tasting fruit. Very silky midpalate, a medium-bodied beauty that goes in search of the land—Châteauneuf's *terroir*. Beautiful finish. Drink now through 2015.–P.M. • $27 • (6/30/2000) • **91**

Châteauneuf-du-Pape 1996: Lean and slightly diluted, with herb, bell pepper and plum flavors. The chewy finish seems unbalanced.–P.M. • $19 • (9/30/1998) • **75**

Châteauneuf-du-Pape 1995 • $26 • (10/15/1997) • **80**
Châteauneuf-du-Pape 1985 • $17 • (10/15/1988) • **85**

Châteauneuf-du-Pape White 1997: Lush, opulent and full-bodied, this wondrous wine seduces you with its classy structure and aromas of butter, spice, toast, pear pie and fruit. Most impressive is the velvety, rich texture. Drink now.–P.M. • $23 • (9/30/1998) • **90**

Châteauneuf-du-Pape White 1996 • $30 • (10/15/1997) • **84**

SENEJAC, BLANC DE

Bordeaux White 1996: Rich, and ready to enjoy. Enticing aromas of butterscotch, apple and pineapple. Full-bodied, with an oily texture and a long aftertaste of vanilla, apple and honey. Drink now.–J.S. • $NA • (1/01/1999) • **88**

Key: SS—Spectator Selection. CS—Cellar Selection. HR—Highly Recommended. $NA—Price not available. (BT)—Barrel tasting. (A)—Auction Price.
For a key to the tasters' initials, see "How to Use These Listings."
Dates in parentheses represent the issues in which the ratings were published.

Bordeaux White Cuvée Charlotte 1997: A lively wine, with lots of grass, apple and lime character. Medium-bodied, with good acidity and a flavorful finish. Well done. Not imported into the U.S. Drink now.–J.S. • $NA • (1/01/1999) • **87**

SENEJAC, CHATEAU

Haut-Médoc 1997: Aromas of berries, walnuts and earth follow through to a medium-bodied palate, with soft tannins and a medium finish. Slightly lean, but good. Best after 2000.–J.S. • $NA • (1/31/2000) • **85**

Haut-Médoc 1988 • $14 • (4/30/1991) • **78**

SENEZ, CHRISTIAN

Brut Champagne NV: A rare style of Champagne that's bright and zingy, with an intense fruit character. Offers fresh, deep, nicely focused lemon-lime flavors and picks up creamy vanilla accents on the lingering finish. Drink now. • $17 • (12/31/1998) • **89**

SENILHAC, CHATEAU

Haut-Médoc 1996: A lovely and caressing '96, with berry and milk chocolate character. Medium-bodied, with medium velvety tannins and a fruity aftertaste. A beauty. Drink now.–J.S. • $17 • (7/31/1999) • **86**

SEPTIMANIE

Maury Mascotte NV • $15 • (1/31/1995) • **80**

SERAFIN PERE & FILS

Charmes-Chambertin 1997: Gorgeous aromas of smoke, game, black cherry and vanilla lead to an elegant, harmonious red. Fragile yet focused and finely wrought, with vibrancy, crispness and a lingering aftertaste. Best from 2001 through 2005.–B.S. • $135 • (9/30/1999) • **89**

Charmes-Chambertin 1996: Best wine of the appellation. Fabulous '96 red, packed with blackberry, cassis and spice, very exotic, yet harmonious, balanced and concentrated, followed by searing intensity of acidity and tannins, finishing up with a saturation of fruit. Best from 2003 through 2010.–B.S. • $120 • (9/30/1998) • **97**

Charmes-Chambertin 1995 • $95 • (11/15/1997) • **96**
Charmes-Chambertin 1994 • $80 • (11/15/1996) • **86**
Charmes-Chambertin 1993 • $90 • (11/15/1995) • **96**
Charmes-Chambertin 1992 • $50 • (12/15/1994) • **89**
Charmes-Chambertin 1989 • $65 • (1/31/1992) • **92**
Gevrey-Chambertin 1995 • $46 • (11/15/1997) • **90**
Gevrey-Chambertin 1994 • $40 • (11/15/1996) • **82**
Gevrey-Chambertin 1990 • $45 • (12/15/1992) • **89**
Gevrey-Chambertin 1988 • $35 • (3/31/1991) • **92**

Gevrey-Chambertin Le Fonteny 1996: Grand red Burgundy of the highest order, this full-bodied, dark-colored, silky treasure explodes with a rainbow of aromas and flavors that range from rose petals, violets and tar to cassis and blackberries. Ripe tannins make it accessible now, but it should hold for years. Drink now through 2010.–P.M. • $75 • (9/30/1998) • **94**

Gevrey-Chambertin Le Fonteny 1995 • $60 • (11/15/1997) • **89**
Gevrey-Chambertin Le Fonteny 1993 • $65 • (11/15/1995) • **91**
Gevrey-Chambertin Le Fonteny 1992 • $40 • (12/15/1994) • **85**
Gevrey-Chambertin Le Fonteny 1990 • $63 • (12/15/1992) • **87**
Gevrey-Chambertin Le Fonteny 1989 • $50 • (1/31/1992) • **86**
Gevrey-Chambertin Le Fonteny 1988 • $50 • (5/15/1991) • **92**

Gevrey-Chambertin Les Cazetiers 1997: With wonderful aromas of violet, blackberry and spicy oak, this is quite elegant and sleek, with good intensity and a long, satisfying finish. Stands out among the '97s. Best from 2002 through 2007.–P.M. • $90 • (9/30/1999) • **89**

Gevrey-Chambertin Les Cazetiers 1996: A gorgeous wine displaying classy Pinot character, bursting with rose petals, violets, concentrated blackberry and black currant flavors and some mineral notes. Full-bodied, suave, sophisticated, supple, but also seriously flavorful. Long, intense, silky finish. Drink now through 2010.–P.M. • $80 • (9/30/1998) • **94**

Gevrey-Chambertin Les Cazetiers 1995 • $72 • (11/15/1997) • **90**
Gevrey-Chambertin Les Cazetiers 1994 • $60 • (11/15/1996) • **86**
Gevrey-Chambertin Les Cazetiers 1993 • $70 • (11/15/1995) • **91**
Gevrey-Chambertin Les Cazetiers 1992 • $44 • (12/15/1994) • **86**
Gevrey-Chambertin Les Cazetiers 1990 • $67 (A) • (12/15/1992) • **91**
Gevrey-Chambertin Les Cazetiers 1989 • $54 • (1/31/1992) • **89**
Gevrey-Chambertin Les Cazetiers 1988 • $53 • (5/15/1991) • **91**

FRANCE

Gevrey-Chambertin Les Corbeaux 1996: Lovely, concentrated, jammy fruit here, showing blackberries, spice and a hint of vanilla, with racy acidity and firm yet ripe tannins. Good richness and depth and a lingering raspberry finish. Drink through 2004–B.S. • $75 • (9/30/1998) • **94**

Gevrey-Chambertin Vieilles Vignes 1997: Smoky and citrusy, with game, grilled and mouthpuckering lime, but there's fatness, and it offers black cherry and floral character. Best from 2002 through 2005.–P.M. • $70 • (9/30/1999) • **87**

Gevrey-Chambertin Vieilles Vignes 1996: Hedonistic, decadent, "to-die-for" red Burgundy. Full-bodied yet elegant, the rose petal, violet, blackberry, mineral, cassis and exotic spice notes burst out of the glass and power their way to a long finish. Ripe, solid tannins make it a pleasure now, but it's so balanced it should hold for years. What a wine. Drink now through 2010.–P.M. • $60 • (9/30/1998) • **95**

Gevrey-Chambertin Vieilles Vignes 1994 • $40 • (11/15/1996) • **80**

Gevrey-Chambertin Vieilles Vignes 1993 • $55 • (11/15/1995) • **85**

Gevrey-Chambertin Vieilles Vignes 1992 • $35 • (12/15/1994) • **84**

Gevrey-Chambertin Vieilles Vignes 1990 • $50 • (12/15/1992) • **87**

Gevrey-Chambertin Vieilles Vignes 1989 • $45 • (1/31/1992) • **92**

Gevrey-Chambertin Vieilles Vignes 1987 • $35 • (3/31/1990) • **91**

SERGANT, CHATEAU

Lalande-de-Pomerol 1996: Rather diluted, this has some decent berry and cherry character but a short finish.–J.S. • $16 • (2/28/1999) • **76**

SERGUE, CHATEAU LA

Lalande-de-Pomerol 1999: Very well done. Dark purple, with black licorice, violet and berry aromas. Medium-bodied, with a solid core of tannins and a long finish.–J.S. • $NA • (1/01/2000) (BT) • **85-89**

Lalande-de-Pomerol 1998: Dark-colored, with masses of ripe fruit and new wood. Medium-bodied, with intense vanilla flavors and some strawberry and berry to back them up. A bit too much new wood.–J.S. • $NA • (5/31/1999) (BT) • **85-89**

Lalande-de-Pomerol 1996: Clever winemaking, with some good berry and cherry character, but the oak dominates at the moment. Medium-bodied, with medium tannins and a coconut aftertaste. Drink through 2002–J.S. • $20 • (1/31/1999) • **84**

SERRE, CHATEAU LA

St.-Emilion 1998: Interesting mineral and black currant aromas. Medium-bodied, with some firm tannins and a light finish. Needs a bit more fruit in the midpalate.–J.S. • $NA • (5/31/1999) (BT) • **85-89**

St.-Emilion 1997: Pretty plum and berry character. Medium-bodied, with good fruit, fine tannins and a slightly short finish. Drink now.–J.S. • $NA • (1/31/2000) • **85**

St.-Emilion 1996: Delicious young wine. Very pretty chocolate and berry aromas. Medium-bodied, with velvety tannins and a fresh, fruity aftertaste. Drink now.–J.S. • $30 • (1/31/1999) • **87**

St.-Emilion 1995 • $28 • (1/31/1998) • **91**

St.-Emilion 1990 • $22 • (3/31/1993) • **88**

St.-Emilion 1989: A seductive wine. Dark-ruby color, with red tint. Intense game, berry, cherry and chocolate aromas. Full-bodied, round and soft, and a beautiful, caressing texture. (1989 Bordeaux horizontal tasting). Best after 2001.–J.S. • $NA • (5/31/1999) • **90**

St.-Emilion 1988 • $18 • (6/15/1991) • **80**

St.-Emilion 1985 • $15 • (5/15/1988) • **91**

SERVIN

Chablis 1997: Strange, earthy aromas, even rotten egg notes, make this grassy, herbal Chablis tough to recommend.–P.M. • $15 • (5/31/1999) • **70**

Chablis 1996 • $17 • (8/31/1997) • **83**

Chablis Bougros 1996 • $42 • (5/31/1998) • **90**

Chablis Les Clos 1997: Firm style, with mineral, salty cracker and herbal overtones that combine deliciously with ripe pear, honey and spice flavors to produce a balanced, lovely, vibrant and deeply satisfying Les Clos. Best from 2003 through 2010.–P.M. • $20 • (5/31/1999) • **94**

Chablis Les Clos 1996 • $45 • (5/31/1998) • **90**

Chablis Montée de Tonnerre 1997: Just wonderful, if a bit earthy. Very ripe yet also firmly constructed, this wine bursts with mineral, stone, dried herb character, but tastes honeyed and superintense on the citrus-inspired ending. Drink through 2007–P.M. • $20 • (5/31/1999) • **90**

Chablis Montée de Tonnerre 1996 • $26 • (5/31/1998) • **90**

Chablis Montée de Tonnerre 1995 • $17 • (6/15/1997) • **90**

Chablis Vaillons 1997: Extremely fresh, with a grass, gooseberry and quince character close to that of a good Sauvignon Blanc, this is very well made, full of ripe and clean fruit. Full-bodied, it ends on a delicious, sweet-tasting finish. Drink now through 2003.–P.M. • $20 • (5/31/1999) • **89**

Chablis Vaillons 1996 • $24 • (5/31/1998) • **88**

Chablis Vaillons 1995 • $18 • (6/15/1997) • **72**

SEUIL, CHATEAU DU

Graves 1996: Very light and weedy, with some berry and tobacco character, but diluted and watery on the finish.–J.S. • $20 • (2/28/1999) • **77**

Graves White 1997: The Sauvignon Blanc character shows through, with freshly cut grass, mineral and lemon on the nose and palate. Medium-bodied, with fresh acidity and a crisp finish, but a slightly simple aftertaste. Drink now.–J.S. • $20 • (3/31/1999) • **84**

Graves White 1996: Very vivid, with apple, mineral and stone aromas. Medium-bodied, with fresh acidity and light finish. Promises more on the nose than it delivers on the palate. Drink now.–J.S. • $20 • (3/31/1999) • **84**

SIAURAC, CHATEAU

Lalande-de-Pomerol 1993 • $19 • (1/31/1996) • **77**

Lalande-de-Pomerol 1990 • $19 • (5/15/1994) • **84**

SIGALAS-RABAUD, CHATEAU

Sauternes 1998: Loads of spice, honey and caramel flavors in this full-bodied and zingy young sticky. Super sticky.–J.S. • $NA • (1/01/1999) (BT) • **90-94**

Sauternes 1997: This Sauternes has lovely lemon, apple and pineapple character, with a hint of honey and vanilla. Medium-bodied and medium sweet, with a fresh finish. Pretty. Drink now.–J.S. • $NA • (1/31/2000) • **87**

Sauternes 1986 • $42 • (12/31/1989) • **77**

Sauternes 1985 • $41 • (7/15/1988) • **82**

Sauternes 1983 • $32 Ⓐ • (1/31/1988) • **88**

SIGAUT, HERVE

Chambolle-Musigny 1992 • $NA • (12/15/1994) • **82**

Chambolle-Musigny Les Sentiers 1995 • $39 • (11/15/1997) • **85**

Chambolle-Musigny Les Sentiers 1992 • $NA • (12/15/1994) • **81**

Morey-St.-Denis Les Charrières 1995 • $39 • (11/15/1997) • **85**

SIGNAC, CHATEAU

Côtes du Rhône 1990 • $9 • (11/30/1992) • **84**

Côtes du Rhône-Villages 1998: Lush and round, packed with fruit and serious tannins. A medium- to full-bodied red, with bitter chocolate lacing the blackberry and a wet earth complexity. All that fruit should balance the tough tannins, so cellar a bit. Not imported into the U.S. Drink through 2004–P.M. • $NA • (1/01/1999) • **86**

Côtes du Rhône-Villages Combe d'Enfer 1998: A red with a grip of fruit, tannins and wet earth. Medium-bodied and showing a slightly tough character on the finish, it has personality, and the dried herb and blackberry flavors are enticing. Should soften with the right food. Not imported into the U.S. Drink now through 2003.–P.M. • $NA • (1/01/1999) • **84**

Côtes du Rhône-Villages Cuvée Terra Amata 1998: This fantastic, velvety red shows the hand of a masterful winemaker. Full-bodied, oozing rich, ripe flavors and overflowing with opulent texture, it's fat on the palate but structured on the finish. Black fruit, silky tannins and impressive balance. The wood is counterbalanced by all the fruit. Drink now through 2004.–P.M. • $15 • (12/15/1999) • **91**

SILLAGE DE MALARTIC, LE

Pessac-Léognan 1996: Good sweet-fruit character on the nose and palate. Medium-bodied, with caressing tannins, but slightly diluted on the finish. Second label of Château Malartic-Lagravière. Drink now.–J.S. • $NA • (1/31/1999) • **83**

Pessac-Léognan 1995 • $15 • (1/31/1998) • **80**

Pessac-Léognan White 1996: Some lemon and apple character here, but slightly candied and dull to taste. Barely acceptable.–J.S. • $NA • (1/01/1999) • **73**

SIMONNET-FEBVRE

Chablis 1998: A papery cardboard aroma is dominant in this dry, tough, weak and diluted white. Tasted twice, with consistent notes.–P.M. • $14 • (5/15/2000) • **69**

Chablis 1997: Well made in the village-Chablis genre, with a dash of herbs, mineral and green apple character that makes for a good, balanced, medium-bodied white. Drink now.–P.M. • $14 • (5/31/1999) • **83**

Chablis 1996 • $15 • (8/31/1997) • **91**

Chablis Fourchaume 1998: A delicate '98 Chablis. Smooth, with good focus of mineral, lemon and salt. A touch diluted, but it's clean and flavorful in a light style. Drink now through 2002.–P.M. • $23 • (5/15/2000) • **84**

Chablis Fourchaume 1997: With its interesting combination of flavorful grass, pineapple and wet earth complexity, this is a very idiosyncratic Chardonnay, but it's lush and ripe-tasting, with pear, tropical, spice and salty notes. Balanced finish. Drink now through 2004.–P.M. • $27 • (5/31/1999) • **88**

Chablis Fourchaume 1996 • $23 • (5/31/1998) • **92**

Chablis Fourchaume 1995 • $24 • (6/15/1997) • **79**

Chablis La Forêt 1998: Clean and pure, with a chalky, flinty, minerally character that makes it interesting. Not very ripe, with a slight dilution, but focused and well made. Drink now through 2005.–P.M. • $23 • (5/15/2000) • **84**

Chablis Mont de Milieu 1998: An ager with good intensity. This minerally, chewy, chalky, stony, medium-bodied white is a bit tough and linear now, but has ripe fruit and honey underneath. Best after 2001.–P.M. • $20 • (5/15/2000) • **86**

Chablis Mont de Milieu 1997: So pretty, this medium-bodied Mont de Milieu just caresses the palate with elegant structure, pineapple, lemon and cream notes. Terrific harmony on the succulent finish. Drink now through 2004.–P.M. • $27 • (5/31/1999) • **91**

Chablis Mont de Milieu 1996 • $20 • (8/31/1997) • **86**

Chablis Mont de Milieu 1995 • $22 • (6/15/1997) • **86**

Chablis Montée de Tonnerre 1997: Hard-as-nails now, this medium-bodied '97 is built for the future; it shows great restraint, lots of acidity and good honey, pear, earth, mineral complexity. Cellar. Best from 2003 through 2007.–P.M. • $27 • (5/31/1999) • **88**

Chablis Montée de Tonnerre 1996 • $20 • (5/31/1998) • **89**

Chablis Preuses 1998: A bit woody, with a paint varnish character. Medium-bodied, it lacks harmony, turning chewy and dry on the finish.–P.M. • $35 • (5/15/2000) • **77**

Chablis Preuses 1997: *Terroir*-driven, with a pebbly, minerally character, of medium body and intensity, this wine offers some pretty honey and ripe fruit without much length. Drink now through 2003.–P.M. • $55 • (5/31/1999) • **87**

Chablis Preuses 1996 • $36 • (5/31/1998) • **82**

Chablis Preuses 1995 • $40 • (6/15/1997) • **84**

Chablis Vaillons 1998: Pretty, with a supple texture and a soft structure. Medium-bodied, it makes for a lovely, easygoing drink as the honey and ripe pear swirl around the palate. Smoky, toasty aftertaste. Drink now through 2003.–P.M. • $23 • (5/15/2000) • **86**

Chablis Vaillons 1997: Supple and accessible, showing sweet-tasting fruit, pineapple and pear, but turns bitter and loses focus on the finish. Serve chilled.–P.M. • $26 • (5/31/1999) • **75**

Chablis Vaillons 1996 • $19 • (5/31/1998) • **89**

Chablis Vaillons 1995 • $20 • (6/15/1997) • **80**

Chablis Valmur 1997: Smooth and lush, this charming, medium-bodied, medium-intense white is round and velvety, turns a bit astringent on the finish. Drink now through 2005.–P.M. • $55 • (5/31/1999) • **88**

Petit Chablis 1998: Fresh and vibrant, with a crisp, freshly cut grass, dried herbs aroma that mixes nicely with some ripe pear and honey notes on the palate. Medium-bodied, it's a fun white that's clean and pure. Drink now through 2002.–P.M. • $12 • (1/01/2000) • **84**

Petit Chablis 1996 • $12 • (8/31/1997) • **77**

Petit Chablis 1995 • $NA • (8/31/1996) • **84**

Key: SS—Spectator Selection. CS—Cellar Selection. HR—Highly Recommended. $NA—Price not available. (BT)—Barrel tasting. Ⓐ—Auction Price.
For a key to the tasters' initials, see "How to Use These Listings."
Dates in parentheses represent the issues in which the ratings were published.

SIPP, LOUIS

Alsace Gentil 1997: A soft, floral- and citrus-tasting white, with a rich texture and lemony finish. Straightforward and appealing. Drink now.–B.S. • $11 • (9/15/1998) • **85**

Auxerrois Alsace 1998: Subtle, displaying peach and pear notes accented by mineral; fatness midpalate and a hint of grapefruit peel on the finish. Drink now.–B.S. • $10 • (10/15/1999) • **83**

Gewürztraminer Alsace 1998: Very spicy, refreshing and richly textured, here's an attractive and straightforward Gewürztraminer for early consumption. Drink now.–B.S. • $17 • (10/31/1999) • **82**

Gewürztraminer Alsace Grand Cru Osterberg Cuvée Particulière 1996: An amorphous, dilute white, sweet, but lacking concentration and depth. A second bottle was corky.–B.S. • $25 • (10/31/1999) • **75**

Gewürztraminer Alsace Réserve Personnelle 1996: Full of citrus notes, especially grapefruit, with a hint of roses, this Gewürztraminer stays lively thanks to bright acidity and finishes on a dry, spicy note. Drink now.–B.S. • $19 • (9/15/1998) • **86**

Gewürztraminer Alsace Vendanges Tardives 1996: Dry and minerally for a VT, this also shows the requisite honey, litchi and spice flavors and a rich texture before clamping down on the finish. Austere now; may come around with time. Best from 2001 through 2007.–B.S. • $50 • (9/30/1999) • **89**

Muscat Alsace 1997: Ripe and grapey, with a touch of residual sugar, this Muscat is rich, with an underlying austerity and slight bitterness. Finishes dry. Drink now.–B.S. • $13 • (10/15/1999) • **83**

Pinot Blanc Alsace 1998: Modest citrus and earth flavors in a dilute package with a slightly bitter finish.–B.S. • $11 • (10/15/1999) • **78**

Pinot Blanc Alsace 1997: A delicious Pinot Blanc, fresh and lively, sporting apple, mineral and a hint of earth wrapped in a smooth texture. The flavors linger on the finish. Tasted twice, with consistent notes.–B.S. • $10 • (9/15/1998) • **86**

Pinot Blanc Alsace Gold Medal Label 1996: This mouthwatering '96 white combines the bracing acidity of the vintage with ripe, appley flavors and good concentration. Ends in a lip-smacking style with a hint of earth.–B.S. • $10 • (9/15/1998) • **85**

Riesling Alsace 1998: Reserved, offering firm support for the peach, quince and mineral flavors, with a rich midpalate and refreshing citrus on the finish. Drink now through 2001.–B.S. • $13 • (10/15/1999) • **86**

Riesling Alsace 1997: Full of spice and mineral aromas, adding white peach and white pepper on the palate, this Riesling shows focus, delicacy, balance and a steely finish. Best with food. Drink now.–B.S. • $12 • (9/15/1998) • **86**

Riesling Alsace Gold Medal Label 1996: A generous Riesling, round and full of apple and almond aromas and flavors and richly textured, though not very expressive. A touch hot on the finish. Drink now through 2001.–B.S. • $16 • (9/15/1998) • **86**

Riesling Alsace Grand Cru Kirchberg de Ribeauvillé 1996: For fans of steely Riesling. Very young and unevolved, displaying ripe peach and a stony character, great presence on the palate and an expansive finish. Still, it's austere and raw with acidity, so give it time. Drink through 2008–B.S. • $19 • (9/15/1998) • **89**

Riesling Alsace Grand Cru Kirchberg de Ribeauvillé Cuvée Particulière 1997: Almond, honey and spice notes combine with a broad profile and firm structure. Fragrant, yet seems to be holding something in reserve, so be patient. Honey lingers on the aftertaste. Drink through 2005–B.S. • $22 • (10/15/1999) • **88**

Riesling Alsace Réserve Personnelle 1997: Showing almond and spice notes, yet the overall impression is slightly dull and maturing quickly. This was the better of two bottles, with significant bottle variation.–B.S. • $18 • (10/15/1999) • **79**

Tokay Pinot Gris Alsace 1996: Ripe and round, with peach and smoke aromas and flavors that are well defined. Underscored by lively acidity, finishing with a grapefruit accent. Drink now through 2001.–B.S. • $19 • (9/15/1998) • **88**

Tokay Pinot Gris Alsace Gold Medal Label 1996: Apricot and mandarin lend an exotic character to this rich Pinot Gris that starts off nicely, then turns austere and slightly tart on the finish. Drink through 2003–B.S. • $14 • (9/15/1998) • **84**

Tokay Pinot Gris Alsace Grand Cru Kirchberg de Ribeauvillé Cuvée Particulière 1996: Middle of the road, not too concentrated or exciting, although correct in its varietal character of apricot and honey. Drink now.–B.S. • $25 • (10/31/1999) • **84**

Tokay Pinot Gris Alsace Réserve Personnelle 1996: This is very flat and soft for a '96 Pinot Gris. Tastes dilute and vapid.–B.S. • $21 • (10/31/1999) • **75**

Tokay Pinot Gris Alsace Sélection de Grains Nobles 1996: Big and full-bore, with a racy underpinning, this SGN shows marzipan, citrus and mature notes that turn crisp and awkward on the finish. Not for everyone. Best from 2001 through 2007.–B.S. • $65 • (10/31/1999) • **87**

Tokay Pinot Gris Alsace Sélection de Grains Nobles 1994: Fresh and vibrant, this rattles the palate with its acidity, keeping the smoke and peach flavors at the forefront. Sweet, but everything is well balanced, and the finish keeps pumping out the flavors. Drink now through 2002.–B.S. • $40 • (9/15/1998) • **88**

Tokay Pinot Gris Alsace Vendanges Tardives 1996: Exotic, showing quince and truffle and a firm, almost racy backbone, here's a rich Pinot Gris VT of depth and complexity. Should be a perfect foil for foie gras. Drink through 2005–B.S. • $44 • (10/31/1999) • **90**

SIRAN, CHATEAU

Margaux 1998: Berry and mineral aromas and flavors throughout. Medium- to full-bodied, with well-integrated tannins and a long finish. Tough little wine.–J.S. • $NA • (5/31/1999) (BT) • **85-89**

Margaux 1997: Decent berry and cherry character. Medium- to light-bodied. Light tannins. Drink now.–J.S. • $50 • (1/31/2000) • **83**

Margaux 1996: A lean and hard wine, but clean and fresh. Aromas of red currant and berry follow through to the palate, with medium tannins and a slightly hard finish. Needs a bit of age to mellow. Best after 2000.–J.S. • $35 • (1/31/1999) • **87**

Margaux 1995 • $25 • (1/31/1998) • **93**

Margaux 1994 • $25 • (1/31/1997) • **79**

Margaux 1993 • $23 Ⓐ • (1/31/1996) • **85**

Margaux 1991 • $15 • (3/31/1994) • **84**

Margaux 1990 • $30 Ⓐ • (3/31/1993) • **90**

Margaux 1989: Chewy and agreeable '89. Good, dark-ruby color, and smoke, berry and cherry aromas. Medium-bodied, with velvety tannins and a medium finish. Still needs time to open. (1989 Bordeaux horizontal tasting). Best after 2000.–J.S. • $33 Ⓐ • (5/31/1999) • **88**

Margaux 1988 • $30 Ⓐ • (6/30/1991) • **88**

Margaux 1985 • $15 • (9/30/1988) • **90**

Margaux 1982: Not as good as I hoped. Slightly rustic. Dark brick-red color, with a black center and an amber rim. Smoke, berry and earth aromas. Medium- to full-bodied, with very velvety tannins but a slightly dry finish. (1982 Bordeaux horizontal tasting). Drink now.–J.S. • $29 Ⓐ • (11/30/1998) • **85**

SIRENE DE GISCOURS, LA

Margaux 1996: Light and fruity, with good berry and cherry character. Medium- to light-bodied, with light tannins and a fruity finish. Delicious. Drink now through 2004.–J.S. • $14 • (1/31/1999) • **82**

Margaux 1995 • $14 • (1/31/1998) • **85**

SIRIUS

Bordeaux 1995 • $12 • (1/31/1998) • **86**

Bordeaux 1988 • $15 • (8/31/1991) • **77**

SIRUGUE & FILS, JEAN-LOUIS

Côte de Nuits-Villages Clos de la Belle Marguerite 1993 • $15 • (11/15/1995) • **83**

Côte de Nuits-Villages Clos de la Belle Marguerite 1990 • $10 • (6/15/1993) • **82**

Côte de Nuits-Villages Clos de la Belle Marguerite 1988 • $16 • (3/31/1991) • **83**

Gevrey-Chambertin 1993 • $25 • (11/15/1995) • **83**

Gevrey-Chambertin 1989 • $20 • (8/31/1992) • **80**

SMITH-HAUT-LAFITTE, CHATEAU

Pessac-Léognan 1999: Ripe berry and plum skin aromas. Medium-bodied, with well-integrated tannins and a smoky berry aftertaste.–J.S. • $NA • (1/01/2000) (BT) • **85-89**

Pessac-Léognan 1998: A slightly one-dimensional young red, with berry and mushroom character. Medium-bodied, with somewhat austere tannins and a medium finish. Too much wood.–J.S. • $NA • (5/31/1999) (BT) • **85-89**

Pessac-Léognan 1997: A wine with lovely tobacco, toasted oak and berry character. Medium in body, with silky tannins and a long, flavorful finish. Smith-Haut-Lafitte is really doing well. Drink now through 2004.–J.S. • $37 • (1/31/2000) • **88**

Pessac-Léognan 1996: Attractive aromas of chocolate and blackberry. Medium-bodied, with velvety tannins, but they turn slightly tough and dry on the finish. Too much new wood? Promises more on the nose than it delivers on the palate, like so many '96s. Best after 2000.–J.S. • $35 Ⓐ • (1/31/1999) • **86**

Pessac-Léognan 1995 • $38 Ⓐ • (1/31/1998) • **90**

Pessac-Léognan 1994 • $23 Ⓐ • (1/31/1997) • **86**

Pessac-Léognan 1993 • $25 • (1/31/1996) • **86**

Pessac-Léognan 1992 • $17 • (4/15/1995) • **84**

Pessac-Léognan 1991 • $17 • (3/31/1994) • **83**

Pessac-Léognan 1990 • $22 • (3/31/1993) • **93**

Pessac-Léognan 1989: Not representative of what this estate makes today. Drinkable, but shows a slightly volatile and unclean barrel component with an earthy, highly ripe fruit character. What happened? (1989 Bordeaux horizontal tasting). Drink now.–J.S. • $NA • (5/31/1999) • **78**

Pessac-Léognan 1987 • $15 • (5/15/1990) • **84**

Graves 1985 • $15 • (11/30/1988) • **89**

Graves 1982 • $18 • (8/31/1992) • **81**

Graves 1981 • $18 • (6/01/1984) • **79**

Pessac-Léognan White 1998: Attractive lemon, pineapple and vanilla character. Medium- to full-bodied, with plenty of fruit and a fresh finish. Delicious. Drink now through 2004.–J.S. • $35 • (2/29/2000) • **90**

Pessac-Léognan White 1996: Wonderful and flamboyant. Very ripe apple, banana and vanilla aromas with a hint of meringue. Full-bodied and round, with lots of coconut and fruit character on the finish. Drink now.–J.S. • $53 • (3/31/1999) • **90**

SOCIANDO-MALLET, CHATEAU

Haut-Médoc 1999: Very good concentration for the vintage. Aromatic, with plum, currant and tar character. Medium- to full-bodied, with velvety tannins and a medium finish.–J.S. • $NA • (1/01/2000) (BT) • **85-89**

Haut-Médoc 1998: Fruit aromas, with lots of tar. Medium- to full-bodied, with lots of tannins and a smoke and berry aftertaste. Slightly austere and herbal on the finish.–J.S. • $NA • (5/31/1999) (BT) • **85-89**

Haut-Médoc 1997: Very well done. Beautiful nose of ripe berry and raspberry with a smoky undertone. Medium- to full-bodied, with silky tannins, medium finish. Slightly hollow center palate. Drink now through 2005.–J.S. • $31 • (1/31/2000) • **88**

Haut-Médoc 1996: Dark-colored, with vanilla, spice and smoky fruit flavor. Medium-bodied, with firm tannins and a silky texture. A stylish wine, showing spicy character. Sociando did the business this year. Best after 2001.–J.S. • $30 Ⓐ • (1/31/1999) • **90**

Haut-Médoc 1995 • $32 Ⓐ • (1/31/1998) • **91**

Haut-Médoc 1994 • $21 Ⓐ • (1/31/1997) • **86**

Haut-Médoc 1993 • $25 • (1/31/1996) • **88**

Haut-Médoc 1992 • $20 • (4/15/1995) • **87**

Haut-Médoc 1991 • $17 • (3/31/1994) • **85**

Haut-Médoc 1990 • $55 Ⓐ • (3/31/1993) • **91**

Haut-Médoc 1989: Slightly one-dimensional but fresh and delicious. Dark-ruby color, and a lovely fresh berry, raspberry and floral nose. Medium-bodied, with silky tannins and a medium, fruity aftertaste. Give it a bit more time. (1989 Bordeaux horizontal tasting). Best after 2000.–J.S. • $46 Ⓐ • (5/31/1999) • **90**

Haut-Médoc 1988: One of the great values of the vintage considering its outstanding quality. Fresh aromas of mint and ripe fruit follow through on the palate. Full-bodied and quite tannic; needs time. (1988 Bordeaux horizontal tasting). Best after 2000.–J.S. • $31 Ⓐ • (11/30/1998) • **91**

Haut-Médoc 1987 • $15 • (5/15/1990) • **88**

Haut-Médoc 1986 • $50 • (11/30/1989) • **94**

Haut-Médoc 1985 • $23 • (10/15/1994) • **91**

Haut-Médoc 1984 • $11 • (3/31/1987) • **84**

Haut-Médoc 1983 • $24 • (10/15/1994) • **92**

Haut-Médoc 1982: A seriously good wine in this category, but not as good as I remember. Dark red color, with an inky center. Blackberry and earth aromas. Full-bodied and rich, with berry flavors and a silky finish. (1982 Bordeaux horizontal tasting). Drink now.–J.S. • $64 Ⓐ • (11/30/1998) • **89**

Haut-Médoc 1981 • $23 • (10/15/1994) • **88**

SOCIANDO-MALLET, LA DEMOISELLE DE

Haut-Médoc 1996: Good plum and strawberry aromas. Medium-bodied, with silky tannins and a fruity aftertaste. Elegant, though lacking a midpalate. Second label of Château Sociando-Mallet. Drink now.–J.S. • $15 • (1/31/1999) • **81**

Haut-Médoc 1995 • $15 • (1/31/1998) • **79**

Haut-Médoc 1992 • $17 • (4/15/1995) • **80**

Haut-Médoc 1989 • $21 • (3/15/1992) • **84**

FRANCE

SOLITUDE, DOMAINE DE LA

Pessac-Léognan 1998: A well-made, medium-bodied red, with chewy tannins and ripe berry and cherry character.–J.S. • $NA • (5/31/1999) (BT) • **85-89**

Pessac-Léognan 1996: Good concentration for the vintage, but slightly rustic and herbal. Medium- to full-bodied, with rough tannins and a dried-herb aftertaste. Needs time to mellow. Best after 2000.–J.S. • $NA • (1/31/1999) • **81**

Pessac-Léognan 1993 • $18 • (1/31/1996) • **77**

Pessac-Léognan White 1997: Wonderful apple, banana and fig aromas follow through to the palate. Medium- to full-bodied, with ripe fruit flavors and a medium finish. Needs a slightly firmer midpalate to be outstanding, but it's still delicious. Drink now.–J.S. • $NA • (9/30/1999) • **89**

Pessac-Léognan White 1996: Muscular and exciting. Tight and closed in, with lots to look forward to. Mineral, lemon and spice aromas and flavors go on and on on the palate. Medium- to full-bodied, with firm acidity and a long finish. Drink through 2005–J.S. • $NA • (3/31/1999) • **90**

SORIN, DOMAINE

Bandol 1995 • $25 • (3/31/1998) • **87**

Côtes de Provence 1997: Well defined and peppery-tasting, with red fruit, leather and tobacco notes that linger on the finish. A good, all-around red that would go great with grilled meats. Drink now through 2003.–K.M. • $13 • (6/15/2000) • **88**

Côtes de Provence 1994 • $13 • (10/31/1995) • **86**

Vin de Pays du Var Les Terres Rouges 1998: A medium-bodied, lively-tasting red, with delicious flavors of red plum and cassis plus lovely spice notes. Balanced, harmonious and light for the vintage, with an elegance reminiscent of Pinot Noir. Drink now.–K.M. • $8 • (6/15/2000) • **86**

SORREL, M.

Hermitage 1995: A ripe core of sweet cherry flavor is bright and appealing in this chewy red, but the firm, slightly astringent tannins clamp down on the finish and give it a rustic character. Concentrated, it might show better balance with age. Drink through 2005–T.M. • $33 • (11/15/1998) • **86**

Hermitage 1994 • $40 • (12/15/1996) • **83**

Hermitage Le Gréal 1994 • $60 • (12/15/1996) • **87**

SOUDARS, CHATEAU

Haut-Médoc 1998: Appealing currant and spice aromas. Medium-bodied, with medium tannins. A bit of a letdown on the light finish.–J.S. • $NA • (5/31/1999) (BT) • **80-84**

Haut-Médoc 1997: Too light really, with berry, tobacco character.–J.S. • $NA • (1/31/2000) • **79**

Haut-Médoc 1996: Interesting berry, grape-skin and tea aromas follow through on the palate, but this is slightly short and diluted on the finish.–J.S. • $17 • (1/31/1999) • **82**

Haut-Médoc 1995 • $15 • (1/31/1998) • **78**

Haut-Médoc 1994 • $NA • (1/31/1997) • **79**

Haut-Médoc 1992 • $15 • (4/15/1995) • **74**

Haut-Médoc 1991 • $15 • (3/31/1994) • **79**

Haut-Médoc 1990 • $18 • (3/31/1993) • **84**

Haut-Médoc 1989: A warm, autumnal wine that's ready to drink. Lovely plum, tobacco and berry aromas follow through to a medium-bodied and velvety palate. Medium-round tannins, with a sweet fruit aftertaste. (1989 Bordeaux horizontal tasting).–J.S. • $NA • (5/31/1999) • **85**

Haut-Médoc 1988 • $15 • (4/30/1991) • **88**

Haut-Médoc 1987 • $12 • (11/30/1989) • **77**

Haut-Médoc 1986 • $13 • (11/30/1989) • **79**

SOUFRANDISE, DOMAINE DE LA

Mâcon-Fuissé 1995 • $16 • (5/31/1997) • **86**

Mâcon-Fuissé Le Ronté 1997: Exotic for its gooseberry, kiwi, apricot, lime, grass and honey complexity, it's a bit tart, but the freshness of this medium-bodied white should complement fish. Drink now through 2001.–P.M. • $16 • (5/31/1999) • **85**

Mâcon-Fuissé Le Ronté 1996 • $14 • (5/31/1998) • **85**

Pouilly-Fuissé Clos la Soufrandise 1997: A medium-bodied white that smells and tastes like green apple skins, this is fresh and pure-tasting, and may be just the answer with fresh seafood. Drink now.–P.M. • $19 • (5/31/1999) • **83**

Pouilly-Fuissé Clos la Soufrandise 1996 • $17 • (5/31/1998) • **86**

Pouilly-Fuissé Levrouté 1995 • $29 • (5/31/1997) • **86**

Pouilly-Fuissé Levrouté Vieilles Vignes 1997: Ripe, full-bodied, golden-colored Pouilly, with dried fig, tropical and burnt honey notes. Shows lots of personality, as it's subtly off-dry in its richness on the opulent, clean and balanced finish. Drink now through 2003.–P.M. • $25 • (5/31/1999) • **90**

Pouilly-Fuissé Vieilles Vignes 1997: Firm, even tough in texture, with oak, lemon and green apple character. Some mineral notes smooth out the finish. Should soften with age. Drink through 2003–P.M. • $23 • (5/31/1999) • **82**

Pouilly-Fuissé Vieilles Vignes 1996 • $21 • (5/31/1998) • **89**

Pouilly-Fuissé Vieilles Vignes 1995 • $25 • (5/31/1997) • **87**

SOULEZ, PIERRE & YVES

Savennières Moelleux Clos du Papillon Cuvée d'Avant 1996 • $24 • (6/15/1998) • **88**

SOUMADE, DOMAINE LA

Côtes du Rhône-Villages Rasteau 1995 • $15 • (10/15/1997) • **88**

Côtes du Rhône-Villages Rasteau 1986 • $11 • (2/28/1990) • **82**

Côtes du Rhône-Villages Rasteau Cuvée Confiance 1997: Firm, a medium-bodied '97 red with some grip of fruit, tannins, spice. Rustic, but appealing for its gumption and lingering, pure finish. Drink now through 2002.–P.M. • $22 • (11/15/1999) • **84**

Côtes du Rhône-Villages Rasteau Cuvée Confiance 1996: Ripe, rich and balanced, medium-bodied, flavorful and deeply satisfying, its tannins well-integrated with the plum, black cherry, blackberry and mineral character of this well-made, concentrated wine. 50 cases imported. Drink now through 2004.–P.M. • $20 • (11/15/1998) • **87**

Côtes du Rhône-Villages Rasteau Cuvée Prestige 1997: A '97 with some guts. Ripe and pretty, a supple red with black cherry, smoke and spice flavors that persist to the lingering, firm finish. Drink now.–P.M. • $16 • (11/15/1999) • **84**

Côtes du Rhône-Villages Rasteau Cuvée Prestige 1996: Oak-accented style, with fancy mocha and Oriental spice, plus some black currant and plum. Has personality. Fairly short finish. Drink through 2001–P.M. • $18 • (11/15/1998) • **81**

SOURDAIS, SERGE & BRUNO

Chinon Les Cornuelles Vieille Vigne 1996: The aromas are reticent and brooding, but this monolith is packed with dense, sweet cherry and raspberry notes. Medium- to full-bodied and firmly structured. The tannins are a bit dry on the finish, yet the fruit is there. Needs time to integrate. Drink through 2005–B.S. • $17 • (10/31/1998) • **91**

SOUTARD, CHATEAU

St.-Emilion 1989 • $38 Ⓐ • (9/15/1993) • **87**

St.-Emilion 1985 • $32 Ⓐ • (5/15/1988) • **85**

St.-Emilion 1982 • $NA • (5/15/1989) • **84**

St.-Emilion 1961 • $22 • (4/30/1996) • **85**

SOUTIRAN, A.

Brut Blanc de Blancs Champagne NV: A lean, crisp blanc de blancs, packing a lot of flavor on a sleek frame. Pear, honey and citrus are the main themes, densely textured and long on the finish. Drink now through 2003.–B.S. • $45 • (2/29/2000) • **89**

Brut Champagne NV: A warm, inviting sparkler, full of baked apple and bread dough notes. Medium-bodied and smooth, it finishes in a crisp, matter-of-fact way, with a lingering aftertaste. Drink now through 2002.–B.S. • $40 • (2/29/2000) • **87**

Brut Champagne Millésimé 1995: Aromatic, exuding aromas of baking bread, followed by flavors of cherry and pencil shavings. Firmly structured, with a subtle power, this is a great aperitif. Drink now through 2004.–B.S. • $60 • (2/29/2000) • **89**

Key: SS—Spectator Selection. CS—Cellar Selection. HR—Highly Recommended. $NA—Price not available. (BT)—Barrel tasting. Ⓐ—Auction Price.
For a key to the tasters' initials, see "How to Use These Listings."
Dates in parentheses represent the issues in which the ratings were published.

FRANCE

Brut Rosé Champagne NV: Round and subtly flavored, with strawberry, cherry and currant notes on a soft, easygoing framework. Drink now.–B.S. • $45 • (2/29/2000) • **86**

SPARR, PIERRE

Alsace Cuvée d'Alsace 1997: Very ripe and perfumed, showing rose, raisin, peach and apricot character. Soft and forward, with a touch of citrusy acidity on the finish, it's ideal for summer picnics. Drink now.–B.S. • $9 • (9/15/1999) • **84**

Brut Blanc de Blancs France Marquis de Perlade NV • $10 • (8/31/1997) • **77**

Brut Blanc de Noirs Crémant d'Alsace Réserve NV • $18 • (3/31/1998) • **84**

Brut Crémant d'Alsace Réserve NV • $15 • (5/31/1997) • **83**

Cuvée d'Alsace 1996 • $10 • (3/31/1998) • **82**

Gewürztraminer Alsace Carte d'Or 1997: Well-defined aromas and flavors of roses and tropical fruit in this rich, yet elegant Gewürz. Texture is almost unctuous, with just enough acidity and a touch of grapefruit peel at the end to pull everything into focus.–B.S. • $12 • (9/15/1998) • **87**

Gewürztraminer Alsace Carte d'Or 1996 • $10 • (11/15/1997) • **85**

Gewürztraminer Alsace Grand Cru Brand Sélection de Grains Nobles 1994 • $48/500 ml. • (3/31/1998) • **87**

Gewürztraminer Alsace Grand Cru Brand Vendange Tardive 1996: Textbook Gewürztraminer aromas of rose and litchi mark this lively, elegant VT. On the lean, dry side, with concentrated flavors and firm structure aided by a hint of bitterness on the finish. Drink now through 2004.–B.S. • $42 • (9/30/1999) • **90**

Gewürztraminer Alsace Grand Cru Mambourg Vendange Tardive 1996: Exotic in aroma, mango, papaya, passion fruit and a slight decadence lead off, followed by sweetness on the palate, with honey and spice. More up-front at this stage, it tightens on the finish, but give it time. Drink through 2005–B.S. • $40 • (9/30/1999) • **90**

Gewürztraminer Alsace Grand Cru Sporen 1997: Frankly sweet, this is more like a VT, soft and loosely knit with modest grapefruit and brown sugar flavors, finishing on the coarse side.–B.S. • $26 • (10/31/1999) • **78**

Gewürztraminer Alsace Grand Cru Sporen 1996: Needs time, showing an overpowering character of corrupt fruit, marzipan and marmalade, with a sweet prune/fig note. Austere and a bit tough on the finish. Drink through 2004–B.S. • $28 • (9/30/1999) • **88**

Gewürztraminer Alsace Réserve 1998: Intriguing aromas of smoke, roses, spice and lanolin weave throughout a silky texture in this complex white. Deftly balanced and building in intensity on the palate, this is fascinating stuff. Drink now through 2001.–B.S. • $14 • (9/30/1999) • **88**

Gewürztraminer Alsace Réserve 1997: Like smelling a bouquet of roses, this rich, fleshy white has flavors ranging from apricot to honey, good depth and persistence, and a lasting finish. Drink now.–B.S. • $15 • (9/15/1998) • **87**

Gewürztraminer Alsace Réserve 1996 • $12 • (11/15/1997) • **89**

Muscat Alsace Grand Cru Froehn 1997: The piercing scent and flavor is reminiscent of pine, with a dash of spice and flowers for accent. Richly textured and slightly sweet, it turns dry on the finish. Drink now through 2002.–B.S. • $25 • (10/15/1999) • **86**

Pinot Blanc Alsace Diamant d'Alsace Réserve 1998: Something wrong here. Smells musty. Fizzy, refermenting in bottle. Tasted four times, with consistent notes.–B.S. • $10 • (9/30/1999) • **55**

Pinot Blanc Alsace Diamant d'Alsace Réserve 1997: A crisp, refreshing 1997 Pinot Blanc, with lemon and apple notes and moderate concentration.–B.S. • $10 • (9/15/1998) • **83**

Pinot Blanc Alsace Diamant d'Alsace Réserve 1996 • $8 • (11/15/1997) • **87**

Pinot Gris Alsace Carte d'Or 1998: Apricot and a smoky note highlight this medium-bodied, crisp Pinot Gris. It finishes on the lean side, but it's young, so give it a few months to settle down. Drink through 2003–B.S. • $12 • (10/31/1999) • **85**

Pinot Gris Alsace Carte d'Or 1997: Smoke, peach and nut aromas and flavors are featured in this fat, almost oily white that shows modest concentration and length.–B.S. • $12 • (9/15/1998) • **83**

Pinot Gris Alsace Réserve 1998: A lovely white whose vanilla, peach and smoke flavors fill the mouth. The unctuous texture is balanced by moderate acidity, finishing with a hint of alcohol. Drink now through 2001.–B.S. • $14 • (10/31/1999) • **86**

Pinot Noir Alsace Prestige 1997: Light and brownish in color, with decent forest floor, spice and smoke notes.–B.S. • $20 • (1/01/2000) • **79**

Pinot Noir Alsace Prestige 1995 • $17 • (11/15/1997) • **83**

Pinot Noir Alsace Rouge d'Ottrott 1997: Reminiscent of meat, game and leather with spices for grace notes, bright acidity and good concentration, this offers a distinctly Alsace version of Pinot Noir. Drink now through 2001.–B.S. • $24 • (10/15/1999) • **87**

Riesling Alsace Carte d'Or 1997: There's plenty of lime-scented, apple and mineral character locked up in this vibrant, moderately structured Riesling that shows balance and length. Drink now.–B.S. • $11 • (9/15/1998) • **86**

Riesling Alsace Carte d'Or 1996 • $9 • (11/15/1997) • **87**

Riesling Alsace Grand Cru Altenberg de Bergheim 1996: Lovely aromas of beeswax, apple and honey introduce this upright Riesling; its tart acidity masks the rich texture now but will allow it to age gracefully. Good, spicy aftertaste. Best from 2001 through 2007.–B.S. • $27 • (8/31/1999) • **88**

Riesling Alsace Grand Cru Brand 1997: Dense and rich, with only a hint of quince flavor right now, this white shows good balance and a firm structure, ending on a citrus note. May open with time. Drink now through 2003.–B.S. • $28 • (6/15/2000) • **84**

Riesling Alsace Grand Cru Brand 1996: A ripe, tropical-scented, full-bore Riesling that displays its lanolin and quince flavors on a rich, dense texture underscored by racy acidity. It's lost the flush of youth, yet the flavors are still submerged. Best from 2001 through 2008.–B.S. • $27 • (8/31/1999) • **92**

Riesling Alsace Grand Cru Mambourg 1996: Lean, dry and racy, there's a laser beam of acidity driving the pine, mineral and quince flavors in this *grand cru*. Fresh, concentrated and densely textured, it shows promise for the future. Best from 2001 through 2006.–B.S. • $25 • (10/31/1999) • **89**

Riesling Alsace Grand Cru Schoenenbourg 1996: Rock solid, firm and backward, this racy '96 is packed with lime, mineral and apple flavors that will require years to soften and reveal their charm. Great intensity and focus. Best from 2002 through 2010.–B.S. • $25 • (9/15/1998) • **90**

Riesling Alsace Grand Cru Schoenenbourg Vendange Tardive 1996: Bursting with apricot aromas and flavors, this has an extra dimension of ripeness to the passion fruit and papaya, all held together by a firm acidic backbone. Racy, but the richness beneath will emerge with time. Drink through 2006–B.S. • $39 • (8/31/1999) • **89**

Riesling Alsace Medaille d'Or Réserve 1997: Banana is the dominant aroma, followed by flavors of apple and rosewater. A bit dilute, it ends lean and tart. Drink now through 2001.–B.S. • $13 • (8/31/1999) • **81**

Riesling Alsace Réserve 1998: Broad strokes of almond and apple mark this straightforward, light- to medium-bodied white, picking up a hint of grapefruit peel on the finish. Drink now through 2001.–B.S. • $13 • (5/31/2000) • **84**

Riesling Alsace Réserve 1997: Lively, but this simple white sustains only a one-dimensional apple flavor. Drink now.–B.S. • $12 • (9/15/1998) • **79**

Riesling Alsace Sélection de Grains Nobles 1989 • $98 • (3/31/1998) • **92**

Savagnin Rosé Klevener de Heiligenstein 1996 • $15 • (3/31/1998) • **84**

Tokay Pinot Gris Alsace Carte d'Or 1996 • $10 • (11/15/1997) • **86**

Tokay Pinot Gris Alsace Grand Cru Brand 1997: This has complexity of flavor, and thanks to the moderate acidity and bitter almond finish, the apricot, chamomile and smoke flavors keep pulsing throughout. Drink now through 2002.–B.S. • $27 • (10/31/1999) • **87**

Tokay Pinot Gris Alsace Grand Cru Brand 1996: Very ripe, even tropical, showing apricot, peach and floral aromas and flavors. There's sweetness and a thick texture, but it's well balanced by acidity, finishing almost dry, with a touch of bitterness. Drink now through 2003.–B.S. • $28 • (9/15/1999) • **86**

Tokay Pinot Gris Alsace Grand Cru Brand Sélection de Grains Nobles 1996: VT in style and medium sweet, underscored by good acidity, exuding apricot, passion fruit and pineapple, with hints of citrus. Lean and intense, yet not that long on the finish. Drink now through 2004.–B.S. • $79 • (10/31/1999) • **87**

Tokay Pinot Gris Alsace Grand Cru Mambourg Sélection des Grains Nobles 1996: Focused and ripe, featuring pear, apricot and passion fruit aromas and flavors up front, all on a moderately sweet, rich frame, with enough acidity to keep it all lively. Finishes on a smoky note. Drink now through 2002.–B.S. • $60/500 ml. • (6/15/2000) • **91**

Tokay Pinot Gris Alsace Prestige 1997: Open and forward, this '97 white is clean and offers pear and apricot accented by smoke in a straightforward, generous style. Drink now.–B.S. • $20 • (6/15/2000) • **84**

Tokay Pinot Gris Alsace Prestige 1996: Quite dry and slightly austere in profile, and full of smoke, mineral and peach notes, this has verve and cut with just enough flesh to round it out. Lovely balance and intensity. Drink now through 2006.–B.S. • $22 • (9/15/1999) • **89**

Tokay Pinot Gris Alsace Réserve 1997: Extremely ripe, bordering on late-harvest, this Pinot Gris is unctuous, with pleasant aromas of quince, but ultimately top-heavy and a touch sweet. Drink now.–B.S. • $15 • (9/15/1998) • **82**

Tokay Pinot Gris Alsace Réserve 1996 • $12 • (11/15/1997) • **91**

Tokay Pinot Gris Alsace Sélection de Grains Nobles 1997: Sweet and immediately appealing yet straightforward, showing candied flavors of almond, apple and honey on a soft, up-front structure. Drink now through 2003.–B.S. • $79 • (6/15/2000) • **87**

Tokay Pinot Gris Alsace Vendanges Tardives 1996: An elegant VT, this displays fine structure, excellent balance and nuances of quince, pear and lanolin followed by a long aftertaste. The structure has the upper hand today, but give this the benefit of time. Drink through 2004–B.S. • $40 • (10/31/1999) • **88**

Vin de Table Français Charisma 1997: Round and ripe, with good pear and baked apple flavors, which carry through appealingly to the finish. There are nice white pepper notes mixed in. Made from Chardonnay. Drink now.–K.M. • $26 • (11/15/1999) • **82**

SPIELMANN

Alsace Gentil Cuvée Reservée 1997: Straightforward almond and cherry flavors combine with a rich texture in a balanced, easygoing style. Drink now.–B.S. • $13 • (10/15/1999) • **80**

Gewürztraminer Alsace Blosenberg 1996: Exotic aromas of quince, passion fruit, apricot and grapefruit are supported by firm acidity in this kaleidoscopic white. Dense, rich and long in the mouth, with a distinct white pepper aftertaste. Drink now through 2002.–B.S. • $18 • (10/31/1999) • **88**

Pinot Blanc Alsace Bergheim Réserve 1997: Round and a touch sweet, this is pleasant, without much delineation or depth. Drink now.–B.S. • $15 • (10/15/1999) • **80**

Pinot Blanc Alsace Réserve 1996: On the lean, tart side, with some green apple and lemon flavors.–B.S. • $14 • (9/15/1998) • **78**

Riesling Alsace Grand Cru Kanzlerberg 1996: A live wire of a Riesling, providing plenty of verve and snap without the requisite concentration and depth, though it is difficult to taste at this stage. Best from 2001 through 2008.–B.S. • $23 • (10/15/1999) • **87**

Tokay Pinot Gris Alsace Bergheim Blosenberg 1997: A bit dull, showing mature notes of earth, almond and marzipan. There's good crispness and structure, but a touch of coarseness on the finish.–B.S. • $18 • (10/31/1999) • **79**

STRIFFILING, BERNARD

Morgon Domaine de Croix de Chèvre 1996: This lean, crisp red is rather light-bodied, but the flavors of cherry, spice and smoke show good intensity, and a core of acidity keeps it firm and lively. Drink now.–T.M. • $12 • (7/31/1998) • **84**

STUART, MARIE

Brut Champagne 1995: Fresh, attractive and easy to enjoy, offering bright citrus flavors, a slight sweetness and lively bubbles. Drink now through 2005. • $39 • (11/15/1999) • **87**

SUAU, CHATEAU

Barsac 1998: A wine of good concentration, with lots of spice, honey and fruit character. Full-bodied, sweet and spicy, with a medium finish. Perhaps better next year.–J.S. • $NA • (1/01/1999) (BT) • **85-89**

Barsac 1996: Rather light, with pleasant clover honey, lemon and apple character. Medium body. Lightly sweet. Delicate finish. Drink now.–J.S. • $NA • (5/15/2000) • **85**

Cadillac 1996: Beautiful, with apple, peach and cream aromas and flavors. Full-bodied and medium sweet, with a fresh, delightful finish. Drink now through 2005.–J.S. • $22 • (7/31/1999) • **88**

Premières Côtes de Bordeaux Élevé en Fûts de Chêne 1996: Bright aromas of licorice and berry, with hints of bark. Medium-bodied, with velvety tannins and a light finish. Drink now.–J.S. • $14 • (7/31/1999) • **83**

SUDUIRAUT, CHATEAU

Sauternes 1998: Subtle Sauternes, with spice, honey and botrytis character. Medium-bodied, very sweet, with a fresh finish.–J.S. • $NA • (1/01/1999) (BT) • **90-94**

Sauternes 1997: An outstanding Sauternes, with wonderful aromas of cream, caramel and honey. Full-bodied, with a light sweetness and a long vanilla and fruit finish. A beauty. Best after 2001.–J.S. • $55 • (1/31/2000) • **90**

Sauternes 1995 • $25 Ⓐ • (4/30/1998) • **90**
Sauternes 1990 • $33 Ⓐ • (4/15/1995) • **93**
Sauternes 1989 • $54 Ⓐ • (4/15/1995) • **92**
Sauternes 1986 • $27 Ⓐ • (12/31/1989) • **85**
Sauternes 1985 • $NA • (11/30/1988) • **81**
Sauternes 1984 • $22 • (11/30/1988) • **81**
Sauternes 1983 • $42 Ⓐ • (4/15/1995) • **88**
Sauternes 1982 • $36 Ⓐ • (11/30/1988) • **83**
Sauternes 1979 • $30 • (11/30/1988) • **86**
Sauternes 1978 • $22 • (11/30/1988) • **78**
Sauternes 1976 • $57 Ⓐ • (11/30/1988) • **77**
Sauternes 1975 • $46 Ⓐ • (11/30/1988) • **84**
Sauternes 1972 • $25 • (11/30/1988) • **77**
Sauternes 1970 • $53 Ⓐ • (11/30/1988) • **81**
Sauternes 1969 • $70 • (11/30/1988) • **88**
Sauternes 1959 • $251 Ⓐ • (11/30/1988) • **93**
Sauternes 1947 • $354 Ⓐ • (5/31/1997) • **85**
Sauternes 1928 • $NA • (11/30/1988) • **90**
Sauternes Crème de Tête 1989 • $NA • (4/15/1995) • **96**

Key: SS—Spectator Selection. CS—Cellar Selection. HR—Highly Recommended. $NA—Price not available. (BT)—Barrel tasting. Ⓐ—Auction Price. For a key to the tasters' initials, see "How to Use These Listings."
Dates in parentheses represent the issues in which the ratings were published.

SUNFLOWER VALLEY

Chardonnay Vin de Pays d'Oc 1996 • $7 • (3/31/1998) • **83**
Merlot Vin de Pays d'Oc 1996 • $7 • (3/31/1998) • **82**
Syrah Vin de Pays d'Oc 1996 • $7 • (4/30/1998) • **85**

SURONDE, CHATEAU DE

Quarts de Chaume 1996: An exaggerated style that's nonetheless impressive, this white, almost mahogany in color, is very thick on the palate, with intense honey and dried pineapple flavors. Very sweet, with just enough acidity to keep it balanced. If you like blockbusters, this is for you. Drink now through 2005.–T.M. • $65 • (6/30/1999) • **90**

Quarts de Chaume 1995 • $57 • (5/31/1998) • **90**

Quarts de Chaume Trie Victor & Joseph 1996: This rich, intense white shows a dark gold color and powerful aromas and flavors of raisin, honey and spice. It has impressive ripeness and concentration, and what it lacks in grace it makes up for in power. Drink now through 2010.–T.M. • $75/500 ml. • (6/30/1999) • **92**

Quarts de Chaume Trie Victor & Joseph 1995 • $43/500 ml. • (5/31/1998) • **93**

TABORDET, YVON & PASCAL

Pouilly-Fumé 1996 • $14 • (6/15/1998) • **89**

TAILLEFER, CHATEAU

Pomerol 1998: A big and tannic young wine that puckers the palate. Full-bodied and fruity, with earth and berry character. A bit rustic, but you have to like it.–J.S. • $NA • (5/31/1999) (BT) • **90-94**

Pomerol 1997: Starts off very well. Lots of blackberry and wet earth aromas. Medium-bodied, with firm tannins and a medium to light finish. Best from 2001 through 2004.–J.S. • $NA • (1/31/2000) • **87**

Pomerol 1996: Dark color. Lovely floral, blackberry and cherry aromas. Medium- to full-bodied, with lots of berry, chocolate and spice flavor, but slightly hollow midpalate. Very pretty '96. Impressive for this estate. Best after 2000.–J.S. • $NA • (1/31/1999) • **88**

Pomerol 1995: Dark-colored, with intense aromas of blackberries and dark chocolate. Full-bodied, with big velvety tannins, loads of fruit and a long finish. Amazing quality for this estate. Best from 2004 through 2008.–J.S. • $NA • (9/15/1998) • **91**

Pomerol 1992 • $19 • (4/15/1995) • **77**
Pomerol 1988 • $22 • (6/30/1991) • **87**
Pomerol 1985 • $24 • (6/30/1988) • **81**
Pomerol 1982 • $23 • (5/15/1989) • **85**

TAIN L'HERMITAGE, CAVE DE

Cornas Les Nobles Rives 1996: Smooth and a bit one-dimensional; medium-bodied, with game and red berry character of modest intensity. Slightly short, drying finish.–P.M. • $13 • (8/31/1999) • **79**

Cornas Les Nobles Rives 1995: Refined and elegant, this racy red offers lovely smoke, grilled meat, blackberry and cassis, even a minty, character, and supersupple tannins on a lively framework of good acidity. Well balanced and harmonious. Drink now through 2010.–P.M. • $15 • (11/15/1998) • **92**

Cornas Michel Courtial 1986 • $11 • (7/31/1989) • **89**

Crozes-Hermitage Les Hauts du Fief 1996: Light and diluted, with strawberry and licorice notes and a watery, cherrylike finish.–P.M. • $13 • (10/31/1999) • **72**

Crozes-Hermitage Les Hauts du Fief 1995: Thick and rich, with fresh, vibrant and pure red- and blackberry character. A slight vegetal note creeps up, but overall, it's a fun, fruit-driven wine. Drink now through 2003.–P.M. • $15 • (11/15/1998) • **84**

Crozes-Hermitage Les Nobles Rives 1998: Sweet-tasting and ripe, but veering toward a jammy style (strawberry jam, for instance). Straightforward and fruity. Serve chilled.–P.M. • $12 • (12/15/1999) • **78**

Crozes-Hermitage Les Nobles Rives 1997: Rich, thick, opulent and ripe. Tastes ultrasweet, delivering a slightly hot feel on the palate, but also loads of cassis, raspberry, prune, spice, cinnamon. Tannins are a bit tough on the finish. Will improve with cellaring. Drink through 2003.–P.M. • $12 • (11/15/1998) • **89**

Crozes-Hermitage Les Nobles Rives 1996: Light in color, with a green and herbal aroma profile, delivering modest fruit and mostly tart texture.–P.M. • $12 • (10/15/1998) • **73**

Crozes-Hermitage Les Nobles Rives 1995 • $11 • (10/15/1997) • **75**

Crozes-Hermitage White Les Nobles Rives 1998: There's ripe fruit here, but it's marred by an odd, crisp, herbaceous matchstick character.–P.M. • $13 • (8/31/1999) • **75**

Crozes-Hermitage White Les Nobles Rives 1996: Elegant and racy, with citrus-spiked acidity nicely balanced by ripe fruit (pear, tropical, applesauce and glazed bitter orange). Medium-bodied, with a lingering and succulent finish. Drink now.–P.M. • $12 • (10/15/1998) • **86**

Hermitage Les Nobles Rives 1996: Already tastes of mature flavors—game, mushroom, leather. Pleasant and vibrant, with a long, elegant finish. Drink now through 2002.–P.M. • $30 • (9/15/1999) • **87**

Hermitage Les Nobles Rives 1995: Made in a crafty new-oak style, with lots of floral, toasted bread, currant and blackberry character. Medium-bodied and suave, with velvety, ripe tannins, it has good intensity on the finish, partly due to the smoked wood flavors. Drink now through 2007.–P.M. • $29 • (11/15/1998) • **92**

Hermitage Michel Courtial 1986 • $15 • (3/31/1990) • **89**

Hermitage White Les Nobles Rives 1998: A gorgeous white that's almost tannic, with a showy, toasty, smoky, lemony way. Offers loads of fruit, honey and fancy wood accents. Full-bodied and well made, it should improve with time. Not imported into the U.S. Drink now through 2008.–P.M. • $NA • (1/01/2000) • **90**

Hermitage White Les Nobles Rives 1997: The fruit has soaked up the heavy oak like a sponge, so expect toasty, burning, smoked barrel flavors along with the taste of grapes. Hot finish, too.–P.M. • $30 • (8/31/1999) • **79**

Hermitage White Les Nobles Rives 1996: Very lush and ripe, honeyed as can be, showing a supple texture that's to die for. Offers layers of honey, peach, pineapple and dried figs in an almost ethereal package. Full-bodied, with a long, harmonious finish.–P.M. • $29 • (9/15/1998) • **93**

St.-Joseph Les Nobles Rives 1998: Lovely ripeness in this sweet-tasting, medium-bodied St.-Joseph. Sings of blackberry flavors supported by black pepper, cinnamon and Earl Grey notes. Well-integrated tannins and acidity make for a balanced, lingering finish. Drink now through 2003.–P.M. • $15 • (12/15/1999) • **87**

St.-Joseph Les Nobles Rives 1997: Ripe and sweet-tasting, a satisfying wine, packed with wild berry and blueberry, showing a real *goût de terroir*. Fans out with the most velvety tannins, delivering plenty of wet earth and currant on the lingering finish. Drink now through 2006.–P.M. • $15 • (11/15/1998) • **90**

St.-Joseph Les Nobles Rives 1996: Fresh, zesty, vibrant and quite sweet-tasting, this is a food wine. Of medium body, with nice raspberry, floral and black cherry character. A bit short on the finish. Drink now through 2002.–P.M. • $15 • (11/15/1998) • **86**

St.-Joseph Les Nobles Rives 1995 • $15 • (10/15/1997) • **72**

St.-Joseph White Les Nobles Rives 1998: Tastes fresh and zesty, with lemon, almond and pear; a fairly rustic wine, but juicy nonetheless. Drink now.–P.M. • $16 • (8/31/1999) • **84**

St.-Joseph White Les Nobles Rives 1996: Seductive, ripe and clean, showing delicious dried pineapple, fresh apricot, mandarin orange and lemon zest character, a full body, a soft texture and an oily finish. A good aperitif at room temperature. Drink now.–P.M. • $15 • (11/15/1998) • **89**

St.-Péray Les Nobles Rives 1997: Fresh and balanced, this smooth-textured white delivers decent pear, hay, wet stone notes. Drink now.–P.M. • $11 • (11/15/1998) • **83**

TAITTINGER

Brut Blanc de Blancs Champagne Comtes de Champagne 1993: An elegant style. Crisp fruit flavors blend with subtle spicy-toasty accents and a rich mousse. Drink now through 2001. • $172 • (10/15/1999) • **89**

Brut Blanc de Blancs Champagne Comtes de Champagne 1990: A fresh and vibrant Champagne, with fresh dough aromas, bright lemon and butter flavors and a lively texture that seems to propel the flavors to a lingering finish. Delicious. Drink now through 2003. • $130 Ⓐ • (12/15/1998) • **90**

Brut Champagne La Française NV: Substantive, with a posh texture and ample fruit flavors accented by vanilla and almond on the lingering finish. Tasted twice, with consistent notes. Drink now. • $42 • (9/15/1999) • **89**

Brut Champagne Millésimé 1992: An inviting, rich-textured brut with ample pear and citrus flavors accented by honey and toast. Fine balance keeps it singing on the finish. Drink now through 2001. • $55 • (10/15/1999) • **89**

Brut Champagne Millésimé 1991 • $52 • (11/30/1997) • **87**

Brut Champagne Millésimé 1990 • $52 • (11/15/1996) • **90**

Brut Rosé Champagne Comtes de Champagne 1993: Ripe fruit flavors distinguish this bright copper-colored rosé. It's dramatic and generous in flavor, firm and well balanced, with a promising future. Drink through 2005 • $71 Ⓐ • (10/15/1999) • **89**

Brut Rosé Champagne Comtes de Champagne 1991 • $150 • (12/31/1996) • **87**

Brut Rosé Champagne Prestige NV: Truly vibrant and refreshing, an intensely fruity Champagne with bright cherry and cranberry flavors, lively bubbles and a lingering tangy finish. Drink now through 2001. • $51 • (10/15/1999) • **89**

TAIX, PATRICE

Cabernet Sauvignon Vin de Pays des Côtes de Thongue Charnu 1998: Quite chewy, with a slightly lifted aroma. Flavors of cherry and red plum have cinnamon notes. Drink now.–K.M. • $7 • (6/15/2000) • **82**

Merlot Vin de Pays des Côtes de Thongue Charnu 1998: Firm and expressive, with nice concentration and flavors of plum, chocolate and espresso. Brickish notes liven up the finish. Drink now.–K.M. • $7 • (6/15/2000) • **84**

TALBOT, CHATEAU

St.-Julien 1999: Very grapey aromas, with hints of licorice and berry. Medium- to full-bodied, with good tannins, but falls away quickly on the finish.–J.S. • $NA • (1/01/2000) (BT) • **85-89**

St.-Julien 1998: A bit lean for Talbot, but shows some good blackberry character. Slightly herbal fruit. Medium-bodied, with a medium finish and somewhat aggressive tannins.–J.S. • $NA • (5/31/1999) (BT) • **85-89**

St.-Julien 1997: A rather meager wine with decent cherry and herbal character. Not very good for Talbot. Tasted twice, with consistent notes. Drink now.–J.S. • $33 • (1/31/2000) • **81**

St.-Julien 1996: Pretty aromas of berries and wet earth. Full-bodied, with firm tannins and a long aftertaste of mineral and spice. Closed and firm at the moment; needs time to open. Best after 2003.–J.S. • $31 Ⓐ • (1/31/1999) • **90**

St.-Julien 1995 • $38 Ⓐ • (1/31/1998) • **87**

St.-Julien 1994 • $38 Ⓐ • (1/31/1997) • **87**

St.-Julien 1993 • $30 Ⓐ • (1/31/1996) • **86**

St.-Julien 1992 • $20 • (4/15/1995) • **75**

St.-Julien 1991 • $22 • (3/31/1994) • **78**

St.-Julien 1990 • $55 Ⓐ • (3/31/1993) • **93**

St.-Julien 1989: A round and velvety-textured '89 just starting to reach its peak. Slightly rustic. Dark-ruby color. Blackberry and dried red berries. Full-bodied, with chewy tannins and a chocolate, plum aftertaste. (1989 Bordeaux horizontal tasting).–J.S. • $58 Ⓐ • (5/31/1999) • **88**

St.-Julien 1988: Perhaps this is an off-bottle, because I remember this as tasting a lot better. Impressive ripe fruit on the nose and palate, but with a slightly wet wool and old wood character. (1988 Bordeaux horizontal tasting). Drink now.–J.S. • $52 Ⓐ • (11/30/1998) • **82**

St.-Julien 1987 • $19 • (5/15/1990) • **85**

St.-Julien 1986 • $80 Ⓐ • (5/31/1989) • **91**

St.-Julien 1985 • $54 Ⓐ • (10/15/1994) • **90**

St.-Julien 1984 • $19 • (5/15/1987) • **80**

St.-Julien 1983 • $28 • (10/15/1994) • **90**

St.-Julien 1982: Not what I expected from the '82 Talbot, which is usually outstanding. Dark ruby center, with a garnet edge. Berry, mushroom and leaf character. Full-bodied, with sweet, ripe fruit and plenty of tobacco and cherry aftertaste. At its peak. (1982 Bordeaux horizontal tasting). Drink now.–J.S. • $99 Ⓐ • (11/30/1998) • **86**

St.-Julien 1981 • $36 Ⓐ • (10/15/1994) • **85**

St.-Julien 1979 • $NA • (10/15/1989) • **84**

St.-Julien 1961 • $101 Ⓐ • (4/30/1996) • **88**

St.-Julien 1959 • $437 Ⓐ • (10/15/1990) • **86**

St.-Julien 1947 • $144 Ⓐ • (5/31/1997) • **83**

St.-Julien 1945 • $325 • (11/30/1995) • **81**

TALMARD, DOMAINE

Mâcon-Chardonnay 1997: Ripe and fresh, offering pineapple, mango, honey and pear tart notes, turning a bit tart on the finish. Drink now through 2001.–P.M. • $10 • (5/31/1999) • **85**

Mâcon-Chardonnay 1995 • $9 • (1/31/1997) • **74**

TALUAU, JOEL & CLARISSE

St.-Nicolas de Bourgueil 1985 •$12 • (4/15/1988) • **71**

St.-Nicolas de Bourgueil Cuvée du Domaine 1995 • $15 • (6/15/1997) • **85**

St.-Nicolas de Bourgueil Cuvée du Domaine 1993 • $15 • (12/15/1995) • **83**

TANESSE, CHATEAU

Bordeaux White 1998: Plenty of apple, cream and celery character. Medium-bodied, with good acidity and a light, very fresh finish. Drink now.–J.S. • $NA • (2/29/2000) • **85**

Premières Côtes de Bordeaux 1997: Yikes. Diluted. Some berry character, but hard to get excited about overall.–J.S. • $NA • (1/31/2000) • **74**

Premières Côtes de Bordeaux 1994 • $10 • (1/31/1997) • **70**

Premières Côtes de Bordeaux 1992 • $NA • (4/15/1995) • **79**

TARDIEU-LAURENT

Bandol Vieilles Vignes 1995: Smells like pipe-tobacco and tastes of dried red cherry and plum, with some interesting smoky notes as well. A rustic style that packs plenty of tannin, but it's still lively despite its age. Should go great with grilled meats and poultry. Finishes on a leathery, gamy note. Drink through 2005–K.M. • $30 • (12/31/1999) • **87**

Châteauneuf-du-Pape 1997: At first it's supersoft in the '97 style, but the finish has a surprising tannin presence that's encouraging. Medium-bodied, with black fruit and licorice. Hold a bit. Best from 2001 through 2005.–P.M. • $46 • (12/15/1999) • **86**

Châteauneuf-du-Pape 1995 • $40 • (10/15/1997) • **93**

Châteauneuf-du-Pape Vieilles Vignes 1996: Showing pretty cassis and plum notes, this has some intensity; tastes of new oak and is very toasty, with a fat midpalate. International-style finish. Drink now through 2001.–P.M. • $45 • (8/31/1999) • **80**

Cornas Coteaux 1996: Full yet lively, bursting with cassis, game, leather, smoke and spice notes. Crisp acidity and a metallic feel take over at midpalate, however, giving the wine zest but not much smoothness on the mouthpuckering finish. Drink now through 2002.–P.M. • $37 • (8/31/1999) • **82**

Cornas Vieilles Vignes 1997: Too oaky and overdone. Thick and rich, showing licorice, red berry and plum character. Has fresh acidity on the palate and sawdust from the obvious oak treatment. The woody finish may need time to come around. Best from 2002 through 2007.–P.M. • $57 • (11/30/1999) • **85**

Cornas Vieilles Vignes 1996: Elegant and well made, even exotic, with violet, rose petal and cassis flavors. Medium-bodied, with lovely silky texture and refined tannins, it leads into a focused, vibrant, clean finish, where subtle toasted oak notes are kept deftly in check. Drink now through 2003.–P.M. • $56 • (8/31/1999) • **91**

Cornas Vieilles Vignes 1995 • $53 • (10/15/1997) • **95**

Côte-Rôtie 1997: A heartbreaker. Combining finesse and power, this beautiful Syrah shows delectable earth, game, blackberry, smoke and baconlike aromas and flavors. Sweet fruit suggests old vines or low yields, and the wood is kept cleverly in check. Floral notes emerge on the finish to deliver the *coup de coeur*. Drink now through 2003.–P.M. • $70 • (11/30/1999) HR • **94**

Côte-Rôtie 1996: A pretty red, with game, wild berry, smoke and black truffle complexity. Medium-bodied, its zesty, fresh-tasting acidity mingles with supple tannin structure to provide an enchanting, focused, crisp, succulent finish accented by floral and smoky black pepper notes. Drink now through 2005.–P.M. • $60 • (9/15/1999) • **89**

Côtes du Rhône Cuvée Guy Louis 1995 • $25 • (10/15/1997) • **90**

Côtes du Rhône Guy Louis 1997: A lovely, thick, dense, even opulent Côtes du Rhône. Impressive for its round tannins, ripe fruit and blend of freshly ground Arabica coffee and mocha notes. The crafty use of oak works because the wine tastes balanced. Drink now through 2003.–P.M. • $23 • (12/15/1999) • **87**

Côtes du Rhône Guy Louis 1996: A stylish, medium-bodied red with a fancy oak treatment, its toasty, smoky blackberry aromas and flavors are showy but fairly attractive. Peppery, fresh finish. Drink now through 2003.–P.M. • $21 • (11/15/1999) • **84**

Côtes du Rhône Guy Louis 1995 • $25 • (10/15/1997) • **90**

Crozes-Hermitage Vieilles Vignes 1997: Delicious balance defines this beautiful, full-bodied wine. Thick and dense but still elegant, it quickens the pulse as it blends oak, earth, black fruit and ripe tannins in a modern but still authentically Rhône-like style. Deep, deep juice. Drink now through 2010.–P.M. • $NA • (12/15/1999) • **93**

Crozes-Hermitage Vieilles Vignes 1995 • $23 • (10/15/1997) • **90**

Gigondas 1997: Delicious. Generously oaked, this is beautifully made for the international markets, delivering fancy violet, floral, blackberry and toasted wood notes. Opulent and ripe, with well-integrated tannins. Best from 2002 through 2010.–P.M. • $36 • (12/15/1999) • **89**

Gigondas Vieilles Vignes 1995 • $40 • (10/15/1997) • **92**

Hermitage 1997: A serious Syrah, well made in a crafty, international style. The mocha, chocolate and spice dominate for now, but the texture is opulent and the massive tannins are ripe and silky, so this full-bodied blockbuster should be a beauty in a few years. Best from 2003 through 2010.–P.M. • $72 • (11/30/1999) • **93**

Hermitage 1996: A dream of a wine, ethereal in its cloudlike lightness yet deeply anchored in its *terroir*. Medium-bodied, the succulent red berry and blackberry notes take the leading role in this dramatic interpretation of the juicy and pure '96 vintage, with the subtle spicy oak, gamy, smoky character charging up the lingering, balanced finish. Drink now through 2003.–P.M. • $66 • (9/15/1999) • **94**

Hermitage 1995 • $61 • (10/15/1997) • **91**

St.-Joseph Vieilles Vignes 1997: Sensational. Reserved on the nose, thick and deeply rich on the palate, this ambushes the senses with silky tannins. Explodes with vivid, concentrated flavors that take in fancy oak but mostly old-vine sort of intensity—wet earth, black pepper and blackberries. A pure, unadulterated "little" Syrah in its own quality orbit. Drink now through 2020.–P.M. • $32 • (12/15/1999) • **91**

St.-Joseph Vieilles Vignes 1995 • $45 • (10/15/1997) • **90**

Vacqueyras 1995 • $23 • (10/15/1997) • **91**

Vacqueyras Vieilles Vignes 1997: Medium-bodied, with black fruit, light tannins and toasted oak and mocha flavors. Turns quite chewy and interesting on the finish. Drink now through 2002.–P.M. • $27 • (12/15/1999) • **85**

TARGE, CHATEAU DE

Saumur-Champigny 1995 • $15 • (6/15/1997) • **86**

TARIQUET, DOMAINE DU

Chardonnay Vin de Pays des Côtes de Gascogne 1997: Apple and citrus flavors dominate this straightforward Chardonnay, with an herbal, buttery note on the finish. Drink now.–K.M. • $9 • (11/15/1998) • **79**

Chardonnay Vin de Pays des Côtes de Gascogne 1996 • $9 • (4/30/1998) • **80**

Gros Manseng Vin de Pays des Côtes de Gascogne Cuvée Tardive 1997: Fresh and focused, with lively green peach, mineral and lime flavors and a nice touch of sweetness. Pleasant herbal notes chime in on the finish. Drink now.–K.M. • $12 • (10/15/1999) • **84**

Gros Manseng Vin de Pays des Côtes de Gascogne Cuvée Tardive 1996 • $10 • (4/30/1998) • **84**

Sauvignon Blanc Vin de Pays des Côtes de Gascogne 1996 • $8 • (4/30/1998) • **84**

Sauvignon Vin de Pays des Côtes de Gascogne 1998: A nice introduction to Sauvignon Blanc, with herbal and citrus flavors and a crisp finish with appealing grassy notes. Clean-tasting and balanced. Drink now.–K.M. • $8 • (10/15/1999) • **84**

Sauvignon Vin de Pays des Côtes de Gascogne 1997: Quite assertive, with herbal and grassy flavors and a nice, rich texture. Crisp and clean, with a lingering finish. Drink now.–K.M. • $8 • (9/30/1998) • **84**

Ugni Blanc-Colombard Vin de Pays des Côtes de Gascogne 1998: Straightforward, with citrusy, herbal-grassy flavors and a touch of sweetness. Drink now.–K.M. • $7 • (10/15/1999) • **81**

Ugni Blanc-Colombard Vin de Pays des Côtes de Gascogne 1996 • $7 • (4/30/1998) • **79**

TARLANT

Brut Champagne Cuvée Louis NV • $46 • (11/15/1997) • **85**

Key: SS—Spectator Selection. CS—Cellar Selection. HR—Highly Recommended. $NA—Price not available. (BT)—Barrel tasting. (A)—Auction Price.
For a key to the tasters' initials, see "How to Use These Listings."
Dates in parentheses represent the issues in which the ratings were published.

Brut Champagne Dosage Zéro NV • $33 • (11/15/1997) • **82**
Brut Champagne Réserve NV • $29 • (12/31/1997) • **84**

TARREYRO, CHATEAU

Côtes de Castillon 1997: Light-bodied, with dried herb aromas, fruit flavors and a light finish. Slightly diluted.–J.S. • $10 • (10/31/1999) • **79**

TARROUX, R.

Vin de Pays de l'Hérault Mas St.-Laurent Cretace 1998: Vibrant, with lovely berry and intense iron and brick flavors. Finishes with touches of mocha, chocolate and mineral. Tempting now, but needs time to come together. Best from 2001 through 2004.–K.M. • $7 • (6/15/2000) • **85**

TARTUGUIERE, CHATEAU

Médoc 1995 • $9 • (1/31/1998) • **84**

TATOUX, J.

Brouilly Garnache 1994 • $10 • (10/31/1995) • **84**

TAUPENOT-MERME, DOMAINE

Chambolle-Musigny 1990 • $22 • (11/30/1994) HR • **90**
Charmes-Chambertin 1990 • $58 • (11/30/1994) • **91**
Gevrey-Chambertin Bel-Air 1990 • $30 • (1/31/1995) • **81**
Morey-St.-Denis 1990 • $22 • (11/30/1994) • **88**

TAUZIA, CHATEAU DU

Buzet 1994: There are juicy notes to this straightforward red, with plum, cherry and some leather flavors. Drink now.–K.M. • $9 • (5/31/1999) • **82**

TAUZINAT L'HERMITAGE, CHATEAU

St.-Emilion 1998: Some decent berry character, but also slightly herbal. Medium- to light-bodied, with medium tannins and a short finish.–J.S. • $NA • (5/31/1999) (BT) • **80-84**

TAYAC, CHATEAU | Bourg

Côtes de Bourg 1996: A bit mean and lean, with berry and bark aromas. Light- to medium-bodied, with firm tannins and a medium finish. Drink now.–J.S. • $13 • (10/31/1999) • **83**
Côtes de Bourg 1990 • $12 • (6/15/1993) • **78**
Côtes de Bourg 1988 • $10 • (1/31/1992) • **78**
Côtes de Bourg Clos du Pain de Sucre 1997: Verging on rosé, this is light-bodied, with fruit, but slightly metallic and very diluted. Barely drinkable.–J.S. • $10 • (10/31/1999) • **73**
Côtes de Bourg Clos du Pain de Sucre 1995 • $9 • (10/15/1997) • **84**
Côtes de Bourg Cuvée Réservée 1995: Aromatic, with loads of berry on the nose. Medium-bodied, with tannins, but slightly diluted and unfocused on the palate. Drink now.–J.S. • $18 • (10/31/1999) • **82**
Côtes de Bourg Cuvée Réservée 1994: This has good tobacco, cherry and berry character, with soft tannins and a medium finish. Drink now.–J.S. • $15 • (10/31/1999) • **88**
Côtes de Bourg Prestige 1995: Plenty of cherry and raspberry aromas, with hints of mint. Medium-bodied, with firm tannins and a silky finish. Slightly one-dimensional, but a good glass of claret. Drink now through 2001.–J.S. • $25 • (10/31/1999) • **84**
Côtes de Bourg Rubis du Prince Noir 1993 • $12 • (10/15/1997) • **83**
Côtes de Bourg Saturny's 1996: Light, weedy, earthy and diluted. Barely acceptable.–J.S. • $13 • (10/31/1999) • **72**

TAYAC, CHATEAU | Medoc

Margaux 1997: A bit lean, but some good berry and mineral character. Light finish. Drink now.–J.S. • $NA • (1/31/2000) • **80**

TEMPE, MARC

Gewürztraminer Alsace Grand Cru Mambourg Sélection de Grains Nobles 1996: A burnt quality to the aromas, along with honey, caramel and coconut, yet the palate is clean and fresh, offering more caramel and fine underlying acidity. Long and intense, leaving an aftertaste of coconut and pineapple, this is a beauty. Drink now through 2006.–B.S. • $100/500ml. • (9/30/1999) • **92**
Gewürztraminer Alsace Grand Cru Mambourg Vendange Tardive 1996: Sweet, lush and bursting with honey, caramel and litchi, this is a delicious VT, never heavy, and supported by firm acidity and a hint of bitterness on the finish. Drink now through 2002.–B.S. • $75 • (9/30/1999) • **89**
Gewürztraminer Alsace Rimelsberg Vendange Tardive 1996: A fascinating wine. Floral, lanolin and honey aromas are followed by sweet honey and butterscotch on the palate. Light, ethereal and firmly structured, finishing on a clean, grapefruit note. Drink through 2005–B.S. • $59 • (9/30/1999) • **90**
Gewürztraminer Alsace Rodelsberg 1997: Extravagant and lush, this hefty Gewürztraminer displays honey, vanilla, cooked pear and licorice mixed with a soft structure. Trails off on the finish. Drink now.–B.S. • $35 • (6/15/2000) • **84**
Gewürztraminer Alsace Rodelsberg 1996: Fabulous aromas of grapefruit, smoke and apricot, while searing acidity on the palate signals the '96 vintage. This is fairly dry, elegant and intense, tailing off on the finish. Drink now through 2003.–B.S. • $29 • (9/30/1999) • **86**
Pinot Blanc Alsace Priegel 1997: Gorgeous, rich and broad, with depth to the peach, smoke and mineral flavors. Really long and harmonious. Drink now. –B.S. • $24 • (6/15/2000) • **90**
Pinot Blanc Alsace Priegel 1996: Quince, apricot and honey are the hallmarks of this ripe, round Pinot Blanc. Begins on a fruity note, then quickly shuts down courtesy of firm acidity and a crisp finish. Drink now.–B.S. • $21 • (9/15/1999) • **84**
Pinot Blanc Alsace Zellenberg 1997: Nuances of vanilla, spice and a hard candy flavor render this atypical, yet there's good integration in this round, soft Pinot Blanc, ending with a nuttiness. Drink now.–B.S. • $18 • (6/15/2000) • **85**
Pinot Blanc Alsace Zellenberg 1996: This shows just how good the '96s are. Ripe, round and mouthcoating, with apple, peach and citrus notes and a hint of sweetness on the finish, bolstered by snappy acidity. Drink now.–B.S. • $18 • (9/15/1999) • **87**
Riesling Alsace Burgreben 1996: Redolent of quince, almond and stone, with a slightly sweet, rich flavor profile that's well matched by bracing acidity. Moderate concentration and length. Best from 2001 through 2007.–B.S. • $29 • (8/31/1999) • **89**
Riesling Alsace Zellenberg 1997: Intriguing aromas and flavors of quince, mineral and caramel or bread pudding on a medium-bodied frame. Lively acidity for a '97, with a lingering finish. Drink now through 2002.–B.S. • $20 • (6/15/2000) • **87**
Riesling Alsace Zellenberg 1996: Dry and lean, this is not a flavorful '96 at this stage, offering bitter almond and quinine. It may come around. Try through 2005.–B.S. • $19 • (8/31/1999) • **86**
Sylvaner Alsace Zellenberg 1996: Deep-colored and ripe, showing quince, apple and citrus flavors that belie the racy structure. A fine Sylvaner, delicious as an aperitif or with light appetizers. Drink now through 2001.–B.S. • $16 • (9/15/1999) • **87**
Tokay Pinot Gris Alsace Zellenberg Vendange Tardive 1996: There are honey flavors and oxidation in this sweet, soft Pinot Gris VT. Lacks the structure of the vintage and comes off flat, with a weak finish. Drink now.–B.S. • $59 • (10/31/1999) • **81**

TEMPIER, DOMAINE

Bandol 1996: Firm and generous, with pretty flavors of red cherry and spice. A vibrant wine, balanced and focused, finishing on delightful notes of orange peel and pepper. Drink now.–K.M. • $21 • (11/15/1998) • **87**
Bandol 1995 • $22 • (12/15/1997) • **83**
Bandol 1994 • $23 • (9/30/1997) • **87**
Bandol 1984 • $15 • (12/15/1987) • **79**
Bandol 1983 • $16 • (8/31/1987) • **78**
Bandol 1981 • $15 • (8/31/1986) • **73**
Bandol Cuvée Spéciale 1995 • $24 • (12/15/1997) • **86**
Bandol Cuvée Spéciale 1994 • $25 • (9/30/1997) • **83**
Bandol Cuvée Spéciale Cabassaou 1996: An impressive red from southern France, loaded with raspberry, blackberry and bittersweet chocolate flavors. Luscious yet focused, with ripe, well-integrated tannins and a solid backbone of acidity. Interesting mushroom and earth notes chime in on the finish, which goes on and on. Best from 2001 through 2006.–K.M. • $35 • (12/31/1999) • **91**
Bandol Cuvée Spéciale Cabassaou 1995 • $45 • (3/31/1998) • **91**
Bandol Cuvée Spéciale La Migoua 1996: A deep, full-bodied red with layers of muscular flavors, including raspberry, bittersweet chocolate and cranberry framed by dusty mineral notes, and with a solid backbone of

FRANCE

acidity that adds to its power. Flavors intensify on the finish to a crescendo of spice and chocolate. Tempting now, but will gain with time. Drink through 2005–K.M. • $28 • (10/31/1999) • **91**

Bandol Cuvée Spéciale La Migoua 1995 • $28 • (3/31/1998) • **86**
Bandol Cuvée Spéciale La Migoua 1994 • $28 • (9/30/1997) • **87**
Bandol Cuvée Spéciale La Migoua 1987 • $22 • (10/31/1990) • **86**
Bandol Cuvée Spéciale La Tourtine 1996: A gorgeous and powerful French red, from Provence, with loads of ripe plum, berry and chocolate flavors and deliciously rich spice elements like cardamom and clove. Nicely sculpted, with a deft balance and some herbal touches. The flavors go on and on; a wine to sink your teeth into. Drink through 2008–K.M. • $28 • (10/31/1999) HR • **92**
Bandol Cuvée Spéciale La Tourtine 1995 • $28 • (3/31/1998) • **87**
Bandol Cuvée Spéciale La Tourtine 1994 • $28 • (9/30/1997) • **89**
Bandol Cuvée Spéciale La Tourtine 1987 • $22 • (10/31/1990) • **82**

TERME, CHATEAU MARQUIS DE

Margaux 1996: Good fruit character, with plenty of new wood on the nose. Medium-bodied, with firm tannins and a caressing finish, but rather hollow midpalate. Best after 2000.–J.S. • $25 • (1/31/1999) • **85**
Margaux 1995: Lots of ripe fruit and new wood. Mineral, chocolate and spice galore. Full-bodied, with velvety tannins and a lovely, silky finish. Hard to resist now, but will improve with age. Best from 2001 through 2008.–J.S. • $30 • (9/15/1998) • **90**
Margaux 1988: A pretty and delicious Margaux, with ripe berry and chocolate aromas and flavors, medium body and fine tannins. Ready to drink. (1988 Bordeaux horizontal tasting).–J.S. • $NA • (11/30/1998) • **88**
Margaux 1986 • $23 • (6/30/1989) • **79**
Margaux 1982: Elegant, delicious wine. Medium ruby-garnet color, with mineral, berry and perfume aromas. Medium-bodied, with fine tannins and a lovely, sweet fruit aftertaste. (1982 Bordeaux horizontal tasting). Drink now.–J.S. • $NA • (11/30/1998) • **88**
Margaux 1961 • $NA • (4/30/1996) • **82**

TERME, DOMAINE DU

Côtes du Rhône 1995 • $10 • (10/15/1997) • **78**
Gigondas 1995: Ripe and rich, full-bodied and supple in texture, with plenty of fine, sweet tannins on an elegant framework that displays pretty layers of plum, spice, licorice and earth. Drink now through 2005.–P.M. • $19 • (10/15/1998) • **87**
Gigondas 1994 • $17 • (10/15/1997) • **84**
Gigondas 1993 • $17 • (10/15/1996) • **89**

TERRASSE, CHATEAU LA

Bordeaux Supérieur 1989 • $8 • (3/31/1991) • **79**
Bordeaux Supérieur La Terrasse sur la Rivière 1993 • $9 • (8/31/1995) • **85**

TERRASSES DE GUILHEM, LES

Merlot Vin de Pays de l'Hérault 1995 • $9 • (3/31/1998) • **78**
Vin de Pays de l'Hérault Red 1996 • $9 • (3/31/1998) • **82**
Vin de Pays de l'Herault Red 1993 • $7 • (3/15/1994) • **84**
Vin de Pays de l'Hérault White 1996 • $9 • (2/28/1998) • **85**

TERRES VINEUSES, DOMAINE DES

Corton-Charlemagne 1995 • $60 • (1/31/1998) • **81**
Corton Renardes 1995 • $45 • (1/31/1998) • **72**

TERRIERE, CHATEAU DE LA

Beaujolais-Villages Cuvée du Souzy Vieilles Vignes 1996 • $13 • (9/15/1997) • **83**
Beaujolais-Villages Vieilles Vignes 1997: This rustic red offers smoky, gamy flavors, with some underlying cherry and a hint of spritz on the palate. Light-bodied, but still quite intense.–T.M. • $12 • (2/28/1999) • **77**

Key: SS—Spectator Selection. CS—Cellar Selection. HR—Highly Recommended. $NA—Price not available. (BT)—Barrel tasting. Ⓐ—Auction Price. For a key to the tasters' initials, see "How to Use These Listings."
Dates in parentheses represent the issues in which the ratings were published.

Brouilly 1997: Earthy and dull, this round red shows game and smoke flavors, and depth, but it lacks fruit and crispness.–T.M. • $15 • (2/28/1999) • **78**
Brouilly 1996 • $16 • (7/31/1997) • **85**
Brouilly Cuvée Jules du Souzy Vieilles Vignes 1997: This tender red shows delicate but lively cherry, chocolate and light smoke flavors, with soft tannins and just enough acidity for grip. Though hardly muscular, it has good focus and length. Drink now.–T.M. • $20 • (2/28/1999) • **84**
Brouilly Cuvée Jules du Souzy Vieilles Vignes 1995 • $18 • (7/31/1997) • **88**
Régnié 1997: Though light-bodied, this red has good intensity of flavor, with game, smoke, cherry and chocolate notes that linger on the finish. Drink now.–T.M. • $15 • (2/28/1999) • **84**
Régnié 1996 • $14 • (9/15/1997) • **84**

TERROIR CLUB

Cabernet Sauvignon Vin de Pays d'Oc Les Marionnettes 1997: Herbal and stemmy-tasting, with modest dried plum and cherry flavors.–K.M. • $8 • (11/15/1998) • **77**
Chardonnay Vin de Pays d'Oc Les Marionnettes 1997: Straightforward, with apple flavors and spicy notes on the finish. Drink now.–K.M. • $8 • (11/15/1998) • **81**
Merlot Vin de Pays d'Oc Les Marionnettes 1997: A good red table wine that's modestly fruity and well balanced, showing plum and smoke character and light tannins. Drink now. • $8 • (10/31/1998) • **81**
Sauvignon Blanc Vin de Pays d'Oc Les Marionnettes 1997: A lively white, showing characteristic cut grass, citrus and melon character and a rich texture. Drink now.–B.S. • $8 • (10/15/1998) • **82**
Syrah Vin de Pays d'Oc Les Marionnettes 1996: Ample fruit flavor and an easy-drinking texture make this medium-bodied red appealing. Drink now. • $9 • (10/15/1998) • **83**

TERROIR DE LAGRAVE

Gaillac 1994 • $10 • (5/15/1997) • **84**
Gaillac Doux 1994 • $13 • (5/31/1997) • **80**
Gaillac Cuvée Sigolène 1993 • $12 • (4/30/1997) • **81**

TERTRE, CHATEAU DU

Margaux 1999: Fine and elegant, with a solid core of ripe fruit and very fine tannins. Medium-bodied, it goes on and on. Very good indeed.–J.S. • $NA • (1/01/2000) (BT) • **85-89**
Margaux 1998: Slightly herbal and metallic character. Medium-bodied, with firm tannins and a medium finish.–J.S. • $NA • (5/31/1999) (BT) • **80-84**
Margaux 1997: Aromas of plums and strawberries follow through to a medium-bodied palate with light tannins. Fresh finish. Drink now.–J.S. • $22 • (1/31/2000) • **83**
Margaux 1996: A reasonable '96, with mint and berry character on the nose and palate. Medium- to light-bodied, with light tannins and a light, fruity finish. Best after 2000.–J.S. • $18 • (1/31/1999) • **81**
Margaux 1995 • $32 • (1/31/1998) • **85**
Margaux 1991 • $17 • (3/31/1994) • **77**
Margaux 1989 • $29 • (3/15/1992) • **90**
Margaux 1988 • $31 Ⓐ • (6/30/1991) • **86**
Margaux 1986 • $22 • (6/15/1989) • **89**
Margaux 1985 • $31 Ⓐ • (6/30/1988) SS • **93**
Margaux 1983 • $39 Ⓐ • (7/16/1986) • **91**
Margaux 1982: A burly Margaux. Dark ruby, inky color, with a slight garnet edge. Lovely berry, coffee and tobacco aromas. Full-bodied, with lots of ripe berry and cherry and a hint of wet earth. Full tannins. Slightly astringent finish. (1982 Bordeaux horizontal tasting). Best after 2000.–J.S. • $40 Ⓐ • (11/30/1998) • **88**

TERTRE DAUGAY, CHATEAU

St.-Emilion 1999: Delicate berry and plum aromas. Medium-bodied, with soft tannins and a pretty berry aftertaste.–J.S. • $NA • (1/01/2000) (BT) • **85-89**
St.-Emilion 1998: Plenty of mineral, spice and licorice. Full-bodied, with well-integrated tannins and a long, sweet fruit finish. Finesse and class mark this young wine.–J.S. • $NA • (5/31/1999) (BT) • **90-94**
St.-Emilion 1996: Tightly knit wine, with clean fruit flavors, but slightly tough. Blackberry and mineral character on the nose and palate. Medium-bodied, with tight tannins and a medium finish.–J.S. • $50 • (1/31/1999) • **83**
St.-Emilion 1995 • $44 • (1/31/1998) • **90**
St.-Emilion 1989 • $29 • (4/30/1992) • **83**

St.-Emilion 1988 • $20 • (4/30/1991) • **85**

TERTRE ROTEBOEUF, CHATEAU

St.-Emilion 1996: A well-crafted '96 with a good dark-ruby color and berry, cherry and spice aromas. Medium-bodied, with fine tannins and a fresh and fruity but slightly dry aftertaste. A bit too much new wood. Best after 2003.–J.S. • $87 Ⓐ • (6/30/1999) • **87**

St.-Emilion 1995: Intense aromas of plums and spices. Medium- to full-bodied, with round, velvety tannins and a long, flavorful finish. Flavor-intense, with masses of toasted oak. New World-style Bordeaux. Drink through 2005–J.S. • $104 Ⓐ • (9/15/1998) • **91**

St.-Emilion 1990 • $239 Ⓐ • (6/15/1993) • **83**

St.-Emilion 1989: A blockbuster of a young wine, oozing with cedar, berry, vanilla and chocolate. Full-bodied, adding a long, rich fruit aftertaste. Built for aging in a modern style. (1989 Bordeaux horizontal tasting). Best after 2005.–J.S. • $180 Ⓐ • (5/31/1999) • **93**

St.-Emilion 1988: One of the more balanced vintages for this pumped-up style. Complex aromas of berry, tobacco and chocolate, with a hint of spice. Full-bodied, with a rich, decadent palate and plenty of velvety tannins. Will improve with age but hard to resist now. (1988 Bordeaux horizontal tasting). Best after 2000.–J.S. • $105 Ⓐ • (11/30/1998) • **93**

St.-Emilion 1987 • $36 Ⓐ • (2/15/1990) • **83**

St.-Emilion 1986 • $87 Ⓐ • (6/30/1989) • **90**

St.-Emilion 1985 • $103 Ⓐ • (6/30/1988) • **89**

St.-Emilion 1983 • $61 Ⓐ • (5/16/1986) • **81**

St.-Emilion 1982 • $46 Ⓐ • (9/16/1985) • **85**

TETE, JEAN

Beaujolais-Villages Château des Alouettes 1997: This soft, straightforward red shows light cherry and spicy flavors with soft tannins and pleasantly crisp acidity. A quaffing wine with enough grip for lighter foods. Drink now.–T.M. • $10 • (8/31/1998) • **80**

TETE, LOUIS

Brouilly Domaine de Chatelan 1997: Black cherry flavors with herbal and spicy accents give personality, and the structure is firm and balanced. Nice with lighter foods. Drink now.–T.M. • $13 • (8/31/1998) • **84**

Fleurie La Madone 1997: This red is light in body but has a lively presence on the palate, thanks to vibrant acidity and a distinctive gamy note that adds depth to the berry and cherry fruit flavors. Drink now.–T.M. • $14 • (8/31/1998) • **84**

Juliénas Les Capitans 1997: Gamy aromas and followed by gamy, plum and herbal flavors with a firm structure. Nice balance of bright acidity and tannic grip. Good intensity for the vintage. A fine match with food.–T.M. • $13 • (8/31/1998) • **86**

Morgon Les Charmes 1997: This fleshy red offers well-defined black cherry and smoke flavors. Has good fruit concentration and pleasant roundness on the palate.–T.M. • $13 • (7/31/1998) • **84**

Régnié 1997: Light and diluted, with simple strawberry and herbal flavors that turn bitter. Drink now.–T.M. • $11 • (8/31/1998) • **76**

TETE, MICHEL

Beaujolais-Villages Domaine du Clos du Fief 1995 • $12 • (9/15/1996) • **83**

Juliénas Domaine du Clos du Fief 1995 • $16 • (9/15/1996) • **86**

Juliénas Domaine du Clos du Fief 1992 • $16 • (6/15/1994) • **90**

Juliénas Domaine du Clos du Fief Cuvée Prestige 1997: Look out—serious Beaujolais here, from the deep, almost brooding aromas of ripe black cherry and earth to the dense fruit flavors capped by a long finish. It's all held together by a solid structure. Drink now through 2002.–B.S. • $16 • (10/15/1999) • **88**

Juliénas Domaine du Clos du Fief Cuvée Prestige 1996 • $20 • (5/31/1998) • **90**

Juliénas Domaine du Clos du Fief Cuvée Prestige 1995 • $20 • (7/31/1997) • **88**

Juliénas Domaine du Clos du Fief Cuvée Prestige 1993 • $20 • (7/31/1995) • **83**

TEYSSIER, CHATEAU

Bordeaux 1998: A lovely, fresh red for early drinking, with grape and berry aromas and hints of crushed strawberry. Medium-bodied, with light tannins and a fresh, fruity finish. Drink now.–J.S. • $9 • (7/31/1999) • **83**

Montagne-St.-Emilion 1997: Pretty plum and raspberry aromas with a hint of pepper. Medium-bodied, with medium tannins and a dark chocolate, mineral character. Slight dilution. Drink now through 2002.–J.S. • $NA • (1/31/2000) • **84**

Puisseguin-St.-Emilion 1998: A bit lean, but shows lovely fruit flavors and fine tannins. Medium-bodied, with a medium finish.–J.S. • $NA • (5/31/1999) (BT) • **80-84**

Puisseguin-St.-Emilion 1996: Not bad for this château, considering the vintage. Good berry and earth aromas turn slightly vegetal on the palate. Medium-bodied, with delicate tannins and a medium finish. Drink now.–J.S. • $20 • (1/31/1999) • **82**

Puisseguin-St.-Emilion 1995 • $NA • (1/31/1998) • **86**

Puisseguin-St.-Emilion 1994 • $NA • (1/31/1997) • **77**

Puisseguin-St.-Emilion 1993 • $NA • (1/31/1996) • **78**

THENARD

Montrachet 1995: A tart, crisp wine, with lime, cilantro and herbal character. Full-bodied, with a slightly flinty and eucalyptus quality, the oak dominates now. Best after 2010.–P.M. • $NA • (8/31/1998) • **80**

THEVENET, JEAN-CLAUDE

Mâcon-Pierreclos 1997: Very crisp, with some decent pear and honey flavors, although the overall feel is one of a tough wine of modest ripeness.–P.M. • $NA • (5/31/1999) • **76**

Mâcon-Pierreclos 1996 • $13 • (8/31/1997) • **90**

St.-Véran Clos de l'Ermitage Cuvée Vieilles Vignes 1997: Nice suppleness here thanks to the ripe, honeyed, pearlike character, while bitter wet hay and blanched almond notes dominate the lingering finish. Drink now.–P.M. • $NA • (5/31/1999) • **84**

St.-Véran Vieilles Vignes 1996 • $18 • (5/31/1998) • **85**

THEVENET, JEAN-PAUL

Morgon Vieilles Vignes 1997: Ripe flavors of cherry and red berry are clean and well defined, with enough tannins and acidity for balance. Clean and pure, it's a good match for food. Drink now.–T.M. • $22 • (12/31/1998) • **85**

Morgon Vieilles Vignes 1996: Distinctive, but won't please everyone. A bit cloudy, and the spritzy attack suggests it's unfiltered. Offers sweet and spicy character of good concentration. Drink now.–T.M. • $22 • (8/31/1998) • **83**

Morgon Vieilles Vignes 1995 • $23 • (9/15/1997) • **87**

THEVENOT-MACHAL, JACQUES

Meursault 1997: A bit odd, with an herbal, cardboardy, dry character.–P.M. • $32 • (5/31/1999) • **73**

Meursault 1996: Buttery and slightly herbal but elegant all the same, with vibrant mineral character on the midpalate. Delivers a touch of honey and lots of toasted oak and spicy curry flavors. Best after 2005.–P.M. • $38 • (8/31/1998) • **87**

Meursault 1995 • $26 • (5/31/1997) • **70**

Meursault Charmes 1998: A bit lean, this crisp Chardonnay delivers modest ripe fruit and mostly citrusy notes. Drink now through 2002.–P.M. • $48 • (5/31/2000) • **80**

Meursault Charmes 1997: A hard, modestly fruity Meursault. Shows decent pear, mandarin and green apple, with a firm structure. Dries a bit on the tough finish. Drink now through 2003.–P.M. • $45 • (5/31/1999) • **80**

Meursault Charmes 1996: Ripe and thick, but a bit overdone with all those butterscotch, buttery, leesy and piecrust flavors. Full-bodied, full-throttle style, showing also some pear and toasted oak. Lacks the elegance of many '96s. Best after 2005.–P.M. • $47 • (8/31/1998) • **83**

Meursault Charmes 1995 • $30 • (8/31/1997) • **96**

Meursault Poruzot 1998: Lacks a bit of elegance, but it's a thick, full-bodied, almost late-harvest kind of Chardonnay. Pleasant, with lots of honey, apple tart and quince-jam flavors. Drink now through 2002.–P.M. • $48 • (5/31/2000) • **85**

Meursault Poruzot 1997: Woody, with a cardboard character, this rustic Chardonnay has a drying finish. 58 cases imported.–P.M. • $45 • (5/31/1999) • **71**

Meursault Poruzot 1995 • $30 • (8/31/1997) • **83**

Puligny-Montrachet 1997: Earthy and bitter-tasting, with strange stewed cabbage and wet cardboard notes.–P.M. • $32 • (5/31/1999) • **70**

Puligny-Montrachet 1995 • $25 • (8/31/1997) • **90**

Puligny-Montrachet Les Charmes 1998: An almost late-harvest style of Chardonnay, tasting a bit of cooked apples and overripe fruit, with dried apricot and wet earth notes, too. Round and full-bodied, but a bit lacking

FRANCE

in midpalate concentration, although it has a lingering finish. Drink now through 2005.–P.M. • $34 • (5/31/2000) • **86**

Puligny-Montrachet Les Charmes 1997: An ultrarich, ripe, thick, dense and silky '97. Full-bodied and golden-colored like a late-harvest white, it coats the palate with lemon, honey, pear and tropical flavors but remains elegant on the smooth, seamless, subtly oaked finish. Drink now through 2007.–P.M. • $35 • (5/31/1999) • **94**

Puligny-Montrachet Les Folatières 1997: A bit hot and burning, with butter, butterscotch and cooked pear aromas and flavors in a low-acidity, flabby, astringent wine.–P.M. • $47 • (5/31/1999) • **72**

Puligny-Montrachet Les Folatières 1995 • $30 • (8/31/1997) • **92**

Volnay-Santenots 1996: Herbal and stemmy on the nose, followed by sweet red cherries and a hint of vanilla from new oak. Still, the overall impression is tough and astringent. Drink through 2003–B.S. • $45 • (9/30/1998) • **80**

Volnay-Santenots 1988 • $36 • (11/15/1990) • **89**

THIBAULT, JEAN-BAPTISTE

Sancerre La Duschesne 1996: Alluring aromas of citrus and honey give way to a full-bodied wine with apple, melon and mineral flavors. Firm and well defined. Drink now.–T.M. • $16 • (9/15/1998) • **85**

THIBERT PERE & FILS

Mâcon-Fuissé 1996 • $19 • (8/31/1997) • **85**

THIEULEY, CHATEAU

Bordeaux White Sec 1998: A very rustic Sauvignon style, with cut grass, hay and melon character. Medium-bodied, with fresh acidity and a clean, lively finish. Drink now.–J.S. • $9 • (6/30/2000) • **84**

THOLOMIES, DOMAINE DE

Merlot Vin de Pays d'Oc 1997: A quaffable red from the south of France, with cherry and tobaccolike flavors and soft, herbal notes on the finish. Drink now.–K.M. • $12 • (2/28/1999) • **83**

THOMAS

Pouilly-Fuissé 1996 • $18 • (5/31/1998) • **76**

Pouilly-Fuissé Vieilles Vignes 1996 • $25 • (5/31/1998) • **86**

St.-Véran 1997: Crisp, superfresh, with lots of acidity, offering green apple and a tart mouthfeel. Might mellow with food. Try with oysters?–P.M. • $15 • (5/31/1999) • **80**

St.-Véran 1995 • $NA • (8/31/1996) • **78**

St.-Véran Cuvée No. 2 1996 • $15 • (5/31/1998) • **85**

St.-Véran Cuvée No. 718 1996 • $12 • (5/31/1998) • **84**

St.-Véran Vieilles Vignes 1997: Round and ripe, with floral, quince jam, almond and pear notes, this medium-bodied and pure St-Véran has a slight grassy and wet hay character that anchors it in the appellation. Drink now.–P.M. • $20 • (5/31/1999) • **84**

St.-Véran Vieilles Vignes 1996 • $18 • (5/31/1998) • **87**

St.-Véran Vieilles Vignes 1995 • $NA • (8/31/1996) • **88**

THOMAS, PAUL

Sancerre Chavignol Les Comtesses 1997: Light herbal and bright citrus flavors dominate; the texture is quite round but the flavors are all lean and sharp. Shows typicity, but lacks generosity. Drink now through 2002.–T.M. • $14 • (9/15/1999) • **84**

Sancerre Chavignol Les Comtesses 1996: This firm, crisp white is full-bodied for Sancerre, with a creamy texture and ripe flavors of almond, melon and herb. Well focused, if a bit austere, it has the muscle to match poultry and other light meats. Drink now.–T.M. • $18 • (2/28/1999) • **85**

Key: SS—Spectator Selection. CS—Cellar Selection. HR—Highly Recommended. $NA—Price not available. (BT)—Barrel tasting. (A)—Auction Price.
For a key to the tasters' initials, see "How to Use These Listings."
Dates in parentheses represent the issues in which the ratings were published.

THOMAS, LUCIEN

Sancerre Clos de la Crêle 1998: Strong herbaceous and smoky aromas are distinctive and may be off-putting to some, but show local character and follow through with austere, well-structured flavors of pear, toast and mineral. A traditional style. Drink now through 2003.–T.M. • $18 • (2/29/2000) • **89**

THOMAS & FILS, ANDRE

Gewürztraminer Alsace 1996: Ripe, floral and bursting with tropical fruit notes, this exuberant Gewürz has personality along with a rich texture, concentration and bright acidity.–B.S. • $18 • (9/15/1998) • **85**

Gewürztraminer Alsace Vieilles Vignes 1996: Ripe and exuberant, this is full of spice and crème brûlée notes, with a rich, full body and moderate length. Drink now.–B.S. • $25 • (9/15/1998) • **85**

Pinot Blanc Alsace 1996: Smells ripe and appealing, tastes of almond, peach and a touch of honey, with a big-boned structure and a slightly coarse, tannic finish. Drink now.–B.S. • $15 • (8/31/1998) • **82**

Pinot Blanc Alsace Sand 1996: A bold, ripe, "in your face" style with almond, peach and tropical accents, moderate acidity and lush texture that closes up on the finish. Drink now.–B.S. • $18 • (8/31/1998) • **84**

Riesling Alsace 1996: Like a laser beam of apple and mineral, this is austere and racy, finishing with a touch of almond. Needs food to show off its fruit. Drink through 2006–B.S. • $17 • (8/31/1998) • **89**

THOMAS & FILS, DOMAINE

Sancerre Ultimus 1997: A powerhouse. This bold white shows ripeness and concentration, with pear and melon flavors that are round but remain intensely dry, accented with berry and mineral notes. Long, complex finish. Can easily match with weighty dishes. Drink now through 2005. –T.M. • $26 • (2/29/2000) • **92**

THOMAS-LABAILLE

Sancerre Les Monts Damnés 1998: This refreshing white offers a good balance of crisp acidity and ripe fruit, with pear, anise and herb flavors. Vibrant enough to carry most fish dishes. Drink now.–T.M. • $15 • (2/29/2000) • **87**

Sancerre Les Monts Damnés 1997: Both full-bodied and crisp, with generous flavors of almonds and pears and an underlying citrusy acidity that keeps it lively and balanced. Give it time. Best after 2000.–T.M. • $16 • (9/15/1999) • **87**

THOMAS-MOILLARD, DOMAINE

Beaune Grèves 1996: Good richness and depth, yet the flavors are modest, tasting of herbs and cherries, and the finish is tough. Drink through 2004–B.S. • $30 • (9/30/1998) • **80**

Beaune Grèves 1995 • $28 • (11/15/1997) • **85**

Beaune Grèves 1994 • $33 • (11/15/1996) • **74**

Beaune Grèves 1990 • $40 • (12/15/1992) • **91**

Beaune Grèves 1989 • $28 • (1/31/1992) • **89**

Beaune Grèves 1986 • $14 • (12/31/1988) • **80**

Beaune Grèves 1985 • $25 • (3/15/1987) • **89**

Beaune Grèves 1984 • $12 • (2/15/1987) • **87**

Bonnes Mares 1986 • $45 • (11/15/1988) • **86**

Bonnes Mares 1984 • $35 • (5/31/1987) • **92**

Clos Vougeot 1994 • $65 • (11/15/1996) • **83**

Corton Clos du Roi 1996: The vanilla and cherry aromas and flavors are subtle, unlike the tannins, which currently shroud everything in this savage, masculine red. Though massive, the lasting impression is sweetness. Best from 2002 through 2008.–B.S. • $49 • (9/30/1998) • **89**

Corton Clos du Roi 1995 • $43 • (11/15/1997) • **91**

Corton Clos du Roi 1994 • $47 • (11/15/1996) • **90**

Corton Clos du Roi 1989 • $41 • (1/31/1992) • **85**

Corton Clos du Roi 1984 • $24 • (5/31/1987) • **87**

Hautes-Côtes de Nuits 1996: Crisp and herbal, with a silky midpalate, but the flavors turn toward asparagus and bell pepper, with an oddly hot, matchstick finish.–P.M. • $15 • (9/30/1998) • **75**

Nuits-St.-Georges 1994 • $35 • (11/15/1996) • **84**

Nuits-St.-Georges Clos de Thorey 1996: Balanced and round, this supple wine shows lovely red- and blackberry character. What it lacks in depth it makes up in charm. Medium in body, lush in texture, the tannins are ripe. Drink now through 2003.–P.M. • $40 • (9/30/1998) • **83**

Nuits-St.-Georges Clos de Thorey 1995 • $39 • (1/31/1998) • **85**
Nuits-St.-Georges Clos de Thorey 1994 • $42 • (11/15/1996) • **82**
Nuits-St.-Georges Clos de Thorey 1990 • $50 • (12/15/1992) • **79**
Nuits-St.-Georges Clos de Thorey 1989 • $35 • (1/31/1992) • **89**
Nuits-St.-Georges Clos de Thorey 1988 • $50 • (12/31/1990) • **89**
Nuits-St.-Georges Clos de Thorey 1987 • $27 • (12/15/1989) • **88**
Nuits-St.-Georges Clos de Thorey 1986 • $28 • (11/15/1988) • **78**
Nuits-St.-Georges Clos de Thorey 1985 • $38 • (5/31/1987) • **89**
Nuits-St.-Georges Clos de Thorey 1984 • $24 • (5/31/1987) • **84**
Nuits-St.-Georges Clos de Thorey 1983 • $19 • (9/16/1985) • **84**
Savigny-lès-Beaune 1990 • $20 • (12/15/1992) • **88**
Vosne-Romanée Malconsorts 1996: A bit simple but supple, this chewy, full-bodied Pinot displays a distinctive wet earth, mineral, stone character, then shoots off some pretty blackberry notes. It has the firm tannin structure to age. Best after 2005.–P.M. • $48 • (9/30/1998) • **84**
Vosne-Romanée Malconsorts 1995 • $43 • (3/31/1998) • **85**
Vosne-Romanée Malconsorts 1994 • $47 • (11/15/1996) • **80**
Vosne-Romanée Malconsorts 1989 • $60 • (1/31/1992) • **93**
Vosne-Romanée Malconsorts 1988 • $50 • (3/31/1991) • **88**
Vosne-Romanée Malconsorts 1987 • $30 • (8/31/1989) • **91**
Vosne-Romanée Malconsorts 1986 • $29 • (10/31/1988) • **88**
Vosne-Romanée Malconsorts 1985 • $44 Ⓐ • (7/31/1988) • **95**
Vosne-Romanée Malconsorts 1984 • $28 • (5/31/1987) • **80**

THORIN, MAISON

Beaujolais-Villages 1988 • $7 • (5/31/1989) • **79**
Beaujolais-Villages Château du Bost 1995 • $9 • (4/30/1997) • **86**
Beaujolais-Villages Domaine Le Moulin 1997: Gamy, smoky notes add depth to this firm but fruity red. Black cherry and leafy notes are well defined. Though a bit austere, it has local character.–T.M. • $8 • (8/31/1998) • **83**
Bourgogne 1994 • $13 • (4/30/1997) • **79**
Bourgogne White 1995 • $12 • (4/30/1997) • **78**
Brouilly Domaine de la Croix Briante 1995 • $16 • (4/30/1997) • **83**
Brouilly Les Jarrons 1997: Light and simple, this thin red gives berry and strawberry flavors, then turns dry on the finish. Drink now.–T.M. • $10 • (8/31/1998) • **77**
Châteauneuf-du-Pape 1986 • $13 • (11/30/1988) • **87**
Côtes du Rhône Les Antiques 1995 • $10 • (12/15/1996) • **83**
Fleurie Les Muriennes 1995 • $18 • (4/30/1997) • **89**
Morgon Les Creusots 1997: Quite light for a Morgon, this offers simple strawberry and cherry flavors, with light tannins and little depth. Best now, lightly chilled as an aperitif.–T.M. • $10 • (8/31/1998) • **79**
Moulin-à-Vent Château des Jacques 1988 • $16 • (5/31/1989) • **88**
Moulin-à-Vent Domaine des Pierres Roses 1997: Ripe fruit flavors of plums and cassis gain complexity from meaty, menthol and cedar notes in this rich, sturdy red. It has plenty of muscle to stand up to food, and to develop with bottle age. Drink now.–T.M. • $12 • (8/31/1998) • **88**
Moulin-à-Vent Domaine des Pierres Roses 1995 • $18 • (4/30/1997) • **88**
Pommard 1986 • $24 • (2/28/1990) • **75**

TIJOU, PIERRE-YVES

Coteaux du Layon-Chaume Château Soucherie 1995 • $25 • (5/15/1997) • **88**
Coteaux du Layon Château Soucherie Vieilles Vignes 1996: Little if any botrytis here, but the apple, honey and mineral aromas and flavors show very good concentration and length. Drink now through 2001.–B.S. • $24 • (11/15/1998) • **88**
Coteaux du Layon-Chaume Cuvée Clémentine 1993 • $20 • (5/15/1996) • **89**
Savennières Clos des Perrières 1996: Lithe and high-toned, this sinewy white displays honeysuckle, thistle, chamomile, limestone and white peach flavors that are well cut and defined. Elegant and racy throughout, it should age nicely. Drink now through 2005.–B.S. • $23 • (6/15/2000) • **91**

TIMBERLAY, CHATEAU

Bordeaux Supérieur 1997: A pleasant and fruity '97, if rather diluted. Light-bodied, with light tannins and a chocolate aftertaste. Drink now.–J.S. • $NA • (1/31/2000) • **80**
Bordeaux Supérieur 1995 • $12 • (1/31/1998) • **81**
Bordeaux Supérieur 1994 • $10 • (1/31/1997) • **79**
Bordeaux Supérieur 1991 • $10 • (3/31/1994) • **70**
Bordeaux White Cuvée Prestige 1998: Good lemon and apple character, with a hint of new oak. Medium-bodied, with fresh fruit and a light finish. Drink now.–J.S. • $NA • (2/29/2000) • **85**
Bordeaux White Cuvée Prestige 1996: Aromas of apple, cream and vanilla continue to the medium-bodied palate, with fresh acidity, but rather light and diluted on the finish. Drink now.–J.S. • $7 • (3/31/1999) • **82**

TINEL-BLONDELET, F.

Pouilly-Fumé L'Arret Buffatte 1997: Broad but dull. This white has power, even tannin, but lacks fruit and liveliness. Might show better against a cream sauce or in contrast with an herbal dish.–T.M. • $19 • (6/30/1999) • **78**

TIRECUL LA GRAVIERE, CHATEAU

Monbazillac 1997: Lots of blanched almond, lemon and biscuit character, picking up maple syrup, honey and fruit flavors. Medium-bodied. Fruity finish. Drink now.–J.S. • $35/500 ml. • (5/15/2000) • **87**
Monbazillac Cuvée Madame 1997: Thick, rich and honeylike. Beautiful aromas of honey, spice and coconut with lots of dried apricot. Full-bodied, very thick and sweet, with loads of pineapple, honey and toffee character on the palate. Drink now.–J.S. • $130/500 ml. • (5/15/2000) • **92**

TOLLOT-BEAUT & FILS

Aloxe-Corton 1997: Toasty oak introduces this fat, round '97 red, whose smooth texture and moderate intensity carry the plum and vanilla flavors to a pleasant conclusion. Lingering aftertaste. Drink now through 2004.–B.S. • $37 • (9/30/1999) • **89**
Aloxe-Corton 1996: Concentrated, but it tastes a bit unripe, with a slight herbaceous, bell-pepper character that is fought off by spice, licorice and oak accents. Medium-bodied, with good length.–P.M. • $38 • (9/30/1998) • **84**
Aloxe-Corton 1995 • $35 • (11/15/1997) • **81**
Aloxe-Corton 1994 • $37 • (11/15/1996) • **82**
Aloxe-Corton 1993 • $29 • (11/15/1995) • **86**
Aloxe-Corton 1992 • $27 • (12/15/1994) • **82**
Aloxe-Corton 1991 • $NA • (1/31/1994) • **82**
Aloxe-Corton 1990 • $38 • (12/15/1992) • **93**
Aloxe-Corton 1989 • $41 • (1/31/1992) • **90**
Aloxe-Corton 1985 • $35 • (3/15/1988) • **89**
Aloxe-Corton Les Vercots 1997: Nice integration of spice and cherry and a hint of earth mark this rich, chewy '97. Balanced to the tannic side, but shows potential. Drink now through 2004.–B.S. • $23 Ⓐ • (9/30/1999) • **85**
Aloxe-Corton Les Vercots 1996: What a joy to taste! Beautiful, spicy Pinot fruit, raspberries and cherries and hints of earth and mineral are in this elegant, refined '96. The structure is so integrated and fine that you almost don't notice the silky tannins. Well done. Drink through 2005–B.S. • $42 • (9/30/1998) • **89**
Aloxe-Corton Les Vercots 1995 • $40 • (11/15/1997) • **80**
Aloxe-Corton Les Vercots 1994 • $40 • (11/15/1996) • **83**
Aloxe-Corton Les Vercots 1993 • $37 • (11/15/1995) • **89**
Beaune Clos du Roi 1997: Balanced like few '97s, with very nice ripe, rich black fruit. Shows a voluptuous mouthfeel, with lovely blackberry, cassis, subtle toast and plum character. Drink now through 2005.–P.M. • $42 • (9/30/1999) • **89**
Beaune Clos du Roi 1996: Pure strawberries and cherries and some sweet vanilla give fragrance and pretty flavors to this big, unevolved '96. The lively acidity, ripe tannins and fruit are in place, but they need time to integrate. Best from 2001 through 2007.–B.S. • $42 • (9/30/1998) • **89**
Beaune Clos du Roi 1995 • $40 • (11/15/1997) • **90**
Beaune Clos du Roi 1994 • $40 • (11/15/1996) • **87**
Beaune Clos du Roi 1993 • $35 • (11/15/1995) • **88**
Beaune Clos du Roi 1992 • $30 • (12/15/1994) • **85**
Beaune Clos du Roi 1991 • $30 • (1/31/1994) • **87**
Beaune Clos du Roi 1990 • $48 • (12/15/1992) • **90**
Beaune Clos du Roi 1989 • $52 • (1/31/1992) • **91**
Beaune Clos du Roi 1988 • $53 • (2/28/1991) • **86**
Beaune Grèves 1997: Beautiful. Very round, ripe and balanced. Pretty blackberry, currant and wild berry flavors fold nicely into a smooth, succulent finish that remains unusually long and fresh for a '97. Drink now through 2007.–P.M. • $29 Ⓐ • (9/30/1999) • **89**
Beaune Grèves 1996: Seductive spice and tangy red fruit notes are displayed in this attractive Beaune, which shows elegance and balance. A structured and serious Pinot Noir. Drink through 2003–B.S. • $42 • (9/30/1998) • **86**
Beaune Grèves 1995 • $35 • (11/15/1997) • **79**
Beaune Grèves 1994 • $30 • (11/15/1996) • **83**
Beaune Grèves 1993 • $35 • (11/15/1995) • **87**
Beaune Grèves 1992 • $30 • (12/15/1994) • **79**
Beaune Grèves 1991 • $30 • (1/31/1994) • **82**

FRANCE

TOLLOT-BEAUT & FILS

Beaune Grèves 1990 • $40 • (12/15/1992) • **92**
Beaune Grèves 1989 • $44 • (1/31/1992) • **90**
Bourgogne White 1997: Thick for this Bourgogne Blanc appellation, this is supple and ripe, with honey, pear and deftly toasted oak. Pleasant finish. Drink now.–P.M. • $25 • (9/30/1999) • **84**
Bourgogne White 1995 • $20 • (8/31/1997) • **90**
Chorey-lès-Beaune 1997: Soft and ripe, but lacking a bit of focused intensity, this shows earth, cherry and toast character. Drink now through 2002.–P.M. • $17 Ⓐ • (9/30/1999) • **83**
Chorey-lès-Beaune 1996: Tar, smoke and cassis aromas and flavors yield to stiff, solid tannins. Good flavors, but lacks a bit of charm. Best from 2000.–B.S. • $22 • (9/30/1998) • **85**
Chorey-lès-Beaune 1995 • $22 • (11/15/1997) • **77**
Chorey-lès-Beaune 1994 • $20 • (11/15/1996) • **80**
Chorey-lès-Beaune 1993 • $18 • (11/15/1995) • **87**
Chorey-lès-Beaune 1992 • $15 • (12/15/1994) • **83**
Chorey-lès-Beaune 1990 • $26 • (12/15/1992) • **86**
Chorey-lès-Beaune 1989 • $28 • (1/31/1992) • **87**
Chorey-lès-Beaune 1988 • $25 • (12/31/1990) • **88**
Chorey-lès-Beaune 1985 • $18 • (4/15/1988) • **83**
Corton 1997: This has a big, toasty, smoky oak aroma, with plum and spice notes and wet earth. Very exotic, full-bodied and dense, displaying *terroir* and a solid tannic structure. Long, intense finish. Best after 2002.–B.S. • $63 • (9/30/1999) • **89**
Corton 1996: Flamboyant. Almost too oaky for the fruit, but the balance is saved by an attractive midpalate ripeness. Displays layers of black cherry, mocha, spice and raspberry flavors. A bit chewy, even slightly coarse, it has a juicy and succulent finish. Best after 2003.–P.M. • $62 • (9/30/1998) • **88**
Corton 1995 • $70 • (11/15/1997) • **84**
Corton 1994 • $70 • (11/15/1996) • **87**
Corton 1993 • $57 • (11/15/1995) • **91**
Corton 1992 • $45 • (12/15/1994) • **82**
Corton 1990 • $53 Ⓐ • (12/15/1992) • **94**
Corton 1989 • $67 • (1/31/1992) • **90**
Corton 1986 • $45 • (8/31/1989) • **87**
Corton 1985 • $75 • (3/15/1988) • **97**
Corton Bressandes 1997: Plenty of oak, almost raspberry in character, yet the wine builds in intensity and is concentrated, elegant, almost tender. Moderate tannins, with cooked cherry and licorice flavors. Drink now through 2003.–B.S. • $63 • (9/30/1999) • **91**
Corton Bressandes 1995 • $70 • (11/15/1997) • **87**
Corton Bressandes 1994 • $70 • (11/15/1996) • **88**
Corton Bressandes 1993 • $57 • (11/15/1995) • **90**
Corton Bressandes 1992 • $45 • (12/15/1994) • **85**
Corton Bressandes 1991 • $48 • (2/28/1995) • **89**
Corton Bressandes 1990 • $40 • (2/28/1995) • **96**
Corton Bressandes 1989 • $58 • (2/28/1995) • **94**
Corton Bressandes 1988 • $59 • (2/28/1995) • **92**
Corton Bressandes 1987 • $33 • (2/28/1995) • **86**
Corton Bressandes 1986 • $40 • (2/28/1995) • **83**
Corton Bressandes 1985 • $NA • (2/28/1995) • **88**
Corton Bressandes 1983 • $NA • (2/28/1995) • **83**
Corton Le Corton 1991 • $45 • (1/31/1994) • **91**
Corton-Charlemagne 1997: Medium in intensity and body, this pretty white harmoniously unfolds its grass, dried herb, green apple and toasty spices nicely, without much fuss. Drink now through 2003.–P.M. • $77 Ⓐ • (9/30/1999) • **87**
Corton-Charlemagne 1996: Heavily oaked but beautifully crafted, thick and ripe, showing a muscular frame but also a seductive charm, this racy wine bursts with grassy, honeyed, earthy, toasted oak and pear aromas and flavors. Full-bodied, still a bit aggressive, it needs time. Best from 2005.–P.M. • $90 • (8/31/1998) • **92**
Corton-Charlemagne 1995 • $77 Ⓐ • (8/31/1997) • **94**
Savigny-lès-Beaune Lavières 1997: Firm, focused, ripe and spicy, this '97 red offers plenty of cherry flavors on a light framework supported by firm tannins. Drink now through 2004.–B.S. • $32 • (9/30/1999) • **87**
Savigny-lès-Beaune Lavières 1996: Well made and supple, this harmonious red displays some nice toasted oak, mocha and plum character. Of medium body and quite suave, it has a crisp acidity on the lively finish. Best from 2002 through 2006.–P.M. • $32 • (9/30/1998) • **85**
Savigny-lès-Beaune Lavières 1995 • $32 • (11/15/1997) • **85**
Savigny-lès-Beaune Lavières 1994 • $30 • (11/15/1996) • **84**
Savigny-lès-Beaune Lavières 1993 • $25 • (11/15/1995) • **90**
Savigny-lès-Beaune Lavières 1992 • $24 • (12/15/1994) • **84**
Savigny-lès-Beaune Lavières 1991 • $22 • (1/31/1994) • **82**
Savigny-lès-Beaune Lavières 1990 • $35 • (12/15/1992) • **90**
Savigny-lès-Beaune Lavières 1989 • $38 • (1/31/1992) • **90**

TONNELLES, CHATEAU LES

Fronsac 1998: A rather lean claret but with decent berry and cherry character. Light- to medium-bodied, with a short finish. Drink now.–J.S. • $10 • (10/31/1999) • **80**

TORTOISE CREEK

Chardonnay-Viognier Vin de Pays d'Oc Les Amoureux 1998: Good flavors of peach and white pepper make this a nice change of pace in white wine. Smooth, with a pleasantly fruity finish. Drink now.–K.M. • $7 • (12/31/1999) • **83**
Chardonnay-Viognier Vin de Pays d'Oc Les Amoureux 1997: A straightforward white, with apple and lemon flavors and peach notes on the finish. –K.M. • $7 • (12/15/1998) • **79**
Chardonnay-Viognier Vin de Pays d'Oc Les Amoureux 1996 • $7 • (4/30/1998) • **78**
Merlot-Cabernet Vin de Pays d'Oc Les Amoureux 1998: A medium-bodied, juicy-tasting red, with blackberry, dark cherry and nice brickish and roasted flavors. Drink now through 2002.–K.M. • $7 • (2/29/2000) • **84**
Merlot-Cabernet Vin de Pays d'Oc Les Amoureux 1997: A focused and nicely concentrated red wine, with dark plum and red cherry flavors that combine with peppery notes. This intense wine will benefit from some aging. Drink through 2001–K.M. • $6 • (9/30/1998) • **86**
Syrah-Mourvèdre Vin de Pays d'Oc Les Amoureux 1998: Youthful and balanced, with plenty of good fruity flavors of red cherry and berry, along with notes of smoke and game. Peppery notes linger on the finish. Drink now.–K.M. • $7 • (12/31/1999) • **84**
Syrah-Mourvèdre Vin de Pays d'Oc Les Amoureux 1997: A juicy, grapey and very young wine, with exuberant fruit flavors and a soft texture. A blend: 70 percent Syrah, 30 percent Mourvèdre. Drink now. • $6 •(9/30/1998) • **82**
Syrah-Mourvèdre Vin de Pays d'Oc Les Amoureux 1996 • $6 • (4/30/1998) • **83**

TOUMALIN, CHATEAU

Canon-Fronsac 1997: A bit lean and tough, with some berry and cherry character. Medium- to light-bodied, with herbal tannins. Drink now.–J.S. • $NA • (1/31/2000) • **82**
Canon-Fronsac 1996: Light and diluted, with some berry character, but weedy and herbal on the aftertaste.–J.S. • $17 • (1/31/1999) • **78**
Canon-Fronsac 1995 • $18 • (1/31/1998) • **88**
Canon-Fronsac 1990 • $14 • (3/31/1993) • **74**
Canon-Fronsac 1989: Medium-red color, with a garnet edge. Soft, round and pleasant. (1989 Bordeaux horizontal tasting). Drink now.–J.S. • $NA • (5/31/1999) • **81**

TOUR, CHATEAU DE LA | BORDEAUX

Bordeaux Supérieur 1992 • $8 • (11/15/1994) • **77**
Bordeaux Supérieur Reserve du Château 1997: Lovely aromas of blackberries, black olives and cherries. Medium-bodied, with silky tannins and a short finish. A bit lean really. Best after 2000.–J.S. • $NA • (1/31/2000) • **84**
Bordeaux Supérieur Réserve du Château 1995 • $16 • (1/31/1998) • **88**
Bordeaux Supérieur Réserve du Château 1994 • $15 • (1/31/1997) • **84**
Bordeaux Supérieur Réserve du Château 1993 • $15 • (1/31/1996) • **79**

TOUR, CHATEAU DE LA | BURGUNDY

Clos Vougeot 1997: Very oaky, with olive, earth and plum notes, this '97 red evokes *terroir* in its firm, unyielding profile. Solidly tannic and dense, it has concentration, fat, pointed tannins and a licorice aftertaste. Best from 2001 through 2008.–B.S. • $85 • (9/30/1999) • **93**
Clos Vougeot 1996: A big red, full of black cherries, cassis and spicy oak, moderately rich, backed by a muscular framework of bright acidity and fine tannins. Best from 2001 through 2006.–B.S. • $65 • (9/30/1998) • **93**
Clos Vougeot 1995 • $79 • (11/15/1997) • **73**
Clos Vougeot 1994 • $62 • (11/15/1996) • **81**
Clos Vougeot 1993 • $53 • (11/15/1995) • **84**
Clos Vougeot 1992 • $51 • (12/15/1994) • **87**

Key: SS—Spectator Selection. CS—Cellar Selection. HR—Highly Recommended. $NA—Price not available. (BT)—Barrel tasting. Ⓐ—Auction Price. For a key to the tasters' initials, see "How to Use These Listings."
Dates in parentheses represent the issues in which the ratings were published.

Clos Vougeot 1991 • $60 • (1/31/1994) • **84**
Clos Vougeot 1990 • $45 • (12/15/1992) • **94**
Clos Vougeot 1988 • $50 • (11/30/1990) • **91**
Clos Vougeot 1987 • $50 • (2/15/1991) • **84**
Clos Vougeot 1985 • $60 • (6/15/1988) • **90**

TOUR, MARQUIS DE LA

Brut France NV: An attractive sparkler, offering pear and vanilla in a light-bodied, crisp presentation. Drink now.–B.S. • $7 • (2/29/2000) • **84**

TOUR BELLEVUE, CHATEAU

Haut-Médoc 1996: Smells like boiled cabbage with some cherry aroma. Medium-bodied, with light tannins and an earthy, herbal aftertaste. Barely acceptable.–J.S. • $12 • (1/31/1999) • **72**
Haut-Médoc 1995 • $9 • (1/31/1998) • **79**

TOUR BLANCHE, CHATEAU LA

Sauternes 1998: Incredibly ripe, with loads of honey, spice and dried fruit character already. Full-bodied and very sweet, with a long, spicy finish. Really outstanding.–J.S. • $NA • (1/01/1999) (BT) • **90-94**
Sauternes 1997: A subtle, sweet wine, with intense aromas of honey, almond, spice and vanilla. Full-bodied and very sweet, with a lovely, ripe tropical fruit character. Super. Best after 2001.–J.S. • $50 • (1/31/2000) • **92**
Sauternes 1990 • $40 Ⓐ • (4/15/1995) • **88**
Sauternes 1989 • $43 Ⓐ • (4/15/1995) • **92**
Sauternes 1988 • $40 Ⓐ • (4/15/1995) • **89**
Sauternes 1987 • $23 • (6/15/1990) • **82**
Sauternes 1986 • $26 • (4/15/1995) • **84**
Sauternes 1985 • $32 • (7/15/1988) • **85**
Sauternes 1983 • $32 • (4/15/1995) • **88**

TOUR BOISEE, DOMAINE LA

Grenache Minervois 1996: Has modest dried cherry and brown sugar flavors, but turns sharp and acidic on the finish.–K.M. • $10 • (12/31/1999) • **73**
Minervois 1990 • $8 • (3/15/1994) • **82**
Minervois Cuvée Marie-Claude 1995: Lovely and fruity, with gobs of blueberry, dark plum and dark cherry flavors. This has a bacony aroma and a nice chewy texture. A wine of character and gusto that finishes on appealing game and chocolate notes. Drink now through 2003.–K.M. • $15 • (10/31/1998) • **90**
Minervois Cuvée Marie-Claude 1990 • $11 • (3/15/1994) • **88**

TOUR CALON, CHATEAU

Montagne-St.-Emilion 1990 • $13 • (8/31/1995) • **82**
Montagne-St.-Emilion 1989 • $13 • (11/30/1992) • **78**
Montagne-St.-Emilion 1986 • $10 • (9/30/1989) • **81**

TOUR CARNET, CHATEAU LA

Haut-Médoc 1999: Wonderful plum and berry with crushed raspberry character. Medium- to full-bodied, with a good core of fruit and lovely tender and velvety tannins. Well done for this estate.–J.S. • $NA • (1/01/2000) (BT) • **85-89**
Haut-Médoc 1995 • $15 • (1/31/1998) • **87**
Haut-Médoc 1992 • $17 • (4/15/1995) • **76**
Haut-Médoc 1991 • $15 • (3/31/1994) • **71**
Haut-Médoc 1989: Open and delicious now. Shows spice, cedar, tobacco and chocolate character throughout. Full-bodied, with velvety tannins and a caressing finish. Will improve, but why wait? (1989 Bordeaux horizontal tasting).–J.S. • $NA • (5/31/1999) • **89**
Haut-Médoc 1988 • $15 • (8/31/1991) • **82**
Haut-Médoc 1985 • $22 • (12/31/1988) • **71**
Haut-Médoc 1945 • $130 • (3/16/1986) • **88**

TOUR D'AURON, CHATEAU

Bordeaux Supérieur 1995 • $9 • (1/01/1998) • **73**

TOUR-DE-BY, CHATEAU LA

Médoc 1998: Rather lean and mean, with medium body, moderate berry, herbal character and a medium finish.–J.S. • $NA • (5/31/1999) (BT) • **80-84**
Médoc 1997: Very light, with some plum and cedar character, but short and slightly dry.–J.S. • $NA • (1/31/2000) • **79**
Médoc 1996: A slightly herbal and metallic wine, with light body, light tannins and a diluted finish. Hard to get excited about.–J.S. • $NA • (2/28/1999) • **78**
Médoc 1995: Pure milk chocolate, with currants. Medium-bodied, with medium tannins and a long, fruity finish. Hard not to drink it now. Best from 2001 through 2004.–J.S. • $15 • (9/15/1998) • **88**
Médoc 1992 • $11 • (4/15/1995) • **73**
Médoc 1991 • $11 • (3/31/1994) • **74**
Médoc 1990 • $12 • (3/31/1993) • **82**
Médoc 1989: A bit rustic but there's good ripeness to this wine. Medium-ruby to brick-red in color. Aromas of plums, berries, bark. Medium- to full-bodied, with intense ripe fruit flavors, velvety tannins and a dusty finish. Drink now. (1989 Bordeaux horizontal tasting).–J.S. • $NA • (5/31/1999) • **86**
Médoc 1988 • $13 • (6/15/1991) • **86**
Médoc 1987 • $10 • (11/30/1989) • **79**
Médoc 1986 • $12 • (2/15/1989) • **84**
Médoc 1983 • $18 • (10/16/1985) • **78**
Médoc 1982 • $20 • (8/31/1992) • **85**
Médoc Cuvée de Prestige 1998: Aromas of tar that verge on herbalness. Medium-bodied, with medium tannins and a short finish. Rather rustic at this stage. May move up a notch next year.–J.S. • $NA • (5/31/1999) (BT) • **80-84**
Médoc Cuvée Prestige 1982 • $20 • (8/31/1992) • **89**

TOUR DE MIRAMBEAU, CHATEAU

Bordeaux Cuvée Passion 1996: A sleek and well-crafted '96. Attractive aromas of violets, berries and spice. Medium-bodied, with firm tannins and a long, fruity aftertaste. Impressive for this appellation. Best after 2001.–J.S. • $NA • (1/31/1999) • **86**
Bordeaux Cuvée Passion 1995 • $NA • (1/01/1997) • **87**
Bordeaux Supèrieur 1997: A bit boring, with aromas of coffee, berry and chocolate. Medium-bodied, with fine tannins and a light finish. Drink now.–J.S. • $14 • (6/15/2000) • **84**
Bordeaux White 1999: Stone, honey and grass character. Medium-bodied, with fresh acidity and a long pear and grapefruit finish. Drink now.–J.S. • $9 • (1/01/2000) • **85**
Bordeaux White Cuvée Passion 1996: Lots of Sauvignon character, with celery and grass aromas and flavors. Medium-bodied, with fresh acidity and a long, delicious finish. Like a very good Loire Sauvignon Blanc. Drink now.–J.S. • $NA • (1/01/1999) • **86**
Entre-Deux-Mers 1999: Attractive aromas of pear, honey and apple. Medium-bodied, with fresh acidity and a clean finish. Drink now.–J.S. • $9 • (6/15/2000) • **85**
Sémillon Bordeaux Supèrieur Noble 1995: Fresh and lightly sweet, with lemon, cream and coconut. Light finish. A bit dull. Drink now.–J.S. • $30 • (1/01/2000) • **81**

TOUR DE MONS, CHATEAU LA

Margaux 1998: A cool '98, with mineral, mint and hints of fruit. Medium-bodied, with medium tannins and a light finish.–J.S. • $NA • (5/31/1999) (BT) • **80-84**
Margaux 1997: A light wine, but shows some pretty berry and cherry character with a hint of spice. Drink now.–J.S. • $28 • (1/31/2000) • **82**
Margaux 1996: Some good fruit flavors, but slightly one-dimensional, with medium body, medium tannins and a berry finish.–J.S. • $22 • (1/31/1999) • **83**
Margaux 1995: Beautiful, pure aromas of red fruits and light earth. Medium-bodied and silky, with fine tannins and a ripe fruit finish. Elegant. Drink through 2005–J.S. • $28 • (9/15/1998) • **88**
Margaux 1992 • $15 • (4/15/1995) • **75**
Margaux 1991 • $15 • (3/31/1994) • **82**
Margaux 1990 • $20 • (3/31/1993) • **89**
Margaux 1989: Sleek and fine, predicting a bright future. Good, deep-ruby color. Wonderful aromas of berries and exotic spices. Full-bodied and very firm, with racy tannins and a long, silky finish. (1989 Bordeaux horizontal tasting). Best after 2000.–J.S. • $NA • (5/31/1999) • **90**
Margaux 1986 • $19 • (11/30/1989) • **90**
Margaux 1982: Delicious red wine, showing dark ruby-garnet color with a black center. Berry, wet earth aromas. Medium-bodied, with silky tannins and a fresh, dark-chocolate aftertaste. (1982 Bordeaux horizontal tasting). Drink now.–J.S. • $NA • (11/30/1998) • **86**

FRANCE

Margaux 1945 • $200 • (3/16/1986) • **89**

TOUR DU MAYNE, CHATEAU

Haut-Médoc 1996: Slightly funky character, but well textured. Alluring cherry and dried herb on the nose. Medium-bodied, with medium tannins and an aftertaste of berry and earth. Best after 2000.–J.S. • $12 • (1/31/1999) • **81**
Haut-Médoc 1995 • $9 • (1/31/1998) • **85**

TOUR DU MOULIN, CHATEAU

Fronsac 1997: Pretty aromas of licorice, berry and cherry. Medium-bodied, with polished tannins and a light and fruity finish. Drink now.–J.S. • $NA • (1/31/2000) • **85**

TOUR-DU-PIN-FIGEAC, CHATEAU LA

St.-Emilion 1988 • $24 • (7/15/1991) • **77**
St.-Emilion 1982: Slightly overdone. Very dark ruby-garnet color. Complex aromas of fruit, dark chocolate and cedar. Full-bodied and very tannic, with almost burnt flavors. Extremely ripe and alcoholic. Drink now. (1982 Bordeaux horizontal tasting).–J.S. • $NA • (11/30/1998) • **87**

TOUR-HAUT-BRION, CHATEAU LA

Pessac-Léognan 1999: Dark-colored, with loads of berry, currant and tobacco aromas. Full- to medium-bodied, with chewy tannins. A bit hollow in the center palate.–J.S. • $NA • (1/01/2000) (BT) • **85-89**
Pessac-Léognan 1998: Very impressive young La Tour. Opulent aromas of currants, chocolate and toasted oak follow through to a full-bodied palate, with velvety tannins and a fruity finish. A beautiful, rich young wine.–J.S. • $NA • (5/31/1999) (BT) • **90-94**
Pessac-Léognan 1996: A light and watery '96, with some ripe fruit character and firm tannins, but it's too diluted to be anything more than average. Much worse than when tasted from barrel.–J.S. • $30 Ⓐ • (1/31/1999) • **78**
Pessac-Léognan 1995 • $43 Ⓐ • (1/31/1998) • **88**
Pessac-Léognan 1990 • $82 Ⓐ • (3/31/1993) • **93**
Pessac-Léognan 1989: A slightly rustic but powerful wine. Impressive. Deep, dark-ruby color. Complex and rich aromas of grilled meat, chocolate and berries with a leafy highlight. Full-bodied and very tannic. Puckers your mouth. Needs time to mellow. Best after 2004. (1989 Bordeaux horizontal tasting). –J.S. • $77 Ⓐ • (5/31/1999) • **92**
Pessac-Léognan 1988 • $30 • (6/15/1991) CS • **91**
Pessac-Léognan 1987 • $22 • (5/15/1990) • **87**
Graves 1985 • $69 Ⓐ • (2/15/1989) • **86**
Graves 1983 • $45 Ⓐ • (3/15/1987) • **90**
Graves 1982: A subtle yet rich wine. Dark red, with an inky center and an amber edge. Beautiful cigar-box, berry and cherry aromas. Full-bodied and very ripe, with sweet fruit and wonderful autumnal flavors. Long, with silky texture. Drink now. (1982 Bordeaux horizontal tasting).–J.S. • $104 Ⓐ • (11/30/1998) • **94**
Graves 1979 • $30 • (11/15/1991) • **85**
Graves 1975 • $152 Ⓐ • (11/15/1991) • **84**
Graves 1970 • $109 Ⓐ • (11/15/1991) • **84**
Graves 1966 • $62 Ⓐ • (11/15/1991) • **84**
Graves 1964 • $110 • (11/15/1991) • **83**
Graves 1962 • $60 • (11/30/1987) • **85**
Graves 1961 • $782 Ⓐ • (4/30/1996) • **88**
Graves 1959 • $172 Ⓐ • (11/15/1991) • **84**
Graves 1958 • $150 • (11/15/1991) • **85**
Graves 1957 • $125 • (11/15/1991) • **86**
Graves 1955 • $300 • (11/15/1991) • **87**
Graves 1953 • $300 • (11/15/1991) • **86**
Graves 1947 • $630 • (11/15/1991) • **91**
Graves 1945 • $650 • (11/30/1995) • **85**
Graves 1943 • $230 • (11/15/1991) • **85**
Graves 1940 • $190 • (11/15/1991) • **83**
Graves 1929 • $500 • (11/15/1991) • **85**

Key: SS—Spectator Selection. CS—Cellar Selection. HR—Highly Recommended. $NA—Price not available. (BT)—Barrel tasting. Ⓐ—Auction Price. For a key to the tasters' initials, see "How to Use These Listings."
Dates in parentheses represent the issues in which the ratings were published.

TOUR HAUT-CAUSSAN, CHATEAU

Médoc 1997: Plum, chocolate and black licorice aromas. Medium-bodied, with velvety tannins and a fresh fruit finish. Slightly hollow center palate. Drink now.–J.S. • $NA • (1/31/2000) • **85**
Médoc 1996: Loads of grape, raspberry and mineral aromas in this red. Medium-bodied, with firm tannins, but slightly hollow in the midpalate. From an estate that always makes very good wine. Best after 2000.–J.S. • $18 • (1/31/1999) • **86**
Médoc 1995: A bit closed but shows promise. Intense aromas of blackberries, violets and oak. Full- to medium-bodied, with silky tannins and a pretty texture. Needs time. Best from 2001 through 2006.–J.S. • $21 • (9/15/1998) • **89**
Médoc 1992 • $14 • (4/15/1995) • **82**
Médoc 1991 • $14 • (3/31/1994) • **81**
Médoc 1990 • $17 • (3/31/1993) • **89**
Médoc 1989: A big, slightly rustic red but delicious to drink now. Medium-brick-red in color, intense raisin and dried cherry aromas. Full-bodied and chewy, with lots of tannins and a thick, round mouthfeel. A bit alcoholic on the finish. (1989 Bordeaux horizontal tasting).–J.S. • $NA • (5/31/1999) • **88**
Médoc 1988 • $13 • (7/15/1991) • **79**
Médoc 1987 • $11 • (11/30/1989) • **80**
Médoc 1986 • $14 • (11/30/1989) • **88**
Médoc 1984 • $10 • (2/15/1988) • **80**
Médoc 1982 • $16 • (8/31/1989) • **90**

TOUR LEOGNAN, CHATEAU LA

Pessac-Léognan 1996: Attractive blackberry and cherry character, with medium body, fine tannins and a fresh, slightly short finish. Second label of Château Carbonnieux. Drink now.–J.S. • $26 • (1/31/1999) • **85**
Pessac-Léognan 1995 • $NA • (1/31/1998) • **86**
Pessac-Léognan 1990 • $21 • (3/31/1993) • **87**
Pessac-Léognan 1986 • $11 • (2/15/1989) • **85**

TOUR-PRIGNAC, CHATEAU

Médoc 1996: Some plum and berry character, with a hint of dried herbs. Medium-bodied, with medium tannins and a dried-herb finish. A bit boring. Drink now.–J.S. • $12 • (1/31/1999) • **82**
Médoc 1995 • $10 • (1/31/1998) • **86**
Médoc 1989 • $9 • (7/15/1992) • **75**

TOUR ST.-ANDRE, CHATEAU

Lalande-de-Pomerol 1997: Pleasant berry and cherry character. Medium-bodied, with soft tannins and a fruity finish. Lovely. Drink now.–J.S. • $NA • (1/01/2000) • **85**

TOUR VIEILLE, DOMAINE LA

Collioure Puig Ambeille 1998: Quite ripe, with roasted and red plum flavors and a slightly drying finish. Drink now.–K.M. • $17 • (6/15/2000) • **83**

TOURELLES DE LONGUEVILLE

Pauillac 1996: A slightly boring '96, with berry and wet-earth character and a hint of herb on the nose and palate. Second label of Château Pichon-Longueville-Baron. Best after 2000.–J.S. • $27 • (1/31/1999) • **82**
Pauillac 1995 • $25 • (1/31/1998) • **87**
Pauillac 1994 • $25 • (1/31/1997) • **85**
Pauillac 1993 • $20 • (1/31/1996) • **78**
Pauillac 1992 • $16 • (4/15/1995) • **70**
Pauillac 1991 • $16 • (3/31/1994) • **78**
Pauillac 1990 • $22 • (3/31/1993) • **90**
Pauillac 1989 • $27 • (3/15/1992) • **94**

TOURETTE, CHATEAU LA

Pauillac 1998: Aromas of minerals and dried berries. Medium-bodied, with polished tannins and a hollow midpalate. Well crafted.–J.S. • $NA • (5/31/1999) (BT) • **85-89**
Pauillac 1996: Very good stuff here. Dark-colored, with wonderful aromas of cinnamon and berries. Medium- to full-bodied, with firm tannins and a silky texture, a complement of ripe fruit in the aftertaste. Best after 2001.–J.S. • $15 • (1/31/1999) • **88**

Pauillac 1995 • $22 • (1/31/1998) • **89**
Pauillac 1994 • $22 • (1/31/1997) • **84**

TOURNONS, CELLIER DES

Mâcon-Villages La Boisserolle 1995 • $9 • (1/31/1997) • **75**

TOURS, CHATEAU DES | BEAUJOLAIS

Brouilly 1998: Shows cherry flavor, with an earthy note and a firm structure underneath. The finish is a touch green and astringent.–B.S. • $13 • (10/15/1999) • **79**
Brouilly 1996 • $11 • (9/15/1997) • **84**
Brouilly 1995 • $14 • (8/31/1996) • **86**
Brouilly 1993 • $12 • (6/30/1994) • **86**

TOURS, CHATEAU DES | RHONE

Côtes du Rhône Réserve 1997: Light in color but thickly layered, with wonderful ripe texture accented by wet earth and a hard-to-define mix of spice, berry and black fruit flavors. Traditional in style, but what a lovely, balanced, full-bodied, sweet-tasting mouthfeel. Drink now through 2001.–P.M. • $14 • (11/15/1999) • **88**
Côtes du Rhône Réserve 1995 • $12 • (10/15/1997) • **75**
Côtes du Rhône Réserve 1994 • $12 • (12/15/1996) • **76**
Côtes du Rhône Réserve 1993 • $12 • (9/30/1995) • **86**
Côtes du Rhône Réserve 1992 • $10 • (11/30/1994) • **76**
Côtes du Rhône Réservé 1990 • $12 • (4/15/1993) • **81**
Côtes du Rhône Réserve 1989 • $12 • (3/15/1991) • **80**
Côtes du Rhône White Réserve 1997: Woody, a bit oxidized and odd, tasting of burnt butter. Tart finish.–P.M. • $14 • (11/15/1999) • **74**
Vacqueyras Réserve 1997: Rich, plummy and minerally, this tannic but ripe "high-visibility" red shows plenty of presence and flavors and delivers bang for the bucks. A blood-orange, get-tough attack on the finish must be mitigated with appropriated foods. Drink now through 2003.–P.M. • $23 • (12/15/1999) • **85**
Vacqueyras Rèserve 1991 • $15 • (3/31/1994) • **85**
Vacqueyras Réservé 1990 • $34 Ⓐ • (4/15/1993) • **79**
Vacqueyras Réserve 1989 • $15 • (10/15/1991) • **85**

TOURS, DOMAINE DES

Vin de Pays de Vaucluse 1994 • $8 • (12/15/1996) • **78**
Vin de Pays de Vaucluse 1993 • $8 • (11/15/1995) • **84**
Vin de Pays de Vaucluse 1990 • $7 • (4/15/1993) • **82**
Vin de Pays de Vaucluse 1989 • $8 • (3/31/1991) • **78**

TOURTEAU-CHOLLET, CHATEAU

Graves 1996: Offers some grass and lime character, but shows slightly candied fruit on the finish. Medium-bodied, with medium acidity.–J.S. • $12 • (3/31/1999) • **78**

TOUZOT, JEAN

Mâcon-Villages 1997: Tart, astringent, lean, with modest fruit.–P.M. • $10 • (5/31/1999) • **70**
Mâcon-Villages 1996 • $11 • (5/31/1998) • **82**
Mâcon-Villages 1995 • $NA • (8/31/1996) • **77**

TRANCHAND, PHILIPPE

Beaujolais-Villages 1997: Cherry and leather, reminiscent of Chianti, hold court in this firm, slightly rustic Beaujolais-Villages. Maturing, yet still lively and interesting, with a lingering finish. Drink now.–B.S. • $9 • (10/15/1999) • **84**
Fleurie La Madone 1997: Weedy, herbal notes dominate this angular red, with raisin and dried cherry flavors and dry tannins. A rustic style that lacks concentration and polish.–T.M. • $15 • (10/15/1999) • **77**

TRAPADIS, DOMAINE DU

Côtes du Rhône 1998: Has character. Medium-bodied and tannic, its dark color, flavorful fruit and ripe tannins give it personality. Lingering, slightly rustic finish. Drink now through 2003.–P.M. • $11 • (12/15/1999) • **85**
Côtes du Rhône 1997: Light and simple, with anise, cedar and cherry notes and a dry finish.–P.M. • $11 • (11/15/1999) • **77**
Côtes du Rhône 1996: Astringent and green, with mature notes, hints of red berry, licorice and spice. Light-bodied, dry on the finish.–P.M. • $12 • (11/15/1998) • **71**
Côtes du Rhône 1995 • $11 • (9/15/1997) • **85**
Côtes du Rhône-Villages Rasteau 1998: A dark, fruity '98. Supple, with good focus of dried herbs and clean red berries and blackberries. The oak flavors add intrigue to the toasty, smoky complexity. Ripe tannins. Drink now through 2004.–P.M. • $14 • (12/15/1999) • **86**
Côtes du Rhône-Villages Rasteau 1997: Fruity and crisp, with black cherry, plum and spice character, rather rustic and one-dimensional. Finishes a bit hot.–P.M. • $14 • (11/15/1999) • **79**
Côtes du Rhône-Villages Rasteau 1996: Ripe and succulent, with loads of plum, coffee and spice, but also a slight herbaceousness. Medium to full in body, fairly generous, but the finish is slightly hot. Drink now.–P.M. • $14 • (11/15/1998) • **80**
Côtes du Rhône-Villages Rasteau 1995 • $13 • (9/15/1997) • **87**
Côtes du Rhône-Villages Rasteau Harys 1998: A beautiful '98, dense and thick, opulent in its texture, offering lovely blackberry and black pepper character. Lots of ripe tannins make this inky-dark red accessible now, or hold if you wish. Drink now through 2003.–P.M. • $24 • (12/15/1999) • **89**
Côtes du Rhône-Villages Rasteau Préstige 1998: Amazing quality for this appellation. Ripe, rich, seductive and smooth, it's just lovely, with good acidity and fruit and smooth tannins. The sort of full-bodied red you want to have around the house. Balanced finish, with fresh herbs and blackberries. Delicious. Drink now through 2003.–P.M. • $19 • (12/15/1999) • **87**
Côtes du Rhône-Villages Rasteau Préstige 1997: Nice and fresh, with some lively red berry aromas, a ripe character and an earthy subtext that makes it distinctive. Drink now.–P.M. • $18 • (11/15/1999) • **82**
Côtes du Rhône-Villages Rasteau Préstige 1996: This oak-aged wine is generous and ripe, offering plenty of plum, mocha, currant and blueberry flavors. Balanced, of medium to full body, its tannins are smooth although the lingering, smoky finish is chewy. Drink now.–P.M. • $18 • (11/15/1998) • **85**
Côtes du Rhône-Villages Rasteau Prestige 1995 • $17 • (9/15/1997) • **90**

TRAPET, JEAN & JEAN-LOUIS

Chambertin 1996: Lovely expression of black cherries, earth and violets in this supple, moderately concentrated red, whose acidity and tannins are muscular. Good, lingering aftertaste. Best from 2002 through 2008.–P.M. • $100 • (9/30/1998) • **90**
Chambertin 1995 • $76 • (11/15/1997) • **87**
Chambertin 1994 • $NA • (11/15/1996) • **55**
Chambertin 1993 • $NA • (5/15/1996) • **92**
Chapelle-Chambertin 1995 • $62 • (11/15/1997) • **87**
Chapelle-Chambertin 1994 • $NA • (11/15/1996) • **85**
Chapelle-Chambertin 1993 • $NA • (5/15/1996) • **87**
Gevrey-Chambertin 1996: A red cherry note pervades this elegant, firmly structured wine, with a straightforward appeal and a modest finish. Drink through 2004–B.S. • $32 • (9/30/1998) • **84**
Gevrey-Chambertin 1993 • $NA • (5/15/1996) • **85**
Gevrey-Chambertin 1991 • $23 • (3/15/1994) • **80**
Gevrey-Chambertin Cuvée Vieilles Vignes 1995 • $25 • (11/15/1997) • **85**
Gevrey-Chambertin Petite Chapelle 1996: Blackberries, plums and a smoky note show in this straightforward red, whose tannins are dry on the finish. Best from 2000.–B.S. • $35 • (9/30/1998) • **86**
Gevrey-Chambertin Petite Chapelle 1994 • $NA • (11/15/1996) • **81**
Latricières-Chambertin 1996: This leans more toward the red-fruit spectrum, accented by earth and game. A healthy dose of tannins adds a rigidness, with moderate concentration and intensity. Best from 2002.–B.S. • $75 • (9/30/1998) • **87**
Latricières-Chambertin 1995 • $62 • (11/15/1997) • **89**
Latricières-Chambertin 1993 • $NA • (5/15/1996) • **86**
Latricières-Chambertin 1991 • $49 • (3/15/1994) • **85**
Marsannay 1996: A bit herbal, with modest red berry flavor, this turns tough, dry and astringent on the palate.–P.M. • $20 • (9/30/1998) • **77**

TREMBLAY, GERARD

Chablis 1997: Bitter and astringent.–P.M. • $14 • (5/31/1999) • **70**
Chablis Beauroy 1997: Lovely, with a salty, minerally, floral, melon character, this is really fruity and attractive, with a lingering, crisp finish. Drink now through 2001.–P.M. • $19 • (5/31/1999) • **87**

FRANCE

TREMBLAY, GERARD

Chablis Fourchaume 1997: Fairly intense, with lemony, grassy, herbal and spicy notes, there's good intensity here, if not much harmony. Disjointed, astringent finish. Drink now.–P.M. • $20 • (5/31/1999) • **80**
Chablis Fourchaume 1995 • $NA • (6/15/1997) • **85**
Chablis Montmain 1997: Supple but bitter, tasting a bit oxidized and woody, the fruit struggles to come through a blanket of cedar and spice.–P.M. • $19 • (5/31/1999) • **78**
Chablis Montmain 1995 • $17 • (6/15/1997) • **78**
Chablis Valmur 1997: Lots of butter, butterscotch, overripe apple and floral aromas make this Chablis a bit overdone.–P.M. • $36 • (5/31/1999) • **73**

TREMONT, DOMAINE DE

Chénas 1997: This modestly concentrated red has nice chunky fruit that borders on plum, with a hint of tannins at the end.–B.S. • $16 • (10/31/1998) • **84**
Chénas 1996 • $15 • (1/01/1998) • **87**

TRENEL & FILS

Beaujolais-Villages 1997: There's some pretty cherry flavor in this light, supple red, still fresh and appealing. A pleasant quaffer; serve lightly chilled. Drink now.–T.M. • $9 • (5/15/1999) • **83**
Beaujolais-Villages 1990 • $10 • (9/15/1991) • **81**
Beaujolais-Villages 1988 • $9 • (5/31/1989) • **78**
Chénas 1988 • $14 • (5/31/1989) • **86**
Chiroubles 1988 • $12 • (5/31/1989) • **83**
Côte de Brouilly 1990 • $15 • (9/15/1991) • **82**
Fleurie Clos des Moriers 1998: Overtly gamy notes dominate the cherry flavors in this straightforward, slightly bitter red.–T.M. • $15 • (3/31/2000) • **78**
Fleurie Clos des Moriers 1997: Dr. Jekyll and Mr. Hyde. Lovely berry and smoky flavors show impressive concentration, but gamy, reductive aromas, a slight but harsh spritz and dry tannins detract.–T.M. • $17 • (5/15/1999) • **74**
Fleurie Clos des Moriers 1988 • $14 • (5/31/1989) • **86**
Mâcon Blanc-Villages 1995 • $NA • (8/31/1996) • **80**
Mâcon-Villages 1997: Quite woody, showing some decent ripe fruit, spice and grilled bread notes. Chewy, crisp finish.–P.M. • $10 • (5/31/1999) • **79**
Mâcon-Villages 1996 • $NA • (8/31/1997) • **85**
Morgon Côte du Py 1998: This broad-textured red offers ripe flavors of kirsch and cassis, with sharp-edged acidity and firm tannins. A juicy wine that will go well with food. Drink now through 2001.–T.M. • $13 • (3/31/2000) • **87**
Morgon Côte du Py 1988 • $17 • (5/31/1989) • **92**
Moulin-à-Vent Domaine de la Tour du Bief 1997: This beefy red offers the ripe fruit and firm structure typical of its appellation, with round plum and licorice flavors and enough tannin to stand up to hearty dishes, yet it's still fresh and accessible. Drink now.–T.M. • $17 • (5/15/1999) • **87**
Moulin-à-Vent La Rochelle 1988 • $17 • (5/31/1989) • **90**
Régnié 1988 • $12 • (5/31/1989) • **83**
St.-Amour 1988 • $15 • (5/31/1989) • **87**
St.-Véran 1997: Smooth and ripe, focusing on delicious fruit not fancy oak, this delivers some apple, pear, honey, wet hay, dried herbs. Medium-bodied, the finish is a tad bitter. Drink now.–P.M. • $12 • (5/31/1999) • **83**
St.-Véran 1996 • $12 • (5/31/1998) • **76**
St.-Véran 1995 • $NA • (8/31/1996) • **83**

TREVALLON, DOMAINE DE

Coteaux d'Aix-en-Provence Les Baux 1987 • $18 • (3/31/1990) • **78**
Coteaux d'Aix-en-Provence Les Baux 1986 • $21 • (4/15/1989) • **87**
Coteaux d'Aix-en-Provence Les Baux 1985 • $13 • (2/29/1988) • **82**
Vin de Pays des Bouches du Rhône 1996: A distinctive red, with mineral, brick and dried plum flavors. Focused and still fairly crisp, with a meaty aroma and a lingering finish of coffee and dried plum. A blend of Cabernet Sauvignon and Syrah. Drink now.–K.M. • $32 • (10/15/1999) • **87**
Vin de Pays des Bouches du Rhône 1995: Big and brawny, with a nice polish to it as well, this has intense dark plum, red cherry and currant flavors, with meaty notes mixed in. Still quite fresh despite its age, with a lovely finish of berry and coffee, and a good wallop of tannins to boot. Impressive. Drink now through 2003.–K.M. • $28 • (1/01/1999) • **89**

Key: SS—Spectator Selection. CS—Cellar Selection. HR—Highly Recommended. $NA—Price not available. (BT)—Barrel tasting. Ⓐ—Auction Price. For a key to the tasters' initials, see "How to Use These Listings."
Dates in parentheses represent the issues in which the ratings were published.

TRIBUT, LAURENT

Chablis 1998: Delicate, ripe and tasting of honey, butter, cream and apple tart. Well made and accessible on release, with a medium body and a smooth finish. Drink now through 2001.–P.M. • $24 • (5/15/2000) • **84**
Chablis 1997: A bit disjointed, showing a rather neutral character and modest fruit, but a dry, lean finish.–P.M. • $23 • (5/31/1999) • **79**
Chablis 1996 • $22 • (5/31/1998) • **88**
Chablis Beauroy 1998: Seductive. All balance and finesse, with ripe pear, honey, lemon, spice and mineral character. Medium-bodied, it's firm on the palate, with a tight structure and good concentration. Delightful. Drink now through 2005.–P.M. • $33 • (5/15/2000) • **88**
Chablis Beauroy 1997: Pure, crisp Chardonnay, light to medium in body, without any obvious taste of oak, it has a good balance of medium-intense ripe fruit and mineral notes. Drink now through 2001.–P.M. • $33 • (5/31/1999) • **87**
Chablis Beauroy 1995 • $30 • (6/15/1997) • **87**
Chablis Côte de Léchet 1998: A steely, crisp, fruity wine, rather open and aromatic but lacking in mineral concentration. Light- to medium-bodied, with green apple and a citrusy finish. Drink now through 2003.–P.M. • $33 • (5/15/2000) • **80**
Chablis Côte de Léchet 1997: Superclean, polished and showing beautiful mineraliness, with vanilla bean, lemon and a pebbly character that anchors this medium-bodied, vibrant Chablis nicely in the local *terroir*. Cellar. Best from 2002 through 2008.–P.M. • $33 • (5/31/1999) • **89**
Chablis Côte de Léchet 1996 • $30 • (5/31/1998) • **79**
Chablis Côte de Léchet 1995 • $30 • (6/15/1997) • **85**

TRICON, OLIVIER

Chablis 1995 • $NA • (8/31/1996) • **83**

TRIENNES, DOMAINE DE

Cabernet Sauvignon Vin de Pays du Var 1995: A mature red, with dried cherry and leather flavors and tealike notes on the finish. Drink now.–K.M. • $15 • (12/31/1999) • **80**
Cabernet Sauvignon Vin de Pays du Var 1994 • $15 • (12/15/1996) • **86**
Merlot Vin de Pays du Var 1995: Tired, with only modest dried cherry flavors and wispy brown sugar notes on the finish.–K.M. • $19 • (12/31/1999) • **77**
Merlot Vin de Pays du Var 1994 • $18 • (12/15/1996) • **82**
Syrah Vin de Pays du Var 1996: Pleasant, with dried cherry and berry flavors, leather and cedar on the finish. Drink now.–K.M. • $15 • (12/31/1999) • **83**
Vin de Pays du Var Reserve 1995: Charry flavors and rhubarb notes dominate this tired red. Syrah and Cabernet Sauvignon. Past its prime.–K.M. • $19 • (12/31/1999) • **74**
Viognier Vin de Pays du Var 1997: Full-bodied and thick, this French white offers honey, peach and chamomile tea flavors augmented by an earthy note. Finishes with a slight pleasant bitterness. Drink now.–B.S. • $20 • (11/15/1999) • **85**

TRIGNON, CHATEAU DU

Côtes du Rhône 1997: Quite earthy, a medium-bodied red with nice red berry flavors. A bit tannic, even rustic, but pure and clean. Drink now through 2002.–P.M. • $11 • (12/15/1999) • **80**
Côtes du Rhône 1996: Crisp, with a chewy core of cherry, butter, strawberry and red pepper. Light-bodied, with an herbal finish.–P.M. • $10 • (11/15/1998) • **73**
Côtes du Rhône 1995 • $10 • (10/15/1997) • **79**
Côtes du Rhône Blanc de Blancs 1998: Fresh on the nose, a light-bodied white with beeswax (or is it cardboard?) and honey character. Lacks a bit of ripe, focused fruit.–P.M. • $11 • (12/15/1999) • **78**
Côtes du Rhône Blanc de Blancs 1997: Pleasant, with litchi, melon, cherry, lemon and mineral flavors. Medium-bodied, with a round midpalate and a supple, elegant finish. Drink now.–P.M. • $10 • (11/15/1998) • **80**
Côtes du Rhône Blanc de Blancs 1996 • $10 • (10/15/1997) • **84**
Côtes du Rhône Cuvée du Bois des Dames 1997: A soft '97. Smoke and raspberries emerge in this round red of decent intensity and length.–P.M. • $12 • (11/15/1999) • **79**
Côtes du Rhône-Villages Rasteau 1997: Straightforward but supple, with black cherry, anise, vanilla and spice. Good fresh finish. Drink now.–P.M. • $15 • (11/15/1999) • **80**

Côtes du Rhône-Villages Rasteau 1996: Has personality, and some good, warm fruit, but it's also slightly herbal, earthy, tarry and spicy—in a less-than-harmonious way. Drink now through 2002.–P.M. • $14 • (11/15/1998) • **80**
Côtes du Rhône-Villages Rasteau 1995 • $15 • (10/15/1997) • **72**
Côtes du Rhône-Villages Rasteau 1993 • $13 • (11/15/1995) • **72**
Côtes du Rhône-Villages Sablet 1997: Supple in tannin, ripe and medium-bodied, showing a peppery black cherry character on an attractively appealing finish that has some grip. Drink now.–P.M. • $15 • (11/15/1999) • **83**
Côtes du Rhône-Villages Sablet 1996: A subtle wine, showing plum, Provençal herbs and floral notes that are quite attractive. Medium-bodied, with supple tannins. Drink through 2001–P.M. • $14 • (11/15/1998) • **85**
Côtes du Rhône-Villages White Sablet 1997: Shows some cedar, apple and fruit cocktail character, fat and a bit flabby.–P.M. • $14 • (11/15/1998) • **76**
Côtes du Rhône-Villages White Sablet 1996 • $14 • (10/15/1997) • **72**
Côtes du Rhône White Cuvée Célestine 1998: Harmonious and well made, showing ripe fruit but also a good balance between oak and acidity. Thick and full-bodied. Drink now through 2003.–P.M. • $20 • (12/15/1999) • **83**
Gigondas 1997: Spicy on the palate, with a tough, tannic structure and wet earth and mocha notes. Fresh fruit lingers on the firm finish. Tasted twice, with consistent notes. Drink now through 2001.–P.M. • $20 • (10/31/1999) • **80**
Gigondas 1995 • $20 • (10/15/1997) • **85**
Viognier Côtes du Rhône 1998: Nice sorbetlike freshness, sweet and ripe, with loads of apricot, floral and peach aromas. Exciting, full and balanced. Very civilized and well done. Smooth from start to finish. Drink now through 2002.–P.M. • $22 • (12/15/1999) • **89**
Viognier Côtes du Rhône 1997: Lovely aromas of peach, apricot, honeysuckle and ripe pear, but also a canned pineapple note. Full-bodied and rich, with a tart, blanched almond flavor that brings zest to an otherwise buttery, hot finish. Drink now.–P.M. • $20 • (11/15/1998) • **82**
Viognier Côtes du Rhône 1996 • $22 • (10/15/1997) • **88**

TRIMBACH

Gewürztraminer Alsace 1998: Ripe and muted aroma for this varietal, showing citrus and mineral. Subtle peach and melon flavors grow into an attractive finish, with good balance and length. Drink now.–B.S. • $15 • (6/15/2000) • **85**
Gewürztraminer Alsace Hors Choix Sélection de Grains Nobles 1989 • $NA • (11/15/1990) • **97**
Gewürztraminer Alsace Sélection de Grains Nobles 1994: Elegant and refined, showing hard candy, honey and a touch of citrus tightly integrated with the lean, sinewy structure. Lovely intensity, balance and length. Drink now through 2004.–B.S. • $115 • (6/15/2000) • **90**
Gewürztraminer Alsace Vendanges Tardives 1997: Ripe and clean, with honey and citrus nuances in a straightforward, rich style. Just off dry; try with Muenster cheese. Drink now through 2002.–B.S. • $60 • (6/15/2000) • **86**
Pinot Blanc Alsace 1998: A broad, anise-tinged white, with apple and citrus notes, turning focused and lemony on the finish. Nicely balanced. Drink now.–B.S. • $10 • (6/15/2000) • **84**
Pinot Blanc Alsace 1996: Ripe and fruity, yet vivid, showing green apple and citrus, with modest depth and concentration. Drink now.–B.S. • $12 • (9/15/1998) • **82**
Pinot Gris Alsace Hommage à Georgette Trimbach 1996: A serious Pinot Gris, ripe and full of apricot and pear notes, yet also firmly structured and built for the long haul. The upright backbone emerges on the finish; do be patient. Best from 2001 through 2005.–B.S. • $60 • (6/15/2000) • **89**
Pinot Gris Alsace Réserve 1997: Straightforward and smooth, showing lovely almond, peach and smoke flavors, all balanced and lingering on the finish. Drink now.–B.S. • $16 • (6/15/2000) • **85**
Pinot Gris Alsace Réserve Personnelle 1997: Austere and racy, with a firm structure locking up the floral, peach and mineral flavors. Powerful, it needs time for the fruit to emerge. Best after 2000.–B.S. • $30 • (6/15/2000) • **87**
Pinot Gris Alsace Réserve Personnelle 1996: A bit muted today, this white displays citrus and mineral notes, a hint of sweetness and plenty of crisp lemony acidity for balance. The flavors may emerge with time. This was the better of two samples. Drink now through 2003.–B.S. • $30 • (10/31/1999) • **84**
Pinot Gris Alsace Sélection de Grains Nobles 1989: A mature SGN, this has lost some thickness, yet offers plenty of marzipan, honey, apricot and vanilla combined with a lively structure. Long, long finish. Drink now through 2005.–B.S. • $70/375 ml. • (10/31/1999) • **90**
Pinot Noir Alsace Réserve 1993 • $15 • (10/15/1996) • **76**
Pinot Noir Alsace Réserve Personnelle 1990 • $29 • (10/15/1996) • **82**
Riesling Alsace 1997: Lean and crisp, exuding floral, apple and mineral aromas. Very clean and direct, with a moderate finish. Drink now.–B.S. • $15 • (6/15/2000) • **84**
Riesling Alsace Cuvée Frédéric Émile 1996: Subtle, showing ripe quince, peach, spring meadow and mineral aromas and flavors, all married to a rich yet restrained framework. Racy acidity is balanced by a density and clarity of flavor, with the quince and mineral expanding on the finish. Drink now through 2006.–B.S. • $30 • (6/15/2000) • **90**
Riesling Alsace Cuvée Frédéric Émile Sélection de Grains Nobles 1989 • $NA • (11/15/1990) • **90**
Tokay Pinot Gris Alsace Hors Choix Sélection de Grains Nobles 1989 • $NA • (11/15/1990) • **99**
Tokay Pinot Gris Alsace Réserve Sélection de Grains Nobles 1989 • $NA • (11/15/1990) • **90**

TRIMOULET, CHATEAU

St.-Emilion 1996: Medium-bodied, with good cherry and chocolate character, soft tannins and a medium finish. Drink now.–J.S. • $34 • (7/31/1999) • **85**
St.-Emilion 1990 • $20 • (9/15/1993) • **86**
St.-Emilion 1988 • $16 • (6/15/1991) HR • **91**
St.-Emilion 1982 • $15 • (5/15/1989) • **81**

TRINQUEVEDEL, CHATEAU DE

Tavel 1998: This is earthy, totally weird and drying on the palate, with modest fruit and a bitter aftertaste. Sorry—we tried but couldn't get the point.–P.M. • $11 • (12/15/1999) • **75**

TRIPOZ, DIDIER

Charnay-lès-Mâcon Clos des Tournons 1996 • $9 • (8/31/1997) • **87**
Mâcon-Charnay Clos des Tournons 1995 • $NA • (8/31/1996) • **86**
Mâcon-Villages 1996 • $15 • (8/31/1997) • **78**

TROCADERO, JEAN-PAUL

Brut Blanc de Blancs France Tête de Cuvée NV • $NA • (1/01/1998) • **76**

TROCARD, CHATEAU

Bordeaux Supèrieur 1997: Light, green and watery. More like herbal tea than wine.–J.S. • $12 • (1/01/2000) • **73**
Bordeaux Supérieur 1988 • $9 • (1/31/1992) • **83**
Bordeaux Supèrieur Monrepos 1997: Aromas of raspberry and currant. Medium-bodied, with silky tannins and a light, watery finish. Drink now.–J.S. • $16 • (6/15/2000) • **81**

TROIS CROIX, CHATEAU LES

Fronsac 1999: Plenty of berry, smoke and mineral character. Medium-bodied, with fresh tannins and a clean finish. Well done.–J.S. • $NA • (1/01/2000) (BT) • **85-89**
Fronsac 1997: Pretty mint, violet and cherry character. Medium-bodied, with fine tannins and a short finish. Drink now.–J.S. • $NA • (1/31/2000) • **85**

TROLLAT, RAYMOND

St.-Joseph 1996: This firm, chewy red shows well-defined flavors of black cherry, smoke and bacon, with black pepper and licorice accents. The tannins are muscular but support the fruit without overwhelming it. Drink through 2005–T.M. • $20 • (11/15/1998) • **88**
St.-Joseph 1994 • $NA • (11/30/1996) • **87**
St.-Joseph 1992 • $15 • (5/31/1994) • **83**
St.-Joseph 1991 • $15 • (5/31/1994) • **88**

TRONQUOY-LALANDE, CHATEAU

St.-Estèphe 1998: Plenty of cherry and tar character. Medium- to full-bodied and velvety, with a good core of fruit and a medium finish. Well done for this estate.–J.S. • $NA • (5/31/1999) (BT) • **85-89**
St.-Estèphe 1997: Plum and green tobacco character throughout. Medium-bodied, with velvety tannins and a medium finish. Drink now through 2005.–J.S. • $14 • (1/31/2000) • **86**
St.-Estèphe 1996: Dark-colored, with blackberry, mineral and spice aromas. Medium-bodied, with well-integrated tannins and a caressing texture, but slightly hollow in the midpalate.–J.S. • $16 • (1/31/1999) • **86**
St.-Estèphe 1995 • $20 • (1/31/1998) • **89**

TRONQUOY-LALANDE, CHATEAU

St.-Estèphe 1994 • $18 • (1/31/1997) • **82**
St.-Estèphe 1993 • $21 • (1/31/1996) • **79**
St.-Estèphe 1991 • $17 • (3/31/1994) • **79**
St.-Estèphe 1988 • $14 • (7/15/1991) • **84**
St.-Estèphe 1987 • $13 • (11/30/1989) • **84**
St.-Estèphe 1986 • $15 • (11/30/1989) • **92**
St.-Estèphe 1982 • $20 • (11/30/1989) • **86**

TROPLONG-MONDOT, CHATEAU

St.-Emilion 1999: Pleasant violet , plum and raspberry aromas. Medium-bodied, with medium to full tannins and a plummy aftertaste. Nicely made.–J.S. • $NA • (1/01/2000) (BT) • **85-89**
St.-Emilion 1998: Racy, with spice, cherry and raspberry character. Medium- to full-bodied, with full, polished tannins and a long finish. Loads of wood, but who cares? It's damn good.–J.S. • $NA • (5/31/1999) (BT) • **90-94**
St.-Emilion 1997: Lovely fruit on the nose of this young wine, with lots of plum, tobacco and berry aromas. Medium-bodied, with polished tannins, but slightly short on the finish. Best after 2000.–J.S. • $45 • (1/31/2000) • **87**
St.-Emilion 1996: Plenty of crushed berry and spice on the nose. Full-bodied, with full, slightly drying tannins, but good berry and chocolate flavors on the finish. Perhaps slightly overwooded. Best after 2001.–J.S. • $34 Ⓐ • (1/31/1999) • **88**
St.-Emilion 1995 • $54 Ⓐ • (1/31/1998) • **92**
St.-Emilion 1994 • $38 Ⓐ • (1/31/1997) • **92**
St.-Emilion 1993 • $34 Ⓐ • (1/31/1996) • **88**
St.-Emilion 1992 • $26 Ⓐ • (4/15/1995) • **88**
St.-Emilion 1991 • $20 • (3/31/1994) • **81**
St.-Emilion 1990 • $150 Ⓐ • (3/31/1993) • **91**
St.-Emilion 1989: Seductive. Gorgeously perfumed, loads of raspberry and floral aromas. Full-bodied, with velvety tannins and a delicious blackberry and dark chocolate aftertaste. Best after 2005. (1989 Bordeaux horizontal tasting).–J.S. • $106 Ⓐ • (5/31/1999) • **93**
St.-Emilion 1988: People always talk about the great new vintages of Troplong and forget about wines such as this, with a good, dark ruby color and an array of aromas from blackberry to milk chocolate. Medium-bodied, with full, velvety tannins and a superfruity and caressing finish. Will improve with age. Drink through 2006. (1988 Bordeaux horizontal tasting).–J.S. • $43 Ⓐ • (11/30/1998) • **90**
St.-Emilion 1986 • $39 Ⓐ • (6/30/1989) • **88**
St.-Emilion 1985 • $45 Ⓐ • (6/30/1988) • **88**
St.-Emilion 1982: A bit tough and overextracted. Medium brick-red color, with an inky center. Blackberry, wet earth and mineral character. Medium- to full-bodied, very tannic and slightly hard. (1982 Bordeaux horizontal tasting). Drink now.–J.S. • $53 Ⓐ • (11/30/1998) • **88**
St.-Emilion 1961 • $NA • (4/30/1996) • **85**

TROTANOY, CHATEAU

Pomerol 1999: Clean and fruity, with berry, cherry and green tobacco character. Medium to light body. Fine tannins.–J.S. • $NA • (1/01/2000) (BT) • **85-89**
Pomerol 1998: Hard to remember a young Trot as exciting as this. Electrifying aromas of crushed grapes, berries and cinnamon. Full-bodied, with masses of chewy tannins and a long, long finish. Fabulous wine.–J.S. • $NA • (5/31/1999) (BT) • **95-99**
Pomerol 1997: A fine and silky red with extremely attractive berry and tobacco character. Medium-bodied, with a caressing finish. A beauty. Drink now through 2004.–J.S. • $65 • (1/31/2000) • **89**
Pomerol 1996: Plenty of blackberry and dried herb. Medium-bodied, with fine tannins and an aftertaste of berry and wet earth. Not one of the great Trotanoys, but a pretty glass of Pomerol. Drink now through 2002.–J.S. • $88 • (1/31/1999) • **86**
Pomerol 1995 • $75 • (1/31/1998) HR • **97**
Pomerol 1994 • $62 • (1/31/1997) • **90**
Pomerol 1993 • $50 • (1/31/1996) CS • **91**
Pomerol 1992 • $42 • (4/15/1995) • **82**
Pomerol 1990 • $46 • (5/15/1994) • **92**
Pomerol 1989: All in elegance and finesse. Medium-ruby color at the center; a brick-red edge. Aromas of berries, raisins and sliced mushrooms. Full-bodied and chewy, with lots of round tannins and a tobacco, berry aftertaste. Best after 2001. (1989 Bordeaux horizontal tasting).–J.S. • $NA • (5/31/1999) • **92**
Pomerol 1988: A classy, elegant wine with everything in the right place. Mineral, spice and berry aromas follow through to the palate. Full-bodied, with lovely, caressing, velvety tannins and a long, sweet, ripe fruit finish. (1988 Bordeaux horizontal tasting). Best after 2001.–J.S. • $NA • (11/30/1998) • **93**
Pomerol 1987 • $NA • (10/15/1988) • **88**
Pomerol 1986 • $70 • (5/15/1994) • **82**
Pomerol 1985 • $75 • (10/15/1994) • **86**
Pomerol 1983 • $55 • (10/15/1994) • **86**
Pomerol 1982: Not quite as grand as I remember, but still a rich, pretty Pomerol. Dark ruby-garnet color, with tobacco, cherry and earth character. Full-bodied and concentrated, with firm tannins and a long, ripe fruit and dark chocolate finish. Drink now. (1982 Bordeaux horizontal tasting).–J.S. • $246 Ⓐ • (11/30/1998) • **93**
Pomerol 1981 • $73 • (10/15/1994) • **94**
Pomerol 1980 • $NA • (10/15/1988) • **83**
Pomerol 1979 • $60 Ⓐ • (10/15/1989) • **88**
Pomerol 1978 • $94 Ⓐ • (10/15/1988) • **83**
Pomerol 1976 • $NA • (10/15/1988) • **86**
Pomerol 1975 • $178 Ⓐ • (10/15/1988) • **84**
Pomerol 1971 • $258 Ⓐ • (10/15/1988) • **90**
Pomerol 1970 • $284 Ⓐ • (10/15/1988) • **95**
Pomerol 1967 • $83 Ⓐ • (10/15/1988) • **84**
Pomerol 1966 • $112 Ⓐ • (10/15/1988) • **92**
Pomerol 1964 • $185 • (5/15/1994) • **83**
Pomerol 1962 • $NA • (10/15/1988) • **88**
Pomerol 1961 • $444 • (4/30/1996) • **90**
Pomerol 1959 • $312 Ⓐ • (10/15/1988) • **92**
Pomerol 1955 • $NA • (10/15/1988) • **94**
Pomerol 1953 • $300 • (10/15/1988) • **86**
Pomerol 1952 • $NA • (10/15/1988) • **83**
Pomerol 1949 • $1,450 • (5/15/1994) • **92**
Pomerol 1947 • $NA • (10/15/1988) • **80**
Pomerol 1945 • $2,015 Ⓐ • (10/15/1988) • **98**
Pomerol 1934 • $450 • (5/15/1994) • **83**
Pomerol 1928 • $600 • (10/15/1988) • **95**
Pomerol 1926 • $900 • (5/15/1994) • **86**
Pomerol 1924 • $NA • (10/15/1988) • **89**

TROTTEVIEILLE, CHATEAU

St.-Emilion 1999: Attractive aromas of plum skin and berry. Medium-bodied, with medium fine tannins, but falls slightly short on the finish.–J.S. • $NA • (1/01/2000) (BT) • **85-89**
St.-Emilion 1998: Floral and fresh, with fine tannins and a delicious medium-bodied palate. Needs a bit more fruit concentration.–J.S. • $NA • (5/31/1999) (BT) • **85-89**
St.-Emilion 1997: Attractive plum and fresh mushroom aromas. Medium-bodied, with soft tannins and a light, fruity finish. Drink now.–J.S. • $NA • (1/31/2000) • **84**
St.-Emilion 1996: Aromas of milk chocolate and berry. Medium-bodied, with firm tannins and chocolate and pepper flavors. Needs a bit more fruit concentration. Austere. Best after 2000.–J.S. • $28 • (1/31/1999) • **84**
St.-Emilion 1995 • $38 Ⓐ • (1/31/1998) • **83**
St.-Emilion 1992 • $18 • (4/15/1995) • **71**
St.-Emilion 1991 • $18 • (3/31/1994) • **82**
St.-Emilion 1990 • $48 Ⓐ • (3/31/1993) • **91**
St.-Emilion 1989: A wine of wonderful fruit but a slightly odd, earthy character; still delicious. Medium-ruby color and a garnet tint. Very ripe fruit, presenting funky barrel aromas that verge on mushroom. Full-bodied, with full, velvety tannins. Long, sweet fruit finish. Drink now. (1989 Bordeaux horizontal tasting).–J.S. • $41 Ⓐ • (5/31/1999) • **87**
St.-Emilion 1988 • $36 Ⓐ • (4/30/1991) • **85**
St.-Emilion 1982 • $48 Ⓐ • (8/31/1992) • **89**
St.-Emilion 1962 • $30 • (11/30/1987) • **75**

TUILERIE, DOMAINE LA | LOIRE

Pouilly-Fumé 1998: This round, creamy-textured white offers broad flavors of apple and almond and has a core of lemony acidity, but it lacks harmony and depth. Drink now.–T.M. • $19 • (6/30/1999) • **84**
Pouilly-Fumé 1997 • $14 • (6/15/1998) • **84**

Key: SS—Spectator Selection. CS—Cellar Selection. HR—Highly Recommended. $NA—Price not available. (BT)—Barrel tasting. Ⓐ—Auction Price.
For a key to the tasters' initials, see "How to Use These Listings."
Dates in parentheses represent the issues in which the ratings were published.

TUILIERE, DOMAINE LA | RHONE

Côtes du Ventoux 1998: Ripe and dark in color, showing some black fruit, but the aromas and flavors seem a bit dull for now, with spice and oak accents showing better. Drink now.–P.M. • $8 • (11/15/1999) • **80**

Côtes du Ventoux 1997: Dark in color, bursting with compacted red berry and blackberry character and some smoky, wet earth complexity, all in a fresh package. Crisp finish. Drink now.–P.M. • $9 • (11/15/1999) • **82**

Côtes du Ventoux 1996: This dark, tannic red from the Southern Rhône shows good depth and structure for the appellation, not to mention the price, with well-defined flavors of black cherry, black pepper and herb. Crisp and clean, tastily tart on the finish. A lively wine for grilled foods. Drink now.–T.M. • $7 • (11/15/1998) • **86**

Vin de Pays des Côtes de Gascogne 1996 • $6 • (5/15/1998) • **82**

TUQUE, DOMAINE DE LA

Buzet 1995: Quite appealing for its balance, with a well-integrated combination of dried cherry and red plum flavors. Smooth, warm, bricklike notes on the silky finish. Drink now.–K.M. • $9 • (5/31/1999) • **85**

Buzet 1992 • $10 • (12/15/1997) • **84**

Buzet 1990 • $10 • (7/31/1996) • **84**

TURCAUD, CHATEAU

Bordeaux 1994 • $9 • (10/15/1997) • **84**

TURGY, MICHEL

Brut Blanc de Blancs Champagne Le Mesnil Réserve Sélection NV • $25 • (4/30/1998) • **85**

USSEGLIO & FILS, PIERRE

Châteauneuf-du-Pape 1998: A dark-colored red, extracted for maximum show, with an exotic floral, cassis and blackberry character, but little charm. Tastes hard and slightly hot, with drying tannins on the finish. Best from 2002 through 2008.–P.M. • $28 • (6/30/2000) • **84**

Châteauneuf-du-Pape 1997: A *terroir*-driven, traditional Châteauneuf—gamy, leathery and plummy. Smells of the aromas after a storm over the pebbles in the area's vineyards. Medium-bodied and tannic, but balanced with the ripeness of the flavors. The fat mouthfeel makes it a winner despite a slightly rustic finish. Best from 2001 through 2008.–P.M. • $22 • (12/15/1999) • **90**

Châteauneuf-du-Pape 1996: Impressive for a '96. Full-bodied and yummy, showing a lovely combination of plum, leather, smoke and wet earth aromas. The tannins turn a bit tough, but there's enough fruit here to warrant cellaring until all the pieces come together. Best from 2003 through 2010.–P.M. • $22 • (12/15/1999) • **89**

Châteauneuf-du-Pape 1990 • $16 • (4/15/1993) • **85**

Châteauneuf-du-Pape Cuvée de mon Aïeul 1998: Very ripe, with prune and plum. Full-bodied and soft, this traditional Châteauneuf offers leather, wet earth and roasted chestnuts. Well made and flavorful. Drink now through 2015.–P.M. • $39 • (6/30/2000) • **93**

VACHERON, DOMAINE

Sancerre 1996 • $18 • (3/31/1998) • **86**

Sancerre Red 1995 • $19 • (5/31/1998) • **85**

Sancerre Red 1993 • $20 • (6/15/1997) • **78**

Sancerre Red Belle Dame 1995 • $35 • (5/31/1998) • **85**

VAISSE, A.

Fleurie Grille-Midi 1994 • $12 • (10/31/1995) • **87**

VAL D'ORBIEU

Cabernet Sauvignon Vin de Pays d'Oc Réserve St.-Martin 1997: Tough and dried out, with herbal and tobacco notes.–K.M. • $7 • (11/15/1998) • **76**

Cabernet Sauvignon Vin de Pays d'Oc Réserve St.-Martin 1996 • $8 • (6/30/1997) • **84**

Cabernet Sauvignon Vin de Pays d'Oc Réserve St.-Martin Mevushal 1997: Medium-bodied, with dried cherry and leather flavors. Drink now.–K.M. • $10 • (11/15/1998) • **79**

Cabernet Sauvignon Vin de Pays de l'Aude Réserve St.-Martin 1989 • $7 • (10/31/1992) • **77**

Chardonnay Vin de Pays d'Oc Réserve St.-Martin 1997: Nice freshness to this Chardonnay, with juicy and spicy flavors and almond notes. A bit soft in the middle, but still tasty. Drink now.–K.M. • $7 • (11/15/1998) • **84**

Chardonnay Vin de Pays d'Oc Réserve St.-Martin 1996 • $8 • (6/30/1997) • **84**

Chardonnay Vin de Pays d'Oc Réserve St.-Martin Mevushal 1997: Ripe and round, with apple and peach flavors, buttery notes on the finish. Drink now.–K.M. • $10 • (11/15/1998) • **83**

Corbières Les Deux Rives 1996: Light, with berrylike aromas and cherry and berry flavors. Drink now.–K.M. • $NA • (10/31/1998) • **80**

Corbières Les Deux Rives 1995 • $7 • (9/30/1997) • **77**

Corbières White Les Deux Rives 1997: This white from the south of France has ripe apple and peach flavors, with spicy notes as well. Drink now.–K.M. • $7 • (10/31/1998) • **82**

Corbières White Les Deux Rives 1996 • $7 • (10/31/1997) • **78**

Grenache Blanc-Chardonnay Vin de Pays d'Oc Réserve St.-Martin Sélection Blanc 1997: Shows modest green apple flavors which turn a bit diluted in the end.–K.M. • $5 • (11/15/1998) • **78**

Marsanne Vin de Pays d'Oc Réserve St.-Martin 1997: A fairly soft white, with peachy aromas and flavors, some nice spicy notes as well. Drink now.–K.M. • $7 • (11/15/1998) • **82**

Merlot Vin de Pays d'Oc Réserve St.-Martin 1997: A basic red wine that starts out with generous fruit aromas but turns lean, dry and tannic on the palate. • $7 • (10/31/1998) • **77**

Merlot Vin de Pays d'Oc Réserve St.-Martin 1996 • $8 • (6/30/1997) • **82**

Merlot Vin de Pays d'Oc Réserve St.-Martin 1993 • $7 • (11/30/1994) • **77**

Merlot Vin de Pays d'Oc Réserve St.-Martin 1991 • $7 • (3/15/1994) • **80**

Merlot Vin de Pays d'Oc Réserve St.-Martin 1990 • $7 • (9/30/1992) • **81**

Merlot-Cabernet Vin de Pays d'Oc Réserve St.-Martin Sélection Rouge 1997: Basic red wine, with thin herb and tomato flavors and a firm texture. Drink now. • $5 • (10/31/1998) • **75**

Minervois 1989 • $8 • (12/31/1991) • **80**

Mourvèdre Vin de Pays d'Oc Réserve St.-Martin 1996: A nice meaty aroma, with flavors of dried plum, leather and tea make this a lively, medium-bodied red. Finishes with notes of dried cherry and spice. Drink now.–K.M. • $7 • (11/15/1998) • **84**

Mourvèdre Vin de Pays d'Oc Réserve St.-Martin 1995 • $8 • (6/30/1997) • **87**

Mourvèdre Vin de Pays d'Oc Réserve St.-Martin 1991 • $7 • (3/15/1994) • **83**

Muscat de St.-Jean-de-Minervois NV: A solid dessert wine. Pleasant orange and spice aromas and nice tangerine and lime flavors are balanced by good, bright acidity. Finishes a bit short. Drink now.–K.M. • $10/375 ml. • (12/31/1998) • **83**

Muscat de St.-Jean-de-Minervois Petit Grains NV • $14 • (1/31/1995) • **87**

Muscat Vin de Pays d'Oc Réserve St.-Martin 1996 • $8 • (8/31/1997) • **83**

Sauvignon Blanc Vin de Pays d'Oc Réserve St.-Martin 1996 • $8 • (6/30/1997) • **81**

Syrah Vin de Pays d'Oc Réserve St.-Martin 1995 • $8 • (6/30/1997) • **84**

Syrah Vin de Pays d'Oc Réserve St.-Martin 1991 • $7 • (3/15/1994) • **82**

Syrah Vin de Pays d'Oc Réserve St.-Martin 1990 • $7 • (9/30/1992) • **79**

Syrah Vin de Pays d'Oc Rosé Réserve St.-Martin 1997: Melony aromas and flavors dominate this straightforward rosé. The finish is slightly cloying.–K.M. • $7 • (11/15/1998) • **78**

Syrah Vin de Pays d'Oc Rosé Réserve St.-Martin 1996 • $8 • (6/30/1997) • **85**

Vin de Pays d'Oc La Cuvée Mythique 1995: A high-toned red, with nice up-front flavors of dried cherry and spice, but they fade a bit on the finish. Drink now.–K.M. • $16 • (12/15/1998) • **82**

Vin de Pays d'Oc La Cuvée Mythique 1994 • $17 • (6/30/1997) • **84**

Vin de Pays d'Oc La Cuvée Mythique 1990 • $NA • (6/30/1994) • **88**

Vin de Pays de l'Aude Sélection Rouge Cuvée No. 3 1990 • $5 • (9/30/1992) • **78**

Viognier Vin de Pays d'Oc Réserve St.-Martin 1997: This has decent melon and peach flavors and oniony notes on the finish.–K.M. • $10 • (12/15/1998) • **79**

Viognier Vin de Pays d'Oc Réserve St.-Martin 1996 • $10 • (8/31/1997) • **83**

VAL DES BRUYERES, DOMAINE

Merlot Vin de Pays d'Oc 1997: Ripe plum and tobacco flavors dominate this dark and somewhat murky red, which has some rhubarb notes on the finish. Drink now.–K.M. • $7 • (10/31/1999) • **81**

Merlot Vin de Pays d'Oc 1996 • $7 • (3/31/1998) • **77**

Sauvignon Blanc Vin de Pays d'Oc 1998: This white has citrusy and limelike flavors, but it turns a bit tough and drying on the finish.–K.M. • $8 • (11/15/1999) • **78**

VAL JOANIS, CHATEAU

Côtes du Lubéron 1995: A sharp, fruity wine with an odd floral, balsamic vinegar, leather and pepper combination.–P.M. • $9 • (11/15/1998) • **77**

Côtes du Lubéron 1993 • $8 • (10/15/1996) • **82**

Côtes du Lubéron 1992 • $8 • (11/15/1995) • **84**

Côtes du Lubéron 1988 • $7 • (6/30/1990) • **82**

Côtes du Lubéron Les Griottes 1996: A straightforward red, with berry character and a slight dilution. Crisp finish.–P.M. • $16 • (11/15/1999) • **77**

Côtes du Lubéron Les Griottes 1995: Pure and clean, this well-defined, medium-bodied wine has pretty floral, plum aromas, but turns a bit dry on the palate. Tannins clamp down on the finish. Might improve. Drink now through 2001.–P.M. • $19 • (11/15/1998) • **82**

Côtes du Lubéron Les Griottes 1992 • $16 • (10/15/1996) • **85**

Côtes du Lubéron Les Griottes 1990 • $15 • (9/30/1995) • **87**

Côtes du Lubéron Rosé 1998: Earthy and incredibly acidic. The tartness and mouthpuckering taste overwhelm. Unbalanced.–P.M. • $12 • (11/15/1999) • **72**

Côtes du Lubéron Rosé 1997: Nice surprise, offering medium body and a spice, chocolate and cream character along with strawberry notes. Rounder than most rosés, it has personality if not much class. Drink now.–P.M. • $10 • (2/28/1999) • **83**

Côtes du Lubéron White 1998: Stinky, earthy and tart. What happened?–P.M. • $12 • (11/15/1999) • **70**

Côtes du Lubéron White 1997: Fresh, with some floral, appleskin, honey and almond notes. Clean and crisp, with a medium-bodied finish. Not complex or big, just a fine little wine for everyday drinking. Drink now.–P.M. • $10 • (2/28/1999) • **82**

Côtes du Lubéron White Les Aubépines 1998: A bit odd, with cardboard and tart notes.–P.M. • $16 • (11/15/1999) • **75**

Vin de Pays de Vaucluse 1998: Lively, focused and lingering aromas and flavors of berry, plum and wet earth mark this fresh, vibrant, medium-bodied red. Crisp on the finish. Drink now.–P.M. • $7 • (11/15/1999) • **82**

Vin de Pays de Vaucluse 1997: Starts out lovely, with black pepper, cherry, leather and plum notes. Good grip on the palate, turning rustic on the tough finish. Needs hearty food. Drink now.–P.M. • $7 • (2/28/1999) • **82**

Vin de Pays de Vaucluse Rosé 1998: Tastes a bit candied, with a sweetish flavor that speaks of cherries and raspberries but also cotton candy. Tart finish.–P.M. • $7 • (11/15/1999) • **77**

Vin de Pays de Vaucluse White 1998: Straightforward, with tart lime and green apple character; a little white that's zesty.–P.M. • $7 • (11/15/1999) • **78**

Vin de Pays de Vaucluse White 1997: Seems overfiltered and overcropped. More water than wine, with little fruit.–P.M. • $7 • (2/28/1999) • **72**

VAL ST.-JEAN, DOMAINE

Cabernet Sauvignon Vin de Pays des Côtes de Thongue 1996: Sweet cherry and tealike flavors make this an awkward-tasting wine.–K.M. • $7 • (11/15/1998) • **74**

Chardonnay Vin de Pays des Côtes de Thongue 1997: Smells and tastes rustic and slightly oxidized. Not recommended. Tasted twice, with consistent notes.–B.S. • $7 • (12/15/1998) • **68**

Merlot Vin de Pays des Côtes de Thongue 1996: A harsh red, with menthol flavors and not much else. Not recommended. Tasted twice, with consistent notes.–K.M. • $7 • (12/15/1998) • **64**

Merlot Vin de Pays des Côtes de Thongue 1994 • $8 • (12/15/1996) • **57**

VALANDRAUD, CHATEAU DE

St.-Emilion 1999: A very, very pretty wine, with lovely fruit and berry character and hints of tobacco. Full-bodied, with well-integrated tannins and a fresh finish. Solid core of fruit.–J.S. • $NA • (1/01/2000) (BT) • **90-94**

St.-Emilion 1998: Wonderful polished tannins along with mineral and spice character in this baby. Full-bodied yet reserved, with a long finish. Supple, supple, supple. A move in the right direction.–J.S. • $NA • (5/31/1999) (BT) • **90-94**

St.-Emilion 1997: Lots of ripe fruit, with tobacco, cherry and plum character. Medium- to full-bodied, with velvety tannins and a long finish. Shows a surprising degree of harmony. Drink now through 2003.–J.S. • $429 • (1/31/2000) • **90**

St.-Emilion 1996: A solid red, with good fruit, but slightly one-dimensional and hollow in the midpalate. Aromas of blackberries and raspberries, and hints of new wood. Medium-bodied, with good, ripe berry flavor, medium tannins and a vanilla, tobacco aftertaste. Lots of wood here. Best after 2000.–J.S. • $396 Ⓐ • (1/31/1999) • **88**

St.-Emilion 1995 • $329 Ⓐ • (1/31/1998) • **93**

St.-Emilion 1994 • $224 Ⓐ • (1/31/1997) • **91**

St.-Emilion 1993 • $161 Ⓐ • (1/31/1996) • **89**

VALCOMBE, CHATEAU

Côtes du Ventoux La Cerisaie 1996: Straightforward, light-bodied, with spice, leather, plum, black cherry character. Lacks in length, turning sour on the drying finish.–P.M. • $13 • (11/15/1998) • **78**

Côtes du Ventoux La Cerisaie 1995 • $10 • (10/15/1997) • **78**

Côtes du Ventoux La Cerisaie 1994 • $NA • (10/15/1996) • **78**

Côtes du Ventoux La Sereine 1997: Fancy oak treatment lifts this red into its own orbit. Violet, smoke, cassis and ultrasmooth tannins give it an international taste. But it is craftily made and rates high on the pleasure scale, as the finesse of the silky finish lingers on the sensual aftertaste. Drink now through 2004.–P.M. • $24 • (12/15/1999) • **90**

Côtes du Ventoux Les Genévrières 1997: A deceptive *terroir* wine. Tasting of strawberry juice and wet earth, this is light in color and body, but then something nice happens: It shows balance and "fat" midpalate, making you want another sip. The finish is deceptively long. Drink now through 2005.–P.M. • $17 • (12/15/1999) • **88**

Côtes du Ventoux Les Griottes 1998: Totally delicious. This thick, dense, sweet-tasting fruit bomb combines wet earth and spice with blackberry and cassis. The tannins are massive but so ripe that this full-bodied wine melts like cream in the mouth. Good acidity balances the slight hotness on the finish. Drink now through 2004.–P.M. • $10 • (12/15/1999) • **90**

Côtes du Ventoux Les Griottes 1996: A crisp red, with plum, cherry and pepper character. Lacks focus and turns tough, even bitter, on the finish.–P.M. • $10 • (2/28/1999) • **78**

Côtes du Ventoux Signature 1998: Light and a bit diluted, showing cherry and strawberry and drying tannins.–P.M. • $9 • (12/15/1999) • **73**

Côtes du Ventoux Signature 1997: A lovely, harmonious, everyday wine, showing warm fruit, black pepper, currant, plum and vibrant wild raspberry character. Medium-bodied and complex, with supple tannins, it's enjoyable now.–P.M. • $7 • (11/15/1998) • **88**

Côtes du Ventoux White La Cerisaie 1996 • $13 • (10/15/1997) • **80**

Côtes du Ventoux White Les Genévrières 1998: Very honeyed, voluptuous in texture, showing wonderful ripeness. A wine that suggests either low yields or late harvest. Coats the palate, turning you on to almost botrytized, dried fruit concentration. Thick and dense on the finish. A marvel from beginning to end. Drink now through 2007.–P.M. • $19 • (12/15/1999) • **90**

Côtes du Ventoux White Les Genévrières 1997: Too much oak and not enough fruit combine for a fairly tart, tough, medium-bodied white. Hard finish doesn't help.–P.M. • $20 • (2/28/1999) • **76**

Syrah Côtes du Ventoux 1995 • $10 • (12/15/1996) • **85**

VALENTIN, CHATEAU

Margaux 1994 • $22 • (4/30/1997) • **82**

VALETTE

Pouilly-Fuissé Clos Reyssié Réserve Particulière 1996: Distinctive, oaky style, with heavy butterscotch, caramel and lemon notes, but there's intense fruit beneath that brings lots of bright, burning character to this medium-bodied '96. Not for the faint of heart. Best from 2002 through 2006.–P.M. • $60 • (5/31/1999) • **88**

Pouilly-Fuissé Clos Reyssié Réserve Particulière 1995 • $40 • (5/31/1997) • **92**

Pouilly-Fuissé Le Clos de Monsieur Noly Vieilles Vignes Reserve 1995: Stunning. Very ripe, late-harvest, off-dry style, with honey, butter, dried apricot, lemon, fig, mocha, raisin and spice flavors. Coats the palate and revs up the engine on the silky, intense finish. Flavors suggest this opulent Chardonnay was made from grapes affected by botrytis. Drink now through 2007.–P.M. • $70 • (5/31/1999) • **94**

VALLEE, CHATEAU LA

Montagne-St.-Emilion 1995 • $NA • (1/01/1997) • **79**

Key: SS—Spectator Selection. CS—Cellar Selection. HR—Highly Recommended. $NA—Price not available. (BT)—Barrel tasting. Ⓐ—Auction Price. For a key to the tasters' initials, see "How to Use These Listings."
Dates in parentheses represent the issues in which the ratings were published.

VALLONGUE, CHATEAU DE

Coteaux d'Aix-en-Provence Les Baux 1988 • $11 • (12/15/1991) • **73**
Coteaux d'Aix-en-Provence Les Baux Cuvée Murielle 1993 • $18 • (6/30/1997) • **77**

VALLOUIT, L. DE

Châteauneuf-du-Pape 1989 • $16 • (12/31/1991) • **77**
Côte-Rôtie 1997: A straightforward, fruity red. A bit diluted, showing red berry, black pepper and stewed tomato character.–P.M. • $29 • (11/30/1999) • **78**
Côte-Rôtie 1989 • $30 • (1/31/1992) • **89**
Côte-Rôtie 1985 • $20 • (10/15/1987) • **75**
Côtes du Rhône St.-Vincent 1990 • $7 • (6/15/1992) • **82**
Gigondas 1989 • $13 • (1/31/1992) • **89**
Hermitage 1997: This gamy, interesting Syrah, with animal (horse stable) character, stands out among the '97s for its intensity and personality. Loads of black pepper and allspice character, with a plum and black cherry finale. Not very elegant, but try with a hunk of meat. Drink now through 2003.–P.M. • $29 • (11/30/1999) • **87**
Hermitage 1983 • $12 • (5/01/1986) • **79**
Hermitage White 1997: A bit flat, with a dry, woody character overwhelming the fruit. Sour finish.–P.M. • $31 • (11/30/1999) • **75**
St.-Joseph 1989 • $13 • (1/31/1992) • **76**
Vin de Pays des Collines Rhodanienn Les Sables 1989 • $6 • (12/31/1991) • **81**
Vin de Pays des Collines Rhodanienn Les Sables 1988 • $5 • (6/30/1990) • **78**

VARIERE, CHATEAU LA

Bonnezeaux 1996: Delicious. The exotic crème brûlée and tropical notes show the botrytis element that gives this sweet wine extra dimension. Honey and mineral flavors round out the spectrum, while the vibrant acidity cleanses on the finish. Marries richness with elegance. Drink now through 2008.–B.S. • $30 • (11/15/1998) • **92**

VATAN, EDMOND

Sancerre Clos La Néore 1996 • $23 • (6/15/1998) • **80**

VATTAN, PAUL

Sancerre Domaine de St.-Romble Grande Cuvée 1997: Still lively and fresh, this Loire white offers ripe pear and almond flavors, with intriguing accents of anise, mineral and herb. Displays harmony, balance and length. Drink now through 2003.–T.M. • $12 • (2/29/2000) HR • **90**

VAUFUGET, DOMAINE DE

Vouvray 1996: Chamomile and wildflower aromas turn a little earthy on the palate in this broad, rich white, whose razor-sharp acidity and chalky finish tie the package up neatly. Drink through 2000.–B.S. • $10 • (11/15/1998) • **82**

VEDEAU, MAUREL

Merlot Vin de Pays d'Oc Domaine Ste.-Brune 1996: Full-bodied, assertive in flavor and tannic enough to need cellaring, this concentrated Merlot is built like a Bordeaux. Has lots of fruit flavor on an austere texture that should soften with time. Drink now through 2001. • $7 • (10/31/1998) • **85**
Terret Vin de Pays de l'Hérault Domaine de la Done 1997: A crisp white, with concentrated apple and lemon flavors and cinnamon notes on the finish. Drink now.–K.M. • $7 • (11/15/1998) • **83**
Vin de Pays d'Oc Mas de Gal 1995: A focused red, with intense cherry, plum and currant flavors and tobacco and herb notes mixed in. Tightly wound and packing plenty of punch, with chocolaty and spicy flavors on the finish. Drink through 2004–K.M. • $10 • (11/30/1998) • **87**

VELANGES, DOMAINE DES

Mâcon-Davayé 1996 • $NA • (8/31/1997) • **86**
Mâcon-Davayé 1995 • $9 • (5/31/1997) • **76**
Pouilly-Fuissé 1996 • $13 • (5/31/1998) • **80**
St.-Véran 1996 • $9 • (5/31/1998) • **80**
St.-Véran 1995 • $10 • (5/31/1997) • **80**
St.-Véran Cuvée Hors Classé 1996 • $11 • (5/31/1998) • **80**
St.-Véran Cuvée Hors Classé 1995 • $12 • (5/31/1997) • **88**

VENOGE, DE

Brut Blanc de Blancs Champagne NV • $38 • (12/31/1990) • **86**
Brut Blanc de Blancs Champagne 1990: The rich, mellow flavors of a Meursault are combined with the bright acidity and uplifting effervescence of great Champagne. Lemon, pear, vanilla and toast flavors last on the finish. Drink now through 2005. • $39 • (11/15/1999) • **91**
Brut Blanc de Noirs Champagne 1990 • $35 • (11/15/1996) • **85**
Brut Champagne Cordon Bleu Sélect NV: Crisp, vibrant, appetizing fruit flavors and an engaging, palate-cleansing freshness characterize this well-balanced, lively Champagne. Drink now. • $26 • (12/31/1998) • **88**
Brut Champagne des Princes 1992: Solid quality and crisp style distinguish this dry, subtly flavored and very young Champagne. All the pieces seem in place for aging: fine balance, vibrant but lean fruit flavors and hints of buttery complexity. Drink through 2003 • $70 • (12/31/1998) • **89**
Brut Champagne des Princes 1990 • $79 • (12/31/1997) • **94**
Brut Champagne Millésimé 1990: A powerful, unusual Champagne that's compelling, but not for everyone. Its assertive, earthy-toasty aromas are distinctive, and the ripe, honeyed flavors are deep and delicious. Drink now through 2005. • $39 • (11/15/1999) • **90**
Brut Rosé Champagne NV: Lean and refreshing, light copper in color, with modest cherry and herb aromas and a tangy texture that cleanses the palate. Drink now. • $33 • (11/30/1998) • **86**
Brut Rosé Champagne Princesse NV • $35 • (11/30/1997) • **88**
Demi-Sec Champagne NV • $27 • (11/30/1997) • **88**

VERDIGNAN, CHATEAU

Haut-Médoc 1998: Aromas of blackberries and tar. Medium-bodied, with soft tannins and a medium finish. Slightly one-dimensional, but very good.–J.S. • $NA • (5/31/1999) (BT) • **85-89**
Haut-Médoc 1997: Decent tobacco and plum character, but rather lean. Drink now.–J.S. • $NA • (1/31/2000) • **80**
Haut-Médoc 1996: A refined 1996. Dark ruby-purple in color, with blackberry, cherry and chocolate aromas and flavors. Medium-bodied, with silky tannins and a fruit, chocolate and berry aftertaste. Drink now.–J.S. • $15 • (6/30/1999) • **85**
Haut-Médoc 1995 • $15 • (1/31/1998) • **83**
Haut-Médoc 1994 • $15 • (1/31/1997) • **85**
Haut-Médoc 1992 • $14 • (4/15/1995) • **75**
Haut-Médoc 1991 • $14 • (3/31/1994) • **80**
Haut-Médoc 1990 • $17 • (3/31/1993) • **85**
Haut-Médoc 1989: Tasted from magnum. Fresh and well made. Best Verdignan ever. Dark-ruby in color and a red edge. Lots of berry, mint and cherry aromas to this. Full-bodied, very chewy, with lots of ripe tannins and a long, long, fruity finish. Best after 2000. (1989 Bordeaux horizontal tasting). –J.S. • $NA • (5/31/1999) • **90**
Haut-Médoc 1988 • $15 • (4/30/1991) • **86**
Haut-Médoc 1987 • $15 • (11/30/1989) • **78**
Haut-Médoc 1986 • $15 • (11/30/1989) • **76**
Haut-Médoc 1985 • $15 • (2/15/1988) • **81**
Haut-Médoc 1982 • $16 • (8/31/1992) • **80**

VERGET

Bâtard-Montrachet 1998: Balanced and very Puligny-like, here is a wine with vanilla, hazelnut and tropical flavors. Ripe, velvety and full-bodied, it makes for a lovely drink. Drink now through 2010.–P.M. • $179 • (5/31/2000) • **91**
Bâtard-Montrachet 1996: Fantastic, supple midpalate mouthfeel, but beware—this is a very oaky, international-style Chardonnay with loads of butterscotch, butter and caramel aromas and flavors. Rated on its incredibly rich, ripe, fat texture and excellent concentration and length, it's clearly a classic white Burgundy; but the overdone oak detracts. The finish tastes oaky, leesy and like a pear pie with a dollop of whipped cream. Best from 2005.–P.M. • $219 Ⓐ • (8/31/1998) • **93**
Bâtard-Montrachet 1995 • $180 • (5/31/1997) • **99**
Bourgogne White 1998: Good fruit and acidity make this a lively, medium-bodied white, delivering some honey, pear and spice. Drink now through 2001.–P.M. • $13 • (5/31/2000) • **82**
Bourgogne White 1996 • $16 • (5/31/1998) • **89**
Chablis 1997: Buttery but also very fresh and fruity, the ripe tropical and pear notes fold nicely into the sweet-tasting acidity to produce a long, delicious charmer. Enjoy. Drink now through 2002.–P.M. • $20 • (5/31/1999) • **90**
Chablis 1996 • $20 • (5/31/1998) • **91**
Chablis Bougros 1997: Ripe, rich, creamy, buttery, showy and just terrific, this cascades along the palate with all the subtlety of lava flowing down

FRANCE

the flank of Mt. Vesuvius, popping with toasted oak, nuts, lemon and ultraripe fruit and roaring to a long, spectacular finish. Best from 2004 through 2012.–P.M. • $50 • (5/31/1999) • **94**

Chablis Bougros 1996: Showy Chablis. Well made and exotic, in a heavily toasted style, showing wonderful lemon, honey, spice and mocha complexity and excellent fresh acidity. Bursts with intense flavors that perk up the palate, but doesn't show quite the round, smooth finesse of the higher-scoring *grands crus*. Drink now.–P.M. • $80 Ⓐ • (8/31/1998) • **93**

Chablis Fourchaume 1997: Ripe and full-bodied, this is a showy Chablis but, make no mistake, it's rich and very satisfying, offering great balance between the deftly toasted oak, fine fruit and lovely spice. Long finish. Best from 2003 through 2010.–P.M. • $31 • (5/31/1999) • **93**

Chablis Fourchaume 1995 • $29 • (6/15/1997) • **80**

Chablis Fourchaume Vieilles Vignes 1998: Oaky-style. Toast, smoke, floral notes in a medium-bodied Chablis that smells and tastes of wood. The crispness on the palate and finish makes you wish for more ripe, sweet fruit.–P.M. • $42 • (5/15/2000) • **79**

Chablis Fourchaume Vieilles Vignes 1997: Nicely oaked, with toasted bread, hazelnut and distinctive spice and butter notes; medium-bodied, the fruit is a bit dominated by the fancy wood. Drink now through 2005.–P.M. • $45 • (5/31/1999) • **86**

Chablis Fourchaume Vieilles Vignes 1996: A lot of wine for the buck here. Intriguing new-wave Chablis, oaky but also clean and pure, with a lime-honey combination that seduces the palate. Ripe, unctuous, opulent and fat, also offering lots of palate-cleansing acidity, this full-bodied Chablis delivers plenty of toasted spice, mocha, coffee, butter, caramel, pear tart, leesy, milky-yogurt complexity. Thick yet zesty finish. Perhaps the most balanced of Verget's Chablis. Best from 2005 through 2015.–P.M. • $43 • (8/31/1998) • **96**

Chablis Montée de Tonnerre 1996 • $36 Ⓐ • (5/31/1998) • **96**

Chablis Montée de Tonnerre 1995 • $29 • (6/15/1997) HR • **92**

Chablis Vaillons 1998: Clean and pure, with a pronounced butter and cream character followed by nice lemon and toasted oak notes. Medium-bodied, not very opulent, but with a vibrant finish. Drink now through 2006.–P.M. • $32 • (5/15/2000) • **87**

Chablis Vaillons 1997: So unusual, it's lovable, with all that honey, green olive, toasted oak, smoke, apricot jam, etc., it's indescribably genuine and therefore great. Try it, and fall in love. Drink now through 2010.–P.M. • $28 • (5/31/1999) • **94**

Chablis Vaillons 1996 • $48 Ⓐ • (5/31/1998) • **98**

Chablis Valmur 1996: A beautiful Chablis, atypical because of the toasted oak, but the wood isn't out of proportion to the opulent texture, the marvelous lime-honey flavors and the excellent acidity. Full-bodied and balanced, it's silky and stays clean, pure and vibrant on the long, deliciously lively finish. Still, expect heavy-duty, full-throttle Burgundian treatment in this heavily toasted Chardonnay. Drink now through 2010.–P.M. • $86 Ⓐ • (8/31/1998) • **94**

Chablis Valmur 1995 • $168 Ⓐ • (6/15/1997) • **91**

Chablis Vaudésir 1996: Un-Chablisienlike Chablis, this is unctuous and decadent to the extreme. Full-bodied, made in a very oaky style, it delivers loads of clean, ripe fruit, a sexy lemon-honey combination, good acidity and lots of toasted, spicy, mocha and coffee complexity. International style, but a good one; its thick midpalate is a winning feature. Perhaps the silkiest of Verget's Chablis. Best after 2003.–P.M. • $51 • (8/31/1998) • **96**

Chassagne-Montrachet 1996 • $38 Ⓐ • (5/31/1998) • **87**

Chassagne-Montrachet Franchemont 1998: Odd white. Very yellow in color, with butter, butterscotch, dried fruit and a slight malic aroma. A bit diluted at midpalate. Turns slightly dry on the finish.–P.M. • $44 • (5/31/2000) • **74**

Chassagne-Montrachet La Maltroie Cuvée Vieilles Vignes 1995 • $44 • (8/31/1997) • **94**

Chassagne-Montrachet La Romanée 1997: This '96 Chassagne tastes very oaky, with a pronounced toastiness and vanilla bean, cream, grilled pineapple and crème brûlée notes. Heavily toasted finish. Drink now through 2002.–P.M. • $63 • (9/30/1999) • **86**

Chassagne-Montrachet La Romanée 1996: Lots of new wood, some mineral and vanilla character accompany the ripe fruit, making this a voluptuous wine of finesse and elegance. Shows also some lovely lime-lemon flavors. Full-bodied, it grows on you, delivering plenty of character on the sophisticated finish. Best from 2005.–P.M. • $91 Ⓐ • (8/31/1998) • **88**

Key: SS—Spectator Selection. CS—Cellar Selection. HR—Highly Recommended. $NA—Price not available. (BT)—Barrel tasting. Ⓐ—Auction Price.
For a key to the tasters' initials, see "How to Use These Listings."
Dates in parentheses represent the issues in which the ratings were published.

Chassagne-Montrachet Les Chaumes 1997: Almost late harvest in character, with butterscotch, balsamic vinegar (volatile acidity?), raspberry, lime and honey. Tart finish.–P.M. • $43 • (9/30/1999) • **79**

Chassagne-Montrachet Morgeot 1996: Fairly ripe and quite fruity, a nice little Chardonnay that's clean and pure, offering spice, vanilla, mineral and pear, and lots of new oak, character. Of medium body, it sparkles with vibrancy on the slightly rustic finish. Best from 2003.–P.M. • $55 • (8/31/1998) • **86**

Chassagne-Montrachet Morgeot Cuvée Vieilles Vignes 1995 • $46 • (8/31/1997) • **93**

Corton-Charlemagne 1998: A medium-bodied white Burgundy showing a crisp, chalky, chewy side. Lacks a bit of opulence, turns a bit tough on the finish. Drink now through 2003.–P.M. • $103 • (5/31/2000) • **82**

Corton-Charlemagne 1997: Lots of butter and butterscotch smother the aromas, but the concentration makes for a fairly round mouthfeel, with very toasty, spicy, hot-curry flavors on the lemony finish.–P.M. • $115 • (9/30/1999) • **79**

Corton-Charlemagne 1996: Outstanding '96, offering a good marriage of smooth texture and lemon-honey-toasted oak intensity. Medium-bodied, quite racy, this is like a mini-volcano that errupts with flavors—flavors that need time to settle down. Still, very oaky for the fruit. Best after 2005.–P.M. • $122 Ⓐ • (8/31/1998) • **90**

Ladoix White 1996 • $24 • (5/31/1998) • **79**

Mâcon-Villages Tête de Cuvée 1998: Oaky but flavorful, with some prune and apple character. Medium-bodied, it turns a bit astringent on the finish. Drink now through 2001.–P.M. • $14 • (5/31/2000) • **80**

Mâcon-Villages Tête de Cuvée 1997: Crisp but fairly rich, with a round, ripe mouthfeel, delivering clean citrus, grass, wet hay notes. Tasted twice, with consistent notes. Drink now.–P.M. • $15 • (5/31/1999) • **80**

Mâcon-Villages Tête de Cuvée 1996 • $15 • (5/31/1998) • **88**

Mâcon-Villages Tête de Cuvée 1995 • $13 • (5/31/1997) • **86**

Meursault Les Casse-Têtes 1995 • $35 • (5/31/1997) • **91**

Meursault Les Charmes Cuvée Vieilles Vignes 1996: Rich and ripe, full-bodied, with loads of everything—butterscotch, ripe fruit, mineral, opulence and silky texture. Could have been overdone with all that malic, chocolate stuff, but a refined, mouthpuckering citrus thread gives it backbone from start to seductive finish. Best from 2005.–P.M. • $75 • (8/31/1998) • **90**

Meursault Les Charmes Cuvée Vieilles Vignes 1995 • $65 • (5/31/1997) • **91**

Meursault Les Poruzots 1997: An "American" Meursault, with a popcorn, butterscotch and butter character that wipes out the *terroir*. A tough, heavily oaked, yellowish, international-style Chardonnay, but it does have body and ripeness—just not class. Tart finish. Drink now through 2002.–P.M. • $77 • (9/30/1999) • **80**

Meursault Les Poruzots 1995 • $50 • (5/31/1997) • **93**

Meursault Les Tillets 1997: Tastes satisfying, with a good, round mouthfeel but a slight butterscotch and cooked apple character. The finish turns a bit crisp, almost tart, with loads of wood tannins. Drink now through 2002.–P.M. • $53 Ⓐ • (9/30/1999) • **80**

Meursault Les Tillets 1996: Sleek and refined, a linear, medium-bodied Meursault of subtle mineral, toasted oak and pear character. Chewy, chalky, almost tannic finish suggests it needs cellaring to show it all. Best from 2005.–P.M. • $42 • (8/31/1998) • **88**

Pouilly-Fuissé Tête de Cuvée 1998: Gorgeous. Thick and seductive, beautifully toasty, with smoke, roasted hazelnut, pineapple, dark chocolate and ripe fruit. Full-bodied, supple and creamy in texture, it's a delight from start to finish. Drink now through 2005.–P.M. • $28 • (5/31/2000) • **90**

Pouilly-Fuissé Tête de Cuvée 1997: What a beauty. Ultrasmooth, yet racy from a lemony texture laced with honey and lovely ripe fruit, this one of the cleanest Pouilly tasted from '97, displaying a minerally concentration on the finish, and not even the slightest astringency, it's that balanced. Drink now through 2005.–P.M. • $18 • (5/31/1999) • **93**

Pouilly-Fuissé Tête de Cuvée 1996 • $15 • (5/31/1998) HR • **93**

Pouilly-Fuissé Tête de Cuvée 1995 • $15 • (5/31/1997) • **86**

Puligny-Montrachet Les Enseignères 1997: Very ripe yet very crisp, it makes for an awkward taste sensation, with apricot, petrol, butterscotch, flint and cooked fruit notes. Crisp, drying finish.–P.M. • $47 • (9/30/1999) • **79**

Puligny-Montrachet Les Enseignères 1996: Super winemaking defines this seductive Puligny, with wonderful mineral, vanilla bean, stone dust and lime notes, well-dosed oak accents that bring out a certain malic, milky character, and delightful, impressively ripe tropical fruit. Full-bodied, with smooth, palate-coating texture, ending in a vibrant, balanced, lime-infused finish. Drink now through 2005.–P.M. • $64 Ⓐ • (8/31/1998) • **95**

Puligny-Montrachet Les Enseignères 1995 • $21 Ⓐ • (5/31/1997) • **94**

Puligny-Montrachet Sous le Puits 1997: Very, very oaky. Hard to warm up to this hard white, with exaggerated toastiness backed by roasted pine nut, toasted coconut and grilled banana notes. Clamps down with a crisp, lemony finish. Best from 2001 through 2007.–P.M. • $48 Ⓐ • (9/30/1999) • **87**

Puligny-Montrachet Sous le Puits 1995 • $39 Ⓐ • (8/31/1997) • **88**

St.-Aubin Premier Cru 1996 • $29 Ⓐ • (5/31/1998) • **91**

St.-Romain 1996 • $21 • (5/31/1998) • **76**

St.-Véran 1997: Lively and fresh, a tightly wound white, sparkling with lemon, green apple and hints of pear, honey and toasted bread. Firm finish is slightly astringent for now, but there is ripe fruit beneath that suggests it will come together. Needs time. Drink through 2003–P.M. • $18 • (5/31/1999) • **88**

St.-Véran 1996 • $13 • (5/31/1998) • **90**

St.-Véran 1995 • $13 • (5/31/1997) • **84**

St.-Véran Tête de Cuvée 1998: Offering nice texture, with ripe, sweet-tasting fruit flavors and some dried herb, grassy character. Fresh and balanced, but lacks a bit of complexity and depth. Drink now through 2001.–P.M. • $16 • (5/31/2000) • **84**

St.-Véran Tête de Cuvée 1997: Delicious. Polished and velvety, with plenty of subtle butter, cream, lemon and ripe pear character, this full-bodied charmer is clean and pure, with a seductive honey accent on the finish. Drink through 2005.–P.M. • $20 • (5/31/1999) • **92**

Santenay White 1998: Satisfying in its full body and thick texture, but it's also elegant and racy from citrus and green apple, rendered a bit more complex by butterscotch and honey. Drink now through 2003.–P.M. • $20 • (5/31/2000) • **85**

Santenay White 1996 • $24 • (5/31/1998) • **87**

VERGET DU SUD

Côtes du Lubéron White 1998: A fresh, "little" wine, the sort of young white you can guzzle down. Offers lemon, green apple and more lemon. Very clean but with little complexity. Drink now.–P.M. • $11 • (12/15/1999) • **80**

VERGNES, CHATEAU DES

Bordeaux 1994 • $10 • (4/30/1997) • **81**

VERNAY, GEORGES

Condrieu 1997: This superb Condrieu, just slightly off-dry yet fresh, offers a marvelous concentration of fruit that shows many different facets: pear tart, apricot, honey, toast, spice, cream and dried prune. Long, toasty finish. Drink now through 2010.–P.M. • $45 • (11/15/1998) • **93**

Condrieu Coteaux de Vernon 1997: An ultrathick, full-bodied Condrieu, very soft, but showing sweet honey, apricot and vanilla notes alongside the minerally, stony character. Good balance despite the minimum acidity. Drink now through 2001.–P.M. • $68 • (8/31/1999) • **89**

Condrieu Coteaux de Vernon 1996: A beautiful Condrieu, showing sweet flavors of dried fruit, fresh peach and apricot, floral scents and a honeyed character. Full-bodied, but still restrained and elegant, with good acidity. The silky texture comes through on the finale, which lasts nicely. Drink now through 2005.–P.M. • $60 • (10/15/1998) • **92**

Condrieu Les Chaillées de l'Enfer 1997: A fantastic late-harvest Viognier, dripping with off-dry honey, floral and peach character, layered with spice, smoke and crème brûlée flavors; this packs it thick, but it turns out decently intense and long on the finish. Drink now through 2001.–P.M. • $65 • (8/31/1999) • **90**

Condrieu Les Chaillées de l'Enfer 1996: Seemingly impressive with all that fat, ripe character, but it turns a bit dry and hard on the finish. Slightly green and herbal, it lacks the sort of opulence and especially sweet character you expect from Condrieu in a top vintage like '96.–P.M. • $52 • (11/15/1998) • **84**

Condrieu Les Terrasses de l'Empire 1998: Butter, honey and ripe fruit character rises from the glass and coats the palate. Lovely, medium-bodied and balanced, this is sheer pleasure to drink. Long, harmonious aftertaste. Drink now through 2002.–P.M. • $39 • (12/15/1999) • **88**

Côte-Rôtie 1995: Light in color, earthy, with horse saddle, chestnut character. Medium-bodied.–P.M. • $35 • (9/15/1998) • **72**

Côte-Rôtie 1994 • $35 • (10/15/1997) • **82**

Côte-Rôtie 1991 • $30 • (5/31/1994) • **84**

Côte-Rôtie Maison Rouge 1996: Odd, tasting of raw beef but also of sweet red berry, with some game and vanilla notes thrown in. Turns tart on the green finish.–P.M. • $43 • (9/15/1999) • **76**

St.-Joseph 1996: It's earthy, but what terrific palate-caressing texture. Delivers layers of crisp, lemon-spiked acidity, wild raspberry, spicy oak—and yes, a bit of leather and animal character—in a most ripe, distinctive package, with supple tannins. Drink now through 2004.–P.M. • $15 • (11/15/1998) • **89**

VERSET, NOEL

Cornas 1997: A fruit bomb, expansive and rich, bordering on game, violets, ink and blackberry. The structure relies more on tannin than acidity, and it will come to the fore soon. Drink now through 2006.–B.S. • $35 • (1/01/2000) • **93**

Cornas 1994 • $35 • (10/15/1997) • **89**

Cornas 1993 • $24 • (10/15/1995) • **85**

Cornas 1987 • $23 • (3/31/1990) • **88**

Cornas 1986 • $25 • (1/31/1989) • **86**

VERTAY, PAUL

Brut Champagne NV • $NA • (1/01/1997) • **85**

VESSELLE, GEORGES

Brut Champagne Cuvée Juline Grand Cru NV • $NA • (12/31/1993) • **87**

Brut Champagne Grand Cru NV • $NA • (12/31/1991) • **86**

VESSIGAUD PERE & FILS

Mâcon-Fuissé 1997: A straightforward Chardonnay of modest fruit complexity, medium-bodied and tasting slightly dull.–P.M. • $19 • (5/31/1999) • **76**

Mâcon-Fuissé 1996 • $16 • (5/31/1998) • **87**

Pouilly-Fuissé Vieilles Vignes 1997: Delicious, but it's so ripe that it tastes off-dry. After the honeysuckle, ripe melon and toast, it turns on the volume on the smoky finish. A full-bodied, very yellow-hued Chardonnay—almost California-style. Drink now.–P.M. • $31 • (5/31/1999) • **88**

Pouilly-Fuissé Vieilles Vignes 1996 • $27 • (5/31/1998) • **90**

Pouilly-Fuissé Vieilles Vignes 1995 • $14 • (5/31/1997) • **84**

VEUVE CLICQUOT

Brut Champagne NV: A fine example of a dry, sophisticated brut, this is an elegant style of Champagne whose understated apple and butter flavors are well balanced by crisp acidity. Drink now through 2001. • $45 • (12/31/1998) • **87**

Brut Champagne La Grande Dame 1990: Assertive and buttery style, dry and bold in flavor, but with the lively effervescence and toasty finish for balance. Drink now through 2002. • $115 Ⓐ • (10/15/1999) • **90**

Brut Champagne Vintage Reserve 1991: A mouthfilling texture and lean but attractive flavors of apple, butter and vanilla make this appealing. Light-bodied for a vintage Champagne. Drink now through 2001. • $60 • (10/15/1999) • **86**

Brut Champagne Vintage Reserve 1990: A generous, buttery-tasting Champagne that's beginning to show an attractive maturity in its intricate flavors. Medium-bodied, quite dry, but smooth in texture and distinctive for its mineral, butter and caramel flavors. Drink now. • $58 Ⓐ • (12/15/1998) • **92**

Brut Rosé Champagne Réserve 1990: A complete and full-flavored rosé from a great year, showing all the elements we like—ripe fruit flavors, vibrant acidity, complex aromas and a lingering finish. Drink now through 2005. • $70 • (10/15/1999) • **89**

Demi-Sec Champagne NV: Straightforward and sweet, this has sugary flavors, a soft mousse and a honeyed finish. Enjoyable and uncomplicated in character. Drink now. • $45 • (12/31/1998) • **82**

VEUVE DU VERNAY

Brut Blanc de Blancs France NV • $9 • (5/31/1997) • **78**

VEYRY, CHATEAU

Côtes de Castillon 1998: Perfumes jump out of the glass. Full-bodied yet compact, with fine tannins and a long, long finish. Fabulous for the appellation. Almost outstanding.–J.S. • $NA • (5/31/1999) (BT) • **85-89**

VEZELAY, HENRY DE

Bourgogne Vézelay Cuvée Henry de Vézelay 1997: Like pineapple juice, a bit sweet and simple, with lemon flavor on the finish.–P.M. • $15 • (9/30/1999) • **79**

VICHON MEDITERRANEAN

Cabernet Sauvignon Vin de Pays d'Oc 1996: A fresh, simple red, with enough fruit to be satisfying and just enough tannin to balance food. Drink now. • $10 • (9/30/1998) • **82**
Cabernet Sauvignon Vin de Pays d'Oc 1995 • $10 • (6/30/1997) • **82**
Chardonnay Vin de Pays d'Oc 1996: For fans of a crisper style of Chardonnay. Nice green apple and citrus nuances, mixed in with mineral notes. Lingering lemon-lime finish. Drink now.–K.M. • $10 • (9/30/1998) • **83**
Chasan Vin de Pays d'Oc 1996: Crisp, with mineral, apple and anise flavors that linger on the finish. Drink now.–K.M. • $11 • (11/15/1998) • **82**
Merlot Vin de Pays d'Oc 1996: A solid, light-bodied red, with cherry candy aromas and flavors peppered with herbal nuances. Finishes short.–B.S. • $10 • (10/15/1998) • **78**
Merlot Vin de Pays d'Oc 1995 • $9 • (5/31/1997) • **82**
Syrah Vin de Pays d'Oc 1995 • $10 • (7/31/1997) • **84**

VICTOR, LES CAVES

Simple Pêche France Sparkling NV • $9 • (5/31/1997) • **83**

VIDAL-FLEURY, J.

Châteauneuf-du-Pape White 1996 • $23 • (10/15/1997) • **81**
Cornas 1990 • $27 • (5/31/1994) • **80**
Cornas 1989 • $10 • (6/15/1992) • **81**
Cornas 1988 • $20 • (1/31/1991) • **85**
Côte-Rôtie 1990 • $30 • (5/31/1994) • **88**
Côte-Rôtie Côte Blonde La Chatillonne 1993 • $42 • (11/30/1996) • **84**
Côte-Rôtie Côte Blonde La Chatillonne 1990 • $42 • (5/31/1994) • **92**
Côte-Rôtie Côte Blonde La Chatillonne 1988 • $42 • (3/15/1994) • **87**
Côte-Rôtie Côte Blonde La Chatillonne 1984 • $26 • (10/31/1987) • **73**
Côte-Rôtie Côtes Brune et Blonde 1996: Interesting, with a mineral-laden character and red berry notes accented by plum, raisin and licorice. Of medium body, it dries a bit on the chewy finish.–P.M. • $40 • (9/15/1998) • **79**
Côte-Rôtie Côtes Brune et Blonde 1994 • $38 • (11/30/1996) • **88**
Côte-Rôtie Côtes Brune et Blonde 1992 • $38 • (11/30/1996) • **84**
Côte-Rôtie Côtes Brune et Blonde 1989 • $28 • (3/15/1994) • **87**
Côte-Rôtie Côtes Brune et Blonde 1988 • $30 • (10/15/1990) • **88**
Côte-Rôtie Côtes Brune et Blonde 1985 • $25 • (3/15/1990) • **90**
Côte-Rôtie Côtes Brune et Blonde 1945 • $NA • (3/15/1990) • **85**
Côte-Rôtie Côtes Brune et Blonde 1934 • $NA • (3/15/1990) • **85**
Côtes du Rhône 1995 • $9 • (10/15/1997) • **88**
Côtes du Rhône 1994 • $9 • (10/15/1996) • **84**
Côtes du Rhône 1992 • $9 • (10/15/1996) • **78**
Côtes du Rhône 1990 • $8 • (4/30/1994) • **85**
Côtes du Rhône 1988 • $9 • (12/15/1990) • **85**
Côtes du Rhône White 1996 • $10 • (10/15/1997) • **83**
Côtes du Rhône-Villages 1994 • $10 • (10/15/1997) • **85**
Côtes du Ventoux 1994 • $8 • (10/15/1996) • **83**
Côtes du Ventoux 1990 • $7 • (6/30/1994) • **84**
Crozes-Hermitage 1996: An exotic Crozes, with distinctive aromas and flavors of violet, rose petal, blueberry, cassis bush, wet earth and jammy prune and plum. Medium-bodied, with a crisp, even racy texture and a succulent finish. A bit herbal. Best from 2002 through 2007.–P.M. • $13 • (10/15/1998) • **85**
Crozes-Hermitage 1994 • $14 • (11/30/1996) • **88**
Crozes-Hermitage 1992 • $14 • (11/30/1996) • **82**
Crozes-Hermitage 1990 • $10 • (5/31/1994) • **87**
Crozes-Hermitage 1988 • $13 • (12/31/1990) • **86**
Crozes-Hermitage 1986 • $10 • (5/31/1988) • **78**
Crozes-Hermitage 1985 • $11 • (10/31/1987) CS • **92**
Crozes-Hermitage White 1997: A distinctive but slightly rustic white, with an oily mouthfeel, mineral, pear, smoke and stone dust notes, good acidity and a lingering finish. Medium- to full-bodied, the flavors turn a bit diffuse on the slightly bitter finish. Drink now.–P.M. • $15 • (10/15/1998) • **84**
Gigondas 1990 • $19 • (10/15/1996) • **84**
Gigondas 1985 • $13 • (10/31/1987) • **86**
Hermitage 1985 • $22 • (10/31/1987) • **89**
Hermitage 1945 • $NA • (3/15/1990) • **80**
Hermitage 1937 • $NA • (3/15/1990) • **91**
Muscat de Beaumes-de-Venise Réserve 1995 • $13/375 ml. • (10/15/1996) • **87**
St.-Joseph 1994 • $17 • (11/30/1996) • **85**
St.-Joseph 1991 • $17 • (11/30/1996) • **86**
St.-Joseph 1990 • $14 • (5/31/1994) • **85**
St.-Joseph 1988 • $14 • (1/31/1991) • **84**
Vacqueyras 1994 • $11 • (10/15/1997) • **84**
Vacqueyras 1991 • $13 • (10/15/1996) • **86**
Vacqueyras 1990 • $9 • (3/31/1994) • **86**
Vacqueyras 1988 • $14 • (12/15/1990) • **89**

VIEILLE CURE, CHATEAU LA

Fronsac 1998: A bright and exciting wine, with loads of floral and raspberry character. Full-bodied, with well-integrated tannins and a long, long finish. A real beauty for this estate.–J.S. • $NA • (5/31/1999) (BT) • **90-94**
Fronsac 1997: Slightly simple but good clean fruit character, with medium body and a fresh finish. Drink now through 2003.–J.S. • $33 • (1/31/2000) • **85**
Fronsac 1996: Good Fronsac for the vintage. Lovely intensity of cherry, blackberry and mineral character on the nose and palate. Medium-bodied, with light tannins and a light finish.–J.S. • $20 • (1/31/1999) • **84**
Fronsac 1995 • $20 • (1/31/1998) • **89**
Fronsac 1994 • $19 • (1/31/1997) • **87**
Fronsac 1993 • $19 • (1/31/1996) • **79**
Fronsac 1992 • $15 • (4/15/1995) • **79**
Fronsac 1990 • $19 • (3/31/1993) • **88**
Fronsac 1989: Chunky '89, with lots of dark chocolate and berry character. Medium- to full-bodied, adding chewy tannins and a medium finish. Slightly one-dimensional, but a seriously good glass of wine. Drink now. (1989 Bordeaux horizontal tasting). –J.S. • $NA • (5/31/1999) • **88**
Fronsac 1988 • $19 • (10/31/1991) • **81**
Fronsac 1987 • $14 • (5/15/1990) • **82**
Fronsac 1986 • $15 • (5/15/1991) • **81**
Fronsac 1985 • $15 • (12/31/1988) • **88**
Fronsac 1982 • $15 • (8/31/1992) • **84**

VIEILLE FERME, LA

Côtes du Lubéron White 1997: Oxidized and heavy, with a pronounced cooked apple character, it turns bitter on the finish.–P.M. • $8 • (11/15/1998) • **75**
Côtes du Rhône Réserve 1992 • $10 • (11/30/1994) • **85**
Côtes du Rhône Réserve 1990 • $8 • (8/31/1992) • **87**
Côtes du Rhône Réserve 1989 • $9 • (3/15/1991) • **87**
Côtes du Rhône Réserve 1988 • $8 • (12/15/1990) • **84**
Côtes du Ventoux 1996 • $8 • (10/15/1997) • **84**
Côtes du Ventoux 1995 • $8 • (10/15/1997) • **85**
Côtes du Ventoux 1994 • $7 • (12/15/1996) • **84**
Côtes du Ventoux 1992 • $7 • (11/30/1994) • **84**
Côtes du Ventoux 1990 • $7 • (4/15/1993) • **78**
Côtes du Ventoux 1988 • $8 • (6/30/1990) • **78**

VIEILLE JULIENNE, DOMAINE DE LA

Châteauneuf-du-Pape 1997: Round at first, teasing with some decent fruit complexity, but then turns a bit short on the straightforward, slightly smoky finish. Drink now through 2002.–P.M. • $30 • (8/31/1999) • **81**
Châteauneuf-du-Pape 1996: Round and fruity, with lightish tannins and modest licorice, currant and cherry notes. Fairly straightforward. Drink now through 2002.–P.M. • $20 • (11/15/1998) • **81**
Châteauneuf-du-Pape 1995: Very pretty and seductive, with black cherry, black pepper, spice, black olive and blackberry aromas and flavors. Full-bodied, with a succulent finish. Drink now through 2005.–P.M. • $20 • (9/30/1998) • **89**
Châteauneuf-du-Pape 1994 • $20 • (9/15/1997) • **87**
Châteauneuf-du-Pape 1990 • $17 • (4/15/1993) • **91**
Châteauneuf-du-Pape 1972 • $20 • (11/15/1987) • **73**
Châteauneuf-du-Pape Vieilles Vignes 1996: Smooth and fresh, with pretty blackberry, black cherry, cedar and chocolate notes, it's elegant but slightly diluted on the finish. Drink now through 2003.–P.M. • $28 • (11/15/1998) • **85**
Côtes du Rhône Vieilles Vignes 1997: Light-flavored, with attractive ripe fruit and spicy mocha notes. A straightforward red with some round texture.–P.M. • $20 • (11/15/1999) • **79**

Key: SS—Spectator Selection. CS—Cellar Selection. HR—Highly Recommended. $NA—Price not available. (BT)—Barrel tasting. Ⓐ—Auction Price.
For a key to the tasters' initials, see "How to Use These Listings."
Dates in parentheses represent the issues in which the ratings were published.

VIEUX-CHATEAU-CERTAN

Pomerol 1999: Lots of blackberry and orange peel aromas. Medium- to full-bodied, with well-integrated tannins and a medium finish. Delicious. –J.S. • $NA • (1/01/2000) (BT) • **85-89**
Pomerol 1998: Big, powerful and chewy young wine. Wonderful crushed raspberries and blackberries. Full-bodied, with a solid core of fruit. Velvety tannins. Greatest young VCC I have ever tasted.–J.S. • $NA • (5/31/1999) (BT) • **95-99**
Pomerol 1997: A tight and very fine wine. Good color. Subtle mineral, violet and berry aromas, with a hint of tobacco. Full- to medium-bodied, with silky tannins and a long finish. Best after 2001.–J.S. • $51 Ⓐ • (1/31/2000) • **90**
Pomerol 1996: A harmonious, well-made wine. Extremely attractive berry and cherry aromas, with hints of tobacco and oak. Medium-bodied, with medium-soft tannins and an aftertaste of berry and herb.–J.S. • $55 Ⓐ • (1/31/1999) • **88**
Pomerol 1995 • $58 Ⓐ • (1/31/1998) • **95**
Pomerol 1994 • $41 Ⓐ • (1/31/1997) • **89**
Pomerol 1993 • $39 Ⓐ • (1/31/1996) • **82**
Pomerol 1992 • $27 Ⓐ • (4/15/1995) • **75**
Pomerol 1990 • $87 Ⓐ • (3/31/1993) • **89**
Pomerol 1989: A decadent, rich wine. Intense aromas of earth, tobacco, mushrooms and meat. Full-bodied and very powerful, with lots of ripe fruit and a long, silky finish. Needs time. (1989 Bordeaux horizontal tasting). Best after 2005.–J.S. • $68 Ⓐ • (5/31/1999) • **91**
Pomerol 1988: A bit simple for this château but still a good red. Medium-bodied, with fine tannins and chocolate and berry flavors. Drink now through 2005. (1988 Bordeaux horizontal tasting). –J.S. • $64 Ⓐ • (11/30/1998) • **87**
Pomerol 1987 • $24 Ⓐ • (5/15/1990) • **84**
Pomerol 1986 • $81 Ⓐ • (6/15/1989) • **93**
Pomerol 1985 • $77 Ⓐ • (10/15/1994) • **90**
Pomerol 1983 • $53 Ⓐ • (10/15/1994) • **90**
Pomerol 1982: A lovely and harmonious red. Beautiful cherry, floral and berry character. Full-bodied, with velvety tannins and long, focused berry and milk chocolate flavors. Drink now or hold. (1982 Bordeaux horizontal tasting).–J.S. • $108 Ⓐ • (11/30/1998) • **91**
Pomerol 1981 • $47 Ⓐ • (10/15/1994) • **87**
Pomerol 1979 • $48 Ⓐ • (10/15/1989) • **87**
Pomerol 1961 • $270 Ⓐ • (4/30/1996) • **86**
Pomerol 1959 • $NA/1.5 liter • (10/15/1990) • **91**
Pomerol 1947 • $999 Ⓐ • (7/31/1997) • **87**
Pomerol 1945 • $299 Ⓐ • (11/30/1995) • **91**

VIEUX CHATEAU CHAMPS DE MARS

Côtes de Castillon 1997: Pretty plum and berry character, with a hint of green tobacco. Medium-bodied, with velvety tannins and a pretty, fruity finish. Best from 2001 through 2006.–J.S. • $17 • (1/31/2000) • **86**
Côtes de Castillon 1995 • $15 • (1/01/1998) • **83**

VIEUX-CHATEAU-NEGRIT

Montagne-St.-Emilion 1995 • $12 • (10/15/1997) • **81**

VIEUX CHENE, DOMAINE DU

Côtes du Rhône-Villages 1995 • $NA • (10/15/1997) • **85**
Vin de Pays de Vaucluse 1990 • $7 • (1/31/1992) • **77**

VIEUX DONJON, LE

Châteauneuf-du-Pape 1995: Odd, with a barnyardlike aroma, an intense mouthfeel and a bitter finish. Does have ripe, sweet tannins on the midpalate.–P.M. • $39 Ⓐ • (11/15/1998) • **78**
Châteauneuf-du-Pape 1990 • $58 Ⓐ • (4/15/1993) • **86**
Châteauneuf-du-Pape 1989 • $17 • (10/15/1991) • **85**
Châteauneuf-du-Pape 1988 • $16 • (10/15/1991) • **85**
Châteauneuf-du-Pape 1986 • $15 • (10/15/1991) • **88**
Châteauneuf-du-Pape 1985 • $16 • (2/15/1988) • **79**
Châteauneuf-du-Pape 1984 • $14 • (10/31/1987) • **79**
Châteauneuf-du-Pape 1981 • $NA • (10/15/1991) • **89**
Châteauneuf-du-Pape White 1997: Offers plenty of vanilla and butter flavors, with crisp underlying acidity, but the light apple and herb flavors are muted. Slightly bitter on the finish. Better with food. Drink now through 2002.–T.M. • $23 • (11/15/1998) • **84**

VIEUX GABIRAN, CHATEAU

Bordeaux Supérieur 1996: A very light Bordeaux, with cherry and earth character. Light and fruity on the finish.–J.S. • $10 • (7/31/1999) • **78**
Bordeaux Supérieur 1988 • $11 • (4/30/1991) • **84**

VIEUX-GUINOT, CHATEAU DU

St.-Emilion 1982: Tasted from magnum. Out of balance. Medium brick-red color, wth a ruby center. Mushroom and ripe fruit aromas. Medium-bodied and round, with ripe fruit and light tannins, but slightly alcoholic. (1982 Bordeaux horizontal tasting.)–J.S. • $NA/1.5 liter • (11/30/1998) • **79**

VIEUX LAZARET, DOMAINE DU

Châteauneuf-du-Pape 1997: A round-textured, medium-bodied red, with a roasted nut, plum and cherry character. Light finish. Drink now through 2002.–P.M. • $18 • (8/31/1999) • **81**
Châteauneuf-du-Pape 1995: Brown in color, with brown sugar flavors that are quite astringent. Dull and disappointing.–T.M. • $17 • (11/15/1998) • **72**
Châteauneuf-du-Pape 1989 • $16 • (10/15/1991) • **85**
Châteauneuf-du-Pape 1986 • $14 • (1/31/1989) • **89**
Châteauneuf-du-Pape 1985 • $12 • (10/15/1991) • **82**
Châteauneuf-du-Pape White 1998: Fresh, young and medium-bodied, this easy, fruity white delivers floral and peach aromas, with a juicy, limelike flavor on the vibrant finish. Drink now through 2002.–P.M. • $19 • (12/15/1999) • **80**
Châteauneuf-du-Pape White 1997: Ripe yet rather juicy, subtle and pleasant. A well-made, full-bodied, tropical-flavored white. Drink now through 2002.–P.M. • $20 • (9/30/1999) • **87**
Côtes du Ventoux 1998: Light, diluted and herbal.–P.M. • $8 • (12/15/1999) • **70**

VIEUX-MAILLET, CHATEAU

Pomerol 1998: Polished and well crafted, with spice, vanilla and ripe fruit character. Medium-bodied, with a fine texture and a medium finish. Slightly hollow midpalate.–J.S. • $NA • (5/31/1999) (BT) • **85-89**

VIEUX MOULIN, LE

Bordeaux 1996: Some dried-cherry character in this diluted red, with slightly unripe fruit flavors. Medium- to light-bodied. Short finish. Drink now.–J.S. • $NA • (1/31/1999) • **80**

VIEUX PREZAT, CHATEAU

Médoc 1996: Slightly simple, but a silky red with fine tannins. Medium-bodied, with cherry flavors and a mineral aftertaste. The silky texture draws you back. Second label of Château Pontet. Best after 2001.–J.S. • $NA • (1/31/1999) • **85**

VIEUX SARPE, CHATEAU

St.-Emilion 1996: A simple wine that is vivid and delicious now. Fresh and lively berry aromas. Medium-bodied, with well-integrated tannins and a dried cherry aftertaste. Drink now through 2002.–J.S. • $NA • (1/31/1999) • **85**
St.-Emilion 1995: Elegant and silky, with vanilla, berry and milk chocolate aromas and flavors. Medium-bodied, with fine tannins and a medium, fruity finish. Drink through 2005–J.S. • $NA • (9/15/1998) • **87**
St.-Emilion 1982 • $NA • (5/15/1989) • **83**

VIEUX ST.-SORLIN, DOMAINE DU

Mâcon-La Roche Vineuse 1995 • $14 • (5/31/1997) • **76**

VIEUX TELEGRAPHE, DOMAINE DU

Châteauneuf-du-Pape 1990 • $53 Ⓐ • (2/28/1993) SS • **89**
Châteauneuf-du-Pape 1989 • $46 Ⓐ • (10/15/1991) • **87**
Châteauneuf-du-Pape 1988 • $37 Ⓐ • (10/15/1991) • **85**
Châteauneuf-du-Pape 1987 • $32 • (9/30/1990) • **81**
Châteauneuf-du-Pape 1986 • $31 Ⓐ • (10/15/1991) • **90**
Châteauneuf-du-Pape 1985 • $30 • (10/15/1991) • **82**
Châteauneuf-du-Pape 1984 • $16 • (9/30/1987) • **89**
Châteauneuf-du-Pape 1983 • $58 Ⓐ • (10/15/1991) • **85**

Châteauneuf-du-Pape 1981 • $35 • (10/15/1991) • **80**

Châteauneuf-du-Pape La Crau 1996: Pleasant. Fairly light in color and texture, this supple, fruity, balanced Châteauneuf has smooth tannins, with licorice, currant and mocha flavors. Medium-bodied. Drink now through 2003.–P.M. • $29 • (11/15/1998) • **86**

Châteauneuf-du-Pape La Crau 1995: Dark in color and quite earthy, this full-bodied red shows plenty of personality and intensity, with loads of blackberry, wet earth and cedar character, but the tannins are very tough. Slightly hot finish. Best from 2002 through 2008.–P.M. • $30 • (9/30/1998) • **88**

Châteauneuf-du-Pape Vieux Mas des Papes 1998: Supple and ripe, with smooth and sweet tannins. Medium-bodied, offering good black and red fruit character, with a mineral complexity. Tannins clamp down on the finish. Best from 2003 through 2015.–P.M. • $26 • (6/30/2000) HR • **91**

Châteauneuf-du-Pape Vieux Mas des Papes 1997: Very ripe, fat in texture, with good concentration of luxurious plum and black fruit and a wet earth taste that continues on the lingering and balanced smoky finish, this Rhône red is simply beautiful. Drink now through 2005.–P.M. • $30 • (8/31/1999) HR • **91**

Châteauneuf-du-Pape Vieux Mas des Papes 1993 • $17 • (10/15/1995) • **86**

Châteauneuf-du-Pape White 1996 • $33 • (10/15/1997) • **78**

Châteauneuf-du-Pape White La Crau 1997: Vibrant yet full-bodied and rich, offering tropical, lemon and floral aromas, with a subtle, buttery and deliciously lingering finish. Delicate oak is folded in oh-so-gently. Drink now through 2002.–P.M. • $32 • (9/30/1999) • **90**

VIGNEAU-CHEVREAU

Vouvray Moelleux 1996 • $20 • (6/15/1998) • **83**

Vouvray Moelleux 1996: Still fresh and quite sweet, this white offers textbook flavors of apple, quince, almond and spice. Balanced and clean, with moderate sweetness that's soft but not cloying, it has the structure to improve with age. Drink now through 2005.–T.M. • $23 • (6/30/1999) • **88**

Vouvray Moelleux Cuvée Château Gaillard 1996 • $25 • (6/15/1998) • **86**

VIGNELAURE, CHATEAU

Coteaux d'Aix-en-Provence 1992 • $12 • (1/01/1998) • **80**

Coteaux d'Aix-en-Provence 1981 • $10 • (10/01/1984) • **89**

Coteaux d'Aix-en-Provence Rosé 1996 • $9 • (9/30/1997) • **79**

VIGNERONS ARDECHOIS

Cabernet Sauvignon Vin de Pays des Coteaux de l'Ardèche 1997: Clean and pure, with red plum and currant flavors. A bit assertive, this needs a little time to calm down. Ends on an herbal note. Best after 2000.–K.M. • $7 • (2/28/1999) • **82**

Merlot Vin de Pays des Coteaux de l'Ardèche 1997: Lively and interesting, with olive, currant and bell pepper flavors. Has a nice focus, turnimg a bit chewy on the finish. Drink now.–K.M. • $7 • (2/28/1999) • **84**

Red Vin de Pays des Coteaux de l'Ardèche 1988 • $5 • (4/30/1990) • **79**

Viognier-Chardonnay Vin de Pays des Coteaux de l'Ardèche 1997: Offers nice creamy texture, with tropical fruit flavors and hints of rosewater, but it flattens out in the end.–K.M. • $10 • (2/28/1999) • **78**

VIGNERONS D'ESTEZARGUES, CAVES DES

Côtes du Rhône-Villages Domaine de Périllière 1995 • $10 • (10/15/1997) • **85**

Côtes du Rhône-Villages Domaine de Périllière Vieilles Vignes 1997: Interesting, with green olive, dill and cassis bush character. Medium-bodied, supple, a bit rustic on the finish. The ripe fruit will hold until the tannins soften. Drink through 2002.–P.M. • $11 • (11/15/1998) • **86**

VIGNERONS D'IGE, LES

Mâcon-Igé 1997: Diluted, with a cardboard character, turning tart on the finish.–P.M. • $9 • (5/31/1999) • **70**

Mâcon-Igé 1995 • $NA • (8/31/1996) • **84**

Mâcon-Igé Château London 1995 • $NA • (8/31/1996) • **77**

Key: SS—Spectator Selection. CS—Cellar Selection. HR—Highly Recommended. $NA—Price not available. (BT)—Barrel tasting. Ⓐ—Auction Price.
For a key to the tasters' initials, see "How to Use These Listings."
Dates in parentheses represent the issues in which the ratings were published.

St.-Véran 1997: Decent fruit and grassy floral notes give this light-bodied Mâcon some interest, but it turns a bit herbal and sharp on the finish.–P.M. • $11 • (5/31/1999) • **78**

St.-Véran 1996 • $11 • (5/31/1998) • **81**

St.-Véran 1995 • $NA • (8/31/1996) • **77**

VIGNERONS DE BAIXAS, CAVE DE

Côtes du Roussillon-Villages dom Brial 1995: Overripe and a little stewy-tasting, with mineral, ripe plum and meat notes.–K.M. • $10 • (11/30/1998) • **77**

VIGNERONS DE BEAUMES DE VENISE

Muscat de Beaumes-de-Venise Carte Or 1996 • $NA • (1/01/1998) • **84**

Muscat de Beaumes-de-Venise Muscat des Papes NV • $25 • (1/01/1998) • **79**

VIGNERONS DE BUZET, LES

Buzet Baron d'Ardeuil 1995: Dark cherry and ripe plum flavors are overlaid with an appealing leathery note. Well made, with some spicy elements on the finish. Drink now.–K.M. • $10 • (5/31/1999) • **83**

Buzet Baron d'Ardeuil 1994: Has a nice fine-grained texture to it, with dried cherry and leather flavors, and some bittersweet chocolate note on the finish. Drink now.–K.M. • $10 • (1/01/1999) • **83**

Buzet Baron d'Ardeuil 1992 • $11 • (12/15/1997) • **84**

Buzet Baron d'Ardeuil 1991 • $11 • (12/15/1997) • **87**

Buzet Baron d'Ardeuil 1990 • $10 • (7/31/1996) • **85**

Buzet Château de Bougigues 1995: Dried cherry, plum and green olive flavors dominate this medium-bodied red. Drink now.–K.M. • $9 • (5/31/1999) • **82**

César Buzet Grande Réserve 1989: A ripe and brooding red, with dark plum and dark cherry flavors and anise and leather notes. Full-bodied, with a mature quality, though it still packs some tannins. Needs a hearty meal. Drink now through 2002.–K.M. • $28 • (6/30/1999) • **86**

César Buzet Grande Réserve 1988 • $18 • (12/15/1997) • **89**

Merlot Buzet Tradition 1996: A straightforward, rather light-tasting red with dried cherry and leather flavors and a gravelly, minerally note on the finish. Drink now.–K.M. • $7 • (5/31/1999) • **81**

Merlot Buzet Tradition 1995 • $8 • (11/15/1997) • **72**

Merlot Buzet Tradition 1993 • $7 • (7/31/1996) • **82**

VIGNERONS DE L'ARBRESLE

Beaujolais Roche Catin 1998: Cherry and cinnamon flavors mark this light, straightforward red, with soft tannins and a clean finish. Drink now.–T.M. • $8 • (3/31/2000) • **82**

VIGNERONS DE LA MEDITERRANEE, LES

Vin de Pays d'Oc Le Pas de Deux de François Gimie 1996: Not very lively, with only modest dried cherry and spice flavors.–K.M. • $11 • (11/30/1998) • **75**

VIGNERONS DE MANCEY, CAVE DES

Bourgogne Cuvée Spéciale Vieille en Fûts de Chêne 1993 • $9 • (5/15/1996) • **79**

Mâcon-Villages 1995 • $NA • (8/31/1996) • **82**

Mâcon-Villages Vieilles Vignes 1997: Hard and tough on the palate, with modest ripe fruit, tasting dry and astringent.–P.M. • $12 • (5/31/1999) • **72**

Mâcon-Villages Vieilles Vignes 1995 • $NA • (8/31/1996) • **76**

VIGNERONS DE SAUMUR, CAVE DES

Saumur Cuvée Tradition 1996 • $7 • (5/31/1998) • **86**

Saumur Cuvée Tradition 1995 • $7 • (6/15/1997) • **84**

Saumur White Cuvée Tradition 1996 • $6 • (5/31/1998) • **76**

Saumur-Champigny Cuvée Tradition 1996 • $9 • (5/31/1998) • **85**

Saumur-Champigny Cuvée Tradition 1995 • $9 • (6/15/1997) • **84**

VIGNERONS DE ST.-FELIX DE LODEZ

Coteaux du Languedoc La Cardabelle de St.-Felix 1995 • $NA • (5/31/1998) • **85**

VIGNERONS DE ST.-GERVAIS

Syrah Côtes du Rhône-Villages 1996 • $10 • (5/15/1998) • **88**

VIGNERONS DES TROIS TERROIRS

Chardonnay Vin de Pays d'Oc Domaine Fontenelles 1998: A mediocre Chardonnay, with dull, woody flavors that turn tough on the finish.–K.M. • $7 • (11/15/1999) • **73**

VIGNERONS DU MONT-VENTOUX, LES

Côtes du Ventoux Chais du Grillon 1996: This ripe red offers round flavors of cooked cherry, raisin and herb, with moderate tannins and a sweetly herbal finish. Generous but lacks focus. Drink now.–T.M. • $10 • (11/15/1998) • **81**

VIGNOBLES BARDE

Cabernet Sauvignon Bergerac Cuvée Angeline 1995 • $9 • (12/15/1996) • **84**
Merlot Bergerac Cuvée Angeline 1995 • $9 • (12/15/1996) • **80**

VIGOUROUX, GEORGES

Cahors 1993 • $12 • (5/15/1998) • **82**
Cahors 1990 • $17 • (5/15/1998) • **85**
Cahors Château de Haute-Serre 1989: Still lively but definitely mature-tasting, with dried cherry, licorice and mineral flavors and a nice roasted note. Flavors gain focus on the finish, which is accented by notes of tea and spice. Drink now.–K.M. • $19 • (4/30/2000) • **87**
Cahors Château de Haute-Serre Géron Dadine Cuvée Prestige 1990 • $20 • (5/15/1998) • **85**
Cahors Gouleyant 1998: A rustic red, with some good plummy and spicy flavors. Earthy notes on the finish. Drink now.–K.M. • $8 • (4/30/2000) • **83**
Cahors Gouleyant 1997: Nice brooding quality to this red, with black currant and dark cherry flavors and hints of tobacco throughout. There's a good backbone of acidity, some tannins as well. Flavors linger appealingly on the finish. Drink through 2004–K.M. • $8 • (8/31/1999) • **85**
Cahors Gouleyant 1996 • $8 • (5/15/1998) • **83**

VILLA BEL-AIR, CHATEAU

Graves 1996: Some fresh fruit and mineral character, but the diluted palate takes away from the overall quality of the wine. Medium- to light-bodied, with light tannins. Short finish.–J.S. • $18 • (1/31/1999) • **76**
Graves 1995 • $12 • (1/31/1998) • **79**
Graves 1994 • $12 • (1/31/1997) • **75**
Graves 1993 • $NA • (1/31/1996) • **78**
Graves 1992 • $NA • (4/15/1995) • **70**
Graves White 1998: Plenty of apple and mango character, with a hint of new wood, but slightly diluted on the finish. Drink now.–J.S. • $18 • (2/29/2000) • **82**
Graves White 1997: Lots of gooseberry and apple aromas, with hints of vanilla. Medium-bodied, with a compacted fruit structure and a medium finish. Well made. Drink now.–J.S. • $17 • (9/30/1999) • **85**
Graves White 1996: Very woody, with some apple and allspice but overall rather subdued and lacking in character. Medium- to light-bodied, with a light finish. This estate is improving, but has a way to go. Drink now.–J.S. • $NA • (1/01/1999) • **81**

VILLAMONT, HENRI DE

Bourgogne 1989 • $11 • (3/31/1991) • **78**
Chambolle-Musigny 1988 • $39 • (2/15/1991) • **83**
Mâcon-Pierreclos 1996 • $10 • (5/31/1998) • **81**
Mâcon-Villages 1996 • $10 • (5/31/1998) • **79**
Pouilly-Fuissé 1996 • $17 • (5/31/1998) • **74**
Pouilly-Fuissé Domaine Carette 1996 • $17 • (5/31/1998) • **80**
St.-Véran 1996 • $13 • (5/31/1998) • **55**
Savigny-lès-Beaune Le Village 1988 • $18 • (3/31/1991) • **80**

VILLARD, FRANCOIS

Condrieu Coteaux de Poncins 1996: This beautiful Condrieu is ripe, thick and full-bodied, showing banana cake, honey, apricot, floral and vanilla cream flavors. Smooth, attractive finish. Drink now through 2005.–P.M. • $50 • (11/15/1998) • **89**
Condrieu Les Terrasses du Palat 1996: This decadent Condrieu delivers an exciting sweet-and-dry character, with melon, apricot, honey, cream and pie tart flavors. Elegant, balanced and harmonious from start to finish. Drink now through 2005.–P.M. • $50 • (11/15/1998) • **94**
Condrieu Quintessence 1997: This late-harvest Condrieu tastes of dry apricot, raisin and honey, with a slight petrol note for added complexity. Full-bodied and sweet, but you may wish for a bit more acidity. Drink now through 2010.–P.M. • $80 • (11/15/1998) • **86**
Condrieu Quintessence 1996 • $60 • (10/15/1997) • **90**
Côte-Rôtie La Brocarde 1996: Inky in color, this is darker than many Côte-Rôties, and at first whiff you know it's special. Fans out with ripe fruit, subtle oak nuances and lots of distinctive smoked bacon, plum, spice, blackberry and Provençal herbs on the palate, all nicely framed by sweet tannins. Full-bodied, with a long, slightly smoky finish. Drink now through 2007.–P.M. • $40 • (11/15/1998) • **94**
Côte-Rôtie La Brocarde 1995 • $35 • (10/15/1997) • **92**
St.-Joseph Côtes de Mairlant 1995 • $16 • (10/15/1997) • **89**
St.-Joseph Reflet 1995 • $30 • (10/15/1997) • **88**
St.-Joseph White Côtes de Mairlant 1996: Overdone, with a burnt butter and milk character. Full-bodied and ripe, but lacks the fresh fruit to carry it through.–P.M. • $20 • (11/15/1998) • **75**

VILLARS, CHATEAU

Fronsac 1997: Interesting aromas of dried cherries and berries. Medium-bodied, with firm tannins. Slightly lean finish, but well done. Drink now through 2002.–J.S. • $NA • (1/31/2000) • **85**
Fronsac 1990 • $17 • (3/31/1993) • **83**
Fronsac 1989 • $16 • (6/15/1993) • **78**

VILLEGEORGE, CHATEAU

Haut-Médoc 1993 • $NA • (1/31/1996) • **79**
Haut-Médoc 1991 • $13 • (3/31/1994) • **81**
Haut-Médoc 1989 • $14 • (3/15/1992) • **79**
Haut-Médoc 1982 • $18 • (8/31/1992) • **84**

VILLEMAURINE, CHATEAU

St.-Emilion 1997: A bit simple, but shows pretty plum and berry character. Medium-bodied, with soft tannins and a light finish. Drink now.–J.S. • $NA • (1/31/2000) • **84**
St.-Emilion 1996: Diluted. Some berry character, but the palate is light-bodied and watery on the finish.–J.S. • $22 • (1/31/1999) • **79**
St.-Emilion 1995 • $20 • (1/31/1998) • **82**
St.-Emilion 1994 • $18 • (1/31/1997) • **79**
St.-Emilion 1993 • $16 • (1/31/1996) • **79**
St.-Emilion 1992 • $13 • (4/15/1995) • **79**
St.-Emilion 1991 • $13 • (3/31/1994) • **77**
St.-Emilion 1990 • $28 • (3/31/1993) • **92**
St.-Emilion 1989: Well done. Inky color. Gorgeous aromas of blackberries, raspberries and spices. Full-bodied, with extremely chewy tannins. It builds, and then persists sensationally on the palate. (1989 Bordeaux horizontal tasting). –J.S. • $NA • (5/31/1999) • **93**
St.-Emilion 1982 • $40 • (8/31/1992) • **93**

VILLENEUVE, CHATEAU DE

Saumur White 1996: Lovely herb-inflected aromas of quince and crisp acidity so common in the '96s provide focus and clarity. Nice depth and intensity, just tailing off a little on the finish. Drink now.–B.S. • $11 • (11/15/1998) • **85**

VILLENEUVE, DOMAINE DE

Châteauneuf-du-Pape Les Vieilles Vignes 1995: A beauty. The aromas are terrific, displaying an earthy quality mingled with blackberry, toasted walnut, white truffle and mineral-laden, lead pencil character. But it's the lush, velvety texture, backed by firm and solid tannins, that impresses the most. And the finish! It's ripe yet elegant. A world-class Rhône that's worth laying down in the cellar for a while. Best from 2005 through 2012.–P.M. • $NA • (9/30/1998) • **96**

VILLERAMBERT JULIEN, CHATEAU

Minervois 1995: Exotic and enticing aromas of bacon and leather usher in this full-bore red from the south of France. Concentrated and powerful, with

FRANCE

dried cherry and wild herb flavors. This is a massive wine that needs some time to come together. Drink through 2005–K.M. • $12 • (10/31/1998) • **89**

Minervois Cuvée Trianon 1989 • $15 • (12/15/1991) • **73**

VILMART

Brut Blanc de Blancs Champagne NV • $63 • (12/31/1997) • **84**

Brut Champagne Coeur de Cuvée 1992: More lively than many 1992s, this has ripe tropical fruit flavors, vibrant acidity and good depth. Drink now through 2001. • $97 • (10/15/1999) • **88**

Brut Champagne Coeur de Cuvée 1991 • $66 • (11/30/1997) • **86**

Brut Champagne Cuvée Création 1992: Seductive, with abundant vanilla, honey and pear flavors and a slightly soft texture. Nicely mature. Drink now. • $95 • (10/15/1999) • **88**

Brut Champagne Cuvée du Nouveau Monde NV • $63 • (11/30/1997) • **89**

Brut Champagne Grand Cellier NV: Generously fruity in flavor, refreshing in texture. Bright and well balanced overall. Drink now. • $55 • (9/15/1999) • **88**

VIN DU SOLEIL

Merlot Vin de Pays d'Oc 1995 • $8 • (4/30/1997) • **79**

VINCENT & FILS, J.J.

Mâcon-Villages Domaine de Champ Brûlé 1997: Soft and perfumed, with a slight dilution, showing modest fruit and a tart finish. Serve chilled.–P.M. • $13 • (5/31/1999) • **73**

Mâcon-Villages Domaine de Champ Brûlé 1996 • $12 • (5/31/1998) • **74**

Pouilly-Fuissé 1997: Interesting. Good ripeness, and if a bit reduced on the nose (an icebox aroma), underneath is lovely clean fruit, honey and mineral character that coats the palate in a silky envelope. Drink through 2004–P.M. • $18 • (5/31/1999) • **86**

Pouilly-Fuissé 1996 • $16 • (5/31/1998) • **84**

Pouilly-Fuissé 1995 • $15 • (1/31/1997) • **84**

St.-Véran Domaine des Morats 1997: Delicious combination of lemon, butter, toasted oak and honey makes this medium-bodied, sophisticated St-Véran worth hunting down. The oak accents fold nicely into the finish. Drink now through 2002.–P.M. • $14 • (5/31/1999) • **89**

St.-Véran Domaine des Morats 1996 • $17 • (5/31/1998) • **75**

VINIVAL

Rosé d'Anjou Vitrine du Monde 1997: This soft, lush rosé offers vibrant cherry and strawberry flavors in a round, off-dry style. A refreshing quaff; drink now, very cold.–T.M. • $6 • (8/31/1998) • **83**

Sauvignon Blanc Touraine Vitrine du Monde 1997: Ripe apples and a grassy element are attractive in this moderately concentrated white that turns broad but not heavy, finishing with a bitter almond flavor. Drink now.–B.S. • $6 • (11/15/1998) • **83**

VIOLOT-GUILLEMARD, CHRISTOPHE

Beaune Clos des Mouches 1997: Ripe cherry and plum notes seem evolved, and there's chewy, licorice fruit. Light, with firm tannins on the finish. Drink through 2006–B.S. • $36 • (9/30/1999) • **79**

Pommard Clos Orgelot 1997: Here's a '97 red Burgundy whose simple cooked cherry and plum flavors combine with a round profile and smooth texture.–B.S. • $39 • (9/30/1999) • **79**

Pommard Epenots 1997: This thick, ripe red Burgundy shows a delicacy of rose petal, cherry and plum aromas, but the flavors turn a bit cooked and jammy on the pasty, somewhat heavy finish. Drink now through 2002.–P.M. • $39 • (9/30/1999) • **84**

St.-Romain Red Sous le Château 1997: Already advanced and slightly anemic, though there are solid tannins.–B.S. • $16 • (9/30/1999) • **78**

Key: SS—Spectator Selection. CS—Cellar Selection. HR—Highly Recommended. $NA—Price not available. (BT)—Barrel tasting. Ⓐ—Auction Price. For a key to the tasters' initials, see "How to Use These Listings." **Dates in parentheses represent the issues in which the ratings were published.**

VIOLOT-GUILLEMARD, THIERRY

Beaune Clos des Mouches 1997: A touch volatile, yet with good intensity and concentrated cherry flavors on a lean, firm framework. Drying tannins. Best from 2001 through 2005.–B.S. • $36 • (9/30/1999) • **83**

Pommard La Platière 1997: Toasty and smoky, this delicate red Burgundy has a vivid, clean and lovely midpalate filled with succulent red berry and blackberry flavors that remain focused on the long, delicious finish. Drink now through 2005.–P.M. • $39 • (9/30/1999) • **88**

Pommard Rugiens 1997: A bit advanced, this medium-bodied red tastes of forest underbrush, tea leaf and mushroom. Dry finish.–P.M. • $42 • (9/30/1999) • **78**

VIORNERY, GEORGES

Brouilly 1998: This lean red offers pretty berry and cherry flavors. Has firm tannins, but lacks concentration and finishes a bit dry. Drink now.–T.M. • $15 • (11/15/1999) • **80**

Brouilly 1996: A year of bottle age has given this sinuous red appealing smoky and spicy accents to go with the cherry and berry flavors; the wine is still fresh and firm. A good example of the appellation. Drink now.–T.M. • $13 • (8/31/1998) • **85**

Brouilly 1995 • $13 • (6/30/1997) • **84**

Côte de Brouilly 1998: This chewy red offers solid cherry, licorice and light herb flavors backed by just enough tannin for food. Clean and fresh. Drink now.–T.M. • $15 • (11/15/1999) • **83**

Côte de Brouilly 1996 • $15 • (6/15/1998) • **87**

Côte de Brouilly 1990 • $13 • (10/31/1991) • **88**

VIRANEL, CHATEAU

St.-Chinian 1996: A smooth and mature-tasting red wine. Red plum flavors dominate, with an appealing roasted note blended in. Medium-bodied and balanced, with a slightly peppery finish. Drink now.–K.M. • $9 • (4/30/1999) • **84**

VIRE, CAVE DE

Mâcon-Viré 1995 • $NA • (8/31/1996) • **73**

Mâcon-Viré Les Charlottes 1995 • $11 • (6/30/1997) • **79**

VIRGINIE DE VALANDRAUD

St.-Emilion 1994 • $NA • (1/31/1997) • **82**

VISSOUX, DOMAINE DU

Beaujolais Cuvée Traditionnêlle 1995 • $13 • (9/15/1997) • **83**

Beaujolais Cuvée Traditionnêlle 1994 • $12 • (9/15/1996) • **83**

Fleurie Poncié 1997: This ambitious red offers smoky, gamy aroma and ripe flavors of plums and cassis with cedar and tobacco notes. It's balanced, with moderate tannins and a silky texture. Not your typical Beaujolais. Drink now.–T.M. • $20 • (1/01/2000) • **87**

Moulin-à-Vent Rochegrès 1997: Smoke, spice and dried cherry aromas and flavors are distinctive and harmonious in this supple yet rich red. A fine effort in a difficult vintage. Drink now.–T.M. • $20 • (1/01/2000) • **88**

VITALLIS, CHATEAU

Pouilly-Fuissé 1997: Crisp and straightforward, with a rustic, grass and wet hay character. A bit bitter on the finish, it's still zesty, if not complex.–P.M. • $20 • (5/31/1999) • **79**

Pouilly-Fuissé 1996 • $15 • (5/31/1998) • **85**

Pouilly-Fuissé Vieilles Vignes 1997: Some honey, spice and fruit notes in a medium-bodied package, but lacks a bit of elegance. A bit tough on the finish too. Drink now.–P.M. • $30 • (5/31/1999) • **81**

VIVIER, CHATEAU LE

Médoc 1998: Slightly unripe, with medium to light body, light tannins and a diluted finish.–J.S. • $NA • (5/31/1999) (BT) • **75-79**

Médoc 1997: Light and fruity red; some berry character but very light.–J.S. • $NA • (1/31/2000) • **79s**

Médoc 1996: Decent aromas of plums and berries. Medium-bodied, with light tannins and a watery finish.–J.S. • $15 • (1/31/1999) • **77**

Médoc 1995 • $15 • (1/31/1998) • **87**

VIVIERS DE SENEJAC, LES

Bordeaux White 1997: A white with lots of mineral and fennel character. Medium-bodied, with light fruit and a chalky, slightly short finish. Second wine of Sénéjac.–J.S. • $NA • (9/30/1999) • **79**
Bordeaux White 1996: Old style of white Bordeaux with a rustic, candied-fruit character. Medium- to light-bodied, with a dull aftertaste. Hard to like.–J.S. • $NA • (1/01/1999) • **77**

VOARICK, EMILE

Mercurey Clos de Paradis 1994 • $NA • (11/15/1996) • **77**
Mercurey Clos du Roi 1994 • $NA • (11/15/1996) • **72**

VOARICK, MICHEL

Aloxe-Corton 1993 • $30 • (1/01/1995) • **82**
Aloxe-Corton 1990 • $26 • (12/15/1992) • **79**
Corton Le Clos du Roi 1994 • $NA • (11/15/1996) • **81**
Corton Le Clos du Roi 1993 • $60 • (11/15/1995) • **85**
Corton Le Clos du Roi 1990 • $36 • (12/15/1992) • **75**
Corton Les Bressandes 1990 • $36 • (12/15/1992) • **73**
Corton Les Languettes 1994 • $NA • (11/15/1996) • **70**
Corton Les Renardes 1993 • $60 • (11/15/1995) • **86**
Pernand-Vergelesses 1993 • $20 • (11/15/1995) • **85**
Romanée St.-Vivant 1990 • $76 • (12/15/1992) • **69**

VOCORET & FILS

Chablis 1998: The tropical character makes this fun. Light-bodied and a bit spritzy, with honey and lemon, it's crisp but ripe-tasting. Nicely done. Drink now through 2001.–P.M. • $15 • (5/15/2000) • **84**
Chablis 1997: Remarkably intense and rich for a village Chablis, this outstanding white kicks with life, boasting a round mouthfeel and a lovely combination of honey, pear, spice and toast flavors of good complexity and, above all, great length. Drink now.–P.M. • $15 • (5/31/1999) HR • **91**
Chablis 1995 • $NA • (8/31/1996) • **87**
Chablis Blanchot 1998: Pleasant, with mineral, lemon and green apple character. Light- to medium-bodied, delivering vibrancy on the finish. Drink now through 2002.–P.M. • $35 • (5/15/2000) • **83**
Chablis Blanchot 1995 • $40 • (6/15/1997) • **90**
Chablis La Forêt 1998: Tough, with wet earth and matchstick character. Medium-bodied and crisp, it turns a bit sour, with green apple and citrus flavors on the mouthpuckering finish. Drink now through 2003.–P.M. • $20 • (5/15/2000) • **80**
Chablis Mont de Milieu 1997: Zesty, vibrant, clean, with good ripe fruit, honey and spice—there's plenty to like in this full-bodied, silky-textured Chablis. Delicious finish. Drink now through 2007.–P.M. • $NA • (5/31/1999) • **91**
Chablis Montée de Tonnerre 1998: A bit on the grassy side, but fresh and lively, with dried herb, melon and ripe pear, a spritzy feel and much vibrancy on the finish. Drink now through 2003.–P.M. • $20 • (5/15/2000) • **83**
Chablis Montée de Tonnerre 1997: Clean and honeyed, very much in the '97 style, this medium-bodied charmer is sweet-tasting and ripe, with pear and quince jam flavors. Immediately appealing. Drink now.–P.M. • $22 • (5/31/1999) • **87**
Chablis Montée de Tonnerre 1995 • $22 • (6/15/1997) • **87**
Chablis Montmains 1997: Exciting. Full-bodied, with a deft dose of lemon, toasted bread, dried herbs and honey, it delivers balance and great length on the finish. Best from 2003 through 2010.–P.M. • $22 • (5/31/1999) • **94**
Chablis Vaudésir 1997: A bit herbal, with a slightly grassy, bitter character. Presents some sweet-tasting honey and (overly) toasted oak, with a tough, astringent finish.–P.M. • $32 • (5/31/1999) • **78**

VOGE, ALAIN

Cornas 1991 • $25 • (5/31/1994) • **86**
Cornas Cuvée Barriques 1990 • $25 • (4/15/1993) • **87**
Cornas Cuvée Vieilles Vignes 1996: An amazing wine that catapults the senses into a different orbit. Layers upon layers of pure cassis and wild berry flavors are married with the prettiest of oak-inspired violet, jasmine and Earl Grey tea notes. Ripe yet elegant, with the finest of tannins, it coats the palate in a creamlike texture that ends on a superbalanced, mineral-laden finish. Drink now through 2010.–P.M. • $40 • (10/15/1998) • **96**
Cornas Cuvée Vieilles Vignes 1995: Medium-bodied, with velvety tannins and terrific acidity to keep it together. Offers excellent harmony and a symphony of flavors—grilled meat, mineral, spice, mocha, blackberry and black cherry. Suave as can be on the finish. Drink now through 2005.–P.M. • $40 • (11/15/1998) • **92**
Cornas Cuvée Vieilles Vignes 1993 • $34 • (10/15/1996) • **86**
Cornas Cuvée Vieilles Vignes 1992 • $34 • (10/15/1996) • **86**
Cornas Cuvée Vieilles Vignes 1991 • $27 • (5/31/1994) • **86**
Cornas Cuvée Vieilles Vignes 1990 • $27 • (5/31/1994) • **83**
Cornas Cuvée Vieilles Vignes 1989 • $32 • (4/15/1993) • **83**
Cornas Les Vieilles Fontaines 1996: Smooth and tasty but a bit diluted, showing blackberry, black pepper and lemonlike flavors, this medium-bodied red is ready on release.–P.M. • $65 • (11/30/1999) • **84**
St.-Péray Mélodie William 1997: Clean and butterscotchlike, with almond and—unfortunately—wet cardboard character. Turns a bit dry on the finish.–P.M. • $20 • (12/15/1999) • **76**
St.-Péray Mélodie William 1996: Clean and pure, with a core of good lemony acidity backed by ripe pear, grilled pineapple and fresh fig flavors. Medium-bodied, remarkably oily in texture, it's balanced, with a lingering finish. Drink now.–P.M. • $20 • (11/15/1998) • **87**

VOGUE, COMTE GEORGES DE

Bonnes Mares 1997: Supple and natural-tasting, not pumped up but delivering waves of medium-intense flavors of red berry, blackberry, spice and smoke that gain velocity and power as they hurdle to a lingering finish. Drink now through 2004.–P.M. • $185 • (9/30/1999) • **87**
Bonnes Mares 1996: Big red, with lots of mineral, toasted oak and compacted fruit; seemingly ungenerous for now, it's a *terroir*-driven Pinot that's hibernating and will need time. But all the pieces are there, including a racy quality. Best from 2005 through 2012.–P.M. • $137 Ⓐ • (5/15/1999) • **90**
Bonnes Mares 1995 • $136 Ⓐ • (11/15/1997) • **91**
Bonnes Mares 1994 • $75 • (11/15/1996) • **82**
Bonnes Mares 1993 • $86 Ⓐ • (11/15/1995) • **94**
Bonnes Mares 1992 • $85 • (12/15/1994) • **88**
Bonnes Mares 1991 • $163 Ⓐ • (1/31/1994) • **93**
Bonnes Mares 1990 • $234 Ⓐ • (12/15/1992) • **99**
Bonnes Mares 1989 • $93 • (1/31/1992) • **94**
Bonnes Mares 1988 • $81 Ⓐ • (3/31/1991) • **89**
Bonnes Mares 1987 • $35 Ⓐ • (7/15/1990) • **87**
Bonnes Mares 1979 • $48 • (11/16/1984) • **88**
Bonnes Mares 1976 • $69 Ⓐ • (11/16/1984) • **90**
Bonnes Mares 1972 • $125 • (11/16/1984) • **79**
Bonnes Mares 1971 • $307 Ⓐ • (11/16/1984) • **88**
Bonnes Mares 1959 • $373 Ⓐ • (11/16/1984) • **83**
Bonnes Mares 1955 • $285 • (11/16/1984) • **91**
Bonnes Mares 1949 • $500/1.5 liter • (11/16/1984) • **90**
Bonnes Mares Avery Bottling 1959 • $NA • (11/16/1984) • **87**
Bonnes Mares Grivolet 1934 • $NA • (11/16/1984) • **82**
Chambolle-Musigny 1997: Rich and almost chunky, full of black cherry, earth and mineral, this is round and balanced, losing a bit of concentration midpalate. Moderate aftertaste of cherry and spice. Drink now through 2004.–B.S. • $60 • (9/30/1999) • **87**
Chambolle-Musigny 1996: Clean and fairly crisp, offering good balance between acidity, fruit and tannins. Nice blackberry and toasted, smoky flavors. Best from 2002 through 2010.–P.M. • $41 Ⓐ • (5/15/1999) • **86**
Chambolle-Musigny 1995 • $77 Ⓐ • (11/15/1997) • **85**
Chambolle-Musigny 1994 • $50 • (11/15/1996) • **82**
Chambolle-Musigny 1993 • $60 • (11/15/1995) • **88**
Chambolle-Musigny 1992 • $45 • (12/15/1994) • **83**
Chambolle-Musigny 1991 • $47 • (1/31/1994) • **88**
Chambolle-Musigny 1990 • $45 • (12/15/1992) • **90**
Chambolle-Musigny 1989 • $44 • (1/31/1992) • **89**
Chambolle-Musigny Les Amoureuses 1996: Ripe and full-bodied, with a distinct Mars candy bar, mocha, vanilla, blackberry flavor. Impressively supple and ripe, with fat tannins that coat the palate in a near *grand cru* way. Best from 2005 through 2015.–P.M. • $188 • (5/15/1999) • **93**
Chambolle-Musigny Les Amoureuses 1995 • $139 Ⓐ • (11/15/1997) • **94**
Chambolle-Musigny Les Amoureuses 1994 • $75 • (11/15/1996) • **85**
Chambolle-Musigny Les Amoureuses 1993 • $125 • (11/15/1995) • **94**
Chambolle-Musigny Les Amoureuses 1992 • $105 Ⓐ • (12/15/1994) • **83**
Chambolle-Musigny Les Amoureuses 1991 • $90 • (1/31/1994) • **87**
Chambolle-Musigny Les Amoureuses 1990 • $134 Ⓐ • (12/15/1992) • **94**
Chambolle-Musigny Les Amoureuses 1989 • $93 • (1/31/1992) • **93**
Chambolle-Musigny Les Amoureuses 1988 • $62 Ⓐ • (2/28/1991) • **89**
Chambolle-Musigny Les Amoureuses 1987 • $74 • (3/31/1990) • **87**

VOGUE, COMTE GEORGES DE

Chambolle-Musigny Les Amoureuses 1971 • $85 • (11/16/1984) • **86**
Chambolle-Musigny Les Amoureuses 1970 • $55 • (11/16/1984) • **78**
Chambolle-Musigny Premier Cru 1996: Delicious and charming. Balanced and sweet-tasting, with lovely red- and blackberry notes, a fresh, vibrant midpalate, full body, and deftly dosed oak accents on the smooth finish. Drink now through 2006.–P.M. • $110 • (5/15/1999) • **91**
Chambolle-Musigny Premier Cru 1995 • $100 • (11/15/1997) • **88**
Musigny 1953 • $200 • (11/16/1984) • **81**
Musigny 1952 • $200 • (11/16/1984) • **85**
Musigny 1949 • $600 • (11/16/1984) • **98**
Musigny 1945 • $1600/1.5 liter • (11/16/1984) • **96**
Musigny 1937 • $650 • (11/16/1984) • **93**
Musigny 1934 • $600 • (11/16/1984) • **95**
Musigny Cuvée Vieilles Vignes 1997: Complex, velvety and muscular. Rich and pure, with mineral and wet earth notes, this clean, full-bodied, sweet-tasting, dark-colored red Burgundy is well worth hunting down. Gorgeous backbone of fresh citrus and acidity, but also loads of mellow spice, mocha, coffee and oak-inspired character. The chewy but balanced finish needs time. Best from 2003 through 2010. • $250 • (1/01/2000) • **92**
Musigny Cuvée Vieilles Vignes 1996: Harmony defined. Full-bodied and without a glitch, here's a red Burgundy so supple it caresses the palate, all the while delivering a mineral, *terroir*-driven character that's simply spectacular. Best from 2005 through 2015.–P.M. • $336 Ⓐ • (5/15/1999) CS • **96**
Musigny Cuvée Vieilles Vignes 1994 • $72 Ⓐ • (11/15/1996) • **88**
Musigny Cuvée Vieilles Vignes 1993 • $248 Ⓐ • (11/15/1995) CS • **96**
Musigny Cuvée Vieilles Vignes 1992 • $95 Ⓐ • (12/15/1994) • **85**
Musigny Cuvée Vieilles Vignes 1991 • $328 Ⓐ • (2/28/1995) • **96**
Musigny Cuvée Vieilles Vignes 1990 • $370 Ⓐ • (2/28/1995) • **99**
Musigny Cuvée Vieilles Vignes 1989 • $201 Ⓐ • (2/28/1995) • **93**
Musigny Cuvée Vieilles Vignes 1988 • $119 Ⓐ • (2/28/1995) • **90**
Musigny Cuvée Vieilles Vignes 1987 • $125 Ⓐ • (2/28/1995) • **87**
Musigny Cuvée Vieilles Vignes 1986 • $100 • (2/28/1995) • **87**
Musigny Cuvée Vieilles Vignes 1985 • $198 Ⓐ • (2/28/1995) • **87**
Musigny Cuvée Vieilles Vignes 1979 • $114 • (11/16/1984) • **87**
Musigny Cuvée Vieilles Vignes 1976 • $119 • (11/16/1984) • **86**
Musigny Cuvée Vieilles Vignes 1972 • $218 Ⓐ • (11/16/1984) • **80**
Musigny Cuvée Vieilles Vignes 1971 • $345 Ⓐ • (11/16/1984) • **90**
Musigny Cuvée Vieilles Vignes 1966 • $448 Ⓐ • (11/16/1984) • **92**
Musigny Cuvée Vieilles Vignes 1962 • $550/1.5 liter • (11/16/1984) • **90**
Musigny Cuvée Vieilles Vignes 1961 • $534 Ⓐ • (11/16/1984) • **93**
Musigny Cuvée Vieilles Vignes 1959 • $1,150 Ⓐ • (11/16/1984) • **89**
Musigny Cuvée Vieilles Vignes 1957 • $255 • (8/31/1990) • **95**
Musigny Cuvée Vieilles Vignes 1947 • $NA • (5/31/1997) • **91**

VOILLARD, JOEL

Côte de Nuits-Villages 1995 • $19 • (11/15/1997) • **78**

VOULTE GASPARET, CHATEAU LA

Corbières 1990 • $10 • (3/15/1994) • **85**
Corbières Cuvée Réservée 1996: Nice intensity, with cherry and plum flavors, but also a muddled stewed quality. Drink now.–K.M. • $12 • (11/30/1998) • **80**
Corbières Cuvée Réservée 1994 • $14 • (5/31/1997) • **82**

VRAI CANON BOUCHE, CHATEAU

Canon-Fronsac 1998: Lean really, but has decent berry, earthy character, medium body and medium tannins, with a short finish.–J.S. • $NA • (5/31/1999) (BT) • **80-84**
Canon-Fronsac Cuvée Prestige 1996: Fresh, with some pleasant berry and green tobacco character, but it lacks definition and fruit on the palate. Medium- to light-bodied, with a diluted finish. Drink now.–J.S. • $NA • (1/31/1999) • **80**

Key: SS—Spectator Selection. CS—Cellar Selection. HR—Highly Recommended. $NA—Price not available. (BT)—Barrel tasting. Ⓐ—Auction Price.
For a key to the tasters' initials, see "How to Use These Listings."
Dates in parentheses represent the issues in which the ratings were published.

VRANKEN

Brut Champagne Demoiselle Cuvée 2000 NV: Straightforward apple and lemon flavors animate this crisp, rather lean Champagne. Drink now. • $30 • (10/15/1999) • **85**
Brut Champagne Demoiselle Cuvée 21 NV: Fruity, smooth and straightforward. It has crisp citrus and apple flavors and a firm texture. Drink now. • $120 • (10/15/1999) • **87**
Brut Champagne Demoiselle Grande Cuvée NV: A good example of a lighter style of Champagne, this elegant, well-balanced bubbly combines fresh flavors with lively acidity and a velvety texture. Drink now. • $28 • (12/31/1998) • **88**
Brut Champagne Demoiselle Tête de Cuvée NV • $NA • (12/31/1993) • **86**
Brut Champagne Demoiselle Tête de Cuvée 1990: This vibrant, zingy style of Champagne boasts bright lemon and apple flavors, a firm but smooth texture and a tangy finish. Pure fruit flavor at its best. Drink now through 2001. • $45 • (12/31/1998) • **89**
Brut Champagne Grande Cuvée NV • $NA • (12/31/1991) • **86**
Brut Champagne Monopole Grand Prestige Cuvée 2000 NV: Excellent in a very dry, crisp style. Focused on a lemony flavor and a tight, tangy texture that opens on the finish. Drink now. • $60 • (9/15/1999) • **88**
Brut Rosé Champagne Demoiselle Tête de Cuvée NV: A fresh-flavored, brightly balanced, reddish pink Champagne that's refreshing in texture and straightforward in taste. Drink now. • $45 • (11/30/1998) • **83**
Brut Rosé Champagne Tête de Cuvée NV • $40 • (9/30/1997) • **85**

VRAYE-CROIX-DE-GAY, CHATEAU LA

Pomerol 1999: Some good plum and cherry character, with light tannins and a fresh finish. A bit diluted.–J.S. • $NA • (1/01/2000) (BT) • **80-84**
Pomerol 1998: A bit rustic, but very concentrated. Crushed berries galore. Full-bodied, with loads of berry, raisin and earth flavors, velvety tannins and a long finish.–J.S. • $NA • (5/31/1999) (BT) • **90-94**
Pomerol 1997: Rather diluted, with some berry character, but short. Drink now.–J.S. • $NA • (1/31/2000) • **80**
Pomerol 1996: Pretty tobacco and cherry character, but very light on the palate. Light-bodied, with a watery finish. Not as good as I remember. Drink now.–J.S. • $NA • (1/31/1999) • **83**
Pomerol 1995: Slightly one-dimensional but ripe and fruity. Medium-bodied, with medium, velvety tannins and a fruity finish, which could use more fresh fruit. Tasted better in barrel. Drink through 2003–J.S. • $NA • (9/15/1998) • **86**
Pomerol 1982: A big surprise; better than I remember. Dark ruby-garnet color. Wild raspberry, milk chocolate and berry aromas. Full-bodied and tannic, it needs time to mellow. Drink through 2006 (1982 Bordeaux horizontal tasting).–J.S. • $NA • (11/30/1998) • **90**

WANTZ, CHARLES

Gewürztraminer Alsace Réserve Particulière 1996: An intriguing smoky note gives way to pear and tropical fruit in this attractive white. Fine acidity keeps the flavors moving across the palate, and the finish is mouthwatering, with a touch of bitter grapefruit.–B.S. • $17 • (9/15/1998) • **87**
Pinot Blanc Alsace Réserve Particulière 1998: Lean and almost tart, with an attractive mineral note, it trails off on the finish. Drink now.–B.S. • $11 • (6/15/2000) • **82**
Pinot Blanc Alsace Réserve Particulière 1996: A seamless Pinot Blanc that exhibits floral, peach and stony elements, well integrated with the rich texture and bright acidity. Flavors linger on the firm finish. Drink now through 2001.–B.S. • $12 • (8/31/1998) • **87**
Riesling Alsace Réserve Particulière 1998: A concentrated, subdued Riesling, with almond, lanolin, apple and lemon notes, it seems compact and tight now. Lovely harmony and length on the finish. Drink now through 2005.–B.S. • $12 • (5/31/2000) • **87**
Riesling Alsace Réserve Particulière 1996: Reserved and sophisticated, this is full of peach and spice flavors and has a stony character that carries through to the long finish. Everything is there in just the right proportions. Drink now through 2008.–B.S. • $12 • (8/31/1998) • **88**

WEINBACH

Gewürztraminer Alsace Altenbourg Cuvée d'Or Quintessence de Grains Nobles 1997: Full-bodied and opulent, this has crowd-pleasing spice, honey and sweetness; seems a bit one-dimensional today, but shows good balance and a long, honeyed finish. Drink now through 2004.–B.S. • $183/375 ml. • (10/31/1999) • **91**

Gewürztraminer Alsace Altenbourg Cuvée Laurence 1998: A palate-coating white, viscous yet not heavy, displaying clover honey, licorice and lemon verbena on the palate, remaining spry and lively through the grapefruity finish. Needs time. Drink through 2004–B.S. • $79 • (10/31/1999) • **90**

Gewürztraminer Alsace Altenbourg Cuvée Laurence 1997: Subtle in its approach, this Gewürztraminer has a floral top note and an underlying mineral element. It's suave and delicious, full of honey tones allied to a thick texture. Should improve with time. Drink through 2002.–B.S. • $70 • (4/30/1999) • **89**

Gewürztraminer Alsace Altenbourg Cuvée Laurence 1996 • $58 • (11/15/1997) • **91**

Gewürztraminer Alsace Cuvée Laurence 1998: Fans of opulent, fragrant Gewürztraminer take note, it doesn't get much better than this. With rose and honey, dashes of litchi and spice for good measure, this shows some restraint and lively acidity to keep it all light on its feet and refreshing. Drink now through 2002.–B.S. • $58 • (10/31/1999) • **91**

Gewürztraminer Alsace Cuvée Laurence 1997: A drier style, with firmness and a spicy edge to the litchi and grapefruit flavors. Balanced and richly textured, this grows on you, and despite an austere finish, there's a lingering aftertaste of litchi. Drink now.–B.S. • $52 • (4/30/1999) • **88**

Gewürztraminer Alsace Cuvée Laurence 1996 • $48 • (11/15/1997) • **87**

Gewürztraminer Alsace Cuvée Théo 1998: Fat and luscious, exhibiting honey, citrus and lanolin aromas and flavors with good supporting structure and a long, spicy aftertaste. Drink now through 2001.–B.S. • $41 • (10/31/1999) • **90**

Gewürztraminer Alsace Cuvée Théo 1997: This is floral and ripe, offering litchi, orange peel and rose flavors, lively acidity and a supple, glycerinlike texture. It's harmonious, with a lingering finish. Drink now.–B.S. • $37 • (4/30/1999) • **87**

Gewürztraminer Alsace Cuvée Théo 1996 • $35 • (11/15/1997) • **86**

Gewürztraminer Alsace Grand Cru Furstentum Cuvée Laurence 1996 • $67 • (11/15/1997) • **92**

Gewürztraminer Alsace Grand Cru Furstentum Vendanges Tardives 1997: Absolutely gorgeous, unctuous without being heavy, this white displays the elegant side of Gewürztraminer, with all the classic rose petal, litchi and spice flavors. Drink now through 2003.–B.S. • $93 • (10/31/1999) • **91**

Gewürztraminer Alsace Quintessence de Grains Nobles 1989 • $275 • (11/15/1990) • **87**

Gewürztraminer Alsace Réserve Personnelle 1998: So intensely flavored, this Gewürztraminer evokes licorice notes in addition to the litchi and floral elements. Fairly dry, yet deftly balanced between power and elegance. Drink now through 2001.–B.S. • $31 • (10/31/1999) • **87**

Gewürztraminer Alsace Réserve Personnelle 1997: This elegant, slightly austere version shows aromas of honey and candied ginger, while grapefruit notes emerge on the palate. Medium-bodied and quite dry, with a touch of grapefruit peel on the finish. Drink now through 2002.–B.S. • $29 • (4/30/1999) • **86**

Gewürztraminer Alsace Réserve Personnelle 1996 • $28 • (11/15/1997) • **86**

Gewürztraminer Alsace Sélection de Grains Nobles 1997: Exhibits more of the rose and floral side of Gewürztraminer, very elegant, too, with concentration and finesse and a long finish. A bit monolithic, but give it time to integrate the sweetness. Best from 2001 through 2007.–B.S. • $133/375 ml. • (10/31/1999) • **91**

Gewürztraminer Alsace Vendanges Tardives 1996: Moderate sweetness marks this ripe, fleshy, late-harvest Gewürztraminer, whose honey, guava and orange notes are backed by crisp acidity and a subtle, lingering finish. Shows depth and harmony rather than overt sweetness. Drink now through 2003.–B.S. • $100 • (4/30/1999) • **87**

Muscat Alsace Réserve 1998: Floral, spicy and bracing, here's a dry Muscat with good concentration, balance and length of flavor. Mineral notes linger on the aftertaste. Drink now through 2001.–B.S. • $39 • (10/31/1999) • **86**

Muscat Alsace Réserve 1997: Pungent in aroma, showing Eastern spices and litchi, this Muscat is richly textured and balanced toward the soft side. Drink now.–B.S. • $39 • (3/31/1999) • **85**

Muscat Alsace Réserve 1996 • $35 • (11/15/1997) • **86**

Pinot Blanc Alsace Réserve 1998: A delicious Pinot Blanc, offering melon, peach and a nutty, earthy component, supported by juicy acidity and a lush texture. Drink now.–B.S. • $24 • (10/31/1999) • **85**

Pinot Blanc Alsace Réserve 1997: A powerful, full-bodied Pinot Blanc exhibiting plenty of ripe, peachy aromas and flavors accented by minerals. Rich in texture, with good acidity, this needs time to integrate. Drink now through 2002.–B.S. • $24 • (3/31/1999) • **87**

Pinot Blanc Alsace Réserve 1996 • $23 • (11/15/1997) • **85**

Riesling Alsace Cuvée Ste.-Cathérine 1998: The aromas are a bit muted, yet there's plenty of ripe peach, apricot and mineral flavors in this luscious, yet delicately wrought Riesling. It has a sense of grace and harmony, along with fine concentration and length on the finish. Drink now through 2005.–B.S. • $52 • (10/31/1999) • **90**

Riesling Alsace Cuvée Ste.-Cathérine 1997: Wonderful depth of flavor. A combination of stone and citrus fruits mingle with a mineral element and a rich texture, providing complexity and length. There's enough acidity and a fillip of bitterness to keep everything in focus. Drink now through 2007.–B.S. • $51 • (3/31/1999) • **92**

Riesling Alsace Cuvée Ste.-Catherine 1996 • $49 • (11/15/1997) • **88**

Riesling Alsace Cuvée Théo 1998: Fine breadth, richness and depth to the grapefruit, peach and mineral components in this young Riesling. Has a firm structure and a lingering finish. Drink now through 2004.–B.S. • $33 • (10/31/1999) • **88**

Riesling Alsace Cuvée Théo 1997: Aromatic and refined, displaying citrus, spice and peach nuances, polished texture and moderate structure. Harmonious, its flavors linger gracefully on the finish. Tasted twice, with consistent notes. Drink now through 2004.–B.S. • $33 • (4/30/1999) • **88**

Riesling Alsace Cuvée Théo 1996 • $32 • (11/15/1997) • **90**

Riesling Alsace Grand Cru Schlossberg 1998: Wow. A smoky, nutty component leaps from the glass, backed by apricot and a beguiling spice and mineral element. Elegant, firmly structured, quite dry and quietly forceful, this is a beautiful white that lingers on the palate. Drink now through 2005.–B.S. • $42 • (10/31/1999) • **90**

Riesling Alsace Grand Cru Schlossberg 1997: A '97 of considerable cut and verve, relying more on earth and mineral notes, barely hinting at peach and black currant flavors. Well structured, it has length and appeal. Drink now through 2005.–B.S. • $42 • (3/31/1999) • **90**

Riesling Alsace Grand Cru Schlossberg 1996 • $40 • (11/15/1997) • **89**

Riesling Alsace Grand Cru Schlossberg Cuvée Ste.-Cathérine 1998: A touch of sweetness complements the ripe, complex layers of smoke, apricot, honey and mineral notes on a full, rich frame. Fine underlying acidity keeps the flavors focused and persistent through the finish. Not quite as good as a tank sample reviewed earlier, so give it time to integrate. Drink through 2003.–B.S. • $65 • (5/31/2000) • **89**

Riesling Alsace Grand Cru Schlossberg Cuvée Ste.-Cathérine 1996 • $61 • (11/15/1997) HR • **92**

Riesling Alsace Grand Cru Schlossberg Cuvée Ste.-Cathérine Cuvée du Centenaire 1997: Stunning. An incredible young Riesling that offers a panoply of smoke, peach, grapefruit, vanilla and stone aromas and flavors married to a velvety texture and full-bodied structure. Good but lowish acidity and a long finish. Feels more like a white Burgundy. Drink now through 2006.–B.S. • $65 • (3/31/1999) • **93**

Riesling Alsace Grand Cru Schlossberg Cuvée Ste.-Cathérine L'Inédit 1998: A touch of sweetness adds depth and viscosity to the opulent apricot, mineral and spice notes, but there's a vibrant acidity lurking in the shadows. This intense, vivacious white needs some time for all its charms to be revealed. Drink through 2007–B.S. • $79 • (10/31/1999) • **91**

Riesling Alsace Grand Cru Schlossberg Sélection de Grains Nobles 1997: Orange, apricot and mineral are the highlights in this delicate, vibrant Riesling SGN. Succulent, yet almost too delicate, it fades a bit on the finish, but it's hard to argue with this attractive presentation. Give it the benefit of the doubt. Drink now through 2005.–B.S. • $171/375 ml. • (10/31/1999) • **89**

Riesling Alsace Grand Cru Schlossberg Vendanges Tardives 1997: Ripe, honeyed and focused, displaying a hint of sweetness. Elegant and pretty, overall, if a little one-dimensional at this stage. Drink through 2005–B.S. • $95/500 ml. • (10/31/1999) • **88**

Riesling Alsace Réserve Personnelle 1998: Ripe, floral notes turn to peach and citrus in this bracing '98 Riesling. Turns a bit lean at the end, but should match well with food. Drink now through 2003.–B.S. • $25 • (10/31/1999) • **86**

Riesling Alsace Réserve Personnelle 1997: An exotic style, full of peach, apricot and smoke flavors, all very ripe, mouthfilling and balanced by moderate acidity. Forward, but with good length and medium structure. Drink now through 2005.–B.S. • $25 • (3/31/1999) • **89**

Riesling Alsace Réserve Personnelle 1996 • $24 • (11/15/1997) • **88**

Riesling Alsace Sélection de Grains Nobles 1989 • $NA • (11/15/1990) • **96**

Sylvaner Alsace Réserve 1998: Smoky, nutty aromas take on a citrus nuance on the palate in this refreshing, lively version of Sylvaner. Good richness and a lingering finish, too. Drink now.–B.S. • $20 • (10/31/1999) • **85**

Sylvaner Alsace Réserve 1997: A lot of fragrance and delicacy is coaxed from Sylvaner in this beguiling version. It hints at peach, herbs and nuts, with richness and a dollop of earth on the aftertaste. Drink now.–B.S. • $20 • (3/31/1999) • **86**

Sylvaner Alsace Réserve 1996 • $19 • (11/15/1997) • **86**

FRANCE

WEINBACH

Tokay Pinot Gris Alsace Altenbourg Cuvée Laurence 1998: Evoking a smoky, nutty character, this is rich, round and open before the bright acidity sneaks up on the finish. Apricot and mineral notes add to the mix. Needs time to integrate. Drink through 2004–B.S. • $77 • (10/31/1999) • **88**

Tokay Pinot Gris Alsace Altenbourg Cuvée Laurence 1997: Gorgeous Pinot Gris, bursting with apricot, crème brûlée, smoke and mineral character, balancing a fat, fleshy texture with lively acidity and intensity that pumps the flavors through to the long, satisfying finish. Drink now through 2005.–B.S. • $69 • (4/30/1999) • **92**

Tokay Pinot Gris Alsace Altenbourg Cuvée Laurence 1996 • $65 • (11/15/1997) • **90**

Tokay Pinot Gris Alsace Cuvée d'Or Quintessence de Grains Nobles 1997: Thick and ripe, like dessert in a glass, this offers plenty of honey, coconut and beeswax in a balanced, vivacious presentation. The structure should allow it to age for years. Drink through 2007–B.S. • $183/375 ml. • (10/31/1999) • **90**

Tokay Pinot Gris Alsace Cuvée d'Or Sélection de Grains Nobles 1995 • $NA/375 ml. • (11/15/1997) • **92**

Tokay Pinot Gris Alsace Cuvée Laurence 1998: Bursting with apricot, licorice and honey, this is a richly textured, openly knit Pinot Gris with plenty of character and depth. Moderate length. Tasted twice, with consistent notes. Drink now through 2002.–B.S. • $65 • (10/31/1999) • **88**

Tokay Pinot Gris Alsace Cuvée Laurence 1997: Good acidity in this '97 Pinot Gris adds brightness to the apricot, smoke and nut flavors. Rich and fleshy, it has weight and power but only moderate structure. Good length of flavor on the finish. Drink now through 2001.–B.S. • $65 • (4/30/1999) • **89**

Tokay Pinot Gris Alsace Cuvée Laurence 1996 • $62 • (11/15/1997) • **89**

Tokay Pinot Gris Alsace Cuvée Ste.-Cathérine 1998: Lean for the varietal, and showing a touch of carbon dioxide, this nonetheless has lanolin, peach and spice flavors, a deft balance, and intensity that continues through the finish. Drink now through 2003.–B.S. • $56 • (10/31/1999) • **88**

Tokay Pinot Gris Alsace Cuvée Ste.-Cathérine 1997: Lush-smelling, with honey and ginger nuances and crème brûlée on the palate. Developed in flavor, with a crispness that stems as much from a citrus-peel note as from the moderate acidity. Not a blockbuster, but attractive. Tasted twice, with consistent notes. Drink now through 2002.–B.S. • $55 • (5/15/1999) • **85**

Tokay Pinot Gris Alsace Cuvée Ste.-Catherine 1996 • $52 • (11/15/1997) • **88**

Tokay Pinot Gris Alsace Sélection de Grains Nobles 1996: Extremely aromatic and pure, displaying apple and pear, this is a supple, elegant, racy SGN, very concentrated. A beautiful expression of the grape and the style. This baby will impress even more in the future. Best from 2001 through 2008.–B.S. • $149/375 ml. • (10/31/1999) • **94**

Tokay Pinot Gris Alsace Sélection de Grains Nobles 1989 • $NA • (11/15/1990) • **95**

Tokay Pinot Gris Alsace Vendanges Tardives 1997: Smoky, rich and mouth-filling while retaining elegance and panache, this is gorgeous, full of honey and apricot with a bright underlying structure. Needs time to integrate. Drink through 2006–B.S. • $88 • (10/31/1999) • **90**

Tokay Pinot Gris Alsace Vendanges Tardives 1996: This displays ripe peach and apricot flavors, with a hint of orange for accent. Very pretty and accessible, but concentrated and underscored with a vibrant acidity that keeps the flavors pulsing through the finish. Drink now through 2005.–B.S. • $98 • (4/30/1999) • **92**

WHEELER

Merlot Vin de Pays d'Oc 1995 • $15 • (4/30/1997) • **81**

WILLM, ALSACE

Alsace Gentil 1997: Soft and rich, this white has immediate appeal due to its floral and spice aromas, peach, rose and grapefruit flavors, and hint of mineral on the finish. A blend of Sylvaner, Pinot Blanc, Riesling, Pinot Gris and Muscat. Drink now.–B.S. • $7 • (8/31/1998) • **85**

Brut Crémant d'Alsace NV: An attractive sparkling white offering broad flavors of honey and beeswax, almost more reminiscent of Chenin Blanc than of Pinot Blanc. Drink now.–B.S. • $15 • (3/31/1999) • **84**

Gewürztraminer Alsace 1998: Full of nectarine, orange and grapefruit flavors, this '98 has a fat profile, with just enough acidity to keep it in check. Drink now.–B.S. • $12 • (10/31/1999) • **84**

Key: SS—Spectator Selection. CS—Cellar Selection. HR—Highly Recommended. $NA—Price not available. (BT)—Barrel tasting. Ⓐ—Auction Price.
For a key to the tasters' initials, see "How to Use These Listings."
Dates in parentheses represent the issues in which the ratings were published.

Gewürztraminer Alsace 1997: Extremely floral, with rose character accented by banana and almond. Broad and soft around the edges, relying on a hint of bitterness for balance, finishing with a bit of alcohol. Drink now.–B.S. • $12 • (4/30/1999) • **83**

Gewürztraminer Alsace Grand Cru Clos Gaensbroennel Willm 1996: Very ripe, even pungent on the nose, showing tropical fruit and a slight vegetal or green tea nuance, this turns flat midpalate. Lacks a bit of acidity, but finishes solidly on a buttery lanolin note. Drink now through 2001.–B.S. • $25 • (10/31/1999) • **88**

Pinot Blanc Alsace 1998: Broad and nutty in character, showing fatness in texture and a firm underlying structure in a straightforward, appealing style. Drink now.–B.S. • $9 • (9/30/1999) • **84**

Pinot Blanc Alsace 1997: Rich and fat, this has peach and cream flavors, with an earthiness creeping in by the finish. Has moderate acidity and a hint of bitterness at the end. Drink now through 2001.–B.S. • $9 • (3/31/1999) • **83**

Pinot Gris Alsace 1998: Lively, showing orange, peach and mineral flavors in a medium-bodied, easygoing style. Drink now through 2001.–B.S. • $10 • (10/31/1999) • **84**

Pinot Gris Alsace 1997: Fat and rich, but lacks the structure and focus to keep the quince and smoke character lively and interesting. Relies on a slight bitterness at the end for balance. Drink now.–B.S. • $10 • (4/30/1999) • **84**

Riesling Alsace 1996: Already showing some development, this '96 Riesling is full of raspberry aromas and flavors, in addition to almond notes and a dry stoniness. Rich and densely textured, with good length. Drink through 2008–B.S. • $10 • (1/01/1999) • **87**

WOLFBERGER

Gewürztraminer Alsace 1998: Sweet and very loose-knit in structure, offering honey flavors and a soft texture.–B.S. • $19 • (10/31/1999) • **77**

Gewürztraminer Alsace Grand Cru Altenberg de Bergheim 1997: Rich, round and full-bodied, this '97 Gewürztraminer has litchi and honey notes and a structure balanced toward the soft side. The flavors carry through to the finish. Drink now.–B.S. • $40 • (10/31/1999) • **86**

Gewürztraminer Alsace Grand Cru Eichberg 1996: Soft, easy drinking, with good varietal character, but not much depth or excitement.–B.S. • $35 • (10/31/1999) • **78**

Gewürztraminer Alsace Grand Cru Florimont 1997: Ripe, soft and inviting, with an appealing mineral character augmenting the honey and litchi. Good lingering finish of mineral. Drink now.–B.S. • $35 • (10/31/1999) • **87**

Gewürztraminer Alsace Grand Cru Katschbourg 1997: Open and loose-knit, showing apricot, honey and grapefruit. Medium-bodied, with a bitterness that detracts slightly from the finish. Drink now.–B.S. • $35 • (10/31/1999) • **84**

Pinot Blanc Alsace W de Wolfberger 1997: There's a hint of pear and spice, but essentially this is nondescript.–B.S. • $16 • (10/15/1999) • **75**

Pinot d'Alsace Alsace 1998: Focused and lemony, there's a touch of sweetness to round out the crisp structure, with a hint of bitter grapefruit on the juicy finish. Drink now.–B.S. • $14 • (10/31/1999) • **84**

Riesling Alsace 1997: Apple, peach and stone notes are the hallmarks of this ripe, yet steely Riesling whose firm structure is offset by a rich texture and slight sweetness. Drink now through 2001.–B.S. • $18 • (10/15/1999) • **86**

Riesling Alsace Grand Cru Eichberg 1997: A hint of residual sugar marks this soft, flavorful white, whose lanolin and quince notes turn crisp on the finish. Drink now through 2001.–B.S. • $35 • (10/15/1999) • **84**

Riesling Alsace Grand Cru Eichberg 1996: Ripe, yet the overall impression is dull, with almond and marzipan flavors, finishing with acidity that stands apart from the whole.–B.S. • $35 • (10/15/1999) • **79**

Riesling Alsace Grand Cru Florimont 1997: Elegant, showing pine forest and apple notes, balance and backbone, with medium-body and -intensity. Drink now through 2002.–B.S. • $35 • (10/15/1999) • **85**

Riesling Alsace Grand Cru Hengst 1997: The aromas are reticent, though there's richness and acidity matching the red berry and almond flavors, before finishing weakly. A bit awkward, but may come together with time. Drink through 2003.–B.S. • $37 • (10/15/1999) • **86**

Riesling Alsace Grand Cru Hengst 1996: Rich and firmly structured, showing quince and passion fruit aromas and flavors on a loose-knit structure. Good intensity, but ready soon. Drink through 2002.–B.S. • $37 • (10/15/1999) • **84**

Tokay Pinot Gris Alsace Grand Cru Rangen 1997: Ripe and fat, yet the apricot and stone flavors go nowhere, finishing flat and short. Drink now through 2001.–B.S. • $64 • (10/31/1999) • **82**

Tokay Pinot Gris Alsace Grand Cru Steingrubler 1997: On the light side, elegant and floral, this Pinot Gris is well balanced, though it could use a bit more concentration and depth. Drink now.–B.S. • $37 • (10/31/1999) • **84**

YON-FIGEAC, CHATEAU

St.-Emilion 1996: A well-crafted red for the vintage. Plenty of toasted oak on the nose, though there is some fruit too. Medium-bodied, with velvety tannins and a light finish. Drink now.–J.S. • $NA • (1/31/1999) • **85**
St.-Emilion 1995: Gorgeous aromas and flavors of chocolate, berry and toasted oak. Medium-bodied, with velvety tannins and a long aftertaste. Unctuous wine. Drink through 2005–J.S. • $30 • (9/15/1998) • **88**
St.-Emilion 1990 • $24 • (3/31/1993) • **86**
St.-Emilion 1982 • $25 • (5/15/1989) • **87**

YON ST.-MARTIN, CHATEAU

St.-Emilion 1995: Simple and ready. Delicate aromas of dried cherries and sand. Light- to medium-bodied, with light, silky tannins and a fruity finish. Drink now.–J.S. • $NA • (9/15/1998) • **80**

YQUEM, CHATEAU D'

Sauternes 1994: A very good but not outstanding Yquem. Yellow-gold color. Intense aromas of petrol, spice and honey, with dried apricot. Full-bodied, very sweet, with a green apple and honey character; petrol character comes through on the finish. Better with age. Best after 2005.–J.S. • $200 • (5/15/2000) • **87**
Sauternes 1993: Rather weak for Yquem. Light gold color. Lemon tea, almond and honey character. Medium-bodied, medium sweet, with some spicy flavors and an herbal, sorbetlike finish. Drink now.–J.S. • $225 • (5/15/2000) • **86**
Sauternes 1991: Lacks a bit of elegance for Yquem. Light gold in color, with honey, marmalade, dried apricot and vanilla aromas and flavors. Full-bodied, rather fat really, with an oily texture. Medium-sweet, with a burnt almond and molasses finish. A bit rustic. This might improve with age, but why wait? Drink now.–J.S. • $150 • (1/01/1999) • **88**
Sauternes 1990 • $223 Ⓐ • (1/31/1997) CS • **97**
Sauternes 1989: Very classy and beautiful, packed with botrityzed flavors. Marvelous blend of vanilla, cream, tobacco-box notes, with a lot of oak on it for now but also loads of pure, clean and elegant fruit. An infant that will age for a long time. (Yquem vertical tasting—and all listings below from the 5/15/1999 issue). Best after 2020.–P.M. • $211 Ⓐ • (5/15/1999) • **97**
Sauternes 1988 • $219 Ⓐ • (4/15/1995) • **94**
Sauternes 1987: From what's considered an average vintage in Sauternes, this is a surprisingly good Yquem. Lively, with good acidity, of medium body and with lemon, pineapple, orange and chocolate notes. It reveals its vintage pedigree in the slightly pedestrian finish. Drink now through 2010.–P.M. • $121 Ⓐ • (5/15/1999) • **88**
Sauternes 1986: From an outstanding year in Sauternes, this Yquem has some honey character but fails to take off. It's a bit flat on the nose, lacking in acidity, turns a little dry on finish.. Drink now through 2010.–P.M. • $236 Ⓐ • (5/15/1999) • **83**
Sauternes 1985: A charming Yquem that's round, thick, dense and very honeyed. But it doesn't taste of botrytized, dried fruit flavors (the château tried to wait for noble rot and harvested late, into December). While creamy and opulent, it's also refined. Best after 2015.–P.M. • $132 Ⓐ • (5/15/1999) • **94**
Sauternes 1984: This wine was produced with the help of cryoextraction. It's well made, quite dense on the palate, with good sweetness. Lacks the botrytis aromas and flavors that normally give length to Yquems made in years with abundant noble rot. Drink now.–P.M. • $100 Ⓐ • (5/15/1999) • **84**
Sauternes 1983 • $266 Ⓐ • (4/15/1995) • **98**
Sauternes 1982: From an average vintage in Sauternes, this is a rich, honeyed Yquem with attractive pear and lemon notes. The aromas are somewhat odd (volatile acidity?) and it lacks a bit of freshness and finesse, turning a bit burning on the finish. Best after 2010.–P.M. • $177 Ⓐ • (5/15/1999) • **85**
Sauternes 1981: Rich and just sweet, without the acid-creating, botrytized notes normally found in Yquem. A slight paint varnish, dull character on the nose, and it tastes a bit heavy-handed, but it came somewhat to life and tasted better with goat cheese. Drink now through 2005.–P.M. • $171 Ⓐ • (5/15/1999) • **80**
Sauternes 1980: A good year for Sauternes, a very good vintage for Yquem. Fresh, with lemon, grapefruit and quince notes, this is lovely and *sympathique*, with honey tones but not much botrytis concentration. Drink now through 2010.–P.M. • $177 Ⓐ • (5/15/1999) • **86**
Sauternes 1979: Lovely, elegant in style, this balanced Yquem seduces with tropical, dried apricot and creamy-smooth flavors. Medium-bodied, it weighs softly on the palate, then kicks in with a persistent finish. Drink now through 2020.–P.M. • $151 Ⓐ • (5/15/1999) • **93**
Sauternes 1978: A burly Yquem, slightly drying, with lots of crème brûlée, toasted nut and raisin flavors. The mocha-tasting finish is long and persistent, but lacks a bit of class. Drink now through 2010.–P.M. • $NA • (5/15/1999) • **83**
Sauternes 1977: Light-bodied and light-tasting, with a floral aroma and flavor, this is pretty on the palate but turns a bit tart and short on the finish. Drink now through 2010.–P.M. • $NA • (5/15/1999) • **80**
Sauternes 1976: This is silky and beautifully creamy in the mouth. Medium-bodied, there's nothing heavy or big here, just a sense of harmony. So ethereal, it's the sort of wine one could drink almost every night. Drink now through 2030.–P.M. • $332 Ⓐ • (5/15/1999) • **96**
Sauternes 1975: A celebrated vintage. Thick, rich and powerful, this Yquem is packed with an immense concentration of flavors. Tastes almost tannic, tough and unyielding (like many '75 red Bordeaux), but the rough, awkward edges should smooth out with time. Best after 2020.–P.M. • $425 Ⓐ • (5/15/1999) • **95**
Sauternes 1973 $NA • (5/15/1999) • **75**
Sauternes 1971 • $410 Ⓐ • (5/15/1999) • **93**
Sauternes 1970 • $199 Ⓐ • (5/15/1999) • **84**
Sauternes 1969 • $NA • (5/15/1999) • **85**
Sauternes 1968 • $282 Ⓐ • (5/15/1999) • **79**
Sauternes 1967 • $649 Ⓐ • (5/15/1999) • **100**
Sauternes 1966 • $238 Ⓐ • (5/15/1999) • **84**
Sauternes 1965 • $185 Ⓐ • (5/15/1999) • **92**
Sauternes 1963 • $NA • (5/15/1999) • **83**
Sauternes 1962 • $NA • (5/15/1999) • **75**
Sauternes 1961 • $263 Ⓐ • (5/15/1999) • **65**
Sauternes 1959 • $958 Ⓐ • (5/15/1999) • **97**
Sauternes 1958 • $435 Ⓐ • (5/15/1999) • **87**
Sauternes 1957 • $589 Ⓐ • (5/15/1999) • **90**
Sauternes 1956 • $418 Ⓐ • (5/15/1999) • **90**
Sauternes 1955 • $551 Ⓐ • (5/15/1999) • **88**
Sauternes 1954 • $543 Ⓐ • (5/15/1999) • **90**
Sauternes 1953 • $516 Ⓐ • (5/15/1999) • **78**
Sauternes 1950 • $514 Ⓐ • (5/15/1999) • **93**
Sauternes 1949 • $927 Ⓐ • (5/15/1999) • **94**
Sauternes 1948 • $626 Ⓐ • (5/15/1999) • **88**
Sauternes 1947 • $1,080 Ⓐ • (5/15/1999) • **97**
Sauternes 1946 • $407 Ⓐ • (5/15/1999) • **80**
Sauternes 1945 • $1,049 Ⓐ • (5/15/1999) • **95**
Sauternes 1944 • $768 Ⓐ • (5/15/1999) • **79**
Sauternes 1943 • $669 Ⓐ• (5/15/1999) • **88**
Sauternes 1942 • $554 Ⓐ• (5/15/1999) • **82**
Sauternes 1941 • $NA • (5/15/1999) • **91**
Sauternes 1940 • $414 Ⓐ • (5/15/1999) • **88**
Sauternes 1939 • $448 Ⓐ • (5/15/1999) • **89**
Sauternes 1938 • $862 Ⓐ • (5/15/1999) • **95**
Sauternes 1937 • $1,546 Ⓐ • (5/15/1999) • **94**
Sauternes 1936 • $672 Ⓐ • (5/15/1999) • **84**
Sauternes 1935 • $461 Ⓐ • (5/15/1999) • **81**
Sauternes 1934 • $799 Ⓐ • (5/15/1999) • **83**
Sauternes 1933 • $NA • (5/15/1999) • **72**
Sauternes 1932 • $NA • (5/15/1999) • **85**
Sauternes 1931 • $NA • (5/15/1999) • **74**
Sauternes 1929 • $1,058 Ⓐ • (5/15/1999) • **97**
Sauternes 1928 • $1,028 Ⓐ • (5/15/1999) • **89**
Sauternes 1927 • $NA • (5/15/1999) • **85**
Sauternes 1926 • $NA • (5/15/1999) • **72**
Sauternes 1925 • $NA • (5/15/1999) • **86**
Sauternes 1924 • $547 Ⓐ • (5/15/1999) • **74**
Sauternes 1923 • $NA • (5/15/1999) • **70**
Sauternes 1922 • $NA • (5/15/1999) • **83**
Sauternes 1921 • $2,228 Ⓐ • (5/15/1999) • **74**
Sauternes 1920 • $908 Ⓐ • (5/15/1999) • **86**
Sauternes 1919 • $805 Ⓐ • (5/15/1999) • **55**
Sauternes 1918 • $NA • (5/15/1999) • **90**
Sauternes 1917 • $NA • (5/15/1999) • **74**
Sauternes 1916 • $NA • (5/15/1999) • **60**
Sauternes 1914 • $632 Ⓐ • (5/15/1999) • **83**
Sauternes 1913 • $NA • (5/15/1999) • **86**
Sauternes 1912 • $NA • (5/15/1999) • **82**
Sauternes 1911 • $563 Ⓐ • (5/15/1999) • **81**
Sauternes 1909 • $1,416 Ⓐ • (5/15/1999) • **70**
Sauternes 1908 • $703 Ⓐ • (5/15/1999) • **75**
Sauternes 1907 • $NA • (5/15/1999) • **55**
Sauternes 1906 • $1,311 Ⓐ • (5/15/1999) • **90**

YQUEM, CHATEAU D'

Sauternes 1905 • $NA • (5/15/1999) • **89**
Sauternes 1904 • $902 Ⓐ • (5/15/1999) • **79**
Sauternes 1903 • $NA • (5/15/1999) • **89**
Sauternes 1902 • $NA • (5/15/1999) • **77**
Sauternes 1901 • $802 Ⓐ • (5/15/1999) • **84**
Sauternes 1900 • $3,421 Ⓐ• (5/15/1999) • **83**
Sauternes 1899 • $1,401 Ⓐ • (5/15/1999) • **91**
Sauternes 1896 • $1,687 Ⓐ • (5/15/1999) • **95**
Sauternes 1895 • $NA • (5/15/1999) • **65**
Sauternes 1894 • $NA • (5/15/1999) • **70**
Sauternes 1893 • $1,706 Ⓐ • (5/15/1999) • **83**
Sauternes 1892 • $747 Ⓐ • (5/15/1999) • **55**
Sauternes 1891 • $1,133 Ⓐ • (5/15/1999) • **55**
Sauternes 1890 • $1,738 Ⓐ • (5/15/1999) • **90**
Sauternes 1888 • $NA • (5/15/1999) • **77**
Sauternes 1887 • $NA • (5/15/1999) • **75**
Sauternes 1886 • $NA • (5/15/1999) • **87**
Sauternes 1876 • $NA • (5/15/1999) • **88**
Sauternes 1875 • $NA • (5/15/1999) • **96**
Sauternes 1874 • $1,265 Ⓐ • (5/15/1999) • **93**
Sauternes 1870 • $2,300 Ⓐ • (5/15/1999) • **89**
Sauternes 1869 • $3,371 Ⓐ • (5/15/1999) • **96**
Sauternes 1868 • $1,426 • (5/15/1999) • **83**
Sauternes 1865 • $NA • (5/15/1999) • **83**
Sauternes 1864 • $6,325 Ⓐ • (5/15/1999) • **76**
Sauternes 1861 • $NA • (5/15/1999) • **95**
Sauternes 1859 • $NA • (5/15/1999) • **100**
Sauternes 1858 • $NA • (5/15/1999) • **92**
Sauternes 1851 • $NA • (5/15/1999) • **90**
Sauternes 1848 • $NA • (5/15/1999) • **65**
Sauternes 1847 • $11,500 Ⓐ • (5/15/1999) • **99**
Sauternes 1846 • $NA • (5/15/1999) • **80**
Sauternes 1841 • $NA • (5/15/1999) • **87**
Sauternes 1840 • $NA • (5/15/1999) • **99**
Sauternes 1838 • $12,035 Ⓐ • (5/15/1999) • **83**
Sauternes 1834 • $NA • (5/15/1999) • **100**
Sauternes 1831 • $7,161 • (5/15/1999) • **98**
Sauternes 1828 • $NA • (5/15/1999) • **84**
Sauternes 1825 • $7,161 • (5/15/1999) • **80**
Sauternes 1822 • $3,751 • (5/15/1999) • **74**
Sauternes 1818 • $NA • (5/15/1999) • **91**

Sauternes 1814: This 185-year-old Yquem demonstrates the amazing quality found in some pre-phylloxera wines. The product of a good vintage in Sauternes, it tastes of cream, cooked apricot, vanilla and crème brûlée. Silky and supersmooth on the lemony finish.–P.M. • $NA • (5/15/1999) • **98**

Sauternes 1811: The famous "Comet Vintage" yielded this perfect Sauternes that's the pinnacle of Yquem. Full-bodied and very smooth in texture, it offers an exotic combination of whipped cream and freshly crushed raspberry, rolling over the palate with incredible finesse to end on a dreamlike, velvety finish. Drink now through 2020.–P.M. • $NA • (5/15/1999) • **100**

Sauternes 1802: From a very good vintage, but this once-beautiful Yquem is a has-been. Showing lovely dried apricots on the nose, you can sit and sniff it with great pleasure, but it falls short on the palate, with a tough, cedary finish that disappoints.–P.M. • $NA • (5/15/1999) • **80**

Sauternes 1787: Celebrated "Thomas Jefferson" bottle that tastes authentic, with good acidity and some faded fruit. Must have been monumental a century ago. Dark-colored but not at all oxidized, this medium-bodied, 212-year-old wine, from a vintage believed to have been very good in Sauternes, is clean and delivers wet earth, chestnut, prune and plum notes. Turns a bit dry and tart on the finish. If you have a bottle, don't drink it; keep it for posterity, like a fine Picasso. (From a bottle with the orignal cork and with "Th.J." marked on the glass.)–P.M. • $NA • (5/15/1999) • **81**

Sauternes 1784: The ultimate trophy wine. This famous, 215-year-old "Thomas Jefferson" bottle is a beauty by every standard. So young—like some of the outstanding Yquems from the mid-1800s—it shows no oxidation. From a vintage considered very good in Sauternes, it offers delicious tropical, dried apricot, honey and truffle aromas and flavors, and a round and harmonious, still-sweet finish. A mythical, beautiful bottle that should be kept with great care—and not drunk. (From a bottle with the original cork and with "Th.J." marked on the glass.)–P.M. • $49,005 • (5/15/1999) • **93**

Key: SS—Spectator Selection. CS—Cellar Selection. HR—Highly Recommended. $NA—Price not available. (BT)—Barrel tasting. Ⓐ—Auction Price.
For a key to the tasters' initials, see "How to Use These Listings."
Dates in parentheses represent the issues in which the ratings were published.

ZIND-HUMBRECHT

Gewürztraminer Alsace Grand Cru Gueberschwihr Goldert 1997: Extremely ripe and maybe slightly desiccated grapes add concentration to this orange marmalade-flavored white. Soft and lush, yet beautifully balanced and long on flavor. Needs time to integrate residual sugar and structure. Drink through 2004–B.S. • $46 • (9/30/1999) • **91**

Gewürztraminer Alsace Grand Cru Gueberschwihr Goldert 1996: So aromatic, the accents almost suggest mint and pine, then the flavors fan out to reveal honey, grapefruit and black currant set against a velvety texture and lively backbone. This goes beyond the grape, expressing its site beautifully. Drink now through 2004.–B.S. • $52 • (4/30/1999) • **93**

Gewürztraminer Alsace Grand Cru Rangen de Thann Clos St.-Urbain 1996: Difficult to taste, evoking more mineral and soil characteristics than fruit, this is impressive for its ripe, concentrated coffee and butterscotch character, but it's also quite heady and a bit awkward. Given its pedigree, be patient and you won't be disappointed. Drink now through 2002.–B.S. • $78 • (4/30/1999) • **89**

Gewürztraminer Alsace Grand Cru Rangen de Thann Clos St.-Urbain Sélection de Grains Nobles 1994 • $225/375 ml. • (10/15/1997) • **91**

Pinot Gris Alsace Grand Cru Rangen de Thann Clos St.-Urbain Sélection de Grains Nobles 1993 • $450 • (10/15/1996) • **88**

Gewürztraminer Alsace Grand Cru Wintzenheim Hengst 1997: What exuberance. Intense, bold and a bit awkward today, yet laudable for its spice, smoke and apple aromas and flavors, displayed on a lush, mouthfilling texture with good balancing acidity, high alcohol and a touch of bitterness on the finish. Drink now through 2002.–B.S. • $46 • (9/30/1999) • **90**

Gewürztraminer Alsace Grand Cru Wintzenheim Hengst 1996: Raspberry and strawberry aromas highlight the grapefruit and orange flavors in this muscular, intense white. Rich and concentrated, with flavors and structure so vivid, they leave the palate resonating for minutes. Drink now through 2004.–B.S. • $52 • (4/30/1999) • **92**

Gewürztraminer Alsace Gueberschwihr 1996: Beguiling. Ample and round, this white shows purity of character, evoking passion fruit and honey. The structure seems derived more from alcohol and shows a slight bitterness, though it has good acidity and a haunting finish. Drink now through 2002.–B.S. • $27 • (4/30/1999) • **90**

Gewürztraminer Alsace Herrenweg de Turckheim 1997: An extrovert, from the deep gold color and exotic, smoky aroma to intense flavors of honey, crème brûlée and orange. Rich and concentrated but deftly balanced, creamy and long on the palate, with a bit of heat on the finish. Drink now.–B.S. • $32 • (9/30/1999) • **89**

Gewürztraminer Alsace Herrenweg de Turckheim 1996: Full of character. A green glint in the color and a gorgeous flinty aroma depict a young wine, as does the palate. Aromatic and intensely flavored, showing floral and mineral elements, this is firm and dry, with finesse, strength and a long, stony, almost austere finish. Drink now through 2004.–B.S. • $28 • (4/30/1999) • **92**

Gewürztraminer Alsace Hunawihr Clos Windsbuhl 1997: Intriguing, displaying class, focus and added depth from the *terroir*. The flavors range from spice and citrus to smoke and crème brûlée, all on a very dry, minerally, structured framework. Drink now through 2002.–B.S. • $46 • (10/31/1999) • **89**

Gewürztraminer Alsace Hunawihr Clos Windsbuhl 1996: Delicious. Floral-scented and honeyed, this is thick and concentrated, full of tropical fruit and marmalade flavors supported by firm acidity and heady alcohol. The finish just goes on and on. Drink now through 2002.–B.S. • $54 • (4/30/1999) • **91**

Gewürztraminer Alsace Turckheim 1996: Appealing rose petal and litchi character marks this '96 white, whose structure is crisp and finish is lean, despite a rich midpalate. Just a touch of heat on the finish. Drink now through 2001.–B.S. • $22 • (4/30/1999) • **86**

Gewürztraminer Alsace Turckheim Heimbourg 1997: Jekyll and Hyde. Ripe, rich and exotic with flowers, honey and spice up front, but followed by an austere mineral component and ending with some heat. I'd give it the benefit of the doubt. Drink now through 2001.–B.S. • $46 • (9/30/1999) • **89**

Gewürztraminer Alsace Turckheim Heimbourg Vendange Tardive 1996: Brimming with smoky, minerally accents that augment the passion fruit and marmalade flavors, this dense, exuberant VT is firmly structured and shows a lot of finesse and elegance, finishing on the dry side. Drink now through 2006.–B.S. • $65 • (4/30/1999) • **91**

Gewürztraminer Alsace Witzenheim 1996: Musk, sandalwood, rich leather and litchi commingle in this exotic '96. Full-bodied and vibrant, it offers complexity and concentration, yet finishes a touch hot. Drink now through 2001.–B.S. • $23 • (4/30/1999) • **88**

Muscat Alsace Grand Cru Gueberschwihr Goldert 1997: Has a complexity rarely found in Muscat. The violet, spice and mineral flavors are entwined in an elegant, concentrated structure. Subtle, yet intense, it shows pedigree and

FRANCE

class. Tasted twice, with consistent notes. Drink now through 2001.–B.S. • $19 Ⓐ • (10/31/1999) • **87**

Muscat Alsace Grand Cru Gueberschwihr Goldert 1996: A rich, powerful Muscat, displaying tropical fruit, vanilla, grape and floral nuances on a soft, lush texture, with good acidity for balance. The spicy component carries through to the finish. Well done. Drink now through 2002.–B.S. • $32 • (3/31/1999) • **88**

Pinot d'Alsace Alsace 1997: Delicious from start to finish, this gorgeous white bursts with ripe peach, smoke, nut and citrus character. Complex, fresh and beautifully balanced, this is textbook Alsace, a perfect introduction to the region. Drink now through 2001.–B.S. • $22 • (9/15/1999) • **90**

Pinot d'Alsace Alsace 1996: A live-wire Pinot Blanc, bone dry, racy and expressive, offering apple, lemon, smoke and tropical fruit nuances on a lean, wiry frame. It's rich and dense, with concentrated flavors that bode well for both food and aging. Drink now through 2004.–B.S. • $22 • (3/31/1999) • **89**

Pinot Gris Alsace Grand Cru Rangen de Thann Clos St.-Urbain 1997: Quite dry and with a hint of CO2, this is lean and intense, with exotic tropical fruit and spice that need time to unfold. Really shows *terroir* more than varietal character. Drink through 2005–B.S. • $56 • (10/31/1999) • **90**

Pinot Gris Alsace Grand Cru Rangen de Thann Clos St.-Urbain 1996: Stunning. Effusive aromas of guava, honey, orange peel and smoke burst forth from the glass. On the palate, it's lush and creamy, underscored by firm acidity and a slight walnutty bitterness that plays off the lingering sweetness. Tre- mendous harmony and length. Drink now through 2005.–B.S. • $58 • (4/30/1999) HR • **95**

Pinot Gris Alsace Herrenweg de Turckheim 1997: Fine concentration, richness and character on a soft, open texture, featuring smoky apricot notes. The lack of acidity shows on the finish, as the flavors lack length and persistence. Drink now through 2001.–B.S. • $28 • (10/31/1999) • **89**

Pinot Gris Alsace Hunawihr Clos Windsbuhl 1997: Austere on the nose, yet bold and ripe on the palate, showing loads of mineral, apricot and smoke flavors. Balanced on the soft side, it lacks a bit of zip today. Drink now through 2001.–B.S. • $46 • (10/31/1999) • **87**

Pinot Gris Alsace Hunawihr Clos Windsbuhl 1996: Saturated with ripe guava and smoke flavors, this '96 white is luscious and vibrant. The firm backbone drives the flavors, ending on orange peel and grapefruit notes that resonate on the palate. Drink now through 2005.–B.S. • $47 • (4/30/1999) • **91**

Pinot Gris Alsace Turckheim Clos Jebsal 1997: Bold, broad-shouldered and firmly structured, this pulls out all the stops, offering ripe apricot, smoke and lanolin aromas and flavors, full body and full-throttle intensity. Excellent length and depth. Drink through 2006–B.S. • $44 • (10/31/1999) • **92**

Pinot Gris Alsace Turckheim Clos Jebsal 1996: Richly textured and sugar-tinged, this showcases the opulent side of '96 Pinot Gris. The peach, butterscotch and cinnamon flavors are supported by solid acidity, and the finish is almost dry. Drink now through 2004.–B.S. • $47 • (4/30/1999) • **90**

Pinot Gris Alsace Turckheim Clos Jebsal Sélection de Grains Nobles 1995: Intriguing. Aromas of acetone (from botrytis), coffee, white chocolate and spice turn to orange and vanilla in the mouth. Racy, but tails off on the finish and just misses the concentration and intensity to be outstanding. Still, a lovely wine, and it should improve with age. Drink now through 2005.–B.S. • $150/375 ml. Ⓐ • (4/30/1999) • **89**

Pinot Gris Alsace Turckheim Clos Jebsal Sélection des Grains Nobles 1994 • $185/375 ml. • (10/15/1997) • **90**

Pinot Gris Alsace Turckheim Clos Jebsal Sélection des Grains Nobles 1993 • $375 • (10/15/1996) • **95**

Pinot Gris Alsace Turckheim Heimbourg 1997: Although rich, this is leaner than most '97s, displaying compact flavors of mineral and pear, a good supporting structure and a slight coarseness on the finish today. May improve with time. Drink now through 2002.–B.S. • $38 • (10/31/1999) • **87**

Pinot Gris Alsace Turckheim Heimbourg 1996: This really lights up the palate. Lots of power in this ripe, dense Pinot Gris. The crème brûlée, violet and guava flavors are deep and intense, set against an ironlike structure that blazes with minerality on the finish. Drink now through 2008.–B.S. • $42 • (4/30/1999) • **93**

Pinot Gris Alsace Turckheim Heimbourg Sélection de Grains Nobles 1995: Wow. Mix apricot compote, maple syrup and piña colada and, voilà, you have this scintillating dessert wine. Obvious botrytis exacerbates both the aromas and flavors and concentrates the acidity, keeping it lively and fresh. Elegant overall, rather than thick and sweet. Best from 2001 through 2010.–B.S. • $80/375 ml. • (5/15/1999) • **92**

Pinot Gris Alsace Turckheim Heimbourg Sélection de Grains Nobles 1994 • $185/375 ml. • (10/15/1997) • **90**

Pinot Gris Alsace Turckheim Heimbourg Sélection de Grains Nobles 1993 • $250/500 ml. • (11/15/1996) • **95**

Pinot Gris Alsace Vieilles Vignes 1997: This notches it up for a '97. There's residual sugar and it's soft and open, but bursting with luscious apricot, citrus, mineral and smoke aromas and flavors. Surprisingly well balanced, given the richness and ripeness, with a smoky aftertaste. Drink now through 2001.–B.S. • $36 • (10/31/1999) • **90**

Pinot Gris Alsace Wintzenheim Rotenberg 1997: Smoke, peach and licorice flavors are underscored by a lively framework in this dry, full-bodied, focused Pinot Gris. A mineral character weaves throughout. Shows great balance and harmony. Drink now through 2003.–B.S. • $38 • (10/31/1999) • **89**

Pinot Gris Alsace Wintzenheim Rotenberg Sélection de Grains Nobles 1993 • $250/500 ml. • (11/15/1996) • **92**

Pinot Gris Alsace Wintzenheim Rotenberg Vendange Tardive 1996: Clean and pure in its aromas and flavors, this '96 VT is on the dry side, with finely etched acidity and crème brûlée, marmalade and citrus character. Very elegant, it holds your interest through the lingering finish. Best from 2001 through 2007.–B.S. • $56 • (4/30/1999) • **92**

Riesling Alsace Grand Cru Rangen de Thann Clos St.-Urbain 1997: Full, lush and concentrated, this spicy, smoky, peach-flavored Riesling literally defies gravity. Full-bodied yet light on its feet, round yet laser-focused, it unravels its complex flavors seductively. Drink through 2005–B.S. • $56 • (8/31/1999) • **91**

Riesling Alsace Grand Cru Rangen de Thann Clos St.-Urbain 1996: Dry, intense and austere, with an internal power and elegance that expresses its *terroir*, this '96 white is densely textured, smelling and tasting of flint, minerals and chamomile. Superb harmony, finesse and length. Best from 2002 through 2012.–B.S. • $62 Ⓐ • (3/31/1999) • **92**

Riesling Alsace Grand Cru Turckheim Brand 1997: Totally exotic, bursting with apricot, passion fruit and orange, this Alsace Riesling is ripe and focused, its opulence supported by grapefruitlike acidity and concentrated flavors. Full, flamboyant and intense, with a great finish, it's one of the wines of the vintage. Drink now through 2006.–B.S. • $54 • (8/31/1999) HR • **93**

Riesling Alsace Grand Cru Turckheim Brand 1996: Almost hypnotic for the spice, mineral and red berry perfumes that burst from the glass, this lovely white delivers exotic flavors of passion fruit and mineral on a framework that's lean and intense yet rich and full-bodied simultaneously, followed by an endless finish. Drinkable now, but it will only get better. Best from 2001 through 2010.–B.S. • $52 • (3/31/1999) CS • **94**

Riesling Alsace Gueberschwihr 1997: Beautiful aromas, understated and pure, evoking spring flowers and peaches, while on the palate, peach, citrus and mineral mingle with the fleshy texture and moderate structure. Drink now through 2003.–B.S. • $24 • (8/31/1999) • **89**

Riesling Alsace Herrenweg de Turckheim 1997: A potpourri of tropical fruit and spice underscored by mineral, this bone-dry Riesling shows the range of flavors possible in '97. Ripe, concentrated and complex, it coats the palate with pineapple, orange and vanilla cream flavors, with plenty of bright acidity for balance. Drink now through 2005.–B.S. • $28 • (8/31/1999) • **90**

Riesling Alsace Herrenweg de Turckheim 1996: Racy and dense, this '96 white shows exotic red berry and grapefruit aromas and flavors and a firmly structured profile that needs time to integrate all its components. Well balanced and complex, it has a long aftertaste. Best from 2001 through 2010.–B.S. • $28 • (3/31/1999) • **90**

Riesling Alsace Hunawihr Clos Windsbuhl 1997: The scent is pure roses, while the lean, compact yet densely textured flavors indicate that this tightly wound Riesling needs time to reveal its charms. Drink through 2005–B.S. • $44 • (8/31/1999) • **90**

Riesling Alsace Hunawihr Clos Windsbuhl 1996: This big, full-bodied, assertive white combines quince and peach notes with an intense mineral character. It's round and viscous, yet finishes dry, with firm underlying acidity. So intense and long, it reverberates on the palate. Best from 2002 through 2010.–B.S. • $47 • (3/31/1999) • **92**

Riesling Alsace Turckheim 1997: Firm and focused, here's a Riesling with verve and style to set off the peach, smoke and mineral aromas and flavors. Builds in intensity to a long, mineral-flavored aftertaste. Drink now through 2004.–B.S. • $29 • (8/31/1999) • **89**

Riesling Alsace Wintzenheim 1997: Rich, vibrant and spicy, with exotic smoke, apricot and cooked apple aromas and flavors. With just a hint of sweetness, deftly balanced by mouthwatering acidity, this is lip-smacking, ending on an apricot note. Drink now through 2003.–B.S. • $22 • (8/31/1999) • **88**

Riesling Alsace Wintzenheim Clos Häuserer 1997: Packs a lot of flavors and character on a light framework. Ripe, smoky apricot and mineral elements mingle in a wine that starts out rich, then closes up on the finish thanks to the taut structure. Needs time. Drink now through 2004.–B.S. • $29 • (8/31/1999) • **90**

■ ■ ■ ■

ZIND-HUMBRECHT

Riesling Alsace Wintzenheim Clos Häuserer 1996: Wonderfully aromatic, displaying stony, smoky red berry notes followed by peach and red berry flavors. Brilliantly cut, like a fine diamond, this has a purity, clarity and grace, a lasting finish, but a structure that demands time. Best from 2002 through 2012.–B.S. • $29 • (3/31/1999) • **91**

Tokay Pinot Gris Alsace Grand Cru Rangen de Thann Clos St.-Urbain Sélection de Grains Nobles 1989 • $300 • (11/15/1990) • **85**

Tokay Pinot Gris Alsace Wintzenheim Rotenberg Sélection de Grains Nobles 1991 • $300 • (8/31/1995) • **94**

FRANCE

Germany

In contrast to their tongue-twisting names and complicated official nomenclature, the sensory appeal of German wines is instantaneous. Combining abundant fruit with lively, refreshing crispness, German wines have a knack for charming the palates of novices and experts in equal measure. In the last decade of the 20th century, Germany had an unbroken string of very good to outstanding vintages, enjoying more successful harvests than any other region in Europe. Yet, while German Riesling, Gewürztraminer, Scheurebe and Sylvaner appear to be gaining recognition, demand is still limited, making them good values for consumers.

1. Mosel-Saar-Ruwer
2. Nahe
3. Rheingau
4. Rheinhessen
5. Pfalz

GERMAN WINE TERMINOLOGY

The terminology of German wine labels is strictly defined and regulated by the German government. The lowest official level, Qualitätswein (QbA), allows the addition of sugar to the grape must (chaptalization) prior to fermentation. While QbAs can be refreshing and pleasant, most are targeted at a mass audience.

All of the better German wines are classified as Qualitätswein mit Pradikat (QmP). These wines are divided into six levels of quality based on ripeness and natural sugar levels at harvest. Kabinetts are the entry-level QmP wines; most are moderately sweet, with a tangy acidity at the finish. Ranking just above Kabinett is Spätlese, which means late harvest. Generally richer than Kabinett because of its higher natural sugar level, Spätlese is sometimes vinified in the very dry "trocken" style or the slightly less dry "halbtrocken" style. These are the German wines that are most similar to white table wines produced elsewhere, though some find them quite austere.

Auslese, made from specially selected bunches of late harvest grapes, is almost always sweet. Sweeter still, Beerenauslese is made from hand-selected, over-ripe individual grapes, usually affected by "noble rot." Rarest of all is Trockenbeerenauslese (TBA), an intensely sweet wine made only from grapes actually shriveled by noble rot. The latter two types clearly rank among the greatest sweet wines in the world, and can age for decades. A special category is Eiswein, produced when grapes are allowed to freeze on the vine and then pressed immediately after picking; the ice crystals inside remain behind with the skins, and the juice that drains off has an exceptional concentration of flavor and sugar. Eiswein's flavor is unaffected by noble rot.

GERMAN WINE REGIONS

German wine regions produce distinctive styles of wines owing to their unique conditions of soil and climate. Most of the important regions are located in what used to be called West Germany.

Rheingau

This is Germany's most aristocratic wine region, and historically its finest. Yet, with some notable exceptions, wine estates in the Rheingau have been chronic under-achievers, despite having superb vineyards and a favorable climate. Most were overproducing and harvesting too early. However, a new generation of Rheingau producers is now leading a quality revolution. Recently, two of the area's leading wine estate associations, VDP-Rheingau and Charta Rheingau, merged under the VDP-Rheingau name. Composed of 50 top Rheingau estates covering more than 2,500 acres of vineyards, the new organization represents about one-third of the vineyards in the region. Members use lower-yielding clones to improve fruit quality and adhere to strict standards of vineyard management. As a result, the Rheingau is once again producing powerful wines with excellent aging potential.

Mosel-Saar-Ruwer

One regional name encompasses all three vineyard areas, which produce Rieslings noted for their spritely fruit. The Middle Mosel (Mittelmosel) is perhaps the most famous wine region of Germany, and encompasses the familiar Piesporter Michelsberg and Bernkasteler Doktor (though many less-renowned Mosels offer better value). Traditionally, the Mosel harvest must be a few weeks later than that of the Rhine due to a chillier climate; in years when the grapes don't fully ripen, Mosels can be charmless. But in the great years, few wines are as complete. Ruwer and Saar wines tend to be steelier and harder than Mosels, though in years of great ripeness, they, too, can excel.

The Prüm estate in the Bernkastel district on the Mosel river.

Nahe

Although the Nahe includes a large number of uninteresting vineyards, it also has steep, volcanic hillside vineyards that produce richly flavorful wines. Wines from these vineyards can be undervalued compared to the better-known Mosels and Rheingaus.

As in the Rheingau, a group of leading Nahe estates recently established a classification for its best vineyard sites. These sites include Monzingen, Schlossböckelheim, Oberhausen, Niederhausen, Norheim, Traisen, Altenbamberg, Bad Münster am Stein, Bad Kreuznach, Wintzenheim, Bretzenheim, Wallhausen, Roxheim, Windesheim, Guldental, Langenlonsheim, Laubenheim, Dorsheim and Münster-Sarmsheim. Under the new VDP-Nahe guidelines, wines which carry the above vineyard names must be produced from 100 percent handpicked, 100 percent Riesling grapes only from those sites, and approved for quality through a blind tasting conducted by members of the association. In addition, rules are set for maximum yields, grape ripeness and finished wine shipment dates. Results so far have been impressive.

Rheinhessen

Rheinhessen's best vineyards are in the district of Nierstein; its wines have a distinctive flavor of smoked meat. Ripeness levels run high here compared with the rest of Germany, so Kabinetts and other light wines are less common. Other parts of Rheinhessen produce more than 50 percent of Germany's popular, sweetish, budget-priced Liebfraumilch.

Pfalz

The southernmost of the well-known German regions and one of the most picturesque; many of its wines are sold directly to local tourists. The wines tend to be rich and earthy, with generous fruit. Lighter Pfalz wines are sometimes bottled in full liter sizes, often at very attractive prices.

CHOOSING GERMAN WINES

While useful, the strict German wine laws are hardly infallible. Since many great vineyards have several owners, consumers must look for growers who are meticulous about quality and who own the most favored sites of certain vineyards. We suggest you seek out shops where there are specialists in the somewhat arcane field of German wines, or choose the wines recommended by a respected wine publication such as *Wine Spectator*.

ABTEIHOF ST.-NICOLAUS

Riesling Kabinett Rheingau Hattenheimer Wisselbrunnen 1997: An attractive kabinett, peachy in flavor, with nuances of red berries and almonds. Just off-dry and elegant in profile. Its fruitiness is offset by cool minerality and juicy acidity. Drink now through 2003.–B.S. • $10 • (5/15/1999) • **87**

Riesling QbA Rheingau Johannisberger Erntebringer 1997: Quite sweet, with simple apple flavors and a tart acidity on the short finish.–B.S. • $9/1 liter • (2/28/1999) • **76**

Riesling Spätlese Halbtrocken Rheingau Geisenheimer Kilzberg 1997: Petrol and almond are the highlights of this rigid white. It's lean and racy, with a moderate finsih. Drink through 2005.–B.S. • $14 • (2/28/1999) • **84**

Riesling Spätlese Rheingau Johannisberger Vogelsang 1997: This '97 white offers apple, almond and grapefruit elements on a sleek, delicate framework. It's moderately concentrated. Drink now through 2004.–B.S. • $12/500 ml. • (2/28/1999) • **85**

BADISCHER WINZERKELLER

Gewürztraminer Spätlese Baden Tuniberg Merdinger Bühl 1996: A simple white, with little varietal character or depth.–B.S. • $16 • (10/15/1998) • **75**

Müller-Thurgau Kabinett Baden Tuniberg Niederrimsinger Attilafelsen 1996: Soft, with floral and peach aromas and flavors and modest concentration.–B.S. • $10 • (10/15/1998) • **78**

Pinot Gris Baden Dry W Cellars 1996: Seems a little underripe for the varietal, with herb and grass flavors on a lean frame.–B.S. • $8 • (10/15/1998) • **77**

QbA Baden Dry NV: A basic dry white, with modest citrus character.–B.S. • $6 • (10/15/1998) • **75**

Ruländer Kabinett Baden Kaiserstuhl Leiselheimer Vulkanfelsen 1997: A basic white, off dry, showing baked apple and a hint of butterscotch.–B.S. • $10 • (10/15/1998) • **74**

BALBACH

Riesling Auslese Rheinhessen Nierstein Hipping 1996 • $NA • (11/30/1997) • **84**

Riesling Beerenauslese Rheinhessen Niersteiner Pettenthal 1989 • $NA • (12/15/1990) • **84**

Riesling Eiswein Rheinhessen Nierstein Ölberg 1998: Like a full moon on water, this illuminates the palate in a warm glow of peach, vanilla and citrus. Gentle in its approach, yet well supported by tangy acidity. Great harmony and expression. Drink now through 2010.–B.S. • $63/375 ml. • (2/29/2000) • **95**

Riesling Eiswein Rheinhessen Nierstein Ölberg 1996 • $NA/375 ml. • (11/30/1997) • **89**

Riesling Kabinett Rheinhessen Nierstein Pettenthal 1996 • $NA • (11/30/1997) • **85**

BASSERMANN-JORDAN

Riesling Auslese Pfalz Deidesheimer Hohenmorgen 1998: Exciting. Almost searing in intensity thanks to the electric structure, which lends a vibrancy to the apricot and citrus flavors. Fine length of flavor on the finish. Drink now through 2008.–B.S. • $25/375 ml. • (2/29/2000) • **90**

Riesling Auslese Pfalz Deidesheimer Hohenmorgen 1996 • $36 • (11/30/1997) • **87**

Riesling Auslese Pfalz Forster Kirchenstück 1998: Ripe and juicy, this literally bursts with apricot, lime and mineral notes. Elegant and slender, with a lingering finish, it would make a fine aperitif. Drink now through 2005.–B.S. • $45 • (1/01/2000) • **88**

Riesling Auslese Pfalz Ruppertsberger Reiterpfad 1997: Concentrated, elegant and well proportioned, this offers honey, grapefruit and apricot aromas and flavors supported by vibrant acidity. Long, satisfying finish. Best from 2001 through 2007.–B.S. • $27/375 ml. • (2/28/1999) • **90**

Riesling Beerenauslese Pfalz Ruppertsberger Reiterpfad 1998: Rich and juicy, this well-defined BA is balanced and lovely, exhibiting apricot, pear and spice flavors that linger on the finish. Drink now through 2008.–B.S. • $92/375 ml. • (2/29/2000) • **89**

Riesling Beerenauslese Rheinhessen Deidesheimer Kieselberg 1990 • $150 • (12/15/1991) • **93**

Riesling Eiswein Pfalz Forster Ungeheuer 1996 • $119/375 ml. • (11/30/1997) • **90**

Riesling Kabinett Pfalz 1998: Elegant, balanced and firmly structured, this is a beguiling Pfalz kabinett, offering rich peach and citrus notes and a moderate finish. Drink now through 2003.–B.S. • $14 • (1/01/2000) • **87**

Riesling Kabinett Pfalz Deidesheimer Leinhöhle 1996 • $16 • (11/30/1997) • **83**

Riesling Kabinett Pfalz Deidesheimer Paradiesgarten 1998: A winner. Has weight, richness and stylishness framing the peach and spice notes well, supported by a tangy acidity. Drink now through 2004.–B.S. • $14 • (2/29/2000) • **89**

Riesling Kabinett Pfalz Forster Jesuitengarten 1998: Totally off the charts for a kabinett! Very ripe and intense, with a sweet-tart component to the grapefruit, apricot and passion fruit flavors, buoyed by a searing acidity. More like a spätlese and a fine one at that. Best from 2001 through 2007.–B.S. • $18 • (2/29/2000) • **91**

Riesling Kabinett Pfalz Forster Jesuitengarten 1997: A medium-bodied white, with power, moderate structure and quince, nectarine and vanilla aromas and flavors. Rich and smooth in texture, it finishes crisply. Needs time to integrate. Drink through 2008.–B.S. • $17 • (2/28/1999) • **89**

Riesling QbA Trocken Pfalz 1997: On the austere side despite good concentration and ripe peach and mineral flavors. Has firm acidity for support, ending with a dry, stony character. For fans of the dry style. Drink now through 2003.–B.S. • $13 • (2/28/1999) • **84**

Riesling Spätlese Pfalz Forster Jesuitengarten 1998: Slender, delicate and airy in texture, this Riesling floats across the palate, its peach, lime and mineral notes seemingly weightless. Drink now through 2006.–B.S. • $26 • (1/01/2000) • **88**

Riesling Spätlese Pfalz Forster Jesuitengarten 1997: Showing a soft texture, this is elegant in stature, with succulent peach flavors. A grapefruit note echoes on the finish. Drink now through 2006.–B.S. • $27 • (2/28/1999) • **88**

Riesling Spätlese Pfalz Forster Jesuitengarten 1996 • $26 • (11/30/1997) • **87**

Riesling Spätlese Pfalz Forster Kirchenstück 1998: A thoroughbred, focused and pure, filling its lightweight, flexible frame with lime, peach and mineral notes. Beautifully balanced, with a lingering finish. Best from 2001 through 2007.–B.S. • $24 • (2/29/2000) • **90**

Riesling Spätlese Pfalz Forster Kirchenstück 1996 • $20 • (4/30/1998) • **86**

Riesling Spätlese Pfalz Ruppertsberger Nussbien 1996 • $26 • (11/30/1997) • **87**

Riesling Spätlese Trocken Pfalz Forster Freundstück 1998: A big, bold Riesling that starts off with ripe peach and spice notes then turns aggressive from the midpalate to the finish. Firmly structured, it needs time to integrate. Best from 2002 through 2008.–B.S. • $23 • (1/01/2000) • **88**

Riesling Trocken Pfalz 1996 • $13 • (11/30/1997) • **86**

BECKER, BRÜDER DR.

Riesling Auslese Rheinhessen Dienheimer Falkenberg 1997: An odd cellar- or cask-note marks this auslese, whose flavor is a one-note peach. Pretty simple and rustic in style; disappointing for this level. Drink now.–B.S. • $NA • (5/15/2000) • **84**

Riesling Spätlese Rheinhessen Dienheimer Tafelstein 1997: Lovely aromatics range from spices to red berries in this spätlese that leans toward the dry end of the spectrum. Firmly structured, with a rich texture, this is balanced and should develop well. Drink now through 2007.–B.S. • $14 • (2/28/1999) • **86**

Scheurebe Kabinett Rheinhessen Dienheimer Tafelstein 1997: Rather neutral in aroma and flavor, showing some grapefruit notes and vibrant acidity. –B.S. • $10 • (5/15/1999) • **79**

BENDER, ERICH

Gewürztraminer Spätlese Pfalz Bissersheimer Held 1996: Good varietal character, exhibiting roses and litchi in a grapey, easy-drinking style.–B.S. • $11 • (10/15/1998) • **82**

BERNHARD, CH.W.

Riesling Kabinett Halbtrocken Rheinhessen Freilaubersheimer Rheingrafenberg 1997: On the dry side of halbtrocken, firm and spicy, this is harmonious and elegant, a fine companion for light fish, chicken and vegetable dishes. Drink now through 2005.–B.S. • $11 • (2/28/1999) • **84**

Riesling Spätlese Rheinhessen Hackenheimer Kirchberg 1997: An added ripeness gives this '97 appeal. It's forward in style, more open and less structured, tailing off a bit on the finish. Drink now through 2004.–B.S. • $12 • (2/28/1999) • **87**

Scheurebe Kabinett Rheinhessen Hackenheimer Kirchberg 1997: Peach and citrus flavors are pleasant, if on the light side, allied to a juicy texture in this easy-drinking white. Try now.–B.S. • $11 • (5/15/1999) • **81**

BIFFAR, JOSEF

Riesling Auslese Pfalz Deidesheimer Kalkofen 1996 • $31 • (11/30/1997) • **84**

BIFFAR, JOSEF

Riesling Auslese Pfalz Deidesheimer Kieselberg 1997: A gentle, silky white, exhibiting vanilla, honeysuckle and peach, combined with a moderate sweetness and soft but sufficient acidity. Drink now through 2005.–B.S. • $30 • (2/28/1999) • **88**

Riesling Auslese Pfalz Deidesheimer Kieselberg 1996 • $34 • (11/30/1997) • **90**

Riesling Auslese Pfalz Deideshiemer Mäushöhle 1996: There's zip here, along with intensity to the grapefruit, nutmeg and lemon, in a compact style, without a lot of complexity. Firmly structured, it turns lean on the finish. May come around with time. Drink now through 2004.–B.S. • $NA • (5/15/2000) • **86**

Riesling Auslese Pfalz Wachenheimer Goldbächel 1998: Distinctive aromas and flavors of lanolin and beeswax augment the peach and spice in this round, vibrant white, with just a hint of astringency on the finish. Drink now through 2006.–B.S. • $47 • (2/29/2000) • **89**

Riesling Eiswein Pfalz Deidesheimer Mäushöhle 1996 • $NA/375 ml. • (11/30/1997) • **93**

Riesling Kabinett Pfalz Deidesheimer Kieselberg 1997: Ripe and well crafted, this delicious kabinett is rich, spicy and full of forward peach, vanilla and guava aromas and flavors on a creamy texture with surprisingly lively structure. Finishes a bit coarse, but may smooth out over time. Drink now through 2007.–B.S. • $13 • (2/28/1999) • **89**

Riesling Kabinett Pfalz Deidesheimer Kieselberg 1996 • $13 • (11/30/1997) • **85**

Riesling Kabinett Trocken Pfalz Deidesheimer Mäushöhle 1996 • $17 • (11/30/1997) • **85**

Riesling Kabinett Trocken Pfalz Wachenheimer Gerümpel 1997 • $NA • (1/01/1998) • **88**

Riesling Spätlese Halbtrocken Pfalz Deidesheimer Mäushöhle 1996 • $21 • (11/30/1997) • **88**

Riesling Spätlese Pfalz Deidesheimer Kalkofen 1998: Round and broad, this '98 white is redolent of almond, peach and a hint of licorice, all kept together by lively acidity. Drink now through 2005.–B.S. • $32 • (2/29/2000) • **89**

Riesling Spätlese Pfalz Deidesheimer Kieselberg 1997: Rich and creamy, this '97 spätlese offers vanilla custard and tropical fruit nuances bolstered by racy acidity. Plenty of power, with some in reserve. Excellent length. Best from 2002 through 2010.–B.S. • $25 • (2/28/1999) • **91**

Riesling Spätlese Pfalz Deideshiemer Mäushöhle 1996: Exotic aromas of passion fruit and papaya are backed by the hallmark '96 acidity, which comes screeching in midpalate and runs the show through the finish. Best from 2001 through 2006.–B.S. • $NA • (5/15/2000) • **88**

Riesling Spätlese Pfalz Wachenheimer Altenburg 1997: Full of almond, petrol and mineral flavors, this is a powerful, muscular white that's on the dry side for this style. Rich and distinctive, it leaves a dry, spicy impression. Best from 2001 through 2007.–B.S. • $24 • (2/28/1999) • **90**

Riesling Spätlese Pfalz Wachenheimer Gerümpel 1996 • $26 • (11/30/1997) • **85**

Riesling Spätlese Pfalz Wachenheimer Goldbächel 1996 • $26 • (11/30/1997) • **86**

Riesling Spätlese Trocken Pfalz Deidesheimer Mäushöhle 1997 • $NA • (1/01/1998) • **83**

Riesling Trockenbeerenauslese Pfalz Deidesheimer Kieselberg 1994 • $107 • (11/30/1995) • **87**

BLUE NUN

QbA Rheinhessen 1996: Noticeably sweet, with flavors of peach. Soft and slightly dilute, yet there's also an herbal, earthy component.–B.S. • $6 • (5/15/1999) • **74**

BREUER, GEORG

Riesling Auslese Gold Cap Rheingau Rüdesheimer Berg Schlossberg 1996 • $100/375 ml. • (11/30/1997) • **88**

Riesling Auslese Gold Cap Rheingau Rüdesheimer Bischofsberg 1998: Fabulous. A supercharged young Riesling, ripe, and with an added dimension of botrytis, this is concentrated, dense and smells of freshly ploughed earth, along with flavors of apricot, honey and mineral. Best from 2001 through 2010.–B.S. • $130 • (2/29/2000) • **91**

Riesling Beerenauslese Gold Cap Rheingau Rüdesheimer Bischofsberg 1995 • $43/375 ml. • (4/30/1997) • **92**

Riesling Beerenauslese Rheingau Rüdesheimer Bischofsberg 1993 • $NA • (11/30/1994) • **86**

Riesling Beerenauslese Rheingau Rüdesheimer Bischofsberg 1992 • $123 • (11/30/1993) • **79**

Riesling Beerenauslese Rheingau Rüdesheimer Bischofsberg 1990 • $100 • (12/15/1991) • **97**

Riesling QbA Rheingau Montosa Charta 1998: Bold and powerful, on the austere side of the style spectrum, showing almond and stone notes. Structured and concentrated, this should come alive with, say, stuffed pork loin. Drink now through 2005.–B.S. • $22 • (2/29/2000) • **85**

Riesling QbA Rheingau Montosa Charta 1997: This fleshy, succulent white begins with a rich texture and turns toward the dry, crisp side on the finish. Attractive for its peach flavors. Drink now through 2004.–B.S. • $20 • (2/28/1999) • **86**

Riesling QbA Rheingau Montosa Charta 1996 • $20 • (11/30/1997) • **90**

Riesling QbA Rheingau Rauenthaler Nonnenberg 1996: Real concentration here, offering aromas and flavors of apricot and quince with hints of orange and mineral. Dry and forceful, with firm yet integrated acidity, a rich texture and fine length. Drink now through 2005.–B.S. • $38 • (5/15/1999) • **88**

Riesling QbA Rheingau Rüdesheimer 1997: Structured, with a firm, authoritative personality, this white has apple and almond flavors. Finishes on an austere note. Drink now through 2004.–B.S. • $16 • (2/28/1999) • **84**

Riesling QbA Rheingau Rüdesheimer Berg Schlossberg 1996: Ripe, with silky-smooth texture, this shows apricot, mineral and earth aromas and flavors, concentration and structure, fine balance. There's a slight austerity that begins midpalate and goes to the finish. Drink now through 2006.–B.S. • $50 • (5/15/1999) • **89**

Riesling Trocken Rheingau Rüdesheim Estate 1996 • $15 • (11/30/1997) • **86**

Riesling Trockenbeerenauslese Rheingau Rüdesheimer Bischofsberg 1993 • $NA • (11/30/1994) • **87**

BUHL, REICHSRAT VON

Riesling Auslese Gold Cap Pfalz Forster Ungeheuer 1996 • $27 • (11/30/1997) • **90**

Riesling Auslese Pfalz Forster Ungeheuer (AP 25) 1998: An extra dimension of ripeness and perhaps botrytis add an exotic note to this brilliant, focused white. Sweet enough to cover the underlying acidity, yet never cloying or heavy, with a clean apricot aftertaste. Drink now through 2007.–B.S. • $17/375 ml. • (2/29/2000) • **92**

Riesling Auslese Pfalz Forster Ungeheuer (AP 41) 1998: Wonderful harmony and grace. Extremely perfumed, exuding violet and rose on the nose, followed by apricot and passion fruit flavors that exhibit great clarity, all supported by a vibrant backbone and well-integrated sweetness. Drink now through 2008.–B.S. • $40 • (2/29/2000) • **93**

Riesling Auslese Pfalz Forster Ungeheuer (AP 27) 1997: This has richness, apricot and honey aromas and flavors and balance, but it's not very exciting. Drink now through 2005.–B.S. • $28/375 ml. • (2/28/1999) • **88**

Riesling Auslese Pfalz Forster Ungeheuer (AP 28) 1997: The honeyed sweetness in this '97 auslese is balanced by a citrus note and bracing acidity. Compact and unyielding now, so give it time. Drink through 2006.–B.S. • $40/375 ml. • (2/28/1999) • **90**

Riesling Auslese Pfalz Forster Ungeheuer 1996 • $27 • (11/30/1997) • **87**

Riesling Beerenauslese Pfalz Forster Pechstein 1990 • $75 • (12/15/1991) • **78**

Riesling Beerenauslese Pfalz Forster Ungeheuer 1998: Pure and focused, offering peach and honey in a streamlined, elegant presentation. Very smooth and integrated. Drink now through 2008.–B.S. • $90/375 ml. • (2/29/2000) • **90**

Riesling Beerenauslese Pfalz Forster Ungeheuer 1997: Wow. An incredible amount of flavor is packed into this medium-bodied, sleek frame. Botrytized notes of dried apricot as well as honey, lime, flowers and butterscotch are displayed against a vivid backdrop of acidity. A marvelous taste experience. Give this baby time. Best from 2003 through 2015.–B.S. • $90/375 ml. • (2/28/1999) • **95**

Riesling Eiswein Pfalz Forster Jesuitengarten 1996 • $89/375 ml. • (11/30/1997) • **92**

Riesling Eiswein Pfalz Forster Ungeheuer 1998: A delicious eiswein. Compelling flavors of apricot, herb and grapefruit glide effortlessly across the palate, buoyed on a snappy structure. Wonderful balance and intensity of flavor. Drink now through 2009.–B.S. • $98/375 ml. • (2/29/2000) • **94**

Riesling Halbtrocken Pfalz Deidesheimer 1996 • $12 • (11/30/1997) • **87**

Riesling Kabinett Pfalz Armand 1998: Spicy and rich, this '98 Riesling starts off round, with peach and a piquant citrus note, ending crisply. Drink now through 2004.–B.S. • $15 • (2/29/2000) • **85**

Key: SS—Spectator Selection. CS—Cellar Selection. HR—Highly Recommended. $NA—Price not available. (BT)—Barrel tasting. Ⓐ—Auction Price. For a key to the tasters' initials, see "How to Use These Listings." **Dates in parentheses represent the issues in which the ratings were published.**

Riesling Kabinett Pfalz Armand 1997: A soft, luscious '97, full of dried apricot, passion fruit, piecrust and spice. So forward and delicious it's hard to resist now, but it has deceptively good structure. Drink now through 2005.–B.S. • $15 • (2/28/1999) • **87**

Riesling Kabinett Pfalz Armand 1996 • $15 • (11/30/1997) • **88**

Riesling Kabinett Trocken Pfalz Deidesheimer Kieselberg 1998: An oblique white, dry and leaning toward the chamomile, verbena and mineral side of the flavor spectrum. Drink now.–B.S. • $17 • (1/01/2000) • **82**

Riesling Kabinett Trocken Pfalz Deidesheimer Kieselberg 1997: Smells of ripe peach and apricot, with forward flavors of peach, citrus and mineral. Medium-bodied, rich and supple, with a lemon and mineral finish. Very well balanced and attractive. Drink now through 2004.–B.S. • $17 • (5/15/1999) • **86**

Riesling QbA Halbtrocken Pfalz Deidesheimer 1998: Rich and spicy, full of peach, ginger and citrus, all underscored by a firm, bracing acidity. Fine length. Needs food. Drink now through 2003.–B.S. • $12 • (1/01/2000) • **86**

Riesling QbA Halbtrocken Pfalz Deidesheimer 1997: Ripe apricot flavors are balanced by a lively spiciness in this off-dry, medium-bodied white. Nicely balanced, it's a good introduction to dry Riesling. Drink now through 2003.–B.S. • $12 • (2/28/1999) • **83**

Riesling Spätlese Halbtrocken Pfalz Forster Pechstein 1997: Suave and harmonious, this '97 off-dry spätlese combines ripe apricot and mineral notes with a firm structure and a seamless texture. Has a nutty component and a long finish. Drink now through 2007.–B.S. • $21 • (2/28/1999) • **88**

Riesling Spätlese Halbtrocken Pfalz Forster Pechstein 1996 • $19 • (11/30/1997) • **85**

Riesling Spätlese Pfalz Forster Kirchenstück 1998: Terrific. Tasting like auslese ripeness, this '98 spätlese has an extra dimension. Soft, lush and full of apricot and honey, the sweetness gives it a monolithic feel, but there's enough acidity for balance. Drink now through 2006.–B.S. • $24 • (2/29/2000) • **92**

Riesling Spätlese Pfalz Forster Kirchenstück 1997: More like an auslese in ripeness, this has dried apricot, guava and grapefruit, beautifully displayed on a delicate framework. Concentrated, with a long aftertaste. Drink now through 2007.–B.S. • $22 • (2/28/1999) • **91**

Riesling Spätlese Pfalz Forster Kirchenstück 1996 • $21 • (11/30/1997) • **84**

Riesling Spätlese Trocken Pfalz Forster Pechstein 1998: *Erstes Gewächs.* Some citrus peel notes initially, along with accents of clove and nutmeg. Excellent density and persistence, on a solid structure that's monolithic and backward now. A powerful young wine, lively and very long on the finish. Drink now.–B.S. • $40 • (2/29/2000) • **92**

Riesling Spätlese Trocken Pfalz Forster Ungeheuer 1998: Focused and balanced, this '98 delivers apricot and peach on a lean, solid structure. Best from 2001 through 2006.–B.S. • $22 • (1/01/2000) • **87**

Riesling Spätlese Trocken Pfalz Forster Ungeheuer 1997: Rich and spicy, with bright acidity, lanolin and dough flavors and residual carbon dioxide. A little backward and austere on the finish, but it shows good focus. Best from 2001 through 2006.–B.S. • $21 • (2/28/1999) • **84**

Riesling Spätlese Trocken Pfalz Forster Ungeheuer 1996 • $20 • (11/30/1997) • **87**

Riesling Spätlese Trocken Pfalz Ruppertsberger Reiterpfad 1998: *Erstes Gewächs.* Ripe and broad, with forthcoming aromas of pineapple, apricot and spice. Packs a lot of ripe fruit on a sinewy frame, supported by fine acidity and ending with a lingering aftertaste of grapefruit peel. Drink now through 2008.–B.S. • $30 • (2/29/2000) • **90**

Riesling Spätlese Trocken Pfalz Ruppertsberger Reiterpfad 1997: Very ripe and full of nectarine character, this is a dry white in a rich, soft, forward style. Judging from the dry, slightly coarse finish, it needs time to integrate. Best from 2001 through 2006.–B.S. • $29 • (2/28/1999) • **86**

Riesling Trockenbeerenauslese Pfalz Forster Ungeheuer 1996 • $183/375 ml. • (11/30/1997) • **93**

BÜRKLIN-WOLF, DR.

Gewürztraminer QbA Trocken Pfalz 1997: Penetrating aromas of white pepper and roses introduce this white whose litchi and rose flavors marry well with its corpulence. The finish is dry and crisp, keeping it all balanced. Drink now.–B.S. • $25 • (5/15/1999) • **87**

Muskateller Auslese Pfalz 1998: Very ripe and concentrated, bursting with apricot, honey and orange marmalade notes. Despite its sweetness, it retains a sense of elegance and harmony. Well done. Drink now through 2003.–B.S. • $22/375 ml. • (5/15/2000) • **88**

Muskateller Trockenbeerenauslese Pfalz Wachenheimer Luginsland 1995 • $89/375 ml. • (11/30/1996) • **78**

Muskateller Trockenbeerenauslese Pfalz Wachenheimer Luginsland 1992 • $75/375 ml. • (11/30/1993) • **95**

Riesling Auslese Pfalz Ruppertsberger Gaisböhl 'R' 1997: A big, broad, ripe auslese, not that sweet, offering honey, apricot and guava aromas and flavors tinged with almond. Clean and bright, it has a lingering mineral note on the finish. To be released in 2002. Tasted twice, with consistent notes. Drink through 2008.–B.S. • $NA • (2/28/1999) • **89**

Riesling Beerenauslese Pfalz Ruppertsberger Gaisböhl 1997: Superconcentrated and unctuous, this '97 BA offers plenty of honey and apricot aromas and flavors, backed by refreshing acidity that keeps it lively. Long nectarine aftertaste. Delicious now, but will improve. Drink through 2012.–B.S. • $181 • (2/28/1999) • **94**

Riesling Beerenauslese Pfalz Wachenheimer Gerümpel 1996 • $72/375 ml. • (11/30/1997) • **91**

Riesling Beerenauslese Pfalz Wachenheimer Gerümpel 1990 • $130/375 ml. • (12/15/1991) • **96**

Riesling Beerenauslese Pfalz Wachenheimer Gerümpel 1989 • $NA • (12/15/1990) • **95**

Riesling Beerenauslese Pfalz Wachenheimer Goldbächel 1994 • $75 • (11/30/1995) • **92**

Riesling Beerenauslese Pfalz Wachenheimer Goldbächel 1988 • $30 • (9/30/1989) • **87**

Riesling Beerenauslese Pfalz Wachenheimer Rechbächel 1989 • $95/375 ml. • (12/15/1990) • **93**

Riesling Eiswein Pfalz Wachenheimer Gerümpel 1996 • $185/375 ml. • (11/30/1997) • **88**

Riesling Kabinett Pfalz Forster 1998: This '98 white notches up the sweetness a bit, remaining focused courtesy of a snappy structure and a dense texture. Sweet-tart apricot right now, so be patient. Best from 2001 through 2005.–B.S. • $13 • (2/29/2000) • **89**

Riesling Kabinett Pfalz Forster 1997: Gorgeous. Exhibiting peach, violet and tropical fruit nuances, this white is concentrated and solidly supported by bracing acidity and power that carries through the finish. Young and unevolved, this shows great potential. Best from 2001 through 2008.–B.S. • $12 • (2/28/1999) • **90**

Riesling Kabinett Pfalz Wachenheimer Rechbächel 1996 • $13 • (11/30/1997) • **86**

Riesling Kabinett Trocken Pfalz Deidesheimer 1997: The floral and peach aromas and flavors and medium weight strike a nice balance in this dry white, supported by a rich texture and elegant structure. Finishes just a little on the austere side. Drink now through 2003.–B.S. • $NA • (2/28/1999) • **86**

Riesling QbA Pfalz Cuvée Christian 1998: A delicate QbA, this is almost dry, spicy and creamy-smooth. Light and airy in its approach, it tails off a little on the finish. Drink now through 2003.–B.S. • $15 • (2/29/2000) • **84**

Riesling QbA Pfalz Forster 1996 • $10 • (11/30/1997) • **85**

Riesling Spätlese Halbtrocken Pfalz Wachenheimer 1997: This white is rich and concentrated, with a dry, spicy character and subtle flavors of peach and mineral. Persistent, if not very expressive in flavor. Best from 2001 through 2006.–B.S. • $20 • (2/28/1999) • **83**

Riesling Spätlese Halbtrocken Pfalz Wachenheimer Gerümpel 1996 • $16 • (11/30/1997) • **87**

Riesling Spätlese Pfalz Forster 1998: An elegant spätlese, exuding peach and spice on an open framework. Deceptively dense and lively, with a long finish. Drink now through 2007.–B.S. • $23 • (2/29/2000) • **89**

Riesling Spätlese Pfalz Forster 1997: A broad, almond-flavored '97, with a creamy texture accented by a lanolin component. Has power and a firm backbone. Finishes on a citrus note. Drink now through 2006.–B.S. • $22 • (2/28/1999) • **89**

Riesling Spätlese Pfalz Wachenheimer 1998: Very ripe, showing concentrated apricot, spice and citrus flavors matched with bright acidity. Vanilla aftertaste. Well structured and multidimensional. Drink now through 2006. –B.S. • $22 • (2/29/2000) • **91**

Riesling Spätlese Pfalz Wachenheimer Gerümpel 1996 • $16 • (11/30/1997) • **88**

Riesling Spätlese Trocken Pfalz Deidesheimer Hohenmorgen 1998: (First Growth) Ripe, bold and richly textured, this dry spätlese delivers peach and pear notes and a white pepper nuance. Full-bodied, with vibrant acidity. Drink now through 2004.–B.S. • $43 • (2/29/2000) • **90**

Riesling Spätlese Trocken Pfalz Forst Kirchenstück 1996 • $25 • (11/30/1997) • **89**

Riesling Spätlese Trocken Pfalz Ruppertsberger Gaisböhl 1998: (First Growth) This stunning dry Riesling carries all the elements beautifully, from the peach and spice aromas and flavors to the round velvet feel and firm finish. Best from 2001 through 2007.–B.S. • $34 • (2/29/2000) • **90**

Riesling Spätlese Trocken Pfalz Wachenheimer Rechbächel 1998: Lean, dense and tangy, this is a dry spätlese for the table. Pear and chamomile notes ride the racy acidity to a lingering finish. Drink now through 2005.–B.S. • $30 • (1/01/2000) • **87**

BÜRKLIN-WOLF, DR.

Riesling Trockenbeerenauslese Pfalz Ehrenfelser Wachenheimer Mandelgarten 1990 • $NA • (12/15/1991) • **93**

Riesling Trockenbeerenauslese Pfalz Forster Kirchenstück 1994 • $211 • (11/30/1995) • **96**

Riesling Trockenbeerenauslese Pfalz Ruppertsberger Linsenbusch 1988 • $9 • (9/30/1989) • **79**

Riesling Trockenbeerenauslese Pfalz Wachenheimer Gerümpel 1997: Thick, sweet and palate-coating, yet remains lively and displays pure flavors of apricot and honey, glints of citrus. Its overall soft impression ensures immediate enjoyment, but this will gain complexity with time. Drink now through 2015.–B.S. • $324 • (2/28/1999) • **93**

Riesling Trockenbeerenauslese Pfalz Wachenheimer Luginsland 1989 • $165 • (12/15/1990) • **95**

Scheurebe Beerenauslese Pfalz 1991 • $120 • (12/15/1992) • **93**

Scheurebe Beerenauslese Pfalz Wachenheimer Gerümpel 1995 • $49/375 ml. • (11/30/1996) • **90**

Scheurebe Trockenbeerenauslese Pfalz Wachenheimer Mandelgarten 1989: Wow. An intense dessert wine with aromas and flavors of spearmint, fresh bay leaf, caramel and apricot. Very sweet, with searing acidity that keeps the wine fresh, and possibly ageless. Needs a dessert to match its acidity. Drink now through 2010.–B.S. • $200 • (5/15/1999) • **90**

CASTELL, SCHLOSS

Riesling QbA Franken 1998: Dry, rich and concentrated, here's a spicy white that combines nectarine notes with a hint of earthiness, backed by a firm structure. Drink now through 2003.–B.S. • $15 • (5/15/2000) • **84**

CHRISTOFFEL, JOH. JOS.

Riesling Auslese Mosel-Saar-Ruwer Ürziger Würzgarten 1998: Very pure and focused, with an open texture and transparency. Lime and slate take center stage, backed by a crisp, appley acidity. Best from 2001 through 2008.–B.S. • $31 • (1/01/2000) • **89**

Riesling Auslese * Mosel-Saar-Ruwer Ürziger Würzgarten 1998: Delicate and perfumed, this '98 auslese shows a touch of herb, red fruit and almonds, augmenting the lime and mineral. Sleek and focused, like a violin crescendo. Best from 2002 through 2010.–B.S. • $38 • (2/29/2000) • **91**

Riesling Auslese ** Mosel-Saar-Ruwer Ürziger Würzgarten 1998: A compact, finely etched Riesling, hinting at lime and mineral, riding a rapierlike structure. Really racy on the finish, it needs time to integrate. Best from 2002 through 2010.–B.S. • $44 • (2/29/2000) • **90**

Riesling Auslese * Mosel-Saar-Ruwer Ürziger Würzgarten 1998:** Plenty of lime, passion fruit and slate mark this slim white. Its creamy texture is balanced by the firm structure, finishing with a mouthwatering tang. Best after 2001.–B.S. • $62/375 ml. • (2/29/2000) • **92**

Riesling Beerenauslese Mosel-Saar-Ruwer Ürziger Würzgarten 1994 • $NA • (11/30/1995) • **84**

Riesling Eiswein Mosel-Saar-Ruwer Ürziger Würzgarten 1998: A live wire, this literally crackles with acidity, citrus and mineral flavors and a lean, trim texture. Needs time to settle down and reveal its charms. Best from 2001 through 2008.–B.S. • $156/375 ml. • (2/29/2000) • **91**

Riesling Kabinett Mosel-Saar-Ruwer Erdener Treppchen 1998: Densely textured, bursting with floral, talc, peach and citrus aromas and flavors, here's a young Riesling whose concentration and firm structure bode well for the future. Fine length. Best from 2001 through 2006.–B.S. • $19 • (2/29/2000) • **90**

Riesling Kabinett Mosel-Saar-Ruwer Ürziger Würzgarten 1998: A solid kabinett, offering lime and apple notes, with a touch of cheesiness today. Well-structured, balanced and lively, with a moderate finish. Drink now through 2003.–B.S. • $19 • (2/29/2000) • **87**

Riesling QbA Halbtrocken Mosel-Saar-Ruwer 1998: Slate and earth are the main themes in an attractive way that plays off the lively structure. The finish is lean. Drink now through 2003.–B.S. • $18 • (1/01/2000) • **82**

Riesling QbA Mosel-Saar-Ruwer 1998: Easygoing and delicious, this zippy, elegant white exhibits a lot of mineral and spice, in addition to lime and apple. Drink now through 2003.–B.S. • $18 • (1/01/2000) • **85**

Riesling Spätlese Mosel-Saar-Ruwer Ürziger Würzgarten 1998: Rich, showing peach, lime and herb notes and lively acidity, all on a dense, creamy texture. Decent finish. Drink now through 2003.–B.S. • $23 • (2/29/2000) • **89**

Key: SS—Spectator Selection. CS—Cellar Selection. HR—Highly Recommended. $NA—Price not available. (BT)—Barrel tasting. (A)—Auction Price.
For a key to the tasters' initials, see "How to Use These Listings."
Dates in parentheses represent the issues in which the ratings were published.

CHRISTOFFEL ERBEN, JOH. JOS.

Riesling Auslese Mosel-Saar-Ruwer Ürziger Würzgarten 1996 • $17 • (11/30/1997) • **87**

Riesling Auslese * Mosel-Saar-Ruwer Ürziger Würzgarten 1996 • $20 • (11/30/1997) • **88**

Riesling Auslese ** Mosel-Saar-Ruwer Ürziger Würzgarten 1996 • $23 • (11/30/1997) • **89**

Riesling Auslese * Mosel-Saar-Ruwer Ürziger Würzgarten 1996** • $32 • (11/30/1997) • **87**

Riesling Eiswein Mosel-Saar-Ruwer Ürziger Würzgarten 1993 • $65 • (11/30/1994) • **90**

Riesling Eiswein Mosel-Saar-Ruwer Ürziger Würzgarten 1992 • $43/375 ml. • (11/30/1993) • **87**

Riesling Kabinett Mosel-Saar-Ruwer Erdener Treppchen 1996 • $11 • (11/30/1997) • **87**

Riesling Kabinett Mosel-Saar-Ruwer Ürziger Würzgarten 1996 • $11 • (11/30/1997) • **86**

Riesling Spätlese Mosel-Saar-Ruwer Erdener Treppchen 1996 • $13 • (11/30/1997) • **85**

CRUSIUS

Riesling Auslese Nahe Schlossböckelheimer Felsenberg 1996 • $34 • (11/30/1997) • **82**

Riesling Beerenauslese Nahe Traiser 1996 • $98/500 ml. • (11/30/1997) • **85**

Riesling Beerenauslese Nahe Traiser Rotenfels 1994 • $NA • (11/30/1995) • **79**

Riesling Eiswein Nahe Traiser Rotenfels 1992 • $195/F • (11/30/1993) • **94**

Riesling Eiswein Nahe Traiser 1996 • $150/500 ml. • (11/30/1997) • **95**

Riesling Kabinett Nahe Niederhäuser Felsensteyer 1996 • $19 • (11/30/1997) • **82**

Riesling QbA Nahe Norheimer 1996 • $12 • (11/30/1997) • **78**

Riesling Spätlese Nahe Traiser Bastei 1996 • $23 • (11/30/1997) • **85**

Riesling Trockenbeerenauslese Nahe Traiser Bastei 1994 • $NA • (11/30/1995) • **80**

DARTING, KURT

Gewürztraminer Spätlese Pfalz Dürkheimer Nonnengarten 1998: More like an auslese in ripeness, this has good concentration and balance between the sweetness and succulent acidity. The flavors lean toward litchi, papaya and apricot and linger on the finish. Drink now.–B.S. • $30 • (5/15/2000) • **88**

Huxelrebe Auslese Pfalz Forster Schnepfenflug 1998: Charming, this white welcomes the palate with an open, easygoing structure upon which the apricot and nectarine flavors float. Not a lot of depth or length. Drink now.–B.S. • $24 • (5/15/2000) • **84**

Huxelrebe Beerenauslese Pfalz Forster Schnepfenflug 1998: Deeply colored, this dessert wine delivers a hedonistic mix of honey, caramel and apricot on a corpulent frame. Straightforward, with a modest finish. Not imported into the U.S. Drink now.–B.S. • $NA/500 ml. • (1/01/2000) • **86**

Rieslaner Auslese Pfalz Dürkheimer Nonnengarten 1998: A forward style, with plenty of fruit up front. Floral and nectarine aromas and flavors are well integrated with the round, bright structure. Tails off a little on the finish. Drink now through 2003.–B.S. • $29 • (5/15/2000) • **87**

Rieslaner Auslese Pfalz Dürkheimer Nonnengarten 1996 • $21 • (11/30/1997) • **84**

Rieslaner Beerenauslese Pfalz Dürkheimer Nonnengarten 1992 • $17/F • (11/30/1993) • **86**

Rieslaner Beerenauslese Pfalz Ungsteiner Bettelhaus 1996 • $23/500 ml. • (11/30/1997) • **91**

Rieslaner Trockenbeerenauslese Pfalz Ungsteiner Bettelhaus 1992 • $28/375 ml. • (11/30/1993) • **92**

Riesling Auslese Pfalz Ungsteiner Herrenberg 1998: Opulent, smooth and inviting, marrrying pure apricot and citrus flavors with a vivid and dense structure. Good, lingering aftertaste. Drink now through 2007.–B.S. • $26 • (2/29/2000) • **91**

Riesling Auslese Pfalz Ungsteiner Herrenberg 1997: Lime, peach and mineral elements are intertwined with a sleek, racy structure. The sweetness is masked by a lot of acidity, giving this style and finesse. Excellent finish. Drink now through 2007.–B.S. • $18 • (2/28/1999) • **90**

Riesling Auslese Pfalz Ungsteiner Herrenberg 1996 • $18 • (11/30/1997) • **85**

Riesling Kabinett Pfalz Dürkheimer Hochbenn 1998: A brilliant kabinett. Slim and zippy, with well-defined cardamom, lime and apricot notes that never veer off the course of vibrant acidity. Ends in a cascade of tropical fruit and citrus. Drink now through 2006.–B.S. • $15 • (2/29/2000) • **90**

Riesling Kabinett Pfalz Ungsteiner Bettelhaus 1997: A delicious kabinett from the Pfalz. Lush yet firm, forward yet complex, with talcum powder, tropical fruit and spice nuances, this '97 white will only get better with age. Long, long finish. Drink now through 2007.–B.S. • $11 • (2/28/1999) • **89**

Riesling Kabinett Pfalz Ungsteiner Bettelhaus 1996 • $11 • (11/30/1997) • **90**

Riesling Spätlese Pfalz Dürkheimer Michelsberg 1998: Luscious peach notes are augmented by citrus and a juicy texture. Delicious now, yet it should age well judging by the crisp acidity. Drink now through 2006.–B.S. • $17 • (2/29/2000) • **90**

Riesling Spätlese Pfalz Dürkheimer Spielberg 1997: Reminiscent of peaches and cream, with a hint of floral nuance, all riding on a rich yet airy texture. Enough acidity to balance everything. Excellent finish. Drink now through 2005.–B.S. • $12 • (2/28/1999) • **89**

Riesling Spätlese Pfalz Dürkheimer Spielberg 1996 • $12 • (11/30/1997) • **89**

Scheurebe Spätlese Pfalz Dürkheimer Spielberg 1998: Lithe and firm, exhibiting plenty of grapefruit, rose, litchi and apricot, solidly built and densely textured from start to finish. Fine length. Drink now through 2002.–B.S. • $17 • (5/15/2000) • **89**

Scheurebe Spätlese Pfalz Dürkheimer Spielberg 1996 • $11 • (11/30/1997) • **87**

DIEL, SCHLOSSGUT

Riesling Auslese Gold Cap Nahe Dorsheimer Goldloch 1998: Auction wine. Ripe, racy and shimmering with snappy apricot ands citrus notes. A touch of honey rounds out the flavors, and all is supported by tangy acidity. Maybe a hint of botrytis here. Drink now through 2010.–B.S. • $NA/375 ml. • (1/01/2000) • **93**

Riesling Auslese Gold Cap Nahe Dorsheimer Pittermännchen 1998: Auction wine. Lovely succulent apricot and citrus aromas and flavors, with an underpinning of firm acidity that leaves a mouthwatering finish. Beautifully put together. Best from 2001 through 2009.–B.S. • $NA/375 ml. • (1/01/2000) • **91**

Riesling Auslese Nahe 1996 • $41/375 ml. • (11/30/1997) • **91**

Riesling Auslese Nahe Dorsheimer Burgberg 1998: Gorgeous auslese, elegant, pure and racy while dense with peach and mineral flavors. Well-delineated and marked by a strong, upright framework, this should be a beauty in time. Best from 2001 through 2010.–B.S. • $46 • (2/29/2000) • **91**

Riesling Auslese Nahe Dorsheimer Burgberg 1997: A light, tender auslese, yet ripe and sleek, with a heart of red currants and peaches and a backbone of steel, all tightly wound for the long haul. Best from 2003 through 2010.–B.S. • $41 • (2/28/1999) • **90**

Riesling Auslese Nahe Dorsheimer Pittermännchen 1998: A fastball across the plate, this '98 shows flesh and power. The apricot and honey notes are effusive, kept bright by a firm acidity. Very harmonious and long. Drink now through 2007.–B.S. • $52 • (2/29/2000) • **92**

Riesling Auslese Nahe Dorsheimer Pittermännchen 1997 • $NA • (1/01/1998) • **91**

Riesling Beerenauslese Gold Cap Nahe 1994 • $NA • (11/30/1995) • **87**

Riesling Beerenauslese Gold Cap Nahe 1993 • $158 • (11/30/1994) • **94**

Riesling Eiswein Gold Cap Nahe 1995 • $NA/375 ml. • (11/30/1996) • **92**

Riesling Eiswein Long Gold Cap Nahe 1996 • $332/375 ml. • (11/30/1997) • **94**

Riesling Eiswein Nahe 1998: Intense, concentrated and packed with pure apricot and mineral flavors and a strong backbone of citrusy acidity. Harmonious enough to enjoy now, but built to age. Drink now through 2012.–B.S. • $100/375 ml. • (2/29/2000) • **93**

Riesling Eiswein Nahe 1995 • $260/375 ml. • (11/30/1996) • **91**

Riesling Eiswein Nahe 1994 • $142 • (11/30/1995) • **90**

Riesling Eiswein Nahe 1993 • $191 • (11/30/1994) • **93**

Riesling Eiswein Nahe 1992 • $104/375 ml. • (11/30/1993) • **93**

Riesling Eiswein Nahe 1991 • $176 • (12/15/1992) • **89**

Riesling Eiswein Nahe 1990 • $NA • (12/15/1991) • **94**

Riesling Kabinett Nahe Dorsheimer Burgberg 1998: Intriguing. Like a peach embedded in slate; it's there, but you have to work through the stone first. Delicately proportioned, fading gracefully on the finish. Drink now through 2002.–B.S. • $21 • (1/01/2000) • **84**

Riesling Kabinett Nahe Dorsheimer Burgberg 1997: Solid and a bit immovable, this white nonetheless has an intense mineral character, with apricot and coconut accents. Densely textured, suave and long on the finish, this is a beauty. Best from 2002 through 2008.–B.S. • $21 • (2/28/1999) • **90**

Riesling Kabinett Nahe Dorsheimer Goldloch 1998: Plump and juicy, like biting into a peach that's been drizzled with lime. Balanced on the soft side, making pleasant drinking now. Drink now through 2003.–B.S. • $23 • (2/29/2000) • **84**

Riesling Kabinett Nahe Dorsheimer Goldloch 1997 • $NA • (1/01/1998) • **89**

Riesling Kabinett Nahe Dorsheimer Goldloch 1996 • $20 • (11/30/1997) • **87**

Riesling Kabinett Nahe Dorsheimer Pittermännchen 1997 • $NA • (1/01/1998) • **89**

Riesling Kabinett Nahe Dorsheimer Pittermännchen 1996 • $20 • (11/30/1997) • **88**

Riesling QbA Nahe 1998: Extremely elegant, smelling like lime blossoms and minerals, changing to grapefruit and earth on the palate. Good firm structure. Drink now through 2002.–B.S. • $20 • (1/01/2000) • **83**

Riesling QbA Nahe 1997: Fresh and delicious, this bursts with lemon-lime and peach aromas and flavors in an elegant, moderately intense manner. Drink now through 2002.–B.S. • $15 • (2/28/1999) • **86**

Riesling QbA Nahe 1996 • $15 • (11/30/1997) • **87**

Riesling QbA Nahe Dorsheimer Goldloch 1997 • $NA • (1/01/1998) • **84**

Riesling Spätlese Gold Cap Nahe Dorsheimer Burgberg 1998: Auction wine. More like an auslese in quality, this is rich, packed with apricot compote and honey flavors accented by mandarin orange. A little top-heavy now, it requires time for the sweetness and acidity to integrate. Best from 2002 through 2010.–B.S. • $NA • (1/01/2000) • **90**

Riesling Spätlese Nahe Dorsheimer Burgberg 1997: A crisp, racy white, exhibiting peach and almond aromas and flavors that keep pulsing through the firm finish. Best from 2002 through 2007.–B.S. • $27 • (2/28/1999) • **89**

Riesling Spätlese Nahe Dorsheimer Burgberg 1996 • $25 • (11/30/1997) • **88**

Riesling Spätlese Nahe Dorsheimer Goldloch 1998: Combines richness and intensity, and the peach and mineral notes have some zip behind them. Well balanced, long on the finish. Drink now through 2006.–B.S. • $31 • (2/29/2000) • **89**

Riesling Spätlese Nahe Dorsheimer Goldloch 1997 • $NA • (1/01/1998) • **90**

Riesling Spätlese Nahe Dorsheimer Goldloch 1996 • $32 • (11/30/1997) • **87**

Riesling Spätlese Nahe Dorsheimer Pittermännchen 1998: Ripe and succulent, here's a '98 Riesling bursting with apricot and mineral elements on a moderate structure. Drink now through 2005.–B.S. • $34 • (2/29/2000) • **88**

Riesling Spätlese Nahe Dorsheimer Pittermännchen 1997 • $NA • (1/01/1998) • **91**

Riesling Spätlese Nahe Dorsheimer Pittermännchen 1996 • $28 • (11/30/1997) • **86**

Riesling Trocken Nahe 1997 • $NA • (1/01/1998) • **87**

DÖNNHOFF, H.

Riesling Auslese Nahe Niederhäuser Hermannshöhle 1998: An intense, nervy white, finely detailed in its lime and mineral flavors that are tightly wound yet persistent. Lean and crisp on the finish. Best from 2001 through 2006.–B.S. • $38/375 ml. • (2/29/2000) • **90**

Riesling Auslese Nahe Niederhäuser Hermannshöhle 1996 • $27/375 ml. • (11/30/1997) • **89**

Riesling Auslese Nahe Oberhäuser Brücke 1998: A delightful combination of intense apricot, peach, lime and mineral aromas and flavors, all nicely displayed on a vibrant framework, with a rich, silky texture. Best from 2001 through 2007.–B.S. • $41/375 ml. • (2/29/2000) • **91**

Riesling Auslese Nahe Oberhäuser Brücke 1996 • $26/375 ml. • (11/30/1997) • **86**

Riesling Beerenauslese Nahe Oberhäuser Brücke 1995 • $49/375 ml. • (11/30/1996) • **93**

Riesling Eiswein Nahe Oberhäuser Brücke 1996 • $93/375 ml. • (11/30/1997) • **90**

Riesling Eiswein Nahe Oberhäuser Brücke 1995 • $129/375 ml. • (11/30/1996) • **91**

Riesling Eiswein Nahe Oberhäuser Brücke 1994 • $127 • (11/30/1995) • **94**

Riesling Eiswein Nahe Oberhäuser Brücke 1992 • $NA • (11/30/1993) • **96**

Riesling Eiswein Nahe Oberhäuser Felsenberg 1993 • $135 • (11/30/1994) • **92**

Riesling Kabinett Nahe Oberhäuser Leistenberg 1998: Sleek and pristine, this racehorse of a white focuses its peach, lime and spice notes through the vibrant acidity. Lightweight yet intense with flavor. Drink now through 2005.–B.S. • $25 • (2/29/2000) • **87**

Riesling QbA Nahe 1998: Seductive aromas of red fruit and spice introduce this lean, intensely flavored white. Apple and mineral notes linger on the finish. Drink now through 2003.–B.S. • $18 • (1/01/2000) • **86**

Riesling QbA Nahe 1996 • $12 • (11/30/1997) • **85**

Riesling Spätlese Nahe Niederhäuser Hermannshöhle 1998: Frankly sweet, yet offset by a crisp acidity that carries the apricot and citrus flavors to a brisk conclusion. The apricot notes linger. Needs time to come together. Drink now through 2004.–B.S. • $40 • (1/01/2000) • **87**

Riesling Spätlese Nahe Niederhäuser Hermannshöhle 1996 • $23 • (11/30/1997) • **85**

Riesling Spätlese Nahe Norheimer Kirschheck 1996 • $21 • (11/30/1997) • **87**

DÖNNHOFF, H.

Riesling Spätlese Nahe Oberhäuser Brücke 1998: A soft, inviting style, exhibiting floral, sweet corn and nectarine aromas and flavors, all on a lively framework. Finishes with crisp apple and mineral notes. Drink now through 2005.–B.S. • $40 • (2/29/2000) • **88**

Riesling Spätlese Nahe Schlossböckelheimer Kupfergrube 1998: Closed at this stage, offering moderate mineral and peach, this '98 white shows density, great texture, harmony and length. Be patient. Drink through 2003.–B.S. • $38 • (2/29/2000) • **88**

Riesling Trockenbeerenauslese Nahe Niederhäuser Hermannshöhle 1994 • $168 • (11/30/1995) • **96**

EBERBACH, STAATSWEINGÜTER KLOSTER

Riesling Auslese Rheingau Erbacher Marcobrunn 1997: There's an extra dimension of ripeness, yet this retains elegance thanks to its brisk acidity, which also drives the apricot and honey flavors. Ripe and forward, with a lingering finish. Drink now through 2007.–B.S. • $40 • (2/28/1999) • **90**

Riesling Auslese Rheingau Rauenthaler Baiken 1996: Electrifyingly fresh, with apples and pears galore. Full-bodied and medium sweet, with zingy acidity and a long, long finish. Drink through 2005.–J.S. • $18/375 ml. • (7/31/1998) • **92**

Riesling Auslese Rheingau Rüdesheimer Berg Schlossberg 1998: Delicate, with the firm and reticent Rheingau manner, this auslese seems to be balanced toward the dryish side, keeping its fruit buttoned up. Grainy texture on the finish. Best after 2001.–B.S. • $43 • (1/01/2000) • **88**

Riesling Beerenauslese Rheingau Rauenthaler Baiken 1993• $NA • (11/30/1994) • **92**

Riesling Kabinett Halbtrocken Rheingau Erbacher Siegelsberg 1997: All the elements are harmonious in this suave peach- and spice-flavored white. On the dry side, with medium body and lively acidity. Drink now through 2003.–B.S. • $15 • (2/28/1999) • **85**

Riesling Kabinett Rheingau Erbacher Marcobrunn 1998: Spicy, exuding cinnamon and ginger, apple and grapefruit in a broad, firmly structured presentation. Fine texture and purity. Best from 2001 through 2004.–B.S. • $21 • (2/29/2000) • **88**

Riesling Kabinett Rheingau Rauenthaler Baiken 1996: Plenty of apple and peach in this young Riesling. Medium-bodied and lightly sweet, with a fresh finish. Slightly simple for this great vineyard.–J.S. • $16 • (7/31/1998) • **85**

Riesling Kabinett Rheingau Steinberger 1998: Sleek, focused and minerally, this elegant '98 Riesling is full of pure citrus, quince and mineral. Best from 2001 through 2004.–B.S. • $18 • (2/29/2000) • **88**

Riesling Kabinett Rheingau Steinberger 1996: Light flinty and mineral aromas and flavors. Medium to light in body, with strong acidity and a fresh finish. A bit young, but impressive. Drink through 2004.–J.S. • $17 • (7/31/1998) • **87**

Riesling QbA Rheingau Steinberger 1998: Lovely peach and citrus elements in this rich '98. Vibrant, smooth and harmonious, it holds the flavors to a lingering aftertaste. Drink now through 2003.–B.S. • $13 • (2/29/2000) • **85**

Riesling QbA Rheingau Steinberger 1996: Attractive aromas of cream and apple, with floral undertones. Medium-bodied and off-dry, with lemon and apricot flavors and a fresh finish. Delicious. Drink now.–J.S. • $12 • (7/31/1998) • **87**

Riesling Spätlese Rheingau Erbacher Marcobrunn 1996: Outstanding intensity, with lots of apricot and apple aromas. Medium- to full-bodied. Medium sweet, with a lively and flavorful finish. Super wine. Drink now through 2005.–J.S. • $24 • (7/31/1998) • **91**

Riesling Spätlese Rheingau Hochheimer Domdechaney 1996: Elegant aromas of tropical and citrus fruits. Medium-bodied and off-dry, with a medium finish. Better on the nose than on the palate. Drink now.–J.S. • $18 • (7/31/1998) • **85**

Riesling Spätlese Rheingau Hochheimer Kirchenstück 1997: Rich, elegant and well defined, this '97 offers aromas and flavors of apricot and passion fruit. Its moderate acidity shows a grapefruit component, with a minerally finish. Drink now through 2005.–B.S. • $20 • (2/28/1999) • **88**

Riesling Spätlese Rheingau Rauenthaler Baiken 1998: Suave and smoothly textured, this exudes breadth and an intense minerality. Needs time for the peach and residual sugar to integrate with the structure. Best from 2001 through 2005.–B.S. • $26 • (2/29/2000) • **87**

Key: SS—Spectator Selection. CS—Cellar Selection. HR—Highly Recommended. $NA—Price not available. (BT)—Barrel tasting. (A)—Auction Price.
For a key to the tasters' initials, see "How to Use These Listings."
Dates in parentheses represent the issues in which the ratings were published.

Riesling Spätlese Rheingau Rauenthaler Baiken 1997: Rich and medium-bodied, this '97 has weight and density as well as lively acidity to carry the peach and lemon-lime flavors. Drink now through 2004.–B.S. • $25 • (2/28/1999) • **86**

Riesling Spätlese Rheingau Rauenthaler Baiken 1996: Aromas of white peach and apple flow from the glass. Medium-bodied and off-dry, with crisp acidity and a medium finish. Slight dilution on the midpalate. Drink now.–J.S. • $22 • (7/31/1998) • **85**

Riesling Spätlese Rheingau Rüdesheimer Berg Rottland 1996: Intensely flavored wine, oozing with apricot tart aromas. Medium-bodied and lightly sweet, with lively acidity and a long aftertaste. Drink now.–J.S. • $18 • (7/31/1998) • **90**

Riesling Spätlese Rheingau Steinberger 1997: A robust, broad style of Riesling, with earth, apricot and orangepeel flavors, concentration and citrusy freshness at the end. Drink now through 2004.–B.S. • $32 • (2/28/1999) • **87**

EHLEN, STEPHAN

Riesling Kabinett Mosel-Saar-Ruwer Erdener Treppchen 1998: Lime and slate aromas and flavors are attractive in this delicate white, which ends with a touch of greenness. Drink now through 2004.–B.S. • $13 • (2/29/2000) • **83**

Riesling Kabinett Mosel-Saar-Ruwer Erdener Treppchen 1996 • $12 • (4/30/1998) • **85**

EMRICH-SCHÖNLEBER

Riesling Auslese Gold Cap * Nahe Monzinger Halenberg 1998:** Auction wine. An extra dimension of ripeness lends the tropical fruit and lime flavors an exotic nuance. Tangy acidity balances the sweetness, allowing the juicy fruit to come to the fore. Fine length. Best from 2002 through 2010.–B.S. • $NA/500 ml. • (1/01/2000) • **91**

Riesling Auslese Gold Cap * Nahe Monzinger Halenberg 1997:** Auction wine. Delicate in style, this white has a transparency and a silk frame from which its lime and mineral flavors hang. Bolstered by tart acidity, but the ripe peach notes win in the end. Best from 2001 through 2007.–B.S. • $NA/500 ml. • (2/28/1999) • **92**

Riesling Auslese Nahe Monzinger Halenberg 1998: Ripe and sweet in character, but it's all bracing acidity now. The quince, lime and mineral flavors remain submerged, yet there's a density and a persistence that echo on the finish. Best from 2001 through 2007.–B.S. • $21/375 ml. • (2/29/2000) • **88**

Riesling Eiswein Nahe Monzinger Halenberg 1998: A gorgeous eiswein, brilliant and shimmering with peach, citrus and mineral nuances that are well integrated with the crystalline structure and creamy texture. Well done. Best from 2001 through 2008.–B.S. • $97/375 ml. • (2/29/2000) • **91**

Riesling Kabinett Nahe Monzinger Frühlingsplätzchen 1998: Like biting into a Granny Smith apple, this '98 Riesling is fresh, crisp and inviting. Balanced, with modest concentration and length. Drink now through 2003.–B.S. • $18 • (2/29/2000) • **84**

Riesling Kabinett Nahe Monzinger Frühlingsplätzchen 1997: Dry in style, very elegant and reserved, here's a Nahe kabinett that's well balanced, with almond, spice and mineral flavors and a firm backbone. Likable despite its cool personality. Best from 2001 through 2006.–B.S. • $18 • (2/28/1999) • **87**

Riesling QbA Halbtrocken Nahe Monzinger 1998: Aromatic, showing peach and citrus in a balanced, direct manner. Finishes short. Drink now.–B.S. • $14 • (2/29/2000) • **80**

Riesling QbA Halbtrocken Nahe Monzinger 1997: A touch of sweetness rounds out the aromas and texture in this succulent '97. Floral, peach and mineral are the hallmarks, balanced by firm acidity. Drink now through 2005.–B.S. • $13 • (2/28/1999) • **86**

Riesling QbA Nahe Monzinger 1997: A straightforward '97 Riesling, showing peach and almond notes, bright acidity and a dry finish. Drink now through 2004.–B.S. • $13 • (2/28/1999) • **86**

Riesling Spätlese Nahe Monzinger Frühlingsplätzchen 1997: Seamless. Expressive of its site, this spätlese shows earth and stone flavors, a hint of peach and a firm underlying structure. Has good richness midpalate and an excellent finish. Best from 2001 through 2006.–B.S. • $24 • (2/28/1999) • **90**

Riesling Spätlese Nahe Monzinger Halenberg 1998: Seems backward and unevolved at this stage, hinting at lime and mineral aromas and flavors. Very sleek and intense, played out against a transparent backdrop. Needs time. Best from 2001 through 2006.–B.S. • $25 • (2/29/2000) • **87**

Riesling Spätlese Nahe Monzinger Halenberg 1997: This is singing now. All elegance and finesse, with a crystalline structure and citrus, peach and

GERMANY

mineral flavors, this white is vibrant and delicious. Drink now through 2007.–B.S. • $24 • (2/28/1999) • **89**

EYMAEL, ROBERT

Riesling Auslese Gold Cap Mosel-Saar-Ruwer Erdener Prälat 1998: Lean and wiry, this is spry, lively and densely textured, showing lime and spice notes and a creamy element. Drink now through 2004.–B.S. • $45 • (2/29/2000) • **90**

Riesling Auslese Gold Cap Mosel-Saar-Ruwer Ürziger Würzgarten 1997: Auction wine. A serious auslese, with superripe flavors of honey, orange and apricot against a minerally backdrop, an unctuous texture and a bright acidity that offsets the sweetness. Long, spicy finish. Best from 2002 through 2010.–B.S. • $NA/375 ml. • (2/28/1999) • **92**

Riesling Auslese Mosel-Saar-Ruwer Erdener Prälat 1997: Distinctive aromas and flavors of lime, pomegranate and orange mingle in this delicate, bright auslese. On the soft side, showing sweetness, moderate concentration and a dilute finish. Tasted twice, with consistent notes. Drink now through 2004.–B.S. • $22/375 ml. • (2/28/1999) • **86**

Riesling Auslese Mosel-Saar-Ruwer Ürziger Würzgarten 1997: Not showing a lot of character, but there's richness, density, a firm structure and an earthy element to match the peach and lime. Offers a long finish and shows promise. Best from 2002 through 2010.–B.S. • $31 • (2/28/1999) • **90**

Riesling Kabinett Mosel-Saar-Ruwer Erdener Treppchen 1997: Begins with floral aromas, then turns to almond and a hint of petrol on the palate, all in an attractive, easy-drinking package. Finishes short. Drink now.–B.S. • $15 • (2/28/1999) • **82**

Riesling Kabinett Mosel-Saar-Ruwer Ürziger Würzgarten Astor 1998: A snappy young white that shows apple and a hint of peach, as well as mineral notes, all on a crisp framework. Good length. Drink now through 2003.–B.S. • $15 • (2/29/2000) • **86**

Riesling Kabinett Mosel-Saar-Ruwer Ürziger Würzgarten Astor 1997: The aromas are muted now, but there are lovely slate and peach flavors interwoven with a rich, dense texture and juicy acidity. Not a blockbuster, but beautifully put together. Drink now through 2005.–B.S. • $15 • (2/28/1999) • **87**

Riesling QbA Mosel-Saar-Ruwer 1998: Simple and lushly textured, with moderate acidity for support, this white displays an apple note that lingers. Drink now through 2002.–B.S. • $12 • (2/29/2000) • **82**

Riesling QbA Mosel-Saar-Ruwer 1997: An off-dry style, showing peach, lime and mineral in an elegant presentation that's juicy and easy-drinking. Very well balanced and put together. Drink now through 2002.–B.S. • $11 • (2/28/1999) • **85**

Riesling Spätlese Mosel-Saar-Ruwer Erdener Treppchen 1997: Intense, pungent and spicy, this white transmits its slate soil origins, with a lot of flavor packed into the sleek, crystalline framework. Needs time to integrate. Drink through 2006–B.S. • $21 • (2/28/1999) • **90**

Riesling Spätlese Mosel-Saar-Ruwer Ürziger Würzgarten 1998: A powerful spätlese, this offers an amazing silkiness, harmony and bracing framework, with peach, lime and slate persisting to a long aftertaste. Tasted twice, with consistent notes. Best from 2001 through 2006.–B.S. • $21 • (2/29/2000) • **91**

Riesling Spätlese Mosel-Saar-Ruwer Ürziger Würzgarten 1997: A delicious Mosel spätlese, evoking apples, peaches, touches of spice and slate, all displayed on a succulent, vibrant framework that has concentration and length. Drink now through 2004.–B.S. • $21 • (2/28/1999) • **88**

FINKENAUER, CARL

Riesling Spätlese Nahe Kreuznacher Gutenthal 1998: Still suffering from bottling, this Riesling nonetheless has slate and lime character on a vibrant, scintillating structure. Needs time to sort itself out. Drink now through 2004.–B.S. • $17 • (2/29/2000) • **87**

FISCHER, DR.

Riesling Beerenauslese Mosel-Saar-Ruwer Ockfener Bockstein 1990 • $NA • (12/15/1991) • **88**

Riesling Eiswein Mosel-Saar-Ruwer Wawerner Herrenberg 1990 • $NA • (12/15/1991) • **88**

Riesling Kabinett Mosel-Saar-Ruwer Ockfener Bockstein 1998: A lean, tight kabinett with plenty of mineral notes, Granny Smith apple and citrus flavors. Leaves a puckering sensation, yet it's attractive overall. Best from 2001 through 2004.–B.S. • $13 • (1/01/2000) • **84**

Riesling QbA Mosel-Saar-Ruwer Ockfener Bockstein 1998: A nice delicacy to the peach, citrus and mineral flavors held together by moderate acidity. Tasty. Drink now through 2002.–B.S. • $10 • (2/29/2000) • **85**

FITZ-RITTER

Riesling Kabinett Halbtrocken Pfalz Dürkheimer Abtsfronhof 1998: Starts out subtly, building in intensity to a long, satisfying conclusion. Dense and smoothly wrought, extremely harmonious and balanced, with a lingering finish. Drink now through 2003.–B.S. • $12 • (2/29/2000) • **87**

Riesling Spätlese Trocken Pfalz Dürkheimer Abtsfronhof 1998: Lean and trim, with residual carbon dioxide, this dry spätlese offers knees and elbows today, courtesy of the bracing structure. Needs food. Best after 2001.–B.S. • $13 • (1/01/2000) • **83**

FRIEDRICH-WILHELM-GYMNASIUM

Riesling Auslese Mosel-Saar-Ruwer Graacher Himmelreich 1997: Rich and forward, this has simple peach and mineral flavors intertwined with generous character and a soft structure. For early drinking. Drink now through 2004.–B.S. • $24 • (2/28/1999) • **84**

Riesling Beerenauslese Mosel-Saar-Ruwer Graacher Himmelreich 1989 • $150 • (12/15/1990) • **90**

Riesling Kabinett Mosel-Saar-Ruwer Graacher Himmelreich 1997: Seems a little green and herbal. Shows richness midpalate, with straightforward apple flavors and a moderate finish.–B.S. • $12 • (2/28/1999) • **79**

Riesling Kabinett Mosel-Saar-Ruwer Neumagener Rosengärtchen 1997: Already petrolly, this seems advanced, but has a vibrant structure and finishes a little awkwardly, with a marzipan note and an astringent feel.–B.S. • $12 • (2/28/1999) • **78**

Riesling Spätlese Mosel-Saar-Ruwer Graacher Himmelreich 1997: A simple white showing modest peach and apple flavors and balancing acidity. Drink now.–B.S. • $16 • (2/28/1999) • **83**

Riesling Spätlese Mosel-Saar-Ruwer Trittenheimer Apotheke 1997: A solid spätlese, showing peach and hints of coconut, a soft structure and moderate intensity and concentration followed by a green apple finish. Drink now through 2004.–B.S. • $16 • (2/28/1999) • **85**

FÜRST LOWENSTEIN

Riesling Beerenauslese Rheingau 1994 • $NA • (11/30/1995) • **83**

GALLAIS, LE

Riesling Auslese Gold Cap Mosel-Saar-Ruwer Wiltinger braune Kupp 1996 • $NA/375 ml. • (11/30/1997) • **92**

Riesling Beerenauslese Mosel-Saar-Ruwer Wiltinger braune Kupp 1994 • $NA • (11/30/1995) • **90**

Riesling Beerenauslese Mosel-Saar-Ruwer Wiltingener braune Kupp 1990 • $NA • (12/15/1991) • **96**

Riesling Beerenauslese Mosel-Saar-Ruwer Wiltingener braune Kupp 1989 • $NA • (12/15/1990) • **91**

Riesling Kabinett Mosel-Saar-Ruwer Wiltinger braune Kupp 1996 • $21 • (11/30/1997) • **83**

Riesling Spätlese Mosel-Saar-Ruwer Wiltinger braune Kupp 1997: More like a '96 in character, this austere, lean white smells like roses and stones, while on the palate there are complex flavors of peach, citrus and mineral, tightly wound and married to a steely framework. Young and unevolved, this baby needs time. From Egon Müller. Best from 2002 through 2010.–B.S. • $33 • (2/28/1999) • **92**

Riesling Spätlese Mosel-Saar-Ruwer Wiltinger braune Kupp 1996 • $33 • (11/30/1997) • **81**

Riesling Trockenbeerenauslese Mosel-Saar-Ruwer Wiltingener braune Kupp 1989 • $NA • (12/15/1990) • **95**

GÄNZ, DR.

Riesling Eiswein Nahe Guldentaler Sonnenberg 1998: Delicately flavored with peach and honey, this subtle eiswein rides a wave of laserlike acidity to the lingering finale. Muted today, it's structured to age. Best from 2001 through 2008.–B.S. • $59/375 ml. • (1/01/2000) • **88**

Riesling Spätlese Halbtrocken Nahe Guldentaler Sonnenberg 1998: This '98 off-dry white is packed with spice and stone flavors, along with nectarine and passion fruit. Good weight and power drive the flavors to a fine conclusion. Drink now through 2004.–B.S. • $17 • (1/01/2000) • **86**

Riesling Spätlese Trocken Nahe Tradition 1997: Austere and dry, this delivers herb and candied lemon peel aromas, with flavors of candied lemon, vanilla custard and mineral. Medium-bodied, with a soft structure and lingering finish. Drink now through 2002.–B.S. • $NA • (5/15/2000) • **85**

GRAF VON NEIPPERG

Lemberger Spätlese Trocken Württemberg Schwaigerner Ruthe 1990 • $20 • (3/31/1995) • **77**

Rotwein QbA Württemberg 1993 • $10 • (3/31/1995) • **80**

Schwarzriesling Kabinett Trocken Württemberg Neipperger Schlossberg 1992 • $14 • (3/31/1995) • **78**

GRAFF, CARL

Riesling Auslese Mosel-Saar-Ruwer Erdener Prälat 1997: Prematurely developed, with an insipid sweetness that sits apart from the pine and almond flavors. Tasted twice, with consistent notes.–B.S. • $14 • (5/15/1999) • **72**

Riesling Auslese Mosel-Saar-Ruwer Ürziger Würzgarten 1997: Already showing petrol, marzipan and a forest-floor character. A poor example of an estate Riesling auslese. Tasted twice, with consistent notes.–B.S. • $13 • (5/15/1999) • **70**

Riesling QbA Mosel-Saar-Ruwer Piesporter Michelsberg 1997: Apple, peach and mineral aromas and flavors lean toward a tinned fruit character, but it's light and refreshing.–B.S. • $7 • (1/01/1999) • **78**

Riesling Spätlese Mosel-Saar-Ruwer Wehlener Sonnenuhr 1997: Simple, showing just an insipid canned fruit character. A very weak effort from a great vineyard site.–B.S. • $9 • (1/01/1999) • **74**

GRANS-FASSIAN

Riesling Auslese Gold Cap * Mosel-Saar-Ruwer Leiwener Laurentiuslay 1998:** Really ripe and exotic, showing slight botrytis notes of pineapple, dried apricot and honey, all on a focused, fiber-optic framework. A bit lean and tight today, it should come together in time. Best from 2002 through 2010.–B.S. • $35/375 ml. • (2/29/2000) • **92**

Riesling Auslese Gold Cap Mosel-Saar-Ruwer Trittenheimer Apotheke 1998: Fine aromas and flavors of vanilla custard and lime, but not very expressive at this point. Has good structure and length, ending a little pinched. Best after 2000.–B.S. • $58/375 ml. • (1/01/2000) • **87**

Riesling Eiswein Mosel-Saar-Ruwer 1993 • $250 • (11/30/1994) • **93**

Riesling Eiswein Mosel-Saar-Ruwer 1992 • $NA • (11/30/1993) • **93**

Riesling Kabinett Mosel-Saar-Ruwer Trittenheimer Altärchen 1998: Lovely character in this creamy, lime-tinged '98. Vibrant and elegant, with concentrated fruit and fine length on the finish, leaving a piecrust aftertaste. Well done. Drink now through 2005.–B.S. • $16 • (2/29/2000) • **89**

Riesling Spätlese Mosel-Saar-Ruwer Trittenheimer Apotheke 1998: Big and creamy, with a pineapple aroma and flavor augmenting the apple and lime. Bracing for its firm backbone of acidity, and lingering on the palate. Drink now through 2005.–B.S. • $24 • (2/29/2000) • **89**

GRIMM, GEBRÜDER

Riesling Kabinett Rheingau Rüdesheimer Burgweg 1998: A pronounced citrus aroma marks this white. Concentrated, yet the citrus and mineral notes and firm structure are disjointed. May come together. Best after 2000.–B.S. • $15 • (1/01/2000) • **81**

Riesling Spätlese Rheingau Rüdesheimer Berg Rottland 1998: Starts off rich and spicy, after which a tidal wave of bracing acidity sweeps across the palate. Backward, it requires patience–or fish, poultry and pork dishes. Best after 2000.–B.S. • $23 • (2/29/2000) • **87**

GUNDERLOCH

Riesling Auslese Gold Cap Rheinhessen Nackenheim Rothenberg 1998: Wow! An incredible juxtaposition of sweetness and searing acidity supports the exotic aromas of dried apricot, fig and honey, all in an ethereal presentation that just melts away on the palate. This enters like a lion and exits like a lamb. Drink now through 2010.–B.S. • $40/375 ml. • (2/29/2000) • **93**

Riesling Auslese Gold Cap Rheinhessen Nackenheimer Rothenberg 1997: Smooth and suave, like a vanilla custard dessert, this '97 is rich, sweet and concentrated without getting heavy or cloying due to its brilliant, crystalline structure. Flavors of warm brioche, honey, piecrust and nectarine wash over the palate, ending in a long aftertaste. Drink now through 2012.–B.S. • $75 • (2/28/1999) • **93**

Riesling Auslese Gold Cap Rheinhessen Nackenheim Rothenberg 1996 • $75 • (11/30/1997) • **86**

Riesling Auslese Rheinhessen Nackenheim Rothenberg 1998: Extremely aromatic, yet very focused and packed with dried apricot, lime and mineral notes. Though dense and concentrated, it needs time for all the elements to integrate. Best from 2002 through 2010.–B.S. • $33 • (2/29/2000) • **92**

Riesling Auslese * Rheinhessen Nackenheim Rothenberg 1998:** Distinctive. A touch of carbon dioxide here, but it doesn't flatten the exuberance of this dryish, powerful Riesling auslese. There's a keen, spicy edge to the mineral and lime notes, and the finish goes on and on. Best from 2001 through 2010.–B.S. • $40 • (2/29/2000) • **91**

Riesling Auslese Rheinhessen Nackenheimer Rothenberg 1997: Difficult to assess. Very ripe, yet full-bodied and drier in style, this is packed with smoke, peach and spice flavors, vibrant acidity and alcohol that dominates on the finish. Impressive, but needs time to come together. Try through 2006.–B.S. • $33 • (2/28/1999) • **91**

Riesling Auslese * Rheinhessen Nackenheimer Rothenberg 1997:** A drier style of auslese. Pungent with red berries, almonds and smoke, this is ripe and assertive, with a succulent texture and bright acidity. A touch of alcohol on the finish lends a slight coarseness now, but there's plenty of ripe fruit to match. Gunderloch's three stars here indicate a traditional winemaking style in which fermantation is allowed to complete naturally. Drink through 2005.–B.S. • $40 • (2/28/1999) • **91**

Riesling Auslese Rheinhessen Nackenheim Rothenberg 1996 • $33 • (11/30/1997) • **82**

Riesling Beerenauslese Gold Cap Rheinhessen Nackenheim Rothenberg 1998: Wonderfully rich and sweet, yet extremely elegant, this dessert-style Riesling glides across the palate effortlessly, then wave upon wave of flavor follows. The firm backbone is covered by the sweetness today, but this should age beautifully. Drink now through 2012.–B.S. • $123/375 ml. • (2/29/2000) • **94**

Riesling Beerenauslese Rheinhessen Nackenheim Rothenberg 1996 • $99/375 ml. • (11/30/1997) • **93**

Riesling Beerenauslese Rheinhessen Nackenheim Rothenberg 1994 • $96 • (11/30/1995) • **90**

Riesling Beerenauslese Rheinhessen Nackenheim Rothenberg 1993 • $90 • (11/30/1994) • **90**

Riesling Beerenauslese Rheinhessen Nackenheim Rothenberg 1992 •$74/375 ml. • (11/30/1993) • **99**

Riesling Kabinett Rheinhessen Jean-Baptiste 1998: Delicious, erupting in a cascade of juicy grapefruit, peach and spice displayed on a lively structure. Balanced, it finishes on a lingering mineral note. Drink now through 2005.–B.S. • $15 • (2/29/2000) • **88**

Riesling Kabinett Rheinhessen Jean-Baptiste 1997: A little sulfur smell now, with ripe peach, spice and mineral flavors underneath. Slightly hard also (again, from the sulfur), this has the elements but needs time to integrate. Drink through 2006.–B.S. • $15 • (2/28/1999) • **85**

Riesling Kabinett Rheinhessen Jean-Baptiste 1996 • $15 • (11/30/1997) • **87**

Riesling QbA Rheinhessen Diva 1997: Pungent aromas and flavors of red berries and spice are the hallmarks of this softly textured, lush '97 that's distinctive and immediately appealing. Drink now through 2003.–B.S. • $17 • (2/28/1999) • **85**

Riesling QbA Rheinhessen Dry 1998: Pure, focused and opulent for a dry Riesling, this suave white boasts spring blossom, peach and spice notes, all finely balanced and with power in reserve. Drink now through 2008.–B.S. • $14 • (1/01/2000) • **89**

Riesling QbA Rheinhessen Dry 1997: A fresh Riesling, with earth and spice character, rich texture and bright acidity. It finishes dry. Drink now through 2005.–B.S. • $15 • (2/28/1999) • **83**

Riesling Spätlese Rheinhessen Nackenheim Rothenberg 1998: Bursting with ripe, juicy peach, apricot, spice and citrus. Just delicious for its effortless balance, seamless texture and elegance. Drink now through 2005.–B.S. • $24 • (2/29/2000) • **90**

Riesling Spätlese Rheinhessen Nackenheim Rothenberg 1997: This spätlese puts it all together. Beautifully focused, ripe flavors of apricot, spice, smoke and mineral ride a wave of acidity through to the long finish. It's concentrated yet transparent, giving the flavors clarity. Drink now through 2007.–B.S. • $24 • (2/28/1999) • **91**

Riesling Spätlese Rheinhessen Nackenheim Rothenberg 1996 • $24 • (11/30/1997) • **88**

Riesling Trockenbeerenauslese Gold Cap Rheinhessen Nackenheim Rothenberg 1998: So pure, so ethereal, so harmonious, it's hard to believe this is so sweet. Young, it's already exhibiting great balance and resolution

Key: SS—Spectator Selection. CS—Cellar Selection. HR—Highly Recommended. $NA—Price not available. (BT)—Barrel tasting. (A)—Auction Price. For a key to the tasters' initials, see "How to Use These Listings." **Dates in parentheses represent the issues in which the ratings were published.**

between the sugar and acidity, combining honey, apricot, green tea and mineral tones without much (any?) botrytis. The aftertaste lasts forever. Best from 2002 through 2020.–B.S. • $251/375 ml. • (2/29/2000) • **97**

Riesling Trockenbeerenauslese Rheinhessen Nackenheim Rothenberg 1996 • $251/375 ml. • (11/30/1997) HR • **100**

Riesling Trockenbeerenauslese Rheinhessen Nackenheim Rothenberg 1994 • $NA • (11/30/1995) • **95**

Riesling Trockenbeerenauslese Rheinhessen Nackenheim Rothenberg 1992 • $153/375 ml. • (11/30/1993) • **100**

GYSLER

Huxelrebe Beerenauslese Rheinhessen Weinheimer Kapellenberg 1994: Showing some maturity, yet there'a a good core of acidty keeping this elegant dessert wine lively and driving the butter, apricot and lime flavors. Fine mouthwatering finish. Drink now through 2002.–B.S. • $32 • (1/01/2000) • **88**

Riesling Eiswein Rheinhessen Weinheimer Hölle 1997 • $NA/500 ml. • (1/01/1998) • **93**

Riesling Eiswein Rheinhessen Weinheimer Hölle 1997: Racy and focused, with a core of peach, quince and mineral exhibiting density and length, this Riesling eiswein is a winner. It's tight and elegant right now, so be patient. Best from 2001 through 2007.–B.S. • $78/500 ml. • (5/15/2000) • **91**

Riesling Spätlese Halbtrocken Rheinhessen Weinheimer Hölle 1998: A distinctive nutty character introduces this austere, crisp white. Severe in its approach, without much fruit or personality. Drink now.–B.S. • $14 • (1/01/2000) • **80**

Riesling Spätlese Rheinhessen Weinheimer Hölle 1997: Rich and succulent, this white offers complex aromas and flavors of vanilla custard, peach and mineral in an open, easygoing way. The vibrant acidity is deceptive, with a grapefruit element on the finish. Drink now through 2006.–B.S. • $10 • (2/28/1999) • **89**

Riesling Spätlese Rheinhessen Weinheimer Mandelberg 1998: This '98 screams with acidity, making it difficult to unearth the apricot and smoke notes, but be patient—there's a lot going on here in a compact, austere style. Best from 2002 through 2010.–B.S. • $14 • (2/29/2000) • **87**

Riesling Trocken Rheinhessen Weinheimer Mandelberg 1997 • $NA • (1/01/1998) • **87**

HAAG, FRITZ

Riesling Auslese Gold Cap Mosel-Saar-Ruwer Brauneberger Juffer-Sonnenuhr 1998: Sleek and airy, showing intense lime and mineral on a gossamer texture. Elegant and concentrated, this is appealing now but should age well. Drink now through 2007.–B.S. • $65 • (2/29/2000) • **91**

Riesling Auslese Gold Cap Mosel-Saar-Ruwer Brauneberger Juffer-Sonnenuhr (AP 9) 1997: Elegant and forward, with ripe apricot, tropical fruit and mineral nuances, this '97 auslese vibrates on the palate. Smooth and succulent, with a lingering aftertaste of lime and honey. Best from 2002 through 2008.–B.S. • $65 • (2/28/1999) • **92**

Riesling Auslese Mosel-Saar-Ruwer Brauneberger Juffer-Sonnenuhr 1998: Lightweight and elegant, with peach and lime, this takes on a spicy quality midpalate. Clean and racy, yet a bit closed on the finish, so give it time. Best from 2001 through 2006.–B.S. • $41 • (2/29/2000) • **89**

Riesling Auslese Mosel-Saar-Ruwer Brauneberger Juffer-Sonnenuhr (AP 6) 1997: Lovely ripe fruit character, with aromas of peach and apricot that carry through to the finish. The rich texture retains a juiciness courtesy of the well-integrated acidity. Best from 2002 through 2008.–B.S. • $40 • (2/28/1999) • **90**

Riesling Kabinett Mosel-Saar-Ruwer 1998: A delicate style, shot through with zingy lime flavors and some mineral notes for complexity. Drink now through 2004.–B.S. • $18 • (2/29/2000) • **85**

Riesling Kabinett Mosel-Saar-Ruwer 1997: A straightforward Mosel kabinett, elegant and balanced, with restrained apple and citrus flavors, moderate concentration and finish. Drink now through 2004.–B.S. • $18 • (2/28/1999) • **83**

Riesling Kabinett Mosel-Saar-Ruwer Brauneberger Juffer 1996 • $15 • (4/30/1998) • **88**

Riesling Kabinett Mosel-Saar-Ruwer Brauneberger Juffer-Sonnenuhr 1998: Lovely kabinett. Rich and snappy, showing lime, peach and mineral aromas and flavors, quite focused and intense, ending with a touch of honey. Drink now through 2004.–B.S. • $22 • (2/29/2000) • **88**

Riesling Kabinett Mosel-Saar-Ruwer Brauneberger Juffer-Sonnenuhr 1997: Very zippy, offering lime, apple and slate accented by vanilla and almond, this complex kabinett packs all those flavors into a lithe, sinewy structure. Ends on an appley note. Drink through 2005.–B.S. • $22 • (2/28/1999) • **89**

Riesling QbA Mosel-Saar-Ruwer 1998: Lean, dense and structured, showing more earth and mineral than fruit at this stage. Still, it might come alive with food. Drink now through 2003.–B.S. • $15 • (2/29/2000) • **86**

Riesling QbA Mosel-Saar-Ruwer 1997: Austere in style, lean and intense, yet with a density you could almost cut with a knife; the peach and mineral flavors are hard-etched into a firm structure. Drink through 2005.–B.S. • $15 • (2/28/1999) • **85**

Riesling Spätlese Mosel-Saar-Ruwer Brauneberger Juffer-Sonnenuhr 1998: Lean and racy, full of peach, apple and slate notes woven into the ice-smooth texture. Just a touch on the tart side, yet the picture of elegance. Best after 2001.–B.S. • $30 • (2/29/2000) • **89**

Riesling Spätlese Mosel-Saar-Ruwer Brauneberger Juffer-Sonnenuhr 1997: Just what you want in a Mosel spätlese: ripe, succulent peach- and lime-tinged aromas and flavors, juicy acidity and a rich texture that makes it all seem so effortless. Drink now through 2006.–B.S. • $26 • (2/28/1999) • **91**

HAAG, WILLI

Riesling Auslese Gold Cap Mosel-Saar-Ruwer Brauneberger Juffer-Sonnenuhr (AP 10) 1997: Forward and open-knit. Purity of fruit is the hallmark of this '97 auslese, offering light peach, slate and lime flavors, with moderate structure and a modest finish. Drink now through 2003.–B.S. • $32 • (5/15/2000) • **87**

Riesling Kabinett Mosel-Saar-Ruwer Brauneberger Juffer (AP 4) 1998: Round and fleshy, reeking of slate with accents of vanilla and cream, this is a big kabinett, almost opulent, backed by a solid structure and a dense texture. Be patient with this baby. Drink through 2005.–B.S. • $15 • (2/29/2000) • **90**

Riesling QbA Mosel-Saar-Ruwer (AP 1) 1998: Juicy and concentrated, this QbA shows apricot and passion fruit on a lively backbone of acidity. A touch on the sweet side, but simply delicious. Drink now through 2002.–B.S. • $12 • (2/29/2000) • **87**

Riesling Spätlese Mosel-Saar-Ruwer Brauneberger Juffer (AP 5) 1998: Ripe, yet underscored by a firm structure, the almond, passion fruit and honey glide across the palate. There's density and expression, ending in an aftertaste of tropical fruit and mineral. Best from 2001 through 2008.–B.S. • $15 • (2/29/2000) • **88**

Riesling Spätlese Mosel-Saar-Ruwer Brauneberger Juffer-Sonnenuhr (AP 6) 1998: Very exotic, exhibiting honey, apricot and citrus. Starts out rich and powerful, then the firm backbone washes the palate with bracing acidity. Needs time to come together. Best from 2001 through 2006.–B.S. • $18 • (2/29/2000) • **89**

HAART, JOHANN

Riesling Auslese Mosel-Saar-Ruwer Piesporter Goldtröpfchen 1996 • $24/500 ml. • (4/30/1998) • **88**

Riesling Spätlese Mosel-Saar-Ruwer Piesporter Goldtröpfchen 1996 • $16 • (4/30/1998) • **83**

HAART, REINHOLD

Riesling Auslese Gold Cap Mosel-Saar-Ruwer Piesporter Goldtröpfchen 1998: Auction wine. Stunning for its ripeness and concentration, this Riesling auslese offers dried apricot, fig, honey and citrus notes, all bonded to a bright, racy structure. Packs in a lot of flavor on a lean frame. Best from 2001 through 2010.–B.S. • $NA/375 ml. • (1/01/2000) • **93**

Riesling Auslese Mosel-Saar-Ruwer Piesporter Domherr 1998: Bursting with slate, passion fruit and lime, all underscored by a firm acidity, this elegant auslese hits a home run. Fine density and length of flavor. Difficult to keep your hands off it now. Drink now through 2009.–B.S. • $36 • (2/29/2000) • **92**

Riesling Auslese Mosel-Saar-Ruwer Piesporter Goldtröpfchen 1997: An absolutely gorgeous auslese, even with botrytis—rare for '97—that adds an extra dimension to the honeyed apricot flavors in this unctuous, concentrated nectar. So delicious you want to drink it now, but it will only get better. Best from 2003 through 2012.–B.S. • $38 • (2/28/1999) • **94**

Riesling Auslese Mosel-Saar-Ruwer Piesporter Goldtröpfchen (AP 8) 1996 • $36 • (11/30/1997) • **89**

Riesling Auslese Mosel-Saar-Ruwer Piesporter Goldtröpfchen (AP 11) 1996 • $NA/375 ml. • (11/30/1997) • **91**

Riesling Beerenauslese Mosel-Saar-Ruwer Piesporter Goldtröpfchen 1996 • $162 • (11/30/1997) • **93**

Riesling Beerenauslese Mosel-Saar-Ruwer Piesporter Goldtröpfchen 1995 • $NA • (11/30/1996) • **85**

Riesling Beerenauslese Mosel-Saar-Ruwer Piesporter Goldtröpfchen 1994 • $NA • (11/30/1995) • **94**

■ ■ ■ ■

HAART, REINHOLD

Riesling Eiswein Mosel-Saar-Ruwer Piesporter Goldtröpfchen 1998: Wow! Rich and intense, with a slight herbal edge but also plenty of butterscotch and caramel. The acidity is a little more civilized, balancing all the elements nicely. Best from 2001 through 2009.–B.S. • $140/375 ml. • (2/29/2000) • **92**

Riesling Kabinett Mosel-Saar-Ruwer Piesporter Goldtröpfchen 1998: Fleshy, round and concentrated, this '98 white delivers plenty of slate, lime and peach in a focused manner. A bit more amplitude here also. Drink now through 2004.–B.S. • $19 • (2/29/2000) • **87**

Riesling Kabinett Mosel-Saar-Ruwer Piesporter Goldtröpfchen 1997: A little sulfur aroma is initially evident, but dissipates with air. Underneath that, however, is a crunchy, dense, complex wine with pineapple accents and a racy character. Long, reverberating finish. Drink through 2005.–B.S. • $19 • (2/28/1999) • **89**

Riesling Kabinett Mosel-Saar-Ruwer Piesporter Goldtröpfchen 1996 • $19 • (11/30/1997) • **90**

Riesling QbA Halbtrocken Mosel-Saar-Ruwer 1997: Sulfur dominates the aromas and mutes the flavors at this stage, but this '97 white has richness and clarity, along with apple and nectarine flavors, ending on a subtle, refreshing note. Tasted twice, with consistent notes. Drink through 2005.–B.S. • $15 • (2/28/1999) • **84**

Riesling Spätlese Mosel-Saar-Ruwer Piesporter Goldtröpfchen 1998: Beautiful spätlese. Bold, ripe and dense, this is serious stuff. Apricot, lime and slate combine with a firm yet opulent texture, leading into a long, mineral and citrus finish. Drink now through 2005.–B.S. • $28 • (2/29/2000) • **91**

Riesling Spätlese Mosel-Saar-Ruwer Piesporter Goldtröpfchen 1997: Lime, spice and a fleeting note of red berries are the highlights of this delicate white that exhibits a tensile structure, well-integrated acidity and superlong finish. Drink now through 2006.–B.S. • $28 • (2/28/1999) • **90**

Riesling Spätlese Mosel-Saar-Ruwer Piesporter Goldtröpfchen 1996 • $28 • (11/30/1997) • **91**

Riesling Spätlese Mosel-Saar-Ruwer Wintricher Ohligsberg 1998: Rich and ripe, sporting a hint of botrytis along with peach, lime and slate, a creamy texture and a fleshy profile. The structure carries the flavors to a long aftertaste of peach and licorice. Terrific stuff. Best from 2001 through 2006.–B.S. • $28 • (2/29/2000) • **92**

Riesling Trockenbeerenauslese Mosel-Saar-Ruwer Piesporter Goldtröpfchen 1993 • $NA • (11/30/1994) • **95**

HEDDESDORFF, FREIHERR VON

Riesling Auslese Mosel-Saar-Ruwer Winninger Röttgen 1998: Exuberant from the start, displaying its ripe lime, honey and nectarine flavors on a medium structure, but it doesn't deliver on the end. Drink now through 2004.–B.S. • $25/500 ml. • (2/29/2000) • **88**

Riesling Kabinett Mosel-Saar-Ruwer Winninger Uhlen 1998: This seems like spätlese-level ripeness, and the flavors of lime, honey, mineral and spice are intriguing, all put together on a gossamer structure. Drink now through 2004.–B.S. • $16 • (2/29/2000) • **87**

Riesling Spätlese Mosel-Saar-Ruwer Winninger Uhlen 1998: Textbook aromas and flavors of peach, melon, lime and mineral in this round, concentrated spätlese. Very creamy in texture, with a lingering finish. Great concentration and depth. Drink now through 2006.–B.S. • $20 • (2/29/2000) • **89**

HEGER, DR.

Grauburgunder Spätlese Trocken Baden 1997: Lovely Pinot Gris character in this dry white. Peach is the main element, supported by stone, smoke and a slight nuttiness, all on a firm structure, yet with concentration and generosity. Well made. Drink now through 2002.–B.S. • $28 • (5/15/1999) • **87**

Grauburgunder Spätlese Trocken * Baden 1997:** Distinctive. Heavily marked by new oak, but with enough flesh and richness to match. The aromas and flavors evoke vanilla, apricot and grapefruit, with a thick texture and a hint of bitterness, which along with the acidity keeps it crisp and focused. Drink now through 2003.–B.S. • $32 • (5/15/1999) • **88**

Silvaner Spätlese Trocken * Baden 1997:** Peach and vanilla custard notes mingle with the rich texture in this dry, attractive white. Fine as an aperitif or when dining alfresco. Drink now.–B.S. • $NA • (1/01/1999) • **85**

Key: SS—Spectator Selection. CS—Cellar Selection. HR—Highly Recommended. $NA—Price not available. (BT)—Barrel tasting. Ⓐ—Auction Price. For a key to the tasters' initials, see "How to Use These Listings." **Dates in parentheses represent the issues in which the ratings were published.**

Weissburgunder Spätlese Trocken * Baden 1997:** Intriguing. Marked by new oak, adding smoke and vanilla accents to the citrus and apple flavors; the rich texture absorbs the oak nicely, while the vibrant acidity acts as a perfect foil. An interplay of oak and fruit lingers on the finish. Drink now through 2001.–B.S. • $32 • (5/15/1999) • **88**

HEGER, JOACHIM

Pinot Blanc QbA Trocken Baden 1997: Rich and mouthfilling, this dry white displays apple and grapefruit elements with firm underlying structure. Drink now.–B.S. • $15 • (5/15/1999) • **83**

Pinot Gris QbA Trocken Baden 1997: Broad aromas and flavors of almond and beeswax form the core of this lean, dry white. An interesting spice component lingers, but the wine remains austere. Drink now.–B.S. • $15 • (5/15/1999) • **82**

Pinot Noir QbA Trocken Baden 1997: Don't judge this red by its color. There are surprisingly deep flavors of black cherry, earth and smoky bacon fat, and a bit of alcohol, too. The finish is on the astringent side, but food may fix that. Fine effort. Drink now through 2002.–B.S. • $16 • (5/15/1999) • **85**

HERRNSHEIM, HEYL ZU

QbA Rheinhessen Baron von Heyl 1998: A straightforward, fruity white offering peach and citrus flavors, balanced and elegant. Drink now.–B.S. • $10 • (5/15/2000) • **81**

Riesling Auslese Rheinhessen Niersteiner Pettental 1996 • $22 • (11/30/1997) • **88**

Riesling Kabinett Rheinhessen Nierstein 1998: Like vanilla custard, this '98 white is subtle in aroma, but bursts on the palate with grapefruit, vanilla and white peach flavors. Moderate in length and creamy on the finish. Drink now through 2004.–B.S. • $14 • (2/29/2000) • **87**

Riesling Kabinett Rheinhessen Niersteiner Ölberg Schloss Mathildenhof 1997: Lacks ripeness, with green apple flavors, tart acidity and only modest concentration. A weak effort.–B.S. • $13 • (2/28/1999) • **76**

Riesling Kabinett Rheinhessen Niersteiner Ölberg Schloss Mathildenhof 1996 • $12 • (11/30/1997) • **87**

Riesling Kabinett Trocken Rheinhessen Niersteiner Pettental 1996 • $12 • (11/30/1997) • **87**

Riesling QbA Rheinhessen Niersteiner Spiegelberg 1996 • $9 • (11/30/1997) • **77**

Riesling QbA Rheinhessen Wormser Liebfrauenstift-Kirchenstück 1997: Aromatically, this white exudes spice and pine, with apricot and stony flavors matched to a soft structure and open-knit texture. Drink now.–B.S. • $13 • (5/15/2000) • **83**

Riesling QbA Trocken Rheinhessen Wormser Liebfrauenstift-Kirchenstück 1998: Rich and spicy, exuding a combination of quince and earth notes, fine concentration and length, though a bit austere on the finish. Drink now through 2003.–B.S. • $10 • (2/29/2000) • **85**

Riesling Spätlese Halbtrocken Rheinhessen Niersteiner Pettental 1996 • $17 • (11/30/1997) • **84**

Riesling Spätlese Rheinhessen Niersteiner Brudersberg 1996 • $18 • (11/30/1997) • **88**

Riesling Spätlese Rheinhessen Niersteiner Pettental 1998: Pungent and spicy, smelling and tasting of oak treatment. Broad and rustic in style, but concentrated, interesting and distinctive. Drink now through 2005.–B.S. • $20 • (2/29/2000) • **88**

Riesling Spätlese Rheinhessen Niersteiner Pettental 1997: Rich and round, this white has the underlying power and solid framework to support the almond and quince flavors. Concentrated and dense, with a lingering aftertaste of peach. Best from 2001 through 2007.–B.S. • $20 • (2/28/1999) • **88**

Riesling Spätlese Rheinhessen Wormser Liebfrauenstift-Kirchenstück 1997: Baroque in style, with weight and power and flavors ranging from vanilla custard and almond to lemon and mineral. Firm finish. Drink now through 2004.–B.S. • $19 • (5/15/2000) • **86**

Riesling Spätlese Trocken Rheinhessen Wormser Liebfrauenstift-Kirchenstück 1998: Straightforward, showing subtle grapefruit and peach flavors, with good richness midpalate before falling off quickly. Drink now through 2004.–B.S. • $20 • (1/01/2000) • **86**

Riesling Trocken Rheinhessen Niersteiner 1996 • $11 • (11/30/1997) • **87**

Riesling Trockenbeerenauslese Rheinhessen Niersteiner Olberg 1989 • $50 • (12/15/1990) • **90**

Silvaner QbA Trocken Rheinhessen Nierstein Rosenberg 1997: Ripe, rich and full of apple and lemon flavors, this dry white shows enough flesh to match its firmness. Moderate intensity and a good, lingering finish. Drink now.–B.S. • $13 • (1/01/1999) • **83**

Silvaner Trocken Rheinhessen Niersteiner Rosenberg 1996 • $12 • (11/30/1997) • **81**

HESSEN, PRINZ VON

Riesling Kabinett Rheingau Johannisberger Klaus 1998: Tightly wound, a densely textured, lean and firmly built kabinett. The flavors range from grapefruit to peach and mineral, finishing slightly coarse. Best from 2001 through 2004.–B.S. • $12 • (2/29/2000) • **86**

Riesling QbA Halbtrocken Rheingau Rüdesheimer Bischofsberg 1998: A charmer, this offers fine peach and citrus aromas and flavors, richness and a juicy texture. A touch firm on the finish, but food should tame it. Drink now through 2003.–B.S. • $12 • (1/01/2000) • **84**

Riesling Spätlese Rheingau Johannisberger Klaus 1998: Piquant, this '98 Riesling mixes orange, nectarine and spice to jazz up the palate. Good concentration and density on a vibrant framework. Drink now through 2004.–B.S. • $18 • (2/29/2000) • **88**

HÖVEL, VON

Riesling Auslese Gold Cap Mosel-Saar-Ruwer Oberemmeler Hütte 1998: Auction wine. An extreme style, ripe and a bit top-heavy, although it has plenty of bracing acidity for backbone. The flavors range from dried apricot to caramel. Drink now through 2006.–B.S. • $NA/375 ml. • (1/01/2000) • **87**

Riesling Auslese Gold Cap Mosel-Saar-Ruwer Oberemmeler Hütte 1997: A liquid dessert. Intriguing aromas and flavors of vanilla custard, honey, lime and even mandarin orange weave throughout this suave, ethereal white. Rich, yet focused by intense, citrusy acidity, giving it class and finesse. Best from 2002 through 2012.–B.S. • $35/375 ml. • (2/28/1999) • **92**

Riesling Auslese Mosel-Saar-Ruwer Oberemmeler Hütte 1997: A powerful '97 auslese, this has weight, density and an electric acidity that pumps the peach and apple flavors through the citrusy finish. Needs time to integrate. Best from 2002 through 2010.–B.S. • $30 • (2/28/1999) • **88**

Riesling Auslese Mosel-Saar-Ruwer Scharzhofberger 1997: Has a creamy texture balanced by a racy structure, with lime, peach and slate aromas and flavors all tightly wound. Good, not great, concentration, but don't touch this now, it needs time to integrate. Best from 2002 through 2010.–B.S. • $30 • (2/28/1999) • **89**

Riesling Beerenauslese Mosel-Saar-Ruwer Oberemmeler Hütte 1989 • $88/375 ml. • (12/15/1990) • **93**

Riesling Eiswein Mosel-Saar-Ruwer Oberemmeler Hütte 1995 • $NA/375 ml. • (11/30/1996) • **90**

Riesling Eiswein Mosel-Saar-Ruwer Oberemmeler Hütte 1993 • $NA • (11/30/1994) • **91**

Riesling Eiswein Mosel-Saar-Ruwer Oberemmeler Hütte 1989 • $147/375 ml. • (12/15/1990) • **87**

Riesling Kabinett Mosel-Saar-Ruwer Oberemmeler Hütte 1998: Very elegant, underscored by juicy acidity, while the flavors lean toward warm spices and slate. Not flamboyant, but it grows on you. Drink now through 2004.–B.S. • $16 • (2/29/2000) • **87**

Riesling Kabinett Mosel-Saar-Ruwer Oberemmeler Hütte 1997: There's a purity and definition here, with lovely pineapple, lime and mineral aromas and flavors, along with elegance, harmony and a lingering finish. Drink now through 2004.–B.S. • $16 • (2/28/1999) • **88**

Riesling Kabinett Mosel-Saar-Ruwer Oberemmeler Hütte 1996 • $14 • (11/30/1997) • **87**

Riesling Kabinett Mosel-Saar-Ruwer Scharzhofberger 1998: This is ripe, with a little added depth from the honey and spice notes, along with lime and mineral. Still, it lacks structure and follow through. Drink now through 2003.–B.S. • $16 • (2/29/2000) • **84**

Riesling Kabinett Mosel-Saar-Ruwer Scharzhofberger 1996 • $14 • (11/30/1997) • **87**

Riesling QbA Mosel-Saar-Ruwer Balduin von Hövel 1998: This wine shows serious ripeness for a QbA, exuding pineapple, honey and apricot aromas and flavors. Everything is balanced, and there's just enough acidity to keep it fresh. Drink now through 2003.–B.S. • $12 • (2/29/2000) HR • **89**

Riesling QbA Mosel-Saar-Ruwer Balduin von Hövel 1997: Like a fruit cocktail in flavor, this QbA is simple and direct in a soft, easygoing way. Tasted twice, with consistent notes.–B.S. • $12 • (2/28/1999) • **79**

Riesling QbA Mosel-Saar-Ruwer Balduin von Hövel 1996 • $11 • (11/30/1997) • **82**

Riesling Spätlese Mosel-Saar-Ruwer Oberemmeler Hütte 1998: Auction wine. Some lifted aromas in this elegant, structured '98 and perhaps botrytis, yet the almond and citrus notes seem light, though there's a moderate finish. Drink now through 2003.–B.S. • $NA • (1/01/2000) • **84**

Riesling Spätlese Mosel-Saar-Ruwer Oberemmeler Hütte 1997: Here's a ripe, exotic '97 that's young and backward. Firmly structured, dense and concentrated, it exhibits a lot of power and richness, with an appley finish. Be patient. Best from 2002 through 2009.–B.S. • $19 • (2/28/1999) • **90**

Riesling Spätlese Mosel-Saar-Ruwer Scharzhofberger 1997: Broad, ripe and big-boned for a Mosel, this is full of quince and passion fruit aromas and flavors, with concentration and a creamy texture. A firm, citrusy acidity keeps the elements lively. Drink now through 2006.–B.S. • $19 • (2/28/1999) • **90**

IMMICH-BATTERIEBERG

Riesling Kabinett Mosel-Saar-Ruwer 1998: Moderately concentrated peach and apricot flavors mark this round, straightforward kabinett. Drink now through 2004.–B.S. • $15 • (2/29/2000) • **82**

Riesling QbA Trocken Mosel-Saar-Ruwer 1998: On the earthy side of the flavor spectrum, with some peach and lime peeking through. Nicely balanced, with an underlying firmness. Drink now through 2005.–B.S. • $14/1 liter • (2/29/2000) • **86**

JAKOBY-MATHY

Riesling Auslese Mosel-Saar-Ruwer Kinheimer Rosenberg 1998: Very open, forward and transparent, offering spice, herb and lime, with a firm structure that clamps down on the finish. Best after 2000.–B.S. • $22 • (2/29/2000) • **84**

Riesling Auslese Mosel-Saar-Ruwer Kinheimer Rosenberg 1997: Sleek and firmly structured, this '97 white offers honey and mineral notes accented by peach. Shows good concentration without the extra ripeness of the top wines in this category. Best from 2002 through 2007.–B.S. • $15 • (2/28/1999) • **87**

Riesling Kabinett Mosel-Saar-Ruwer Kinheimer Rosenberg 1998: A straightforward kabinett offering lime, peach and slate flavors balanced by a vibrant structure, with a lingering finish. Drink now through 2003.–B.S. • $14 • (2/29/2000) • **85**

Riesling Kabinett Mosel-Saar-Ruwer Kinheimer Rosenberg 1997: Lean and minerally, this '97 kabinett is tightly wound and elegant. Firmly structured, it needs some time to open. Drink through 2006.–B.S. • $10 • (2/28/1999) • **82**

Riesling Spätlese Mosel-Saar-Ruwer Kinheimer Rosenberg 1998: A tangerine-grapefruit edge livens up this precision-balanced, filigreed white, while a mineral note lurks in the background. Needs some time to integrate. Best from 2001 through 2006.–B.S. • $17 • (2/29/2000) • **88**

Riesling Spätlese Mosel-Saar-Ruwer Kinheimer Rosenberg 1997: On the austere side, offering almond and apple aromas and flavors, this is muted in flavor, though it has a juicy, open structure, finishing on a lemony note. Drink through 2006.–B.S. • $12 • (2/28/1999) • **84**

JOHANNISBERG, SCHLOSS

Riesling Auslese Rheingau 1996 • $74 • (11/30/1997) • **91**

Riesling Beerenauslese Rheingau 1996 • $NA • (11/30/1997) • **92**

Riesling Eiswein Rheingau 1996 • $222 • (11/30/1997) • **93**

Riesling Eiswein Rheingau 1992 • $NA • (11/30/1993) • **85**

Riesling Kabinett Rheingau 1998: Fresh as a spring breeze, with peach and apple flavors displayed on a fleshy frame, with good support. Shows weight and richness. Drink now through 2003.–B.S. • $21 • (5/15/2000) • **86**

Riesling Kabinett Rheingau 1996 • $23 • (11/30/1997) • **88**

Riesling QbA Rheingau 1998: Shows austerity and reserve, yet it's moderately concentrated, exhibiting peach, lemon and mineral notes on a broad frame. Good subtle finish. Drink now through 2003.–B.S. • $17 • (5/15/2000) • **86**

Riesling QbA Rheingau 1996 • $15 • (11/30/1997) • **83**

Riesling Spätlese Rheingau 1998: Bold and fleshy, showing ripe apricot, nectarine and orange notes underscored by piquant acidity, keeping the whole package lively and long on the finish. Needs time. Best from 2001 through 2007.–B.S. • $29 • (5/15/2000) • **88**

Riesling Spätlese Rheingau 1996 • $28 • (11/30/1997) • **90**

Riesling Spätlese Trocken Rheingau 1996 • $27 • (11/30/1997) • **90**

JOHANNISHOF

Riesling Kabinett Rheingau Johannisberger Goldatzel 1998: A lovely Rheingau kabinett. Firm and spicy, complemented by peach, citrus and a juicy texture, all displayed on a tight framework. Forward in character. Drink now through 2004.–B.S. • $15 • (2/29/2000) • **87**

Riesling Kabinett Rheingau Johannisberger Goldatzel 1997: A racy, rich, dense and powerful white, this shows apricot ripeness and an earthy character derived from the vineyard. Sinewy, with a citrus intensity on the long, satisfying finish. Drink now through 2007.–B.S. • $14 • (2/28/1999) • **89**

Riesling Kabinett Rheingau Johannisberger Vogelsang 1997: Distinctive for its rose, almond and candied apple aromas and flavors, this has green apple acidity to keep it lively and elegant. Drink now through 2004.–B.S. • $13 • (2/28/1999) • **85**

Riesling Spätlese Rheingau Johannisberger Klaus 1998: A slender, shimmering '98, offering concentrated grapefruit, mineral and ripe apple notes on a compact structure. Best from 2001 through 2004.–B.S. • $20 • (2/29/2000) • **87**

Riesling Spätlese Rheingau Johannisberger Klaus 1997: This white has focus and a combination of floral and citrus notes wedded to a rich texture. An underlying firmness comes out on the lingering finish. Personality here. Drink through 2007.–B.S. • $19 • (2/28/1999) • **89**

Riesling Spätlese Rheingau Rüdesheimer Berg Rottland 1998: The creamy texture really highlights the lemon, peach and vanilla flavors in this juicy, elegant Riesling. Would make a fine aperitif. Drink now through 2006.–B.S. • $22 • (2/29/2000) • **88**

Riesling Spätlese Rheingau Rüdesheimer Berg Rottland 1997: A beautifully delineated, spicy, stony '97, with ripe peach notes and finely etched acidity. More like a Mosel wine than a typical Rheingau. Drink now through 2006.–B.S. • $22 • (2/28/1999) • **91**

JOST, TONI

Riesling Auslese Mittelrhein Bacharacher Hahn 1998: Difficult to taste from the carbonic gas, but seems to have plenty of ripe apricot and mineral beneath, allied to a sleek, vibrant structure. Needs time. Best from 2002 through 2010.–B.S. • $35/500 ml. • (2/29/2000) • **90**

Riesling Auslese Mittelrhein Bacharacher Hahn 1997: Intense aromas of apricot, but despite its ripeness, this '97 is delicate and airy, lilting across the palate rather than lunging. The flavors are persistent, followed by a lingering aftertaste. Drink now through 2005.–B.S. • $28/500 ml. • (2/28/1999) • **90**

Riesling Auslese Mittelrhein Bacharacher Hahn 1996 • $37 • (4/30/1998) • **90**

Riesling Eiswein Rheingau Wallufer Walkenberg 1998: Seamless and balanced, with a silky texture and bright acidity to frame the peach and lime flavors. Not big or in your face—it just makes you come back for more. Drink now through 2008.–B.S. • $287/500 ml. • (2/29/2000) • **92**

Riesling Kabinett Mittelrhein Bacharacher Hahn 1997: More Mosel in style than Rheingau, this soft, rich and slightly sweet '97 white has immediate appeal thanks to the peach flavor and succulent texture. Drink now through 2003.–B.S. • $17 • (2/28/1999) • **84**

Riesling Kabinett Mittelrhein Bacharacher Hahn 1996 • $17 • (4/30/1998) • **88**

Riesling Spätlese Halbtrocken Mittelrhein 1997 • $NA • (1/01/1998) • **85**

Riesling Spätlese Mittelrhein Bacharacher Hahn 1998: Beautiful slate- and peach-infused Riesling, very tightly wound and built for the long haul. Has a mix of crispness and density, ending in a peach and citrus aftertaste. Drink now through 2008.–B.S. • $31 • (2/29/2000) • **90**

Riesling Spätlese Mittelrhein Bacharacher Hahn 1997: An absolutely delicious spätlese, full of rich, creamy apricot and spice flavors and a supple texture, all supported by a citruslike acidity. It's concentrated and long on the palate. Drink now through 2006.–B.S. • $21 • (2/28/1999) • **90**

Riesling Spätlese Trocken * Mittelrhein Bacharacher Hahn 1997 • $NA • (1/01/1998) • **87**

Riesling Trockenbeerenauslese Mittelrhein Bacharacher Hahn 1993 • $NA • (11/30/1994) • **90**

KARLSMÜHLE

Riesling Auslese Gold Cap Mosel-Saar-Ruwer Kaseler Kehrnagel 1998: Fabulous interplay of ripe apricot, nectarine and mineral aromas and flavors on a velvety swath, supported by a racy structure. Fine length and depth of flavor. Best from 2002 through 2010.–B.S. • $47/500 ml. • (2/29/2000) • **93**

Riesling Auslese Gold Cap Mosel-Saar-Ruwer Lorenzhofer 1997: A gorgeous auslese. Huge aromas of pineapple, passion fruit, vanilla and mineral integrate with the rich, creamy texture and racy structure to create a fantastic taste experience. Superripe yet balanced, this is young and unevolved, so be patient. Best from 2004 through 2012.–B.S. • $30/500 ml. • (2/28/1999) • **93**

Riesling Auslese Mosel-Saar-Ruwer Lorenzhofer 1997: Focused and intense, this streamlined '97 auslese displays lime, peach and mineral flavors, with an orange note on the finish. A live-wire white that shows good ripeness, this is medium-sweet and structured for aging. Best from 2002 through 2008.–B.S. • $28 • (2/28/1999) • **89**

Riesling Eiswein Mosel-Saar-Ruwer Kaseler Kehrnagel 1998: Broad and rich, offering warm, baking apple and maple notes, with a tart citrus acidity supporting the whole. Should be interesting in a few years. Best after 2001.–B.S. • $142/500 ml. • (2/29/2000) • **92**

Riesling Eiswein Mosel-Saar-Ruwer Lorenzhofer 1997: Wow. Here's a racy version, with tart acidity overwhelming the flavors of lemon-lime, vanilla custard and marzipan and really dominating the finish; doubtful that it will be balanced in the future. Best from 2003 through 2020.–B.S. • $71/375 ml. • (2/28/1999) • **87**

Riesling Eiswein Mosel-Saar-Ruwer Lorenzhofer 1993 • $68 • (11/30/1994) • **81**

Riesling Kabinett Mosel-Saar-Ruwer Lorenzhofer Mäuerchen 1997: Bursting with aromas and flavors of ripe, juicy apples and peaches. Very precocious, yet there's no shortage of fine acidity to balance all the elements. Drink now through 2004.–B.S. • $14 • (2/28/1999) • **87**

Riesling Spätlese Mosel-Saar-Ruwer Kaseler Kehrnagel Patheiger 1997: Well made. Smoke, lime and red berry flavors are displayed on a delicate, sleek framework that is dense and firm. A mineral note intermingles from start to lingering finish. Best from 2001 through 2008.–B.S. • $20 • (2/28/1999) • **90**

Riesling Spätlese Mosel-Saar-Ruwer Kaseler Nies'chen 1997: A racehorse. Redolent of apples and almonds, this high-strung '97 Mosel displays screaming acidity, beautiful focus and clarity, dense flavors and a citrusy finish. Not imported into the U.S. Best from 2001 through 2008.–B.S. • $NA • (2/28/1999) • **91**

Riesling Spätlese Mosel-Saar-Ruwer Lorenzhöfer 1998: Very floral and on the sweet side for a spätlese, displaying ripe apricot, passion fruit and pineapple. Richly textured and firm in structure. Drink now through 2006.–B.S. • $25 • (2/29/2000) • **88**

KARP-SCHREIBER

Riesling Kabinett Mosel-Saar-Ruwer Brauneberger Juffer-Sonnenuhr 1997: Delicate and bright. Already beginning to lose its primary fruit and show slate flavors, while the sugar and acidity are integrating. Suggests that some '97s will develop quickly. Drink now through 2003.–B.S. • $19 • (1/01/2000) • **87**

Riesling QbA Mosel-Saar-Ruwer Brauneberger Juffer 1997: A little sweetness here balances the lively acidity, while the lime and mineral notes remain focused. Delicately wrought. Drink now through 2001.–B.S. • $15 • (1/01/2000) • **85**

KARTHÄUSERHOF

Riesling Auslese Mosel-Saar-Ruwer Eitelsbacher Karthäuserhofberg 1997: Lovely ripe apricot and pineapple aromas and flavors combine with a luscious texture and firm backbone in this mouthwatering white. Fine harmony, with pure flavors and a lingering finish. Drink now through 2008.–B.S. • $35 • (2/28/1999) • **89**

Riesling Eiswein Mosel-Saar-Ruwer Eitelsbacher Karthäuserhofberg (AP 33) 1995 • $92/375 ml. • (11/30/1996) • **95**

Riesling Eiswein Mosel-Saar-Ruwer Eitelsbacher Karthäuserhofberg (AP 36) 1995 • $NA/375 ml. • (11/30/1996) • **92**

Riesling Eiswein Mosel-Saar-Ruwer Eitelsbacher Karthäuserhofberg (AP 34) 1993 • $NA • (11/30/1994) • **83**

Riesling Kabinett Halbtrocken Mosel-Saar-Ruwer Eitelsbacher Karthäuserhofberg 1998: Crystal clear and off dry, this white's flavors revolve around mineral and spice, with a touch of almond. Shows density and concentration. Drink now through 2004.–B.S. • $20 • (2/29/2000) • **87**

Riesling Kabinett Halbtrocken Mosel-Saar-Ruwer Eitelsbacher Karthäuserhofberg 1996 • $17 • (11/30/1997) • **83**

Riesling Kabinett Mosel-Saar-Ruwer Eitelsbacher Karthäuserhofberg 1997: A thoroughbred. Intense and spicy, this white is packed with slate, lime and tropical fruit nuances, all tightly wound on a sleek, racy frame. Mouthwatering finish, with an aftertaste of passion fruit. Drink now through 2007.–B.S. • $19 • (2/28/1999) • **90**

Riesling Kabinett Mosel-Saar-Ruwer Eitelsbacher Karthäuserhofberg 1996 • $17 • (1/01/1998) • **90**

Riesling QbA Halbtrocken Mosel-Saar-Ruwer Eitelsbacher Karthäuserhofberg 1998: Round and fruity, this halbtrocken evokes apple, peach and spice flavors, with a firm, citruslike acidity underneath. Drink now through 2003.–B.S. • $15 • (2/29/2000) • **84**

Key: SS—Spectator Selection. CS—Cellar Selection. HR—Highly Recommended. $NA—Price not available. (BT)—Barrel tasting. (A)—Auction Price.
For a key to the tasters' initials, see "How to Use These Listings."
Dates in parentheses represent the issues in which the ratings were published.

Riesling QbA Mosel-Saar-Ruwer Eitelsbacher Karthäuserhofberg 1996 • $14 • (11/30/1997) • **88**

Riesling Spätlese Mosel-Saar-Ruwer Eitelsbacher Karthäuserhofberg 1997: Lovely richness here, peach and apricot flavors and a ripe, juicy acidity. Round and lip-smacking, it's delicious now and should develop well over the medium-term. Drink now through 2005.–B.S. • $25 • (2/28/1999) • **88**

Riesling Spätlese Mosel-Saar-Ruwer Eitelsbacher Karthäuserhofberg 1996 • $24 • (11/30/1997) • **87**

KERPEN, HERIBERT

Riesling Auslese * Mosel-Saar-Ruwer Wehlener Sonnenuhr 1998: Wow. Layers of lime, passion fruit and slate unfold as if suspended in air, like a reduction that's been emulsified. Impeccably balanced and delicate, with a long finish. Drink now through 2008.–B.S. • $32 • (2/29/2000) • **92**

Riesling Auslese Mosel-Saar-Ruwer Wehlener Sonnenuhr 1997: A slim, compact Mosel auslese, sporting citrus flavors of lime and grapefruit. The mix ends up not too sweet, probably due to the zingy acidity, and the flavors persist through the long finish. Best from 2001 through 2007.–B.S. • $21 • (2/28/1999) • **91**

Riesling Auslese ** Mosel-Saar-Ruwer Wehlener Sonnenuhr 1997: Smells like the vanilla of new oak. Could it be? Overall a delicious young auslese, with lime and mineral flavors allied to a racy structure and rich texture. Well balanced and long. Best from 2002 through 2008.–B.S. • $37 • (2/28/1999) • **90**

Riesling Beerenauslese Mosel-Saar-Ruwer Wehlener Sonnenuhr 1990 • $66/375 ml. • (12/15/1991) • **91**

Riesling Eiswein Mosel-Saar-Ruwer Bernkasteler Bratenhöfchen 1992 • $NA • (11/30/1993) • **88**

Riesling Eiswein Mosel-Saar-Ruwer Wehlener Sonnenuhr 1990 • $75/375 ml. • (12/15/1991) • **89**

Riesling Kabinett Mosel-Saar-Ruwer Wehlener Sonnenuhr 1998: Very distinctive, with a slight resinous character along with peach, mineral and a creaminess. May not appeal to everyone. Drink now through 2004.–B.S. • $19 • (2/29/2000) • **87**

Riesling Kabinett Mosel-Saar-Ruwer Wehlener Sonnenuhr 1997: Extremely ripe, with a hint of botrytis(?), this focused white shows pineapple, lime and mineral aromas and flavors, firm structure and a long finish. Drink through 2005.–B.S. • $14 • (2/28/1999) • **88**

Riesling Spätlese Mosel-Saar-Ruwer Bernkasteler Bratenhöfchen 1997: Forward and inviting, there's a clarity to this '97 white, which delivers almond and citrus notes, a refreshing, delicate structure. Drink now through 2004.–B.S. • $16 • (2/28/1999) • **87**

Riesling Spätlese * Mosel-Saar-Ruwer Wehlener Sonnenuhr 1997: This '97 spätlese is like a flower yet to open. Austere in style, and the core of peach and slate flavors is bound up in the dense texture and firm structure. Pure and well focused. Best from 2001 through 2006.–B.S. • $20 • (2/28/1999) • **90**

KESSELER, AUGUST

Riesling Auslese Rheingau Rüdesheimer Berg Schlossberg 1998: This rich auslese has almond and pear notes, with hints of peach, all on a broad profile offset by a lively structure. Drink now through 2005.–B.S. • $73 • (2/29/2000) • **90**

Riesling Auslese Rheingau Rüdesheimer Bischofsberg 1996 • $32/375 ml. • (11/30/1997) • **87**

Riesling Kabinett Rheingau 1998: Straightforward, modest in its apple and almond notes, finishing short and crisp. Drink now.–B.S. • $22 • (2/29/2000) • **80**

Riesling Kabinett Rheingau 1996 • $18 • (11/30/1997) • **88**

Riesling Kabinett Rheingau Rüdesheimer Berg Roseneck 1996 • $22 • (11/30/1997) • **85**

Riesling Kabinett Trocken Rheingau Rüdesheimer Berg Rottland 1998: The ripe apricot and nectarine notes balance the firm, lean structure in this appealing dry Riesling. Should be a good match with food. Drink now through 2004.–B.S. • $26 • (1/01/2000) • **84**

Riesling Kabinett Trocken Rheingau Rüdesheimer Berg Rottland 1997: A tasty Riesling that puts it all together in a dry style. Apple and stone aromas and flavors mingle with rich texture and solid structure. Finishes on a mineral note. Drink through 2005.–B.S. • $23 • (2/28/1999) • **87**

Riesling Kabinett Trocken Rheingau Rüdesheimer Berg Schlossberg 1997: Rich up front, showing a reserved peach flavor, this is dry and firm from the midpalate to the finish. Still, it's attractive, with flavors that linger on the finish. Drink now through 2004.–B.S. • $24 • (2/28/1999) • **85**

Riesling Kabinett Trocken Rheingau Rüdesheimer Bischofsberg 1998: An orange nuance creeps into this dry '98 white, though the main theme is nectarine. A bit stiff, but it may relax with time. Drink now through 2003.–B.S. • $26 • (1/01/2000) • **83**

Riesling QbA Rheingau 1998: A roundness is followed by bracing acidity, washing away the almond, citrus and apple flavors. Crisp finish. May just need time. Drink through 2004.–B.S. • $18 • (2/29/2000) • **84**

Riesling QbA Rheingau 1996 • $15 • (11/30/1997) • **86**

Riesling QbA Rheingau Rüdesheim Berg Schlossberg 1998: *Erstes Gewächs.* Very spicy, reminiscent of Muscat, this is on the dry side and medium-bodied. Has fine balance and length. Drink now through 2005.–B.S. • $53 • (1/01/2000) • **86**

Riesling QbA Trocken Rheingau 1998: Firm and spicy, with a zippy structure and good balance. Starts out with plenty of fruit character, finishing on the lean side. Drink now through 2003.–B.S. • $18 • (2/29/2000) • **83**

Riesling QbA Trocken Rheingau 1997: Dry and powerful. Rich, beautifully balanced and concentrated, expressing mineral and spice, accented by a core of peach flavor. Good length and intensity. Drink now through 2006.–B.S. • $16 • (2/28/1999) • **88**

Riesling Spätlese Rheingau 1998: Lovely interplay between the peach and citrus notes and firm structure, buffered by a richness midpalate. Good length. This grows on you. Drink now through 2005.–B.S. • $33 • (2/29/2000) • **89**

Riesling Spätlese Rheingau 1996 • $25 • (11/30/1997) • **85**

Riesling Spätlese Rheingau Rüdesheimer Berg Roseneck 1997: Somewhat angular in its profile, yet there are rich apple and peach flavors, along with plenty of mineral character and a firm underpinning that dominates the finish at this stage. Best from 2001 through 2006.–B.S. • $30 • (2/28/1999) • **88**

Riesling Spätlese Rheingau Rüdesheimer Berg Rottland 1996 • $36 • (11/30/1997) • **89**

Riesling Spätlese Trocken Rheingau Rüdesheimer Berg Roseneck 1998: Lean and zippy, with a core of ripe, concentrated nectarine and citrus flavors, finishing crisply. Will benefit from a little bottle age and food. Best from 2001 through 2005.–B.S. • $41 • (1/01/2000) • **84**

Riesling Spätlese Trocken Rheingau Rüdesheimer Bischofsberg 1998: Broad-shouldered as German Riesling goes, exhibiting power and concentration on an upright structure. Ripe apricot and almond notes help the balance. Best after 2000.–B.S. • $33 • (1/01/2000) • **85**

Spätburgunder Beerenauslese Rheingau Weissherbst 1997: Very sweet, this late-harvest Pinot Noir displays honey, apricot and spice against a back-drop of racy acidity. Astringency on the finish suggests some skin contact. Interesting, if atypical. Drink now through 2004.–B.S. • $66/375 ml. • (5/15/1999) • **87**

Spätburgunder Trockenbeerenauslese Rheingau Weissherbst 1997: Thick and sweet, this has apricot, quince and passion fruit flavors, very pure and focused, with honey edging in toward the finish. Well balanced, it's unusual and appealing. Drink now through 2007.–B.S. • $213/375 ml. • (5/15/1999) • **89**

KESSELSTATT, REICHSGRAF VON

Riesling Auslese Gold Cap Mosel-Saar-Ruwer Josephshöfer 1996 • $26/375 ml. • (11/30/1997) • **88**

Riesling Auslese Mosel-Saar-Ruwer Bernkasteler Doctor 1997: Very aromatic, showing lime blossom, apricot and mineral notes, followed by a rich yet lively texture that dances on the palate through the mouthwatering finish. Drink now through 2007.–B.S. • $42 • (2/28/1999) • **89**

Riesling Auslese Mosel-Saar-Ruwer Josephshöfer 1998: Austere and firmly structured, this Riesling auslese shows density and an interplay of lime and slate. Could use a touch more ripeness to balance the zing. Best from 2002 through 2010.–B.S. • $22/375 ml. • (2/29/2000) • **88**

Riesling Auslese Mosel-Saar-Ruwer Josephshöfer 1997: Round and softly textured, with honey notes. Though not very expressive in aroma or flavor, it has good underlying acidity and a moderate finish. Best from 2001 through 2005.–B.S. • $24 • (2/28/1999) • **88**

Riesling Auslese Mosel-Saar-Ruwer Piesporter Goldtröpfchen 1997: A racy auslese, augmenting its peach and mineral flavors with a touch of honey, this is pure and transparent in its profile, with a zingy, crystalline finish. Best from 2004 through 2012.–B.S. • $22 • (2/28/1999) • **90**

Riesling Auslese Mosel-Saar-Ruwer Scharzhofberger 1997: Young and a bit muted now but with the rich, succulent character typical of the '97 vintage, this has gorgeous lime and apricot flavors supported by a crisp acid framework and an intense mineral character. Leaves the palate buzzing on the finish. Best from 2002 through 2012.–B.S. • $27 • (2/28/1999) • **92**

Riesling Beerenauslese Mosel-Saar-Ruwer Scharzhofberger 1995 • $NA • (11/30/1996) • **90**

Riesling Beerenauslese Mosel-Saar-Ruwer Scharzhofberger 1989 • $220 • (12/15/1990) • **94**

KESSELSTATT, REICHSGRAF VON

Riesling Eiswein Mosel-Saar-Ruwer Scharzhofberger 1993 • $NA • (11/30/1994) • **89**

Riesling Kabinett Halbtrocken Mosel-Saar-Ruwer Scharzhofberger 1997: Ripe and rich, with lime, spice and mineral aromas and flavors, this is a big kabinett that's firmly structured, despite its rich texture. Fine, lingering finish. Drink now through 2005.–B.S. • $15 • (2/28/1999) • **86**

Riesling Kabinett Mosel-Saar-Ruwer Graacher Himmelreich 1996 • $14 • (11/30/1997) • **86**

Riesling Kabinett Mosel-Saar-Ruwer Josephshöfer 1998: Rich and juicy, this lacks a little focus, giving an impression of softness and diffuseness to the lime, peach and honey notes. Drink now through 2003.–B.S. • $18 • (1/01/2000) • **85**

Riesling Kabinett Mosel-Saar-Ruwer Josephshöfer 1997: Taut and firmly structured, redolent of apple, mineral and a hint of herbs, this needs time to unfold and show more of its fruit character. Good, lingering finish. Drink through 2005.–B.S. • $12 • (2/28/1999) • **86**

Riesling Kabinett Mosel-Saar-Ruwer Josephshöfer 1996 • $15 • (11/30/1997) • **86**

Riesling Kabinett Mosel-Saar-Ruwer Kaseler Nies'chen 1997: Intense and vibrant, rattling the gums with its passion fruit, lime and apple flavors, piquant acidity and dense structure. Fine length too, but it all needs time to come together. Drink through 2006.–B.S. • $12 • (2/28/1999) • **91**

Riesling Kabinett Mosel-Saar-Ruwer Piesporter Goldtröpfchen 1998: Lovely aromas and flavors of peach and red fruits, with a hint of herbs, yet lacks the extra oomph to be really exciting. Drink now through 2003.–B.S. • $18 • (2/29/2000) • **85**

Riesling Kabinett Mosel-Saar-Ruwer Piesporter Goldtröpfchen 1997: A focused white, this delivers clearly defined aromas and flavors of apple and slate, and zingy acidity. Has a sleek, almost transparent profile. Drink now through 2004.–B.S. • $12 • (2/28/1999) • **87**

Riesling Kabinett Mosel-Saar-Ruwer Piesporter Goldtröpfchen 1996 • $15 • (11/30/1997) • **88**

Riesling Kabinett Mosel-Saar-Ruwer Scharzhofberger 1998: Delicious lime, honey and mineral flavors here, displayed against a soft, diffuse backdrop. Firms up on the finish. Drink now through 2004.–B.S. • $18 • (2/29/2000) • **87**

Riesling Kabinett Mosel-Saar-Ruwer Scharzhofberger 1997: Ethereal aromas of lime and spring wildflowers introduce this rich, deftly balanced kabinett, then apple and lime flavors glide across the palate. Absolutely delicious now, but should age well, too. Drink now through 2004.–B.S. • $15 • (2/28/1999) • **88**

Riesling Kabinett Mosel-Saar-Ruwer Scharzhofberger 1996 • $15 • (11/30/1997) • **88**

Riesling Spätlese Mosel-Saar-Ruwer Bernkasteler Doctor 1998: Rich and slightly sweet, this spätlese delivers plenty of peach, honey and herbal nuances. Less structured than many '98s, it should come forward soon. Drink now through 2004.–B.S. • $41 • (1/01/2000) • **87**

Riesling Spätlese Mosel-Saar-Ruwer Graacher Domprobst 1996 • $18 • (11/30/1997) • **88**

Riesling Spätlese Mosel-Saar-Ruwer Josephshöfer 1997: Shows the ripe, rich character of the vintage, with peach and licorice notes. All the elements are balanced and integrated, but it lacks the density and intensity to score outstanding. Drink now through 2006.–B.S. • $16 • (2/28/1999) • **89**

Riesling Spätlese Mosel-Saar-Ruwer Josephshöfer 1996 • $21 • (11/30/1997) • **89**

Riesling Spätlese Mosel-Saar-Ruwer Kaseler Nies'chen 1997: Gorgeous '97 spätlese. Pure, bright floral and peach aromas are accented by mineral on the palate in this crunchy, richly textured white. Almost like biting into a fresh peach. Long aftertaste leaves the mouth watering. Drink now through 2005.–B.S. • $15 • (2/28/1999) • **90**

Riesling Spätlese Mosel-Saar-Ruwer Kaseler Nies'chen 1996 • $18 • (11/30/1997) • **88**

Riesling Spätlese Mosel-Saar-Ruwer Piesporter Goldtröpfchen 1998: Incredibly rich and ripe, showing exotic nuances of dried apricot, coconut and honey. Very light on its feet and densely flavored. Drink now through 2005.–B.S. • $24 • (2/29/2000) • **90**

Riesling Spätlese Mosel-Saar-Ruwer Piesporter Goldtröpfchen 1996 • $15 • (11/30/1997) • **84**

Riesling Spätlese Mosel-Saar-Ruwer Scharzhofberger 1997: Seductive, bursting with succulent lime and apricot aromas and flavors accented by white pepper. In the mouth, it's rich and racy until the refreshing acidity ushers in a long, multidimensional finish. Great stuff. Drink now through 2010.–B.S. • $20 • (2/28/1999) • **93**

Key: SS—Spectator Selection. CS—Cellar Selection. HR—Highly Recommended. $NA—Price not available. (BT)—Barrel tasting. (A)—Auction Price.
For a key to the tasters' initials, see "How to Use These Listings."
Dates in parentheses represent the issues in which the ratings were published.

Riesling Spätlese Mosel-Saar-Ruwer Scharzhofberger 1996 • $19 • (11/30/1997) • **90**

Riesling Trockenbeerenauslese Mosel-Saar-Ruwer Scharzhofberger 1994 • $NA • (11/30/1995) • **91**

Riesling Trockenbeerenauslese Mosel-Saar-Ruwer Scharzhofberger 1989 • $150 • (12/15/1990) • **94**

KIMICH, JULIUS FERDINAND

Riesling Kabinett Pfalz Deidesheimer Herrgottsacker 1996 • $13 • (4/30/1998) • **83**

Riesling Kabinett Pfalz Forster Elster 1996 • $13 • (4/30/1998) • **86**

KLEIN

Grauburgunder Beerenauslese Rheinhessen Niersteiner Spiegelberg 1994: Showing some maturity, this has lost its overt sweetness to complex marmalade, spice and woodsy flavors. Supported by bracing acidity, it combines freshness and mature flavors. A good match for foie gras or blue cheese. Drink now through 2004.–B.S. • $60/500 ml. • (5/15/1999) • **88**

Riesling Eiswein Rheinhessen Niersteiner Bildstock 1994: Beginning to reveal some mature character, this is smoky and minerally, with apricot and almond notes supported by vibrant acidity. It's lost some of the early fatness in texture, gaining complexity and terrific length. Drink now through 2010.–B.S. • $60/375 ml. • (1/01/1999) • **94**

Riesling Eiswein Rheinhessen Niersteiner Bildstock 1989 • $82 • (1/01/1994) • **89**

KNYPHAUSEN, BARON ZU

Riesling Eiswein Rheingau Erbacher Siegelsberg 1996 • $90/500 ml. • (11/30/1997) • **86**

Riesling Kabinett Rheingau 1997: Soft in structure, this easygoing, peachy white is direct and modest on the finish. Drink now through 2002.–B.S. • $13 • (2/28/1999) • **82**

Riesling Kabinett Rheingau Erbacher Steinmorgen 1998: This has weight, offering medium sweetness and an opulent texture, with candied apricot and citrus peel flavors. Drink now.–B.S. • $14 • (2/29/2000) • **84**

Riesling Kabinett Rheingau Erbacher Steinmorgen 1996 • $12 • (11/30/1997) • **85**

Riesling Kabinett Trocken Rheingau Erbacher Steinmorgen 1998: Round and peachy, with a moderately firm structure and a brief finish. Drink now. –B.S. • $14 • (1/01/2000) • **82**

Riesling Kabinett Trocken Rheingau Erbacher Steinmorgen 1997: Concentrated flint and almond aromas and flavors linger on the finish in this '97 kabinett. Dry and firm. Drink now through 2003.–B.S. • $14 • (2/28/1999) • **84**

Riesling QbA Rheingau 1998: Shows ripeness, hinting at apricot in addition to almond and spice notes. A solid framework supports it, with a little less severity than its peers. Drink now through 2003.–B.S. • $11 • (2/29/2000) • **83**

Riesling QbA Rheingau 1997: Austere and on the acidic side, finishing with a marzipan note.–B.S. • $10 • (2/28/1999) • **79**

Riesling QbA Rheingau Charta 1996 • $12 • (11/30/1997) • **85**

Riesling Spätlese Rheingau Erbacher Marcobrunn 1998: Closed and austere, exhibiting earth and almond nuances on a broad framework supported by citrusy acidity. Best after 2000.–B.S. • $33 • (2/29/2000) • **85**

Riesling Spätlese Rheingau Erbacher Marcobrunn 1997: A forward '97, showing peach and honey notes and a rich texture supported by crisp acidity. The flavors don't follow through to the finish. Drink now through 2003.–B.S. • $28 • (2/28/1999) • **83**

Riesling Spätlese Rheingau Erbacher Michelmark feinherb/off-dry 1997: Tastes dry, with spice, mineral and quince notes, a rich texture, concentration and persistence of flavor. Well balanced and long on the finish. Drink now through 2008.–B.S. • $20 • (2/28/1999) • **89**

Riesling Spätlese Rheingau Erbacher Siegelsberg 1998: A straightforward spätlese, combining apple, pear and mineral flavors, all on a creamy texture. Good, crisp acidity on the finish. Drink now through 2005.–B.S. • $29 • (2/29/2000) • **86**

Riesling Spätlese Rheingau Erbacher Steinmorgen 1997: Fairly sweet, this offers concentrated flavors of apple and quince with tropical fruit nuances and has lovely succulence and crispness to balance the sweet, ripe fruit. Drink now through 2005.–B.S. • $35 • (2/28/1999) • **87**

Riesling Spätlese Rheingau Kiedricher Sandgrub 1998: Firm and crisp, like an apple on an autumn day, but it turns lean and tart on the finish. Tasted twice, with consistent notes.–B.S. • $27 • (1/01/2000) • **79**

Riesling Spätlese Rheingau Kiedricher Sandgrub 1997: Very ripe and on the sweeter end of the spätlese spectrum, with flavors of apricot and honey, lively acidity and rich texture. Structured for midterm aging. Drink now through 2004.–B.S. • $20 • (2/28/1999) • **87**

Riesling Spätlese Rheingau Kiedricher Sandgrub 1996 • $19 • (11/30/1997) • **81**

KNYPHAUSEN, FREIHERR ZU

Riesling Beerenauslese Rheingau Erbacher Michelmark 1993 • $88 • (11/30/1994) • **90**

Riesling Kabinett Rheingau 1996 • $12 • (11/30/1997) • **86**

Riesling Kabinett Trocken Rheingau Erbacher Steinmorgen 1996 • $12 • (11/30/1997) • **86**

Riesling QbA Rheingau 1996 • $9 • (11/30/1997) • **80**

Riesling Spätlese Trocken Rheingau Erbacher Steinmorgen 1996• $18 • (11/30/1997) • **82**

Riesling Trockenbeerenauslese Rheingau Erbacher Michelmark 1992 • $230 • (11/30/1993) • **95**

KOCH ERBEN, BÜRGERMEISTER CARL

Riesling Kabinett Rheinhessen Oppenheimer Kreuz 1997: Red berry, cherry and grapefruit accent tinned fruit flavors. Silky in texture and soft in structure but lacks some finesse. Tasted twice, with consistent notes.–B.S. • $10 • (2/28/1999) • **79**

Riesling Spätlese Rheinhessen Oppenheimer Kreuz 1996: Beginning to show some maturity, yet locked up tight in its structure, this racy, quince-, pear- and mineral-nuanced Riesling has a lot going for it—just all knees and elbows today. Best from 2002 through 2006.–B.S. • $16 • (5/15/2000) • **89**

Riesling Trockenbeerenauslese Rheinhessen Oppenheimer Sackträger 1994: Amber in color and smelling of orange peel, apricot and cinnamon, this maturing TBA has lost its initial sweetness and fat, settling into a rhythm between the complex flavors and vibrant acidity. Ends on a walnut and dried citrus note. Drink now through 2010.–B.S. • $105/500 ml. • (5/15/2000) • **91**

KOEHLER-RUPRECHT

Gewürztraminer Spätlese Pfalz Kallstadter Steinacker 1997: Richly textured yet lively and focused, this spicy white has immediate appeal. The lushness is balanced by a characteristic grapefruit peel accent on the finish. Not imported into the U.S. Drink now.–B.S. • $NA • (1/01/1999) • **86**

Muskateller Auslese Pfalz Kallstadter Saumagen 1998: Assertive and spicy, rich in body and well balanced, displaying pine, clove and grapefruit aromas and flavors. Try as an aperitif. Drink now.–B.S. • $44 • (5/15/2000) • **85**

Muskateller Auslese Pfalz Kallstadter Saumagen 1996 • $NA • (11/30/1997) • **88**

Muskateller Beerenauslese Pfalz Kallstadter Saumagen 1992 • $NA • (11/30/1993) • **84**

Muskateller Trockenbeerenauslese Pfalz Kallstadter Saumagen 1994 • $NA • (11/30/1995) • **94**

Riesling Auslese Gold Cap Pfalz Kallstadter Saumagen 1997: There's lovely, concentrated dried apricot, honey and citrus components in this rich, sweet white. The underlying structure is fine, but is overshadowed by the sweetness and fruit. Drink now through 2008.–B.S. • $30 • (2/28/1999) • **91**

Riesling Auslese Pfalz Kallstadter Saumagen 1998: Firm and spicy in a slender mold, this lightweight auslese is well defined, keeping its narrow range of citrus and peach reined in through the finish. Drink now through 2006.–B.S. • $53/375 ml. • (2/29/2000) • **88**

Riesling Auslese Pfalz Kallstadter Saumagen 1997 • $NA • (1/01/1998) • **91**

Riesling Auslese Pfalz Kallstadter Saumagen 1996 • $NA • (11/30/1997) • **85**

Riesling Beerenauslese Pfalz Kallstadter Saumagen 1997: Incredibly fresh aromas of quince and orange lead into an elegant dessert white that carries a distinctive minty element on the palate. Balanced on the rich, soft side, with a hint of astringency on the finish. Drink now through 2010.–B.S. • $75 • (2/28/1999) • **91**

Riesling Beerenauslese Pfalz Kallstadter Saumagen 1994 • $NA • (11/30/1995) • **89**

Riesling Beerenauslese Pfalz Kallstadter Saumagen 1993 • $NA • (11/30/1994) • **84**

Riesling Beerenauslese Pfalz Kallstadter Saumagen 1992 • $NA • (11/30/1993) • **92**

Riesling Eiswein Pfalz Kallstadter Saumagen 1997: Very clean, with pure flavors of peach and almond, moderate concentration and rich mouthfeel. The acidity has a citrusy edge to it, though not particularly bracing. Drink now through 2012.–B.S. • $90 • (2/28/1999) • **89**

Riesling Kabinett Halbtrocken Pfalz Kallstadter Steinacker 1997 • $12 • (1/01/1998) • **88**

Riesling Kabinett Halbtrocken Pfalz Kallstadter Steinacker 1996 • $NA • (11/30/1997) • **89**

Riesling Kabinett Pfalz Kallstadter Steinacker 1996 • $13 • (11/30/1997) • **84**

Riesling Spätlese Halbtrocken Pfalz Kallstadter Saumagen 1997 • $NA • (1/01/1998) • **87**

Riesling Spätlese Halbtrocken Pfalz Kallstadter Saumagen 1996 • $19 • (11/30/1997) • **88**

Riesling Spätlese Pfalz Kallstadter Saumagen 1997 • $NA • (1/01/1998) • **89**

Riesling Spätlese Pfalz Kallstadter Saumagen 1997: Exotic and spicy, here's a Riesling full of vanilla, honey, pineapple and passion fruit, buoyed by succulent acidity and ending on a firm note. Drink now through 2003.–B.S. • $33 • (5/15/2000) • **89**

Riesling Spätlese Pfalz Kallstadter Saumagen 1996 • $NA • (11/30/1997) • **82**

Riesling Trockenbeerenauslese Pfalz Kallstadter Saumagen 1994 • $NA • (11/30/1995) • **90**

Scheurebe Beerenauslese Pfalz Kallstadter Saumagen 1994 • $NA • (11/30/1995) • **87**

Scheurebe Spätlese Pfalz Kallstadter Steinacker 1998: Floral and apricot notes are pure, sweet and ripe, backed by a grapefruit peel character as well as acidity in this focused, elegant, pretty style of Scheurebe. Drink now.–B.S. • $28 • (5/15/2000) • **87**

KREUSCH, LEONARD

Riesling Auslese Mosel-Saar-Ruwer Piesporter Goldtröpfchen 1996 • $15 • (4/30/1998) • **83**

Riesling Auslese Mosel-Saar-Ruwer Piesporter Michelsberg 1996 • $12 • (4/30/1998) • **79**

Riesling Kabinett Mosel-Saar-Ruwer Bernkasteler Kurfürstlay 1998: Smells and tastes a bit dirty, with marzipan and candied fruit.–B.S. • $10 • (1/01/2000) • **74**

Riesling Kabinett Mosel-Saar-Ruwer Piesporter Michelsberg 1996 • $8 • (4/30/1998) • **76**

Riesling QbA Mosel-Saar-Ruwer Piesporter Goldtröpfchen 1996 • $9 • (4/30/1998) • **79**

Riesling Spätlese Mosel-Saar-Ruwer Piesporter Michelsberg 1996 • $10 • (4/30/1998) • **73**

KRUGER-RUMPF

Riesling Auslese Gold Cap Nahe Münsterer Pittersberg 1998: Saturated with apricot, in a round, forward style, yet with enough acidity to keep it lively. Delicious now, should also improve with age. Drink now through 2008.–B.S. • $35 • (2/29/2000) • **91**

Riesling Auslese Gold Cap Nahe Münsterer Pittersberg 1997: An impressive '97 auslese, redolent of red berries and almonds, this is intense and difficult to taste at this stage due to its raw, unharnessed power and exuberance. Its sweetness and structure need time to integrate. Great finish. Best from 2004 through 2012.–B.S. • $25/375 ml. • (2/28/1999) • **94**

Riesling Auslese Nahe Münsterer Dautenpflänzer 1997: A superripe version, showing apricot, mineral and black currant flavors that just melt in your mouth, with the intensity and depth to follow through the finish. Needs time to integrate. Best from 2003 through 2010.–B.S. • $15/375 ml. • (2/28/1999) • **92**

Riesling Auslese Nahe Münsterer Dautenpflänzer 1996 • $20 • (4/30/1998) • **89**

Riesling Eiswein Nahe Münsterer Pittersberg 1998: Ripe and thick, with a vibrant framework keeping everything balanced and lively, this '98 eiswein evokes peach, pear and vanilla custard notes. Approachable now, but will keep. Drink now through 2008.–B.S. • $84/375 ml. • (2/29/2000) • **90**

Riesling Eiswein Nahe Münsterer Pittersberg 1997: Packed with almond, baked piecrust and intense citrus flavors, this balances richness and concentration with a crystalline framework and bracing acidity. Finishes with a long aftertaste of marzipan. Best from 2002 through 2020.–B.S. • $51/375 ml. • (2/28/1999) • **93**

Riesling Kabinett Nahe Münsterer Kapellenberg 1997: A lovely '97, displaying white peach and spice notes, with richness, density and vibrant acidity, all the while maintaining a sense of harmony. Finishes dry. Best from 2001 through 2006.–B.S. • $11 • (2/28/1999) • **86**

Riesling Kabinett Nahe Münsterer Rheinberg 1997: There's intensity along with a rich texture, yet this is very firmly supported by a green apple acidity and carbon dioxide, which will dissipate in time and expand the peach and spice flavors. Best from 2001 through 2006.–B.S. • $12 • (2/28/1999) • **88**

Riesling Spätlese Nahe Münsterer Dautenpflänzer 1998: Huge nose of creamy vanilla, then the apricot and grapefruit emerge on the palate.

Assertive rather than graceful, yet you have to admire its exuberance. Drink now through 2004.–B.S. • $21 • (2/29/2000) • **86**

Riesling Spätlese Nahe Münsterer Dautenpflänzer 1997: A live wire of a white, reverberating with apricot, mineral and coconut aromas and flavors. Full of intensity, with a green apple finish that lingers. Best from 2002 through 2008.–B.S. • $14 • (2/28/1999) • **89**

Riesling Spätlese Nahe Münsterer Dautenpflänzer 1996 • $16 • (4/30/1998) • **89**

Scheurebe Spätlese Nahe Münsterer 1998: Pleasant and simple, with pine and peach flavors on a soft, medium-sweet structure. Drink now through 2001.–B.S. • $20 • (5/15/2000) • **83**

KÜHLING-GILLOT

Riesling Spätlese Rheinhessen Oppenheimer Herrenberg 1996 • $18 • (4/30/1998) • **85**

KUHN, PETER JAKOB

Riesling Spätlese Rheingau Oestricher Lenchen 1998: Compact and on the sweet side for this category, with apricot backed by mouthwatering acidity and opulent texture, it tails off a bit on the finish. Needs time to come together. Drink through 2006.–B.S. • $23 • (2/29/2000) • **89**

KÜNSTLER, FRANZ

Riesling Auslese Gold Cap Rheingau Hochheimer Hölle (AP 6) 1998: Sexy, uninhibited and in your face, this '98 auslese never loses its sense of elegance and harmony. Bursting with apricot, vanilla and lime notes, delivered in a clean, focused manner. Excellent length. Drink now through 2008.–B.S. • $50 • (2/29/2000) • **93**

Riesling Auslese Gold Cap Rheingau Hochheimer Hölle (AP 7) 1998: Auction wine. Deep gold in color, exhibiting ripe apricot and orange peel nuances, with a touch of mushroom. Broad and imposing, yet with a bracing acidity that emerges midpalate through the finish. Needs time. Best from 2001 through 2008.–B.S. • $NA • (1/01/2000) • **91**

Riesling Auslese Trocken Rheingau Hochheimer Hölle 1997: An impressive dry white, this has latent power, ripe apricot-laden flavors and a structure of steel. Ample flesh and depth of flavor prevent it from becoming too austere on the finish of spice and mineral. Best from 2002 through 2010. –B.S. • $59 • (2/28/1999) • **92**

Riesling Auslese Trocken Rheingau Hochheimer Kirchenstück 1998: Cool, reserved and confident, this dry auslese is full of stone, spice and white peach flavors, arrayed on a solid, powerful grid. Kicks in about midpalate with an additional blast of fruit and mineral. Well done. Best from 2002 through 2012.–B.S. • $49 • (2/29/2000) • **92**

Riesling Auslese Trocken Rheingau Hochheimer Stielweg 1998: Reminiscent of Austria's Wachau, this '98 dry Riesling evokes spice, stone and smoke aromas and flavors on a sprightly framework. Like a gray November day in its austerity now, with concentration and flavors ready to emerge with time in the bottle. Best from 2002 through 2010.–B.S. • $45 • (2/29/2000) • **92**

Riesling Auslese Trocken Rheingau Hochheimer Stielweg 1997: A dry version of auslese, showing ripe peach and apricot notes along with broad almond and beeswax elements. Well balanced, featuring plenty of richness and acidity, finishing with a hint of citrus. Drink now through 2007.–B.S. • $42 • (2/28/1999) • **89**

Riesling Beerenauslese Gold Cap Rheingau Hochheimer Hölle 1998: Lovely and exotic-tasting, like butterscotch and apricot, with forest floor components entering the mix. Well balanced and lively, it's drinkable now, but should age nicely. Drink now through 2007.–B.S. • $128 • (2/29/2000) • **93**

Riesling Beerenauslese Rheingau Hochheimer Hölle 1996 • $113/375 ml. • (11/30/1997) • **91**

Riesling Beerenauslese Rheingau Hochheimer Hölle 1994 • $104 • (11/30/1995) • **89**

Riesling Eiswein Rheingau Hochheimer Reichestal 1996 • $195/375 ml. • (11/30/1997) • **94**

Riesling Kabinett Halbtrocken Rheingau 1998: A fruit bomb, this '98 white bursts with lime, spice and peach aromas and flavors, all married to a juicy texture and a vibrant backbone. Easily quaffable. Drink now through 2004.–B.S. • $17 • (1/01/2000) • **86**

Key: SS—Spectator Selection. CS—Cellar Selection. HR—Highly Recommended. $NA—Price not available. (BT)—Barrel tasting. Ⓐ—Auction Price.
For a key to the tasters' initials, see "How to Use These Listings."
Dates in parentheses represent the issues in which the ratings were published.

Riesling Kabinett Rheingau Hochheimer Hölle 1997: Smells and tastes slightly of new wood, with butter and vanilla elements, a thick, creamy texture (for Riesling) and a mealy character. Strives for power over finesse, but is well balanced. Drink now through 2006.–B.S. • $22 • (2/28/1999) • **87**

Riesling Kabinett Rheingau Hochheimer Reichestal 1996 • $18 • (11/30/1997) • **84**

Riesling Kabinett Rheingau Hochheimer Reichesthal 1998: Immediately appealing for its up-front apricot character and juiciness, this is rich and quite sweet, yet balanced and refreshing on the finish. Drink now through 2004.–B.S. • $18 • (2/29/2000) • **88**

Riesling Kabinett Rheingau Hochheimer Reichesthal 1997: A gorgeous kabinett. Seamless from start to finish, it combines white peach and apricot with spice and mineral, richness with succulent acidity. Long aftertaste of citrus and mineral. Drink now through 2007.–B.S. • $18 • (2/28/1999) • **91**

Riesling Kabinett Rheingau Hochheimer Reichesthal Charta 1997: Dry and austere, this has some ripe peach elements and moderate richness but is dominated by lemony acidity and firm structure. The finish is bone-dry and a little tart. For fans of the dry style, or to pair with food. Drink now through 2005.–B.S. • $22 • (2/28/1999) • **82**

Riesling Kabinett Trocken Rheingau 1997 • $NA • (1/01/1998) • **81**

Riesling Kabinett Trocken Rheingau Hochheimer Hölle 1998: Smells sweet, with ripe apricot and peach notes, all on a dry, firm structure, with fine fruit character and balance. The whole package should settle down in a few months. Drink now through 2004.–B.S. • $22 • (1/01/2000) • **85**

Riesling QbA Halbtrocken Rheingau 1997: A stern, medium-weight, off-dry white, displaying peach and nut flavors and a firm backbone. Well made, if a bit lacking in charm. Drink now through 2003.–B.S. • $15 • (2/28/1999) • **85**

Riesling Spätlese Halbtrocken Rheingau Hochheimer Hölle 1997: There's a nice balance of soft peach flavors and firm structure in this rich, mouthfilling '97 white, whose mineral accents linger on the finish. Drink now through 2004.–B.S. • $32 • (2/28/1999) • **86**

Riesling Spätlese Halbtrocken Rheingau Hochheimer Stielweg 1998: Balance and harmony are the hallmarks throughout this '98 Riesling. Full of peach, apricot, spice and mineral notes from start to finish, it ends austerely, yet there's plenty of concentration. Best from 2001 through 2008.–B.S. • $28 • (1/01/2000) • **89**

Riesling Spätlese Rheingau Hochheimer Domdechaney 1998: Serious ripeness, displaying truffle, apricot and auslese-level concentration. Feels like there's good structure underneath, but it's top-heavy now, so give it time. Best from 2001 through 2006.–B.S. • $45 • (2/29/2000) • **90**

Riesling Spätlese Rheingau Hochheimer Domdechaney 1997: Wonderful depth of flavor. This '97 spätlese exhibits a nutty, earthy component contrapuntal to its citrus and apricot. Rich and lavish, this feels like a "small" auslese. Drink now through 2004.–B.S. • $45 • (2/28/1999) • **91**

Riesling Spätlese Rheingau Hochheimer Kirchenstück 1998: Well delineated and densely woven, this spätlese shows lime-tinged peach and mineral notes, with a strong underlying musculature. Fine, subtle length. Drink now through 2006.–B.S. • $32 • (2/29/2000) • **91**

Riesling Spätlese Rheingau Hochheimer Kirchenstück 1997: An aristocrat. Exotic and expressive, offering apricot, orange, grapefruit and hazelnut character, very complex, very concentrated, with the structure to age and develop. You feel the firmness and power on the finish. Drink now through 2010.–B.S. • $32 • (2/28/1999) • **90**

Riesling Spätlese Rheingau Hochheimer Kirchenstück 1996 • $30 • (11/30/1997) • **92**

Riesling Spätlese Trocken Rheingau Hochheimer Hölle 1997: Vanilla and butter notes suggest new oak, an atypical style. Also shows peach and apple flavors, rich on the palate, and a dry, spicy character. Finishes on the austere side. Drink now through 2005.–B.S. • $34 • (2/28/1999) • **85**

Riesling Spätlese Trocken Rheingau Hochheimer Hölle 1996 • $34 • (11/30/1997) • **88**

Riesling Spätlese Trocken Rheingau Hochheimer Stielweg 1998: Gorgeous ripe peach is enhanced by a smoky, stony nuance, etched onto a crystalline structure. Pure, focused and intense, the flavors persist on the palate, ending in a grapefruit and mineral duet. Best from 2001 through 2008. –B.S. • $31 • (2/29/2000) • **90**

Riesling Spätlese Trocken Rheingau Hochheimer Stielweg 1997: Firm and dry, displaying lovely spice and earth character and hints of flowers and stone fruits, this '97 white is well integrated, concentrated and long on the palate. Drink now through 2005.–B.S. • $31 • (2/28/1999) • **88**

Riesling Spätlese Trocken Rheingau Hochheimer Stielweg 1996 • $31 • (11/30/1997) • **85**

Riesling Trocken Rheingau 1997 • $NA • (1/01/1998) • **90**

Riesling Trockenbeerenauslese Rheingau Hochheimer Hölle 1994 • $428 • (11/30/1995) • **90**

Riesling Trockenbeerenauslese Rheingau Hochheimer Hölle 1992 • $NA • (11/30/1993) • **94**

KUNTZ, MARKUS & SYBILLE

Riesling Kabinett Mosel-Saar-Ruwer Bernkastel-Kueser Kardinalsberg 1998: For fans of the dry style. Great nose of dried apricots, mineral and lime, then the dryness shocks the palate. It has concentration, though it turns lean and austere by the finish. Needs food. Best from 2001 through 2005.–B.S. • $17 • (2/29/2000) • **84**

Riesling QbA Trocken Mosel-Saar-Ruwer 1998: Dry and slightly austere, with a firm structure overlaid with peach and lime. A mineral note creeps in on the finish. Drink now through 2004.–B.S. • $12 • (2/29/2000) • **84**

LEITZ, JOSEF

Riesling Auslese Rheingau Rüdesheimer Berg Rottland 1997: Lean and focused, this doesn't have the concentration of the best in the region, but its almond, chamomile and butterscotch flavors are appealing. Drink now through 2007.–B.S. • $41 • (2/28/1999) • **88**

Riesling Auslese Rheingau Rüdesheimer Berg Schlossberg 1998: A ripe, round auslese, full of apricot and grapefruit, backed by tangy acidity. Turns elegant and complex on the finish. Drink now through 2007.–B.S. • $67 • (2/29/2000) • **89**

Riesling Eiswein Rheingau Rüdesheimer Klosterberg 1998: Great tension in this eiswein. Focused, pure and unevolved, this is weightless, yet packed with the essence of peach and offering hints of cream and mineral. Dense and finely textured, with a finish that goes on and on. Best from 2001 through 2012.–B.S. • $127/375 ml. • (2/29/2000) • **97**

Riesling Kabinett Halbtrocken Rheingau Rüdesheimer Bischofsberg 1996 • $15 • (11/30/1997) • **86**

Riesling Kabinett Rheingau Rüdesheimer Magdalenenkreuz 1998: Firm and lean, without a lot of fruit flavor, this '98 ends on a crisp note. Drink now.–B.S. • $16 • (2/29/2000) • **80**

Riesling Kabinett Rheingau Rüdesheimer Magdalenenkreuz 1997: Broad in profile, with lanolin and apple aromas and flavors. Precisely balanced, with moderate sweetness, a rich texture and citrusy acidity. Drink now through 2004.–B.S. • $12 • (2/28/1999) • **84**

Riesling Kabinett Rheingau Rüdesheimer Magdalenenkreuz 1996 • $15 • (11/30/1997) • **87**

Riesling QbA Rheingau Rüdesheimer Drachenstein 1998: Quince and spice highlight this dryish QbA, very attractive and well balanced. Drink now through 2003.–B.S. • $16 • (2/29/2000) • **84**

Riesling QbA Rheingau Rüdesheimer Klosterlay 1997: Lovely, sappy apple, honey and cinnamon flavors, good concentration and structure are followed by a minerally finish. Very well put together. Drink now through 2005.–B.S. • $11 • (2/28/1999) • **87**

Riesling Spätlese Halbtrocken Rheingau 1997: Lean and intense, here's an off-dry '97 white with character. It hints at peach, but reveals more almond, tobacco and citrus, all firmly structured, before turning austere on the finish. Best from 2002 through 2008.–B.S. • $15 • (2/28/1999) • **85**

Riesling Spätlese Rheingau Rüdesheimer Berg Roseneck 1998: Gorgeous spätlese, with spice, apple and peach that tease the palate while bracing acidity keeps everything lively. A crisp apple note lingers on the finish. Best from 2001 through 2007.–B.S. • $29 • (2/29/2000) • **88**

Riesling Spätlese Rheingau Rüdesheimer Berg Roseneck 1997: Rich, ripe and creamy in texture, this '97 white has great presence on the palate, while its flavors remain subdued but linger attractively on the finish. Give it time to develop. Drink now through 2005.–B.S. • $19 • (2/28/1999) • **89**

Riesling Spätlese Rheingau Rüdesheimer Kirchenpfad 1997: Supple and juicy, this white's floral and peach character has clarity and expression on a soft, easy structure. Drink now through 2002.–B.S. • $16 • (2/28/1999) • **86**

LIESER, SCHLOSS

Riesling Auslese ** Mosel-Saar-Ruwer Lieser Niederberg Helden 1998: Sweet, balanced and creamy on the palate, like a vanilla custard or key lime pie. The extra dimension of ripeness is offset by vibrant citrusy acidity in this sleek, ethereal Riesling auslese. Best from 2001 through 2009.–B.S. • $21/375 ml. • (2/29/2000) HR • **91**

Riesling Auslese * Mosel-Saar-Ruwer Lieser Niederberg Helden 1998: Some trapped carbon dioxide flattens this out and lends a quinine note. Still, there's apricot, peach and lime peeking through, all backed by crisp acidity. Vivid yet delicate. Best from 2001 through 2007.–B.S. • $30 • (2/29/2000) • **88**

Riesling Auslese * Mosel-Saar-Ruwer Niederberg Helden 1997:** Tantalizing ripeness, offering honey, apricot and mineral aromas and flavors on a delicate, racy framework, with a lime aftertaste. Beautifully made, with density, but needs time. Best from 2002 through 2012.–B.S. • $31/375 ml. • (2/28/1999) • **92**

Riesling Auslese Mosel-Saar-Ruwer Niederberg Helden 1997: Displaying pure slate and lime, with a pear nuance, this is sweet, rich and on the soft side of the structure spectrum, finishing with a lovely almond aftertaste. Drink now through 2007.–B.S. • $26 • (2/28/1999) • **91**

Riesling Kabinett Mosel-Saar-Ruwer 1998: Gorgeous slate, lime and floral aromas carry through to the finish in this lighter-than -air '98 Riesling. Very pure and transparent. Drink now through 2005.–B.S. • $15 • (2/29/2000) • **89**

Riesling Kabinett Mosel-Saar-Ruwer 1997: Delicate and toned, this is a dense, sinewy wine with a sense of grace, displaying aromas and flavors of quince and slate. Lime and mineral nuances linger on the finish. Drink now through 2006.–B.S. • $14 • (2/28/1999) • **89**

Riesling Kabinett Mosel-Saar-Ruwer 1996 • $14 • (4/30/1998) • **86**

Riesling QbA Mosel-Saar-Ruwer 1998: An intense QbA whose peach, citrus and slate notes have authority, thanks to a dense texture and moderate weight for a Mosel white. Drink now through 2005.–B.S. • $12 • (2/29/2000) • **88**

Riesling QbA Mosel-Saar-Ruwer 1997: Focused, with straightforward apple and earth notes, firm acidity and a lean finish. Tasted twice, with consistent notes. Drink now through 2003.–B.S. • $11 • (2/28/1999) • **81**

Riesling Spätlese Mosel-Saar-Ruwer 1998: Packed with slate, lime and a cheesy note, all tightly wound around a firm, lively backbone. Tails off a bit on the finish. Drink now through 2006.–B.S. • $18 • (1/01/2000) • **87**

Riesling Spätlese Mosel-Saar-Ruwer Niederberg Helden 1998: Wow. This is spicy like a white Graves, showing some lime, spice and red fruit aromas and flavors along with racy acids and intensity. Power and elegance combined. Drink now through 2007.–B.S. • $19 • (2/29/2000) • **91**

Riesling Spätlese Mosel-Saar-Ruwer Niederberg Helden 1997: What crystalline structure and pure flavors in this peach- and mineral-drenched white. It's rich and supple yet has a firm backbone and a hint of herbs on the finish. Drink through 2006.–B.S. • $18 • (2/28/1999) • **91**

LINGENFELDER

Riesling Auslese Pfalz Freinsheimer Goldberg 1998: Richly textured and in a dry style for auslese, it offers apricot, with spice notes lingering in the background. Round and effortlessly balanced. Drink now through 2005. –B.S. • $22/375 ml. • (2/29/2000) • **89**

Riesling Auslese Trocken Pfalz Freinsheimer Goldberg 1996 • $NA • (11/30/1997) • **89**

Riesling Beerenauslese Pfalz Freinsheimer Musikantenbuckel 1997: Smoke, passion fruit and glazed orange peel are the highlights of this rich and lively BA. Focus and firm acidity keep it from becoming cloying, although it has a hint of bitterness on the finish. Drink now through 2010.–B.S. • $26/375 ml. • (2/28/1999) • **90**

Riesling Kabinett Halbtrocken Pfalz Freinsheimer Musikantenbuckel 1998: Lovely spicy character augments the peach and mineral in this focused white, whose open texture and density lead to a lingering finish. Drink now through 2003.–B.S. • $20 • (2/29/2000) • **88**

Riesling Kabinett Halbtrocken Pfalz Freinsheimer Musikantenbuckel 1996 • $12 • (11/30/1997) • **87**

Riesling Spätlese Halbtrocken Pfalz Grosskarlbacher Osterberg 1998: Vibrant, with apricot and fig aromas, picking up grapefruit and mineral on the palate, all backed by a firm, austere framework. Drink now through 2005.–B.S. • $22 • (2/29/2000) • **90**

Riesling Spätlese Halbtrocken Pfalz Grosskarlbacher Osterberg 1997: Assertive aromas of apricot, white pepper and grapefruit lead into a rich, juicy texture supported by mouthwatering acidity. Easy to enjoy now, but will improve. Drink through 2006.–B.S. • $15 • (2/28/1999) • **90**

Riesling Spätlese Halbtrocken Pfalz Grosskarlbacher Osterberg 1996 • $14 • (11/30/1997) • **90**

Riesling Spätlese Pfalz Grosskarlbacher Osterberg 1998: Exotic and concentrated, this Riesling evokes apricot and spice aromas and flavors, supported by a firm structure, with tropical fruit on the long aftertaste. Drink now through 2007.–B.S. • $22 • (2/29/2000) • **90**

Riesling Spätlese Pfalz Grosskarlbacher Osterberg 1997: Generous and ripe, offering peach, passion fruit and citrus aromas and flavors wedded to bright, refreshing acidity. Tails off a bit on the finish. Drink now through 2005.–B.S. • $15 • (2/28/1999) • **88**

Riesling Spätlese Pfalz Grosskarlbacher Osterberg 1996 • $15 • (11/30/1997) • **88**

■ ■ ■ ■

LINGENFELDER

Riesling Trockenbeerenauslese Pfalz Freinsheimer Goldberg 1989 • $100/375 ml. • (12/15/1990) • **96**

Riesling Trockenbeerenauslese Pfalz Grosskarlbacher Osterberg 1989 • $85/375 ml. • (12/15/1990) • **92**

Scheurebe Auslese Pfalz Freinsheimer Goldberg 1997: A dead-ringer for a Gewürztraminer, this offers attractive rose petal, litchi and grapefruit notes, all concentrated, richly textured and supported by moderate acidity. Shows the potential of Scheurebe in the right hands. Drink now through 2002. –B.S. • $22 • (5/15/1999) • **87**

Scheurebe Beerenauslese Pfalz Grosskarlbacher Burgweg 1989 • $65/375 ml. • (12/15/1990) • **88**

Scheurebe Spätlese Halbtrocken Pfalz Grosskarlbacher Burgweg 1997: Full of character, this white is rich and spicy, just off-dry, with lively peach and grapefruit flavors and a stony mineral finish. Drink now through 2001. –B.S. • $15 • (1/01/1999) • **85**

Scheurebe Spätlese Pfalz Freinsheimer Goldberg 1996 • $14 • (11/30/1997) • **87**

Scheurebe Spätlese Trocken Pfalz Freinsheimer Musikantenbuckel 1996 • $14 • (11/30/1997) • **86**

Scheurebe Trockenbeerenauslese Pfalz Grosskarlbacher Burgweg 1990 • $150 • (12/15/1991) • **96**

Spätburgunder Trocken Germany 1996: Serious Pinot here. Dark, ripe and concentrated, beginning with aromas of cherry, spice and a hint of decay, followed by clove-tinged cherry flavors. Very extracted and focused by racy acidity married to a sinewy structure. Good, lingering finish. Drink now through 2004.–B.S. • $21 • (5/15/1999) • **88**

LOEWEN, CARL

Riesling Auslese Mosel-Saar-Ruwer Leiwener Laurentiuslay 1997: Shows an apricot and lime intensity, with just a hint of a vegetal note, racy acidity and good concentration. Tasty, but doesn't exhibit a lot of depth and complexity. Best from 2002 through 2008.–B.S. • $34/500 ml. • (2/28/1999) • **88**

Riesling Auslese Mosel-Saar-Ruwer Thörnicher Ritsch 1997 • $NA/500 ml. • (1/01/1998) • **84**

Riesling Eiswein Mosel-Saar-Ruwer Leiwener Klostergarten 1998: Thickly textured, sweet, and supported by searing acidity, this eiswein shows notes of herbs and apricot. Compact and simple, it lacks the purity of the best in this category. Drink now through 2005.–B.S. • $111/375 ml. • (5/15/2000) • **84**

Riesling Eiswein Mosel-Saar-Ruwer Leiwener Klostergarten 1997 • $NA/375 ml. • (1/01/1998) • **88**

Riesling Spätlese Mosel-Saar-Ruwer Leiwener Laurentiuslay 1998: Struggles between peach and citrus notes and an off-putting tinned-fruit character. Tasted twice, with consistent notes.–B.S. • $25 • (5/15/2000) • **72**

Riesling Spätlese Mosel-Saar-Ruwer Leiwener Laurentiuslay 1997: A combination of earth and canned fruit-cocktail. Disappointing. Tasted twice, with consistent notes.–B.S. • $16 • (2/28/1999) • **74**

LOOSEN, DR.

Riesling Auslese Gold Cap Mosel-Saar-Ruwer Erdener Prälat 1998: A serious auslese. Very concentrated and packed with apricot and honey, it screams across the palate, courtesy of the bracing structure. Finishes with caramel and mineral notes. Give this baby time. Best from 2002 through 2010. –B.S. • $62/375 ml. • (2/29/2000) • **95**

Riesling Auslese Gold Cap Mosel-Saar-Ruwer Erdener Prälat 1997: Very ripe, this has an extra component of sweetness, with vibrant acidity to match. Light and mercurial, showing lime and apricot flavors, but it falls just short of the top of this category. Best from 2002 through 2010.–B.S. • $54 • (2/28/1999) • **90**

Riesling Auslese Gold Cap Mosel-Saar-Ruwer Ürziger Würzgarten 1998: Exotic, with a touch of botrytis, passion fruit and pineapple aromas and flavors and almost sour acidity. Disjointed today, but with good flavors, so be patient. Best after 2001.–B.S. • $59 • (1/01/2000) • **88**

Riesling Auslese Long Gold Cap Mosel-Saar-Ruwer Erdener Prälat 1997: Auction wine. There's an extra dimension of sweetness and concentration in this '97 white, with an herbal note accenting the apricot and tropical fruit. Thick and ripe, yet still light on its feet and well balanced, this is special for the vintage. Best from 2002 through 2012.–B.S. • $360/375 ml. • (2/28/1999) • **94**

Key: SS—Spectator Selection. CS—Cellar Selection. HR—Highly Recommended. $NA—Price not available. (BT)—Barrel tasting. (A)—Auction Price. For a key to the tasters' initials, see "How to Use These Listings." **Dates in parentheses represent the issues in which the ratings were published.**

Riesling Auslese Mosel-Saar-Ruwer Erdener Prälat 1998: A compact, firm style of Mosel auslese, this displays attractive lime and grapefruit flavors in a lightweight presentation. Drink now through 2005.–B.S. • $45 • (2/29/2000) • **91**

Riesling Auslese Mosel-Saar-Ruwer Erdener Prälat 1997: Plenty of sweetness here, with vibrant acidity and a rich texture and straightforward flavors of lime and peach. Lacks the concentration of better Mosel auslesen though. Drink now through 2006.–B.S. • $40 • (1/01/1999) • **87**

Riesling Auslese Mosel-Saar-Ruwer Erdener Prälat 1996 • $49 • (11/30/1997) • **91**

Riesling Auslese Mosel-Saar-Ruwer Erdener Treppchen 1997: Light and airy, this elegant white is like a "formula one" racer: nimble, balanced and sleek. The flavors tend to the lime, apple and quince end of the spectrum, with a firm, lively structure. Best from 2001 through 2009.–B.S. • $29 • (2/28/1999) • **90**

Riesling Auslese Mosel-Saar-Ruwer Ürziger Würzgarten 1998: This seems drier than most auslese, with peach and mineral notes well supported by bracing acidity. A little lean. Best after 2001.–B.S. • $32 • (1/01/2000) • **87**

Riesling Auslese Mosel-Saar-Ruwer Ürziger Würzgarten 1997: Lip-smacking and smelling of freshly baked bread, lime and mineral, this white combines rich peach and apple flavors with a racy structure and an intensity that continues on the fine, fresh aftertaste. Drink now through 2007.–B.S. • $30 • (2/28/1999) • **91**

Riesling Auslese Mosel-Saar-Ruwer Ürziger Würzgarten 1996 • $36 • (11/30/1997) • **90**

Riesling Auslese Mosel-Saar-Ruwer Wehlener Sonnenuhr 1998: Round and expressive, with brightness and backbone, this '98 Riesling bursts with peach, stone and citrus aromas and flavors, finishing crisply. Drink now through 2007.–B.S. • $30 • (2/29/2000) • **88**

Riesling Beerenauslese Mosel-Saar-Ruwer Erdener Treppchen 1996 • $153/375 ml. • (11/30/1997) • **90**

Riesling Beerenauslese Mosel-Saar-Ruwer Wehlener Sonnenuhr 1992 • $377 • (11/30/1993) • **96**

Riesling Eiswein Mosel-Saar-Ruwer Bernkasteler Lay 1998: Assertive, leaning toward vegetal aromas, but the coconut, mango and honey flavors prevail, resulting in a very pretty dessert white, balanced by lively acidity and lingering on the finish. Drink now through 2007.–B.S. • $150/375 ml. • (2/29/2000) • **90**

Riesling Eiswein Mosel-Saar-Ruwer Erdener Prälat 1991 • $537 • (12/15/1992) • **94**

Riesling Kabinett Mosel-Saar-Ruwer Erdener Treppchen 1998: A rich, ripe white, bordering on spätlese in quality, sporting apricot, mineral and light herbal flavors. Racy acidity keeps it balanced, and the feel is silky-smooth. Drink now through 2005.–B.S. • $15 • (2/29/2000) • **88**

Riesling Kabinett Mosel-Saar-Ruwer Erdener Treppchen 1997: Ripe aromas and flavors of lime and passion fruit mark this rich, succulent white. Finishes on white pepper and apple notes. Drink now through 2002.–B.S. • $15 • (2/28/1999) • **86**

Riesling Kabinett Mosel-Saar-Ruwer Wehlener Sonnenuhr 1998: A little awkward. Fascinating aromas and flavors of lime and coconut are displayed on an airy texture, with tart acidity taking over on the finish. Needs time to integrate. Best after 2000.–B.S. • $14 • (1/01/2000) • **84**

Riesling Kabinett Mosel-Saar-Ruwer Wehlener Sonnenuhr 1996 • $17 • (11/30/1997) • **89**

Riesling QbA Mosel-Saar-Ruwer 1998: More mineral aroma and flavor than fruit here, with a hint of green apple on a round, easy-drinking structure. Drink now through 2001.–B.S. • $8 • (2/29/2000) • **84**

Riesling Spätlese Mosel-Saar-Ruwer Erdener Treppchen 1998: A graceful, ethereal Riesling, showing a distinctive mint or rosemary aroma, followed by apricot and citrus on the palate. Very lithe and supple, with a taut structure emerging on the finish. Best from 2001 through 2006.–B.S. • $24 • (2/29/2000) • **89**

Riesling Spätlese Mosel-Saar-Ruwer Erdener Treppchen 1996 • $26 • (11/30/1997) • **86**

Riesling Spätlese Mosel-Saar-Ruwer Ürziger Würzgarten 1998: Starts off big, rich and creamy, with apricot and honey aromas and flavors, turning elegant toward the finish. There's enough crisp acidity to keep it lively. Drink now through 2005.–B.S. • $25 • (2/29/2000) • **90**

Riesling Spätlese Mosel-Saar-Ruwer Ürziger Würzgarten 1997: Auction wine. About as structured as Mosel spätlese gets, this white has flavors of peach, apple and mineral, but doesn't quite have the midpalate depth and concentration to rate outstanding. Drink now through 2005.–B.S. • $22 • (2/28/1999) • **88**

Riesling Spätlese Mosel-Saar-Ruwer Ürziger Würzgarten 1996 • $27 • (11/30/1997) • **90**

Riesling Spätlese Mosel-Saar-Ruwer Ürziger Würzgarten 1996 • $70 • (11/30/1997) • **88**

Riesling Spätlese Mosel-Saar-Ruwer Wehlener Sonnenuhr 1998: Shows a little maturity in addition to the pineapple and slate flavors, with a round and slightly soft impression. Nice creamy texture. Drink now through 2004.–B.S. • $19 • (1/01/2000) • **87**

Riesling Spätlese Mosel-Saar-Ruwer Wehlener Sonnenuhr 1997: Showing some aromatic development, with a hint of petrol accenting the apple and almond flavors, here's a white that's concentrated, flavorful and well balanced, if without the excitement of the best. Drink through 2006.–B.S. • $18 • (2/28/1999) • **88**

Riesling Spätlese Mosel-Saar-Ruwer Wehlener Sonnenuhr 1996 • $23 • (11/30/1997) • **89**

Riesling Trockenbeerenauslese Mosel-Saar-Ruwer Ürziger Würzgarten 1994 • $NA • (11/30/1995) • **96**

Riesling Trockenbeerenauslese Mosel-Saar-Ruwer Wehlener Sonnenuhr 1993 • $NA • (11/30/1994) • **93**

Riesling Trockenbeerenauslese Mosel-Saar-Ruwer Wehlener Sonnenuhr 1991 • $53 • (12/15/1992) • **97**

MATHERN

Riesling Spätlese Nahe Niederhäuser Kertz 1998: Serious spätlese. Fine concentration of tropical fruit, citrus and spice flavors that start off round, turning crisp by the finish. Delicious presentation. Drink now through 2005.–B.S. • $22 • (2/29/2000) • **90**

Riesling Spätlese Nahe Niederhäuser Rosenberg 1998: Lovely flavors of peach, citrus and mineral are delicately delivered on a lightweight frame. Drink now through 2004.–B.S. • $22 • (2/29/2000) • **87**

Riesling Spätlese Nahe Norheimer Kirschheck 1998: A highwire interplay of fruit and structure. Intriguing aromas and flavors of lime, passion fruit and a sweet spicy note combine in this racy white. A touch hard on the finish. Best from 2001 through 2005.–B.S. • $22 • (1/01/2000) • **86**

MERKELBACH, ALFRED

Riesling Auslese Mosel-Saar-Ruwer Ürziger Würzgarten (AP 15) 1998: A model of balance and harmony, displaying vibrant lime, mineral and peach notes on a background of bracing acidity. The intensity of flavor carries through to a long aftertaste. Drink now through 2008.–B.S. • $23 • (2/29/2000) • **91**

Riesling Auslese Mosel-Saar-Ruwer Ürziger Würzgarten (AP 16) 1997: Very floral, with a ripe, rich profile and a juicy peach flavor. Full-bodied for the Mosel, with alcohol and a hint of bitterness on the finish that pulls it slightly off balance, yet impressive for its persistence of flavor. Drink now through 2004.–B.S. • $22 • (2/28/1999) • **88**

Riesling Auslese Mosel-Saar-Ruwer Ürziger Würzgarten (AP 18) 1997: Delicate and flavorful, showing a mix of floral, lime and peach aromas and flavors. Light-bodied yet rich, finishing on a distinct mineral note. Drink now through 2006.–B.S. • $16 • (2/28/1999) • **88**

Riesling Auslese Mosel-Saar-Ruwer Ürziger Würzgarten (AP 11) 1996 • $18 • (4/30/1998) • **88**

Riesling Auslese Mosel-Saar-Ruwer Ürziger Würzgarten (AP 12) 1996 • $18 • (4/30/1998) • **90**

Riesling Kabinett Mosel-Saar-Ruwer Erdener Treppchen 1997: Displays some peach aromas and flavors tinged with lime and mineral. Rich and soft, then turns lean on the finish. Drink now through 2002.–B.S. • $12 • (2/28/1999) • **84**

Riesling Kabinett Mosel-Saar-Ruwer Ürziger Würzgarten (AP 6) 1998: Pure slate, with lime and spice, all buoyed by a vibrant structure. Just lacks a little concentration and length to really sing. Drink now through 2003.–B.S. • $17 • (2/29/2000) • **84**

Riesling Kabinett Mosel-Saar-Ruwer Ürziger Würzgarten 1997: Peach and a hint of mineral here, along with a light, slightly dilute body and soft acidity.–B.S. • $12 • (2/28/1999) • **79**

Riesling Spätlese Mosel-Saar-Ruwer Erdener Treppchen 1997: A white so dense and rich it's creamy in texture; also has a vibrant framework of acidity—both bear the apple and pear flavors to a lingering finish. Drink now through 2006.–B.S. • $13 • (2/28/1999) • **89**

Riesling Spätlese Mosel-Saar-Ruwer Erdener Treppchen (AP 9) 1996 • $15 • (4/30/1998) • **89**

Riesling Spätlese Mosel-Saar-Ruwer Kinheimer Rosenberg 1998: Sleek and spicy, this weaves lime and stone notes around a core of rich fruit, ending with a streak of citrus. Tightly packed and persistent in flavor. Best after 2002.–B.S. • $16 • (2/29/2000) • **88**

Riesling Spätlese Mosel-Saar-Ruwer Ürziger Würzgarten (AP 5) 1998: A vibrant Mosel spätlese, full of ripe and tangy citrus and tropical fruit flavors accented by mineral, all on a firm, finely etched structure. Needs some time to integrate. Best from 2001 through 2006.–B.S. • $19 • (2/29/2000) • **89**

Riesling Spätlese Mosel-Saar-Ruwer Ürziger Würzgarten (AP 12) 1998: A piercing scent of roses and slate highlights this crisp Riesling, whose moderate concentration and elegant structure make a nice overall impression. Drink now through 2004.–B.S. • $20 • (1/01/2000) • **87**

Riesling Spätlese Mosel-Saar-Ruwer Ürziger Würzgarten 1997: A touch on the spicy side, showing straightforward flavors of peach and green apple, short on the finish.–B.S. • $14 • (2/28/1999) • **84**

MERZ

Chardonnay Spätlese Trocken Rheinhessen 1997: A kiss of oak adds interest to this sleek, vivid Chardonnay. Not particularly varietal in character, but delivers citrus and mineral notes in a dry style which should work well with light seafood and chicken dishes. Drink now through 2001.–B.S. • $17 • (5/15/1999) • **84**

Riesling Kabinett Halbtrocken Rheinhessen Ockenheimer Kreuz 1997 • $NA • (1/01/1998) • **80**

Riesling Spätlese Halbtrocken Rheinhessen Ockenheimer Klosterweg 1997: Attractive peach notes combine with a rich texture and citrusy acidity in this off-dry white. Good balance, but a little lean on the finish, where a hint of sweet fruit prevails. Drink now through 2004.–B.S. • $12 • (2/28/1999) • **84**

Riesling Spätlese Trocken Rheinhessen Ockenheimer Hockenmühle 1997: Dry and steely, with earth and lanolin flavors, this shows moderate richness and density, turning austere on the finish. Drink now through 2005.–B.S. • $12 • (2/28/1999) • **83**

Riesling Spätlese Trocken Rheinhessen Ockenheimer Laberstall 1997: Spice and earth notes begin generously before the firm, dry, tart finish kicks in. Drink now through 2007.–B.S. • $12 • (2/28/1999) • **82**

MESSMER, HERBERT

Riesling Kabinett Halbtrocken Pfalz Burrweiler Schlossgarten 1997: Nectarine and tropical fruit are the main themes in this ripe, exotic white. Rich and succulent, with moderate structure, it has immediate appeal. Lingering aftertaste of peaches. Drink now through 2004.–B.S. • $12 • (2/28/1999) • **87**

Riesling Trockenbeerenauslese Pfalz Burrweiler Schäwer 1992 • $42/375 ml. • (11/30/1993) • **94**

Scheurebe Spätlese Pfalz Burrweiler Altenforst 1997: Assertive, Muscat-like aromas announce this grapefruit-flavored white, its slight sweetness balanced by a hint of bitter grapefruit peel. Fresh and lively. Try as an aperitif. Drink now.–B.S. • $16 • (5/15/1999) • **84**

Weissburgunder Beerenauslese Pfalz Burrweiler Schlossgarten 1992 • $23/375 ml. • (11/30/1993) • **86**

MEULENHOF

Riesling Auslese Gold Cap Mosel-Saar-Ruwer Erdener Prälat 1998: Lovely floral, banana and peach aromas and flavors ally with a round, easygoing character. There's deceptive underlying structure and an airy texture. Moderate finish. Drink now through 2006.–B.S. • $28/500 ml. • (2/29/2000) • **89**

Riesling Auslese Gold Cap Mosel-Saar-Ruwer Erdener Prälat 1997: Exotic notes of guava and passion fruit are infused with lime, but there's not the concentration and intensity of the best in this category, with slightly tart acidity and an almond note on the finish. Tasted twice, with consistent notes. Drink now through 2006.–B.S. • $20/500 ml. • (2/28/1999) • **88**

Riesling Auslese Mosel-Saar-Ruwer Erdener Treppchen (AP 12) 1997: This '97 is balanced and harmonious, delicate yet intense. Sports a strong backbone, with lime, peach and mineral flavors and a lingering finish. Drink now through 2010.–B.S. • $17 • (2/28/1999) • **89**

Riesling Beerenauslese Mosel-Saar-Ruwer Erdener Treppchen 1997 • $NA/375 ml. • (1/01/1998) • **93**

Riesling Eiswein Mosel-Saar-Ruwer Erdener Busslay 1996: Already showing some development, this '96 has searing acidity which dominates the moderate richness and interesting smoke and marzipan flavors. Best from 2002 through 2015.–B.S. • $59/375 ml. • (1/01/1999) • **87**

Riesling Kabinett Mosel-Saar-Ruwer Erdener Treppchen (AP 8) 1997: A kabinett of concentration and density, this displays plenty of mineral and spice aromas and flavors in addition to peach. Fresh and lively, but tails off slightly on the finish. Drink now through 2003.–B.S. • $12 • (2/28/1999) • **87**

Riesling Spätlese Mosel-Saar-Ruwer Erdener Treppchen (AP 6) 1998: Delicious. Intriguing, tropical notes of pineapple and passion fruit hold sway in this rich, creamy white. It all comes together thanks to the juicy acidity. Excellent length on the finish. Best from 2001 through 2006.–B.S. • $20 • (2/29/2000) • **91**

Riesling Spätlese Mosel-Saar-Ruwer Erdener Treppchen 1997: Soft and inviting, here's a '97 with violet and talc aromas and flavors that yield to apple on the finish. Open and moderately rich. Drink now through 2004.–B.S. • $14 • (2/28/1999) • **86**

Riesling Spätlese Mosel-Saar-Ruwer Wehlener Sonnenuhr (AP 17) 1998: Rich, dense and creamy, here's a powerful Riesling showing its *terroir*. Needs some time for the earth, lime, apple and peach nuances to come to the fore. Best from 2001 through 2007.–B.S. • $20 • (2/29/2000) • **90**

MILZ-LAURENTIUSHOF

Riesling Auslese Gold Cap Mosel-Saar-Ruwer Trittenheimer Apotheke 1998: Auction wine. This pretty auslese is all delicacy and finesse, yet there's no shortage of apricot, lime and mineral or vibrant structure. Still needs time judging from the tight finish. Best from 2002 through 2008.–B.S. • $NA/500 ml. • (1/01/2000) • **90**

Riesling Auslese Gold Cap Mosel-Saar-Ruwer Trittenheimer Apotheke 1997: Auction wine. Full of lime and apricot aromas and flavors, this has a sleek profile with bracing acidity. Intense but a bit closed in; wait a few years for the components to integrate. Best from 2004 through 2012.–B.S. • $NA/500 ml. • (2/28/1999) • **92**

Riesling Auslese Gold Cap Mosel-Saar-Ruwer Trittenheimer Leiterchen 1998: Auction wine. Dense and creamy, a little monolithic right now, but it shows good underlying power and structure. Could ultimately rate higher. Best from 2002 through 2009.–B.S. • $NA/500 ml. • (1/01/2000) • **89**

Riesling Auslese Gold Cap Mosel-Saar-Ruwer Trittenheimer Leiterchen 1997: Auction wine. Has exemplary concentration and structure. Honey, apricot and maybe a hint of botrytis give nuance to this intensely flavored '97. Firmly structured, it needs time to resolve its crisp acidity. Best from 2002 through 2008.–B.S. • $NA/500 ml. • (2/28/1999) • **91**

Riesling Auslese Mosel-Saar-Ruwer Trittenheimer Felsenkopf 1998: This ripe '98 white shows apricot, spice and mineral notes allied to a bracing, high-acid framework. A really solid base of creamy, lime-tinged fruit lingers on the finish. Best from 2001 through 2008.–B.S. • $35 • (2/29/2000) • **90**

Riesling Eiswein Gold Cap Mosel-Saar-Ruwer Trittenheimer Apotheke 1998: Intense and pure, showing lime, nectarine and passion fruit aromas and flavors that unfold in layers, backed by a firm structure. Lovely harmony and dimension. Best from 2001 through 2007.–B.S. • $68/375 ml. • (2/29/2000) • **94**

Riesling Eiswein Gold Cap Mosel-Saar-Ruwer Trittenheimer Felsenkopf 1998: Delicious. Round and unctuous, with plenty of acidity already well integrated with the fruit and sugar. The flavors are intense, ranging from apricot and honey to citrus. Drink now through 2006.–B.S. • $69/375 ml. • (2/29/2000) • **90**

Riesling Eiswein Mosel Trittenheimer Felsenkopf 1992 • $NA • (11/30/1993) • **90**

Riesling Eiswein Mosel-Saar-Ruwer Trittenheimer Apotheke 1990 • $42/375 ml. • (12/15/1991) • **91**

Riesling Kabinett Mosel-Saar-Ruwer Piesporter Hofberger 1998: Ripe and juicy, this shows peach, floral and a touch of mineral on a lightweight frame, all supported by vibrant acidity. Drink now through 2003.–B.S. • $16 • (2/29/2000) • **86**

Riesling Kabinett Mosel-Saar-Ruwer Piesporter Hofberger 1997: Compact in style, with soft acidity and slightly flat, unfocused flavors of apple and a hint of tarragon or fennel. May be in an awkward stage. Drink through 2004–B.S. • $16 • (2/28/1999) • **83**

Riesling Kabinett Mosel-Saar-Ruwer Trittenheimer Apotheke 1997: A supercharged kabinett, showing ripe aromas and flavors of tropical fruit, lime and slate that begin richly, turn a little austere on the finish. Disjointed now, but should come together with time. Drink through 2005.–B.S. • $16 • (2/28/1999) • **88**

Riesling Kabinett Mosel-Saar-Ruwer Trittenheimer Felsenkopf 1998: Appears soft and open, sporting delicious flavors of lime, honey, slate and a hint of spice. One wishes for a tad more concentration and zip. Drink now through 2003.–B.S. • $17 • (1/01/2000) • **84**

Riesling Kabinett Mosel-Saar-Ruwer Trittenheimer Felsenkopf 1997: Elegant and lively, exhibiting apple and citrus aromas and flavors, juicy acidity and a medium finish. Drink now through 2004.–B.S. • $17 • (2/28/1999) • **87**

Riesling Spätlese Mosel-Saar-Ruwer Neumagener Nusswingert 1997: Plenty of ripeness here, tasting of apricots and tropical fruit, and it has good acidity, but not cut to really sing. Finishes just a tad short. Drink now through 2004.–B.S. • $21 • (2/28/1999) • **87**

Riesling Spätlese Mosel-Saar-Ruwer Piesporter Hofberger 1998: Gorgeous lime and peach notes are augmented by mineral, all displayed on a racy structure. Elegant and totally seductive. Drink now through 2004.–B.S. • $18 • (2/29/2000) • **89**

Riesling Spätlese Mosel-Saar-Ruwer Piesporter Hofberger 1997: Compact and tightly wound, this shows moderate intensity of peach, mineral and spice flavors. Has a very solid backbone of acidity and should develop well. Drink through 2006.–B.S. • $18 • (2/28/1999) • **88**

Riesling Spätlese Mosel-Saar-Ruwer Trittenheimer Apotheke 1998: A powerful spätlese, this is densely textured and flavored, packed with peach, lime and slate. The whole presentation is tied to a steel-girder structure. Excellent length. Best from 2001 through 2008.–B.S. • $21 • (2/29/2000) • **90**

Riesling Spätlese Mosel-Saar-Ruwer Trittenheimer Apotheke 1997: A straight-ahead white with medium concentration, flavors of apple, spice and mineral together with crunchy acidity. Rich and satisfying, and as expressive as the best Mosel spätlesen. Drink now through 2005.–B.S. • $21 • (2/28/1999) • **88**

Riesling Spätlese Mosel-Saar-Ruwer Trittenheimer Felsenkopf 1998: Broad-shouldered and fleshy, this spätlese shows loads of dense ripe peach, apricot and citrus, with accents of slate. Bracing acidity closes everything on the finish, so be patient. Best from 2001 through 2007.–B.S. • $24 • (1/01/2000) • **88**

Riesling Spätlese Mosel-Saar-Ruwer Trittenheimer Felsenkopf 1997: Explodes in the mouth with zippy lime, honey, spice and peach and an intensity that's almost painful. Tangy finish. Very ripe and densely textured, this needs time for the components to integrate. Best from 2002 through 2010.–B.S. • $22 • (2/28/1999) • **91**

Riesling Spätlese Mosel-Saar-Ruwer Trittenheimer Leiterchen 1998: Rich, dense and laserlike in its focus, this '98 spätlese screams across the palate, showing lime mineral and ripe apple notes and a creamy texture. Long, long finish. Best after 2002.–B.S. • $23 • (1/01/2000) • **88**

Riesling Spätlese Mosel-Saar-Ruwer Trittenheimer Leiterchen 1997: A lot going on in this '97 white, with an earthy, red-fruit character. Concentrated and intense, with firm underlying acidity. The aftertaste has intriguing white pepper and green apple notes. Drink through 2006–B.S. • $22 • (2/28/1999) • **90**

MINGES, THEO

Riesling Auslese Pfalz Gleisweiler Hölle 1997: Quite sweet, with richness and body, yet candied citrus and marzipan are the main flavors. Overall, it's sweet and simple. Drink now.–B.S. • $29/500 ml. • (5/15/2000) • **83**

Riesling Eiswein Pfalz Flemlinger Vogelsprung 1996: Broad, thick and sweet, offering vanilla, honey, pineapple and a slight resinous note. On the palate, the initial sweetness is swept aside by a cascade of searing acidity, keeping it lively and balanced. Best from 2001 through 2010.–B.S. • $54/375 ml. • (5/15/2000) • **89**

Riesling Kabinett Pfalz Flemlinger Zechpeter 1997: Has a richness, but also almond and petrol notes and acidity that give the impression of austerity. Compact, with a lingering aftertaste. Drink now through 2003.–B.S. • $11 • (2/28/1999) • **82**

Riesling QbA Halbtrocken Pfalz Flemlinger Bischofskreuz 1997: A simple, apple- and peach-flavored white with modest concentration and a crisp finish.–B.S. • $10/1 liter • (2/28/1999) • **79**

Riesling QbA Pfalz Flemlinger Bischofskreuz 1997: This has good apple and almond character, well integrated with the brisk acidity, in a straightforward, direct style. Drink now through 2003.–B.S. • $10/1 liter • (2/28/1999) • **81**

Riesling Spätlese Pfalz Gleisweiler Hölle 1997: Ripe and juicy, with a honey element and lovely underlying acidity and apricot flavors. Not the most concentrated in this category, but has good persistence of flavor. Drink now through 2005.–B.S. • $14 • (2/28/1999) • **87**

MOLITOR, MARKUS

Riesling Auslese Mosel-Saar-Ruwer Zeltinger Sonnenuhr 1997: A bold white, broad-shouldered for Riesling, showing red berry, peach and mineral nuances supported by a fine structure. A little marred by SO2 today, but

Key: SS—Spectator Selection. CS—Cellar Selection. HR—Highly Recommended. $NA—Price not available. (BT)—Barrel tasting. Ⓐ—Auction Price.
For a key to the tasters' initials, see "How to Use These Listings."
Dates in parentheses represent the issues in which the ratings were published.

will come around with bottle age. Drink through 2007–B.S. • $19 • (5/15/1999) • **90**

Riesling Auslese * Mosel-Saar-Ruwer Zeltinger Sonnenuhr 1997: A lovely auslese. Smells like peaches and cream with underlying honey and mineral notes, all woven into the silky texture. So integrated now you hardly notice the lively backbone, but it's there and carries the flavors to a lengthy finish. Drink now through 2004.–B.S. • $23 • (5/15/1999) • **90**

Riesling Auslese ** Mosel-Saar-Ruwer Zeltinger Sonnenuhr 1997: Auction wine. Seductive. Botrytis takes this to another dimension, offering apricot, lanolin, honey and lime aromas and flavors. Ultrarich and smooth, with a purity and harmony that makes it melt in the mouth. Maintains a sense of delicacy. Drink now through 2005.–B.S. • $NA/375 ml. • (1/01/1999) • **91**

Riesling Auslese * Mosel-Saar-Ruwer Zeltinger Sonnenuhr 1997:** Auction wine. Pungent smelling, displaying orange marmalade, tropical fruits and a smoky note all combined with a thick, sweet character against a backdrop of snappy acidity. Concentrated, intense and elegant, despite the sweetness having the upper hand today. Drink now through 2007.–B.S. • $NA/375 ml. • (1/01/1999) • **93**

Riesling Beerenauslese Mosel-Saar-Ruwer Zeltinger Sonnenuhr 1996 • $67 • (1/01/1998) • **88**

Riesling Kabinett Mosel-Saar-Ruwer Zeltinger Sonnenuhr 1997: Seductive kabinett. Aromas and flavors of spring flowers, peaches and earth combine with juicy acidity and a supportive, though not firm, backbone. Has richness and elegance that carry through the lingering finish. Drink now through 2005.–B.S. • $10 • (5/15/1999) • **88**

Riesling Spätlese Mosel-Saar-Ruwer Bernkasteler Bratenhöfchen 1997: A racy, piquant spätlese, displaying a mélange of mineral, earth, peach and black currant, all finely etched on a texture of velvet. Really packs a lot of intensity into a slim framework. Excellent length. Drink now through 2007.–B.S. • $11 • (5/15/1999) • **90**

Riesling Trockenbeerenauslese * Mosel-Saar-Ruwer Zeltinger Sonnenuhr 1996 • $98 • (1/01/1998) • **88**

MÜLLER, EGON

Riesling Auslese Mosel-Saar-Ruwer Scharzhofberger (AP B) 1996 • $NA/375 ml. • (11/30/1997) • **94**

Riesling Beerenauslese Mosel-Saar-Ruwer Scharzhofberger (AP F) 1995 • $NA/375 ml. • (11/30/1996) • **93**

Riesling Beerenauslese Mosel-Saar-Ruwer Scharzhofberger 1994 • $NA • (11/30/1995) • **93**

Riesling Beerenauslese Mosel-Saar-Ruwer Scharzhofberger 1993 • $NA • (11/30/1994) • **98**

Riesling Beerenauslese Mosel-Saar-Ruwer Scharzhofberger 1991 • $NA • (12/15/1992) • **94**

Riesling Beerenauslese Mosel-Saar-Ruwer Scharzhofberger 1990 • $NA • (12/15/1991) • **97**

Riesling Beerenauslese Mosel-Saar-Ruwer Scharzhofberger 1989 • $NA • (12/15/1990) • **95**

Riesling Beerenauslese Mosel-Saar-Ruwer Scharzhofberger 1988 • $70 • (9/30/1989) • **99**

Riesling Beerenauslese Mosel-Saar-Ruwer Wiltinger Braune Kupp 1993 • $NA • (11/30/1994) • **95**

Riesling Eiswein Mosel-Saar-Ruwer Scharzhofberger (AP 103) 1996 • $NA • (11/30/1997) • **95**

Riesling Eiswein Mosel-Saar-Ruwer Scharzhofberger 1992 • $169 • (11/30/1993) • **95**

Riesling Eiswein Mosel-Saar-Ruwer Scharzhofberger 1989 • $NA • (12/15/1990) • **97**

Riesling Eiswein Mosel-Saar-Ruwer Scharzhofberger 1988 • $NA • (9/30/1989) • **92**

Riesling Kabinett Mosel-Saar-Ruwer Scharzhofberger 1998: Seems advanced in its evolution, with almond, apple and a tart impression on the aftertaste. Not bad though. Drink now.–B.S. • $29 • (2/29/2000) • **82**

Riesling Kabinett Mosel-Saar-Ruwer Scharzhofberger 1997: Packed with slate and herb elements, but also peach and hints of passion fruit, this sleek, delicate white delivers intensity on a tightrope. Succulent and pure—a fine example of Mosel Riesling. Drink now through 2004.–B.S. • $27 • (5/15/1999) • **87**

Riesling Kabinett Mosel-Saar-Ruwer Scharzhofberger 1996 • $27 • (11/30/1997) • **87**

Riesling QbA Mosel-Saar-Ruwer Scharzhof 1998: Delicious QbA, from the peach and slate aromas and flavors to the succulent texture and balancing structure. Good finish, too. Drink now through 2002.–B.S. • $15 • (2/29/2000) • **86**

Riesling QbA Mosel-Saar-Ruwer Scharzhof 1996 • $16 • (11/30/1997) • **88**

Riesling QbA Mosel-Saar-Ruwer Scharzhofberger 1997: Bright, juicy and attractive, this easy-drinking white offers ripe apple and peach notes in a balanced, forward style. Drink now.–B.S. • $15 • (2/28/1999) • **84**

Riesling Spätlese Mosel-Saar-Ruwer Scharzhofberger 1997: Scintillating. Racy and alive, with lime, apricot and slate aromas and flavors, this is packed with intense fruit character. Has density, and a firm backbone to balance everything. The finish goes on and on. Best from 2001 through 2008.–B.S. • $37 • (2/28/1999) • **93**

Riesling Spätlese Mosel-Saar-Ruwer Scharzhofberger 1996 • $37 • (11/30/1997) • **87**

Riesling Trockenbeerenauslese Mosel-Saar-Ruwer Scharzhofberger (AP B) 1995 • $NA/375 ml. • (11/30/1996) • **98**

Riesling Trockenbeerenauslese Mosel-Saar-Ruwer Scharzhofberger 1990 • $NA • (12/15/1991) • **99**

Riesling Trockenbeerenauslese Mosel-Saar-Ruwer Scharzhofberger 1989 • $NA • (12/15/1990) • **100**

MÜLLER, EUGEN

Riesling Auslese Pfalz Forster Kirchenstück 1997: Clean and focused but seems to lack concentration, offering almond flavors and zippy acidity. Good length. May improve with time. Best from 2001 through 2006.–B.S. • $20/500 ml. • (2/28/1999) • **87**

Riesling Eiswein Pfalz Forster Stift 1996: Sweet, ripe and thick, an outstanding eiswein, delivering plenty of ripeness offset by bracing acidity. Apricot, honey, caramel, citrus and spice galore, right through to the long finish. Smoky aftertaste. Drink now through 2005.–B.S. • $76/375 ml. • (5/15/2000) • **91**

Riesling Kabinett Pfalz Forster Mariengarten 1998: Tart and lean, this is tough to taste today. Tight and compact, with not much going on. Best after 2000.–B.S. • $15 • (2/29/2000) • **81**

Riesling Kabinett Pfalz Forster Mariengarten 1997: Effusive aromas of quince, nectarine and vanilla custard introduce this ripe and lively white. Medium-bodied, forceful and compact in profile. Drink now through 2006.–B.S. • $10 • (2/28/1999) • **89**

Riesling Spätlese Halbtrocken Pfalz Forster Pechstein 1998: Lean, with intensity and verve to the citrus and pineapple flavors. Bold and cutting, this needs time. Best from 2001 through 2007.–B.S. • $19 • (2/29/2000) • **88**

Riesling Spätlese Pfalz Forster Ungeheuer 1998: Intriguing. A sleek, ripe '98 white, tinged with lime, peach and mineral notes displayed on a gossamer texture. Good length. Drink now through 2005.–B.S. • $20 • (2/29/2000) • **88**

Scheurebe Spätlese Pfalz Forster Ungeheuer 1997: A floral aroma is followed by tangy, nectarine flavors on a rich, vibrant framework. Overall, it's balanced and appealing. Drink now.–B.S. • $14 • (5/15/1999) • **84**

Scheurebe Trockenbeerenauslese Pfalz Forster Ungeheuer 1992: There's a lot of oxidation augmenting the caramel, marzipan and raisin notes, yet this lacks structure, turning flat and lacking concentration.–B.S. • $54/375 ml. • (5/15/2000) • **78**

MÜLLER, RUDOLF

Gewürztraminer QbA Pfalz 1997: Characteristic varietal flavors of rose, litchi and spice are allied to a sprightly structure and juicy texture. Moderately concentrated, with an almond and ginger aftertaste. Drink now.–B.S. • $8 • (5/15/2000) • **85**

Pinot Blanc QbA Pfalz 1998: Neutral in aroma and flavor, although it's rich and round.–B.S. • $8 • (5/15/2000) • **78**

Riesling QbA Pfalz 1998: The aromas are like Muscat, with slightly sweet lemon and peach notes on a light framework.–B.S. • $8 • (5/15/2000) • **78**

MÜLLER-CATOIR

Muskateller Eiswein Pfalz Haardter Bürgergarten 1993 • $73/375 ml. • (11/30/1994) • **92**

Muskateller Kabinett Trocken Pfalz 1996 • $23 • (11/30/1997) • **88**

Rieslaner Auslese Pfalz Haardter Bürgergarten 1996 • $39/375 ml. • (11/30/1997) • **89**

Rieslaner Auslese Pfalz Mussbacher Eselshaut 1996 • $37/375 ml. • (11/30/1997) • **89**

Rieslaner Beerenauslese Pfalz Haardter Bürgergarten 1998: Exotic and spicy, the pine, passion fruit and citrus notes in this dessert white encase a beam of lively acidity that keeps the wine focused through to the lingering finish. Well made. Drink now through 2003.–B.S. • $110/375 ml. • (5/15/2000) • **90**

Rieslaner Beerenauslese Pfalz Mussbacher Eselshaut 1990 • $39/375 ml. • (12/15/1991) • **96**

MÜLLER-CATOIR

Rieslaner Spätlese Pfalz Mussbacher Eselshaut 1996 • $34 • (11/30/1997) • **91**

Rieslaner Spätlese Trocken Pfalz Mussbacher Eselshaut 1998: Pretty, in a delicate, subtle style. Strongly floral- and cherry-scented, with peach and citrus flavors balanced on an elegant framework. Drink now.–B.S. • $43 • (5/15/2000) • **85**

Rieslaner Trockenbeerenauslese Pfalz Mussbacher Eselshaut 1994 • $75 • (11/30/1995) • **89**

Rieslaner Trockenbeerenauslese Pfalz Mussbacher Eselshaut 1992 • $44/375 ml. • (11/30/1993) • **97**

Rieslaner Trockenbeerenauslese Pfalz Mussbacher Eselshaut 1990 • $53/375 ml. • (12/15/1991) • **97**

Riesling Auslese Pfalz Haardter Bürgergarten 1997: Wonderful intense fruit character in this '97 auslese. Apricot and citrus notes intermingle in this lush but never heavy version, deftly supported by refreshing acidity. Finishes clean as a whistle. Drink now through 2006.–B.S. • $43 • (2/28/1999) • **91**

Riesling Auslese Pfalz Mussbacher Eselshaut 1997: An unabashed auslese, brimming with apricot, vanilla, blood orange and a hint of bergamot wrapped in a soft, juicy-textured package. Delicious and beautifully made. Drink now.–B.S. • $47/375 ml. • (5/15/1999) • **90**

Riesling Beerenauslese Pfalz Mussbacher Eselshaut 1992 • $35/375 ml. • (11/30/1993) • **95**

Riesling Eiswein Pfalz Haardter Bürgergarten 1996 • $94/375 ml. • (11/30/1997) • **91**

Riesling Eiswein Pfalz Haardter Herenletten 1992 • $42/375 ml. • (11/30/1993) • **90**

Riesling Eiswein Pfalz Haardter Herzog 1991 • $122 • (12/15/1992) • **92**

Riesling Kabinett Halbtrocken Pfalz Haardter Bürgergarten 1997: Very aromatic, displaying red berry, spice and almond notes, this is a firm, moderately concentrated white, just off-dry, with a lean finish. Needs time to open up. Drink through 2005.–B.S. • $23 • (2/28/1999) • **84**

Riesling Kabinett Trocken Pfalz 1996 • $24 • (11/30/1997) • **81**

Riesling Spätlese Halbtrocken Pfalz Haardter Bürgergarten 1998: Zippy and transparent, offering peach and grapefruit on a lean, focused framework. Great balance makes it seem effortless. Best after 2001.–B.S. • $40 • (2/29/2000) • **90**

Riesling Spätlese Pfalz Haardter Bürgergarten 1998: Gorgeous ripe peach and apricot are displayed on a pure, crystalline framework, with finely etched acidity, all deftly balanced. Drink now through 2007.–B.S. • $46 • (2/29/2000) • **92**

Riesling Spätlese Pfalz Haardter Herrenletten 1997: Gorgeous. Bursting with lime, peach and apricot, this vibrant white keeps the flavors pulsing across the palate. Elegant and focused, it packs a lot of character into its lightweight frame. Drink now through 2007.–B.S. • $30 • (2/28/1999) • **91**

Riesling Spätlese Pfalz Haardter Herzog 1996 • $31 • (11/30/1997) • **92**

Riesling Spätlese Trocken Pfalz Haardter Bürgergarten 1998: Lean and reductive, with a coil-spring structure and dense texture, all very austere and cool. Great clarity and harmony. Best after 2000.–B.S. • $43 • (2/29/2000) • **88**

Riesling Spätlese Trocken Pfalz Haardter Bürgergarten 1997: A beautiful dry spätlese that's at once ripe and fruity, yet reserved and powerful. Aromas and flavors of guava, hazelnut and earth combine with a rich mouthfeel and a firm backbone. Long finish. Best from 2002 through 2010.–B.S. • $28 • (2/28/1999) • **89**

Riesling Spätlese Trocken Pfalz Haardter Herrenletten 1996 • $29 • (11/30/1997) • **89**

Scheurebe Auslese Pfalz Haardter Mandelring 1998: Expressive and vibrant. Loads of spice, floral and grape aromas and flavors in this assertive white. Medium-sweet and intense, the flavors just keep coming, followed by a long, lingering finish. Drink now through 2001.–B.S. • $50 • (5/15/2000) • **91**

Scheurebe Eiswein Pfalz Haardter Mandelring 1996 • $107/375 ml. • (11/30/1997) • **88**

Scheurebe Eiswein Pfalz Haardter Mandelring 1990 • $NA • (12/15/1991) • **94**

Scheurebe Kabinett Pfalz Haardter Mandelring 1996 • $24 • (11/30/1997) • **90**

Scheurebe Kabinett Trocken Pfalz Haardter Mandelring 1997: Very aromatic, offering peach, litchi and earth tones that continue on the palate right through to the finish. Crisp, dry and well balanced. Drink now.–B.S. • $24 • (5/15/1999) • **84**

Key: SS—Spectator Selection. CS—Cellar Selection. HR—Highly Recommended. $NA—Price not available. (BT)—Barrel tasting. Ⓐ—Auction Price.
For a key to the tasters' initials, see "How to Use These Listings."
Dates in parentheses represent the issues in which the ratings were published.

MUNZINGEN, SCHLOSS

Brut Spätburgunder Baden NV: Fizzy and light-bodied, with pleasant strawberry and cherry flavors, but the bubbles give it a hard edge, altering the silky texture that's an integral part of the Pinot Noir experience.–B.S. • $10 • (10/15/1998) • **83**

NECKERAUER, K.

Portugieser QbA Trocken Pfalz Weisenheimer Rosenbühl 1997: Light in body, yet packs a lot of berry and spice on its lean, lively framework, with a silky feel. Drink now through 2001.–B.S. • $9 • (5/15/1999) • **83**

Riesling Auslese Pfalz Weisenheimer Hasenzeile 1997: Exotic, this dishes up spice, almond and orange aromas and flavors, moderate sweetness and a sense of elegance. Not very expressive, but shows good concentration and length on the finish. Drink now through 2005.–B.S. • $19/500 ml. • (2/28/1999) • **87**

Riesling Kabinett Halbtrocken Pfalz Weisenheimer Hahnen 1997: Floral and fruit-cocktail aromas and flavors highlight this soft white. Pleasant if a little obvious, offering crisp acidity on the finish. Drink now through 2002.–B.S. • $10/1 liter • (2/28/1999) • **80**

Riesling Kabinett Pfalz Weisenheimer Goldberg 1997: An oddball. This kabinett starts round and forward, delivering floral and peach aromas with an intriguing hint of sage, then turns lean and bitter on the finish, though the aftertaste lingers.–B.S. • $11 • (2/28/1999) • **74**

Riesling Spätlese Pfalz Weisenheimer Halde 1997: Deep in color, showing strong marzipan aromas and flavors, this is awkward, with sweetness and soft acidity, becoming lean and astringent on the finish. Tasted twice, with consistent notes.–B.S. • $15 • (2/28/1999) • **74**

Riesling Spätlese Trocken Pfalz Weisenheimer Hahnen 1997: A ripe, full-bodied white, offering quince, almond and spice flavors, viscous texture and a solid structure. All the elements are balanced, and the finish lingers. Drink through 2006–B.S. • $15 • (2/28/1999) • **88**

NICOLAY, PETER

Riesling Auslese Mosel-Saar-Ruwer Erdener Prälat 1997: Delicate, with a lively structure and finely etched aromas and flavors of sweet corn, lime and peach, this white has an intensity that carries through the resonant finish. Best from 2001 through 2009.–B.S. • $47 • (2/28/1999) • **91**

Riesling Auslese Mosel-Saar-Ruwer Erdener Treppchen 1998: A '98 fleshpot. Loose-knit and open in texture, this has a good beginning, with peach and spice notes that diminish slightly through the finish. Drink now through 2003.–B.S. • $38 • (2/29/2000) • **88**

Riesling Auslese Mosel-Saar-Ruwer Ürziger Goldwingert 1998: Flamboyant and ample, with exotic notes of honey and candied citrus peel. A big auslese, with enough structure to balance the elements and keep the lingering finish refreshing. Drink now through 2008.–B.S. • $42 • (2/29/2000) • **89**

Riesling Auslese Mosel-Saar-Ruwer Ürziger Goldwingert 1996 • $30 • (11/30/1997) • **87**

Riesling Beerenauslese Mosel-Saar-Ruwer Ürziger Würzgarten 1992 • $72 • (11/30/1993) • **90**

Riesling Kabinett Mosel-Saar-Ruwer Feinherb Ürziger Würzgarten 1996 • $17 • (11/30/1997) • **86**

Riesling Trockenbeerenauslese Mosel-Saar-Ruwer Ürziger Würzgarten 1989 • $325 • (12/15/1990) • **91**

OHLER'SCHES, P. VON

Riesling Auslese Nahe Münsterer Kapellenberg 1998: This '98 auslese starts off softly, with peach and cinnamon flavors then turns crisp and citrusy on the finish. Moderately structured and a little light. Best from 2001 through 2006.–B.S. • $20 • (2/29/2000) • **86**

Scheurebe QbA Rheinhessen Binger Schlossberg-Schwätzerchen 1997: Not much aroma, but fresh and grapey on the palate, with a citrus edge to the finish.–B.S. • $8/1 liter • (5/15/1999) • **78**

OTHEGRAVEN, VON

Riesling Auslese Gold Cap Mosel-Saar-Ruwer Kanzemer Altenberg (AP 7) 1997: Straightforward, this auslese shows modest honey and peach flavors, good balance and a hint of astringency on the finish. Drink now through 2003.–B.S. • $19/375 ml. • (2/28/1999) • **84**

Riesling Auslese Gold Cap Mosel-Saar-Ruwer Kanzemer Altenberg (AP 14) 1997 • $NA/375 ml. • (1/01/1998) • **78**

Riesling Auslese Mosel-Saar-Ruwer Kanzemer Altenberg (AP 12) 1996 • $30 • (3/31/1998) • **88**

Riesling Auslese Mosel-Saar-Ruwer Kanzemer Altenberg (AP 13) 1996 • $NA/375 ml. • (3/31/1998) • **89**

Riesling Kabinett Mosel-Saar-Ruwer Kanzemer Altenberg 1996 • $14 • (3/31/1998) • **87**

Riesling QbA Mosel-Saar-Ruwer Maximus 1998: Nice ripe aromas of peach and lime are offset by firm acidity. Good themes played out here, yet it's slightly dilute. Drink now.–B.S. • $20 • (2/29/2000) • **83**

Riesling QbA Trocken Mosel-Saar-Ruwer Kanzemer Altenberg 1997: Dry and rich, this shows a lot of lees (the spent yeast sediment) contact, white peach and mineral. Not a lot of zip to it, but it's moderately concentrated, balanced and finishes clean. Drink now through 2002.–B.S. • $27 • (2/28/1999) • **84**

Riesling QbA Trocken Mosel-Saar-Ruwer Maximus 1997: This dry, medium-bodied Mosel displays apple and earth character, good richness and a dry, lingering finish. Well made, it will appeal to fans of the dry style. Tasted twice, with consistent notes. Drink now through 2005.–B.S. • $19 • (2/28/1999) • **85**

Riesling Spätlese Mosel-Saar-Ruwer Kanzemer Altenberg 1996 • $19 • (3/31/1998) • **89**

PAULY-BERGWEILER, DR.

Riesling Auslese Mosel-Saar-Ruwer Bernkasteler alte Badstube 1998: With fine weight on an open, transparent texture, this '98 shows modest lime and mineral notes. Finishes with a slight astringency. Drink now through 2004.–B.S. • $50 • (2/29/2000) • **88**

Riesling Auslese Mosel-Saar-Ruwer Bernkasteler alte Badstube am Doctorberg 1996 • $30 • (11/30/1997) • **86**

Riesling Auslese Mosel-Saar-Ruwer Bernkasteler Lay 1996 • $29 • (11/30/1997) • **84**

Riesling Beerenauslese Mosel-Saar-Ruwer Bernkasteler Alte Badstube am Doctorberg 1993 • $55 • (11/30/1994) • **85**

Riesling Beerenauslese Mosel-Saar-Ruwer Bernkasteler Badstube 1994 • $NA • (11/30/1995) • **84**

Riesling Beerenauslese Mosel-Saar-Ruwer Bernkasteler Badstube 1989 • $60 • (12/15/1990) • **86**

Riesling Beerenauslese Mosel-Saar-Ruwer Bernkasteler Lay 1994 • $33 • (11/30/1995) • **90**

Riesling Beerenauslese Mosel-Saar-Ruwer Wehlener Sonnenuhr 1989 • $70 • (12/15/1990) • **83**

Riesling Eiswein Mosel-Saar-Ruwer Bernkasteler Lay 1996 • $139 • (11/30/1997) • **94**

Riesling Eiswein Mosel-Saar-Ruwer Bernkasteler Lay 1995 • $120 • (11/30/1996) • **90**

Riesling Eiswein Mosel-Saar-Ruwer Graacher Himmelreich 1992 • $NA • (11/30/1993) • **86**

Riesling Eiswein Mosel-Saar-Ruwer Graacher Himmelreich 1989 • $100 • (12/15/1990) • **81**

Riesling Kabinett Mosel-Saar-Ruwer Bernkasteler alte Badstube am Doctorberg 1998: Almond and vanilla-custard aromas are followed by citrus notes, with a creamy texture and a crisp backbone. Not that expressive now, but all the elements are there. Drink through 2004.–B.S. • $21 • (2/29/2000) • **88**

Riesling Kabinett Mosel-Saar-Ruwer Bernkasteler alte Badstube am Doctorberg 1996 • $19 • (11/30/1997) • **85**

Riesling Kabinett Mosel-Saar-Ruwer Bernkasteler Badstube 1998: A rounder, fleshier style, showing peach, lime and herb aromas and flavors. Not as expressive as other Mosel kabinetts today, but there's an underlying weight and power. Best from 2001 through 2006.–B.S. • $18 • (1/01/2000) • **87**

Riesling Kabinett Mosel-Saar-Ruwer Wehlener Sonnenuhr 1997: Distinctive, this exhibits a mealy, biscuity aroma and earthy, mineral accents to the tropical fruit and spicy flavors. Concentrated and dense, it seems more like a spätlese. Structured and powerful, with a lingering finish. Best from 2001 through 2007.–B.S. • $18 • (2/28/1999) • **91**

Riesling Spätlese Mosel-Saar-Ruwer Bernkasteler alte Badstube am Doctorberg 1998: Gorgeous. Ripe, concentrated and elegant, bursting with apricot, lemon curd, violet and mineral aromas and flavors. Soft and plump, for early consumption, yet who can deny the delicious flavors? Drink now through 2003.–B.S. • $27 • (5/15/2000) • **88**

Riesling Spätlese Mosel-Saar-Ruwer Bernkasteler alte Badstube am Doctorberg 1997: The purity of this Riesling is amazing. Packed with apricot, lime and honey notes, buoyed upon a dazzling acid structure, rich and harmonious, it just keeps pumping out the flavors. The finish is long and satisfying. Delicious. Drink now through 2010.–B.S. • $26 • (2/28/1999) • **93**

Riesling Spätlese Mosel-Saar-Ruwer Bernkasteler alte Badstube am Doctorberg 1996 • $25 • (11/30/1997) • **81**

Riesling Spätlese Mosel-Saar-Ruwer Bernkasteler Badstube 1998: Straightforward, with lovely citrus and peach and an appealing earthiness, yet it lacks a bit of intensity, though the finish is fine. Drink now through 2004.–B.S. • $25 • (1/01/2000) • **87**

Riesling Spätlese Mosel-Saar-Ruwer Bernkasteler Badstube 1997: A sleek, graceful '97 Riesling. Superripe, like a small auslese, this has honey, spice and apricot aromas and flavors, beautifully displayed on a transparent yet electric framework. Long finish, with an apple aftertaste. Drink now through 2007.–B.S. • $21 • (2/28/1999) • **92**

Riesling Spätlese Mosel-Saar-Ruwer Bernkasteler Badstube 1996 • $22 • (11/30/1997) • **86**

Riesling Spätlese Mosel-Saar-Ruwer Graacher Himmelreich 1997: The soft, luscious texture and ripe peach flavors in this white cover the firm acidity. Elegant and lively, it should age well. Drink now through 2006.–B.S. • $21 • (2/28/1999) • **88**

Riesling Spätlese Mosel-Saar-Ruwer Wehlener Sonnenuhr 1998: Floral and talc notes are high-toned in this broad, slightly awkward Riesling that has good length, but finishes on the coarse side. Tasted twice, with consistent notes. Drink now through 2004.–B.S. • $19 • (2/29/2000) • **87**

Riesling Spätlese Mosel-Saar-Ruwer Wehlener Sonnenuhr 1997: Fabulous. More like an auslese, this '97 spätlese is rich and zingy yet packed into a lean framework. Pinpoint delineation of lime, grapefruit and slate, intensely displayed on bracing acidity, is followed by a long, long finish. Best from 2002 through 2008.–B.S. • $21 • (2/28/1999) HR • **94**

Riesling Spätlese Mosel-Saar-Ruwer Wehlener Sonnenuhr 1996 • $23 • (11/30/1997) • **88**

Riesling Trockenbeerenauslese Mosel-Saar-Ruwer Bernkasteler Badstube am Doctorberg 1994 • $NA • (11/30/1995) • **86**

Riesling Trockenbeerenauslese Mosel-Saar-Ruwer Bernkasteler Alte Badstube am Doctorberg 1993 • $70 • (11/30/1994) • **84**

PFEFFINGEN

Gewürztraminer Spätlese Pfalz Ungsteiner Honigsäckel 1997: Floral aromas are delicate and haunting, followed by a moderately sweet impression on the palate. Lovely purity to the rose, apricot and spice flavors and fine concentration add to the overall harmony. Drink now.–B.S. • $18 • (5/15/1999) • **89**

Riesling Auslese Gold Cap Pfalz Ungsteiner Weilberg 1998: A lean, compact auslese, offering tightly wound quince and peach flavors and a spicy, clovelike note, maybe even a touch of botrytis that should unfold nicely over time. Drink now through 2007.–B.S. • $17/375 ml. • (2/29/2000) • **90**

Riesling Auslese Gold Cap Pfalz Ungsteiner Weilberg 1997: Impressive for its concentrated flavors of almond, citrus, honey and even a hint of candy, but it lacks focus, finishing with astringency. Drink now through 2005.–B.S. • $17/375 ml. • (2/28/1999) • **86**

Riesling Kabinett Halbtrocken Pfalz Pfeffo 1998: Round and full of apple and pear, this starts out rich, turning to citrus on the finish. Bright acidity keeps it lively. Drink now through 2003.–B.S. • $15 • (2/29/2000) • **85**

Riesling Kabinett Halbtrocken Pfalz Pfeffo 1997: Round, with lush apricot flavors and a soft framework, this is a forward, flattering '97. Drink now through 2003.–B.S. • $15 • (2/28/1999) • **83**

Riesling Kabinett Halbtrocken Pfalz Pfeffo 1996 • $15 • (4/30/1998) • **88**

Riesling Kabinett Pfalz Ungsteiner Honigsäckel 1997: This has ripe dried apricot notes, concentration and intensity allied to a solid structure. Everything pulses through the long finish. Drink now through 2006.–B.S. • $15 • (2/28/1999) • **89**

Riesling Kabinett Trocken Pfalz Ungsteiner Weilberg 1997: This has good body, yet maintains a racy quality from the vibrant acidity. Well concentrated, with flavors of dried peach and apricot. Dry, spicy finish. Drink now through 2005.–B.S. • $15 • (2/28/1999) • **86**

Riesling QbA Trocken Pfalz 1998: A touch on the earthy side, this dry white offers apple and almond flavors, a firm structure and a crisp finish. Try with food. Drink now through 2003.–B.S. • $11 • (2/29/2000) • **82**

Riesling Spätlese Halbtrocken Pfalz Ungsteiner Herrenberg 1998: Huge and thick, with mineral-tinged peach, apple and pear aromas and flavors, this is a monster dry spätlese, accented by spice and herb. So big it's scary. Best from 2001 through 2008.–B.S. • $20 • (2/29/2000) • **90**

Riesling Spätlese Halbtrocken Pfalz Ungsteiner Herrenberg 1997: This has a lees character, denoted by the brioche aromas and flavors and creamy texture, in addition to a pine flavor, making this '97 white distinctive. Rich, powerful and structured, it has a long finish. Best from 2001 through 2007.–B.S. • $20 • (2/28/1999) • **89**

■ ■ ■ ■

PFEFFINGEN

Riesling Spätlese Pfalz Ungsteiner Herrenberg 1998: Difficult to assess. The bracing acidity and astringent feel sit apart from each other, with an earthy streak running through.–B.S. • $20 • (1/01/2000) • **78**

Riesling Spätlese Pfalz Ungsteiner Herrenberg 1997: Focused, structured and powerful, the almond, honey and citrus flavors of this white cruise along the palate. Has wonderful intensity and a promising future. Best from 2002 through 2010.–B.S. • $20 • (2/28/1999) • **92**

Riesling Spätlese Pfalz Ungsteiner Herrenberg 1996 • $20 • (4/30/1998) • **81**

Riesling Spätlese Trocken Pfalz Ungsteiner Herrenberg 1998: Rich and dry, showing the spicy citrus side of Riesling. Austere and slightly tart on the finish. Drink now through 2004.–B.S. • $20 • (2/29/2000) • **84**

Riesling Spätlese Trocken Pfalz Ungsteiner Herrenberg 1997: Showing milky, yeasty flavors, this is lean and austere, offering more texture and body than fruit flavor.–B.S. • $20 • (2/28/1999) • **78**

Scheurebe Auslese Gold Cap Pfalz Ungsteiner Herrenberg 1998: Delicious auslese, full of lemon curd, peach, quince and honey, along with hints of chamomile and a grainy, clover-honeylike texture. Lovely integration and length. Drink now through 2004.–B.S. • $21/375 ml. • (5/15/2000) • **90**

Scheurebe Auslese Gold Cap Pfalz Ungsteiner Herrenberg 1997: Grapefruit and apricot notes mingle in this sweet white, with richness and acidity adding interest overall, despite a hint of vegetal flavor and a slight coarseness to the texture. Drink now through 2002.–B.S. • $21/375 ml. • (5/15/1999) • **82**

Scheurebe Beerenauslese Gold Cap Pfalz Ungsteiner Herrenberg 1998: Exotic and sweet offering apricot, pineapple, passion fruit and citrus underscored by a firm backbone. Still a little awkward at this stage, but has good elements in place. Best from 2001 through 2005.–B.S. • $39/375 ml. • (5/15/2000) • **90**

Scheurebe Beerenauslese Pfalz Ungsteiner Herrenberg 1990 • $35/375 ml. • (12/15/1991) • **93**

Scheurebe Eiswein Gold Cap Pfalz Ungsteiner Herrenberg 1998: Very sweet up front, dominating the character and structure, with straightforward honey and apricot flavors. Round and soft, with some acidity emerging on the finish. Drink now through 2003.–B.S. • $63/375 ml. • (5/15/2000) • **87**

Scheurebe Spätlese Pfalz Ungsteiner Herrenberg 1998: Serious Scheu here, from the honey, grapefruit and apricot notes to the lively structure and intensity of flavors. Fades just a tad on the finish, yet delicious. Drink now through 2001.–B.S. • $20 • (5/15/2000) • **87**

Scheurebe Spätlese Pfalz Ungsteiner Herrenberg 1997: Starts off fairly sweet, displaying concentrated passion fruit, apricot and orange flavors, yet there's good acidity for balance, along with a silky texture. An apricot note lingers. Drink now through 2002.–B.S. • $20 • (5/15/1999) • **86**

PRINZ

Riesling Auslese Rheingau Hallgartener Jungfer (AP 2) 1997: Sleek and racy, this has rapierlike acidity, marshaling its apricot and citrus flavors through to the long, minerally finish. It grows on you. Best from 2002 through 2008.–B.S. • $43/375 ml. • (2/28/1999) • **90**

Riesling Auslese Rheingau Hallgartener Jungfer (AP 10) 1997 • $NA/375 ml. • (1/01/1998) • **92**

Riesling Kabinett Rheingau Hallgartener Jungfer 1998: Ripe and forward, delivering juicy apricot aromas and flavors on a rich texture that turns firm on the finish. Drink now through 2003.–B.S. • $23 • (2/29/2000) • **86**

Riesling Kabinett Rheingau Hallgartener Jungfer 1997: Noticeably sweet for a kabinett, with vibrant acidity driving the apricot, grapefruit and mineral flavors. Moderate in concentration, finishing short. Drink now through 2002.–B.S. • $15 • (2/28/1999) • **83**

Riesling Kabinett Trocken Rheingau Hallgartener Schönhell 1998: Round and generous, this dry '98 has modest grapefruit and apple flavors, ending crisply. Try with food. Drink now through 2003.–B.S. • $23 • (2/29/2000) • **82**

Riesling QbA Halbtrocken Rheingau Hallgartener Hendelberg 1997: Plenty of ripeness in the form of quince aromas and flavors, pleasantly augmented by earth and herb notes. Just off-dry, with a crisp, firm finish. Drink now through 2005.–B.S. • $13 • (2/28/1999) • **87**

Riesling Spätlese Rheingau Hallgartener Jungfer 1998: Straightforward and medium sweet, this '98 Riesling exhibits peach and apple, a bracing structure and a moderate finish. Drink now through 2004.–B.S. • $35 • (2/29/2000) • **86**

Key: SS—Spectator Selection. CS—Cellar Selection. HR—Highly Recommended. $NA—Price not available. (BT)—Barrel tasting. (A)—Auction Price.
For a key to the tasters' initials, see "How to Use These Listings."
Dates in parentheses represent the issues in which the ratings were published.

Riesling Spätlese Rheingau Hallgartener Jungfer (AP 3) 1997 • $NA • (1/01/1998) • **88**

Riesling Spätlese Rheingau Hallgartener Jungfer (AP 4) 1997 • $NA • (1/01/1998) • **87**

PRÜM, JOH. JOS.

Riesling Auslese Gold Cap Mosel-Saar-Ruwer Wehlener Sonnenuhr 1997: Has an extra dimension of ripeness, but lacks the focus and cut of the higher-scoring Mosel auslesen—and gold caps. Apricot and guava flavors hold sway on the rich palate, but it's soft in texture, with just a moderate finish. Drink now through 2005.–B.S. • $44/375 ml. • (2/28/1999) • **90**

Riesling Auslese Long Gold Cap Mosel-Saar-Ruwer Wehlener Sonnenuhr 1998: Simply glorious and dense, with sweet, ripe apricot, passion fruit and honey nuances supported by an acid structure that hurts today but will integrate with the sweetness and preserve the fruit. Great intensity of flavor. Best from 2002 through 2010.–B.S. • $155/375 ml. • (2/29/2000) • **94**

Riesling Auslese Mosel-Saar-Ruwer Graacher Himmelreich 1997: A live wire, this racy, vibrant auslese gets out of the blocks like gangbusters, delivering the purest of lime, slate and apricot flavors in a rich, juicy texture, fading slightly on the finish. May firm up a little with time. Drink through 2010.–B.S. • $34 • (2/28/1999) • **90**

Riesling Auslese Mosel-Saar-Ruwer Wehlener Sonnenuhr 1998: A textbook auslese, literally bursting with apricot, nectarine, lime and mineral. Clean and beautifully balanced, with the sweetness playing off the vivid acidity and silky texture. Already delicious, this should age gracefully. Drink now through 2010.–B.S. • $34 • (2/29/2000) • **93**

Riesling Auslese Mosel-Saar-Ruwer Wehlener Sonnenuhr 1997: Wow. This '97 auslese almost overpowers the sensory receptors with its succulent, pure aromas and flavors of peach, apple and slate, rapierlike acidity and brilliant clarity. But it's never too much, as it remains balanced and harmonious all the way through. Drink now through 2010.–B.S. • $38 • (2/28/1999) • **93**

Riesling Beerenauslese Mosel-Saar-Ruwer Wehlener Sonnenuhr 1989 • $NA • (12/15/1990) • **95**

Riesling Eiswein Mosel-Saar-Ruwer Bernkasteler Johannisbrünchen 1990 • $NA • (12/15/1991) • **96**

Riesling Kabinett Mosel-Saar-Ruwer Wehlener Sonnenuhr 1998: Lush, ripe and sweet, with some trapped carbonic gas, yet this stylish, sleek Riesling is well balanced and redolent of peach and slate. Tasted twice, with consistent notes. Drink now through 2002.–B.S. • $19 • (2/29/2000) • **87**

Riesling Kabinett Mosel-Saar-Ruwer Wehlener Sonnenuhr 1997: An initial burnt-match smell should dissipate with either time in the bottle or aeration in the glass. Underneath is a blast of juicy peach and lime-tinged flavor and a delicate, crystalline framework. Long, mineral finish. Best from 2001 through 2007.–B.S. • $22 • (2/28/1999) • **88**

Riesling QbA Mosel-Saar-Ruwer Dr. M. Prüm 1996 • $11 • (4/30/1998) • **87**

Riesling Spätlese Mosel-Saar-Ruwer Graacher Himmelreich 1997: Amazing sense of purity and grace. Sleek, juicy in texture and concentrated, this Mosel spätlese offers lime, peach and mineral aromas and flavors, all precisely balanced and harmonious. Beautiful finish. Best from 2001 through 2007.–B.S. • $29 • (2/28/1999) • **91**

Riesling Spätlese Mosel-Saar-Ruwer Wehlener Sonnenuhr 1998: Silky-smooth and elegantly wrought, this white's pineapple, lime and stone flavors glide across the palate, concentrated and intense, cascading to a long finish. Drink now through 2006.–B.S. • $28 • (2/29/2000) • **90**

Riesling Spätlese Mosel-Saar-Ruwer Wehlener Sonnenuhr 1997: Brilliant Mosel. A delicious white, full of apple pie, spice and peach aromas and flavors accented by lime and mineral, all on a racy structure. Shows excellent focus and intensity, a succulent texture and a long finish. Drink through 2008.–B.S. • $32 • (2/28/1999) • **92**

PRÜM, S.A.

Riesling Auslese Mosel-Saar-Ruwer Graacher Himmelreich (AP 25) 1998: Subtle apricot and honey aromas and flavors gain a citrus edge as the initial sweetness in this elegant auslese meets the firm underlying acidity. Needs time to integrate. Best from 2001 through 2008.–B.S. • $NA/500 ml. • (2/29/2000) • **88**

Riesling Auslese Mosel-Saar-Ruwer Wehlener Sonnenhur (AP 16) 1998: Like a compressed steel spring, this is all structure. Lightweight and airy, it doesn't exhibit the density and concentration of the best, but it's difficult to evaluate now. Best after 2001.–B.S. • $NA • (2/29/2000) • **89**

Riesling Kabinett Mosel-Saar-Ruwer Wehlener Sonnenuhr 1998: Ripe and tangy, this kabinett displays apricot, lime and a hint of pineapple on a lightweight frame. Shows promise; needs a bit of time to come together. Drink through 2004.–B.S. • $18 • (2/29/2000) • **87**

Riesling QbA Halbtrocken Mosel-Saar-Ruwer 1998: Balanced toward the sweet side, with honey and citrus flavors, this '98 white seems soft initially, yet there's good acidity that provides support. Drink now through 2002.–B.S. • $15 • (2/29/2000) • **83**

Riesling Spätlese Mosel-Saar-Ruwer Wehlener Sonnenuhr (AP 15) 1998: Magnificent. Smells and tastes young, but there's a lot going on here, from the elegantly displayed smoke, slate, lime and apricot notes to the steel framework. Just keeps building and building across the palate. Drink now through 2006.–B.S. • $24 • (2/29/2000) • **92**

REINHARTSHAUSEN, SCHLOSS

Riesling Auslese Gold Cap Rheingau Erbacher Schlossberg 1997: A delicious auslese, ripe and sweet but never cloying, whose apricot, honey and white chocolate flavors are beautifully balanced and proportioned through the long finish. There are no rough edges here. Drink now through 2008.–B.S. • $157 • (2/28/1999) • **93**

Riesling Auslese Gold Cap Rheingau Hattenheimer Wisselbrunnen 1998: Dessert in the glass, showing apricot, cream and honey, with a hint of exotic passion fruit and spice, all held together by a firm backbone. Lingers on the palate for minutes. Drink now through 2010.–B.S. • $158/375 ml. • (2/29/2000) • **96**

Riesling Auslese Rheingau Erbacher Schlossberg 1997: Superripe, this has butterscotch and vanilla accents to the guava and honey. Very exotic, rich and forward, its sweetness covers the acidity, which seems soft but balances everything nicely and peeks through on the long finish. Drink now through 2007.–B.S. • $35 • (2/28/1999) • **91**

Riesling Auslese Rheingau Erbacher Siegelsberg 1996 • $31/375 ml. • (11/30/1997) • **85**

Riesling Auslese Rheingau Hattenheimer Wisselbrunnen 1998: Extremely ripe, forward and delicious, boasting dried apricot, truffle and candied citrus peel flavors, with sufficient acidity support to keep it fresh and balanced. Drink now through 2006.–B.S. • $80 • (2/29/2000) • **90**

Riesling Beerenauslese Rheingau Erbacher Marcobrunn 1992 • $NA • (11/30/1993) • **84**

Riesling Beerenauslese Rheingau Erbacher Siegelsberg 1996 • $119/375 ml. • (11/30/1997) • **87**

Riesling Beerenauslese Rheingau Hattenheimer Wisselbrunnen 1997: Thick and concentrated, offering botrytis accents of honey and orange peel. Silky and persistent on the palate, ending on a note of citrus and cleansing acidity. Moderate length. Drink now through 2008.–B.S. • $255 • (2/28/1999) • **90**

Riesling Beerenauslese Rheingau Hattenheimer Wisselbrunnen 1994 • $NA • (11/30/1995) • **89**

Riesling Beerenauslese Rheingau Hattenheimer Wisselbrunnen 1993 • $NA • (11/30/1994) • **83**

Riesling Beerenauslese Rheingau Hattenheimer Wisselbrunnen 1990 • $100 • (12/15/1991) • **87**

Riesling Eiswein Rheingau Erbacher Michelmark 1993 • $NA • (11/30/1994) • **84**

Riesling Kabinett Halbtrocken Rheingau Hattenheimer Wisselbrunnen 1998: Difficult to judge. There appears to be density and concentration, but trapped carbon dioxide is flattening the aromas and flavors, only hinting at peach and mineral. Best from 2001 through 2005.–B.S. • $24 • (2/29/2000) • **84**

Riesling Kabinett Rheingau Erbacher Schlossberg 1997: Very aromatic, brimming with white pepper and apple aromas and flavors, lively acidity and good weight on the palate. Spice notes echo on the finish. Drink now through 2004.–B.S. • $23 • (2/28/1999) • **86**

Riesling Kabinett Rheingau Erbacher Schlossberg 1996 • $17 • (11/30/1997) • **86**

Riesling Kabinett Trocken Rheingau Erbacher Schlossberg 1998: Austere in flavor, though there's plump texture before it turns lean on the finish. May improve, but there isn't much fruit.–B.S. • $26 • (1/01/2000) • **78**

Riesling Kabinett Trocken Rheingau Erbacher Schlossberg 1997: Perfumed and spicy, this dry kabinett has flesh and richness. Balanced on the soft side, yet with good acidity. Finishes a little lean. Drink now through 2003.–B.S. • $23 • (2/28/1999) • **83**

Riesling QbA Trocken Rheingau 1998: This seems bone-dry, with richness up front and hints of citrus, yet turns lean and austere midpalate through the finish. Where's the fruit? Drink now through 2003.–B.S. • $18 • (2/29/2000) • **80**

Riesling QbA Trocken Rheingau 1997: Very distinctive, displaying slightly smoky almond aromas and flavors and a strong mineral component. Intense and firmly structured, with a lot of power on the finish. Tasted twice, with consistent notes. Drink through 2007–B.S. • $16 • (2/28/1999) • **89**

Riesling Spätlese Rheingau Erbacher Marcobrunn 1998: Very high-toned, full of grapefruit and floral character, all in a lean, compact presentation. Finishes tartly. Best after 2000.–B.S. • $51 • (1/01/2000) • **83**

Riesling Spätlese Rheingau Erbacher Marcobrunn 1997: A solid spätlese that hints of petrol in the aroma, with peach flavor and bright, citrusy acidity. It could use more concentration and ripeness to match the acidity. Drink now through 2004.–B.S. • $44 • (2/28/1999) • **84**

Riesling Spätlese Rheingau Erbacher Siegelsberg 1996 • $27 • (11/30/1997) • **85**

Riesling Spätlese Trocken Rheingau Erbacher Marcobrunn 1998: A Jekyll and Hyde. High-toned apricot aromas and a rich texture up front quickly turn to a firm, citruslike acidity that shuts everything down. Give it a chance. Best after 2000.–B.S. • $51 • (2/29/2000) • **85**

Riesling Spätlese Trocken Rheingau Erbacher Marcobrunn 1997: Dry and spicy in character, with expressive aromas and flavors of nectarine accented by nutmeg and white pepper. Rich and concentrated, it has power, followed by a juicy finish. Drink now through 2006.–B.S. • $43 • (2/28/1999) • **88**

Riesling Spätlese Trocken Rheingau Erbacher Marcobrunn 1996 • $40 • (11/30/1997) • **83**

Riesling Trockenbeerenauslese Rheingau Erbacher Siegelsberg 1996 • $NA/375 ml. • (11/30/1997) • **89**

RESS, BALTHASAR

Riesling Auslese Rheingau Rüdesheimer Berg Rottland 1997: Complex and intriguing for its flint, petrol, red berry and almond character, this has ripeness and elegance, moderate concentration, bright acidity and a lingering finish. Best from 2001 through 2007.–B.S. • $50 • (2/28/1999) • **89**

Riesling Auslese Rheingau Rüdesheimer Berg Schlossberg 1998: Ripe and intense, yet it tastes awkward, with marzipan, toast and a flat character on the finish. Drink now through 2004.–B.S. • $45 • (1/01/2000) • **84**

Riesling Beerenauslese Rheingau Oestricher Doosberg 1996 • $100/500 ml. • (11/30/1997) • **82**

Riesling Eiswein Rheingau Hallgartener Hendelberg 1996 • $NA/500 ml. • (11/30/1997) • **86**

Riesling Kabinett Halbtrocken Rheingau Schloss Reichartshausen 1997: Appealing and off-dry, with juicy yet reserved peach and apple aromas and flavors as well as herb and mineral elements in the background. Good finish. Drink now through 2002.–B.S. • $14 • (2/28/1999) • **83**

Riesling Kabinett Rheingau Hattenheimer Schützenhaus 1997: Authoritative, with a hint of a swagger, but this never loses focus. Shows peach aromas and flavors, but with more smoke and mineral, married to a rich texture and a firm backbone. Fine length of flavor. Drink now through 2007.–B.S. • $10 • (2/28/1999) • **90**

Riesling Kabinett Rheingau Hattenheimer Schützenhaus 1996 • $10 • (11/30/1997) • **87**

Riesling Kabinett Rheingau Schloss Reichartshausen 1996 • $13 • (11/30/1997) • **76**

Riesling QbA Halbtrocken Rheingau Schloss Reichartshausen 1998: Firm and a bit stiff, with almond and citrus notes and a hint of sweetness to balance the structure. Still, it's pretty lean on the finish. Drink now through 2003.–B.S. • $11 • (2/29/2000) • **82**

Riesling QbA Rheingau Hattenheim 1996 • $9 • (11/30/1997) • **79**

Riesling QbA Rheingau Rüdesheimer Berg Schlossberg 1998: More akin to Alsace in its approach, this Riesling is on the dry side. Medium-bodied and muscular, exuding baked apple, spice and lemon flavors. Good length. Try with roast pork. Best from 2001 through 2006.–B.S. • $11 • (2/29/2000) • **88**

Riesling Spätlese Rheingau Hattenheimer Nussbrunnen 1998: Like putting on clothes a size too small, it's hard to reconcile the generous apricot and mineral flavors with the compact structure and slight astringency. Still a pretty array of flavors. Best from 2001 through 2006.–B.S. • $19 • (2/29/2000) • **88**

Riesling Spätlese Rheingau Oestricher Doosberg 1996 • $22 • (11/30/1997) • **87**

Riesling Spätlese Rheingau Rüdesheimer Berg Rottland 1998: Round and ample. Apricot and nectarine plus a hint of almond combine with a moderately solid frame. Picks up citrus and astringence on the finish. Drink now through 2005.–B.S. • $19 • (1/01/2000) • **85**

Riesling Spätlese Rheingau Rüdesheimer Berg Rottland 1996 • $NA • (11/30/1997) • **88**

Riesling Spätlese Rheingau Schloss Reichartshausen 1998: Rheingau's firm, upright personality is tamed by the exuberant peach, mineral and spice in this '98 spätlese. Needs a little time to integrate. Best from 2002 through 2006.–B.S. • $19 • (2/29/2000) • **87**

Riesling Spätlese Rheingau Schloss Reichartshausen 1997: Dense and concentrated, offering apricot and mineral flavors allied to a creamy texture, then finishes on an astringent, crisp note, giving a disjointed impression. May just need time. Drink through 2005.–B.S. • $22 • (2/28/1999) • **86**

Riesling Trocken Rheingau 1996 • $9 • (11/30/1997) • **86**

REUSCHER-HAART

Riesling Auslese Mosel-Saar-Ruwer Piesporter Goldtröpfchen 1997: Richly textured with a soft structure and almond, peach and mineral aromas and flavors followed by a weak finish. A little dilute for this category. Tasted twice, with consistent notes. Drink now through 2004.–B.S. • $21/500 ml. • (2/28/1999) • **84**

Riesling Kabinett Mosel-Saar-Ruwer Piesporter Goldtröpfchen 1997: Wow. A pumped-up kabinett, more like a spätlese, full of rich apricot, passion fruit and sweet corn, all richly textured and supported by lively acidity. Drink through 2005–B.S. • $14 • (2/28/1999) • **89**

Riesling Spätlese Mosel-Saar-Ruwer Piesporter Goldtröpfchen (AP 9) 1997: A broad, rich Riesling, displaying apple, peach and a hint of petrol, this is open and easygoing, with a hint of green apple acidity lurking underneath and on the finish. Drink now through 2005.–B.S. • $17 • (2/28/1999) • **88**

Riesling Spätlese Mosel-Saar-Ruwer Piesporter Goldtröpfchen (AP 12) 1997 • $NA • (1/01/1998) • **89**

REVERCHON, EDMUND

Riesling QbA Mosel-Saar-Ruwer Filzener Herrenberg 1997: Pure slate, showing a round profile and an initial richness that turns firmer on the finish. Ripe quince and lemon add nuance to the flavors. Drink now through 2003.–B.S. • $14 • (5/15/2000) • **86**

RICHTER, MAX FERD.

Riesling Auslese Mosel-Saar-Ruwer Brauneberger Juffer 1997: Apple, peach and citrus notes, but lacks density and concentration. Delicate, it's more like a top spätlese than auslese. Drink now through 2004.–B.S. • $20 • (9/30/1999) • **88**

Riesling Auslese Mosel-Saar-Ruwer Brauneberger Juffer-Sonnenuhr 1998: This pretty auslese is on the soft side, with moderate flavors of peach and lime. Not particularly concentrated or long, but attractive. Drink now through 2003.–B.S. • $26 • (2/29/2000) • **88**

Riesling Auslese Mosel-Saar-Ruwer Graacher Dompropst 1998: Round and forward, delivering peach, citrus and mineral flavors up front, followed by vibrant structure and a mouthwatering citrus finish. Needs time to integrate. Best from 2001 through 2008.–B.S. • $25 • (2/29/2000) • **90**

Riesling Auslese Mosel-Saar-Ruwer Graacher Himmelreich 1997: Intriguing white, shows an element of terroir, an intensity and a creaminess in texture. Not a blockbuster, yet earth, slate and spice aromas and flavors combine deftly with the delicate structure. Drink through 2005.–B.S. • $25 • (9/30/1999) • **89**

Riesling Eiswein Mosel-Saar-Ruwer Mülheimer Helenenkloster 1992 • $NA • (11/30/1993) • **79**

Riesling Eiswein Mosel-Saar-Ruwer Mülheimer Helenenkloster 1990 • $100 • (12/15/1991) • **93**

Riesling Eiswein Mosel-Saar-Ruwer Mülheimer Helenenkloster 1989 • $50/375 ml. • (12/15/1990) • **82**

Riesling Kabinett Halbtrocken Mosel-Saar-Ruwer Graacher Dompropst 1997: A sense of restraint and inner tension plays off the lime, peach and mineral flavors in this off-dry Riesling. Good concentration and length. Drink now through 2003.–B.S. • $17 • (9/30/1999) • **85**

Riesling Kabinett Halbtrocken Mosel-Saar-Ruwer Mülheimer Sonnenlay 1998: Pleasant, if a little simple in its citrus flavor profile. Bright acidity keeps it lively. Drink now through 2002.–B.S. • $16 • (1/01/2000) • **83**

Riesling Kabinett Halbtrocken Mosel-Saar-Ruwer Mülheimer Sonnenlay 1997: The apricot and passion fruit aromas and flavors are offset by a spicy element, all supported by a succulent, citrusy acidity. Finishes austerely and on the dry side. Drink now through 2003.–B.S. • $15 • (9/30/1999) • **85**

Key: SS—Spectator Selection. CS—Cellar Selection. HR—Highly Recommended. $NA—Price not available. (BT)—Barrel tasting. (A)—Auction Price.
For a key to the tasters' initials, see "How to Use These Listings."
Dates in parentheses represent the issues in which the ratings were published.

Riesling Kabinett Mosel-Saar-Ruwer Brauneberger Juffer 1998: A pronounced aroma and flavor of lime marks this soft, approachable Riesling. Moderately structured and dense, with flavors that dissipate quickly on the finish. Drink now through 2003.–B.S. • $17 • (1/01/2000) • **83**

Riesling Kabinett Mosel-Saar-Ruwer Brauneberger Juffer 1997: On the austere side, yet offers dense flavors of slate and lime, backed up by a firm structure. Seems rigid and a little short today, offering more of the site than the grape. Drink through 2004–B.S. • $16 • (9/30/1999) • **86**

Riesling Kabinett Mosel-Saar-Ruwer Brauneberger Juffer 1996 • $15 • (11/30/1997) • **88**

Riesling Kabinett Mosel-Saar-Ruwer Graacher Himmelreich 1998: Exotic aromas of passion fruit and red berries segue into lime and mineral on the palate in this intense, racy Riesling. It has the live-wire structure of a Saar or Ruwer wine. Excellent length. Drink now through 2007.–B.S. • $17 • (2/29/2000) • **91**

Riesling Kabinett Mosel-Saar-Ruwer Graacher Himmelreich 1997: Attractive and immediately appealing for its peach, mineral and citrus aromas and flavors, yet shows very firm structure and lovely balance, tailing off a bit on the finish. Drink now through 2004.–B.S. • $16 • (9/30/1999) • **87**

Riesling Kabinett Mosel-Saar-Ruwer Graacher Himmelreich 1996 • $15 • (11/30/1997) • **87**

Riesling Kabinett Mosel-Saar-Ruwer Wehlener Sonnenhuhr 1998: Straightforward apple and citrus notes are overshadowed by the structure today. A hint of SO2 also. Needs time. Best after 2001.–B.S. • $17 • (1/01/2000) • **85**

Riesling Kabinett Mosel-Saar-Ruwer Wehlener Sonnenhuhr 1997: Not very expressive now. A touch of honey, along with almond and good concentration, yet it turns austere and quite dry on the finish. Drink through 2004–B.S. • $16 • (9/30/1999) • **84**

Riesling Kabinett Mosel-Saar-Ruwer Wehlener Sonnenuhr 1996 • $15 • (11/30/1997) • **88**

Riesling QbA Mosel-Saar-Ruwer 1996 • $11 • (11/30/1997) • **83**

Riesling QbA Mosel-Saar-Ruwer Estate 1997: Very minerally, along with lime, peach and earth notes; zippy, firm and stony, relying more on mineral tones than fruit. Fine intensity and length. Drink now through 2003.–B.S. • $12 • (9/30/1999) • **86**

Riesling QbA Mosel-Saar-Ruwer Mülheimer Sonnenlay 1997: A "drink me" style of white. Round and juicy, bursting with peach and hints of spice and earth. Moderate intensity and length, yet well balanced. Drink now through 2001.–B.S. • $10 • (9/30/1999) • **84**

Riesling Spätlese Mosel-Saar-Ruwer Brauneberger Juffer 1998: Lovely apricot, pineapple and mineral notes are driven by firm structure, despite being tightly wound and somewhat closed on the finish today. Best after 2002.–B.S. • $21 • (2/29/2000) • **90**

Riesling Spätlese Mosel-Saar-Ruwer Brauneberger Juffer-Sonnenuhr 1998: Like a fastball across the plate, the apricot, lime and mineral notes hit home, buoyed by vibrant acidity and good concentration. Drink now through 2005.–B.S. • $21 • (2/29/2000) • **89**

Riesling Spätlese Mosel-Saar-Ruwer Brauneberger Juffer-Sonnenuhr 1996 • $18 • (11/30/1997) • **86**

Riesling Spätlese Mosel-Saar-Ruwer Graacher Dompropst 1996 • $19 • (11/30/1997) • **84**

Riesling Spätlese Mosel-Saar-Ruwer Graacher Dompropst 1997: Flavorful and appealing for its nectarine and lime elements, but it quickly turns dilute before a weak finish.–B.S. • $21 • (9/30/1999) • **80**

Riesling Spätlese Mosel-Saar-Ruwer Veldenzer Elisenberg 1997: Delicate and restrained, offering a balance between the spice, earth and cassis flavors, juicy acidity and silky texture. Light-bodied, yet concentrated. Drink now through 2004.–B.S. • $17 • (9/30/1999) • **87**

Riesling Spätlese Mosel-Saar-Ruwer Wehlener Sonnenuhr 1998: Soft and appealing, with floral and talcum powder aromas and flavors; a soft, forward '98 that's easy to enjoy now. Tasted twice, with consistent notes. Drink now.–B.S. • $21 • (1/01/2000) • **83**

Riesling Spätlese Mosel-Saar-Ruwer Wehlener Sonnenuhr 1997: Gorgeous, from the floral- and lime-inflected flavors and creamy texture to the long citrus and slate finish. Everything is in proportion and backed by succulent acidity. Drink now through 2005.–B.S. • $20 • (9/30/1999) • **89**

Riesling Spätlese Mosel-Saar-Ruwer Wehlener Sonnenuhr 1996 • $18 • (11/30/1997) • **89**

Riesling Trockenbeerenauslese Mosel-Saar-Ruwer Brauneberger Juffer-Sonnenuhr 1992 • $300 • (11/30/1993) • **94**

Riesling Trockenbeerenauslese Mosel-Saar-Ruwer Mülheimer Sonnenlay 1989 • $100/375 ml. • (12/15/1990) • **92**

ROTHROCK

Ortega Beerenauslese Rheinhessen Wormser Liebfrauenmorgen 1997: Sweet, with honeyed crème brûlée aromas and flavors, yet lacks the depth and concentration to surge across the palate. Finishes weak.–B.S. • $15/375 ml. • (10/15/1998) • **80**

Riesling Spätlese Dry Rheinhessen Wormser Liebfrauenmorgen 1996: A pleasant Riesling. Dry and lemony, if without much depth of flavor.–B.S. • $10 • (10/15/1998) • **77**

Riesling Spätlese Rheinhessen Wormser Liebfrauenmorgen 1997: Medium-sweet, with perfumed aromas and candied apple and peach flavors.–B.S. • $10 • (10/15/1998) • **76**

SAARSTEIN, SCHLOSS

Riesling Auslese Gold Cap Mosel-Saar-Ruwer Serriger Schloss Saarsteiner 1997: Lean and vibrant, this is a backward white, with firmly etched lime, peach and smoke flavors, followed by a mouthpuckering finish. All the elements are here but need time to integrate. Best from 2002 through 2009.–B.S. • $45/375 ml. • (2/28/1999) • **91**

Riesling Auslese Mosel-Saar-Ruwer Serriger Schloss Saarsteiner 1997: A lovely Mosel Riesling, offering peach and citrus aromas and flavors displayed on a light, gossamer framework. Racy acidity keeps everything focused and sharp. Herbs linger on the finish. Drink through 2010.–B.S. • $29 • (2/28/1999) • **88**

Riesling Beerenauslese Gold Cap Mosel-Saar-Ruwer Serriger Schloss Saarsteiner 1997: Exotic, bursting with coconut, cream and tropical fruit character which mingles with the rich texture. There's screeching acidity underneath, so give it time to integrate or try as an intermezzo between courses instead of sorbet. Best from 2002 through 2012.–B.S. • $120/375 ml. • (2/28/1999) • **93**

Riesling Beerenauslese Mosel-Saar-Ruwer Serriger Schloss Saarsteiner 1990 • $NA • (12/15/1991) • **94**

Riesling Eiswein Mosel-Saar-Ruwer Serriger Schloss Saarsteiner 1992 • $NA • (11/30/1993) • **92**

Riesling Kabinett Mosel-Saar-Ruwer Serriger Schloss Saarsteiner 1997: Lithe and intense, with slate, lime and peach flavors driven by racy acidity and an explosive personality. Mouthwatering finish. Drink now through 2004.–B.S. • $14 • (2/28/1999) • **88**

Riesling QbA Trocken Mosel-Saar-Ruwer 1997: Austere and a little muted, with slate and apple notes, good density and texture on the palate and a harmonious character. Drink now through 2002.–B.S. • $12 • (2/28/1999) • **83**

Riesling Spätlese Mosel-Saar-Ruwer Serriger Schloss Saarsteiner 1997: Plenty of lime and peach aromas and flavors in this elegant, lightweight '97, buoyed upon a juicy texture and solid, tensile structure. Good, lingering finish of peach. Drink now through 2004.–B.S. • $19 • (2/28/1999) • **88**

SALM-DALBERG, PRINZ ZU

Riesling Auslese Nahe Wallhäuser Johannisberg 1998: Serious richness here. Ripe and clean, showing peach, nectarine and citrus flavors backed by a lively structure. Long apricot aftertaste. Drink now through 2006.–B.S. • $34 • (2/29/2000) • **89**

Riesling Kabinett Nahe Wallhäuser Felseneck 1998: Elegant and racy, this focused white is full of peach, spice and mineral, deftly balanced and subtle on the finish. Drink now through 2003.–B.S. • $18 • (2/29/2000) • **84**

Riesling Spätlese Nahe Roxheimer Berg 1998: Rich and round, this '98 appeals with its ripe apricot and nectarine flavors. The sweetness covers the bright acidity, but it's balanced and lingering on the aftertaste. Drink now through 2004.–B.S. • $22 • (2/29/2000) • **87**

SCHAEFER, WILLI

Riesling Auslese Mosel-Saar-Ruwer Graacher Domprobst 1998: A hummingbird. Crisp and well delineated, this '98 excites the palate with its brisk acidity, carrying the lime and mineral notes to a long finish. Best from 2001 through 2010.–B.S. • $81 • (2/29/2000) • **89**

Riesling Auslese Mosel-Saar-Ruwer Graacher Domprobst (AP 13) 1997: Auction wine. Added ripeness lends a tropical note to the honey and apricot aromas and flavors in this rich, sweet '97 auslese. Vibrant acidity supports everything, though there's not a lot of nuance to the flavors. Drink now through 2006.–B.S. • $NA/375 ml. • (2/28/1999) • **89**

Riesling Auslese Mosel-Saar-Ruwer Graacher Domprobst (AP 14) 1997: A straightforward, delicious auslese, delivering citrus and peach notes in a rich, open style. Juicy acidity keeps the sweetness in check and refreshes on the finish. Drink now through 2006.–B.S. • $32/375 ml. • (2/28/1999) • **88**

Riesling Auslese Mosel-Saar-Ruwer Graacher Domprobst 1996 • $55/375 ml. • (4/30/1998) HR • **95**

Riesling Auslese Mosel-Saar-Ruwer Graacher Himmelreich 1997: A racy, tightly wound '97, exhibiting lime and mineral aromas and flavors. Densely textured and concentrated, with excellent length and the structure for aging. Best from 2002 through 2009.–B.S. • $40 • (2/28/1999) • **90**

Riesling Beerenauslese Mosel-Saar-Ruwer Graacher Domprobst 1997: A thoroughbred. Sleek and racy, this BA evokes citrus, slate and honey, yet hardly seems sweet. It packs dense flavors of lime, passion fruit and kiwi into its lissome frame and just keeps building on the palate to a never-ending finish. Best from 2002 through 2012.–B.S. • $69/375 ml. • (5/15/1999) • **95**

Riesling Beerenauslese Mosel-Saar-Ruwer Graacher Domprobst 1992 • $76 • (11/30/1993) • **94**

Riesling Kabinett Mosel-Saar-Ruwer Graacher Domprobst (AP 3) 1998: Banana and tropical fruit scents mark this '98 Riesling, whose brightness and elegance carry through to the firm finish. Drink now through 2003.–B.S. • $20 • (2/29/2000) • **86**

Riesling Kabinett Mosel-Saar-Ruwer Graacher Domprobst (AP 7) 1997: A solid white with apple and peach aromas and flavors, richness and concentration, and plenty of appley acidity on the long finish. Drink now through 2004.–B.S. • $14 • (2/28/1999) • **86**

Riesling Kabinett Mosel-Saar-Ruwer Graacher Domprobst (AP 8) 1997: A compact, angular '97 kabinett, unrevealing today, but with richness, concentration and a red fruit character. Firm acidity provides backbone and verve. Drink through 2005.–B.S. • $14 • (2/28/1999) • **88**

Riesling Kabinett Mosel-Saar-Ruwer Wehlener Sonnenuhr 1998: Mint or rosemary and banana aromas mark this delicate, vibrant '98 Riesling. Virtually reverberates on the palate, carrying the peach, lime and herb flavors to a moderate finish. Drink now through 2003.–B.S. • $20 • (2/29/2000) • **87**

Riesling QbA Halbtrocken Mosel-Saar-Ruwer Graacher Himmelreich 1998: A solid Mosel QbA, this shows power along with grapefruit, almond and earth flavors. Drink now through 2003.–B.S. • $17 • (1/01/2000) • **83**

Riesling QbA Mosel-Saar-Ruwer Graacher Himmelreich 1998: Lovely peach notes are framed by a vibrant structure, all beautifully balanced and long on the finish. Drink now through 2003.–B.S. • $17 • (2/29/2000) • **87**

Riesling QbA Mosel-Saar-Ruwer Graacher Himmelreich 1997: A delicious QbA with a lot going for it: very good concentration, with ripe, appley flavors and vibrant balancing acidity to offset the richness, and a density that offers promise for the future. Well done. Drink now through 2003.–B.S. • $12 • (2/28/1999) • **87**

Riesling Spätlese Mosel-Saar-Ruwer Graacher Domprobst (AP 4) 1998: Closed, tightly wound and unevolved, this has grapefruit and mineral yet it's not that expressive at this stage. Fine creamy richness underneath. Best after 2000.–B.S. • $25 • (2/29/2000) • **88**

Riesling Spätlese Mosel-Saar-Ruwer Graacher Domprobst (AP 12) 1998: Floral in aroma, turning to peach and mineral on the palate, this '98 spätlese is round and delicious, showing concentration and depth, ending with a crisp note of citrus. Drink now through 2005.–B.S. • $25 • (2/29/2000) • **90**

Riesling Spätlese Mosel-Saar-Ruwer Graacher Domprobst (AP 10) 1997: Reserved today, this nonetheless exhibits good concentration, density and structure, with vibrant acidity, although the apple, herb and peach flavors remain muted. Drink through 2005.–B.S. • $17 • (2/28/1999) • **87**

Riesling Spätlese Mosel-Saar-Ruwer Graacher Domprobst (AP 12) 1997: Lovely piquant acidity adds kick to the lime, mineral and spice aromas and flavors in this elegant '97. Good concentration, and fine length on the finish. Best from 2002 through 2008.–B.S. • $19 • (2/28/1999) • **90**

Riesling Spätlese Mosel-Saar-Ruwer Graacher Himmelreich 1998: A touch spritzy on entry, otherwise smooth and rich, like liquid key-lime pie with a mineral undercurrent. It's bright and lively, with a mouthwatering finish. Drink now through 2005.–B.S. • $23 • (2/29/2000) • **89**

Riesling Spätlese Mosel-Saar-Ruwer Graacher Himmelreich 1997: Richness of texture and harmony are the highlights in this white; its apple, peach and mineral flavors are subdued, yet there's weight and density, a long finish and well-integrated, racy acidity. Drink through 2006.–B.S. • $16 • (2/28/1999) • **89**

Riesling Spätlese Mosel-Saar-Ruwer Graacher Himmelreich 1996 • $17 • (4/30/1998) HR • **91**

SCHÄFER-FRÖHLICH

Riesling QbA Trocken Nahe Bockenauer Felseneck 1998: Dry, lean and spicy in character, offering modest citrus and apple notes.–B.S. • $13 • (1/01/2000) • **77**

SCHLEINITZ, VON

Riesling Auslese Mosel-Saar-Ruwer Koberner Weisenberg 1998: A '98 auslese with substance, this offers ripe apricot, fig and honey, offset by very bracing acidity. A touch coarse on the finish, it needs time to come together. Drink through 2005.–B.S. • $26 • (2/29/2000) • **88**

Riesling Kabinett Mosel-Saar-Ruwer Koberner Weisenberg 1998: A big kabinett, this displays its earth, spice and even a slight herbal element on a dense structure. It's all capped by a long finish. Very tightly wound today, but give it some time. Best from 2001 through 2007.–B.S. • $15 • (2/29/2000) • **88**

Riesling Spätlese Mosel-Saar-Ruwer Koberner Weisenberg 1998: Firm, dense and backward, here's a '98 spätlese offering lime and slate notes on an elegant frame, very clean and pure, with a fine finish. Best from 2001 through 2005.–B.S. • $18 • (2/29/2000) • **88**

SCHMITGES

Riesling Auslese Mosel-Saar-Ruwer Erdener Treppchen 1996 • $24/375 ml. • (9/15/1997) • **80**

Riesling Kabinett Mosel-Saar-Ruwer Erdener Treppchen 1996 • $12 • (9/15/1997) • **80**

Riesling QbA Mosel-Saar-Ruwer 1996 • $10 • (9/15/1997) • **86**

Riesling Spätlese Mosel-Saar-Ruwer Erdener Treppchen 1996 • $18/375 ml. • (9/15/1997) • **80**

Riesling Spätlese Trocken Mosel-Saar-Ruwer Erdener Treppchen 1996 • $18 • (9/15/1997) • **82**

SCHMITT SÖHNE

Riesling QbA Mosel-Saar-Ruwer Classic 1998: A pretty white, offering white peach and apple, with balance and a tart element that sneaks in around the edges. Drink now through 2003.–B.S. • $10 • (2/29/2000) • **81**

SCHMITT-WAGNER, CARL

Riesling Spätlese Mosel-Saar-Ruwer Longuicher Maximiner Herrenberg 1998: Odd-tasting, spritzy, with a plastic flavor. Tasted twice, with consistent notes.–B.S. • $19 • (1/01/2000) • **65**

SCHNEIDER, GEORG ALBRECHT

Riesling Kabinett Rheinhessen Niersteiner Paterberg 1998: Round and velvety, this slightly sweet '98 Riesling shows nectarine and grapefruit notes, finishing with a hint of astringency. Drink now through 2003.–B.S. • $13 • (2/29/2000) • **85**

SCHNEIDER, JAKOB

Riesling Spätlese Nahe Niederhäuser Hermannshöhle 1998: A round, fruity spätlese, all peaches and pears held together by a soft, juicy structure. Drink now through 2003.–B.S. • $22 • (2/29/2000) • **84**

SCHÖNBORN, SCHLOSS

Riesling Auslese Rheingau Erbacher Marcobrunn Gräflich Schönborn'scher Eigenbau 1997: Very floral and spicy Gewürztraminer-like aromas, then the apricot and honey take over on the palate, where this just keeps pumping out the flavors. Elegant, harmonious and vibrant, this is a winner. Drink now through 2007.–B.S. • $65 • (2/28/1999) • **91**

Riesling Beerenauslese Rheingau Hattenheimer Pfaffenberg 1994: Full of mineral, apricot and passion fruit flavors, this tastes sweet, concentrated and structured. A bit closed at this stage, yet intensely flavored and long on the finish. Best from 2001 through 2010.–B.S. • $NA • (9/30/1999) • **94**

Riesling Beerenauslese Rheingau Rüdesheimer Berg Schlossberg 1996: Intense apricot, honey and mineral aromas, with a pronounced earthiness. The wine is lean and wiry, despite the sweetness, with racy acidity and dense flavors of apricot and spice, which carry through to a long finish. (Schloss Schönborn vertical tasting.) Best from 2001 through 2010.–B.S. • $125 • (9/30/1999) • **93**

Riesling Beerenauslese Rheingau Rüdesheimer Berg Schlossberg 1989: Amber-orange in color, and the bouquet mixes beeswax, honey, apricot and orange peel. Full, rich and round, it shows a spicy, hard candy flavor and botrytis character, ending on a note of orange peel. (Schloss Schönborn vertical tasting.) Drink now through 2005.–B.S. • $NA • (9/30/1999) • **87**

Riesling Eiswein Rheingau Hattenheimer Nussbrunnen 1991 • $150 • (12/15/1992) • **90**

Riesling Kabinett Rheingau 1998: Beautiful apricot, rich and smooth, with vibrant acidity keeping it all fresh. Really hangs together nicely. Drink now through 2005.–B.S. • $17 • (2/29/2000) • **88**

Riesling Kabinett Rheingau 1997: Already showing petrol and almond flavors, this is a solid if unexciting white. Drink now.–B.S. • $14 • (2/28/1999) • **80**

Riesling Kabinett Rheingau Erbacher Marcobrunn 1998: Broad and powerful, this Rheingau white shows plenty of peach and spice, with a hint of earth. Well constituted, it's built for the long haul. Best from 2001 through 2007.–B.S. • $19 • (2/29/2000) • **88**

Riesling Kabinett Rheingau Erbacher Marcobrunn 1997: Not very expressive now, this '97 white shows good concentration and length, with pear and almond flavors and a firm structure. Drink through 2005–B.S. • $15 • (2/28/1999) • **84**

Riesling Kabinett Rheingau Hattenheimer Pfaffenberg 1997: An elegant '97, offering almond and orange notes, but without the concentration and intensity of the best. Turns a little coarse on the finish. Drink now through 2002.–B.S. • $14 • (2/28/1999) • **83**

Riesling Kabinett Rheingau Hattenheimer Pfaffenberg 1996: Wonderfully fresh white. Aromas of mango and apple, with hints of pie crust that follow through on the palate. Medium-bodied and lightly sweet, with fresh acidity and a lively finish. Drink now through 2005.–J.S. • $13 • (7/31/1998) • **89**

Riesling Kabinett Rheingau Johannisberger 1997: Offers ripe and focused peach and apricot aromas and flavors, combined with a rich texture, soft structure and tangy finish. (Schloss Schönborn vertical tasting.) Drink now through 2005.–B.S. • $30 • (9/30/1999) • **88**

Riesling Kabinett Rheingau Johannisberger Klaus 1997: This juicy, plump white makes your mouth water with its apricot and citrus notes. Not structured for the long haul. Drink now.–B.S. • $NA • (2/28/1999) • **85**

Riesling QbA Rheingau Erbacher Marcobrunn 1998: Tightly wound, with good density and balance, this is powerful, showing earth and almond flavors followed by a racy finish. Drink now through 2003.–B.S. • $18 • (2/29/2000) • **87**

Riesling QbA Rheingau Erbacher Marcobrunn 1996: Beautiful aromas of pie crust and apple, with hints of peach. Medium-bodied and dry, with a short finish. Promises more on the nose. Drink now.–J.S. • $12 • (7/31/1998) • **85**

Riesling QbA Rheingau Rüdeshiem Berg Schlossberg 1998: A powerful '98 Riesling, sinewy and coiled. Its apple and mineral notes are wrapped in the structure. Judging from the density and length, this should open up nicely. Best from 2001 through 2006.–B.S. • $15 • (2/29/2000) • **87**

Riesling Spätlese Gold Cap Rheingau Erbacher Marcobrunn 1997: Easily auslese in ripeness, this '97 white displays apricot, honey and mineral flavors and is rich and generous in character, with good underlying acidity but without the structure for the long haul. Drink now through 2007.–B.S. • $25 • (2/28/1999) • **89**

Riesling Spätlese Rheingau Erbacher Marcobrunn 1998: More like a '97, showing rich, ripe peach and spice notes, yet there's a firm structure underneath. Very smooth and opulent, with a moderate finish. Drink now through 2004.–B.S. • $30 • (1/01/2000) • **89**

Riesling Spätlese Rheingau Erbacher Marcobrunn 1996: Light aromas of dried apricot and maple syrup. Medium-bodied and off-dry, with good fruit flavors and a medium finish. Drink now.–J.S. • $21 • (7/31/1998) • **86**

Riesling Spätlese Rheingau Geisenheimer Rothenberg-Lothar Franz 1996: Superintense aromas of sliced peach and nectarine. Medium-bodied and lightly sweet, with ripe fruit flavors and a long finish. A beauty. Drink now.–J.S. • $20 • (7/31/1998) • **90**

Riesling Spätlese Rheingau Hattenheimer Pfaffenberg 1998: This gorgeous spätlese combines rich peach and mineral aromas and flavors with a smooth texture and a firm structure bordering on austere. Great purity of flavors. Drink now through 2004.–B.S. • $25 • (2/29/2000) • **91**

Key: SS—Spectator Selection. CS—Cellar Selection. HR—Highly Recommended. $NA—Price not available. (BT)—Barrel tasting. (A)—Auction Price.
For a key to the tasters' initials, see "How to Use These Listings."
Dates in parentheses represent the issues in which the ratings were published.

GERMANY

Riesling Spätlese Rheingau Hattenheimer Pfaffenberg 1997: Restrained and subtle in its delivery, this shows apple, almond and a slight accent of herbs or grass. It has richness and a moderately firm structure. Drink now through 2004.–B.S. • $19 • (2/28/1999) • **86**

Riesling Spätlese Rheingau Hattenheimer Pfaffenberg 1996: A lovely, rich, peachy wine, with undertones of dough and crust. Medium-bodied and lightly sweet, with a soft texture and a long, flavorful aftertaste. Drink now through 2000.–J.S. • $17 • (7/31/1998) • **88**

Riesling Spätlese Rheingau Hattenheimer Pfaffenberg Gräflich Schönborn'scher Eigenbau 1997: Stunning. Auslese in quality, delivering rose and fruit blossom aromas. Soft peach, apricot and floral flavors are ethereal and harmonious, with a crystal-clear expression. It should develop well, but won't be a long-ager. Drink now through 2005.–B.S. • $40 • (2/28/1999) • **90**

Riesling Spätlese Rheingau Hochheimer Domdechaney 1998: A bit angular, showing the earth and almond side of Rheingau, yet it's forceful and persistent in flavor. Should improve with a few months of aging. Best from 2001 through 2005.–B.S. • $23 • (2/29/2000) • **87**

Riesling Trockenbeerenauslese Rheingau 1993 • $NA • (11/30/1994) • **89**

Riesling Trockenbeerenauslese Rheingau Hattenheimer Pfaffenberg 1997: Intense and unctuous, showing a lot of botrytis character, apricot, honey and Eastern-spice flavors. There's good balance here, but more toward the sweet side. Drink now through 2012.–B.S. • $300/500 ml. • (2/28/1999) • **92**

Riesling Trockenbeerenauslese Rheingau Hattenheimer Pfaffenberg 1992 • $325 • (11/30/1993) • **81**

Riesling Trockenbeerenauslese Rheingau Hochheimer 1990 • $NA • (12/15/1991) • **92**

SCHUBERT, C. VON

Riesling Auslese Mosel-Saar-Ruwer Maximin Grünhäuser Abtsberg (AP 57) 1997: Crunchy in texture, thanks to crisp acidity, and moderately rich, displaying lime and stony flavors, with the overall impression that of a tightly wound, austere white. Delicious, but lacks the concentration to rate outstanding. Tasted twice, with consistent notes. Best from 2001 through 2006.–B.S. • $61 • (2/28/1999) • **88**

Riesling Auslese Mosel-Saar-Ruwer Maximin Grünhäuser Abtsberg (AP 55) 1996 • $28/375 ml. • (11/30/1997) • **88**

Riesling Beerenauslese Mosel-Saar-Ruwer Maximin Grünhäuser Abtsberg 1989 • $NA • (12/15/1990) • **99**

Riesling Eiswein Mosel-Saar-Ruwer Maximin Grünhäuser Abtsberg 1990 • $NA • (12/15/1991) • **96**

Riesling Eiswein Mosel-Saar-Ruwer Maximin Grünhäuser Herrenberg 1991 • $120 • (12/15/1992) • **86**

Riesling Kabinett Mosel-Saar-Ruwer Maximin Grünhäuser Abtsberg 1998: Fresh, focused and delicate, this '98 Riesling shows peach, lime and smoky mineral tones that build in intensity through the finish. Good density is matched by a firm structure. Drink now through 2004.–B.S. • $25 • (2/29/2000) • **86**

Riesling Kabinett Mosel-Saar-Ruwer Maximin Grünhäuser Abtsberg 1997: Gorgeous fruit here. Apricot, passion fruit and even red berries are accented by slate and spice in this sleek, racy '97. There's density underscored by vibrant acidity, culminating in a long, multidimensional aftertaste. Drink now through 2006.–B.S. • $25 • (2/28/1999) • **91**

Riesling Kabinett Mosel-Saar-Ruwer Maximin Grünhäuser Abtsberg 1996 • $19 • (11/30/1997) • **86**

Riesling Kabinett Mosel-Saar-Ruwer Maximin Grünhäuser Herrenberg 1996 • $18 • (11/30/1997) • **90**

Riesling QbA Mosel-Saar-Ruwer Maximin Grünhäuser Brüderberg 1996 • $12 • (11/30/1997) • **86**

Riesling QbA Mosel-Saar-Ruwer Maximin Grünhäuser Herrenberg 1996 • $13 • (11/30/1997) • **84**

Riesling Spätlese Mosel-Saar-Ruwer Maximin Grünhäuser Abtsberg 1998: Displays textbook slate, lime and peach aromas and flavors on a transparent but solid backbone of acidity. Just fades a little on the finish, preventing it from rating outstanding. Drink now through 2005.–B.S. • $27 • (2/29/2000) • **89**

Riesling Spätlese Mosel-Saar-Ruwer Maximin Grünhäuser Abtsberg 1997: Wow. Beautifully delineated, pure and zingy. Its lime, peach and slate flavors ride a razor's edge of acidity. Huge intensity of flavors and richness packed into this sleek frame. Best from 2002 through 2010.–B.S. • $27 • (2/28/1999) • **93**

Riesling Spätlese Mosel-Saar-Ruwer Maximin Grünhäuser Abtsberg 1996 • $24 • (11/30/1997) • **89**

Riesling Trockenbeerenauslese Mosel-Saar-Ruwer Maximin Grünhäuser Abtsberg 1994 • $220 • (11/30/1995) • **88**

Riesling Trockenbeerenauslese Mosel-Saar-Ruwer Maximin Grünhäuser Herrenberg 1989 • $NA • (12/15/1990) • **96**

SCHULZ, GERHARD

Riesling Spätlese Mosel-Saar-Ruwer Schweicher Annaberg 1996 • $10 • (4/30/1998) • **72**

SEEBRICH, HEINRICH

Riesling Eiswein Rheinhessen Niersteiner Rosenberg 1996 • $38/375 ml. • (4/30/1998) • **89**

SELBACH, J. & H.

Riesling QbA Mosel-Saar-Ruwer Dry 1997: A simple, crisp white offering modest lime and apple notes that dissipate quickly.–B.S. • $9 • (2/28/1999) • **77**

Riesling Spätlese Mosel-Saar-Ruwer Bernkastel-Kueser Kardinalsberg 1997: Distinctive if atypical, this white smells and tastes like vanilla, with spice and cooked apple notes. Lean and intense, it has screeching acidity and a marzipan note on the finish. Best from 2002 through 2008.–B.S. • $8 • (2/28/1999) • **87**

SELBACH-OSTER

Riesling Auslese Mosel-Saar-Ruwer Graacher Domprobst 1998: Sleek and delineated, offering lime and mineral, like water filtered through slate. There's plenty of substance, polished and smooth as marble. Great length. Best from 2001 through 2010.–B.S. • $44 • (2/29/2000) • **90**

Riesling Auslese Mosel-Saar-Ruwer Zeltinger Sonnenuhr 1998: Like a squeeze of fresh lime, crisp and tangy, intensely wrought with accents of spice. Lightweight and gossamerlike in structure, with a long aftertaste. Drink now through 2008.–B.S. • $22/375 ml. • (2/29/2000) • **91**

Riesling Auslese * Mosel-Saar-Ruwer Zeltinger Sonnenuhr 1998: Red fruit and almond aromas and flavors are distinctive. Has a firm backbone of acidity and good concentration, but it's just a little less expressive than its peers at this stage. Best from 2001 through 2006.–B.S. • $30/375 ml. • (1/01/2000) • **89**

Riesling Auslese * Mosel-Saar-Ruwer Zeltinger Sonnenuhr 1997: A slender ballerina of a white, whose mineral, apple and red berry flavors pirouette on the laserlike acidity to stay vibrant and well delineated. Intense and long on the finish. Best from 2002 through 2012.–B.S. • $32 • (2/28/1999) • **91**

Riesling Auslese ** Mosel-Saar-Ruwer Zeltinger Sonnenuhr 1997: Demonstrates beautiful clarity and focus, a crunchy texture and a grapefruitlike zing on the finish. Laden with spice, apricot and a distinctive sage note. Delicious now, but has the structure to age. Drink through 2008.–B.S. • $33 • (2/28/1999) • **90**

Riesling Auslese * Mosel-Saar-Ruwer Zeltinger Sonnenuhr 1996 • $36/375 ml. • (11/30/1997) • **86**

Riesling Beerenauslese Mosel-Saar-Ruwer Zeltingen-Rachtiger Sonnenuhr 1989 • $56/375 ml. • (12/15/1990) • **91**

Riesling Beerenauslese Mosel-Saar-Ruwer Zeltinger Sonnenuhr 1998: Smooth, showing ripe apricot, passion fruit and nectarine in a stylish, balanced package. Not too sweet and very elegant. Drink now through 2007.–B.S. • $115/375 ml. • (2/29/2000) • **89**

Riesling Beerenauslese Mosel-Saar-Ruwer Zeltinger Sonnenuhr 1995 • $NA/375 ml. • (11/30/1996) • **87**

Riesling Beerenauslese Mosel-Saar-Ruwer Zeltinger Sonnenuhr 1994 • $83 • (11/30/1995) • **93**

Riesling Beerenauslese Mosel-Saar-Ruwer Zeltinger Sonnenuhr 1990 • $75/375 ml. • (12/15/1991) • **91**

Riesling Eiswein Mosel-Saar-Ruwer Bernkasteler Badstube 1998: This riveting white begins with candied citrus peel and Poire William aromas that turn to caramelized brown sugar and maple notes on the palate. A nice juxtaposition of sweet and tart in the crisp structure supports the flavors. Best from 2001 through 2010.–B.S. • $107/375 ml. • (2/29/2000) • **96**

Riesling Eiswein Mosel-Saar-Ruwer Bernkasteler Badstube 1996 • $NA • (11/30/1997) • **90**

Riesling Eiswein Mosel-Saar-Ruwer Bernkasteler Badstube 1990 • $87/375 ml. • (12/15/1991) • **95**

Riesling Eiswein Mosel-Saar-Ruwer Zeltinger Schlossberg 1992 • $61/375 ml. • (11/30/1993) • **86**

Riesling Kabinett Mosel-Saar-Ruwer 1998: Delicious aromas and flavors of pear, apple, slate and lime are matched with a moderate structure and concentration. Drink now through 2003.–B.S. • $17 • (2/29/2000) • **86**

Riesling Kabinett Mosel-Saar-Ruwer Bernkasteler Badstube 1998: Like a piece of slate, this has a slight graininess to its texture, offsetting the lime and herb flavors. Tightly wound, it needs time to resolve the firm structure. Best from 2001 through 2005.–B.S. • $18 • (1/01/2000) • **86**

Riesling Kabinett Mosel-Saar-Ruwer Graacher Domprobst 1996 • $13 • (11/30/1997) • **84**

Riesling Kabinett Mosel-Saar-Ruwer Wehlener Sonnenuhr 1998: A modest, straightforward kabinett, offering almond, lime and apple notes allied to a tart structure. Unusual for this estate, whose quality is typically very high. Tasted twice, with consistent notes.–B.S. • $19 • (1/01/2000) • **79**

Riesling Kabinett Mosel-Saar-Ruwer Zeltinger Schlossberg 1998: Racy and pure, showing textbook floral, lime and mineral flavors and good intensity that keeps the flavors pumping through. Drink now through 2004.–B.S. • $19 • (2/29/2000) • **87**

Riesling Kabinett Mosel-Saar-Ruwer Zeltinger Schlossberg 1997: A tight, compact style, unyielding now, with moderate density and concentration of peach and mineral flavors. Should develop well, but lacks the intensity of the best. Drink through 2005.–B.S. • $13 • (2/28/1999) • **86**

Riesling Spätlese Mosel-Saar-Ruwer 1998: Firm, focused and zippy, this spätlese is full of slate, apple and citrus. There's some stuffing underneath, so give it time. Best from 2001 through 2005.–B.S. • $22 • (1/01/2000) • **86**

Riesling Spätlese Mosel-Saar-Ruwer Bernkasteler Badstube 1998: Crisp yet round, this is bursting with lime, cream and mineral character. Full-bodied for a Mosel spätlese and needing time to come together. Best from 2001 through 2007.–B.S. • $23 • (1/01/2000) • **88**

Riesling Spätlese Mosel-Saar-Ruwer Wehlener Sonnenuhr 1998: Gorgeous spätlese, round, opulent and beautifully balanced, with elements of peach, citrus and mineral. Smooth and inviting, yet possesses a firm backbone of acidity. Long finish. Drink now through 2005.–B.S. • $25 • (2/29/2000) • **90**

Riesling Spätlese Mosel-Saar-Ruwer Wehlener Sonnenuhr 1996 • $20 • (11/30/1997) • **89**

Riesling Spätlese Mosel-Saar-Ruwer Zeltinger Schlossberg 1997: Lean and intense, like an untrained thoroughbred. It's difficult to see beyond the steel structure of this Mosel white, yet there are plenty of apple and peach flavors and a dense texture locked within its firm exterior. Best from 2002 through 2010.–B.S. • $16 • (2/28/1999) • **90**

Riesling Spätlese * Mosel-Saar-Ruwer Zeltinger Sonnenuhr 1998: Crisp and lively, with a rich, creamy texture and a forward approach that make this wine delicious drinking now, with flavors of peach, apricot and lime. Drink now through 2005.–B.S. • $27 • (2/29/2000) • **88**

Riesling Spätlese Mosel-Saar-Ruwer Zeltinger Sonnenuhr 1997: Filigreed and elegant, with a succulent texture and concentrated flavors of lime, peach and mineral, this seductive '97 Riesling is impeccably balanced. Drink now through 2005.–B.S. • $16 • (2/28/1999) • **89**

Riesling Spätlese * Mosel-Saar-Ruwer Zeltinger Sonnenuhr 1997: A brilliant spätlese, offering ripe, focused aromas and flavors of lime, apricot and honey on a delicate and vibrant structure. This has clarity, intensity of character and a long future. Best from 2001 through 2008.–B.S. • $18 • (2/28/1999) • **92**

Riesling Spätlese Trocken Mosel-Saar-Ruwer Zeltinger Sonnenuhr 1998: Lean and dry, with ripe peach, melon and mineral notes, very concentrated and persistent right through the lingering finish. Best from 2001 through 2005.–B.S. • $NA/375 ml. • (1/01/2000) • **87**

Riesling Trockenbeerenauslese Mosel-Saar-Ruwer Zeltingen-Rachtiger Sonnenuhr 1989 • $100/375 ml. • (12/15/1990) • **97**

Riesling Trockenbeerenauslese Mosel-Saar-Ruwer Zeltinger Sonnenuhr 1996 • $NA • (11/30/1997) • **90**

Riesling Trockenbeerenauslese Mosel-Saar-Ruwer Zeltinger Sonnenuhr 1990 • $NA • (12/15/1991) • **93**

SICHEL

Pinot Noir Rotwein Pfalz Dornfelder 1992 • $6 • (3/31/1995) • **77**

Riesling Beerenauslese Rheinpfalz Deidesheimer Hofstück 1988 • $10/375 ml. • (3/15/1990) • **92**

Trockenbeerenauslese Pfalz Kirchheimer Kreuz 1990 • $30/375 ml. • (12/15/1995) • **84**

Key: SS—Spectator Selection. CS—Cellar Selection. HR—Highly Recommended. $NA—Price not available. (BT)—Barrel tasting. (A)—Auction Price.
For a key to the tasters' initials, see "How to Use These Listings."
Dates in parentheses represent the issues in which the ratings were published.

SICHEL SÖHNE

Beerenauslese Rheinpfalz Kirchheimer Kreuz 1992 • $14 • (11/30/1993) • **77**

SIMMERN, LANGWERTH VON

Riesling Auslese Rheingau Hattenheimer Nussbrunnen 1996 • $45 • (11/30/1997) • **91**

Riesling Beerenauslese Rheingau Erbacher Marcobrunn 1992 • $NA • (11/30/1993) • **83**

Riesling Beerenauslese Rheingau Erbacher Marcobrunn 1991 • $152 • (12/15/1992) • **89**

Riesling Beerenauslese Rheingau Erbacher Marcobrunn 1990 • $300 • (12/15/1991) • **91**

Riesling Beerenauslese Rheingau Hattenheimer Nussbrunnen 1990 • $300 • (12/15/1991) • **90**

Riesling Eiswein Rheingau Eltviller Sonnenberg 1991 • $129 • (12/15/1992) • **89**

Riesling Kabinett Rheingau 1996 • $11 • (11/30/1997) • **86**

Riesling Kabinett Rheingau Erbacher Marcobrunn 1996 • $14 • (11/30/1997) • **88**

Riesling Kabinett Rheingau Hattenheimer Mannberg 1996 • $12 • (11/30/1997) • **87**

Riesling Kabinett Rheingau Rauenthaler Baiken 1996 • $13 • (11/30/1997) • **87**

Riesling QbA Rheingau 1996 • $10 • (11/30/1997) • **86**

Riesling Spätlese Rheingau Erbacher Marcobrunn 1996 • $25 • (11/30/1997) • **87**

Riesling Spätlese Rheingau Rauenthaler Baiken 1996 • $23 • (11/30/1997) • **89**

Riesling Trockenbeerenauslese Rheingau Erbacher Marcobrunn 1989 • $NA • (12/15/1990) • **99**

Riesling Trockenbeerenauslese Rheingau Hattenheimer Nussbrunnen 1993 • $NA • (11/30/1994) • **90**

Riesling Trockenbeerenauslese Rheingau Hattenheimer Nussbrunnen 1990 • $500 • (12/15/1991) • **94**

SIMON, BERT

Riesling Auslese Gold Cap Mosel-Saar-Ruwer Serriger Würtzberg 1998: Ripe and concentrated, underscored by zingy acidity that keeps everything defined. Pure apricot, honey and citrus flavors caress the palate, with a texture that's smooth but not heavy. Best from 2001 through 2008.–B.S. • $33 • (2/29/2000) • **91**

Riesling Auslese Gold Cap Mosel-Saar-Ruwer Serriger Herrenberg 1997: Light and airy, showing a vibrant framework and flavors of lime, peach and slate. Full of elegance and finesse, with a crackling texture and a long finish, this displays great terroir and fine winemaking. Drink now through 2006.–B.S. • $27 • (2/28/1999) • **89**

Riesling Beerenauslese Mosel-Saar-Ruwer Serriger Würtzberg 1989 • $53/375 ml. • (12/15/1990) • **93**

Riesling Eiswein Gold Cap * Mosel-Saar-Ruwer Serriger Würtzberg 1998: This super eiswein is redolent of apricot, tropical fruit and smoke. Very intense and bracing, with a long finish. Best from 2001 through 2010.–B.S.
• $53/375 ml. • (2/29/2000) • **92**

Riesling Kabinett Gold Cap Mosel-Saar-Ruwer Serriger Herrenberg 1997: A distinctive white, offering red currant and spice notes, a rich texture and vibrant acidity. An almond aftertaste lingers. Forward and enjoyable now for its bloom of youth. Drink through 2003.–B.S. • $15 • (2/28/1999) • **87**

Riesling Kabinett Mosel-Saar-Ruwer Serriger Herrenberg 1998: Almost pungent aromas of stone and spice here, with concentrated mineral and spice flavors interwoven on an open-knit texture. Good length. Drink now through 2003.–B.S. • $14 • (2/29/2000) • **86**

Riesling QbA Mosel-Saar-Ruwer 1998: Rich and round, an easy-drinking QbA, evoking apple and peach flavors on a soft structure. Drink now through 2002.–B.S. • $11 • (2/29/2000) • **84**

Riesling Spätlese Gold Cap Mosel-Saar-Ruwer Serriger Herrenberg 1997: A distinctive white, its attractive red berry and herb aromas and flavors married to a vivid, slim structure. Good concentration and a hint of astringency on the finish. Drink now through 2004.–B.S. • $18 • (2/28/1999) • **87**

Riesling Spätlese Gold Cap Mosel-Saar-Ruwer Serriger Würtzberg 1998: Tight, lean and racy, this is a coil ready to spring. Full of lime, mineral and intense dried apricot and peach notes displayed on a creamy texture. Very concentrated and long. Drink now through 2005.–B.S. • $16 • (2/29/2000) • **90**

Riesling Trockenbeerenauslese Mosel-Saar-Ruwer Serriger Würtzberg 1989 • $96/375 ml. • (12/15/1990) • **95**

STAATLICHEN WEINBAUDOMANEN

Riesling Beerenauslese Nahe Münsterer Pittersberg 1989 • $41 • (12/15/1990) • **91**

Riesling Beerenauslese Nahe Niederhausener Hermannsberg 1989 • $65 • (12/15/1990) • **87**

Riesling Eiswein Nahe Niederhauser Hermannsberg 1992 • $NA • (11/30/1993) • **91**

Riesling Trockenbeerenauslese Nahe Schlossböckelheimer Kupfergrube 1990 • $250 • (12/15/1991) • **92**

Riesling Trockenbeerenauslese Nahe Schlossböckelheimer Kupfergrube 1989 • $150 • (12/15/1990) • **88**

STRUB, J. & H.A.

Riesling Auslese Rheinhessen Niersteiner Oelberg 1998: Baroque in style, this auslese's sweetness is balanced by a citrusy acidity, while flavors of vanilla, nectarine and mineral hold sway. Good length. Best from 2001 through 2008.–B.S. • $32 • (2/29/2000) • **89**

Riesling Kabinett Rheinhessen Niersteiner 1997: There's a rich, almost chewy texture to this kabinett, as well as apple, almond and mineral flavors, yet it's solidly structured and finishes on the austere side. Needs time to integrate. Drink through 2005.–B.S. • $10/1 liter • (2/28/1999) • **84**

Riesling Kabinett Rheinhessen Niersteiner Brückchen 1997: Good weight and richness in this kabinett, in a softer style, due to the ripe flavors and fat texture covering the acidity that balances the elements. Very aromatic, showing almond and mineral notes. Drink now through 2005.–B.S. • $11 • (2/28/1999) • **84**

Riesling Kabinett Rheinhessen Niersteiner Hipping 1997: Marked by an almondlike character, this '97 white shows richness up front before turning lean and austere on the finish. It has good concentration and density. Drink now through 2006.–B.S. • $12 • (2/28/1999) • **84**

Riesling Kabinett Rheinhessen Niersteiner Ölberg 1997: Very perfumed, with mineral and spice aromas, but still tightly wound and structured on the palate. On the dry side, with a lean finish. Best from 2001 through 2006.–B.S. • $11 • (2/28/1999) • **85**

Riesling Kabinett Rheinhessen Niersteiner Orbel 1997: A compact style, showing peach and almond character, good concentration and a moderate finish. Drink now through 2004.–B.S. • $11 • (2/28/1999) • **82**

Riesling Spätlese Rheinhessen Niersteiner Paterberg 1998: German wake-up call. Lovely ripe apricot and cream aromas and flavors take on a citrus edge at the finish in this vibrant, dense '98. Best from 2002 through 2010.–B.S. • $23 • (2/29/2000) • **87**

Riesling Spätlese * Rheinhessen Niersteiner Paterberg 1998:** A sweet spätlese, round, full of forward apricot married to a bright framework. Finishes on the crisp side, with a lovely succulence. Drink now through 2005.–B.S. • $23 • (2/29/2000) • **88**

Riesling Spätlese Rheinhessen Niersteiner Rosenberg 1998: An extra dimension of ripeness and concentration sets this spätlese apart. Reverberating with lime, peach and stone notes, it ends in a racy fashion. Drink now through 2006.–B.S. • $20 • (2/29/2000) • **89**

TESCH

Riesling Auslese Gold Cap Nahe Langenlonsheimer Königsschild 1997: A racy, nerves-of-steel style, tautly wound at this stage, offering green apple, almond and a hint of tropical fruit before the screaming acidity takes over on the finish. This is a very good auslese, but not at the level of the tops in the region. Best from 2004 through 2012.–B.S. • $49 • (2/28/1999) • **88**

Riesling Auslese Nahe Laubenheimer Karthäuser 1997: Gorgeous concentration of apricot dominates the aroma and palate, yet there's racy acidity underneath, with red fruits and a mineral component that keep on coming. The finish is a bit puckering, but there's plenty of sweetness. Best from 2003 through 2010.–B.S. • $24 • (2/28/1999) • **91**

Riesling Kabinett Trocken Nahe Laubenheimer Krone 1997: Dry, firm and spicy, with good richness midpalate, this turns a little lean on the finish but is pretty well balanced overall. Drink through 2005.–B.S. • $13 • (2/28/1999) • **86**

Riesling Spätlese Nahe Laubenheimer Karthäuser 1997: This has attractive peach and mineral aromas and flavors and a rich texture, but it's on the light side. Drink now through 2004.–B.S. • $18 • (2/28/1999) • **86**

Riesling Spätlese Trocken Nahe Langenlonsheimer Königsschild 1997: Out of sorts now, this smells ripe and rich but remains austere on the palate, dominated by the structure and a tartness. Severe finish. Shows promise based on the nose, but it's a gamble.–B.S. • $18 • (2/28/1999) • **79**

Weissburgunder Spätlese Trocken Nahe 1997: Ripe tropical and nectarine aromas and flavors are amply proportioned and offset by a vibrant structure. The finish is dry and lingering. Drink now.–B.S. • $16 • (5/15/1999) • **85**

THANISCH, DR. H.| MÜLLER-BERGGRAEF

Riesling Auslese Gold Cap Mosel-Saar-Ruwer Berncasteler Doctor 1998: Exotic thanks to botrytis and bracing structure, here's a broad, forward '98 white that's drinkable now but should improve. Drink now through 2006.–B.S. • $35/375 ml. • (2/29/2000) • **90**

Riesling Auslese Mosel-Saar-Ruwer Berncasteler Doctor 1997: Pretty, sweet and clean, displaying honey, lime and spice notes, along with juicy acidity and balance. Better than previously reviewed. Drink now through 2005.–B.S. • $55/375 ml. • (9/30/1999) • **89**

Riesling Auslese Mosel-Saar-Ruwer Berncasteler Doctor 1996 • $55 • (11/30/1997) • **88**

Riesling Auslese Mosel-Saar-Ruwer Bernkasteler Lay 1998: Ripe, honeyed and creamy, this auslese is sweet and intense, with perhaps a hint of botrytis lending the apricot flavor an orange twist. More weight here, backed by firm acidity that needs time to come together. Best from 2001 through 2009.–B.S. • $27 • (2/29/2000) • **93**

Riesling Auslese Mosel-Saar-Ruwer Bernkasteler Lay 1997: Elegant and on the lighter side for an auslese, with clearly defined flavors of lime, apple and mineral that dissipate quickly on the finish. Drink now through 2003.–B.S. • $29 • (2/28/1999) • **84**

Riesling Auslese Mosel-Saar-Ruwer Bernkasteler Lay 1996 • $24 • (11/30/1997) • **85**

Riesling Auslese Mosel-Saar-Ruwer Graacher Himmelreich 1996 • $24 • (11/30/1997) • **85**

Riesling Beerenauslese Mosel-Saar-Ruwer Bernkasteler Doctor 1994 • $NA • (11/30/1995) • **82**

Riesling Beerenauslese Mosel-Saar-Ruwer Bernkasteler Doctor 1989 • $240 • (12/15/1990) • **91**

Riesling Eiswein Mosel-Saar-Ruwer Bernkasteler Doctor 1989 • $190 • (12/15/1990) • **88**

Riesling Kabinett Mosel-Saar-Ruwer Bernkasteler Badstube 1998: Not much aroma at this stage, yet there's crisp, citrusy acidity and white peach notes on the palate, balanced by a smooth texture. Apple lingers on the finish. Drink now through 2003.–B.S. • $13 • (2/29/2000) • **85**

Riesling Kabinett Mosel-Saar-Ruwer Berncasteler Doctor 1997: Loaded with peach and mineral aromas and flavors, dense and richly textured with plenty in reserve. All the elements are well integrated, and the finish long. Drink now through 2005.–B.S. • $27 • (2/28/1999) • **88**

Riesling Kabinett Mosel-Saar-Ruwer Berncasteler Doctor 1996 • $25 • (11/30/1997) • **86**

Riesling Kabinett Mosel-Saar-Ruwer Lieserer Niederberg-Helden 1996 • $15 • (11/30/1997) • **85**

Riesling Kabinett Mosel-Saar-Ruwer Wehlener Sonnenuhr 1997: Ripe and exotic, this displays coconut, mango and lime aromas and flavors allied to mineral in a racy profile. All is balanced and the finish fans out with a lingering aftertaste of mineral. Drink through 2006.–B.S. • $13 • (2/28/1999) • **90**

Riesling Spätlese Mosel-Saar-Ruwer Berncasteler Doctor 1996 • $37 • (11/30/1997) • **87**

Riesling Spätlese Mosel-Saar-Ruwer Bernkasteler Graben 1997: Has lime and pineapple aromas and flavors supported by tangy acidity and concentration. Falls short on the finish. Drink through 2006.–B.S. • $19 • (2/28/1999) • **84**

Riesling Spätlese Mosel-Saar-Ruwer Bernkasteler Graben 1996 • $21 • (11/30/1997) • **86**

Riesling Spätlese Mosel-Saar-Ruwer Bernkasteler Lay 1997: Very racy, showing lemon custard and vanilla flavors; could benefit from more richness and complexity. Drink through 2005.–B.S. • $19 • (2/28/1999) • **86**

Riesling Spätlese Mosel-Saar-Ruwer Brauneberger Juffer 1997: Wiry and vibrant, this white shows mineral, floral and pear aromas and flavors on a rich texture, then a firm mineral character takes over on the finish. Drink now through 2006.–B.S. • $19 • (2/28/1999) • **86**

Riesling Spätlese Mosel-Saar-Ruwer Brauneberger Juffer-Sonnenuhr 1998: An added dimension of ripeness here lends a toffee, butterscotch note, buffering the marblelike structure. Dense and tightly packed from start to finish, this is a winner. Drink now through 2006.–B.S. • $19 • (2/29/2000) • **93**

THANISCH, DR. H. | VDP

Riesling Auslese Gold Cap Mosel-Saar-Ruwer Berncasteler Doctor 1998: A beautiful auslese. Racy, concentrated and full of lime, apricot and teeth-rattling acidity, this builds on the palate to an intense conclusion. Great length and harmony. Best from 2001 through 2010.–B.S. • $60 • (2/29/2000) • **92**

Riesling Auslese Gold Cap Mosel-Saar-Ruwer Berncasteler Doctor (AP 6) 1996 • $110/375 ml. • (11/30/1997) • **88**

Riesling Auslese Long Gold Cap Mosel-Saar-Ruwer Berncasteler Doctor (AP 5) 1996 • $163/375 ml. • (11/30/1997) • **92**

Riesling Beerenauslese Mosel-Saar-Ruwer Bernkasteler Doctor 1990 • $NA • (12/15/1991) • **95**

Riesling Kabinett Gold Cap Mosel-Saar-Ruwer Berncasteler Doctor 1998: Excellent depth of flavor for a kabinett. Lime and mineral are etched onto a bracing structure, yet there's plenty of stuffing on the elegant framework. Best from 2001 through 2006.–B.S. • $29 • (2/29/2000) • **90**

Riesling Kabinett Mosel-Saar-Ruwer Bernkasteler Badstube 1997: Seamless and refined, this kabinett just slips down, its rich peach, spice and mineral flavors buoyed by juicy acidity. There's a purity and definition to the flavors, which linger delicately on the finish. Drink now through 2005.–B.S. • $17 • (2/28/1999) • **89**

Riesling Kabinett Mosel-Saar-Ruwer Bernkasteler Badstube 1996 • $14 • (11/30/1997) • **86**

Riesling Kabinett Mosel-Saar-Ruwer Brauneberger Juffer-Sonnenuhr 1997 • $NA • (1/01/1998) • **90**

Riesling QbA Mosel-Saar-Ruwer 1998: Plenty of mineral character, with an intensity that sets it apart from the pack. Amply proportioned, showing apple and an herbal, earthy note that lingers. Drink now through 2004.–B.S. • $13 • (2/29/2000) • **87**

Riesling Spätlese Gold Cap Mosel-Saar-Ruwer Berncasteler Doctor 1998: Great aromatics, from red berries to almonds and flowers, delicate and finely etched. Turns less interesting on the palate, finishing weakly. Drink now through 2004.–B.S. • $45 • (2/29/2000) • **86**

Riesling Spätlese Gold Cap Mosel-Saar-Ruwer Berncasteler Doctor 1997: A powerhouse for the Mosel, this '97 white is restrained now, just hinting at the lime, peach and ripe apple that will emerge as the racy acidity, residual sweetness and flavors integrate. Just shy on the density and concentration of the very best. Best from 2002 through 2010. • $51 • (2/28/1999) • **91**

Riesling Spätlese Mosel-Saar-Ruwer Bernkasteler Badstube 1998: Refined and concentrated, bursting with lime and mineral notes, all woven into the firm framework. Lingering aftertaste. Drink now through 2005.–B.S. • $20 • (2/29/2000) • **88**

Riesling Spätlese Mosel-Saar-Ruwer Bernkasteler Badstube 1996 • $21 • (11/30/1997) • **86**

Riesling Spätlese Mosel-Saar-Ruwer Berncasteler Doctor 1996 • $51 • (11/30/1997) • **89**

UNCKRICH

Riesling Kabinett Pfalz Kallstadter Saumagen 1997: Forward and juicy, sporting light flavors of apricot, citrus and spice in a fleshy, round body. Drink now.–B.S. • $12 • (5/15/2000) • **84**

Riesling Kabinett Trocken Pfalz Kallstadter Steinacker 1998: Dry and round in profile, offering a modicum of peach and spice notes. A bit dilute in the end. Drink now.–B.S. • $12 • (2/29/2000) • **82**

VALCKENBERG

Gewürztraminer QbA Pfalz 1997: A soft, gentle Gewürztraminer, offering modest honey and spice flavors in an off-dry style. Drink now.–B.S. • $9 • (5/15/1999) • **80**

QbA Rheinhessen Madonna Liebfraumilch 1997: Hints of white pepper aromas and apple flavors combine with light intensity and soft structure in this off-dry white.–B.S. • $7 • (1/01/1999) • **76**

VILLA SACHSEN

Riesling QbA Trocken Rheinhessen 1998: Rich and glossy, if simple in flavor, and balanced on the sweet side.–B.S. • $13/1 liter • (1/01/2000) • **79**

Riesling Spätlese Trocken Rheinhessen Binger Scharlachberg 1998: Terrific Riesling. Intense pineapple, passion fruit and spice awaken the senses in this bone-dry, powerful white. Extremely complex, offering a panorama of ripe fruit, spice and mineral on a sinewy framework. Slightly aggressive now, but this baby needs time. Best from 2003 through 2015.–B.S. • $16 • (2/29/2000) • **92**

VOLLRADS, SCHLOSS

Riesling Auslese Gold Cap Rheingau 1996: Funky aromas of white pepper and earth. Medium-bodied and very sweet, with some ripe fruit character and a slightly cloying finish. Drink now.–J.S. • $38/500 ml. • (7/31/1998) • **85**

Riesling Eiswein Gold Cap Rheingau 1996 • $NA/500 ml. • (11/30/1997) • **92**

Riesling Eiswein Long Gold Cap Rheingau 1996: Fasten your seat belts—this is pungent, intense and has a spine of mouthpuckering acidity. Very sweet and dense, with apricot and orange peel flavors and a lingering finish. Best from 2002 through 2015.–B.S. • $485/500 ml. • (1/01/1999) • **93**

Riesling Kabinett Halbtrocken Rheingau 1998: Floral notes introduce this white, whose soft peach and citrus flavors are supported by a lively acidity. Shows elegance, balance and a lingering finish. Drink now through 2003.–B.S. • $18 • (2/29/2000) • **84**

Riesling Kabinett Halbtrocken Rheingau 1997: Creamy gooseberry aromas signal this rich white. Soft, with a simple citrus character. Finishes on a lemony note. Drink now.–B.S. • $17 • (2/28/1999) • **80**

Riesling Kabinett Halbtrocken Rheingau 1996 • $16 • (11/30/1997) • **83**

Riesling Kabinett Rheingau 1998: Round and soft yet not flabby, showing apple, fig and citrus notes on a creamy texture. Finishes with acidity to cleanse the palate. Good length. Drink now through 2004.–B.S. • $18 • (2/29/2000) • **86**

Riesling Kabinett Rheingau 1997: Pungent yet appealing aromas of mineral and spice yield to rich, concentrated flavors of ripe apple. Fairly sweet yet bright and elegant, this is well made, with a lingering finish. Drink now through 2003.–B.S. • $17 • (2/28/1999) • **86**

Riesling Kabinett Rheingau 1996: Superclean and subtle aromas of mineral and tropical fruit. Medium-bodied and lemony, with intense mineral character and a lively acidity. Needs time. Drink through 2005.–J.S. • $15 • (7/31/1998) • **87**

Riesling Kabinett Trocken Rheingau 1996 • $17 • (11/30/1997) • **85**

Riesling QbA Halbtrocken Rheingau 1997: Starting off soft and round, this has immediate appeal, richness and cooked apple and spice notes. There's good acidity underneath, especially on the finish. Drink now through 2005.–B.S. • $15 • (2/28/1999) • **85**

Riesling QbA Rheingau 1996 • $13 • (11/30/1997) • **84**

Riesling QbA Rheingau Grünsilber 1997: Very fruity, smelling and tasting of canned peaches in a soft texture that lacks a bit of focus.–B.S. • $22 • (2/28/1999) • **78**

Riesling QbA Trocken Rheingau Matuschka-Greiffenclau 1996: Creamy and appley, with fresh fruit aromas and flavors. Medium-bodied and very dry, with crisp acidity and a refreshing finish. Drink now through 2004.–J.S. • $13 • (7/31/1998) • **86**

Riesling Spätlese Halbtrocken Rheingau 1996 • $15 • (11/30/1997) • **85**

Riesling Spätlese Rheingau 1998: Frankly sweet and just a touch cloying. Otherwise this is a pleasant, forward Riesling, full of stone fruit and apple, ending with a slight astringency. Drink now through 2004.–B.S. • $28 • (2/29/2000) • **84**

Riesling Spätlese Rheingau 1997: Elegant, with rich aromas and flavors of tropical fruit and spice, vibrant acidity and a long, lingering aftertaste reminiscent of orange. Drink now through 2005.–B.S. • $27 • (2/28/1999) • **87**

Riesling Spätlese Rheingau 1996 • $24 • (11/30/1997) • **83**

Riesling Trocken Rheingau 1996 • $14 • (11/30/1997) • **85**

WAGNER, DR. HEINZ

Riesling Eiswein Mosel-Saar-Ruwer Saarburger Rausch 1993 • $NA • (11/30/1994) • **83**

Riesling Spätlese Mosel-Saar-Ruwer Ayler Kupp 1996 • $16 • (4/30/1998) • **84**

WALLHAUSEN, SCHLOSS

Riesling Beerenauslese Nahe 1992 • $75 • (11/30/1993) • **86**

Riesling Eiswein Nahe 1992 • $59 • (11/30/1993) • **83**

WEGELER-DEINHARD

Riesling Beerenauslese Mosel-Saar-Ruwer Berncasteler Doctor Geheimrat J 1994 • $NA • (11/30/1995) • **89**

Riesling Beerenauslese Rheingau Oestricher Lenchen Geheimrat J 1994 • $NA • (11/30/1995) • **82**

Riesling Eiswein Mosel-Saar-Ruwer Kaseler Nies'chen 1993 • $NA • (11/30/1994) • **89**

Key: SS—Spectator Selection. CS—Cellar Selection. HR—Highly Recommended. $NA—Price not available. (BT)—Barrel tasting. (A)—Auction Price.
For a key to the tasters' initials, see "How to Use These Listings."
Dates in parentheses represent the issues in which the ratings were published.

Riesling Eiswein Rheingau Geisenheimer Rothenberg 1992 • $70/F • (11/30/1993) • **90**

Riesling Eiswein Rheingau Oestricher Lenchen 1992 • $70/F • (11/30/1993) • **87**

Riesling Trockenbeerenauslese Pfalz Deidesheimer Herrgottsacker Geheimrat J 1994 • $NA • (11/30/1995) • **92**

Riesling Trockenbeerenauslese Pfalz Deidesheimer Herrgottsacker 1989 • $NA • (12/15/1990) • **93**

WEGELER ERBEN, J.

Riesling Auslese Mosel-Saar-Ruwer Bernkasteler Doctor 1998: A live wire, brisk and tightly wound, with full-throttle peach and quince flavors. On the dry side, with a lingering aftertaste of peaches. Drink now through 2007.–B.S. • $67 • (2/29/2000) • **90**

Riesling Auslese Mosel-Saar-Ruwer Bernkasteler Doctor (AP 8) 1997: Very distinctive, from the spice, stone and slight herb aromas and flavors to the dense, almost thick texture and powerful structure, this '97 white grabs your attention and holds it. Well crafted. Best from 2002 through 2010.–B.S. • $70 • (2/28/1999) • **92**

Riesling Auslese Mosel-Saar-Ruwer Bernkasteler Doctor (AP 21) 1997: Has sweetness, but could use more definition and dimension in the honey and apricot flavors. Good underlying backbone and a moderate finish. Drink through 2008–B.S. • $63/375 ml. • (2/28/1999) • **88**

Riesling Auslese Mosel-Saar-Ruwer Bernkasteler Graben 1997: A tasty white, displaying apple, spice and mineral flavors, but doesn't quite flesh out the midpalate with the depth and concentration of the best, despite good balancing acidity. Drink now through 2005.–B.S. • $42 • (2/28/1999) • **87**

Riesling Auslese Mosel-Saar-Ruwer Wehlener Sonnenuhr 1997: A super-charged auslese, this has an extra dimension of ripeness and richness, with apricot and honey flavors, all backed by a vibrant acidity that keeps everything lively and pulsing through the long, long finish. Drink now through 2012.–B.S. • $42/375 ml. • (2/28/1999) • **96**

Riesling Auslese Rheingau Geisenheimer Rothenberg 1996 • $30/500 ml. • (11/30/1997) • **83**

Riesling Eiswein Rheingau Oestricher Lenchen 1996 • $NA/375 ml. • (11/30/1997) • **90**

Riesling QbA Rheingau Rüdesheimer Berg Schlossberg 1996 • $NA • (11/30/1997) • **87**

Riesling Spätlese Mosel-Saar-Ruwer Bernkasteler Doctor (AP 7) 1998: Dense and powerful, here's an intense, concentrated white full of slate and lime, with a creamy texture and a broad profile. Lovely display of fruit that's still tightly wound. Best from 2001 through 2007.–B.S. • $43 • (2/29/2000) • **90**

Riesling Spätlese Mosel-Saar-Ruwer Bernkasteler Doctor (AP 8) 1998: Auction wine. A rich, intense spätlese, full of citrus and mineral up-front, turning to herb nuances toward the finish. Starts off generously, then turns tight and a bit diffuse on the finish. Drink now through 2004.–B.S. • $NA • (1/01/2000) • **90**

Riesling Spätlese Mosel-Saar-Ruwer Bernkasteler Doctor 1997: Stunning. Fine ripeness and concentration in this spätlese, showing pineapple and papaya notes underscored by mineral tones and racy acidity. All the components are in the right place; this will only get better. Best from 2001 through 2007.–B.S. • $42 • (2/28/1999) • **93**

Riesling Spätlese Mosel-Saar-Ruwer Bernkasteler Graben 1996 • $NA • (11/30/1997) • **86**

Riesling Spätlese Mosel-Saar-Ruwer Wehlener Sonnenuhr (AP 9) 1998: Seems more like a small auslese. Ripe and opulent, showing plenty of tropical fruit nuances supported by citrusy acidity and concentration. A bit raw and unevolved now. Tasted twice, with consistent notes. Best from 2001 through 2006.–B.S. • $23 • (2/29/2000) • **88**

Riesling Spätlese Mosel-Saar-Ruwer Wehlener Sonnenuhr (AP 10) 1998: Auction wine. Ripe, concentrated and firmly textured, here'a a '98 spätlese that snaps and crackles on the palate, offering pineapple, lime and stone flavors that just keep coming. Best from 2001 through 2006.–B.S. • $NA • (1/01/2000) • **90**

Riesling Spätlese Mosel-Saar-Ruwer Wehlener Sonnenuhr 1997: Ripe and spicy, with crackling acidity and a lean, intense structure displaying lime, grapefruit and peach flavors. Rich, but stays lively and crisp through the finish. Best from 2001 through 2006.–B.S. • $23 • (2/28/1999) • **90**

Riesling Spätlese Rheingau Charta 1996 • $NA • (11/30/1997) • **89**

Riesling Spätlese Rheingau Geisenheimer Rothenberg 1997: Quite sweet, this white shows almond, marzipan and a touch of orange, enough acidity for balance and a soft, approachable demeanor. Drink now through 2003.–B.S. • $24 • (2/28/1999) • **84**

Riesling Spätlese Rheingau Geisenheimer Rothenbergben 1996 • $20 • (11/30/1997) • **88**

Riesling Spätlese Trocken Rheingau Geheimrat J 1997: A dry, rich, well-balanced white that hints at apricot flavor, with moderate depth, but lacks expressiveness. Drink now through 2003.–B.S. • $31 • (2/28/1999) • **83**

Riesling Spätlese Trocken Rheingau Geheimrat J 1996 • $NA • (11/30/1997) • **88**

Riesling Trocken Rheingau 1996 • $9 • (11/30/1997) • **85**

Riesling Trockenbeerenauslese Rheingau Geisenheimer Rothenberg 1997: Auction wine. Viscous and very concentrated, this '97 TBA offers apricot, crème brûlée, honey and a hint of glazed orange peel. It melts in the mouth, as the vibrant acidity takes over, keeping everything fresh and lively. Drink now through 2020.–B.S. • $NA/375 ml. • (2/28/1999) • **97**

Riesling Trockenbeerenauslese Rheingau Geisenheimer Rothenberg 1996 • $NA/500 ml. • (11/30/1997) • **89**

WEHRHEIM, EUGEN

Huxelrebe Trockenbeerenauslese Rheinhessen Niersteiner Klostergarten 1994: Unctuous, displaying honey, apricot and orange peel aromas and flavors, screeching acidity and a tangy finish.–B.S. • $48/500 ml. • (10/15/1998) • **89**

Riesling Spätlese Rheinhessen Niersteiner Orbel 1998: Clean and ripe, on the sweet side, yet matched by a vibrant acidity. Citrus, peach and mineral hold court in the flavor department. Drink now through 2004.–B.S. • $15 • (2/29/2000) • **86**

WEIL, ROBERT

Riesling Auslese Gold Cap Rheingau Kiedricher Gräfenberg 1998: Auction wine. This monster auslese is thick, concentrated and sweet, yet with a citruslike backbone, exuding lifted aromas and flavors of violet, apricot and orange blossom. Very intense and assertive, with a monumental finish. Best from 2002 through 2012.–B.S. • $NA/375 ml. • (1/01/2000) • **95**

Riesling Auslese Gold Cap Rheingau Kiedricher Gräfenberg 1997: Auction wine. Scintillating auslese. Very ripe and rich, but not overdone, this puts it all together with vanilla, apricot, honey and nectarine character, vibrant acidity and a firm structure. More backward than most in this category, it's built to age. Best from 2002 through 2012.–B.S. • $NA/375 ml. • (2/28/1999) • **95**

Riesling Auslese Gold Cap Rheingau Kiedricher Gräfenberg 1996 • $299/375 ml. • (11/30/1997) • **92**

Riesling Auslese Rheingau Kiedricher Gräfenberg 1998: Rippling with sweet apricot, honey and citrus aromas and flavors that revolve around a core of laserlike acidity, providing the backbone for this intense, sweet white to develop. Long finish. Drink now through 2007.–B.S. • $52/375 ml. • (2/29/2000) • **92**

Riesling Auslese Rheingau Kiedricher Gräfenberg 1997: A '97 auslese that bursts with apricot, peach, orange peel and floral character, all delicately displayed on a gossamer framework. An elegant, ripe dessert-style Riesling that packs a lot of flavor. Drink now through 2006.–B.S. • $49/375 ml. • (2/28/1999) • **93**

Riesling Auslese Rheingau Kiedricher Gräfenberg 1996 • $41/375 ml. • (11/30/1997) • **89**

Riesling Beerenauslese Gold Cap Rheingau Kiedricher Gräfenberg 1997: Auction wine. Monolithic and backward now, this nonetheless has botrytis character, incredible concentration and density and balancing acidity. Never heavy or cloying, with finesse and a lingering finish, but the honey, apricot, spice and orange flavors need time to develop as the sweetness integrates. Best from 2005 through 2025.–B.S. • $NA/375 ml. • (2/28/1999) • **97**

Riesling Beerenauslese Rheingau 1989 • $NA • (12/15/1990) • **98**

Riesling Beerenauslese Rheingau Kiedricher Gräfenberg 1998: Elegance and purity are defined in this '98 BA. Beautifully integrated and silky-smooth, mingling apricot, peach and citrus backed by a firm yet unintrusive structure. A pleasure to drink. Drink now through 2012.–B.S. • $210/375 ml. • (2/29/2000) • **95**

Riesling Beerenauslese Rheingau Kiedricher Gräfenberg 1997: A serious BA with about as much botrytis as there was in 1997, this is silky, vibrant and pure. It glides across the palate with ease, unfolding apricot, citrus, floral and mineral flavors. Great depth of flavor and expression, with a long aftertaste. Drink now through 2015.–B.S. • $194/375 ml. • (2/28/1999) • **96**

Riesling Beerenauslese Rheingau Kiedricher Gräfenberg 1994 • $141 • (11/30/1995) • **96**

Riesling Beerenauslese Rheingau Kiedricher Gräfenberg 1992 • $329 • (11/30/1993) • **95**

Riesling Eiswein Rheingau Kiedricher Gräfenberg 1998: Brisk and inviting, this sprightly dessert wine mixes grapefruit and apricot on a lean frame.

Good balance and length of flavor. Drink now through 2008.–B.S. • $281/375 ml. • (2/29/2000) • **91**

Riesling Eiswein Rheingau Kiedricher Gräfenberg 1997: Amazing flavors of tangerine, mandarin orange, guava and other tropical fruits, incredibly fresh and concentrated, with a silky-smooth texture and harmonious structure. The finish just goes on and on. Yet another classic from this great producer. Drink now through 2020.–B.S. • $258/375 ml. • (2/28/1999) • **97**

Riesling Kabinett Halbtrocken Rheingau 1998: High-toned and a touch spritzy, displaying ripe, concentrated peach and pear. Needs time to integrate. Drink through 2003.–B.S. • $24 • (2/29/2000) • **85**

Riesling Kabinett Halbtrocken Rheingau 1997: A light, off-dry Riesling, displaying ripe apple and almond aromas and flavors. Straightforward in appeal, with a citrusy finish. Drink now through 2002.–B.S. • $22 • (2/28/1999) • **82**

Riesling Kabinett Rheingau 1996 • $19 • (11/30/1997) • **90**

Riesling QbA Trocken Rheingau 1998: Plenty of structure in this lean, firm white. Very dense, with grapefruit flavor and a long finish. Drink now through 2003.–B.S. • $17 • (1/01/2000) • **85**

Riesling QbA Trocken Rheingau 1997: A dry Riesling with balance and elegance, offering nectarine and mineral flavors and a firm structure that will pair well with light seafood and poultry dishes. Drink now through 2005.–B.S. • $17 • (2/28/1999) • **86**

Riesling Spätlese Rheingau 1997: Soft and ripe, here's an immediately appealing '97 white, brimming with peachy Riesling flavors, richly displayed. Drink now through 2003.–B.S. • $31 • (2/28/1999) • **88**

Riesling Spätlese Rheingau Kiedricher Gräfenberg 1998: Stunning. Must be auslese in quality, with rich, ripe apricot, quince and mineral offset by screeching acidity that keeps it all focused and pumping through the long, long finish. Great stuff. Best from 2001 through 2010.–B.S. • $50 • (2/29/2000) • **92**

Riesling Spätlese Rheingau Kiedricher Gräfenberg 1997: A monster spätlese—intense, ripe and concentrated. Surely an auslese in ripeness, it's brimming with peach, apricot, passion fruit and mineral flavors. Elegant and aristocratic in stature, with a long, long finish. Drink now through 2010.–B.S. • $47 • (2/28/1999) • **92**

Riesling Spätlese Rheingau Kiedricher Gräfenberg 1996 • $41 • (11/30/1997) • **92**

Riesling Spätlese Trocken Rheingau 1997: Bursting with peach character, this is round and generous in texture, bolstered by a moderate structure. Finishes with a slight tang of mineral and citrus. Drink now through 2003.–B.S. • $31 • (2/28/1999) • **84**

Riesling Trockenbeerenauslese Gold Cap Rheingau Kiedricher Gräfenberg 1997: Auction wine. A showstopper. Hard to believe these flavors come from a grape. Smells exotic, evoking pure dried peach, apricot, mandarin orange and guava. Never heavy or cloying, its firm backbone of acidity keeps it light on its feet and refreshing on the incredibly long finish. Best from 2005 through 2025.–B.S. • $NA/375 ml. • (2/28/1999) • **98**

Riesling Trockenbeerenauslese Rheingau 1989 • $NA • (12/15/1990) • **93**

Riesling Trockenbeerenauslese Rheingau Kiedricher Gräfenberg 1994 • $291 • (11/30/1995) • **95**

Riesling Trockenbeerenauslese Rheingau Kiedricher Gräfenberg 1992 • $218/375 ml. • (11/30/1993) • **96**

WEINGART, ADOLF

Riesling Auslese Mittelrhein Bopparder Hamm Feuerley 1997: Bursting with apricot, honey and a hint of orange, here's a rich, fruity style, with juicy acidity and forward appeal. The structure is soft for long aging, but you won't want to wait to enjoy this, drink now through 2006.–B.S. • $18 • (2/28/1999) • **91**

Riesling Kabinett Mittelrhein Bopparder Hamm Ohlenberg 1998: Racy and sleek, offering grapefruit and mineral flavors etched into a firm structure; a lot of density packed into a slim frame. Drink now through 2004.–B.S. • $17 • (2/29/2000) • **87**

Riesling QbA Mittelrhein 1997: This elegant '97 white shows a lovely peachy quality and a mineral element supported by a rich texture and balancing acidity. Drink now through 2004.–B.S. • $11 • (2/28/1999) • **86**

Riesling Spätlese Halbtrocken Mittelrhein Bopparder Hamm Feuerley 1997: A lovely halbtrocken, showing floral and spicy aromas and flavors, rich peachy notes on the palate and bright acidity. Firms up on the finish, while remaining succulent. Drink now through 2005.–B.S. • $14 • (2/28/1999) • **87**

Key: SS—Spectator Selection. CS—Cellar Selection. HR—Highly Recommended. $NA—Price not available. (BT)—Barrel tasting. (A)—Auction Price.
For a key to the tasters' initials, see "How to Use These Listings."
Dates in parentheses represent the issues in which the ratings were published.

Riesling Spätlese Mittelrhein Bopparder Hamm Ohlenberg 1997: Mouthwatering flavors of apricot and spice fill the mouth in this rich, opulent '97. Balancing, but lowish acidity keeps everything lively. Drink now through 2003.–B.S. • $14 • (2/28/1999) • **87**

WEINS-PRÜM, DR. F.

Riesling Auslese Mosel-Saar-Ruwer Erdener Prälat 1998: Elegant, balanced and exuding lime, peach and mineral, this approachable '98 spätlese starts off rich, then fades a bit on the finish. Drink now through 2004.–B.S. • $46 • (1/01/2000) • **88**

Riesling Auslese Mosel-Saar-Ruwer Erdener Prälat 1997: Lean, focused and intense, this scintillating '97 exhibits peach and slate aromas and flavors on an electric framework. Fine length on the finish. Best from 2001 through 2009.–B.S. • $45 • (2/28/1999) • **90**

Riesling Auslese Mosel-Saar-Ruwer Graacher Domprobst 1998: Very high-toned and sleek, with focused lime, slate and earth notes,. Very crystalline in structure yet concentrated, with a mineral aftertaste. Best from 2001 through 2008.–B.S. • $29 • (2/29/2000) • **90**

Riesling Auslese Mosel-Saar-Ruwer Wehlener Sonnenuhr 1998: Impressive. Very aromatic, adding spice, herb and red fruit to the mix of citrus and mineral. A live wire that would scorch the palate were it not for the intense flavors. Great finish. Best from 2001 through 2010.–B.S. • $32 • (2/29/2000) • **92**

Riesling Auslese Mosel-Saar-Ruwer Wehlener Sonnenuhr 1997: Juicy and lip-smacking, this white delivers the rich, crunchy texture typical of the '97 vintage. Delicious peach aromas and flavors are supported by crisp, balancing acidity and linger on the finish. Drink now through 2006.–B.S. • $32 • (2/28/1999) • **89**

Riesling Eiswein Gold Cap Mosel-Saar-Ruwer Bernkasteler Johannisbrünnchen 1998: An electric dessert wine, lean and reductive in style, offering quince, pear and citrus notes on a razor's edge of acidity. Best from 2001 through 2008.–B.S. • $90/375 ml. • (2/29/2000) • **90**

Riesling Kabinett Halbtrocken Mosel-Saar-Ruwer Wehlener Sonnenuhr 1998: A little austere, with nice weight and richness, all balanced, although there's not a lot of fruit today and it finishes a bit short. Drink now through 2003.–B.S. • $15 • (1/01/2000) • **85**

Riesling Kabinett Mosel-Saar-Ruwer Graacher Domprobst 1997: Rich, round and appealing, with a soft, floral component and apple and herbal flavors, then turns a bit lean on the finish, ending on a slightly astringent note. Drink now through 2002.–B.S. • $15 • (2/28/1999) • **82**

Riesling Kabinett Mosel-Saar-Ruwer Ürziger Würzgarten 1997: Elegant, with slate character, good concentration and richness midpalate. There's enough acidity to keep it together, but it won't be a long-term wine. Drink now through 2002.–B.S. • $15 • (2/28/1999) • **83**

Riesling Kabinett Mosel-Saar-Ruwer Wehlener Sonnenuhr 1998: Rich and fleshy, this '98 kabinett exhibits power and breadth. The flavors range from piecrust and almond to lime and mineral, all on a firm structure. Drink now through 2004.–B.S. • $15 • (2/29/2000) • **87**

Riesling Kabinett Mosel-Saar-Ruwer Wehlener Sonnenuhr 1997: A delicious white. Shows the round, balanced, easygoing character of the '97 vintage in the Mosel. Ripe and rich, with peach and vanilla custard flavors, lively acidity and a mouthwatering finish. Drink now through 2004.–B.S. • $15 • (2/28/1999) • **89**

Riesling QbA Halbtrocken Mosel-Saar-Ruwer 1998: A straightforward Riesling, offering slate and citrus aromas and flavors. It's all nicely balanced, if a bit short on the finish. Drink now through 2003.–B.S. • $11 • (1/01/2000) • **83**

Riesling QbA Halbtrocken Mosel-Saar-Ruwer 1997: Tasty, showing talc, lemon custard and a bright citrus component. Mouthwatering and juicy, with good concentration and finish. Drink now through 2002.–B.S. • $11 • (2/28/1999) • **84**

Riesling Spätlese Mosel-Saar-Ruwer Erdener Prälat 1998: Seductive spätlese. There's an added dimension of ripeness and intensity to the apricot, lime and stone flavors, while the focused structure keeps the flavors pumping through. Drink now through 2006.–B.S. • $24 • (2/29/2000) • **90**

Riesling Spätlese Mosel-Saar-Ruwer Erdener Prälat 1997: Textbook spätlese. Rich and zingy, full of floral, lime, peach and mineral flavors, all compact, elegant and delicious. Drink now through 2005.–B.S. • $24 • (2/28/1999) • **88**

Riesling Spätlese Mosel-Saar-Ruwer Graacher Domprobst 1998: Rich and round, this has an herbal note beneath the peach and lime that echoes on the finish. Crisp and a bit disjointed today, needing time to integrate. Good finish. Best after 2000.–B.S. • $21 • (2/29/2000) • **88**

Riesling Spätlese Mosel-Saar-Ruwer Graacher Domprobst 1997: Extremely rich and succulent, this '97 white has straightforward peach and citrus notes, ending with a lemon flavor. A little closed-in right now, it may improve with time. Drink through 2006.–B.S. • $21 • (2/28/1999) • **87**

Riesling Spätlese Mosel-Saar-Ruwer Wehlener Sonnenuhr 1998: Succulent and immediately appealing, this '98 spätlese packs a lot of apple, floral and mineral notes into a lightweight frame. Drink now through 2004.–B.S. • $22 • (1/01/2000) • **88**

Riesling Spätlese Mosel-Saar-Ruwer Wehlener Sonnenuhr 1997: A delicious '97 spätlese offering ripe peach and apricot notes, mouthwatering acidity and good richness in a harmonious presentation. Drink now through 2005.–B.S. • $21 • (2/28/1999) • **88**

WELLER-LEHNERT

Riesling Auslese Mosel-Saar-Ruwer Piesporter Goldtröpfchen (AP 6) 1997: A little on the tart side and slightly green in flavor, sporting lime and slate flavors on a delicate structure. Just out of balance today; not up to the best of the vintage. Best from 2001 through 2006.–B.S. • $35 • (9/30/1999) • **86**

Riesling Auslese Mosel-Saar-Ruwer Piesporter Goldtröpfchen (AP 7) 1997: Juicy and round, like biting into a fresh peach. Lime and mineral accents, yet could use a tad more concentration and length. Drink now through 2005.–B.S. • $35/500 ml. • (9/30/1999) • **87**

Riesling Auslese Mosel-Saar-Ruwer Piesporter Goldtröpfchen (AP 8) 1997: More like a small beerenauslese, this is packed with apricot, orange and honey flavors and botrytis character. Really intense, yet light on its feet and supported by enough acidity to keep it all balanced. Drink now through 2010.–B.S. • $35/375 ml. • (9/30/1999) • **92**

Riesling Auslese Mosel-Saar-Ruwer Piesporter Goldtröpfchen (AP 8) 1996: Very ripe, fresh and exotic, with dense, apricot, mango and passion fruit, backed by bracing acidity, which needs to integrate with the residual sugar. Promising. Best from 2001 through 2010.–B.S. • $35 • (1/01/1999) • **89**

Riesling Auslese Mosel-Saar-Ruwer Piesporter Goldtröpfchen (AP 9) 1996: Serious auslese. Very ripe and sweet, smells and tastes like it has a touch of botrytis, from the apricot, orange and honey character. Ethereal and balanced, packing in a lot of flavor on a sleek frame. Drink through 2008.–B.S. • $35/500 ml. • (1/01/1999) • **90**

Riesling Kabinett Mosel-Saar-Ruwer Piesporter Goldtröpfchen (AP 3) 1997: A slate monster, sleek and precise, guided by a crisp structure and dense flavors of lime, mineral and ripe apple. Intense, it grabs your attention and holds it. Drink now through 2004.–B.S. • $19 • (9/30/1999) • **88**

Riesling Kabinett Mosel-Saar-Ruwer Piesporter Goldtröpfchen (AP 14) 1997: A noticeably sweet white with marzipan, honey and slate flavors, good underlying acidity and a slightly short finish. Drink now.–B.S. • $19 • (9/30/1999) • **83**

Riesling Spätlese Mosel-Saar-Ruwer Piesporter Goldtröpfchen (AP 4) 1997: Give this some time to develop. A very distinctive petrol aroma, while lime, peach and mineral are on the palate, almost chewy it's so dense and unevolved. Fine structure too. Best from 2002 through 2007.–B.S. • $25 • (9/30/1999) • **89**

Riesling Spätlese Mosel-Saar-Ruwer Piesporter Goldtröpfchen (AP 5) 1997: Rich, round and easygoing, with plenty of honey, apricot and slate, good concentration and a smooth texture. The citrus acidity comes out on the finish. Drink now through 2004.–B.S. • $25 • (9/30/1999) • **88**

WERNER'SCHES, DOMDECHANT

Riesling Auslese Gold Cap Rheingau Hochheimer Domdechaney 1997: Distinctive, this auslese evokes a candied character, offering vanilla, marzipan and glazed orange-peel aromas and flavors, bracing acidity and a compact profile. Needs time. Drink through 2006.–B.S. • $36 • (2/28/1999) • **89**

Riesling Auslese Gold Cap Rheingau Hochheimer Kirchenstück 1998: Juicy and delicious. Apricot and nectarine aromas and flavors are displayed on a transparent texture, with mouthwatering acidity and a moderate finish. Drink now through 2005.–B.S. • $37 • (2/29/2000) • **90**

Riesling Auslese Trocken Rheingau Hochheimer Stielweg 1998: A brooding, concentrated white, densely textured, with reticent white peach and mineral notes backed by screaming acidity. Very backward and intense. Best from 2002 through 2010.–B.S. • $37 • (2/29/2000) • **89**

Riesling Beerenauslese Gold Cap Rheingau Hochheimer 1997: Racy and elegant, displaying more finesse than viscosity, yet with concentrated flavors of apricot, almond, honey and mineral. Very lively and focused, with excellent length and an aftertaste of dried fig and molasses. Drink now through 2015.–B.S. • $160 • (2/28/1999) • **94**

Riesling Beerenauslese Rheingau Hochheimer 1989 • $NA • (12/15/1990) • **79**

Riesling Beerenauslese Rheingau Hochheimer Domdechaney 1992 • $NA • (11/30/1993) • **80**

Riesling Eiswein Rheingau Hochheimer Domdechaney 1992 • $NA • (11/30/1993) • **84**

Riesling Eiswein Rheingau Hochheimer Domdechaney 1990 • $NA • (12/15/1991) • **93**

Riesling Kabinett Rheingau Hochheimer Hölle 1998: Not particularly expressive, although it has a creamy texture and good balance. Mostly on the citrus side of the flavor range. Best after 2000.–B.S. • $14 • (2/29/2000) • **84**

Riesling Kabinett Rheingau Hochheimer Hölle 1997: A broad-shouldered Rheingau kabinett, exhibiting almond, vanilla and stone aromas and flavors. Densely textured and muscular, with a lingering finish. Best from 2001 through 2007.–B.S. • $13 • (2/28/1999) • **89**

Riesling Spätlese Rheingau Hochheimer Domdechaney 1998: This is smokin', from the spice, pear and nectarine notes to the racy backbone and creamy texture. Awakens the senses in an elegant, energetic way. Drink now through 2005.–B.S. • $21 • (2/29/2000) • **90**

Riesling Spätlese Rheingau Hochheimer Domdechaney 1997: Lean and crisp, showing a lot of citrus character. Though firm and well supported by vibrant acidity, it's concentrated and balanced. Drink now through 2006.–B.S. • $23 • (2/28/1999) • **87**

Riesling Spätlese Rheingau Hochheimer Kirchenstück 1998: Exotic. Thickly textured and creamy, showing ripe pear, peach and quince aromas and flavors allied with a bright, spicy acidity. Eiswein added? Drink now through 2005.–B.S. • $23 • (2/29/2000) • **89**

Riesling Spätlese Rheingau Hochheimer Kirchenstück 1997: Restrained in its approach yet displaying fine ripeness, with peach flavor, bright acidity and a rich, juicy texture all balanced toward the soft side. Drink now through 2005.–B.S. • $21 • (2/28/1999) • **88**

Riesling Spätlese Trocken Rheingau Hochheimer Domdechaney 1998: Sings on the nose and offers plenty of ripe apricot, citrus and mineral, with an underlying support of steel. A little disjointed now, but the elements are there. Best from 2001 through 2006.–B.S. • $23 • (1/01/2000) • **87**

Riesling Spätlese Trocken Rheingau Hochheimer Kirchenstück 1997: Elegant, this dry white shows almond aromas and flavors, a delicate structure and the flesh and fruit to balance. Drink now through 2004.–B.S. • $21 • (2/28/1999) • **82**

Riesling Trockenbeerenauslese Gold Cap Rheingau Hochheimer Kirchenstück 1997: An exotic, vivid version, offering cherry, almond and citrus aromas and flavors in a streamlined package, with a distinct almond finish. Hints of botrytis add complexity. Best from 2002 through 2015.–B.S. • $NA/500 ml. • (2/28/1999) • **93**

Riesling Trockenbeerenauslese Rheingau Hochheimer 1989 • $NA • (12/15/1990) • **84**

WIRSCHING, HANS

Scheurebe Spätlese Trocken Franken Iphöfer Kronsberg 1998: A mix of grapefruit, peach and herbal aromas and flavors in this fruity, yet dry Scheurebe. Well balanced, showing a firm structure and a nutty, lentil note on the finish. Drink now through 2002.–B.S. • $27 • (5/15/2000) • **85**

Silvaner Spätlese Trocken Franken Iphöfer Kronsberg 1998: Smooth and rich, this white starts off with peach notes and a hint of grilled almond, softly structured. Firms up on the finish, with a touch of earthiness and grapefruit peel for structure. Drink now through 2002.–B.S. • $26 • (5/15/2000) • **87**

Traminer Spätlese Franken Iphöfer Kalb 1998: Textbook aromas of rose, litchi and cardamom are followed by honey and grapefruit on the palate. Begins with a rich texture, turning a bit leaner on the finish. Drink now.–B.S. • $31 • (5/15/2000) • **86**

WITTMAN

Albalonga Beerenauslese Rheinhessen Westhofener Steingrube 1998: The essence of pear, augmented by a little honey and citrus. Lush and tangy, with an open-knit structure and lingering finish. Drink now through 2002.–B.S. • $45/500 ml. • (5/15/2000) • **88**

Chardonnay Trockenbeerenauslese Rheinhessen Westhofener Aulerde 1997: Moderately sweet, offering honey and caramel aromas and flavors on a firm structure. Tasty, if not so complex, thick and sweet. Not imported into the U.S. Drink now through 2005.–B.S. • $NA/375 ml. • (1/01/1999) • **88**

Riesling Spätlese Rheinhessen Westhofener Morstein 1997: This '97 spätlese notches it up. An added dimension of ripeness, plus concentrated flavors of smoke, mineral and apricot, combine with a racy, vibrant backbone to tantalize the palate. Fine length. Best from 2002 through 2010.–B.S. • $16 • (2/28/1999) • **91**

Weisser Riesling QbA Trocken Rheinhessen 1998: Austere, showing white peach and citrus notes backed by a crisp structure. Needs food. Drink now through 2003.–B.S. • $20 • (2/29/2000) • **82**

Weisser Riesling Spätlese Trocken Rheinhessen Westhofener Aulerde 1997: Crisp and dry, this has a grapefruit component to its flavor profile, along with hints of peach and mineral. Lovely balance in this style, and cleansing on the finish. Drink now through 2003.–B.S. • $16 • (5/15/1999) • **85**

Weisser Riesling Trockenbeerenauslese Rheinhessen Westhofener Aulerde 1997: A lively, elegant dessert white with restrained aromas and flavors of orange peel. A firm backbone provides support and it finishes with a slight astringence. Best from 2002 through 2015.–B.S. • $65/375 ml. • (2/28/1999) • **89**

WOLF, J.L.

Riesling Auslese Pfalz Deidesheimer Herrgottsacker 1998: Broad and creamy, this '98 auslese covers all the bases, with balancing acidity keeping the peach and almond flavors fresh and persistent. Drink now through 2006.–B.S. • $31 • (2/29/2000) • **88**

Riesling Auslese Pfalz Wachenheimer Belz 1997: Hints at chamomile flowers, with apricot and grapefruit on the nose. The tightly wound, citrusy palate closes on the finish. Disjointed now, but has fine elements. Drink through 2007.–B.S. • $23 • (2/28/1999) • **88**

Riesling Auslese Trocken Pfalz Forster Jesuitengarten 1997: Dry, firm and steely, showing broad, waxy, nutty aromas and flavors, good richness and density and a subtle length, with an aftertaste evocative of roses. Drink through 2006.–B.S. • $NA • (2/28/1999) • **86**

Riesling Beerenauslese Pfalz Wachenheimer Bischofsgarten 1997: A dead ringer for a Gewürztraminer SGN from Alsace, this is very fragrant, smelling of roses and spice, while the palate is soft, luscious and honeyed. A real charmer, but it lacks the structure for long aging. Drink now through 2003.–B.S. • $30/375 ml. • (2/28/1999) • **89**

Riesling Eiswein Pfalz Wachenheimer Gerümpel 1998: Lean and racy, showing violet and pear aromas and a pine or rosemary note on the palate. Not too sweet, finishing crisply. Best after 2000.–B.S. • $113/375 ml. • (2/29/2000) • **88**

Riesling Kabinett Halbtrocken Pfalz Forster Stift 1997: Distinctive for its petrol and lime aromas and flavors and racy character, this '97 off-dry white shows a lot of mineral elements up front, then tails off on the finish. Drink now through 2003.–B.S. • $NA • (2/28/1999) • **83**

Riesling Kabinett Halbtrocken Pfalz Wachenheimer Königswingert 1998: Broad and weighty, showing almond aromas, vanilla custard flavors and a milky feel, all tightly wound. Best from 2001 through 2004.–B.S. • $22 • (2/29/2000) • **86**

Riesling Kabinett Pfalz Forster 1998: Sleek and citrusy, this '98 Pfalz kabinett is closed in, needing time to reveal its peach, grapefruit and spice notes. Good length and structure. Not imported into the U.S. Best from 2001 through 2005.–B.S. • $NA • (1/01/2000) • **88**

Riesling QbA Halbtrocken Pfalz 1997: Tropical fruit highlights this rich, exotic '97, which is medium-bodied, elegant and enticing. It's concentrated and balanced on the soft side. Drink now through 2005.–B.S. • $12 • (2/28/1999) • **85**

Riesling QbA Pfalz 1998: On the dry side and brimming with citrus-tinged, piquant peach and apple, yet it lacks the stuffing to really make it exciting. Drink now through 2003.–B.S. • $NA • (1/01/2000) • **84**

Riesling Spätlese Pfalz Forster Stift 1998: Reductive in style, showing almond and apricot aromas and flavors. Juicy midpalate, it closes up on the finish. Not imported into the U.S. Best from 2001 through 2006.–B.S. • $NA • (1/01/2000) • **87**

Riesling Spätlese Pfalz Wachenheimer Gerümpel 1997: Very citrusy in character, delivering grapefruit and lime in an elegant, zippy way, with moderate concentration. Hint of almond on the aftertaste. Drink now through 2005.–B.S. • $18 • (2/28/1999) • **87**

Riesling Spätlese Trocken Pfalz Forster Jesuitengarten 1998: A blockbuster, concentrated and dense, with licorice, pear, fig and mineral aromas and flavors. Lean and intense, it's a little raw right now, so give it time to settle down. Not imported into the U.S. Best from 2002 through 2010.–B.S. • $NA • (1/01/2000) • **90**

Riesling Spätlese Trocken Pfalz Forster Pechstein 1997: This white shows reserved peach notes and firm acidity, turning even leaner on the finish. Solid, but it fails to excite. Drink now through 2004.–B.S. • $NA • (2/28/1999) • **83**

Key: SS—Spectator Selection. CS—Cellar Selection. HR—Highly Recommended. $NA—Price not available. (BT)—Barrel tasting. (A)—Auction Price.
For a key to the tasters' initials, see "How to Use These Listings."
Dates in parentheses represent the issues in which the ratings were published.

ZILLIKEN

Riesling Auslese Gold Cap Mosel-Saar-Ruwer Saarburger Rausch 1998: Auction wine. Thyme and apricot make for an interesting marriage of flavors in this gum-searing, densely textured auslese. Really high-pitched and tightly coiled, with a ton of slate on the finish. Best from 2001 through 2010.–B.S. • $NA/375 ml. • (1/01/2000) • **91**

Riesling Auslese Gold Cap Mosel-Saar-Ruwer Saarburger Rausch (AP 3) 1997: Auction wine. Wonderful harmony, richness and structure. Still young and unevolved, with classic Mosel flavors of lime, peach and mineral, finishing with a hint of orange. The flavors have intensity, concentration and length. Drink now through 2010.–B.S. • $NA/375 ml. • (2/28/1999) • **91**

Riesling Auslese Gold Cap Mosel-Saar-Ruwer Saarburger Rausch (AP 4) 1997: Auction wine. Rich, with a strong vanilla note whose sweetness gives way to the vibrant backbone. Tasty yet a little simple at this stage; it will improve with bottle age. Drink now through 2004.–B.S. • $NA/375 ml. • (2/28/1999) • **88**

Riesling Auslese Gold Cap Mosel-Saar-Ruwer Saarburger Rausch (AP 6) 1997: Very sleek and focused, this '97 white displays a smoky, stony character that starts off rich before the screeching acidity takes over. Definitely for fans of wines with cut, this needs time to integrate. Best from 2003 through 2012.–B.S. • $60 • (2/28/1999) • **90**

Riesling Auslese Mosel-Saar-Ruwer Saarburger Rausch (AP 5) 1997: Auction wine. Intense, sinewy and stony, this '97 white shows a lot of nerve and style, from its mineral, spice and cream flavors to its reverberating acidity on the long finish. A lot of flavor is packed into the slender frame. Give this baby time. Best from 2003 through 2012.–B.S. • $NA • (2/28/1999) • **90**

Riesling Auslese Mosel-Saar-Ruwer Saarburger Rausch (AP 9) 1997: A tasty, crunchy white, with citrus and apple aromas and flavors augmented by spice, moderate concentration and a crisp, lingering finish. Best from 2002 through 2010.–B.S. • $38 • (2/28/1999) • **90**

Riesling Auslese Mosel-Saar-Ruwer Saarburger Rausch 1996 • $171/375 ml. • (11/30/1997) • **87**

Riesling Beerenauslese Mosel-Saar-Ruwer Saarburger Rausch 1994 • $NA • (11/30/1995) • **84**

Riesling Beerenauslese Mosel-Saar-Ruwer Saarburger Rausch 1993 • $NA • (11/30/1994) • **93**

Riesling Eiswein Long Gold Cap Mosel-Saar-Ruwer Saarburger Rausch (AP 1) 1998: Auction wine. Utterly seductive aromas and flavors of rose, red berry and citrus blossom are packed into a slim, racy frame, with plenty of tart acidity refreshing the finish. Best from 2001 through 2010.–B.S. • $NA/375 ml. • (1/01/2000) • **93**

Riesling Eiswein Long Gold Cap Mosel-Saar-Ruwer Saarburger Rausch (AP 2) 1998: A suave eiswein, whose orange-tinged and floral notes are accented by a mineral and smoke element, all buoyed by a bracing structure that leaves a distinctively tart impression on the finish. Best from 2002 through 2012.–B.S. • $189/375 ml. • (2/29/2000) • **92**

Riesling Eiswein Mosel-Saar-Ruwer Saarburger Rausch 1990 • $NA • (12/15/1991) • **91**

Riesling Eiswein Mosel-Saar-Ruwer Saarburger Rausch 1989 • $NA • (12/15/1990) • **96**

Riesling Eiswein Mosel-Saar-Ruwer Saarburger Rausch 1988 • $NA • (9/30/1989) • **97**

Riesling Halbtrocken Mosel-Saar-Ruwer Zilliken Gutsriesling 1996 • $11 • (11/30/1997) • **86**

Riesling Kabinett Mosel-Saar-Ruwer Ockfener Bockstein 1996 • $14 • (11/30/1997) • **88**

Riesling Kabinett Mosel-Saar-Ruwer Saarburger Rausch 1998: Slightly candied flavors of apple and lime seem dilute in this light, delicate Riesling. Drink now through 2002.–B.S. • $16 • (1/01/2000) • **82**

Riesling Kabinett Mosel-Saar-Ruwer Saarburger Rausch 1997: Intriguing. From the red-fruit aromas and pomegranate flavors to the pineapplelike bite and sleek framework, this is a winner. Really packs a lot of flavor into its compact frame. Great finish. Drink now through 2006.–B.S. • $16 • (2/28/1999) • **92**

Riesling Kabinett Mosel-Saar-Ruwer Saarburger Rausch 1996 • $15 • (11/30/1997) • **87**

Riesling QbA Halbtrocken Mosel-Saar-Ruwer 1998: Toward the dry side, this is full of lime, floral and mineral flavors that show good intensity and length on the finish. Very classy. Drink now through 2005.–B.S. • $12 • (2/29/2000) • **87**

Riesling QbA Halbtrocken Mosel-Saar-Ruwer 1997: Straightforward, this white has a juicy texture, moderate concentration and shows mineral and apple flavors. Drink now.–B.S. • $12 • (2/28/1999) • **80**

Riesling QbA Mosel-Saar-Ruwer 1998: Straightforward, balanced and slightly sweet, with appealing aromas and flavors of apple, mineral and a hint of beeswax. Lovely texture, too. Drink now through 2003.–B.S. • $12 • (2/29/2000) • **85**

Riesling QbA Mosel-Saar-Ruwer Zilliken Gutsriesling 1996 • $11 • (11/30/1997) • **80**

Riesling Spätlese Mosel-Saar-Ruwer Ockfener Bockstein 1997: An aromatic, richly textured white, supported by a firm backbone on which to display its mineral, peach and lime flavors. Drink through 2006.–B.S. • $20 • (2/28/1999) • **88**

Riesling Spätlese Mosel-Saar-Ruwer Saarburger Rausch 1998: Auction wine. Delicious. Textbook aromas and flavors of peach, apricot, lime and mineral are allied to a rich, firm structure. The flavors keep pumping through to the lingering finish. Drink now through 2006.–B.S. • $NA • (1/01/2000) • **89**

Riesling Spätlese Mosel-Saar-Ruwer Saarburger Rausch (AP 8) 1997: Auction wine. Smells of pure apricot and delivers apricot and slate flavors in a racy, minerally style. Firm acidity dominates the finish, so give it time. Best from 2002 through 2008.–B.S. • $NA • (2/28/1999) • **88**

Riesling Spätlese Mosel-Saar-Ruwer Saarburger Rausch (AP 10) 1997: A resonating, juicy spätlese with bright acidity carrying the apple and peach flavors, just shy of the depth and complexity of the best in its category. Drink now through 2003.–B.S. • $21 • (2/28/1999) • **87**

Riesling Spätlese Mosel-Saar-Ruwer Saarburger Rausch 1996 • $21 • (11/30/1997) • **90**

Italy

Italy's greatest wines are on a par with the best of France and the United States, and its everyday wines offer great value. The soul of Italian wine will always be found in its two great, indigenous red grape varieties, Nebbiolo and Sangiovese. No other country has cracked the code for molding these often finicky varieties into great wines, and Italy could easily earn its keep merely by continuing make great Barolo, Barbaresco, Brunello di Montalcino and Chianti. But Italian winemakers are a restive lot, and rather than rest on their laurels, they have plunged ahead on other fronts. Cabernet Sauvignon and Merlot, made in an oak-aged international style, are signature wines at several important estates. Chardonnay's seemingly irresistible tide has been stemmed here, but only because Italian Pinot Grigio has proved popular and profitable beyond anyone's dreams. However the wines of southern Italy (including Apulia, Sicily and Sardinia), while improving, have yet to live up to their great promise. They are Italy's last frontier.

1. **Piedmont**
2. **Veneto**
3. **Trentino-Alto Adige**
4. **Friuli**
5. **Tuscany**
6. **Abruzzo**
7. **Apulia**
8. **Sicily**
9. **Sardinia**

UNDERSTANDING ITALIAN LABELS: THE DOC and DOCG SYSTEMS

Like France, Italy has long had a controlled appellation system, called the DOC *(Denominazioni d'Origine Controllata)*. It is slowly being replaced by a newer system of DOCGs (the G stands for *Garantita*) which imposes stricter controls on quality and authenticity. Over 250 different DOCs and DOCGs have been established, each with detailed rules and regulations covering allowable grape varieties, maximum yields per acre, vineyard quality, soil type, geographic boundaries, minimum standards for aging and other quality factors. While far from perfect, the newer DOCG laws address a glaring defect of the DOC, rigid rules that inhibit legitimate efforts to improve the quality of regional wines through innovations in grape types, aging periods, the use of *barriques* (small wooden casks, typically made of French oak), and other winemaking techniques. An unintended effect of the DOC has been a profusion of so-called *vini da tavola*, unsanctioned wines that do not meet the official standards of the DOC. At many estates, these wines surpass the level of the DOC wines in quality and in price. Because the DOCG emphasizes authenticity of origin over legalistic formalities, winemakers should be freer to work within the DOCG to produce ever-better wines.

ITALIAN WINE REGIONS

It's been said that there's no such thing as Italian food, only Italian regional cuisines. The same can be said of Italian wine. The Piedmontese don't make wine like the Tuscans, who don't make wine like the Apulians, and so on. The key to sorting out the differences is understanding the unique character of Italy's many regions, ranging from the Alpine hills in the North to the heel of the boot in the south.

Tuscany

Tuscany epitomizes the blend of art and science that characterizes Italian winemaking. Though the Tuscan landscape still looks like the background of the Mona Lisa, much has changed behind the graceful facades of her ancient castles and wineries.

At the heart of Tuscany, in terms of both geography and importance, is Chianti. Chianti ranges in style from soft, fruity and quaffable to deeply colored, tannic and ageworthy. At the core of all Chianti is the remarkable Sangiovese grape. Although cultivated throughout much of Italy, only in Tuscany does it achieve its classic style: a delicate, aromatic wine of warmth and depth, with an almost ethereal astringency on the finish.

Chianti Classico, which can only come from the strictly defined Classico zone, is the more structured and ageworthy Chianti. The Classico Riserva designation is reserved for its best wines, which have been aged in oak for a minimum statutory period (once three years, now reduced to 18-24 months). In the past, Chianti Classico tended to show amber highlights fairly early in its development, but this style is rapidly being displaced in favor of one that is more vigorously fruity. Most of the famous Chianti producers have their centers of operation in the Classico zone; among these are Antinori, Ruffino, Felsina and Fontodi. Although the Gallo Negro ("Black Rooster") neck seal is still a well-known fixture in Chianti, several of the best-known producers are not members of that consortium and have chosen to rely solely on the reputation of their own brand.

On a level with Chianti Classico is the much smaller Chianti Rufina zone (not to be confused with the Ruffino winery, in Classico), located in the hills east of Florence. Its most famous name is the Marchesi de' Frecobaldi, known for its Castello di Nippozano, Montesodi and Rèmole bottlings; another top producer is Selvapiana. The Rufina zone surrounds the area called Pomino, an old DOC that was resurrected through the efforts of the Marchesi de' Frescobaldi. Pomino is a curiosity because, historically, it has relied heavily on French grapes for blends. Red Pomino is made from Cabernet, Sangiovese and Merlot, while white Pomino is mostly Chardonnay.

The other Chianti zones—Colli Fiorentino, Pisani, Colli Senesi, Colli Aretini and Montalbano—offer distinct styles. The latter encompasses the Carmignano district, which like Pomino, has a history of blending in substantial portions of Cabernet Sauvignon. The other Chianti regions are not generally *riserva* producers, but they do make appealingly soft and fruity everyday wines meant to be drunk very young.

From southern Tuscany comes Brunello di Montalcino, which, along with Barolo, is Italy's most acclaimed—and often its most expensive—traditional red wine. The only permissible grape for this DOCG is Brunello, a potent clone of the Sangiovese. The austere, age-forever style of Brunello pioneered by Biondi-Santi seems destined for the endangered species list, as modern tastes seem to prefer a less dauntingly structured wine with greater fruit and grapey extract. Besides Biondi-Santi, top producers include Caparzo, Poggio Antico, Conti Costanti, and Castello Banfi. For the budget-conscious or the impatient, the best choice from this region is Rosso di Montalcino, made from young Brunello vines and vinified in a fruitier style after minimal aging.

East of Montalcino, Vino Nobile di Montepulciano is trying set to itself apart from the crowd. Also made from a local clone of Sangiovese, it combines much of the power of a Brunello with the rounder fruitiness of a Chianti Riserva. However, many a Vino Nobile di Montepulciano does not justify its premium asking price.

Tuscany started the *vino da tavola* movement, and has been a hotbed of experimentation and the free borrowing of ideas and techniques from winemakers around the world. The wines that have resulted are known as super Tuscans. The most famous of these, such as Tignanello, Sassicaia, Sammarco, and Fontalloro, are now considered in a class with the top *crus* of Burgundy, Bordeaux and California—and are priced accordingly.

Two different approaches to super Tuscans predominate. The more visible relies heavily on Cabernet Sauvignon vinified in a Bordelais style using small oak barrels. Examples of this type include Sassicaia and Sammarco. Other super Tuscans bring the indigenous Sangiovese to its ultimate expression, a supple core of warm fruit wrapped in an ethereal cloud of bright tannins. Made without the white grapes of traditional Chianti, and sometimes spiced up with Cabernet or Merlot, these extraordinary wines have no parallel outside of Tuscany. Some of the best are Tignanello, Fontalloro, Flaccianello, and Luce, a joint venture between the American Robert Mondavi Winery and the Marchesi de' Frescobaldi.

Piedmont

With its own dialect, unique winemaking philosophy, and vintages that bear little relation to the rest of Italy, Piedmont, in Northwestern Italy, is a world removed both culturally and enologically from the rest of Italy. Yet it would be difficult to name a region where the art of the winemaker flourishes more profoundly than amidst its fog-draped hills. Like Burgundy's, Piedmont's greatness flows from the precarious balance of nature, in which the threat of disaster always looms in even the best vintages; only in the best years do its greatest wines live up to their reputation.

Barolo, sometimes called the king of Piedmont reds, is made from 100 percent Nebbiolo. The mist-shrouded hills of the Barolo region gave Nebbiolo its name—from nebbia, meaning fog. Barolo is a wine of enormous size. Even more than the great wines of Bordeaux and Burgundy, it demands cellaring. When mature, Barolo is brick orange, with aromas of truffles and smoke, and potent earth and tar flavors. Top producers include Aldo Conterno, Ceretto, Pio Cesare, Luciano Sandrone, and Paolo Scavino.

Barbaresco is almost as long-lived and can be every bit as grand as Barolo. Not quite possessed of Barolo's immense strength, Barbaresco is more supple and elegant, making it ready to drink a bit sooner. The leading exponent of Barbaresco has been Angelo Gaja.

Nebbiolo d'Alba is made outside the Barolo and Barbaresco zone. Not subject to a long minimum-aging requirement, most Nebbiolo d'Alba is fruitier and less forbidding than Barolo or Barbaresco, and quite delicious. Nebbiolo delle Langhe is usually declassified Barolo or Barbaresco. Both Nebbiolos can offer exceptional value. Look for wines made by leading Barolo and Barbaresco producers.

Gattinara is from the north of Piedmont, on the other side of Turin from Alba. This wine should rival Barolo and Barbaresco, but due to inconsistent winemaking, it rarely does. At its best, Gattinara is the Margaux of Piedmont, exquisitely delicate and deeply flavored, with a bouquet of truffles, black plum and violets. Budget-conscious lovers of Gattinara should seek out Spanna, taken from the local name for the Nebbiolo grape. Spanna can be superb, rivaling Gattinara at half the cost.

Barbera and Dolcetto, made from the grapes of the same name, are also excellent Piedmont reds. Deliciously fruity in their youth, most are intended for early consumption.

The white Cortese grape is responsible for Gavi, Gavi di Gavi, and Cortese di Gavi. Another fine Piedmont white is made from the Muscat-like Arneis grape. It is finely scented and tart. Chardonnay is making an appearance here, sometimes in a full, oaky style that calls to mind a Meursault.

Other Regions:

Fruili and Trentino-Alto Adige: Although Cabernet Franc, with its distinctive peppery/herbal character, is best known as a major grape of the French districts St.-Emilion and Chinon, it has been cultivated in the Collio region of Friuli for well over a century. The Friuli interpretation emphasizes subtle aromatics allied with a complex, light body. Friuli also makes Merlots that have an abundance of bright fruit, a clean, dry finish and an herbal, almost grassy delicacy unique to this region. Adding Cabernet Sauvignon to the blend accents the herbal notes on the bouquet, and complements the round, red-fruit notes of the Merlot grape.

Friuli and the neighboring region of Trentino-Alto Adige also have shown a knack for producing refreshing, surprisingly complex white wines. German varietals, such as Riesling, Sylvaner, Müller-Thurgau, Pinot Bianco (Weissburgunder) and Gewürztraminer, thrive in the cool, high-altitude vineyards found in these regions. Most are made in a dry, zesty style, often showing a distinctive smokiness on the nose. Sauvignon Blanc and Tocai Friulano (unrelated to the Tokaji of Hungary), show more power and intensity; some are vinified in wood casks, giving an even richer, firmer wine. Pinot Grigio is taken seriously in Friuli, as well. Often it is vinified with extended skin contact, which allows it to take on an appealing coppery tinge and extraordinary intensity. Finally, the indigenous Ribolla Gaialla should not be overlooked. Dry and quite lemony, its firm acidity makes it a perfect match with calamari.

Veneto: The predominant red grape in this region is Corvina, which is typically blended with Rondinella, Molinara and Negrara to produce Valpolicella and Bardolino. Long devoted to rather light versions of these two wines, Veneto is beginning to look more to quality. The ultimate expression of the Corvina grape is Amarone, which requires extensive drying of the grapes on open racks to concentrate the must sufficiently to create a wine of monumental character. Bertani, Anselmi, Bolla and other producers have shown that, aside from the traditional Amarones, there is a lot of unexploited potential for serious Valpolicella and Bardolino, made with far more intensity. The same is true of the white Soave, made mostly from Garganega and Trebbiano.

Abruzzo: This promising region on the Adriatic coast has been plagued by gross overproduction, which has obscured the potential for much better wines if yields are kept under control. Done well, Montepulciano d'Abruzzo (Montepulciano is the grape) can produce a ripe, Rhône-like cousin of Chianti.

Apulia: On the heel of the Italian boot, Apulia is a sunny area that enjoys a moderating influence from the sea. Salice Salentino is a rich, often rustic red that can have real character—perhaps too much for some palates. A lighter version called Rosso del Salento is also making a name for itself.

Sicily: Sicily has proven its potential for bulk production of flavorful, if not terribly complex, red and white table wines. Top bottlings from Corvo and Regaleali suggest that there is also considerable quality potential here.

Sardinia: Another out-of-the-way island, Sardinia produces wines with a gentle ripeness and smooth fruit. The white, made from the obscure Vermentino grape, may have the potential to be the next Pinot Grigio, in terms of mass acceptance and sales.

James Suckling

The harvest for Argiano's super Tuscan wine, Solengo.

ITALIAN VARIETAL WINES

Increasingly in Italy, as in France, grape varieties are getting top billing on wine labels. Below is a quick run-through of the leading types.

Barbera. The best known examples of this red—from Alba and Asti in the Piedmont—can approach Barolo and Barbaresco in power, though rarely in finesse. Increasingly, experiments with low yields and new wood aging suggest star potential.

Chardonnay. Though a few very serious producers, such as Gaja, vinify a Chardonnay that tastes like a Meursault, most Italian Chardonnay is vinified in the style of a Pinot Grigio. This means little or no wood, and lots of cold-fermented, apple-like crispness up front.

Dolcetto. Sometimes referred to as the Beaujolais of Italy, Dolcetto can be a very attractive wine when vinified in a grapey purple nouveau style. Like Barbera, its real future may lie in experiments with lower yields and barrel aging.

Merlot. Of all the classic Bordeaux varietals, Merlot appears to be the greatest commercial success. Often coupled with a regional name, such as Merlot del Piave, the Italians vinify it in a clean, fresh style so that it comes out something like a lightly herbal Chianti. Prices tend to be reasonable.

Pinot Grigio. This white grape is the same as Alsace's Pinot Gris, except that in Italian hands it sells like hot-cakes. Perhaps this is because Italy vinifies it in a light, fresh style with lots of soft fruit. Most of the best comes from Friuli, but it is increasingly being made successfully in other locales as well.

Sangiovese. Arguably Italy's most important grape, this mainstay of Chianti is becoming an important variety on its own. It tends to produce mid-weight, often quite fruity wines, with a characteristic tart, clean finish.

Trebbiano. Now beginning to make a name for itself as a single variety, this is the white grape that was once added to Chianti. It is also a component of many other popular Italian whites, such as Soave and Orvieto, the chief white wine of Umbria.

A MANO

Primitivo Puglia 1998: Seriously good Primitivo—California Zinfandel watch out. This Italian red is dark ruby in color, with aromas of bright berry, raspberry and mint. Medium- to full-bodied, with polished tannins and a fruity, vanilla aftertaste. Worth every penny, and then some. Drink now.–J.S. • $10 • (5/15/2000) • **88**

ABBONA, MARZIANO & ENRICO

Barolo 1986 • $30 • (12/15/1992) • **81**
Barolo Vigneto Terlo Ravera 1990 • $25 • (7/31/1995) • **85**
Barolo Vigneto Terlo Ravera 1989 • $23 • (10/31/1994) • **89**
Dolcetto di Dogliani Papa Celso 1992 • $13 • (6/15/1994) • **84**
Dolcetto di Dogliani Vigneto Doriolo 1993 • $11 • (7/31/1995) • **83**
Nebbiolo d'Alba 1990 • $14 • (6/15/1994) • **89**

ABRATE

Barbera d'Alba Castelvé 1997: A bit of mintiness adds an exotic side to this crisp, tart Barbera. Medium-bodied, with distinct smoke and spring roll flavors on the finish. Lacks a bit of balance.–P.M. • $19 • (11/15/1999) • **78**

Barbera d'Alba Castelvé 1996: Lush, exotic and lovely, clearly fashioned after an international taste of Barbera. Violet, rose petal, plum, spice and toasted oak accents mingle beautifully in this medium-bodied, ripe-tasting and balanced red. Drink now through 2002.–P.M. • $16 • (10/31/1998) • **87**

Barbera d'Alba Ouitin Le Coste 1997: Exploding with grapey, licorice, fresh berry character, but it's incredibly velvety, with smooth tannins, vanilla and toasted complexity and a ripe mouthfeel. Perhaps not "serious" but has "pleasure" written all over it. Drink now through 2003.–P.M. • $16 • (10/31/1998) • **88**

Dolcetto delle Langhe Monregalesi Colin-a di Ciochin 1997: Green and a bit unripe, with bell pepper notes, this light-bodied Dolcetto turns astringent on the finish. Drink now.–P.M. • $11 • (10/31/1998) • **77**

Nebbiolo d'Alba Bricco Rotondo 1997: This maturing, medium-bodied red shows earth, leather and game character. Chewy finish.–P.M. • $19 • (11/15/1999) • **78**

Nebbiolo d'Alba Bricco Rotondo 1996: A bit odd and herbal. Medium-bodied, with unappealing earth, petrol and rubber aromas and flavors. Very dry and chewy on the finish.–P.M. • $14 • (10/31/1998) • **74**

Nebbiolo d'Alba Bricco Rotondo 1995: A crisp but well-defined Nebbiolo, offering a firm texture of concentrated fruit, solid tannins and good length. The sort of medium-bodied wine that will cut through meats, with lovely black cherry, blackberry, spice and dried herbs. Drink now through 2002.–P.M. • $14 • (10/31/1998) • **87**

ACCORNERO & FIGLI, GIULIO

Barbera d'Asti Bricco Battista 1996: Intense but in a supple, thick-bodied and balanced way, this Barbera shows spice, tar and ultraripe black cherry. Exotic, with a mesquite wood fire character on the finish, but a petrol note is a bit too much. Drink now through 2003.–P.M. • $18 • (11/15/1999) • **86**

Barbera del Monferrato Giulin 1997: Tastes better than it smells. The green asparagus aromas turn to a sweet-tasting plum character on the fairly smooth palate. Lacks a bit of class.–P.M. • $14 • (11/15/1999) • **79**

Monferrato Centenario 1996: Full-bodied, displaying olive, dried herb, petrol and blackberry character, with a gorgeous, thick mouthfeel. Oozes with superripe tannins, with a sweet-ripe finish. A hair from outstanding because a petrol scent on the slightly hot ending distracts a bit, at least for now. Drink now through 2005.–P.M. • $28 • (11/15/1999) • **89**

ACINUM

Amarone della Valpolicella 1990 • $30 • (5/31/1998) • **86**
Valpolicella Classico Superiore 1995 • $12 • (5/31/1998) • **85**

Key: SS—Spectator Selection. CS—Cellar Selection. HR—Highly Recommended. $NA—Price not available. (BT)—Barrel tasting. Ⓐ—Auction Price.
For a key to the tasters' initials, see "How to Use These Listings."
Dates in parentheses represent the issues in which the ratings were published.

ADRIANO, MARCO & VITTORIO

Barbaresco 1996: Multilayered and complex, full-bodied and intense, a red wine that enlivens the palate and the imagination. Combines blackberry, earth, horse stable, parmesan, mineral and bitter chocolate notes on the long and balanced finish. Best from 2001 through 2007.–P.M. • $30 • (10/31/1999) • **91**

AGOSTINA, PIERI

Brunello di Montalcino 1994: Elegant Brunello, wonderfully perfumed, with berry, violet and tobacco character. Medium-bodied, with very refined tannins, sweet fruit on the finish. Not imported into the U.S. Drink now through 2005.–J.S. • $NA • (8/31/1999) • **89**
Rosso di Montalcino 1994 • $NA • (11/30/1996) • **85**

AIOLA

Chianti Classico 1993 • $13 • (10/31/1995) • **80**
Chianti Classico 1991 • $NA • (10/31/1993) • **85**
Chianti Classico 1990 • $11 • (9/15/1992) • **81**
Chianti Classico Riserva 1988 • $18 • (9/15/1992) • **79**
Logaiolo 1991 • $18 • (10/31/1995) • **75**
Logaiolo 1990 • $NA • (10/31/1993) • **83**

AJA, L'

Chianti Classico 1994 • $NA • (10/31/1996) • **70**
Chianti Classico 1993 • $NA • (10/31/1995) • **81**
Chianti Classico 1991 • $NA • (10/31/1993) • **82**
Chianti Classico Riserva 1993 • $NA • (10/31/1996) • **77**

ALBOLA, CASTELLO D'

Acciaiolo 1993 • $40 • (5/31/1997) • **86**
Acciaiolo 1990 • $35 • (7/31/1995) • **84**
Acciaiolo 1988 • $40 • (9/15/1991) • **88**
Chianti Classico 1996: Slightly one-dimensional, but with lots of clean and fresh cherry character. Medium-bodied, with light tannins and a crisply fruity aftertaste. Drink now.–J.S. • $10 • (12/15/1998) • **84**
Chianti Classico 1995 • $10 • (12/31/1997) • **83**
Chianti Classico 1994 • $9 • (10/31/1996) • **85**
Chianti Classico 1992 • $9 • (2/28/1995) • **74**
Chianti Classico 1991 • $9 • (10/31/1994) • **80**
Chianti Classico 1990 • $9 • (9/15/1992) • **76**
Chianti Classico 1988 • $10 • (9/15/1991) • **89**
Chianti Classico Riserva 1990 • $13 • (2/28/1995) • **79**
Chianti Classico Riserva 1988 • $15 • (10/31/1993) • **80**
Chianti Classico Riserva 1985 • $12 • (11/30/1989) • **76**
Pinot Grigio Aquileia del Friuli 1997: Subtle apple and peach character, with bright acidity and good concentration and intensity.–B.S. • $10 • (9/30/1998) • **84**
Pinot Nero Toscana Le Marangole 1996: Hard to tell it's Pinot Nero. Rather forward, with berry, vanilla and cedar. Medium- to light-bodied, with soft tannins, a light finish.–J.S. • $25 • (12/15/1998) • **79**
Toscana Acciaiolo 1995: A solid yet slightly rustic red with blackberry, currant and dried herbs through and through. Medium- to full-bodied, with full, chewy tannins and a smoky, herbal finish. The Cabernet Sauvignon dominates this blend, which includes Sangiovese. Seriously good. Drink now.–J.S. • $25 • (12/15/1998) • **88**

ALERAMICI, MARCHESATO DEGLI

Brunello di Montalcino 1994: Berry, vanilla and chocolate aromas and flavors. Medium-bodied, with soft tannins and a delicious finish. A joyous Brunello to drink now.–J.S. • $42 • (8/31/1999) • **87**
Brunello di Montalcino 1993: Good but not going anywhere. Cherry character, with leather highlights on the nose. Medium-bodied, with a slightly austere finish. Drink now.–J.S. • $40 • (12/15/1998) • **81**
Brunello di Montalcino 1992 • $34 • (9/30/1997) • **85**
Brunello di Montalcino 1991 • $35 • (11/30/1996) • **78**
Brunello di Montalcino 1990 • $NA • (10/31/1995) • **86**
Brunello di Montalcino Riserva 1991 • $40 • (9/30/1997) • **78**
Il Galampio Rosso 1993 • $18 • (10/31/1996) • **79**

Rosso di Montalcino 1997: Simple and fruity. Slightly annoying aromas of stems, with berries and earth. Medium-bodied, with light tannins and a light, fruity finish. Drink now.–J.S. • $18 • (9/15/1999) • **81**
Rosso di Montalcino 1996: Delicate and fruity, with cherry and tobacco flavors and silky, fine tannins. A little dry on the finish. Drink now.–J.S. • $17 • (12/15/1998) • **80**
Rosso di Montalcino 1995 • $15 • (9/30/1997) • **84**
Rosso di Montalcino 1994 • $15 • (11/30/1996) • **79**
Rosso di Montalcino 1993 • $NA • (10/31/1995) • **81**

ALESSANDRIA, CRISSANTE

Barolo Capalot 1995: The toasted, violet-scented oak notes give it complexity. The tannins are smooth, and the black fruit is flavorful but neither thick nor rich. Medium-bodied and elegant. Drink now through 2005.–P.M. • $45 • (11/15/1999) • **88**
Barolo Vigna dei Roggeri 1994: A ripe-tasting Nebbiolo that shows fine oak treatment. Palate-coating and complex, with earth, horse stable, blackberry, plum and tar notes. The tannins on the long finish are manageable. Drink now through 2005.–P.M. • $45 • (11/15/1999) • **89**
Rugé 1997: This wonderful red is all seduction and pleasure. Full-bodied, black-colored, thick, opulent and ripe-tasting, it delivers silky-smooth tannins, with toasted oak that burns like a slow fuse to a long finish, where the black fruit explodes. Wow. Drink now through 2005.–P.M. • $32 • (11/15/1999) • **92**

ALESSANDRIA, GIANFRANCO

Barbera d'Alba 1997: Unique. Ultrathick and huge; given time it should deliver a dried herbs, green olive, blackberry complexity, but for now, its petrol-like oaky notes are awkward. Best from 2001 through 2007.–P.M. • $28 • (9/15/1999) • **86**
Barolo 1993 • $30 • (10/31/1997) • **85**

ALESSI

Sangiovese Toscana All'Omo il Vino 1996: A chewy and flavorful Sangiovese. Pleasant aromas of dried cherries, bark and berries. Medium-bodied, with fine tannins and a medium finish. Drink through 2001.–J.S. • $21 • (12/15/1998) • **85**

ALFIERI

Barbera d'Asti Alfiera 1996: Well made, offering succulent fruit, full body and fresh acidity softened by nice toasted oak, mocha and vanilla notes. A nicely balanced food wine, with a succulent, lingering finish. Drink now through 2002.–P.M. • $28 • (11/15/1999) • **88**
Barbera d'Asti Alfiera 1994: Rich and ripe, full-bodied yet refined, showing earth, spice, toasted bread, vanilla, plum and berry character. Intense, but with its good balance between traditional and new, this Barbera can be enjoyed now or cellared. Drink now through 2004.–P.M. • $17 • (10/31/1998) • **88**
Barbera d'Asti Alfiera 1993 • $17 • (10/31/1997) • **80**
Barbera d'Asti La Tota 1997: Spicy oak mingles with red berry notes to present a smooth, maturing Barbera that delivers ripe tannins, medium fruit intensity and a supple finish despite the kick of acidity. Drink now.–P.M. • $19 • (11/15/1999) • **84**
Barbera d'Asti La Tota 1996: Fruity and slightly spritzy, delivering blackberry and cassis, some wet earth. A bit tart, and light to medium in body, it should go well with food. Tasted twice, with consistent notes. Drink now.–P.M. • $17 • (10/31/1998) • **81**
Barbera d'Asti La Tota 1995 • $17 • (10/31/1997) • **75**
Monferrato Il Rosso dei Marchesi 1996 • $12 • (10/31/1997) • **72**
Monferrato San Germano 1994 • $32 • (10/31/1997) • **84**

ALLEGRINI

Amarone della Valpolicella 1985 • $28 • (9/15/1992) • **84**
Amarone della Valpolicella Classico 1995: Wonderfully clean and vibrant, with crushed berry, cherry, spice and raisin on the nose. Full-bodied, with velvety tannins and a long finish. Slightly one-dimensional; give it time. Best after 2002.–J.S. • $58 • (6/15/2000) • **89**
Amarone della Valpolicella Classico Superiore 1990 • $31 • (6/15/1997) CS • **94**
Amarone della Valpolicella Classico Superiore 1980 • $13 • (12/31/1987) • **85**
La Poja 1992 • $22 • (6/30/1998) • **88**
La Poja 1991 • $25 • (6/15/1997) • **86**
La Poja 1986 • $55 • (9/15/1992) • **86**
Recioto della Valpolicella Classico Superiore Amarone 1991: Lean and compact, showing plum and fruitcake character and a tobacco note that turns dry and tannic on the finish. Drink now through 2002.–B.S. • $35 • (7/31/1998) • **83**
Valpolicella Classico 1998: A delicious Valpo for the price. Very grapey and fresh. Medium-bodied, with good fruit, fresh acidity and a clean finish. Delicious. Drink now.–J.S. • $11 • (6/15/2000) • **86**
Valpolicella Classico 1996: A definite earthy note pervades the chocolate and cherry flavors in this smooth, light- to medium-bodied red. Cleansing finish. Drink now.–B.S. • $10 • (7/31/1998) • **84**
Valpolicella Classico 1995 • $10 • (6/15/1997) • **79**
Valpolicella Classico 1991 • $11 • (9/15/1992) • **78**
Valpolicella Classico 1990 • $11 • (9/15/1992) • **82**
Valpolicella Classico Superiore La Grola 1996: Gorgeous and well crafted, with berry, cherry and mint aromas and flavors. Medium-bodied, with fine tannins and a fruity finish. Drink now through 2003.–J.S. • $18 • (6/15/2000) • **89**
Valpolicella Classico Superiore La Grola 1994 • $17 • (6/15/1998) • **87**
Valpolicella Classico Superiore La Grola 1993 • $16 • (6/15/1997) • **85**
Valpolicella Classico Superiore La Grola 1990 • $16 • (12/15/1995) • **88**
Valpolicella Classico Superiore La Grola 1988 • $18 • (9/15/1992) • **82**
Valpolicella Classico Superiore Palazzo della Torre 1996: Rich and polished, with intense plum, mint and tanned leather aromas. Medium- to full-bodied, with velvety tannins and a long, minty berry and cherry aftertaste. A gorgeous red that needs time. Best after 2001.–J.S. • $16 • (6/15/2000) SS • **90**
Valpolicella Classico Superiore Palazzo della Torre 1994 • $15 • (6/15/1998) • **86**
Valpolicella Classico Superiore Palazzo della Torre 1990 • $13 • (12/15/1995) • **84**
Valpolicella Classico Superiore Palazzo della Torre 1988 • $16 • (9/15/1992) • **78**
Valpolicella Classico Superiore Palazzo della Torre 1986 • $16 • (9/15/1992) • **85**
Verona La Poja 1995: A consistent and well-crafted red with lots of potential. Dark ruby, with intense aromas of chocolate, berry and mint. Medium- to full-bodied, with big, velvety tannins and a big finish. Best after 2000. –J.S. • $50 • (6/15/2000) • **91**

ALMONDO, GIOVANNI

Roero Arneis 1996: Intense, with lovely flavors of ripe apple, pear and butterscotch that linger appealingly on the finish. A well-balanced wine that would go well with fish or poultry. Drink now.–K.M. • $16 • (8/31/1998) • **87**

ALTARE, ELIO

Barolo 1992 • $41 • (10/31/1996) • **88**
Barolo 1991 • $30 • (10/31/1995) • **85**
Barolo 1990 • $58 Ⓐ • (10/31/1994) • **81**
Barolo 1988 • $32 • (10/31/1993) • **85**
Barolo 1985 • $24 • (1/31/1990) • **92**
Barolo 1982 • $13 • (6/30/1987) • **88**
Barolo Vigneto Arborina 1990 • $115 • (10/31/1994) • **93**
Barolo Vigneto Arborina 1989 • $45 Ⓐ • (10/31/1993) • **85**
Barolo Vigneto Arborina 1988 • $42 • (10/31/1993) • **88**
Barolo Vigneto Arborina 1982 • $15 • (9/15/1987) • **87**
Cabernet Sauvignon Piedmont La Villa 1992 • $NA • (10/31/1994) • **89**
Nebbiolo Piedmont Vigna Arborina 1992 • $40 • (10/31/1994) • **85**
Nebbiolo Piedmont Vigna Arborina 1987 • $32 • (9/15/1990) • **84**
Nebbiolo Piedmont Vigna Arborina 1986 • $20 • (2/28/1989) • **90**
Nebbiolo Piedmont Vigna Larigi 1987 • $28 • (5/31/1990) • **89**
Vigna Larigi 1992 • $40 • (10/31/1994) • **91**

ALTESINO

Brunello di Montalcino 1994: Good clarity of ripe fruit. Medium-bodied, with fine tannins and a fresh, slightly citrusy finish. Slightly one-dimensional really, but very good. Drink through 2005.–J.S. • $40 • (8/31/1999) • **87**
Brunello di Montalcino 1993: Wonderfully bright, with cherry, blackberry and wet earth aromas. Full-bodied, with velvety, fine tannins and a long, fruity finish. A well-crafted '93 Brunello. Best after 2000.–J.S. • $50 • (12/15/1998) • **89**
Brunello di Montalcino 1992 • $42 • (9/30/1997) • **84**
Brunello di Montalcino 1991 • $40 • (11/30/1996) • **89**
Brunello di Montalcino 1990 • $96 Ⓐ • (10/31/1995) • **87**

ALTESINO

Brunello di Montalcino 1988 • $28 • (4/30/1994) • **91**
Brunello di Montalcino 1982 • $22 • (9/15/1986) • **85**
Brunello di Montalcino 1981 • $22 • (9/15/1986) • **80**
Brunello di Montalcino 1980 • $18 • (9/15/1986) • **91**
Brunello di Montalcino 1979 • $20 • (9/15/1986) • **82**
Brunello di Montalcino Montosoli 1993: A gorgeous, subtle Brunello. Not the powerful style that Altesino's single-vineyard Brunello can be in great years such as 1990, but an outstanding, classy bottle. Floral, blackberry and meat aromas follow through to a medium-bodied palate, with very fine tannins and a zingy finish. Best after 2001.–J.S. • $80 • (12/15/1998) • **91**
Brunello di Montalcino Montosoli 1990 • $137 Ⓐ • (10/31/1995) • **98**
Brunello di Montalcino Montosoli 1988 • $37 • (4/30/1994) • **92**
Brunello di Montalcino Riserva 1993: Perfumed and beautiful. Aromas of roses, berries, fresh mushrooms and grapes follow through to the palate. Full-bodied and velvety, with polished tannins and a fresh finish. Well crafted. Drink now through 2005.–J.S. • $54 • (8/31/1999) • **90**
Brunello di Montalcino Riserva 1990 • $122 Ⓐ • (11/30/1996) • **89**
Brunello di Montalcino Riserva 1988 • $50 • (10/31/1994) • **90**
Brunello di Montalcino Riserva 1983 • $29 • (11/30/1989) • **86**
Brunello di Montalcino Vigna Altesino 1985 • $32 • (9/30/1990) • **91**
Brunello di Montalcino Vigna Altesino 1983 • $26 • (1/31/1990) • **84**
Rosso di Altesino 1989 • $8 • (1/31/1992) • **86**
Rosso di Montalcino 1993 • $17 • (10/31/1995) • **80**
Rosso di Montalcino 1992 • $15 • (4/30/1994) • **81**
Rosso di Montalcino 1991 • $15 • (4/30/1994) • **84**
Rosso di Montalcino 1988 • $15 • (7/15/1991) • **73**
Rosso di Montalcino 1986 • $10 • (7/15/1989) • **80**
Toscana Alte d'Altesi 1995: Plenty of ripe fruit here, also plenty of new wood, with loads of slightly annoying coconut and cedar aromas and flavors. Medium-bodied, with polished tannins. Drink now.–J.S. • $32 • (12/15/1998) • **84**
Toscana Alte d'Altesi 1993 • $18 • (10/31/1996) • **87**
Toscana Alte d'Altesi 1990 • $34 • (10/31/1993) • **86**
Toscana Alte d'Altesi 1988 • $35 • (9/15/1991) • **92**
Toscana Alte d'Altesi 1987 • $35 • (1/31/1992) • **69**
Toscana Alte d'Altesi 1986 • $32 • (7/15/1989) • **85**
Toscana Borgo d'Altesi 1996: Lovely texture, with aromas of berry, green olive and grilled meat. Medium-bodied, with lots of polished tannins and a medium, fruity finish. Made from Cabernet Sauvignon. Drink now.–J.S. • $50 • (11/30/1999) • **88**
Toscana Borgo d'Altesi 1995: Extremely grapey and rich, with ripe berry and black currant aromas that lessen on the palate. Medium-bodied, with medium, fine tannins and a short, silky finish. Drink now.–J.S. • $NA • (12/15/1998) • **87**
Toscana Borgo d'Altesi 1993 • $NA • (10/31/1996) • **88**
Toscana Palazzo Altesi 1996: A fresh and silky red, with light strawberry, plum and almond aromas. Medium-bodied, with medium tannins and a fresh finish. Needs a bit more fruit on the midpalate. Made from Sangiovese. Drink now.–J.S. • $33 • (11/30/1999) • **85**
Toscana Palazzo Altesi 1995: Funky but delicious, this is a stylish red with berry, earth and barnyard aromas and flavors. Medium-bodied, with soft tannins and a fruity finish. Drink now.–J.S. • $30 • (12/15/1998) • **85**
Toscana Palazzo Altesi 1994 • $18 • (10/31/1996) • **80**
Toscana Palazzo Altesi 1993 • $18 • (10/31/1996) • **87**
Toscana Palazzo Altesi 1990 • $26 • (10/31/1993) • **89**
Toscana Palazzo Altesi 1988 • $26 • (9/15/1991) • **90**
Toscana Palazzo Altesi 1987 • $25 • (1/31/1992) • **78**
Toscana Palazzo Altesi 1985 • $23 • (10/31/1990) • **82**
Toscana Palazzo Altesi 1983 • $17 • (2/15/1988) • **88**

AMA, CASTELLO DI

Chianti Classico 1997: A well-crafted, superb Chianti Classico. Totally fruit-driven. Beautiful aromas of plum, leaf and cherry. Medium- to full-bodied, with medium, fine tannins and a silky mouthfeel. Best from 2001 through 2004.–J.S. • $35 • (11/30/1999) • **91**
Chianti Classico 1996: Very good Chianti, with fresh and lively aromas and flavors of dried cherry and strawberry. Medium-bodied, with vivid fruit and zingy acidity, a leanish finish. Drink now.–J.S. • $33 • (12/15/1998) • **85**
Chianti Classico 1995 • $14 • (9/30/1997) • **82**
Chianti Classico 1993 • $15 • (10/31/1995) • **78**
Chianti Classico 1992 • $15 • (2/28/1995) • **85**
Chianti Classico 1990 • $16 • (9/15/1992) • **81**
Chianti Classico 1988 • $18 • (4/15/1991) • **87**
Chianti Classico Bellavista Riserva 1995: Shows loads of blackberries and chocolate on the nose and palate, with masses of velvety tannins. Full-bodied and rich, it goes on and on. Always one of the best Chiantis going, and '95 is no different. Needs time to mellow. Best after 2000.–J.S. • $30 Ⓐ • (12/15/1998) • **90**
Chianti Classico Bellavista Riserva 1994 • $40 • (9/30/1997) • **91**
Chianti Classico Bellavista Riserva 1993 • $40 • (9/30/1997) • **87**
Chianti Classico Bellavista Riserva 1992 • $25 • (10/31/1995) • **82**
Chianti Classico Bellavista Riserva 1991 • $25 • (2/28/1995) • **87**
Chianti Classico Bellavista Riserva 1990 • $NA • (9/30/1997) • **95**
Chianti Classico Bellavista Riserva 1988 • $NA • (9/30/1997) • **94**
Chianti Classico Bellavista Riserva 1986 • $36 • (11/30/1989) • **90**
Chianti Classico Bellavista Riserva 1985 • $NA • (9/30/1997) • **92**
Chianti Classico Bellavista Riserva 1983 • $25 • (12/15/1987) • **90**
Chianti Classico Bertinga 1990 • $34 • (2/28/1995) HR • **93**
Chianti Classico Bertinga 1988 • $34 • (9/15/1992) • **89**
Chianti Classico La Casuccia 1995: Delicious, drink-me-now Chianti, with lovely plum and blackberry aromas and flavors and a hint of chocolate. Medium-bodied, with soft tannins and a plummy aftertaste. Drink now.–J.S. • $46 Ⓐ • (12/15/1998) • **88**
Chianti Classico La Casuccia 1994: A gentle and friendly Chianti. Attractive plummy, cherry, grapey character on the nose and palate. Medium- to full-bodied, with soft, polished tannins and a juicy finish. Drink now.–J.S. • $42 • (12/15/1998) • **87**
Chianti Classico La Casuccia 1993 • $40 • (9/30/1997) • **86**
Chianti Classico La Casuccia 1992 • $25 • (10/31/1995) • **82**
Chianti Classico La Casuccia 1991 • $25 • (2/28/1995) • **86**
Chianti Classico La Casuccia 1990 • $38 • (2/28/1995) • **93**
Chianti Classico La Casuccia 1986 • $40 • (11/30/1989) • **87**
Chianti Classico La Casuccia 1985 • $40 • (9/15/1991) • **89**
Chianti Classico San Lorenzo 1990 • $34 • (2/28/1995) • **90**
Chianti Classico San Lorenzo 1988 • $34 • (9/15/1992) HR • **91**
Chianti Classico San Lorenzo 1986 • $36 • (11/30/1989) • **84**
Chianti Classico San Lorenzo 1985 • $32 • (11/30/1989) • **86**
Toscana Vigna Il Chiuso 1995: Smells rather old and raisiny, with leather, cooked fruit and cheese aromas. Medium-bodied and very ripe. Alcoholic. An overdone Pinot Noir. Not up to Ama's standard.–J.S. • $NA • (11/30/1999) • **78**
Toscana Vigna Il Chiuso 1994: A rustic and raisiny Pinot Nero. Strawberry, tea, stems and raisins on the nose. Medium-bodied, with slightly austere tannins, a drying palate. Disappointing.–J.S. • $23 • (12/15/1998) • **79**
Toscana Vigna Il Chiuso 1993 • $28 • (9/30/1997) • **81**
Toscana Vigna Il Chiuso 1992 • $25 • (10/31/1995) • **73**
Toscana Vigna Il Chiuso 1991 • $25 • (2/28/1995) • **88**
Toscana Vigna Il Chiuso 1990 • $34 • (10/31/1993) • **85**
Toscana Vigna Il Chiuso 1988 • $25 • (9/15/1991) • **90**
Toscana Vigna l'Apparita 1996: This big and concentrated Merlot is more like a raisiny dry Port. Enticing aromas of mushroom, a hint of oak and ripe, almost dried fruit. Full-bodied, with tough, chewy tannins and a long, fruity finish. A bit rustic but outstanding. Best after 2003.–J.S. • $146 • (11/30/1999) • **92**
Toscana Vigna l'Apparita 1995: Wonderful floral, berry and cocoa aromas. Full-bodied, with fine, polished tannins and a long finish with dark chocolate and berry on the aftertaste. A sleek, racy Merlot from a respected winery. Best after 2001.–J.S. • $200 • (12/15/1998) • **92**
Toscana Vigna l'Apparita 1994: Delicious. Very intense aromas of raspberries, currants and crushed berries. Full-bodied, with soft tannins and a delicious, fruity aftertaste. This Merlot is not up to the stunning quality of the '93, but it's still outstanding. Drink now.–J.S. • $130 • (12/15/1998) • **91**
Toscana Vigna l'Apparita 1993 • $77 Ⓐ • (9/30/1997) HR • **96**
Toscana Vigna l'Apparita 1992 • $60 • (10/31/1995) • **88**
Toscana Vigna l'Apparita 1991 • $60 • (2/28/1995) • **92**
Toscana Vigna l'Apparita 1990 • $169 Ⓐ • (10/31/1993) HR • **92**
Toscana Vigna l'Apparita 1988 • $115 Ⓐ • (9/15/1991) • **93**
Toscana Vigna l'Apparita 1986 • $NA • (11/30/1989) • **87**
Toscana Vigna l'Apparita 1985 • $NA • (11/30/1989) • **92**

AMBROSINI, LORELLA

Toscana Riflesso Antico 1996: Decent berry and vanilla character, with hints of cedar. Rather mature already. Medium-bodied, with light tannins and a meaty finish. Drink now.–J.S. • $31 • (11/30/1999) • **81**

Key: SS—Spectator Selection. CS—Cellar Selection. HR—Highly Recommended. $NA—Price not available. (BT)—Barrel tasting. Ⓐ—Auction Price.
For a key to the tasters' initials, see "How to Use These Listings."
Dates in parentheses represent the issues in which the ratings were published.

ITALY

Toscana Riflesso Antico 1995: A bit mature-tasting for a 95, but shows ripe berry, leather and plum aromas and flavors, medium body and soft texture. Drink now.–J.S. • $30 • (12/15/1998) • **82**
Toscana Riflesso Antico 1994 • $29 • (4/30/1998) • **84**
Val di Cornia Armonia 1997: A simple but rather rustic white, with steely pear aromas, medium body, fruit cocktail flavors and medium, fresh finish. Drink now.–J.S. • $13 • (11/30/1999) • **81**
Val di Cornia Red Suvereto Tabaro 95 1998: Not altogether clean, with sweet fruit and turpentine character. Hard to like.–J.S. • $11 • (11/30/1999) • **71**
Val di Cornia Red Suvereto Tabaro 95 1997: Rather rustic in style, with a strawberry, bubble-gum character. Light-bodied, with light tannins and a soft texture.–J.S. • $10 • (12/15/1998) • **79**
Val di Cornia Subertum 1996: Interesting aromas of ripe berry, toasted almond and earth. Medium-bodied, with medium tannins and a light finish. Slightly hollow midpalate. Drink now.–J.S. • $29 • (11/30/1999) • **82**
Val di Cornia Suvereto Subertum 1995: Vanilla character slightly overwhelms this wine, but there's also pleasant berry aromas and flavors. Medium-bodied, with fresh acidity and a coconut aftertaste.–J.S. • $28 • (12/15/1998) • **84**
Val di Cornia Suvereto Subertum 1994 • $25 • (4/30/1998) • **78**
Val di Cornia Suvereto Tabaro 95 1995 • $12 • (4/30/1998) • **82**
Val di Cornia White Suvereto Armonia 1997: I like the almond and mineral, with hints of ripe apple character, in this white. Medium-bodied, with good acidity and a flavorful finish. Drink now.–J.S. • $10 • (12/15/1998) • **83**
Val di Cornia White Suvereto Armonia 1996: Aromas of piecrust, apple and apricots. Medium-bodied, with mineral character and a soft, round-textured finish. A bit rustic, but tasty. Drink now.–J.S. • $10 • (12/15/1998) • **82**
Val di Cornia White Suvereto Tabaro 95 1997: Sulfurous and cloying. Acidic and mouth-drying. Tasted twice, with consistent notes.–J.S. • $10 • (12/15/1998) • **65**
Val di Cornia White Tabaro 95 1998: A pleasant white offering pear and honeycomb aromas with hints of tarragon. Medium-bodied, with lively acidity and minerally pear flavors.–J.S. • $9 • (11/30/1999) • **84**

AMERINI, CANTINA COLLI

Sangiovese Umbria Torraccio 1995 • $25 • (6/15/1998) • **84**

ANFORIO

Barolo 1994: This simple, enjoyable red is fresh, clean and easy, with plummy, grapey aromas and flavors. Medium-bodied, with a soft texture. Drink now.–J.S. • $39 • (6/30/1999) • **81**
Gavi 1997: Attractive aromas of melon, banana and mineral. Medium-bodied, with lots of flavors and a blanched almond, earth and fruit aftertaste. Drink now.–J.S. • $14 • (6/15/1999) • **85**
Roero Arneis 1997: A very pungent white, with intense rose petal and perfume aromas and flavors. Medium-bodied, with fresh acidity and a flavorful finish. Shows a confected quality.–J.S. • $17 • (6/15/1999) • **79**

ANGELINI

Merlot Montello e Colli Asolani 1995 • $9 • (5/31/1998) • **76**
Pinot Grigio Veneto 1996 • $9 • (5/31/1998) • **78**

ANGELINI, TENIMENTI

Chianti Classico Fattoria San Leonino 1997: A light and simple Chianti, with plum, dried cherry and cedar character. Light, fruity finish. Drink now.–J.S. • $16 • (11/30/1999) • **82**
Chianti Classico Fattoria San Leonino 1996: Bright cherry and berry flavors, with an underlying citrusy character. Medium- to light-bodied, with light tannins and a crisp finish. Drink now.–J.S. • $13 • (12/15/1998) • **81**
Chianti Classico Fattoria San Leonino 1995 • $19 • (9/30/1997) • **80**
Chianti Classico Fattoria San Leonino 1991 • $10 • (10/31/1993) • **82**
Chianti Classico Fattoria San Leonino 1990 • $10 • (9/15/1992) • **89**
Chianti Classico Fattoria San Leonino 1988 • $10 • (12/15/1990) • **87**
Chianti Classico Fattoria San Leonino Riserva 1995: A fresh and succulent red for current drinking. Offers pretty aromas of porcini and fruit, a medium body with silky tannins, and a crisp finish. Drink now.–J.S. • $27 • (12/15/1998) • **86**
Chianti Classico Fattoria San Leonino Riserva 1993 • $25 • (12/31/1997) • **87**
Chianti Classico Fattoria San Leonino Riserva 1988 • $19 • (9/15/1992) • **85**
Chianti Classico Monsenese 1995: A bit simple, but offers some good plum and dried cherry character. Medium- to light-bodied, with light tannins, a fresh aftertaste. Drink now.–J.S. • $30 • (12/15/1998) • **82**

Syrah Toscana 1993 • $NA • (9/30/1997) • **90**
Toscana Busillis 1997: Interesting grapefruit and lime aromas and flavors. Medium-bodied, with medium acidity and a short finish. Viognier. Drink now.–J.S. • $NA • (11/30/1999) • **85**
Toscana Busillis 1996: A stylish white, with interesting aromas and flavors of peaches and cream and a hint of cotton candy. Medium-bodied, with fine acidity and a long, fresh finish. Serve very cold. Viognier. Drink now.–J.S. • $NA • (12/15/1998) • **86**
Toscana Salivolpe 1995: A bright and lively Syrah with dried cherry and black pepper character. Medium-bodied, with firm tannins and a crisp finish. Drink now.–J.S. • $50 • (11/30/1999) • **87**
Vino Nobile di Montepulciano La Villa 1996: A clean and fresh wine, with dried cherry and berry character. Medium-bodied, with fresh acidity and a clean finish. Drink now.–J.S. • $42 • (11/30/1999) • **85**
Vino Nobile di Montepulciano La Villa 1995: A balanced, well-crafted red, with blackberry, cherry and tobacco aromas and flavors. Medium-bodied, with medium tannins. Drink now.–J.S. • $33 • (12/15/1998) • **86**

ANGELO, D'

Aglianico del Vulture 1997: Has good pepper and rustic fruit character, but dry and slightly volatile on the finish.–J.S. • $11 • (5/31/2000) • **76**
Aglianico del Vulture 1991 • $15 • (1/31/1996) • **84**
Aglianico del Vulture 1985 • $18 • (9/15/1989) • **70**
Aglianico del Vulture Vigna Caselle Riserva 1990 • $20 • (1/31/1996) • **85**
Basilicata Canneto 1995: Hard. Ethyl acetate. Tasted twice, with consistent notes.–J.S. • $20 • (5/31/2000) • **69**
Canneto 1991 • $25 • (1/31/1996) • **85**

ANGELO, DARIO D'

Montepulciano d'Abruzzo 1996 • $6 • (6/15/1998) • **82**
Montepulciano d'Abruzzo 1993 • $4 • (3/31/1995) • **82**

ANSELMI, ROBERTO

Amarone della Valpolicella 1985 • $19 • (6/30/1991) • **86**
Cabernet Sauvignon Veneto Realda 1989 • $28 • (12/15/1992) • **84**
Cabernet Sauvignon Veneto Realda 1988 • $28 • (9/15/1992) • **78**
Recioto di Soave I Capitelli 1992 • $35 • (4/30/1996) • **90**
Recioto di Soave I Capitelli 1989 • $35 • (9/15/1992) HR • **94**
Recioto di Soave I Capitelli 1988 • $34 • (9/15/1992) CS • **95**
Soave Classico Superiore San Vincenzo 1996 • $10 • (4/30/1998) • **84**

ANTARIO

Barolo Vigneto Castelletto 1993 • $27 • (1/31/1998) • **70**
Gavi Tenuta La Marchesa 1996 • $15 • (8/31/1997) • **85**
Pinot Grigio Venezie 1996 • $10 • (8/31/1997) • **77**

ANTINORI

Bolgheri Guado al Tasso Tenuta Belvedere 1997: A balanced and harmonious young red. Dark ruby color, with loads of grape, berry, mineral and violet aromas. Full-bodied, with loads of blackberry and cherry character, fine tannins and a medium finish. Gorgeous wine. Best after 2005.–J.S. • $52 • (6/15/2000) • **96**
Bolgheri Superiore Guado al Tasso Tenuta Belvedere 1996: An intense, extremely well-structured Tuscan red, showing intense Cabernet character, with currant, spice and mint aromas and flavors. Full in body, with loads of silky tannins and a long, long finish. Finest Guado al Tasso ever. Best after 2002.–J.S. • $52 • (11/30/1999) HR • **94**
Bolgheri Guado al Tasso Tenuta Belvedere 1995: California Zinfandel lovers will go bonkers for this. Very ripe but slightly rustic. Provocative aromas of crushed berry, smoke and raisin. Full-bodied, very round and smooth, with a juicy-fruity aftertaste. Drink now through 2003.–J.S. • $53 Ⓐ • (12/15/1998) • **88**
Bolgheri Guado al Tasso Tenuta Belvedere 1994 • $42 • (9/30/1997) • **81**
Bolgheri Guado al Tasso Tenuta Belvedere 1993 • $68 • (10/31/1996) • **87**
Bolgheri Guado al Tasso Tenuta Belvedere 1992 • $NA • (10/31/1995) • **86**
Bolgheri Guado al Tasso Tenuta Belvedere 1990 • $NA • (2/28/1995) • **89**
Bolgheri Rosato Scalabrone Tenuta Belvedere 1996 • $NA • (9/30/1997) • **83**
Brunello di Montalcino Pian delle Vigne 1995: Gorgeous aromas of Indian spice and ripe berries. Medium- to full-bodied, with silky tannins and a long finish. A bit closed still. Needs time. Antinori's debut Brunello. Best after 2000.–J.S. • $50 • (6/30/2000) • **90**

ANTINORI

Chardonnay Umbria Castello della Sala 1998: A well-made, delicious Chardonnay, with pretty aromas of apple, honey and apricot. Medium-bodied, with ripe fruit and good acidity. Fresh finish. Drink now.–J.S. • $13 • (2/29/2000) • **86**
Chardonnay Umbria Castello della Sala 1996 • $12 • (10/15/1997) • **85**
Chianti Classico 1988 • $11 • (9/15/1991) • **86**
Chianti Classico Badia a Passignano 1996: A pleasant yet simple Chianti with fresh berry and strawberry character, a medium body, light tannins and a fruity, slightly stemmy finish. Drink now.–J.S. • $13 • (12/15/1998) • **82**
Chianti Classico Badia a Passignano 1995 • $13 • (9/30/1997) • **86**
Chianti Classico Badia a Passignano 1994 • $11 • (10/31/1996) • **81**
Chianti Classico Badia a Passignano 1993 • $10 • (2/28/1995) • **83**
Chianti Classico Badia a Passignano 1991 • $9 • (10/31/1993) • **84**
Chianti Classico Badia a Passignano 1990 • $NA • (10/31/1993) • **92**
Chianti Classico Badia a Passignano Riserva 1996: A bit disappointing. Straightforward plum skin and grape aromas, with hints of bark. Medium-bodied, with fine tannins and a racy finish. Slightly diluted midpalate. Drink now.–J.S. • $38 • (11/30/1999) • **84**
Chianti Classico Badia a Passignano Riserva 1995: A joy to taste. Wonderful rose and blackberry aromas follow through on the palate. Medium-bodied, with medium, velvety tannins and a fruity aftertaste. Drink now.–J.S. • $36 • (12/15/1998) • **87**
Chianti Classico Badia a Passignano Riserva 1994 • $30 • (9/30/1997) • **88**
Chianti Classico Badia a Passignano Riserva 1993 • $28 • (10/31/1996) • **87**
Chianti Classico Badia a Passignano Riserva 1991 • $30 • (10/31/1995) • **89**
Chianti Classico Badia a Passignano Riserva 1990 • $30 • (2/28/1995) • **89**
Chianti Classico Badia a Passignano Riserva 1988 • $30 • (4/30/1994) • **88**
Chianti Classico Pèppoli 1997: A Chianti Classico with lively fruit and acidity as well as fine tannins. Medium-bodied, with cherry and raspberry flavors and a fine finish. Drink now through 2001.–J.S. • $20 • (11/30/1999) • **88**
Chianti Classico Pèppoli 1996: Offers pleasant dried cherry and earth aromas and flavors, medium body and medium tannins. Fruity finish. Good texture. Drink now through 2001.–J.S. • $19 • (12/15/1998) • **86**
Chianti Classico Pèppoli 1995 • $19 • (9/30/1997) • **82**
Chianti Classico Pèppoli 1994 • $18 • (10/31/1996) • **84**
Chianti Classico Pèppoli 1993 • $16 • (10/31/1995) • **82**
Chianti Classico Pèppoli 1991 • $NA • (10/31/1993) • **82**
Chianti Classico Pèppoli 1990 • $16 • (2/28/1995) • **84**
Chianti Classico Pèppoli 1988 • $19 • (9/15/1991) • **88**
Chianti Classico Pèppoli 1987 • $17 • (5/15/1990) • **83**
Chianti Classico Pèppoli 1986 • $17 • (7/15/1989) • **90**
Chianti Classico Pèppoli 1985 • $16 • (5/31/1988) • **92**
Chianti Classico Tenute Marchese Antinori Riserva 1996: An extremely well crafted 1996 CC riserva, with beautiful aromas of currant, raspberry and smoky wood. Medium-bodied, with polished tannins and a long, flavorful finish. Drink now through 2001.–J.S. • $35 • (11/30/1999) • **87**
Chianti Classico Tenute Marchese Antinori Riserva 1995: Pretty, well-defined Sangiovese with an abundance of blackberry aromas and flavors. Medium-bodied, with medium tannins and a refreshing aftertaste. Antinori still makes seriously good riserva CC. Drink through 2003.–J.S. • $33 • (12/15/1998) • **88**
Chianti Classico Tenute Marchese Antinori Riserva 1994 • $33 • (9/30/1997) • **87**
Chianti Classico Tenute Marchese Antinori Riserva 1993 • $NA • (9/30/1997) • **87**
Chianti Classico Tenute Marchese Antinori Riserva 1991 • $22 • (10/31/1995) • **87**
Chianti Classico Tenute Marchese Antinori Riserva 1990 • $NA • (9/30/1997) • **69**
Chianti Classico Tenute Marchese Antinori Riserva 1989 • $22 • (10/31/1993) • **82**
Chianti Classico Tenute Marchese Antinori Riserva 1988 • $NA • (9/30/1997) • **86**
Chianti Classico Tenute Marchese Antinori Riserva 1987 • $22 • (9/15/1992) • **85**
Chianti Classico Tenute Marchese Antinori Riserva 1985 • $21 • (10/31/1991) • **88**
Chianti Classico Tenute Marchese Antinori Riserva 1983 • $16 • (11/30/1989) • **90**

Key: SS—Spectator Selection. CS—Cellar Selection. HR—Highly Recommended. $NA—Price not available. (BT)—Barrel tasting. Ⓐ—Auction Price.
For a key to the tasters' initials, see "How to Use These Listings."
Dates in parentheses represent the issues in which the ratings were published.

Chianti Classico Tenute Marchese Antinori Riserva 1982 • $16 • (5/31/1989) • **90**
Chianti Classico Tenute Marchese Antinori Riserva 1980 • $16 • (9/15/1987) • **90**
Chianti Classico Villa Antinori Riserva 1996: Disappointing. Extremely light, with tobacco, cedar, berry and cherry character. Light-bodied, with fine tannins and a short finish. Drink now.–J.S. • $18 • (11/30/1999) • **80**
Chianti Classico Villa Antinori Riserva 1995: Plenty of dried cherry and citrus aromas and flavors. Medium-bodied, with light tannins and a fruity, lively finish. A delicious red for current drinking.–J.S. • $17 • (12/15/1998) • **85**
Chianti Classico Villa Antinori Riserva 1994 • $16 • (9/30/1997) • **86**
Chianti Classico Villa Antinori Riserva 1993 • $13 • (10/31/1996) • **80**
Chianti Classico Villa Antinori Riserva 1990 • $12 • (7/31/1995) • **82**
Chianti Classico Villa Antinori Riserva 1989 • $12 • (1/01/1994) • **82**
Chianti Classico Villa Antinori Riserva 1988 • $11 • (10/31/1993) • **84**
Chianti Classico Villa Antinori Riserva 1987 • $11 • (11/30/1991) • **82**
Merlot Toscana Fattoria La Braccesca 1996: Beautiful, refreshing aromas of blackberry and violet, hints of citrus. Full-bodied and powerful, with full, silky tannins and a long finish. Needs time. New from Antinori's estate in Vino Nobile. Best after 2001.–J.S. • $NA • (12/15/1998) • **89**
Orvieto Classico Campogrande 1998: A lively white. Subtle aromas of honeydew melon and minerals. Medium-bodied, with good acidity and a clean, flavorful finish. Drink now.–J.S. • $10 • (2/29/2000) • **84**
Orvieto Classico Campogrande 1996 • $9 • (10/15/1997) • **83**
Pinot Nero Consola 1990 • $NA • (10/31/1993) • **84**
Pinot Noir Umbria Castello della Sala 1994 • $NA • (10/15/1997) • **83**
Rosso di Montepulciano Fattoria La Braccesca 1997: Clever winemaking. Crushed blackberries with wet earth aromas. Medium-bodied, with medium, polished tannins. Drink now.–J.S. • $NA • (12/15/1998) • **86**
Rosso di Montepulciano Fattoria La Braccesca 1996 • $NA • (9/30/1997) • **85**
Rosso di Montepulciano Fattoria La Braccesca 1993 • $11 • (10/31/1995) • **80**
Sangiovese Toscana Santa Cristina 1998: Crisp and fruity, with plenty of dried cherry character throughout. Light- to medium-bodied, with light tannins and a refreshing finish. Delicious. Drink now.–J.S. • $9 • (10/31/1999) • **83**
Sangiovese Toscana Santa Cristina 1997: There are plenty of raspberry aromas and flavors in this medium-bodied Italian red, along with a soft texture and a light, fruity finish. Focused and clean, it gives you the chance to dig into the wonderful quality of the '97 vintage right away, and for an affordable price. Drink now.–J.S. • $9 • (12/15/1998) • **85**
Sangiovese Toscana Santa Cristina 1995 • $8 • (10/31/1996) • **81**
Santa Cristina 1993 • $7 • (2/28/1995) • **84**
Santa Cristina 1992 • $7 • (7/31/1994) • **83**
Santa Cristina 1991 • $7 • (6/30/1993) • **84**
Santa Cristina 1990 • $7 • (12/15/1992) • **79**
Santa Cristina 1989 • $7 • (7/15/1991) • **80**
Santa Cristina 1988 • $7 • (1/31/1991) • **85**
Sauvignon Blanc Umbria Castello della Sala 1998: A thoroughly pleasant white for summer sipping, with good apple and pineapple character. Medium-bodied, with apple, honey and a hint of ripe canteloupe. Fresh finish. Drink now.–J.S. • $12 • (1/01/1999) • **85**
Sauvignon Blanc Umbria Castello della Sala 1996 • $11 • (10/15/1997) • **83**
Toscana Aleatico 1998: A pleasant, sweet red. Lovely aromas of rose petal, plum and watermelon. Medium-bodied and medium sweet, with a very fruity finish. Try with fresh fruit. Not imported into the U.S. Drink now.–J.S. • $NA • (1/01/1999) • **85**
Toscana Galestro 1997: Fresh and simple, with nice lemon-lime character and just the right amount of mineral flavors. Medium-bodied, with fresh acidity and a clean finish. Drink now.–J.S. • $9 • (12/15/1998) • **83**
Toscana Solaia 1997: A solid, muscular red. Greatest Solaia ever made. Dark ruby in color, with extremely ripe raisin and spice aromas. Full-bodied and very chewy, with loads of polished tannins and a long, long finish that's big and fruity. Best after 2004.–J.S. • $90 • (6/15/2000) CS • **98**
Toscana Solaia 1996: This solid Solaia has a good dark ruby color, with berry, tobacco and a hint of mint to its character. It's medium-bodied, boasts a solid core of fruit and polished tannins. Long finish. Needs bottle age. Best after 2000.–J.S. • $90 • (11/30/1999) CS • **90**
Toscana Solaia 1995: Always a voluptuous and rounded red. Gorgeous blackberry, black currant and lead pencil aromas. Full-bodied, with well integrated, soft tannins. Long, fruity aftertaste. Best after 2000.–J.S. • $129 Ⓐ • (12/15/1998) • **90**
Toscana Solaia 1994 • $99 Ⓐ • (9/30/1997) CS • **93**
Toscana Solaia 1993 • $82 Ⓐ • (10/31/1996) • **86**
Toscana Solaia 1991 • $65 • (10/31/1995) CS • **90**
Toscana Solaia 1990 • $202 Ⓐ • (2/28/1995) CS • **97**
Toscana Solaia 1989 • $113 Ⓐ • (11/15/1993) • **88**

Toscana Solaia 1988 • $164 Ⓐ • (11/15/1993) • **97**
Toscana Solaia 1987 • $NA • (11/15/1993) • **88**
Toscana Solaia 1986 • $144 Ⓐ • (11/15/1993) • **90**
Toscana Solaia 1985 • $257 Ⓐ • (11/15/1993) • **94**
Toscana Solaia 1982 • $182 Ⓐ • (11/15/1993) • **91**
Toscana Tignanello 1997: This is a fabulous wine, young and racy. Very dark ruby. Focused aromas of blackberries, wood and very ripe fruit. Full-bodied, with loads of velvety tannins and a long, long finish. Best after 2003.–J.S. • $51 • (6/15/2000) CS • **95**
Toscana Tignanello 1996: Rather light for a Tignanello. Delicate and refined Sangiovese character, with berry, tobacco and cedar. Light- to medium-bodied, with fine tannins and a delicate, fruity finish. Drink now through 2004.–J.S. • $47 Ⓐ • (11/30/1999) • **87**
Toscana Tignanello 1995: Balanced and delicious, with plenty of blackberry and currant aromas and flavors and just a touch of leafiness. Medium-bodied, with soft tannins and a long, fruity aftertaste. Drink now.–J.S. • $79 Ⓐ • (12/15/1998) • **89**
Toscana Tignanello 1994 • $55 • (9/30/1997) • **89**
Toscana Tignanello 1993 • $40 Ⓐ • (10/31/1996) • **86**
Toscana Tignanello 1991 • $38 • (10/31/1995) • **86**
Toscana Tignanello 1990 • $149 Ⓐ • (2/28/1995) CS • **92**
Toscana Tignanello 1989 • $33 • (10/31/1993) • **87**
Toscana Tignanello 1988 • $121 Ⓐ • (11/15/1993) • **95**
Toscana Tignanello 1987 • $NA • (11/15/1993) • **87**
Toscana Tignanello 1986 • $NA • (11/15/1993) • **87**
Toscana Tignanello 1985 • $174 Ⓐ • (11/15/1993) • **88**
Toscana Tignanello 1983 • $61 Ⓐ • (11/15/1993) • **88**
Toscana Tignanello 1982 • $91 Ⓐ • (7/15/1987) CS • **91**
Toscana Villa Antinori 1997: Apple and celery character comes through on the nose and palate. Medium-bodied, with fresh acidity and a minerally aftertaste. A fresh and delicious white, and a very good value. Drink now.–J.S. • $9 • (12/15/1998) • **84**
Toscana White 1996 • $9 • (10/31/1997) • **78**
Umbria Cervaro della Sala 1997: Here's a big and ripe Chardonnay blend from Italy, with mango, pineapple and toasted oak galore. Full-bodied, very creamy in texture, with lots of fruit character and a long tropical fruit aftertaste. An exotic white. Drink now through 2001.–J.S. • $28 • (2/29/2000) SS • **90**
Vermentino Bolgheri Tenuta Belvedere 1996 • $NA • (9/30/1997) • **85**
Vin Santo 1994: Not a very sweet Vin Santo, but a very fruity one with lots of marmalade, orange peel and nutty character. Full-bodied, with light sweetness and a crisp finish. Delicious as an aperitif. Drink now.–J.S. • $29/500 ml. • (12/15/1998) • **86**
Vino Nobile di Montepulciano Fattoria La Braccesca 1995: Powerful, with cedar, berry and earth aromas and flavors. Medium-bodied, with full tannins. Already a bit mature. Drink now.–J.S. • $NA • (12/15/1998) • **84**
Vino Nobile di Montepulciano Fattoria La Braccesca 1994 • $NA • (9/30/1997) • **81**
Vino Nobile di Montepulciano Fattoria La Braccesca 1993 • $NA • (10/31/1996) • **85**
Vino Nobile di Montepulciano Fattoria La Braccesca 1992 • $18 • (10/31/1995) • **86**

ANTONELLI

Montefalco 1996: Decent plum and fruit character, although also weedy. Medium-bodied, with light tannins and a slight bubbly sensation. Not altogether clean.–J.S. • $14 • (2/29/2000) • **77**
Sagrantino di Montefalco 1995: A fascinating red, with wonderful aromas of orange peel, plum and exotic fruit. Medium- to full-bodied, with velvety tannins and a long, spicy finish. Drink now through 2002.–J.S. • $24 • (2/29/2000) • **88**

APOLLONIO

Copertino 1997: From Italy comes this fresh red at a refreshing price, delivering pleasant, silky tannins, plum and cherry flavors and a clean finish. Drink now.–J.S. • $9 • (5/31/2000) • **86**
Copertino Divoto Riserva 1993: Sour and harsh. Like paint thinner. Tasted twice, with consistent notes.–J.S. • $14 • (5/31/2000) • **65**
Primitivo Salento Terragnolo 1997: Big and rustic, with lots of blackberry and wet earth character. Full-bodied and thick, with medium tannins but a rather one-dimensional finish. Drink now.–J.S. • $10 • (5/31/2000) • **86**
Salento Valle Cupa 1997: Clean and silky, with berry, cedar and tobacco character. Medium-bodied, with light tannins and a light, slightly short finish. Drink now.–J.S. • $8 • (5/31/2000) • **81**
Salice Salentino 1997: A bit lean, though it has decent berry, cherry and cedar character. Light-bodied, with a short finish.–J.S. • $8 • (5/31/2000) • **79**
Squinzano 1998: Light and simple, with good berry and citrus character. Clean finish. A pizza cooler. Not imported into the U.S. Drink now.–J.S. • $NA • (1/01/2000) • **80**

ARGIANO

Brunello di Montalcino 1994: Rather subdued aromas of cherries and tanned leather; the palate shows more intense, similar character, with well-integrated tannins. Drink now.–J.S. • $24 • (8/31/1999) • **87**
Brunello di Montalcino 1993: Floral and slightly herbal on the nose, with undertones of bright fruit. Medium-bodied, with medium, chewy tannins and a tobacco aftertaste. Reminds me more of a Cabernet. Best after 2000.–J.S. • $46 Ⓐ • (12/15/1998) • **86**
Brunello di Montalcino 1992 • $35 • (9/30/1997) • **75**
Brunello di Montalcino 1991 • $35 • (11/30/1996) • **87**
Brunello di Montalcino 1990 • $77 Ⓐ • (10/31/1995) • **90**
Brunello di Montalcino 1988 • $29 • (4/30/1994) • **91**
Brunello di Montalcino 1979 • $11 • (9/15/1986) • **77**
Brunello di Montalcino Riserva 1990 • $134 Ⓐ • (11/30/1996) CS • **95**
Brunello di Montalcino Riserva 1988 • $26 • (10/31/1994) • **88**
Brunello di Montalcino Riserva 1985 • $42 • (12/15/1992) • **88**
Rosso di Montalcino 1997: A wine with well-defined berry and cherry character although slightly one-dimensional. Medium-bodied, with firm tannins and a light finish. Drink now.–J.S. • $26 • (9/15/1999) • **85**
Rosso di Montalcino 1996: Pretty dried cherry aromas, with hints of dried herbs. Medium-bodied, with vanilla undertones and a lightly fruity, velvety finish. Drink now.–J.S. • $19 • (12/15/1998) • **85**
Rosso di Montalcino 1995 • $17 • (9/30/1997) • **87**
Rosso di Montalcino 1994 • $17 • (11/30/1996) • **79**
Rosso di Montalcino 1993 • $19 • (10/31/1995) • **85**
Rosso di Montalcino 1992 • $13 • (10/31/1994) • **77**
Rosso di Montalcino 1991 • $18 • (4/30/1994) • **82**
Toscana Solengo 1997: The best Solengo yet. Rich and thick, with wonderfully complex aromas of berry, vanilla, tobacco and flowers, and full in body, with a complement of finely polished yet velvety tannins. The long, concentrated, fruity finish has currant and toasted oak. Best after 2003.–J.S. • $115 Ⓐ • (11/30/1999) HR • **97**
Toscana Solengo 1996: Wild thing. This Italian red is even better than the wonderful debut 95. It offers exotic and complex aromas of blackberry, violet, crushed raspberry, is full-bodied, and though very tannic, the tannins are coated with ripe fruit, and the long and caressing finish delivers even more fruit. A blend of Sangiovese, Cabernet Sauvignon, Merlot and Syrah. Best after 2000.–J.S. • $115 Ⓐ • (12/15/1998) CS • **95**
Toscana Solengo 1995 • $119 Ⓐ • (12/31/1997) HR • **94**

ARGIOLAS

Isola dei Nuraghi Angialis 1995: Thick and rich, but with a slightly burnt character. Packed with apple, almond and orange peel. Impressive. Drink now.–J.S. • $34/500 ml. • (5/31/2000) • **87**
Isola dei Nuraghi Kore 1997: Well crafted, with sophisticated aromas of blackberry, cherry and currant. Full-bodied, with medium tannins, a silky texture and a long finish. Drink through 2004.–J.S. • $34 • (5/31/2000) • **88**
Turriga 1994: Voluptuous. Gorgeous aromas of coconut, chocolate and ripe berry follow through to a full-bodied, soft and velvety palate. Long, flavorful finish. Just slightly too much new wood. Drink now.–J.S. • $40 • (5/31/2000) • **87**
Turriga 1989 • $22 • (5/31/1995) • **89**

ARNALDO CAPRAI

Grechetto dei Colli Martani Grecante 1998: A zingy and fruity white, with good aromas of lemon, melon and flint. Medium-bodied, with light acidity and a lively, ripe fruit aftertaste. Delicious. Drink now.–J.S. • $12 • (2/29/2000) • **87**
Montefalco 1997: Pretty plum and dried herb character. Light- to medium-bodied, with light tannins and a simple, fruity finish. Drink now.–J.S. • $14 • (2/29/2000) • **83**
Montefalco 1991 • $10 • (8/31/1996) • **81**
Montefalco Riserva 1996: A well-crafted red, with good aromas of dark chocolate and raspberry. Medium- to full-bodied, with silky tannins and a long, fresh aftertaste. Drink now.–J.S. • $40 • (2/29/2000) • **86**
Montefalco Sagrantino 1988 • $15 • (8/31/1996) • **84**

ARNALDO CAPRAI

Montefalco White 1998: Plenty of apple, grapefruit and banana aromas. Medium-bodied, with good ripe fruit and medium acidity. Lovely flavors. Drink now.–J.S. • $11 • (2/29/2000) • **85**

Sagrantino di Montefalco 1996: A '96 with bright aromas of raspberry, violet and mandarin orange. Medium-bodied, with silky tannins and a long, fresh aftertaste. Slightly one-dimensional on the palate, but delicious. Drink now.–J.S. • $45 • (2/29/2000) • **87**

Sagrantino di Montefalco 25 Anni 1996: Racy and lovely, with vivid aromas of cherry and plum skin. Medium-bodied, with firm tannins and a lively, fresh finish. Drink now.–J.S. • $95 • (2/29/2000) • **88**

ASCEVI

Chardonnay Collio 1998: A fine, elegant Chardonnay with white pepper, spice and melon aromas and flavors. Medium-bodied, with good acidity and a clean finish. Drink now.–J.S. • $14 • (3/31/2000) • **86**

Pinot Grigio Collio 1998: A very spicy Pinot Gris, with blanched almonds and peaches. Medium-bodied, with a long, dry white pepper aftertaste. Should stand up to many foods. Drink now.–J.S. • $14 • (3/31/2000) • **86**

Venezia Giulia Le Vigne 1996: A wine with fresh berry character, a light body and a fruity finish. Drink now.–J.S. • $NA • (1/01/2000) • **81**

Venezia Giulia Vigna Verdana 1998: A bit simple, with pleasant melon and appleskin character. Medium-bodied, light finish. Drink now.–J.S. • $17 • (4/30/2000) • **83**

ASCHERI, GIACOMO

Barbaresco 1995: Smooth and supple, if not so complex, this is a pleasant, fruit-driven, plummy Barbaresco. Tannins kick in on the finish for a firm backbone, suggesting it will pair nicely with meats. Drink now through 2005.–P.M. • $25 • (10/31/1998) • **83**

Barbaresco 1992 • $20 • (10/31/1995) • **75**

Barbera d'Alba Vigna Fontanelle 1998: Elegant and firm. Medium-bodied, with a mineral, wet earth, chalk and wild berry character, it's rather lean, but in a balanced way. Try with grilled meat. Drink through 2003.–P.M. • $16 • (11/15/1999) • **85**

Barbera d'Alba Vigna Fontanelle 1997: Supersupple, opulent, with an earthy, cassis, chocolate character. Ripe and full-bodied, it's just delicious as long as you don't mind a touch of barnyard aroma. Balanced. Tannins are velvety. Drink now through 2002.–P.M. • $12 • (10/31/1998) • **92**

Barbera d'Alba Vigna Fontanelle 1995 • $12 • (10/31/1997) • **85**

Barolo 1994: Big, burly, thick and without much elegance. Firm and slightly linear, with plum, mineral, red berry and blackberry flavors. Cellar a bit. Best after 2002.–P.M. • $25 • (10/31/1998) • **81**

Barolo 1993 • $25 • (10/31/1997) • **87**

Barolo Sorano 1995: Rich and full-bodied, with plum, leather, smoke and black cherry flavors. Ripe tannins and moderate acidity make you want to drink up. Drink now through 2005.–P.M. • $40 • (11/15/1999) • **88**

Barolo Vigna dei Pola 1995: Red fruit but a bit herbal in aroma, with mocha, chocolate and spice on the palate. Medium-bodied, with a slightly dry finish.–P.M. • $35 • (11/15/1999) • **78**

Barolo Vigna Farina 1994: A fresh and clean Barolo, with a crisp texture, delivering plum, black cherry, citrus and raspberry character in a fairly lean package. Succulent finish. Drink now through 2003.–P.M. • $40 • (10/31/1998) • **83**

Barolo Vigna Farina 1993 • $35 • (10/31/1997) • **88**

Barolo Vigna Farina 1992 • $NA • (10/31/1996) • **81**

Barolo Vigna Farina 1991 • $30 • (10/31/1995) • **79**

Dolcetto d'Alba Vigna Nirane 1998: A firm, medium-bodied Dolcetto, with lovely currant aromas and spice, game and cassis bush notes. Good, clean acidity makes it a fine match with food. Drink now through 2001.–P.M. • $13 • (7/31/1999) • **85**

Dolcetto d'Alba Vigna Nirane 1997: Smooth and fairly light, this delicate Dolcetto has ripe, sweet-tasting fruit and wet earth complexity. Silky in the midpalate, it turns chewy on the tannic, long finish. A well-made wine that's not overly extracted. Drink now.–P.M. • $14 • (10/31/1998) • **83**

Dolcetto d'Alba Vigna Nirane 1996 • $14 • (10/31/1997) • **84**

Dolcetto d'Alba Vigna S. Anna 1997: Firm but focused, with a tough midpalate but also some nice fruit. Of medium body, it clamps down on the finish. Drink through 2000.–P.M. • $12 • (10/31/1998) • **80**

Key: SS—Spectator Selection. CS—Cellar Selection. HR—Highly Recommended. $NA—Price not available. (BT)—Barrel tasting. (A)—Auction Price.
For a key to the tasters' initials, see "How to Use These Listings."
Dates in parentheses represent the issues in which the ratings were published.

Dolcetto d'Alba Vigna S. Rocco 1998: A "reduced" (gamy) Dolcetto, but also full of nice fruit, with layers that make it very intriguing to drink, as the ripe character folds into the sweet tannins on the balanced finish. Drink now.–P.M. • $15 • (11/15/1999) • **84**

Nebbiolo d'Alba Bricco S. Giacomo 1996: Earthy and tart, this is a tough, light-colored and herbal wine.–P.M. • $16 • (11/15/1999) • **72**

Podere di Montalupa di Bra Red 1996: Oaky, with decent fruit, smelling and tasting of cassis and black cherry. Medium-bodied and a bit dry. Hopefully short-term cellaring will help. Made from Syrah. Best after 2002.–P.M. • $40 • (10/31/1998) • **79**

Podere di Montalupa di Bra White 1997: Distinctive for its peanut butter, chocolate and honey mixture. Medium-bodied and quite soft, it turns a bit flabby and hot on the finish. Made from Viognier.–P.M. • $40 • (10/31/1998) • **76**

AVIGNONESI

Aleatico 1990 • $28 • (2/28/1995) • **86**

Chardonnay Toscana Il Marzocco 1997: This white is slightly dull from the excess of new wood used. Full-bodied, with vanilla and burnt coconut flavors. Medium finish. Drink now.–J.S. • $23 • (11/30/1999) • **80**

Merlot Tuscany 1994 • $62 • (9/30/1997) • **87**

Merlot Tuscany 1993 • $32 • (10/31/1996) HR • **90**

Merlot Tuscany 1992 • $37 • (10/31/1996) • **89**

Merlot Tuscany 1991 • $36 • (10/31/1995) • **88**

Merlot Tuscany 1990 • $55 • (2/28/1995) • **86**

Merlot Tuscany 1989 • $36 • (10/31/1993) • **82**

Merlot Tuscany 1988 • $45 • (9/15/1991) • **93**

Pinot Nero di Valdicapraia 1994 • $37 • (9/30/1997) • **83**

Pinot Nero di Valdicapraia 1993 • $28 • (10/31/1996) • **85**

Pinot Nero di Valdicapraia 1990 • $NA • (10/31/1995) • **86**

Pinot Nero Toscana di Valdicapraia 1997: This ripe, spicy and gamy red is more like a serious Syrah than Pinot Noir. Full-bodied, with velvety tannins and a long, decadent finish. Slightly austere and overdone, but good. Best after 2000.–J.S. • $53 • (11/30/1999) • **86**

Pinot Nero Toscana di Valdicapraia 1996: Good, no-nonsense Pinot Nero. Fresh and simple, with cherry, strawberry and tea aromas and flavors. Medium-bodied, with light tannins and a fresh aftertaste. Drink now.–J.S. • $55 • (12/15/1998) • **85**

Rosso di Montepulciano 1993 • $NA • (10/31/1995) • **74**

Rosso di Montepulciano 1991 • $12 • (11/15/1993) • **80**

Rosso di Montepulciano 1990 • $12 • (12/15/1992) • **84**

Rosso di Montepulciano 1989 • $12 • (4/30/1991) • **83**

Sangiovese Toscana 1996: A fresh and fruity red, with refreshing acidity and lively character. Medium-bodied, delicate on the finish. Drink now.–J.S. • $17 • (12/15/1998) • **83**

Sangiovese Tuscany 1994 • $13 • (10/31/1996) • **78**

Toscana Bianco 1998: Medium-bodied, with fresh acidity and subtle sliced grapefruit character. Clean, fruity aftertaste. Sauvignon Blanc and Chardonnay. Drink now.–J.S. • $14 • (11/30/1999) • **86**

Toscana Bianco 1997: Crisp and lively. Straw and pear on the nose, with hints of celery. Medium-bodied, with fine acidity and a light, refreshing aftertaste. A blend of Sauvignon and Chardonnay. Drink now.–J.S. • $12 • (12/15/1998) • **86**

Toscana Grifi 1996: A serious red with lots of cherry, olive and tobacco character and hints of wood. Medium- to full-bodied, with polished tannins and a long, chewy finish. Best after 2000.–J.S. • $45 • (11/30/1999) • **90**

Toscana Grifi 1995: Solid, well-structured super Tuscan, with plummy, earthy aromas that follow through on the palate. Medium- to full-bodied, with chewy, slightly tough tannins and a mouthpuckering finish. Made from Cabernet Sauvignon. Best after 2000.–J.S. • $45 • (12/15/1998) • **90**

Toscana Grifi 1994 • $43 • (9/30/1997) • **88**

Toscana Grifi 1993 • $45 • (10/31/1996) • **87**

Toscana Grifi 1992 • $37 • (10/31/1996) • **86**

Toscana Grifi 1990 • $36 • (2/28/1995) CS • **91**

Toscana Grifi 1988 • $28 • (11/15/1993) • **93**

Toscana Grifi 1987 • $NA • (11/15/1993) • **87**

Toscana Grifi 1986 • $NA • (11/15/1993) • **88**

Toscana Grifi 1985 • $NA • (11/15/1993) • **90**

Toscana Grifi 1983 • $NA • (11/15/1993) • **90**

Toscana Grifi 1982 • $10 • (6/16/1985) • **87**

Toscana Il Vignola 1996: Interesting very dried fruit flavors, but rather tired and oxidized at this point.–J.S. • $23 • (11/30/1999) • **78**

Toscana Rosso 1997: This delicious red has berry, tobacco and chocolate aromas and flavors. Medium-bodied, with delicate tannins and a fruity vanilla finish. Drink now.–J.S. • $14 • (11/30/1999) • **85**

Toscana Rosso 1996: A straightforward, fresh red, with dried cherry and rose. Medium-bodied, with silky tannins and a crisp, fruity finish. Drink now.–J.S. • $12 • (12/15/1998) • **85**

Tuscana Rosso 1994 • $NA • (10/31/1996) • **80**

Tuscana Rosso 1993 • $13 • (10/31/1995) • **78**

Toscana Toro Desiderio 1996: A big, juicy wine, with intense cherry, meat and tobacco character. Full-bodied and chewy, with a long, caressing finish. Best Toro Desiderio in years. Made from Merlot. Best after 2000.–J.S. • $63 • (11/30/1999) • **90**

Toscana Toro Desiderio 1995: Rich and velvety, with green olive and berry character. Medium- to full-bodied, with full tannins and a fruity, slightly green pepperish aftertaste. Made from Merlot. Drink now.–J.S. • $62 • (12/15/1998) • **87**

Toscana Toro Desiderio 1988 • $39 • (12/15/1992) • **85**

Vino Nobile di Montepulciano 1997: A pretty VN with plum, earth and coffee aromas and flavors. Medium-bodied, with fine tannins and a fresh finish. Drink now.–J.S. • $24 • (6/15/2000) • **86**

Vino Nobile di Montepulciano 1996: Lovely, with subtle tobacco, plum and berry character, light to medium body and silky tannins. Drink now.–J.S. • $27 • (11/30/1999) • **85**

Vino Nobile di Montepulciano 1995: Medium-bodied, with fresh, fruity character, but the crisp acidity makes it a little one-dimensional. Needs food. Drink now.–J.S. • $27 • (12/15/1998) • **83**

Vino Nobile di Montepulciano 1994 • $30 • (9/30/1997) • **84**

Vino Nobile di Montepulciano 1993 • $25 • (10/31/1996) • **80**

Vino Nobile di Montepulciano 1992 • $20 • (10/31/1995) • **76**

Vino Nobile di Montepulciano 1990 • $22 • (2/29/1996) • **85**

Vino Nobile di Montepulciano 1988 • $22 • (12/15/1992) • **86**

Vino Nobile di Montepulciano 1985 • $12 • (2/15/1988) • **86**

Vino Nobile di Montepulciano Riserva 1994: Slightly forward and mature, with tobacco and cedar aromas and flavors. Medium-bodied, with fine tannins and vanilla, cedar and berry on the aftertaste. Drink now.–J.S. • $36 • (12/15/1998) • **83**

Vino Nobile di Montepulciano Riserva 1993 • $36 • (9/30/1997) • **85**

Vino Nobile di Montepulciano Riserva 1988 • $24 • (11/15/1993) • **87**

Vino Nobile di Montepulciano Riserva Grandi Annate 1990 • $36 • (10/31/1995) • **89**

AVIGNONESI-CAPANNELLE

Toscana 50 & 50 1995: Modern, big and well-crafted red. Plenty of sweet berry, plum and cherry aromas. Full-bodied, with lovely silky tannins and a fruity, vanilla aftertaste. Fruit and new toasted oak galore. A joint effort from these two wineries. Drink through 2004.–J.S. • $99 • (11/30/1999) • **90**

AZELIA

Barbera d'Alba Vigneto Punta 1996: Pure, rich and focused, this dark-colored, balanced and supple Barbera screams with life and grapey, slightly herbal aromas, but delivers round tannins, a sweet-tasting finish and plenty of blackberry character dosed cleverly with oak and acidity. Drink now.–P.M. • $28 • (9/15/1999) • **89**

Barolo 1992 • $30 • (10/31/1996) • **85**

Barolo 1991 • $NA • (10/31/1996) • **85**

Barolo Bricco Fiasco 1995: All seduction. Gorgeous balance in this silky, full-bodied, sweet-tasting, modern-style Barolo. Complex mocha, vanilla, floral, blackberry and smoke notes bundle up in a neat, smooth package. Kicks in with a burning intensity on the finish. Drink now through 2003.–P.M. • $58 • (11/15/1999) • **94**

Barolo Bricco Fiasco 1994: Shows ripe fruit character and soft tannins. Medium-bodied, with charming plum, currant and spice character that follows through on the supple but lingering finish. Drink now through 2003.–P.M. • $40 • (10/31/1998) • **84**

Barolo Bricco Fiasco 1993 • $41 • (10/31/1997) • **93**

Barolo Bricco Fiasco 1989 • $24 • (10/31/1994) • **85**

Barolo Bricco Fiasco 1985 • $30 • (7/15/1991) • **81**

Barolo Bricco Punta 1982 • $23 • (11/15/1988) • **92**

Barolo San Rocco 1995: Has a slight unbecoming herbal, olivelike aroma, but it's tender, thick and ripe, offering spice, tar and black fruit character in an impressively intense package. Very lovely, silky roundness on the palate, with chewy tannins on the finish. Drink now through 2005.–P.M. • $58 • (11/15/1999) • **87**

Dolcetto d'Alba Bricco dell'Oriolo 1989 • $9 • (7/15/1991) • **79**

BADIA A COLTIBUONO

Cancelli 1993 • $9 • (12/31/1995) • **85**

Cancelli 1990 • $7 • (10/31/1993) • **78**

Chardonnay Toscana Sella del Boscone 1996: Subtle and Burgundian in style. Pretty apple, earth and oak character in this Chardonnay. Medium-bodied, with fresh acidity and a creamy, appley aftertaste with a hint of straw. An outstanding new wine from Badia a Coltibuono. Drink now.–J.S. • $18 • (12/15/1998) • **90**

Chianti Cetamura 1990 • $8 • (10/31/1993) • **78**

Chianti Cetamura 1988 • $7 • (12/15/1990) • **82**

Chianti Classico 1997: A bright and fruity '97 Chianti Classico, with dried cherry and violet character. Light- to medium-bodied, with light tannins and a fresh finish. Drink now.–J.S. • $21 • (11/30/1999) • **85**

Chianti Classico 1996: Very plummy, with hints of earth and mushroom. Medium-bodied, with crisp acidity and silky texture. Delicious. Drink now.–J.S. • $18 • (12/15/1998) • **86**

Chianti Classico 1995 • $18 • (9/30/1997) • **79**

Chianti Classico 1994 • $15 • (10/31/1996) • **83**

Chianti Classico Riserva 1996: Very delicate and clean, with cherry and berry character and hints of fresh mushroom. Light- to medium-bodied, with silky tannins. Drink now.–J.S. • $35 • (11/30/1999) • **84**

Chianti Classico Riserva 1995: True-blue premium Chianti with plenty of dried cherry and earthy character. Medium-bodied, with good polish to the tannins and a lively, fruity aftertaste. The texture of a very good Burgundy. Drink now through 2003.–J.S. • $28 • (12/15/1998) • **87**

Chianti Classico Riserva 1994 • $20 • (9/30/1997) • **85**

Chianti Classico Riserva 1993 • $28 • (10/31/1996) • **86**

Chianti Classico Riserva 1990 • $25 • (2/28/1995) • **85**

Chianti Classico Riserva 1988 • $20 • (7/31/1995) • **84**

Chianti Classico Riserva 1987 • $15 • (9/15/1992) • **84**

Chianti Classico Riserva 1985 • $16 • (9/15/1991) • **90**

Chianti Classico Riserva 1983 • $15 • (11/30/1989) • **78**

Chianti Classico Riserva 1982 • $13 • (7/31/1988) • **88**

Chianti Classico Roberto Stucchi 1997: A pretty Chianti Classico, with berry, tobacco and fresh mushroom character. Light- to medium-bodied, with light tannins and a fresh finish. Drink now.–J.S. • $22 • (11/30/1999) • **84**

Chianti Classico Roberto Stucchi 1996: Delicate and delicious. Plum, cedar and mushroom on the nose. Medium-bodied, with light tannins and a smooth aftertaste of fresh fruit. Drink now.–J.S. • $18 • (12/15/1998) • **83**

Toscana Le Trappoline 1996: There's ripe fruit in this white, with hints of oak, but some candied character detracts. Medium-bodied, with a creamy texture, a slightly dull finish. Drink now.–J.S. • $10 • (12/15/1998) • **80**

Toscana Sangioveto 1995: Very bright raspberry aromas. Medium-bodied, with medium tannins and a slightly short finish. Needs but a bit more fruit concentration on the center palate to score outstanding. Drink now through 2003.–J.S. • $55 • (12/15/1998) • **88**

Toscana Sangioveto 1994 • $35 • (9/30/1997) • **88**

Toscana Sangioveto 1988 • $40 • (10/31/1993) HR • **94**

Toscana Sangioveto 1985 • $NA • (11/30/1989) • **85**

Toscana Sangioveto 1983 • $20 • (11/30/1989) • **84**

Toscana Sangioveto 1982 • $21 • (9/15/1988) • **83**

Toscana Sangioveto 1981 • $21 • (9/15/1987) • **87**

BADIA DI MORRONA

Chianti I Sodi del Paretaio 1997: A delicious '97 Chianti, with plenty of berry and cherry character. Medium-bodied, with soft tannins and a fresh, fruity aftertaste. Drink now.–J.S. • $NA • (1/01/1999) • **85**

Colli dell'Etruria Centrale VignAalta 1996: A fruity, clean CC, with bright cherry and berry character. Medium-bodied, with fine tannins and a medium finish. Drink now.–J.S. • $NA • (1/01/1999) • **86**

Toscana N'Antia 1996: Rather worrying, with lovely pungent aromas of berry, earth and meat, but it's slightly prickly or bubbly on the palate. Something strange here. Tasted twice, with consistent notes.–J.S. • $NA • (1/01/1999) • **75**

BAGGIOLINO, FATTORIA

Chianti Colli Fiorentini 1996: Light and plummy Sangiovese, with slightly raised acidity and a watery finish. Not much to it.–J.S. • $12 • (12/15/1998) • **78**

Chianti Colli Fiorentini 1994 • $NA • (10/31/1996) • **74**

Chianti Colli Fiorentini 1993 • $NA • (2/28/1995) • **72**

Chianti Colli Fiorentini 1992 • $NA • (2/28/1995) • **83**

Chianti Colli Fiorentini 1990 • $NA • (10/31/1993) • **86**

ITALY

BAGGIOLINO, FATTORIA

Chianti Colli Fiorentini Riserva 1995: Beautiful aromas of dried cherry with hints of citrus and crushed berry. Medium-bodied, with fine tannins and good fruit, but a slightly austere, dry finish. Drink now through 2003.–J.S. • $18 • (12/15/1998) • **84**
Chianti Colli Fiorentini Riserva 1993 • $NA • (10/31/1996) • **78**
Chianti Colli Fiorentini Riserva 1991 • $NA • (10/31/1993) • **85**
Chianti Colli Fiorentini Riserva 1990 • $NA • (2/28/1995) • **87**
Toscana Poggio Brandi 1995: Bubbling over with blackberry and fresh porcini aromas. Medium-bodied, with well-integrated tannins and a polished texture from just the right amount of new oak maturation. Clever winemaking here. Drink now.–J.S. • $24 • (12/15/1998) • **88**
Toscana Poggio Brandi 1993 • $NA • (10/31/1995) • **85**
Toscana Poggio Brandi 1990 • $26 • (2/28/1995) • **86**
Toscana Poggio Brandi 1986 • $19 • (8/31/1991) • **86**
Toscana Poggio Brandi 1985 • $19 • (9/15/1989) • **84**

BAGNOLI

Merlot Grave del Friuli 1996 • $11 • (5/31/1998) • **84**
Merlot Grave del Friuli 1995 • $11 • (12/15/1997) • **84**
Pinot Grigio Grave del Friuli 1996 • $13 • (5/31/1998) • **85**

BANEAR

Cabernet Sauvignon Grave del Friuli 1995 • $12 • (4/30/1998) • **81**
Merlot Grave del Friuli 1995 • $12 • (12/15/1997) • **82**
Pinot Grigio Grave del Friuli 1996 • $12 • (11/15/1997) • **75**

BANFI, CASTELLO

Brunello di Montalcino 1994: A very energetic '94 Brunello, this mouthfilling Italian red is medium- to full-bodied, with full, velvety tannins and a subtle character of spices, ripe fruits and earth that lingers for a long finish. Drink through 2005.–J.S. • $40 • (8/31/1999) SS • **90**
Brunello di Montalcino 1993: Extremely aromatic and pretty, medium-bodied, it's a joy now to drink now but will improve with age. Dark-colored, with a penetrating aroma of blackberries, freshly picked mushrooms and a hint of chocolate. Fine tannins and a long, flavorful aftertaste. Best after 2000.–J.S. • $40 • (12/15/1998) • **90**
Brunello di Montalcino 1992 • $38 • (9/30/1997) • **86**
Brunello di Montalcino 1991 • $NA • (11/30/1996) • **84**
Brunello di Montalcino 1990 • $80 Ⓐ • (10/31/1995) • **93**
Brunello di Montalcino 1986 • $32 • (12/31/1992) CS • **91**
Brunello di Montalcino 1985 • $30 • (10/15/1990) HR • **92**
Brunello di Montalcino 1982 • $28 • (12/15/1987) • **89**
Brunello di Montalcino 1981 • $23 • (3/31/1987) CS • **92**
Brunello di Montalcino 1980 • $20 • (9/15/1986) • **90**
Brunello di Montalcino 1979 • $18 • (4/16/1985) SS • **90**
Brunello di Montalcino Poggio all'Oro Riserva 1993: This red from Italy is big, chewy and delicious. Opens with beautiful, multidimensional aromas of ripe berries, mushrooms and chestnuts, while on the palate, it's full-bodied and very velvety, with a long, long, fruity finish. Needs a little time; best after 2002.–J.S. • $125 • (8/31/1999) CS • **93**
Brunello di Montalcino Poggio all'Oro Riserva 1990 • $123 Ⓐ • (11/30/1996) • **95**
Brunello di Montalcino Poggio all'Oro Riserva 1988 • $32 • (10/31/1994) • **90**
Brunello di Montalcino Poggio all'Oro Riserva 1985 • $37 • (12/15/1991) CS • **92**
Cabernet Sauvignon Sant'Antimo 1996: Slightly rustic, but you have to dig it. Really interesting aromas of black cherry, black licorice and flowers. Full-bodied, with full, chewy tannins and a long tobacco and cherry aftertaste. Best after 2001.–J.S. • $33 • (11/30/1999) • **90**
Cabernet Sauvignon Toscana Tavernelle 1995: A subtle yet rich red, with a racy backbone of acidity. Wonderfully fruity, with plums and crushed berry through and through. Full-bodied, with lovely, well-integrated tannins and a long, silky finish. Cabernet lovers, dig in.–J.S. • $32 • (12/15/1998) • **91**
Cabernet Sauvignon Tuscany Tavernelle 1994 • $27 • (5/31/1997) • **90**
Cabernet Sauvignon Tuscany Tavernelle 1993 • $25 • (10/31/1996) • **89**
Cabernet Sauvignon Tuscany Tavernelle 1992 • $20 • (10/31/1995) • **88**
Cabernet Sauvignon Tuscany Tavernelle 1991 • $22 • (2/28/1995) • **86**

Key: SS—Spectator Selection. CS—Cellar Selection. HR—Highly Recommended. $NA—Price not available. (BT)—Barrel tasting. Ⓐ—Auction Price.
For a key to the tasters' initials, see "How to Use These Listings."
Dates in parentheses represent the issues in which the ratings were published.

Cabernet Sauvignon Tuscany Tavernelle 1990 • $23 • (10/31/1993) • **85**
Cabernet Sauvignon Tuscany Tavernelle 1989 • $23 • (10/31/1993) • **84**
Cabernet Sauvignon Tuscany Tavernelle 1988 • $23 • (9/15/1991) • **87**
Cabernet Sauvignon Tuscany Tavernelle 1985 • $23 • (3/31/1993) • **83**
Cabernet Sauvignon Tuscany Tavernelle 1984 • $18 • (1/31/1988) • **89**
Cabernet Sauvignon Tuscany Tavernelle 1982 • $15 • (8/01/1985) • **88**
Chardonnay Sant'Antimo Fontanelle 1997: Has good ripe fruit but lacks a bit of freshness, with intense aromas of canned pears and honey. Medium-bodied, with light acidity and a round, fruity aftertaste. Slightly candied and milky on the finish. Somewhat disappointing for this producer. Tasted twice, with consistent notes. Drink now.–J.S. • $18 • (11/30/1999) • **84**
Chardonnay Toscana Fontanelle 1996: A well-crafted Chardonnay, with apple, pear and vanilla aromas and flavors which develop a smoky, coconut character. Of medium body, with crisp acidity and a flavorful finish. Delicious. Drink now.–J.S. • $18 • (12/15/1998) • **89**
Chianti Classico Riserva 1989 • $10 • (5/15/1994) • **79**
Chianti Classico Riserva 1988 • $10 • (5/15/1993) • **80**
Col di Sasso 1995 • $7 • (10/31/1996) • **83**
Col di Sasso 1994 • $9 • (11/15/1996) • **81**
Merlot Sant'Antimo Mandrielle 1996: Despite the vegetal nose, it shows good fruit, with lots of plum and dried herb verging on bell pepper aromas. Medium-bodied, with silky tannins and a fruity finish. Drink now.–J.S. • $33 • (11/30/1999) • **84**
Merlot Toscana Mandrielle 1995: Shows good structure for aging. Complex aromas of spices, mint and fruit. Full-bodied and very fruity, with a sleek tannic backbone and a lingering aftertaste. A beautiful Merlot from Tuscany. Best after 2000.–J.S. • $32 • (12/15/1998) • **91**
Merlot Tuscany Mandrielle 1994 • $29 • (5/31/1997) • **89**
Merlot Tuscany Mandrielle 1993 • $29 • (10/31/1996) • **85**
Merlot Tuscany Mandrielle 1992 • $25 • (2/28/1995) • **89**
Merlot Tuscany Mandrielle 1990 • $25 • (2/28/1995) • **87**
Moscadello di Montalcino Vendemmia Tardiva 1996: An extremely pretty, sweet wine, with honey, lemon and apricot character throughout. Medium-bodied and very sweet, with a long finish. Well done. Drink now.–J.S. • $15 • (11/30/1999) • **87**
Pinot Grigio Toscana San Angelo 1998: Strange aromas of aniseed and pear. Medium-bodied, with light fruit and a simple finish. Drink now.–J.S. • $13 • (11/30/1999) • **80**
Pinot Grigio Toscana San Angelo 1997: A subtle and interesting white with blanched almond, mineral and ash aromas and flavors. Medium-bodied, with fresh acidity and a fruity finish. Drink now.–J.S. • $13 • (12/15/1998) • **86**
Pinot Grigio Tuscany San Angelo 1996 • $13 • (9/30/1997) • **86**
Pinot Grigio-Chardonnay Toscana Le Rime 1997: Light and bright, fresh in fruit flavor, perfect for quaffing with any number of foods. Don't wait, drink now. • $9 • (7/31/1998) • **84**
Pinot Nero Sant'Antimo Belnero 1996: A good, simple Pinot Noir. Attractive aromas of berry and strawberry, with a hint of oak. Medium-bodied, with fine, silky tannins and a fruity, caressing finish. Drink now.–J.S. • $33 • (11/30/1999) • **85**
Pinot Nero Toscana Belnero 1995: A very good red, just not so Pinot Nero-like. Lovely cherry and strawberry character. Medium-bodied, with soft tannins and a fresh, fruity finish. Drink now.–J.S. • $32 • (12/15/1998) • **85**
Pinot Nero Tuscany Belnero 1992 • $28 • (10/31/1995) • **85**
Pinot Nero Tuscany Belnero 1990 • $30 • (7/31/1994) • **83**
Pinot Nero Tuscany Belnero 1988 • $NA • (9/15/1991) • **86**
Rosso di Montalcino 1997: Slinky and enticing red. Good level of berry and fresh mushroom character, medium-bodied, with firm yet silky tannins and a long, flavorful finish. Drink now.–J.S. • $21 • (9/15/1999) • **87**
Rosso di Montalcino 1996: Lots of ripe fruit character, with dried berry, cherry and earth aromas. Medium-bodied, with velvety tannins and a long, fruity aftertaste. Juicy Rosso; Banfi's best in years. Drink now.–J.S. • $21 • (12/15/1998) • **87**
Rosso di Montalcino 1995 • $21 • (9/30/1997) • **85**
Rosso di Montalcino 1992 • $9 • (10/31/1994) • **80**
Rosso di Montalcino Centine 1994 • $NA • (11/30/1996) • **83**
Rosso di Montalcino Centine 1993 • $8 • (10/31/1995) • **83**
Rosso di Montalcino Centine 1992 • $10 • (4/30/1994) • **73**
Rosso di Montalcino Centine 1991 • $10 • (4/30/1994) • **77**
Rosso di Montalcino Centine 1990 • $8 • (3/31/1993) • **82**
Rosso di Montalcino Centine 1989 • $8 • (12/15/1992) • **81**
Rosso di Montalcino Centine 1988 • $8 • (12/15/1991) • **81**
Sant'Antimo Centine 1996 • $9 • (9/30/1997) • **82**
Sauvignon Blanc Sant'Antimo Serena 1997: Clean but a little dull for a Sauvignon. Aromas of apple skin, vanilla and honey, with a hint of white pepper. Medium-bodied, with a soft, round texture and a fruity finish. Drink now.–J.S. • $18 • (11/30/1999) • **84**

Sauvignon Blanc Toscana Serena 1996: Intense character of canned asparagus and celery, with wax notes. Full-bodied, rather heavy-handed.–J.S. • $18 • (12/15/1998) • **78**
Syrah Sant'Antimo Colvecchio 1996: A delicious and seriously good Syrah. Aromas of grilled meat, berry and earth follow through to a full-bodied palate, with medium tannins and a plummy, ripe fruit finish. Lovely and succulent. Drink now through 2002.–J.S. • $33 • (11/30/1999) • **89**
Syrah Toscana Colvecchio 1995: Not much Syrah character, but a good red nonetheless. Very ripe strawberry aromas follow through on the palate. Medium-bodied, with good fruit, but not much on the finish. Drink now through 2003.–J.S. • $32 • (12/15/1998) • **84**
Syrah Tuscany Colvecchio 1993 • $29 • (10/31/1996) • **88**
Syrah Tuscany Colvecchio 1992 • $25 • (2/28/1995) • **78**
Syrah Tuscany Colvecchio 1991 • $25 • (2/28/1995) • **87**
Syrah Tuscany Colvecchio 1990 • $30 • (10/31/1993) • **85**
Toscana Centine 1997: This Italian red is not only ready for drinking, it won't strain the budget. It's very ripe style, a bit rustic, with raisin and spice character, medium body, soft tannins and a fresh finish. Go for it. Drink now.–J.S. • $11 • (11/30/1999) • **86**
Toscana Excelsus 1995: Absolutely gorgeous aromas of currant, berry and hints of mints that lighten in intensity on the palate. Medium-bodied, with medium tannins and a fruity finish. Drink now.–J.S. • $50 • (12/15/1998) • **87**
Toscana Excelsus 1993 • $45 • (9/30/1997) • **90**
Toscana Le Rime 1998: Extremely perfumed, with flowers and passion fruit galore. Medium-bodied, with almond and peach pit flavor. Light and fruity finish. Pinot Grigio and Chardonnay. Drink now.–J.S. • $9 • (11/30/1999) • **85**
Toscana Sant'Antimo Summus 1996: Slightly one-dimensional, but I like the fruit. Intense aromas of berry, mint, dried herb and currant. Full-bodied, with velvety tannins and a lovely vanilla, berry and cherry aftertaste. Sangiovese, Cabernet Sauvignon and Syrah. Best after 2001.–J.S. • $47 • (11/30/1999) • **88**
Toscana Summus 1995: A blockbuster red wine from Italy—the best Summus I've ever tasted. Shows an intense blackberry character offset by hints of wet earth. It's full in body, with full, mouthpuckering tannins yet a sweet and fruity aftertaste. Needs some age to come together. Best after 2001.–J.S. • $45 • (12/15/1998) CS • **93**
Toscana Summus 1994 • $40 • (9/30/1997) • **90**
Toscana Summus 1993 • $38 • (10/31/1996) • **90**
Toscana Summus 1990 • $40 • (10/31/1993) • **92**
Toscana Summus 1988 • $NA • (9/15/1991) • **87**

BANFI, VINI

Brachetto d'Acqui Vigneto La Rosa 1998: Lightly sweet, offering candied cherry and strawberry flavors and a hint of dough in a soft, easy-drinking style. Drink now.–B.S. • $15 • (10/15/1999) • **84**
Brut Metodo Tradizionale Classico NV: A straightforward sparkler, round and medium-bodied, a bit one-dimensional in its brioche flavor yet ends cleanly. Drink now.–B.S. • $20 • (10/15/1999) • **84**
Dolcetto d'Acqui Argusto 1995 • $13 • (1/31/1998) • **79**
Gavi Principessa 1996 • $13 • (8/31/1997) • **85**

BANTI, ERIK

Morellino di Scansano Ciabatta 1996: Very pretty aromas of dried cherry and berry. Medium-bodied, with silky tannins and a pepper and berry aftertaste. Drink now.–J.S. • $23 • (11/30/1999) • **86**
Toscana Annoprimo 1997: Lovely intensity of plum and berry aromas and flavors, with a hint of new oak. Medium-bodied, with silky tannins and a ripe fruit finish. A beauty. Made with Sangiovese and a touch of Merlot. Drink now through 2004.–J.S. • $25 • (11/30/1999) • **90**
Toscana Aquilaia 1997: A traditional yet friendly wine. Soft and silky, with pretty berry, tobacco and cedar character and a hint of parmigiana. Medium-bodied, with a caressing texture and a light, fruity finish. Drink now.–J.S. • $18 • (11/30/1999) • **85**
Toscana Carato 1997: A fresh and easy red, with plum and berry aromas and flavors. Medium-bodied, with soft tannins and a fruity finish. Drink now.–J.S. • $12 • (11/30/1999) • **83**

BARACCO DE BARACHO

Barolo 1988 • $26 • (6/30/1993) • **77**

BARALE, FRATELLI

Barolo Castellero 1993 • $NA • (10/31/1997) • **87**

BARBARESCO, PRODUTTORI DEL

Barbaresco 1995: A bitter wine, sour and odd. Not recommended. Tasted twice, with consistent notes.–P.M. • $32 • (10/31/1998) • **65**
Barbaresco 1993 • $27 • (1/31/1998) • **73**
Barbaresco 1991 • $21 • (10/31/1995) • **79**
Barbaresco 1989 • $24 • (10/31/1993) • **76**
Barbaresco 1988 • $24 • (10/31/1993) • **84**
Barbaresco 1986 • $12 • (10/31/1990) HR • **90**
Barbaresco 1984 • $12 • (9/15/1988) • **80**
Barbaresco 1983 • $NA • (9/15/1988) • **85**
Barbaresco 1982 • $NA • (9/15/1988) • **87**
Barbaresco 1979 • $NA • (9/15/1988) • **90**
Barbaresco Asili 1990 • $35 • (10/31/1995) • **81**
Barbaresco Asili 1989 • $32 • (10/31/1993) • **85**
Barbaresco Asili 1988 • $32 • (10/31/1993) • **88**
Barbaresco Asili Riserva 1985 • $27 • (10/31/1990) • **92**
Barbaresco Asili Riserva 1982 • $22 • (9/15/1988) • **89**
Barbaresco Moccagatta 1989 • $29 • (10/31/1994) • **87**
Barbaresco Moccagatta Riserva 1982 • $22 • (9/15/1988) • **89**
Barbaresco Montefico Riserva 1982 • $22 • (9/15/1988) • **85**
Barbaresco Montefico Riserva 1978 • $22 • (9/15/1988) • **92**
Barbaresco Montestefano 1990 • $32 • (10/31/1993) • **78**
Barbaresco Montestefano 1989 • $32 • (10/31/1993) • **87**
Barbaresco Montestefano 1988 • $32 • (10/31/1993) • **89**
Barbaresco Montestefano Riserva 1985 • $25 • (10/31/1990) • **82**
Barbaresco Montestefano Riserva 1982 • $18 • (9/15/1988) • **88**
Barbaresco Ovello 1989 • $29 • (10/31/1994) • **85**
Barbaresco Ovello Riserva 1985 • $25 • (10/31/1990) • **86**
Barbaresco Ovello Riserva 1982 • $22 • (9/15/1988) • **86**
Barbaresco Paje Riserva 1982 • $22 • (9/15/1988) • **91**
Barbaresco Pora 1989 • $29 • (10/31/1994) • **84**
Barbaresco Pora Riserva 1982 • $18 • (9/15/1988) • **91**
Barbaresco Pora Riserva 1979 • $24 • (9/15/1988) • **91**
Barbaresco Rabajà 1990 • $35 • (10/31/1995) • **86**
Barbaresco Rabajà 1989 • $33 • (10/31/1994) • **82**
Barbaresco Rabajà Riserva 1982 • $22 • (9/15/1988) • **89**
Barbaresco Rio Sordo 1990 • $35 • (10/31/1995) • **82**
Barbaresco Rio Sordo 1989 • $29 • (10/31/1994) • **88**
Barbaresco Rio Sordo Riserva 1988 • $30 • (4/15/1994) • **76**
Barbaresco Rio Sordo Riserva 1982 • $22 • (9/15/1988) • **87**
Barbaresco Selezione del Trentennio '30' 1988 • $28 • (4/30/1992) HR • **91**
Nebbiolo delle Langhe 1995 • $14 • (1/31/1998) • **80**
Nebbiolo Langhe 1990 • $10 • (7/31/1992) • **83**
Nebbiolo Langhe 1988 • $9 • (2/28/1991) • **82**

BARBERO, PIETRO

Barbera d'Asti Bricco Verlenga 1997: Very crisp and bitingly acidic, with a green, astringent character that dominates the aftertaste.–P.M. • $20 • (11/15/1999) • **76**
Barbera d'Asti Bricco Verlenga 1996: Ripe, with a raisiny character, but also a lot of mouthpuckering, lemony-tasting acidity. Medium in body, with a good focus on the firm but deliciously clean, natural finish. Should go well with food. Drink now through 2001.–P.M. • $19 • (10/31/1998) • **87**
Barbera d'Asti Camparò 1997: A fruity, pretty wine. Tastes ripe and flavorful, with plenty of red berry, plum and red licorice. Medium-bodied, with a supple balance and a lingering finish. Drink now through 2002.–P.M. • $13 • (11/15/1999) • **86**
Barbera d'Asti Camparò 1996: Has some spritz to it, and some earthy aromas. Displays fruit and concentration, but overall seems rustic, with tart tannins, inelegant flavors.–P.M. • $13 • (10/31/1998) • **78**
Barbera d'Asti La Vignassa 1997: Full of personality and interesting in an odd way. Medium-bodied and a bit earthy, with the primal stink of truffle or horse stable, it also delivers a red berry character, with just enough spice. Drink now through 2003.–P.M. • $35 • (11/15/1999) • **86**
Barbera d'Asti La Vignassa 1996: Oak is the first aroma, but the wine is quite ripe, with cherry, blackberry character, and the acidity keeps it focused for a smoky finish of good balance. Medium-bodied. Cellar awhile. Drink through 2004.–P.M. • $34 • (10/31/1998) • **85**
Barbera d'Asti La Vignassa 1995: Yes, it's oaky and made in an "international style," but one must admire the deep, ripe fruit, the smooth tannins, the full body and opulent texture, and the fresh acidity weaving through. Enticing for its lingering finish, despite the wood. Handsomely crafted and, above all, superbalanced. Drink now through 2002.–P.M. • $35 • (10/31/1998) • **90**

BARBERO, PIETRO

Barbera d'Asti La Vignassa 1994: A mature Barbera, with licorice, forest underbrush, mushroom, also lovely plum and wild berry. A bit dry on the finish.–P.M. • $30 • (10/31/1998) • **80**

Barbera del Monferrato La Sera 1997: There's a nice, clean berry aroma in this straightforward Barbera, with wet earth, cranberry and cherry notes. Lacks a bit of depth, but try with pasta. Drink now.–P.M. • $12 • (11/15/1999) • **80**

Barbera del Monferrato La Sera 1996: Spritzy, and the flavors are light, dominated by strawberry and cherry. Tasted twice, with consistent notes.–P.M. • $12 • (10/31/1998) • **74**

Monferrato Piagé 1997: A straightforward red, with cherry, citrus and herb character in a crisp, medium-bodied package. Not imported into the U.S.–P.M. • $NA • (1/01/1999) • **79**

BARBI

Orvieto Classico 1998: Rich and fruity, with spicy mineral and lemon character. Medium-bodied, with good acidity and a fruity aftertaste. Drink now.–J.S. • $11 • (2/29/2000) • **85**

Toscana Lago di Corbara 1995: An elegant and subtle young red. Beautifully aromatic, with raspberry, cherry and grape aromas. Medium-bodied, with fine tannins and a fresh, silky finish. Best after 2001.–J.S. • $13 • (6/30/1999) • **87**

BARBI, FATTORIA DEI

Brunello di Montalcino 1995: Wonderful berry, strawberry, plum and smoke aromas open to a medium to full body, with well- integrated tannins and a fresh finish. A bright and exciting Brunello. Drink now through 2004.–J.S. • $45 • (6/30/2000) • **90**

Brunello di Montalcino 1994: Promises more on the nose than it gives on the palate, with wonderful aromas of crushed raspberries, flowers and wet earth. Medium-bodied, with firm, polished tannins and a fruity, slightly diluted finish. Drink now.–J.S. • $45 • (8/31/1999) • **86**

Brunello di Montalcino 1992 • $35 • (9/30/1997) • **86**

Brunello di Montalcino 1990 • $67 Ⓐ • (10/31/1995) • **88**

Brunello di Montalcino 1988 • $30 • (4/30/1994) • **81**

Brunello di Montalcino 1982 • $20 • (3/15/1989) • **78**

Brunello di Montalcino 1981 • $20 • (9/15/1986) • **85**

Brunello di Montalcino Blue Label 1993: Slightly rustic in style but you have to appreciate the intensity. Showy aromas of mushrooms and very ripe, almost raisiny fruit. Full-bodied, tannic, chewy on the finish. Best after 2000.–J.S. • $39 • (12/15/1998) • **86**

Brunello di Montalcino Blue Label 1986 • $28 • (8/31/1991) • **84**

Brunello di Montalcino Blue Label 1981 • $20 • (1/31/1991) • **81**

Brunello di Montalcino Riserva 1994: A pleasant and fresh '94 Brunello with berry, spice and tobacco character. Medium-bodied, with silky tannins and a fresh finish. A bit diluted. Drink now.–J.S. • $60 • (6/30/2000) • **84**

Brunello di Montalcino Riserva 1991 • $49 • (9/30/1997) • **87**

Brunello di Montalcino Riserva 1990 • $49 • (11/30/1996) • **91**

Brunello di Montalcino Riserva 1988 • $35 • (10/31/1994) • **85**

Brunello di Montalcino Riserva 1985 • $46 • (11/30/1991) • **87**

Brunello di Montalcino Riserva 1977 • $20 • (9/15/1986) • **86**

Brunello di Montalcino Vigna del Fiore 1995: Decadent style of Brunello. Aromas of raw meat, fruit and freshly cut mushrooms. Full-bodied and chewy, with lots of leather and spice—funky. Drink now.–J.S. • $85 • (6/30/2000) • **88**

Brunello di Montalcino Vigna del Fiore Riserva 1993: What a wonderful Brunello. Gorgeous aromas of crushed currants and berries. Full-bodied, with well-integrated tannins and a long, expressive, fruity aftertaste. Drink now through 2008.–J.S. • $78 • (8/31/1999) • **91**

Brunello di Montalcino Vigna del Fiore Riserva 1991 • $65 • (9/30/1997) • **85**

Brunello di Montalcino Vigna del Fiore Riserva 1990 • $139 Ⓐ • (11/30/1996) • **91**

Brunello di Montalcino Vigna del Fiore Riserva 1988 • $48 • (10/31/1994) • **90**

Brusco dei Barbi 1996 • $10 • (9/30/1997) • **87**

Bruscone dei Barbi 1993 • $NA • (10/31/1996) • **87**

Bruscone dei Barbi 1990 • $12 • (10/31/1993) • **87**

Bruscone dei Barbi 1988 • $27 • (9/15/1991) • **84**

Chianti Il Colle 1995 • $NA • (10/31/1996) • **85**

Key: SS—Spectator Selection. CS—Cellar Selection. HR—Highly Recommended. $NA—Price not available. (BT)—Barrel tasting. Ⓐ—Auction Price. For a key to the tasters' initials, see "How to Use These Listings." **Dates in parentheses represent the issues in which the ratings were published.**

Morellino di Scansano Colombini 1997: Delicious drink-me wine. Attractive aromas of ripe berry, plum and minerals. Medium-bodied, with soft tannins and a lots of fresh fruit character on the finish. Drink now.–J.S. • $21• (6/15/2000) • **85**

Rosso di Montalcino 1997: A good chunky rosso with a slightly raisiny, stemmy character. Medium-bodied, with medium tannins and a fruity finish. A bit rustic really, but very good. Drink now.–J.S. • $9 • (9/15/1999) • **85**

Rosso di Montalcino 1996: A relatively rich Rosso with ripe berry and vanilla aromas and flavors. Medium-bodied, with moderate tannins and a fresh finish. Drink now.–J.S. • $12 • (12/15/1998) • **84**

Rosso di Montalcino 1995 • $15 • (9/30/1997) • **85**

Rosso di Montalcino 1994 • $12 • (11/30/1996) • **86**

Rosso di Montalcino 1993 • $14 • (10/31/1995) • **85**

Rosso di Montalcino 1992 • $12 • (10/31/1994) • **85**

Rosso di Montalcino 1991 • $9 • (4/30/1994) • **80**

Toscana Brigante dei Barbi 1996: A wine with a slightly vegetal, wet earth and berry character. Medium-bodied, with light tannins and a fresh fruit finish. Disappointing for this producer.–J.S. • $39 • (6/15/2000) • **79**

Toscana Brigante dei Barbi 1995: A pretty red in a reserved style. Lovely aromas of mint and blackberries. Medium-bodied, with medium tannins and a chocolaty finish. Drink now.–J.S. • $39 • (12/15/1998) • **87**

Toscana Brigante dei Barbi 1994 • $40 • (9/30/1997) • **87**

Toscana Brusco dei Barbi 1997: Firm and delicious, with tobacco, berry and chocolate character. Medium-bodied, with well-integrated tannins and a chewy finish. Drink now.–J.S. • $14 • (11/30/1999) • **88**

Toscana Brusco dei Barbi 1994 • $12 • (10/31/1996) • **88**

Toscana Brusco dei Barbi 1992 • $10 • (2/28/1995) • **83**

Toscana Brusco dei Barbi 1988 • $12 • (9/15/1991) • **86**

Tuscany 1982 • $20 • (9/15/1986) • **80**

BARGAGLI

Morellino di Scansano Provveditore 1997: The slightly stewed fruit character has plum undertones. Light-bodied, with light tannins and a fresh finish. Not imported into the U.S.–J.S. • $NA • (1/01/1999) • **79**

BAROLO, MARCHESI DI

Barbaresco 1993: Ready to enjoy. Supple and smooth, ripe and delicious, with lovely earth, plum, prune and currant character. Of medium weight, with impressively silky tannins, it's well made and balanced. Drink now through 2005.–P.M. • $15 • (10/31/1998) • **87**

Barbaresco 1990 • $18 • (10/31/1993) • **88**

Barbaresco 1989 • $18 • (10/31/1993) • **87**

Barbaresco Montestefano 1991 • $20 • (10/31/1995) • **77**

Barbaresco Rio Sordo 1988 • $18 • (1/31/1992) • **86**

Barbera d'Alba 1990 • $10 • (10/15/1993) • **70**

Barbera d'Alba Paiagallo 1996: Lean, showing some good fruit and rather pronounced toasted mocha and coffee notes. Lacks a bit of richness. Chewy finish. Drink now.–P.M. • $17 • (9/15/1999) • **80**

Barbera d'Alba Paiagallo 1990 • $12 • (10/15/1993) • **76**

Barbera d'Alba Ruvei 1996: Balanced, supple and light-bodied, with fresh, delicious berry and oak flavors that follow through on the succulent finish. Not much complexity, but a good everyday wine. Drink now.–P.M. • $12 • (10/31/1998) • **82**

Barbera del Monferrato Le Lune 1988 • $6 • (7/15/1991) • **78**

Barolo 1995: Round-tasting at first sip, with lovely floral, tarry, smoky aromas, it turns quite chewy on the aftertaste, as the crisp fruit peeks through the tough tannin blanket of this medium-bodied Barolo. Time might soften it. Best after 2003.–P.M. • $35 • (11/15/1999) • **85**

Barolo 1993: Clean and pure, built on loads of fruit. Medium- to full-bodied, it lacks a bit of harmony from the acidity and hard tannins that give a drying sensation to the finish. Best after 2002.–P.M. • $26 • (10/31/1998) • **83**

Barolo 1992 • $19 • (10/31/1996) • **82**

Barolo 1991 • $20 • (10/31/1995) • **83**

Barolo 1990 • $15 • (10/31/1994) • **79**

Barolo 1989 • $18 • (10/31/1993) • **86**

Barolo 1988 • $18 • (10/31/1993) • **88**

Barolo Brunate 1985 • $29 • (10/15/1990) • **85**

Barolo Brunate 1982 • $14 • (2/15/1989) • **89**

Barolo Cannubi 1989 • $30 • (10/31/1994) • **91**

Barolo Cannubi 1988 • $30 • (10/31/1993) • **85**

Barolo Cannubi 1985 • $29 • (10/15/1990) • **88**

Barolo Castel la Volta 1987 • $20 • (1/31/1992) • **89**

Barolo Coste di Rosé 1985 • $29 • (10/15/1990) • **86**

Barolo III Millennium M 1993: Well made. Balanced, ripe, blending tar and smoke with spice and plum. Has tough tannins, but delivers soil, mineral and wet earth to satisfy the Barolo purist and a supple overall mouthfeel. Drinkable now with red meats, but made for cellaring. Drink now through 2010.–P.M. • $100 • (10/31/1998) • **92**
Barolo Riserva 1993: Interesting, new-wave Barolo, with a eucalyptus edge that makes it distinctive, along with some plum and blackberry character. Toasted and smoky accents need time; tannins are a bit astringent on the finish. Drink through 2007–P.M. • $26 • (10/31/1998) • **89**
Barolo Riserva 1982 • $14 • (2/15/1989) • **87**
Barolo Riserva 1978 • $20 • (2/28/1989) • **86**
Barolo Sarmassa 1989 • $35 • (10/31/1994) • **88**
Barolo Sarmassa 1988 • $30 • (10/31/1993) • **83**
Barolo Valletta 1985 • $29 • (10/15/1990) • **88**
Dolcetto d'Alba Madonna di Como 1998: Distinctive, with a slightly lifted grappa aroma, game and earth notes and a lean, citrusy, mouthpuckering finish.–P.M. • $12 • (7/31/1999) • **77**
Dolcetto d'Alba Madonna di Como 1997: This impressive Dolcetto is true to type, with loads of freshly crushed blackberry, spice and toasted aromas and fine-textured, ripe tannins backed by good acidity. Long, succulent finish. Drink now.–P.M. • $15 • (10/31/1998) • **87**
Dolcetto d'Alba Madonna di Como 1995 • $12 • (10/31/1996) • **79**
Dolcetto d'Alba Madonna di Como 1990 • $10 • (1/31/1992) • **77**
Dolcetto d'Alba Madonna di Como 1989 • $9 • (12/31/1990) • **88**

BARONE

Cabernet Piave 1993 • $6 • (1/31/1996) • **78**
Merlot Piave 1995 • $6 • (3/31/1997) • **80**
Merlot Piave 1994 • $5 • (2/29/1996) • **79**
Merlot Piave 1993 • $6 • (6/15/1996) • **77**

BARONE LA LUMIA

Sicilia Cadetto Signorio 1995: Simple, rustic yet interesting ripe fruit aromas and flavors. Short finish. Not imported into the U.S. Drink now.–J.S. • $NA • (1/01/1999) • **80**
Sicilia Signorio 1997: Rustic but rich. Aromas of peach, ash and mineral open onto a full-bodied palate with very similar character. Quite chewy for a white, with fresh acidity. Drink now.–J.S. • $8 • (6/15/1999) • **85**
Sicilia Signorio 1994: A bit rustic but pleasurable. Ripe and raisiny, with hints of chestnut on the nose. Medium-bodied, with plenty of grapey flavor and a long, ripe fruit finish. Not imported into the U.S. Drink now.–J.S. • $NA • (1/01/1999) • **81**
Sicilia Stemma Signorio 1997: A meager red, with fruity chestnut character but not much else. Not imported into the U.S.–J.S. • $NA • (1/01/1999) • **77**

BARTOLI, MARCO DE

Grillo Sicilia Grappoli 1998: This young white has good apple, vanilla and toasted oak character. Medium-bodied, with light acidity and a woody finish. Tastes a bit like white Rioja. Not imported into the U.S. Drink now.–J.S. • $NA • (1/01/2000) • **83**
Marsala Superiore NV: Why drink fine olorosso Sherry? Intense aromas of caramel, leather and fig, with hints of orange peel. Medium-bodied and off dry, with a spicy, nutty, dried fruit aftertaste. Not imported into the U.S. Drink now.–J.S. • $NA/500 ml. • (1/01/2000) • **90**
Moscato Passito di Pantelleria Bukkuram 1996: A superb dessert wine. Thick and rich like honey, but with spice, butterscotch, caramel and dried apricot coming through on the palate. Full-bodied, sweet and rich, with a long finish. A beauty. Drink now.–J.S. • $39/500 ml. • (5/31/2000) • **92**
Vecchio Samperi NV: Like a great amontillado Sherry. A wonderful aperitif for a winter's night, with toasted walnut, orange peel and honey. Medium- to full-bodied, with very ripe fruit and a long, nutty, fruity aftertaste. Drink now.–J.S. • $30/500 ml. • (5/31/2000) • **90**

BASCIANO, FATTORIA DI

Chianti Paolo Masi 1991 • $6 • (6/15/1993) • **79**
Chianti Rufina 1997: Great value. Gorgeous aromas of violet, berry and raspberry. Medium-bodied, with silky, seamless tannins and a long, fruity finish. A beauty. Drink now through 2001.–J.S. • $9 • (11/30/1999) • **89**
Chianti Rufina 1996: Vibrant cherry and blackberry with hints of vanilla on the nose. Full-bodied and very soft, with delectable, round tannins. Medium finish. A big, juicy red for near-term drinking, it's quite a good value, too. Drink now.–J.S. • $9 • (12/15/1998) • **87**
Chianti Rufina 1995 • $7 • (9/30/1997) • **86**
Chianti Rufina 1994 • $NA • (10/31/1996) • **86**
Chianti Rufina 1993 • $6 • (10/31/1994) • **84**
Chianti Rufina 1991 • $9 • (10/31/1993) • **78**
Chianti Rufina 1990 • $9 • (10/31/1993) • **88**
Chianti Rufina Riserva 1996: A bit rustic, but I like the fruit. Intensely grapey, with hints of vanilla. Medium-bodied, with a chunky fruit and tannin structure. Short finish. Drink now.–J.S. • $13 • (11/30/1999) • **86**
Chianti Rufina Riserva 1995: A racy young wine. Wonderful raspberry and cherry aromas and flavors. Medium-bodied, with fine tannins and a long, fresh aftertaste. Drink now.–J.S. • $12 • (12/15/1998) • **88**
Chianti Rufina Riserva 1994 • $11 • (9/30/1997) • **88**
Chianti Rufina Riserva 1993 • $NA • (10/31/1996) • **88**
Colli della Toscana Centrale I Pini 1997: A sleek and well-crafted red, with blueberry and vanilla character. Medium-bodied, with silky tannins. Drink now.–J.S. • $17 • (11/30/1999) • **86**
Colli della Toscana Centrale I Pini 1996: A balanced red, with silky tannins and luscious berry, cherry and vanilla aromas and flavors. Medium-bodied, with medium tannins and a soft, caressing finish. Thoroughly satisfying. A seriously good value. Drink through 2001.–J.S. • $11 • (12/15/1998) • **88**
Colli della Toscana Centrale I Pini 1995 • $14 • (9/30/1997) • **87**
Colli della Toscana Centrale Vigna Il Corto 1997: Big and slightly awkward yet loaded with fruit and tannin. Full-bodied, with an interesting cherry and bark character, intense and polished tannins and a medium finish. Not imported into the U.S. Best after 2000.–J.S. • $NA • (11/30/1999) • **89**
Colli della Toscana Centrale Vigna Il Corto 1996: Dark-colored, with black cherry and licorice aromas. Full-bodied, with lovely, round tannins and a long, fruity, smoky aftertaste. Quite a mouthful, and a great buy. Drink through 2001.–J.S. • $12 • (12/15/1998) • **88**
Colli della Toscana Centrale I Pini 1995 • $14 • (9/30/1997) • **87**
Toscana Vigna il Corto 1995 • $15 • (9/30/1997) • **89**
Vin Santo del Chianti Rufina 1995: Very pretty aromas of clove, honey, almond and peach. Medium-bodied and medium sweet, with a zingy finish of acidity and creamy flavors. Try with fruit. Not imported into the U.S. Drink now.–J.S. • $NA/375 ml. • (1/01/1999) • **87**

BASTIANICH

Pinot Grigio Colli Orientali del Friuli 1998: A very fresh white, with melon and almond character. Medium-bodied, with fresh acidity and a long, fruity finish. Drink now.–J.S. • $19 • (3/31/2000) • **86**
Tocai Friulano Colli Orientali del Friuli 1998: Very clean and fresh, with appleskin, mineral and piecrust character. Medium-bodied, with a fresh finish. Drink now.–J.S. • $25 • (3/31/2000) • **85**
Tocai Friulano Colli Orientali del Friuli Plus 1998: Subtle and rich, with apple, sliced pear and lemon character. Medium-bodied, with fresh acidity and a mineral aftertaste. Drink now through 2001.–J.S. • $25 • (3/31/2000) • **86**
Vespa 1998: Serious white. Complex. Plenty of ripe melon and apple character in this wine. Full-bodied, with lots of fruit and a long, rich finish. Delicious. Drink now.–J.S. • $27 • (4/30/2000) • **89**
Vespa 1997: Powerful aromas of honey and ripe apple, with similar flavors. Full-bodied and thick, with a medium finish. Slightly one-dimensional, but very good. Best after 2000.–J.S. • $25 • (1/01/2000) • **87**

BATASIOLO, BENI DI

Barbaresco 1996: A bit tough, with hard tannins, showing earth, cherry pit and chalk character. Smacking acidity on the finish. Might improve with time. Drink now through 2004.–P.M. • $26 • (10/31/1999) • **80**
Barbaresco 1995: Subtle beauty. Pure and natural wine, emphasizing fruit over wood, with red berry, cassis, rose petal, plum and prune character in a balanced whole. Of medium to full body, the tannins are well integrated, supple and velvety, yet it delivers a firm grip on the lingering, elegant finish. Drink now through 2007.–P.M. • $19 • (10/31/1998) • **93**
Barbaresco 1993 • $23 • (10/31/1996) • **84**
Barbaresco 1990 • $22 • (10/31/1994) • **80**
Barbaresco 1989 • $18 • (10/31/1994) • **72**
Barbera d'Alba 1997: Crisp and fruity, with good red berry and toast aromas. Medium-bodied, with a fresh aftertaste. Try with pizza or burgers. Drink now through 2001.–P.M. • $11 • (11/15/1999) • **81**
Barbera d'Alba 1996: A crisp, slightly herbal, berryish red. Somewhat astringent, with bell pepper notes on the finish.–P.M. • $10 • (10/31/1998) • **72**
Barbera d'Alba 1994 • $NA • (10/31/1996) • **79**
Barbera d'Alba 1992 • $NA • (10/31/1994) • **76**
Barbera d'Alba 1991 • $10 • (11/15/1993) • **82**
Barbera d'Alba 1988 • $11 • (4/15/1991) • **88**

ITALY

BATASIOLO, BENI DI

Barbera d'Alba Sovrana 1997: Flavorful and fresh, showing tobacco aromas and a racy wild berry character. Medium-bodied, with ripe tannins and acidity for a cleansing, mouthpuckering experience. Drink now through 2002.–P.M. • $18 • (11/15/1999) • **86**
Barbera d'Alba Sovrana 1996: Ripe yet elegant, with clean and pure fruit, this walks a nice tightrope between black fruit, good acidity and spice shadings. Medium-bodied, it's a great, not-too-serious, trattoria-style food wine. Drink now.–P.M. • $18 • (10/31/1998) • **84**
Barbera d'Alba Sovrana 1994 • $19 • (10/31/1997) • **85**
Barbera d'Alba Sovrana 1993 • $NA • (10/31/1996) • **81**
Barbera d'Alba Sovrana 1990 • $18 • (10/31/1994) • **79**
Barolo 1995: A bit rustic, with interesting fruit and wet earth quality. Distinct smoky, spicy, toasted notes. It has grip, with chewy tannins that linger. Drink now through 2005.–P.M. • $24 • (11/15/1999) • **84**
Barolo 1994: Fruit and *terroir* is what you get in this medium-bodied, elegant Barolo. Not showy or oaky, it's a purist's sort of wine, with firm tannins, mineral notes, plum, tar and floral character. Better with cellaring through 2005.–P.M. • $20 • (10/31/1998) • **89**
Barolo 1993 • $20 • (10/31/1997) • **89**
Barolo 1992 • $25 • (10/31/1996) • **81**
Barolo 1991 • $22 • (10/31/1995) • **82**
Barolo 1990 • $22 • (10/31/1994) • **78**
Barolo 1989 • $18 • (10/31/1993) • **81**
Barolo 1988 • $25 • (10/31/1994) • **85**
Barolo 1985 • $15 • (3/31/1990) • **84**
Barolo Bofani 1989 • $25 • (10/31/1994) • **90**
Barolo Boscareto 1995: Supple and silky, this seductive, medium-bodied red shows mineral and blackberry character. The texture is smooth until the tannins clamp down on the lovely finish. Drink now through 2002.–P.M. • $60 • (11/15/1999) • **88**
Barolo Boscareto 1993: Sweet-tasting and sophisticated, ripe and racy, firm, medium-bodied and attractive, with some of the smoothest tannins you can imagine coating your palate with harmony from start to finish. Delivers layers of fresh and pure cassis and blueberry flavors. Best from 2005 through 2010.–P.M. • $46 • (9/15/1998) • **90**
Barolo Boscareto 1991 • $NA • (10/31/1996) • **82**
Barolo Boscareto 1990 • $NA • (10/31/1993) • **74**
Barolo Boscareto 1989 • $28 • (10/31/1994) • **82**
Barolo La Corda della Briccolina 1995: A pretty Barolo that's rather reserved. Full-bodied and fairly ripe, with black fruit, mineral and smoke character. Firm tannins kick in on the intense finish. Needs time in the cellar to show it all, or try with hearty foods. Best from 2003 through 2007.–P.M. • $69 • (11/15/1999) • **88**
Barolo La Corda della Briccolina 1993: Pretty, if a bit straightforward, this fruity Barolo offers some plum and licorice. Tastes youthful and grapey. Drink now through 2002.–P.M. • $50 • (10/31/1998) • **81**
Barolo La Corda della Briccolina 1991 • $60 • (10/31/1996) • **80**
Barolo La Corda della Briccolina 1990 • $40 • (10/31/1994) • **94**
Barolo La Corda della Briccolina 1989 • $38 • (10/31/1993) HR • **94**
Barolo La Corda della Briccolina 1988 • $38 • (10/31/1993) • **90**
Barolo La Corda della Briccolina 1987 • $35 • (1/31/1992) • **84**
Barolo Riserva 1993: Medium-bodied and fairly ripe, showing midpalate softness, it tastes of cherry, plum and oak. A touch diluted on the finish. It's time to open this. Drink now through 2002.–P.M. • $NA • (11/15/1999) • **82**
Barolo Riserva 1986 • $22 • (12/15/1992) • **81**
Barolo Riserva 1982 • $17 • (3/31/1990) • **79**
Dolcetto d'Alba 1998: Ripe-tasting, with floral, mint and cherry notes. Turns a bit tough on the finish.–P.M. • $11 • (11/15/1999) • **76**
Dolcetto d'Alba 1997: Fairly tart, with wet earth, tobacco leaf, spice, cherry pit and black cherry character. Should go well with food, which will soften the finish.–P.M. • $10 • (10/31/1998) • **82**
Dolcetto d'Alba 1996 • $11 • (10/31/1997) • **85**
Dolcetto d'Alba 1995 • $13 • (10/31/1996) • **85**
Dolcetto d'Alba 1990 • $13 • (10/31/1992) • **77**
Dolcetto d'Alba 1989 • $12 • (2/15/1992) • **84**
Dolcetto d'Alba 1988 • $11 • (12/31/1990) • **85**
Dolcetto d'Alba Bricco di Vergne 1997: A vibrant wine of good concentration. Round and ripe, with a core of black cherry, raspberry and wet earth, notable fullness in the midpalate and refined tannins. Intense finish suggests short-term cellaring.–P.M. • $13 • (10/31/1998) • **84**

Key: SS—Spectator Selection. CS—Cellar Selection. HR—Highly Recommended. $NA—Price not available. (BT)—Barrel tasting. (A)—Auction Price.
For a key to the tasters' initials, see "How to Use These Listings."
Dates in parentheses represent the issues in which the ratings were published.

BAVA

Barbaresco 1982 • $23 • (4/30/1991) • **83**
Barbera d'Asti 1985 • $13 • (3/15/1991) • **87**
Barbera d'Asti Arbest 1994: Traditional in style, this well-made, ripe Barbera is packed with wet earth, chocolate, roasted chestnut, plum and blackberry character. Medium to full in body, it delivers an intriguing taste, showing lots of personality. Supple tannins make it accessible on release through 2003.–P.M. • $19 • (10/31/1998) • **87**
Barbera d'Asti Cocconato 1990 • $10 • (4/30/1993) • **75**
Barbera d'Asti Stradivario 1994: A well-made Barbera in a traditional style, showing cedar, tobacco box, wet earth and plum character. Medium-bodied, with a firm mouthfeel and ripe tannins. The balanced finish has a bitter dark chocolate touch. Drink now through 2002.–P.M. • $33 • (10/31/1998) • **85**
Barolo 1985 • $19 • (4/30/1991) • **83**
Monferrato White Alteserre 1996: Displays some buttery notes along with ripe-tasting pear and melon, with a lush, round and delicious mouthfeel. This hedonistic white is balanced and laced with honey on the beautiful, fairly crisp, elegant yet subtly off-dry finish. Good as an aperitif or with fish. Drink now.–P.M. • $22 • (10/31/1998) • **87**

BEL COLLE

Barbaresco 1994 • $22 • (10/31/1997) • **72**
Barbera d'Alba Le Masche 1996: Crisp, hollow and light-colored, with modest fruit and a short finish.–P.M. • $14 • (9/15/1999) • **74**
Barbera d'Alba Le Masche 1995 • $20 • (10/31/1997) • **83**
Barbera d'Alba Le Masche 1989 • $15 • (10/31/1992) • **86**
Barbera d'Alba Vigneti in Verduno 1995 • $13 • (10/31/1997) • **80**
Barolo 1994: Fruity and light, with some cherry, raspberry and herbal character, but tannic, drying and astringent on the short finish.–P.M. • $29 • (10/31/1998) • **71**
Barolo 1993 • $28 • (10/31/1997) • **83**
Barolo Monvigliero 1995: Ripeness mingles with herbaceousness. Tasting of olive, herb and currant character, this medium-bodied red offers a minty note on the finish, which is slightly chewy. Drink now through 2005.–P.M. • $40 • (11/15/1999) • **83**
Barolo Monvigliero 1985 • $20 • (10/15/1990) • **87**
Barolo Riserva 1982 • $15 • (3/31/1990) • **85**
Dolcetto d'Alba Altavilla 1990 • $12 • (10/31/1992) • **81**
Dolcetto d'Alba Borgo Castagni 1997: A bit herbaceous, with bell pepper notes. Slightly diluted, light-bodied, with modest cherry character, but dries out on the finish.–P.M. • $14 • (7/31/1999) • **73**
Dolcetto d'Alba Borgo Castagni in Verduno 1996 • $12 • (10/31/1997) • **85**
Dolcetto d'Alba Madonna Como 1990 • $14 • (10/31/1992) • **79**

BELISARIO

Verdicchio di Matelica Cambrugiano Riserva 1998: Impressive. Wonderful clarity in this white, with floral, stone and melon character. Medium- to full-bodied, with plenty of acidity and a long aftertaste of mineral, flint and melon. Delicious. Drink now.–J.S. • $13 • (2/29/2000) • **89**
Verdicchio di Matelica I Ritratti 1998: An aromatic and lively Italian white, emitting scents of flowers and honey with hints of melon, this is medium-bodied, with fresh acidity and a crisp finish. The no-risk price belies its drinkability. Ready now.–J.S. • $8 • (2/29/2000) • **86**
Verdicchio di Matelica Vigneti del Cerro 1998: A delicious white, with lots of ripe fruit, showing pineapple and mango character. Full-bodied and round, with good apple and peach flavors and a medium finish. Drink now.–J.S. • $10 • (2/29/2000) • **87**

BELLANOVA

Sicilia Red 1995 • $8/1.5 liter • (4/30/1997) • **81**

BELLARINA, PODERE

Brunello di Montalcino 1993: Slightly mature and tired at this stage—not a good sign. Chocolate and dried cherry aromas. Medium-bodied, with light tannins and a fruity finish. Drink now.–J.S. • $40 • (12/15/1998) • **81**

BELLAVISTA

Solesine 1994 • $45 • (12/15/1997) HR • **91**

ITALY

Solesine 1993 • $43 • (3/31/1997) • **90**
Solesine 1986 • $30 • (5/15/1989) • **92**
Terre de Franciacorta 1994 • $17 • (12/15/1997) • **86**

BELLINI, CANTINE

Chianti Rufina Fattoria Monte 1994: Clean, simple and slightly austere, with berry and cherry character, but it's rather light and short on the palate. Medium-bodied, with a short finish. Drink now.–J.S. • $NA • (1/01/1999) • **80**

Toscana Le Lodole 1997: A joy to drink, with lovely cherry, raspberry and strawberry galore. Medium-bodied, with light tannins and a fresh, fruity finish. Drink now.–J.S. • $NA • (1/01/1999) • **87**

BENANTI

Edèlmio 1996: Lovely, with aromas of peach and pear and a hint of mineral. Medium-bodied, with good fruit and a vanilla and butter finish. Drink now.–J.S. • $19 • (5/31/2000) • **85**

Etna Bianco di Caselle 1998: Very fresh and lively, with lemon-lime and mineral character. Medium-bodied, with a long finish. Drink now.–J.S. • $12 • (5/31/2000) • **85**

Etna Rosso di Verzela 1997: A good red, with plum and berry character. Medium-bodied, with light tannins and a fruity finish. Drink now.–J.S. • $13 • (5/31/2000) • **81**

Etna Rovittello 1996: Very clean, with lots of berry, plum and floral character throughout. Medium- to full-bodied, with soft tannins and a fresh finish. Drink now.–J.S. • $29 • (5/31/2000) • **87**

Lamorèmio 1996: Big and thick, with impressive currant, berry, mint and violet aromas. Full-bodied, with loads of polished tannins and a long finish. A little more finesse would make it outstanding, but it's serious all the same. Best after 2001.–J.S. • $29 • (5/31/2000) • **89**

BENOTTO

Barbera d'Asti Balau 1996: A rich, thick Barbera, with pronounced oak accented by a slight petrol aroma, some pretty black cherry, blackberry flavors, and a supple mouthfeel ending in a fresh, succulent finish. Drink now through 2002.–P.M. • $13 • (1/01/1999) • **86**

Barbera d'Asti Rupestris 1996: A big oak job here, with the wood aromas smothering the fruit—at least for now—but you do get a round, thick mouthfeel and some plum and blackberry notes on the toasty, mocha-tasting, fresh finish. Drink now through 2003.–P.M. • $23 • (1/01/1999) • **87**

Dolcetto Monferrato Plissè 1998: Lovely, subtle harmony. Chalk dust, stone, plum and blackberry character, with light smoke and toasted spices, all in a supersupple texture. This medium-bodied red fans out its seductive charm to a long finish. Drink now through 2003.–P.M. • $12 • (1/01/1999) • **89**

Dolcetto Monferrato Plissè 1996: Beautiful aromas and flavors range from cassis to game, spice and smoke (as well as, unfortunately, a slightly lifted, unbecoming balsamic vinegar note) make this medium-bodied, flavorful Dolcetto very distinctive.–P.M. • $12 • (1/01/1999) • **79**

Monferrato Gamba di Pernice 1998: Straightforward, but with pleasant cherry, spice and licorice notes. Medium-bodied, it shows a round mouth-feel. Tastes young, with a juicy finish.–P.M. • $13 • (1/01/1999) • **79**

Monferrato Nebieul 1996: Lively, with a nice, clean cherry and raspberry character that also shows toasted oak. Medium-bodied, with a persistent, grilled meat character on the finish. Drink now through 2003.–P.M. • $13 • (1/01/1999) • **80**

BERETTA, CECILIA

Amarone della Valpolicella Classico Terre di Cariano 1990 • $40 • (5/31/1998) • **88**

Amarone della Valpolicella Classico Terre di Cariano 1985 • $26 • (9/30/1995) • **89**

Valpolicella Classico Superiore Terre di Cariano 1993 • $15 • (4/30/1998) • **87**
Valpolicella Classico Vigneti di Marano 1995 • $11 • (4/30/1998) • **84**
Valpolicella Superiore Roccolo di Mizzole 1992 • $8 • (12/15/1995) • **84**

BERETTA, GUSSALLI

Extra Brut Franciacorta Lo Sparviere NV • $25 • (1/31/1997) • **83**
Franciacorta Lo Sparviere Vino del Cacciatore 1991 • $20 • (3/31/1997) • **82**

BERGADANO, ENRICO

Barolo 1993 • $NA • (10/31/1997) • **83**

BERSANO

Barbaresco 1995: A bit mature already, tasting of forest underbrush with a mushroom note. Tannins turn harsh on the finish. Old-fashioned.–P.M. • $33 • (10/31/1998) • **77**

Barbaresco 1994: Some modest fruit and spice, but overall there's a bit of balsamic vinegar character that leads to a tart finish and suggests it has peaked.–P.M. • $25 • (10/31/1998) • **72**

Barbaresco 1993 • $30 • (1/31/1998) • **73**
Barbaresco 1991 • $16 • (10/31/1995) • **78**
Barbaresco 1975 • $NA • (9/15/1988) • **76**
Barbaresco 1971 • $NA • (9/15/1988) • **78**
Barbaresco 1964 • $NA • (9/15/1988) • **85**

Barbaresco Mantico 1996: Very open and forward now, and a touch light on the midpalate, but still pleasant. This medium-bodied Barbaresco has medium intensity, but what's there—blackberry, spice and wet earth—tastes balanced. Drink now through 2006.–P.M. • $35 • (10/31/1999) • **86**

Barbera d'Asti 1996: Light in color and body, lean and rather crisp, with unripe fruit flavors that turn astringent on the finish. Lacks harmony.–P.M. • $10 • (10/31/1998) • **73**

Barbera d'Asti 1995 • $9 • (1/31/1998) • **75**
Barbera d'Asti 1992 • $NA • (10/31/1995) • **80**

Barbera d'Asti Costalunga 1997: This straightforward Barbera has bright, medium-intense fruit but not much complexity. Turns a bit hot and astringent on the finish.–P.M. • $12 • (11/15/1999) • **79**

Barbera d'Asti Generala 1997: Fresh fruit blends with toasted oak in this rather firm, medium-bodied red. The wood dominates the fruit and leaves an astringent bitterness on the finish, along with cassis and smoke. Drink now.–P.M. • $50 • (11/15/1999) • **80**

Barbera d'Asti Vigna Cremosina 1997: Rather thick and full-bodied, this tannic red has plenty of ripe plum and red berry, but it turns a bit tough on the finish. Best from 2001 through 2005.–P.M. • $26 • (11/15/1999) • **85**

Barbera d'Asti Vigna Cremosina 1995: Light in color, body and flavor, this earthy, slightly funky wine misses the point. Not much fruit or suppleness. Lean finish.–P.M. • $18 • (10/31/1998) • **72**

Barbera Piemonte 1998: Fruity and light-bodied, offering red berry and earth character. Supple tannins make it ready to enjoy. Drink now.–P.M. • $8 • (11/15/1999) • **80**

Barbera Piemonte 1997: Light in body but very grapey and youthful, this Nouveau-style Barbera offers freshly crushed berry flavors, supple tannins and a succulent, juicy finish. Serve slightly chilled.–P.M. • $7 • (10/31/1998)• **84**

Barolo 1993 • $35 • (1/31/1998) • **84**
Barolo 1991 • $18 • (10/31/1995) • **78**
Barolo 1985 • $10 • (10/15/1990) • **79**
Barolo 1974 • $NA • (9/15/1988) • **79**
Barolo 1971 • $NA • (9/15/1988) • **77**
Barolo 1964 • $NA • (9/15/1988) • **80**

Barolo Nirvasco 1995: Light and diluted, with a fruity character but a crisp finish.–P.M. • $38 • (11/15/1999) • **78**

Barolo Vigna Badarina 1995: A Barolo with finesse. Tastes of mocha and chocolate bars, but with ripe plum and blackberry. A touch diluted. Drink now through 2005.–P.M. • $55 • (11/15/1999) • **86**

Barolo Vigna Badarina 1993: Overtly oaky, with a milk chocolate kind of character. Medium to full in body, with a lush texture and pretty spice, red berry and blackberry aromas and flavors. Balanced, fleshy and attractive, though not superintense. Drink now through 2005.–P.M. • $35 • (10/31/1998) • **87**

Barolo Vigna Badarina 1990 • $30 • (10/31/1995) • **87**
Castellengo 1986 • $16 • (4/15/1991) • **88**

Cortese Piemonte 1997: Nice and fruity on the nose, it falls short on the palate, offering subdued floral, pear and melon notes that turn a bit dull on the supple but uninspiring finish. Drink now.–P.M. • $7 • (10/31/1998) • **79**

Dolcetto d'Alba 1997: Light in color and body, with decent strawberry and raspberry character. Pleasant, but a bit short on the finish. Drink now. –P.M. • $15 • (10/31/1998) • **79**

Dolcetto d'Alba 1994 • $12 • (10/31/1995) • **78**

Dolcetto d'Alba Coldelfosso 1998: Simple, tart and herbal.–P.M. • $14 • (11/15/1999) • **72**

Gavi 1997: Very dry, even a bit herbal and grassy, with an undertow of butter and butterscotch. Medium-bodied and quite supple, this has an uncompromising personality, with mineral and stone notes. Should match well with food given its acidity. Drink now.–P.M. • $12 • (10/31/1998) • **84**

BERSANO

Gavi 1996 • $12 • (1/31/1998) • **83**
Monferrato Pomona 1997: An attractive, medium-bodied red, with clean, vibrant red berry and blackberry character. Shows an intensity as the toasted oak notes pick up velocity on the smoky finish. Drink now through 2003.–P.M. • $60 • (11/15/1999) • **86**

BERTANI

Amarone della Valpolicella Classico Superiore 1985 • $45 • (6/15/1996) • **90**
Amarone della Valpolicella Classico Superiore 1983 • $40 • (11/15/1994) • **87**
Amarone della Valpolicella Classico Superiore 1980 • $40 • (9/15/1992) • **87**
Bardolino Classico Superiore 1990 • $9 • (9/15/1992) • **84**
Catullo 1990 • $12 • (11/15/1994) • **79**
Catullo 1986 • $13 • (9/15/1992) • **81**
Recioto della Valpolicella Amarone Classico Superiore 1988 • $59 • (5/31/1998) • **88**
Valpolicella Valpantena Secco-Bertani 1995 • $10 • (4/30/1998) • **86**
Valpolicella Valpantena Secco-Bertani 1993 • $10 • (6/15/1997) • **79**
Valpolicella Valpantena Secco-Bertani 1992 • $10 • (6/15/1996) • **87**
Valpolicella Valpantena Secco-Bertani 1988 • $9 • (11/15/1994) • **76**

BERTELLI

Barbera d'Asti 1994 • $NA • (10/31/1997) • **72**
Barbera d'Asti Giarone 1993 • $40 • (10/31/1996) • **80**
Barbera d'Asti Giarone 1990 • $NA • (10/31/1994) • **78**
Barbera d'Asti Montetusa 1996: A stunning red that's exotically flavored. Inky black in color, full-bodied, its multifaceted personality shows layers of violet, rose petal, plum, cassis, mineral and wet earth, with subtle oak accents on the long finish. The tannins are supple. Drink now through 2005.–P.M. • $NA • (10/31/1998) • **92**
Barbera d'Asti Montetusa 1995: Showing violet, spice and black currant, this lively, vibrant medium-bodied red delights with its fruitiness, mingled with some smoky, toasted flavors and good acidity. Drink now through 2005.–P.M. • $44 • (10/31/1998) • **85**
Barbera d'Asti Montetusa 1994 • $NA • (10/31/1997) • **90**
Barbera d'Asti San Antonio Vieilles Vignes 1996: Seriously classy. Thick, dense, ripe and fairly new oakish, yet packed with lively fruit and good acidity, this craftily made red is incredibly concentrated, inky dark in color, ultrasmooth. Imagine violets, rose petals, tar, plum, cherry trees in full bloom, ripe wild strawberries. Drink now through 2007.–P.M. • $45 • (10/31/1998) • **92**
Barbera d'Asti San Antonio Vieilles Vignes 1993 • $40 • (10/31/1996) • **79**
Giarone 1991 • $NA • (10/31/1994) • **78**
I Fossaretti 1995: Something wrong here. Of four samples provided, two were dark in color, but tasted metallic and odd. The other two were corky.–P.M. • $45 • (10/31/1998) • **58**
I Fossaretti 1993 • $40 • (10/31/1996) • **89**
I Fossaretti 1985 • $34 • (12/31/1990) • **92**
Montetusa 1990 • $NA • (10/31/1994) • **80**
St. Marsan 1996: Both samples provided were corky.–P.M. • $44 • (10/31/1998) • **55**
St. Marsan 1995 • $45 • (10/31/1997) • **90**
St. Marsan 1994 • $38 • (10/31/1996) • **91**

BERUTTI, PIETRO

Barbera d'Alba La Spinona 1996: New-oakish style, with violet and toasted oak dominating the fruit. Burns a bit as the tannins seem tough and astringent. Drink now.–P.M. • $13 • (10/31/1998) • **79**
Dolcetto d'Alba La Spinona Vigneto Qualin 1997: Light-bodied and a bit odd, with woodsy, underbrush aromas and flavors. Bitter finish. Drink now.–P.M. • $11 • (10/31/1998) • **74**

BIANCHI

Gattinara Vigneto Valferana 1995: Very good, with attractive aromas of berry and vanilla and a hint of raspberry. Medium-bodied, with lots of vanilla and coconut from the new wood maturation. A biological wine. Drink now through 2002.–J.S. • $18 • (6/15/2000) • **86**
Nebbiolo Colline Novaresi 1997: A bit fruity but rather vegetal and funky. Crawls in the mouth. Tasted twice, with consistent notes.–J.S. • $12 • (6/15/2000) • **65**

BIANCHI, A.

Chianti Classico Regina Riserva 1990 • $20 • (11/15/1996) • **79**

BIBBIANO, TENUTA

Chianti Classico Montornello 1997: Light, fruity and easy, with plum and cedar character. Drink now.–J.S. • $20 • (11/30/1999) • **81**
Chianti Classico Montornello 1996: A very ripe style of Chianti, but I like it. Intense aromas of raisin and dried fruit. Medium-bodied, with well-integrated tannins and a ripe fruit and tobacco finish. A bit rustic. Drink now.–J.S. • $16 • (11/30/1999) • **83**
Chianti Classico Montornello 1995: Typical Sangiovese character of dried cherry, with an underlying citrus quality. Medium-bodied, with slightly dry tannins and a short finish. Tasted twice, with consistent notes. Drink now. –J.S. • $19 • (12/15/1998) • **81**
Chianti Classico Montornello 1993 • $NA • (10/31/1995) • **85**
Chianti Classico Vigna del Capannino Riserva 1996: Not a big red, but with very pretty plum and earth aromas and flavors. Medium-bodied, with silky tannins and a fresh finish. Drink now.–J.S. • $22 • (11/30/1999) • **86**
Chianti Classico Vigna del Capannino Riserva 1995: Delicious, well-crafted red. Lovely cherry and smoky character on the nose and palate. Medium-bodied, with round, succulent tannins and a ripe fruit aftertaste. Drink now through 2002.–J.S. • $20 • (12/15/1998) • **87**
Chianti Classico Vigna del Capannino Riserva 1993 • $NA • (10/31/1996) • **80**
Chianti Classico Vigna del Capannino Riserva 1990 • $NA • (2/28/1995) • **86**

BIGI

Orvieto Classico 1998: Fresh and easy, with light apple, fruit cocktail and mineral character. Light finish. Not much to it. Drink now.–J.S. • $9 • (2/29/2000) • **80**
Orvieto Classico Superiore Tenuta di Corbara 1998: Medium-bodied, with aromas of mineral, earth and smoke and a spicy pear-drop flavor. Slightly dull finish. Needs a bit more freshness, but good.–J.S. • $11 • (2/29/2000) • **79**
Orvieto Classico Torricella 1998: Simple, with lemon and white pepper character plus hints of apple. Medium-bodied, with good acidity and a fruity finish. Drink now.–J.S. • $12 • (2/29/2000) • **81**
Sangiovese Umbria 1997: Light, simple and diluted, with berry character and spice. Hard to get excited about.–J.S. • $10 • (2/29/2000) • **79**
Sangiovese Umbria Tenuta di Corbara 1998: A good, fruity red, with delicious plum and berry character, medium body and light, silky tannins. Drink now.–J.S. • $12 • (2/29/2000) • **84**
Vino Nobile di Montepulciano 1985 • $12 • (11/30/1990) • **81**

BINDELLA

Toscana Vallocaia 1996: Too much new oak maturation this year? Very grapey, with plum and cherry undertone on the nose. Medium-bodied, with lots of new oak tannins as well as its own. A bit dry on the finish. Drink now.–J.S. • $30 • (11/30/1999) • **84**
Toscana Vallocaia 1995: A thoroughly well-crafted red. Builds on your palate with interesting tobacco, berry and porcini aromas and flavors. Medium in body, with a caressing finish. Best after 2000.–J.S. • $30 • (12/15/1998) • **89**
Vallocaia 1994 • $30 • (9/30/1997) • **86**
Vallocaia 1993 • $23 • (10/31/1996) • **84**
Vallocaia 1990 • $23 • (11/30/1994) • **82**
Vallocaia 1989 • $25 • (11/30/1994) • **89**
Vino Nobile di Montepulciano 1995: A round red, with leaf, berry and cherry aromas and flavors. Medium-bodied, with medium tannins and a soft finish. Drink now.–J.S. • $15 • (12/15/1998) • **81**
Vino Nobile di Montepulciano 1994 • $16 • (9/30/1997) • **81**
Vino Nobile di Montepulciano 1990 • $14 • (2/29/1996) • **83**
Vino Nobile di Montepulciano Riserva 1993 • $23 • (9/30/1997) • **82**
Vino Nobile di Montepulciano Riserva 1990 • $22 • (2/29/1996) • **89**
Vino Nobile di Montepulciano Riserva 1985 • $27 • (10/31/1990) • **68**
Vino Nobile di Montepulciano Rubentino 1996: A very good Vino Nobile, with attractive plum, earth and bright cherry character. Medium-bodied,

Key: SS—Spectator Selection. CS—Cellar Selection. HR—Highly Recommended. $NA—Price not available. (BT)—Barrel tasting. (A)—Auction Price. For a key to the tasters' initials, see "How to Use These Listings."
Dates in parentheses represent the issues in which the ratings were published.

with a solid core of fruit and a complement of tannins. Better with a little age. Best after 2000.–J.S. • $18 • (11/30/1999) • **88**

BIONDI-SANTI

Brunello di Montalcino 1994: A traditional, slightly tough wine, with interesting aromas of rose, berry and dried cherry. Medium-bodied, with slightly hard tannins and a short finish. High acidity. Best after 2002.–J.S. • $85 • (11/30/1999) • **83**
Brunello di Montalcino 1993: Shows interesting white pepper and cherry aromas and flavors, but it's unbalanced and short on the palate. Medium-bodied, with a hint of raisins and a very tart finish. The acidity is too high to get better with age. Drink now.–J.S. • $42 • (12/15/1998) • **80**
Brunello di Montalcino 1990 • $58 • (11/30/1996) • **87**
Brunello di Montalcino 1988 • $65 • (4/30/1994) • **81**
Brunello di Montalcino Il Greppo 1990 • $50 • (10/31/1996) • **79**
Brunello di Montalcino Il Greppo 1983 • $66 • (11/30/1989) • **91**
Brunello di Montalcino Il Greppo 1982 • $45 • (10/15/1988) • **92**
Brunello di Montalcino Il Greppo 1981 • $40 • (9/15/1986) • **93**
Brunello di Montalcino Il Greppo 1980 • $40 • (9/15/1986) • **88**
Brunello di Montalcino Il Greppo 1978 • $45 • (9/15/1986) • **70**
Brunello di Montalcino Riserva 1993: A disaster for Biondi-Santi. Slightly odd aromas of old wood and bark, with ripe fruit. Medium-bodied, with light tannins and a dry finish. Going nowhere.–J.S. • $160 • (11/30/1999) • **77**
Brunello di Montalcino Riserva 1990 • $230 • (11/30/1996) • **92**
Brunello di Montalcino Riserva 1988 • $145 • (10/31/1994) • **87**
Brunello di Montalcino Riserva 1985 • $173 Ⓐ • (3/31/1992) • **82**
Brunello di Montalcino Riserva 1982 • $80 • (10/15/1988) CS • **94**
Rosso di Montalcino Il Greppo 1984 • $23 • (8/31/1988) • **83**

BIONDI-SANTI, JACOPO

Colli della Toscana Centrale Schidione 1995: A bit of a letdown for this wine. Blackberries with hints of dried herbs. Medium-bodied, with light tannins and a slightly diluted center palate, but shows good fruit character. Drink now.–J.S. • $100 • (11/30/1999) • **83**
Colli della Toscana Centrale Schidione 1993 • $107 • (9/30/1997) • **90**
Toscana Sassoalloro 1997: This pretty, well-crafted red has vivid aromas of dried cherry, strawberry and raspberry. Medium- to full-bodied, with fine tannins and a medium finish. Drink now.–J.S. • $35 • (11/30/1999) • **88**
Toscana Sassoalloro 1995: A wine with lovely harmony of fruit and tannins. Aromas of currants, tar and oak follow through on the palate. Medium-bodied, with well-integrated tannins. Drink now.–J.S. • $32 Ⓐ • (12/15/1998) • **88**
Toscana Sassoalloro 1994 • $28 • (9/30/1997) • **88**
Toscana Sassoalloro 1991 • $NA • (2/28/1995) • **87**

BISOL & FIGLI, DESIDERIO

Prosecco di Valdobbiadene Crede NV • $19 • (12/31/1997) • **85**

BOATINA, LA

Cabernet Sauvignon Collio 1997: A medium-bodied Cabernet Sauvignon with polished tannins but a slightly dry and austere finish. Will it improve with age? Drink now through 2002.–J.S. • $20 • (5/15/2000) • **83**
Chardonnay Collio 1998: Delicious white. Fresh aromas of peaches and apples. Medium-bodied, with lovely fruit and cookie flavors. Medium finish. Drink now.–J.S. • $15 • (3/31/2000) • **86**
Collio Pertè 1998: A delicious white with blanched almonds, cream and pie pastry character. Medium-bodied, with a creamy texture. Slightly overripe but very good. Not a wine to age. Drink now.–J.S. • $29 • (4/30/2000) • **88**
Collio Picol Maggiore 1994: Slightly vegetal, with some currant character. Medium-bodied, with firm tannins and a slightly lean finish. Better with food. Drink now.–J.S. • $25 • (5/15/2000) • **81**
Merlot Collio 1997: A Merlot with bright berry and cherry character. Medium-bodied, with polished tannins and a fruity finish, although a slightly hollow center palate. Best after 2000.–J.S. • $18 • (5/15/2000) • **85**
Merlot Collio 1993 • $11 • (6/15/1996) • **75**
Pinot Bianco Collio 1998: A very fresh white with appleskin, lemon and mineral character. Medium-bodied, with a clean finish. Drink now.–J.S. • $16 • (4/30/2000) • **86**
Pinot Grigio Collio 1998: Thick, with good concentration of almond and marzipan character. Full-bodied, with good fruit, but a bit dull on the finish. Drink now.–J.S. • $16 • (3/31/2000) • **82**
Pinot Grigio Collio 1996 • $16 • (6/30/1998) • **86**
Sauvignon Collio 1998: Not very Sauvignon-like but there are very pretty almond, honey, spice and pineapple aromas to this white. Medium-bodied, with good acidity and a long apple-mineral aftertaste. Well done. Drink now.–J.S. • $16 • (4/30/2000) • **86**
Tocai Friulano Collio 1998: A white with plenty of apple, coconut and pineapple skin. Medium-bodied, with light acidity and a fresh finish. Drink now.–J.S. • $16 • (4/30/2000) • **85**
Verduzzo 1989 • $17 • (1/31/1992) • **84**

BOCCE, FATTORIA LE

Chianti Classico 1997: This has extremely ripe fruit, with raisin, fig and berry aromas. Full-bodied, with velvety tannins and a fruity finish. A bit rustic. Drink now through 2002.–J.S. • $13 • (11/30/1999) • **86**
Chianti Classico 1996: A very raisiny almost burnt character on the nose. Medium-bodied, overextracted, with dry tannins and raisiny flavors.–J.S. • $12 • (12/15/1998) • **73**
Chianti Classico 1995 • $12 • (9/30/1997) • **80**
Chianti Classico 1994 • $11 • (10/31/1996) • **83**
Chianti Classico 1993 • $9 • (10/31/1995) • **84**
Chianti Classico 1992 • $9 • (2/28/1995) • **80**
Chianti Classico 1991 • $13 • (10/31/1993) • **81**
Chianti Classico 1990 • $11 • (9/15/1992) HR • **90**
Chianti Classico Riserva 1995: Not serious, but delicious. An extremely floral and fruity red. Medium-bodied, with light tannins and a fruity finish. Drink now.–J.S. • $16 • (12/15/1998) • **85**
Chianti Classico Riserva 1993 • $16 • (9/30/1997) • **86**
Chianti Classico Riserva 1991 • $14 • (10/31/1995) • **84**
Chianti Classico Riserva 1990 • $15 • (2/28/1995) • **85**
Chianti Classico Riserva 1988 • $16 • (9/15/1992) • **86**
Toscana Vigna del Paladino 1995: A good Sangiovese with plenty of ripe fruit character, crisp acidity and a refreshing finish. Body is medium to light, tannins are fine. Drink now.–J.S. • $17 • (12/15/1998) • **84**
Vigna del Paladino 1990 • $NA • (10/31/1993) • **84**

BOGLIETTI, ENZO

Barbera d'Alba 1993 • $16 • (3/31/1997) • **81**
Barbera d'Alba Vigna dei Romani 1993 • $30 • (3/31/1997) • **88**
Barolo Vigna delle Brunate 1992 • $38 • (1/01/1997) • **80**
Barolo Vigna delle Brunate 1991 • $32 • (1/01/1997) • **83**
Dolcetto d'Alba 1995 • $17 • (5/31/1997) • **85**
Nebbiolo delle Langhe 1993 • $13 • (5/31/1997) • **80**

BOLLA

Amarone della Valpolicella 1985 • $22 • (9/15/1992) • **85**
Amarone della Valpolicella Classico 1995: Cheesy and earthy, with very ripe fruit. Full-bodied and thick, but very raisiny and aggressive. Not completely clean. Not my glass of Amarone. Tasted twice, with consistent notes.–J.S. • $45 • (5/15/2000) • **78**
Amarone della Valpolicella Classico 1994: Promises a little more on the nose than the palate, but delicious nonetheless. Wonderful ripe berry, light raisin and rose aromas. Medium-bodied, with light tannins and a fresh, light finish. Drink now.–J.S. • $40 • (1/01/2000) • **85**
Amarone della Valpolicella Classico 1990 • $30 • (5/31/1998) • **89**
Amarone della Valpolicella Classico 1989 • $20 • (1/31/1997) SS • **91**
Amarone della Valpolicella Classico 1988 • $18 • (6/15/1996) CS • **91**
Amarone della Valpolicella Classico 1986 • $18 • (10/31/1994) • **85**
Bardolino 1995 • $8 • (1/31/1997) • **77**
Bardolino 1990 • $8 • (1/31/1992) • **79**
Bardolino Classico 1993 • $7 • (10/31/1994) • **81**
Bardolino Classico 1991 • $8 • (9/15/1992) • **81**
Cabernet Sauvignon Creso 1994: Dominated by new toasted oak at the moment, but there's some interesting plum character beneath. Medium-bodied, with medium tannins and a fresh finish. Too much new oak. Drink now.–J.S. • $28 • (5/15/2000) • **82**
Cabernet Sauvignon Creso 1993: Attractive floral and berry aromas and flavors. Medium-bodied, with light tannins, almond and fruit flavors and an easy, light finish. A Cabernet beginning to fade. Drink now.–J.S. • $30 • (1/01/2000) • **84**
Cabernet Sauvignon Veneto Creso 1991 • $26 • (6/15/1998) • **88**
Chardonnay 1996 • $8 • (6/15/1997) • **83**
Creso 1987 • $33 • (3/31/1993) • **86**
Creso 1986 • $33 • (3/31/1993) • **87**
Merlot Piave 1996 • $8 • (6/15/1997) • **81**

ITALY

BOLLA

Merlot Piave 1995 • $8 • (1/31/1997) • **77**
Merlot Piave 1994 • $8 • (1/31/1996) • **82**
Merlot Piave 1993 • $7 • (10/31/1994) • **83**
Merlot Venezie Colforte 1998: Pretty combination of plums, berries and vanilla throughout. Medium-bodied, with light tannins and a fresh finish. Easy-drinking. Drink now.–J.S. • $14 • (5/15/2000) • **84**
Merlot Venezie Colforte 1996 • $30 • (4/30/1998) • **84**
Pinot Grigio 1996 • $7 • (6/15/1997) • **82**
Pinot Grigio Venezie 1998: Rather candied, with spice and fruit. Light finish. Dull.–J.S. • $8 • (3/31/2000) • **77**
Recioto di Soave 1990 • $NA • (9/15/1992) • **83**
Sangiovese di Romagna 1995 • $8 • (3/31/1997) • **82**
Sangiovese di Romagna 1994 • $6 • (2/29/1996) • **82**
Soave Classico 1998: A pleasant white, with peach and melon character. Medium-bodied, with a fresh, clean finish. Drink now.–J.S. • $8 • (3/31/2000) • **83**
Soave Classico 1996 • $8 • (6/15/1997) • **79**
Soave Classico Tufaie 1998: Rather subdued on the nose, but showing lovely apple, honey and mineral flavors. Medium-bodied, with a fresh finish. Drink now.–J.S. • $10 • (3/31/2000) • **85**
Soave Classico Tufaie 1996 • $15 • (6/30/1998) • **85**
Valpolicella 1997: Medium-bodied, with a fresh and delicate character of watermelon, berry and dried cherry. Crisp finish. Drink now.–J.S. • $8 • (6/30/1999) • **83**
Valpolicella 1996 • $8 • (6/15/1997) • **78**
Valpolicella 1990 • $8 • (9/15/1992) • **75**
Valpolicella Classico 1995 • $8 • (1/31/1997) • **82**
Valpolicella Classico Le Poiane 1995: A delicious Valpo, with plenty of floral and blackberry character. Medium-bodied, with light yet silky tannins and a long, fruity finish. Drink now.–J.S. • $12 • (1/01/2000) • **86**
Valpolicella Classico Le Poiane 1994 • $30 • (4/30/1998) • **85**
Valpolicella Classico Vigneti di Jago 1987 • $13 • (9/15/1992) • **81**
Valpolicella Classico Vigneti di Jago 1986 • $12 • (12/31/1990) • **78**
Valpolicella Vigneti di San Vito 1990 • $NA • (9/15/1992) • **78**

BOLLINI

Cabernet Sauvignon Grave del Friuli 1989 • $12 • (2/28/1995) • **74**
Cabernet Sauvignon Grave del Friuli 1987 • $11 • (12/15/1992) • **76**
Cabernet Sauvignon Trentino Reserve Selection 1989 • $15 • (4/30/1994) • **80**
Chardonnay Trentino 1996 • $11 • (12/15/1997) • **84**
Merlot Trentino 1996 • $11 • (4/30/1998) • **82**
Merlot Trentino 1992 • $8 • (2/28/1995) • **77**
Merlot Trentino 1990 • $9 • (12/15/1992) • **77**
Merlot Trentino Reserve Selection 1994 • $16 • (12/15/1997) • **84**
Merlot Trentino Reserve Selection 1990 • $15 • (4/30/1994) • **86**
Pinot Grigio Grave del Friuli Reserve Selection 1997: Very fruity, with grapefruit, melon and lemon character. Medium-bodied, with lively acidity and a clean, refreshing finish. Delicious. Drink now.–J.S. • $16 • (5/15/2000) • **86**
Pinot Grigio Grave del Friuli Reserve Selection 1996 • $15 • (5/15/1998) • **86**
Pinot Grigio Trentino 1997 • $11 • (5/31/1998) • **85**
Pinot Grigio Trentino 1996 • $10 • (7/31/1997) • **83**

BOLOGNA, GIACOMO

Barbera d'Asti Ai Suma 1996: Incredible. Purple-black in color, full-bodied, hedonistically rich and so ripe it tastes almost like a late-harvest with residual sugar. Bursts with clean, pure and vibrant cassis flavors accented by deftly dosed toasted oak. Very youthful on the superharmonious, smooth and fruity finish. The quality matches the reputation of this cult wine. Bravo! Drink now.–P.M. • $40 Ⓐ • (10/31/1998) • **93**
Barbera d'Asti Ai Suma 1995 • $40 Ⓐ • (10/31/1997) • **87**
Barbera d'Asti Braida 1993 • $38 • (10/31/1996) • **82**
Barbera d'Asti Bricco dell'Uccellone 1996: Crisp, intense and medium-bodied, with tart cherry flavors. Shows a minerally component, but it's a tough customer now, with distinct acidity accompanying the red berries. Time might soften it, though it should cozy up to lots of food. Best from 2001 through 2006.–P.M. • $40 • (11/15/1999) • **83**
Barbera d'Asti Bricco dell'Uccellone 1995: This modern style of Barbera shows lovely plum, violet and cassis flavors, all presented in a deftly oaked, medium-bodied package that comes together harmoniously on the ripe-tasting, deliciously smooth finish. Drink now through 2003.–P.M. • $30 • (10/31/1998) • **88**
Barbera d'Asti Bricco della Bigotta 1994 • $40 • (10/31/1997) • **83**
Barbera d'Asti Bricco della Bigotta 1991 • $NA • (1/01/1994) • **83**
Barbera di Rocchetta Tanaro Bricco dell'Uccellone 1993 • $38 • (10/31/1996) • **82**
Barbera Piedmont Bricco dell' Uccellone 1991 • $47 • (1/01/1994) • **82**
Barbera Piedmont Bricco dell' Uccellone 1988 • $45 • (3/15/1991) • **91**
Barbera Piedmont Bricco dell' Uccellone 1987 • $45 • (3/15/1991) • **88**
Barbera Piedmont Bricco dell' Uccellone 1986 • $38 • (3/15/1991) • **89**
Barbera Piedmont Bricco dell' Uccellone 1985 • $33 • (8/31/1989) • **88**
Barbera Piedmont Bricco della Bigotta 1988 • $40 • (3/15/1991) • **92**
Barbera Piedmont Bricco della Bigotta 1987 • $34 • (3/15/1991) • **88**
Barbera Piedmont Bricco della Bigotta 1986 • $34 • (3/15/1991) • **88**
Brachetto d'Acqui 1987 • $16 • (3/31/1990) • **84**
Monferrato Il Bacialé 1997: Herbal and stemmy, offering sweet-tasting character but also a vegetal undertow. Sour finish.–P.M. • $18 • (11/15/1999) • **75**
Monferrato Il Bacialé 1996: Unpretentious, fresh and slightly spritzy, this earthy, fruit-driven, youthful-tasting, ripe wine is pleasant to drink now slightly chilled, as you can enjoy the pepper, plum and blackberry aromas and flavors. Succulent finish.–P.M. • $18 • (10/31/1998) • **84**

BONCI, VALLEROSA

Verdicchio dei Castelli di Jesi Classico San Michele 1996 • $10 • (10/15/1997) • **83**

BORGHINI BALDOVINETTI

Armaiolo di San Fabiano 1991: This red is slightly rustic, but it still has good structure, showing blackberry, black pepper and dried spice aromas. Full-bodied, chewy and fresh for a '91, with full tannins and a smoked almond, earth and fruit aftertaste. Drink now.–J.S. • $32 • (1/01/1999) • **86**
Toscana Armaiolo di San Fabiano 1995: An elegant Tuscan red. Pretty raspberry and cherry aromas follow through on the palate. Medium-bodied, with light to medium tannins and a fresh finish. Drink now.–J.S. • $34 • (6/30/1999) • **85**

BORGO AL CASTELLO

Primitivo Tarantino Mother Zin 1996 • $10 • (1/01/1998) • **85**

BORGO CONVENTI

Braida Nuova 1994: A well-polished, rich red, with an impressive dark ruby color and complex aromas of blackberry, earth and violet. Full-bodied, with full, silky tannins and a long, caressing finish. A blend of Cabernet Sauvignon, Cabernet Franc and Merlot. Drink now through 2004.–J.S. • $40 • (1/01/2000) • **89**
Chardonnay Collio 1998: Good melon and apple character in this medium-bodied Chardonnay. Fresh finish. Drink now.–J.S. • $19 • (3/31/2000) • **85**
Chardonnay Collio Colle Russian 1997: Very good Chardonnay character, with apple, pineapple and toasted oak. Medium-bodied, round and rich, with a medium finish. Drink now.–J.S. • $30 • (3/31/2000) • **88**
Merlot Collio 1998: Fresh and fruity Merlot with berry, olive and cherry character. Medium body. Light tannins, caressing finish. Drink now.–J.S. • $20 • (5/15/2000) • **85**
Merlot Collio 1997: This wine shows a good core of fruit and a very herbal character. Medium-bodied, with medium, firm tannins and a short finish. Drink now.–J.S. • $22 • (1/01/2000) • **85**
Merlot Collio 1987 • $15 • (3/31/1989) • **84**
Pinot Grigio Collio 1998: A pleasant and fresh white, with pear and apple character. Medium-bodied, with a clean finish. Drink now.–J.S. • $19 • (3/31/2000) • **86**
Pinot Grigio Collio 1997: Light aromas of pear, flowers and lemon. Medium-bodied, with lemon and mineral character, but slightly bitter on the finish. Drink now.–J.S. • $20 • (1/01/2000) • **81**
Sauvignon Collio 1998: Very intense canned asparagus and green, stemmy character. Hard to get excited about. –J.S. • $19 • (4/30/2000) • **74**
Tocai Friulano Collio 1998: Medium-bodied, with canned fruit cocktail character. A bit diluted on the finish.–J.S. • $19 • (3/31/2000) • **79**
Venezia Giulia Braida Nuova 1996: A bit too much herbal Cabernet character in this wine, but it's medium-bodied, with a rounded texture and a fresh finish. Drink now.–J.S. • $40 • (5/15/2000) • **82**

Key: SS—Spectator Selection. CS—Cellar Selection. HR—Highly Recommended. $NA—Price not available. (BT)—Barrel tasting. Ⓐ—Auction Price.
For a key to the tasters' initials, see "How to Use These Listings."
Dates in parentheses represent the issues in which the ratings were published.

BORGO MAGREDO

Cabernet Sauvignon Grave del Friuli 1994 • $8 • (6/15/1996) • **82**
Cabernet Sauvignon Grave del Friuli 1990 • $NA • (2/28/1995) • **72**
Cabernet Sauvignon Grave del Friuli Braida Vieri 1997: Some olive and chocolate character to this fresh young wine. Turns a bit bubbly and simple on the palate.–J.S. • $10 • (5/15/2000) • **78**
Chardonnay Grave del Friuli 1996 • $9 • (5/31/1998) • **78**
Chardonnay Grave del Friuli Braida Longa 1998: A delicious Chardonnay. Lovely aromas of flowers and apple follow through to a medium-bodied palate, with good acidity and a fruity, piecrust aftertaste. Drink now. –J.S. • $10 • (2/29/2000) • **86**
Merlot Grave del Friuli 1998: A rather weedy red with some berry character. Medium body. Light, fruity finish.–J.S. • $10 • (5/15/2000) • **79**
Merlot Grave del Friuli 1996 • $9 • (5/31/1998) • **84**
Merlot Grave del Friuli 1995 • $9 • (3/31/1997) • **83**
Merlot Grave del Friuli 1994 • $8 • (2/29/1996) • **75**
Merlot Grave del Friuli Braida Moral 1997: Fresh and grapey, with hints of herbs and wet earth. Medium-bodied, with light tannins and a crisp finish. Drink now.–J.S. • $10 • (5/15/2000) • **82**
Pinot Grigio Grave del Friuli 1998: Beautiful freshness of mineral, honey and apple defines this white from northeast Italy. It's medium in body, with lively acidity and a long mineral finish. Very good indeed, and won't strain the budget. Drink now.–J.S. • $10 • (2/29/2000) • **87**
Pinot Grigio Grave del Friuli 1996 • $9 • (5/31/1998) • **84**
Pinot Grigio Grave del Friuli Braida Gaia 1998: Fresh and gorgeous. Lovely spice, honey and apple aromas. Medium- to full-bodied, with delicious fruit flavors and a long, clean finish. Drink now.–J.S. • $11 • (2/29/2000) • **88**
Refosco Grave del Friuli 1994 • $8 • (4/30/1996) • **77**
Sauvignon Grave del Friuli 1996 • $9 • (6/15/1998) • **84**
Tocai Friulano Grave del Friuli 1996 • $9 • (5/31/1998) • **81**

BORGO SCOPETO, TENUTA

Chardonnay Toscana Violette 1997: Apple aromas, tinged with a rich, maple syrup, almond and smoke, and similar flavors. Medium-bodied, with moderate acidity and a creamy finish. A very good, clean Chardonnay, just a bit too much oak. Drink now.–J.S. • $15 • (12/15/1998) • **86**
Chardonnay Toscana Violette 1996 • $NA • (9/30/1997) • **85**
Chianti Classico 1996: Impressive for its gorgeous aromas of ripe strawberry and rasperry, with a hint of chocolate. Medium-bodied, with fine tannins and a light finish. Drink now.–J.S. • $12 • (12/15/1998) • **86**
Chianti Classico 1994 • $12 • (9/30/1997) • **86**
Chianti Classico 1993 • $12 • (10/31/1996) • **75**
Chianti Classico 1992 • $NA • (2/28/1995) • **78**
Chianti Classico 1991 • $10 • (10/31/1994) • **79**
Chianti Classico Riserva 1995: Pretty aromas of plums and pepper follow through on the palate. Of medium body, with medium tannins and high acidity. Slightly austere, dry finish. Drink now.–J.S. • $24 • (12/15/1998) • **85**
Chianti Classico Riserva 1993 • $23 • (10/31/1996) • **86**
Chianti Classico Riserva 1990 • $22 • (10/31/1994) • **83**

BORGOGNO, LODOVICO

Barbaresco Virna Riserva 1990: Shows prune and dried cherry flavors, but turns astringent on the fading finish. Very disappointing for a '90. Past its prime.–K.M. • $38 • (8/31/1998) • **78**
Barolo Preda Sarmassa 1993 • $NA • (10/31/1997) • **85**
Barolo Virna 1993: Astringent, with faded prune flavors and a brown-sugar note on the finish. Past its prime.–K.M. • $30 • (8/31/1998) • **74**
Barolo Virna Riserva 1990: Mature before its time, with fading flavors. Smooth but simple. Disappointing for the vintage. Past its prime.–K.M. • $43 • (8/31/1998) • **79**

BORGOGNO & FIGLI, GIACOMO

Barbaresco Riserva 1990 • $22 • (6/15/1997) • **86**
Barbera d'Alba 1990 • $10 • (6/15/1994) • **88**
Barolo 1995: A big, ripe and round Barolo, offering a kick of fresh acidity to accompany the red berry, plum, smoke and toast notes unfolding on the harmonious but tannic finish. Drink now through 2003.–P.M. • $30 • (11/15/1999) • **84**
Barolo 1988 • $20 • (6/15/1994) • **88**

BORTOLUZZI

Chardonnay Isonzo del Friuli 1998: A Chardonnay with lots of apple pie and cream character. Medium- to full-bodied, with a round texture and a long, flavorful finish. Drink now.–J.S. • $14 • (3/31/2000) • **87**
Chardonnay Isonzo del Friuli 1996 • $14 • (6/15/1998) • **83**
Merlot Collio 1998: A fresh and easy red. Lovely perfumes of violets and cherries follow through to a medium-bodied palate with light tannins. Clean finish. Drink now.–J.S. • $16 • (5/15/2000) • **83**
Merlot Collio 1995 • $14 • (6/15/1998) • **84**
Pinot Grigio Isonzo del Friuli 1998: Lovely floral and apple character. Medium- to full-bodied, with lots of fruit and a long, clean, crisp finish. Drink now through 2001.–J.S. • $14 • (3/31/2000) • **87**
Sauvignon Isonzo del Friuli 1998: A ripe Sauvignon with lovely pineapple, honey and apple character. Medium- to full-bodied, with lots of fruit and a long, long finish. Drink now.–J.S. • $14 • (4/30/2000) • **88**

BOSCAINI, PAOLO

Amarone della Valpolicella Classico Ca' de Loi 1993: Well done, in a traditional style. Prune, spice and coffee notes seem a bit advanced, but the wine shows some of the rich, supple texture and grip of Amarone. Drink now through 2000.–B.S. • $45 • (7/31/1998) • **84**
Amarone della Valpolicella Classico Ca' de Loi 1988 • $39 • (6/15/1997) • **89**
Amarone della Valpolicella Classico Marano 1994: Good richness, almost finding that slippery, glycerin groove on the palate to carry the coffee and plum flavors, but still finishes tannic. Drink now through 2002.–B.S. • $29 • (7/31/1998) • **85**
Amarone della Valpolicella Classico Marano 1988 • $23 • (9/15/1992) • **83**
Pinot Grigio Alto Adige Firmiano 1997: Delicate peach and apple flavors marry with a medium-bodied texture that turns firm on the finish, with an almond aftertaste.–B.S. • $15 • (7/31/1998) • **81**
Pinot Grigio Valdadige La Cros 1997: Refreshing and lemony, this almond-flavored Pinot Grigio draws elegance from firm acidity. Slightly bitter finish. Drink now.–B.S. • $12 • (7/31/1998) • **81**
Santa Stefano de le Cane 1993 • $16 • (6/15/1997) • **83**
Santo Stefano de le Cane 1988 • $15 • (9/15/1992) • **80**
Santo Stefano Vino di Ripasso 1994: A complex wine whose cherry, woodsy and spicy aromas and flavors are muted today, and while it's concentrated and long on the finish, it seems to lack the extra focus and clarity to really stand out. May improve with time; try through 2000.–B.S. • $16 • (7/31/1998) • **84**
Soave Classico Superiore Monteleone 1997: Aromas are mute in this young white, but there are quince and mineral notes, and body on the palate. Picks up a touch of honey on the finish. Drink now.–B.S. • $11 • (7/31/1998) • **82**
Valpolicella Classico San Ciriaco 1997: A fresh, fruity, soft style of Valpolicella for early drinking. Its cherry flavor and gentle structure finish with a pleasant austerity. Drink now.–B.S. • $14 • (7/31/1998) • **82**
Valpolicella Classico San Ciriaco 1995 • $14 • (6/15/1997) • **78**
Valpolicella Classico Superiore Marano 1996: On the lean side, this has decent concentration and balance, but finishes a little tough. Food should smooth it out. Drink now.–B.S. • $11 • (7/31/1998) • **81**
Valpolicella Classico Superiore Marano 1990 • $10 • (9/15/1992) • **81**

BOSCARELLI, PODERI

Chianti Colli Senesi 1993 • $15 • (3/31/1997) • **79**
Rosso di Montepulciano 1992 • $14 • (8/31/1995) • **82**
Toscana Marchesi de Ferrari Corradi 1997: A thoroughly pleasant Sangiovese, with berry and tobacco aromas and flavors. Medium-bodied, with fine tannins and a plummy aftertaste. Drink now.–J.S. • $15 • (11/30/1999) • **85**
Toscana Marchesi de Ferrari Corradi 1995: A velvety red that gives plenty of immediate pleasure but will improve with bottle age. Fresh floral and blackberry aromas. Medium-bodied,with round tannins and a fruity, caressing finish. Drink now.–J.S. • $43 • (12/15/1998) • **88**
Toscana Marchesi de Ferrari Corradi 1994 • $NA • (9/30/1997) • **85**
Toscana Marchesi de Ferrari Corradi 1993 • $39 • (3/31/1997) • **87**
Toscana Marchesi de Ferrari Corradi 1985 • $30 • (2/15/1989) • **92**
Toscana Marchesi de Ferrari Corradi 1983 • $29 • (6/30/1988) • **85**
Vino Nobile di Montepulciano 1996: This drink-me Nobile has plenty of plum and berry character, with hints of earth and leather. Medium-bodied, with silky tannins and a medium finish. Drink now through 2001.–J.S. • $27 • (11/30/1999) • **87**

BOSCARELLI, PODERI

Vino Nobile di Montepulciano 1995: A pretty and well-made Nobile, with fresh berry and chocolate character. Medium-bodied, with fine tannins and a long finish. Drink now.–J.S. • $27 • (12/15/1998) • **87**
Vino Nobile di Montepulciano 1994 • $25 • (9/30/1997) • **86**
Vino Nobile di Montepulciano 1990 • $22 • (2/29/1996) • **89**
Vino Nobile di Montepulciano 1981 • $10 • (7/01/1986) • **71**
Vino Nobile di Montepulciano del Nocio Riserva 1993 • $NA • (3/31/1997) • **81**
Vino Nobile di Montepulciano del Nocio Riserva 1985 • $15 • (6/15/1990) • **76**
Vino Nobile di Montepulciano del Nocio Riserva 1981 • $11 • (10/31/1986) • **70**
Vino Nobile di Montepulciano Vigna del Nocio 1996: Very well structured, with aromas of dried cherry, bark and tobacco. Medium- to full-bodied, with velvety tannins and a fruity finish. Needs a bit of age. Drink now.–J.S. • $40 • (11/30/1999) • **89**
Vino Nobile di Montepulciano Vigna del Nocio 1995: Superb. Superplummy, with a lot of berry and ripe fruit character. Medium- to full-bodied, with fine tannins and a fruity aftertaste. This can age. Proves serious Vino Nobile does exist. Best after 2001.–J.S. • $37 • (12/15/1998) • **91**

BOSCO NESTORE

Montepulciano d'Abruzzo Riserva 1994: A medium-bodied red, with peppery, floral, cherrylike character, a smooth texture and light tannins. Drink now. • $10 • (8/31/1998) • **83**

BOSSI, CASTELLO DI

Chianti Classico 1996: Intense raspberry aromas and flavors in this red, which seems to be holding a bit in reserve. Medium-bodied, with medium yet refined tannins. Moderate finish. Drink now.–J.S. • $14 • (12/15/1998) • **87**
Chianti Classico 1995 • $NA • (9/30/1997) • **84**
Chianti Classico 1994 • $NA • (10/31/1996) • **77**
Chianti Classico 1993 • $NA • (10/31/1995) • **84**
Chianti Classico Berardo Riserva 1995: A sexy young red. Gorgeous perfumed, floral and raspberry aromas. Medium-bodied, with medium, velvety tannins and a long, caressing finish. Best after 2000.–J.S. • $20 • (12/15/1998) • **89**
Chianti Classico Berardo Riserva 1994 • $19 • (9/30/1997) • **84**
Chianti Classico Berardo Riserva 1993 • $17 • (10/31/1996) • **82**
Chianti Classico Berardo Riserva 1991 • $NA • (10/31/1995) • **79**
Toscana Corbaia 1995: A seriously polished, well-made red, oozing with currant and cassis aromas. Medium- to full-bodied, with firm tannins and a slightly austere finish. Needs time. Best after 2000.–J.S. • $30 • (12/15/1998) • **89**
Toscana Corbaia 1994 • $NA • (9/30/1997) • **88**
Toscana Corbaia 1993 • $NA • (10/31/1996) • **86**
Toscana Corbaia 1990 • $32 • (12/31/1995) • **89**
Toscana Corbaia 1988 • $NA • (10/31/1995) • **84**

BOTROMAGNO

Gravina 1998: Riesling fans (and their wallets) will like this Italian white. It's extremely aromatic, with lemon, lime and floral aromas and a hint of aniseed. Medium-bodied, with good acidity and a long, lively, fruity finish. Delicious. Drink now.–J.S. • $9 • (5/31/2000) • **86**

BRACCESCA, LA

Merlot Toscana 1997: Extremely floral, with loads of violet, orchid and berry aromas. Medium- to full-bodied, with well-integrated tannins and a medium finish. Pretty mineral and berry flavors. Best after 2000.–J.S. • $57 • (6/15/2000) • **89**
Vino Nobile di Montepulciano 1997: A wine with good fruit but slightly diluted at the end. Good dark ruby color, with blackberry, cherry and licorice aromas. Full- to medium-bodied, with velvety tannins and lots of ripe fruit. Lacks a bit of definition. Drink now.–J.S. • $26 • (6/15/2000) • **87**
Vino Nobile di Montepulciano 1996: A good Vino Nobile bubbling over with cassis, violet and fruit. Medium-bodied, with velvety tannins and a medium finish. Lacks a bit of fruit midpalate. Best after 2000.–J.S. • $26 • (11/30/1999) • **86**

Key: SS—Spectator Selection. CS—Cellar Selection. HR—Highly Recommended. $NA—Price not available. (BT)—Barrel tasting. Ⓐ—Auction Price.
For a key to the tasters' initials, see "How to Use These Listings."
Dates in parentheses represent the issues in which the ratings were published.

BRANCAIA, PODERE LA

Chianti Classico 1996: A beautiful Chianti of blackberry, mushroom and plum character. Medium-bodied, with medium, soft tannins and a fruity aftertaste. Drink now.–J.S. • $15 • (12/15/1998) • **86**
Toscana Brancaia 1996: A harmonious and mouth-caressing red, this is complex, with berry, mint, raspberry and cherry character. Medium-bodied, with velvety tannins and a ripe fruit finish. Still a little tight. Drink now.–J.S. • $40 • (11/30/1999) • **89**
Toscana Brancaia 1995 • $NA • (9/30/1997) • **85**
Toscana Brancaia 1993 • $NA • (10/31/1996) • **87**
Toscana Brancaia 1991 • $NA • (2/28/1995) • **86**

BRANDOLINI D'ADDA, CONTI

Merlot Grave del Friuli Vistorta 1995 • $17 • (5/31/1998) • **86**
Merlot Grave del Friuli Vistorta 1993 • $14 • (1/01/1997) • **86**
Merlot Grave del Friuli Vistorta 1992 • $14 • (4/30/1996) • **88**

BREZZA & FIGLI, GIACOMO

Barbera d'Alba Cannubi 1996: Very crisp, a bit herbal and metallic, lacking the round richness of a top Barbera. Tart finish.–P.M. • $20 • (9/15/1999) • **71**
Barbera d'Alba Cannubi 1995: An intense, earthy style of Barbera, packed with berry, grilled meat and smoke flavors. Medium-bodied and quite crisp, even a bit lean. Juicy finish. Drink now through 2001.–P.M. • $NA • (10/31/1998) • **80**
Barbera d'Alba Cannubi 1993 • $NA • (10/31/1996) • **86**
Barbera d'Alba Cannubi 1991 • $NA • (10/31/1994) • **77**
Barbera d'Alba Cannubi Muscatel 1996: Full of fresh and succulent red berry aromas and flavors, plus an earthy whiff, this is rather crisp in style but a good match for food. Drink now through 2001.–P.M. • $20 • (9/15/1999) • **82**
Barbera d'Alba Cannubi Muscatel 1995: Straightforward and a bit diluted, with somewhat dry tannins and an earth and red berry character. Disjointed finish.–P.M. • $15 • (10/31/1998) • **76**
Barolo Bricco Sarmassa 1993: Shows cedar, tobacco-box and tea leaf flavors, but little in the way of ripe, rich, sweet fruit. The firm backbone of acidity and tannins suggests an ager. Drink now through 2005.–P.M. • $43 • (10/31/1998) • **82**
Barolo Cannubi 1995: A slight herbal note creeps into the otherwise good red berry and blackberry character of this medium-bodied, crisp Barolo.–P.M. • $50 • (11/15/1999) • **79**
Barolo Cannubi 1994: Fruity, with cherry and raspberry notes, but also some herbal character, it turns quite astringent on the finish.–P.M. • $NA • (10/31/1998) • **77**
Barolo Cannubi 1991 • $30 • (10/31/1995) • **86**
Barolo Cannubi 1991 • $NA • (10/31/1996) • **88**
Barolo Cannubi 1990 • $40 • (10/31/1995) • **88**
Barolo Cannubi 1989 • $NA • (10/31/1994) • **88**
Barolo Sarmassa 1994: Firm and tough, but with a good grip of mineral and wet earth character, some plum and black cherry. A fairly austere, medium-bodied style. Tannins are slightly bitter on the finish. Drink through 2005.–P.M. • $NA • (10/31/1998) • **83**
Barolo Sarmassa 1993 • $NA • (10/31/1997) • **87**
Barolo Sarmassa 1991 • $NA • (10/31/1996) • **90**
Dolcetto d'Alba San Lorenzo 1998: This well-made Dolcetto is satisfying in a clean way. Nice balance, hinting at spice and mocha, showing lively, ripe red berry flavors. Drink now.–P.M. • $18 • (11/15/1999) • **83**
Dolcetto d'Alba San Lorenzo 1997: Rather straightforward, with mouthpuckering acidity, firm tannins and modest fruit. Tough finish.–P.M. • $16 • (10/31/1998) • **79**
Dolcetto d'Alba San Lorenzo 1996: This typical Dolcetto is quite firm, but contact with air makes it lusher. Offers some vivid, lively berry, earth and dried herb flavors. Clean and pure, slightly tough on the finish, this will cut through cheesy pizza. Drink now.–P.M. • $13 • (10/31/1998) • **85**
Dolcetto d'Alba San Lorenzo 1993 • $13 • (10/31/1995) • **87**

BROLIO

Chardonnay Toscana Torricella 1996: A lot of wood. Some orange peel and apple aromas and flavors, but the new oak barrels really dominate. Full-bodied. Chalk and apple on the finish. A bit dull for a Chardonnay. Drink now.–J.S. • $20 • (12/15/1998) • **82**

ITALY

Chianti Classico 1997: A grapey Chianti, with hints of wet earth and licorice. Medium-bodied, with silky tannins and an aftertaste of chocolate and tobacco. Drink now through 2001.–J.S. • $14 • (10/31/1999) • **86**

Chianti Classico 1996: A straightforward Chianti with dried cherry and light floral aromas and flavors. Light in body and tannin, crisp on the finish. Drink now.–J.S. • $13 • (12/15/1998) • **82**

Chianti Classico 1995 • $13 • (9/30/1997) • **86**

Chianti Classico 1994 • $10 • (10/31/1996) • **85**

Chianti Classico 1990 • $11 • (9/15/1992) • **87**

Chianti Classico 1988 • $10 • (9/15/1991) • **84**

Chianti Classico 1987 • $12 • (10/31/1991) • **84**

Chianti Classico del Barone Riserva 1983 • $11 • (11/30/1989) • **85**

Chianti Classico del Barone Riserva 1983 • $26 • (10/31/1994) • **81**

Chianti Classico del Barone Riserva 1978 • $11 • (6/01/1985) • **90**

Chianti Classico Riserva 1994 • $17 • (9/30/1997) • **88**

Chianti Classico Riserva 1993 • $14 • (10/31/1996) • **86**

Chianti Classico Riserva 1990 • $13 • (1/01/1996) • **87**

Chianti Classico Riserva 1988 • $13 • (10/31/1994) • **87**

Chianti Classico Riserva 1985 • $12 • (9/15/1991) • **86**

Chianti Classico Riserva 1983 • $10 • (5/15/1990) • **80**

Sangiovese Tuscany 1993 • $9 • (2/28/1995) • **80**

Sangiovese Tuscany 1991 • $9 • (7/31/1994) • **85**

Toscana Casalferro 1996: An outstanding Sangiovese from Brolio, with complex aromas of porcino, crushed berry and cherry and loads of toasted French oak. Full-bodied, with layers of velvety tannins and a long, long finish. Big and rich. Needs time. Best after 2000.–J.S. • $37 • (11/30/1999) • **90**

Toscana Casalferro 1995: Extremely polished. Deep and rich aromas of ripe berry, with a hint of meat. Medium- to full-bodied, with ultrapolished tannins and a long, caressing finish. Drink now.–J.S. • $29 • (12/15/1998) • **88**

Toscana Casalferro 1994 • $28 • (9/30/1997) • **86**

Toscana Casalferro 1993 • $28 • (10/31/1996) • **87**

BROVIA, FRATELLI

Barbera d'Alba Sorì del Drago 1997: Dark chocolate, black cherry and raspberry flavors are delicious in this solid, medium-bodied Barbera. Supple tannins make it approachable on release. Drink now through 2002.–P.M. • $22 • (11/15/1999) • **86**

Barbera d'Alba Sorì del Drago 1996: A sophisticated, international-style Barbera, with loads of oak influence helping to soften the harsh edges. Vanilla, mocha and chocolate notes complement lovely ripe plum and blackberry flavors. Full-bodied, with a long, smoky, toasted finish. Drink now through 2004.–P.M. • $16 • (10/31/1998) • **87**

Barbera d'Alba Sorì del Drago 1993 • $14 • (10/31/1995) • **83**

Barolo 1993: Pretty, with good structure and acidity, a firm tannic backbone and plenty of clean, pure cassis and blackberry flavors. Medium-bodied, it veers toward the lean side because of its chewy tannins, but the fruit is there to balance it. Best after 2005.–P.M. • $40 • (10/31/1998) • **86**

Barolo 1990 • $NA • (10/31/1995) • **83**

Barolo 1989 • $NA • (10/31/1994) • **83**

Barolo Garblèt Sué 1993: Medium-bodied and a bit herbal, with decent plum and cherry flavors, but the tannins are rather hard and unyielding on the tough, greenish finish.–P.M. • $32 • (10/31/1998) • **77**

Barolo Garblèt Sué 1991 • $34 • (10/31/1996) • **79**

Barolo Monprivato 1990 • $44 • (10/31/1995) • **88**

Barolo Monprivato 1989 • $NA • (10/31/1994) • **80**

Barolo Rocche dei Brovia 1995: Odd. Herbal notes blend with ripe red berry character in this medium-bodied red. Lacks a bit of depth, but has decently smooth tannins on the finish. Drink now through 2002.–P.M. • $52 • (11/15/1999) • **82**

Barolo Rocche dei Brovia 1993 • $40 • (10/31/1997) • **82**

Barolo Rocche dei Brovia 1991 • $38 • (10/31/1996) • **78**

Barolo Rocche dei Brovia 1989 • $NA • (10/31/1994) • **87**

Barolo Rocche dei Brovia 1988 • $30 • (10/31/1993) • **82**

Barolo Villero 1995: Medium-bodied, with red berry character but also attractive licorice, tar and plum flavors. Decent length. The tannins might soften a bit with short-term cellaring. Drink now through 2003.–P.M. • $50 • (11/15/1999) • **85**

Barolo Villero 1993 • $40 • (10/31/1997) • **89**

Barolo Villero 1991 • $38 • (10/31/1996) • **88**

Dolcetto d'Alba Ciabòt del Re 1997: Fairly supple mouthfeel, with licorice, tar and black cherry character. Ripe, smoky, somewhat tough finish.–P.M. • $18 • (10/31/1998) • **82**

Dolcetto d'Alba Solatio Brovia 1996: This mind-blowing masterpiece of a Dolcetto—which tastes like an international-style red even though it's seen no new oak—mingles clean, pure, vibrant but ripe fruit with the supple, thick texture of olive oil. Gliding over the palate and coating it with spice, mocha, blackberry, fig and plum, it has an oak-scented, toasted, smoky finish. Talk about a silky wine. Drink now through 2002.–P.M. • $26 • (10/31/1998) • **93**

Dolcetto d'Alba Vignavillej 1995 • $15 • (10/31/1997) • **79**

Dolcetto d'Alba Vignavillej 1993 • $13 • (10/31/1995) • **80**

Nebbiolo d'Alba Valmaggione 1993 • $18 • (10/31/1997) • **79**

Roero Arneis 1997: Very pretty and distinctive, showing lovely wet hay, green hazelnut, pistachio, marzipan and pear pie character. Light to medium in body, with clean, juicy length. Good ripeness on the bone-dry, chewy, very likable finish. It grows on you. Drink now.–P.M. • $16 • (10/31/1998) • **87**

BRUNELLI

Amarone della Valpolicella Classico 1996: Dark ruby in color, with powerful aromas of smoked almond, berry and raisin. Medium-bodied, with velvety tannins and a medium finish. A rather one-dimensional Amarone. Drink now.–J.S. • $60 • (1/01/2000) • **87**

Amarone della Valpolicella Classico 1995: A blockbuster, seriously dark, with intense aromas of smoke, raisin, berry and grilled meat. Full-bodied and incredibly fruity, slightly sweet, with loads of flavor and chewy tannins. An alternative to vintage Port, but would go well with large hunks of grilled meat as well as cheese. Drink now through 2010.–J.S. • $60 • (1/01/2000) • **91**

Amarone della Valpolicella Classico Campo del Titari 1996: Wonderfully rich, big red. Very intense aromas of crushed berries, mint and strawberries with a hint of wet earth. Full-bodied and chewy, with soft, round tannins and a long, flavorful finish. Better with age but hard to resist now. Drink now through 2010.–J.S. • $55 • (5/15/2000) • **91**

Garganega Veneto Passito Re Sol 1994: A pleasant, lightly sweet dessert wine. Dark yellow color, with almond, walnut and peach aromas. Medium-bodied, off dry, with a peach, honey aftertaste and a hint of caramel. Drink now.–J.S. • $20/500 ml. • (4/30/2000) • **85**

Valpolicella Classico Superiore 1997: Simple and fresh red with plum, watermelon character. Light body. Fresh finish. Not imported into the U.S. Drink now.–J.S. • $NA • (1/01/2000) • **82**

Valpolicella Classico Superiore Pàriondo 1997: Big, chewy Valpo, but a bit too rustic for me. Loads of plum, tobacco and raisin character. Full-bodied and very ripe, with chewy tannins and a medium finish. Drink now.–J.S. • $18 • (5/15/2000) • **84**

BRUNELLI, GIANNI

Brunello di Montalcino 1995: A bit funky, but good with food. Very plummy with hints of earth and herbal on the nose. Medium- to full-bodied, with round tannins and a fruity, earthy finish. Chewy at this stage. Best after 2000.–J.S. • $58 • (6/30/2000) • **86**

Brunello di Montalcino 1994: Not a big wine, but very fine with a delicate fruit and tannin structure. Lovely berry, tobacco aftertaste. Medium-bodied. Drink now. Not imported into the U.S.–J.S. • $NA • (1/01/1999) • **86**

Brunello di Montalcino 1993: Still a bit austere and coarse, yet shows enticing aromas of raspberries and flowers, a joy to smell. Medium-bodied, with firm tannins and a slightly hard finish. Needs time to mellow. Best after 2000. Not imported into the U.S.–J.S. • $NA • (12/15/1998) • **87**

BUCCELLATO, ROMOLO

Cerasuolo di Vittoria Il Cigno Nero 1995: Interesting plum skin and berry aromas. Medium-bodied, with fresh acidity, light tannins and a long finish. Drink now.–J.S. • $NA • (1/01/2000) • **82**

Grillo Sicilia Tre Vigne 1998: Has interesting aromas of pineapple, honey and apple, with hints of dried apricot, but slightly oxidized. Shame.–J.S. • $NA • (1/01/2000) • **78**

Sicilia Villa Surdi 1998: Rather diluted and weedy, with ripe fruit.–J.S. • $NA • (1/01/2000) • **77**

BUCCIARELLI

Chianti Classico 1997: A Chianti Classico with a solid core of delicious raspberry and cherry flavors. Medium-bodied, with well-integrated, medium tannins and a long finish. Drink through 2003.–J.S. • $15 • (11/30/1999) • **88**

Chianti Classico Riserva 1996: This has berry and cherry character, but it's rather light and watery on the finish. Tasted twice, with consistent notes. –J.S. • $22 • (11/30/1999) • **77**

BUCCIARELLI

Colli della Toscana Centrale Gandino 1996: Very well crafted, with pretty aromas of crushed berry and raspberry. Medium- to full-bodied, with medium, silky tannins and a caressing mouthfeel. Sangiovese. Drink now. Not imported into the U.S.–J.S. • $NA • (1/01/1999) • **87**

BUON DONNO

Chianti Classico 1996: Good berry and dried cherry aromas and flavors, with a hint of mushroom. Medium-bodied, with light tannins and a refreshing finish. Drink now.–J.S. • $15 • (12/15/1998) • **84**
Chianti Classico 1994 • $NA • (10/31/1996) • **78**
Chianti Classico 1993 • $NA • (10/31/1995) • **79**
Chianti Classico 1992 • $NA • (2/28/1995) • **70**
Chianti Classico Riserva 1993 • $NA • (10/31/1996) • **83**

BUONINSEGNA, LA

Toscana 1995: Blackberry and strawberry aromas follow through on the palate. Light to medium in body, with light tannins and a fresh finish. Drink now.–J.S. • $20 • (12/15/1998) • **83**
Toscana 1993 • $NA • (9/30/1997) • **81**

BURACCHI

Rosso di Montepulciano 1996 • $NA • (9/30/1997) • **84**
Vino Nobile di Montepulciano 1994 • $NA • (9/30/1997) • **83**
Vino Nobile di Montepulciano Riserva 1993 • $NA • (9/30/1997) • **80**

BUSSO, PIERO

Barbaresco Vigna Borgese 1996: This pretty Barbaresco shows nice elegance. Focused and minerally, with ripe berry, plum and smoke and ripe tannins. Seductive length. Fresh and vibrant from good acidity. Best from 2003 through 2010.–P.M. • $35 • (10/31/1999) • **88**
Barbera d'Alba Vigna Majano 1997: Sweet-tasting and minerally, with a wet earth and chalk character. Medium-bodied, showing nice blueberry, black cherry and plum flavors. Lacks a bit of richness on the finish. Drink now through 2002.–P.M. • $20 • (11/15/1999) • **82**

BUZZINELLI, CARLO

Merlot Collio 1995 • $13 • (6/30/1998) • **85**
Pinot Bianco Collio 1996 • $13 • (6/15/1998) • **83**
Pinot Grigio Collio 1996 • $13 • (6/30/1998) • **86**
Tocai Friulano Collio 1996: Loads of almond character in this crisp white that has both concentration and balance. Finishes with a hint of grapefruit peel. Drink now.–B.S. • $13 • (7/31/1998) • **86**

CA' BOLANI

Merlot Aquileia del Friuli 1996: Attractive berry, cherry and spice flavors grace this elegant, moderately concentrated red. Finishes on the crisp side. Drink now.–B.S. • $12 • (7/31/1998) • **83**
Sauvignon Aquileia del Friuli 1997: A pungent, herbal, gooseberry style of Sauvignon. Leaner than some '97s, yet still has body, with a touch of earthiness. Drink now.–B.S. • $12 • (7/31/1998) • **82**
Sauvignon Aquileia del Friuli Aristós 1997: Full of citrus, gooseberry and grass aromas and flavors, all well integrated with bright acidity and medium body. Drink now.–B.S. • $19 • (7/31/1998) • **85**
Venezia Giulia White Opimio Aristós 1997: Light and dilute, showing modest grass and herb aromas and flavors and crisp acidity. Contains Tocai, Chardonnay. Drink now.–B.S. • $19 • (7/31/1998) • **80**

CA' DE MONTE

Barolo 1990 • $16 • (2/28/1995) • **88**
Dolcetto d'Alba 1993 • $8 • (7/31/1995) • **83**

Key: SS—Spectator Selection. CS—Cellar Selection. HR—Highly Recommended. $NA—Price not available. (BT)—Barrel tasting. (A)—Auction Price.
For a key to the tasters' initials, see "How to Use These Listings."
Dates in parentheses represent the issues in which the ratings were published.

CA' DEI FRATI

Lugana Brolettino 1996: New oak adds exotic nuances of nutmeg and vanilla to the apple and citrus flavors, supported by zippy acidity. On the lean, racy side, though it has good concentration and balance. Drink now.–B.S. • $18 • (9/30/1998) • **86**
Lugana I Frati 1996: Very tart, verging on cidery, with some spicy notes, too. Quite a mouthful, but doesn't quite come together.–K.M. • $14 • (8/31/1998) • **79**

CA' DEL BOSCO

Brut Franciacorta NV: A rather neutral sparkling wine, but clean. Light-bodied, with a lemony aftertaste. Drink now.–J.S. • $62 • (5/31/2000) • **81**
Franciacorta 1992 • $NA • (2/29/1996) • **78**
Franciacorta 1988 • $11 • (1/31/1992) • **81**
Franciacorta 1987 • $16 • (12/31/1990) • **77**
Franciacorta 1985 • $11 • (9/15/1988) • **83**
Maurizio Zanella 1991 • $40 • (2/29/1996) • **88**
Maurizio Zanella 1990 • $34 • (7/31/1993) • **85**
Maurizio Zanella 1988 • $32 • (9/30/1991) HR • **93**
Maurizio Zanella 1987 • $40 • (12/31/1990) • **88**
Maurizio Zanella 1985 • $38 • (9/15/1988) • **92**
Pinéro 1988 • $50 • (1/31/1992) • **83**
Pinéro 1987 • $69 • (6/15/1990) • **82**
Rosso del Sebino Maurizio Zanella 1995: An impressive young red, deeply colored, showing a camphor note in the aromas followed by flavors of black cherry and plum. Lush on the palate and concentrated, it finishes with very firm tannins and a hint of sweet fruit. Drink now through 2004.–B.S. • $82 • (9/30/1998) • **86**
Terre de Franciacorta 1997: A fresh and easy-to-drink Chardonnay, with enticing aromas of apple, vanilla and mineral. Medium-bodied, with light acidity and a simple, fruity aftertaste. Drink now.–J.S. • $20 • (6/15/1999) • **84**
Terre de Franciacorta 1996: Promises more on the nose than it delivers on the palate, but give it some time. Medium-bodied, with complex aromas of apple, dough and vanilla, cut wood flavors and hints of pineapple and melon. Short finish.–J.S. • $20 • (6/15/1999) • **87**
Terre de Franciacorta 1995: Crushed grapes with floral undertones througout this red. Light- to medium-bodied, with light tannins and a fruity finish. Drink now.–J.S. • $20 • (6/30/1999) • **81**
Terre de Franciacorta 1994 • $20 • (12/15/1997) • **88**
Terre de Franciacorta Pinéro 1994 • $65 • (12/15/1997) • **88**

CA' DEL RE

Barbera d'Alba 1997: This youthful, grapey red is wonderfully ripe, tasting almost sweet, with lots of raspberry, plum, black cherry, and blackberry flavors. Medium-bodied and delicious for guzzling down now.–P.M. • $15 • (10/31/1998) • **87**
Barbera d'Alba 1996 • $10 • (10/31/1997) • **90**
Dolcetto d'Alba 1997: Very ripe-tasting and light-bodied, offering a swirl of delicate and delicious raspberry, strawberry, cherry, apple juice and plummy jam character. All the flavors come together like a perfect sorbet, with a dollop of spice. Enjoy this harmonious, Nouveau-style Dolcetto on release.–P.M. • $15 • (10/31/1998) • **86**

CA' MONTINI

Veneto Barricato 1997: Lots of wood in this young wine, with loads of vanilla and apple character. Oily on the palate and full-bodied, with pineapple flavors and a thick texture. Drink now.–J.S. • $25 • (1/01/2000) • **83**

CA' ROME DI ROMANO MARENGO

Barbaresco 1996: The fruit is fresh and pure—black currant comes to mind—and the oak is so subtle that this medium-bodied red feels like a feather on the palate, except for the firm tannins on the balanced finish. Best from 2004 through 2010.–P.M. • $55 • (10/31/1999) • **90**
Barbaresco 1995: Supple and soft, but lacking a bit of fruit concentration, this is balanced and attractive. Fairly complex aromas of earth, animal, blackberry, tar and roses. Drink now through 2003.–P.M. • $40 • (10/31/1998) • **81**
Barbaresco 1993 • $39 • (10/31/1996) • **81**
Barbaresco 1990 • $28 • (10/31/1994) • **83**
Barbaresco 1989 • $30 • (10/31/1993) • **85**

Barbaresco 1985 • $28 • (1/31/1990) • **88**

Barbaresco Maria di Brun 1996: Crisp in texture, with cranberry and cherry notes. Medium-bodied, showing mocha and vanilla on the finish, which has tough, chewy tannins. Drink now through 2003.–P.M. • $64 • (10/31/1999) • **80**

Barbaresco Maria di Brun 1995: This light-colored, smooth Barbaresco is a bit diluted and earthy-funky, showing some red berry, licorice and wet earth notes. Fairly delicate and medium-bodied, with supple tannins.–P.M. • $47 • (10/31/1998) • **75**

Barbaresco Maria di Brun 1993 • $50 • (10/31/1997) • **86**

Barbaresco Maria di Brun 1990 • $40 • (10/31/1994) • **89**

Barbaresco Maria di Brun 1989 • $43 • (10/31/1993) • **86**

Barbaresco Maria di Brun 1985 • $37 • (1/31/1990) • **92**

Barbera d'Alba La Gamberaja 1996: Balanced and delicious, very nice and supple, with the edges softened by deft oak treatment. Medium-bodied, it shows good acidity and plenty of smoky, toasted spice, chocolate and berry character. Drink now through 2003.–P.M. • $NA • (10/31/1998) • **87**

Barolo 1993 • $44 • (10/31/1997) • **77**

Barolo 1985 • $35 • (10/15/1990) • **89**

Barolo Rapet 1995: Lots of fresh berries jump out of the glass, delivering a lemony, citrusy character. Crisp finish. Drink now through 2003.–P.M. • $58 • (11/15/1999) • **80**

Barolo Rapet 1990 • $35 • (10/31/1994) • **87**

Barolo Rapet 1989 • $32 • (10/31/1994) • **82**

Barolo Rapet 1988 • $36 • (10/31/1993) • **83**

Barolo Vigna Ceretta 1995: A bit herbaceous, but showing rose petal notes and bursts of cassis flavors. Turns tough on the finish, but time should help.–P.M. • $42 • (11/15/1999) • **79**

Dapruvé 1997: Gamy and earthy, with limelike acidity that seems tart.–P.M. • $28 • (11/15/1999) • **75**

Dapruvé 1993 • $34 • (10/31/1997) • **78**

Dapruvé 1989 • $24 • (4/15/1994) • **80**

CA' RUGATE

Recioto di Soave La Perlara 1997: Sticky yet likable, with pretty aromas of honey, dried almond and straw. Medium- to full-bodied and medium sweet, with lots of ripe fruit, dried apricot flavors and a fresh finish. Drink now.–J.S. • $30/500 ml. • (3/31/2000) • **88**

Recioto di Soave La Perlara 1995 • $19/500 ml. • (6/15/1998) • **88**

Soave Classico 1998: Lots of ripe fruit and spicy character here. Medium-bodied, with light honey and cream flavors and a fresh finish. Drink now.–J.S. • $12 • (3/31/2000) • **85**

Soave Classico 1996 • $12 • (6/15/1998) • **85**

Soave Classico Monte Alto 1998: Big and rich. Late-harvest style, but dry. Lots of spice, roasted almond and apricot character. Full-bodied and slightly rustic. Needs food. Drink now.–J.S. • $17 • (3/31/2000) • **87**

Soave Classico Monte Alto 1996 • $13 • (6/15/1998) • **87**

CA'VIOLA

Dolcetto d'Alba Barturot 1998: A ripe-tasting Dolcetto, with sweet tannins and succulent black cherry, plum and wet earth intensity. Full-bodied and seductively balanced. From an acclaimed Dolcetto star. Drink now through 2001.–P.M. • $19 • (11/15/1999) • **87**

Dolcetto d'Alba Barturot 1997: This complex, dark-colored Dolcetto is packed with black fruit character, spice and smoke, but above all a ripe-tasting texture, round tannins and a fresh, lively, seductive finish that beckons for another sip. Great quality as expected from a recognized star, Giuseppe Caviola. Drink now through 2001.–P.M. • $18 • (11/15/1999) • **90**

Langhe Bric du Luv 1996: Amazing quality. Here's what a really ripe and balanced Piedmont red tastes like. It's black as night and as thick and opulent as wine gets, oozing black fruit, with violet and rose petal. The flavors are folded into velvety tannins. Good acidity makes it taste harmonious on the long finish. Drink now through 2005.–P.M. • $35 • (11/15/1999) • **93**

CA'VIT

Merlot Trentino 1997 • $8 • (6/30/1998) • **84**

Merlot Trentino 1994 • $9 • (6/15/1997) • **78**

Merlot Trentino Riserva 1991 • $8 • (2/28/1995) • **85**

Pinot Grigio Venezie 1997 • $8 • (6/30/1998) • **86**

Teroldego Rotaliano Riserva 1991 • $8 • (2/28/1995) • **77**

Teroldego Venezie Novello Terrazze della Luna 1999: The slight spritziness and smoky, gamy notes suggest a wine that hasn't quite come together; the fruit is good but the wine lacks harmony.–T.M. • $7 • (1/01/2000) • **78**

Trentino Vino Santo 1988 • $NA/500 ml. • (1/01/1997) • **87**

CABUTTO

Barbera d'Alba Bricco delle Viole 1997: A bit tough, with some light herbal notes creeping into the crisp red berry flavors.–P.M. • $20 • (9/15/1999) • **79**

Barbera d'Alba Bricco delle Viole 1996: Crisp and lean, with a somewhat herbal character, this is a tough wine to warm up to. Shows modest ripe fruit and tastes astringent on the finish.–P.M. • $18 • (10/31/1998) • **75**

Barbera d'Alba Bricco delle Viole 1995 • $16 • (10/31/1997) • **80**

Barolo Riserva del Fondatore 1990: Interesting. A bit earthy yet quite fruity, with plum, black cherry, currant and spice. Impressively ripe, this full-bodied red fills the palate with delicious waves of flavors and a lingering finish. Give this time to show it all. Best after 2005.–P.M. • $80 • (10/31/1998) • **88**

Barolo Vigna La Volta 1995: Bright fruit bursts in the glass, but the cranberry and cherry aromas are a bit lifted. Medium-bodied, made in a crisp style, with blackberry and herb notes and a tart finish.–P.M. • $43 • (11/15/1999) • **78**

Barolo Vigna La Volta 1994: An attractive '94 Barolo, with earth, plum, currant and cherry aromas and flavors. Of medium body and intensity, with ripe character, fresh acidity and a lingering herbaceous finish. Drink now through 2003.–P.M. • $36 • (10/31/1998) • **84**

Barolo Vigna La Volta 1993 • $32 • (10/31/1997) • **85**

Dolcetto d'Alba Superiore Elevato in Piccole Botti 1996: The dark color announces what this is made of: deep flavors, supple and ripe tannins and a sophisticated barriques treatment accented by the violet, plum, cassis, mocha and toasted oak notes. Everything blends beautifully in this smooth, harmonious, medium-bodied wine. Terrific. Drink now.–P.M. • $20 • (10/31/1998) • **89**

Dolcetto d'Alba Vigna La Volta 1998: Wonderful, tasting of freshly crushed wild raspberries. This medium-bodied beauty is balanced, with sweet-tasting fruit, smooth texture and pure, clean aromas and flavors of cassis, game and spice that deepen with each sip. Drink now.–P.M. • $14 • (7/31/1999) • **89**

Dolcetto d'Alba Vigna La Volta 1996 • $13 • (10/31/1997) • **86**

Langhe 1996: A bit earthy and forward, this smells of horse saddle and forest underbrush and shows plum, with a crisp level of acidity on the mouthpuckering finish.–P.M. • $35 • (11/15/1999) • **79**

Langhe 1995: Both modern and traditional, dishing up chestnut undertones to the ripe plum, berry and black cherry flavors. Really delicious as it unfolds its sweet-tasting fruit accented by subtle oak, which turns a bit toasted on the slightly dry finish, suggesting a modern mind-set along with respect for tradition. Drink now through 2003.–P.M. • $32 • (10/31/1998) • **87**

Langhe 1994 • $30 • (10/31/1997) • **81**

CACCHIANO, CASTELLO DI

Chianti Classico 1996: Light and simple, with dried cherry character and a fresh finish. Short. Drink now.–J.S. • $15 • (11/30/1999) • **80**

Chianti Classico 1994 • $NA • (10/31/1996) • **75**

Chianti Classico 1993 • $13 • (10/31/1995) • **80**

Chianti Classico 1992 • $10 • (2/28/1995) • **74**

Chianti Classico 1991 • $14 • (10/31/1993) • **87**

Chianti Classico 1990 • $14 • (10/31/1993) • **87**

Chianti Classico 1988 • $14 • (9/15/1991) • **90**

Chianti Classico 1985 • $10 • (10/31/1988) • **87**

Chianti Classico Millennio Riserva 1995: A chewy and fruity Chianti Classico. Bright cherry and floral aromas. Medium-bodied, with velvety tannins and a long, fruity finish. Harmonious wine. Drink now through 2004.–J.S. • $35 • (11/30/1999) • **89**

Chianti Classico Millennio Riserva 1990 • $17 • (2/28/1995) • **89**

Chianti Classico Millennio Riserva 1988 • $18 • (9/15/1992) • **86**

Chianti Classico Millennio Riserva 1985 • $18 • (9/15/1990) • **80**

Toscana RF 1995: Wonderful aromas of cherries, blackberries and licorice. Medium- to full-bodied, with silky tannins and a fresh finish. A beauty. Sangiovese and Merlot. Drink now through 2002.–J.S. • $14 • (11/30/1999) • **89**

Toscana RF 1993 • $25 • (10/31/1995) • **84**

Toscana RF 1990 • $25 • (2/28/1995) • **90**

Toscana RF 1988 • $20 • (9/15/1991) • **90**

Toscana RF 1986 • $16 • (6/15/1990) • **85**

Toscana RF 1985 • $15 • (8/31/1988) • **91**

ITALY

CAGGIANO, CANTINE ANTONIO

Aglianico d'Irpinia Salae Domini 1997: Good, simple red. Raspberry and berry aromas follow through to a medium-bodied palate, with fine tannins and a short finish. Drink now.–J.S. • $33 • (1/31/2000) • **83**

Aglianico d'Irpinia Tauri 1997: Like a good, simple Côtes du Rhône. Some attractive black pepper and fruit aromas and flavors. Medium-bodied, with light tannins and a fresh finish. Drink now.–J.S. • $17 • (1/31/2000) • **85**

Fiagre 1998: Delicious white. Lovely pear, lemon and mineral aromas. Medium-bodied, with soft texture and a fruity finish. Drink now.–J.S. • $17 • (1/31/2000) • **87**

Mel 1997: Pretty little sweet wine. Aromas of banana, pineapple and almonds. Medium-bodied, medium sweet with a lovely lemon, cream and spice finish. Not imported into the U.S. Drink now.–J.S. • $NA/500 ml. • (1/31/2000) • **88**

Taurasi Vigna Macchia dei Goti 1995: Interesting, spicy red. Aromas of ripe fruit and tar follow through to a medium-bodied palate, with medium tannins and a medium, spicy, peppery finish. Drink now.–J.S. • $40 • (1/31/2000) • **86**

CALATRASI

Catarratto-Trebbiano Sicilia Terrale 1998: Good mineral and ash character, with a citrus undertone. Medium-bodied, with a light finish. Drink now.–J.S. • $7 • (5/31/2000) • **81**

Chardonnay Puglia Terrale 1998: Good apple and honey character, but a little subdued for a Chardonnay. Medium-bodied, with good (though perhaps too much) acidity and a simple, fruity finish. Drink now.–J.S. • $7 • (5/31/2000) • **84**

Nero d'Avola-Sangiovese Sicilia Terrale 1998: Earthy and already tired, with plum flavor.–J.S. • $7 • (5/31/2000) • **74**

Primitivo Puglia Terrale 1998: A solid Italian red, with plum and berry character and a hint of meatiness. It's full-bodied, with medium tannins and a fruity finish. Very good wine at a painless price. Drink now through 2002.–J.S. • $7 • (5/31/2000) • **87**

Sicilia Red Terrale 1996 • $6 • (2/28/1998) • **84**
Sicilia White Terrale 1996 • $6 • (10/31/1997) • **83**
Terrale Red 1995 • $6 • (1/01/1997) • **85**
Terrale Red 1994 • $5 • (1/31/1996) • **82**
Terrale Red 1993 • $5 • (5/31/1995) • **84**

CALBELLO

Rosso di Montalcino 1997: A delicious and simple rosso. Aromas of ripe plum follow through to a medium-bodied palate, with light tannins and a fresh finish. Drink now.–J.S. • $30 • (11/30/1999) • **84**

Toscana Ardingo 1997: Slightly overdone but delicious. Dark ruby red in color, with loads of jam, berry and vanilla aromas and flavors. Full-bodied, with soft tannins and a fruity raisin aftertaste. Drink now.–J.S. • $42 • (11/30/1999) • **84**

CALLE, LE

Montecucco 1998: This red is gloriously fruity, with delicious aromas of plum, berry and raspberry. Full-bodied, with a chunky, thick texture. Not imported into the U.S. Drink through 2003–J.S. • $NA • (11/30/1999) • **89**

CALONICA, LA

Sangiovese Toscana 1997: A light and simple Sangiovese, with cherry and orange peel character, light body and fresh acidity. Drink now.–J.S. • $11 • (11/30/1999) • **81**

Toscana Girifalco 1996: A stylish Italian red. Deep and dark blackberry character, with a good dose of new wood. Medium-bodied, with polished tannins and a long, grapey aftertaste. Drink now.–J.S. • $32 • (12/15/1998) • **88**

Toscana Girifalco 1995 • $29 • (9/30/1997) • **88**

Vino Nobile di Montepulciano 1996: Medium-bodied, with berry and bark aromas, soft tannins and a fruity finish. Hollow midpalate and a bit dull. Drink now.–J.S. • $22 • (11/30/1999) • **82**

Vino Nobile di Montepulciano 1995: A pretty, balanced Vino Nobile, with chocolate, berry and bark character. Medium-bodied, with medium, velvety tannins and a fresh finish. Drink now.–J.S. • $25 • (12/15/1998) • **86**

Vino Nobile di Montepulciano 1993 • $16 • (9/30/1997) • **85**

CAMERANO

Barolo 1993 • $NA • (10/31/1997) • **83**

CAMIGLIANO, CASTELLO DI

Brunello di Montalcino 1995: Some good fruit; attractive raisin and ripe fruit character. Medium-bodied, with dried cherry, toasted oak character and a slightly short finish. A bit lean. Drink now.–J.S. • $50 • (6/30/2000) • **85**

Brunello di Montalcino 1994: A yummy red. Intense aromas of blackberries, cherries and cedar. Medium-bodied, with fine tannins and a long, sweet, ripe fruit aftertaste. This property is improving. Drink now through 2004.–J.S. • $42 • (8/31/1999) • **87**

Brunello di Montalcino 1992 • $NA • (9/30/1997) • **82**
Brunello di Montalcino 1991 • $29 • (11/30/1996) • **79**
Brunello di Montalcino 1990 • $NA • (10/31/1995) • **85**
Brunello di Montalcino 1988 • $NA • (4/30/1994) • **89**

Brunello di Montalcino Riserva 1993: Big and compacted, with plenty of ripe fruit and polished tannins. Full body. Mineral, berry and cherry flavors on the finish. Rather tough still. Best after 2001.–J.S. • $65 • (8/31/1999) • **90**

Brunello di Montalcino Riserva 1991 • $NA • (9/30/1997) • **83**
Brunello di Montalcino Riserva 1990 • $NA • (11/30/1996) • **88**
Brunello di Montalcino Riserva 1977 • $11 • (8/01/1985) • **85**

Brunello di Montalcino Villa I Lecci 1993: Aromas of leather and berry. Medium-bodied, with dry tannins and a rather dry finish. Not going anywhere.–J.S. • $40 • (12/15/1998) • **78**

Cabernet Sauvignon Sant'Antimo 1998: Well made but slightly hard, with a good dark color and mint, berry and chocolate aromas. Medium in body, finish and tannins, which are slightly hard. Best after 2000. Not imported into the U.S.–J.S. • $NA • (1/01/2000) • **87**

Rosso di Montalcino 1998: Clean and simple, with berry and dried cherry character. Light-bodied, with a fresh finish. Not imported into the U.S. Drink now.–J.S. • $NA • (1/01/2000) • **82**

Rosso di Montalcino 1997: Fresh and silky rosso. Currants and berries exude from the glass. Medium-bodied, with light silky tannins and a fresh fruit aftertaste. Drink now.–J.S. • $18 • (9/15/1999) • **85**

Rosso di Montalcino 1995 • $NA • (9/30/1997) • **86**
Rosso di Montalcino 1994 • $NA • (11/30/1996) • **79**
Rosso di Montalcino 1993 • $NA • (10/31/1995) • **81**
Rosso di Montalcino 1991 • $NA • (4/30/1994) • **80**

Rosso di Montalcino Villa I Lecci 1996: A grapey, almost minty red on both nose and palate. Medium-bodied, with fine tannins and a fruity finish. A bit simple, but delicious. Drink now.–J.S. • $18 • (12/15/1998) • **84**

Toscana Poderuccio 1998: A pretty, young wine, with beautiful aromas of plum, berry and mineral. Medium-bodied, with berry, mint and cherry flavors, very polished tannins and a caressing finish. Not imported into the U.S. Best after 2000.–J.S. • $NA • (1/01/2000) • **89**

CAMPANILE

Pinot Grigio Grave del Friuli 1997 • $11 • (6/30/1998) • **85**
Pinot Grigio Grave del Friuli 1996 • $11 • (6/15/1997) • **85**

CAMPOGIOVANNI

Brunello di Montalcino 1994: A wine with class. Bright and vivid aromas of berries, plums and the forest. Medium- to full-bodied, with well-integrated tannins and a long, beautiful finish. Drink now through 2006.–J.S. • $39 • (8/31/1999) • **88**

Brunello di Montalcino 1993: Delicious and delectable. Medium-bodied, with pretty strawberry and cherry aromas, fine tannins and a succulent, fruity aftertaste. Drink now.–J.S. • $40 • (12/15/1998) • **87**

Brunello di Montalcino 1992 • $30 • (9/30/1997) • **80**
Brunello di Montalcino 1991 • $30 • (11/30/1996) • **89**
Brunello di Montalcino 1990 • $33 • (10/31/1995) • **95**
Brunello di Montalcino 1988 • $36 • (4/30/1994) • **90**
Brunello di Montalcino 1986 • $28 • (11/30/1991) HR • **92**
Brunello di Montalcino 1985 • $24 • (9/30/1990) • **85**
Brunello di Montalcino 1982 • $22 • (7/31/1988) CS • **92**
Brunello di Montalcino Vigna del Quercione Riserva 1990 • $84 • (11/30/1996) • **97**

Key: SS—Spectator Selection. CS—Cellar Selection. HR—Highly Recommended. $NA—Price not available. (BT)—Barrel tasting. (A)—Auction Price.
For a key to the tasters' initials, see "How to Use These Listings."
Dates in parentheses represent the issues in which the ratings were published.

ITALY

CAMPOSILIO

Toscana 1996: A bit tough right now, but it has attractive aromas of plum and berry, with a hint of earth. Medium-bodied, with chewy tannins and a medium, slightly austere finish. Drink now. Not imported into the U.S.–J.S. • $NA • (1/01/1999) • **83**

CAMPRIANO

Chianti Colli Senesi 1997: Rather earthy and a bit funky, with a chestnut and fruit character. Light-bodied, with light tannins and a slightly dry finish. Fading already.–J.S. • $10 • (12/15/1998) • **78**

Chianti Colli Senesi 1996: A fresh and delicate '96 Chianti with dried cherry and plum character. Medium- to light-bodied, with light tannins and a crisp finish. Drink now.–J.S. • $10 • (12/15/1998) • **82**

Chianti Colli Senesi 1994 • $NA • (10/31/1995) • **83**

Val d'Arbia 1997: Good, no-nonsense white, with pretty melon, mineral and grapefruit aromas, a medium body with fresh acidity and a zingy, lemony finish. Drink now.–J.S. • $9 • (12/15/1998) • **82**

CANALE, TENUTA

Chianti Classico 1996 • $15 • (1/01/1998) • **74**

Chianti Classico 1995 • $NA • (9/30/1997) • **86**

Chianti Classico 1994 • $NA • (10/31/1996) • **80**

Chianti Classico Riserva 1993 • $30 • (10/31/1996) • **74**

Sinfonia 1993 • $NA • (10/31/1996) • **78**

Toscana Poesia 1996 • $13 • (1/01/1998) • **68**

CANALICCHIO DI SOPRA

Brunello di Montalcino 1994: A reserved wine, with light plum, berry, cedar and mushroom character. Medium-bodied, with soft tannins and a sweet, fruity finish. Drink now.–J.S. • $55 • (8/31/1999) • **88**

Brunello di Montalcino 1992 • $NA • (9/30/1997) • **80**

Brunello di Montalcino 1991 • $NA • (11/30/1996) • **83**

Brunello di Montalcino 1990 • $45 • (10/31/1995) • **88**

Brunello di Montalcino 1988 • $36 • (4/30/1994) • **80**

Brunello di Montalcino Le Gode di Montosoli 1994: A refreshing '94, with sweet fruit and silky tannins. Medium-bodied. Crisp and delicious. Lovely finish. Drink now.–J.S. • $60 • (8/31/1999) • **87**

Brunello di Montalcino Le Gode di Montosoli 1991 • $NA • (11/30/1996) • **76**

Brunello di Montalcino Le Gode di Montosoli Riserva 1988 • $35 • (10/31/1994) • **88**

Brunello di Montalcino Riserva 1988 • $NA • (10/31/1994) • **88**

Rosso di Montalcino 1997: Plenty of strawberry and cherry in this. Medium-bodied, with lovely, succulent fruit character and a soft, velvety texture. Drink now.–J.S. • $20 • (9/15/1999) • **87**

Rosso di Montalcino 1995 • $22 • (9/30/1997) • **85**

Rosso di Montalcino 1994 • $NA • (11/30/1996) • **85**

Rosso di Montalcino 1993 • $19 • (10/31/1995) • **88**

Rosso di Montalcino 1991 • $NA • (4/30/1994) • **82**

Rosso di Montalcino Canalichio 1997: Clean and silky rosso with focused berry and plum character. Medium-bodied, with pleasant tannins and a short finish. Needs a bit more fruit on the finish. Drink now.–J.S. • $20 • (9/15/1999) • **86**

Rosso di Montalcino Le Gode di Montosoli 1994 • $NA • (11/30/1996) • **86**

CANDIDO, FRANCESCO

Salice Salentino Riserva 1996: Pleasant, with pepper, cherry and plumskin character. Medium-bodied, with a fruity finish. At its peak. Drink now.–J.S. • $7 • (5/31/2000) • **81**

Salice Salentino Riserva 1988 • $8 • (7/31/1993) • **84**

CANELLA

Prosecco di Conegliano NV: Floral and apple aromas and flavors mark this Prosecco, and a slight sweetness gives it a round, soft structure. Drink now.–B.S. • $12 • (7/31/1998) • **82**

CANNETO

Vino Nobile di Montepulciano 1996: A good, straightforward Nobile, with berry, cherry and mineral character. Medium-bodied, with light tannins and a fresh finish. Drink now.–J.S. • $22 • (1/01/1999) • **84**

CANTAGALLO, TENUTA

Carleto 1996 • $16 • (9/30/1997) • **86**

Chianti Montalbano 1996: A delicious Sangiovese, with ripe plum and raspberry aromas. Full-bodied, with velvety tannins and a long, fruity aftertaste with hints of smoke and nuts. Drink now through 2002.–J.S. • $10 • (12/15/1998) • **86**

Chianti Montalbano 1995 • $10 • (9/30/1997) • **81**

Chianti Montalbano Riserva 1994: Impressive for this appellation. Expressive aromas of blackberries, porcini and forests. Medium-bodied, with soft tannins and a delicious aftertaste of blackberry and smoke. Drink now.–J.S. • $18 • (12/15/1998) • **87**

Chianti Montalbano Riserva 1993 • $17 • (9/30/1997) • **86**

Colli della Toscana Centrale Carleto 1997: Some pineapple and waxy character in this ripe and slightly oxidized white. Full-bodied, with a slightly candied finish.–J.S. • $17 • (12/15/1998) • **79**

Gioveto 1995 • $15 • (9/30/1997) • **79**

CAPACCIA, PODERE

Chianti Classico 1994 • $NA • (9/30/1997) • **85**

Chianti Classico 1990 • $NA • (10/31/1993) • **84**

Chianti Classico 1988 • $NA • (9/15/1991) • **89**

Chianti Classico Riserva 1996: An aromatic, zingy CC, with very pretty berry, cherry and toasted oak character. Medium-bodied, with light tannins and a crisp, high acidity. Needs food. Drink now.–J.S. • $NA • (1/01/1999) • **85**

Chianti Classico Riserva 1993 • $NA • (10/31/1996) • **78**

Chianti Classico Riserva 1988 • $NA • (9/15/1992) • **86**

Chianti Classico Riserva 1985 • $NA • (9/15/1991) • **88**

Colli della Toscana Centrale Querciagrande 1995: A rich and delicious wine with layers of blackberry, cherry, a meaty, earthy character. Full-bodied, with velvety texture and a long, fruit finish. Drink now. Not imported into the U.S.–J.S. • $NA • (11/30/1999) • **90**

Colli della Toscana Centrale Querciagrande 1994 • $NA • (9/30/1997) • **85**

Colli della Toscana Centrale Querciagrande 1993 • $NA • (10/31/1996) • **85**

Colli della Toscana Centrale Querciagrande 1990 • $NA • (10/31/1993) • **88**

CAPANNA

Brunello di Montalcino 1993: Rather mature-looking, but good. Medium ruby in color, with a brick edge. Medium- to full-bodied and rich, with smoke and dried raisin aromas, lots of ripe fruit and a round texture. Drink now.–J.S. • $40 • (12/15/1998) • **84**

Brunello di Montalcino 1991 • $30 • (11/30/1996) • **74**

Brunello di Montalcino 1990 • $NA • (10/31/1995) • **83**

Brunello di Montalcino 1988 • $NA • (4/30/1994) • **84**

Brunello di Montalcino Riserva 1991 • $40 • (9/30/1997) • **79**

Brunello di Montalcino Riserva 1990 • $55 • (11/30/1996) • **85**

Brunello di Montalcino Riserva 1988 • $NA • (10/31/1994) • **90**

Rosso di Montalcino 1996: Some ripe fruit, but with a rubbery undertone. Medium-bodied, with firm tannins and a short, hard finish. Tasted twice, with consistent notes.–J.S. • $15 • (12/15/1998) • **74**

Rosso di Montalcino 1995 • $12 • (9/30/1997) • **83**

Rosso di Montalcino 1994 • $15 • (11/30/1996) • **85**

Rosso di Montalcino 1993 • $NA • (10/31/1995) • **82**

Rosso di Montalcino 1992 • $NA • (4/30/1994) • **79**

Rosso di Montalcino 1991 • $NA • (4/30/1994) • **80**

CAPANNA FATTOI

Brunello di Montalcino 1991 • $NA • (11/30/1996) • **80**

Brunello di Montalcino Riserva 1990 • $47 • (11/30/1996) • **85**

Brunello di Montalcino Riserva 1988 • $NA • (10/31/1994) • **92**

Rosso di Montalcino 1994 • $19 • (11/30/1996) • **77**

CAPANNELLE

2000 NV: This is an eccentric blend of various vintages from 1990 to 1995, yet it's fresh and lively, with plenty of plum and dried cherry character.

Full-bodied, with medium tannins and a crisp finish. Delicious Sangiovese. Drink through 2005.–J.S. • $250/1.5 liter • (11/30/1999) • **90**

Barrique 1995: A good amount of berry character in this, with notes of herbs and vanilla. Medium-bodied, with soft tannins and a hint of dilution at the finish. Drink now.–J.S. • $25 • (11/30/1999) • **85**

Barrique 1988 • $NA • (10/31/1993) • **86**

Tuscany 1988 • $NA • (10/31/1993) • **85**

CAPARZO

Brunello di Montalcino 1995: A harmonious and fine wine. Plenty of pretty plum, strawberry and berry aromas open to a medium-bodied palate, with fine tannins and a long finish. Drink now through 2008.–J.S. • $55 • (6/30/2000) • **90**

Brunello di Montalcino 1994: Attractive plum and cherry character in this, with medium body, medium round tannins and a fresh, fruity finish. Why wait? Drink now.–J.S. • $55 • (8/31/1999) • **87**

Brunello di Montalcino 1993: Pleasant and easy to drink, but with a bit too much new wood. A bit lacking in concentration, but with pretty, round tannins and a soft finish. Tasted twice, with consistent notes. Drink now.–J.S. • $53 • (12/15/1998) • **80**

Brunello di Montalcino 1991 • $41 • (11/30/1996) • **87**

Brunello di Montalcino 1990 • $93 Ⓐ • (10/31/1995) • **91**

Brunello di Montalcino 1988 • $30 • (4/30/1994) • **91**

Brunello di Montalcino 1985 • $34 • (7/15/1991) • **83**

Brunello di Montalcino 1982 • $NA • (9/15/1986) • **95**

Brunello di Montalcino 1981 • $18 • (9/15/1986) • **90**

Brunello di Montalcino 1980 • $23 • (9/15/1986) • **88**

Brunello di Montalcino La Casa 1995: A fine, elegant and long Brunello. Floral and aromatic with a red licorice character. Medium body. Very polished and fine tannins, with a fresh finish. Give it time. Best after 2002.–J.S. • $85 • (6/30/2000) CS • **91**

Brunello di Montalcino La Casa 1994: Very good Brunello for the vintage. Subtle aromas of tobacco, cherry and cedar. Medium-bodied, with a lovely silky texture and a long cherry, berry aftertaste. Delicious. Drink now through 2003.–J.S. • $82 • (1/01/2000) • **89**

Brunello di Montalcino La Casa 1993: A harmonious and very good Brunello, with plenty of blackberry and cherry aromas. Medium-bodied, with firm tannins and a smoky, chocolaty finish. Best after 2000.–J.S. • $75 • (12/15/1998) • **88**

Brunello di Montalcino La Casa 1991 • $76 • (11/30/1996) • **86**

Brunello di Montalcino La Casa 1990 • $113 Ⓐ • (10/31/1995) CS • **95**

Brunello di Montalcino La Casa 1988 • $60 • (4/30/1994) • **94**

Brunello di Montalcino La Casa 1985 • $53 • (7/15/1991) • **88**

Brunello di Montalcino La Casa 1982 • $50 • (11/30/1989) • **67**

Brunello di Montalcino La Casa 1981 • $50 • (6/15/1990) • **83**

Brunello di Montalcino La Casa 1979 • $27 • (9/15/1986) • **89**

Brunello di Montalcino Rio Cassero 1992 • $50 • (9/30/1997) • **82**

Brunello di Montalcino Riserva 1994: Incredibly fresh 1994. Hard to believe, but you have to like it. Medium-bodied, with a good core of ripe fruit and silky tannins. Drink now through 2002.–J.S. • $63 • (6/30/2000) • **88**

Brunello di Montalcino Riserva 1993: Pleasant '93 riserva, with berry, chestnut and meat character. Medium-bodied, with silky tannins and a crisp finish. Drink now.–J.S. • $70 • (8/31/1999) • **86**

Brunello di Montalcino Riserva 1990 • $115 Ⓐ • (11/30/1996) • **93**

Brunello di Montalcino Riserva 1988 • $55 • (10/31/1994) • **92**

Brunello di Montalcino Riserva 1981 • $23 • (6/15/1990) • **70**

Moscadello di Montalcino Vendemmia Tardiva 1997: Delicious. Dark yellow with a gold tint. Wonderful aromas of toffee, almond, honey and dried apricot. Medium-bodied and medium sweet, with an almond and sweet fruit aftertaste. Not imported into the U.S. Drink now.–J.S. • $NA/375 ml. • (1/01/2000) • **88**

Rosso di Montalcino 1997: Pretty floral and blackberry aromas, but the palate is rather light and diluted, with a short finish. Drink now.–J.S. • $20 • (9/15/1999) • **82**

Rosso di Montalcino 1996: A lovely zingy red, with dried cherry, berry aromas and flavors, medium body and a crisp finish. Harmonious. Delicious pasta wine. Drink now.–J.S. • $19 • (12/15/1998) • **85**

Rosso di Montalcino 1995 • $15 • (9/30/1997) • **86**

Rosso di Montalcino 1994 • $20 • (11/30/1996) • **85**

Key: SS—Spectator Selection. CS—Cellar Selection. HR—Highly Recommended. $NA—Price not available. (BT)—Barrel tasting. Ⓐ—Auction Price. For a key to the tasters' initials, see "How to Use These Listings." **Dates in parentheses represent the issues in which the ratings were published.**

Rosso di Montalcino 1993 • $13 • (10/31/1995) • **83**

Rosso di Montalcino 1991 • $15 • (4/30/1994) • **85**

Rosso di Montalcino 1988 • $14 • (4/30/1991) • **81**

Rosso di Montalcino 1986 • $10 • (9/30/1989) • **86**

Rosso di Montalcino La Caduta 1997: A wine with fresh fruit, tobacco and cedar character. Medium body. Medium finish. Tasted twice, with consistent notes. Drink now.–J.S. • $33 • (6/15/2000) • **85**

Rosso di Montalcino La Caduta 1996: This has solid Sangiovese character, with cherry and floral aromas and flavors. Medium-bodied, with a good core of fruit, light tannins and a fresh finish. Drink now.–J.S. • $33 • (11/30/1999) • **86**

Rosso di Montalcino La Caduta 1995 • $20 • (9/30/1997) • **87**

Rosso di Montalcino La Caduta 1994 • $20 • (11/30/1996) • **85**

Rosso di Montalcino La Caduta 1993 • $18 • (10/31/1995) • **87**

Rosso di Montalcino La Caduta 1991 • $NA • (4/30/1994) • **83**

Sant'Antimo Le Grance 1996: Attractive aromas of apple and toasted almond. Medium-bodied, with honey and vanilla flavors and a fresh aftertaste. Drink now.–J.S. • $20 • (11/30/1999) • **86**

Toscana Cà del Pazzo 1995: A pretty Cabernet. The dried cherry and floral character follows through to the medium-bodied, firm palate. Fresh acidity, medium tannins. Drink now through 2004.–J.S. • $34 • (11/30/1999) • **88**

Toscana Cà del Pazzo 1994: Best Cà del Pazzo in years. A flavor-intensive, youthful red, delicious and well crafted. Intense aromas of strawberry and raspberry tart. Medium-bodied, with very silky tannins and a long, fruity aftertaste. Made from Cabernet Sauvignon. Drink now.–J.S. • $29 • (12/15/1998) • **89**

Toscana Cà del Pazzo 1993 • $30 • (9/30/1997) • **87**

Toscana Cà del Pazzo 1992 • $28 • (10/31/1995) • **87**

Toscana Cà del Pazzo 1990 • $25 • (10/31/1993) • **86**

Toscana Cà del Pazzo 1987 • $24 • (8/31/1991) • **85**

Toscana Cà del Pazzo 1985 • $28 • (5/15/1990) • **77**

Toscana Le Crete 1998: A bit one-dimensional, but showing good, flinty sliced apple character, medium body and a fresh finish. Chardonnay and Trebbiano. Drink now.–J.S. • $10 • (11/30/1999) • **85**

CAPEZZANA

Barco Reale Conte Contini Bonacossi 1998: Don't let the slight bubbles put you off. This easy-drinking Sangiovese is light and fresh, with pretty strawberry and cherry aromas and flavors. Drink now.–J.S. • $15 • (11/30/1999) • **81**

Barco Reale Conte Contini Bonacossi 1997: Very grapey, with hints of strawberry on the nose and palate. Light-bodied, with bright fruit and a crisp finish. Drink now.–J.S. • $12 • (12/15/1998) • **84**

Barco Reale Conte Contini Bonacossi 1996 • $12 • (9/30/1997) • **81**

Barco Reale Conte Contini Bonacossi 1995 • $10 • (10/31/1996) • **85**

Barco Reale Conte Contini Bonacossi 1994 • $NA • (10/31/1995) • **75**

Barco Reale Conte Contini Bonacossi 1993 • $10 • (7/31/1995) • **84**

Barco Reale Conte Contini Bonacossi 1987 • $12 • (7/15/1991) • **78**

Carmignano Conte Contini Bonaccossi Riserva 1996: A pretty Carmignano, with bright raspberry and cherry aromas. Medium-bodied, with delicate tannins and a berry and vanilla aftertaste. Delicate finish. Drink now.–J.S. • $40 • (11/30/1999) • **85**

Carmignano Conte Contini Bonaccossi Riserva 1995: Shows impressive aromas of cassis, blackberries and milk chocolate. Medium-bodied, with velvety tannins and a fruity finish. Touch of dilution at the end. Drink now.–J.S. • $40 • (11/30/1999) • **87**

Carmignano Conte Contini Bonaccossi Riserva 1990 • $30 • (1/01/1997) • **87**

Carmignano Conte Contini Bonaccossi Riserva 1985 • $25 • (7/15/1991) • **83**

Carmignano Conte Contini Bonacossi 1997: This moreish wine has beautiful aromas of berry, cherry and raspberry, with a hint of vanilla. Medium- to full-bodied, with supersilky tannins and a long, sweet fruit aftertaste. Drink now through 2002.–J.S. • $22 • (11/30/1999) • **91**

Carmignano Conte Contini Bonacossi 1996: One of the best Carmignanos I have tasted in years. Lovely refined aromas of blackberry and cherry, with hints of flowers. Medium-bodied, with moderate tannins and a chewy finish. Drink through 2001.–J.S. • $NA • (12/15/1998) • **90**

Carmignano Conte Contini Bonacossi 1994 • $17 • (10/31/1996) • **80**

Carmignano Conte Contini Bonacossi 1989 • $12 • (8/31/1995) • **82**

Carmignano Conte Contini Bonacossi 1986 • $15 • (7/15/1991) • **81**

Carmignano Rosato Vin Ruspo 1996 • $NA • (9/30/1997) • **86**

Carmignano Trefiano Vittorio Contini Bonacossi 1996: Not a bad Carmignano, but needs a bit more fruit. Earthy berry aromas and flavors. Medium-bodied, with light tannins and a slightly diluted finish. Drink now.–J.S. • $18 • (11/30/1999) • **81**

Carmignano Trefiano Vittorio Contini Bonacossi 1995 • $35 • (9/30/1997) • **87**

Carmignano Trefiano Vittorio Contini Bonacossi 1994 • $35 • (10/31/1996) • **78**
Chardonnay Toscana Conti Contini 1998: Apple and leaf character on the nose follows through to the palate. Medium-bodied, with a round texture and a fruity finish. Rather simple. Drink now.–J.S. • $10 • (11/30/1999) • **83**
Chardonnay Toscana Conti Contini 1996 • $9 • (9/30/1997) • **69**
Chianti Montalbano Conte Contini Bonacossi 1997: Fresh, and literally bubbling with new fruit character. Medium- to light-bodied, with light tannins and a refreshing finish. A delicious young Chianti, as always. Chill before serving. Drink now.–J.S. • $11 • (12/15/1998) • **83**
Chianti Montalbano Conte Contini Bonacossi 1996 • $10 • (9/30/1997) • **83**
Chianti Montalbano Conte Contini Bonacossi 1995 • $10 • (10/31/1996) • **79**
Chianti Montalbano Conte Contini Bonacossi 1994 • $8 • (10/31/1995) • **81**
Chianti Montalbano Conte Contini Bonacossi 1993 • $8 • (7/31/1995) • **84**
Chianti Montalbano Conte Contini Bonacossi 1990 • $9 • (9/15/1992) • **81**
Chianti Montalbano Conte Contini Bonacossi 1988 • $8 • (10/31/1991) • **79**
Sangiovese Conti Contini 1993 • $9 • (10/31/1995) • **86**
Sangiovese Toscana Conti Contini 1995 • $10 • (9/30/1997) • **82**
Sangiovese Toscana Conti Contini 1994 • $9 • (10/31/1996) • **82**
Toscana Ghiaie della Furba 1997: An excellent Cabernet, with all the berry, currant and spice character you can expect. Full-bodied, with lovely tannins and a long currant and vanilla aftertaste. Best after 2000.–J.S. • $50 • (11/30/1999) • **91**
Toscana Ghiaie della Furba 1995 • $39 • (9/30/1997) • **87**
Toscana Ghiaie della Furba 1994 • $35 • (10/31/1996) • **87**
Toscana Ghiaie della Furba 1990 • $NA • (10/31/1995) • **86**
Toscana Ghiaie della Furba 1988 • $34 • (12/15/1992) • **69**
Toscana Ghiaie della Furba 1987 • $30 • (12/15/1991) • **79**
Toscana Ghiaie della Furba 1985 • $20 • (1/31/1990) • **91**
Vin Santo di Carmignano Riserva 1991: Wonderful and subtle aromas of nectarine, peach and light caramel. Medium-bodied and medium-sweet, with an oily texture and lots of ripe fruit and butter flavors on the finish. Drink now.–J.S. • $20/375 ml. • (12/15/1998) • **87**

CAPICHERA

Assajé 1998: A bit earthy, but with interesting strawberry and plum character. Medium-bodied, soft and funky on the finish. Not imported into the U.S. Drink now.–J.S. • $NA • (1/01/2000) • **83**
Vermentino di Gallura 1998: Clean and easy, with lemon and white pepper flavors. Light-bodied, with a fresh finish. Not imported into the U.S.–J.S. • $NA • (1/01/2000) • **79**
Vermentino di Gallura Vendemmia Tardiva 1998: A fresh and easy dry white, with melon and apple flavors. Medium-bodied, with a fresh finish. Not imported into the U.S. Drink now.–J.S. • $NA • (1/01/2000) • **85**

CAPPALLOTTO, TENUTA

Barolo Sôrì Paradiso 1995: Tough and slightly lean, with plum, rose and paraffin aromas and flavors. Medium-bodied and astringent, with fresh acidity. If you like mean and lean, here's your wine. Drink now through 2001.–J.S. • $60 • (6/15/2000) • **82**

CAPPELLA, PODERE LA

Chianti Classico Querciolo Riserva 1996: Good crushed cherry and berry character. Light- to medium-bodied, with light tannins and a slightly diluted finish. Drink now.–J.S. • $18 • (11/30/1999) • **81**
Toscana Corbezzolo 1996: A new producer to me. From organically grown Sangiovese. Intense aromas of violet, berry and toasted oak. Full-bodied, with loads of velvety tannins and a medium finish. Needs bottle age. Best after 2000.–J.S. • $36 • (11/30/1999) • **90**
Toscana Tancredi di Rossini 1997: A stylish white, with plenty of character and lovely aromas of grapefruit and lime. Medium-bodied, with good acidity and a long, tropical fruit finish. Made from Vermintino. Drink now.–J.S. • $17 • (11/30/1999) • **87**

CAPPELLANO

Barbera d'Alba Vigneto Gabutti 1992 • $NA • (10/31/1994) • **79**
Barbera d'Alba Vigneto Storico Gabutti 1996: Tar and spice add lovely complexity to this smooth-edged Barbera. Softened a bit by oak, it delivers a ripe mouthfeel, with plum and blackberry character. Balanced and seductive. Drink now.–P.M. • $NA • (10/31/1998) • **85**
Barolo 1992 • $NA • (10/31/1996) • **84**
Barolo 1991 • $NA • (10/31/1995) • **78**
Barolo 1990 • $NA • (10/31/1994) • **85**
Barolo 1989 • $NA • (10/31/1994) • **86**
Barolo 1988 • $32 • (10/31/1993) • **91**
Barolo Gabutti 1991 • $42 • (10/31/1995) • **86**
Barolo Gabutti 1990 • $42 • (10/31/1995) • **90**
Barolo Gabutti 1989 • $NA • (10/31/1994) • **93**
Barolo Otin Fiorin Collina Gabutti 1993 • $45 • (10/31/1997) • **86**
Barolo Otin Fiorin Collina Gabutti 1992 • $NA • (10/31/1996) • **88**
Barolo Otin Fiorin Franco Vigneto Storico Gabutti 1994: Full-bodied and rich, yet elegant, with a grip of wet earth, licorice, mineral and grilled flavors, the blackberry character emerges to makes this a distinctive and intense Barolo. Chewy finish. Best from 2005 through 2010.–P.M. • $NA • (10/31/1998) • **88**
Barolo Otin Fiorin Vigneto Storico Gabutti 1994: Tough, with some licorice, black fruit and wet earth. The tannins are firm, but dry a bit on the finish. Tasted twice, with consistent notes.–P.M. • $NA • (10/31/1998) • **79**
Langhe Augusto 1996: Welcome to a well-made, international-style red from Piedmont, from a good grower. Redolent with exciting, concentrated, pure cassis and blackberry flavors. Quite generous, the tannins are massive and tough, but the overall mouthfeel is opulent, the finish smoothed by lovely toasted bread, vanilla, smoky character.–P.M. • $NA • (10/31/1998) • **90**
Nebbiolo d'Alba 1994: Smooth, with smoke and licorice, this is an easy-to-like wine for drinking tonight. Offers some red fruit and a slightly chewy finish. A bit simple perhaps, but will complement food. Drink now.–P.M. • $NA • (10/31/1998) • **80**

CAPPELLETTI

Monferrato Rosso di Malì 1997: Really earthy and smelling of a sweaty horse, it turns tart on the palate.–P.M. • $17 • (11/15/1999) • **74**

CAPPUCCINA, LA

Recioto di Soave Arzìmo 1996: A very ripe dessert wine, but slightly overdone, with smoked almond and dried apricot character. Medium-bodied and off dry, with a dry finish. A bit unbalanced. Drink now.–J.S. • $25/500 ml. • (3/31/2000) • **84**
Recioto di Soave Arzìmo 1994 • $25/500 ml. • (5/31/1998) • **90**
Sauvignon Verona 1998: A ripe and intense white but not very Sauvignon-like. Lemon, apple and tropical fruit character with hints of straw. Medium-bodied, with good acidity and a rich, fruity aftertaste. Drink now through 2003.–J.S. • $11 • (4/30/2000) • **86**
Sauvignon Verona 1996 • $12 • (6/15/1998) • **84**
Soave 1998: Powerful and rich, with lots of dried fruit aromas, particularly apricot. Medium-bodied, with a dry and firm structure. Medium finish. Drink now.–J.S. • $9 • (3/31/2000) • **86**
Soave 1996 • $10 • (4/30/1998) • **83**
Soave Superiore Fontégo 1998: Lots of apples and spices in this young white. Full-bodied, with plenty of ripe fruit but a slightly short finish. Needs food. Drink now.–J.S. • $12 • (3/31/2000) • **86**
Soave Superiore Fontégo 1996 • $12 • (4/30/1998) • **83**
Soave Superiore San Brizio 1996: Big and very ripe, with wonderful aromas of almond, lime and honey. Full-bodied, with lots of fruit and an oily, thick texture. Drink now.–J.S. • $19 • (1/01/2000) • **87**
Verona Campo Buri 1996: Interesting currant, pepper and spice aromas follow through to a medium-bodied palate, with fine tannins and a fruity finish. Cabernet Franc and Cabernet Sauvignon Drink now through 2003.–J.S. • $21 • (5/15/2000) • **87**
Verona Madégo 1997: Not much to this really. Plum, chocolate, weedy character. Medium- to light-bodied, with light tannins and a weedy finish.–J.S. • $13 • (5/15/2000) • **79**
Verona Madégo 1996: There seems to be a serious red wine here, but the horsey, barnyard aromas and flavors dominate. Disappointing. Tasted twice, with consistent notes. A blend: 40 percent Cabernet Sauvignon, 40 percent Merlot, 20 percent Cabernet Franc.–B.S. • $12 • (7/31/1998) • **69**

CARDETO

Orvieto Classico Superiore Febeo 1998: A simple white that delivers pear and white pepper character throughout. Light in body and finish. Not imported into the U.S.–J.S. • $NA • (1/01/2000) • **79**
Orvieto Classico Superiore Jazz 1998: A simple white, with a pear-drop, slightly candied character. Light in body and finish. Not imported into the U.S.–J.S. • $NA • (1/01/2000) • **78**
Orvieto Classico Vendemmia Tardiva 1997: Pleasant, with aromas and flavors of canned peaches in syrup and a hint of clove character. Medium-bodied

and medium sweet. Drink now. Not imported into the U.S.–J.S. • $NA • (1/01/2000) • **84**

Umbria Fantasie del Cardeto 1996: A very ripe '96, with loads of tobacco, chocolate and spice character. Full-bodied, with chewy tannins and a fruity finish. Slightly hollow midpalate, but very good indeed. Drink now. Not imported into the U.S.–J.S. • $NA • (1/01/2000) • **86**

CARLINA, TENUTA

Brunello di Montalcino La Togata 1994: A little hard to believe, it's so dark and rich in flavor. But it's serious wine. Full-bodied, with chewy tannins and gamy, berry flavors. Medium aftertaste. Almost outstanding. Drink through 2005–J.S. • $49 • (8/31/1999) • **89**

Brunello di Montalcino La Togata 1991 • $NA • (11/30/1996) • **85**

Toscana Azzurreta 1996: Delicious. Intriguing plum skin and mushroom aromas follow through to the medium-bodied palate. Silky tannins and a medium, fruity finish. Not imported into the U.S. Drink now.–J.S. • $NA • (1/01/1999) • **85**

CARNASCIALE

Il Caberlot 1993 • $NA • (9/30/1997) • **81**

CARNEVALE, GIORGIO

Barbera d'Asti de la Rocchetta 1995 • $19 • (1/31/1998) • **77**

Barbera d'Asti il Crottino 1994 • $29 • (1/31/1998) • **70**

Brachetto d'Acqui Dolce 1996 • $28 • (12/31/1997) • **86**

Dolcetto d'Alba 1996 • $17 • (1/31/1998) • **83**

Gavi 1996 • $17 • (1/31/1998) • **81**

Moscato d'Asti 1996 • $17 • (12/31/1997) • **84**

Moscato d'Asti Sorì 1996 • $25 • (12/31/1997) • **85**

CAROBBIO

Chianti Classico 1997: This pretty '97 Chianti has interesting aromas of dried cherry, green tobacco and cigar box. Medium-bodied, with soft tannins and a fruity, caressing aftertaste. Drink now.–J.S. • $24 • (11/30/1999) • **88**

Chianti Classico 1996: Fruity and smooth, with alluring aromas of raspberry and cedar. Medium-bodied, with silky tannins and a fruity aftertaste. Drink now.–J.S. • $20 • (12/15/1998) • **87**

Chianti Classico 1992 • $NA • (2/28/1995) • **80**

Chianti Classico 1990 • $NA • (10/31/1993) • **90**

Chianti Classico Riserva 1996: An aromatic wine, with light body and subtle aromas of plum, tobacco and cedar. Medium-bodied, with light tannins and a light finish. Drink now.–J.S. • $35 • (11/30/1999) • **83**

Chianti Classico Riserva 1995: Wonderfully fresh blackberry and wet earth aromas. Of medium body, with silky tannins and a fruity finish. Delicious. Drink now.–J.S. • $33 • (12/15/1998) • **85**

Chianti Classico Riserva 1993 • $NA • (10/31/1996) • **87**

Chianti Classico Riserva 1991 • $NA • (10/31/1995) • **87**

Chianti Classico Riserva 1990 • $NA • (2/28/1995) • **89**

Leone del Carobbio 1993 • $NA • (10/31/1996) • **87**

Toscana Pietraforte 1995: An attractive Cabernet. Excellent aromas of black currant and cherry, with touches of dried herbs. Full-bodied, with lots of ripe, round tannins and just the right amount of new oak to give complexity. Slightly short on the finish.–J.S. • $40 • (12/15/1998) • **89**

CAROSO

Montepulciano d'Abruzzo Riserva 1992 • $12 • (7/31/1997) • **84**

CARPENE MALVOLTI

Prosecco di Conegliano NV: Almond flavors combine with a rich texture in this balanced, slightly sweet bubbly that finishes on a crisp note. Drink now.–B.S. • $15 • (7/31/1998) • **83**

Key: SS—Spectator Selection. CS—Cellar Selection. HR—Highly Recommended. $NA—Price not available. (BT)—Barrel tasting. (A)—Auction Price. For a key to the tasters' initials, see "How to Use These Listings."
Dates in parentheses represent the issues in which the ratings were published.

CARPINETO

Brut Chardonnay Farnito NV: Unique, this smells of vanilla and clove, feels a little dilute on the palate, then turns austere and very dry on the finish. Not for everyone. Drink now.–B.S. • $26 • (10/15/1999) • **83**

Cabernet Sauvignon Toscana Farnito 1996: Lots of black currant but with a hint of herbaceousness, which I am not keen on. Full-bodied, with angular tannins and a long finish. A bit coarse. Needs time. Best after 2001.–J.S. • $30 • (5/31/2000) • **85**

Cabernet Sauvignon Toscana Farnito 1995: Fabulous aromas of blackberry, black currant and mint. Full-bodied, full of tannins, yet polished and reserved. Slightly closed on the finish but should give more fruit with time. A top-notch Cabernet nearly every vintage. Best after 2000.–J.S. • $25 • (12/15/1998) • **91**

Chardonnay Colli della Toscana Centrale Farnito 1997: A simple, dry Chardonnay, with attractive pear and melon character, medium body and fresh acidity. Drink now.–J.S. • $28 • (11/30/1999) • **83**

Chardonnay Toscana Farnito 1996: A rather exotic wine, a cross between a Rhône Valley white and a California Chardonnay. Fresh aromas and flavors of pears and apples, hints of vanilla and nuts. Medium-bodied, with moderate acidity and a fruity, vanilla finish. Drink now.–J.S. • $20 • (12/15/1998) • **87**

Chianti Classico 1997: Rather odd, with bubbly carbon dioxide. Reserved and medium-bodied, with light vanilla and berry character and a fruity finish. Tasted twice, with consistent notes.–J.S. • $17 • (11/30/1999) • **79**

Chianti Classico 1996: A delicious and balanced Chianti with berry and raspberry aromas, a medium body, light tannins and a bright fruit aftertaste. Drink now.–J.S. • $16 • (12/15/1998) • **84**

Chianti Classico 1995 • $15 • (9/30/1997) • **86**

Chianti Classico 1994 • $14 • (10/31/1996) • **78**

Chianti Classico 1993 • $10 • (10/31/1995) • **82**

Chianti Classico 1992 • $9 • (2/28/1995) • **83**

Chianti Classico 1988 • $12 • (9/15/1991) • **87**

Chianti Classico Riserva 1996: This CC riserva has good structure for the vintage, with tobacco, dried fruit and chocolate aromas and flavors. Medium-bodied, with medium tannins and a juicy, Cabernet-like finish. Drink now.–J.S. • $24 • (11/30/1999) • **87**

Chianti Classico Riserva 1995: A big, rich Chianti that tastes more of Cabernet Sauvignon than Sangiovese at the moment, with black currant, berry and herbs on the nose and palate. Medium-bodied, with moderate tannins and a fruity aftertaste. Drink now.–J.S. • $20 • (12/15/1998) • **85**

Chianti Classico Riserva 1994 • $18 • (9/30/1997) • **87**

Chianti Classico Riserva 1993 • $16 • (10/31/1996) • **81**

Chianti Classico Riserva 1990 • $13 • (2/28/1995) • **87**

Chianti Classico Riserva 1988 • $14 • (9/15/1992) • **85**

Chianti Classico Riserva 1985 • $19 • (9/15/1991) • **89**

Sauvignon Toscana Farnito 1996: Subtle and delicious. Pretty aromas of gooseberry, melon and apple. Medium-bodied, with a creamy texture and ripe fruit flavors. Crisp and fruity on the aftertaste. Drink now.–J.S. • $20 • (12/15/1998) • **86**

Toscana Dogajolo 1998: A bright and bubbly red, with simple dried cherry aromas and flavors, light body and a fresh finish. Drink now.–J.S. • $12 • (11/30/1999) • **82**

Toscana Dogajolo 1996 • $11 • (9/30/1997) • **85**

Toscana Farnito 1994 • $20 • (9/30/1997) • **90**

Toscana Farnito 1991 • $18 • (2/28/1995) • **87**

Toscana Farnito 1990 • $18 • (10/31/1993) • **93**

Vino Nobile di Montepulciano Riserva 1994: A little herbal in character; could be a Sonoma Valley Cab. Medium-bodied, with medium tannins and an herbal, fruity finish. Shy on Sangiovese character. Drink now.–J.S. • $23 • (12/15/1998) • **82**

CARRAIA, LA

Orvieto Classico Poggio Calvelli 1998: Fresh and easy, with an intense character of lemon peel and mineral. Medium-bodied, with good acidity and a long, flavorful finish. Drink now.–J.S. • $8 • (2/29/2000) • **85**

Sangiovese Umbria 1995: A good, fruity wine, with dried cherry and floral character. Medium-bodied, with light tannins and a fresh finish. Not imported into the U.S. Drink now.–J.S. • $NA • (1/01/2000) • **84**

Umbria Fobiano 1997: A well-crafted red. Tobacco, berry and cherry aromas, with hints of oak. Full-bodied, with a wonderful intensity of fruit and milk chocolate character and notes of dried herb. Silky tannins. Medium finish. Best after 2001.–J.S. • $37 • (2/29/2000) • **88**

CARRETTA

Barbaresco Cascina Bordino 1993 • $23 • (10/31/1997) • **77**
Barolo Poderi Cannubi 1993 • $23 • (10/31/1997) • **76**
Barolo Poderi Cannubi 1988 • $23 • (3/31/1993) • **75**
Barolo Poderi Cannubi 1985 • $26 • (1/31/1992) • **82**
Dolcetto d'Alba Vigna Tavoleto 1996 • $12 • (10/31/1997) • **76**
Langhe 1995 • $NA • (10/31/1997) • **86**
Nebbiolo d'Alba Bric Paradiso 1990 • $19 • (4/30/1993) • **82**
Nebbiolo d'Alba Bric Paradiso 1989 • $15 • (7/31/1992) • **78**
Nebbiolo d'Alba Bric Tavoleto 1994 • $13 • (10/31/1997) • **75**
Nebbiolo d'Alba Bric Tavoleto 1988 • $15 • (7/31/1992) • **75**
Quercia Bric 1990 • $21 • (3/31/1993) • **87**
Quercia Bric 1989 • $20 • (1/31/1992) • **84**

CASA D'AMBRA

Epomeo Frassitelli 1998: Rather simple, with apple skin, pear and mineral character. Medium-bodied. Fresh finish. Drink now. Not imported into the U.S.–J.S. • $NA • (1/01/2000) • **82**
Ischia Forastera 1998: Fresh and delicious, with lemon, mineral and honeydew melon character throughout. Medium-bodied, with a light finish. Drink now. Not imported into the U.S.–J.S. • $NA • (1/01/2000) • **86**
Ischia Per'e Palummo 1998: Light, simple and fruity, with a plum, black pepper character and a fresh finish. Slightly diluted. Drink now. Not imported into the U.S.–J.S. • $NA • (1/01/2000) • **80**
Tenuta Montecorvo 1998: Delicious and easy to drink. Attractive aromas of roses, berries and minerals. Light-bodied, with light tannins and a fruity, fresh finish. Drink now. Not imported into the U.S.–J.S. • $NA • (1/01/2000) • **82**

CASA, LA

Merlot Piave 1995 • $9 • (3/31/1997) • **78**

CASA DI BACCO, LA

Chardonnay Lison-Pramaggiore 1998: Oxidized, with some apple and marzipan character but dull. Not imported into the U.S.–J.S. • $NA • (1/01/2000) • **77**
Pinot Grigio Lison-Pramaggiore 1998: Apple and cream character has a hint of marzipan. Medium-bodied, with light acidity and a slightly dull finish.–J.S. • $11 • (3/31/2000) • **78**
Sauvignon Lison-Pramaggiore 1998: Off dry and odd, with candied fruit cocktail and a plastic finish. Tasted twice, with consistent notes. Not imported into the U.S.–J.S. • $NA • (1/01/2000) • **68**
Veneto Orientale Hallowine 1998: Fizzy and unpleasant, with sweet cloying fruit character. Tasted twice, with consistent notes.–J.S. • $10 • (4/30/2000) • **68**

CASA DI PESCATORI

Sicilia Red 1998: A no-nonsense red from Sicily, with berry character. Light- to medium-bodied, with light tannins and a fresh finish. Drink now.–J.S. • $6 • (5/31/2000) • **82**
Sicilia White 1998: Simple and slightly oxidized, with a pepper and celery character.–J.S. • $6 • (5/31/2000) • **78**

CASA EMMA

Chianti Classico 1997: A fresh and fruity Chianti Classico, with dried cherry and plum character. Medium-bodied, with light tannins and a fruity finish. I had hoped for a little more from this producer in '97. Drink now.–J.S. • $15 • (11/30/1999) • **85**
Chianti Classico 1996: A fresh and vibrant Chianti with dried cherry and mushroom character. Medium-bodied, with light tannins and a fruity, fresh aftertaste. Drink now.–J.S. • $15 • (12/15/1998) • **85**
Chianti Classico 1995 • $15 • (9/30/1997) • **81**
Chianti Classico 1994 • $NA • (10/31/1996) • **86**
Chianti Classico 1993 • $NA • (10/31/1995) • **85**
Chianti Classico 1992 • $NA • (2/28/1995) • **77**
Chianti Classico 1991 • $NA • (10/31/1993) • **83**
Chianti Classico Riserva 1996: Really well done for the vintage. A pleasing combination of raspberry, violet and vanilla. Medium-bodied, with medium tannins and a fruity finish. Drink now.–J.S. • $40 • (11/30/1999) • **88**
Chianti Classico Riserva 1995: Extremely plummy, with undertones of tar. Medium-bodied, with moderate tannins and a slightly one-dimensional, fruity aftertaste. Drink now.–J.S. • $35 • (12/15/1998) • **86**
Chianti Classico Riserva 1994 • $35 • (9/30/1997) • **89**
Chianti Classico Riserva 1993 • $NA • (10/31/1996) • **87**
Chianti Classico Riserva 1990 • $NA • (2/28/1995) • **87**
Toscana Soloìo 1996: An eye-catching red with everything in the right proportions. Tastes more like Cabernet than Merlot, though. Extremely focused and rich, with blackberry and raspberry aromas. Full-bodied, with big, velvety tannins and a long, caressing finish. Drink now.–J.S. • $37 • (12/15/1998) • **87**
Toscana Soloìo 1994 • $NA • (9/30/1997) • **88**

CASA GIRELLI

Chardonnay Puglia Canaletto Winemaker's Choice 1998: Medium-bodied, round and fruity, with pineapple skin and cream aromas. A bit simple, but delicious. Drink now.–J.S. • $10 • (5/31/2000) • **80**
Merlot Canaletto 1995 • $7 • (6/15/1997) • **83**
Merlot Canaletto 1994 • $7 • (6/15/1996) • **79**
Merlot Canaletto 1993 • $6 • (7/31/1995) • **78**
Merlot Veneto Canaletto Winemaker's Choice 1998: A chewy young wine with lots of grapey character, thick tannins and a medium finish. Needs a bit more fruit in the center palate. Good value. Drink now.–J.S. • $10 • (5/15/2000) • **85**
Montepulciano d'Abruzzo Canaletto 1993 • $6 • (3/31/1995) • **83**
Montepulciano d'Abruzzo Canaletto Winemaker's Choice 1997: Good dried cherry, plum and tobacco character. Medium-bodied, with medium tannins and a fruity finish. Drink now.–J.S. • $10 • (4/30/2000) • **82**
Moscato Rosa Trentino i Mesi 1991 • $29 • (6/15/1996) • **84**
Pinot Grigio Trentino i Mesi 1996 • $10 • (12/15/1997) • **79**
Pinot Grigio Venezie Canaletto Winemaker's Choice 1998: Lovely perfumes of flowers, mineral and apricot. Medium-bodied, with lots of flavor and a lively, fresh finish. Well done. Drink now.–J.S. • $10 • (3/31/2000) • **85**
Pinot Grigio-Garganega Canaletto 1996 • $7 • (6/15/1997) • **84**
Pinot Nero Trentino i Mesi 1988 • $10 • (2/15/1991) • **81**
Sangiovese Marche Fontella 1996 • $7 • (2/28/1998) • **77**

CASA MARTELLETTI

Barbera d'Asti Gli Scaglioni 1997: A bright Barbera, with distinct mocha, spice and wild berry aromas and flavors. Flavorful in a pungent way, it's medium-bodied, with crisp acidity on the finish. Drink now through 2002.–P.M. • $16 • (11/15/1999) • **85**
Dolcetto d'Alba Camürot 1998: Has nice wet earth, red berry and plum character, but also green, herbal notes and a toughness that clamps down on the finish.–P.M. • $14 • (11/15/1999) • **78**

CASA SOLA

Chianti Classico 1997: Medium-bodied, with interesting berry and bark aromas and light tannins. Fresh vanilla and berry aftertaste. Drink now. –J.S. • $17 • (11/30/1999) • **85**
Chianti Classico 1996: Some attractive berry and vanilla aromas and flavors. Medium-bodied, with soft tannins and a short, slightly dry finish. Drink now.–J.S. • $15 • (12/15/1998) • **81**
Chianti Classico 1993 • $NA • (10/31/1995) • **81**
Chianti Classico Riserva 1995: Some decent berry character but very dry and austere on the palate. Medium-bodied, with a short finish. Tasted twice, with consistent notes.–J.S. • $25 • (12/15/1998) • **75**
Toscana Montarsiccio 1995: A plummy, minty red with fine tannins which give a caressing texture, but its slightly austere and dry on the finish. Drink now.–J.S. • $40 • (12/15/1998) • **84**

CASA VINICOLA TRIACCA

Chianti Classico La Madonnina 1997: A solid CC normale, with good berry and dried cherry character and a hint of earth. Medium-bodied, with light tannins and a fresh finish. Drink now.–J.S. • $13 • (11/30/1999) • **85**
Chianti Classico La Madonnina 1996: Pretty blackberry and cherry aromas and flavors weave through and through. Medium- to light-bodied, with well-integrated tannins and a caressing finish. Drink now.–J.S. • $11 • (12/15/1998) • **85**
Chianti Classico La Madonnina Riserva 1996: A bit lean but showing attractive berry, cedar and cigar box character. Medium-bodied, with

slightly astringent tannins and a firm finish. Needs to mellow a bit. Best after 2000.–J.S. • $15 • (11/30/1999) • **86**

Chianti Classico La Madonnina Riserva 1995: Luscious. Beautiful blackberry aromas. Medium- to full-bodied, with wonderfully smooth tannins and a long, fruity aftertaste. Drink now through 2005.–J.S. • $15 • (12/15/1998) • **88**

Chianti Classico La Madonnina Vigna La Palaia 1996: A slinky and fine modern Chianti. Dark ruby in color, it's bubbling over with ripe berry, wet earth and smoke character. Full-bodied and very racy, with polished tannins and a medium finish. Drink now.–J.S. • $17 • (11/30/1999) • **87**

Toscana Il Mandorlo 1995: A rich yet slightly rustic red. Dark color. Intense grapey, berry character. Full-bodied and chewy. Cabernet Sauvignon and Sangiovese. Drink now.–J.S. • $18 • (11/30/1999) • **87**

Vino Nobile di Montepulciano Santa Venere 1996: Very grapey, with hints of raisin. Light- to medium-bodied, with a burnt fruit and earth component. Slightly rustic. Drink now.–J.S. • $15 • (11/30/1999) • **81**

CASAL THAULERO

Abbazia di Propezzano 1986 • $19 • (7/15/1991) • **89**

Colli Aprutini Abbazia di Propezzano 1992: A very flavorful, ripe-tasting, even sweetish red wine, with ample prune, herb and tomato flavors and moderate tannins. Big and broad in character. Drink now. • $10 • (8/31/1998) • **82**

Montepulciano d'Abruzzo 1993 • $6 • (2/29/1996) • **82**

Montepulciano d'Abruzzo 1989 • $6 • (6/30/1991) • **81**

Montepulciano d'Abruzzo 1988 • $5 • (5/31/1990) • **80**

Montepulciano d'Abruzzo Orsetto 1996: A light, dry red, with fresh raspberry and plum flavors and spicy accents. Easy in texture, with little tannin. Drink now. • $7 • (8/31/1998) • **82**

CASALE DAVIDDI

Vino Nobile di Montepulciano 1996: Plenty of rose and berry on the nose. Medium-bodied, with silky tannins and a caressing finish. Needs a bit more fruit concentration to be outstanding. Drink now.–J.S. • $23 • (11/30/1999) • **87**

Vino Nobile di Montepulciano 1995: Clean and fresh, showing dried cherry and mineral aromas and flavors. Medium-bodied and silky, with a lot of fresh fruit character. Well done. Drink now.–J.S. • $18 • (12/15/1998) • **87**

Vino Nobile di Montepulciano Riserva 1995: A silky and cedary wine with good dried cherry character, medium body and a crisp finish. At its peak. Not imported into the U.S. Drink now.–J.S. • $NA • (1/01/1999) • **85**

CASALE DEL GIGLIO

Cabernet Sauvignon Lazio 1996: Dark, with wonderful perfumes of berry, raspberry, mint and currant. Full-bodied, with loads of polished tannins and a long, fruity finish. A big and juicy Cab. Best after 2001.–J.S. • $25 • (4/30/2000) • **88**

Chardonnay Lazio 1998: Clean, with apple skin, lime and mineral character. Medium-bodied, with fresh acidity and a light finish. Drink now.–J.S. • $18 • (4/30/2000) • **82**

Lazio Madreselva 1995: Attractive berry, dried herb and currant aromas. Full-bodied and very velvety, with chewy tannins and a long finish. A bit tough and rustic, but good. Cabernet and Merlot. Best after 2000.–J.S. • $35 • (4/30/2000) • **86**

Lazio Satrico 1998: Delicious and fresh, with good aromas of pineapple, pear and mango. Medium-bodied, with medium acidity and a ripe fruit aftertaste. Trebbiano and Chardonnay. Not imported into the U.S. Drink now.–J.S. • $NA • (1/01/2000) • **85**

Merlot Lazio 1997: Doesn't taste much like Merlot, but it's a solid wine for current drinking. Lots of good ripe berry, with a firm backbone of acidity and a fruity finish. Drink now.–J.S. • $20 • (1/01/2000) • **81**

Petit Verdot Lazio 1997: A fresh and fruity red, with pleasant strawberry and cherry character, medium body and a light finish. Drink now.–J.S. • $22 • (1/01/2000) • **82**

Sauvignon Lazio 1998: Subdued, with pear and peach character and a hint of apricot. Medium-bodied, with good fruit flavors, medium acidity and a lemony aftertaste. Drink now.–J.S. • $18 • (4/30/2000) • **84**

Shiraz Lazio 1997: Decent Syrah character, but a little lean, with a good dark color, violet and floral aromas and hints of ripe fruit. Medium-bodied, with firm tannins and a slightly austere finish. Drink now.–J.S. • $23 • (1/01/2000) • **83**

CASALOSTE

Chianti Classico 1997: This decadent, rich, exotic Chianti is ripe and earthy, with plenty of fruit. Full-bodied, with velvety tannins and a superripe fruit finish. Drink now through 2002.–J.S. • $25 • (11/30/1999) • **90**

Chianti Classico 1996: Juicy and ripe, with cherry and chestnut aromas and flavors. Medium-bodied, with earth and fruit flavors, a fruity finish. Delicious.–J.S. • $25 • (12/15/1998) • **85**

Chianti Classico 1995 • $NA • (9/30/1997) • **81**

Chianti Classico 1994 • $NA • (10/31/1996) • **85**

Chianti Classico 1993 • $NA • (10/31/1995) • **79**

Chianti Classico 1993 • $14 • (10/31/1996) • **81**

Chianti Classico Don VincEnzo Riserva 1995: Serious CC riserva. It shows a very bright character of crushed berries, minerals and other fruits. Medium-bodied, with medium velvety tannins and a lovely fruity, slightly vanilla aftertaste. Drink now through 2001.–J.S. • $NA • (11/30/1999) • **88**

Chianti Classico Riserva 1996: A good, simple Sangiovese, with dried cherry and berry character. Light-bodied, with light tannins and a fresh finish. Drink up. Drink now.–J.S. • $37 • (11/30/1999) • **82**

Chianti Classico Riserva 1995: Very pretty raspberry and cherry and aromas and flavors on a medium-bodied palate, with soft, succulent tannins and a long, ripe fruit aftertaste. Delicious. Drink now through 2001.–J.S. • $40 • (12/15/1998) • **88**

Chianti Classico Riserva 1994 • $NA • (9/30/1997) • **86**

Chianti Classico Riserva 1993 • $18 • (10/31/1996) • **85**

CASALTE, FATTORIA LE

Rosso di Montepulciano 1996: Light and fruity, with tobacco, berry and cherry aromas and flavors. Drink now.–J.S. • $11 • (12/15/1998) • **81**

Vino Nobile di Montepulciano 1995: Medium-bodied, with lots of cherry and bark aromas and flavors and a slightly tough finish. Traditional in style. Needs food. Better with age?–J.S. • $24 • (12/15/1998) • **80**

Vino Nobile di Montepulciano 1993 • $NA • (9/30/1997) • **80**

CASANOVA DI NERI

Brunello di Montalcino 1995: Elegant and well-done. Pretty plum and berry aromas with hints of flowers. Medium-bodied, with silky tannins and a fresh, fruity finish. Drink now.–J.S. • $44 • (6/30/2000) • **87**

Brunello di Montalcino 1993: Not huge but delicious, bringing to mind grilled steak. Blackberry and bark aromas follow through to a firm and zingy palate of ripe fruit, fine tannins and fresh acidity. Drink now.–J.S. • $44 • (12/15/1998) • **87**

Brunello di Montalcino 1991 • $35 • (11/30/1996) • **85**

Brunello di Montalcino 1990 • $33 • (10/31/1995) • **90**

Brunello di Montalcino 1988 • $27 • (4/30/1994) • **82**

Brunello di Montalcino Cerreto Alto Riserva 1990 • $72 • (11/30/1996) • **93**

Brunello di Montalcino Riserva 1993: Delicate and seductive aromas of berries, flowers and smoke introduce a wine that builds on the palate, delivering pleasure. Medium- to full-bodied, with ripe and silky tannins and a long, sweet fruit aftertaste. Drink now through 2008.–J.S. • $87 • (8/31/1999) • **91**

Brunello di Montalcino Riserva 1988 • $NA • (10/31/1994) • **92**

Brunello di Montalcino Tenuta Nuova 1995: This is a blockbuster—the real thing. Very ripe and earthy with lots of wonderful fruit and wet leaves. Full-bodied, with velvety tannins and a long finish. Drink through 2008.–J.S. • $49 • (6/30/2000) HR • **94**

Brunello di Montalcino Tenuta Nuova 1994: A very fresh and fruity '94 Brunello, with currant, licorice and cherry character. Medium-bodied, with round tannins and a grapey, fruity finish. Slightly monolithic, but solid. Drink through 2005.–J.S. • $52 • (8/31/1999) • **88**

Brunello di Montalcino Tenuta Nuova 1993: A serious and tightly knit red. Very plummy, with wet earth undertones. Medium- to full-bodied, with firm tannins and a long, rich aftertaste. A new, very rich wine from this producer. Needs bottle age. Best after 2001.–J.S. • $50 • (12/15/1998) • **90**

Rosso di Montalcino 1997: Some really delicious bright berry and cherry flavors, but slightly earthy and rustic. Medium-bodied, with soft tannins. Caressing finish. Drink now.–J.S. • $27 • (9/15/1999) • **86**

Key: SS—Spectator Selection. CS—Cellar Selection. HR—Highly Recommended. $NA—Price not available. (BT)—Barrel tasting. (A)—Auction Price. For a key to the tasters' initials, see "How to Use These Listings."
Dates in parentheses represent the issues in which the ratings were published.

ITALY

Rosso di Montalcino 1996: Chunky, with plenty of berry and cherry aromas and flavors. Medium-bodied, with medium tannins and finish. Slightly one-dimensional, but delicious. Drink now.–J.S. • $16 • (12/15/1998) • **86**

Rosso di Montalcino 1995 • $13 • (9/30/1997) • **83**

Rosso di Montalcino 1994 • $14 • (11/30/1996) • **81**

Rosso di Montalcino 1993 • $NA • (10/31/1995) • **84**

Rosso di Montalcino 1991 • $14 • (4/30/1994) • **84**

CASCINA BALLARIN

Barolo 1993 • $NA • (10/31/1997) • **79**

CASCINA BONGIOVANNI

Barolo 1995: A bit simple but showing clean, vibrant fruit, with a smoky edge. Licorice and raspberry on the light finish. Drink now through 2003.–P.M. • $42 • (11/15/1999) • **84**

Barolo 1993 • $40 • (10/31/1997) • **91**

Barolo Pernanno 1995: Firm and succulent, this medium-bodied, clean Barolo provides ripe flavors and a herbal note, with bright fruit, crisp acidity and firm tannins. Drink now through 2005.–P.M. • $51 • (11/15/1999) • **85**

Dolcetto d'Alba 1995 • $18 • (10/31/1997) • **90**

Langhe Falletto 1996: Just gorgeous. Silky in texture, with clean, pure blackberry and cassis flavors, turning fresh and crisp. Full-bodied, it's refined and focused throughout. The tannins are ultraripe on the finish. Drink now through 2005.–P.M. • $40 • (11/15/1999) • **92**

CASCINA CASTLET

Barbera d'Asti 1997: Earthy aromas are funky, and the character is herbal and astringent on the palate. Light-bodied, showing only modest red berry fruit. Dry finish.–P.M. • $15 • (10/31/1998) • **74**

Barbera d'Asti 1995 • $NA • (1/01/1997) • **82**

Barbera d'Asti Litina 1996: Delicate, with raspberry, strawberry and floral notes. Light-bodied, it lacks a bit of intensity. Serve slightly chilled with light dishes. Drink now.–P.M. • $17 • (10/31/1998) • **80**

Barbera d'Asti Passum 1996: Racy and well made, showing lovely, well-defined blackberry and cassis flavors, a supersmooth palate thanks to ripe tannins and a lingering, clean, balanced finish. Neither heavy nor overly oaky, this delightful wine would be a delicious companion to many foods. Drink now.–P.M. • $26 • (10/31/1998) • **88**

Barbera d'Asti Policalpo 1994 • $NA • (1/01/1997) • **88**

Barbera del Monferrato Goj 1996: Very odd, this spritzy, light-bodied red tastes of strawberry juice and olives. Tasted twice, with consistent notes.–P.M. • $13 • (10/31/1998) • **60**

Monferrato Policalpo 1996: Quite strange. Earthy and funky, with mushroom, forest underbrush, plum and herb notes mingling together. Very dry finish.–P.M. • $25 • (10/31/1998) • **72**

CASCINA CORSALETTO

Dolcetto di Dogliani Cursalet 1996: A bit green, but this vivacious Dolcetto delivers ripe fruit, green olive and earth complexity. The sweet finish makes it end better than it starts. Drink now.–P.M. • $25 • (10/31/1998) • **82**

Dolcetto di Dogliani Vigneto Maestra 1996: Ripe and sweet, but it has an herbal undertow, with a drying mouthfeel and an astringent finish.–P.M. • $25 • (10/31/1998) • **75**

CASCINA GALLETO

Dolcetto d'Alba 1996 • $NA • (10/31/1997) • **83**

CASCINA LA BARBATELLA

Barbera d'Asti 1994 • $9 • (10/31/1996) • **85**

Barbera d'Asti Superiore Vigna dell'Angelo 1993 • $16 • (10/31/1996) • **86**

CASCINA LA PERTICA

Bianco Le Sincette 1996 • $12 • (2/28/1998) • **83**

Riviera del Garda Bresciano Chiaretto Le Sincette 1996 • $12 • (12/15/1997) • **80**

Rosso Le Zalte 1994 • $18 • (12/15/1997) • **90**

CASCINA LUISIN

Barbaresco 1994: This impressively round and silky red is a bit earthy, with a surprising salami aroma and vanilla bean, cream, milk chocolate and blackberry character. Supple, but lacking a bit in complexity. Drink now.–P.M. • $28 • (10/31/1998) • **80**

Barbaresco 1993 • $NA • (10/31/1996) • **85**

Barbaresco Rabajà 1995: Impressive for its inky-dark color, extracted quality—it explodes with blackberry and cassis—and lovely, fruit-packed mouthfeel. Vibrant and succulent, it lacks only a bit of finesse and *terroir*. Very hard finish; hopefully time will smooth it. Best after 2003.–P.M. • $31 • (10/31/1998) • **84**

Barbaresco Rabajà 1994: Soft and pleasant, with spice, mocha and chocolate notes mingling with the red berry flavors in a light- to medium-bodied package. Supple tannins. Drink now through 2004.–P.M. • $28 • (10/31/1998) • **81**

Barbaresco Rabajà 1993 • $NA • (10/31/1996) • **70**

Barbaresco Sorì Paolin 1996: A bit one-dimensional in the aroma spectrum. It's ripe and full-bodied, but an herbal character weaves its distracting web through the tar and red berry notes. Tough, chewy tannins.–P.M. • $29 • (8/31/1999) • **79**

Barbaresco Sorì Paolin 1995: Fairly supple and easygoing, with black cherry character but also some herbaceousness. Medium-bodied, but quite tannic and lean.–P.M. • $31 • (10/31/1998) • **76**

Barbera d'Alba Asili 1997: Crisp but succulent, with sweet-tasting red berry character, but it turns a bit herbaceous.–P.M. • $17 • (9/15/1999) • **79**

Barbera d'Alba Asili 1996: This beautiful Barbera is a bit earthy yet lush and supple, with ripe fruit and smooth tannins, all presented in a balanced, medium-bodied package. The seductive and long finish is accented by complex plum and smoky, toasted oak notes. Drink now through 2005.–P.M. • $14 • (10/31/1998) • **88**

Barbera d'Alba Asili Barrique 1996: Nice ripe mouthfeel, with smoke, black cherry, mineral notes, but a slight herbal character creeps in. Turns overly crisp on the finish. Drink now.–P.M. • $13 • (9/15/1999) • **80**

Barbera d'Alba Asili Barrique 1995: Exciting, showing lots of clean, pure fruit and earth, with spice, mocha and chocolate flavors. Of medium body, this fans out on the palate with supple tannins. The balanced finish ends on a succulent note. Drink now through 2002.–P.M. • $NA • (10/31/1998) • **86**

Dolcetto d'Alba Bric Trifüla 1997: Crisp and juicy, but also a bit herbal and slightly diluted, with decent cherry, currant and smoke notes. Tart, lean finish.–P.M. • $14 • (11/15/1999) • **78**

Dolcetto d'Alba Bric Trifüla 1996: Beautiful harmony. Dark-colored and flavorful, packed with pure and clean berry flavors, this medium-bodied Dolcetto impresses with its ripe tannins and dovetailing, supple finish. Drink now.–P.M. • $14 • (10/31/1998) • **86**

CASELLE, FATTORIA LE

Chianti 1998: This good, simple Chianti has dried cherry, berry and wet earth aromas and flavors. Light- to medium-bodied, with light tannins and a fresh finish. Drink now.–J.S. • $10 • (11/30/1999) • **83**

Toscana Bramasole 1998: A little earthy, but with good berry and cherry character. Medium-bodied, with soft tannins and a light, chewy finish. Drink now.–J.S. • $15 • (11/30/1999) • **84**

CASINA DI CORNIA

Cabernet Sauvignon Toscana L'Amaranto 1996: A pretty, ripe, well-made Cabernet, with raspberry and mint aromas and flavors. Medium-bodied, with well-integrated tannins and a caressing, polished texture on the finish. Drink now.–J.S. • $25 • (12/15/1998) • **87**

Chianti Classico 1996: A simple and fruity CC with plum and tea character, medium to light body and light tannins. Fresh acidity on the finish. Drink now.–J.S. • $15 • (12/15/1998) • **81**

Chianti Classico 1994 • $17 • (10/31/1996) • **72**

Chianti Classico Riserva 1996: Clean but light. Plum, cedar and redwood aromas follow through to a light- to medium-bodied palate and a diluted finish. Drink now.–J.S. • $NA • (11/30/1999) • **80**

L'Amaranto 1994 • $17 • (10/31/1996) • **88**

CASISANO-COLOMBAIO

Brunello di Montalcino 1995: Very good wine from a new name. Loads of fruit on the nose with cherries, berries and plums. Full-bodied, with cherry, vanilla pods and earth flavors. Punchy tannins and a long, long finish. Drink now through 2006.–J.S. • $50 • (6/30/2000) • **89**

Brunello di Montalcino 1990 • $NA • (10/31/1995) • **87**

Rosso di Montalcino 1993 • $NA • (10/31/1995) • **78**

CASON HIRSCHPRUNN

Mitterberg Bianco Contest 1996: A serious white, with pretty, complex aromas of pineapple, apple and pie crust plus a hint of vanilla. Full-bodied, with excellent fruit concentration and a lively finish. Pinot Grigio, Chardonnay and other white varieties. Drink now through 2003.–J.S. • $28 • (6/15/2000) • **90**

Mitterberg Bianco Etelle 1997: Delicious, with lemon, cookie and mineral aromas. Medium-bodied, with fresh acidity and a long, flavorful finish. Drink now.–J.S. • $13 • (6/15/2000) • **88**

Mitterberg Bianco Etelle 1996: New oak provides most of the character in this delicately structured white. Overall, it's lean and slightly astringent on the finish. Drink now.–B.S. • $15 • (7/31/1998) • **83**

Mitterberg Rosso Casòn 1996: Delicious, with good berry, herb and olive character. Medium-bodied, with velvety tannins and a sweet fruit aftertaste. Drink now through 2002.–J.S. • $30 • (6/15/2000) • **85**

Mitterberg Rosso Casòn 1995: A lovely red, full of cherry, black currant and smoky, spicy oak aromas and flavors set off by a firm yet elegant structure and tangy acidity. Fruit and oak keep pulsing on the finish. Drink now through 2000.–B.S. • $30 • (7/31/1998) • **88**

Mitterberg Rosso Casòn 1994: What a beauty. Exhibits cassis, cedar and roasted coffee and vanilla aromas and flavors, while its elegance and power are draped like a finely tailored Italian suit. So suave and supple it seduces you, yet it should get even better over the next few years. Best through 2004.–B.S. • $30 • (7/31/1998) • **89**

Mitterberg Rosso Corolle 1995: Interesting, with rhubarb, leather and fruit character plus roasted coffee. Medium-bodied, with light tannins, but a bit short on the finish. Drink now.–J.S. • $16 • (6/15/2000) • **83**

Mitterberg Rosso Corolle 1994: Sporting herb and cherry, this has density, structure and moderate concentration. Cassis, cherry and cedar are the flavor highlights, lightly framed by oak and velvety tannins. Drink now through 2001.–B.S.• $17 • (7/31/1998) • **86**

CASSERO, VIGNA DEL

Brunello di Montalcino Riserva 1990 • $NA • (11/30/1996) • **88**

CASTEL RUGGERO

Chianti Classico 1995 • $NA • (9/30/1997) • **82**

Chianti Classico 1994 • $NA • (10/31/1996) • **88**

Chianti Classico 1993 • $NA • (10/31/1995) • **85**

Chianti Classico 1988 • $NA • (9/15/1991) • **86**

Chianti Classico Riserva 1993 • $NA • (10/31/1996) • **89**

CASTELGREVE

Chianti Classico 1995 • $NA • (9/30/1997) • **81**

Chianti Classico 1993 • $10 • (10/31/1995) • **80**

Chianti Classico 1992 • $9 • (2/28/1995) • **82**

Chianti Classico 1991 • $9 • (10/31/1993) • **82**

Chianti Classico 1990 • $10 • (9/15/1992) • **78**

Chianti Classico Fascia Rossa Riserva 1994: At its peak now for a Chianti, with tobacco, berry and ripe plum character. Medium-bodied, with caressing tannins and a slightly short, dry finish. Not imported into the U.S. Drink now.–J.S. • $NA • (1/01/1999) • **83**

Chianti Classico Riserva 1996: A pretty '96 CC riserva, with light aromas of berry, mushroom and meat. Medium-bodied, with sweet, ripe fruit flavors and a medium, silky tannin structure. Drink now.–J.S. • $18 • (11/30/1999) • **85**

Chianti Classico Riserva 1994 • $NA • (9/30/1997) • **86**

Chianti Classico Riserva 1993 • $15 • (10/31/1996) • **77**

Chianti Classico Riserva 1991 • $13 • (10/31/1995) • **82**

Chianti Classico Riserva 1990 • $12 • (2/28/1995) • **85**

Key: SS—Spectator Selection. CS—Cellar Selection. HR—Highly Recommended. $NA—Price not available. (BT)—Barrel tasting. Ⓐ—Auction Price. For a key to the tasters' initials, see "How to Use These Listings."
Dates in parentheses represent the issues in which the ratings were published.

Vin Santo di Chianti Classico 1993: Very pretty aromas of almond, honey, cream and passion fruit. Medium-bodied and off-dry, with a slightly harsh and medicinal finish. Too bad. Not imported into the U.S.–J.S. • $NA • (1/01/1999) • **78**

CASTELL'IN VILLA

Chianti Classico 1990 • $NA • (10/31/1993) • **84**

Chianti Classico 1988 • $13 • (9/15/1991) • **88**

Chianti Classico 1986 • $13 • (9/15/1990) • **79**

Chianti Classico 1985 • $12 • (6/30/1989) • **86**

Chianti Classico Il Poggiale Riserva 1996: A good, no-nonsense CC riserva, with attractive plum and cedar aromas and flavors. Medium-bodied, with light tannins and a fresh finish. Not imported into the U.S. Drink now. –J.S. • $NA • (1/01/1999) • **85**

Chianti Classico Riserva 1988 • $NA • (10/31/1993) • **79**

Chianti Classico Riserva 1982 • $18 • (11/30/1990) • **86**

Santa Croce 1988 • $NA • (10/31/1993) • **92**

CASTELLARE DI CASTELLINA

Chianti Classico 1997: Medium-bodied, with a good amount of dried cherry and spice character and polished tannins. A bit more fruit on the short finish would move it up. Drink now.–J.S. • $20 • (11/30/1999) • **85**

Chianti Classico 1996: Delicate and fruity, with a pleasant cherry and chocolate character. Medium- to light-bodied, with light tannins and a fresh finish. Drink now.–J.S. • $15 • (12/15/1998) • **84**

Chianti Classico 1995 • $16 • (9/30/1997) • **80**

Chianti Classico 1994 • $16 • (10/31/1996) • **84**

Chianti Classico 1993 • $18 • (10/31/1995) • **80**

Chianti Classico 1991 • $12 • (10/31/1993) • **81**

Chianti Classico 1990 • $14 • (9/15/1992) • **82**

Chianti Classico 1989 • $14 • (9/15/1992) • **82**

Chianti Classico 1988 • $13 • (11/30/1990) • **82**

Chianti Classico 1987 • $11 • (11/30/1989) • **81**

Chianti Classico 1986 • $11 • (10/15/1989) • **82**

Chianti Classico 1985 • $11 • (3/31/1988) • **85**

Chianti Classico Il Poggiale Riserva 1995: A subtle red with cedar, berry and tobacco aromas and flavors. Medium-bodied, with well-integrated tannins and a caressing, silky texture. Well crafted; would score higher if a bit more concentrated. Drink now.–J.S. • $30 • (12/15/1998) • **85**

Chianti Classico Il Poggiale Riserva 1993 • $30 • (9/30/1997) • **86**

Chianti Classico Riserva 1996: Pleasant. Aromas of berry and grilled meat in this red. Light- to medium-bodied, with light tannins and a crisp finish. Drink now.–J.S. • $29 • (11/30/1999) • **84**

Chianti Classico Riserva 1995: Fading fast, with very little fruit left. Light-bodied, with some vanilla character and a very dry finish. Tasted twice, with consistent notes.–J.S. • $20 • (12/15/1998) • **75**

Chianti Classico Riserva 1994 • $22 • (9/30/1997) • **84**

Chianti Classico Riserva 1993 • $22 • (10/31/1996) • **82**

Chianti Classico Riserva 1991 • $21 • (10/31/1995) • **85**

Chianti Classico Riserva 1990 • $20 • (2/28/1995) • **84**

Chianti Classico Riserva 1988 • $23 • (9/15/1992) • **83**

Chianti Classico Riserva 1986 • $11 • (11/30/1989) • **86**

Chianti Classico Riserva 1985 • $17 • (9/15/1991) • **77**

Colli della Toscana Centrale Canonico 1996: An obvious style. Loads of vanilla and smoky wood aromas, with hints of ripe fruit. Medium-bodied, with moderate acidity and a chalk, wood and fruit finish. Drink now.–J.S. • $21 • (12/15/1998) • **80**

Colli della Toscana Centrale Coniale 1995: Very smoky, ripe fruit character. Full-bodied, with very polished tannins and coconut, toasted oak and fruit on the finish. Needs time to come together. Outstanding Cabernet. Best after 2000.–J.S. • $32 • (11/30/1999) • **90**

Colli della Toscana Centrale Coniale 1994: A delicious wine, close to outstanding, with subtle currant and smoke character. Medium-bodied, with fine tannins and a fruity and caressing aftertaste. Cabernet Sauvignon. Drink now.–J.S. • $35 • (12/15/1998) • **89**

Colli della Toscana Centrale Coniale 1993 • $35 • (9/30/1997) • **90**

Colli della Toscana Centrale Coniale 1988 • $35 • (9/15/1991) • **92**

Colli della Toscana Centrale Coniale 1987 • $31 • (10/31/1990) • **87**

Colli della Toscana Centrale I Sodi di San Niccolò 1995: A solid, well-built red with smoke, dried cherry and mineral character throughout. Medium-bodied, with medium, velvety tannins and a medium, fruity finish. Harmonious. Drink now.–J.S. • $45 • (11/30/1999) • **90**

Colli della Toscana Centrale I Sodi di San Niccolò 1994: A lean and slightly hard style for this wine, with bright, pretty blackberry and cherry aromas that have hints of dark chocolate. Medium-bodied, with fresh, very crisp acidity and a medium, fruity finish. Best after 2001.–J.S. • $41 • (11/30/1999) • **87**

Colli della Toscana Centrale I Sodi di San Niccolò 1993: An outstanding Sangiovese. Terrific structure, with a hidden reserve of blackberry, mushroom and raspberry character. Full-bodied yet reserved, with fine tannins and a long finish. Still needs time. Best after 2000.–J.S. • $37 • (12/15/1998) • **92**

Colli della Toscana Centrale I Sodi di San Niccolò 1991 • $42 • (10/31/1995) • **87**

Colli della Toscana Centrale I Sodi di San Niccolò 1990 • $240 Ⓐ • (2/28/1995) • **88**

Colli della Toscana Centrale I Sodi di San Niccolò 1988 • $35 • (9/15/1991) • **88**

Colli della Toscana Centrale I Sodi di San Niccolò 1987 • $32 • (4/15/1991) • **86**

Colli della Toscana Centrale I Sodi di San Niccolò 1986 • $25 • (11/30/1989) • **94**

Colli della Toscana Centrale I Sodi di San Niccolò 1985 • $25 • (5/31/1988) • **96**

Colli della Toscana Centrale I Sodi di San Niccolò 1983 • $20 • (5/31/1988) • **87**

Colli della Toscana Centrale I Sodi di San Niccolò 1982 • $20 • (9/15/1987) • **89**

Colli della Toscana Centrale I Sodi di San Niccolò 1981 • $20 • (9/15/1987) • **87**

Colli della Toscana Centrale Spartito 1996: Rather oxidized and tired, with apple and lime character. Medium-bodied, with a short finish. Not imported into the U.S.–J.S. • $NA • (1/01/1999) • **77**

CASTELLARI BERGAGLIO

Gavi di Gavi 1997: Delicious. A subtle and squeaky-clean white, with sliced apple and light spice aromas. Medium-bodied, with fine acidity and a delicious ash, mineral and light fruit aftertaste. Not imported into the U.S. Drink now.–J.S. • $NA • (1/01/1999) • **86**

Gavi di Rovereto 1997: Shows slightly synthetic character along with the fruit cocktail aromas and flavors. Not imported into the U.S.–J.S. • $NA • (1/01/1999) • **78**

Gavi Pilin 1996: A Gavi with aspirations that doesn't quite make it. Aromas of pineapple and cream follow through to a full-bodied and soft palate. Round and caressing texture, but rather short and uninteresting on the finish. Not imported into the U.S. Drink now.–J.S. • $NA • (1/01/1999) • **84**

CASTELLARIN

Cabernet Sauvignon Grave del Friuli 1995 • $9 • (4/30/1998) • **78**

Chardonnay Venezia Giulia 1996 • $9 • (12/15/1997) • **80**

Merlot Grave del Friuli 1995 • $9 • (12/15/1997) • **79**

Pinot Grigio Venezia Giulia 1996 • $9 • (11/15/1997) • **84**

CASTELLI MARTINOZZI

Brunello di Montalcino 1988 • $NA • (4/30/1994) • **79**

Rosso di Montalcino 1991 • $NA • (4/30/1994) • **84**

CASTELLINA, LA

Chianti Classico 1997: Simple, light and fruity, with cherry and plum character, medium body and a light finish. Drink now.–J.S. • $14 • (11/30/1999) • **82**

Reale 1995: Too much wood. Some decent fruit, but it turns dry and lean on the finish.–J.S. • $32 • (11/30/1999) • **79**

CASTELLUCCIO

Le More 1992 • $19 • (2/29/1996) • **85**

Ronco dei Ciliegi 1990 • $35 • (2/29/1996) • **77**

Ronco della Simia 1991 • $35 • (2/29/1996) • **75**

Ronco delle Ginestre 1990 • $27 • (2/29/1996) • **79**

CASTELVECCHIO

Cabernet Franc 1991 • $15 • (6/15/1996) • **79**

CASTIGLION DEL BOSCO

Brunello di Montalcino 1995: Lots of raspberry, plum and wet-earth character. Medium-bodied, with polished tannins, but a bit dry. Too much new oak? Still, it shows good fruit with a medium finish. Drink now.–J.S. • $54 • (6/30/2000) • **86**

Brunello di Montalcino 1994: A bit rustic but very good. Aromas of raisins and earth are slightly funky, but the palate shows a delicious ripe fruit character, medium fine tannins and a light, fruity finish. Drink now.–J.S. • $55 • (8/31/1999) • **85**

Brunello di Montalcino 1993: A pretty, ready-to-drink Brunello, with an attractive amount of ripe berry and chocolate character. Medium-bodied, with fine tannins and a medium finish. Not imported into the U.S. Drink now.–J.S. • $NA • (12/15/1998) • **87**

Brunello di Montalcino 1991 • $NA • (11/30/1996) • **84**

Brunello di Montalcino 1990 • $NA • (10/31/1995) • **76**

Brunello di Montalcino 1979 • $14 • (4/30/1987) • **93**

Brunello di Montalcino Riserva 1993: A clean, well-crafted riserva '93, with fine tannins and a medium body. Fruity, slightly raisiny palate. Drink now.–J.S. • $75 • (8/31/1999) • **86**

Brunello di Montalcino Riserva 1990 • $NA • (11/30/1996) • **87**

Rosso di Montalcino 1997: A subtle and well-crafted rosso. Lovely aromas of plums, flowers and wet earth follow through to the palate. Medium-bodied, with soft tannins and a pretty, flavorful finish. Drink now.–J.S. • $16 • (9/15/1999) • **88**

Rosso di Montalcino 1996: Slightly diluted still decent. Aromas of fruit, hay and mint. Medium-bodied, with light tannins and a fresh and fruity finish. Not imported into the U.S. Drink now.–J.S. • $NA • (12/15/1998) • **80**

Rosso di Montalcino 1994 • $NA • (11/30/1996) • **70**

Rosso di Montalcino 1988 • $11 • (7/15/1991) • **82**

CATALDI MADONNA

Alto Tirino Malandrino 1997: Pretty, bright fruit has lots of berry and raspberry character. Medium-bodied, with polished tannins and a fresh finish. Drink now through 2002.–J.S. • $78 • (4/30/2000) • **86**

Montepulciano d'Abruzzo 1997: Intense dried cherry and grape aromas. Medium-bodied, with good, clean fruit flavors, light tannins and a fruity finish. Drink now.–J.S. • $14 • (4/30/2000) • **84**

Montepulciano d'Abruzzo 1995 • $14 • (2/28/1998) • **86**

Montepulciano d'Abruzzo Cerasuolo Piè delle Vigne 1998: Delicious, with fresh fruit and a simple finish. Rather fun, but very light in body. Drink now.–J.S. • $13 • (4/30/2000) • **84**

Montepulciano d'Abruzzo Tonì 1995: Velvety and very fruity, with bright plum and cherry character. Full-bodied, with soft tannins and a fresh finish. Delicious. Drink now through 2003.–J.S. • $30 • (4/30/2000) • **87**

Trebbiano d'Abruzzo 1996 • $13 • (12/31/1997) • **78**

CAVALCHINA

Bardolino Superiore Santa Lucia 1997: Delicious Bardolino. Bright plum and black cherry aromas. Medium-bodied, with compacted fruit and firm tannins.–J.S. • $14 • (5/15/2000) • **86**

Bianco di Custoza 1998: Slightly oxidized, with almond and melon character. Light-bodied and crisp on the finish.–J.S. • $12 • (2/29/2000) • **77**

Bianco di Custoza 1997: A fresh, crisp and pure white, more than worth the modest asking price. Superbly balanced, the concentrated flavors of apple and grass, with mineral accents, linger on the finish. From Northeast Italy, it shows what can be done in a less-than-famous appellation. Drink now.–B.S. • $10 • (7/31/1998) • **86**

Bianco di Custoza Amadeo 1996: A touch of oak adds breadth and richness to this peach-flavored, deftly balanced, velvety-textured white that evokes honey and vanilla on the finish. Has the body and weight for light foods. Drink now.–B.S. • $13 • (7/31/1998) • **88**

Bianco di Custoza Amedeo 1997: Medium-bodied, with very interesting mineral, apple, pear and mango aromas and a perfumed aftertaste. Drink now.–J.S. • $15 • (1/01/2000) • **85**

CAVALIERE, IL

Chianti Rufina Frascole 1996: Straightforward and clean, with decent dried cherry and berry character. Medium- to light-bodied, with light tannins and a crisp finish. Drink now.–J.S. • $9 • (12/15/1998) • **80**

CAVALLOTTO

Barbaresco Vigna San Giuseppe Riserva 1985 • $22 • (2/28/1991) HR • **90**

Barbera d'Alba Bricco Boschis Vigna del Cuculo 1996: Distinguished and racy, offering nice toasted spice along with lipsmacking red- and blackberry character. Grapey, yet has depth, good balance and well-integrated tannins, with a smoky finish that lingers. Drink now through 2002.–P.M. • $12 • (10/31/1998) • **85**

Barbera d'Alba Bricco Boschis Vigna del Cuculo 1993 • $14 • (10/31/1997) • **80**

Barbera d'Alba Bricco Boschis Vigna del Cuculo 1991 • $NA • (10/31/1994) • **84**

Barolo 1991 • $29 • (10/31/1995) • **82**

Barolo 1988 • $NA • (10/31/1994) • **87**

ITALY

CAVALLOTTO

Barolo Bricco Boschis Vigna San Giuseppe 1993: Distinctively minty, turning a bit tough with drying tannins, but it tastes ripe, with plum, black cherry and licorice. Astringent finish.–P.M. • $40 • (10/31/1998) • **77**
Barolo Bricco Boschis Vigna San Giuseppe 1988 • $15 • (10/31/1993) • **77**
Barolo Bricco Boschis Vigna San Giuseppe Riserva 1990 • $39 • (10/31/1995) • **87**
Dolcetto d'Alba Bricco Boschis 1996 • $14 • (10/31/1997) • **82**
Dolcetto d'Alba Bricco Boschis Vigna Scot 1997: Very youthful, with almost barrel samplelike earthy notes, but underneath are ripe tannins, ripe fruit and good intensity. The finish is chewy and a bit hard.–P.M. • $12 • (10/31/1998) • **80**
Dolcetto d'Alba Mallera 1987 • $10 • (3/15/1989) • **83**

CAVAZZA

Cabernet Colli Berici 1996 • $11 • (6/15/1998) • **80**

CECCHI

Chianti Classico 1997: A good, simple Chianti Classico, with delicious cherry character verging on raisins and fresh acidity. Not imported into the U.S. Drink now.–J.S. • $12 • (1/01/1999) • **83**
Chianti Classico 1995 • $10 • (5/31/1997) • **84**
Chianti Classico 1994 • $9 • (10/31/1996) • **84**
Chianti Classico 1993 • $7 • (10/31/1995) • **80**
Chianti Classico 1992 • $8 • (10/31/1994) • **86**
Chianti Classico 1990 • $11 • (9/15/1992) • **85**
Chianti Classico Teuzzo 1997: Blackberry and wild cherry aromas grab your attention. Medium-bodied, with soft tannins. The long, fruity finish has hints of toasted oak. Drink now through 2001.–J.S. • $27 • (11/30/1999) • **88**
Chianti Classico Teuzzo 1993 • $NA • (10/31/1995) • **81**
Chianti Classico Teuzzo 1990 • $NA • (10/31/1993) • **84**
Chianti Classico Teuzzo Riserva 1995: Has lovely perfumes of bark and dried cherry, but lets you down on the palate. Medium-bodied, with fine tannins but a slightly dry finish. Drink now.–J.S. • $27 • (12/15/1998) • **84**
Chianti Classico Teuzzo Riserva 1993 • $21 • (9/30/1997) • **80**
Chianti Classico Villa Cerna 1997: A bit rustic, but with attractive berry and plum character. Medium-bodied, with light tannins and a fruity finish. Not imported into the U.S. Drink now.–J.S. • $NA • (1/01/1999) • **83**
Chianti Classico Villa Cerna 1990 • $NA • (9/15/1992) • **89**
Chianti Classico Villa Cerna 1988 • $10 • (9/15/1991) • **89**
Chianti Classico Villa Cerna Riserva 1996: A '96 riserva with a good core of fruit. Medium-bodied with medium tannins and a slightly short finish. Drink now.–J.S. • $19 • (11/30/1999) • **84**
Chianti Classico Villa Cerna Riserva 1995: Floral and cherry aromas fill the glass, with more on the nose than it gives on the palate. Medium-bodied, with fine tannins and a slightly dry, too woody finish. Drink now.–J.S. • $15 • (12/15/1998) • **83**
Chianti Classico Villa Cerna Riserva 1994 • $NA • (9/30/1997) • **86**
Chianti Classico Villa Cerna Riserva 1991 • $19 • (10/31/1995) • **79**
Chianti Classico Villa Cerna Riserva 1990 • $15 • (2/28/1995) • **76**
Chianti Classico Villa Cerna Riserva 1988 • $NA • (9/15/1992) • **88**
Chianti Classico Villa Cerna Riserva 1985 • $16 • (9/15/1991) • **87**
Morellino di Scansano Val delle Rose 1997: This Morellino shows wonderful berry, plum and cherry character. Medium-bodied, with medium, silky tannins and a fresh, fruity finish. Drink now through 2002.–J.S. • $15 • (11/30/1999) • **87**
Morellino di Scansano Val delle Rose Riserva 1996: A pretty, perfumed Morellino, with plum, berry and toasted oak character. Medium-bodied, with silky tannins and a medium finish. Needs a bit of age. Best after 2000.–J.S. • $20 • (11/30/1999) • **87**
Sangiovese Toscana 1998: Already showing maturity, but with pleasant plum and tobacco character throughout. Light- to medium-bodied, with light tannins and a short finish. Drink now.–J.S. • $9 • (11/30/1999) • **80**
Sangiovese Toscana 1995 • $8 • (9/30/1997) • **85**
Toscana Sangiovese Tuscany 1993 • $6 • (7/31/1995) • **82**
Toscana La Gavina 1997: Plenty of Cabernet Sauvignon character in this wine. Mint, berry and tobacco aromas are underlined with earth. Full-bodied, with masses of tannins and a long, mouthpuckering finish. Not imported into the U.S. Best after 2000.–J.S. • $NA • (11/30/1999) • **90**
Toscana La Gavina 1988 • $NA • (9/15/1991) • **91**
Toscana Spargolo 1997: Delicious and soft, with loads of plum, berry and vanilla character. Medium- to full-bodied, with caressing tannins and a long, fruity finish. Give it a bit of bottle age. Best after 2001.–J.S. • $38 • (11/30/1999) • **91**
Toscana Spargolo 1995: Rather simple, with berry, cherry and floral aromas and flavors, a medium to light body and a fresh finish. Drink now.–J.S. • $38 • (12/15/1998) • **83**
Toscana Spargolo 1991 • $29 • (10/31/1995) • **89**
Toscana Spargolo 1988 • $36 • (10/31/1993) • **89**
Toscana Spargolo 1985 • $36 • (1/31/1992) • **78**
Toscana Spargolo 1983 • $25 • (3/15/1991) • **75**
Toscana Spargolo 1982 • $12 • (9/30/1989) • **68**
Vernaccia di San Gimignano 1998: Lots of melon and light mineral aromas in this white. Medium-bodied, with good fruit and a light white pepper and fruit aftertaste. Drink now.–J.S. • $10 • (11/30/1999) • **84**
Vernaccia di San Gimignano 1997: Smells a bit like cooked pasta without sauce. Also hints of melon. Medium-bodied, with moderate acidity, a rather dull finish.–J.S. • $10 • (12/15/1998) • **77**
Vernaccia di San Gimignano 1996 • $9 • (9/30/1997) • **83**
Vino Nobile di Montepulciano 1991 • $12 • (2/29/1996) • **83**
Vino Nobile di Montepulciano 1987 • $13 • (3/31/1992) • **77**

CELLOLE

Chianti Classico Riserva 1990 • $NA • (2/28/1995) • **87**

CENNATOIO

Cabernet Sauvignon Toscana Rosso Fiorentino 1995: Shows a slightly odd herbal character buttressed with new oak. Medium body, light finish. Better with age? Drink now.–J.S. • $50 • (12/15/1998) • **81**
Chianti Classico 1997: A delicious, fruit-forward Chianti. Lovely dried cherry and cedar aromas follow through to a medium-bodied palate, with light tannins and a fresh, crisp finish. Drink now.–J.S. • $22 • (11/30/1999) • **85**
Chianti Classico 1996: Blackberry and bark character on the nose and palate. Medium-bodied, with light tannins and a light, fruity finish. A good Chianti but normally this producer makes something a little more concentrated. Drink now.–J.S. • $23 • (12/15/1998) • **83**
Chianti Classico 1995 • $NA • (9/30/1997) • **85**
Chianti Classico 1994 • $14 • (10/31/1996) • **84**
Chianti Classico 1993 • $13 • (10/31/1995) • **85**
Chianti Classico 1992 • $12 • (2/28/1995) • **76**
Chianti Classico 1990 • $10 • (10/31/1993) • **83**
Chianti Classico O'Leandro Riserva 1995: Super well-balanced CC riserva. Wonderfully plummy, with hints of wet earth. Medium-bodied, with medium, velvety tannins and a fruity, beautiful aftertaste. Drink now through 2005.–J.S. • $42 • (11/30/1999) • **89**
Chianti Classico O'Leandro Riserva 1994: Attractive aromas of ripe berry, earth, and mushroom. Medium-bodied, with medium tannins and a smoky vanilla aftertaste. Perhaps a tad too much new French oak maturation, but still delicious. Drink now.–J.S. • $44 • (12/15/1998) • **85**
Chianti Classico Riserva 1996: A bit lean but with good berry, dried cherry and cedar character. Light- to medium-bodied, with light tannins and a fresh finish. Slightly disappointing for this producer. Drink now.–J.S. • $35 • (11/30/1999) • **81**
Chianti Classico Riserva 1995: Plenty of cherry and chocolate aromas and flavors, with caressing, rounded tannins and a sweet fruit, smoke and berry character on the finish. Always a very good riserva Chianti. Drink now through 2002.–J.S. • $38 • (12/15/1998) • **88**
Chianti Classico Riserva 1994 • $NA • (9/30/1997) • **90**
Chianti Classico Riserva 1993 • $21 • (10/31/1996) • **85**
Chianti Classico Riserva 1990 • $17 • (2/28/1995) • **87**
Rosso Fiorentino 1994 • $NA • (9/30/1997) • **86**
Rosso Fiorentino 1993 • $32 • (10/31/1996) • **84**
Rosso Fiorentino 1991 • $26 • (2/28/1995) • **87**
Rosso Fiorentino 1990 • $10 • (10/31/1993) • **83**
Sangiovese Toscana Etrusco 1996: A beautiful, balanced Sangiovese, with pretty blackberry, fresh mushroom and dried cherry character. Medium-bodied, with silky tannins and a fresh fruit finish. Drink now.–J.S. • $60 • (11/30/1999) • **88**
Sangiovese Toscana Etrusco 1995: Wonderfully soft and caressing, with lovely milk chocolate and berry character in a medium-bodied package. Not for long-term aging, but delicious. Drink now.–J.S. • $54 • (12/15/1998) • **87**
Toscana Etrusco 1994 • $NA • (9/30/1997) • **87**

Key: SS—Spectator Selection. CS—Cellar Selection. HR—Highly Recommended. $NA—Price not available. (BT)—Barrel tasting. Ⓐ—Auction Price. For a key to the tasters' initials, see "How to Use These Listings."
Dates in parentheses represent the issues in which the ratings were published.

Toscana Etrusco 1993 • $32 • (10/31/1996) • **89**
Toscana Etrusco 1991 • $26 • (2/28/1995) • **88**
Toscana Etrusco 1990 • $11 • (10/31/1993) • **89**
Toscana All'Omo il Vino 1997: A Chianti with plenty of dried cherry character and very lively acidity. Medium-bodied, with light tannins and a crisp finish. Slightly simple. Drink now.–J.S. • $22 • (11/30/1999) • **83**
Toscana Arcibaldo 1995: There's pretty and caressing tannins in this wine, but the green pepper and herbal character of the Cabernet is overpowering. Medium body. Best after 2000.–J.S. • $NA • (12/15/1998) • **81**
Toscana Arcibaldo 1994 • $NA • (9/30/1997) • **89**
Toscana Mammolo 1995: Very open and fruity, with a bounteous strawberry and raspberry character. Medium body. Medium, round tannins and a fruity aftertaste. Drink now.–J.S. • $50 • (12/15/1998) • **88**
Toscana Mammolo 1994 • $NA • (9/30/1997) • **88**
Toscana Mammolo 1993 • $32 • (10/31/1996) • **87**
Vin Santo di Chianti Classico Occhio di Pernice 1991: Aromas of almond, rose petal and dried red fruit. Medium-bodied, very high in acidity and harsh on the finish. Hard to get excited about. Not imported into the U.S. –J.S. • $NA • (1/01/1999) • **79**
Vin Santo di Chianti Classico Uvae 1998: Aromas of salted almond, buttered popcorn and clove honey. Very high in acidity, with a popcorn and cider flavor. Difficult to appreciate. Not imported into the U.S.–J.S. • $NA/375 ml. • (1/01/1999) • **72**

CENTOLANI

Brunello di Montalcino Pietranera 1994: Well crafted Brunello. Crushed berries, raspberries and light earth character throughout. Medium- to full-bodied with polished tannins and a long, fruity finish. Drink now.–J.S. • $65 • (8/31/1999) • **88**
Brunello di Montalcino Tenuta Friggiali 1995: Well-crafted Brunello. Wonderfully fresh and floral aromas with undertones of plum and cherry. Full- to medium-bodied, with velvety tannins and a long, long finish. Best after 2002.–J.S. • $54 • (6/30/2000) • **91**
Brunello di Montalcino Tenuta Friggiali 1994: Very fine indeed. Bright berry, violet and cherry aromas continue to a compacted, medium-bodied palate, with fine, silky tannins and a long, long finish. Drink now.–J.S. • $54 • (8/31/1999) • **89**
Brunello di Montalcino Tenuta Friggiali 1993: A luscious, rich wine. Medium- to full-bodied, with aromas of crushed raspberry and cherry, velvety, ripe tannins and a long aftertaste. Best after 2000.–J.S. • $38 • (12/15/1998) • **88**
Brunello di Montalcino Tenuta Friggiali 1990 • $NA • (10/31/1995) • **88**
Brunello di Montalcino Tenuta Friggiali 1988 • $NA • (4/30/1994) • **87**
Pietrafocaia 1993: A solid Sangiovese, showing blackberry, chestnut and berry. Medium-bodied, with velvety tannins and a fresh and fruity aftertaste. Still needs some time to mellow. Drink through 2003.–J.S. • $NA • (12/15/1998) • **87**
Rosso di Montalcino Pietranera 1997: Promises more on the nose than it delivers on the palate. Attractive blackberry and plum aromas. Medium-bodied, with chocolate and berry flavors and a short finish. Drink now.–J.S. • $25 • (9/15/1999) • **83**
Rosso di Montalcino Tenuta Friggiali 1997: Straightforward, good Sangiovese with dried cherry and berry character, medium body and a fresh finish. Drink now.–J.S. • $20 • (9/15/1999) • **83**
Rosso di Montalcino Tenuta Friggiali 1996: A bit hot and alcoholic, but offers decent berry and cherry character. Light-bodied, with a light finish.–J.S. • $19 • (12/15/1998) • **79**
Rosso di Montalcino Tenuta Friggiali 1995 • $NA • (9/30/1997) • **82**
Rosso di Montalcino Tenuta Friggiali 1993 • $NA • (10/31/1995) • **82**
Rosso di Montalcino Tenuta Friggiali 1991 • $NA • (4/30/1994) • **78**

CERBAIA

Brunello di Montalcino 1994: A bit lean but shows good fruit beneath the tannins; blackberry with minty and cherry undertones. Medium- to full-bodied, with polished tannins and a firm, silky finish. Drink now.–J.S. • $40 • (8/31/1999) • **86**
Brunello di Montalcino 1988 • $NA • (4/30/1994) • **82**
Brunello di Montalcino Riserva 1993: A little meager really, and funky in style. Aromas of dried cherries and leather with hints of earth. Medium-bodied, with light tannins and a crisp, slightly drying finish. Drink now.–J.S. • $55 • (8/31/1999) • **82**
Brunello di Montalcino Vigna Cerbaia 1995: A drink-me Brunello. Lovely ripe berry aromas with hints of mushroom and violets. Medium-bodied, with soft tannins and a rich aftertaste. Delicious. Drink now.–J.S. • $60 • (6/30/2000) • **87**
Rosso di Montalcino 1991 • $NA • (4/30/1994) • **84**

CERBAIE, CASANUOVA DELLA

Brunello di Montalcino 1994: Lovely perfumed aromas of flowers, berries and minerals. Medium-bodied, with silky tannins and a fresh but slightly short finish. Drink now.–J.S. • $45 • (8/31/1999) • **85**
Brunello di Montalcino 1993: Some pretty aromas, with rose petal and fruit character, but a tight and slightly dry palate. Drink now.–J.S. • $44 • (12/15/1998) • **80**

CERBAIOLA

Brunello di Montalcino Salvioni 1995: A rich and decadent Brunello with earth and mushroom aromas and hints of ripe fruit. Medium- to full-bodied, with soft tannins and a ripe fruit finish. Drink now.–J.S. • $87 • (6/30/2000) • **87**
Brunello di Montalcino Salvioni 1994: Pretty aromas of fruit, meat and smoke. Medium-bodied, with fine tannins and a fruity, spicy finish. Thoroughly delicious now.–J.S. • $99 • (8/31/1999) • **88**
Brunello di Montalcino Salvioni 1986 • $60 • (12/15/1992) • **93**
Rosso di Montalcino Salvioni 1997: A wine with grapey, spicy character throughout. Medium-bodied, with chewy tannins and a medium finish. Slightly monolithic. Drink now.–J.S. • $40 • (9/15/1999) • **85**

CERBAIONA

Brunello di Montalcino 1994: Slightly mature already, but with pretty strawberry, leather and berry character. Medium-bodied, with light tannins and an earthy, funky aftertaste. Better than when previously reviewed, but beware of significant bottle variation. Drink now.–J.S. • $108 • (11/30/1999) • **82**
Brunello di Montalcino 1993: Surprisingly supple. Very ripe and raisiny on the nose. Full-bodied and round-textured, with caressing tannins and a delicate finish. Drink now.–J.S. • $105 • (12/15/1998) • **87**
Brunello di Montalcino 1988 • $50 • (4/30/1994) • **80**
Brunello di Montalcino 1985 • $60 • (11/30/1991) • **71**
Rosso di Montalcino 1988 • $21 • (1/31/1992) • **82**
Toscana 1997: A very pretty Sangiovese, with cigar box, berry and tobacco aromas and flavors. Medium-bodied, with fine tannins and a fresh finish. A lively, fruity wine. Drink now.–J.S. • $45 • (11/30/1999) • **87**

CERETTO

Arneis Langhe Blange' 1997: Very spritzy, yet impressive for its dry, clean and pure character. Displays vanilla bean, wet earth, green apple and cured ham aromas and flavors. Long finish. Surprise your guests by serving this as an aperitif. Drink now.–P.M. • $18 • (10/31/1998) • **83**
Arneis Langhe Blange' 1996 • $15 • (8/31/1997) • **84**
Barbaresco Asij 1996: Ripe, with voluptuous fruit, stylishly dressed up in refined tannins, flirting with the taste buds, this is a balanced, understated, medium-bodied beauty that tastes of toasted spices, red berries, wet earth, and melts on the palate with silky grace. Best from 2003 through 2006.–P.M. • $42 • (8/31/1999) • **91**
Barbaresco Asij 1995: A delicate Barbaresco, light in color and body but showing pretty raspberry, wild strawberry and cherry character. Fine tannins and a lingering finish. Drink now through 2003.–P.M. • $40 • (10/31/1998) • **83**
Barbaresco Asij 1993 • $25 • (10/31/1996) • **86**
Barbaresco Asij 1991 • $23 • (10/31/1995) • **74**
Barbaresco Asij 1990 • $53 Ⓐ • (10/31/1994) • **80**
Barbaresco Asij 1989 • $23 • (10/31/1993) • **85**
Barbaresco Asij 1988 • $23 • (10/31/1993) • **77**
Barbaresco Asij 1987 • $22 • (7/15/1991) • **86**
Barbaresco Asij 1985 • $15 • (1/31/1990) • **64**
Barbaresco Asili 1996: Complex and powerful, big and full-bodied, but surprisingly fresh and crisp. A lovely wine, very flavorful, offering barrique-like toasty, grilled, violet notes, accented by blackberry and tar character. Ripe but firm and chewy tannins need time. Best from 2003 through 2010.–P.M. • $105 • (8/31/1999) • **90**
Barbaresco Asili 1995: International style and very woody. Shows dark color and lots of earth, fruit and tannins, married nicely to oak-infused mocha and toasted bread notes. Lead pencil, mineral, stone dust, blackberry and

ITALY

cassis flavors set up a long, delicious finish. Drink now through 2005.–P.M. • $50 • (10/31/1998) • **85**
Barbaresco Asili 1994 • $65 • (10/31/1997) • **75**
Barbaresco Asili 1993 • $50 • (10/31/1996) • **85**
Barbaresco Asili 1990 • $69 Ⓐ • (10/31/1994) • **79**
Barbaresco Asili 1989 • $61 • (10/31/1993) • **87**
Barbaresco Asili 1988 • $61 • (10/31/1993) • **75**
Barbaresco Asili 1987 • $40 • (4/30/1991) • **89**
Barbaresco Asili 1986 • $35 • (4/15/1990) • **85**
Barbaresco Asili 1985 • $67 Ⓐ • (8/31/1989) • **89**
Barbaresco Asili 1984 • $15 • (9/15/1988) • **80**
Barbaresco Asili 1982 • $19 • (9/15/1988) • **87**
Barbaresco Asili 1978 • $NA • (3/01/1986) • **90**
Barbaresco Asili 1976 • $NA • (9/15/1988) • **89**
Barbaresco Asili 1974 • $NA • (3/01/1986) • **90**
Barbaresco Fasêt 1996: Authentic Nebbiolo of great finesse. Light-colored and delicate, a full-boded Barbaresco that speaks a true Piedmont voice, from the lovely rose petal and smoky tar notes to the ripe fruit, crisp acidity, silky tannins and classy balance. Drink now through 2010.–P.M. • $70 • (8/31/1999) • **93**
Barbaresco Fasêt 1995: Fresh and vibrant, mingling citrus, blackberry, cassis bush and some herbal notes, but this medium-bodied wine lacks finesse with its hard tannins, dry finish. Drink now through 2003.–P.M. • $45 • (10/31/1998) • **77**
Barbaresco Fasêt 1993 • $53 • (10/31/1996) • **87**
Barbaresco Fasêt 1990 • $44 • (10/31/1994) • **86**
Barbaresco Fasêt 1989 • $44 • (10/31/1993) • **82**
Barbaresco Fasêt 1988 • $44 • (10/31/1993) • **79**
Barbaresco Fasêt 1987 • $31 • (7/15/1991) • **89**
Barbaresco Fasêt 1985 • $31 • (1/31/1990) • **87**
Barbera d'Alba Piana 1997: Ripe but quite crisp and mouthpuckering, it's a bit dull on the palate, at least for now, tasting of mocha, red berry and citrus flavors. Not imported into the U.S. Drink now.–P.M. • $NA • (1/01/1999) • **82**
Barbera d'Alba Piana 1995 • $29 • (10/31/1997) • **86**
Barbera d'Alba Piana 1993 • $17 • (10/31/1995) • **83**
Barbera d'Alba Piana 1991 • $17 • (11/15/1993) • **76**
Barbera d'Alba Piana 1990 • $17 • (4/30/1993) • **70**
Barbera d'Alba Piana 1989 • $18 • (10/31/1992) • **87**
Barolo Bricco Rocche 1995: Only in Piedmont. This sensational, brick-colored Barolo is exotic from rose petal, tar, smoke and red fruit. Round, velvety and refined, with a full body, sweet tannins, a toasted character and a balanced finish that shout *grande vino*. Drink now through 2010.–P.M. • $140 • (11/15/1999) • **93**
Barolo Bricco Rocche 1990 • $101 Ⓐ • (10/31/1994) • **88**
Barolo Bricco Rocche 1986 • $110 • (4/30/1991) • **89**
Barolo Bricco Rocche 1985 • $80 Ⓐ • (3/31/1990) • **86**
Barolo Bricco Rocche 1982 • $134 Ⓐ • (9/15/1988) • **91**
Barolo Bricco Rocche 1980 • $31 Ⓐ • (3/01/1986) • **90**
Barolo Brunate 1995: A well-made, balanced, subtle wine, with Barolo's classic tar, rose petal and black fruit character. Full-bodied, with a ripe texture that charms, but expect a jolt of refined yet tough tannins on the chewy finish. Drink now through 2005.–P.M. • $70 • (11/15/1999) • **94**
Barolo Brunate 1994: Very soft and pleasant, medium-bodied, with little structure but a decent amount of spice, mocha, coffee, plum and black cherry notes. Slightly diluted. Drink now through 2003.–P.M. • $60 • (10/31/1998) • **80**
Barolo Brunate 1993 • $49 • (10/31/1997) • **88**
Barolo Brunate 1990 • $44 • (10/31/1994) • **77**
Barolo Brunate 1989 • $70 Ⓐ • (10/31/1993) • **86**
Barolo Brunate 1988 • $44 • (10/31/1993) • **81**
Barolo Brunate 1986 • $40 • (4/30/1991) • **80**
Barolo Brunate 1985 • $115 Ⓐ • (1/31/1990) • **92**
Barolo Brunate 1983 • $27 • (7/31/1989) • **85**
Barolo Brunate 1979 • $NA • (3/01/1986) • **86**
Barolo Brunate 1978 • $NA • (9/15/1988) • **86**
Barolo Brunate 1967 • $100 • (10/20/1987) • **90**
Barolo Cannubi 1971 • $NA • (3/01/1986) • **85**
Barolo Prapò 1995: Like a long-simmering fuse, this full-bodied, heavily oaked Nebbiolo builds up to an explosive finish. Concentrated and supple, it burns with intensity from all that high-grade, toasted oak, spicy mocha, rich blackberry, tar and smoke. Drink through 2010.–P.M. • $70 • (11/15/1999) • **92**
Barolo Prapò 1994: Light in body and rather lean, with only decent fruit. Turns a bit astringent and dry on the slightly diluted finish.–P.M. • $65 • (10/31/1998) • **78**
Barolo Prapò 1993 • $50 • (10/31/1997) • **83**
Barolo Prapò 1990 • $67 Ⓐ • (10/31/1994) • **88**
Barolo Prapò 1989 • $54 • (10/31/1993) • **82**
Barolo Prapò 1988 • $54 • (10/31/1993) • **84**
Barolo Prapò 1986 • $50 • (2/28/1991) • **91**
Barolo Prapò 1985 • $82 Ⓐ • (3/31/1990) • **78**
Barolo Prapò 1983 • $31 • (7/31/1989) • **86**
Barolo Prapò 1978 • $NA • (3/01/1986) • **95**
Barolo Prapò 1976 • $80 • (9/15/1988) • **82**
Barolo Prapò 1971 • $100 • (10/30/1987) • **88**
Barolo Zonchera 1995: Odd. Perfumed and sweet-tasting, with a matured, oxidative quality to the truffle, wet forest floor and raspberry aromas, but the toasted oak, rose petal and ripe fruit concentration is good. Chunky tannins on the finish. Drink now.–P.M. • $42 • (11/15/1999) • **80**
Barolo Zonchera 1994: Quite disjointed, a bit green and herbal in flavor, with a coarse, chewy texture and an astringent finish. Hard to tell if it will ever come around.–P.M. • $30 • (10/31/1998) • **74**
Barolo Zonchera 1992 • $25 • (10/31/1996) • **81**
Barolo Zonchera 1991 • $23 • (10/31/1995) • **76**
Barolo Zonchera 1989 • $23 • (10/31/1994) • **88**
Barolo Zonchera 1988 • $23 • (10/31/1993) • **87**
Barolo Zonchera 1987 • $23 • (8/31/1991) • **86**
Barolo Zonchera 1985 • $16 • (6/15/1990) • **82**
Barolo Zonchera 1984 • $16 • (9/15/1988) • **83**
Barolo Zonchera 1982 • $16 • (6/30/1987) • **90**
Cabernet Sauvignon Langhe La Bernardina Da Uve 1996: A classy Piedmont red, with ultrasmooth tannins. Supple, full-bodied and ripe, with a gorgeous blackberry, earth, horse blanket, leather and toasted oak combination that glides to an immensely pleasurable, harmonious finish. Drink now through 2005.–P.M. • $60 • (11/15/1999) • **93**
Cabernet Sauvignon Langhe La Bernardina Da Uve 1995: Fabulous. Strikes great balance between new wave and tradition. Racy and full-bodied, it's opulent in structure, exploding with deep and complex violet, plum and cassis character accented by clever use of fancy oak to infuse it with spice and chocolate. It also captures the mineral-laden, iron-rich, lead pencil complexity of the local soil, making this a *terroir*-anchored red. Everything is in place, from the velvety tannins to the hedonistic finish. Drink now through 2010.–P.M. • $50 • (10/31/1998) • **95**
Langhe Cabernet Sauvignon La Bernardina Da Uve 1991 • $26 • (2/28/1995) • **93**
Chardonnay Langhe La Bernardina Da Uve 1996: Distinctive and delicious, clean and pure, very ripe and full-bodied. Apricot, peach, melon, honey and lemon are accented by toasted oak, which brings out a chewy, almost tannic side. Could age, but with food it has the stuffing to stand up and speak for itself. Well made. Drink now through 2003.–P.M. • $35 • (10/31/1998) • **88**
Dolcetto d'Alba Rossana 1998: Quite earthy—"reduced" and animallike—but there is plenty of supple wine underneath that's nice to drink. Drink now.–P.M. • $18 • (11/15/1999) • **80**
Dolcetto d'Alba Rossana 1997: Fresh and grapey, with nice cherry and raspberry flavors, a bit of spice and earth, this balanced Dolcetto is very attractive.–P.M. • $20 • (10/31/1998) • **83**
Dolcetto d'Alba Rossana 1996 • $19 • (10/31/1997) • **83**
Dolcetto d'Alba Rossana 1994 • $17 • (10/31/1995) • **81**
Dolcetto d'Alba Rossana 1990 • $18 • (10/31/1992) • **83**
Dolcetto d'Alba Rossana 1989 • $16 • (4/30/1991) • **79**
Dolcetto d'Alba Rossana 1987 • $12 • (3/15/1989) • **86**
Dolcetto d'Alba Rossana 1985 • $11 • (3/15/1989) • **77**
La Bernardina Monsordo Red 1996: This classy, international-style Piedmont red seduces with gorgeous violet, floral, toasted oak and black currant aromas and flavors. An earthy, Syrah-like note adds complexity. Full-bodied and thick, it remains racy from a good level of acidity and has a lovely, fresh, clean finish. Made from Syrah. Drink now through 2005.–P.M. • $50 • (11/15/1999) • **94**
La Bernardina Monsordo Red 1995: Just wonderful. Superripe yet racy and sophisticated. Bursting with plum, red berry and blackberry character accented by deftly dosed toasted oak accents, this coats the palate with its refined tannins and leads to a marvelous finish packed with spice, mocha, chocolate and wild raspberry. Intense but lovely on release because it's so

Key: SS—Spectator Selection. CS—Cellar Selection. HR—Highly Recommended. $NA—Price not available. (BT)—Barrel tasting. Ⓐ—Auction Price.
For a key to the tasters' initials, see "How to Use These Listings."
Dates in parentheses represent the issues in which the ratings were published.

supple and balanced. Made from Syrah. Drink now through 2009.–P.M. • $50 • (10/31/1998) • **93**

La Bernardina Monsordo Red 1994 • $36 • (10/31/1997) • **89**

La Bernardina Monsordo Red 1991 • $26 • (2/28/1995) • **93**

La Bernardina Monsordo White 1996: Bone-dry and slightly grassy, with butter and spice character. Chewy and tough on the palate, but at least it's clean and pure. Green, citrusy finish. Made from Viognier.–P.M. • $35 • (10/31/1998) • **77**

Moscato d'Asti I Vignaioli di Santo Stefano 1997: Sweet, concentrated and lightly fizzy, this displays grape, spice and honey aromas and flavors, an easygoing structure and rich texture. Try with fresh fruit desserts. Drink now.–B.S. • $17 • (10/15/1999) • **85**

Moscato d'Asti I Vignaioli di Santo Stefano 1996 • $16 • (8/31/1997) • **84**

Nebbiolo d'Alba Lantasco 1990 • $19 • (4/30/1993) • **87**

Nebbiolo d'Alba Lantasco 1989 • $16 • (10/31/1992) • **81**

Nebbiolo d'Alba Lantasco 1988 • $18 • (4/30/1991) • **81**

Pinot Nero Langhe La Bernardina Da Uve 1996: A bit earthy, showing some horse stable aromas, this is light reddish in color, medium-bodied, delivering some decent Pinot Noir character. Some attractive licorice and red berry notes, but lacks the depth of a top Pinot as it turns a bit tough and herbal on the finish. Drink now through 2003.–P.M. • $45 • (11/15/1999) • **85**

Pinot Nero Langhe La Bernardina Da Uve 1995: Intense, with good concentration of fruit and wet earth, along with massive toasted oak accents. Medium-bodied and ripe, although the finish is very woody. Drink now through 2003.–P.M. • $50 • (10/31/1998) • **83**

CERRO, FATTORIA DEL

Merlot Toscana Poggio Golo 1997: Very subtle and well done, with gorgeous, bright berry, raspberry and mineral character. Full-bodied, yet showing very polished tannins and a long finish. A beauty. Not imported into the U.S. Best after 2000.–J.S. • $NA • (1/01/2000) • **90**

Rosso di Montepulciano 1998: A good, dark-colored rosso di Montepulciano, with raspberry and cherry aromas. Light- to medium-bodied, with light tannins, vanilla and oak character and a medium finish. Drink now.–J.S. • $13 • (11/30/1999) • **85**

Rosso di Montepulciano 1997: Why buy Vino Nobile when you have something like this? Excellent value. Floral aromas follow through on the palate. Medium-bodied, with well-proportioned tannins and a medium finish. Slightly rough now. Drink now.–J.S. • $10 • (12/15/1998) • **87**

Rosso di Montepulciano 1996 • $11 • (9/30/1997) • **86**

Rosso di Montepulciano 1992 • $9 • (7/31/1994) • **83**

Sangiovese Toscana Manero 1995: Wonderful aromas of plum, raspberry and cinnamon. Medium- to full-bodied, with very well integrated tannins and a long, silky finish. Very fine indeed. Not imported into the U.S. Best after 2001.–J.S. • $NA • (1/01/2000) • **90**

Vino Nobile di Montepulciano 1996: A very fine Nobile, with subtle aromas of cherry and berry and hints of flowers. Medium-bodied, with silky tannins and a medium finish. Drink now.–J.S. • $17 • (11/30/1999) • **87**

Vino Nobile di Montepulciano 1995: Very good indeed. Chocolate, berry and vanilla character on the nose and palate. Medium-bodied, with firm tannins and a long, silky finish. Drink now.–J.S. • $17 • (12/15/1998) • **88**

Vino Nobile di Montepulciano 1994 • $16 • (9/30/1997) • **83**

Vino Nobile di Montepulciano 1990 • $14 • (5/31/1995) • **74**

Vino Nobile di Montepulciano Riserva 1995: Extremely well-crafted Nobile, with good concentration. Intense aromas of raspberries, blackberries and strawberries. Medium- to full-bodied, with plenty of fruit, medium tannins and a vanilla and cherry aftertaste. Drink now through 2003.–J.S. • $22 • (11/30/1999) • **89**

Vino Nobile di Montepulciano Riserva 1993 • $24 • (9/30/1997) • **87**

Vino Nobile di Montepulciano Riserva 1988 • $16 • (7/31/1994) • **85**

Vino Nobile di Montepulciano Vigneto Antica Chiusina 1995: A balanced and well-crafted Nobile with aging potential. Excitingly vivid aromas of blackberries, raspberries and mint. Full-bodied, with superintegrated tannins and a long, long finish. Best after 2000.–J.S. • $35 • (11/30/1999) • **90**

Vino Nobile di Montepulciano Vigneto Antica Chiusina 1993 • $25 • (9/30/1997) • **82**

Vino Nobile di Montepulciano Vigneto Antica Chiusina 1990 • $19 • (2/29/1996) • **87**

CERVETERI, CANTINA COOPERATIVA DI

Cerveteri Rosso Vigna Grande 1995 • $19 • (6/15/1998) • **88**

CESARE, PIO

Arneis Langhe 1997: A medium-bodied white, with flavors of white peach and almond and a nice spicy edge. Drink now.–K.M. • $23 • (8/31/1998) • **84**

Arneis Langhe 1996 • $20 • (12/31/1997) • **84**

Barbaresco 1996: Medium-bodied, clean and elegant, the acidity is crisp, the flavors fresh. A Nebbiolo that needs a bit of cellaring to soften the hard angles of raw tannins. Best after 2002.–P.M. • $NA • (11/15/1999) • **87**

Barbaresco 1994: Seductive, beginning to show some truffle and mushroom along with the plum and blackberry. Very supple tannins make it quite hedonistic. Add the oak-made chocolate, tar and mocha notes, and you have a lovely wine. Lacks a bit of length (as expected from a '94), but still well made. Drink now through 2005.–P.M. • $42 • (10/31/1998) • **85**

Barbaresco 1993 • $37 • (10/31/1997) • **77**

Barbaresco 1992 • $33 • (10/31/1996) • **77**

Barbaresco 1991 • $32 • (10/31/1995) • **82**

Barbaresco 1990 • $28 • (10/31/1994) • **89**

Barbaresco 1989 • $NA • (10/31/1994) • **81**

Barbaresco 1988 • $34 • (10/31/1993) • **83**

Barbaresco Bricco 1993 : Deeply satisfying, very sweet and ripe, with lush tannins, this opulent Barbaresco stands out for its hedonistic qualities. Offers plum, tar, rose petal and blackberry notes, all flowing harmoniously to a seamless finish. Much better than previously reviewed. Drink now through 2005.–P.M. • $92 • (9/15/1998) • **91**

Barbaresco Il Bricco 1995: Beautiful balance defines this great Nebbiolo. Rather traditional in style, with a light color and some earthy aromas, it turns silky smooth and ripe on the palate. Full-bodied, with a delicious lingering finish of wild berry, black fruit, toast and chocolate flavors. Tempting now, but better to cellar. Best from 2001 through 2005.–P.M. • $NA • (11/15/1999) • **93**

Barbaresco Il Bricco Riserva 1990 • $52 • (10/31/1995) • **88**

Barbera d'Alba 1996: Delicate, sweet- and plummy-tasting, with soft tannins and pretty rose petal, earth and black cherry notes fanning out seductively on the palate. The supple finish offers good length. Drink now.–P.M. • $17 • (10/31/1998) • **85**

Barbera d'Alba 1995 • $15 • (10/31/1997) • **85**

Barbera d'Alba 1993 • $13 • (10/31/1996) • **86**

Barbera d'Alba 1991 • $10 • (10/31/1994) • **86**

Barbera d'Alba 1989 • $17 • (10/15/1993) • **83**

Barbera d'Alba 1987 • $12 • (4/15/1991) • **81**

Barbera d'Alba 1985 • $12 • (11/15/1988) • **78**

Barbera d'Alba Fides 1996: Ripe and full, showing smooth texture and supple tannins, with lovely red- and blackberry flavors. Medium-bodied, the finish is juicy, even crisp. Drink now through 2002.–P.M. • $NA • (11/15/1999) • **87**

Barolo 1995: On the light side perhaps, but accessible on release. A bit earthy and light in color, but it's easy to enjoy for its pleasing tannins, balance and clean fruit. Elegant structure opens up to all sorts of wild berry, chalk, mineral notes. Drink now through 2004.–P.M. • $NA • (11/15/1999) • **89**

Barolo 1994: This deliciously harmonious, supple, velvety Barolo offers some pretty fruit and spice, with licorice, toasted bread and smoke notes on the lingering finish. Medium-bodied, and quite delicate. Drink now through 2005.–P.M. • $39 • (10/31/1998) • **86**

Barolo 1993 • $34 • (10/31/1997) • **86**

Barolo 1992 • $24 • (10/31/1996) • **85**

Barolo 1990 • $28 • (10/31/1994) • **88**

Barolo 1989 • $28 • (10/31/1994) • **86**

Barolo 1988 • $28 • (10/31/1993) • **83**

Barolo 1987 • $27 • (12/15/1992) • **82**

Barolo 1985 • $38 • (5/15/1991) • **89**

Barolo 1983 • $NA • (9/15/1988) • **88**

Barolo 1982 • $NA • (9/15/1988) • **91**

Barolo 1981 • $NA • (9/15/1988) • **87**

Barolo 1978 • $NA • (9/15/1988) • **85**

Barolo 1974 • $NA • (9/15/1988) • **77**

Barolo 1971 • $NA • (9/15/1988) • **80**

Barolo Ornato 1995: The tannins are well integrated but still showing a certain toughness normal for '95. Medium-bodied, it's more elegant than concentrated, with a slight chocolate character. Also shows blackberry, wet earth and smoky tobacco-leaf notes. Tempting now, but better to cellar. Best after 2002.–P.M. • $NA • (11/15/1999) • **90**

Barolo Ornato 1993: Impressive. This inky black, thick, ripe, rich and supple Barolo is balanced and appealing from start to finish. Full-bodied, it delivers spice and oak-scented aromas (mocha, coffee and grilled meat) plus good acidity and firm tannins that coat the palate on the chewy finish.

ITALY

Even better than when tasted from the barrel. Drink now through 2005.–P.M. • $92 • (9/15/1998) • **93**

Barolo Ornato 1990 • $41 • (10/31/1994) • **95**

Barolo Ornato 1988 • $NA • (10/31/1993) • **90**

Barolo Ornato Riserva 1985 • $48 • (5/15/1991) HR • **91**

Barolo Riserva 1982 • $31 • (11/15/1988) • **86**

Barolo Riserva 1980 • $19 • (2/15/1987) • **72**

Barolo Riserva 1978 • $19 • (10/01/1984) SS • **89**

Chardonnay Langhe Piodilei 1996: Full-bodied and very ripe and round in the mouth, it has decent citrus-spiked acidity but is shot down by overdone perfumes and an inelegant finish that's a bit short. Packed with butter, honey and toasted oak notes, but not much *terroir*. Good try, though. Drink now.–P.M. • $39 • (10/31/1998) • **80**

Chardonnay Piemonte 1997: Light-bodied, with violet, honey, melon, vanilla and butter notes. The perfumey aroma seems a bit odd, but this is still distinctive, with a supple finish.–P.M. • $18 • (10/31/1998) • **79**

Cortese di Gavi 1997: Woody, soft and supple, with butterscotch and not-totally-clean flavors. Flavors of wet hay, cedar and melon. Very distinctive, but in a strange way.–P.M. • $20 • (10/31/1998) • **74**

Dolcetto d'Alba 1997: Flat and a bit dull, it tastes somewhat diluted, although it has modest strawberry and cherry flavors. Serve chilled. –P.M. • $19 • (10/31/1998) • **76**

Dolcetto d'Alba 1996 • $13 • (10/31/1997) • **82**

Dolcetto d'Alba 1992 • $10 • (7/31/1995) • **83**

Dolcetto d'Alba 1991 • $18 • (10/31/1992) • **81**

Dolcetto d'Alba 1985 • $10 • (10/31/1986) • **71**

Moscato d'Asti 1996: Sweet and balanced, with pleasant peach flavors augmented by a slight spritz. Drink now, chilled, as an apéritif.–K.M. • $23 • (8/31/1998) • **85**

Nebbiolo d'Alba 1996: Nice ripe plum, cherry and red berry flavors seduce the palate and balance the tannic structure. Well made and delicious, true to type for a Nebbiolo. Medium-bodied, with a firm finish. Should be terrific with all sorts of tannic-taming foods. Drink now through 2002.–P.M. • $23 • (10/31/1998) • **87**

Ornato 1983 • $16 • (3/31/1988) • **82**

Rosso 1989 • $12 • (1/31/1992) • **83**

CESARI, UMBERTO

Albana di Romagna Colle del Re Passito 1993 • $27/500 ml. • (4/30/1997) • **83**

Albana di Romagna Passito Colle del Re 1994: Lots of late-harvest character, with aromas of burnt almond, spice and dried fig and apricot. Full-bodied and medium sweet, with a fruit finish. Drink now.–J.S. • $25/500 ml. • (4/30/2000) • **87**

Chardonnay Emilia Laurento 1997: Rather unusual. Interesting aromas of pineapple skin, white pepper and vanilla. Medium-bodied, with coconut, toasted oak and apple flavors. Medium acidity. Drink now.–J.S. • $16 • (2/29/2000) • **85**

Emilia Liano 1995: Good ruby color, with lovely perfumes of flowers and blackberry. Medium-bodied, with velvety tannins and a good shot of new wood on the finish. A bit too much new oak, but delicious. A blend of Sangiovese and Cabernet Sauvignon. Drink now.–J.S. • $15 • (1/01/2000) • **85**

Liano 1992 • $12 • (3/31/1997) • **84**

Sangiovese di Romagna Riserva 1996: Good color, with berry and chocolate and a slightly volatile nose. Medium-bodied, with light tannins and a crisp finish. Drink now.–J.S. • $11 • (1/01/2000) • **81**

Sangiovese di Romagna Riserva 1995 • $10 • (6/15/1998) • **81**

Sangiovese di Romagna Riserva 1993 • $10 • (3/31/1997) • **79**

Sangiovese di Romagna Riserva 1992 • $10 • (2/29/1996) • **83**

Sangiovese di Romagna Superiore Ca' Grande 1995 • $8 • (3/31/1997) • **80**

CESARI & FIGLI, FRANCO

Amarone della Valpolicella Il Bosco 1988 • $30 • (9/30/1995) • **85**

Barolo Vigna Cerreta 1990 • $NA • (10/31/1995) • **79**

Key: SS—Spectator Selection. CS—Cellar Selection. HR—Highly Recommended. $NA—Price not available. (BT)—Barrel tasting. (A)—Auction Price. For a key to the tasters' initials, see "How to Use These Listings." **Dates in parentheses represent the issues in which the ratings were published.**

CEUSO

Sicilia Custera 1997: A red with aspirations. Medium-bodied, with silky tannins and a berry and milk chocolate aftertaste. Best after 2000.–J.S. • $32 • (5/31/2000) • **86**

Sicilia Custera 1996: A very ripe and traditional red, with dried fruit, raisin and nut character. Full-bodied, with soft tannins and a long, slightly dry finish. A bit rustic. Drink now.–J.S. • $32 • (1/01/2000) • **83**

CHIARLO, MICHELE

Barbaresco 1996: New wave and new-oakish, but lovely, ripe, opulent Barbaresco, packed with berry and plum, delivering a minty, minerally layer along with crisp acidity on the lingering, chewy finish. Needs time for the tough tannins to settle down. Best from 2004 through 2010.–P.M. • $51 • (8/31/1999) • **89**

Barbaresco 1995: Delicate and fruity, medium-bodied, appealing for its clean and pure red- and blackberry, tar, rose petal and lightly spicy notes. Complex and balanced, but not a blockbuster, just very pretty. Drink now through 2003.–P.M. • $35 • (10/31/1998) • **86**

Barbaresco 1993 • $28 • (10/31/1996) • **89**

Barbaresco 1992 • $24 • (10/31/1995) • **81**

Barbaresco 1990 • $25 • (10/31/1994) • **85**

Barbaresco 1989 • $23 • (10/31/1993) • **81**

Barbaresco 1988 • $23 • (10/31/1993) • **85**

Barbaresco Asili 1996: Clean and ripe, elegant in build, there's good sweet fruit character here, with a fresh black currant, plum and even subtle minty character. Silky midpalate turns into a tough-tannin finish, with a smoky, herbal overtone and some astringency. Drink now through 2003.–P.M. • $79 • (8/31/1999) • **87**

Barbaresco Asili 1995: Dark-colored, but fairly lean, showing lots of cassis, blackberry and black cherry character. Turns a bit dry and tough on the finish. Tasted twice, with consistent notes.–P.M. • $72 • (10/31/1998) • **78**

Barbaresco Rabajà 1996: Beautiful. Aromatically exciting, with floral (roses come to mind) scents, this full-bodied, rich yet racy Barbaresco saturates the palate with sweet-tasting plum and red- and blackberry, and combines crisp acidity with ripe but tough tannins for a finale worthy of the grand '96 vintage. Best from 2006 through 2016.–P.M. • $79 • (8/31/1999) • **94**

Barbaresco Rabajà 1995: Elegant and refined, this lovely wine has subtle fruit and supple tannins. Wonderful red berry and blackberry notes and hints of toasted oak, spice and chocolate complete this medium-bodied package that delivers pleasure from start to finish. Delicious. Drink now through 2007.–P.M. • $65 • (9/15/1998) • **90**

Barbaresco Rabajà 1993 • $57 • (6/15/1997) • **85**

Barbaresco Rabajà 1990 • $48 • (10/31/1994) • **90**

Barbaresco Rabajà 1989 • $48 • (10/31/1993) • **91**

Barbaresco Rabajà 1988 • $48 • (10/31/1993) • **90**

Barbera d'Asti 1997: A vibrant style of Barbera, with pronounced spicy oak along with black cherry flavors. The tannins are rounded and ripe, but expect a shot of tart acidity on the finish. Drink now through 2001.–P.M. • $11 • (11/15/1999) • **84**

Barbera d'Asti 1996: Fresh but a bit earthy. Light-bodied, with strawberry, raspberry and mocha notes, a crisp texture and a delicate finish. Should go well with pizza and pasta. Drink now.–P.M. • $11 • (10/31/1998) • **81**

Barbera d'Asti 1995 • $10 • (3/31/1997) • **84**

Barbera d'Asti 1993 • $9 • (10/31/1994) • **85**

Barbera d'Asti 1991 • $9 • (1/01/1994) • **79**

Barbera d'Asti 1990 • $9 • (10/15/1993) • **91**

Barbera d'Asti La Court 1996: Vanilla, lemon and raspberry combine for a rather unusual blend in this medium-intense, obviously oaked, medium-bodied Barbera. Lacks a bit of focus, but tastes clean. Drink now.–P.M. • $30 • (11/15/1999) • **84**

Barbera d'Asti Superiore 1994 • $10 • (10/31/1996) • **83**

Barbera d'Asti Superiore Valle del Sole 1994 • $25 • (10/31/1997) • **87**

Barbera d'Asti Superiore Valle del Sole 1993 • $22 • (10/31/1996) • **86**

Barbera d'Asti Superiore Valle del Sole 1990 • $22 • (6/30/1993) • **87**

Barbera d'Asti Superiore Valle del Sole 1989 • $19 • (10/15/1993) • **86**

Barbera d'Asti Superiore Valle del Sole 1988 • $19 • (10/31/1992) • **83**

Barbera d'Asti Superiore Valle del Sole 1987 • $19 • (2/15/1992) • **84**

Barbera d'Asti Superiore Valle del Sole 1986 • $18 • (3/15/1991) • **86**

Barilot 1994 • $34 • (1/31/1998) • **84**

Barilot 1993 • $30 • (10/31/1996) • **86**

Barilot 1991 • $28 • (1/01/1997) • **86**

Barilot 1990 • $25 • (10/31/1994) • **85**

Barilot 1987 • $31 • (6/15/1994) • **86**

Barilot 1986 • $31 • (12/15/1992) • **73**

Barolo 1995: Well made in a supple way. Ripe and full-bodied, with firm but sweet tannins and herb, wild berry, smoke, toast and mocha notes. Drink now through 2001.–P.M. • $48 • (11/15/1999) • **86**
Barolo 1994: Quite sweet-tasting, with plum and cherry notes struggling to emerge in this rather tannic, slightly herbal, medium-bodied red of modest concentration. Give it time. Best after 2000.–P.M. • $33 • (10/31/1998) • **80**
Barolo 1993 • $34 • (10/31/1997) • **85**
Barolo 1992 • $28 • (10/31/1996) • **85**
Barolo 1991 • $24 • (10/31/1995) • **85**
Barolo 1990 • $25 • (10/31/1994) • **85**
Barolo 1989 • $23 • (10/31/1993) • **91**
Barolo 1988 • $23 • (10/15/1993) SS • **92**
Barolo 1987 • $22 • (12/15/1992) • **86**
Barolo Brunate 1990 • $47 • (10/31/1994) • **92**
Barolo Brunate 1989 • $47 • (10/31/1993) • **89**
Barolo Brunate 1988 • $47 • (10/31/1993) • **89**
Barolo Cannubi 1995: Clean, pure red berry and blackberry fruit is the backbone of this well-made, medium-bodied, smoky, spicy, modern-style Barolo, but it also tastes a bit herbal and turns up the tannin on the chewy finish. Drink now through 2005.–P.M. • $97 • (11/15/1999) • **89**
Barolo Cannubi 1993 • $77 • (10/31/1997) • **88**
Barolo Cannubi 1991 • $60 • (10/31/1995) • **86**
Barolo Cannubi 1990 • $56 • (10/31/1994) • **74**
Barolo Cerequio 1995: Showing crisp, freshly crushed red berry, with some lightly toasted, petrollike wet earth notes. Medium-bodied, dark in color, clean on the lingering finish. Tough tannins—will they soften? Give it some time. Best after 2000.–P.M. • $88 • (11/15/1999) • **87**
Barolo Cerequio 1993 • $77 • (10/31/1997) • **86**
Barolo Cerequio 1991 • $60 • (10/31/1995) • **88**
Barolo Cerequio 1990 • $56 • (10/31/1994) • **93**
Barolo Cerequio 1989 • $54 • (10/31/1993) • **87**
Barolo Cerequio 1988 • $36 Ⓐ • (3/31/1993) • **88**
Barolo Granduca 1985 • $20 • (2/28/1991) • **89**
Barolo Riserva 1993: Impressively dark, with good ripeness, this is full-bodied yet packed with high acidity and mouthpuckeringly fresh on the midpalate. Wood plays second fiddle, with plum, cassis and tart tannins coming through on the tough finish. Best after 2005.–P.M. • $50 • (10/31/1998) • **86**
Barolo Riserva 1990 • $47 • (10/31/1996) • **89**
Barolo Rocche di Castiglione 1990 • $47 • (10/31/1994) • **85**
Barolo Rocche di Castiglione 1989 • $44 • (10/31/1993) • **90**
Barolo Rocche di Castiglione 1988 • $44 • (10/31/1993) • **89**
Barolo Rocche di Castiglione Riserva 1985 • $43 • (1/31/1992) • **88**
Barolo Rocche di Castiglione Riserva 1983 • $30 • (2/28/1991) • **78**
Barolo Vigna Rionda di Serralunga 1993 • $64 • (10/31/1997) • **90**
Barolo Vigna Rionda di Serralunga 1990 • $47 • (10/31/1994) • **90**
Barolo Vigna Rionda di Serralunga 1989 • $47 • (10/31/1993) • **89**
Barolo Vigna Rionda di Serralunga 1988 • $47 • (10/31/1993) • **85**
Barolo Vigna Rionda di Serralunga Riserva 1986 • $45 • (12/15/1992) • **84**
Barolo Vigna Rionda di Serralunga Riserva 1985 • $39 • (2/28/1991) • **81**
Barolo Vigna Rionda di Serralunga Riserva 1983 • $36 • (2/28/1991) • **87**
Barolo Vigna Rionda di Serralunga Riserva 1982 • $32 • (1/31/1990) • **89**
Countacc! 1993 • $61 • (1/31/1998) • **87**
Countacc! 1990 • $52 • (10/31/1994) • **87**
Dolcetto d'Alba 1993 • $NA • (1/01/1995) • **82**
Gavi 1996 • $14 • (1/31/1998) • **73**
Gavi Rovereto 1997: Diluted. More like water than wine, tasting of...perhaps watermelon. It comes in a tall, heavy, fancy designer bottle—why?–P.M. • $24 • (10/31/1998) • **70**
Gavi Rovereto 1996 • $23 • (1/31/1998) • **78**
Langhe Barilot 1996: Fresh and focused. Medium-bodied, with oak treatment balanced by lively red berry and blackberry character. Good intensity and vibrant acidity. A bit lean on the finish. Drink now through 2005.–P.M. • $36 • (11/15/1999) • **87**
Monferrato Countacc! 1996: Smooth and round, perhaps lacking a bit of really ripe and focused fruit. Oak notes weave into the acidity and fresh fruit. Drink now through 2002.–P.M. • $62 • (11/15/1999) • **82**
Monferrato White Plenilunio 1996: Light-bodied, showing decent acidity. The grassy lime flavor brings it to life, but it soon turns chewy, then dries a bit on the finish. A blend of Sauvignon Blanc, Chardonnay and Cortese. Not available in the U.S. Drink now.–P.M. • $NA • (10/31/1998) • **80**
Moscato d'Asti Nivole 1996 • $9/375 ml. • (7/31/1997) • **86**

CHIESA DI S. RESTITUTA, LA

Brunello di Montalcino 1988 • $32 • (4/30/1994) • **85**
Brunello di Montalcino Vigna San Pietro Riserva 1988 • $NA • (10/31/1994) • **83**
Red 1990 • $NA • (10/31/1993) • **94**
Rosso di Montalcino 1992 • $NA • (10/31/1994) • **83**
Rosso di Montalcino 1991 • $14 • (4/30/1994) • **83**

CHIONETTI & FIGLIO, QUINTO

Dolcetto di Dogliani Briccolero 1997: Well made, balanced and concentrated. Medium- to full-bodied, with blackberry, black cherry, even mineral character and round, supple tannins. Fresh, vibrant finish. Drink now.–P.M. • $18 • (7/31/1999) • **88**
Dolcetto di Dogliani Briccolero 1996: A beautiful Dolcetto, tasting of earth, mineral and red berry notes. A charmer of medium body, it delivers some silky tannins. Harmonious finish. Drink now through 2001.–P.M. • $18 • (10/31/1998) • **86**
Dolcetto di Dogliani Briccolero 1994 • $15 • (10/31/1996) • **84**
Dolcetto di Dogliani Briccolero 1989 • $16 • (4/30/1991) • **87**
Dolcetto di Dogliani San Luigi 1993 • $NA • (10/31/1995) • **81**

CHIUSE, LE

Brunello di Montalcino 1995: Very nice, but promises a bit more on the nose than delivers on the palate. Pretty aromas of wet leaves, plums and berries. Full-bodied, with velvety tannins and a medium finish. Drink now.–J.S. • $50 • (6/30/2000) • **87**

CIABOT BERTON

Barbera d'Alba 1996 • $18 • (10/31/1997) • **73**
Barbera d'Alba Bricco San Biagio 1997: Smoothed by fancy oak treatment, it blends mocha with cranberry and blueberry in a supple package. Medium-bodied, with a toasted finish. Drink now through 2001.–P.M. • $26 • (11/15/1999) • **81**
Barbera d'Alba Bricco San Biagio 1996: Lots of wine in this lush package, but the flavors are odd, veering toward petrol, rubber and earthiness. Not recommended. Tasted twice, with consistent notes.–P.M. • $19 • (10/31/1998) • **60**
Barbera d'Alba Bricco San Biagio 1995 • $18 • (10/31/1997) • **88**
Barbera d'Alba Bricco San Biagio 1994 • $NA • (10/31/1996) • **80**
Barbera d'Alba Bricco San Biagio 1993 • $NA • (10/31/1996) • **87**
Barolo 1995: A balanced Barolo, with lovely ripe fruit—plum, blackberry, cassis—along with a floral, mint, licorice and tar complexity that fans out with good intensity. Deliciously persistent finish. Drink now through 2005.–P.M. • $34 • (11/15/1999) • **89**
Barolo 1994: Odd and a bit stinky, with oil, petrol and rubber aromas dominating the wet earth, dried herb, mineral and tar notes. Medium-bodied.–P.M. • $27 • (10/31/1998) • **75**
Barolo 1993 • $24 • (10/31/1997) • **84**
Barolo 1991 • $NA • (10/31/1995) • **71**
Barolo 1990 • $NA • (10/31/1995) • **80**
Barolo 1988 • $28 • (12/15/1992) • **85**
Barolo Roggeri 1995: Good fruit in a silky package. This seductive, modern-style Barolo tastes of toasted oak and shows blackberry, violet and smoke notes. A medium-bodied Nebbiolo, with character and length. Could hold, but tempting now. Drink through 2005.–P.M. • $46 • (11/15/1999) • **90**
Barolo Roggeri 1994: Odd, of medium body and intensity. A bit metallic and earthy, with herbal notes, cassis bush and plum character.–P.M. • $34 • (10/31/1998) • **77**
Barolo Roggeri 1993 • $28 • (10/31/1997) • **92**
Dolcetto d'Alba 1996 • $11 • (10/31/1997) • **82**
Dolcetto d'Alba 1993 • $NA • (10/31/1995) • **79**
Dolcetto d'Alba 1990 • $12 • (3/31/1993) • **83**
Dolcetto d'Alba Rutuin 1996: Delightful. Ripe, thick, and fairly acidic, this is a joy to drink, with its vivid cassis, wet earth, lemon, cherry, plum and chocolate flavors. A bit chewy, but who cares? The tannins are ripe and the finish is deftly toasted. Should be a super match with food. Drink now through 2002.–P.M. • $14 • (10/31/1998) • **88**
Dolcetto d'Alba Rutuin 1993 • $NA • (10/31/1995) • **84**
Nebbiolo delle Langhe 1988 • $12 • (3/31/1993) • **82**

CIACCI PICCOLOMINI D'ARAGONA

Brunello di Montalcino 1990 • $35 • (10/31/1995) • **93**
Brunello di Montalcino 1984 • $25 • (6/15/1990) • **91**
Brunello di Montalcino Riserva 1988 • $50 • (10/31/1994) • **91**

CIACCI PICCOLOMINI D'ARAGONA

Brunello di Montalcino Vigna di Pianrosso 1994: Very aromatic wine, with dried berries and cherries throughout. Medium- to full-bodied, with very soft, round tannins and a long, long finish. An absolute joy to drink. Drink now.–J.S. • $50 • (8/31/1999) • **90**

Brunello di Montalcino Vigna di Pianrosso 1993: Delicate and traditional, with floral, berry and leather aromas and flavors. Medium in body, with medium tannins and a light, crisp finish. Drink now.–J.S. • $53 • (12/15/1998) • **85**

Brunello di Montalcino Vigna di Pianrosso 1988 • $40 • (4/30/1994) • **88**

Rosso di Montalcino 1992 • $15 • (10/31/1994) • **80**

Rosso di Montalcino 1988 • $16 • (4/30/1991) • **82**

Rosso di Montalcino Vigna della Fonte 1997: Attractive berry and floral character to this medium-bodied, fruity rosso. Medium finish. Drink now.–J.S. • $23 • (9/15/1999) • **84**

Rosso di Montalcino Vigna della Fonte 1996: Rich for a Rosso '96, with raisin and berry aromas and flavors. Medium-bodied, with velvety tannins and a shortish finish. A bit hard at the end. Drink now.–J.S. • $20 • (12/15/1998) • **84**

Rosso di Montalcino Vigna della Fonte 1993 • $17 • (10/31/1995) • **87**

Rosso di Montalcino Vigna della Fonte 1991 • $16 • (4/30/1994) • **81**

CIELO

Chardonnay Veneto 1997: A solid, appealing Chardonnay, with apple and lemon character. Drink now.–B.S. • $6 • (9/30/1998) • **83**

Chardonnay Veneto 1996 • $6 • (4/30/1998) • **82**

Merlot Veneto 1997: A straightforward, juicy Merlot, with cherry and tomato flavors that lean toward the spicy side, almost like tomato sauce. Moderate richness and depth. Drink now.–B.S. • $6 • (9/30/1998) • **82**

Merlot Veneto 1996 • $6 • (4/30/1998) • **77**

Merlot Veneto 1995 • $6 • (4/30/1997) • **77**

Merlot Veneto 1992 • $5 • (10/31/1994) • **82**

Pinot Grigio Veneto 1997: A lovely Pinot Grigio at a bygone price, sporting floral, apple and peach character, good concentration and balance, ending with a mouthwatering finish. Drink this appealing Italian white now.–B.S. • $6 • (9/30/1998) • **85**

Pinot Grigio Veneto 1996 • $6 • (5/15/1998) • **78**

CIGLIUTI

Asti Briccoserra 1997: Clean and vibrant, this refreshing red has smoke, toast and blackberry flavors, all presented in a balanced package. Persistent, slightly chewy finish. Drink now through 2003.–P.M. • $43 • (11/15/1999) • **87**

Barbaresco Serraboella 1996: Ultrasmooth, with an opulent texture, this full-bodied Barbaresco is deftly oaked as it seduces with mocha, vanilla and espresso aromas and flavors, ripe tannins and good, medium-intense fruit. Tannins clamp down on the finish, so cellar. Best after 2003.–P.M. • $55 • (10/31/1999) • **88**

Barbaresco Serraboella 1995: Impressive dark color in this extracted, tannic wine. Shows plenty of lively, pure fruit, with an earthy undertone that blows off after a while. Medium-bodied and succulent, with a slightly drying finish. Time should tame it. Best after 2003.–P.M. • $46 • (10/31/1998) • **83**

Barbaresco Serraboella 1994 • $45 • (10/31/1997) • **87**

Barbaresco Serraboella 1986 • $20 • (8/31/1989) • **86**

Barbera d'Alba Serraboella 1996: A true-to-type Barbera, with earth, cedar and black cherry aromas and flavors. Medium-bodied and quite tough, this fairly rustic wine should hold up to spicy and flavorful food. Drink now through 2002.–P.M. • $21 • (10/31/1998) • **83**

Barbera d'Alba Serraboella 1993 • $NA • (10/31/1995) • **80**

Barbera d'Alba Serraboella 1989 • $15 • (11/30/1991) • **87**

Dolcetto d'Alba Serraboella 1997: Ripe-tasting, with sweet tannins that make it irresistible. Beautifully balanced, of medium body, it delivers lovely spice, black cherry, raspberry, vanilla and a slight toasty character, but it's a touch herbal on the otherwise good finish.–P.M. • $18 • (10/31/1998) • **86**

Dolcetto d'Alba Serraboella 1993 • $NA • (10/31/1995) • **78**

Langhe Bricco Serra 1996: Purple-black, full-bodied and oaky as can be, this hugely extracted red delivers layers of ripe plum, wild raspberry and cassis, with nuances of spice and mocha. The acidity saves it from being overdone, and it ends on a lingering, creamlike finish. An international-style wine. Drink now.–P.M. • $35 • (10/31/1998) • **89**

Key: SS—Spectator Selection. CS—Cellar Selection. HR—Highly Recommended. $NA—Price not available. (BT)—Barrel tasting. Ⓐ—Auction Price.
For a key to the tasters' initials, see "How to Use These Listings."
Dates in parentheses represent the issues in which the ratings were published.

CINCIOLE, LE

Chianti Classico 1997: A good, chewy CC, with plenty of dried cherry and citrus character. Medium-bodied, with chewy tannins and crisp acidity on the finish. Drink now.–J.S. • $18 • (11/30/1999) • **86**

Chianti Classico 1996: Fresh and fruity, with light but very clean dried cherry flavors. Light-bodied, with crisp acidity and a fresh finish. Serve chilled.–J.S. • $18 • (12/15/1998) • **80**

Chianti Classico 1995 • $16 • (9/30/1997) • **83**

Chianti Classico 1994 • $16 • (10/31/1996) • **86**

Chianti Classico 1993 • $NA • (10/31/1995) • **88**

Chianti Classico Valle del Pozzo Riserva 1996: Lovely, sweet strawberry, cherry and berry character. Medium-bodied, with medium, velvety tannins and a fresh fruit finish. Drink now.–J.S. • $18 • (11/30/1999) • **87**

Chianti Classico Valle del Pozzo Riserva 1995: Fresh and fruity, with dried cherry and plum aromas and flavors, a light body, light tannins and a crisp finish. Drink now.–J.S. • $25 • (12/15/1998) • **80**

Chianti Classico Valle del Pozzo Riserva 1994 • $26 • (9/30/1997) • **83**

Chianti Classico Vecchie Vigne Riserva 1994: Beautiful to sniff. Very floral in aroma, with rose and lily and undertones of fruit. Medium- to full-bodied, with medium tannins and a crisp finish. Subtle and rich. From old vines. Drink now.–J.S. • $28 • (12/15/1998) • **89**

CIPRESSAIA, TENUTA LA

Chianti Colli Fiorentini 1997: A very ripe red that verges on raisins. Medium-bodied, with soft tannins and a cherry and coffee aftertaste. Lacks freshness. Not imported into the U.S. Drink now.–J.S. • $NA • (1/01/1999) • **81**

CISPIANO

Chianti Classico 1996: Hard to believe this is a Chianti. It's big and chunky, with loads of blackberry, currant and mint character. Full-bodied, with well-integrated tannins and a long aftertaste of ripe fruit. Tasted twice, with consistent notes. Drink now.–J.S. • $14 • (12/15/1998) • **87**

Chianti Classico 1993 • $17 • (10/31/1996) • **84**

Chianti Classico 1990 • $NA • (10/31/1993) • **85**

Chianti Classico Riserva 1995: Good concentration of fruit, though a bit one-dimensional. Loads of ripe blackberry and currant bush aromas. Medium-bodied, with firm tannins and an intense berry finish with a stemmy note. Drink now.–J.S. • $21 • (12/15/1998) • **85**

Chianti Classico Riserva 1991 • $28 • (3/31/1997) • **81**

Toscana Red 1995: Interesting. Tastes more like a '97. Rather rustic. Full-bodied and very grapey, with masses of fruit, verging on raisiny, and tannins. California Zinfandel lovers will like this one. Drink now.–J.S. • $26 • (12/15/1998) • **85**

CLERICO, DOMENICO

Barbera d'Alba 1991 • $15 • (11/15/1993) • **80**

Barbera d'Alba 1990 • $14 • (12/15/1992) • **84**

Barbera d'Alba 1988 • $12 • (3/15/1991) • **84**

Barolo 1984 • $13 • (8/31/1988) • **85**

Barolo Briccoto Bussia 1990 • $40 • (10/31/1994) • **90**

Barolo Ciabot Mentin Ginestra 1995: Good fruit mingles with spice, dried herb and licorice in this satisfying, medium-bodied, medium complex, clean Barolo. Ripe but very chewy tannins should soften with time. Drink now through 2003.–P.M. • $60 • (11/15/1999) • **88**

Barolo Ciabot Mentin Ginestra 1994: Overly oaky for the fruit. Light to medium in body, it offers mocha, spice, coffee, toasted oak, plum and black cherry. Lean, with a chewy finish. Drink now.–P.M. • $46 Ⓐ • (10/31/1998) • **80**

Barolo Ciabot Mentin Ginestra 1993 • $44 • (10/31/1997) • **91**

Barolo Ciabot Mentin Ginestra 1992 • $32 • (10/31/1996) • **92**

Barolo Ciabot Mentin Ginestra 1991 • $30 • (10/31/1995) • **85**

Barolo Ciabot Mentin Ginestra 1989 • $72 Ⓐ • (10/31/1993) HR • **92**

Barolo Ciabot Mentin Ginestra 1988 • $45 • (10/31/1993) • **89**

Barolo Ciabot Mentin Ginestra 1985 • $27 • (4/15/1990) CS • **92**

Barolo Ciabot Mentin Ginestra 1983 • $19 • (12/15/1987) • **88**

Barolo Pajana 1995: Excellent. Layered with tar, toasted oak, currant and herb, this full-bodied Barolo comes together beautifully on the ripe, round midpalate, as the concentration becomes obvious. Supple tannins, balanced finish. Drink now through 2003.–P.M. • $60 • (11/15/1999) • **92**

Barolo Pajana 1994: Round and pleasant, with mocha, spice and modest red berry character, this medium-bodied wine turns a bit dry on the finish.

ITALY

Tasted twice, with consistent notes. Drink now through 2002.–P.M. • $45 • (10/31/1998) • **82**
Barolo Pajana 1993 • $44 • (10/31/1997) • **93**
Barolo Pajana 1992 • $32 • (10/31/1996) • **90**
Barolo Pajana 1991 • $28 • (10/31/1995) • **84**
Barolo Pajana 1990 • $115 Ⓐ • (10/31/1994) • **90**
Dolcetto d'Alba 1994 • $13 • (10/31/1995) • **85**
Langhe Arte 1996: Ripe and full-bodied, with olive, dried herb and a roasted, sweet-tasting yellow bell pepper character. Opulent but also chewy, with blackberry flavors that zing along. Drink now through 2005.–P.M. • $40 • (11/15/1999) • **88**
Langhe Arte 1995: Elegant but very oaky, and a bit dry on the finish. With less wood, the plum and berry character could have tasted great. Maybe short-term cellaring will help.–P.M. • $35 • (10/31/1998) • **80**
Langhe Arte 1992 • $26 • (10/31/1994) • **86**
Langhe Arte 1989 • $30 • (12/15/1992) • **89**
Langhe Arte 1988 • $26 • (2/28/1991) • **90**
Langhe Arte 1987 • $22 • (1/31/1990) • **78**
Langhe Arte 1986 • $22 • (2/15/1989) • **88**
Langhe Arte 1985 • $22 • (1/31/1988) • **91**

COCCI GRIFONI

Falerio dei Colli Ascolani 1996 • $8 • (5/15/1998) • **82**
Falerio dei Colli Ascolani Vigneti San Basso 1996 • $10 • (5/15/1998) • **82**
Rosso Piceno Superiore 1994: Generous flavor and rich texture, with rustic earthy, smoky, tomatolike flavors and firm tannins. Not pretty, but nice and solid. A blend: 60 percent Sangiovese and 40 percent Montepulciano. Drink now. • $9 • (8/31/1998) • **84**
Rosso Piceno Superiore Vigna Messieri 1995: A good but rather austere red that's dry and somewhat tannic, with a distinctive range of smoke, spice, black cherry flavors. A blend of Sangiovese and Montepulciano. Drink now. • $15 • (8/31/1998) • **84**

COGNO, ELVIO

Barbera d'Alba Bricco del Merlo 1997: Gorgeous. Plays the field, from floral-violet notes to black currant, smoke and game, this dark-colored, full-bodied red with its refined tannins also delivers a punch of crisp, mouthpuckering Barbera character on the finish—but the balance is there. Drink now through 2004.–P.M. • $32 • (9/15/1999) • **91**
Barbera d'Alba Bricco del Merlo 1996: Stands out for its black color, thick texture and opulent body. This barrique style of Barbera is so woody that the mocha, spice and toasted oak overwhelms the fruit, but it's full-bodied, supple and satisfying if you like oak. Drink now through 2002.–P.M. • $24 • (10/31/1998) • **87**
Barbera d'Alba Bricco del Merlo 1995 • $23 • (10/31/1997) • **87**
Barbera d'Alba Bricco del Merlo 1991 • $15 • (7/31/1995) • **85**
Barolo Ravera 1995: A burly, full-bodied Barolo, with a good grip of ripe fruit, solid tannins and spicy complexity. Clean and powerful, it delivers a core of mineral, plum and lead pencil complexity that should blossom with cellaring. Drink now through 2003.–P.M. • $54 • (11/15/1999) • **89**
Barolo Ravera 1994: Very supple and ready to drink, with nice plum, cherry, citrus and blackberry flavors. Clean and pure, well made and velvety. Impressive from start to finish. Should improve with cellaring given its length and acidity. Drink now through 2006.–P.M. • $39 • (10/31/1998) • **88**
Barolo Ravera 1993 • $41 • (10/31/1997) • **76**
Dolcetto d'Alba Vigna del Mandorlo 1998: A Dolcetto of the highest level. Full-bodied, coating the palate with well-integrated tannins as well as mocha, chocolate and mostly black cherry and tar. For this varietal, there's amazing richness on the opulent finish. Tastes unfiltered. A perfect forebear of what the great '98 vintage might bring us. Drink now through 2001.–P.M. • $17 • (11/15/1999) • **92**
Dolcetto d'Alba Vigna del Mandorlo 1997: Lovely fruit in this clean, vibrant Dolcetto, showing cassis bush and a slight herbal note, with enough balance to enjoy it fully. Drink now.–P.M. • $16 • (7/31/1999) • **84**
Langhe Montegrilli 1997: Smooth in texture, offering toasted oak aromas and olive and black fruit flavors. Medium-bodied, with a roundness on the heavily toasted finish. Has a fresh appeal. Drink now through 2001.–P.M. • $36 • (11/15/1999) • **85**
Langhe Montegrilli 1996: A muscular, brooding, ripe and thick red, showing loads of plum, tar, violet, rose petal, red berry and blackberry flavors. Full-bodied, it's layered with toasted oak notes that turn smoky on the long, tough finish. The tannins are firm and ripe, but give them time to soften. Best after 2003.–P.M. • $28 • (10/31/1998) • **88**
Langhe Montegrilli 1995 • $27 • (10/31/1997) • **89**

COL D'ORCIA

Brunello di Montalcino 1995: Chewy red. Bright cherry, smoke and spice aromas. Medium-bodied, with velvety tannins, soft texture and a fruity finish. Drink now through 2003.–J.S. • $45 • (6/30/2000) • **87**
Brunello di Montalcino 1994: A silky '94 Brunello, with fine tannins and plenty of berry, tea and cedar flavors. Medium body. Delicate, sweet fruit finish. Drink now.–J.S. • $32 • (8/31/1999) • **87**
Brunello di Montalcino 1993: Slightly one-dimensional, but well made and balanced. Medium-bodied, with chocolate and cherry aromas and flavors, firm tannins and a refreshing finish. Best after 2000.–J.S. • $35 • (12/15/1998) • **88**
Brunello di Montalcino 1992 • $35 • (9/30/1997) • **88**
Brunello di Montalcino 1991 • $NA • (11/30/1996) • **80**
Brunello di Montalcino 1990 • $NA • (10/31/1995) • **87**
Brunello di Montalcino 1988 • $30 • (4/30/1994) • **86**
Brunello di Montalcino 1985 • $23 • (11/30/1990) • **88**
Brunello di Montalcino 1981 • $22 • (9/15/1986) • **70**
Brunello di Montalcino 1979 • $15 • (9/15/1986) CS • **94**
Brunello di Montalcino Poggio al Vento Riserva 1993: A rich and slightly decadent Brunello, with plum, meat and mushroom aromas. Full-bodied and very ripe, with powerful tannins and a long, rich finish. Still needs a bit of age. Drink through 2005.–J.S. • $70 • (11/30/1999) • **90**
Brunello di Montalcino Poggio al Vento Riserva 1990 • $64 • (9/30/1997) • **84**
Brunello di Montalcino Poggio al Vento Riserva 1988 • $NA • (4/30/1994) • **92**
Brunello di Montalcino Poggio al Vento Riserva 1982 • $40 • (4/15/1991) • **89**
Brunello di Montalcino Riserva 1991 • $48 • (9/30/1997) • **86**
Brunello di Montalcino Riserva 1990 • $NA • (11/30/1996) • **89**
Brunello di Montalcino Riserva 1988 • $27 • (10/31/1994) • **90**
Brunello di Montalcino Riserva 1981 • $22 • (7/31/1988) • **89**
Chianti Gineprone 1993 • $10 • (9/30/1997) • **79**
Moscadello di Montalcino Pascena Vendemmia Tardiva 1995: This delicious dessert wine has impressive aromas of ripe pear, beeswax and flowers. Medium-bodied and medium sweet, with plenty of sweet pineapple and fruit character. Long finish. Drink now through 2002.–J.S. • $33 • (11/30/1999) • **88**
Olmaia 1995: A chewy Cabernet. Intense aromas of red licorice, with hints of dried herbs. Full-bodied, with lots of tannins and a medium finish. Best after 2000.–J.S. • $48 • (11/30/1999) • **90**
Olmaia 1994: An outstanding red, verging on classic quality. Inky-colored, with a powerful bouquet of currant, lead pencil and tar. Full-bodied, with full, well-polished tannins. The finish goes on and on. Just a tad more concentration of fruit at midpalate would give it a classic rating. Needs some time to mellow. Col d'Orcia is making great Cabernet at the moment. Best after 2001.–J.S. • $43 • (12/15/1998) • **94**
Olmaia 1993 • $39 • (9/30/1997) • **91**
Olmaia 1992 • $NA • (10/31/1996) • **88**
Olmaia 1990 • $19 • (2/28/1995) • **96**
Rosso degli Spezieri 1995 • $NA • (3/31/1997) • **85**
Rosso di Montalcino 1997: Pleasant, fresh, fruity and simple. Medium- to light-bodied, with light fruit and a delicate finish. Drink now.–J.S. • $13 • (9/15/1999) • **81**
Rosso di Montalcino 1996: A light and simple Rosso with a slightly herbal flavor. Light-bodied, with a light finish. Rather disappointing for this producer.–J.S. • $10 • (12/15/1998) • **77**
Rosso di Montalcino 1995 • $14 • (9/30/1997) • **83**
Rosso di Montalcino 1994 • $14 • (11/30/1996) • **86**
Rosso di Montalcino 1993 • $NA • (10/31/1995) • **74**
Rosso di Montalcino 1992 • $11 • (10/31/1994) • **81**
Rosso di Montalcino 1991 • $11 • (4/30/1994) • **78**
Rosso di Montalcino 1988 • $9 • (4/30/1991) • **84**
Toscana Rosso degli Spezieri 1998: Light- to medium-bodied, with pretty, bright cherry and berry aromas and flavors, light tannins and a fresh finish. Drink now through 2001.–J.S. • $11 • (11/30/1999) • **83**
Toscana Rosso degli Spezieri 1997: Fresh and delicious, with cherry, grape and pear aromas and flavors. Medium-bodied, with light tannins and a fresh finish. Drink now.–J.S. • $10 • (12/15/1998) • **84**

COLDISOLE

Rosso di Montalcino 1997: Extremely ripe, almost raisiny character. Full-bodied, with medium tannins and a long, baked, slightly burnt cherry pie finish. Slightly rustic, but you've got to like it. Not imported into the U.S. Drink now.–J.S. • $NA • (11/30/1999) • **88**

COLLA, PODERI

Barbaresco 1994 • $38 • (10/31/1997) • **84**
Barbaresco 1993 • $37 • (10/31/1996) • **88**
Barbaresco Tenuta Roncaglia 1995: Soft, smooth and drinkable tonight, with uncomplex red berry, banana and spice flavors. The tannins kick in on the end, giving it a welcome edge for food.–P.M. • $39 • (10/31/1998) • **85**
Barbera d'Alba 1996: Of medium intensity, this Barbera is smoothed by some vanilla and mocha notes. Mild red berry character, light finish. Drink now.–P.M. • $19 • (10/31/1998) • **80**
Barbera d'Alba 1995 • $18 • (10/31/1997) • **83**
Barbera d'Alba 1994 • $19 • (10/31/1996) • **81**
Barbera d'Alba 1993 • $NA • (10/31/1995) • **82**
Barbera d'Alba 1993 • $17 • (10/31/1996) • **79**
Barolo Bussia Dardi Le Rose 1994: Round and supple. Full-bodied, with smoke, tar, plum and wet earth, one can only appreciate the well-integrated tannins and opulent mouthfeel. The vanilla and milk chocolate notes suggest it's seen some barriques. Drink now through 2003.–P.M. • $37 • (10/31/1998) • **87**
Barolo Bussia Dardi Le Rose 1993 • $45 • (10/31/1997) • **85**
Nebbiolo d'Alba 1996: Simple and light-bodied, with licorice and strawberry notes, light tannins and not much length. Served slightly chilled. Drink now.–P.M. • $20 • (10/31/1998) • **79**

COLLAVINI

Cabernet Grave del Friuli 1996: Good intensity of cassis and Cabernet character. Medium-bodied, with soft tannins and a delicious fruity aftertaste. Drink now.–J.S. • $12 • (6/30/1999) • **83**
Cabernet Grave del Friuli Roncaccio 1997: Some good ripe fruit in this red, but slightly overdone, with an austere and dry finish. Medium body. Medium fruit. Too much wood? Tasted twice, with consistent notes.–J.S. • $13 • (5/15/2000) • **79**
Cabernet Grave del Friuli Roncaccio 1993 • $9 • (6/15/1996) • **82**
Cabernet Grave del Friuli Roncaccio 1991 • $8 • (2/28/1995) • **82**
Cabernet Sauvignon Collio Trebes 1993 • $12 • (5/31/1996) • **86**
Cabernet Sauvignon Grave del Friuli Roncaccio 1991 • $8 • (2/28/1995) • **82**
Chardonnay Isonzo del Friuli dei Sassi Cavi 1998: Very pleasant Chardonnay; I like the apple and mineral character in this fruity white. Medium-bodied. Fresh finish. Drink now.–J.S. • $13 • (3/31/2000) • **85**
Chardonnay Isonzo del Friuli dei Sassi Cavi 1997: A fruity and refreshing young white, with sliced melon and apple aromas and flavors, medium body and clean acidity. Drink now.–J.S. • $13 • (6/15/1999) • **80**
Chardonnay Isonzo del Friuli dei Sassi Cavi 1996 • $12 • (12/15/1997) • **83**
Colli Orientali del Friuli Romandolo 1993 • $17 • (5/31/1996) • **84**
Merlot Collio 1996: An easy, soft and fruity Merlot, with berry and cherry aromas and flavors. Medium-bodied, with a fruity finish. Drink now.–J.S. • $12 • (6/30/1999) • **82**
Merlot Collio Pubrida 1993 • $12 • (6/15/1996) • **79**
Merlot Collio Riserva di Casa 1997: Loads of wood on this simple Merlot, with vanilla, cherry character. Medium body. Soft texture. Drink now.–J.S. • $13 • (5/15/2000) • **81**
Merlot Collio Riserva di Casa 1995 • $12 • (12/15/1997) • **80**
Merlot Grave del Friuli Campo Olivio 1993 • $9 • (6/15/1996) • **78**
Merlot Grave del Friuli Campo Olivio 1991 • $7 • (2/28/1995) • **80**
Merlot Grave del Friuli Campo Olivio 1991 • $7 • (2/28/1995) • **80**
Pinot Grigio Collio Vendemmia Tardiva 1998: A pleasant dry white, with apple, melon and honey character. Medium-bodied, with a fresh finish. Drink now.–J.S. • $12 • (3/31/2000) • **84**
Pinot Grigio Collio Villa di Canlungo Vendemmia Tardiva 1997: There's decent melon character but also an annoying plastic and geranium note. Medium-bodied and dry, with a fruity but short aftertaste.–J.S. • $13 • (6/15/1999) • **77**
Pinot Grigio Collio Villa di Canlungo Vendemmia Tardiva 1996 • $12 • (5/15/1998) • **85**
Refosco dal Peduncolo Rosso Grave del Friuli Pucino 1996 • $10 • (4/30/1998) • **83**
Refosco dal Peduncolo Rosso Grave del Friuli Pucino 1994 • $9 • (6/15/1996) • **79**
Refosco del Peduncolo Rosso Grave del Friuli Pucino 1997: Light, fruity and delicious, like a decent Beaujolais. Drink now.–J.S. • $12 • (6/30/1999) • **80**
Sauvignon Blanc Collio 1998: Good apple and pear character. Medium-bodied, with good fruit and a light finish. A bit simple really. Drink now.–J.S. • $13 • (4/30/2000) • **83**
Sauvignon Collio 1997: A clean and simple wine, with apple, white pepper and grapefruit aromas and flavors. Medium-bodied, with a light finish, it doesn't taste much like Sauvignon Blanc. Drink now.–J.S. • $13 • (6/15/1999) • **80**
Schioppettino Colli Orientali del Friuli Turian 1993 • $20 • (6/15/1996) • **83**

COLLE, IL

Brunello di Montalcino 1992 • $NA • (9/30/1997) • **73**
Brunello di Montalcino 1991 • $NA • (11/30/1996) • **71**
Brunello di Montalcino 1990 • $NA • (10/31/1995) • **85**
Brunello di Montalcino Riserva 1990 • $NA • (11/30/1996) • **85**
Rosso di Montalcino 1995 • $NA • (9/30/1997) • **75**
Rosso di Montalcino 1993 • $NA • (10/31/1995) • **83**

COLLE BERETO

Chianti Classico 1994 • $17 • (9/30/1997) • **78**
Chianti Classico Riserva 1994 • $24 • (9/30/1997) • **80**
Chianti Classico Riserva 1993 • $NA • (10/31/1996) • **76**
Il Cénno 1990 • $27 • (12/31/1995) • **91**
Il Tòcco 1993 • $40 • (9/30/1997) • **78**
Tuscany White 1996 • $11 • (9/30/1997) • **82**

COLLELUNGO

Chianti Classico 1997: Captivating aromas of crushed berry have hints of orange peel. Medium- to full-bodied, with silky tannins and a long, fruity finish. Clever winemaking here. Drink now through 2001.–J.S. • $22 • (11/30/1999) • **88**
Chianti Classico Roveto 1997: Very powerful for a Chianti, with lots of ripe fruit and toasted oak—and it works. Medium- to full-bodied, with silky tannins and a long, long finish. A new producer to watch. Drink now.–J.S. • $45 • (11/30/1999) • **90**

COLLEMATTONI

Brunello di Montalcino 1995: Lovely floral and ripe fruit aromas. Medium-bodied, with well-integrated tannins and a long, long silky finish. A beauty. Not imported into the U.S. Drink now through 2003.–J.S. • $NA • (6/30/2000) • **89**
Rosso di Montalcino 1995 • $NA • (9/30/1997) • **85**

COLLI AMERINI, CANTINA

Chardonnay Umbria Rocca Nerina 1997: Butterscotch and toasted oakcharacter, with hints of ripe fruit. Medium-bodied, with medium acidity and a fruity finish. Good Chardonnay. Drink now.–J.S. • $20 • (2/29/2000) • **85**
Colli Amerini Superiore Carbio 1996: Very raisiny, with burnt fruit character. Full-bodied, alcoholic and tannic. Astringent and slightly overextracted.–J.S. • $20 • (2/29/2000) • **76**
Sangiovese Umbria Torraccio 1996: Very earthy, barnyardy character in this wine, and slightly dry. Not imported into the U.S.–J.S. • $NA • (1/01/2000) • **72**

COLLI RIPANI, CANTINA

Falerio dei Colli Ascolani Brezzolino 1997: Not very refined but interesting to taste, with peach and earth character. Medium-bodied and round, with a flavorful finish. Drink now.–J.S. • $8 • (6/15/1999) • **82**
Marches Leo Ripanus 1995: This red is already mature, with a light ruby color and strawberry and leather aromas and flavors. Light-bodied, with light tannins and a fresh, crisp, toasted oak finish. Drink now.–J.S. • $12 • (6/30/1999) • **80**
Rosso Piceno Castellano 1994: A delicious red. Pretty aromas of roasted chestnut, berry and flowers open onto a medium-bodied palate. Fine tannin structure and fresh acidity. Drink now.–J.S. • $9 • (6/30/1999) • **85**

Key: SS—Spectator Selection. CS—Cellar Selection. HR—Highly Recommended. $NA—Price not available. (BT)—Barrel tasting. Ⓐ—Auction Price.
For a key to the tasters' initials, see "How to Use These Listings."
Dates in parentheses represent the issues in which the ratings were published.

ITALY

COLLOSORBO

Brunello di Montalcino 1994: Elegant and enjoyable. Attractive aromas of berries and oyster mushrooms follow through to a medium-bodied palate with fine tannins and a medium, fruity finish. Drink now.–J.S. • $50 • (8/31/1999) • **87**

Brunello di Montalcino 1993: Rather mature-looking. Toasty oak and vanilla, with ripe berry and meat aromas. Medium-bodied, with firm tannins and a tart finish. Drink now.–J.S. • $33 • (12/15/1998) • **80**

Brunello di Montalcino 1991 • $NA • (11/30/1996) • **85**

Rosso di Montalcino 1997: A profusion of dried cherry and fresh mushroom character in this rosso. Medium- to full-bodied, with firm yet silky tannins and a medium-fruity finish. Lovely texture. Drink now.–J.S. • $25 • (9/15/1999) • **88**

Rosso di Montalcino 1996: Beautifully perfumed, with violet and rose and undertones of fruit. Medium-bodied, with fine tannins and a fruity finish. Drink now.–J.S. • $15 • (12/15/1998) • **86**

Rosso di Montalcino 1994 • $NA • (11/30/1996) • **82**

COLMELLO DI GROTTA

Chardonnay Isonzo del Friuli 1996 • $13 • (6/15/1998) • **82**

Pinot Grigio Isonzo del Friuli 1996 • $13 • (6/15/1998) • **81**

Sauvignon Isonzo del Friuli 1996 • $13 • (6/15/1998) • **81**

COLOGNOLE

Chianti Rufina 1997: This simple Chianti has clean berry and cherry character. Medium-bodied, with light tannins and a fresh finish. Drink now.–J.S. • $12 • (11/30/1999) • **82**

Chianti Rufina 1995 • $10 • (9/30/1997) • **78**

Chianti Rufina 1994 • $NA • (10/31/1996) • **78**

Chianti Rufina 1993 • $8 • (10/31/1995) • **78**

Chianti Rufina del Don Riserva 1995: A pleasant, grapey red with a hint of earthiness. Medium-bodied, with light, soft tannins and a crisp finish. Drink now.–J.S. • $20 • (12/15/1998) • **84**

Chianti Rufina del Don Riserva 1994 • $18 • (9/30/1997) • **79**

Chianti Rufina del Don Riserva 1993 • $12 • (10/31/1996) • **83**

Toscana Quattro Chiacchiere 1996: Lots of new wood, with vanilla and coconut, hints of pear and apple character. Medium-bodied, with moderate acidity and a light, fruity finish. Drink now.–J.S. • $16 • (12/15/1998) • **80**

COLOMBINI, DONATELLA CINELLI

Brunello di Montalcino 1994: Not typical but very good. Lots of mint, olive and Cabernet-like character. Medium- to full-bodied, with firm, silky tannins and a medium finish. Well-built red. Best after 2000.–J.S. • $44 • (8/31/1999) • **88**

Brunello di Montalcino 1993: A refreshing Brunello, with milk chocolate and berry through and through, but a bit austere. Medium-bodied, with medium, chewy tannins and a fruity yet slightly hard finish. Better with age? Not imported into the U.S.–J.S. • $42 • (12/15/1998) • **82**

Brunello di Montalcino Progetto Prime Donne 1994: Deep aromas of black licorice, berry and sliced porcini mushrooms. Medium-bodied, with chewy tannins and a ripe, almost raisiny finish. A bit rustic, but impressive. Drink now.–J.S. • $50 • (8/31/1999) • **87**

Brunello di Montalcino Progetto Prime Donne 1993: This is a racy, young Brunello that needs time. Subtle aromas of berries, minerals and wet earth. Full-bodied and tannic, with zingy acidity. Outstanding debut wine from the daughter of the owners of Fattoria de Barbi. Not imported into the U.S. Best after 2002.–J.S. • $48 • (12/15/1998) • **90**

Chianti Superiore Fattoria Il Colle 1998: Lovely, ripe Sangiovese character, with chocolate, ripe plum and tobacco. Medium-bodied, with silky tannins and a long, fruity finish. Drink now through 2001.–J.S. • $12 • (5/31/2000) • **86**

Rosso di Montalcino 1998: Very clean, with dried cherry and plum character. Medium-bodied, with light tannins and a fresh finish. Drink now.–J.S. • $20 • (5/31/2000) • **85**

Toscana Fattoria Il Colle Leone Rosso 1998: A bit simple, but very fresh and fruity, with dried cherry and light mineral character. Medium-bodied, with fine tannins. Drink now through 2001.–J.S. • $12 • (5/31/2000) • **85**

COLOMBO, CANTINE

Salento 1995 • $7 • (1/01/1998) • **80**

COLOSI

Malvasia delle Lipari Passito di Salina 1997: A wonderful Malvasia, with gorgeous aromas of apricot, flowers and honey and a hint of perfume. Full-bodied and medium sweet, with a long violet and lilac aftertaste. Drink now.–J.S. • $23 • (5/31/2000) • **91**

Malvasia delle Lipari Passito di Salina 1989 • $20/375 ml. • (3/31/1992) • **81**

Passito di Pantelleria 1998: A unique dessert wine, with a golden amber color and intense aromas of dried apricot, dried pineapple and marmalade. Medium sweet, with an oily texture and a long, spicy lime skin aftertaste. A bit more sweetness would make it outstanding. Drink now.–J.S. • $96/500 ml. • (5/31/2000) • **89**

Sicilia Red Cariddi 1997: Fresh and straightforward, with pepper, cherry and berry character. Medium-bodied, with light tannins and a fruity finish. Drink now.–J.S. • $10 • (5/31/2000) • **85**

Sicilia White Cariddi 1998: Rather perfumed, with a off-dry palate and a simple finish. Not very exciting.–J.S. • $10 • (5/31/2000) • **77**

COLPETRONE

Montefalco 1997: A slightly tough wine, with interesting plum skin, floral and berry character. Medium-bodied, with medium, firm tannins and a slightly austere finish. Drink now through 2002.–J.S. • $15 • (2/29/2000) • **83**

Sagrantino di Montefalco 1996: Serious winemaking. Dark ruby in color, with bright aromas of crushed berry and raspberry. Full-bodied, with lots of tannins and a long, long finish. Give it time. Best after 2000.–J.S. • $28 • (2/29/2000) • **89**

COLTERENZIO

Alto Adige Cornell Cornelius 1995: Gorgeous currant and berry aromas, with hints of mint. Full-bodied, with well-compacted fruit, firm, chewy tannins and a medium finish. Cabernet and Merlot. Best after 2000.–J.S. • $38 • (6/15/2000) • **90**

Chardonnay Alto Adige Cornell 1997: A New World Chardonnay from an Old World area. Wonderful aromas of lemon meringue and vanilla, with hints of cedar. Full-bodied, with lots of flavor and a long, fruity aftertaste. Drink now.–J.S. • $24 • (6/15/2000) • **90**

Merlot Alto Adige 1997: Medium-bodied, with plum, earth and mushroom character, light tannins and a herb and berry aftertaste. A good Merlot for current drinking. Drink now.–J.S. • $11 • (6/15/2000) • **85**

Mitterberg Bianco Cornell Cornelius 1996: A moreish white, with gorgeous aromas of pineapple, peach and honeysuckle. Medium- to full-bodied, with a round texture, pretty fruit flavors and a medium finish. Pinot Bianco, Chardonnay and Pinot Grigio. Drink now.–J.S. • $18 • (6/15/2000) • **88**

Pinot Bianco Alto Adige Praedium Weisshaus 1998: Pretty floral and mineral aromas follow through to a medium-bodied palate, with good acidity and a creamy apple finish. Drink now.–J.S. • $15 • (6/15/2000) • **87**

Pinot Bianco Alto Adige Praedium Weisshaus 1996 • $17 • (5/31/1998) • **86**

Pinot Bianco Terlaner Thurnerhof 1998: Clean and fruity, with apple, lemon and pear character. Medium-bodied, with a light finish. Drink now.–J.S. • $15 • (6/15/2000) • **83**

Pinot Grigio Alto Adige 1998: This superclean white from Northeast Italy is a delicious value, offering lovely mineral, apple and cream character in a medium-bodied presentation, with firm acidity and a fruity yet subtle finish. Drink now.–J.S. • $11 • (6/15/2000) • **87**

Pinot Grigio Alto Adige Praedium Puiten 1998: Has interesting Pinot Grigio character of grapefruit and sweat. Medium-bodied, with good acidity and a round texture. Drink now.–J.S. • $15 • (6/15/2000) • **86**

Pinot Grigio Alto Adige Praedium Puiten 1996 • $17 • (5/31/1998) • **85**

CONCADORO

Chianti Classico 1990 • $NA • (10/31/1993) • **88**

Chianti Classico Riserva 1995: A fresh and fruity Sangiovese, with a slightly chewy style. Medium-bodied, with good tannin backbone and a fresh and fruity finish. Drink now.–J.S. • $20 • (11/30/1999) • **86**

Chianti Classico Riserva 1990 • $NA • (2/28/1995) • **74**

CONCILIIS, DE

Aglianico Paestum Temparubra 1998: A good easy-drinking red, delivering berry, floral and salty character. Medium-bodied, with light tannins and a fresh finish. Drink now.–J.S. • $12 • (1/31/2000) • **82**

Paestum Donnaluna 1998: Interesting aromas of pears, blanched almonds and honeydew. Medium-bodied, with light acidity and a fruity finish. Light and simple. Drink now.–J.S. • $12 • (1/31/2000) • **84**

Paestum Naima 1997: Stunner. Very dark ruby color. Intense aromas of blackberries, raspberries and violets. Full-bodied and very tight, with loads of tannin and a long finish. Chewy. Shows outstanding structure, but needs time to come around. Best after 2001.–J.S. • $27 • (1/31/2000) • **91**

Paestum Passito RA 1997: A pure beauty. This dry red is bubbling over with plum, strawberry and cherry aromas. Full-bodied, with an excellent concentration of pure fruit. So vivid. Best after 2001.–J.S. • $45/375 ml. • (1/31/2000) • **90**

Paestum Perella 1997: A subtle, fruity wine that builds on your palate. Pleasurable character of pear drop, honey and flowers. Medium-bodied, with good tropical fruit flavors including passion fruit and mango. Clean finish. Drink now.–J.S. • $16 • (1/31/2000) • **88**

Paestum Zero 1997: Outrageous. Dark ruby color. Fabulous aromas of flowers, berries and crushed raspberries with a complement of subtle oak. Full-bodied, very chewy, with loads of polished tannins, new oak and a long finish. California Cab lovers will go nuts over this. Best after 2001.–J.S. • $55 • (1/31/2000) • **92**

CONCILIO

Brut Clarius NV: This extremely fresh and delicious Chardonnay-based sparkling wine is a bit simple but very good indeed, especially for the money. Lovely, creamy texture, with apple and biscuit character and good acidity. Drink now.–J.S. • $10 • (5/31/2000) • **85**

Cabernet Sauvignon Trentino 1994: An initial whiff of barnyard gives way to spicy, leafy character reminiscent of Cabernet Franc from the Loire. Firm, slightly austere, but expressive and distinctive, though the gamy note isn't for everyone. Drink now.–B.S. • $13 • (9/30/1998) • **84**

Cabernet Sauvignon Trentino Riserva 1996: Medium-bodied, with a good berry and currant character that's slightly green. Slightly acidic and lean on the finish, with a mineral undertone. Drink now.–J.S. • $14 • (6/15/2000) • **81**

Chardonnay Trentino 1998: Simple and fruity, with apple and mineral character. Medium-bodied, with a light finish. Drink now.–J.S. • $9 • (6/15/2000) • **84**

Chardonnay Trentino 1997: A nice mouthful of apple and spice, showing medium body and richness, ending with a vanilla note. Drink now.–B.S. $9 • (9/30/1998) • **84**

Chardonnay Trentino Barrel Select 1996: A good Chardonnay, with almond, honey and apple flavors. Medium-bodied, with medium acidity and a walnut aftertaste. Drink now.–J.S. • $14 • (6/15/2000) • **85**

Gewürztraminer Trentino 1998: Delicious apple, spice and marmalade character. Medium-bodied, with good acidity and a tasty finish. Not imported into the U.S. Drink now.–J.S. • $NA • (1/01/2000) • **86**

Gewürztraminer Trentino 1998: Delicious apple, spice and marmalade character. Medium-bodied, with good acidity and a tasty finish. Not imported into the U.S. Drink now.–J.S. • $NA • (1/01/2000) • **86**

Merlot Trentino 1998: Like unfermented grape juice. Thick and syrupy. Tasted twice, with consistent notes.–J.S. • $9 • (6/15/2000) • **69**

Merlot Trentino 1990 • $10 • (12/15/1992) • **70**

Merlot Trentino Riserva 1996: Delicious Merlot character, with currant, coffee and cereal undertones. Medium-bodied, with soft tannins and a fresh finish. Drink now.–J.S. • $14 • (6/15/2000) • **85**

Merlot Trentino Riserva 1995: Delicious red, displaying cherry notes and spice from new oak. Good depth of flavor, balanced and firmly structured, all in an elegant package.–B.S. • $13 • (9/30/1998) • **86**

Pinot Grigio Trentino Contessa Manci 1998: Lovely, with peach, apple and cream aromas and flavors. Medium-bodied, with good acidity and a clean finish. Drink now.–J.S. • $14 • (6/15/2000) • **86**

Pinot Grigio Trentino Contessa Manci 1997: A straightforward white, with good almond and earth flavors and lemony acidity. Drink now.–B.S. • $13 • (9/30/1998) • **83**

Pinot Noir Trentino Riserva 1996: A decent Pinot, with attractive aromas of lemon rind, leather and plum. Medium-bodied, with light tannins, fresh acidity and a fruity finish. Slightly diluted midpalate. Drink now.–J.S. • $14 • (6/15/2000) • **82**

Sauvignon Trentino 1998: Pleasant, with good fruit flavors and grass, grapefruit and mineral character throughout. Medium-bodied, with a fresh finish. Not imported into the U.S. Drink now.–J.S. • $NA • (1/01/2000) • **84**

Sauvignon Trentino 1998: Pleasant, with good fruit flavors and grass, grapefruit and mineral character throughout. Medium-bodied, with a fresh finish. Not imported into the U.S. Drink now.–J.S. • $NA • (1/01/2000) • **84**

Teroldego Rotaliano Braide 1997: Yummy. Dark ruby, with wonderfully ripe plum, cherry and dark chocolate aromas. Medium-bodied, with firm tannins and a succulent plum aftertaste. Not imported into the U.S. Drink now through 2002.–J.S. • $NA • (1/01/2000) • **88**

Teroldego Rotaliano Braide 1997: Yummy. Dark ruby, with wonderfully ripe plum, cherry and dark chocolate aromas. Medium-bodied, with firm tannins and a succulent plum aftertaste. Not imported into the U.S. Drink now through 2002.–J.S. • $NA • (1/01/2000) • **88**

Trentino Mori Vecio 1996: Complex aromas of currant, berry, spice and vanilla. Full-bodied, with firm tannins and a long finish. Slightly diluted midpalate. Best after 2000.–J.S. • $14 • (6/15/2000) • **88**

CONTADI CASTALDI

Brut Franciacorta NV • $19 • (5/15/1998) • **81**

Terre de Franciacorta 1996: The aromas and flavors evoke freshly crushed berries in this light-bodied, bright red. Firm, with moderate acidity and tannins, but enjoy it for its fruit.–B.S. • $11 • (9/30/1998) • **83**

Terre de Franciacorta White 1996 • $10 • (5/15/1998) • **85**

CONTERNO, ALDO

Barbera d'Alba 1996: This impressive Barbera, made in a traditional style, shouts "Piedmont earth" and shows chestnut, mineral, blackberry and wet earth character that fans out on the palate. Excellent concentration. Supple on the palate and vivid on the delicious finish. Drink now through 2003.–P.M. • $27 • (10/31/1998) • **91**

Barbera d'Alba 1993 • $NA • (10/31/1995) • **80**

Barbera d'Alba Conca Tre Pile 1990 • $22 • (4/30/1993) • **91**

Barbera d'Alba Conca Tre Pile 1989 • $21 • (10/31/1992) • **91**

Barbera d'Alba Monforte Bussia 1997: A pretty wine but lacks a bit of depth. Smooth and elegant, medium-bodied, with a wet earth, coffee and tobacco-leaf character that folds nicely into the fresh red berry flavors. Drink now through 2001.–P.M. • $37 • (11/15/1999) • **85**

Barolo 1994: Light and delicate, with sweet-tasting raspberry, strawberry and mocha. A bit uncharacteristic for Barolo, but approachable thanks to supple tannins and a round mouthfeel. Finishes a bit short. Drink now.–P.M. • $68 • (10/31/1998) • **80**

Barolo 1993 • $99 • (10/31/1997) • **87**

Barolo 1991 • $62 • (10/31/1995) • **81**

Barolo Bussia Soprana 1995: Light-bodied, a bit diluted, a crisp wine in a lean style, with some drying tannins on the tough finish. A blend of grapes from Conterno's lesser vineyards.–P.M. • $80 • (11/15/1999) • **78**

Barolo Bussia Soprana 1989 • $91 Ⓐ • (10/31/1993) • **86**

Barolo Bussia Soprana 1988 • $102 Ⓐ • (10/31/1993) • **87**

Barolo Bussia Soprana 1985 • $40 • (9/15/1990) • **87**

Barolo Bussia Soprana 1983 • $25 • (9/15/1988) • **85**

Barolo Bussia Soprana 1982 • $18 • (9/15/1987) • **85**

Barolo Granbussia 1990 • $120 • (10/31/1995) • **90**

Barolo Granbussia Riserva 1985 • $211 Ⓐ • (12/15/1992) • **85**

Barolo Granbussia 1982 • $NA • (9/15/1988) • **93**

Barolo Romirasco 1993: Elegant and polished, this sophisticated and supple '93 has good fruit, acidity and oak balance. Full-bodied and balanced, offering lots of complexity, with tar, spice and blackberry character. The smooth, seamless finish is just delicious. Drink now through 2005.–P.M. • $90 • (9/15/1998) • **90**

Barolo Vigna Cicala 1995: Classy aromas of wild berries, smoke and dried herbs are appealing. Medium to full in body, with a clean, rather crisp frame, it has a enough concentration of ripe and rich fruit to suggest cellaring for extra complexity. The mineral, soillike taste of *terroir* is impressive on the long finish. Best after 2002.–P.M. • $105 • (11/15/1999) • **90**

Barolo Vigna Cicala 1993 • $125 • (10/31/1997) • **94**

Barolo Vigna Cicala 1990 • $120 Ⓐ • (10/31/1994) • **83**

Barolo Vigna Cicala 1988 • $52 • (10/31/1993) HR • **93**

Barolo Vigna Cicala 1985 • $40 • (6/15/1990) • **90**

Barolo Vigna Cicala 1982 • $94 Ⓐ • (9/15/1987) • **86**

Barolo Vigna Colonello 1990 • $115 Ⓐ • (10/31/1994) • **92**

Barolo Vigna Colonello 1989 • $96 Ⓐ • (10/31/1993) • **89**

Barolo Vigna Colonello 1988 • $57 • (3/31/1993) • **90**

Barolo Vigna Colonello 1985 • $40 • (6/15/1990) • **84**

Key: SS—Spectator Selection. CS—Cellar Selection. HR—Highly Recommended. $NA—Price not available. (BT)—Barrel tasting. Ⓐ—Auction Price. For a key to the tasters' initials, see "How to Use These Listings."
Dates in parentheses represent the issues in which the ratings were published.

Dolcetto d'Alba 1995 • $22 • (10/31/1997) • **84**
Dolcetto d'Alba 1987 • $12 • (9/15/1990) • **84**
Dolcetto d'Alba 1985 • $10 • (5/15/1987) • **77**
Dolcetto d'Alba Bussia 1993 • $20 • (10/31/1995) • **85**
Dolcetto d'Alba Bussia Soprana 1990 • $18 • (10/31/1992) • **84**
Langhe Quartetto 1997: Built around fancy wood treatment, this is dark in color, medium-bodied, smooth and very extracted. Nice balance to the violet, toasty, spice and black currant flavors, with vibrant acidity on the lingering finish. Drink now through 2003.–P.M. • $50 • (11/15/1999) • **87**
Langhe White Bussiador 1996: This perfumey, violet-scented wine is smooth on the palate but tastes more of oak than *terroir*. Medium-bodied, with spice, floral, lemon and honey notes and a supple, balanced finish. Drink now through 2002.–P.M. • $40 • (10/31/1998) • **81**
Nebbiolo delle Langhe Bussia Conca Tre Pile 1985 • $13 • (11/15/1988) • **85**
Nebbiolo delle Langhe Il Favot 1997: Forward, with earth, horse saddle, mocha and toasted oak character. Tastes a bit burning from the charred wood, but the tannins are supple. Lacks a bit of ripeness.–P.M. • $59 • (11/15/1999) • **79**
Nebbiolo delle Langhe Il Favot 1996: Quite intense, with lots of fruit but also intense tannins and toast, grilled meat, truffle and tobacco box notes. New and traditional mingle nicely in this interesting, barrique-aged, medium-bodied red. Not for everyone, but cognoscenti will enjoy it as a reflection of Piedmont. Drink now through 2004.–P.M. • $45 • (10/31/1998) • **91**
Nebbiolo delle Langhe Il Favot 1995 • $60 • (10/31/1997) • **83**
Nebbiolo delle Langhe Il Favot 1992 • $NA • (10/31/1994) • **89**
Nebbiolo delle Langhe Il Favot 1988 • $32 • (3/31/1993) • **89**
Nebbiolo delle Langhe Il Favot 1983 • $13 • (5/31/1990) • **84**

CONTERNO, GIACOMO

Barbera d'Alba 1997: Rich and dense, but also a bit herbal, with black fruit character. Medium-bodied, with good intensity and smacking acidity. Herbaceous finish. Drink now.–P.M. • $22 • (10/31/1998) • **78**
Barbera d'Alba 1992 • $15 • (11/15/1993) • **82**
Barbera d'Alba Cascina Francia 1994 • $NA • (10/31/1996) • **80**
Barbera d'Alba Cascina Francia 1991 • $15 • (11/15/1993) • **81**
Barolo 1993: Smelling of steel, tough despite some midpalate concentration, with an herbal and astringent finish. Tasted twice, with consistent notes.–P.M. • $110 • (10/31/1998) • **70**
Barolo 1985 • $23 • (4/15/1990) • **87**
Barolo 1983 • $23 • (9/15/1988) • **88**
Barolo 1982 • $25 • (9/15/1988) • **90**
Barolo Bussia Munie 1993 • $NA • (10/31/1997) • **79**
Barolo Cascina Francia 1989 • $NA • (10/31/1993) • **86**
Barolo Cascina Francia 1988 • $40 • (10/31/1993) • **82**
Barolo Monfortino Reserva 1982 • $57 • (6/30/1987) • **91**
Dolcetto d'Alba 1997: Incredibly tannic, in a rustic style. Fairly sweet-tasting, but it smells of bell pepper and artichokes, and these herbal notes come back on the drying finish.–P.M. • $20 • (10/31/1998) • **72**
Dolcetto d'Alba 1994 • $NA • (10/31/1995) • **85**

CONTERNO, PAOLO

Barbera d'Alba Ginestra 1997: Very plummy and ripe. Full-bodied, balanced and fresh, it's almost minty, showing good fruit and focus. Drink now through 2002.–P.M. • $20 • (11/15/1999) • **89**
Barolo Ginestra 1995: This delicious, international-style Barolo shows depth, concentration and complexity, starting with the opulent mouthfeel and continuing through layers of ripe black fruit, mineral, wet earth and smoke notes. Rich, thick and very satisfying, with a persistent, balanced finish. Drink now through 2007.–P.M. • $75 • (11/15/1999) • **94**

CONTERNO-FANTINO

Barbera d'Alba Vignota 1997: Intense, round and impressively concentrated. Offers green olive, dried herb, even herbaceous character. But the texture is fine, and it's not very oaky, just showing a vanilla aroma. A bit green on the chewy finish. Drink now through 2002.–P.M. • $20 • (9/15/1999) • **85**
Barbera d'Alba Vignota 1996: Earthy and a bit funky, smelling of horse stable and leather, it has a smooth mouthfeel and berry character. Medium-bodied, it's rather light on the finish.–P.M. • $18 • (10/31/1998) • **75**
Barbera d'Alba Vignota 1995 • $19 • (10/31/1997) • **76**
Barbera d'Alba Vignota 1994 • $18 • (10/31/1996) • **87**
Barbera d'Alba Vignota 1993 • $16 • (10/31/1995) • **76**
Barbera d'Alba Vignota 1992 • $NA • (10/31/1994) • **86**
Barbera d'Alba Vignota 1991 • $14 • (11/15/1993) • **78**
Barbera d'Alba Vignota 1990 • $15 • (7/31/1995) • **87**
Barbera d'Alba Vignota 1989 • $20 • (3/15/1991) • **86**
Barolo Sorì Ginestra 1995: Built piece by careful piece, with a supple, compacted mouthfeel and a silky yet intense midpalate. A full-bodied ager, with solid tannins and dried herbs, wet soil and black fruit. Full-bodied, ripe and balanced despite a slight herbal note. Drink now through 2003.–P.M. • $61 • (11/15/1999) • **91**
Barolo Sorì Ginestra 1994: This impressive, full-bodied, opulent Nebbiolo is thick, ripe and seductive. Packed with lovely blackberry, currant and sweet black cherry flavors, along with a touch of tar, mineral, lead pencil and spice. Lots of fine tannins on the lingering finish. Drink now through 2010.–P.M. • $45 • (9/15/1998) • **92**
Barolo Sorì Ginestra 1993 • $45 • (10/31/1997) • **86**
Barolo Sorì Ginestra 1992 • $37 • (10/31/1996) • **76**
Barolo Sorì Ginestra 1991 • $32 • (10/31/1995) • **84**
Barolo Sorì Ginestra 1990 • $40 • (10/31/1994) • **96**
Barolo Sorì Ginestra 1989 • $31 • (10/31/1993) • **83**
Barolo Sorì Ginestra 1988 • $30 • (10/31/1993) • **80**
Barolo Sorì Ginestra Riserva 1982 • $24 • (1/31/1990) • **84**
Barolo Vigna del Gris 1995: Crisp, even tart, with a slight balsamic vinegar/lifted nose that makes it a bit odd, but the smoky, spicy, toasty red berry notes allow this medium-bodied Barolo to save face. Drink now through 2005.–P.M. • $61 • (11/15/1999) • **80**
Barolo Vigna del Gris 1993 • $45 • (10/31/1997) • **77**
Barolo Vigna del Gris 1990 • $36 • (10/31/1994) • **93**
Barolo Vigna del Gris 1989 • $29 • (10/31/1993) • **88**
Barolo Vigna del Gris 1988 • $28 • (10/31/1993) • **80**
Dolcetto d'Alba Bricco Bastia 1997: A typically clean Dolcetto. Fresh and crisp, with good red berry character, a rather lean texture and a juicy, acidic finish. Not nearly as good as when reviewed last year. Drink now.–P.M. • $17 • (7/31/1999) • **80**
Dolcetto d'Alba Bricco Bastia 1996 • $18 • (10/31/1997) • **81**
Dolcetto d'Alba Bricco Bastia 1995 • $17 • (10/31/1996) • **84**
Dolcetto d'Alba Bricco Bastia 1994 • $15 • (10/31/1995) • **85**
Langhe Monprá 1996: Fresh and lively. Medium-bodied, delivering spice, toast, smoke and blackberry flavors, it offers a crisp mouthfeel that should go well with food. Drink now through 2003.–P.M. • $43 • (11/15/1999) • **84**
Langhe Monprá 1995 • $41 • (10/31/1997) • **85**
Langhe Monprá 1993 • $36 • (1/01/1997) • **84**
Langhe Monprá 1992 • $35 • (10/31/1995) • **80**
Langhe Monprá 1991 • $35 • (10/31/1994) • **86**
Langhe Monprá 1990 • $32 • (4/15/1994) • **88**
Langhe Monprá 1989 • $30 • (10/31/1992) • **87**
Langhe Monprá 1988 • $27 • (3/15/1991) • **91**
Langhe White Bastía 1996: Smells like a barrique-aged, new-world Chardonnay, with violet, toasted oak, honey, melon and tropical flavors. A bit overdone on the oak side, and a bit flat on the burning, slightly hot finish, which lacks clear definition to rate higher. Okay as an aperitif. Drink now.–P.M. • $30 • (10/31/1998) • **80**
Nebbiolo delle Langhe Ginestrino 1990 • $19 • (2/28/1995) • **85**

CONTRATTO, GIUSEPPE

Barbaresco 1995: Fresh and vibrant, with freshly cut rosemary and thyme, blueberry and cassis, and good acidity that leads to a mouthpuckering and rather tannic finish. Not opulent, this medium-bodied red should go well with food.–P.M. • $45 • (10/31/1998) • **84**
Barbera d'Asti Bricco della Fanciullaccia 1995 • $NA • (3/31/1997) • **80**
Barbera d'Asti Pian del Re 1996: Slightly spritzy, a Nouveau-style Barbera, very light and all fruit, but little depth and complexity.–P.M. • $10 • (10/31/1998) • **79**
Barbera d'Asti Pian del Re 1994 • $17 • (3/31/1997) • **86**
Barbera d'Asti Solus Ad 1996: International-style, with loads of spice, mocha and barrique-inspired grilled flavors. Attractively full in body and smooth in texture—until the crisp, tart finish kicks in. Drink now through 2002.–P.M. • $45 • (10/31/1998) • **82**
Barbera d'Asti Solus Ad 1995: Fairly light, showing raspberry and strawberry character, supple tannins and a juicy finish. Serve slightly chilled.–P.M. • $45 • (10/31/1998) • **79**
Barbera d'Asti Solus Ad 1994 • $38 • (10/31/1997) • **87**
Barolo 1983 • $10 • (3/31/1990) • **75**
Barolo Cerequio Tenuta Secolo 1993: Polished and lovely, this full-bodied wine is full of nice, ripe fruit (plum, cassis and black cherry) and touches of tar, grilled meat, mocha and spice from just-so oak accents. Well made from start to finish, delivering nice, clean, pure fruit aromas. Firm tannins

need time to soften. Better than previously reviewed. Best after 2005.–P.M. • $50 • (10/31/1998) • **88**

Barolo del Centenario Riserva 1978 • $18 • (5/16/1986) • **86**

Gavi Le Arnelle 1996: Simple and straightforward, with modest citrus and pine flavors and dull fruit-cocktail notes on the finish.–K.M. • $17 • (8/31/1998) • **78**

CONTUCCI

Vino Nobile di Montepulciano 1995 • $NA • (1/01/1998) • **71**

Vino Nobile di Montepulciano Pietra Rossa 1995 • $NA • (1/01/1998) • **77**

Vino Nobile di Montepulciano Riserva 1994 • $NA • (1/01/1998) • **69**

COPERTINO, CANTINA SOCIALE COOPERATIVA DEL

Copertino Reserva 1993 • $10 • (4/30/1997) • **79**

Copertino Riserva 1994 • $8 • (1/01/1998) • **84**

COPPO

Barbera d'Asti Camp du Rouss 1997: Thickly oaked and richly layered, tasting of roasted coffee, vanilla, mocha and blackberry. Here's a full-bodied, smooth-tasting, international-style red, although the crisp acidity on the finish is unmistakably Barbera-like. Drink now through 2003.–P.M. • $18 • (11/15/1999) • **87**

Barbera d'Asti Camp du Rouss 1996: Very pretty, with ripe, sweet fruit, silky tannins, excellent acidity, and yes, some obvious oak-treatment. But it's medium-bodied, balanced and delightful. Drink now through 2002.–P.M. • $16 • (10/31/1998) • **84**

Barbera d'Asti Camp du Rouss 1995 • $19 • (10/31/1997) • **75**

Barbera d'Asti Camp du Rouss 1993 • $15 • (7/31/1995) • **86**

Barbera d'Asti Camp du Rouss 1991 • $13 • (10/31/1994) • **75**

Barbera d'Asti Camp du Rouss 1990 • $13 • (10/31/1994) • **85**

Barbera d'Asti Camp du Rouss 1988 • $21 • (3/15/1991) • **88**

Barbera d'Asti Camp du Rouss 1986 • $19 • (3/31/1990) • **87**

Barbera d'Asti L'Avvocata 1997: Vanilla- and mocha-scented oak notes and a petrol aroma overwhelm this red, leaving the fruit to fend for itself. But it's full in body, with a crisp finish that should help with food. Drink now through 2001.–P.M. • $12 • (11/15/1999) • **80**

Barbera d'Asti Pomorosso 1996: A stellar Barbera that cruises across the palate like a meteor sprinkling magic dust—violet, roses, wild berry and cassis flavors. Elegant, ripe and rich, this is a multifaceted, full-bodied, cleverly oaked Piedmont red. Drink through 2004–P.M. • $48 • (11/15/1999) • **92**

Barbera d'Asti Pomorosso 1995: Fairly traditional, with roasted chestnut, mocha, earth and plum character. Medium-bodied, displaying lovely concentration of fruit and supple tannins. The firm finish suggests matching with meat dishes. Drink now through 2003.–P.M. • $45 • (10/31/1998) • **86**

Barbera d'Asti Pomorosso 1994 • $44 • (10/31/1997) • **93**

Barbera d'Asti Pomorosso 1993 • $43 • (10/31/1996) • **89**

Barbera d'Asti Pomorosso 1990 • $33 • (10/31/1994) • **90**

Barbera d'Asti Pomorosso 1989 • $30 • (10/31/1994) • **79**

Barbera d'Asti Pomorosso 1987 • $41 • (3/15/1991) • **90**

Barbera d'Asti Pomorosso 1986 • $41 • (3/15/1991) • **84**

Barbera Le Taccole 1994 • $11 • (7/31/1995) • **79**

Dolcetto d'Alba 1989 • $11 • (7/15/1991) • **81**

Mondaccione 1996: Weak and slightly diluted, with a tart, tough mouthfeel. Tough tannins.–P.M. • $28 • (11/15/1999) • **77**

Mondaccione 1995: A red that emphasizes fruit and the Piedmont soil over oak. Medium-bodied, with a delicate structure, offering delicious, ripe raspberry, cherry and blackberry flavors, with a touch of roasted chestnut on the clean, lingering finish. Drink now.–P.M. • $28 • (10/31/1998) • **87**

Mondaccione 1994 • $27 • (10/31/1997) • **76**

Mondaccione 1990 • $30 • (10/31/1994) • **83**

Mondaccione 1988 • $34 • (1/31/1992) • **73**

Mondaccione 1987 • $13 • (3/31/1990) • **87**

Key: SS—Spectator Selection. CS—Cellar Selection. HR—Highly Recommended. $NA—Price not available. (BT)—Barrel tasting. Ⓐ—Auction Price.
For a key to the tasters' initials, see "How to Use These Listings."
Dates in parentheses represent the issues in which the ratings were published.

Piemonte White Monteriolo 1996: A soft and slightly off-dry Chardonnay, showing butter, pear and spice character. Kicks in with acidity on the finish. Drink now.–P.M. • $35 • (10/31/1998) • **79**

CORDERO DI MONTEZEMOLO

Barbera d'Alba Monfalletto 1997: As black as the darkest ink, this oaky Barbera is impressive for its velvety texture, smoky, spicy, tarry notes and nice black fruit character. Full-bodied and balanced, the ripe tannins can't fail to impress. So sweet, it almost tastes as if it had residual sugar. A showy wine, with an opulent finish. Drink now through 2003.–P.M. • $16 • (10/31/1998) • **92**

Barbera d'Alba Monfalletto 1996: Has the texture of thick cream and shows a lot of refined, smooth tannins. Full-bodied, ripe and complex, with blackberry, plum, mocha, coffee and spice aromas and flavors, this international-style red manages to stay loyal to this varietal, offering good acidity and a wet earth quality on the lovely finish. Drink now through 2005.–P.M. • $18 • (10/31/1998) • **90**

Barbera d'Alba Monfalletto 1992 • $18 • (10/31/1994) • **85**

Barolo 1990 • $40 • (10/31/1994) • **82**

Barolo 1988 • $NA • (10/31/1993) • **81**

Barolo 1980 • $16 • (12/15/1987) CS • **91**

Barolo Enrico VI 1994: Starts out okay, but the herbal, green, herbaceous notes take over. Medium-bodied and a bit metallic on the dry finish.–P.M. • $39 • (10/31/1998) • **78**

Barolo Enrico VI 1993 • $24 • (10/31/1997) • **79**

Barolo Enrico VI 1990 • $40 • (10/31/1994) • **91**

Barolo Enrico VI 1989 • $NA • (10/31/1993) • **88**

Barolo Enrico VI 1988 • $NA • (10/31/1993) • **78**

Barolo Enrico VI 1983 • $20 • (9/15/1988) • **86**

Barolo Enrico VI 1982 • $20 • (9/15/1988) • **88**

Barolo Enrico VI 1981 • $NA • (9/15/1988) • **88**

Barolo Enrico VI 1980 • $NA • (9/15/1988) • **85**

Barolo Monfalletto 1994: Fairly dark in color, with currant and blackberry notes but also a slight herbaceousness that comes back on the finish. Too bad, because this is a full-bodied, rather ripe wine. Might improve.–P.M. • $33 • (10/31/1998) • **79**

Barolo Monfalletto 1993 • $30 • (10/31/1997) • **81**

Barolo Monfalletto 1984 • $NA • (9/15/1988) • **88**

Barolo Monfalletto 1983 • $17 • (2/28/1989) • **85**

Barolo Monfalletto 1980 • $11 • (1/31/1987) • **91**

Barolo Monfalletto 1979 • $NA • (9/15/1988) • **82**

Barolo Monfalletto 1978 • $NA • (9/15/1988) • **84**

Barolo Monfalletto 1975 • $NA • (9/15/1988) • **77**

Barolo Monfalletto 1971 • $NA • (9/15/1988) • **85**

Dolcetto d'Alba Monfalletto 1997: A bit herbal and slightly dull, with only modest pure fruitiness. A bit dry on the finish. Drink now.–P.M. • $13 • (10/31/1998) • **78**

Dolcetto d'Alba Monfalletto 1996 • $12 • (10/31/1997) • **84**

Dolcetto d'Alba Monfalletto 1994 • $NA • (10/31/1995) • **81**

CORFECCIANO URBANA, FATTORIA

Chianti Riserva 1995: A wine at its peak, with very leathery, raisin and spice aromas. Medium-bodied, with thick tannins and a raisiny finish. A bit rustic. Drink now.–J.S. • $NA • (1/01/1999) • **82**

CORINO

Barbera d'Alba Vigna Giachini 1989 • $14 • (11/30/1991) • **91**

Barbera d'Alba Vigna Pozzo 1993 • $28 • (10/31/1996) • **85**

Barbera d'Alba Vigna Pozzo 1990 • $30 • (11/15/1993) • **92**

Barolo Vigna Giachini 1994: New-wave style, with violet, mocha and toasted bread character masking the *terroir*, at least for now. Fairly full-bodied, turning a bit bitter on the finish. Drink now through 2005.–P.M. • $37 • (10/31/1998) • **80**

Barolo Vigna Giachini 1993 • $35 • (10/31/1997) • **84**

Barolo Vigna Giachini 1992 • $30 • (10/31/1996) • **81**

Barolo Vigna Giachini 1992 • $30 • (10/31/1996) • **81**

Barolo Vigna Giachini 1991 • $30 • (10/31/1995) • **79**

Barolo Vigna Giachini 1990 • $81 Ⓐ • (10/31/1994) • **90**

Barolo Vigna Giachini 1988 • $45 • (10/31/1993) • **93**

Barolo Vigneto Rocche 1994: Barrique-o-rama, packed with violet, smoke and new wood flavors, astringent tannins, toasted bread finish. May improve with cellaring.–P.M. • $40 • (10/31/1998) • **79**

Barolo Vigneto Rocche 1993 • $35 • (10/31/1997) • **90**

Barolo Vigneto Rocche 1992 • $28 • (10/31/1996) • **86**
Barolo Vigneto Rocche 1991 • $NA • (10/31/1995) • **79**
Barolo Vigneto Rocche 1990 • $45 • (10/31/1994) • **91**
Dolcetto d'Alba Vigna Giachini 1990 • $14 • (3/31/1993) • **84**

CORNAREA

Roero Arneis 1996 • $18 • (12/31/1997) • **78**

CORREGGIA, MATTEO

Barbera d'Alba 1994 • $31 • (10/31/1996) • **83**
Barbera d'Alba Bricco Marun 1994 • $28 • (10/31/1997) • **90**
Barbera d'Alba Bricco Marun 1993 • $30 • (10/31/1995) • **86**
Barbera d'Alba Bricco Marun 1993 • $30 • (10/31/1996) • **84**
Barbera d'Alba Bricco Marun 1991 • $29 • (10/31/1994) • **83**
Barbera d'Alba Bricco Marun 1990 • $20 • (10/31/1994) • **86**
Bracchetto Langhe 1992 • $12 • (10/31/1994) • **82**
Nebbiolo d'Alba La Val dei Preti 1993 • $28 • (10/31/1995) • **85**
Nebbiolo d'Alba La Val dei Preti 1992 • $28 • (10/31/1995) • **81**
Nebbiolo d'Alba La Val dei Preti 1991 • $19 • (10/31/1995) • **86**

CORTACCIA, CANTINA SOCIALE DI

Chardonnay Alto Adige Anime 1998: A bit oxidized, with a pear drop character. Medium-bodied, with an almond aftertaste.–J.S. • $10 • (6/15/2000) • **78**
Chardonnay Alto Adige Anime 1997 • $10 • (5/31/1998) • **81**
Pinot Grigio Alto Adige Anime 1998: Rather flat, with apple character and almond. Short, slightly oxidized finish.–J.S. • $10 • (6/15/2000) • **78**
Pinot Grigio Alto Adige Anime 1997 • $10 • (5/31/1998) • **83**

CORTE CARIANO

Amarone della Valpolicella Classico 1996: Aromas of ripe plums, berries and Sultana. Full-bodied, with chewy tannins and compacted fruit. Plenty of concentration but slightly one-dimensional and monolithic. Give it time. Best after 2002.–J.S. • $29 • (1/01/2000) • **88**
Recioto della Valpolicella Classico 1997: Bright berry, cherry and raspberry aromas. Full-bodied and off dry, with lovely berry and tar character. Try with a hard cheese. Drink now.–J.S. • $NA/500 ml. • (1/01/2000) • **86**
Valpolicella Classico Superiore 1997: Lots of pretty flavors in this red, with berry, milk chocolate character. Medium body. Soft texture. Sweet fruit finish. Drink now through 2001.–J.S. • $10 • (1/01/2000) • **86**

CORTE PAVONE

Brunello di Montalcino 1995: A fresh and silky Brunello with dried cherry and mineral aromas. Medium body. Fine tannins. Delicious. Drink now through 2002.–J.S. • $35 • (6/30/2000) • **87**
Brunello di Montalcino 1994: Very pretty violet, berry and cherry aromas continue onto the palate, with polished tannins, medium body and a fresh finish, although slightly diluted. Drink now.–J.S. • $35 • (8/31/1999) • **86**
Brunello di Montalcino 1993: Looks slightly mature, but it's very fresh on the palate. Complex aromas of grilled meat and ripe fruit. Has full to medium body, with firm yet polished tannins. Best after 2000.–J.S. • $50 • (12/15/1998) • **87**
Brunello di Montalcino 1991 • $NA • (9/30/1997) • **86**
Brunello di Montalcino Riserva 1990 • $NA • (9/30/1997) • **89**

CORTE SANT'ALDA

Amarone della Valpolicella 1992 • $42 • (5/31/1998) • **85**
Amarone della Valpolicella 1986 • $19 • (9/15/1992) • **85**
Amarone della Valpolicella 1986 • $23 • (9/15/1992) • **79**
Recioto della Valpolicella 1995: Only a hint of sweetness on entry, where the dried cherry, prune and orange peel flavors augment the rich, firm texture; finishing on a clean, dry, astringent note. Drink now through 2000.–B.S. • $16/375 ml. • (7/31/1998) • **84**
Soave Campi Magri 1996 • $13 • (6/15/1998) • **82**
Valpolicella 1996 • $12 • (6/15/1998) • **81**
Valpolicella 1991 • $9 • (9/15/1992) • **83**
Valpolicella 1988 • $11 • (9/15/1992) • **82**
Valpolicella Metius 1988 • $17 • (9/15/1992) • **85**
Valpolicella Superiore 1994 • $15 • (6/15/1998) • **85**
Valpolicella Superiore 1993 • $10 • (6/15/1996) • **85**
Valpolicella Superiore Mithas 1994 • $21 • (5/31/1998) • **87**

CORTESE, GIUSEPPE

Barbaresco 1982 • $19 • (12/15/1988) • **85**
Barbaresco Rabajà 1996: Traditional style. Tough wine, but the ripeness and clarity of *terroir* are there. Quite crisp, but the body is full, the flavors rather intense and sweet-tasting—with cherry and olive as components. For aficionados of unyielding Nebbiolo. Best from 2003 through 2010.–P.M • $37 • (8/31/1999) • **87**
Barbaresco Rabajà 1995: Crisp and a bit herbal, with a cassis bush note, this is a bit hard. Vibrant and lively, but lacks harmony. Tough tannins on the astringent finish. Drink now through 2003.–P.M. • $34 • (10/31/1998) • **79**
Barbaresco Rabajà 1986 • $19 • (9/15/1990) • **89**
Barbaresco Rabajà 1983 • $18 • (1/31/1990) • **75**
Barbaresco Rabajà 1981 • $12 • (8/31/1989) • **72**
Barbera d'Alba 1997: Not a showy wine, but elegant, racy and clean; mocha, spice, chocolate and ground coffee notes provide foreground to fresh red berry flavors in this medium-bodied, focused, rather lean red. Drink now through 2001.–P.M. • $14 • (9/15/1999) • **89**
Barbera d'Alba 1996: Fresh and vibrant, with cassis bush, olive and dried herb notes. Of light to medium body, its tannins are rather crisp, making for a mouthpuckering finish. Drink now.–P.M. • $13 • (10/31/1998) • **80**
Barbera d'Alba 1995 • $11 • (10/31/1997) • **79**
Barbera d'Alba 1990 • $12 • (2/15/1992) • **71**
Barbera d'Alba 1989 • $11 • (7/15/1991) • **86**
Barbera d'Alba 1988 • $9 • (3/15/1991) • **86**
Barbera d'Alba Morassina 1997: Dark-colored and succulent, full-bodied and rich, packed with vanilla, toasted oak accents and red- and black-fruit flavors. It's both smooth from the fine tannins and crisp from the proper acidity level. Good with food. Drink now.–P.M. • $15 • (9/15/1999) • **88**
Barbera d'Alba Morassina 1995 • $16 • (10/31/1997) • **82**
Dolcetto d'Alba 1991 • $15 • (12/15/1992) • **84**
Dolcetto d'Alba 1989 • $10 • (12/31/1990) • **83**
Dolcetto d'Alba 1988 • $8 • (3/31/1990) • **78**
Dolcetto d'Alba Trifolera 1998: Surprisingly full on the palate for a young Dolcetto, with mocha, spice and red berry flavor. Clean and fresh, with ripe, sweet tannins on a zesty finish. Drink now through 2001.–P.M. • $14 • (7/31/1999) • **87**
Dolcetto d'Alba Trifolera 1997: A fantastic Dolcetto, totally pure and traditional in style, showing earth and ripe blackberry character. There is no obvious oak, just amazing fruit and supple, sweet-tasting tannins. The texture is smooth and thick like double cream, and the finish is just seamless. Delicious on release through 2000.–P.M. • $13 • (10/31/1998) • **91**
Dolcetto d'Alba Trifolera 1996 • $11 • (10/31/1997) • **88**
Nebbiolo delle Langhe Vigna in Rabajà 1990 • $15 • (7/31/1992) • **83**
Nebbiolo delle Langhe Vigna in Rabajà 1988 • $13 • (2/28/1991) • **80**

CORTI, LE

Chianti Classico 1997: A Chianti Classico with a very good concentration of plum skin and berry character. Medium-bodied, with silky tannins and a fruity finish. Drink now through 2002.–J.S. • $15 • (11/30/1999) • **87**
Chianti Classico 1996: Light and bubbly, with dried cherry character, a light to medium body, light tannins and a crisp and fruity aftertaste. Drink now.–J.S. • $14 • (12/15/1998) • **82**
Chianti Classico 1995 • $15 • (10/31/1997) • **84**
Chianti Classico 1994 • $20 • (10/31/1996) • **82**
Chianti Classico 1993 • $NA • (10/31/1995) • **81**
Chianti Classico 1992 • $11 • (10/31/1995) • **79**
Chianti Classico 1991 • $9 • (10/31/1994) • **77**
Chianti Classico 1990 • $14 • (10/31/1993) • **85**
Chianti Classico Cortevecchia Riserva 1996: Plenty of ripe fruit on the nose, with hints of raisin and berry, but it turns slightly dry and austere on the light- to medium-bodied palate. Tasted twice, with consistent notes. Drink now.–J.S. • $27 • (11/30/1999) • **83**
Chianti Classico Cortevecchia Riserva 1995: Wonderful raspberry and blackberry aromas, similar if less-intense flavors. Medium-bodied, with caressing tannins. Slightly short on the finish. Drink now through 2002.–J.S. • $23 • (12/15/1998) • **85**
Chianti Classico Cortevecchia Riserva 1994 • $25 • (9/30/1997) • **88**
Chianti Classico Cortevecchia Riserva 1993 • $NA • (10/31/1996) • **87**
Chianti Classico Don Tommaso 1997: Incredibly concentrated for a Chianti. Full-bodied, with loads of berry, tobacco and cherry character and a long,

long aftertaste of chocolate and red fruit. Goes on and on. Drink now through 2001.–J.S. • $35 • (11/30/1999) • **91**

Chianti Classico Don Tommaso 1996: Seriously well-made for a regular Chianti. Blackberry and wet earth aromas and flavors. Medium-bodied, with soft tannins and a smoky, fruity aftertaste. Drink now.–J.S. • $32 • (12/15/1998) • **87**

Chianti Classico Don Tommasso 1994 • $32 • (10/31/1996) • **86**

Masso Tondo 1985 • $20 • (4/30/1989) • **86**

CORZANO E PATERNO, FATTORIA

Chianti Terre di Corzano 1997: A thoroughly delicious Chianti, with excellent aromas of ripe plum and berry. Medium-bodied, with velvety tannins and a lovely, sweet fruit aftertaste. Drink now through 2003.–J.S. • $19 • (11/30/1999) • **88**

Chianti Terre di Corzano 1996: Delicious and well-made Chianti, sporting attractive bright berry and cherry aromas and flavors. Medium-bodied, with crisp acidity and a fruity, grapey aftertaste. Drink now.–J.S. • $17 • (12/15/1998) • **85**

Chianti Terre di Corzano Riserva 1995: Some good ripe fruit character in this, also rather chewy. Medium-bodied, with full tannins, a medium finish. Needs time to mellow. Drink now.–J.S. • $21 • (12/15/1998) • **86**

Toscana Il Corzano 1996: A solid 1996, with ripe fruit aromas and hints of tobacco and grilled meat. Medium-bodied, with chunky tannins and a medium finish. Needs a bit more fruit midpalate to be outstanding. Drink now through 2001.–J.S. • $35 • (11/30/1999) • **88**

Toscana Il Corzano 1995: Subtle, yet outstanding in structure. Reminds me of Heitz Martha's Vineyard, but with Tuscan acidity. Dark-colored, adding intense black currant and eucalyptus aromas. Medium- to full-bodied, with a superfine tannic structure and a long, caressing finish. Best after 2000.–J.S. • $32 • (12/15/1998) • **90**

Vin Santo 1993: A good, traditional vin santo, dark yellow with an amber hue, with aromas of dried apricot and nuts. Medium-bodied and medium sweet, with a lovely, creamy, salty, nutty aftertaste. Not imported into the U.S. Drink now.–J.S. • $NA/375 ml. • (1/01/1999) • **87**

COS

Cerasuolo di Vittoria 1998: Lots of bright berry and raspberry on the nose. Medium-bodied, with fresh acidity and a crisp finish. Delicious. Drink now through 2002.–J.S. • $18 • (5/31/2000) • **86**

Cerasuolo di Vittoria Sciri 1997: Bright, with lots of dried cherry and plum character. Medium-bodied, with medium tannins and a fruity finish. Drink now through 2001.–J.S. • $30 • (5/31/2000) • **87**

Sicilia Ramingallo 1998: Basic, with good, ripe fruit character, but slightly flabby and lacking in freshness.–J.S. • $16 • (5/31/2000) • **79**

COSER, FABIO

Collio Vigna del Lauro 1996 • $16 • (5/31/1998) • **82**

Pinot Grigio Collio Vigna del Lauro 1996 • $16 • (5/31/1998) • **86**

Sauvignon Collio Vigna del Lauro 1996 • $16 • (5/15/1998) • **84**

Tocai Friulano Collio Vigna del Lauro 1996 • $16 • (5/31/1998) • **82**

COSI

Pinot Grigio Valdadige 1996 • $10 • (11/15/1997) • **84**

COSIMI, E. ROBERTO

Brunello di Montalcino Il Poggiolo 1995: Very ripe, Portlike. Loads of black licorice, berry and mint. Medium-bodied, with very ripe fruit, almost raisiny, and smoky flavors. Medium finish. A bit rustic. Drink now through 2004.–J.S. • $56 • (6/30/2000) • **87**

Brunello di Montalcino Il Poggiolo 1994: Aromatic, but light and simple '94 Brunello, with tobacco, cherry and berry character. Light-bodied, with a short finish. Drink now.–J.S. • $38 • (8/31/1999) • **81**

Brunello di Montalcino Il Poggiolo 1993: Delivers more on the nose than the palate. Rich aromas of ripe fruit, porcini and tanned leather. Medium-bodied, with fine tannins and a slightly short finish. Drink now.–J.S. • $90 • (12/15/1998) • **84**

Brunello di Montalcino Il Poggiolo 1992 • $35 • (9/30/1997) • **82**

Brunello di Montalcino Il Poggiolo 1991 • $30 • (11/30/1996) • **88**

Brunello di Montalcino Il Poggiolo 1990 • $NA • (10/31/1995) • **77**

Brunello di Montalcino Il Poggiolo 1988 • $39 • (4/30/1994) • **86**

Brunello di Montalcino Il Poggiolo 1985 • $34 • (11/30/1990) • **93**

Brunello di Montalcino Il Poggiolo Beato 1994: Lovely perfumes of new wood, chocolate and fruit follow through to a medium-bodied palate. Fine tannins, slightly too woody on the finish. A little less new wood would be nice. Drink now.–J.S. • $55 • (8/31/1999) • **85**

Brunello di Montalcino Il Poggiolo Beato 1993: A very good 1993 Brunello. Loads of blackberries and raspberries on the nose, with a hint of earth. Full-bodied and chewy, with lots of polished tannins and a long, flavorful finish.–J.S. • $150 • (12/15/1998) • **88**

Brunello di Montalcino Il Poggiolo Beato 1992 • $35 • (9/30/1997) • **88**

Brunello di Montalcino Il Poggiolo Riserva 1990 • $55 • (11/30/1996) • **92**

Brunello di Montalcino Il Poggiolo Riserva 1988 • $NA • (10/31/1994) • **75**

Brunello di Montalcino Il Poggiolo Sassello 1995: Very fresh style for a 95 Brunello. Slightly too refreshed? Violets, crushed berry with hints of earth on the nose. Medium-bodied, with silky tannnins and a fresh fruit finish. Slightly unbalanced, but very good. Best after 2000.–J.S. • $91 • (6/30/2000) • **86**

Brunello di Montalcino Il Poggiolo Sassello 1994: Really woody, with masses of vanilla and cut wood character. Medium-bodied. Tannic and dry on the finish. Tasted twice, with consistent notes.–J.S. • $52 • (8/31/1999) • **78**

Brunello di Montalcino Il Poggiolo Sassello 1991 • $39 • (11/30/1996) • **89**

Brunello di Montalcino Il Poggiolo Sassello 1990 • $NA • (10/31/1995) • **86**

Brunello di Montalcino Il Poggiolo Sassello 1988 • $NA • (4/30/1994) • **83**

Brunello di Montalcino Il Poggiolo Sassello Riserva 1991 • $55 • (9/30/1997) • **87**

Brunello di Montalcino Il Poggiolo Sassello Riserva 1990 • $70 • (11/30/1996) • **93**

Cabernet Sauvignon Toscana Il Poggiolo Sassandra 1996: A gamy, earthy character mingles with the ripe fruit. Medium-bodied, with velvety tannins and a fresh, fruity aftertaste. Slightly hollow center-palate, but still delicious. Tastes more like Syrah. Drink now.–J.S. • $34 • (12/15/1998) • **84**

Carmignano Il Poggiolo Riserva 1985 • $16 • (5/15/1990) • **80**

Rosso di Montalcino Il Poggiolo 1991 • $NA • (4/30/1994) • **78**

Rosso di Montalcino Il Poggiolo Sassello 1997: Some good berry and cherry character in this, but rather subdued in style. Medium-bodied, with light tannins and a fruity finish. Drink now.–J.S. • $55 • (9/15/1999) • **83**

Rosso di Montalcino Il Poggiolo Sassello 1996: A stylish wine. Intense aromas of smoke and berry. Medium-bodied, with plenty of good fruit and a long, green tobacco finish. Drink now.–J.S. • $22 • (12/15/1998) • **85**

Rosso di Montalcino Il Poggiolo Sassello 1995 • $19 • (9/30/1997) • **90**

Rosso di Montalcino Il Poggiolo Sassello 1994 • $NA • (11/30/1996) • **85**

Rosso di Montalcino Il Poggiolo Sassello 1993 • $NA • (10/31/1995) • **65**

Rosso di Montalcino Il Poggiolo Sassello 1992 • $14 • (8/31/1995) • **86**

COSIMI, RODOLFO

Toscana Bottaccio 1996: Very ripe, with blackberry and cherry aromas, there's good fruit in this, if needing a little more focus on the palate. Full-bodied, with soft, round tannins and a fruity aftertaste with a hint of new wood. Slightly diluted finish. Drink now through 2002.–J.S. • $31 • (12/15/1998) • **84**

Toscana Bottaccio 1992 • $20 • (5/31/1997) • **86**

Toscana Bottaccio 1990 • $NA • (10/31/1996) • **86**

Toscana Gypsy 1997: Simple and fruity, with some mineral and melon character, fresh acidity and a light finish. Comes in a strange, bright blue bottle.–J.S. • $18 • (12/15/1998) • **80**

Toscana Olivetaccio 1997: Some good grapey character, with a slight rustic note; fruity, with light body and an earthy berry aftertaste.–J.S. • $32 • (12/15/1998) • **78**

Toscana Sasso Nero 1997: Plenty of bright fruit, as expected in a young and simple Sangiovese. Medium to light in body, with light tannins and a fruity aftertaste. Drink now.–J.S. • $16 • (12/15/1998) • **81**

COSTANTI, CONTI

Brunello di Montalcino 1995: A racy and fine Brunello with plum, berry and smoky character. Full-bodied, with well-integrated tannins and a long finish. Well-done from this producer. Drink through 2008.–J.S. • $61 • (6/30/2000) • **92**

Brunello di Montalcino 1994: Vivid aromas of blackberries and flowers follow through to a medium-bodied, silky palate. Lovely sweet fruit on the finish. Drink now.–J.S. • $58 • (8/31/1999) • **88**

Key: SS—Spectator Selection. CS—Cellar Selection. HR—Highly Recommended. $NA—Price not available. (BT)—Barrel tasting. Ⓐ—Auction Price.
For a key to the tasters' initials, see "How to Use These Listings."
Dates in parentheses represent the issues in which the ratings were published.

ITALY

Brunello di Montalcino 1993: A good, rather traditional Brunello with delicious plummy aromas. Medium in body, with soft tannins and a succulent, fruity finish. Drink now.–J.S. • $54 • (12/15/1998) • **85**
Brunello di Montalcino 1992 • $49 • (9/30/1997) • **79**
Brunello di Montalcino 1991 • $48 • (11/30/1996) • **87**
Brunello di Montalcino 1990 • $54 • (10/31/1995) • **93**
Brunello di Montalcino 1988 • $45 • (4/30/1994) • **88**
Brunello di Montalcino 1987 • $40 • (12/15/1992) • **88**
Brunello di Montalcino 1982 • $32 • (7/31/1988) • **81**
Brunello di Montalcino 1980 • $17 • (9/15/1986) • **89**
Brunello di Montalcino Riserva 1993: A wine with a future. Intense aromas of raspberries, dark chocolate and cherries. Full-bodied and very velvety, with round, ripe tannins and a delicious finish. Best after 2000.–J.S. • $81 • (8/31/1999) • **90**
Brunello di Montalcino Riserva 1990 • $75 • (11/30/1996) • **93**
Brunello di Montalcino Riserva 1988 • $NA • (10/31/1994) • **89**
Rosso di Montalcino 1996: A harmonious red, with chocolate and blackberry aromas and flavors. Light-bodied, with light tannins, a fresh finish. Drink now.–J.S. • $25 • (12/15/1998) • **82**
Rosso di Montalcino 1995 • $26 • (9/30/1997) • **85**
Rosso di Montalcino 1994 • $22 • (11/30/1996) • **86**
Rosso di Montalcino 1993 • $NA • (10/31/1995) • **85**
Rosso di Montalcino 1991 • $21 • (4/30/1994) • **81**
Rosso di Montalcino Calbello 1997: Beautiful, pure Sangiovese fruit. Aromas of dried cherries, violets, roses and plums. Full-bodied and very firm, with lots of silky tannins and a long finish. A seriously built rosso that needs time. Drink now.–J.S. • $30 • (9/15/1999) • **90**
Vermiglio 1991 • $NA • (10/31/1995) • **80**

CROCEDIMEZZO

Brunello di Montalcino 1995: A very earthy and funky red with saddle leather and ripe fruit character. A bit too much for me, but drinkable. Not imported into the U.S.–J.S. • $NA • (1/01/2000) • **79**
Brunello di Montalcino 1994: A subtle, early-drinking Brunello, flowing with plum and berry character. Medium-bodied, with fine, delicate tannins and a berry, grapey aftertaste. Not imported into the U.S. Drink now.–J.S. • $NA • (1/01/1999) • **86**
Rosso di Montalcino 1997: Lots of plum and berry character to this, with silky tannins and a long, long finish. A friendly and inviting wine. Not imported into the U.S. Drink now.–J.S. • $NA • (1/01/1999) • **87**

CROCIANI

Rosso di Montepulciano 1997: Very fresh and delicious, with grape and violet aromas. Medium-bodied, with light tannins and a crisp aftertaste. Needs food. Drink now.–J.S. • $12 • (12/15/1998) • **84**
Vino Nobile di Montepulciano 1995: Slightly raised acidity, with violet and berry character. Light- to medium-bodied, with a dry finish.–J.S. • $18 • (12/15/1998) • **78**
Vino Nobile di Montepulciano Riserva 1994: Round, with good berry and cherry character. Medium-bodied, with a velvety texture and a medium finish. Drink now.–J.S. • $24 • (12/15/1998) • **85**

DAL FORNO, ROMANO

Amarone della Valpolicella Vigneti del Monte Lodoletta 1987 • $47 • (9/15/1992) • **89**
Recioto della Valpolicella 1988 • $47 • (9/15/1997) • **83**
Valpolicella Superiore 1987 • $20 • (9/15/1992) • **86**
Valpolicella Superiore 1986 • $20 • (4/30/1992) • **84**

DECUGNANO DEI BARBI

Orvieto Classico 1997: Pretty serious stuff for Orvieto. Stylish and fresh, this white has lovely floral, peach and honey aromas. Medium-bodied, with lemon and grapefruit flavors and fresh acidity on the finish. Drink now.–J.S. • $15 • (6/15/1999) • **87**
Orvieto Classico Barbi 1997: A pleasant, easy-to-drink Italian white, with bright aromas and flavors of pear, melon and apple. Medium-bodied, with fresh acidity and a simple, fruity aftertaste. Drink now.–J.S. • $9 • (6/15/1999) • **82**
Orvieto Classico IL 1997: A seriously rich Orvieto, with plenty of mineral and melon character. Medium-bodied, with good acidity and a solid core of fruit that builds on the palate. Long, fruity aftertaste. Drink now.–J.S. • $24 • (6/15/1999) • **89**
Orvieto Classico Superiore 1998: A bit reserved, with aromas of lemon, honey and white pepper. Full-bodied and chewy, with good fruit and a medium finish. Drink now.–J.S. • $20 • (2/29/2000) • **86**
Umbria IL 1995: Slightly one-dimensional but very well made red, showing a solid core of fruit. Intensely grapey, with hints of blackberry and vanilla that follow through to a medium- to full-bodied palate. Velvety tannins. Best after 2000.–J.S. • $23 • (6/30/1999) • **87**

DEI

Rosso di Montepulciano 1998: A lovely, well-focused and fresh Sangiovese, with berry, plum and bark aromas and flavors. Light- to medium-bodied, with light tannins and a fruity finish. Drink now.–J.S. • $15 • (11/30/1999) • **85**
Rosso di Montepulciano 1997: Slightly austere, with some decent blackberry and dried cherry character. Medium- to light-bodied, with firm tannins, a fresh finish. Drink now.–J.S. • $15 • (12/15/1998) • **80**
Rosso di Montepulciano 1996 • $13 • (9/30/1997) • **82**
Toscana Santa Catharina 1996: Perfumed and fruity, with mint and dried herb undertones. Light- to medium-bodied, with light polished tannins and a fresh fruit finish. Cabernet Sauvignon, Prugnolo, Syrah. Drink now.–J.S. • $36 • (11/30/1999) • **85**
Toscana Santa Catharina 1995 • $35 • (9/30/1997) • **88**
Toscana Santa Catharina 1994 • $35 • (10/31/1996) • **89**
Vino Nobile di Montepulciano 1996: Very light for a Vino Nobile, with aromas of plum and light earth. Light- to medium-bodied, with light tannins and a short finish. Drink now.–J.S. • $26 • (11/30/1999) • **82**
Vino Nobile di Montepulciano 1995: An interesting red, with citrus and berry character, but slightly mature. Medium-bodied, with light tannins and high, crisp acidity. Shy on freshness. Drink now.–J.S. • $25 • (12/15/1998) • **81**
Vino Nobile di Montepulciano 1994 • $20 • (9/30/1997) • **81**
Vino Nobile di Montepulciano 1993 • $25 • (10/31/1996) • **84**
Vino Nobile di Montepulciano Riserva 1995: Stylish wine. Fascinating aromas of ripe fruit, ginger and cumin. Medium-bodied, with soft tannins and a long, spicy finish. Delicious. Drink now.–J.S. • $35 • (11/30/1999) • **88**
Vino Nobile di Montepulciano Riserva 1994: Pretty Nobile. Lovely and elegant berry and cherry character, with silky tannins and a caressing finish. Medium-bodied. Drink now.–J.S. • $30 • (12/15/1998) • **89**
Vino Nobile di Montepulciano Riserva 1993 • $28 • (9/30/1997) • **88**
Vino Nobile di Montepulciano Riserva 1991 • $23 • (10/31/1996) • **84**
Vino Nobile di Montepulciano Riserva 1985 • $13 • (4/15/1990) • **85**

DELIZIA, LA

Cabernet Sauvignon Grave del Friuli Morasutti 1996 • $5 • (4/30/1998) • **84**
Chardonnay Grave del Friuli Morasutti 1996 • $5 • (4/30/1998) • **80**
Le Delizie di Krizia Red 1989 • $18 • (12/15/1994) • **75**
Merlot Grave del Friuli Morasutti 1995 • $5 • (4/30/1998) • **74**
Pinot Grigio Venezie Morasutti 1997 • $5 • (6/15/1998) • **81**

DELLA STAFFA

Chardonnay Alto Adige 1997: Simple and light. Appley and slightly candied aromas follow through to a medium-bodied palate, with a chalky, short aftertaste.–J.S. • $15 • (6/15/1999) • **78**
Pinot Grigio Alto Adige 1997: Not very impressive on nose or palate, but there's decent melon and apple character, with fresh acidity and a light, slightly candied finish. Drink now.–J.S. • $15 • (6/15/1999) • **83**

DELTETTO

Barbera d'Alba Bramè 1997: Very toasted and a bit herbal, with vanilla, grilled and chocolate notes. Medium-bodied, with distinct acidity and an astringent finish. Not imported into the U.S.–P.M. • $NA • (1/01/1999) • **79**
Barbera d'Alba Bramè 1996: Supple and smooth, this oak-styled, medium-bodied Barbera has pronounced acidity and succulent red berry fruit, with a straightforward finish.–P.M. • $13 • (10/31/1998) • **79**
Dolcetto d'Alba 1997: Dull and a bit flat, showing little of anything except plywood notes. A bit green and unripe. May be suffering from bottle shock, as it is a 1997.–P.M. • $12 • (10/31/1998) • **75**
Roero Arneis S. Michele 1997: A lovely Arneis, showing juicy citrus, melon, pear and orange aromas and flavors. Round in texture, turning very harmonious on the palate and the long finish. Drink now.–P.M. • $13 • (10/31/1998) • **87**
Roero Braja 1997: The obvious oak (sawdust and sandalwood) can't hide the lack of serious fruit. Medium-bodied, it offers a fresh drink that's chewy on the finish.–P.M. • $16 • (11/15/1999) • **78**

Roero Braja 1996: Quite nice and very accessible on release, with smooth tannins and delicate raspberry, plum, licorice and floral notes. Not much depth, but quaffable. Drink now.–P.M. • $14 • (10/31/1998) • **82**
Roero Madonna dei Boschi 1997: Not a big wine, but worth having. Medium-bodied, it shows mocha and chocolate character, with a supple, ripe texture. Focused red berry flavors on the midpalate lead to a lovely, balanced finish. Drink now through 2002.–P.M. • $17 • (11/15/1999) • **87**
Roero Madonna dei Boschi 1996: Light and a bit diluted, offering a fairly dull flavor profile. Turns a bit dry on the finish.–P.M. • $14 • (10/31/1998) • **77**

DESSILANI

Barbera Piemonte 1993 • $9 • (3/31/1997) • **84**
Barbera Piemonte 1990 • $8 • (10/31/1992) • **83**
Caramino Riserva 1985 • $13 • (9/15/1990) • **79**
Spanna 1990 • $9 • (2/28/1995) • **79**
Spanna Riserva 1988 • $11 • (2/28/1995) • **83**

DIEVOLE

Chianti Classico 1997: Superbright berry aromas have hints of mineral in this medium- to full-bodied beauty, with medium, silky tannins and an intensely fruity finish. Drink now through 2001.–J.S. • $16 • (11/30/1999) • **89**
Chianti Classico 1996: Aromatic and delectable, with a profuse ripe plum, floral and spice character. Medium-bodied, with soft tannins and a fruity, crisp finish. Hard to resist. Dievole continues to make wonderful Chianti. Drink through 2001.–J.S. • $15 • (12/15/1998) • **87**
Chianti Classico 1995 • $12 • (9/30/1997) • **86**
Chianti Classico 1994 • $11 • (10/31/1996) • **86**
Chianti Classico 1990 • $10 • (9/15/1992) • **85**
Chianti Classico 1988 • $13 • (9/15/1991) • **85**
Chianti Classico Dieulele 1990 • $24 • (10/31/1993) • **84**
Chianti Classico Dieulele 1988 • $22 • (4/15/1991) HR • **91**
Chianti Classico Novecentenario 1090-1990 1995: A rather big and ponderous wine with plenty of fruit, if lacking in complexity. Wonderful aromas of blackberry and dark chocolate. Medium-bodied, with moderate tannins and a fruity aftertaste; albeit a large shot of new, coconut-flavored oak masks some of the quality. Best through 2001.–J.S. • $NA • (12/15/1998) • **86**
Chianti Classico Novecento 1996: A joyful and well-made Chianti. Plum and berry aromas follow through to a medium-bodied palate, with polished tannins and a medium finish. Drink now.–J.S. • $29 • (11/30/1999) • **87**
Chianti Classico Rinascimento 1993 • $16 • (10/31/1996) • **85**
Chianti Classico Riserva 1996: A pretty combination of subtle berry and new wood, although slightly monolithic. Medium- to full-bodied, with polished tannins and a medium finish. Doesn't taste much like Sangiovese, but a good red. Drink now.–J.S. • $20 • (11/30/1999) • **86**
Chianti Classico Riserva 1995: Steely, well-built Chianti. Gorgeous floral and blackberry aromas follow through on the palate. Medium- to full-bodied, with solid tannins and a crisp and focused, fruit finish. Drink now.–J.S. • $22 • (12/15/1998) • **89**
Chianti Classico Riserva 1994 • $18 • (9/30/1997) • **86**
Chianti Classico Riserva 1993 • $18 • (10/31/1996) • **84**
Chianti Classico Riserva 1988 • $18 • (9/15/1992) • **88**
Chianti Classico Vigna Campi Nuovi 1988 • $15 • (4/15/1991) • **82**
Chianti Classico Vigna Campi Nuovi 1987 • $10 • (11/30/1990) • **84**
Chianti Classico Vigna Petrignano 1988 • $12 • (1/31/1992) • **84**
Chianti Classico Vigna Sessina 1988 • $12 • (1/31/1992) • **84**
Malvasia Toscana 1998: Aromas of mineral stand out in this wine, with hints of fruit. Medium-bodied, with fresh acidity and a crisp finish. Drink now.–J.S. • $12 • (11/30/1999) • **84**
Malvasia Toscana 1997: Fresh and easy, with some pear and honeysuckle aromas and flavors. Medium-bodied, with light acidity, light finish. Drink now.–J.S. • $12 • (12/15/1998) • **80**
Plenum Secundus 1997: Intense aromas of berry and black licorice, with a hint of wet earth. Full-bodied and very grapey, with lots of fruit, medium tannins and a very fruity finish. Slightly hollow midpalate, like it didn't completely blend. Made from a 50/50 blend of Barbera from Piedmont's Dezzani and Sangiovese from Tuscany's Dievole. Best after 2000.–J.S. • $49 • (4/30/2000) • **89**

Key: SS—Spectator Selection. CS—Cellar Selection. HR—Highly Recommended. $NA—Price not available. (BT)—Barrel tasting. Ⓐ—Auction Price. For a key to the tasters' initials, see "How to Use These Listings." **Dates in parentheses represent the issues in which the ratings were published.**

Sangiovese Toscana Rosato 1998: A decent rosé, with strawberry and almond character throughout. Medium-bodied. The light finish has a slightly musty undertone. Drink now.–J.S. • $12 • (11/30/1999) • **81**
Toscana Broccato 1996: There's good bright berry and plum skin character in this medium-bodied, light-tannined red. Shows a very pleasant freshness, with structure for aging. Slightly austere finish. Drink now through 2001.–J.S. • $26 • (11/30/1999) • **87**
Toscana Broccato 1995: A rich, voluptuous, modern-style red. Gorgeous plum, vanilla and berry aroma and flavors. Full-bodied, with supersmooth tannins and a long, smoky, fruity aftertaste.–J.S. • $24 • (12/15/1998) • **88**
Toscana Broccato 1994 • $14 • (9/30/1997) • **87**
Toscana Broccato 1987 • $19 • (12/15/1991) • **86**
Toscana Duemila Dievole 1997: This is a hell of a wine even though the packaging is a bit bizarre. Full-bodied, with amazing aromas of blackberry, cherry and tobacco and masses of caressing, velvety tannins. The finish lasts for minutes on your palate. Best after 2001.–J.S. • $175/1.5 liter • (11/30/1999) • **95**
Toscana Rinascimento 1996: Not a big wine, but with wonderfully bright dried cherry and berry character. Medium-bodied, with light tannins and a fresh finish. Slightly lean and austere. Drink now.–J.S. • $19 • (11/30/1999) • **85**
Toscana Rinascimento 1994 • $14 • (9/30/1997) • **88**
Val d'Arbia 1996 • $12 • (9/30/1997) • **80**

DOLIANOVA, CANTINE DI

Cannonau di Sardegna Dolia 1997: Rather stewed fruit character and a papery aftertaste. Tasted twice, with consistent notes.–J.S. • $8 • (5/31/2000) • **75**
Monica di Sardegna Dolia 1997: Dried cherry character has light mineral and floral notes. Medium-bodied, with light to medium tannins and a fresh finish. Slightly austere. Drink now.–J.S. • $9 • (5/31/2000) • **84**
Vermentino di Sardegna Dolia 1998: Spritzy, with a fruit cocktail character. Simple. Tasted twice, with consistent notes.–J.S. • $8 • (5/31/2000) • **77**

DOMENICO DE BERTIOL

Prosecco di Conegliano NV: Quite frothy and smelling like vanilla, this is peachy in flavor, soft and slightly sweet, yet with enough citrus bite to leave the mouth watering. Drink now.–B.S. • $13 • (10/15/1999) • **82**

DONNAFUGATA

Contessa Entellina Tancredi 1996: Big and rich, with a slight cooked fruit and tar character. Full-bodied and tarry, with a chewy finish. Drink now.–J.S. • $24 • (5/31/2000) • **82**
Passito di Pantelleria Ben Ryé 1998: Shows a wonderful richness of honey, lemon, apricot and grapefruit. Full-bodied and medium sweet, with a very lively palate and a long blanched almond and honey aftertaste. Drink now.–J.S. • $26 • (5/31/2000) • **89**
Sicilia Il Bianco 1998: A good, clean white, with lemon, lime and mineral character. Medium-bodied, with good acidity and a fresh finish. Drink now.–J.S. • $9 • (5/31/2000) • **82**
Sicilia Il Rosato 1998: Medium-bodied, with candied watermelon aromas. Oxidized and tired.–J.S. • $9 • (5/31/2000) • **72**
Sicilia Il Rosso 1997: A traditional, simple red, with attractive ripe berry and plum character, but slightly nutty. Medium-bodied, with light tannins and a fruity finish. Drink now.–J.S. • $9 • (5/31/2000) • **82**

DOSIO

Barolo Fossati 1993 • $NA • (10/31/1997) • **85**

DUCHI DI CASTELLUCCIO

Montepulciano d'Abruzzo 1994 • $13/1.5 liter • (3/31/1997) • **84**

ECCO DOMANI

Merlot Venezie 1996: A fleshy red, almost chewy, sporting cherry, spice and licorice flavors, all well balanced and with moderate structure. Finishes quickly.–B.S. • $10 • (9/30/1998) • **83**
Pinot Bianco Venezie 1996 • $10 • (5/15/1998) • **85**
Pinot Nero Venezie 1996 • $10 • (4/30/1998) • **82**
Sangiovese Toscana 1996 • $10 • (4/30/1998) • **83**

EINAUDI, LUIGI

Barbera d'Alba 1995 • $15 • (10/31/1997) • **88**
Barbera Langhe 1994 • $16 • (10/31/1996) • **77**
Barbera Langhe 1992 • $13 • (10/31/1994) • **78**
Barbera Piemonte 1997: Clean and fruity, with supple tannins. Medium-bodied, it lacks complexity but makes for a fun drink, with red berry and spice character. Drink now through 2001.–P.M. • $20 • (11/15/1999) • **84**
Barbera Piemonte 1995: Fairly mature, with plum, spicy oak, vanilla, mocha and earth notes and supple (even soft) tannins. Lovely mouthfeel, with a soft glow to it on the lush, seductive finish. Drink now.–P.M. • $14 • (10/31/1998) • **85**
Barolo 1995: A bit on the hard side at first, it turned more supple in the glass. The pure red berry aromas are pretty, and there's clean cassis and toasted oak character on the firm, lean finish. Enough concentration for aging. Drink now through 2003.–P.M. • $49 • (11/15/1999) • **87**
Barolo 1994: Well made and intriguing, this Barolo of the earth includes plenty of fruit. Supple and ripe yet medium-bodied, it's a bit earthy, with animal ("reduced"), plum and red berry notes. Silky on the midpalate, suggesting good concentration and good winemaking. Tempting now, but should age. Best after 2000.–P.M. • $32 • (10/31/1998) • **87**
Barolo 1993 • $41 • (10/31/1997) • **83**
Barolo 1992 • $41 • (10/31/1996) • **82**
Barolo 1991 • $37 • (10/31/1995) • **81**
Barolo 1989 • $43 • (10/31/1994) • **71**
Barolo 1988 • $30 • (12/15/1992) • **83**
Barolo 1982 • $23 • (6/30/1987) • **81**
Barolo Costa Grimaldi 1995: Beautiful. Shows lovely mineral, lead pencil and *terroir* concentration, with a solid tannin structure. This muscular Barolo stays the course with clean, ripe fruit flavors and deftly dosed toasted oak. An ager that needs time to soften up. Best from 2003 through 2010.–P.M. • $52 • (11/15/1999) • **94**
Barolo Nei Cannubi 1995: There's excellent ripeness way underneath, but the crisp flavors and texture make this medium-bodied red a tough customer to warm up to. Might improve with age.–P.M. • $61 • (11/15/1999) • **78**
Dolcetto di Dogliani 1997: A powerhouse. Very dark in color and explosive in aroma, with spice, floral, black currant and dried herb character. A bit herbal and tough on the aftertaste. Might come together with age. Drink now through 2001.–P.M. • $17 • (7/31/1999) • **80**
Dolcetto di Dogliani 1996: Medium-bodied, with ripe tannins and a mineral-laden, lead pencil character that suggests *terroir*. Traditional in style, very well made, delivering pure, clean berry notes. Plenty of firm tannins on the long finish suggest it can improve with short-term cellaring. Drink now. –P.M. • $12 • (10/31/1998) • **87**
Dolcetto di Dogliani 1995 • $14 • (10/31/1997) • **79**
Dolcetto di Dogliani 1994 • $14 • (10/31/1996) • **78**
Dolcetto di Dogliani 1993 • $12 • (10/31/1995) • **80**
Dolcetto di Dogliani 1990 • $11 • (10/31/1992) • **87**
Dolcetto di Dogliani I Filari 1997: Fresh and grapey, with a cedar, mocha and coffee complexity. A Dolcetto that appears to have been aged a bit in oak. Medium-bodied, with firm, chewy tannins. (It was aged one year in wood.) Should improve with age. Drink now through 2002.–P.M. • $26 • (7/31/1999) • **84**
Dolcetto di Dogliani I Filari 1996: Full-bodied and packed with personality, this thick and ripe Dolcetto impresses with its tannins, which are supple in the midpalate and go into high gear on the firm finish. A bit herbal, it's accented by wet earth and mineral notes and buttressed by good acidity. Drink now through 2003.–P.M. • $21 • (10/31/1998) • **88**
Dolcetto di Dogliani I Filari 1995 • $20 • (10/31/1996) • **83**
Dolcetto di Dogliani Vigna Tecc 1997: Smooth and rich, with sweet-tasting tannins. Turns chewy on the finish as the spice, wet earth and black fruit flavors tighten. Drink now through 2002.–P.M. • $20 • (7/31/1999) • **86**
Dolcetto di Dogliani Vigna Tecc 1996: Thick and dense, inky dark in color, ripe yet packed with pure, clean, laser-sharp berry character that plays without obstruction from any obvious oak. A lovely mineral-laden note surfaces on the firmly tannic finish, which suggests cellaring. Drink now.–P.M. • $16 • (10/31/1998) • **90**
Dolcetto di Dogliani Vigna Tecc 1995 • $18 • (10/31/1997) • **82**
Dolcetto di Dogliani Vigna Tecc 1994 • $18 • (10/31/1996) • **81**
Dolcetto di Dogliani Vigna Tecc 1993 • $16 • (10/31/1995) • **84**
Langhe 1996: Nicely balanced and full-bodied, with good, ripe fruit, supple tannins, loads of charred oak and petrollike flavors—and enough acidity to carry the whole ship forward to a focused finish. Drink now through 2005.–P.M. • $44 • (11/15/1999) • **89**
Langhe 1995: Fairly smooth, showing vanilla and chocolate candy bar flavors. A bit earthy and slightly dry, turning a bit light and short on the finish. Tasted twice, with consistent notes.–P.M. • $39 • (10/31/1998) • **79**
Nebbiolo delle Langhe 1991 • $17 • (2/28/1995) • **79**

ENO-FRIULIA

Cabernet Sauvignon Collio 1988 • $12 • (7/15/1991) • **76**
Chardonnay Collio 1997: Apple aromas and flavors and a crisp structure are light and lacking in concentration. Drink now.–B.S. • $12 • (7/31/1998) • **78**
Merlot Collio 1996: Not much aroma and the flavors are light, showing only modest herb and berry. Drink now.–B.S. • $12 • (7/31/1998) • **78**
Merlot Collio 1988 • $12 • (4/30/1991) • **82**
Pinot Bianco Collio 1997: Beautifully displayed apple, peach, lemon and nut aromas and flavors typical of this varietal, with vibrant acidity and fine balance. Drink now.–B.S. • $12 • (7/31/1998) • **86**
Pinot Grigio Collio 1997: Delicious from start to finish. Tastes like quince and nuts, with a rich texture. Bright acidity keeps everything lively and fresh through the lingering finish.–B.S. • $12 • (7/31/1998) • **85**
Sauvignon Isonzo del Friuli 1997: Broad and waxy in both aroma and flavor, this white shows richness and weight but isn't very expressive. Good, crisp finish. Drink now.–B.S. • $12 • (7/31/1998) • **83**
Tocai Friulano Collio 1997: Open and easygoing. Already rich and inviting. Low in acidity, showing banana and peach flavors, with a hint of almond peeking through. Drink now.–B.S. • $12 • (7/31/1998) • **84**

FALCHINI, RICCARDO

Campora 1991 • $50 • (1/31/1997) • **89**
Chianti Colli Senesi Titolato Colombaia 1996: Nicely balanced, with bright fruit, hints of black pepper, lively acidity and modest tannins. Easy to enjoy. Drink now. • $9 • (7/31/1998) • **85**
Chianti Colli Senesi Titolato Colombaia 1995 • $9 • (3/31/1997) • **86**
Paretaio 1994: Rugged, with modest fruit and spice framed by tight tannins. Full-bodied and a bit tough in texture. Needs rich food. Drink now. • $17 • (9/30/1998) • **83**
Paretaio 1993 • $17 • (1/31/1997) • **83**
Toscana Campora 1989 • $50 • (1/01/1998) • **77**
Vernaccia di San Gimignano Vigna a Solatio 1996: Crisp in texture, lightly peachy and appley in flavor, this medium-weight white should be versatile with food. Drink now. • $9 • (7/31/1998) • **82**
Vin Santo di Caratello 1990 • $16/500 ml. • (5/31/1997) • **85**

FALCONE, IL

Toscana Boccalupo 1996: A good amount of crushed raspberry and cherry in this wine. Medium-bodied, with firm tannins and a medium finish. Slight dilution on the midpalate. Drink now.–J.S. • $25 • (11/30/1999) • **85**
Val di Cornia Falcorosso 1998: Sour and undrinkable, with rather strange aromas of fruit and incense. Tasted twice, with consistent notes.–J.S. • $12 • (11/30/1999) • **65**

FALESCO

Est! Est!! Est!!! di Montefiascone Poggio dei Gelsi 1998: Clean and well made, with lemon rind and mineral character and a hint of ripe pear. Medium-bodied, with a light finish. Drink now.–J.S. • $10 • (4/30/2000) • **82**
Est! Est!! Est!!! di Montefiascone Poggio dei Gelsi 1996: Fresh and fruity with appealing flavors of honeydew melon. Drink now.–K.M. • $10 • (8/31/1998) • **81**
Grechetto Umbria 1998: Lots of pear and lanolin character in this wine. Medium-bodied, with light apple flavors. Drink now.–J.S. • $14 • (2/29/2000) • **81**
Grechetto Umbria 1996: A lumbering and somewhat funky white, with oniony character. Tasted twice, with consistent notes.–K.M. • $12 • (8/31/1998) • **73**
Lazio Montiano 1997: A sexy and very polished Italian red. Dark, with mint, cherry, tobacco and vanilla. Medium- to full-bodied, with silky tannins and a long, fruity, minty aftertaste. Pure Merlot. Drink now through 2005.–J.S. • $39 • (4/30/2000) HR • **91**
Merlot Aprilia 1993 • $13 • (1/31/1996) • **84**
Merlot Umbria 1996 • $14 • (6/15/1998) • **84**
Montiano Latium 1995 • $30 • (6/15/1998) HR • **91**
Umbria Vitiano 1998: Plum, green tobacco and earth character. Medium-bodied, with medium, chewy tannins and a tough finish. Slightly astringent. Drink now.–J.S. • $11 • (2/29/2000) • **82**

Vitiano 1996 • $10 • (6/15/1998) • 85

FANTI

Brunello di Montalcino 1994: Very aromatic Brunello, with chocolate and berry character and a hint of grilled meat. Medium- to full-bodied, with soft yet fine tannins and a sweet fruit finish. A beauty. Drink now.–J.S. • $50 • (8/31/1999) • **88**
Brunello di Montalcino 1993: A delicious traditional-style Brunello which gives more on the nose than in the mouth, its aromas of flowers and white pepper intertwined with ripe fruit. Medium-bodied, with soft tannins and a short, chestnut aftertaste. Drink now.–J.S. • $42 • (12/15/1998) • **85**
Brunello di Montalcino 1991 • $NA • (11/30/1996) • **85**
Brunello di Montalcino 1990 • $NA • (10/31/1995) • **87**
Brunello di Montalcino 1988 • $NA • (4/30/1994) • **79**
Brunello di Montalcino Riserva 1993: A serious Brunello that needs more age. Complex aromas of blackberries, wet earth and porcini. Full-bodied, with loads of flavor and a well-integrated backbone of velvety tannins. Medium finish. Best after 2000.–J.S. • $70 • (8/31/1999) • **90**
Rosso di Montalcino 1997: Delivers bright blackberry and cherry character, with a hint of mint. Medium-bodied, with silky tannins and a fruity finish. Drink now.–J.S. • $19 • (9/15/1999) • **87**
Rosso di Montalcino 1996: Easy to like this wine. Grapey and floral, with medium body, medium, velvety tannins and a fruity finish. Drink now.–J.S. • $16 • (12/15/1998) • **84**
Rosso di Montalcino 1994 • $NA • (11/30/1996) • **84**
Rosso di Montalcino 1993 • $NA • (10/31/1995) • **84**
Rosso di Montalcino 1991 • $NA • (4/30/1994) • **82**

FANTINEL

Cabernet Franc Grave del Friuli F Sigillo Oro 1997 • $12 • (6/15/1998) • **85**
Cabernet Sauvignon Grave del Friuli 1996 • $15 • (6/15/1998) • **87**
Cabernet Sauvignon Grave del Friuli Vigneti Sant'Helena 1997: A delicious Cabernet, with lovely cassis character, blackberry flavors and hints of wet earth. Medium-bodied, with fine tannins and a long, fruity aftertaste. Drink now.–J.S. • $18 • (1/01/2000) • **86**
Chardonnay Collio Vigneti Sant'Helena 1997: Fresh, with lemon, lime and clove character. Medium-bodied, with good acidity and a fresh finish. Drink now.–J.S. • $18 • (1/01/2000) • **84**
Merlot Grave del Friuli Barone Rosso 1997 • $9 • (6/15/1998) • **86**
Pinot Bianco Grave del Friuli F Sigillo Oro 1997 • $12 • (6/15/1998) • **82**
Pinot Grigio Collio 1997 • $15 • (6/15/1998) • **88**
Pinot Grigio Collio Vigneti Sant'Helena 1998: A bit strange, with almond, geranium and herb character. Medium-bodied, with a dull finish. Tasted twice, with consistent notes.–J.S. • $18 • (3/31/2000) • **78**
Pinot Grigio Friuli-Venezia Giulia Paron Mario Montecristo 1998: Attractive peach and lemon rind aromas and flavors. Medium-bodied, with good acidity and a fruity finish. Drink now.–J.S. • $10 • (3/31/2000) • **85**
Pinot Grigio Grave del Friuli Montecristo 1996: Already mature, showing slightly oxidized, marzipan character and sharp acidity.–B.S. • $9 • (7/31/1998) • **78**
Sauvignon Grave del Friuli F Sigillo Oro 1996: Smells like marzipan and clove, with dilute, nonvarietal flavors. Finishes on the metallic side.–B.S. • $12 • (7/31/1998) • **76**

FARINA, REMO

Amarone della Valpolicella Classico 1993 • $23 • (5/31/1998) • **84**
Amarone della Valpolicella Classico 1983 • $13 • (3/31/1990) • **70**
Bianco di Custoza 1996 • $8 • (5/15/1998) • **82**
Soave Classico Superiore 1996 • $8 • (6/15/1998) • **84**
Valpolicella Classico Superiore 1995 • $8 • (4/30/1998) • **82**

FARINA, STEFANO

Barbaresco 1996: Plum is the dominant flavor in this full-bodied, ripe, sweet-tasting wine. Well made, with fresh acidity making it clean and long on the chewy finish. Best from 2002 through 2010.–P.M. • $27 • (10/31/1999) • **88**
Barbaresco 1995: A lovely wine that stresses fruit, fruit and more fruit. Dark in color, with a super marriage of plum, blackberry, truffle, licorice and cassis, it has a ripe, sweet midpalate and massive but fairly supple tannins. Full-bodied, it should improve with age and turn into a real gem. Best from 2002 through 2005.–P.M. • $24 • (9/15/1998) • **91**
Barbaresco 1994 • $18 • (10/31/1997) • **73**
Barbaresco 1993 • $19 • (10/31/1996) • **88**
Barbaresco 1989 • $15 • (10/31/1994) • **79**
Barbera d'Alba 1998: A bit reduced and earthy, even slightly spritzy, a lightish Barbera made in a nouveau style. Chill and serve at a picnic. Drink now.–P.M. • $9 • (11/15/1999) • **80**
Barbera d'Alba 1997: Typical Barbera, fresh and lively, with pure and vibrant red berry character. Of medium body, it's fairly tart, but should match food. Drink now.–P.M. • $9 • (10/31/1998) • **82**
Barbera d'Alba 1996: Quite light, with juicy, red berry flavors accented by pronounced acidity. Shows ripe character on the subtle smoky, toasted finish.–P.M. • $12 • (10/31/1998) • **79**
Barbera d'Alba 1995 • $9 • (10/31/1997) • **85**
Barbera d'Alba 1994 • $9 • (10/31/1996) • **84**
Barolo 1995: It smells and tastes plummy, almost jammy, with a blackberry, somewhat spiritlike character. Medium-bodied, with a supple tannin texture. Drink now through 2003.–P.M. • $24 • (11/15/1999) • **85**
Barolo 1994: A bit earthy, with truffle or mushroom character that stands out amid the currant and blackberry flavors. Slightly coarse, with firm, rough tannins, yet has complexity, with animal, spice and oak accents. Drink now through 2005.–P.M. • $25 • (10/31/1998) • **85**
Barolo 1993 • $24 • (10/31/1997) • **78**
Barolo 1992 • $22 • (10/31/1996) • **86**
Barolo 1990 • $18 • (7/31/1995) • **88**
Barolo 1989 • $16 • (6/15/1994) HR • **90**
Barolo Franco Fiorina 1994: Elegant, bordering on light, with some wet earth and mineral, some red berry too, accessible tannins and a clean, firm finish. Nothing opulent, but should go well with food. Drink now through 2002.–P.M. • $21 • (10/31/1998) • **84**
Chianti La Ginestra 1992 • $6 • (7/31/1994) • **77**
Dolcetto d'Alba 1998: A bit simple, as the strawberry and earth notes get a bit lost. Tart finish.–P.M. • $9 • (11/15/1999) • **76**
Dolcetto d'Alba 1997: Not very intense, but it grows on you as it unfolds its delicate, sweet-tasting flavors, smooth tannins and soft finish. Drink now.–P.M. • $12 • (10/31/1998) • **80**
Dolcetto d'Alba 1996 • $10 • (10/31/1997) • **86**
Dolcetto d'Alba 1995 • $10 • (10/31/1996) • **87**
Dolcetto d'Alba 1991 • $10 • (6/15/1994) • **78**
Il Brumaio NV: Dark and brooding, complex and balanced. A full-bodied, hot-weather red, tasting of plum, mineral, smoked wood and leather, with fine tannins but a chewy finish. Drink now through 2002.–P.M. • $9 • (11/15/1999) • **88**

FARNESE

Montepulciano d'Abruzzo 1996 • $6 • (7/31/1997) • **78**
Montepulciano d'Abruzzo 1993 • $5 • (2/29/1996) • **85**
Sangiovese Abruzzi 1995 • $6 • (7/31/1997) • **85**
Trebbiano d'Abruzzo 1996 • $6 • (5/31/1997) • **83**

FARNETA, TENUTA DI

Toscana Bentivoglio 1995: A pretty and delicious Tuscan red, with dried cherry and berry aromas and hints of mushroom and leather. Medium-bodied, with fine tannins and a fresh and fruity aftertaste. Drink now through 2003.–J.S. • $14 • (6/30/1999) • **86**
Toscana Buongoverno 1994: Slightly dilute and herbal red. Medium-bodied, with light tannins and a grassy, tarragon aftertaste. Tastes unripe.–J.S. • $32 • (6/30/1999) • **78**

FARNETELLA, CASTELLO DI

Chianti Colli Senesi 1997: Lots of ripe berry and plum character. Medium-bodied, with light tannins and a light, fruity finish. Drink now.–J.S. • $14 • (11/30/1999) • **84**
Chianti Colli Senesi 1996: Firm and crisp, with berry, bark and earth aromas and flavors. Medium-bodied, with light tannins and slightly hard acidity. Drink now.–J.S. • $12 • (12/15/1998) • **84**
Chianti Colli Senesi 1995 • $13 • (9/30/1997) • **83**

Key: SS—Spectator Selection. CS—Cellar Selection. HR—Highly Recommended. $NA—Price not available. (BT)—Barrel tasting. Ⓐ—Auction Price. For a key to the tasters' initials, see "How to Use These Listings." **Dates in parentheses represent the issues in which the ratings were published.**

Chianti Colli Senesi 1992 • $10 • (2/28/1995) • **81**
Chianti Colli Senesi 1991 • $10 • (2/28/1995) • **81**
Poggio Granoni 1993: Lovely, soft and ready. A voluptuous and generous wine, showing plum, berry and mocha on the nose and palate. Medium-bodied, with velvety tannins and a delicious finish. Drink now through 2001.–J.S. • $NA • (12/15/1998) • **88**
Sauvignon Toscana 1997: Wild aromas of passion fruit, pineapple and honey. Medium-bodied, with fresh acidity and a long lime and kiwi fruit aftertaste. Drink now.–J.S. • $22 • (11/30/1999) • **88**
Sauvignon Toscana 1996: A pretty and elegant Sauvignon. Lovely aromas of peaches, melons and cream. Medium-bodied, with fresh acidity and a lively, fruity aftertaste. Drink now.–J.S. • $18 • (12/15/1998) • **87**
Toscana Nero di Nubi 1995: Interesting Pinot Noir character, but a bit raisiny and rustic. Aromas of strawberry and leather, with hints of earth and funk. Medium-bodied, with dry fruit flavors, medium tannins and a slightly austere finish. Drink now.–J.S. • $NA • (11/30/1999) • **80**
Toscana Nero di Nubi 1994: A bit too mature, with too much funk. Medium-bodied, with velvety tannins and a decadent finish.–J.S. • $28 • (12/15/1998) • **79**

FASSATI

Rocca delle Querce 1995 • $NA • (9/30/1997) • **80**
Rosso di Montepulciano Selciaia 1997: Milk chocolate and black pepper on the nose and palate. Medium-bodied, with firm tannins, a medium finish. Drink now.–J.S. • $10 • (12/15/1998) • **84**
Rosso di Montepulciano Selciaia 1996 • $8 • (9/30/1997) • **81**
Rosso di Montepulciano Selciaia 1995 • $8 • (9/30/1997) • **80**
Rosso di Montepulciano Selciaia 1994 • $8 • (1/01/1997) • **83**
Torre al Fante 1994: Slightly rustic aromas of berry, raisin and burnt almond. Medium- to full-bodied, with chewy tannins and a raisiny finish. Tastes more like a wine from southern Italy than Tuscany. Not imported into the U.S. Drink now.–J.S. • $NA • (1/01/1999) • **82**
Torre al Fante 1993: Extremely well-crafted, with superpolished tannins and pretty berry and cherry character. Medium- to full-bodied, with an inviting finish. A blend of Sangiovese and Prugnolo Gentile. Not imported into the U.S. Best after 2000.–J.S. • $NA • (12/15/1998) • **88**
Vino Nobile di Montepulciano 1993 • $11 • (9/30/1997) • **83**
Vino Nobile di Montepulciano 1991 • $20 • (1/01/1997) • **79**
Vino Nobile di Montepulciano Pasiteo 1996: A soft and delicious red, impressive for this producer. Dark, with intense coffee, chocolate and ripe fruit character. Medium-bodied, with velvety tannins and an opulent fruity finish. Drink now through 2002.–J.S. • $15 • (11/30/1999) • **88**
Vino Nobile di Montepulciano Pasiteo 1995: Rich and powerful. Full-bodied and a little herbal, with loads of berry, cherry and mineral aromas and very polished tannins. Is there Cabernet Sauvignon in this? Best after 2000.–J.S. • $15 •(12/15/1998) • **86**
Vino Nobile di Montepulciano Riserva 1994: Modern style with berry, mineral and new wood character. Medium-bodied, with well-integrated tannins and a fine finish. Drink now.–J.S. • $25 • (12/15/1998) • **88**
Vino Nobile di Montepulciano Riserva 1985 • $22 • (11/30/1989) • **86**
Vino Nobile di Montepulciano Salarco Riserva 1995: Very ripe berry character, with a good amount of barnyard. Medium-bodied and soft, with round tannins and an earthy, fruity aftertaste. Drink now.–J.S. • $25 • (11/30/1999) • **85**
Vino Nobile di Montepulciano Salarco Riserva 1991 • $16 • (9/30/1997) • **84**

FATTOI

Brunello di Montalcino 1995: A wine with plenty of ripe fruit and a fresh mushroom and chestnut aroma. Medium-bodied, with dried cherry character and a medium finish. A bit one dimensional. Drink now through 2004.–J.S. • $60 • (6/30/2000) • **83**
Brunello di Montalcino 1994: Aromas of wood and fruit follow through to the palate. Medium-bodied, with pleasant fruit and fine tannins, but slightly diluted in the midpalate. A nice early-drinking wine. Drink now.–J.S. • $50 • (8/31/1999) • **84**
Brunello di Montalcino 1993: Medium-bodied, with lovely cherry and plum aromas, fine tannins and a fruity, fresh finish. A typical, well-crafted '93 that's a joy to drink now.–J.S. • $48 • (12/15/1998) • **88**
Brunello di Montalcino 1992 • $45 • (9/30/1997) • **84**
Rosso di Montalcino 1997: Vivid and clean, with berry, cherry and plum character. Medium-bodied, with firm and silky tannins and a long and fruity finish. Almost outstanding. Drink now through 2002.–J.S. • $27 • (9/15/1999) • **89**
Rosso di Montalcino 1996: Delicious. Perfumed berry and dried cherry aromas, with hints of violet. Medium-bodied, with lovely berry flavors and a zingy, fresh finish. Drink now.–J.S. • $21 • (12/15/1998) • **86**
Rosso di Montalcino 1995 • $21 • (9/30/1997) • **85**

FATTORI & GRANEY

Soave Classico Superiore 1998: Pretty aromas of flowers, lemon and cream. Medium-bodied, with lovely fresh fruit and a medium, clean, fresh finish. Drink now.–J.S. • $NA • (1/01/2000) • **85**

FELLUGA, LIVIO

Chardonnay Venezie Esperto 1996: Bright and lively, with a firm structure, this white's character leans toward spice and licorice.–B.S. • $12 • (9/30/1998) • **82**
Merlot Colli Orientali del Friuli 1995 • $23 • (6/15/1998) • **84**
Merlot Colli Orientali del Friuli 1993 • $17 • (2/29/1996) • **85**
Merlot Collio 1988 • $16 • (7/15/1991) • **84**
Merlot Venezie Esperto 1995 • $14 • (12/15/1997) • **83**
Pinot Grigio Colli Orientali del Friuli 1996 • $19 • (5/31/1998) • **84**
Pinot Grigio Venezie Esperto 1996 • $14 • (12/15/1997) • **83**
Tocai Friulano Colli Orientali del Friuli 1996: Delightful, combining floral and almond flavors with freshness and elegance. Perfect as an aperitif. Drink now.–B.S. • $19 • (7/31/1998) • **85**

FELLUGA, MARCO

Carantan 1993 • $27 • (6/30/1998) • **88**
Carantan 1990 • $20 • (6/15/1996) • **78**
Carantan 1988 • $36 • (4/30/1992) • **88**
Chardonnay Collio 1998: A Chardonnay with plenty of apple, mineral and honey character. Medium-bodied, with fresh acidity and a long, long finish. Drink now.–J.S. • $13 • (2/29/2000) • **87**
Friuli-Venezia Giulia Carantan 1995: A captivating young wine with all the style of a serious Médoc red. Fabulous aromas and flavors of cassis, mint and rose. Full-bodied, with very well-integrated tannins and a long, caressing finish. Cabernet Sauvignon and Merlot.–J.S. • $28 • (6/30/1999) • **90**
Merlot Collio 1993 • $11 • (6/15/1996) • **82**
Molamatta 1996 • $16 • (6/30/1998) • **84**
Pinot Bianco Collio 1998: Lovely intensity of apple, mineral and melon character. Medium-bodied, with good acidity and a long finish. A joy to taste. Drink now.–J.S. • $13 • (2/29/2000) • **88**
Pinot Grigio Collio 1998: Subtle aromas of apple, mineral and blanched almonds. Medium-bodied, with fine acidity and a long, clean finish. Delicious. Drink now.–J.S. • $13 • (2/29/2000) • **86**
Tocai Friulano Collio 1998: Interesting aromas and flavors of ash, honey and appleskin. Medium-bodied, with fresh acidity and a long, ripe fruit finish. Slightly dull. Drink now.–J.S. • $13 • (3/31/2000) • **84**
Venezia Giulia Molamatta 1998: Extremely crisp and clean, with aromas and flavors of honey and tropical fruit. Medium-bodied. Fresh finish. Tocai Friulano and Ribolla Gialla. Drink now.–J.S. • $14 • (1/01/2000) • **87**

FELSINA, FATTORIA DI

Berardenga Maestro Raro 1994: A rather rich and decadent Port-like Cabernet, with very ripe plum, earth, and cheese aromas and flavors. Full-bodied, with velvety tannins and a long, gamy finish. Fat and soft. Drink now.–J.S. • $50 • (11/30/1999) • **87**
Berardenga Maestro Raro 1993: An unctuous, rich Cabernet Sauvignon. Blackberry and plenty of milk chocolate character. Medium-bodied, with soft tannins and a smooth texture on the finish. Drink now through 2001.–J.S. • $40 • (12/15/1998) • **89**
Berardenga Maestro Raro 1989 • $38 • (10/31/1993) • **83**
Berardenga Maestro Raro 1988 • $38 • (10/31/1993) • **91**
Chardonnay Toscana Berardenga I Sistri 1997: A very interesting white for Tuscany, with complex yet reserved aromas of pineapple, mango and vanilla. Medium- to full-bodied, with a good dose of new wood and a long, fruity finish. Drink now through 2001.–J.S. • $27 • (11/30/1999) • **90**
Chardonnay Toscana Berardenga I Sistri 1996: Harmonious Chardonnay with just the right amount of toasted oak to balance the ripe fruit flavors. Medium-bodied, with moderate acidity and a long aftertaste of vanilla, apple and tropical fruit. Drink now.–J.S. • $23 • (12/15/1998) • **89**
Chianti Classico Berardenga 1997: Just as expected from Felsina: a superb Chianti Classico, displaying lots of cherry, berry and wet earth character.

ITALY

The wine is medium-bodied, with medium, silky tannins and a long, flavorful finish. Drink now through 2001.–J.S. • $22 • (11/30/1999) SS • **91**

Chianti Classico Berardenga 1996: A delicious Chianti, with lovely blackberry and cherry aromas and flavors. Medium-bodied, with soft tannins and a fruity aftertaste. Lovely texture. Drink now.–J.S. • $17 • (12/15/1998) • **88**

Chianti Classico Berardenga 1995 • $18 • (9/30/1997) • **88**

Chianti Classico Berardenga 1994 • $14 • (10/31/1996) • **88**

Chianti Classico Berardenga 1992 • $12 • (2/28/1995) • **84**

Chianti Classico Berardenga 1990 • $12 • (9/15/1992) • **91**

Chianti Classico Berardenga 1988 • $13 • (9/15/1991) • **89**

Chianti Classico Berardenga Rancia Riserva 1995: Very well made, from one of the Chianti's best vineyards. Loads of plum and roses on the nose. Medium- to full-bodied, with well-integrated yet chewy tannins and a caressing, silky texture. Another winner from Felsina. Best after 2000.–J.S. • $32 • (12/15/1998) • **90**

Chianti Classico Berardenga Rancia Riserva 1994 • $35 • (9/30/1997) • **92**

Chianti Classico Berardenga Rancia Riserva 1993 • $28 • (10/31/1996) • **89**

Chianti Classico Berardenga Rancia Riserva 1993 • $33 • (9/30/1997) • **92**

Chianti Classico Berardenga Rancia Riserva 1990 • $28 • (2/28/1995) SS • **93**

Chianti Classico Berardenga Rancia Riserva 1990 • $NA • (9/30/1997) • **88**

Chianti Classico Berardenga Rancia Riserva 1988 • $NA • (9/30/1997) • **90**

Chianti Classico Berardenga Rancia Riserva 1985 • $NA • (9/30/1997) • **87**

Chianti Classico Berardenga Rancia Riserva 1983 • $17 • (12/15/1988) • **91**

Chianti Classico Berardenga Riserva 1994 • $23 • (9/30/1997) • **90**

Chianti Classico Berardenga Riserva 1993 • $NA • (1/31/1996) • **87**

Chianti Classico Berardenga Riserva 1990 • $18 • (2/28/1995) • **90**

Chianti Classico Berardenga Riserva 1988 • $17 • (9/15/1992) • **92**

Chianti Classico Berardenga Riserva 1985 • $15 • (9/15/1991) • **86**

Chianti Classico Berardenga Riserva 1983 • $12 • (11/30/1989) • **87**

Toscana Fontalloro 1995: Fresh and chunky red. Well-structured and balanced. A bounty of dark chocolate and ripe cherries on the nose and palate. Medium- to full-bodied, with soft, silky tannins and a long, clean fruit finish. Drink now through 2004.–J.S. • $NA • (11/30/1999) • **90**

Toscana Fontalloro 1994: A strong and very tannic young wine, showing ripe berry with hints of smoke and mocha. Medium-bodied, with chewy tannins and a long finish. Drink now.–J.S. • $44 • (12/15/1998) • **89**

Toscana Fontalloro 1993 • $40 • (9/30/1997) • **90**

Toscana Fontalloro 1990 • $38 • (2/28/1995) • **91**

Toscana Fontalloro 1988 • $NA • (11/15/1993) • **93**

Toscana Fontalloro 1986 • $NA • (11/15/1993) • **89**

Toscana Fontalloro 1985 • $24 • (9/15/1988) • **91**

Toscana Fontalloro 1983 • $NA • (11/15/1993) • **88**

Toscana Fontalloro 1982 • $NA • (11/15/1993) • **92**

FENOCCHIO, RICCARDO

Barolo Pianpolvere Soprano 1991 • $32 • (10/31/1995) • **84**

Barolo Pianpolvere Soprano 1990 • $40 • (10/31/1995) • **79**

Barolo Pianpolvere Soprano 1988 • $30 • (10/31/1993) • **80**

Barolo Pianpolvere Soprano 1982 • $26 • (7/31/1989) • **74**

Dolcetto d'Alba Pianpolvere Soprano 1993 • $14 • (10/31/1995) • **80**

FERRARI

Brut Rosé Trento NV • $20 • (1/31/1997) • **83**

Brut Trento NV • $19 • (1/31/1997) • **80**

FERRARIS, ROBERTO

Barbera d'Asti Nobbio 1997: Great intensity in this sweet- and ripe-tasting, voluptuous, full-bodied Barbera. With its plum, vanilla, blackberry and grilled game character, it's seductive through to the smoky, spicy, slightly hot finish. Try with barbecued chicken and hot sauce. Drink now through 2003.–P.M. • $16 • (11/15/1999) • **93**

Key: SS—Spectator Selection. CS—Cellar Selection. HR—Highly Recommended. $NA—Price not available. (BT)—Barrel tasting. (A)—Auction Price. For a key to the tasters' initials, see "How to Use These Listings."
Dates in parentheses represent the issues in which the ratings were published.

FEUDI DI SAN GREGORIO

Aglianico d'Irpinia Rubrato 1997: Shows plenty of crushed cherries and berries on the nose, with a hint of dusty earth. Medium-bodied, with light tannins and a fruity, lightly spicy aftertaste. Drink now.–J.S. • $15 • (1/31/2000) • **86**

Albente 1998: Shows amazing aromas of peaches and honey, with hints of mineral. Full- to medium-bodied, with intense flavors and a long, long finish. Give it some time to develop.–J.S. • $11 • (1/31/2000) • **91**

Falanghina del Sannio Beneventano 1998: Very pretty. Loads of mineral, honey and honeysuckle. Medium-bodied, with crisp acidity and a long aftertaste of mineral and citrus. Drink now.–J.S. • $15 • (1/31/2000) • **88**

Fiano di Avellino 1998: A bit fat and oily, but loaded with cream, honey, apple and tropical fruit character. Full-bodied, round and rich, with a concentrated fruit finish. Drink now.–J.S. • $20 • (1/31/2000) • **88**

Fiano di Avellino Pietracalda Vendemmia Tardiva 1998: A big and powerful late-harvest wine, dry and ready to go with food. Full-bodied, with loads of almond, honey and honeydew melon. Long and spicy in the mouth. Like a top Pinot Gris late-harvest from Alsace. Drink now through 2005. –J.S. • $30 • (1/31/2000) • **91**

Greco di Tufo 1998: Zingy and fresh, like a beautiful Riesling. Piecrust and lemon character throughout, with medium body and a crisp finish. Drink now.–J.S. • $18 • (1/31/2000) • **88**

Greco di Tufo Cutizzi 1997: Big, ripe and showy wine, with melon, honey and cream aromas and flavors. Full-bodied, with similar character on the palate. Bit fat. Long finish.–J.S. • $18 • (1/31/2000) • **89**

Greco di Tufo Cutizzi Vendemmia Tardiva 1998: Gushing with fresh melon, pear and honey character. Medium-bodied, lightly sweet, with a piecrust, apple and cream aftertaste. A lovely, light sweet wine; more for sipping on its own than for drinking with dessert. Drink now.–J.S. • $23 • (1/31/2000) • **88**

Irpinia Campanaro 1998: Big, thick, rich and powerful, with loads of pineapple and hints of vanilla. Full-bodied, dry, with a long, oily and superfruity finish. A rather extreme, ripe style, but delicious. Drink now.–J.S. • $33 • (1/31/2000) • **89**

Irpinia Campanaro 1997: A bit clumsy and fat, but very interesting just the same. Full-bodied, with lots of vanilla, oak and apple character and hints of mineral. Drink now.–J.S. • $34 • (1/01/2000) • **86**

Irpinia Privilegio 1997: A classy, moreish, sweet wine. Gorgeous cream, apple, honey and apricot aromas. Full-bodied, sweet and fresh, with a long, creamy, tropical fruit aftertaste. Drink now through 2005.–J.S. • $50/500 ml. • (1/31/2000) • **92**

Irpinia Serpico 1997: A decadent, flamboyant, glorious red from southern Italy. Appealing aromas of plums, cumin and other spices lead to a full-bodied wine, with smoke, berry and spice flavors and a medium tannin structure. Caressing texture. Best after 2000.–J.S. • $49 • (1/31/2000) HR • **92**

Irpinia Serpico 1996: A big, well-structured red for aging. An abundance of berry, olive and herbal aromas, with hints of spices. Full-bodied, with loads of velvety tannins and a long, long, fruity finish. Best after 2001.–J.S. • $57 • (1/01/2000) • **91**

Irpinia Syriacus 1997: This wine takes no prisoners. Rhône Rangers celebrate. A big and ripe wine with masses of raisin, spice, tobacco and grilled meat character. Full-bodied, with tons of extract, tannin and fruit. Not to mention the alcohol. Give this baby time. Not imported into the U.S. Best after 2002.–J.S. • $NA • (1/31/2000) • **95**

Taurasi 1995: Lovely aromas of ripe blackberries and subtle spices. Medium-bodied, with velvety tannins and a long, smoky, fruity finish. Drink now through 2003.–J.S. • $35 • (1/31/2000) • **88**

Taurasi 1991 • $26 • (1/31/1996) • **88**

Taurasi Piano di Montevergine 1995: A brutish red that grabs your attention. Very ripe and powerful, with plum, raisin, grilled meat and spices. Full-bodied, with chewy tannins and a long, long finish. Best after 2000.–J.S. • $48 • (1/31/2000) • **90**

FIANO, FATTORIA DI

Chianti Ugo Bing 1996: A delicious, simple Chianti, with wonderful ripe raspberry and plum aromas. Medium-bodied, with chunky fruit structure and a long chocolate and berry aftertase. Not imported into the U.S. Drink now.–J.S. • $NA • (1/01/1999) • **85**

FILIGARE, LE

Chianti Classico 1997: Pretty fresh plum and dried cherry character. Medium-bodied, with light tannins and a fresh, fruity finish. Lovely, refreshing acidity. Drink now.–J.S. • $18 • (11/30/1999) • **88**

Chianti Classico 1990 • $NA • (10/31/1993) • **88**

Chianti Classico 1988 • $NA • (9/15/1991) • **91**
Chianti Classico Riserva 1996: Medium-bodied, with blackberry and spice throughout, silky tannins and a medium, fruity finish. A bit more fruit concentration would be nice. Drink now through 2001.–J.S. • $28 • (11/30/1999) • **85**
Chianti Classico Riserva 1995: A sophisticated red with layers of blackberry, violet and smoke character. Medium-bodied, with very smooth tannins and a succulent finish. Drink through 2004.–J.S. • $27 • (12/15/1998) • **89**
Chianti Classico Riserva 1994 • $28 • (4/30/1998) • **88**
Chianti Classico Riserva 1988 • $18 • (9/15/1992) • **90**
Toscana Podere Le Rocce 1996: A delicious and caressing red, with interesting black currant and hints of wet earth. Medium-bodied, with well-integrated tannins and a fruity finish. Drink now through 2001.–J.S. • $38 • (11/30/1999) • **89**
Toscana Podere Le Rocce 1994 • $38 • (4/30/1998) • **88**
Toscana Podere Le Rocce 1990 • $NA • (10/31/1993) • **93**

FILIPUTTI, WALTER

Colli Orientali del Friuli Poiesis 1996 • $26 • (5/31/1998) • **83**
Pinot Grigio Venezia Giulia 1996 • $26 • (5/31/1998) • **79**
Ribolla Gialla Colli Orientali del Friuli 1996 • $26 • (5/31/1998) • **83**
Sauvignon Colli Orientali del Friuli 1996 • $26 • (6/15/1998) • **83**

FIORIAE, LE

Chianti Classico 1994 • $NA • (10/31/1996) • **76**
Chianti Classico 1992 • $NA • (2/28/1995) • **75**
Chianti Classico Riserva 1990 • $NA • (2/28/1995) • **80**

FIORINA, FRANCO

Barbaresco 1996: Very open and forward, ripe and plummy. Appealingly sweet-tasting, full-bodied and showing excellent grip of tannins, fruit and *terroir* without a distracting fancy oak character. Long, chewy, licoricelike finish. Drink now through 2010.–P.M. • $27 • (10/31/1999) • **89**
Barbaresco 1995: Accessible Barbaresco, with smooth tannins and straightforward red berry aromas and flavors, it has good acidity to balance and make it food-friendly. Drink now through 2002.–P.M. • $19 • (10/31/1998) • **84**
Barbera d 'Alba 1998: Fruity and a bit spritzy, with cherry, raspberry and strawberry character. Serve this straightforward, light-bodied, delicate red chilled at a picnic.–P.M. • $9 • (11/15/1999) • **79**
Barolo 1995: Forward and ready, with little grip but plum, chocolate and black cherry notes. Tastes a bit like jam, with the tannins clamping down on the finish. Drink now through 2003.–P.M. • $27 • (11/15/1999) • **85**
Barolo 1982 • $22 • (5/31/1988) • **79**
Dolcetto d 'Alba 1998: A bit rough and crisp, but there is modest fruit, with wet earth character.–P.M. • $9 • (11/15/1999) • **77**
Dolcetto d 'Alba 1997: Light and a bit diluted, showing modest strawberry and raspberry character, a short finish.–P.M. • $9 • (10/31/1998) • **75**
Dolcetto d 'Alba 1990 • $14 • (10/31/1992) • **83**
Dolcetto d 'Alba 1989 • $13 • (4/30/1991) • **83**
Freisa Langhe 1989 • $16 • (7/15/1991) • **78**

FIRESTEED

Barbera d 'Asti 1995 • $8 • (1/31/1998) • **79**

FIRRIATO

Catarratto-Chardonnay Sicilia Santagostino 1998: A pleasant, no-nonsense Chardonnay, with apple, pineapple and straw character. Medium-bodied, with good fruit and a light finish. Not imported into the U.S. Drink now.–J.S. • $NA • (1/01/2000) • **83**
Grillo-Chardonnay Sicilia Altavilla della Corte 1998: Delicious, with apple, mineral and straw character. Medium-bodied, with hints of apricot and a fresh fruit aftertaste. Drink now.–J.S. • $12 • (5/31/2000) • **87**
Nero d 'Avola-Cabernet Sauvignon Sicilia Altavilla della Corte 1997: Interesting aromas of dark chocolate and strawberry. Medium-bodied, with firm tannins and a medium finish. A bit lean but well done. Best after 2000.–J.S. • $12 • (5/31/2000) • **86**
Nero d 'Avola-Syrah Sicilia Santagostino 1997: Lovely and soft, with berry, Merlot and chocolate character. Medium- to full-bodied, with round tannins and a long, fruity vanilla finish. Impressive. Not imported into the U.S. Drink now through 2003.–J.S. • $NA • (1/01/2000) • **87**

FOGNANO, FATTORIA DI

Chianti Colli Senesi Talosa 1988 • $8 • (11/30/1990) • **88**
Rosso di Montepulciano Talosa 1989 • $11 • (1/31/1992) • **79**
Vino Nobile di Montepulciano Talosa 1995: Good ripe fruit, but shows a little too much chestnut. Medium-bodied, with good acidity. Needs food.–J.S. • $16 • (12/15/1998) • **79**
Vino Nobile di Montepulciano Talosa 1994 • $13 • (9/30/1997) • **75**
Vino Nobile di Montepulciano Talosa Riserva 1993 • $17 • (9/30/1997) • **84**
Vino Nobile di Montepulciano Talosa Riserva 1988 • $16 • (7/31/1994) • **84**
Vino Nobile di Montepulciano Talosa Riserva 1986 • $15 • (7/15/1991) • **84**

FOLONARI

Merlot delle Venezie 1996: Aromas and flavors express the herbal, minty side of this grape. Finishes with astringency. Drink now.–B.S. • $7 • (7/31/1998) • **77**
Merlot-Sangiovese Veneto 1997 • $7 • (6/15/1998) • **83**
Pinot Grigio delle Venezie 1997 • $7 • (6/15/1998) • **79**
Pinot Grigio-Chardonnay delle Venezie 1997 • $7 • (6/30/1998) • **84**
Rosso del Salento 1995: Extremely flawed. Has maderized, medicinal, cooked celery flavors. Tasted twice, with consistent notes. • $6 • (9/30/1998) • **58**
Valpolicella NV: A light red wine with appealing cherry flavors and nice spicy notes on the finish. Drink now.–K.M. • $9/1.5 liter • (7/31/1998) • **80**

FONTANA CANDIDA

Frascati Superiore 1996 • $6 • (10/15/1997) • **78**
Merlot 1994 • $8 • (1/31/1996) • **83**
Merlot Venezie 1997: Light- to medium-bodied, with alluring plum and berry character, fresh acidity and a fruity finish. Drink now.–J.S. • $8 • (1/01/2000) • **81**
Pinot Grigio Venezie 1996 • $8 • (12/15/1997) • **85**
Villa Fontana 1993 • $6 • (5/31/1995) • **82**

FONTANABIANCA

Barbaresco Sorì Burdin 1996: A masterful opus. This full-bodied, ripe, harmonious piece of art tastes as if it comes from the old school even though it aged in small oak barrels. Plays full string on the most adorable, sweet-tasting fruit and baby-fat tannins. Even better than when tasted from barrel last year. Drink now through 2015.–P.M. • $45 • (8/31/1999) • **95**
Barbaresco Sorì Burdin 1995: Exotic, with ginger, violet, rose petal, mint—you name it. This racy Nebbiolo shows lots of pure floral, plum and blackberry character supported by spice notes. Medium-bodied and ripe, with a firm, classy structure. Tannins clamp down on the finish. Best from 2003 through 2007.–P.M. • $34 • (9/15/1998) • **90**
Barbaresco Sorì Burdin 1993 • $30 • (10/31/1997) • **85**
Barbera d 'Alba 1996: Racy, dark as ink, this shows clean, pure, laser-sharp berry notes along with wet earth, allowing the fruit to express itself. Medium-bodied, with a long, succulent finish. Drink now through 2003.–P.M. • $15 • (10/31/1998) • **88**
Chardonnay Langhe 1997: Shows honey and butter, with a round quality on the midpalate, but it turns a bit dull on the uninteresting finish. Drink now.–P.M. • $13 • (10/31/1998) • **79**
Dolcetto d 'Alba Vigneto Bordini 1998: Clean and balanced in a light, fruity way, showing coarse tannins but also pure fruit. A good effort at harmony in a Dolcetto. Drink now.–P.M. • $15 • (11/15/1999) • **83**
Dolcetto d 'Alba Vigneto Bordini 1997: Intriguing, with some smoke, licorice and spice notes, it fills the palate with ripe tannins and fair blackberry, black cherry concentration. Balanced finish.–P.M. • $14 • (10/31/1998) • **84**
Dolcetto d 'Alba Vigneto Bordini 1996 • $14 • (10/31/1997) • **84**

FONTANAFREDDA

Asti Dolce NV • $11 • (5/31/1997) • **79**
Barbaresco 1995: Light but supple, with raspberry and strawberry, it also has a pronounced mushroom element that leads to a drying midpalate and finish.–P.M. • $22 • (10/31/1998) • **73**
Barbaresco 1989 • $18 • (10/31/1994) • **79**
Barbaresco 1988 • $12 • (10/31/1993) • **75**
Barbaresco 1983 • $12 • (9/15/1988) • **80**
Barbaresco 1982 • $NA • (9/15/1988) • **81**
Barbaresco 1978 • $NA • (9/15/1988) • **86**

FONTANAFREDDA

Barbaresco Coste Rubin 1995: Smooth and elegant. A light-style Barbaresco that tastes of cherry, raspberry and strawberry, then turns a bit astringent from the tough tannins on the finish.–P.M. • $24 • (10/31/1998) • **78**
Barbera d 'Alba 1994 • $11 • (10/31/1996) • **74**
Barbera d 'Alba 1993 • $11 • (10/31/1995) • **79**
Barbera d 'Alba 1990 • $10 • (7/31/1995) • **83**
Barbera d 'Alba Raimonda 1996: One of Fontanafredda 's best wines in years. Full-bodied, with ripe tannins and rich fruit, some mineral, smoky, black fruit character. Quite impressive, with a long, silky finish. Drink now. –P.M. • $15 • (10/31/1998) • **86**
Barbera d 'Alba Raimonda 1995 • $14 • (10/31/1997) • **77**
Barbera d 'Alba Raimonda 1990 • $9 • (11/15/1993) • **78**
Barolo 1992 • $21 • (10/31/1996) • **74**
Barolo 1990 • $16 • (10/31/1994) • **89**
Barolo 1989 • $16 • (10/31/1994) • **84**
Barolo 1988 • $13 • (10/31/1993) • **85**
Barolo 1983 • $16 • (9/15/1988) • **83**
Barolo 1982 • $16 • (9/15/1988) • **84**
Barolo 1978 • $13 • (2/16/1984) • **80**
Barolo di Serralunga d 'Alba 1992 • $29 • (10/31/1996) • **82**
Barolo di Serralunga d 'Alba 1990 • $20 • (10/31/1995) • **86**
Barolo di Serralunga d 'Alba 1989 • $20 • (10/31/1994) • **89**
Barolo di Serralunga d 'Alba 1988 • $17 • (10/31/1993) • **85**
Barolo Galarey 1993 • $27 • (10/31/1997) • **76**
Barolo San Pietro 1982 • $42 • (9/15/1988) • **85**
Barolo Serralunga d'Alba 1993 • $33 • (10/31/1997) • **77**
Barolo Vigna Gattinera 1990 • $39 • (10/31/1995) • **81**
Barolo Vigna Gattinera 1989 • $NA • (10/31/1994) • **67**
Barolo Vigna La Delizia 1993: Smells a bit herbal, but picks up some plum on the palate before returning to a green olive, asparagus sort of character.–P.M. • $56 • (10/31/1998) • **72**
Barolo Vigna La Delizia 1989 • $39 • (10/31/1994) • **90**
Barolo Vigna La Rosa 1993: A bit odd, with some funky, earthy aromas and flavors, tasting a bit herbal. Astringent finish.–P.M. • $60 • (10/31/1998) • **70**
Barolo Vigna La Rosa 1989 • $39 • (10/31/1994) • **81**
Barolo Vigna La Rosa 1982 • $40 • (2/15/1988) CS • **90**
Barolo Vigna La Villa 1989 • $39 • (10/31/1994) • **91**
Barolo Vigna La Villa Paiagallo 1993: Traditional, mature Barolo. Delivers some good character, with chestnut, underbrush, mushroom and wet earth character, also nice ripe fruit and notes of vanilla and spice. Has firm grip on the palate, balanced finish. Drink now through 2005.–P.M. • $NA • (10/31/1998) • **85**
Barolo Vigna La Villa Paiagallo 1990 • $39 • (10/31/1995) • **85**
Barolo Vigna La Villa Paiagallo 1989 • $NA • (10/31/1993) • **85**
Barolo Vigna Lazzarito 1993: Mature, with mushroom, underbrush notes, and slightly oxidized, but shows also some plum and blackberry character. A bit astringent on the finish. Drink now.–P.M. • $60 • (10/31/1998) • **79**
Barolo Vigna Lazzarito 1990 • $39 • (10/31/1995) • **87**
Barolo Vigna Lazzarito 1982 • $42 • (9/15/1988) • **90**
Diano d'Alba Vigna La Lepre 1997: There 's a spicy, bitter black-chocolate undertow to the cranberry notes in this fairly tart red. Not imported into the U.S.–P.M. • $NA • (10/31/1998) • **79**
Dolcetto d'Alba 1995 • $12 • (10/31/1996) • **77**
Dolcetto d'Alba 1993 • $11 • (10/31/1995) • **80**
Dolcetto d'Alba di Treiso 1997: Fairly straightforward, with decent red berry flavors, turning a bit tannic on the light-bodied finish. Drink now.–P.M. • $15 • (10/31/1998) • **78**
Dolcetto d'Alba di Treiso 1996 • $13 • (10/31/1997) • **82**
Dolcetto d'Alba di Treiso 1995 • $13 • (10/31/1996) • **76**
Dolcetto d'Alba di Treiso 1993 • $NA • (10/31/1995) • **84**
Dolcetto d'Alba di Treiso 1992 • $12 • (6/15/1994) • **86**

FONTERUTOLI, CASTELLO DI

Brancaia 1994 • $35 • (9/30/1997) • **87**
Brancaia 1990 • $24 • (10/31/1993) • **91**
Chianti Classico 1995 • $17 • (9/30/1997) • **85**
Chianti Classico 1994 • $13 • (10/31/1996) • **85**
Chianti Classico 1993 • $13 • (10/31/1995) • **81**
Chianti Classico 1992 • $13 • (2/28/1995) • **85**

Key: SS—Spectator Selection. CS—Cellar Selection. HR—Highly Recommended. $NA—Price not available. (BT)—Barrel tasting. Ⓐ—Auction Price. For a key to the tasters' initials, see "How to Use These Listings."
Dates in parentheses represent the issues in which the ratings were published.

Chianti Classico 1991 • $13 • (10/31/1993) • **88**
Chianti Classico 1990 • $13 • (9/15/1992) • **89**
Chianti Classico 1988 • $14 • (11/30/1990) • **85**
Chianti Classico 1987 • $11 • (11/30/1989) • **90**
Chianti Classico 1986 • $11 • (1/31/1989) • **85**
Chianti Classico 1985 • $11 • (11/30/1989) • **88**
Chianti Classico Ser Lapo Riserva 1995 • $NA • (1/01/1997) • **89**
Chianti Classico Ser Lapo Riserva 1994 • $17 Ⓐ • (9/30/1997) • **89**
Chianti Classico Ser Lapo Riserva 1993 • $31 • (10/31/1996) • **87**
Chianti Classico Ser Lapo Riserva 1991 • $25 • (10/31/1995) • **84**
Chianti Classico Ser Lapo Riserva 1990 • $26 • (2/28/1995) • **86**
Chianti Classico Ser Lapo Riserva 1988 • $20 • (9/15/1992) • **90**
Chianti Classico Ser Lapo Riserva 1986 • $25 • (11/30/1990) • **88**
Chianti Classico Ser Lapo Riserva 1985 • $18 • (9/15/1991) • **87**
Chianti Classico Ser Lapo Riserva 1983 • $15 • (1/31/1989) • **88**
Concerto 1994 • $40 • (9/30/1997) • **86**
Concerto 1993 • $38 • (10/31/1996) • **88**
Concerto 1991 • $30 • (10/31/1995) • **88**
Concerto 1990 • $27 • (10/31/1993) • **88**
Concerto 1986 • $35 • (3/15/1991) • **87**
Concerto 1985 • $25 • (2/15/1989) • **84**
Concerto 1983 • $15 • (11/30/1989) • **86**
Siepi 1995 • $50 • (9/30/1997) • **88**
Siepi 1994 • $47 • (10/31/1996) • **81**
Siepi 1993 • $30 • (10/31/1995) • **94**
Siepi 1992 • $30 • (10/31/1995) • **90**
Toscana Badiola 1996 • $14 • (4/30/1998) • **88**
Toscana Badiola 1994 • $NA • (10/31/1996) • **80**

FONTEVINO

Brunello di Montalcino Villa dei Lecchi 1992 • $21 • (9/30/1997) • **86**
Brunello di Montalcino Villa dei Lecchi 1991 • $NA • (11/30/1996) • **79**
Brunello di Montalcino Villa dei Lecchi 1990 • $NA • (10/31/1995) • **83**
Brunello di Montalcino Villa dei Lecchi Riserva 1991 • $24 • (9/30/1997) • **79**
Brunello di Montalcino Villa dei Lecchi Riserva 1990 • $NA • (11/30/1996) • **83**
Brunello di Montalcino Villa dei Lecchi Riserva 1988 • $NA • (10/31/1994) • **79**
Rosso di Montalcino Villa dei Lecchi 1995 • $18 • (9/30/1997) • **85**
Rosso di Montalcino Villa dei Lecchi 1994 • $NA • (11/30/1996) • **79**
Rosso di Montalcino Villa dei Lecchi 1993 • $NA • (10/31/1995) • **85**
Villa dei Lecchi Vigna di Bellaria 1993 • $NA • (10/31/1996) • **84**

FONTI, FATTORIA LE

Chianti Classico 1996: Plum and mushroom aromas, with hints of horse hair. Medium-bodied, rather astringent, with a diluted, slightly raisiny finish. Too rustic for me.–J.S. • $15 • (12/15/1998) • **77**
Chianti Classico 1995 • $14 • (10/31/1997) • **86**
Chianti Classico Riserva 1995: Sleek and racy, with berry and dried cherry aromas and flavors, fine tannins. Finishes moderately. Great complement to meats. Drink now.–J.S. • $22 • (12/15/1998) • **86**
Toscana Vito Arturo 1995: A beautifully aromatic Sangiovese, with ripe berry and raspberry character. Medium-bodied, with medium, velvety tannins and a fresh finish. Drink now.–J.S. • $28 • (12/15/1998) • **86**

FONTODI

Chianti Classico 1997: The best Chianti normale of the vintage. This fantastic wine emits terrific aromas of plum and blackberry, with hints of vanilla. It 's full-bodied and very chewy, with an ultralong finish. Drink now.–J.S. • $23 • (11/30/1999) SS • **92**
Chianti Classico 1996: The way a young Chianti should be. Bright and beautiful aromas of crushed raspberry and cherry. Medium-bodied, with soft, fine tannins and a long, sweet berry aftertaste. Not for aging, but for serious imbibing. Enjoy. Drink now.–J.S. • $18 • (12/15/1998) • **89**
Chianti Classico 1995 • $18 • (9/30/1997) • **88**
Chianti Classico 1994 • $15 • (10/31/1996) • **88**
Chianti Classico 1993 • $12 • (10/31/1995) • **86**
Chianti Classico 1992 • $13 • (2/28/1995) • **85**
Chianti Classico 1991 • $12 • (10/31/1993) • **87**
Chianti Classico 1990 • $16 • (9/15/1992) • **87**
Chianti Classico 1989 • $13 • (11/30/1991) • **89**
Chianti Classico 1988 • $13 • (9/15/1991) SS • **91**
Chianti Classico Riserva 1996: Pretty, with a plum, tobacco and raspberry character that follows through to the palate. Medium-bodied, with velvety

tannins and a fruity, plummy finish that 's slightly short. Drink now.–J.S. • $28 • (11/30/1999) • **87**

Chianti Classico Riserva 1995: Everything 's in the right place. Beautiful aromas of crushed plums and meat. Medium-bodied, with firm tannins and a long, silky-textured finish. Drink now.–J.S. • $28 • (12/15/1998) • **90**

Chianti Classico Riserva 1994 • $23 • (9/30/1997) • **88**

Chianti Classico Riserva 1993 • $19 • (10/31/1996) • **89**

Chianti Classico Riserva 1991 • $18 • (10/31/1995) • **90**

Chianti Classico Riserva 1990 • $20 • (2/28/1995) • **89**

Chianti Classico Riserva 1988 • $18 • (10/31/1993) • **89**

Chianti Classico Riserva 1985 • $16 • (9/15/1991) • **93**

Chianti Classico Vigna del Sorbo Riserva 1995: A well-structured red built for aging, with plenty of ripe berry and spice aromas and flavors. Medium- to full-bodied, with silky tannins and a fresh aftertaste. Drink now.–J.S. • $42 • (12/15/1998) • **90**

Chianti Classico Vigna del Sorbo Riserva 1994 • $30 • (9/30/1997) • **90**

Chianti Classico Vigna del Sorbo Riserva 1994 • $30 • (9/30/1997) • **90**

Chianti Classico Vigna del Sorbo Riserva 1993 • $28 • (10/31/1996) • **90**

Chianti Classico Vigna del Sorbo Riserva 1993 • $28 • (9/30/1997) • **90**

Chianti Classico Vigna del Sorbo Riserva 1990 • $27 • (2/28/1995) • **91**

Chianti Classico Vigna del Sorbo Riserva 1990 • $NA • (9/30/1997) • **89**

Chianti Classico Vigna del Sorbo Riserva 1988 • $28 • (10/31/1993) HR • **92**

Chianti Classico Vigna del Sorbo Riserva 1988 • $NA • (9/30/1997) • **90**

Chianti Classico Vigna del Sorbo Riserva 1985 • $NA • (9/30/1997) • **86**

Colli della Toscana Centrale Flaccianello 1996: All class and elegance. Bright aromas of blackberry, currant and red forest fruit. Medium- to full-bodied, with silky tannins and a long, enjoyable finish. Drink now.–J.S. • $50 • (11/30/1999) • **90**

Colli della Toscana Centrale Flaccianello 1995: Built for aging. Extremely well made, with concentrated aromas of dried berry, fruit and spices. Full-bodied, with full tannins which are wonderfully fine-tuned and well-integrated. Long, long fruity finish. Best after 2000.–J.S. • $50 • (12/15/1998) • **92**

Colli della Toscana Centrale Flaccianello 1994 • $46 Ⓐ • (9/30/1997) • **88**

Colli della Toscana Centrale Flaccianello 1993 • $35 • (10/31/1996) • **89**

Colli della Toscana Centrale Flaccianello 1991 • $32 • (2/28/1995) • **90**

Colli della Toscana Centrale Flaccianello 1990 • $NA • (11/15/1993) • **90**

Colli della Toscana Centrale Flaccianello 1988 • $NA • (11/15/1993) • **92**

Colli della Toscana Centrale Flaccianello 1987 • $NA • (11/15/1993) • **88**

Colli della Toscana Centrale Flaccianello 1986 • $NA • (11/15/1993) • **90**

Colli della Toscana Centrale Flaccianello 1985 • $NA • (11/15/1993) • **90**

Colli della Toscana Centrale Flaccianello 1983 • $NA • (11/15/1993) • **83**

Colli della Toscana Centrale Flaccianello 1982 • $NA • (11/15/1993) • **85**

Pinot Nero Colli della Toscana Centrale Case Via 1997: Incredibly raisiny, verging on burnt, with tobacco and game flavors. Medium-bodied. Overripe and overdone.–J.S. • $38 • (11/30/1999) • **79**

Pinot Nero Colli della Toscana Centrale Case Via 1996: Very good fruit concentration here, although I wouldn't say it's very Pinot Nero-like; more like Gamay. Intense aromas of dried cherry, blackberry and grape. Medium-bodied, with fine tannins and a fresh and fruity aftertaste. Drink now.–J.S. • $NA • (12/15/1998) • **86**

Pinot Nero Colli della Toscana Centrale Case Via 1995 • $32 •(9/30/1997) • **87**

Pinot Nero Colli della Toscana Centrale Case Via 1994 • $40 • (10/31/1996) • **87**

Pinot Nero Colli della Toscana Centrale Case Via 1993 • $35 • (10/31/1995) • **87**

Pinot Nero Colli della Toscana Centrale Case Via 1992 • $30 • (2/28/1995) • **83**

Pinot Nero Colli della Toscana Centrale Case Via 1990 • $35 • (10/31/1993) • **88**

Syrah Colli della Toscana Centrale Case Via 1996: Dark, brilliant ruby color. Extremely fruity, with loads of blackberry and a hint of wet earth on the nose. Medium-bodied with medium, velvety tannins and a short finish. Slight dilution midpalate. Drink now.–J.S. • $44 • (11/30/1999) • **87**

Syrah Colli della Toscana Centrale Case Via 1995: Exciting Syrah. Very dark-purple, with a profusion of black pepper and very ripe fruit on the nose and palate. Full-bodied, with full but very soft tannins and a long, peppery aftertaste. Drink now.–J.S. • $40 • (12/15/1998) • **91**

Syrah Colli della Toscana Centrale Case Via 1994 • $38 • (9/30/1997) • **88**

Syrah Colli della Toscana Centrale Case Via 1993 • $35 • (10/31/1996) • **88**

Syrah Colli della Toscana Centrale Case Via 1992 • $NA • (10/31/1995) • **86**

Syrah Colli della Toscana Centrale Case Via 1991 • $30 • (2/28/1995) • **90**

Syrah Colli della Toscana Centrale Case Via 1990 • $28 • (10/31/1993) • **93**

FORADORI

Atesino Granato 1995 • $45 • (6/30/1998) • **87**

Atesino Karanar 1995 • $37 • (6/30/1998) • **87**

Granato 1996: A unique and challenging red, with an amazing inky color. Aromas of mint, berry and violet jump from the glass. Medium- to full-bodied, with polished, silky tannins and a medium berry and citric finish. Beautifully crafted. Drink now through 2005.–J.S. • $49 • (1/01/2000) • **91**

Granato di Mezzolombardo 1988 • $33 • (1/31/1992) • **86**

Pinot Bianco Trentino Sgarzon 1996 • $33 • (5/31/1998) • **83**

Teroldego Rotaliano 1997: A bit simple but delicious, with attractive aromas of plum, cherry and berry. Medium-bodied, with fresh fruit and fine tannins. Drink now.–J.S. • $20 • (6/15/2000) • **85**

Teroldego Rotaliano 1996 • $19 • (6/30/1998) • **86**

Teroldego Rotaliano Granato 1997: An unbelievably great red. Black in color, with amazing aromas of berry, cherry, tar and mint. Full-bodied and wonderfully polished, with a silky texture and an ultralong aftertaste. Best after 2004.–J.S. • $50 • (6/15/2000) • **95**

Teroldego Rotaliano Sgarzon 1994 • $33 • (6/30/1998) • **87**

Teroldego Rotaliano Vigneto Morel 1988 • $16 • (1/31/1992) • **69**

Vigneti delle Dolomiti Ailanpa 1997: Smell and enjoy the complex aromas of spearmint, berry and Indian spice. Medium-bodied, with well-integrated tannins and a medium finish. Syrah. Not imported into the U.S. Drink now through 2002.–J.S. • $NA • (6/15/2000) • **89**

Vigneti delle Dolomiti Karanar 1997: Pretty, with interesting aromas of mineral, berry, cherry and earth. Medium-bodied, with velvety tannins and a light, fruity fnish. Not imported into the U.S. Drink now.–J.S. • $NA • (1/01/2000) • **87**

Vigneti delle Dolomiti Karanar 1997: Pretty, with interesting aromas of mineral, berry, cherry and earth. Medium-bodied, with velvety tannins and a light, fruity fnish. Not imported into the U.S. Drink now.–J.S. • $NA • (1/01/2000) • **87**

Vigneti delle Dolomiti Myrto 1998: A lovely, stylish wine, with pretty aromas of toasted oak, grapefruit and melon. Medium-bodied, with good acidity and a long mineral and ripe fruit aftertaste. Drink now.–J.S. • $30 • (6/15/2000) • **87**

FORMENTINI, CONTI

Cabernet Franc Collio 1997: A good Cabernet Sauvignon with mint, berry and cherry character. Medium body. Fine tannins and a fruity finish. Best after 2000.–J.S. • $14 • (5/15/2000) • **87**

Cabernet Franc Collio 1994 • $13 • (5/31/1996) • **86**

Chardonnay Collio Torre di Tramontana 1997: Very well made, with apple and lightly toasted oak. Medium-bodied, with a hint of mineral on the nose and palate, good acidity and a long finish. Not imported into the U.S. Drink now through 2002.–J.S. • $NA • (1/01/2000) • **87**

Merlot Collio 1997: A Merlot with attractive berry, olive and herb character, medium body and light tannins. Short finish, though. Drink now.–J.S. • $14 • (5/15/2000) • **84**

Merlot Collio 1996 • $13 • (4/30/1998) • **75**

Merlot Collio Tajut 1997: A rich and powerful red with lots of velvety tannins, new wood and ripe fruit giving a coffee, cherry and toasted oak character. Full body. Long finish. More like Australia than Italy but outstanding quality. Drink now.–J.S. • $35 • (5/15/2000) • **90**

Pinot Grigio Collio 1998: Lots of focused mineral, pineapple and coconut character. Medium- to full-bodied, with good acidity and a long, fruity finish. Drink now through 2002.–J.S. • $14 • (3/31/2000) • **88**

FORNACE, LA

Brunello di Montalcino 1995: Well done. Enticing aromas of berries, red licorice and flowers. Medium- to full-bodied, with very firm tannins and lively acidity. A bit astringent and chewy at this stage. Needs time. Best after 2001.–J.S. • $45 • (6/30/2000) • **90**

Brunello di Montalcino 1994: Plenty of strawberry and earth aromas and flavors. Medium-bodied, with silky tannins and a short finish. Not imported into the U.S. Drink now.–J.S. • $NA • (1/01/1999) • **86**

Rosso di Montalcino 1997: Lovely blackberry, chocolate and plum aromas. Medium-bodied, with loads of fruit and superfine tannins. A beauty. Not imported into the U.S. Drink now.–J.S. • $NA • (1/01/1999) • **88**

FORNACINA

Brunello di Montalcino 1995: Very barnyardy with hints of V8 juice. Medium-bodied, with soft tannins. Better on the palate than the nose. Tasted twice, with consistent notes.–J.S. • $49 • (6/30/2000) • **78**

Brunello di Montalcino Riserva 1994: Lots of plum and smoke aromas follow through to a medium-bodied palate, with silky tannins and a light finish. Drink now.–J.S. • $69 • (6/30/2000) • **85**

ITALY

FORO

Chianti 1998: Not much to it, but it 's clean and fruity for a simple Chianti. Light finish. Drink now.–J.S. • $8 • (11/30/1999) • **80**

Chianti Classico 1997: A light and simple Chianti, with berry, tobacco and cedar character. Light- to medium-bodied, with an austere finish. Lacks fruit.–J.S. • $8 • (11/30/1999) • **79**

FORTUNA, LA

Brunello di Montalcino 1995: This is built for aging. Bright berry, tobacco and meat aromas in this 1995. Full-bodied and very tight, with silky tannins and a long, long finish. Super red. Best after 2002.–J.S. • $59 • (6/30/2000) • **92**

Brunello di Montalcino 1994: A good all around '94 Brunello with pleasant berry, mushroom and chocolate character. Medium-bodied, with medium to light tannins and a fruity finish. Slightly diluted center-palate. Not imported into the U.S. Drink now.–J.S. • $NA • (1/01/1999) • **85**

Brunello di Montalcino 1990 • $NA • (10/31/1995) • **84**

Brunello di Montalcino Riserva 1993: Alluring. Enticing aromas of new wood and ripe berries follow through to the palate. Full-bodied, round and soft, with ripe tannins and a long, fruity vanilla aftertaste. Perhaps a bit too much new wood, but delicious. Drink now through 2008.–J.S. • $50 • (8/31/1999) • **89**

Rosso di Montalcino 1997: A lovely rosso, silky and caressing, with ripe berry and plum flavors and a long, long finish. A real beauty. Drink now.–J.S. • $24 • (9/15/1999) • **89**

Rosso di Montalcino 1993 • $NA • (10/31/1995) • **82**

FRANCO, NINO

Brut Prosecco di Valdobbiadene NV: Big and fruity, with lots of pear and melon character. Full-bodied, with a creamy texture. Drink now.–J.S. • $14 • (5/31/2000) • **86**

Prosecco di Valdobbiadene NV: More bread dough and almond than fruit in this rich, creamy sparkler, with a soft and just slightly cloying finish. Drink now.–B.S. • $16 • (7/31/1998) • **81**

Prosecco di Valdobbiadene Primo Franco 1998: Pleasant, with grape and pear character, a creamy texture and a rather sweet finish. Drink now.–J.S. • $16 • (5/31/2000) • **81**

Prosecco di Valdobbiadene Rustico NV: Clean and fruity, with a creamy texture and a lemon and melon aftertaste. Drink now.–J.S. • $11 • (5/31/2000) • **84**

Prosecco di Valdobbiadene Sassi Bianchi 1996: Yes, that 's right, a dry Prosecco. An oddity, showing bitter almond and cherry notes, good richness and an acidic, astringent structure. Drink now.–B.S. • $10 • (7/31/1998) • **79**

Prosecco di Valdobbiadene Sassi Bianco 1998: A still Prosecco that is very clean and fresh, with appleskin, lemon and mineral character. Medium-bodied, with good acidity and a crisp finish. Drink now.–J.S. • $10 • (4/30/2000) • **84**

FRASCOLE

Chianti Rufina 1997: A pretty wine, with lovely berry, cherry and bark character. Medium-bodied, with a fruity finish. Not imported into the U.S. Drink now.–J.S. • $NA • (1/01/1999) • **85**

FRESCOBALDI, MARCHESI DE '

Brunello di Montalcino Castelgiocondo 1995: A seductive and sleek wine. Lots of tobacco, earth and plum aromas. Full-bodied and incredibly silky and long. Caresses your palate. Drink now through 2005.–J.S. • $55 • (6/30/2000) • **91**

Brunello di Montalcino Castelgiocondo 1994: A bit simple for this producer, with mineral and berry character on the nose and palate. Medium- to light-bodied, with firm tannins and a short finish. Drink now.–J.S. • $53 • (8/31/1999) • **85**

Key: SS—Spectator Selection. CS—Cellar Selection. HR—Highly Recommended. $NA—Price not available. (BT)—Barrel tasting. Ⓐ—Auction Price. For a key to the tasters' initials, see "How to Use These Listings."
Dates in parentheses represent the issues in which the ratings were published.

Brunello di Montalcino Castelgiocondo 1993: Extremely fine Brunello, one of the best ever from this producer. Bright cherry, berry and grilled meat aromas. Medium- to full-bodied, with firm yet polished tannins and a long finish. Built for aging. Best after 2001.–J.S. • $47 • (12/15/1998) • **90**

Brunello di Montalcino Castelgiocondo 1992 • $40 • (9/30/1997) • **80**

Brunello di Montalcino Castelgiocondo 1991 • $29 • (11/30/1996) • **81**

Brunello di Montalcino Castelgiocondo 1990 • $30 • (10/31/1995) • **92**

Brunello di Montalcino Castelgiocondo 1988 • $32 • (4/30/1994) • **85**

Brunello di Montalcino Castelgiocondo Riserva 1993: A delicious, well-crafted Brunello, with plum, berry and cherry aromas that have hints of bark. Medium-bodied, with silky tannins and a medium finish. Drink now through 2003.–J.S. • $115 • (11/30/1999) • **90**

Brunello di Montalcino Castelgiocondo Riserva 1990 • $85 • (11/30/1996) • **89**

Brunello di Montalcino Castelgiocondo Riserva 1988 • $NA • (10/31/1994) • **90**

Brunello di Montalcino Frescobaldi-Ferré Riserva 1993: The rather campy packaging makes you think it 's not up to much, but the wine is excellent. Impressive aromas of blackberry, cherry and wet earth follow through to a full-bodied palate, with loads of polished tannins and a long finish. Mouthpuckering. Give it time. Best after 2001.–J.S. • $450/1.5 liter • (11/30/1999) • **93**

Cabernet Sauvignon Toscana Mormoreto 1996: An elegant, compacted Cabernet, with wonderful ripe berry, raspberry and blackberry aromas. Medium-bodied, with seamless tannins, a polished texture and a medium, fruity finish. Drink now.–J.S. • $47 • (11/30/1999) • **90**

Cabernet Sauvignon Toscana Mormoreto 1995: A chunky Cabernet with good currant and berry character underlined with an earthy element. Medium- to full-bodied, with full tannins and a medium finish. Drink now.–J.S. •$42 • (12/15/1998) • **88**

Cabernet Sauvignon Toscana Mormoreto 1994 • $33 • (9/30/1997) • **90**

Cabernet Sauvignon Mormoreto 1993 • $34 • (10/31/1996) • **87**

Cabernet Sauvignon Mormoreto 1991 • $32 • (2/28/1995) • **90**

Cabernet Sauvignon Mormoreto 1990 • $32 • (2/28/1995) • **88**

Cabernet Sauvignon Mormoreto 1988 • $NA • (11/15/1993) • **94**

Cabernet Sauvignon Mormoreto 1988 • $30 • (11/30/1989) • **93**

Cabernet Sauvignon Mormoreto 1986 • $NA • (11/15/1993) • **91**

Cabernet Sauvignon Mormoreto 1985 • $NA • (11/15/1993) • **90**

Cabernet Sauvignon Mormoreto 1983 • $NA • (11/15/1993) • **90**

Castelgiocondo Lamaione 1993 • $21 • (10/31/1996) • **90**

Castelgiocondo Lamaione 1992 • $18 • (2/28/1995) • **89**

Castelgiocondo Lamaione 1991 • $18 • (2/28/1995) • **90**

Chianti 1989 • $6 • (4/15/1991) • **70**

Chianti 1988 • $5 • (11/30/1989) • **85**

Chianti Castiglioni 1998: Good aromas of plum skin and flowers. Light- to medium-bodied, with light tannins and a fruity finish. A bit simple, really. Drink now.–J.S. • $13 • (11/30/1999) • **83**

Chianti Rèmole 1996 • $8 • (12/31/1997) • **78**

Chianti Rèmole 1994 • $7 • (10/31/1995) • **79**

Chianti Rèmole 1993 • $7 • (2/28/1995) • **78**

Chianti Rufina Castello di Nipozzano Riserva 1996: Aromas of plum, tobacco and grilled meat. Medium-bodied, with silky tannins and a medium finish. Slightly hollow midpalate. Drink now.–J.S. • $20 • (11/30/1999) • **85**

Chianti Rufina Castello di Nipozzano Riserva 1995: Plenty of fresh currant and berry aromas and flavors here, if a bit one-dimensional. Medium-bodied, with fine tannins and a fresh finish. Drink now.–J.S. • $23 Ⓐ • (12/15/1998) • **86**

Chianti Rufina Castello di Nipozzano Riserva 1994 • $15 • (9/30/1997) • **88**

Chianti Rufina Castello di Nipozzano Riserva 1993 • $15 • (10/31/1996) • **86**

Chianti Rufina Castello di Nipozzano Riserva 1992 • $14 • (10/31/1995) • **85**

Chianti Rufina Castello di Nipozzano Riserva 1991 • $14 • (10/31/1993) • **88**

Chianti Rufina Castello di Nipozzano Riserva 1990 • $14 • (2/28/1995) • **85**

Chianti Rufina Castello di Nipozzano Riserva 1989 • $14 • (5/15/1994) • **80**

Chianti Rufina Castello di Nipozzano Riserva 1988 • $15 • (9/15/1992) • **86**

Chianti Rufina Castello di Nipozzano Riserva 1986 • $11 • (9/15/1990) • **82**

Chianti Rufina Castello di Nipozzano Riserva 1985 • $11 • (11/30/1989) • **88**

Chianti Rufina Castello di Nipozzano Riserva 1983 • $10 • (11/30/1989) • **89**

Chianti Rufina Montesodi 1997: An amazing Chianti rufina, with tar, tobacco and cherry aromas. Full-bodied, with polished, velvety tannins and a long, fruity finish. A beauty. To be released June 2000. Drink now through 2001.–J.S. • $50 • (11/30/1999) • **91**

Chianti Rufina Montesodi 1996: Complex aromas of spices, blackberry and black currant. Full-bodied and chewy, with plenty of polished tannins and a silky finish. Harmonious and very ripe; better than the 95. Drink now.–J.S. • $47 • (12/15/1998) • **90**

Chianti Rufina Montesodi 1995: A generous amount of blackberry and milk chocolate on the nose, less on the palate. Medium-bodied, with full tannins

and a slightly austere finish. Better with bottle age. Drink now.–J.S. • $47 • (12/15/1998) • **86**
Chianti Rufina Montesodi 1993 • $34 • (10/31/1996) • **84**
Chianti Rufina Montesodi 1993 • $34 • (9/30/1997) • **79**
Chianti Rufina Montesodi 1991 • $32 • (10/31/1995) • **86**
Chianti Rufina Montesodi 1990 • $32 • (2/28/1995) • **91**
Chianti Rufina Montesodi 1990 • $NA • (9/30/1997) • **90**
Chianti Rufina Montesodi 1988 • $32 • (10/31/1994) CS • **90**
Chianti Rufina Montesodi 1988 • $NA • (9/30/1997) • **90**
Chianti Rufina Montesodi 1985 • $NA • (9/30/1997) • **85**
Chianti Rufina Montesodi 1982 • $28 • (12/15/1988) • **86**
Chianti Rufina Rèmole 1992 • $7 • (4/30/1994) • **85**
Chianti Rufina Rèmole 1991 • $7 • (10/31/1993) • **81**
Chianti Rufina Rèmole 1990 • $7 • (9/15/1992) • **86**
Merlot Toscana Castelgiocondo Lamaione 1997: Unbelievable. A monster Merlot. Dark, with stunning aromas of exotic spice, ripe berry and vanilla. Full-bodied and very concentrated, with masses of ripe fruit and tannins. Best after 2003.–J.S. • $NA • (11/30/1999) • **96**
Merlot Toscana Castelgiocondo Lamaione 1996: A subtle, pure Merlot, with plenty of dried cherry, plum and tobacco and a bit of mint on the nose. Medium-bodied, with very polished, silky tannins and a fresh fruit finish. Drink now.–J.S. • $45 • (11/30/1999) • **90**
Merlot Toscana Castelgiocondo Lamaione 1995: Offers subtle aromas of berries and dark chocolate, then sneaks up and grabs you by the tongue, telling you to pay attention. Full-bodied with masses of tannins, yet they 're polished and succulent. Best after 2000.–J.S. • $42 • (12/15/1998) • **91**
Merlot Toscana Castelgiocondo Lamaione 1994 • $25 • (9/30/1997) • **87**
Pomino Tenuta di Pomino 1996: A delicate, elegant red, with bright berry and strawberry aromas. Light- to medium-bodied, with fine tannins and a light, fruity finish. Drink now.–J.S. • $27 • (11/30/1999) • **85**
Pomino Tenuta di Pomino 1995: Big and juicy, with wild floral and grapey aromas. Medium-bodied, with soft tannins and plenty of grapey, succulent fruit on the finish. Drink now.–J.S. • $22 • (12/15/1998) • **86**
Pomino Tenuta di Pomino 1994 • $18 • (9/30/1997) • **87**
Pomino Tenuta di Pomino 1993 • $18 • (10/31/1996) • **80**
Pomino Tenuta di Pomino 1992 • $17 • (10/31/1995) • **83**
Pomino Tenuta di Pomino 1991 • $17 • (2/28/1995) • **80**
Pomino Tenuta di Pomino 1988 • $17 • (10/31/1993) • **82**
Pomino Tenuta di Pomino 1986 • $14 • (1/31/1990) • **87**
Pomino Tenuta di Pomino 1985 • $12 • (9/15/1988) SS • **93**
Pomino Tenuta di Pomino Il Benefizio 1998: Very pretty apple, honey and pineapple aromas follow through to a medium-bodied palate, with fresh acidity and a long, flavorful finish. A beauty. Chardonnay and Pinot Grigio. Drink now.–J.S. • $NA • (11/30/1999) • **89**
Pomino White Tenuta di Pomino Il Benefizio 1997: Quite likable for its vibrant, fruity style. A fresh, lively white with banana and pineapple flavors, medium body and tangy finish. Drink now. • $17 • (7/31/1998) • **85**
Pomino White Tenuta di Pomino Il Benefizio 1996 • $13 • (9/30/1997) • **85**
Rosso di Montalcino Castelgiocondo Campo ai Sassi 1997: A good, simple rosso. Ripe berry and very earthy, slightly decadent aromas. Medium-bodied, with velvety tannins and a fresh fruit finish. Slightly diluted in the midpalate. Not imported into the U.S. Drink now.–J.S. • $NA • (1/01/1999) • **83**
Rosso di Montalcino Castelgiocondo Campo ai Sassi 1996 • $NA • (9/30/1997) • **86**
Rosso di Montalcino Castelgiocondo Campo ai Sassi 1995 • $15 • (9/30/1997) • **74**
Rosso di Montalcino Castelgiocondo Campo ai Sassi 1993 • $15 • (10/31/1995) • **83**
Rosso di Montalcino Castelgiocondo Campo ai Sassi 1992 • $15 • (10/31/1994) • **79**
Rosso di Montalcino Castelgiocondo Campo ai Sassi 1991 • $15 • (4/30/1994) • **77**
Sangiovese Toscana Pater 1996 • $9 • (4/30/1998) • **84**
Sangiovese Toscana Pater 1995 • $8 • (1/31/1997) • **82**
Sangiovese Toscana Pater 1994 • $NA • (10/31/1995) • **81**
Toscana Albizzia 1998: Subtle aromas of apple, mineral and pie crust. Medium-bodied, with good acidity and a pleasant lemon and vanilla aftertaste. Not imported into the U.S. Drink now.–J.S. • $NA • (1/01/1999) • **86**
Toscana Albizzia 1996 • $8 • (4/30/1998) • **76**
Toscana Rèmole 1998: A simple, well-made Sangiovese. A little light but very fresh and fruity, with delicate tannins and a crisp finish. Drink now.–J.S. • $9 • (11/30/1999) • **82**

FRIMAIO

Chianti Classico 1997: A solid CC, with cherry and plum character. Medium-bodied, with medium tannins and a fruity finish. Slightly one-dimensional. Drink now through 2001.–J.S. • $NA • (1/01/1999) • **85**
Chianti Classico 1994 • $NA • (10/31/1996) • **85**

FUGA, TENUTA LA

Brunello di Montalcino 1994: Attractive plum and earth character. Medium-bodied, with firm tannins, crisp acidity and a slightly austere finish. A bit lean, but enjoyable. Drink now.–J.S. • $50 • (8/31/1999) • **85**
Brunello di Montalcino 1993: A seriously good Brunello, with complex aromas of stone, berry and chocolate. Full-bodied, with extremely well-integrated tannins and a caressing, fruity finish. Wonderful harmony and structure. Drink now through 2008.–J.S. • $43 • (12/15/1998) • **90**
Brunello di Montalcino 1991 • $45 • (11/30/1996) • **86**
Brunello di Montalcino 1990 • $NA • (10/31/1995) • **81**
Brunello di Montalcino Riserva 1994: A firm wine, yet slightly lean, with berry and violet aromas and flavors. Medium body. Fresh finish. Drink now.–J.S. • $64 • (6/30/2000) • **86**
Brunello di Montalcino Riserva 1993: Bubbling over with fruity character, from ripe plums to crushed berries. Full-bodied yet silky-textured, with lovely fruit and a long, sweet fruit finish. All in harmony. Drink now through 2010.–J.S. • $65 • (8/31/1999) • **92**
Brunello di Montalcino Riserva 1991 • $51 • (9/30/1997) • **86**
Brunello di Montalcino Riserva 1990 • $50 • (11/30/1996) • **87**
Rosso di Montalcino 1997: A solid core of ripe berry and dried cherry flavors to this medium-bodied wine, with firm tannins and a fresh fruit finish. Drink now.–J.S. • $27 • (9/15/1999) • **85**
Rosso di Montalcino 1995 • $17 • (9/30/1997) • **79**
Rosso di Montalcino 1994 • $20 • (11/30/1996) • **78**
Rosso di Montalcino 1993 • $NA • (10/31/1995) • **80**
Rosso di Montalcino 1992 • $NA • (4/30/1994) • **79**

FULIGNI, EREDI

Brunello di Montalcino Vigneti dei Cottimelli 1995: Great wine as usual. Gorgeous, generous plum, berry and dried cherry aromas with hints of flowers. Full-bodied, with big, polished tannins and a long, long finish. Goes on and on. Drink now through 2006.–J.S. • $60 • (6/30/2000) • **93**
Brunello di Montalcino Vigneti dei Cottimelli 1994: A real beauty, with dried cherry, plum, earth and light oak on the nose and palate. Medium-bodied, with very fine tannins and a long, slinky and caressing finish. Drink now through 2005.–J.S. • $80 • (8/31/1999) • **90**
Brunello di Montalcino Vigneti dei Cottimelli 1993: Fuligni shows how to build a proper Brunello. Seductive and moreish, it offers violet and berry on the nose, with hints of porcini. Full-bodied, with soft tannins, a velvety texture and flavors that go on and on. Delicious. Drink now through 2008.–J.S. • $50 • (12/15/1998) • **91**
Brunello di Montalcino Vigneti dei Cottimelli 1992 • $45 • (9/30/1997) • **83**
Brunello di Montalcino Vigneti dei Cottimelli 1991 • $46 • (11/30/1996) • **86**
Brunello di Montalcino Vigneti dei Cottimelli 1990 • $46 • (10/31/1995) • **90**
Brunello di Montalcino Vigneti dei Cottimelli 1989 • $39 • (11/30/1994) • **88**
Brunello di Montalcino Vigneti dei Cottimelli 1988 • $NA • (4/30/1994) • **91**
Brunello di Montalcino Vigneti dei Cottimelli Riserva 1993: Such class and complexity. Super. Dark ruby-colored, with vivid aromas of blackberries and roses and hints of grilled porcini. Full-bodied, with wonderfully silky full tannins and a long, long aftertaste. Drink through 2008.–J.S. • $54 • (8/31/1999) • **93**
Brunello di Montalcino Vigneti dei Cottimelli Riserva 1990 • $75 • (11/30/1996) • **91**
Brunello di Montalcino Vigneti dei Cottimelli Riserva 1988 • $NA • (10/31/1994) • **95**
Rosso di Montalcino Ginestreto Vigneti dei Cottimelli 1996: Raspberry, cherry and flowers flow from the glass. Medium-bodied, with fine tannins and loads of refined, subtle fruit and floral flavors on the aftertaste. Beautiful, always one of the best Rossos. Drink now.–J.S. • $26 • (12/15/1998) • **89**
Rosso di Montalcino Ginestreto Vigneti dei Cottimelli 1995 • $27 • (9/30/1997) • **87**
Rosso di Montalcino Ginestreto Vigneti dei Cottimelli 1994 • $24 • (11/30/1996) • **87**
Rosso di Montalcino Ginestreto Vigneti dei Cottimelli 1993 • $20 • (10/31/1995) • **89**

FULIGNI, EREDI

Rosso di Montalcino Ginestreto Vigneti dei Cottimelli 1992 • $NA • (10/31/1994) • **79**
Rosso di Montalcino Ginestreto Vigneti dei Cottimelli 1991 • $NA • (4/30/1994) • **87**
Toscana Rosso San Jacopo 1997: A new wine from one of the best producers in Brunello. Big, chewy and chocolaty, with masses of berry and plum character. Full-bodied and mouthpuckering, with lots of tannins and a long finish. Pure Sangiovese pleasure. Give it time. Best after 2001.–J.S. • $35 • (11/30/1999) • **92**

FURLAN CASTELCOSA

Castelcosa Grigio 1996 • $12 • (5/15/1998) • **85**
Chardonnay Venezie 1996 • $12 • (4/30/1998) • **85**
Grigio Venezia Giulia 1997: There 's an attractive grassy, herbal note in this white, atypical for the variety but appealing for its crisp, frank presentation. Drink now.–B.S. • $NA • (9/30/1998) • **81**
Merlot Friuli 1994 • $14 • (9/15/1997) • **79**
Merlot Venezie 1995 • $15 • (4/30/1998) • **61**
Picolit Colli Orientali del Friuli 1992 • $39/500 ml. • (5/15/1997) • **84**

GABBIANO, CASTELLO DI

Cabernet Sauvignon Colli della Toscana Centrale 1990: A slightly burnt bell pepper character marks this wine. Medium-bodied, with dry tannins and a smoky, green pepper finish.–J.S. • $25 • (12/15/1998) • **77**
Chianti 1997: Fresh and fruity, with berry, strawberry character. Light-bodied, with light tannins and a fresh finish. Drink now.–J.S. • $10 • (12/15/1998) • **80**
Chianti 1996 • $10 • (9/30/1997) • **80**
Chianti Classico 1995 • $12 • (9/30/1997) • **80**
Chianti Classico 1990 • $9 • (4/30/1994) • **81**
Chianti Classico Gold Label Riserva 1990 • $9 • (6/15/1993) • **77**
Chianti Classico Gold Label Riserva 1988 • $12 • (6/15/1993) • **87**
Chianti Classico Gold Label Riserva 1986 • $20 • (11/30/1994) • **88**
Chianti Classico Gold Label Riserva 1985 • $20 • (6/15/1993) • **82**
Chianti Classico Gold Label Riserva 1982 • $21 • (11/30/1989) • **79**
Chianti Classico Gold Label Riserva 1981 • $18 • (2/15/1988) • **81**
Chianti Classico Riserva 1993 • $15 • (9/30/1997) • **83**
Chianti Classico Riserva 1990 • $15 • (2/28/1995) • **86**
Chianti Classico Riserva 1985 • $19 • (4/30/1994) • **82**
Chianti Classico Riserva 1983 • $19 • (9/15/1992) • **78**
Chianti Classico Riserva 1982 • $11 • (7/31/1988) • **84**
Chianti Classico Titolato 1996: A little tired, with berry and chestnut character and a slight, tanned leather element. Light in body, tannin and finish.–J.S. • $12 • (12/15/1998) • **78**
Chianti Classico Titolato Riserva 1994: Already a bit tired. Leather, berry and cherry character. Medium- to light-bodied, with light tannins and a light finish.–J.S. • $17 • (12/15/1998) • **79**
Il Cavaliere 1988 • $9 • (12/15/1992) • **78**
Merlot Colli della Toscana Centrale 1993: Tastes more like Cabernet than Merlot, but has plenty of pretty aromas of currant, dried herbs and berries. Full-bodied, with well-integrated, polished tannins and a long, fruit and mint finish. A beauty. Drink through 2001.–J.S. • $25 • (12/15/1998) • **87**
Merlot Tuscany 1988 • $55 • (7/15/1991) • **86**
perAnia 1990 • $30 • (9/30/1997) • **88**
perAnia 1988 • $31 • (10/31/1996) • **78**
perAnia 1986 • $30 • (12/15/1992) • **72**
perAnia 1985 • $30 • (1/31/1990) • **93**
perAnia 1983 • $25 • (7/15/1987) • **83**
R & R 1986 • $38 • (1/31/1991) • **90**
R & R 1985 • $30 • (3/31/1990) • **91**
Toscana 1994 • $8 • (9/30/1997) • **76**
Toscana Galestro 1996 • $8 • (9/30/1997) • **81**
Toscana Rosso 1996: Light, simple and fruity, with hints of leather on the nose and palate.–J.S. • $8 • (12/15/1998) • **78**

Key: SS—Spectator Selection. CS—Cellar Selection. HR—Highly Recommended. $NA—Price not available. (BT)—Barrel tasting. Ⓐ—Auction Price. For a key to the tasters' initials, see "How to Use These Listings."
Dates in parentheses represent the issues in which the ratings were published.

GAGLIARDO, GIANNI

Barbera d'Alba La Matta 1995 • $14 • (10/31/1997) • **89**
Barolo 1993 • $25 • (10/31/1997) • **81**
Barolo 1992 • $25 • (10/31/1996) • **88**
Barolo Batié 1990 • $28 • (6/15/1994) • **87**
Barolo La Serra 1989 • $26 • (6/15/1994) • **85**
Barolo Preve 1994: Distinctive and attractive, showing lovely, fresh fruit—plum, wild berry, currant—along with tar and smoke. Very good Barolo, of medium body, good intensity. Cellar to smooth the tannins and improve the aromas. Drink through 2005.–P.M. • $40 • (10/31/1998) • **87**
Barolo Preve 1993 • $40 • (10/31/1997) • **86**
Barolo Preve 1991 • $40 • (10/31/1996) • **88**
Barolo Preve 1990 • $35 • (10/31/1995) • **91**
Dolcetto d'Alba 1996 • $13 • (10/31/1997) • **82**
Dolcetto d'Alba 1995 • $13 • (10/31/1996) • **79**
Dolcetto d'Alba 1994 • $13 • (10/31/1995) • **82**
Dolcetto d'Alba Paulin 1998: With the essence of freshly crushed grapes, this Dolcetto bursts with succulent red berry and blackberry flavors. There is nothing complex in this juicy, balanced guzzler, so enjoy on release. Not imported into the U.S.–P.M. • $NA • (1/01/1999) • **87**
Dolcetto d'Alba Paulin 1995 • $20 • (10/31/1996) • **86**
Favorita Langhe Casá 1996 • $13 • (12/31/1997) • **84**
Nebbiolo delle Langhe Batié 1995: Odd, with a smoky, matchstick aroma. The wine turns very dry on the finish. Tasted twice, with consistent notes. Not imported into the U.S.–P.M. • $NA • (1/01/1999) • **60**
Nebbiolo delle Langhe Batié 1994: Straightforward, with a metallic edge, this tastes a bit unripe, showing some strawberry and raspberry notes. Drying tannins on the short finish.–P.M. • $30 • (10/31/1998) • **73**
Nebbiolo delle Langhe Batié 1993 • $30 • (10/31/1997) • **85**
Nebbiolo delle Langhe Batié 1992 • $29 • (10/31/1996) • **85**

GAGLIOLE, ANTICO PODERE

Colli della Toscana Centrale 1998: Interesting aromas of toasted oak, orange peel and apple skin. Full-bodied and very woody, with fruit and a long, long vanilla and toothpick finish. A bit too much wood. Drink now.–J.S. • $40 • (11/30/1999) • **82**
Colli della Toscana Centrale 1996: Not as superb as the 95, but outstanding all the same. Chunky, with blackberry and tobacco and hints of cedar on the nose and palate. Medium-bodied, medium in tannins, chewy-textured on the finish. Drink now.–J.S. • $42 • (12/15/1998) • **90**
Colli della Toscana Centrale 1995: Tantilizing aromas of rose, plum and cherry. Medium-bodied, with very fine yet powerful tannins and a fresh and subtle finish that 's slightly austere now. A serious wine to watch. The new Solaia? A blend of Sangiovese and Cabernet Sauvignon. Drink now.–J.S. • $33 • (12/15/1998) • **92**
Toscana 1997: A tough and powerful red built for aging, with reserved aromas of berry and mint. Full-bodied, with a powerful, compacted fruit and tannin structure. Long, long finish. Best after 2000.–J.S. • $60 • (11/30/1999) • **92**

GAIERHOF

Cabernet Sauvignon Trentino 1994 • $13 • (5/31/1998) • **88**
Moscato Goldmuskateller Trentino 1995 • $13 • (10/31/1997) • **83**
Pinot Grigio Trentino Torre di Luna 1996 • $12 • (12/15/1997) • **83**
Teroldego Rotaliano 1994 • $13 • (4/30/1998) • **84**
Teroldego Rotaliano 1988 • $11 • (9/30/1991) • **75**

GAJA

Barbaresco 1996: Aromatically reserved at this stage, it holds back its charm, teasing with layers of mineral, blackberry, plum, spice and wet earth. It may unleash much power and complexity with age, as it 's firm, full-bodied and ripe. Best from 2003 through 2010.–P.M. • $120 • (10/31/1999) • **90**
Barbaresco 1995: Most impressive. Hard to tell it apart from the single-vineyard *crus* because it 's so massive while also offering an incredibly dense texture. Shows mineral, stonelike, spicy and black currant character, while some new oak plays subtly in the background. Firm tannins on the finish. Best from 2005 through 2015.–P.M. • $115 Ⓐ • (10/31/1998) • **94**
Barbaresco 1994 • $70 • (10/31/1997) • **91**
Barbaresco 1993 • $86 Ⓐ • (10/31/1996) • **87**
Barbaresco 1991 • $49 • (10/31/1994) • **88**

Barbaresco 1990 • $165 Ⓐ • (10/31/1993) • **94**
Barbaresco 1989 • $90 Ⓐ • (10/31/1993) • **88**
Barbaresco 1988 • $101 Ⓐ • (10/31/1993) • **87**
Barbaresco 1986 • $70 Ⓐ • (1/31/1990) CS • **92**
Barbaresco 1985 • $162 Ⓐ • (12/15/1988) CS • **95**
Barbaresco 1983 • $35 • (9/15/1989) • **93**
Barbaresco 1982 • $168 Ⓐ • (9/15/1989) • **93**
Barbaresco 1981 • $NA • (9/15/1989) • **90**
Barbaresco 1980 • $14 • (7/01/1985) • **88**
Barbaresco 1979 • $NA • (9/15/1989) • **89**
Barbaresco 1978 • $141 Ⓐ • (9/15/1989) • **93**
Barbaresco 1976 • $NA • (9/15/1989) • **91**
Barbaresco 1974 • $125 Ⓐ • (9/15/1989) • **89**
Barbaresco 1971 • $NA • (9/15/1989) • **86**
Barbaresco 1967 • $NA • (9/15/1989) • **83**
Barbaresco 1964 • $114 Ⓐ • (9/15/1989) • **87**
Barbaresco 1961 • $383 Ⓐ • (9/15/1989) • **92**

Barbaresco Costa Russi 1996: Here 's a wine that transcends cultures, regions and varietals. La Tâche in Piedmont? Rutherford Cabernet? Balanced, with the sort of ripe, clean, pure fruit that most wine lovers (and winemakers) would kill for. Focused, opulent and elegant, packed with lightly toasted, slightly petrollike aromas and loads of cassis and blackberry flavors. Very firm, so cellar. Best from 2003 through 2026.–P.M. • $180 • (10/31/1999) • **97**

Barbaresco Costa Russi 1995: Fantastic, world-class, silky-as-they-come red. Thick and dense, extracted but without heaviness, this elegant Barbaresco is packed to the brim with velvety tannins, red- and blackberry flavors and some tasteful, toasted, spicy notes. Palate-coating, smooth and long Nebbiolo. Drink now through 2015.–P.M. • $190 • (10/31/1998) • **96**

Barbaresco Costa Russi 1993 • $115 Ⓐ • (10/31/1996) • **93**
Barbaresco Costa Russi 1990 • $225 Ⓐ • (10/31/1993) • **98**
Barbaresco Costa Russi 1989 • $155 Ⓐ • (10/15/1993) CS • **96**
Barbaresco Costa Russi 1988 • $138 Ⓐ • (10/31/1993) • **92**
Barbaresco Costa Russi 1986 • $152 Ⓐ • (1/31/1990) • **89**
Barbaresco Costa Russi 1985 • $233 Ⓐ • (12/15/1988) • **96**
Barbaresco Costa Russi 1982 • $161 Ⓐ • (9/15/1988) • **91**

Barbaresco Sorì San Lorenzo 1996: The Romanée-Conti of Piedmont. An extraordinary red. Thick and ripe, with an elegant structure that makes it eerily balanced. Oozes blackberry, violet, mineral, smoke and petrol notes. Refined, with sweet tannins, it 's tempting now if you don 't mind a grip on the finish. Drink through 2016.–P.M. • $200 • (10/31/1999) CS • **97**

Barbaresco Sorì San Lorenzo 1995: International in style to the extent that it's amazingly dense and filled with silky, ripe, fat tannins that just balloon on the palate, but it's clearly Piedmontese in all that mineral, blood orange, lead-pencil and intriguing red- and blackberry character. Refined and elegant despite its full-bodied, rich personality. Slightly smoky, toasted complexity on the blackberry-packed finish. Drink now through 2015.–P.M. • $190 • (10/31/1998) • **96**

Barbaresco Sorì San Lorenzo 1993 • $115 Ⓐ • (10/31/1996) • **92**
Barbaresco Sorì San Lorenzo 1990 • $380 Ⓐ • (10/31/1993) • **96**
Barbaresco Sorì San Lorenzo 1989 • $212 Ⓐ • (9/15/1993) HR • **98**
Barbaresco Sorì San Lorenzo 1988 • $159 Ⓐ • (10/31/1993) • **93**
Barbaresco Sorì San Lorenzo 1986 • $89 • (1/31/1990) • **91**
Barbaresco Sorì San Lorenzo 1985 • $246 Ⓐ • (12/15/1988) • **96**
Barbaresco Sorì San Lorenzo 1983 • $NA • (9/15/1988) • **90**

Barbaresco Sorì Tildìn 1996: This Piedmont beauty is dark in color and beautifully compacted on the midpalate, where it displays gorgeous blackberry, black cherry, mint and spicy oak notes. Tannins are firm and ripe. A serious red that needs time. Best from 2002 through 2008.–P.M. • $200 • (10/31/1999) CS • **95**

Barbaresco Sorì Tildìn 1993 • $115 Ⓐ • (10/31/1996) CS • **94**
Barbaresco Sorì Tildìn 1990 • $295 Ⓐ • (10/31/1993) • **100**
Barbaresco Sorì Tildìn 1989 • $236 Ⓐ • (10/15/1993) CS • **96**
Barbaresco Sorì Tildìn 1988 • $143 Ⓐ • (10/31/1993) • **93**
Barbaresco Sorì Tildìn 1986 • $134 Ⓐ • (1/31/1990) • **93**
Barbaresco Sorì Tildìn 1985 • $276 Ⓐ • (12/15/1988) • **97**
Barbaresco Sorì Tildìn 1983 • $95 • (9/15/1988) • **89**
Barbaresco Sorì Tildìn 1982 • $187 Ⓐ • (9/15/1989) • **94**
Barbaresco Sorì Tildìn 1981 • $NA • (9/15/1989) • **87**
Barbaresco Sorì Tildìn 1979 • $NA • (9/15/1989) • **89**
Barbaresco Sorì Tildìn 1978 • $NA • (9/15/1989) • **90**
Barbaresco Sorì Tildìn 1973 • $153 Ⓐ • (9/15/1989) • **88**
Barbaresco Sorì Tildìn 1971 • $NA • (9/15/1989) • **91**
Barbaresco Sorì Tildìn 1970 • $NA • (9/15/1989) • **78**
Barbera d'Alba Vignarey 1992 • $42 • (10/31/1995) • **81**
Barbera d'Alba Vignarey 1990 • $40 • (10/15/1993) • **89**
Barbera d'Alba Vignarey 1987 • $35 • (4/15/1991) • **88**
Barbera d'Alba Vignarey 1986 • $27 • (3/15/1991) • **88**
Barbera d'Alba Vignarey 1984 • $13 • (2/15/1987) • **82**
Barolo Gromis Conteisa Cerequio 1991 • $NA • (10/31/1996) • **84**
Barolo Gromis Conteisa Cerequio 1990 • $NA • (10/31/1996) • **88**
Barolo Gromis Conteisa Cerequio 1989 • $NA • (10/31/1996) • **90**

Barolo Sperss 1995: Power and charm combine in this exotic, black-colored, beautifully perfumed, balanced Barolo. Sure, it 's a barrique-boosted Nebbiolo, but look at the exquisite result: sweet tannins, full body, exciting violet, blackberry, mint, smoke and tar notes, and a rock-solid but harmonious finish. Best from 2003 through 2010.–P.M. • $135 • (11/15/1999) • **94**

Barolo Sperss 1994: New-wave Barolo, with toasted oak, violet and spicy mocha character. Well made, showing black fruit and supple tannins. Chewy tannins on the smoky finish. Drink now through 2005.–P.M. • $86 Ⓐ • (10/31/1998) • **88**

Barolo Sperss 1993 • $54 Ⓐ • (10/31/1997) • **88**
Barolo Sperss 1991 • $115 Ⓐ • (10/31/1995) • **86**
Barolo Sperss 1989 • $185 Ⓐ • (10/31/1993) • **96**
Barolo Sperss 1988 • $142 Ⓐ • (9/15/1993) CS • **94**

Cabernet Sauvignon Darmagi 1995: Stunning. Black in color, velvety in texture, ripe, sweet and bursting with black currant and blackberry aromas and flavors accented by subtle smoke, vanilla and spicy oak accents, this full-bodied wine just waltzes around your palate. The acidity, toasted oak and pure, fresh fruit keep the wine dancing on the firm finish. Best from 2003 through 2012.–P.M. • $NA • (10/31/1998) • **95**

Cabernet Sauvignon Darmagi 1988 • $60 • (12/15/1992) HR • **92**
Cabernet Sauvignon Darmagi 1986 • $76 • (1/31/1990) • **94**
Cabernet Sauvignon Darmagi 1985 • $70 • (3/15/1989) CS • **94**
Cabernet Sauvignon Darmagi 1983 • $51 • (7/15/1988) • **91**
Dolcetto Langhe 1994 • $22 • (10/31/1995) • **88**
Nebbiolo d'Alba Vignaveja 1985 • $30 • (2/15/1989) • **87**
Nebbiolo d'Alba Vignaveja 1983 • $16 • (2/15/1987) SS • **94**
Sito Moresco 1991 • $30 • (10/31/1994) • **88**

Sitorey 1996: International in style. Inky in color, massively extracted, tasting of ink and oak. But it's supple on the palate, with nice blackberry character and acidity. Heavyish finish. Might rate outstanding with time. Best from 2003 through 2008.–P.M. • $45 • (10/31/1998) • **87**

Sitorey 1993 • $45 • (10/31/1995) • **84**
Sitorey 1991 • $35 • (10/31/1994) • **85**

GALARDI, FATTORIA

Terra di Lavoro 1997: A fabulously crafted and powerful young wine with lots of class. Wonderful aromas of crushed berries and flowers, with hints of spice. Full-bodied, with lots of polished tannins, notes of spice and toasted oak. Loads of fruit on the finish. Best after 2001.–J.S. • $45 • (1/31/2000) • **93**

Terra di Lavoro 1994 • $29 • (6/15/1998) • **84**

GALLINA, PIERINO

Barbera d'Alba 1996: With funky aromas, spritzy mouthfeel, this tastes odd and not very clean. Tasted twice, with consistent notes.–P.M. • $12 • (10/31/1998) • **68**

Dolcetto d'Alba 1997: Light and pretty, delicate, with raspberry and cherry flavors, light tannins. A balanced, lunch-type wine for everyday drinking . Drink now.–P.M. • $12 • (10/31/1998) • **82**

GANCIA

Asti NV • $12 • (5/31/1997) • **84**
Barolo 1993 • $75 • (10/31/1997) • **78**

Barolo Cannubi Ca ' dei Gancia 1993: Fairly good intensity in this oak-aged wine, offering spice, mocha, coffee, plum, prune and wet earth aromas and flavors. Medium-bodied, with nice complexity, but the finish is very woody. Not available in the U.S. Best after 2002.–P.M. • $NA • (10/31/1998) • **83**

Barolo Cannubi Ca ' dei Gancia 1992 • $NA • (10/31/1996) • **83**
Barolo Cannubi Ca ' dei Gancia 1990 • $65 • (10/31/1994) • **93**
Barolo Cannubi Ca ' dei Gancia 1989 • $65 • (10/31/1993) • **96**

Brut NV: Apple, lemon and a hint of earth are the flavors in this light-bodied, focused sparkling wine from Italy. With an intriguing nutty aftertaste, it leaves the palate refreshed, at a refreshing price. Drink now.–B.S. • $11 • (10/15/1999) • **86**

Il Defino 1991 • $NA • (10/31/1995) • **81**
Rosso Spumante NV • $10 • (5/15/1998) • **81**

ITALY

GATTAVECCHI

Chianti Colli Senesi 1994 • $15 • (9/30/1997) • **65**
Chianti Colli Senesi 1990 • $8 • (4/30/1992) • **80**
Rosso di Montepulciano 1997: Attractive strawberry and cherry character. Medium-bodied, with light, silky tannins and a fresh finish. Drink now.–J.S. • $11 • (11/30/1999) • **85**
Vino Nobile di Montepulciano 1996: Medium-bodied, with plum and cherry throughout, velvety tannins and a fruity, minty finish. Slightly austere aftertaste. Better with a bit more age. Drink now.–J.S. • $20 • (11/30/1999) • **87**
Vino Nobile di Montepulciano 1994 • $19 • (9/30/1997) • **78**
Vino Nobile di Montepulciano 1990 • $14 • (2/29/1996) • **80**
Vino Nobile di Montepulciano 1988 • $14 • (12/15/1992) • **83**
Vino Nobile di Montepulciano dei Padri Serviti Riserva 1995: Aromas of plums and berries, with hints of cedar, follow through on the palate. Medium- to light-bodied, with light tannins and a fresh finish. Drink now.–J.S. • $24 • (11/30/1999) • **83**
Vino Nobile di Montepulciano dei Padri Serviti Riserva 1993 • $22 • (9/30/1997) • **82**
Vino Nobile di Montepulciano dei Padri Serviti Riserva 1985 • $11 • (11/30/1989) • **81**

GATTINARA, SERGIO

Gattinara 1994: Like a chocolate milkshake with mocha powder on top. Medium-bodied, with intense midpalate black fruit character. Lacks a bit of finesse and class as it clamps down on the burning finish.–P.M. • $30 • (11/15/1999) • **79**

GEOGRAFICO

Brunello di Montalcino 1985 • $30 • (7/15/1991) • **80**
Chianti Classico 1997: A Chianti with plenty of fresh cherry character and a hint of almond. Medium-bodied, with soft tannins and a fresh finish. Drink now.–J.S. • $16 • (11/30/1999) • **85**
Chianti Classico 1996: Rather light. Some pleasant strawberry and plum aromas and flavors, but it's light in body and very short on the finish. At least it's clean.–J.S. • $15 • (12/15/1998) • **78**
Chianti Classico 1995 • $13 • (9/30/1997) • **77**
Chianti Classico 1994 • $10 • (10/31/1996) • **82**
Chianti Classico 1993 • $9 • (10/31/1995) • **83**
Chianti Classico 1992 • $10 • (2/28/1995) • **82**
Chianti Classico 1991 • $10 • (10/31/1993) • **82**
Chianti Classico 1990 • $12 • (9/15/1992) • **87**
Chianti Classico 1988 • $10 • (11/30/1991) • **78**
Chianti Classico Castello di Fagnano 1991 • $12 • (10/31/1993) • **75**
Chianti Classico Castello di Fagnano 1989 • $10 • (1/31/1992) • **70**
Chianti Classico Castello di Fagnano 1988 • $10 • (10/31/1991) • **86**
Chianti Classico Contessa di Radda 1997: Medium-bodied, with good berry and blackberry character, fine tannins and a fresh finish. Drink now through 2001.–J.S. • $17 • (11/30/1999) • **86**
Chianti Classico Contessa di Radda 1988 • $14 • (9/15/1992) • **88**
Chianti Classico Contessa di Radda 1987 • $11 • (10/31/1991) • **80**
Chianti Classico Tenuta Montegiachi Riserva 1996: A little light and diluted, but with pretty berry, strawberry and cedar character. Light-bodied, with fine tannins and a fresh, fruity finish. An enjoyable red. Drink now.–J.S. • $22 • (11/30/1999) • **83**
Chianti Classico Tenuta Montegiachi Riserva 1995: A seamless red with delicious blackberry and dried cherry aromas and flavors. Medium-bodied, with soft tannins and a caressing, light finish. Drink now.–J.S. • $21 • (12/15/1998) • **86**
Chianti Classico Tenuta Montegiachi Riserva 1994 • $20 • (9/30/1997) • **83**
Chianti Classico Tenuta Montegiachi Riserva 1993 • $20 • (10/31/1996) • **82**
Chianti Classico Tenuta Montegiachi Riserva 1990 • $NA • (2/28/1995) • **83**
Chianti Classico Tenuta Montegiachi Riserva 1986 • $15 • (10/31/1991) • **79**
Toscana Capitolare di Biturica 1996: The slightly unripe Cabernet diminishes the overall quality. Bright cherry, berry and violet aromas have a slightly herbal note. Medium-bodied, with firm tannins and a medium finish. Slightly hollow midpalate. Cabernet Sauvignon and Sangiovese. Drink now.–J.S. • $23 • (11/30/1999) • **84**
Toscana Capitolare di Biturica 1995: Another simple yet juicy Sangiovese, with berry, cherry and chocolate character. Medium- to light-bodied, with light tannins and a fresh finish. Drink now.–J.S. • $26 • (12/15/1998) • **84**
Toscana Capitolare di Biturica 1994 • $24 • (9/30/1997) • **86**
Toscana Capitolare di Biturica 1993 • $23 • (10/31/1996) • **84**
Toscana Capitolare di Biturica 1990 • $27 • (2/28/1995) • **88**
Toscana Capitolare di Biturica 1988 • $26 • (10/31/1993) • **91**
Toscana Capitolare di Biturica 1986 • $21 • (8/31/1991) • **85**
Vernaccia di San Gimignano 1998: Slightly oxidized, with almond, honey and rock candy character. Medium-bodied, with a simple finish.–J.S. • $10 • (11/30/1999) • **79**
Vernaccia di San Gimignano 1997: Simple and a bit candied, with marzipan aromas and flavors, high acidity and a tart finish.–J.S. • $9 • (12/15/1998) • **76**
Vernaccia di San Gimignano 1996 • $10 • (9/30/1997) • **83**
Vino Nobile di Montepulciano Cerraia 1994 • $17 • (10/31/1997) • **68**
Vino Nobile di Montepulciano Cerraia 1986 • $15 • (7/15/1991) • **85**

GERLA, LA

Brunello di Montalcino 1994: Pretty crushed berry and mushroom character. Medium-bodied, with polished tannins and a slightly austere and dry finish. Still, a very good bottle. Drink now.–J.S. • $27 • (8/31/1999) • **85**
Brunello di Montalcino 1993: A balanced, attractive, modern-style Brunello. Alluring aromas of blackberry and violet. Medium-bodied, with medium, firm tannins and a long, refreshing aftertaste. Best after 2000.–J.S. • $24 • (12/15/1998) • **88**
Brunello di Montalcino 1991 • $30 • (11/30/1996) • **85**
Brunello di Montalcino 1990 • $NA • (10/31/1995) • **84**
Brunello di Montalcino 1988 • $30 • (4/30/1994) • **86**
Brunello di Montalcino Riserva 1993: A pretty and thoroughly drinkable '93 riserva with mineral, crushed berry character. Medium-bodied, with fine tannins and a fresh fruit aftertaste. Drink now.–J.S. • $35 • (8/31/1999) • **87**
Brunello di Montalcino Riserva 1991 • $44 • (9/30/1997) • **83**
Brunello di Montalcino Riserva 1990 • $37 • (11/30/1996) • **91**
Brunello di Montalcino Riserva 1988 • $NA • (10/31/1994) • **89**
Rosso di Montalcino 1996: Surprisingly rich for a Rosso. A bit simple, but with serious dark color and violet and berry aromas. Medium-bodied, with lots of grapey character. Finishes moderately, with a velvety texture. Drink through 2001.–J.S. • $16 • (12/15/1998) • **86**
Rosso di Montalcino 1995 • $17 • (9/30/1997) • **82**
Rosso di Montalcino 1994 • $13 • (11/30/1996) • **84**
Rosso di Montalcino 1991 • $12 • (4/30/1994) • **84**
Toscana Birba 1996: Lots of new wood on this Sangiovese, giving it loads of coconut and vanilla character. Medium-bodied, with silky tannins. Tastes a bit like a Rioja. Drink now.–J.S. • $11 • (12/15/1998) • **84**
Toscana Birba 1995 • $NA • (9/30/1997) • **86**
Toscana Birba 1994 • $NA • (10/31/1996) • **85**
Toscana Birba 1990 • $NA • (10/31/1993) • **87**
Toscana Birba 1989 • $NA • (10/31/1993) • **84**

GERMANO, ETTORE

Barolo 1991 • $NA • (10/31/1995) • **81**
Barolo Cerretta 1993 • $NA • (10/31/1997) • **76**

GHISOLFI, ATTILIO

Barbera d'Alba 1990 • $18 • (10/15/1994) • **86**
Barbera d'Alba Vigna Lisi 1995: A delicious, distinctive red. Rich, ripe and medium-bodied, with spice, hot pepper, petrol and mocha character. Supple tannins make this a round and appealing wine that's hotly intense on the finish. Drink now through 2003.–P.M. • $20 • (11/15/1999) • **89**
Barbera d'Alba Vigna Lisi 1994 • $20 • (1/31/1998) • **76**
Barolo Bricco Visette 1995: Classy, with subtle aromas and a ripe mouthfeel, offering pretty layers of rose petal, tar, black fruit and wet earth. Full-bodied, with well-integrated tannins and a slight vanilla note on the finish. Drink now through 2005.–P.M. • $38 • (11/15/1999) • **90**
Dolcetto d'Alba 1991 • $12 • (10/15/1994) • **84**
Langhe Carlin 1997: Medium-bodied and straightforward, showing toasted oak, smoke and red berry quality. Short, crisp finish. Drink now.–P.M. • $25 • (11/15/1999) • **80**

Key: SS—Spectator Selection. CS—Cellar Selection. HR—Highly Recommended. $NA—Price not available. (BT)—Barrel tasting. Ⓐ—Auction Price.
For a key to the tasters' initials, see "How to Use These Listings."
Dates in parentheses represent the issues in which the ratings were published.

ITALY

GHIZZANO, TENUTA DI

Chianti 1997: A bit lean but offers some nice, clean berry and cherry aromas and flavors. Light tannins and a slightly dry finish. Drink now.–J.S. • $14 • (12/15/1998) • **80**
Chianti 1996 • $10 • (4/30/1998) • **85**
Toscana Veneroso 1997: A well-structured red. Impressive ripe berry and cherry aromas follow through to a full-bodied palate, with compacted, polished tannins and a long tobacco and berry aftertaste. A blend of Cabernet Sauvignon, Sangiovese and Merlot. Best after 2000.–J.S. • $28 • (11/30/1999) • **90**
Toscana Veneroso 1996: Clean and fruity. Dark, with lots of grape, raspberry and violet character. Full-bodied, with fine tannins and a good amount of fruit. Needs a bit more on the finish. Drink now.–J.S. • $32 • (11/30/1999) • **86**
Toscana Veneroso 1995: Lots of plum skin and berry aromas and flavors. Medium-bodied, with light tannins and a very ripe, almost raisiny aftertaste. Slightly overdone. Drink now.–J.S. • $26 • (12/15/1998) • **83**
Veneroso 1994 • $22 • (9/30/1997) • **86**

GIACOSA, BRUNO

Barbaresco 1996: Fine craftsmanship behind this traditional Barbaresco. Gorgeous, ripe fruit and round body lead to a silky midpalate, with rose petal, roasted chestnut, plum, cherry and mineral complexity. Great balance, with firm but ripe tannins clamping down the finish. Best from 2003 through 2006.–P.M. • $65 • (8/31/1999) • **93**
Barbaresco 1995: Intriguing. Supple and ripe-tasting, with animal, grilled meat, black pepper and plum flavors. Of medium body, it's quite round in the midpalate, then kicks in with a firm tannic structure on the chewy finish. Stays balanced throughout. Drink now through 2007.–P.M. • $18 Ⓐ • (10/31/1998) • **87**
Barbaresco 1985 • $42 • (8/31/1989) • **84**
Barbaresco 1983 • $24 • (7/31/1987) • **88**
Barbaresco Asili 1993 • $NA • (10/31/1996) • **90**
Barbaresco Asili 1990 • $NA • (10/31/1994) • **92**
Barbaresco Gallina di Neive 1995: Delicate, light-bodied but pleasant, showing mineral, mint, plum and blackberry character along with a rustic chestnut note. Tannins creep up at the end. Drink now through 2005.–P.M. • $95 • (10/31/1998) • **88**
Barbaresco Gallina di Neive 1986 • $40 • (8/31/1991) • **88**
Barbaresco Gallina di Nieve 1990 • $NA • (10/31/1994) • **86**
Barbaresco Gallina di Nieve 1989 • $NA • (10/31/1993) • **79**
Barbaresco Santo Stefano di Neive 1996: Unmistakably traditional Piedmont—in the best sense—this Italian red offers pleasure all around. There's some mocha blended with chestnut, full-throttle, supersweet and ripe black fruit, a full mouthfeel, plus a grip of refined but muscular tannins for the decade or two ahead. Drink now through 2020.–P.M. • $100 • (8/31/1999) CS • **95**
Barbaresco Santo Stefano di Neive 1995: Complex, light- to medium-bodied, offering mineral, lead pencil and wet earth, with lots of polished tannins and lovely fruit. Very light in color, it caresses the palate and grows when in contact with air, showing a deceptive personality. Drink now through 2010.–P.M. • $115 • (9/15/1998) • **90**
Barbaresco Santo Stefano di Neive 1993 • $48 Ⓐ • (10/31/1996) • **89**
Barbaresco Santo Stefano di Neive 1990 • $125 Ⓐ • (10/31/1994) • **83**
Barbaresco Santo Stefano di Neive 1986 • $51 Ⓐ • (8/31/1991) • **83**
Barbaresco Santo Stefano di Neive 1982 • $98 Ⓐ • (9/15/1988) • **92**
Barbaresco Santo Stefano di Neive Riserva 1985 • $154 Ⓐ • (8/31/1991) • **77**
Barbaresco Santo Stefano di Neive Riserva 1982 • $155 Ⓐ • (9/15/1988) • **90**
Barbera d'Alba Altavilla 1993 • $17 • (10/31/1995) • **82**
Barbera d'Alba Altavilla 1990 • $18 • (10/15/1993) • **77**
Barbera d'Alba Altavilla 1987 • $12 • (3/15/1991) • **73**
Barbera d'Alba Altavilla 1986 • $12 • (3/15/1991) • **77**
Barolo 1990 • $91 Ⓐ • (10/31/1995) • **84**
Barolo 1980 • $19 • (9/15/1987) • **78**
Barolo 1978 • $31 • (9/16/1984) • **88**
Barolo Collina Rionda 1993 • $110 • (10/31/1997) • **89**
Barolo Collina Rionda 1989 • $NA • (10/31/1994) • **78**
Barolo Collina Rionda 1985 • $74 Ⓐ • (4/30/1991) • **86**
Barolo Falletto 1993 • $90 • (10/31/1997) • **87**
Barolo Falletto 1989 • $NA • (10/31/1994) • **84**
Barolo Le Rocche di Castiglione Falletto 1982 • $38 • (7/31/1989) • **80**
Barolo Riserva 1982 • $65 • (1/31/1990) • **72**
Barolo Rocche 1982 • $41 • (9/15/1988) • **90**
Barolo Villero 1989 • $NA • (10/31/1994) • **81**
Barolo Villero 1988 • $39 • (10/31/1993) • **70**
Barolo Villero 1983 • $29 • (1/31/1989) • **85**
Dolcetto d'Alba 1997: A maturing Dolcetto, with a candied wet leaf character and a somewhat drying texture. Tart, herbal-tasting finish.–P.M. • $14 • (7/31/1999) • **72**
Dolcetto d'Alba 1989 • $12 • (2/28/1991) • **88**
Dolcetto d'Alba Falletto 1996 • $14 • (10/31/1997) • **84**

GIACOSA, CARLO

Barbaresco 1992 • $20 • (1/01/1997) • **79**
Barbaresco Montefico 1996: Medium-bodied, dark in color, with lively cassis intensity, there's a racy quality to this Nebbiolo. Has ripe but firm tannins and succulent acid structure, but it's a bit herbal and has a crisp finish.–P.M. • $35 • (8/31/1999) • **79**
Barbaresco Montefico 1995: Supple, ripe-tasting, of medium body and concentration, showing smoky, toasted, spicy character. Fairly lush in texture, it delivers also a fresh, vibrant, fruit-driven structure. Tannins clamp down on the finish. Drink now through 2005.–P.M. • $25 • (10/31/1998) • **80**
Barbaresco Montefico 1993 • $26 • (1/01/1997) • **79**
Barbaresco Narin 1996: Oh, the balance in this fleshy red. Nothing is out of place as the supple tannins, full fruit, violet-scented toasted oak flavors and racy acidity roam with great class around the palate, then land with a whisper on the succulent finish. Best from 2003 through 2006.–P.M. • $35 • (8/31/1999) • **93**
Barbaresco Narin 1995: A round, supple, well-made Barbaresco, offering toasted oak, mocha, spice, wet earth, blackberry and floral notes. Medium-bodied, it kicks in with firm tannins on the medium intense finish. Best after 2002.–P.M. • $25 • (10/31/1998) • **85**
Barbaresco Narin 1993 • $26 • (1/01/1997) • **82**
Barbera d'Alba Lina 1997: Supple in texture and thick in body, it charms with its underlying lemony-acid raciness, and captures nicely the subtle oak flavors and ripe fruit. Long, delicious finish. Drink now through 2002.–P.M. • $28 • (9/15/1999) • **90**
Barbera d'Alba Vigna Mucin 1997: Lovely. Young and grapey, smelling a bit earthy as if it were a barrel sample in need of racking, but the intense ripe fruit, integrated acidity and smooth tannins make it a balanced, pleasant wine. Drink now.–P.M. • $15 • (9/15/1999) • **87**
Dolcetto d'Alba Vigna Cuchet 1998: Fruity and lively, with wet earth, currant and black cherry character. Light-bodied, it's clean and crisp on the firm finish. Drink now.–P.M. • $15 • (7/31/1999) • **82**
Dolcetto d'Alba Vigna Cuchet 1997: Thick-textured and creamy, with lots of fresh berry character, this is utterly delicious to drink now, thanks to its balanced and supple finish. Drink now.–P.M. • $15 • (10/31/1998) • **85**
Dolcetto d'Alba Vigna Cuchet 1995 • $14 • (1/01/1997) • **77**
Nebbiolo delle Langhe 1997: A bit diluted, with herbal, toasty flavors and a tart finish.–P.M. • $28 • (11/15/1999) • **75**

GILLARDI, GIOVANNI & BATTISTA

Harys 1995: Packed with earth and *terroir* and tasting of mineral and lead pencil, this elegant, racy red has a superminty character unusual for a Piedmont wine. Medium-bodied, with fine-textured yet tough tannins that need time. A blend: 80 percent Syrah, 20 percent Cabernet. Best after 2005.–P.M. • $30 • (10/31/1998) • **89**

GINESTRE, LE

Barbera d'Alba Pian Romualdo 1996: Balanced and ripe, with a character of plum, herbs, black cherry and other black fruits. Shows quite some acidity, for a mouthpuckering finish. Drink now.–P.M. • $12 • (10/31/1998) • **81**
Barolo 1994: Distinctive, with an appealing wet earth, mineral character and good concentration of subtle smoke, tar and plum notes. The tannins are smooth, the structure firm. Medium-bodied, it lingers on the balanced finish. Drink now through 2002.–P.M. • $26 • (10/31/1998) • **86**
Dolcetto d'Alba Madonna Como 1996: Deliciously ripe, with black currant, wild berry and a touch of wet earth, this is grapey and medium-bodied, with just enough tannin for the fruit. Balanced, sweet-tasting finish.–P.M. • $13 • (10/31/1998) • **85**
Nebbiolo delle Langhe 1996: Beautiful fruit in this medium-bodied Nebbiolo, stressing blackberry, black cherry and wild strawberry. Very attractive, with a bit of wet earth complexity. Supple tannins make it good drinking tonight.–P.M. • $15 • (10/31/1998) • **85**

ITALY

GINI

Chianti Classico 1994 • $NA • (10/31/1996) • **86**
Recioto di Soave Col Foscarin 1989 • $22/375 ml. • (9/15/1992) • **83**
Soave Classico Superiore 1996 • $15 • (6/30/1998) • **86**
Soave Classico Superiore La Froscà 1996 • $16 • (6/30/1998) • **87**

GINI, CANTINE

Chianti Il Novecento Riserva 1996: This elegant Chianti shows a medium-bodied palate, with fine tannins and a fresh, silky texture. Drink now.–J.S. • $16 • (11/30/1999) • **85**

Toscana Messere 1997: This medium-bodied Sangiovese has plenty of ripe fruit and raisin character, with light tannins and fresh acidity. Drink now.–J.S. • $20 • (11/30/1999) • **83**

GIOIOSA, LA

Cabernet Veneto La Villa Veneta 1998: Nice, simple and fruity, with grapey, cherry character and a fresh finish. Drink now.–J.S. • $7 • (5/15/2000) • **81**

Chardonnay Veneto La Villa Veneta 1998: A simple white, with melon and honey character, light body and a light finish.–J.S. • $7 • (2/29/2000) • **79**

Merlot Veneto 1996: Plenty of menthol and spice notes in this moderately concentrated, medium-weight red that finishes slightly coarse.–B.S. • $5 • (7/31/1998) • **83**

Merlot Veneto La Villa Veneta 1998: A fresh and fruity red with grapey, cherry flavors, light body, light tannins and a crisp finish. Not much Merlot character.–J.S. • $7 • (5/15/2000) • **79**

Pinot Grigio Veneto 1997: Light and slightly spritzy. A basic white with modest apple and almond flavors. Drink now.–B.S. • $5 • (7/31/1998) • **76**

Pinot Grigio Veneto La Villa Veneta 1998: Decent fruit, with peaches and cream character. Medium-bodied, with a light finish.–J.S. • $7 • (2/29/2000) • **79**

GIOVELLO

Merlot Veneto 1996 • $7 • (4/30/1998) • **68**
Merlot Veneto 1995 • $6 • (1/01/1997) • **81**
Pinot Grigio Veneto 1996 • $7 • (5/15/1998) • **79**

GIRIBALDI

Barbaresco 1991: A bit diluted, with light tannins and a tart texture, this lacks the concentration and ripeness you expect in a fine Nebbiolo. Short finish.–P.M. • $27 • (10/31/1998) • **73**

Barbera d'Alba 1997: Like a barrel sample. Medium-bodied, with grape and crushed berry flavors and plum notes, this is a joy to taste. Drinks like a Nouveau Beaujolais-style wine. Very ripe and full-bodied, it's delicious now.–P.M. • $13 • (10/31/1998) • **85**

Barolo 1993: Very traditional in style, this medium-bodied red has chestnut, wet earth, tar and black cherry notes and dry tannins. Offers fairly good midpalate concentration. Maybe time will soften the finish. Best after 2003.–P.M. • $27 • (10/31/1998) • **81**

Dolcetto d'Alba Vigna Cason 1997: Thick-textured but rather firm. A traditional Dolcetto that delivers good acidity and plenty of black cherry, cedar and wet earth character that should hold up nicely at the table.–P.M. • $15 • (10/31/1998) • **83**

Favorita Langhe 1997: This medium-bodied, supple, fruity white (made of the local variety Favorita) has good ripeness and plays on the almond, pear, apple, pineapple and melon register with a deft touch. Chill as an aperitif. Drink now.–P.M. • $15 • (10/31/1998) • **82**

Nebbiolo d'Alba 1995: Light, with delicate raspberry and strawberry aromas and flavors, light tannins and a fairly short finish. Serve slightly chilled. Drink now.–P.M. • $14 • (10/31/1998) • **79**

Pinot Nero Oltrepò Pavese 1997: Light and pleasant, off-dry white with a spritzy texture. Shows some pear, fig and melon flavors. Quite lovely in its type, with a slight bitter almond bite on the finish to give a bit of length. Enjoy now as an aperitif.–P.M. • $10 • (8/31/1998) • **80**

Key: SS—Spectator Selection. CS—Cellar Selection. HR—Highly Recommended. $NA—Price not available. (BT)—Barrel tasting. Ⓐ—Auction Price.
For a key to the tasters' initials, see "How to Use These Listings."
Dates in parentheses represent the issues in which the ratings were published.

Roero 1996: A light Nouveau style, with raspberry and strawberry notes and a slightly spritzy texture. Serve chilled as a picnic wine. Drink now.–P.M. • $15 • (10/31/1998) • **79**

Roero Arneis 1997: Dry, minerally and taut, with good personality and stone, wet earth and citrus character. Fairly lean and light-bodied, yet clean and pure. A refreshing departure from many wobbly Piedmont whites. Drink now.–P.M. • $15 • (10/31/1998) • **84**

GONDI, MARCHESE

Chianti Rufina 1990 • $NA • (10/31/1993) • **85**

Chianti Rufina San Giuliano 1996: Strange, with a rather vegetal and burnt fruit character. Medium-bodied, with light tannins and a slightly hard, peppery finish. Tasted twice, with consistent notes. Not imported into the U.S.–J.S. • $NA • (12/15/1998) • **76**

Chianti Rufina Tenuta di Bossi Riserva 1995: A sleek and slender red with lovely, bright berry character and well-knit tannins. Caresses the palate while entertaining it with fresh fruit. Medium-bodied. Not imported into the U.S. Drink now.–J.S. • $NA • (12/15/1998) • **87**

Chianti Rufina Tenuta di Bossi Riserva 1994 • $NA • (9/30/1997) • **79**
Chianti Rufina Tenuta di Bossi Riserva 1993 • $NA • (9/30/1997) • **79**

Colli dell 'Etruria Centrale Tenuta di Bossi 1997: Interesting mineral, honeydew and floral aromas. Medium-bodied, with fresh acidity and a light-flavored, crisp finish. Not imported into the U.S. Drink now.–J.S. • $NA • (12/15/1998) • **81**

Colli dell 'Etruria Centrale Tenuta di Bossi 1996 • $NA • (9/30/1997) • **80**
Mazzaferrata 1993 • $NA • (9/30/1997) • **86**

GORELLI

Brunello di Montalcino 1995: Best wine ever from Gorelli. Delicate aromas of plums, orange peel and lemons with hints of violets. Full-bodied and very fine. Super silky tannins and a long, long finish. Wonderful. Drink now through 2006.–J.S. • $53 • (6/30/2000) • **93**

Brunello di Montalcino 1994: Wonderfully made. Subtle and complex aromas and flavors of plums, flowers and minerals. Medium- to full-bodied, with superintegrated tannins and a long, caressing finish. Will improve with age. Drink now through 2003.–J.S. • $50 • (8/31/1999) • **90**

Brunello di Montalcino 1993: Rather mature-tasting. Brick-red in color, with a light vanilla, fruit and floral bouquet. Medium in body, with firm tannins and a slightly dry finish. Drink now.–J.S. • $50 • (12/15/1998) • **81**

Brunello di Montalcino 1992 • $35 • (9/30/1997) • **85**
Brunello di Montalcino 1991 • $32 • (11/30/1996) • **86**
Brunello di Montalcino 1990 • $NA • (10/31/1995) • **87**
Brunello di Montalcino 1988 • $NA • (4/30/1994) • **87**

Rosso di Montalcino 1997: Good rosso with straightforward berry and cherry character. Medium-bodied, with fine tannins and a fresh finish. Drink now.–J.S. • $25 • (9/15/1999) • **84**

Rosso di Montalcino 1996: A lovely, balanced Rosso, with floral and berry aromas and flavors. Medium-bodied, with delicate tannins and a fresh finish. Drink now.–J.S. • $20 • (12/15/1998) • **86**

Rosso di Montalcino 1995 • $20 • (9/30/1997) • **89**
Rosso di Montalcino 1994 • $15 • (11/30/1996) • **84**
Rosso di Montalcino 1993 • $NA • (10/31/1995) • **86**
Rosso di Montalcino 1992 • $NA • (10/31/1994) • **80**
Rosso di Montalcino 1991 • $NA • (4/30/1994) • **82**

GRACCIANO DELLA SETA, TENUTA DI

Rosso di Montepulciano 1997: Promises more on the nose than it delivers on the palate, with aromas of dried berry and cherry. Medium-bodied, with crisp acidity and a short finish. Drink now.–J.S. • $10 • (12/15/1998) • **83**

Rosso di Montepulciano 1995 • $10 • (9/30/1997) • **87**

Vino Nobile di Montepulciano 1995: A balanced, easy-to-drink 1995 Nobile, with plenty of berry and tobacco aromas and flavors. Medium-bodied, with medium tannins and a light finish. Drink now.–J.S. • $17 • (12/15/1998) • **84**

Vino Nobile di Montepulciano 1994 • $14 • (9/30/1997) • **81**

Vino Nobile di Montepulciano Rovisci Riserva 1996: A bit tired and light, with tobacco, cedar and berry character. Light-bodied, with a drying finish. Not imported into the U.S.–J.S. • $NA • (1/01/1999) • **79**

Vino Nobile di Montepulciano Rovisci Riserva 1995: A very modern style, with a bit too much new wood. Medium- to full-bodied, with fine tannins and a vanilla and toasty oak finish. Drink now.–J.S. • $23 • (12/15/1998) • **85**

Vino Nobile di Montepulciano Rovisci Riserva 1993 • $17 • (9/30/1997) • **71**

GRASSO, ELIO

Barbera d'Alba Vigna Martina 1992 • $18 • (10/31/1995) • **82**
Barbera Langhe Vigna Martina 1990 • $20 • (9/15/1993) • **81**
Barolo 1991 • $24 • (10/31/1995) • **81**
Barolo Gavarini Vigna Chiniera 1990 • $30 • (10/31/1994) • **87**
Barolo Gavarini Vigna Rüncot 1988 • $30 • (9/15/1993) • **84**
Barolo Ginestra Vigna Casa Maté 1990 • $58 Ⓐ • (10/31/1994) • **85**
Barolo Ginestra Vigna Casa Maté 1988 • $30 • (9/15/1993) • **82**
Dolcetto d'Alba Gavarini Vigna dei Grassi 1989 • $18 • (7/15/1991) • **76**
Gavarini 1989 • $20 • (7/15/1991) • **83**

GRASSO, SILVIO

Barolo 1993 • $30 • (10/31/1997) • **89**
Barolo Bricco Luciani 1993 • $33 • (10/31/1997) • **86**
Barolo Ciabot Manzoni 1993 • $35 • (10/31/1997) • **90**

GRATTAMACCO

Bolgheri 1995: Irresistable. Blackberry and currant aromas jump out of the glass. Medium- to full-bodied, with velvety tannins and a long, fruity finish. A juicy, chewy beauty. A big step forward for this producer. Drink now.–J.S. • $40 • (12/15/1998) • **90**
Bolgheri 1994 • $NA • (9/30/1997) • **86**
Bolgheri Superiore 1996: Grattamacco can do no wrong. Gorgeous aromas of raspberry and fruits of the forest, with hints of earth. Medium- to full-bodied, with a solid core of ripe fruit and well-integrated tannins. Drink now through 2004.–J.S. • $45 • (11/30/1999) • **91**
Bolgheri White 1998: Refreshing aromas of peach, apple and lemon. Full-bodied, with good acidity and a spicy, honeyed aftertaste. Drink now.–J.S. • $18 • (11/30/1999) • **87**
Bolgheri White 1996 • $NA • (9/30/1997) • **84**
Tuscany 1990 • $NA • (10/31/1993) • **93**
Tuscany 1989 • $NA • (10/31/1993) • **86**
Tuscany 1988 • $NA • (9/15/1991) • **87**
Tuscany 1986 • $25 • (12/15/1992) • **72**

GRESY, MARCHESI DI

Barbaresco Camp Gros Martinenga 1996: Another beautiful '96 from Marchesi di Gresy. Elegant, with a refined tannin structure, offering ripe blackberry in a medium-bodied package. Piedmont wet earth, mineral and stone dust character needs time to integrate. Don't expect much midpalate richness, but the finesse charms. Best from 2002 through 2008.–P.M. • $75 • (10/31/1999) • **88**
Barbaresco Camp Gros Martinenga 1995: Distinctive Barbaresco, showing wet earth, flint, mineral and blood orange character. Delicate in body, supple in texture, with good ripe fruit. The tannins kick in on the finish, but they're well-integrated and rather sweet. Drink now through 2003.–P.M. • $60 • (10/31/1998) • **85**
Barbaresco Camp Gros Martinenga 1990 • $60 • (10/31/1993) • **90**
Barbaresco Camp Gros Martinenga 1989 • $60 • (10/31/1993) • **78**
Barbaresco Camp Gros Martinenga 1988 • $60 • (10/31/1993) • **82**
Barbaresco Camp Gros Martinenga 1985 • $58 • (1/31/1989) • **92**
Barbaresco Camp Gros Martinenga 1983 • $30 • (9/15/1988) • **88**
Barbaresco Camp Gros Martinenga 1982 • $26 • (9/15/1988) • **89**
Barbaresco Gaiun Martinenga 1996: It's official: Marchesi di Gresy is back after a few disappointing years. This complex, ripe and intense Nebbiolo shows beautiful blackberry, fig, tobacco and raspberry notes. Full-bodied, anchored in mineral and wet earth *terroir* roots that bring the flavors to a long, succulent, tannic finish. Best from 2004 through 2008.–P.M. • $75 • (10/31/1999) • **92**
Barbaresco Gaiun Martinenga 1995: Offering blueberry, cranberry and floral notes, but also some harsh tannins, this medium- to full-bodied wine is a bit disjointed, at least now. Has good concentration, so time might work. Best from 2002 through 2005.–P.M. • $60 • (10/31/1998) • **82**
Barbaresco Gaiun Martinenga 1990 • $91 Ⓐ • (10/31/1994) • **83**
Barbaresco Gaiun Martinenga 1989 • $61 • (10/31/1994) • **86**
Barbaresco Gaiun Martinenga 1988 • $60 • (10/31/1993) • **83**
Barbaresco Gaiun Martinenga 1986 • $64 • (9/15/1990) • **90**
Barbaresco Gaiun Martinenga 1985 • $55 • (1/31/1989) CS • **95**
Barbaresco Gaiun Martinenga 1983 • $30 • (9/15/1988) • **84**
Barbaresco Gaiun Martinenga 1982 • $26 • (9/15/1988) • **87**
Barbaresco Camp Gros Martinenga 1979 • $NA • (9/15/1988) • **88**
Barbaresco Martinenga 1996: Elegant and refined, this medium-bodied Barbaresco focuses on wet earth, mineral and chalk notes, with fresh, grapey red berries. Linear, clean, pure finish. Best from 2002 through 2006.–P.M. • $50 • (10/31/1999) • **89**
Barbaresco Martinenga 1995: Fairly crisp, a bit hot, but has decent fruit and mouthfeel, with red berry and lemony notes. Tough tannins on the finish. –P.M. • $45 • (10/31/1998) • **77**
Barbaresco Martinenga 1994 • $40 • (10/31/1997) • **79**
Barbaresco Martinenga 1992 • $41 • (10/31/1995) • **78**
Barbaresco Martinenga 1991 • $41 • (10/31/1995) • **81**
Barbaresco Martinenga 1990 • $40 • (10/31/1994) • **82**
Barbaresco Martinenga 1989 • $36 • (10/31/1994) • **82**
Barbaresco Martinenga 1988 • $30 • (10/31/1993) • **80**
Barbaresco Martinenga 1986 • $56 • (9/15/1990) • **88**
Barbaresco Martinenga 1985 • $39 • (1/31/1989) • **90**
Barbaresco Martinenga 1984 • $20 • (9/15/1988) • **84**
Barbaresco Martinenga 1983 • $20 • (9/15/1988) • **87**
Barbaresco Martinenga 1982 • $20 • (9/15/1988) • **86**
Barbaresco Martinenga 1979 • $NA • (9/15/1988) • **81**
Barbaresco Martinenga 1978 • $NA • (9/15/1988) • **89**
Dolcetto d'Alba Monte Aribaldo 1998: A nice Dolcetto, with earth, bark, dried herb and red berry character, presented in a rather intense package that lingers on the finish. Drink now.–P.M. • $15 • (11/15/1999) • **83**
Dolcetto d'Alba Monte Aribaldo 1997: Lovely. Ripe and sweet-tasting, with cherry, raspberry and currant, supple tannins and good balance. (A bit spritzy, though.) Light- to medium-bodied, charming; try with meals.–P.M. • $14 • (10/31/1998) • **85**
Dolcetto d'Alba Monte Aribaldo 1996 • $14 • (10/31/1997) • **84**
Dolcetto d'Alba Monte Aribaldo 1994 • $NA • (10/31/1995) • **84**
Dolcetto d'Alba Monte Aribaldo 1993 • $NA • (10/31/1995) • **80**
Langhe Villa Martis 1996: Attractive and balanced. Nice plum and black fruit flavors coexist in this medium-bodied, rather supple red. It has just enough toasted and smoky notes to add interest. Drink now through 2002.–P.M. • $19 • (11/15/1999) • **87**
Langhe Villa Martis 1995: Metallic and herbal notes dominate in this medium-bodied red. Astringent finish.–P.M. • $17 • (10/31/1998) • **71**
Langhe Villa Martis 1994 • $17 • (10/31/1997) • **75**
Langhe Virtus 1996: Clean, ripe and polished. A balanced red, with focused black fruit flavors, smooth tannins and a deft dosage of oak. Not showy, just full of pleasure, with a lingering, smoky finish. Drink now through 2003.–P.M. • $30 • (11/15/1999) • **88**
Langhe Virtus 1995: A serious red, appealing for its fresh acidity, ripe, clean fruit and, above all, sweet, round tannins. What appears to be barrique influence creeps in, but it's OK, the wine has structure and enough red- and blackberry concentration support fancy oak. Balanced and very silky finish. Drink now through 2005.–P.M. • $27 • (10/31/1998) • **90**
Langhe Virtus 1991 • $25 • (10/31/1994) • **83**
Nebbiolo delle Langhe Martinenga 1998: Like a spoonful of chocolate mousse, this is all mocha and spice, with raspberry and black cherry. Supple tannins clamp down on the ripe, lingering finish. Drink now through 2004.–P.M. • $18 • (11/15/1999) • **88**
Nebbiolo Martinenga 1986 • $11 • (10/15/1988) • **82**

GREVEPESA, CASTELLI DEL

Chianti Classico 1994 • $NA • (10/31/1996) • **76**
Chianti Classico Castelgreve Riserva 1988 • $10 • (9/15/1992) • **79**
Chianti Classico Castello di Bibbione 1995: Good Chianti, if not exciting. Dried cherry with tanned leather character. Medium-bodied, with medium tannins and a mouthpuckering acidity and dryness on the finish. Not imported into the U.S. Drink now.–J.S. • $NA • (1/01/1999) • **80**
Chianti Classico Clemente VII 1997: A pleasant Chianti, with dried cherry and plum character. Light- to medium-bodied, with a crisp finish. Drink now.–J.S. • $13 • (11/30/1999) • **84**
Chianti Classico Clemente VII 1996: Delivers pretty chocolate and berry aromas and flavors, with a medium body, soft tanins and a fresh aftertaste. Zingy acidity. Drink now.–J.S. • $11 • (12/15/1998) • **85**
Chianti Classico Clemente VII 1995 • $11 • (9/30/1997) • **75**
Chianti Classico Clemente VII 1993 • $NA • (10/31/1995) • **79**
Chianti Classico Clemente VII 1988 • $8 • (9/15/1992) • **81**
Chianti Classico Clemente VII Riserva 1996: A pleasant, mature Sangiovese, with tobacco, cedar and plum character. Medium-bodied, with light tannins and a crisp finish. Not imported into the U.S. Drink now.–J.S. • $NA • (1/01/1999) • **83**

ITALY

GREVEPESA, CASTELLI DEL

Chianti Classico Clemente VII Riserva 1995: Straightforward Sangiovese with dried cherry aromas and flavors, medium to light body and a crisp finish. Drink now.–J.S. • $18 • (12/15/1998) • **81**

Chianti Classico Clemente VII Riserva 1994 • $18 • (9/30/1997) • **78**

Chianti Classico L 'Alberello di Lamole 1997: Gorgeous aromas of blackberry, plum and black cherry. Medium-bodied, with lovely silky tannins and a crisp, lively finish. Not imported into the U.S. Drink through 2001.–J.S. • $NA • (1/01/1999) • **87**

Chianti Classico L 'Alberello di Lamole 1996: Straightforward and fruity, with dried cherry character, medium body, light tannins and a crisp finish. Drink now.–J.S. • $17 • (12/15/1998) • **84**

Chianti Classico L 'Alberello di Lamole 1990 • $NA • (10/31/1993) • **76**

Chianti Classico Lamole 1995: A very fine, subtle wine. Aromatic, with blackberry and floral character. Medium-bodied, with lovely fruit and a light, silky-textured finish. Not imported into the U.S. Drink now.–J.S. • $NA • (11/30/1999) • **87**

Chianti Classico Monte Firidolfi 1995: Simple red, with dried cherry character throughout. Light-bodied, with a fresh finish. Drink now.–J.S. • $20 • (11/30/1999) • **81**

Chianti Classico Monte Firidolfi 1993: Barely holding on now, with some plum character but mostly cedar and parmesan tones.–J.S. • $19 • (12/15/1998) • **75**

Chianti Classico Panzano 1994: An elegant and succulent red, with delicious berry, chocolate and vanilla character. Medium-bodied, with light tannins and a fresh finish. Drink now.–J.S. • $19 • (12/15/1998) • **83**

Chianti Classico Panzano 1988 • $11 • (9/15/1992) • **84**

Chianti Classico Pianacci 1995: Fresh blackberry and dried cherry aromas. Medium-bodied, with fresh fruit and a crisp finish. Slightly one-dimensional. Not imported into the U.S. Drink now.–J.S. • $NA • (1/01/1999) • **82**

Chianti Classico Sant 'Angolo Vico L 'Abate 1994: Slightly overdone. Shows intense dried cherry, with a hint of raisins. Full-bodied, with mouthpuckering tannins, a very dry on the finish. Drink now.–J.S. • $19 • (12/15/1998) • **81**

Chianti Classico Sant 'Angolo Vico L 'Abate 1988 • $NA • (9/15/1991) • **88**

Chianti Classico Vigna Elisa 1995: Some decent dried cherry and mineral character in this light-bodied Chianti Classico. Slightly austere finish. Drink now.–J.S. • $20 • (11/30/1999) • **82**

Chianti Classico Vigna Elisa 1993: Light-bodied, with plum and cedar character, light tannins and a light finish. Simple. Drink now.–J.S. • $19 • (12/15/1998) • **81**

Chianti Classico Vigna Elisa 1988 • $13 • (9/15/1992) • **85**

Magiòlo 1990 • $NA • (10/31/1993) • **84**

Toscana Coltifredi 1995: Good but needs more fruit. Focused blackberry, mint and dried cherry character. Medium-bodied, with light silky tannins and a slightly short finish. Not imported into the U.S. Drink now.–J.S. • $NA • (11/30/1999) • **85**

Toscana Coltifredi 1988 • $21 • (10/31/1993) • **85**

Toscana Gualdo al Luco 1995: A lot of minty, blackberry character. Full-bodied and chewy, with lots of fruit and lots of new wood. Still needs time; shows promise. Best after 2000.–J.S. • $37 • (11/30/1999) • **88**

Toscana Gualdo al Luco 1993 • $NA • (9/30/1997) • **82**

GROTTA DEL SOLE, CANTINE

Falanghina dei Campi Flegrei 1998: Lively and delicious white. Lovely aromas of pears, honey and melons. Medium-bodied, with honeysuckle, mineral flavors and a fresh finish. Drink now.–J.S. • $14 • (1/31/2000) • **86**

Greco di Tufo 1998: Beautifully rich wine with tropical fruit, honeycomb and mineral character. Full-bodied, with a creamy texture and a long, mineral finish. Drink now.–J.S. • $16 • (1/31/2000) • **90**

Lacryma Christi del Vesuvio 1997: Vivid aromas of ripe plums, black licorice and spices. Full-bodied, with velvety tannins and a cedar, berry aftertaste. Round and delicious. Drink now.–J.S. • $13 • (1/01/1999) • **87**

Lacryma Christi del Vesuvio White 1998: Lots of mineral and melon character in this medium-bodied, very fresh white. Subtle honeyed and mineral finish. Drink now.–J.S. • $13 • (1/31/2000) • **87**

Piedirosso dei Campi Flegrei 1998: Shows a good intensity of cherry skin and spice character on the nose, but it's slightly one-dimensional on the palate. Medium-bodied, with medium tannins and a light finish. Drink now.–J.S. • $14 • (1/31/2000) • **84**

Key: SS—Spectator Selection. CS—Cellar Selection. HR—Highly Recommended. $NA—Price not available. (BT)—Barrel tasting. Ⓐ—Auction Price. For a key to the tasters' initials, see "How to Use These Listings."
Dates in parentheses represent the issues in which the ratings were published.

GUALDO DEL RE

Toscana Federico Primo 1996: Big and rich, with decadent aromas of ripe fruit, tobacco and meat. Full-bodied and loaded with fruit and round, velvety tannins. Long, long finish. Merlot and Sangiovese. Best after 2000.–J.S. • $30 • (11/30/1999) • **91**

Val di Cornia Red Suvereto 1998: Slightly earthy, but with decent dried cherry and berry character. Light-bodied, with fresh acidity and a light tannin structure. Drink now.–J.S. • $12 • (11/30/1999) • **82**

Val di Cornia Suvereto 1996: An earthy, rustic flavor marks this smooth, broad-textured, low-tannin, easy-drinking red. Good, but not everyone's cup of tea. Ready now. • $12 • (7/31/1998) • **83**

Val di Cornia Suvereto 1995 • $NA • (10/31/1996) • **78**

Val di Cornia Suvereto Riserva 1996: Lovely clarity of fruit from nose to palate, with plum, berry and a hint of mushroom. Medium-bodied, with silky tannins. A joy to taste. Drink now through 2003.–J.S. • $28 • (11/30/1999) • **90**

Val di Cornia Suvereto Riserva 1994: A substantial red, full-bodied and full of character. Has deep color, firm tannins and a distinctive flavor profile that's earthy in an appealing way. Lingering finish. Drink now through 2001. • $27 • (7/31/1998) • **87**

Val di Cornia White Suvereto 1998: A light and aromatic white, with pie crust and pear character. Light-bodied, with a light, bubbly palate and a fresh finish. Drink now.–J.S. • $12 • (11/30/1999) • **83**

Vermentino Toscana Valentina 1998: Light and easy, with pear, almond and melon aromas and flavors. Light- to medium-bodied, with fresh acidity and a light finish. Drink now.–J.S. • $12 • (11/30/1999) • **84**

GUICCIARDINI, CONTE FERDINANDO

Castello di Poppiano Tricorno 1995: Slightly disjointed. Some berry character surfaces from the cut grass and earth. Medium-bodied, with masses of vanilla, cream character and a caressing finish. Sangiovese, Cabernet, Nebbiolo and Barbera. Drink now.–J.S. • $22 • (11/30/1999) • **83**

Castello di Poppiano Tricorno 1993: Shows chocolate and mocha character, with hints of fruit. Medium-bodied, with soft tannins and a slightly dry finish. Chestnut and cedar aftertaste. Starting to get tired, but still interesting. A blend of many grapes, including Sangiovese, Nebbiolo, Barbera and Cabernet Sauvignon. Drink now.–J.S. • $22 • (12/15/1998) • **85**

Castello di Poppiano Tricorno 1990 • $24 • (10/31/1996) • **88**

Castello di Poppiano Tricorno 1987 • $18 • (7/31/1994) • **86**

Chianti Colli Fiorentini Castello di Poppiano Riserva 1995: Simple, with plum, cedar and tobacco character throughout. Medium- bodied, with soft tannins and a fruity finish. Already at its peak. Drink now.–J.S. • $13 • (11/30/1999) • **82**

Chianti Colli Fiorentini Castello di Poppiano Riserva 1993: Some decent cherry and berry aromas and flavors but starting to dry out. Light body with light tannins.–J.S. • $13 • (12/15/1998) • **77**

Chianti Colli Fiorentini Castello di Poppiano Riserva 1986 • $10 • (5/15/1994) • **88**

Chianti Colli Fiorentini Il Cortile del Castello di Poppiano 1996: A rather lean Chianti. Plummy, with a hint of herb. Medium-bodied, with light tannins and a slightly austere finish. Slightly grassy. Drink now.–J.S. • $10 • (11/30/1999) • **83**

Chianti Colli Fiorentini Il Cortile del Castello di Poppiano 1995: A delicate wine with pleasant dried cherry and almond aromas and flavors. Medium- to light-bodied, with light tannins, a fresh finish. Drink now.–J.S. • $9 • (12/15/1998) • **84**

Chianti Colli Fiorentini Il Cortile del Castello di Poppiano 1994 • $9 • (10/31/1997) • **86**

Chianti Colli Fiorentini Il Cortile del Castello di Poppiano 1993 • $10 • (10/31/1996) • **77**

Chianti Colli Fiorentini Il Cortile del Castello di Poppiano 1990 • $8 • (5/15/1995) • **88**

Colli dell 'Etruria Centrale Castello di Poppiano Sassaia del Virginio 1997: Simple apple and pear aromas and flavors to this, with moderate acidity, but it's slightly dull and candied. Old style.–J.S. • $8 • (12/15/1998) • **78**

Colli dell 'Etruria Centrale Vin Santo della Torre Grande Castello di Poppiano 1994: Like an amontillado sherry, but slightly unclean. Dry and hard in acidity. Difficult to like.–J.S. • $18 • (11/30/1999) • **72**

Sangiovese Colli della Toscana Centrale Castello di Poppiano Tosco Forte 1997: Medium-bodied, with interesting berry, strawberry and spice character and light tannins. A bit light on the fresh, fruity finish. Not imported into the U.S. Drink now.–J.S. • $NA • (1/01/1999) • **85**

Sangiovese Colli della Toscana Centrale Castello di Poppiano Tosco Forte 1996: A slightly raisiny, stemmy red with lots of alcohol. Medium-bodied, with a hot, slightly diluted finish.–J.S. • $15 • (12/15/1998) • **78**

Sangiovese Colli della Toscana Centrale Castello di Poppiano Tosco Forte 1995 • $12 • (10/31/1997) • **83**

Syrah Colli della Toscana Centrale Castello di Poppiano 1997: This straightforward Syrah is bright, fruity and delicious, with strawberry, berry and plum character. Medium-bodied, with soft tannins and a fruity aftertaste. Not imported into the U.S. Drink now.–J.S. • $NA • (1/01/1999) • **86**

Syrah Colli della Toscana Centrale Castello di Poppiano 1996: Interesting, but very herbal, extremely grapey too, with notes of earth and game. Medium-bodied, with polished tannins but a grassy character comes through on the finish. Young vines? Drink now.–J.S. • $12 • (12/15/1998) • **84**

Syrah Colli della Toscana Centrale Castello di Poppiano 1995 • $12 • (10/31/1997) • **84**

Syrah Toscana Castello di Poppiano 1994 • $15 • (10/31/1996) • **84**

Vernaccia Colli della Toscana Centrale Castello di Poppiano 1998: Good concentration of fruit, with aromas of dried fruit such as pear and pineapple. Medium-bodied, dry yet slightly confected, with a mineral and honey finish. Drink now.–J.S. • $11 • (11/30/1999) • **85**

GUICCIARDINI STROZZI

Chianti Colli Senesi Terre del Principe 1995 • $11 • (3/31/1997) • **77**

Chianti Colli Senesi Titolato Strozzi 1997: A deliciously fruity young Chianti. Crushed berry and raspberry aromas. Medium-bodied, with medium tannins and a grapey, berry aftertaste. Drink now.–J.S. • $12 • (12/15/1998) • **85**

Terre del Principe Vin Santo 1991 • $17/375 ml. • (5/31/1997) • **83**

Toscana 994 Millanni 1997: This attractive red has lots of toasted, smoky oak and fruit. Medium-bodied, with medium-silky tannins and a fruity finish. Drink now.–J.S. • $75 • (11/30/1999) • **86**

Toscana 994 Millanni 1996: A fine, well-crafted red. Incredibly floral on the nose, with rose and gardenia and a hint of fruit. Medium-bodied, with well-integrated tannins and a caressing texture. Drink now.–J.S. • $65 • (11/30/1999) • **89**

Toscana 994 Millanni 1995: Interesting minty character, with berry highlights. Medium-bodied, with very firm and slightly austere tannins. A tad too much new oak and volatility for me, making the wine too dry.–J.S. • $56 • (12/15/1998) • **83**

Toscana Millanni 1994 • $42 • (9/30/1997) • **89**

Toscana Selvascura 1997: A mouthpuckering yet soft and rustic Merlot, with intense aromas of blackberry, plum and smoke. Full-bodied and powerful, with lots of fruit and tannins. Give it time. Best after 2000.–J.S. • $40 • (11/30/1999) • **90**

Toscana Selvascura 1996: Shows lots of good ripe fruit but it's a bit austere at the moment from the new oak. Wonderful, dark color, with loads of blackberry and black currant aromas. Medium-bodied, with full, slightly dry tannins. Drink now.–J.S. • $25 • (12/15/1998) • **87**

Toscana Sòdole 1997: Soft and rich, with very ripe plum and spice character. Full-bodied, with velvety tannins and a long chocolate, berry and cherry aftertaste. Made from Sangiovese. Drink now.–J.S. • $70 • (11/30/1999) • **90**

Toscana Sòdole 1996: A rich and flamboyant wine. Blackberry and cherry with hints of tanned leather and smoke on the nose. Full-bodied, with chewy tannins and a long, ripe fruit finish. Slightly hollow at midpalate. Drink now.–J.S. • $30 • (12/15/1998) • **88**

Toscana Sòdole 1994 • $26 • (9/30/1997) • **88**

Vernaccia di San Gimignano Perlato 1998: Pretty aromas of apple, straw and honey. Full-bodied, with good acidity and pineapple flavors. Oily finish. Drink now.–J.S. • $12 • (11/30/1999) • **87**

Vernaccia di San Gimignano Perlato 1997: Good concentration of fruit for a Vernaccia, with lots of almond, cream and pear and hints of ash. Medium-bodied, with fresh acidity and a fruity aftertaste. Drink now.–J.S. • $16 • (12/15/1998) • **85**

Vernaccia di San Gimignano Terre del Principe San Biagio Riserva 1997: Interesting character of lemon, orange and almond. Medium-bodied, with fresh acidity and a crisp finish. Drink now.–J.S. • $70 • (11/30/1999) • **84**

Vernaccia di San Gimignano Titolato Strozzi 1997: Fresh and fruity, with light mineral and pear aromas and flavors, light body and crisp acidity. Drink now.–J.S. • $12 • (12/15/1998) • **80**

HAAS, FRANZ

Chardonnay Alto Adige Kris 1996 • $9 • (6/15/1998) • **79**

Heart Kris 1997: Light, fresh and fruity, with pleasant berry and cherry aromas and flavors. Drink now.–J.S. • $11 • (6/15/2000) • **81**

Pinot Grigio Venezie Kris 1998: Good mineral and apple character. Medium-bodied, with honey and a medium, slightly pear drop aftertaste. Drink now.–J.S. • $11 • (6/15/2000) • **85**

HADERBURG

Chardonnay Alto Adige Stainhauser 1996: Sweaty, earthy, cheesy aromas and flavors are dominant. Not recommended. Tasted twice, with consistent notes.–B.S. • $15 • (7/31/1998) • **65**

I DUE CIPRESSI

Brunello di Montalcino 1990 • $28 • (10/31/1995) • **87**

Brunello di Montalcino 1989 • $28 • (7/31/1995) • **82**

Rosso di Montalcino 1993 • $14 • (10/31/1995) • **84**

Rosso di Montalcino 1992 • $14 • (8/31/1995) • **85**

Vino Nobile di Montepulciano 1992 • $11 • (10/31/1995) • **76**

Vino Nobile di Montepulciano 1991 • $11 • (2/29/1996) • **78**

INAMA

Chardonnay Veneto 1997: A pretty little number. An aromatic and zingy white, with subtle green apple, celery and mineral aromas. Medium-bodied, with fresh acidity and a long aftertaste. Drink now.–J.S. • $NA • (6/15/1999) • **87**

Chardonnay Veneto Campo dei Tovi 1997: Plenty going on in the glass with this Chardonnay. Aromas of melon, toasted oak and earth follow through to a medium- to full-bodied palate with apple and dough flavors. Long aftertaste. Subtle and very interesting. Drink now through 2002.–J.S. • $30 • (6/15/1999) • **90**

Sauvignon Veneto Vulcaia 1997: A stylish white, with aromas of apple, leaf and mineral. Medium-bodied, with fresh acidity and a clean apple, earth and herb finish. Drink now.–J.S. • $33 • (6/15/1999) • **85**

Soave Classico Superiore 1997: Subtle yet captivating, this lovely Soave has wonderful straw, apple, melon and honey aromas. Medium-bodied, with compacted fruit and a long honey, clove and lilac aftertaste. Drink now.–J.S. • $15 • (6/15/1999) • **88**

Soave Classico Superiore Vigneti di Foscarino 1997: This is an exaggerated, late-harvest style that works. Hard to believe it's Soave. Full-bodied and powerful, with spice, pineapple and burnt almond character, good acidity and a long finish. Like a top Pinot Gris from Alsace. Drink now.–J.S. • $21 • (6/15/1999) • **91**

Soave Classico Vigneto du Lot 1997: Overripe pineapple and butter character turns to butterscotch, vanilla and cream. Full-bodied, with a round texture and a buttery finish. Drink now.–J.S. • $27 • (6/15/1999) • **82**

Veneto Vulcaia Fumé 1997: A delicious Sauvignon Blanc in a full-throttle style. Gold in color, this has intense aromas of toasted oak and baked bread, with an underlying nutty character. Big and rich, with apple, butterscotch and honey. A bit mature, but great for current drinking.–J.S. • $33 • (6/15/1999) • **89**

Vulcaia Apres 1997: Aromas of nut, fruit, herb and toasted oak. Medium-bodied and medium sweet, with a dusty, musty finish. A late-harvest wine made with unnoble rot as well as the noble stuff. Drink now.–J.S. • $NA • (1/01/1999) • **82**

ISOLE E OLENA

Antiche Tenute 1989 • $6 • (8/31/1991) • **80**

Antiche Tenute 1988 • $6 • (9/15/1989) • **83**

Cabernet Sauvignon Toscana Collezione de Marchi 1996: A cerebral, wonderfully textured Cabernet. Dark, with loads of currant, mint and dried herb aromas. Medium- to full-bodied, with smooth, silky tannins and a long currant, berry and raspberry aftertaste. Best after 2000.–J.S. • $40 • (11/30/1999) • **91**

Cabernet Sauvignon Toscana Collezione de Marchi 1995: Gorgeous Cabernet Sauvignon from Isole, with lovely harmony and fruit. Smells like fresh-picked blueberries. Medium-bodied, with full, polished tannins and a long, succulent finish. Drink now.–J.S. • $40 • (12/15/1998) • **90**

Cabernet Sauvignon Tuscany Collezione de Marchi 1994 • $32 • (9/30/1997) • **90**

Cabernet Sauvignon Tuscany Collezione de Marchi 1993 • $32 • (10/31/1996) • **91**

Cabernet Sauvignon Tuscany Collezione de Marchi 1991 • $30 • (2/28/1995) • **90**

Cabernet Sauvignon Tuscany Collezione de Marchi 1990 • $30 • (10/31/1993) • **95**

Cabernet Sauvignon Tuscany Collezione de Marchi 1988 • $40 • (9/15/1991) • **94**

ITALY

ISOLE E OLENA

Chardonnay Toscana Collezione de Marchi 1997: Always one of the best whites of Tuscany. Gorgeous aromas of apple, pineapple and coconut, with hints of orange peel. Full-bodied, with very ripe fruit and a lovely infusion of vanilla and coconut character. Drink now through 2001.–J.S. • $23 • (11/30/1999) • **91**

Chardonnay Toscana Collezione de Marchi 1996: Big and rich, with lots of ripe apple, pineapple and tropical fruit character as well as just the right amount of smoky oak. Full-bodied, with fresh acidity and a long, flavorful finish. California Chardonnay lovers will go for this. Will improve with age but don't wait. Drink now.–J.S. • $25 • (12/15/1998) • **90**

Chianti Classico 1997: Medium-bodied, with lots of plum and berry character, soft tannins and a fruity finish. Very pretty indeed, although slightly one-dimensional. Drink now.–J.S. • $18 • (11/30/1999) • **86**

Chianti Classico 1996: A fresh and floral young Chianti, its crisp acidity and light tannins making it enjoyable now. Medium body. Fresh finish.–J.S. • $15 • (12/15/1998) • **85**

Chianti Classico 1995 • $13 • (9/30/1997) • **85**

Chianti Classico 1994 • $14 • (10/31/1996) • **87**

Chianti Classico 1993 • $12 • (10/31/1996) • **86**

Chianti Classico 1992 • $12 • (2/28/1995) • **79**

Chianti Classico 1991 • $13 • (10/31/1993) • **82**

Chianti Classico 1990 • $12 • (9/15/1992) • **90**

Chianti Classico 1988 • $9 • (11/30/1990) • **89**

Collezione de Marchi I 'Eremo 1990 • $NA • (10/31/1993) • **89**

Collezione de Marchi I 'Eremo 1988 • $NA • (9/15/1991) • **90**

Syrah Toscana Collezione de Marchi 1996: A drink-me-now Syrah, with enjoyable fruit, though it needs more on the palate. Vivid aromas of cherry and plum, with a hint of game and earth. Medium-bodied, with medium yet soft, velvety tannins and a light finish. Drink now through 2002.–J.S. • $35 • (11/30/1999) • **87**

Syrah Toscana Collezione de Marchi 1995: Like a very good Crozes-Hermitage but with a touch of Tuscan acidity. Subtle blackberry and gamy aromas and flavors. Medium-bodied, with full, soft tannins and a deliciously fruity aftertaste. Drink now.–J.S. • $35 • (12/15/1998) • **87**

Syrah Tuscany Collezione de Marchi 1994 • $34 • (9/30/1997) • **89**

Syrah Tuscany Collezione de Marchi 1993 • $32 • (10/31/1996) • **88**

Toscana Cepparello 1997: This blockbuster of a Sangiovese shows layers of ripe fruit on the palate, with loads of ripe tannins and a long, fruity finish. Truly monumental for this producer and appellation. Breathtaking. Best after 2002.–J.S. • $38 • (11/30/1999) • **96**

Toscana Cepparello 1996: Extremely grapey, with highlights of raspberries and mint. Medium-bodied, with silky, polished tannins from clever small-barrel maturation. Long, caressing finish. A gorgeous wine now but be patient, you will be rewarded. This super Tuscan is always a beauty.–J.S. • $45 • (12/15/1998) • **90**

Toscana Cepparello 1995 • $33 Ⓐ • (9/30/1997) • **91**

Toscana Cepparello 1994 • $32 • (9/30/1997) • **87**

Toscana Cepparello 1993 • $32 • (10/31/1996) • **91**

Toscana Cepparello 1991 • $28 • (2/28/1995) • **86**

Toscana Cepparello 1990 • $51 Ⓐ • (11/15/1993) • **91**

Toscana Cepparello 1989 • $NA • (11/15/1993) • **85**

Toscana Cepparello 1988 • $NA • (11/15/1993) • **92**

Toscana Cepparello 1986 • $NA • (11/15/1993) • **85**

Toscana Cepparello 1985 • $NA • (11/15/1993) • **90**

Toscana Cepparello 1983 • $NA • (11/15/1993) • **90**

Toscana Cepparello 1982 • $NA • (11/15/1993) • **94**

Vin Santo NV • $17/375 ml. • (3/31/1990) • **93**

Vin Santo 1993: A clean and zingy Vin Santo, with subtle aromas of cream, caramel and custard and hints of pie crust. Medium-bodied and medium sweet, with lovely cream and apple flavors and a sweet honey aftertaste. Drink now.–J.S. • $20/375 ml. • (12/15/1998) • **89**

JERMANN

Chardonnay Venezia Giulia 1998: Attractive apple and cream aromas follow through to a medium-bodied palate with good acidity and a ripe fruit aftertaste. Drink now through 2001.–J.S. • $27 • (3/31/2000) • **86**

Moscato Rosa del FVG Vigna Bellina 1993 • $29 • (1/01/1997) • **83**

Moscato Rosa del FVG Vigna Bellina 1989 • $26 • (3/15/1991) • **81**

Pinot Bianco Venezia Giulia 1996 • $23 • (6/15/1998) • **83**

Key: SS—Spectator Selection. CS—Cellar Selection. HR—Highly Recommended. $NA—Price not available. (BT)—Barrel tasting. Ⓐ—Auction Price. For a key to the tasters' initials, see "How to Use These Listings." **Dates in parentheses represent the issues in which the ratings were published.**

Pinot Grigio Venezia Giulia 1998: Very pretty apple, apricot and spice character in this young white. Medium- to full-bodied, with good acidity and a long finish. Delicious. Drink now through 2002.–J.S. • $27 • (3/31/2000) • **87**

Riesling Venezie Afix 1998: Stylish and fresh. Intense lemon, lime and mineral character in this Riesling. Medium-bodied, with fresh acidity and a clean, crisp finish. Drink now.–J.S. • $29 • (4/30/2000) • **86**

Sauvignon Venezia Giulia 1998: A superclean white with fresh cut apple, pineapple and leafy character. Medium body. Zingy finish. Drink now.–J.S. • $27 • (4/30/2000) • **86**

Sauvignon Venezia Giulia 1996 • $24 • (6/15/1998) • **84**

Traminer Aromatico Venezie 1998: Pleasant white, with appleskin and melon character. Medium-bodied, with light acidity and a good spicy finish. Not imported into the U.S. Drink now.–J.S. • $NA • (1/01/2000) • **83**

Venezia Giulia Capo Martino 1997: A curious wine, with aromas of lemon, aniseed and fennel. Medium-bodied, with good acidity and a luscious apple, spice and honey finish. Interesting and fun to taste. Drink now.–J.S. • $51 • (1/01/2000) • **87**

Venezia Giulia Dreams 1997: Very attractive. Pineapple and tropical fruit aromas follow through to a medium-bodied palate with good acidity. Slightly diluted on the fruity finish, but very good indeed. Drink now.–J.S. • $52 • (1/01/2000) • **87**

Venezia Giulia Vinnae 1998: A wine with lovely apple, straw and honey aromas. Medium-bodied, with ripe fruit flavors and a long finish. Delicious. Drink now through 2001.–J.S. • $26 • (4/30/2000) • **87**

Venezia Giulia Vinnae da Vinnaioli 1996 • $23 • (6/15/1998) • **86**

Venezia Giulia Vintage Tunina 1998: A wine of finesse and character. Medium-bodied, with spicy honey and pineapple character. Lively and rich finish. Subdued now; better with a bit of bottle age. Best after 2000.–J.S. • $44 • (4/30/2000) • **88**

KEBER, EDI

Merlot Collio Riserva 1995 • $26 • (5/31/1998) • **87**

Merlot Collio Riserva 1993 • $22 • (3/31/1997) • **88**

Pinot Grigio Collio 1996: Floral, talcum powder flavors are allied to a firm structure that ends up slightly astringent. Drink now.–B.S. • $23 • (7/31/1998) • **77**

KRIZIA

Cabernet Franc Colli Orientali del Friuli 1994 • $21 • (4/30/1998) • **79**

LAGARIA

Chardonnay Atesino 1996 • $9 • (10/15/1997) • **79**

Merlot Atesino 1996 • $8 • (6/15/1998) • **82**

Pinot Grigio Venezie 1996 • $9 • (10/15/1997) • **82**

LAGEDER, ALOIS

Cabernet Alto Adige Löwengang 1995: Rich and decadent, with fascinating aromas of flowers, berry and chocolate. Medium-bodied, with soft tannins and a long, flavorful finish. Drink now.–J.S. • $33 • (6/15/2000) • **88**

Cabernet Alto Adige Löwengang 1994: Starts off with herbal, berry aromas; deeper plum and vanilla flavors emerge on the palate. Shows good concentration, depth and harmony, and a touch of astringency on the finish. Drink now through 2000.–B.S. • $32 • (7/31/1998) • **87**

Cabernet Alto Adige Riserva 1996: Delicious currant and berry character, with a hint of herb. Medium-bodied with medium tannins and a fruity finish. Drink now.–J.S. • $16 • (6/15/2000) • **85**

Cabernet Alto Adige Riserva 1989 • $15 • (3/31/1994) • **80**

Cabernet Sauvignon Alto Adige Cor Römigberg 1995: Rich and dark, with black currant, mint and smoke. Medium-bodied, with polished tannins. The pretty berry and cherry aftertaste has a hint of chocolate. Best after 2001.–J.S. • $52 • (6/15/2000) • **91**

Cabernet Sauvignon Alto Adige Cor Römigberg 1994: Gorgeous Cabernet Sauvignon from start to finish. Sweet, ripe cassis and black cherry flavors are accented by toasty, vanilla-laced oak—the deep character supported by ample, ripe tannins and an intensity that persists long after the wine is swallowed. From Northeast Italy. Drink now through 2004 .–B.S. • $45 • (7/31/1998) HR • **91**

Cabernet Sauvignon Alto Adige Cor Römigberg 1993 • $48 • (6/30/1998) HR • **90**

Chardonnay Alto Adige 1998: Very clean and crisp, with lots of apple and citrus character. Medium-bodied, with good acidity and a creamy texture. Drink now.–J.S. • $13 • (6/15/2000) • **85**

Chardonnay Alto Adige Buchholz 1997: Lively and crisp, with a steely style. Medium-bodied and very clean, with a long lemon, cream and sliced apple aftertaste. Very well done. Drink now.–J.S. • $15 • (6/15/2000) • **88**

Chardonnay Alto Adige Löwengang 1996: Very good, with lovely pineapple and mineral aromas. Medium-bodied, with creamy lemon flavors and a fresh finish. Drink now.–J.S. • $32 • (6/15/2000) • **88**

Gewürztraminer Alto Adige 1998: Promises more on the nose. Light in style, with wonderful aromas of sliced peaches, grapefruit and cantaloupe. Medium-bodied, with medium acidity and a slightly short finish. Drink now.–J.S. • $15 • (6/15/2000) • **85**

Lagrein Alto Adige Lindenburg 1996: Plenty of good licorice, spice and berry character. Medium-bodied, with silky tannins, good fruit and a short finish. Drink now.–J.S. • $14 • (6/15/2000) • **85**

Merlot Alto Adige 1997: Has a decent amount of berry, leather and spice. Medium-bodied, with plum, leather and a light finish. Drink now.–J.S. • $14 • (6/15/2000) • **83**

Merlot Alto Adige 1994 • $13 • (6/15/1996) • **81**

Merlot Alto Adige 1990 • $13 • (3/31/1994) • **82**

Mitterberg Bianco Dornach 1997: Very clean and fresh, with apple and lemon aromas and flavors. Medium-bodied, with an appley finish. Chardonnay, Pinot Grigio and Pinot Bianco. Drink now.–J.S. • $18 • (6/15/2000) • **87**

Mitterberg Bianco Dornach 1996 • $19 • (6/30/1998) • **86**

Pinot Bianco Alto Adige 1998: Plenty of green apple, cream and pear character. Medium-bodied, with good acidity and an appley finish. Drink now.–J.S. • $13 • (6/15/2000) • **84**

Pinot Bianco Alto Adige Haberlehof 1997: Superclean, with lemon, lime, flint and mineral character. Medium-bodied, with fresh acidity and a long finish. A delicious, subtle wine. Drink now.–J.S. • $17 • (6/15/2000) • **86**

Pinot Grigio Alto Adige 1998: Slightly strange aromas of apple, with wax and paraffin. Medium-bodied, hard and short. Disappointing. Tasted twice, with consistent notes.–J.S. • $14 • (6/15/2000) • **79**

Pinot Grigio Alto Adige Benefizium Porer 1998: Attractive aromas of honeydew melon, apple and pear. Medium-bodied, with good acidity and a light, flinty finish. Drink now.–J.S. • $17 • (6/15/2000) • **85**

Pinot Grigio Alto Adige Benefizium Porer 1997: Delicious and steely, with lots of mineral, lemon and fresh apple. Full-bodied with a flinty character and a long, crisp finish. Drink now.–J.S. • $17 • (1/01/2000) • **87**

Pinot Grigio Alto Adige Benefizium Porer 1997: Delicious and steely, with lots of mineral, lemon and fresh apple. Full-bodied with a flinty character and a long, crisp finish. Drink now.–J.S. • $17 • (1/01/2000) • **87**

Pinot Grigio Alto Adige Benefizium Porer 1996: Bright and focused, showing concentrated apple, herb and vanilla notes augmented by firm structure and mineral detailing. Clove accentuates the aftertaste.–B.S. • $18 • (7/31/1998) • **86**

Pinot Nero Alto Adige Krafuss 1996: One of the best Pinot Noirs from Italy I have ever tasted. Beautiful plum, berry and cedar aromas follow through to a medium-bodied palate, with soft tannins and a fresh finish. Drink now.–J.S. • $30 • (6/15/2000) • **88**

Sauvignon Terlaner Lehenhof 1998: Wonderfully subtle, with mineral, apple and lime character. Medium-bodied, with good acidity and a peach and light honey aftertaste. Drink now.–J.S. • $19 • (6/15/2000) • **87**

Sauvignon Terlaner Lehenhof 1997: An intense style of Sauvignon, with aromas of sweat, lime and grapefruit. Medium-bodied, with crisp acidity and a long finish. Drink now.–J.S. • $19 • (1/01/2000) • **86**

LAMBARDI

Brunello di Montalcino 1995: Always value for the money. Very focused and fresh with cherries, violets, minerals and spices. Full-bodied, with compacted fruit and firm tannins. Still too young. Best after 2000.–J.S. • $48 • (6/30/2000) • **90**

Brunello di Montalcino 1994: A real and tender '94 Brunello that shows focused berry, cherry and slightly earthy aromas and flavors. Medium-bodied. Fine tannins. Caressing texture. Drink now.–J.S. • $33 • (8/31/1999) • **88**

Brunello di Montalcino 1993: The '93 Lambardi Brunello is rich, round and wonderful. It shows berry, tobacco and spice aromas and flavors, full body and soft, comforting tannins. Delicious. People in Montalcino have been saying good things about this small, inexpensive producer, and what they're saying is all true. Drink now.–J.S. • $34 • (12/15/1998) • **90**

Rosso di Montalcino 1997: All in finesse, with berry, dried cherry and strawberry character. Medium-bodied, with fine tannins and a medium, crisp finish. Drink now.–J.S. • $20 • (9/15/1999) • **85**

LAMBERTI

Amarone della Valpolicella Corte Rubini 1990 • $20 • (6/15/1996) • **87**

Amarone della Valpolicella Corte Rubini 1985 • $19 • (9/15/1992) • **80**

Recioto della Valpolicella Amarone Corte Rubini 1993: Plenty of tobacco-scented plum flavors on a tight, compact frame that finishes up dry and astringent. Tasted twice, with consistent notes. Drink now through 2000. –B.S. • $23 • (7/31/1998) • **84**

Valpolicella Vigneti di Ca ' Bolcana 1991 • $9 • (9/15/1992) • **74**

LAMBORGHINI

Colli del Trasimeno Trescone 1997: A simple wine, with attractive floral and berry aromas. Light- to medium-bodied, with light tannins and a slightly austere finish. Not imported into the U.S. Drink now.–J.S. • $NA • (1/01/2000) • **81**

Umbria Campoleone 1997: Really a blockbuster. Like a great Pomerol from the 1950s. Black and purple in color, with intense aromas of blackberry, cherry, licorice and mint. Full-bodied and mouthpuckering, with masses of tannins and tons of fruit. Give it time. Not imported into the U.S. Best after 2004.–J.S. • $40 • (2/29/2000) • **95**

LAMOLE DI LAMOLE

Chianti Classico 1997: Light- to medium-bodied, with pretty, bright berry character, light tannins and a lively, fruity finish. Drink now.–J.S. • $12 • (11/30/1999) • **84**

Chianti Classico 1996: A pretty, easy-to-drink Chianti, with bright grape, raspberry and cherry aromas and flavors. Medium-bodied, with soft tannins and a fresh finish. Drink now.–J.S. • $13 • (12/15/1998) • **85**

Chianti Classico 1995 • $12 • (9/30/1997) • **80**

Chianti Classico 1994 • $15 • (9/30/1997) • **82**

Chianti Classico 1991 • $14 • (10/31/1993) • **86**

Chianti Classico 1990 • $12 • (9/15/1992) • **73**

Chianti Classico 1988 • $12 • (9/15/1991) • **90**

Chianti Classico Riserva 1996: A very fine, well-structured riserva. Loads of fruit on the nose, from crushed berry to watermelon. Medium-bodied, with well-integrated tannins and a long, silky finish. Drink now through 2003.–J.S. • $20 • (11/30/1999) • **87**

Chianti Classico Riserva 1995: A wine without any rough spots, this is smooth and caressing, with plenty of dried cherry and berry character, a medium body and a delicate tannin structure. Drink now.–J.S. • $17 • (12/15/1998) • **87**

Chianti Classico Riserva 1993 • $17 • (9/30/1997) • **85**

Chianti Classico Riserva 1988 • $17 • (9/15/1992) • **82**

Chianti Classico Vigneto di Campolungo Riserva 1994: Delicious, with pretty aromas of dried cherry and flowers. Medium-bodied, with velvety tannins and a fruity, delicious aftertaste. Drink now.–J.S. • $30 • (11/30/1999) • **86**

Chianti Classico Vigneto di Campolungo Riserva 1993 • $27 • (9/30/1997) • **87**

Chianti Classico Vigneto di Campolungo Riserva 1985 • $20 • (4/30/1990) • **90**

LANCIOLA

Chardonnay Toscana Terricci 1997: Tastes more like Sauvignon than Chardonnay with its cut grass, celery and honeydew melon character. Medium-bodied, with well-integrated acidity and a fruity, mineral aftertaste. Drink now.–J.S. • $31 • (12/15/1998) • **83**

Chianti Classico 1994 • $NA • (9/30/1997) • **65**

Chianti Classico Le Masse di Greve 1996: Pretty blackberry and cherry aromas. Medium-bodied, with slightly austere tannins, a dry finish. Tasted twice, with consistent notes.–J.S. • $15 • (12/15/1998) • **79**

Chianti Classico Le Masse di Greve 1995 • $16 • (9/30/1997) • **80**

Chianti Classico Le Masse di Greve 1991 • $16 • (3/31/1997) • **79**

Chianti Classico Le Masse di Greve Riserva 1995: A little dry and slightly tired. Has some plum and berry character, a hint of oak, but it turns dry on the aftertaste. Tasted twice, with consistent notes.–J.S. • $19 • (12/15/1998) • **77**

Chianti Classico Le Masse di Greve Riserva 1994 • $20 • (9/30/1997) • **87**

Chianti Classico Le Masse di Greve Riserva 1993 • $20 • (9/30/1997) • **81**

Chianti Colli Fiorentini 1997: This young wine has interesting berry, earth and funk character. Medium-bodied, with soft tannins and a sweet fruit finish. A little loosely knit, but enjoyable. Drink now.–J.S. • $12 • (11/30/1999) • **83**

ITALY

LANCIOLA

Chianti Colli Fiorentini 1996: Rather odd aromas and flavors of wet paper and fruit. Medium-bodied and dry. Barely acceptable. Tasted twice, with consistent notes.–J.S. • $12 • (12/15/1998) • **70**

Chianti Colli Fiorentini 1995 • $11 • (9/30/1997) • **84**

Chianti Colli Fiorentini 1993 • $11 • (3/31/1997) • **82**

Chianti Colli Fiorentini Riserva 1995: Beautiful to taste. Enticing aromas of berries, meats and leather. Medium-bodied, with medium, velvety tannins and a very long and caressing finish. Impressive for this appellation. Drink through 2005.–J.S. • $17 • (12/15/1998) • **87**

Chianti Colli Fiorentini Riserva 1994 • $15 • (9/30/1997) • **85**

Chianti Le Masse di Greve Riserva 1996: A focused Chianti, with lots of cherry and berry character. Medium-bodied, with light tannins and a fresh finish. Drink now.–J.S. • $13 • (11/30/1999) • **86**

Toscana Terricci 1995: Very good super Tuscan, with bright berry and plum aromas and flavors. Medium- to full-bodied, with well-integrated tannins and a long minty, berry aftertaste. Drink now.–J.S. • $30 • (12/15/1998) • **87**

LASTRA, LA

Chianti Colli Senesi 1997: A simple Chianti, with plum character, light body and a fresh finish.–J.S. • $12 • (11/30/1999) • **79**

Toscana Rovaio 1996: A thoroughly polished, fine wine, with gorgeous aromas of berry, violet, plum and mint. Medium-bodied, with medium, silky tannins and a long, long finish. Give this time. Made from Sangiovese, Cabernet Sauvignon and Merlot. Best after 2000.–J.S. • $30 • (11/30/1999) • **90**

Vernaccia di San Gimignano 1997: Medium-bodied, with canned fruit cocktail aromas and a slightly candied, unfresh finish. Hard to get excited about.–J.S. • $14 • (11/30/1999) • **78**

Vernaccia di San Gimignano Riserva 1996: A bit confected, with strawberry, apple and fruit cocktail aromas and flavors. Medium-bodied, with fresh acidity and a light finish. Drink now.–J.S. • $20 • (11/30/1999) • **82**

LATINI, IL

Premium 1994 • $NA • (9/30/1997) • **87**

Red 1994 • $20 • (9/30/1997) • **81**

LAVACCHIO, FATTORIA

Chardonnay Colli della Toscana Centrale 1998: Pleasant aromas of lemon, banana peel and apple. Medium-bodied, with medium acidity and a fruity, chalky finish. Not imported into the U.S. Drink now.–J.S. • $NA • (1/01/1999) • **86**

Chardonnay Colli della Toscana Centrale 1997: A good, clean Chardonnay, with lots of apple, cider and honey aromas. Medium-bodied, with medium acidity and a fruity finish. Not imported into the U.S. Drink now.–J.S. • $NA • (1/01/1999) • **85**

Chianti Rufina 1997: Strangely, it's not as good as the '96, but it is pleasant, with plum, cedar and berry character. Light-bodied, with light tannins and a fresh finish. Not imported into the U.S. Drink now.–J.S. • $NA • (1/01/1999) • **80**

Chianti Rufina 1996: Fresh and fruity, with delicate cherry and hints of plum and cedar on the nose and palate. Medium-bodied, with bright cherry flavors and a light, refreshing finish. Not imported into the U.S. Drink now.–J.S. • $NA • (1/01/1999) • **83**

Chianti Rufina Riserva 1996: Disappointing. Has decent fruit, but it's rather rustic and herbal, with grassy undertones. Medium-bodied, with light tannins and an earthy finish. Not imported into the U.S.–J.S. • $NA • (1/01/1999) • **78**

Colli della Toscana Centrale Cortigiano 1997: A seriously good wine from an unknown producer, this has lots of berry, green tobacco and cherry character. Full-bodied, with sleek and racy tannins and a lovely, fruity, crisp finish. Not imported into the U.S. Drink now through 2002.–J.S. • $NA • (11/30/1999) • **88**

Colli della Toscana Centrale Cortigiano 1996: Pretty on the nose, with vivid aromas of raspberry and wild cherry. Medium-bodied, with full, slightly hard tannins and a slightly austere finish. Needs time to mellow. A blend of Cabernet and Merlot. Not imported ito the U.S.–J.S. • $NA • (12/15/1998) • **86**

Key: SS—Spectator Selection. CS—Cellar Selection. HR—Highly Recommended. $NA—Price not available. (BT)—Barrel tasting. (A)—Auction Price.
For a key to the tasters' initials, see "How to Use These Listings."
Dates in parentheses represent the issues in which the ratings were published.

Toscana Oro del Cedro 1998: An impressive late-harvest Traminer, with lovely aromas of vanilla, honey and dried apricot. Full-bodied and very sweet, with loads of spicy honey flavors. Very good acidity and a long finish. Not imported into the U.S. Drink now through 2005.–J.S. • $NA/500 ml. • (1/01/1999) • **90**

LECCIA, CASTELLO LA

Chianti Classico 1997: This superbly crafted Chianti Classico is dark ruby in color, with intense aromas of blackberry, raspberry and spice. Medium- to full-bodied, with very well integrated tannins and a long, spicy finish. Drink now through 2001.–J.S. • $16 • (1/01/1999) • **89**

Chianti Classico 1995: More on the nose than the palate, with alluring blackberry and floral character. Medium-bodied, with fine tannins and a light, slightly austere finish. Drink now.–J.S. • $16 • (12/15/1998) • **83**

Chianti Classico 1994: An elegant Chianti, with aromas and flavors of cedar, berry and tanned leather. Medium-bodied, with fine tannins and a light, fruity finish. Drink now.–J.S. • $14 • (12/15/1998) • **84**

Chianti Classico 1991 • $10 • (2/28/1995) • **86**

Chianti Classico 1990 • $NA • (9/15/1992) • **88**

Chianti Classico Riserva 1995: Plenty of dried cherry and floral character. Medium-bodied, with well-integrated polished tannins and a toasted oak, berry and cherry aftertaste. Give it a bit of time. Drink now.–J.S. • $25 • (11/30/1999) • **87**

Toscana Bruciagna 1996: Extremely well done, with subtle and complex aromas of berry, cedar and cigar box. Medium-bodied, with lovely, polished tannins and a long finish. A beauty. Drink now through 2004.–J.S. • $30 • (11/30/1999) • **89**

LENARDO, DI

Cabernet Grave del Friuli Vigne dai Vieris 1998: Light and fruity Cabernet with herbal and cherry character. Medium- to light-bodied, with light tannins and a fruity finish. Drink now.–J.S. • $9 • (5/15/2000) • **82**

Chardonnay Grave del Friuli Musque 1998: Good almond, apple and honey character in this medium-bodied white, though it could use a tiny bit more acidity on the finish. Drink now.–J.S. • $9 • (2/29/2000) • **84**

Chardonnay Grave del Friuli Woody 1998: Too much wood. Strange aromas of clove follow through to the palate. Not imported into the U.S.–J.S. • $NA • (1/01/2000) • **79**

Merlot Grave del Friuli Vigne San Martin 1998: Fresh and fruity red with delicious berry and plum character. Medium body. Light tannins and crisp finish. Drink now.–J.S. • $9 • (5/15/2000) • **83**

Pinot Bianco Grave del Friuli 1998: Plenty of fruit cocktail character. Medium-bodied, with light acidity and a short finish. Slightly dull. Drink now.–J.S. • $9 • (2/29/2000) • **80**

Pinot Grigio Grave del Friuli 1998: A good Pinot Grigio, with aromas of very ripe apple and honey. Full-bodied, with lots of fruit but a slightly dull finish. Drink now.–J.S. • $9 • (2/29/2000) • **84**

Refosco dal Peduncolo Rosso Grave del Friuli Vigne San Martin 1998: Fresh and easy red with a touch of CO2 and a light, crisp finish. No big deal but pleasant enough. Drink now.–J.S. • $9 • (5/15/2000) • **81**

Ronco Nolè 1997: Pretty aromas of minerals, mint and currants. Medium-bodied, with firm tannins and a lovely harmony of fruit and wood. Medium finish. Not imported into the U.S. Drink now through 2002.–J.S. • $NA • (1/01/2000) • **86**

Santa Paziena Le Madri 1998: There's a good core of fruit to this wine, with pineapple and cream character. Fresh finish. Drink now through 2001.–J.S. • $6 • (4/30/2000) • **85**

Sauvignon Blanc Grave del Friuli Vigne dai Vieris 1998: A delicious, simple Sauvignon. Clean, fresh and fruity, with honey and apple character and a crisp finish. Drink now.–J.S. • $9 • (2/29/2000) • **85**

Tocai Friulano Grave del Friuli 1998: Lots of ripe pineapple and banana character, but it falls a bit short on the finish. Medium-bodied, with good acidity and a short finish. Drink now.–J.S. • $9 • (3/31/2000) • **84**

LENTO, CANTINE

Greco di Bianco 1996 • $14 • (10/15/1997) • **87**

LEONARDINI

Cabernet Sauvignon 1995 • $8 • (1/01/1997) • **82**

Cabernet Sauvignon Veneto 1991 • $7 • (11/15/1994) • **78**

Merlot Piave 1995 • $8 • (1/31/1997) • **81**

Merlot Veneto 1991 • $7 • (11/15/1994) • **74**

Montepulciano d'Abruzzo 1991 • $6 • (3/31/1995) • **73**
Valpolicella 1990 • $5 • (4/30/1992) • **81**

LEONARDO DA VINCI

Brunello di Montalcino 1991 • $35 • (5/31/1997) • **87**
Chianti 1995 • $6 • (3/31/1997) • **80**
Chianti Classico 1994 • $8 • (3/31/1997) • **79**
Chianti Classico Riserva 1991 • $11 • (3/31/1997) • **84**
Chianti Leonardo 1998: Pretty dried cherry and bark aromas. Light- to medium-bodied, with pleasant fruit and a light finish. Drink now.–J.S. • $8 • (11/30/1999) • **83**
Chianti San Zio 1997: Delicious and silky, with pretty dried cherry and tobacco character. Medium-bodied, with soft tannins and a fresh finish. Drink now.–J.S. • $20 • (11/30/1999) • **85**
Rosso di Montalcino 1994 • $13 • (5/31/1997) • **85**
Toscana Santo Ippolito 1997: A little dull, despite the good dark ruby color and interesting aromas of blackberry and licorice. Medium-bodied, with soft tannins and a short finish. Drink now.–J.S. • $15 • (11/30/1999) • **84**

LEONE DE CASTRIS

Copertino 1996 • $8 • (1/01/1998) • **83**
Locorotondo White 1996 • $7 • (5/15/1998) • **78**
Salice Salentino Maiana 1995 • $8 • (1/01/1998) • **85**
Salice Salentino Riserva 1994 • $12 • (1/01/1998) • **86**

LEQUIO, OTTAVIO

Barbaresco 1995: This chewy, medium-bodied red has pretty toasted oak, but also tastes a bit tough, with a slight herb and cassis bush character that takes on a crisp edge.–P.M. • $29 • (10/31/1999) • **78**

LEQUIO, UGO

Barbaresco Gallina 1995: This medium-bodied Barbaresco offers some modest fruit, dry tannins and a short, mouthpuckering finish. Drink now through 2003.–P.M. • $20 • (10/31/1998) • **76**
Barbaresco Gallina 1994: Good acidity and fresh fruit aromas make for a lively, vibrant Barbaresco, medium-bodied and balanced, with blood orange, blackberry, cranberry and mineral flavors. A bit dry and short on the finish. Drink now through 2005.–P.M. • $18 • (10/31/1998) • **84**
Barbaresco Gallina 1993: Smooth and supple, with spice, mocha and mushroom character, the oak accents bring out toasted bread, black pepper and blackberry notes. A pleasant, modern-style. Drink now through 2005.–P.M. • $20 • (10/31/1998) • **85**
Barbera d'Alba Gallina 1996: Ultraripe, dense and sweet-tasting, this fills the palate, melting like vanilla sauce, blending black fruit with spice and tar. Balanced and delicious. Just a slight herbal touch, but amazing quality for a '96 Barbera.–P.M. • $9 • (10/31/1998) • **88**
Barbera d'Alba Gallina 1995: Good, with fresh berry flavor, smacking acidity and a crisp finish. Not overly herbal, just a bit. Tasted twice, with consistent notes. Drink now.–P.M. • $9 • (10/31/1998) • **80**

LIBRANDI

Cirò Classico 1997: Looks and tastes old, with ripe fruit but a rather dry finish.–J.S. • $10 • (5/31/2000) • **76**
Cirò Duca Sanfelice Riserva 1995: Has good ripe fruit, but rather old and slightly earthy-tasting.–J.S. • $17 • (5/31/2000) • **78**
Val di Neto Gravello 1993: A bit tired already, with an amber hue. Aromas of raisin and tobacco have a hint of cedar. Light finish. Rather old style.–J.S. • $28 • (5/31/2000) • **79**
Val di Neto Gravello 1989 • $20 • (5/31/1995) • **87**
Val di Neto Passito Le Passule 1994: Lots of honey character, with burnt almond and clove honey. Medium-bodied and medium sweet, with lively acidity and a spicy finish. Drink now.–J.S. • $29/500 ml. • (5/31/2000) • **88**

LILLIANO, CASTELLO DI

Chianti Classico 1997: A balanced and pretty CC, with plum and berry aromas and flavors, medium body and a fresh finish. Drink now.–J.S. • $12 • (11/30/1999) • **85**
Chianti Classico 1995 • $11 • (9/30/1997) • **87**
Chianti Classico 1994 • $10 • (10/31/1996) • **86**
Chianti Classico 1993 • $NA • (10/31/1995) • **87**
Chianti Classico 1990 • $11 • (9/15/1992) • **89**
Chianti Classico 1988 • $10 • (11/30/1990) • **81**
Chianti Classico Riserva 1995: A delicious, early drinking red. Pretty autumnal aromas of cherries and grilled meats. Medium-bodied, with light, delicate tannins and a fruity finish. Drink now through 2003.–J.S. • $28 • (12/15/1998) • **86**
Chianti Classico Riserva 1994 • $25 • (9/30/1997) • **88**
Chianti Classico Riserva 1993 • $24 • (10/31/1996) • **88**
Chianti Classico Riserva 1990 • $22 • (2/28/1995) • **86**
Chianti Classico Riserva 1988 • $NA • (9/15/1992) • **89**
Chianti Classico Riserva 1985 • $14 • (11/30/1989) • **89**
Colli della Toscana Centrale Anagallis 1997: This is an ultrafine Sangiovese. Dark ruby in color, with bright aromas of raspberry, cherry, violet and rose. Full-bodied, with refined tannins and a superlong aftertaste. Best after 2000.–J.S. • $34 • (11/30/1999) • **93**
Colli della Toscana Centrale Anagallis 1995: A subtle, classy red. Blackberry with hints of earth pour from the glass. Medium-bodied, with a wonderful intensity of ripe fruit and fine tannins. Beautiful Sangiovese. Best after 2000.–J.S. • $31 • (12/15/1998) • **89**
Colli della Toscana Centrale Anagallis 1994 • $28 • (9/30/1997) • **87**
Colli della Toscana Centrale Anagallis 1993 • $28 • (10/31/1996) • **87**
Colli della Toscana Centrale Anagallis 1990 • $25 • (2/28/1995) • **88**
Colli della Toscana Centrale Anagallis 1987 • $25 • (12/15/1992) • **85**
Colli della Toscana Centrale Anagallis 1985 • $34 • (3/31/1990) • **86**
Colli della Toscana Centrale Vignacatena 1995: A blockbuster, no-holding-back red with loads of ripe fruit, black olive and tar aromas and flavors. Full-bodied, with full tannins and a long, superfruity aftertaste. Rather Port-like, really. Merlot. Try with cheese. Drink now.–J.S. • $38 • (12/15/1998) • **90**

LILLIANO, FATTORIA DI

Chianti Colli Fiorentini 1997: Another simple, fresh and grapy red with light to medium body, light tannins and a crisp finish. Not imported into the U.S. Drink now.–J.S. • $NA • (1/01/1999) • **83**
Toscana Bruzzico 1997: Slightly austere and dry on the palate, but with decent blackberry and bark character. Light body and finish. Not imported into the U.S. Drink now.–J.S. • $NA • (1/01/1999) • **81**

LIMITI, DINO

Marino Campo Fattore 1998: A captivating wine for the region, with aromas of very ripe apricot. Medium-bodied, with a good concentration of fruit and a fresh backbone of acidity. Drink now.–J.S. • $12 • (4/30/2000) • **86**

LISINI

Brunello di Montalcino 1995: A rather lean Brunello with some berry and tobacco character. Medium-bodied, with a short and slightly dry finish, yet pleasant. Slightly disappointing for this producer. Drink now.–J.S. • $49 • (6/30/2000) • **81**
Brunello di Montalcino 1994: Plenty of crushed berries and cherries, with hints of cut wood. Medium-bodied, with firm yet soft tannins and a medium finish. Drink now.–J.S. • $45 • (8/31/1999) • **87**
Brunello di Montalcino 1993: A solid, racy young Brunello, built for aging. Grapes, violets and berries on the nose. Medium- to full-bodied, with firm tannins and a lengthy finish. Best after 2002.–J.S. • $45 • (12/15/1998) • **90**
Brunello di Montalcino 1991 • $41 • (11/30/1996) • **88**
Brunello di Montalcino 1988 • $36 • (4/30/1994) • **80**
Brunello di Montalcino 1985 • $33 • (8/31/1991) • **81**
Brunello di Montalcino 1983 • $22 • (7/31/1989) • **73**
Brunello di Montalcino 1982 • $25 • (1/31/1989) • **84**
Brunello di Montalcino 1975 • $30 • (9/15/1986) • **78**
Brunello di Montalcino Ugolaia Riserva 1994: Interesting aromas of fruit, grain and wood bark. Medium-bodied, with a spicy, chestnut flavor and medium-fine tannins. Delicious. Drink now through 2001.–J.S. • $94 • (6/30/2000) • **87**
Brunello di Montalcino Ugolaia Riserva 1993: A balanced and well-defined Brunello. Vivid aromas of blackberries, wet earth and forest with hints of flowers. Medium- to full-bodied, with well-integrated tannins and a medium finish. Drink now through 2006.–J.S. • $65 • (8/31/1999) • **88**
Brunello di Montalcino Ugolaia Riserva 1991 • $105 • (9/30/1997) • **89**
Brunello di Montalcino Ugolaia Riserva 1990 • $99 • (11/30/1996) • **90**
Brunello di Montalcino Ugolaia Riserva 1988 • $NA • (10/31/1994) • **86**

ITALY

Rosso di Montalcino 1996: Impressive harmony to this Rosso, with chocolate, berry and cherry aromas and flavors. Medium-bodied, with well-integrated tannins and a refreshing aftertaste. Very pretty indeed. Drink now.–J.S. • $19 • (12/15/1998) • **87**

Rosso di Montalcino 1995 • $23 • (9/30/1997) • **87**

Rosso di Montalcino 1994 • $15 • (11/30/1996) • **85**

Rosso di Montalcino 1988 • $14 • (4/30/1991) • **79**

LIVON

Refosco dal Peduncolo Rosso Riul Colli Orientali del Friuli 1988 • $11 • (1/31/1992) • **79**

Schioppettino 1988 • $13 • (1/31/1992) • **86**

Schioppettino 1987 • $18 • (4/15/1990) • **81**

Tiareblù 1991 • $35 • (5/31/1998) • **84**

Tocai Friulano Collio 1996 • $13 • (6/15/1998) • **84**

LOGGIA, FATTORIA LA

Chianti Classico Riserva 1990 • $17 • (2/28/1995) • **85**

Nearco 1990 • $NA • (10/31/1993) • **85**

LOMBARDO, ANTONINO

Chianti Colli Senesi 1996 • $11 • (9/30/1997) • **82**

Rosso di Montepulciano 1998: This chunky young 1998 has a good dark color and vivid plum skin and berry aromas. Medium-bodied, with medium tannins and a fruity finish. Drink now.–J.S. • $15 • (11/30/1999) • **86**

Rosso di Montepulciano 1997: Good blackberry and cherry aromas and flavors. Medium-bodied, with light tannins and a crisp yet slightly austere finish. Drink now.–J.S. • $15 • (12/15/1998) • **81**

Rosso di Montepulciano 1996 • $13 • (9/30/1997) • **83**

Vino Nobile di Montepulciano 1997: Good but simple. Interesting aromas of grapeskins and flowers. Medium-bodied, with medium tannins and a grapey finish. Drink now.–J.S. • $24 • (6/15/2000) • **84**

Vino Nobile di Montepulciano 1996: Has decent fruit, but it's slightly weedy. Light- to medium-bodied, with light tannins and a fresh finish. Drink now.–J.S. • $23 • (11/30/1999) • **81**

Vino Nobile di Montepulciano 1995: Superclean, with lots of lively cherry and berry aromas and flavors. Medium-bodied, with well-integrated tannins. Drink now.–J.S. • $20 • (12/15/1998) • **87**

Vino Nobile di Montepulciano 1994 • $20 • (9/30/1997) • **87**

Vino Nobile di Montepulciano Riserva 1995: Very strange and unpleasant vegetal and varnish character. Tasted twice, with consistent notes.–J.S. • $27 • (11/30/1999) • **68**

Vino Nobile di Montepulciano Riserva 1994: A bit rustic, with berry, tomato character, but the tannins are well-integrated and the fruit ripe. Drink now.–J.S. • $25 • (12/15/1998) • **83**

Vino Nobile di Montepulciano Riserva 1993 • $23 • (9/30/1997) • **84**

LOSI

Chianti Classico Pontignanello 1997: A good '97 CC, with berry, plum and tobacco aromas and flavors. Medium-bodied, with soft tannins and a fruity finish. Drink now.–J.S. • $13 • (11/30/1999) • **85**

Chianti Classico Pontignanello 1996: Fresh and grapey, with bubbly fruit flavors, medium to light body and a crisp finish. Serve slightly chilled, with pasta.–J.S. • $12 • (12/15/1998) • **83**

Chianti Classico Pontignanello Riserva 1996: Hard to get excited about. Slightly mature-looking brick red, with earth, berry and barnyard aromas. Medium-bodied, with prune and berry character and a light, slightly dry finish.–J.S. • $16 • (11/30/1999) • **78**

Chianti Classico Pontignanello Riserva 1995: Simple dried cherry and watermelon aromas and flavors. Medium-bodied, with crisp acidity and delicate tannins. Slightly diluted finish. Drink now.–J.S. • $16 • (12/15/1998) • **82**

Key: SS—Spectator Selection. CS—Cellar Selection. HR—Highly Recommended. $NA—Price not available. (BT)—Barrel tasting. Ⓐ—Auction Price. For a key to the tasters' initials, see "How to Use These Listings."
Dates in parentheses represent the issues in which the ratings were published.

LUCE

Toscana Luce della Vite 1996: A polished, beautiful wine, with lovely aromas of ripe berry, tobacco and bark. Medium-bodied, with a solid core of fruit and caressing, velvety tannins. Slightly short finish. Drink now through 2003.–J.S. • $55 • (11/30/1999) • **89**

Toscana Luce della Vite 1995: Loads of crushed berry and milk chocolate aromas. Medium-bodied, very polished, with ultrafine tannins and a long, long finish. A slinky, sexy red, like a supermodel strolling down the catwalk. Best Luce to date. Drink now.–J.S. • $63 • (12/15/1998) • **93**

Toscana Luce della Vite 1994 • $55 • (9/30/1997) • **89**

Toscana Luce della Vite 1993 • $55 • (9/30/1997) • **90**

Toscana Lucente La Vite 1996: Slightly one-dimensional but enjoyable, with aromas of blackberry and green tobacco. Medium-bodied, with soft tannins and a fruity finish. Drink now.–J.S. • $25 • (11/30/1999) • **84**

Toscana Lucente La Vite 1995: Straightforward, with accentuated acidity. Pretty aromas of blackberry, chocolate and plum. Medium in body, tart and fresh in style, with a berry, bark aftertaste. Drink now.–J.S. • $26 • (12/15/1998) • **85**

LUCIA, DE

Falanghina Sannio 1998: Medium-bodied, with lime and apple skin character and fresh acidity. Drink now.–J.S. • $NA • (1/01/2000) • **80**

Greco Sannio 1998: Medium-bodied, with interesting pear, melon and ash character, medium acidity and a light finish. Drink now.–J.S. • $NA • (1/01/2000) • **83**

Solopaca Vassallo 1998: Plenty of ripe crushed berry on the nose, but with a bubbling, unstable palate. Tasted twice, with consistent notes.–J.S. • $NA • (1/01/2000) • **69**

LUCIA, GALASSO

Don Giovanni di Giovanni Crosato Il Rosso 1994 • $25 • (5/31/1996) • **85**

LUCIANI

Brunello di Montalcino 1991 • $39 • (11/30/1996) • **86**

Brunello di Montalcino Riserva 1990 • $50 • (11/30/1996) • **90**

LUNGAROTTI

Cabernet Sauvignon Lombardy 1983 • $18 • (5/15/1991) • **85**

Cabernet Sauvignon Torgiano 1995: The green Cabernet character is hard to like. Smells of cut grass and plums. Medium-bodied, with light tannins and a weedy, grassy aftertaste.–J.S. • $18 • (2/29/2000) • **79**

Cabernet Sauvignon Umbria 1979 • $11 • (2/15/1987) • **79**

Pinot Grigio Bianco dell 'Umbria 1996 • $12 • (8/31/1997) • **78**

Pinot Grigio Umbria 1998: A simple white, with pear and lemon character and a hint of white pepper. Light in body and finish. Drink now.–J.S. • $12 • (2/29/2000) • **80**

Sangiovese Umbria 1995 • $16 Ⓐ • (4/30/1997) • **84**

Torgiano Rubesco 1996: A juicy, traditional young red, with lots of fruit and black pepper. Medium in body, it's straightforward and polished. Drink now.–J.S. • $12 • (6/30/1999) • **87**

Torgiano Rubesco 1996: Berry, plum and tobacco character. Light-bodied, with a fruity finish. Drink now.–J.S. • $12 • (2/29/2000) • **80**

Torgiano Rubesco 1993 • $11 • (8/31/1996) • **84**

Torgiano Rubesco 1988 • $13 • (9/15/1992) • **83**

Torgiano Rubesco 1987 • $11 • (5/15/1991) • **83**

Torgiano Rubesco 1985 • $11 • (9/15/1989) • **74**

Torgiano Rubesco Monticchio Riserva 1990: A pretty, mature, traditional red. Interesting aromas of blackberry and tobacco, with hints of bark. Medium-bodied, with soft tannins and a lovely, velvety finish. Drink now through 2004.–J.S. • $35 • (2/29/2000) • **87**

Torgiano Rubesco Monticchio Riserva 1982 • $25 • (9/15/1992) • **71**

Torgiano Rubesco Monticchio Riserva 1980 • $27 • (7/15/1991) • **84**

Torgiano Rubesco Monticchio Riserva 1978 • $23 • (9/15/1989) • **82**

Torgiano Torre di Giano 1998: A stylish white, with aromas of straw, apple and spice. Medium-bodied, with lots of peach and fruity stone character. Medium finish. Drink now.–J.S. • $11 • (2/29/2000) • **85**

Torgiano Vino Santo 1991 • $13 • (8/31/1996) • **88**

Torgiano Vino Santo 1988 • $15 • (7/31/1993) • **84**

Torgiano White Torre di Giano 1996 • $11 • (8/31/1997) • **79**

Umbria San Giorgio 1990: Good ripe fruit, but drying out slightly. Attractive aromas of blackberry and plum, with an herbal undertone. Medium-bodied, with chewy tannins and a crisp finish that's a bit tough and austere. Drink now.–J.S. • $49 • (2/29/2000) • **84**

Umbria San Giorgio 1988: A fully mature, funky red, with plum, tanned leather and milk chocolate aromas and flavors. Medium-bodied, with fine tannins and a silky texture, though it's slightly earthy, tart and cheesy on the finish. Drink now.–J.S. • $42 • (6/30/1999) • **82**

Umbria San Giorgio 1986 • $30 • (4/30/1997) • **86**

Umbria San Giorgio 1985 • $30 • (5/31/1995) • **85**

Umbria San Giorgio 1982 • $34 • (7/15/1991) • **77**

Umbria San Giorgio 1979 • $18 • (3/15/1987) • **75**

Umbria San Giorgio 1978 • $19 • (4/16/1985) • **84**

Umbria Vino Santo 1993: A solid traditional vin santo, with salted almond, butterscotch and caramel character. Full-bodied and medium sweet, with a clean finish. Very well done. Drink now.–J.S. • $15 • (2/29/2000) • **87**

LUWA

Ribolla Gialla Collio 1998: Interesting aromas of almonds, honey and peaches. Medium-bodied, with good acidity and a long, fruity finish. Drink now.–J.S. • $15 • (4/30/2000) • **85**

Sauvignon Collio 1998: Promises more on the palate. Intense aromas of honey, peach and passion fruit. Medium-bodied, with nice ripe fruit and a medium finish. Drink now.–J.S. • $15 • (4/30/2000) • **85**

MACCHIOLE, LE

Bolgheri Messorio 1996: Slightly overdone, emphasizing the herbal, almost bell pepper character in the young vines. Full-bodied and velvety, with cut grass aromas, cherry and berry flavors and lots of extracted, slightly austere tannins. May be better with age? Best after 2001.–J.S. • $100 • (11/30/1999) • **85**

Bolgheri Paleo 1995: Slightly disjointed, with a pleasingly caressing texture, but it's slightly herbal and dry on the finish.–J.S. • $60 • (12/15/1998) • **79**

Bolgheri Scrio 1996: A beautiful Syrah, with wonderful blackberry, cherry and smoke aromas. Full-bodied and very soft and velvety, with a long, long finish. Very well crafted. Bravo.–J.S. • $75 • (11/30/1999) • **90**

Paleo 1993 • $30 • (10/31/1996) • **81**

Toscana Le Contessine 1998: A solid, clean white, with delicious pineapple, white pepper and apple character. Medium-bodied, with good acidity and a fruity finish. Not imported into the U.S. Drink now.–J.S. • $NA • (1/01/1999) • **86**

Toscana Messorio 1995: Juicy, rich and decadent. Deep, dark and brooding, with currant and berry oozing from the glass. Full-bodied, with well-integrated tannins and a lovely mint, berry and cherry aftertaste. Why drink only Pomerols if you love super Merlot? Try this.–J.S. • $95 • (12/15/1998) • **91**

Toscana Paleo 1997: A white with ripe pineapple, honey and vanilla character. Medium-bodied, with a milk texture and a light finish. Needs a bit more freshness. Drink now.–J.S. • $40 • (11/30/1999) • **82**

Toscana Scrio 1995: Tastes like a very good Syrah; would give many Northern Rhône reds a run for their money. Intense aromas of blackberries and earth, with a hint of barnyard. Medium-bodied, with ripe fruit and round tannins. Long, fruity aftertaste. Drink now.–J.S. • $70 • (12/15/1998) • **87**

MACHIAVELLI, ANTICA FATTORIA

Chianti Classico 1994 • $NA • (10/31/1996) • **82**

Chianti Classico Vigna di Fontalle Riserva 1994: Still holding on but showing light fruit and earth character. Medium-bodied, with light tannins and a slightly austere finish. Not imported into the U.S. Drink now.–J.S. • $NA • (1/01/1999) • **82**

Chianti Classico Vigna di Fontalle Riserva 1993 • $15 • (10/31/1996) • **85**

Chianti Classico Vigna di Fontalle Riserva 1990 • $23 • (2/28/1995) • **84**

Chianti Classico Vigna di Fontalle Riserva 1988 • $21 • (10/31/1993) • **87**

Chianti Classico Vigna di Fontalle Riserva 1986 • $16 • (10/31/1991) • **84**

Chianti Classico Vigna di Fontalle Riserva 1985 • $15 • (9/15/1991) • **91**

Pinot Nero Toscana Il Principe 1996: Very floral, with rose, fruit and mineral character. Medium-bodied, with velvety tannins and a medium finish. Doesn't taste much like Pinot Noir, but still a good red. Not imported into the U.S. Drink now.–J.S. • $NA • (1/01/1999) • **85**

Pinot Nero Toscana Il Principe 1995: Pleasantly balanced and fruity, with a good amount of ripe berry and plum character and rounded tannins. Doesn't taste much like Pinot Nero but it's very good. Not imported into the U.S. Drink now.–J.S. • $NA • (12/15/1998) • **85**

Podere Solatio del Tani 1993 • $NA • (10/31/1996) • **85**

Ser Niccolo` Solatìo del Tani 1994: Doesn't taste much like Cabernet, but it's silky and drinkable, with tobacco, berry and oak. Medium-bodied, with medium tannins, a succulent finish. Not imported into the U.S. Drink now.–J.S. • $NA • (12/15/1998) • **84**

Toscana Il Piano 1998: Melon and fruit cocktail aromas. Medium-bodied, with flinty honey flavors and a refreshing finish. A bit vulgar, though. Not imported into the U.S. Drink now.–J.S. • $NA • (1/01/1999) • **83**

Toscana Il Piano 1997: Attractive aromas and flavors of apple, cream and smoky oak. Medium-bodied, with fresh acidity and a pear and apple aftertaste. A white produced from black Canaiolo grapes. Not imported into the U.S. Drink now.–J.S. • $NA • (12/15/1998) • **86**

Toscana Ser Niccolo` Solatìo del Tani 1995: Good texture, but slightly boring. Aromas of plums and mushrooms follow through to a medium-bodied palate, with polished tannins and a light finish. Not imported into the U.S. Drink now.–J.S. • $NA • (1/01/1999) • **84**

MACI

Chardonnay Salento Tenute La Mea 1998: Fresh, with mineral and lemon rind aromas and flavors. Medium-bodied, with a fresh finish. Drink now.–J.S. • $15 • (5/31/2000) • **82**

Salento Bella Mojgan 1997: Has plenty of ripe fruit character but a bit too much new wood. Medium- to full-bodied, with medium tannins and a long vanilla aftertaste. Drink now.–J.S. • $29 • (5/31/2000) • **82**

Salento Chiaro di Luna 1998: Very soapy and dull. Not much Chardonnay character.–J.S. • $11 • (5/31/2000) • **75**

Salento Frà Diavolo 1997: Like a dry Port. Big, powerful and rustic. Full-bodied and chewy, it's slightly overdone but impressive. If you like late-harvest Zinfandel, try this. Drink now.–J.S. • $23 • (5/31/2000) • **84**

Salento Lume di Candela 1997: Medium-bodied, with plenty of fruit and light tannins. Plum and cherry character throughout. Drink now.–J.S. • $11 • (5/31/2000) • **83**

Salento Rosato Gote Rubizze 1998: Decent plum and berry character, but it's a rather tired rosé.–J.S. • $11 • (5/31/2000) • **75**

Salento Rosato Tenute La Mea 1998: Looks and tastes tired. Past its prime.–J.S. • $15 • (5/31/2000) • **71**

Salento Sire 1997: A bit raisiny and thick, but has good fruit. Full-bodied, with soft tannins and a simple finish. Slightly overdone. Drink now.–J.S. • $27 • (5/31/2000) • **81**

Salice Salentino Tenute La Mea 1997: There's lots of ripe fruit here, balanced by berry, cherry and licorice character. It's a full-bodied wine, with velvety tannins and a long finish. This, Maci's simple red, is the best of the winery's current releases, and the price makes it a no-brainer. Best after 2000.–J.S. • $10 • (5/31/2000) • **87**

Salice Salentino Terrae di Marta 1998: Good, clean apple, pineapple and mineral character. Medium-bodied, with a fresh finish. Drink now.–J.S. • $18 • (5/31/2000) • **84**

Sauvignon Salento Tenute La Mea 1998: Plenty of lemon, lime and almond character. Medium-bodied, with fresh fruit and a crisp finish. Drink now.–J.S. • $15 • (5/31/2000) • **85**

MACIOCHE, LE

Brunello di Montalcino 1994: A bit lean really, but shows some attractive dried cherry and leather character. Medium-bodied, with firm tannins and a short finish. Drink now.–J.S. • $45 • (8/31/1999) • **84**

Brunello di Montalcino 1993: A delicious Brunello for current drinking. Blackberries and plums on the nose and palate. Medium-bodied, with soft tannins and a fresh finish. Not imported into the U.S. Drink now.–J.S. • $40 • (12/15/1998) • **85**

Brunello di Montalcino 1992 • $35 • (9/30/1997) • **82**

Brunello di Montalcino 1991 • $32 • (11/30/1996) • **87**

Rosso di Montalcino 1997: Something has gone horribly wrong here. Stemmy, rubbery and dirty; undrinkable. Tasted twice, with consistent notes.–J.S. • $18 • (9/15/1999) • **55**

Rosso di Montalcino 1996: Slightly diluted, but shows some bright plum and berry character. Medium-bodied, with light tannins and a fresh, light finish. Not imported into the U.S.–B.S. • $17 • (12/15/1998) • **81**

Rosso di Montalcino 1994 • $17 • (11/30/1996) • **86**

MACULAN

Breganze Brentino 1995 • $14 • (6/15/1998) • **85**

MACULAN

Breganze Brentino 1994 • $13 • (6/15/1997) • **82**
Breganze Brentino 1990 • $12 • (9/15/1992) • **79**
Breganze Brentino 1986 • $10 • (3/31/1989) • **85**
Breganze di Breganze Bianco 1998: A pleasant white, with fresh apple, peach and mineral character. Medium-bodied, with a light finish. Drink now.–J.S. • $14 • (2/29/2000) • **84**
Breganze di Breganze Bianco 1996 • $14 • (6/30/1998) • **83**
Breganze di Breganze Rosso 1991 • $11 • (9/15/1992) • **72**
Breganze Torcolato 1998: Delicious, with lovely aromas of pear, coconut and marzipan. Medium-bodied, with good sweetness and a long apricot and mango aftertaste. Drink now.–J.S. • $30/375 ml. • (6/15/2000) • **89**
Breganze Torcolato 1997: A subtle sweet wine with lemon, passion fruit, honey and spices. Full-bodied, medium sweet, with a fresh and elegant aftertaste. Refreshing. Mellow. Drink now.–J.S. • $29/375 ml. • (4/30/2000) • **90**
Breganze Torcolato 1995 • $46 • (6/30/1998) HR • **91**
Breganze Torcolato Acininobili Riserva 1997: Slightly subdued on the nose, but it comes through big time in the mouth. Aromas of butterscotch, honey and pear intermingle with dried pineapple and coconut. Medium-bodied and very sweet, with a maple syrup, honey and almond aftertaste. Best after 2000.–J.S. • $95/375 ml. • (6/15/2000) • **91**
Breganze Torcolato Acininobili Riserva 1995: Wild juice. Rockin' aromas of dried fruit and exotic Indian spices. Full-bodied, medium sweet, with a long, intense aftertaste of lime, passion fruit and cinnamon. Drink now.–J.S. • $95/375 ml. • (1/01/2000) • **94**
Cabernet Breganze Fratta 1997: A wine that aspires to be great. Dark, with intense blackberry and cassis and hints of toasted wood. Full-bodied, with a very velvety texture and a medium finish. A bit fat and lacking in tannin backbone, but polished and enjoyable. Drink now through 2005.–J.S. • $85 • (1/01/2000) • **88**
Cabernet Breganze Fratta 1996: Serious Cabernet. Beautiful aromas of black olives, fruit and cigar box. Full-bodied and very concentrated, with lots of chewy, velvety tannins and a long finish. Best after 2002.–J.S. • $70 • (1/01/2000) • **90**
Cabernet Breganze Fratta 1994: Good definition and depth of black cherry and cedar flavors provide extra dimension in this mature, supple red. Softly textured yet well balanced, with a hint of tannin on the finish. Tasted twice, with consistent notes. Drink now.–B.S. • $29 • (9/30/1998) • **86**
Cabernet Breganze Fratta 1990 • $39 • (9/15/1992) • **92**
Cabernet Breganze Fratta 1986 • $29 • (3/31/1989) • **92**
Cabernet Sauvignon Breganze Ferrata 1996: Well-crafted red with currant bush, mint and light oak aromas. Full-bodied, with silky tannins and a medium finish. Needs a bit more oomph at the end to be outstanding. Best after 2000.–J.S. • $53 • (5/15/2000) • **88**
Cabernet Sauvignon Breganze Palazzotto 1990 • $24 • (9/15/1992) • **77**
Cabernet Sauvignon Veneto 1994 • $20 • (6/15/1998) • **88**
Cabernet Sauvignon Veneto 1993 • $NA • (1/01/1997) • **84**
Cabernet Sauvignon Veneto Ferrata 1994 • $NA • (1/01/1997) • **83**
Cabernet Sauvignon Veneto Palazzotto 1987 • $30 • (1/31/1992) • **82**
Cabernet Sauvignon Veneto Palazzotto 1986 • $19 • (3/31/1989) • **71**
Chardonnay Breganze Ferrata 1997: Delicious and rich, with toasted oak, honey and apple aromas that follow through to the palate. Medium-bodied, with fresh acidity and a clean finish. Drink now.–J.S. • $39 • (1/01/2000) • **88**
Chardonnay Breganze Riale 1997: Fresh and well made, with almond, apple and honey character. Medium-bodied, with good acidity and a long, flavorful finish. Delicious. Drink now through 2001.–J.S. • $15 • (1/01/2000) • **88**
Dindarello 1991 • $28 • (9/15/1992) • **84**
Dindarello 1989 • $24 • (7/15/1991) • **84**
Merlot Breganze Brentino 1997: Fine red. Very pretty berry and mint aromas. Medium-bodied, with fine tannins and a fresh and silky finish. Drink now through 2003.–J.S. • $15 • (5/15/2000) • **87**
Merlot Breganze Marchesante 1996: Sleek Merlot. Perfumed berry and smoky aromas follow through to a medium-bodied palate with firm tannins and a medium finish. Best after 2000.–J.S. • $43 • (5/15/2000) • **88**
Merlot Breganze Marchesante 1995 • $26 • (6/15/1998) • **87**
Merlot Breganze Marchesante 1994 • $NA • (1/01/1997) • **86**
Moscato Veneto Dindarello 1998: Delicious sweet wine, with honey, apricot and cream character. Full-bodied, with a lovely balance of ripe fruit and acidity. Long finish. Luscious Muscat. Drink now through 2002.–J.S. • $17/375 ml. • (4/30/2000) • **90**

Key: SS—Spectator Selection. CS—Cellar Selection. HR—Highly Recommended. $NA—Price not available. (BT)—Barrel tasting. Ⓐ—Auction Price.
For a key to the tasters' initials, see "How to Use These Listings."
Dates in parentheses represent the issues in which the ratings were published.

Torcolato 1994 • $47 • (1/01/1997) • **85**
Torcolato 1990 • $44 • (9/15/1992) • **87**
Torcolato 1990 • $19/375 ml. • (1/31/1995) HR • **92**
Torcolato 1988 • $35 • (4/15/1991) • **91**
Veneto Prato di Canzio 1997: Apple, pear and floral aromas follow through to the palate. Medium-bodied, with a fresh finish. Drink now.–J.S. • $23 • (1/01/2000) • **87**

MAJO NORANTE, DI

Aglianico Terra degli Osci Contado 1996: This big red shows lots of cherry and raisin character. Full-bodied, with medium velvety tannins and a fruity finish. A bit monolithic but interesting. Drink now.–J.S. • $13 • (4/30/2000) • **84**
Cabernet Terra degli Osci 1998: Pretty blackberry and dark chocolate aromas. Medium-bodied, with lots of chocolate and berry flavors and a long finish. A beauty. Drink now.–J.S. • $7 • (4/30/2000) • **87**
Molise Biblos 1998: Oxidized, with butterscotch and caramel character. Dull palate. Barely acceptable.–J.S. • $11 • (4/30/2000) • **73**
Moscato Apianae da uva Reale 1992 • $16/500 ml. • (1/01/1997) • **84**
Passito Apianae 1994: Promises more on the nose than the palate, with aromas of flowers, apple, lemon and honey. Medium-bodied and slightly sweet, with a lemon and orange zest flavor and a light finish. Drink now.–J.S. • $17/500 ml. • (4/30/2000) • **86**
Sangiovese Terra degli Osci 1998: A good, simple red, with berry, currant and mint character. Medium-bodied, with medium tannins and a light, fruity finish. Drink now.–J.S. • $7 • (4/30/2000) • **84**
Terra degli Osci Ramitello 1996: Big and slightly rough, but very good, with licorice, raisins and vanilla. Full-bodied and chewy, with plenty of ripe fruit. Give it time. Best after 2001.–J.S. • $12 • (4/30/2000) • **87**

MANDORLO, IL

Chianti Classico 1997: Delicious, with subtle aromas of plum, porcini mushroom and cherry. Medium-bodied, with compacted fruit and tannins. The flavorful finish has a caressing texture. Drink now through 2001.–J.S. • $15 • (11/30/1999) • **87**
Chianti Classico Riserva 1995: Appealing aromas of cherries and plums. Medium-bodied, with silky tannins and a medium finish. Needs a bit more fruit in the center palate but delicious. Drink now.–J.S. • $21 • (11/30/1999) • **85**

MANORA

Barbera del Monferrato Collezione 1996: Light-bodied, with herbal crispness, dry, tart tannins and a licorice, candied taste. Green finish.–P.M. • $26 • (11/15/1999) • **71**
Barbera del Monferrato Collezione 1995: This hedonistic Barbera oozes with ripe and rich berry, chocolate, vanilla, chestnut and plum character that melts in the mouth. Full-bodied, with wonderfully integrated tannins and a seductive but firm finish that gives it a lot of personality. Will go well with dishes that require a big red. Drink now through 2005.–P.M. • $12 • (10/31/1998) • **91**
Barbera del Monferrato Pais 1997: Ripe, with cassis, cherry and herb character, this Barbera packs lots of punch and not much class, except for the round tannins. A bit green on the finish. Drink now through 2001.–P.M. • $14 • (11/15/1999) • **83**
Barbera del Monferrato Pais 1996: Extremely earthy and gamy, with only modest cherry flavors. Past its prime.–K.M. • $15 • (8/31/1998) • **74**
Collezione 1994 • $24 • (10/31/1997) • **76**
Monferrato Palo Alto 1996: Ripe, with sweet fruit and petrol, charred oak, cassis bush and olive notes. Supple tannins. Drink now through 2002.–P.M. • $45 • (11/15/1999) • **84**
Monferrato Palo Alto 1995: A delicious international style of red, with loads of mocha, spice, coffee and plum. Good acidity keeps it alive and vibrant, while the ripe tannins offer supple texture on the toasted, smoky, grilled finish. A blend of Pinot Noir, Merlot, Cabernet Sauvignon and Barbera. Drink now through 2003.–P.M. • $35 • (10/31/1998) • **87**
Palo Alto 1994 • $38 • (10/31/1997) • **85**

MANZANO, FATTORIA DI

Chardonnay Toscana Podere Fontarca 1998: Very good Chardonnay, with plenty of apple and spice character. Medium-bodied, with toasted almond flavors and a long, appley finish. Delicious. Drink now.–J.S. • $30 • (11/30/1999) • **88**

Chardonnay Toscana Podere Fontarca 1997: As ripe in fruit as it is fresh on the palate. Full-bodied, with crisp acidity and a long apple, pineapple and oak finish. Needs a bit of time. Drink through 2001.–J.S. • $35 • (12/15/1998) • **89**
Podere Fontarca 1996 • $NA • (9/30/1997) • **89**
Podere il Vescovo 1996 • $NA • (9/30/1997) • **84**
Sangiovese Toscana 1995: Shows an interesting mix of grape and mineral aromas and flavors. Medium-bodied, with chewy tannins and a long, long finish. Slightly hollow midpalate but still a good drink. A new wine from this up-and-coming producer. Drink now.–J.S. • $NA • (12/15/1998) • **87**
Sangiovese Tuscany Podere Migliara 1997: Silky and seductive, with fine tannins and plenty of berry, tobacco and dark chocolate character. Medium body and finish. Best after 2000.–J.S. • $65 • (11/30/1999) • **89**
Syrah Toscana Podere il Bosco 1997: This breathtaking, superbly structured Syrah is dark ruby in color, with intense aromas of pepper, red meat and berry. Full-bodied, with masses of velvety tannins and a long, long finish of chocolate, berry and game. Why buy Guigal anymore? Best after 2001.–J.S. • $63 • (11/30/1999) • **96**
Syrah Toscana Podere il Bosco 1996: A chunky, fruity Syrah with deliciously enticing plum and milk chocolate character, hints of spice and game. Medium- to full-bodied, with velvety tannins and a fresh and fruity finish. Not as good as the 95, but a beautiful bottle all the same. Drink now through 2003.–J.S. • $62 • (12/15/1998) • **89**
Syrah Toscana Podere il Bosco 1995 • $NA • (9/30/1997) • **92**
Syrah Toscana Podere il Bosco 1994 • $32 • (10/31/1996) • **89**
Syrah Toscana Podere il Bosco 1992 • $NA • (10/31/1995) • **90**
Vin Santo 1992: Very sweet, with buttered popcorn, honey and dried fruit on the nose. Medium-bodied, with a lovely nut, honey and cream aftertaste. Not imported into the U.S. Drink now.–J.S. • $NA/375 ml. • (1/01/1999) • **86**

MANZONE, GIOVANNI

Barbera d'Alba Gramolere 1990 • $19 • (11/15/1993) • **90**
Barbera d'Alba La Serra 1995: Crisp, light in color and light-bodied, with zingy acidity and mocha, toast and spicy oak notes. Good though not supple finish. A good match with trattoria foods. Drink now.–P.M. • $20 • (11/15/1999) • **80**
Barbera d'Alba La Serra 1994: A crisp Barbera, with juicy and succulent texture, cassis bush and black cherry notes, a touch of mocha and toasted oak on the finish. With food, it should get softer around the edges. Drink now through 2001.–P.M. • $20 • (10/31/1998) • **84**
Barolo Bricat 1995: A pretty little red, with decent red berry flavors and mineral and toasted oak notes. Tannins kick in on the finish. Drink now through 2003.–P.M. • $45 • (11/15/1999) • **86**
Barolo Bricat 1994: Elegant, offering plum, smoke and currant, but mostly a fruity, smooth midpalate and well-integrated, sweet tannins. Of medium body, the finish is balanced. Drink now through 2005.–P.M. • $37 • (10/31/1998) • **87**
Barolo Gramolere 1995: A bit herbal, with a crisp taste but a tart finish. Slightly diluted.–P.M. • $43 • (11/15/1999) • **77**
Barolo Gramolere 1994: Beautiful. Quite ripe and sweet-tasting, showing wet earth, plum, tar and some smoke, very balanced and delicious. Medium-bodied, with mineral notes on the finish, which displays some firm tannins. Drink now through 2005.–P.M. • $35 • (10/31/1998) • **89**
Barolo Gramolere 1993 • $48 Ⓐ • (10/31/1997) • **88**
Barolo Gramolere 1991 • $28 • (10/31/1995) • **82**
Barolo Gramolere 1990 • $35 • (10/31/1994) • **86**
Barolo Gramolere 1989 • $35 • (10/31/1993) • **89**
Barolo Gramolere 1988 • $35 • (10/31/1993) • **85**
Barolo Gramolere Riserva 1993: Beautiful and pure Barolo in a classic style, with much complexity stemming from tar, smoke, floral and plum notes. Rich, but also shows finesse thanks to well-integrated tannins. Fresh acidity gives a palate-cleansing length to the chewy finish. Drink now through 2008.–P.M. • $40 • (10/31/1998) • **91**
Barolo Perno S. Stefano 1995: Elegant and pleasant, with flavorful cherry, raspberry and tar notes. Medium-bodied, without much richness, but balanced in a sleek way. Smooth tannins. Drink now through 2002.–P.M. • $45 • (11/15/1999) • **87**
Dolcetto d'Alba Gramolere 1990 • $14 • (3/31/1993) • **76**
Dolcetto d'Alba La Serra 1997: A bit herbal, with tart character on the hard finish.–P.M. • $15 • (11/15/1999) • **77**
Dolcetto d'Alba La Serra 1996: Very earthy and funky, but also round and ripe on the palate, it has lovely wild raspberry, floral and currant character. Quite tannic.–P.M. • $15 • (10/31/1998) • **79**
Langhe Tris 1996: Good harmony between acidity and pure blackberry flavors. Medium-bodied, this red is firm and lively on the palate, with a vibrant, food-friendly texture on the lingering finish. Drink now through 2003.–P.M. • $26 • (11/15/1999) • **87**
Langhe Tris 1995: A bit herbal, with cassis bush and olive character. Medium-bodied and crisp, with a chewy finish. Drink now through 2005.–P.M. • $25 • (11/15/1999) • **84**

MARAI, FOSS

Cabernet Piave 1990 • $9 • (1/31/1992) • **76**
Cabernet Sauvignon Piave Nono Gío 1992 • $38 • (6/15/1996) • **82**

MARCA, LA

Cabernet Sauvignon Piave 1994 • $6 • (6/15/1998) • **83**
Cabernet Sauvignon Piave 1993 • $6 • (5/31/1996) • **83**
Chardonnay Piave 1996 • $6 • (5/31/1998) • **76**
Merlot Piave 1995 • $6 • (5/31/1998) • **76**
Merlot Piave 1993 • $6 • (6/15/1996) • **78**
Merlot Piave Novello del Veneto 1995 • $6 • (2/29/1996) • **80**
Merlot Piave Novello del Veneto 1994 • $6 • (1/31/1996) • **83**
Pinot Grigio Veneto 1996 • $6 • (5/31/1998) • **79**

MARCARINI

Barbera d'Alba Ciabot Camerano 1988 • $18 • (3/15/1991) • **90**
Barolo Brunate 1994: Funky and odd-smelling, astringent, it's not what you expect in a Barolo.–P.M. • $32 • (10/31/1998) • **70**
Barolo Brunate 1993 • $30 Ⓐ • (10/31/1997) • **85**
Barolo Brunate 1992 • $27 • (10/31/1996) • **78**
Barolo Brunate 1991 • $26 • (10/31/1995) • **77**
Barolo Brunate 1990 • $26 • (10/31/1994) • **91**
Barolo Brunate 1989 • $67 Ⓐ • (10/31/1993) • **91**
Barolo Brunate 1988 • $27 • (10/31/1993) • **85**
Barolo Brunate 1985 • $35 • (3/31/1990) • **90**
Barolo Brunate 1983 • $23 • (9/15/1988) • **89**
Barolo Brunate 1982 • $18 • (9/15/1988) • **90**
Barolo Brunate 1979 • $NA • (9/15/1988) • **88**
Barolo Brunate 1978 • $NA • (9/15/1988) • **80**
Barolo Brunate 1971 • $NA • (9/15/1988) • **89**
Barolo Brunate 1964 • $100 • (9/15/1988) • **96**
Barolo La Serra 1994: A bit simple, with a pronounced herbal overtone and some bitter tannins. Medium-bodied, there are modest red berry flavors.–P.M. • $32 • (10/31/1998) • **79**
Barolo La Serra 1993 • $41 • (10/31/1997) • **86**
Barolo La Serra 1992 • $27 • (10/31/1996) • **76**
Barolo La Serra 1991 • $26 • (10/31/1995) • **77**
Barolo La Serra 1990 • $26 • (10/31/1994) • **88**
Barolo La Serra 1988 • $27 • (10/31/1993) • **77**
Barolo La Serra 1983 • $17 • (9/15/1988) • **87**
Barolo La Serra 1982 • $18 • (9/15/1988) • **91**
Barolo La Serra 1978 • $18 • (9/16/1984) • **79**
Dolcetto d'Alba Boschi di Berri 1989 • $23 • (4/30/1991) • **89**
Dolcetto d'Alba Boschi di Berri 1988 • $17 • (3/31/1990) • **86**
Dolcetto d'Alba Boschi di Berri 1987 • $13 • (3/15/1989) • **89**
Dolcetto d'Alba Fontanazza 1997: More complex than most Dolcettos, this is redolent with currant, blackberry and spicy complexity. Medium-bodied, it tastes very young now, and a bit chewy, but the tannins are ripe and there's plenty of fruit concentration to suggest cellaring it a bit. Drink through 2002.–P.M. • $13 • (10/31/1998) • **88**
Dolcetto d'Alba Fontanazza 1996 • $13 • (10/31/1997) • **89**
Dolcetto d'Alba Fontanazza 1995 • $13 • (10/31/1996) • **75**
Dolcetto d'Alba Fontanazza 1991 • $12 • (7/31/1995) • **84**
Dolcetto d'Alba Fontanazza 1990 • $13 • (10/31/1992) • **85**
Dolcetto d'Alba Fontanazza 1989 • $13 • (4/30/1991) • **84**
Dolcetto d'Alba Fontanazza 1988 • $11 • (3/31/1990) • **87**
Nebbiolo delle Langhe Lasarin 1989 • $10 • (4/30/1991) • **84**
Nebbiolo delle Langhe Lasarin 1988 • $10 • (3/31/1990) • **84**

MARCARINO

Barbaresco Campo Quadro 1989 • $NA • (10/31/1994) • **85**
Barbera d'Alba Vigneto Zocco 1996: Elegant style, modestly oaked and lightly concentrated, with an herbal, red berry character. Light-bodied.–P.M. • $19 • (9/15/1999) • **78**
Dolcetto d'Alba Campo Re 1997: Shows clean fruit, with wild berry, cherry character, good balance and fresh lemony acidity. Medium-bodied, it

ITALY

delivers some dry tannins on the finish, but should go well with antipasta and other light Italian dishes.–P.M. • $15 • (10/31/1998) • **83**

MARCELLINA, LA

Chianti Classico 1997: This shows a very good fruit concentration, with dominant aromas and flavors of fig, raisin and cherry. Medium-bodied, with velvety tannins and a chewy finish. Not imported into the U.S. Drink through 2002.–J.S. • $NA • (1/01/1999) • **87**

Chianti Classico Comignole 1997: Fruity and lively, with black cherry and berry character from nose to palate. Medium-bodied, with fresh acidity and silky tannins. Drink now.–J.S. • $23 • (11/30/1999) • **87**

Toscana Camporosso 1995: Berries, flowers and cedar abound on the nose and palate. Medium-bodied, with medium tannins and a slightly short finish. A bit austere. Sangiovese and Cabernet. Not imported into the U.S. Drink now.–J.S. • $NA • (1/01/1999) • **86**

MAREGA, GIORGIO

Chardonnay Collio 1998: Quite creamy and fruity, with apple, banana and lemon character. Medium body. Good fresh acidity. Drink now.–J.S. • $15 • (3/31/2000) • **86**

Chardonnay Collio 1997: Very good, with fresh aromas and flavors of apple, almond and honey. Medium-bodied, with good acidity and a long, flavorful finish. Delicious. Drink now.–J.S. • $15 • (1/01/2000) • **88**

Friuli-Venezia Giula Holbar Red 1993 • $25 • (5/31/1998) • **88**

Friuli-Venezia Giulia Vendemmia Tardiva Holbar 1995: Almond and lemon aromas with a hint of candied fruit. Medium-bodied, dry, with a slightly dull lime finish. A bit tired at this point. Drink now.–J.S. • $25 • (4/30/2000) • **80**

Holbar Red 1994: Good herbal, berry and tobacco character throughout. Medium-bodied, with soft tannins and a fruity finish. Merlot, Cabernet Sauvignon and Gamay. Drink now.–J.S. • $25 • (5/15/2000) • **84**

Holbar Red 1991 • $22 • (4/30/1996) • **85**

Malvasia Collio Vendemmia Tardiva 1997: Pleasant dry white with delicious lemon, mineral and melon character. Medium body. Fresh acidity. Drink now.–J.S. • $25 • (4/30/2000) • **85**

Pinot Bianco Collio 1998: Superfresh apple, pineapple and honey aromas. Full-bodied, with lots of superclean fruit and a long finish. Wonderful Pinot Bianco. Drink now.–J.S. • $15 • (4/30/2000) • **88**

Pinot Bianco Collio 1996 • $14 • (6/15/1998) • **84**

Pinot Bianco Venezie 1997: Clean and well made, with mineral, lemon and lime character. Medium-bodied, with light acidity and a clean finish. Drink now.–J.S. • $15 • (1/01/2000) • **84**

Pinot Grigio Collio 1996 • $14 • (5/31/1998) • **87**

Pinot Grigio Venezie 1997: Lots of ripe fruit, with apple, cream and toasted oak character. Medium-bodied, with good acidity and a long, flavorful aftertaste. Very good. Drink now.–J.S. • $15 • (1/01/2000) • **86**

Tocai Friulano Collio 1998: Medium-bodied, with good mineral, honey and appleskin character and fresh acidity. Slight marzipan finish. Drink now.–J.S. • $15 • (3/31/2000) • **82**

Tocai Friulano Collio 1997: Decent apple and lemon character, with a hint of straw, but slightly earthy on the finish. Light body.–J.S. • $15 • (1/01/2000) • **78**

Tocai Friulano Collio 1996 • $14 • (6/15/1998) • **83**

Venezie Red 1998: A thin red with some earth and berry character. Watery. Not imported into the U.S.–J.S. • $NA • (1/01/2000) • **78**

Venezie Red 1997: Very light and watery, with decent strawberry and cherry character.–J.S. • $NA • (1/01/2000) • **78**

Venezie White 1998: Delicious white, with apple, cream and a hint of blanched almond. Medium-bodied, with good acidity and a fruity finish. Not imported into the U.S. Drink now through 2002.–J.S. • $15 • (1/01/2000) • **87**

MARENCO & FIGLI, ALDO

Barbera Piemonte Pirona 1997: This has good fruit and tar, smoke and spice character, with a blend of crisp acidity and a rather nice mouthfeel. Should go well with food. Drink now through 2001.–P.M. • $17 • (11/15/1999) • **82**

Key: SS—Spectator Selection. CS—Cellar Selection. HR—Highly Recommended. $NA—Price not available. (BT)—Barrel tasting. Ⓐ—Auction Price.
For a key to the tasters' initials, see "How to Use These Listings."
Dates in parentheses represent the issues in which the ratings were published.

Dolcetto di Dogliani Parlapà 1997: Intense grape and red berry character leaves a bit of tartness on the slightly herbaceous finish.–P.M. • $17 • (11/15/1999) • **79**

MARENGO, GIACOMO

Chianti Castello di Rapale 1997: Fruity and delicious, with bright cherry, berry and strawberry character. Medium-bodied, with light tannins and a fresh finish. Drink now.–J.S. • $12 • (11/30/1999) • **85**

Chianti Le Tornaie 1997: A medium-bodied Chianti, with attractive cherry and wet earth character, light tannins and a fresh finish. Drink now.–J.S. • $11 • (11/30/1999) • **84**

Chianti Tenuta del Fondatore La Commenda 1995: Simple and fruity, with light raspberry and plum character. Light-bodied, light tannins. Delicious and fresh. Drink now.–J.S. • $23 • (11/30/1999) • **82**

Toscana Tenuta del Fondatore Stroncoli 1996: You've got to like the plum, berry and dried cherry aromas in this wine. Medium-bodied, with silky tannins and a crisp, fruity finish. Slightly one-dimensional but delicious. Made from Sangiovese and Cabernet Sauvignon. Drink now.–J.S. • $30 • (11/30/1999) • **86**

MARIANNA

Coda di Volpe Irpinia 1998: Shows vivid aromas of apple and minerals, with hints of lemon and cream. Medium-bodied, with good acidity and a long, flavorful finish. Drink now.–J.S. • $9 • (1/31/2000) • **88**

Fiano di Avellino 1998: A wine with focused mineral, steel and fruit character. Medium-bodied, with lively acidity and a fresh, mineral aftertaste. Yummy. Drink now.–J.S. • $15 • (1/31/2000) • **87**

Fiano di Avellino Ghirlandaio 1996: Candied and dull, with some geranium and fruit character. Barely acceptable. Tasted twice, with consistent notes.–J.S. • $20 • (1/31/2000) • **74**

Greco di Tufo 1998: A fresh and delicious young white, with citrus, honey and light mineral character. Medium-bodied, light finish. Drink now.–J.S. • $13 • (1/31/2000) • **85**

Irpinia 1996: Light and watery, with some fruit, but hard to like really.–J.S. • $9 • (1/31/2000) • **74**

Irpinia Moro di Pietra 1996: Good grapey, floral aromas, with light body, spicy flavors and a light finish. But it's diluted.–J.S. • $15 • (1/31/2000) • **78**

MARLUNGHE

Merlot Colli Euganei 1994 • $11 • (5/31/1996) • **84**

MARRONETO, IL

Brunello di Montalcino 1995: A bit lean, but good flavors. Aromas of bark and plum with hints of fresh mushrooms. Medium-bodied, with dried-herb and berry flavors and firm tannins. Fresh finish. Drink now.–J.S. • $60 • (6/30/2000) • **84**

Brunello di Montalcino 1993: Very mature. Light ruby, with an amber hue. Light-bodied, with delicate berry and vanilla aromas and flavors and a light finish.–J.S. • $48 • (12/15/1998) • **78**

Brunello di Montalcino 1988 • $NA • (4/30/1994) • **80**

MARTINETTI, FRANCO

Barbera d'Asti Superiore Montruc 1994 • $NA • (10/31/1996) • **85**

MARTINI DI CIGALA

Chianti Classico San Giusto a Rentennano 1995 • $NA • (9/30/1997) • **86**
Chianti Classico San Giusto a Rentennano 1991 • $NA • (10/31/1993) • **77**
Chianti Classico San Giusto a Rentennano 1990 • $16 • (10/31/1993) • **85**
Chianti Classico San Giusto a Rentennano Riserva 1994 • $NA • (9/30/1997) • **87**
Chianti Classico San Giusto a Rentennano Riserva 1988 • $23 • (9/15/1992) • **84**
Chianti Classico San Giusto a Rentennano Riserva 1985 • $17 • (11/30/1989) • **91**
Chianti Classico San Giusto a Rentennano Riserva 1983 • $11 • (11/15/1987) • **87**
Percarlo San Giusto a Rentennano 1993 • $NA • (9/30/1997) • **88**
Percarlo San Giusto a Rentennano 1990 • $37 • (10/31/1993) • **87**
Percarlo San Giusto a Rentennano 1989 • $21 • (10/31/1993) • **81**
Percarlo San Giusto a Rentennano 1986 • $24 • (11/30/1989) • **88**
Percarlo San Giusto a Rentennano 1985 • $25 • (2/15/1989) • **92**
Percarlo San Giusto a Rentennano 1983 • $13 • (9/15/1987) • **77**

MARWOOD

Brut NV • $9 • (5/15/1998) • **85**
Dolce Select NV: Quite sweet, appealing but simple in flavor, like spumoni in a bottle. Drink now. • $9 • (7/31/1998) • **78**

MASCARELLO, BARTOLO

Barbera d'Alba 1993 • $10 • (10/31/1995) • **81**
Barolo 1991 • $45 • (10/31/1995) • **83**
Barolo 1989 • $NA • (10/31/1994) • **76**
Barolo 1988 • $35 • (10/31/1993) • **87**
Barolo 1983 • $27 • (5/31/1988) • **88**
Dolcetto d'Alba 1993 • $10 • (10/31/1995) • **81**
Dolcetto d'Alba Vigne Monrobiolo-Rué-Giardino 1996: Slightly earthy, in an uncompromising style, this is firm, tough and tannic, but also has good vibrant fruit to keep your interest. A mineral edge comes through on the mouthpuckeringly fresh, firm finish. Drink now.–P.M. • $18 • (10/31/1998) • **84**

MASCARELLO & FIGLIO, GIUSEPPE

Barbaresco Marcarini 1988 • $32 • (10/31/1993) HR • **94**
Barbaresco Marcarini 1985 • $30 • (8/31/1989) • **85**
Barbera d'Alba Fasana 1987 • $10 • (3/15/1991) • **80**
Barbera d'Alba Superiore Ginestra 1987 • $11 • (3/15/1991) • **85**
Barbera d'Alba Superiore Santo Stefano di Perno 1987 • $13 • (9/15/1990) • **83**
Barolo 1982 • $28 • (6/30/1987) • **81**
Barolo 1978 • $19 • (9/16/1984) • **91**
Barolo Belvedere 1985 • $35 • (6/15/1990) CS • **93**
Barolo Bricco 1988 • $38 • (10/31/1993) • **84**
Barolo Bricco Castiglione Falleto 1991 • $NA • (10/31/1996) • **78**
Barolo Dardi 1982 • $18 • (9/15/1987) • **87**
Barolo Monprivato 1991 • $NA • (10/31/1996) • **86**
Barolo Monprivato 1990 • $79 Ⓐ • (10/31/1995) • **78**
Barolo Monprivato 1989 • $42 • (10/31/1993) • **85**
Barolo Monprivato 1988 • $42 • (10/31/1993) • **82**
Barolo Monprivato 1986 • $47 • (7/15/1991) • **88**
Barolo Monprivato 1985 • $53 • (6/15/1990) • **86**
Barolo Monprivato 1983 • $28 • (7/15/1988) • **85**
Barolo Monprivato 1982 • $22 • (9/15/1987) • **87**
Barolo Monprivato 1981 • $NA • (9/15/1988) • **84**
Barolo Monprivato 1980 • $NA • (9/15/1988) • **76**
Barolo Monprivato 1979 • $61 Ⓐ • (9/15/1988) • **83**
Barolo Monprivato 1978 • $NA • (9/15/1988) • **86**
Barolo Monprivato 1974 • $NA • (9/15/1988) • **91**
Barolo Monprivato 1971 • $NA • (9/15/1988) • **81**
Barolo Monprivato 1970 • $NA • (9/15/1988) • **80**
Barolo Monprivato Falletto 1983 • $23 • (7/31/1989) • **80**
Barolo Santo Stefano di Perno 1985 • $35 • (10/15/1990) HR • **94**
Barolo Villero 1983 • $17 • (10/15/1988) • **77**
Dolcetto d'Alba Bricco 1993 • $12 • (10/31/1995) • **79**
Dolcetto d'Alba Bricco Ravera 1988 • $10 • (9/15/1990) • **82**
Dolcetto d'Alba Gagliassi 1989 • $13 • (7/15/1991) • **85**
Dolcetto d'Alba Gagliassi 1987 • $10 • (3/31/1990) • **80**
Grignolino Monferrato Casalese Besso 1988 • $10 • (1/31/1990) • **75**
Nebbiolo d'Alba San Rocco 1988 • $16 • (7/31/1992) • **82**
Nebbiolo d'Alba San Rocco 1986 • $15 • (9/15/1990) • **85**

MASCIARELLI

Montepulciano d'Abruzzo 1995 • $6 • (2/28/1998) • **83**
Montepulciano d'Abruzzo 1993 • $6 • (2/29/1996) • **85**
Montepulciano d'Abruzzo 1992 • $6 • (3/31/1995) • **86**
Montepulciano d'Abruzzo Villa Gemma Riserva 1992 • $30 • (2/28/1998) • **88**

MASI

Amarone della Valpolicella Classico 1996: Clean, with fresh, focused aromas of plum and berry. Medium-bodied, with silky tannins and a pretty, fruity finish. Drink now.–J.S. • $38 • (6/15/2000) • **87**
Amarone della Valpolicella Classico 1994: Cherry, menthol and vanilla hold court in this slim version of Amarone. Lacks the richness and fruit on the back of the palate to match the tannin and alcohol. Good effort in a difficult vintage. Better than when previously reviewed. Drink now.–B.S. • $28 • (7/31/1998) • **84**
Amarone della Valpolicella Classico 1993 • $25 • (4/30/1997) • **86**
Amarone della Valpolicella Classico 1991 • $28 • (5/31/1996) • **83**
Amarone della Valpolicella Classico 1990 • $25 • (5/31/1996) • **86**
Amarone della Valpolicella Classico 1989 • $28 • (11/15/1994) • **85**
Amarone della Valpolicella Classico 1988 • $36 • (5/31/1996) • **81**
Amarone della Valpolicella Classico 1981 • $15 • (10/31/1988) • **84**
Amarone della Valpolicella Classico Campolongo di Torbe 1993: Superb. Dark ruby, with chocolate, blackberry, game and raspberry aromas. Full-bodied and extremely intense, with loads of ripe fruit and big, soft, velvety tannins. Best after 2003.–J.S. • $60 • (6/15/2000) CS • **93**
Amarone della Valpolicella Classico Campolongo di Torbe 1990 • $47 • (4/30/1997) • **92**
Amarone della Valpolicella Classico Campolongo di Torbe 1988 • $36 • (5/31/1996) • **84**
Amarone della Valpolicella Classico Campolongo di Torbe 1983 • $26 • (4/15/1988) • **85**
Amarone della Valpolicella Classico Mazzano 1993: Big and earthy, with funky aromas of ripe fruit, raisin, axle grease and tar. Full-bodied, thick and peppery, with a long raisin and varnish finish. Not completely clean, but impressive nonetheless. Drink now.–J.S. • $70 • (6/15/2000) • **87**
Amarone della Valpolicella Classico Mazzano 1990 • $50 • (5/31/1998) CS • **92**
Amarone della Valpolicella Classico Mazzano 1988 • $54 • (5/31/1996) • **84**
Amarone della Valpolicella Classico Mazzano 1986 • $58 • (5/31/1996) • **88**
Amarone della Valpolicella Classico Mazzano 1985 • $66 • (5/31/1996) • **90**
Amarone della Valpolicella Classico Mazzano 1983 • $70 • (5/31/1996) • **89**
Amarone della Valpolicella Classico Mazzano 1980 • $26 • (10/31/1988) • **88**
Amarone della Valpolicella Classico Mazzano 1979 • $91 • (5/31/1996) • **88**
Amarone della Valpolicella Classico Mazzano 1977 • $99 • (5/31/1996) • **89**
Amarone della Valpolicella Classico Mazzano 1976 • $99 • (5/31/1996) • **87**
Amarone della Valpolicella Classico Mazzano 1974 • $133 • (5/31/1996) • **89**
Amarone della Valpolicella Classico Mazzano 1971 • $NA • (5/31/1996) • **84**
Amarone della Valpolicella Classico Mazzano 1969 • $NA • (5/31/1996) • **91**
Amarone della Valpolicella Classico Mazzano 1964 • $290 • (5/31/1996) • **92**
Amarone della Valpolicella Classico Mazzano 1958 • $NA • (5/31/1996) • **92**
Amarone della Valpolicella Classico Mazzano 1941 • $NA • (5/31/1996) • **88**
Amarone della Valpolicella Classico Serègo Alighieri Vaio Armaron 1995: A fine red. Extremely floral, with blackberry and violet aromas. Full-bodied, with polished, silky tannins and a long, long finish. A beauty. Best after 2001.–J.S. • $45 • (6/15/2000) • **90**
Amarone della Valpolicella Classico Serègo Alighieri Vaio Armaron 1993: Complex aromas of mint, meat, spice, gunpowder and dried fruit. Medium- to full-bodied, with silky tannins and a sweet fruit aftertaste. Drink now through 2005.–J.S. • $55 • (6/15/2000) • **88**
Amarone della Valpolicella Classico Serègo Alighieri Vaio Armaron 1991: Starts off rich, with prune and chocolate, then this full-bodied red turns tannic, finishing on a hot (alcoholic) note. Good Amarone character without the fat and texture of the best vintages. Drink now.–B.S. • $65 • (7/31/1998) • **86**
Amarone della Valpolicella Classico Serègo Alighieri Vaio Armaron 1990 • $57 • (5/31/1998) • **90**
Amarone della Valpolicella Classico Serègo Alighieri Vaio Armaron 1988 • $55 • (5/31/1996) • **90**
Bardolino 1994 • $9 • (1/31/1997) • **78**
Bardolino 1993 • $15 • (4/30/1996) • **78**
Bardolino Classico Superiore 1992 • $8 • (10/31/1994) • **83**
Bardolino Classico Superiore 1990 • $8 • (9/15/1992) • **78**
Bardolino Classico Superiore 1988 • $9 • (5/15/1991) • **82**
Bardolino Classico Superiore La Vegrona 1990 • $15 • (4/30/1996) • **79**
Campofiorin 1994 • $17 • (5/31/1998) • **85**
Campofiorin 1993 • $15 • (4/30/1997) • **86**
Campofiorin 1991 • $14 • (5/31/1996) • **84**
Campofiorin 1990 • $13 • (10/31/1996) • **78**
Campofiorin 1988 • $15 • (9/15/1992) • **79**
Campofiorin 1985 • $12 • (9/15/1990) • **77**
Recioto della Valpolicella 1991 • $28 • (4/30/1996) • **80**
Recioto della Valpolicella Recioto Amabile Serègo Alighieri 1994 • $50 • (5/31/1998) • **88**
Soave Classico Superiore 1997 • $8 • (6/30/1998) • **84**
Toar 1993 • $20 • (4/30/1997) • **88**
Toar 1992 • $15 • (4/30/1996) • **89**
Toar 1991 • $20 • (5/31/1995) • **86**
Valpolicella 1993 • $14 • (12/15/1995) • **84**
Valpolicella Classico Serègo Alighieri Rosso delle Possessioni 1998: An impressive Valpolicella that needs time but shows promise, with aromas of

black currant, mint and berry. Full-bodied and very well balanced, with good length, a silky texture and fine tannins. Best after 2000.–J.S. • $15 • (6/15/2000) • **88**

Valpolicella Classico Superiore 1996: Shows more of the plum, leather and menthol flavors of Valpolicella in a slightly traditional style, with moderate concentration and structure and a baked-earth finish. Drink now.–B.S. • $8 • (7/31/1998) • **82**

Valpolicella Classico Superiore 1995 • $8 • (4/30/1998) • **78**

Valpolicella Classico Superiore 1994 • $9 • (1/31/1997) • **84**

Valpolicella Classico Superiore 1992 • $8 • (11/15/1994) • **80**

Valpolicella Classico Superiore 1991 • $8 • (10/15/1994) • **86**

Valpolicella Classico Superiore 1989 • $8 • (9/15/1992) • **82**

Valpolicella Classico Superiore Serègo Alighieri 1994 • $17 • (5/31/1998) • **84**

Valpolicella Classico Superiore Serègo Alighieri 1993 • $15 • (4/30/1997) • **87**

Valpolicella Classico Superiore Serègo Alighieri 1991 • $14 • (4/30/1996) • **82**

Valpolicella Classico Superiore Serègo Alighieri 1988 • $18 • (9/15/1992) • **82**

Verona Bianco Serègo Alighieri 1996: An exuberant white that has weight and presence on the palate. Fruit flavors are subtle, finishing with a grapefruit peel note. 70 percent Garganega, 30 percent Sauvignon. Drink now.–B.S. • $16 • (7/31/1998) • **81**

Verona Campofiorin 1996: Bright and fruity, with silky tannins and a long, long finish. Subtle and very fine indeed, with plum and berry. Drink now.–J.S. • $NA • (6/15/2000) • **88**

MASI, RENZO

Toscana Erta e China 1997: A pretty, balanced Sangiovese and Cabernet Sauvignon blend. Intriguing aromas of plum skin and fresh mushroom have a hint of flowers. Medium- to full-bodied, with velvety tannins and a fruity, minty aftertaste. Best after 2000.–J.S. • $9 • (11/30/1999) • **90**

Toscana Erta e China 1996: The Cabernet dominates this blend, which also includes Sangiovese. Black-colored, with lots of currant, berry and dried herb aromas. Full-bodied, with velvety tannins and hints of ripe fruit and new oak. Drink now.–J.S. • $8 • (12/15/1998) • **87**

MASO POLI

Pinot Grigio Trentino 1996 • $14 • (5/31/1998) • **82**

Pinot Nero Trentino 1995 • $19 • (6/30/1998) • **80**

Pinot Nero Trentino 1994 • $19 • (6/30/1998) • **81**

Trentino Costa Erta 1996 • $19 • (5/31/1998) • **80**

MASSA, LA

Chianti Classico 1997: A joyous, aromatic wine. Dark, with amazing aromas of ripe blackberry and licorice. Medium-bodied, with medium tannins and a soft, medium-fruity finish. Needs more backbone to be outstanding. Drink now.–J.S. • $23 • (11/30/1999) • **89**

Chianti Classico 1996: Seriously good Chianti. Plenty of fruit concentration, with lots of blackberry and cherry aromas and flavors. Medium-bodied, with medium, fine tannins and a fruity aftertaste. Drink now through 2003.–J.S. • $13 • (12/15/1998) • **88**

Chianti Classico 1995 • $20 • (9/30/1997) • **84**

Chianti Classico 1994 • $15 • (10/31/1996) • **85**

Chianti Classico 1993 • $14 • (10/31/1995) • **82**

Chianti Classico 1992 • $12 • (2/28/1995) • **84**

Chianti Classico 1990 • $NA • (10/31/1993) • **89**

Chianti Classico Giorgio Primo 1997: More like a serious claret than Chianti in style, but really superb. Dark ruby in color, with aromas of blackberry, wet earth, currant and mint plus lots of new oak. Full-bodied, with super-polished tannins and a medium finish. Drink through 2003.–J.S. • $49 • (11/30/1999) • **92**

Chianti Classico Giorgio Primo 1996: A bit lean but with good fruit and silky, polished tannins. Enticing aromas of plum, berry and spice. Medium-bodied, with a crisp finish. Falls away slightly on the aftertaste. Drink now.–J.S. • $47 • (11/30/1999) • **88**

Chianti Classico Giorgio Primo 1995: Bright in style, with beautiful perfumes and fresh fruit aromas of ripe plums and flowers. Medium-bodied, with very polished tannins. Lively acidity on the aftertaste. Drink now.–J.S. • $26 Ⓐ • (12/15/1998) • **88**

Key: SS—Spectator Selection. CS—Cellar Selection. HR—Highly Recommended. $NA—Price not available. (BT)—Barrel tasting. Ⓐ—Auction Price.
For a key to the tasters' initials, see "How to Use These Listings."
Dates in parentheses represent the issues in which the ratings were published.

Chianti Classico Giorgio Primo 1994 • $18 • (9/30/1997) • **87**

Chianti Classico Giorgio Primo 1992 • $57 • (10/31/1995) • **88**

Chianti Classico Giorgio Primo Riserva 1993 • $30 • (10/31/1996) • **87**

Chianti Classico Giorgio Primo Riserva 1990 • $17 • (2/28/1995) • **91**

MASSE DI GREVE, LE

Chianti Classico 1997: I love the clarity of ripe Sangiovese in this fruit-driven CC. Medium-bodied, with fine tannins and a long, fruity finish. Drink now.–J.S. • $18 • (11/30/1999) • **88**

Chianti Classico Riserva 1996: Harmonious and delicious, with lovely aromas of crushed berry and cherry. Medium-bodied, with silky tannins and a long, fresh finish. Drink now through 2001.–J.S. • $22 • (11/30/1999) • **87**

MASSOLINO

Barbera d'Alba 1993 • $NA • (10/31/1995) • **84**

Barolo 1995: A still-reserved '95 that shows good mineral and wet earth character—serious *terroir* here—and a ripe, complex structure built on firm but well-integrated tannins and deep flavors. Drink now through 2005.–P.M. • $48 • (11/15/1999) • **86**

Barolo 1994: Quite intense, with a hard structure, fairly ripe and sweet tannins and a good combination of earth, horse, plum, black cherry and tar notes. Medium- to full-bodied, it turns a bit tough on the finish. Best after 2003.–P.M. • $35 • (10/31/1998) • **87**

Barolo 1992 • $NA • (10/31/1996) • **79**

Barolo 1990 • $30 • (10/31/1995) • **77**

Barolo Sorì Vigna Rionda 1991 • $NA • (10/31/1996) • **84**

Barolo Vigna Margheria 1995: A tough customer. This Barolo has red berry, plum, smoke and rose petal character. Full-bodied, with good concentration, it kicks in with nice, pure wet earth intensity on the finish. Best after 2000.–P.M. • $60 • (11/15/1999) • **86**

Barolo Vigna Margheria 1991 • $NA • (10/31/1996) • **85**

Barolo Vigna Margheria 1990 • $37 • (10/31/1995) • **78**

Barolo Vigna Parafada 1995: Clean and supple, with nice tar, smoke, plum, green olive and fresh tomato complexity. Medium-bodied, with a succulent finish of manageably firm tannins. Drink now through 2005.–P.M. • $58 • (11/15/1999) • **88**

Barolo Vigna Parafada 1993 • $45 • (10/31/1997) • **89**

Barolo Vigna Parafada 1991 • $NA • (10/31/1996) • **83**

Barolo Vigna Parafada 1990 • $39 • (10/31/1995) • **83**

Barolo Vigna Rionda 1990 • $40 • (10/31/1995) • **85**

Dolcetto d'Alba Vigna Barilot 1996: Exciting and racy, bursting with clean, pure cassis character accented by dried herbs, mint and earth. Medium-bodied, very dark in color and supersupple on the palate, thanks to lots of fine-tuned, ripe tannins. Drink now.–P.M. • $15 • (10/31/1998) • **87**

Dolcetto d'Alba Vigna Barilot 1993 • $NA • (10/31/1995) • **81**

MASTROBERARDINO

Aglianico d'Irpinia Avellanio 1997: A thoroughly delicious red. Plenty of dried cherry, carnations and other flowers on the nose. Medium-bodied, with light tannins and a lovely, fruity, black pepper aftertaste. Drink now.–J.S. • $20 • (1/31/2000) • **86**

Avellanio Red 1992 • $10 • (7/31/1994) • **77**

Avellanio Red 1991 • $12 • (3/31/1993) • **83**

Avellanio Red 1989 • $11 • (7/15/1991) • **87**

Falanghina Beneventano Sirèum 1998: A bit clumsy, but shows character. Ripe fruit with honey and almond throughout this full-bodied wine. Round and rich, with a long, marzipan finish. Drink now.–J.S. • $18 • (1/31/2000) • **86**

Fiano di Avellino More Maiorum 1996: Concentrated, cerebral white. Captivating aromas of peach, honey and mineral. Medium-bodied, with a subtle pie crust, creamy flavor and a long finish. Drink now through 2003.–J.S. • $47 • (1/31/2000) • **90**

Fiano di Avellino Radici 1998: A young and powerful white. Mineral, citrus and steely character. Medium-bodied, with plenty of fruit, medium acidity and a flavorful finish. Drink now.–J.S. • $26 • (1/31/2000) • **90**

Greco di Tufo 1998: A very ripe white, with peach, pineapple and pie crust character. Medium- to full-bodied, with a fresh finish. Drink now.–J.S. • $25 • (1/31/2000) • **87**

Irpinia Anthères Liquoroso NV: A very sweet, full-bodied red with barbecue sauce, pepper and earth character. Plenty of volatile acidity. Not really clean.–J.S. • $35 • (1/31/2000) • **72**

Irpinia Mastro 1998: A seriously good late-harvest-style dry white. Very attractive ripe fruit aromas of apricots and orange peel, with hints of

ITALY

mineral. Full-bodied, dry, with a blanched almond and ripe fruit finish. Not imported into the U.S. Drink now.–J.S. • $NA • (1/31/2000) • **89**

Irpinia Mastro Rosso 1998: Lots of bright berry and black pepper character, like a solid Grenache. Medium-bodied, with light tannins and a fruity finish. Drink now.–J.S. • $11 • (1/31/2000) • **85**

Irpinia Melizie Vino Passito 1996: Slightly strange aromas of peaches, herbs and sugar-coated lemon rinds, with hints of volatile acidity. Full-bodied, medium sweet, with a honeyed finish. A bit rustic, but interesting. Not imported into the U.S. Drink now.–J.S. • $NA • (1/01/1999) • **85**

Irpinia Rosato Lacrimarosa 1998: One of the great rosés of the world. Loads of character yet fine and elegant. Subtle aromas of light plum, mineral, pomace and white pepper. Medium-bodied, with a lovely strawberry and mineral aftertaste that persists on the finish. Drink now.–J.S. • $17 • (1/31/2000) • **90**

Lacryma Christi del Vesuvio 1998: Delicious young wine. Aromas of plums, earth and spice follow through to a medium-bodied palate, with fine tannins and a short finish. Needs a bit more fruit on the midpalate. Drink now through 2002.–J.S. • $28 • (1/31/2000) • **87**

Lacryma Christi del Vesuvio 1991 • $15 • (7/31/1993) • **84**

Lacryma Christi del Vesuvio 1989 • $14 • (7/15/1991) • **89**

Lacryma Christi del Vesuvio White 1998: Here's an extremely well-made Italian white that's a dead-ringer for Riesling, with honey, mineral and pie crust aromas and flavors. It's medium-bodied, with lots of fruit and a flavorful finish. Drink now.–J.S. • $19 • (1/31/2000) SS • **89**

Mastro Rosso 1994 • $10 • (1/31/1996) • **79**

Taurasi 1987 • $19 • (9/15/1992) • **80**

Taurasi 1986 • $18 • (7/15/1991) • **87**

Taurasi 1982 • $13 • (7/15/1987) • **75**

Taurasi Radici 1995: A well-crafted red. Bright aromas of cherries and raspberries, with hints of mineral and spice. Medium- to full-bodied, with polished tannins and a long aftertaste of black pepper and cherry. Drink now through 2005.–J.S. • $47 • (1/31/2000) • **89**

Taurasi Radici 1990 • $22 • (3/31/1997) • **85**

Taurasi Radici 1989 • $20 • (1/31/1996) • **87**

Taurasi Radici 1988 • $21 • (7/31/1994) • **88**

Taurasi Riserva 1987 • $18 • (7/31/1994) • **78**

Taurasi Riserva 1985 • $22 • (6/30/1991) • **84**

Taurasi Riserva 1981 • $21 • (2/15/1989) • **78**

Taurasi Riserva 1980 • $15 • (9/15/1989) • **75**

Taurasi Riserva 1977 • $28 • (10/16/1984) CS • **92**

MASTROJANNI

Brunello di Montalcino 1994: Needs a bit more freshness, but still a good glass of Brunello. Slightly mature-looking, with a garnet hue. Aromas of tobacco, earth and plum. Medium-bodied, with fine tannins and a light fruit and cedar aftertaste. Drink now.–J.S. • $40 • (8/31/1999) • **84**

Brunello di Montalcino 1993: A rich, ripe Brunello, with loads of smoke, berry and meat aromas and flavors. Medium-bodied, with round tannins and a long, succulent finish. Plenty of alcohol—perhaps a tad too much. Drink now.–J.S. • $45 • (12/15/1998) • **87**

Brunello di Montalcino 1991 • $33 • (3/31/1997) • **85**

Brunello di Montalcino 1990 • $27 • (10/31/1995) • **94**

Brunello di Montalcino 1988 • $30 • (4/30/1994) • **90**

Brunello di Montalcino 1982 • $17 • (6/15/1990) • **87**

Brunello di Montalcino 1979 • $17 • (9/15/1986) • **72**

Brunello di Montalcino Riserva 1993: Fine and elegant. Intense aromas of fresh cherries with undertones of flowers. Medium- to full-bodied,with fine tannins and a lovely fresh finish. Drink now through 2009.–J.S. • $50 • (8/31/1999) • **92**

Brunello di Montalcino Riserva 1990 • $90 • (11/30/1996) • **91**

Brunello di Montalcino Riserva 1988 • $50 • (10/31/1994) • **91**

Brunello di Montalcino Schiena d'Asino 1993: A bit simple but attractive. Aromas of dried cherries and plum skins flow from the glass. Medium-bodied, with medium tannins and a light, fresh finish. Drink now through 2005.–J.S. • $55 • (8/31/1999) • **87**

Brunello di Montalcino Schiena d'Asino 1990 • $90 • (3/31/1997) • **88**

Rosso di Montalcino 1996: Good aromas of grapes and berries. Medium-bodied, with ripe fruit and round tannins. A tad alcoholic on the finish, and tough. Needs a little time to mellow. Drink through 2001.–J.S. • $22 • (12/15/1998) • **83**

Rosso di Montalcino 1995 • $18 • (9/30/1997) • **84**

Rosso di Montalcino 1991 • $13 • (8/31/1995) • **84**

Rosso di Montalcino 1987 • $10 • (7/15/1991) • **79**

San Pio 1992 • $18 • (10/31/1996) • **85**

MAZZEI

Chianti Classico Castello di Fonterutoli 1997: A delicious, soft Chianti, with extremely plummy aromas and hints of bark. Medium-bodied, with velvety tannins and a vanilla, berry and tobacco aftertaste. Drink now.–J.S. • $22 • (11/30/1999) • **88**

Chianti Classico Castello di Fonterutoli 1996: Good plummy, berry character in this easy-to-like Chianti. Medium-bodied, with light tannins and a fresh and fruity aftertaste. Smooth texture. Winery formerly known as Castello di Fonterutoli. Drink now.–J.S. • $17 • (12/15/1998) • **85**

Chianti Classico Castello di Fonterutoli Riserva 1996: Good intensity of ripe fruit for the vintage. Crushed raspberry and dried cherry character, with hints of smoky oak. Medium-bodied, with medium, silky tannins and a fresh finish. Drink now.–J.S. • $42 • (11/30/1999) • **88**

Chianti Classico Castello di Fonterutoli Riserva 1995: A well-made riserva CC. Black currant, with a hint of dried herbs on the nose. Medium-bodied, with velvety tannins and a grapey, fruity aftertaste. Drink now.–J.S. • $42 • (12/15/1998) • **86**

Morellino di Scansano Belguardo 1998: This seriously good Morellino has a wonderful dark ruby color, with intense aromas of berry, cherry and grilled meat. Full-bodied, with well-integrated, silky tannins and a medium finish. Drink now through 2001.–J.S. • $20 • (11/30/1999) • **88**

Morellino di Scansano Belguardo 1997: This shows richness and class. Dark color, with wonderful blackberry, mineral and raspberry character. Full-bodied, with velvety tannins and a long, fruity finish. From the Mazzei family of Castello di Fonterutoli. Best through 2001.–J.S. • $18 • (12/15/1998) • **88**

Toscana Badiola 1997: A simple, no-nonsense red, with dried cherry and orange peel character. Light- to medium-bodied, with crisp acidity and a simple finish. Drink now.–J.S. • $14 • (11/30/1999) • **82**

Toscana Badiola 1996: Clean and firm, with blackberry and cherry aromas and flavors. Medium body. A bit shy on fruit concentration at midpalate but delicious all the same. Drink now.–J.S. • $14 • (12/15/1998) • **86**

Toscana Brancaia 1995: Wonderfully concentrated on the nose, with plum and berry character. Medium-bodied, with succulent and fruity flavors and a soft texture. A gorgeous red for drinking now.–J.S. • $39 • (12/15/1998) • **87**

Toscana Siepi 1996: A gorgeous red, with beautiful crushed raspberry and currant and a hint of spice. Full-bodied, with a solid core of fruit and polished tannins. Super finish. Sangiovese and Merlot. Drink now through 2003.–J.S. • $66 • (11/30/1999) • **90**

MAZZI

Amarone della Valpolicella Classico Punta di Villa 1994 • $45 • (6/15/1998) • **86**

Valpolicella Classico Superiore 1996 • $20 • (6/15/1998) • **78**

Valpolicella Classico Superiore Poiega 1995 • $20 • (6/15/1998) • **84**

Valpolicella Colle Crosetta 1988 • $17 • (9/15/1992) • **82**

Valpolicella Poiega 1988 • $20 • (9/15/1992) • **82**

Valpolicella Poiega 1986 • $20 • (9/15/1992) • **86**

Valpolicella Superiore 1988 • $12 • (9/15/1992) • **79**

MEDICI ERMETE

Concerto Lambrusco Reggiano 1994 • $14 • (12/15/1995) • **81**

MELETO, CASTELLO DI

Chianti Classico 1997: A Chianti bubbling over with bright berry and strawberry character. Medium-bodied, with light tannins and a fruity finish. Not imported into the U.S. Drink now.–J.S. • $NA • (1/01/1999) • **83**

Chianti Classico Riserva 1996: A well-done CC, with aromas of blackberry and mint that follow through to the palate. Medium-bodied, with fine tannins, a good amount of new wood and a medium finish. Not imported into the U.S. Drink now.–J.S. • $NA • (1/01/1999) • **87**

Toscana Fiore 1997: This wine shows enchanting aromas of dried cherry and spice, with hints of raisin. Medium-bodied, with sweet fruit and light tannins. Not imported into the U.S. Drink now.–J.S. • $NA • (1/01/1999) • **85**

MELINI

Chianti Borghi d'Elsa 1992 • $13 • (7/31/1995) • **74**

Chianti Borghi d'Elsa 1990 • $7 • (7/31/1992) • **84**

Chianti Borghi d'Elsa 1989 • $7 • (10/31/1991) • **81**

Chianti Classico Isassi 1997: Pretty weak for the vintage. This mature red is garnet in color, with light plum and cherry aromas. Light-bodied, with fresh acidity and a light finish.–J.S. • $13 • (11/30/1999) • **78**
Chianti Classico Isassi 1995 • $13 • (9/30/1997) • **80**
Chianti Classico Isassi 1994 • $12 • (10/31/1996) • **78**
Chianti Classico Isassi 1990 • $10 • (10/31/1993) • **83**
Chianti Classico Isassi 1989 • $10 • (9/15/1992) • **81**
Chianti Classico Isassi 1988 • $9 • (9/15/1991) • **89**
Chianti Classico La Selvanella Riserva 1993 • $15 • (10/31/1996) • **84**
Chianti Classico La Selvanella Riserva 1991 • $20 • (4/30/1998) • **78**
Chianti Classico La Selvanella Riserva 1990 • $13 • (2/28/1995) • **79**
Chianti Classico La Selvanella Riserva 1988 • $14 • (10/31/1993) • **85**
Chianti Classico La Selvanella Riserva 1987 • $13 • (9/15/1992) • **83**
Chianti Classico Laborel Riserva 1990 • $11 • (2/28/1995) • **78**
Chianti Classico Laborel Riserva 1987 • $11 • (12/15/1992) • **85**
Chianti Classico Laborel Riserva 1986 • $10 • (10/31/1991) • **83**
Chianti Classico Massovecchio Riserva 1995: Some interesting character, but slightly hard and austere. Shows tobacco, herb and berry. Medium-bodied, with medium tannins and a slightly dry finish. Drink now.–J.S. • $30 • (11/30/1999) • **86**
Toscana I Coltri Vigna 1 1995: A charming and delicious red. Vivid aromas of dried cherries and cherries. Medium- to full-bodied, with soft tannins and a long, fruity finish. A beauty. Sangiovese and Cabernet Sauvignon. Drink now.–J.S. • $25 • (11/30/1999) • **87**
Toscana I Coltri Vigna 1 1993 • $21 • (10/31/1996) • **77**
Toscana I Coltri Vigna 1 1990 • $20 • (12/31/1995) • **85**
Toscana I Coltri Vigna 1 1988 • $19 • (11/30/1994) • **86**
Toscana I Coltri Vigna 1 1986 • $20 • (12/15/1992) • **85**
Toscana I Coltri Vigna 2 1995: Impressive concentration but slightly too herbal. Intense bright berry character, with hints of dried herbs. Medium- to full-bodied, with silky tannins and plenty of herbal and berry character on the finish. Cabernet Sauvignon and Sangiovese. Drink now.–J.S. • $25 • (11/30/1999) • **87**
Toscana I Coltri Vigna 2 1994 • $24 • (4/30/1998) • **82**
Toscana I Coltri Vigna 2 1993 • $21 • (10/31/1996) • **86**
Toscana I Coltri Vigna 2 1990 • $20 • (12/31/1995) • **90**
Toscana I Coltri Vigna 2 1988 • $19 • (11/30/1994) • **90**
Toscana I Coltri Vigna 2 1986 • $20 • (12/15/1992) • **83**
Vernaccia di San Gimignano Le Grillaie 1998: Plenty of subtle tropical fruit character in this white, with pineapple, passion fruit and honey aromas and flavors. Full-bodied and rich, with good acidity and a medium, fruity finish. Drink now.–J.S. • $17 • (11/30/1999) • **87**
Vernaccia di San Gimignano Le Grillaie 1997: Refreshing and sophisticated, this is seriously good quality for a Vernaccia. Bright aromas of apples, nectarines, peaches and cream. Medium-bodied, with crisp acidity and a lively, fruity aftertaste. Drink now.–J.S. • $22 • (12/15/1998) • **87**
Vernaccia di San Gimignano Le Grillaie 1996 • $17 • (9/30/1997) • **86**
Vino Nobile di Montepulciano Riserva 1985 • $10 • (4/15/1990) • **82**

MEO, DI

Fiano di Avellino 1997: Some decent lemon, lime and mineral character, but dull and chalky on the palate.–J.S. • $26 • (1/31/2000) • **77**
Greco di Tufo 1997: A dull, slightly oxidized, candied white with almond and honey character.–J.S. • $20 • (1/31/2000) • **77**
Taurasi 1994: Pleasant yet simple, fruity, with spicy, peppery and cherry character. Medium-bodied, with light tannins and a fruity finish. Drink now.–J.S. • $38 • (1/31/2000) • **84**

MEZZACORONA

Cabernet Sauvignon Trentino 1995 • $8 • (6/15/1998) • **85**
Chardonnay Trentino 1997 • $8 • (6/15/1998) • **77**
Merlot Trentino 1996 • $8 • (6/15/1998) • **83**
Merlot Trentino 1993 • $8 • (6/15/1996) • **81**
Merlot Trentino 1991 • $8 • (4/30/1994) • **82**
Merlot Trentino 1990 • $8 • (9/15/1992) • **81**
Pinot Grigio Trentino 1997 • $8 • (6/15/1998) • **84**
Pinot Nero Trentino 1995 • $8 • (6/30/1998) • **79**
Teroldego Rotaliano Vigneto Sottodossi 1993 • $15 • (6/15/1996) • **83**

Key: SS—Spectator Selection. CS—Cellar Selection. HR—Highly Recommended. $NA—Price not available. (BT)—Barrel tasting. (A)—Auction Price. For a key to the tasters' initials, see "How to Use These Listings."
Dates in parentheses represent the issues in which the ratings were published.

Teroldego Rotaliano Vigneto Sottodossi 1992 • $17 • (2/28/1995) • **84**

MICCINE, LE

Chianti Classico 1997: Rather light for a '97, with pleasant berry and cherry character and a light, slightly diluted finish.–J.S. • $NA • (1/01/1999) • **79**
Chianti Classico da Gino 1997: A delicate Chianti Classico. Aromas of blackberry and raspberry follow through to a medium-bodied palate, with light tannins and a fresh finish. Drink now.–J.S. • $NA • (1/01/1999) • **84**
Red da Gino 1994 • $NA • (9/30/1997) • **85**
Red L 'Aura 1996 • $NA • (9/30/1997) • **77**

MIONETTO

Marca Trevigiana Novello 1999: Silky, supple and sweet. Strawberry, licorice and cinnamon flavors are distinctive but lack the grapey freshness typical of Nouveau. Drink now.–T.M. • $8 • (1/01/2000) • **84**

MOCALI

Brunello di Montalcino 1994: Delicious and harmonious. Vivid aromas of strawberry, chocolate and wet earth. Medium-bodied, with fresh fruit flavors, fine tannins and a fruity finish. Drink now.–J.S. • $32 • (8/31/1999) • **88**
Brunello di Montalcino 1993: Gorgeous aromas of blackberries and flowers. Medium to full in body, with firm, chewy tannins and a long, raspberry aftertaste. Slightly austere at this stage but very good indeed. Best after 2001.–J.S. • $32 • (12/15/1998) • **89**
Brunello di Montalcino 1992 • $29 • (9/30/1997) • **84**
Brunello di Montalcino 1991 • $NA • (11/30/1996) • **81**
Brunello di Montalcino 1990 • $NA • (10/31/1995) • **88**
Brunello di Montalcino Riserva 1993: Pretty cherry and spice aromas with hints of flowers. Medium-bodied, with fine tannins and a fresh, fruity finish. A lovely, delicate and delicious wine. Not imported into the U.S. Drink now.–J.S. • $NA • (1/01/1999) • **86**
Brunello di Montalcino Riserva 1991 • $40 • (9/30/1997) • **88**
Rosso di Montalcino 1997: Light, fresh and fruity, with some vanilla and cherry character. Light- to medium-bodied, with a lean finish. Needs a bit more fruit concentration considering the vintage. Drink now.–J.S. • $15 • (9/15/1999) • **81**
Rosso di Montalcino 1996: Pretty wine. Wonderful perfumes of flowers and fruit. Medium-bodied, with juicy, fruity flavors and a long finish with a hint of vanilla. Drink now.–J.S. • $18 • (12/15/1998) • **87**
Rosso di Montalcino 1995 • $15 • (9/30/1997) • **85**
Rosso di Montalcino 1994 • $NA • (11/30/1996) • **85**

MOCCAGATTA

Barbaresco Basarin 1996: International in style, but complex and beautifully made, this full-bodied seducer uses its fancy oak origins to tap into Piedmont's register: flavorful black fruit (with violet, mint and currant notes), ripe but tough tannins, racy acidity and, especially, the mineral *terroir*. Has the stuffing to age. Best from 2006 through 2010.–P.M. • $42 • (8/31/1999) • **95**
Barbaresco Basarin 1995: Very new-oakish style, but it's well made, with a lush and supple frame delivering silky tannins and lots of floral, cassis, toast, roasted walnut and cigar-box aromas that burn like a good Havana on the finish. Distinctive and delicious.–P.M. • $33 • (10/31/1998) • **89**
Barbaresco Basarin 1994 • $30 • (10/31/1997) • **77**
Barbaresco Basarin 1993 • $29 • (10/31/1996) • **87**
Barbaresco Basarin 1992 • $26 • (10/31/1995) • **79**
Barbaresco Basarin 1991 • $24 • (10/31/1994) • **85**
Barbaresco Basarin 1990 • $26 • (10/31/1993) • **90**
Barbaresco Basarin 1989 • $25 • (10/31/1993) • **82**
Barbaresco Basarin 1988 • $24 • (10/31/1994) • **74**
Barbaresco Basarin 1987 • $23 • (7/15/1991) • **86**
Barbaresco Bric Balin 1996: Balanced, beautifully made Barbaresco, showing lots of ripe fruit, sweet tannins and racy acidity. Full-bodied, some toasted, spicy vanilla notes make a subtle presence on the plummy aftertaste.–P.M. • $45 • (8/31/1999) • **93**
Barbaresco Bric Balin 1995: When a Barbaresco gets it right, like this one, you can only marvel at the full body, the complex spice, red berry, earth and currant flavors, the thick, ripe and silky midpalate, and yes, the finish with its firm backbone of tannins. Drink through 2007.–P.M. • $35 • (10/31/1998) • **93**
Barbaresco Bric Balin 1994 • $33 • (10/31/1997) • **77**
Barbaresco Bric Balin 1993 • $31 • (10/31/1997) • **85**

ITALY

Barbaresco Bric Balin 1992 • $28 • (10/31/1995) • **83**
Barbaresco Bric Balin 1991 • $28 • (10/31/1994) • **87**
Barbaresco Bric Balin 1990 • $31 • (10/31/1993) • **93**
Barbaresco Bric Balin 1989 • $28 • (10/31/1994) • **83**
Barbaresco Bric Balin 1988 • $28 • (10/31/1993) • **89**
Barbaresco Bric Balin 1987 • $28 • (7/15/1991) • **89**
Barbaresco Vigna Cole 1996: Fantastic. Nebbiolo doesn't get much fuller, more opulent or silkier than this ripe and classy Barbaresco. Dark but not black in color, it focuses on an intriguing blend of roses, chestnut, tar, black cherry, wet earth and vanilla. Healthy dose of tannins on the finish. Best from 2003 through 2010.–P.M. • $48 • (8/31/1999) • **95**
Barbaresco Vigna Cole 1995: Pretty, offering milky chocolate, red berry, spice, mocha and ground coffee aromas and flavors. Fresh acidity mingles in this full-bodied wine, making it opulent but also fresh.–P.M. • $40 • (10/31/1998) • **88**
Barbaresco Vigna Cole 1994 • $38 • (10/31/1997) • **85**
Barbaresco Vigna Cole 1993 • $34 • (10/31/1996) • **87**
Barbaresco Vigna Cole 1992 • $27 • (10/31/1995) • **82**
Barbaresco Vigna Cole 1991 • $26 • (10/31/1994) • **83**
Barbaresco Vigna Cole 1990 • $33 • (10/31/1993) • **88**
Barbaresco Vigna Cole 1989 • $27 • (10/31/1993) • **89**
Barbaresco Vigna Cole 1988 • $25 • (10/31/1993) • **78**
Barbera d'Alba 1991 • $12 • (11/15/1993) • **81**
Barbera d'Alba 1989 • $14 • (3/15/1991) • **89**
Barbera d'Alba Basarin 1994 • $27 • (10/31/1997) • **88**
Barbera d'Alba Basarin 1993 • $23 • (10/31/1996) • **89**
Barbera d'Alba Basarin 1991 • $NA • (10/31/1994) • **80**
Barbera d'Alba Basarin 1990 • $25 • (11/15/1993) • **84**
Dolcetto d'Alba 1997: Crafty winemaking. Charming and exotic, with wild berry and violet, this is a Dolcetto that reaches for sophistication. Along with smacking acidity and some chewy tannins, it has a slight herbal scent but the finish tastes ripe.–P.M. • $16 • (10/31/1998) • **87**
Dolcetto d'Alba Buschet 1996 • $14 • (10/31/1997) • **84**
Dolcetto d'Alba Buschet 1991 • $14 • (3/31/1993) • **82**

MOLETTO

Cabernet Franc Lison-Pramaggiore 1997: A fresh, light-bodied red, with a good amount of strawberry and cherry character and a light, crisp finish. Drink now.–J.S. • $12 • (1/01/2000) • **80**
Cabernet Franc Lison-Pramaggiore 1995 • $12 • (6/30/1998) • **83**
Chardonnay Piave 1996 • $11 • (12/15/1997) • **83**
Colmello 1994: Rich, concentrated and harmonious, with intense aromas of ripe berry and flowers and hints of raisin. Full-bodied and chewy, with lots of fruit on the finish. Drink now through 2003.–J.S. • $20 • (1/01/2000) • **87**
Colmello Bianco 1996: Simple, with apple and lemon character. Medium-bodied, with light acidity and a crisp finish. Drink now.–J.S. • $20 • (1/01/2000) • **81**
Merlot Piave 1997: A pleasant Merlot from the Veneto. Blackberry and floral aromas follow through to a medium-bodied palate, with light tannins and a short finish. Drink now.–J.S. • $11 • (1/01/2000) • **82**
Merlot Piave 1995 • $13 • (11/15/1997) • **77**
Pinot Grigio Piave 1997 • $10 • (6/30/1998) • **83**
Pinot Grigio Piave 1996 • $11 • (5/15/1998) • **83**
Veneto Colmello Rosso 1991 • $22 • (4/30/1998) • **87**

MOLINO, FRANCO

Barolo Bricco Zuncai 1993 • $NA • (10/31/1997) • **74**

MOLINO, MAURO

Acanzio 1993 • $24 • (5/31/1997) • **88**
Acanzio 1989 • $15 • (1/31/1992) • **85**
Barolo Vigna Conca 1992 • $35 • (1/01/1997) • **81**
Barolo Vigna Conca 1986 • $29 • (2/28/1991) • **87**
Barolo Vigna Conca 1985 • $25 • (3/31/1990) • **82**
Dolcetto d'Alba 1989 • $14 • (2/28/1991) • **87**
Dolcetto d'Alba 1988 • $12 • (3/31/1990) • **82**
Nebbiolo delle Langhe 1989 • $12 • (7/31/1992) • **83**
Nebbiolo delle Langhe 1988 • $12 • (3/31/1990) • **84**
Pinotu 1989 • $20 • (8/31/1991) • **84**

MONASTERO, CASTELLO DI

Chardonnay Toscana Solo 1997: An elegant and delicious wine, with aromas of apple, cantaloupe and lemon. Medium-bodied, with a lovely balance of wood and fruit and a creamy aftertaste. Drink now.–J.S. • $18 • (11/30/1999) • **86**
Chianti Classico 1997: This young CC has pretty plum, wood and earth character. Medium-bodied, with light tannins and a medium finish. Drink now.–J.S. • $14 • (11/30/1999) • **84**
Chianti Classico Riserva 1995: Lots of bright berry character, but also loads of new toasted oak. Medium-bodied, with medium tannins and a vanilla, berry aftertaste. Slightly too much new wood in a CC for me, but good quality. Drink now.–J.S. • $24 • (11/30/1999) • **84**
Sangiovese Toscana 1997: Rather light and forward for a '97 Sangiovese, with a slightly watery finish.–J.S. • $10 • (11/30/1999) • **78**

MONCHIERO

Barbera d'Alba 1996: Dark-colored, but very crisp, showing some cherry, lime and cassis bush notes. Of medium body, it should soften a bit with food. Drink now.–P.M. • $13 • (10/31/1998) • **83**
Barbera d'Alba MonBirone 1997: Spice, smoke, chocolate, bark—you can taste the barriques here. With time, this medium-bodied Barbera ought to come around and lay on the ripe plum and focused wild berry notes. Best from 2001 through 2003.–P.M. • $18 • (11/15/1999) • **86**
Barolo Montanello Riserva 1993: Elegant, yet fairly ripe, with plum and blackberry character. Rather tannic but showing good wet earth and smoke notes. Nice to smell now, better to drink in a few years.–P.M. • $24 • (10/31/1998) • **86**
Dolcetto d'Alba 1997: This Dolcetto really is *dolce* (sweet), in a ripe way that's very pleasant. Light- to medium-bodied, it kicks in with black cherry, wild berry and cassis bush aromas and flavors, ending in a lingering, tannic finish.–P.M. • $13 • (10/31/1998) • **84**

MONSANTO, FATTORIA

Chardonnay Toscana Fabrizio Bianchi 1997: A delicious and subtle Chardonnay, with honey, cream, vanilla and apple character. Medium-bodied, with good acidity and a fresh finish. Drink now.–J.S. • $21 • (11/30/1999) • **87**
Chardonnay Toscana Fabrizio Bianchi 1996: Apple skin and melon aromas, with hints of oak. Medium-bodied, with moderate acidity and a creamy finish. Offers decent fruit character, but slightly dull overall. Drink now.–J.S. • $16 • (12/15/1998) • **84**
Chianti Classico Il Poggio Riserva 1995: A warm and inviting wine, with berry, tobacco and meat aromas and flavors. Medium-bodied, with soft tannins and a medium finish. Slightly traditional in style but delicious all the same. Drink now.–J.S. • $45 • (11/30/1999) • **88**
Chianti Classico Il Poggio Riserva 1985 • $58 Ⓐ • (3/31/1990) • **80**
Chianti Classico Il Poggio Riserva 1983 • $23 • (11/30/1989) • **86**
Chianti Classico Il Poggio Riserva 1982 • $23 • (6/30/1989) • **88**
Chianti Classico Il Poggio Riserva 1981 • $17 • (11/30/1989) • **82**
Chianti Classico Il Poggio Riserva 1979 • $16 • (9/15/1987) • **93**
Chianti Classico Riserva 1996: Monsanto always makes a very good riserva CC. A subtle and elegant red, with lovely plum, cherry and tobacco aromas. Medium-bodied, with medium firm tannins and a long, fresh finish. Drink now through 2004.–J.S. • $21 • (11/30/1999) • **88**
Chianti Classico Riserva 1995: Full-bodied, rich, traditional-style Chianti, with intense autumnal character of smoked almond, chestnut, fresh mushroom and ripe fruit. Medium- to full-bodied, with firm tannins and fresh acidity. Decant if drinking now. Best after 2000.–J.S. • $16 • (12/15/1998) • **90**
Chianti Classico Riserva 1994 • $17 • (9/30/1997) • **86**
Chianti Classico Riserva 1991 • $17 • (10/31/1995) • **82**
Chianti Classico Riserva 1990 • $19 • (10/31/1993) • **86**
Chianti Classico Riserva 1988 • $16 • (9/15/1992) • **86**
Chianti Classico Riserva 1987 • $16 • (12/15/1992) • **68**
Chianti Classico Riserva 1986 • $15 • (4/15/1991) • **85**
Chianti Classico Riserva 1985 • $10 • (11/30/1989) • **89**
Chianti Classico Riserva 1982 • $10 • (2/15/1988) • **72**
Fabrizio Bianchi Vigneto Scanni 1988 • $30 • (9/15/1991) • **82**
Fabrizio Bianchi Vigneto Scanni 1988 • $30 • (10/31/1993) • **85**
Fabrizio Bianchi Vigneto Scanni 1985 • $33 • (12/15/1992) • **74**
Nemo 1994 • $33 • (10/31/1997) • **88**
Nemo 1993 • $30 • (10/31/1996) • **87**
Nemo 1990 • $29 • (2/28/1995) • **88**
Nemo 1988 • $30 • (9/15/1991) • **91**

MONSANTO, FATTORIA

Nemo 1986 • $33 • (12/15/1992) • **84**
Nemo 1983 • $28 • (9/15/1990) • **87**
Sangiovese Fabrizio Bianchi 1993 • $26 • (7/31/1997) • **90**
Tinscvil 1993 • $30 • (10/31/1996) • **85**
Tinscvil 1990 • $21 • (2/28/1995) • **81**
Tinscvil 1988 • $22 • (3/31/1993) • **71**
Tinscvil 1986 • $32 • (1/31/1993) • **83**
Tinscvil 1985 • $22 • (9/15/1990) • **88**

MONTALCINO, CANTINA DI

Brunello di Montalcino 1995: A ripe and soft Brunello with violet, berry and cherry aromas. Medium-bodied, with velvety tannins and a short finish. Slightly hollow midpalate, but delicious. Drink now through 2003.–J.S. • $45 • (6/30/2000) • **87**

Brunello di Montalcino 1994: A good '94. Light aromas of berries, leaves and earth. Medium-bodied, with medium tannins and a plummy aftertaste. Drink now through 2003.–J.S. • $40 • (8/31/1999) • **84**

Brunello di Montalcino 1993: A pleasant, drink-now Brunello. Good, brick-red color, with blackberry, dried cherry and black pepper aromas. Medium-bodied, with medium, silky tannins.–J.S. • $34 • (12/15/1998) • **86**

Chianti Riserva 1995: Pretty plum and berry character in this young red. Medium-bodied, with medium, fine tannins and a light finish. Drink now.–J.S. • $10 • (12/15/1998) • **84**

Rosso di Montalcino 1997: Very grapey, with hints of berries and raisins. Medium-bodied, with light tannins and a short, fresh finish. A bit rustic. Drink now.–J.S. • $22 • (9/15/1999) • **82**

Rosso di Montalcino 1996: A fruit-driven Rosso, with peppery, fruity character. Medium-bodied, with medium tannins and a caressing finish. Seriously good from the cooperative of Montalcino. Drink now.–J.S. • $12 • (12/15/1998) • **84**

Toscana Poggio del Sasso 1996: A big red, slightly overdone. Black-colored, with fruit and spices on the nose and palate. Full-bodied and very concentrated. Finishes dry and tannic. Drink now.–J.S. • $16 • (12/15/1998) • **84**

Toscana Villa di Corsano 1997: A solid and delicious red, with plenty of blackberry and plum aromas and flavors. Medium-bodied, with light tannins and a fruity finish. Drink now.–J.S. • $20 • (11/30/1999) • **84**

Toscana Villa di Corsano 1996: Boasts plenty of delicious fruit. Bright floral, grape and berry aromas. Full-bodied, with loads of grapey fruit character and silky tannins. Drink through 2002.–J.S. • $20 • (12/15/1998) • **86**

MONTE ANTICO

Red 1991 • $9 • (12/31/1995) • **89**
Red 1990 • $9 • (7/31/1995) • **80**

Toscana 1996: Italy still abounds with bargains—like this traditional Tuscan red for current drinking. Delicious, with plenty of plum, berry and mushroom character, medium body, velvety tannins and a soft finish. Drink now.–J.S. • $10 • (11/30/1999) • **86**

MONTE BERNARDI

Chianti Classico 1995 • $NA • (9/30/1997) • **82**
Chianti Classico 1994 • $25 • (10/31/1996) • **80**
Chianti Classico 1993 • $NA • (10/31/1995) • **80**
Chianti Classico Riserva 1994 • $NA • (9/30/1997) • **80**
Sa 'Etta 1994 • $32 • (10/31/1996) • **80**
Sa 'Etta 1993 • $32 • (10/31/1996) • **76**

MONTECALVI

Alta Valle della Greve 1995 • $36 • (10/31/1997) • **90**

Toscana 1996: A beauty for the vintage. Vivid aromas of violet, berry and raspberry. Medium-bodied, with a good core of fruit and medium, silky tannins. Drink now.–J.S. • $44 • (11/30/1999) • **88**

Key: SS—Spectator Selection. CS—Cellar Selection. HR—Highly Recommended. $NA—Price not available. (BT)—Barrel tasting. (A)—Auction Price. For a key to the tasters' initials, see "How to Use These Listings." **Dates in parentheses represent the issues in which the ratings were published.**

MONTECCHIA, LA

Cabernet Colli Euganei Bandiera 1996: A simple fruity red with plum and berry character and a hint of earth. Light- to medium-bodied, with light tannins. Short finish. Drink now.–J.S. • $20 • (5/15/2000) • **80**

Cabernet Veneto Godimondo 1998: Interesting red. Plenty of currant and blackberry aromas in this wine. Medium-bodied, with a peppery fruit character and a long, soft finish. Drink now through 2002.–J.S. • $19 • (5/15/2000) • **86**

Chardonnay Colli Euganei Montecchia 1998: Pretty combination of fruit, spices and toasted oak. Medium-bodied, with good fruit and a lovely pie crust and apple aftertaste. Drink now.–J.S. • $20 • (3/31/2000) • **86**

Colli Euganei 1996: A bit diluted, with some decent fruit but slightly green. Aromas of plums with a hint of green tobacco. Light- to medium-bodied, with light tannins and a short finish. Merlot and Cabernet. Drink now.–J.S. • $12 • (5/15/2000) • **80**

Colli Euganei Montecchia 1996: Sleek and fruity, with pleasant berry and plum character, medium body, light finish. Merlot, Cabernet Sauvignon, Cabernet Franc and Raboso. Drink now.–J.S. • $29 • (5/15/2000) • **81**

Colli Euganei Passito Fior d'Arancio 1996: Shows lovely ripe fruit on the nose but turns volatile and acidic on the finish. Unclean. Tasted twice, with consistent notes. Not imported into the U.S.–J.S. • $NA/500 ml. • (1/01/2000) • **68**

Merlot Colli Euganei Bandiera 1997: A red with plenty of bright berry and chocolate character. Medium-bodied, with silky tannins and a fresh finish. Delicious. Drink now.–J.S. • $18 • (5/15/2000) • **85**

Pinot Bianco Colli Euganei 1998: Strange candied character to this young white, with a lemon-lime undertone.–J.S. • $15 • (4/30/2000) • **77**

Veneto Vendemmia Tardiva Raboso 1997: Big and powerful red with lots of berry, cherry character. Full-bodied, dry and very chewy, with lots of tannin and ripe fruit. A bit one-dimensional, but the purity of fruit is impressive. Not imported into the U.S. Drink now through 2002.–J.S. • $NA • (1/01/2000) • **87**

MONTECCHIO, FATTORIA DI

Chianti Classico 1995 • $13 • (9/30/1997) • **80**
Chianti Classico Riserva 1994 • $18 • (9/30/1997) • **82**
Pietracupa 1995 • $18 • (9/30/1997) • **87**

MONTELLORI, FATTORIA

Chianti Moro 1998: A little stemmy and earthy, but with good, ripe berry character. Light- to medium-bodied, with light tannins and a fresh finish. Drink now.–J.S. • $10 • (11/30/1999) • **80**

Chianti Moro 1996: Seriously good Chianti. Lovely dried cherry and raspberry aromas. Medium-bodied, with well-integrated tannins and a caressing finish. Can age a few years, but why wait? Drink now.–J.S. • $11 • (12/15/1998) • **86**

Chianti Moro 1995: Has a lovely balance of ripe fruit and fine tannins. Medium-bodied, with light tannins and a light finish. Drink now.–J.S. • $NA • (12/15/1998) • **85**

Chianti Moro 1990 • $8 • (5/15/1993) • **80**
Chianti Putto 1988 • $6 • (11/30/1989) • **83**

Sauvignon Toscana Sant 'Amato 1997: Celery and grassy aromas and flavors. Medium-bodied, with moderate acidity and an herbal aftertaste. Drink now.–J.S. • $NA • (12/15/1998) • **82**

Toscana Bonfiglio 1997: A ponderous white with loads of new wood that dominates the fruit. Full-bodied and fat, with some acidity and a vanilla and ripe apple finish. A bit dull.–J.S. • $NA • (12/15/1998) • **81**

Toscana Castelrapiti 1995: Aromas of dried cherry, with some blackberry and earth. Medium-bodied, with well-integrated tannins and a fresh but slightly short finish. A delicious wine for current drinking.–J.S. • $31 • (12/15/1998) • **84**

Toscana Moro 1997: Medium-bodied, with lots of cherry, plum and floral aromas, fine tannins and a fruity, silky finish. Needs a bit more fruit concentration to be outstanding. Interesting blend of Malvasia Nera and Cabernet Sauvignon. Drink through 2004.–J.S. • $14 • (11/30/1999) • **88**

Toscana Salamartano 1997: This gorgeous Bordeaux blend has ripe fruit throughout, with berry, plum and blackberry character and a hint of smoke. Full-bodied, with masses of caressing, polished tannins and a long, long finish. A real beauty. Best after 2000.–J.S. • $43 • (11/30/1999) • **93**

Toscana Salamartano 1996: This beautifully crafted red is seamless in structure, with pretty aromas of ripe fruit and smoky oak. Medium-bodied, with polished tannins and a round, caressing mouthfeel. Merlot and Cabernet Sauvignon. Best after 2000.–J.S. • $44 • (11/30/1999) • **90**

Toscana Salamartano 1995: Good berry character, but it could use a bit more fruit to give more texture. Medium-bodied, with firm tannins and a short, slightly hard finish. Drink now.–J.S. • $39 • (12/15/1998) • **83**

MONTERINALDI, CASTELLO DI

Chianti Classico 1996: What you expect in a very good CC. Pretty berry and violet aromas with hints of chocolate. Medium-bodied, with light tannins and a crisp, fruity aftertaste. Drink now.–J.S. • $12 • (12/15/1998) • **85**
Chianti Classico Riserva 1995: Very elegant Sangiovese, with lovely cherry and blackberry aromas, a medium body and a light, crisp finish. Delicious. Drink now.–J.S. • $18 • (12/15/1998) • **85**

MONTEVERTINE

Il Novantuno di Sergio Manetti 1991: Still holding on for a '91, with pretty dried cherry and floral character throughout. Medium-bodied, with a silky finish. A declassified Le Pergole Torte. (Montevertine vertical tasting). Drink now.–J.S. • $NA • (11/30/1999) • **84**
Il Sodaccio 1995: A ponderous and rich wine. Some pretty plum, tobacco, vanilla and berry aromas and flavors. Medium in body, with fresh acidity and a chocolate and tobacco aftertaste. An abundance of oak on the finish. Drink now through 2006.–J.S. • $29 Ⓐ • (12/15/1998) • **87**
Il Sodaccio 1994 • $42 • (9/30/1997) • **86**
Il Sodaccio 1990 • $32 • (10/31/1993) • **83**
Il Sodaccio 1988 • $35 • (9/15/1991) • **91**
Il Sodaccio 1987 • $32 • (1/31/1991) • **87**
Il Sodaccio 1986 • $30 • (9/30/1989) • **90**
Il Sodaccio 1985 • $25 • (3/15/1989) • **91**
Il Sodaccio 1983 • $20 • (2/15/1987) • **93**
Le Pergole Torte 1996: A seductive red, with subtle aromas yet a powerful structure. Medium-bodied, with berry, tea, tobacco and cigar box on the nose and a medium finish. Slightly mouthpuckering from the dense, silky tannins. Needs bottle age. Best after 2000.–J.S. • $73 • (11/30/1999) • **90**
Le Pergole Torte 1995: Vibrant aromas of rose, blackberry and honeysuckle. Full-bodied yet extremely elegant, with ultrafine tannins and a long, long finish. A serious and seductive red. (Montevertine vertical tasting, as are all Le Pergole notes below). Best after 2000.–J.S. • $NA • (11/30/1999) • **92**
Le Pergole Torte 1994: Elegant and delectable, with tobacco and cherry aromas and flavors. Medium-bodied, with silky tannins and a long and fruity finish. Will age, but why wait? Drink now.–J.S. • $NA • (11/30/1999) • **90**
Le Pergole Torte 1993: Very impressive for the vintage. Milk chocolate and ripe berry character throughout. Medium-bodied, with silky tannins and a long fruity, chocolate aftertaste. This is racy. Drink now through 2004.–J.S. s• $NA • (11/30/1999) • **91**
Le Pergole Torte 1992: A rather hollow and short wine, but it shows interesting dried cherry and mushroom character. Medium-bodied, with a light finish. Drink now.–J.S. • $NA • (11/30/1999) • **85**
Le Pergole Torte 1990: Dark ruby in color, with bright raspberry and earth aromas. Medium- to Full-bodied, with well-integrated tannins and a long, caressing finish. Drink now through 2005.–J.S. • $NA • (11/30/1999) • **93**
Le Pergole Torte 1988: Aromatic and refined. Attractive aromas of chocolate, blackberries and cherries. Full-bodied yet elegant and silky-textured, with a berry and cherry aftertaste. A real beauty. Drink now.–J.S. • $NA• (11/30/1999) • **92**
Le Pergole Torte 1987: A delicious and refined red. Plenty of fresh cherry and milk chocolate character. Medium- to full-bodied, with a velvety texture and a long, sweet fruit aftertaste. Drink now.–J.S. • $NA • (11/30/1999) • **89**
Le Pergole Torte 1986: Succulent and delicious. Autumnal aromas of ripe cherry and tobacco with hints of mushroom. Medium-bodied, with fine silky tannins and a cherry, vanilla aftertaste. Drink now.–J.S. • $NA • (11/30/1999) • **88**
Le Pergole Torte 1985: Very fine indeed. Dark ruby in color, with intense blackberry and mint aromas. Full-bodied, with chewy tannins and a wonderful, concentrated fruit aftertaste. Silky and pleasurable. Drink now. –J.S. • $NA • (11/30/1999) • **93**
Le Pergole Torte 1983: A well-defined red with wonderful harmony and definition. Medium-ruby color with an amber edge. Milk chocolate and berry aromas. Medium- to full-bodied, with firm tannins and a long, sweet fruit aftertaste. Drink now.–J.S. • $NA • (11/30/1999) • **90**
Le Pergole Torte 1980: This is a surprise as the vintage was never that great, but the wine shows lovely ripe fruit with lots of cherry, cedar character and a long, fresh finish. Drink now.–J.S. • $NA • (11/30/1999) • **87**
Le Pergole Torte Riserva 1990: A big and powerful wine but very harmonious. Intense aromas of crushed red berries and blackberries with hints of dark chocolate. Full-bodied, with a very velvety texture and a long, fruity, caressing finish. Drink now through 2010.–J.S. • $NA • (11/30/1999) • **95**
Pian del Ciampolo 1996: An extremely fine red, with fascinating aromas of plum, berry, tea and flowers. Medium-bodied, with delicate tannins and a caressing, subtle, fruity finish. Drink now.–J.S. • $26 • (11/30/1999) • **86**
Pian del Ciampolo 1995: Simple and delicious. Extremely floral and citrusy on the nose. Medium-bodied, with well-integrated tannins and a fresh, crisp finish. Perfect with pasta. Drink now.–J.S. • $26 • (12/15/1998) • **85**
Pian del Ciampolo 1993 • $21 • (10/31/1996) • **83**
Red 1983 • $15 • (2/15/1987) • **85**
Riserva 1996: Like a lovely Pinot Noir, with tobacco, tea and berry aromas. Medium-bodied, with light, silky tannins and a lovely, smooth texture. Drink now.–J.S. • $40 • (11/30/1999) • **87**
Riserva 1995: Like a fine Burgundy, this Sangiovese shows a lovely balance of delicate fruit and fine tannins. Medium-bodied, with light to medium silky tannins and a fresh, fruity aftertaste. Drink now.–J.S. • $37 • (12/15/1998) • **88**
Riserva 1994 • $38 • (9/30/1997) • **84**
Riserva 1993 • $35 • (10/31/1996) • **88**
Riserva 1991 • $23 • (2/28/1995) • **85**
Riserva 1990 • $30 • (10/31/1993) • **86**
Riserva 1988 • $30 • (9/15/1991) • **90**
Riserva 1987 • $30 • (3/15/1991) • **91**
Riserva 1986 • $26 • (9/30/1989) • **86**
Riserva 1982 • $18 • (2/15/1987) • **84**
Riserva 1981 • $15 • (8/31/1986) • **90**
Sangioveto 1985 • $17 • (8/31/1988) • **89**
Sergio Manetti 1989 • $NA • (11/15/1993) • **85**
Vin Santo NV • $20 • (2/15/1987) • **89**

MONTEVETRANO

Colli di Salerno 1997: One of Southern Italy's greatest reds ever. Intense aromas of blackberries, mint, grilled meat and raisins rise from the glass. The wine is full-bodied, with masses of mouthpuckering tannins, but a long, fruity finish. A wonderful Bordeaux-style blend. Best from 2001 through 2006.–J.S. • $60 • (1/31/2000) HR • **95**

MONTRESOR

Amarone della Valpolicella Classico Capitel della Crosara 1995: A well-crafted Amarone, with captivating aromas of rose, violet and berry. Medium-bodied, with extremely well-polished tannins and a long, caressing finish. Drink now through 2003.–J.S. • $55 • (1/01/2000) • **88**
Bianco di Custoza Fattoria di Cavalcaselle Vigneto Monte Fiera 1998: A wine with interesting tropical fruit and spice character. Medium-bodied, with a marzipan and fruit character, a medium finish. Drink now.–J.S. • $18 • (4/30/2000) • **83**
Merlot-Cabernet Veneto Santomío 1997: A bit austere, but with decent flavors of red licorice and raspberry. Medium-bodied, with medium firm tannins and a short finish. Drink now.–J.S. • $25 • (1/01/2000) • **81**
Valpolicella Classico Capitel della Crosara 1997: Bubbling over with strawberry and citrus. Light and simple.–J.S. • $13 • (1/01/2000) • **79**

MORIS FARMS

Morellino di Scansano 1998: Slightly rustic, but showing lots of ripe plum and earth character. Medium-bodied, with medium, velvety tannins and a fruity finish. Drink now.–J.S. • $15 • (5/31/2000) • **84**
Morellino di Scansano 1997: A big and burly young Sangiovese with lots of grapey character, verging on raisin. Full-bodied, a bit rustic, but admirable concentration of fruit. A producer and an area to watch. Drink through 2001.–J.S. • $NA • (12/15/1998) • **85**
Morellino di Scansano Riserva 1995: A soft and polished Sangiovese from Scansano, with plenty of dried cherry and berry character. Medium-bodied, with fine tannins and a medium finish. Thoroughly delicious. Drink now through 2003.–J.S. • $26 • (11/30/1999) • **88**
Toscana Avvoltore 1997: Loads of new wood in this, but it's delicious, with amazing aromas of chocolate, cherry and coconut. Medium-bodied, with polished tannins and a vanilla and toasted oak finish. A touch less wood would make it outstanding. A blend of Sangiovese and Cabernet with a splash of Syrah. Drink now through 2002.–J.S. • $40 • (11/30/1999) • **89**

MURAGLIA ESTATE, LA

Chianti Colli Senesi 1994 • $9 • (3/31/1997) • **79**

MUSTILLI

Aglianico di Sant 'Agata dei Goti Vigna Cesco di Nece 1995: A fresh, fruity and youthful wine. Plenty of crushed berry and floral aromas. Medium-bodied, with good acidity, light tannins and a fresh finish. Drink now.–J.S. • $19 • (1/31/2000) • **85**

Campania Red NV: Lots of character to this Campania vino da tavola. Bright aromas of dried cherries, violets and black pepper. Full-bodied, with loads of fruit, medium tannins and a spicy finish. Drink now through 2003.–J.S. • $10 • (1/31/2000) • **87**

Greco di Sant 'Agata dei Goti 1998: Some slightly oxidized character, but shows decent lemon fruit with a steely mineral aftertaste.–J.S. • $14 • (1/31/2000) • **79**

Greco di Sant 'Agata dei Goti Primicerio 1998: Decent lemon and leaf character, with decent acidity, but slightly dull and boring.–J.S. • $19 • (1/31/2000) • **79**

Piedirosso di Sant 'Agata dei Goti 1997: Plenty of dried cherry and berry character on the nose, but the palate is slightly diluted. Medium-bodied, with a boiled sweet berry character and a light finish. Drink now.–J.S. • $17 • (1/31/2000) • **80**

Sant 'Agata dei Goti Conte Artus 1997: Lots of floral and berry character on the nose, but a bit short on the palate. Light- to medium-bodied, with a slightly austere finish. Too much new wood? Drink now.–J.S. • $18 • (1/31/2000) • **84**

NADA, FIORENZO

Barbaresco 1996: Phenomenal quality for a communal wine. Dark-colored and richly textured, packed with earth, rose and black fruit. Talk about unadulterated purity of fruit and *terroir*. Massive, refined tannins clamp down on the finish. Best from 2003 through 2010.–P.M. • $53 • (10/31/1999) • **94**

Barbaresco 1994 • $44 • (10/31/1997) • **86**

Barbaresco 1993 • $43 • (10/31/1996) • **86**

Dolcetto d'Alba 1997: Succulent, with lively red berry character, supple tannins and smooth acidity. Balanced and delicious. Drink now through 2001.–P.M. • $18 • (11/15/1999) • **86**

Langhe Seifile 1996: A real beauty. As dark as ink, it reveals little in the aromas except a hint that this wine is deep. Full-bodied, ultrasmooth and packed with well-integrated oak that's deftly toasted and an intriguing petrol note. Plenty of concentration of black fruit, with round tannins. Drink now through 2005.–P.M. • $60 • (11/15/1999) • **95**

NARDI, SILVIO

Brunello di Montalcino 1995: A wine with lots of stewed-fruit character, like cherry pie. Slightly overdone. Full-bodied, thick and chewy—almost syrupy. Better with age? Tasted twice, with consistent notes. Best from 2001 through 2003.–J.S. • $49 • (6/30/2000) • **84**

Brunello di Montalcino 1994: Interesting aromas of berries and tea with earthy undertones. Medium-bodied, with silky tannins and a fruity, delicious aftertaste. Drink now.–J.S. • $39 • (8/31/1999) • **87**

Brunello di Montalcino 1993: Blackberry and cherry aromas, with undertones of wet earth. Medium- to full-bodied, with well-integrated tannins and a long, fresh fruit finish. Drink through 2005.–J.S. • $35 • (12/15/1998) • **88**

Brunello di Montalcino 1992 • $28 • (9/30/1997) • **86**

Brunello di Montalcino 1991 • $26 • (11/30/1996) • **79**

Brunello di Montalcino 1990 • $25 • (7/31/1995) • **86**

Brunello di Montalcino 1988 • $33 • (4/30/1994) • **86**

Brunello di Montalcino Riserva 1993: Amazingly fresh aromas of crushed berries and flowers, with a hint of wood. Full-bodied, with velvety tannins and a long chocolate-berry aftertaste. Slightly monolithic on the finish. Give it time. Best after 2001.–J.S. • $52 • (8/31/1999) • **90**

Brunello di Montalcino Riserva 1988 • $36 • (10/31/1994) • **79**

Brunello di Montalcino Vigneto Manichiara 1995: Seductive wine with violets, minerals and spices that highlight the fruit. Full-bodied, with plenty of velvety tannins and a long, spicy finish. A beauty. A new single-vineyard Brunello from Nardi. Drink now through 2005.–J.S. • $66 • (6/30/2000) • **91**

Rosso di Montalcino 1997: A delightful rosso. Bright and vivid, with roses, violets and ripe fruit character. Medium-bodied, with fine tannins and a medium, fruity finish. Drink now.–J.S. • $18 • (9/15/1999) • **87**

Rosso di Montalcino 1996: Impressive Rosso from Nardi with very good concentration of fruit. Deep-colored, with blackberry and mineral aromas. Full-bodied, with chewy tannins and a long finish. Needs some bottle age. Drink through 2001.–J.S. • $12 • (12/15/1998) • **88**

Rosso di Montalcino 1995 • $15 • (9/30/1997) • **87**

Rosso di Montalcino 1994 • $12 • (11/30/1996) • **82**

Rosso di Montalcino 1993 • $13 • (10/31/1995) • **84**

Rosso di Montalcino 1992 • $13 • (10/31/1994) • **78**

NEGRI, NINO

Valtellina 5 Stelle Sfursat 1994 • $36 • (6/15/1997) • **88**

Valtellina Superiòre Inferno 1990 • $13 • (2/28/1995) • **78**

Valtellina Superiòre Inferno 1989 • $NA • (10/31/1996) • **77**

Valtellina Superiòre Le Botti d'Oro 1989 • $13 • (2/28/1995) • **77**

Valtellina Superiòre Riserva 1986 • $20 • (2/28/1995) • **86**

NEIRANO

Barbera d'Asti 1995 • $10 • (10/31/1997) • **80**

Barbera d'Asti 1994 • $8 • (10/31/1996) • **77**

Barbera d'Asti Superiòre Le Croci 1994 • $NA • (10/31/1996) • **85**

Cantico Red NV • $6 • (1/31/1998) • **76**

Cantico White NV • $6 • (1/31/1998) • **78**

NEIVE, CASTELLO DI

Barbaresco Santo Stefano 1995: A solid Barbaresco, quite dark in color, with cassis, blackberry, plum and floral notes as well as spice and toasted oak accents. This medium-bodied, intense package leaves a trail of flavors on the lingering, tannic finish. Drink now through 2005.–P.M. • $30 • (10/31/1998) • **88**

Barbaresco Santo Stefano 1994: Light in color and body and lacking a bit of fruit, with modest raspberry, strawberry and currant. Diluted and a bit dry on the short finish.–P.M. • $20 • (10/31/1998) • **76**

Barbaresco Santo Stefano 1990 • $20 • (10/31/1994) • **88**

Barbaresco Santo Stefano 1989 • $20 • (10/31/1993) • **90**

Barbaresco Santo Stefano 1988 • $23 • (10/31/1993) • **77**

Barbaresco Santo Stefano 1987 • $20 • (12/31/1990) • **79**

Barbaresco Santo Stefano 1982 • $27 • (9/15/1988) • **86**

Barbera d'Alba Mattarello 1996: Great grape quality here, but the new super-toasted oak detracts. Expect heavily roasted walnuts, charred pine nuts and toasted bread to dominate the otherwise nice blackberry and cassis flavors. Drink through 2005.–P.M. • $NA • (10/31/1998) • **84**

Barbera d'Alba Messoirano 1988 • $11 • (7/15/1991) • **83**

Barbera d'Alba Santo Stefano 1995: The color of a rosé, this is light in body and dilute. Not much to it.–P.M. • $13 • (10/31/1998) • **70**

Dolcetto d'Alba Basarin 1997: Crisp and flavorful, focusing on cranberry, cherry and olive notes that give a succulent, juicy character to this light-bodied red. A bit herbal but fresh. Try with Italian food. Drink now.–P.M. • $14 • (10/31/1998) • **80**

Dolcetto d'Alba Basarin 1990 • $15 • (12/15/1992) • **85**

Dolcetto d'Alba Basarin 1989 • $12 • (2/28/1991) • **80**

Dolcetto d'Alba Basarin 1987 • $11 • (3/15/1989) • **80**

Dolcetto d'Alba Valtorta 1986 • $12 • (8/31/1988) • **73**

Langhe White Montebertotto 1997: This Arneis with personality delights with almond and earth aromas, delivering a full-bodied, round-textured mouthfeel and some delicious cedar, citrus and wet hay character. Balanced, with a pleasant, fairly long finish. Enjoy with light dishes.–P.M. • $14 • (10/31/1998) • **85**

NICOLIS

Amarone della Valpolicella Classico 1991 • $27 • (11/15/1997) • **79**

Amarone della Valpolicella Classico Ambrosan 1992: A modern style, beginning to mature into caramel and nut aromas and flavors, accented by prune, vanilla and balsamic vinegar. Still on the lean, tough side, but the sweet fruit and warmth win out in the end. Drink now.–B.S. • $44 • (7/31/1998) • **87**

Valpolicella Classico Superiòre Seccal 1993: Smoky aromas turn to plum and licorice in this mature Valpolicella; acidity and dry tannins make it rough around the edges. Good length though, and food should tame it. Drink now.–B.S. • $17 • (7/31/1998) • **84**

Key: SS—Spectator Selection. CS—Cellar Selection. HR—Highly Recommended. $NA—Price not available. (BT)—Barrel tasting. (A)—Auction Price. For a key to the tasters' initials, see "How to Use These Listings." **Dates in parentheses represent the issues in which the ratings were published.**

ITALY

NITTARDI, CASANUOVA DI

Chianti Classico 1997: A blast of vivid fruit from the start, with loads of blackberry, plum and orange peel character. Medium-bodied, with velvety tannins and a medium finish. A beauty. Drink now.–J.S. • $20 • (11/30/1999) • **87**

Chianti Classico 1996: Plummy and lively, with pretty fruit on the nose and palate. Medium-bodied, with fine tannins and a fresh, crisp finish. Nittardi always delivers very good Chianti. Drink now.–J.S. • $15 • (12/15/1998) • **86**

Chianti Classico 1995 • $18 • (9/30/1997) • **86**

Chianti Classico 1994 • $12 • (10/31/1996) • **82**

Chianti Classico 1993 • $12 • (10/31/1995) • **85**

Chianti Classico 1992 • $NA • (2/28/1995) • **82**

Chianti Classico 1990 • $NA • (9/15/1992) • **80**

Chianti Classico Riserva 1996: A wine with unfulfilled aspirations. Good dark color for a CC. Aromas of dried cherry and herb. Medium-bodied, with medium tannins and a short, slightly austere finish. Drink now.–J.S. • $28 • (11/30/1999) • **83**

Chianti Classico Riserva 1995: Not an ager, it's delicious now. Floral aromas follow through to the palate. Medium-bodied, with delicate tannins and a fresh finish.–J.S. • $24 • (12/15/1998) • **85**

Chianti Classico Riserva 1994 • $25 • (9/30/1997) • **87**

Chianti Classico Riserva 1993 • $NA • (10/31/1996) • **86**

Chianti Classico Riserva 1990 • $NA • (2/28/1995) • **86**

Chianti Classico Riserva 1988 • $NA • (9/15/1992) • **80**

Toscana Biondi di Nittardi 1998: Good, simple apple and lemon character in this white. Medium-bodied, with a fruity finish. Drink now.–J.S. • $14 • (11/30/1999) • **82**

Toscana Biondo di Nittardi 1996 • $12 • (4/30/1998) • **84**

NOARNA, CASTEL

Cabernet Sauvignon Trentino Mercuria 1997: Good ruby color, with crushed raspberry and cherry character. Medium-bodied, with light to medium tannins and a slightly diluted finish. Drink now.–J.S. • $16 • (1/01/2000) • **82**

Cabernet Trentino Romeo 1995: Lots of mint, wet earth and eucalyptus character. Medium-bodied, with well-integrated tannins and a light finish. Slightly diluted. Drink now.–J.S. • $22 • (1/01/2000) • **80**

Cabernet Vallagarina Vigna Romeo 1989 • $22 • (12/15/1992) • **72**

Chardonnay Trentino Campo Grande 1997: Full of ripe pineapple and cream aromas and flavors. Medium-bodied, with good fruit and a fresh finish that's a bit simple. Drink now.–J.S. • $19 • (6/15/2000) • **85**

Nosiola Trentino Casot 1997: Candied, with geranium character. Unpleasant. Oxidized. Tasted twice, with consistent notes.–J.S. • $12 • (6/15/2000) • **68**

Sauvignon Trentino 1997: Very fresh, with lemon, apple and grapefruit. Medium-bodied, with plenty of fruit and a crisp finish. Drink now.–J.S. • $12 • (6/15/2000) • **86**

Vallagarina Bianco di Castelnuovo 1997: Good apple, mineral and very ripe pear aromas. Medium-bodied, with fresh acidity and a clean finish. Drink now.–J.S. • $16 • (6/15/2000) • **84**

NOTTOLA

Vino Nobile di Montepulciano 1997: A pretty, balanced red with mineral, mint and berry character. Medium body. Medium finish. Drink now.–J.S. • $22 • (6/15/2000) • **87**

Vino Nobile di Montepulciano 1996: Not the cleanest wine, but offers pretty fruit, with violet, berry, tar and funky aromas. Medium-bodied, with firm tannins. Tasted twice, with consistent notes.–J.S. • $NA • (12/15/1998) • **78**

Vino Nobile di Montepulciano 1995: A delicious drink-now Nobile, with generous milk chocolate and berry character. Full-bodied and velvety, with lovely tannins and ripe fruit. You have to like it.–J.S. • $21 • (12/15/1998) • **89**

Vino Nobile di Montepulciano 1994: Pure, vibrant black cherry flavor gives focus and life. Delicious, smooth, full-bodied, firm with acidity and tannin but accessible. Drink now. • $21 • (7/31/1998) • **88**

NOVACELLA, ABBAZIA DI

Gewürztraminer Alto Adige Valle Isarco 1996 • $19 • (5/31/1998) • **84**

Lagrein Alto Adige Valle Isarco 1996 • $16 • (6/30/1998) • **84**

Moscato Rosa Alto Adige 1996 • $19/375 ml. • (5/31/1998) • **88**

Müller-Thurgau Alto Adige Valle Isarco 1996 • $16 • (5/31/1998) • **83**

Sylvaner Alto Adige Valle Isarco 1996 • $15 • (5/31/1998) • **84**

NOZZOLE

Chardonnay Toscana Le Bruniche 1998: Pretty Chardonnay character, with honey, lemon and apple aromas and a hint of vanilla. Medium-bodied, with good acidity and a lovely, creamy finish. Well done. Drink now through 2003.–J.S. • $13 • (11/30/1999) • **87**

Chardonnay Toscana Le Bruniche 1997: A simple Chardonnay with apple and mineral aromas and flavors. Medium-bodied, with crisp acidity and a light, fruity aftertaste. Drink now.–J.S. • $10 • (12/15/1998) • **84**

Chardonnay Toscana Le Bruniche 1996 • $12 • (9/30/1997) • **79**

Chianti Classico La Forra 1995 • $NA • (9/30/1997) • **83**

Chianti Classico La Forra 1994 • $NA • (9/30/1997) • **80**

Chianti Classico La Forra 1990 • $13 • (10/31/1993) • **88**

Chianti Classico La Forra Riserva 1994 • $29 • (9/30/1997) • **84**

Chianti Classico La Forra Riserva 1993 • $30 • (10/31/1996) • **82**

Chianti Classico La Forra Riserva 1990 • $22 • (2/28/1995) • **86**

Chianti Classico La Forra Riserva 1988 • $23 • (10/31/1993) • **82**

Chianti Classico La Forra Riserva 1987 • $NA • (11/30/1989) • **88**

Chianti Classico La Forra Riserva 1985 • $21 • (9/15/1992) • **84**

Chianti Classico La Forra Riserva 1982 • $20 • (10/31/1991) • **77**

Chianti Classico Riserva 1996: A light and delicious CC riserva. Attractive raspberry and earth aromas follow through to a medium-bodied palate, with light tannins and a fresh finish. Not imported into the U.S. Drink now.–J.S. • $NA • (1/01/1999) • **85**

Chianti Classico Riserva 1993 • $15 • (10/31/1996) • **77**

Chianti Classico Riserva 1991 • $12 • (2/28/1995) • **77**

Chianti Classico Riserva 1990 • $12 • (2/28/1995) • **85**

Chianti Classico Riserva 1989 • $12 • (10/31/1993) • **82**

Chianti Classico Riserva 1988 • $14 • (9/15/1992) • **81**

Chianti Classico Riserva 1985 • $13 • (9/15/1991) • **88**

Toscana Il Pareto 1996: Wonderful aromas of blackberry, licorice and chocolate. Medium-bodied, with velvety tannins and a long, chewy finish. Needs a tiny more fruit on the midpalate to be outstanding. Best after 2000.–J.S. • $72 • (11/30/1999) • **89**

Toscana Il Pareto 1995: Beautiful grape and boysenberry aromas and flavors. Medium-bodied, with full, round tannins and a long vanilla and berry aftertaste. A softer, more accessible style than is usual for this wine; a bit obvious but delicious. Drink now.–J.S. • $40 • (12/15/1998) • **88**

Toscana Il Pareto 1993 • $45 • (10/31/1995) • **92**

Toscana Il Pareto 1990 • $41 • (1/01/1994) • **96**

Toscana Il Pareto 1989 • $30 • (10/31/1993) • **85**

Toscana Il Pareto 1988 • $28 • (6/15/1993) • **91**

NUOVA CAPPELLETTA

Barbera del Monferrato 1997: Fairly earthy, with berry and sweaty saddle character. Medium-bodied and rich, but not totally clean. Not imported into the U.S.–J.S. • $NA • (1/01/2000) • **77**

Barbera del Monferrato Minola 1996: Good fruit and oak, with minty berry character. Light- to medium-bodied, with a light finish. Slightly lean and losing its fruit. Not imported into the U.S. Drink now.–J.S. • $NA • (1/01/2000) • **80**

Barbera del Monferrato Minola 1995: Still showing good fruit, with plum, mint and berry character. Medium-bodied, with polished tannins and a slightly dry finish. Not imported into the U.S. Drink now.–J.S. • $NA • (1/01/2000) • **83**

Grignolino del Monferrato 1998: Fresh, fruity, rustic and very light. Not imported into the U.S.–J.S. • $NA • (1/01/2000) • **78**

OBERTO, ANDREA

Barbera d'Alba Giada 1993 • $26 • (3/31/1997) • **89**

Barbera d'Alba Giada 1992 • $24 • (10/31/1995) • **84**

Barbera d'Alba Vigneto Boiolo 1997: This fruit volcano is amazing—just unadulterated red berry and blackberry aromas and flavors, with a slight green olive, herbal tone. Pulls it off without any help from obvious-tasting oak. The tannins, acidity and succulent, juicy texture bring it into balance. Can hold. Drink now through 2003.–P.M. • $18 • (9/15/1999) • **90**

Barolo 1994: A light, weak '94 Barolo. Lacks structure and offers only modest fruit on a supple but superficial frame.–P.M. • $20 • (10/31/1998) • **77**

Barolo 1993 • $20 • (10/31/1997) • **86**

Barolo 1992 • $32 • (1/01/1997) • **79**

Barolo 1991 • $30 • (1/01/1997) • **79**

Barolo Vigneto Rocche 1995: Seductive. Silky in texture, with beautifully round tannins, this is a light-colored, full-bodied, ripe Barolo with a lot of red berry, roasted chestnut, tar and floral character. Drink now through 2005.–P.M. • $42 • (11/15/1999) • **93**

Barolo Vigneto Rocche 1994: A light-bodied Barolo, with modest strawberry, cherry, plum and spice character.–P.M. • $22 • (10/31/1998) • **77**

Barolo Vigneto Rocche 1993 • $22 • (10/31/1997) • **80**

Barolo Vigneto Rocche 1992 • $25 • (10/31/1996) • **77**

Dolcetto d'Alba 1996 • $11 • (10/31/1997) • **79**

Dolcetto d'Alba Vigneto San Francesco 1994 • $15 • (10/31/1995) • **75**

Dolcetto d'Alba Vigneto Vantrino Albarella 1997: Should cut into dishes with sauces, but expect a lean, tart red with a bitter aftertaste.–P.M. • $17 • (7/31/1999) • **75**

Nebbiolo delle Langhe Vigneto Albarella 1994 • $16 • (1/01/1997) • **78**

OBERTO, EGIDIO

Barolo La Serra 1993 • $NA • (10/31/1997) • **75**

OCONE

Aglianico del Sannio Beneventano 1987 • $17 • (5/31/1995) • **78**

Aglianico del Taburno 1995: Rich aromas of ripe fruit and meat follow through to a medium-bodied palate, with soft tannins, good acidity and a peppery finish. Where's the grilled steak to go with it? Drink now through 2004.–J.S. • $18 • (1/31/2000) • **87**

Aglianico del Taburno Diomede 1996: A fruity, delicious red with some complexity. Intriguing aromas of berries, nutmeg, cumin and other dried spices. Medium-bodied, with good acidity, light tannins and a fresh finish. Drink now.–J.S. • $18 • (1/31/2000) • **86**

Aglianico del Taburno Vigna Pezza La Corte 1995: Already showing some maturity, with plummy, meaty and cedary aromas. Medium-bodied, with silky tannins and a short, slightly dry finish. Not imported into the U.S. Drink now.–J.S. • $NA • (1/01/1999) • **83**

Coda di Volpe del Taburno 1998: Pretty, aromatic wine but the bitter character on the palate detracts from the overall quality. Medium-bodied, with a lime, almond flavor. Unattractive finish. Not imported into the U.S. Drink now.–J.S. • $NA • (1/01/1999) • **80**

Falanghina del Taburno 1998: Rather minerally and steely, with a burnt match character. Diluted finish. Hard to like. Tasted twice, with consistent notes.–J.S. • $NA • (1/31/2000) • **72**

Falanghina del Taburno Vigna del Monaco 1998: Very crisp style of white, with lime, steely mineral character. Medium-bodied, with fresh acidity and a clean finish. Drink now.–J.S. • $14 • (1/31/2000) • **86**

Greco del Taburno 1998: Interesting aromas of roses, honey and melons. Medium-bodied, with lots of fruit and a mineral and citrus character on the finish. Slightly waxy. Drink now.–J.S. • $16 • (1/31/2000) • **84**

Piedirosso del Taburno 1998: A polished, delicious young red. Dark in color, with intense crushed raspberries and black pepper. Medium-bodied, with polished tannins and a pretty, delicate berry aftertaste. Needs more of a center palate to be outstanding. Drink now through 2002.–J.S. • $14 • (1/31/2000) • **87**

ODDERO, FRATELLI

Barbaresco 1995: This dark-colored, flavorful, explosively fruity wine charms with its freshly crushed, vibrant, clean and pure blackberry and cassis flavors. The tannins clamp down, though, on the slightly unbalanced finish. Best after 2005.–P.M. • $30 • (10/31/1998) • **84**

Barbaresco 1993 • $19 • (10/31/1996) • **86**

Barbaresco 1989 • $15 • (3/31/1993) • **85**

Barbaresco 1982 • $15 • (9/15/1988) • **84**

Barbera d'Alba 1996: This racy, medium-bodied Barbera is true to type. Wonderfully extracted, inky-purple in color, with good acidity, pure berry character and an earthy note that adds complexity. Expect firm tannins on the long finish. A good match with food. Drink now through 2001.–P.M. • $13 • (10/31/1998) • **86**

Barbera d'Alba 1995 • $14 • (10/31/1997) • **86**

Barbera d'Alba 1994 • $NA • (10/31/1996) • **83**

Barbera d'Alba Carbea 1997: International-style Barbera, heavily oaked in fancy wood, with violet, rose petal and cassis aromas as well as spice and blackberry flavors. Full-bodied, it stays elegant though, with supple tannins and balanced acidity. Drink through 2005.–P.M. • $NA • (9/15/1999) • **87**

Barbera d'Asti 1997: Smooth and supple at first, with ripe fruit and sweet tannins, accented by smoky, spicy notes. Delivers a crisp, clean kick on the lingering finish. Drink now through 2002.–P.M. • $20 • (11/15/1999) • **85**

Barolo 1995: A straightforward Nebbiolo, medium-bodied and juicy, with stewed tomato, herb and cherry notes and dry tannins.–P.M. • $40 • (11/15/1999) • **78**

Barolo 1994: Exciting and quite exotic, with loads of cassis, dried herbs and fresh thyme and rosemary. Very intense, it explodes on the palate, offering great fruit concentration backed by doses of mocha and coffee accents from the subtle application of oak. Medium to full in body, with supple tannins and a very long finish. Needs time. Best after 2004.–P.M. • $30 • (10/31/1998) • **88**

Barolo 1992 • $24 • (10/31/1996) • **82**

Barolo 1991 • $17 • (10/31/1995) • **79**

Barolo 1989 • $16 • (10/31/1994) • **82**

Barolo 1983 • $15 • (9/15/1988) • **85**

Barolo 1982 • $14 • (6/30/1987) • **91**

Barolo Mondoca di Bussia Soprana 1993 • $29 • (10/31/1997) • **90**

Barolo Mondoca di Bussia Soprana 1990 • $30 • (10/31/1995) • **69**

Barolo Rocche dei Riviera di Castiglione 1995: Herbal and dry, with a stewed tomato and stewed prune character. Harsh tannins. From vines hit by the hailstorms of '95?–P.M. • $46 • (11/15/1999) • **70**

Barolo Rocche dei Riviera di Castiglione 1993 • $58 • (10/31/1997) • **85**

Barolo Rocche di Castiglione 1995: A distinctive red that drinks beautifully thanks to a full body, a ripe texture and sweet tannins, but the display of roasted peanut, green tea leaf, anise, cassis bush and slight herbaceousness lacks class. Drink now through 2005.–P.M. • $46 • (11/15/1999) • **82**

Barolo Vigna Rionda 1993 • $58 • (10/31/1997) • **74**

Barolo Vigna Rionda 1990 • $30 • (10/31/1995) • **72**

Dolcetto d'Alba 1997: Sparkles with vivacious cassis, blueberry and cranberry character and a slight green olive overtone. Full-bodied and appealing, with supple tannins and a silky midpalate, turning quite crisp on the slightly smoky, cedary finish. Should be great with pizza and pasta. Has the stuffing to improve with cellaring through 2002.–P.M. • $14 • (10/31/1998) • **86**

Dolcetto d'Alba 1996 • $14 • (10/31/1997) • **83**

Dolcetto d'Alba 1995 • $14 • (10/31/1996) • **82**

Dolcetto d'Alba 1989 • $9 • (4/30/1991) • **78**

Nebbiolo delle Langhe 1990 • $NA • (10/31/1994) • **79**

ODDERO, MASSIMO

Vino del Notaio 1997: Modern and international in style. The violet-scented wood is almost impenetrable now. But underneath this ambitious, dark-colored, full-bodied red brew extracted blackberry and cassis flavors. The fresh acidity holds it all together on the hard finish. Best from 2001 through 2005.–P.M. • $24 • (11/15/1999) • **88**

OLIVETO

Chianti 1990 • $6 • (3/31/1993) • **79**

Rosso di Montalcino Il Roccolo 1997: Stunning aromas of berries, strawberries and flowers. Medium- to full-bodied, with super well-integrated tannins and a long finish. A tad more fruit concentration in the midpalate would push it to outstanding, but it's a joy to taste nevertheless. Drink now through 2002.–J.S. • $25 • (9/15/1999) • **89**

OLMO, PODERE

Chianti Classico Riserva 1994 • $18 • (9/30/1997) • **79**

ORMANNI

Chianti Classico 1997: A very ripe style of Chianti, with plum skin and raisin aromas and flavors. Medium-bodied, with light tannins and a fruity finish. Slightly overdone. Drink now.–J.S. • $17 • (11/30/1999) • **84**

Chianti Classico Riserva 1995: Attractive berry, cedar and vanilla character. Medium-bodied, with silky tannins and a medium finish. Needs a bit more fruit concentration. Drink now.–J.S. • $26 • (11/30/1999) • **85**

Colli della Toscana Centrale Julius 1997: A big, monolithic red, with lots of cherry, berry and tobacco character and hints of herb and mineral. Medium-bodied, with chewy tannins and a medium finish. Needs a bit of time. Best after 2000.–J.S. • $33 • (11/30/1999) • **88**

Key: SS—Spectator Selection. CS—Cellar Selection. HR—Highly Recommended. $NA—Price not available. (BT)—Barrel tasting. (A)—Auction Price. For a key to the tasters' initials, see "How to Use These Listings."
Dates in parentheses represent the issues in which the ratings were published.

ORNELLAIA, TENUTA DELL'

Bolgheri Ornellaia 1996: Ornellaia is superb this year. One of the best in years, with currant and blackberry and hints of mint. Full-bodied, with excellent tannin structure and a lovely, sweet berry aftertaste. Best after 2000.–J.S. • $74 • (11/30/1999) • **94**

Bolgheri Ornellaia 1995: A wine that emphasizes finesse rather than power. Plenty of dried herb and berry character, with a hint of mint. Medium- to full-bodied, with velvety tannins and a long, long finish. Greatest Ornellaia in years. Best after 2000.–J.S. • $65 • (12/15/1998) • **91**

Bolgheri Ornellaia 1994 • $56 • (9/30/1997) • **85**

Bolgheri Ornellaia 1993 • $50 • (10/31/1996) • **88**

Bolgheri Ornellaia 1992 • $44 • (10/31/1995) • **85**

Bolgheri Ornellaia 1991 • $38 • (2/28/1995) • **86**

Bolgheri Ornellaia 1990 • $42 • (11/15/1993) • **96**

Bolgheri Ornellaia 1989 • $NA • (11/15/1993) • **87**

Bolgheri Ornellaia 1988 • $NA • (11/15/1993) • **93**

Bolgheri Ornellaia 1987 • $NA • (11/15/1993) • **88**

Bolgheri Ornellaia 1986 • $NA • (11/15/1993) • **92**

Bolgheri Ornellaia 1985 • $NA • (11/15/1993) • **87**

Sauvignon Toscana Poggio alla Gazze 1998: A ripe and intense Sauvignon Blanc with aromas of apricots and melons and hints of flint. Full-bodied, with lots of fruit and a long, fresh finish. Delicious. Drink now through 2001.–J.S. • $25 • (11/30/1999) • **89**

Sauvignon Toscana Poggio alla Gazze 1997: Subtle aromas of gooseberry, nectarine and grass. Medium-bodied, with lovely, lively acidity and a long, long grassy-fruity finish. Why bother with Sancerre? This is a beautiful Sauvignon; what Cloudy Bay is to New Zealand. Drink now.–J.S. • $24 • (12/15/1998) • **91**

Sauvignon Toscana Poggio alla Gazze 1996 • $NA • (9/30/1997) • **88**

Toscana Le Volte 1997: A good, straightforward red, with light strawberry, cherry and tobacco character. Medium-bodied, with fine tannins and a fresh finish. Drink now through 2001.–J.S. • $20 • (11/30/1999) • **85**

Toscana Le Volte 1996: Smells like Zinfandel with very ripe fruit, verging on raisiny, with similar flavors. Rather rustic. Full-bodied, with chewy tannins. Sweet fruit finish. Drink now.–J.S. • $18 • (12/15/1998) • **82**

Toscana Le Volte 1995 • $17 • (10/31/1997) • **83**

Toscana Le Volte 1993 • $13 • (2/28/1995) • **82**

Toscana Le Volte 1992 • $13 • (2/28/1995) • **78**

Toscana Le Volte 1991 • $14 • (10/31/1993) • **87**

Toscana Masseto 1996: Masseto is superb as usual. The wine of the vintage, with an impressive dark color. Fabulous aromas of berries and mint follow through to a full-bodied palate, with polished tannins and a long finish. Big and chewy. Drink now.–J.S. • $201 • (11/30/1999) • **95**

Toscana Masseto 1995: An amazingly massive Merlot. Like a top '89 Pomerol but with a wonderful backbone of acidity and that unique Tuscan style. Intense aromas of blackberry, olive and herbs, with hints of the sea. Full-bodied, very tannic, with masses of fruit and structure. Best after 2003.–J.S. • $150 • (12/15/1998) • **95**

Toscana Masseto 1994 • $137 Ⓐ • (9/30/1997) • **92**

Toscana Masseto 1993 • $144 Ⓐ • (10/31/1996) • **91**

Toscana Masseto 1992 • $110 Ⓐ • (2/28/1995) • **93**

Toscana Masseto 1991 • $79 Ⓐ • (2/28/1995) • **91**

Toscana Masseto 1990 • $235 Ⓐ • (10/31/1993) • **90**

Toscana Masseto 1989 • $134 Ⓐ • (10/31/1993) • **83**

Toscana Masseto 1988 • $212 Ⓐ • (9/15/1991) • **90**

PACENTI, SIRO

Brunello di Montalcino 1995: Gorgeous and opulent. Ripe and decadent style with meaty, berry and earthy character. Full-bodied and velvety, with licorice and berry flavors. Full finish. Drink through 2006.–J.S. • $50 • (6/30/2000) • **92**

Brunello di Montalcino 1994: Aromas of cherries and plums open to a medium-bodied palate, with silky tannins and a medium, fruity finish. A thoroughly pleasing Brunello. Drink now.–J.S. • $50 • (8/31/1999) • **88**

Brunello di Montalcino 1993: Chunky and fruity, with cherry and blackberry through and through. Medium- to full-bodied, with polished yet chewy tannins and a medium finish. Best after 2001.–J.S. • $50 • (12/15/1998) • **90**

Brunello di Montalcino 1991 • $36 • (11/30/1996) • **89**

Brunello di Montalcino 1990 • $36 • (10/31/1995) • **92**

Brunello di Montalcino 1988 • $31 • (4/30/1994) • **90**

Brunello di Montalcino Riserva 1990 • $40 • (11/30/1996) • **90**

Rosso di Montalcino 1997: This is an incredibly well-structured rosso. Full-bodied, with silky tannins and a long berry, cherry and floral aftertaste. Superb. Why buy Brunello with rosso like this? Drink now.–J.S. • $25 • (9/15/1999) • **90**

Rosso di Montalcino 1996: Beautiful aromas of dried cherries and flowers follow through to a medium body with fine tannins and plenty of fresh fruit and acidity on the finish. Delicious; Pacenti always delivers a wonderful rosso. Drink now.–J.S. • $20 • (12/15/1998) • **88**

Rosso di Montalcino 1995 • $12 • (9/30/1997) • **88**

Rosso di Montalcino 1994 • $16 • (11/30/1996) • **86**

Rosso di Montalcino 1993 • $18 • (10/31/1995) • **90**

Rosso di Montalcino 1991 • $16 • (4/30/1994) • **84**

Rosso di Montalcino 1989 • $14 • (4/30/1992) • **87**

PACINA

Chianti Colli Senesi 1995: Juicy and grapey, with plenty of fruit and round, succulent tannins. A little short on the finish, but this medium-bodied red is a delight to taste. Drink now.–J.S. • $14 • (12/15/1998) • **85**

Chianti Colli Senesi 1994 • $15 • (9/30/1997) • **82**

PAGGIO

Pinot Grigio Alto Adige 1996 • $10 • (12/15/1997) • **83**

PAGLIARESE

Capitolare di Biturica Il Neri 1991 • $NA • (10/31/1995) • **87**

Capitolare di Biturica Il Neri 1990 • $NA • (2/28/1995) • **88**

Chianti Classico 1993 • $NA • (10/31/1995) • **86**

Chianti Classico 1992 • $9 • (2/28/1995) • **80**

Chianti Classico 1991 • $9 • (10/31/1993) • **78**

Chianti Classico 1990 • $11 • (9/15/1992) • **80**

Chianti Classico Boscardini Riserva 1988 • $15 • (9/15/1992) • **88**

Della Provincia di Siena Camerlengo 1991 • $NA • (10/31/1995) • **85**

PAITIN

Barbaresco Sorì Paitin 1996: Ripe and sweet-tasting, with good fruit. Medium-bodied, it smells a bit earthy. Below the surface, the attractive black fruit and ripe tannins bode well for the future. Best from 2002 through 2006.–P.M. • $45 • (10/31/1999) • **86**

Barbaresco Sorì Paitin 1995: Lovely, balanced and ripe, with delicious red berry, floral, toast and earth intensity. Tannins are firm but well integrated in this medium-bodied Nebbiolo, which turns slightly smoky and toasted, offering more complexity as it airs. Seductive finish.–P.M. • $37 • (10/31/1998) • **92**

Barbaresco Sorì Paitin 1994 • $29 • (10/31/1997) • **72**

Barbaresco Sorì Paitin 1993 • $27 • (10/31/1996) • **83**

Barbaresco Sorì Paitin 1991 • $20 • (10/31/1995) • **85**

Barbaresco Sorì Paitin 1985 • $14 • (3/31/1990) • **88**

Barbera d'Alba Campolive 1997: Quite oaky, with smoky aromas and chocolate and toast flavors. Medium-bodied, with supple tannins. A plum and red berry character surfaces on the finish. Drink now through 2002.–P.M. • $23 • (11/15/1999) • **83**

Barbera d'Alba Campolive 1996: Elegant and racy, with some not-so-subtle, toasted oak-infused floral aromas, it offers Barbera's usual crisp acidity, with its lemon tang, plus some cassis bush and grapey blueberry notes. Good with food.–P.M. • $16 • (10/31/1998) • **86**

Barbera d'Alba Campolive 1995 • $16 • (10/31/1997) • **84**

Barbera d'Alba Campolive 1993 • $NA • (10/31/1996) • **85**

Barbera d'Alba Sorì Paitin 1989 • $10 • (11/30/1991) • **88**

Barbera d'Alba Sorì Paitin 1988 • $8 • (3/15/1991) • **83**

Dolcetto d'Alba Sorì Paitin 1998: Smells a bit odd and tastes a bit tough. –P.M. • $16 • (11/15/1999) • **75**

Dolcetto d'Alba Sorì Paitin 1997: Darker and more concentrated than most, a good effort. Medium-bodied, with ripe tannins, a lush mouthfeel, licorice, floral, cassis and wild berry character. A bit simple on the finish. Drink now.–P.M. • $15 • (10/31/1998) • **83**

Dolcetto d'Alba Sorì Paitin 1996 • $14 • (10/31/1997) • **91**

Dolcetto d'Alba Sorì Paitin 1991 • $12 • (9/30/1993) • **80**

PALAGIO, IL

Chardonnay Tuscany 1996 • $NA • (9/30/1997) • **81**

Chianti Classico 1995 • $NA • (9/30/1997) • **83**

Chianti Classico 1994 • $NA • (10/31/1996) • **83**

Chianti Classico 1993 • $NA • (10/31/1995) • **82**

Chianti Classico 1992 • $NA • (2/28/1995) • **79**

PALAGIO, IL

Chianti Classico Riserva 1991 • $NA • (10/31/1995) • **86**
Chianti Classico Riserva 1990 • $NA • (2/28/1995) • **86**

PALAMA

Salento Metiusco 1998: A good, fruity wine, with peppery, plummy character. Medium-bodied, with a fresh finish. Drink now.–J.S. • $13 • (5/31/2000) • **84**
Salice Salentino Rosato Albarossa 1998: Dull, with plum character. Hard to get excited about.–J.S. • $8 • (5/31/2000) • **78**
Salice Salentino Rosso Albarossa 1997: A bit raisiny and short, but with decent fruit.–J.S. • $9 • (5/31/2000) • **78**

PALAZZETTA, LA

Brunello di Montalcino 1995: A seriously crafted wine. Intense aromas of berries, blackberries, flowers and mint. Full-bodied, with polished tannins and a chocolate, berry and currant aftertaste. Best from 2001 through 2004.–J.S. • $68 • (6/30/2000) • **90**
Brunello di Montalcino 1994: A very solid '94. Wonderfully fresh and fruity for the vintage with crushed blackberries, cherries and dark chocolate. Medium- to full- bodied, with well-integrated tannins and a long finish. Modern wine. Drink now.–J.S. • $54 • (8/31/1999) • **88**
Brunello di Montalcino 1991 • $NA • (11/30/1996) • **85**
Brunello di Montalcino 1988 • $NA • (4/30/1994) • **84**
Rosso di Montalcino 1995 • $NA • (9/30/1997) • **87**
Rosso di Montalcino 1994 • $NA • (11/30/1996) • **81**
Rosso di Montalcino 1991 • $14 • (4/30/1994) • **83**

PALAZZINO, PODERE IL

Chianti Classico 1997: A soft and fruity Chianti, with ripe plum, earth and berry character. Medium- to full-bodied, with a fruity finish. Slightly hollow midpalate. Drink now.–J.S. • $18 • (11/30/1999) • **86**
Chianti Classico 1996: Clean and fresh, with strawberry and cherry flavors, a light body and a light finish. Crisp and refreshing. Drink now.–J.S. • $18 • (12/15/1998) • **80**
Chianti Classico 1990 • $16 • (10/31/1993) • **90**
Chianti Classico 1988 • $16 • (9/15/1991) • **90**
Chianti Classico 1987 • $12 • (3/31/1990) • **67**
Chianti Classico 1985 • $11 • (11/30/1987) SS • **93**
Chianti Classico Grasso Sanese 1996: Delicious now. Elegant aromas of berry, cherry and flowers. Medium-bodied, with light tannins, crisp acidity and a fruity finish. Drink now.–J.S. • $35 • (11/30/1999) • **86**
Chianti Classico Grosso Sanese 1995: Good, ripe berry aromas with a barnyard and earth undertone. Medium-bodied and round, with a slightly dry, woody finish that detracts. Tasted twice, with consistent notes. Drink now.–J.S. • $35 • (12/15/1998) • **81**
Chianti Classico Grosso Sanese 1994 • $35 • (9/30/1997) • **84**
Chianti Classico Riserva 1987 • $15 • (12/15/1992) • **85**
Chianti Classico Riserva 1985 • $22 • (9/15/1991) • **88**
Chianti Classico Riserva 1983 • $21 • (11/15/1987) • **80**
Grosso Sanese 1990 • $35 • (10/31/1993) HR • **93**
Grosso Sanese 1988 • $29 • (3/15/1991) • **88**
Grosso Sanese 1987 • $25 • (11/30/1989) • **90**
Grosso Sanese 1986 • $22 • (2/15/1989) • **87**
Grosso Sanese 1985 • $13 • (12/15/1987) • **94**

PALAZZO

Brunello di Montalcino 1994: Light and simple, with berry and dried cherry character, light body and a citrusy, crisp yet slightly astringent finish. Not imported into the U.S.–J.S. • $NA • (1/01/1999) • **79**
Rosso di Montalcino 1997: Not really giving much other than a grapey, grappalike aroma and flavor. Medium-bodied, with silky tannins and a short finish. Hard to get excited about. Drink now.–J.S. • $NA • (1/01/1999) • **83**
Rosso di Montalcino 1993 • $NA • (10/31/1995) • **84**

Key: SS—Spectator Selection. CS—Cellar Selection. HR—Highly Recommended. $NA—Price not available. (BT)—Barrel tasting. Ⓐ—Auction Price. For a key to the tasters' initials, see "How to Use These Listings."
Dates in parentheses represent the issues in which the ratings were published.

PALAZZO VECCHIO, FATTORIA DI

Rosso di Montepulciano 1996: A delicious red. Blackberry and cherry aromas, with peppery highlights. Medium-bodied, with firm tannins. Drink now.–J.S. • $18 • (12/15/1998) • **85**
Vino Nobile di Montepulciano 1995: A bit austere, with berry and green tobacco character. Medium-bodied, with fine tannins and a light finish. Drink now.–J.S. • $21 • (12/15/1998) • **84**
Vino Nobile di Montepulciano 1994 • $15 • (9/30/1997) • **77**
Vino Nobile di Montepulciano Riserva 1993 • $23 • (9/30/1997) • **79**

PALAZZOLA, LA

Merlot Umbria 1997: An aromatic red, with vivid fruit ranging from crushed raspberry to red berry. Medium-bodied, with silky tannins and a fresh, fruity aftertaste. Drink now.–J.S. • $43 • (2/29/2000) • **88**

PALAZZONE, IL

Brunello di Montalcino 1991 • $NA • (9/30/1997) • **86**
Brunello di Montalcino 1990 • $NA • (10/31/1995) • **88**
Rosso di Montalcino 1995 • $NA • (9/30/1997) • **85**

PALLADINO

Barbera d'Alba 1995: Shows spice and brown-sugar flavors, with notes of dried cherry, but it's light and nearly dried out. Past its prime.–K.M. • $11 • (8/31/1998) • **76**
Barolo 1993 • $NA • (10/31/1997) • **83**
Barolo Vigna S. Bernardo 1992: Light, with modest cherry flavors and an astringent finish. Past its prime.–K.M. • $25 • (8/31/1998) • **75**
Gavi 1996: A delicious white wine with plenty of character. Crisp and gutsy, with bracing citrus flavors and nicely nuanced almond and vanilla notes. Drink now.–K.M. • $14 • (8/31/1998) • **86**
Nebbiolo d'Alba 1994: Smooth but fairly light, with decent dried cherry and spice flavors. Drink now.–K.M. • $14 • (8/31/1998) • **80**

PANCRAZI, MARCHESI

Pinot Nero Toscana Villa di Bagnolo 1997: The best Pinot Noir in Italy. A bit reserved on the nose but still showing lovely tea, berry and plum skin character. Medium-bodied, with superfine, silky tannins and a long, fruity finish. Really grows on you. A beauty. Drink now.–J.S. • $39 • (11/30/1999) • **90**
Pinot Nero Toscana Villa di Bagnolo 1996: Strawberry, raspberry and game aromas and flavors. Medium-bodied, with medium tannins and plenty of fruit flavors. A bit short on the finish. Very good Pinot Nero, if not as good as past vintages. Drink now.–J.S. • $36 • (12/15/1998) • **87**
Pinot Nero Toscana Villa di Bagnolo 1995: Spicy and peppery, with strawberry and leather character. Medium-bodied, with medium tannins and a spicy aftertaste. The best Pinot Nero in Italy at the moment. Drink now.–J.S. • $32 • (12/15/1998) • **88**
Pinot Nero Toscana Villa di Bagnolo 1994 • $32 • (9/30/1997) • **90**
Toscana San Donato 1997: Really stylish and fun, with wonderful aromas of cherry, berry and orange peel. Medium-bodied, with loads of flavor, silky tannins and a long, lively finish. Sangiovese. Drink now through 2001. –J.S. • $15 • (11/30/1999) • **89**
Toscana San Donato 1996: A fruity Sangiovese with good berry and tea leaf character. Medium-bodied, with well-integrated tannins and a fresh finish. Drink now.–J.S. • $13 • (12/15/1998) • **85**
Toscana San Donato 1995 • $17 • (9/30/1997) • **85**

PANERETTA, CASTELLO DELLA

Chianti Classico 1996: Good blackberry and cherry character, but a slightly austere, rather dry finish. Still, there's good ripe fruit to it. Medium-bodied. Drink now.–J.S. • $13 • (12/15/1998) • **84**
Chianti Classico 1993 • $NA • (10/31/1996) • **79**
Chianti Classico 1992 • $NA • (2/28/1995) • **79**
Chianti Classico 1991 • $NA • (10/31/1993) • **85**
Chianti Classico 1990 • $NA • (10/31/1993) • **84**
Chianti Classico 1988 • $NA • (9/15/1991) • **79**
Chianti Classico Riserva 1996: Rich and slightly rustic yet delicious. Well done for a 1996, with very pretty blackberry, cherry, cedar and earth

character. Full-bodied, with very ripe fruit flavors, medium tannins and a long finish. Drink now.–J.S. • $20 • (5/31/2000) • **87**

Chianti Classico Riserva 1995: A very woody red, with smoke, vanilla and ripe fruit aromas and flavors. Medium-bodied, with an intense coconut, slightly dry aftertaste. Drink now.–J.S. • $20 • (12/15/1998) • **82**

Chianti Classico Riserva 1990 • $NA • (2/28/1995) • **86**

Chianti Classico Riserva 1988 • $NA • (9/15/1992) • **80**

Chianti Classico Riserva 1985 • $NA • (9/15/1991) • **92**

Chianti Classico Torre a Destra Riserva 1996: Has very good fruit, but a bit too much wood makes this dry and austere. Medium-bodied, with polished tannins and a dry finish. Going nowhere but down. Tasted twice, with consistent notes.–J.S. • $24 • (5/31/2000) • **78**

Chianti Classico Torre a Destra Riserva 1995: A well-defined young red. Showy aromas of blackberry and vanilla. Medium-bodied, with well-integrated, silky tannins and a long, fruity finish. Drink now.–J.S. • $NA • (12/15/1998) • **87**

Toscana 1596-1996 1996: A serious 1996, with wonderfully ripe aromas of plum, berry and mint. Full-bodied, with silky tannins and a long smoke, coffee and blackberry aftertaste. Drink now through 2003.–J.S. • $36 • (5/31/2000) • **90**

Toscana 1596-1996 1995: A big mouthful of a red with loads of fruit. Attractive aromas of blackberry, mint and blueberry. Full in body, with juicy, round tannins and a long, long aftertaste of ripe fruit. Best after 2000.–J.S. • $40 • (12/15/1998) • **90**

Toscana Terrine 1996: A very well crafted red. Very pretty aromas of milk chocolate and raspberry follow through to a full-bodied palate, with firm, well-knit tannins and a long, long finish. Drink through 2003.–J.S. • $26 • (5/31/2000) • **90**

Toscana Terrine 1995: Blackberry and chocolate aromas flow over the rim of the glass. Full-bodied, with supervelvety tannins and a long, long aftertaste. A real beauty; hard not to drink now it's so rich and opulent.–J.S. • $30 • (12/15/1998) • **88**

Toscana Terrine 1993 • $NA • (10/31/1996) • **88**

Toscana Terrine 1990 • $NA • (2/28/1995) • **85**

PANIZZI, GIOVANNI

Chianti Colli Senesi 1996: A good Chianti, with dried cherry and tobacco aromas and flavors. Medium-bodied, with lovely acidity and fine tannins. Fresh on the finish. Drink now.–J.S. • $12 • (12/15/1998) • **84**

Toscana Ceraso 1997: Rather light, but deliciously fruity with lovely strawberry and dried cherry aromas and flavors. More like a simple, good-quality red Burgundy than a Tuscan red. Drink now.–J.S. • $10 • (12/15/1998) • **80**

Toscana Il Bianco di Gianni 1996: Pleasant and fresh, with honey and apple aromas and flavors. Medium-bodied, with fresh acidity and a light honey aftertaste. Drink now.–J.S. • $21 • (12/15/1998) • **82**

Vernaccia di San Gimignano 1997: A simple, fruity white with almond, melon and apple aromas and flavors. Medium-bodied, with a chalky texture and a fresh melon finish. Drink now.–J.S. • $15 • (12/15/1998) • **85**

Vernaccia di San Gimignano 1996 • $15 • (4/30/1998) • **87**

Vernaccia di San Gimignano Riserva 1996: Serious Vernaccia, with lovely apple, pineapple character, hints of vanilla. Medium-bodied, with a green apple skin flavor and undertones of coconut. Fresh finish. Drink now.–J.S. • $28 • (12/15/1998) • **88**

PAOLIS, CASTEL DE

I Quattro Mori 1994 • $45 • (4/30/1997) • **88**

PARADISO, IL

Brunello di Montalcino 1990 • $NA • (10/31/1995) • **70**

Rosso di Montalcino 1993 • $NA • (10/31/1995) • **82**

Rosso di Montalcino 1991 • $NA • (4/30/1994) • **82**

PARUSSO, ARMANDO

Barbera d'Alba 1988 • $12 • (3/15/1991) • **85**

Barbera d'Alba Bricco di Pugnana 1990 • $20 • (10/15/1993) • **91**

Barbera d'Alba Bricco di Pugnana 1989 • $18 • (10/31/1992) • **88**

Barbera d'Alba Ornati 1997: *Grand Cru* Burgundy? No, Barbera d'Alba. This is just mind-boggling—thick and dense, velvety-textured like a Richebourg, with plenty of cassis, blackberry and black cherry to satisfy (an herbal note too). Drink now through 2001.–P.M. • $22 • (10/31/1998) • **90**

Barbera d'Alba Ornati 1996: Exotic, with violet, plum and wild raspberry character. Medium-bodied, of medium intensity, with supple, oak-softened tannins that carry on to a lush yet fresh finish. Drink now.–P.M. • $20 • (10/31/1998) • **85**

Barbera d'Alba Ornati 1995 • $17 • (10/31/1997) • **88**

Barbera d'Alba Ornati 1994 • $17 • (10/31/1996) • **77**

Barbera d'Alba Ornati 1993 • $18 • (10/31/1996) • **87**

Barbera d'Alba Ornati 1992 • $17 • (10/31/1994) • **75**

Barbera d'Alba Superiòre 1989 • $11 • (10/31/1992) • **84**

Barolo 1994: Very light in color, browning already. Watery, with neutral aromas and an astringent, tough finish.–P.M. • $30 • (10/31/1998) • **71**

Barolo 1993 • $28 • (10/31/1997) • **76**

Barolo 1990 • $27 • (10/31/1994) • **90**

Barolo 1985 • $27 • (4/30/1991) • **84**

Barolo Bussia 1990 • $70 Ⓐ • (1/01/1994) • **79**

Barolo Bussia 1989 • $38 • (10/31/1994) • **92**

Barolo Bussia Vigna Munie 1995: Intriguing and balanced, with wet earth, cedar and rock dust complexity followed by a lightly smoky, toasted mocha character. Sweet, round, ripe fruit and tannins caress the palate. Refined, superlong finish. Drink now through 2005.–P.M. • $53 • (11/15/1999) • **94**

Barolo Bussia Vigna Munie 1994: Pure and exuberant. Smells of tar, roses and plum and tastes very ripe, with earth and mineral character laced into the fruit. Supersupple on the midpalate, gliding to a long, succulent and firm finish. One of the most structured Barolos of the vintage. Best from 2003 through 2010.–P.M. • $40 • (10/31/1998) • **88**

Barolo Bussia Vigna Munie 1993 • $37 • (10/31/1997) • **88**

Barolo Bussia Vigna Munie 1992 • $30 • (10/31/1996) • **85**

Barolo Bussia Vigna Rocche 1995: Light-colored, elegant and refined, made in a subtle style. Medium-bodied, with lovely ripeness and delicate wet earth, floral, toast, plum and blackberry complexity. Firm but sweet tannins. Drink now through 2005.–P.M. • $60 • (11/15/1999) • **91**

Barolo Bussia Vigna Rocche 1994: So woody that the oak treatment overwhelms the fruit, leaving the wine a bit dry. Still, there are plenty of aromas and flavors: good fruit, seductive rose petal, violet, mocha and spice. Very toastlike finish. Best after 2003.–P.M. • $40 • (10/31/1998) • **84**

Barolo Bussia Vigna Rocche 1993 • $40 • (10/31/1997) • **85**

Barolo Bussia Vigna Rocche 1992 • $35 • (10/31/1996) • **77**

Barolo Bussia Vigna Rocche 1991 • $30 • (10/31/1996) • **87**

Barolo Bussia Vigna Rocche 1988 • $35 • (10/31/1993) • **87**

Barolo Mariondino 1995: A ripe Barolo with a pure berry thread that gives it vibrancy, Shows earth, game, smoke and a solid tannin structure. Long, juicy finish. Drink now through 2003.–P.M. • $48 • (11/15/1999) • **87**

Barolo Mariondino 1990 • $71 Ⓐ • (10/31/1994) • **68**

Barolo Mariondino 1989 • $30 • (10/31/1993) • **87**

Barolo Mariondino 1988 • $25 • (10/31/1993) • **90**

Barolo Mariondino 1986 • $23 • (4/30/1991) • **83**

Barolo Piccole Vigne 1995: Medium-bodied, it's supple but a bit one-dimensional in the overall impression, lacking a bit of intensity and length despite decent fruit. Drink now through 2003.–P.M. • $40 • (11/15/1999) • **84**

Bricco Rovella 1992 • $15 • (1/01/1994) • **76**

Dolcetto d'Alba 1997: Fairly ripe, offering licorice, raspberry candy and strawberry flavors. Tannins kick in on the slightly drying finish. A bit unbalanced.–P.M. • $15 • (10/31/1998) • **80**

Dolcetto d'Alba 1994 • $12 • (10/31/1995) • **80**

Langhe Red Bricco Rovella 1996: Beautiful for its velvety texture, ripe tannins, lovely blackberry and black currant flavors, this elegant, full-bodied wine just melts to a seamless finish. Hopefully, the wood won't overwhelm the fruit as it ages. Drink now through 2005.–P.M. • $32 • (10/31/1998) • **92**

Langhe Red Bricco Rovella 1995: Decadent. A marvelous swirl of ripe plum, red berry and blackberry flavors, subtle oak notes and supersupple, sweet tannins. The earth of Piedmont takes central stage in this well-made, terrific, full-bodied blend of Barbera and Nebbiolo despite the mocha and coffee bean notes that strike on the rich finish. Drink now through 2006.–P.M. • $30 • (10/31/1998) • **91**

Langhe White Bricco Rovella 1996: Very lush, rich and ripe, with a supple mouthfeel, butter, pear, honey and mocha-chocolate flavors. Slightly hot finish. Overdone.–P.M. • $28 • (10/31/1998) • **79**

Mariondino 1991 • $11 • (10/31/1994) • **80**

Mariondino 1990 • $14 • (10/31/1992) • **86**

Nebbiolo delle Langhe 1988 • $11 • (7/31/1992) • **79**

PASOLINI

Chardonnay Toscana Le Macchie 1996: Barely acceptable, with oxidized toasted oak flavors and a dull finish.–J.S. • $25 • (11/30/1999) • **71**

ITALY

Chianti Classico Badia a Sicelle Riserva 1995: Shows slightly raised acidity with a varnish character. Medium-bodied, with light tannins and a hard, acidic finish. Slight problem here.–J.S. • $24 • (11/30/1999) • **72**

Chianti Montòli Riserva 1995: Hard and austere, with some dried plum character but it's woody and earthy on the finish.–J.S. • $30 • (11/30/1999) • **78**

PATERNO, FATTORIA DI

Vino Nobile di Montepulciano 1996: A silky and fruity red, with well-knit tannins, medium body and a strawberry and berry aftertaste. Drink now.–J.S. • $22 • (11/30/1999) • **86**

Vino Nobile di Montepulciano 1994 • $NA • (9/30/1997) • **85**

Vino Nobile di Montepulciano Riserva 1993 • $NA • (9/30/1997) • **86**

PATERNOSTER

Aglianico del Vulture 1997: Decent peppery character, but slightly light in body and tannin, with a fruity finish. Drink now.–J.S. • $34 • (5/31/2000) • **81**

Aglianico del Vulture 1994 • $20 • (6/15/1997) • **87**

Aglianico del Vulture 1987 • $16 • (1/31/1992) • **82**

Aglianico del Vulture Don Anselmo Riserva del Fondatore 1994: Like a very good Zinfandel. This young wine has extremely intense black pepper character. Full-bodied, with firm tannins and a long, long finish. Drink now through 2003.–J.S. • $34 • (5/31/2000) • **88**

Aglianico del Vulture Don Anselmo Riserva del Fondatore 1985 • $32 • (9/15/1992) • **81**

PAVIA & FIGLI, AGOSTINO

Barbera d'Asti Bricco Blina 1997: Racy, exotic and savage, with ripe, clean plum and blackberry character, lovely floral aromas and a fresh, medium-bodied texture. On top, there's a sense of elegance. Drink now.–P.M. • $11 • (1/01/1999) • **85**

Barbera d'Asti La Marescialla 1997: Fancy winemaking, the use of fancy oak and excellent, ripe, concentrated fruit combine in this full-bodied Barbera for a smooth, complex red. Round mouthfeel, with vanilla, mocha and toast notes, with a crisp, citrusy finish. Not imported into the U.S. Drink now through 2001.–P.M. • $18 • (11/15/1999) • **90**

Barbera d'Asti Moliss 1997: Ripe, supple and fruity, with raspberry and cranberry character and some herb, smoke and pepper notes, this light-bodied Barbera is a charmer; without much depth, but fun to drink now. –P.M. • $13 • (1/01/1999) • **82**

PECCHENINO, FRATELLI

Dolcetto di Dogliani Pizabo 1994 • $NA • (10/31/1995) • **86**

PECORARI, FRANCESCO

Isonzo Lis Neris 1991 • $20 • (2/29/1996) • **80**

Lis Neris 1990 • $20 • (10/15/1994) • **89**

Verduzzo Friulano Tal Luc 1994 • $20 • (1/01/1996) • **85**

PECORARI, PIERPAOLO

Merlot Isonzo del Friuli Baolar 1995 • $19 • (5/31/1998) • **79**

Pinot Grigio Isonzo del Friuli 1996 • $21 • (6/30/1998) • **88**

Pinot Grigio Isonzo del Friuli Olivers 1996 • $19 • (5/31/1998) • **83**

Sauvignon Isonzo del Friuli Kolàus 1996: Atypical. Deep yellow-green in color, with smoky, nutty, mature aromas that persist on the palate right through to the long finish. Rich and full-bodied, but oak is the dominant theme. Drink now.–B.S. • $19 • (7/31/1998) • **84**

PELISSERO

Barbaresco 1996: A bit tough and herbal. Medium-bodied, offering some cassis bush character, it tastes hard and crisp, but does have some redeeming sweet fruit. Drink through 2003.–P.M. • $60 • (8/31/1999) • **83**

Barbaresco 1995: Interesting and structured, with firm tannins, decent fruit. Fairly angular, though, with earth, plum, blackberry and tar notes. Dry finish.–P.M. • $39 • (10/31/1998) • **79**

Barbaresco 1994 • $32 • (10/31/1997) • **86**

Barbaresco 1992 • $NA • (10/31/1995) • **82**

Barbaresco Vanotu 1996: Very supple and round, a full-bodied, international-style Barbaresco. The fruit is a bit dulled by a cover of toasted, spicy wood, whose vanilla and mocha flavors fight off the ripe berry character, at least for now. Drink now through 2003.–P.M. • $70 • (8/31/1999) • **88**

Barbaresco Vanotu 1995: Gorgeous. Ripe yet elegant and racy, with laser-sharp red- and blackberry flavors that marry beautifully with subtle oak accents. Full-bodied, it has a fresh, vibrant midpalate, with lots of fine, sweet tannins. The finish is seamless and lasting—the earth, violet, rose petal, plum and smoky notes go on and on. Drink through 2005.–P.M. • $48 • (9/15/1998) • **91**

Barbaresco Vanotu 1994 • $42 • (10/31/1997) • **86**

Barbaresco Vanotu 1993 • $19 • (10/31/1996) • **81**

Barbaresco Vanotu 1991 • $19 • (10/31/1995) • **76**

Barbaresco Vanotu 1990 • $NA • (11/30/1994) • **87**

Barbera d'Alba Casot 1997: Ripe and supple, almost sweet-tasting, with seductive plum and blackberry character, but it also shows a hint of herbaceousness. Drink now.–P.M. • $18 • (9/15/1999) • **85**

Barbera d'Alba Piani 1996: Wonderfully seductive, with lush texture and complex flavors. Full-bodied, it's layered with toasted oak, spice and mocha accents but also has blackberry and plum character. Ripe tannins coat the palate and smooth out the long, smoky finish. Drink through 2002–P.M. • $19 • (10/31/1998) • **88**

Barbera d'Alba Piani 1995 • $19 • (10/31/1997) • **80**

Barbera d'Alba Piani 1994 • $NA • (10/31/1996) • **84**

Barbera d'Alba Piani 1993 • $12 • (7/31/1995) • **84**

Barbera d'Alba Ronchi 1990 • $11 • (4/30/1993) • **87**

Dolcetto d'Alba Augenta 1994 • $8 • (10/31/1996) • **85**

Dolcetto d'Alba Augenta 1993 • $12 • (7/31/1995) • **84**

Dolcetto d'Alba Munfrina 1996 • $16 • (10/31/1997) • **76**

Dolcetto d'Alba Munfrina 1994 • $NA • (10/31/1995) • **84**

Dolcetto d'Alba Munfrina 1991 • $12 • (4/30/1993) • **83**

PERVINI

Apulia Bizantino 1993: An elegant red, firmly textured and well balanced, this has serious structure, with light but satisfying cherry and plum flavors. Drink now. • $9 • (8/31/1998) • **85**

PESCAIA, LA

Brunello di Montalcino 1995: Light and rustic Brunello with berry, earth and slightly varnishlike character. Hard to get excited about. Not imported into the U.S.–J.S. • $NA • (1/01/2000) • **79**

Brunello di Montalcino 1990 • $NA • (10/31/1995) • **79**

Brunello di Montalcino 1988 • $NA • (4/30/1994) • **80**

Rosso di Montalcino 1993 • $NA • (10/31/1995) • **78**

Rosso di Montalcino 1991 • $NA • (4/30/1994) • **77**

PETROGNANO

Pomino 1995: Aromatic, with loads of ripe currant, light raisin and berry character. Full-bodied, with round, soft tannins and a long, long fruity finish. A big, voluptuous juicy red. A name to watch from Pomino; from the owners of Rufina's Selvapiana. Drink now.–J.S. • $NA • (12/15/1998) • **89**

Pomino 1993 • $NA • (10/31/1995) • **85**

PETROIO, FATTORIA DI

Chianti Classico 1997: Outstanding quality for a Chianti Classico *normale*, with fabulous aromas of berry, raspberry and a hint of earth. Medium-bodied, with full, silky tannins and a finish that builds on your palate. Drink now through 2001.–J.S. • $10 • (11/30/1999) • **90**

Chianti Classico 1996: Alluring aromas of blackberry, raspberry and flowers. Medium-bodied, with delicate tannins and a fruity, fresh aftertaste. This estate always makes delicious Chianti. Drink now.–J.S. • $9 • (12/15/1998) • **86**

Chianti Classico 1995 • $9 • (9/30/1997) • **84**

Chianti Classico 1994 • $NA • (10/31/1996) • **84**

Chianti Classico 1993 • $NA • (10/31/1995) • **80**

Chianti Classico 1992 • $NA • (2/28/1995) • **73**

Chianti Classico 1991 • $NA • (10/31/1995) • **65**

Key: SS—Spectator Selection. CS—Cellar Selection. HR—Highly Recommended. $NA—Price not available. (BT)—Barrel tasting. (A)—Auction Price. For a key to the tasters' initials, see "How to Use These Listings."
Dates in parentheses represent the issues in which the ratings were published.

Chianti Classico 1988 • $NA • (9/15/1991) • **83**
Chianti Classico Cru Montetondo 1990 • $NA • (10/31/1993) • **86**
Chianti Classico Cru Montetondo 1988 • $NA • (9/15/1991) • **90**
Chianti Classico Riserva 1996: Slightly simple but showing delicious dried cherry and strawberry character. Medium-bodied, with light tannins and a fresh finish. Drink now.–J.S. • $20 • (11/30/1999) • **83**
Chianti Classico Riserva 1995: Well-balanced Sangiovese with dried cherry and citrus character. Medium-bodied, with delicate tannins and a crisp finish. Drink now.–J.S. • $13 • (12/15/1998) • **87**
Chianti Classico Riserva 1994 • $15 • (9/30/1997) • **83**
Chianti Classico Riserva 1993 • $NA • (10/31/1996) • **86**
Chianti Classico Riserva 1990 • $NA • (2/28/1995) • **79**
Chianti Classico Riserva 1988 • $17 • (10/31/1993) • **84**
L 'Unico di Petroio 1990 • $NA • (10/31/1993) • **87**
Toscana Poggio al Mandorlo 1996: Dried cherry and raspberry aromas and flavors are simple and bright. Light- to medium-bodied, with light tannins and a fresh finish. Drink now.–J.S. • $7 • (12/15/1998) • **84**

PETROLO, FATTORIA

Chianti 1991 • $NA • (10/31/1993) • **85**
Chianti 1990 • $NA • (10/31/1993) • **80**
Chianti Colli Aretini 1995 • $10 • (9/30/1997) • **81**
Chianti Colli Aretini 1993 • $10 • (10/31/1996) • **78**
Chianti Colli Aretini Riserva 1993 • $20 • (10/31/1996) • **78**
Chianti Colli Fiorentini 1993 • $NA • (10/31/1995) • **80**
Chianti Riserva 1991 • $NA • (2/28/1995) • **84**
Toscana Galatrona 1997: A big and juicy Merlot, with loads of blackberry, cherry and mint as well as new oak character and hints of tar. Full-bodied, with full, polished tannins. Voluptuous and sexy, but needs time to calm down. Best after 2000.–J.S. • $50 • (11/30/1999) • **94**
Toscana Galatrona 1995: Very polished Merlot, as well cut as an Armani suit. Violets and currants with an underlying cherry character on the nose. Medium- to full-bodied, with fine tannins and a caressing texture. Best after 2000.–J.S. • $50 • (12/15/1998) • **90**
Toscana Galatrona 1994 • $NA • (9/30/1997) • **91**
Toscana Terre di Galatrona 1997: This pretty Sangiovese-based red has aromas of plum, green tobacco and earth. Medium-bodied, with polished tannins and a delicate finish. Drink now through 2001.–J.S. • $15 • (11/30/1999) • **86**
Toscana Terre di Galatrona 1996: Delicious and succulent, subtle in style. Aromatically lively, with crushed berry and light earth character. Of medium body, with delicate tannins and fresh acidity. Drink now.–J.S. • $17 • (12/15/1998) • **87**
Toscana Torrione 1997: An exotic and voluptuous Sangiovese. Wonderfully ripe on the nose, with masses of plums, berries and figs, and hints of new oak. Full-bodied and chewy, with tons of fruit and velvety tannins. Long, long finish. Massive. Best after 2000.–J.S. • $42 • (11/30/1999) • **94**
Toscana Torrione 1996: An outstanding Sangiovese, with gorgeous aromas of crushed berry and flowers and hints of toasted oak. Full-bodied, with chewy tannins and a solid core of fruit. Very classy. Best after 2000.–J.S. • $40 • (11/30/1999) • **91**
Toscana Torrione 1995: Rich and concentrated, with lots of tobacco, berry and cherry aromas and flavors. Full-bodied, with ultrafine tannins and a long, succulent finish. Drink through 2003.–J.S. • $38 • (12/15/1998) • **90**
Toscana Torrione 1994 • $32 • (9/30/1997) • **88**
Toscana Torrione 1993 • $NA • (10/31/1996) • **87**
Toscana Torrione 1991 • $NA • (2/28/1995) • **86**
Toscana Torrione 1990 • $NA • (10/31/1993) • **90**

PIAN CORNELLO

Brunello di Montalcino 1995: Extremely fresh '95 with crushed cherries and berries—almost too fresh. Medium-bodied, with firm tannins and a medium finish. A bit lean, but very good. Drink now through 2003.–J.S. • $NA • (1/01/2000) • **87**
Brunello di Montalcino 1994: Pretty floral and berry aromas follow through to a medium-bodied palate, with fresh fruit, delicate tannins and a refreshing finish. A lovely Brunello for current drinking.–J.S. • $NA • (8/31/1999) • **86**
Brunello di Montalcino 1993: Very mature, with leather and tea flavors, hints of ripe fruit. Medium-bodied, with fine tannins and a slightly austere finish.–J.S. • $42 • (12/15/1998) • **79**
Brunello di Montalcino 1992 • $30 • (9/30/1997) • **88**
Rosso di Montalcino 1996: A simple, no-nonsense rosso with berry and vanilla character. Light-bodied, with light tannins and a light finish. Drink now.–J.S. • $21 • (12/15/1998) • **81**
Rosso di Montalcino 1995 • $14 • (9/30/1997) • **86**
Rosso di Montalcino 1991 • $NA • (4/30/1994) • **80**

PICCINI

Chianti Classico 1997: A simple and light Chianti, with dried cherry character, light body and fresh acidity. Drink now.–J.S. • $9 • (11/30/1999) • **80**
Chianti Classico 1995 • $NA • (9/30/1997) • **83**
Chianti Classico 1994 • $10 • (10/31/1996) • **77**
Chianti Classico 1992 • $7 • (2/28/1995) • **79**
Chianti Classico 1991 • $6 • (6/15/1993) • **75**
Chianti Classico 1990 • $8 • (6/15/1993) • **79**
Chianti Classico Riserva 1994 • $NA • (9/30/1997) • **77**
Chianti Classico Riserva 1993 • $13 • (10/31/1996) • **73**
Chianti Classico Riserva 1990 • $10 • (2/28/1995) • **79**
Toscana Patriarca 1997: Raisiny and overdone. Has interesting fruit character, but lacks freshness.–J.S. • $16 • (11/30/1999) • **79**
Toscana Solicello 1995: Delicious. Loads of dry cherry character. Medium-bodied, with silky tannins and a crisp finish. A bit simple. Drink now.–J.S. • $9 • (12/15/1998) • **84**
Vernaccia di San Gimignano 1997: Fresh and crisp, with lemon, mineral and light spice aromas and flavors. Medium-bodied, with refreshing acidity and a light finish. Drink now.–J.S. • $7 • (12/15/1998) • **80**

PICCOLA, VIGNA

Chianti Classico 1994 • $NA • (10/31/1996) • **84**

PIERAZZUOLI, ENRICO

Carmignano Le Farnete Riserva 1996: An outstanding Carmignano, with wonderful aromas of crushed berry and raspberry. Full-bodied, with compacted tannins, ripe fruit flavors and a long, silky finish. Very fine indeed. Best after 2000.–J.S. • $30 • (11/30/1999) • **89**
Carmignano Le Farnete Riserva 1993 • $27 • (4/30/1998) • **85**
Chianti Classico Matronèo 1996: A fine-textured yet decadent wine, with aromas of game, berry and bark. Medium-bodied, with silky tannins and a light, earthy, fruity finish. Drink now.–J.S. • $15 • (11/30/1999) • **87**
Chianti Classico Matronèo 1994 • $15 • (4/30/1998) • **86**
Chianti Classico Matronèo Riserva 1991 • $26 • (4/30/1998) • **86**
Chianti Montalbano 1997: A fresh and soft red, with pleasant plum and dried cherry character. Medium-bodied, with a fruity finish. Drink now.–J.S. • $10 • (11/30/1999) • **85**
Chianti Montalbano Riserva 1996: A lean and fresh red, with cherry, berry and vanilla aromas and flavors. Medium-bodied, with silky tannins and a lively finish. Well crafted. Drink now.–J.S. • $20 • (11/30/1999) • **86**

PIERI, AGOSTINA

Rosso di Montalcino 1996: Big and rich for a rosso, but impressive. Aromas of freshly picked cherries. Medium-bodied, with velvety tannins and a long, fruity finish. Not imported into the U.S. Drink through 2001.–J.S. • $NA • (12/15/1998) • **87**

PIEROPAN, LEONILDO

Recioto di Soave La Colombare 1991 • $21 • (4/30/1996) • **79**
Recioto di Soave La Colombare 1989 • $29 • (9/15/1992) • **87**
Recioto di Soave Le Colombare 1994 • $23/500 ml. • (6/15/1998) • **87**
Soave Classico Superiòre 1996 • $13 • (6/15/1998) • **87**
Soave Classico Superiòre Vigneto Calvarino 1996 • $16 • (6/30/1998) • **87**

PIETRA PINTA

Chardonnay Lazio 1998: Good, clean pear and lemon character, with a hint of mineral. Light- to medium-bodied, with a light, fresh finish. Not very Chardonnay-like. Drink now.–J.S. • $10 • (4/30/2000) • **81**
Colle Amato 1997: Wonderful class and finesse. Black in color, with an amazing nose of crushed raspberry, mint and berry. Full-bodied, with beautifully polished tannins and a long, long finish. Cabernet Sauvignon. Not imported into the U.S. Best after 2000.–J.S. • $NA • (4/30/2000) • **90**
Cori Costa Vecchia 1998: Fruit-driven, with loads of bright berry, cherry and currant aromas. Medium-bodied, with medium tannins and a slightly short finish. Not imported into the U.S. Drink now.–J.S. • $NA • (1/01/2000) • **85**

PIETROSO

Brunello di Montalcino 1995: A drink-me-now Brunello. Pretty aromas of plums, tobacco, cedar and flowers follow through to a medium-bodied palate, with medium-fine tannins, fresh acidity and a clean finish. Drink now.–J.S. • $NA • (1/01/2000) • **86**

Brunello di Montalcino 1994: Pleasant, early-drinking Brunello. Looks slightly mature but shows fresh and rich berry, earth and chocolate character. Medium-bodied, with firm, medium tannins and a short finish. Not imported into the U.S. Drink now.–J.S. • $NA • (1/01/1999) • **85**

Brunello di Montalcino 1988 • $NA • (4/30/1994) • **89**

PIEVE DEL VESCOVO

Colli del Trasimeno Lucciaio 1996: Tough and lean, with good aromas of plum and mineral. Medium-bodied, with tough tannins and a slightly austere finish. Best after 2000.–J.S. • $22 • (2/29/2000) • **84**

Colli del Trasimeno Piovano 1998: Loaded with raspberry character but slightly one-dimensional. Medium-bodied, with light tannins and a fresh finish. Drink now.–J.S. • $11 • (2/29/2000) • **85**

PIEVE SANTA RESTITUTA

Brunello di Montalcino Rennina 1994: A very good but slightly lean '94 Brunello. Medium-bodied, with berry and fresh mushroom flavors and a refreshing finish. Drink now.–J.S. • $72 • (8/31/1999) • **86**

Brunello di Montalcino Rennina 1993: Lean and racy in style, with a beautiful bouquet of plum and dried cherry. Medium-bodied, with silky tannins and a slightly simple finish. Drink now.–J.S. • $70 • (12/15/1998) • **86**

Brunello di Montalcino Rennina 1990 • $168 Ⓐ • (10/31/1995) • **85**

Brunello di Montalcino Sugarille 1993: Traditional in style, but shows wonderful cherry, tobacco and porcini aromas. Medium- to full-bodied, with well-integrated, chewy tannins and a fresh, medium-fruity finish. Best after 2000.–J.S. • $95 • (12/15/1998) • **88**

PIGHIN, FRATELLI

Pinot Grigio Collio 1996 • $19 • (11/15/1997) • **84**

Pinot Grigio Grave del Friuli 1996 • $12 • (11/15/1997) • **86**

PIRA

Barolo 1994: Pleasantly balanced and infused with oak, with plenty of mocha, toasted wood and coffee mill notes along with chewy but fairly ripe tannins. Medium-bodied and slightly diluted, it turns a bit dry on the finish. Best after 2000.–P.M. • $42 • (10/31/1998) • **80**

Barolo 1993 • $45 • (10/31/1997) • **84**

Barolo 1990 • $40 • (10/31/1995) • **85**

Barolo Cannubi 1995: This serious, big-bodied Nebbiolo has classic Barolo complexity: layers of smoke, wet earth, tar, roses and black fruit. Has ripe but firm tannins, but the silky concentration is such that this should age gracefully. Best from 2003 through 2010.–P.M. • $70 • (11/15/1999) • **92**

PLANETA

Cabernet Sauvignon Sicilia 1997: A modern, well-made Cab. Delicious, with plum and berry aromas and flavors that have undertones of new oak. Medium-bodied, with polished tannins and a medium finish. Best after 2000.–J.S. • $34 • (5/31/2000) • **88**

Chardonnay Sicilia 1998: Here's an Italian white that tastes like a village Meursault from Lafon; very impressive. Golden in color, with very ripe pineapple and apricot aromas plus hints of vanilla and dough. Full in body, with lots of unctuous fruit and a long, long finish. Drink now through 2003.–J.S. • $30 • (5/31/2000) HR • **91**

Merlot Sicilia 1997: Outstanding. Gorgeous fresh fruit, with mineral, berry and floral aromas. Full-bodied, with full, silky tannins and a tight, well-knit finish. Very fine indeed. Best after 2001.–J.S. • $38 • (5/31/2000) • **90**

Sicilia Red La Segreta 1998: A pretty, fresh and well-made red from Italy at a no-quibble price, this is medium-bodied, with lots of strawberry and berry character, light tannins and a fresh finish. Drink now.–J.S. • $10 • (5/31/2000) • **86**

Sicilia Santa Cecilia 1997: A very attractive and very real wine, with loads of strawberry character and hints of vanilla oak and spice. Medium- to full-bodied, with firm tannins and a medium finish. Well made. Nero d'Avola. Drink now through 2004.–J.S. • $38 • (5/31/2000) • **88**

Sicilia White La Segreta 1998: Simple and fruity, with apple, mineral and a little lime. Medium-bodied, with light acidity and a fresh finish. Drink now.–J.S. • $14 • (5/31/2000) • **85**

PLOZNER

Chardonnay Grave del Friuli 1998: A very good, superclean Chardonnay, offering extremely fresh sliced apple character with hints of cream. Medium- to full-bodied, with lots of fruit and a long ripe apple aftertaste. Drink now.–J.S. • $11 • (3/31/2000) • **85**

Chardonnay Grave del Friuli 1996: Already mature, this Chardonnay shows more almond aromas and flavors than fruit, but it's concentrated and racy. Finishes tart. Drink now.–B.S. • $11 • (7/31/1998) • **81**

Chardonnay Grave del Friuli Barriques 1996: Stylish, with interesting dried apricot, apple and vanilla character. Medium-bodied, with good acidity and a fruity finish. Drink now.–J.S. • $17 • (1/01/2000) • **87**

Merlot Grave del Friuli 1997: Very earthy, with barnyard character. Too much. Medium-bodied, with soft tannins.–J.S. • $10 • (5/15/2000) • **75**

Merlot Grave del Friuli 1996 • $10 • (1/01/1998) • **64**

Merlot Grave del Friuli 1993 • $10 • (6/15/1996) • **77**

Pinot Grigio Grave del Friuli 1998: A solid, clean white, with apple, honey and mineral character. Medium-bodied, with a fresh finish. Drink now.–J.S. • $13 • (3/31/2000) • **85**

Pinot Grigio Grave del Friuli 1996 • $12 • (6/15/1998) • **80**

Sauvignon Grave del Friuli 1998: Interesting aromas of mineral, sliced pears and peaches. Medium-bodied, with fresh acidity and a light finish. Drink now.–J.S. • $11 • (4/30/2000) • **84**

Tocai Friulano Grave del Friuli 1998: Lots of mineral and apple character, with a hint of honey. Medium-bodied, with light fruit and a crisp finish. Drink now.–J.S. • $10 • (3/31/2000) • **84**

Tocai Friulano Grave del Friuli 1996 • $10 • (6/15/1998) • **83**

PODERINA, LA

Brunello di Montalcino 1995: Dark colored and very fruity and minty. Tastes a lot like Cabernet. Full-bodied and very polished, with a long, long finish. A serious wine with lots of oak, but is it Brunello? Best after 2001.–J.S. • $45 • (6/30/2000) • **89**

Brunello di Montalcino 1994: Incredibly fresh and rich for the vintage, with mint, berry and raspberry character. Full-bodied, with well-integrated polished tannins and a long caressing finish with hints of new wood. A modern, well-crafted wine. Drink through 2005.–J.S. • $48 • (8/31/1999) • **90**

Brunello di Montalcino 1993: A beefy Brunello. Dark-colored, with mineral, mint and berry aromas. Full-bodied, with firm tannins and a long finish. Best after 2000.–J.S. • $43 • (12/15/1998) • **88**

Brunello di Montalcino 1992 • $40 • (9/30/1997) • **87**

Brunello di Montalcino 1991 • $NA • (11/30/1996) • **79**

Brunello di Montalcino 1990 • $NA • (10/31/1995) • **86**

Brunello di Montalcino 1988 • $32 • (4/30/1994) • **91**

Brunello di Montalcino Riserva 1993: A big, modern Brunello with a Bordeaux-like style. Very vivid, fresh character of blackberries and currants. Full-bodied, with polished tannins and a long, minty, slightly toasted finish. Best after 2001.–J.S. • $69 • (8/31/1999) • **90**

Brunello di Montalcino Riserva 1990 • $NA • (11/30/1996) • **83**

Brunello di Montalcino Riserva 1988 • $32 • (10/31/1994) • **88**

Moscadello di Montalcino 1997: A pretty late-harvest white, with aromas of ripe pear, melon and honey. Medium-bodied and medium sweet, with a long, fruity finish. Very clean and well made. Drink now.–J.S. • $22/375 ml. • (11/30/1999) • **86**

Moscadello di Montalcino Vendemmia Tardiva 1998: Stylish but not very sweet for a dessert wine. Plenty of Moscato character, with orange peel and spice aromas. Medium-bodied and lightly sweet, with a lemon, lime and clove aftertaste. Not imported into the U.S. Drink now.–J.S. • $NA/375 ml. • (1/01/2000) • **86**

Rosso di Montalcino 1997: A stylish rosso. Dark, inky color. Intense aromas of blackberries, plums and cherries with hints of wood. Medium-bodied, with polished tannins and a unique aftertaste of chocolate-covered cherries. Slightly too much wood on the finish to be outstanding, but comes close. Drink now through 2002.–J.S. • $20 • (9/15/1999) • **89**

Rosso di Montalcino 1994 • $NA • (11/30/1996) • **75**

Key: SS—Spectator Selection. CS—Cellar Selection. HR—Highly Recommended. $NA—Price not available. (BT)—Barrel tasting. Ⓐ—Auction Price.
For a key to the tasters' initials, see "How to Use These Listings."
Dates in parentheses represent the issues in which the ratings were published.

ITALY

POGGERINO

Bugialla 1991 • $NA • (2/28/1995) • **93**
Bugialla 1990 • $20 • (10/31/1993) • **91**
Chianti Classico 1997: A silky and fine Chianti, with ripe plum and berry character throughout. Medium-bodied, with soft tannins and a long, fruity aftertaste. A beauty. Drink now through 2001.–J.S. • $27 • (11/30/1999) • **89**
Chianti Classico 1996: A lively and intense Chianti Classico. Bright violet and strawberry aromas. Medium-bodied, with delicate tannins and a refreshing, fruity aftertaste. Drink now.–J.S. • $22 • (12/15/1998) • **88**
Chianti Classico 1995 • $22 • (9/30/1997) • **85**
Chianti Classico 1994 • $22 • (10/31/1996) • **87**
Chianti Classico 1993 • $NA • (10/31/1995) • **88**
Chianti Classico 1992 • $NA • (2/28/1995) • **83**
Chianti Classico 1991 • $16 • (10/31/1993) • **84**
Chianti Classico 1990 • $14 • (9/15/1992) • **91**
Chianti Classico 1988 • $13 • (11/30/1991) • **78**
Chianti Classico Bugialla Riserva 1996: Slightly overdone with oak but still fruity and caressing on the palate, with lots of coconut and toasted oak along with berry and cherry character. Medium-bodied, with fine yet velvety tannins and a fruity finish. Needs time in the bottle. Drink through 2003.–J.S. • $46 • (11/30/1999) • **88**
Chianti Classico Bugialla Riserva 1995: Extremely stylish. Intensely floral, with ripe fruit and hints of citrus. Medium-bodied, with medium, fine tannins and a long, superfruity finish that reminds me of peaches. Lovely seductive texture. Drink now through 2003.–J.S. • $50 • (12/15/1998) • **90**
Chianti Classico Bugialla Riserva 1994 • $42 • (9/30/1997) • **90**
Chianti Classico Bugialla Riserva 1993 • $28 • (9/30/1997) • **90**
Chianti Classico Bugialla Riserva 1990 • $NA • (9/30/1997) • **92**
Chianti Classico Bugialla Riserva 1988 • $20 • (9/30/1997) • **86**
Chianti Classico Bugialla Riserva 1985 • $NA • (9/30/1997) • **76**
Toscana Primamateria 1997: A rich and well-structured red, with loads of coffee, raisin and berry character. Full-bodied, with loads of velvety tannins and a long, ripe fruit finish. Made for aging. Drink through 2005.–J.S. • $120/1.5 liter • (11/30/1999) • **91**

POGGIO, IL

Sangiovese di Romagna Superiore 1995 • $NA/1.5 liter • (3/31/1997) • **80**

POGGIO AL MULINO

Toscana Pancarta 1997: Full-bodied, with fascinating aromas of blackberry, black licorice and spices. Very chewy, with lots of tannins and a long tobacco, ripe fruit and chocolate finish. Made by the same winemaker as Riecine. Not imported into the U.S. Best after 2003.–J.S. • $NA • (11/30/1999) • **89**

POGGIO AL SOLE

Chianti Classico 1997: Silky and fruity, with attractive dried cherry and berry character and a hint of tobacco. Medium body and finish. Not imported into the U.S. Drink now.–J.S. • $NA • (1/01/1999) • **86**
Chianti Classico 1996: Delicate and fruity, with plum and cherry character. Medium-bodied, with light tannins and a fruity, crisp finish. Not imported into the U.S. Drink now.–J.S. • $NA • (12/15/1998) • **83**
Chianti Classico 1992 • $NA • (2/28/1995) • **84**
Chianti Classico 1988 • $NA • (9/15/1991) • **91**
Chianti Classico Casasilia 1996: This racy, rockin' '96 Chianti Classico riserva has a good dose of new wood, but the ripe fruit supports it. Medium- to full-bodied, with firm tannins and a closed finish. Needs bottle age. Not imported into the U.S. Best after 2000.–J.S. • $NA • (11/30/1999) • **88**
Chianti Classico Casasilia 1995: Seriously good, single-vineyard Chianti. Wonderfully perfumed with blackberry, cherry and black licorice. Medium-bodied, with extremely well-integrated tannins and a flavorful yet subtle aftertaste of fruit and mushroom. Not imported into the U.S. Drink now.–J.S. • $NA • (12/15/1998) • **89**
Chianti Classico Riserva 1995: Pretty blackberry and chocolate aromas and flavors. Medium-bodied, with silky tannins and fruity structure. Polished and caressing texture on the finish. Not imported into the U.S. Drink now.–J.S. • $NA • (12/15/1998) • **87**
Chianti Classico Riserva 1990 • $NA • (2/28/1995) • **86**
Chianti Classico Riserva 1988 • $NA • (9/15/1992) • **81**
Chianti Classico Riserva 1985 • $NA • (9/15/1991) • **88**
Toscana Seraselva 1996: Impressive aromas of blackberry, smoke and mint. Medium-bodied, with silky tannins and a minty finish. A bit austere but well crafted. Made from Merlot and Cabernet. Not imported into the U.S. Drink now.–J.S. • $NA • (11/30/1999) • **88**

POGGIO AL SORBO

Chianti Classico 1995 • $16 • (4/30/1998) • **81**
Chianti Classico 1990 • $15 • (9/15/1992) • **84**
Chianti Classico Riserva 1994 • $21 • (4/30/1998) • **73**
Chianti Classico Riserva 1990 • $15 • (2/28/1995) • **79**
Le Robbiaie 1991 • $17 • (7/31/1994) • **79**

POGGIO ANTICO

Brunello di Montalcino 1994: A welcoming '94 Brunello. Warm and ripe fruit aromas with hints of vanilla. Medium-bodied, with velvety tannins and a fruity, soft and friendly finish. Drink now.–J.S. • $54 • (8/31/1999) • **87**
Brunello di Montalcino 1993: Poggio Antico always makes elegant and subtle Brunellos, and the '93 is no different. Plenty of dried fruit and tobacco. Medium-bodied, with firm tannins and a very ripe fruit finish. Best after 2000.–J.S. • $48 • (12/15/1998) • **88**
Brunello di Montalcino 1992 • $50 • (9/30/1997) • **85**
Brunello di Montalcino 1991 • $46 • (11/30/1996) • **86**
Brunello di Montalcino 1990 • $85 Ⓐ • (10/31/1995) • **91**
Brunello di Montalcino 1989 • $42 • (11/30/1994) • **90**
Brunello di Montalcino 1988 • $35 • (4/30/1994) • **91**
Brunello di Montalcino 1987 • $45 • (12/15/1992) • **87**
Brunello di Montalcino 1986 • $40 • (8/31/1991) HR • **91**
Brunello di Montalcino 1985 • $36 • (11/30/1990) CS • **95**
Brunello di Montalcino 1982 • $25 • (11/30/1989) • **92**
Brunello di Montalcino 1979 • $13 • (9/15/1986) • **72**
Brunello di Montalcino Riserva 1993: A silky and easy riserva giving immediate pleasure. Pretty aromas of dried cherries and flowers. Medium-bodied, with fine tannins and a fresh and fruity aftertaste. Tasted twice, with consistent notes. Drink now.–J.S. • $74 • (8/31/1999) • **87**
Brunello di Montalcino Riserva 1990 • $101 Ⓐ • (11/30/1996) • **93**
Brunello di Montalcino Riserva 1988 • $56 • (10/31/1994) • **85**
Brunello di Montalcino Riserva 1986 • $62 • (12/15/1992) • **89**
Brunello di Montalcino Riserva 1985 • $125 Ⓐ • (8/31/1991) • **93**
Rosso di Montalcino 1993 • $25 • (10/31/1995) • **83**
Rosso di Montalcino 1992 • $25 • (10/31/1994) • **84**
Rosso di Montalcino 1991 • $24 • (4/30/1994) • **83**
Rosso di Montalcino 1989 • $21 • (8/31/1991) • **85**
Toscana Altero 1993: Surprisingly light for Altero, but fruity and pleasant. Light-bodied, with light plum and cedar flavors and a simple finish. Slightly dry texture. Drink now.–J.S. • $50 • (12/15/1998) • **80**
Toscana Altero 1990 • $33 • (2/28/1995) • **82**

POGGIO BONELLI

Chianti Classico 1997: This good, straightforward Chianti Classico has berry and mushroom character, medium body and a fresh finish. Drink now.–J.S. • $18 • (11/30/1999) • **86**
Chianti Classico 1996: Intriguing, with a cherry, earth and burnt wood character. Medium-bodied, with soft tannins and a fruity finish. Drink now.–J.S. • $14 • (12/15/1998) • **85**
Chianti Classico 1993 • $NA • (10/31/1996) • **79**
Chianti Classico 1990 • $NA • (10/31/1993) • **88**
Chianti Classico Riserva 1996: A pleasant and balanced wine, with tobacco, berry and cherry aromas and flavors. Medium-bodied, with silky tannins and a medium, fruity finish. Slightly austere. Drink now.–J.S. • $24 • (11/30/1999) • **85**
Chianti Classico Riserva 1995: Sleek and racy CC riserva. Lots of currant and violet on the nose. Medium-bodied, with extremely well-knit tannins and a medium finish. Drink now.–J.S. • $20 • (12/15/1998) • **88**
Toscana Tramonto d'Oca 1995: Silky, sexy red. Very intense aromas of ripe fruit with hints of game and dried fruit. Full-bodied and tannic, with a silky texture and an extremely ripe aftertaste. A beauty. Drink now.–J.S. • $28 • (12/15/1998) • **90**
Toscana Tramonto d'Oca 1990 • $NA • (10/31/1993) • **89**

POGGIO DI SOTTO

Brunello di Montalcino 1993: Traditional and delicious. No new wood near this wine, but it's big and voluptuous. Wonderfully perfumed with roses,

ITALY

berries and fruits of the woods. Full-bodied and flavorful, with succulent tannins and a long finish. Best after 2000.–J.S. • $67 • (12/15/1998) • **90**
Brunello di Montalcino 1991 • $45 • (11/30/1996) • **82**
Rosso di Montalcino 1994 • $30 • (11/30/1996) • **84**
Rosso di Montalcino 1993 • $NA • (10/31/1995) • **83**
Rosso di Montalcino 1991 • $NA • (4/30/1994) • **83**

POGGIO REALE

Chianti Rufina Riserva 1990 • $NA • (2/28/1995) • **88**

POGGIO SALVI

Chianti Colli Senesi 1997: A decent, fruity Chianti, with blackberry and hints of licorice and earth. Medium-bodied, with a slightly raisiny character, light tannins and a fruity finish. Drink now.–J.S. • $15 • (11/30/1999) • **81**
Chianti Colli Senesi 1996: A perfumed red with floral and blackberry character. Medium-bodied, with light tannins and a light and fruity finish. Delicious with simple foods. Drink now.–J.S. • $12 • (12/15/1998) • **85**
Toscana Campo del Bosco 1997: A simple and clean red, with plum and berry character, light body and a short, fruity finish. A bit lean. Drink now.–J.S. • $25 • (11/30/1999) • **80**
Toscana Campo del Bosco 1995: Light, silky and easy to drink, more like a refreshing Pinot Noir. Delicate strawberry and tea character, with a light to medium body, light tannins and a crisp finish. Drink now.–J.S. • $22 • (12/15/1998) • **83**
Toscana Lavischio 1995: A simple, bubbly red, with cherry and berry character. Medium body. Light tannins. Refreshing and quaffable; serve lightly chilled.–J.S. • $17 • (12/15/1998) • **84**
Toscana Lavischio 1995 • $26 • (9/30/1997) • **87**
Toscana Refola 1998: Lovely aromas of lemon, lime, spice and honey. Medium-bodied and dry, with mineral and honey flavors and a medium finish. Sauvignon and Trebbiano. Not imported into the U.S. Drink now.–J.S. • $NA • (1/01/1999) • **87**
Toscana Refola 1997: A simple, easy white, with clean apple and lemon-lime aromas and flavors. Medium-bodied, with fresh acidity and a lively aftertaste. Drink now.–J.S. • $12 • (12/15/1998) • **83**

POGGIO SAN POLO

Brunello di Montalcino 1994: Amazing for the vintage. Electrifying '94 Brunello with berry, spice and chocolate character. Full-bodied, with supersilky tannins and a long, sweet fruit aftertaste. Drink now through 2006.–J.S. • $NA • (8/31/1999) • **90**
Brunello di Montalcino 1993: Though there's plenty of plum and cherry character, this is a little simple on the palate. Medium-bodied, with velvety tannins and a fresh fruit finish. Drink now.–J.S. • $48 • (12/15/1998) • **85**
Brunello di Montalcino 1992 • $48 • (9/30/1997) • **82**
Brunello di Montalcino 1991 • $45 • (11/30/1996) • **85**
Brunello di Montalcino 1989 • $24 • (7/31/1995) • **91**
Brunello di Montalcino Riserva 1990 • $70 • (11/30/1996) • **91**
Rosso di Montalcino 1996: Very grapey, with berry and stemmy aromas and flavors. Medium-bodied, moderately tannic, fresh on the finish. A bit simple. Drink now.–J.S. • $28 • (12/15/1998) • **84**
Rosso di Montalcino 1994 • $20 • (11/30/1996) • **82**
Rosso di Montalcino 1990 • $15 • (8/31/1995) • **88**
Rubio 1994 • $15 • (10/31/1996) • **87**

POGGIO SCALETTE, PODERE

Alta Valle della Greve Il Carbonaione 1997: A super, well-crafted red, with wonderful aromas of violet, berry and fresh oak. Full-bodied and very silky, with plenty of fruit and a long, caressing finish. Drink through 2004.–J.S. • $60 • (11/30/1999) • **92**
Toscana Il Carbonaione 1996: A fine, well-made red with lots of dried cherry, plum, smoke, game, vanilla and berry aromas and flavors and a long, pepper and fruit aftertaste. Full-bodied, with well-integrated tannins. Drink now.–J.S. • $55 • (12/15/1998) • **91**

Key: SS—Spectator Selection. CS—Cellar Selection. HR—Highly Recommended. $NA—Price not available. (BT)—Barrel tasting. Ⓐ—Auction Price.
For a key to the tasters' initials, see "How to Use These Listings."
Dates in parentheses represent the issues in which the ratings were published.

Toscana Il Carbonaione 1995: A soft and fruity mouthful that amazes with its fresh, crushed berry character. Full-bodied, oozing with raspberry and blackberry flavors, its tannins are big, soft and velvety. Long aftertaste. –J.S. • $55 • (12/15/1998) • **93**
Toscana Il Carbonaione 1994 • $55 • (9/30/1997) • **90**
Toscana Il Carbonaione 1993 • $55 • (9/30/1997) • **93**
Toscana Il Carbonaione 1992 • $40 • (10/31/1996) • **90**

POGGIOLINO, IL

Chianti Classico 1997: Medium-bodied, with focused violet and blackberry character and fresh, lively acidity. Delicious with food. Drink now.–J.S. • $14 • (11/30/1999) • **86**
Chianti Classico 1996: Impressively concentrated for a regular Chianti Classico. Good cherry and earthy mushroom aromas. Full-bodied, chewy, with lots of ripe fruit flavors and a long, smoky, earthy, meaty aftertaste. Drink now.–J.S. • $15 • (12/15/1998) • **87**
Chianti Classico 1994 • $14 • (4/30/1998) • **87**
Chianti Classico 1993 • $NA • (10/31/1996) • **78**
Chianti Classico 1988 • $15 • (5/15/1993) • **83**
Chianti Classico Riserva 1996: Pretty raspberry and cherry aromas follow through to a medium-bodied palate, with light tannins and a fresh finish. Drink now.–J.S. • $14 • (11/30/1999) • **85**
Chianti Classico Riserva 1995: A delicious, youthful riserva. Intense aromas of strawberry and violet. Medium-bodied, with light tannins and a crisp and lively finish. Will improve, but why wait? Drink now.–J.S. • $23 • (12/15/1998) • **87**
Chianti Classico Riserva 1994 • $21 • (4/30/1998) • **87**
Chianti Classico Riserva 1988 • $NA • (9/15/1992) • **83**
Chianti Classico Riserva 1985 • $NA • (9/15/1991) • **84**
Colli dell 'Italia Centrale Rosato 1997: Delivers strawberry character, hints of almonds and cream. Medium-bodied, with crisp acidity and a fruity aftertaste. Like a good Tavel. Drink now.–J.S. • $10 • (12/15/1998) • **85**
Toscana Le Balze 1997: A fruity and enjoyable red, with pretty aromas of raspberry, plum and violet. Medium-bodied, with light tannins and a crisp finish. From Sangiovese. Drink now.–J.S. • $28 • (11/30/1999) • **87**
Toscana Le Balze 1995: Pungent style of wine. Plenty of plum, berry and smoke character. Medium-bodied, with soft tannins and a rich, earthy finish. Drink now.–J.S. • $24 • (11/30/1999) • **87**
Toscana Le Balze 1990 • $25 • (1/01/1998) • **78**

POGGIONE, IL

Brunello di Montalcino 1994: A subtle red with aromas of blackberries and earth. Medium-bodied, with fine tannins and a caressing finish of fruit and earth. Drink now.–J.S. • $51 • (8/31/1999) • **86**
Brunello di Montalcino 1993: Never big and brutish, Il Poggione's top wines are always velvety and caressing, like this 1993 Brunello. Berry, tobacco and leather aromas and flavors prevail. Medium-bodied, with caressing tannins. Drink now.–J.S. • $48 • (12/15/1998) • **87**
Brunello di Montalcino 1992 • $40 • (9/30/1997) • **85**
Brunello di Montalcino 1991 • $37 • (11/30/1996) • **80**
Brunello di Montalcino 1990 • $38 • (10/31/1995) • **87**
Brunello di Montalcino 1988 • $42 • (4/30/1994) • **86**
Brunello di Montalcino 1982 • $30 • (9/15/1988) • **88**
Brunello di Montalcino 1981 • $28 • (9/15/1986) • **93**
Brunello di Montalcino Riserva 1993: Already tired. Ruby-garnet in color, with berry, cedar, earth and meat aromas, hints of chestnut. Medium-bodied, with hard tannins and a short, dry finish. Tasted twice, with consistent notes.–J.S. • $67 • (8/31/1999) • **79**
Brunello di Montalcino Riserva 1990 • $47 • (11/30/1996) • **91**
Brunello di Montalcino Riserva 1988 • $48 • (10/31/1994) • **90**
Brunello di Montalcino Riserva 1979 • $35 • (9/15/1986) • **79**
Brunello di Montalcino Riserva 1978 • $35 • (7/01/1984) SS • **92**
Rosso di Montalcino 1997: Rather simple and mature '97 rosso with berry, tobacco and grapefruit character. Light- to medium-bodied, with a crisp finish. Drink now.–J.S. • $23 • (9/15/1999) • **81**
Rosso di Montalcino 1996: Typical, light '96 Rosso, with berry and tobacco aromas and flavors, light to medium body and a light finish. Drink now.–J.S. • $21 • (12/15/1998) • **81**
Rosso di Montalcino 1995 • $18 • (9/30/1997) • **87**
Rosso di Montalcino 1994 • $17 • (11/30/1996) • **86**
Rosso di Montalcino 1993 • $17 • (10/31/1995) • **79**
Rosso di Montalcino 1992 • $17 • (8/31/1995) • **87**
Rosso di Montalcino 1991 • $18 • (4/30/1994) • **82**
Rosso di Montalcino 1985 • $17 • (3/31/1988) • **85**

Toscana San Leopoldo 1997: A pleasant, fruity red with light to medium body, fresh acidity and a light tannin structure. Drink now.–J.S. • $41 • (6/15/2000) • **83**

Toscana San Leopoldo 1996: Balanced and yummy youthful Sangiovese, with dried cherry and plum aromas and flavors. Medium-bodied, with fine tannins and a crisp, fruity finish. Drink through 2003.–J.S. • $38 • (12/15/1998) • **87**

POGGIOPIANO, FATTORIA

Chianti Classico 1997: Medium-bodied, with attractive aromas of blackberry and earth, silky tannins and a light, slightly diluted finish. Drink now.–J.S. • $21 • (11/30/1999) • **84**

Chianti Classico 1996: Perfumed aromas of flowers and red fruits. Medium-bodied, with well-integrated, chewy tannins and a long, fruity aftertaste. A very good wine from a rising producer. Drink now.–J.S. • $40 • (12/15/1998) • **86**

Toscana Rosso di Sera 1997: A big, boisterous Sangiovese, with loads of blackberry, spice and toasted oak character. Full-bodied, with a thick, velvety tannin structure and a long finish. A beauty. Best after 2000.–J.S. • $44 • (11/30/1999) • **92**

Toscana Rosso di Sera 1996: I have never tasted a wine from this estate; this is a big and rough young red with a lot of character and heart. Wonderful multilayered aromas of flowers and ripe fruits follow through on the palate. Full-bodied, roughly tannic, with lots of fruit on the finish. Like a top California red from the 1970s. Stellar Sangiovese. Drink now.–J.S. • $22 • (12/15/1998) • **90**

POJER & SANDRI

Atesino Essenzia 1995: Intense and fragrant, the exotic citrus-peel, passion fruit and pineapple jump out of the glass. Elegant and racy, it might be better as an aperitif. Tasty, with tannins on the finish. Drink now through 2002.–B.S. • $40/375 ml. • (7/31/1998) • **88**

Atesino Rosso Faye 1994: Deep color and gorgeous aroma, like a good St.-Emilion. Roasted coffee and vanilla accent the plum and herb flavors. Medium-bodied, turns austere on the finish. 70 percent Lagrein. Drink now.–B.S. • $32 • (7/31/1998) • **87**

Chardonnay Trentino Di Faedo 1996: Displays body and concentration but the aromas and flavors remain submerged. Good length on the finish; may just need a few months to open. Drink now.–B.S. • $16 • (7/31/1998) • **84**

Müller-Thurgau Trentino 1996: Plenty of peach and mineral character in this rich, fruity white, underscored by lively acidity and a tangy finish. Shows what can be done with this grape.–B.S. • $16 • (7/31/1998) • **85**

Nosiola Trentino 1996: A clean, crisp, easy-drinking white, showing apple and herb flavors and a firm, mouthwatering finish. Good aperitif. Drink now.–B.S. • $16 • (7/31/1998) • **82**

Pinot Nero Trentino 1994: Shows some age in the color, with spicy balsamic vinegar, brown sugar and woodsy flavors, smooth texture and lightly tannic finish. Good effort with a difficult grape. Drink now.–B.S. • $28 • (7/31/1998) • **80**

Sauvignon Atesino 1996: Citrus and tropical notes abound in this rich, juicy white, its flavors lingering on the mouthwatering finish. Drink now.–B.S. • $16 • (7/31/1998) • **85**

Traminer Trentino 1996: The rose character is very pure, but a carbon dioxide element initially masks both aroma and flavor in this racy white. Short aeration brings out more floral, spicy, tropical fruit. Best to decant. Drink now.–B.S. • $16 • (7/31/1998) • **82**

POLIZIANO

Elegia 1995 • $35 • (9/30/1997) • **89**
Elegia 1994 • $NA • (10/31/1996) • **85**
Rosso di Montepulciano 1998: Good stuff that starts off with a bang. Intriguing aromas of blackberry and dried cherry. Medium-bodied, with a solid core of fruit, medium tannins and a light finish. Not imported into the U.S. Drink now.–J.S. • $NA • (1/01/1999) • **86**

Rosso di Montepulciano 1990 • $10 • (12/15/1992) • **83**
Vino Nobile di Montepulciano 1996: A seamless Vino Nobile. Plum and mineral aromas flow out of the glass. Full-bodied, with a solid core of fruit, polished tannins and a long finish. Not imported into the U.S. Drink now through 2003.–J.S. • $NA • (11/30/1999) • **90**

Vino Nobile di Montepulciano 1995: A firm, well-crafted red, with berry, cherry and green tobacco aromas and flavors. Medium-bodied, with firm tannins and a fresh finish. Drink now.–J.S. • $26 • (12/15/1998) • **86**

Vino Nobile di Montepulciano 1989 • $13 • (3/31/1993) • **84**
Vino Nobile di Montepulciano 1988 • $12 • (12/15/1991) • **81**
Vino Nobile di Montepulciano 1987 • $12 • (3/15/1991) • **84**
Vino Nobile di Montepulciano 1985 • $13 • (9/15/1988) • **89**
Vino Nobile di Montepulciano Vigna Asinone 1996: The best wine of the vintage from Montepulciano. Attractive aromas of raspberry and cream follow through to the full-bodied palate, with loads of polished tannins and a long, mouthpuckering finish. Needs time to open and mellow. Not imported into the U.S. Best after 2000.–J.S. • $NA • (11/30/1999) • **91**

Vino Nobile di Montepulciano Vigna Asinone 1995: A wine with racy mineral and berry character and a hint of mint. Full-bodied, with well-integrated tannins and a long, racy finish. An outstanding Tuscan red by anyone's standards, and a Vino Nobile at that. Best after 2001.–J.S. • $42 • (12/15/1998) • **90**

Vino Nobile di Montepulciano Vigneto Caggiole 1994 • $27 • (9/30/1997) • **87**
Vino Nobile di Montepulciano Vigneto Caggiole Riserva 1988 • $23 • (6/30/1993) • **82**

PONTORMO

Chianti 1994 • $6 • (10/31/1996) • **80**

PORTA ROSSA

Barbaresco 1995: Nicely made, with ripe fruit, firm structure and massive tannins that are tough but sweet enough to suggest they'll come together with bottle age. Medium in body, subtle in style, it should pair well with red meat.–P.M. • $34 • (10/31/1998) • **87**

Barolo 1994: A bit tough and odd, with some not-so-clean aromas and flavors. Too bad, because there's good fruit beneath. Turns dry on the finish.–P.M. • $36 • (10/31/1998) • **76**

Barolo Riserva 1985 • $26 • (1/31/1992) • **87**
Barolo Vigna Delizia Riserva 1982 • $25 • (8/31/1991) • **87**
Diano d'Alba Vigna Bruni 1996: Light and a bit simple, with strawberry and cherry notes, the tannins turn astringent on the tough finish. Drink now.–P.M. • $17 • (10/31/1998) • **75**

Diano d'Alba Vigna Bruni 1990 • $14 • (3/31/1992) • **84**
Diano d'Alba Vigna Bruni 1988 • $25 • (2/15/1991) • **85**
Nebbiolo d'Alba 1995: Light in color and delicate in texture, with chestnut, wet earth and cherry pit character, it has some distinction despite its lean body. Interesting wine. Drink now.–P.M. • $17 • (10/31/1998) • **81**

PRA' DI PRADIS

Pinot Grigio Collio 1996 • $18 • (5/15/1998) • **84**
Stukara 1993 • $23 • (9/15/1997) • **80**
Tocai Friulano Collio 1996 • $13 • (4/30/1998) • **87**

PRAVINI

Merlot Trentino 1995 • $9 • (4/30/1998) • **86**

PREMIOVINI

Sangiovese di Romagna Plauto 1997: Clean and lean red, with plenty of fresh raspberry character. Light- to medium-bodied, with firm, slightly drying tannins and a short finish. Drink now.–J.S. • $7 • (6/30/1999) • **81**

PRENDINA, LA

Cabernet Sauvignon Alto Mincio Falcone 1995: Black currant and cherry accented with a hint of cedar offer good Cabernet character in this elegant, well-defined red. It's supple, with a dollop of tannin for structure.–B.S. • $25 • (9/30/1998) • **84**

Merlot Alto Mincio 1995: There's a touch of minty herbs along with cherry character in this simple, pleasant Merlot. Tightens up on the finish. Drink now.–B.S. • $15 • (9/30/1998) • **81**

PRINCIC, DORO

Merlot Collio 1995 • $18 • (6/15/1998) • **87**
Tocai Friulano Collio 1996 • $15 • (6/15/1998) • **85**

PRINCIPATO

Merlot-Cabernet Sauvignon Rosso della Vallagarina 1994 • $6 • (6/15/1997) • **82**

PRINCIPIANO, FERDINANDO

Barbera d'Alba Pian Romualdo 1996: Smells and tastes like concentrated dark chocolate, with wonderful, ripe, rich black fruit plus spice and smoke character. Balanced, velvety finish. Drink now through 2003.–P.M. • $35 • (11/15/1999) • **87**

Barolo Boscareto 1995: Decent in the fruit department, but not very complex. Round in the mouth, with plum, black cherry and toasted oak filling out the package. A touch herbaceous. Drink now through 2003.–P.M. • $49 • (11/15/1999) • **84**

Dolcetto d'Alba Sant 'Anna 1998: This has a kirschlike note, but the wine is supple and harmonious enough to go with rustic foods. A wet earth note is appealing. Drink now.–P.M. • $17 • (11/15/1999) • **80**

PROMESSA

Primitivo Puglia 1997: A very, very ripe wine, with raisin, pepper and plum character. Thick and full-bodied. Slightly short finish. A little simple really. Drink now.–J.S. • $8 • (5/15/2000) • **82**

PROVENZA

Brut Lugana Ca ' Maiöl 1998: Barely drinkable. Lemon and bug killer character.–J.S. • $11 • (5/31/2000) • **70**

PRUNETO

Chianti Classico 1996: Rather mature color of brick red. Tea, dried cherry and tobacco character. Light body and finish. Drying out.–J.S. • $20 • (11/30/1999) • **78**

PRUNOTTO

Barbaresco 1996: Some ripe fruit, but it's dominated by herbal, bell pepper aromas and flavors and dry tannins.–P.M. • $41 • (8/31/1999) • **71**

Barbaresco 1995: A bit earthy but otherwise ripe and opulent, with lots of clean, pure berry character. Medium-bodied, with lots of firm tannins, but it has the stuffing to age harmoniously. Best from 2002 through 2005.–P.M. • $34 • (10/31/1998) • **87**

Barbaresco 1994 • $29 • (10/31/1997) • **85**
Barbaresco 1993 • $20 • (10/31/1996) • **84**
Barbaresco 1991 • $25 • (10/31/1995) • **79**
Barbaresco 1990 • $NA • (10/31/1994) • **81**
Barbaresco 1989 • $21 • (10/31/1994) • **85**
Barbaresco 1988 • $17 • (10/31/1994) • **87**
Barbaresco 1987 • $27 • (3/31/1992) • **70**

Barbaresco Bric Turot 1996: Juicy red, quite mouthpuckeringly crisp and lacking the layered, round suppleness expected in this vintage. Slightly herbal aftertaste.–P.M. • $89 • (8/31/1999) • **77**

Barbaresco Montestefano 1993 • $30 • (10/31/1996) • **88**
Barbaresco Montestefano 1990 • $58 Ⓐ • (10/31/1994) • **85**
Barbaresco Montestefano 1989 • $35 • (10/31/1994) • **85**
Barbaresco Montestefano 1987 • $37 • (3/31/1992) • **76**
Barbaresco Montestefano 1986 • $37 • (12/31/1990) • **86**
Barbaresco Montestefano 1985 • $29 • (3/31/1990) • **87**
Barbaresco Rabajà Riserva 1982 • $19 • (7/31/1987) • **81**
Barbera d'Alba 1993 • $NA • (10/31/1996) • **77**
Barbera d'Alba 1991 • $11 • (11/15/1993) • **74**
Barbera d'Alba Fiulot 1996 • $11 • (10/31/1997) • **89**
Barbera d'Alba Fiulot 1994 • $NA • (10/31/1996) • **85**
Barbera d'Alba Fiulot 1993 • $10 • (10/31/1994) • **79**
Barbera d'Alba Fiulot 1992 • $8 • (11/15/1993) • **80**

Barbera d'Alba Pian Romualdo 1997: Fresh and crisp and tasting of lots of clean red berry character, this wine is ripe and balanced, making it fun to drink (there's no obvious oak here) and sniff—if you don't mind a hint of earthy stable aroma. Drink now.–P.M. • $26 • (9/15/1999) • **86**

Barbera d'Alba Pian Romualdo 1996: Ripe yet succulent, this fresh Barbera has a lot going on. Offers some toasted flavors, along with blueberry, cranberry and cherry. Fairly tart finish. Drink now.–P.M. • $24 • (10/31/1998) • **84**

Key: SS—Spectator Selection. CS—Cellar Selection. HR—Highly Recommended. $NA—Price not available. (BT)—Barrel tasting. Ⓐ—Auction Price.
For a key to the tasters' initials, see "How to Use These Listings."
Dates in parentheses represent the issues in which the ratings were published.

Barbera d'Alba Pian Romualdo 1994 • $18 • (10/31/1997) • **86**
Barbera d'Alba Pian Romualdo 1993 • $22 • (10/31/1995) • **85**
Barbera d'Alba Pian Romualdo 1991 • $19 • (10/31/1994) • **77**
Barbera d'Alba Pian Romualdo 1990 • $19 • (10/31/1994) • **81**
Barbera d'Alba Pian Romualdo 1989 • $19 • (7/31/1995) • **85**
Barbera d'Alba Pian Romualdo 1988 • $19 • (11/15/1993) • **80**
Barbera d'Alba Pian Romualdo 1987 • $14 • (9/15/1990) • **81**

Barbera d'Asti Costamiòle 1996: Very ripe-tasting, this oozes sweet tannins, smooth texture, full body and layers of toasted oak. It still tastes fresh thanks to clean red berry flavors and decent acidity. Drink now through 2001.–P.M. • $56 • (11/15/1999) • **91**

Barbera d'Asti Fiulot 1998: A simple, irresistible pleasure. Purple in color, with youthful, grapey aromas like a nouveau-style Barbera. Fresh, vibrant and ripe-tasting, this is pure, balanced, "guzzle me" stuff. Enjoy it a bit chilled. Drink now.–P.M. • $14 • (11/15/1999) • **87**

Barolo 1995: There's good concentration, but it tastes herbal and odd, with green, asparagus and basil aromas and flavors, tough tannins and a tough finish.–P.M. • $41 • (11/15/1999) • **77**

Barolo 1994: A clean, pure, fruit-driven Barolo. Medium-bodied, with an undertow of fresh herb, citrus, plum and red berry flavors. Supple, round and ripe tannins make it delicious now, but it has depth to hold in the cellar. Drink now through 2005.–P.M. • $29 • (10/31/1998) • **86**

Barolo 1993 • $27 • (10/31/1997) • **87**
Barolo 1992 • $27 • (10/31/1996) • **82**
Barolo 1991 • $27 • (10/31/1995) • **80**
Barolo 1990 • $29 • (10/31/1994) • **86**
Barolo 1989 • $27 • (10/31/1993) • **90**
Barolo 1988 • $27 • (9/30/1993) HR • **93**
Barolo 1987 • $27 • (3/31/1992) • **85**
Barolo 1985 • $31 • (3/31/1990) • **82**

Barolo Bussia 1995: Very fresh style, succulent and lively, with a crisp, herbal red berry edge. Medium-bodied, it turns a bit dry and simple on the green, tart finish.–P.M. • $66 • (11/15/1999) • **75**

Barolo Bussia 1993 • $50 • (10/31/1997) • **90**
Barolo Bussia 1990 • $53 Ⓐ • (10/31/1994) • **88**
Barolo Bussia 1989 • $37 • (10/31/1994) • **89**
Barolo Bussia 1988 • $35 • (11/30/1994) • **85**
Barolo Bussia 1986 • $39 • (3/31/1992) • **78**
Barolo Bussia 1985 • $38 • (9/15/1990) • **92**
Barolo Bussia 1983 • $NA • (9/15/1988) • **88**
Barolo Bussia 1982 • $25 • (9/15/1988) • **91**
Barolo Bussia 1978 • $NA • (9/15/1988) • **86**
Barolo Bussia 1974 • $NA • (9/15/1988) • **80**
Barolo Bussia 1971 • $NA • (9/15/1988) • **90**
Barolo Bussia 1967 • $NA • (9/15/1988) • **82**
Barolo Bussia 1964 • $NA • (9/15/1988) • **80**
Barolo Bussia 1961 • $NA • (9/15/1988) • **91**

Barolo Cannubi 1995: A dark-colored, extracted Nebbiolo, with crisp cassis bush, herb, green olive and spice character. Appealingly ripe midpalate. Medium-bodied, it should improve with age given its concentration. Drink now through 2003.–P.M. • $66 • (11/15/1999) • **88**

Barolo Cannubi 1990 • $NA • (10/31/1994) • **81**
Barolo Cannubi 1989 • $37 • (10/31/1994) • **83**
Barolo Cannubi 1985 • $32 • (3/31/1990) • **85**
Barolo Cannubi 1983 • $26 • (9/15/1988) • **85**
Barolo Cannubi 1982 • $25 • (9/15/1988) • **75**
Barolo Cannubi 1978 • $NA • (9/15/1988) • **78**
Barolo Ginestra di Monforte d'Alba Riserva 1980 • $13 • (6/30/1987) • **78**

Dolcetto d'Alba 1998: What Dolcetto should be: fresh and lovely, with pure fruit in a lively but balanced package. This medium-bodied Italian red is full of pretty raspberry, black cherry and floral notes, with sweet tannins. Drink now.–P.M. • $16 • (7/31/1999) HR • **88**

Dolcetto d'Alba 1997: A rather delicate wine that grows on you. Soft and supple, it delivers some good blueberry and cherry flavors and finishes kicking with life. Drink now.–P.M. • $15 • (10/31/1998) • **83**

Dolcetto d'Alba 1996 • $14 • (10/31/1997) • **85**
Dolcetto d'Alba 1990 • $11 • (9/30/1993) • **80**
Dolcetto d'Alba 1989 • $11 • (2/15/1992) • **83**
Dolcetto d'Alba 1985 • $10 • (3/15/1989) • **84**

Dolcetto d'Alba Mosesco 1997: What you expect from a satisfying Dolcetto. A pretty, medium-bodied red, with black cherry and cassis character. Succulent finish. Drink now.–P.M. • $18 • (7/31/1999) • **86**

Dolcetto d'Alba Mosesco 1990 • $15 • (9/30/1993) • **82**
Nebbiolo d'Alba 1993 • $19 • (10/31/1995) • **83**

Nebbiolo d'Alba Occhetti 1997: Shows decent fruit, but it's a bit light-bodied and earthy, with smoke, raspberry and cherry character. Drink now.–P.M. • $26 • (11/15/1999) • **80**

Nebbiolo d'Alba Occhetti 1996: Packed with red berry and blackberry flavors, and with chewy tannins. Well made, if a touch rustic and herbal with cassis bush, this should be great with pizza and pasta. Drink now.–P.M. • $23 • (10/31/1998) • **85**

Nebbiolo d'Alba Occhetti 1995 • $21 • (10/31/1997) • **80**

Nebbiolo d'Alba Occhetti 1994 • $18 • (10/31/1996) • **87**

Nebbiolo d'Alba Occhetti 1990 • $17 • (7/31/1995) • **82**

Roero 1986 • $10 • (6/30/1988) • **82**

PUGNANE

Barbera d'Alba 1993 • $NA • (10/31/1996) • **83**

PUIATTI, GIOVANNI

Cabernet Franc Isonzo del Friuli 1997: Leafy, berry aromas and flavors mark this Cabernet Franc, reminiscent of Chinon, though softer in structure. Offers nice sappy fruit, and it's well balanced. Drink now.–B.S. • $15 • (7/31/1998) • **85**

Chardonnay Isonzo del Friuli 1997: Still youthful, displaying apple and nut flavors on a bright, elegant framework. Finishes short. Drink now.–B.S. • $15 • (7/31/1998) • **82**

Merlot Isonzo del Friuli 1997: Deeply colored, with a grapey character and soft texture. Appealing, and designed for early consumption. Drink now.–B.S. • $15 • (7/31/1998) • **82**

Pinot Grigio Isonzo del Friuli 1997: A lovely expression of Pinot Grigio, displaying peach, nut and smoke character, rich texture and vibrant acidity. Picks up a stoniness on the finish.–B.S. • $15 • (7/31/1998) • **85**

Sauvignon Isonzo del Friuli 1997: More emphasis on body and power than on aromatics, yet subtle gooseberry and melon flavors prevail in the end. –B.S. • $15 • (7/31/1998) • **84**

PUIATTI, VITTORIO

Cabernet Sauvignon Toscana Fattoria Casavecchia Carfino 1995: Fresh, with lively dried cherry, raspberry and a hint of herb. Medium-bodied, with light tannins and a crisp finish. Drink now through 2001.–J.S. • $30 • (5/31/2000) • **84**

Chardonnay Collio 1998: Some melon and mango character to this, but slightly dull. Medium-bodied. Light finish.–J.S. • $20 • (3/31/2000) • **79**

Chianti Classico Fattoria Casavecchia Il Sogno 1995: Bubbly. A bit thin and odd. Tasted twice, with consistent notes.–J.S. • $16 • (5/31/2000) • **69**

Chianti Classico Fattoria Casavecchia Nerissa Riserva 1995: Medium-bodied, with focused plum and raspberry character, good acidity and a silky finish. Best after 2002.–J.S. • $22 • (5/31/2000) • **87**

Merlot Collio 1989 • $26 • (1/31/1992) • **78**

Merlot Toscana Fattoria Casavecchia Capetino 1995: Pleasant and fresh, with dried cherry and tobacco character. Medium-bodied, with light tannins and a crisp finish. Drink now.–J.S. • $30 • (5/31/2000) • **84**

Pinot Grigio Collio 1998: Delicious, with lovely mineral, lemon rind and melon character. Medium-bodied, with fresh acidity and a long, clean finish. Drink now.–J.S. • $20 • (3/31/2000) • **84**

Pinot Grigio Collio 1997: Bubble-gum character is followed by a rich, stony palate. Soft in texture already. Drink now.–B.S. • $18 • (7/31/1998) • **82**

Pinot Nero Collio 1997: A light Pinot Noir, slightly lean. Clean tea, berry and leather character. A bit mature already. Drink now.–J.S. • $20 • (5/15/2000) • **80**

Pinot Nero Collio 1989 • $26 • (9/15/1992) • **70**

Ribolla Collio 1998: A clean wine but rather neutral, with lemon and melon character, a light body and a fresh finish. Drink now.–J.S. • $20 • (4/30/2000) • **80**

Sauvignon Collio 1998: Slightly subdued on the nose but shows lots of fruit on the palate. Medium-bodied, with gooseberry and grapefruit character. Very fresh finish. Drink now.–J.S. • $20 • (4/30/2000) • **85**

Sauvignon Collio 1997: Ripe peach aromas and flavors are married to a powerful structure and an almost viscous texture, yet there's just enough acidity—and a touch of bitterness at the end—to balance it all. Drink now.–B.S. • $18 • (7/31/1998) • **85**

Tocai Friulano Collio 1998: A very clean and simple white, with apple and citrus character. Light in body and finish.–J.S. • $20 • (3/31/2000) • **79**

PUNSET

Barbaresco 1996: An elegant, medium-bodied Nebbiolo, beautifully balanced in an unoaked way, offering lovely purity of fruit and ripe tannins plus the expected kick of acidity to help it age, even though it's approachable now. Best from 2003 through 2010.–P.M. • $40 • (10/31/1999) • **87**

Barbaresco 1995: Beautiful—from the first whiff to the last sip. Traditional in style, this combines the earth of Piedmont, with its mineral and stony tannins, with tar, smoke, cherry pit, blackberry and cigar-box notes. The subtlety of the wine, its firm but dense structure, grows on you as it cascades to an attention-grabbing finish. Aficionados will enjoy it now, but best to cellar to let the aromas gain. Drink now through 2007.–P.M. • $35 • (10/31/1998) • **93**

Barbaresco 1994 • $20 • (10/31/1997) • **71**

Barbaresco 1993 • $20 • (10/31/1997) • **79**

Barbaresco 1989 • $17 • (6/15/1994) HR • **90**

Barbaresco Campo Quadro 1996: One-dimensional and a bit herbal, with cherry notes, but there's a lemony, citrusy, crisp side to this light-bodied Nebbiolo. Tasted twice, with consistent notes.–P.M. • $45 • (10/31/1999) • **77**

Barbaresco Campo Quadro 1995: Funky, not totally clean, this tastes a bit unripe, with cherry and lemon notes. Dry tannins. Not recommended. Tasted twice, with consistent notes.–P.M. • $48 • (10/31/1998) • **68**

Barbaresco Campo Quadro 1994 • $29 • (10/31/1997) • **80**

Barbera d'Alba 1997: Crisp, acidic and rather lean style, with modest depth; offers some cranberry, cherry and strawberry notes in a superficial package.–P.M. • $16 • (9/15/1999) • **77**

Barbera d'Alba 1996: Light and fruity, but also a bit diluted and simple, with strawberry, raspberry and cassis notes. Turns a bit tart on the finish.–P.M. • $13 • (10/31/1998) • **78**

Barbera d'Alba 1994 • $12 • (10/31/1997) • **76**

Barbera d'Alba 1990 • $14 • (4/30/1993) • **87**

Dolcetto d'Alba 1997: Slightly spritzy, fruity and light-bodied, with some fresh currant and cherry notes, and a lemony taste on the fresh finish. Drink now.–P.M. • $16 • (10/31/1998) • **81**

Dolcetto d'Alba 1995 • $12 • (10/31/1997) • **85**

Dolcetto d'Alba 1991 • $12 • (4/30/1993) • **76**

PUPILLE, FATTORIA LE

Morellino di Scansano 1998: Le Pupille does it again. Dark ruby in color, with intense aromas of crushed cherry and berry and a hint of wet earth. Medium-bodied, with medium, velvety tannins and a fruity finish. A beauty. Drink now through 2001.–J.S. • $16 • (11/30/1999) • **89**

Morellino di Scansano 1997: A stylish and wonderful wine, with terrific character and real quality for the money. Vivid blackberry and tar aromas. Medium-bodied, with velvety tannins. Alluring mocha and berry character on the long finish. Drink now.–J.S. • $12 • (12/15/1998) • **89**

Morellino di Scansano 1996 • $13 • (9/30/1997) • **85**

Morellino di Scansano 1995 • $10 • (10/31/1996) • **89**

Morellino di Scansano 1989 • $13 • (10/31/1993) • **84**

Morellino di Scansano Poggio Valente 1997: A brick house of a Sangiovese, with fabulous aromas of concentrated cherry and berry and a hint of mineral. Full-bodied, with loads of fruit, velvety tannins and a long, long finish. Best after 2000.–J.S. • $38 • (11/30/1999) • **92**

Morellino di Scansano Riserva 1997: This Tuscan red is gorgeous. Emitting beautiful aromas of blackberry, wet earth and toasted oak, it's full-bodied and very polished, with fine tannins and a fresh, delicious finish. Needs time. Best after 2000.–J.S. • $19 • (5/31/2000) HR • **91**

Morellino di Scansano Riserva 1996: A bit too woody. Medium-bodied, with ripe fruit and masses of vanilla. Slightly dry finish. Drink now.–J.S. • $28 • (11/30/1999) • **84**

Morellino di Scansano Riserva 1995: An extremely well-crafted, elegant red. Concentrated aromas of crushed blackberry and chocolate. Medium-bodied, with well-integrated tannins and a long, silky finish. Drink now.–J.S. • $17 • (12/15/1998) • **90**

Morellino di Scansano Riserva 1993 • $20 • (9/30/1997) • **87**

Morellino di Scansano Riserva 1988 • $NA • (10/31/1993) • **85**

Morellino di Scansano Riserva 1986 • $16 • (6/30/1991) • **86**

Toscana Saffredi 1997: Wow. Stunning Cabernet aromas of mint, dried herb, cassis and tobacco flow from this Tuscan red. It's full-bodied, with loads of flavor and masses of tannins, yet all is in balance. Just give it time to come together. Best after 2002.–J.S. • $80 • (11/30/1999) HR • **95**

Toscana Saffredi 1995: Bold aromas of plum, blackberry, earth and tobacco. Full-bodied, with layers of velvety tannins and a caressing texture. From "the" producer in an up-and-coming region. Best after 2000.–J.S. • $34 • (12/15/1998) • **91**

PUPILLE, FATTORIA LE

Toscana Saffredi 1994 • $46 • (9/30/1997) • **84**
Toscana Saffredi 1993 • $40 • (10/31/1996) • **89**
Toscana Saffredi 1990 • $40 • (2/28/1995) • **88**
Toscana Saffredi 1989 • $NA • (10/31/1993) • **86**
Toscana Saffredi 1988 • $NA • (10/31/1993) • **91**
Toscana Vin Santo SolAlto 1996: Complex and gorgeous, a sweet wine with subtle aromas of nectarines, cream and honey. Full-bodied and very sweet, with lively acidity and a long, sweet and fruity finish. A joy to taste. Drink now.–J.S. • $NA/375 ml. • (12/15/1998) • **91**
Toscana Vin Santo SolAlto 1995: Gorgeous apple, honeycomb and butterscotch aromas. Medium-bodied, medium sweet, with plenty of botrytis spice and honey flavors. Fresh finish. Sticky-wine lovers should search this out; lovely with fresh fruit as dessert. Drink now through 2005.–J.S. • $13/375 ml. • (12/15/1998) • **90**
Toscana Vin Santo 1991 • $32 • (9/30/1997) • **91**

QUERCE, FATTORIA LA

Chianti Classico Caratello 1995 • $14 • (9/30/1997) • **82**
Chianti Classico Caratello 1991 • $9 • (10/31/1993) • **79**
Chianti Classico Caratello 1988 • $9 • (12/15/1990) • **77**
Chianti Classico Caratello 1985 • $10 • (11/30/1987) • **83**

QUERCECCHIO

Brunello di Montalcino 1990 • $NA • (10/31/1995) • **80**
Brunello di Montalcino 1988 • $NA • (4/30/1994) • **79**
Brunello di Montalcino Riserva 1988 • $NA • (10/31/1994) • **88**
Rosso di Montalcino 1993 • $NA • (10/31/1995) • **77**
Rosso di Montalcino 1991 • $NA • (4/30/1994) • **81**

QUERCETO, CASTELLO DI

Chianti Classico 1996: A rather light and slightly mature Sangiovese, with plum, cedar and tobacco character. Light body and finish. Hurry and drink this now.–J.S. • $11 • (11/30/1999) • **80**
Chianti Classico 1994 • $12 • (9/30/1997) • **86**
Chianti Classico 1992 • $9 • (10/31/1995) • **82**
Chianti Classico 1990 • $14 • (10/31/1993) • **85**
Chianti Classico 1989 • $15 • (9/15/1992) • **84**
Chianti Classico 1988 • $14 • (9/15/1991) • **86**
Chianti Classico Cento 1995: A fresh and delicious Chianti, with plum and hints of earth on the nose and palate. Medium-bodied, with silky tannins and a ripe fruit finish. Drink now.–J.S. • $24/1.5 liter • (11/30/1999) • **87**
Chianti Classico Il Picchio Riserva 1994: This needs drinking. Medium-bodied, with red licorice, berry and plum skin aromas, light tannins and a slightly watery finish. Drink now.–J.S. • $26 • (11/30/1999) • **80**
Chianti Classico Il Picchio Riserva 1990 • $27 • (10/31/1995) • **88**
Chianti Classico Il Picchio Riserva 1988 • $NA • (9/15/1992) • **83**
Chianti Classico Riserva 1994: Still fresh but a bit thin. Attractive berry and bark aromas follow through to the light- to medium-bodied palate, with fine tannins and a fresh finish. Drink now.–J.S. • $17 • (11/30/1999) • **82**
Chianti Classico Riserva 1990 • $14 • (2/28/1995) • **87**
Chianti Classico Riserva 1988 • $19 • (9/15/1992) • **86**
Chianti Classico Riserva 1985 • $16 • (11/30/1989) • **91**
Colli della Toscana Centrale Cignale 1995: A thoroughly enjoyable red. Intriguing aromas of cherries and tobacco. Medium-bodied, with silky tannins and a medium, fruity finish. Not imported into the U.S. Drink now through 2003.–J.S. • $NA • (11/30/1999) • **88**
Colli della Toscana Centrale Cignale 1993 • $NA • (9/30/1997) • **89**
Colli della Toscana Centrale Cignale 1989 • $35 • (10/31/1993) • **80**
Colli della Toscana Centrale Cignale 1988 • $40 • (2/28/1995) • **87**
Colli della Toscana Centrale Cignale 1987 • $36 • (2/28/1995) • **89**
Colli della Toscana Centrale Il Querciolaia 1995: Serious winemaking. Aromas of minerals and black licorice, with hints of fruit. Medium-bodied, with well-integrated polished tannins and a long, silky finish. Drink now.–J.S. • $37 • (11/30/1999) • **89**
Colli della Toscana Centrale Il Querciolaia 1988 • $40 • (9/15/1991) • **88**
Colli della Toscana Centrale Il Querciolaia 1986 • $35 • (11/30/1989) • **85**
Colli della Toscana Centrale Il Querciolaia 1985 • $30 • (2/15/1989) • **85**
Colli della Toscana Centrale La Corte 1995: Wonderfully rich and decadent on the nose, with ripe berry, tobacco and earthy character. Full-bodied, with velvety tannins and a medium finish. A bit tight still; give it time. Best after 2000.–J.S. • $33 • (11/30/1999) • **89**
Colli della Toscana Centrale La Corte 1993 • $30 • (9/30/1997) • **89**
Colli della Toscana Centrale La Corte 1988 • $30 • (7/31/1995) • **80**
Colli della Toscana Centrale La Corte 1985 • $20 • (11/30/1989) • **93**
Colli della Toscana Centrale La Corte 1983 • $17 • (11/30/1989) • **83**

QUERCIA AL POGGIO

Chianti Classico 1996: Bright aromas of strawberry, leather and citrus. Medium-bodied, with fresh acidity and a light, fruity aftertaste. Already starting to fade.–J.S. • $14 • (12/15/1998) • **79**
Chianti Classico 1990 • $NA • (10/31/1993) • **85**
Chianti Classico Riserva 1995: Well-crafted, delicate red. Beautiful dried cherry and plum character. Medium-bodied, with rounded tannins and a fruity, smooth-textured finish. Drink now.–J.S. • $18 • (12/15/1998) • **86**
Chianti Classico Riserva 1988 • $NA • (10/31/1993) • **80**

QUERCIABELLA, AGRICOLA

Chianti Classico 1997: A thick and structured Chianti, its aromas of very ripe fruit, bark and wet earth leading to a medium- to full-bodied palate, with full, chewy tannins and a big finish. Needs bottle age. Drink through 2002.–J.S. • $20 • (11/30/1999) SS • **90**
Chianti Classico 1996: A lively and well-structured red. Plenty of crushed blueberry on the nose and palate. Medium-bodied, with sleek tannins and a silky texture. Drink now.–J.S. • $19 • (12/15/1998) • **87**
Chianti Classico 1995 • $17 • (9/30/1997) • **85**
Chianti Classico 1994 • $13 • (10/31/1996) • **85**
Chianti Classico 1988 • $13 • (9/15/1991) • **90**
Chianti Classico Riserva 1996: A serious '96 CC. Blackberry, bark and wet earth character gives this wine a sophisticated style, with medium body, velvety tannins and a long finish. Drink now through 2003.–J.S. • $36 • (11/30/1999) • **89**
Chianti Classico Riserva 1995: Good blackberry and fruity aromas. Medium-bodied, with polished tannins but a slightly short, austere finish. Tasted twice, with consistent notes. Drink now.–J.S. • $30 • (12/15/1998) • **83**
Chianti Classico Riserva 1994 • $25 • (9/30/1997) • **88**
Chianti Classico Riserva 1993 • $NA • (10/31/1996) • **83**
Chianti Classico Riserva 1991 • $NA • (10/31/1995) • **84**
Chianti Classico Riserva 1988 • $20 • (9/15/1992) • **90**
Chianti Classico Riserva 1985 • $17 • (9/15/1991) • **89**
Toscana Batàr White 1997: A good Chardonnay, with pretty aromas of toasted oak, almond and apple. Medium-bodied, with apple pie and vanilla flavors and a medium finish. Drink now.–J.S. • $55 • (11/30/1999) • **87**
Toscana Batàr White 1996: Very woody—like a white Rioja—with some waxy, apple skin character, too. Still, it's stylish and rather interesting on the finish. Medium-bodied. Drink now.–J.S. • $55 • (12/15/1998) • **85**
Toscana Camartina 1995: A big and juicy red. Always a blockbuster. Dark in color, with chocolate, berry and cherry character. Full-bodied and very chewy, with loads of fruit and tannins. Long finish. Cabernet. Needs time. Best after 2002.–J.S. • $55 • (11/30/1999) • **93**
Toscana Camartina 1994: A massive super Tuscan red, though slightly coarse. California Cab lovers rejoice. Terrific aromas of black currants, cherries and dried herbs. Full-bodied, with full, velvety tannins and masses of fruit. Long, slightly austere finish. Best after 2001.–J.S. • $45 • (12/15/1998) • **93**
Toscana Camartina 1993 • $40 • (9/30/1997) • **86**
Toscana Camartina 1991 • $NA • (10/31/1995) • **85**

QUERCIAVALLE

Armonia 1995 • $35 • (9/30/1997) • **87**
Chianti Classico 1996: Ripe plum aromas, with hints of earthiness. Light to medium in body, with soft tannins and a simple, sweetish finish. A bit cloying.–J.S. • $20 • (12/15/1998) • **78**
Chianti Classico 1995 • $15 • (9/30/1997) • **82**
Chianti Classico 1994 • $13 • (10/31/1996) • **81**
Chianti Classico Querciavalle 1990 • $10 • (7/31/1994) • **85**
Chianti Classico Riserva 1995: Old-style, with slightly cheesy, leathery and plummy aromas and flavors. Medium-bodied, with light tannins and finish. A bit tired.–J.S. • $30 • (12/15/1998) • **77**
Chianti Classico Riserva 1994 • $22 • (9/30/1997) • **84**

Key: SS—Spectator Selection. CS—Cellar Selection. HR—Highly Recommended. $NA—Price not available. (BT)—Barrel tasting. Ⓐ—Auction Price.
For a key to the tasters' initials, see "How to Use These Listings."
Dates in parentheses represent the issues in which the ratings were published.

Chianti Classico Riserva 1993 • $18 • (10/31/1996) • **76**
Val d'Arbia 1997: Aromas and flavors of canned fruit salad dominate. Medium-bodied, with moderate acidity. Hard to like.–J.S. • $13 • (12/15/1998) • **77**

QUINTARELLI, GIUSEPPE

Amarone della Valpolicella Classico 1991 • $98 • (6/15/1998) • **92**
Valpolicella Classico Superiore 1991 • $28 • (6/15/1998) • **84**

RAGOSE, LE

Amarone della Valpolicella 1991 • $48 • (5/31/1998) • **85**

RAINOLDI

Valtellina Fruttaio Ca ' Rizzieri Sfursat 1996: Medium-bodied, dry and mouthpuckering, with rather funky, burnt fruit aromas. Drinkable, but not very fresh.–J.S. • $33 • (1/01/2000) • **76**
Valtellina Superiòre Il Crespino 1996: Attractive floral and berry aromas follow through to the palate, but it's slightly short and watery at the end.–J.S. • $25 • (1/01/2000) • **79**
Valtellina Superiòre Inferno 1995: Decent floral and berry character. Light-bodied, with some fruit, but slightly dry and short on the finish.–J.S. • $14 • (1/01/2000) • **79**
Valtellina Superiòre Inferno Barrique 1995: Old and uninteresting. Grapey, jammy aromas turn rather sour and dried out. Barely holding on. Tasted twice, with consistent notes.–J.S. • $23 • (1/01/2000) • **71**

RAMPA DI FUGNANO, LA

Chianti Colli Senesi Via dei Franchi 1997: Fresh and fruity, with lots of grape and plum character and fresh acidity. Light body and finish. Drink now.–J.S. • $12 • (11/30/1999) • **82**
Colli della Toscana Centrale Bombereto 1997: Slightly rustic but showing impressively vivid aromas of ripe plum and berry. Better than the '96. Full-bodied, with chewy tannins that are slightly dry on the finish. Still, there's plenty of fruit. Best after 2001.–J.S. • $21 • (11/30/1999) • **87**
Colli della Toscana Centrale Bombereto 1996: A very ripe, strong, slightly rustic wine. Very peppery, with lots of ripe fruit. Full-bodied and chewy, with a raisin and pepper aftertaste. Drink now through 2001.–J.S. • $21 • (11/30/1999) • **84**
Colli della Toscana Centrale Gisele 1997: This outstanding new-wave Merlot is the essence of ripe berries. Black in color, with incredible aromas of crushed raspberry, currant and berry and a hint of mint. Full-bodied, with lots of concentrated fruit and ripe tannins. Built for aging. Best after 2004.–J.S. • $45 • (11/30/1999) • **91**
Vernaccia di San Gimignano Alata 1998: A white with herbal, almost geraniumlike aromas and hints of lemon rind. Medium-bodied, with fresh acidity and a light finish. Drink now.–J.S. • $14 • (11/30/1999) • **81**
Vernaccia di San Gimignano Privato 1998: A white with fresh and enjoyable aromas of pear, flowers and melon. Medium-bodied, with good acidity and a delicious flint, blanched almond and melon aftertaste. Drink now.–J.S. • $23 • (11/30/1999) • **87**

RAMPOLLA, CASTELLO DEI

Chianti Classico 1995 • $20 • (9/30/1997) • **80**
Chianti Classico 1994 • $18 • (10/31/1996) • **83**
Chianti Classico 1992 • $17 • (10/31/1995) • **75**
Chianti Classico 1989 • $17 • (12/15/1992) • **80**
Chianti Classico 1988 • $14 • (9/15/1992) • **87**
Chianti Classico 1987 • $15 • (4/15/1991) • **84**
Chianti Classico Riserva 1996: A bit earthy and mouthpuckering but with lots of ripe fruit and structure for a Chianti. Full-bodied, with berry, green tobacco and cherry character and full tannins. Slightly monolithic and rustic. Best after 2000.–J.S. • $37 • (11/30/1999) • **87**
Chianti Classico Riserva 1995: Rich and decadent, with tobacco, berry and leafy aromas and flavors. Medium to full in body, with medium, velvety tannins and a smoky, fruity aftertaste. Drink now.–J.S. • $35 • (12/15/1998) • **87**
Chianti Classico Riserva 1994 • $34 • (9/30/1997) • **85**
Chianti Classico Riserva 1993 • $31 • (10/31/1996) • **81**
Chianti Classico Riserva 1991 • $28 • (10/31/1995) • **86**
Chianti Classico Riserva 1990 • $25 • (2/28/1995) • **88**
Chianti Classico Riserva 1988 • $19 • (5/15/1993) • **88**
Chianti Classico Riserva 1985 • $16 • (4/30/1990) • **81**
Toscana Sammarco 1996: A thoroughly caressing and delicious red. Very pretty, with rose, berry, plum and coffee aromas. Full-bodied, with soft and velvety tannins and a long, ripe fruit finish. Drink now through 2005.–J.S. • $65 • (11/30/1999) • **91**
Toscana Sammarco 1995: A big, juicy and voluptuous red with lots of everything. Intense aromas of berry, currant and chocolate follow through to the full-bodied palate. Loads of concentrated fruit and velvety tannins. Long, long finish. Best after 2001.–J.S. • $NA • (12/15/1998) • **93**
Toscana Sammarco 1994 • $65 • (9/30/1997) • **92**
Toscana Sammarco 1993 • $58 • (10/31/1996) CS • **90**
Toscana Sammarco 1991 • $58 • (10/31/1995) • **87**
Toscana Sammarco 1990 • $94 Ⓐ • (10/31/1995) • **91**
Toscana Sammarco 1986 • $46 • (3/15/1991) • **76**
Toscana Sammarco 1985 • $124 Ⓐ • (11/30/1989) • **90**
Toscana Sammarco 1983 • $28 • (9/15/1988) • **88**
Toscana Vigna d'Alceo 1997: Even better than the superb 1996, this young wine has an amazing amount of pure fruit. A thick and rich Cabernet, with loads of tar, green tobacco, currant and fruit character. Full-bodied, with chewy tannins and a tobacco and wet earth aftertaste. Seriously well structured yet wonderfully harmonious. Best after 2003.–J.S. • $85 • (11/30/1999) • **97**
Toscana Vigna d'Alceo 1996: A new wine from Rampolla, potentially the Château Mouton-Rothschild of Tuscany. A fabulous, superbly structured red, overflowing with black currant, lead pencil and mint aromas. Full-bodied, with layers of velvety tannins and a long aftertaste of ripe fruit and spearmint. Gorgeous. A blend of Cabernet Sauvignon and Petit Verdot. Best after 2004.–J.S. • $NA • (12/15/1998) • **95**
Trebbiano Toscana Vendemmia Tardiva 1998: A good late-harvest white from Tuscany, with interesting aromas of dried pineapple, apricot and fresh fruit. Medium-bodied and medium sweet, with slightly raised acidity and a lively finish. Not imported into the U.S. Drink now.–J.S. • $NA • (1/01/1999) • **85**
Trebbiano Toscana Vendemmia Tardiva 1996: Break out the foie gras for this wine. Like a light-bodied Sauternes with hints of hay on the nose and palate. Medium-bodied, medium sweet, with raisin and allspice character. Fresh finish. Drink now.–J.S. • $NA • (12/15/1998) • **87**

RAPITALA

Alcamo 1996 • $NA • (10/15/1997) • **79**

RASCIONI CECCONELLO

Toscana Poggio Capitana 1994: Not completely clean, with earthy barnyard aromas dominating the nose and a dry, slightly tough palate.–J.S. • $22 • (6/30/1999) • **76**
Toscana Poggio Ciliegio 1996: Has intense ripe berry character, but it's very, very oaky, with a dry, almost papery aftertaste. Tasted twice, with consistent notes.–J.S. • $29 • (6/30/1999) • **75**

RATTI, RENATO

Barbaresco 1994 • $29 • (1/31/1998) • **85**
Barbaresco 1990 • $26 • (10/31/1994) • **85**
Barbaresco 1989 • $31 • (10/31/1994) • **73**
Barbera d'Alba Torriglione 1997: Exotic. Lovely violet, grilled and toasted scents blend on the palate with wild berry, ginger and cacao. Medium- to full-bodied, with a chewy texture that should smooth out with cellaring or the right food. Drink through 2003.–P.M. • $NA • (11/15/1999) • **89**
Barbera d'Alba Torriglione 1994 • $18 • (10/31/1997) • **88**
Barbera Piedmont 1995 • $13 • (1/31/1998) • **79**
Barolo 1993 • $35 • (1/31/1998) • **86**
Barolo 1990 • $31 • (10/31/1994) • **85**
Barolo 1989 • $28 • (10/31/1994) • **79**
Barolo 1985 • $23 • (9/15/1990) • **85**
Barolo 1983 • $20 • (10/15/1988) • **87**
Barolo 1982 • $17 • (6/30/1987) CS • **93**
Barolo 1980 • $10 • (2/15/1987) • **83**
Barolo Conca Marcenasco 1993 • $60 • (10/31/1997) • **85**
Barolo Conca Marcenasco 1988 • $NA • (10/31/1993) • **78**
Barolo Marcenasco 1995: More elegant than powerful, showing delicate mineral, smoke, game and red berry character. Balanced and just delicious. Integrated and ripe tannins give length and backbone to this medium-bodied red. Drink now through 2005.–P.M. • $NA • (11/15/1999) • **89**
Barolo Marcenasco 1994: Light-bodied and a bit dry, with only modest fruit character and lacking in ripe flavors.–P.M. • $48 • (10/31/1998) • **76**

ITALY

RATTI, RENATO

Barolo Marcenasco 1993 • $40 • (10/31/1997) • **90**
Barolo Marcenasco 1992 • $31 • (10/31/1996) • **83**
Barolo Marcenasco 1991 • $33 • (10/31/1995) • **84**
Barolo Marcenasco 1990 • $36 • (10/31/1994) • **91**
Barolo Marcenasco 1989 • $40 • (10/31/1994) • **87**
Barolo Marcenasco 1988 • $NA • (10/31/1993) • **84**
Barolo Marcenasco 1985 • $37 • (10/15/1990) • **82**
Barolo Marcenasco 1982 • $23 • (6/30/1987) • **90**
Barolo Marcenasco 1981 • $15 • (6/30/1987) • **84**
Barolo Marcenasco Rocche 1995: A bit on the light side, with chocolate, rose petal, tar, forest underbrush and black cherry notes. Rather elegant, coming to maturity. Not imported into the U.S. Drink now through 2002.–P.M. • $NA • (1/01/1999) • **82**
Barolo Marcenasco Rocche 1993 • $60 • (10/31/1997) • **86**
Barolo Marcenasco Rocche 1989 • $NA • (10/31/1993) • **81**
Barolo Marcenasco Rocche 1988 • $NA • (10/31/1993) • **79**
Barolo Marcenasco Rocche 1983 • $30 • (1/31/1989) • **86**
Barolo Marcenasco Rocche 1981 • $19 • (6/30/1987) • **88**
Cabernet Sauvignon Piedmont 1989 • $25 • (6/15/1994) • **83**
Dolcetto d'Alba 1998: A bit herbal, with crisp flavors. Not imported into the U.S.–P.M. • $14 • (1/01/1999) • **77**
Dolcetto d'Alba 1997: Very pretty, supple and smooth, this is a delight to drink for all the fresh berry and subtle oak accents. Medium in body, refined in texture, with a ripe, plummy character on the lingering finish. Drink now.–P.M. • $16 • (10/31/1998) • **88**
Dolcetto d'Alba 1996 • $14 • (10/31/1997) • **78**
Dolcetto d'Alba 1995 • $13 • (10/31/1996) • **89**
Dolcetto d'Alba 1993 • $10 • (7/31/1995) • **86**
Dolcetto d'Alba Colombè 1998: A bit gamy but with pretty berry notes, a sweet tannin structure and appealing chalk dust, olive and cherry pit flavors. Not imported into the U.S. Drink now.–P.M. • $16 • (1/01/1999) • **84**
Dolcetto d'Alba Colombè 1997: Clean, juicy and fresh, with vibrant berry, a bit of wet earth, mocha, spice and freshly ground coffee beans. Of medium body, with a fairly crisp finish. Tasted twice, with consistent notes. Drink now.–P.M. • $18 • (10/31/1998) • **81**
I Cedri V 1995: A firm and focused Italian red made in an international style, with an appealing core of sweet cherry, plum and spice flavors. Smooth and rich, with a nice gamy note on the finish. Drink now through 2002.–K.M. • $33 • (8/31/1998) • **87**
Monferrato Villa Pattono 1997: Medium-bodied, with appealing licorice, blackberry, black cherry and tar notes. A fresh character on the finish adds to its personality. Not imported into the U.S. Drink now through 2002.–P.M. • $NA • (1/01/1999) • **85**
Nebbiolo d'Alba 1993 • $18 • (10/31/1995) • **82**
Nebbiolo d'Alba Occhetti 1995 • $16 • (10/31/1997) • **79**
Villa Pattono V 1995: A rich, sculpted red, with appealing spice, chocolate and sweet cherry flavors and a pleasant finish. A blend of Barbera, Freisa, Merlot and Cabernet. Drink now through 2001.–K.M. • $31 • (8/31/1998) • **84**
Villa Pattono IV 1994 • $22 • (10/31/1997) • **85**
Villa Pattono 1993 • $23 • (10/31/1996) • **74**
Villa Pattono 1989 • $18 • (10/31/1994) • **83**

RAVIZZA, VISCONTI CASSINIS

Barbera del Monferrato Cantico della Crosia 1997: A well-made, round, dense Barbera. The toasted oak is nicely balanced by ripe black fruit and a floral character. Medium-bodied, with supple tannins, nice acidity and a lingering, smoky finish. Not imported into the U.S. Drink now through 2002.–P.M. • $NA • (1/01/1999) • **87**
Barbera del Monferrato Superiòre 1997: Fruity and flavorful. Light-bodied, with a pungent cranberry and spice character and strong, almost hot chili pepper flavors on the finish. Drink now through 2001.–P.M. • $15 • (11/15/1999) • **81**
Barbera del Monferrato Volpulva 1998: Sweet cassis, blackberry and bell pepper flavors burst forth in this medium-bodied, chewy and flavorful red. Not imported into the U.S. Drink now through 2002.–P.M. • $NA • (1/01/1999) • **80**
Monferrato L 'Uccelletta 1997: Light-colored and a bit washed up, this tastes diffused and confused, with sweet flavors of licorice and strawberry. Not imported into the U.S.–P.M. • $NA • (1/01/1999) • **73**

Key: SS—Spectator Selection. CS—Cellar Selection. HR—Highly Recommended. $NA—Price not available. (BT)—Barrel tasting. (A)—Auction Price. For a key to the tasters' initials, see "How to Use These Listings."
Dates in parentheses represent the issues in which the ratings were published.

Monferrato Rubello 1997: Fresh and vibrant, with black cherry, floral and cassis bush character. Good acidity combined with toast and spice character make for a flavorful ensemble. Drink now through 2003.–P.M. • $18 • (11/15/1999) • **87**

REDI

Rosso di Montepulciano Argo et Non Briareo 1998: Rather light and simple, with dried cherry and cedar character and a slight cooked-fruit aftertaste. –J.S. • $16 • (11/30/1999) • **79**
Rosso di Montepulciano Argo et Non Briareo 1997: A delicious young red. Very grapey, with a peppery component. Medium-bodied, with velvety tannins and a chocolaty aftertaste. Drink now.–J.S. • $14 • (12/15/1998) • **85**
Toscana Riccio 1997: An interesting, pleasant, fruity white. Cream, butter and banana aromas, with a hint of dough. Medium-bodied, with fresh acidity and a clean, appley aftertaste. A blend of Grechetto, Viognier and Sauvignon. Drink now.–J.S. • $20 • (12/15/1998) • **85**
Vin Santo 1990: A thick and rich Vin Santo, with almond, honey and orange peel character. Full-bodied and very sweet, with a medium finish. A bit clumsy, but showing very good concentration. Not imported into the U.S. Drink now through 2002.–J.S. • $NA/375 ml. • (1/01/1999) • **87**
Vino Nobile di Montepulciano Briareo 1996: A lovely and fresh Sangiovese, with cherry and plum aromas and flavors. Medium-bodied, with fine tannins and a fresh finish. Drink now through 2001.–J.S. • $35 • (11/30/1999) • **85**
Vino Nobile di Montepulciano Briareo 1995: Good fruit but slightly rustic, with bright cherry and strawberry aromas and flavors. Medium-bodied, with a hint of cut grass and velvety tannins. Drink now.–J.S. • $33 • (12/15/1998) • **84**
Vino Nobile di Montepulciano Briareo 1994 • $NA • (9/30/1997) • **87**
Vino Nobile di Montepulciano Riserva 1995: Thoroughly pleasant Vino Nobile. Lots of plum, berry and hints of mint in this red. Medium-bodied, with silky tannins and a fresh finish. Drink now.–J.S. • $28 • (11/30/1999) • **85**
Vino Nobile di Montepulciano Riserva 1994: Round and easy, with tobacco, berry and cherry aromas and flavors. Medium-bodied, with a soft finish. Drink now.–J.S. • $23 • (12/15/1998) • **83**

REGNI, GIORGIO

Chianti Classico 1996: Supercharged Chianti. Very fruity, with crushed raspberries oozing from the glass. Medium- to full-bodied, with firm yet polished tannins and a long, fruity, slightly peppery finish. Drink now through 2002.–J.S. • $18 • (12/15/1998) • **87**
Chianti Classico 1994 • $28 • (10/31/1996) • **83**
Chianti Classico 1993 • $NA • (10/31/1995) • **84**
Chianti Classico 1992 • $13 • (2/28/1995) • **86**
Chianti Classico 1990 • $NA • (10/31/1993) • **90**
Chianti Classico 1988 • $19 • (9/15/1991) • **83**
Chianti Classico Riserva 1995: Blueberry and floral aromas, with hints of porcini. Medium-bodied, with fine tannins. Seems to need a little more fruit on the finish but very good all the same. Drink now.–J.S. • $28 • (12/15/1998) • **86**
Chianti Classico Riserva 1990 • $25 • (2/28/1995) • **93**
Chianti Classico Riserva 1985 • $20 • (9/15/1991) • **92**
Toscana Convivio 1995: Interesting minty, blackberry, herbal and cherry character with hints of tar. Medium-bodied, with moderate tannins and a delicate, fruity finish. Slightly disappointing for this producer. Drink now.–J.S. • $50 • (12/15/1998) • **83**
Toscana Convivio 1991 • $30 • (2/28/1995) • **91**
Toscana Convivio 1990 • $NA • (10/31/1993) • **93**

RICASOLI, BARONE

Chianti 1998: Dried cherry and smoked almond aromas. Light- to medium-bodied, with light tannins and a fruity finish. Drink now.–J.S. • $11 • (11/30/1999) • **83**
Chianti 1997: Very clean and fruity, with cherry and mineral notes throughout. Light-bodied, with light tannins and a fresh, fruity aftertaste. Drink now.–J.S. • $9 • (12/15/1998) • **83**
Chianti 1996 • $8 • (9/30/1997) • **83**
Chianti 1995 • $7 • (10/31/1996) • **79**
Chianti 1994 • $7 • (10/31/1995) • **80**
Chianti 1993 • $7 • (2/28/1995) • **79**
Chianti 1990 • $6 • (11/30/1991) • **81**
Chianti 1989 • $7 • (4/15/1991) • **83**
Chianti Classico 1994 • $8 • (10/31/1996) • **85**

Chianti Classico 1993 • $8 • (10/31/1995) • **81**
Chianti Classico Riserva 1994 • $14 • (9/30/1997) • **85**
Chianti Classico Riserva 1993 • $11 • (10/31/1996) • **85**
Chianti Classico Riserva 1990 • $12 • (10/31/1995) • **82**
Chianti Classico Rocca Guicciardi Riserva 1996: Upfront and fruity, with pretty blackberry and floral character and hints of earth. Medium-bodied, with medium tannins, fresh acidity and a fruity finish. Drink now through 2002.–J.S. • $18 • (11/30/1999) • **87**
Chianti Classico Rocca Guicciardi Riserva 1995: There's an enticing blueberry and cherry quality to this wine, with medium body, light tannins and a crisp finish. Drink now.–J.S. • $18 • (12/15/1998) • **86**
Chianti Classico San Ripolo 1997: A subtle, simple Chianti, with plenty of dried cherry and blackberry character. Medium-bodied, with fine tannins, crisp acidity and a caressing texture. Drink now.–J.S. • $16 • (11/30/1999) • **85**
Chianti Classico San Ripolo 1996: Simple and fruity, with light body, fresh fruit and crisp acidity. Serve slightly chilled. Drink now.–J.S. • $12 • (12/15/1998) • **80**
Chianti Classico San Ripolo 1995 • $10 • (9/30/1997) • **85**
Chianti Classico San Ripolo 1988 • $10 • (10/31/1991) • **84**
Chianti Classico San Ripolo 1987 • $10 • (4/15/1991) • **79**
Orvieto Classico 1997 • $8 • (1/01/1998) • **81**
Orvieto Classico 1996 • $8 • (10/31/1997) • **78**
Sangiovese Toscana Formulae 1997: This good, no-nonsense Sangiovese '97 has pretty dried cherry character. Light- to medium-bodied, with a fresh finish. Drink now.–J.S. • $14 • (11/30/1999) • **83**
Sangiovese Toscana Formulae 1996: A round and fruity red with just a touch of vanilla. Light- to medium-bodied, with light tannins and a slightly diluted finish. Drink now.–J.S. • $13 • (12/15/1998) • **82**
Sangiovese Toscana Formulae 1995 • $12 • (7/31/1997) • **85**
Tremalvo 1987 • $18 • (12/15/1991) • **87**
Vin Santo 1990: Dark gold, with an amber hue. Intense aromas of dried fruit, marmalade and cedar. Slightly oxidized but nothing out of the norm. Medium-bodied and medium sweet, with a smoke, apricot and cedar aftertaste. Not the sweetest Vin Santo I have had, but traditional in style and delicious. Drink now.–J.S. • $12/375 ml. • (12/15/1998) • **87**

RIECINE

Chianti Classico 1997: A moreish, juicy CC, with pretty aromas of plum, berry and bark. Medium- to full-bodied, with well-integrated tannins and a rich finish. Lovely harmony. Drink now through 2001.–J.S. • $23 • (11/30/1999) • **90**
Chianti Classico 1996: Stunning aromas in this young wine; absolutely gorgeous vivid aromas of cherries, blueberries and hints of new oak. Medium-bodied, with fine tannins and a silky texture. Drink now through 2002.–J.S. • $20 • (12/15/1998) • **89**
Chianti Classico 1995 • $20 • (9/30/1997) • **87**
Chianti Classico 1994 • $22 • (10/31/1996) • **86**
Chianti Classico 1992 • $NA • (2/28/1995) • **80**
Chianti Classico 1991 • $21 • (10/31/1993) • **86**
Chianti Classico 1990 • $22 • (9/15/1992) • **80**
Chianti Classico 1988 • $22 • (4/30/1991) • **89**
Chianti Classico 1987 • $20 • (4/30/1991) • **83**
Chianti Classico Riserva 1996: A very good CC, with vivid aromas of crushed raspberry and cherry. Medium-bodied, with well-integrated tannins and a medium finish. Drink now through 2001.–J.S. • $40 • (11/30/1999) • **86**
Chianti Classico Riserva 1995: Depth of fruit on the nose and palate, ranging from blackberry to chocolate. Full-bodied, with chunky, chewy tannins covered with ripe and exciting fruit. A gorgeous, voluptuous red. Best after 2000.–J.S. • $35 • (12/15/1998) • **90**
Chianti Classico Riserva 1994 • $33 • (9/30/1997) • **88**
Chianti Classico Riserva 1993 • $34 • (10/31/1996) • **87**
Chianti Classico Riserva 1991 • $35 • (10/31/1995) • **88**
Chianti Classico Riserva 1990 • $NA • (2/28/1995) • **88**
Chianti Classico Riserva 1988 • $24 • (9/15/1992) • **82**
Chianti Classico Riserva 1985 • $19 • (9/15/1991) • **87**
Toscana La Gioia 1997: Super class in a glass. Wonderful aromas of berry, cherry, raspberry and mint. Full-bodied, with very fine tannins and a long, long aftertaste of ripe fruit and mint. Drink through 2005.–J.S. • $53 • (11/30/1999) • **93**
Toscana La Gioia 1996: Extremely well crafted—as always. Dark, with beautiful aromas of berry, raspberry and mint. Full-bodied, with velvety tannins and a fruit and berry aftertaste. Best after 2000.–J.S. • $53 • (11/30/1999) • **90**
Toscana La Gioia 1995: Silky and caressing, with violet and berry, a hint of vanilla character. Medium body and tannins, racy finish. Riecine is an estate on the rise, and its super Tuscan Sangiovese has always been first rate. Drink through 2006.–J.S. • $45 • (12/15/1998) • **90**
Toscana La Gioia 1994 • $40 • (9/30/1997) • **90**
Toscana La Gioia 1993 • $41 • (10/31/1996) • **89**
Toscana La Gioia 1991 • $42 • (10/31/1995) • **89**
Toscana La Gioia 1990 • $45 • (10/31/1995) • **90**
Toscana La Gioia 1988 • $65 • (9/15/1991) • **91**
Toscana La Gioia 1987 • $45 • (4/30/1991) • **82**

RIETINE

Chianti Classico 1997: Plenty of blackberry and boysenberry character in this Chianti. Medium-bodied, with silky tannins and a very good fruit concentration. Tasted twice, with consistent notes. Drink now through 2001.–J.S. • $13 • (11/30/1999) • **87**
Chianti Classico 1996: An exemplary young Chianti. Attractive aromas of crushed plum and raspberry open to a medium-bodied palate with delicate tannins and a fruity aftertaste. Drink now.–J.S. • $11 • (12/15/1998) • **85**
Chianti Classico 1995 • $NA • (9/30/1997) • **86**
Chianti Classico 1994 • $NA • (10/31/1996) • **79**
Chianti Classico 1992 • $NA • (10/31/1995) • **83**
Chianti Classico Riserva 1995: Seriously good for a riserva. Wonderful aromas of bright crushed raspberries and hints of wet earth. Full-bodied, with polished silky tannins and a lovely fruity finish. Could use a bit more fruit concentration. Drink now.–J.S. • $17 • (11/30/1999) • **88**
Chianti Classico Riserva 1994: Very good. Still rather closed, but showing some alluring dried cherry and berry with hints of vanilla. Medium-bodied, with firm tannins and a fresh and fruity finish. Drink now through 2001. –J.S. • $16 • (12/15/1998) • **87**
Chianti Classico Riserva 1991 • $NA • (10/31/1995) • **84**
Colli della Toscana Centrale White 1997: Some good apple and almond aromas and flavors in this white. Medium-bodied, with moderate acidity and a mineral aftertaste. Drink now.–J.S. • $10 • (12/15/1998) • **83**
Colli della Toscana Centrale Tiziano 1995: Big, juicy, chewy young red. Dark-colored, with masses of cassis, mint and spice character. Full-bodied, with lots of fruit and velvety tannins. Long finish. Drink through 2003. –J.S. • $16 • (11/30/1999) • **90**
Colli della Toscana Centrale Tiziano 1994: An extremely well-crafted red. Essence of raspberry and cream aromas. Full-bodied, with well-integrated tannins and a silky finish. I always like this wine. Drink through 2001. –J.S. • $25 • (12/15/1998) • **90**
Colli della Toscana Centrale Tiziano 1993 • $NA • (9/30/1997) • **88**
Colli della Toscana Centrale Tiziano 1990 • $NA • (10/31/1995) • **85**
Toscana White 1998: A bit one-dimensional, with vanilla and apple skin character. Medium-bodied, with medium acidity. Drink now.–J.S. • $11 • (11/30/1999) • **84**
Toscana White 1996 • $NA • (9/30/1997) • **82**

RIGHETTI, LUIGI

Amarone della Valpolicella Capitel de Roari 1983 • $16 • (2/15/1989) • **90**
Amarone della Valpolicella Classico Capitel de ' Roari 1991 • $20 • (6/15/1998) • **85**
Amarone della Valpolicella Classico Capitel de Roari 1990 • $20 • (4/30/1996) HR • **90**
Valpolicella Classico Superiòre Campolieti 1994 • $11 • (6/15/1998) • **84**
Valpolicella Classico Superiòre Campolieti 1993 • $10 • (12/15/1995) • **85**
Veneto Valcaia 1994 • $17 • (5/31/1998) • **86**

RINALDI, GIUSEPPE

Barolo 1992 • $NA • (10/31/1996) • **78**
Barolo Brunate 1991 • $NA • (10/31/1996) • **86**
Barolo Brunate Le Coste 1994: A bit neutral in aroma, with some chestnut, walnut, tar and plum flavors. Lots of drying tannins on the finish.–P.M. • $46 • (10/31/1998) • **78**
Barolo Brunate Riserva 1989 • $38 • (10/31/1994) • **80**

RINALDI & FIGLI, FRANCESCO

Barbaresco 1985 • $23 • (9/15/1990) • **87**
Barbaresco 1983 • $16 • (1/31/1989) • **79**
Barbera d'Alba 1996 • $12 • (10/31/1997) • **81**

RINALDI & FIGLI, FRANCESCO

Barbera d'Alba 1993 • $13 • (10/31/1995) • **85**
Barbera d'Alba 1991 • $12 • (9/30/1993) • **86**
Barbera d'Alba 1989 • $13 • (10/31/1992) • **89**
Barbera d'Alba 1987 • $10 • (3/15/1991) • **87**
Barolo 1988 • $23 • (9/15/1993) • **79**
Barolo 1986 • $22 • (7/15/1991) • **83**
Barolo 1983 • $NA • (9/15/1988) • **84**
Barolo 1982 • $16 • (9/15/1988) • **83**
Barolo 1978 • $12 • (9/16/1984) • **89**
Barolo 1947 • $NA • (5/31/1997) • **74**
Barolo Brunate Riserva 1988 • $30 • (10/31/1993) • **71**
Barolo Brunate Riserva 1985 • $24 • (7/15/1991) • **89**
Barolo Brunate Riserva 1982 • $27 • (6/30/1987) • **79**
Barolo Cannubbio 1995: Bright cassis, wild raspberry and blackberry burst out of this vibrant, crisp, full-bodied Barolo. Made in a bright, pure style, with firm tannins on the juicy, vanilla- and mocha-scented finish. Best after 2001.–P.M. • $58 • (11/15/1999) • **87**
Barolo Cannubbio 1993: Delicious, with plenty of ripe fruit and good balance and intensity. Medium-bodied, it delivers plum, fig and blackberry, with a touch of oak-influenced spice and mocha. Supple and ripe tannins are the best part of this lovely, well-made package. Drink now through 2005.–P.M. • $46 • (10/31/1998) • **89**
Barolo Cannubbio 1990 • $NA • (10/31/1994) • **89**
Barolo Cannubbio 1989 • $NA • (10/31/1994) • **79**
Barolo Cannubbio 1988 • $30 • (10/31/1993) • **83**
Barolo Cannubbio 1985 • $25 • (6/15/1990) • **78**
Barolo Cannubbio 1982 • $16 • (10/31/1987) • **75**
Barolo La Brunata 1995: Well made. Nice, ripe fruit in this Barolo, with cassis jam, black cherry and blackberry character. Toasted spice and mocha notes kick in on the attractive, multidimensional finish. Drink now through 2005.–P.M. • $48 • (11/15/1999) • **89**
Barolo La Brunata 1993: A well-made Barolo, not overly extracted, delivering supple tannins and ripe fruit in a medium-bodied package. With its currant, plum and black cherry notes—and little obvious oak—it's pleasant to try now, but can hold. Drink now through 2003.–P.M. • $42 • (10/31/1998) • **88**
Dolcetto d'Alba 1989 • $12 • (7/15/1991) • **80**
Dolcetto d'Alba Roussot 1991 • $12 • (9/30/1993) • **76**
Dolcetto d'Alba Roussot 1990 • $13 • (10/31/1992) • **78**
Dolcetto d'Alba Roussot 1988 • $10 • (7/15/1991) • **78**

RIO GRANDE

Chardonnay Umbria Colle delle Montecchie 1998: A flavorful white, with attractive pear and melon aromas. Medium-bodied, with lots of good flavors and a long, intense aftertaste of peach and other fruit. Tasted twice, with consistent notes. Not imported into the U.S. Drink now through 2001.–J.S. • $NA • (1/01/2000) • **87**
Chardonnay Umbria Colle delle Montecchie 1996 • $8 • (6/15/1998) • **79**
Umbria Casa Pastore 1997: Loads of crushed raspberry and plum on the nose. Full-bodied, with lovely ripe berry and pepper flavors, medium tannins and a long finish. Tasted twice, with consistent notes. Not imported into the U.S. Best after 2000.–J.S. • $NA • (1/01/2000) • **87**
Umbria Casa Pastore 1995 • $24 • (6/15/1998) • **83**

RIPA, FATTORIA LA

Chianti Classico 1997: A beautifully crafted Chianti Classico, with enticing aromas of plum, fresh mushroom and berry. Medium-bodied, with a compact, rich fruit structure and lovely, velvety tannins. Drink now through 2001.–J.S. • $14 • (11/30/1999) • **88**
Chianti Classico 1996: Light and fruity, with a somewhat diluted but clean dried cherry character and a fresh finish.–J.S. • $12 • (12/15/1998) • **78**
Chianti Classico 1995 • $14 • (9/30/1997) • **78**
Chianti Classico 1994 • $12 • (10/31/1996) • **78**
Chianti Classico 1993 • $10 • (10/31/1995) • **77**
Chianti Classico Riserva 1996: Interesting aromas of bark, berry and cherry. Medium-bodied, with well-integrated tannins and a medium, fruity finish. Drink now.–J.S. • $20 • (11/30/1999) • **84**

Key: SS—Spectator Selection. CS—Cellar Selection. HR—Highly Recommended. $NA—Price not available. (BT)—Barrel tasting. (A)—Auction Price.
For a key to the tasters' initials, see "How to Use These Listings."
Dates in parentheses represent the issues in which the ratings were published.

Chianti Classico Riserva 1995: Refreshing and fruity, with very fine, delicate tannins, focused fruit and a crisp finish. Delicious. Drink now.–J.S. • $16 • (12/15/1998) • **85**
Chianti Classico Riserva 1993 • $19 • (10/31/1996) • **77**
Colli della Toscana Centrale Bianco della Lega 1997: A simple, somewhat rustic white, with watermelon and mineral character. Light-bodied, with moderate acidity and a slightly cloying aftertaste.–J.S. • $10 •(12/15/1998) • **78**
Colli della Toscana Centrale Bianco della Lega 1996 • $12 • (9/30/1997) • **82**
Colli della Toscana Centrale Santa Brigida 1997: A serious red, with loads of currant, berry and mint character jumping out of the glass. Full-bodied, with polished, silky tannins and a medium finish. Best after 2000.–J.S. • $21 • (11/30/1999) • **90**
Colli della Toscana Centrale Santa Brigida 1995: An up-front, drink-me-now wine. Incredibly aromatic, with grapes and cherry gushing from the glass. Medium in body, with light to medium tannins and a fresh finish.–J.S. • $16 • (12/15/1998) • **87**
Colli della Toscana Centrale Santa Brigida 1993 • $17 • (10/31/1996) • **82**
Colli della Toscana Centrale Santa Brigida 1990 • $15 • (10/31/1995) • **73**

RISECCOLI, TENUTA DI

Chianti Classico 1997: Blackberry and dried mushroom character galore. Medium-bodied, with soft tannins and a fruity finish. Drink now.–J.S. • $17 • (11/30/1999) • **85**
Chianti Classico Riserva 1996: A straightforward '96 Chianti, with berry and bark character, medium body, light tannins and a light finish. Drink now.–J.S. • $25 • (11/30/1999) • **83**
Toscana Saeculum 1996: Slightly one-dimensional, but with a good level of fruit for the vintage. Dark ruby, with dried herb and currant aromas. Medium-bodied, with plenty of tannins and a medium finish. Slightly hollow midpalate. Drink now.–J.S. • $40 • (11/30/1999) • **85**

RITRATTI

Pinot Nero Trentino 1991 • $12 • (2/28/1995) • **78**

RIVETTI, FRATELLI

Barbera d'Alba Cairel 1990 • $12 • (6/15/1994) • **82**
Nebbiolo d'Alba Vigneto Rainè 1990 • $14 • (6/15/1994) • **86**

RIVETTI & FIGLI, GIUSEPPE

Barbaresco Vigneto Gallina Vürsù 1996: Well made in a modern, new-wave style, tasting of toasted, violet-scented, grilled barriques, with mocha and vanilla but also ripe, lush fruit. Quite extracted and tannic, with a chewy finish. Drink now through 2004.–P.M. • $60 • (10/31/1999) • **91**
Barbaresco Vigneto Starderi Vürsù 1996: Toasted in a "new-wave" style, with violet, smoke and blackberry notes. Full-bodied, harshly tannic and highly extracted, from the dark saturated color to the concentrated flavors and sweet-tasting but firm finish. Hopefully time will soften the tough tannins. Best from 2003 through 2010.–P.M. • $60 • (10/31/1999) • **87**

RIZZARDI, GUERRIERI

Amarone della Valpolicella Classico 1990 • $22 • (6/15/1996) HR • **90**
Amarone della Valpolicella Classico 1988 • $20 • (9/15/1992) • **75**
Bardolino Tacchetto 1991 • $12 • (9/15/1992) • **83**
Valpolicella Classico Poiega 1990 • $8 • (9/15/1992) • **80**
Valpolicella Classico Poiega 1988 • $9 • (12/15/1989) • **82**
Valpolicella Classico Superiore 1991 • $9 • (4/30/1994) • **80**
Valpolicella Classico Superiore Villa Rizzardi Poiega 1993 • $7 • (6/15/1996) • **85**

RIZZO, LUIGI

Barolo 1947 • $NA • (5/31/1997) • **84**

ROAGNA, ALFREDO & GIOVANNI

Barbaresco 1995: Serious winemaking. Ripe and sweet-tasting, this firm Barbaresco shows tough tannins and distinctive flavors of currant, blackberry, mineral and wet earth, with a slight smoky quality. Has the concentration and acidity to age graciously. Long, delicious finish. Best from 2005 through 2010.–P.M. • $44 • (10/31/1998) • **91**

Barbaresco 1988 • $33 • (10/31/1994) • **72**
Barbaresco 1986 • $26 • (7/15/1991) • **86**
Barbaresco 1985 • $27 • (2/28/1989) • **89**
Barolo La Rocca e La Pira Riserva 1993: Wonderfully deep fruit aromas mingle with smoke, tar and wet earth in this dense but elegant Barolo. Ripe but not overdone, the subtle oak accents shine the spotlight on *terroir* and ripe fruit. Tannins are firm but also ripe and sweet. Drink now through 2010.–P.M. • $46 • (10/31/1998) • **93**
Opera Prima Imbottigliato il 15 Novembre NV • $17 • (12/31/1987) • **82**
Opera Prima IV NV • $23 • (7/31/1989) • **76**

ROCCA, ALBINO

Barbaresco Loreto 1993 • $25 • (10/31/1996) • **75**
Barbaresco Loreto 1991 • $22 • (10/31/1994) • **82**
Barbaresco Vigneto Brich Ronchi 1996: A beauty that fans out with aromas of roasted chestnut, rose petal, tar, olive and blackberry. With its opulent, silky mouthfeel and gorgeous balance, this shows a master marrying Piedmont's new and traditional styles. Takes on a tough edge on the finish. Drink now through 2003.–P.M. • $53 • (10/31/1999) • **92**
Barbaresco Vigneto Brich Ronchi 1995: Elegant and racy, with a good balance of fruit and refined tannins. Emphasizes fruit rather than wood, although it shows some spice and oak-flavored mocha character along with the currant and blackberry notes. The tannins clamp down a bit on the harmonious finish. Best after 2002.–P.M. • $35 • (10/31/1998) • **87**
Barbaresco Vigneto Brich Ronchi 1994 • $35 • (10/31/1997) • **85**
Barbaresco Vigneto Brich Ronchi 1993 • $30 • (10/31/1996) • **91**
Barbaresco Vigneto Brich Ronchi 1991 • $23 • (10/31/1994) • **83**
Barbaresco Vigneto Loreto 1996: A big, burly, heavily extracted, dark-colored red, with tough tannins. The cranberry, cassis bush and olive flavors are intense but a bit on the crisp side. Dries a bit on the finish. –P.M. • $50 • (10/31/1999) • **79**
Barbaresco Vigneto Loreto 1995: Subtle and elegant, this lovely red has ripe fruit, showing blackberry, cassis and plum character, with a wet earth and spice complexity. Medium-bodied, with a good tannin structure that needs a few years to soften. Best after 2002.–P.M. • $30 • (10/31/1998) • **86**
Barbaresco Vigneto Loreto 1994 • $30 • (10/31/1997) • **75**
Barbera d'Alba Gepin 1997: Wonderfully exotic, exploding with violet, rose, wild raspberry and spice complexity, with smartly dosed acidity. Fresh and succulent, but also smooth and round, the balance here is really impressive and the toasted finish long. Drink now through 2002.–P.M. • $23 • (9/15/1999) • **93**
Barbera d'Alba Gepin 1996: Strikes an excellent balance between oak and fruit, tannins and acidity. Supple and lush, it stays loyal to its region, with a wet earth, mineral-laden character mingling with some ripe plum and blackberry notes. Spice and mocha accents sneak in on the subtle, chewy but long finish. Drink now through 2005.–P.M. • $21 • (10/31/1998) • **91**
Barbera d'Alba Gepin 1995 • $16 • (10/31/1997) • **87**
Barbera d'Alba Gepin 1994 • $12 • (10/31/1996) • **86**
Dolcetto d'Alba Vignalunga 1998: Wild and savage, with dried herb, cassis and sweet plum character, this medium-bodied Dolcetto sings, honing in on wet earth and spice. The chewy, substantial finish keeps the balance. Drink now through 2001.–P.M. • $16 • (11/15/1999) • **86**
Dolcetto d'Alba Vignalunga 1997: Delicious, balanced and ripe, yet showing elegance, with blackberry and black cherry notes, some earth, mineral and spice, all presented in a well-made package full of firm tannins. Drink now. –P.M. • $16 • (10/31/1998) • **87**
Dolcetto d'Alba Vignalunga 1996 • $15 • (10/31/1997) • **92**
Dolcetto d'Alba Vignalunga 1993 • $11 • (10/31/1996) • **85**

ROCCA, BRUNO

Barbaresco 1991 • $42 • (10/31/1994) • **86**
Barbaresco Coparossa 1996: Full-bodied, nicely oaked wine, layered with smoke and toasted notes, chewy tannins and some pretty fruit. Opulent, ripe mouthfeel is impressive, but the tannins are really tough on the finish. Tasted twice, with consistent notes. Drink now through 2003.–P.M. • $60 • (8/31/1999) • **87**
Barbaresco Coparossa 1995: Ripe and concentrated yet very elegant and racy, it bursts with floral, violet and rose petal aromas, tastes of blackberry and wet earth. The thick texture remains fresh and vibrant on the lingering finish. Of medium body, with firm tannins. Best from 2003 through 2010.–P.M. • $40 • (9/15/1998) • **90**
Barbaresco Rabajà 1996: New-oakish, modernist kind of Barbaresco, with the toasted violet notes in the driver's seat, towing some richly flavored and extracted gamy, smoky, spicy blackberry notes. But it ends with tough, drying tannins that just might—your call—soften with age. Drink now through 2005.–P.M. • $60 • (8/31/1999) • **87**
Barbaresco Rabajà 1995: International in style, pumped up with fancy oak, but it's the ripe fruit that seduces: plenty of jammy plum and red berry and blackberry character, plus the smoky, toasted mocha and spice flavors. Tannins are supple and ripe, and the finish is lovely. Well made. Drink now through 2008.–P.M. • $44 • (9/15/1998) • **90**
Barbaresco Rabajà 1994: This full-bodied wine smells of new oak but tastes very round and supple, with a good amount of blackberry, black cherry and spice. The tannins are quite tough, but this is clearly built for the long term, although today it's overly woody. Best from 2003 through 2007. –P.M. • $44 • (10/31/1998) • **84**
Barbaresco Rabajà 1993 • $40 • (10/31/1996) • **90**
Barbaresco Rabajà 1992 • $40 • (10/31/1995) • **80**
Barbaresco Rabajà 1989 • $45 • (10/31/1993) • **92**
Barbera d'Alba 1996: A rich, ripe Barbera, fanning out in the mouth with green olive and red berry flavors, moving on to a supple finish that's fresh but not overly acidic. Drink now through 2001.–P.M. • $30 • (9/15/1999) • **87**
Barbera d'Alba 1995: This wonderful *terroir*-driven Barbera, though strong and concentrated like a reduced sauce, shows well-defined earth, leather, mineral and blackberry aromas and flavors. Of medium to full body, it bursts with character, but its tannins are fine-textured and supple and it manages a graceful finish. Drink now through 2003.–P.M. • $20 • (10/31/1998) • **89**
Barbera d'Alba 1994 • $20 • (10/31/1996) • **85**
Barbera d'Alba 1993 • $20 • (10/31/1995) • **86**
Barbera d'Alba 1991 • $22 • (10/31/1994) • **88**
Dolcetto d'Alba Vigna Trifolé 1996: A light and fruity red, with berry, cherry and tobacco flavors and a nice combination of leather and spice notes on the finish. Drink now.–K.M. • $14 • (8/31/1998) • **83**
Nebbiolo delle Langhe Fralù 1996: Fairly round, with plum and black cherry character backed by oak. Lacks a bit of ripeness, and the tannins turn slightly dry on the finish, making this a bit disjointed, at least for now. Best after 2000.–P.M. • $15 • (10/31/1998) • **79**
Nebbiolo delle Langhe Fralù 1993 • $15 • (10/31/1995) • **78**

ROCCA BERNARDA

Merlot Colli Orientali del Friuli Centis 1996: Has a pleasant soft texture that caresses your palate, but a slightly weedy character detracts a bit. Medium body. Velvety finish. Drink now.–J.S. • $23 • (5/15/2000) • **81**
Pinot Grigio Colli Orientali del Friuli 1996 • $14 • (5/31/1998) • **83**
Sauvignon Colli Orientali del Friuli 1996 • $14 • (6/15/1998) • **87**
Tocai Friulano Colli Orientali del Friuli 1997: Has ripe fruit but slightly oxidized, with marzipan character. Tasted twice, with consistent notes.–J.S. • $13 • (1/01/2000) • **78**
Tocai Friulano Colli Orientali del Friuli 1996 • $13 • (6/15/1998) • **83**

ROCCA DELLE MACIE

Chianti Classico 1997: A pleasant, plummy wine, with light body and crisp acidity. Serve slightly chilled. Drink now.–J.S. • $12 • (11/30/1999) • **81**
Chianti Classico 1996: Plum and nectarine aromas and flavors. Medium-bodied, with light tannins and a fresh aftertaste. Drink now.–J.S. • $11 • (12/15/1998) • **83**
Chianti Classico 1995 • $10 • (3/31/1997) • **79**
Chianti Classico 1994 • $9 • (3/31/1997) • **81**
Chianti Classico 1992 • $NA • (2/28/1995) • **76**
Chianti Classico 1991 • $9 • (10/31/1993) • **85**
Chianti Classico 1990 • $10 • (9/15/1992) • **88**
Chianti Classico 1987 • $NA • (11/30/1989) • **82**
Chianti Classico 1986 • $NA • (11/30/1989) • **80**
Chianti Classico Riserva 1996: A very pleasant Chianti, with subtle cherry, raspberry and bark aromas and flavors. Medium-bodied, with well-integrated tannins and a fresh finish. Drink now.–J.S. • $22 • (11/30/1999) • **85**
Chianti Classico Riserva 1995: A bit diluted, with some berry and herbal character. Light-bodied, with a short, slightly hot finish.–J.S. • $19 • (12/15/1998) • **76**
Chianti Classico Riserva 1994 • $16 • (9/30/1997) • **86**
Chianti Classico Riserva 1993 • $11 • (3/31/1997) • **85**
Chianti Classico Riserva 1990 • $13 • (2/28/1995) • **75**
Chianti Classico Riserva 1985 • $14 • (9/15/1991) • **77**
Chianti Classico Tenuta di Fizzano Riserva 1996: A wine with very ripe plum and spice character that verges on raisin. Medium-bodied, with full tannins and a chewy, slightly dry finish. A bit too much new wood maturation? Best after 2000.–J.S. • $24 • (11/30/1999) • **84**

■ ■ ■ ■

ROCCA DELLE MACIE

Chianti Classico Tenuta di Fizzano Riserva 1995: A bit rustic but well structured. Very grapey, with a light, dried herb character. Full-bodied, with chewy tannins and an herbal, berry aftertaste. Best after 2001.–J.S. • $24 • (12/15/1998) • **85**
Chianti Classico Tenuta di Fizzano Riserva 1994 • $19 • (9/30/1997) • **86**
Chianti Classico Tenuta di Fizzano Riserva 1993 • $13 • (3/31/1997) • **85**
Chianti Classico Tenuta di Fizzano Riserva 1987 • $NA • (11/30/1989) • **89**
Chianti Classico Tenuta di Fizzano Riserva 1985 • $NA • (11/30/1989) • **88**
Chianti Classico Tenuta di Fizzano Riserva 1982 • $16 • (3/31/1989) • **87**
Chianti Classico Tenuta di Sant 'Alfonso 1996: Pleasant texture to this, but it's way overripe, with raisin and berry throughout. Medium-bodied, with an alcoholic finish. Tasted twice, with consistent notes.–J.S. • $NA • (12/15/1998) • **76**
Chianti Classico Tenuta di Sant 'Alfonso 1995 • $NA • (9/30/1997) • **81**
Chianti Classico Tenuta di Sant 'Alfonso 1993 • $NA • (3/31/1997) • **82**
Chianti Classico Tenuta di Sant 'Alfonso 1992 • $NA • (2/28/1995) • **78**
Chianti Classico Tenuta di Sant 'Alfonso 1988 • $NA • (9/15/1991) • **89**
Chianti Vernaiolo 1998: Bright, fresh and fruity. Light- to medium-bodied, with light tannins and a crisp finish. Not imported into the U.S. Drink now.–J.S. • $NA • (1/01/1999) • **81**
Orvieto Classico 1998: Has pear fruit, but it's slightly candied, with medium body and a dull finish. Drink now.–J.S. • $10 • (1/01/1999) • **80**
Orvieto Classico 1997 • $10 • (1/01/1998) • **84**
Sangiovese Toscana Rubizzo 1998: A delicious red, with attractive ripe plum and berry aromas. Medium-bodied, with light tannins and a fruity, spicy finish. Drink now through 2001.–J.S. • $11 • (11/30/1999) • **85**
Sangiovese Toscana Rubizzo 1997: Smooth and fruity, with attractive blackberry and tobacco character. Medium-bodied, with light yet velvety tannins and a caressing finish. Here's your chance to taste the quality of the 1997 vintage soon and at a good price. Drink now.–J.S. • $10 • (12/15/1998) • **86**
Sangiovese Toscana Rubizzo 1995 • $8 • (3/31/1997) • **85**
Sangiovese Toscana Rubizzo 1994 • $6 • (1/31/1997) • **85**
Sangiovese Toscana Rubizzo 1993 • $10 • (2/28/1995) • **77**
Toscana Roccato 1996: A well-structured 1996, with blackberry, cherry and smoke character. Medium- to full-bodied, with full, polished tannins and a medium finish. Needs time. Best after 2000.–J.S. • $35 • (11/30/1999) • **87**
Toscana Roccato 1995: Straightforward dried cherry and berry aromas and flavors. Medium-bodied, with medium, polished tannins and a fruity finish. Drink now.–J.S. • $31 • (12/15/1998) • **86**
Toscana Roccato 1994 • $26 • (9/30/1997) • **88**
Toscana Roccato 1993 • $18 • (1/31/1997) • **87**
Toscana Roccato 1990 • $30 • (2/28/1995) • **87**
Toscana Roccato 1988 • $NA • (9/15/1991) • **90**
Toscana Ser Gioveto 1996: Extremely well done for this vintage and producer. Delicate aromas of raspberry, mint and violet. Medium- to full-bodied, with well-integrated tannins and a medium, caressing finish. Drink now.–J.S. • $25 • (11/30/1999) • **88**
Toscana Ser Gioveto 1995: A bit rustic, showing blackberry and tanned leather aromas with hints of green herbs. Medium in body, tannins and finish. Drink now.–J.S. • $23 • (12/15/1998) • **83**
Toscana Ser Gioveto 1994 • $19 • (9/30/1997) • **81**
Toscana Ser Gioveto 1993 • $13 • (3/31/1997) • **85**
Toscana Ser Gioveto 1990 • $16 • (2/28/1995) • **82**
Toscana Ser Gioveto 1989 • $15 • (10/31/1993) • **76**
Toscana Ser Gioveto 1987 • $NA • (11/30/1989) • **90**
Toscana Ser Gioveto 1986 • $15 • (2/15/1989) • **84**
Toscana Ser Gioveto 1985 • $15 • (11/30/1989) • **88**
Vernaccia di San Gimignano 1998: Pretty, fresh and lively, with lime, honey and melon aromas. Medium-bodied, with fresh acidity and a fruity finish. Drink now.–J.S. • $12 • (11/30/1999) • **85**
Vernaccia di San Gimignano 1997: Light aromas of watermelon, apple and minerals. Medium-bodied, with blanched almond and fruit flavors and a crisp finish. Drink now.–J.S. • $8 • (12/15/1998) • **83**

ROCCA DI CASTAGNOLI

Buriano 1993 • $NA • (9/30/1997) • **89**
Buriano 1990 • $28 • (10/31/1993) • **86**
Cabernet Sauvignon Toscana Buriano 1996: An outstanding Cabernet from Chianti Classico, with subtle harmony. Very dark ruby in color, with intense aromas of blackberry, raspberry and vanilla. Full-bodied, with velvety tannins and a long, rich aftertaste. Best after 2000.–J.S. • $40 • (11/30/1999) • **90**
Cabernet Sauvignon Toscana Buriano 1995: Lots of raspberry and fresh-cut wood on the nose. Medium- to full-bodied, with very polished tannins and a slightly astringent, woody aftertaste that gives a green flavor. Best after 2000.–J.S. • $40 • (12/15/1998) • **83**
Chianti Classico 1997: Good intensity of dried cherry and berry character. Medium-bodied, with medium tannins and a fresh finish. Drink now.–J.S. • $15 • (11/30/1999) • **87**
Chianti Classico 1996: Lots of dried cherry and bark character. Medium-bodied, with light tannins and a crisp, refreshing finish. Drink now.–J.S. • $20 • (12/15/1998) • **85**
Chianti Classico 1995 • $19 • (9/30/1997) • **87**
Chianti Classico 1993 • $NA • (10/31/1996) • **78**
Chianti Classico 1991 • $17 • (10/31/1995) • **80**
Chianti Classico 1990 • $14 • (2/28/1995) • **86**
Chianti Classico Capraia Riserva 1996: Really good for the vintage. Dark and packed to the brim with fruit. Aromas of crushed berry, raspberry and oak follow through to a medium- to full-bodied palate, with velvety tannins. A bit more fruit on the medium finish would make it outstanding. Drink now.–J.S. • $20 • (11/30/1999) • **89**
Chianti Classico Capraia Riserva 1995: Fresh, plummy aromas and flavors in this medium- to light-bodied red. It's light on tannins and easy to enjoy. Drink now.–J.S. • $19 • (12/15/1998) • **84**
Chianti Classico Capraia Riserva 1993 • $20 • (10/31/1996) • **78**
Chianti Classico Capraia Riserva 1988 • $NA • (9/15/1992) • **84**
Chianti Classico Poggio a' Frati Riserva 1996: Rather light on the palate, with interesting, lovely aromas of freshly cut mushroom and berry. Medium-bodied, with light tannins and a crisp finish. Drink now.–J.S. • $23 • (11/30/1999) • **83**
Chianti Classico Poggio a' Frati Riserva 1995: A delicate and enchanting young red, with subtle aromas of spices and berries. Medium-bodied, with light tannins and a fresh, crisp finish. Drink now.–J.S. • $29 • (12/15/1998) • **86**
Chianti Classico Poggio a' Frati Riserva 1993 • $27 • (9/30/1997) • **87**
Chianti Classico Poggio a' Frati Riserva 1990 • $22 • (10/31/1995) • **87**
Chianti Classico Poggio a' Frati Riserva 1988 • $21 • (9/15/1992) • **87**
Chianti Classico Poggio a' Frati Riserva 1985 • $NA • (9/15/1991) • **84**
Toscana Le Pergoline White 1998: A rather eccentric white, with aromas of overripe apple and lime. Medium-bodied, with mineral and lemon peel flavors and a slightly effervescent finish. Not imported into the U.S. Drink now.–J.S. • $NA • (1/01/1999) • **80**
Toscana Le Pergoline White 1997: A rather delicious white, with stone, apple and spice aromas and flavors. Medium-bodied, with fresh acidity and a light, refreshing finish. Not imported into the U.S. Drink now.–J.S. • $NA • (12/15/1998) • **85**
Toscana Le Pergoline White 1996 • $13 • (9/30/1997) • **83**
Toscana Stielle 1996: Very well crafted, a solid '96 with an abundance of ripe berry, chocolate and cherry character. Medium- to full-bodied, with velvety tannins and a medium finish. Drink now.–J.S. • $25 • (11/30/1999) • **88**
Toscana Stielle 1995: A modern, well-made red, with attractive, crushed berry aromas that follow through on the palate. Medium-bodied, with medium tannins and a light finish. Drink through 2003.–J.S. • $35 • (12/15/1998) • **87**
Toscana Stielle 1993 • $33 • (9/30/1997) • **86**
Toscana Stielle 1991 • $NA • (10/31/1995) • **87**
Toscana Stielle 1990 • $33 • (10/31/1995) • **90**
Toscana Stielle 1988 • $28 • (10/31/1993) • **82**

ROCCA DI MONTEGROSSI

Chianti Classico 1997: Simple and easy, with plum, cedar and tobacco. Light body and finish. Not much to it for a '97. Drink now.–J.S. • $19 • (11/30/1999) • **80**
Chianti Classico 1995 • $15 • (9/30/1997) • **83**
Chianti Classico 1994 • $17 • (10/31/1996) • **78**
Chianti Classico 1991 • $NA • (10/31/1993) • **76**
Chianti Classico 1990 • $16 • (10/31/1993) • **88**
Chianti Classico San Marcellino Riserva 1996: A light and simple Sangiovese, with berry and tobacco character throughout. Short and slightly diluted finish.–J.S. • $32 • (11/30/1999) • **79**
Chianti Classico San Marcellino Riserva 1995: A pretty Chianti. Lovely aromas of dried cherry and rose follow through to a medium-bodied palate, with light tannins and a fresh, crisp finish. Drink now.–J.S. • $37 • (6/30/1999) • **85**
Chianti Classico San Marcellino Riserva 1993 • $NA • (9/30/1997) • **83**

Key: SS—Spectator Selection. CS—Cellar Selection. HR—Highly Recommended. $NA—Price not available. (BT)—Barrel tasting. Ⓐ—Auction Price.
For a key to the tasters' initials, see "How to Use These Listings."
Dates in parentheses represent the issues in which the ratings were published.

ITALY

Chianti Classico San Marcellino Riserva 1987 • $17 • (5/15/1993) • **78**
Toscana Geremia 1996: Good fruit but slightly lean, with pleasant dried cherry and slight vanilla character. Light- to medium-bodied, with light tannins and a slightly austere finish. Drink now.–J.S. • $40 • (11/30/1999) • **80**
Toscana Geremia 1995: Oozing with blackberry and cherry aromas. Medium- to full-bodied, with smooth, fine tannins and a fruity finish. Drink through 2004.–J.S. • $45 • (12/15/1998) • **88**
Toscana Geremia 1993 • $30 • (10/31/1996) • **87**
Vin Santo 1993: Extremely ripe fruit, with a dried apricot and almost burnt brown sugar character. Full-bodied and very sweet, with a lovely, silky texture. Eccentric and delicious. Like crème brûlée in the bottle. Drink now.–J.S. • $30/375 ml. • (11/30/1999) • **90**
Vin Santo 1992: A fresher, more modern style of Vin Santo, perfect with fruit. Concentrated aromas of honey, caramel and peach. Medium-bodied and medium sweet, with a long, sweet and fruity aftertaste. Drink now. –J.S. • $30/375 ml. • (12/15/1998) • **87**

ROCCHE COSTAMAGNA

Barbera d'Alba 1995 • $17 • (10/31/1997) • **87**
Barbera d'Alba 1988 • $12 • (3/15/1991) • **90**
Barbera d'Alba Annunziata 1997: Earthy and a bit green. Medium-bodied, with a bell pepper character along with cherry.–P.M. • $20 • (11/15/1999) • **78**
Barbera d'Alba Annunziata 1996: Fresh and juicy, succulent, medium-bodied, with cassis bush, black cherry and blackberry character. Tastes a bit herbal and acidic on the finish, but should pair well with food. Drink now through 2003.–P.M. • $18 • (10/31/1998) • **81**
Barbera d'Alba Rocche di la Morra 1993 • $16 • (10/31/1996) • **75**
Barbera d'Alba Rocche di la Morra 1992 • $NA • (10/31/1994) • **78**
Barbera d'Alba Rocche di la Morra 1991 • $14 • (4/30/1993) • **84**
Barbera d'Alba Rocche di la Morra 1990 • $17 • (10/31/1992) • **86**
Barolo Bricco Francesco 1995: Sweet and appealing, medium-bodied and fun, with a soft midpalate of raspberry and cranberry, kicking in with a lively, fresh and chewy finish that's a bit toasted. Drink now through 2003. –P.M. • $34 • (11/15/1999) • **86**
Barolo Bricco Francesco 1994: Well made. Full in body and smooth in texture, with a good combination of black fruit, toasted, spicy, peppery flavors and a smoky finish. There is concentration here, and massive, supple tannins. Best from 2003 through 2008.–P.M. • $43 • (10/31/1998) • **88**
Barolo Rocche dell 'Annunziata 1995: A bit green and herbal, with a crisp, tough finish.–P.M. • $31 • (11/15/1999) • **77**
Barolo Rocche dell 'Annunziata 1994: Seamless '94 Barolo, thick yet elegant, supple as they come, with well-integrated ripe tannins, good balance of acidity, concentrated and ripe black fruit and what appears to be slightly toasted oak. Lingers with wild berries, plum, smoke, and raspberries. A very good effort for this difficult vintage. Drink now through 2005. –P.M. • $35 • (10/31/1998) • **89**
Barolo Rocche dell 'Annunziata 1993 • $32 • (10/31/1997) • **87**
Barolo Rocche di la Morra 1991 • $29 • (10/31/1996) • **79**
Barolo Rocche di la Morra 1990 • $NA • (10/31/1994) • **89**
Barolo Rocche di la Morra 1989 • $20 • (10/31/1994) • **89**
Barolo Rocche di la Morra 1988 • $26 • (12/15/1992) • **87**
Barolo Rocche di la Morra 1985 • $25 • (2/28/1991) • **72**
Barolo Vigna San Francesco 1993 • $38 • (10/31/1997) • **87**
Barolo Vigna San Francesco 1991 • $37 • (10/31/1996) • **87**
Barolo Vigna San Francesco 1990 • $NA • (10/31/1994) • **90**
Dolcetto d'Alba 1997: Fruity, grapey, lovely. Balanced, with ripe currant and blackberry flavors, this has sweet tannins that make for a supple finish. –P.M. • $14 • (10/31/1998) • **87**
Dolcetto d'Alba 1996 • $12 • (10/31/1997) • **83**
Dolcetto d'Alba 1993 • $13 • (10/31/1995) • **81**
Dolcetto d'Alba 1991 • $15 • (4/30/1993) • **78**
Dolcetto d'Alba 1989 • $12 • (4/30/1991) • **83**
Nebbiolo delle Langhe Roccardo 1989 • $13 • (4/30/1991) • **85**
Rocche delle Rocche 1990 • $17 • (3/31/1993) • **81**

ROCCHE DEI MANZONI

Barbera d'Alba Sorito Mosconi 1996: Super-Barbera. Rich, dense and amazingly smooth. Tar, black fruit, smoke and spice plus distinct fresh acidity beneath the wood give plenty of complexity. Smoky on the finish, the lingering taste is one of fruit and length. Drink now.–P.M. • $25 • (10/31/1998) • **89**
Barbera d'Alba Vigna La Cresta 1995 • $25 • (10/31/1997) • **81**
Barbera d'Alba Vigna La Cresta 1994 • $16 • (10/31/1996) • **84**
Barbera d'Alba Vigna La Cresta 1993 • $NA • (10/31/1995) • **85**
Barolo Riserva 1990 • $35 • (10/31/1995) • **89**
Barolo Riserva 1989 • $NA • (10/31/1994) • **88**
Barolo Vigna Big 1995: Sure, it's international in its fancy toasted oak treatment, but this is so well done, supple and flavorful, with lush fruit, a silky texture and a focused cassis, blackberry and smoke character. Drink now through 2002.–P.M. • $75 • (11/15/1999) • **93**
Barolo Vigna Big 1993 • $25 • (10/31/1997) • **86**
Barolo Vigna Big Riserva 1990 • $NA • (10/31/1995) • **83**
Barolo Vigna Big Riserva 1989 • $NA • (10/31/1994) • **87**
Barolo Vigna Cappella di S. Stefano 1995: Clever winemaking delivers subtle, deftly oaked barrique notes—toasted, smoky, grilled aromas—while letting the ripe fruit character unfold in a smooth package that shows complexity and class. Long, satisfying finish. Drink now through 2003. –P.M. • $85 • (11/15/1999) • **93**
Barolo Vigna d'la Roul 1995: Heavy on the smoke and tar, this tastes Piedmont-like despite the international oak treatment. Supple and full-bodied, with lovely blackberry and anise and a good mix of ripe, chewy tannins and lively acidity. Drink now through 2003.–P.M. • $75 • (11/15/1999) • **89**
Barolo Vigna d'la Roul 1993 • $25 • (10/31/1997) • **83**
Barolo Vigna d'La Roul Riserva 1990 • $NA • (10/31/1995) • **90**
Barolo Vigna d'La Roul Riserva 1989 • $NA • (10/31/1994) • **92**
Barolo Vigna Rocche 1994: Like velvet on the palate. This barrique-treated Barolo sings with smoke and floral flavors, but the wood is subtle and the wine remains elegant, allowing fruit and earth to take center stage on the balanced, ripe-tasting, just-lovely finish. Drink now through 2005.–P.M. • $45 • (10/31/1998) • **90**
Barolo Vigna Rocche 1993 • $22 • (10/31/1997) • **88**
Bricco Manzoni 1996: Charismatic and sexy. A brilliant, inky-black, superripe yet elegant VdT that bursts with flavors. The oak is subtle but the black fruit is not, the tannins are silky-smooth and it kicks in on the finish with good acidity. Drink now through 2005.–P.M. • $NA • (11/15/1999) • **92**
Bricco Manzoni 1995: Smooth and silky, this full-bodied wine folds in its rose petal, tar, smoke and blackberry flavors elegantly, without obvious oak. Good acidity and the fresh fruit make it delicious with food; ripe tannins and good balance make it accessible upon release, but it will hold for years. Drink now through 2007.–P.M. • $26 • (10/31/1998) • **89**
Bricco Manzoni 1994 • $25 • (10/31/1997) • **83**
Bricco Manzoni 1990 • $25 • (10/31/1994) • **74**
Dolcetto d'Alba Vigna Matinera 1997: Straightforward and a bit diluted, with modest fruit, licorice notes and astringent tannins.–P.M. • $18 • (10/31/1998) • **77**
Dolcetto d'Alba Vigna Rocche 1995 • $NA • (10/31/1996) • **79**
Langhe Quatr Nas 1996: Black-colored, and everything fits in a godlike pattern of balance and seduction. With plenty of sweet tannins and ripe flavors, it bursts with exotic black fruit. Drink now through 2005.–P.M. • $NA • (11/15/1999) • **94**
Pinonero di Valentino 1994 • $22 • (10/31/1997) • **83**

RODANO

Chianti Classico 1996: Light and watery, with some berry and plum character, but it's slightly earthy and cheesy on the finish.–J.S. • $14 • (12/15/1998) • **74**
Chianti Classico 1994 • $15 • (10/31/1996) • **71**
Chianti Classico 1993 • $12 Ⓐ • (10/31/1995) • **78**
Chianti Classico 1990 • $10 • (10/31/1993) • **87**
Chianti Classico Riserva Viacosta 1990 • $20 • (10/31/1995) • **84**
Chianti Classico Viacosta Riserva 1995: A delicate and crisp Sangiovese, with cherry, bark and earth character, medium body and aftertaste. Drink now.–J.S. • $26 • (12/15/1998) • **82**
Toscana Monna Claudia 1995: Ripe, almost raisiny in character, with underlying aromas and flavors of tanned leather. Medium in body and tannins, slightly dry on the finish. Drink now.–J.S. • $32 • (12/15/1998) • **82**
Toscana Monna Claudia 1988 • $NA • (10/31/1995) • **86**

ROMANDIOLA

Sangiovese di Romagna Superiore Il Pavone d'Oro 1993 • $8 • (2/29/1996) • **84**

ROMANO, CLELIA

Fiano di Avellino Colli di Lapio 1998: Solid Fiano. Perplexing aromas of fruit and dust, with hints of ash. Medium-bodied, with fresh acidity and a lemon, ash finish. Drink now.–J.S. • $23 • (1/31/2000) • **87**

ITALY

ROMEO

Vino Nobile di Montepulciano 1996: A lovely autumnal wine, with pretty aromas of plum, rose and cherry. Medium-bodied, with well-integrated tannins and sweet fruit on the finish. Subtle and delicate. Drink now.–J.S. • $26 • (11/30/1999) • **86**

ROMITORIO, CASTELLO

Brio 1992 • $10 • (2/28/1995) • **84**

Brunello di Montalcino 1995: Big, ripe and chewy. Good dark color. Meaty, ripe-fruit and tanned-leather aromas. Full-bodied, with velvety tannins and a long, long finish. Best after 2000.–J.S. • $38 • (6/30/2000) • **91**

Brunello di Montalcino 1994: Just sniff and enjoy. Aromas of berries and lilies flow from the glass. Medium-bodied, with firm and polished tannins, yet slightly dry on the finish (a bit too much new wood maturation?). Drink now.–J.S. • $43 • (8/31/1999) • **87**

Brunello di Montalcino 1993: Dark-colored, with meaty, cooked fruit aromas. Full-bodied, tannic, with astringent acidity. A bit overdone. Age may tame it a bit. Drink now through 2005.–J.S. • $40 • (12/15/1998) • **81**

Brunello di Montalcino 1988 • $30 • (11/30/1994) • **91**

Romito del Romitorio 1993 • $25 • (10/31/1995) • **91**

Romito del Romitorio 1992 • $20 • (11/30/1994) • **88**

Rosso di Montalcino San Giovese 1996: Typically fresh and fruity, with plenty of berry and ripe fruit character, a medium body and light tannins. A bit simple, but delicious. Drink now.–J.S. • $20 • (12/15/1998) • **84**

RONCHI DI MANZANO

Cabernet Sauvignon Colli Orientali del Friuli 1997: Very good fruit, but it turns rubbery and unpleasant on the palate. Tasted twice, with consistent notes.–J.S. • $14 • (5/15/2000) • **68**

Chardonnay Colli Orientali del Friuli 1998: Wonderful spiciness to this white. Aromas of apples, honey and cream with hints of pineapple. Medium-bodied, with good fruit and an intense canned peach aftertaste. Drink now.–J.S. • $15 • (3/31/2000) • **85**

Colli Orientali del Friuli Rosazzo Bianco 1998: Ripe fruit character jumps from the glass here, with pineapple, cream and apple aromas. Full-bodied, with lots of character and a long, long finish. Drink now through 2002.–J.S. • $24 • (4/30/2000) • **89**

Colli Orientali del Friuli Rosazzo Rosso Ronc di Rosazzo 1997: Wonderful bright berry character with hints of toasted oak. Medium-bodied, with velvety tannins and a medium finish. Slightly hollow midpalate, but very fine indeed. Best after 2000.–J.S. • $21 • (5/15/2000) • **87**

Merlot Colli Orientali del Friuli 1997: A delicious Merlot with berry, currant and mineral character and a hint of mint. Medium-bodied, with silky tannins and a long finish. Drink now through 2002.–J.S. • $14 • (5/15/2000) • **86**

Merlot Colli Orientali del Friuli Ronc di Subule 1996: Wonderful aromas of raspberries and plums, with a hint of spice. Medium-bodied, with soft tannins and a short finish. A bit hollow in the midpalate. Best after 2000.–J.S. • $26 • (5/15/2000) • **86**

Picolit Colli Orientali del Friuli Ronc di Rosazzo 1997: A clean and well-made wine with blanched almond, mineral and floral character. Medium-bodied, off-dry, with a fresh finish. Not really sweet enough for dessert but pleasant as an aperitif. Drink now.–J.S. • $33/375 ml. • (4/30/2000) • **86**

Pinot Grigio Colli Orientali del Friuli 1998: A pretty white, with almond, pineapple and light peach character. Medium-bodied, with good acidity and a ripe fruit aftertaste. Drink now through 2002.–J.S. • $15 • (3/31/2000) • **87**

Refosco dal Peduncolo Rosso Colli Orientali del Friuli 1997: A very aromatic wine that oozes with blackberries, olives and plums. Medium-bodied, with soft tannins and a leafy, berry aftertaste. Drink now.–J.S. • $15 • (5/15/2000) • **86**

Sauvignon Colli Orientali del Friuli 1998: Superripe aromas of pineapple, peaches and minerals. Medium-bodied, with good acidity and a long, spicy fruit aftertaste. Well done. Drink now through 2001.–J.S. • $15 • (4/30/2000) • **88**

Key: SS—Spectator Selection. CS—Cellar Selection. HR—Highly Recommended. $NA—Price not available. (BT)—Barrel tasting. Ⓐ—Auction Price. For a key to the tasters' initials, see "How to Use These Listings."
Dates in parentheses represent the issues in which the ratings were published.

Tocai Friulano Colli Orientali del Friuli Superiore 1998: Clean and lively, with mineral and bay leaf character. Medium-bodied, with a short white pepper finish. Needs more ripe fruit. Drink now.–J.S. • $17 • (3/31/2000) • **83**

Venezia Giulia Le Zuccule 1996: Attractive plum and chocolate character. Medium-bodied, with velvety tannins and a fresh, fruity finish. A bit diluted midpalate, but delicious. Merlot and Cabernet Sauvignon. Drink now. –J.S. • $26 • (5/15/2000) • **86**

Verduzzo Friulano Colli Orientali del Friuli Ronc di Rosazzo 1997: Aromas of very ripe pineapple, honey and vanilla. Full-bodied, off-dry, highly extracted, with loads of spice, honey and lemon flavors. Flavor packed. Drink now.–J.S. • $24/375 ml. • (4/30/2000) • **89**

RONCO DEI TASSI

Collio Fosarin 1998: Very fresh and clean on the nose. Medium-bodied, with a very good intensity of pineapple, banana and apple flavors. Drink now. –J.S. • $16 • (4/30/2000) • **88**

Pinot Grigio Collio 1998: Plenty of mineral and almond character, with a hint of apple. Medium- to full-bodied, with good acidity and a fruity finish. Drink now.–J.S. • $16 • (3/31/2000) • **86**

Sauvignon Collio 1998: Shows lots of apple, almond and honey character. Very fresh. Medium in body, with good acidity and a long, crisp finish. Drink now.–J.S. • $16 • (4/30/2000) • **87**

Tocai Friulano Collio 1998: Rich on the nose, with honey, lime and slate character. Medium-bodied, with good acidity and a light finish. Drink now.–J.S. • $16 • (3/31/2000) • **86**

RONCO DEL GNEMIZ

Chardonnay Colli Orientali del Friuli 1996: A full-throttle Chardonnay, with lots of almond, apple, pineapple and toasted oak character. Medium- to full-bodied, with good acidity and a long, flavorful finish. Drink now through 2001.–J.S. • $38 • (1/01/2000) • **90**

Müller-Thurgau 1996 • $19 • (6/15/1998) • **84**

Pinot Grigio Colli Orientali del Friuli 1998: A fresh and spicy white, with hints of melon and earth. Medium-bodied, with light acidity and a slightly hot finish. A bit lean. Drink now.–J.S. • $20 • (2/29/2000) • **83**

Pinot Grigio Colli Orientali del Friuli 1997: Interesting apple, lime and floral character, but also a bit like canned fruit cocktail. Medium-bodied, almost off-dry, with a fresh finish. Slightly disappointing for this producer. Drink now.–J.S. • $22 • (1/01/2000) • **81**

Pinot Grigio Colli Orientali del Friuli 1996 • $17 • (6/15/1998) • **82**

Rosso del Gnemiz 1988 • $28 • (9/15/1992) • **85**

Rosso del Gnemiz 1986 • $15 • (3/31/1989) • **80**

Schioppettino Colli Orientali del Friuli 1995: Youthful and powerful. Fresh aromas of blackberries, licorice and fruit. Medium- to full-bodied, with compacted fruit and tannins and a long, chewy finish. Still needs some time. Best after 2000.–J.S. • $37 • (5/15/2000) • **89**

Tocai Friulano Colli Orientali del Friuli 1998: Has ripe fruit character, but it's slightly dull and candied on the palate. Hard to get excited about. Tasted twice, with consistent notes.–J.S. • $20 • (3/31/2000) • **78**

Tocai Friulano Colli Orientali del Friuli 1997: Clean apple, mineral and lemon aromas follow through to a medium-bodied palate, with good acidity and a canned pear aftertaste. Better aromas than flavors. Drink now.–J.S. • $22 • (1/01/2000) • **83**

Tocai Friulano Colli Orientali del Friuli 1996 • $17 • (6/15/1998) • **84**

ROSSO, GIGI

Barbaresco Vigneto Viglino 1995: Light in color like a rosé, with a diluted texture, this watery wine tastes of strawberries and cherries. Dry on the herbal finish.–P.M. • $40 • (10/31/1998) • **70**

Barbera d'Alba 1995 • $11 • (10/31/1997) • **78**

Barbera d'Alba Vino del Buon Ricordo 1996: A smooth and balanced Barbera, with wet earth, stone dust and chalk character accented by pure fruit. Well made, medium-bodied, delicious and respectful of the traditional style. Good acidity on the succulent finish bodes well for matching with food. Drink now through 2002.–P.M. • $18 • (10/31/1998) • **86**

Barbera d'Alba Vino del Buon Ricordo 1995 • $15 • (10/31/1997) • **76**

Barbera d'Alba Vino del Buon Ricordo 1994 • $NA • (10/31/1996) • **78**

Barolo Arione 1994: A delicate Barolo, showing ripe, sweet-tasting fruit in a light-bodied package. Offers plum, wild raspberry and cherry character and a lingering, fresh finish. Supple tannins. Drink now.–P.M. • $40 • (10/31/1998) • **81**

Barolo Arione 1993 • $23 • (10/31/1997) • **80**

Barolo Arione Sôrì dell 'Ulivo 1993: A bit light and superficial for Barolo, this light-colored wine has straightforward flavors. Drying tannins on the finish don't help.–P.M. • $55 • (10/31/1998) • **77**
Barolo Arione Sôrì dell 'Ulivo 1990 • $NA • (10/31/1996) • **92**
Dolcetto d'Alba Rocca Giovino 1995 • $NA • (10/31/1996) • **77**
Dolcetto di Diano d'Alba Moncolombetto 1997: Aromatically attractive, with rose petal, rosemary and other fragrant herbs but also a slight herbal side. This thick-textured, full-bodied Dolcetto has ripe and lush tannins, but the finish is a bit dry. Drink now.–P.M. • $15 • (10/31/1998) • **82**
Dolcetto di Diano d'Alba Moncolombetto 1996 • $12 • (10/31/1997) • **80**
Dolcetto di Diano d'Alba Moncolombetto 1995 • $NA • (10/31/1996) • **85**
Dolcetto di Diano d'Alba Vigna Vecchia del Pinnacolo 1997: Fairly tart, light-bodied Dolcetto, with cassis and cherry notes. Nice balance between acidity and smooth tannins. Fresh finish.–P.M. • $15 • (10/31/1998) • **83**
Nebbiolo d'Alba Rocca Giovino 1996: Light and diluted. Watery and straw-berry-scented, with a short, drying finish.–P.M. • $18 • (10/31/1998) • **70**

ROTARI

Brut Blanc de Noirs Trento NV • $13 • (6/15/1997) • **76**
Brut Trento Arte Italiana NV • $13 • (6/15/1997) • **83**

RUFFINO

Brunello di Montalcino Tenuta Il Greppone Mazzi 1995: Dried berry and tanned leather aromas. Sweet and ripe fruit with a rustic finish. Medium-bodied, with firm tannins and a tobacco and cherry aftertaste. Drink now.–J.S. • $66 • (6/30/2000) • **87**
Brunello di Montalcino Tenuta Il Greppone Mazzi 1994: Rather eccentric wine with raisin, berry and Ovaltine-like aromas. Slightly volatile. Medium- to full-bodied with lots of fruit and an intensely fruity, rich finish. A bit too raisiny and funky for me, but some may love it. Not imported into the U.S. Drink now.–J.S. • $NA • (1/01/1999) • **84**
Brunello di Montalcino Tenuta Il Greppone Mazzi 1993: Plummy aromas verge on raisiny. Ripe and traditional. Medium- to full-bodied, with a lot of alcohol and fruit. Round and velvety in texture. Drink now.–J.S. • $55 • (12/15/1998) • **87**
Brunello di Montalcino Tenuta Il Greppone Mazzi 1991 • $35 • (11/30/1996) • **83**
Brunello di Montalcino Tenuta Il Greppone Mazzi 1990 • $35 • (10/31/1995) • **87**
Brunello di Montalcino Tenuta Il Greppone Mazzi 1982 • $30 • (9/15/1986) • **90**
Brunello di Montalcino Tenuta Il Greppone Mazzi 1981 • $25 • (9/15/1986) • **70**
Brunello di Montalcino Tenuta Il Greppone Mazzi Riserva 1991 • $50 • (9/30/1997) • **78**
Brunello di Montalcino Tenuta Il Greppone Mazzi Riserva 1990 • $50 • (11/30/1996) • **93**
Brunello di Montalcino Tenuta Il Greppone Mazzi Riserva 1988 • $40 • (10/31/1994) • **85**
Brunello di Montalcino Tenuta Il Greppone Mazzi Riserva 1987 • $38 • (11/30/1993) • **81**
Brunello di Montalcino Tenuta Il Greppone Mazzi Riserva 1986 • $33 • (12/15/1992) • **84**
Toscana Chardonnay Toscana Cabreo La Pietra 1997: If you like new oak, this is for you. Aromas of almond, pie crust and citrus open to a full-bodied palate, with lots of toasted oak and medium fruit. Long coconut and toasted oak finish. Drink now.–J.S. • $22 • (11/30/1999) • **87**
Chardonnay-Pinot Grigio Toscana Libaio 1998: Always a great value. Solid aromas of apples and cream. Medium-bodied, with good fruit and a lovely toasted-oak aftertaste. Drink now.–J.S. • $10 • (10/31/1999) • **86**
Chardonnay-Pinot Grigio Toscana Libaio 1997: Interesting and subtle white. Fresh aromas of canteloupe and tropical fruits. Medium-bodied, with fresh acidity and an interesting aftertaste of mineral and citrus, with an almond hint. Shows wonderful character for a super price. Drink now.–J.S. • $9 • (12/15/1998) • **86**
Chianti 1995 • $8 • (11/15/1996) • **84**
Chianti 1994 • $NA • (10/31/1995) • **80**
Chianti 1991 • $8 • (5/15/1993) • **79**
Chianti 1990 • $8 • (1/31/1992) • **77**
Chianti Classico Aziano 1997: Already tired. Light ruby-garnet in color, with a plummy, cheesy character and a light palate.–J.S. • $13 • (11/30/1999) • **78**
Chianti Classico Aziano 1995 • $12 • (10/31/1996) • **81**
Chianti Classico Aziano 1994 • $12 • (10/31/1996) • **78**
Chianti Classico Aziano 1992 • $10 • (2/28/1995) • **72**
Chianti Classico Aziano 1991 • $11 • (10/31/1993) • **78**
Chianti Classico Aziano 1990 • $10 • (9/15/1992) • **88**
Chianti Classico Aziano 1989 • $10 • (4/30/1992) • **79**
Chianti Classico Aziano 1988 • $11 • (9/15/1991) • **83**
Chianti Classico Ducale Gold Label Riserva 1995: Simple and fruity; no-nonsense red. Light- to medium-bodied, with dried cherry and earth character. Drink now.–J.S. • $38 • (11/30/1999) • **84**
Chianti Classico Ducale Gold Label Riserva 1993 • $NA • (9/30/1997) • **88**
Chianti Classico Ducale Gold Label Riserva 1990 • $25 • (9/30/1997) • **85**
Chianti Classico Ducale Gold Label Riserva 1988 • $25 • (9/30/1997) • **79**
Chianti Classico Ducale Gold Label Riserva 1986 • $24 • (5/15/1993) • **87**
Chianti Classico Ducale Gold Label Riserva 1985 • $NA • (9/30/1997) • **86**
Chianti Classico Ducale Gold Label Riserva 1983 • $17 • (11/30/1989) • **84**
Chianti Classico Ducale Gold Label Riserva 1982 • $20 • (5/31/1989) • **80**
Chianti Classico Ducale Gold Label Riserva 1979 • $16 • (9/30/1986) • **70**
Chianti Classico Ducale Gold Label Riserva 1978 • $NA • (11/30/1989) • **82**
Chianti Classico Ducale Gold Label Riserva 1977 • $NA • (9/16/1985) • **89**
Chianti Classico Ducale Gold Label Riserva 1975 • $NA • (9/16/1985) • **86**
Chianti Classico Ducale Gold Label Riserva 1971 • $NA • (9/16/1985) • **85**
Chianti Classico Ducale Gold Label Riserva 1958 • $NA • (9/16/1985) • **82**
Chianti Classico Ducale Riserva 1996: Mature and cedary in style but enjoyable. Pretty strawberry and cedar aromas follow through to a light- to medium-bodied palate, with light tannins and a crisp finish. At its peak. Drink now.–J.S. • $22 • (11/30/1999) • **84**
Chianti Classico Ducale Riserva 1995 • $16 • (9/30/1997) • **81**
Chianti Classico Ducale Riserva 1993 • $15 • (10/31/1996) • **82**
Chianti Classico Ducale Riserva 1990 • $15 • (2/28/1995) • **84**
Chianti Classico Ducale Riserva 1989 • $14 • (4/30/1994) • **83**
Chianti Classico Ducale Riserva 1988 • $15 • (9/15/1992) • **82**
Chianti Classico Ducale Riserva 1987 • $14 • (9/15/1992) • **86**
Chianti Classico Ducale Riserva 1986 • $16 • (10/31/1991) • **89**
Chianti Classico Ducale Riserva 1985 • $13 • (9/15/1991) • **90**
Chianti Classico Ducale Riserva 1979 • $16 • (9/16/1985) • **80**
Chianti Classico Santedame 1997: Very light for a '97. Light in color, with delicate cherry and berry character. Fresh finish. Rather lean. Drink now.–J.S. • $17 • (11/30/1999) • **80**
Chianti Classico Santedame 1996: Offers attractive cherry and earth character, but slightly austere. Light to medium in body, with fresh acidity, finishing on the dry side. Drink now.–J.S. • $16 • (12/15/1998) • **80**
Chianti Classico Santedame 1995 • $14 • (9/30/1997) • **87**
Chianti Classico Santedame 1994 • $12 • (10/31/1996) • **82**
Chianti Classico Santedame 1993 • $NA • (10/31/1995) • **79**
Chianti Classico Santedame 1991 • $14 • (10/31/1993) • **85**
Chianti Classico Santedame 1990 • $14 • (10/31/1993) • **87**
Chianti Classico Santedame 1988 • $NA • (9/15/1991) • **88**
Libaio 1996 • $10 • (9/30/1997) • **87**
Orvieto Classico 1998: Rather candied and slightly oxidized, with a lime and herb character. Rather disappointing.–J.S. • $7 • (2/29/2000) • **76**
Orvieto Classico Abboccato 1998: Clean and fresh melon aromas, with hints of mineral. Light-bodied and off-dry, with a flinty melon aftertaste. A decent aperitif. Drink now.–J.S. • $8 • (2/29/2000) • **80**
Sangiovese Toscana Torgaio 1995 • $8 • (1/31/1997) • **83**
Sangiovese Toscana Torgaio 1994 • $NA • (10/31/1995) • **81**
Sangiovese Toscana Torgaio 1992 • $10 • (10/31/1993) • **83**
Toscana Cabreo Il Borgo 1996: Rather light for this wine, but pretty. Very fresh and vivid aromas of dried cherry and flowers. Medium-bodied, with light tannins and crisp acidity. Tasted twice, with consistent notes. Drink now.–J.S. • $30 • (11/30/1999) • **86**
Toscana Cabreo Il Borgo 1995 • $28 • (9/30/1997) • **90**
Toscana Cabreo Il Borgo 1994 • $28 • (9/30/1997) • **87**
Toscana Cabreo Il Borgo 1993 • $NA • (10/31/1995) • **87**
Toscana Cabreo Il Borgo 1990 • $NA • (10/31/1993) • **92**
Toscana Cabreo Il Borgo 1988 • $NA • (9/15/1991) • **90**
Toscana Cabreo Il Borgo 1987 • $27 • (12/15/1992) • **82**
Toscana Cabreo Il Borgo 1985 • $21 • (9/30/1989) • **90**
Toscana Fonte al Sole 1998: Rather light yet good. A simple quaffing red, with plenty of cherry character. Serve slightly chilled. Drink now.–J.S. • $10 • (11/30/1999) • **81**
Toscana Nero del Tondo 1996: A good Pinot Noir, though very delicate in style. Light aromas of tobacco, strawberry and cedar. Light- to medium-bodied, with light tannins and a fresh finish. Not imported into the U.S. Drink now.–J.S. • $NA • (1/01/1999) • **85**
Toscana Nero del Tondo 1995 • $NA • (9/30/1997) • **85**
Toscana Nero del Tondo 1994 • $NA • (9/30/1997) • **87**
Toscana Nero del Tondo 1993 • $NA • (10/31/1995) • **85**
Toscana Nero del Tondo 1988 • $18 • (9/15/1991) • **88**
Vino Nobile di Montepulciano Lodola Nuova 1996: Good fruit but slightly short. Vivid aromas of dried cherry, with hints of bark and mushroom. Medium-bodied, with silky tannins and a earthy, slightly austere finish. Drink now.–J.S. • $18 • (11/30/1999) • **84**

Vino Nobile di Montepulciano Lodola Nuova 1995: A friendly and round Nobile, with chocolate and berry aromas and flavors. Medium-bodied, with medium tannins and a fresh finish. Drink now.–J.S. • $15 • (12/15/1998) • **85**

Vino Nobile di Montepulciano Lodola Nuova 1991 • $NA • (10/31/1995) • **84**

Vino Nobile di Montepulciano Lodola Nuova 1989 • $12 • (7/31/1994) • **82**

RUGGERI & C.

Prosecco di Valdobbiadene NV: Crisp and clean, with a floral character, finishing short. Drink now.–B.S. • $14 • (7/31/1998) • **80**

Prosecco di Valdobbiadene Giustino B. 1996: Intriguing floral and almond aromas are followed by apple flavors, all richly interwoven with fine acidity that leaves a clean finish. Almond notes echo on the aftertaste. Drink now.–B.S. • $19 • (7/31/1998) • **86**

Prosecco di Valdobbiadene S. Stefano NV: A tasty sparkler. The honey and citrus flavors are subtle, but the texture is rich, balanced by acidity that carries everything to a cleansing finish. Drink now.–B.S. • $15 • (7/31/1998) • **84**

RUGGERO, CASTEL

Chianti Classico 1997: A pretty Chianti, with raspberry and cherry aromas and flavors. Medium-bodied, with light tannins and a bright berry aftertaste. Drink now.–J.S. • $18 • (11/30/1999) • **86**

RUSSIZ SUPERIORE

Cabernet Franc Collio 1996: Plenty of ripe Cabernet Franc character, with subtle hints of dried herb and wet earth. Medium-bodied, with light, caressing tannins and a fruity finish. Drink now.–J.S. • $20 • (6/30/1999) • **87**

Cabernet Franc Collio 1995: Broad-shouldered, showing cherry and plum, good concentration and weight, but it's a little rigid, lacking the nuance and complexity of the best.–B.S. • $20 • (7/31/1998) • **86**

Cabernet Franc Collio 1986 • $15 • (9/15/1988) • **83**

Collio Degli Orzoni Riserva 1994: A very fine, silky red, with lovely aromas of mint, berry and currant that follow through to a medium-bodied and very well-structured palate. Fine tannins and a medium finish. Needs time to mellow. Best after 2001.–J.S. • $35 • (6/30/1999) • **88**

Collio Degli Orzoni Riserva 1993 • $30 • (6/30/1998) • **89**

Collio Degli Orzoni Riserva 1990 • $30 • (6/15/1996) • **83**

Merlot Collio 1996: A light- to medium-bodied Merlot, with berry, tobacco and herb character and light tannins. A bit too weedy. Drink now.–J.S. • $20 • (6/30/1999) • **81**

Merlot Collio 1993 • $18 • (5/31/1996) • **86**

Merlot Collio 1989 • $27 • (4/30/1992) • **86**

Merlot Collio 1986 • $14 • (9/15/1988) • **80**

Pinot Bianco Collio 1998: Very good Pinot Bianco. Wonderful aromas of peaches and cream with hints of pie crust. Full-bodied, with lots of fruit yet still reserved. Firm acidity, fresh finish. Drink now.–J.S. • $19 • (4/30/2000) • **87**

Pinot Bianco Collio 1996 • $20 • (6/15/1998) • **86**

Pinot Grigio Collio 1998: Plenty of ripe fruit. More like fruit juice than wine. A bit simple, with melon flavors. Medium in body and finish. Drink now.–J.S. • $19 • (3/31/2000) • **84**

Sauvignon Collio 1998: Fruit-driven white, with spicy grapefruit flavors. Medium-bodied, with good fruit character and a firm finish. Drink now.–J.S. • $19 • (4/30/2000) • **85**

Tocai Friulano Collio 1998: Sets the standard for Tocai Friulano. Aromas of apple and cream, with hints of spice. Full-bodied, with loads of ripe fruit and a long, long finish. A beauty. Drink now.–J.S. • $19 • (3/31/2000) • **89**

Tocai Friulano Collio 1996 • $20 • (6/15/1998) • **85**

S. BIAGIO

Barolo 1993 • $NA • (10/31/1997) • **77**

Key: SS—Spectator Selection. CS—Cellar Selection. HR—Highly Recommended. $NA—Price not available. (BT)—Barrel tasting. (A)—Auction Price. For a key to the tasters' initials, see "How to Use These Listings." **Dates in parentheses represent the issues in which the ratings were published.**

S. LORENZO, CASTEL

Barbera Piedmont Bios 1997: Delicious, showing mineral, blood orange and wild strawberry character. Good acidity helps cleanse the palate. Good concentration, but turns a bit dry. Drink now through 2003.–P.M. • $12 • (10/31/1998) • **85**

S. STEFANO

Chianti Classico 1993 • $NA • (10/31/1995) • **72**

SACCARDI

Chianti Classico 1993 • $10 • (3/31/1997) • **84**

Chianti Classico 1990 • $10 • (10/31/1994) • **87**

Chianti Classico 1987 • $10 • (5/15/1990) • **75**

Chianti Classico Riserva 1993 • $15 • (3/31/1997) • **81**

Chianti Classico Riserva 1988 • $13 • (10/31/1994) • **85**

Chianti Classico Riserva 1983 • $12 • (5/15/1990) • **87**

SAFFIRIO, JOSETTA

Barolo 1992 • $NA • (10/31/1996) • **85**

Barolo 1991 • $NA • (10/31/1996) • **88**

Barolo 1987 • $40 • (12/15/1992) • **87**

SALA, LA

Chianti Classico 1997: Light, fresh and fruity, with good acidity and a berry and dried cherry finish. Drink now.–J.S. • $15 • (11/30/1999) • **81**

Chianti Classico 1996: A bit rustic, but shows some really good fruit character. Grapey in aroma, with hints of dried fruit. Medium-bodied, with raisin, licorice and berry flavors, light tannins and a slightly alcoholic finish. Drink now.–J.S. • $12 • (12/15/1998) • **82**

Chianti Classico 1995 • $13 • (9/30/1997) • **79**

Chianti Classico 1994 • $13 • (10/31/1996) • **80**

Chianti Classico 1993 • $NA • (10/31/1995) • **79**

Chianti Classico 1991 • $NA • (10/31/1995) • **81**

Chianti Classico 1990 • $NA • (10/31/1993) • **84**

Chianti Classico Riserva 1996: A well-crafted CC riserva, with plum skin and berry aromas. Medium-bodied, with medium tannins and a pretty vanilla and fruit aftertaste. Drink now.–J.S. • $24 • (11/30/1999) • **86**

Chianti Classico Riserva 1995: A straightforward Sangiovese with dried cherry aromas and flavors, medium body, fresh acidity and a light finish. Drink now.–J.S. • $23 • (12/15/1998) • **84**

Chianti Classico Riserva 1994 • $18 • (9/30/1997) • **86**

Chianti Classico Riserva 1993 • $18 • (10/31/1996) • **77**

Chianti Classico Riserva 1990 • $NA • (2/28/1995) • **85**

Colli della Toscana Centrale Campo all 'Albero 1996: A soft and delicious red, with ripe fruit and grilled meat aromas. Medium-bodied, with soft tannins and a medium finish. Needs a bit more fruit concentration to be outstanding. Drink now.–J.S. • $32 • (11/30/1999) • **86**

Colli della Toscana Centrale Campo all 'Albero 1995: A big, fruity, show-me red. Gorgeous blackberry and raspberry aromas. Full-bodied, with velvety tannins and a long, ripe fruit aftertaste. Drink now.–J.S. • $30 • (12/15/1998) • **88**

Colli della Toscana Centrale Campo all 'Abero 1994 • $22 • (9/30/1997) • **87**

Colli della Toscana Centrale Campo all 'Abero 1993 • $22 • (10/31/1996) • **85**

Colli della Toscana Centrale Campo all 'Abero 1990 • $NA • (2/28/1995) • **90**

Il Bianco 1996 • $8 • (9/30/1997) • **84**

SALAPARUTA, DUCA DI

Duca Enrico 1992 • $45 • (6/15/1997) • **89**

Duca Enrico 1990 • $40 • (1/01/1997) • **90**

Duca Enrico 1987 • $38 • (11/30/1994) • **89**

Duca Enrico 1984 • $27 • (9/15/1989) • **92**

Sicilia Ala 1998: Interesting in small doses. Very sweet, with a dark amber color and intense aromas of marzipan, coffee and allspice. Tastes like amaretto. Not imported into the U.S. Drink now.–J.S. • $NA/500 ml. • (1/01/2000) • **86**

Sicilia Colomba Platino 1998: Good, with lemon, cream and light mineral character. Medium-bodied, with a fruity finish. Drink now.–J.S. • $13 • (5/31/2000) • **81**

Sicilia Duca Enrico 1995: Has wonderfully ripe fruit, but very nutty, with walnut and chestnut character. Full-bodied and soft, with a long finish. A bit traditional but delicious. Drink now through 2001.–J.S. • $58 • (5/31/2000) • **85**

Sicilia Red Corvo 1997: A traditional red, with chestnut and berry character. Medium-bodied, with light tannins and a fruity finish. Drink now.–J.S. • $10 • (5/31/2000) • **82**

Sicilia Terre d'Agala 1996: Very ripe and thick, with raisin, walnut and old wood character. Full-bodied, thick and slightly short. A bit funky, but good. Needs food. Drink now.–J.S. • $13 • (5/31/2000) • **81**

Sicilia White Corvo 1998: Fresh and zingy, with lemon rind and mineral character. Medium-bodied, with lively acidity. Drink now.–J.S. • $10 • (5/31/2000) • **84**

Terre d'Agala 1993 • $13 • (5/15/1997) • **88**

Terre d'Agala 1989 • $11 • (5/31/1995) • **80**

SALCETINO

Chianti Classico 1991 • $NA • (10/31/1993) • **78**

Chianti Classico Lucarello Riserva 1996: A bit light but with intriguing aromas of fruit, bark and smoke. Medium-bodied, with light tannins and a smoky finish. Not imported into the U.S. Drink now.–J.S. • $NA • (1/01/1999) • **83**

Chianti Classico Salcineto 1997: A solid '97 Chianti, with very pretty aromas of raspberry and cherry. Medium-bodied, with medium tannins and a fruity, crisp finish. Drink now.–J.S. • $20 • (11/30/1999) • **87**

SALCHETO

Rosso di Montepulciano 1997: A young, lively wine that needs some bottle age. Very grapey in aroma with peppery undertones. Medium-bodied, with medium, firm tannins and a long finish. Drink now.–J.S. • $17 • (12/15/1998) • **85**

Rosso di Montepulciano 1996: Dried cherry and hints of vanilla on the nose. Medium-bodied, with polished tannins and a fresh aftertaste. Drink now.–J.S. • $17 • (12/15/1998) • **84**

Vino Nobile di Montepulciano 1996: Delicious, with lovely cherry, vanilla and berry character and a soft, velvety texture. Medium-bodied, with a ripe fruit finish. Drink now.–J.S. • $28 • (11/30/1999) • **86**

Vino Nobile di Montepulciano 1995: Young and lively for a 1995. Dark-colored, with grapey and stemmy aromas and flavors. Medium-bodied, with medium tannins and a fresh finish. Drink now through 2001.–J.S. • $25 • (12/15/1998) • **88**

Vino Nobile di Montepulciano Riserva 1995: Maybe a bit too much new wood, but delicious. Beautiful plum, berry, and violet aromas and flavors. Full-bodied and very soft, with masses of new wood, giving it a vanilla ice cream and berry aftertaste. Drink now through 2002.–J.S. • $36 • (11/30/1999) • **87**

SALETTE, LE

Amarone della Valpolicella Classico La Marega 1990 • $29 • (6/15/1998) • **87**

Amarone della Valpolicella La Marega 1988 • $25 • (9/15/1992) • **81**

Valpolicella Ca ' Carnocchio 1989 • $NA • (9/15/1992) • **81**

Valpolicella Classico I Progni 1991 • $12 • (9/15/1992) • **72**

Valpolicella Classico Superiore I Progni 1993 • $12 • (1/01/1998) • **72**

Valpolicella Classico Superiore I Progni 1989 • $12 • (9/15/1992) • **79**

SALICUTTI, PODERE

Rosso di Montalcino 1997: Amazing new wine—and made from organic vineyards. A blockbuster, with masses of berry, dark chocolate and vanilla flavors. Full-bodied, with velvety tannins and a long finish. Lots of new wood, but done just right. Stunning. Drink now.–J.S. • $26 • (9/15/1999) • **91**

SALLE, CASTELLO DI

Montepulciano d'Abruzzo 1995 • $17 • (2/28/1998) • **85**

Montepulciano d'Abruzzo 1985 • $15 • (6/15/1990) • **84**

SALUSTRI

Toscana Santa Marta 1997: A beautifully balanced red, with berry, cherry and raspberry character. Medium-bodied, with silky tannins and a medium, fruity finish. Not imported into the U.S. Drink now.–J.S. • $NA • (1/01/1999) • **87**

SALVIANO

Orvieto Classico 1996 • $12 • (2/28/1998) • **85**

SAN BONIFACIO

Pinot Grigio Veneto 1998: Plenty of apple, mineral and melon character. Medium-bodied, with fresh acidity and a clean, flavorful finish. Drink now.–J.S. • $10 • (3/31/2000) • **84**

SAN DONATO, FATTORIA DI

Chianti Colli Senesi 1997: Loaded with blackberry and crushed raspberry aromas. Medium-bodied, with light tannins and a deliciously fruity finish. Drink now.–J.S. • $9 • (12/15/1998) • **85**

Toscana Poggio alle Corti 1996: Some lemon and canteloupe character. Medium-bodied, with moderate acidity and a light finish. A bit dull.–J.S. • $14 • (12/15/1998) • **79**

Toscana Rosato Donna Miolanne 1996: Some decent fruit in this rosé but there's a bit of an herbal undertone to it. Medium-bodied, with fresh acidity and a strawberry, leafy aftertaste. Drink now.–J.S. • $NA • (12/15/1998) • **80**

Vernaccia di San Gimignano 1997: Big and powerful Vernaccia. A ripe white with interesting almond, peach and ripe fruit character. Medium- to full-bodied, with moderate acidity and a spicy aftertaste. Needs food. Drink now.–J.S. • $NA • (12/15/1998) • **86**

Vernaccia di San Gimignano 1996: Fruity and simple. Perfumed, with pear blossom and other flowers. Medium-bodied, with white pepper, chalk and fruit flavors and a light finish. Drink now.–J.S. • $NA • (12/15/1998) • **81**

SAN FABIANO CALCINAIA

Chianti Classico 1997: Fresh and fruity, with dried berry and tobacco character. Medium-bodied, with light tannins and a fresh finish. Drink now.–J.S. • $18 • (11/30/1999) • **86**

Chianti Classico 1996: Impressive concentration of blackberry and cherry aromas. Medium-bodied, with well-integrated tannins and a silky, caressing texture on the finish. Drink now through 2003.–J.S. • $13 • (12/15/1998) • **87**

Chianti Classico 1995 • $13 • (9/30/1997) • **86**

Chianti Classico 1994 • $13 • (10/31/1996) • **83**

Chianti Classico 1992 • $11 • (2/28/1995) • **76**

Chianti Classico 1991 • $12 • (10/31/1993) • **84**

Chianti Classico 1990 • $9 • (10/31/1993) • **85**

Chianti Classico 1988 • $12 • (9/15/1991) • **84**

Chianti Classico Cellole Riserva 1996: Extremely well crafted for the vintage, with very pretty aromas of raspberry and flowers. Medium-bodied, with well-integrated tannins and a caressing texture. Drink now.–J.S. • $28 • (11/30/1999) • **87**

Chianti Classico Cellole Riserva 1995: Hard to resist. Lots of crushed berry character. Medium-bodied, with moderate tannins and an aftertaste of berry, chocolate and spice. Drink now.–J.S. • $20 • (12/15/1998) • **86**

Chianti Classico Cellole Riserva 1994 • $NA • (9/30/1997) • **87**

Chianti Classico Cellole Riserva 1993 • $18 • (10/31/1996) • **81**

Chianti Classico Cellole Riserva 1990 • $16 • (10/31/1993) • **86**

Chianti Classico Cellole Riserva 1988 • $15 • (9/15/1991) • **83**

Chianti Classico Cellole Riserva 1985 • $13 • (11/30/1989) • **91**

Chianti Classico Il Grigio Riserva 1995: Pretty and aromatic, with roses, berries and milk chocolate. Light- to medium-bodied, with light tannins and a slightly diluted finish. Drink now.–J.S. • $22 • (12/15/1998) • **84**

Chianti Classico Riserva 1988 • $NA • (9/15/1992) • **85**

Chianti Classico Riserva 1985 • $NA • (9/15/1991) • **84**

Toscana Cerviolo Red 1997: Can't keep my hands off this. Full-bodied, with gorgeous velvety tannins, loads of berry, cherry and vanilla character and a caressing texture. Wonderful blend of Sangiovese, Cabernet and Merlot. Best after 2000.–J.S. • $36 • (11/30/1999) • **92**

Toscana Cerviolo Red 1996: Dark-colored and deeply aromatic, showing black currants, dark chocolate and mint. Full-bodied, with similar character on the palate. Long, caressing finish. A beautiful blend of Cabernet and Merlot. Drink now.–J.S. • $32 • (12/15/1998) • **90**

Toscana Cerviolo Red 1995 • $22 • (9/30/1997) • **87**

Toscana Cerviolo Red 1993 • $18 • (10/31/1996) • **87**

Toscana Cerviolo Red 1991 • $15 • (2/28/1995) • **88**

Toscana Cerviolo Red 1990 • $13 • (10/31/1993) • **89**

■ ■ ■ ■

SAN FABIANO CALCINAIA

Toscana Cerviolo Red 1988 • $14 • (12/31/1992) • **81**
Toscana Cerviolo Red 1986 • $19 • (3/31/1990) • **82**
Toscana Cerviolo White 1998: A rather exaggerated style of Chardonnay, but I like it. Deep yellow in color and very rich, with toasted oak, coconut and dried pineapple character. Full-bodied, with a smooth, caressing texture and a long toasted almond and vanilla aftertaste. Not an ager. Drink now. –J.S. • $17 • (11/30/1999) • **86**

SAN FELICE

Chardonnay Toscana Ancherona 1997: Aromas of peach, lemon and vanilla are really interesting. Medium-bodied, with apricot and dried fruit on the palate. Medium finish. Needs a bit more acidity, but delicious. Drink now. –J.S. • $18 • (11/30/1999) • **86**
Chardonnay Toscana Ancherona 1996: Subtle, with apple, cream and smoke character, developing into ripe and tropical fruit flavors. Medium body. Moderate acidity. Long, delicious aftertaste. Also contains Sauvignon. Drink now.–J.S. • $18 • (12/15/1998) • **88**
Chianti Classico 1997: Attractive blackberry and cherry character. Medium-bodied, with light tannins and a fruity vanilla aftertaste. Drink now.–J.S. • $13 • (10/31/1999) • **85**
Chianti Classico 1996: Lots of fresh berry character in this light-bodied yet delicious young red. Delicate and fruity, with light tannins and crisp acidity. Drink now.–J.S. • $12 • (12/15/1998) • **84**
Chianti Classico 1995 • $12 • (9/30/1997) • **85**
Chianti Classico 1994 • $12 • (10/31/1996) • **80**
Chianti Classico 1993 • $11 • (10/31/1995) • **80**
Chianti Classico 1992 • $10 • (2/28/1995) • **80**
Chianti Classico 1991 • $13 • (10/31/1993) • **80**
Chianti Classico 1990 • $11 • (9/15/1992) • **87**
Chianti Classico Campo del Civettino 1990 • $NA • (10/31/1993) • **83**
Chianti Classico Campo del Civettino 1988 • $NA • (9/15/1991) • **84**
Chianti Classico Il Grigio Riserva 1996: Shows the good, mature cedar, plum and leather character you expect in a Sangiovese. Medium-bodied, with a light finish. Drink now.–J.S. • $18 • (11/30/1999) • **84**
Chianti Classico Il Grigio Riserva 1994 • $16 • (9/30/1997) • **83**
Chianti Classico Il Grigio Riserva 1993 • $15 • (10/31/1996) • **80**
Chianti Classico Il Grigio Riserva 1991 • $16 • (10/31/1995) • **86**
Chianti Classico Il Grigio Riserva 1990 • $16 • (2/28/1995) • **85**
Chianti Classico Il Grigio Riserva 1988 • $16 • (9/15/1992) • **86**
Chianti Classico Il Grigio Riserva 1987 • $13 • (1/31/1992) • **83**
Chianti Classico Il Grigio Riserva 1985 • $10 • (9/15/1990) • **86**
Chianti Classico Il Grigio Riserva 1983 • $12 • (11/30/1989) • **85**
Chianti Classico Il Grigio Riserva 1982 • $11 • (5/31/1988) • **90**
Chianti Classico Poggio Rosso Riserva 1996: A chunky Chianti Classico riserva. Dark, with captivating aromas of licorice and blackberry. Full-bodied, with polished tannins and a medium finish. Slightly monolithic. Drink now.–J.S. • $29 • (11/30/1999) • **89**
Chianti Classico Poggio Rosso Riserva 1995: Best Chianti riserva of the vintage. Beautiful blackberry and wet earth with a hint of fresh mushrooms. Medium- to full-bodied, with intense fruit flavors, extremely well-integrated tannins and a just-right note of smoky oak. Drink through 2005. –J.S. • $30 • (12/15/1998) • **91**
Chianti Classico Poggio Rosso Riserva 1994 • $27 • (9/30/1997) • **90**
Chianti Classico Poggio Rosso Riserva 1993 • $30 • (9/30/1997) • **90**
Chianti Classico Poggio Rosso Riserva 1990 • $24 • (9/30/1997) • **92**
Chianti Classico Poggio Rosso Riserva 1988 • $18 • (9/30/1997) • **89**
Chianti Classico Poggio Rosso Riserva 1987 • $23 • (6/30/1993) • **68**
Chianti Classico Poggio Rosso Riserva 1986 • $24 • (1/31/1992) • **86**
Chianti Classico Poggio Rosso Riserva 1985 • $20 Ⓐ • (9/30/1997) • **89**
Chianti Classico Poggio Rosso Riserva 1983 • $17 • (11/30/1989) • **87**
Chianti Classico Poggio Rosso Riserva 1982 • $15 • (9/15/1990) • **81**
Chianti Classico Poggio Rosso Riserva 1981 • $15 • (8/31/1988) • **87**
Chianti Classico Poggio Rosso Riserva 1978 • $14 • (3/15/1987) • **73**
Predicato di Bitùrica 1985 • $28 • (12/15/1991) • **82**
Predicato di Bitùrica 1983 • $22 • (11/30/1989) • **87**
Predicato di Bitùrica 1982 • $19 • (1/31/1988) SS • **92**
Toscana Belcaro White 1998: Plenty of lemon and mineral character in this good-quality white. Medium-bodied, with a fruity finish. Sauvignon Blanc and Vermentino. Drink now.–J.S. • $11 • (11/30/1999) • **85**
Toscana Belcaro White 1997: This wine has some character. Fresh apple, melon and lemon rind aromas. Medium-bodied, with fresh acidity and a fruity, mineral, blanched almond finish. A blend of Vermentino and Sauvignon. Drink now.–J.S. • $12 • (12/15/1998) • **85**
Toscana Belcaro White 1996 • $11 • (9/30/1997) • **85**
Toscana Vigorello 1996: Dark, with plenty of blackberry and spice and hints of dried herb. Full-bodied, with velvety tannins, a ripe fruit and smoke character and a medium finish. Needs a bit more fruit midpalate to be outstanding. Drink now.–J.S. • $27 • (11/30/1999) • **88**
Toscana Vigorello 1995: Berry and cherry character with a slight herbal tint. Medium-bodied, with medium, silky tannins and an aftertaste of berry. Slightly green Cabernet Sauvignon character comes out. Best after 2000.–J.S. • $28 • (12/15/1998) • **86**
Toscana Vigorello 1994 • $24 • (9/30/1997) • **89**
Toscana Vigorello 1993 • $27 • (10/31/1996) • **88**
Toscana Vigorello 1990 • $NA • (10/31/1993) • **91**
Toscana Vigorello 1988 • $NA • (11/15/1993) • **88**
Toscana Vigorello 1987 • $25 • (6/15/1993) • **87**
Toscana Vigorello 1986 • $NA • (11/15/1993) • **91**
Toscana Vigorello 1985 • $18 • (9/15/1990) • **89**
Toscana Vigorello 1983 • $NA • (11/15/1993) • **91**
Toscana Vigorello 1982 • $NA • (11/15/1993) • **92**
Toscana Vigorello 1981 • $13 • (1/31/1988) • **84**
Toscana Vigorello 1980 • $12 • (2/28/1987) SS • **95**
Vin Santo Val d'Arbia in Pincis 1993: Slightly oxidized and nutty on the nose, but the palate is sweet, with almond, dried orange and honey flavors. A very good traditional Vin Santo. Try with a fruit tart. Drink now.–J.S. • $34/375 ml. • (11/30/1999) • **87**
Vin Santo Val d'Arbia in Pincis 1990: A beautiful, superclean Vin Santo, with almond, burnt orange and caramel character through and through, yet it's fresh and balanced, with lovely sweetness and good acidity. Drink now.–J.S. • $32/375 ml. • (12/15/1998) • **89**

SAN FILIPPO

Brunello di Montalcino 1990 • $NA • (10/31/1995) • **85**

SAN FRANCESCO, FATTORIA

Cirò Classico 1998: A bit old and tired, with berry and cedar character, but short and slightly dry.–J.S. • $10 • (5/31/2000) • **79**
Cirò Classico Donna Madda 1997: Has good ripe fruit but a rather dry, austere, peppery finish. Hard to get excited about. Tasted twice, with consistent notes.–J.S. • $19 • (5/31/2000) • **78**
Cirò Classico Ronco dei Quattroventi 1997: Pleasant and fruity, with vanilla and tobacco character. Medium-bodied, with light tannins and a slightly dry finish. Drink now.–J.S. • $26 • (5/31/2000) • **81**

SAN GERVASIO

Bianco Pisano di San Torpè Casima de 'Venti 1998: Slightly candied aromas of pear drops and fruit cocktail. Medium-bodied, with a short, slightly watery finish. Not imported into the U.S.–J.S. • $NA • (1/01/1999) • **79**
Bianco Pisano di San Torpè Recinaio Vin Santo 1995: Not altogether clean, but with decent ripe fruit character and aromas of ripe peach, butterscotch and almond. Medium-bodied and medium sweet, with high acidity and a volatile almond finish. Not imported into the U.S.–J.S. • $NA/500 ml. • (1/01/1999) • **79**
Chianti Le Stoppie 1998: Enticing, bright berry and cherry aromas and flavors. Light- to medium-bodied, with light tannins and a fruity finish. Delicious. Not imported into the U.S. Drink now.–J.S. • $NA • (1/01/1999) • **84**
Colli dell 'Etruria Centrale Rosato Aprico 1998: Loads of strawberry character in this rosé with a floral undertone. Medium-bodied, with fresh acidity and a fruity finish. Not imported into the U.S. Drink now.–J.S. • $NA • (1/01/1999) • **83**
Toscana A Sirio Red 1997: A harmonious and lovely red, with gorgeous blackberry and cherry aromas. Medium-bodied, with chewy tannins and a solid core of berry fruit on the finish. Made with Sangiovese and a splash of Cabernet Sauvignon. Drink now.–J.S. • $32 • (11/30/1999) • **88**

SAN GIORGIO

Brunello di Montalcino 1995: Opulent and very ready-to-drink Brunello. Aromas of sandlewood and fruit. Full-bodied, with soft tannins and a ripe

Key: SS—Spectator Selection. CS—Cellar Selection. HR—Highly Recommended. $NA—Price not available. (BT)—Barrel tasting. Ⓐ—Auction Price. For a key to the tasters' initials, see "How to Use These Listings."
Dates in parentheses represent the issues in which the ratings were published.

fruit, tobacco aftertaste. Limited U.S. availability. Drink now.–J.S. • $NA • (1/01/2000) • **87**

Brunello di Montalcino 1994: Clear and focused, with berry, dried cherry, chocolate and light earth character. Medium- to full-bodied, with velvety tannins and a sweet fruit finish. A beauty. Best now through 2005.–J.S. • $50 • (8/31/1999) • **89**

Brunello di Montalcino 1991 • $NA • (9/30/1997) • **78**

Brunello di Montalcino 1990 • $28 • (10/31/1995) • **89**

Brunello di Montalcino 1988 • $25 • (7/31/1995) • **86**

Rosso di Montalcino 1997: Well-crafted, modern rosso. Aromas of berries, strawberries and new wood galore. Medium-bodied, with silky tannins and a fresh fruit aftertaste. Drink now.–J.S. • $NA • (1/01/1999) • **85**

SAN GIOVANNI

Fiano Paestum 1998: Pleasant aromas of ripe tangerine and almond follow through to a medium-bodied palate, with light acidity and a fresh, fruity finish. Slight dilution midpalate. Drink now.–J.S. • $NA • (1/01/2000) • **84**

SAN GIUSEPPE

Pinot Grigio Veneto 1997 • $9 • (6/30/1998) • **78**

Pinot Nero Veneto 1996 • $9 • (6/30/1998) • **78**

SAN GIUSEPPE, PODERE

Toscana Red 1997: A lovely Sangiovese, with harmonious cherry, plum and berry character. Medium-bodied, with medium tannins and a fresh finish. Not imported into the U.S. Drink now.–J.S. • $NA • (1/01/1999) • **87**

SAN GUIDO, TENUTA

Bolgheri-Sassicaia Sassicaia 1996: A well-structured Sass, with plenty of blackberry and dried herb character. Full-bodied, with plenty of ripe tannins and a currant bush and herb finish. Give it time to develop. Best after 2001.–J.S. • $110 • (11/30/1999) • **91**

Bolgheri-Sassicaia Sassicaia 1995: Best Sassicaia since the '90. Rich in currant, blackberry, dried herbs and tanned leather on the nose and palate. Medium- to full-bodied, with very soft yet fine tannins and a long, caressing finish. Hard to resist now. Drink now.–J.S. • $95 • (12/15/1998) • **90**

Bolgheri-Sassicaia Sassicaia 1994 • $78 • (9/30/1997) • **88**

Sassicaia 1993 • $96 Ⓐ • (10/31/1996) • **85**

Sassicaia 1992 • $85 Ⓐ • (7/31/1996) • **78**

Sassicaia 1991 • $82 Ⓐ • (7/31/1996) • **81**

Sassicaia 1990 • $90 • (7/31/1996) • **93**

Sassicaia 1989 • $131 Ⓐ • (7/31/1996) • **88**

Sassicaia 1988 • $234 Ⓐ • (7/31/1996) • **97**

Sassicaia 1987 • $92 • (7/31/1996) • **86**

Sassicaia 1986 • $105 Ⓐ • (7/31/1996) • **84**

Sassicaia 1985 • $679 Ⓐ • (7/31/1996) • **99**

Sassicaia 1984 • $96 Ⓐ • (7/31/1996) • **82**

Sassicaia 1983 • $143 Ⓐ • (7/31/1996) • **88**

Sassicaia 1982 • $187 Ⓐ • (7/31/1996) • **90**

Sassicaia 1981 • $183 Ⓐ • (7/31/1996) • **89**

Sassicaia 1980 • $134 Ⓐ • (7/31/1996) • **77**

Sassicaia 1979 • $173 Ⓐ • (7/31/1996) • **83**

Sassicaia 1978 • $133 • (7/31/1996) • **95**

Sassicaia 1977 • $NA • (7/31/1996) • **85**

Sassicaia 1976 • $79 • (7/31/1996) • **65**

Sassicaia 1975 • $99 • (7/31/1996) • **90**

Sassicaia 1974 • $NA • (7/31/1996) • **83**

Sassicaia 1972 • $NA • (7/31/1996) • **85**

Sassicaia 1971 • $NA • (7/31/1996) • **78**

Sassicaia 1970 • $NA • (7/31/1996) • **83**

Sassicaia 1968 • $550 • (7/31/1996) • **88**

SAN LEONARDO, TENUTA

Merlot Trentino 1997: Fruity, with berry and herb character. Medium-bodied, with light to medium tannins and a fresh finish. Drink now.–J.S. • $20 • (6/15/2000) • **84**

Merlot Trentino 1995 • $18 • (5/31/1998) • **83**

Merlot Trentino 1994 • $18 • (6/15/1997) • **84**

Trentino San Leonardo 1996: A beautiful Bordeaux blend, with currant bush, mint and mineral aromas plus a touch of new oak. Full-bodied, with polished tannins and a long, long finish. Best after 2002.–J.S. • $50 • (6/15/2000) • **90**

Trentino San Leonardo 1995: A monster of a red. This stunning Bordeaux-style blend from Italy is inky in color and exhibits incredible concentration of black currant and dried herb character. It's full-bodied and superconcentrated, with masses of velvety tannins and a long, long finish. Best after 2003.–J.S. • $50 • (6/30/1999) HR • **93**

Trentino San Leonardo 1994 • $47 • (1/01/1998) • **87**

Trentino San Leonardo 1993 • $47 • (6/15/1997) • **84**

Trentino San Leonardo 1991 • $38 • (6/15/1997) • **84**

Trentino San Leonardo 1990 • $40 • (1/01/1998) • **89**

Trentino San Leonardo 1986 • $33 • (12/15/1992) • **86**

Trentino San Leonardo 1985 • $35 • (12/15/1992) • **82**

Trentino San Leonardo 1983 • $35 • (12/15/1992) • **79**

SAN LUIGI

Chianti Colli Senesi 1997: A bit light and diluted, but with pleasant dried cherry and cedar character.–J.S. • $NA • (1/01/2000) • **78**

Chianti Colli Senesi 1994 • $11 • (10/31/1997) • **85**

Toscana 1996: Medium-bodied, with aromas of dried cherry and red licorice, light tannins and a crisp, very fruity finish. Drink now.–J.S. • $NA • (1/01/2000) • **85**

SAN MARTINO

Salice Salentino Red 1993: A mellow and soft red. Aromas of plum and earth with hints of ash follow through to a medium-bodied palate, with clean grape flavors and a soft finish. Drink now.–J.S. • $9 • (6/30/1999) • **83**

SAN MICHELE

Chianti 1991 • $7 • (7/31/1995) • **75**

Chianti Classico Tenuta La Gabbiola 1997: A solid, chunky red, with plum, berry and cappuccino aromas and flavors. Medium-bodied, with silky tannins and a caressing texture on the fruity finish. Not imported into the U.S. Drink now through 2001.–J.S. • $NA • (11/30/1999) • **88**

Chianti Classico Tenuta La Gabbiola Riserva 1995: Good, clean '95 riserva. Plenty of bright raspberry aromas. Medium-bodied, with firm tannins and a crisp finish. Slightly tough really. Not imported into the U.S. Drink now.–J.S. • $NA • (1/01/1999) • **85**

Chianti Colli Fiorentini 1997: Subtle aromas of raspberry, earth and spice. Medium-bodied, with medium, velvety tannins and a ripe fruit finish. Not imported into the U.S. Drink now.–J.S. • $NA • (1/01/1999) • **85**

SAN POLO IN ROSSO, CASTELLO DI

Cetinaia 1990 • $NA • (3/31/1997) • **86**

Cetinaia 1986 • $27 • (12/15/1992) • **82**

Chianti Classico 1993 • $NA • (3/31/1997) • **85**

Chianti Classico 1985 • $10 • (11/30/1989) • **67**

Chianti Classico Riserva 1991 • $NA • (3/31/1997) • **87**

Chianti Classico Riserva 1988 • $15 • (9/15/1992) • **85**

Chianti Classico Riserva 1986 • $14 • (9/15/1992) • **75**

Chianti Classico Riserva 1985 • $14 • (11/30/1989) • **78**

SAN VINCENTI

Chianti Classico 1995 • $17 • (9/30/1997) • **85**

Chianti Classico 1990 • $NA • (10/31/1993) • **68**

Chianti Classico Podere di Stignano 1997: A rustic wine, with peppery, spicy character and hints of raisin. Medium-bodied, with rich fruit and a medium finish. Drink now.–J.S. • $17 • (11/30/1999) • **85**

Chianti Classico Podere di Stignano 1996: A sleek and well-made Chianti Classico. Bright strawberry and cherry aromas. Medium-bodied, with well-integrated tannins and a fresh finish. Drink now through 2003.–J.S. • $16 • (12/15/1998) • **86**

Chianti Classico Podere di Stignano 1991 • $13 • (10/31/1995) • **74**

Chianti Classico Podere di Stignano Riserva 1996: Slightly one-dimensional but very clean, with aromas of flowers and dried cherry. Medium-bodied, with medium tannins and a fresh finish. Drink now.–J.S. • $19 • (11/30/1999) • **85**

Chianti Classico Podere di Stignano Riserva 1995: Wonderfully floral, with loads of mint, berry and currant flavors. Medium- to full-bodied, with a silky texture. Needs some time to mellow. Drink now.–J.S. • $20 • (12/15/1998) • **87**

Chianti Classico Podere di Stignano Riserva 1994 • $18 • (9/30/1997) • **86**

Chianti Classico Podere di Stignano Riserva 1988 • $17 • (10/31/1995) • **81**

ITALY

SAN VINCENTI

Colli dell 'Etruria Centrale 1996 • $13 • (9/30/1997) • **78**

Toscana Stignano 1997: Pretty, well-crafted red. Medium-dark ruby color. Plum, berry and smoke aromas. Medium- to full-bodied, with velvety tannins and a fresh fruit finish. Drink now.–J.S. • $30 • (6/15/2000) • **87**

Toscana Stignano 1996: Sleek and racy. Dark ruby in color, with berry, raspberry and mint aromas. Medium- to full-bodied, with silky tannins and a long, caressing aftertaste. A beauty. Not imported into the U.S. Best after 2000.–J.S. • $NA • (11/30/1999) • **88**

SANDRONE, LUCIANO

Barbera d'Alba 1997: Stunning Barbera. Flawless in its texture, full-bodied and with silky, round, ripe tannins. A wine that focuses on red berry and blackberry flavors, with just-so acidity and controlled oak doses that bring in just enough spice, mocha and coffee notes. Clever winemaking. Drink now through 2002.–P.M. • $23 • (9/15/1999) • **94**

Barbera d'Alba 1996: Sophisticated, medium-bodied, with a supple texture, ripe fruit and smooth tannins, this balanced red packs in the berry flavors with subtle oak accents and earthy, wet soil, *terroir* notes. The lingering, chewy finish suggests it could improve with cellaring. Best after 2000. –P.M. • $15 • (10/31/1998) • **88**

Barbera d'Alba 1994 • $24 • (10/31/1996) • **86**

Barbera d'Alba 1991 • $22 • (11/15/1993) • **77**

Barolo 1984 • $14 • (8/31/1988) • **82**

Barolo 1983 • $20 • (12/15/1987) • **90**

Barolo 1982 • $15 • (6/30/1987) • **94**

Barolo Cannubi Boschis 1995: A firm, slightly herbal style of '95 Barolo, but it's concentrated, with good, ripe fruit and lovely toast, smoke and mocha character. The long finish has a tough tannic edge, but give it time. Hit by hail? Tasted twice, with consistent notes. Drink now through 2002.–P.M. • $85 • (11/15/1999) • **87**

Barolo Cannubi Boschis 1994: Very light in color, Beaujolais-like in texture and aromas, with strawberry, asparagus, herb and cherry flavors and a touch of mocha and coffee. Tasted twice, with consistent notes.–P.M. • $55 Ⓐ • (10/31/1998) • **76**

Barolo Cannubi Boschis 1993 • $88 Ⓐ • (10/31/1997) • **82**

Barolo Cannubi Boschis 1992 • $45 • (10/31/1996) • **87**

Barolo Cannubi Boschis 1991 • $57 Ⓐ • (10/31/1995) • **84**

Barolo Cannubi Boschis 1990 • $274 Ⓐ • (10/31/1994) • **96**

Barolo Cannubi Boschis 1989 • $217 Ⓐ • (10/31/1993) CS • **95**

Barolo Cannubi Boschis 1988 • $152 Ⓐ • (10/31/1993) • **92**

Barolo Cannubi Boschis 1986 • $34 • (12/31/1990) • **89**

Barolo Cannubi Boschis 1985 • $30 • (1/31/1990) • **92**

Barolo Le Vigne 1990 • $NA • (10/31/1994) • **98**

Dolcetto d'Alba 1997: Balanced and supple in texture, with sweet-tasting fruit that seduces, it's a medium-bodied red, with wet earth and black cherry. Delicious, fresh, crisp and fruity finish. Better than when previously reviewed. Drink now.–P.M. • $20 • (7/31/1999) • **86**

Dolcetto d'Alba 1990 • $14 • (3/31/1992) • **87**

Dolcetto d'Alba 1989 • $12 • (7/15/1991) • **87**

Nebbiolo d'Alba Valmaggiore 1996: Starts out with decent fruit, offering raspberry and cherry character, but turns a bit light, lean and dry on the palate and the finish.–P.M. • $15 • (10/31/1998) • **77**

Nebbiolo d'Alba Valmaggiore 1994 • $NA • (10/31/1996) • **84**

SANT'AGATA

Barbera d'Asti Superiore 1997: Fruity and a bit effervescent, made in a fresh, nouveau style. Good balance. Serve chilled at a picnic.–P.M. • $10 • (11/15/1999) • **79**

Barbera d'Asti Superiore 1996: A clean, vibrant, fruit-driven Barbera, with subtle oak-infused mocha notes. Not big in body, but supple enough on the palate and the finish, with plenty of good berry concentration. Enjoy with a nice meal. Drink now.–P.M. • $12 • (11/15/1999) • **85**

Barbera d'Asti Superiore Cavalé 1997: Ripe and just delicious. Full-bodied, with lots of plum, black cherry and dried currant flavors, it sparkles with life, showing a deft balance of acidity and very approachable tannins. Drink now through 2002.–P.M. • $24 • (11/15/1999) • **89**

Barbera d'Asti Superiore Cavalé 1996: This oak bomb delivers mocha, spice and ground coffee, but the fruit is plentiful and pretty, the acidity vibrant. The seductive package is supported by fabulously ripe, intense red berry, plum and even fig character. Rich, vibrant finish. Drink now through 2002.–P.M. • $23 • (11/15/1999) • **92**

Barbera d'Asti Superiore Piatin 1997: Nice quality. Smooth, jammy, rich and ripe, medium- to full-bodied, offering raspberry jam, plum, fresh fig and charred toast notes. Lingering finish. Drink now through 2003.–P.M. • $18 • (11/15/1999) • **86**

Barbera d'Asti Superiore Piatin 1996: Juicy, with clean raspberry character and distinct spice, oak, wet leaf and forest notes. Elegant, with a crisp finish. Drink now.–P.M. • $17 • (11/15/1999) • **84**

Grignolino Asti Miravalle 1997: Lighter than a rosé in color, with a diluted midpalate and tart flavors.–P.M. • $14 • (11/15/1999) • **72**

Monferrato Monterovere 1997: Smooth and ripe-tasting, with fancy toasted oak blending into the blackberry and cassis flavors. Medium-bodied and nicely balanced. Drink now through 2002.–P.M. • $20 • (11/15/1999) • **86**

Monferrato Monterovere 1996: Rather fresh and vibrant, leaner than some in this category, this red is balanced enough to be enjoyed with food. Smoky, with toasted oak, black cherry and watermelon flavors. Drink now through 2002.–P.M. • $18 • (11/15/1999) • **84**

Ruchè di Castagnole Monferrato Na' Vota 1998: Tastes like a nouveau-styled red—young and juicy—showing cherry, licorice and plum flavors. Sweet-tasting and medium-bodied, it lacks depth and complexity. Drink now.–P.M. • $20 • (11/15/1999) • **83**

Ruchè di Castagnole Monferrato Na' Vota 1997: Light-bodied and fresh, showing a grape, crushed raspberry and cassis berry character. Crisp finish.–P.M. • $19 • (11/15/1999) • **79**

SANT'ANDREA

Chianti Classico Panzanello 1996: A little high in acidity, with light body, light tannins and a fruity, slightly diluted aftertaste. Not much to it.–J.S. • $13 • (12/15/1998) • **75**

Chianti Classico Panzanello 1995: Slightly simple, but delicious. Dried cherry and dried flower aromas. Medium-bodied, moderate tannins, a crisp finish. Drink now.–J.S. • $13 • (12/15/1998) • **84**

SANT'ANTONIO, TENUTA

Amarone della Valpolicella Campo dei Gigli 1995: A pleasant, medium-bodied Amarone with earth, raisin and spice aromas and flavors. Drink now.–J.S. • $55 • (5/15/2000) • **84**

Cabernet Sauvignon Veneto Capitello 1997: Some people may like this big, rustic, slightly sweet red, but I can't come to grips with its green, grassy, sweet and cloying character.–J.S. • $45 • (5/15/2000) • **78**

Cabernet Sauvignon Veneto Torre di Mellotti 1997: Big, chewy and powerful, with raisin, violet and wet earth character. Full body. Chewy tannins. A bit rustic, but with impressive concentration. Best after 2000.–J.S. • $26 • (5/15/2000) • **86**

Chardonnay Veneto Capitello 1997: Has a rather exaggerated milky vanilla aroma but good fruit. Medium-bodied, with decent acidity and a medium finish. Drink now.–J.S. • $27 • (1/01/2000) • **84**

Chardonnay Veneto Passito Colori d'Autunno 1996: Best sweet Chardonnay I have ever tasted. Aromas of orange peel, caramel and butterscotch ooze from the glass. Full-bodied and very thick, like syrup. Very sweet, with a long, flavorful finish. An exceptional wine. Drink now.–J.S. • $29/375 ml. • (3/31/2000) • **93**

Valpolicella Superiore Monti Garbi 1997: Fruity and harmonious, with plum and cherry character, medium body and soft tannins. Fruity finish. Drink now.–J.S. • $22 • (5/15/2000) • **85**

SANTA ANASTASIA, ABBAZIA

Sicilia Litra 1997: Pretty fruit character here, with berry, mint and dark chocolate aromas. Full-bodied, with masses of silky tannins and a long, long finish. Slightly astringent and dry; needs a bit more fruit on the finish to be outstanding. Best after 2000.–J.S. • $32 • (5/15/2000) • **88**

Sicilia Passomaggio 1998: A wine with good berry and pepper character. Light- to medium-bodied, with light tannins and a fruity finish. Drink now.–J.S. • $13 • (5/15/2000) • **82**

Sicilia Passomaggio 1996: A fresh but simple red, with herbal, raspberrylike and vegetal flavors. Smooth texture, light tannins. 65 percent Nero d'Avola, 20 percent Merlot and 15 percent Cabernet. Drink now. • $13 • (8/31/1998) • **81**

Sicilia 1996: Direct, simple fruit flavors and a fresh, lively texture, light on the tannins. Light-bodied and easy to enjoy. 85 percent Nero d'Avola and 15 percent Cabernet Sauvignon. Drink now. • $10 • (8/31/1998) • **83**

Key: SS—Spectator Selection. CS—Cellar Selection. HR—Highly Recommended. $NA—Price not available. (BT)—Barrel tasting. Ⓐ—Auction Price.
For a key to the tasters' initials, see "How to Use These Listings."
Dates in parentheses represent the issues in which the ratings were published.

Sicilia Red Santa Anastasia 1998: Slightly astringent but with some good berry, raisin and tobacco character. Medium body, light tannins, a slightly dry finish.–J.S. • $9 • (5/15/2000) • **80**
Sicilia White Santa Anastasia 1998: A good, simple white, with lemon and white pepper character. Fresh finish.–J.S. • $8 • (5/15/2000) • **81**
Sicilia Zurrica 1998: Plenty of ripe fruit in this white, with peaches, honey and mineral character. Medium body. Fruity finish. Drink now.–J.S. • $12 • (5/15/2000) • **85**

SANTA ANITA

Pinot Grigio Veneto 1996 • $9 • (5/15/1998) • **75**

SANTA MARGHERITA

Merlot Lison-Pramaggiore Selva Maggiore 1990 • $12 • (12/15/1992) • **79**
Pinot Grigio Alto Adige 1997: Shows some delicate citrus and mineral flavors, but overall this white is light and simple. Drink now.–B.S. • $18 • (7/31/1998) • **81**

SANTA SOFIA

Amarone della Valpolicella Classico Gioé 1990 • $45 • (6/15/1998) • **86**
Amarone della Valpolicella Classico Superiore 1988 • $30 • (9/30/1995) • **85**
Amarone della Valpolicella Classico Superiore 1986 • $28 • (10/31/1994) • **82**
Amarone della Valpolicella Classico Superiore 1984 • $29 • (9/15/1992) • **86**
Bardolino Classico 1996: A bracing, light red with modest cherry aromas and flavors and a crisp finish. Drink now.–B.S. • $9 • (7/31/1998) • **79**
Bardolino Classico Superiore 1989 • $8 • (9/15/1992) • **71**
Pinot Grigio Valdadige Vigneto Fratte 1996 • $10 • (6/30/1998) • **84**
Soave Classico Montefoscarino 1996 • $9 • (6/30/1998) • **82**
Valpolicella Classico 1996: Leather and plum aromas and flavors suggest use of ripasso in this traditional Veronese red. Light-bodied, with a pronounced acidity that should match well with light foods. Drink now.–B.S. • $9 • (7/31/1998) • **83**
Valpolicella Classico 1995 • $10 • (9/15/1997) • **82**
Valpolicella Classico Superiore 1992 • $8 • (12/15/1995) • **80**
Valpolicella Classico Superiore 1989 • $9 • (9/15/1992) • **78**
Valpolicella Classico Superiore Montegradella 1995: Rich and concentrated, displaying ripe, sweet cherry and menthol notes, spicy accents on the finish. Some firm tannins provide support.–B.S. • $15 • (7/31/1998) • **85**

SANTADI, CANTINA SOCIALE DI

Carignano del Sulcis Grotta Rossa 1995: This hearty, rustic, full-bodied red has a nice blast of smoky, meaty flavor. Robust and simple. Drink now. • $10 • (8/31/1998) • **80**
Carignano del Sulcis Rocca Rubia Riserva 1996: Good concentration of fruit to this, but there's an odd tea bag and earthy character. A bit funky.–J.S. • $18 • (5/15/2000) • **74**
Carignano del Sulcis Rocca Rubia Riserva 1993: A mellow, ripe-tasting, easy-drinking red wine that's full-bodied but not too tannic, with flavors reminiscent of cherries and roast meats. Drink now. • $17 • (8/31/1998) • **83**
Carignano del Sulcis Superiore Terre Brune 1995: Slightly raised volatile acidity, with a nail polish character, yet it's ripe and rich with tobacco and cherry, too. Too bad.–J.S. • $39 • (5/15/2000) • **77**
Terre Brune 1993: An enticingly rich red wine in an international style. It has luxurious spicy, oaky aromas, a velvety texture and concentrated flavors of cherry, cedar and chocolate. Drink now through 2002. • $30 • (8/31/1998) • **90**
Terre Brune 1992 • $35 • (1/01/1997) • **88**
Terre Brune 1991 • $30 • (1/01/1997) • **86**
Valli di Porto Pino Araja 1997: Pretty, plummy red with hints of herbs. Good fruit, medium tannins and a chocolate and earth finish. Not imported into the U.S. Drink now through 2003.–J.S. • $NA • (1/01/2000) • **83**
Valli di Porto Pino Shardana 1996: Pretty red. Good intensity of berry, chocolate and violet character on the nose. Medium-bodied, with velvety tannins, hints of vanilla and a fresh fruit finish. Best after 2000.–J.S. • $20 • (5/15/2000) • **87**

SANTANGELO

Montepulciano d'Abruzzo Colli del Moro 1992 • $10 • (2/29/1996) • **87**

SANTI

Amarone della Valpolicella 1993 • $33 • (6/15/1998) • **86**
Amarone della Valpolicella 1988 • $20 • (11/15/1994) • **85**
Amarone della Valpolicella 1985 • $20 • (9/15/1992) • **84**
Merlot Veneto 1995 • $12 • (6/15/1998) • **82**
Pinot Grigio Trentino Vigneto Sortesele 1996 • $12 • (6/15/1998) • **85**
Valpolicella Classico Solane 1993 • $8 • (12/15/1995) • **86**

SANTO STEFANO

Asti NV: A medium-sweet, effervescent white redolent of pine, grapefruit and roses. Soft and round, if not so expressive. Drink now.–B.S. • $10 • (10/15/1999) • **82**

SARTORI

Amarone della Valpolicella Classico 1993: Modest herb, cherry and leather, but dull and tired overall, with tough tannins. Drink now.–B.S. • $31 • (7/31/1998) • **79**
Amarone della Valpolicella Classico 1991 • $25 • (6/15/1997) • **86**
Amarone della Valpolicella Classico 1990 • $19 • (1/31/1997) • **87**
Amarone della Valpolicella Classico Superiore 1982 • $11 • (11/15/1988) • **79**
Amarone della Valpolicella Corte Bra 1991 • $37 • (6/15/1997) • **87**
Bardolino Classico Superiore 1994 • $7 • (6/15/1997) • **77**
Chardonnay Grave del Friuli 1997 • $9 • (6/15/1998) • **81**
Merlot Grave del Friuli 1995 • $9 • (6/30/1998) • **80**
Merlot Grave del Friuli 1994 • $8 • (6/15/1997) • **84**
Merlot Grave del Friuli 1989 • $6 • (12/15/1992) • **80**
Pinot Grigio Grave del Friuli 1997 • $9 • (6/30/1998) • **83**
Pinot Grigio Grave del Friuli 1996 • $8 • (6/15/1997) • **80**
Recioto di Soave 1995 • $26/375 ml. • (6/15/1998) • **86**
Recioto di Soave 1994 • $30/375 ml. • (6/15/1997) • **85**
Regolo 1993 • $15 • (6/30/1998) • **87**
Regolo 1992 • $20 • (6/15/1997) • **79**
Soave Classico Superiore 1997 • $8 • (6/15/1998) • **84**
Valpolicella Classico Superiore 1996: Straightforward cherry character in this velvety red lends immediate appeal, followed by a crisp finish. Drink now.–B.S. • $8 • (7/31/1998) • **83**
Valpolicella Classico Superiore 1994 • $7 • (6/15/1997) • **80**
Valpolicella Classico Superiore 1990 • $6 • (9/15/1992) • **80**

SASSETTI, LIVIO

Brunello di Montalcino Pertimali 1994: Starts off a little earthy but with air, showing lovely ripe plum, berry and cherry character. Medium-bodied, with soft tannins and a ripe fruit finish. Delicious. Drink now.–J.S. • $45 • (11/30/1999) • **88**
Brunello di Montalcino Pertimali 1993: A funky Brunello for those who like traditional, earthy reds. Full-bodied, with a silky texture and loads of berry, game and leather flavors. Caresses the palate. Drink now through 2003. –J.S. • $43 Ⓐ • (12/15/1998) • **90**
Brunello di Montalcino Pertimali 1991 • $32 • (11/30/1996) • **79**
Brunello di Montalcino Pertimali 1988 • $45 • (4/30/1994) • **86**
Brunello di Montalcino Pertimali 1985 • $41 • (11/30/1990) • **83**
Brunello di Montalcino Pertimali 1982 • $25 • (1/31/1988) • **77**
Rosso di Montalcino Pertimali 1994 • $16 • (11/30/1996) • **85**
Rosso di Montalcino Pertimali 1991 • $17 • (4/30/1994) • **78**
Rosso di Montalcino Pertimali 1987 • $13 • (1/31/1991) • **84**
Vigna dei Fili di Seta 1994 • $37 • (10/31/1996) • **70**

SATTA, MICHELE

Bolgheri Bianco 1996 • $NA • (9/30/1997) • **83**
Bolgheri Piastraia 1997: Bramble berries and cherries ooze out of the glass. Medium-bodied, with soft tannins and a fruity finish. Delicious. Drink now.–J.S. • $45 • (11/30/1999) • **87**
Bolgheri Piastraia 1996: An aromatic and pretty young red with lovely violet and berry character. Medium in body, with light tannins and a fruity after-taste. Drink now.–J.S. • $40 • (12/15/1998) • **85**
Bolgheri Piastraia 1995 • $40 • (9/30/1997) • **85**
Bolgheri Piastraia 1994 • $38 • (9/30/1997) • **85**
Bolgheri Rosato 1997: A fresh and pleasing rosé, with attractive strawberry and floral aromas and flavors, light body and a crisp and fruity finish. Delicious. Drink now.–J.S. • $18 • (12/15/1998) • **84**
Bolgheri Rosato 1996 • $NA • (9/30/1997) • **82**

■ ■ ■ ■

SATTA, MICHELE

Diambra 1996 • $NA • (9/30/1997) • **82**

Toscana Vigna al Cavaliere 1997: Really beautiful. This super Sangiovese is dark, with intense blueberry and cherry character and a hint of Indian spice. Medium- to full-bodied, with silky tannins and a long, fruity finish. Drink now.–J.S. • $45 • (11/30/1999) • **91**

Toscana Vigna al Cavaliere 1995: Pretty, pure Sangiovese. Lovely strawberry and tea on the nose and palate, with hints of smoke. Medium-bodied, with medium, soft tannins and a fruity finish. Delicious. Drink now through 2003.–J.S. • $42 • (12/15/1998) • **87**

Toscana Vigna al Cavaliere 1994 • $35 • (9/30/1997) • **78**

Vermentino Bolgheri Costa di Giulia 1996 • $16 • (9/30/1997) • **78**

Vermentino Toscana Costa di Giulia 1998: A simple white, with apple, almond and honey character. Medium-bodied, with decent fruit and a honey aftertaste. Drink now.–J.S. • $18 • (11/30/1999) • **84**

Vermentino Toscana Costa di Giulia 1997: Clean aromas and flavors of pears and melons. Medium-bodied, with fresh acidity and a fruity aftertaste. Pleasant and refreshing. Drink now.–J.S. • $18 • (12/15/1998) • **83**

SAVIGNOLA PAOLINA

Chianti Classico 1997: An extremely well made Chianti, with complex aromas of blackberry, cherry and raspberry and a hint of earth. Medium-bodied, with a lovely, silky tannin structure and a fresh, fruity aftertaste. Drink now through 2001.–J.S. • $16 • (11/30/1999) • **89**

Chianti Classico 1995 • $13 • (9/30/1997) • **83**

Chianti Classico 1994 • $12 • (10/31/1996) • **77**

Chianti Classico Riserva 1996: A delicate Chianti, with berry, plum and light oak aromas and flavors. Light-bodied, with medium tannins and a short finish. Drink up. Drink now.–J.S. • $25 • (11/30/1999) • **82**

Chianti Classico Riserva 1995: Well balanced, elegant Sangiovese, with floral, plum and raspberry aromas and flavors. Medium-bodied, with very smooth tannins and a caressing texture. Tasted twice, with consistent notes. Drink now.–J.S. • $24 • (12/15/1998) • **87**

Chianti Classico Riserva 1994 • $20 • (9/30/1997) • **79**

Chianti Classico Riserva 1993 • $19 • (10/31/1996) • **79**

Chianti Classico Riserva 1990 • $NA • (2/28/1995) • **86**

Toscana Red 1994 • $10 • (9/30/1997) • **79**

SCARBOLO

Chardonnay Grave del Friuli 1998: A lovely Chardonnay with lots of apple, cream, milk and pineapple character. Medium-bodied, with a round texture and a long finish. Drink now.–J.S. • $11 • (3/31/2000) • **87**

Merlot Grave del Friuli 1998: Weedy Merlot with a cabbage patch and fruit character. Hard to like. Tasted twice, with consistent notes.–J.S. • $11 • (5/15/2000) • **76**

Merlot Grave del Friuli Campo del Viotto 1995: Soft and delicious Merlot with plum and tobacco character. Medium body. Fresh finish. Drink now.–J.S. • $20 • (5/15/2000) • **83**

Pinot Grigio Grave del Friuli 1998: Rather dull and short, with apple and almond character.–J.S. • $11 • (3/31/2000) • **76**

Sauvignon Grave del Friuli 1998: Good apple and almond character. Medium body. Fresh finish. Drink now.–J.S. • $11 • (4/30/2000) • **82**

Tocai Friulano Grave del Friuli 1998: Simple, with honey and apple character. Slightly candied finish.–J.S. • $11 • (3/31/2000) • **79**

SCARLATTA

Montepulciano d'Abruzzo 1993 • $4 • (2/29/1996) • **81**

SCAVINO, PAOLO

Barbera d'Alba 1992 • $13 • (10/31/1995) • **88**

Barbera d'Alba 1991 • $30 • (10/31/1994) • **87**

Barbera d'Alba 1990 • $40 • (10/15/1993) • **89**

Barbera d'Alba Affinato in Carati 1995: Blends ripe fruit with well-crafted oak nuances. Bursting with violet, rose petal, cassis, blackberry and plum notes, this full-bodied, supple and seductive red offers plenty of fine-textured tannins. The smoky, toasted, long-lasting finish is fresh and succulent. Drink now through 2005.–P.M. • $35 • (10/31/1998) • **91**

Barbera d'Alba Affinato in Carati 1994 • $30 • (10/31/1997) • **92**

Barbera d'Alba Affinato in Carati 1993 • $30 • (10/31/1996) • **87**

Barolo 1985 • $21 • (10/15/1990) • **88**

Barolo 1983 • $NA • (9/15/1988) • **85**

Barolo 1982 • $NA • (9/15/1988) • **88**

Barolo Bric dël Fiasc 1995: This wonderful, modern-style, full-bodied '95 Barolo packs in layers of mocha, vanilla, cigar box and red fruit notes. Shows ripe flavors and tannins and a long, impressive finish. Drink now through 2008.–P.M. • $68 • (11/15/1999) • **93**

Barolo Bric dël Fiasc 1994: This serious, modern-style Barolo has a fancy oak treatment that gives it lots of polish and elegance. Great balance defines this '94, as it delivers layers of toasted oak, spice, mocha, coffee mill, plum and blackberry notes, ending on a velvety—what else?—toasted, smoky finish. Drink now through 2007.–P.M. • $53 • (9/15/1998) • **90**

Barolo Bric dël Fiasc 1993 • $53 • (10/31/1997) • **92**

Barolo Bric dël Fiasc 1990 • $86 Ⓐ • (10/31/1994) • **93**

Barolo Bric dël Fiasc 1989 • $96 Ⓐ • (10/31/1993) CS • **95**

Barolo Bric dël Fiasc 1988 • $45 • (10/31/1993) • **87**

Barolo Bric dël Fiasc 1985 • $39 • (6/15/1990) • **90**

Barolo Cannubi 1995: Balanced. A pleasant dose of vanilla and mocha gives this full-bodied, smooth Nebbiolo a capuccino and chocolate milkshake flavor. The fruit is ripe, the tannins round, the depth attractive. Drink now through 2006.–P.M. • $68 • (11/15/1999) • **92**

Barolo Cannubi 1994: Seductively round and supple, with a soft texture and ripe tannins, this medium-bodied red charms with its spice, mocha, plum and currant character. Who said a young Barolo has to rip your tongue out? Very balanced, with good length. Lovely. Drink now through 2002.–P.M. • $53 • (10/31/1998) • **88**

Barolo Cannubi 1993 • $53 • (10/31/1997) • **92**

Barolo Cannubi 1992 • $45 • (10/31/1996) • **88**

Barolo Cannubi 1991 • $30 • (10/31/1995) • **85**

Barolo Cannubi 1990 • $115 Ⓐ • (10/31/1994) • **93**

Barolo Cannubi 1989 • $123 Ⓐ • (10/31/1993) • **94**

Barolo Cannubi 1988 • $45 • (10/31/1993) • **86**

Barolo Cannubi 1985 • $30 • (1/31/1990) • **74**

Barolo Rocche dell 'Annunziata 1995: Impressively structured and rather reserved despite the full-throttle fancy oak treatment, this international Barolo has a lovely, ripe fruit concentration to balance the seductive mocha, coffee and vanilla notes. Amazingly sweet and supple tannins, but needs time to show it all. Drink now through 2010.–P.M. • $80 • (11/15/1999) • **94**

Barolo Rocche dell 'Annunziata 1993: A modern-style Barolo, with loads of oak-infused spice, mocha and coffee mill aromas—yet also ripe and sweet-tasting, with plum, blackberry and fig flavors and lovely, supple tannins. Full-bodied and well made. Drink now through 2007.–P.M. • $69 • (9/15/1998) • **94**

Barolo Rocche dell 'Annunziata Riserva 1990 • $65 • (10/31/1995) • **90**

Dolcetto d'Alba Vigneto dël Fiasc 1996 • $17 • (10/31/1997) • **90**

Dolcetto d'Alba Vigneto dël Fiasc 1995 • $17 • (10/31/1996) • **89**

Dolcetto d'Alba Vigneto dël Fiasc 1994 • $13 • (10/31/1995) • **84**

SCHIOPETTO

Cabernet Franc Collio 1993 • $15 • (6/15/1997) • **87**

Chardonnay Colli Orientali del Friuli Podere dei Blumeri 1998: An intense, persistent white. Fresh like a mountain stream, with mineral, honey and light tropical fruit aromas. Medium-bodied, with lots of fruit and a long, long finish. Drink now.–J.S. • $29 • (2/29/2000) • **90**

Merlot Collio 1997: Weird wine. Intense aromas of asparagus and earth. Medium-bodied, with soft tannins and a short, slightly austere finish. Stick to his glorious whites.–J.S. • $25 • (5/15/2000) • **78**

Pinot Bianco Collio 1998: Fascinating aromas of apple skin, flowers and mineral. Medium-bodied, with plenty of apple flavors and a medium finish. Drink now.–J.S. • $29 • (2/29/2000) • **86**

Pinot Bianco Collio 1996 • $30 • (6/15/1998) • **85**

Pinot Grigio Colli Orientali del Friuli Podere dei Blumeri 1998: A very subtle white, with lovely aromas of tropical fruit from pineapple to banana. Medium-bodied, with light acidity and a mineral and honey aftertaste. Drink now.–J.S. • $29 • (2/29/2000) • **89**

Pinot Grigio Collio 1998: Lots of racy, mineral character, with intense aromas of flint and fruit. Medium-bodied, with good acidity and a long apple and melon aftertaste. Drink now.–J.S. • $30 • (3/31/2000) • **88**

Sauvignon Collio 1998: A perfumed Sauvignon, with very pretty aromas of rose and gooseberry. Medium- to full-bodied, with plenty of mineral

Key: SS—Spectator Selection. CS—Cellar Selection. HR—Highly Recommended. $NA—Price not available. (BT)—Barrel tasting. Ⓐ—Auction Price.
For a key to the tasters' initials, see "How to Use These Listings."
Dates in parentheses represent the issues in which the ratings were published.

ITALY

character and a fruity finish. Slightly one-dimensional. Drink now.–J.S. • $29 • (2/29/2000) • **86**

Tocai Friulano Collio 1998: Pretty, with aromas of light gooseberry and flowers. Medium-bodied, with plenty of good fruit and a fresh finish. Drink now.–J.S. • $29 • (3/31/2000) • **87**

Tocai Friulano Collio 1996 • $29 • (6/15/1998) • **86**

SCOLCA, LA

Dolcetto di Dogliani 1997: Unusual game and wet forest floor aromas mark this mature yet not fresh Dolcetto. Tastes a bit candied, with licorice, cherry and brown sugar notes.–P.M. • $11 • (7/31/1999) • **75**

Gavi Black Label 1996: Not much here, with only modest fruit-cocktail flavors. Tasted twice, with consistent notes.–K.M. • $41 • (8/31/1998) • **72**

SCRIMAGLIO

Barbaresco 1993 • $19 • (1/31/1998) • **71**

Barbaresco Bricco Loreto 1995: An elegant Barbaresco in a traditional, crisp style, this Piedmont red delivers, with finesse, ripe tannins, amazing ripe and sweet fruit, a clean finish and—the best for last—lovely mineral, *terroir*, wet earth complexity. Best from 2003 through 2010.–P.M. • $32 • (8/31/1999) HR • **93**

Barbera d'Asti 1998: Like a nouveau Barbera, all youth and strawberries and raspberries. Fresh and light, supple and balanced, this is a good wine to serve chilled at picnic time. Drink now.–P.M. • $8 • (11/15/1999) • **84**

Barbera d'Asti Acse 1998: Beautiful. Dark ruby in color, full-bodied and opulent, this explodes with flavors that range from a slight earthiness and dark chocolate to blackberry and currant. Smooth and elegant on the finish. Drink now through 2003.–P.M. • $30 • (11/15/1999) • **89**

Barbera d'Asti Bricco Sant 'Ippolito 1997: Smooth and ripe, with a cedar, black cherry and spice character. Turns chewy and firms up on the finish, with a slightly hot aftertaste. Drink now through 2002.–P.M. • $14 • (11/15/1999) • **81**

Barbera d'Asti Bricco Sant 'Ippolito 1996: Like biting into milk chocolate. This oaky style of Barbera is balanced and supple, with a game, mocha and red berry character. Light-bodied and fairly simple, but pleasant. Drink now.–P.M. • $14 • (11/15/1999) • **83**

Barbera d'Asti Superiòre 1993 • $10 • (3/31/1997) • **84**

Barbera d'Asti Superiòre Bricco Sant 'Ippolito 1995 • $13 • (1/31/1998) • **86**

Barbera d'Asti Superiòre Crôutin Riserva Personale 1997: A crisp, tart Barbera, but it develops cacao and toasted notes to support the racy berry character. Medium-bodied, it lacks a bit of length but should soften with Italian food. Drink now through 2001.–P.M. • $25 • (11/15/1999) • **81**

Barbera d'Asti Superiòre Crôutin Riserva Personale 1996: This has a ripe, supple texture, but the fruit lacks complexity. Still, petrol, smoke, cigar and black fruit character makes it attractive. Drink now.–P.M. • $25 • (11/15/1999) • **80**

Barbera d'Asti Superiòre Crôutin Riserva Personale 1995 • $25 • (1/31/1998) • **84**

Barbera d'Asti Superiòre Crôutin Riserva Personale 1990 • $36 • (3/31/1997) • **87**

Barbera d'Asti Superiòre Crôutin Riserva Personale 1989 • $32 • (3/31/1997) • **81**

Barbera d'Asti Superiòre Crôutin Riserva Personale 1988 • $32 • (5/31/1997) • **78**

Barbera d'Asti Superiòre Vigneto Roccanivo 1997: Chewy and attractive, this medium-bodied red has plenty of fresh, vibrant fruit, toasted spice and just enough acidity to keep things interesting on the finish. Drink now through 2002.–P.M. • $10 • (11/15/1999) • **85**

Barbera d'Asti Superiòre Vigneto Roccanivo 1996: This has character, from the juicy fruit to the chewy tannins, passing by the spicy, oaky, smoky notes. But it fails to convince, as the midpalate seems a bit dilute.–P.M. • $10 • (11/15/1999) • **79**

Dolcetto d'Alba 1997: A crisp, light-bodied red, with cherry, smoke and matchstick notes. Turns spicy and fruity on the tart finish.–P.M. • $10 • (7/31/1999) • **77**

Dolcetto d'Alba 1996 • $10 • (1/31/1998) • **87**

Dolcetto d'Alba 1995 • $13 • (5/31/1997) • **78**

Gavi 1996 • $10 • (1/31/1998) • **84**

Roero Arneis 1996 • $13 • (10/15/1997) • **84**

SEBASTE

Barolo 1995: Light in color and in body, showing silky texture but little volume or richness, it turns astringent on the finish.–P.M. • $45 • (11/15/1999) • **75**

Barolo 1985 • $NA • (9/15/1988) • **90**

Barolo 1984 • $NA • (9/15/1988) • **85**

Barolo 1983 • $NA • (9/15/1988) • **86**

Barolo 1982 • $NA • (9/15/1988) • **91**

Barolo 1979 • $NA • (9/15/1988) • **85**

Barolo Bussia 1995: Traditional. Very light in color, almost like a rosé. Decent ripe berries and sweet tannins try to compensate for a weak structure. Drying tannins.–P.M. • $55 • (11/15/1999) • **79**

Barolo Bussia 1993: Ripe and attractive, with plenty of plum, spice, coffee and blackberry flavors, this harmonious, medium-bodied red delivers a supple package that is a pleasure to discover. Drink now through 2005. –P.M. • $38 • (10/31/1998) • **86**

Barolo Bussia 1988 • $30 • (6/15/1994) • **87**

Barolo Bussia 1987 • $25 • (6/30/1993) • **78**

Barolo Bussia Riserva 1984 • $17 • (7/31/1989) • **84**

Barolo Bussia Riserva 1982 • $15 • (11/15/1987) • **90**

Bricco Viole 1995: An international, new oakish style, with vanilla, grilled meat and toast aromas. The ripe black fruit works, letting this full-bodied red come through tasting balanced. Long, smoky finish. Drink now through 2003.–P.M. • $18 • (11/15/1999) • **87**

Bricco Viole 1994: Very traditional, with roasted chestnut, plum, violet and wet earth, yet ripe and concentrated, offering a unique mineral-laden, lead pencil character. The quality of the ripe fruit is truly wonderful, and the tannins are within civilized boundaries on the long, sweet-tasting finish. A blend: 50 percent Barbera, 50 percent Nebbiolo.–P.M. • $18 • (10/31/1998) • **90**

Bricco Viole 1993 • $16 • (10/31/1997) • **78**

Bricco Viole 1989 • $20 • (6/15/1994) • **86**

Bricco Viole 1988 • $19 • (6/30/1993) • **79**

Bricco Viole 1986 • $16 • (1/31/1989) • **89**

Bricco Viole 1985 • $13 • (10/31/1987) • **91**

Dolcetto d'Alba Monrobiolo di Bussia 1997: Aromatically a bit dull, but fairly sweet-tasting on the palate, although it turns herbaceous on the finish.–P.M. • $14 • (7/31/1999) • **77**

Dolcetto d'Alba Monrobiolo di Bussia 1992 • $16 • (6/15/1994) • **83**

Nebbiolo delle Langhe Passo delle Viole 1998: Looks and tastes like a red wine cut with water. Tart finish.–P.M. • $20 • (11/15/1999) • **72**

Nebbiolo delle Langhe Passo delle Viole 1997: Earthy and funky, as if it needs a good racking. There is some nice berry beneath.–P.M. • $14 • (10/31/1998) • **73**

Nebbiolo delle Langhe Passo delle Viole 1996 • $13 • (10/31/1997) • **79**

SEGHESIO, ALDO & RICCARDO

Barbera d'Alba 1994 • $14 • (10/31/1996) • **79**

Barbera d'Alba 1989 • $12 • (11/30/1991) • **81**

Barbera d'Alba Vigneto della Chiesa 1996: Gorgeous. Full-bodied, rich and ripe but with excellent acidity, this velvety fruit bomb explodes with lovely red berry and blackberry flavors, accented by toasted oak. Impresses with the smoothest tannins, ripe fruit and balance you can imagine in a Barbera. Drink now.–P.M. • $15 • (10/31/1998) • **91**

Barolo Bussia-Pianpolvere 1986 • $28 • (1/31/1992) • **84**

Barolo Castelletto 1989 • $NA • (10/31/1994) • **88**

Barolo Vigneto La Villa 1995: This full-bodied red took time to open up, but the ripe, sweet black currant character hidden below the wet earth, smoke and cedar blanket is stunning in its purity. A firm wine, with the depth and complexity to age. Drink now through 2005.–P.M. • $48 • (11/15/1999) • **94**

Barolo Vigneto La Villa 1994: Lots of oak, violet and rose aromas, with toast and smoke notes and fairly ripe fruit, but the tough, hard tannins ambush the palate. Still an impressive effort for the vintage. Has the stuffing to age, and cellaring should soften it. Best after 2004.–P.M. • $40 • (10/31/1998) • **88**

Barolo Vigneto La Villa 1993 • $40 • (10/31/1997) • **83**

Barolo Vigneto La Villa 1992 • $33 • (10/31/1996) • **88**

Barolo Vigneto La Villa 1991 • $NA • (10/31/1995) • **81**

Bouquet 1996: Has a lovely texture, but an herbal character seems to dominate. Round and full-bodied, sweet and ripe-tasting, this fruity red has lots going on, including olive, black currant and red bell pepper notes. Drink now through 2003.–P.M. • $30 • (11/15/1999) • **87**

Dolcetto d'Alba 1989 • $12 • (11/30/1991) • **77**

Dolcetto d'Alba Vigneto della Chiesa 1997: Well made and beautifully balanced. Light but pretty, with good fresh fruit and decent intensity but also some fairly firm, even tart tannins. Mineral and wet earth overtones make it interesting. Drink now.–P.M. • $15 • (10/31/1998) • **85**

Dolcetto d'Alba Vigneto della Chiesa 1996 • $15 • (10/31/1997) • **84**

Dolcetto d'Alba Vigneto della Chiesa 1995 • $14 • (10/31/1996) • **84**

Dolcetto d'Alba Vigneto della Chiesa 1994 • $NA • (10/31/1995) • **79**

SEGHESIO, ALDO & RICCARDO

Nebbiolo Ruri 1989 • $14 • (1/31/1992) • **84**

SELLA & MOSCA, TENUTE

Alghero Le Arenarie 1998: Very herbal, with a canned asparagus and cut grass character. Hard to get excited about.–J.S. • $12 • (5/31/2000) • **77**

Alghero Marchese di Villamarina 1995: Pleasant Cabernet character shows tobacco, mint and dried herb. Medium-bodied, with medium tannins and a fruity finish. Drink now.–J.S. • $38 • (5/31/2000) • **86**

Alghero Marchese di Villamarina 1990 • $36 • (6/15/1997) • **84**

Alghero Tanca Farrà 1994: Medium-bodied, with raisin and nut aromas, light tannins and a slightly cooked finish. Already fading a bit. Cabernet and Cannonau.–J.S. • $18 • (5/31/2000) • **79**

Cannonau di Sardegna Riserva 1996: Something wrong here. Papery character. Dry. Tasted twice, with consistent notes.–J.S. • $13 • (5/31/2000) • **68**

Isola dei Nuraghi Ráim 1996: Simple, with berry and plum character plus dried fruit. Medium-bodied, with a fruity finish. Lacks a bit of freshness. Merlot and Carignano.–J.S. • $12 • (5/31/2000) • **79**

Vermentino di Gallura Superiòre Monteoro 1998: Simple, with mineral, pepper and pear drop flavors. Medium-bodied, with good acidity and a short finish. Slightly oxidized. Tasted twice, with consistent notes.–J.S. • $14 • (5/31/2000) • **78**

Vermentino di Sardegna La Cala 1998: Medium-bodied, with lovely lemon and mineral character, good acidity and a fresh apricot finish. Subtle. Drink now.–J.S. • $11 • (5/31/2000) • **84**

Vermentino di Sardegna La Cala 1996 • $9 • (9/15/1997) • **82**

SELVA, TENUTA DELLA

Chianti 1997: A delicious Chianti, with plum skin and spice character, medium body and a crisp, fruity finish. Drink now.–J.S. • $11 • (11/30/1999) • **86**

Chianti 1995 • $NA • (1/01/1998) • **74**

Colli della Toscana Centrale Selvino 1997: A crisp wine with wet earth and raspberry aromas. Medium-bodied, with good acidity, light tannins and a fresh finish. Need food. Drink now.–J.S. • $26 • (6/15/2000) • **85**

Colli della Toscana Centrale Selvino 1996: Earthy and soft, with plum, berry and cherry character. Slightly barnyardy. Medium body. Fresh finish. Drink now.–J.S. • $24 • (1/01/2000) • **80**

Colli della Toscana Centrale Selvino 1996: Earthy and soft, with plum, berry and cherry character. Slightly barnyardy. Medium body. Fresh finish. Drink now.–J.S. • $24 • (1/01/2000) • **80**

Colli della Toscana Centrale Selvino 1995: Good berry and leather character, although slightly lean. Medium-bodied, with silky tannins and a medium finish. Drink now.–J.S. • $26 • (11/30/1999) • **85**

Colli della Toscana Centrale Selvino 1994 • $NA • (1/01/1998) • **86**

Colli della Toscana Centrale Selvino 1993: Intense cherry aromas have hints of varnish. Medium-bodied, with light tannins and a raised acidity that makes the wine slightly hard.–J.S. • $23 • (11/30/1999) • **78**

Colli della Toscana Centrale Selvino 1991 • $NA • (1/01/1998) • **82**

Colli della Toscana Centrale Selvino 1990 • $NA • (1/01/1998) • **78**

Colli della Toscana Centrale Usannella 1997: Wonderful intensity of plum and cedar character, with a hint of vanilla on the nose. Medium-bodied, with delicate tannins and a fresh finish. Drink now through 2003.–J.S. • $14 • (11/30/1999) • **87**

Pinot Nero Colli della Toscana Centrale Castello della Selva 1997: A very good Pinot Noir. Like a good village Burgundy. Medium-bodied, with pretty strawberry and berry character, delicate tannins and a fresh, fruity aftertaste. Drink now through 2002.–J.S. • $12 • (11/30/1999) • **88**

Usannella 1995 • $NA • (1/01/1998) • **71**

SELVAPIANA

Chianti Classico Riserva 1985 • $11 • (11/30/1989) • **89**

Chianti Classico Riserva 1983 • $10 • (11/30/1989) • **86**

Chianti Classico Riserva 1982 • $10 • (11/30/1989) • **87**

Chianti Rufina 1997: A pretty Chianti, with plum, berry and earth character and a hint of tar. Medium-bodied, with a soft, round texture. Drink now.–J.S. • $17 • (11/30/1999) • **86**

Key: SS—Spectator Selection. CS—Cellar Selection. HR—Highly Recommended. $NA—Price not available. (BT)—Barrel tasting. Ⓐ—Auction Price. For a key to the tasters' initials, see "How to Use These Listings." **Dates in parentheses represent the issues in which the ratings were published.**

Chianti Rufina 1996: Pretty blackberry and earth aromas and flavors in this medium-bodied red, with fine tannins and a fresh finish. Selvapiana always delivers fresh and fruity Chiantis. Drink now.–J.S. • $11 • (12/15/1998) • **85**

Chianti Rufina 1995 • $14 • (9/30/1997) • **88**

Chianti Rufina 1994 • $11 • (9/30/1997) • **86**

Chianti Rufina 1992 • $10 • (2/28/1995) • **82**

Chianti Rufina 1991 • $12 • (10/31/1993) • **87**

Chianti Rufina 1990 • $13 • (9/15/1992) • **92**

Chianti Rufina Bucerchiale Riserva 1995: Interesting raspberry, strawberry and wet earth character. Medium-bodied, with good blackberry flavor and fine tannins. Racy, lively finish. Very approachable vintage for Bucerchiale, but a joy to drink. Drink now.–J.S. • $20 • (12/15/1998) • **89**

Chianti Rufina Bucerchiale Riserva 1994 • $NA • (9/30/1997) • **86**

Chianti Rufina Bucerchiale Riserva 1993 • $24 • (9/30/1997) • **88**

Chianti Rufina Bucerchiale Riserva 1990 • $20 • (9/30/1997) • **91**

Chianti Rufina Bucerchiale Riserva 1988 • $25 • (9/30/1997) • **89**

Chianti Rufina Bucerchiale Riserva 1985 • $NA • (9/30/1997) • **92**

Chianti Rufina Fornace Riserva 1995: In-your-face red with its raisin and ripe berry aromas, but doesn't give much on the palate. Full-bodied, with soft tannins and a short finish. Seems slightly closed now. Best after 2000.–J.S. • $32 • (12/15/1998) • **87**

Chianti Rufina Fornace Riserva 1993 • $35 • (10/31/1996) • **87**

Chianti Rufina Riserva 1996: A rich, full-throttle wine. Impressive for the vintage. Very ripe, with dried fig, Moroccan spice and light raisin. Full-bodied and chewy, with a long, ripe fruit finish. Drink now through 2002.–J.S. • $25 • (11/30/1999) • **89**

Chianti Rufina Riserva 1995: A lush and smooth young red. Dark purple, and charged with grapey, currant and mint aromas. Medium- to full-bodied, with velvety, soft tannins and a long, fruity finish. Best after 2000.–J.S. • $18 • (12/15/1998) • **88**

Chianti Rufina Riserva 1993 • $17 • (10/31/1996) • **85**

Chianti Rufina Riserva 1990 • $15 • (2/28/1995) • **89**

Vin Santo del Chianti Rufina 1993: A beautiful Vin Santo. Amber-gold in color, with wonderful aromas of vanilla, honey and orange peel and hints of maple syrup. Full-bodied and medium sweet, with a honey texture and a long almond and apricot finish. Drink now.–J.S. • $27 • (11/30/1999) • **89**

Vin Santo del Chianti Rufina 1991: More like an oloroso Sherry than table wine. Cloudy. Shows apple, almond and nutty character on the nose and palate, with hints of butter. Medium-bodied, lightly sweet. Better as an aperitif than for dessert. Drink now.–J.S. • $NA/375 ml. • (12/15/1998) • **85**

SELVOLE

Barullo 1991 • $16 • (10/31/1995) • **87**

Barullo 1990 • $15 • (2/28/1995) • **78**

Chianti Classico 1994 • $13 • (10/31/1996) • **83**

Chianti Classico 1993 • $10 • (10/31/1995) • **80**

Chianti Classico 1988 • $NA • (9/15/1991) • **78**

Chianti Classico Lanfredini Riserva 1993 • $17 • (10/31/1996) • **82**

Chianti Classico Lanfredini Riserva 1991 • $13 • (10/31/1995) • **86**

Chianti Classico Lanfredini Riserva 1990 • $14 • (2/28/1995) • **75**

Chianti Classico Lanfredini Riserva 1985 • $NA • (9/15/1991) • **77**

SERAFINO

Barolo Riserva 1947 • $NA • (5/31/1997) • **87**

SERENA, LA

Brunello di Montalcino 1995: A bit funky with burned nuts, wood and ripe fruit character. Full-bodied, chewy and chocolatey. Slightly unclean barrels? Drink now.–J.S. • $65 • (6/30/2000) • **84**

Brunello di Montalcino 1994: Extremely fresh, with strawberries and raspberries popping out of the glass. Medium-bodied, with light tannins and a fruity finish. A bit diluted in the midpalate. Drink now.–J.S. • $44 • (8/31/1999) • **85**

Brunello di Montalcino 1988 • $NA • (4/30/1994) • **89**

Rosso di Montalcino 1997: Gorgeous dried cherry, plum and floral character. Medium- to full-bodied, with velvety tannins and a medium, fruity finish. Drink now through 2003.–J.S. • $26 • (9/15/1999) • **89**

SERRISTORI, CONTI

Chianti Classico Riserva 1993 • $NA • (10/31/1996) • **80**

SESTA, TENUTA DI

Brunello di Montalcino 1994: Enticing, elegant wine with berry, grilled meat and cherry character. Medium-bodied, with fine tannins and a sweet, fresh finish. Drink now.–J.S. • $35 • (8/31/1999) • **86**

Brunello di Montalcino 1993: A gorgeous, drink-me-now Brunello, with very pretty aromas of milk chocolate and fruit. Medium-bodied, with round, velvety tannins and a long, flavorful finish. Drink now.–J.S. • $34 • (12/15/1998) • **89**

Brunello di Montalcino 1988 • $42 • (4/30/1994) • **79**

Brunello di Montalcino Campo della Spinaia 1992 • $32 • (10/31/1997) • **86**

Rosso di Montalcino 1997: A good, straightforward rosso with plenty of berry and cherry character. Medium-bodied, with light tannins and a fruity finish. Drink now.–J.S. • $18 • (9/15/1999) • **84**

Rosso di Montalcino 1996: Fresh and grapey, with aromas and flavors of berry and cherry. Medium-bodied, with chewy tannins and a long, fruity finish. Impressive for the vintage. Drink now.–J.S. • $15 • (12/15/1998) • **85**

Rosso di Montalcino 1991 • $NA • (4/30/1994) • **75**

SESTI

Brunello di Montalcino 1995: This is a beautiful, direct wine. Very ripe aromas of plums, berries and earth. Full-bodied, with lovely round tannins and a long, long berry and milk chocolate aftertaste. Not imported into the U.S. Best after 2000.–J.S. • $NA • (6/30/2000) • **90**

SETTEN, TENUTA

Cabernet Franc Piave 1994 • $11 • (6/15/1997) • **84**

Prosecco della Marca Trevigiana NV • $10 • (5/31/1997) • **84**

SETTIMO, AURELIO

Barolo Vigna Rocche 1993 • $NA • (10/31/1997) • **84**

Barolo Vigna Rocche 1982 • $19 • (5/31/1988) • **83**

Barolo Vigna Rocche 1980 • $17 • (5/31/1988) • **73**

SOLARIA

Brunello di Montalcino 1995: A new name doing seriously well. A modern, rich and wonderful Brunello. Beautifully ripe with fresh plum, cherry and blackberry aromas. Full-bodied and round, with velvety tannins and a fabulous, ripe fruit finish. No known U.S. importer. Best after 2001.–J.S. • $NA • (6/30/2000) • **91**

Brunello di Montalcino 1994: An easy, early-drinking Brunello with lots of vanilla and berry character. Medium-bodied, with medium soft tannins and a caressing finish. Not imported into the U.S. Drink now.–J.S. • $NA • (1/01/1999) • **85**

Rosso di Montalcino 1997: An autumnal style of rosso with berry and tobacco character throughout. Medium-bodied, with soft tannins and a fresh, fruity aftertaste. Not imported into the U.S. Drink now.–J.S. • $NA • (1/01/1999) • **86**

SOLATIONE

Chianti Classico 1996: Standard Chianti, with pleasant berry and cherry aromas and flavors. Light- to medium-bodied, with light tannins and a fresh finish. Drink now.–J.S. • $15 • (12/15/1998) • **85**

Chianti Classico 1994 • $13 • (4/30/1998) • **79**

Chianti Classico Riserva 1995: A bit rustic, but shows plenty of fruit. Very ripe berry, almost raisiny, character on the nose. Medium-bodied, with soft tannins and a delicious finish with sweet fruit flavors. Drink now.–J.S. • $28 • (12/15/1998) • **83**

Chianti Classico Riserva 1993 • $20 • (4/30/1998) • **88**

Vin Santo di Chianti Classico 1994: Very raisiny, with hints of kerosene and nut. Medium-bodied and lightly sweet, with a nut, butter and ripe fruit aftertaste. Drink now.–J.S. • $28/375 ml. • (12/15/1998) • **84**

SOLDERA

Brunello di Montalcino Case Basse 1994: A disappointment from Soldera. Simple and fruity, with plum, berry and cedar character. Light-bodied, with light tannins and a crisp, slightly dry finish.–J.S. • $150 • (11/30/1999) • **76**

Brunello di Montalcino Case Basse 1993: Soldera Brunellos are always big and rich but this '93 is extremely polished and refined. Blackberry, cherry and violet aromas. Medium-bodied, with fine, silky tannins and a long, long finish. Best after 2000.–J.S. • $150 • (12/15/1998) • **91**

Brunello di Montalcino Case Basse 1990 • $326 Ⓐ • (10/31/1995) • **84**

Brunello di Montalcino Case Basse 1988 • $150 • (4/30/1994) • **92**

Brunello di Montalcino Case Basse 1985 • $90 • (7/15/1991) • **89**

Brunello di Montalcino Case Basse Riserva 1993: A big mistake for Soldera. Earthy and mushroomy on the nose, with a hint of ripe fruit and buttered popcorn. Medium-bodied with a raised acidity and a dry, volatile finish. –J.S. • $200 • (11/30/1999) • **71**

Brunello di Montalcino Case Basse Riserva 1990 • $273 Ⓐ • (11/30/1996) • **92**

Intistiei 1987 • $68 • (1/31/1992) • **87**

SOLDO

Pinot Grigio Veneto 1997: Modest apple and earth flavors in this light, dilute white. Drink now.–B.S. • $NA • (9/30/1998) • **75**

SOLOPACA, CANTINA SOCIALE DI

Aglianico Solopaca 1995: Intriguing, but lacks a bit of freshness. Looks slightly mature for a '95, with a brick-red hue to the ruby color. Aromas of raisins and perfume follow through to a medium-bodied palate, with an orange peel and citrus finish. Drink now.–J.S. • $NA • (1/01/2000) • **85**

Solopaca Superiòre 1995: Lovely, focused aromas of plums, berries and roses, with a hint of wood. Medium- to full-bodied, with compacted fruit and silky tannins. Long and delicious finish. Very good structure, although it's still not showing all it has. Drink through 2005.–J.S. • $NA • (1/01/2000) • **89**

SONNINO, FATTORIA

Chianti Castello di Montespertoli 1998: Simple and slightly spritzy, with lots of dried cherry character. Rather rustic but enjoyable. Drink now.–J.S. • $9 • (11/30/1999) • **81**

Chianti Castello di Montespertoli 1997: A pleasant and fruity red, with light body, fresh acidity and a crisp finish. Drink now.–J.S. • $9 • (11/30/1999) • **82**

Chianti Castello di Montespertoli 1996 • $NA • (9/30/1997) • **81**

Chianti Castello di Montespertoli 1994 • $NA • (10/31/1996) • **79**

Chianti Castello di Montespertoli 1993 • $NA • (2/28/1995) • **79**

Chianti Castello di Montespertoli 1992 • $NA • (2/28/1995) • **79**

Chianti Castello di Montespertoli 1991 • $NA • (10/31/1993) • **80**

Chianti Castello di Montespertoli 1990 • $NA • (10/31/1993) • **78**

Chianti Colli Fiorentini Castello di Montespertoli 1996: Standard Chianti. Some pleasant berry and cherry aromas and flavors. Medium- to light-bodied, with light tannins and a fresh finish. Rather short. Drink now.–J.S. • $12 • (12/15/1998) • **81**

Chianti Colli Fiorentini Castello di Montespertoli 1995 • $11 • (9/30/1997) • **86**

Chianti Colli Fiorentini Castello di Montespertoli 1994 • $NA • (10/31/1996) • **85**

Chianti Colli Fiorentini Castello di Montespertoli 1993 • $NA • (10/31/1995) • **85**

Toscana Cantinino Vigneto di Fezzana 1996: Although a little hard from firm tannins and tough acidity, it's a delicious and interesting wine, with cherry and tobacco character throughout. Drink now.–J.S. • $16 • (11/30/1999) • **85**

Toscana Cantinino Vigneto di Fezzana 1995: Rich and generous, with plenty of plum and spice aromas and flavors. Medium-bodied, with soft, smooth tannins and a velvety finish. Drink now.–J.S. • $26 • (12/15/1998) • **87**

Toscana Cantinino Vigneto di Fezzana 1993 • $NA • (10/31/1996) • **75**

Toscana Cantinino Vigneto di Fezzana 1990 • $NA • (10/31/1993) • **85**

Toscana Cantinino Vigneto di Fezzana 1988 • $NA • (10/31/1993) • **83**

Toscana San Leone 1997: Rather eccentric in character, but enjoyable. Very exaggerated aromas of toasted coffee bean and cherry, with a hint of herb and raisin. Full-bodied, with extremely well polished tannins and a long, smoky finish. Merlot and Sangiovese. Best after 2000.–J.S. • $25 • (11/30/1999) • **86**

Toscana San Leone 1996: Rather coarse and overripe. Some good smoky, berry, raisin and chocolate character, but a slight cooked fruit component in the aftertaste. Medium-bodied, with full tannins and an alcoholic finish.–J.S. • $26 • (12/15/1998) • **79**

Toscana San Leone 1994 • $NA • (10/31/1996) • **86**

Toscana San Leone 1993 • $NA • (10/31/1995) • **88**

SORAVAL

Chardonnay Trentino 1996 • $15 • (5/31/1998) • **84**

Merlot Trentino 1996 • $13 • (5/31/1998) • **85**

SORDO, GIOVANNI

Barbera d'Alba 1997: A straightforward, rather balanced Barbera. Medium-bodied, with wild berry and coffee notes. Chewy finish.–P.M. • $11 • (11/15/1999) • **78**

Barbera d'Alba 1996: This ripe Barbera is smoky and petrollike, with intense black fruit. Medium- to full-bodied, with a slightly chewy finish. Drink now through 2003.–P.M. • $11 • (11/15/1999) • **86**

Barolo 1995: Delicate and pure, with gorgeous balance. Light in color, with medium (almost light) body, it has an attractive sweet-tasting quality and appealing silkiness joined by lovely red berry, smoke and mineral notes. Not showy but pleasurable, here's an authentic Piedmont red that grows and grows on the ethereal finish. Drink now through 2007.–P.M. • $30 • (11/15/1999) • **92**

Barolo Riserva 1993: A bit crisp, with green fruit and a slightly herbal aftertaste. Tough tannins.–P.M. • $40 • (11/15/1999) • **76**

SORGENTI, FATTORIA LE

Chianti Colli Fiorentini 1998: A wonderful dark ruby color for an early-drinking red, showing bright berry and chocolate aromas. Medium-bodied, with light tannins and a caressing texture on the fruity finish. Drink now. –J.S. • $10 • (11/30/1999) • **84**

Toscana Scirus Red 1998: Wonderful Cab-Merlot blend. Black color. Wonderful aromas of currants, berries and cherries. Medium- to full-bodied, with velvety tannins and a long, sweet fruit finish. Needs time. Best after 2002. –J.S. • $25 • (6/15/2000) • **90**

SORTE, LA

Amarone della Valpolicella Classico Vigneti di Jago 1988 • $41 • (5/31/1998) • **89**
Valpolicella Classico Superiòre 1991 • $7 • (10/15/1994) • **83**

SOTTIMANO

Barbaresco Fausoni Vigna del Salto 1996: Rich, ripe, full-bodied, a deftly oaked Barbaresco offering espresso and cappuccino aromas and flavors and loads of wine for your buck as it fans out its minty, smoky, black currant and grilled meat character. Expect massive but ripe tannins to keep you chewing. Best from 2005 through 2010.–P.M. • $40 • (8/31/1999) • **90**

SPADAFORA

Sicilia Divino 1998: Decent ripe fruit, but rather rustic, with lemon and candied fruit.–J.S. • $15 • (5/31/2000) • **78**

Sicilia Red Don Pietro 1997: Slightly herbal but showing good fruit. Medium-bodied, with medium tannins and a light finish. Drink now.–J.S. • $19 • (5/31/2000) • **81**

Sicilia Schietto 1997: A big and very rich red, with loads of intense tar and blackberry character. Full-bodied and very chewy, with lots of fruit and a long, long finish. Impressive. Cabernet Sauvignon. Drink now through 2005.–J.S. • $35 • (5/31/2000) • **90**

Sicilia Vigna Virzì 1998: A bit earthy, with ripe fruit and barnyard aromas. Medium-bodied, with slightly raised acidity. Hard.–J.S. • $15 • (5/31/2000) • **78**

Sicilia White Don Pietro 1998: Medium-bodied, with white pepper, dried apricot and ash character, good acidity and a fresh finish. Grows on you. Drink now.–J.S. • $15 • (5/31/2000) • **81**

SPADIO E PIECORTE

Chianti Classico 1997: Easy, with light cherry and berry character. Light-bodied, with a fresh finish. Not imported into the U.S. Drink now.–J.S. • $NA • (1/01/1999) • **80**

SPALLETTI

Chianti 1996 • $9 • (4/30/1998) • **84**
Chianti 1995 • $8 • (3/31/1997) • **82**

Key: SS—Spectator Selection. CS—Cellar Selection. HR—Highly Recommended. $NA—Price not available. (BT)—Barrel tasting. (A)—Auction Price.
For a key to the tasters' initials, see "How to Use These Listings."
Dates in parentheses represent the issues in which the ratings were published.

Chianti 1993 • $8 • (7/31/1995) • **82**
Chianti 1992 • $NA • (2/28/1995) • **77**
Chianti Rufina 1993 • $NA • (10/31/1995) • **83**

Chianti Rufina Poggio Reale Riserva 1996: Fresh and fruity, with strawberry and cherry character. Medium-bodied, with light tannins and a fresh finish. Drink now.–J.S. • $NA • (11/30/1999) • **83**

Chianti Rufina Poggio Reale Riserva 1993 • $19 • (9/30/1997) • **81**
Chianti Rufina Poggio Reale Riserva 1990 • $NA • (10/31/1995) • **80**
Palazzo al Campo 1994 • $NA • (10/31/1995) • **82**
Sangiovese Toscana Palazzo al Campo 1995 • $13 • (12/31/1997) • **79**
Vernaccia di San Gimignano 1996 • $10 • (9/30/1997) • **78**

SPERI, FRATELLI

Amarone della Valpolicella Classico 1991 • $34 • (1/31/1997) • **85**
Valpolicella Classico Superiòre Vigneto La Roverina 1994 • $12 • (4/30/1997) • **83**
Valpolicella Classico Superiòre Vigneto La Roverina 1993 • $12 • (6/15/1996) • **86**
Valpolicella Classico Superiòre Vigneto La Roverina 1991 • $8 • (4/30/1994) • **83**

SPESSA, CASTELLO DI

Collio Conte di Spessa 1995: Impressive 1995. Black in color, with an intense aroma of flowers, ripe fruit and perfume. Full-bodied and very chewy, yet refined and polished. A bit tight right now,so give it time. Merlot, Cabernet Sauvignon and Cabernet Franc. Best after 2000.–J.S. • $32 • (5/15/2000) • **91**

Pinot Bianco Collio 1998: Subtle aromas of apple, pineapple and spice. Medium-bodied, with good mineral and fruit character and a zingy finish. Well done for Pinot Bianco. Drink now.–J.S. • $23 • (4/30/2000) • **87**

Pinot Grigio Collio 1998: Delicious aromas of ripe apple, almond and pear. Full-bodied and rich, with perhaps a touch of residual sugar and a long, flavorful finish. Drink now.–J.S. • $23 • (3/31/2000) • **87**

Sauvignon Collio 1998: Very rich white with loads of pineapple character. Full-bodied, with lots of fruit and a long finish. Slightly thick and oily, but very good indeed. Drink now.–J.S. • $23 • (4/30/2000) • **87**

Tocai Friulano Collio 1998: Lovely, showing very good peach and mineral character and a hint of melon. Medium-bodied and round, with a light, fruity finish. Drink now.–J.S. • $23 • (3/31/2000) • **86**

SPORTOLETTI

Assisi 1998: Very bright and fruity, bubbling over with raspberries and cherries. Medium-bodied, with light tannins and a very fruity finish. Like an energetic young Beaujolais. Delicious. Drink now.–J.S. • $11 • (2/29/2000) • **85**

Grechetto Assisi 1998: A fat and oily white, with aromas of ripe apple and tropical fruit. Full-bodied and rather thick, with a long mango and spice finish. Needs a bit more acidity, but rich and interesting. Drink now. –J.S. • $11 • (2/29/2000) • **85**

Umbria Red Villa Fidelia 1997: A very bright and fruity red, with loads of plum character. Medium-bodied, with chunky fruit and medium tannins. Very ripe. Drink now.–J.S. • $28 • (2/29/2000) • **89**

Umbria White Villa Fidelia 1997: A soft and fruity white, with aromas of apple, lemon and straw. Medium-bodied, with ripe fruit and fresh acidity. The milky aftertaste has hints of vanilla. Drink now.–J.S. • $19 • (2/29/2000) • **85**

STIVAL

Merlot Veneto Le Rive 1995 • $12 • (6/30/1998) • **79**
Merlot Veneto Orientale 1993 • $6 • (1/31/1996) • **72**

STRA & FIGLIO, GIOVANNI

Barolo 1993 • $NA • (10/31/1997) • **70**

STRACCALI

Chianti 1998: A simple Chianti, with dried cherry and cedar aromas and flavors, light body and a fresh, slightly austere finish. Drink now.–J.S. • $8 • (11/30/1999) • **82**

Chianti 1997: Simple and fruity, with a nice combination of dried cherry and bark on the nose and palate. Light-bodied, with light tannins and a fresh finish. Drink now.–J.S. • $9 • (12/15/1998) • **82**

Chianti 1996 • $6 • (9/30/1997) • **84**
Chianti 1994 • $7 • (3/31/1997) • **86**
Chianti 1993 • $7 • (2/28/1995) • **73**
Chianti Classico 1992 • $NA • (2/28/1995) • **79**
Chianti Classico 1991 • $NA • (10/31/1993) • **83**
Chianti Classico 1990 • $6 • (9/15/1992) • **79**
Chianti Classico Riserva 1990 • $NA • (2/28/1995) • **71**
Chianti Classico Riserva 1988 • $NA • (9/15/1992) • **81**
Chianti Vernaiolo 1997: Simple, fresh and fruity with hints of earth and grapes. Light-bodied, with light tannins and finish.–J.S. • $7 • (12/15/1998) • **79**
Chianti Vernaiolo 1991 • $6 • (10/31/1993) • **83**
Orvieto Classico 1998: A good, clean Tuscan white, with citrus and mineral aromas and flavors. Medium-bodied, with good acidity and a fruity finish. Drink now.–J.S. • $7 • (1/01/1999) • **85**
Sangiovese Toscana 1998: A simple and fruity Sangiovese, with dried cherry and plum character, medium body and a caressing mouthfeel. Delicious. Drink now.–J.S. • $8 • (11/30/1999) • **83**
Sangiovese Toscana 1996 • $6 • (9/30/1997) • **81**
Sangiovese Toscana 1995: Delicious plum- and berry-infused red, with soft tannins and a crisp finish. Medium body. Serve lightly chilled. Drink now. –J.S. • $7 • (12/15/1998) • **83**

STRUZZIERO

Fiano di Avellino 1998: Lots of almond and apple character. Medium-bodied, with chunky apple and pineapple character and a fresh finish. A bit simple really, but delicious. Drink now.–J.S. • $22 • (1/31/2000) • **85**
Greco di Tufo 1998: A bit cloying, but some decent fruit. Aromas of blanched almonds, clove honey and dried tarragon. Medium-bodied, with light acidity and a slightly sweet, fruity finish. Drink now.–J.S. • $15 • (1/31/2000) • **84**
Greco di Tufo VillaGiulia 1998: Lively, well-made white. Lovely aromas of minerals, honey and almonds. Medium-bodied, with a good intensity of fruit and a long, lively finish. Drink now.–J.S. • $18 • (1/31/2000) • **88**
Taurasi Campoceraso Riserva 1995: A bit hard, with a slightly raised volatile acidity and hints of varnish. Medium-bodied, with ripe fruit and a short finish. Tasted twice, with consistent notes.–J.S. • $25 • (1/31/2000) • **79**
Taurasi Riserva 1977 • $22 • (8/31/1986) CS • **93**

STURM

Refosco dal Peduncolo Rosso 1993 • $14 • (5/31/1996) • **84**
Refosco del Peduncolo Rosso Venezie 1996: Delicious, from the fresh blackberry and raspberry character to the lush richness on the palate. Bright acidity keeps it lively. Perfect summer red.–B.S. • $15 • (7/31/1998) • **87**

TALENTI

Brunello di Montalcino Pian di Conte 1995: Good Brunello. Aromas of strawberry patch and earth. Medium- to full-bodied, with soft tannins and a smooth finish. Straightforward. Drink now.–J.S. • $49 • (6/30/2000) • **85**
Brunello di Montalcino Pian di Conte 1994: Rather advanced, mature in style, with plum, cedar and tobacco character. Light-bodied, with a crisp finish. Not a wine to age.–J.S. • $45 • (8/31/1999) • **76**
Brunello di Montalcino Pian di Conte 1993: Offers some enticing flavors, if a bit raisiny and overripe. Medium-bodied and slightly astringent, with a ripe fruit aftertaste. Drink now.–J.S. • $50 • (12/15/1998) • **82**
Brunello di Montalcino Pian di Conte 1992 • $NA • (9/30/1997) • **77**
Brunello di Montalcino Pian di Conte 1991 • $37 • (11/30/1996) • **83**
Brunello di Montalcino Pian di Conte 1990 • $NA • (10/31/1995) • **88**
Brunello di Montalcino Pian di Conte 1988 • $40 • (4/30/1994) • **90**
Brunello di Montalcino Pian di Conte 1982 • $NA • (9/15/1986) • **90**
Brunello di Montalcino Pian di Conte 1981 • $NA • (9/15/1986) • **88**
Brunello di Montalcino Pian di Conte Riserva 1994: A wine with pretty plum and cherry aromas with hints of Indian spice. Medium body. Fresh tannins and a light finish. Drink now.–J.S. • $45 • (6/30/2000) • **84**
Brunello di Montalcino Pian di Conte Riserva 1993: Looks and smells mature but tastes vibrant and delicious. Slightly light garnet in color, but shows lovely tobacco, cherry and tree bark aromas. Medium-bodied, with velvety, polished tannins and a caressing finish. Well done. Drink now.–J.S. • $65 • (8/31/1999) • **88**
Brunello di Montalcino Pian di Conte Riserva 1990 • $60 • (11/30/1996) • **87**
Brunello di Montalcino Pian di Conte Riserva 1988 • $NA • (10/31/1994) • **94**
Rosso di Montalcino Pian di Conte 1997: Slightly diluted but fresh and fruity right through the finish, with berry, vanilla and cedar character. Light-bodied. Drink now.–J.S. • $19 • (9/15/1999) • **82**
Rosso di Montalcino Pian di Conte 1996: Rather light, with some pleasant berry and vanilla character. Light- to medium-bodied, with a short finish. Drink now.–J.S. • $20 • (12/15/1998) • **80**
Rosso di Montalcino Pian di Conte 1995 • $15 • (9/30/1997) • **83**
Rosso di Montalcino Pian di Conte 1994 • $14 • (11/30/1996) • **84**
Rosso di Montalcino Pian di Conte 1993 • $NA • (10/31/1995) • **79**
Rosso di Montalcino Pian di Conte 1992 • $NA • (10/31/1994) • **79**
Rosso di Montalcino Pian di Conte 1991 • $18 • (4/30/1994) • **81**
Toscana Rosso 1997: A fruity and delicious '97 Sangiovese with dark cherry and raspberry aromas and flavors. Medium-bodied, with light yet smooth tannins and a fresh, fruity finish. From the winemaker of Il Poggione and Talenti in Montalcino. Drink now.–J.S. • $40 • (12/15/1998) • **85**

TASCA D'ALMERITA

Cabernet Sauvignon Sicilia 1997: Subtle aromas of plum, black currant and berry follow through to a medium-bodied palate, with fine tannins and a fruity, medium finish. A well-made Cab for current drinking. Drink now.–J.S. • $50 • (5/31/2000) • **87**
Chardonnay Sicilia 1997: Oily and slightly flabby, with apple, vanilla, cream and butterscotch. Full-bodied, round and delicious. At its peak. Tasted twice, with consistent notes. Drink now.–J.S. • $55 • (5/31/2000) • **84**
Sicilia Red Regaleali 1997: A good, simple red, with plum and berry character, light body and a fresh finish. Drink now.–J.S. • $10 • (5/31/2000) • **81**
Sicilia Rosso del Conte 1997: Aromas of ripe red fruit and dried tobacco. Medium-bodied, with a cooked fruit character and a slightly papery finish. Tasted twice, with consistent notes.–J.S. • $10 • (5/31/2000) • **76**
Sicilia White Regaleali 1998: Clean and fresh, with lime, apricot and mineral character. Medium-bodied, with a fresh finish. Delicious. Drink now.–J.S. • $10 • (5/31/2000) • **85**

TAURINO, DR. COSIMO

Brindisi Patriglione 1981 • $14 • (12/31/1990) • **85**
Brindisi Patriglione Riserva 1979 • $12 • (3/31/1989) • **82**
Notarpanaro 1985 • $10 • (3/31/1994) • **81**
Salice Salentino Riserva 1995: A rustic, mature-tasting red, with peppery, herbal, leathery accents to the narrow cherry flavor. Lean, moderately tannic. • $9 • (8/31/1998) • **78**
Salice Salentino Riserva 1994: A hearty, straightforward red that's easy to enjoy. It blends spicy, earthy aromas with solid cherry and berry flavors, a smooth texture and moderate tannins. Drink now. • $9 • (8/31/1998) • **84**
Salice Salentino Riserva 1990 • $9 • (1/31/1996) • **82**
Salice Salentino Riserva 1988 • $9 • (3/31/1994) • **80**

TEDESCHI

Amarone della Valpolicella 1993 • $32 • (5/31/1998) • **82**
Amarone della Valpolicella Capitel Monte Fontana 1988 • $NA • (9/15/1992) • **85**
Amarone della Valpolicella Capitel Monte Olmi 1993 • $24 • (5/31/1998) • **83**
Amarone della Valpolicella Capitel Monte Olmi 1988 • $40 • (9/15/1992) • **84**
Valpolicella Capitel del Nicalò 1989 • $14 • (9/15/1992) • **82**
Veneto Capitel San Rocco 1993 • $16 • (5/31/1998) • **82**
Veneto Capitel San Rocco 1988 • $NA • (9/15/1992) • **78**
Veneto Capitel San Rocco 1983 • $11 • (2/15/1989) • **84**

TEO COSTA

Barbera d'Alba Castellinaldo 1995: Like biting into a handful of sweet, ripe cherries. Plenty of nice spicy flavors linger on the finish. Pretty and rich, with lots of punch. Drink now through 2001.–K.M. • $24 • (8/31/1998) • **87**
Barbera d'Alba Sanmicè 1996: Pleasant and light, with berry, cherry and game flavors. Slightly spritzy. Drink now.–K.M. • $12 • (8/31/1998) • **81**
Dolcetto Langhe Trifulot 1996: Light and a bit spritzy, with leather and dried cherry flavors. Slightly astringent finish. Drink now.–K.M. • $12 • (8/31/1998) • **78**
Favorita Langhe Costabianca 1996: Citrus flavors are attractive, but the wine lacks intensity. Slightly spritzy. Drink now.–K.M. • $12 • (8/31/1998) • **79**
Langhe Costarossa 1996: Very spritzy, with bitter, lean cherry flavors. Astringent finish. Not recommended. Tasted twice, with consistent notes. –K.M. • $12 • (8/31/1998) • **67**

Roero Arneis Ajnaldi Bianc 1996: A medium-bodied white, with good peach character and spicy notes on the finish. Drink now.–K.M. • $20 • (8/31/1998) • **83**

Roero Arneis Serramiana 1996: Thin and dried out, with earthy aromas and flavors. Not much fun.–K.M. • $16 • (8/31/1998) • **72**

Roero Batajot 1996: A bit hard around the edges, with some simple mint and sweet cherry flavors.–K.M. • $15 • (8/31/1998) • **78**

TERLANO, CANTINA SOCIALE

Pinot Grigio Alto Adige 1996 • $12 • (5/15/1998) • **83**

TERRABIANCA

Campaccio Barriques 1993 • $31 • (9/30/1997) • **85**

Campaccio Barriques 1991 • $NA • (10/31/1995) • **80**

Campaccio Barriques 1990 • $33 • (2/28/1995) • **84**

Campaccio Barriques 1988 • $31 • (9/15/1991) • **87**

Campaccio Barriques Speciale 1993 • $58 • (9/30/1997) • **90**

Chianti Classico Riserva 1991 • $NA • (10/31/1995) • **84**

Chianti Classico Scassino 1992 • $12 • (2/28/1995) • **78**

Chianti Classico Scassino 1991 • $16 • (10/31/1993) • **85**

Chianti Classico Scassino 1990 • $13 • (9/15/1992) • **90**

Chianti Classico Vigna della Croce Riserva 1995: Good simple Sangiovese. Attractive plum and dried cherry character, persisting to the palate. Medium-bodied, with a stemmy, slightly green finish. Drink now.–J.S. • $26 • (11/30/1999) • **83**

Chianti Classico Vigna della Croce Riserva 1994: Gentle and pleasing. Attractive strawberry and chocolate aromas. Medium-bodied, with rounded tannins and a creamy, light vanilla and fruit aftertaste. Drink now.–J.S. • $23 • (12/15/1998) • **88**

Chianti Classico Vigna della Croce Riserva 1993 • $27 • (9/30/1997) • **85**

Chianti Classico Vigna della Croce Riserva 1990 • $40 Ⓐ • (2/28/1995) • **87**

Chianti Classico Vigna della Croce Riserva 1988 • $25 • (9/15/1992) • **88**

Scassino 1994 • $16 • (1/31/1997) • **79**

Toscana Campaccio 1995: Likable red but slightly hard, with silky tannins and dried herbs and berries on the palate. Medium-bodied, with firm tannins and a medium finish. Drink now.–J.S. • $31 • (11/30/1999) • **86**

Toscana Campaccio 1994: Strong herbal Cabernet character comes through, but it's well-crafted. Interesting aromas of currant, dried herb and eucalyptus verging on bell pepper. Medium-bodied, with firm tannins and a chewy finish. Drink through 2001.–J.S. • $28 • (12/15/1998) • **87**

Toscana Campaccio 1993: Good concentration of fruit, but bell pepper and grass aromas and flavors mar the overall quality. Medium-bodied, with medium, polished tannins and a fruity finish. Drink now.–J.S. • $50 • (12/15/1998) • **84**

Toscana Campaccio 1991 • $NA • (10/31/1995) • **80**

Toscana Campaccio 1990 • $77 Ⓐ • (10/31/1993) • **88**

Toscana Piano del Cipresso 1995: Rather disjointed. Slightly herbal aromas, with some berry and earth. Medium-bodied, with chewy tannins and a slightly aggressive finish. Will it mellow with time? Drink now.–J.S. • $31 • (11/30/1999) • **83**

Toscana Piano del Cipresso 1994: Weedy, burnt bell pepper character dominates. Watery and unpleasant. What in the world happened here? Not recommended. Tasted twice, with consistent notes.–J.S. • $28 • (12/15/1998) • **69**

Toscana Piano del Cipresso 1993 • $31 • (9/30/1997) • **88**

Toscana Piano del Cipresso 1991 • $NA • (10/31/1995) • **87**

Toscana Piano del Cipresso 1990 • $48 Ⓐ • (10/31/1993) • **86**

Toscana Piano del Cipresso 1988 • $29 • (9/15/1991) • **83**

TERRE CORTESI MONCARO

Esino Red Terrazzo 1998: Bright and fruity character, with crushed berry. Medium-bodied, with a fresh fruit finish. Drink now.–J.S. • $7 • (4/30/2000) • **84**

Esino White Terrazzo 1998: Has pear character but is slightly dull.–J.S. • $7 • (4/30/2000) • **79**

Key: SS—Spectator Selection. CS—Cellar Selection. HR—Highly Recommended. $NA—Price not available. (BT)—Barrel tasting. Ⓐ—Auction Price.
For a key to the tasters' initials, see "How to Use These Listings."
Dates in parentheses represent the issues in which the ratings were published.

Rosso Cònero Terrazzo C 1997: Captivating blackberry and raspberry aromas. Medium-bodied, with silky tannins and a fruity finish. Elegant and well done. Drink now through 2002.–J.S. • $12 • (4/30/2000) • **87**

Verdicchio dei Castelli di Jesi Classico Carosello 1998: Fresh melon and apple character. Medium-bodied, with fresh acidity and a fruity finish. Delicious. Drink now.–J.S. • $8 • (4/30/2000) • **84**

Verdicchio dei Castelli di Jesi Terrazzo V 1998: Lemon, spice and mineral character. Medium-bodied, with good acidity and a fruity, fresh finish. Drink now.–J.S. • $12 • (4/30/2000) • **85**

TERRE DA VINO

Barolo Paesi Tuoi 1993 • $NA • (10/31/1997) • **77**

TERRE DEL BAROLO

Barolo 1993 • $29 • (10/31/1997) • **78**

TERRE DEL CEDRO

Emilia Avi 1997: Lots of ripe berry, tobacco and toasted oak. Medium-bodied, with medium velvety tannins and a slightly astringent finish. Drink now.–J.S. • $32 • (4/30/2000) • **85**

Sangiovese di Romagna 1998: Simple and light-bodied, with light plum, strawberry and floral character. Serve slightly chilled. Drink now.–J.S. • $10 • (4/30/2000) • **80**

Sangiovese di Romagna Riserva Zarricante 1997: A bit simple and rustic, but with good ripe fruit character and smoky undertones. Full-bodied, with chewy, slightly dry tannins. Needs food. Drink now.–J.S. • $22 • (4/30/2000) • **82**

Trebbiano di Romagna Vintàn 1998: Smells a bit like chicken broth. Light and slightly oxidized. Strange, really. Not imported into the U.S.–J.S. • $NA • (1/01/2000) • **75**

TERRE DI GINESTRA

Sicilia Red 1995 • $9 • (6/15/1998) • **85**

Sicilia Red 1994 • $9 • (4/30/1997) • **86**

Sicilia White 1996 • $9 • (5/15/1998) • **82**

TERREDORA

Aglianico d'Irpinia 1998: Intriguing aromas of plum skin and red berries with hints of cumin. Medium-bodied, with light tannins and a spicy, peppery finish. Drink now.–J.S. • $12 • (1/31/2000) • **84**

Aglianico d'Irpinia Il Principio 1998: Very fruity, with green tobacco character. Full-bodied, with velvety tannins and a long finish. Slightly one-dimensional but very good. Drink now through 2003.–J.S. • $12 • (5/31/2000) • **85**

Aglianico d'Irpinia Il Principio 1997: Bubbling over with ripe blackberry, grilled meat and cumin aromas. Full-bodied, with velvety tannins and a long finish. Outstanding. Give it a bit more time in the bottle. Best after 2001.–J.S. • $20 • (1/31/2000) • **90**

Fiano di Avellino 1998: Exciting fruit in this very youthful, lively white from Italy, with honey, citrus and mineral character. It's full in body, with lots of fruit and a long, long finish. Drink now through 2004.–J.S. • $20 • (1/31/2000) HR • **90**

Fiano di Avellino Campo Re 1998: Bright and fruity white, with apple, melon and honey character. Medium-bodied, with good acidity and a fresh finish. Not imported into the U.S. Drink now.–J.S. • $NA • (1/31/2000) • **88**

Greco di Tufo Loggia della Serra 1998: An outstanding, balanced white with a captivating character of mineral, honey and lemon. Full-bodied, with fresh acidity and a long aftertaste of mineral and fruit. Drink now.–J.S. • $19 • (1/31/2000) • **90**

Greco di Tufo Loggia della Serra 1996 • $20 • (12/31/1997) • **84**

Taurasi 1996: Well crafted, with ripe berry, black pepper and spice character. Medium- to full-bodied, with firm tannins and a long finish. Slightly austere. Give it time. Best after 2000.–J.S. • $23 • (5/31/2000) • **87**

Taurasi Fatica Contadina 1995: Lovely aromas of plums, mineral and spices follow through to a medium-bodied palate, with fine, polished tannins and a slightly short, austere finish; needs a bit more fruit on the finish. Not imported into the U.S. Drink now.–J.S. • $NA • (1/01/1999) • **86**

TERRENO

Chianti Classico 1997: Plenty of black cherry and berry character, bubbling over with ripe plum. Full-bodied, with medium tannins and a fruity finish. Drink now.–J.S. • $17 • (11/30/1999) • **87**

Chianti Classico 1995 • $20 • (9/30/1997) • **79**

Chianti Classico Riserva 1996: Pretty aromas of blackberry and flowers. Medium-bodied, with lovely berry and cherry flavors, fine tannins and a silky finish. Best after 2000.–J.S. • $22 • (11/30/1999) • **87**

Chianti Classico Riserva 1995: Very pretty, with loads of blackberry and dark chocolate, hints of earth on the nose and palate. Medium-bodied, with fine tannins and a fresh finish. Drink now.–J.S. • $24 • (12/15/1998) • **87**

Sangiovese-Cabernet Toscana Pierfrancesco 1997: Slightly one-dimensional but delicious. Aromas of cherry, smoke and earth follow through to a medium-bodied palate, with lively acidity, light tannins and a fruity finish. Not imported into the U.S. Drink now.–J.S. • $NA • (1/01/1999) • **85**

TERRICCI

Antiche Terre de 'Ricci 1994 • $NA • (9/30/1997) • **77**

Antiche Terre de 'Ricci 1986 • $23 • (5/15/1990) • **83**

Antiche Terre de 'Ricci 1985 • $22 • (3/15/1989) • **91**

TERRICCIO, TENUTA DEL

Toscana Con Vento 1998: A solid white, with gorgeous aromas of ripe peach, honey and vanilla. Full-bodied, with chalk, apple and tropical fruit character and a medium finish. Not imported into the U.S. Drink now.–J.S. • $NA • (1/01/1999) • **87**

Toscana Con Vento 1997: Lots of pear and celery character in this fresh white. Medium-bodied, with crisp acidity and more celery and fruit on the aftertaste. Mostly Sauvignon. Drink now.–J.S. • $NA • (12/15/1998) • **83**

Toscana Con Vento 1996 • $16 • (9/30/1997) • **88**

Toscana Lupicaia 1996: Less polished than the '95, more like the stupendous '93. I like it. Chunky, ripe and rich Cabernet character. Gorgeous plum, blackberry and wet earth aromas. Full-bodied, with velvety tannins and a long, ripe fruit aftertaste. Drink now.–J.S. • $85 • (12/15/1998) • **91**

Toscana Lupicaia 1995: Seductive and elegant. Extremely aromatic, with berries and floral character. Medium- to full-bodied, with well-integrated tannins and a caressing, silky finish. Needs time. A Cabernet Sauvignon blend. Best after 2000.–J.S. • $NA • (12/15/1998) • **90**

Toscana Lupicaia 1993 • $58 • (5/31/1997) • **93**

Toscana Rondinaia 1998: A pleasant, slightly earthy wine, with very ripe apple aromas and a hint of cheese. Medium-bodied, with vanilla, cream and green apple flavors. Hints of straw and herb on the finish. Not imported into the U.S. Drink now.–J.S. • $NA • (1/01/1999) • **84**

Toscana Rondinaia 1997: Aromas of freshly cut pears, cream and peaches. Medium-bodied, with a creamy texture and a long, refreshing aftertaste of citrus fruits. Always an interesting white. Drink now.–J.S. • $NA • (12/15/1998) • **87**

Toscana Rondinaia 1996 • $16 • (9/30/1997) • **88**

Toscana Saluccio 1998: Pretty aromas of pie crust, honey and apple. Medium-bodied, with apple, almond and wood character and hints of herb. Lacks a little freshness. Not imported into the U.S. Drink now.–J.S. • $NA • (1/01/1999) • **84**

Toscana Saluccio 1996: Beautiful aromas of pears, honeysuckle and vanilla with hints of apples. Medium-bodied, with fresh fruit flavors and a long aftertaste. A tribute to the potential of white wine-making in Tuscany. Mostly Chardonnay. Drink now.–J.S. • $NA • (12/15/1998) • **90**

Toscana Tassinaia 1997: A big and chewy wine that needs time. A bit rustic, it tastes a bit like Zinfandel, with very ripe berry and a hint of game and spice. Full-bodied and peppery, with a long, velvety, tannic aftertaste. Best after 2000.–J.S. • $62 • (11/30/1999) • **89**

Toscana Tassinaia 1996: A slender yet seductive red, with plenty of plum skin and berry character. Medium-bodied, with fine tannins and a fresh, fruity aftertaste. Drink now.–J.S. • $60 • (12/15/1998) • **88**

Toscana Tassinaia 1995 • $29 • (9/30/1997) • **87**

Toscana Tassinaia 1994 • $36 • (10/31/1996) • **84**

Toscana Tassinaia 1993 • $NA • (10/31/1995) • **90**

Toscana Tassinaia 1992 • $NA • (10/31/1995) • **86**

TERUZZI & PUTHOD

Toscana Carmen Puthod White 1998: A subtle white, with lemon peel, honey and melon character and hints of mineral. Medium-bodied, with a crisp and fruity finish. Drink now.–J.S. • $16 • (11/30/1999) • **87**

Toscana Terre di Tufi White 1998: One of the best dry whites of Tuscany as always, with plenty of apple, cut wood and cream aromas and flavors. Full-bodied, with firm acidity and a medium finish. A bit closed right now. Drink now.–J.S. • $20 • (11/30/1999) • **89**

Toscana Terre di Tufi White 1997: Pretty aromas of apple, vanilla and spice, with a hint of pie crust. Full-bodied, with lively fruit flavors and fresh acidity. The ripe and exotic fruit character is still slightly reserved; give it time to open. Drink now.–J.S. • $22 • (12/15/1998) • **88**

Vernaccia di San Gimignano 1998: A white with pretty honeydew and almond character throughout. Medium-bodied, with fresh acidity and a fruity finish. Drink now.–J.S. • $11 • (11/30/1999) • **86**

Vernaccia di San Gimignano 1996 • $12 • (9/30/1997) • **84**

Vigna Peperino 1986 • $11 • (1/31/1990) • **68**

Vigna Peperino 1985 • $11 • (10/31/1988) • **92**

TIARE

Cabernet Franc Collio 1998: Some good fruit on the nose, but slightly weedy. Medium-bodied, with light tannins and a weedy finish. Hard to get excited about.–J.S. • $17 • (5/15/2000) • **78**

Cabernet Sauvignon Isonzo del Friuli 1998: Soft, fruity and very obvious, with lots of cherry and vanilla character. Medium body. Light tannins. Fruity finish. Drink now.–J.S. • $17 • (5/15/2000) • **81**

Chardonnay Collio 1998: Interesting aromas of rose and mineral. Medium-bodied, with an intense mineral flavor and a slightly alcoholic finish. A bit out of balance. Not imported into the U.S. Drink now.–J.S. • $NA • (1/01/2000) • **81**

Cormontium 1996: Wonderful aromas of apricot jam, marmalade and coconut. Medium-bodied, with medium sweetness and a long, long finish. A delicious dessert wine. Drink now.–J.S. • $17/500 ml. • (6/15/2000) • **87**

Merlot Isonzo del Friuli 1998: Pretty aromas of crushed roses and plums. Medium-bodied and chewy, with lots of ripe tannins but slightly austere and short on the finish. Drink now.–J.S. • $16 • (5/15/2000) • **83**

Pinot Grigio Collio 1998: Medium-bodied, with mineral and apple character, fresh acidity and an ashy aftertaste. Drink now.–J.S. • $15 • (3/31/2000) • **84**

Pinot Nero Collio 1998: A pleasant, fruity red with lots of plum and cherry character, a medium body and a fresh finish. Doesn't taste much like Pinot Noir. Drink now.–J.S. • $17 • (5/15/2000) • **83**

Ronco della Tiare Red 1996: A bit lean but there's some beautiful plum and berry character here, with polished tannins and hints of new oak on the finish. Well made. Cabernet Sauvignon, Merlot and Schioppettino. Drink now through 2002.–J.S. • $19 • (5/15/2000) • **85**

TIEFENBRUNNER

Cabernet Sauvignon Alto Adige Linticlarus 1996: Very good, with a nice dark color and lots of black currant bush and eucalyptus aromas. Full-bodied, with chewy tannins and a long finish. Needs time. Best after 2003.–J.S. • $25 • (6/15/2000) • **89**

Cabernet Sauvignon Alto Adige Linticlarus 1992 • $13 • (2/29/1996) • **83**

Chardonnay Alto Adige Linticlarus 1996: Lovely cream and apple aromas, with a hint of mineral. Medium-bodied, with good acidity and a clean, citric aftertaste. Drink now.–J.S. • $23 • (6/15/2000) • **85**

Feldmarscall von Fenner zu Fennberg 1998: Very aromatic, with mineral, lime and lemon character. Medium-bodied, with zingy acidity. Drink now.–J.S. • $32 • (6/15/2000) • **86**

Merlot Alto Adige 1997: Decent plum and cherry character, with hints of flowers. Medium-bodied, with fine tannins and a light, fruity finish. A bit lean. Drink now.–J.S. • $17 • (6/15/2000) • **85**

Pinot Bianco Alto Adige 1998: Simple and clean, with a lemon-lime and slightly herbal character. Light-bodied, with a fresh finish. Drink now. –J.S. • $12 • (6/15/2000) • **83**

Pinot Bianco Alto Adige 1996 • $11 • (6/15/1998) • **82**

Pinot Grigio Alto Adige 1998: Clean and fresh white, with light melon and apple skin character. Light body. Fresh finish. Drink now.–J.S. • $12 • (4/30/2000) • **82**

Pinot Grigio Alto Adige 1996 • $11 • (6/15/1998) • **85**

Sauvignon Alto Adige Kirchleiten 1998: Subtle, with interesting aromas of peach, honey and mineral. Medium-bodied, with delicious fruit and a fine, elegant finish. Drink now.–J.S. • $19 • (6/15/2000) • **88**

TIEZZI, ENZO

Brunello di Montalcino 1995: A bit rustic, but very good. Aromas of ripe fruit, raisins and meat with hints of cedar. Medium- to full-bodied, with chewy tannins and a ripe fruit aftertaste. Limited U.S. availability. Drink now.–J.S. • $NA • (1/01/2000) • **87**
Brunello di Montalcino 1994: This is all in finesse. Wonderful aromas of plums, strawberries and flowers with hints of oak. Medium-bodied, with superfine tannins and a long, long, silky finish. Drink now through 2004.–J.S. • $45 • (8/31/1999) • **88**
Brunello di Montalcino 1993: A big, juicy, traditional-style Brunello. Plenty of ripe fruit character, with highlights of chocolate. Medium-bodied, with medium, velvety tannins and a long finish. Slightly disjointed at the moment. Best after 2000.–J.S. • $29 Ⓐ • (12/15/1998) • **88**
Brunello di Montalcino 1992 • $32 • (9/30/1997) • **84**
Brunello di Montalcino 1991 • $30 • (11/30/1996) • **80**
Brunello di Montalcino 1990 • $NA • (10/31/1995) • **85**
Cerrino 1994 • $NA • (10/31/1996) • **76**
Rosso di Montalcino 1995 • $12 • (9/30/1997) • **86**
Rosso di Montalcino 1994 • $12 • (11/30/1996) • **82**
Rosso di Montalcino 1993 • $NA • (10/31/1995) • **85**

TINAZZI

Bardolino Classico 1994 • $9 • (11/15/1997) • **74**
Soave Classico 1996 • $9 • (4/30/1998) • **81**
Valpolicella Classico Superiòre 1992 • $9 • (11/15/1997) • **82**

TOMMASI

Amarone della Valpolicella Classico 1993: Ripe, with prune and leather notes that persist to the slightly curt finish, this starts off rich and soft but lacks midpalate concentration. Drink now.–B.S. • $30 • (9/30/1998) • **83**
Amarone della Valpolicella Classico 1990 • $42 • (4/30/1997) • **88**
Amarone della Valpolicella Classico 1989 • $23 • (1/31/1997) • **88**
Amarone della Valpolicella Classico 1988 • $23 • (1/31/1997) • **86**
Pinot Grigio Valdadige Le Rosse 1997 • $13 • (6/30/1998) • **84**
Recioto della Valpolicella Classico 1993: Just slightly sweet, this has only modest plum flavors, but the texture is like drinking faded velvet. Drink now.–B.S. • $28 • (9/30/1998) • **84**
Recioto di Soave Classico 1995: Honey and walnut aromas and flavors are light and airy in this medium-sweet dessert wine. It's balanced and lively, with an astringency reminiscent of walnuts on the finish. Drink now through 2005.–B.S. • $28 • (9/30/1998) • **87**
Valpolicella Classico Superiòre Rafael 1995: Check out the deal on this ripe Italian red with its plummy aromas, flavors of plums and leather, all richly textured. Medium in body, with a moderate finish, it's best now.–B.S. • $10 • (9/30/1998) • **85**
Valpolicella Classico Superiòre Ripasso 1995: There's fine depth of flavor and a chewy texture to this licorice- and plum-flavored red. It's in the ripasso style, displaying some mouthcoating tannins, but it scores points for exuberance. Drink now through 2002.–B.S. • $20 • (9/30/1998) • **86**
Valpolicella Classico Vigneto del Campo Rafael 1993 • $10 • (1/31/1997) • **87**

TORRACCIA, LA

Chianti Classico 1995 • $NA • (9/30/1997) • **80**
Chianti Classico 1994 • $NA • (9/30/1997) • **85**
Chianti Classico Il Tarocco 1997: Aromatic, with fig, berry and ripe fruit. Full-bodied, with soft tannins and a long, fruity finish. Succulent. Not imported into the U.S. Drink now.–J.S. • $NA • (1/01/1999) • **85**
Chianti Classico Il Tarocco 1993 • $11 • (9/30/1997) • **86**
Chianti Classico Il Tarocco Riserva 1996: A typical light 1996 CC riserva. Floral and dried cherry aromas follow through to a medium-bodied palate, with light tannins and a crisp finish. Not imported into the U.S. Drink now.–J.S. • $NA • (1/01/1999) • **84**
Chianti Classico Il Tarocco Riserva 1993 • $14 • (9/30/1997) • **80**
Colli della Toscana Centrale Lucciolaio 1996: A pretty wine, with subtle aromas of raspberry and toasted oak. Medium-bodied, with well-integrated tannins and a silky finish. Sangiovese and Cabernet Sauvignon. Not imported into the U.S. Drink now.–J.S. • $NA • (1/01/1999) • **86**
Colli della Toscana Centrale Lucciolaio 1994 • $25 • (9/30/1997) • **79**
Colli della Toscana Centrale Solitario White 1997: A simple and easy white, with sliced apple and melon characer. Medium-bodied, with a fresh finish. Not imported into the U.S. Drink now.–J.S. • $NA • (1/01/1999) • **82**

TORRE, LA

Brunello di Montalcino 1994: Decent dried cherry and earth character, but slightly short and light on the palate. Still there's some sweet fruit to the wine. Drink now.–J.S. • $43 • (8/31/1999) • **82**
Brunello di Montalcino 1993: A drink-me Brunello with berry and slightly raisiny aromas and flavors, a medium body and soft tannins. Drink through 2003.–J.S. • $38 • (12/15/1998) • **81**
Brunello di Montalcino 1991 • $31 • (11/30/1996) • **85**
Brunello di Montalcino 1990 • $NA • (10/31/1995) • **85**
Brunello di Montalcino 1985 • $30 • (4/15/1991) • **78**
Rosso di Montalcino 1997: Interesting aromas of walnuts and fruits. Medium-bodied, with firm tannins and a slightly austere finish. Needs more fruit. Drink now.–J.S. • $20 • (9/15/1999) • **84**
Rosso di Montalcino 1996: Simple and fruity, with some dried cherry character, light tannins and a fresh finish. Serve slightly chilled. Drink now.–J.S. • $16 • (12/15/1998) • **80**

TORRE ROSAZZA

Cabernet Sauvignon Colli Orientali del Friuli Ronco della Torre 1996: A bit too herbal and weedy for me. Shows a full body, with lots of tannin and a slightly short finish. For fans of herbal Cabernets. Best after 2000.–J.S. • $22 • (5/15/2000) • **81**
Cabernet Sauvignon Colli Orientali del Friuli Ronco della Torre 1994 • $19 • (5/31/1998) • **79**
Chardonnay Colli Orientali del Friuli 1998: A pleasant, well-made white. Fresh aromas of apple, with a hint of banana. Medium-bodied, with medium acidity and a round, caressing mouthfeel. Drink now.–J.S. • $13 • (2/29/2000) • **86**
Chardonnay Colli Orientali del Friuli 1996 • $14 • (5/31/1998) • **83**
Merlot Colli Orientali del Friuli L 'Altromerlot 1996: Good Merlot. Aromas of cigar tobacco and plums. Medium-bodied, with good fruit and a tobacco quality on the finish. Medium tannins. Best after 2000.–J.S. • $30 • (5/15/2000) • **87**
Merlot Colli Orientali del Friuli L 'Altromerlot 1993 • $27 • (5/31/1998) • **85**
Merlot Colli Orientali del Friuli L 'Altromerlot 1992 • $20 • (2/29/1996) • **88**
Pinot Bianco Colli Orientali del Friuli Ronco delle Magnolie 1997: Superfresh, lively and intense, with very ripe aromas of lemon, apple, straw and tropical fruit. Medium- to full-bodied, with lots of flavor and a long, long finish. Drink now through 2001.–J.S. • $17 • (1/01/2000) • **89**
Pinot Grigio Colli Orientali del Friuli 1998: A serious Pinot Grigio, with beautiful aromas of pineapple, almond and cookies. Full-bodied, with an excellent concentration of ripe fruit and a long, long finish. Drink now.–J.S. • $13 • (2/29/2000) • **88**
Pinot Grigio Colli Orientali del Friuli 1996 • $14 • (5/31/1998) • **81**
Pinot Nero Colli Orientali del Friuli 1993 • $13 • (4/30/1996) • **83**

TORREGIORGI

Barbaresco 1990 • $NA • (10/31/1995) • **82**

TORRESELLA

Cabernet Veneto 1996 • $9 • (6/15/1998) • **78**
Chardonnay Veneto 1996 • $9 • (6/15/1998) • **74**
Merlot 1993 • $9 • (1/31/1996) • **81**
Merlot Lison-Pramaggiore 1995: A good, middleweight Merlot with decent herbal and dried cherry flavors. Turns tough on the finish. Drink now.–K.M. • $9 • (7/31/1998) • **80**
Merlot Veneto 1996 • $9 • (5/31/1998) • **74**
Pinot Grigio Veneto 1998: Clean and simple, with citrus and mineral character. Light finish. Drink now.–J.S. • $9 • (3/31/2000) • **80**
Pinot Grigio Veneto 1996 • $9 • (5/31/1998) • **79**

Key: SS—Spectator Selection. CS—Cellar Selection. HR—Highly Recommended. $NA—Price not available. (BT)—Barrel tasting. Ⓐ—Auction Price.
For a key to the tasters' initials, see "How to Use These Listings."
Dates in parentheses represent the issues in which the ratings were published.

TORTI, DINO

Barbera Oltrepò Pavese 1997: Has a good amount of ripe berry and blackberry character. Medium-bodied, with too much new wood on the palate. Overdone. Not imported into the U.S.–J.S. • $NA • (1/01/2000) • **79**

TOSCOLO

Chianti Classico 1993 • $10 • (10/31/1996) • **74**
Chianti Classico 1990 • $8 • (4/30/1994) • **85**

TRACOLLE

Chianti Classico 1997: Focused and fresh, with bright berry and bark aromas. Medium-bodied, with velvety tannins and a delightful finish. Drink now.–J.S. • $12 • (11/30/1999) • **85**
Chianti Classico 1996: A bit lean, but showing some fresh fruit on the nose and palate. Light-bodied, with light tannins and a slightly austere finish. Drink now.–J.S. • $11 • (12/15/1998) • **81**
Chianti Classico 1993 • $NA • (10/31/1995) • **71**
Chianti Classico 1988 • $NA • (9/15/1991) • **69**

TRAVAGLINI

Gattinara 1994: Displays an earthy horse stable character, with lovely rose petal and blackberry notes—an exciting combination. Medium-bodied, it tastes balanced and floats to a delectable finish. Drink now through 2003. –P.M. • $29 • (1/01/1999) • **89**
Gattinara 1993 • $20 • (1/31/1998) • **73**
Gattinara 1986 • $18 • (1/31/1992) • **82**
Gattinara Numerata 1985 • $26 • (1/31/1992) • **84**
Gattinara Riserva 1993: Has personality, with intense, ripe flavors of black fruit (including plum) and smoke, toast, tar and floral notes. The persistent finish is marked by a good dose of chewy tannins. Drink through 2005.–P.M. • $34 • (1/01/1999) • **88**
Gattinara Riserva 1990 • $29 • (1/31/1998) • **80**
Spanna 1988 • $10 • (7/15/1991) • **83**

TRAVIGNOLI

Chianti Rufina 1997: A decent Chianti rufina, with berry and tobacco aromas and flavors that are slightly too earthy. Medium-bodied, with soft tannins. Drink now.–J.S. • $12 • (11/30/1999) • **80**
Chianti Rufina Riserva 1996: Interesting ripe berry and barnyard character. Medium-bodied, with light tannins and a light finish. Needs more fresh fruit. Drink now.–J.S. • $9 • (11/30/1999) • **81**
Colli della Toscana Centrale Tegolaia 1996: A young Cabernet, still in diapers but beautiful. Dark-colored, with deep and rich aromas of currant and blackberry. Full-bodied, with velvety tannins and a long fruity aftertaste. Best after 2000.–J.S. • $23 • (12/15/1998) • **89**
Toscana 1998: A fun white, with white pepper, honey and peach character. Medium-bodied, with good acidity and a fruity finish. Delicious. Drink now.–J.S. • $5 • (11/30/1999) • **85**
Vin Santo del Chianti Rufina Riserva 1990: Acidic and harsh, with dried fruit character, but it's rather green and vegetal. Barely drinkable.–J.S. • $20/500 ml. • (11/30/1999) • **71**

TREROSE, TENUTA

Toscana Flauto 1996: A medium-bodied Sauvignon Blanc, with simple apple and straw flavors, a hint of vanilla and a light finish. Drink now.–J.S. • $NA • (12/15/1998) • **81**
Toscana Renaio 1998: A straightforward and fruity Chardonnay, with hints of mineral and chalk. Medium-bodied, with good fruit and a pleasant aftertaste. Not imported into the U.S. Drink now.–J.S. • $NA • (1/01/1999) • **85**
Vino Nobile di Montepulciano 1996: Pretty and caressing. Strawberry and cherry, with a hint of earth. Light- to medium-bodied, with medium tannins and a slightly short finish. A bit austere. Drink now.–J.S. • $21 • (11/30/1999) • **84**
Vino Nobile di Montepulciano 1995: A modern Vino Nobile, with focused aromas and flavors of berry and vanilla. Medium-bodied, with fine tannins and a long finish. Delicious. Drink now.–J.S. • $20 • (12/15/1998) • **86**
Vino Nobile di Montepulciano 1988 • $16 • (12/15/1992) • **86**
Vino Nobile di Montepulciano 1986 • $16 • (7/15/1991) • **80**
Vino Nobile di Montepulciano 1985 • $11 • (11/15/1988) • **90**
Vino Nobile di Montepulciano Riserva 1995: Rich aromas of plums, berries and tea. Medium-bodied, with well-integrated tannins and a fresh finish. Slightly short. Drink now.–J.S. • $NA • (11/30/1999) • **84**
Vino Nobile di Montepulciano Riserva 1993 • $60 • (12/31/1997) • **81**
Vino Nobile di Montepulciano Riserva 1985 • $19 • (7/15/1991) • **85**
Vino Nobile di Montepulciano Simposio 1995: Simple Sangiovese character, with dried cherries on the nose and palate. Light- to medium-bodied, with crisp acidity and a light finish. Drink now.–J.S. • $NA • (11/30/1999) • **81**
Vino Nobile di Montepulciano Simposio 1988 • $40 • (12/15/1992) • **88**

TRINORO, TENUTA DI

Toscana 1997: The Tuscan answer to new-wave St.-Emilions. A wine loaded with big, velvety tannins and ripe fruit. Full-bodied and chewy, with a long plum and cherry aftertaste. Very impressive. Best after 2002.–J.S. • $130 • (11/30/1999) • **93**

TUA RITA

Toscana Giusto di Notri 1997: A decadent red, with intense aromas of berry and herb and a hint of meat. Full-bodied, with lots of soft tannins. The delicious aftertaste has succulent ripe fruit, tobacco and toasted oak. Drink now through 2002.–J.S. • $75 • (11/30/1999) • **90**
Toscana Giusto di Notri 1996: Gorgeous, fat and fruity. Shows everything it has right away. Dark-colored, with intense, grapey, blackberry and raspberry aromas. Full-bodied, packed with fruit and velvety tannins. Long, long finish. California Cab lovers should dig this. A blend of Cabernet and Merlot. Drink now through 2003.–J.S. • $50 • (12/15/1998) • **91**
Toscana Perlato del Bosco 1997: A pretty and delicious Sangiovese. Plenty of plum, berry and fresh mushroom character in this youthful red. Medium-bodied, with silky tannins and a rich finish. Drink now through 2003.–J.S. • $30 • (11/30/1999) • **88**
Toscana Redigaffi 1997: A mind-blowing Merlot. Black in color, with superrich aromas of crushed berry, currant and a hint of grilled meat. Full-bodied, with masses of chewy yet ripe tannins and an amazing mint, berry, violet and earth aftertaste. Best after 2003.–J.S. • $100 • (11/30/1999) • **97**
Toscana Redigaffi 1996: A Tuscan rendition of a top-growth St.-Emilion. Fabulous aromas of currant, lead pencil and raspberry. Full-bodied, beautifully crafted, with polished tannins and a long mint, berry and cherry finish. Made from Merlot.–J.S. • $70 • (12/15/1998) • **93**

UCCELLIERA, FATTORIA

Brunello di Montalcino 1995: Pretty plum, berry and floral aromas with hints of strawberries. Medium-bodied, with fine tannins and a fruity, autumnal aftertaste. Drink now.–J.S. • $53 • (6/30/2000) • **87**
Brunello di Montalcino 1994: Rather simple really, but clean and well done, with dried cherry and chocolate character. Light to medium in body and tannins. A light, fruity finish. Drink now.–J.S. • $45 • (8/31/1999) • **85**
Brunello di Montalcino 1993: Pretty berry and tobacco character, but with earth and bothersome funk on the nose. Medium-bodied, with soft tannins and a tart finish. Drink now.–J.S. • $40 • (12/15/1998) • **81**
Brunello di Montalcino 1991 • $32 • (11/30/1996) • **80**
Rosso di Montalcino 1997: Delicious rosso. Pretty dried cherries and violets on the nose. Medium-bodied, with light tannins and a fresh and fruity finish. Drink now.–J.S. • $20 • (9/15/1999) • **84**
Rosso di Montalcino 1996: Wonderful balance of ripe fruit and silky tannins. Medium- to full-bodied, with well-integrated tannins and a long aftertaste of ripe berry, cherry and earth. Drink now.–J.S. • $18 • (12/15/1998) • **87**
Rosso di Montalcino 1994 • $15 • (11/30/1996) • **80**

UCCELLIERA DI POGGIANTI, FATTORIA

Castellaccio Red 1993 • $26 • (9/30/1997) • **89**
Toscana Red Castellaccio 1995: A smooth, enjoyable red. Plums with hints of cream on the nose. Medium-bodied, with soft tannins and a long, caressing finish. Drink now.–J.S. • $NA • (1/01/1999) • **87**
Toscana White Castellaccio 1996: Hard to get excited about this white. Medium-bodied, with fruit cocktail flavors and a bubbly finish.–J.S. • $NA • (1/01/1999) • **78**

UMANI RONCHI

Marches Le Busche 1997: This delicious wine has melon, apple and straw character, with hints of vanilla. Medium-bodied and very fresh, with a long honey and straw aftertaste. Drink now.–J.S. • $19 • (6/15/1999) • **85**

■ ■ ■ ■

UMANI RONCHI

Marches Pelago 1995: Extremely oaky red; tastes more like a Rioja than an Italian. Medium-bodied and slightly astringent, with vanilla, coconut and hints of fruit. Overdone.–J.S. • $45 • (6/30/1999) • **79**

Montepulciano d'Abruzzo 1997: Interesting blackberry and fresh mushroom character to this red. Light- to medium-bodied, with a light, fruity aftertaste.–J.S. • $7 • (6/30/1999) • **79**

Montepulciano d'Abruzzo 1994 • $6 • (3/31/1997) • **78**

Montepulciano d'Abruzzo 1989 • $5 • (2/15/1991) • **75**

Montepulciano d'Abruzzo Jorio 1996: This big, drink-me-now red is dark ink-colored, with an explosion of superripe fruit and floral components. Full-bodied, with soft tannins and a grapey, simple aftertaste. Drink now. –J.S. • $11 • (6/30/1999) • **86**

Montepulciano d'Abruzzo Jorio 1995 • $11 • (6/15/1998) • **86**

Pelago 1994 • $46 • (5/15/1998) • **87**

Rosso Cònero 1995 • $6 • (4/30/1997) • **78**

Rosso Cònero Cúmaro 1995: A burly, youthful red that Zin or Rhône lovers will enjoy. Inky in color, with a blast of spice, earth and wild berry. Full-bodied and velvety, with loads of fruit and funk on the finish. Best after 2000.–J.S. • $23 • (6/30/1999) • **88**

Rosso Cònero Cúmaro 1994 • $17 • (6/15/1998) • **88**

Rosso Cònero Cúmaro 1988 • $22 • (9/15/1992) • **83**

Rosso Cònero San Lorenzo 1996: Lovely roses and crushed berries on the nose follow through to the palate in this light and fruity red. Drink now. –J.S. • $11 • (6/30/1999) • **84**

Rosso Cònero San Lorenzo 1994 • $10 • (6/15/1998) • **81**

Rosso Cònero San Lorenzo 1993 • $9 • (3/31/1997) • **84**

Sangiovese Marches Medoro 1997: A simple and fruity red, with berry and blackberry character, medium body and a fresh finish. Drink now.–J.S. • $9 • (6/30/1999) • **82**

Verdicchio dei Castelli di Jesi Classico Superiore Casal di Serra 1997: This juicy and fruity white has apple, almond and honeydew character with a mineral undertone. Medium-bodied, with good acidity and a fruity finish. Delicious. Drink now.–J.S. • $12 • (6/15/1999) • **85**

Verdicchio dei Castelli di Jesi Classico Superiore Casal di Serra 1996: A buttery-tasting wine with ripe apple and peach flavors. Turns a bit sharp on the finish, but still enjoyable. Drink now.–K.M. • $10 • (8/31/1998) • **82**

Verdicchio dei Castelli di Jesi Classico Superiore Villa Bianchi 1997: A no-nonsensé, fresh and fruity white with apple and mineral character. Light- to medium-bodied, with a clean finish. Drink now.–J.S. • $10 • (6/15/1999) • **81**

UNTEREBNERHOF, TENUTA

Pinot Grigio Alto Adige 1996: Slightly corky? A sour, earthy edge fights with the nutty, quince flavors. Otherwise rich, with a firm structure and astringent finish. This was the better of two bottles.–B.S. • $12 • (7/31/1998) • **72**

VAJRA, G.D.

Barbera d'Alba 1992 • $NA • (10/31/1994) • **81**

Barbera d'Alba Bricco delle Viole 1997: Herbal, with a sharp, tart, berrylike character followed by a green bell pepper note.–P.M. • $40 • (11/15/1999) • **77**

Barbera d'Alba Bricco delle Viole 1996: Shows good black fruit and wet earth flavors, but a musty note and a drying finish detract. Tasted twice, with consistent notes.–P.M. • $26 • (10/31/1998) • **65**

Barbera d'Alba Bricco delle Viole 1993 • $35 • (10/31/1995) • **82**

Barbera d'Alba Bricco delle Viole Riserva 1985 • $22 • (7/31/1989) • **83**

Barolo 1994: Straightforward, juicy, with plum and licorice and a supple texture but not much depth. Slight herbal note on the finish.–P.M. • $32 • (10/31/1998) • **78**

Barolo 1990 • $28 • (10/31/1994) • **64**

Barolo 1988 • $NA • (10/31/1993) • **85**

Barolo 1982 • $14 • (3/15/1987) • **91**

Barolo Bricco delle Viole 1995: This has good ripeness right off the bat. Black fruit mingles with attractive mocha, chocolate and oak notes. Full-bodied, with tannins that turn firm and chewy but remain manageable. Drink now through 2005.–P.M. • $40 • (11/15/1999) • **88**

Barolo Bricco delle Viole 1982 • $19 • (8/31/1988) • **91**

Barolo Fossati 1985 • $34 • (12/31/1990) • **91**

Key: SS—Spectator Selection. CS—Cellar Selection. HR—Highly Recommended. $NA—Price not available. (BT)—Barrel tasting. (A)—Auction Price. For a key to the tasters' initials, see "How to Use These Listings."
Dates in parentheses represent the issues in which the ratings were published.

Dolcetto d'Alba 1997: Light-bodied, fairly green, with wet earth, cedar, cherry pit and raspberry flavors. Its light tannin structure should cozy up to pizza and other trattoria dishes. Drink now.–P.M. • $14 • (10/31/1998) • **81**

Dolcetto d'Alba 1996 • $13 • (10/31/1997) • **84**

Dolcetto d'Alba Coste & Fossati 1998: Impressively inky black and extracted, with attractive tar, licorice, blackberry and smoke aromas and flavors. Showy, full of fruit and not easily ignored. Drink now through 2001.–P.M. • $20 • (11/15/1999) • **85**

Dolcetto d'Alba Coste & Fossati 1997: Well made. Ripe and supple, deliciously packed with floral, currant and blackberry flavors, this wine is worth the hunt as it remains balanced and seductive from start to finish.–P.M. • $18 • (10/31/1998) • **88**

Dolcetto d'Alba Coste & Fossati 1996 • $20 • (10/31/1997) • **91**

Dolcetto d'Alba Coste & Fossati 1994 • $19 • (10/31/1995) • **85**

Langhe Kyè 1997: A bit chewy. Medium-bodied and dark in color, with black cherry and red berry flavors. A bit overdone, with a tough, petrollike character. Time might tame it. Best from 2001 through 2005.–P.M. • $25 • (11/15/1999) • **81**

Langhe Rosso 1997: Very pretty, light-hearted red wine, smacking with fresh acidity, raspberry and wild strawberry. Tannins are fairly smooth already; enjoy now, slightly chilled.–P.M. • $10 • (10/31/1998) • **85**

Nebbiolo delle Langhe 1998: Nice structure of fruit, acidity, tannins and oak. The balance makes this medium-bodied, smoky red a lovely drink in the near future. Drink now through 2002.–P.M. • $16 • (11/15/1999) • **87**

Nebbiolo delle Langhe 1997: Fresh, lush and fruity, with raspberry, black cherry and touches of spice and smoke. Will be super with trattoria food. Balanced, with velvety tannins. Well made and delicious from start to finish, without pretension. Drink now.–P.M. • $18 • (10/31/1998) • **87**

Nebbiolo delle Langhe 1996 • $14 • (10/31/1997) • **80**

VAL DI SUGA

Brunello di Montalcino 1995: Slightly lean, but shows clean fruit. Lots of smoke, plum and ash aromas. Medium- to full-bodied, with fine tannins and a fresh finish. Slightly overwooded? Turns a bit dry. Drink now.–J.S. • $42 • (6/30/2000) • **83**

Brunello di Montalcino 1994: Subtle aromas of berries, cedar and creamed coffee. Medium-bodied, with firm tannins and a medium fruity finish. Slightly one-dimensional. Drink now.–J.S. • $38 • (8/31/1999) • **86**

Brunello di Montalcino 1993: Brick-red in color, with amber edges. Aromas and flavors of leather, cedar and dried fruit. Medium-bodied, with a dry finish.–J.S. • $33 • (12/15/1998) • **75**

Brunello di Montalcino 1992 • $38 • (9/30/1997) • **85**

Brunello di Montalcino 1991 • $33 • (11/30/1996) • **82**

Brunello di Montalcino 1990 • $NA • (10/31/1995) • **86**

Brunello di Montalcino 1988 • $26 • (4/30/1994) • **78**

Brunello di Montalcino 1985 • $23 • (9/30/1990) • **88**

Brunello di Montalcino Riserva 1993: Enticingly decadent aromas of berries, bark, earth and game. Full-bodied, with firm, slightly tough tannins but plenty of fruit on the finish. Needs time still. Drink now.–J.S. • $55 • (8/31/1999) • **90**

Brunello di Montalcino Riserva 1991 • $48 • (9/30/1997) • **82**

Brunello di Montalcino Riserva 1990 • $45 • (11/30/1996) • **84**

Brunello di Montalcino Riserva 1988 • $NA • (10/31/1994) • **87**

Brunello di Montalcino Riserva 1986 • $27 • (11/30/1993) • **87**

Brunello di Montalcino Riserva 1982 • $20 • (11/30/1989) • **89**

Brunello di Montalcino Vigna del Lago 1995: Modern and well-made. Lovely aromas of raspberries, smoke and vanilla. Full-bodied, with powerful, silky tannins, ripe fruit and a vanilla aftertaste. Lots of new wood, but needs a bit more bottle age to mellow out. Best after 2001.–J.S. • $92 • (6/30/2000) • **89**

Brunello di Montalcino Vigna del Lago 1993: A designer Brunello, with a showy, voluptuous style and complex aromas of blackberry, chocolate and flowers. Full-bodied and polished, with fine tannins and a long, chocolaty finish. Best after 2001.–J.S. • $83 • (12/15/1998) • **90**

Brunello di Montalcino Vigna del Lago 1990 • $70 • (11/30/1996) • **87**

Brunello di Montalcino Vigna del Lago 1988 • $52 • (4/30/1994) • **90**

Brunello di Montalcino Vigna del Lago 1986 • $52 • (11/30/1993) HR • **91**

Brunello di Montalcino Vigna del Lago 1985 • $52 • (7/15/1991) • **90**

Brunello di Montalcino Vigna Spuntali 1993: Loaded with new wood. Vanilla and berry aromas follow through to the palate. Medium- to full-bodied, with polished tannins and a fruity, toasted oak finish. A bit too much new oak for me, but some good fruit under it all. Drink now.–J.S. • $91 • (8/31/1999) • **87**

Brunello di Montalcino Vigna Spuntali 1990 • $70 • (11/30/1996) • **89**

Brunello di Montalcino Vigna Spuntali 1988 • $52 • (7/31/1995) • **88**

Rosso di Montalcino 1997: Light and simple, with berry and tobacco character, light to medium body and a fresh finish. Drink now.–J.S. • $20 • (9/15/1999) • **81**

Rosso di Montalcino 1996: Straightforward, with berry and tobacco character, light to medium body and a simple finish. Drink now.–J.S. • $16 • (12/15/1998) • **81**

Rosso di Montalcino 1995 • $17 • (9/30/1997) • **79**

Rosso di Montalcino 1994 • $16 • (11/30/1996) • **86**

Rosso di Montalcino 1993 • $NA • (10/31/1995) • **77**

Rosso di Montalcino 1991 • $12 • (4/30/1994) • **80**

Rosso di Montalcino 1988 • $10 • (4/30/1991) • **87**

VALDICAVA

Brunello di Montalcino 1994: Superaromatic, with currants, violets, dried cherries and fresh wet earth. Full-bodied, with well-integrated silky tannins and a long, sweet fruit finish. A thoroughly harmonious red. Drink now through 2006.–J.S. • $NA • (8/31/1999) • **90**

Brunello di Montalcino 1993: Medium-bodied, tannic and slightly austere, with lots of dried fruits and nuts and a hot finish. Slightly overdone. Drink now.–J.S. • $NA • (12/15/1998) • **81**

Brunello di Montalcino 1991 • $NA • (11/30/1996) • **85**

Brunello di Montalcino 1990 • $NA • (10/31/1995) • **80**

Brunello di Montalcino 1988 • $28 • (4/30/1994) • **86**

Brunello di Montalcino Madonna del Piano Riserva 1993: A joy to drink. A lovely and multidimensional red with berry, floral and forestlike aromas. Full-bodied, with fine tannins and a long, long, wonderfully sweet fruit aftertaste. Drink now through 2008.–J.S. • $100 • (8/31/1999) • **90**

Brunello di Montalcino Madonna del Piano Riserva 1990 • $NA • (11/30/1996) • **93**

Brunello di Montalcino Madonna del Piano Riserva 1988 • $NA • (10/31/1994) • **85**

Rosso di Montalcino 1997: A big, concentrated style with intense blackberry, grilled meat and tobacco character. Full-bodied. Full, velvety tannins. A bit rustic, but if you like Syrah or Zinfandel, go for this. Drink now through 2003.–J.S. • $24 • (9/15/1999) • **88**

Rosso di Montalcino 1996: Very perfumed, with floral, berry and cherry aromas. Medium- to full-bodied, with chunky tannins and a long, fruity finish. Drink now through 2001.–J.S. • $23 • (12/15/1998) • **87**

Rosso di Montalcino 1995 • $NA • (9/30/1997) • **83**

Rosso di Montalcino 1994 • $NA • (11/30/1996) • **87**

Rosso di Montalcino 1993 • $NA • (10/31/1995) • **84**

Rosso di Montalcino 1991 • $15 • (4/30/1994) • **78**

VALDINERA

Barbera d'Alba Ca ' Rusa Barriques 1997: Very oaky, full-bodied and thick, this is distinctive Barbera in a very woody yet fresh and crisp style, showing some clean red berry flavors. Maybe time will bring it all together, but it seems a bit clumsy for now. Not imported into the U.S. Drink through 2004.–P.M. • $NA • (1/01/1999) • **85**

Nebbiolo d'Alba Sontuoso 1996: Herbal. Light in color and body, with a tart finish. Not imported into the U.S.–P.M. • $NA • (1/01/1999) • **73**

VALDIPIATTA, TENUTA

Rosso di Montepulciano 1998: A simple and enjoyable red, with plum skin and cedar aromas and flavors. Light-bodied, with light tannins and a crisp finish. Drink now.–J.S. • $13 • (11/30/1999) • **81**

Rosso di Montepulciano 1996: Medium-bodied, with aromas of ripe plum and raspberry, medium tannins and a slightly austere finish. Drink now. –J.S. • $12 • (12/15/1998) • **82**

Rosso di Montepulciano 1995 • $13 • (9/30/1997) • **68**

Toscana Trefonti 1996: A bit lean but clean, with plenty of black cherry, fresh mushroom and cherry aromas. Medium-bodied, with well-integrated tannins, medium fruit and a slightly short finish. Drink now through 2001. –J.S. • $31 • (11/30/1999) • **85**

Toscana Trefonti 1995: Thick and rich, with loads of berry and black olive aromas and flavors. Full-bodied, with velvety tannins. Slightly monolithic, but wonderfully good. Best after 2001.–J.S. • $31 • (12/15/1998) • **89**

Toscana Trefonti 1994 • $30 • (9/30/1997) • **88**

Toscana Trincerone 1997: A fabulous Sangiovese, with aromas of violet, berry and cherry. Medium- to full-bodied, with velvety tannins and a long aftertaste of chocolate and cherry. Best after 2001.–J.S. • $33 • (11/30/1999) • **92**

Vino Nobile di Montepulciano 1996: A beauty. Dark ruby in color, with aromas of raspberry, currant and berry that leap out of the glass. Medium-bodied, with velvety tannins and a medium, fruity finish. Drink now through 2002.–J.S. • $21 • (11/30/1999) • **88**

Vino Nobile di Montepulciano 1995: A firm and racy Nobile, with good, clean fruit flavors and silky tannins. Medium-bodied, with medium tannins. Drink now.–J.S. • $21 • (12/15/1998) • **87**

Vino Nobile di Montepulciano Riserva 1995: Intriguing aromas of spices, berries and fruit. Full-bodied, with very polished tannins and a silky finish. A bit closed now but shows potential. Drink now.–J.S. • $32 • (11/30/1999) • **89**

Vino Nobile di Montepulciano Riserva 1994: Alluring Nobile. Plenty of chocolate and berry character. Medium- to full-bodied, with velvety tannins and caressing texture. Drink now.–J.S. • $27 • (12/15/1998) • **88**

Vino Nobile di Montepulciano Riserva 1993 • $27 • (9/30/1997) • **78**

VALENTINO

Dolcetto di Dogliani La Scolca 1997: Very extracted for Dolcetto; full-bodied, it offers good concentration, with earthy red berry and blackberry character. Wonderful balance and fine tannins. Nice upon release, but the toughish finish should improve with short-term cellaring.–P.M. • $NA • (10/31/1998) • **83**

VALFIERI

Barbaresco 1989 • $16 • (4/15/1994) • **77**

Barbaresco 1986 • $12 • (9/15/1990) • **82**

Barolo 1990 • $NA • (10/31/1994) • **83**

Barolo 1985 • $13 • (10/15/1990) HR • **90**

Dolcetto d'Alba 1988 • $9 • (12/31/1990) • **81**

VALGIANO, TENUTA DI

Colline Lucchesi Giallo dei Muri 1998: Simple, fruity and delicate, with lime and lemon on an effervescent palate. Drink now.–J.S. • $19 • (11/30/1999) • **80**

Colline Lucchesi Giallo dei Muri 1997: An interesting white in the Toscana style. Plenty of apple, honey and melon, with hints of stone and mineral. Medium body. Fresh acidity. Refreshing and spicy aftertaste. Drink now.–J.S. • $19 • (12/15/1998) • **86**

Colline Lucchesi Rosso dei Palistorti 1997: An eccentric style of wine, with interesting aromas of cranberry and plum. Medium-bodied, with medium, ripe tannins and a game and berry aftertaste. Drink now.–J.S. • $21 • (11/30/1999) • **88**

Colline Lucchesi Rosso dei Palistorti 1996: A little unclean, with chestnut, cheese and fruit character. Light-bodied, with light tannins and a short finish.–J.S. • $22 • (12/15/1998) • **77**

Toscana Scasso dei Cesari 1997: A joy to taste, this red has scrumptious aromas of blackberry, cherry and Indian spice. Full-bodied and very velvety, with wonderful ripe fruit on the finish. Best after 2000.–J.S. • $28 • (11/30/1999) • **91**

Toscana Scasso dei Cesari 1995: Gives you what it's got right away. Pretty aromas and flavors of dried berries and spices. Medium in body, with fine tannins and crisp acidity on the finish. Delicious. Drink now through 2003.–J.S. • $28 • (12/15/1998) • **88**

VALIANO

Chianti Classico 1994 • $11 • (10/31/1996) • **78**

Chianti Classico 1992 • $8 • (2/28/1995) • **79**

Chianti Classico Casarossa 1997: A straightforward Chianti, with light fruit and pepper flavors. Light-bodied, with carbon dioxide on the finish.–J.S. • $18 • (11/30/1999) • **79**

Chianti Classico Poggio Teo 1997: Pretty aromas of plum, berry and watermelon. Light- to medium-bodied, with light tannins and a fruity finish. Rather simple and easy. Drink now.–J.S. • $18 • (11/30/1999) • **84**

Chianti Classico Poggio Teo 1996: Somewhat disjointed now, this lacks charm. Very ripe on the nose. Medium-bodied, with raisiny, black pepper flavors and a short, slightly alcoholic finish.–J.S. • $20 • (12/15/1998) • **79**

Chianti Classico Poggio Teo 1995 • $NA • (9/30/1997) • **77**

Chianti Classico Riserva 1995: Good quality, but short. Dried cherry with hints of leather. Medium-bodied, with light tannins and a slightly dry finish. Drink now.–J.S. • $20 • (12/15/1998) • **81**

Chianti Classico Riserva 1994 • $NA • (9/30/1997) • **83**

Chianti Classico Riserva 1993 • $15 • (10/31/1996) • **84**

VALLAROM

Cabernet Sauvignon Trentino 1988 • $27 • (12/15/1992) • **80**
Pinot Nero Trentino 1990 • $25 • (7/31/1993) • **74**

VALLE CHIARA, ABBAZIA DI

Dolcetto d'Ovada 1990 • $11 • (4/30/1993) • **80**
Dolcetto d'Ovada 1989 • $13 • (7/15/1991) • **79**
Torre Albarola 1988 • $24 • (1/31/1992) • **87**

VARALDO

Barbaresco Bricco Libero 1996: Just sniff and enjoy. Refined tannins, subtle toasted oak and a ripe fruit, tar, smoke and black truffle character lurk in the wings. This elegant, medium-bodied Barbaresco is all balance and satisfaction, with a smooth landing of a finish. Drink now through 2010.–P.M. • $60 • (10/31/1999) • **92**
Barbaresco La Gemma 1996: Light in color and fruity in flavors, this straightforward Nebbiolo displays drying tannins and red berry and earth. Finishes really tough.–P.M. • $NA • (10/31/1999) • **79**
Barbaresco Sorì Loreto 1996: Very plummy. The ripe cassis and crisp red berries of this medium-bodied Barbaresco storm the palate, delivering a vibrant, slightly smoky finish. Needs time. Best from 2002 through 2010.–P.M. • $60 • (10/31/1999) • **87**
Barbera d'Alba 1997: Dense and opulent-textured for a Barbera. Full-bodied, with depth and complexity, showing black fruit, supple tannins, deft oak notes and even a touch of petrol. Tempting now, but will improve. Drink through 2004.–P.M. • $38 • (11/15/1999) • **88**
Barbera d'Alba 1996: A crisp but aromatically interesting Barbera. Light- to medium-bodied, with coffee, spice and toast aromas supporting lovely fruit. Rather vibrant and lean. Should cozy up to food. Drink now through 2002.–P.M. • $34 • (11/15/1999) • **80**
Barolo Vigna di Aldo 1995: This medium-bodied Barolo has very good concentration of black fruit, with an interesting structure. Shows chewy, ripe tannins and lightly smoky, toasted notes. Drink now through 2004.–P.M. • $63 • (11/15/1999) • **88**
Dolcetto d'Alba 1998: Flowers and even cassis and raspberries offer interest at first, but this lacks deep, authentic roots.–P.M. • $18 • (11/15/1999) • **77**
Dolcetto d'Alba 1997: A bit simple, with modest fruit.–P.M. • $18 • (11/15/1999) • **78**
Langhe Freisa 1998: Tough, even tart, with drying tannins and cool fruit.–P.M. • $22 • (11/15/1999) • **74**
Langhe Freisa 1997: Maturing and forward, with mushroom, earth and forest underbrush character, showing cherry notes on the crisp finish.–P.M. • $22 • (11/15/1999) • **76**

VARRAMISTA

Toscana 1996: A solid and fruity red, with interesting dried berry, cocoa and cherry character. Medium- to full-bodied, with velvety tannins and a long, ripe fruit and berry aftertaste. Sangiovese and Syrah. Drink through 2003.–J.S. • $48 • (11/30/1999) • **88**

VECCHIE TERRE DI MONTEFILI

Chianti Classico 1997: An elegant, earthy style of CC, with attractive blackberry and raspberry aromas. Medium-bodied, with berry and nut flavors and a soft texture. Drink now.–J.S. • $22 • (11/30/1999) • **87**
Chianti Classico 1995 • $23 • (9/30/1997) • **85**
Chianti Classico 1994 • $20 • (10/31/1996) • **88**
Chianti Classico 1993 • $NA • (10/31/1995) • **85**
Chianti Classico 1992 • $20 • (2/28/1995) • **85**
Chianti Classico 1990 • $20 • (10/31/1993) • **86**
Chianti Classico 1988 • $20 • (9/15/1991) • **90**
Chianti Classico 1986 • $14 • (4/30/1990) • **85**
Chianti Classico Anfiteatro Riserva 1988 • $24 • (9/15/1992) • **89**
Chianti Classico Anfiteatro Riserva 1985 • $NA • (9/15/1991) • **90**

Key: SS—Spectator Selection. CS—Cellar Selection. HR—Highly Recommended. $NA—Price not available. (BT)—Barrel tasting. (A)—Auction Price. For a key to the tasters' initials, see "How to Use These Listings."
Dates in parentheses represent the issues in which the ratings were published.

Colli della Toscana Centrale Anfiteatro 1996: A wonderfully aromatic wine, with gorgeous aromas of crushed berry, plum and chocolate. Medium-bodied, with medium, silky tannins, crisp acidity and a fresh fruit finish. Needs a bit more fruit midpalate to be outstanding. Drink now.–J.S. • $60 • (11/30/1999) • **87**
Colli della Toscana Centrale Anfiteatro 1994 • $50 • (9/30/1997) • **89**
Colli della Toscana Centrale Anfiteatro 1993 • $50 • (10/31/1996) • **90**
Colli della Toscana Centrale Anfiteatro 1991 • $32 • (10/31/1995) • **90**
Colli della Toscana Centrale Anfiteatro 1990 • $40 • (11/30/1994) • **89**
Colli della Toscana Centrale Bruno di Rocca 1996: I expected a little more out of this, but it's good quality. Dark, with blueberry and dried herb character. Medium-bodied, with a good level of tannins, but slightly short and diluted on the finish. Drink now.–J.S. • $60 • (11/30/1999) • **85**
Colli della Toscana Centrale Bruno di Rocca 1994 • $50 • (9/30/1997) • **88**
Colli della Toscana Centrale Bruno di Rocca 1993 • $50 • (10/31/1996) • **84**
Colli della Toscana Centrale Bruno di Rocca 1992 • $NA • (10/31/1995) • **87**
Colli della Toscana Centrale Bruno di Rocca 1991 • $40 • (11/30/1994) • **87**
Colli della Toscana Centrale Bruno di Rocca 1990 • $NA • (10/31/1993) • **89**
Colli della Toscana Centrale Bruno di Rocca 1989 • $NA • (10/31/1993) • **87**
Colli della Toscana Centrale Vigna Regis 1997: An extremely woody white, with loads of apple pie, coconut and apricot character. Full-bodied, with loads of oak and a long, rich vanilla aftertaste. Lacks a touch of freshness. Drink now.–J.S. • $37 • (11/30/1999) • **86**

VEGA, AZIENDA AGRICOLA

Greco di Tufo d'Antiche Terre 1996: A fairly rich white with plenty of punch. Distinctive flavor of sweet onions, with a slightly buttery note. Flavors linger on the finish with a nice touch of clove. Not for everyone though. Drink now.–K.M. • $15 • (8/31/1998) • **84**

VELETTE, TENUTA LE

Orvieto Classico 1998: Lots of lemon and lime character, with hints of apricot. Medium-bodied, with light acidity and a fruity finish. Delicious. Drink now.–J.S. • $10 • (2/29/2000) • **86**
Orvieto Classico Superiòre Lunato 1998: Refreshing and delicious, with intriguing aromas of melon, mineral and honey. Medium-bodied, with medium acidity and a fruity, slightly spicy finish. Drink now.–J.S. • $15 • (2/29/2000) • **87**
Umbria Calanco 1996: A good but rather simple red. Pretty aromas of plum, with hints of herb and vanilla. Medium- to full-bodied, with soft tannins and a fruity finish. Drink now.–J.S. • $35 • (2/29/2000) • **84**
Umbria Traluce 1998: This ripe white has lots of character, with aromas of grapefruit, apricot and dried fruit. Medium-bodied, with good acidity and a ripe fruit aftertaste. Sauvignon Blanc. Drink now.–J.S. • $15 • (2/29/2000) • **86**

VENEGAZZU

Brut Prosecco del Montello e Colli Asolani Loredan Gasparini NV: Dry, with a grapefruit note accented by cherry, this is appealing, on the soft side yet well balanced. Drink now.–B.S. • $12 • (10/15/1999) • **83**
Cabernet Sauvignon Montello e Colli Asolani Loredan Gasparini 1998: Light, simple and fruity. Slightly thin yet pleasant.–J.S. • $11 • (6/15/2000) • **79**
Colli Trevigiani Della Casa 1997: Crawling. Rubbery. Yuck. Tasted twice, with consistent notes.–J.S. • $26 • (6/15/2000) • **60**
Colli Trevigiani Loredan Gasparini Capo di Stato 1997: Sexy juice, with decadent aromas of earth, ripe fruit and flowers. Full-bodied, with very well integrated tannins and a long, ripe fruit finish. A beauty that needs bottle age. Best after 2001.–J.S. • $36 • (6/15/2000) • **90**
Della Casa 1993 • $23 • (6/15/1997) • **87**
Della Casa 1992 • $20 • (6/15/1996) • **83**
Della Casa 1990 • $15 • (9/15/1992) • **85**
Della Casa 1985 • $25 • (3/31/1990) • **91**
Della Casa 1983 • $25 • (2/15/1989) • **86**
Della Casa 1982 • $15 • (7/15/1987) • **82**
Della Casa 1980 • $10 • (2/15/1987) • **72**
Loredan Gasparini 1990 • $NA • (10/31/1996) • **83**
Loredan Gasparini Capo di Stato 1994 • $41 • (6/15/1997) • **87**
Loredan Gasparini Capo di Stato 1992 • $33 • (5/31/1996) • **88**
Loredan Gasparini Capo di Stato 1990 • $33 • (5/31/1995) • **83**

ITALY

VENICA & VENICA

Bottaz 1993 • $21 • (4/30/1998) • **85**
Merlot Collio Perilla 1993 • $21 • (12/15/1997) • **86**
Pinot Bianco Collio 1996 • $15 • (11/15/1997) • **84**
Tocai Friulano Collio 1996 • $15 • (4/30/1998) • **85**

VENTURELLI

Chardonnay Garda 1996: Quite earthy, with an astringent finish. Not recommended. Tasted twice, with consistent notes.–K.M. • $10 • (8/31/1998) • **68**
Groppello Garda Classico Adamo 1996: Hints of licorice and cherry, but an oxidized note and browning color suggest that this is on the downside. Past its prime.–B.S. • $10 • (9/30/1998) • **76**
Groppello Garda Classico Selezione 1996: Showing some brown color, but still has spicy cherry notes and tangy acidity. Drink now.–B.S. • $9 • (9/30/1998) • **80**
Lugana Selezione 1996: Crisp, lemony and fresh, light-bodied, with a hint of earth on the finish. Made from Trebbiano. Drink now.–B.S. • $9 • (9/30/1998) • **79**
Merlot Garda 1996: Inviting aromas of cherries, spices and licorice continue on the palate in this crisp, focused red. Modestly concentrated, its finish tails off quickly. Drink now.–B.S. • $8 • (9/30/1998) • **83**

VERBENA

Brunello di Montalcino 1988 • $NA • (4/30/1994) • **75**
Rosso di Montalcino 1991 • $NA • (4/30/1994) • **83**

VERDUNO, CASTELLO DI

Barbaresco Rabajà 1993 • $NA • (10/31/1996) • **82**
Barbaresco Rabajà 1990 • $NA • (10/31/1994) • **80**
Barbera d'Alba Bricco del Cuculo 1993 • $NA • (10/31/1995) • **79**
Barbera d'Alba Bricco del Cuculo 1992 • $NA • (10/31/1994) • **80**
Barolo Massara 1993 • $NA • (10/31/1997) • **85**
Barolo Massara 1990 • $NA • (10/31/1994) • **81**

VERRAZZANO, CASTELLO DI

Chianti Classico 1997: A lively Chianti that needs a bit of bottle age. Bright aromas of blackberry and dried cherry. Medium-bodied, with medium tannins and a chewy, crisp aftertaste. Drink now.–J.S. • $23 • (11/30/1999) • **88**
Chianti Classico 1996: Slightly rustic, but loaded with ripe fruit character. Medium-bodied, with lively dried cherry, a hint of raisin, soft tannins and a fruity aftertaste. Drink now.–J.S. • $18 • (12/15/1998) • **85**
Chianti Classico 1995 • $11 • (9/30/1997) • **82**
Chianti Classico 1994 • $13 • (10/31/1996) • **84**
Chianti Classico 1993 • $9 • (10/31/1995) • **86**
Chianti Classico 1992 • $10 • (2/28/1995) • **84**
Chianti Classico 1991 • $10 • (10/31/1993) • **84**
Chianti Classico 1990 • $9 • (10/31/1993) • **88**
Chianti Classico 1988 • $8 • (9/15/1991) • **85**
Chianti Classico Cinquecentenario di Verrazzano Riserva 1985 • $NA • (9/15/1991) • **83**
Chianti Classico Riserva 1996: Pretty floral and blackberry aromas and flavors, with medium body, light tannins and a light finish. Drink now. –J.S. • $39 • (11/30/1999) • **84**
Chianti Classico Riserva 1995: Can't complain about this. Pretty aromas and flavors of dried cherry, with chocolate tones. Medium-bodied, with moderate tannins and a succulent finish. Drink now through 2003.–J.S. • $21 • (12/15/1998) • **85**
Chianti Classico Riserva 1994 • $15 • (9/30/1997) • **84**
Chianti Classico Riserva 1993 • $18 • (10/31/1996) • **79**
Chianti Classico Riserva 1991 • $9 • (10/31/1995) • **86**
Chianti Classico Riserva 1988 • $NA • (9/15/1992) • **84**
Toscana Bottiglia Particolare 1996: Bright aromas of grape, raspberry and mint. Medium-bodied, with medium tannins and a fresh finish. Slightly one-dimensional and hollow, but very fresh. Not imported into the U.S. Drink now.–J.S. • $NA • (1/01/1999) • **85**
Toscana Bottiglia Particolare 1995: A deliciously fruity and well-crafted red, with enticing aromas of crushed berries. Medium-bodied, with medium, fine tannins and a subtle aftertaste of fruit. Drink now through 2003.–J.S. • $43 • (12/15/1998) • **88**
Toscana Sassello 1997: A wonderful Sangiovese, with a super structure. Ink in color, with intense aromas of crushed blackberry, mint, currant and cherry. Full-bodied, with loads of silky tannins and a long berry, currant and mint finish. Best after 2000.–J.S. • $50 • (11/30/1999) • **92**
Toscana Sassello 1995: Delicious and juicy, superfruity. Bright aromas of strawberry and violet open to a medium-bodied wine with medium, velvety tannins and a long, fruity aftertaste. Drink now.–J.S. • $45 • (12/15/1998) • **88**
Toscana Sassello 1994 • $17 • (9/30/1997) • **87**
Toscana Sassello 1993 • $25 • (10/31/1996) • **88**
Toscana Sassello 1990 • $NA • (10/31/1993) • **92**

VESCOVINO, IL

Chianti Classico Vigna Piccola 1997: A clean and delicious Chianti, with lots of berry and dried cherry character. Medium-bodied, with light, fine tannins and a fresh finish. Drink now.–J.S. • $19 • (11/30/1999) • **87**
Chianti Classico Vigna Piccola 1996: Delicious and vibrant Chianti Classico. Bright, fruity aromas and flavors of cherry, strawberry and plum skin. Medium-bodied, with delicate tannins and a crisp and lively fruit finish. Drink now.–J.S. • $17 • (12/15/1998) • **87**
Il Merlotto 1994 • $NA • (9/30/1997) • **86**
Il Merlotto 1993 • $NA • (10/31/1996) • **80**
Toscana Il Merlotto 1996: A subtle red, with lovely blackberry, cherry and tobacco aromas and flavors. Medium-bodied, with light, silky tannins and a delicate, fruity, crisp finish. Sangiovese and Cabernet Sauvignon. Drink now through 2001.–J.S. • $35 • (11/30/1999) • **87**
Toscana Il Merlotto 1995: A straightforward red with attractive berry and dried cherry character. Medium-bodied. Light tannins and a light, fruity finish.–J.S. • $31 • (12/15/1998) • **84**

VESCOVO, GIANNI

Cabernet Sauvignon Isonzo del Friuli 1998: Some pleasant cherry and berry character. Medium in body, with light tannins and a slightly austere, thin finish. Not much to it really. Young vines?–J.S. • $12 • (5/15/2000) • **79**
Cabernet Sauvignon Isonzo del Friuli 1997: A very grassy Cabernet with a cooked beet character. Medium-bodied. Hard to like.–J.S. • $12 • (1/01/2000) • **74**
Pinot Grigio Isonzo del Friuli I Fiori 1998: Has citrusy character, but a bit soapy in aroma. Medium-bodied, with a crisp finish.–J.S. • $10 • (3/31/2000) • **79**
Refosco dal Peduncolo Rosso Isonzo del Friuli 1998: Intense wet earth character in this light and simple red, with fresh fruit and a light finish. Like a pleasant, light Beaujolais. Drink now.–J.S. • $10 • (5/15/2000) • **81**
Refosco dal Peduncolo Rosso Isonzo del Friuli I Fiori 1997: Unclean, with bacterial spoilage. Like a farm yard on a hot summer day. Tasted twice, with consistent notes.–J.S. • $12 • (1/01/2000) • **65**
Schioppettino Isonzo del Friuli 1998: A light-bodied wine, its perfumed aromas having hints of pepper and cut grass. Light body. Fresh finish. A bit green really.–J.S. • $12 • (5/15/2000) • **79**
Schioppettino Isonzo del Friuli 1997: A light and fruity red, with light body, light tannins and a fresh finish. Drink now.–J.S. • $12 • (1/01/2000) • **80**
Tocai Friulano Isonzo del Friuli I Fiori 1998: Rather odd, with canned fruit cocktail character. Light finish.–J.S. • $10 • (3/31/2000) • **77**

VIALA

Chardonnay Venezie 1996 • $6 • (12/15/1997) • **85**
Sangiovese Ravenna 1996 • $6 • (2/28/1998) • **78**

VIBERTI, ERALDO

Barbera d'Alba Vigna Clara 1995: Shows mocha, spice and toast notes, with the fruit struggling to emerge in this medium-bodied, fairly supple, international-style red. Balanced finish. Drink now through 2002.–P.M. • $28 • (10/31/1998) • **83**
Barolo 1994: Shows some pronounced barrique-induced toasted oak, spice and mocha aromas and flavors. The wood overwhelms the fruit, and the finish is slightly dry.–P.M. • $39 • (10/31/1998) • **77**
Barolo 1991 • $NA • (10/31/1996) • **84**

VIBERTI, GIOVANNI

Barbera d'Alba Bricco Airoli 1997: Beautiful. Well made in an international style. Medium-bodied, with violet, game, toasted oak and black currant notes, good acidity, a fresh, persistent length and supple tannins. Drink through 2001.–P.M. • $25 • (11/15/1999) • **88**

Barbera d'Alba Bricco Airoli 1996: This fantastic Barbera, made in an international style, shows beautiful cassis, violet, plum and spice. Very dark in color and full in body, with a lush, supple and opulent texture that caresses the palate. Fans out with loads of flavors on the superharmonious, velvety, dreamlike finish. Drink now through 2005.–P.M. • $25 • (10/31/1998) • **92**

Barbera d'Alba Bricco Airoli 1994 • $23 • (10/31/1997) • **82**

Barolo 1995: Exotic. Pretty fruit and nice violet, rose petal and toasted oak aromas build complexity in this lingering, medium-bodied Barolo. The tannins are ripe but turn chewy on the finish. Drink now through 2005. –P.M. • $45 • (11/15/1999) • **89**

Barolo 1994: Just delicious. This full-bodied red has loads of complex character, with ripe, charming, seductive plum, wild raspberry and black cherry notes. And how about the blackberry, spice, tar, rose petal and cigar box aromas? Seductive on the balanced finish. Drink now through 2005.–P.M. • $40 • (9/15/1998) • **90**

Barolo 1993 • $35 • (10/31/1997) • **89**

Barolo Bricco delle Viole 1993 • $NA • (10/31/1997) • **83**

Barolo La Volta Riserva 1993 • $NA • (10/31/1997) • **90**

Barolo San Pietro 1993 • $NA • (10/31/1997) • **88**

Chardonnay Piemonte Juant Lucas Vineyards 1997: Full-bodied but lacking in personality, tasting of butterscotch, wood and little fruit. Short finish. –P.M. • $24 • (10/31/1998) • **73**

Dolcetto d'Alba Toni 'd Giuspin 1998: Medium-bodied and rather full on the palate, showing appealing softness, with spice, game and berry flavors. Drink now.–P.M. • $20 • (11/15/1999) • **80**

Dolcetto di Diano d'Alba Toni 'd Giuspin 1995 • $NA • (10/31/1997) • **80**

Langhe Pramorasso 1998: Straightforward, with an earthy edge, a crisp texture and a short finish.–P.M. • $32 • (11/15/1999) • **75**

VICCHIOMAGGIO, CASTELLO DI

Chianti Classico La Prima Riserva 1996: A delicious CC riserva, with good color and floral and plum aromas. Medium-bodied, with light to medium tannins and a slightly chewy finish. Drink now.–J.S. • $30 • (11/30/1999) • **86**

Chianti Classico La Prima Riserva 1995: A pretty, elegant red with fresh mushroom and dried cherry character, medium body, fine tannins, a fresh finish. Drink now.–J.S. • $30 • (12/15/1998) • **86**

Chianti Classico La Prima Riserva 1994 • $29 • (9/30/1997) • **86**

Chianti Classico La Prima Riserva 1993 • $23 • (10/31/1996) • **83**

Chianti Classico La Prima Riserva 1991 • $NA • (10/31/1995) • **86**

Chianti Classico La Prima Riserva 1985 • $20 • (9/15/1991) • **86**

Chianti Classico Petri Riserva 1996: Already at its peak, with plum, berry and cedar aromas and flavors. Light- to medium-bodied, with light tannins and a delicate finish. Slightly diluted. Drink now.–J.S. • $23 • (11/30/1999) • **82**

Chianti Classico Petri Riserva 1995: Big and jammy. Lacks sophistication, but is rich in style. Brilliant aromas of blackberry, currant and raspberry. Full-bodied, with chewy yet silky tannins and a long, ripe fruit aftertaste. Drink now.–J.S. • $22 • (12/15/1998) • **88**

Chianti Classico Petri Riserva 1994 • $22 • (9/30/1997) • **83**

Chianti Classico Petri Riserva 1993 • $17 • (10/31/1996) • **80**

Chianti Classico Petri Riserva 1991 • $NA • (10/31/1995) • **81**

Chianti Classico Petri Riserva 1990 • $NA • (2/28/1995) • **85**

Chianti Classico Petri Riserva 1988 • $NA • (9/15/1992) • **87**

Chianti Classico San Jacopo 1997: A good, simple Chianti, with plum and black pepper character. Medium-bodied, with soft tannins and a fruity finish. Drink now.–J.S. • $15 • (11/30/1999) • **83**

Chianti Classico San Jacopo 1995 • $12 • (9/30/1997) • **81**

Chianti Classico San Jacopo 1991 • $9 • (10/31/1993) • **80**

Chianti Classico San Jacopo 1990 • $9 • (10/31/1993) • **87**

Toscana Ripa della More 1996: I like the plum skin, berry and wet bark character in this wine. Well done. Medium-bodied, with medium tannins and a caressing finish. Delicious. Drink now.–J.S. • $36 • (11/30/1999) • **88**

Toscana Ripa della More 1995: Elegant and silky. Interesting aromas of cherry with hints of mushroom. Light- to medium-bodied, with cherry and lightly smoky flavors and a light finish. Drink now.–J.S. • $35 • (12/15/1998) • **84**

Toscana Ripa delle More 1994 • $31 • (9/30/1997) • **87**

Key: SS—Spectator Selection. CS—Cellar Selection. HR—Highly Recommended. $NA—Price not available. (BT)—Barrel tasting. Ⓐ—Auction Price.
For a key to the tasters' initials, see "How to Use These Listings."
Dates in parentheses represent the issues in which the ratings were published.

Toscana Ripa delle More 1993 • $NA • (10/31/1996) • **76**

Toscana Ripa delle More 1991 • $NA • (10/31/1995) • **88**

Toscana Ripa delle More 1990 • $NA • (10/31/1993) • **91**

Toscana Ripa delle Mandorle 1996: Pretty Sangiovese. Loads of dried cherry and raspberry character. Medium-bodied, with medium, velvety tannins and a flavorful finish. Drink now through 2002.–J.S. • $20 • (12/15/1998) • **87**

Toscana Ripa delle Mandorle 1995 • $19 • (12/31/1997) • **81**

VICENTINI ORGNANI, FRANCESCO

Chardonnay Grave del Friuli 1996 • $14 • (5/31/1998) • **79**

Merlot Grave del Friuli 1996 • $14 • (5/31/1998) • **81**

Merlot Grave del Friuli Braide Cjasa 1992 • $18 • (3/31/1997) • **87**

Pinot Grigio Grave del Friuli 1996 • $14 • (5/15/1998) • **84**

VICO, GIACOMO

Barbera d'Alba 1993 • $NA • (10/31/1996) • **83**

VIETTI

Barbaresco 1993 • $33 • (10/31/1996) • **89**

Barbaresco 1985 • $28 • (7/31/1989) • **81**

Barbaresco 1982 • $15 • (7/31/1987) • **84**

Barbaresco Della Localita ' Rabajà 1986 • $18 • (10/31/1990) • **87**

Barbaresco Masseria 1996: Seductive and full-bodied, with a smooth texture, ripe, sweet-tasting fruit and medium-intense tar, rose petal and vanilla notes. Fairly delicate, but beautifully balanced. Drink now through 2008.–P.M. • $45 • (10/31/1999) • **91**

Barbaresco Masseria 1995: Ripe and complex, with wet earth, tobacco, spice and smoky flavors mingling with the red berry and blackberry, this is pretty hedonistic despite a tannic bite. Mineral character on the finish adds to its depth. Drink now through 2007.–P.M. • $55 • (9/15/1998) • **91**

Barbaresco Masseria 1990 • $26 • (10/31/1994) • **82**

Barbaresco Masseria 1989 • $34 • (10/31/1993) • **84**

Barbaresco Masseria 1988 • $34 • (10/31/1993) • **78**

Barbera d'Alba Pian Romualdo 1991 • $20 • (11/15/1993) • **83**

Barbera d'Alba Pian Romualdo 1990 • $20 • (11/15/1993) • **85**

Barbera d'Alba Pian Romualdo 1989 • $19 • (11/30/1991) • **83**

Barbera d'Alba Pian Romualdo 1988 • $15 • (3/15/1991) • **79**

Barbera d'Alba Scarrone 1997: A big Barbera, thick and ripe, veering a bit to simple licorice flavors, but delivering also some delicate raspberry and a heavy oakiness. The refined tannins are seductive. Drink now.–P.M. • $18 • (9/15/1999) • **85**

Barbera d'Alba Scarrone 1995 • $22 • (10/31/1997) • **81**

Barbera d'Alba Scarrone 1992 • $15 • (10/31/1994) • **85**

Barbera d'Alba Scarrone 1990 • $11 • (11/15/1993) • **84**

Barbera d'Alba Scarrone 1989 • $13 • (3/15/1991) • **85**

Barbera d'Alba Scarrone 1987 • $11 • (8/31/1989) • **86**

Barbera d'Alba Scarrone Vigna Vecchia 1997: Who knew Barbera produced this quality? Here's an inky-looking, pitch-black, oily, ripe Italian red that breaks the quality barrier with its sweet, pure fruit concentration. Shows silky tannins, with plum, blackberry, smoke and subtle spice character and hints of petrol from all that oak. It's fresh but not overly acidic on the balanced, smooth and succulent finish. Drink now through 2002.–P.M. • $25 • (9/15/1999) HR • '95

Barbera d'Asti La Crena 1996: A rich, opulent style of Barbera that oozes oily texture, with a distinct oaky character balanced by ripe blackberry and plum. It has a supple tannin structure and turns elegant on the long, clean finish, with a good dose of acidity. Drink now through 2002.–P.M. • $25 • (11/15/1999) • **91**

Barbera d'Asti Tre Vigne 1997: Clearly oaked by barriques, as evident by all that vanilla, mocha and milk chocolate character, but it's impressively smooth and ripe, with the fruit and acidity bulging below the wood blanket. Full-bodied and balanced, with a long, fresh finish. Drink now through 2002.–P.M. • $18 • (11/15/1999) • **90**

Barolo 1991 • $30 • (10/31/1995) • **84**

Barolo 1990 • $NA • (10/31/1994) • **82**

Barolo 1978 • $12 • (9/16/1984) • **84**

Barolo Brunate 1995: This gorgeous '95 is ripe yet solid, with layers of seductive oak-infused mocha, vanilla, roasted coffee, cappuccino and blackberry. Full-bodied, with smooth tannins, it's all silk on the palate. Harmonious finish. Drink now through 2005.–P.M. • $60 • (11/15/1999) • **93**

Barolo Brunate 1994: Medium-bodied and earthy, yet showing pretty plum, cherry and raspberry character, with mocha, spice and coffee notes on the

smoky, toasted finish. A bit tough and chewy; best after 2002.–P.M. • $60 • (10/31/1998) • **80**
Barolo Brunate 1993 • $59 • (10/31/1997) • **88**
Barolo Brunate 1990 • $37 • (10/31/1994) • **79**
Barolo Brunate 1989 • $30 • (10/31/1993) • **91**
Barolo Bussia 1982 • $20 • (9/15/1987) • **89**
Barolo Castiglione 1993 • $40 • (10/31/1997) • **88**
Barolo Lazzarito 1995: This extreme "modernist" style of Barolo, pumped up in the toasted oak department, is packed with mocha and roasted coffee bean character. Delivers ripe fruit and a full mouthfeel accented by dark chocolate on the smoky, delectably supple finish. Drink now through 2005. –P.M. • $60 • (11/15/1999) • **90**
Barolo Lazzarito 1994: Very oaky, with vanilla, mocha and spice flavors cutting through the plum and red berry. Medium-bodied, with smoky, toasted notes on the finish. Drink now through 2002.–P.M. • $60 • (10/31/1998) • **80**
Barolo Lazzarito 1993 • $60 • (10/31/1997) • **86**
Barolo Lazzarito 1990 • $37 • (10/31/1994) • **85**
Barolo Rocche 1995: Rather light in aroma but impressively oily in texture, offering plum, raspberry, smoke and olive notes. Pleasantly ripe on the midpalate, then kicks in with crisp acidity and sweet but firm tannins on the concentrated finish. Drink now through 2005.–P.M. • $65 • (11/15/1999) • **92**
Barolo Rocche 1990 • $60 • (10/31/1995) • **85**
Barolo Rocche 1989 • $40 • (10/31/1994) • **83**
Barolo Rocche 1988 • $50 • (10/31/1993) • **78**
Barolo Rocche 1982 • $45 • (7/31/1989) • **85**
Barolo Rocche 1980 • $NA • (9/15/1988) • **87**
Barolo Rocche 1979 • $NA • (9/15/1988) • **79**
Barolo Rocche 1978 • $NA • (9/15/1988) • **92**
Barolo Rocche 1971 • $NA • (9/15/1988) • **86**
Barolo Rocche 1961 • $NA • (9/15/1988) • **93**
Barolo Villero Riserva 1982 • $45 • (9/15/1988) • **89**
Dolcetto d'Alba Bussia 1994 • $12 • (10/31/1995) • **80**
Dolcetto d'Alba Bussia 1990 • $11 • (11/30/1991) • **85**
Dolcetto d'Alba Bussia 1989 • $12 • (2/28/1991) • **85**
Dolcetto d'Alba Disa 1988 • $12 • (9/15/1990) • **87**
Dolcetto d'Alba Lazzarito 1998: Whoa. A wondrous, young, supple, inky-black red, all smooth with sweet tannins, this is a joy to taste, almost flawless in its silky structure. Very fruity, not supercomplex, but who cares? Outstanding example of the potential of Dolcetto in '98. Drink now through 2002.–P.M. • $18 • (11/15/1999) • **90**
Fioretto 1988 • $25 • (6/30/1993) • **84**
Fioretto 1987 • $17 • (6/15/1990) • **85**

VIGNALE, IL

Amarone della Valpolicella Classico 1994: Pleasant and plummy, with firm tannins and pronounced acidity; the structure and alcohol on the finish dominate the modest fruit. Drink now.–B.S. • $20 • (7/31/1998) • **83**
Gavi 1996: An attempt at a serious style, with loads of ripe pear and butter flavors. Turns a bit coarse on the finish, but still quite enjoyable. Drink now.–K.M. • $15 • (8/31/1998) • **83**
Soave Classico 1997 • $10 • (6/15/1998) • **83**
Valpolicella Classico Superiore 1996: Offers light cherry and leather aromas and flavors, yet is basically austere and tannic.–B.S. • $10 • (7/31/1998) • **79**

VIGNALTA

Cabernet Sauvignon Colli Euganei 1990 • $18 • (9/15/1992) • **88**
Colli Euganei Rosso 1994 • $14 • (5/31/1996) • **85**
Colli Euganei Rosso 1993 • $14 • (5/31/1996) • **87**
Gemola 1993 • $18 • (5/31/1996) • **86**
Gemola 1991 • $18 • (5/31/1996) • **89**
Gemola 1990 • $18 • (9/15/1992) • **85**
Gemola 1988 • $22 • (9/30/1991) • **81**
Merlot Veneto 1988 • $18 • (4/15/1991) • **80**
Moscato Fior d'Arancio Apianae 1992 • $18/375 ml. • (1/01/1997) • **87**
Moscato Fior d'Arancio Apianae 1991 • $22 • (1/31/1995) • **76**
Moscato Fior d'Arancio Apianae 1990 • $24/375 ml. • (9/15/1992) • **85**

VIGNAMAGGIO

Chianti Classico 1996: Bright and beautiful, with dried cherry, raspberry and blackberry aromas. Medium-bodied, with fine tannins and a fruity, delicious aftertaste. One of the best Chiantis from here in a long time. Drink now.–J.S. • $17 • (12/15/1998) • **87**
Chianti Classico 1995 • $16 • (9/30/1997) • **84**
Chianti Classico 1992 • $14 • (2/28/1995) • **84**
Chianti Classico 1990 • $13 • (9/15/1992) • **90**
Chianti Classico 1988 • $17 • (9/15/1991) • **85**
Chianti Classico 1986 • $12 • (5/15/1990) • **85**
Chianti Classico 1985 • $11 • (8/31/1988) • **86**
Chianti Classico Castello di Mona Lisa Riserva 1995: A very good, no-nonsense riserva. Attractive floral and blackberry character. Medium-bodied, with a fresh, fruity, citrusy quality and a crisp finish. Drink now.–J.S. • $26 • (12/15/1998) • **85**
Chianti Classico Castello di Mona Lisa Riserva 1994 • $25 • (9/30/1997) • **81**
Chianti Classico Castello di Mona Lisa Riserva 1993 • $24 • (3/31/1997) • **86**
Chianti Classico Castello di Mona Lisa Riserva 1990 • $17 • (2/28/1995) • **88**
Chianti Classico Castello di Mona Lisa Riserva 1988 • $16 • (10/31/1994) HR • **91**
Chianti Classico Castello di Mona Lisa Riserva 1986 • $20 • (10/31/1991) • **88**
Chianti Classico Castello di Mona Lisa Riserva 1985 • $17 • (9/15/1991) • **89**
Chianti Classico Castello di Mona Lisa Riserva 1983 • $14 • (5/15/1990) • **85**
Chianti Classico Terre di Prenzano 1995 • $12 • (9/30/1997) • **82**
Gerardino 1993 • $36 • (9/30/1997) • **88**
Gerardino 1991 • $NA • (2/28/1995) • **79**
Gerardino 1990 • $NA • (2/28/1995) • **88**
Gerardino 1987 • $NA • (11/30/1989) • **92**
Gerardino 1986 • $NA • (11/30/1989) • **91**
Gerardino 1985 • $18 • (1/31/1992) • **87**
Toscana Obsession Red 1996: This vivid Tuscan red has a bounty of dried cherry and raspberry aromas and flavors. Medium- to full-bodied, with polished tannins and a tobacco, spice and wood finish. Best after 2000.–J.S. • $63 • (6/30/1999) • **89**
Tuzcany 1993 • $NA • (9/30/1997) • **84**
Tuscany 1990 • $NA • (10/31/1993) • **94**

VIGNAVECCHIA

Canvalle 1993 • $NA • (9/30/1997) • **83**
Canvalle 1992 • $NA • (10/31/1995) • **78**
Canvalle 1991 • $NA • (10/31/1995) • **78**
Canvalle 1990 • $NA • (10/31/1993) • **91**
Chianti Classico 1995 • $NA • (9/30/1997) • **80**
Chianti Classico 1993 • $NA • (10/31/1995) • **74**
Chianti Classico 1991 • $NA • (10/31/1993) • **79**
Chianti Classico 1990 • $12 • (10/31/1993) • **74**
Chianti Classico 1988 • $11 • (10/31/1991) • **83**
Chianti Classico Riserva 1996: A well-crafted, fresh CC riserva, with really pretty blueberry and raspberry aromas. Medium-bodied, with silky tannins and a fresh finish. Drink now.–J.S. • $14 • (11/30/1999) • **86**
Chianti Classico Riserva 1995: Plenty of plum and fresh mushroom character. Medium-bodied, with medium, silky tannins and a fresh finish. Drink now.–J.S. • $12 • (12/15/1998) • **85**
Chianti Classico Riserva 1991 • $NA • (10/31/1995) • **76**
Chianti Classico Riserva 1990 • $NA • (2/28/1995) • **78**
Colli della Toscana Centrale Canvalle 1996: More Cabernet in style than Sangiovese, but subtle, with plenty of herb, berry and currant Cabernet character. Medium-bodied, with silky tannins and a medium finish. Drink now through 2005.–J.S. • $25 • (11/30/1999) • **88**
Colli della Toscana Centrale Canvalle 1995: Delicious Sangiovese. Plenty of black cherry and dark chocolate aromas and flavors. Medium-bodied, with fine tannins and a light finish. Drink now.–J.S. • $25 • (12/15/1998) • **85**
Raddese 1990 • $NA • (2/28/1995) • **87**
Reddege 1993 • $NA • (9/30/1997) • **84**

VIGNE DAL LEON

Merlot 1989 • $15 • (5/31/1996) • **85**

VIGNE DI CA NOVA, LE

Dolcetto d'Alba Monforte d'Alba 1998: Has wonderful ripe fruit but smells cheesy. Bad barrels?–J.S. • $NA • (1/01/2000) • **71**
Dolcetto d'Alba Superiòre Barrique 1996: Surprisingly fresh and interesting for an aged Dolcetto. Aromas of mineral, meat and fruit follow through to the medium-bodied palate. Fresh finish. Drink now.–J.S. • $NA • (1/01/2000) • **85**
Langhe Canova Noir 1996: The intensely earthy and unpleasant nose puts me off, though it opens to ripe fruit, medium body and a round texture. Too old for Dolcetto.–J.S. • $NA • (1/01/2000) • **78**

ITALY

VIGNOLE, TENUTA DI

Chianti Classico 1997: A delicious Chianti Classico, with subtle aromas of cherry, wet earth and citrus. Medium-bodied, with silky tannins and a fruity finish. Drink now.–J.S. • $13 • (11/30/1999) • **86**

Chianti Classico 1994 • $NA • (10/31/1996) • **81**

Chianti Classico 1993 • $NA • (10/31/1995) • **83**

Chianti Classico 1992 • $NA • (2/28/1995) • **82**

Chianti Classico 1990 • $NA • (10/31/1993) • **85**

Chianti Classico 1988 • $NA • (9/15/1991) • **90**

Chianti Classico Riserva 1996: Gorgeous aromas of blackberry and chocolate. Medium-bodied, with well-integrated tannins and a delicious, sweet fruit finish. Drink now through 2003.–J.S. • $22 • (11/30/1999) • **87**

Vin Santo di Chianti Classico 1995: Very salty, with raisin and dried apricot aromas. Medium-bodied and off-dry, with very high acidity and a nutty finish. A dry-style Vin Santo that tastes more like an amontillado Sherry. Not imported into the U.S.–J.S. • $NA/500 ml. • (1/01/1999) • **79**

VILLA ABA

Cabernet Sauvignon Grave del Friuli 1995 • $12 • (4/30/1998) • **82**

Chardonnay Grave del Friuli 1996 • $12 • (12/15/1997) • **79**

Merlot Grave del Friuli 1995 • $12 • (12/15/1997) • **82**

Pinot Bianco Grave del Friuli 1996 • $12 • (11/15/1997) • **78**

Pinot Grigio Grave del Friuli 1996 • $12 • (11/15/1997) • **85**

Ribolla Gialla Colli Orientali del Friuli 1996 • $15 • (4/30/1998) • **83**

Schioppettino Grave del Friuli 1994 • $26 • (4/30/1998) • **87**

VILLA ARCENO

Chianti Classico 1990 • $NA • (10/31/1993) • **83**

VILLA ARTIMINO

Barco Reale 1998: A fresh and fruity red, with plum and cherry character. Medium-bodied, with a fruity finish. Delicious. Drink now.–J.S. • $11 • (11/30/1999) • **83**

Carmignano 1996: Has pretty fruit, but it's rather dry and hard, with slightly high acidity. Rather disappointing after such a good riserva 1995.–J.S. • $14 • (11/30/1999) • **78**

Carmignano Medicea Riserva 1995: Very rich, plummy and meaty. Full-bodied, with plenty of soft tannins and a long, fruity finish. Delicious. Drink now.–J.S. • $19 • (11/30/1999) • **87**

Chianti 1998: A bit light and diluted but clean and fresh, with cherry character and a lemony finish.–J.S. • $10 • (11/30/1999) • **79**

VILLA BORGHETTI

Amarone della Valpolicella Classico 1995: A bit too much barnyard and berry character. Medium-bodied, with a soft texture. Too cheesy.–J.S. • $27 • (6/15/2000) • **77**

Valpolicella Classico 1989 • $7 • (4/30/1992) • **78**

Valpolicella Classico Vigneti in Marano 1996: Simple, with berry and floral character, light body and a fruity finish. Drink now.–J.S. • $9 • (6/15/2000) • **80**

VILLA BOSCOROTONDO

Chianti Classico 1993 • $8 • (10/31/1996) • **81**

Chianti Classico 1990 • $NA • (9/15/1992) • **81**

VILLA BRANCA

Chianti Classico 1997: An extremely silky and fruity CC that caresses your palate. Medium-bodied, with a fresh finish. A bit simple. Drink now.–J.S. • $12 • (11/30/1999) • **85**

Key: SS—Spectator Selection. CS—Cellar Selection. HR—Highly Recommended. $NA—Price not available. (BT)—Barrel tasting. Ⓐ—Auction Price.
For a key to the tasters' initials, see "How to Use These Listings."
Dates in parentheses represent the issues in which the ratings were published.

VILLA BUONASERA

Chianti Classico 1993 • $NA • (10/31/1995) • **78**

Chianti Classico Riserva 1991 • $NA • (10/31/1995) • **69**

VILLA CAFAGGIO

Chianti Classico 1997: A delicious, fruity wine, with beautiful aromas of cherry and berry. Medium-bodied, with silky tannins and a fruity finish. Drink now.–J.S. • $16 • (11/30/1999) • **88**

Chianti Classico 1996: Bright and fruity in aroma and flavor, with strawberry, cherry and melon character. Medium-bodied, with light tannins, a fresh finish. A bit light for this producer. Drink now.–J.S. • $15 • (12/15/1998) • **83**

Chianti Classico 1995 • $15 • (9/30/1997) • **83**

Chianti Classico 1994 • $15 • (10/31/1996) • **81**

Chianti Classico 1993 • $9 • (10/31/1995) • **82**

Chianti Classico 1990 • $14 • (10/31/1993) • **82**

Chianti Classico 1989 • $13 • (9/15/1992) • **84**

Chianti Classico 1988 • $10 • (11/30/1990) • **83**

Chianti Classico 1983 • $11 • (9/15/1987) • **91**

Chianti Classico Riserva 1996: Really elegant, with delicate, silky tannins and a lovely fruit structure. Medium-bodied, with a delicious berry, plum and toasted oak finish. Drink now.–J.S. • $29 • (11/30/1999) • **87**

Chianti Classico Riserva 1995: Refined and delectable CC riserva. Pretty strawberry and cherry aromas and flavors. Medium-bodied, with fine tannins and a fresh, fruity aftertaste. Drink now.–J.S. • $26 • (12/15/1998) • **87**

Chianti Classico Riserva 1994 • $27 • (9/30/1997) • **87**

Chianti Classico Riserva 1993 • $NA • (10/31/1996) • **80**

Chianti Classico Riserva 1990 • $17 • (2/28/1995) • **87**

Chianti Classico Riserva 1988 • $18 • (9/15/1992) • **91**

Chianti Classico Riserva 1986 • $18 • (12/15/1990) • **86**

Chianti Classico Riserva 1985 • $13 • (9/15/1991) • **91**

Chianti Classico Riserva 1983 • $10 • (5/31/1988) • **80**

Chianti Classico Solatio Basilica Riserva 1995: Well-crafted Chianti Classico. Cherry and plum character throughout. Medium-bodied, with medium tannins and a soft, fruity finish. Drink now.–J.S. • $39 • (11/30/1999) • **87**

Solatio Basilica 1990 • $32 • (10/31/1993) • **87**

Solatio Basilica 1985 • $20 • (8/31/1991) • **83**

Toscana Cortaccio 1997: A generous and rich wine that needs time to soften. Black color. Amazing aromas of crushed berries, mint, tar and dark chocolate. Full-bodied, with voluptuous and velvety tannins. Long finish. Best after 2004.–J.S. • $50 • (6/15/2000) • '95

Toscana Cortaccio 1995: A seamless, well-made red. Fabulous aromas of blackberry, raspberry and plum. Medium-bodied, with silky tannins and a fresh, crisp, fruity finish. Beautiful Cabernet Sauvignon character. Drink now.–J.S. • $45 • (12/15/1998) • **90**

Toscana Cortaccio 1994 • $46 • (9/30/1997) • **88**

Toscana Cortaccio 1993 • $40 • (3/31/1997) • **90**

Toscana Cortaccio 1990 • $32 • (10/31/1993) • **91**

Toscana San Martino 1997: Big and powerful wine, but very tight. Very dark color. Intense blackberry, raspberry and floral character. Full-bodied, with very chewy tannins. Best after 2005.–J.S. • $50 • (6/15/2000) CS • '95

Toscana San Martino 1996: A lovely, soft wine, with velvety tannins and plenty of plum, cherry and tobacco character. Medium body and finish. This Sangiovese is always good. Drink now through 2004.–J.S. • $40 • (11/30/1999) • **88**

Toscana San Martino 1995: Quite perfumed, with rose, violet and light fruit character. Medium- to full-bodied, with fine tannins and a long aftertaste of tobacco and fruit. Will improve with age but why wait? Drink now through 2003.–J.S. • $41 • (12/15/1998) • **89**

Toscana San Martino 1994 • $41 • (9/30/1997) • **88**

Toscana San Martino 1993 • $30 • (10/31/1996) • **88**

Toscana San Martino 1990 • $31 • (10/31/1993) • **89**

Toscana San Martino 1985 • $20 • (9/30/1989) • **79**

VILLA CALCINAIA

Chianti Classico 1997: This red has a good core of berry and cherry character. Medium-bodied, with silky tannins and a fresh finish. Drink now.–J.S. • $13 • (11/30/1999) • **86**

Chianti Classico 1996: Unctuous, with aromas of raspberry and cherry, a hint of milk chocolate. Medium- to full-bodied, with lovely ripe fruit and smooth, round tannins. Drink now through 2003.–J.S. • $15 • (12/15/1998) • **88**

Chianti Classico 1992 • $8 • (2/28/1995) • **73**

Chianti Classico 1988 • $12 • (9/15/1991) • **89**

Chianti Classico Riserva 1996: An aromatic wine that promises more on the nose than the palate, with plum and berry character and a hint of black pepper. Medium-bodied, with firm tannins and a slightly austere finish. Drink now.–J.S. • $15 • (11/30/1999) • **83**

Chianti Classico Riserva 1994: Barely holding on, with a light, slightly watery structure, strawberry and cherry character. Tasted twice, with consistent notes.–J.S. • $16 • (12/15/1998) • **75**

Chianti Classico Riserva 1993 • $NA • (9/30/1997) • **83**

Chianti Classico Riserva 1990 • $NA • (2/28/1995) • **84**

Toscana Casarsa Red 1996: Slightly mature-looking but delicious, with aromas of plum and cigar box that follow through to a medium-bodied palate. Light tannins and a crisp, smoked almond finish. Sangiovese and Merlot. Not imported into the U.S. Drink now.–J.S. • $NA • (1/01/1999) • **85**

Toscana Casarsa Red 1995: A crisp and fruity red with dried cherry and citrus character. Light- to medium-bodied, with light tannins, a delicate finish. Drink now.–J.S. • $NA • (12/15/1998) • **82**

Toscana Comitale White 1998: Very cool, with intriguing aromas of peach and spice that follow through to the palate. Medium-bodied, with good acidity and a toasted oak and honey aftertaste. Chardonnay and Traminer. Not imported into the U.S. Drink now.–J.S. • $NA • (1/01/1999) • **87**

VILLA CAPODILISTA

Colli Euganei Rosso 1996 • $9 • (6/30/1998) • **82**

Merlot Colli Euganei 1996 • $17 • (6/30/1998) • **83**

VILLA CASALE

Chianti Classico La Cappella 1997: Tastes more like California Cabernet than Chianti Classico, but very good. Big, rich and full-bodied, with lots of berry, chocolate and vanilla character and a long finish. Best after 2000.–J.S. • $NA • (1/01/2000) • **89**

VILLA CERVIA

Montepulciano d'Abruzzo 1995 • $6 • (1/01/1998) • **85**

Montepulciano d'Abruzzo 1993 • $5 • (2/29/1996) • **84**

Montepulciano d'Abruzzo 1992 • $4 • (3/31/1995) • **84**

VILLA CILNIA

Chianti Colli Aretini 1997: A bit weedy, with plum and slightly metallic, unripe flavors. Light body and finish. Not imported into the U.S.–J.S. • $NA • (1/01/1999) • **77**

Chianti Colli Aretini 1990 • $10 • (1/31/1992) • **86**

Chianti Colli Aretini 1989 • $10 • (4/30/1991) • **85**

Chianti Colli Aretini 1988 • $10 • (4/15/1991) • **89**

Chianti Colli Aretini Riserva 1995: A pleasant red, with aromas of plum and chocolate. Medium-bodied, with soft tannins and a sweet fruit finish. Not imported into the U.S. Drink now.–J.S. • $NA • (1/01/1999) • **82**

Chianti Colli Aretini Riserva 1986 • $18 • (10/31/1991) • **76**

Colli della Toscana Centrale Vocato 1995: Slightly herbal, but with pretty berry and rosemary aromas. Medium-bodied, with dried cherry and herb flavors, silky tannins and a fruity finish. Not imported into the U.S. Drink now.–J.S. • $NA • (1/01/1999) • **85**

Colli della Toscana Centrale Vocato 1986 • $11 • (5/15/1989) • **86**

Le Vignacce 1988 • $24 • (9/15/1991) • **89**

Le Vignacce 1986 • $19 • (11/30/1989) • **90**

Le Vignacce 1985 • $20 • (7/15/1989) • **88**

VILLA DEL BORGO

Cabernet Sauvignon Grave del Friuli 1998: Good aromas of currants and minerals with a hint of blackberries. Medium-bodied, with firm tannins but a slightly short finish. A bit lean really. Drink now.–J.S. • $8 • (5/15/2000) • **83**

Cabernet Sauvignon Grave del Friuli 1996: Assertive aromas of cherry candy, vanilla and earth carry through on the palate to a decent finish. Light and quaffable. Drink now.–B.S. • $7 • (7/31/1998) • **82**

Chardonnay Grave del Friuli 1998: A lovely, creamy-textured wine with subtle pineapple and pear character and a touch of mineral. Medium body. Fresh, fruity finish. Drink now.–J.S. • $8 • (3/31/2000) • **86**

Merlot Grave del Friuli 1998: Simple, bright and fruity, with berry, floral character and a fresh finish. Drink now.–J.S. • $8 • (5/15/2000) • **81**

Merlot Grave del Friuli 1997: Light-bodied and straightforward, with a touch of earthiness adding dimension to the plum and spice. Some may find it too earthy. Drink now.–B.S. • $7 • (7/31/1998) • **80**

Pinot Grigio Grave del Friuli 1998: Lots of apple, cream and almond character to this lovely medium-bodied white from Northeast Italy, along with a caressing texture and a fruity finish. Quite a nice ensemble for so low a price. Drink now.–J.S. • $8 • (3/31/2000) • **86**

Pinot Grigio Grave del Friuli 1997: Shy aromas. The flavors are peachlike, and there's body, though this young white is straightforward and a touch earthy. Drink now.–B.S. • $7 • (7/31/1998) • **80**

Sangiovese di Romagna San Patrignano 1996: A light, fresh red marked by modest cherry and raspberry flavors. Low in tannins, easy to quaff. Drink now. • $7 • (8/31/1998) • **81**

Sauvignon Grave del Friuli 1998: Good mineral and green apple skin character, with a spice note. Medium body. Fresh finish with hints of grassiness. Drink now.–J.S. • $8 • (4/30/2000) • **86**

Sauvignon Grave del Friuli 1997: Good Sauvignon character, with the grassy, citrusy elements of the Loire and the richness, though not the assertiveness, of New Zealand. If only it had a little more concentration. Finishes short. Drink now.–B.S. • $7 • (7/31/1998) • **83**

Tocai Friulano Grave del Friuli 1998: Pretty and clean, with lots of mineral and almond character. Medium-bodied, with a light, fresh finish. Drink now.–J.S. • $8 • (3/31/2000) • **85**

VILLA DI VETRICE

Chianti Classico 1991 • $8 • (10/31/1993) • **75**

Chianti Rufina 1997: This chewy Sangiovese has plenty of ripe berry and plum character, with a hint of earth. Medium- to full-bodied, with velvety tannins and a sweet fruit aftertaste. A bit funky but good. Tasted twice, with consistent notes. Drink now.–J.S. • $10 • (11/30/1999) • **84**

Chianti Rufina Riserva 1995: Good simple Chianti. Aromas of violets and berries follow through to a medium-bodied palate, with fresh acidity and a fruity finish. Drink now.–J.S. • $14 • (11/30/1999) • **84**

Chianti Rufina Signor Grato Riserva 1990: A bit rustic but with decent fruit, this is at its peak, with aromas of raisin and earth. Medium-bodied, with plum and dried fruit character and a light finish. Drink now.–J.S. • $22 • (11/30/1999) • **83**

VILLA LA PAGLIAIA

Chianti Classico 1991 • $NA • (10/31/1993) • **86**

VILLA LA SELVA

Colli della Toscana Centrale Felciaia 1997: A sleek and racy young red, with pretty aromas of ripe blackberry and cherry plus a hint of oak. Full-bodied yet compacted, with polished, silky tannins and a fruity finish. Best after 2000.–J.S. • $24 • (5/31/2000) HR • **90**

Colli della Toscana Centrale Felciaia 1996: Elegant and smooth. Bright berry and mineral character throughout. Medium-bodied, with silky tannins and a long finish. Drink now.–J.S. • $24 • (11/30/1999) • **87**

Colli della Toscana Centrale Felciaia 1995: A fruity, mushroomy nose follows through to a medium-bodied palate, with polished tannins and a short finish. Needs some bottle age. Drink now.–J.S. • $23 • (12/15/1998) • **86**

Colli della Toscana Centrale Felciaia 1994 • $24 • (9/30/1997) • **82**

Colli della Toscana Centrale Felciaia 1993 • $23 • (1/31/1997) • **88**

Colli della Toscana Centrale Selvamaggio 1996: Good dark color, with currant and a minty, slightly herbal Cabernet character. Medium- to full-bodied, with polished, velvety tannins and a medium finish. Best after 2000.–J.S. • $26 • (5/31/2000) • **86**

Colli della Toscana Centrale Selvamaggio 1994: Some interesting currant and berry character here, but an underlying herbalness detracts. Medium-bodied, with plenty of polished tannins and a fruity, herbal aftertaste. Drink now.–J.S. • $25 • (12/15/1998) • **85**

Colli della Toscana Centrale Selvamaggio 1993 • $25 • (9/30/1997) • **89**

Colli della Toscana Centrale Selvamaggio 1992 • $25 • (1/31/1997) • **86**

Vin Santo Vigna del Papa 1994: A nice Vin Santo to sip on its own. Amber-orange in color, with aromas of salted nuts and honey. Medium-bodied and lightly sweet, with nut, orange peel and honey flavors. Pretty. Drink now.–J.S. • $22/500 ml. • (11/30/1999) • **85**

VILLA MAISANO

Chianti Classico 1995 • $14 • (9/30/1997) • **80**

Chianti Classico Riserva 1994 • $21 • (9/30/1997) • **76**

VILLA MATILDE

Aglianico Passito 1998: Bizarre but wonderful. Like a spice-infused Port. Inky in color. Sweet and spicy, with amazing aromas of spices from cinnamon to cumin, and loads of ripe fruit. Full-bodied, with a long, velvety, tannic finish that delivers masses of fruit. Not imported into the U.S. Best after 2001.–J.S. • $NA/375 ml. • (1/31/2000) • **90**

Campania Rosato Terre Cerase 1998: Delicious rosé. Wonderful aromas of strawberries and berries, with hints of pomace. Medium-bodied, with lovely fresh fruit and a long, crisp finish. Not imported into the U.S. Drink now.–J.S. • $NA • (1/01/1999) • **86**

Cecubo Red 1996: A well-crafted red. Plenty of plum, berry and cherry character in this one. Medium-bodied, with a good core of fruit and a long, fruity finish with polished tannins. Drink now through 2005.–J.S. • $27 • (1/31/2000) • **88**

Falerno del Massico 1997: Really delicious. Burgundy-like, with plum, strawberry and floral aromas, with hints of new wood. Medium-bodied, with silky tannins and a fruity, toasted oak finish. Tasted twice, with consistent notes. Drink now.–J.S. • $18 • (1/31/2000) • **88**

Falerno del Massico White 1998: Shows wonderful honey, mineral and spice character. Medium-bodied, with fresh acidity and a citrus aftertaste. Delicious. Drink now.–J.S. • $14 • (1/31/2000) • **87**

Falerno del Massico White Vigna Caracci 1998: Plenty of pear and melon character in this white, with a medium-bodied palate, fresh acidity and a clean finish. Not imported into the U.S. Drink now.–J.S. • $NA • (1/01/1999) • **85**

Vigna Camarato 1997: Harmonious and caressing. Attractive aromas of ripe plums, earth and leather, almost decadent. Medium-bodied, with velvety tannins and a medium-long, sweet fruit finish. Not imported into the U.S. Drink now through 2003.–J.S. • $NA • (1/31/2000) • **89**

Vigna Camarato 1995: Loads of wood in this, perhaps a bit too much, but it shows wonderful ripeness and richness. Full-bodied, with soft tannins and a medium, slightly drying finish. Tasted twice, with consistent notes. Drink now.–J.S. • $35 • (1/01/2000) • **87**

VILLA MONTE RICO

Toscana 1995: Beautifully defined, with alluring aromas of plum, berry and milk chocolate. Medium- to full-bodied, with round, smooth tannins and a long, fruity finish. Drink now.–J.S. • $30 • (12/15/1998) • **90**

Tuscany Red 1994 • $NA • (9/30/1997) • **80**

VILLA PIGNA

Rozzano 1990 • $13 • (5/31/1995) • **87**

Vellutato 1990 • $7 • (5/31/1995) • **85**

VILLA PILLO

Cabernet Sauvignon Toscana 1997: This good, simple Cabernet is very clean, with cherry and green tobacco and a hint of oak. Medium-bodied, with medium tannins and a fresh finish. Drink now.–J.S. • $18 • (11/30/1999) • **85**

Cabernet Sauvignon Toscana 1996: A big and powerful Cabernet with lots of fruit, but there's an underlying green and herbal note. Full-bodied, with full tannins, a moderate finish. A bit coarse. Drink now.–J.S. • $19 • (12/15/1998) • **83**

Chardonnay Toscana 1997: A good, simple Chardonnay with fresh aromas and flavors of apple, blanched almond and minerals. Medium-bodied, with crisp acidity and a long, zingy aftertaste. Drink now.–J.S. • $14 • (12/15/1998) • **84**

Chardonnay Toscana 1996 • $13 • (10/31/1997) • **82**

Merlot Toscana 1997: An enjoyable Merlot, with good berry and dried cherry character. Medium-bodied, with silky tannins and a light finish. Drink now.–J.S. • $20 • (11/30/1999) • **85**

Merlot Toscana 1996: A bit disjointed now, but shows decent fruit. Very ripe, with berry and currant bush character. Full-bodied, slightly austere in tannin, slightly alcoholic on the finish. Drink now.–J.S. • $19 • (12/15/1998) • **83**

Merlot Toscana 1995 • $15 • (10/31/1997) • **88**

Syrah Toscana 1997: Very good Syrah character. Good dark color, with lovely ripe berry and raspberry aromas. Medium-bodied, with velvety tannins and a long, spicy, chocolaty, gamy finish. Drink now through 2003.–J.S. • $18 • (11/30/1999) • **88**

Syrah Toscana 1996: A peppery wine with a game and earth undertone. Medium-bodied, with soft tannins and a long, succulent aftertaste. Like a good Côtes du Rhône. Drink now.–J.S. • $19 • (12/15/1998) • **86**

Syrah Toscana 1995 • $13 • (10/31/1997) • **87**

Toscana Borgoforte 1996: Slightly diluted and weedy. Shows some berry character, but generally lacking in body, ripe fruit and definition.–J.S. • $12 • (12/15/1998) • **75**

Toscana Borgoforte 1995 • $12 • (10/31/1997) • **81**

Toscana Borgoforte 1994 • $10 • (10/31/1996) • **82**

Toscana Vivaldaia 1997: Has good currant character, but it's slightly too herbal. Medium-bodied, with medium tannins and a rosemary and dried herb finish. Drink now.–J.S. • $20 • (11/30/1999) • **84**

Toscana Vivaldaia 1996: Bright aromas of cherry and black currant, with herbal hints that build on the palate. Medium in body, with fine tannins, a grassy finish. Rustic Cabernet character detracts. Drink now.–J.S. • $20 • (12/15/1998) • **80**

Toscana Vivaldaia 1995 • $17 • (10/31/1997) • **85**

Vin Santo 1991 • $17/375 ml. • (10/31/1997) • **90**

Vin Santo di Chianti 1994: Intense aromas of lemon peel and salted almond, with head-jolting acidity. Nice to smell but hard to taste.–J.S. • $26/375 ml. • (11/30/1999) • **76**

Vin Santo di Chianti 1992: A traditional Vin Santo, with a sweet dried fruit, salt and almond character. Medium-bodied and medium sweet, with a fresh caramel aftertaste. Drink now.–J.S. • $20/375 ml. • (12/15/1998) • **86**

VILLA POGGIO SALVI

Brunello di Montalcino 1995: Big and powerful. Plum skin, berry and incense aromas. Full-bodied, with velvety tannins and a long, long finish. Best Poggio Salvi I have ever had. Best after 2002.–J.S. • $55 • (6/30/2000) • **92**

Brunello di Montalcino 1994: Pretty chocolate and berry aromas. Medium-bodied, with soft tannins and a fresh, fruity finish. Delicious. Drink now.–J.S. • $52 • (8/31/1999) • **87**

Brunello di Montalcino 1993: A drink-now Brunello, and drink now you should. Enticing blackberry and tobacco aromas of seductively fine character. Medium-bodied, with fine tannins and a refreshing aftertaste.–J.S. • $46 • (12/15/1998) • **87**

Brunello di Montalcino 1991 • $NA • (11/30/1996) • **87**

Brunello di Montalcino 1990 • $45 • (10/31/1995) • **91**

Brunello di Montalcino 1988 • $42 • (4/30/1994) • **88**

Brunello di Montalcino 1985 • $30 • (11/30/1990) • **83**

Brunello di Montalcino 1981 • $20 • (10/15/1988) • **88**

Brunello di Montalcino 1979 • $15 • (3/15/1987) • **88**

Brunello di Montalcino Riserva 1988 • $45 • (10/31/1994) • **90**

Brunello di Montalcino Riserva 1981 • $35 • (11/30/1990) • **85**

Moscadello di Montalcino Aurico 1996: Slightly high volatile acidity on the nose, with buttered popcorn and almond. Medium-bodied and medium sweet, with a slightly sour finish. Hard to appreciate.–J.S. • $50/375 ml. • (5/31/2000) • **78**

Rosso di Montalcino 1997: Really delicious. Very fruity and aromatic, with lots of plums and dried cherries. Medium-bodied, with soft tannins and a fresh and fruity finish. Drink now.–J.S. • $24 • (9/15/1999) • **86**

Rosso di Montalcino 1994 • $15 • (11/30/1996) • **86**

VILLA ROCCA

Amarone della Valpolicella Classico 1989 • $10 • (11/15/1994) • **78**

VILLA RUSSIZ

Pinot Bianco Collio 1998: Very perfumed aromas, with lilac and honey character. Medium- to full-bodied, with good flavors but a rather short finish. Drink now.–J.S. • $21 • (4/30/2000) • **87**

Pinot Grigio Collio 1998: A clean and lively white. Medium-bodied, with spice and honey character and a fresh finish. Drink now.–J.S. • $21 • (3/31/2000) • **85**

Sauvignon Collio 1998: Intense aromas of stones, almond skins and fruit. Medium-bodied, with plenty of fruit and a long, appley aftertaste. Drink now.–J.S. • $21 • (4/30/2000) • **87**

Key: SS—Spectator Selection. CS—Cellar Selection. HR—Highly Recommended. $NA—Price not available. (BT)—Barrel tasting. Ⓐ—Auction Price.
For a key to the tasters' initials, see "How to Use These Listings."
Dates in parentheses represent the issues in which the ratings were published.

Sauvignon Collio de la Tour 1998: A delicious white. Apple and lemon character with a hint of earth. Medium body. Dry, with a rich finish. Drink now.–J.S. • $29 • (4/30/2000) • **86**

Tocai Friulano Collio 1998: Interesting apple, mineral and citrus character. Medium- to full-bodied, with lots of straw and honey flavors. Long finish. Very good indeed. Drink now.–J.S. • $21 • (3/31/2000) • **88**

VILLA S. ANNA

Chianti Colli Senesi 1997: A very good red, with delicious plum, berry and chocolate character. Medium-bodied, with medium, velvety tannins and a ripe fruit and vanilla aftertaste. Drink now through 2001.–J.S. • $15 • (11/30/1999) • **86**

Chianti Colli Senesi 1994 • $15 • (10/31/1996) • **79**

Chianti Colli Senesi 1992 • $15 • (10/31/1995) • **80**

Chianti Colli Senesi Riserva 1992 • $16 • (10/31/1996) • **80**

Toscana Vigna Il Vallone 1995: Harmonious red. Lovely silky Cabernet, with berry, mint and tobacco aromas and flavors. Medium-bodied, with medium tannins and a fruity finish. Prugnolo Gentile and Cabernet Sauvignon. Drink now.–J.S. • $25 • (11/30/1999) • **88**

Toscana Vigna Il Vallone 1993 • $25 • (10/31/1996) • **85**

Toscana Vigna Il Vallone 1992 • $23 • (10/31/1995) • **86**

Vino Nobile di Montepulciano 1996: A harmonious and delicate Sangiovese, with berry, cherry and plum character. Medium-bodied, with medium, well-knit tannins and a fresh finish. Drink now through 2002.–J.S. • $24 • (11/30/1999) • **85**

Vino Nobile di Montepulciano 1995: A well-crafted wine, with cherry and vanilla aromas and flavors. Medium-bodied, with fresh acidity and a lovely creamy berry aftertaste. Drink now.–J.S. • $23 • (12/15/1998) • **87**

Vino Nobile di Montepulciano 1994 • $20 • (9/30/1997) • **82**

VILLA SANDI

Cabernet Sauvignon Piave 1997: A bit harsh, with a slightly grassy, green character, but well concentrated. Medium- to full-bodied, with firm, slightly coarse tannins and a medium finish. Best after 2000.–J.S. • $10 • (5/15/2000) • **83**

Chardonnay Piave 1998: Decent peaches and cream character, but slightly dull on the finish. Medium body.–J.S. • $10 • (2/29/2000) • **79**

Marca Trevigiana Marinali 1996: Intense green grass and green bean character coupled with some berriness. Full-bodied and chewy, with slightly unripe and austere tannins. Needs time to mellow. Best after 2000.–J.S. • $20 • (5/15/2000) • **80**

Merlot Piave 1997: A hard wine, with some plum character and cut wood. Medium-bodied, with hard tannins and a short finish. Give it some time. Best after 2000.–J.S. • $10 • (5/15/2000) • **83**

Merlot Piave 1996: A solid Merlot, with black cherry and plum notes and a hint of herb, all on a medium-bodied structure. Sinewy tannins emerge on the finish. Drink now.–B.S. • $8 • (7/31/1998) • **84**

Pinot Grigio Piave 1998: Simple, with peach character and a light, crisp finish.–J.S. • $10 • (2/29/2000) • **79**

Pinot Grigio Piave 1997: A filigree white, with a translucent texture supporting the peachy, nutty, minerally flavors. Piquant acidity keeps it lively and focused. Drink now.–B.S. • $8 • (7/31/1998) • **84**

Prosecco di Valdobbiadene NV: Delicious. Fresh and fruity, with melon and grapefruit character, fine bead and a dry finish. Drink now.–J.S. • $11 • (5/31/2000) • **86**

Veneto Rosso 1995: An austere, tobacco- and cedar-flavored red, this has a lean, sinewy structure and needs food to tame the stiff tannins. A blend of Cabernet Sauvignon and Cabernet Franc. Drink now.–B.S. • $12 • (7/31/1998) • **83**

VILLA TERLINA

Barbera d'Asti Gradale 1997: This beautiful Barbera tastes succulent from the natural acidity but also complex from the oak-inspired spice, mocha and smoke. Red berry flavors moderate the balance in this medium-bodied, focused red. Long finish. Not imported into the U.S. Drink now through 2003.–P.M. • $NA • (11/15/1999) • **88**

VILLA VITTORIA

Chianti 1994 • $6 • (10/31/1996) • **83**

Valpolicella 1995 • $5 • (1/31/1997) • **76**

VILLADORIA

Barbera d'Alba 1998: Rather lean but with decent berry and leather character. The light to medium finish is dry. Where's the fruit? Not imported into the U.S.–J.S. • $NA • (1/01/2000) • **78**

Barbera d'Alba Superiòre 1997: Very fresh, with lots of violet and mineral. Medium-bodied, with silky tannins and a fresh finish. A bit lean but delicious. Drink now.–J.S. • $12 • (6/15/2000) • **83**

Barbera d'Alba Superiòre 1996: Lovely aromas of toffee and berry. Medium-bodied, with light fruit and a leather and toffee finish. Slightly dry. Drink now.–J.S. • $13 • (6/15/2000) • **83**

Barbera d'Alba Superiòre 1992 • $NA • (10/31/1995) • **82**

Barolo 1995: Subtle plum, vanilla and cinnamon aromas. Medium-bodied, with firm tannins and a fresh finish. Best after 2000.–J.S. • $30 • (6/15/2000) • **84**

Barolo 1993 • $21 • (10/31/1997) • **79**

Barolo 1991 • $NA • (10/31/1995) • **86**

Barolo Riserva 1993: This friendly Barolo has pretty aromas of leather, cedar and tobacco, with a hint of plum. Medium-bodied, with silky tannins, crisp acidity and a slightly short, dry finish. Drink now.–J.S. • $32 • (6/15/2000) • **84**

Barolo Riserva 1990: Mature, with plum, mushroom and cedar character. Medium-bodied, with spicy flavors and an earthy finish. Drink now through 2001.–J.S. • $84 • (6/15/2000) • **82**

Barolo Riserva 1988 • $NA • (10/31/1995) • **85**

Barolo Riserva Spéciale 1978 • $14 • (8/31/1986) • **73**

Bricco Magno 1995: Aromatic, with tanned leather and floral character along with fruit. Medium-bodied, with fine tannins and a fresh, ripe fruit finish. Pleasant. Drink now.–J.S. • $17 • (6/15/2000) • **85**

Nebbiolo d'Alba 1997: Thick and ripe, with tobacco, berry and earth character. Medium-bodied, with slightly dry tannins. Drying out a bit. Not imported into the U.S.–J.S. • $NA • (1/01/2000) • **79**

VILLALTA

Amarone della Valpolicella Classico 1988 • $18 • (9/30/1995) • **80**

Amarone della Valpolicella Classico I Comunali 1991 • $25 • (6/15/1997) • **87**

VINI E MOSTI ROSSI, CONSORZIO PRODUTTORI

Primitivo di Manduria Dolce Naturale Il Madrigale 1997: Remember late-harvest Zinfandel? Here it is and beautiful, oozing with berry, cherry and smoke character. Full-bodied and very sweet, with a long, fruity finish. An alternative to Port. Best after 2001.–J.S. • $NA • (1/01/2000) • **88**

Primitivo di Manduria Il Sonnetto 1997: Like a good, simple Zin, with loads of ripe fruit character but an annoying amount of carbon dioxide on the palate. Medium-bodied and soft, with a fruity aftertaste. Not imported into the U.S.–J.S. • $NA • (1/01/2000) • **79**

VINO DEI PADRI, IL

Barbera d'Asti 1998: Dark, with plum skin, violet and berry character. Medium-bodied, with good fruit, polished and light tannins and a clean finish. Drink now.–J.S. • $13 • (6/15/2000) • **85**

Barbera d'Asti 1997: Demonstrates the potential of the '97 vintage. Beautiful, pure, refined, it tastes uncompromisingly natural, with oak-influenced spice granting center stage to a harmonious symphony of mineral, wild berry, currant and spice flavors. Drink now through 2003.–P.M. • $13 • (10/31/1998) • **90**

Barbera d'Asti Barrique 1998: Loads of minty plum character. Medium-bodied, with good fruit, light tannins and a fresh finish. Drink now. –J.S. • $16 • (6/15/2000) • **84**

Dolcetto d'Acqui 1998: Light, with strawberry and cherry character. Light-bodied and clean, with a fresh finish.–J.S. • $12 • (6/15/2000) • **79**

Dolcetto d'Acqui 1997: Smooth style of Dolcetto, with chocolate, mocha and milk flavors adding complexity to the red berry character. Smooth tannins. Drink now.–P.M. • $13 • (10/31/1998) • **81**

Freisa d'Asti 1998: Lovely and fresh, with floral and berry character. Medium-bodied, with good acidity and a light finish. Drink now.–J.S. • $13 • (6/15/2000) • **83**

Grignolino d'Asti 1998: Very light, with an ashlike character. Hard to get excited about.–J.S. • $13 • (6/15/2000) • **75**

Ruchè di Castagnole Monferrato NV: A strange mix of cut grass and raspberry. Medium-bodied, with polished tannins but a slightly aggressive finish. Rather cloying.–J.S. • $17 • (6/15/2000) • **79**

ITALY

VISTARENNI

Chianti Classico 1997: This pleasant, solid Sangiovese has a good dark ruby color and enticing aromas of blackberry and blueberry, with hints of smoke. It's medium in body, with silky, medium tannins and a fruity finish. Add to its charms: it's well priced. Drink now.–J.S. • $10 • (11/30/1999) • **87**
Chianti Classico 1996: Pretty strawberry and cherry aromas, but a light palate. Light-bodied, with light tannins and a crisp finish. Serve slightly chilled. Drink now.–J.S. • $12 • (12/15/1998) • **82**
Chianti Classico 1995 • $12 • (9/30/1997) • **76**
Chianti Classico 1992 • $NA • (2/28/1995) • **80**
Chianti Classico 1991 • $11 • (10/31/1993) • **75**
Chianti Classico 1990 • $NA • (9/15/1992) • **83**
Chianti Classico 1988 • $11 • (9/15/1991) • **86**
Chianti Classico 1987 • $10 • (10/15/1989) • **89**
Chianti Classico 1986 • $18 • (7/31/1989) • **78**
Chianti Classico Riserva 1996: A thoroughly enjoyable Chianti Classico, with cherry and blackberry character. Medium-bodied, with soft tannins and a lovely chocolate and fruit aftertaste. Drink now.–J.S. • $15 • (11/30/1999) • **86**
Chianti Classico Riserva 1995: Lots of lively, bubbly dried cherry and raspberry character. Light to medium in body, with light tannins and a fresh finish. Drink now.–J.S. • $15 • (12/15/1998) • **84**
Chianti Classico Riserva 1993 • $16 • (9/30/1997) • **80**
Chianti Classico Riserva 1990 • $NA • (2/28/1995) • **87**
Chianti Classico Riserva 1985 • $NA • (9/15/1991) • **81**
Chianti Classico Vigneto Assòlo 1990 • $18 • (9/15/1992) • **88**
Chianti Classico Vigneto Assòlo 1988 • $16 • (9/15/1991) • **78**
Codirosso 1993 • $24 • (9/30/1997) • **89**
Codirosso 1990 • $NA • (2/28/1995) • **87**
Codirosso 1986 • $22 • (11/30/1989) • **90**
Toscana Codirosso 1996: An elegant, good red, with vivid aromas of cherry, blackberry and earth. Medium-bodied, with silky tannins and a medium finish. Drink now.–J.S. • $22 • (11/30/1999) • **86**
Toscana Codirosso 1995: Dried cherry and plum aromas and flavors. Medium-bodied, with velvety tannins and a long, fruity finish. Underlying crisp acidity makes it fresh and enjoyable. Drink now through 2003.–J.S. • $24 • (12/15/1998) • **87**

VITICCIO

Chianti Classico 1997: Don't let the value price fool you—this is a delicious, even slightly decadent Chianti Classico, with very ripe plum and tobacco on the nose, medium body, well-knit medium tannins and a savory, fruity aftertaste. Drink now through 2001.–J.S. • $11 • (11/30/1999) • **87**
Chianti Classico 1996: Has a lot going for it. Violet and berry character, with a hint of black pepper. Medium-bodied, with chewy tannins and a delicious, fruity aftertaste. Will improve with age, but why wait? Drink now through 2003.–J.S. • $10 • (12/15/1998) • **87**
Chianti Classico 1995 • $11 • (9/30/1997) • **84**
Chianti Classico 1993 • $10 • (10/31/1995) • **80**
Chianti Classico 1991 • $10 • (10/31/1993) • **83**
Chianti Classico 1990 • $11 • (9/15/1992) SS • **90**
Chianti Classico 1988 • $10 • (4/30/1992) • **81**
Chianti Classico Riserva 1996: An aromatic red, with plenty of dried cherry and floral character. Medium-bodied, with light tannins and a short finish. Slightly austere. Not imported into the U.S. Drink now.–J.S. • $NA • (1/01/1999) • **84**
Chianti Classico Riserva 1995: Elegant and moreish. Floral, raspberry and violet aromas. Medium-bodied, with soft tannins and a succulent, fruit aftertaste with hints of berry and milk chocolate. Drink now.–J.S. • $15 • (12/15/1998) • **87**
Chianti Classico Riserva 1993 • $20 • (10/31/1996) • **86**
Chianti Classico Riserva 1991 • $16 • (10/31/1995) • **85**
Chianti Classico Riserva 1990 • $NA • (2/28/1995) • **87**
Chianti Classico Riserva 1988 • $15 • (9/15/1992) • **88**
Chianti Classico Riserva 1985 • $11 • (11/30/1989) • **85**
Chianti Classico Riserva 1978 • $13 • (11/30/1987) • **78**
Chianti Classico Riserva 1975 • $14 • (11/15/1987) • **71**

Key: SS—Spectator Selection. CS—Cellar Selection. HR—Highly Recommended. $NA—Price not available. (BT)—Barrel tasting. Ⓐ—Auction Price.
For a key to the tasters' initials, see "How to Use These Listings."
Dates in parentheses represent the issues in which the ratings were published.

Toscana Monile 1995: Offers a lovely texture, but it's slightly herbal and austere. Medium-bodied, with velvety tannins and a tobacco, green herb and fruit aftertaste. Best after 2000.–J.S. • $34 • (12/15/1998) • **84**
Toscana Monile 1994 • $40 • (9/30/1997) • **88**
Toscana Monile 1993 • $40 • (10/31/1996) • **82**
Toscana Monile 1991 • $33 • (2/28/1995) • **90**
Toscana Prunaio 1995: Plenty of crushed raspberry and minty character. Medium- to full-bodied, with lots of tannins and a polished finish. Slightly too woody, but wonderful fruit. Best after 2000.–J.S. • $33 • (12/15/1998) • **88**
Toscana Prunaio 1994 • $35 • (9/30/1997) • **84**
Toscana Prunaio 1993 • $38 • (10/31/1996) • **87**
Toscana Prunaio 1990 • $34 • (10/31/1993) • **90**
Toscana Prunaio 1988 • $28 • (3/31/1992) • **88**
Toscana Prunaio 1986 • $31 Ⓐ • (3/31/1990) SS • **92**
Toscana Prunaio 1985 • $18 • (4/30/1989) • **88**

VITICOLTORI RIUNITI DEI COLLI EUGANEI

Cabernet Colli Euganei 1997: A simple, fruity red. Pretty boysenberry and crushed strawberry aromas follow through to a medium-bodied palate. Short finish. Drink now.–J.S. • $6 • (1/01/2000) • **80**
Colli Euganei White 1997: A fresh and simple white, with apple and lime character, medium body and a crisp finish. Delicious. Drink now.–J.S. • $NA • (1/01/2000) • **82**
Merlot Colli Euganei 1997: A lovely, soft and fruity red, with light tannins and a caressing mouthfeel. Drink now.–J.S. • $6 • (1/01/2000) • **81**
Pinot Bianco Colli Euganei 1998: Aromas of baked apple pie with a bit of cream. Medium-bodied, with lots of fruit flavors and a spicy, slightly candied finish. Drink now.–J.S. • $8 • (4/30/2000) • **82**
Tocai Colli Euganei Italico 1998: Apple and pineapple skin aromas follow through to a medium-bodied palate with white pepper and spicy character. A bit simple. Drink now.–J.S. • $6 • (4/30/2000) • **83**

VITIGLIANO

Chianti Classico 1995 • $NA • (9/30/1997) • **84**
Chianti Classico 1991 • $10 • (10/31/1993) • **86**
Chianti Classico La Casina del Diavolo Riserva 1994 • $NA • (9/30/1997) • **81**

VOERZIO, GIANNI

Barolo La Serra 1991 • $NA • (10/31/1995) • **86**
Dolcetto d'Alba Ciabòt della Luna 1995 • $NA • (10/31/1996) • **88**
Dolcetto d'Alba Ciabòt della Luna 1994 • $NA • (10/31/1995) • **84**

VOERZIO, ROBERTO

Barolo 1985 • $18 • (1/31/1990) • **87**
Barolo 1983 • $15 • (9/15/1988) • **88**
Barolo 1982 • $12 • (9/15/1988) • **90**
Barolo Brunate 1992 • $30 • (10/31/1996) • **81**
Barolo Cerequio 1991 • $48 • (6/30/1997) • **84**
Barolo La Serra 1991 • $NA • (10/31/1995) • **85**
Barolo La Serra di La Morra 1982 • $12 • (7/31/1987) • **91**
Dolcetto d'Alba 1990 • $12 • (1/31/1992) • **82**
Dolcetto d'Alba Pria S. Francesco Croera 1994 • $NA • (10/31/1996) • **86**
Dolcetto d'Alba Pria S. Francesco Croera 1991 • $12 • (10/31/1992) • **81**
Dolcetto d'Alba Priavino 1990 • $14 • (12/15/1992) • **86**
Dolcetto d'Alba Priavino 1988 • $11 • (12/31/1990) • **87**
Nebbiolo delle Langhe Croera Fossati 1990 • $13 • (10/31/1992) • **80**
Vignaserra 1988 • $24 • (3/31/1992) • **85**
Vignaserra 1987 • $18 • (8/31/1991) • **85**

VOLPAIA, CASTELLO DI

Balifico 1995: Polished, elegant wine. Pretty raspberry and floral aromas, with hints of vanilla. Medium-bodied, with lovely silky tannins and a long, caressing finish. Drink now through 2003.–J.S. • $40 • (11/30/1999) • **88**
Balifico 1994 • $30 • (9/30/1997) • **87**
Balifico 1993 • $30 • (10/31/1996) • **90**
Balifico 1991 • $26 • (10/31/1995) • **83**
Balifico 1987 • $25 • (12/15/1992) • **80**
Balifico 1986 • $19 • (4/30/1989) • **83**
Balifico 1985 • $21 • (11/30/1989) • **91**
Chianti Borgianni 1992 • $8 • (7/31/1995) • **81**

Chianti Classico 1997: The best simple Chianti from Volpaia I have ever tasted. Soft and generous, with lovely tobacco, cherry and smoke character. Medium- to full-bodied, with well-knit tannins and a long finish. Drink now through 2003.–J.S. • $18 • (11/30/1999) • **89**
Chianti Classico 1996: Bright aromas of blackberry and spices. Medium-bodied, with well-integrated tannins and a fresh and silky finish. All in finesse. Extremely delicious. Very impressive from Volpaia. Drink now through 2003.–J.S. • $16 • (12/15/1998) • **88**
Chianti Classico 1995 • $15 • (9/30/1997) • **79**
Chianti Classico 1994 • $15 • (10/31/1996) • **83**
Chianti Classico 1993 • $11 • (10/31/1995) • **84**
Chianti Classico 1992 • $10 • (2/28/1995) • **76**
Chianti Classico 1991 • $11 • (10/31/1993) • **80**
Chianti Classico 1990 • $16 • (9/15/1992) • **88**
Chianti Classico 1989 • $12 • (9/15/1992) • **79**
Chianti Classico 1988 • $14 • (9/15/1991) • **85**
Chianti Classico 1987 • $16 • (11/30/1989) • **85**
Chianti Classico 1986 • $10 • (3/31/1990) • **75**
Chianti Classico 1985 • $10 • (6/30/1989) SS • **90**
Chianti Classico Riserva 1996: Elegant and fine, with lovely berry, tobacco and cherry character. Medium-bodied, with fine tannins and a fruit and tobacco aftertaste. Drink now through 2001.–J.S. • $24 • (11/30/1999) • **86**
Chianti Classico Riserva 1995: A very subtle and refined Chianti, fresh and fruity, with plenty of dried cherry and floral aromas and flavors. Medium in body, fresh on the finish. Drink now through 2003.–J.S. • $22 • (12/15/1998) • **85**
Chianti Classico Riserva 1994 • $19 • (9/30/1997) • **82**
Chianti Classico Riserva 1993 • $20 • (10/31/1996) • **82**
Chianti Classico Riserva 1991 • $14 • (10/31/1995) • **84**
Chianti Classico Riserva 1990 • $14 • (2/28/1995) • **86**
Chianti Classico Riserva 1988 • $22 • (9/15/1992) • **81**
Chianti Classico Riserva 1987 • $14 • (9/15/1992) • **84**
Chianti Classico Riserva 1985 • $13 • (9/15/1991) • **84**
Chianti Classico Riserva 1983 • $12 • (5/31/1989) • **87**
Chianti Classico Riserva 1982 • $11 • (9/15/1987) • **84**
Chianti Classico Riserva 1981 • $NA • (9/15/1987) • **86**
Chianti Classico Riserva 1977 • $NA • (9/15/1987) • **81**
Chianti Classico Riserva 1970 • $NA • (9/15/1987) • **85**
Coltassala 1995: A subtle, pretty wine. Interesting aromas of mint, fruit and earth. Medium-bodied, with polished tannins and a long, caressing finish. Drink now through 2002.–J.S. • $40 • (11/30/1999) • **87**
Coltassala 1994 • $30 • (9/30/1997) • **87**
Coltassala 1993 • $30 • (10/31/1996) • **87**
Coltassala 1991 • $26 • (10/31/1995) • **83**
Coltassala 1990 • $26 • (11/30/1994) SS • **92**
Coltassala 1988 • $NA • (11/15/1993) • **89**
Coltassala 1987 • $NA • (11/15/1993) • **86**
Coltassala 1986 • $NA • (11/15/1993) • **87**
Coltassala 1985 • $NA • (11/15/1993) • **90**
Coltassala 1983 • $22 • (9/15/1988) • **86**
Coltassala 1982 • $NA • (11/15/1993) • **90**
Coltassala 1981 • $NA • (9/15/1987) • **90**
Val d'Arbia 1996 • $10 • (9/30/1997) • **80**

VOLPE PASINI

Chardonnay Colli Orientali del Friuli 1998: Very clean and aromatic, with floral and mineral character. Medium-bodied, with fresh acidity and a fruity finish. Slightly short. Drink now.–J.S. • $12 • (3/31/2000) • **83**
Chardonnay Colli Orientali del Friuli Zuc di Volpe Selezione 1997: Gorgeous aromas of flowers and fruit, with hints of honey. Medium-bodied, with good acidity and a long, spicy almond aftertaste. Drink now through 2002.–J.S. • $20 • (3/31/2000) • **86**
Colli Orientali del Friuli Zuc di Volpe Le Roverelle 1997: I like the lemon, mineral and honey aromas of this wine. Medium-bodied, with chunky fruit and a fresh aftertaste. Drink now through 2002.–J.S. • $28 • (4/30/2000) • **87**
Merlot Colli Orientali del Friuli 1998: A solid Merlot with plum and blackberry character and a solid core of fruit on the palate. Medium body. Medium tannins. Chewy finish. Best after 2000.–J.S. • $12 • (5/15/2000) • **87**
Merlot Colli Orientali del Friuli Villa Volpe 1993 • $11 • (6/15/1996) • **80**
Pinot Bianco Colli Orientali del Friuli Zuc di Volpe 1998: Attractive aromas of melons and pears follow through to a medium-bodied palate with a mineral and almost aniseed character on the finish. Drink now.–J.S. • $20 • (4/30/2000) • **85**
Pinot Bianco Colli Orientali del Friuli Zuc di Volpe 1996 • $17 • (5/31/1998) • **79**
Pinot Grigio Colli Orientali del Friuli 1998: Subdued, with pretty aromas of almond and spice and hints of melon. Medium-bodied, with light fruit and a clean, fresh aftertaste. Drink now.–J.S. • $12 • (3/31/2000) • **83**
Pinot Grigio Colli Orientali del Friuli Zuc di Volpe 1998: Clean, with attractive peach and mineral character. Medium-bodied, with good fruit and a fresh finish. Drink now.–J.S. • $18 • (3/31/2000) • **85**
Pinot Grigio Colli Orientali del Friuli Zuc di Volpe 1996 • $16 • (5/31/1998) • **84**
Refosco Colli Orientali del Friuli Zuc di Volpe 1990 • $20 • (6/15/1996) • **81**
Ribolla Gialla Colli Orientali del Friuli 1998: Plenty of apple and melon character. Medium-bodied, with fresh acidity and a clean finish. Drink now.–J.S. • $12 • (4/30/2000) • **84**
Ribolla Gialla Colli Orientali del Friuli Zuc di Volpe 1998: Some lemon and spice character but slightly dull on the palate, with medium body and a light citrus finish. Drink now.–J.S. • $18 • (4/30/2000) • **81**
Ribolla Gialla Colli Orientali del Friuli Zuc di Volpe 1996 • $16 • (5/31/1998) • **82**
Tocai Friulano Colli Orientali del Friuli 1998: Medium-bodied, with pineapple and resin aromas. Slightly candied finish. Drink now.–J.S. • $12 • (3/31/2000) • **80**
Tocai Friulano Colli Orientali del Friuli Zuc di Volpe 1998: Despite a good core of ripe fruit, this seems slightly oxidized, with marzipan character. Short finish.–J.S. • $18 • (3/31/2000) • **78**
Tocai Friulano Colli Orientali del Friuli Zuc di Volpe 1996 • $16 • (5/31/1998) • **83**

ZAMO & PALAZZOLO

Merlot Colli Orientali del Friuli 1994 • $8 • (6/15/1997) • **83**
Merlot Colli Orientali del Friuli 1993 • $16 • (2/29/1996) • **84**

ZARDETTO

Brut Prosecco NV: Here's a value worth celebrating: a thick, full-bodied sparkler with a bountiful honeydew character, light bead and fresh finish. Drink now.–J.S. • $10 • (5/31/2000) • **86**
Brut Prosecco di Conegliano NV: Light and bubbly, with modest earth and apple flavors. Drink now.–B.S. • $12 • (7/31/1998) • **78**

ZEMMER, PETER

Gewürztraminer Alto Adige 1997: Rose petal and litchi aromas are here, as are pronounced mineral and herb elements, lending elegance to the rich texture and lingering flavors. Bitter grapefruit finish, with a lingering note of roses. Drink now.–B.S. • $13 • (7/31/1998) • **85**
Lagrein Dunkel Alto Adige 1995: Plenty of acidity and tannins in this lean, medium-bodied red, with tobacco, plum and cedar flavors and an intensity that pulses through the finish.–B.S. • $12 • (7/31/1998) • **83**
Merlot Alto Adige 1995: Good depth and concentration of cherry, plum and spice in this bright, focused Merlot. The components are in balance and the plum notes resonate on the finish.–B.S. • $12 • (7/31/1998) • **85**
Pinot Grigio Alto Adige 1997: Nutty, leesy aromas segue into almond, quince and stone flavors. Good body and intensity.–B.S. • $10 • (7/31/1998) • **83**

ZENATO

Amarone della Valpolicella Classico 1993: Dark ruby in color, with intense aromas of raisin, raspberry and wet earth and hints of meat. Medium- to full-bodied, with fine tannins and a medium finish. Needs a bit more length at the end to be outstanding. Drink now.–J.S. • $53 • (1/01/2000) • **88**
Amarone della Valpolicella Classico 1990 • $30 • (6/15/1997) • **90**
Amarone della Valpolicella Classico 1988 • $25 • (9/30/1995) • **86**
Amarone della Valpolicella Classico 1986 • $25 • (6/15/1997) • **87**
Amarone della Valpolicella Classico 1983 • $28 • (6/15/1997) • **86**
Amarone della Valpolicella Classico 1981 • $11 • (3/15/1989) • **81**
Amarone della Valpolicella Classico Sergio Zenato Riserva 1990: Big and rich. Loads of dried fruit, raisins and Indian spices on the nose. Full-bodied and chewy, with round tannins and a long, spicy chocolate aftertaste. A beauty. Drink now through 2005.–J.S. • $65 • (5/15/2000) • **92**
Amarone della Valpolicella Classico Sergio Zenato Riserva 1988 • $48 • (5/31/1998) HR • **93**
Amarone della Valpolicella Classico Signature Label 1983 • $35 • (6/15/1996) • **88**
Bardolino Classico Superiòre 1990 • $8 • (9/15/1992) • **81**
Bardolino Classico Superiòre 1989 • $8 • (7/15/1991) • **78**
Bardolino Novello 1996 • $8 • (6/15/1997) • **80**
Chardonnay Veneto Sergio Zenato Riserva 1997: A bit subdued, but with plenty of apple, lemon and light vanilla character. Full-bodied, with firm

acidity and a medium finish. Give it time. Best from 2001 through 2003.–J.S. • $22 • (1/01/2000) • **88**

Lugana San Benedetto 1998: A beauty—well done, and at a great price, too. This Italian white smells lovely, like an apple pie. It's full-bodied, with lots of intense fruit flavors, good acidity and a long, spicy finish. Drink now.–J.S. • $10 • (2/29/2000) • **88**

Lugana San Benedetto 1996 • $12 • (5/31/1998) • **85**

Lugana Sergio Zenato Riserva 1997: Well made, with apple, honey and straw character throughout. Medium-bodied, with fresh acidity and a reserved, fruity aftertaste. Drink now through 2002.–J.S. • $22 • (1/01/2000) • **87**

Merlot Venezie 1996: An extremely floral red (roses, carnations), with berry character. Medium-bodied, with well-integrated tannins and a fresh finish. Delicious. Drink now.–J.S. • $12 • (1/01/2000) • **85**

Pinot Grigio Veneto 1996 • $9 • (6/15/1998) • **84**

Valpolicella Classico Superiore 1996: A bit lean but with good, clean berry and strawberry character. Light- to medium-bodied, with crisp acidity. Drink now.–J.S. • $10 • (1/01/2000) • **82**

Valpolicella Classico Superiore 1994 • $9 • (6/15/1997) • **83**

Valpolicella Classico Superiore 1990 • $9 • (9/15/1992) • **84**

Valpolicella Classico Superiore 1988 • $8 • (4/30/1992) • **83**

Valpolicella Classico Superiore Ripassa 1996: An extremely serious Valpo. Dark ruby, with blackberry, raspberry and violet character. Full-bodied, with loads of fruit and polished tannins. Drink now.–J.S. • $16 • (1/01/2000) • **88**

Valpolicella Classico Superiore Ripassa 1994 • $15 • (5/31/1998) • **86**

Valpolicella Classico Superiore Ripassa 1993 • $15 • (6/15/1997) • **87**

Valpolicella Classico Superiore Ripassa 1992 • $15 • (4/30/1996) • **87**

ZONIN

Amarone della Valpolicella 1994: Prune, licorice, tobacco and a touch of mint are the aromas and flavors in this Amarone with personality. There's a nice glycerinlike feel midpalate, slightly dry tannins on the finish. Good effort in a difficult vintage. Drink now through 2005.–B.S. • $22 • (9/30/1998) • **87**

Amarone della Valpolicella Il Maso 1991 • $17 • (9/30/1995) • **86**

Amarone della Valpolicella Il Maso 1990 • $16 • (9/30/1995) • **89**

Amarone della Valpolicella Il Maso 1988 • $16 • (9/15/1992) • **82**

Bardolino Classico 1991 • $7 • (9/15/1992) • **82**

Berengario Red 1993: Showing mature notes of cooked plum and spice, this has a ripe, pruny character that ends with some pretty stiff tannins. Best now while there's still fruit. 60 percent Cabernet Sauvignon, 40 percent Merlot.–B.S. • $21 • (9/30/1998) • **83**

Berengario Barrel Aged 1989 • $24 • (3/31/1993) • **85**

Berengario Barrel Aged 1988 • $30 • (1/31/1992) • **84**

Merlot Veneto 1995 • $7 • (9/15/1997) • **78**

Merlot-Cabernet del Friuli 1992 • $6 • (2/28/1995) • **82**

Merlot-Cabernet del Friuli 1991 • $6 • (4/30/1994) • **75**

Merlot-Cabernet Aquileia del Friuli 1990 • $8 • (9/15/1992) • **74**

Merlot-Cabernet del Friuli 1989 • $6 • (1/31/1992) • **78**

Montepulciano d'Abruzzo 1995 • $7 • (7/31/1997) • **82**

Montepulciano d'Abruzzo 1993 • $6 • (2/29/1996) • **79**

Montepulciano d'Abruzzo 1992 • $6 • (3/31/1995) • **77**

Montepulciano d'Abruzzo 1991 • $7 • (7/31/1993) • **80**

Montepulciano d'Abruzzo 1990 • $7 • (9/15/1992) • **83**

Montepulciano d'Abruzzo 1988 • $6 • (6/30/1991) • **80**

Pinot Grigio Umbria 1997: A broad style, whose earth, apple and citrus notes have weight on the palate. Finishes with a hint of bitter almond. Drink now.–B.S. • $9 • (9/30/1998) • **81**

Recioto di Gambellara 1990 • $20 • (9/15/1992) • **75**

Valpolicella Classico Il Maso 1990 • $8 • (9/15/1992) • **82**

White Merlot Veneto 1996 • $7 • (12/15/1997) • **75**

ZORZETTIG, LIVIO

Cabernet Franc Colli Orientali del Friuli 1998: A simple and fruity Cabernet Franc with berry, eucalyptus and herb character. Medium-bodied, with soft tannins and a light finish. Drink now.–J.S. • $12 • (5/15/2000) • **81**

Chardonnay Colli Orientali del Friuli 1998: A straightforward Chardonnay, with lovely apple, honey and cream character. Medium-bodied, with good acidity and a fruity finish. Drink now.–J.S. • $10 • (2/29/2000) • **85**

Merlot Colli Orientali del Friuli 1998: An aromatic red, with blackberries, currants and earth character. Medium-bodied, soft and fruity, with a simple, fruity finish. Drink now.–J.S. • $12 • (5/15/2000) • **83**

Picolit Colli Orientali del Friuli 1998: A subtle and balanced sweet white. Medium-bodied, lightly sweet, with almond, floral, lemon and honey flavors. Fresh finish. Drink now.–J.S. • $32/500 ml. • (4/30/2000) • **85**

Pinot Bianco Colli Orientali del Friuli 1998: Plenty of apple and cream character in this stand-up Pinot Bianco. Medium-bodied, with good intensity and a long, flavorful finish. Drink now.–J.S. • $10 • (2/29/2000) • **86**

Pinot Grigio Colli Orientali del Friuli 1998: A good Pinot Grigio, with aromas of almond and spice plus hints of apple. Medium-bodied, with good fruit and a flavorful finish. Slightly one-dimensional. Drink now.–J.S. • $10 • (2/29/2000) • **85**

Ribolla Gialla Colli Orientali del Friuli 1998: Starts off nicely, with spicy dried apricot aromas. Medium-bodied, with good acidity, but it loses a bit at the finish. Drink now.–J.S. • $10 • (2/29/2000) • **85**

Savignon Colli Orientali del Friuli 1998: A very perfumed Sauvignon, with lemon, leaf and floral aromas. Medium-bodied, with plenty of fruit and a crisp finish. A bit simple on the palate. Drink now.–J.S. • $10 • (2/29/2000) • **85**

Key: SS—Spectator Selection. CS—Cellar Selection. HR—Highly Recommended. $NA—Price not available. (BT)—Barrel tasting. Ⓐ—Auction Price. For a key to the tasters' initials, see "How to Use These Listings." **Dates in parentheses represent the issues in which the ratings were published.**

New Zealand

If you think New Zealand wines are suddenly appearing all around you, rest assured, you aren't imagining things. Exports to the U.S. have been soaring, and New Zealand has moved onto the American scene with a wave of distinctive Sauvignon Blancs and Chardonnays and even some stylish reds. Since only the best wines typically make it to the United States, the quality of these wines is reassuringly consistent. In addition, prices are reasonable for wines of this quality, with many wines scoring 85 points or higher in *Wine Spectator* tastings priced under $15.

1. Hawke's Bay
2. Gisborne
3. Auckland/Kumeu
4. Martinborough/ Wairarapa
5. Marlborough
6. Nelson
7. Canterbury
8. Central Otago

THE REGION

New Zealand is farther south than most of the winegrowing regions of its closest neighbor, Australia, and therefore cooler. No vineyard lies more than 80 miles from the ocean, and the maritime influence makes for some of the coolest winegrowing regions on earth. In sunny years, the long, cool growing season allows the grapes to achieve full ripeness while retaining vibrant acidity. In the past some wines have been marred by vegetal, unripe flavors, but modern New Zealand bottlings are crisp, vibrant wines that emphasize bright fruit flavors.

Ten main wine regions, comprising more than 25,000 acres of vineyard are spread across the island nation's two main land masses. The South Island is dominated by the heavily-planted Marlborough region, with the less-familiar Nelson, Canterbury and Central Otago regions gaining in importance. On the North Island, Auckland, Gisborne, Hawkes Bay and Martinborough are the most important wine regions. Because New Zealand is very much an emerging wine-producing area, it is hard to generalize about the particular characteristics of any one region. Soil types are still being analyzed and microclimates are still being defined, in the ongoing task of matching grape varieties to the sites to which they are best suited.

GRAPE VARIETIES

New Zealand first captured world attention with its Sauvignon Blancs, especially those from the Marlborough region of the South Island, which are often compared to Sancerre or Pouilly-Fumé, France's finest Sauvignon Blancs. But New Zealanders have sought to create a style of their own, one that combines Old World complexity with a California-like richness. New Zealand Sauvignons display flavors of lime and other citrus fruits, green apple, pear, and an exotic note of passion fruit, the last being the most distinctly original New Zealand flavor. Cloudy Bay is the best known of New Zealand's Sauvignon Blancs, with Babich, Brancott, Chancellor, Gibbston Valley, Goldwater, Jackson, Lawson's Dry Hills, Martinborough, Te Mata, Sinclair and Villa Maria also proving to be outstanding.

As important as Sauvignon Blanc has become, Chardonnay may have equal, if not greater, potential. Chardonnay is the more widely planted variety, and the best North Island grapes produce wines that

Late autumn in the Brancott Estate vineyard, Marlborough.

Kevin Judd/Cephas

smoothly integrate classic Chardonnay flavors with New Zealand's signature zing of lemon and passion fruit. Though oak is used as an accent, most New Zealand Chardonnays are fruit-driven, with flavors evoking peach, pear, orange, apricot, fig, apple, quince or pineapple. Among the best Chardonnay producers is Kumeu River, a 25,000-case high-end winery whose best offerings can hold their own with the stars of Burgundy and California.

Although Chardonnay and Sauvignon Blanc currently account for two-thirds of New Zealand's offerings in the United States, several other varieties are making a bid, albeit with mixed results. Pinot Noir is currently the most widely planted red variety, with Cabernet Sauvignon and Merlot gaining a foothold in the Hawkes Bay region. The best are crisp, fruity and complex, but because of the islands' cool, windy, maritime climate, late ripeners such as Cabernet Sauvignon and Merlot will always have to struggle to reach full flavor. Cool-climate-loving Pinot Noir seems a better bet. Excellent Pinot Noirs have come from Marlborough, Martinborough and Central Otago, and the hope is that many more will soon follow.

ATA RANGI

Pinot Noir Martinborough 1997: Fresh, focused and framed by spicy oak, this has berry and black cherry flavors at the intense core. The oak notes are a bit loud at this point, but should integrate with time in the cellar. Drink through 2004.–H.S. • $45 • (5/15/1999) • **88**

Pinot Noir Martinborough 1995 • $50 • (6/15/1997) • **86**

Pinot Noir Martinborough 1991 • $NA • (5/15/1994) • **81**

BABICH

Cabernet Sauvignon Hawkes Bay 1989 • $10 • (7/15/1991) • **74**

Chardonnay Gisborne 1999: Bright and refreshing, with nectarine and citrus flavors that linger on the sprightly finish. Gets better with each sip. Drink now through 2004.–H.S. • $11 • (2/29/2000) • **88**

Chardonnay Hawkes Bay Irongate 1998: Broad and generous, not at all heavy, but it piles the mineral, spice and tobacco overtones onto the basic pear and hazelnut flavors. Everything lingers neatly on the finish. Drink now through 2007.–H.S. • $22 • (2/29/2000) • **91**

Chardonnay Hawkes Bay The Patriarch 1998: Packs a rainbow of juicy flavors onto a taut, lithe frame, letting the apple, pear, walnut and earth notes cascade impressively over the palate. A stylish wine with plenty to offer. Drink through 2006.–H.S. • $28 • (6/15/1999) • **91**

Irongate Hawkes Bay 1990 • $NA • (5/15/1994) • **79**

Merlot Hawkes Bay Gimblett Road Vineyard Winemakers Reserve 1998: Lean and lithe, with pretty raspberry and earthy mineral flavors in profusion on the supple finish. Drink now through 2004.–H.S. • $16 • (3/31/2000) • **86**

Pinot Gris Marlborough 1998: Ripe and smooth, with pretty melon, honey and gentle spice flavors on a creamy texture. Don't wait. Drink now.–H.S. • $10 • (6/15/1999) • **88**

Pinot Noir Henderson Valley 1992 • $NA • (5/15/1994) • **77**

Riesling Marlborough 1998: Bright and refreshing for its jazzy green apple, floral and spice flavors that remain lively, with clean acidity on the gently sweet finish. Drink now through 2002.–H.S. • $10 • (6/15/1999) • **87**

Sauvignon Blanc Marlborough 1999: Crisp and fruity, with apricot and pear flavors on a lean frame, hinting at herb and anise seed on the finish. Drink now.–H.S. • $11 • (2/29/2000) • **86**

Sauvignon Blanc Marlborough 1998: Zesty and brimming with fruit describes this Kiwi Sauvignon Blanc—a lively mouthful of apricot, citrus, pear, and fennel flavors that keep bouncing merrily through the finish. Drink now.–H.S. • $10 • (5/15/1999) SS • **90**

Sauvignon Blanc Marlborough Wakefield Downs Vineyard Winemakers Reserve 1999: Light, bright and refreshing for its open-textured apple and citrus flavors that linger on the straightforward finish. Drink now.–H.S. • $15 • (2/29/2000) • **86**

Syrah Hawkes Bay Gimblett Road Vineyard Winemakers Reserve 1998: Ripe and generous, appealing for its supple texture and lovely black cherry, violet and anise flavors that linger gently on the smooth finish. Drink now through 2005.–H.S. • $16 • (3/31/2000) • **88**

Syrah Hawkes Bay Mara Estate Gimblett Road 1997: This crisp style of Syrah emphasizes racy acidity and pretty blackberry and spice flavors that linger attractively on the finish. Drink now through 2004.–H.S. • $17 • (6/15/1999) • **86**

Syrah Hawkes Bay Mara Estate Gimblett Road 1996: Crisp, juicy style of Syrah featuring berry and mint flavors that linger brightly on the tart finish. Drink now.–H.S. • $16 • (5/15/1999) • **85**

BRANCOTT

Chardonnay Gisborne Ormond Estate 1998: Has a hard edge up front to the bright pineapple and melon flavors, finishing with pretty citrus notes and a broader texture. Drink now through 2003.–H.S. • $25 • (2/29/2000) • **87**

Chardonnay Gisborne Reserve 1998: Bright, jazzy and lively, with citrus-scented pear, guava and apple flavors that practically jump out on the finish. The texture remains silky and refined throughout. Drink now through 2003.–H.S. • $16 • (1/31/2000) • **90**

Chardonnay Gisborne Reserve 1997: On the lighter side, this supple white wine has pretty spice and honey overtones to the delicate pineapple and citrus flavors. Appealing for its tangy freshness. 2,000 cases imported. Drink now.–H.S. • $15 • (1/31/1999) • **88**

Chardonnay Marlborough Renwick Estate 1998: Ripe, round and full of personality. A lush mouthful of pear, nectarine, spice and citrus flavors that pick up extra notes of fresh herb and mineral on the long, long finish. Drink now through 2007.–H.S. • $25 • (2/29/2000) • **92**

Merlot Marlborough Reserve 1997: Smooth in texture and generous in flavor, with extra-ripe currant, plum, tobacco and spice that linger on the soft finish. Drink now through 2002.–H.S. • $16 • (1/31/2000) • **85**

Merlot Marlborough Reserve 1996: Supple and generous with its berry and herb flavors, with polished texture on the finish, making it feel creamy and light. Drink now through 2002.–H.S. • $15 • (5/15/1999) • **87**

Pinot Noir Marlborough Reserve 1998: Velvety and spicy, with pretty black cherry and vanilla notes leading, picking up a caramel note on the soft finish. Drink now.–H.S. • $16 • (1/31/2000) • **81**

Sauvignon Blanc Marlborough Brancott Estate 1998: Bright and jazzy, reverberating with citrus, passion fruit and apple flavors, plus just a touch of herb on the lively finish. A quintessential Kiwi Sauvignon. Drink now.–H.S. • $26 • (2/29/2000) • **91**

Sauvignon Blanc Marlborough Reserve 1998: Subtler than most Kiwi Sauvignon Blancs. Light and pretty, with apple and passion fruit aromas and flavors, an open texture and a harmonious finish. Drink now.–H.S. • $16 • (6/15/1999) • **88**

Sauvignon Blanc Marlborough Reserve 1997 • $16 • (5/15/1998) • **88**

CAIRNBRAE

Chardonnay Marlborough 1998: Vibrant citrus, pear and almond flavors characterize this distinctive Chardonnay. With its pinpoint balance of acidity and richness, it's delightful already. Drink now through 2003.–H.S. • $13 • (5/31/1999) • **88**

Riesling Marlborough 1998: Bright, racy and dry, with a pretty range of peach, apple and floral aromas and flavors that zig and zag nicely across the palate. Drink now through 2005.–H.S. • $13 • (6/15/1999) • **89**

Riesling Marlborough Noble 1999: A stunning dessert wine. Apricot, honey and citrus notes play off the racy acidity and elegant texture. Lacks a bit on the finish, yet very appealing. Drink now through 2003.–B.S. • $18/375 ml. • (6/15/2000) • **89**

Sauvignon Blanc Marlborough The Stones 1999: Bright and juicy. A lively mouthful of fresh apple, lime and leafy green aromas and flavors that lingers nicely on the crisp finish. Drink now.–H.S. • $13 • (12/31/1999) • **88**

Sauvignon Blanc Marlborough The Stones 1998: A straightforward white, offering hints of white pepper and green apple in a juicy mix of mineral and citrus flavors. Drink now.–H.S. • $13 • (5/31/1999) • **86**

CALLAHAN HILL

Sauvignon Blanc Marlborough 1998: Odd flavors, but lean and silky in texture, with a strong peppermint and herb character up front and only a hint of citrus on the finish. Drink now.–H.S. • $10 • (11/15/1999) • **80**

CHANCELLOR

Sauvignon Blanc Waipara 1997: Unmistakably Sauvignon Blanc, with gooseberry and citrus flavors that expand and linger on the lively finish. Drink now.–H.S. • $18 • (5/31/1999) • **90**

Sauvignon Blanc Waipara Mt. Cass Road 1998: Bright, refreshing and surprisingly elegant, offering pretty apple, passion fruit, herb and pepper flavors that linger nicely on the long finish. Drink now.–H.S. • $19 • (11/30/1999) • **91**

CLOUDY BAY

Cabernet-Merlot New Zealand 1991 • $NA • (5/15/1994) • **75**

Chardonnay Marlborough 1997: Bright and crisp, with a floral edge to the tart pineapple and mineral flavors. 1,000 cases imported. Drink now through 2001.–H.S. • $23 • (5/15/1999) • **86**

Sauvignon Blanc Marlborough 1999: Lively and balanced, this broader, rounder version of Sauvignon Blanc offers grapefruit, lime, pear and melon notes, with a hint of earth. Has good depth, a crunchy texture and a long finish. Drink now.–B.S. • $24 • (6/15/2000) • **89**

Sauvignon Blanc Marlborough 1998: This New Zealand white displays an impressive range of flavors—green apple, sweet pea, citrus and celery—balanced on an elegant frame, all coming together harmoniously on the tart, silky-textured finish. Delicious. Drink now.–H.S. • $18 • (5/15/1999) SS • **92**

Sauvignon Blanc Marlborough 1997: Bright and jazzy on the palate, with beautifully folded layers of quince, passion fruit and grapefruit flavors on a surprisingly smooth, silky frame. This New Zealand white is lovely already. Drink now. 7,000 cases imported.–H.S. • $18 • (10/31/1998) HR • **91**

COOPERS CREEK

Cabernet Sauvignon Huapai 1990 • $12 • (8/31/1993) • **83**

Cabernet Sauvignon Huapai 1989 • $10 • (4/15/1992) • **79**

Cabernet-Merlot Huapai 1991 • $NA • (5/15/1994) • **77**

Cabernet-Merlot Huapai Reserve 1995: Smooth and polished, generous with its bright berry flavors and earth, mineral and herb shadings. Harmonious and distinctive, this has come together nicely. Drink now through 2002.–H.S. • $28 • (10/15/1999) • **88**

Chardonnay Gisborne 1998: Smooth, polished and refreshing for its juicy pineapple, citrus and vanilla-almond flavors that wrap up neatly on the silky finish. Drink now through 2004.–H.S. • $12 • (6/15/1999) • **90**

Chardonnay Hawkes Bay 1998: Ripe, aromatic and round, this is nicely proportioned to show off pear, hazelnut and vanilla-smoke flavors that expand and linger on the subtle finish. Gorgeously balanced. Drink now through 2005.–H.S. • $15 • (6/15/1999) • **88**

Chardonnay Hawkes Bay Swamp Reserve 1997: Ripe in flavor and open in texture, with a generous mouthful of pear, fig and spice flavors that linger nicely on the rich, deftly balanced finish. But really, "swamp"? Oh, yummy. Drink now through 2005.–H.S. • $25 • (6/15/1999) • **90**

Merlot Hawkes Bay 1998: Crisp and juicy, with pretty blackberry and spice flavors that remain light and fragrant on the finish. Drink now through 2002.–H.S. • $14 • (6/15/1999) • **86**

Merlot Hawkes Bay 1992 • $NA • (5/15/1994) • **70**

Pinot Noir Hawkes Bay 1998: Light and refreshing for its delicate plum and currant flavors that linger on the soft finish. Drink now through 2002.–H.S. • $14 • (6/30/1999) • **85**

Riesling Hawkes Bay 1998: Light, dry and refreshing for its grapefruit, nectarine and floral aromas and flavors. Harmonious and appealing. Drink now through 2003.–H.S. • $10 • (6/15/1999) • **86**

Sauvignon Blanc Marlborough 1999: Lean and crisp up front, but with ripe flavors that round it out nicely. Offers pretty apricot, citrus and passion fruit flavors that open up beautifully as they move toward the finish. Drink now.–H.S. • $13 • (2/29/2000) • **88**

Sauvignon Blanc Marlborough 1997: Here's an affordable opportunity to check out a variety the wine world's buzzing about—New Zealand Sauvignon Blanc. This one's intensely flavorful, with juicy pear, guava and herb notes threading through the crisp, citrusy flavors. Drink now.–H.S. • $10 • (6/15/1999) • **87**

CORBANS

Cabernet-Merlot Hawkes Bay Private Bin 1995 • $21 • (2/28/1998) • **86**

Cabernet Sauvignon Hawkes Bay Private Bin 1996: Has ripe flavors, supple texture and a sense of refinement, with blueberry, currant and sage flavors fading only slightly on the smooth finish. Drink now through 2002.–H.S. • $18 • (5/15/1999) • **88**

Cabernet Sauvignon Hawkes Bay Private Bin Premium Selection 1994 • $18 • (12/15/1997) • **81**

Chardonnay Marlborough Select 1997: Bright and juicy, with a raw, leafy edge to the citrusy apple flavors, the fruit lingering on the finish. Drink now.–H.S. • $16 • (5/15/1999) • **87**

Merlot Marlborough Private Bin 1991 • $15 • (5/15/1994) • **88**

Merlot-Cabernet Marlborough Select 1997: Smooth, generous and fruit-rich, with lovely blackberry, plum and spicy smoky notes that linger enticingly on the supple finish. Drink now through 2003.–H.S. • $16 • (5/15/1999) • **89**

Sauvignon Blanc Marlborough Private Bin 1997: Crisp in texture, with juicy citrus, gooseberry and celery flavors packed into a lean frame, echoing on the lively finish. Drink now.–H.S. • $16 • (5/15/1999) • **88**

Sauvignon Blanc Marlborough Select 1998: Bright and green, with lime, celery and green apple notes on a tart, juicy structure. Echoes fruit on the zesty finish. Drink now.–H.S. • $16 • (5/15/1999) • **88**

CRAWFORD, KIM

Cabernet Franc Hawkes Bay Wicken 1998: Light, crisp and fragrant, with blueberry and mineral flavors that finish a bit softer than they start. Drink now.–H.S. • $17 • (5/15/1999) • **85**

Key: SS—Spectator Selection. CS—Cellar Selection. HR—Highly Recommended. $NA—Price not available. (BT)—Barrel tasting. Ⓐ—Auction Price.
For a key to the tasters' initials, see "How to Use These Listings."
Dates in parentheses represent the issues in which the ratings were published.

Chardonnay Gisborne Tietjen 1998: Ripe and aromatic, a smooth-textured mouthful of pear and exotic spices, finishing round and generous. Drink now through 2002.–H.S. • $20 • (5/15/1999) • **89**

Chardonnay Gisborne Tietjen 1997 • $20 • (6/30/1998) • **91**

Chardonnay Marlborough Unoaked 1998: Juicy and fresh, a pretty wine with generous citrus and apple flavors, hinting at orange peel on the soft finish. Drink now.–H.S. • $15 • (5/15/1999) • **86**

Chardonnay Marlborough Unoaked 1997 • $15 • (6/30/1998) • **86**

Chardonnay New Zealand Unoaked 1999: Light, bright and appealing for its lively apple and spice flavors. Finishes with a nice vanilla and pepper note. Drink now through 2003.–H.S. • $15 • (12/31/1999) • **86**

Merlot Hawkes Bay Te Awanga 1998: Smooth and round, with pretty berry, plum and black olive flavors that mingle with style and polish on the finish. Delicious already. Drink now through 2007.–H.S. • $20 • (12/31/1999) • **89**

Pia New Zealand White 1998: Broader and richer than most New Zealand Chardonnays, this has plenty of pear, violet and caramel flavors that echo fragrantly on the finish. Drink now through 2004.–H.S. • $25 • (12/31/1999) • **88**

Riesling Marlborough Dry 1999: Crisp and lively, generous with lime, mineral and floral flavors around the core of citrus. Drink now through 2005.–H.S. • $15 • (12/31/1999) • **87**

Sauvignon Blanc Awatere Valley 1998: Supple and soft, this gently spicy wine mixes pretty oak flavors with ripe fig and pineapple, the fruit echoing on the finish. Drink now.–H.S. • $20 • (5/15/1999) • **88**

Sauvignon Blanc Marlborough 1999: Lean and lively, with a strong layer of decaying flowers and citrusy flavors that finish soft. Drink now.–H.S. • $15 • (12/31/1999) • **80**

Sauvignon Blanc Marlborough 1998: Light and frisky, lively, with green apple and lime flavors that linger gently on the finish. Drink now.–H.S. • $15 • (5/15/1999) • **87**

Sauvignon Blanc Marlborough 1997 • $15 • (6/30/1998) • **89**

Tané New Zealand Red 1998: The package suggests that this will be a big, raw-boned red, but it's actually smooth, polished and refined. Offers lovely plum, berry and spicy oak aromas and flavors that cascade beautifully through the elegant finish. Drink now through 2006.–H.S. • $30 • (12/31/1999) • **90**

DASHWOOD

Sauvignon Blanc Marlborough 1998: Round in texture, with a lively core of citrus and sweet pea aromas and flavors. Feels closed-in at this point. Drink now.–H.S. • $13 • (11/15/1999) • **86**

Sauvignon Blanc Marlborough 1997 • $14 • (6/30/1998) • **87**

DOCTORS CREEK

Chardonnay Marlborough 1998: Bright and appealing for its pretty apricot and citrus flavors that linger on a light frame. Drink now.–H.S. • $16 • (5/15/1999) • **85**

Merlot Marlborough 1998: Crisp and bright, here's a jazzy Merlot with ripe blackberry and currant flavors on a tart frame. Drink now.–H.S. • $17 • (5/15/1999) • **86**

ESK VALLEY

Cabernet-Merlot Hawkes Bay 1992 • $NA • (5/15/1994) • **78**

Cabernet-Merlot Hawkes Bay Reserve 1991 • $NA • (5/15/1994) • **86**

FAIRHALL DOWNS

Chardonnay Marlborough 1998: Light and juicy, with pretty apple and spice flavors that linger on the soft, silky finish. Drink now.–H.S. • $20 • (3/31/2000) • **85**

Sauvignon Blanc Marlborough 1999: Light and open-textured, this is a pretty wine with spicy nectarine and herb flavors. Drink now.–H.S. • $18 • (3/31/2000) • **86**

Sauvignon Blanc Marlborough 1998: Light and vibrant, this lithe, fresh wine is packed with citrus, passion fruit and pineapple flavors that linger delicately on the finish. Drink now.–H.S. • $16 • (11/15/1999) • **89**

Sauvignon Blanc Marlborough 1997: This jazzy, vibrant white has racy passion fruit, lime, herb and white pepper aromas and flavors. Finishes bright and juicy. Drink now.–H.S. • $16 • (6/30/1999) • **88**

FOREFATHERS

Sauvignon Blanc Marlborough 1998: Fresh and open-textured, with pretty apricot, herb and pear flavors on a modest scale. Drink now.–H.S. • $15 • (5/15/1999) • **86**

FORREST

Chardonnay Marlborough 1998: Fresh and open-textured, refreshing for its guileless apple, pear and citrus flavors that ride through the finish. Drink now through 2003.–H.S. • $16 • (3/31/2000) • **88**

Chardonnay Marlborough 1997: A lively, jazzy mouthful of lime-scented apple, quince and spice flavors that remain bright and appealing through the finish. Drink now through 2002.–H.S. • $15 • (10/31/1998) • **90**

Riesling Marlborough Botrytized 1997: Ripe and juicy. A lively mouthful of sweet apricot, citrus and floral flavors that remain golden through the finish. Drink through 2002.–H.S. • $18/375 ml. • (11/15/1998) • **89**

Sauvignon Blanc Marlborough 1999: Fresh and appealing for its silky texture and pretty citrus, sweet corn and apple flavors. Drink now.–H.S. • $16 • (1/31/2000) • **86**

Sauvignon Blanc Marlborough 1998: Bright and focused, a lively mouthful of tangy green apple, citrus and mineral flavors that echo on the generous finish. Drink now.–H.S. • $13 • (5/15/1999) • **88**

Sauvignon Blanc Marlborough 1997: Bright and vivid, its lively citrus, passion fruit and pear flavors swirl attractively through the silky finish.–H.S. • $13 • (10/31/1998) • **88**

FRAMINGHAM

Riesling Marlborough Classic 1998: Fresh and juicy. A dry wine with pretty honey-scented apple and peach flavors that linger on the harmonious finish. Drink now through 2003.–H.S. • $14 • (5/15/1999) • **88**

Riesling Marlborough Classic 1997 • $14 • (5/15/1998) • **87**

Sauvignon Blanc Marlborough 1998: Bright in flavor, crisp in texture, with melon, passion fruit and almond echoing on the open finish. Drink now.–H.S. • $14 • (5/15/1999) • **85**

Sauvignon Blanc Marlborough 1997 • $18 • (12/31/1997) • **87**

GIBBSTON VALLEY

Pinot Noir Central Otago 1996: A smooth-textured Pinot, fresh and lively, with pretty plum and currant flavors and spicy overtones of nutmeg and vanilla. Modest tannins don't get in the way. Drink now through 2001.–H.S. • $28 • (11/15/1998) • **86**

Sauvignon Blanc Marlborough 1997 • $19 • (5/31/1998) • **90**

GIESEN

Chardonnay Canterbury Barrel Selection Reserve 1997: Ripe, earthy and polished in texture, this medium-weight wine packs in plenty of apple, spice and cream flavors that linger nicely. Distinctive for its range of flavors and elegant balance. Drink now through 2003.–H.S. • $24 • (12/31/1999) • **90**

Chardonnay Canterbury-Marlborough School Road 1998: Crisp and citrusy, it's a lean wine with racy acidity and a refreshing finish that lingers in a bracing sort of way. Drink now through 2002.–H.S. • $14 • (3/31/2000) • **87**

Chardonnay Marlborough School Road 1997: Bright and zingy, with floral, Riesling-like overtones to the Chardonnay flavors. Finishes with a nice touch of spice. Drink now through 2002.–H.S. • $14 • (11/15/1998) • **88**

Noble School Road Late Harvest Canterbury 1998: Sweet and silky, a lovely dessert wine, with peach, melon, vanilla and floral flavors that linger effortlessly on the light structure. Made from Riesling and Müller-Thurgau. Drink now.–H.S. • $16/500 ml. • (11/15/1999) • **89**

Noble School Road Late Harvest Canterbury 1997: Sweet and focused, reminiscent of golden raisins and honey. Nicely balanced, with citrusy acidity. Could develop well with cellaring. Made from a blend of Riesling and Müller-Thurgau. Drink now through 2008.–H.S. • $18/500 ml. • (6/30/1999) • **91**

Pinot Noir Canterbury 1998: Light and crisp, with pretty strawberry notes and a hint of herb on the chewy finish. Drink now through 2003.–H.S. • $16 • (12/31/1999) • **83**

Pinot Noir Canterbury Barrel Selection Reserve 1996: Has a sense of freshness and brightness, illuminating the currant and spice flavors as they echo on the jazzy finish. Needs to settle down. Drink through 2002.–H.S. • $25 • (10/31/1998) • **88**

Riesling Canterbury 1998: Bracingly tart, with jazzy apple and floral flavors that are definitively Riesling. Drink now through 2002.–H.S. • $11 • (5/15/1999) • **89**

Riesling Canterbury 1997: Bright, vivid and generous, a jazzy mouthful of pineapple, citrus and floral flavors that linger on the crisp, open-textured finish. Drink now through 2002.–H.S. • $12 • (11/15/1998) • **90**

Sauvignon Blanc Marlborough 1999: Light, bright and refreshing, more citrusy than herbal, with pretty lemon and tangerine notes echoing on the delicate finish. Drink now.–H.S. • $12 • (1/01/2000) • **87**

Sauvignon Blanc Marlborough 1998: Bright and refreshing, with pretty nectarine and green apple flavors, finishing fresh and juicy. Drink now.–H.S. • $11 • (1/31/1999) • **86**

Sauvignon Blanc Marlborough 1997 • $12 • (3/31/1998) • **88**

GOLDWATER

Cabernet-Merlot Waiheke Island 1997: Light and supple, with pretty plum, currant and sage flavors that linger on the delicately dry finish. Drink now through 2003.–H.S. • $54 • (1/31/2000) • **85**

Cabernet-Merlot Waiheke Island 1996: Smooth and refined, nicely balanced to add polish to a food-wine match. Has a leathery component, echoes berry and mint on the velvety finish. Drink now through 2002.–H.S. • $25 • (5/15/1999) • **85**

Cabernet-Merlot Waiheke Island 1994 • $50 • (10/15/1997) • **88**

Cabernet-Merlot Waiheke Island 1990 • $30 • (5/15/1994) • **84**

Cabernet-Merlot Waiheke Island 1985 • $27 • (7/15/1988) • **73**

Chardonnay Marlborough Roseland 1998: Lively and refreshing, racy, with lime, floral and apple flavors that resonate on the vibrant finish. Stylish without weight. Drink now through 2002.–H.S. • $20 • (3/31/2000) • **88**

Chardonnay Marlborough Roseland 1997: Bright and lively, with herb and lime notes around the edges of the green apple flavors, all lingering jauntily on the finish. Drink now through 2001.–H.S. • $20 • (5/15/1999) • **87**

Merlot Waiheke Island Esslin 1998: Silky in texture and distinctly herbal, with a decadent edge to the modest black cherry and sage flavors. Drink now through 2002.–H.S. • $70 • (1/31/2000) • **87**

Merlot Waiheke Island Esslin 1997: Ripe and spicy, a generous mouthful of blackberry, tobacco, earth and dusty sage flavors that remain concentrated on the solid finish. Drink now through 2003.–H.S. • $80 • (5/15/1999) • **88**

Sauvignon Blanc Marlborough Dog Point 1999: Fresh and lively describe this young New Zealand white, offering up bright apple, nectarine and citrus flavors that linger enticingly on the racy finish. Yummy now.–H.S. • $19 • (1/31/2000) SS • **90**

Sauvignon Blanc Marlborough Dog Point 1998: This young white from New Zealand is bracingly fresh and appealing for its passion fruit, apple and herb flavors that linger on the palate and echo on the finish. Drink now.–H.S. • $19 • (5/15/1999) SS • **90**

GROVE MILL

Chardonnay Marlborough 1998: Bright and jazzy yet supple and generous at the core, offering nutmeg- and vanilla-scented peach, pear and citrus flavors that linger enticingly. Drink now through 2005.–H.S. • $20 • (2/29/2000) • **90**

Chardonnay Marlborough 1997: Crisp, focused and generous, its citrus, apple and green melon flavors lingering nicely on the lively finish. Drink now through 2001.–H.S. • $20 • (1/31/1999) • **87**

Pinot Gris Marlborough 1999: Bright and vivid in flavor, silky in texture, with pretty pear and spice flavors that linger on the smooth finish. Drink now.–H.S. • $20 • (3/31/2000) • **88**

Riesling Marlborough 1999: So fruity and generous that it seems almost sweet, this off-dry white offers big sprays of apple, apricot, floral and mineral flavors that last on the long finish. Drink now through 2005.–H.S. • $15 • (2/29/2000) • **90**

Riesling Marlborough 1998: Fresh and tasty, with yummy green apple, peach, citrus and floral flavors in classic proportion on an off-dry frame. Drink through 2001.–H.S. • $15 • (1/31/1999) • **89**

Riesling Marlborough 1997 • $14 • (3/31/1998) • **90**

Sauvignon Blanc Marlborough 1999: Fresh and lively, with a modest level of citrus and sweet pea aromas and flavors. Finishes juicy and crisp. Drink now.–H.S. • $18 • (1/31/2000) • **85**

Sauvignon Blanc Marlborough 1998: Bright, racy and appealing for its floral and gooseberry flavors, shaded with nice leesy notes, persisting on the jazzy finish. Much more flavorful than a previously reviewed bottle. Drink now.–H.S. • $18 • (6/15/1999) • **87**

Sauvignon Blanc Marlborough 1997 • $17 • (3/31/1998) • **90**

HIGHFIELD

Chardonnay Marlborough 1997: A tart wine, lively, with an earthy streak running through the citrus and bread flavors. Drink now through 2001.–H.S. • $15 • (5/15/1999) • **81**

Merlot Marlborough 1995 • $11 • (6/15/1997) • **83**

Pinot Noir Marlborough Elstree Reserve 1997: Light, fresh and generous with its plum and berry flavors as they sail through the just-firm-enough finish. Fruit echoes attractively on the aftertaste. Drink now through 2002.–H.S. • $29 • (5/15/1999) • **88**

Riesling Marlborough Elstree Brut Reserve 1998: Dry, crisp and zingy, with lime and grapefruit flavors shaded with hints of Bosc pear and floral notes on the finish. Drink now through 2008.–H.S. • $16 • (11/15/1999) • **87**

Riesling Marlborough Waipara 1998: Light and dry, with an earthy, slightly metallic edge to the apple flavors. Drink now.–H.S. • $13 • (5/15/1999) • **82**

Sauvignon Blanc Marlborough 1998: Light in texture, with an herbal edge to the tarry citrus flavors. Drink now.–H.S. • $14 • (5/15/1999) • **84**

Sauvignon Blanc Marlborough 1997: Smooth in texture, with distinctive passion fruit, fennel and apple flavors swirling through the generous finish. Not as tart as some. Drink now.–H.S. • $14 • (1/31/1999) • **87**

HUIA

Brut Marlborough NV: Crisp, focused and silky underneath the fine-textured bubbles, offering immediately appealing pear, spice and toast flavors that linger. Drink now.–H.S. • $29 • (3/31/2000) • **88**

Sauvignon Blanc Marlborough 1998: Lean, silky and impressively smooth in texture, with strongly floral and peppery flavors. Nice apple notes on the finish. Drink now.–H.S. • $18 • (11/15/1999) • **86**

HUNTAWAY

Gewürztraminer Marlborough Reserve 1998: Light and appealing, with an earthy, slightly soapy edge to the modest fruit flavors. Drink now.–H.S. • $15 • (5/15/1999) • **81**

HUNTER'S

Cabernet Sauvignon Marlborough 1990 • $NA • (5/15/1994) • **77**

Chardonnay Marlborough 1997: Ripe flavors on a razor-sharp frame. Snazzy for its green apple, quince and spice flavors that linger on the well-modulated finish. Drink now.–H.S. • $22 • (2/29/2000) • **88**

Pinot Noir Marlborough 1992 • $NA • (5/15/1994) • **76**

Sauvignon Blanc Marlborough 1997: Bright and bracing, jazzy and lively, with citrus and apple flavors, echoing leafy and herbal notes on the finish.–H.S. • $20 • (5/15/1999) • **88**

ISABEL

Chardonnay Marlborough 1997: Open-textured and generous with its apple, citrus and honey flavors on a racy, refreshingly tart frame, finishing ripe and focused. Drink now through 2002.–H.S. • $21 • (5/15/1999) • **89**

Pinot Noir Marlborough 1997: Ripe in flavor and open-textured, with fine-grained tannins weaving through the generous black cherry, red currant and spice notes. Drink now through 2003.–H.S. • $27 • (5/15/1999) • **88**

Riesling Marlborough 1999: Light and fragrant, with floral and lime flavors, finishing crisp and lively. Drink now through 2008.–H.S. • $15 • (2/29/2000) • **86**

Sauvignon Blanc Marlborough 1999: A fresh, straightforward style of Sauvignon Blanc, featuring tangerine, lime and apple flavors, with a hint of green pepper on the finish. Drink now.–H.S. • $18 • (2/29/2000) • **85**

Sauvignon Blanc Marlborough 1998: Fresh and lively, with racy green apple and herb flavors that last on the finish. Drink now.–H.S. • $18 • (5/15/1999) • **86**

JACKSON

Chardonnay Marlborough 1998: Crisp in texture, with exotic tropical fruit, pear and citrus flavors that linger on the bright finish. Drink now through 2003.–H.S. • $17 • (2/29/2000) • **89**

Key: SS—Spectator Selection. CS—Cellar Selection. HR—Highly Recommended. $NA—Price not available. (BT)—Barrel tasting. (A)—Auction Price.
For a key to the tasters' initials, see "How to Use These Listings."
Dates in parentheses represent the issues in which the ratings were published.

Chardonnay Marlborough 1997: A lush mouthful of bracingly refreshing fruit, with lemony pear and apricot flavors on a razor's edge of mouthwatering acidity. Drink now.–H.S. • $19 • (5/15/1999) • **89**

Chardonnay Marlborough Reserve 1997: Smooth in texture, refreshing for its light pear and citrus flavors that pick up hints of honey and mineral as the finish lingers. Drink now through 2002.–H.S. • $29 • (5/15/1999) • **88**

Riesling Marlborough Dry 1998: Dry, with jaunty apple and floral flavors, finishing juicy and fresh. Drink now.–H.S. • $18 • (5/15/1999) • **82**

Sauvignon Blanc Marlborough 1999: Lean and crisp, this jazzy mouthful of pear, herb and grass aromas and flavors lingers on the citrusy finish. Drink now.–H.S. • $NA • (1/31/2000) • **87**

Sauvignon Blanc Marlborough 1998: So youthful, light and lively it almost feels raw, but it's brimming with citrus and apricot notes. Drink now.–H.S. • $18 • (5/15/1999) • **86**

Sauvignon Blanc Marlborough 1997: Lively, jazzy and fresh, delicious and lean, here's a pretty mouthful of pear, apple, passion fruit and herb flavors. Finish goes on and on. 4,000 cases imported. Drink now.–H.S. • $15 • (1/31/1999) • **90**

JINDALEE

Merlot Murray Darling Region 1998: Light and crisp, this pretty wine has tart berry and mineral flavors that linger on the fresh finish. Drink now through 2002.–H.S. • $10 • (9/30/1999) • **85**

KEMBLEFIELD

Chardonnay Hawkes Bay 1997: Ripe and round, a lovely mouthful of peach, vanilla and tropical fruit flavors that echo on the finish. Not a big wine, it's light and gentle. 600 cases imported. Drink now through 2002.–H.S. • $15 • (5/15/1999) • **90**

Gewürztraminer Hawkes Bay 1997: Has pretty Gewürz aromas and flavors, with a streak of honey running through the modestly sweet pineapple and pear, finishing with a touch of rose petal. Drink now.–H.S. • $10 • (5/15/1999) • **88**

Merlot Hawkes Bay 1997: Ripe and generous, a silky-textured mouthful of pretty blackberry and currant, finishing generous and smooth, with more than a hint of spicy oak. Drink now through 2001.–H.S. • $15 • (5/15/1999) • **87**

Sauvignon Blanc Hawkes Bay 1997: Has more polish than most Kiwi Sauvignons, but a bit less flavor as well, with pretty apple and herb notes. Drink now.–H.S. • $12 • (5/15/1999) • **82**

KUMEU RIVER

Chardonnay Kumeu 1998: Bright and refreshing, remarkably lively, offering pretty apple, pear and intriguingly peppery vanilla flavors that expand on the open-textured finish. Shows restraint (for a Kumeu River wine), but the flavors linger long. Drink now through 2003.–H.S. • $33 • (1/31/2000) • **91**

Chardonnay Kumeu 1997: Crisp, bright and generous with its pear, apple and spice flavors, smoothly integrated with hints of vanilla and lemon on the lively finish. Balanced to open up with short-term cellaring; try now through 2003.–H.S. • $33 • (2/28/1999) • **90**

Chardonnay Kumeu Brajkovich Signature Series 1997: Lean, crisp and juicy, with a lively core of nectarine and mineral flavors that keep echoing on the long, tart finish. Drink now through 2002.–H.S. • $15 • (5/15/1999) • **88**

Chardonnay Kumeu Maté's Vineyard 1998: Juicy and elegant. A mouthwatering wine that layers apple, citrus and spice flavors on a delicate frame. Fruit echoes nicely on the finish. Drink now through 2002.–H.S. • $42 • (1/31/2000) • **90**

Chardonnay Kumeu Maté's Vineyard 1997: A ripe and rich New Zealand Chardonnay, beautifully focused to show off its range of pear, lime, orange and mocha flavors and the hints of passion fruit that chime in on the supple finish. Drink now.–H.S. • $42 • (2/28/1999) CS • **92**

Merlot-Cabernet Kumeu 1987 • $18 • (12/31/1990) • **87**

Pinot Noir Kumeu 1998: Distinctively aromatic, this ripe, round Pinot has layers of currant, spice and earth notes plus, unfortunately, a touch of burnt coffee on the generous finish. It will be interesting to see how this develops. Drink through 2005.–H.S. • $35 • (1/31/2000) • **87**

Sauvignon Blanc Kumeu 1997: Lean and herbal, with a raw edge to the citrus, sage and green onion flavors, which remain light through the finish. Drink now.–H.S. • $19 • (5/15/1999) • **84**

LAKE CHALICE

Merlot-Cabernet Marlborough Platinum 1997: Packs a lot of flavor onto a lean but smooth-surfaced structure, with the meaty, smoky berry and herb flavors echoing for a distinctive finish. Not for every taste. Drink through 2005.–H.S. • $24 • (5/31/1999) • **86**

Sauvignon Blanc Marlborough 1997: Bright and jazzy, with a buzz of spice and herb running through the fresh apple flavor and emerging on the finish. Drink now.–H.S. • $17 • (1/31/1999) • **84**

Sauvignon Blanc Marlborough Platinum 1998: Has a spicy edge and a round texture, reflective of barrel fermentation, but not a strong woody character. Citrus and apple come through nicely on the soft finish. Drink now.–H.S. • $23 • (11/15/1999) • **86**

LAWSON'S DRY HILLS

Pinot Noir Marlborough 1997: Supple and smooth, this is generous with its raspberry and smoke flavors. Nicely balanced and seamless through the finish. Drink now through 2002.–H.S. • $24 • (1/31/1999) • **88**

Sauvignon Blanc Marlborough 1999: Lean and lively, here's a racy style of Sauvignon that emphasizes the mineral and floral side of the grape. Finishes crisp. Drink now.–H.S. • $15 • (12/31/1999) • **88**

Sauvignon Blanc Marlborough 1998: Fresh and juicy, with pretty apple and citrus flavors and hints of herb. Drink now.–H.S. • $17 • (1/31/1999) • **85**

Sauvignon Blanc Marlborough 1997 • $14 • (6/30/1998) • **92**

LONGRIDGE

Cabernet-Merlot Hawkes Bay 1997: Lean and racy, with a streak of spice and mint running through the pretty blueberry and currant flavors. Velvety and polished on the finish. Drink now through 2002.–H.S. • $10 • (5/15/1999) • **87**

Cabernet-Merlot Hawkes Bay 1997: Light in weight and chewy in texture, offering a nice range of cherry and herb flavors that linger on the gentle finish. Drink now through 2003.–H.S. • $10 • (1/31/2000) • **84**

Cabernet-Merlot Hawkes Bay 1992 • $9 • (5/15/1994) • **78**

Chardonnay Hawkes Bay 1998: From New Zealand comes this jazzy Chardonnay of impressive value, delivering a lively and refreshing medley of apple, lemon and lime aromas and flavors that linger brightly on the finish. Drink now.–H.S. • $10 • (5/15/1999) • **87**

Chardonnay Hawkes Bay 1998: Ripe and spicy, firm in texture, offering a solid beam of pear, pineapple and nutmeg flavors that echo on the finish. Drink now through 2003.–H.S. • $10 • (3/31/2000) • **88**

Merlot Hawkes Bay 1991 • $10 • (8/31/1993) • **80**

Sauvignon Blanc Hawkes Bay 1998: Light and racy, with an onion skin note along with the zesty green apple and floral flavors. Drink now.–H.S. • $10 • (5/15/1999) • **84**

LYNSKEYS

Pinot Noir Marlborough Wairau Peaks 1998: Bright in flavor and open-textured. A jazzy mouthful of currant, plum, spice and toast flavors that linger effortlessly on the supple finish. Drink now through 2003.–H.S. • $33 • (2/29/2000) • **87**

MARTINBOROUGH

Chardonnay Martinborough 1998: Light and bright, jazzy, with citrus and pear flavors that finish with a flourish of peppery floral notes. Drink now.–H.S. • $27 • (3/31/2000) • **87**

Chardonnay Martinborough 1997: Ripe and spicy, with rich, honey-scented apple and almond flavors that echo brightly on the crisp finish. Drink now through 2001.–H.S. • $27 • (5/31/1999) • **87**

Pinot Noir Martinborough 1998: Light and appealing for its pretty blackberry and cherry on a soft, refined frame. Drink now through 2003.–H.S. • $NA • (1/31/2000) • **84**

Pinot Noir Martinborough 1997: Ripe in flavor, smooth and refined in texture, with pretty currant and blackberry flavors segueing into a crisp finish, where the flavors sail nicely. Drink now through 2003.–H.S. • $27 • (5/31/1999) • **88**

Pinot Noir Martinborough 1996 • $27 • (6/15/1998) • **87**

Pinot Noir Martinborough 1995 • $28 • (4/30/1997) • **86**

Pinot Noir Martinborough 1992 • $NA • (5/15/1994) • **80**

Pinot Noir Martinborough Reserve 1994 • $36 • (11/15/1997) • **88**

Riesling Martinborough Late Harvest 1996 • $19/375 ml. • (3/31/1998) HR • **94**

MATARIKI

Anthology Hawkes Bay Red 1997: Light and silky, a pretty wine on a modest scale, offering plum and spice flavors that echo on the delicate finish. Drink now.–H.S. • $25 • (1/31/2000) • **83**

Chardonnay Hawkes Bay 1998: Fresh, ripe and juicy. A lean wine with a nice mix of pear, honey and citrus flavors that linger and gain in generosity on the finish. Drink now through 2003.–H.S. • $25 • (3/31/2000) • **89**

Chardonnay Hawkes Bay 1997: Bright and jazzy, with orange and lime overtones to the apple and honey flavors at the core. Silky finish. Drink now through 2002.–H.S. • $25 • (1/01/2000) • **88**

Sauvignon Blanc Hawkes Bay 1997: A crisp, citrusy style, with a fresh anise note wafting through the flavor profile. Finishes lean and tight. Needs food. Drink now.–H.S. • $19 • (2/29/2000) • **86**

MATUA

Cabernet-Merlot Hawkes Bay 1998: Ripe and generous, this supple mouthful of plum, currant, dried tomato and coffee notes swirls nicely through the silky finish. Seductive already. Best after 2000.–H.S. • $17 • (1/31/2000) • **89**

Cabernet-Merlot Hawkes Bay 1996: Crisp and appealing for its mature plum, earth and herb flavors that linger gently on the finish. Drink now through 2003.–H.S. • $12 • (5/15/1999) • **85**

Cabernet-Merlot Hawkes Bay 1995 • $NA • (5/15/1997) • **85**

Cabernet-Merlot Hawkes Bay Ararimu 1996: Ripe and generous with its berry and sage flavors, this rich and supple wine has enough tannin to want a few seasons in the cellar. Drink through 2005.–H.S. • $35 • (5/15/1999) • **88**

Chardonnay Eastern Bays 1998: Light and refreshing, with a minty, leafy edge to the modest apple flavors. Drink now.–H.S. • $15 • (5/15/1999) • **85**

Chardonnay Gisborne Judd Estate 1997: Smooth in texture, bright in flavor, long and generous, this lively wine is brimming with apple, citrus and spice flavors that echo beautifully. Delicious. Drink now through 2004.–H.S. • $19 • (5/15/1999) • **90**

Chardonnay Gisborne Judd Estate Innovator 1997: Bright and jazzy, very lively, with apple, lemon, melon and spice flavors that linger enticingly on the delicate finish. Immensely appealing already. Drink now through 2004.–H.S. • $25 • (5/15/1999) • **91**

Chardonnay Waimauku Ararimu 1997: Smooth and polished, rich and spicy, a lively medley of orange, spice, grapefruit and pear flavors that linger seductively on the finish. Drink now through 2003.–H.S. • $35 • (5/15/1999) • **91**

Merlot Hawkes Bay Smith-Dartmoor Estate 1996: Supple and silky, with pretty berry and spice flavors, reminiscent of Pinot Noir, which linger nicely. Drink now through 2001.–H.S. • $19 • (5/15/1999) • **85**

Muscat Late Harvest Hawkes Bay 1996 • $NA/375 ml. • (5/15/1997) • **89**

Muscat Late Harvest Hawkes Bay 1991 • $NA • (5/15/1994) • **86**

Pinot Noir Waimauku 1995 • $NA • (5/15/1997) • **85**

Sauvignon Blanc Hawkes Bay 1999: Lean and spicy, with a peppery edge to its softish apple and vanilla flavors. Drink now.–H.S. • $13 • (3/31/2000) • **85**

Sauvignon Blanc Hawkes Bay 1998: Fresh and appealing for its juicy nectarine and green apple flavors, shaded lightly with herbal notes. Drink now.–H.S. • $15 • (5/15/1999) • **86**

Sauvignon Blanc Hawkes Bay 1997: Light, refreshing, mildly aromatic, with a delicate herbal edge to the citrusy apple flavors. Drink now.–H.S. • $15 • (5/15/1999) • **86**

Sauvignon Blanc Hawkes Bay Matheson Reserve 1998: Crisp and juicy, nicely laced with touches of honey and spice, finishing with a hint of citrus. Not your typical Kiwi Sauvignon Blanc, but a lively drink. Drink now.–H.S. • $16 • (3/31/2000) • **86**

Sauvignon Blanc Waimauku Reserve 1997: Light and refreshing, with pretty floral notes around a core of fresh apple flavor. Drink now.–H.S. • $16 • (5/15/1999) • **84**

MILLS REEF

Sauvignon Blanc Hawkes Bay Reserve 1998: Crisp and citrusy, with modest flavors of lime and herb. Feels subdued for a Kiwi Sauvignon Blanc, but has plenty of charm. Drink now.–H.S. • $16 • (5/31/1999) • **84**

MISSION

Cabernet Sauvignon Hawkes Bay 1997 • $13 • (6/15/1998) • **84**

Cabernet-Merlot Hawkes Bay 1997 • $13 • (6/15/1998) • **84**

Chardonnay Hawkes Bay 1997 • $15 • (5/31/1998) • **86**

Sauvignon Blanc Hawkes Bay 1997 • $12 • (5/31/1998) • **87**

MORTON

Brut New Zealand NV • $NA • (5/15/1994) • **83**
Cabernet-Merlot Hawkes Bay Black Label 1991 • $NA • (5/15/1994) • **76**
Cabernet-Merlot Hawkes Bay White Label 1992 • $NA • (5/15/1994) • **74**
Chardonnay Hawkes Bay Riverview 1997: Bright and juicy, fresh, with apple and citrus flavors that persist on the lively finish. Drink now through 2002.–H.S. • $24 • (5/15/1999) • **88**
Chardonnay Hawkes Bay White Label 1997: Bright and fruity, it's a zippy white with plenty of lemony acidity behind the apple flavors. Drink now.–H.S. • $16 • (5/15/1999) • **86**
Merlot Hawkes Bay Black Label 1995: Firm in texture, with a pickle-barrel note chiming in with the solid blackberry and toast flavors. Finishes with a hard edge. Best after 2000.–H.S. • $32 • (5/15/1999) • **83**
Merlot-Cabernet Hawkes Bay Black Label 1995: Smooth and distinctive for its mint and herbal berry flavors. Has a sense of refinement and harmony on the finish. Drink now through 2002.–H.S. • $32 • (5/15/1999) • **85**
Pinot Noir Hawkes Bay White Label 1996: Light and silky, with pretty cherry and tea aromas and flavors that linger gently on the fine-textured finish. Drink now.–H.S. • $16 • (5/15/1999) • **83**
Riesling Marlborough White Label 1998: Has an interesting earthy edge to the modest apple flavors. Finishes dry. Drink now.–H.S. • $12 • (5/15/1999) • **80**
Sauvignon Blanc Hawkes Bay 1997: Bright and fresh, with juicy apple, anise and quince flavors on a jazzy frame. Flavors persist nicely. 8,000 cases imported. Drink now.–H.S. • $13 • (1/31/1999) • **88**
Sauvignon Blanc Hawkes Bay Colefield 1997: Fresh and fruity, a simple wine with pretty peach and green apple flavors. Not especially varietal, but charming. Drink now.–H.S. • $20 • (5/15/1999) • **85**
Sauvignon Blanc Hawkes Bay White Label 1998: Distinctive for its bright fruit. An intense wine focusing on apple, pear and citrus flavors that linger beautifully on the finish. Drink now.–H.S. • $13 • (5/15/1999) • **88**

MOUNT RILEY

Cabernet-Merlot Hawkes Bay-Marlborough 1997: Smooth, polished and generous with its fresh plum, currant and delicate mint flavors, which persist on the harmonious finish. Drink now through 2005.–H.S. • $12 • (6/30/1999) • **87**
Chardonnay Wairau Valley 1997: Delivers a lot of polish and focus for the price. Lovely for its integration of subtle hazelnut-scented pear and mineral flavors, with a racy edge of acidity on the finish. Drink now through 2004.–H.S. • $12 • (6/30/1999) • **89**
Sauvignon Blanc Marlborough 1998: Bright and refreshing, with clean melon, citrus and pear flavors that linger on the lively finish. Drink now.–H.S. • $15 • (6/30/1999) • **87**

NAUTILUS

Chardonnay Marlborough 1998: Fresh and spicy. A bright mouthful of peach, apple and vanilla-spice notes that linger on the lively finish. Drink now through 2003.–H.S. • $18 • (2/29/2000) • **89**
Chardonnay Marlborough 1997: Smooth in texture, with a nice tension in the balance between ripe fig and honey flavors and citrus and green apple notes that linger on the finish. Drink now through 2002.–H.S. • $16 • (5/15/1999) • **90**
Sauvignon Blanc Marlborough 1999: Bright and refreshing, like biting into a crisp green apple sprinkled with lime juice, finishing with a floral, slightly herbal fillip. Drink now.–H.S. • $16 • (3/31/2000) • **89**
Sauvignon Blanc Marlborough 1998: Fresh and open-textured, with appealing apple and herb flavors that linger softly on the finish. Drink now.–H.S. • $15 • (5/15/1999) • **86**

NEUDORF

Chardonnay Moutere 1998: Light in texture, this is a jazzy wine with pretty floral and citrus flavors. Drink now.–H.S. • $NA • (3/31/2000) • **87**
Pinot Noir Moutere 1992 • $NA • (5/15/1994) • **79**

Key: SS—Spectator Selection. CS—Cellar Selection. HR—Highly Recommended. $NA—Price not available. (BT)—Barrel tasting. Ⓐ—Auction Price. For a key to the tasters' initials, see "How to Use These Listings."
Dates in parentheses represent the issues in which the ratings were published.

Sauvignon Blanc Marlborough 1999: Fresh and appealing for its citrusy pear flavors, opening up on the finish with pretty passion fruit notes that linger. Drink now.–H.S. • $21 • (3/31/2000) • **89**
Sauvignon Blanc Nelson 1997: Earthy and decadent floral flavors on a crisp frame, finishing with tart intensity. Drink now.–H.S. • $17 • (5/15/1999) • **85**

NGA WAKA

Chardonnay Martinborough 1997: Crisp and citrusy, with a lovely wrapping of spice and vanilla around the grapefruit flavors at the center. Drink now through 2003.–H.S. • $25 • (12/15/1999) • **88**
Sauvignon Blanc Martinborough 1999: Bright and appealing for its citrus, apple and herb flavors that refrain from shouting, instead forming an almost refined wine. Drink now.–H.S. • $20 • (12/15/1999) • **88**

NOBILO

Cabernet Sauvignon Hawkes Bay Reserve 1990 • $NA • (5/15/1994) • **62**
Chardonnay Gisborne Fall Harvest 1998: Fresh and generous. A pretty mouthful of green apple, with a touch of honey on the bright, tangy finish. 10,000 cases imported. Drink now.–H.S. • $10 • (1/31/1999) • **85**
Pinotage Huapai 1991 • $NA • (5/15/1994) • **83**
Pinotage Huapai 1988 • $15 • (7/15/1991) • **82**
Sauvignon Blanc Marlborough Fall Harvest 1998: Fresh and lively, with pretty pear, honey and passion fruit flavors that open up and linger on the jazzy finish. 15,000 cases imported. Drink now.–H.S. • $10 • (1/31/1999) • **87**
White Cloud Hawkes Bay 1998: Soft and light, with pretty citrus, cream and apple flavors on a delicate frame. A blend of Sauvignon Blanc and Müller-Thurgau. 25,000 cases imported. Drink now.–H.S. • $7 • (1/31/1999) • **84**

OBSIDIAN

Cabernet-Merlot Waiheke Island 1997: Lean and lively, this jazzy wine has pretty black cherry and raspberry flavors that linger on the finish. Needs to lose the scratchy tannins. Best after 2000.–H.S. • $38 • (6/15/1999) • **87**

OLD COACH ROAD

Chardonnay Nelson Unoaked 1997: Bright and sharp, with lively peach, apple and mineral flavors on a lean frame. Try with seafood. Drink now through 2001.–H.S. • $13 • (5/15/1999) • **86**
Pinot Noir-Cabernet Nelson Classic 1997: Light and simple, an appealing red with modest berry flavors on a crisp frame. Drink now.–H.S. • $13 • (5/31/1999) • **81**
Sauvignon Blanc Nelson 1998: Light and refreshing, with pretty pear, herb and mineral flavors on a steely frame. Drink now.–H.S. • $12 • (5/15/1999) • **85**

OMAKA SPRINGS

Cabernet-Merlot Marlborough 1997: Herbal, vegetal flavors on a polished, silky frame. Not for everyone, but well made within the style. Drink now through 2002.–H.S. • $13 • (11/15/1998) • **85**
Chardonnay Marlborough 1998: Juicy and bright, with lively citrus, green apple and vanilla-spice notes on the vibrant finish. Immensely appealing. Drink now.–H.S. • $13 • (5/15/1999) • **87**
Merlot Marlborough 1998: Firm in texture, with a velvety veneer that lets the ripe blackberry and tar flavors come through nicely on the finish. Drink now through 2002.–H.S. • $15 • (5/15/1999) • **86**
Sauvignon Blanc Marlborough 1998: A lively wine, fresh and juicy, with pretty apple and citrus flavors. Drink now.–H.S. • $13 • (5/15/1999) • **87**
Sauvignon Blanc Marlborough 1997: Vivid and zingy, with citrus, pear and anise flavors cascading along the smooth-textured finish. Flavors linger attractively.–H.S. • $13 • (10/31/1998) • **88**

PALLISER

Chardonnay Martinborough Noble 1997: Dark gold in color, with classic botrytis character in the deeply honeyed aromas. Sweet, but with plenty of acidity to keep the balance on the rich finish. Drink now through 2007.–H.S. • $17/375 ml. • (5/15/1999) • **92**
Pinot Noir Martinborough 1997: Smooth and generous, a pretty mouthful of currant, plum and floral flavors that linger on the velvety finish. Drink now through 2003.–H.S. • $24 • (5/15/1999) • **87**
Pinot Noir Martinborough 1996 • $23 • (5/15/1998) • **87**
Pinot Noir Martinborough 1995 • $NA • (5/15/1997) • **84**

Pinot Noir Martinborough 1992 • $NA • (5/15/1994) • **78**

Sauvignon Blanc Martinborough 1999: A laser beam of grapefruit and grass, bordering on peach, all firmly structured and balanced, with a mouthwatering finish. Drink now.–B.S. • $17 • (6/15/2000) • **86**

Sauvignon Blanc Martinborough 1998: Bright and juicy, with pretty apricot and citrus flavors that echo nicely on the open-textured finish. Drink now.–H.S. • $19 • (5/15/1999) • **85**

Sauvignon Blanc Martinborough 1997 • $17 • (5/15/1998) • **88**

PASK, C.J.

Cabernet-Merlot Hawkes Bay Gimblett Road 1992 • $NA • (5/15/1994) • **73**

Cabernet-Merlot Hawkes Bay Roy's Hill 1996: Smooth in texture, with herb and tobacco flavors that keep ringing, along with tart berry and citrus on the finish. Drink now through 2002.–H.S. • $11 • (5/15/1999) • **83**

Pinot Noir Hawkes Bay 1996: Crisp and juicy, with pretty currant and plum flavors lurking behind a veil of firm tannins. Feels like it can open up with cellaring. Drink through 2003.–H.S. • $13 • (5/15/1999) • **85**

PROVIDENCE

Matakana 1994 • $75 • (3/31/1998) • **81**

REDWOOD VALLEY

Rhine Riesling Late Harvest Nelson 1991 • $NA • (5/15/1994) • **91**

RONGOPAI

Chardonnay Late Harvest Te Kauwhata Botrytised Reserve 1991 • $NA • (5/15/1994) • **88**

Riesling Late Harvest Te Kauwhata Botrytised Reserve 1993 • $NA • (5/15/1994) • **92**

RIPPON

Pinot Noir Central Otago 1996: A pretty wine despite some raspy acidity, light and crisp, with plum and berry flavors and a mint note on the finish. Best after 2000.–H.S. • $27 • (5/31/1999) • **81**

ROWLAND

Pinot Noir Central Otago Jill's Vineyard 1997: Fresh, firm and focused to show off its gamy black cherry and herb notes. Polished texture on the finish lets the flavors unfold. Drink through 2003.–H.S. • $22 • (5/15/1999) • **87**

SACRED HILL

Cabernet-Merlot Hawkes Bay Basket Press Reserve 1997: Distinctive for its supple texture, light for a Cabernet-Merlot blend, with pretty berry, smoke and herb flavors lingering on the smooth finish. Drink now through 2002.–H.S. • $16 • (5/15/1999) • **86**

Chardonnay Hawkes Bay 1997: Bright, fresh and appealing for its harmonious, beautifully integrated citrus, apple and spice flavors that swirl and linger on the elegant finish. Drink now through 2004.–H.S. • $23 • (5/15/1999) • **89**

Chardonnay Hawkes Bay Barrel Fermented 1998: Soft and ripe, with a thick layer of dusky spice flavors between the pear and vanilla notes. Drink now through 2002.–H.S. • $22 • (1/31/2000) • **87**

Chardonnay Hawkes Bay Riflemans 1997: Smooth, spicy and distinctive for its ripe fig and citrus flavors that open nicely as the finish crisps up. Drink now through 2003.–H.S. • $39 • (5/15/1999) • **88**

Chardonnay Hawkes Bay Whitecliff 1997: Light and fragrant, this zippy mouthful of citrus, apple and spice flavors remains focused through the delicate finish. Drink now through 2001.–H.S. • $22 • (12/15/1998) • **86**

Chardonnay Marlborough-Hawkes Bay Whitecliff 1998: Light and juicy, with a spicy, earthy edge to the basic apple flavors. Drink now through 2002.–H.S. • $17 • (1/31/2000) • **86**

Merlot Hawkes Bay Broken Stone 1995: Minty, herbal notes stand out in this generally supple, oak-spicy red, with hints of tomato on the light finish. Drink now.–H.S. • $32 • (12/15/1998) • **82**

Merlot Hawkes Bay Whitecliff 1997: Bright and flavorful, with pretty raspberry and spice. Finishes with pure fruit and a touch of chewy tannin. Drink now.–H.S. • $16 • (12/15/1998) • **87**

Merlot-Cabernet Hawkes Bay Basket Press Reserve 1996: Light and supple, with pretty spice, herb, vanilla and berry flavors in modest proportions that echo on the finish. Drink now.–H.S. • $22 • (12/15/1998) • **85**

Sauvignon Blanc Hawkes Bay Whitecliff 1998: Bright, silky and lively, with pretty citrus and fresh anise flavors that remain zingy through the finish. Drink now.–H.S. • $17 • (1/01/2000) • **86**

Sauvignon Blanc New Zealand Whitecliff 1997 • $16 • (5/15/1998) • **86**

ST. CLAIR

Chardonnay Marlborough 1998: Ripe, focused and juicy, with pear, guava and citrus flavors that remain rich as they linger on the crisp finish. Framed with a fine layer of oak, this is already delicious. Drink now through 2005.–H.S. • $15 • (6/15/1999) • **90**

Chardonnay Marlborough Unoaked 1998: Lean and bright. A juicy wine with pretty nectarine, apple and floral aromas and flavors that linger on the fruit-centered finish. Drink now through 2001.–H.S. • $14 • (5/15/1999) • **87**

Chardonnay Omaka Valley Omaka Reserve 1998: Ripe, spicy and bracing, offering plush pear, grapefruit and honey flavors on a sharp edge of racy acidity. Drink through 2005.–H.S. • $19 • (6/15/1999) • **89**

Merlot Marlborough 1998: Lean and racy, with a grip of acidity around the ripe currant and blackberry. Has a hint of smoke on the finish. Drink through 2004.–H.S. • $15 • (6/15/1999) • **87**

Merlot Marlborough Rapaura Road 1998: Light and open-textured, especially fragrant, with spicy plum and raspberry lingering on the polished finish. Drink now through 2003.–H.S. • $22 • (3/31/2000) • **86**

Riesling Marlborough 1998: Fragrant, with pretty citrus and nectarine aromas and flavors on a slightly raw, if off-dry, texture. Invigorating. Drink now through 2003.–H.S. • $12 • (6/15/1999) • **87**

Riesling Marlborough 1997 • $12 • (6/30/1998) • **90**

Sauvignon Blanc Marlborough 1997: Tart and juicy, with an interesting leesy edge to the green apple and citrus flavors that linger on the bright finish. Drink now.–H.S. • $13 • (5/15/1999) • **88**

Sauvignon Blanc Marlborough Awatere Reserve 1998: This well-mannered Sauvignon Blanc is light and crisp, with lively, citrusy apple and herb flavors in a fresh style. Drink now.–H.S. • $18 • (11/15/1999) • **87**

ST. JEROME

Cabernet-Merlot Henderson 1994: Herbal, vegetal aromas and flavors wind through the modest blackberry and tobacco character. Has plenty to offer in its style. Best now through 2003.–H.S. • $35 • (6/15/1999) • **85**

SANCTUARY, THE

Chardonnay Marlborough 1997: Light and crisp, with anise and other spices adding nuance to the basic apple character. Drink now.–H.S. • $13 • (1/31/1999) • **85**

Sauvignon Blanc Marlborough 1999: Light, lean and juicy, with pretty apple, citrus and mineral flavors that remain tight through the finish. Drink now. –H.S. • $13 • (2/29/2000) • **86**

Sauvignon Blanc Marlborough 1997: Bright and jazzy describes this vibrant mouthful of apple, passion fruit and citrus flavors that linger appreciably on the invigorating finish. A quality quaff and a good price, too. Drink now.–H.S. • $13 • (1/31/1999) HR • **89**

SCHUSTER, DANIEL

Chardonnay Canterbury 1997: Citrusy, floral flavors are distinctive but a little strange, with an aftertaste more reminiscent of flower stalks than fruit.–H.S. • $15 • (11/15/1999) • **78**

Pinot Noir Canterbury 1998: Smooth and elegant, with pretty plum and currant flavors that hint at spiciness on the long, silky finish. Drink now through 2005.–H.S. • $15 • (12/31/1999) • **87**

SCOTT, ALLAN

Chardonnay Marlborough 1998: Ripe in flavor, racy in structure, with pretty citrus-laced pear and spice flavors lingering on the smoothly integrated finish. Drink now through 2005.–H.S. • $18 • (10/15/1999) • **89**

Chardonnay Marlborough 1997: Bright, ripe and generous with its apple, green peach and green mango flavors, shading them with orange and spice notes on the round finish. Drink now through 2001.–H.S. • $18 • (10/31/1998) • **89**

Riesling Marlborough 1998: Dry and aromatic, with pretty green apple, peach and peppermint aromas and flavors that linger enticingly on the bracing finish. Drink now through 2002.–H.S. • $13 • (5/15/1999) • **88**

Riesling Marlborough 1997 • $15 • (2/28/1998) • **87**

Sauvignon Blanc Marlborough 1999: Strong flavors of rose petal, herb and grass permeate this crisp, citrusy white. Odd, but ultimately refreshing. Drink now.–H.S. • $16 • (12/31/1999) • **86**

Sauvignon Blanc Marlborough 1998: Fresh, appealing for its jazzy citrus and melon flavors, this feels almost delicate, with a spray of flavors opening on the finish. Drink now.–H.S. • $16 • (1/31/1999) • **87**

Sauvignon Blanc Marlborough 1997 • $17 • (1/31/1998) • **89**

Sauvignon Blanc Marlborough Vineyard Select 1999: Crisp and focused, offering gooseberry, grass and a hint of earth, turning austere on the finish. Drink now.–B.S. • $11 • (6/15/2000) • **81**

SEIFRIED

Chardonnay Nelson 1998: Fresh and open-textured, a pretty wine, with apple, pear and citrus flavors that linger on the appealing finish. Drink now through 2002.–H.S. • $17 • (1/31/2000) • **86**

Gewürztraminer Nelson 1998: Bright and refreshing for its pineapple, white pepper and floral aromas and flavors. Finishes dry. Drink now.–H.S. • $11 • (5/15/1999) • **86**

Pinot Noir Nelson 1998: Light in color and weight, with spice and weak coffee notes and just a hint of strawberry on the earthy finish. Drink now.–H.S. • $17 • (1/31/2000) • **80**

Pinot Noir Nelson 1996: Light in color and flavor, but nicely proportioned to show off its berry, orange peel and rose petal elements. Finish could be stronger. Drink now through 2001.–H.S. • $17 • (5/15/1999) • **85**

Sauvignon Blanc Nelson 1999: Light and bright, with fresh apple and sweet pea flavors on a modest scale. Drink now.–H.S. • $13 • (1/31/2000) • **85**

Sauvignon Blanc Nelson 1998: Tart and citrusy, with a celery leaf and fennel edge to the racy green apple character. Flavors persist on the lively finish. Drink now.–H.S. • $12 • (5/15/1999) • **87**

SELAKS

Ice Wine Marlborough 1995 • $13/375 ml. • (2/28/1997) • **83**

Ice Wine Premium Selection Marlborough 1999: Sweet and generous with its apricot, spice and honey flavors that remain focused through the lingering finish. A gentle wine with deftly balanced sweetness. Riesling and Gewürztraminer. Drink now.–H.S. • $15/375 ml. • (2/29/2000) • **90**

Riesling Marlborough Ice Wine Premium Selection 1998: Frankly sweet, with honeyed pineapple and Golden Delicious apple flavors on a lean, refined frame. Could have more oomph on the finish. Drink now through 2002.–H.S. • $14/375 ml. • (5/15/1999) • **87**

Sauvignon Blanc Marlborough Drylands Winemakers Reserve 1999: Amazingly delicate, creating a virtual halo of flavor around passion fruit, green apple, gooseberry and all those good tart tastes. Flavors linger enticingly. Drink now.–H.S. • $18 • (1/31/2000) • **90**

Sauvignon Blanc Marlborough Premium Selection 1999: Crisp and fragrant, this Kiwi white delivers a riot of floral and tropical fruit flavors, favoring passion fruit, lime and spicy rose petal notes. Delicious, and affordable, too. Drink now.–H.S. • $13 • (1/31/2000) HR • **91**

Sauvignon Blanc Marlborough Premium Selection 1998: Light, bright and refreshing, a pretty mouthful of citrus and herb flavors that echo on the finish. Drink now.–H.S. • $12 • (5/15/1999) • **86**

SERESIN

Chardonnay Marlborough 1998: Crisp and bright up front, with sappy pear and floral flavors that finish with grace and refinement. Drink now through 2004.–H.S. • $22 • (11/30/1999) • **87**

Chardonnay Marlborough 1997: Light, bright and refreshing for its pretty pear and apple character. Has an earthy streak that evolves into pretty honey and caramel notes on the finish. Drink now through 2001.–H.S. • $22 • (5/31/1999) • **90**

Key: SS—Spectator Selection. CS—Cellar Selection. HR—Highly Recommended. $NA—Price not available. (BT)—Barrel tasting. Ⓐ—Auction Price. For a key to the tasters' initials, see "How to Use These Listings." **Dates in parentheses represent the issues in which the ratings were published.**

Chardonnay Marlborough Limited Release Reserve 1997: Earthy and tangy, with tart pineapple and toffee notes ringing on the finish. Drink through 2002.–H.S. • $26 • (5/31/1999) • **86**

Pinot Noir Marlborough 1997: Light in texture, with modest berry character and hints of root beer sneaking into the aromas and flavors. Fruit persists on the finish. Drink now through 2001.–H.S. • $38 • (5/31/1999) • **86**

Sauvignon Blanc Marlborough 1998: Bright and racy, with pretty lime and mineral flavors on a tart frame. A lively drink. 900 cases imported. Drink now.–H.S. • $19 • (5/31/1999) • **87**

SHEPHERDS RIDGE

Merlot Hawkes Bay 1998: Crisp and appealing without having any sharp edges, folding its ripe, smoky black currant flavors around a smooth frame. Drink now through 2002.–H.S. • $13 • (1/31/2000) • **86**

Sauvignon Blanc Marlborough 1999: Bright, jazzy and yummy, with passion fruit, citrus and pear aromas and flavors on a racy frame, this New Zealand white is quite impressive for the price. Lean, lithe and exciting. Drink now. –H.S. • $12 • (1/31/2000) • **90**

SHERWOOD ESTATE

Pinot Noir Canterbury-Marlborough Reserve 1998: Light and silky, offering delicate raspberry and sweet leather flavors that linger enticingly on the crisp finish. Drink now through 2002.–H.S. • $17 • (2/29/2000) • **86**

SHINGLE PEAK

Chardonnay Marlborough 1997: Crisp in texture, with odd celery and green pepper notes sneaking in among the citrus and apple. Drink now.–H.S. • $14 • (5/15/1999) • **83**

Pinot Gris Marlborough 1998: Bright and refreshing, brimming with lemon, pear and spice flavors that linger on the generous finish. Drink now.–H.S. • $15 • (3/31/2000) • **88**

Pinot Gris Marlborough 1997: Light, soft and pretty, with melon and spice character. Drink now, while it's fresh.–H.S. • $14 • (5/15/1999) • **85**

Pinot Noir Marlborough 1998: Light and silky, a pretty red, with modest blackberry and vanilla flavors. Drink now through 2002.–H.S. • $16 • (1/31/2000) • **82**

Pinot Noir Marlborough 1997: Ripe in flavor, light and supple in texture, with pretty stewed-plum and mineral flavors that finish soft. Drink now through 2001.–H.S. • $15 • (5/15/1999) • **85**

Riesling Marlborough 1998: Light, tart and minerally, with pretty apricot and peach notes floating around the edges. Drink now.–H.S. • $17 • (5/15/1999) • **85**

Riesling Marlborough Botrytis 1997: Ripe, racy and flavorful, with pineapple, pear and honey character. Balanced, with jazzy lime and tart berry on the persistent finish. Yummy now. Best from 2001 through 2010.–H.S. • $23/375 ml. • (6/30/1999) • **91**

Sauvignon Blanc Marlborough 1999: This bright, vibrant wine offers layers of citrus, nectarine and apple flavors that linger on the jazzy finish. Drink now.–H.S. • $15 • (3/31/2000) • **88**

Sauvignon Blanc Marlborough 1998: A pretty wine, rife with apple and citrus flavors, finishing with echoes of the fruit on a generous frame. Drink now.–H.S. • $15 • (5/15/1999) • **87**

SINCLAIR

Sauvignon Blanc Marlborough 1997: Aromatic with peach, passion fruit and delicate herbal tones and pretty, citrus-centered flavors, all echoing on the artfully balanced finish. Drink now through 2001.–H.S. • $15 • (5/15/1999) • **91**

SPENCER HILL

Chardonnay Marlborough Brentwood Vineyard 1998: A medium-weight Chardonnay, not exuberant but offering some dusky spiced apple and honey notes that linger on the finish. Drink now.–H.S. • $19 • (12/31/1999) • **85**

Sauvignon Blanc New Zealand Evan's Vineyard Moutere 1998: Subdued for a New Zealand Sauvignon, but with some pretty herb and apple flavors on a simple frame. Drink now.–H.S. • $16 • (12/31/1999) • **82**

Sauvignon Blanc New Zealand Evan's Vineyard Moutere 1997: Softer and spicier than most Kiwi Sauvignon Blancs, showing distinct flavors reminiscent of barrel fermentation, finishing with pretty orange, honey and vanilla notes among the herbs. Drink now.–H.S. • $15 • (10/31/1998) • **86**

STONELEIGH

Cabernet Sauvignon Marlborough 1991 • $NA • (5/15/1994) • **75**

Chardonnay Marlborough 1998: Light and fruity, a zesty wine bubbling over with citrusy flavors; somewhat reminiscent of Sauvignon Blanc. Drink now.–H.S. • $10 • (5/15/1999) • **87**

Sauvignon Blanc Marlborough 1999: This New Zealand-grown value boasts an intriguing range of flavors, with a profile centering around apricot, orange and lime and a distinctly herbal character sneaking in on the finish. Drink now.–H.S. • $11 • (2/29/2000) • **87**

Sauvignon Blanc Marlborough 1998: New Zealand's Sauvignon Blancs are making a splash, and this one provides an affordable test-drive. It's bright and racy, delivering a bracing mouthful of citrus, herb and green apple flavors that linger on the tart finish. Enjoy now.–H.S. • $10 • (5/15/1999) • **86**

STONYRIDGE

Cabernets Larose Waiheke Island 1995 • $50 • (4/30/1997) • **87**

TASMAN BAY

Chardonnay Marlborough 1998: Silky and polished, with a spicy edge to the pretty pear and lime flavors, harmonious and balanced on the lingering finish. Drink now through 2003.–H.S. • $15 • (1/31/2000) • **89**

Chardonnay Marlborough 1997: Starts off crisp, but gains in generosity as the pear, nectarine and spice flavors pick up speed on the finish. Nicely done.–H.S. • $16 • (10/31/1998) • **86**

Sauvignon Blanc Marlborough 1998: Light and herbal, with citrusy flavors and peppery overtones reminiscent of dying flower petals. Drink now.–H.S. • $13 • (12/31/1999) • **84**

Sauvignon Blanc Nelson Oak Aged 1997 • $14 • (5/31/1998) • **88**

TE AWA FARM

Cabernet Sauvignon-Merlot-Cabernet Franc Hawkes Bay Longlands 1997: Smooth and pretty, with generous raspberry and chocolate notes singing on the elegant finish. Drink now through 2002.–H.S. • $15 • (5/15/1999) • **86**

Cabernet-Merlot Hawkes Bay Longlands 1996 • $15 • (2/28/1998) • **88**

Cabernet-Merlot-Cabernet Franc Hawkes Bay Longlands 1998: Ripe, round and generous with its plum and spice flavors, finishing with a nice hint of toasty oak and a touch of herb. Harmonious and complete. Best after 2000.–H.S. • $15 • (12/31/1999) • **87**

Chardonnay Hawkes Bay Frontier 1998: Light and appealing for its modest scale and pretty apple and spice flavors that linger on the gentle finish. Drink now.–H.S. • $22 • (12/31/1999) • **85**

Merlot Hawkes Bay Boundary 1996: An elegant, refined red with pretty red pepper-scented currant and spice flavors, picking up a hint of tomato on the supple finish. Drink now through 2004.–H.S. • $22 • (1/31/1999) • **88**

Merlot Hawkes Bay Longlands 1998: Firm in texture, with chewy tannins around a core of floral and berry flavors. Has a dill-like edge, finishing with a sense of refinement. Drink now through 2004.–H.S. • $15 • (12/31/1999) • **86**

Merlot Hawkes Bay Longlands 1997: Ripe and focused, delivering a generous mouthful of blackberry, currant, chocolate and spice flavors. Everything lingers enticingly on the plush finish. Drink now through 2004.–H.S. • • (5/15/1999) • **89**

Merlot Hawkes Bay Longlands 1996 • $15 • (2/28/1998) • **87**

Sauvignon Blanc Hawkes Bay Longlands 1998: Zesty and refreshing, with citrus-scented pear and herb flavors that linger appreciably on the open-textured finish. Drink now.–H.S. • $12 • (5/15/1999) • **87**

TE KAIRANGA

Chardonnay Martinborough Reserve 1997: Bright and lively, brimming with crisp apple and tart pineapple flavors that linger on the refreshing finish. Drink now through 2004.–H.S. • $20 • (1/31/2000) • **88**

Pinot Noir Martinborough 1996: Firm in texture, light, with bright blackberry and currant flavors and a hint of mushroom under a layer of chewy tannin. Best after 2000.–H.S. • $16 • (5/15/1999) • **86**

Pinot Noir Martinborough Reserve 1997: Appealingly light and velvety, with a nice core of ripe currant and blackberry flavors that linger on the open-textured finish. Drink now through 2003.–H.S. • $24 • (1/31/2000) • **88**

TE MATA

Cabernet-Merlot Hawkes Bay 1998: Ripe, lively and remarkably elegant and refined, this has distinctive herb- and cedar-scented currant and raspberry flavors that keep spilling over on the long finish. Drink now through 2010.–H.S. • $20 • (11/15/1999) • **90**

Cabernet-Merlot Hawkes Bay Coleraine 1991 • $NA • (5/15/1994) • **87**

Chardonnay Hawkes Bay 1998: Fresh and juicy, this lively mouthful of citrus and nectarine flavors lingers on the beautifully focused finish. A vivid wine linked with refinement. Drink now through 2004.–H.S. • $20 • (11/15/1999) • **90**

Sauvignon Blanc Hawkes Bay Castle Hill 1997: Crisp and lively, with beautifully focused, apricot-scented apple and passion fruit flavors that remain balanced and open-textured through the finish. Drink now.–H.S. • $17 • (5/15/1999) • **90**

TERRACE VIEW

Cabernet-Merlot Hawkes Bay 1997: Bright and crisp, with racy, up-front raspberry, currant and herb flavors that persist on the lively finish. Drink now through 2002.–H.S. • $12 • (5/15/1999) • **87**

Chardonnay Hawkes Bay 1997: Light, supple and refreshing for its nectarine, citrus and vanilla flavors that linger on the gentle finish. Drink now.–H.S. • $12 • (5/15/1999) • **86**

Sauvignon Blanc Hawkes Bay 1998: An odd, earthy-musty note intrudes on the herbal pear flavors. Not pleasant. Tasted twice, with consistent notes.–H.S. • $10 • (11/15/1999) • **70**

THORNBURY

Chardonnay Hawkes Bay 1998: Silky and vibrant, not a big style but showing refinement with its sappy apple and almond flavors and lithe frame. Drink now through 2004.–H.S. • $17 • (10/15/1999) • **87**

Merlot Hawkes Bay 1998: Bright and racy, this jazzy red offers mint- and bay leaf-scented berry and plum flavors that linger lightly on the finish. Drink now.–H.S. • $24 • (10/15/1999) • **87**

Sauvignon Blanc Marlborough 1999: Lively in flavor and delicate in texture, offering lovely passion fruit, citrus, floral and spice flavors that echo nicely on the long finish. Drink now.–H.S. • $17 • (12/31/1999) • **90**

Sauvignon Blanc Marlborough 1998: Ripe in flavor and bracing in texture, this vibrant wine has tiers of passion fruit, citrus, apple and herb flavors that linger impressively on the graceful finish. Drink now.–H.S. • $23 • (11/15/1999) • **88**

TOHU

Chardonnay Gisborne 1999: Bright and refreshing, brimming with peach, melon and grapefruit flavors that remain lively through the jazzy finish. Drink now through 2005.–H.S. • $16 • (12/31/1999) • **88**

Sauvignon Blanc Gisborne 1999: A softer style of Sauvignon, offering pretty melon and herb flavors on a medium frame. Drink now.–H.S. • $15 • (12/31/1999) • **86**

TRINITY HILL

Cabernet-Merlot Hawkes Bay Gimblett Road 1997: Ripe in flavor, chewy in texture, concentrating its currant, berry and herb flavors on a frame bristling with fine-textured tannins. Needs time to come together. 56 cases imported. Best after 2001.–H.S. • $30 • (5/31/1999) • **88**

Chardonnay Hawkes Bay Gimblett Road 1997: Bright and zingy, with crisp texture and a dusky spice edge to the apple cider flavors. Picks up a lovely honeyed note on the delicate finish. 30 cases imported. Drink now through 2001.–H.S. • $30 • (5/31/1999) • **88**

Chardonnay Hawkes Bay Shepherds Croft 1998: Smooth and round, a nice, open-textured white, with pretty nectarine and floral flavors that echo on the finish. Drink now through 2002.–H.S. • $18 • (1/31/2000) • **86**

Merlot-Cabernet Franc-Syrah Hawkes Bay Shepherds Croft 1998: A crisp, earthy red, with interesting currant and herb flavors, finishing with a dusty character. Best after 2000.–H.S. • $18 • (11/30/1999) • **83**

Riesling Wairarapa 1999: Lean and crisp, with simple floral and mineral flavors lingering on the soft finish. Drink now.–H.S. • $16 • (2/29/2000) • **80**

Sauvignon Blanc Hawkes Bay Shepherds Croft 1999: Light, bright and zingy, this is appealing for its pure apple, citrus and pear flavors that linger on the bright finish. Drink now.–H.S. • $16 • (1/31/2000) • **88**

TRINITY HILL

Syrah Hawkes Bay Gimblett Road 1998: Smooth, silky and generous with its grapey blackberry flavors. Has a nice touch of smoke on the polished finish. Appealing now; best from 2001 through 2006.–H.S. • $37 • (1/31/2000) • **88**

Sauvignon Blanc Marlborough Private Bin 1999: Crisp, refreshing and lively, with citrus, green pear and sweet pea aromas and flavors. Lingers nicely on the crisp finish. Drink now.–H.S. • $NA • (1/31/2000) • **88**

UNISON

Hawkes Bay 1998: Lean and smooth, with a strong minty-herbal component coursing through the berry and chocolate flavors. A blend of Merlot, Cabernet Sauvignon and Syrah. Drink now through 2003.–H.S. • $25 • (12/15/1999) • **86**

VAVASOUR

Cabernet Sauvignon Marlborough Reserve 1991 • $NA • (5/15/1994) • **84**

Chardonnay Awatere Valley 1997: Light, bright and juicy, its pretty citrus, green pineapple and vanilla notes harmonizing nicely on the crisp finish. Drink now through 2004.–H.S. • $24 • (5/15/1999) • **87**

Pinot Noir New Zealand Reserve 1992 • $NA • (5/15/1994) • **74**

Riesling Awatere Valley 1998: Lean and tart, this dry style has strong floral and mineral overtones to the green apple flavor. Drink now through 2004.–H.S. • $17 • (11/15/1999) • **84**

Sauvignon Blanc Awatere Valley 1998: Fresh and generous with its apple and citrus flavors, this offers distinctive leafy overtones and hints of black pepper and spicy oak around the edges. Drink now.–H.S. • $20 • (11/15/1999) • **87**

Sauvignon Blanc Awatere Valley 1997: Tart and lively, with racy gooseberry and green apple flavor that just doesn't quit. A full-steam-ahead Sauvignon, not for every taste. Drink now.–H.S. • $20 • (5/15/1999) • **87**

Sauvignon Blanc Awatere Valley Single Vineyard 1997: Light and fragrant, lively, with green apple and passion fruit flavors that ease gently into the slightly raw finish. Drink now.–H.S. • $23 • (5/15/1999) • **86**

VILLA MARIA

Cabernet Sauvignon Auckland Reserve 1986 • $30 • (7/15/1988) • **74**

Cabernet Sauvignon Hawkes Bay Private Bin 1992 • $NA • (5/15/1994) • **74**

Cabernet Sauvignon Hawkes Bay Reserve 1990 • $NA • (5/15/1994) • **78**

Cabernet-Merlot Hawkes Bay Cellar Selection 1996: Bright and flavorful, showing nicely focused currant and plum flavors on a crisp background, finishing with a supple texture. Tempting now.Drink through 2005.–H.S. • $20 • (5/15/1999) • **88**

Cabernet-Merlot Hawkes Bay Reserve 1991 • $NA • (5/15/1994) • **84**

Chardonnay Marlborough Reserve 1998: Elegant, silky and ripe, this lovely mouthful of pear, nutmeg, vanilla and floral flavors lingers enticingly on the long, gentle finish. Beautifully built to age gracefully. Drink through 2008.–H.S. • $30 • (1/31/2000) • **91**

Chardonnay Marlborough Reserve 1997: Bright in flavor, appealing for its focused green apple and spice tones that echo, with hints of lime and mineral, on the finish. 250 cases imported. Drink now through 2001.–H.S. • $30 • (5/15/1999) • **89**

Chardonnay New Zealand Private Bin 1998: Crisp and lively, with pretty pear and toast flavors, finishing with a citrusy edge. Drink now.–H.S. • $14 • (5/15/1999) • **85**

Merlot-Cabernet Hawkes Bay Cellar Selection 1995 • $20 • (7/31/1997) • **83**

Merlot-Cabernet Hawkes Bay Reserve 1995 • $37 • (7/31/1997) • **87**

Riesling Marlborough Private Bin 1998: Fresh and vibrant, juicy, with apple, pear, citrus and white pepper aromas and flavors. Finishes smooth and open-textured. Drink now through 2004.–H.S. • $11 • (5/15/1999) • **89**

Sauvignon Blanc Hawkes Bay Private Bin 1998: Bright and fruity, with straightforward apple, peach and passion fruit flavors that stay fresh through the finish. Drink now.–H.S. • $11 • (5/15/1999) • **87**

Sauvignon Blanc Marlborough Cellar Selection 1997: Refreshingly juicy, with pretty floral overtones adding nuance to the passion fruit, apple and pineapple flavors on a remarkably elegant frame, all overflowing into the finish. Drink now.–H.S. • $18 • (5/15/1999) HR • **90**

Sauvignon Blanc Marlborough Clifford Bay Reserve 1998: Fresh and lively, with nice hints of gooseberry and citrus on a bracingly tart frame. Needs food to balance. Drink now.–H.S. • $26 • (5/31/1999) • **87**

WAIHEKE

Cabernet-Merlot Waiheke Island te motu 1996: Firm in texture and pure in flavor, centering around lovely currant, plum and delicately spicy flavors that remain vibrant through the supple finish. Drink through 2010.–H.S. • $48 • (6/15/1999) • **90**

WAIMARAMA

Cabernet-Merlot Hawkes Bay 1992 • $NA • (5/15/1994) • **81**

WAIRAU RIVER

Riesling Marlborough Botrytised Reserve 1998: Sweet and silky, with pretty pineapple, tangerine, honey and spice flavors and just a hint of a vinegar note on the finish. Has a sense of balance and elegance. Drink now through 2010.–H.S. • $50/375 ml. • (11/15/1999) • **92**

Sauvignon Blanc Marlborough 1997 • $20 • (6/30/1998) • **89**

Sauvignon Blanc Marlborough Reserve 1997: Unusual for New Zealand with its spicy, barrel-fermentation flavors and polished texture. There's enough racy herb and citrus notes to keep it interesting, and it finishes with style. Drink now.–H.S. • $28 • (5/15/1999) • **89**

WHITEHAVEN

Pinot Noir Marlborough 1997: Crisp and juicy, with anise-scented currant and plum flavors on a racy frame. Tannins don't get in the way. Has a sense of refinement. Drink through 2004.–H.S. • $19 • (5/15/1999) • **86**

Sauvignon Blanc Marlborough 1998: Light and jazzy, with pretty herb and melon flavors up front and a nice hint of citrus on the finish. Drink now.–H.S. • $15 • (6/30/1999) • **86**

WITHER HILLS

Chardonnay Marlborough 1998: Crisp and refreshing, this simple style has green apple and floral flavors. Feels a bit raw, but should settle down quickly. Drink now through 2002.–H.S. • $18 • (1/31/2000) • **86**

Sauvignon Blanc Marlborough 1998: Herbal, minty aromas make this distinctive, and the fresh apple flavors weave through the sweetish finish. Drink now.–H.S. • $14 • (1/31/2000) • **84**

Key: SS—Spectator Selection. CS—Cellar Selection. HR—Highly Recommended. $NA—Price not available. (BT)—Barrel tasting. (A)—Auction Price. For a key to the tasters' initials, see "How to Use These Listings."
Dates in parentheses represent the issues in which the ratings were published.

Portugal

Portugal's claim to greatness rests on Port, and, in all likelihood, always will. However, the singular status of this magnificent fortified, sweet wine should not obscure the ever-improving reputation of Portugal's dry table wines. At their best, they are smooth, full-bodied and ready to drink upon release. With warm and inviting flavors, wines of good to very good quality at bargain prices have become a Portuguese specialty.

Portugal has also been making notable strides at the high end of the price scale. Who would have predicted just a few years back that Portugal would attract an international array of superstar winemakers, and that the most successful efforts, mostly from the Bairrada and Douro regions, would be attracting cult followings? It's strong evidence that, although Portugal's full quality potential is not close to be being realized, it is now considered among the most promising viticultural frontiers in Europe, if not the world.

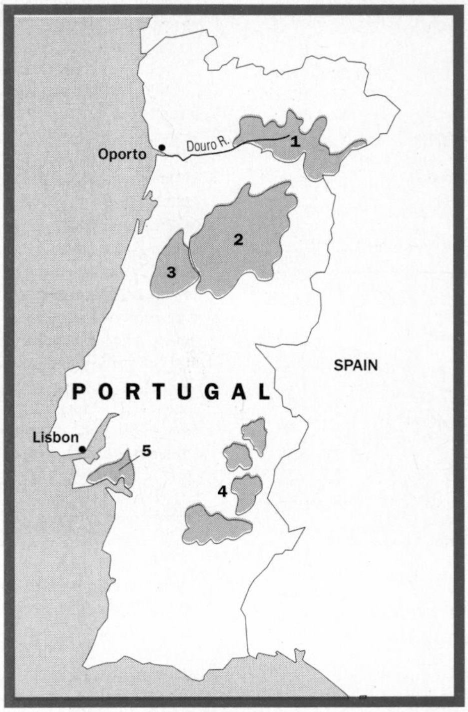

1. Douro
2. Dão
3. Bairrada
4. Alentejo
5. Setubal

PORT

Although many inferior imitations are produced around the world, true Port comes from only from the Douro region of Portugalóan area of steeply terraced hillside vineyards in the upper Douro River valley, stretching from a point about 40 miles east of Oporto all the way to the Spanish border. After vinification and fortification, most new Port is transferred to the shippers' lodges in Oporto for aging and bottling.

True Port is made in several styles, each with differing characteristics. Most of the Ports produced are wood Ports, which means that all significant aging takes place in wood barrels before bottling. Wood Ports are ready to drink upon release and do not require aging in the consumer's cellar. The two basic types of wood Ports are ruby Port and tawny Port. Both are usually blends of different vintages (and are thus designated non-vintage or NV).

As their names suggest, a chief difference between ruby and tawny ports is the color. Ruby is red in color, offering vigorous fruit that tastes fresh and shows little evidence of oxidation. It tends to be a younger wine than tawny, and is intended to be enjoyed for its freshness, vivacity, and smoothness. Tawny has a light orange/brown color and a more mature character than does ruby Port. The aromas and flavors typically display notes of caramel, orange peel and hazelnuts. Serious tawnies are aged for decades in wood barrels before being bottled and released, and designations of 10, 20 or 30 years old are not uncommon. Fine, aged tawny is a wine of civilized distinction, to be enjoyed in the company of good friends and good conversation.

The most revered and collectible Port is vintage Port. Although vintage Port spends its first two years in wood casks, it is not considered a wood Port. The critical maturation takes place in the bottle, typically over a period of decades in a cool cellar. To be worthy of the term "vintage Port," these wines can only be made in the best years, when the grapes achieve a special ripeness and intensity. Port shippers will then "declare" a vintage, meaning that the best of their production will be made in the unique style of vintage Port—fiery when young, mellow and tender in maturity—and released with a vintage date. The decision to declare a vintage is up to the individual Port house, but there tends to be a high degree of unanimity among the major houses, because houses that declare a vintage too often are regarded by their fellow vintners with derision, if not contempt. Oporto is a clubby community, where personal standing and reputation contribute more to quality than government edict and regulation.

To resist pressure to release more vintage port than is warranted by the quality of the harvest, many important houses have turned to making so-called "single quinta" Ports. These vintage-dated wines are made exactly like vintage Port, but are generally produced in slightly lesser vintages and come from a single estate. Although they sell for significantly less than vintage Port, the quality is often very close, because the grapes are carefully selected from the best vineyards owned or controlled by the house. In their way, single quinta ports are among the finest wine values in the world today.

The fastest growing category of Port is late-bottled vintage Port, or LBV. LBV is a vintage Port bottled later than normal, usually after undergoing about four to six years of wood aging, instead of the two years of vintage Port. The added wood aging softens the rough edges a bit, and good LBV is usually ready to drink upon release, without the need to decant the wine to remove sediment.

James Suckling

Quinta do Roriz, a historic property on the Douro River.

DRY PORTUGUESE WINES

Although the quality potential of the dry red wines of Portugal has long been recognized, progress was stymied by the domination of large merchant firms and lackadaisical winemaking cooperatives. It took small, ambitious producers to prove what Portugal could do when a true commitment to quality was adopted.

Several regions have emerged as leaders. The Dão region, midway between the cities of Oporto and Lisbon, has the longest history of producing good table wines, but from the 1940s through the 1980s quality suffered under a rigid, government-controlled cooperative system. Wineries are now allowed to buy grapes directly from growers and vinify the wines themselves, and quality is improving markedly here as the influence of the old cooperatives fades. Most Dão is red, but about a third is white. Dão reds age well, and it is not unusual to find them drinking well after more than a decade in the bottle.

Though overshadowed by the fame of Port, the dry red wines of the Douro can be delectably potent. Red Douro is made from the same grapes as Port; unlike Port, the grapes are allowed to finish their fermentation in the normal way, without the addition of brandy (which stops the fermentation process before all sugar has been turned to alcohol.) Douro reds take wood aging well. White wines from the Douro can be pleasant, but they rarely satisfy as fully as the reds.

The Bairrada district, located between the Douro and the Dão, has a favorable climate moderated by the Atlantic Ocean. It is producing some truly impressive wines in a big, Rhône-like style. Most wines are made from the Baga grape that is unique to Bairrada, though Touriga Nacional, one of the grapes that forms the backbone of vintage Port, is now being blended in to add color, depth and complexity.

Until recently, the vast Alentejo region in Southern Portugal was known mostly for its light rosés. However, that has changed with the arrival of the Domaines Rothschild (Lafite). Its stylish Quinta do Carmo is very much in the aristocratic "R" (for Rothschild) mold.

Ironically, Portugal's best-known dry white wine, Vinho Verde, which literally means "green wine," is one of its least reliable. Vinho Verde can in fact be red or white, as the "greenness" refers to the youth of the wine rather than its color (although most of the Vinho Verde that is exported is white). White Vinho Verde, made primarily from the Loureiro grape and less often the Alvarinho, can be a delightful aperitif wine, low in alcohol and nicely crisp and citrusy. The red can also be good, but is often rough around the edges. The best bet is to buy from a reputable producer.

ABRIGADA, QUINTA DE

Alenquer 1992 • $8 • (9/15/1996) • **87**

ALIANCA, CAVES

Alentejo Alabastro 1996 • $8 • (8/31/1997) • **78**
Alentejo Alabastro 1995 • $9 • (5/31/1997) • **86**
Alentejo Alabastro 1994 • $8 • (3/31/1996) • **78**
Alentejo Alabastro 1993 • $7 • (4/30/1995) • **84**
Alentejo Quinta da Terrugem 1997: Medium-bodied and smooth, with good concentration of red plum, cedar and spice flavors. Finishes on a smoky note. Drink now.–K.M. • $30 • (6/30/2000) • **85**
Alentejo Quinta da Terrugem 1996: A spicy aroma and flavor dominates this medium-bodied red, with dried cherry notes and tough tannins on the finish.–K.M. • $29 • (1/31/2000) • **79**
Bairrada Angelus Reserva 1994 • $5 • (9/15/1997) • **82**
Bairrada Garrafeira 1995: Firm and still quite tannic, with cherry, leather and tarlike flavors. Finishes with notes of coffee and ripe cherry. Drink now.–K.M. • $14 • (2/28/1999) • **84**
Bairrada Garrafeira 1991 • $10 • (8/31/1997) • **74**
Bairrada Garrafeira 1984 • $10 • (4/15/1994) • **78**
Bairrada Reserva 1996: A smooth, medium-bodied Portuguese red, with ripe dark cherry and leather flavors and a slight stewiness on the finish. Drink now.–K.M. • $6 • (2/28/1999) • **82**
Bairrada Reserva 1994 • $6 • (5/31/1997) • **84**
Bairrada Reserva 1992 • $6 • (4/30/1996) • **77**
Bairrada Reserva 1991 • $6 • (4/30/1995) • **80**
Bairrada Reserva 1990 • $6 • (3/31/1994) • **86**
Bairrada Reserva 1989 • $5 • (6/15/1993) • **79**
Bical Bairrada Galeria 1996 • $8 • (8/31/1997) • **75**
Borba Quinta da Terrugem 1995: Vanilla and a resinous note add dimension to the wild berry character in this firmly structured red that has a chewy texture, but lacks the concentration to repay long cellaring.–B.S. • $22 • (10/15/1998) • **84**
Cabernet Sauvignon Beiras Galeria 1997: Smooth and approachable, with dark plum, berry and black olive flavors. Smoky notes on the finish. Drink now.–K.M. • $10 • (6/30/2000) • **84**
Cabernet Sauvignon Beiras Galeria 1996: A straightforward Cabernet dominated by green olive, with herb and red plum flavors. A bit astringent on the finish. Drink now.–K.M. • $13 • (2/28/1999) • **81**
Cabernet Sauvignon Beiras Galeria 1994 • $10 • (8/31/1997) • **83**
Cabernet Sauvignon Beiras Galeria 1993 • $10 • (4/30/1995) • **79**
Cabernet Sauvignon Beiras Galeria 1991 • $10 • (4/15/1994) • **83**
Chardonnay Beiras Galeria 1997: This full-bodied Portuguese white tastes mature and almost oxidized, with buttery aromas and flavors. Drink now.–K.M. • $13 • (2/28/1999) • **81**
Chardonnay Beiras Galeria 1996 • $10 • (8/31/1997) • **80**
Dão Garrafiera 1989 • $6 • (4/30/1995) • **85**
Dão Particular 1996: This has appealing spice aromas, but it's made in a rustic, almost backward style, with flavors of brick, dark plum and leather and cherry notes on the finish. Drink through 2001.–K.M. • $15 • (2/28/1999) • **83**
Dão Particular 1995: A solid red, rustic in character, with a firm backbone and dusty tannins supporting the cherry and cedar notes. Dry finish.–B.S. • $13 • (10/15/1998) • **81**
Dão Particular 1994 • $10 • (8/31/1997) • **84**
Dão Particular 1992 • $10 • (3/31/1996) • **78**
Dão Reserva 1997: Muddled and stewy-tasting, with dried cherry flavors.–K.M. • $7 • (1/31/2000) • **74**
Dão Reserva 1992 • $5 • (4/30/1995) • **85**
Dão Reserva 1990 • $5 • (4/15/1994) • **82**
Dão Reserva 1989 • $5 • (6/15/1993) • **78**
Douro Foral 1996: Pleasant black cherry and plum notes are supported by just-right acidity and tannins in this balanced Portuguese red. The flavors linger lightly on the finish. A good wine, a good deal.–B.S. • $6 • (10/15/1998) • **84**
Douro Foral 1992 • $8 • (3/31/1996) • **82**
Douro Foral 1991 • $5 • (4/30/1995) • **86**
Douro Foral Garrafeira 1990 • $6 • (4/30/1995) • **87**
Douro Foral Garrafeira 1989 • $6 • (1/31/1995) • **77**
Douro Foral Grande Escolha 1997: A red with an edge. Currant and crushed red berry flavors dominate this lively, medium-bodied wine. Just oozes red plum on the finish, with tobacco notes. Drink now.–K.M. • $15 • (1/31/2000) • **85**
Douro Foral Grande Escolha 1995: A ripe and chewy red that's appealing for its freshness. Good concentration, with plum and dark cherry flavors and cedary elements. Drink now through 2001.–K.M. • $13 • (2/28/1999) • **86**
Douro Foral Grande Escolha 1994 • $12 • (8/31/1997) • **73**
Douro Foral Reserva 1997: Pepper, plum and berry flavors dominate this smooth-tasting red, which ends on notes of spice and mincemeat. Drink now.–K.M. • $6 • (6/30/2000) • **84**
Douro Foral Reserva 1995 • $5 • (8/31/1997) • **79**
Douro Foral Reserva 1994 • $5 • (5/31/1997) • **86**
Douro Foral Reserva 1992 • $5 • (3/31/1996) • **78**
Palmela Particular 1992 • $10 • (8/31/1997) • **78**
Palmela Particular 1991 • $10 • (3/31/1996) • **77**
Terras do Sado Tagra 1998: A thin red, with stewy and menthol flavors and rhubarb notes on the finish.–K.M. • $6 • (1/31/2000) • **77**
Tinta Roriz Estremadura Quinta da Cortezia 1998: Luscious, rich and made in an international style, with plenty of ripe plum and chocolate flavors. A plush red, not particularly complex but a lovely mouthful. Finishes on a soft note of warm cherry pie. Drink now.–K.M. • $33 • (1/31/2000) • **86**
Touriga Nacional Estremadura Quinta da Cortezia 1998: Concentrated and finely sculpted, with loads of ripe plum, dark cherry, berry and spice flavors. Made in a international style yet still well balanced, with a nice minty element throughout and meaty notes. Chocolate and spice notes linger on the finish. Drink now through 2002.–K.M. • $30 • (6/30/2000) • **89**
Touriga Nacional Estremadura Quinta da Cortezia 1997: An impressive effort from Portugal. Thick and well structured, with loads of fruit and leather flavors. Quite young-tasting, with notes of red plum, cherry, currant and bittersweet chocolate. Balanced, with a good backbone of acidity and berry and game notes that linger on the finish. Drink through 2004.–K.M. • $24 • (2/28/1999) • **88**
Trás-Os-Montes Terra Boa 1998: Wow. Check out the deal on this juicy and jammy-tasting red from Portugal, with its fresh berry and pepper flavors that linger on the finish, along with warm brickish notes. Drink now.–K.M. • $6 • (1/31/2000) • **84**

ALVES DE SOUSA, DOMINGOS

Douro Quinta da Gaivosa 1994 • $16 • (8/31/1997) • **87**
Douro Quinta do Vale da Raposa 1995 • $7 • (8/31/1997) • **80**

ARRUDA DOS VINHOS

Arruda 1990 • $NA • (9/15/1996) • **83**
Estremadura Comenda de Sant'lago 1994 • $NA • (9/15/1996) • **83**

AVELAR, QUINTA DO

Bucelas 1997: A cheesy aroma and sharp fruit cocktail flavors don't add up to much. Unbalanced.–K.M. • $NA • (1/01/1999) • **73**

AVELEDA

Douro Charamba 1996: Medium-bodied, with decent red plum and peppery flavors that linger on the finish. Drink now.–K.M. • $5 • (9/30/1999) • **82**
Douro Charamba 1995 • $5 • (8/31/1997) • **81**
Douro Charamba 1992 • $6 • (4/30/1995) • **86**
Vinho Verde NV: A piney, resinous quality defines this wine, which comes off a bit exaggerated but still flavorful. Green peachy notes chime in on the finish. Drink now.–K.M. • $6 • (10/15/1999) • **82**
Vinho Verde Casal Garcia NV: Light, with green apple flavors, citrusy notes on the finish. Drink now.–K.M. • $5 • (1/01/1999) • **81**
Vinho Verde Grinalda NV: A floral aroma and flavor dominates this spicy white, which also has good green apple flavors and some backbone. Drink now.–K.M. • $8 • (10/15/1999) • **84**
Vinho Verde Loureiro 1998: A straightforward white, with flavors of peach and mineral and even some herbal notes. Drink now.–K.M. • $7 • (10/15/1999) • **82**
Vinho Verde Loureiro da Aveleda 1996 • $7 • (8/31/1997) • **80**
Vinho Verde Quinta da Aveleda NV: A bit thin-tasting, with green apple flavors and peachy notes.–K.M. • $7 • (10/15/1999) • **78**
Vinho Verde Trajadura 1998: A basic white, with some decent spicy, appley flavors, but it's a bit coarse around the edges.–K.M. • $7 • (10/15/1999) • **79**
Vinho Verde Trajadura da Aveleda 1996 • $7 • (10/15/1997) • **75**

BARROS

Douro Vilar da Galeira 1995 • $NA • (8/31/1997) • **84**

Late Bottled Port 1994: Rather simple, but good, with raisin and leather aromas and a touch of bark. Medium-bodied and lightly sweet, with a hot finish. Drink now.–J.S. • $16 • (7/31/1999) • **82**
Late Bottled Port 1992 • $16 • (2/28/1998) • **86**
Tawny Port 20-year-old NV • $35 • (2/28/1990) • **96**
Vintage Port 1997: Serious black color. Amazing aromas of black truffles, earth and sweet berries. Full-bodied, medium-sweet, with loads of soft tannins. Long finish. A beauty. Well-done Barros. Best after 2007.–J.S. • $40 • (2/29/2000) • **88**
Vintage Port 1995 • $22 • (4/30/1998) • **87**
Vintage Port 1994 • $20 • (4/30/1997) • **86**
Vintage Port 1991 • $NA • (7/31/1994) • **79**
Vintage Port Quinta D. Matilde 1996: A chewy young Port with berry, earth and plum aromas and flavors. Medium-bodied, with medium to full tannins and a moderate finish. Could do with a bit more fresh fruit. Best after 2003.–J.S. • $32 • (2/28/1999) • **85**
White Port Lagrima NV • $9 • (8/31/1997) • **85**

BLANDY'S

Bual Madeira 5 Years Old NV • $20 • (11/30/1997) • **87**
Malmsey Madeira 10 Years Old NV • $34 • (11/30/1997) • **88**
Malmsey Madeira 15 Years Old NV • $45 • (11/30/1997) • **89**
Malmsey Madeira 5 Years Old NV • $20 • (11/30/1997) • **86**
Sercial Madeira 5 Years Old NV • $20 • (11/30/1997) • **86**
Verdelho Madeira 5 Years Old NV • $20 • (11/30/1997) • **89**

BORBA, ADEGA COOPERATIVA DE

Alentejo 1992 • $5 • (4/30/1995) • **83**
Alentejo Borba 1994 • $5 • (4/30/1996) • **78**
Alentejo Borba 1991 • $5 • (4/15/1994) • **82**
Alentejo Convento da Vila 1995 • $4 • (5/31/1997) • **83**
Alentejo Convento da Vila 1994 • $4 • (4/30/1996) • **79**
Alentejo Convento da Vila 1992 • $4 • (4/15/1994) • **78**
Alentejo Convento da Vila Reserva 1993 • $7 • (5/31/1997) • **76**
Alentejo Reserva 1996: A workmanlike red, with smoke and red plum flavors and cedary notes on the finish. Drink now.–K.M. • $14 • (6/30/2000) • **82**
Alentejo Reserva 1989 • $9 • (4/15/1994) • **77**
Alentejo Reserva 1988 • $7 • (4/15/1994) • **80**
Alentejo Vila Morena 1994 • $5 • (4/30/1996) • **82**
Borba 1996: Like biting into a chocolate-covered cherry, this red is round and appealing, with just a hint of tannins at the end.–B.S. • $5 • (10/15/1998) • **82**
Borba 1995 • $5 • (5/31/1997) • **84**
Borba Reserva 1994: Has a plum and licorice character, chewy texture and good depth, and all the components are integrated. The flavors linger on the finish. Drink now.–B.S. • $9 • (10/15/1998) • **85**
Borba Reserva 1992 • $8 • (5/31/1997) • **85**
Borba Special Reserva Cork Label 1994: Still fresh and lively. A lush black cherry and plum element, soft tannins and balancing acidity make for a pleasant mouthful.–B.S. • $11 • (10/15/1998) • **84**

BORGES

Dão Meia Encosta 1996: Highlights of red cherry and raspberry are elegantly displayed, with lively acidity and a touch of black pepper on the finish. Drink now.–B.S. • $7 • (10/15/1998) • **84**
Dão White Meia Encosta 1996: Crisp, a bit tart, with herbal and peachy flavors. Drink now.–K.M. • $7 • (8/31/1998) • **78**
Late Bottled Port 1992 • $16 • (2/28/1998) • **85**
Vinho Verde Gatão NV: Simple and slightly sweet, with modest green peach flavors. Drink now.–K.M. • $6 • (8/31/1998) • **79**
Vintage Port 1994 • $25 • (9/15/1997) • **81**

BROADBENT

Madeira 5 Years Old Reserve NV: Dark in color, and sweet, this is full, rich and satisfying, with burnt caramel and smoke notes. The sweetness is balanced by vibrant acidity, ending on a clean, almost salty tang. Drink now.–B.S. • $17 • (7/31/1999) • **88**
Madeira Fine Rich NV: Amber-brown in color, with aromas and flavors of coffee and caramel, this is medium sweet and a bit spirity (alcohol), with a nut and coffee aftertaste. Drink now.–B.S. • $13 • (7/31/1999) • **82**
Madeira Rainwater NV: Here's a good introduction to Madeira. Appealing, straightforward flavors of caramel are followed by a tangy acidity and a walnut note on the finish. Drink now.–B.S. • $13 • (7/31/1999) • **85**
Malmsey Madeira 10 Years Old NV: Coffee and toffee are the main themes in this sweet Malmsey. The flavor is reminiscent of crème brûlée and it lacks concentration, ending fairly simple and hot. Drink now.–B.S. • $28 • (7/31/1999) • **84**
Terrantez Madeira Old Reserve NV: Intriguing scents of musk and autumn woods segue into nut and mineral flavors in this elegant, forceful wine. Medium sweet, it builds in intensity, finishing with a bracing acidity. A touch alcoholic yet delicious. Drink now.–B.S. • $48 • (7/31/1999) • **90**

BURMESTER

Late Bottled Port 1989 • $23 • (2/28/1998) • **80**
Late Bottled Port Extra Selected 1994: Intense aromas of raisin and pepper are slightly burning. Full-bodied, sweet and thick, with lots of berry character on the finish. A bit monolithic. Drink now.–J.S. • $30 • (7/31/1999) • **86**
Late Bottled Port Extra Selected 1992 • $21 • (2/28/1998) • **87**
Late Bottled Port Extra Selected 1991 • $NA • (2/28/1998) • **88**
Late Bottled Port Quinta do Carmo 1992 • $NA • (2/28/1998) • **85**
Tawny Port 20-year-old NV • $40 • (2/28/1990) • **95**
Vintage Port 1995 • $22 • (4/30/1998) • **88**
Vintage Port 1994 • $NA • (4/30/1997) • **82**
Vintage Port 1992 • $NA • (6/15/1995) • **85**
Vintage Port 1991 • $NA • (7/31/1994) • **86**
Vintage Port Extra Selected 1997: Fresh and floral, with sweet fruit and a good backbone of tannins. Medium body. Long, chewy finish. Best after 2006.–J.S. • $50 • (2/29/2000) • **89**
Vintage Port Quinta do Nova 1992 • $NA • (6/15/1995) • **87**
Vintage Port Quinta Nova de Nossa Senhora do Carmo 1997: A good, peppery young vintage Port, with medium body, medium tannins and a fresh finish. Best after 2004.–J.S. • $60 • (2/29/2000) • **88**
Vintage Port Quinta Nova de Nossa Senhora do Carmo 1996: A rustic and burly young wine showing a hint of nuttiness. Full-bodied and very sweet, with an alcoholic and musty finish. Could improve, but the funky character detracts from the overall quality now. Best after 2002.–J.S. • $49 • (2/28/1999) • **82**
Vintage Port Quinta Nova de Nossa Senhora do Carmo 1995 • $43 • (4/30/1998) • **80**

CALCOS DO TANHA

Douro 1996: A good, medium-bodied red, with beefy flavors and chocolaty notes. Plum and smoke notes emerge on the slightly drying finish. Drink now with food.–K.M. • $13 • (4/30/2000) • **83**

CALEM

Late Bottled Port 1994: A vivid LBV, with berry, violet and plum character. Medium-bodied, with a soft, caressing texture. Lovely. Drink now.–J.S. • $17 • (7/31/1999) • **88**
Late Bottled Port 1992 • $18 • (2/28/1998) • **79**
Tawny Port 20 Años NV • $35 • (4/15/1990) • **83**
Touriga Nacional Vintage Port 1996: Best young Cálem ever. Inky-colored, with amazing aromas of blackberry, cheery and Christmas puddin. Full-bodied, medium-sweet, with loads of tannins. Has grip. A new single varietal wine from Cálem. Best after 2003.–J.S. • $40 • (2/28/1999) • **91**
Vintage Character Port NV • $16 • (3/15/1994) • **79**
Vintage Port 1997: Black color, with gorgeous aromas of blackberries, cherries and flowers. Full-bodied and medium-sweet, with velvety tannins and a touch of pepper on the long, fruity finish. Best Cálem ever? Best after 2007.–J.S. • $67 • (2/29/2000) • **93**
Vintage Port 1994 • $40 • (4/30/1997) • **79**
Vintage Port 1991 • $NA • (7/31/1994) • **80**
Vintage Port Quinta da Foz 1995 • $19 • (4/30/1998) • **86**
Vintage Port Quinta do Foz 1992 • $NA • (6/15/1995) • **86**
Vintage Port Quinta do Sagrado 1994 • $38 • (4/30/1997) • **89**

Key: SS—Spectator Selection. CS—Cellar Selection. HR—Highly Recommended.
$NA—Price not available. (BT)—Barrel tasting. (A)—Auction Price.
For a key to the tasters' initials, see "How to Use These Listings."
Dates in parentheses represent the issues in which the ratings were published.

CANTANHEDE, ADEGA COOPERATIVA DE

Baga Bairrada Marquês de Marialva Reserva 1995: Distinctive aromas and flavors of wild berries, black pepper and cardamom enliven this dry, tannic red, whose flavors linger on the finish.–B.S. • $12 • (10/15/1998) • **84**

Bairrada Marquês de Marialva Reserva 1994: A dry, rustic red, whose cherry and almond flavors show briefly before the tannins supersede. Past its prime.–B.S. • $5 • (10/15/1998) • **76**

CARMO, QUINTA DO

Alentejo 1996: Dark smoke and cassis notes give way to a firm and focused red that finishes on a bittersweet chocolate note. Should unwind more with either food or short-term cellaring. Drink now through 2001.–T.M. • $25 • (3/31/2000) • **85**

Alentejo 1995: This chewy red shows good intensity, with plum, briar, coffee and game flavors and firm yet ripe tannins. It's both bitter and sweet, but has balance and a distinctive character. Drink now through 2002.–T.M. • $25 • (12/31/1998) • **87**

Alentejo 1994 • $24 • (8/31/1997) • **76**

Alentejo 1993 • $23 • (7/31/1997) • **86**

Alentejo 1988 • $20 • (4/15/1994) • **84**

Alentejo 1987 • $20 • (6/15/1993) • **80**

Alentejo Dom Martinho 1996: Earth, currant, raspberry and coffee notes run through this medium-weight red, with light cedar shadings on the supple finish. Drink now.–T.M. • $14 • (3/31/2000) • **84**

Alentejo Dom Martinho 1995: There's a nice smoky, meaty flavor to this medium-bodied red. Smooth and supple, with a chocolaty note on the balanced finish. Drink now.–K.M. • $12 • (12/31/1998) • **83**

CARVALHO, RIBEIRO & FERREIRA

Dão Quinta do Serrado 1991 • $7 • (4/15/1994) • **84**

Dão Quinta do Serrado 1990 • $7 • (4/15/1994) • **82**

Dão Quinta do Serrado 1989 • $7 • (4/15/1994) • **76**

Douro Reserva 1990 • $NA • (4/30/1995) • **83**

Ribatejo Serradayres 1993 • $7 • (3/31/1996) • **83**

Ribatejo Serradayres 1989 • $5 • (4/15/1994) • **81**

Tràs-os-Montes Garrafeira 1990 • $14 • (3/31/1996) • **74**

CASA CADAVAL

Cabernet Sauvignon Ribatejo 1994 • $12 • (10/15/1997) • **78**

Pinot Noir Ribatejo 1994 • $12 • (10/15/1997) • **79**

Ribatejo 1995 • $9 • (10/15/1997) • **82**

Trincadeira Preta Ribatejo 1994 • $12 • (10/15/1997) • **87**

CASA DE SANTAR

Dão 1997: A stewy red, with muddled flavors and herbal notes on the finish.–K.M. • $7 • (10/31/1999) • **74**

Dão 1996: A balanced, medium-bodied red with interesting animal and red fruit flavors. On the mature side, with rich and spicy notes of cardamom on the finish. Drink now.–K.M. • $7 • (9/30/1999) • **84**

Dão 1994: Mature, showing modest plum and cedar notes. Balanced toward the tannic side. Drink now.–B.S. • $5 • (10/15/1998) • **80**

Dão 1992 • $8 • (8/31/1997) • **77**

Dão 1990 • $7 • (3/31/1996) • **72**

Dão Reserva 1996: This red shows muted plum character and woodsy notes, richly textured and with moderate structure, giving an integrated impression.–B.S. • $9 • (10/15/1998) • **83**

Dão Reserva 1994 • $11 • (8/31/1997) • **79**

Dão Reserva 1992 • $10 • (3/31/1996) • **82**

Dão White 1998: Refreshing and lively, with peachy aromas and flavors that make it a pleasant quaff. Great for a summer picnic. Drink now.–K.M. • $7 • (8/31/1999) • **84**

Dão White 1997: This light white has pineapple and almond flavors and herbal elements on the finish.–K.M. • $5 • (12/31/1998) • **78**

CASA DE VILA VERDE

Vinho Verde 1998: This has some lemon and almond flavors, with butter notes on the finish. Drink now.–K.M. • $9 • (10/31/1999) • **80**

CASA FERREIRINHA

Douro Barca-Velha 1991: A brooding and fairly intense red that still has some spark despite its age, with focused raspberry, plum and leather flavors. Still has plenty of tannin, as well as mature flavors. Powerful and distinctive. Drink now through 2003.–K.M. • $65 • (9/30/1999) • **88**

Douro Reserva 1989: Mature, with good complexity, leather and red berry flavors and nice minerally, smoky notes. Still going strong despite its age, with plenty of blood and iron on the finish. Drink now.–K.M. • $45 • (1/31/2000) • **87**

Douro Vinha Grande 1994 • $22 • (7/31/1997) • **87**

Douro Vinha Grande 1990 • $10 • (4/15/1994) • **83**

CASAL MIRANDA

Vinho Verde NV: Perfumed, with a green, almost minty note and citrus accents, this is crisp and bracing. Drink now.–B.S. • $4 • (10/15/1998) • **80**

CHURCHILL

Late Bottled Port 1994: A very fresh LBV, with violet, berry and cherry character. Medium-bodied and medium sweet, with a fresh fruit aftertaste. Delicious. Drink now.–J.S. • $23 • (7/31/1999) • **89**

Late Bottled Port Traditional 1990 • $19 • (1/31/1996) • **85**

Late Bottled Port Traditional 1988 • $17 • (11/15/1994) • **87**

Ruby Port VC Reserve NV • $11 • (11/15/1994) • **86**

Vintage Character Port Finest NV • $19 • (4/15/1991) • **83**

Vintage Character Port Finest Reserve NV • $17 • (3/15/1994) • **87**

Vintage Port 1997: A bit lean, but shows a good backbone of tannins. Good aromas and flavors of pepper and berry. Medium-bodied, with a mouth-puckering finish. Lacks a bit of grip. Best after 2005.–J.S. • $75 • (2/29/2000) • **87**

Vintage Port 1994 • $35 • (4/30/1997) • **93**

Vintage Port 1991 • $35 • (7/31/1994) • **91**

Vintage Port Agua Alta 1996: This is a big glass of young Port. It's got grip. Intense grapey, berry and violet aromas and flavors. Full bodied and medium-sweet with plenty of tannins and a fruity but tannic finish. Best after 2006.–J.S. • $NA • (2/28/1999) • **91**

Vintage Port Agua Alta 1995 • $40 • (4/30/1998) • **91**

Vintage Port Agua Alta 1992 • $35 • (6/15/1995) • **89**

COCKBURN

Late Bottled Port 1994: Impressive concentration of dried fruit in this LBV. Mature in style but delicious, with raisinskin and bark character. Full-bodied and chewy, with lots of berry and Christmas pudding flavors. A joy. Drink now.–J.S. • $20 • (7/31/1999) • **88**

Late Bottled Port Anno 1992 • $20 • (2/28/1998) • **81**

Late Bottled Port Anno 1990 • $17 • (1/31/1996) • **85**

Ribatejo Serradayres 1996: Mature-tasting, with brown sugar flavors and plummy notes; leathery flavors linger on the finish.–K.M. • $7 • (9/30/1999) • **78**

Ribatejo Serradayres 1994: A licorice note augments the cherry and cedar flavors in this medium-bodied, sinewy red, with chewiness and persistence on the palate. Drink now.–B.S. • $7 • (10/15/1998) • **83**

Ribatejo White Serradayres 1996: A plodding white wine, with modest fruit cocktail and ripe apple flavors.–K.M. • $7 • (12/31/1998) • **75**

Ruby Port Fine NV • $10 • (3/31/1988) • **85**

Ruby Port No. 25 NV • $8 • (3/31/1988) • **85**

Tawny Port 10 years old NV • $24 • (1/31/1996) • **88**

Tawny Port 20 year old NV • $35 • (2/28/1990) • **86**

Tawny Port Directors' Reserve 20 years old NV • $43 • (1/31/1996) • **86**

Vintage Character Port Special Reserve NV • $16 • (11/15/1994) • **84**

Vintage Port 1997: A bit lean, with some good berry, herbal and cherry character. Medium-bodied, with medium tannins and a light, sweet finish. Rather light for Cockburn. Best after 2004.–J.S. • $65 • (2/29/2000) • **85**

Vintage Port 1994 • $22 Ⓐ • (4/30/1997) • **92**

Vintage Port 1991 • $36 • (7/31/1994) • **88**

Vintage Port Quinta da Canias 1995 • $39 • (4/30/1998) • **90**

Vintage Port Quinta da Canias 1992 • $35 • (6/15/1995) • **89**

COSSART GORDON

Bual Madeira 5 Years Old NV • $21 • (11/30/1997) • **88**

Bual Madeira 10 Years Old NV • $35 • (11/30/1997) • **87**

COSSART GORDON

Bual Madeira 15 Years Old NV • $45 • (11/30/1997) • **89**

COTTO, QUINTA DO

Douro 1996: A focused and well-concentrated red with flavors of dark cherry, coffee, plum and blackberry. Smooth, with a good backbone of acidity and a touch of ripeness. Coffee and spice notes linger on the finish. Luscious, and finely crafted. Drink now through 2001.–K.M. • $15 • (1/01/1999) • **87**
Douro 1995 • $13 • (4/30/1998) • **87**
Douro 1992 • $10 • (4/30/1995) • **88**
Douro 1991 • $10 • (4/15/1994) • **87**
Douro Grande Escolha 1995 • $50 • (4/30/1998) • **90**
Douro Grande Escolha 1994 • $40 • (4/30/1996) • **87**
Douro Grande Escolha 1990 • $40 • (4/30/1995) • **90**
Douro Grande Escolha 1987 • $18 • (12/31/1990) • **81**
Douro White 1996 • $12 • (4/30/1998) • **85**

COUTEIRO-MOR

Alentejo 1994 • $5 • (8/31/1997) • **73**
Alentejo Colheita Seleccionada 1994 • $7 • (8/31/1997) • **78**

COVELA, QUINTA DE

Rios do Minho White 1996 • $8 • (9/15/1997) • **83**
Vinho de Mesa Tinto 1995 • $12 • (8/31/1997) • **79**

CRASTO, QUINTA DO

Douro 1995 • $11 • (7/31/1997) • **86**
Douro Reserva 1994 • $15 • (7/31/1997) • **89**
Late Bottled Port 1992 • $19 • (2/28/1998) • **87**
Late Bottled Port Traditional Unfiltered 1994: Rather floral, with a berry and mineral undertone. Medium-bodied and medium sweet, with a balance of tannins and a sweet aftertaste. Very good indeed. Drink now.–J.S. • $24 • (7/31/1999) • **86**
Vintage Port 1997: Racy, young vintage Port. Intense aromas of raspberries and wet earth. Full-bodied and medium-sweet, with chewy tannins and a ripe, raisiny aftertaste. Best after 2007.–J.S. • $56 • (2/29/2000) • **90**
Vintage Port 1996: Elegant and well made. Dark ruby colored with floral, berry aromas which follow through to a medium-bodied palate. Medium sweet with fine tannins and a fresh aftertaste. For early drinking. Drink now through 2003.–J.S. • $40 • (1/01/1999) • **86**
Vintage Port 1995 • $33 • (4/30/1998) • **90**
Vintage Port 1994 • $35 • (4/30/1997) • **93**

CROFT

Late Bottled Port 1994: This cool and refreshing LBV has violets and berries throughout. Medium-bodied, with fine tannins and a lovely fruit finish. A bit simple, but delicate and refined. Drink now.–J.S. • $25 • (7/31/1999) • **87**
Late Bottled Port 1991 • $20 • (2/28/1998) • **83**
Tawny Port 20 year old NV • $38 • (2/28/1990) • **76**
Vintage Port 1994 • $37 Ⓐ • (4/30/1997) • **96**
Vintage Port 1991 • $30 Ⓐ • (7/31/1994) • **94**
Vintage Port Quinta da Roêda 1997: Outstanding quality. Black color, with an amazing nose of blueberries, cherries and wet earth. Full-bodied, with loads of soft, velvety tannins, medium sweetness and a medium finish. Best after 2007.–J.S. • $83 • (2/29/2000) • **92**
Vintage Port Quinta da Roêda 1995 • $45 • (4/30/1998) • **91**

DELAFORCE

Late Bottled Port 1991 • $21 • (2/28/1998) • **86**
Tawny Port His Eminence's Choice NV • $9 • (4/16/1985) • **86**
Tawny Port His Eminence's Choice Reserve NV • $19 • (1/31/1996) • **80**
Vintage Character Port NV • $NA • (3/15/1994) • **81**
Vintage Port 1994 • $18 Ⓐ • (4/30/1997) • **92**

Key: SS—Spectator Selection. CS—Cellar Selection. HR—Highly Recommended. $NA—Price not available. (BT)—Barrel tasting. Ⓐ—Auction Price.
For a key to the tasters' initials, see "How to Use These Listings."
Dates in parentheses represent the issues in which the ratings were published.

Vintage Port 1992 • $16 Ⓐ • (6/15/1995) • **90**
Vintage Port Quinta da Corte 1997: A fruit bomb. Superb single-quinta wine. Excellent dark color, with intense currant, berry and claretlike aromas. Full-bodied, with a big, racy backbone of tannins. Lovely, sweet finish. Best after 2007.–J.S. • $78 • (2/29/2000) • **95**
Vintage Port Quinta da Corte 1995 • $40 • (4/30/1998) • **92**
Vintage Port Quinta da Corte 1991 • $29 • (7/31/1994) • **87**

DOW

Late Bottled Port 1994: Very grapey in style, with hints of violet and floral character. Medium-bodied and medium sweet, with fruit and wet earth on the finish. A bit rustic. Drink now.–J.S. • $17 • (7/31/1999) • **83**
Late Bottled Port 1991 • $20 • (2/28/1998) • **84**
Tawny Port 10 year old NV • $23 • (1/31/1996) • **89**
Tawny Port 20 year old NV • $42 • (1/31/1996) • **89**
Tawny Port 30 year old NV • $73 • (1/31/1996) • **89**
Tawny Port Boardroom NV • $18 • (1/31/1996) • **82**
Tawny Port Fine Tawny NV • $10 • (1/31/1996) • **82**
Vintage Character Port NV • $10 • (3/31/1988) • **89**
Vintage Character Port AJ Vintage Character NV • $19 • (3/15/1994) • **79**
Vintage Character Port AJS NV • $17 • (6/15/1993) • **83**
Vintage Port 1997: This is an exceptionally aromatic young vintage Port, with wonderful floral, berry and violet character. Full-bodied and very firm, with a racy tannin structure. Mouth-gripping, it's close to classic quality. (Dow vertical tasting).–J.S. • $NA • (12/31/1999) (BT) • **90-94**
Vintage Port 1994: A blackstrap, powerful Port. Black, with intense aromas of raspberries, raisins, flowers and stems. Full-bodied and medium sweet, with a long, rich finish. Tannins pull at your palate. A wine for the future.—Dow vertical. Best after 2008.–J.S. • $57 Ⓐ • (12/31/1999) • **97**
Vintage Port 1991: One of the great buys in young vintages of Dow. Dark and powerful, its aromas of ripe berry, cherry and raspberry open to a full-bodied palate, with firm tannins and a long, sweet finish. (Dow vertical tasting). Best after 2005.–J.S. • $45 Ⓐ • (12/31/1999) • **91**
Vintage Port Quinta do Bomfim 1996: Elegant and silky young vintage Port with cherry, berry and plum aromas and flavors. Medium-bodied, with medium tannins and a fresh finish. Would be outstanding with a bit more oomph. Best after 2003.–J.S. • $NA • (2/28/1999) • **86**
Vintage Port Quinta do Bomfim 1995 • $38 • (4/30/1998) • **90**
Vintage Port Quinta do Bomfim 1992 • $30 • (6/30/1995) • **92**
Vintage Port Quinta do Bomfim 1990 • $31 • (1/31/1993) • **86**
Vintage Port Quinta do Bomfim 1989 • $24 • (11/30/1991) CS • **90**

DUFF GORDON

Vintage Port 1995 • $40 • (4/30/1998) • **87**
Vintage Port 1994: A late arrival '94 for the U.S. market. Inky colored with plenty of crushed raspberry and orange peel character on the nose. Full-bodied and sweet, with big, soft tannins and a long, chocolatey aftertaste. Best from 2005 through 2015.–J.S. • $40 • (1/01/1999) • **89**

ESPORAO, HERDADE DO

Alentejo Monte Velho 1996 • $8 • (9/15/1997) • **80**
Alentejo Monte Velho 1992 • $7 • (3/31/1996) • **82**
Alentejo White Monte Velho 1996 • $7 • (9/15/1997) • **83**
Reguengos 1993 • $12 • (10/15/1997) • **85**

FEIST

Douro 1995: Balanced and ready to drink, with red plum, dried cherry and leather notes. Drink now.–K.M. • $8 • (9/30/1999) • **83**
Late Bottled Port 1994: Earthy and spicy but a bit oxidized, with pepper, leather and cedar character. Medium-bodied, sweet and juicy, with a nutty finish. Tastes older than it is. Drink now.–J.S. • $18 • (7/31/1999) • **81**
Vintage Port 1997: Pleasant, soft young Port. Good aromas of grape skins and mineral follow through to a medium-bodied palate, with soft tannins and a medium finish. Best after 2003.–J.S. • $28 • (2/29/2000) • **86**
Vintage Port 1995 • $25 • (4/30/1998) • **90**
Vintage Port 1991 • $26 • (7/31/1994) • **83**

FELGUEIRAS, COOPERATIVA AGRICOLA DE

Vinho Verde NV • $5 • (8/31/1997) • **82**

FERREIRA

Douro Barca Velha 1983 • $35 • (4/15/1994) • **89**
Late Bottled Port 1994: More on the nose than the palate, with powerful and rich aromas of berry, cherry and plum and hints of wet earth. Medium-bodied and medium sweet, with a light, fruity finish. Drink now.–J.S. • $20 • (7/31/1999) • **86**
Late Bottled Port 1991 • $19 • (2/28/1998) • **86**
Tawny Port Duque de Bragança 20 Years Old NV • $49 • (1/31/1996) • **73**
Tawny Port Quinta do Porto 10 Years Old NV • $25 • (1/31/1996) • **81**
Vintage Port 1997: Very pretty aromas of raspberries, violets and cherries. Full-bodied and very sweet, with big, soft tannins and a long, velvety, sweet fruit finish. Best after 2008.–J.S. • $49 • (2/29/2000) • **91**
Vintage Port 1995 • $37 • (4/30/1998) • **90**
Vintage Port 1994 • $42 • (4/30/1997) • **89**
Vintage Port 1991 • $19 • (7/31/1994) • **91**

FEUERHEERD

Vintage Port 1997: Wonderful aromas of licorice, plums and violets. Medium- to full-bodied, with silky tannins and a fresh, sweet fruit finish. Needs a bit more punch at the end to be outstanding. Best after 2005.–J.S. • $36 • (2/29/2000) • **88**
Vintage Port 1995 • $28 • (4/30/1998) • **87**

FONSECA

Late Bottled Port 1994: Big and raisiny, with a burnt fruit character. Full-bodied, thick, sweet and hot, with a slightly astringent finish. A very fat and rustic style that's not completely pleasurable. Drink now.–J.S. • $20 • (7/31/1999) • **84**
Late Bottled Port 1991 • $18 • (2/28/1998) • **81**
Late Bottled Port 1989 • $18 • (1/31/1996) • **85**
Late Bottled Port 1988 • $17 • (11/15/1994) • **84**
Tawny Port 10 year-old NV • $23 • (1/31/1996) • **86**
Tawny Port 20 year-old NV • $44 • (1/31/1996) • **84**
Tawny Port 40 year-old NV • $114 • (1/31/1996) • **86**
Vintage Character Port Bin 27 NV • $16 • (3/15/1994) • **85**
Vintage Port 1997: A young Port, with good, dark color and mineral and raspberry character. Medium- to full-bodied, with a solid core of fruit and a firm, silky finish. This is outstanding, but I expected a little more from Fonseca; not as impressive as when tasted from barrel. Tasted twice, with consistent notes. Best after 2006.–J.S. • $83 • (2/29/2000) • **91**
Vintage Port 1994 • $132 Ⓐ • (4/30/1997) CS • **100**
Vintage Port 1992 • $84 Ⓐ • (6/15/1995) CS • **96**
Vintage Port 1991 • $NA • (7/31/1994) • **93**
Vintage Port Guimaraens 1996: Lovely ripe wine with lots of berry and cherry aromas and flavors. Medium bodied and very sweet with soft tannins and a fresh fruit finish. Best after 2002.–J.S. • $NA • (2/28/1999) • **87**
Vintage Port Guimaraens 1995 • $39 • (4/30/1998) CS • **92**
Vintage Port Guimaraens 1991 • $35 • (7/31/1994) • **93**
Vintage Port Quinta do Panascal 1996: Supergrapey, with wet earth and stones on the nose. Full-bodied, medium-sweet, with lots of tannins. Long and racy on the finish. A serious young Port. Best Panascal ever. Best after 2005.–J.S. • $NA • (2/28/1999) • **90**

FONSECA, JOSE MARIA DA

Alentejo Garrafeira 1988 • $13 • (4/15/1994) • **82**
Alentejo Garrafeira AP 1987 • $13 • (4/15/1994) • **85**
Alentejo José de Sousa Mayor 1994: Traditional style, with mature red plum, dried cherry and sandalwood flavors. Smooth and soft on the finish. Drink now.–K.M. • $22 • (10/31/1999) • **83**
Alentejo José de Sousa Tinto Velho 1996: High-toned, with nice raspberry and spice flavors, rhubarb notes on the finish. Mature. Drink now.–K.M. • $11 • (10/31/1999) • **84**
Alentejo Morgado do Reguengo 1989 • $8 • (4/15/1994) • **81**
Arrábida Garrafeira CO 1990 • $20 • (5/31/1997) • **82**
Arrábida Garrafeira CO 1982 • $14 • (12/31/1990) • **83**
Arrábida Garrafeira TE 1990 • $19 • (1/01/1997) • **78**
Arrábida Garrafeira TE 1988 • $NA • (4/15/1994) • **67**
Dão Casa da Insua 1988 • $9 • (1/01/1995) • **76**
Dão Terras Altas 1991 • $9 • (5/31/1997) • **77**
Dão Terras Altas 1990 • $7 • (4/15/1994) • **79**
Moscatel Roxo Setúbal 20 Years NV • $50/500 ml. • (5/31/1997) • **90**
Moscatel Setúbal 1990 • $14 • (5/31/1997) • **86**
Moscatel Setúbal 20 Years NV • $42 • (5/31/1997) • **92**
Muscat Terras do Sado João Pires 1998: Strange sour herb and menthol flavors don't add up to much.–K.M. • $9 • (4/30/2000) • **71**
Palmela Garrafeira RA 1987 • $20 • (5/31/1997) • **85**
Palmela Garrafeira RA 1982 • $14 • (12/31/1990) • **88**
Periquita Azeitão 1989 • $5 • (1/31/1993) • **80**
Periquita Terras do Sado 1994 • $8 • (8/31/1997) • **78**
Periquita Terras do Sado 1993 • $9 • (5/31/1997) • **76**
Periquita Terras do Sado 1990 • $7 • (4/15/1994) • **84**
Periquita Terras do Sado Classico 1992 • $21 • (10/15/1997) • **83**
Portalegre d'Avillez 1991 • $12 • (5/31/1997) • **88**
Portalegre d'Avillez 1990 • $12 • (5/31/1997) • **87**
Reguengos José de Sousa Garrafeira 1991 • $20 • (5/31/1997) • **83**
Reguengos José de Sousa Garrafeira 1990 • $20 • (5/31/1997) • **85**
Reguengos José de Sousa Tinto Velho 1993 • $12 • (8/31/1997) • **75**
Reguengos José de Sousa Tinto Velho 1992 • $12 • (5/31/1997) • **85**
Requengos Tinto Velho de Monsarax Colheita 1986 • $10 • (12/31/1990) • **82**
Terras do Sado Pasmados 1990 • $12 • (1/01/1997) • **85**
Terras do Sado Pasmados 1989 • $9 • (4/15/1994) • **78**
Terras do Sado Quinta de Camarate 1990 • $12 • (1/01/1997) • **79**
Terras do Sado Quinta de Camarate 1989 • $10 • (4/15/1994) • **68**
Touriga Nacional-Touriga Francesa Terras do Sado Primum 1997: Intense and fairly rich, with an impressive concentration of red cherry and cranberry flavors and some spice and cedar notes chiming in the finish. Supple and balanced. Tempting now, but should improve with short-term aging. Drink now through 2003.–K.M. • $16 • (10/31/1999) • **87**

GILBERT

Vintage Port 1995 • $45 • (4/30/1998) • **85**
Vintage Port 1994 • $NA • (4/30/1997) • **86**
Vintage Port 1992 • $NA • (6/15/1995) • **85**
Vintage Port 1991 • $NA • (7/31/1994) • **85**

GOULD CAMPBELL

Vintage Port 1997: Pretty berry and mineral aromas, with a full-bodied palate that builds. Excellent backbone of tannins. Medium sweetness. Gould Campbell is consistently outstanding. Best after 2005.–J.S. • $45 • (2/29/2000) • **90**
Vintage Port 1994 • $55 • (4/30/1997) • **92**
Vintage Port 1991 • $35 • (7/31/1994) • **92**

GRAHAM

Late Bottled Port 1994: Bright raspberry and violet aromas and flavors. Medium-bodied and medium sweet, with a raspberry and cherry aftertaste. Delicious. Drink now.–J.S. • $18 • (7/31/1999) • **87**
Late Bottled Port 1991 • $21 • (2/28/1998) • **87**
Tawny Port 10 years old NV • $24 • (1/31/1996) SS • **91**
Tawny Port 20 year-old NV • $45 • (1/31/1996) • **88**
Tawny Port 30 year-old NV • $75 • (1/31/1996) • **87**
Tawny Port 40 years old NV • $122 • (1/31/1996) • **87**
Tawny Port Fine Tawny NV • $12 • (1/31/1996) • **78**
Vintage Character Port Six Grapes NV • $21 • (3/15/1994) • **81**
Vintage Port 1997: Lovely claretlike aromas of plums, cherries and spices. Full- to medium-bodied, with a solid core of silky tannins and a long, medium-sweet finish. Very refined. A solid Graham. Best after 2007.–J.S. • $78 • (2/29/2000) • **90**
Vintage Port 1994 • $68 Ⓐ • (4/30/1997) • **95**
Vintage Port 1991 • $37 Ⓐ • (7/31/1994) • **93**
Vintage Port Malvedos 1996: Good deep-ruby color, with an attractive plummy, grapey character. Medium-bodied and medium-sweet, with fresh acidity and fruit that hide the tannins. Needs more tannin backbone. Best after 2002.–J.S. • $NA • (2/28/1999) • **87**
Vintage Port Malvedos 1995 • $29 Ⓐ • (4/30/1998) • **89**
Vintage Port Malvedos 1992 • $39 • (6/30/1995) • **91**
Vintage Port Malvedos 1988 • $26 • (1/31/1991) HR • **93**
Vintage Port Malvedos Centenary 1990 • $32 • (1/31/1993) • **82**

HENRIQUES & HENRIQUES

Bual Madeira 10 Years Old NV • $35 • (11/30/1997) • **93**
Madeira Monte Seco NV • $15 • (11/30/1997) • **84**
Madeira Rainwater NV • $15 • (11/30/1997) • **84**

HENRIQUES & HENRIQUES

Malmsey Madeira 10 Years Old NV • $35 • (11/30/1997) • **91**
Malmsey Madeira 5 Years Old NV • $18 • (11/30/1997) • **85**
Sercial Madeira 10 Years Old NV • $35 • (11/30/1997) • **89**
Sercial Madeira 5 Years Old NV • $18 • (11/30/1997) • **87**
Verdelho Madeira 10 Years Old NV • $35 • (11/30/1997) • **91**
Verdelho Madeira 5 Years Old NV • $18 • (11/30/1997) • **88**

HENRIQUES, VINHOS JUSTINO

Boal Madeira 10 Years Old NV: Sweet, rich and expansive, this evokes caramel and butterscotch, thickly textured and matched by a tangy framework of acidity. Moderate length on the finish. Drink now.–B.S. • $30 • (10/31/1999) • **88**
Madeira Fine Rich 5 Years Old NV: A full-fledged dessert wine, giving caramel, floral and spice flavors that turn to tobacco and walnut on the aftertaste. The firm structure and astringent finish balance all the elements well. Drink now.–B.S. • $14 • (10/31/1999) • **88**
Madeira Old Reserve 10 Years Old NV: Frankly sweet, here's a spicy, grapey wine, thick and somewhat cloying, but it finishes with some astringency, leaving a dry, chalky impression. Lacks harmony. Drink now.–B.S. • $30 • (10/31/1999) • **84**
Malmsey Madeira 10 Years Old NV: Round and supple at start, turning dry and astringent, exuding flavors of toffee, brown sugar and a burnt element. Plenty of power and persistence on the finish. Tasted twice, with consistent notes. Drink now.–B.S. • $30 • (11/15/1999) • **89**
Sercial Madeira 10 Years Old NV: Suggestion of caramel and brown sugar aromas lead into soft, slightly sweet, richly textured wine with straightforward caramel and vanilla flavors. Touch hot on the finish. Drink now.–B.S. • $30 • (11/15/1999) • **86**
Verdelho Madeira 10 Years Old NV: Sweet, yet appears to lack the concentration to match the bracing acidity and alcohol. Lovely nutty, toffee flavors and a hint of dried fig on the finish, a little awkward. Tasted twice, with consistent notes. Drink now.–B.S. • $30 • (11/15/1999) • **88**

HUTCHESON

Vintage Port 1997: A pleasant and easy '97, with plum, cherry and berry character. Medium-bodied, very sweet, with a light finish. Best after 2003. –J.S. • $35 • (2/29/2000) • **82**
Vintage Port 1991 • $19 • (7/31/1994) • **81**

INFANTADO, QUINTA DO

Late Bottled Port 1994: A thick and rich style, slightly heavy, with a serious concentration of blackberry and boysenberry character and a hint of earth. Medium- to full-bodied, with lots of sweet fruit and a slightly raisiny finish. Drink now.–J.S. • $24 • (7/31/1999) • **85**
Tawny Port 10 Years Old NV • $32 • (9/15/1997) • **87**
Vintage Port 1992 • $40 Ⓐ • (6/15/1995) • **90**
Vintage Port 1991 • $25 • (7/31/1994) • **85**
Vintage Port 1989 • $35 • (7/31/1993) • **81**

J.P. VINHOS

Alentejo Herdade de Santa Marta 1996: Smooth and mature, with dried cherry and dark plum plus chewy and leathery notes on the finish. Drink now.–K.M. • $9 • (6/30/2000) • **81**
Alentejo Herdade de Santa Marta 1995: Mature. Dried cherry and smoke flavors linger on the finish, with spicy and brickish notes. Drink now. –K.M. • $9 • (6/30/2000) • **83**
Alentejo Herdade de Santa Marta 1994: Tired and stewy-tasting, with murky brown sugar tones. Tasted twice, with consistent notes.–K.M. • $8 • (7/31/1999) • **67**
Alentejo Herdade de Santa Marta 1993 • $9 • (3/31/1996) • **83**
Alentejo Herdade de Santa Marta 1991 • $10 • (4/15/1994) • **85**
Alentejo Tinto da Anfora 1995: Smooth, subtle and still lively despite its age, with appealing berry, dried cherry and smoke aromas and flavors. Try with grilled meats. Drink now.–K.M. • $12 • (6/30/2000) • **85**

Key: SS—Spectator Selection. CS—Cellar Selection. HR—Highly Recommended. $NA—Price not available. (BT)—Barrel tasting. Ⓐ—Auction Price. For a key to the tasters' initials, see "How to Use These Listings." **Dates in parentheses represent the issues in which the ratings were published.**

Alentejo Tinto da Anfora 1992: Smells like a mélange of sweet spices—sandalwood, cinnamon, cedar—while the flavors offer sweet plum notes before turning dry and a little austere on the finish. There's a hint of caramel, too. Drink now.–B.S. • $10 • (7/31/1999) • **83**
Alentejo Tinto da Anfora 1991 • $10 • (3/31/1996) • **84**
Alentejo Tinto da Anfora 1990 • $9 • (4/15/1994) • **79**
Cabernet Sauvignon Terras do Sado Quinta da Bacalhôa 1996: Very aromatic, though not typical of Cabernet Sauvignon, displaying sweet, plummy flavors accented with sandalwood and vanilla, all supported by lively acidity and stiff tannins. Plenty of sweet fruit lingers on the aftertaste. Drink now through 2003.–B.S. • $16 • (7/31/1999) • **86**
Cabernet Sauvignon Terras do Sado Quinta da Bacalhôa 1995 • $14 • (7/31/1997) • **85**
Cabernet Sauvignon Terras do Sado Quinta da Bacalhôa 1992 • $14 • (3/31/1996) • **85**
Cabernet Sauvignon Terras do Sado Quinta da Bacalhôa 1991 • $15 • (4/30/1995) • **83**
Cabernet Sauvignon Terras do Sado Quinta da Bacalhôa 1990 • $15 • (4/15/1994) • **81**
Chardonnay Terras do Sado Cova da Ursa 1997: Already mature-tasting, despite its youth, with butter and ripe apple flavors. Notes of white pepper on the finish. Drink now.–K.M. • $NA • (1/01/1999) • **82**
Estremadura Tinta Miúda 1997: A smoky-tasting red, with currant and red plum flavors accented by bacon and herb notes on the finish. Drink now.–K.M. • $NA/500 ml. • (1/01/1999) • **83**
Merlot Terras do Sado Má Partilha 1996: A medium-bodied red with well-defined red plum and tobacco flavors, peppery and chocolaty notes on the finish. Drink now.–K.M. • $NA • (1/01/1999) • **83**
Moscatel Roxo Setúbal 1988: Fairly rich and smooth, with loads of apricot, honey, caramel flavor. A fortified style of dessert wine. Mature; ready to drink.–K.M. • $NA/500 ml. • (1/01/1999) • **87**
Palmela Garrafeira 1988 • $8 • (1/01/1997) • **74**
Terras do Sado Má Partilha 1991 • $19 • (1/01/1997) • **84**
Terras do Sado Meia Pipa 1994: A rustic and mature-tasting red, with plenty of dried cherry and leather flavors and a stewy note. Not for everyone. Drink now.–K.M. • $NA • (1/01/1999) • **81**
Terras do Sado Quinta de Santo Amaro 1992 • $8 • (4/15/1994) • **78**
Terras do Sado White Catarina 1998: Quite oaky and buttery-tasting, but not much else, with drying tannins on the finish.–K.M. • $9 • (6/30/2000) • **76**
Terras do Sado White Catarina 1997: An overdone style, with buttery notes and tealike flavors that don't quite mesh in the end. A blend of Chardonnay and Fernão Pires.–K.M. • $8 • (8/31/1999) • **77**

KOPKE

Late Bottled Port 1994: Medium-bodied and very sweet, with raisin and spice character and chocolate, pepper and sweet-and-sour flavors on the finish. Lacks a bit of freshness. Drink now.–J.S. • $20 • (7/31/1999) • **84**
Port Varsity NV • $7 • (3/31/1988) • **72**
Tawny Port 20 year old NV • $30 • (2/28/1990) • **88**
Vintage Port 1997: Very soft and plummy young Port, with delicious ripe fruit character, medium to full body and a long, sweet finish. Serious Kopke. Best after 2006.–J.S. • $35 • (2/29/2000) • **89**
Vintage Port 1995 • $30 • (4/30/1998) • **86**
Vintage Port 1994 • $NA • (4/30/1997) • **86**
Vintage Port 1991 • $NA • (7/31/1994) • **82**
Vintage Port Quinta São Luiz 1996: A very grapey young Port with lots of jam and chocolate character. Medium- to full-bodied, very sweet, with big, soft tannins and a fruity finish. Best after 2002.–J.S. • $30 • (2/28/1999) • **88**

KROHN

Late Bottled Port 1994: Intense aromas of black pepper and raisin, but then a slight letdown. Medium-bodied and medium sweet, with soft tannins and a light, slightly alcoholic finish. Drink now.–J.S. • $20 • (7/31/1999) • **83**
Late Bottled Port 1987 • $19 • (2/28/1998) • **84**
Late Bottled Port 1985 • $23 • (2/28/1998) • **79**

LAGOALVA, QUINTA DA

Ribatejo 1994 • $10 • (10/15/1997) • **81**
Ribatejo 1992 • $9 • (4/30/1996) • **75**
Ribatejo 1991 • $7 • (4/15/1994) • **83**

Ribatejo Cima 1995: There's a beefy flavor to this wine, and some dried cherry notes as well. Smooth and straightforward. Drink now.–K.M. • $NA • (1/01/1999) • **81**

Ribatejo Cima 1992 • $9 • (4/30/1996) • **83**

Ribatejo Cima 1991 • $10 • (4/15/1994) • **86**

LEACOCK'S

Madeira Rainwater NV • $14 • (11/30/1997) • **82**

MARTINEZ

Late Bottled Port 1994: A bit earthy and funky, with raisinskin character. Medium-bodied and not very sweet, with a hot finish. Tough to get excited about. Drink now.–J.S. • $17 • (7/31/1999) • **80**

Late Bottled Port 1992 • $17 • (2/28/1998) • **81**

Tawny Port 20 year old Directors NV • $25 • (2/28/1990) • **93**

Vintage Port 1997: Good aromas and flavors of pepper, raisin and ripe fruit in this young vintage Port. Medium-bodied, medium-sweet, with a fresh aftertaste. Not as good as when tasted from barrel. Best after 2005.–J.S. • $77 • (2/29/2000) • **87**

Vintage Port 1994 • $30 • (4/30/1997) • **95**

Vintage Port 1991 • $NA • (7/31/1994) • **85**

Vintage Port Quinta da Chousa 1995 • $39 • (4/30/1998) • **79**

Vintage Port Quinta da Eira Velha 1997: A ripe and round style of vintage Port, with lovely, fat, sweet tannins, medium body and a velvety finish. Lacks a bit of grip. Not as good as when tasted from barrel. Best after 2004.–J.S. • $68 • (2/29/2000) • **87**

Vintage Port Quinta da Eira Velha 1995 • $45 • (4/30/1998) • **90**

Vintage Port Quinta da Eira Velha 1994 • $30 • (4/30/1997) • **97**

Vintage Port Quinta da Eira Velha 1992 • $NA • (6/15/1995) • **89**

MATO MIRANDA, QUINTA DE

Ribatejo 1992 • $6 • (3/31/1996) • **84**

MELGACO, QUINTAS DE

Alvarinho Vinho Verde Couto de Frades 1998: There's a nice zippiness here, augmented by lime, stone and some green peach flavors. Crisp finish. Drink now.–K.M. • $13 • (10/31/1999) • **84**

Alvarinho Vinho Verde Couto de Frades 1997: Peachy aromas and green peach flavors dominate this racy Portuguese white. Nicely concentrated, though a tad coarse on the finish. Drink now.–K.M. • $11 • (1/01/1999) • **83**

Alvarinho Vinho Verde QM 1998: Peachy, with citrus accents and a nice herbal note on the finish. Clean and refreshing. Drink now.–K.M. • $13 • (10/31/1999) • **83**

Alvarinho-Trajadura Vinho Verde Torre de Menagem 1998: A basic white, with citrus flavors and some minerallike accents. Finishes on an earthy note.–K.M. • $10 • (10/31/1999) • **78**

MINHO, QUINTA DO

Vinho Verde Vinha Verde 1997: Simple and vinous, with modest apple and citrus flavors. A little fizz on the finish.–K.M. • $8 • (1/01/1999) • **78**

MONCAO, ADEGA COOPERATIVA REGIONAL DE

Vinho Verde Danaide 1998: A bit coarse, with canned and tropical fruit flavors.–K.M. • $5 • (6/30/2000) • **77**

Vinho Verde Danaide 1997: A well-made Vinho Verde. Clean, refreshing and lemony, with moderate richness and lively acidity. Drink now.–B.S. • $5 • (10/15/1998) • **83**

Vinho Verde Muralhas de Monção NV • $7 • (5/15/1997) • **82**

Vinho Verde Muralhas de Monção 1998: Has modest citrus and green apple flavors, with a good dose of acidity. Smoky notes on the finish. Drink now.–K.M. • $8 • (6/30/2000) • **83**

Vinho Verde Muralhas de Monção 1996: A citrusy-tasting, refreshing white, with simple, clean flavors. Drink now.–B.S. • $7 • (10/15/1998) • **81**

MONTEIRO, A.M. ESTEVES

Vinho Verde Arca Nova 1998: Crisp and fairly refreshing, with lively apple and green peach flavors, some zip on the finish. Drink now.–K.M. • $6 • (10/15/1999) • **83**

MURGAS, QUINTA DAS

Estremadura 1989 • $8 • (4/30/1996) • **79**

NAVEGA, ANTONIO AFONSO

Bairrada Quinta do Carvalhinho 1990 • $NA • (4/15/1994) • **80**

Bairrada Quinta do Carvalhinho Garrafeira 1990 • $14 • (9/15/1997) • **84**

Bairrada Quinta do Carvalhinho Reserva 1991 • $10 • (4/30/1996) • **78**

Cabernet Sauvignon Beiras Quinta do Carvalhinho 1995: Already mature, even over-the-hill, with prune and tealike flavors and a lifted aroma.–K.M. • $13 • (1/01/1999) • **77**

NIEPOORT

Douro Redoma 1991 • $12 • (3/31/1996) • **85**

Late Bottled Port 1994: A harmonious and delicate LBV. Shows a touch of class, with aromas of berry, violet and spice. Medium-bodied and medium sweet, with a long, caressing aftertaste. Drink now.–J.S. • $19 • (7/31/1999) • **88**

Late Bottled Port 1992 • $17 • (2/28/1998) • **86**

Tawny Port 10 years old NV • $28 • (1/31/1996) • **88**

Tawny Port 20 years old NV • $47 • (1/31/1996) • **91**

Tawny Port 30 years old NV • $100 • (1/31/1996) • **81**

Tawny Port Fine Tawny NV • $17 • (1/31/1996) • **84**

Vintage Character Port NV • $NA • (3/15/1994) • **86**

Vintage Port 1997: The greatest modern vintage of Niepoort. Shows a black color and intense aromas of crushed berries and wet earth, with a slight stemminess. Full-bodied and mouthpuckering, this young bodybuilder of a Port has loads of fruit and powerful tannins. Amazingly long finish. Best after 2009.–J.S. • $45 • (2/29/2000) CS • **98**

Vintage Port 1994 • $45 • (4/30/1997) • **91**

Vintage Port 1992 • $33 • (6/15/1995) • **90**

Vintage Port 1991 • $NA • (7/31/1994) • **85**

NOVA DE NOSSA SENHORA DO CARMO, QUINTA

Trás-Os-Montes Tavedo Terras Durienses 1995: Ripe and pruny, smelling and tasting like a Valpolicella made by the ripasso method, this has good concentration and character, though its rusticity won't appeal to everyone.–B.S. • $9 • (10/15/1998) • **83**

NOVAL, QUINTA DO

Late Bottled Port 1994: An excellent, youthful ruby, with vibrant berry, mineral and wet earth character. Medium- to full-bodied and medium sweet, with a lingering, sweet fruit finish. Very good indeed. Drink now.–J.S. • $19 • (7/31/1999) • **88**

Late Bottled Port 1991 • $18 • (2/28/1998) • **80**

Tawny Port 20 year old NV • $32 • (2/28/1990) • **82**

Vintage Character Port Noval LB NV • $18 • (3/15/1994) • **86**

Vintage Port 1997: Black color. Loads of ripe berry, mineral and wet earth character, with a hint of green tobacco. Full-bodied, medium-sweet, with a supersolid core of tannins. Long, long finish. The greatest Quinta do Noval in decades. Best after 2009.–J.S. • $85 • (2/29/2000) • **97**

Vintage Port 1995 • $55 • (4/30/1998) • **90**

Vintage Port 1994 • $50 • (4/30/1997) • **95**

Vintage Port 1991 • $25 • (7/31/1994) • **87**

Vintage Port Nacional 1997: Not quite as great as the 100-point '94, but really superb. Black color, with intense aromas of mineral, blueberries and blackberries. Full-bodied and very sweet, with layers of big, velvety tannins and a long, long finish. Truly impressive. Best after 2009.–J.S. • $750 • (2/29/2000) CS • **99**

Vintage Port Nacional 1996: Port of the vintage. Inky-colored, with aromas of boysenberry, raspberry sauce. Full-bodied, medium sweet, with superracy tannins and a long, long finish. This is a very serious vintage Port. Bravo. Best after 2008.–J.S. • $533 • (2/28/1999) • **94**

Vintage Port Nacional 1994 • $739 Ⓐ • (4/30/1997) CS • **100**

PORTUGAL

NOVAL, QUINTA DO

Vintage Port Nacional 1991 • $180 • (6/15/1998) CS • **93**

Vintage Port Quinta do Roriz 1995 • $45 • (4/30/1998) • **90**

Vintage Port Quinta do Silval 1995 • $45 • (4/30/1998) • **88**

Vintage Port Quinto do Silval 1997: Impressive berry, violet and grape skin aromas. Full-bodied, with a solid core of silky tannins and a long, caressing finish. Well done. Even better than when tasted from barrel. Best after 2006.–J.S. • $50 • (2/29/2000) • **91**

OFFLEY

Late Bottled Port 1990 • $19 • (2/28/1998) • **88**

Late Bottled Port 1988 • $19 • (11/15/1994) • **86**

Late Bottled Port Traditional 1994: A fresh and vibrant LBV, with berry, violet and cherry aromas. Medium-bodied, with firm tannins and a sleek and fruity finish. Well crafted. Drink now or hold for a few years.–J.S. • $22 • (7/31/1999) • **88**

Tawny Port 20 year old Baron Forrester NV • $35 • (2/28/1990) • **89**

Vintage Character Port Boa Vista Reserve NV • $14 • (3/15/1994) • **75**

Vintage Character Port Boa Vista Special Reserve NV • $10 • (3/31/1988) • **75**

Vintage Port 1997: Good, dark color. Lovely berry, cherry and spice aromas. Full- to medium-bodied, with firm tannins and a medium finish. Good grip at the end. Subtle. Best after 2007.–J.S. • $46 • (2/29/2000) • **89**

Vintage Port Boa Vista 1995 • $35 • (4/30/1998) • **86**

Vintage Port Boa Vista 1994 • $30 • (4/30/1997) • **84**

OSBORNE

Late Bottled Port 1994: Here's an excellent alternative to vintage Port. This LBV is rich and concentrated, with fresh berry, cherry and plum character. Full-bodied and medium-sweet, with a long, sweet fruit finish. Outstanding for this producer. Better in 2001, but who can wait? Drink now.–J.S. • $15 • (7/31/1999) HR • **90**

Late Bottled Port 1991 • $15 • (2/28/1998) • **77**

Vintage Port 1997: A young, pretty Port, with delicious berry and floral character. Medium-bodied and medium-sweet, with a firm tannin structure. Best after 2006.–J.S. • $40 • (2/29/2000) • **87**

Vintage Port 1995 • $30 • (4/30/1998) • **87**

Vintage Port 1994 • $30 • (4/30/1997) • **91**

Vintage Port 1992 • $28 • (6/15/1995) • **88**

PACO, QUINTA DO

Vinho Verde Paço de Teixeiró 1997: Spice and butter flavors mark this amber-colored wine, but not much else. Turns hollow on the finish. Tasted twice, with consistent notes.–K.M. • $12 • (10/15/1999) • **74**

Vinho Verde Paço de Teixeiró 1996 • $12 • (4/30/1998) • **83**

PANCAS, QUINTA DE

Alenquer 1990 • $7 • (4/15/1994) • **85**

Cabernet Sauvignon Alenquer 1991 • $7 • (4/15/1994) • **85**

Cabernet Sauvignon Estremadura 1995 • $11 • (8/31/1997) • **81**

Cabernet Sauvignon Estremadura 1992 • $NA • (4/30/1995) • **83**

Cabernet Sauvignon Estremadura Special Selection 1995: This crisp red offers well-defined berry and plum flavors, with firm but well-integrated tannins and balanced acidity. It's a juicy wine that brings you back for another sip. Drink now through 2001.–T.M. • $30 • (12/31/1998) • **86**

PARROTES, QUINTA DE

Alenquer 1995 • $8 • (8/31/1997) • **73**

Alenquer 1992 • $7 • (3/31/1996) • **83**

Alenquer 1991 • $NA • (4/30/1995) • **84**

Periquita Alenquer 1990 • $6 • (4/15/1994) • **83**

Key: SS—Spectator Selection. CS—Cellar Selection. HR—Highly Recommended. $NA—Price not available. (BT)—Barrel tasting. Ⓐ—Auction Price. For a key to the tasters' initials, see "How to Use These Listings."
Dates in parentheses represent the issues in which the ratings were published.

PASSADOURO, QUINTA DO

Vintage Port 1997: A very grapey '97, with loads of ripe fruit, firm tannins and a long, caressing finish. Subtle and long. Better than when tasted from barrel. Best after 2007.–J.S. • $45 • (2/29/2000) • **90**

Vintage Port 1996: Surprisingly mature in color, with a red hue to the dark ruby. Full-bodied and sweet, with peppery flavors, fine tannins and a fruity finish. Very claret-like in structure. Best after 2002.–J.S. • $54 • (2/28/1999) • **86**

Vintage Port 1995 • $54 • (4/30/1998) • **86**

Vintage Port 1994 • $45 • (4/30/1997) • **88**

Vintage Port 1992 • $NA • (6/15/1995) • **88**

PATO, LUIS

Bairrada 1988 • $16 • (4/15/1994) • **84**

Bairrada Oak Aged 1988 • $17 • (4/15/1994) • **85**

Bairrada Quinta do Ribeirinho 1990 • $7 • (4/15/1994) • **84**

Bairrada Quinta do Ribeirinho Primeira Escolha 1995 • $12 • (9/15/1997) • **87**

Bairrada Vinha Barrosa 1995 • $32 • (9/15/1997) • **89**

Bairrada Vinha Pan 1995 • $32 • (9/15/1997) • **87**

Bairrada Vinhas Velhas 1995 • $22 • (10/15/1997) • **88**

Bairrada Vinhas Velhas 1990 • $12 • (4/15/1994) • **86**

PELLADA, QUINTA DA

Dão 1992 • $10 • (4/30/1995) • **80**

PIRES, JOAO

Muscat Terras do Sado 1997: This light white has modest flavors of quince and canned pineapple.–K.M. • $10 • (1/01/1999) • **77**

POCAS, PORTO

Late Bottled Port 1994: Superfruity and aromatic, with violet, cherry and blackberry. Medium-bodied and medium sweet, with silky tannins and a fruity aftertaste. Delicious. Drink now.–J.S. • $20 • (7/31/1999) • **87**

Vintage Port 1997: Ripe and raisiny Port, with a solid core of fruit and tannins. Medium-sweet, with good grip on the finish. Not as good as when tasted from barrel. Best after 2005.–J.S. • $NA • (2/29/2000) • **88**

Vintage Port 1996: Perfumed, aromatic with fruity, plum character. Medium-bodied, medium-sweet, with silky, easy tannins and a delicate finish. Best after 2002.–J.S. • $NA • (2/28/1999) • **85**

Vintage Port 1995 • $30 • (4/30/1998) • **86**

Vintage Port 1994 • $51 • (4/30/1997) • **86**

Vintage Port 1991 • $NA • (7/31/1994) • **84**

PORTA DA RAVESSA

Redondo 1995 • $8 • (8/31/1997) • **80**

Redondo 1990 • $4 • (4/15/1994) • **82**

PORTALEGRE, ADEGA COOPERATIVA DE

Alentejo 1990 • $11 • (4/15/1994) • **80**

Alentejo Conventual 1995 • $13 • (9/15/1997) • **84**

Alentejo Conventual 1992 • $12 • (3/31/1996) • **76**

Alentejo Conventual 1990 • $9 • (4/15/1994) • **78**

Alentejo Terras do Baco 1996 • $10 • (10/15/1997) • **78**

PRIMAVERA, CAVES

Bairrada Colheita 1990 • $5 • (3/31/1996) • **76**

Dão 1989 • $5 • (4/15/1994) • **74**

PROVAM

Alvarinho Vinho Verde Portal do Fidalgo 1999: Juicy and fresh, with apple flavors and nice mineral and and spice notes. Drink now.–K.M. • $14 • (6/30/2000) • **84**

Alvarinho Vinho Verde Portal do Fidalgo 1997: Ripe and mature-tasting, with pear and apple flavors, some spicy notes mixed in. Drink now.–K.M. • $12 • (10/15/1999) • **82**

QUARLES HARRIS

Vintage Port 1997: A young Port, with plenty of black pepper and cherry character. Full- to medium-bodied, with lots of sweet fruit and a velvety tannin structure. Best after 2005.–J.S. • $NA • (2/29/2000) • **90**
Vintage Port 1994 • $55 • (4/30/1997) • **87**

RAMOS-PINTO

Douro 1994 • $11 • (7/31/1997) • **88**
Douro Duas Quintas 1996: Looking for a good red at a great price? This nicely balanced and fairly rich wine from Portugal fits the bill, with warm, brickish flavors of plum, chocolate and spice and peppery notes on the finish. Smooth and seductive, it's drinkable tonight.–K.M. • $11 • (9/30/1999) • **86**
Douro Duas Quintas 1995: Supple and youthful, with well-defined plum, dark cherry and leather flavors. Chocolate and pepper notes linger on the finish. Medium-bodied, well-balanced wine. Drink now.–K.M. • $11 • (1/01/1999) • **87**
Douro Duas Quintas 1994: This has more finesse than most Portuguese reds. Very fresh, showing black currant and plum aromas and flavors that are harmonious and wed to a firm yet elegant structure. Well done. Drink now through 2001.–B.S. • $11 • (7/31/1999) • **87**
Douro Duas Quintas 1992 • $9 • (9/15/1996) • **82**
Douro Duas Quintas 1991 • $7 • (4/15/1994) • **82**
Douro Duas Quintas Reserva 1994: A finely sculpted red, with rich, ripe flavors of plum, raspberry and dark cherry and plenty of spice. Has a lovely aroma of cassis and a nice broad frame. Dark chocolate and mocha flavors chime in on the finish. Drink now through 2002.–K.M. • $27 • (1/31/2000) • **88**
Douro Duas Quintas Reserva 1992 • $16 • (3/31/1996) • **86**
Douro Duas Quintas Reserva 1991 • $18 • (7/31/1997) • **87**
Late Bottled Port 1992 • $20 • (2/28/1998) • **89**
Late Bottled Port Traditional 1994: Round in texture, with intense aromas of ripe plum and berry, a hint of earth and soft tannins. Medium sweet finish. A little hot but delicious. Drink now.–J.S. • $20 • (7/31/1999) • **85**
Tawny Port 10 Year Old Quinta da Ervamoira NV • $25 • (1/31/1996) • **86**
Tawny Port 20 Year Old Quinta do Bom-Retiro NV • $48 • (1/31/1996) HR • **93**
Tawny Port 30 years old NV • $65 • (1/31/1996) • **90**
Tràs-os-Montes Quinta dos Bons Ares 1992 • $NA • (1/01/1996) • **84**
Vintage Character Port Quinta da Urtiga NV • $17 • (3/15/1994) • **86**
Vintage Port 1997: Good floral, earthy, spicy character. Medium- to full-bodied, with sweet fruit and a medium finish. Best after 2006.–J.S. • $39 • (2/29/2000) • **88**
Vintage Port 1995 • $35 • (4/30/1998) • **83**
Vintage Port 1994 • $36 Ⓐ • (4/30/1997) • **87**
Vintage Port 1991 • $26 • (7/31/1994) • **86**
Vintage Port Quinta da Ervamoira 1994 • $50 • (4/30/1997) • **88**

REAL VINICOLA

Dão 1990 • $6 • (4/30/1995) • **79**
Douro Evel 1994 • $7 • (8/31/1997) • **83**
Douro Evel 1990 • $6 • (4/30/1995) • **84**
Douro Evel Grande Escolha 1996: Heady with plum and vanilla aromas, this full-bodied red makes an impact on the palate with its ripe plum and spice notes. Rustic in style, it finishes with heat and drying tannins. Drink now through 2002.–B.S. • $35 • (7/31/1999) • **84**
Douro Porca de Murça Reserva 1996: An assertive style, with fairly tart cranberry and currant flavors and spicy notes mixed in. Flavorful, but a bit rough-hewn, with an unripe finish. Hard to say if it will come around. Try after 2000.–K.M. • $12 • (7/31/1999) • **81**

REGUENGOS DE MONSARAZ, COOPERATIVA

Alentejo Terras d'el Rei NV • $4 • (4/30/1995) • **80**
Alentejo Terras d'el Rei 1994 • $4 • (4/30/1996) • **78**
Aragonês Alentejo 1998: Gorgeous blueberry and dark plum flavors dominate this medium-bodied Aragonês (Tempranillo), which has a nice touch of elegance and richness and a bright structure. Spicy notes linger on the finish. Drink now.–K.M. • $16 • (6/30/2000) • **87**
Reguengos 1997: A soft, grapey red, full of spice and red berry character, finishing with a currant note. Fresh and quaffable. Drink now.–B.S. • $5 • (10/15/1998) • **83**
Reguengos 1994 • $5 • (4/30/1996) • **85**
Reguengos 1992 • $5 • (4/30/1995) • **84**
Reguengos 1990 • $5 • (4/15/1994) • **71**
Reguengos Garrafeira dos Sócios 1990 • $12 • (4/30/1995) • **83**
Reguengos Monsaraz 1997: Light and grapey, with banana and strawberry character, this is made in an *en primeur* style. Drink now.–B.S. • $6 • (10/15/1998) • **80**
Reguengos Reserva 1990 • $8 • (4/30/1995) • **78**
Reguengos Terras d'el Rei 1992 • $4 • (4/15/1994) • **77**
Reguengos Terras d'el Rei Garrafeira 1987 • $10 • (4/15/1994) • **77**
Reguengos White Monsaraz 1997: There's moderate weight and richness here, along with peach and almond flavors. Drink now.–B.S. • $6 • (10/15/1998) • **81**

ROMANIERA

Vintage Port Quinta das Liceiras 1992 • $NA • (6/15/1995) • **89**

ROMEIRA, QUINTA DA

Arinto Bucelas 1998: This soft white offers broad, rather flat flavors of beeswax and almonds, with just enough lemony acidity to give it a refreshing edge.–T.M. • $8 • (4/30/2000) • **79**
Arinto Bucelas 1997: A medium-bodied white from Portugal, with pear and apple flavors, and a touch of citrus on the finish. Drink now.–K.M. • $8 • (8/31/1999) • **83**
Bucelas Morgado de Sta.-Catherina 1998: An exaggerated style. Quite caramellike in taste, with waxy, doughy and spicy flavors.–K.M. • $9 • (4/30/2000) • **78**
Bucelas Morgado de Sta.-Catherina 1997: This has apple flavors, butter notes and a somewhat coarse finish.–K.M. • $10 • (8/31/1999) • **79**
Palmela Tradição 1998: Smooth and supple, with dried plum and leather flavors and hints of clove and cinnamon. Drink now.–K.M. • $7 • (4/30/2000) • **84**
Palmela Tradição 1996: Fading dried cherry and rhubarb flavors dominate this mature red. Past its prime.–K.M. • $7 • (10/31/1999) • **77**

ROSA, QUINTA DE LA

Douro 1997: Exuberant grape and plum notes lead to a light-bodied red, with raspberry nuances and a dusty finish. Drink now.–T.M. • $13 • (3/31/2000) • **84**
Douro 1992 • $8 • (4/15/1994) • **83**
Douro 1991 • $10 • (4/15/1994) • **85**
Late Bottled Port 1994: This Port has very ripe fruit but is slightly disjointed, with aromas of baked fruit and raisin. Full-bodied and very sweet, with berry on the slightly dry finish. Drink now.–J.S. • $21 • (7/31/1999) • **81**
Late Bottled Port 1992 • $21 • (2/28/1998) • **86**
Vintage Character Port Finest Reserve NV • $15 • (3/15/1994) • **84**
Vintage Port 1997: Pretty aromas of violets and berries. Full- to medium-bodied, with medium tannins and a fruity finish. Very attractive young Port. Best after 2006.–J.S. • $45 • (2/29/2000) • **89**
Vintage Port 1996: Dark-colored, with cherry, cinnamon and berry aromas. Medium-bodied, lightly sweet, with a good amount of chewy tannins but lacking a lot of fruit on the finish. Best after 2004.–J.S. • $45 • (2/28/1999) • **86**
Vintage Port 1995 • $39 • (4/30/1998) • **85**
Vintage Port 1994 • $40 • (4/30/1997) • **86**
Vintage Port 1992 • $NA • (6/15/1995) • **88**
Vintage Port 1991 • $NA • (7/31/1994) • **86**
Vintage Port 1988 • $18 • (4/15/1992) • **85**

ROYAL OPORTO

Late Bottled Port 1994: Distinctive bark, plum and raisin aromas reappear on the palate. Slightly hot and alcoholic finish. A bit tiring and old-tasting. Drink now.–J.S. • $15 • (7/31/1999) • **82**
Tawny Port 20 year old NV • $25 • (2/28/1990) • **77**
Vintage Port 1997: An earthy and rich wine, with berry, cherry and a touch of volatile acidity. Medium- to full-bodied, with velvety tannins and a long finish. Not as good as when tasted from barrel. Tasted twice, with consistent notes. Best after 2007.–J.S. • $65 • (2/29/2000) • **88**
Vintage Port 1996: Good dark color, with intense blackberry, light raisin and cherry aromas. Full-bodied, medium-sweet, with very good grip. Long, long finish. Best Royal Oporto in years. Best after 2004.–J.S. • $35 • (2/28/1999) • **86**

ROZES

Late Bottled Port 1994: Superfresh and fragrant, with currant, berry and cherry aromas. Medium-bodied and medium sweet, with a silky, crisp and titillating finish. Serious LBV. Drink now.–J.S. • $19 • (7/31/1999) • **88**
Late Bottled Port 1992 • $18 • (2/28/1998) • **85**
Ruby Port Infanta Isabel 10 years old NV • $20 • (1/31/1996) • **85**
Vintage Port 1997: Lovely, concentrated nose of plums, berries and cherries. Full-bodied, very sweet, with velvety tannins and a sweet fruit finish. Even better than when tasted from barrel. Best after 2006.–J.S. • $45 • (2/29/2000) • **88**
Vintage Port 1995 • $45 • (4/30/1998) • **88**
Vintage Port 1994 • $NA • (1/01/1997) • **86**
Vintage Port 1991 • $23 • (7/31/1994) • **87**

SAES, QUINTA DE

Dão 1995 • $10 • (10/15/1997) • **81**
Dão 1992 • $10 • (4/30/1996) • **82**
Dão 1990 • $9 • (4/15/1994) • **84**
Dão Maxiais 1996: This wine has game, leather and tealike flavors, with some dried cherry notes mixed in and an aroma of cardamom. A bit rustic, but enjoyable. Drink now.–K.M. • $10 • (1/01/1999) • **84**
Dão Reserva 1996: A juicy red, on the light side, with plenty of appealing berry and currant flavors. Finishes with some pepper and leather notes. Drink now.–K.M. • $12 • (1/01/1999) • **82**
Dão White Maxiais 1997: A crisp, lean white with some green apple and gooseberry flavors. Finishes on a fairly tart and slightly spicy note. Drink now.–K.M. • $10 • (1/01/1999) • **82**

SANDEMAN

Late Bottled Port 1994: A delicious, spicy LBV. Very good indeed. Black pepper and ripe fruit aromas follow through to a medium-bodied palate. Medium sweet, with a delicate, fruity aftertaste. Drink now.–J.S. • $32 • (7/31/1999) • **88**
Late Bottled Port 1991 • $25 • (2/28/1998) • **82**
Tawny Port 20 years old NV • $42 • (1/31/1996) HR • **91**
Vintage Character Port Founders Reserve NV • $17 • (3/15/1994) • **81**
Vintage Port 1994 • $22 Ⓐ • (4/30/1997) • **85**
Vintage Port Vau Vintage 1997: Dark purple in color, with wonderful violet, berry and cherry aromas. Full-bodied, medium-sweet, with a solid core of fruit and tannins. Long finish. Subtle. Best Sandeman since the 1960s. Best after 2008.–J.S. • $42 • (2/29/2000) • **92**

SANTA JOANA

Alentejo 1997: A light- to medium-bodied red, with red plum and leather flavors. Slightly stewy note on the finish. Drink now.–K.M. • $7 • (9/30/1999) • **82**
Bairrada Reserva 1996: Modest red plum flavors are framed by some fairly drying tannins, with an earthy note on the finish.–K.M. • $6 • (9/30/1999) • **79**
Douro Reserva 1996: A good, juicy, medium-bodied red, with currant and plum and even some raspberry flavors mixed in. Lively and quaffable; great for a barbecue. Drink now.–K.M. • $6 • (9/30/1999) • **84**
Vinho Verde NV: The aromas and flavors are on the earthy side, but this light-bodied white has snap. Drink now.–B.S. • $5 • (10/15/1998) • **78**

SAO JOAO, CAVES

Bairrada Frei João 1989 • $6 • (4/30/1995) • **73**
Bairrada Frei João Reserva 1985 • $13 • (4/30/1995) • **85**
Bairrada Frei João Reserva 1983 • $13 • (4/15/1994) • **81**
Bairrada Reserva 1983 • $14 • (4/15/1994) • **79**
Dão Porta dos Cavaleiros 1988 • $6 • (4/30/1995) • **79**
Dão Porta dos Cavaleiros 1984 • $12 • (4/30/1995) • **78**
Dão Porta dos Cavaleiros Reserva 1985 • $12 • (4/15/1994) • **85**
Dão Reserva 1985 • $14 • (4/30/1995) • **84**

Key: SS—Spectator Selection. CS—Cellar Selection. HR—Highly Recommended. $NA—Price not available. (BT)—Barrel tasting. Ⓐ—Auction Price. For a key to the tasters' initials, see "How to Use These Listings."
Dates in parentheses represent the issues in which the ratings were published.

SAO PEDRO

Tawny Port 10 Years Old NV • $40 • (9/15/1997) • **88**

SETENCOSTAS, QUINTA DAS

Alenquer 1996: Sweet cherry and spice flavors dominate this quaffable red. Medium-bodied and exuberant, with some cola and cardamom notes on the finish. Drink now.–K.M. • $10 • (1/01/1999) • **83**
Alenquer White 1996: There are some nice mineral and stony notes in this medium-bodied white from Portugal, mixed in with assertive grapefruit and green apple flavors. This is a clean-tasting, well-structured wine with plenty of backbone; drink with fish. Drink now.–K.M. • $10 • (1/01/1999) • **87**

SILVA, C. DA

Vintage Port Presidential 1997: Odd, with earthy and stinky aromas and a slightly sour flavor. This is funky and flawed. Much worse than when tasted from barrel, although it was funky then. Tasted twice, with consistent notes.–J.S. • $23 • (2/29/2000) • **69**

SKEFFINGTON

Late Bottled Port 1994: A simple LBV, with a pronounced grapey, boiled sweets character. Medium-bodied and very sweet, with a silky, easy finish. Drink now.–J.S. • $18 • (7/31/1999) • **82**
Vintage Port 1997: A bit lean, with berry and mineral character. Medium-bodied, with firm tannins and a medium, sweet finish. Not nearly as good as when tasted from barrel. Not imported into the U.S. Best after 2004.–J.S. • $NA • (1/01/2000) • **84**

SMITH WOODHOUSE

Vintage Character Port Lodge Reserve NV • $15 • (6/15/1993) • **82**
Vintage Port 1997: Good, dark color, with raisin, grape and dried cherry aromas. Big and chewy, with lots of fruit and full tannins. Long finish. Smith is the stuff. Best after 2007.–J.S. • $50 • (2/29/2000) • **90**
Vintage Port 1994 • $21 Ⓐ • (4/30/1997) • **86**
Vintage Port 1992 • $33 • (6/15/1995) • **88**
Vintage Port 1991 • $22 Ⓐ • (7/31/1994) • **87**
Vintage Port Madalena 1996: Loads of wet earth, berry, violet and cherry aromas and flavors. Medium bodied and very sweet with chocolate and lots of berry fruit on the finish. Best after 2004.–J.S. • $NA • (2/28/1999) • **89**
Vintage Port Madalena 1995 • $32 • (4/30/1998) CS • **92**

SOGRAPE

Alentejo Vinha do Monte 1998: A lively and fruity red, with plenty of blueberry and raspberry flavors and notes of cardamom on the finish. Drink now.–K.M. • $9 • (6/30/2000) • **85**
Alentejo Vinha do Monte 1996: Easy-drinking, with soft, up-front cherry and raspberry flavors, fresh acidity and juicy texture.–B.S. • $11 • (10/15/1998) • **83**
Alentejo Vinha do Monte 1994 • $10 • (8/31/1997) • **84**
Alentejo Vinha do Monte 1992 • $9 • (3/31/1996) • **85**
Alentejo Vinha do Monte 1991 • $9 • (4/30/1995) • **86**
Alvarinho Vinho Verde Morgadio da Torre 1998: Firm, with green apple and lime flavors, and spicy notes on the finish. A nice change of pace in a white wine. Drink now.–K.M. • $10 • (10/15/1999) • **84**
Aragonês Alentejo Herdade do Peso 1997: Plenty of muscle and concentration in this warm-tasting red, with a hummus aroma and flavors of dark plum, raspberry and spice, which linger on the finish. Aragonês is the Portuguese name for Tempranillo. Drink now.–K.M. • $32 • (6/30/2000) • **88**
Bairrada Nobilis 1995: Candied fruit and a tough overall presentation in this traditionally styled red. Drink now.–B.S. • $9 • (10/15/1998) • **78**
Beiras Terra Franca 1996: A basic, neutral red, with modest berry flavors.–B.S. • $7 • (10/15/1998) • **76**
Dão Duque de Viseu 1996: Soft, ripe and peppery, this offers plum and spice flavors yet lacks focus. Firmly structured, with moderate tannins, this would go well with grilled meats. Drink now.–B.S. • $10 • (7/31/1999) • **82**
Dão Duque de Viseu 1995: This red begins with a velvety feel, turning slightly astringent on the finish. Attractive for its cherry and vanilla flavors, underlying firmness, bright acidity and focus. Drink now.–B.S. • $13 • (10/15/1998) • **86**

Dão Duque de Viseu 1994 • $9 • (8/31/1997) • **83**
Dão Duque de Viseu 1992 • $9 • (3/31/1996) • **87**
Dão Duque de Viseu 1990 • $10 • (4/15/1994) • **85**
Dão Grão Vasco 1994 • $5 • (8/31/1997) • **83**
Dão Grão Vasco 1992 • $5 • (3/31/1996) • **81**
Dão Grão Vasco 1990 • $7 • (4/15/1994) • **77**
Dão Quinta dos Carvalhais 1995: A lovely red, deeply colored, showing spicy cherry character, a firm yet integrated structure and supple texture. Very harmonious and fresh, with lingering cherry and cedar notes. Drink now.–B.S. • $45 • (10/15/1998) • **88**
Dão Reserva 1985 • $11 • (4/15/1994) • **83**
Dão White Duque de Viseu 1999: A well-rounded and smooth white, with flavors of peach, almond and spice that linger on the finish. Drink now.–K.M. • $9 • (6/30/2000) • **84**
Dão White Duque de Viseu 1996 • $8 • (7/31/1997) • **85**
Douro Mateus Signature 1993 • $7 • (8/31/1997) • **81**
Douro Mateus Signature 1992 • $6 • (4/30/1996) • **80**
Douro Mateus Signature 1989 • $9 • (4/15/1994) • **80**
Douro Reserva 1997: Medium-bodied, firm and focused, with flavors of red plum, berry and even a little dark cherry and spice. Hearty, with peppery notes on the finish. Drink now.–K.M. • $13 • (6/30/2000) • **87**
Douro Reserva 1996: A brawny red, showing depth to the black cherry and plum aromas and flavors. Solidly built yet balanced, with cherry notes echoing on the finish. Drink now.–B.S. • $13 • (7/31/1999) • **85**
Douro Reserva 1992 • $10 • (3/31/1996) • **85**
Douro Reserva 1990 • $10 • (4/30/1995) • **89**
Douro Reserva 1987 • $11 • (4/15/1994) • **83**
Douro Vila Regia 1990 • $7 • (4/15/1994) • **78**
Encruzado Dão Quinta dos Carvalhais 1997: An interesting and well-made wine from the Encruzado grape, with butter and apple flavors that linger, with caramel notes, on the finish. Enjoy with fish or fowl. Drink now.–K.M. • $27 • (8/31/1999) • **87**
Touriga Nacional Dão Quinta dos Carvalhais 1996: Bright, lively and concentrated, a red whose violet, plum and spice flavors are densely textured with firm acidity and beefy tannins. Tastes like a dry Port and should improve with age. Drink through 2004.–B.S. • $39 • (7/31/1999) • **88**
Vinho Verde Gazela NV • $4 • (8/31/1997) • **81**

SOPE DA ENCOSTA

Ribatejo 1994 • $6 • (3/31/1996) • **78**

TAYLOR FLADGATE

Late Bottled Port 1994: Has berry character, but it's slightly funky, with old wood and earth notes. Medium- to full-bodied and medium sweet, with silky tannins and an earth and berry aftertaste. Drink now.–J.S. • $21 • (7/31/1999) • **84**
Late Bottled Port 1991 • $18 • (2/28/1998) • **80**
Late Bottled Port 1989 • $16 • (1/31/1996) • **87**
Late Bottled Port 1988 • $17 • (11/15/1994) • **85**
Port First Estate NV • $14 • (4/15/1992) • **81**
Tawny Port 10 Year Old NV • $22 • (1/31/1996) • **84**
Tawny Port 20 Year Old NV • $42 • (1/31/1996) • **84**
Tawny Port 40 Year Old NV • $102 • (1/31/1996) • **86**
Vintage Character Port First Estate Lugar das Lages NV • $16 • (3/15/1994) • **85**
Vintage Port 1997: Beautiful. A young Port, with very pretty blackberry, violet and cherry character. Full-bodied, with velvety tannins and a long, long finish. Very well done. Best after 2007.–J.S. • $83 • (2/29/2000) • **94**
Vintage Port 1994 • $120 Ⓐ • (4/30/1997) CS • **100**
Vintage Port 1992 • $115 Ⓐ • (6/15/1995) • **95**
Vintage Port Quinta de Terra Feita 1996: An elegant, well-crafted young Port, with gorgeous aromas of flowers and ripe blackberries. Full-bodied, medium-sweet, with lots of fine, racy tannins and a long, silky aftertaste. Best after 2004.–J.S. • $NA • (2/28/1999) • **90**
Vintage Port Quinta de Terra Feita 1995 • $NA • (4/30/1998) • **90**
Vintage Port Quinta de Vargellas 1996: Intense aromas of crushed grapes and berries. Full-bodied, with excellent fruit and tannin intensity. Long finish shows violets, fruit and grape character. Vargellas is always impressive. Best after 2006.–J.S. • $NA • (2/28/1999) • **92**
Vintage Port Quinta de Vargellas 1995 • $32 Ⓐ • (4/30/1998) CS • **92**
Vintage Port Quinta de Vargellas 1991 • $38 Ⓐ • (7/31/1994) • **94**
Vintage Port Quinta de Vargellas Vinha Velha 1995 • $200 • (4/30/1998) • **95**
Vintage Port Special Quinta 1947 • $NA • (7/31/1997) • **94**

TEDO, QUINTA DO

Late Bottled Port 1994: Good, clean berry and mineral character. Medium-bodied and medium sweet, with a short, slightly austere finish. Drink now.–J.S. • $20 • (7/31/1999) • **82**
Port Finest Reserve NV: Grapey and rich, with black pepper and light raisin character. Medium- to full-bodied, with velvety tannins. Ripe fruit on the medium sweet, slightly hot finish. Drink now.–J.S. • $17 • (1/01/1999) • **85**
Vintage Port 1995: An aromatic '95 that needs more time to come around. Intensely grapey, with berry and wet earth character. Medium-bodied, with fine tannins and a fresh finish. Best after 2000.–J.S. • $NA • (1/01/1999) • **87**
Vintage Port Traditional Single Quinta 1997: A young Port, with raisin, spice and plum character. Medium-bodied, with racy, firm tannins and a fresh fruit finish. Best after 2005.–J.S. • $45 • (2/29/2000) • **87**

TEODOSIO, CAVES DOM

Arinto Tomar Quinta de S. João Batista 1996 • $7 • (8/31/1997) • **82**
Bairrada Teodósio 1994 • $7 • (8/31/1997) • **71**
Bairrada Teodósio 1990 • $8 • (8/31/1997) • **84**
Bairrada Vinhas da Faia 1995: Leafy and somewhat stemmy-tasting, this thin and tired red has only some sour cherry flavors.–K.M. • $8 • (7/31/1999) • **72**
Cartaxo Falcão de Cima 1996 • $7 • (10/15/1997) • **75**
Cartaxo Quinta d'Almargem Garrafeira 1995: This smells like it's going to be sweet, with caramel and lightly oxidized aromas and flavors like a tawny Port, but it's dry and quite tannic. An odd style that may appeal to some.–B.S. • $15 • (7/31/1999) • **78**
Cartaxo Quinta do Bairro Falcão 1995 • $7 • (8/31/1997) • **83**
Cartaxo Quinta do Bairro Falcão 1993 • $8 • (3/31/1996) • **82**
Cartaxo Quinta do Bairro Falcão 1992 • $NA • (4/30/1995) • **75**
Cartaxo Quinta do Bairro Falcão 1991 • $6 • (4/15/1994) • **84**
Dão Cardeal 1995 • $7 • (8/31/1997) • **85**
Dão Cardeal 1991 • $7 • (3/31/1996) • **84**
Dão Cardeal 1989 • $5 • (4/30/1995) • **85**
Dão Cardeal Reserva 1990 • $9 • (8/31/1997) • **86**
Dão Cardeal Reserva 1983 • $10 • (8/31/1997) • **80**
Dão White Cardeal 1997: Green apple and citrus flavors dominate this modest white.–K.M. • $7 • (8/31/1999) • **79**
Douro Terra das Fragas 1994 • $8 • (8/31/1997) • **84**
Estremoz Casaleiro Garrafeira 1992 • $NA • (4/30/1995) • **78**
Estremoz Casaleiro Garrafeira 1990 • $NA • (4/30/1995) • **76**
Estremoz Casaleiro Garrafeira 1985 • $NA • (4/30/1995) • **83**
Estremoz Casaleiro Garrafeira 1980 • $NA • (4/30/1995) • **73**
Fernão Pires Tomar Quinta de S. João Batista 1999: Peachy aromas and flavors dominate this white, which finishes with crunchy green apple notes. Drink now.–K.M. • $10 • (6/30/2000) • **83**
Fernão Pires Tomar Quinta de S. João Batista 1996 • $7 • (8/31/1997) • **84**
Palmela Almargem 1995: Dried out and charry-tasting, with only modest plum flavors and an astringent finish. Tasted twice, with consistent notes.–K.M. • $10 • (7/31/1999) • **67**
Palmela Almargem 1992 • $8 • (8/31/1997) • **73**
Periquita Tomar Quinta de S. João Batista 1996: Balanced, with pleasant, sweet cherry and spice flavors. Medium-bodied and ready to drink. A lively red that will go well with meaty or spicy dishes. Drink now.–K.M. • $7 • (7/31/1999) • **83**
Periquita Tomar Quinta de S. João Batista Reserva 1995: A nice expression of a traditonal Portuguese red, with flavors of cherry, spice and a little cola. Light- to medium-bodied, with hints of orange peel on the finish. Drink now.–K.M. • $12 • (6/30/2000) • **84**
Ribatejo Casaleiro 1997: A milky aroma and sweet cherry and spice flavors dominate this soft red.–K.M. • $9 • (6/30/2000) • **76**
Ribatejo Casaleiro 1996: Smooth and slightly spicy, with stewy notes. Medium-bodied, with red plum and leather flavors, though they turn a bit bitter on the finish.–K.M. • $7 • (1/01/1999) • **76**
Santarém Cabeça de Toiro Reserva 1992 • $8 • (8/31/1997) • **81**
Santarém Cabeça de Toiro Reserva 1991 • $10 • (3/31/1996) • **79**
Tomar Quinta de S. João Batista 1994 • $7 • (8/31/1997) • **85**
Tomar Quinta de S. João Batista 1992 • $8 • (3/31/1996) • **82**
Tomar Quinta de S. João Batista 1991 • $NA • (4/30/1995) • **76**
Tomar Quinta de S. João Batista Reserva 1995: Nice and juicy, with appealing berry and cherry flavors. Leathery notes on the finish. Drink now.–K.M. • $12 • (1/01/1999) • **82**
Tomar Quinta de S. João Batista Reserva 1992 • $8 • (8/31/1997) • **79**

TERRA DE LOBOS

Ribatejo 1992 • $5 • (4/30/1995) • **86**

TUKE HOLDSWORTH

Vintage Port 1994 • $33 • (4/30/1997) • **88**

UNIAO VINICOLA

Madeira Colombo Old Reserve 10 Years Old NV: Good richness and concentration from the aromas to the finish, all on an off-dry, elegant framework. Smoke and citrus peel flavors turn to a nutty, briny aftertaste that's refreshing and intriguing, leaving a bite at the end.–B.S. • $20 • (4/30/1999) • **87**

Madeira Colombo Rainwater NV: Amber, with a rust tint, this is light-bodied and straightforward, showing caramel notes that turn to walnut on the aftertaste. A touch alcoholic on the finish.–B.S. • $10 • (4/30/1999) • **81**

VALDARCOS, CAVES

Bairrada Garrafeira 1987 • $NA • (4/15/1994) • **79**

Bairrada Reserva 1995: A smooth and mature red, with dried cherry and sandalwood flavors that linger on the finish. Drink now.–K.M. • $7 • (6/30/2000) • **83**

Bairrada Reserva 1989 • $NA • (4/15/1994) • **78**

Dão Reserva 1996: Has modest red fruit flavors, with drying tannins on the finish.–K.M. • $7 • (6/30/2000) • **78**

VALE DA MINA, QUINTA

Late Bottled Port Seixo de Ansiães 1994: A bit hot and rustic. Medium-bodied and very sweet, with a raisiny, earthy aftertaste. Drink now.–J.S. • $20 • (7/31/1999) • **82**

Vintage Port 1995 • $NA • (4/30/1998) • **84**

VALE DONA MARIA, QUINTA DO

Vintage Port 1997: Sleek and racy, with plenty of fine tannins and ripe fruit. Full-bodied, with long, sweet cherry and berry character. Very good indeed. Best after 2006.–J.S. • $50 • (2/29/2000) • **90**

VELHAS, CAVES

Alentejo 1991 • $6 • (4/15/1994) • **76**

Almeirim Garrafeira 1995: Rhubarb and tea flavors don't add up to much in this dull red.–K.M. • $12 • (1/01/1999) • **71**

Almeirim Garrafeira 1993 • $12 • (10/15/1997) • **78**

Almeirim Garrafeira 1990 • $12 • (4/30/1996) • **82**

Bairrada 1992 • $9 • (9/15/1996) • **82**

Bairrada 1990 • $8 • (4/30/1995) • **82**

Bairrada 1989 • $8 • (4/15/1994) • **82**

Bairrada Garrafeira 1990 • $12 • (9/15/1997) • **84**

Bairrada Garrafeira 1985 • $12 • (4/30/1996) • **83**

Dão 1990 • $8 • (4/30/1995) • **86**

Dão 1989 • $8 • (4/15/1994) • **85**

Dão Reserva 1994: Mature and smooth, with nice dried cherry and spice flavor. Brown sugar notes linger on the finish. Drink now.–K.M. • $8 • (1/01/1999) • **83**

Dão Reserva 1985 • $10 • (4/30/1995) • **85**

Douro Lagar Velho 1992 • $8 • (8/31/1997) • **84**

Douro Lagar Velho Reserva 1990 • $10 • (8/31/1997) • **85**

Palmela Romeira Garrafeira 1994: Past its prime, with brown sugar and dried cherry flavors. Minty notes linger on the finish.–K.M. • $11 • (1/01/1999) • **78**

Palmela Romeira Garrafeira 1992 • $8 • (9/15/1996) • **83**

Palmela Romeira Garrafeira 1991 • $11 • (10/15/1997) • **73**

Palmela Romeira Garrafeira 1990 • $7 • (4/30/1995) • **84**

Palmela Romeira Garrafeira 1989 • $11 • (9/15/1996) • **81**

Ribatejo Romeira Garrafeira 1988 • $12 • (4/30/1996) • **80**

Ribatejo Romeira Garrafeira 1982 • $11 • (4/15/1994) • **79**

Ribatejo Romeira Garrafeira 1980 • $12 • (4/15/1994) • **70**

VESUVIO, QUINTA DO

Vintage Port 1997: A fresh and dark Port, with lovely floral, berry and cherry aromas. Full-bodied, medium-sweet, with a firm backbone of tannins and plum and tobacco on the finish. Best after 2007.–J.S. • $80 • (2/29/2000) • **90**

Vintage Port 1996: Impressive. Dark purple in color, with lots of pretty plum, floral and berry aromas. Full-bodied, with very racy tannins and a long, long, fruity finish. Reserved, it needs time. Best after 2004.–J.S. • $60 • (2/28/1999) • **90**

Vintage Port 1995 • $60 • (4/30/1998) CS • **95**

Vintage Port 1994 • $35 Ⓐ • (4/30/1997) • **96**

Vintage Port 1992 • $49 • (6/15/1995) • **94**

Vintage Port 1991 • $53 Ⓐ • (7/31/1994) • **91**

VILARINHO DO BAIRRO, ADEGA COOPERATIVA DE

Bairrada Lar de Forno Reserva 1994 • $5 • (8/31/1997) • **79**

VIMOMPOR

Alvarinho Vinho Verde Quinta da Pedra 1996 • $12 • (10/15/1997) • **73**

Vinho Verde Senhoria 1996 • $6 • (10/15/1997) • **79**

WARRE

Late Bottled Port 1984 • $24 • (2/28/1998) • **89**

Tawny Port 20 year old Nimrod NV • $38 • (2/28/1990) • **84**

Tawny Port 10 year-old Sir William NV • $25 • (1/31/1996) • **82**

Tawny Port Very Finest Rare Nimrod NV • $24 • (4/15/1991) • **85**

Vintage Character Port Warrior Finest Reserve NV • $14 • (3/15/1994) • **80**

Vintage Port 1997: Aromas of minerals, berries and wet earth jump out of the glass. Full-bodied and very chewy, with lots of fruit and a long finish. A tough young wine. Warre is flexing its muscles here. Best after 2008.–J.S. • $55 • (2/29/2000) • **94**

Vintage Port 1994 • $44 Ⓐ • (4/30/1997) • **95**

Vintage Port 1991 • $34 Ⓐ • (7/31/1994) • **91**

Vintage Port Quinta da Cavadinha 1996: Smells like claret, with currants and berries. Medium-bodied, medium-sweet, showing well-integrated tannins and a moderate finish. Best after 2003.–J.S. • $24 • (2/28/1999) • **87**

Vintage Port Quinta da Cavadinha 1995 • $34 Ⓐ • (4/30/1998) CS • **92**

Vintage Port Quinta da Cavadinha 1992 • $26 • (6/30/1995) • **91**

Key: SS—Spectator Selection. CS—Cellar Selection. HR—Highly Recommended. $NA—Price not available. (BT)—Barrel tasting. Ⓐ—Auction Price. For a key to the tasters' initials, see "How to Use These Listings."
Dates in parentheses represent the issues in which the ratings were published.

South Africa

Ever since the trade embargo aimed at the former apartheid government ended in 1991, South Africa has tried to provide reasons—other than novelty—to try its many wines. While the initial wave of stringy Pinotage, brutish Cabernet Sauvignon and charmless Chenin Blanc was not exactly encouraging, it must be remembered that in the early 1990s South Africa's winemakers had been cut off from much of world for several decades and were considerably "off their game." Today, the situation is far more positive. Recent releases are fresher and more concentrated, and the best can make a respectable run at competitors from around the world.

1. Swartland
2. Constantia
3. Stellenbosch
4. Paarl
5. Franschhoek
6. Walker Bay
7. Robertson

GRAPE VARIETIES

As in most of the New World, South African wines are varietally labeled, meaning that they are labeled by the predominant grape in the blend (which must constitute at least 75% of the finished wine). Chardonnay thrives here, producing beautifully balanced wines that call to mind a cross between the subtle mineral-like charm of French white Burgundy and the bolder style of Chardonnays from Australia, Washington and, to a degree, California. The most widely planted white variety is Chenin Blanc, called "Steen" locally, which is undependable but which can produce some excellent buys for $8 or less. When not over-oaked, Sauvignon Blanc serves up bright New World fruit accented with tropical notes.

South Africa's trademark red, called Pinotage, is a cross between Pinot Noir and Cinsault. It is a bit of an acquired taste, often exhibiting a varietal-specific burnt almond note on the finish. At its best, Pinotage can produce powerful, long-lived reds with vigorous black-fruit flavors. Shiraz (or Syrah, as it's called in France), Cabernet Sauvignon and Merlot are also thriving. Shiraz may be the most exciting red wine of all, because it combines generous (but not jammy) fruit flavors with smoky, meaty accents and firm tannins that are more reminiscent of the Rhône than of Australia. While some Cabernets and Merlots may be best enjoyed for their intense fruit character, others are defined by a spicy, new-oak lushness.

WINE REGIONS

Most of South Africa's quality vineyards are located on or near the country's coastal southern tip, and benefit from cool Atlantic breezes in the same way that Carneros in California is cooled by Pacific breezes. Stellenbosch, an ocean-cooled coastal district just 15 miles from Cape Town, is one of South Africa's oldest grape-growing regions and produces many of its best red wines. Yields are low, and the demand for good Stellenbosch wines always seems to exceed supply. The adjacent district of Paarl also accounts for several of the best wines and best-known wineries. Another 40 miles to the southeast, Walker Bay has produced successful wines from the Burgundian varieties Chardonnay and Pinot Noir.

South Africa's inland wine regions are generally hotter and drier, and the wineries must irrigate their vineyards. Yields are large, quality is ordinary, and most of the wine made here is destined for domestic consumption. However, several estates and cooperatives produce some notable Chardonnays and dessert wines. In the future, we can expect more good wines from this richly diverse country.

ALLESVERLOREN

Cabernet Sauvignon Swartland Region 1989 • $15 • (9/30/1995) • **89**

AMANI

Sauvignon Blanc Stellenbosch 1998: Delicious, full of peach, melon, gooseberry and herb flavors matched to a light, vibrant framework. A citrus note completes the package. Drink now.–B.S. • $12 • (4/30/2000) • **87**

AVENIR, L'

Pinotage Stellenbosch 1998: Broad and warm, this masculine red is reminiscent of a fine Châteauneuf with its plum, hot brick and wild herb aromas and flavors. Open and immediately appealing, there's balance and a chewiness to the texture. Drink now through 2003.–B.S. • $17 • (4/30/2000) • **89**

BACKSBERG

Cabernet Sauvignon Paarl 1996: Full-bodied and firm-textured, this hearty, concentrated Cabernet has ripe fruit flavors accented by buttery, spicy oak. Just tannic enough. Drink now through 2001. • $13 • (11/30/1998) • **86**
Cabernet Sauvignon Paarl 1995 • $12 • (4/30/1998) HR • **88**
Cabernet Sauvignon Paarl 1993 • $12 • (7/31/1996) • **88**
Cabernet Sauvignon Paarl 1992 • $10 • (3/31/1995) • **85**
Cabernet Sauvignon Paarl 1990 • $11 • (6/30/1994) • **88**
Cabernet Sauvignon-Merlot Paarl Klein Babylonstoren 1996: Soft and appealing, this red offers chocolate aromas and flavors, yet the fruit lacks full ripeness, showing an herbal quality and astringence on the finish. Food will help. Drink now.–B.S. • $18 • (4/30/2000) • **81**
Chardonnay Paarl 1997: Quite oaky, almost sweet in style, with butterscotch, smoke and candy apple flavors, a smooth texture and a lingering finish. Drink now. • $13 • (11/30/1998) • **81**
Klein Babylonstoren Paarl 1992 • $13 • (12/31/1995) • **84**
Klein Babylonstoren Paarl 1991 • $13 • (9/30/1995) • **78**
Merlot Paarl 1997: On the wild side, with a minty aroma and flavors of leather, red plum and chocolaty spice. Concentrated and fairly rich, with minty notes that linger on the finish. Quite a mouthful. Drink now through 2001.–K.M. • $13 • (9/15/1999) • **86**
Merlot Paarl 1996: A serious Merlot, supporting its concentrated cherry flavors with a firm texture and accents of smoke, mineral and herb that linger on the finish. Drink now through 2002. • $13 • (11/15/1998) • **86**
Merlot Paarl 1995 • $12 • (4/30/1998) • **85**
Merlot Paarl 1994 • $12 • (1/31/1997) • **85**
Merlot Paarl 1993 • $10 • (6/15/1995) • **87**
Pinotage Paarl 1997: This Pinotage goes for the gusto, packing in bold flavors of plum, rosemary, black olive, cedar and smoke. But the texture is tannic and dry, and the finish is overtly smoky. Drink now. • $11 • (9/15/1999) • **83**
Pinotage Paarl 1994 • $10 • (5/15/1997) • **85**
Pinotage Paarl 1993 • $10 • (7/31/1996) • **87**
Pinotage Paarl 1992 • $8 • (6/15/1995) • **86**
Pinotage Paarl 1990 • $10 • (2/15/1993) • **86**
Shiraz Paarl 1997: Generous fruit flavors and a firm but smooth texture make this an inviting, full-bodied red. It has peppery, plummy accents, moderate tannins and a lingering finish. Drink now through 2002. • $13 • (9/15/1999) • **86**
Shiraz Paarl 1996: A hearty, jammy, wild and exuberant red, with ripe blackberry and raspberry flavors, good balance and firm but soft tannins. Drink now. • $13 • (11/30/1998) • **86**
Shiraz Paarl 1995 • $12 • (4/30/1998) • **89**
Shiraz Paarl 1993 • $12 • (5/15/1997) • **89**
Shiraz Paarl 1992 • $10 • (4/30/1996) • **85**
Shiraz Paarl 1991 • $10 • (9/30/1995) • **84**

BAOBAB

Cabernet Sauvignon Western Cape 1997: Has some ripe plum and dark cherry flavors, but a charred, dry finish.–K.M. • $9 • (3/31/1999) • **78**
Chardonnay Western Cape 1997: A bit coarse, with decent fig and ripe pear flavors. White pepper notes linger on the finish.–K.M. • $9 • (2/28/1999) • **78**
Chenin Blanc Western Cape 1997: A cloying aroma and a pineappley flavor are the lone hallmarks of this modest white.–K.M. • $7 • (3/31/1999) • **77**
Merlot Western Cape 1997: Muddled, with some faint plum flavor that is quickly overwhelmed by a charry, astringent finish.–K.M. • $9 • (3/31/1999) • **73**
Sauvignon Blanc Western Cape 1997: Flat and soft. There's little fruit and not much acidity; it offers almond and tarragon flavors that lack varietal definition.–T.M. • $8 • (2/28/1999) • **77**

BEAUMONT

Ariane Walker Bay 1998: An extracted attempt, with ripe prune, coffee and chocolate flavors and a firm, chewy texture. Verging on top-heavy, but it stays together. Should be better with food. Drink now.–B.S. • $15 • (1/01/2000) • **86**
Chardonnay Walker Bay 1997: Tart and tightly wound, this tastes more like a still blanc de blancs Champagne, offering citrus, green apple and nutmeg. Crisp, minerally finish. Needs food. Drink now through 2001.–B.S. • $15 • (12/31/1999) • **84**
Chenin Blanc Walker Bay 1997: Maturing with personality, this offers notes of butterscotch, pine, apple and lemon in a crisp, compact style. Subtle finish. Drink now.–B.S. • $9 • (12/31/1999) • **83**
Goutte d'Or Walker Bay 1997: Strongly in the dessert camp, this bursts with smoke, apricot and crème brûlée notes. Rich and round, it doesn't quite follow through on the finish, where a vegetal element lingers. Drink now.–B.S. • $17/375 ml. • (11/15/1999) • **82**
Pinotage Walker Bay 1998: Lovely berry aromas, with some meaty tones beneath. The spicy oak emerges on the palate, along with black cherry. Turns a little charry on the finish, with some stiff tannins. Best from 2001 through 2004.–B.S. • $14 • (4/30/2000) • **85**

BECK, GRAHAM

Chardonnay Robertson Lonehill 1997 • $10 • (6/15/1998) • **83**
Shiraz-Cabernet Sauvignon Robertson 1996: An appealing, light, fruity-tasting, almost sweet red, with abundant cherry and raspberry flavors and light tannins. Drink now. • $10 • (7/31/1998) • **84**

BELLINGHAM

Cabernet Sauvignon Paarl 1997: Plenty of lush toasty oak frames the cherry and chocolate flavors in this delicate red. Balanced on the oaky side, with a lingering yet firm finish. Drink now.–B.S. • $30 • (12/15/1999) • **85**
Merlot Coastal Region 1996 • $11 • (6/15/1998) • **79**
Pinotage Paarl 1997: Smells and tastes like ripe plums, with a veneer of sweet vanilla from the oak, yet it's firm and lean at the core, ending on a minerally note. Needs time and food. Best from 2001 through 2004.–B.S. • $30 • (4/30/2000) • **85**
Pinotage Paarl 1990 • $10 • (2/15/1993) • **80**
Sauvignon Blanc Coastal Region 1997 • $10 • (6/15/1998) • **84**
Syrah Coastal Region 1996: Round and generous, delivering plenty of smoke, plum, vanilla and leather aromas and flavors on a full-bodied, structured frame. Good complexity persists on the finish. Drink now.–B.S. • $30 • (4/30/2000) • **85**

BEYERSKLOOF

Pinotage Stellenbosch 1996 • $11 • (10/15/1997) • **84**
Pinotage Stellenbosch 1995 • $10 • (7/31/1996) • **82**
Stellenbosch 1997: Young and unevolved, this brooding giant of a red is densely textured and complex, boasting roasted black cherry, plum, vanilla and cedar flavors. Lovely focus and vibrance drives the fruit, with fine grip on the finish. Cabernet Sauvignon and Merlot. Drink through 2006.–B.S. • $28 • (4/30/2000) • **91**

BLAAUWKLIPPEN

Cabernet Sauvignon Stellenbosch 1989 • $20 • (9/30/1995) • **84**
Cabernet Sauvignon Stellenbosch Reserve Guild Auction Label 1989 • $24 • (9/30/1995) • **88**
Zinfandel Stellenbosch 1990 • $16 • (6/30/1995) • **75**
Zinfandel Stellenbosch Reserve 1990 • $20 • (6/30/1995) • **79**

Key: SS—Spectator Selection. CS—Cellar Selection. HR—Highly Recommended. $NA—Price not available. (BT)—Barrel tasting. (A)—Auction Price. For a key to the tasters' initials, see "How to Use These Listings."
Dates in parentheses represent the issues in which the ratings were published.

BLOUPUNT

Chardonnay Montagu Unwooded 1997: A straightforward Chardonnay with simple, herbaceous flavors, coarse texture and short finish. • $11 • (9/15/1999) • **77**

Chardonnay Montagu Wooded 1997: A simple, basic Chardonnay, with very light fruit flavors and rather full but coarse body. • $13 • (9/15/1999) • **77**

BODEGA

Cabernet Sauvignon Paarl 1993: Rich in fruit flavor, this Bordeaux-style Cabernet is broad and expansive in texture yet amply supported by tannins. Complex, attractive and long on the finish. Should continue to mellow. Drink now through 2002. • $16 • (11/30/1998) • **88**

Merlot Paarl 1994: A beefy overtone dominates, with mineral and dried plum notes. Finishes with appealing herbal flavors. Drink now.–K.M. • $15 • (12/15/1998) • **84**

BOLAND WYNKELDER

Cabernet Sauvignon Paarl 1995 • $11 • (3/31/1998) • **84**

Cabernet Sauvignon Paarl 1992 • $10 • (9/15/1997) • **84**

Pinotage Paarl 1995 • $NA • (8/31/1997) • **83**

Vintage Port Paarl 1992 • $15 • (3/31/1998) • **84**

BONHEUR, LE

Cabernet Sauvignon Simonsberg-Stellenbosch 1995: Very ripe flavors of plum—almost prune—along with mint and cedar combine with good concentration and solid structure for a rustic, intense style. Drink now through 2001.–B.S. • $18 • (12/15/1999) • **85**

Cabernet Sauvignon Simonsberg-Stellenbosch 1991: This unusual, nearly mature wine gets better as you sip. Herbal aromas give way to bright cherry-currant flavors, and the texture turns silky on the finish. Drink now. • $17 • (9/30/1998) • **85**

Chardonnay Simonsberg-Stellenbosch 1997: Mature, this Chardonnay offers almond, baked apple and nut flavors accented by vanilla and nutmeg. Crisp, with richness midpalate and a lingering finish. Drink now.–B.S. • $11 • (5/15/2000) • **88**

BOPLAAS

Port South Africa 1989 • $NA • (9/30/1995) • **82**

Ruby Port Calitzdorp Cape NV: A sweet, soft, after-dinner wine that has fresh, light plum flavors, full body and a sweet finish. Drink now. • $8 • (9/15/1999) • **81**

Tawny Port Western Cape Cape Tawny NV: This medium-weight tawny has a nice toffee aroma followed by a walnut-accented midpalate, but a slightly coarse and hot finish. Drink now.–B.S. • $12 • (1/01/2000) • **84**

Vintage Port Calitzdorp Reserve 1996: An ambitious vintage Port that's flavorful and satisfying. Has a deep color, ripe-raisiny aromas, full body and a lingering finish. Drink now through 2005. • $30 • (9/15/1999) • **85**

Vintage Port South Africa Cape Vintage 1996: Raisin, molasses and slightly stemmy aromas and flavors run through this medium-weight, somewhat rustic Port. Slightly hot finish but the flavors push through. Drink now.–B.S. • $13 • (1/01/2000) • **86**

BOSCHENDAL

Sauvignon Blanc Coastal Region 1999: Modest herbal flavors, with an earthy streak. Ends on a bitter note.–B.S. • $12 • (4/30/2000) • **79**

Sauvignon Blanc Coastal Region 1998: Firm, crisp and well defined, with grassy aromas, pleasant flavors of gooseberry and citrus and some herbal notes. Good structure and backbone, with a lingering finish. Drink now.–.M. • $12 • (3/31/1999) • **84**

Sauvignon Blanc Coastal Region Grand Cuvée 1998: Ripe and juicy, exhibiting nectarine and gooseberry, with a touch of almond. Mature and enjoyable, with a butterscotch aftertaste. Drink now.–B.S. • $15 • (4/30/2000) • **84**

BOUCHARD FINLAYSON

Pinot Noir Walker Bay 1994 • $NA • (6/15/1995) • **84**

Pinot Noir Walker Bay 1993 • $NA • (6/15/1995) • **85**

BOUWLAND

Cabernet Sauvignon-Merlot Stellenbosch 1997: A fresh and flavorful red blend that's light on its feet and ready to enjoy. The bright cherry and plum flavors are backed by crisp acidity and moderate tannins. Drink now. • $10 • (9/15/1999) • **87**

BOVLEI WINERY

Cabernet Sauvignon Wellington 1992 • $NA • (6/30/1995) • **81**

Grand Rouge Wellington 1992 • $NA • (6/30/1995) • **85**

Pinotage Wellington 1994 • $NA • (6/30/1995) • **81**

Shiraz Wellington 1991 • $NA • (6/30/1995) • **75**

BRAMPTON

Cabernet Sauvignon-Merlot Stellenbosch 1998: Marked by aromatic new oak, with cherry notes vying for attention over the freshly cut wood and coffee. It's an elegant package, ending with wood tannins. Drink now.–B.S. • $15 • (4/30/2000) • **84**

Cabernet Sauvignon-Merlot Stellenbosch 1997: Focused aromas and flavors of black currant, cherry and vanilla highlight this elegant, supple red. Merlot provides flesh midpalate, with Cabernet prevailing on the firm finish. Drink now.–B.S. • $15 • (12/15/1999) • **86**

Cabernet Sauvignon-Merlot Stellenbosch 1996: An elegant, silky style that shows off the Bordeaux grapes' cherry and currant flavors beautifully. Not too tannic, bright with acidity and perfectly balanced. Drink now through 2002. • $15 • (9/30/1998) • **88**

Chardonnay Stellenbosch 1998: An exotic style of Chardonnay whose apricot and smoke notes float on the soft, pillowy framework. Firms up a little on the finish. Drink now.–B.S. • $15 • (5/15/2000) • **81**

Chardonnay Stellenbosch 1997: A bit woody and lean, with modest apple and citrus flavors. Tasted twice, with consistent notes.–K.M. • $15 • (9/30/1998) • **77**

Sauvignon Blanc Stellenbosch 1999: Moderate flavors of gooseberry and earth and an austere character add up to a simple white. Drink now.–B.S. • $15 • (4/30/2000) • **80**

Sauvignon Blanc Stellenbosch 1997: Not shy, this wine has plenty of aggressive Sauvignon character, with a heavy dose of herbal, grassy aromas and flavors, full body and a lingering finish. Drink now. • $15 • (8/31/1998) • **85**

BREDELL'S

Shiraz Stellenbosch 1997: An assertive sweet oak character and a juniper note augment the raspberry and leather in this bold, full-bodied red. Exuberant, it ends with a coffee, soy flavor. Not for the faint of heart. Drink now through 2002.–B.S. • $17 • (4/30/2000) • **86**

Vintage Port Stellenbosch Limited Release 1991 • $NA • (9/30/1995) • **87**

BRENTHURST

Cabernet Sauvignon-Merlot Coastal Region 1996: Showing maturity, here's a red in the Bordeaux camp, exuding coffee, mineral, black currant and cedar in an elegant package. Minty finish. Drink now through 2001.–B.S. • $20 • (5/15/2000) • **86**

BUITENVERWACHTING

Chardonnay Constantia 1998: Medium-bodied, this exhibits depth and concentration to the pear, spice and vanilla aromas and flavors, along with a solid structure and a lingering finish. Drink now.–B.S. • $20 • (12/31/1999) • **85**

Christine Constantia 1989 • $20 • (9/30/1995) • **88**

Grand Vin Constantia 1990 • $22 • (9/30/1995) • **77**

Sauvignon Blanc Constantia 1999: Crisp and lean, displaying a citrus note along with grassy, herbal accents. Focused and elegant, ending with a lingering chalky sensation. Drink now.–B.S. • $18 • (4/30/2000) • **84**

Sauvignon Blanc Constantia 1998: Ripe, with grapefruit and fig notes and decent acidity underneath. Light-bodied, turning crisp and grassy on the moderate finish. Drink now.–B.S. • $17 • (1/01/2000) • **83**

Sauvignon Blanc Constantia 1997: Nicely balanced, crisp and lively in texture and almost elegant in style, this reminds one of Sancerre. The bright grapefruit and apple flavors linger on the finish. Drink now. • $18 • (8/31/1998) • **86**

CAPE COUNTRY

Cabernet Sauvignon South Africa 1991 • $6 • (6/30/1994) • **75**
Pinotage Coastal Region 1990 • $6 • (6/30/1994) • **78**
Pinotage Coastal Region 1989 • $5 • (2/15/1993) • **77**

CAPE INDABA

Cabernet Sauvignon Coastal Region 1998: Berry and plum aromas and flavors align with a soft texture, picking up spice notes and a firm edge on the finish. Drink now.–B.S. • $10 • (12/15/1999) • **82**
Chardonnay Western Cape 1999: Fresh and light-bodied, this straightforward, peach- and pear-flavored white has a candied quality. Finishes on the short side.–B.S. • $11 • (5/15/2000) • **79**
Chardonnay Western Cape 1998: An attractive Chardonnay that's lush in texture, subtle in flavor and lasting on the finish. Well balanced and appealing. Drink now. • $9 • (5/15/1999) • **84**
Chenin Blanc Western Cape 1999: A touch earthy, with beeswax, honey and apple flavors prevailing on a bright, firm structure. Drink now.–B.S. • $8 • (5/15/2000) • **84**
Chenin Blanc Western Cape 1998: A dry, straightforward white wine with modest flavors of baked apple. • $7 • (5/15/1999) • **79**
Pinotage Coastal Region 1998: A hearty young red that reminds of a Côtes du Rhône with its peppery, berrylike character and dry, moderately tannic texture. Drink now. • $10 • (5/15/1999) • **84**
Pinotage Coastal Region 1995 • $9 • (4/30/1996) • **84**
Sauvignon Blanc Robertson 1998: Fragrant and fresh, this Sauvignon has plenty of ripe citrus and herb flavor, a soft texture and clean finish. Drink now. • $8 • (5/15/1999) • **84**
Sauvignon Blanc Western Cape 1999: Ripe and nutty-tasting, with a hint of butterscotch married to a soft, medium-bodied structure. Drink now.–B.S. • $9 • (4/30/2000) • **82**

CAPE RIVER ISLE

Cabernet Sauvignon Western Cape 1997: A big, full-bodied Cabernet, with warm, generous fruit flavors of moderate intensity, ample tannins and seemingly high alcohol. Drink now. • $9 • (9/30/1998) • **85**
Pinotage Breede River Valley 1996: Like a light-bodied Côtes du Rhône, this has lean plum, herb and smoke character, with soft tannins and an easy texture.–P.M. • $9 • (11/15/1998) • **79**

CATHEDRAL CELLARS

Cabernet Franc Western Cape 1996 • $14 • (1/01/1998) • **85**
Cabernet Sauvignon Coastal Region 1995 • $14 • (6/15/1998) • **84**
Cabernet Sauvignon Coastal Region 1994 • $12 • (9/30/1997) • **86**
Cabernet Sauvignon Coastal Region 1993 • $12 • (1/31/1997) • **84**
Cabernet Sauvignon Coastal Region 1992 • $10 • (6/15/1995) • **85**
Cabernet Sauvignon Coastal Region 1990 • $11 • (6/30/1994) • **85**
Chardonnay Coastal Region 1997: Toasty oak aromas and flavors distinguish this round-textured and sufficiently fruity Chardonnay. Has generosity and complexity. Drink now. • $12 • (11/30/1998) • **85**
Merlot Coastal Region 1995 • $14 • (6/15/1998) • **78**
Merlot Coastal Region 1994 • $12 • (5/15/1997) • **82**
Pinotage Coastal Region 1996: An easy-to-drink, medium-bodied red. Generous, bright cherry and plum flavors are backed by soft tannins and linger on the finish. Drink now.–P.M. • $14 • (11/15/1998) • **87**
Pinotage Coastal Region 1993 • $12 • (5/31/1997) • **88**
Pinotage Coastal Region 1992 • $10 • (9/30/1995) • **80**
Sauvignon Blanc Coastal Region 1998: Alive with crisp citrus and herb aromas and flavors, this is a fresh, bright white that's easy to drink. Drink now. • $12 • (11/30/1998) • **85**
Shiraz Western Cape 1996: A vibrant, full-flavored Shiraz oozing with blackberry and cherry notes and accented by subtle oak. It's full-bodied, but not too tannic. Drink now. • $14 • (11/30/1998) • **88**
Steen Western Cape 1998: The subdued apple and honey flavors in this smooth-textured wine grow on you with each sip. Drink now. • $7 • (11/30/1998) • **83**

Key: SS—Spectator Selection. CS—Cellar Selection. HR—Highly Recommended. $NA—Price not available. (BT)—Barrel tasting. (A)—Auction Price.
For a key to the tasters' initials, see "How to Use These Listings."
Dates in parentheses represent the issues in which the ratings were published.

Triptych Coastal Region Red 1995: Solid, flavorful and polished, this has rich black cherry flavors accented by vanilla and cedar, smooth but firm tannins and a lingering finish. A blend of Cabernet Sauvignon, Merlot and Cabernet Franc. Drink now through 2001. • $14 • (11/30/1998) • **87**
Triptych Coastal Region Red 1994 • $14 • (1/01/1998) • **78**
Triptych Coastal Region Red 1992 • $10 • (9/30/1995) • **82**
Triptych Coastal Region Red 1990 • $11 • (6/30/1994) • **84**

CENTAURUS

Cabernet Sauvignon Durbanville 1991 • $12 • (4/30/1996) • **84**
Pinotage Durbanville 1991 • $12 • (4/30/1996) • **83**
Zinfandel Stellenbosch 1991 • $11 • (7/31/1996) • **70**

CHAMONIX

Cabernet Sauvignon Franschhoek 1995: Crisp and quite tannic in texture but bright with cherry flavor, making for a flavorful yet rather tart experience overall. Will it mellow with time? Drink now. • $19 • (11/30/1998) • **83**
Merlot Coastal Region 1995: Dense and fairly rich, with an inviting aroma of red fruit, good blackberry, cassis and currant flavors, a solid backbone of acidity and plenty of tannins. Drink through 2001–K.M. • $19 • (12/15/1998) • **86**

CHATEAU LIBERTAS

Red Coastal Region 1996: Thin, light in color and browning at the rim, this tastes stewed and herbal, with an astringent finish.–B.S. • $10 • (4/30/2000) • **79**
Red Coastal Region 1988 • $10 • (6/30/1994) • **75**

CHEETAH VALLEY

Cabernet Sauvignon Paarl Reserve 1993 • $9 • (7/31/1996) • **87**
Chardonnay Western Cape 1997: Clean fruit flavors, uncomplicated pear and grapefruit notes with hints of vanilla, and a polished, silky texture make this South African quite appealing, as does its reasonable price. Drink now. • $10 • (7/31/1998) • **86**
Merlot Western Cape 1997: Light and appealing, with fresh strawberry and cherry flavors, an easy-drinking texture and little tannin. Fun for quaffing. Drink now. • $10 • (7/31/1998) • **84**
Merlot Western Cape 1993 • $9 • (1/31/1997) • **83**
Pinotage Paarl Reserve 1993 • $9 • (7/31/1996) • **86**
Pinotage Western Cape 1997: A light, fresh red, with cherry-berry flavors, very little tannin and a sweet finish. Drink now. • $10 • (7/31/1998) • **81**
Pinotage Western Cape 1994 • $9 • (5/15/1997) • **83**
Vintage Port Western Cape 1994 • $14 • (6/15/1998) • **82**

CLOS CABRIERE

Brut Franschhoek Pierre Jourdan Cuvée Belle Rose NV: A fruit-scented bubbly, offering berry and cherry notes, round and smoothly textured, with a crisp, refreshing finish. Drink now.–B.S. • $25 • (1/01/2000) • **85**
Brut Franschhoek Valley Pierre Jourdan NV • $14 • (2/28/1995) • **78**
Brut Franschhoek Valley Pierre Jourdan Sauvage NV • $20 • (2/28/1995) • **85**

CLOS MALVERNE

Auret Stellenbosch Red 1995 • $15 • (4/30/1998) • **78**
Auret Stellenbosch Red 1989 • $20 • (10/15/1992) • **77**
Cabernet Sauvignon Stellenbosch 1995 • $14 • (3/31/1998) • **88**
Cabernet Sauvignon Stellenbosch 1994 • $14 • (1/31/1997) • **84**
Cabernet Sauvignon Stellenbosch 1989 • $16 • (10/15/1992) • **77**
Cabernet Sauvignon Stellenbosch Basket Pressed 1997: Ripe, with a nice density to it, but the overtly gamy and herbal flavors are not for the faint of heart. This was the better of two samples, with significant bottle variation. Drink now through 2001.–K.M. • $15 • (9/15/1999) • **82**
Pinotage Stellenbosch 1996: Ah, so this is what Pinotage can do. Abundantly fruity, richly textured, densely colored, lightly tannic and easy to enjoy. Drink now. • $12 • (7/31/1998) • **87**
Pinotage Stellenbosch 1995 • $12 • (1/01/1997) • **81**
Pinotage Stellenbosch 1990 • $10 • (2/15/1993) • **87**
Pinotage Stellenbosch Basket Pressed 1998: Wonderfully ripe and grapey, this tastes like crushed fruit in a glass. Deep in color and flavor, with bold blackberry and cherry notes that linger on the finish. The firm texture is

not too tannic. Two new samples were consistent and much better than previously reviewed, but beware of bottle variation. Drink now through 2001. • $14 • (9/15/1999) • **88**

Pinotage Stellenbosch Basket Pressed Reserve 1997: A complex aroma of smoke, spices and berries draws you into this ripe, mature, full-bodied Pinotage. It's substantive but smooth, with a lingering finish. Drink now. • $15 • (9/15/1999) • **86**

Pinotage Stellenbosch Reserve 1996: Distinctive in flavor and rich in texture, this offers unusual concentration and complexity. Packed with ripe plum and blackberry notes and accented by earthy, aniselike undertones. Ample but soft tannins make it appealing. Drink now through 2001.–P.M. • $15 • (11/15/1998) • **89**

Sauvignon Blanc Stellenbosch 1999: Broad, infused with ripe peach and melon, showing butterscotch, almond and citrus on an open structure. Drink now.–B.S. • $12 • (4/30/2000) • **84**

CLUVER, PAUL

Pinot Noir Elgin 1998: An expressive Pinot Noir, showing a slightly charred note along with cherry and spice. Generous yet a little awkward, but may come together. Drink now through 2001.–B.S. • $23 • (5/15/2000) • **81**

Sauvignon Blanc Elgin 1998: There's a lively, succulent structure in this mature white, yet the grass and melon notes are diffuse, lacking concentration. Still, a good quaff. Drink now.–B.S. • $17 • (4/30/2000) • **82**

DE TRAFFORD

Cabernet Sauvignon Stellenbosch 1996: Lovely Cabernet character. Cool, fresh and well defined in aroma and flavor, showing concentration and an elegant structure. Black currant, licorice and olive flavors linger on the finish. Drink now through 2002.–B.S. • $25 • (4/30/2000) • **87**

DELAIRE

Chardonnay Stellenbosch 1998: This simple white is shy on concentration and freshness.–B.S. • $23 • (12/31/1999) • **76**

Chardonnay Stellenbosch 1997: A harmonious, smooth-textured Chardonnay from a label new to the United States. It seamlessly blends subtle nutmeg, vanilla and butter nuances with lively pear and apple notes. Has fine balance and a lingering finish. Drink now. • $27 • (8/31/1998) • **89**

Sauvignon Blanc Stellenbosch 1999: Broad and forward in style, with peach, melon and grapefruit flavors. Enough acidity to keep it fresh. A good aperitif. Drink now.–B.S. • $18 • (4/30/2000) • **84**

Sauvignon Blanc Stellenbosch 1998: With textbook aromas and flavors of freshly cut grass and gooseberry, this subtle Sauvignon also shows good weight, a clean, ripe mouthfeel and lingering juicy acidity. Nicely done. Drink now.–B.S. • $17 • (1/01/2000) • **87**

Sauvignon Blanc Stellenbosch 1997: Shows a smoky edge, mixed with some applelike flavors. Tasted twice, with consistent notes.–K.M. • $19 • (9/30/1998) • **76**

DELHEIM

Cabernet Sauvignon Stellenbosch 1998: Suave, brimming with toasty, roasted plum and black cherry. Smooth as velvet and supported by fine tannins. Not a blockbuster, but well integrated. Drink now through 2002.–B.S. • $16 • (5/15/2000) • **88**

Edelspatz Noble Late Harvest Stellenbosch 1998: Sweet, bursting with apricot and honey on a thick texture, here's an appealing, if one-dimensional, dessert white. Riesling and Bukettraube. Drink now.–B.S. • $19/375 ml. • (5/15/2000) • **85**

Gewürztraminer Stellenbosch 1998: Textbook rose petal and litchi notes remain focused in this light, slim version of Gewürztraminer. Drink now.–B.S. • $13 • (5/15/2000) • **82**

Grand Reserve Stellenbosch 1991 • $18 • (6/15/1995) • **87**

Heerenwijn Stellenbosch 1998: A juicy white offering apple and pear flavors on a moderately rich, bright framework. Drink now.–B.S. • $10 • (5/15/2000) • **82**

Merlot Stellenbosch 1997: Incredibly ripe, bold and zingy, this broad-shouldered red exudes plum, coffee, spice and a roasted character on a firm structure that shows mineral on the finish. Still youthful, it should marry well with grilled meats. Drink now through 2003.–B.S. • $17 • (5/15/2000) • **88**

Pinotage Stellenbosch 1998: Distinctive, with a savage, feral nuance augmenting the plum, smoke and leather aromas and flavors. Broad and rich on the palate, it's balanced and lingering on the finish. Drink now through 2001.–B.S. • $16 • (5/15/2000) • **87**

Pinotage Stellenbosch 1989 • $10 • (2/15/1993) • **81**

Roodenwijn Stellenbosch Dry Red 1994 • $8 • (9/30/1995) • **78**

Shiraz Stellenbosch 1998: Gorgeous aromas of violets, raspberries, blackberries, coffee and vanilla give way to intense, freshly crushed berry flavors wrapped in a silky coating. Young, vibrant and concentrated, this holds promise for the future. Great length. Drink now through 2003.–B.S. • $17 • (4/30/2000) • **89**

Shiraz Stellenbosch 1991 • $10 • (9/30/1995) • **77**

DESTINARE

Cabernet Sauvignon Franschhoek Valley 1995 • $8 • (6/15/1998) • **76**

Grand Rouge Franschhoek Valley 1996: A simple, fruity red that might be best chilled. Light but jammy cherry and strawberry flavors, with a slightly sweet finish. • $8 • (7/31/1998) • **78**

Grand Rouge Franschhoek Valley 1995 • $7 • (7/31/1996) • **83**

Merlot Worcester 1996 • $8 • (6/15/1998) • **76**

DIAMOND BAY

Cabernet Sauvignon Western Cape 1998: Starts out soft and slightly jammy, in an easy-drinking style. Lacks a bit of focus and balance, turning astringent on the finish. Drink now.–B.S. • $10 • (4/30/2000) • **82**

Chardonnay Western Cape 1999: Smells like a Riesling with its strong petrol note. The smoky, eucalyptus character overwhelms the fruit, leaving this white awkward.–B.S. • $10 • (5/15/2000) • **77**

Pinotage Western Cape 1998: A very good quality South African Pinotage, this is dark and smells of cherry candy and vanilla, with plenty of cherry and plum to support the oak. Fresh and very forward in style, it's a nice quaff for the price. Drink now through 2004.–B.S. • $10 • (4/30/2000) • **86**

DROSTDYHOF

Merlot Coastal Region 1992 • $10 • (9/30/1995) • **86**

Pinotage Coastal Region SFW 1989 • $8 • (2/15/1993) • **87**

EIKENDAL

Cabernet Sauvignon Stellenbosch 1994 • $16 • (4/30/1998) • **85**

Chardonnay Stellenbosch 1997 • $15 • (4/30/1998) • **84**

Merlot Stellenbosch 1996 • $15 • (6/15/1998) • **84**

Merlot Stellenbosch 1995 • $16 • (8/31/1997) • **80**

ELLIS, NEIL

Cabernet Sauvignon Jonkershoek Valley 1997: Assertive, exhibiting black currant, cedar and spice notes, with an overlay of vanilla oak and firm structure allied to a lean texture. Needs food. Best from 2001 through 2004.–B.S. • $25 • (4/30/2000) • **84**

Cabernet Sauvignon Stellenbosch 1997: Lavishly oaked, exhibiting green olive, black currant and leafy underbrush aromas and flavors. Very firmly structured, it ends on an astringent component. Best from 2001 through 2004.–B.S. • $18 • (4/30/2000) • **84**

Cabernet Sauvignon Stellenbosch 1995 • $17 • (6/15/1998) • **88**

Cabernet Sauvignon Stellenbosch 1994 • $16 • (9/15/1997) • **87**

Cabernet Sauvignon Stellenbosch 1993 • $18 • (12/31/1995) • **84**

Cabernet Sauvignon Stellenbosch 1992 • $14 • (3/31/1995) • **82**

Cabernet Sauvignon Stellenbosch 1990 • $13 • (6/30/1994) • **86**

Cabernet Sauvignon-Merlot Stellenbosch Inglewood 1998: Focused and lively, showing juicy cherry and strawberry aromas and flavors on a lightweight frame. Drink now.–B.S. • $11 • (4/30/2000) • **83**

Chardonnay Elgin 1998: The apple and pear flavors hold their own against the buttery, spicy oak in this lively, attractive Chardonnay. Good concentration, balance and length, if not a lot of terroir. Drink now.–B.S. • $16 • (5/15/2000) • **86**

Chardonnay Elgin 1997: A good, lip-smacking Chardonnay, with vibrant pear, apple and citrus flavors. Finishes with a nice butterscotch note. Drink now.–K.M. • $15 • (9/30/1998) • **85**

Sauvignon Blanc Groenkloof 1999: Simply delicious. Rich and vibrant, bursting with peach, melon, grass and stone notes woven into the dense texture. Balanced, with a lingering finish. Drink now.–B.S. • $14 • (4/30/2000) • **88**

Sauvignon Blanc Groenkloof 1998: Ripe in flavor and jazzy in texture, this is a good example of its type. It's generous but well balanced, emphasizing tangy grapefruit and herb flavors that linger on the finish. Better than when previously reviewed. Drink now. • $14 • (6/15/1999) • **86**

Sauvignon Blanc Groenkloof 1997 • $12 • (6/15/1998) • **87**

Sauvignon Blanc-Chenin Blanc Stellenbosch Inglewood 1999: Fresh and appealing, this soft white has plenty of juicy melon, citrus and grass flavors that dovetail nicely on the finish. Drink now.–B.S. • $9 • (4/30/2000) • **85**

Shiraz Stellenbosch Jonkershoek Valley 1997: Aromatic, this shows more oak than fruit on the nose, though the palate offers berry and cherry notes. Elegant, soft and well put together, it tails off a little on the finish. Drink now.–B.S. • $25 • (4/30/2000) • **84**

FAIRVIEW ESTATE

Pinotage Coastal Region 1998: Round and lushly textured, with good underlying firmness and a gamy edge to the plum and spice flavors. Good complexity and a lingering finish. Drink now through 2003.–B.S. • $13 • (4/30/2000) • **87**

Pinotage Paarl 1997: Emphasizing the raspberry and cherry side of Pinotage, this precocious fruit-bomb is irresistible for its succulent flavors and vibrant structure. Drink now.–B.S. • $13 • (4/30/2000) • **87**

Sémillon Paarl Cyril Back 1998: An oaky style of Sémillon, showing plenty of vanilla and nutmeg along with melon and herb. Rich and medium-bodied, with a touch of bitterness from the wood. Drink now through 2001.–B.S. • $14 • (11/15/1999) • **84**

Shiraz Coastal Region Cyril Back 1997: The raspberry flavor fights with a cardboard note in this modest, tough, short red.–B.S. • $16 • (4/30/2000) • **78**

Shiraz Paarl 1996: There's a slight raisiny note to the ripe cherry, yet here's a broad, muscular Shiraz wearing its maturity well. The cherry segues into licorice and coffee on the finish. Try with barbecue. Drink now through 2001.–B.S. • $14 • (4/30/2000) • **86**

Shiraz Paarl 1992 • $8 • (9/30/1995) • **83**

Shiraz Paarl Reserve 1993: Mature, but with freshness, along with mint, raspberry, plum and spice flavors. Shows good concentration and intensity in a full, structured profile, with intrusive tannins that turn dry on the finish. Drink now.–B.S. • $NA • (1/01/2000) • **86**

Shiraz-Merlot Paarl 1991 • $8 • (9/30/1995) • **85**

Viognier Paarl 1998: This full-bore, assertive white is lavishly oaked, showing butterscotch and spice notes. The peach notes fight hard, but in the end the oak gets the upper hand. Will appeal to fans of oak. Drink now.–B.S. • $16 • (11/15/1999) • **84**

Zinfandel Paarl Cyril Back 1997: Plenty of spicy berry flavors accented with musk are wrapped in sweet oak. Medium-bodied, with good concentration, its rich fruit lingers on the finish along with a freshly cut wood element. Drink now.–B.S. • $19 • (1/01/2000) • **86**

FLEUR DU CAP

Cabernet Sauvignon Coastal Region 1992: Mature, displaying slight oxidation and mushroom aromas and flavors, a hint of cherry and dry, tough tannins. The fruit is drying out.–B.S. • $12 • (12/15/1999) • **76**

Cabernet Sauvignon Coastal Region 1989 • $12 • (1/31/1997) • **80**

Chardonnay Coastal Region 1998: The flavors are more like baked apple or pear, mixed with a lean profile and a touch of bitterness. Drink now.–B.S. • $9 • (12/31/1999) • **81**

Merlot Coastal Region 1997: A blast of pure cherry leads into a straightforward, spice-flavored red on a compact, firm frame. Stiff tannins on the finish beg for food. Drink now through 2001.–B.S. • $11 • (5/15/2000) • **83**

Merlot Coastal Region 1996: Offers mature wood, spice and cinnamon notes before giving way to a palate of mature, subtle fruit that gets out-muscled by some dry tannins. Drink now.–B.S. • $11 • (1/01/2000) • **82**

Merlot Coastal Region 1994 • $11 • (6/30/1997) • **82**

Merlot Coastal Region 1992 • $8 • (6/15/1995) • **84**

Merlot Coastal Region 1991 • $8 • (1/01/1994) • **78**

Noble Late Harvest Coastal Region 1996: This dessert wine is beautifully balanced, evoking honey and citrus aromas and flavors on a sleek frame. Light on its feet, it would pair well with foie gras or a lightly sweet dessert. Made from 100 percent Chenin Blanc. Drink now through 2002.–B.S. • $13/375 ml. • (11/15/1999) • **87**

Pinotage Coastal Region 1993: Focused, though not that expressive, offering cherry and leather flavors backed by stiff tannins. A bit awkward but not bad, and food will help tame the tannins. Drink now.–B.S. • $12 • (4/30/2000) • **84**

Pinotage Coastal Region 1992 • $11 • (5/31/1997) • **83**

Pinotage Coastal Region 1991 • $9 • (1/01/1997) • **80**

Pinotage Coastal Region 1990 • $9 • (9/30/1995) • **78**

Pinotage Coastal Region 1989 • $9 • (6/15/1995) • **84**

Pinotage Coastal Region 1988 • $10 • (2/15/1993) • **88**

Sauvignon Blanc Coastal Region 1998: Shows soft grapefruit and faint tangerine flavors before finishing a tad dilute. Lacks zip. Tasted twice, with consistent notes.–B.S. • $9 • (1/01/2000) • **78**

FORRESTER, KEN

Chenin Blanc Stellenbosch 1998: Broad and richly structured, there's concentration to the almond and apple flavors, yet it's soft and tails off on the finish. Drink now.–B.S. • $10 • (12/31/1999) • **83**

Chenin Blanc Stellenbosch 1997: An intriguing chamomile note is backed by honey and a hint of citrus in this smooth, satisfying white. Vibrant acidity adds a tangy feel to the finish. Drink now.–B.S. • $10 • (1/01/1999) • **85**

Chenin Blanc Stellenbosch Petit Chenin 1999: Attractive, in a moderately firm, rich style, evoking flavors of chamomile, almond and baked apple. Citrus notes peek through on the finish. Drink now.–B.S. • $6 • (5/15/2000) • **83**

Fumé Blanc Stellenbosch 1998: Mature, this white offers new oak nuances, lending a butterscotch element to the melon and citrus flavors. The wood character dominates, and the palate is on the dilute side. Drink now.–B.S. • $13 • (4/30/2000) • **82**

Grenache-Syrah Stellenbosch 1998: Juicy, vivid berry aromas burst from the glass in this elegant red. Laced with currant and herbal flavors supported by a firm structure, with some astringency at the end. Drink now through 2001.–B.S. • $17 • (1/01/2000) • **85**

GLEN CARLOU

Cabernet Sauvignon Paarl 1993 • $20 • (6/15/1995) • **88**

Chardonnay Paarl 1998: Out of South Africa comes this delicious Chardonnay at a good price. Vibrant, concentrated and integrated, its apple, pear and fig flavors take center stage while vanilla and nutmeg play supporting roles. Long, refreshing finish. Drink now through 2001.–B.S. • $14 • (5/15/2000) SS • **90**

Chardonnay Paarl 1997: A spicy, complex, tantalizing Chardonnay with lots to sink your teeth into. This South African white's layers of pear, vanilla, nutmeg and pineapple begin in the aroma, carry onto the palate, last through the lingering finish. Drink now through 2000. • $15 • (7/31/1998) HR • **90**

Grand Classique Paarl Red 1997: A big mouthful of plum and cherry, with vanilla and cinnamon accents allied to a firm, lean framework. The vanilla-tinged fruit emerges on the finish. Well balanced and concentrated, this should develop well. Drink now through 2003.–B.S. • $18 • (5/15/2000) • **89**

Grande Classique Paarl Reserve Red 1993 • $16 • (5/15/1997) • **85**

Grande Classique Paarl Reserve Red 1992 • $22 • (9/30/1995) • **88**

Les Trois Paarl Red 1993 • $17 • (9/30/1995) • **89**

Merlot Paarl 1995 • $13 • (4/30/1997) • **87**

Merlot Paarl 1993 • $18 • (6/15/1995) • **89**

Pinot Noir Paarl 1994 • $18 • (6/15/1995) • **87**

GOOD HOPE WINES

Chairman's Selection Durbanville Red 1992 • $11 • (4/30/1996) • **84**

Merlot Klein Karoo 1992 • $9 • (4/30/1996) • **78**

Pinotage Paarl 1994 • $9 • (4/30/1996) • **85**

GRANGEHURST

Cabernet Sauvignon Stellenbosch 1992 • $16 • (6/15/1995) • **90**

Pinotage Stellenbosch 1997: Thick and polished, this international-style red boasts plum and chocolate accented by spicy oak. Medium-bodied, with soft tannins and a sweet fruit finish. Drink now through 2002.–B.S. • $25 • (4/30/2000) • **86**

Pinotage Stellenbosch 1992 • $15 • (6/15/1995) • **89**

GROOT CONSTANTIA

Cabernet Sauvignon Constantia 1992 • $12 • (12/31/1995) • **81**

Cabernet Sauvignon Constantia 1990 • $12 • (6/30/1994) • **78**

Merlot Constantia 1992 • $12 • (12/31/1995) • **79**

Pinotage Constantia 1993 • $10 • (7/31/1996) • **77**

Key: SS—Spectator Selection. CS—Cellar Selection. HR—Highly Recommended. $NA—Price not available. (BT)—Barrel tasting. (A)—Auction Price. For a key to the tasters' initials, see "How to Use These Listings."
Dates in parentheses represent the issues in which the ratings were published.

Pinotage Constantia 1992 • $9 • (9/30/1995) • **78**
Pinotage Constantia 1990 • $8 • (6/30/1994) • **75**
Pinotage Constantia 1989 • $7 • (2/15/1993) • **81**
Rood Constantia Red 1990 • $7 • (6/30/1994) • **80**
Shiraz Constantia 1996: Rather lean, featuring aromas of cedar, smoke and black pepper, flavors of blackberry, a medium body and moderate tannins. Better than previously reviewed. Drink now. • $12 • (9/15/1999) • **83**
Shiraz Constantia 1995: A sturdy red, with attractive oaky aromas, modest fruit flavors, a firm texture and a lean flavor profile. • $12 • (9/30/1998) • **79**
Shiraz Constantia 1991 • $10 • (1/01/1997) • **81**
Shiraz Constantia 1989 • $9 • (6/30/1994) • **84**

HAMILTON RUSSELL

Chardonnay Walker Bay 1998: There's purity and depth to the pear, butter and spicy oak aromas of this South African white, augmented by nutmeg and vanilla on the palate, with plenty of fruit beneath. It's elegant, focused and intensely flavored, and has beautiful oak shadings on the finish. Drink through 2003–B.S. • $18 • (12/31/1999) HR • **90**
Chardonnay Walker Bay 1997: Forward and appealing, this begins with pineapple, pear and spice notes allied to a creamy texture, supported by both acidity and oak tannins. Falls off slightly on the finish. Drink now.–B.S. • $18 • (1/01/1999) • **88**
Pinot Noir Walker Bay 1995 • $15 • (4/30/1998) • **80**
Pinot Noir Walker Bay 1992 • $16 • (6/30/1995) • **82**

HARTENBERG

Chardonnay Stellenbosch 1997: Plenty of nutty, spicy overtones, yet it seems to have lost a little zip, with the oak gaining the upper hand over the fruit. Past its prime.–B.S. • $18 • (5/15/2000) • **83**
Merlot Stellenbosch 1995: A pure-tasting red, with good cherry and plum flavors and mineral notes. Finishes with chocolaty notes. Focused and flavorful, but needs a bit more time to open up. Drink now.–K.M. • $24 • (12/15/1998) • **86**
Shiraz Stellenbosch 1995: A mature Shiraz whose earthy, leathery aromas, ripe fruit flavors and rounded texture all make it appealing to adventurous palates. Drink now. • $24 • (11/30/1998) • **85**
Weisser Riesling Stellenbosch 1998: Petrol and pine are the main themes in this soft, light Riesling. An inkling of honey emerges on the palate.–B.S. • $13 • (5/15/2000) • **79**

HAUTE-CABRIERE

Pinot Noir Franschhoek 1998: This silky, light-bodied, moderately concentrated red has smoky berry and cherry aromas and flavors. The smoky note builds on the finish. Drink now through 2001.–B.S. • $30 • (5/15/2000) • **83**
Pinot Noir Franschhoek 1997: Verging on rosé in color, this light-bodied but tough Pinot shows a faint strawberry flavor overridden by stemmy, spicy notes.–B.S. • $30 • (1/01/2000) • **78**

HAUTE PROVENCE

Angels' Tears Coastal Region White 1997 • $9 • (4/30/1998) • **80**

HIDDEN VALLEY

Pinotage Stellenbosch 1997: Ambitious. An international-style red—from the dark color, lavishly oaked black cherry and plum flavors to the rich, lush texture. Firm tannins and acidity make for a crisp finish. Drink now through 2003.–B.S. • $35 • (4/30/2000) • **88**

HOOPENBURG

Cabernet Sauvignon Coastal Region 1997: A drinkable red that's short on ripeness and Cabernet character. It's medium-bodied and slightly tannic, with indistinct flavors. • $14 • (9/15/1999) • **78**
Chardonnay Coastal Region 1998: Almond and apple notes take on a slightly candied character in this straightforward, compact white. It's lively, with some oaky nuances and an astringency on the finish. Drink now.–B.S. • $13 • (5/15/2000) • **84**
Chardonnay Western Cape 1997: Not showy, yet smooth and complex. An elegant Chardonnay, with light but nicely integrated flavors of pear, vanilla and butter that linger on the finish. Drink now. • $13 • (9/15/1999) • **87**
Merlot Stellenbosch 1998: A light and appealing Merlot, with fresh berry, oak and herb flavors and an agreeably soft texture. Drink now. • $13 • (9/15/1999) • **84**
Pinot Noir Coastal Region 1998: A charming but substantive Pinot Noir with delicious strawberry and cherry flavors. Light tannins and fresh acidity make it a pleasure. Drink now. • $15 • (9/15/1999) • **86**
Pinotage Coastal Region 1998: A ripe, fruit-driven red wine to drink now. It's slightly earthy in aroma, generous with its cherry and berry flavors and not too tannic. Drink now. • $13 • (9/15/1999) • **84**
Sauvignon Blanc Coastal Region 1998: A light, soft, fresh white wine that is pleasantly fruity and herbal in flavor. This is clean and simple in style. Drink now. • $10 • (9/15/1999) • **81**

IMPALA

Merlot Western Cape 1996 • $10 • (11/15/1997) • **83**

JACOBSDAL

Pinotage Stellenbosch 1995: Bottle age gives this red a leather and game edge to the cherry notes. Firmly structured, with a chewy licorice character. Needs food. Tasted three times, with noticeable bottle variation. Drink now.–B.S. • $15 • (5/15/2000) • **87**
Pinotage Stellenbosch 1988 • $10 • (2/15/1993) • **86**

JARDIN

Cabernet Sauvignon-Merlot Stellenbosch Chameleon 1997: Turning brickish in color, this mature Cab blend shows supple currant and cassis, finishing on a nice smoky, tarry note. Drink now.–B.S. • $16 • (1/01/2000) • **86**
Chardonnay Stellenbosch 1998: Subtle, with moderate intensity to the pear, vanilla and nutmeg flavors, all in a lithe, elegant package. Spice notes linger on the finish. Drink now.–B.S. • $17 • (12/31/1999) • **82**
Chardonnay-Sauvignon Blanc Stellenbosch Chameleon 1998: Shows more of Chardonnay's character than Sauvignon's, with pear and vanilla flavors that peter out on the dull finish, leaving just a simple buttery note. Drink now.–B.S. • $16 • (1/01/2000) • **80**
Merlot Stellenbosch 1997: Mint and chocolate aromas lead into a plush, well-rounded Merlot featuring plum, spice and black cherry flavors all kept honest by a faint herbal note. Lingering finish. Drink now.–B.S. • $17 • (1/01/2000) • **85**

KAAPZICHT

Cabernet Sauvignon Stellenbosch 1997: Cherry and raspberry flavors up front catch your attention, but overall it's a bit awkward. Firmly structured, with intensity and personality, it may come together with time. Drink now through 2002.–B.S. • $20 • (5/15/2000) • **85**
Merlot Stellenbosch Wooded 1997: Pure fruit quality, extremely ripe, evoking raspberry, cherry and spice, well integrated with the medium-weight and lively structure. Delicious. Drink now through 2002.–B.S. • $18 • (5/15/2000) • **87**
Pinotage Stellenbosch Steytler 1998: A fruit bomb, bright and buoyed by light tannins wrapped around a core of raspberry and wild berry flavors. On the lean side, this should go well with simple grilled food. Drink now through 2001.–B.S. • $32 • (5/15/2000) • **86**
Shiraz Stellenbosch Wooded 1997: Exuding violets and raspberries, this is a pretty Shiraz, taking on allspice, juniper and leather notes on the palate. Elegant, dense and creamy, it's not what you expect, yet it's very attractive. Drink now through 2001.–B.S. • $18 • (4/30/2000) • **87**

KANONKOP

Cabernet Sauvignon Stellenbosch 1995: A diamond in the rough. This is a seriously gorgeous Cabernet with great fruit concentration, super balance and a feeling of harmony and grace. No gimmicks here, just wonderful Cabernet flavors that fill the mouth and linger on the finish. Drink now through 2004. • $27 • (5/15/1999) • **91**
Cabernet Sauvignon Stellenbosch 1991 • $20 • (9/30/1995) • **81**
Cabernet Sauvignon Stellenbosch 1990 • $20 • (9/30/1995) • **82**
Kadette Stellenbosch Red 1997: Flavorful, well balanced and bright, this lively Bordeaux-style blend of Cabernet and Merlot is appealing to the palate, marrying ripe fruit flavors, a tangy texture and firm tannins. Drink now through 2001. • $10 • (5/15/1999) • **87**
Kadette Stellenbosch Red 1996 • $11 • (3/31/1998) • **83**
Kadette Stellenbosch Red 1995 • $10 • (8/31/1997) • **87**

KANONKOP

Paul Sauer Stellenbosch Red 1995: Seductive Cabernet with beautifully spicy aromas, ripe fruit flavors and a velvety texture. It's tannic and full-bodied, but so generous with the black cherry and vanilla notes that you hardly notice. A blend of Cabernet Sauvignon, Cabernet Franc and Merlot. Tasted twice, with consistent notes. Drink now through 2002. • $29 • (5/15/1999) • **90**

Paul Sauer Stellenbosch Red 1993 • $26 • (8/31/1997) • **89**

Paul Sauer Stellenbosch Red 1991 • $25 • (6/15/1995) • **90**

Pinotage Stellenbosch Red 1998: This pure, modern-styled red offers blackberry with a hint of spice on a smooth, solidly built structure. The tannins leave a bittersweet chocolate impression. Drink now through 2001.–B.S. • $25 • (5/15/2000) • **87**

Pinotage Stellenbosch 1997: A truly ambitious red wine. An inky-dark color, pronounced oak aromas and concentrated fruit flavors combine with very firm tannins. Too young to enjoy now—but time should reveal its concentration and complexity. Best after 2001. • $25 • (5/15/1999) • **88**

Pinotage Stellenbosch 1995 • $20 • (8/31/1997) SS • **91**

Pinotage Stellenbosch 1993 • $14 • (6/15/1995) • **88**

Pinotage Stellenbosch 1990 • $10 • (2/15/1993) • **84**

Pinotage Stellenbosch Reserve 1993 • $18 • (9/30/1995) • **91**

Pinotage Stellenbosch Reserve 1992 • $17 • (9/30/1995) • **87**

KANU

Merlot Stellenbosch Limited Release 1998: Thick, ripe and extracted, this is impressive for its plum and chocolate flavors, full body and fleshy texture. The oak emerges on the finish, leaving vanilla and coarse tannins behind. Needs food. Drink now through 2003.–B.S. • $24 • (5/15/2000) • **87**

KLEIN CONSTANTIA

Cabernet Sauvignon-Merlot Constantia Marlbrook 1996: Gorgeous. Full of lavish oak shadings that display coffee, tobacco and vanilla to augment the black cherry and plum. Concentrated, intense and beautifully balanced, with a long finish. Drink now through 2004.–B.S. • $23 • (5/15/2000) • **90**

Chardonnay Constantia 1997: Mature, showing candied apple and spice elements combined with a bright, elegant structure. Drink now.–B.S. • $18 • (5/15/2000) • **83**

Sauvignon Blanc Constantia 1998: Big, bold and exotic, delivering passion fruit, clove and cardamom flavors on a loosely knit structure. The finish lacks a little focus. Drink now.–B.S. • $16 • (4/30/2000) • **83**

Sauvignon Blanc Constantia Botrytis Noble Late Harvest 1996: Not much Sauvignon Blanc character, but this is piquant and full of orange marmalade, backed by vibrant acidity and a rich texture. Not too sweet, it has a long citrus-preserve finish. Drink now.–B.S. • $23/375 ml. • (5/15/2000) • **88**

KLEINBOSCH

Cabernet Sauvignon Paarl 1993 • $7 • (9/15/1997) • **81**

Cinsaut-Cabernet Sauvignon Paarl 1995 • $6 • (10/15/1997) • **83**

Pinotage Paarl 1995 • $6 • (10/15/1997) • **83**

Red Paarl 1996 • $6 • (10/15/1997) • **83**

KUMALA

Cabernet Sauvignon Stellenbosch Reserve 1998: Soft and smooth, this Cabernet combines black cherry, herb and plum aromas and flavors. Crisp, mildly tannic finish. Drink now.–B.S. • $27 • (5/15/2000) • **83**

Cabernet Sauvignon-Shiraz Western Cape 1999: Light and fruity, similar to a basic Bordeaux in its soft, cherry- and herb-tinged flavors. Drink now.–B.S. • $9 • (5/15/2000) • **80**

Chardonnay Western Cape 1999: Essentially light and dilute, showing spice and not much varietal character.–B.S. • $8 • (5/15/2000) • **75**

Merlot Stellenbosch Reserve 1998: Ripe and smoky, this distinctive red boasts plum, leather and spice flavors in a gentle, fleshy way, with just a hint of tannins on the finish. Drink now through 2001.–B.S. • $27 • (5/15/2000) • **86**

Sémillon-Chardonnay Western Cape 1999: Round and succulent, this white mixes melon and herb notes with a hint of earth. Straightforward, with a modest finish. Drink now.–B.S. • $7 • (5/15/2000) • **82**

Key: SS—Spectator Selection. CS—Cellar Selection. HR—Highly Recommended. $NA—Price not available. (BT)—Barrel tasting. (A)—Auction Price.
For a key to the tasters' initials, see "How to Use These Listings."
Dates in parentheses represent the issues in which the ratings were published.

KWV

Abraham Perold Paarl 1996: Fresh cut wood and raspberry aromas and flavors signal a bold, extroverted red boasting juicy berry flavors and a vibrant, solid structure. Medium-bodied, with a coating of tannins on the finish. 100 percent Shiraz. Drink now.–B.S. • $80 • (4/30/2000) • **86**

Cabernet Sauvignon Western Cape 1996: A smooth and satisfying wine at a satisfying price, this South African Cabernet offers lots of juicy plum and cherry flavors, a moderately tannic, velvety texture and a lingering finish. Drink now. • $8 • (9/30/1998) • **86**

Cabernet Sauvignon Western Cape 1995 • $14 • (6/15/1998) • **84**

Chardonnay Western Cape 1998: This light-bodied Chardonnay has an attractive overlay of toasty oak flavor but could use more fruit character to back it up. Drink now. • $8 • (9/15/1999) • **80**

Chardonnay Western Cape 1997 • $8 • (6/15/1998) • **79**

Cream Sherry South Africa Full NV • $7 • (6/30/1995) • **86**

Merlot Western Cape 1995 • $14 • (6/15/1998) • **75**

Merlot Western Cape 1994 • $8 • (1/31/1997) • **85**

Noble Late Harvest Coastal Region 1988 • $10 • (6/30/1995) • **84**

Pinotage Western Cape 1998: Generous fruit flavors and a rich texture make this South African red eminently drinkable, and its price tag is easy to swallow, too. It has ripe cherry and plum notes, vanilla accents and an agreeably soft balance. Drink now. • $9 • (9/15/1999) • **86**

Pinotage Western Cape 1996: Like a good Aussie Shiraz, with abundant fruit flavors, light oak accents, modest tannins and an almost sweet blackberry finish. Drink now. • $9 • (7/31/1998) • **84**

Renasans Pale Medium Dry Sherry South Africa NV • $7 • (6/30/1995) • **84**

Roodeberg Coastal Region Red 1991 • $7 • (6/30/1995) • **77**

Roodeberg Coastal Region Red 1989 • $7 • (6/30/1994) • **78**

Ruby Port South Africa Full NV • $7 • (9/30/1995) • **81**

Sauvignon Blanc Western Cape 1997 • $7 • (6/15/1998) • **81**

Shiraz Western Cape 1997: Supple, with sweet and spicy flavors of red cherry, chocolate and clove. Medium-bodied, with a light, almost mapley finish. Drink now.–K.M. • $8 • (3/31/1999) • **82**

Shiraz Western Cape 1996: Straightforward, ripe and appealing. Medium-bodied, with fresh plum and blackberry flavors and light tannins. Easy to enjoy. Drink now. • $8 • (7/31/1998) • **84**

Steen Western Cape 1997 • $7 • (6/15/1998) • **84**

Tawny Port South Africa Full NV • $7 • (9/30/1995) • **84**

LAIBACH

Cabernet Sauvignon Stellenbosch 1998: Very oaky in style, showing coffee, butterscotch and spice along with modest plum flavors. The soft attack dissipates slightly before finishing a tad astringent. May improve with time. Drink now through 2001.–B.S. • $19 • (5/15/2000) • **82**

Cabernet Sauvignon-Merlot Stellenbosch 1997: Ripe and vigorous. Cherry, cedar, vanilla and mineral aromas and flavors feel round, though it firms up on the finish. Toasty oak complements the aftertaste. Drink now through 2001.–B.S. • $20 • (5/15/2000) • **87**

Dry Red Stellenbosch 1997: Black cherry, roasted coffee and herb combine with a medium body and a soft structure in this mature red. Cabernet Sauvignon, Merlot and Cinsault. Drink now.–B.S. • $10 • (5/15/2000) • **80**

LANDSKROON

Cabernet Sauvignon Paarl Estate Wine 1990 • $11 • (1/31/1995) • **82**

Pinotage Paarl 1994 • $NA • (9/30/1995) • **84**

Pinotage Paarl Estate Wine 1990 • $10 • (2/15/1993) • **83**

LANZERAC

Pinotage Stellenbosch 1996: Seems to be fading. The plum and tobacco notes take on a dryness midpalate and the structure looks to outlast the modest fruit. Past its prime.–B.S. • $20 • (4/30/2000) • **79**

LEBENSRAUM

Chardonnay Breede River 1997: Standard-issue, with modest fruit flavors and a certain richness of texture. Not bad, just a bit simple, rough around the edges. • $15 • (7/31/1998) • **78**

Chenin Blanc Breede River 1997: This hearty but simple white has apricot and apple flavors, a tart texture and a short finish. • $10 • (7/31/1998) • **78**

Sémillon Breede River 1997: A rich texture and a lingering finish add interest to this subtly flavored, well-balanced white. Not a blockbuster, but intriguing for its fig, melon and apple nuances. • $13 • (7/31/1998) • **85**

LEUWEN JAGT, DE

Cabernet Franc Paarl 1993 • $11 • (9/30/1995) • **84**

LIEVLAND

DVB Stellenbosch 1992 Red • $19 • (12/31/1995) • **84**
Lievlander Stellenbosch Red 1997: High-toned cedar and herbal shadings on the nose give way to an elegant Cab blend, with sweet cherry and currant flavors accented by an interesting sanguine note. Drink now through 2001.–B.S. • $13 • (1/01/2000) • **85**
Lievlander Stellenbosch Red 1995 • $8 • (11/15/1997) • **87**
Lievlander Stellenbosch Red 1994 • $9 • (7/31/1996) • **87**
Shiraz Stellenbosch 1997: Reminiscent of a fine Northern Rhône red in its roasted, plum, leather and game profile, resting on a finely integrated and vibrant structure. A blast of coffee and spice come through on the aftertaste. Drink now through 2005.–B.S. • $19 • (4/30/2000) • **89**
Shiraz Stellenbosch 1994 • $19 • (5/15/1997) • **85**
Shiraz Stellenbosch 1991 • $18 • (4/30/1996) • **81**

LONGRIDGE

Cabernet Sauvignon Coastal Region 1993 • $16 • (7/31/1996) • **83**
Cabernet Sauvignon Stellenbosch 1998: Balanced on the soft side, this berry, mineral and herb-flavored Cabernet picks up vanilla nuances before turning firm on the finish. Drink now.–B.S. • $20 • (5/15/2000) • **85**
Cabernet Sauvignon-Pinotage Western Cape Bay View 1994 • $10 • (7/31/1996) • **77**
Chardonnay Stellenbosch 1998: Mature, open-knit aromas of grilled hazelnut, nutmeg and vanilla lead into a soft, buttery Chardonnay that sports more toast flavor than pure fruit. Manages to stay focused on the finish. For fans of this style. Drink now.–B.S. • $19 • (1/01/2000) • **86**
Chardonnay Western Cape Bay View 1998: Very appealing, displaying butterscotch, nutmeg and tropical flavors and moderate richness, all balanced, with a lingering finish. Drink now.–B.S. • $10 • (12/31/1999) • **84**
Chenin Blanc Western Cape Bay View 1997: Initial floral and talc aromas, then a hint of resin or freshly cut wood creeps in from the oak treatment, which dominates the fruit in this soft, delicate white. Drink now.–B.S. • $9 • (12/31/1999) • **81**
Merlot Coastal Region Bay View 1995 • $9 • (7/31/1996) • **80**
Merlot Stellenbosch 1998: Soft, ripe, freshly crushed cherry takes center stage, with vanilla, chocolate and plum in supporting roles. Overall, it's elegant and concentrated, ending on a firm, tannic note. Drink now through 2002.–B.S. • $20 • (5/15/2000) • **88**
Merlot Western Cape Bay View 1998: This Merlot's dill and chocolate aromas precede a medium-bodied, plummy wine, with soft texture and finish. Drink now.–B.S. • $10 • (1/01/2000) • **83**
Pinotage Stellenbosch 1998: Dark and plummy, yet a soapy note detracts from the aroma, and the finish is tough and tannic.–B.S. • $20 • (5/15/2000) • **78**
Pinotage Western Cape Bay View 1998: Already showing some brownish tint, this smells cooked and woody. Modest cedary flavors and an astringent finish.–B.S. • $10 • (4/30/2000) • **76**
Pinotage Western Cape Bay View 1994 • $9 • (7/31/1996) • **83**

LOUISVALE

Cabernet Sauvignon-Merlot Stellenbosch Dominique 1997: Lean and focused, with a firm structure and a grainy texture supporting the cedar, coffee and plum notes. Good intensity and persistence of flavor through the finish. Drink now through 2001.–B.S. • $20 • (5/15/2000) • **87**
Chardonnay Stellenbosch 1997: Broad and appley, with mature flavors of smoke and clove allied to a rich texture and lively structure. Good accompaniment to grilled fish or chicken. Drink now.–B.S. • $20 • (5/15/2000) • **87**

LOVEREN, VAN

Cabernet Sauvignon-Shiraz Robertson 1997: A gutsy red, with enough flavor of cherry, black pepper and smoke to remind one of a Côtes du Rhône. Not too tannic, with a smooth texture. Drink now. • $10 • (11/30/1998) • **84**
Chardonnay Robertson Spes Bona 1997 • $10 • (3/31/1998) • **80**
Gewürztraminer Robertson Special Late Harvest 1997 • $9 • (4/30/1998) • **75**
Muscadel Robertson Blush Blanc de Noir 1997 • $7 • (3/31/1998) • **82**
Pinot Gris Robertson 1997 • $9 • (4/30/1998) • **77**

MALAN FAMILY

Cabernet Sauvignon-Merlot Stellenbosch Adelberg 1999: Soft, round and easygoing, this simple red offers cherry and berry flavors.–B.S. • $7 • (4/30/2000) • **79**

MEERLUST

Cabernet Sauvignon Stellenbosch 1991 • $22 • (6/15/1995) • **89**
Cabernet Sauvignon Stellenbosch 1986 • $16 • (11/30/1994) • **78**
Merlot Stellenbosch 1996: Firm, offering chocolate with spice accents married to a medium-bodied, moderately tannic structure. Cherry and tobacco linger on the finish. Tasted twice, with consistent notes. Drink now.–B.S. • $28 • (5/15/2000) • **85**
Merlot Stellenbosch 1995: This medium-bodied red has plenty of pleasant cherry, sweet oak and spicy flavors. Ends on a slightly piney note. Drink now.–K.M. • $22 • (3/31/1999) • **83**
Merlot Stellenbosch 1994: An austere but interesting style of Merlot that has a firm texture and good acidity to match lean, mature plum and cherry flavors. Drink now. • $22 • (9/30/1998) • **84**
Merlot Stellenbosch 1993 • $22 • (6/30/1997) • **86**
Merlot Stellenbosch 1991 • $22 • (1/31/1997) • **84**
Merlot Stellenbosch 1989 • $16 • (6/15/1995) • **84**
Pinot Noir Stellenbosch Reserve 1997: Beginning to brown, with a gorgeous spicy berry aroma followed by forest floor, decaying berry and smoke flavors. Silky and dense on the palate, this is ready to enjoy. Drink now.–B.S. • $30 • (5/15/2000) • **85**
Rubicon Stellenbosch Red 1995: Purity and grace are the hallmarks in this maturing raspberry- and cassis-flavored red, though there's plenty of structure and muscle to back it up. Firms up on the finish. Cabernet Sauvignon, Merlot and Cabernet Franc. Drink now through 2005.–B.S. • $30 • (4/30/2000) • **89**
Rubicon Stellenbosch Red 1994: This Bordeaux blend has softened slightly, offering mature flavors of cherry and chocolate with a hint of spice. Has the texture of crushed velvet, with firm, slightly coarse tannins. Drink now.–B.S. • $30 • (12/15/1999) • **85**
Rubicon Stellenbosch Red 1992 • $22 • (6/30/1997) • **85**
Rubicon Stellenbosch Red 1991 • $22 • (1/31/1997) • **87**
Rubicon Stellenbosch Red 1989 • $16 • (6/30/1995) • **88**

MEINERT, MARTIN

Cabernet Sauvignon-Merlot Stellenbosch 1997: Traditional in style, this red delivers green olive, dill and cherry notes on a bed of woolly tannins. Good concentration. Drink now through 2002.–B.S. • $20 • (5/15/2000) • **84**
Merlot Stellenbosch 1997: Herbaceous, offering dill, eucalyptus and cedar with a tannic, astringent profile. Good concentration, followed by a vanilla finish. Drink now through 2003.–B.S. • $18 • (5/15/2000) • **84**

MIDDELVLEI

Pinotage Stellenbosch 1998: Appealing for its ripe, vanilla-tinged character, this rich, firm red delivers tangy black cherry wrapped in moderate tannins. Drink now.–B.S. • $17 • (5/15/2000) • **85**
Pinotage Stellenbosch 1996: Slightly rustic in style, though there's no shortage of ripe, chewy cherry and licorice notes in this lively, well-defined red. The tannins are a bit rough, so try with grilled meat. Drink now.–B.S. • $17 • (4/30/2000) • **86**
Pinotage Stellenbosch 1991 • $13 • (5/15/1997) • **84**
Pinotage Stellenbosch 1990 • $10 • (9/30/1995) • **76**
Pinotage Stellenbosch 1989 • $10 • (2/15/1993) • **78**
Pinotage-Merlot Stellenbosch 1998: A bright cherry aroma and flavor holds sway, while the supporting notes are vanilla and plum. Round and fleshy, with mouthcoating tannins and sweet fruit on the finish. Drink now through 2001.–B.S. • $17 • (5/15/2000) • **86**
Pinotage-Merlot Stellenbosch 1995: A sturdy straightforward red, with fresh cherry flavors, earthy overtones and a firm, tannic texture. Drink now.–P.M. • $15 • (11/15/1998) • **84**
Shiraz Stellenbosch 1998: Simple, forward flavors of blackberry and black cherry on a moderately concentrated, firm backbone. Finishes short. Drink now through 2001.–B.S. • $16 • (5/15/2000) • **83**

Shiraz Stellenbosch 1996: Mature in aroma and flavor, displaying dried fruit, dried herb and resinous components. There's elegance and fine structure. Drink now.–B.S. • $16 • (4/30/2000) • **84**

Shiraz Stellenbosch 1991: Intriguing and harmonious. Mature, but still lively with fruit. Shows an elegant texture, with subtle berry, cedar, spice and smoke flavors that linger on the finish. Drink now. • $14 • (9/30/1998) • **87**

Shiraz Stellenbosch 1990 • $14 • (4/30/1996) • **78**

MORGENHOF

Merlot Stellenbosch 1993 • $14 • (6/30/1995) • **87**

MOTTE, LA

Cabernet Sauvignon Franschhoek Valley 1992 • $NA • (9/30/1995) • **83**

Cabernet Sauvignon Franschhoek Valley 1991 • $18 • (6/30/1997) • **84**

Cabernet Sauvignon Franschhoek Valley 1989 • $15 • (6/15/1995) • **86**

Cabernet Sauvignon Franschhoek Valley 1987 • $15 • (1/01/1994) • **74**

Estate Red Franschhoek Valley 1994: A solid, appetizing red, with enough lively cherry and spice flavor to keep your interest. Light tannins and a smooth texture make it easy to enjoy. Drink now. • $15 • (9/30/1998) • **84**

Estate Red Franschhoek Valley 1992 • $15 • (6/30/1997) • **85**

Estate Red Franschhoek Valley 1990 • $11 • (6/15/1995) • **86**

Millenium Red Franschhoek Valley 1992 • $11 • (9/30/1995) • **81**

Shiraz Franschhoek Valley 1992 • $NA • (9/30/1995) • **87**

MULDERBOSCH

Chardonnay Stellenbosch 1997: An intriguing Chardonnay in the style of a white Burgundy. Subtle but exotic aromas of toast, lime and vanilla lead to a rich texture and generous flavors of pear and almond that linger on the finish. Drink now through 2001. • $24 • (5/15/1999) • **90**

Chardonnay Stellenbosch Barrel Fermented 1998: Thick and broad, with good underlying structure, this white's pear, fig and hazelnut flavors power across the palate in a cohesive, focused fashion. The finish is expansive and multidimensional. Drink now through 2001.–B.S. • $38 • (5/15/2000) • **90**

Faithful Hound Stellenbosch Red 1996: High-octane red wine that's full-bodied and ripe in flavor but not too tannic to enjoy. Combines pleasant plummy aromas and flavors with spicy, oaky accents. Cabernet Sauvignon, Merlot, Malbec and Cabernet Franc. Drink now through 2001. • $23 • (5/15/1999) • **86**

Faithful Hound Stellenbosch Red 1995: An honest, well-made red, with enough concentration and a firm-enough texture to suggest it can age. It combines fresh fruit flavors with intriguing smoky, meaty accents that linger on the finish. Full-bodied and tannic. A blend: 41 percent Merlot, 35 percent Cabernet Sauvignon, 12 percent Malbec, 12 percent Cabernet Franc. Drink now through 2001. • $19 • (7/31/1998) • **87**

Faithful Hound Stellenbosch Red 1994 • $17 • (8/31/1997) • **88**

Faithful Hound Stellenbosch Red 1993 • $15 • (9/30/1995) • **82**

Sauvignon Blanc Stellenbosch 1999: Delicious. A lean, racy white, this Sancerre look-alike offers grapefruit, freshly cut grass and a stony accent on a firm backbone, adding up to a pleasurable, resonant experience. Drink now.–B.S. • $20 • (5/15/2000) • **88**

Sauvignon Blanc Stellenbosch 1998: Smooth in texture and well balanced, this appealing Sauvignon has a subtle combination of grapefruit, herb and mineral flavors that reminds one of white Bordeaux. Drink now. • $19 • (5/15/1999) • **85**

Sauvignon Blanc Stellenbosch 1997 • $19 • (12/15/1997) • **86**

NEDERBURG

Baronne Coastal Region Red 1989 • $10 • (6/30/1995) • **77**

Cabernet Sauvignon Paarl 1991 • $10 • (9/30/1995) • **76**

Cabernet Sauvignon Paarl 1989 • $10 • (6/30/1994) • **84**

Cabernet Sauvignon Western Cape Reserve 1996: Cooked fruit aromas and flavors mark this soft red, which finishes on the astringent side.–B.S. • $21 • (12/15/1999) • **78**

Chardonnay Western Cape Reserve 1998: Very attractive. A little residual sugar, yet there's enough acidity for balance, as well as fig, vanilla and tropical fruit aromas and flavors. Finishes with a refreshing astringency. Drink now.–B.S. • $15 • (12/31/1999) • **85**

Edelrood Paarl Red 1989 • $10 • (6/30/1995) • **77**

Pinotage Paarl 1990 • $10 • (9/30/1995) • **73**

Pinotage Paarl 1988 • $10 • (6/30/1994) • **73**

Sauvignon Blanc Western Cape Reserve 1998: An intriguing smoky note augments the melon and nectarine flavors in this focused style that shows fine balance, with a crisp finish. Drink now.–B.S. • $15 • (4/30/2000) • **85**

Sauvignon Blanc-Cape Riesling-Chardonnay Western Cape Lyric 1999: This simple white blend is round, with a modest apple note.–B.S. • $10 • (4/30/2000) • **78**

Shiraz-Cabernet Sauvignon Paarl Auction Reserve 1992: Mature. Plum, cherry, licorice and herb aromas and flavors are outgunned by the dry tannins in this ambitious, but tiring red. Drink up.–B.S. • $24 • (4/30/2000) • **80**

NEETHLINGSHOF

Cabernet Sauvignon Stellenbosch 1992 • $10 • (9/30/1997) • **76**

Cabernet Sauvignon Stellenbosch 1990 • $10 • (9/30/1995) • **84**

Merlot Stellenbosch 1994 • $10 • (9/15/1997) • **85**

Merlot Stellenbosch 1993 • $10 • (9/30/1995) • **72**

Neethlingsrood Stellenbosch Red 1992 • $10 • (10/15/1997) • **76**

Pinotage Stellenbosch 1993 • $10 • (10/15/1997) • **78**

Shiraz Stellenbosch 1993 • $10 • (11/15/1997) • **73**

Shiraz Stellenbosch 1992 • $10 • (9/30/1995) • **81**

Weisser Riesling Stellenbosch Noble Late Harvest 1995 • $22/375 ml. • (9/30/1997) • **89**

NITIDA

Cabernet Sauvignon Durbanville 1998: Ripe, smoky licorice and plum aromas and flavors combine with a medium body and stiff tannins. Chewy and full of personality, if a bit rustic. Drink now through 2001.–B.S. • $14 • (4/30/2000) • **87**

Cabernet Sauvignon Durbanville 1997: A medicinal menthol smell and stewed fruit character end on an astringent note.–B.S. • $15 • (12/15/1999) • **77**

Chardonnay Durbanville 1999: A concentrated, mouthfilling white, its pear and fig flavors framed in butterscotch. It's lively and balanced, with a refreshing finish. Drink now through 2001.–B.S. • $13 • (5/15/2000) • **87**

Chardonnay Durbanville 1998: An attractive, light-bodied Chardonnay, offering buttered, ripe apples, with a touch of nutmeg. More oaky on the palate. Finishes short. Drink now.–B.S. • $13 • (12/31/1999) • **80**

Merlot-Cabernet Franc Durbanville 1998: Light- to medium-bodied, showing bright cherry, olive and cedar aromas and flavors on a firm backbone. Try with roast chicken. Drink now.–B.S. • $12 • (5/15/2000) • **84**

Pinotage Durbanville 1998: Distinctive, but not for everyone. A heady red, smelling of earth, plum and horse stable. Medium-bodied frame, moderately firm, ending with an iron note. Drink now through 2001.–B.S. • $13 • (4/30/2000) • **83**

Sauvignon Blanc Durbanville 1999: Assertive aromas of grapefruit, herb and mineral introduce this crisp, moderately concentrated Sauvignon Blanc. Tails off on the finish. Drink now.–B.S. • $11 • (4/30/2000) • **83**

Sauvignon Blanc Durbanville 1998: Shows the traditional hay and gooseberry, followed by grapefruit and lemon zest flavors. Light-bodied and soft. Drink now.–B.S. • $11 • (1/01/2000) • **81**

Sauvignon Blanc Durbanville 1997: Aromas of hay, earth and cat's pee announce this Sauvignon, that also offers soft grapefruit and lemon flavors before a slightly earthy finish. Drink now.–B.S. • $11 • (1/01/2000) • **82**

Shiraz Coastal Region 1997: Textbook flavors of plum, wild berry, smoke and game mark this solid, balanced red that sports a licoricelike chewiness on the finish. Moderate concentration, yet appealing. Drink now.–B.S. • $15 • (4/30/2000) • **85**

Shiraz Durbanville 1998: Thick and meaty, showing plum, smoke and a touch of leather, this medium-bodied red remains bright and focused throughout. Solidly structured, it's delicious now, yet can age, too. Drink now through 2002.–B.S. • $14 • (4/30/2000) • **85**

ORMARINS, L'

Chardonnay Franschhoek Valley 1997: A forward style, showing plenty of oak and butter flavor mixed in with nice pear and green peach accents. Finishes on a smoky note. Drink now through 2001.–K.M. • $13 • (5/15/1999) • **84**

Fumé Blanc Franschhoek Valley 1997: Hanging in, this has a modicum of fruit but should have been drunk up long ago. The oak imprint lends a buttery caramel element. Past its prime.–B.S. • $10 • (4/30/2000) • **81**

Key: SS—Spectator Selection. CS—Cellar Selection. HR—Highly Recommended. $NA—Price not available. (BT)—Barrel tasting. (A)—Auction Price. For a key to the tasters' initials, see "How to Use These Listings."
Dates in parentheses represent the issues in which the ratings were published.

OVERGAAUW

Cabernet Sauvignon Stellenbosch 1990 • $15 • (9/30/1995) • **86**
Cabernet Sauvignon Stellenbosch Landgoedwyn 1987 • $16 • (10/15/1992) • **75**
Merlot Stellenbosch Landgoedwyn 1988 • $13 • (10/15/1992) • **77**

PETITE FERME, LA

Blanc Fumé Franschhoek 1997: A lean, austere white, with light lemon and apple flavors and a very tart balance. • $9 • (11/30/1998) • **77**
Sauvignon Blanc Franschhoek 1997 • $9 • (1/01/1998) • **87**

PLAISIR DE MERLE

Cabernet Sauvignon Paarl 1996: Mature, from the slightly browning color to the sweet prune and cedar notes. There's still some lushness here, but an overly smoky element on the finish gets in the way. Drink now.–B.S. • $23 • (1/01/2000) • **82**
Chardonnay Paarl 1997: Mature, showing pear and spice aromas and flavors on a lean, lively frame. Drink now.–B.S. • $18 • (5/15/2000) • **83**
Merlot Paarl 1996: Browning in color, with mature tea and menthol aromas followed up by root beer and licorice root flavors. A tad astringent on the finish. Past its prime.–B.S. • $23 • (1/01/2000) • **78**
Sauvignon Blanc Paarl 1998: There's a nice smoky note on the nose, along with tropical apricot and pineapple. Also shows some nut and grass notes. Moderate finish. Drink now.–B.S. • $16 • (1/01/2000) • **82**

RED HILL

Cabernet Sauvignon Coastal Region 1996 • $8 • (12/15/1997) • **78**
Pinotage Coastal Region 1996 • $8 • (3/31/1998) • **75**
Pinotage Coastal Region 1993 • $6 • (9/30/1995) • **82**
Shiraz Coastal Region 1996 • $8 • (12/15/1997) • **82**

RICHE, ETIENNE LE

Cabernet Sauvignon Stellenbosch 1998: A solid, vigorous Cabernet that delivers characteristic black currant and cedar notes, with a hint of plum backed by firm tannins and acidity. Flavors linger on the finish. Drink now through 2002.–B.S. • $19 • (4/30/2000) • **85**
Cabernet Sauvignon Stellenbosch Reserve 1998: Top-quality French oak delivers the kicker in this stylish, international red. A core of black cherry and cassis is cloaked in lush green olive, vanilla and clove, adding up to sweet fruit and oak on an elegant, dense structure. Tasty. Drink now through 2004.–B.S. • $28 • (4/30/2000) • **89**
Cabernet Sauvignon-Merlot Stellenbosch 1998: Light-bodied and well defined. The cherry flavors in this succulent red burst on the palate, maintaining an intensity through the finish. Drink now.–B.S. • $15 • (4/30/2000) • **85**

ROBERT'S ROCK

Cabernet Sauvignon-Merlot Western Cape 1997: Straightforward, with herbal and weedy aromas and flavors in a light-bodied presentation.–B.S. • $7 • (4/30/2000) • **78**
Chenin Blanc-Chardonnay Western Cape 1998: A good, sturdy white, with enough apple, herb and spice flavors to give it substance. Soft in texture. Drink now. • $5 • (11/30/1998) • **84**
Shiraz-Malbec Western Cape 1998: Polished, with sweet plum and vanilla on a medium-bodied frame, turning slightly coarse and astringent on the finish. Drink now.–B.S. • $7 • (4/30/2000) • **83**
Shiraz-Malbec Western Cape 1997: A medium-bodied red with roasted flavors of red plum and cherry and a gamy aroma. Notes of white pepper on the finish. Drink now.–K.M. • $6 • (3/31/1999) • **83**

ROOIBERG

Cabernet Sauvignon Robertson 1992 • $8 • (9/30/1995) • **69**
Pinotage Robertson 1992 • $8 • (6/15/1995) • **84**
Port Eilandia Cape Ruby 1994 • $15 • (9/15/1997) • **87**
Port Robertson 1993 • $NA • (1/01/1997) • **78**
Shiraz Breede River Valley 1993 • $10 • (8/31/1997) • **83**
Shiraz Goree 1989 • $11 • (4/15/1992) • **82**
Shiraz Vinkrivier 1991 • $9 • (6/30/1994) • **84**

ROOSENVELDT

Cabernet Sauvignon Franschhoek Valley 1993 • $14 • (4/30/1996) • **83**
Merlot Franschhoek Valley 1994 • $14 • (4/30/1996) • **87**

ROZENDAL FARM

Jonkershoek 1996: Starts out smooth and elegant, offering plum and olive flavors accented by roast coffee. The stiff tannins come to the fore from mid-palate to the finish. Drink now through 2003.–B.S. • $25 • (5/15/2000) • **84**
Red Stellenbosch 1990 • $18 • (6/30/1995) • **78**
Red Stellenbosch 1989 • $18 • (6/15/1995) • **86**

RUST EN VREDE

Cabernet Sauvignon Stellenbosch 1995: Pure Cabernet aromas of black currant and cedar lead to an elegant, soft, easy-drinking style, with medium body and concentration. Persistent in flavor, with just a hint of tannin on the finish. Drink now through 2001.–B.S. • $22 • (4/30/2000) • **86**
Cabernet Sauvignon Stellenbosch 1989 • $20 • (11/30/1994) • **87**
Estate Wine Stellenbosch Red 1992 • $25 • (1/31/1997) • **85**
Estate Wine Stellenbosch Red 1991 • $25 • (6/15/1995) • **89**
Estate Wine Stellenbosch Red 1990 • $NA • (11/30/1994) • **88**
Merlot Stellenbosch 1998: Firm and elegant, showing green olive, cedar, vanilla and cherry flavors. Lacks a little integration, ending with astringence. Drink now.–B.S. • $15 • (5/15/2000) • **80**
Merlot Stellenbosch 1996 • $12 • (9/15/1997) • **84**
Merlot Stellenbosch 1994 • $12 • (1/31/1997) • **83**
Merlot Stellenbosch 1993 • $12 • (12/31/1995) • **80**
Merlot Stellenbosch 1992 • $11 • (9/30/1995) • **73**
Merlot Stellenbosch 1991 • $12 • (11/30/1994) • **84**
Shiraz Stellenbosch 1996: Austere and peppery, with plum, leather and a tart, tight finish. Needs food. Tasted twice, with consistent notes. Drink now through 2001.–B.S. • $20 • (5/15/2000) • **83**
Shiraz Stellenbosch 1995: With generous flavor and lush texture, this is an easygoing, medium-bodied red, spicy-oaky in aroma, ripe in flavor and just tannic enough. Drink now. • $16 • (9/30/1998) • **87**
Shiraz Stellenbosch 1994 • $16 • (5/15/1997) • **88**
Shiraz Stellenbosch 1991 • $16 • (1/01/1997) • **83**
Shiraz Stellenbosch 1990 • $15 • (4/30/1996) • **83**
Shiraz Stellenbosch 1989 • $16 • (11/30/1994) • **85**
Stellenbosch 1996: This red makes a statement. Fresh, bold and extravagantly oaked, exuding vanilla, coffee and toast elements, backed by a core of rich, concentrated plum and black currant. Lovely acidity keeps it all lively, and the long finish bodes well for the future. Cabernet Sauvignon, Merlot and Shiraz. Best from 2001 through 2008.–B.S. • $32 • (4/30/2000) HR • **92**
Tinta Barocca Stellenbosch 1994 • $11 • (1/31/1997) • **76**
Tinta Barocca Stellenbosch 1993 • $10 • (7/31/1996) • **85**

RUSTENBERG

Cabernet Sauvignon Stellenbosch Red 1990 • $12 • (9/30/1995) • **84**
Cabernet Sauvignon Stellenbosch 1988 • $14 • (10/15/1992) • **74**
Cabernet Sauvignon-Merlot Stellenbosch 1991 • $12 • (9/30/1995) • **76**
Chardonnay Stellenbosch 1998: Slightly candied apple notes don't quite mesh with the smoky clove elements from the oak in this disjointed, straightforward white.–B.S. • $21 • (12/31/1999) • **78**
Dry Red Stellenbosch 1991 • $11 • (9/30/1995) • **82**
Five Soldiers Stellenbosch 1998: Medium-bodied and nutty, showing richness and focus. The vanilla, pear, smoke and nut flavors ally themselves to a creamy texture and the oak is well-integrated, leaving a complex, balanced impression. Chardonnay. Drink now through 2001.–B.S. • $34 • (5/15/2000) • **89**
Gold Label Stellenbosch Red 1990 • $17 • (9/30/1995) • **84**
Peter Barlow Stellenbosch 1997: The compact, solid structure puts a viselike grip on the black cherry, cedar and pencil-shaving core in this modern Pauillac-styled Cab. Has a lovely sense of harmony and incredible length, so be patient. Drink now through 2004.–B.S. • $39 • (5/15/2000) • **89**
Rustenberg Gold Stellenbosch Red 1989 • $19 • (10/15/1992) • **82**
Sauvignon Blanc Stellenbosch 1999: Straightforward, offering modest melon and nectarine flavors on a soft structure. Drink now.–B.S. • $20 • (4/30/2000) • **82**
Stellenbosch 1997: Deep and satisfying, from the dark color to the exquisite cherry, black currant and vanilla aromas and flavors. Elegant, it packs a lot

of flavors into a lithe frame, with serious structure and a lingering finish. Cabernet Sauvignon, Merlot and Cabernet Franc. Drink now through 2003.–B.S. • $29 • (4/30/2000) • **88**

Stellenbosch 1996: Thick and concentrated, here's a red packed with cherry, plum and cedar flavors. Intense and long, with a moderate tannic structure, if not great focus. A blend of Cabernet Sauvignon, Merlot and Cabernet Franc. Drink now.–B.S. • $28 • (12/15/1999) • **87**

SAVANHA

Cabernet Sauvignon Western Cape Agulhas Bank 1996 • $11 • (6/15/1998) • **78**

Chenin Blanc Western Cape Barrel Fermented 1997: A simple, sturdy white, with vague apple flavors and a slightly coarse texture. • $7 • (7/31/1998) • **75**

Merlot Western Cape 1995 • $10 • (1/31/1997) • **87**

Merlot-Cabernet Sauvignon Rosé Western Cape Barrel Fermented 1997: Not a bad rosé. Nicely dry, with light berry flavors and a sense of body and substance that lasts on the finish. Drink now. • $7 • (7/31/1998) • **84**

Pinotage Western Cape 1996 • $11 • (5/31/1997) • **85**

Pinotage-Cabernet Sauvignon Western Cape 1996 • $11 • (5/31/1997) • **84**

Sauvignon Blanc Western Cape 1997: Nice texture, with citrus and herbal notes mixed in. A quaffable white with an edge to it. Drink now.–K.M. • $7 • (7/31/1998) • **80**

Sauvignon Blanc Western Cape Benguela Current 1997: Simple and fruity, with bright grapefruit and apple, but a bit soft in texture, short on the finish. • $7 • (7/31/1998) • **77**

Shiraz Western Cape 1996 • $11 • (5/31/1997) • **84**

SAXENBURG

Cabernet Sauvignon Stellenbosch 1996: Vibrant, fruity and inviting, marked by cherry and plum notes and well supported by acidity. Has the fine balance of a Pinot Noir. Drink now. • $14 • (9/30/1998) • **86**

Cabernet Sauvignon Stellenbosch 1995 • $15 • (9/30/1997) • **87**

Cabernet Sauvignon Stellenbosch Private Collection 1995: A serious, dark-colored and tannic Cabernet that's tough to drink now. It's a gamble whether the generous black cherry and raspberry flavors will last until the texture smooths out, but it might be worth the risk. Best after 2001. • $25 • (6/15/1999) • **87**

Chardonnay Stellenbosch Private Collection 1998: A full-bodied, smooth-textured Chardonnay that goes for the gusto. Rich and assertive, from the toasty aromas through the ripe pear flavors accented by vanilla and smoky oak to the lingering finish. Drink now through 2001. • $15 • (6/15/1999) • **88**

Chardonnay Stellenbosch Private Collection 1997: An elegant wine, with plenty of luscious pear, apple and spice flavor that lingers appealingly on the finish. Drink now.–K.M. • $24 • (9/30/1998) • **86**

Merlot Stellenbosch 1996 • $14 • (6/15/1998) • **86**

Merlot Stellenbosch 1995 • $13 • (9/30/1997) • **86**

Merlot Stellenbosch Private Collection 1997: A deep-colored, rich-textured Merlot, with smoky, plummy flavors, moderate tannins and firm acidity. A bit lean in fruit, but enjoyable. Drink now through 2001. • $17 • (6/15/1999) • **83**

Pinotage Stellenbosch 1996: Quite flavorful but extreme in style, with ripe, almost sweet cherry flavors competing with smoky overtones. Light in tannin, medium in body. Drink now. • $14 • (7/31/1998) • **80**

Pinotage Stellenbosch 1995 • $13 • (10/15/1997) • **89**

Pinotage Stellenbosch 1994 • $12 • (7/31/1996) • **84**

Pinotage Stellenbosch Private Collection 1997: Perfectly charming. A generous, easygoing red, with ample berry and cherry flavors, a rich texture and a lingering finish. Drink now. • $15 • (6/15/1999) • **87**

Sauvignon Blanc Stellenbosch 1998: A serious style of Sauvignon, like a white Bordeaux. Full-bodied, with a broad, smooth texture and subtle grapefruit flavors accented by herb and spice. Drink now. • $9 • (11/30/1998) • **88**

Shiraz Stellenbosch 1995 • $18 • (11/15/1997) • **88**

Shiraz Stellenbosch 1994 • $16 • (7/31/1996) • **88**

Shiraz Stellenbosch Private Collection 1997: A generous, flavor-packed red with luscious ripe blackberry and pepper notes, smooth tannins and a lingering finish. Tasted twice, with consistent notes. Drink now through 2001. • $22 • (9/15/1999) • **88**

Shiraz Stellenbosch Private Collection 1996: A gutsy, distinctive Shiraz that's so good it reminds me of Crozes-Hermitage from France. Blends intriguing pepper, beef, smoke and blackberry flavors on a firm but supple texture. Drink now. • $25 • (9/30/1998) • **90**

Shiraz Stellenbosch Private Collection 1993 • $16 • (4/30/1996) • **90**

Shiraz Stellenbosch Special Release 1997: Suave and charming, with forward plum, black cherry and spice flavors on a smooth, moderately structured frame. Drink now through 2001.–B.S. • $50 • (4/30/2000) • **86**

SIMONSIG

Cabernet Sauvignon Stellenbosch 1996: Mature aromas of cedar and cigar box give way to a firm but still lush Cabernet, with currant, prune and bittersweet chocolate notes. Slightly charry on the finish though. Drink now.–B.S. • $14 • (1/01/2000) • **84**

Cabernet Sauvignon Stellenbosch 1989 • $14 • (10/15/1992) • **84**

Chardonnay Stellenbosch 1998: Exotic, perhaps from botrytis, this Chardonnay relies on intense peach, spring blossom and hazelnut notes with a touch of oak for spice. Beautifully displayed on a rich, suave framework, with a lingering aftertaste of butterscotch. Drink now through 2001.–B.S. • $13 • (5/15/2000) • **89**

Chardonnay Stellenbosch 1997: Straightforward in its approach, this Chardonnay shows a smoky note in addition to ripe apple. Lively and rich in texture. Drink now.–B.S. • $14 • (12/31/1999) • **83**

Chenin Blanc Stellenbosch 1999: Crisp, dry and balanced, here's an apple and citrus-flavored white to complement either fish in cream sauces or light chicken preparations. Drink now.–B.S. • $7 • (5/15/2000) • **85**

Chenin Blanc Stellenbosch 1998: This delicious and affordable white wine comes courtesy of South Africa, its straightforward floral and apple aromas and flavors married to a rich texture, with enough underlying acidity to keep everything fresh and lively. Drink now.–B.S. • $7 • (12/31/1999) • **86**

Gewürztraminer Stellenbosch 1998: Here's a broad, rich, thickly textured white that evokes floral, vanilla custard and raisin flavors. It shows balance and finishes on a spicy note. Drink now.–B.S. • $9 • (11/15/1999) • **83**

Pinotage Stellenbosch 1998: This has lovely purity of flavors, showing violet, raspberry, cherry and spice, with just a hint of gaminess stealing its virtue. Elegant and persistent in flavor right through to the long finish. Drink now through 2003.–B.S. • $13 • (4/30/2000) HR • **89**

Pinotage Stellenbosch 1989 • $11 • (10/15/1992) • **82**

Pinotage Stellenbosch Private Reserve 1989 • $NA • (2/15/1993) • **87**

Sauvignon Blanc Stellenbosch 1999: Ripe and suave, with an almost grainy texture to the mineral, grass and peach flavors. Good intensity and a firm structure keep it all focused through the long finish. Drink now.–B.S. • $11 • (4/30/2000) • **86**

Shiraz Stellenbosch 1997: Rustic in style, this Shiraz offers a modicum of berry and licorice notes, with more structure than flesh, ending with some firm tannins. Best with food. Drink now through 2002.–B.S. • $13 • (4/30/2000) • **84**

Shiraz Stellenbosch 1996: Traditional. Round, open and maturing, this red exhibits smoke, plum and leather elements, underscored by a firm, almost lean framework, with a hint of dill on the finish. Drink now.–B.S. • $14 • (1/01/2000) • **84**

Tiara Stellenbosch 1997: Vigorous and concentrated, this ripe red displays meat, plum, coffee and leather notes accented by spice. Medium-bodied, it turns a touch astringent on the finish. Cabernet Sauvignon and Merlot. Drink now through 2001.–B.S. • $20 • (4/30/2000) • **86**

Tiara Stellenbosch 1996: Bordeaux-like, showing cedar, black currant and smoke notes on a medium-bodied frame. Dusty tannins and a lingering cedar note complete the package. Drink now through 2002.–B.S. • $20 • (1/01/2000) • **84**

SIMONSVLEI WYNKELDER

Cabernet Sauvignon-Merlot Coastal Region 1995 • $9 • (9/30/1997) • **80**

Pinotage Coastal Region Reserve 1995 • $13 • (8/31/1997) • **85**

SINNYA

Cabernet Sauvignon-Merlot Robertson 1998: Ripe on the nose, with smoke, plum and currant aromas that are sweet and straightforward on the palate, but bracing acidity and a metallic note detract from the overall presentation. Drink now.–B.S. • $11 • (1/01/2000) • **80**

Cabernet Sauvignon-Merlot Robertson 1997: Smoky, oaky accents give definition to this medium-bodied, well-balanced and easy-textured red, with ripe plum and cherry flavors at its core. A blend: 59 percent Cabernet Sauvignon, 41 percent Merlot. Drink now. • $11 • (9/30/1998) • **84**

Key: SS—Spectator Selection. CS—Cellar Selection. HR—Highly Recommended. $NA—Price not available. (BT)—Barrel tasting. Ⓐ—Auction Price. For a key to the tasters' initials, see "How to Use These Listings."
Dates in parentheses represent the issues in which the ratings were published.

Chardonnay Robertson 1998: A light, commercial style of Chardonnay, with modest apple flavors.–B.S. • $11 • (12/31/1999) • **78**

Chardonnay Robertson 1997: A light-textured, easygoing Chardonnay, with ample fruit flavors and a sense of freshness. Drink now. • $11 • (11/30/1998) • **83**

SLALEY

Shiraz Stellenbosch Hunting Family Reserve 1997: Lovely international-style Shiraz, balancing raspberry and violet aromas and flavors and smoky, vanilla-laced oak. Very pretty, vibrant and full of palate-saturating berry flavors. Long, lingering finish. Drink now.–B.S. • $20 • (4/30/2000) • **87**

SORGVLIET

Grand Vin Rouge Stellenbosch 1992 • $7 • (9/30/1995) • **87**

SPRINGBOK

Cabernet Sauvignon Coastal Region 1994 • $7 • (1/31/1997) • **84**
Cabernet Sauvignon Coastal Region 1992 • $7 • (9/30/1995) • **73**
Cabernet Sauvignon Coastal Region 1991 • $7 • (1/01/1994) • **79**
Cabernet Sauvignon Coastal Region 1990 • $7 • (6/30/1994) • **82**
Cabernet Sauvignon Western Cape 1995 • $8 • (9/30/1997) • **85**
Merlot Western Cape 1995 • $8 • (9/30/1997) • **87**
Merlot Western Cape 1994 • $7 • (1/31/1997) • **83**
Pinotage Coastal Region 1993 • $7 • (4/30/1996) • **87**
Pinotage Coastal Region 1991 • $6 • (9/30/1995) • **74**
Pinotage Coastal Region 1990 • $7 • (6/30/1994) • **80**
Pinotage Coastal Region 1989 • $7 • (2/15/1993) • **82**
Pinotage Western Cape 1995 • $9 • (10/15/1997) • **86**
Shiraz Coastal Region 1994 • $7 • (5/15/1997) • **86**
Shiraz Coastal Region 1989 • $7 • (6/30/1994) • **74**
Shiraz Western Cape 1996 • $8 • (9/15/1997) • **84**

STELLENRYCK

Cabernet Sauvignon Coastal Region 1993: This medium-bodied red shows black currant and cedar notes that dissolve into a dry, tannic finish.–B.S. • $16 • (12/15/1999) • **79**

Cabernet Sauvignon Coastal Region 1992: A bit tired, with red cherry flavors and some leafy, tobaccolike notes. Hints of pepper on the finish, but dried out. Past its prime.–K.M. • $16 • (3/31/1999) • **78**

Cabernet Sauvignon Coastal Region 1991 • $16 • (5/31/1997) • **87**
Cabernet Sauvignon Coastal Region 1989 • $13 • (6/15/1995) • **87**
Cabernet Sauvignon Coastal Region 1988 • $13 • (11/30/1994) • **82**

Chardonnay Coastal Region 1999: More spice than fruit in this medium-bodied Chardonnay. The oak tannins and moderate acidity carry the vanilla, butter and nutmeg flavors to a modest conclusion. Drink now.–B.S. • $12 • (5/15/2000) • **84**

Chardonnay Coastal Region 1998: Dense and almost chewy in texture, this white shows pear and peach flavors as well as serious oak treatment, lending a fine structure and a toasty green olive and butterscotch finish. Drink now.–B.S. • $12 • (1/01/2000) • **83**

Chardonnay Coastal Region 1997: Ripe and round, with nice ripe pear flavors and buttery notes. A bit heavy-handed, but flavorful. Drink now.–K.M. • $11 • (5/15/1999) • **83**

STELLENZICHT

Cabernet Sauvignon Stellenbosch 1994 • $15 • (10/15/1997) • **87**
Merlot Stellenbosch 1994 • $15 • (9/15/1997) • **81**
Merlot-Cabernet Franc Stellenbosch 1994 • $15 • (9/30/1997) • **83**
Syrah Stellenbosch 1994 • $35 • (9/15/1997) • **92**

SWARTLAND

Cabernet Sauvignon Swartland Region 1998: A touch of herb augments the black currant and cherry flavors and juicy texture in this straightforward red. Drink now.–B.S. • $11 • (12/15/1999) • **83**

Cabernet Sauvignon Swartland Region 1993 • $9 • (9/30/1995) • **85**
Dry Red Swartland Region NV • $7 • (9/30/1995) • **81**

Merlot Swartland Region 1998: Some light herbal notes offset the soft plum and candied black cherry flavors. A simple quaffer. Drink now.–B.S. • $11 • (1/01/2000) • **81**

Merlot Swartland Region 1997: A satisfying Merlot, with deep color, intriguing tobacco and herb aromas, rich plum and tomato flavors and soft tannins. Drink now. • $10 • (7/31/1998) • **85**

Merlot Swartland Region 1996 • $11 • (5/15/1997) • **84**
Merlot Swartland Region 1995 • $10 • (4/30/1996) • **87**

Pinotage Swartland Region 1998: Rich, this relies on cherry and cardamom notes up front, turning a little lean and tannic on the finish. Cedar and smoke complete the aftertaste. Drink now through 2002.–B.S. • $10 • (4/30/2000) • **84**

Pinotage Swartland Region 1996 • $9 • (5/15/1997) • **84**
Pinotage Swartland Region 1995 • $9 • (4/30/1996) • **83**
Pinotage Swartland Region 1994 • $6 • (9/30/1995) • **83**

Shiraz Swartland Region 1997: Thick and mouthfilling, yet the flavor is one-dimensional, evoking cooked plums with a hint of rubber.–B.S. • $10 • (4/30/2000) • **79**

Shiraz Swartland Region 1992 • $9 • (9/30/1995) • **80**

Steen Swartland Region 1999: A fresh, lean, unoaked style of Chenin Blanc, displaying moderate apple and butterscotch notes that fade on the finish. Drink now.–B.S. • $8 • (5/15/2000) • **83**

THELEMA

Cabernet Sauvignon Stellenbosch 1996: Lean and well integrated, showing plum and eucalyptus, with a backbone of stiff tannins. Though not completely ripe, it's concentrated and stylish. The best of three samples tasted, with significant bottle variation. Drink now through 2001.–B.S. • $28 • (5/15/2000) • **85**

Cabernet Sauvignon Stellenbosch 1995: A grand Cabernet, from the deep mahogany color to the complex aromas of cedar and spice to the rich fruit flavors and lingering finish. Close to Napa in style. Drink now through 2001. • $26 • (5/15/1999) • **88**

Cabernet Sauvignon Stellenbosch 1994 • $30 • (9/15/1997) • **90**
Cabernet Sauvignon Stellenbosch 1993 • $20 • (8/31/1997) • **89**
Cabernet Sauvignon Stellenbosch 1991 • $19 • (6/15/1995) • **89**
Cabernet Sauvignon Stellenbosch 1990 • $18 • (1/31/1995) • **87**
Cabernet Sauvignon Stellenbosch Reserve 1991 • $22 • (9/30/1995) • **91**
Cabernet Sauvignon-Merlot Stellenbosch 1992 • $20 • (6/15/1995) • **90**

Chardonnay Stellenbosch 1998: Plenty of character in this medium-bodied white, whose oak-tinged spiciness augments the apple flavor. Finishes with a slight astringence. Drink now.–B.S. • $28 • (12/31/1999) • **87**

Chardonnay Stellenbosch 1997: Wow. This is a richly concentrated, deftly made Chardonnay that's packed with ripe fruit flavors and layered with creamy, spicy accents that linger on the finish. Full-bodied, almost sweet in its ripeness, but still balanced. Drink now through 2001. • $21 • (5/15/1999) • **91**

Merlot Stellenbosch 1996: An odd bread dough note runs through this mature Merlot, with a simple cola flavor and a soft, wispy finish. Drinkable, but fading fast.–B.S. • $28 • (1/01/2000) • **78**

Merlot Stellenbosch 1995: A sturdy Merlot that's tannic, rather tart and tight in texture, with underlying plum and herb flavors of moderate intensity. Too stiff to enjoy now, but will perhaps improve with age. Best after 2000. • $23 • (5/15/1999) • **82**

Merlot Stellenbosch 1994 • $24 • (9/15/1997) • **89**

Sauvignon Blanc Stellenbosch 1999: This straightforward Sauvignon Blanc shows vanilla, melon and hints of grass. It's light-bodied and a bit soft on the finish. Drink now.–B.S. • $22 • (4/30/2000) • **82**

Sauvignon Blanc Stellenbosch 1998: A sturdy Sauvignon Blanc that is full-bodied, generous in texture, with solid herb and sweet-pea flavors. Drink now. • $17 • (5/15/1999) • **83**

Sauvignon Blanc Stellenbosch 1997 • $19 • (12/15/1997) • **85**

TRILLENNIUM

Cabernet Sauvignon Western Cape 1997: A whiff of acetone on the nose turns soft and herbal, with black olive, dill and modest cherry flavors. Moderately structured, with vanilla on the finish. Made from a blend of 100 different barrels of Cabernet from various South African producers.–B.S. • $135/1.5 liter • (4/30/2000) • **79**

UITERWYK

Pinotage Stellenbosch 1992 • $12 • (9/30/1995) • **88**

VEENWOUDEN

Classic Red Paarl 1995: A robust but bright red, with lots of oak and good fruit flavor to back it up. Deep-colored and firm-textured, with full tannins.

A blend of Cabernet Sauvignon, Merlot, Cabernet Franc and Malbec. Drink now. • $30 • (9/30/1998) • **87**

Classic Red Coastal Region 1994 • $30 • (4/30/1997) • **83**

Merlot Coastal Region 1994 • $30 • (4/30/1997) • **85**

Merlot Coastal Region 1993 • $NA • (9/30/1995) • **87**

Merlot Paarl 1995: An inviting Merlot, whose mellow cherry and plum flavors are accented with cedar and mint. It has firm but smooth tannins and a light, mature character. Drink now. • $30 • (9/30/1998) • **85**

Vivat Bacchus Paarl 1996: A flavorful but unusual red, showing expressive, earthy aromas and flavors of cedar, cherry and prune. Full-bodied, with firm but smooth tannins. Drink now. • $30 • (11/30/1998) • **84**

VERGELEGEN

Sauvignon Blanc Coastal Region 1999: Pleasant, yet the grassy, herbal flavors disappear quickly, with a slight bitterness completing the profile. Drink now.–B.S. • $13 • (4/30/2000) • **81**

VILLIERA ESTATE

Brut South Africa Tradition Carte Rouge NV • $14 • (7/31/1995) • **81**

Cabernet Sauvignon Paarl 1993 • $NA • (9/30/1995) • **77**

Cabernet Sauvignon-Merlot Paarl Cru Monro 1997: Fresh, full of concentrated cherry, coffee and currant flavors, all densely textured and buoyed by ripe, firm tannins. Fades just a little on the finish. Drink now through 2001.–B.S. • $18 • (5/15/2000) • **86**

Chenin Blanc Paarl 1999: Rich and broad, showing vanilla, nutmeg and pear notes, this round, easy-drinking white reminds one of a Chardonnay from the Mâconnais. Drink now.–B.S. • $10 • (5/15/2000) • **84**

Chenin Blanc-Sauvignon Blanc Paarl Blue Ridge Blanc 1999: Round and appley, this rich white is soft and appealing. Good as an aperitif. Drink now.–B.S. • $10 • (5/15/2000) • **82**

Cru Monro Red Limited Release Oak Matured Paarl 1993 • $16 • (9/30/1995) • **88**

Cru Monro Red Limited Release Paarl 1992 • $16 • (9/30/1995) • **89**

Fumé Blanc Paarl 1999: This oak-influenced Sauvignon Blanc matches melon and gooseberry notes with vanilla on a crisp, lightweight frame. Good, lingering finish. Drink now.–B.S. • $14 • (4/30/2000) • **84**

Merlot Paarl 1993 • $15 • (6/15/1995) • **89**

Merlot Paarl 1992 • $15 • (6/15/1995) • **86**

Pinotage Paarl 1998: More structure than flavor in this densely textured, tangy red, whose cherry notes struggle with the underlying tannins. Drink now through 2002.–B.S. • $15 • (5/15/2000) • **84**

Sauvignon Blanc Paarl 1999: Broad, this offers herb and melon in an open-knit texture, with enough acidity to keep it balanced. Drink now.–B.S. • $13 • (4/30/2000) • **84**

VRIESENHOF

Cabernet Sauvignon Stellenbosch 1990 • $12 • (6/30/1994) • **75**

Kallista Stellenbosch Red 1991 • $14 • (6/15/1995) • **87**

Kallista Stellenbosch Red 1989 • $13 • (6/30/1994) • **75**

WARWICK

Cabernet Franc Stellenbosch 1993 • $15 • (6/30/1995) • **85**

Cabernet Sauvignon Stellenbosch 1995 • $14 • (3/31/1998) • **88**

Cabernet Sauvignon Stellenbosch 1992 • $15 • (1/31/1997) • **82**

Cabernet Sauvignon Stellenbosch 1991 • $15 • (6/30/1995) • **85**

Merlot Stellenbosch 1997: Herbal and woodsy elements here, along with a core of bright cherry flavor. It's on the leaner side for Merlot and wrapped in some serious tannins, so give it at least six months to settle down. Best from 2001 through 2004.–B.S. • $17 • (5/15/2000) • **86**

Merlot Stellenbosch 1992 • $15 • (6/30/1995) • **78**

Trilogy Stellenbosch Red 1995 • $18 • (3/31/1998) • **87**

Trilogy Stellenbosch Red 1994 • $18 • (9/30/1997) • **84**

Trilogy Stellenbosch Red 1992 • $17 • (6/30/1995) • **83**

Key: SS—Spectator Selection. CS—Cellar Selection. HR—Highly Recommended. $NA—Price not available. (BT)—Barrel tasting. (A)—Auction Price. For a key to the tasters' initials, see "How to Use These Listings."
Dates in parentheses represent the issues in which the ratings were published.

WATERFORD

Shiraz Stellenbosch Kevin Arnold 1998: Distinctive and problematic. International in style and well structured, with concentrated black cherry and spice flavors, yet overt, jumbled coffee, chocolate and animal aromas dominate. Drink now through 2002.–B.S. • $25 • (5/15/2000) • **84**

WELTEVREDE

Gewürztraminer Robertson 1999: Ripe apricots and a smoky element ally themselves to a lean structure in this personable, round white. The smoke flavor carries through to the finish. Drink now.–B.S. • $10 • (5/15/2000) • **83**

Muscat de Hambourg Robertson 1997: Sweet and grapey yet never thick or cloying, though the alcohol shows on the finish, which turns a little coarse. Try with blue cheeses. Drink now.–B.S. • $10 • (5/15/2000) • **84**

WETSHOF, DE

Chardonnay Robertson Bateleur 1997: Not a typical, oaky Chardonnay. This is subtle, almost austere in style, with understated fig and mineral flavors, crisp acidity and a lingering finish. Better than previously reviewed. Drink now. • $20 • (9/15/1999) • **86**

Chardonnay Robertson Bon Vallon 1999: A straightforward, quaffable white displaying moderate pineapple and pear aromas and flavors on a lightweight frame. Drink now.–B.S. • $10 • (5/15/2000) • **81**

Chardonnay Robertson Bon Vallon 1998: Easy to enjoy. Generous flavors of pear and pineapple fill out this medium-bodied, smooth-textured Chardonnay and linger on the finish. Drink now. • $10 • (9/15/1999) • **85**

Chardonnay Robertson Bon Vallon 1997 • $10 • (3/31/1998) • **83**

Chardonnay Robertson Lesca 1998: Lean, bracing and citrusy, this Chardonnay is reminiscent of a Chablis with its lemon, honey and flinty notes. Fresh and lingering, it's a white for light foods. Drink now through 2001.–B.S. • $13 • (5/15/2000) • **85**

Chardonnay Robertson Lesca 1997 • $12 • (4/30/1998) • **84**

WILDEBOSCH

Cabernet Sauvignon Western Cape 1996: A solid but simple Cabernet, with light plum and cherry flavors, mild tannins and a pleasant, fruity aftertaste. Drink now. • $8 • (9/30/1998) • **82**

Cinsault-Ruby Cabernet Western Cape 1996: Like a Beaujolais, this light, appealing red has fresh plum and strawberry flavors and a soft texture. Drink now. • $8 • (11/30/1998) • **82**

ZONNEBLOEM

Cabernet Sauvignon Stellenbosch 1997: Muddled and lacking direction, with modest stewed plum flavor.–B.S. • $10 • (4/30/2000) • **78**

Cabernet Sauvignon Stellenbosch 1989 • $11 • (6/30/1994) • **82**

Chardonnay Stellenbosch 1999: An elegant version, this Chardonnay exudes pineapple and even orange aromas and flavors, remaining bright and focused through the lingering finish. Could use a tad more concentration. Drink now.–B.S. • $10 • (5/15/2000) • **83**

Merlot Stellenbosch 1991 • $10 • (9/30/1995) • **76**

Pinotage Stellenbosch 1997: Simple stewed plum flavors lack focus, and it finishes short.–B.S. • $10 • (4/30/2000) • **78**

Pinotage Stellenbosch 1990 • $10 • (6/30/1994) • **75**

Pinotage Stellenbosch Vintner's Selection 1988 • $10 • (2/15/1993) • **82**

Shiraz Stellenbosch 1989 • $10 • (6/30/1994) • **71**

Spain

Dismissed as a backwater of Western European winemaking just a few years ago, Spain has transformed itself into one of the most exciting wine regions in the world. Gone is the stubbornly nationalistic devotion to tired-tasting wines with minimal appeal outside the Iberian peninsula. In its place is an energetic willingness to assimilate new winemaking ideas from around the world into the best of the old traditions. At long last, Spain is on its way to becoming a full-fledged member of the modern wine world.

1. **Rioja**
2. **Ribera del Duero**
3. **Priorat**
4. **Navarra**
5. **Penedès**
6. **Rias Baixas**
7. **Rueda**
8. **Jerez**

Its potential is seemingly limitless. With almost three million acres under vine, Spain has more vineyards than Italy or France. Spain is also a wine culture, with a per capita consumption five times that of the U.S. Its winegrowers are steeped in the knowledge of their individual soils and microclimates, giving them the same intimacy with the land as the French and the Italians. The combination of ready markets, native expertise and a new infusion of private and governmental investment means that Spanish wines have entered the 21st century with the full set of credentials needed to achieve world-class status.

SPANISH GRAPE VARIETIES

Most of Spain's best red wines have been based on a single grape—Tempranillo—which gained fame as the principal grape of Rioja. However, it is far more widely planted than it might appear, due to its multiplicity of names. Elsewhere in Spain it goes by Tinto del Pais ("the country red"), Cencibel, Ojo de Liebre, Tinto Fino, Tinto de Toro, and Ull de Llebre, according to local custom. It is also a much better grape variety than is usually acknowledged. Its reputation has been tarnished by the fact that, except in Rioja and Ribera del Duero, it tends to be over-cropped and lacking in concentration. Even in Rioja, excessive aging in American oak has masked its vibrant fruit. However, Tempranillo's image has dramatically improved now that winemakers such as Ribera's Alejandro Fernandez have used it to make imposing wines with dark color, firm structure and rich, ripe red fruit flavors. The list of top quality Tempranillo-based wines is growing exponentially.

Other red varieties are also showing dramatic improvement. These include Garnacha (the Spanish name for Grenache), Cabernet Sauvignon and Syrah. Among whites, the hot newcomer is the Albariño, with the more traditional Viura also making noticeable gains in quality and freshness.

SPANISH WINE REGIONS

Spain's wine laws are similar to those of the French appellation system, with the best vineyard regions delimited into approximately 50 *Denominacíons de Origen.* The DO regions specify geographic boundaries, permitted grape varieties, maximum yields and alcoholic strengths for each region. Rioja and Ribera del Duero have already made names for themselves, but less familiar regions, especially Navarra, Priorato, Somontano, Jumilla, Cariñena, Costers del Segre, La Mancha and Toro, are poised for wide recognition. For white wines, Galicia appears to have broken through to general acclaim.

Rioja

The modern history of Rioja dates back to the last century, when French *vignerons* from Bordeaux fled the phylloxera epidemic and set up house in this northerly region of Spain. Rioja contains three sub-regions: Rioja

Alta, Rioja Alavesa, and Rioja Baja. The first two lie in the west of the region, while the latter, the hottest and driest of the three, is in the eastern part.

Basic Rioja, most often sold as *"crianza"* (wood-aged), is marked by the vanilla and smoky tones of American oak layered over the spicy notes of Tempranillo. Most *crianza* should be drunk within three years of the vintage. Above the *crianza* level are the *reservas* and *gran reservas*. Both are selections from the best vats of the harvest and are usually made only in better years. *Gran reservas*, which spend the most time in oak, can be profound, provided one has cultivated a taste for the traditional wood-dominated, autumnal flavors and aromas of older Rioja. Top Rioja producers include Marqués de Riscal, Finca Allende, Remelluri, Martinez Bujanda, Marqués de Murrieta and CUNE, among others.

James Suckling

Decorative wall tiles at the Contino winery in Rioja.

Ribera del Duero

The Ribera del Duero region to the south of Rioja has for decades been producing wines from Tempranillo (called Tinto Fino here) that rival the world's best. Its greatest wine is the rare and expensive Vega Sicilia. Using older wood barrels and lengthy aging, Vega Sicilia shows the continued vitality of the traditional approach, and has similarities to great Rioja. A newer, more exuberantly fruity style is epitomized by Bodegas Alejandro Fernandez's Pesquera, which is aged in new French and American oak. It has more in common with a vigorous young Bordeaux than with Vega Sicilia. Other standouts from the region include Dominio de Pingus and Flor de Pingus, made by Danish immigrant Peter Sisseck, Bodegas y Viñedos Alion and Fernandez's Condado de Haza.

Emerging Regions

Spain's Priorat region, located about 85 miles southwest of Barcelona, has emerged as a hot new appellation, producing potently ripe and powerful reds that have attracted a cult following. Most of the new vines are Garnacha, with smaller amounts of Cabernet Sauvignon and Syrah filling out the blends. Notable reds from other regions include the robust reds from Navarra, and the Torres winery's classic Grans Muralles, made from a blend of four varieties—Garnacha Tinta, Monastrell, Samsó and Garró—grown on a 235-acre estate at an altitude of nearly 1,500 feet in the mountains of Catalonia.

Emerging regions are also the best place to look for bargains in the under-$15 price range. Navarra, Somontano, Jumilla, Cariñena, Costers del Segre, Toro and La Mancha all make remarkably delicious reds in the budget category.

SPANISH WHITE WINES

Some of the most impressive Spanish white wines come from Galicia, located just north of Portugal. Galicia's most exciting sub-region now is the Rias Baixas. Its principal grape, the Albariño, offers an intensity and complexity that calls to mind a cross between a French Viognier and an Alsace Riesling. In addition, white Riojas and Ruedas, made from the native Viura grape, now emphasize lemony fruit and freshness and are often quite good.

CAVA

Spain's immensely popular sparkling wine, called Cava, is made in some of the most technologically advanced, mechanized wineries anywhere in the world. It must spend a minimum of nine months in bottle, and many spend between one and three years. Though rarely the equal of French Champagne, the wines can be delightfully fresh and frothy, and the prices are reasonable.

SHERRY

Sherry, a fortified wine from Andalusia, offers many styles from which to choose. Manzanillas and Finos are pale, dry and delicate, and are perfect with tapas, the traditional Spanish delicacy. Amontillados are made both sweet and dry, and show more nutty, mature flavors. Dessert Sherries, such as Osborne's Oloroso Abocado Solera India, usually made from super-ripe, sweet Pedro Ximenez grapes, can provide an unforgettably luxurious tasting experience.

AGAPITO RICO

Jumilla Carchelo 1998: Plum and cherry flavors are clean and straightforward in this balanced red. Restrained, but has the stuffing to match with food. Drink now through 2002.–T.M. • $9 • (11/15/1999) • **84**
Monastrell Jumilla Carchelo 1997: This jammy red blend from Spain delivers ripe flavors of plum, chocolate and smoke, thick on the palate, with full but mild tannins. More exuberant than complex, but it makes for flavorful near-term drinking at an unbeatable price. Drink now through 2001.–T.M. • $8 • (10/31/1998) • **84**
Monastrell Jumilla Carchelo 1996 • $8 • (6/30/1997) • **84**
Monastrell Jumilla Carchelo 1995 • $8 • (4/30/1996) • **82**
Monastrell Jumilla Carchelo 1994 • $7 • (4/30/1995) • **81**
Monastrell Jumilla Carchelo 1993 • $6 • (12/15/1994) • **82**
Syrah Jumilla Carchelo 1998: Black cherry, game and black pepper flavors are true to the grape variety in this bright, polished red. Sturdy, crisp, straightforward and clean. Drink now through 2003.–T.M. • $12 • (11/15/1999) • **86**

AGE, BODEGAS

La Mancha Vega Serena 1993 • $5 • (2/28/1995) • **80**
Rioja Siglo 1988 • $9 • (3/31/1993) • **74**
Rioja Siglo Crianza 1991 • $7 • (3/31/1996) • **76**
Rioja Siglo Crianza 1990 • $8 • (1/31/1995) • **84**
Rioja Siglo Crianza 1989 • $7 • (4/15/1994) • **84**
Rioja Siglo Gran Reserva 1984 • $12 • (3/31/1993) • **84**
Rioja Siglo Reserva 1988 • $12 • (11/15/1997) • **87**
Rioja Siglo Reserva 1986 • $10 • (4/30/1995) • **86**
Rioja Siglo Reserva 1985 • $10 • (3/31/1993) • **77**

AGNET, L'

Priorat 1997: This ripe red is generous yet well defined, with alluring plum, raspberry and smoke flavors that are harmonious and fresh. It's less aggressive than many of the bruisers from this region. Drink now through 2005.–T.M. • $11 • (10/31/1998) • **88**

ALAVESAS, BODEGAS

Rioja Solar de Samaniego 1995 • $8 • (11/15/1997) • **79**
Rioja Solar de Samaniego Crianza 1992 • $10 • (11/15/1997) • **82**
Rioja Solar de Samaniego Reserva 1989 • $14 • (11/15/1997) • **83**

ALBET I NOYA

Cabernet Sauvignon Penedès 1997: This generous red shows a round texture over firm tannins. The flavors lean toward the herb and black olive side of Cabernet, with plum and coffee notes underneath. In the international style. Drink now through 2004.–T.M. • $18 • (6/15/2000) • **85**
Cabernet Sauvignon Penedès 1995 • $15 • (1/01/1998) • **86**
Cabernet Sauvignon Penedès 1994 • $15 • (10/31/1997) • **87**
Cabernet Sauvignon Penedès 1993 • $15 • (8/31/1996) • **78**
Cabernet Sauvignon Penedès 1992 • $14 • (4/30/1995) • **83**
Cabernet Sauvignon Penedès 1991 • $14 • (4/15/1994) • **82**
Syrah Penedès 1997: This rich red shows vibrant black cherry, chocolate and game notes. Full-bodied yet graceful, with plenty of ripe tannins for structure and a vibrant acidity that brings you back for another sip. Drink now through 2002.–T.M. • $18 • (6/15/2000) • **89**
Tempranillo Penedès 1995 • $15 • (11/15/1997) • **86**
Tempranillo Penedès 1994 • $15 • (11/15/1997) • **85**
Tempranillo Penedès 1993 • $15 • (8/31/1996) • **85**

ALION, BODEGAS Y VINEDOS

Ribera del Duero Reserva 1995: This modern-style red shows plenty of toasty vanilla flavors up front, but there's a solid core of ripe blackberry and black cherry, too. The texture is plush, but crisp acidity keeps the wine lively. It's a polished, impressive mix of suppleness and weight. Tasted twice, with consistent notes. Drink now through 2005.–T.M. • $35 • (10/31/1999) • **92**
Ribera del Duero Reserva 1994: This rich, ripe red offers deep fruit, plenty of new oak, a plush texture and great balance, with alluring flavors of blackberry, vanilla and toast, great concentration and a long, fruity finish. Seductive now, but has the potential to improve with age. Drink now through 2010.–T.M. • $35 • (11/30/1998) • **94**
Ribera del Duero Reserva 1993 • $25 • (6/15/1997) • **87**
Ribera del Duero Reserva 1992 • $22 • (7/31/1996) HR • **90**
Ribera del Duero Reserva 1991 • $20 • (4/15/1995) • **92**

ALLENDE, FINCA

Rioja 1996: A lush and deep red from Spain, with ripe fruit flavors of blackberry and cassis, rich notes of chocolate and toast from new oak and a muscular structure that remains balanced and approachable through the long, spicy finish. A fine example of modern Rioja, it's also a good buy at this price and score. Drink now through 2006.–T.M. • $17 • (10/31/1999) HR • **90**
Rioja Crianza 1995: This deep-colored red shows good concentration, with ripe blackberry and black cherry flavors accented by chocolate and coffee notes, firm tannins and bright acidity. A good example of the modern style. Drink through 2005.–T.M. • $15 • (11/30/1998) • **88**

ALTO ARAGON, VINEDOS Y CRIANZAS DEL

Cabernet Sauvignon-Merlot Somontano Enate 1998: Lush and fruity. This plum- and cherry-stuffed red doesn't have the tannic structure to age, but it delivers a mouthful of pleasure now. Drink now.–T.M. • $10 • (4/30/2000) • **85**
Tempranillo-Cabernet Sauvignon Somontano Crianza 1996: This supple red has well-focused berry and cherry flavors, with just enough tannin to keep it firm with food. Drink now.–T.M. • $12 • (4/30/2000) • **83**

AMEZOLA DE LA MORA, BODEGAS

Rioja Señorio Amezola Reserva 1989 • $13 • (4/15/1995) • **87**
Rioja Viña Amezola Crianza 1990 • $10 • (4/30/1995) • **85**

ANGUERA, JOAN D'

Tarragona Finca L'Argata 1997: Lush plum, black cherry and chocolate flavors are round and soft in this accessible red. It has good balance and a clean, spicy finish. Drink now through 2002.–T.M. • $20 • (11/15/1999) • **84**
Tarragona Finca L'Argata 1996: Cherry and vanilla flavors are direct, clean and firm in this lively, straightforward red. Has the grip for food. Drink now through 2003.–T.M. • $19 • (12/15/1999) • **84**
Tarragona La Planella 1998: This fruity red is frank and fresh, with light, firm tannins framing black cherry and plum flavors that taste a bit like fruit juice. A pleasant quaffer. Drink now through 2001.–T.M. • $13 • (11/15/1999) • **82**
Tarragona La Planella 1997: Round and fruity. Pretty black cherry, plum and chocolate flavors are bright and soft in this lush red. Straightforward yet balanced and clean. Drink now through 2002.–T.M. • $12 • (11/15/1999) • **83**

ARAGONESAS, BODEGAS

Campo de Borja Coto de Hayas Crianza 1995: Vanilla, sweet cherry and earth notes mingle uneasily in this drying red. Has some lingering sweetness, but tastes a bit disjointed.–T.M. • $7 • (12/15/1999) • **77**

ARGUESO, HEREDEROS DE

Manzanilla Jerez San León NV: Fascinating. Very tangy, from the first whiff to the intense finish, this manzanilla displays aromas and flavors of nuts and cooked apples allied to an almost creamy texture with buttery overtones. Drink now.–B.S. • $13 • (12/15/1998) HR • **91**

ARROYO, BODEGA S.

Ribera del Duero Arroyo Crianza 1996: Vivid berry and cherry flavors have intensity without weight in this light-structured but engaging red, which has enough acidity to keep it lively with food. Drink now through 2002.–T.M. • $27 • (10/31/1999) • **84**
Ribera del Duero Bodega San Jorge Arroyo 1998: This light, tart red has little fruit but dry tannins, and bears almost no resemblance to Ribera as I know it.–T.M. • $14 • (10/31/1999) • **74**
Ribera del Duero Bodega San Jorge Arroyo 1996 • $7 • (10/31/1997) • **85**
Ribera del Duero Bodega San Jorge Arroyo 1995 • $7 • (10/31/1997) • **84**
Ribera del Duero Bodega San Jorge Arroyo Crianza 1995: This chewy red offers cherry, raisin and earth flavors, with hard tannins and a slightly cooked note on the finish. Rich but a bit simple. Drink now through 2003.–T.M. • $23 • (10/31/1999) • **82**

ARROYO, BODEGA S.

Ribera del Duero Bodega San Jorge Arroyo Crianza 1994 • $12 • (10/31/1997) • **89**

Ribera del Duero Bodega San Jorge Arroyo Reserva 1991: This supple red is still quite fresh, with lively flavors of cherries, raisins and licorice and a polished texture with round tannins. Though not very concentrated or complex, it's balanced and graceful. Drink now.–T.M. • $35 • (10/31/1999) • **86**

ARROYO, BODEGAS ISMAEL

Ribera del Duero Mesoñeros de Castilla Crianza 1991 • $14 • (4/30/1995) • **89**

Ribera del Duero Mesoñeros de Castilla Crianza 1990 • $14 • (4/15/1994) SS • **90**

Ribera del Duero Val Sotillo 1996: This powerful red offers lush blackberry and vanilla aromas, a thick, full-bodied texture rich with blackberry, cassis, chocolate and light herb flavors and a fresh, lingering finish. Balanced enough to drink now; has the stuffing to improve through 2004.–T.M. • $22 • (10/31/1998) • **91**

Ribera del Duero Val Sotillo Crianza 1995 • $19 • (4/30/1998) HR • **92**

Ribera del Duero Val Sotillo Crianza 1994 • $19 • (10/31/1997) HR • **91**

Ribera del Duero Val Sotillo Gran Reserva 1990 • $60 • (10/31/1997) • **91**

Ribera del Duero Val Sotillo Gran Reserva 1989 • $60 • (7/31/1996) • **85**

Ribera del Duero Val Sotillo Reserva 1995: This beauty marries concentration with elegance. Layered flavors of plum, tobacco, coffee and mineral are mouthfilling but not heavy, backed by firm but round tannins and a long, spicy finish. Drink now through 2009.–T.M. • $53 • (10/31/1999) • **91**

Ribera del Duero Val Sotillo Reserva 1994: This impressive red combines ripe fruit and luscious texture in a marriage of regional flavors and international-style structure. Polished and velvety on the palate, with expressive flavors of plum, coffee, licorice and herb. Drink now through 2010.–T.M. • $39 • (11/30/1998) • **91**

Ribera del Duero Val Sotillo Reserva 1991 • $30 • (7/31/1996) • **90**

Ribera del Duero Val Sotillo Reserva 1990 • $25 • (4/30/1995) • **89**

Ribera del Duero Val Sotillo Reserva 1989 • $27 • (4/15/1994) • **87**

ARTADI

Rioja Crianza 1994 • $12 • (2/28/1998) • **86**

Rioja Grandes Añadas Reserva 1994: Beautifully sculpted, this red is rich yet tender, concentrated yet elegant, with ripe flavors of raspberry and blackberry, sweet toasted oak notes and a silky texture that simply glides into a long finish. Not a typical Rioja, but irresistible. Drink now through 2008.–T.M. • $130 • (2/29/2000) • **93**

Rioja Pagos Viejos Reserva 1995: Ripe and rich. This concentrated red is inky dark in color and thick on the palate, with muscular tannins, smoky oak and ripe fruit flavors of cassis, plum and prune. Has a firm balance, a long finish and definite aging potential. Another outstanding example of the modern style. Drink now through 2010.–T.M. • $50 • (2/29/2000) • **90**

Rioja Pagos Viejos Reserva 1994: Rich yet tender, this velvety red offers ripe flavors of blackberry and cassis, with oaky accents of toast and vanilla. Round, ripe tannins caress the palate, while jammy fruit lingers on the finish. A beautiful example of the modern style. Drink now through 2006.–T.M. • $45 • (2/29/2000) • **91**

Rioja Viña el Pison Reserva 1995: Alluring flavors of raspberry jam and milk chocolate give this red a velvety appeal. Sweet and beautifully textured, with ripe fruit and lavish oak, though a bit short on the finish. Drink now through 2004.–T.M. • $65 • (2/29/2000) • **89**

Rioja Viñas de Gain Crianza 1996: This deeply colored, round-textured red offers ripe flavors of plum and black cherry, with accents of coffee and licorice. The tannins are soft, but there's enough grip to stand up to food. Drink now through 2003.–T.M. • $18 • (2/29/2000) • **86**

Rioja Viñas de Gain Crianza 1995: Firm and polished, this concentrated red shows an impressive structure of ripe fruit and tannins. Roasted flavors of plum, prune and toast veer toward the earthy side of the spectrum. Tasted twice, with consistent notes. Drink now through 2003.–T.M. • $18 • (2/29/2000) • **83**

Key: SS—Spectator Selection. CS—Cellar Selection. HR—Highly Recommended. $NA—Price not available. (BT)—Barrel tasting. (A)—Auction Price. For a key to the tasters' initials, see "How to Use These Listings."
Dates in parentheses represent the issues in which the ratings were published.

ARZOBISPO, COOPERATIVA AGRICOLA VILLAR DEL

Valencia Cerro Gordo 1993 • $4 • (12/15/1997) • **76**

Valencia Cerro Gordo Crianza 1996: Sweet cherry and vanilla flavors are expressive but taste a bit candied in this supple red. Firmer tannins emerge on the finish and give the wine enough grip for food.–T.M. • $4 • (11/15/1999) • **79**

ARZUAGA, BODEGAS

Ribera del Duero Crianza 1995: This brooding, muscular red shows dark aromas and flavors of coffee, smoke, tar and game. The solid tannins overwhelm the modest fruit flavors, but plum and cassis emerge on the finish. Concentrated but closed now. Best after 2000.–T.M. • $23 • (10/31/1998) • **88**

Ribera del Duero Crianza 1994 • $20 • (4/30/1998) • **86**

Ribera del Duero Reserva 1995: This rich red is dense but not aggressive. Its ripe flavors of plum, chocolate and spice are smooth and harmonious, with spice and cedar notes that linger on the finish. Showing development now, it has a good future. Drink now through 2005.–T.M. • $55 • (11/15/1999) • **87**

Ribera del Duero Reserva 1994: This powerful red is beginning to mature now, with cedar and tobacco notes joining the ripe flavors of plum, prune and coffee. Thick on the palate, with muscular tannins that give way to a long, spicy finish. A blockbuster style that needs food for balance. Drink through 2010.–T.M. • $45 • (10/31/1998) • **92**

AS LAXAS, BODEGAS

Albariño Rias Baixas 1998: Crisp and quite full-bodied, this well-focused white offers pear, smoke and light herb flavors that have zest and grip. Good with food. Drink now.–T.M. • $15 • (11/15/1999) • **85**

Albariño Rias Baixas 1997: This full-bodied white offers creamy vanilla and hazelnut aromas and ripe flavors of apples and melons. Despite its power, it's clean and refreshing, with crisp acidity and a citrusy finish.–T.M. • $15 • (11/15/1998) • **84**

Albariño Rias Baixas 1996 • $15 • (5/31/1998) • **79**

Albariño Rias Baixas Bãgoa do Miño NV: This white cuts as cleanly as a sharp knife, leaving behind crisp lemon and herb flavors, with a slightly leesy note on the finish. A bit tart on its own, it should soften with food. From the 1998 vintage, though not listed anywhere on the bottle. Drink now.–T.M. • $20 • (11/15/1999) • **83**

Albariño Rias Baixas Bãgoa do Miño 1997: Pretty floral aromas give way to intense yet delicate lemon, pineapple and light vanilla flavors in this vibrant white. Works as an aperitif or with lighter dishes. Drink now.–T.M. • $20 • (11/15/1998) • **86**

Albariño Rias Baixas Don Bernardo 1997: Lovely aromas of lime and vanilla follow through on the palate, light and delicate, clean and refreshing, with an almond-scented finish. Though not powerful, this makes an attractive apéritif. Drink now.–T.M. • $10 • (11/15/1998) • **84**

AYALA LETE E HIJOS, R. DE

Rioja Viña Santurnia Crianza 1994 • $7 • (5/31/1998) • **86**

AYUSO, BODEGAS

La Mancha 1990 • $6 • (12/15/1992) • **81**

La Mancha Estola Crianza 1987 • $10 • (12/15/1992) • **78**

La Mancha Estola Reserva 1993: Vanilla and light berry flavors are soft and sweet in this light, traditional-style red. Simple but well integrated and still fresh. Drink now.–T.M. • $6 • (10/31/1998) • **82**

La Mancha Estola Reserva 1991: This simple red offers light cherry and tea flavors, with light tannins that are starting to dry out on the finish. It's harmonious, but nearing the end of the road. Drink now.–T.M. • $7 • (10/31/1998) • **81**

La Mancha Estola Reserva 1985 • $10 • (2/15/1992) • **80**

La Mancha Viña Q NV: Light and lean, this simple red offers berry and herb flavors, with hints of smoke and dust. The tannins are light yet astringent.–T.M. • $4 • (10/31/1998) • **78**

AZPILICUETA, BODEGAS FELIX

Rioja Gran Reserva 1982 • $36 • (3/31/1996) • **82**

BAJAMAR, MARQUES DE

Navarra 1995 • $6 • (11/15/1997) • **82**
Navarra White 1996 • $6 • (11/15/1997) • **78**

BALBAS, BODEGAS

Ribera del Duero 1988 • $15 • (9/30/1991) • **88**
Ribera del Duero 1987 • $14 • (9/30/1990) • **81**
Ribera del Duero 1986 • $15 • (7/31/1989) • **87**
Ribera del Duero 1985 • $13 • (9/15/1988) • **83**
Ribera del Duero Crianza 1995: This red is vivid and harmonious from start to finish. Blackberry, vanilla and licorice flavors are clean and well defined against bright acidity and firm tannins. Though not overly powerful, it shows impressive elegance. Drink now through 2003.–T.M. • $14 • (10/31/1998) • **89**
Ribera del Duero Reserva 1994: This thick, muscular red is ripe and rich, with plum, prune and coffee flavors that emerge through powerful tannins. Not graceful yet balanced, it should soften with food and time. Drink through 2010.–T.M. • $22 • (10/31/1998) • **88**

BARBIER, RENE

Cabernet Sauvignon Penedès 1994 • $7 • (10/31/1997) • **84**
Cabernet Sauvignon Penedès Mediterranean Select 1990 • $7 • (3/31/1996) • **80**
Merlot Penedès 1993 • $7 • (10/31/1997) • **84**
Merlot Penedès Mediterranean Select 1992 • $7 • (3/31/1996) • **84**
Penedès Family Reserve NV • $6 • (4/15/1994) • **75**
Penedès Mediterranean Red NV: Ripe plum and tobacco aromas are generous, but the wine turns lighter on the palate, with scratchy tannins and modest cherry and herb flavors. A light, almost citrusy acidity keeps it fresh. Drink now.–T.M. • $5 • (11/30/1998) • **83**
Penedès Mediterranean Rosé NV: This rosé is almost light red in color, with light but noticeable tannins and red berry and apple flavors. It's a bit clumsy, but will stand up to food. Drink now.–T.M. • $5 • (11/30/1998) • **82**
Penedès Mediterranean White NV: This bright, friendly white has fruity, almost candied flavors of orange, lemon and lime, with vanilla accents and a round, soft texture kept crisp by tart acidity. Drink now.–T.M. • $5 • (11/15/1998) • **84**
Priorat Clos Mogador 1997: This big wine carries its ripe fruit and firm tannins with grace and polish; flavors of plum, licorice and herbs are lush and well-integrated. Accessible now, but has the stuffing to age. Drink now through 2007.–T.M. • $45 • (4/30/2000) • **90**
Priorat Clos Mogador 1996: Coffee, chocolate and prune flavors are expressive and powered by high alcohol in this heady, firm red. It's dark and spicy, with a silky texture and firm, underlying tannins. This was the better of two bottles, with significant bottle variation. Drink now through 2010.–T.M. • $34 Ⓐ • (9/15/1999) • **88**
Priorat Clos Mogador 1995: A rich, inky black wine, with dark flavors of bitter chocolate, nutmeg, plum, prune and coffee. It fills the palate, yet the muscular tannins are well integrated. The finish is a bit hot but long and spicy. A big wine that needs time to show its best. Best after 2002.–T.M. • $43 Ⓐ • (10/31/1998) • **92**
Priorat Clos Mogador 1994 • $35 • (10/31/1997) • **91**
Priorat Clos Mogador 1993 • $35 • (1/01/1997) • **90**
Priorat Clos Mogador 1992 • $35 • (1/01/1997) • **87**
Priorat Clos Mogador 1991 • $35 • (4/30/1995) • **90**
Priorat Clos Mogador 1990 • $35 • (4/15/1994) • **87**
Tempranillo Penedès 1993 • $7 • (11/15/1997) • **79**

BARCELO, HIJOS DE ANTONIO

Castilla y Leon Peñascal 1996: This light red is balanced and subtle, with cherry, light vanilla and herbal flavors backed by moderate tannins. Has just enough grip for food. Drink now.–T.M. • $6 • (12/15/1999) • **83**
Castilla y Leon Peñascal 1995: This expressive Spanish red boasts lively flavors of blueberry, cherry and chocolate, and firm but ripe tannins that add backbone without astringency. A modern-style wine, with appealing flavors and good balance, only its price tag is an atavism. Drink now.–T.M. • $6 • (11/30/1998) • **85**
Castilla y Leon Peñascal 1994 • $6 • (11/15/1997) • **84**
Ribera del Duero Viña Mayor 1996 • $6 • (10/31/1997) • **87**
Ribera del Duero Viña Mayor 1994 • $7 • (10/15/1996) • **78**
Ribera del Duero Viña Mayor 1992 • $6 • (4/15/1994) • **75**
Ribera del Duero Viña Mayor 1991 • $7 • (1/31/1993) • **86**
Ribera del Duero Viña Mayor Crianza 1996: Rather light and soft, this plump red offers pretty cherry and light vanilla flavors that dissipate quickly on the finish. A quaffable wine for current drinking.–T.M. • $11 • (10/31/1999) • **84**
Ribera del Duero Viña Mayor Crianza 1995: This rustic red has ripe, almost roasted flavors of plum, prune and coffee, with herb and tobacco accents and tough tannins. A good match for grilled game. Drink now through 2005.–T.M. • $9 • (11/30/1998) • **85**
Ribera del Duero Viña Mayor Crianza 1994 • $8 • (10/31/1997) • **85**
Ribera del Duero Viña Mayor Crianza 1992 • $8 • (7/31/1996) • **85**
Ribera del Duero Viña Mayor Crianza 1991 • $8 • (4/30/1995) • **86**
Ribera del Duero Viña Mayor Crianza 1990 • $7 • (2/15/1992) • **83**
Ribera del Duero Viña Mayor Crianza 1989 • $9 • (12/15/1993) • **83**
Ribera del Duero Viña Mayor Reserva 1994: This strong, balanced red offers clean flavors of black cherry and plum, with notes of coffee and licorice, backed by firm tannins in a balanced, graceful package. This Spanish wine is food-friendly now, should become more expressive with age. Enjoy through 2004.–T.M. • $13 • (10/31/1998) SS • **90**
Ribera del Duero Viña Mayor Reserva 1991 • $11 • (7/31/1996) • **83**
Ribera del Duero Viña Mayor Reserva 1989 • $11 • (4/15/1994) • **81**
Tempranillo Castilla y Leon Realeza 1997: Sweet vanilla aromas give way to round, lush flavors of vanilla, berry and cherry in this frank, appealing red. Not complex, but draws you back for another sip. Drink now.–T.M. • $6 • (10/31/1998) • **84**

BARONIA DE TURIS

Moscatel Valencia NV • $6 • (11/15/1997) • **80**

BERBERANA, BODEGAS

Brut Cava Marino NV • $9 • (10/31/1997) • **80**
Rioja Carta de Oro Crianza 1989 • $9 • (8/31/1993) • **85**
Rioja Carta de Oro Crianza 1988 • $10 • (3/31/1992) • **78**
Rioja Carta de Oro Crianza 1987 • $10 • (3/31/1992) • **87**
Rioja Carta de Plata 1989 • $9 • (3/31/1992) • **77**
Rioja Carta de Plata 1988 • $8 • (9/30/1991) • **83**
Rioja Crianza 1991 • $9 • (1/31/1996) • **82**
Rioja d'Avalos 1994 • $8 • (1/31/1996) • **80**
Rioja Dragon Label 1995 • $10 • (10/15/1997) • **84**
Rioja Dragon Label 1994 • $10 • (6/30/1996) • **86**
Rioja Dragon Label 1993 • $10 • (1/31/1996) • **83**
Rioja Dragon Label 1992 • $10 • (4/30/1995) • **84**
Rioja Gran Reserva 1988: This rich red has good structure, but the flavors are thick and a bit dull, with coffee and prune notes over chewy tannins. Spice and cedar accents add interest, but the finish is dry and short. Drink now through 2002.–T.M. • $18 • (11/30/1998) • **84**
Rioja Gran Reserva 1987 • $18 • (10/15/1997) • **87**
Rioja Gran Reserva 1985 • $17 • (9/30/1996) HR • **89**
Rioja Gran Reserva 1983 • $15 • (1/31/1996) • **85**
Rioja Gran Reserva 1982 • $24 • (11/30/1991) • **88**
Rioja Gran Reserva 1980 • $18 • (10/31/1988) • **82**
Rioja Gran Reserva 1975 • $13 • (3/31/1992) • **88**
Rioja Gran Reserva 1973 • $20 • (3/31/1992) • **89**
Rioja Preferido 1992 • $6 • (8/31/1993) • **78**
Rioja Reserva 1994: This traditional-style red offers a core of plum flavor, with mineral, earth and tobacco accents. Has a silky texture, moderate tannins and lively acidity. Drink now.–T.M. • $15 • (12/15/1999) • **83**
Rioja Reserva 1990 • $13 • (12/15/1997) • **83**
Rioja Reserva 1988 • $11 • (1/31/1996) • **87**
Rioja Reserva 1986 • $11 • (3/31/1992) • **81**
Rioja Reserva 1985 • $13 • (3/31/1992) • **82**
Rioja Reserva 1983 • $12 • (3/31/1992) • **82**
Rioja Reserva 1982 • $20 • (3/31/1992) • **85**
Tempranillo Rioja Crianza 1995: The light color belies its firm structure, but its cherry and light spice flavors don't have much impact or persistence. A good red for fish dishes. Drink now.–T.M. • $10 • (11/30/1999) • **82**
Tempranillo Rioja Crianza 1994 • $10 • (11/30/1997) • **84**
Tempranillo Rioja Crianza 1992 • $10 • (9/15/1996) • **84**
Tempranillo Rioja d'Avalos 1996: This rich but unbalanced red is sweet, with very toasty oak and ripe fruit flavors that are assertive but lack freshness and verve.–T.M. • $8 • (11/30/1998) • **79**
Tempranillo Rioja d'Avalos 1995 • $8 • (10/15/1997) • **84**
Tempranillo Rioja Dragon Label 1996: An assertive vanilla character gives this red a typical Rioja accent, with black cherry and plum flavors. Smooth and rather light, but has intensity. Drink now through 2001.–T.M. • $10 • (11/30/1998) • **84**

BERBERANA, BODEGAS

Viño de Mesa Marino NV • $6 • (4/30/1996) • **78**

BERONIA, BODEGAS

Rioja Crianza 1994 • $9 • (11/15/1997) • **81**
Rioja Crianza 1990 • $8 • (4/30/1995) • **79**
Rioja Crianza 1989 • $8 • (4/15/1994) • **77**
Rioja Gran Reserva 1985 • $23 • (5/31/1998) • **86**
Rioja Gran Reserva 1981 • $18 • (1/31/1996) • **83**
Rioja Gran Reserva 1980 • $18 • (4/15/1994) • **85**
Rioja Reserva 1991 • $13 • (5/31/1998) • **80**
Rioja Reserva 1985 • $11 • (4/15/1994) • **80**
Rioja Reserva 1982 • $12 • (3/31/1990) • **82**
Viura Rioja 1996 • $9 • (10/31/1997) • **84**
Viura Rioja Barrel Fermented 1996 • $11 • (10/31/1997) • **85**

BILBAINAS, BODEGAS

Rioja La Vicalanda de Viña Pomal Reserva 1995: Round and ripe, this polished wine offers plummy, smoky and meaty flavors that are balanced and clean. It has a pleasing plumpness, kept in focus by ripe tannins. A good food wine, it should age well. Drink now through 2004.–T.M. • $20 • (11/30/1999) • **88**

Rioja La Vicalanda de Viña Pomal Reserva 1994 • $21 • (1/01/1998) • **84**
Rioja Viña Pomal Crianza 1990 • $13 • (3/31/1996) • **85**
Rioja Viña Pomal Gran Reserva 1980 • $26 • (4/15/1994) • **83**
Rioja Viña Pomal Gran Reserva 1978 • $20 • (3/31/1990) • **88**

Rioja Viña Pomal Reserva 1994: Ripe, firm and balanced, this solid red has a rich core of plum flavor, with accents of chocolate, tobacco and spice. Has enough tannin for grip, yet stays lively and light through the long finish. Drink now through 2002.–T.M. • $15 • (12/15/1999) • **86**

Rioja Viña Pomal Reserva 1988 • $29 • (3/31/1996) • **80**
Rioja Viña Pomal Reserva 1985 • $12 • (4/15/1994) • **84**

BILBAO, BODEGAS RAMON

Rioja Crianza 1995: Traditional style. This red offers dried cherry, leather and spice flavors on a lean frame, with firm tannins and bright acidity that will work well with food. Drink now through 2003.–T.M. • $11 • (1/01/2000) • **86**

Rioja Gran Reserva 1989: This traditional-style red offers dried cherry, floral and cedar flavors, nicely harmonious, a supple texture and just enough tannin for grip. The finish is long and sweet. Drink now.–T.M. • $30 • (1/01/2000) • **86**

Rioja Reserva 1994: Supple and elegant, this red shows complex, mature flavors of cherry, tea and cinnamon, yet remains lively and focused. Best with lighter dishes. Drink now through 2003.–T.M. • $20 • (1/01/2000) • **87**

BLAGUEURS, DOMAINE DES

Grenache Navarra Grenache Village 1996: This plush, international-style beauty is lively and rich, with pure blackberry and black cherry flavors, firm, ripe tannins, a core of fresh acidity and good concentration and balance. Drink now through 2004.–T.M. • $13 • (11/30/1998) • **88**

BOADA, BODEGAS

Ribera del Duero Crianza 1994: Firm and focused. This well-structured red offers ripe plum, black cherry and coffee flavors, with muscular tannins and a clean finish. Has the balance to improve with age. Drink now through 2005.–T.M. • $17 • (12/15/1999) • **87**

Ribera del Duero Crianza 1991 • $15 • (11/30/1997) • **84**

Ribera del Duero Reserva 1989: Solid, ripe, mature. Flavors of raisins, cedar and tobacco are traditional but focused in this sturdy, tannic red. Still has life, but the flavors are quite evolved. Drink now.–T.M. • $35 • (10/31/1999) • **85**

Ribera del Duero Reserva 1985 • $30 • (10/31/1997) • **86**

Key: SS—Spectator Selection. CS—Cellar Selection. HR—Highly Recommended. $NA—Price not available. (BT)—Barrel tasting. Ⓐ—Auction Price.
For a key to the tasters' initials, see "How to Use These Listings."
Dates in parentheses represent the issues in which the ratings were published.

BORJA, AGRICOLA DE

Campo de Borja Borsao 1998: Blackberry, plum and vanilla flavors are vivid in this round, supple red, but have a sweet-tart note reminiscent of hard candies. Distinctive. Drink now.–T.M. • $6 • (12/15/1999) • **81**

Campo de Borja Borsao 1997: Bright and fruity, this red shows youthful exuberance, with grapey flavors, crisp acidity and light tannins. It resembles a young Beaujolais in style and freshness. Drink now.–T.M. • $6 • (11/30/1998) • **81**

Campo de Borja Borsao 1993 • $4 • (4/30/1995) • **81**

Campo de Borja Borsao Crianza 1996: Ripe berry and cherry flavors are framed by intense sweet vanilla notes in this supple red. It's sweet and soft, but has a fruity appeal. Drink now.–T.M. • $8 • (12/15/1999) • **83**

Campo de Borja Viña Borgia 1998: Supple and perfumed. Floral, berry and vanilla notes are soft and sweet in this gentle red that has just enough grip for lighter foods. Drink now.–T.M. • $5 • (12/15/1999) • **83**

BRETON, BODEGAS

Rioja Alba de Bretón Reserva 1995: This concentrated red marries lively, rather tart cherry and cassis flavors with muscular tannins and smoky vanilla oak flavors. It needs a thick steak, or time in the bottle, to harmonize its intense but disparate elements. Drink through 2005.–T.M. • $65 • (11/30/1999) • **88**

Rioja Dominio de Conte Reserva 1995: Ripe and concentrated. Rich flavors of plum, prune and chocolate are backed by firm, ripe tannins in this muscular red, with enough acidity for balance. A powerful wine with a good future. Drink now through 2004.–T.M. • $35 • (11/30/1999) • **88**

Rioja Dominio de Conte Reserva 1994: This powerful red is packed with ripe, almost jammy flavors of black raspberry, licorice and vanilla. The tannins are full yet well integrated. An exuberant wine that will marry well with hearty dishes. Drink now through 2005.–T.M. • $30 • (10/31/1998) • **87**

Rioja Dominio de Conte Reserva 1991 • $26 • (8/31/1996) • **87**
Rioja Dominio de Conte Reserva 1990 • $24 • (1/31/1996) • **84**

Rioja Loriñon Crianza 1996: Ripe, almost jammy flavors of blackberries and plums shine through this red; the texture is round but not heavy or dull, with moderate tannins and enough acidity for balance. Drink now through 2004.–T.M. • $13 • (10/31/1999) • **86**

Rioja Loriñon Crianza 1995: This vivid red is lively and harmonious, with bright plum and cherry flavors backed by notes of coffee and hazelnut. The tannins are firm yet well integrated, and crisp acidity keeps the wine fresh. Well made in the modern style. Drink now through 2003.–T.M. • $11 • (11/30/1998) • **87**

Rioja Loriñon Crianza 1994 • $10 • (6/30/1997) • **86**
Rioja Loriñon Crianza 1991 • $10 • (3/31/1996) • **81**
Rioja Loriñon Crianza 1990 • $9 • (4/30/1995) • **86**
Rioja Loriñon Crianza 1989 • $9 • (4/15/1994) • **87**
Rioja Loriñon Crianza 1988 • $10 • (1/31/1992) • **83**

Rioja Loriñon Reserva 1995: This elegant red marries fine, firm structure with restrained but deep flavors of tobacco, cedar, licorice and plum. Subtle but complete, it grows on you with every sip. Drink now through 2004.–T.M. • $20 • (11/30/1999) • **88**

Rioja Loriñon Reserva 1994: This ripe, muscular red is rich on the palate, with full, firm tannins and good concentration. Though the fruit flavors are subdued now, there's plenty of plum, prune and spice character that will increase with time. Drink through 2005.–T.M. • $20 • (10/31/1998) • **88**

Rioja Loriñon Reserva 1991 • $17 • (10/15/1997) • **88**
Rioja Loriñon Reserva 1989 • $17 • (4/30/1995) • **82**
Rioja Loriñon Reserva 1987 • $15 • (12/15/1993) • **77**

Rioja White Loriñon Barrel Fermented 1998: This rich white offers ripe apple and apricot flavors with pleasant floral overtones, framed by sweet vanilla and cream notes from oak aging. A fine example of the international style that is making inroads in Rioja. Drink now.–T.M. • $12 • (10/31/1999) • **87**

Rioja White Loriñon Barrel Fermented 1996 • $10 • (10/31/1997) • **85**

CABEZA, BODEGAS NUESTRA SENORA DE LA

Cencibel-Cabernet Sauvignon La Mancha Casa Gualda 1996: This modest red offers straightforward flavors of cherries and herbs, with light, balanced flavors and a fresh finish. A pleasant complement to a light meal. Drink now.–T.M. • $8 • (10/31/1998) • **82**

CACERES, MARQUES DE

Rioja 1992 • $12 • (3/31/1996) • **83**
Rioja 1991 • $10 • (3/31/1995) • **84**
Rioja 1989 • $9 • (3/31/1993) • **86**
Rioja Crianza 1995: This light, crisp red offers simple cherry and herb flavors, with light tannins and a bit too much acidity for balance. A good red for fish dishes. Drink now.–T.M. • $12 • (11/30/1999) CS • **81**
Rioja Crianza 1994 • $12 • (10/15/1997) • **86**
Rioja Crianza 1990 • $10 • (4/15/1994) • **84**
Rioja Crianza 1989 • $9 • (4/15/1994) • **84**
Rioja Gran Reserva 1989: Supple yet focused, this spicy red still shows a deep, youthful color, along with flavors of dried cherries, chocolate, cocoa and herbs. It has enough structure to match with food, and a long, spicy finish. Drink now through 2003.–T.M. • $25 • (12/15/1999) • **88**
Rioja Gran Reserva 1987 • $23 • (11/30/1997) • **88**
Rioja Gran Reserva 1986 • $25 • (3/31/1996) • **83**
Rioja Gran Reserva 1982 • $25 • (3/31/1992) • **89**
Rioja Gran Reserva 1975 • $26 • (3/31/1992) • **89**
Rioja Gran Reserva 1973 • $30 • (3/31/1992) • **83**
Rioja Reserva 1992: This red still has a youthful color and ripe flavors of cherry and plum, and shows good balance and a clean finish. Though it seems modest in structure and depth, it may still improve with age. Drink now through 2003.–T.M. • $18 • (12/15/1999) • **85**
Rioja Reserva 1991: This dense red is still youthful, with muscular tannins and ripe, even roasted flavors of plum, prune and chocolate. A bit heavy-handed on its own, it has the power to match with richer foods. 5,000 cases imported. Drink now through 2003.–T.M. • $17 • (11/30/1998) • **88**
Rioja Reserva 1990 • $17 • (10/15/1997) • **86**
Rioja Reserva 1989 • $20 • (3/31/1996) • **87**
Rioja Reserva 1986 • $12 • (4/15/1994) • **88**
Rioja Reserva 1985 • $19 • (3/31/1992) • **87**
Rioja Reserva 1982 • $25 • (3/31/1992) • **83**
Rioja Reserva 1981 • $20 • (3/31/1990) • **69**
Rioja Rosado 1998: This pale, subtle rosé has a nice balance of herbal and mineral notes, and it's fresh and dry. Berry flavors are light but clean. Drink now.–T.M. • $6 • (10/31/1999) • **83**
Rioja Rosado 1997: Light and fresh, this delicate rosé offers clean, crisp flavors of strawberry and raspberry and makes a pleasant quaff. 4,000 cases imported. Drink now.–T.M. • $7 • (10/31/1998) • **83**
Rioja White 1998: Floral and vanilla notes give this Spanish white an appealing hint of sweetness and a pillowy-soft texture, supported by enough citrusy acidity to keep the balanced. A nice aperitif at a very nice price. Drink now.–T.M. • $6 • (10/31/1999) • **84**
Rioja White 1997: Smoky, toasty accents are alluring in this snappy white, with lemony acidity that keeps it lively. The apple flavors are modest, but the wine is balanced and fresh. Drink now.–T.M. • $7 • (11/30/1998) • **84**
Rioja White 1996 • $7 • (10/31/1997) • **81**
Rioja White Satinela 1997: This unusual white is round and soft, offering distinctive tropical fruit flavors that are almost sweet and slightly cloying, with accents of vanilla and butter.–T.M. • $7 • (11/30/1998) • **78**
Rioja White Satinela 1996 • $7 • (10/31/1997) • **78**

CACHAZO, BODEGAS ANGEL LORENZO

Rueda Martivillí 1996 • $10 • (4/30/1998) • **78**
Sauvignon Blanc Rueda Martivillí 1998: This crisp white shows good varietal character, with notes of herb and grapefruit. Round with much concentration, balanced without much length. Drink now.–T.M. • $8 • (10/31/1999) • **83**
Sauvignon Blanc Rueda Martivillí 1997: This clean, fresh white offers lively acidity and light apple and citrus flavors, with hints of vanilla. Not complex, yet easy to drink. Drink now.–T.M. • $8 • (11/30/1998) • **82**
Verdejo Rueda Martivillí 1998: This lively white marries a round texture with crisp flavors of green apple and an intriguing almond note. The absence of oak lets the fruit shine through. Drink now.–T.M. • $9 • (10/31/1999) • **85**

CACHAZO, BODEGAS FELIX LORENZO

Rueda Gran Cardiel 1996 • $7 • (10/31/1997) • **84**
Verdejo Rueda Carrasviñas 1997: Sharp and thin, this maturing white offers lemony acidity and very little fruit.–T.M. • $11 • (10/31/1999) • **77**
Verdejo Rueda Carrasviñas 1996: This straightforward white is light and clean, with light notes of almond and licorice and a tart core of acidity. Try with shellfish. Drink now.–T.M. • $11 • (11/30/1998) • **80**

CALATAYUD, BODEGAS MIGUEL

Valdepeñas Vegaval Plata Crianza 1996: Supple and straightforward, this red offers pleasant cherry and light chocolate flavors in an easy-drinking style. Drink now.–T.M. • $10 • (4/30/2000) • **82**
Valdepeñas Vegaval Plata Crianza 1995: This maturing red still has enough ripe fruit to balance the slightly drying tannins, with plum, raisin and tobacco flavors. Best with food. Drink now.–T.M. • $10 • (1/31/2000) • **83**
Valdepeñas Vegaval Plata Reserva 1989: Though the region isn't known for age-worthy reds, this wine is still rich and fruity, with plum, smoke and game flavors and firm, chunky tannins. It has the stuffing to match up to food. Drink now.–T.M. • $10 • (10/31/1998) • **85**
Valdepeñas Vegaval Plata Reserva 1987 • $10 • (4/30/1996) • **79**
Viño de Mesa Viña Almazán NV: This light red shows dried cherry and raisin flavors, with light tannins, crisp acidity and a dry finish.–T.M. • $6 • (10/31/1998) • **79**

CALLEJO, BODEGAS FELIX

Ribera del Duero Crianza 1994 • $14 • (10/31/1997) • **84**
Ribera del Duero Crianza 1991 • $14 • (7/31/1996) • **82**
Ribera del Duero Cuatro Meses en Barrica 1996 • $12 • (11/15/1997) • **85**
Ribera del Duero Cuatro Meses en Barrica 1992 • $12 • (7/31/1996) • **85**
Ribera del Duero Gran Reserva 1989 • $30 • (7/31/1996) • **85**
Ribera del Duero Joven 1996 • $8 • (10/31/1997) • **79**
Ribera del Duero Reserva 1991 • $20 • (7/31/1996) • **86**
Ribera del Duero Reserva 1989 • $25 • (7/31/1996) • **83**
Ribera del Duero Viña Pilar 1994 • $8 • (7/31/1996) • **79**

CAMPO, COOPERATIVA DEL

Calatayud Viña Alarba 1997: Ripe, round flavors of plums, smoke and licorice are fresh and forward in this plump, gamy red, with round tannins and soft acidity. Drink now.–T.M. • $6 • (10/31/1998) • **82**
Calatayud Viña Alarba 1995 • $5 • (10/31/1997) • **84**

CAMPO VIEJO, BODEGAS

Rioja 1988 • $NA • (3/31/1992) • **83**
Rioja Albor 1996 • $6 • (12/15/1997) • **82**
Rioja Albor 1992 • $6 • (4/30/1995) • **81**
Rioja Albor 1991 • $6 • (4/15/1994) • **85**
Rioja Crianza 1995: A gamy, earthy character dominates the light berry flavor in this rustic red, with dry tannins and a dry finish.–T.M. • $9 • (11/30/1998) • **77**
Rioja Crianza 1990 • $7 • (1/31/1995) • **78**
Rioja Crianza 1989 • $8 • (4/15/1994) • **77**
Rioja Crianza Commemorative Label 1992 • $7 • (1/31/1996) • **73**
Rioja Gran Reserva 1989: This ripe red offers warm, spicy flavors of raisin, tobacco and cola. Round on the palate, with light but firm tannins. Generous yet quite delicate, with a sweet finish. Drink now.–T.M. • $20 • (11/30/1998) • **85**
Rioja Gran Reserva 1988 • $20 • (10/15/1997) • **86**
Rioja Gran Reserva 1981 • $NA • (3/31/1992) • **83**
Rioja Gran Reserva 1980 • $15 • (9/30/1991) • **88**
Rioja Gran Reserva 1978 • $14 • (9/30/1990) • **83**
Rioja Marqués de Villamagna Gran Reserva 1989: Alluring spicy aromas give way to cola, raisin and tea flavors typical of mature traditional Rioja. It's still fresh, with a pleasant silky texture. Drink now through 2001.–T.M. • $30 • (10/31/1998) • **84**
Rioja Marqués de Villamagna Gran Reserva 1987 • $30 • (10/15/1997) • **85**
Rioja Marqués de Villamagna Gran Reserva 1982 • $20 • (3/31/1992) • **81**
Rioja Marqués de Villamagna Gran Reserva 1978 • $19 • (11/15/1991) • **84**
Rioja Marqués de Villamagna Gran Reserva 1975 • $20 • (3/31/1992) • **88**
Rioja Marqués de Villamagna Gran Reserva 1973 • $25 • (3/31/1992) • **74**
Rioja Marqués de Villamagna Gran Reserva 1970 • $28 • (3/31/1992) • **87**
Rioja Reserva 1990 • $12 • (11/15/1997) • **87**
Rioja Reserva 1989 • $10 • (4/30/1995) • **79**
Rioja Reserva 1987 • $NA • (4/15/1994) • **77**
Rioja Viña Alcorta 1985 • $10 • (9/30/1990) • **85**
Rioja Viña Alcorta Crianza 1989 • $7 • (4/30/1995) • **83**
Rioja Viña Alcorta Reserva 1987 • $10 • (4/30/1995) • **78**
Rioja Viña Alcorta Reserva 1982 • $NA • (11/15/1987) • **87**
Rioja White Albor 1996 • $6 • (10/31/1997) • **80**

CAN FEIXES

Chardonnay Penedès 1998: A blast of oak, an electric shock of acidity and a fruit bowl of apple, melon and pineapple flavors aren't quite in harmony, but this lively white shows appealing character. Drink now.–T.M. • $30 • (4/30/2000) • **88**

Penedès Blanc Selecció 1998: This crisp, slightly spritzy white offers light peach and herbal flavors. It's a bit lean and green, but refreshing with food. Drink now.–T.M. • $9 • (12/31/1999) • **82**

Penedès Blanc Selecció 1997: Light and crisp, this refreshing white shows lemon-lime and light pineapple flavors, with bright acidity. A good aperitif or shellfish wine. Drink now.–T.M. • $9 • (11/30/1998) • **84**

Penedès Negre Selecció 1995: With assertive flavors of coffee and bacon and very firm tannins, this wine shows more power than finesse. It's quite austere, but may bloom with time. Drink through 2004.–T.M. • $15 • (11/30/1998) • **83**

Penedès Negre Selecció 1991 • $12 • (4/15/1994) • **82**

CAN RAFOLS DELS CAUS

Penedès Caus Lubis 1994: This inky red is richly concentrated, with sweet, Port-like flavors of very ripe fruit, chocolate and prunes. The muscular tannins turn a bit dry on the finish; though not polished, it's powerful. Drink now through 2004.–T.M. • $55 • (12/31/1999) • **88**

Penedès Gran Caus 1994: Still youthful, this inky red marries firm tannins and a supple texture, ripe plum flavors and crisp acidity. It's balanced and elegant, with the concentration to improve with cellaring. Drink now through 2003.–T.M. • $23 • (12/31/1999) • **90**

Penedès Gran Caus 1989 • $14 • (4/15/1994) • **80**

Penedès Gran Caus 1988 • $20 • (10/31/1997) • **85**

Penedès Gran Caus 1986 • $12 • (4/30/1989) • **77**

Penedès Gran Caus 1985 • $12 • (10/15/1988) • **77**

Penedès Petit Caus 1997: This generous red offers ripe plum and black cherry flavors, with accents of chocolate and coffee. Has a round, rich texture, yet remains crisp and clean through the long finish. Drink now through 2002.–T.M. • $10 • (12/31/1999) • **88**

Penedès White Gran Caus 1997: Oaky notes of smoke, toast and vanilla dominate; the modest but appealing apple and melon flavors struggle to emerge through the forest. For fans of oak. Drink now.–T.M. • $15 • (12/31/1999) • **84**

CANALS CANALS, RAMON

Brut Nature Cava Duran NV: Fairly tart, but has a pleasant mouthfeel along with green peach and apple flavors, a touch of mineral on the finish. Drink now.–K.M. • $6 • (12/15/1999) • **82**

CAPCANES

Garnatxa-Syrah Tarragona Mas Donís Vinyes Velles 1996: This round, soft red offers ripe plum and chocolate flavors, integrated tannins and a clean, fruity finish. A modest wine with a fresh character. Drink now.–T.M. • $8 • (11/30/1998) • **83**

Tarragona Costers del Gravet 1997: Lush and lively. Ripe plum flavors are accented with spice in this fleshy red. It's generous but accessible. Drink now.–T.M. • $18 • (4/30/2000) • **84**

Tarragona Mas Donís Barrica 1997: There are pretty cherry and chocolate flavors in this supple red, but it turns a bit lean and dry on the finish. Better with food. Drink now.–T.M. • $10 • (4/30/2000) • **82**

CASA-JUAN, BODEGAS

Rioja Cuarteto 1998: Gamy aromas and flavors and noticeable spritz mar the bright berry flavor at the core of this light, fresh red. Not imported into the U.S.–T.M. • $NA • (1/01/1999) • **77**

Rioja Soneto 1997: This muscular red shows a deep, youthful color, firm tannins and plump, ripe black cherry and plum flavors. A successful example of the modern style. Not imported into the U.S. Drink now through 2003.–T.M. • $NA • (1/01/1999) • **87**

CASTANO, BODEGAS

Yecla Colección 1996: This meaty red shows some richness, with ripe plum and prune flavors and firm tannins. It's a bit clumsy, but should smooth with food. Drink now.–T.M. • $20 • (1/31/2000) • **84**

Yecla Hécula 1997: This simple wine shows exuberant grapey flavors and dry tannins; not complex, but will stand up to food. Drink now.–T.M. • $14 • (1/31/2000) • **81**

Yecla Hécula 1994: Floral and herbal aromas give way to herbal and berry flavors in this lean, slightly astringent red. The fruit lingers on the finish, and the wine could bloom with food. Drink through 2000.–T.M. • $9 • (10/31/1998) • **82**

Yecla Hécula Crianza 1994: This round red has a pleasant texture, firm yet plush, and shows ripe plum and earth flavors. It's straightforward, but clean and fresh. Drink now.–T.M. • $12 • (10/31/1998) • **82**

Yecla Pozuelo Crianza 1995: Maturing now, this straightforward red shows dried fruit, spice and cedar flavors, with drying tannins on the short finish. A slight but pleasant bitterness keeps it refreshing. Drink now.–T.M. • $12 • (11/15/1999) • **82**

Yecla Pozuelo Reserva 1993: Fading now, this light, soft red is dominated by sweet vanilla and cedar flavors from oak aging, with light dried cherry and berry notes that just keep it lively.–T.M. • $16 • (11/15/1999) • **79**

Yecla Pozuelo Reserva 1990 • $10 • (8/31/1996) • **82**

Yecla Viña Las Gruesas 1997: Sweet vanilla, dried cherry and cinnamon flavors mingle in this chewy red. Has a solid structure and a clean, short finish, but is already showing signs of maturity. Drink now through 2001.–T.M. • $8 • (11/15/1999) • **83**

Yecla Viña Las Gruesas Selección 1996: Dried cherry, raisin and prune flavors give this wine an intriguing, if slightly disconcerting, sweetness to go along with its smooth, almost creamy texture. A rich red with a traditional character. Drink now through 2002.–T.M. • $8 • (11/15/1999) • **84**

Yecla White Viña Las Gruesas 1998: This round white is fresh but fairly neutral in character, with light apple and pine flavors marred by a musty note.–T.M. • $8 • (11/15/1999) • **77**

Yecla White Viña Las Gruesas 1996: This firm-textured, broadly flavored white tastes of apples and fennel, with hints of vanilla on the finish. It's thick and a bit cloying, but has the weight to match with food. Drink now.–T.M. • $8 • (11/15/1998) • **82**

CASTELLBLANCH

Brut Cava Extra NV • $6 • (5/15/1994) • **78**

Extra Brut Cava NV: Rather neutral in flavor, with hints of apple, toast and earth. The mousse is soft, the finish dry and a touch earthy.–T.M. • $6 • (11/30/1998) • **79**

CASTILLA, HDOS. CAMILO

Navarra Beltran Crianza 1996: Rich with extract and ripe flavors of plum and prune. Lavish oak notes of toast and coffee are dominant right now; should balance more with age. Try through 2003.–T.M. • $14 • (11/15/1999) • **85**

Navarra Beltran Crianza 1995: Expressive chocolate and meaty aromas give way to a thick texture and ripe flavors of plums, chocolate and toast in this muscular red. Has the structure to stand up to food, enough acidity to keep it lively. Drink now through 2005.–T.M. • $13 • (11/30/1998) • **88**

CASTILLA, SENORIO DE

Ribera del Duero Mayor de Castilla 1997: Aromas of smoke and bitter herb, with dark flavors of cherry and coffee. The texture combines a hint of spritz, dry tannins.–T.M. • $9 • (10/31/1998) • **76**

Ribera del Duero Mayor de Castilla Crianza 1994: This velvety red offers ripe flavors of raspberry, black cherry and chocolate. Sweet and approachable, it has moderate tannins and good acidity for balance. Drink now through 2003.–T.M. • $13 • (10/31/1998) • **87**

CASTILLO, CASA

Monastrell Jumilla 1997: This light, round red offers dark flavors of plum, bacon and earth, with light but firm tannins and a tobacco-scented finish. Assertive, though a bit rustic. Drink now.–T.M. • $9 • (11/30/1998) • **81**

Key: SS—Spectator Selection. CS—Cellar Selection. HR—Highly Recommended. $NA—Price not available. (BT)—Barrel tasting. (A)—Auction Price. For a key to the tasters' initials, see "How to Use These Listings."
Dates in parentheses represent the issues in which the ratings were published.

CASTILLO DE MALUENDA

Calatayud Viña Alarba 1998: This chunky red offers black cherry and licorice flavors, with rather harsh tannins that turn slightly bitter on the finish. Perhaps better with food.–T.M. • $5 • (12/15/1999) • **77**

Grenache Calatayud Viña Alarba Old Vines 1998: Ripe plum, pepper and earth flavors are quite rich in this rustic red. Shows a hearty exuberance; good with peasant dishes. Drink now through 2002.–T.M. • $6 • (12/15/1999) • **82**

CASTILLO DE MONJARDIN, BODEGAS

Cabernet Sauvignon-Merlot Navarra Crianza 1996: Polished, with a smooth texture, rich flavors of chocolate, plum, raisin and earth and just enough tannin for grip; shows a deft, international style. Drink now through 2002.–T.M. • $10 • (11/15/1999) • **86**

Chardonnay Navarra 1998: An appealing snap of acidity gives life to the apple and melon flavors of this fruity white. It's straightforward but has nice balance and focus. Drink now.–T.M. • $9 • (10/15/1999) • **82**

Chardonnay Navarra Barrel Fermented 1996: Racy acidity and sweet vanilla flavors are bold in this fruity white, giving it an awkward sweet-and-sour character. Tasted twice, with consistent notes.–T.M. • $11 • (11/15/1999) • **78**

Merlot Navarra Crianza 1996: This rustic red offers smoky, earthy and herbal flavors, with cherry and raisin notes. It's firm, with a crisp acidity, and turns a bit dry on the finish. Drink now through 2002.–T.M. • $11 • (10/31/1999) • **82**

Navarra 1997: A simple red, almost rosé in color and structure, with hints of berries and bitter herbs. Best chilled.–T.M. • $8 • (11/15/1999) • **77**

Navarra Reserva 1994: Well-integrated cherry, spice, cedar and light earth flavors, with firm tannins. Achieves balance of refinement and muscle. A good match with food. Drink now through 2002.–T.M. • $19 • (11/15/1999) • **87**

Navarra Rosado 1998: Tastes more like fruit juice than wine, with citrusy acidity and a slight candylike sweetness. Quite full-bodied and would make a good Sangria.–T.M. • $8 • (10/15/1999) • **78**

CENTRO ESPANOLAS, BODEGAS

La Mancha Allozo Gran Reserva 1992: Still lively, this traditional-style red shows mineral, coffee, smoke and light cherry flavors on a lean frame, with a slightly dry finish. Drink now.–T.M. • $22 • (6/15/2000) • **82**

Tempranillo La Mancha Allozo 1998: Smoky and earthy notes are expressive but rather bitter in this firm red. It has enough tannin for food, but not quite enough fruit for pleasure.–T.M. • $8 • (11/15/1999) • **78**

Tempranillo La Mancha Allozo 1996: This fleshy red shows ripe plum and raisin flavors, but lacks definition and crispness, and the tannins turn dry on the finish.–T.M. • $9 • (10/31/1998) • **79**

Tempranillo La Mancha Allozo Crianza 1994: Sweet cherry, cola and spice flavors give this red an assertive personality. Firm tannins should soften with food.–T.M. • $12 • (10/31/1998) • **84**

Tempranillo La Mancha Allozo Reserva 1993: Still youthful and fresh, this red offers a core of sweet cherry inside a shell of firm tannins. Balanced and clean.–T.M. • $20 • (10/31/1998) • **84**

CERROSOL, BODEGAS

Rueda Fermentado en Barrica 1998: This modern-style white shows round fruit flavors of melons and apples with some vanilla notes and a soft, clean finish. Drink now.–T.M. • $18 • (12/31/1999) • **84**

Verdejo Rueda 1998: Tropical fruit aromas give way to round but surprisingly crisp flavors of green apples and grapefruit in this fresh white. Clean acidity and the absence of oak make it a refreshing quaff. Drink now.–T.M. • $9 • (12/31/1999) • **84**

CHENEAU, PAUL

Brut Blanc de Blancs Cava NV: This has some nice doughy and toasty flavors, with some spicy notes, and a touch of sweetness on the finish. A good workman-like bubbly.–K.M. • $10 • (12/15/1999) • **84**

CHIVITE, BODEGAS JULIAN

Chardonnay Navarra Gran Feudo 1998: Sturdy, and has the body to match with food, but the flavors are muted, except for vanilla-oak notes. Balanced and firm. Drink now.–T.M. • $10 • (10/15/1999) • **82**

Chardonnay Navarra Gran Feudo 1997: This solid white has a firm structure, a round texture and fresh acidity, but the flavors are modest, with hints of toast, hazelnut and apple. Has the weight to match with food. Drink now.–T.M. • $8 • (11/30/1998) • **83**

Navarra 125 Aniversario 1988 • $19 • (4/15/1995) • **85**

Navarra Coleccion 125 Gran Reserva 1992: Ripe, almost jammy flavors of plum and prune are sweet and thick in this maturing red. It has a soft, voluptuous texture and accents of herb and toast that linger on the finish. Drink now.–T.M. • $25 • (11/30/1998) • **85**

Navarra 125 Aniversario Gran Reserva 1988 • $25 • (8/31/1996) • **87**

Navarra 125 Aniversario Gran Reserva 1985 • $31 • (8/31/1993) • **82**

Navarra Coleccion 125 Reserva 1995: Spicy cinnamon and cedar notes are pleasant in this silky, maturing red, accenting light cherry and berry flavors. Like a traditional Rioja in style. Drink now.–T.M. • $25 • (11/15/1999) • **83**

Navarra Coleccion 125 Reserva 1994: There's concentration and good balance in this red; the plum and herb flavors are straightforward but fresh, and the tannins are well integrated. The finish is short but clean. Drink now.–T.M. • $25 • (10/31/1998) • **84**

Navarra Coleccion 125 Reserva 1992 • $14 • (5/15/1997) • **85**

Navarra Gran Feudo Crianza 1996: Firm, smooth structure, but earthy notes dominate the cherry and herbal flavors and turn a bit bitter on the finish. Better with food.–T.M. • $10 • (11/15/1999) • **79**

Navarra Gran Feudo Crianza 1994: Sweet aromas of dried fruits and spices give way to a light but firm-textured palate with simple raisin and cinnamon flavors. It's balanced in a traditional style. Drink now.–T.M. • $8 • (11/30/1998) • **82**

Navarra Gran Feudo Crianza 1993 • $8 • (8/31/1996) • **84**

Navarra Gran Feudo Crianza 1991 • $7 • (4/30/1995) • **85**

Navarra Gran Feudo Crianza 1990 • $8 • (4/15/1994) • **83**

Navarra Gran Feudo Reserva 1994: This polished red offers straightforward flavors of cherries and herbs, with a smooth texture and well-integrated tannins. It's modest but balanced. Drink now.–T.M. • $10 • (10/31/1998) • **83**

Navarra Gran Feudo Reserva 1992 • $12 • (11/15/1997) • **83**

Navarra Gran Feudo Reserva 1991 • $10 • (8/31/1996) • **86**

Navarra Reserva 1991 • $10 • (4/15/1994) • **86**

Navarra Reserva 1990 • $9 • (4/15/1994) • **85**

Navarra Reserva 1988 • $10 • (12/15/1993) • **79**

Navarra Reserva 1987 • $10 • (6/15/1993) • **81**

Navarra Rosado Gran Feudo 1998: Crisp in texture but rather neutral in flavor, this rosé offers light cherry and watermelon, with fresh acidity and a short finish. Drink now.–T.M. • $8 • (10/15/1999) • **81**

Navarra Rosado Gran Feudo 1997: This dark-colored rosé offers assertive flavors of raspberry and tart cherry. Clean and refreshing, with crisp acidity and a light, pleasant bitterness on the finish. Drink now.–T.M. • $7 • (10/31/1998) • **84**

Navarra Rosado Gran Feudo 1996 • $8 • (10/31/1997) • **83**

Navarra Viña Marcos 1995 • $7 • (10/31/1997) • **83**

Navarra Viña Marcos 1992 • $NA • (4/15/1994) • **78**

Navarra Viña Marcos 1991 • $6 • (6/15/1993) • **77**

Navarra White Coleccion 125 Fermentado en Barrica 1996: Lavish oak treatment has given this full-bodied white lush aromas and flavors of coffee, chocolate and toast. There's enough tropical fruit and citrus flavor to keep it lively on the finish. Drink now.–T.M. • $40 • (11/15/1998) • **86**

Tempranillo Navarra Viña Marcos 1997: This firm red shows good structure and balance for food, with herb and cherry flavors and an unfortunate light charred note. Try with grilled foods.–T.M. • $6 • (11/30/1998) • **82**

CILLAR DE SILOS

Ribera del Duero Crianza 1996: Lush and harmonious, this velvety red is packed with plum, cassis, smoke and mineral flavors. Rich yet not heavy, firm yet not overly tannic, it's a nice match with grilled meats. Drink now through 2004.–T.M. • $22 • (10/31/1999) • **87**

CIMS DE PORRERA

Priorat Clàssic 1996: Seamless and pure. This beautifully integrated red has the texture of crushed velvet, rich, clean flavors of blackberries and plums and rich yet smooth tannins that add weight without harshness. Delicious now, but built for graceful aging. Drink through 2010.–T.M. • $37 Ⓐ • (9/15/1999) • **90**

CODORNIU

Brut Blanc de Blancs Cava NV • $12 • (5/31/1997) • **86**

Brut Cava NV: More sophisticated than the usual Cava, this Spanish sparkler offers rich, mature toast and vanilla notes. It's round and almost sweet on the palate, yet sports a firm backbone of acidity that keeps it crisp and food-friendly. A nice all-around choice, affordable and ready to drink. Drink now.–T.M. • $10 • (11/30/1998) • **86**

Brut Chardonnay Cava Cuvée Raventós NV: Lean and winey-tasting, with some green lime and citrus flavors that end on a minerally note. Drink now.–K.M. • $13 • (12/15/1999) • **81**

COMARCAL VIRGEN DE LA VEGA, BODEGA COOPERATIVA

Ribera del Duero Rauda Crianza 1995: Very ripe flavors of black cherry, raisin and chocolate are rich and chewy in this firm, tannic red, while a streak of tart acidity keeps it lively, if a bit off balance. A gutsy wine that needs food to harmonize. Drink through 2004.–T.M. • $17 • (11/30/1998) • **85**

CONCAVINS, BODEGAS

Cabernet Sauvignon Conca de Barberá Santara Carbonell 1995: This deeply colored red shows vibrant flavors of raspberry, cola and mint, with firm but well-integrated tannins providing ample structure. Distinctive and voluptuous, it brings you back for another sip. 1,500 cases imported. Drink now through 2003.–T.M. • $18 • (11/30/1998) • **87**

Cabernet Sauvignon-Merlot Conca de Barberá Santara 1996: There's plenty of up-front cherry and chocolate flavor in this juicy red, but it thins out on the palate and finishes with drying tannins. Will show more harmony with food. 3,500 cases imported. Drink now.–T.M. • $9 • (11/30/1998) • **81**

Chardonnay Conca de Barberá Santara 1997: Soft and creamy, this lush white offers round, soft flavors of vanilla, honey and apple tart, full and heavy. Though low in acidity for food, it will appeal to fans of oak. 4,500 cases imported. Drink now.–T.M. • $7 • (11/15/1998) • **83**

Tempranillo Conca de Barberá Santara 1997: This light, simple red gains interest from its core of sweet strawberry flavor that brightens on the palate, then fades quickly and cleanly. A lovely afternoon sipper. Drink now.–T.M. • $6 • (10/31/1998) • **82**

Viura-Chardonnay Conca de Barberá Santara 1997: Ripe and broad, this fruity white offers apple, melon and lemon flavors, straightforward but with intensity. Vanilla and citrus notes linger on the clean finish. 1,000 cases imported to the U.S. Drink now.–T.M. • $6 • (11/15/1998) • **83**

CONDADO DE HAZA

Ribera del Duero 1997: This inky red is rich with ripe flavors of plum and prune backed by meat and mineral notes that give it a rustic but appealing earthiness. Tannins tend to dominate, and this turns a bit dry on the finish. May need time. Tasted twice, with consistent notes. Best after 2001.–T.M. • $20 • (11/30/1999) • **85**

Ribera del Duero 1996: A rich Spanish red of concentration and density, with massive tannins that hardly even register, and ripe cassis, kirsch and meat flavors that are Port-like intexture and depth. Shows tremendous potential, but it's so intense now; it needs time in the bottle and air in the glass. Best after 2005.–T.M. • $20 • (11/30/1998) SS • **92**

Ribera del Duero Alenza Crianza 1996: This polished red is shy right now, but the structure is beautiful, balanced and harmonious, with toasty oak, blueberry and accents of mineral and earth. It has good concentration, but the tannins are well integrated. Accessible now, it will only improve. Drink now through 2010.–T.M. • $72 Ⓐ • (10/31/1999) • **92**

Ribera del Duero Alenza Crianza 1995: An impressive debut release for this Spanish red. Vivid aromas are Port-like, with notes of chocolate, plum and spices; on the palate, the wine is rich and deep, with mouthcoating tannins and a solid core of ripe plum flavor. Great concentration, great balance—this is a keeper. Drink through 2005.–T.M. • $100 • (8/31/1998) HR • **92**

Ribera del Duero Crianza 1995 • $17 • (11/30/1997) SS • **90**

Ribera del Duero Crianza 1994 • $15 • (6/15/1997) • **89**

CONSEJO DE LA ALTA

Rioja Alta Rio 1998: This soft red offers a nice combination of ripe plum flavor and spicy, peppery accents. Round and supple, with enough acidity to keep it lively. Fresh and flavorful. Drink now through 2002.–T.M. • $14 • (11/30/1999) • **86**

Key: SS—Spectator Selection. CS—Cellar Selection. HR—Highly Recommended. $NA—Price not available. (BT)—Barrel tasting. Ⓐ—Auction Price. For a key to the tasters' initials, see "How to Use These Listings."
Dates in parentheses represent the issues in which the ratings were published.

Rioja Alta Rio Crianza 1996: This vibrant red has a solid core of cherry and plum flavors, nicely accented with chocolate, tobacco and light herbal notes. It's firm yet accessible, balanced and round. Drink now through 2006.–T.M. • $12 • (10/31/1999) • **87**

Rioja Alta Rio Reserva 1994: This firm red boasts a solid structure and ripe flavors of plum, dried fig, coffee and cocoa. It's balanced and clean, and an intriguing spicy note emerges on the finish. Drink now through 2004.–T.M. • $15 • (12/15/1999) • **87**

CONTINO

Rioja Crianza 1995: Ripe, sweet plum and raisin flavors gain interest from oaky notes of toast and vanilla, and a spicy accent enlivens the finish. Balanced and fresh, with just enough structure for food. Drink now.–T.M. • $25 • (10/31/1998) • **86**

Rioja Reserva 1995: This smooth red offers ripe flavors of plum, raisin and sweet chocolate, with ripe tannins and low acidity. It's rich yet gentle, an easy quaff that brings you back for another sip. Drink now.–T.M. • $45 • (11/30/1999) • **86**

Rioja Reserva 1990 • $22 • (10/15/1997) • **85**

Rioja Reserva 1989 • $16 • (8/31/1996) • **84**

Rioja Reserva 1988 • $16 • (4/30/1995) • **84**

Rioja Reserva 1987 • $15 • (4/15/1994) • **88**

Rioja Reserva 1985 • $14 • (12/15/1990) • **88**

Rioja Reserva 1984 • $12 • (3/31/1990) • **84**

Rioja Reserva 1983 • $13 • (3/31/1992) • **89**

Rioja Reserva 1982 • $12 • (3/31/1992) • **92**

Rioja Reserva 1980 • $11 • (1/31/1987) • **83**

CORRAL, BODEGAS

Rioja Don Jacobo Crianza 1993 • $9 • (11/15/1997) • **83**

Rioja Don Jacobo Crianza 1989 • $7 • (4/30/1995) • **86**

Rioja Don Jacobo Crianza 1988 • $7 • (4/15/1994) • **87**

Rioja Don Jacobo Gran Reserva 1983 • $16 • (4/15/1994) • **80**

Rioja Don Jacobo Reserva 1985 • $11 • (4/15/1994) • **85**

Rioja Don Jacobo Reserva 1981 • $11 • (3/31/1990) • **86**

COSTERS DEL SIURANA

Priorat Clos de L'Obac 1997: This distinctive red offers alluring, exotic floral and fruit flavors, with notes of cherry, lilac, vanilla and spice. It's quite delicate on the palate, though light, firm tannins keep it structured enough for food. Drink now through 2002.–T.M. • $49 • (11/30/1999) • **87**

Priorat Clos de L'Obac 1996: Vivid and elegant, this polished red offers well-defined flavors of raspberry, cherry, toast and smoke, with harmonious tannins and acidity that keep the wine in balance. More graceful than muscular, but has the structure to age. Drink now through 2010.–T.M. • $44 • (10/31/1998) • **90**

Priorat Clos de L'Obac 1995 • $45 • (11/30/1997) • **93**

Priorat Clos de L'Obac 1994 • $40 • (6/15/1997) • **92**

Priorat Clos de L'Obac 1993 • $NA • (1/01/1997) • **86**

Priorat Clos de L'Obac 1992 • $NA • (1/01/1997) • **86**

Priorat Clos de L'Obac 1991 • $NA • (1/01/1997) • **88**

Priorat Clos de L'Obac 1990 • $30 • (8/31/1996) • **86**

Priorat Clos de L'Obac 1989 • $NA • (1/01/1997) • **82**

Priorat Dolç de L'Obac 1997: Distinctive and harmonious. Made in a dessert style, with noticeable sweetness, it's full of chocolate, plum and dried cherry flavors, silky and full on the palate. An interesting substitute for vintage Port. Drink now through 2010.–T.M. • $80/500 ml. • (9/15/1999) • **91**

Priorat Dolç de L'Obac 1996: This powerful red tastes like young vintage Port. It's thick on the palate, with very sweet plum and chocolate flavors and ripe tannins, finishing with cola, alcohol and spice notes. More a dessert wine than a table wine, it's distinctive and delightful. Drink now through 2005.–T.M. • $80/500 ml. • (10/31/1998) • **91**

Priorat Dolç de L'Obac 1994 • $75 • (9/15/1997) • **94**

Priorat Miserere 1996: This polished red offers intense, pure raspberry flavors, with notes of chocolate, clove and licorice. Tannins are firm yet well integrated, and a bright core of acidity keeps it lively. Not as rich as the best of the region, but shows uncommon elegance. Drink through 2004.–T.M. • $36 • (10/31/1998) • **88**

Priorat Miserere 1995 • $35 • (4/30/1998) • **91**

Priorat Miserere 1994 • $35 • (1/01/1998) • **89**

Priorat Miserere 1993 • $30 • (8/31/1996) • **85**

Priorat Miserere 1990 • $30 • (4/30/1995) • **91**

COTO DE RIOJA, EL

Rioja Coto de Imaz Gran Reserva 1991: Ripe and sweet, this maturing red shows a nice blend of ripe fruit and spice, with cedar and raisin notes. Balanced and clean. Drink now through 2003.–T.M. • $30 • (2/29/2000) • **87**

Rioja Coto de Imaz Reserva 1995: This muscular red offers concentrated flavors of plum, prune, vanilla and chocolate. Has firm tannins and lively acidity, with pleasant spice on the finish. Not graceful, but impressive. Drink now through 2005.–T.M. • $17 • (2/29/2000) • **87**

Rioja El Coto Crianza 1997: Supple and spicy. This light red offers simple cherry and berry flavors, with pleasant cedar and spice notes on the clean finish. Not concentrated, but harmonious. Drink now.–T.M. • $11 • (2/29/2000) • **84**

COVIDES

Brut Cava Xènius Reserva NV: Nicely structured, this sparkling wine offers a lively mousse and crisp acidity, but the appley flavors are simple and a bit coarse.–T.M. • $10 • (4/30/2000) • **79**

COVISA

Elena Talier La Pyramida Somontano 1994 • $6 • (8/31/1996) • **84**

CRIANZA, BODEGAS DE

Rioja Valserrano Reserva 1991: This maturing red shows harmony and elegance, with raisin, cedar, tobacco and vanilla flavors that float on the palate over firm, slightly dry tannins. A fine example of the traditional style. Drink now through 2003.–T.M. • $16 • (11/30/1998) • **86**

CRISTOBAL, BODEGAS LOPEZ

Ribera del Duero Crianza 1996: Juicy fruit and a firm tannic backbone combine to give this wine both punch and balance. Black cherry, cedar and mineral flavors are focused and should bloom with time. Drink now through 2005.–T.M. • $18 • (4/30/2000) • **88**

CUADRADO-GARCIA, HNOS.

Ribera del Duero Finca Villacreces Crianza 1996: Ripe, muscular and rich, this inky red offers vivid flavors of plums, cassis, tobacco and minerals, backed by very firm tannins, kept lively by crisp acidity. Yet it remains focused and harmonious, and is even accessible now. Drink now through 2008.–T.M. • $27 • (4/30/2000) • **91**

Ribera del Duero Finca Villacreces Crianza 1994: Polished, almost silky on the palate, with blackberry flavors and a tangy acidity that keeps it lively. The tannins are well integrated, the finish clean. A distinctive wine that draws you back for another sip. Drink now through 2003.–T.M. • $25 • (8/31/1998) • **87**

CUNE

Rioja Clarete Crianza 1996: Smooth and soft, this maturing red offers dried cherry, raisin and tobacco flavors that are thick and sweet on the palate. Turns a bit cloying on the finish. Drink now.–T.M. • $12 • (11/30/1999) • **82**

Rioja Clarete Crianza 1990 • $8 • (4/15/1994) • **81**

Rioja Imperial Gran Reserva 1991: This focused, traditional red offers plum, berry, mineral and earth notes. Harmonious but a bit austere, it's not big, but has the balance to match with lighter dishes. Drink now through 2003.–T.M. • $40 • (6/15/2000) • **86**

Rioja Imperial Gran Reserva 1990: Harmonious and elegant, this maturing but still firm red shows typical flavors of dried cherry, vanilla, cedar and spice. Well integrated and backed by firm but ripe tannins. Clean and still quite fresh. Drink now through 2005.–T.M. • $36 • (11/30/1998) • **88**

Rioja Imperial Gran Reserva 1989 • $33 • (11/30/1997) • **87**

Rioja Imperial Gran Reserva 1988 • $33 • (11/15/1997) • **86**

Rioja Imperial Gran Reserva 1986 • $25 • (4/15/1994) • **86**

Rioja Imperial Gran Reserva 1985 • $25 • (4/15/1994) • **89**

Rioja Imperial Gran Reserva 1982 • $22 • (3/31/1992) • **86**

Rioja Imperial Gran Reserva 1981 • $26 • (3/31/1992) • **82**

Rioja Imperial Gran Reserva 1978 • $15 • (3/31/1990) • **70**

Rioja Imperial Gran Reserva 1975 • $24 • (3/31/1992) • **84**

Rioja Imperial Gran Reserva 1973 • $28 • (3/31/1990) • **85**

Rioja Imperial Reserva 1991: This round, plump, lively red offers mature flavors of dried cherry, raisin and cedar, with plenty of vanilla oak influence and light tannins that turn a bit dry on the sweet, lingering finish. Drink now.–T.M. • $27 • (11/30/1998) • **86**

Rioja Imperial Reserva 1986 • $NA • (3/31/1992) • **87**

Rioja Reserva 1994: Ripe fruit and new oak give prune, coffee and cola flavors to this round, fleshy red. It's exuberant yet still fresh, with ripe, soft tannins and a clean, sweet finish. Drink now through 2002.–T.M. • $19 • (10/31/1998) • **85**

Rioja Reserva 1991 • $15 • (11/15/1997) • **77**

Rioja Reserva 1986 • $10 • (4/15/1994) • **76**

Rioja Viña Real Crianza 1996: Compact and balanced, this polished red offers cherry, raisin, tobacco and spice flavors. Smooth on the palate, with gentle tannins and just enough acidity to keep it lively. Drink now through 2001.–T.M. • $14 • (11/30/1999) • **84**

Rioja Viña Real Crianza 1995: Ripe cherry and light vanilla flavors give this light red a sweet, quaffable appeal, with silky tannins and a fresh finish. Drink now.–T.M. • $13 • (10/31/1998) • **83**

Rioja Viña Real Crianza 1992 • $10 • (11/15/1997) • **84**

Rioja Viña Real Crianza 1990 • $9 • (4/30/1995) • **84**

Rioja Viña Real Crianza 1989 • $9 • (4/15/1994) • **87**

Rioja Viña Real Crianza 1988 • $10 • (3/31/1992) • **87**

Rioja Viña Real Crianza 1987 • $10 • (3/31/1992) • **86**

Rioja Viña Real Gran Reserva 1990: Cherry, raisin, tobacco and cola flavors run through this maturing red. Chunky and firm, with slightly drying tannins and a spicy finish. Good with roasted meats. Drink now.–T.M. • $30 • (11/30/1998) • **84**

Rioja Viña Real Gran Reserva 1986 • $19 • (4/30/1995) • **77**

Rioja Viña Real Gran Reserva 1985 • $18 • (4/15/1994) • **91**

Rioja Viña Real Gran Reserva 1981 • $17 • (3/31/1990) • **88**

Rioja Viña Real Gran Reserva 1973 • $24 • (3/31/1992) • **84**

Rioja Viña Real Gran Reserva 1970 • $24 • (3/31/1992) • **85**

Rioja Viña Real Reserva 1994: Good concentration, with thick, mouth-coating tannins and ripe flavors of plum, licorice and smoke. An underlying mineral note adds backbone to this rich and harmonious wine. Drink now through 2005.–T.M. • $26 • (11/30/1999) • **88**

Rioja White Monopole 1997: This solid white offers a rich, full-bodied texture, deep flavors of toasted almond and pear and a soft but clean finish. A more traditional approach to white Rioja. Drink now through 2002.–T.M. • $14 • (10/31/1999) • **86**

CURROS, LOS

Brut Rueda Cantosán NV: A robust bubbly, with appealing spicy flavors and a nice mature quality. A little rough around the edges, but still quite enjoyable. Drink now.–K.M. • $8 • (8/31/1998) • **84**

Rueda Tierra Buena 1997: This simple white is neutral in flavor and blunt in texture, without much fruit or personality. Makes an acceptable spritzer. Drink now.–T.M. • $6 • (11/30/1998) • **77**

Rueda Tierra Buena 1996: This awkward white is a mismatched marriage of herbal, candied and odd fishy flavors. Not recommended. Tasted twice, with consistent notes.–T.M. • $5 • (11/30/1998) • **69**

Rueda Viña Cantosán 1996 • $9 • (10/31/1997) • **82**

Verdejo Rueda Viña Cantosán 1997: Soft floral aromas and light flavors of apple and herb give this easygoing white a gentle appeal. Makes a pleasant aperitif. Drink now.–T.M. • $10 • (11/30/1998) • **81**

Viño de Mesa de Castilla y Leon Yllera 1995: Balanced and fresh, if a bit light, this red shows clean black cherry and licorice flavors. A modest accompaniment to food. Made from Tempranillo aged to Crianza requirements. Drink now through 2002.–T.M. • $10 • (11/15/1999) • **84**

Viño de Mesa de Castilla y Leon Yllera Gran Selección 1986: This clean, light red is silky on the palate, with light cherry, raisin and tea flavors, then turns a bit dry on the finish. Will make a nice match with lighter dishes. Made from Tempranillo aged to Gran Reserva requirements. Drink now.–T.M. • $75 • (11/15/1999) • **83**

Viño de Mesa de Castilla y Leon Yllera Red Label NV • $24 • (11/15/1997) • **81**

Viño de Mesa de Castilla y Leon Yllera White Label NV • $9 • (5/15/1998) • **84**

DOMECQ, PEDRO

Amontillado Jerez 51-1a NV • $83 • (2/28/1998) • **89**

Palo Cortado Jerez Sibarita NV • $83 • (2/28/1998) • **90**

Pedro Ximenez Jerez Venerable NV • $83 • (2/28/1998) • **93**

DOMECQ, BODEGAS

Rioja Marqués de Arienzo Crianza 1995: This ripe red shows plum, raisin, chocolate and tobacco flavors, with firm tannins and a chewy texture. A bit heavy-handed, but it can stand up to hearty dishes. Drink now through 2004.–T.M. • $12 • (11/30/1999) • **85**

Rioja Marqués de Arienzo Crianza 1994: Appealing spicy, toasty aromas give way to cherry and herb flavors in this round, soft red. It has light tannins and delivers more flesh than structure. Drink now.–T.M. • $12 • (11/30/1998) • **82**

Rioja Marqués de Arienzo Gran Reserva 1991: This traditional red offers a silky texture, with ripe flavors of cherry, cedar, tobacco and spice backed by firm tannins that give it the grip to match with food. Well knit and harmonious. Drink now through 2001.–T.M. • $25 • (12/15/1999) • **87**

Rioja Marqués de Arienzo Gran Reserva 1989: This lighter, traditional-style, silky red offers spicy raisin and cola flavors with herb and light earth accents. Firm tannins turn a bit dry on the finish. Drink now.–T.M. • $24 • (10/31/1998) • **84**

Rioja Marqués de Arienzo Gran Reserva 1982 • $23 • (3/31/1992) • **83**

Rioja Marqués de Arienzo Gran Reserva 1981 • $18 • (3/31/1992) • **84**

Rioja Marqués de Arienzo Gran Reserva 1978 • $18 • (3/31/1990) • **78**

Rioja Marqués de Arienzo Gran Reserva 1976 • $18 • (11/15/1989) • **88**

Rioja Marqués de Arienzo Reserva 1994: Maturing now, this light red offers tobacco, cedar and raisin flavors, with notes of cola and spice. Turns a bit dry on the finish. Drink now.–T.M. • $15 • (12/15/1999) • **82**

Rioja Marqués de Arienzo Reserva 1992: Pretty floral and vanilla aromas float over the rustic raisin and leather flavors in this dry, maturing red. Shows spicy complexity, but winds up astringent and short. Drink now.–T.M. • $16 • (11/30/1998) • **81**

Rioja Marqués de Arienzo Reserva 1985 • $12 • (3/31/1992) • **84**

Rioja Marqués de Arienzo Reserva 1983 • $12 • (5/31/1991) • **84**

Rioja Marqués de Arienzo Reserva 1981 • $12 • (7/31/1989) • **83**

Rioja Marqués de Arienzo Reserva Especial 1994: This firm red shows good grip, with meat, licorice and mint flavors. The fruit is a bit muted now, but there's good concentration and balance. Drink now through 2005.–T.M. • $35 • (1/31/2000) • **86**

DURON, BODEGAS

Ribera del Duero Crianza 1995: Herbal and vegetal flavors are prominent in this chewy red, with cherry and raisin notes underneath. It has concentration, but not much finesse. Drink now through 2003.–T.M. • $15 • (10/31/1999) • **84**

Ribera del Duero Gran Reserva 1991: Fresh cherry and licorice flavors shine through this round, polished red. It tastes younger than its age, remains harmonious and graceful. Spice and cedar flavors linger on the finish. Drink now through 2002.–T.M. • $28 • (10/31/1999) • **87**

Ribera del Duero Gran Reserva 1990 • $21 • (11/15/1997) • **87**

Ribera del Duero Reserva 1991 • $19 • (11/15/1997) • **86**

EGUREN, BODEGAS

Tempranillo Viño de la Tierra Manchuela 1998: This juicy red offers a core of ripe black cherry flavor, with strong chocolaty and spicy notes and light but firm tannins for structure. Balanced and lively. Drink now through 2003.–T.M. • $8 • (11/15/1999) • **85**

Viño de la Tierra Manchuela Reinares 1998: Soft and clean, with simple but appealing berry and cherry flavors and just enough tannin for grip.–T.M. • $7 • (1/31/2000) • **78**

EGUREN, DOMINIO DE

Spain Protocolo 1997: This light red mingles tart cherry and vanilla flavors with firm, slightly drying tannins. Fresh and bitter, it needs food to soften it. Drink now.–T.M. • $5 • (11/15/1999) • **81**

Key: SS—Spectator Selection. CS—Cellar Selection. HR—Highly Recommended. $NA—Price not available. (BT)—Barrel tasting. Ⓐ—Auction Price.
For a key to the tasters' initials, see "How to Use These Listings."
Dates in parentheses represent the issues in which the ratings were published.

1890, BODEGAS

Jumilla Castillo San Simón 1997: This light, simple red offers pretty strawberry flavors, with hints of spice. It has very light tannins and finishes short and clean.–T.M. • $5 • (10/31/1998) • **79**

Jumilla Castillo San Simón Gran Reserva 1989: A nutty aroma reminiscent of an amontillado Sherry gives this Spanish red a distinctive appeal. Not for fans of the international style, it's a delicious expression of traditional virtues. Well worth trying. Drink now.–T.M. • $10 • (10/31/1998) • **86**

Jumilla Castillo San Simón Reserva 1992: This ripe red offers prune, game and coffee flavors, plump yet backed by firm, dry tannins, then turns raisiny-sweet on the finish. It has concentration, but it's a bit clumsy. Drink now.–T.M. • $8 • (10/31/1998) • **81**

Jumilla Mayoral 1997: This plush, soft red offers ripe cherry and sweet vanilla flavors in a generous, velvety texture. Simple yet appealing. Drink now.–T.M. • $6 • (10/31/1998) • **82**

Jumilla Mayoral Crianza 1996: This supple Spanish red overflows with ripe, sweet flavors of cherry and vanilla. Smooth and harmonious, with pretty spice notes on the finish. A good example of the traditional style. Drink now.–T.M. • $9 • (11/15/1999) • **85**

Tempranillo Jumilla Don Luciano 1998: This light red has a core of sweet cherry, but it tastes candied and turns bitter on the finish.–T.M. • $5 • (12/15/1999) • **73**

EIRAS, ADEGAS DAS

Albariño Rias Baixas Abadia de San Campio 1996 • $12 • (11/15/1997) • **86**

EL CEP

Brut Cava Marqués de Gelida NV: Fruit cocktail flavors dominate this wine; slightly cloying on the finish.–K.M. • $9 • (12/15/1999) • **78**

Brut Cava Marqués de Gelida Gran Seleccio NV • $9 • (2/28/1998) • **78**

EL GRIFO

Malvasia Lanzarote Dulce 1998: This silky white is very sweet but not much more, with hints of rose water and orange peel. Serve well chilled. Drink now.–T.M. • $13 • (10/31/1999) • **82**

Malvasia Lanzarote Dulce 1997: This full-bodied, slightly heavy-handed white is quite sweet, with melon, cooked apple, floral and herb notes. A distinctive wine with more power than grace. Drink now.–T.M. • $13 • (11/30/1998) • **83**

EL MESON, BODEGAS

Rioja Selección Especial NV: This polished, subdued red offers ripe cherry and light spice flavors. Round on the palate, with little tannin, finishing on a light earthy note. Simple but harmonious. Drink now.–T.M. • $9 • (11/30/1998) • **83**

ELEZ, FINCA

Chardonnay Viño de la Tierra Manuel Manzaneque 1996: A sturdy frame of oak gives powerful toasty and smoky flavors but overshadows the light apple flavor. Still, crisp acidity gives it some life. For fans of oak. Drink now.–T.M. • $20 • (11/15/1999) • **83**

Viño de la Tierra Manuel Manzaneque 1995: A firm red, a bit austere in its flavors, with notes of cedar, tobacco and licorice, but the structure is solid and balanced. It should shine with food. A blend of Cabernet Sauvignon, Merlot and Tempranillo. Drink now through 2003.–T.M. • $16 • (11/15/1999) • **86**

Viño de la Tierra Manuel Manzaneque Crianza 1994: This highly extracted red has muscular tannins and lots of extraction, but the flavors are austere, even bitter, with earth, licorice and tobacco notes. May bloom with food. Drink now through 2003.–T.M. • $20 • (11/15/1999) • **84**

ETXANIZ TXAKOLINA

Getariako Txakolina Txomin Etxaniz 1996 • $15 • (2/28/1998) • **83**

FALSET-MARCA

Grenache Tarragona Étim 1998: Plush and fruity, this round red is stuffed with plum, cherry and black pepper flavors, all up front, but with just enough tannin for grip. Drink now through 2001.–T.M. • $11 • (6/15/2000) • **83**

Tarragona Castell de Falset 1997: Licorice and floral notes add interest to this fruit-filled red. The black cherry flavors are ripe and clean, and the wine is firm and balanced. Drink now through 2002.–T.M. • $17 • (6/15/2000) • **86**

FARINA, BODEGAS

Castilla y Leon Fin del Duero 1990 • $12 • (3/31/1995) • **85**

Toro 1998: This muscular red from Spain offers solid drinking at a deceptively low price. It shows deep color and high extraction, with firm tannins and deep but muted plum and licorice flavors. Balanced, but needs time to soften. Drink through 2005.–T.M. • $8 • (11/15/1999) • **86**

Toro 1997: This round, chewy red offers black cherry, meat and smoke flavors, ripe fruit balanced by a pleasant bitterness, moderate tannins and a smoky finish. Drink now through 2001.–T.M. • $7 • (10/31/1998) • **83**

Toro 1994 • $7 • (4/30/1995) • **81**

Toro 1993 • $6 • (1/31/1995) • **74**

Toro 1992 • $6 • (8/31/1993) • **75**

Toro 1990 • $9 • (10/15/1992) • **81**

Toro Colegiata 1998: This rustic red offers earthy, slightly bitter flavors and rough tannins, but a core of pure cherry flavor keeps it interesting. Best with food. Drink now through 2001.–T.M. • $8 • (11/15/1999) • **83**

Toro Colegiata 1996: This lean red shows light berry and herb flavors inside a hard shell of tannin. Tough on the palate, bitter on the finish.–T.M. • $8 • (10/31/1998) • **78**

Toro Colegiata 1993 • $9 • (1/31/1995) • **77**

Toro Colegiata 1991 • $7 • (4/30/1995) • **63**

Toro Colegiata 1990 • $9 • (4/15/1994) • **77**

Toro Dama de Toro Reserva 1991: This polished red offers harmonious flavors of dried cherry, cedar and herb, with firm tannins that turn a bit dry on the finish. Should soften with food. Drink now through 2002.–T.M. • $12 • (10/31/1998) • **84**

Toro Dama de Toro Reserva 1990: Still lively and fruity, this round red shows plum, licorice and coffee flavors, with firm but well-integrated tannins and a clean, fruity finish. Ripe and well balanced, it's a good match with grilled meats. Drink now through 2004.–T.M. • $12 • (10/31/1998) • **87**

Toro Dama de Toro Reserva 1989 • $10 • (4/15/1994) • **83**

Toro Fin del Rio Reserva 1991: There's a core of cherry and plum flavors in this maturing red, and the cedar and tobacco accents add complexity. The tannins are a bit dry, but the finish lingers, with spice and raisin notes. Drink now.–T.M. • $14 • (10/31/1998) • **85**

Toro Gran Colegiata Crianza 1995: Bitter smoky and earthy aromas and flavors are accentuated by the tannic and spritzy texture. Tasted twice, with consistent notes. Past its prime.–T.M. • $12 • (11/30/1998) • **72**

Toro Gran Colegiata Crianza 1990 • $10 • (1/31/1995) • **81**

Toro Gran Colegiata Crianza 1989 • $11 • (4/15/1994) • **83**

Toro Gran Colegiata Gran Reserva 1987: Vanilla and raisin flavors give this mature red the character of an old Rioja, though it's rounder and more tannic than its northern cousins. A good if somewhat rustic example of the traditional style. Drink now.–T.M. • $20 • (10/31/1998) • **82**

Toro Gran Colegiata Reserva 1991: Coffee and cola aromas give way to raisin and dried cherry flavors in this smooth, maturing red. It's harmonious and shows complexity, but the drying finish suggests it's time to drink up.–T.M. • $15 • (10/31/1998) • **83**

Toro Gran Colegiata Reserva 1988 • $12 • (4/30/1995) • **79**

Toro Gran Colegiata Reserva 1987 • $12 • (3/31/1995) • **80**

Toro Gran Colegiata Reserva 1986 • $20 • (3/31/1995) • **76**

Toro Reserva 1987 • $12 • (10/15/1992) • **80**

Toro Viño Primero 1995 • $8 • (4/30/1996) • **77**

Toro White Colegiata 1998: This lively white offers a jumble of strong flavors, from bitter almond to candy apple. Full-bodied, with good acidity, it needs food to tame it. Drink now.–T.M. • $8 • (11/15/1999) • **80**

Toro White Colegiata 1997: This firm, slightly tart white shows expressive flavors of almond and herb, but there's not much fruit to balance the acidity. Austere yet refreshing. Drink now.–T.M. • $8 • (10/31/1998) • **82**

Viño de la Tierra de Zamora 1997: Like biting into a ripe plum, this red is juicy and fruity, with a light but pleasing astringency. Not complex, but definitely quaffable. Drink now.–T.M. • $6/1 liter • (11/15/1999) • **83**

Viño de la Tierra de Zamora 1996: Round and soft, this straightforward red offers ripe plum and cherry flavors, with hints of vanilla, moderate tannins and a clean, short finish. Easy to quaff. Drink now.–T.M. • $7/1 liter • (11/30/1998) • **80**

Viño de la Tierra de Zamora Gran Peromato Reserva 1995: Sweet cherry and milk chocolate flavors are light but appealing in this balanced red. The moderate tannins provide backbone for lighter dishes. Drink now.–T.M. • $7 • (12/15/1999) • **83**

Viño de la Tierra de Zamora Peromato 1996: Cherry, light chocolate and licorice flavors are clean and balanced in this fresh red. It's lively and has just enough grip for food. Drink now through 2002.–T.M. • $6 • (12/15/1999) • **83**

Viño de la Tierra de Zamora White 1998: Soft in texture and floral in aroma, this pillowy white shows delicacy, but it's a bit simple. The finish is clean but short.–T.M. • $6/1 liter • (11/15/1999) • **79**

Viño de la Tierra de Zamora White 1997: This deeply colored, full-bodied white is round and rather dull, with soft flavors of cooked apple and pear. Past its prime.–T.M. • $7/1 liter • (11/30/1998) • **76**

Viño de la Tierra Gran Peromato 1992: Ripe, jammy cherry and raisin flavors are rich, lively and sweet in this tannic red. A bit heavy-handed and cloying on the finish.–T.M. • $7 • (11/30/1998) • **79**

Viño de la Tierra Gran Peromato 1991 • $5 • (2/28/1995) • **81**

Viño de la Tierra Gran Peromato 1990 • $6 • (4/30/1996) • **82**

Viño de la Tierra Gran Peromato 1989 • $9 • (2/28/1995) • **82**

Viño de la Tierra Peromato 1995: Smoke and herb flavors dominate this light, dry, rustic red. Chewy and turning a bit sour on the palate, this may soften with food.–T.M. • $6 • (11/30/1998) • **79**

Viño de la Tierra Peromato 1992 • $6 • (2/28/1995) • **79**

Viño de la Tierra Peromato 1991 • $5 • (4/15/1994) • **79**

Viño de la Tierra Peromato 1990 • $6 • (4/15/1994) • **77**

FAUSTINO MARTINEZ, BODEGAS

Rioja 1989 • $10 • (3/31/1993) • **83**

Rioja Crianza 1996: Firm and focused, this chewy red offers plum, chocolate and coffee flavors, with a solid tannin structure and a clean, spicy finish. A nice blend of modern structure and traditional flavors. Drink now through 2004.–T.M. • $16 • (5/31/2000) • **87**

Rioja Faustino I Gran Reserva 1993: Rich and dark. This ripe red offers coffee, prune and earth flavors in a firm, focused package. Turns a bit dry on the finish; best with food. Drink now through 2002.–T.M. • $28 • (5/31/2000) • **84**

Rioja Faustino I Gran Reserva 1988 • $20 • (11/15/1997) • **81**

Rioja Faustino I Gran Reserva 1987 • $16 • (4/15/1994) • **82**

Rioja Faustino I Gran Reserva 1986 • $21 • (3/31/1993) • **86**

Rioja Faustino I Gran Reserva 1982 • $25 • (3/31/1992) • **82**

Rioja Faustino I Gran Reserva 1981 • $12 • (10/31/1988) • **88**

Rioja Faustino I Gran Reserva 1978 • $NA • (3/31/1992) • **76**

Rioja Faustino I Gran Reserva 1973 • $NA • (3/31/1992) • **82**

Rioja Faustino I Gran Reserva 1970 • $43 Ⓐ • (3/31/1992) • **89**

Rioja Faustino V Reserva 1995: This plush yet focused red shows intense flavors of smoky cedar, cherry and spice, with firm tannins and a tart spark of acidity. Balanced and clean. Drink now through 2004.–T.M. • $17 • (5/31/2000) • **87**

Rioja Faustino V Reserva 1992 • $11 • (11/15/1997) • **83**

Rioja Faustino V Reserva 1991 • $10 • (3/31/1996) • **84**

Rioja Faustino V Reserva 1989 • $10 • (4/15/1994) • **83**

Rioja Faustino V Reserva 1988 • $14 • (3/31/1993) • **81**

Rioja Faustino V Reserva 1987 • $13 • (1/31/1992) • **81**

Rioja Faustino V Reserva 1986 • $16 • (3/31/1992) • **86**

Rioja Faustino V Reserva 1985 • $18 • (3/31/1992) • **82**

Rioja Faustino VII 1998: This supple, rather delicate red displays harmonious flavors of cherry, tobacco and spice, delicate and alluring. Refreshing. Drink now.–T.M. • $12 • (5/31/2000) • **84**

Rioja Faustino VII 1995 • $8 • (11/15/1997) • **81**

Rioja Faustino VII 1993 • $8 • (9/30/1996) • **86**

Rioja Faustino VII 1991 • $6 • (1/31/1995) • **81**

Rioja Faustino VII 1990 • $7 • (4/15/1994) • **81**

Rioja Faustino VII 1988 • $9 • (1/31/1992) • **85**

Rioja White Faustino V 1998: Light and simple, this white is crisp enough to be refreshing, but too neutral in flavor to be very interesting.–T.M. • $12 • (6/15/2000) • **79**

Rioja White Faustino V 1996 • $9 • (5/31/1998) • **81**

FERNANDEZ, BODEGAS ALEJANDRO

Ribera del Duero Pesquera 1976: More advanced in color and flavor than is the '75 Reserva, showing an amber rim, aromas of raisins and cedar and sweet flavors of dried cherry and vanilla. It's lean and still firm, more like a traditional Spanish red, and should be drunk now. (Pesquera vertical tasting, as are all notes below dated 11/30/1998). –T.M. • $11 • (11/30/1998). • **88**

Ribera del Duero Pesquera Crianza 1996: Alluring aromas of plums and spices give way to bright fruit flavors of plums and cherries, with notes of tobacco and licorice. It's balanced, with firm tannins and bright acidity.

Tasted three times, with consistent notes, but I expect it will show better with time. Drink now through 2006.–T.M. • $28 • (10/31/1999) • **86**

Ribera del Duero Pesquera Crianza 1995: This big, rich red from Spain is years away from its peak; now it's muscular but mute, showing only glimpses of its ripe black fruit and complex spices under an iron bed of tannins. Impressive concentration and fine balance promise that patience will be rewarded. Best after 2002.–T.M. • $24 • (10/31/1998) SS • **92**

Ribera del Duero Pesquera Crianza 1994: Still in its infancy, but promises to develop into a real powerhouse. It's thick and tannic, muscular and closed, even a bit clumsy now, as the powerful tannins and coffee and chocolate oak notes mask the roasted, jammy fruit flavors of cassis and plum. Best after 2005.–T.M. • $22 • (11/30/1998) • **93**

Ribera del Duero Pesquera Crianza 1993: This tender, polished wine reflects a difficult vintage, offering less-than-normal concentration for Pesquera. But the fruit flavors are still ripe, showing notes of plums and cherries, and the oak influence really stands out, adding flavors of cocoa, chocolate and toast. It's accessible now, and should reach maturity by 2003. –T.M. • $20 • (11/30/1998) • **89**

Ribera del Duero Pesquera Crianza 1991 • $18 • (4/15/1994) • **91**

Ribera del Duero Pesquera Crianza 1990 • $20 • (12/15/1993) • **89**

Ribera del Duero Pesquera Crianza 1989 • $24 Ⓐ • (4/15/1992) CS • **91**

Ribera del Duero Pesquera Crianza 1988: Still quite young, with a deep garnet color and ripe, jammy blackberry flavor on the palate, but it's thick and not very expressive, marked by vanilla and toasty oak, with a dry, tannic finish. Accessible now, may improve with another three to five years in bottle.–T.M. • $17 • (11/30/1998) • **88**

Ribera del Duero Pesquera Crianza 1987 • $17 • (9/30/1990) • **84**

Ribera del Duero Pesquera Crianza 1986 • $20 • (4/30/1989) • **91**

Ribera del Duero Pesquera Crianza 1985 • $16 • (4/30/1988) • **89**

Ribera del Duero Pesquera Crianza 1984 • $14 • (10/15/1987) • **89**

Ribera del Duero Pesquera Crianza 1983 • $12 • (11/15/1987) • **94**

Ribera del Duero Pesquera Crianza 1982 • $12 • (11/15/1987) • **89**

Ribera del Duero Pesquera Crianza 1979 • $11 • (11/15/1987) • **90**

Ribera del Duero Pesquera Crianza 1978 • $11 • (11/15/1987) • **89**

Ribera del Duero Pesquera Crianza 1975 • $10 • (11/15/1987) • **88**

Ribera del Duero Pesquera Gran Reserva 1990: A huge wine, still young and even a bit unformed, but with great ripeness, concentration and potential. Ripe aromas of roasted plums, chocolate and game give way to round, jammy flavors of plums, prunes, tobacco and spices backed up by plenty of toasty, vanilla oak notes. Still clumsy now, it should show well with five to 10 years in the cellar.–T.M. • $35 • (11/30/1998) • **92**

Ribera del Duero Pesquera Gran Reserva 1986: Tasted from magnum. The '86 Gran Reserva offers a very deep, youthful garnet color, and the aromas show an alluring midpoint between youth and maturity, with fresh blackberry and floral notes mingling with spice, toast and vanilla accents. It's rich on the palate, but soft and tender, as ripe tannins beautifully support the sweet blackberry and black cherry flavors. Delicious now, but should improve for another five to 10 years.–T.M. • $35 • (11/30/1998) • **93**

Ribera del Duero Pesquera Gran Reserva 1985: This wine's extra time in oak (compared with the '85 Reserva) seems to have done more harm than good. It has a lighter color, with more garnet at the rim and, while it's still vigorous on the palate, there's less fruit and more tannin. Flavors range from cherry and raisin to cedar and spice and, though it's a bit tough on the palate, the long finish is sweet and fruity. Drink now or hold for up to three years.–T.M. • $35 • (11/30/1998) • **89**

Ribera del Duero Pesquera Janus Gran Reserva 1991: This powerful red is ripe and roasted, thick on the palate, with extraordinary concentration of ripe plum, prune, chocolate and mineral flavors. In a bit of a dumb phase now, it clearly has the stuffing and balance to last. Best after 2005.–T.M. • $134 Ⓐ • (11/30/1998) • **95**

Ribera del Duero Pesquera Janus Gran Reserva 1986: Compared with the '86 Gran Reserva, the '86 Janus shows more extraction and concentration but less focus and definition. It has rich, muscular tannins, plenty of cherry and berry flavors and a long finish spiced with menthol and vanilla. While impressive for its power, I preferred the balance of the '86 Gran Reserva. Drink now or hold for up to five years.—Pesquera vertical.–T.M. • $75 • (11/30/1998) • **90**

Ribera del Duero Pesquera Janus Gran Reserva 1982: This mature red shows ripe cherry and raisin flavors, with rich chocolate and tobacco notes and bright acidity. The tannins are firm but well integrated, and the long finish is scented with cedar, tobacco and raisin. A rustic wine with a lot of heart. Drink now through 2002.–T.M. • $75 • (11/30/1998) • **88**

Ribera del Duero Pesquera Janus Reserva 1994: This massive wine resembles a young Port in its extraordinary concentration of ripe, sweet fruit, thick texture and potential for long aging. Closed now, it only hints at the richness of ripe fruit that hides behind the iron tannins and lavish oak. Few Spanish reds attain this degree of power and intensity; with time, it should also develop the harmony and elegance the country's best wines are know for. Best after 2008.–T.M. • $116 Ⓐ • (11/30/1998) • **96**

Ribera del Duero Pesquera Janus Reserva 1982 • $93 Ⓐ • (9/15/1988) • **94**

Ribera del Duero Pesquera Reserva 1995: A Spanish red of brute force, this powerful wine shows a deep color, ripe aromas of plum and prune and plenty of chocolate and toasty oak flavors. Full-bodied and packed with ripe tannins, it's a muscular wine of good pedigree that should develop well. Best after 2002.–T.M. • $41 Ⓐ • (10/31/1999) CS • **90**

Ribera del Duero Pesquera Reserva 1994: Tasted from magnum. Compared with the '94 Crianza, the Reserva is just as rich but even better balanced, with richer fruit flavors that are expressive and powerful yet harmonious on the palate. Shows plenty of chocolate and toasty oak flavors, and the full-bodied tannins are ripe and well integrated. A blockbuster, yet still a beauty. Best after 2005.–T.M. • $46 Ⓐ • (11/30/1998) • **94**

Ribera del Duero Pesquera Reserva 1993: Tasted from magnum. In this light vintage, the extra oak-aging seems to have worked against the wine, leaving it rather lean on the palate, with light fruit flavors of raspberry and cherry, and tea and raisin notes on the finish. Already maturing, it may peak within five years.–T.M. • $30 • (11/30/1998) • **87**

Ribera del Duero Pesquera Reserva 1992: This muscular red has great intensity, with ripe, rich flavors of cassis, plums and prunes over very firm tannins. Lavish oaking adds deep chocolate and coffee notes. Right now, its power emphasizes the alcohol and structure, obscuring the fruit and complexity, but it should harmonize with five to eight more years in the bottle.–T.M. • $26 • (11/30/1998) • **92**

Ribera del Duero Pesquera Reserva 1991: Tasted from magnum. Offers an irresistible youthful exuberance, with a plush layer of baby fat over a muscular, firm structure. Vanilla oak flavors are sweet and luscious, marrying well with ripe, well-defined flavors of blackberry and cherry; the tannins are ripe and firm, giving the wine balance and the potential to improve for 10 to 15 years in the bottle.–T.M. • $26 • (11/30/1998) • **91**

Ribera del Duero Pesquera Reserva 1990 • $25 • (4/15/1994) • **89**

Ribera del Duero Pesquera Reserva 1989: Tasted from magnum. Deep, intense garnet color. Though still a bit closed, its aromas range from plum to tobacco and menthol. Thick and ripe on the palate, it offered spicy plum and prune flavors with herbal and tobacco accents. Has plenty of oak and tannin; drinkable now, it should improve for five to eight years.–T.M. • $25 • (11/30/1998) • **91**

Ribera del Duero Pesquera Reserva 1987: Still shows a slight lack of concentration, compared with typical Pesqueras, but the flavors are quite intense, ranging widely from plum and black cherry to licorice, tobacco and menthol. It's soft and plush on the palate, perhaps peaking now, but can still age for three to five more years.–T.M. • $20 • (11/30/1998) • **88**

Ribera del Duero Pesquera Reserva 1986 • $25 • (9/30/1990) • **92**

Ribera del Duero Pesquera Reserva 1985: This shows a youthful character, with a deep ruby color and fresh aromas of plums and black cherries. The palate is packed with harmonious, fresh fruit flavors and accents of cedar and vanilla. Well integrated and rich, this is a well focused wine with a long finish. Drinkable now, but will develop for five more years, at least.–T.M. • $25 • (11/30/1998) • **91**

Ribera del Duero Pesquera Reserva 1984: Tasted from magnum. This wine's character is atypical for Pesquera. It shows gamy and light vegetal aromas, less concentration than usual on the palate and leans toward flavors of toast and tar rather than fruity notes. Drink now or hold for up to three years.–T.M. • $32 Ⓐ • (11/30/1998) • **86**

Ribera del Duero Pesquera Reserva 1982: Shows some age in its medium-ruby color and amber rim, and while it lacks Pesquera's usual concentration it displays elegance and length. Sweet cherry, vanilla and tea aromas and flavors are well defined and silky on the palate, with light but firm tannins and a vanilla-accented finish. Drink now.–T.M. • $45 Ⓐ • (11/30/1998) • **89**

Ribera del Duero Pesquera Reserva 1978: Shows a deep-ruby color, little amber, and its flavors are still young, with aromas of blackberry, cherry and licorice and flavors of cherry, raisin and tobacco. It's full-bodied, and still quite fruity, though it turns a bit dry on the finish. Drinkable now, but can hold for up to five more years.–T.M. • $11 • (11/30/1998) • **89**

Ribera del Duero Pesquera Reserva 1975: Clearly showing maturity, but it is still a big, firm wine, with well-defined flavors of plum, tar and tobacco, and, while the wood is still very present, the overall structure is clean and long. Will drink well for three to five more years.–T.M. • $10 • (11/30/1998) • **90**

Key: SS—Spectator Selection. CS—Cellar Selection. HR—Highly Recommended. $NA—Price not available. (BT)—Barrel tasting. Ⓐ—Auction Price.
For a key to the tasters' initials, see "How to Use These Listings."
Dates in parentheses represent the issues in which the ratings were published.

FILLABOA, GRANJA

Albariño Rias Baixas 1996 • $14 • (5/31/1998) • **82**

FOREST CREEK

Merlot Utiel-Requena Rio Valley 1995: Perfumed with aromas of strawberry and watermelon, this red turns a bit darker on the palate, with notes of plum and tobacco and just enough tannin for grip. Fruity and almost sweet, it's an easy-sipping wine. Drink now.–T.M. • $7/L • (11/30/1998) • **84**

FORNELOS, LAGAR DE

Albariño Rias Baixas Lagar de Cervera 1996 • $15 • (10/31/1997) • **85**

FREIXENET

Brut Cava Carta Nevada NV: Slightly sweet-tasting, with some minerally and earthy flavors that linger on the finish.–K.M. • $8 • (12/15/1999) • **79**
Brut Cava Cordon Negro NV: The vanilla, cream and apple flavors show intensity in this richly textured sparkler. It has more depth than many Cavas, yet remains fresh and fruity, with a slightly sweet finish. Drink now.–T.M. • $9 • (11/30/1998) • **85**
Brut Cava Estate NV: Nice and fruity, with a pleasant effervescence and a clean finish. Has appealing green apple and mineral flavors and green peach notes. Drink now.–K.M. • $15 • (12/15/1999) • **83**
Brut de Noirs Cava NV: This rosé, with a lovely pink-salmon color, though quite dry on the palate, shows flavors of watermelon, strawberry and raspberry. An appealing quaff for a lazy afternoon. Drink now.–T.M. • $10 • (11/30/1998) • **84**
Cava Spumante NV: This vivid, noticeably sweet sparkler tastes strongly of Muscat, with orange, mango and lemon-lime flavors unusual for cava.–T.M. • $10 • (11/30/1998) • **78**
Extra Dry Cava Cordon Negro NV: This fruity sparkler offers simple but appealing floral, peach and pear flavors, with a hint of sweetness and a soft mousse. A pleasant afternoon quaffer. Drink now.–T.M. • $9 • (11/30/1998) • **80**
Semi-Seco Cava Carta Nevada NV: Round and fruity, this exuberant sparkler offers noticeably sweet, canned fruit flavors of peach and pear. Just enough acidity to maintain a fresh, easy-drinking balance. Drink now.–T.M. • $8 • (11/30/1998) • **81**

FUENTES, J.M.

Priorat Gran Clos 1996: Richly concentrated yet beautifully balanced, this harmonious red is packed with delicious cherry, blackberry and vanilla flavors accented by notes of toast, cola and spice. The tannins are firm but polished, the alcohol high but well integrated, the wine powerful yet graceful. Drink now through 2008.–T.M. • $38 • (11/30/1999) • **92**
Priorat Gran Clos 1995 • $35 • (6/30/1998) • **87**

FUENTESPINA, BODEGAS

Ribera del Duero 1998: This straightforward red has cherry, raisin and chocolate flavors, with rather drying tannins.–T.M. • $12 • (1/31/2000) • **78**
Ribera del Duero Crianza 1996: Quite light and dilute for the vintage. This lean red shows herbal and tobacco flavors and finishes dry and short.–T.M. • $17 • (1/31/2000) • **76**
Ribera del Duero Pagos Viejos Reserva Especial 1995: Ripe and jammy. Rich, soft flavors of cooked plums and prunes are thick, but lack focus and freshness. Drink now through 2003.–T.M. • $65 • (1/31/2000) • **82**
Ribera del Duero Reserva 1995: Jammy and soft. This plump red shows cooked plum, herb and cedar flavors, fairly rich but without much focus. Drink now through 2002.–T.M. • $25 • (1/31/2000) • **80**

GALEGAS, ADEGAS

Albariño Rias Baixas D. Pedro de Soutomaior 1997: Lemon and apple flavors are clean and balanced in this straightforward white. Though neutral in character, it has the body and acidity to accompany lighter dishes. Drink now.–T.M. • $11 • (11/15/1998) • **82**
Albariño Rias Baixas D. Pedro de Soutomaior 1996 • $11 • (5/31/1998) • **81**
Rias Baixas Veigadares 1996: This straightforward white has good body and balance, and lemony acidity keeps it fresh, but aside from a light vanilla note on the finish, the flavors are rather neutral. Drink now.–T.M. • $18 • (11/15/1998) • **83**

GANDIA

Cabernet Sauvignon Utiel-Requena Hoya Valley 1996: This soft red offers berry and herb flavors, gentle and unfocused, with light, slightly drying tannins. It's fresh and simple.–T.M. • $5 • (12/15/1998) • **79**
Cabernet Sauvignon Utiel-Requena Hoya Valley 1994 • $5 • (10/31/1997) • **79**
Cabernet Sauvignon Utiel-Requena 1993 • $6 • (4/30/1995) • **78**
Ceremonia Crianza Utiel-Requena 1996: Polished and firm, this ripe red offers plum, mineral and cedar flavors, with a firm structure and a clean finish. Drink now through 2003.–T.M. • $NA • (1/01/2000) • **84**
Chardonnay Utiel-Requena Hoya Valley 1997: This simple white is almost neutral on the palate, with light apple and herb flavors and a short finish.–T.M. • $5 • (12/15/1998) • **76**
Grenache Rosé Utiel-Requena Hoya Valley 1996 • $5 • (6/30/1997) • **79**
Hoya de Cadenas Utiel-Requena Reserva 1989 • $7 • (4/30/1996) • **74**
Marques de Chivé Utiel-Requena 1989 • $6 • (4/15/1994) • **81**
Merlot Utiel-Requena Hoya Valley 1996: This firm red shows some cherry flavor, but austere beef and mineral notes leave it a bit tough.–T.M. • $5 • (12/15/1998) • **78**
Merlot Utiel-Requena Hoya Valley 1994 • $5 • (10/31/1997) • **82**
Merlot Utiel-Requena 1993 • $6 • (4/30/1995) • **83**
Sauvignon Blanc Utiel-Requena Hoya Valley 1996 • $6 • (6/30/1997) • **84**
Tempranillo Utiel-Requena Hoya Valley 1993: Round and soft, this plush red offers simple but juicy flavors of cherry, plum and chocolate, with soft tannins and low acidity. An agreeable, easy-drinking wine. Drink now.–T.M. • $5 • (11/30/1998) • **83**
Tempranillo Utiel-Requena Hoya Valley 1992 • $5 • (10/31/1997) • **81**

GLORIAN, DAPHNE

Priorat Clos Erasmus 1997: Alluring aromas of violets, cassis and cinnamon give way to lush, polished flavors of black fruits and spices. Though made in a plush international-style, this red retains the distinctive flavors of the region. It's a beauty. Tasted twice, with consistent notes. Drink now through 2008.–T.M. • $44 • (4/30/2000) • **93**
Priorat Clos Erasmus 1996: This shows the distinctive flavors of modern Priorat: ripe, juicy fruit flavors of blackberries and raspberries, heady alcohol and firm yet harmonious tannins. Coffee and chocolate flavors add depth. It's rather hard now; give it time. Best after 2001.–T.M. • $81 Ⓐ • (9/15/1999) • **92**
Priorat Clos Erasmus 1995: This impressive Spanish red attacks the palate so subtly, you think it's delicate—until it overwhelms the taste buds with licorice, coffee, plum, berry and spice flavors. Massive tannins deliver the knockout punch. A big wine that needs time to breathe. Worth the hunt. Best after 2000.–T.M. • $86 Ⓐ • (10/31/1998) HR • **94**
Priorat Clos Erasmus 1993 • $70 Ⓐ • (9/15/1997) • **88**

GODEVAL, BODEGAS

Valdeorras Viña Godeval 1998: This crisp white has nice grip, and the peach, pine and mineral flavors are focused and clean. A nice marriage of ripe fruit and firm acidity, this is a natural match with shellfish. Drink now.–T.M. • $13 • (11/15/1999) • **83**
Valdeorras Viña Godeval 1996: Though light-bodied, this crisp white offers expressive floral and fruity flavors, with notes of pear and piecrust. A pleasant aperitif. Drink now.–T.M. • $13 • (11/30/1998) • **83**

GORMAZ, BODEGAS

Ribera del Duero Crianza 1996: This round red is dominated by oak, with strong, slightly clumsy flavors of coffee, chocolate and coconut and rather harsh wood tannins, though there is plum underneath.–T.M. • $16 • (10/31/1999) • **77**
Ribera del Duero Joven 1998: The light structure of this red makes it accessible for current drinking, yet it still packs a wallop of flavor, with notes of black cherry, licorice and smoke. A better-than-average example of the vino joven style. Drink now through 2002.–T.M. • $12 • (10/31/1999) • **84**

GRANDES BODEGAS

Ribera del Duero Marques de Velilla 1996 • $8 • (10/31/1997) • **84**
Ribera del Duero Marqués de Velilla Crianza 1996: This ripe, thick red offers sweet flavors of plum, cherry jam and raisin. Full-bodied, with rich tannins and a sweet, chocolate-scented finish. A bit rustic, but with good concentration. Drink through 2004.–T.M. • $13 • (10/31/1998) • **87**

Ribera del Duero Marqués de Velilla Reserva 1994: This ripe, jammy red is almost sweet, with flavors of chocolate, vanilla and even maple to accompany the cherry and blackberry notes, yet it's not heavy. Firm but evanescent tannins and a clean, fresh finish. Drink now through 2003.–T.M. • $26 • (10/31/1998) • **89**

GRANDES VINOS Y VINEDOS

Cariñena Monasterio de las Viñas Gran Reserva 1988: An amazingly deep color and rich structure for its age and pedigree. Not complex, but offers a ripe, spicy character, good balance and sweet fruit flavors. Drink now.–T.M. • $14 • (11/15/1999) • **86**

Cariñena Monasterio de las Viñas Reserva 1990: Prune and licorice flavors are ripe and soft in this jammy red. Ripe tannins give some grip, but it's a bit soft and sweet for food. Drink now.–T.M. • $11 • (11/15/1999) • **81**

Cariñena Viña Rotura NV: This light, soft red offers simple flavors of berries, raisins and herbs. Try slightly chilled.–T.M. • $5 • (1/31/2000) • **77**

Cariñena White Valdeflor NV: This bold white is spritzy, with candied citrus, smoke and bitter almond flavors. Not for the faint of heart.–T.M. • $6 • (11/15/1999) • **79**

Tempranillo Cariñena Monasterio de las Viñas Crianza 1994: This soft, fruity red offers overripe flavors of plums, with a meaty texture and herbal accents.–T.M. • $7 • (1/31/2000) • **78**

GREDOS, CASTILLO DE

Viño de Mesa NV: This soft, light red offers simple flavors of cooked cherry and herb, with light tannins and a short, raisiny finish.–T.M. • $4 • (11/30/1998) • **77**

GRINON, MARQUES DE

Cabernet Sauvignon Viño de Mesa de Toledo Dominio de Valdepusa 1995 • $22 • (4/30/1998) • **84**

Cabernet Sauvignon Viño de Mesa Dominio de Valdepusa 1993 • $22 • (10/31/1997) • **76**

Castilla y Leon Durius 1993 • $9 • (4/30/1996) • **83**

Castilla y Leon Durius 1991 • $9 • (3/31/1995) • **78**

Rioja 1996: This silky red offers cherry, coffee and light spice flavors over light but firm tannins. Balanced and fresh. Good definition and enough grip to match with food. Drink now through 2001.–T.M. • $10 • (11/30/1998) • **84**

Rioja 1995 • $10 • (10/15/1997) • **87**

Rioja 1994 • $10 • (6/30/1996) • **88**

Rioja 1991 • $10 • (4/30/1995) • **86**

Rioja Colección Personal Reserva 1993: Alluring vanilla and spice aromas give way to darker flavors of game, plum and tar in a firmly structured red that turns dry on the finish. Has power, but a bit unbalanced now; give it time to harmonize. Best after 2000.–T.M. • $19 • (11/30/1998) • **85**

Rioja Colección Personal Reserva 1990 • $18 • (10/15/1997) • **89**

Rioja Colección Personal Reserva 1988 • $15 • (4/30/1995) • **88**

Syrah Viño de Mesa de Toledo Dominio de Valdepusa 1996: Crisp, focused and harmonious, this red packs vivid flavors of black cherry, licorice, spice and smoke into a lean, graceful structure that faithfully echoes the Northern Rhône. Drink now through 2002.–T.M. • $21 • (10/31/1999) • **87**

Syrah Viño de Mesa de Toledo Dominio de Valdepusa 1995 • $22 • (4/30/1998) • **84**

Syrah Viño de Mesa Dominio de Valdepusa 1993 • $26 • (9/30/1996) • **85**

Viño de Mesa de Castilla y Leon Durius 1995: Sweet cherry and chocolate flavors are appealing but get lost in the thick tannins of this muscular red. Ripe and clean, it may unwind with food. Drink through 2004.–T.M. • $9 • (11/30/1998) • **82**

Viño de Mesa de Castilla y Leon White Durius 1996: Toasty, smoky oak notes dominate this white, though it has a core of ripe melon and apple flavors. Just enough acidity for balance. Drink now.–T.M. • $9 • (11/30/1998) • **82**

Viño de Mesa de Toledo 1985 • $12 • (2/28/1990) • **86**

Viño de Mesa Dominio de Valdepusa 1992 • $19 • (4/30/1995) • **87**

Viño de Mesa Durius 1994 • $9 • (7/31/1997) • **83**

Viño de Mesa Durius Colección Personal 1994 • $15 • (10/31/1997) • **83**

Key: SS—Spectator Selection. CS—Cellar Selection. HR—Highly Recommended. $NA—Price not available. (BT)—Barrel tasting. Ⓐ—Auction Price. For a key to the tasters' initials, see "How to Use These Listings."
Dates in parentheses represent the issues in which the ratings were published.

GUELBENZU, BODEGAS

Garnacha Navarra Jardin 1998: Gamy and earthy flavors dominate this austere red, while a hint of spritz unsettles the palate. The finish is bitter and short.–T.M. • $9 • (11/15/1999) • **74**

Garnacha Navarra Jardin 1996 • $8 • (10/31/1997) • **75**

Navarra 1996: The smoky, toasty oak in this round red dominates the core of ripe plum and cherry flavors. It's firm, with well-integrated tannins, and should stand up with food. Drink through 2005.–T.M. • $12 • (10/31/1998) • **85**

Navarra 1995 • $10 • (10/31/1997) • **86**

Navarra 1994 • $10 • (4/30/1996) • **84**

Navarra 1992 • $9 • (4/30/1995) • **84**

Navarra 1990 • $10 • (12/15/1993) • **82**

Navarra 1989 • $11 • (4/15/1992) • **87**

Navarra Evo 1994 • $20 • (10/31/1997) • **80**

Navarra Evo 1993 • $20 • (6/15/1997) • **86**

Navarra Evo 1992 • $17 • (4/30/1995) • **87**

Navarra Evo 1989 • $20 • (4/15/1992) • **85**

Navarra Evo Crianza 1996: Toasty oak and sweet plum flavors are vivid and clean in this well-balanced red. Has depth and grip and nicely marries traditional flavors and international style. Drink now through 2003.–T.M. • $22 • (11/15/1999) • **87**

Navarra Evo Crianza 1995: There's plenty of oak here, with assertive coffee, chocolate and toast character and just enough plum and black cherry flavor for balance. It's thick and tannic, with a toasty finish. Drink through 2005.–T.M. • $20 • (10/31/1998) • **85**

Navarra Jardin 1995 • $8 • (8/31/1996) • **84**

Navarra Lautus 1996: This ambitious red is full-bodied, with lots of smoky, toasty oak, muscular tannins and ripe flavors of plum and licorice. Still a bit hard, it should develop well. Best from 2001 through 2005.–T.M. • $55 • (11/15/1999) • **87**

GUTIERREZ DE LA VEGA, BODEGAS

Alicante Casta Diva Cosecha Miel 1995 • $20/500 ml. • (5/15/1997) • **84**

Muscat Alicante Casta Diva Miel 1997: Soft, silky and sweet, this shows very ripe flavors of raisins, dates and walnuts. Distinctive but a bit heavy. Drink now.–T.M. • $20/500 ml. • (10/31/1999) • **82**

HIDALGO, VINICOLA

Amontillado Jerez Viejo NV: Caramel, toffee and a touch of orange pekoe tea mark this dry, firm Sherry. Grows nutty on the palate, showing good length and character. Drink now.–B.S. • $79 • (10/31/1999) • **89**

Manzanilla Jerez La Gitana NV: Nutty, honeyed, resinous aromas and flavors are followed by a round, medium- to full-bodied structure. It shows good intensity, and a walnut note kicks in on the finish. Drink now.–B.S. • $11 • (12/15/1998) • **89**

Oloroso Jerez Viejo NV: Great aromas, like the sea air on the isle of Skye, with salt tang, peat and a wet earth note. Dry and finely etched on the palate, forceful and intensely flavored, this has balance and personality in spades. Drink now.–B.S. • $110 • (10/31/1999) • **92**

Palo Cortado Jerez Viejo NV: A streak of iodine runs through this lean, bracing Sherry. Molasses and a walnutlike finish add complexity, and it's concentrated. Excellent depth to the aftertaste. Drink now.–B.S. • $130 • (10/31/1999) • **90**

IBERNOBLE

Ribera del Duero 1997: This rustic red offers plum flavor, but it tastes muddy and stewed, and there's a strong barnyard aroma (brett?) that persists through the finish.–T.M. • $14 • (10/31/1999) • **76**

Ribera del Duero 1996 • $14 • (10/31/1997) • **82**

Ribera del Duero Crianza 1996: Bright and spicy, this vivid red offers berry, cherry and cassis flavors, with accents of licorice and spice. The tannins are firm yet stay in the background. The wine seems a bit unsettled now, yet it has all the right elements. Drink now through 2003.–T.M. • $25 • (11/30/1999) • **87**

Ribera del Duero Crianza 1995: This red offers ripe flavors of blackberry and black cherry, with a lively streak of acidity. The moderate tannins are well integrated and the finish is fresh and fruity. 2,500 cases imported. Drink now through 2004.–T.M. • $24 • (10/31/1998) • **88**

Ribera del Duero Crianza 1994 • $22 • (10/31/1997) • **88**

Ribera del Duero Crianza 1992 • $15 • (4/30/1996) • **78**

Ribera del Duero Crianza 1989 • $15 • (4/30/1995) • **87**

Ribera del Duero Reserva 1994: There's sweet coffee and chocolate oak framing in this maturing red, but the fruit, though bright and laced with cherry, doesn't quite fill out the tannic frame. A bit rustic and simple. Drink now through 2003.–T.M. • $45 • (11/30/1999) • **86**

Ribera del Duero Reserva 1992: Cherry and herb flavors are thick but a bit muddied in this blunt red. Quite concentrated but lacking in definition, this is a rustic style that needs food for balance. 2,500 cases imported. Drink now.–T.M. • $38 • (10/31/1998) • **84**

Ribera del Duero Reserva 1991 • $38 • (10/31/1997) • **92**

Ribera del Duero Reserva 1986 • $27 • (4/30/1995) • **87**

IJALBA, VINA

Rioja Ijalba Reserva 1990 • $16 • (10/15/1996) • **88**

Rioja Livor 1994 • $10 • (10/15/1996) • **77**

Rioja Múrice Crianza 1992 • $13 • (10/15/1996) • **79**

INVIOSA, BODEGAS

Tierra de Barros Lar de Barros Gran Reserva 1994: This ripe, clean red has a core of attractive black cherry flavor, but firm tannins dominate the palate. Needs food to come into balance. Drink now.–T.M. • $17 • (11/30/1998) • **80**

Tierra de Barros Lar de Barros Reserva 1996: Sweet cherry and berry flavors are backed by firm tannins in this light-bodied red. The sweet fruit flavors are fresh and clean, and it has enough grip for food. Drink now.–T.M. • $9 • (10/31/1998) • **83**

Tierra de Barros Lar de Barros Reserva 1994 • $10 • (6/30/1997) • **85**

Tierra de Barros Lar de Barros Reserva 1992 • $10 • (8/31/1996) • **83**

Tierra de Barros Lar de Barros Reserva 1991 • $9 • (4/30/1995) • **79**

Tierra de Barros Lar de Barros Reserva 1990 • $10 • (12/15/1994) • **82**

Tierra de Barros Lar de Barros Reserva 1989 • $9 • (12/15/1993) • **86**

Tierra de Barros Lar de Barros Reserva 1988 • $10 • (4/15/1992) • **79**

IRUN, MARQUES DE

Rueda Superior 1996: Toast and hazelnut flavors suggest oak aging, but there's not much fruit in this white, though it is clean and balanced. A modest accompaniment to lighter dishes. Drink now.–T.M. • $8 • (11/30/1998) • **82**

Tempranillo Viño de la Tierra 1996: This round, soft red shows ripe plum, raisin and light earth flavors, with just enough tannin for grip. A hint of sweet vanilla lingers on the finish. Drink now.–T.M. • $7 • (10/31/1998) • **83**

Tempranillo Viño de Mesa de Castilla y Leon 1998: Overly earthy and barnyardy flavors mar this thin, bitter red. Tasted twice, with consistent notes.–T.M. • $7 • (12/15/1999) • **67**

Verdejo Rueda 1998: An austere white of fairly neutral flavors, with a hint of earthiness. Tasted twice, with consistent notes. Drink now.–T.M. • $8 • (12/15/1999) • **78**

LABASTIDA, UNION DE COSECHEROS DE

Rioja Manuel Quintano Reserva 1994: This ripe red offers plenty of coffee and toasty flavors from oak, with a core of ripe fruit backed by polished tannins. An austere wine made in the modern style. Drink now through 2004.–T.M. • $NA • (1/01/2000) • **85**

Rioja Montebuena 1996 • $7 • (11/15/1997) • **83**

Rioja Solagüen Crianza 1994 • $10 • (11/15/1997) • **83**

Rioja Solagüen Crianza 1990 • $9 • (6/30/1997) • **87**

Rioja Solagüen Gran Reserva 1985: This chewy red offers raisin, coffee and light earth flavors. Thick on the palate, with firm, slightly dry tannins. Spice notes emerge on the finish, but the structure is outlasting the fruit. Drink now.–T.M. • $27 • (11/30/1998) • **84**

Rioja Solagüen Reserva 1989 • $10 • (6/30/1997) • **86**

Rioja Solagüen Reserva 1985 • $10 • (4/15/1994) • **85**

Rioja White Montebuena 1996 • $7 • (10/31/1997) • **82**

LAN, BODEGAS

Rioja Crianza 1995: Shows traditional Rioja flavors of dried cherry, vanilla and tea, with raisin and light earth notes and soft tannins. Finishes dry and earthy.–T.M. • $11 • (11/30/1998) • **79**

Rioja Crianza 1994 • $9 • (5/31/1998) • **84**

Rioja Gran Reserva 1991: Firm and still very fresh, this well-structured red has ripe plum and blackberry flavors backed by ripe, full tannins and plenty of crisp acidity. Clean, balanced and intense, it should improve with cellaring. Try through 2008.–T.M. • $21 • (11/30/1998) • **89**

Rioja Gran Reserva 1987 • $15 • (5/31/1998) • **85**

Rioja Lancorta Crianza 1989 • $9 • (1/31/1995) • **84**

Rioja Reserva 1994: Cola, raisin and spice flavors are ripe and distinctive in this fleshy red, and firm tannins give way to a fresh, fruity finish. Oaky notes are dominant, but there is a core of ripe fruit. Drink now through 2003.–T.M. • $15 • (10/31/1998) • **86**

Rioja Reserva 1988 • $12 • (5/31/1998) • **87**

Rioja Viña Lanciano Reserva 1994: Plum, blackberry, vanilla and nutmeg flavors are rich and ripe in this fleshy yet firm red. The tannins are big but well integrated, and the finish is clean and long. A balanced, expressive wine that's accessible now through 2010.–T.M. • $22 • (10/31/1998) • **89**

Rioja Viña Lanciano Reserva 1991 • $17 • (5/31/1998) • **85**

LAR DE LARES

Tierra de Barros Gran Reserva 1989 • $16 • (4/30/1996) • **78**

Tierra de Barros Gran Reserva 1982 • $14 • (6/15/1991) HR • **90**

LASANTA, HERENCIA

Rioja Crianza 1995: Smoke and berry aromas give way to smooth flavors of cherry, tobacco and vanilla in this soft, harmonious red. Though no powerhouse, it has enough structure for food and enough complexity to hold your interest. Drink now through 2004.–T.M. • $12 • (11/30/1998) • **87**

Rioja Reserva 1994: This well-structured red is firm and full on the palate, and the black cherry and cola flavors have the depth to stand up to muscular tannins. A bit hollow now, but should fill in with time. Drink through 2004.–T.M. • $15 • (10/31/1998) • **86**

Tempranillo Rioja Crianza 1996: Raisin and cedar flavors show maturity in this smooth red. Has sweetness from oak yet enough acidity to keep it lively. Its balance makes it a good companion for dinner. Drink now through 2001.–T.M. • $14 • (11/30/1999) • **85**

LEON, JEAN

Cabernet Sauvignon Penedès 1988 • $26 • (3/31/1996) • **85**

Cabernet Sauvignon Penedès 1987 • $15 • (4/15/1994) • **84**

Cabernet Sauvignon Penedès 1984 • $12 • (3/31/1991) • **77**

Cabernet Sauvignon Penedès Reserva 1991: This full-bodied red shows a dark color and muscular tannins, but the impressive structure leaves little room for the core of blackberry, licorice and herb flavors. Best after 2000.–T.M. • $25 • (11/30/1998) • **85**

Cabernet Sauvignon Penedès Reserva 1990 • $24 • (10/31/1997) • **86**

Cabernet Sauvignon Penedès Reserva 1982 • $31 • (3/31/1996) • **84**

Cabernet Sauvignon Penedès Reserva 1979 • $34 • (3/31/1996) • **85**

LEY, BARON DE

Rioja Reserva 1995: Vivid blackberry and blueberry flavors are atypical but appealing in this bold red, with its sweet vanilla oaky flavors and full tannins. An international style that lacks polish and finesse. Best from 2001 through 2005.–T.M. • $NA • (1/01/1999) • **86**

Rioja Reserva 1994: Ripe, sweet flavors of raisin and chocolate are rich, if a bit clumsy, in this fleshy red. Hard tannins turn slightly metallic on the finish. There's concentration here, but not much harmony. Drink through 2003.–T.M. • $16 • (10/31/1998) • **83**

Rioja Reserva 1986 • $10 • (4/15/1994) • **84**

Rioja White 1998: Austere and refreshing. This crisp white offers muted flavors of grapefruit, herbs and bitter almond, with a vivid streak of acidity that will clean the palate after food. Drink now.–T.M. • $8 • (10/31/1999) • **84**

Rioja White 1997: This crisp, well-balanced Spanish white has good weight on the palate and delivers round flavors of pear and almond. It's a bit austere in style, but with the body and freshness to complement food, it's an affordable match for party fare. Drink now.–T.M. • $8 • (11/30/1998) • **85**

LEZCANO, BODEGAS Y VINEDOS

Cigales Rosado Docetañidos 1997: The deep color and noticeable tannins make this bizarre rosé nearly a red; it has murky, earthy flavors and a rustic, grainy finish.–T.M. • $9 • (10/15/1999) • **77**

Cigales Rosado Docetañidos 1996: Deep color and ripe flavors of cherry and plum mark this round, slightly heavy-handed rosé. Enough grip for food.–T.M. • $10 • (11/30/1998) • **79**

LLANOS, BODEGAS LOS

Valdepeñas Pata Negra Gran Reserva 1991: Chocolate and coffee aromas give way to a polished wine, with moderate structure and flavors of plum, raisin and chocolate. Mature, but will still match well with lighter dishes. Tempranillo and Garnacha. Drink now.–T.M. • $9 • (11/30/1998) • **83**

Valdepeñas Señorio de los Llanos Crianza 1997: Earthy and vegetal notes dominate the light cherry flavors in this traditional red. Firm, turning a bit dry on the finish.–T.M. • $7 • (6/15/2000) • **78**

Valdepeñas Señorio de los Llanos Crianza 1996: This supple red shows light cherry flavors, with enough spicy accents to give kick. Balanced and clean. Drink now.–T.M. • $6 • (12/15/1999) • **83**

Valdepeñas Señorio de los Llanos Gran Reserva 1994: Drying now, this mature red offers dried cherry, earth and cedar flavors. It's got body, but little finesse. Past its prime.–T.M. • $8 • (1/31/2000) • **79**

Valdepeñas Señorio de los Llanos Gran Reserva 1990: Herbal and earthy flavors mingle with some dried cherry and raisin flavor, but the tannins shut down the finish. Past its prime.–T.M. • $8 • (11/30/1998) • **76**

Valdepeñas Señorio de los Llanos Gran Reserva 1984 • $13 • (1/31/1993) • **85**

Valdepeñas Señorio de los Llanos Reserva 1996: Round and supple, this red offers straightforward cherry and spice notes, with a fruity sweetness that's simple but appealing. Drink now.–T.M. • $8 • (6/15/2000) • **81**

Valdepeñas Señorio de los Llanos Reserva 1993: This maturing red offers aromas of tea and spice, with raisin, tea and cedar flavors. The light tannins are beginning to dry out, but for now the wine is balanced and fairly fresh. Drink now.–T.M. • $6 • (11/30/1998) • **82**

LOPEZ, BODEGAS PENALBA

Brut Nature Cava NV: An exaggerated style, with oxidized, Sherry-like flavors and some buttery notes.–K.M. • $12 • (12/15/1999) • **75**

Ribera del Duero Torre Albéniz Reserva 1995: This ripe red shows good concentration, with full-bodied flavors of plum, raisin, coffee and tobacco. The tannins are muscular but still harmonious, and the finish is long and spicy. Solid, not subtle. Drink now through 2003.–T.M. • $23 • (10/31/1999) • **85**

Ribera del Duero Torre Albéniz Reserva 1992: This balanced, well-structured red is still fresh and young, with black cherry, chocolate and tobacco flavors. The tannins are firm yet well integrated, and the finish is fresh and clean. Drink now through 2005.–T.M. • $22 • (11/30/1998) • **88**

Ribera del Duero Torremilanos Crianza 1996: This rustic red shows old-fashioned earth and barnyard flavors that dominate the underlying plum and berry, but it has a solid chunkiness that could work with food. Drink now through 2004.–T.M. • $16 • (10/31/1999) • **82**

Ribera del Duero Torremilanos Crianza 1995: Plum, cherry, vanilla and toast flavors mingle in this firm yet approachable red. Has good balance and density, though showing more oak than fruit, with a clean finish that brings you back for another sip. Drink through 2008.–T.M. • $13 • (11/30/1998) • **88**

Ribera del Duero Torremilanos Gran Reserva 1990: This lush red offers an alluring marriage of ripe blackberry and toasty oak with ripe, round tannins. Balanced and deep, though not at all heavy, this drinking beautifully now and should continue to improve. Drink now through 2004.–T.M. • $20 • (11/30/1998) • **90**

Ribera del Duero Torremilanos Gran Reserva 1989: Maturing now, this chunky red shows ripe flavors of dried cherry, plum and raisin, with cedar and tobacco notes and thick, firm tannins. Shows good concentration and can stand up to the richest foods. Drink now through 2008.–T.M. • $28 • (11/30/1998) • **89**

Ribera del Duero Torremilanos Reserva 1994: Supple and fruity, this bright red offers sweet cherry and vanilla flavors, pleasant on the palate, turning a bit candied on the finish. Drink now.–T.M. • $24 • (10/31/1999) • **81**

Ribera del Duero Torremilanos Reserva 1991: Gorgeous oak flavors of vanilla, toast and chocolate give this red an immediate appeal, and the solid core of black cherry and plum adds depth and balance. Ripe and polished on the palate, with a sweet vanilla finish. Drink now through 2003.–T.M. • $20 • (11/30/1998) • **90**

Key: SS—Spectator Selection. CS—Cellar Selection. HR—Highly Recommended. $NA—Price not available. (BT)—Barrel tasting. Ⓐ—Auction Price. For a key to the tasters' initials, see "How to Use These Listings." **Dates in parentheses represent the issues in which the ratings were published.**

LOPEZ DE HEREDIA VINA TONDONIA, R.

Rioja Bosconia Full Red 1993: This pale, supple red offers light flavors of cherry and cedar, with tart acidity and a drying finish. A light wine from a weak vintage.–T.M. • $18 • (12/15/1999) • **76**

Rioja Bosconia Full Red 1992: This mature red offers traditional Rioja flavors of dried cherry, tea and leather. A spicy elegance is undermined by the dry finish. Best with food. Drink now.–T.M. • $15 • (11/30/1998) • **82**

Rioja Bosconia Full Red 1987 • $NA • (4/30/1995) • **83**

Rioja Viña Bosconia Crianza 1990 • $15 • (12/15/1997) • **83**

Rioja Viña Bosconia Gran Reserva 1976 • $14 • (3/31/1990) • **72**

Rioja Viña Bosconia Gran Reserva 1973 • $15 • (12/31/1987) • **75**

Rioja Viña Bosconia Gran Reserva 1973 • $14 • (3/31/1990) • **80**

Rioja Viña Bosconia Reserva 1986 • $13 • (3/31/1992) • **79**

Rioja Viña Bosconia Reserva 1983 • $13 • (3/31/1992) • **78**

Rioja Viña Cubillo 1995: Cherry, cedar and earth flavors mark this straightforward red. Well balanced but a bit rustic in character, it's better with hearty food. Drink now through 2002.–T.M. • $14 • (11/30/1999) • **82**

Rioja Viña Cubillo 1994: Strawberry, vanilla and light herb flavors mark this traditional-style red. It's light on the palate, but has astringent tannins. Drink now.–T.M. • $10 • (11/30/1998) • **80**

Rioja Viña Cubillo 1993 • $10 • (11/15/1997) • **79**

Rioja Viña Cubillo Crianza 1992 • $10 • (12/15/1997) • **80**

Rioja Viña Tondonia Gran Reserva 1981 • $NA • (3/31/1992) • **79**

Rioja Viña Tondonia Gran Reserva 1978 • $35 • (10/15/1997) • **85**

Rioja Viña Tondonia Gran Reserva 1976 • $37 • (4/30/1995) • **82**

Rioja Viña Tondonia Gran Reserva 1973 • $44 • (3/31/1992) • **87**

Rioja Viña Tondonia Gran Reserva 1970 • $44 • (3/31/1992) • **75**

Rioja Viña Tondonia Reserva 1993: This supple red offers traditional flavors of dried cherry, spice and leather. Lively acidity supplies the structure. Light, but shows elegance. Drink now.–T.M. • $29 • (6/15/2000) • **85**

Rioja Viña Tondonia Reserva 1992: Dried cherry, cola, cedar and spice flavors are clean but subdued in this modest red. Has just enough tannin for grip. Drink now.–T.M. • $22 • (12/15/1999) • **81**

Rioja Viña Tondonia Reserva 1991: Coffee and leather notes mingle with light raisin and dried cherry flavors in this maturing red. Light on the palate, with dry tannins that dominate the finish. Drink now.–T.M. • $18 • (11/30/1998) • **80**

Rioja Viña Tondonia Reserva 1990 • $17 • (11/15/1997) • **85**

Rioja Viña Tondonia Reserva 1989 • $17 • (10/15/1997) • **86**

Rioja Viña Tondonia Reserva 1987 • $10 • (4/15/1994) • **77**

Rioja Viña Tondonia Reserva 1985 • $13 • (3/31/1992) • **86**

LOZANO, JUAN RAMON

La Mancha Oristan Gran Reserva 1992: Still fruity, this gentle red shows floral and berry flavors, with just enough tannin for grip. Drink now.–T.M. • $13 • (6/15/2000) • **81**

La Mancha Oristan Reserva 1995: This soft red shows light cherry, herb and cedar notes. Generous, but turns a bit metallic on the finish.–T.M. • $10 • (6/15/2000) • **78**

LUBERRI, BODEGAS

Rioja Alavesa 1998: Roasted coffee and dark chocolate flavors have appeal in this brooding red, but a bitter, gamy note and light spritz detract from the pleasure.–T.M. • $9 • (11/30/1999) • **78**

Rioja Alavesa 1996 • $7 • (5/31/1998) • **83**

Rioja Altún Crianza 1996: This fleshy red is rich with coffee, plum and prune flavors that might turn flabby, except the firm tannins and lively acidity bring it into balance. An exaggerated style, but full of pleasure. Drink now through 2003.–T.M. • $16 • (11/30/1999) • **89**

LURTON, J. & F.

Rueda Hermanos Lurton 1998: Soft in texture yet vivid in flavor, this distinctive white offers floral, almond and citrus notes, with a generous mouthfeel and good balance. Drink now.–T.M. • $6 • (4/30/2000) • **84**

Tempranillo Viño de Mesa de Castilla y Leon Hermanos Lurton 1995 • $6 • (11/15/1997) • **80**

Tempranillo Viño de Mesa de Castilla y Leon Hermanos Lurton Crianza 1994 • $9 • (11/15/1997) • **83**

Tempranillo Viño de Mesa Hermanos Lurton 1998: Firm and fresh, this fruity red offers a nice burst of cherry and licorice flavors, unencumbered by wood and more refreshing for that. Drink now.–T.M. • $6 • (4/30/2000) • **82**

SPAIN

Viño de Mesa de Valladolid Rosado Hermanos Lurton 1996 • $6 • (10/31/1997) • **82**

LUSCO DO MINO

Albariño Rias Baixas Lusco 1998: This distinctive white adds floral and light banana notes to the citrus and herb flavors typical of the variety. Delicate yet still firm. Drink now.–T.M. • $22 • (11/15/1999) • **86**

Albariño Rias Baixas Lusco 1997: This big white is full-bodied yet crisp, with lemon and grapefruit flavors given roundness and depth by notes of pear, vanilla and herb. Bold but balanced, it's refreshing yet rich enough for food. Drink now.–T.M. • $20 • (11/30/1998) • **87**

Albariño Rias Baixas Lusco 1996 • $20 • (9/15/1997) • **85**

LUSTAU, EMILIO

Amontillado Jerez Almacenista del Puerto J.L. Gonzalez Obregon NV • $21 • (7/31/1994) • **86**

Amontillado Jerez Amacenista Fino Alberto Lorente Piaget NV • $20 • (7/31/1994) • **87**

Amontillado Jerez Bodega Vieja 100 Años NV: Offers butterscotch and treacle aromas before unfolding on the palate with rich flavors of bitter chocolate, grilled almond and eventually walnut. Very harmonious and balanced, with a dry finish. Drink now.–B.S. • $40 • (12/15/1998) • **90**

Amontillado Jerez Don Rafael Solera Gran Reserva NV: Assertive, with an oxidative character underlying the chocolate, marmite, walnut and smoke flavors. Full-bodied and quite dry, it finishes with a strong walnut note that may not appeal to everyone. Drink now.–B.S. • $20 • (12/15/1998) • **91**

Amontillado Jerez Escuadrilla Solera Reserva NV • $10 • (7/31/1994) • **85**

Amontillado Jerez Los Arcos Solera Reserva NV • $10 • (7/31/1994) • **89**

Amontillado Jerez Single Cask El Carro NV: Smooth and easygoing, with caramel and crême brûlée notes that transform to walnuts and molasses on the finish. On the dry side, with an astringent texture, this lacks the dimension of the best, but is concentrated and tasty nonetheless. Drink now.–B.S. • $35 • (12/15/1998) • **88**

Cream Jerez Capataz Andres Solera Reserva NV • $10 • (4/15/1994) • **79**

Cream Jerez Superior Solera Reserva NV • $10 • (4/15/1994) • **83**

Fino Jerez Almacenista Fino del Puerto J. L. Gonzalez Obregon NV • $13 • (7/31/1994) • **86**

Fino Jerez Jarana Solera Reserva NV: Warm cardamom and nutmeg accents add complexity to the grilled almond and apple flavors. The richness and intensity are underscored by crispness, and the flavors keep pumping through the long, tangy finish. Drink now.–B.S. • $11 • (12/15/1998) • **90**

Manzanilla Jerez Almacenista Amontillada Manuel Cuevos Jurado NV • $21 • (7/31/1994) • **86**

Manzanilla Jerez Almacenista Pasada Manuel Cuevos Jurado NV • $20 • (7/31/1994) • **87**

Manzanilla Jerez Papirusa Solera Reserva NV • $10 • (7/31/1994) • **83**

Moscatel Jerez Emilin Solera Resrva NV • $13 • (7/31/1994) • **86**

Oloroso Jerez Almacenista Pata de Gallina Juan Garcia NV • $22 • (7/31/1994) • **87**

Oloroso Jerez del Tonel 100 Años NV: Definitely sweet, this full-bodied, dessert-style Sherry displays raisin, caramel and honey notes, with enough acidity and astringency on the finish for balance. Not a lot of complexity, but very appealing. Drink now.–B.S. • $40 • (12/15/1998) • **87**

Oloroso Jerez Don Nuño Solera Reserva NV • $13 • (7/31/1994) • **82**

Oloroso Jerez Dry Single Cask NV • $37 • (6/30/1997) • **88**

Oloroso Jerez East India Solera NV • $15 • (7/31/1994) • **80**

Oloroso Jerez Emperatriz Eugenia Rare Solera NV • $22 • (7/31/1994) • **78**

Oloroso Jerez Single Cask Almacenista Maria Luisa Coveñas NV: Very distinctive aromas of herb, dough and malting barley combine with moderate sweetness. Medium-bodied and somewhat one-dimensional, with a coarse finish. Drink now.–B.S. • $35 • (12/15/1998) • **84**

Oloroso Jerez Single Cask Almacenista Pilar Aranda NV: Moderately sweet, showing good concentration and persistence of caramel, chocolate and nut flavors, yet it's a bit spirity, pulling the whole slightly out of balance. Good length. Drink now.–B.S. • $35 • (10/31/1999) • **87**

Palo Cortado Jerez Almacenista Vides NV: Caramel, tobacco and nut aromas and flavors pervade this rich, tangy Sherry. Moderately sweet and medium-bodied, with a bracing finish. Drink now.–B.S. • $35 • (12/15/1998) • **88**

Palo Cortado Jerez Bodega Capataz NV: There's verve and cut here from acidity, along with ample body and an exotic character that exhibits orange peel, vanilla, caramel and walnut. On the dry side, the finish goes on and on. Drink now.–B.S. • $37 • (12/15/1998) • **90**

Palo Cortado Jerez Peninsula Solera Reserva NV • $13 • (7/31/1994) • **80**

Pedro Ximénez Jerez Murillo 100 Años NV: If you're looking for a wine that envelops your palate with sweet, concentrated, dried Muscat and fruitcake flavors, this is for you. Full, ultrarich and smooth, it's almost too much, but the acidity saves the day on the finish. Very long aftertaste. Drink now.–B.S. • $40 • (12/15/1998) • **90**

Pedro Ximenez Jerez San Emilio Solera Reserva NV • $13 • (7/31/1994) • **84**

San Bartolome Jerez Dry Solera Gran Reserva NV • $18 • (6/30/1997) • **87**

LUZON, FINCA

Jumilla 1998: Meaty and gamy flavors are dark and strong in this red. Its velvety texture has a very firm tannic underpinning, turning a bit dry and bitter on the finish. Drink now through 2001.–T.M. • $9 • (11/15/1999) • **82**

MAGANA, BODEGAS

Merlot Navarra Viña Magaña Reserva 1989 • $14 • (4/30/1995) • **77**

Merlot Navarra Viña Magaña Reserva 1985 • $35 • (4/15/1994) • **78**

Navarra Dingus Finca Paso de la Reina 1994: Herbal, musty flavors and a very dry, paint-varnishlike finish. Not recommended. Tasted twice, with consistent notes.–T.M. • $10 • (11/30/1998) • **57**

Navarra Eventum Finca Paso de la Reina Crianza 1991 • $10 • (9/15/1996) • **78**

Navarra Eventum Finca Paso de la Reina Crianza 1990 • $9 • (4/30/1995) • **88**

Navarra Viña Magaña Gran Reserva 1982 • $30 • (4/15/1994) • **74**

Navarra Viña Magaña Reserva 1990: Maturing, deeply colored and quite firm in texture, offering cedar, spice, cherry and raisin flavors; balanced and clean. Spice notes linger on the finish. Drink now.–T.M. • $23 • (11/15/1999) • **85**

MAHLER-BESSE

Jumilla Roquero 1998: Soft and spicy, this straightforward red offers focused cherry and tobacco flavors, ripe and accessible. Monastrell. Debut Spanish wines from this Bordeaux négociant. Drink now.–T.M. • $9 • (4/30/2000) • **82**

Jumilla Roquero Reserva 1994: Flavors of tobacco and bitter herbs are a bit harsh in this tannic red, but there are cherry notes. Might soften with gutsy food. Monastrell.–T.M. • $12 • (4/30/2000) • **77**

MALUMBRES, BODEGAS VICENTE

Navarra Crianza 1996: Well knit, offering ripe cherry and light spicy flavors; supple, with firm tannins and lively acidity for balance. Will match well with food. Drink now through 2002.–T.M. • $12 • (11/15/1999) • **85**

Navarra Special Blend Crianza 1996: Ripe plum, chocolate and sweet vanilla flavors are lush, but supported by firm tannins in this concentrated red. A bit clumsy, but solid and likable. Drink now through 2002.–T.M. • $15 • (11/15/1999) • **86**

MARINO, A. Y B.

Navarra Crianza 1996: Dark and rich, this smooth red shows plenty of vanilla flavors from oak, with ripe plum and raisin notes, a nice velvety texture and a clean, slightly bitter finish. Drink now through 2002.–T.M. • $15 • (11/15/1999) • **86**

Navarra Crianza 1995: Smooth, velvety texture marries ripe flavors of plum, black cherry, toast and vanilla. Firm yet not heavy on the palate, with juicy acidity. A blend of Cabernet Sauvignon and Merlot. Drink now through 2002.–T.M. • $15 • (11/15/1999) • **87**

Navarra Palacio de Muruzabal Reserva 1992 • $26 • (11/15/1997) • **78**

MARQUESA, BODEGAS DE LA

Rioja Valserrano Crianza 1995: A nice marriage of concentration and grace, this red is ripe, firm and fresh, offering flavors of ripe black cherry and plum, with well-integrated notes of smoke and coffee. Polished, balanced and should age well. Drink through 2005.–T.M. • $13 • (11/30/1998) • **88**

MARTINEZ BUJANDA, BODEGAS

Garnacha Rioja Reserva 1991: Alluring aromas of dried fruit and spice follow through on the palate in this very traditional Rioja. Light raisin and vanilla flavors add sweetness to the silky palate. For fans of the old style. Drink now.–T.M. • $25 • (11/30/1998) • **84**

Rioja Conde de Valdemar 1989 • $9 • (12/15/1993) • **81**

■ ■ ■ ■

MARTINEZ BUJANDA, BODEGAS

Rioja Conde de Valdemar Crianza 1996: Rich, yet firm and well-integrated, this red from Spain offers concentrated plummy, woody and spicy flavors that fill the mouth and linger on the finish; a lot of wine for so moderate a price. A great match with roasted meats. Drink now through 2003.–T.M. • $10 • (11/30/1999) • **88**
Rioja Conde de Valdemar Crianza 1995: Toasty oak character has grip and weight in this firm red, more so than the black cherry flavors. Still, the wine has life and depth, with notes of smoke and herb that linger on the finish. Drink now through 2004.–T.M. • $9 • (11/30/1998) • **84**
Rioja Conde de Valdemar Crianza 1994 • $9 • (11/15/1997) • **82**
Rioja Conde de Valdemar Crianza 1993 • $9 • (10/15/1996) • **84**
Rioja Conde de Valdemar Crianza 1992 • $10 • (1/31/1996) • **82**
Rioja Conde de Valdemar Crianza 1991 • $9 • (4/30/1995) • **85**
Rioja Conde de Valdemar Crianza 1990 • $9 • (3/31/1994) • **87**
Rioja Conde de Valdemar Crianza 1988 • $9 • (3/31/1993) • **85**
Rioja Conde de Valdemar Gran Reserva 1992: Supple and straightforward. Flavors of cherry and vanilla are clean and simple in this maturing red. It's well balanced and modest in character, but why produce a gran reserva from a weak vintage? Drink now.–T.M. • $25 • (12/15/1999) • **80**
Rioja Conde de Valdemar Gran Reserva 1991: Elegant and delicate, this silky red offers traditional flavors of dried berry, cedar and vanilla. Light-bodied, yet with good intensity over light but rather dry tannins. The long, spicy finish is delightful. Drink now through 2002.–T.M. • $20 • (11/30/1998) • **87**
Rioja Conde de Valdemar Gran Reserva 1990 • $21 • (11/15/1997) • **87**
Rioja Conde de Valdemar Gran Reserva 1989 • $20 • (3/31/1996) • **89**
Rioja Conde de Valdemar Gran Reserva 1987 • $20 • (1/31/1996) • **83**
Rioja Conde de Valdemar Gran Reserva 1985 • $21 • (4/15/1994) HR • **90**
Rioja Conde de Valdemar Gran Reserva 1982 • $22 • (11/30/1991) • **89**
Rioja Conde de Valdemar Gran Reserva 1981 • $24 • (3/31/1992) • **89**
Rioja Conde de Valdemar Gran Reserva 1975 • $NA • (3/31/1992) • **87**
Rioja Conde de Valdemar Gran Reserva 1973 • $30 • (3/31/1992) • **86**
Rioja Conde de Valdemar Gran Reserva 1970 • $NA • (3/31/1992) • **89**
Rioja Conde de Valdemar Reserva 1994: Raisin and cooked plum flavors are a bit overripe in this jammy red, with sweet vanilla flavors that hint at cough syrup. Ambitious but clumsy. Drink now through 2003.–T.M. • $15 • (11/30/1999) • **81**
Rioja Conde de Valdemar Reserva 1993: Unusually plump and chewy for Rioja, this rustic red is packed with ripe flavors of blackberry and plum, with vanilla and toast accents and a thick texture backed by firm tannins. A good match with grilled meats. Drink now through 2005.–T.M. • $12 • (11/30/1998) • **86**
Rioja Conde de Valdemar Reserva 1992 • $14 • (11/15/1997) • **80**
Rioja Conde de Valdemar Reserva 1991 • $12 • (3/31/1996) • **84**
Rioja Conde de Valdemar Reserva 1990 • $12 • (4/30/1995) • **89**
Rioja Conde de Valdemar Reserva 1987 • $12 • (12/15/1993) • **84**
Rioja Conde de Valdemar Reserva 1986 • $10 • (3/31/1992) • **83**
Rioja Conde de Valdemar Reserva 1983 • $14 • (3/31/1992) • **88**
Rioja Conde de Valdemar Reserva 1982 • $NA • (3/31/1992) • **89**
Rioja Crianza 1990 • $9 • (4/15/1994) • **87**
Rioja Crianza 1989 • $9 • (4/15/1994) • **85**
Rioja Finca Valpiedra Reserva 1995: This assertive red marries firm, slightly angular tannins, very crisp acidity and strong flavors of coffee, plum, licorice and toast. A bit unsettled now, it should come together with time. Best from 2002 through 2007.–T.M. • $28 • (11/30/1999) • **87**
Rioja Finca Valpiedra Reserva 1994: This dark-colored red offers ripe, sweet flavors of blackberry, plum, cola and vanilla, with a fleshy texture and firm yet well-integrated tannins. Though not typical in profile, it's delicious. Drink now through 2004.–T.M. • $23 • (10/31/1998) • **88**
Rioja Garnacha Reserva 1990 • $25 • (3/31/1996) • **82**
Rioja Garnacha Reserva 1989 • $22 • (4/30/1995) • **86**
Rioja Gran Reserva 1990: This silky red follows the traditional style, with high-toned flavors of cherry, tea, vanilla and spice, and light tannins that turn a bit dry on the finish. Harmonious but a bit lean. Drink now.–T.M. • $26 • (11/30/1998) • **84**
Rioja Gran Reserva 1985 • $21 • (4/15/1994) • **90**
Rioja Reserva 1990 • $26 • (3/31/1996) • **87**
Rioja Reserva 1989 • $12 • (4/15/1994) • **88**
Rioja Reserva 1987 • $12 • (4/15/1994) • **79**
Rioja Reserva Especial 1989 • $25 • (4/30/1995) • **87**

Key: SS—Spectator Selection. CS—Cellar Selection. HR—Highly Recommended. $NA—Price not available. (BT)—Barrel tasting. (A)—Auction Price.
For a key to the tasters' initials, see "How to Use These Listings."
Dates in parentheses represent the issues in which the ratings were published.

Rioja Rosado Valdemar 1998: Clean and spicy, this juicy rosé has more subtlety than most, with floral and cinnamon notes that linger on the finish. It's crisp and dry. Drink now.–T.M. • $8 • (10/31/1999) • **84**
Rioja Rosado 1997: Fresh and clean, this sinuous rosé has notes of smoke and herb that wind through the delicate cherry and berry flavors. Drink now.–T.M. • $9 • (10/31/1998) • **84**
Rioja Rosado Conde de Valdemar 1996 • $8 • (9/15/1997) • **85**
Rioja Valdemar 1998: This juicy red offers bright plum and grape flavors. Simple but clean, with light tannins for grip. Try it slightly chilled. Drink now.–T.M. • $9 • (11/30/1999) • **83**
Rioja Valdemar 1997: Earthy and gamy aromas give way to dark flavors of toast and herb in this round, slightly bitter red. Tender, but lacks fruit.–T.M. • $6 • (11/30/1998) • **79**
Rioja Valdemar 1991 • $7 • (3/31/1993) • **83**
Rioja Valdemar 1989 • $7 • (6/30/1990) • **83**
Rioja White Valdemar 1997: This round, crisp white is made in the modern style, with bright flavors of apple and peach and snappy acidity. Simple yet clean and refreshing. Drink now.–T.M. • $6 • (11/30/1998) • **83**

MAS IGNEUS

Priorat Barranc del Closos 1997: Juicy, grapey flavors gain interest from smoky, herbal and gamy notes in this round red. The tannins are soft, but the finish is slightly hot and dry. Try with grilled meats. Much better than the spritzy, bitter samples of last year. Drink now through 2003.–T.M. • $12 • (9/15/1999) • **84**
Priorat 1997: This ripe, crisp red offers juicy raspberry flavors accented by attractive notes of smoke and game. It's lighter than the best new Priorats, but has plenty of personality. Drink now through 2003.–T.M. • $35 • (9/15/1999) • **85**

MAS MARTINET VITICULTORS

Priorat Clos Martinet 1995: Pretty berry and cherry flavors give this red an immediate appeal, and coffee and tobacco accents add complexity. It lacks the power of the best Priorats, but has good balance and focus. Drink now through 2005.–T.M. • $42 • (9/15/1999) • **87**
Priorat Clos Martinet 1994 • $40 • (12/15/1997) • **88**
Priorat Martinet Bru 1995 • $17 • (6/30/1998) • **86**

MASACHS, JOSEP

Brut Blanc de Blancs Cava NV: Not much in this wine, which has canned fruit aromas and flavors. Ends on a cloying note.–K.M. • $8 • (12/15/1999) • **74**
Brut Cava Reserva NV: An oniony aroma and flavor doesn't add up to much.–K.M. • $9 • (12/15/1999) • **71**

MASIA BARRIL

Priorat 1996 • $17 • (6/30/1998) • **84**
Priorat Tipico 1991 • $16 • (12/15/1997) • **73**

MAURO, BODEGAS

Ribera del Duero 1991 • $22 • (4/30/1995) • **83**
Ribera del Duero 1990 • $22 • (4/15/1994) • **83**
Ribera del Duero 1987 • $17 • (10/15/1990) • **82**
Ribera del Duero 1986 • $17 • (3/31/1990) • **76**
Ribera del Duero 1985 • $15 • (3/31/1990) • **88**
Ribera del Duero 1984 • $16 • (3/31/1990) • **78**
Ribera del Duero 1983 • $15 • (10/15/1987) • **82**
Viño de Mesa de Castilla y Leon 1996: Dark chocolate and coffee flavors are alluring in this muscular red, and the firm structure keeps them focused. There's not much fruit, but this could match well with rich meat dishes. Drink now through 2004.–T.M. • $27 • (11/15/1999) • **85**
Viño de Mesa de Castilla y Leon 1995 • $25 • (5/15/1998) • **85**
Viño de Mesa de Castilla y Leon San Román 1997: Polish and concentration combine in this focused red. Oak, black cherry, tobacco and mineral notes are complex and harmonious and linger on the finish. Nice sophistication here. Drink now through 2005.–T.M. • $34 • (4/30/2000) • **89**
Viño de Mesa de Castilla y Leon Selección Especial 1991 • $36 • (5/15/1998) • **89**
Viño de Mesa de Castilla y Leon Terreus Pago de Cueva Baja 1996: This flashy red pushes all the buttons: deep color, strong toast and vanilla aromas from new oak, sweet velvety fruit flavors and a luscious texture, with enough acidity to keep it refreshing on the finish. It's a beautiful

wine, though it doesn't have much to do with Spain. Drink now through 2006.–T.M. • $80 • (11/15/1999) • **90**

MEDRANO, VINOS

Spain Prologo 1998: This fresh, soft red offers straightforward cherry, chocolate and bitter coffee flavors. Supple and clean. A nice quaffing wine. Drink now.–T.M. • $4 • (11/15/1999) • **83**

MEIN, VINA

Ribeiro 1996: This red is amazingly youthful in color and character, but the raw fruit and oak flavors lack harmony and balance. Hard and tart.–T.M. • $18 • (12/15/1999) • **77**

Ribeiro White 1998: This white has a lovely, racy elegance. Lime, pineapple and mineral flavors are focused and expressive, and the balance is exquisite. Mouthwatering on its own or perfect with lighter fish dishes. Drink now.–T.M. • $13 • (11/15/1999) • **88**

Ribeiro White 1997: Time in the bottle has mellowed and deepened this white but, alas, has not really improved it. Shows typical mineral and apple flavors, but has lost verve and freshness. Drink now.–T.M. • $16 • (11/15/1999) • **84**

Ribeiro White 1996: Vanilla oak and tropical fruit flavors give this white a lush appeal, while citrusy acidity keeps it clean and refreshing. An international-style wine that aims for pleasure rather than distinction. Drink now.–T.M. • $13 • (11/15/1998) • **85**

MOLI COLOMA

Brut Cava Sumarroca NV • $8 • (7/31/1996) • **83**

Brut Cava Sumarroca Reserva NV: A straightforward cava that's firm and focused, with a mineral and pencil-lead aroma and flavors of apple and green fig. Spicy notes linger on the finish. Drink now.–K.M. • $9 • (12/15/1999) • **83**

Brut Nature Cava Sumarroca NV • $9 • (7/31/1995) • **81**

Chardonnay Penedès Sumarroca 1998: This light white is crisp, showing vibrant apple and lemon flavors, but earthy and vegetal notes mar the pleasure.–T.M. • $8 • (10/31/1999) • **74**

Extra Brut Cava Sumarroca NV: Simple, with some herbal and oniony flavors that linger on the finish.–K.M. • $9 • (12/15/1999) • **77**

Merlot Penedès Sumarroca 1998: This soft, supple red offers straightforward plum,. herbal and chocolate flavors. Modest but pleasant. Drink now.–T.M. • $8 • (12/31/1999) • **82**

Muscat Penedès Sumarroca 1998: A dry Muscat in an Alsace style, light and quite crisp, with exuberant peach and honeysuckle aromas and simpler herbal flavors. Clean and fresh. Drink now.–T.M. • $8 • (12/31/1999) • **83**

Penedès Sumarroca 1997: Cedar, cherry and tobacco flavors run through this smooth red. It's balanced, if somewhat muted in style. 100 percent Tempranillo. Drink now.–T.M. • $8 • (1/01/2000) • **83**

MONASTERIO, BODEGAS

Ribera del Duero Hacienda Monasterio Crianza 1996: Two scoops of sweet, vanilla-accented oak don't cover up the lush plum and cassis flavors in this flashy, international-style red. It may lack typicity, but it's delicious. Drink now through 2003.–T.M. • $25 • (4/30/2000) • **89**

MONASTERIO DE TENTUDIA

Tierra de Barros 1992: The strawberry and cinnamon character is appealing in this light red, but it's simple and a bit dry on the palate. Drink now.–T.M. • $12 • (10/31/1998) • **81**

Tierra de Barros Reserva 1990: This straightforward red is balanced and still lively, with simple but appealing flavors of cherry, vanilla and spice that linger on the finish. Not powerful, but has the character to match with food. Drink now.–T.M. • $12 • (11/30/1998) • **84**

MONASTERIO, HACIENDA

Ribera del Duero 1995: This lush, velvety Spanish red offers a wide range of flavors, from chocolate and toast to plums, cherries and tobacco. The tannins are firm and well integrated, the concentration rich, yet the structure graceful. Should bloom with some time in the bottle. A blend of Tempranillo, Cabernet, Merlot and Malbec. The first vintage under new winemaker Peter Sisseck. Drink through 2002.–T.M. • $30 • (8/31/1998) SS • **90**

Ribera del Duero 1992 • $23 • (4/30/1996) • **88**

MONISTROL, MARQUES DE

Brut Cava Reserva 1992 • $10 • (5/15/1997) • **78**
Brut Rosé Cava NV • $10 • (5/15/1997) • **79**
Cabernet Sauvignon Penedès 1992 • $9 • (11/30/1997) • **84**
Merlot Penedès 1993 • $9 • (12/15/1997) • **83**

MONT-MARCAL

Brut Cava Reserva NV: Straightforward, with green apple and mineral flavors and some creamy notes on the finish. Drink now.–K.M. • $11 • (12/15/1999) • **82**
Cabernet Sauvignon Penedès 1989 • $9 • (12/15/1993) • **82**
Penedès 1988 • $8 • (3/31/1991) • **83**
Penedès Reserva 1989 • $10 • (10/31/1997) • **84**

MONTE VANNOS

Ribera del Duero 1994 • $11 • (4/30/1996) • **77**
Ribera del Duero 1992 • $10 • (4/15/1994) • **86**
Ribera del Duero 1991 • $10 • (12/15/1992) • **77**
Ribera del Duero Reserva 1989 • $16 • (2/28/1995) • **85**
Ribera del Duero Reserva Baños de Valdearados 1985 • $28 • (1/31/1993) • **84**

MONTEBACO

Ribera del Duero Crianza 1996: A firm texture and bright acidity give this wine a lively character. It shows crisp berry and cherry flavors and a slightly dry finish. It has local character, albeit in a minor key. Drink now.–T.M. • $19 • (10/31/1999) • **80**

MONTECILLO, BODEGAS

Rioja Gran Reserva 1985: This deeply colored red offers delectable, complex aromas of mineral, blood, tobacco and spice, but the flavors are meager and the finish is dry. Perhaps once a great wine, it has just enough left to intrigue and inspire. Serve with gentle food and patience. Drink now.–T.M. • $36 • (12/15/1999) • **86**
Rioja Gran Reserva 1978 • $30 • (3/31/1990) • **85**
Rioja Gran Reserva 1975 • $29 • (12/15/1988) • **85**
Rioja Gran Reserva 1973 • $30 • (4/30/1995) • **80**
Rioja Gran Reserva 1970 • $45 • (1/31/1996) • **87**
Rioja Primera Seleccion 1995 • $14 • (12/15/1997) • **78**

Rioja Reserva 1995: This full-throttle Spanish red is rich and dark, with chocolate, coffee and toasty oak flavors, yet has a solid layer of ripe fruit for balance, and a fine mix of firm tannins and bright acidity. The finish is long and fine. Drink now through 2009.–T.M. • $15 • (5/31/2000) SS • **90**

Rioja Reserva 1994: Bright and polished, this balanced red shows well-defined vanilla, black cherry and mint flavors, backed by ripe tannins and very fresh acidity. Harmonious and long. Drink now through 2004.–T.M. • $17 • (12/15/1999) • **88**

Rioja Reserva 1991: Chewy for a Rioja, this maturing red offers gamy and roasted fruit aromas, with ripe flavors of plum, prune and tobacco. The tannins are still firm but well integrated, and traditional notes of spice and cedar emerge on the finish. Drink now.–T.M. • $17 • (11/30/1998) • **87**
Rioja Reserva 1989 • $12 • (10/15/1997) • **86**

Rioja Viña Cumbrero Crianza 1997: Ripe and jammy. This juicy red is rich with black cherry, licorice and black pepper flavors, round and thick on the palate. Drink now through 2003.–T.M. • $10 • (5/31/2000) • **84**

Rioja Viña Cumbrero Crianza 1996: This lean Spanish red delivers good drinking at a decent price. It has good grip, a core of cherry surrounded by assertive earthy, herbal and smoky flavors, and it's a bit dry. The finish is long and clean, and the wine should go well with grilled foods. Drink now through 2003.–T.M. • $10 • (10/31/1999) • **85**

Rioja Viña Cumbrero Crianza 1995: Ripe red fruit aromas and flavors, along with characteristic notes of spice and cedar make this silky red from Spain a harmonious combination of modern and traditional style, with good availability and low price as bonuses. It's fresh, clean and long on the finish. Drink now through 2002.–T.M. • $9 • (11/30/1998) • **87**
Rioja Viña Cumbrero Crianza 1994 • $8 • (10/15/1997) • **86**
Rioja Viña Cumbrero Crianza 1993 • $9 • (12/15/1997) • **83**
Rioja Viña Cumbrero Crianza 1991 • $7 • (3/31/1996) • **84**
Rioja Viña Cumbrero Crianza 1990 • $7 • (4/30/1995) • **87**
Rioja Viña Cumbrero Crianza 1989 • $7 • (4/15/1994) • **84**
Rioja Viña Cumbrero Crianza 1988 • $NA • (3/31/1992) • **89**

MONTECILLO, BODEGAS

Rioja Viña Monty Gran Reserva 1991: Browning in color, this mature red shows tea, leather and raisin flavors, silky on the palate but a bit dry on the finish. Drink now.–T.M. • $20 • (5/31/2000) • **81**

Rioja Viña Monty Gran Reserva 1989: This light-bodied red shows mature flavors of raisin, vanilla and tea, with firm tannins and a lingering spicy finish. For fans of the traditional style. Drink now.–T.M. • $19 • (11/30/1998) • **82**

Rioja Viña Monty Gran Reserva 1987 • $16 • (10/15/1997) • **88**

Rioja Viña Monty Gran Reserva 1986 • $16 • (4/30/1995) • **73**

Rioja Viña Monty Gran Reserva 1985 • $15 • (3/31/1994) HR • **89**

Rioja Viña Monty Gran Reserva 1982 • $14 • (3/31/1992) • **87**

Rioja Viña Monty Gran Reserva 1981 • $13 • (3/31/1992) • **88**

Rioja Viña Monty Gran Reserva 1978 • $28 • (3/31/1992) • **82**

Rioja Viña Monty Gran Reserva 1975 • $28 • (3/31/1992) • **86**

Rioja Viña Monty Gran Reserva 1973 • $35 • (3/31/1992) • **85**

Rioja Viña Monty Gran Reserva 1970 • $40 • (3/31/1992) • **87**

MONTEVANNOS, BODEGAS

Ribera del Duero 1996 • $11 • (10/31/1997) • **77**

Ribera del Duero 1995 • $13 • (10/31/1997) • **79**

Ribera del Duero Crianza 1994 • $13 • (10/31/1997) • **86**

Ribera del Duero Reserva 1992 • $21 • (10/31/1997) • **84**

MONTSARRA

Brut Cava NV: Fairly tight, with some modest green apple flavors, which turn a bit astringent on the finish.–K.M. • $12 • (12/15/1999) • **79**

Brut Nature Cava NV • $10 • (5/15/1997) • **81**

In Fraganti Penedès 1995 • $9 • (10/15/1996) • **81**

MORALES, BODEGAS HNOS.

La Mancha Gran Creacion Crianza 1992 • $7 • (4/30/1995) • **84**

La Mancha Viña Quintana Crianza 1996: Dried cherry and raisin notes give this supple red a sweet, almost candied character. Soft and velvety on the palate, with a short, sweet finish.–T.M. • $8 • (11/15/1999) • **79**

Tempranillo-Cabernet Sauvignon La Mancha Gran Creacion Crianza 1995: Cherry, vanilla and spice flavors in this lush red; though it's light in structure, it does have a firm tannic backbone. Integrates traditional flavors into a modern structure. Drink now through 2002.–T.M. • $8 • (11/15/1999) • **85**

MORGADIO, ADEGAS

Albariño Rias Baixas 1998: Lean and crisp. Light citrus and herb flavors are pleasant but rather faint in this sharp white. Needs food to soften. Drink now.–T.M. • $20 • (11/15/1999) • **82**

Albariño Rias Baixas 1997: This lively white is lighter than many Albariños, but shows characteristic almond, pineapple and citrus flavors, clean and refreshing. It makes an appealing apéritif. Drink now.–T.M. • $17 • (11/15/1998) • **84**

Albariño Rias Baixas 1996 • $17 • (10/31/1997) • **87**

Albariño Rias Baixas Torre Fornelos 1998: Fresh and balanced, this white offers clean citrus, pear and herb flavors. Straightforward, yet with a sharp focus through the clean finish. Drink now.–T.M. • $12 • (11/15/1999) • **84**

Albariño Rias Baixas Torre Fornelos 1997: This lively, fruity white from Spain is stuffed with flavors of pineapple, mango and coconut, round and juicy on the palate, clean and refreshing on the finish. It's versatile enough to work as an aperitif or with food, vivid enough to make a lasting impression, affordable, and drinkable now.–T.M. • $10 • (11/15/1998) • **88**

MORO, BODEGAS EMILIO

Ribera del Duero Crianza 1996: This exuberant red offers vivid flavors of blackberry, cherry and chocolate, with firm yet well-integrated tannins and a streak of bright acidity. Though not huge, it's balanced and lively. Drink through 2005.–T.M. • $20 • (11/30/1998) • **87**

Key: SS—Spectator Selection. CS—Cellar Selection. HR—Highly Recommended. $NA—Price not available. (BT)—Barrel tasting. Ⓐ—Auction Price.
For a key to the tasters' initials, see "How to Use These Listings."
Dates in parentheses represent the issues in which the ratings were published.

MOURE, ADEGAS

Mencía Ribeira Sacra Abadia da Cova 1996 • $6 • (11/15/1997) • **81**

Mencía Ribeira Sacra Abadia da Cova Selección Especial NV: Rather bitter and earthy, this soft red is austere and short.–T.M. • $15 • (1/31/2000) • **74**

MUERZA, BODEGAS

Rioja Vega Crianza 1996: Plump yet lively, this chewy red offers smoky and earthy flavors that frame a core of light, rather tart cherry. A bit rustic; best with food. Drink now through 2002.–T.M. • $14 • (11/30/1999) • **83**

Rioja Vega Crianza 1995: This thick, slightly jammy red offers ripe cherry, raisin and chocolate flavors, with chunky tannins and just enough acidity to keep it lively. A bit rustic, but will stand up to food. Drink now through 2004.–T.M. • $10 • (11/30/1998) • **84**

Rioja Vega Crianza 1994 • $10 • (11/30/1997) • **88**

Rioja Vega Crianza 1993 • $11 • (6/30/1997) • **84**

Rioja Vega Crianza 1990 • $9 • (12/15/1994) • **84**

Rioja Vega Crianza 1989 • $9 • (4/15/1994) • **85**

Rioja Vega Crianza 1986 • $10 • (3/31/1991) • **75**

MUGA, BODEGAS

Rioja 1990 • $13 • (3/31/1995) • **82**

Rioja 1986 • $12 • (5/31/1991) • **81**

Rioja 1985 • $12 • (3/31/1990) • **83**

Rioja Prado Enea Gran Reserva 1991: This generous, traditional red is rich, with alluring aromas and flavors of plum, cola, spice and chocolate. Has a plump texture backed by firm tannins, and remains lively through the long finish. Drink now through 2003.–T.M. • $35 • (12/15/1999) • **89**

Rioja Prado Enea Gran Reserva 1989: This rich red is maturing, with coffee, cedar and tobacco notes swirling around the plum and raisin flavors, but it still has enough bright acidity to keep it vivid. A chunky, generous wine, with the structure to age further. Tasted twice, with consistent notes. Drink through 2006.–T.M. • $32 • (11/30/1998) • **87**

Rioja Prado Enea Gran Reserva 1985 • $35 • (4/30/1995) • **87**

Rioja Prado Enea Gran Reserva 1982 • $83 Ⓐ • (11/30/1991) • **84**

Rioja Prado Enea Gran Reserva 1981 • $77 Ⓐ • (4/30/1989) • **80**

Rioja Prado Enea Gran Reserva 1976 • $24 • (3/31/1990) • **84**

Rioja Reserva 1995: This spicy red has a food-friendly structure, firm but balanced. Subdued cherry flavors are less prominent than cola, cedar and herb notes, which will appeal to fans of the more traditional style. Drink now through 2002.–T.M. • $15 • (12/15/1999) • **87**

Rioja Reserva 1994: Alluring coffee, spice and plum aromas follow through on the palate in this well-structured red. Elegant yet well defined, it has both concentration and balance. Tasted twice, with consistent notes. Drink now through 2002.–T.M. • $14 • (10/31/1998) • **87**

Rioja Reserva 1992 • $14 • (2/28/1998) • **84**

Rioja Reserva 1991 • $13 • (8/31/1996) • **80**

Rioja Reserva 1989 • $13 • (4/15/1994) • **85**

Rioja Reserva 1988 • $13 • (4/15/1994) • **87**

Rioja Rosado 1998: Pale yet quite full-bodied, this rosé marries juicy berry flavors with slightly bitter notes that balance the noticeable sweetness. Clean and fresh. Drink now.–T.M. • $9 • (10/31/1999) • **82**

Rioja Torre Muga Reserva 1995: Beautifully aromatic, with notes of cassis, lilacs, coffee and spices, this sinuous red is polished and elegant, yet dense with fruit, oak and earthy flavors that linger and expand on the long finish. An extraordinary marriage of typicity and sophistication. Drink now through 2010.–T.M. • $55 • (5/31/2000) HR • **95**

Rioja Torre Muga Reserva 1994: This red marries elegance and concentration, with ripe plum and blackberry flavors, toasty, cola-scented oak notes and lovely spice accents. A bit tightly wound now, it should be gorgeous with a bit of age. Drink through 2010.–T.M. • $50 • (10/31/1998) • **90**

Rioja Torre Muga Reserva 1991 • $42 Ⓐ • (2/28/1998) CS • **91**

Rioja White Barrel Fermented 1998: Lavish oak treatment has given this white rich vanilla, cream and toast flavors. The oak tends to dominate the bright apple and peach, but good acidity keeps the wine lively. Drink now.–T.M. • $11 • (10/31/1999) • **85**

Rioja White Barrel Fermented 1996 • $10 • (2/28/1998) • **84**

MURIEL, BODEGAS

Rioja Barón de Barbón Reserva 1994: Maturing now, this traditional-style red offers dried cherry, tobacco and spice flavors. Has intensity, but needs food to soften the lean, dry tannins under the ripe fruit. Drink now through 2001.–T.M. • $19 • (11/30/1998) • **83**

Rioja Gran Reserva 1985: This mature red shows flavors of raisin, coffee and leather, with astringent tannins that ease up on the finish, allowing pretty spice and cola notes to emerge. Rustic, but has richness and depth. Drink now through 2002.–T.M. • $20 • (11/30/1998) • **85**

Rioja Reserva 1991: Sweet, slightly candied cherry and vanilla flavors mark this atypical red. Fresh and firm yet lacking in depth and harmony. Distinctive and pleasant, but tough to match with food. Drink now.–T.M. • $14 • (11/30/1998) • **82**

Rioja Viña Muriel Crianza 1995: Raisin, dried cherry and burnt vanilla notes run through this awkward red, and the tannins are very dry.–T.M. • $10 • (11/30/1998) • **74**

MURRIETA, BODEGAS MARQUES DE

Rioja 1985 • $17 • (2/28/1990) • **87**

Rioja Castillo Ygay Gran Reserva Especial 1989: This ink-colored wine is still vivid and youthful, with a bright streak of acidity enlivening the dried cherry, raisin and cola flavors. The tannins are firm but ripe and fresh. More power than subtlety, but plenty of stuffing to develop with age. Drink now through 2008.–T.M. • $35 • (11/30/1998) • **90**

Rioja Castillo Ygay Gran Reserva Especial 1970: This ripe red is still rich and vibrant, with a core of cherry and a velvety texture that indicate it still has life. The exotic coffee, walnut and orange peel flavors remind me of a fine Oloroso Sherry. An essential taste experience for fans of traditional Rioja. Drink now.–T.M. • $160 • (12/15/1999) • **93**

Rioja Castillo Ygay Gran Reserva Especial 1968 • $85 • (3/31/1990) • **92**

Rioja Castillo Ygay Gran Reserva Especial 1952 • $150 • (3/31/1990) • **94**

Rioja Crianza 1991 • $11 • (12/15/1994) • **86**

Rioja Crianza 1990 • $10 • (4/15/1994) • **88**

Rioja Gran Reserva 1983 • $20 • (4/15/1994) • **88**

Rioja Gran Reserva 1982 • $60 • (4/15/1994) • **89**

Rioja Gran Reserva 1978 • $30 • (3/31/1992) • **87**

Rioja Gran Reserva 1975 • $35 • (3/31/1992) • **93**

Rioja Gran Reserva 1973 • $30 • (3/31/1992) • **89**

Rioja Gran Reserva 1970 • $NA • (3/31/1992) • **83**

Rioja Reserva 1990 • $15 • (4/30/1995) • **81**

Rioja Reserva 1988 • $12 • (4/15/1994) • **87**

Rioja Reserva 1986 • $20 • (3/31/1992) • **88**

Rioja Reserva 1985 • $20 • (3/31/1992) • **90**

Rioja Reserva 1983 • $13 • (3/31/1992) • **85**

Rioja Reserva 1982 • $39 • (3/31/1992) • **84**

Rioja Reserva 1981 • $39 • (3/31/1992) • **88**

Rioja Reserva 1980 • $27 • (3/31/1990) • **83**

Rioja White Ygay Colección 2100 1996: An assertive toasty, smoky character dominates the light apple flavor in this aggressive white. Though rather light-bodied to carry so much oak, it does have snappy acidity.–T.M. • $10 • (11/30/1998) • **79**

Rioja Ygay Colección 2100 1997: Round and soft, this maturing red offers traditional flavors of cherry, cola and vanilla. Spicy and sweet, it has a velvety texture, with light tannins and low acidity. Drink now.–T.M. • $11 • (11/30/1999) • **83**

Rioja Ygay Colección 2100 1996: This fresh red has a light, lively texture, but flavors of coffee, black cherry and earth give it a darker edge. Firm tannins and a fresh finish. Drink now.–T.M. • $12 • (11/30/1998) • **82**

Rioja Ygay Dalmau Reserva 1994: Assertive cassis, blackberry and vanilla flavors give a distinctive personality to this red. The structure is more modest, with medium body and moderate tannins, but it has the balance and depth to evolve well. A new wine from Murrieta that contains 10 percent Cabernet Sauvignon in addition to Tempranillo and Garnacha. Aged in oak for 36 months. Drink now through 2005.–T.M. • $90 • (12/15/1999) • **88**

Rioja Ygay Reserva 1995: This vivid red is rich with spice, cedar and light herb flavors, anchored by a core of cherry. Generous on the palate, but the tannins are light, the acidity lively. Drink now.–T.M. • $20 • (12/15/1999) • **87**

Rioja Ygay Reserva 1992 • $15 • (10/15/1997) • **85**

Rioja Ygay Reserva Especial 1994: Gamy and earthy flavors are backed by firm tannins in this assertive red, while tart cherry emerges on the finish. Shows more extraction than finesse, but can match with hearty dishes. Drink now through 2005.–T.M. • $24 • (11/30/1999) • **85**

Rioja Ygay Reserva Especial 1991: Expressive yet a bit heavy-handed, this lively red marries bright cherry and cranberry flavors with toasty oak and firm tannins in a style that aims more for power than elegance. Has the stuffing to age. Best after 2000.–T.M. • $23 • (11/30/1998) • **87**

Rioja Ygay Reserva Especial 1989 • $20 • (11/15/1997) SS • **89**

NAVARRA, VINICOLA

Cabernet Sauvignon Navarra Las Campanas 1989 • $8 • (4/15/1994) • **80**

Navarra Las Campanas Crianza 1995: Berry and spice notes are well defined and slightly sweet in this traditional-style red. It has light but firm tannins and a vanilla-scented finish. Drink now through 2002.–T.M. • $8 • (10/31/1998) • **83**

Navarra Las Campanas Crianza 1994 • $8 • (11/15/1997) • **84**

Navarra Las Campanas Crianza 1991 • $7 • (4/30/1996) • **83**

Navarra Las Campanas Crianza 1990 • $7 • (4/15/1994) • **84**

Navarra Rosado Las Campanas 1996 • $7 • (9/15/1997) • **80**

NEKEAS, BODEGA

Cabernet Sauvignon-Tempranillo Navarra Vega Sindoa 1997: Pleasant, sweet vanilla oak flavors dominate this round red, supported by cherry and licorice notes. It has tannin, but the overall impression is soft and sweet. Drink now.–T.M. • $8 • (11/15/1999) • **83**

Cabernet Sauvignon-Tempranillo Navarra Vega Sindoa 1996: Plum, coffee and herb flavors mingle nicely in this firm, rich red. It's balanced and shows some concentration, just needs some time in the bottle to unwind. Drink through 2005.–T.M. • $7 • (10/31/1998) • **86**

Cabernet Sauvignon-Tempranillo Navarra Vega Sindoa 1995 • $7 • (6/15/1997) • **88**

Cabernet Sauvignon-Tempranillo Navarra Vega Sindoa 1993 • $6 • (8/31/1996) • **81**

Chardonnay Navarra Vega Sindoa Barrel Fermented 1998: This compact, thick-textured white offers flavors from a slice of lemon meringue pie—citrus, cream and vanilla, with a hint of smoke from the oven. It's clean and fresh. Drink now.–T.M. • $9 • (11/15/1999) • **84**

Chardonnay Navarra Vega Sindoa Barrel Fermented 1997: Ripe and smooth, this offers plenty of vanilla and cream flavor, with enough apple and melon to keep it in balance. It's clean and refreshing. Drink now.–T.M. • $9 • (11/15/1998) • **84**

Chardonnay Navarra Vega Sindoa Barrel Fermented 1996 • $9 • (10/31/1997) • **84**

Chardonnay Navarra Vega Sindoa Cuvée Allier Barrel Fermented 1998: Toasty, smoky oak flavors dominate this supple white, with notes of apple and herbs adding interest. Smooth and soft. Drink now.–T.M. • $11 • (10/15/1999) • **81**

Chardonnay Navarra Vega Sindoa Cuvée Allier Barrel Fermented 1997: This smells like a lumberyard. Round and polished on the palate, with plenty of toast, coffee and vanilla flavor, but little fruit or acidity for balance. May appeal to fans of oak. Drink now.–T.M. • $9 • (11/15/1998) • **83**

Grenache Navarra Vega Sindoa El Chaparral Old Vines 1998: This round, supple red is chock-full of cherry, berry and light herb flavors. Clean and balanced, with just enough grip for food. A textbook example of the varietal in a light style. Drink now through 2002.–T.M. • $11 • (11/15/1999) • **86**

Grenache Navarra Vega Sindoa El Chaparral Old Vines 1997: Fleshy and fresh, this rich, almost jammy red shows ripe plum, cassis and tar flavors, with a slight bitter toastiness and firm tannins. A bit clumsy now, but should improve. Drink through 2003.–T.M. • $8 • (11/30/1998) • **84**

Merlot Navarra Vega Sindoa 1997: This soft red leans toward the earthy, herbal side of the variety's character, with soft tannins and a clean finish. It has just enough fruit flavor to keep it balanced and quaffable. Drink now.–T.M. • $10 • (10/31/1999) • **81**

Merlot Navarra Vega Sindoa 1996: This firm red has a core of ripe plum, but smoky, meaty notes give it a slightly burnt flavor. Fresh and balanced, with moderate tannins. Harmonious with grilled meats.–T.M. • $7 • (11/30/1998) • **81**

Merlot Navarra Vega Sindoa 1995 • $9 • (6/15/1997) • **89**

Merlot Navarra Vega Sindoa 1993 • $10 • (8/31/1996) • **85**

Navarra Rosado Vega Sindoa 1996 • $7 • (2/28/1998) • **82**

Tempranillo Navarra Vega Sindoa 1996: This chewy red offers ripe black cherry and sweet vanilla aromas and flavors, with firm tannins and fresh acidity. Well extracted yet still fresh, with plenty of structure to marry with food. Drink now.–T.M. • $7 • (10/31/1998) • **85**

Tempranillo-Merlot Navarra Vega Sindoa 1998: This thick-textured red offers sweet cherry and light herb flavors that are round on the palate but a bit dry on the finish. A sturdy wine that will stand up to food. Drink now through 2001.–T.M. • $6 • (11/15/1999) • **83**

Tempranillo-Merlot Navarra Vega Sindoa 1997: Aromas of dark smoke and earth follow through on the palate, dominating the lighter cherry and berry flavors in this firm red. It has some concentration and may round out with time. Drink now through 2003.–T.M. • $6 • (10/31/1998) • **84**

NEKEAS, BODEGA

Viura-Chardonnay Navarra Vega Sindoa 1998: Floral and litchi notes are distinctive in this round, soft white. It has the body of Chardonnay, with spicy and herbal flavors from Viura. Drink now.–T.M. • $5 • (10/15/1999) • **80**
Viura-Chardonnay Navarra Vega Sindoa 1996 • $6 • (10/31/1997) • **85**

NEVADA HILLS

Chardonnay Utiel-Requena 1997: This wine lacks focused fruit flavor and varietal character. Tastes more manufactured than grown.–T.M. • $6 • (10/31/1999) • **74**

NIEVA, VINEDOS DE

Sauvignon Rueda 1998: Canned fruit cocktail flavors show little varietal character in this thick, rather clumsy white.–T.M. • $10 • (10/31/1999) • **76**
Verdejo Rueda 1998: Very crisp, yet still with good weight on the palate, this clean, refreshing white is almost neutral in flavor, with hints of apple and herb. A good aperitif or shellfish wine. Drink now.–T.M. • $10 • (10/31/1999) • **83**

NUESTRA SENORA DE LAS VINAS, BODEGA COOPERATIVA

Toro Viña Bajoz 1997: This light-bodied red shows game, bacon fat and black cherry flavors, with fresh acidity and light tannins. A pleasant quaffer in the Beaujolais style. Drink now.–T.M. • $9 • (11/30/1998) • **83**
Toro Viña Bajoz 1996: Shows ripe plum, earth and chocolate flavors, but a streak of bitterness and astringent tannin gives it a rustic, clumsy character. Might soften with food.–T.M. • $9 • (10/31/1998) • **79**

OCHOA, BODEGAS

Cabernet Sauvignon Navarra Crianza 1994: There are ripe plum, raisin and chocolate flavors in this chewy red, and solid tannins add structure. Though not very expressive, it's compact and harmonious. Drink now through 2003.–T.M. • $12 • (11/30/1998) • **84**
Merlot Navarra Crianza 1996: This red is soft and generous, with true varietal flavors of ripe plum and bright herb notes. Clean and supple. Drink now.–T.M. • $14 • (11/15/1999) • **84**
Merlot Navarra Crianza 1995: Shows some concentration, but the earthy, candied flavors are awkward and unbalanced. Tasted twice, with consistent notes.–T.M. • $12 • (11/30/1998) • **73**
Moscatel Navarra 1997: This exuberant white offers apricot, honey and vanilla flavors, with vivid notes of lemon meringue pie in a sweet but lively wine that's bright and balanced. Drink now.–T.M. • $14/500 ml. • (11/30/1998) • **87**
Navarra 1998: Earthy and gamy flavors dominate this austere red, and a slight spritz accents the bitter finish.–T.M. • $8 • (11/15/1999) • **74**
Navarra 1997: Black cherry, licorice and cola flavors are distinctive; the tannins are firm, but the texture is smooth, with floral notes emerging on the finish. A bit tight now. Drink through 2003.–T.M. • $7 • (10/31/1998) • **84**
Navarra 1988 • $8 • (9/30/1991) • **83**
Navarra 1987 • $14 • (9/30/1991) • **79**
Navarra Gran Reserva 1991: This light, silky red, maturing now, tastes a bit washed-out, with light herbal, spicy and earthy notes and soft tannins. Past its prime.–T.M. • $18 • (11/15/1999) • **81**
Navarra Gran Reserva 1988: Still quite fresh, this smooth, velvety red offers black cherry, raisin and date flavors, with notes of spice and herb. Balanced and quite deep, with firm, round tannins. A harmonious wine that should continue to age well. A blend of Cabernet Sauvignon and Tempranillo. Drink now through 2003.–T.M. • $16 • (11/30/1998) • **87**
Navarra Reserva 1994: Ripe and soft. Plum, raisin and vanilla flavors run through this velvety red. Sweet and fruity, a bit rustic but generous. A second sample was corky. Cabernet Sauvignon and Tempranillo. Drink now.–T.M. • $16 • (12/31/1999) • **84**
Navarra Reserva 1992: This red shows light cherry, raspberry and sweetened coffee flavors. Velvety on the palate, yet with firm tannins underneath that will stand up to food. It's maturing nicely, but still fresh. Drink now through 2001.–T.M. • $14 • (11/30/1998) • **84**

Key: SS—Spectator Selection. CS—Cellar Selection. HR—Highly Recommended. $NA—Price not available. (BT)—Barrel tasting. Ⓐ—Auction Price.
For a key to the tasters' initials, see "How to Use These Listings."
Dates in parentheses represent the issues in which the ratings were published.

Navarra Reserva 1985 • $10 • (4/15/1994) • **83**
Navarra Reserva 1982 • $14 • (9/30/1991) • **73**
Navarra Reserva 1980 • $11 • (4/15/1989) • **85**
Navarra Rosado 1998: Pretty strawberry aromas gain richness on the palate, where notes of herb and anise kick in. Fresh yet quite full-bodied, it's a nice match with food. Drink now.–T.M. • $10 • (10/15/1999) • **84**
Navarra Rosado 1997: Soft and silky, this deep rosé shows crisp flavors of tart cherry and strawberry, with a hint of bitterness on the finish. A nice aperitif. Drink now.–T.M. • $10 • (10/31/1998) • **83**
Tempranillo Navarra 1990 • $10 • (4/15/1994) • **82**
Tempranillo Navarra Crianza 1996: This round, smooth red offers sweet cherry, raisin and cola flavors, with polished tannins and a smoky finish. Drink now.–T.M. • $13 • (11/15/1999) • **83**
Tempranillo Navarra Crianza 1995: This silky red is delicate yet assertive, with alluring aromas of vanilla, spice and berry and sweet fruit flavors over light yet firm tannins. Made in a traditional style, it's evanescent, yet the flavors stay with you. Drink now.–T.M. • $12 • (10/31/1998) • **84**

OLARRA, BODEGAS

Rioja Añares Crianza 1995: Smoky and gamy aromas and flavors give this red a rustic character, but the wine shows good concentration and balance, and a core of ripe fruit emerges on the finish. Drink now through 2004.–T.M. • $9 • (11/30/1999) • **84**
Rioja Añares Gran Reserva 1983 • $19 • (3/31/1992) • **75**
Rioja Añares Gran Reserva 1982 • $27 • (11/30/1991) • **75**
Rioja Añares Gran Reserva 1981 • $25 • (3/31/1992) • **76**
Rioja Añares Reserva 1994: This red shows plum and vanilla flavors, with floral and berry notes that add a filigree to the sturdy tannins and thick texture. It sacrifices harmony for a vivid personality. Drink now through 2002.–T.M. • $13 • (12/15/1999) • **85**
Rioja Añares Reserva 1985 • $25 • (3/31/1992) • **83**
Rioja Añares Reserva 1983 • $12 • (2/28/1990) • **73**
Rioja Cerro Añon Gran Reserva 1983 • $19 • (3/31/1992) • **83**
Rioja Cerro Añon Gran Reserva 1982 • $27 • (11/30/1991) • **71**
Rioja Cerro Añon Gran Reserva 1981 • $25 • (3/31/1992) • **87**
Rioja Cerro Añon Gran Reserva 1973 • $NA • (3/31/1992) • **81**
Rioja Cerro Añon Gran Reserva 1970 • $NA • (3/31/1992) • **75**
Rioja Cerro Añon Reserva 1994: Plum, prune, walnut and tobacco notes mingle in this round red. The silky texture is backed by firm tannins, and spicy notes linger on the finish. Drink now.–T.M. • $13 • (12/15/1999) • **84**
Rioja Cerro Añon Reserva 1985 • $NA • (3/31/1992) • **73**
Rioja Otoñal 1997: This light red is supple and a bit diluted, with soft flavors of dried cherry, herb and cedar that linger on a sweet, spicy finish. Delicate, but has personality. Drink now.–T.M. • $6 • (11/30/1999) • **82**
Rioja White Otoñal 1997: Rich and smooth. Pear, almond and honey flavors are round and soft in this big white, but the wine is dry and has a lively underlying acidity. Drink now.–T.M. • $6 • (11/30/1999) • **84**

OLIVARES, BODEGAS

Monastrell Spain Dulce 1996: Exotic and exuberant. Velvety and quite sweet, this rich red offers ripe flavors of blackberry and cassis, with accents of chocolate, cola and mint. More alcoholic than tannic, it's a seductive way to finish a meal. Not imported into the U.S. Drink now through 2005.–T.M. • $NA • (1/01/2000) • **88**

ONA, TORRE DE

Rioja Barón de Oña Reserva 1992 • $14 • (5/31/1998) • **78**
Rioja Barón de Oña Reserva 1991 • $14 • (2/28/1998) • **82**
Rioja Barón de Oña Reserva 1989 • $15 • (8/31/1996) • **76**

ONDARRE, BODEGAS

Rioja Gran Reserva 1989: Coffee, prune and licorice flavors are dark and rich in this plump red. Round and gentle, with supple tannins and a short, spicy finish. Drink now.–T.M. • $18 • (12/15/1999) • **83**
Rioja Mayor de Ondarre Reserva 1994: Ripe and thick, this sturdy red offers plum, prune, coffee and herb flavors, more chewy than elegant but a good match for hearty dishes. Has good balance and should improve in the bottle. Drink now through 2004.–T.M. • $30 • (12/15/1999) • **86**
Rioja Reserva 1994: Vivid sweet-and-sour flavors of cherry and berry are bold but unbalanced in this lively red. Still youthful in color and structure, so perhaps it will come together with time. Drink now through 2003.–T.M. • $12 • (12/15/1999) • **82**

ONIX

Priorat 1998: This vibrant red shows a purple color so bright it glows in the glass. Vivid aromas of crushed blackberry follow through on the fresh, juicy palate. The tannins are modest, the texture supple. An irresistible quaff. Drink now through 2001.–T.M. • $10 • (11/30/1999) • **86**
Priorat 1997: This rich, velvety wine offers vibrant flavors of ripe raspberry and raspberry liqueur, with accents of clove and nutmeg. Generous on the palate, with ripe, round tannins. Drink now through 2002.–T.M. • $9 • (10/31/1998) • **87**
Priorat 1995 • $8 • (10/31/1997) • **87**
Priorat 1992 • $7 • (4/15/1994) • **84**
Priorat Collita 1992 • $7 • (4/30/1995) • **86**

OSBORNE, BODEGAS

Amontillado Jerez Coquinero NV: Crisp and tangy, this offers a nutty character and a hint of brine in a straightforward manner, with soft richness midpalate. Moderate length on the finish. Drink now.–B.S. • $14 • (10/31/1999) • **87**
Amontillado Jerez La Honda NV • $24 • (7/31/1994) • **84**
Amontillado Jerez Medium NV: Amber in color, this shows caramel and butterscotch aromas and flavors that turn to walnuts on the long finish. Supple and rich on the palate, slightly sweet and medium-bodied, with lively acidity. Drink now.–B.S. • $8 • (12/15/1998) • **86**
Cream Jerez NV: Fabulous nose. There's interesting, mature wax and lanolin notes along with a woodsy caramel note. Concentrated, medium-bodied and harmonious. The firm structure keeps it lively and interesting. Drink now.–B.S. • $14 • (11/15/1999) • **92**
Fino Jerez Pale Dry NV: Lovely aromas of almond, wildflowers, apple and a hint of the sea are followed by a rich texture and complex apple, almond and butter flavors. Broad and full for fino, with a long aftertaste. Drink now.–B.S. • $8 • (12/15/1998) • **89**
Manzanilla Jerez NV: Elegant yet persistent, this outstanding Sherry combines a broad structure with subtle and lingering mineral, flint, petrol and vanilla flavors. Quality this high at a price this low is increasingly rare—enjoy. Drink now.–B.S. • $8 • (12/15/1998) • **90**
Oloroso Jerez Abocado Solera India NV • $33 • (7/31/1994) • **90**
Oloroso Jerez Amoroso Solera Alonso El Sabio NV • $37 • (7/31/1994) • **84**
Oloroso Jerez Dark Mahogany Solera BC 200 NV • $37 • (7/31/1994) • **86**
Oloroso Jerez Dry Bailen NV: Caramel and chocolate notes are supported by a chiseled framework that keeps the flavors pumping through. Starts off round, then finishes very dry, leaving a mouthwatering sensation. Excellent aperitif. Drink now.–B.S. • $14 • (10/31/1999) • **89**
Oloroso Jerez Medium 10RF NV: A lovely Sherry, this is sweet, round and full of caramel flavor, yet there's plenty of structure and zingy acidity to offset the initial sweetness, leaving a dry sensation and a nutty aftertaste. Drink now.–B.S. • $14 • (10/31/1999) SS • **91**
Palo Cortado Jerez Abocado Solera PP NV • $33 • (7/31/1994) • **89**
Pedro Ximénez Jerez 1827 NV: So thick you could almost cut it with a knife. Very sweet and cloying, definitely for fans of intensely sweet dessert wines. Flavors border on grape, dried fig, molasses and toffee. Impressive, though a touch heavy and short. Drink now.–B.S. • $16 • (10/31/1999) • **88**

PADIN, BODEGAS PABLO

Albariño Rias Baixas Segrel 1997: This brassy white shows nut and canned fruit flavors that suggest it's already aging, though it remains crisp enough to match with food. A smoky note on the finish adds interest.–T.M. • $15 • (11/15/1999) • **79**
Albariño Rias Baixas Segrel 1996 • $14 • (5/31/1998) • **86**
Rias Baixas Segrel Especial 1996 • $18 • (5/31/1998) • **88**

PALACIO, BODEGAS

Rioja Cosme Palacio y Hermanos 1997: Ripe and round, this velvety Spanish red is rich, with plum, sweet chocolate and spice flavors, light tannins and a gentle, lingering finish. Drink now through 2002.–T.M. • $10 • (11/30/1999) • **86**
Rioja Cosme Palacio y Hermanos 1989 • $13 • (9/30/1992) • **84**
Rioja Cosme Palacio y Hermanos 1988 • $13 • (9/30/1992) • **84**
Rioja Cosme Palacio y Hermanos 1987 • $13 • (3/31/1990) • **83**
Rioja Glorioso Gran Reserva 1982 • $19 • (11/30/1991) • **84**
Rioja Glorioso Gran Reserva 1981 • $20 • (3/31/1993) • **85**
Rioja Glorioso Gran Reserva 1978 • $15 • (2/28/1989) • **88**
Rioja Glorioso Reserva 1982 • $18 • (3/31/1990) • **79**
Rioja Glorioso Reserva 1981 • $10 • (2/28/1989) • **83**

PALACIO DE LA VEGA

Cabernet Sauvignon Navarra Reserva 1993 • $18 • (10/31/1997) • **86**
Merlot Navarra Crianza 1994 • $16 • (10/31/1997) • **88**
Navarra Crianza 1994 • $12 • (11/30/1997) • **85**
Navarra Crianza 1991 • $NA • (4/15/1994) • **83**
Navarra Rosado 1996 • $9 • (9/15/1997) • **83**
Tempranillo Navarra 1996 • $9 • (11/15/1997) • **85**
Tempranillo Navarra Reserva 1993 • $16 • (11/15/1997) • **85**

PALACIOS, ALVARO

Priorat Finca Dofí 1996: A good balance of ripeness and crispness gives definition to this powerful red. Raspberry and cassis flavors are clean and firm, backed by powerful tannins and high alcohol. It's aromatic and long on the finish, but needs time to harmonize and reach its full potential. Best from 2002 through 2010.–T.M. • $50 • (9/15/1999) • **92**
Priorat Finca Dofí 1995 • $86 Ⓐ • (6/30/1998) • **93**
Priorat Finca Dofí 1994 • $62 Ⓐ • (9/15/1997) HR • **92**
Priorat Finca Dofí 1990 • $35 • (8/31/1993) • **85**
Priorat Finca Dofí 1989 • $40 • (1/31/1992) • **89**
Priorat L'Ermita 1996: Elegant and focused, this firm, graceful red offers crisp black cherry and cassis flavors, with lead pencil and cigar box accents, much like a fine Bordeaux. Not a blockbuster, it's impressive for its excellent backbone and definition. Best after 2002.–T.M. • $230 Ⓐ • (9/15/1999) • **92**
Priorat L'Ermita 1995 • $183 Ⓐ • (6/30/1998) • **97**
Priorat L'Ermita 1994 • $238 Ⓐ • (9/15/1997) • **94**
Priorat Les Terrasses 1997: Supple yet intense, this red offers plenty of raspberry and black cherry flavors, with accents of cinnamon and toast. It has enough tannin to match with food, and a long, seductive finish. Drink now through 2004.–T.M. • $30 • (4/30/2000) • **89**
Priorat Les Terrasses 1996: Plenty of ripe, fresh fruit in this red, with flavors of black cherries, blackberries and plums, along with accents of toast and coffee. Yet it remains smooth and graceful on the palate, with well-integrated tannins and a long, fruity finish. Drink now through 2005.–T.M. • $25 • (9/15/1999) • **90**
Priorat Les Terrasses 1995 • $20 • (6/30/1998) • **88**

PALACIOS REMONDO, BODEGAS

Garnacha Rioja Rosado Herencia Remondo 1996 • $8 • (2/28/1998) • **84**
Rioja 2 Viñedos Finca Los Riscos Finca La Montesa Reserva 1994: Plum, tobacco and spice flavors are round yet firm in this generous red. Has plenty of tannin for structure, yet remains gentle and fruity on the palate, with a clean finish. Drink now through 2003.–T.M. • $75 • (11/30/1999) • **85**
Rioja Herencia Remondo 1996: This maturing red has a solid core of cherry flavor, with herb and cedar accents. The tannins are polished, and the wine has enough weight to match well with food. Drink now through 2002.–T.M. • $14 • (11/30/1999) • **85**
Rioja Herencia Remondo 1985 • $NA • (3/31/1990) • **81**
Rioja Herencia Remondo 1982 • $NA • (11/15/1987) • **90**
Rioja Herencia Remondo Crianza 1994 • $10 • (2/28/1998) • **85**
Rioja Herencia Remondo Gran Reserva 1987 • $25 • (5/31/1998) • **88**
Rioja Herencia Remondo Gran Reserva 1982 • $13 • (1/31/1992) • **78**
Rioja Herencia Remondo Gran Reserva 1975 • $NA • (3/31/1992) • **79**
Rioja Herencia Remondo Gran Reserva 1973 • $NA • (3/31/1992) • **77**
Rioja Herencia Remondo Reserva 1992 • $14 • (2/28/1998) • **81**
Rioja Herencia Remondo Reserva 1986 • $10 • (3/31/1992) • **79**
Rioja White Plácet Finca La Montesa 1997: Though big and bright, this round white has a canned fruit quality that's cloying on the palate. It has some appealing elements, but lacks balance.–T.M. • $16 • (10/31/1999) • **78**
Tempranillo Rioja Herencia Remondo 1996 • $8 • (2/28/1998) • **78**
Viura Rioja Herencia Remondo 1996 • $8 • (2/28/1998) • **83**

PARIENTE, JOSE

Verdejo Rueda II Victorias 1998: Lively and focused, this crisp white offers vivid green apple, citrus and light herb flavors, with richer undertones of lanolin and cream. A nice combination of delicacy and power. Not imported into the U.S. Drink now.–T.M. • $NA • (1/01/1999) • **86**

PARXET

Alella Marqués de Alella Allier 1996: This round, soft white shows a deep gold color and ripe flavors of cooked apple and butter, but a streak of citrusy acidity keeps it balanced. A distinctive wine, best on its own. Drink now.–T.M. • $12 • (11/30/1998) • **81**

Alella Marqués de Alella Clasico 1997: Floral aromas give way to light flavors of peach and bitter herb, kept lively by a fair amount of spritz. Clean and refreshing, this white is like a ready-made spritzer. Drink now.–T.M. • $10 • (11/30/1998) • **83**

Alella Marqués de Alella Clasico 1996 • $10 • (10/31/1997) • **83**

Brut Cava Millennium MM Gran Reserva NV: Toasty, but not complex, with some nice spicy and minerally flavors, which linger on the finish. Drink now.–K.M. • $21 • (12/15/1999) • **81**

Brut Cava Reserva NV: Quite toasty-tasting, with some apple and nutty flavors and a charry note on the finish. This has a nice richness, and would go well with food.–K.M. • $15 • (12/15/1999) • **85**

Brut Nature Cava NV: This straightforward sparkler offers light apple and toast flavors, a well-integrated mousse and a crisp finish. Has enough weight to match with food. Drink now.–T.M. • $15 • (11/30/1998) • **81**

Brut Nature Cava 77 NV: Foamy and fruity, more assertive than harmonious, with ripe apple, toast and light earth flavors that turn slightly rubbery on the finish. Tasted twice, with consistent notes.–T.M. • $60 • (11/30/1998) • **78**

Brut Nature Cava 79 NV: Tired and funky-tasting, with cheesy flavors on the finish.–K.M. • $64 • (12/15/1999) • **72**

Brut Nature Chardonnay Cava NV: Rather harsh, with aggressive mousse and bitter flavors of apple skins and seeds. Drink now.–T.M. • $20 • (11/30/1998) • **74**

Semi-Seco Cava Reserva NV: Cloyingly sweet, with canned peach flavors and an odd, rubbery-metallic finish.–K.M. • $13 • (12/15/1999) • **77**

PARXET, BODEGAS

Ribera del Duero Tionio 1996: This muscular wine shows impressive concentration, but it's closed and a bit clumsy now. Offers ripe plum, green olive, vanilla and licorice flavors, very firm tannins and crisp acidity; when all comes into harmony, could be a real winner. Drink through 2001.–T.M. • $15 • (8/31/1998) • **88**

PASANAU GERMANS

Priorat Finca La Planeta 1996: This massive yet well-crafted red shows rich flavors of chocolate, coffee, plum, black cherry and herb. Muscular tannins are well integrated into the generous texture. Clean and long, it should bloom with time. Drink through 2005.–T.M. • $29 • (10/31/1998) • **91**

PATERNINA, BODEGAS FEDERICO

Rioja 1998: Soft and supple, this traditionally styled red offers sweet cherry, vanilla and spice flavors on a smooth, light frame. Drink now.–T.M. • $7 • (11/30/1999) • **84**

Rioja 1997: This smooth, light red offers pretty cherry and spice flavors, with notes of vanilla and toast and just enough tannin for grip. It's balanced and clean, and the spice lingers on the finish. Drink now through 2001.–T.M. • $7 • (11/30/1998) • **83**

Rioja Banda Azul Crianza 1996: This traditional-style red is silky-smooth, with light but focused flavors of cherry, tobacco and spice that linger on the finish. Though light, it has enough grip for food. Drink now.–T.M. • $11 • (11/30/1999) • **85**

Rioja Banda Azul Crianza 1994 • $8 • (10/15/1997) • **84**

Rioja Banda Azul Crianza 1993 • $9 • (3/31/1996) • **78**

Rioja Clos Crianza 1996: Opulent toast and coffee flavors show oak influence, while juicy plum and cherry notes lurk beneath. The tannins are a bit dry now, but there is impressive stuffing here. Best from 2001 through 2006.–T.M. • $53 • (5/31/2000) • **87**

Rioja Gran Reserva 1987 • $20 • (3/31/1996) • **76**

Rioja Viña Vial Reserva 1991 • $14 • (3/31/1996) • **79**

Key: SS—Spectator Selection. CS—Cellar Selection. HR—Highly Recommended. $NA—Price not available. (BT)—Barrel tasting. Ⓐ—Auction Price. For a key to the tasters' initials, see "How to Use These Listings." **Dates in parentheses represent the issues in which the ratings were published.**

PAZO DE BARRANTES, BODEGAS

Albariño Rias Baixas 1996 • $20 • (5/31/1998) • **87**

PAZO DE SENORANS

Albariño Rias Baixas 1996 • $15 • (5/31/1998) • **88**

PAZO DE VILLAREI

Albariño Rias Baixas 1997: Pineapple and vanilla flavors mingle happily in this round, creamy-textured white, ripe and even sweet on the finish, but with plenty of lemony acidity for crispness. A vivid and refreshing wine. Drink now.–T.M. • $14 • (11/15/1998) • **87**

Albariño Rias Baixas 1996 • $13 • (9/15/1997) • **86**

PERELADA, CASTILLO

Brut Cava Fleur de Nuit NV: Light and doughy-tasting, with some nice apple and green pear flavors and a fruity aroma. Drink now.–K.M. • $8 • (12/15/1999) • **83**

Cabernet Sauvignon Empordà-Costa Brava 1991 • $10 • (4/30/1996) • **80**

Empordà-Costa Brava Crianza 1993 • $7 • (4/30/1996) • **77**

Empordà-Costa Brava Reserva 1990 • $9 • (4/30/1996) • **80**

Extra Brut Cava Gran Claustro 1996: Tastes tired, with woody and buttery flavors and a cheesy finish.–K.M. • $16 • (12/15/1999) • **76**

PEREZ PASCUAS, BODEGAS HNOS.

Ribera del Duero Viña Pedrosa 1996: Aromas of toasty, smoky oak carry through on the palate, joined by flavors of coffee and prune and a polished texture, with firm but well-integrated tannins. Not a powerful wine, but it has harmony and intensity. Drink now through 2005.–T.M. • $20 • (10/31/1998) • **87**

Ribera del Duero Viña Pedrosa Crianza 1996: Strong toasty and chocolate oak flavors dominate this juicy red, backed by lively cherry and berry notes. The wine is a bit thick and heavy now, but crisp acidity keeps it clean. Best from 2002 through 2010.–T.M. • $28 • (10/31/1999) • **87**

Ribera del Duero Viña Pedrosa Crianza 1994 • $27 • (1/01/1998) • **93**

Ribera del Duero Viña Pedrosa Crianza 1992 • $23 • (4/30/1996) • **87**

Ribera del Duero Viña Pedrosa Crianza 1991 • $20 • (4/30/1995) • **78**

Ribera del Duero Viña Pedrosa Crianza 1990 • $16 • (4/15/1994) • **88**

Ribera del Duero Viña Pedrosa Crianza 1989 • $18 • (4/15/1992) • **86**

Ribera del Duero Viña Pedrosa Crianza 1988 • $16 • (5/31/1991) • **82**

Ribera del Duero Viña Pedrosa Crianza 1987 • $15 • (9/30/1990) • **77**

Ribera del Duero Viña Pedrosa Crianza 1986 • $14 • (3/31/1990) • **88**

Ribera del Duero Viña Pedrosa Crianza 1985 • $16 • (9/15/1988) • **83**

Ribera del Duero Viña Pedrosa Gran Reserva 1992: Supple and still quite lively, this red offers perfumed cherry and berry aromas and sweet fruit flavors that lose focus on the finish, which is both dry and tart. Drink now.–T.M. • $84 • (10/31/1999) • **81**

Ribera del Duero Viña Pedrosa Reserva 1995: Light and polished for a Ribera, this silky red offers cherry, herb and cedar flavors, with light but firm tannins and a clean, crisp finish. Not a powerhouse, but elegant. Drink now through 2002.–T.M. • $48 • (10/31/1999) • **85**

Ribera del Duero Viña Pedrosa Reserva 1994: Chocolate, cola and cherry flavors are rich and alluring in this ripe, velvety red, while the moderate tannins and bright acidity keep it approachable. Well balanced and fresh. Drink now through 2004.–T.M. • $38 • (10/31/1998) • **88**

Ribera del Duero Viña Pedrosa Reserva 1990 • $50/1.5 liter • (4/30/1996) • **77**

PIEDEMONTE, BODEGAS

Cabernet Sauvignon Navarra Crianza 1996: Rustic, leaning toward the earthy, herbal side of the varietal spectrum, with light cherry flavor and firm tannins. Not showy, it might bloom with food. Drink now through 2002.–T.M. • $16 • (11/15/1999) • **83**

Cabernet Sauvignon Navarra Crianza 1995: Pretty floral and berry aromas follow through on the light yet tannic palate, giving this almost rosélike flavors on a red-wine structure. Though the marriage is awkward, this has distinctive character. Drink now through 2001.–T.M. • $9 • (11/30/1998) • **84**

Cabernet Sauvignon Navarra Crianza 1994 • $8 • (10/31/1997) • **86**

Cabernet Sauvignon Navarra Oligitum 1995 • $6 • (10/31/1997) • **87**

Chardonnay Navarra 1997: Heavy oak gives this thick white loads of sweet vanilla flavor, and a core of lemony acidity keeps it lively, but there's not much fruit.–T.M. • $10 • (11/15/1998) • **78**

SPAIN

Merlot Navarra 1998: This round red is juicy and soft, with very light tannins, simple grapey and plummy flavors and a bracing herbal accent. An easy quaff that is best lightly chilled. Drink now.–T.M. • $13 • (10/31/1999) • **83**

Merlot Navarra 1997: This bright, fresh red offers a core of tart cherry flavors, with accents of smoke and herb. It's a bit lean, with light tannins that have just enough grip for food. Drink now.–T.M. • $7 • (10/31/1998) • **83**

Merlot Navarra Oligitum 1995 • $6 • (10/31/1997) • **84**

Moscatel Navarra 1998: This rich white has a lively balance of tart orange, sweet honey and spice notes, bold and clean. Strawberry and mango add cake to the icing. Drink now.–T.M. • $24/500 ml. • (10/31/1999) • **87**

Moscatel Navarra 1997: This soft white offers plenty of sweetness, with light lemon custard flavors. It's clean and balanced, but has little distinctive character. A nice match for sugar cookies or other sweet pastries. Drink now.–T.M. • $10/500 ml. • (11/30/1998) • **83**

Navarra Albero 1997: This plump red offers ripe flavors of plums, smoke and herbs, with light gamy notes. It has round tannins and fresh acidity, and a clean, fruity finish. Drink now through 2001.–T.M. • $7 • (10/31/1998) • **83**

Navarra Coupage Crianza 1994 • $8 • (10/31/1997) • **87**

Navarra Crianza 1996: This fleshy red offers raisin, coffee and cola flavors; sweet and a bit clumsy. Quaffable but turns cloying after a glass or two.–T.M. • $14 • (11/15/1999) • **78**

Navarra Crianza 1995: This modest red offers straightforward flavors of cherry, toast and tobacco, with firm tannins and a clean, short finish. A modest but solid accompaniment to food. Drink now through 2002.–T.M. • $9 • (11/30/1998) • **83**

Navarra Noble 1996: Plum and chocolate notes are fresh and solid in this lively red. Balanced and fresh, with appealing hints of game and mint. A chewy wine that makes a solid match with food. Drink now through 2001.–T.M. • $7 • (11/30/1998) • **85**

Navarra Oligitum 1995 • $6 • (10/31/1997) • **85**

Navarra Reserva 1994: Sweet vanilla and cola flavors from oak dominate this smooth red. Light cherry and herbal notes are buried beneath the wood. Drink now.–T.M. • $19 • (11/15/1999) • **81**

Navarra Rosado 1997: Though delicate in color and texture, this pale rosé shows an assertive, smoky, bitter note that dominates the light berry flavors.–T.M. • $6 • (11/30/1998) • **77**

Navarra Seleccion 1998: A supple, juicy red packed with ripe black cherry and plum flavors, with sweet vanilla accents. Lively acidity keeps it refreshing. Drink now.–T.M. • $12 • (11/15/1999) • **84**

Navarra White 1997: Round and soft, this white shows earthy and odd, almost fishy flavors, without much fruit or depth.–T.M. • $6 • (11/15/1998) • **73**

Tempranillo Navarra Oligitum 1996 • $6 • (10/31/1997) • **82**

PINGUS, DOMINIO DE

Ribera del Duero 1996: A gentle giant. This inky, massive wine coats the palate with rich, ripe flavors of plum, prune and cassis and plenty of oaky notes of chocolate and coffee. Despite high alcohol, it remains velvety and balanced. Try it with a big steak now, or hold to tame it. Best after 2003.–T.M. • $276 Ⓐ • (11/30/1999) • **95**

Ribera del Duero Flor de Pingus 1996: Muscular and rich. This big red is jammy, with plum, cassis, chocolate and licorice flavors that coat the palate and enrobe the underlying tannins. Powerful and thick, it's not graceful now but certainly impressive. Best from 2001 through 2007.–T.M. • $38 Ⓐ • (11/30/1999) • **90**

PINORD, BODEGAS

Cabernet Sauvignon Penedès Chateldon Gran Reserva 1993: Maturing now, this supple red offers cedar, tobacco and spicy flavors, yet retains a core of cherry and raisin. The tannins turn a bit dry on the finish, but the wine should bloom with food. Drink now.–T.M. • $19 • (12/31/1999) • **86**

Cabernet Sauvignon Penedès Chateldon Reserva 1995: Maturing nicely, this supple red has pretty cherry flavors and is developing cedar, spice and tobacco notes that linger on the finish. It's still fresh and will show nicely with food. Drink now.–T.M. • $12 • (12/31/1999) • **85**

Chardonnay Penedès 1998: Voluptuous, offering generous flavors of ripe melon, vanilla and cream, with sweet oak and low acidity, yet the finish is crisp enough to marry the wine with food. Drink now.–T.M. • $10 • (12/31/1999) • **87**

Chardonnay Penedès Barrel Fermented 1997: Rivals old-school California with its lavish sweet oak and extremely ripe fruit flavors, but it sacrifices elegance for opulence and falls short of balance. Drink now.–T.M. • $10 • (12/31/1999) • **79**

Penedès Clos de Torribas Crianza 1996: Floral, berry and toast flavors have distinctive personality, but tend to get lost behind very firm tannins. Still, it has the structure for food. Drink now.–T.M. • $8 • (1/01/2000) • **82**

PIQUERAS, BODEGAS

Almansa Castillo de Almansa Crianza 1988 • $NA • (4/15/1994) • **82**

Almansa Castillo de Almansa Reserva 1994: Soft on the palate and dry on the finish, this shows light cherry and herb flavors. Fading.–T.M. • $10 • (6/15/2000) • **77**

Almansa Castillo de Almansa Reserva 1993: Still deep in color and youthful in texture, this red offers ripe cherry and plum flavors, with accents of earth and tobacco. Has firm tannins and bright acidity, and should show well with food. Drink now.–T.M. • $NA • (11/30/1998) • **83**

PIRINEOS, BODEGA

Macabeo Somontano Montesierra 1997: This round, fresh white offers clean flavors of apple and pear. Not complex, but balanced and juicy. A pleasant, albeit modest, complement to food. Drink now.–T.M. • $6 • (11/30/1998) • **83**

Macabeo Somontano Vendimia Tardia 1997: This firm white shows ripe melon and pear flavors, with a backbone of tart acidity and hints of vanilla and honey. Fruity, yet quite dry, despite the late harvest designation. Drink now.–T.M. • $10 • (11/30/1998) • **83**

Moristel Somontano 1998: Ripe flavors of juicy plum and black cherry are round and sweet in this modern-style red. Has enough body to match with food. Drink now through 2002.–T.M. • $9 • (11/15/1999) • **84**

Moristel Somontano Montesierra 1997: Herbal and earthy notes mingle with simple, sweet-and-sour fruit flavors in this fleshy red. Tannins are light but firm.–T.M. • $6 • (11/30/1998) • **78**

Moristel Somontano Montesierra 1996 • $7 • (10/31/1997) • **83**

Moristel Somontano Montesierra 1995 • $6 • (8/31/1996) • **79**

Moristel Somontano Montesierra 1993 • $5 • (1/31/1995) • **78**

Moristel Somontano Montesierra 1988 • $6 • (3/31/1990) • **81**

Somontano Montesierra 1998: Soft and fruity. Simple but lively grape and cherry flavors and a supple texture make this red an easy quaffer. Drink now.–T.M. • $6 • (11/15/1999) • **82**

Somontano Montesierra Crianza 1996: This sturdy red is rich with ripe plum and toasty oak flavors. Balanced and well structured, it has more exuberance than refinement, but should settle down with food. A blend of Tempranillo and Moristel (Mourvèdre). Drink now through 2004.–T.M. • $11 • (11/15/1999) • **85**

Somontano Montesierra Crianza 1995: This appealing red offers well-defined flavors of black cherry and blackberry, with sweet vanilla accents, firm tannins, bright acidity and a velvety mouthfeel. A drink-me wine in the modern style. Enjoy through 2000.–T.M. • $10 • (11/30/1998) • **86**

Somontano Señorio de Lazán Reserva 1995: Smooth and polished, this international-style red offers toasty oak and ripe plum flavors, with a plush texture and a firm backbone. Licorice and spice notes on the finish add interest. A blend of Tempranillo, Cabernet Sauvignon and Moristel (Mourvèdre). Drink now through 2004.–T.M. • $15 • (11/15/1999) • **87**

POBOLEDA

Priorat 1996 • $10 • (6/30/1998) • **84**

PORTOMARIN, BODEGAS

Ribeiro White Trisquel 1998: Light and crisp, with a refreshing hint of spritz, this simple white offers herb and bitter almond flavors and a clean, dry finish. Drink now.–T.M. • $8 • (11/15/1999) • **81**

POVEDA, SALVADOR

Monastrell Alicante Reserva 1989 • $8 • (4/30/1996) • **80**

Monastrell Alicante Reserva 1988 • $9 • (4/15/1994) • **83**

Monastrell Alicante Viña Vermeta Reserva 1994: This exuberant wine is lively with cherry and woodsy aromas, but turns simple and candied on the palate.–T.M. • $11 • (4/30/2000) • **75**

Monastrell Alicante Viña Vermeta Reserva 1990: This maturing red offers light raisin and candied cherry flavors, with accents of spice and licorice. The tannins are very soft, the texture almost like fruit juice.–T.M. • $8 • (11/30/1998) • **79**

Moscatel Alicante Extra NV: This thick, honeyed white shows round flavors of raisin, rose water and tarragon in an interesting blend that's more perfumed than strictly sweet. Has good intensity and distinctive character. Drink now.–T.M. • $10 • (11/30/1998) • **85**

PRIMICIA, BODEGAS

Rioja Viña Diezmo Crianza 1994 • $10 • (11/15/1997) • **86**
Rioja Viña Diezmo Gran Reserva 1989: This luscious red is packed with ripe flavors of plum and prune, backed by chocolate and coffee notes and ripe, round tannins. A generous, muscular wine that can stand up to the richest dishes. Drink now through 2008.–T.M. • $18 • (11/30/1998) • **87**
Rioja Viña Diezmo Reserva 1991: This brooding red has good balance and hidden depth. Still showing youthful power, it offers dark flavors of coffee, leather and herb, with layers of ripe plum and prune supported by muscular tannins. Give it time. Best after 2002.–T.M. • $14 • (11/30/1998) • **88**
Rioja Viña Diezmo Reserva 1989 • $14 • (11/15/1997) • **85**

PRINCIPE DE VIANA, BODEGAS

Cabernet Sauvignon Navarra 1989 • $8 • (3/31/1991) • **83**
Cabernet Sauvignon Navarra Crianza 1994: This light red offers straightforward flavors of cherry, raisin and cedar, with light but firm tannins. Focused but narrow, it's maturing, but remains clean and balanced. Drink now through 2001.–T.M. • $10 • (11/30/1998) • **82**
Cabernet Sauvignon Navarra Crianza 1990 • $8 • (4/15/1994) • **82**

PROTOS, BODEGAS

Ribera del Duero 1996 • $9 • (11/15/1997) • **84**
Ribera del Duero Crianza 1996: Thick texture and firm tannins don't always mean concentration. In this chewy red, they accompany stewed fruit flavors and a muddled finish.–T.M. • $28 • (10/31/1999) • **78**
Ribera del Duero Crianza 1994 • $17 • (11/15/1997) • **89**
Ribera del Duero Gran Reserva 1991: Maturing now, this traditional-style red is smooth and solid, with dried cherry, cigar box and spicy flavors that linger on the finish. Still has the structure to match food. Drink now through 2003.–T.M. • $72 • (10/31/1999) • **88**
Ribera del Duero Gran Reserva 1990: Alluring floral and spicy aromas give way to cherry, cedar and spice flavors in this maturing red, but dry tannins nearly overwhelm the fruit. Drink now.–T.M. • $40 • (10/31/1998) • **83**
Ribera del Duero Gran Reserva 1989 • $40 • (11/15/1997) • **87**
Ribera del Duero Gran Reserva Especial 1989: This muscular red offers sturdy, mature flavors of cedar, earth and tobacco, but a musty note detracts and it's a bit clumsy and dry on the finish. Will show better with hearty food. Decant before serving. Tasted three times, with considerable bottle variation, so beware. Drink now through 2003.–T.M. • $220/1.5 liter • (11/30/1999) • **82**
Ribera del Duero Reserva 1995: This round, generous red is packed with candied cherry and chocolate flavors. Almost sweet, with big, soft tannins and a coffee-scented finish. Not a typical Ribera, but appealing. Drink now through 2002.–T.M. • $42 • (10/31/1999) • **83**

PUERTO, MARQUES DEL

Rioja Crianza 1996: Lively flavors of black cherry, licorice and tobacco are harmonious, and good acidity keeps them lively in this round red. Supple and clean. Drink now through 2002.–T.M. • $11 • (11/30/1999) • **84**
Rioja Crianza 1995: This red offers light flavors of raisin and cooked fruit, with notes of herb and vanilla. Sweet on the palate, but the tannins are a bit dry and the finish is short. Drink now through 2002.–T.M. • $11 • (11/30/1998) • **80**
Rioja Crianza 1994 • $9 • (11/15/1997) • **85**
Rioja Crianza 1988 • $12 • (3/31/1993) • **85**
Rioja Gran Reserva 1985 • $16 • (4/30/1995) • **86**
Rioja Gran Reserva 1978 • $20 • (3/31/1990) • **85**
Rioja Reserva 1994: Cherry and berry flavors are tangy and bright in this approachable red, with light vanilla and spice notes that add interest. Good definition and just enough tannin for grip, with a pleasant, fruity finish. Drink now through 2002.–T.M. • $NA • (11/30/1998) • **84**
Rioja Reserva 1991 • $13 • (11/15/1997) • **83**
Rioja Reserva 1987 • $10 • (4/30/1995) • **83**

Key: SS—Spectator Selection. CS—Cellar Selection. HR—Highly Recommended. $NA—Price not available. (BT)—Barrel tasting. (A)—Auction Price.
For a key to the tasters' initials, see "How to Use These Listings."
Dates in parentheses represent the issues in which the ratings were published.

Rioja Roman Paladino Gran Reserva 1975 • $35 • (11/15/1997) • **78**
Rioja Rosado 1998: This vibrant, fruity rosé has a neon-scarlet color of startling appeal. The cherry flavors are deep, and there's even grip on the clean, dry finish. Drink now.–T.M. • $9 • (10/31/1999) • **85**
Rioja Rosado 1997: This light, clean rosé offers simple cherry and berry flavors. Light on the palate, with just enough acidity to keep it lively. A pleasant quaff. Drink now.–T.M. • $9 • (10/31/1998) • **83**
Rioja White 1998: Almond and herbal flavors shine through this muscular white. Has the structure to stand up to food, but a slight sweet-sour note turns a bit cloying on the finish. Drink now.–T.M. • $9 • (10/31/1999) • **81**

PUIG & ROCA, CELLERS

Cabernet Sauvignon Penedès Augustus 1991 • $11 • (3/31/1995) • **84**
Chardonnay Penedès Augustus 1997: Strong, sweet vanilla flavors from oak almost compensate for the underlying vegetal notes, but in the end, it lacks the acidity to draw you back for a second glass.–T.M. • $20 • (4/30/2000) • **76**

RAIMAT

Cabernet Sauvignon Costers del Segre 1989 • $8 • (1/31/1993) • **81**
Cabernet Sauvignon Costers del Segre 1988 • $8 • (12/15/1992) • **80**
Cabernet Sauvignon Costers del Segre 1986 • $10 • (3/31/1990) • **81**
Cabernet Sauvignon Costers del Segre El Moli Reserva 1994: This polished red achieves a fine balance of supple fruit and firm tannins, with complex flavors of black cherry, tobacco and herb that linger on the finish. It speaks of both the grape variety and the terroir. Drink now through 2008.–T.M. • $29 • (12/15/1999) • **89**
Cabernet Sauvignon Costers del Segre Mas Castell Reserva 1994: Rich and meaty. This dark, highly extracted red leans towards the earthy, herbal side of the variety, with muscular tannins and a clean, firm finish. Best from 2001 through 2006.–T.M. • $29 • (12/15/1999) • **87**
Cabernet Sauvignon Costers del Segre Vallcorba Reserva 1994: Still deeply colored and youthful, this polished red shows plush texture and lush fruit flavors of the international style, with plum, toast and spice notes. Harmonious and refined. Drink now through 2003.–T.M. • $30 • (11/15/1999) • **87**
Costers del Segre Abadia 1989 • $8 • (4/15/1994) • **83**
Merlot Costers del Segre 1990 • $8 • (4/15/1994) • **79**
Tempranillo Costers del Segre 1996: Round and soft, this generous red offers plum, chocolate and licorice flavors, lush and even a bit sweet. A warm and fuzzy style, perhaps better with dessert than a hearty main course. Drink now through 2002.–T.M. • $14 • (12/15/1999) • **84**
Tempranillo Costers del Segre 1995: A crisp, fresh and well-defined red, offering bright cherry, smoke and light chocolate flavors, balanced and vibrant. Though not muscular, it can stand up to lighter meat dishes, and draws you back for another sip. Drink now.–T.M. • $15 • (9/15/1999) • **85**
Tempranillo Costers del Segre 1990 • $8 • (4/15/1994) • **85**

RAMIREZ, BODEGAS

Rioja Ramírez de la Piscina Crianza 1996: Silky and supple. This elegant red offers pretty cherry and black cherry flavors, with well-integrated tannins and notes of spice on the finish. A drink-me wine. Drink now through 2002.–T.M. • $12 • (10/31/1999) • **85**
Rioja Ramírez de la Piscina Crianza 1995: Distinctive and intense, but lacks balance. Flavors range from cherry and coffee to red licorice and tarragon, while the plush texture gives way to astringent tannins. May improve with time.–T.M. • $9 • (11/30/1998) • **79**
Rioja Ramírez de la Piscina Reserva 1994: This supple red offers traditional flavors of dried cherries and spice, with notes of earth and leather. It's balanced and harmonious and has enough grip for food. Drink now through 2003.–T.M. • $16 • (5/31/2000) • **85**

RAVENTOS ROSELL, JOAN

Cabernet Sauvignon Penedès Heretat Vall-Ventós Crianza 1997: This juicy red shows distinctive character, with cherry, cola and tobacco flavors, bright acidity and fine tannins. Supple enough for drinking now, firm enough for food. Drink now.–T.M. • $15 • (12/31/1999) • **85**
Chardonnay Penedès Heretat Vall-Ventós 1997: Oaky flavors of toast and smoke dominate this straightforward white. While the bright acidity keeps it lively, there's little fruit for balance.–T.M. • $12 • (10/31/1999) • **79**
Merlot Penedès Heretat Vall-Ventós 1997: Already browning, this red is tired and flat, with simple cedar and cola notes. Tasted twice, with consistent notes.–T.M. • $14 • (1/01/2000) • **74**

REAL, BODEGAS MARCO

Cabernet Sauvignon Navarra Homenaje 1996: Earth and cedar flavors dominate this lean red. It's tart and a bit spritzy, too. Tasted twice, with consistent notes. Past its prime.–T.M. • $10 • (12/31/1999) • **75**

Navarra Homenaje Crianza 1995: Firm, offering tart cherry, cola and light earthy flavors backed by muscular tannins. It's lively and tightly wound, and should bloom with food. Drink now through 2002.–T.M. • $10 • (11/15/1999) • **86**

Navarra Homenaje Reserva 1994: A juicy red, packed with ripe plum and blackberry flavors, accented by lively acidity and sweet vanilla notes. Round but not heavy; balanced and clean. Drink now through 2002.–T.M. • $12 • (11/15/1999) • **88**

REAL SITIO DE VENTOSILLA, BODEGAS

Ribera del Duero Pradorey 1996 • $7 • (5/15/1998) • **78**

REMELLURI, LA GRANJA NUESTRA SENORA DE

Rioja 1996: This ambitious red from Spain has a deep, opaque color, deep, almost charred aromas of coffee and toast and is firmly tannic on the palate, with ripe flavors of coffee, plum, prune and licorice. The wood notes are dominant now, but it has the concentration to improve with age. Best after 2002.–T.M. • $20 • (10/31/1999) SS • **90**

Rioja 1995: This firm, polished red offers ripe plum, licorice and toast flavors. Harmonious and showing good intensity. Moderate tannins are well integrated, and the fruit comes out on the finish. Drink now through 2001.–T.M. • $18 • (10/31/1998) • **87**

Rioja 1994 • $16 • (2/28/1998) • **88**
Rioja 1993 • $16 • (1/01/1997) • **84**
Rioja 1989 • $NA • (3/31/1992) • **82**
Rioja 1988 • $NA • (3/31/1992) • **75**
Rioja 1986 • $11 • (12/15/1990) • **87**
Rioja 1985 • $10 • (3/31/1990) • **88**
Rioja 1983 • $12 • (3/31/1990) • **77**
Rioja 1982 • $12 • (3/31/1990) • **82**
Rioja Gran Reserva 1990 • $40 • (2/28/1998) • **88**
Rioja Gran Reserva 1989 • $40 • (12/15/1997) • **82**
Rioja Gran Reserva 1985 • $40 • (3/31/1992) • **84**
Rioja Gran Reserva 1982 • $40 • (11/30/1991) • **87**
Rioja Reserva 1990 • $14 • (4/30/1995) • **88**
Rioja Reserva 1989 • $14 • (4/15/1994) • **83**
Rioja Reserva 1987 • $14 • (3/31/1992) • **76**
Rioja Reserva 1986 • $14 • (3/31/1992) • **78**

Rioja White 1997: This big white is crisply balanced, with green apple and melon flavors that are attractive but dominated by oak. Give it time to open up, as there's enough acidity to provide a lively complement to seafood or poultry. Drink now through 2002.–T.M. • $23 • (11/30/1999) • **87**

REMIREZ DE GANUZA, BODEGAS FERNANDO

Rioja 1995: This muscular red shows a deep color, a thick texture, firm tannins and solid flavors of vanilla, plum and raisin. Balanced if not graceful, it can stand up to hearty foods. Drink now through 2003.–T.M. • $50 • (12/15/1999) • **87**

Rioja Reserva 1994: This rich, modern-style red has good structure, with ripe plum and blackberry flavors, sweet vanilla oak notes and round, firm tannins. Fresh, with the depth to age. Drink now through 2005.–T.M. • $50 • (11/30/1998) • **86**

RETUERTA, ABADIA

Viño de Mesa de Castilla y Leon 1996: This is packed with flavor, offering blackberry, black pepper, game and licorice notes. The tannins have just enough grip for food. Intriguing, with a distinctive personality. Tasted twice, with consistent notes. Drink now.–T.M. • $24 • (11/30/1998) • **86**

Viño de Mesa de Castilla y Leon Cuvée El Campanario 1996: Firm and polished, this wine is closed right now but shows concentration and balance, with notes of toast, coffee and cassis. Modern in style, it comes off as a bit too sculpted. Tasted three times, with consistent notes. Drink through 2005.–T.M. • $49 • (11/30/1998) • **87**

Viño de Mesa de Castilla y Leon Cuvée El Palomar 1996: Coffee and cocoa flavors are expressive but overshadow the ripe plum in this chunky, rather austere red. Rich and firm, but a bit drying on the finish. Tasted twice, with consistent notes. Drink through 2002.–T.M. • $43 • (11/30/1998) • **83**

Viño de Mesa de Castilla y Leon Pago Negralada 1996: This nicely sculpted, stylish red has well-integrated new oak and ripe flavors of plum, chocolate and mineral. The tannins are firm but unobtrusive, and the finish is clean and lingering. Drink now through 2005.–T.M. • $100 • (11/15/1999) • **88**

Viño de Mesa de Castilla y Leon Pago Valdebellón 1996: This dense, polished red offers ripe plum, chocolate and coffee flavors. Rich and a bit soft, with a sweet chocolate finish, good concentration and round, well-integrated tannins. Made from Cabernet Sauvignon. Drink now through 2004.–T.M. • $100 • (11/15/1999) • **88**

Viño de Mesa de Castilla y Leon Primicia 1998: This straightforward red shows good structure, with firm, balanced tannins and a clean, fresh texture, but the flavors are a bit muted, showing light black cherry and herb notes. A blend of Tempranillo, Cabernet and Merlot. Drink through 2003.–T.M. • $10 • (11/15/1999) • **84**

Viño de Mesa de Castilla y Leon Rívola 1998: Bright black cherry and black pepper flavors are clean and focused in this vibrant red. Lively and balanced, with a fresh, spicy finish. Drink now through 2003.–T.M. • $12 • (11/15/1999) • **87**

Viño de Mesa de Castilla y Leon Rívola 1997: Black cherry, black pepper and tobacco notes are firm and well defined in this austere red. Light-bodied, with a clean finish. Tasted twice, with consistent notes. Drink now.–T.M. • $10 • (11/30/1998) • **81**

Viño de Mesa de Castilla y Leon Rívola 1996 • $10 • (5/15/1998) • **87**

REYES, BODEGAS

Ribera del Duero Teófilo Reyes 1997: Alluring mineral, dark fruit and tobacco aromas give way to more subdued but still harmonious flavors of plums and herbs, with enough acidity to keep it lively. Drink now through 2003.–T.M. • $27 • (4/30/2000) • **87**

Ribera del Duero Teófilo Reyes 1996: This muscular red has plenty of concentration, with its dark color, mouthfilling tannins and ripe, almost stewed flavors of prune, plum and coffee. Clumsy and almost bitter on the finish, it's hard to foresee a good future. A far cry from the '94 and '95 vintages. Tasted three times, with consistent notes. Best after 2000.–T.M. • $26 • (11/30/1998) • **83**

Ribera del Duero Teófilo Reyes 1995 • $25 • (5/15/1998) • **91**
Ribera del Duero Teófilo Reyes 1994 • $25 • (6/15/1997) CS • **95**

RIBERA, VINICOLA DE LA

Tarragona Mediterráneo NV • $4 • (11/15/1997) • **76**

RIBERALTA, BODEGAS

Ribera del Duero Vega Izan 1992 • $7 • (4/30/1995) • **75**
Ribera del Duero Vega Izan 1991 • $7 • (2/28/1995) • **72**

Ribera del Duero Vega Izan Crianza 1994: In a traditional style that resembles Rioja, this is a lighter red with cherry, smoky, tea and spicy flavors, light tannins and a spicy, slightly dry finish. Drink now.–T.M. • $13 • (8/31/1998) • **84**

Ribera del Duero Vega Izan Crianza 1991 • $11 • (2/28/1995) • **83**

Ribera del Duero Vega Izan Joven 1996: Light-bodied for Ribera, with dry tannins, a hint of spritz on the finish.–T.M. • $8 • (8/31/1998) • **77**

RICAVI

Rioja 1997: Light and silky, this modest red offers pretty berry and light vanilla flavors, with light tannins and a clean, short finish. A pleasant quaff. Drink now.–T.M. • $7 • (11/30/1998) • **81**

Rioja 1994 • $6 • (4/30/1996) • **81**
Rioja 1993 • $6 • (4/30/1995) • **82**
Rioja 1992 • $5 • (4/15/1994) • **78**
Rioja Crianza 1991 • $8 • (4/30/1996) • **83**
Rioja Crianza 1990 • $7 • (4/30/1995) • **81**

RIOJA ALTA, LA

Rioja 890 Gran Reserva 1982 • $65 • (11/30/1997) • **86**
Rioja 890 Gran Reserva 1981 • $65 • (6/30/1996) • **86**
Rioja 890 Gran Reserva 1978 • $50 • (4/30/1995) • **89**
Rioja 890 Gran Reserva 1973 • $55 • (3/31/1992) • **77**

RIOJA ALTA, LA

Rioja 904 Gran Reserva 1989: Atypical but alluring. Distinctive floral, cranberry and orange peel notes give this wine personality, and it's still quite racy on the palate, with enough grip to stand up to food. Drink now.–T.M. • $38 • (12/15/1999) • **87**
Rioja 904 Gran Reserva 1987 • $35 • (11/15/1997) • **86**
Rioja 904 Gran Reserva 1985 • $66 Ⓐ • (6/30/1996) • **82**
Rioja 904 Gran Reserva 1982 • $NA • (3/31/1992) • **84**
Rioja 904 Gran Reserva 1981 • $29 • (3/31/1992) • **82**
Rioja 904 Gran Reserva 1976 • $17 • (3/31/1990) • **90**
Rioja 904 Gran Reserva 1975 • $NA • (3/31/1992) • **82**
Rioja 904 Gran Reserva 1973 • $10 • (9/30/1986) • **84**
Rioja 904 Gran Reserva 1970 • $NA • (3/31/1992) • **75**
Rioja Viña Alberdi Reserva 1995: This ripe red offers jammy cherry, coffee and earth flavors, with more intensity than definition. Good with hearty dishes. Drink now through 2004.–T.M. • $13 • (5/31/2000) • **83**
Rioja Viña Alberdi Reserva 1994 • $14 • (5/31/1998) • **84**
Rioja Viña Alberdi Reserva 1993 • $13 • (11/15/1997) • **76**
Rioja Viña Alberdi Reserva 1992 • $14 • (10/15/1996) • **84**
Rioja Viña Alberdi Reserva 1991 • $13 • (6/30/1996) • **78**
Rioja Viña Alberdi Reserva 1989 • $12 • (4/15/1994) • **77**
Rioja Viña Alberdi Reserva 1988 • $11 • (4/15/1994) • **86**
Rioja Viña Alberdi Reserva 1987 • $12 • (3/31/1992) • **79**
Rioja Viña Alberdi Reserva 1986 • $12 • (3/31/1992) • **83**
Rioja Viña Alberdi Reserva Lot 2 1989 • $12 • (4/30/1995) • **82**
Rioja Viña Arana Reserva 1991 • $18 • (5/31/1998) • **85**
Rioja Viña Arana Reserva 1988 • $21 Ⓐ • (6/30/1996) • **83**
Rioja Viña Arana Reserva 1986 • $16 • (4/30/1995) • **82**
Rioja Viña Arana Reserva 1985 • $15 • (4/15/1994) • **76**
Rioja Viña Ardanza Reserva 1990: This mature red shows traditional flavors of coffee and brown sugar, with notes of cola and raisin. Still quite generous on the palate, but lacks the fruit to carry it much longer. Drink now.–T.M. • $25 • (12/15/1999) • **86**
Rioja Viña Ardanza Reserva 1989 • $22 • (6/30/1996) • **79**
Rioja Viña Ardanza Reserva 1987 • $40 Ⓐ • (4/15/1994) • **72**
Rioja Viña Ardanza Reserva 1986 • $32 Ⓐ • (4/15/1994) • **85**
Rioja Viña Ardanza Reserva 1985 • $18 • (3/31/1992) • **85**
Rioja Viña Ardanza Reserva 1983 • $31 Ⓐ • (3/31/1992) • **81**
Rioja Viña Ardanza Reserva 1982 • $17 • (3/31/1992) • **84**

RIOJANAS, BODEGAS

Rioja Monte Real Gran Reserva 1985 • $22 • (4/15/1994) • **88**
Rioja Monte Real Gran Reserva 1982 • $19 • (3/31/1992) • **82**
Rioja Monte Real Gran Reserva 1981 • $19 • (4/15/1994) • **89**
Rioja Monte Real Gran Reserva 1975 • $NA • (4/15/1994) • **78**
Rioja Monte Real Gran Reserva 1973 • $NA • (4/15/1994) • **85**
Rioja Monte Real Reserva 1995: Alluring aromas of spice and cedar follow through on the silky palate in this traditional red. There's enough cherry flavor to keep it lively and enough tannin to stand up to food. Drink now through 2003.–T.M. • $15 • (11/30/1999) • **86**
Rioja Monte Real Reserva 1985 • $NA • (3/31/1992) • **87**
Rioja Monte Real Reserva 1986 • $14 • (4/15/1994) • **77**
Rioja Puerta Vieja Crianza 1988 • $9 • (4/15/1994) • **80**
Rioja Viña Albina Gran Reserva 1985 • $22 • (4/15/1994) • **83**
Rioja Viña Albina Gran Reserva 1982 • $19 • (3/31/1992) • **87**
Rioja Viña Albina Gran Reserva 1981 • $19 • (3/31/1992) • **86**
Rioja Viña Albina Gran Reserva 1975 • $NA • (3/31/1992) • **85**
Rioja Viña Albina Gran Reserva 1973 • $NA • (3/31/1992) • **81**
Rioja Viña Albina Reserva 1986 • $14 • (4/15/1994) • **82**
Rioja Viña Albina Reserva 1985 • $NA • (3/31/1992) • **78**

RISCAL, MARQUES DE

Rioja 1945: Very minty, with cherry, berry and mineral notes. Full-bodied and tannic. A tough and powerful, muscular and strong wine. Like the Château Latour 1945. Still has ages to go. Will outlive us all. (Marqués de Riscal vertical tasting—and all listings below from the 7/31/1998 issue). –J.S. • $NA • (7/31/1998) • **99**
Rioja 1938: Slightly simple, but very silky and fine. A caressing old wine, with mint, berry and chocolate notes and a fine coffee finish. Delicious. –J.S. • $NA • (7/31/1998) • **88**
Rioja 1936: Slightly lifted, with some volatile acidity, but fresh and easy. A bit simple, but ripe and full, with tea-tinged chocolate notes. Medium-bodied, with smooth tannins and a silky finish.–J.S. • $NA • (7/31/1998) • **87**
Rioja 1924: A deep ruby wine, with lovely berry, mineral and cigar-box aromas. Full-bodied and mouthfilling, with a supervelvety and long finish. A seamless, sexy wine. Wonderful.–J.S. • $NA • (7/31/1998) • **98**
Rioja 1918: Gorgeous aromas of dried berries, with smoke, floral and chocolate notes. Medium-bodied, with fresh, fine tannins. Lacks a bit of body, but shows a very fine, short finish.–J.S. • $NA • (7/31/1998) • **91**
Rioja 1898: Not a perfect bottle, but very impressive, with loads of dried raisin and ripe fruit character. Full-bodied, with slightly high acidity but a long and silky finish. Outstanding for staying alive for so long.–J.S. • $NA • (7/31/1998) • **90**
Rioja 1897: Fabulous aromas of milk chocolate, with fruit and mint flavors. A full-bodied, silky wine with a long, long finish. Stunning.–J.S. • $NA • (7/31/1998) • **96**
Rioja 1879: A dusty, funky old wine, but rather cuddly and enjoyable, with mushroom, spice and berry character, mint and meat flavors. Medium- to full-bodied, with medium tannins and a soft texture. Warming finish.–J.S. • $NA • (7/31/1998) • **87**
Rioja Barón de Chirel Reserva 1988 • $36 • (4/30/1995) • **90**
Rioja Barón de Chirel Reserva 1986 • $36 • (4/15/1994) • **90**
Rioja Gran Reserva 1982 • $NA • (11/30/1991) • **84**
Rioja Gran Reserva 1981 • $18 • (11/15/1997) • **78**
Rioja Gran Reserva 1964: A gorgeous wine, with violet and other floral aromas and flavors. Full-bodied and firmly tannic, yet harmonious and long. A truly great wine, like layered silk.–J.S. • $NA • (7/31/1998) • **98**
Rioja Gran Reserva 1958: Very fine Burgundian style. Medium- to light-bodied, with vanilla, cocoa and berry aromas. Fine tannins, with fresh acidity and a long, delicious finish. An elegant, easy wine.–J.S. • $NA • (7/31/1998) • **88**
Rioja Gran Reserva 1952: Lovely notes of raspberry, dried cherry, coffee and dark chocolate. Full- to medium-bodied, with fine tannins and a chocolaty coconut flavor. Really gorgeous. A very silky, elegant, fine supermodel of a wine.–J.S. • $NA • (7/31/1998) • **93**
Rioja Reserva 1994: Perfumed with spice and floral aromas, this red combines intensity and delicacy, with light but well-defined flavors of cherry, chocolate, herb and cedar. The tannins are light but firm, and herb and spice notes linger on the finish. Tasted twice, with consistent notes. Drink now through 2001.–T.M. • $12 • (11/30/1998) • **86**
Rioja Reserva 1992 • $12 • (11/15/1997) • **81**
Rioja Reserva 1991 • $13 • (3/31/1996) • **85**
Rioja Reserva 1990 • $13 • (1/31/1996) • **82**
Rioja Reserva 1989 • $11 • (4/30/1995) • **90**
Rioja Reserva 1988 • $12 • (4/15/1994) • **83**
Rueda 1996 • $7 • (10/31/1997) • **85**

RODA, BODEGAS

Rioja Roda I Reserva 1995: Combining traditional flavors and modern structure, this rich red offers cedar, smoke and ripe plum flavors, with firm tannins and good concentration. Despite its power, it remains smooth and harmonious. Drink now through 2005.–T.M. • $50 • (11/30/1999) • **90**
Rioja Roda I Reserva 1994: This polished red marries extraction and elegance, with a firm structure and well-balanced flavors of plum, toast and spice that linger on the clean, fresh finish. Drink now through 2005.–T.M. • $45 • (10/31/1998) • **88**
Rioja Roda II Reserva 1995: This ambitious, international-style red shows a deep color, muscular tannins and plenty of extraction, with smoky oak, coffee, ripe plum and vanilla flavors that are bold and rich. It lacks harmony now, but should come together with time. Best after 2001.–T.M. • $37 • (11/30/1999) • **88**

RODERO, BODEGAS

Ribera del Duero Carmelo Rodero Gran Reserva 1991 • $80 • (1/01/1998) • **87**
Ribera del Duero Carmelo Rodero Reserva 1995: Rich and chewy, this red offers ripe plum and black cherry flavors, overlaid with assertive, smoky espresso notes that turn a bit bitter on the finish. Needs food for balance. Drink now through 2003.–T.M. • $40 • (10/31/1999) • **86**
Ribera del Duero Carmelo Rodero Reserva 1994: Firm and harmonious. Alluring aromas of blackberry, vanilla and smoke follow through on the palate in this polished, well-balanced red. There's good intensity, though it seems to be holding back now. Drink through 2010.–T.M. • $40 • (11/30/1998) • **89**

Key: SS—Spectator Selection. CS—Cellar Selection. HR—Highly Recommended. $NA—Price not available. (BT)—Barrel tasting. Ⓐ—Auction Price.
For a key to the tasters' initials, see "How to Use These Listings."
Dates in parentheses represent the issues in which the ratings were published.

Ribera del Duero Val Ribeño Crianza 1996: This rich red is thick with oak, showing intense espresso and smoky, almost charred flavors that dominate plum and herb notes. The tannins are thick and chewy but not dry. A bruiser that needs food for balance. Best from 2002 through 2010.–T.M. • $25 • (10/31/1999) • **86**

Ribera del Duero Val Ribeño Crianza 1995: This assertive red shows gamy and toasty aromas and flavors, with firm tannins and crisp acidity. The notes of plum and berry are clean but a bit subdued. Best with food. Drink now through 2002.–T.M. • $25 • (11/30/1998) • **85**

Ribera del Duero Val Ribeño Crianza 1994: A firm red, lively and polished on the palate, with expressive flavors of chocolate, smoke and game, and more subdued notes of plum and black cherry. Has enough structure and the right balance for food. Drink now through 2004.–T.M. • $25 • (11/30/1998) • **87**

ROMERO, BODEGA

Navarra La Cruceta Crianza 1994 • $7 • (4/30/1996) • **81**
Navarra La Cruceta Crianza 1993 • $6 • (4/30/1995) • **79**
Navarra La Cruceta Crianza 1990 • $8 • (4/30/1995) • **84**
Navarra Señorio de Yaniz 1993 • $4 • (3/31/1995) • **75**
Navarra Via Corel 1993 • $6 • (4/30/1996) • **82**
Navarra Via Corel 1992 • $5 • (4/30/1995) • **83**

ROTLLAN TORRA

Priorat Amadis 1996: Smooth and solid, this polished red offers harmonious flavors of black cherry, chocolate and cola that glide on silky tannins and linger on the finish. Gentle on the palate, this brings you back for another sip. Drink now through 2004.–T.M. • $45 • (11/30/1999) • **88**

Priorat Balandra 1996: Bursting with ripe cherry and blackberry, this round red remains soft and even delicate on the palate. Accents of smoke and dried herbs add interest, and the jammy flavors linger on the finish. Drink now through 2003.–T.M. • $30 • (9/15/1999) • **87**

Priorat Gran Reserva 1991: This rustic red is fully mature, with flavors of dried cherries, raisins, cedar and earth. A bit dry and musty on the finish.–T.M. • $19 • (9/15/1999) • **77**

Priorat Reserva 1994: Maturing now, this soft red shows berry, dried cherry, tobacco and earth flavors, gentle but lacking life and grip, though some spicy flavors emerge on the finish. Drink now.–T.M. • $15 • (9/15/1999) • **82**

ROVIRA, BODEGAS PEDRO

Brut Nature Cava Brut de Belart NV • $12 • (10/31/1997) • **84**

Muscat Tarragona Novell 1996: This round, soft white is rather neutral, with candle wax and light vanilla notes. A light, citrusy acidity just keeps it alive.–T.M. • $9 • (11/30/1998) • **79**

Tarragona Catalonia Reserva 1988 • $9 • (11/15/1997) • **76**
Tarragona Gran Corpas 1989 • $6 • (8/31/1993) • **79**
Tarragona Gran Reserva 1987 • $18 • (11/15/1997) • **79**
Tarragona Gran Reserva 1982 • $10 • (3/31/1993) • **86**

Tarragona Marqués de Campo Real Crianza 1993: This light, silky red offers dried cherry, vanilla and spice flavors, with light tannins that turn a bit dry on the finish. Fully mature.–T.M. • $6 • (11/30/1998) • **77**

Tarragona Marqués de Campo Real Crianza 1991 • $6 • (11/15/1997) • **77**
Tarragona Rosado Seco Marqués de Campo Real 1996 • $6 • (10/31/1997) • **84**
Tarragona Señorio del Mar 1989 • $NA • (4/15/1994) • **70**
Tarragona Señorio del Mar Crianza 1991 • $6 • (11/15/1997) • **78**

Tarragona Viña Mater Reserva 1991: Mature flavors of nut, raisin and spice give this light red a traditional character. Light tannins turn dry on the finish. Past its prime.–T.M. • $9 • (11/30/1998) • **77**

Tarragona Viña Mater Reserva 1989 • $9 • (11/15/1997) • **79**
Tarragona White Marqués de Campo Real Blanc de Blancs 1996 • $6 • (10/31/1997) • **79**
Tarragona White Señorio del Mar Blanc de Blancs 1996 • $6 • (10/31/1997) • **79**
Terra Alta Negre de Belart 1992 • $9 • (11/15/1997) • **77**

Terra Alta White Alta Mar Blanc de Nectar 1997: Sweet toffee and floral aromas and flavors remind one of penny candy in this simple white. If you like gumdrops, this is your wine.–T.M. • $7 • (11/30/1998) • **77**

RUIZ, SANTIAGO

Rias Baixas 1997: This round white seems prematurely aged, with a deep gold color, aromas of nuts and honey and flavors of cooked apples and vanilla. Quite rich, but finishes a bit flat. Drink now.–T.M. • $25 • (11/15/1998) • **80**

Rias Baixas 1996 • $19 • (5/31/1998) • **85**

SALCEDA, VINA

Rioja 1990 • $11 • (4/30/1995) • **83**
Rioja Conde de la Salceda Gran Reserva 1987 • $23 • (6/30/1997) • **78**

Rioja Crianza 1995: Alluring aromas and flavors of black cherry, chocolate and herb mingle in this light-bodied yet firmly tannic red. Ripe and well structured, but a light earthy note detracts. Drink now through 2003.–T.M. • $14 • (11/30/1998) • **82**

Rioja Crianza 1994: This generous red offers ripe flavors of roasted plum and prune, with vanilla and coffee accents. It has ample structure, but tastes a bit coarse. Should smooth out with food. Drink now.–T.M. • $14 • (11/30/1998) • **81**

Rioja Crianza 1993 • $13 • (6/30/1997) • **84**
Rioja Crianza 1991 • $11 • (3/31/1996) • **85**
Rioja Crianza 1989 • $10 • (4/15/1994) • **83**
Rioja Cuvée Especial 25 Aniversario Reserva 1987 • $16 • (4/30/1995) • **84**
Rioja Gran Reserva 1985 • $20 • (4/15/1994) • **89**

SALNESUR, BODEGAS

Albariño Rias Baixas Condes de Albarei 1997: This assertive white delivers pure, intense flavors of pineapple, lime and almond, with vibrant acidity and just a hint of spritz on the palate. It's clean and very refreshing. Drink now.–T.M. • $12 • (11/15/1998) • **87**

Albariño Rias Baixas Condes de Albarei 1996 • $13 • (5/31/1998) • **87**

SAN ESTEBAN, BODEGA COOP.

Rufete Viño de Mesa de Castilla y Leon Tiriñuelo NV: This light, astringent red tastes like it hasn't quite finished its business. Shows grapey, bitter and herbal flavors, with drying tannins.–T.M. • $8 • (11/15/1999) • **77**

SAN VICENTE, SENORIO DE

Tempranillo Rioja 1996: Ambitious. This deeply colored, highly extracted red has a muscular structure, with mouthfilling tannins that dominate coffee and smoke flavors, which in turn dominate the core of ripe plum, tobacco, licorice and prune flavors. Give it time and watch it soar. Best after 2002.–T.M. • $28 • (10/31/1999) • **92**

Tempranillo Rioja 1995: Lavish flavors of chocolate, coffee and toasted nut, but only hints of raisin and plum. Medium-bodied, with firm oak tannins drying on the finish, this comes off as clumsy in the end. An ambitious conundrum. Tasted three times, with consistent notes. Drink through 2005.–T.M. • $26 • (11/30/1998) • **84**

Tempranillo Rioja 1994 • $25 • (2/28/1998) • **92**
Tempranillo Rioja Reserva 1991 • $25 • (2/28/1998) • **87**

SANZ, VINOS

Rueda Superior Montesol 1998: Lively acidity gives this bracing white its backbone, while citrus and herbal flavors make it a good match with shellfish dishes. Drink now.–T.M. • $11 • (4/30/2000) • **84**

SARDA, BODEGAS J.

Brut Cava NV • $10 • (10/31/1997) • **81**
Brut Cava Extra Reserva NV • $16 • (3/31/1993) • **80**

Cabernet Sauvignon Penedès 1992: Fading now, this supple red offers light floral, vanilla and dried cherry flavors. Shows some elegance, but turns a bit dry on the finish. Drink now.–T.M. • $10 • (12/31/1999) • **83**

Chardonnay Penedès 1996 • $9 • (10/31/1997) • **83**
Moscatel Spain NV • $9 • (11/15/1997) • **78**
Tempranillo Penedès Viña Sardà 1993 • $6 • (12/15/1997) • **78**

SCALA DEI

Priorat Cartoixa Gran Reserva 1987 • $18 • (4/15/1994) • **83**
Priorat Cartoixa Gran Reserva 1978 • $25 • (4/15/1994) • **86**
Priorat El Cipres 1995 • $8 • (10/31/1997) • **85**
Priorat El Cipres 1994 • $10 • (8/31/1996) • **84**
Priorat El Cipres 1993 • $8 • (4/30/1995) • **82**
Priorat Negre Crianza 1991 • $9 • (4/30/1995) • **85**
Priorat Negre Crianza 1989 • $10 • (4/15/1994) • **85**

SEGURA VIUDAS

Brut Cava Aria NV: A well-balanced bubbly, with a fine mousse, flavors of apple and green peach and rich spicy notes on the finish. Drink now.–K.M. • $10 • (12/15/1999) • **84**

Brut Cava Aria Estate NV • $10 • (7/31/1996) • **84**

Brut Cava Heredad Reserva NV: A floral aroma and flavor dominates this focused wine, with toasty and green peach flavors. Ends on a slightly rubbery note.–K.M. • $13 • (12/15/1999) • **82**

Brut Cava Reserva NV: This lightly sweet sparkler offers simple flavors of apple and canned peach, but stays lively thanks to a fresh mousse and crisp acidity. A quaffable aperitif. Drink now.–T.M. • $7 • (11/30/1998) • **80**

Extra Dry Cava Aria NV: Toast, butter and cooked apple flavors give this soft sparkler a pielike character. Dry on the palate, with a lean texture and a soft mousse.–T.M. • $9 • (11/30/1998) • **78**

SENDA GALIANA, BODEGAS Y VINAS

Rioja Conde Alegre 1997: This lean red is light-bodied yet dry, with astringent tannins and simple cherry and cedar flavors.–T.M. • $9 • (11/30/1999) • **78**

Rioja Conde Allegre 1997: This red is very light, with simple, diluted flavors of berry and herb, almost no tannin and a short, herbal finish.–T.M. • $7 • (11/30/1998) • **78**

Rioja Conde Allegre 1993 • $5 • (4/30/1995) • **81**

Rioja Crianza 1995: This traditional red is light in color and body, with strawberry and light cherry flavors and hints of vanilla on the finish. Firm tannins leave it a bit unbalanced. Drink now through 2002.–T.M. • $12 • (11/30/1998) • **80**

Rioja Crianza 1990 • $7 • (3/31/1996) • **72**

Rioja Crianza 1989 • $7 • (1/31/1995) • **79**

Rioja Reserva 1991: Haunting aromas of cedar and cinnamon give way to mature but lively flavors of dried cherry, cedar, vanilla and spice in this firm but balanced red. A bit lean, but has good intensity and a lingering finish. Drink now through 2003.–T.M. • $14 • (11/30/1998) • **86**

Rioja Reserva 1989 • $10 • (3/31/1996) • **83**

Rioja Reserva 1987 • $10 • (3/31/1995) • **81**

SERRA, JAUME

Brut Cava Cristalino NV: Offers green peach and almond flavors, with a touch of creaminess, turning a tad sharp on the finish. Drink now.–K.M. • $8 • (12/15/1999) • **81**

Brut Cava Reserva NV: A nice attempt at a serious style, with toasty aromas and flavors and ripe fruit notes, with a heady spiciness that lingers on the finish. Drink now.–K.M. • $15 • (12/15/1999) • **86**

Extra Dry Cava Cristalino NV: Fruity and a touch sweet, with fruit cocktail flavors and creamy notes on the finish.–K.M. • $8 • (12/15/1999) • **79**

Merlot Penedès 1991 • $13 • (6/15/1993) • **72**

Penedès Crianza 1992 • $7 • (3/31/1996) • **83**

Penedès Crianza 1991 • $6 • (4/30/1995) • **71**

Penedès Crianza 1989 • $8 • (3/31/1993) • **83**

Penedès Reserva 1988 • $9 • (4/15/1994) • **79**

Seco Cava Reserva NV: Quite ripe-tasting, with pear and baked apple flavors, which end on a slightly candied note. Drink now.–K.M. • $10 • (12/15/1999) • **81**

Tempranillo Penedès 1996: Already browning at the edges, this traditional-style wine offers tobacco, tea and raisin flavors, simple and rather meager. Tasted twice, with consistent notes. Past its prime.–T.M. • $6 • (1/01/2000) • **75**

Tempranillo Penedès 1994 • $6 • (11/15/1997) • **82**

Tempranillo Penedès 1993 • $5 • (3/31/1996) • **82**

Tempranillo Penedès 1992 • $5 • (4/30/1995) • **75**

Tempranillo Penedès 1991 • $5 • (4/30/1995) • **76**

Tempranillo Penedès 1990 • $6 • (3/31/1993) • **71**

Tempranillo Penedès 1988 • $6 • (4/15/1992) • **80**

SIERRA CANTABRIA, BODEGAS

Rioja 1992 • $5 • (4/15/1994) • **77**

Rioja 1991 • $8 • (6/30/1996) • **81**

Key: SS—Spectator Selection. CS—Cellar Selection. HR—Highly Recommended. $NA—Price not available. (BT)—Barrel tasting. (A)—Auction Price.
For a key to the tasters' initials, see "How to Use These Listings."
Dates in parentheses represent the issues in which the ratings were published.

Rioja Codice 1997: Soft and round though a bit light, this red offers cherry, plum and sweet vanilla flavors, with gentle tannins and a spicy finish. Drink now.–T.M. • $8 • (11/30/1999) • **84**

Rioja Codice 1995 • $7 • (12/15/1997) • **77**

Rioja Codice 1993 • $7 • (6/30/1996) • **81**

Rioja Codice 1992 • $6 • (4/15/1994) • **79**

Rioja Codice 1990 • $6 • (4/15/1994) • **84**

Rioja Codice 1989 • $6 • (4/15/1992) • **77**

Rioja Codice 1988 • $6 • (6/15/1991) • **78**

Rioja Crianza 1996: This round red offers sweet plum and prune flavors, with chocolate and date accents. The structure is round and supple, with a touch of heat on the finish. Drink now through 2002.–T.M. • $11 • (10/31/1999) • **82**

Rioja Crianza 1995: Aromas of coffee and chocolate give way to flavors of dried cherry, coffee and tobacco in this straightforward, slightly rustic red. Its chewy, tough texture should soften with food. Drink now through 2002.–T.M. • $9 • (11/30/1998) • **82**

Rioja Crianza 1994 • $9 • (10/15/1997) • **84**

Rioja Crianza 1989 • $7 • (4/30/1995) • **85**

Rioja Gran Reserva 1987 • $18 • (12/15/1997) • **82**

Rioja Gran Reserva 1982 • $35 • (4/15/1994) • **78**

Rioja Reserva 1990 • $14 • (10/15/1997) • **84**

Rioja Reserva 1987 • $11 • (4/30/1995) • **82**

Rioja Rosado Codice 1998: This big-boned rosé offers juicy watermelon and strawberry flavors with a bit of sweetness, bold but slightly candied. It has personality; enjoy well chilled. Drink now.–T.M. • $8 • (10/31/1999) • **82**

Rioja White Codice 1996 • $8 • (10/31/1997) • **83**

SIU

Priorat 1998: Vivid, juicy flavors of blackberry and currant are backed by firm tannins in this lively red. Notes of earth and chocolate accent the fruit, and though the structure is big enough for food, the wine turns light and silky on the finish. Drink now through 2003.–T.M. • $45 • (11/30/1999) • **88**

Priorat 1997: Raspberry, cherry and chocolate flavors mingle in this firm, rich red. The tannins and alcohol are dominant now, but should soften with time. Drink through 2005.–T.M. • $30 • (10/31/1998) • **86**

SOLABAL, BODEGA Y VINEDOS

Rioja Crianza 1995: This dark, thick red resembles Cabernet more than Tempranillo, with ripe plum and licorice flavors and muscular tannins. Shows admirable concentration, but lacks grace. Drink through 2008–T.M. • $10 • (11/30/1998) • **84**

SOLAR, CASA

Tempranillo Viño de la Tierra 1997: Smoky and earthy flavors dominate light cherry notes in this supple red. It has lively acidity and just enough grip for food. Drink now.–T.M. • $5 • (11/15/1999) • **80**

Tempranillo Viño de la Tierra 1995: The berry and vanilla flavors in this round red are almost sweet, yet remain balanced and fresh, with firm tannins and a clean finish. Drink now.–T.M. • $4 • (10/31/1998) • **84**

Viño de la Tierra 1994: Ripe cherry, light herb and chocolate flavors are jammy and almost sweet in this fleshy red. Soft on the palate, with just enough tannin for grip. Drink now.–T.M. • $5 • (11/30/1998) • **80**

Viño de Mesa Oro 1994: Very light in body, with rather dilute flavors of tea, raisin and vanilla. Past its prime.–T.M. • $6 • (11/30/1998) • **78**

Viño de Mesa Plata 1994 • $5 • (10/31/1997) • **83**

Viño de Mesa White NV: Thin and dull. There's little fruit or life in this smooth white, which offers hints of apple and herb.–T.M. • $5 • (11/15/1999) • **77**

SOLAR DE CARRION

Rioja 1996: Neutral in character, with light notes of berry, herb and earth, light but drying tannins and a short finish.–T.M. • $6 • (11/30/1998) • **79**

Rioja Crianza 1994: Dried raisin and prune flavors and coffee-scented oak accents give this red a sweet character that favors ripeness over balance. Just enough tannin for grip. Drink now.–T.M. • $9 • (11/30/1998) • **81**

SOLAR DE LIBANO

Rioja Reserva 1992 • $15 • (11/15/1997) • **78**

SOLAR DE URBEZO, BODEGAS

Cariñena Viña Urbezo 1997: This has good structure and concentration, with ripe roasted plum and prune flavors and accents of smoke and game. Drink now.–T.M. • $13 • (10/31/1998) • **84**

TAPADA, BODEGAS LA

Godello Valdeorras Guitian 1998: Crisp and clean, this white offers grapefruit and mineral flavors, with a pleasant bitterness that makes it quite refreshing. A nice aperitif or shellfish wine. Drink now.–T.M. • $14 • (11/15/1999) • **83**

Godello Valdeorras Guitian 1996: Toast aromas and flavors dominate the light melon in this light-bodied white. Soft and a bit dry on the finish.–T.M. • $13 • (11/30/1998) • **79**

Godello Valdeorras Guitian Fermentado en Barrica 1997: Oak has added sweet vanilla flavors to the crisp citrus and mineral notes that form its core. It's still fresh and clean, but a certain purity has been compromised. For fans of oak. Drink now.–T.M. • $25 • (11/15/1999) • **83**

TERRAS GAUDA, BODEGAS

Albariño Rias Baixas O Rosal 1998: Deeply colored and heavy on the palate, this rich white shows apple and herb flavors. Has power but lacks the typical vivacity. Drink now.–T.M. • $17 • (11/15/1999) • **83**

Rias Baixas O Rosal 1996 • $12 • (11/15/1997) • **88**

THOMAS, JULIAN

Cabernet Sauvignon Utiel-Requena 1996: Modest cherry and herb flavors float over drying tannins in this fresh but still awkward red. A simple wine that needs food to soften. Drink now.–T.M. • $5 • (11/30/1998) • **80**

Chardonnay Utiel-Requena Corral Valley 1997: Thick and rather dull, this ripe white offers flavors of cooked apples and melon, with plenty of sweet vanilla.–T.M. • $6 • (11/15/1999) • **78**

Merlot Utiel-Requena Corral Valley 1996: A touch of sweet vanilla adds interest to this balanced, straightforward red. It's round and soft, with simple cherry flavor, finishing fresh and clean. Drink now.–T.M. • $5 • (10/31/1998) • **82**

TORELLO, AGUSTI

Brut Cava Gran Reserva NV: Fruity and almost peachy, with apple flavors mixed in. Turns just a tad cloying on the finish. The youngest wine in the blend is 5 years old. Drink now.–K.M. • $16 • (8/31/1998) • **81**

Cava Kripta Gran Reserva NV: Assertive in aroma and flavor, showing toast, earth and honey on a broad, easy-drinking structure. Good, lingering finish. Drink now.–B.S. • $60 • (1/01/2000) • **83**

TORO ALBALA, BODEGAS

Montilla-Moriles Pedro Ximénez NV: Very thick and sweet, it pours like motor oil and tastes of raisin, fig and honey. Intense and concentrated, but there's very little acidity for relief, and it grows cloying after a couple of sips. Drink now.–T.M. • $20 • (11/30/1999) • **83**

Montilla-Moriles Viejisimo NV: Dry and rather bitter, with an overt stale note that reminds me of spoiled butter. I'm not sure it's flawed, but it's not my cup of tea. From a solera established in 1922, producing about 1,000 cases per year.–T.M. • $30 • (11/30/1999) • **74**

TORRE DEL VEGUER, BODEGAS

Cabernet Sauvignon Penedès 1996: A light red of weedy flavors that turn sour on the finish. Not recommended. Tasted twice, with consistent notes.–T.M. • $16 • (11/30/1998) • **68**

TORRE ORIA

Brut Cava Reserve NV: Quite lean, with some quince flavors and a rubbery note on the finish.–K.M. • $11 • (12/15/1999) • **75**

Brut Nature Cava NV: A tart and fairly austere wine, with flavors of pineapple and tinny notes on the finish.–K.M. • $14 • (12/15/1999) • **78**

Brut Nature Cava Centenario NV: This wine has good up-front flavors of apple and green peach, with some smoky and cinnamon notes, thinning out on the finish. Drink now.–K.M. • $27 • (12/15/1999) • **82**

Demi-Sec Rosé Cava NV: A sickly sweet rosé with bubbles.–K.M. • $13 • (12/15/1999) • **75**

Utiel-Requena 1996: Light but still fresh, this red offers berry and floral notes, with hints of licorice and tobacco. A pleasant quaff. Drink now.–T.M. • $10 • (1/31/2000) • **83**

Utiel-Requena Dominio del Derramador Reserve 1993: Pretty berry, vanilla and floral notes give an appealing delicacy to this light, firm red. It's fresh and clean, with a lingering finish. Drink now.–T.M. • $13 • (1/31/2000) • **84**

Utiel-Requena Grand Reserve 1991: Still lively, this sturdy red offers jammy plum and raisin flavors, with firm, slightly drying tannins. Try with grilled meats. Drink now.–T.M. • $16 • (1/31/2000) • **84**

TORRES

Cabernet Sauvignon Penedès Gran Coronas Reserva 1995: Plum, berry and black olive flavors are balanced and clean in this firm red. Shows good varietal character and the structure to match well with food. Drink now.–T.M. • $18 • (1/01/2000) • **86**

Cabernet Sauvignon Penedès Gran Coronas Reserva 1994: Cherry, raisin and chocolate notes are light but fresh in this straightforward red. Firm tannins give it enough grip to match with food. Balanced but rather subdued in character. Drink now through 2001.–T.M. • $15 • (11/30/1998) • **81**

Cabernet Sauvignon Penedès Gran Coronas Reserva 1993 • $15 • (10/31/1997) • **80**

Cabernet Sauvignon Penedès Gran Coronas Reserva 1991 • $15 • (4/30/1995) • **86**

Chardonnay Conca de Barberá Milmanda 1997: Vivid and complex. This lively white offers fresh flavors of lime, pineapple, toast and spice, well defined and harmonious. Drink now through 2002.–T.M. • $44 • (11/15/1999) • **89**

Chardonnay Penedès Gran Viña Sol 1998: Rich yet racy, this white marries deep smoky and toasty flavors from oak with ripe tropical fruit flavors, balanced by crisp acidity. Bold flavors linger on the finish. Contains 15 percent Parellada. Drink now through 2002.–T.M. • $11 • (11/15/1999) • **87**

Chardonnay Penedès Gran Viña Sol 1996 • $11 • (6/30/1997) • **84**

Conca de Barberá Grans Muralles 1996: This deep-colored red has a mouth-filling texture, subtle yet muscular; sweet, ripe fruit lingers on the finish. A combination of refinement and depth. A blend of Garnacha, Garró, Samsó (Cariñena) and Monastrell. Drink now through 2004.–T.M. • $75 • (11/15/1999) • **90**

Merlot Penedès Las Torres 1996: Round and soft, this simple red offers straightforward cherry and herb flavors, with very light tannins and a short but clean finish. Drink now.–T.M. • $12 • (10/31/1998) • **80**

Merlot Penedès Las Torres 1994 • $11 • (1/01/1997) • **84**

Merlot Penedès Las Torres 1993 • $12 • (4/15/1995) • **81**

Merlot Penedès Las Torres 1992 • $12 • (4/15/1994) • **82**

Merlot Penedès Las Torres 1990 • $12 • (11/15/1991) • **86**

Merlot Penedès Las Torres 1989 • $13 • (10/15/1990) • **82**

Merlot Penedès Las Torres 1988 • $10 • (3/31/1990) • **83**

Penedès Coronas 1990 • $8 • (2/28/1995) • **78**

Penedès Coronas 1989 • $8 • (4/15/1992) • **81**

Penedès Coronas 1988 • $7 • (6/15/1991) • **81**

Penedès Gran Coronas 1985 • $11 • (11/30/1988) • **89**

Penedès Gran Coronas Mas La Plana Black Label 1994: Luscious chocolate, plum and cassis aromas follow through on the palate of this ripe, generous red. Well structured yet lively, with deep flavors and a polished texture. Should improve with age; try now through 2008.–T.M. • $39 • (11/30/1998) • **88**

Penedès Gran Coronas Mas La Plana Black Label 1990 • $34 • (4/15/1994) • **88**

Penedès Gran Coronas Mas La Plana Black Label 1987 • $33 • (12/15/1992) • **85**

Penedès Gran Coronas Mas La Plana Black Label 1985 • $32 • (10/15/1990) • **85**

Penedès Gran Coronas Mas La Plana Black Label 1983 • $26 • (3/31/1990) • **85**

Penedès Gran Coronas Mas La Plana Black Label 1982 • $29 • (6/15/1988) • **85**

Penedès Gran Coronas Mas La Plana Black Label 1981 • $23 • (10/15/1987) • **83**

Penedès Gran Coronas Mas La Plana Black Label 1978 • $65 • (2/16/1986) • **85**

Penedès Gran Coronas Reserva 1988 • $15 • (4/15/1994) • **79**

Penedès Gran Coronas Reserva 1987 • $15 • (4/15/1992) • **84**

Penedès Gran Coronas Reserva 1986 • $12 • (11/30/1989) • **86**

Penedès Gran Coronas Reserva 1985 • $12 • (3/31/1990) • **77**

Penedès Gran Sangre de Toro 1989 • $13 • (12/15/1993) • **84**

Penedès Gran Sangre de Toro Reserva 1996: This smooth, ripe red is rich with chocolate, coffee, prune and herb flavors. Generous and fleshy. Drink now through 2002.–T.M. • $11 • (6/15/2000) • **85**

Penedès Gran Sangre de Toro Reserva 1995: This fleshy red shows good varietal character, with berry, black pepper and herbal flavors, vivid and well defined. Not a muscular wine, but has enough grip for food. Drink now.–T.M. • $11 • (12/31/1999) • **86**

Penedès Gran Sangre de Toro Reserva 1994: This tough red shows flavors of cherry, green bean and coffee. Dark and a bit austere, with very firm tannins and some concentration. May unwind with food. Drink now.–T.M. • $11 • (11/30/1998) • **82**
Penedès Gran Sangre de Toro Reserva 1993 • $11 • (10/31/1997) • **84**
Penedès Gran Sangre de Toro Reserva 1991 • $11 • (8/31/1996) • **83**
Penedès Gran Sangre de Toro Reserva 1988 • $11 • (12/15/1992) • **82**
Penedès Gran Sangre de Toro Reserva 1987 • $10 • (11/15/1991) • **83**
Penedès Gran Sangre de Toro Reserva 1986 • $10 • (10/15/1990) • **83**
Penedès Sangre de Toro 1996: This pillowy red shows bright cherry, berry and herbal flavors, with a soft texture and almost no tannin. It's vivid, but evanescent. Try slightly chilled. Drink now.–T.M. • $7 • (12/31/1999) • **84**
Penedès Sangre de Toro 1990 • $8 • (4/15/1994) • **85**
Penedès Sangre de Toro 1989 • $7 • (4/15/1992) • **82**
Penedès Sangre de Toro 1988 • $7 • (3/31/1991) • **82**
Penedès Viña Magdala 1986 • $14 • (11/15/1991) • **82**
Penedès Viña Magdala 1984 • $11 • (7/31/1989) • **76**
Penedès White Fransola 1996 • $17 • (4/30/1998) • **84**
Penedès White Milmanda 1996: Round and smooth, this offers toast, cream and vanilla oak flavors, with modest apple and melon notes and soft acidity. Drink now.–T.M. • $44 • (11/15/1998) • **82**
Penedès White San Valentin 1996: A rather heavy white, off-dry, showing apple and melon flavors. Simple and a bit clumsy. Made from Parellada. –T.M. • $8 • (12/15/1999) • **78**
Penedès White Viña Esmeralda 1998: This fragrant dry white has a pleasant delicacy, with subtle but focused flavors of peach and citrus and floral notes that linger on the finish. A lovely aperitif. A blend of Muscat d'Alexandria and Gewürztraminer. Drink now.–T.M. • $10 • (12/15/1999) • **85**
Penedès White Viña Esmeralda 1997: Vivid and exotic, this lush yet crisp mix of tropical fruit and citrus flavors is enticing and refreshing. A delightful aperitif. A blend of Muscat of Alexandria and Gewürztraminer. Drink now. –T.M. • $11 • (11/30/1998) • **85**
Penedès White Viña Sol 1997: This straightforward white offers flavors of apples and herbs, clean but simple. A nice aperitif. Drink now.–T.M. • $7 • (12/15/1999) • **79**
Pinot Noir Penedès Mas Borras 1993 • $18 • (11/30/1997) • **84**
Pinot Noir Penedès Mas Borras 1991 • $20 • (12/15/1994) • **76**
Pinot Noir Penedès Mas Borras 1990 • $20 • (4/15/1994) • **78**
Pinot Noir Penedès Mas Borras 1989 • $20 • (11/15/1991) • **79**
Pinot Noir Penedès Mas Borras 1988 • $18 • (10/15/1990) • **79**
Riesling Penedès Waltraud 1998: This dry white shows light flavors of herbs and peaches, with good acidity. Turns a bit cloying on the finish.–T.M. • $13 • (12/15/1999) • **77**
Sauvignon Blanc Penedès Fransola 1998: This soft white wine is rich with pear, vanilla and almond notes, held together by a slender thread of citrusy acidity. Bold if simple flavors make it a good quaffing wine. Drink now. –T.M. • $22 • (6/15/2000) • **84**
Tempranillo Penedès Coronas 1996: This soft red doesn't have much structure, but the cherry, tobacco and cedar flavors are focused and quite rich. Maturing now, it's balanced and clean. Drink now.–T.M. • $11 • (1/01/2000) • **83**

UGARTE, HEREDAD

Rioja 1998: Toast and vanilla flavors from oak dominate this round red, but there are pleasant plum and spice notes and a firm tannic backbone for balance. For fans of oak. Drink now through 2002.–T.M. • $13 • (11/30/1999) • **84**
Rioja Crianza 1996: This soft red has bright flavors of plum and black cherry, with cola and toast accents that add sweetness to the finish. The tannins are gentle but firm enough for food. Drink now.–T.M. • $16 • (11/30/1999) • **84**
Rioja Reserva 1994: Ripe and concentrated. Rich flavors of plum, prune, coffee and earth have good weight in this firm red, and there's enough acidity to keep it lively. A slight earthiness gives it a rustic edge. Drink now through 2002.–T.M. • $24 • (12/15/1999) • **86**

VALDAMOR

Albariño Rias Baixas 1996 • $15 • (5/31/1998) • **82**

Key: SS—Spectator Selection. CS—Cellar Selection. HR—Highly Recommended. $NA—Price not available. (BT)—Barrel tasting. (A)—Auction Price. For a key to the tasters' initials, see "How to Use These Listings."
Dates in parentheses represent the issues in which the ratings were published.

VALDESPINO

Amontillado Jerez Hartley & Gibson's NV • $7 • (7/31/1994) • **83**
Cream Jerez Argüeso NV • $14 • (7/31/1994) • **88**
Cream Jerez Diez y Ocho NV: Intriguing scents, from spring flowers to crème brûlée and honey. This is a sweet, dessert-style Sherry, full in body and loaded with caramel and molasses flavors. Long and caressing on the palate, with a lingering aftertaste. Drink now.–B.S. • $18 • (12/15/1998) • **89**
Cream Jerez Hartley & Gibson's NV • $7 • (1/01/1994) • **80**
Fino Jerez Hartley & Gibson's NV • $7 • (7/31/1994) • **79**
Fino Jerez Inocente NV • $13 • (7/31/1994) • **86**
Oloroso Jerez Rare Oloroso Siglo XX NV • $NA • (7/31/1994) • **70**

VALDESTRADA, CASTILLO DE

Tierra de Barros 1991: This maturing red offers light flavors of dried cherries, tea and herbs, with a hint of sweet vanilla on the finish. The tannins are light but still firm; the wine is balanced, if not complex. Drink now.–T.M. • $17 • (10/31/1998) • **83**
Tierra de Barros Gran Reserva 1987: Earthy and tough, this red still has a core of cherry flavor, but it's drying now and needs food to soften. Probably won't improve.–T.M. • $17 • (11/30/1998) • **78**

VALDUBON, BODEGAS

Ribera del Duero 1998: This deeply colored yet light-bodied red is supple yet crisp, with dark flavors of black cherry, smoke and earth. The light tannins turn a bit dry on the finish. Not imported into the U.S. Drink now through 2002.–T.M. • $NA • (1/01/1999) • **82**

VALDUERO, BODEGAS

Ribera del Duero Crianza 1994: This thick, syrupy red offers ripe (almost overripe) flavors of plums, prunes, cedar and herbs, with big tannins and little acidity. Has more power than grace, but there's character and tradition here. Drink now through 2003.–T.M. • $15 • (10/31/1999) • **88**
Ribera del Duero Gran Reserva 1986: Old wine. Brown color, earth and raisin flavors, sweet on the palate and dry on the finish. Past its prime.–T.M. • $75 • (10/31/1999) • **77**
Ribera del Duero Reserva 1991: Tastes older than its age, but still delivers a silky texture and attractive flavors of raisins, truffles, cedar and earth. A traditional wine that wants drinking now. Drink now.–T.M. • $25 • (10/31/1999) • **87**

VALDUMIA

Albariño Rias Baixas 1997: Light, yet with good intensity, this white is firm and refreshing, offering apple, melon and almond flavors with a crisp core of acidity. It's harmonious and quite long. Drink now.–T.M. • $15 • (11/15/1998) • **85**
Albariño Rias Baixas 1996 • $12 • (11/30/1997) • **87**

VALLFORMOSA

Brut Cava NV: This has nice appley and spicy flavors, with cloying notes on the finish.–K.M. • $10 • (12/15/1999) • **82**
Brut Cava Metodo Tradicional NV • $10 • (10/31/1997) • **83**
Cabernet Sauvignon Penedès 1990 • $13 • (10/31/1997) • **85**
Penedès Gran Baron Crianza 1988 • $6 • (4/15/1994) • **78**
Penedès Gran Reserva 1992: Milk chocolate and toast flavors mingle with sweet berry notes in this smooth, oaky red. Still lively, with a spicy finish. Drink now.–T.M. • $15 • (11/30/1998) • **83**
Penedès Gran Reserva 1989 • $16 • (11/15/1997) • **83**
Penedès Vall Fort Crianza 1994 • $8 • (11/15/1997) • **82**
Penedès Vall Fort Crianza 1990 • $7 • (4/15/1994) • **81**
Penedès Vall Reserva 1994: This offbeat red offers distinctive flavors of watermelon, milk chocolate, tarragon and almond that are lively and firm. What it lacks in depth it makes up in expressiveness. Drink now through 2001.–T.M. • $12 • (11/30/1998) • **83**
Penedès Vall Reserva 1990 • $12 • (10/31/1997) • **83**

VALMINOR, ADEGAS

Albariño Rias Baixas 1997: Almond, banana and mango flavors are rich, even thick, in this ripe white wine. It's creamy on the palate, soft and

SPAIN

round, with a buttery vanilla finish. Just enough acidity for balance. Drink now.–T.M. • $16 • (11/15/1998) • **84**

VALORIA, VINA

Rioja 1991 • $8 • (4/30/1995) • **78**
Rioja 1989 • $8 • (4/15/1994) • **75**
Rioja Crianza 1995: This supple red offers plenty of juicy fruit flavors without much in the way of tannin or body. Balanced and fresh, with plum, black cherry and vanilla notes accented by smoke and herbs. Drink now through 2003.–T.M. • $14 • (11/30/1998) • **85**
Rioja Crianza 1994 • $11 • (11/30/1997) • **84**
Rioja Crianza 1987 • $12 • (4/15/1994) • **76**
Rioja Reserva 1992: Vivid aromas of vanilla, spice and tea follow through on the round, soft palate, adding interest to the raisin and leather flavors. Dry tannins emerge on the finish. Drink now.–T.M. • $18 • (11/30/1998) • **83**
Rioja Reserva 1985 • $15 • (4/15/1994) • **85**

VALTRAVIESO, BODEGAS Y VINEDOS

Ribera del Duero Crianza 1996: Deeply colored and velvety on the palate, this lush red offers intriguing flavors of licorice, mint, chocolate and plum. Nicely integrated, fresh and juicy, with just enough tannin for grip. Drink now through 2004.–T.M. • $35 • (10/31/1999) • **87**
Ribera del Duero Crianza 1995: Flavors of coffee, licorice and prunes start out soft and velvety, but the wine turns quite firm on the finish, with spicy, leathery notes. Well concentrated, but tastes a bit flat right now. Drink now.–T.M. • $21 • (8/31/1998) • **85**
Ribera del Duero Gran Valtravieso Reserva 1994: Powerful yet restrained. Lovely aromas of plum, prune and chocolate give way to a lush palate, with very ripe cassis and chocolate flavors wrapped around muscular yet well-integrated tannins. Deceptively polished now, it has the structure to age well. Drink now through 2010.–T.M. • $150 • (10/31/1999) • **91**

VARGAS, BODEGAS Y VINEDOS DEL MARQUES DE

Rioja Privada Reserva 1994: Traditional flavors of sweet vanilla and red berry show modern concentration and freshness in this rich, ripe wine. It's generous yet polished, with firm tannins and a sweet finish. Drink now through 2004.–T.M. • $48 • (10/31/1998) • **89**
Rioja Reserva 1994: A silky texture and firm structure give this red elegance, while ripe yet fresh black cherry and spice flavors contribute depth. Though not muscular, it has excellent balance. Drink now through 2002.–T.M. • $19 • (10/31/1998) • **87**

VEGA DE LA REINA, BODEGAS

Viño de Mesa de Castilla y Leon 1991: Fading now, this light, supple red offers dried cherry, cedar and spicy notes. Remarkably harmonious for its age, this is a fine example of the traditional style. Drink now.–T.M. • $10 • (12/15/1999) • **84**
Viño de Mesa de Castilla y Leon 1985 • $15 • (4/15/1994) • **82**

VEGA SAUCO, BODEGA

Toro 1996: This polished red offers pleasing ripe plum and cherry flavors, with accents of smoke and licorice, ripe, firm tannins and a clean, lingering finish. Harmonious and well structured. Drink now through 2003.–T.M. • $9 • (10/31/1998) • **87**

VEGA SICILIA, BODEGAS

Ribera del Duero Unico Gran Reserva 1986: Muscular but not overbearing, this big Spanish red marries ripe fruit and plenty of oak, with a nice mix of plum, chocolate, licorice and spice flavors backed by firm, well-integrated tannins. Harmonious and long on the finish, it's stylish yet with traditional character. Drink now through 2008.–T.M. • $184 Ⓐ • (11/15/1999) HR • **95**
Ribera del Duero Unico Gran Reserva 1985 • $140 Ⓐ • (7/31/1996) • **88**
Ribera del Duero Unico Gran Reserva 1983 • $NA • (4/30/1995) • **89**
Ribera del Duero Unico Gran Reserva 1981 • $148 Ⓐ • (5/15/1998) HR • **93**
Ribera del Duero Unico Gran Reserva 1980 • $NA • (12/15/1992) • **86**
Ribera del Duero Unico Gran Reserva 1979 • $139 Ⓐ • (3/31/1990) • **95**
Ribera del Duero Unico Gran Reserva 1976 • $NA • (4/30/1989) • **91**
Ribera del Duero Unico Gran Reserva 1974 • $144 Ⓐ • (4/15/1994) • **87**
Ribera del Duero Unico Gran Reserva 1973 • $NA • (3/31/1990) • **90**
Ribera del Duero Unico Gran Reserva 1970 • $272 Ⓐ • (4/30/1995) • **92**
Ribera del Duero Unico Gran Reserva 1962 • $283 Ⓐ • (3/31/1990) • **89**
Ribera del Duero Unico Reserva Especial NV • $209 Ⓐ • (4/15/1995) • **88**
Ribera del Duero Valbuena 3.° Reserva 1986 • $47 • (12/15/1990) • **90**
Ribera del Duero Valbuena 3.° Reserva 1985 • $55 • (3/31/1990) CS • **92**
Ribera del Duero Valbuena 3.° Reserva 1984 • $28 • (4/30/1989) • **79**
Ribera del Duero Valbuena 3.° Reserva 1983 • $22 • (10/15/1988) • **88**
Ribera del Duero Valbuena 3.° Reserva 1982 • $25 • (10/15/1988) • **90**
Ribera del Duero Valbuena 5.° Reserva 1994: This expressive wine is rich with fragrance and deep on the palate. It features a mouthwatering mix of very ripe plum and prune flavors, chocolate and smoke notes, firm but not aggressive tannins and clean acidity. Though still young, it's almost impossible to resist. Tasted twice, with consistent notes. Drink now through 2010.–T.M. • $70 • (11/15/1999) • **94**
Ribera del Duero Valbuena 5.° Reserva 1993: This elegant racehorse is showing age, but it's not tiring as it heads around the track. Its lean, crisp texture carries lively cherry, currant and cedar flavors, with firm but not overbearing tannins and a bright streak of acidity. Drink now through 2004.–T.M. • $65 • (12/15/1999) • **89**
Ribera del Duero Valbuena 5.° Reserva 1992 • $75 • (6/15/1997) • **88**
Ribera del Duero Valbuena 5.° Reserva 1991 • $70 • (7/31/1996) • **87**
Ribera del Duero Valbuena 5.° Reserva 1990 • $60 • (4/30/1995) • **86**
Ribera del Duero Valbuena 5.° Reserva 1988 • $75 • (4/15/1994) • **90**
Ribera del Duero Valbuena 5.° Reserva 1984 • $49 • (3/31/1990) • **90**
Ribera del Duero Valbuena 5.° Reserva 1982 • $35 • (10/15/1988) • **91**

VENTA D'AUBERT

Viño de la Tierra Domus 1996: This lively red has some pop, with juicy flavors of cherries, berries and licorice, and just enough tannin to keep them in line. It's crisp and clean, and the fruit lingers on the finish. Not imported into the U.S. Drink now through 2003.–T.M. • $NA • (1/01/1999) • **88**

VICTORIANAS, BODEGAS

Tempranillo Viño de la Tierra Manchuela 1997: Berry, herb and cedar notes are focused but light in this simple red. Well balanced and clean. Drink now.–T.M. • $6 • (6/15/2000) • **81**
Viura Viño de la Tierra Manchuela 1998: This smooth white is crisp and clean, though rather neutral in flavor, with pear and herb notes on the finish. A refreshing aperitif. Drink now.–T.M. • $6 • (6/15/2000) • **82**

VIDAL, ANGEL RODRIGUEZ

Verdejo Rueda Martinsancho 1998: Appealing floral and green apple aromas give way to a round, rather soft texture, with notes of pear and almond. Though well focused, it fades on the finish. Drink now.–T.M. • $12 • (10/31/1999) • **83**
Verdejo Rueda Martinsancho 1996 • $10 • (2/28/1998) • **84**

VILARINO-CAMBADOS, BODEGAS

Albariño Rias Baixas Burgáns 1998: Ripe and luscious, this rich white from Spain is redolent of pears, peaches and melons, full-bodied yet clean and refreshing. The lively fruit makes an impact; the wine stays balanced and harmonious. More than worth the modest asking price. Drink now.–T.M. • $9 • (12/15/1999) • **89**
Albariño Rias Baixas Burgáns 1997: This vivid Spanish white offers a vibrant mix of vanilla oak and ripe tropical fruit, yet maintains a crisp profile, with a core of citrusy acidity. It has intensity without weight, a great balance of sweet and tart, and a long, clean finish. A lot to offer at this price. Drink now.–T.M. • $9 • (11/15/1998) • **89**
Albariño Rias Baixas Burgáns 1996 • $10 • (9/15/1997) • **88**
Albariño Rias Baixas Martin Códax 1998: The rich texture of this big white is kept lively by a core of fresh acidity, allowing the ripe pear, butter and honeyed flavors to linger lushly on the finish. Balanced and clean. Drink now.–T.M. • $13 • (12/15/1999) • **88**
Albariño Rias Baixas Martin Códax 1997: Firm and full-bodied, this muscular white delivers more structure than flavor now, but the concentration and balance are evident, and the wine should open with time. It has ripe notes of pear, melon and almond, austere but deep. Drink through 2002.–T.M. • $13 • (11/15/1998) • **89**
Albariño Rias Baixas Martin Códax 1996 • $13 • (9/15/1997) • **83**

VILARINO-CAMBADOS, BODEGAS

Albariño Rias Baixas Martin Códax Gallaecia 1996: Assertive but unbalanced, with canned fruit flavors, a bitter almond note and tart acidity. Tasted twice, with consistent notes. Past its prime.–T.M. • $17 • (11/15/1998) • **76**

Albariño Rias Baixas Organistrum 1997: Melon and toasty vanilla notes show ripeness and maturity yet remain balanced in this generous white. With a broader range of flavors than many Albariños, it brings you back for another sip. Drink now.–T.M. • $17 • (11/15/1999) • **87**

VILARNAU, CASTELL DE

Brut Cava NV • $12 • (10/31/1997) • **83**
Brut Cava de Bruts NV • $12 • (7/31/1996) • **85**
Demi-Sec Cava NV • $11 • (7/31/1996) • **79**

VILLAR, BODEGA HERMANOS DEL

Rueda Oro de Castilla 1996 • $9 • (2/28/1998) • **83**

Verdejo Rueda Oro de Castilla 1998: This assertive white offers rich flavors of pineapple and pear, with a pleasant sweet fruitiness and just enough acidity to keep it lively. Drink now.–T.M. • $9 • (10/31/1999) • **84**

VINA, CASA DE LA

Cencibel Valdepeñas 1997: This fresh, grapey red is straightforward and clean, with simple fruit flavors and light yet firm tannins that brings you back for another sip. A nice match for lighter dishes. Drink now.–T.M. • $5 • (11/30/1998) • **83**

Cencibel Valdepeñas 1996 • $5 • (11/15/1997) • **83**

VINAS DEL VERO

Cabernet Sauvignon Somontano 1997: A muscular red with good structure, firm tannins and concentration on the palate. Flavors lean toward herbal, with green bean and tobacco notes alongside cherry. Drink now through 2003.–T.M. • $8 • (11/15/1999) • **83**

Cabernet Sauvignon Somontano 1996: This deeply colored red has a core of ripe plum, but oak-influenced chocolate and coffee notes and very firm tannins make it heavy and a bit dull on the palate. Rich but clumsy. Drink through 2003.–T.M. • $7 • (11/30/1998) • **84**

Cabernet Sauvignon Somontano 1995 • $7 • (10/31/1997) • **84**
Cabernet Sauvignon Somontano 1994 • $8 • (6/15/1997) • **87**
Cabernet Sauvignon Somontano Reserva 1991 • $8 • (9/30/1996) • **83**

Chardonnay Somontano 1998: This chunky white has acceptable balance, but it's almost neutral in flavor, with hints of apple and vanilla and a short, soft finish.–T.M. • $8 • (10/31/1999) • **79**

Chardonnay Somontano 1997: Thick and clumsy, with cooked apple and vegetal flavors, toasty notes and a streak of tart acidity.–T.M. • $7 • (11/15/1998) • **76**

Chardonnay Somontano Barrel Select 1998: This straightforward white has light flavors of apple and citrus, with just enough acidity to keep it lively. Drink now.–T.M. • $8 • (10/31/1999) • **80**

Chardonnay Somontano La Piedra Barrel Select 1996 • $8 • (12/15/1997) • **82**

Merlot Somontano 1997: This ripe red offers bright plum and black cherry flavors, with light herbal accents, on a soft yet full-bodied frame. A pleasant quaffing wine with just enough grip for food. Drink now.–T.M. • $8 • (12/31/1999) • **84**

Merlot Somontano 1995 • $8 • (6/15/1997) • **86**
Merlot Somontano 1994 • $8 • (9/30/1996) • **83**
Merlot Somontano Saint Marc 1993 • $8 • (12/31/1995) • **86**
Pinot Noir Somontano Saint Marc Estate 1991 • $10 • (4/30/1995) • **78**
Somontano Duque de Azara Crianza 1992 • $8 • (1/01/1997) • **79**

Somontano Gran Vos Reserva 1995: This ripe red is concentrated yet balanced, with rich cassis and plum flavors backed by smoky oak and licorice notes. Firm yet velvety on the palate, it finishes clean and long. Drink now through 2004.–T.M. • $13 • (11/15/1999) • **88**

Somontano Gran Vos Reserva 1993: This muscular red is rich with tannin and toasty oak but a bit light on fruit, with cherry and light herb flavors. Expressive, but a bit tough. Drink now through 2002.–T.M. • $18 • (11/30/1998) • **83**

Somontano La Pyramida 1996 • $5 • (10/15/1997) • **84**

Somontano Saint Marc 1990 • $9 • (4/15/1994) • **86**
Somontano Saint Marc Duque de Azara Crianza 1991 • $9 • (4/30/1996) • **83**
Somontano Saint Marc Estate Reserva Especial 1991 • $9 • (4/30/1996) • **81**
Somontano Saint Marc Reserva Especial 1990 • $9 • (4/15/1994) • **86**

Somontano White Clarión 1997: Orange and peach flavors give this wine panache, and bright acidity keeps it lively. It's clean and refreshing, if not complex, and draws you back for another sip. Drink now.–T.M. • $14 • (11/15/1998) • **83**

Tempranillo Somontano Joven 1994 • $9 • (8/31/1996) • **77**

VINEDOS Y BODEGAS, BODEGAS

Ribera del Duero Matarromera 1995 • $31 • (6/15/1997) • **87**

VINEGRA, BODEGAS

Rioja Don Teófilo I Crianza 1994 • $17 • (5/31/1998) • **86**

Rioja Don Teófilo I Reserva 1994: An uneasy marriage of sweet, ripe plum and prune flavors with very tart acidity throws this thick wine off balance. An ambitious effort that hasn't quite come together. Best after 2001.–T.M. • $40 • (12/15/1999) • **84**

VINOS DE LA GRANJA, COMPANIA DE

Garnacha Navarra Alma 1998: Rich, sweet flavors of cherry, raisin and chocolate run though this round, supple red. Bright and quaffable, it has just enough grip to keep it balanced. Drink now through 2002.–T.M. • $8 • (11/15/1999) • **85**

Navarra Alma 1996 • $7 • (11/15/1997) • **83**

Rueda Basa 1998: Crisp and clean, this white shows green apple and citrus flavors that are delicate against the full-bodied structure. More refreshing than distinctive. Drink now.–T.M. • $7 • (10/31/1999) • **83**

Rueda Basa 1997: Assertive grassy aromas turn herbal and even a bit vegetal on the palate. A very exaggerated style.–T.M. • $7 • (11/30/1998) • **78**

Rueda Basa 1996 • $7 • (10/31/1997) • **86**

Key: SS—Spectator Selection. CS—Cellar Selection. HR—Highly Recommended. $NA—Price not available. (BT)—Barrel tasting. (A)—Auction Price.
For a key to the tasters' initials, see "How to Use These Listings."
Dates in parentheses represent the issues in which the ratings were published.

Other International

BULGARIA

ASHTON ESTATES

Cabernet Sauvignon Rousse Valley 1995: Lean, with cranberry and tea flavors.–K.M. • $5 • (10/31/1998) • **74**
Merlot Rousse Valley 1995 • $5 • (1/01/1998) • **82**

COASTAL CELLARS

Merlot Rousse Valley 1995 • $6 • (2/28/1997) • **80**

DALINA, CHATEAU

Cabernet Sauvignon Russe 1998: Pruney aromas are followed by light currant and cherry notes. Finishes on a slightly medicinal note.–B.S. • $5 • (1/01/2000) • **77**
Cabernet Sauvignon Russe 1997: A fresh, simple red, with bright cherry flavors, light tannins and good acidity. Drink now. • $5 • (10/31/1998) • **82**
Cabernet Sauvignon Russe 1996 • $4 • (10/31/1997) • **82**
Cabernet Sauvignon Russe 1995 • $5 • (6/30/1997) • **78**
Cabernet Sauvignon Russe 1994 • $5 • (12/31/1995) • **82**
Cabernet Sauvignon Russe 1993 • $4 • (12/31/1994) • **80**
Cabernet Sauvignon Russe 1992 • $4 • (1/01/1995) • **84**
Chardonnay Russe 1998: A simple white, with figgy and buttery flavors and a tinny edge on the finish.–K.M. • $5 • (1/01/2000) • **76**
Chardonnay Russe 1997: Floral and herbal-tasting, with a resinous quality.–K.M. • $5 • (10/31/1998) • **78**
Chardonnay Russe 1996 • $4 • (10/31/1997) • **76**
Merlot Russe 1998: Strawberry, rhubarb notes on the nose, with some thin, weedy flavors, and just a wisp of plummy fruit on the drying finish.–B.S. • $5 • (1/01/2000) • **78**
Merlot Russe 1997: Quite tart, with sour cherry flavors on the finish.–K.M. • $5 • (10/31/1998) • **71**
Merlot Russe 1996 • $4 • (11/15/1997) • **79**
Merlot Russe 1995 • $5 • (1/01/1997) • **79**
Merlot Russe 1994 • $5 • (12/31/1995) • **83**
Merlot Russe 1993 • $4 • (12/31/1994) • **84**

MARITSA

Merlot Haskovo 1995 • $7 • (12/31/1997) • **74**

MENADA

Cabernet Sauvignon Oriahovitsa Private Reserve 1991 • $8 • (8/31/1997) • **79**
Cabernet Sauvignon Oriahovitsa Reserve 1992 • $6 • (8/31/1997) • **70**
Cabernet Sauvignon-Merlot Oriahovitsa Private Reserve 1990 • $8 • (8/31/1997) • **71**
Merlot Stara Zagora 1995 • $6 • (8/31/1997) • **80**

VINI

Cabernet Sauvignon Sliven 1992 • $8 • (12/31/1997) • **69**
Cabernet Sauvignon Sliven Reserve 1995: This medium-weight red verges on stewy, with rhubarb and coffee flavors, before finishing on a slight raisiny note. Hanging in there, barely.–T.M. • $7 • (3/31/2000) • **79**
Merlot Sliven 1997: Candied cherry and herbal notes run through this light-weight Merlot. The finish is a tad astringent.–T.M. • $6 • (3/31/2000) • **78**
Merlot Sliven 1995 • $6 • (11/15/1997) • **84**

CANADA

BLUE MOUNTAIN | BRITISH COLUMBIA

Pinot Blanc Okanagan Valley Reserve 1998: Pleasant, showing nuances of vanilla, apple skin and spice laid out on a vibrant structure. Drink now.–B.S. • $20 • (6/30/2000) • **82**
Pinot Gris Okanagan Valley 1996: Lean and racy, with new oak rounding off the edges, offering peach and nutmeg flavors. Concentrated, with a butterscotch aftertaste. Drink now.–B.S. • $24 • (6/15/2000) • **85**
Pinot Noir Okanagan Valley 1995: Light-textured, with earth and herb overtones backed by pretty, bright cherry and anise flavors. The finish is long though a little bitter, with a solid dollop of toasty oak. Drink now through 2003. Not imported into the U.S. • $NA • (10/15/1999) • **86**

BURROWING OWL | BRITISH COLUMBIA

Chardonnay Okanagan Valley 1997: Well balanced and elegant, with bright pear and apple flavors, this offers a certain weightiness on the palate, which helps carry the finish. It's fairly luscious, framed by sweet oak. Drink now through 2002. • $19 • (6/15/1999) • **89**
Pinot Gris Okanagan Valley 1998: Lovely. Violet in aroma, with flavors of peach and apricot displayed on an elegant, focused framework. Well done. Drink now.–B.S. • $13 • (6/15/2000) • **86**
Pinot Gris Okanagan Valley 1997: A blend of bright acidity and good viscosity, with mild melon and herb flavors. Finishes light, with a hint of grapefruit. Drink now. • $18 • (10/15/1999) • **82**

CALONA | BRITISH COLUMBIA

Chardonnay Okanagan Valley Artist Series 1997: Tightly wound, with layers of pear, citrus and herb, this wine is firm yet elegant, framed in plenty of oak, but the balance is good and it should improve nicely with time. Drink now through 2003. Not imported into the U.S. • $NA • (6/15/1999) • **88**
Merlot British Columbia Burrowing Owl Vineyard Private Reserve 1995: Tasting tired already, this is quite vegetal, serving up green bean and asparagus flavors. Rustic tannins don't help. Not imported into the U.S. • $NA • (10/15/1999) • **72**
Pinot Blanc Okanagan Valley Artist Series 1997: A moderately concentrated, spice-tinged white whose apple and pear notes are carried by the bright acidity. Drink now.–B.S. • $8 • (6/30/2000) • **83**

CAVE SPRING | ONTARIO

Chardonnay Niagara Peninsula Cave Spring Vineyards 1997: Showing concentration and intensity, this white relies more on fruit character, with oak nuances. Bright and lively, offering pear and spice flavors and finishing long. Drink now.–B.S. • $10 • (6/15/1999) • **86**
Riesling Niagara Peninsula Off Dry 1998: Distinctive. Fine varietal character, though the petrol aroma is advanced for a young Riesling, with flavors of cooked apple, petrol and lemon. Drink now.–B.S. • $8 • (6/15/2000) • **83**
Riesling Niagara Peninsula Reserve 1997: A soft, dry, floral-scented white, with apple blossom and grapefruit flavors. An underlying firmness keeps it balanced and fresh. Finishes on a citrus note. Drink now.–B.S. • $11 • (6/15/1999) • **84**

CHATEAU DES CHARMES | ONTARIO

Chardonnay Niagara Peninsula Paul Bosc Estate Vineyard 1997: Firm, vibrant and well integrated, this Chardonnay is like a rich lemon cake, with floral and nutty flavors. Beautiful texture and harmony carry through to the long finish. Drink now through 2002.–B.S. • $20 • (6/30/2000) • **88**

CANADA

Chardonnay Niagara Peninsula St.-Davids Bench Vineyard 1996: Floral, citrus and mineral aromas show good concentration, but oak and fruit clash on the awkward finish. From a winery with a good track record, but lacks the harmony of the best Ontario Chardonnays in this tasting. Drink now.–B.S. • $9 • (10/15/1999) • **80**

Riesling Niagara Peninsula Ice Wine Paul Bosc Estate Vineyard 1997: Delicious. Combines intense, extracted honey and apricot flavors with vibrant acidity, offering the sweet/sour character typical of ice wine. Persistent yet delicate, and long on the finish, this is a winner. Drink now through 2003.–B.S. • $56/375 ml. • (6/15/1999) • **90**

Riesling Niagara Peninsula Late Harvest 1997: Lovely aromas of honey and apricot introduce this soft, concentrated dessert wine. Its sweetness is balanced by lively acidity, leaving a fresh, cleansing impression on the palate. Drink now.–B.S. • $12/375 ml. • (6/15/1999) • **87**

CREEKSIDE | Ontario

Sauvignon Blanc Niagara Peninsula 1998: Lovely grass, herb and gooseberry notes turn softer on the palate than the aromas indicate. Loses a little focus by the end, but tasty. Drink now.–B.S. • $11 • (6/30/2000) • **83**

D'ANGELO | Ontario

Vidal Blanc Lake Erie North Shore Ice Wine 1998: Plush and seemingly on the soft side, with honey and passion fruit aromas and flavors that dissipate quickly at this stage. An up-front, sweet wine that may just need time to come together. Drink through 2001.–B.S. • $40 • (6/30/1999) • **88**

GEHRINGER BROTHERS | British Columbia

Pinot Blanc Okanagan Valley Private Reserve 1998: A gentle, softly structured white reminiscent of candy apple and almond, with a lingering finish. Drink now.–B.S. • $13 • (6/30/2000) • **81**

Pinot Gris Okanagan Valley Private Reserve 1998: Good varietal character in this Pinot Gris, leaning toward the violet candy and tinned pear end of the flavor spectrum on an elegant frame. Drink now.–B.S. • $13 • (6/15/2000) • **82**

Pinot Gris Okanagan Valley Private Reserve 1997: Showing hints of grapefruit, lemon and apple flavors, this refreshingly tangy wine also has a smooth side. The finish is moderate yet clean, with a slight mineral edge. Drink now. Not imported into the U.S.–J.L. • $NA • (10/15/1999) • **86**

Riesling Okanagan Valley Icewine 1997: Bright edges balance the thick, oily texture of this big wine. Honey is the dominant flavor, with an aftertaste that includes peach and pear. Drink now through 2005. Not imported into the U.S. • $NA/375 ml. • (10/15/1999) • **88**

GRAY MONK | British Columbia

Chardonnay Okanagan Valley Unwooded 1997: An effusively fruity wine that's balanced by bright acidity, its lemon, lime, mandarin orange, nectarine and apple flavors weave an intricate tapestry on the palate. On the finish, it's long and exotic, ending with a steely edge. Unusual. Not imported into the U.S. Drink now through 2001. • $NA • (6/15/1999) • **89**

Riesling Okanagan Valley 1998: Just off dry, with a nice spiciness augmenting the peach and apple notes. A touch lean, it finishes short. Drink now.–B.S. • $11 • (6/15/2000) • **81**

HAWTHORNE MOUNTAIN | British Columbia

Ehrenfelser Okanagan Valley Icewine 1997: Starts off with pretty peach aromas that extend to the palate. Honey and spice notes carry through to the long finish. The texture is a bit less viscous than some of the competition's, which can be refreshing. Drink now through 2005. • $50/375 ml. • (6/30/1999) • **89**

Gewürztraminer British Columbia 1997: Marked by bright grapefruit, herb and steely mineral notes, this crisp and refreshing wine is focused and fairly elegant. Clean, moderate finish. Drink now.–H.S. • $13 • (6/30/1999) • **88**

Riesling British Columbia 1998: A hint of sweetness rounds out this simple, apple- and almond-flavored white. Drink now.–B.S. • $13 • (6/15/2000) • **82**

Key: SS—Spectator Selection. CS—Cellar Selection. HR—Highly Recommended. $NA—Price not available. (BT)—Barrel tasting. Ⓐ—Auction Price.
For a key to the tasters' initials, see "How to Use These Listings."
Dates in parentheses represent the issues in which the ratings were published.

Riesling British Columbia 1997: Slightly sweet and exhibiting peach, apple and honey flavors supported by a firm, dense structure, this has developed nicely. Drink now.–B.S. • $10 • (6/15/2000) • **83**

HENRY OF PELHAM | Ontario

Chardonnay Niagara Peninsula Barrel Fermented 1998: Fresh and fruity, with apple and pear notes augmented by a good use of oak that leaves a buttery aftertaste. Drink now.–B.S. • $23 • (6/30/2000) • **84**

Chardonnay Niagara Peninsula Barrel Fermented 1997: Vanilla and nutmeg from new oak integrate nicely with the rich texture. Charming and elegant in style, with apple and honey flavors. Spicy oak echoes on the finish. Drink now.–B.S. • $18 • (6/30/1999) • **86**

Riesling Niagara Peninsula Ice Wine 1997: Gorgeous aromas of citrus blossom, honey and apricot introduce a sweet, racy dessert wine that dances across the palate. Concentrated, complex and focused, it remains nimble and keeps pumping out the flavors. Long, rich finish. Drink now through 2005.–B.S. • $55/375 ml. • (6/15/1999) • **92**

Riesling Niagara Peninsula Late Harvest Select 1995: Honey and crème brûlée are the main themes, buoyed on a thick, concentrated texture but never cloying. Nutmeg and cinnamon accents add interest. Drink now through 2001.–B.S. • $15/375 ml. • (6/15/1999) • **88**

HERNDER ESTATE WINES | Ontario

Chardonnay Niagara Peninsula Barrel Fermented 1997: A mouthful of Chardonnay, this medium-bodied, pear- and nutmeg-flavored version floats on its plush texture. Warm, lingering finish. Drink now.–B.S. • $12 • (6/30/2000) • **84**

HESTER CREEK | British Columbia

Pinot Blanc Okanagan Valley 1997: Supple and smooth, with fresh apple, pear, tangerine and cinnamon overtones. Elegant in profile, with good acidity and a moderate finish. Drink now. Not imported into the U.S. • $NA • (6/15/1999) • **87**

Pinot Blanc Okanagan Valley Signature Release 1997: Quite tart, with a strong lemony edge and herbal overtones. A bit shocking at first, but with oysters or Dover sole it should sing. Clean and bright on the finish. Drink now. Not imported into the U.S. • $NA • (10/15/1999) • **85**

HILLEBRAND | Ontario

Vidal Blanc Niagara Peninsula Ice Wine Trius 1997: There's a brilliance to the apricot and citrus peel flavors from the racy acidity that lends an ethereal quality. Light on its feet, with intensity but not the depth for keeping. Drink now through 2001.–B.S. • $45/375 ml. • (6/30/1999) • **90**

INNISKILLIN | Ontario

Cabernet Sauvignon Niagara Peninsula Klose Vineyard 1991 • $15 • (5/15/1995) • **82**

Chardonnay Niagara Peninsula Reserve 1997: Well done. Like a ripe Chablis, this white delivers honey, melon and the tiniest bit of apricot, interwoven with a lively, densely textured framework. If there's new oak, it's very discreet and takes a backseat to the fruit. Drink now.–B.S. • $10 • (6/30/1999) • **86**

Ice Wine Niagara Peninsula Brae Burn Vineyard 1990 • $46/375 ml. • (4/15/1995) • **76**

Ice Wine Ontario 1992 • $33/375 ml. • (4/15/1995) • **80**

Ice Wine Ontario Brae Burn Estate 1989 • $71/375 ml. • (4/15/1995) • **76**

Pinot Noir Niagara Peninsula Founder's Show Reserve 1995: Minty, earthy aromas segue into spicy cherry flavors in this firm, lean red. Silky in texture, but the fruit is overshadowed by the structure. Finishes lean. Drink now.–B.S. • $15 • (6/15/1999) • **80**

Pinot Noir Niagara Peninsula Reserve 1992 • $15 • (5/15/1995) • **77**

Pinot Noir Niagara Peninsula Reserve 1991 • $15 • (5/15/1995) • **82**

Vidal Blanc Niagara Peninsula Icewine Oak Aged 1996: Gingerbread, cinnamon and apricot aromas and flavors and a hint of truffle signify a complex, maturing dessert wine. Lively acidity and concentration transport the fruit and spice mélange to a satisfying conclusion. Drink now through 2001.–B.S. • $75/375 ml. • (6/30/1999) • **92**

INNISKILLIN OKANAGAN | British Columbia

Chardonnay Okanagan Valley Reserve 1996: Somewhat austere, this features mineral-like flavors, and a hint of crisp apple on the finish. Quite clean and bright. Refreshing. Drink now. • $28 • (6/15/1999) • **85**

Ice Wine Okanagan Valley 1994 • $NA • (5/15/1996) • **86**

JACKSON-TRIGGS | British Columbia

Chardonnay Okanagan Valley Grand Reserve 1997: Modest apple and spice flavors take on resinous tones that detract from its overall appeal.–B.S. • $12 • (6/30/2000) • **78**

Riesling Okanagan Valley Ice Wine Proprietors' Grand Reserve 1996: Zippy and somehow light despite the rich sweetness. Quite honeyed, with fresh peach and lemon overtones. A touch of ginger lingers on the palate, with a finish that is long and rewarding. Drink now through 2006. • $70/375 ml. • (10/15/1999) • **91**

Riesling Okanagan Valley Proprietors' Reserve 1997: A light, bright style with subtle green apple and honey notes. Dry, however, with a moderate, flinty finish. Drink now. • $17 • (6/15/1999) • **84**

KITTLING RIDGE | Ontario

Ice Wine Limited Release Niagara Peninsula 1996 • $45/375 ml. • (12/31/1997) • **88**

KONZELMANN | Ontario

Vidal Blanc Niagara Peninsula Ice Wine 1997: Thick, rich and vibrant, this has all the elements of ice wine, with apricot, honey, almond and candied orange peel flavors that persist through the finish. Showing great intensity, this needs time for the sweetness and structure to integrate. Drink through 2003.–B.S. • $45/375 ml. • (6/30/1999) • **92**

MAGNOTTA | Ontario

Vidal Blanc Niagara Peninsula Ice Wine 1995 • $47/375 ml. • (12/31/1997) • **86**

MALIVOIRE | Ontario

Chardonnay Niagara Peninsula 1998: A vibrant, densely textured Chardonnay, showing apple, citrus, toast and nutmeg flavors. Quite oaky, with a richness that carries it well, all on a spritely frame. Drink now. Not imported into the U.S.–B.S. • $NA • (1/01/2000) • **85**

MISSION HILL | British Columbia

Chardonnay Okanagan Valley Barrel Select Grand Reserve 1997: A bit earthy on the nose, this wine serves up tangy lemon, lime and mineral accents punctuated by grassy overtones that remind one more of Sauvignon Blanc than Chardonnay. It's crisp and refreshing, however, and begs for a plate of raw oysters. Drink now. • $18 • (6/15/1999) • **87**

Chardonnay Okanagan Valley Barrel Select Grand Reserve 1996: Quite bright, with a flinty, mineral edge. Leans toward citrus flavors—lemon, orange and grapefruit come to mind. Lightly oaked and refreshing, with a moderate finish. Drink now through 2001. • $18 • (6/15/1999) • **86**

Gewürztraminer Okanagan Valley Icewine Grand Reserve 1997: Floral, fig and Muscat raisin aromas and flavors mark this amber-colored sweetie. Not so concentrated or complex, but its forward fruit and soft texture make it immediately appealing. Drink now.–B.S. • $65/375 ml. • (10/15/1999) • **89**

Gewürztraminer Okanagan Valley Private Reserve 1998: Borders on Muscat in aroma, yet there's good richness and interplay of apricot and orange, with a hint of earth. Drink now.–B.S. • $8 • (6/15/2000) • **82**

Pinot Blanc Okanagan Valley Private Reserve 1997: Starts with grassy aromas more redolent of Sauvignon Blanc than Pinot Blanc. On the palate, it is equally distinctive, focusing on mineral, herb, grass, fig and gooseberry notes. Finishes long and clean. Drink now. • $13 • (6/15/1999) • **88**

Pinot Gris Okanagan Valley Barrel Select Grand Reserve 1997: A full-bodied white, with plenty of citrus, green apple and tropical fruit flavors. Tangy acidity and a long, fresh, minerallike finish round out this assertive yet balanced and elegant wine. Drink now through 2003. • $15 • (6/15/1999) • **88**

Pinot Gris Okanagan Valley Barrel Select Grand Reserve 1996: A richly styled wine, with lots of sweet oak backed by pear, apricot and herb flavors. Has depth and structure, sitting firmly on the palate and finishing with a stony, slightly tart edge. Drink now through 2002. • $15 • (6/15/1999) • **89**

Pinot Noir Okanagan Valley Barrel Select Grand Reserve 1997: Light cherry and herb flavors form the core of this tight wine. Rustic tannins seem to shut down the finish fairly quickly. • $18 • (10/15/1999) • **79**

Riesling Okanagan Valley Icewine Grand Reserve 1997: Thick and viscous, with a vegetal note augmenting the apricot, honey and orange peel flavors. It's so sweet, you hardly notice the vibrant acidity beneath, yet it comes through on the long, clean finish. Drink now through 2004.–B.S. • $65/375 ml. • (10/15/1999) • **88**

Vidal Blanc Okanagan Valley Icewine 1995: Richly textured, with honey and peach flavors at the fore. Bright acidity lends nice balance, but a touch of earthiness and a metallic edge temper the attributes. Drink now. • $40 • (10/15/1999) • **83**

PELEE ISLAND | Ontario

Pinot Gris Ontario 1997: A firm structure supports the rich texture and almond and smoke flavors in this reserved white. Finishes with a hint of bitterness. Drink now.–B.S. • $9 • (6/15/1999) • **82**

PELLER ESTATES | Ontario

Chardonnay Niagara Peninsula Founder's Series 1997: Broad and open-knit, this white shows cooked apple, spice and a hint of earth, turning buttery on the finish. Drink now.–B.S. • $10 • (6/30/2000) • **83**

Merlot Okanagan Valley Limited Showcase 1994: The texture is plush, almost weighty, though the flavors are quite herbal and smoky, with pretty black currant and chocolate notes. The finish is long but somewhat bitter. Drink now. Not imported into the U.S.–J.L. • $NA • (10/15/1999) • **84**

Niagara Peninsula Vidal Ice Wine 1991 • $38 • (4/15/1995) • **80**

Pinot Noir Okanagan Valley Limited Showcase 1994: Smoky, tarry and vegetal. This tired wine was probably not much better in its youth. Not imported into the U.S. • $NA • (10/15/1999) • **69**

Vidal Blanc Niagara Peninsula Ice Wine 1996 • $NA/375 ml. • (12/31/1997) • **88**

Vidal Blanc Ontario Late Harvest 1996 • $NA/375 ml. • (12/31/1997) • **83**

PILLITTERI ESTATES | Ontario

Gewürztraminer Niagara Peninsula Ice Wine 1997: Wow. This is packed with pear and apricot aromas and flavors on a structure that's sweet and lively. Light- to medium-bodied, with flavors that just keep coming. Delicious. Drink now.–B.S. • $45/375 ml. • (6/30/1999) • **89**

QUAILS' GATE | British Columbia

Chardonnay Okanagan Valley Family Reserve 1996: Over the top, this mélange of clove, nutmeg, vanilla and butterscotch is too heavy and candied for this palate, despite lively acidity underneath. May appeal to fans of new oak. Drink now.–B.S. • $25 • (6/30/2000) • **85**

Chenin Blanc Okanagan Valley Limited Release 1998: Fresh, floral and peachy, this off-dry white delivers soft fruitiness on an easygoing structure. A good quaffer. Drink now.–B.S. • $9 • (6/30/2000) • **83**

Pinot Noir Okanagan Valley Family Reserve 1995: Kicks off with rich plum, cherry and earth aromas, but on the palate it shows bright acidity, herbal aspects and a certain lean edge. Finishes a bit tart. Drink now. Not imported into the U.S. • $NA • (10/15/1999) • **81**

Riesling British Columbia Ice Wine 1993 • $33 • (4/15/1995) • **86**

Riesling Okanagan Valley Dry Limited Release 1998: Elegant and well defined, this fresh, pure Riesling glides across the palate, with apple, peach and honey notes that linger. Well done. Drink now.–B.S. • $9 • (6/15/2000) • **86**

SOUTHBROOK | Ontario

Cabernet Sauvignon Ontario Lailey Vineyard 1997: More like Cabernet Franc, emphasizing leaf, black currant and cherry aromas and tobacco flavors, with smoky accents. Fresh and crisp, this would be a fine partner at the table. Drink now through 2002.–B.S. • $18 • (6/15/1999) • **82**

Chardonnay Niagara Peninsula Triomphe 1997: Subtle, offering hazelnut, pear and chamomile flavors accented by vanilla, building on the palate to a warm finish. Nutmeg and vanilla linger on the aftertaste. Drink now.–B.S. • $18 • (6/30/2000) • **85**

Chardonnay Ontario Barrel Fermented 1997: Starts soft and rich, with attractive aromas and flavors of pear, nutmeg and vanilla, but it lacks focus. Turns lean and slightly astringent on the finish. Drink now.–B.S. • $10 • (10/15/1999) • **81**

STONEY RIDGE | ONTARIO

Cabernet Franc Niagara Peninsula Butler's Grant Vineyard Reserve 1997: Black currant and cherry are the main themes in this forward, vibrant and balanced red. Its structure is deceptively firm, but more like a gymnast than a weightlifter. Drink now. Limited availablility in the U.S.–B.S. • $11 • (10/15/1999) • **85**

Chardonnay Niagara Peninsula Butler's Grant Vineyard Reserve 1997: Fans of fat, buttery Chardonnay will love this. There's plenty of fig, apple and honey flavors to match the spicy oak. Smooth and concentrated, showing a sense of elegance, fine balance and a lingering finish. Drink now. Limited availability in the U.S.–B.S. • $13 • (10/15/1999) • **89**

Chardonnay Ontario Cuesta Estates Old Vines 1997: Big, bold and in the oak camp, this has breadth, depth and length, with modest apple and fig flavors and ple ıty of butterscotch and spice. The creamy, thick texture and long, long finish sets this apart. Drink now through 2001. Not imported into the US. –B.S. • $NA • (1/01/2000) • **87**

SUMAC RIDGE | BRITISH COLUMBIA

Black Sage Vineyard Meritage Okanagan Valley 1996: Bright cherry and subtle anise notes are followed by hints of herb and a bit of smoke. The texture is lean, with firm tannins and a moderate finish. Should round out with time. A blend of Cabernet Sauvignon, Merlot and Cabernet Franc. Best from 2001 through 2006. • $25 • (6/30/1999) • **85**

Brut British Columbia Stellar's Jay NV: Toast and citrus aromas lead off, with honeyed tones in the background. Fresh, smooth and creamy on the palate, marked by bright acidity and tangy lemon-lime and apple flavors. Finishes moderately, with a crisp mineral edge. Drink now. • $22 • (6/30/1999) • **88**

Meritage Okanagan Valley 1997: Mild melon, herb and citrus flavors are pleasant, but don't really stand up to the dominant oak. Clean, light-textured finish. A blend of Sauvignon Blanc and Sémillon. Drink now. • $24 • (10/15/1999) • **82**

Merlot Okanagan Valley 1995: Showing green bean and other unripe flavors, also hinting at more pleasant anise and black currant notes. Firm and a bit tart, this needs steak to round it out. • $18 • (10/15/1999) • **76**

Pinot Blanc Okanagan Valley 1997: A juicy, racy blend of citrus and peach flavors, firmly structured with enough acidity to keep it all on track. The finish is moderate, with a bright, lemony aftertaste. Drink now. • $11 • (6/15/1999) • **87**

Pinot Blanc Okanagan Valley Private Reserve 1998: For fans of new oak. A vehicle for the toast, butter and nutmeg flavors of oak. Light-bodied, with hints of lemon, all displayed on a rich texture. Drink now.–B.S. • $13 • (6/30/2000) • **84**

Sauvignon Blanc Okanagan Valley Black Sage Vineyard 1997: Bright and fragrant, showing classic varietal hints of melon, fig, sweet pea, citrus and a touch of gooseberry. Firm and zingy on the palate, it finishes with a fresh, clean mineral edge. Drink now through 2001. • $15 • (6/30/1999) • **89**

SUMMERHILL | BRITISH COLUMBIA

Brut British Columbia Cipes Brut NV • $NA • (7/31/1995) • **81**

Ehrenfelser British Columbia Pyramid Aged 1997: Quite peachy on the nose, this brightly textured wine has a bit of sweetness nicely offset by a bracing, lemony finish. A fine aperitif. Drink now through 2002. • $13 • (6/30/1999) • **86**

Pinot Blanc British Columbia Pyramid Aged 1997: Bright and tangy, with crisp melon, citrus, mineral and apple flavors. This is a firm, tight white that could benefit from oysters or other rich seafood. Long on the finish and quite refreshing. Drink now through 2002. • $11 • (6/30/1999) • **88**

Pinot Noir British Columbia 1993 • $NA • (6/30/1995) • **81**

Pinot Noir British Columbia Pyramid Aged 1997: Extremely light in color and texture. Sour cherry flavors favor the "sour" aspect, followed by herbs. A tangy wine that could use more ripeness.–J.L. • $17 • (10/15/1999) • **75**

Riesling British Columbia Ice Wine 1992 • $33 • (4/15/1995) • **86**

Key: SS—Spectator Selection. CS—Cellar Selection. HR—Highly Recommended. $NA—Price not available. (BT)—Barrel tasting. (A)—Auction Price.
For a key to the tasters' initials, see "How to Use These Listings."
Dates in parentheses represent the issues in which the ratings were published.

THIRTY BENCH | ONTARIO

Cabernet Franc Niagara Peninsula Beamsville Bench 1995: Smoky bacon fat aromas and flavors and tough tannins overwhelm the fruit in this light-bodied red. It's ambitious, but the fruit will likely never gain the upper hand. Not imported into the U.S.–B.S. • $NA • (10/15/1999) • **79**

TINHORN CREEK | BRITISH COLUMBIA

Gewürztraminer Okanagan Valley 1998: Straightforward flavors of rose and grapefruit on a crisp, firm structure. Drink now.–B.S. • $10 • (6/15/2000) • **83**

Kerner Okanagan Valley Icewine 1996: Thick, rich and spicy, this sweet dessert white shows straightforward flavors of apricot and mandarin orange. Everything is kept lively by the acidity, which refreshes on the finish. Drink now. Not imported into the U.S.–B.S. • $NA/375 ml. • (10/15/1999) • **89**

VINELAND ESTATES | ONTARIO

Gewürztraminer Niagara Peninsula Frontier Vineyard Reserve 1998: Disjointed, with white pepper aroma, candied pear flavor and a sweet/tart taste.–B.S. • $18 • (6/15/2000) • **78**

Riesling Niagara Peninsula St.-Urban Vineyard Dry 1997: This pleasant white is soft in its approach, yet has balancing acidity. Aromas and flavors remain subtle, hinting at apple.–B.S. • $10 • (10/15/1999) • **78**

Riesling Niagara Peninsula Semi-Dry 1998: Almond, petrol and baked apple notes hold sway in this off-dry, crisp Riesling. Good depth and richness keep the flavors interesting and lingering. Drink now.–B.S. • $7 • (6/15/2000) • **84**

Vidal Blanc Niagara Peninsula Ice Wine 1992 • $32 • (4/15/1995) • **81**

Vidal Blanc Niagara Peninsula Ice Wine 1989 • $85 • (4/15/1995) • **70**

WILD GOOSE | BRITISH COLUMBIA

Gewürztraminer British Columbia 1997: Slight spice and litchi aromas and tangy acidity are backed by peach and melon flavors. Somewhat weighty on the finish. Drink now. Not imported into the U.S. • $NA • (10/15/1999) • **85**

Pinot Blanc Okanagan Valley 1998: Hard to cozy up to the earth and tinned pear notes.–B.S. • $11 • (6/30/2000) • **77**

WILLOW HEIGHTS | ONTARIO

Cabernet Franc Niagara Peninsula Reserve 1995: There's decent black cherry and chocolate notes, but strong diesel and earth aromas and flavors dominate and the finish is dry. Not imported into the U.S.–B.S. • $NA • (10/15/1999) • **76**

Chardonnay Niagara Peninsula Beamsville Bench Reserve 1998: Broad and appealing, this white offers baked apple, spice and earth flavors on a medium-bodied framework. Drink now. Not imported into the US.–B.S. • $NA • (1/01/2000) • **84**

Pinot Noir Niagara Peninsula Reserve 1994: Seductive aromas of spicy cherry introduce a silky, cherry- and berry-flavored red that has chewy concentration, purity and firm structure. Maybe a bit too firm on the finish. Drink now. Not imported into the U.S. –B.S. • $NA • (10/15/1999) • **85**

CROATIA

GRGIC VINA

Plavac Mali Dingac 1997: Similar to Zin in its raspberry and plum aromas and flavors, yet very muscular, with chewy tannins that lack finesse. A good pasta wine. From Mike Grgich's new Croatian winery. Drink now through 2001.–B.S. • $23 • (1/01/2000) • **83**

Posip Cara 1997: Like an Aligoté for it's crisp, lemon zest aroma and pineapple flavor, with a nice waxy note on the finish. Refreshing. Drink now.–T.M. • $20 • (1/01/2000) • **82**

■ GREECE ■

BOUTARI

Agiorgitiko Nemea 1996: Lean, with some dried plum flavors and tobacco notes. Tannic finish. Drink now.–K.M. • $24 • (10/31/1999) • **80**
Agiorgitiko Nemea 1994: Cherry and leather flavors, with a charred note. Balanced, but not very generous.–K.M. • $24 • (8/31/1998) • **76**
Goumenissa 1993 • $11 • (5/15/1996) • **83**
Greece Red Kretikos 1996: Bordering on rosé in color, with a slightly lifted nose, and cooked strawberry notes that fade on the drying finish. Made from Kotsifali and Mandilaria.–B.S. • $9 • (1/01/2000) • **74**
Greece Samos NV • $14 • (5/15/1997) • **85**
Merlot-Xinomavro Vin de Pays d'Imathia 1996: Well focused, with good plum and dried cherry flavors and an assertive herbal component. A bit austere in the end, but still enjoyable. Drink with grilled meats. Drink now.–K.M. • $18 • (10/31/1999) • **83**
Merlot-Xinomavro Vin de Pays d'Imathia 1994 • $15 • (12/31/1997) • **81**
Merlot-Xinomavro Vin de Pays d'Imathia 1993 • $15 • (5/15/1997) • **85**
Naoussa 1994 • $8 • (5/15/1997) • **75**
Naoussa 1993 • $8 • (5/15/1996) • **84**
Naoussa Grande Reserve 1994: Like a traditional Rioja, with browning color and flavors of dilute tea that are fading fast. Very disappointing. Made from Xinomavro. Past its prime.–B.S. • $15 • (1/01/2000) • **75**
Naoussa Grande Reserve 1992 • $13 • (5/15/1997) • **76**
Naoussa Grande Reserve 1990 • $13 • (5/15/1996) • **82**
Nemea 1997: There's a nice core of red plum flavors to this red, along with some herbal notes. A good wine for pizza. Made from Agiorgitiko. Drink now.–K.M. • $9 • (10/31/1999) • **82**
Nemea 1993 • $8 • (5/15/1996) • **82**
Paros 1995 • $9 • (12/31/1997) • **82**
Paros 1993 • $13 • (5/15/1996) • **78**
Santorini 1996 • $11 • (12/31/1997) • **78**
Vin de Pays d'Arcadia White 1996: Has a somewhat sweet cloying taste, with fruit-cocktail flavors. A blend of Roditis and Moschofilero.–K.M. • $NA • (8/31/1998) • **74**
Vin de Pays de Pallini White Laoutari 1997: An almond and pine-scented white, with fresh herbal notes on the palate. Light and refreshing on the finish. Drink now.–B.S. • $10 • (1/01/1999) • **82**

KOURTAKIS, D

Nemea Kouros 1993 • $8 • (1/31/1997) • **78**
Vin de Crete Kourtaki 1994 • $7 • (1/31/1997) • **81**

LAZARIDI, DOMAINE CONSTANTIN

Amethystos Red Greece 1994 • $15 • (1/31/1997) • **83**

LIMNOS

Muscat de Lemnos Grand Cru Greece NV • $10 • (5/15/1997) • **86**

OINOTHEKIE

Dafnis Greece NV • $19 • (1/31/1997) • **85**
Greece Red Dafnis 1994 • $19 • (4/30/1998) • **85**
Oinopolis Greece NV • $15 • (4/30/1997) • **78**

SKOURAS

Chardonnay Vin de Pays de Péloponnèse 1996 • $14 • (4/30/1998) • **79**
Matinia White Megas Oenos 1996 • $12 • (4/30/1998) • **81**
Nemea Red Megas Oenos 1995 • $17 • (4/30/1998) • **83**
Nemea Red Megas Oenos 1994 • $18 • (8/31/1997) • **86**
Nemea Red Megas Oenos 1993 • $16 • (1/31/1997) • **88**
Saint George Nemea 1994 • $11 • (8/31/1997) • **83**
Saint George Nemea 1993 • $9 • (1/31/1997) • **84**
Vin de Pays de Péloponnèse Cambello 1996 • $7 • (8/31/1997) • **78**
Vin de Pays de Péloponnèse Cambello 1995 • $6 • (1/31/1997) • **83**
Viognier Vin de Pays de Péloponnèse Cuvée Larsinós 1996 • $18 • (4/30/1998) • **78**

SPILIOTOPOULOS, CHRISTOS

Dimitra Geromilos Farms Greece 1994 • $14 • (1/31/1997) • **78**

■ HUNGARY ■

BAKONDI

Eger Egri Bikavér 1993 • $12 • (7/31/1997) • **78**

BELA, VINCZE

Merlot Egri 1997: A light and somewhat tired red dominated by herbal flavors, with a stewy note on the finish.–K.M. • $14 • (11/15/1999) • **76**

BODROG VARHEGY

Tokay Aszú 3 Puttonyos 1988 • $16 • (9/15/1995) • **83**
Tokay Aszú 3 Puttonyos Citadella 1988 • $14/500 ml. • (10/31/1997) • **87**
Tokay Aszú 5 Puttonyos Citadella 1988 • $20/500 ml. • (10/31/1997) • **86**
Tokay Aszú 5 Puttonyos Messzelátö Dúlö 1988 • $20 • (9/15/1995) • **81**
Tokay Szamorodni Citadella Sweet 1988 • $8/500 ml. • (10/31/1997) • **84**

CASTLE HILL CELLARS

Cabernet Sauvignon Villány Barrique 1994 • $8 • (12/31/1997) • **75**
Merlot Villány Barrique 1994 • $8 • (12/31/1997) • **70**

DEGENFELD, GROF

Tokay Hárslevelú´ 1997: Just off dry, showing peach and citrus notes in a light, refreshing style. Drink now.–B.S. • $13 • (1/01/2000) • **82**

DISZNOKO

Tokay Aszú 3 Puttonyos 1990 • $NA • (9/15/1995) • **77**
Tokay Aszú 4 Puttonyos 1993 • $25/500 ml. • (12/31/1997) • **85**
Tokay Aszú 4 Puttonyos 1992 • $21 • (4/30/1997) • **89**
Tokay Aszú 4 Puttonyos 1989 • $NA • (9/15/1995) • **80**
Tokay Aszú 5 Puttonyos 1993 • $32/500 ml. • (12/31/1997) • **94**
Tokay Aszú 5 Puttonyos 1992 • $27 • (4/30/1997) • **90**
Tokay Aszú 5 Puttonyos 1988 • $18 • (9/15/1995) • **86**
Tokay Aszú 6 Puttonyos 1993 • $40/500 ml. • (12/31/1997) • **87**
Tokay Aszú 6 Puttonyos 1992 • $32 • (4/30/1997) • **94**
Tokay Aszú 6 Puttonyos 1989 • $NA • (9/15/1995) • **84**
Tokay Aszú Eszencia 1993 • $NA/500 ml. • (12/31/1997) • **95**
Tokay Aszú Eszencia 1988 • $NA • (9/15/1995) • **83**
Tokay Eszencia 1992 • $NA/500 ml. • (12/31/1997) • **90**
Tokay Szamorodni Edes 1993 • $20/500 ml. • (12/31/1997) • **89**
Tokay Szamorodni Száraz 1990 • $NA • (9/15/1995) • **82**

DUNAVAR

Merlot Hungary 1996 • $5 • (10/31/1997) • **78**

HETSZOLO

Tokay Aszú 5 Puttonyos Dessewffy 1988 • $NA • (9/15/1995) • **80**
Tokay Fordítás Dessewffy 1990 • $NA • (9/15/1995) • **81**

HICKORY RIDGE

Chardonnay Gyongyos 1996: A lean, straightforward wine that reminds more of Sauvignon. Simple in character, rather green in flavor. Drink now. • $6 • (8/31/1998) • **78**

IGRISTOJE

Hungary Sparkling Dry NV • $12 • (12/31/1997) • **78**
Hungary Sparkling Semi-Dry NV • $12 • (12/31/1997) • **81**

HUNGARY

JOSEF, KAISER FRANZ

Furmint Tokay 1997: Distinctive, with ripe apple and matchstick flavors, some lemony notes as well. Try it for a change of pace. Drink now. Kosher.–K.M. • $9/500 ml. • (1/01/1999) • **82**

LEGLI, OTTO

Chardonnay Balaton 1997: An earthy white, with canned fruit flavors and a green finish.–K.M. • $14 • (1/01/2000) • **74**

OREMUS

Furmint Tokay Late Harvest 1996: Lovely caramel and citrus notes accented by a hint of oxidation and supported by a bracing structure add up to an enjoyable, medium-sweet dessert wine. Orange marmalade flavors echo on the finish. Drink now through 2005.–B.S. • $NA/375 ml. • (1/01/2000) • **89**

Furmint Tokay Late Harvest 1995 • $NA/375 ml. • (1/01/1998) • **74**

Furmint Tokay Mandolás 1998: Floral and tropical fruit aromas signal sweetness, yet this is dry and spicy on the palate, showing grapefruit, clove and vanilla nuances. A bit awkward on the finish. Drink now.–B.S. • $NA • (1/01/2000) • **80**

Tokay Aszú 5 Puttonyos 1994: Gorgeous. The orange marmalade, honey and nut aromas and flavors hang together beautifully on the racy structure. Wonderful concentration and intensity, with a long finish. Drink now through 2006.–B.S. • $NA/500 ml. • (1/01/2000) • **91**

Tokay Aszú 5 Puttonyos 1993 • $22/500 ml. • (12/31/1997) • **90**

Tokay Aszú 5 Puttonyos 1989 • $22/500 ml. • (12/31/1997) • **90**

Tokay Aszú 5 Puttonyos 1988 • $NA • (9/15/1995) • **82**

PAJZOS, CHATEAU

Sárga Muskotály Tokay Late Harvest 1997: Very modern in style, displaying fresh apricot compote and sweetness. A little one-dimensional at this stage, with the sweetnness covering the vibrant acidity. Best from 2001 through 2005.–B.S. • $80/375 ml. • (1/01/2000) • **87**

Tokay Aszú 4 Puttonyos 1988 • $NA • (9/15/1995) • **79**

Tokay Aszú 5 Puttonyos 1993 • $35/500 ml. • (12/31/1997) • **90**

Tokay Aszú 5 Puttonyos 1988 • $21 • (9/15/1995) • **82**

Tokay Esszencia 1993 • $400/500 ml. • (12/31/1997) • **99**

PETERS' HILL

Bátaapáti Estate Special Reserve Möcsényi 1995 • $7 • (5/15/1998) • **83**

Chardonnay Möcsényi Bátaapáti Estate 1996 • $7 • (10/31/1997) • **70**

Tramini Möcsényi Bátaapáti Estate 1996 • $7 • (4/30/1998) • **75**

ROYAL TOKAJI WINE CO., THE

Tokay Aszú 5 Puttonyos 1990 • $NA • (9/15/1995) • **86**

Tokay Aszú 5 Puttonyos Betsek 1991 • $48/500 ml. • (8/31/1996) • **88**

Tokay Aszú 5 Puttonyos Betsek 1990 • $50/500 ml. • (8/31/1996) • **89**

Tokay Aszú 5 Puttonyos Birsalmás 1993 • $53/500 ml. • (12/31/1997) • **94**

Tokay Aszú 5 Puttonyos Birsalmás 1991 • $48/500 ml. • (8/31/1996) • **87**

Tokay Aszú 5 Puttonyos Birsalmás 1990 • $50 • (9/15/1995) • **87**

Tokay Aszú 5 Puttonyos Blue Label 1993 • $32/500 ml. • (12/31/1997) • **92**

Tokay Aszú 5 Puttonyos Blue Label 1991 • $32/500 ml. • (8/31/1996) • **89**

Tokay Aszú 5 Puttonyos Bojta 1991 • $28/500 ml. • (8/31/1996) • **84**

Tokay Aszú 5 Puttonyos Bojta 1990 • $28 • (9/15/1995) • **88**

Tokay Aszú 5 Puttonyos Nyulászó 1991 • $65/500 ml. • (8/31/1996) • **91**

Tokay Aszú 5 Puttonyos Nyulászó 1990 • $65 • (9/15/1995) • **89**

Tokay Aszú 5 Puttonyos Red Label 1993 • $28/500 ml. • (12/31/1997) HR • **95**

Tokay Aszú 5 Puttonyos Szt. Tamás 1991 • $65/500 ml. • (8/31/1996) • **90**

Tokay Aszú 6 Puttonyos Nyulászó 1993 • $77/500 ml. • (12/31/1997) • **94**

Tokay Aszú 6 Puttonyos Szt. Tamás 1993 • $77/500 ml. • (12/31/1997) • **95**

Tokay Aszú Essencia 1993 • $135/500 ml. • (12/31/1997) • **97**

Key: SS—Spectator Selection. CS—Cellar Selection. HR—Highly Recommended. $NA—Price not available. (BT)—Barrel tasting. (A)—Auction Price. For a key to the tasters' initials, see "How to Use These Listings." **Dates in parentheses represent the issues in which the ratings were published.**

VESZTERGOMBI

Cabernet Sauvignon Szekszárdi 1997: Juicy-tasting, with nice zip. Made in a lighter style, with pleasant spice notes and red plum and cherry flavors. Clean and fairly well balanced. Drink now.–K.M. • $14 • (11/15/1999) • **83**

Merlot Szekszárdi 1997: There's a nice ripe texture to this red. Cherry and red plum flavors linger with tobaccolike notes on the finish. Drink now.–K.M. • $14 • (11/15/1999) • **83**

ZOLTAN, GUNZER

Kékfrankos-Cabernet Sauvignon-Kékoportó-Merlot Villány Günzer Cuvée 1997: This has nice peppery flavors, with dried cherry notes, but turns a bit drying on the midpalate.–K.M. • $14 • (11/15/1999) • **78**

■ ISRAEL ■

CARMEL

Almog King David Israel NV • $6 • (1/01/1998) • **75**

Blanc de Blancs Israel NV: This bubbly shows pleasant peach and tropical fruit flavors, but turns simple on the candied finish. Drink now.–K.M. • $9 • (9/15/1998) • **78**

Cabernet Sauvignon Israel Carmel Vineyards 1996: This shows a definite cinnamon edge, with plum and berry flavors. Finishes on a smoky note. Drink now.–K.M. • $11 • (9/30/1998) • **79**

Cabernet Sauvignon Israel Private Collection 1995: Smoke and prune flavors dominate this tired Cabernet. Past its prime.–K.M. • $20 • (9/30/1998) • **76**

Cabernet Sauvignon Samson Valley Wines 1996: Straightforward, with a touch of sweetness, this is a pleasant, medium-bodied red showing plum and berry flavors.–K.M. • $9 • (9/30/1998) • **81**

Chardonnay Galil Private Collection 1997: Dominated by a caramel flavor that turns smoky and coarse on the finish.–K.M. • $11 • (9/30/1998) • **79**

Chateau Richon King David Israel Red NV • $8 • (1/01/1998) • **72**

Chateau Richon King David Israel White NV • $8 • (1/01/1998) • **76**

Chenin Blanc Samson Carmel Vineyards 1997: A bit dull, with modest apple and peach flavors. Drink now.–K.M. • $9 • (9/30/1998) • **75**

Cream Red Israel NV • $4 • (1/01/1998) • **76**

Cream White Israel NV • $4 • (1/01/1998) • **76**

Emerald Riesling Israel Private Collection 1997: A lumbering, off-dry wine, with pleasant peach and ripe apple flavors.–K.M. • $11 • (9/30/1998) • **81**

Emerald Riesling Shomron Valley Wines 1997: Shows decent peach and apricot flavors, but finishes on a slight cloying note.–K.M. • $9 • (9/30/1998) • **78**

French Colombard Israel Adulan 1997: Definitely sweet, with peachy flavors that linger on the finish. Drink now.–K.M. • $8 • (9/30/1998) • **77**

Kadmon Israel NV • $10/500 ml. • (1/01/1998) • **82**

Muscat Samson Private Collection NV: Reminiscent of Vin Santo, with crème brûlée flavors and a nice richness. Smooth and elegant. Flavors linger appealingly on the finish. Drink now.–K.M. • $12/375 ml. • (9/30/1998) • **84**

Petite Sirah Shomron Valley Wines 1997: A plummy red, with berry flavors and a gamy note on the finish. Drink now.–K.M. • $9 • (9/30/1998) • **79**

Sauvignon Blanc Israel Carmel Vineyards Dan 1997: Simple and straightforward, with ripe apple and peach flavors and an herbal note on the finish.–K.M. • $9 • (9/30/1998) • **78**

Sémillon Shomron Valley Wines 1997: A peachy flavor dominates this simple white wine. Drink now, well chilled.–K.M. • $8 • (9/30/1998) • **77**

Valley Wines Israel NV • $6 • (1/01/1998) • **72**

CASTEL, DOMAINE DU

Grand Vin Haute-Judée 1995: A walk on the wild side, with appealing charred and plummy flavors and sweet-spicy notes. Spicy flavors linger appealingly on the finish. Drink now.–K.M. • $33 • (9/30/1998) • **85**

DALTON

Merlot Israel 1997: Focused, with concentrated red plum and cherry flavors and plenty of herbal and leathery notes mixed in. A well-honed, medium-bodied red with herbal and pepper notes that linger on the finish. Drink now through 2001. Kosher.–K.M. • $19 • (1/01/1999) • **85**

GAMLA

Cabernet Sauvignon Galil 1995: Ripe and plummy, with nice balance and smooth texture, has fine tannins and well-integrated dark chocolate and spice notes. An elegant wine, with a nice minty touch on the finish. Drink now through 2001.–K.M. • $12 • (9/30/1998) • **86**
Cabernet Sauvignon Galil 1990 • $12 • (12/15/1994) • **83**
Cabernet Sauvignon Galil 1989 • $12 • (12/15/1994) • **78**
Cabernet Sauvignon Galil 1988 • $10 • (7/15/1993) • **77**
Cabernet Sauvignon Galil Special Reserve 1995: A straightforward red, with sweet cherry and chocolate flavors. Drink now.–K.M. • $15 • (9/30/1998) • **82**
Cabernet Sauvignon Galil Special Reserve 1986 • $12 • (3/31/1991) • **83**
Cabernet Sauvignon Galilee 1996: Red plum and herb flavors are overwhelmed by a charred quality. Dries out on the finish. Kosher.–K.M. • $NA • (1/01/1999) • **79**
Chardonnay Galil 1996: Pineapple and tropical flavors dominate this white from Israel, with candied flavors on the finish. Kosher.–K.M. • $NA • (1/01/1999) • **79**
Sauvignon Blanc Galil 1996: A spicy Sauvignon, with appealing honey, nutmeg and fig flavors and a lingering finish. A little flat in the middle, but still enjoyable. Drink now.–K.M. • $9 • (9/30/1998) • **82**
Sauvignon Blanc Galil Late Harvest 1988 • $14 • (3/31/1991) • **75**

GOLAN HEIGHTS

Cabernet Sauvignon Galil 1995: A firmly structured Cabernet, with pleasant cherry and tea flavors and spicy notes on the finish. Drink now.–K.M. • $13 • (9/30/1998) • **84**
Cabernet Sauvignon Galil 1992 • $13 • (4/30/1997) • **85**
Cabernet Sauvignon Galil 1989 • $12 • (12/15/1994) • **81**
Cabernet Sauvignon Galil 1987 • $12 • (4/15/1992) • **83**
Cabernet Sauvignon Galil 1986 • $11 • (3/31/1991) • **85**
Golan Village Red Galil 1996: Soft and fruity, with pleasant berry and pepper flavors, straightforward and quaffable. A blend of Gamay, Pinot Noir and Syrah. Drink now.–K.M. • $9 • (9/30/1998) • **82**
Golan Village Red Galil 1994 • $10 • (4/30/1997) • **82**
Sauvignon Blanc Galil 1996: This white is dominated by fig and melon flavors, with some spicy notes on the finish. Drink now.–K.M. • $9 • (9/30/1998) • **79**

MARGALIT

Cabernet Sauvignon Israel Special Reserve 1993: Thick and rich, with dark plum and cherry flavors and a charred note. Finishes on notes of tea, prune and chocolate. An ambitious effort, but overripe. Drink through 2001. Not available in the U.S.–K.M. • $NA • (9/30/1998) • **84**
Merlot Israel 1995: Smooth, ripe and leathery, with appealing dried plum and cherry flavors. Shows a pleasing violet aroma and a mature taste. Well balanced, with a brown-sugar finish. Drink now. Not available in the U.S. –K.M. • $NA • (9/30/1998) • **87**

YARDEN

Blanc de Blancs Galil NV • $NA • (1/01/1998) • **86**
Brut Galil NV • $NA • (1/01/1998) • **83**
Cabernet Sauvignon Galil 1995: Delicious, with ripe plum, berry and cherry flavors and gorgeous chocolate notes throughout. A well-balanced and concentrated wine with plenty of punch. Drink now.–K.M. • $21 • (9/30/1998) • **88**
Cabernet Sauvignon Galil 1993 • $20 • (4/30/1997) • **88**
Cabernet Sauvignon Galil 1990 • $18 • (12/15/1994) • **82**
Cabernet Sauvignon Galil 1989 • $18 • (12/15/1994) • **79**
Cabernet Sauvignon Galil 1986 • $14 • (6/30/1990) • **79**
Cabernet Sauvignon Galil 1985 • $14 • (6/30/1990) • **82**
Chardonnay Galil 1996: Lush and rich, with layers of ripe flavor that ooze with honey, butterscotch and crème brûlée. This is a full-bodied Chardonnay, with a touch of elegance and spicy flavors that linger on the finish. Drink now.–K.M. • $15 • (9/30/1998) • **86**
Katzrin Red Israel 1993: Chocolate and cherry flavors dominate this overripe wine, turning minty on the finish. Drink now.–K.M. • $25 • (9/30/1998) • **79**
Merlot Galil 1995: There's a nice thickness to this wine, with red plum, cherry and herb flavors. Finishes with chocolate and leather notes and some tannins. Drink now.–K.M. • $17 • (9/30/1998) • **84**
Merlot Galil Special Reserve 1988 • $14 • (3/31/1991) • **77**
Merlot Galil Special Reserve 1986 • $12 • (6/30/1990) • **79**
Merlot Galilee 1996: A bit tired-tasting, with sour cherry flavors and charry notes on the finish. Kosher.–K.M. • $NA • (1/01/1999) • **77**
Mt. Hermon Red Galil 1995 • $10 • (4/30/1997) • **86**
Mt. Hermon Red Galil 1989 • $7 • (3/31/1991) • **70**
Muscat Galil 1996: Sweet and peachy, with a spicy flavor on the finish. Drink now.–K.M. • $13/500 ml. • (9/30/1998) • **81**
Sauvignon Blanc Galil 1996: Crisp and forward, with rich fig flavors and a spicy finish. There's a nice power to it, and an appealing earthy note as well. Drink now.–K.M. • $13 • (9/30/1998) • **84**

■ LEBANON ■

KEFRAYA, CHATEAU

Comte de M... Lebanon 1996: Quite rich, with a sweet-spicy quality, this wine has loads of red plum, ripe cherry and black fig flavors, along with plenty of leather, bacon and cardamom. A supple and voluptuous red that lingers with milk chocolate on the finish. A blend of Cabernet Sauvignon, Mourvèdre and Syrah. Drink now through 2003.–K.M. • $60 • (2/28/1999) • **88**

■ MEXICO ■

MONTE XANIC

Cabernet Sauvignon-Merlot Valle de Guadalupe 1995: Prune, plum and coffee notes dominate this somewhat clumsy, overripe red. It's concentrated and ambitious, but lacks delineation. Drink now.–T.M. • $17 • (1/01/2000) • **82**
Sauvignon Blanc-Sémillon Valle de Guadalupe Viña Kristel 1997: Shows some resinous, waxy notes, some clove and orange peel as well. Comes off a bit top-heavy though. Drink now.–T.M. • $9 • (1/01/2000) • **80**

SANTO THOMAS, BODEGAS DE

Cabernet Sauvignon Baja California 1995: Ripe and smoky, with plum and leather flavors that linger on the finish. A bit lumbering, it ends on a tealike note. Drink now.–K.M. • $15 • (2/28/1999) • **80**
Tempranillo Baja California 1996: A rustic wine, with a thick, overripe texture and charry, pruny flavors. Earthy finish.–K.M. • $8 • (2/28/1999) • **73**

■ REPUBLIC OF GEORGIA ■

GWS

Alexandreuli Republic of Georgia Khvanchkara Semi-Sweet NV: A sweet style, with flavors of berry, cherry and cola and an herbal note on the finish.–K.M. • $15/500 ml. • (4/30/1999) • **77**
Rkatsiteli Kakheti Balanchine 1997: Baked apple and cinnamon aromas dominate this white, which turns foxy on the dull finish.–K.M. • $8 • (2/28/1999) • **77**
Rkatsiteli Kakheti Old Tbilisi 1997: A medium-bodied white with flavors of pineapple and spice, and a slightly rubbery note on the finish.–K.M. • $7 • (2/28/1999) • **78**
Saperavi Kakheti 1997: Some decent grapey and juicy aromas, but they turn quite tart on the lean finish.–K.M. • $10 • (2/28/1999) • **77**
Saperavi Kakheti Akhasheni 1997: Sweet, with red plum and black currant flavors. Medium-bodied, with a clean finish. Serve chilled. Drink now. –K.M. • $13 • (4/30/1999) • **82**
Saperavi Kakheti Balanchine 1997: Straightforward and juicy, with berry and cherry flavors and peppery notes on the finish.–K.M. • $8 • (4/30/1999) • **78**
Saperavi Kakheti Kindzmarauli Semi-Sweet 1997: A pleasant mix, with bright flavors of sweet berry and plum and agreeable spicy notes. Reminiscent of Lillet; serve it well chilled or on the rocks. Drink now.–K.M. • $14 • (4/30/1999) • **83**
Saperavi Kakheti Pirosmani Semi-Sweet 1997: A cloying red, with simple plum and red berry flavors.–K.M. • $10 • (4/30/1999) • **78**
Saperavi Republic of Georgia Chinebuli Finest Ruby NV: Brown, sweet, with flavors of maple syrup and raisins. A rough-hewn dessert-style wine.–K.M. • $13 • (4/30/1999) • **79**
Tsolikauri Lechkhumi Tvishi Semi-Sweet 1997: A floral aroma and pineapple-like flavors don't add up to much.–K.M. • $13 • (4/30/1999) • **72**

■ ROMANIA ■

HICKORY RIDGE

Chardonnay Hincesti 1996 • $6 • (5/15/1998) • **69**

VALEVERDE

Cabernet Sauvignon Valea Calugareasca 1995: Lean and thin, with tomato and rhubarblike flavors.–K.M. • $5 • (3/31/1999) • **71**
Merlot Valea Calugareasca 1995: Has some thin, dried cherry and plum flavors, finishing with a slight gamy note.–K.M. • $5 • (3/31/1999) • **76**
Pinot Grigio Valea Calugareasca 1997: An oxidized aroma and canned fruit flavors don't add up to much.–K.M. • $5 • (3/31/1999) • **71**

VAMPIRE

Cabernet Sauvignon Dealu Mare 1991 • $7 • (12/31/1995) • **79**
Cabernet Sauvignon Dealu Mare Private Reserve 1995: Has a candied aroma, with some red plum flavors, but they're overwhelmed by the charry, harsh texture.–K.M. • $10 • (3/31/1999) • **73**
Merlot Dealu Mare 1991 • $7 • (12/31/1995) • **76**
Merlot Dealu Mare Private Reserve 1995: The faint cherry and herbal flavors fade away on the dried out finish. Past its prime.–K.M. • $10 • (3/31/1999) • **72**

■ SWITZERLAND ■

AUVERNIER, CHATEAU D'

Neuchâtel Rosé Oeil de Perdrix 1996 • $17 • (2/28/1998) • **79**
Neuchâtel White 1996 • $17 • (2/28/1998) • **85**
Pinot Gris Neuchâtel 1996 • $18 • (2/28/1998) • **88**

BADOUX, HENRI

Aigle White Les Murailles 1996 • $28 • (2/28/1998) • **84**

BONVIN, CHARLES

Dôle Valais Matterhorn Mont Cervin 1995 • $14 • (2/28/1998) • **82**
Humagne Rouge Valais Les Cépages 1995 • $21 • (2/28/1998) • **78**
Valais Cuvée d'Or 1995 • $NA/375 ml. • (2/28/1998) • **87**
Valais Cuvée Rouge 1995 • $24 • (2/28/1998) • **86**

BOVARD

Calamin Cuvée Spéciale 1997: Well delineated, this Swiss white from Chasselas offers apple, mineral and chamomile aromas and flavors in a crisp style. Its moderate acidity and intensity will match well with food. Drink now.–B.S. • $25 • (9/15/1999) • **85**
Dézaley Medinette 1997: Aromas of honey and spring blossoms are augmented by citrus on the palate in this round, soft-textured white made from Chasselas; a hint of bitterness on the finish keeps it focused. Drink now.–B.S. • $28 • (9/15/1999) • **84**
Sauvignon Villette 1997: Very tropical in aroma and flavor, displaying passion fruit, ripe melon, vanilla and a hint of herbs. Round and opulent for Sauvignon Blanc, with a lingering aftertaste of vanilla from the new oak treatment. Drink now through 2001.–B.S. • $33 • (9/15/1999) • **87**

GERMANIER-BALAVAUD

Amigne Vétroz 1996 • $24 • (2/28/1998) • **88**
Amigne Vétroz Mitis 1994 • $32/375 ml. • (2/28/1998) • **89**
Syrah Valais 1995 • $36 • (2/28/1998) • **84**

GILLIARD, ROBERT

Dôle Monts 1996 • $19 • (2/28/1998) • **79**
Fendant Sion Les Murettes 1996 • $18 • (2/28/1998) • **69**
Fendant Valais 1996 • $15 • (2/28/1998) • **73**

Key: SS—Spectator Selection. CS—Cellar Selection. HR—Highly Recommended. $NA—Price not available. (BT)—Barrel tasting. (A)—Auction Price. For a key to the tasters' initials, see "How to Use These Listings."
Dates in parentheses represent the issues in which the ratings were published.

MONTMOLLIN, DOMAINE DE

Neuchâtel Rosé Oeil de Perdrix 1996 • $19 • (2/28/1998) • **71**
Neuchâtel White 1996 • $17 • (2/28/1998) • **86**
Pinot Noir Neuchâtel 1995 • $21 • (2/28/1998) • **80**

PROVINS VALAIS

Cornalin Valais Cuvée du Grand Métral 1995 • $29 • (2/28/1998) • **83**
Dôle Valais Chanteauvieux 1995 • $16 • (2/28/1998) • **78**
Fendant Valais Pierrafeu 1996 • $16 • (2/28/1998) • **80**
Humagne Rouge Valais Cuvée du Grand Métral 1995 • $26 • (2/28/1998) • **78**

ROUVINEZ

Dôle Valais de Sierre 1995 • $19 • (2/28/1998) • **81**
Fendant Valais de Sierre 1996 • $17 • (2/28/1998) • **85**
Valais Red Le Tourmentin 1995 • $34 • (2/28/1998) • **84**

TAMBORINI, CARLO

Merlot Ticino Collivo Riserva 1995 • $25 • (2/28/1998) • **82**
Merlot Ticino Comano 1995 • $25 • (2/28/1998) • **85**
Merlot Ticino San Zeno Riserva 1994 • $20 • (2/28/1998) • **81**
Merlot Ticino Vigna Vecchia 1995 • $25 • (2/28/1998) • **83**

TESTUZ, JEAN & PIERRE

Dézaley White L'Arbalette 1996 • $30 • (2/28/1998) • **86**

UVAVINS

La Côte Red Les Rocards 1995 • $18 • (2/28/1998) • **82**
Morges White Vieilles Vignes 1996 • $17 • (2/28/1998) • **85**

VALSANGIACOMO

Merlot Ticino Riserva di Bacco 1994 • $18 • (2/28/1998) • **77**
Merlot Ticino Rubro 1993 • $34 • (2/28/1998) • **87**

VARONE

Fendant Sion Soleil du Valais 1996 • $16 • (2/28/1998) • **79**
Valais White Hermitage Grand Glarier 1996 • $22 • (2/28/1998) • **89**

■ UKRAINE ■

MASSANDRA

Pink Muscat Crimea 2 Year Old NV: Pretty, sweet aperitif wine. Amber-rust colored. Lots of honey, marmalade and fruit character. Medium-bodied and lightly sweet, with fresh fruit and a honey-almond aftertaste. Drink now.–J.S. • $23/500 ml. • (10/15/1999) • **87**
Pinot Gris Crimea 2 Year Old NV: Delicious sweet wine. Amber-rust colored. Fruit cake with lots of dried fruits on the nose. Medium-bodied and lightly sweet, with a wonderful intensity of caramel and dried fruit character. Fresh finish. Drink now.–J.S. • $23/500 ml. • (10/15/1999) • **90**
Tokay Crimea 2 Year Old NV: Intense aromas of dried apricots and butterscotch. Medium-bodied, medium sweet, with an almond, honey finish. A bit rustic. Drink now.–J.S. • $35/500 ml. • (10/15/1999) • **86**
White Muscat Crimea 2 Year Old NV: A delicious wine. Loads of butterscotch and lemon with hints of meringue. Medium- to full-bodied, lightly sweet, with plenty of mandarin orange and cream character.–J.S. • $23/500 ml. • (10/15/1999) • **88**

■ URUGUAY ■

LURTON, J. & F.

Tannat-Merlot Uruguay Casilla Dorada 1998: Overripe (pruny) on the nose, but with dark plum and mineral flavors that are typical for Tannat. Lacks focus, with a crisp finish. Drink now.–B.S. • $12 • (1/01/2000) • **80**

■ YUGOSLAVIA ■

HICKORY RIDGE

Merlot Vranje 1995 • $NA • (6/15/1998) • **78**

USA

American wines are labeled primarily by the grape variety (Chardonnay, for instance) that makes up all or most (the legal minimum is 75%) of the wine in the bottle. This method differs from the classic European approach, which is based primarily on geographic locations and/or appellations, such as Bordeaux and the Rhône. Instead of being limited to a few grape types or an inflexible aging scheme under an appellation law, American winemakers are free to experiment and plant whatever grape variety they wish. This flexibility in choosing what wines to make and how to make them has allowed American wines made from Chardonnay, Cabernet Sauvignon, Merlot, Pinot Noir and other grape varieties to challenge their European models in almost every arena.

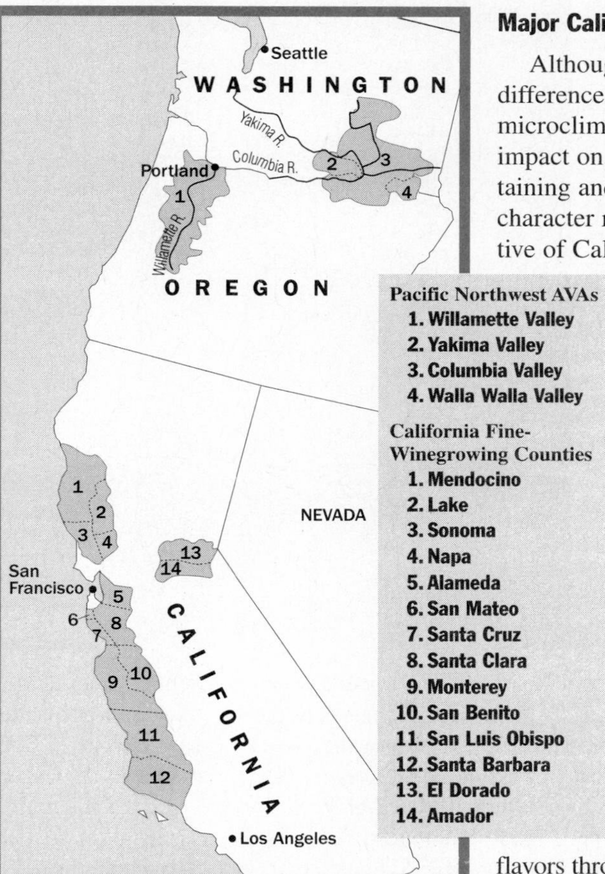

CALIFORNIA

California produces about 90 percent of the wine made in the U.S. Although the California industry formerly relied on the mass production of low-end generic wines, for example, those that used to be labeled "Chablis" or "Burgundy," these are being steadily displaced by varietally labeled wines based on classic European grapes, such as Cabernet Sauvignon, Chardonnay, Pinot Noir, Merlot and Sauvignon Blanc. Large wineries in California (and Washington) have had great success selling Chardonnay and other well-known varietals, often at less than $10. At the same time, California uses the same varieties—but from the choicest locations, such as Napa Valley, Sonoma County and Santa Barbara—to produce top-of-the-line bottlings that compete head-to-head with the best wines of Europe in price and quality. While overall prices of California wines have risen steadily in response to increased consumer demand for upscale wines, quality has more than kept up with price.

Major California Grape Varieties

Although regional soil differences and variations in microclimate have a significant impact on wine flavors, maintaining and enhancing varietal character remains a key objective of California winemaking. Thus, knowledge of the leading grape varieties grown in California is a prerequisite to understanding the state's wines.

Chardonnay: California Chardonnay displays flavors of fresh-cut yellow fruit, especially apples, melon, pineapple and other tropical fruits. Winemakers build more complexity into these flavors through the use of such techniques as barrel fermentation, *sur lie* aging and malolactic fermentation. California Chardonnays tend to be more full-bodied and plump than French Chardon-nay wines such as white Burgundy. Chardonnay is now being planted in cooler areas, leading to wines with less alcohol and a better balance of fruit and acidity. Leading Chardonnay appellations include Sonoma Valley, Alexander Valley, Russian River Valley, Carneros, Napa Valley and Santa Barbara. As Chardonnay prices have zoomed, vintners are increasingly looking toward other regions, such as Monterey County, Mendocino and Lodi for quality fruit at lower prices.

Cabernet Sauvignon: California Cabernet displays the classic varietal characteristics of fresh herbs, cedar, cassis, mint, black currant and violets. In the cooler areas, it can take on a distinct vegetal/bell pepper characteristic, which is increasingly viewed as undesirable. For many years, it was thought that California Cabernet was sufficiently soft and complex that it did not benefit from blending with other varietals. While some of the best California Cabernets are still made from 100 percent Cabernet Sauvignon, the trend in recent years has been to add Merlot and other Bordeaux varietals such as Petit Verdot and Cabernet Franc. The term Meritage applies to Bordeaux-style blends of these varieties, typically with less than 75% Cabernet Sauvignon.

A vineyard in Monterey County, California.

Kent Hanson

Top quality Cabernet Sauvignons today are aged in small barrels, of both French and American oak, to add appealing vanilla and spice notes. Although several areas of the state now produce top-notch Cabernet, Napa Valley is responsible for the majority of the best examples.

Zinfandel: The most widely planted red grape in California, Zinfandel lends itself to an enormous variety of styles, ranging from the rosé style called "white" Zinfandel at one extreme, to inky black late-harvest Zinfandels at the other. Red Zinfandel has a zesty, spicy varietal character, and is loaded with notes of raspberry, plum and red-berry fruit. Winemakers often choose to emphasize one or more of these characteristics. Thus, some Zinfandels are made in a medium-weight, claret style that emphasizes the grape's subtler elements and innate fruitiness. Amador County and a few other regions specialize in blockbusters, characterized by high levels of tannin, extract, and alcohol. Another popular style emphasizes Zinfandel's grapey, Beaujolais character.

Sauvignon Blanc. Also known as Fumé Blanc, California Sauvignon Blanc is an often underappreciated and usually bargain-priced white. Some California Sauvignon Blancs are made in a Loire style, and offer strong grassy, herbal, mineral and citrus (particularly grapefruit) tastes with minimal or no oak flavors. A more recent trend, most evident in Napa Valley, has been to emphasize barrel fermentation, lees stirring, and blending with Sémillon, all of which yields a rich style closer to that of a white Bordeaux. Leaf thinning, a technique in which vine leaves are selectively removed to allow more sunlight to reach the grape bunches, is now widely used to produce riper, better-balanced Sauvignon Blancs.

Merlot: Though once thought of as a blending grape, California Merlot has now emerged as a hot new variety on its own. Merlot has been called the "kinder, gentler" alternative to Cabernet Sauvignon: it is softer than the latter, and offers more cherry, plum and red fruit flavors. In California, as elsewhere, Merlot is often blended with Cabernet Sauvignon and other Bordeaux grapes to add complexity to the finished wine. Merlot seems to thrive mainly in the regions where Cabernet Sauvignon does best; the finest California examples tend to be from Napa and Sonoma.

Pinot Noir: While many early California Pinot Noirs were clumsy and lacked the elegance expected of a good Pinot Noir, that is no longer the case. Today, good California Pinot Noir has layers of pure strawberry, raspberry and other red and black fruits that expand across the palate on the finish. Pinot Noir seems to have found a natural home in the cooler regions of California, including Carneros, Russian River Valley and Santa Barbara.

Rhône varieties: The term "Rhône Rangers" is applied to numerous California winemakers who are working with grape varieties that originated in France's Rhône Valley. The thinking is that California's Mediterranean-like climate is ideally suited to these varieties. Among the red wines, Syrah seems to be achieving the most acclaim at the moment, displaying dense red berry fruit with hints of bacon fat, tar and spice. Mourvèdre displays characteristics similar to Syrah, but with a bit more earthiness and dustier tannins on the finish. Among whites, Viognier is showing exceptional promise. Its primary characteristics are peach and honeysuckle notes, with an alcoholic fullness and gentle roundness on the finish.

MAJOR CALIFORNIA WINE REGIONS

Napa Valley

Undoubtedly the best-known wine region of California, Napa Valley produces a star-studded array of fine wines. More than 35,000 acres of Napa Valley are planted with vines today. Chardonnay and Cabernet Sauvignon account for about half of this total, with Merlot increasingly displacing old plantings of Sauvignon Blanc and Riesling.

Napa Valley encompasses a wide range of microclimates and soil types. The northern portion of the Valley, near Calistoga, is the warmest, while the southern end, near Carneros and extending up through Yountville, is cooler, owing to the moderating influence of the San Pablo Bay. Many of Napa's best-known wineries—and some of the area's oldest wineries—Beaulieu, Robert Mondavi, Beringer and Louis Martini are situated in the central part of the Valley, around Oakville, Rutherford and St. Helena. Many of the best vineyards are situated on the so-called benchlands (or outlying foothills) of Rutherford and Oakville, which are recognized for producing classic, long-lived Cabernet Sauvignon.

Several subregions of Napa have developed individual winemaking identities. The Stags Leap District, east of Yountville, is known for its supple, Bordeaux-like Cabernets. It is home to Stag's Leap Wine Cellars, Stags' Leap Winery, Shafer Vineyards, Pine Ridge, Chimney Rock, S. Anderson and others. Carneros, which straddles the southern ends of Napa and Sonoma, has developed a reputation for Burgundy-style wines made from Pinot Noir and Chardonnay. Merlot also does well here, somewhat surprisingly in view of the cool climate. Well-known Carneros wineries include Acacia, Bouchaine, Saintsbury and Carneros Creek.

In recent years, several regions in the hilly mountainsides of the Valley have attracted special recognition. Howell Mountain, located to the northeast of St. Helena, has volcanic soil that produces especially rich wines. Howell Mountain wineries such as Dunn and La Jota have established well-deserved reputations for producing powerful Cabernets and Zinfandels. To the west of Yountville is Mount Veeder, a part of the Mayacamas Mountains, which has become known for Cabernet Sauvignon, Chardonnay and Sauvignon Blanc. Leading Mount Veeder wineries include Mayacamas Vineyards, Mount Veeder Winery, Hess Collection and Chateau Potelle. Further north in the Mayacamas Mountains, Diamond Creek and Philip Togni are highly respected.

Sonoma County

Sonoma County presents a more varied picture than does the Napa Valley. Geographically diverse, with numerous microclimates, it supports many grape varieties and wine styles. The historic heart of Sonoma County is the Sonoma Valley, where many of its oldest wineries are located. Cabernet Sauvignon has fared well here, as has Zinfandel, while Chardonnay and Pinot Noir seem especially well suited to the southern part of the Sonoma Valley. Leading wineries of Sonoma Valley include Kenwood, B.R. Cohn, Kunde, Laurel Glen, Glen Ellen and Sebastiani, although the latter two also get grapes from elsewhere throughout the state.

Alexander Valley is planted mostly to Cabernet Sauvignon and Chardonnay. Its Cabernets are often marked by a hint of eucalyptus, while its Chardonnays tend to be full and rich. In addition to luxury-priced Cabernets and Chardonnays, Jordan Winery produces a luxury sparkling wine cuvée called J at a nearby sister facility. The region's other well-known wineries include Alexander Valley Vineyards, Murphy-Goode, Simi and Stonestreet.

Dry Creek Valley parallels Alexander Valley, but has a warmer microclimate. Zinfandel grows well in its benchland soil, but Cabernet and Merlot are making significant inroads. Among whites, Sauvignon Blanc does particularly well here. Leading wineries include Dry Creek Vineyard, Mazzocco, Quivira and Preston.

Because of its proximity to the ocean, the Russian River Valley's climate is cool and damp, which for some years discouraged extensive planting. However, Pinot Noir and Chardonnay seem to thrive under these conditions, which can be likened to those of Burgundy. Russian River Valley also encompasses two smaller

At Silver Oak in Napa Valley.

subregions that are attracting increasing attention, Chalk Hill and Green Valley. Both excel in Chardonnay, and Green Valley has been developed by Iron Horse Vineyards as a source of high-quality sparkling wines.

Santa Barbara County

In northern Santa Barbara County, the Santa Maria Valley is becoming well-known for Pinot Noir and Chardonnay; both varieties take on a special intensity and richness of fruit here. Au Bon Climat, Byron, Wild Horse and Cambria are among the leading producers. In southern Santa Barbara, the Santa Ynez Valley has also shown an affinity for cool-climate varieties, including Pinot Noir and Chardonnay. The Sanford & Benedict Vineyard in the eastern part of the Valley supplies grapes for some of Sanford Winery's best wines, and supplies other wineries as well. Also in Santa Barbara, experiments with Syrah have produced excellent results; Zaca Mesa's is one of the best.

Other Regions

Just north of Napa lies Lake County, which has become an important producer of Chardonnay, Cabernet, Sauvignon Blanc, Merlot and Pinot Noir. Lake County is the home of Kendall-Jackson Winery and Guenoc Winery, among others. Located just to the west of Lake County, Mendocino is home to a wide array of wineries—Fetzer, Parducci and Steele are the best-known—many of which sell excellent varietals at modest prices.

The areas of Santa Clara, Monterey and Saint Luis Obispo contain a vast number of fine properties. Important viticultural regions in these areas include the Santa Cruz Mountains, Livermore Valley, Carmel, Arroyo Seco, Paso Robles and Edna Valley. These regions produce a full range of varietal types and make wines that often reach the highest levels of quality.

WASHINGTON

Washington has built its reputation on stylish Merlot, Cabernet Sauvignon and Cabernet-based blends, and bright, lush Chardonnay. In addition, some very impressive late-harvest Riesling, Sémillon and Gewürztraminer dessert wines are made here. With over 140 wineries and 24,000 acres of *vinifera* vineyards, Washington ranks second behind California in total wine production and is its most serious competitor in quality.

Most Washington wineries are located in the Columbia River Valley appellation, which includes the smaller Yakima Valley and Walla Walla Valley AVAs within its borders. Columbia Valley vineyards are protected from the Pacific Northwest rains by the Cascade Mountains, which prevent precipitation from moving into the state's interior. This "rain shadow" provides hundreds of days of sunshine each year and allows winemakers to irrigate the vines in precisely desired amounts. Solar angle is also a quality factor, as Washington's latitude, roughly 46 degrees north, is the same as the great winegrowing regions of Bordeaux and Burgundy in France. As in France, however, northerly ice storms can be a problem. In some years, devastating frosts have cut the state's grape crop by as much as 40 percent, leaving many wineries stranded.

While there are many fine vineyards throughout the state, those in the Walla Walla Valley may be Washington's best kept secret. The wineries here—Leonetti, Woodward Canyon, Waterbrook, L'Ecole No. 41, Glen Fiona and Canoe Ridge—all produce top-quality wines on a small scale, and consistently rank among the best in the state. However, big is far from bad in Washington; the large Chateau Ste. Michelle and Columbia Crest wineries both produce notably fine wines in all price categories. At the Yakima-based Columbia winery, winemaker David Lake offers his signature series of fine wines, including Cabernet Sauvignon from the Otis, Red Willow and Sagemoor Vineyards, and top-notch Chardonnay, Sémillon and Syrah. These and other wines have won Washington wines many loyal customers and collectors.

OREGON

Oregon has staked its reputation on Pinot Noir, a challenging grape variety even in its homeland of France, where it produces the great red wines of the Côte d'Or. Just as red Burgundy is often a hit or miss proposition, so, too, is Oregon Pinot Noir. At its best, it comes as close to the silky power of red Burgundy as Pinot Noir from anywhere else in the world. Good years have a classic balance, producing wines with magnificently perfumed aromas and clean, pure, focused flavors. As in Burgundy, however, only about one vintage in three is truly exceptional.

Most Oregon wineries are in the Willamette Valley. A break in the coastal mountain range permits the cool Pacific Ocean breezes to enter the valley, providing natural air-conditioning and maintaining the proper temperatures for the optimum maturation of Pinot Noir. Willamette Valley also makes a fair amount of Chardonnay and other white wines, most notably Pinot Gris and Pinot Blanc, all of which can be bright, fruity and well made.

Two smaller regions in the warmer southern part of the state also show promise. Rogue Valley, just across the California border, has made good-to-very-good Merlot, Pinot Gris and Viognier, as well as attractively plummy Syrah. Umpqua Valley, south of the Willamette, is growing everything from Cabernet Franc and Malbec to Tempranillo and Dolcetto, with considerable success.

Oregon has yet to achieve the stature of California or the consistency of Washington. However, it is clearly a region capable of producing world-class wine, and is worthy of keen interest among lovers of fine wine.

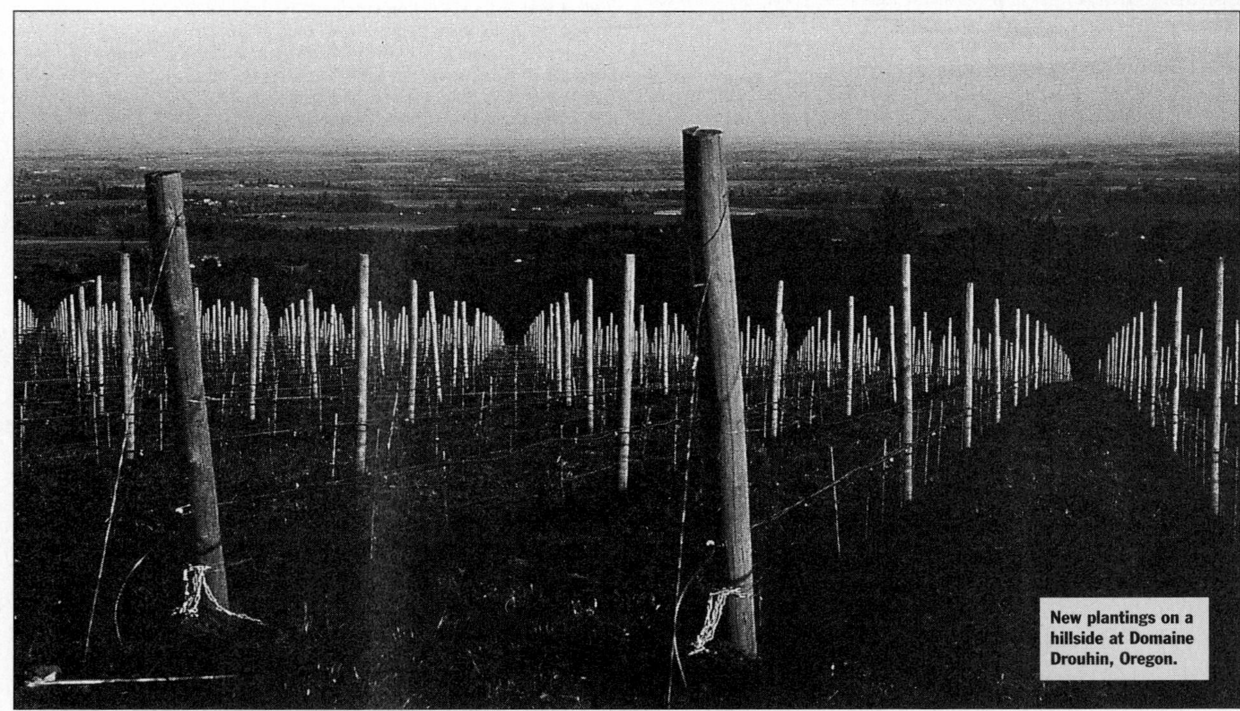

New plantings on a hillside at Domaine Drouhin, Oregon.

Doreen Wynja

ABACELA | OREGON

Cabernet Franc Umpqua Valley 1997: Firm in texture, almost chewy, with an earthy streak weaving through the supple blackberry and spice flavors that linger on the harmonious finish. Drink now through 2005.–H.S. • $23 • (12/31/1999) • **88**

Cabernet Sauvignon Umpqua Valley 1997: Firm in texture, supporting some pretty bayleaf-scented berry and currant flavors, finishing with fine-grained tannins. Needs to develop some richness. Contains 77 percent Cabernet Sauvignon, also Malbec, Merlot, Cabernet Franc and Petit Verdot. Best after 2001.–H.S. • $21 • (12/31/1999) • **86**

Dolcetto Umpqua Valley 1997: A bit denser and tougher than an Italian Dolcetto, but it has the requisite raspberry and strawberry. Drink with hearty food. Drink now through 2001.–H.S. • $18 • (5/15/2000) • **84**

Malbec Umpqua Valley 1997: Ripe and generous, this rustic, raw-boned red has raucous plum and raspberry flavors that keep jumping on the finish. Needs to settle down. Drink through 2001.–H.S. • $13 • (12/31/1999) • **85**

Merlot Umpqua Valley 1997: Firm in texture, it's a lighter style of Merlot, with modest stewed plum and coffee flavors lingering on the finish. Tasted twice, with consistent notes. Drink now through 2003.–H.S. • $17 • (12/31/1999) • **83**

Syrah Umpqua Valley 1997: Smells great, with spicy, peppery nuances to the rich berry aromas, but it turns lean and minty on the palate, finishing with more herb and wood than fruit. Best from 2001 through 2004.–H.S. • $21 • (5/15/2000) • **85**

Tempranillo Umpqua Valley 1997: Brightly focused blackberry and mineral flavors and firm, nicely integrated tannins make this eminently worth drinking. Not much about Umpqua Valley looks like Spain's Rioja, the home of Tempranillo, but this wine suggests that the grape might have found another home in Oregon. Drink now through 2002.–H.S. • $28 • (12/31/1999) • **87**

Vintner's Blend Umpqua Valley 1997: Thick, juicy and spicy, with predominant black pepper and dark plum flavors. Firm, tannic finish. Carignane, Graciano, Syrah and others. Drink now through 2002.–H.S. • $9 • (5/15/2000) • **85**

ABREU | CALIFORNIA

Cabernet Sauvignon Napa Valley Madrona Ranch 1994: Massive, rich and deeply flavored, packed with complex currant, mineral, spice, sage and cedary oak flavors and chewy but polished tannins. This one will require some patience. Best from 2002 through 2010.–J.L. • $201 Ⓐ • (1/01/1999) • **96**

Cabernet Sauvignon Napa Valley Madrona Ranch 1992 • $95 Ⓐ • (1/01/1998) • **93**

Cabernet Sauvignon Napa Valley Madrona Ranch 1991 • $45 • (1/01/1998) • **93**

Cabernet Sauvignon Napa Valley Madrona Ranch 1989 • $67 Ⓐ • (1/01/1998) • **91**

Cabernet Sauvignon Napa Valley Madrona Ranch 1987 • $25 • (7/31/1991) • **89**

ABUNDANCE | CALIFORNIA

Chardonnay Central Coast French Camp Vineyard Lot 95-96 Vintner's Preferred NV • $10 • (9/30/1997) • **84**

Sangiovese California 1994 • $10 • (7/31/1997) • **80**

Sangiovese California Lot #1-Mer 1996: Black cherry and herb notes come to the fore in this light-style wine. Finishes dry, with an unusual touch of menthol and a shade-too-much oak. Drink now. • $10 • (2/28/1999) • **80**

ACACIA | CALIFORNIA

Cabernet Sauvignon Napa Valley 1984 • $15 • (12/15/1986) • **75**

Chardonnay California Caviste 1996: A slight metallic edge to the simple pear and pineapple flavors. Turns a little tinny on the finish. The last vintage of this wine. Drink now.–J.L. • $12 • (7/31/1998) • **81**

Chardonnay Carneros 1998: With excellent purity of fruit, this California white boasts ripe, spicy apple, pear, melon and honeysuckle. It's clean and fruity on the finish, with perfumy, elegant, floral notes. Drink now through 2005.–J.L. • $21 • (4/30/2000) SS • **89**

Chardonnay Carneros 1997: Sleek, racy and elegant, with spicy, grassy pear, apple, melon and citrus flavors that dance on the palate. Wonderful sense of harmony and tenderness. Drink now through 2002.–J.L. • $21 • (8/31/1999) • **89**

Chardonnay Carneros 1996 • $20 • (5/31/1998) • **85**

Merlot Napa Valley 1984 • $15 • (2/28/1987) • **83**

Pinot Noir Carneros 1997: A racy style, with ripe cherry, wild berry, anise, raspberry and spice, firming up at midpalate, then turning tannic. Needs short-term cellaring. Drink through 2005–J.L. • $22 • (9/15/1999) • **87**

Pinot Noir Carneros 1996 • $20 • (1/31/1998) • **87**

Pinot Noir Carneros 1995 • $19 • (7/31/1997) • **88**

Pinot Noir Carneros 1994 • $18 • (4/30/1996) • **89**

Pinot Noir Carneros 1993 • $15 • (6/30/1995) • **83**

Pinot Noir Carneros Beckstoffer Vineyard 1996: Ripe, spicy, supple, with polished cherry, berry and plum flavors, it's a touch tannic now, but a little time in the cellar should soften the tannins. Drink through 2005.–J.L. • $44 • (9/15/1999) • **87**

Pinot Noir Carneros Beckstoffer Vineyard 1995: Ripe, with juicy, spicy black cherry, wild berry, plum and cedary notes. It's intense and concentrated, rich and complex. Drink now through 2003.–J.L. • $40 • (2/28/1999) • **91**

Pinot Noir Carneros Reserve 1996: A pleasing if tight array of up-front, ripe black cherry, raspberry and spice, with enough tannin and substance to merit short-term cellaring. Drink through 2004–J.L. • $32 • (9/15/1999) • **87**

Pinot Noir Carneros Reserve 1995 • $30 • (2/28/1998) • **90**

Pinot Noir Carneros Reserve 1993 • $25 • (4/30/1996) • **86**

Pinot Noir Carneros St. Clair Vineyard 1996: Spicy, with a peppery edge to the modest plum and cherry flavors, it's elegant and polished, with pretty oak and a long, complex aftertaste. Drink now through 2004.–J.L. • $44 • (9/15/1999) • **87**

Pinot Noir Carneros St. Clair Vineyard Reserve 1994 • $38 • (3/31/1998) • **88**

Pinot Noir Napa Valley 1991 • $7 • (2/28/1993) • **75**

Pinot Noir Napa Valley Carneros 1998: Very complete and enticing, this Pinot Noir has ripe, focused black cherry, plum, berry and cedar notes. It finishes with touches of wild blackberry and spice. The tannins are mild, making it drinkable now. Drink now through 2007.–J.L. • $25 • (4/30/2000) HR • **88**

Pinot Noir Napa Valley Carneros 1991 • $15 • (2/28/1994) • **83**

Pinot Noir Napa Valley Carneros 1990 • $15 • (2/28/1993) • **80**

Pinot Noir Napa Valley Carneros 1989 • $14 • (11/15/1991) • **71**

Pinot Noir Napa Valley Carneros 1988 • $14 • (2/28/1991) • **89**

Pinot Noir Napa Valley Carneros 1987 • $13 • (2/15/1990) • **87**

Pinot Noir Napa Valley Carneros 1986 • $15 • (6/15/1988) • **88**

Pinot Noir Napa Valley Carneros 1985 • $12 • (12/15/1987) • **84**

Pinot Noir Napa Valley Carneros 1984 • $11 • (12/15/1986) SS • **95**

Pinot Noir Napa Valley Carneros Iund Vineyard 1991 • $21 • (2/28/1994) • **82**

Pinot Noir Napa Valley Carneros Iund Vineyard 1984 • $15 • (3/15/1987) • **81**

Pinot Noir Napa Valley Carneros Iund Vineyard 1983 • $16 • (8/31/1986) • **77**

Pinot Noir Napa Valley Carneros Iund Vineyard 1982 • $15 • (7/16/1984) CS • **91**

Pinot Noir Napa Valley Carneros Lee Vineyard 1983 • $16 • (8/31/1986) • **89**

Pinot Noir Napa Valley Carneros Lee Vineyard 1982 • $15 • (7/16/1984) • **90**

Pinot Noir Napa Valley Carneros Madonna Vineyard 1986 • $18 • (6/15/1988) • **88**

Pinot Noir Napa Valley Carneros Madonna Vineyard 1985 • $16 • (12/15/1987) • **88**

Pinot Noir Napa Valley Carneros Madonna Vineyard 1984 • $16 • (3/15/1987) • **88**

Pinot Noir Napa Valley Carneros Madonna Vineyard 1983 • $16 • (8/31/1986) • **93**

Pinot Noir Napa Valley Carneros St. Clair Vineyard 1991 • $25 • (2/28/1994) • **83**

Pinot Noir Napa Valley Carneros St. Clair Vineyard 1990 • $21 • (2/28/1993) • **84**

Pinot Noir Napa Valley Carneros St. Clair Vineyard 1989 • $21 • (10/31/1991) • **86**

Pinot Noir Napa Valley Carneros St. Clair Vineyard 1988 • $20 • (2/28/1991) HR • **91**

Pinot Noir Napa Valley Carneros St. Clair Vineyard 1987 • $18 • (2/15/1990) • **89**

Pinot Noir Napa Valley Carneros St. Clair Vineyard 1986 • $18 • (6/15/1988) • **91**

Pinot Noir Napa Valley Carneros St. Clair Vineyard 1985 • $16 • (12/15/1987) • **91**

Pinot Noir Napa Valley Carneros St. Clair Vineyard 1984 • $16 • (11/30/1986) • **93**

Pinot Noir Napa Valley Carneros St. Clair Vineyard 1983 • $15 • (10/01/1985) CS • **95**

Pinot Noir Napa Valley Carneros St. Clair Vineyard 1982 • $15 • (7/16/1984) • **89**

Pinot Noir Napa Valley Carneros St. Clair Vineyard Reserve 1992 • $25 • (6/30/1995) • **87**

Pinot Noir Napa Valley Carneros Winery Lake Vineyard 1983 • $15 • (11/16/1985) • **78**

Pinot Noir Napa Valley Carneros Winery Lake Vineyard 1982 • $15 • (7/16/1984) • **90**

Viognier Carneros 1997: Brassy in color, with vivid aromas and flavors, offering a riot of wildflower, pear and spice plus something reminiscent of fresh white corn. Finishes dry, with a bit of a bite from alcohol. Drink now.–H.S. • $25 • (11/30/1999) • **87**

Zinfandel Napa Valley Caviste 1992 • $11 • (10/15/1994) • **85**

Zinfandel Napa Valley Caviste 1991 • $12 • (9/30/1993) • **87**

Zinfandel Napa Valley Caviste 1990 • $12 • (10/15/1992) • **86**

Key: SS—Spectator Selection. CS—Cellar Selection. HR—Highly Recommended. $NA—Price not available. (BT)—Barrel tasting. Ⓐ—Auction Price.
For a key to the tasters' initials, see "How to Use These Listings."
Dates in parentheses represent the issues in which the ratings were published.

Zinfandel Napa Valley Old Vines 1993 • $10 • (10/15/1995) • **85**

ACADEMY, THE | OREGON

Cabernet Sauvignon Rogue Valley 1996: Ripe, generous and supple, offering pretty plum and currant flavors wrapped with chocolate and vanilla notes on the silky finish. Already approachable. Drink now through 2005.–H.S. • $15 • (6/15/1999) • **88**
Cabernet Sauvignon Rogue Valley 1995 • $16 • (5/15/1998) • **86**
Merlot Rogue Valley 1996 • $16 • (5/15/1998) • **86**

ACORN | CALIFORNIA

Zinfandel Russian River Valley Alegría Vineyards Heritage Vines 1997: Young and grapey, with a yeasty edge that detracts from the sweet black cherry flavors.–J.L. • $23 • (11/15/1999) • **77**

ADASTRA | CALIFORNIA

Chardonnay Napa Valley Carneros 1998: A touch tinny, with a thin band of metallic camphor flavors.–J.L. • $25 • (5/31/2000) • **78**
Chardonnay Napa Valley Carneros 1997: Full-bodied, with firm acidity. Minerals and ripe pear, melon and apple lend complexity. Sleek and steely, quite classy and refreshing. Long finish. Drink now through 2003. • $25 • (7/31/1999) • **90**
Chardonnay Napa Valley Carneros 1996 • $22 • (12/31/1997) • **88**
Merlot Napa Valley Carneros 1996: Tight, with a smoky, charred edge to the core of coffee, plum and currant, it fans out and turns spicy and tannic. Drink now through 2003.–J.L. • $27 • (12/31/1998) • **85**

ADELAIDA | CALIFORNIA

Cabernet Sauvignon Paso Robles 1995: Tangy currant and blackberry flavors are framed in moderately ripe tannins and a bit too much smoky oak. The finish is herbal and a little bitter—nothing that couldn't be fixed with a nice juicy steak, however. Drink now through 2005. • $21 • (2/28/1999) • **84**
Cabernet Sauvignon Paso Robles 1988 • $15 • (11/15/1992) • **87**
Cabernet Sauvignon Paso Robles 1987 • $14 • (2/28/1991) • **89**
Cabernet Sauvignon Paso Robles 1983 • $12 • (12/15/1989) • **75**
Cabernet Sauvignon San Luis Obispo County 1994 • $21 • (5/31/1998) • **88**
Cabernet Sauvignon San Luis Obispo County 1993 • $19 • (8/31/1997) • **90**
Cabernet Sauvignon San Luis Obispo County 1992 • $19 • (11/15/1996) • **88**
Cabernet Sauvignon San Luis Obispo County 1991 • $19 • (11/30/1996) • **89**
Cabernet Sauvignon San Luis Obispo County 1990 • $22 • (11/15/1993) • **81**
Calitage Paso Robles 1994: Smells of fresh raspberry, giving way to currant, plum and spice on the palate. Fairly bright, with firm tannins and a smoky edge at the moderate finish. A blend of Cabernet Sauvignon, Merlot, Cabernet Franc, Zinfandel. Drink now through 2004. • $28 • (6/15/1999) • **88**
Pinot Noir Paso Robles 1996: Rich coffee and chocolate notes kick off this ripe, full-bodied wine. The finish is a little short, but the ensemble of black cherry, toast, anise and herb flavors remains quite tasty. Lacks Pinot's more delicate side. Drink now through 2004. • $30 • (5/31/1999) • **87**
Pinot Noir Paso Robles HMR Vineyards 1995: Shows depth on the nose, with rich, dark plum and blackberry aromas. On the palate, it has a tight, tart edge. Drink now. • $30 • (9/15/1998) • **81**
Pinot Noir Paso Robles HMR Vineyards 1994 • $24 • (12/15/1996) • **84**
Pinot Noir San Luis Obispo County 1993 • $24 • (11/30/1996) • **87**
Sangiovese San Luis Obispo County 1995: Ripe and chewy, with a solid mouthful of cherry and spice flavors that linger on the finish. Drink now through 1999 .–H.S. • $24 • (7/31/1998) • **85**
Sangiovese San Luis Obispo County 1994 • $24 • (11/30/1997) • **83**
Sangiovese San Luis Obispo County 1993 • $23 • (4/30/1996) • **87**
Syrah Paso Robles 1996: Sports a peppery component which highlights a deep, rich black currant core. Acidity is a bit bright and rustic tannins may need a little time to smooth out, but the ensemble remains quite attractive. Drink through 2005 • $24 • (2/28/1999) • **87**
Zinfandel Late Harvest Paso Robles 1992 • $18 • (4/30/1996) • **84**
Zinfandel Paso Robles 1997: Struggles a little between ripe berry flavors and a spicy sage profile on a crisp frame. Drink now.–J.L. • $21 • (6/15/2000) • **81**
Zinfandel Paso Robles 1994 • $19 • (8/31/1997) • **87**
Zinfandel Paso Robles 1993 • $17 • (12/15/1996) • **89**
Zinfandel Paso Robles 1989 • $12 • (10/15/1992) • **83**
Zinfandel Paso Robles 1988 • $12 • (4/30/1991) • **88**
Zinfandel San Luis Obispo County 1996: Redolent of raspberry, cherry, plum, spice and sweet oak, this is a tangy Zin, with a long, bright finish. Tannins are firm but mild. Drink now. • $19 • (2/28/1999) • **87**
Zinfandel San Luis Obispo County 1992 • $16 • (4/30/1996) • **87**
Zinfandel San Luis Obispo County 1991 • $14 • (10/15/1994) • **87**
Zinfandel San Luis Obispo County 1990 • $14 • (9/30/1993) • **82**

ADELSHEIM | OREGON

Chardonnay Oregon 1998: Crisp and earthy, with a smoky, herbal edge to the basic citrus and apple pie flavors. Drink now.–H.S. • $16 • (5/15/2000) • **82**
Chardonnay Yamhill County Reserve 1998: Supple and generous, with appealing citrus, peach and apple flavors that ride smoothly through the refreshing finish. Drink now.–H.S. • $25 • (5/15/2000) • **86**
Chardonnay Yamhill County Reserve 1997: Soft and generous, with nicely modulated spice, smoke, apple and lemon flavors. Drink now.–H.S. • $20 • (4/30/1999) • **85**
Pinot Blanc Oregon 1998: Light and refreshing, with honey-scented apple and mineral flavors that linger on the finish. Drink now.–H.S. • $13 • (3/31/2000) • **87**
Pinot Blanc Oregon 1997: Fresh, if a little raw, with nectarine and melon flavors that linger on the gentle finish. Drink now.–H.S. • $14 • (4/30/1999) • **85**
Pinot Gris Oregon 1998: Aromatic with spicy notes, but it's tart and citrusy with a lively finish. Needs food to balance. Drink now.–H.S. • $14 • (4/30/2000) • **82**
Pinot Noir Oregon 1998: A lean, lithe Pinot packed with juicy berry and plum flavors, which pick up exotic spice notes on the tingly finish. Stylish, with fine tannins, this wants only short-term cellaring. Best from 2001 through 2007.–H.S. • $25 • (4/30/2000) • **89**
Pinot Noir Oregon 1997: Firm and ripe for the vintage, with pretty black cherry and toast flavors that linger on the modestly chewy finish. Drink through 2002–H.S. • $20 • (4/30/1999) • **85**
Pinot Noir Oregon 1996 • $20 • (5/15/1998) • **85**
Pinot Noir Oregon 1995 • $NA • (2/28/1997) • **80**
Pinot Noir Oregon 1991 • $15 • (2/28/1993) • **84**
Pinot Noir Oregon 1987 • $13 • (2/15/1990) • **72**
Pinot Noir Oregon 1985 • $25 • (2/15/1990) • **75**
Pinot Noir Polk County 1986 • $15 • (6/15/1988) • **87**
Pinot Noir Polk County Seven Springs Vineyard 1996: Light in texture, dark in flavor, with blackberry, currant and anise notes lingering on the finish with crisp tannins. Drink through 2002–H.S. • $30 • (4/30/1999) • **85**
Pinot Noir Polk County Seven Springs Vineyard 1992 • $23 • (10/31/1994) • **89**
Pinot Noir Polk County Seven Springs Vineyard 1990 • $20 • (2/28/1993) • **85**
Pinot Noir Polk County The Eola Hills 1987 • $16 • (2/15/1990) • **70**
Pinot Noir Willamette Valley Ridgecrest Vineyards 1997: Light, supple and pretty, with open-textured raspberry and spice flavors that linger gently on the finish. Drink now through 2002.–H.S. • $35 • (4/30/1999) • **86**
Pinot Noir Willamette Valley Ridgecrest Vineyards 1996 • $40 • (5/15/1998) • **88**
Pinot Noir Willamette Valley 1988 • $13 • (4/15/1991) • **89**
Pinot Noir Yamhill County 1985 • $16 • (6/15/1987) • **88**
Pinot Noir Yamhill County 1983 • $40 • (2/15/1990) • **70**
Pinot Noir Yamhill County Elizabeth's Reserve 1996: A supple texture and gamy flavors give this medium-weight Pinot a distinct appeal, with slightly volatile currant flavors lurking in the background. Drink now through 2003.–H.S. • $40 • (4/30/2000) • **85**
Pinot Noir Yamhill County Elizabeth's Reserve 1991 • $23 • (11/30/1994) • **85**
Pinot Noir Yamhill County Elizabeth's Reserve 1990 • $25 • (2/28/1993) • **83**
Pinot Noir Yamhill County Elizabeth's Reserve 1987 • $19 • (2/15/1990) • **73**

ADLER FELS | CALIFORNIA

Cabernet Sauvignon Napa Valley 1980 • $10 • (10/01/1984) • **74**
Chardonnay Russian River Valley Aquarius Vineyard Reserve 1998: Sour lemon-lime flavors and a dull earthy note. Drink now.–J.L. • $16 • (6/15/2000) • **80**
Chardonnay Sonoma County 1996 • $14 • (3/31/1998) • **82**
Chardonnay Sonoma County Coleman Reserve 1996 • $16 • (3/31/1998) • **86**
Fumé Blanc Sonoma County 1997: Fairly smooth, showing a fine blend of citrus, gooseberry, melon, herb and mineral flavors. The texture is mild, with a moderate finish. Drink now. • $12 • (6/15/1999) • **87**
Fumé Blanc Sonoma County 1996 • $11 • (5/15/1998) • **80**
Gewürztraminer Sonoma County 1996 • $11 • (7/31/1997) • **86**
Sangiovese Mendocino County 1995 • $16 • (9/15/1997) • **79**
Sangiovese Mendocino County 1994 • $16 • (12/15/1996) • **87**
Sauvignon Blanc Sonoma County 1997: Quite herbal, with a gooseberry edge. Has character and plays up the varietal. Brightly textured, with grapefruit, lemon and mineral flavors. Finishes clean and long. Drink now. • $11 • (5/31/1999) • **89**

ADRIAN FOG | CALIFORNIA

Pinot Noir Anderson Valley Floodgate Vineyard 1998: Smooth, ripe and polished, with a pretty array of plum, black cherry, wild berry and floral notes, picking up a touch of herb and cedar. Finishes with supple tannins. Drink now through 2008.–J.L. • $45 • (4/30/2000) • **90**

AETNA SPRINGS | CALIFORNIA

Cabernet Sauvignon Napa Valley 1991 • $18 • (5/15/1994) • **81**
Chardonnay Rutherford 1998: Heavy lemon and earth notes are simple and straightforward. Drink now.–J.L. • $18 • (6/15/2000) • **81**

AIRLIE | OREGON

Chardonnay Willamette Valley 1997: Light and crisp, with pretty apple and slate aromas and flavors that echo on the bright finish. Drink now through 2002.–H.S. • $10 • (3/31/2000) • **84**
Pinot Gris Willamette Valley 1998: Bright in flavor and silky in texture, with pretty pear, cream and melon flavors lingering with a little unexpected elegance. Drink now.–H.S. • $11 • (3/31/2000) • **86**
Pinot Noir Willamette Valley 1996: Light in color and body, with pretty plum and chocolate notes echoing on the fragile finish. Drink now.–H.S. • $11 • (3/31/2000) • **83**
Pinot Noir Willamette Valley 1994 • $11 • (7/31/1996) • **82**
Pinot Noir Willamette Valley 1993 • $10 • (1/31/1996) • **80**
Pinot Noir Willamette Valley 1992 • $10 • (11/30/1994) • **78**
Pinot Noir Willamette Valley 1990 • $10 • (2/28/1993) • **60**

ALBAN | CALIFORNIA

Grenache Edna Valley Alban Estate Vineyard 1997: Dark, intense and concentrated, with black cherry, plum and wild berry flavors, turning firm and intricate on the finish. Drink now through 2005.–J.L. • $28 • (3/31/2000) • **88**
Grenache Edna Valley Alban Estate Vineyard 1996: Ripe and jammy, with a good core of acidity to balance things out. Serves up wild cherry, raspberry, black currant, herb and spice flavors in a smooth, refreshing blend. Drink now through 2002. • $29 • (10/31/1998) • **89**
Grenache Edna Valley Alban Estate Vineyard 1995 • $28 • (3/31/1998) • **88**
Grenache Edna Valley Alban Estate Vineyard 1994 • $28 • (8/31/1997) • **85**
Grenache Edna Valley 1993 • $28 • (4/30/1996) • **86**
Syrah Edna Valley Lorraine 1997: Immense color. Dark, rich and concentrated, with juicy, opulent plum, wild berry, black cherry, anise and spice. Finishes with a wall of flavors and rich tannins. Drink now through 2008.–J.L. • $35 • (1/31/2000) • **93**
Syrah Edna Valley Reva 1997: Inky in color, superrich and deeply fruity, with tiers of blackberry, black cherry, currant and wild berry turning smooth and plush on the long, complex finish. Best from 2001 through 2008.–J.L. • $25 • (11/15/1999) • **93**
Syrah Edna Valley Alban Estate Reva 1996: Complex if a bit earthy in style, with herb, cherry, wild berry and leather notes. Finishes with dry, earthy coffee and mineral notes. Drink through 2005–J.L. • $24 • (11/30/1998) • **88**
Syrah Edna Valley Alban Estate Reva 1995 • $21 • (3/31/1998) • **89**
Syrah Edna Valley Reva 1994 • $18 • (8/31/1997) • **88**
Syrah Edna Valley Reva 1993 • $18 • (6/15/1996) • **87**
Viognier Central Coast 1998: Spicy, with an herb, cedar and celery edge to the ripe pear, fig and apple flavors. Gains complexity on the finish. Drink now through 2003.–J.L. • $20 • (1/31/2000) • **87**
Viognier Edna Valley Alban Estate Vineyard 1998: Solid if lacking in focus, with coarse melon, honeysuckle and pear flavors of modest depth and proportion. Drink now through 2004.–J.L. • $28 • (1/31/2000) • **86**

ALBINI | CALIFORNIA

Merlot Russian River Valley 1996: Opens with pretty plum and smoke aromas, but the follow-through is slightly bitter and vegetal. Finishes moderately, with hints of black currant and herb. Drink now through 2002. • $23 • (10/15/1999) • **82**
Merlot Sonoma County 1995 • $21 • (5/31/1998) • **86**

Key: SS—Spectator Selection. CS—Cellar Selection. HR—Highly Recommended. $NA—Price not available. (BT)—Barrel tasting. (A)—Auction Price.
For a key to the tasters' initials, see "How to Use These Listings."
Dates in parentheses represent the issues in which the ratings were published.

Merlot Sonoma County 1994 • $19 • (7/31/1997) • **86**

ALDERBROOK | CALIFORNIA

Cabernet Sauvignon Sonoma County 1997: Shows some bitterness up front, with herbal overtones. Improves measurably, however, as hints of black currant, licorice, tar and herbs emerge, then linger on a moderate finish. Tannins are firm. Drink through 2005 • $16 • (10/15/1999) • **86**
Cabernet Sauvignon Sonoma County 1996: Quite young and fruity, with a leathery, menthol note at the fore. Licorice and herbs form the flavor core, backed by charry oak notes. Drink now through 2004. • $16 • (11/15/1998) • **84**
Cabernet Sauvignon Sonoma County 1995 • $16 • (8/31/1997) • **89**
Cabernet Sauvignon Dry Creek Valley 1994 • $17 • (5/15/1997) • **86**
Chardonnay Dry Creek Valley 1997: Well balanced, open-textured and ripe with pear, citrus, fig and melon flavors that linger on the clean, fleshy finish. Drink now.–J.L. • $14 • (6/30/1999) • **88**
Chardonnay Dry Creek Valley 1996 • $13 • (2/28/1998) SS • **89**
Chardonnay Dry Creek Valley Dorothy's Vineyard 1996: Ripe and fruity, with spicy pear, fig and citrus notes. Picks up pretty toasty oak on the finish, where the flavors are crisp and elegant. Drink now through 2002.–J.L. • $23 • (6/30/1999) • **89**
Gewürztraminer Russian River Valley McIlroy Vineyard 1997: Fresh, open-textured and soft, with pretty orange and spice flavors that linger on the dry finish. Drink now.–H.S. • $12 • (11/30/1998) • **85**
Gewürztraminer Russian River Valley Saralee's Vineyard 1996 • $11 • (11/30/1997) • **85**
Merlot Sonoma County 1997: Kicks off with smoke and anise flavors, shows a little burnt toast, and finishes off with a burst of oak and plum. Pleasant enough, but not really well-integrated. Drink now. • $20 • (10/15/1999) • **83**
Merlot Sonoma County 1996: Fairly supple, with a core of black cherry, licorice, herb and spice flavors. Well balanced, it shows some finesse. Drink now through 2004. • $19 • (9/30/1998) • **87**
Merlot Sonoma County Kunde Vineyard 1995 • $20 • (4/30/1998) • **86**
Merlot Sonoma County Kunde Vineyard 1994 • $22 • (12/31/1996) • **86**
Muscat de Frontignan Sonoma Valley Late Harvest Kunde Vineyard 1995 • $24/375 ml. • (12/31/1996) • **87**
Muscat de Frontignan Sonoma County Late Harvest Kunde Vineyard 1994 • $20/375 ml. • (10/31/1996) • **92**
Pinot Noir Russian River Valley 1997: Showing some tea and earth notes up front. On the palate, the wine offers a waxy texture that supports a blend of stemmy, herbal and cherry flavors. Finishes moderately. Drink now. • $20 • (9/15/1999) • **83**
Pinot Noir Russian River Valley 1996 • $18 • (3/31/1998) • **86**
Pinot Noir Russian River Valley 1995 • $18 • (12/31/1996) • **87**
Pinot Noir Russian River Valley 1994 • $15 • (1/31/1996) • **87**
Sauvignon Blanc Dry Creek Valley 1997: Shows intriguing hints of fresh-cut hay and melon, then fleshes out nicely, blending pretty mineral, herb, lemon and grapefruit elements, finishing moderately. Good wine, good price. Drink now. • $10 • (5/15/1999) • **87**
Sauvignon Blanc Dry Creek Valley 1996 • $11 • (6/30/1997) • **86**
Sauvignon Blanc Dry Creek Valley Late Harvest 1989 • $24/375 ml. • (6/15/1992) • **88**
Viognier Russian River Valley 1997: Tangy acidity and a mineral edge make this a good match for Pacific oysters and other seafoods. Lemon and lime are in evidence as well. Drink now. • $18 • (11/15/1998) • **86**
Viognier Russian River Valley Timbervine Ranch Alta Vina 1996 • $18 • (12/15/1997) • **86**
Zinfandel Dry Creek Valley 1993 • $14 • (10/15/1995) • **85**
Zinfandel Russian River Valley Gamba Vineyard 1997: Attractive for its bright, snappy cherry, wild berry, plum and spice character, turning crisp and tannic. Drink now through 2002.–J.L. • $22 • (5/15/1999) • **87**
Zinfandel Russian River Valley Gamba Vineyard 1996 • $20 • (3/31/1998) • **89**
Zinfandel Russian River Valley Gamba Vineyard 1995 • $20 • (12/31/1996) • **92**
Zinfandel Sonoma County 1994 • $16 • (9/15/1996) • **89**
Zinfandel Sonoma County George's Vineyards 1997: A delicious orchestration of fruit and oak, offering ripe, complex black cherry, plum and wild berry flavors and pretty toasty, spicy oak that adds texture and dimension. Drink now through 2002.–J.L. • $25 • (5/15/1999) • **92**
Zinfandel Sonoma County OVOC 1997: Supple and elegant, with ripe, spicy black cherry, wild berry and raspberry, finishing with pretty toasty oak flavors. Drink now through 2002.–J.L. • $18 • (5/15/1999) • **88**
Zinfandel Sonoma County OVOC 1996 • $16 • (5/31/1998) • **87**
Zinfandel Sonoma County Old Vine Old Clone 1995 • $14 • (4/30/1997) • **89**

ALEXANDER VALLEY FRUIT & TRADING CO. CALIFORNIA

Zinfandel Alexander Valley Late Harvest 1991 • $12 • (10/31/1995) • **85**
Zinfandel Alexander Valley Late Harvest 1990 • $12 • (10/15/1994) • **82**
Zinfandel Dry Creek Valley 1992 • $9 • (10/15/1994) • **81**

ALEXANDER VALLEY VINEYARDS CALIFORNIA

Cabernet Franc Alexander Valley Wetzel Family Estate 1996 • $20 • (3/31/1998) • **86**
Cabernet Sauvignon Alexander Valley 1989 • $13 • (8/31/1992) • **87**
Cabernet Sauvignon Alexander Valley 1988 • $12 • (9/30/1991) • **88**
Cabernet Sauvignon Alexander Valley 1987 • $12 • (5/31/1990) • **87**
Cabernet Sauvignon Alexander Valley 1986 • $NA • (12/15/1988) • **86**
Cabernet Sauvignon Alexander Valley 1985 • $11 • (11/15/1987) HR • **92**
Cabernet Sauvignon Alexander Valley 1984 • $11 • (5/15/1987) SS • **93**
Cabernet Sauvignon Alexander Valley 1983 • $11 • (1/01/1986) • **87**
Cabernet Sauvignon Alexander Valley 1982 • $10 • (2/01/1986) • **84**
Cabernet Sauvignon Alexander Valley 1982 • $10 • (11/01/1984) SS • **92**
Cabernet Sauvignon Alexander Valley Library Reserve 1986 • $18 • (6/15/1993) • **80**
Cabernet Sauvignon Alexander Valley Wetzel Family Estate 1996: A rustic range of well-integrated, juicy black cherry, mineral and herb flavors that linger on the finish, where the tannins are mild. Drink now.–J.L. • $18 • (11/15/1998) • **86**
Cabernet Sauvignon Alexander Valley Wetzel Family Estate 1995 • $16 • (11/15/1997) • **82**
Cabernet Sauvignon Alexander Valley Wetzel Family Estate 1994 • $15 • (11/15/1997) • **87**
Cabernet Sauvignon Alexander Valley Wetzel Family Estate 1993 • $15 • (3/31/1997) • **84**
Cabernet Sauvignon Alexander Valley Wetzel Family Estate 1992 • $14 • (5/31/1995) • **86**
Cabernet Sauvignon Alexander Valley Wetzel Family Estate 1991 • $13 • (11/15/1993) • **84**
Cabernet Sauvignon Alexander Valley Wetzel Family Estate 1990 • $14 • (6/15/1993) • **88**
Cabernet Sauvignon Alexander Valley Wetzel Family Estate 1987 • $NA • (12/15/1997) • **89**
Chardonnay Alexander Valley 1997: Smooth, with a modest core of creamy citrus flavors. Drink now.–J.L. • $15 • (1/31/1999) • **85**
Chardonnay Alexander Valley Wetzel Family Estate 1996 • $13 • (11/30/1997) • **84**
Chardonnay Alexander Valley Wetzel Family Reserve 1997: Rich and toasty, with honeyed orange, lemon and peach flavors marked by complex spicy oak notes. Drink now.–H.S. • $20 • (6/15/1999) • **88**
Chardonnay Alexander Valley Wetzel Family Reserve 1996 • $24 • (5/31/1998) • **86**
Chenin Blanc Alexander Valley Wetzel Family Estate Dry 1996: Dry and spicy, with exotic melon, apple and allspice flavors, marked by resiny fruit. Drink now.–H.S. • $9 • (12/15/1998) • **86**
Cyrus Alexander Valley 1996: Complex, with a pretty core of cedary green olive and berryish fruit, finishing with a touch of herb and currant. Tannins are mild. Drink now through 2006.–J.L. • $45 • (5/31/2000) • **88**
Cyrus Alexander Valley 1995: Ripe and juicy, with pretty, complex black cherry, plum, wild berry, herb, sage and tea flavors that are smooth and polished. Finishes with supple, integrated tannins and a touch of herb. Debut vintage for this blend of Cabernet Sauvignon, Merlot and Cabernet Franc. Drink now through 2008.–J.L. • $35 • (2/29/2000) • **90**
Gewürztraminer North Coast New Gewürz 1997 • $9 • (3/31/1998) • **84**
Merlot Alexander Valley Wetzel Family Estate 1997: Ripe and flavorful, featuring a core of mineral, cassis and herb flavors that linger on the supple finish. Drink now through 2003 .–J.L. • $18 • (9/15/1999) • **87**
Merlot Alexander Valley Wetzel Family Estate 1996: Ripe and spicy, showing plum, blackberry, cherry and cedary oak flavors before the tannins weigh in—and they're dominant. Best to cellar short-term. Drink through 2004–J.L. • $17 • (9/30/1998) • **83**
Merlot Alexander Valley Wetzel Family Estate 1995 • $17 • (6/30/1997) • **86**
Merlot Alexander Valley Wetzel Family Estate 1993 • $15 • (5/15/1996) • **83**
Merlot Alexander Valley Wetzel Family Estate 1992 • $15 • (7/31/1995) • **86**
Merlot Alexander Valley Wetzel Family Estate 1991 • $14 • (9/15/1994) • **77**
Merlot Alexander Valley 1990 • $13 • (3/31/1993) • **87**
Merlot Alexander Valley 1989 • $13 • (11/15/1991) • **84**
Merlot Alexander Valley 1985 • $11 • (10/31/1987) • **88**
Pinot Noir Alexander Valley Wetzel Family Estate 1997: Offers light cherry and tea notes with a mild-mannered finish and soft tannins. Drink now. • $15 • (2/28/1999) • **81**
Pinot Noir Alexander Valley Wetzel Family Estate 1996 • $13 • (12/15/1997) • **84**
Pinot Noir Alexander Valley Wetzel Family Estate 1990 • $11 • (2/28/1994) • **83**
Pinot Noir Alexander Valley 1989 • $10 • (10/31/1991) • **65**
Syrah Alexander Valley Vyborny Vineyards 1995 • $17 • (12/15/1997) • **83**
Syrah Alexander Valley Wetzel Family Estate 1997: A little restrained at first but opens up to reveal a layered core of strawberry, blackberry and herbs. The oak is a little overbearing, however, and the finish is only moderately smooth. Drink now through 2002. • $20 • (2/28/1999) • **83**
Zinfandel Alexander Valley Sin Zin 1997: Soft-textured, with earthy, gamy flavors and notes of tart cherry, spice and herb. Drink now.–H.S. • $15 • (5/15/1999) • **84**
Zinfandel Alexander Valley Sin Zin 1993 • $13 • (10/15/1995) • **78**
Zinfandel Alexander Valley Sin Zin 1989 • $11 • (10/15/1992) • **76**

ALMADEN | CALIFORNIA

White Zinfandel California Premium Varietal NV • $NA/1.5 liter • (5/15/1998) • **80**

ALPEN | CALIFORNIA

Chardonnay Trinity County 1996: Simple and slightly sweet, with citrus, pear and tart apple. Some light tannins on the finish. • $7 • (7/31/1998) • **81**

ALTAMURA | CALIFORNIA

Cabernet Sauvignon Napa Valley 1996: A complex array of ripe cherry, plum and blackberry, with pretty toasty oak and anise shadings on a medium- to full-bodied frame. Finishes with elegant fruit and mild tannins. Drink now through 2007.–J.L. • $50 • (4/30/2000) • **88**
Cabernet Sauvignon Napa Valley 1995: Ripe, smooth and smoky, with wild berry, black cherry, currant, plum and spice flavors deliciously woven together in a supple, complex, concentrated style. Tannins weigh in on the finish. Drink through 2007–J.L. • $40 • (5/31/1999) • **93**
Cabernet Sauvignon Napa Valley 1994 • $33 • (12/15/1997) • **91**
Cabernet Sauvignon Napa Valley 1993 • $25 • (2/28/1997) • **92**
Cabernet Sauvignon Napa Valley 1992 • $28 • (8/31/1996) HR • **92**
Cabernet Sauvignon Napa Valley 1991 • $25 • (5/31/1996) • **88**
Cabernet Sauvignon Napa Valley 1990 • $25 • (9/15/1995) • **88**
Cabernet Sauvignon Napa Valley 1988 • $18 • (11/15/1992) • **85**
Sangiovese Napa Valley 1995: Tight and firm, with an earthy core of wild berry, black cherry, cedar and sage-laced fruit, turning dry and tannic on the finish. Drink now through 2001.–J.L. • $28 • (12/15/1998) • **87**
Sangiovese Napa Valley 1994 • $22 • (11/30/1997) HR • **92**
Sangiovese Napa Valley 1993 • $18 • (4/30/1996) • **90**
Sangiovese Napa Valley-Monterey 1996: Struggles to find its focus, with wet earth, cedar and slightly sour-tasting wood flavors masking the plummy fruit. Tasted twice, with consistent notes. Drink now through 2004.–J.L. • $28 • (1/31/2000) • **82**

AMADOR FOOTHILL | CALIFORNIA

Sangiovese Shenandoah Valley 1994 • $12 • (7/31/1997) • **85**
Sangiovese Shenandoah Valley Festa Dell'Uva 1993 • $12 • (11/30/1995) • **80**
Sangiovese Shenandoah Valley Festa Dell'Uva 1992 • $12 • (9/15/1994) • **79**
Zinfandel Fiddletown Eschen Vineyard 1991 • $10 • (10/15/1994) • **78**
Zinfandel Fiddletown Eschen Vineyard 1990 • $10 • (9/30/1993) • **82**
Zinfandel Fiddletown Eschen Vineyard 1988 • $10 • (10/15/1992) • **73**
Zinfandel Shenandoah Valley Ferrero Vineyard 1996: Lean, showing tart cherry and herb flavors with a dry, woody finish.–J.L. • $12 • (6/30/1999) • **79**
Zinfandel Shenandoah Valley Ferrero Vineyard 1991 • $10 • (10/15/1995) • **83**
Zinfandel Shenandoah Valley Ferrero Vineyard 1990 • $10 • (9/30/1993) • **82**
Zinfandel Shenandoah Valley Ferrero Vineyard Special Selection 1989 • $10 • (3/31/1992) • **81**
Zinfandel Shenandoah Valley Grand-Père Vineyard 1990 • $10 • (9/30/1993) • **83**
Zinfandel Shenandoah Valley Grand-Père Vineyard 1989 • $10 • (10/15/1992) • **79**
Zinfandel Shenandoah Valley Grand-Père Vineyard Special Selection 1988 • $10 • (8/31/1991) • **75**

AMBERHILL | CALIFORNIA

Cabernet Sauvignon California 1996: Pleasant, with plum and berry notes and a hefty dose of oak. Drink now. • $10 • (10/31/1998) • **80**

Chardonnay California 1998: An atypical Chardonnay, with apple, mineral and sweet pea notes, showing good focus. Drink now.–J.L. • $10 • (6/15/2000) • **84**

Chardonnay California 1997: Toasty oak, spice, fig and citrus notes are pleasant. Drink now.–J.L. • $8 • (11/30/1998) • **82**

Sauvignon Blanc California 1997: A pleasant wine, with moderate body and gentle orange and melon flavors, but it shuts down early on the palate. Drink now. • $6 • (2/28/1999) • **83**

AMETHYST | CALIFORNIA

Nebbiolo-Sangiovese Napa Valley Carneros Vinalia 1995: Leads off with cinnamon and spice on the nose. It's pretty astringent on the palate, however, though hints of black cherry and anise come through nicely, with a moderate finish. Should smooth out in a few years. Made by Acacia veterans Larry Brooks and Mike Richmond. Nebbiolo and Sangiovese. Drink through 2005 • $23 • (2/28/1999) • **86**

Nebbiolo-Sangiovese Napa Valley Carneros Vinalia 1994 • $22 • (1/01/1998) • **84**

AMICI | CALIFORNIA

Cabernet Sauvignon Napa Valley 1995: Fairly soft, with plum, spice and oak tones to the fore. Finishes with a slightly bitter herbal edge. Drink now through 2002. • $20 • (10/31/1998) • **83**

Cabernet Sauvignon Napa Valley 1994 • $22 • (5/31/1998) • **86**

Cabernet Sauvignon Napa Valley 1993 • $18 • (10/15/1997) • **86**

AMITY | OREGON

Gamay Noir Oregon 1996 • $9 • (5/15/1998) • **80**

Gewürztraminer Oregon Dry 1996 • $10 • (4/30/1998) • **87**

Gewürztraminer Oregon Juliard Vineyard Late Harvest 1992 • $8 • (4/30/1997) • **90**

Pinot Blanc Willamette Valley 1998: Polished and refined. Beautifully balanced to show off its creamy apple and melon flavors, which linger on the delicate finish. Drink now.–H.S. • $12 • (3/31/2000) • **88**

Pinot Blanc Willamette Valley 1997: Soft in texture, with some slightly sour notes in the melon and almond melody.–H.S. • $12 • (2/28/1999) • **77**

Pinot Blanc Willamette Valley Helmick Vineyards 1996 • $12 • (5/15/1998) • **85**

Pinot Noir Oregon 1997: Very light in color, almost rosé, with earthy strawberry and spice notes on a delicate frame. Drink now.–H.S. • $13 • (6/15/1999) • **81**

Pinot Noir Oregon 1995 • $16 • (5/15/1998) • **82**

Pinot Noir Oregon 1992 • $10 • (11/30/1994) • **83**

Pinot Noir Oregon 1988 • $10 • (5/31/1991) • **82**

Pinot Noir Oregon Eco-Wine Cattrall Brothers Vineyards 1998: Ripe, rich and generous, with an interesting gamy streak running through the cherry, strawberry and floral flavors. Drink now through 2002.–H.S. • $13 • (3/31/2000) • **85**

Pinot Noir Oregon Eco Wine 1995 • $12 • (2/28/1997) • **72**

Pinot Noir Oregon Gamay Noir 1988 • $9 • (2/15/1990) • **84**

Pinot Noir Oregon Winemaker's Reserve 1985 • $NA • (2/15/1990) • **80**

Pinot Noir Oregon Winemaker's Reserve 1983 • $30 • (2/15/1990) • **75**

Pinot Noir Willamette Valley 1996: Light, almost fragile, with pretty strawberry and cream flavors that emerge smoothly on the polished finish. Drink now.–H.S. • $16 • (2/28/1999) • **86**

Pinot Noir Willamette Valley 1994 • $16 • (2/28/1997) • **90**

Pinot Noir Willamette Valley 1993 • $16 • (2/28/1997) • **81**

Pinot Noir Willamette Valley 1987 • $15 • (2/15/1990) • **81**

Pinot Noir Willamette Valley 1986 • $13 • (2/15/1990) • **74**

Pinot Noir Willamette Valley 1985 • $25 • (2/15/1990) • **85**

Pinot Noir Willamette Valley Estate 1987 • $25 • (2/15/1990) • **79**

Pinot Noir Willamette Valley Estate 1985 • $25 • (2/15/1990) • **79**

Pinot Noir Willamette Valley Estate 1983 • $30 • (2/15/1990) • **76**

Pinot Noir Willamette Valley Sunnyside Vineyard 1995 • $18 • (5/15/1998) • **86**

Pinot Noir Willamette Valley Winemaker's Reserve 1994: Firm in texture, with generous black cherry and berry flavors that wind through a layer of firm but not excessive tannins on the finish. Has presence and impressive length. Drink now.–H.S. • $30 • (5/15/1999) • **87**

Pinot Noir Willamette Valley Winemaker's Reserve 1993 • $35 • (5/15/1998) • **85**

Pinot Noir Willamette Valley Winemaker's Reserve 1988 • $25 • (2/28/1993) • **80**

Pinot Noir Willamette Valley Winemaker's Reserve 1987 • $30 • (2/15/1990) • **83**

Riesling Oregon Dry 1996 • $9 • (5/15/1998) • **80**

Riesling Oregon Late Harvest Juliard Vineyard 1996 • $10 • (5/15/1998) • **86**

AMIZETTA | CALIFORNIA

Cabernet Sauvignon Napa Valley 1985 • $16 • (5/31/1988) • **70**

Merlot Napa Valley 1997: Spicy mint and bay leaf aromas lead to a supple, polished wine, with currant, berry and plum notes. Finishes with fine tannins. Tasty now, but worthy of short-term cellaring. Best from 2001 through 2005.–J.L. • $38 • (3/31/2000) • **88**

ANAPAMU | CALIFORNIA

Cabernet Sauvignon Monterey County 1994 • $10 • (2/28/1997) • **78**

Chardonnay Central Coast 1998: Buttery, with peach, apricot and candied vanilla flavors on the finish. Drink now.–J.L. • $16 • (6/15/2000) • **83**

Chardonnay Central Coast 1997: A smoky, toasty, butterscotch-flavored style, with ripe melon and citrus flavors that linger on the finish. Drink now.–J.L. • $14 • (8/31/1999) • **84**

Chardonnay Central Coast 1996 • $12 • (6/30/1998) • **86**

Pinot Noir Central Coast 1997: Supple, with flavorful Syrah-like, earthy, spicy plum and cherry flavors. Drink now.–J.L. • $14 • (9/15/1999) • **84**

Pinot Noir Monterey County 1995 • $12 • (1/31/1998) • **87**

Syrah Central Coast 1998: A bit minty, with blueberry, blackberry and bubblegum notes that show pleasant depth. Drink now through 2003.–J.L. • $16 • (6/15/2000) • **84**

ANCIEN | CALIFORNIA

Chardonnay Carneros 1998: Tangy, with floral and peach and notes of cedar shavings. Turns a bit dilute on the finish. Drink now.–J.L. • $30 • (6/30/2000) • **85**

Chardonnay Carneros 1997: Complex and concentrated, with rich spice, pear, fig, tangerine and exotic nutmeg aromatics. A tasty wine now and should only get better in the next year or so. Drink through 2002.–J.L. • $28 • (4/30/1999) • **90**

Pinot Noir Carneros 1998: Firm, with blueberry and red currant notes wrapped in some healthy tannins. Drink now.–J.L. • $30 • (6/30/2000) • **87**

Pinot Noir Carneros 1997: Richly textured, with subtle, concentrated black cherry, vanilla and spice flavors and hints of citrus. An earthy nuance carries through on the focused finish. Best from 2000 through 2005.–J.L. • $28 • (8/31/1999) • **88**

Pinot Noir Carneros 1996: Sustained by ripe cherry, plum and wild berry, with full-bodied tannins and rich mineral, leather and spicy nuances on the finish. Has enough tannin to merit short-term cellaring.–J.L. • $25 • (8/31/1998) • **87**

Pinot Noir Carneros 1995 • $23 • (7/31/1997) • **88**

Pinot Noir Carneros 1994 • $21 • (9/15/1996) • **90**

Pinot Noir Carneros 1993 • $18 • (4/30/1996) • **87**

Pinot Noir Sonoma Mountain Steiner Vineyard 1997: Tight, firm and tannic, with an earthy, cedary edge to the racy blackberry and cherry flavors, finishing with mineral and herb notes. Needs a little time to soften. Best from 2001 through 2006.–J.L. • $36 • (1/31/2000) • **87**

ANDERSON, S. | CALIFORNIA

Blanc de Noirs Napa Valley 1995: Intriguing nose, with hints of cherry, citrus and herbs. On the palate, the wine serves up tiny bubbles and a core of toasty hazelnut, pear, lemon and apricot flavors. A touch of bitterness at the end. Drink now through 2002. • $28 • (10/15/1999) • **89**

Blanc de Noirs Napa Valley 1994: Crisp, fresh toasty aromas blend well in this full-bodied wine. Rich in well-defined toast, hazelnut, cherry and citrus flavors. Clean and refreshing on the finish. Drink now through 2002. • $25 • (12/15/1998) • **90**

Blanc de Noirs Napa Valley 1993 • $23 • (11/30/1997) • **90**

Blanc de Noirs Napa Valley 1992 • $22 • (11/30/1996) SS • **91**

Blanc de Noirs Napa Valley 1991 • $23 • (12/31/1995) • **88**

Blanc de Noirs Napa Valley 1990 • $20 • (11/30/1994) SS • **90**

Key: SS—Spectator Selection. CS—Cellar Selection. HR—Highly Recommended. $NA—Price not available. (BT)—Barrel tasting. (A)—Auction Price.
For a key to the tasters' initials, see "How to Use These Listings."
Dates in parentheses represent the issues in which the ratings were published.

Brut Napa Valley 1995: Crisp and lemony, this is a bit tight but nonetheless refreshing. Serves up a fine blend of citrus, green apple and herb flavors and finishes moderately. Drink now through 2002. • $28 • (10/15/1999) • **87**
Brut Napa Valley 1994: Toasty, doughy notes up front meet hazelnut, bright lemon and grapefruit flavors and a pretty, peppery finish. Sleek and elegant; could improve in the bottle. Try now through 2002. • $26 • (12/15/1998) • **89**
Brut Napa Valley 1993 • $24 • (4/30/1998) SS • **92**
Brut Napa Valley 1992 • $24 • (11/30/1997) • **91**
Brut Napa Valley 1991 • $20 • (9/15/1996) • **89**
Brut Napa Valley 1990 • $23 • (11/30/1995) • **88**
Brut Napa Valley Reserve 1990 • $32 • (11/30/1997) • **87**
Cabernet Sauvignon Stags Leap District 1996: An elegant, understated style, with pretty black cherry, currant, cedar and tar notes, turning dry and tannic. Best from 2001 through 2006.–J.L. • $25 • (9/15/1999) • **86**
Cabernet Sauvignon Stags Leap District 1994 • $24 • (10/31/1997) • **89**
Cabernet Sauvignon Stags Leap District 1993 • $22 • (11/15/1996) • **87**
Cabernet Sauvignon Stags Leap District Richard Chambers Vineyard 1998: Smooth, ripe and polished, with a rich core of plum, currant, cherry and berryish flavor, plush and rich in texture.–J.L. • $NA • (8/31/1999) (BT) • **90-94**
Cabernet Sauvignon Stags Leap District Richard Chambers Vineyard 1997: Complex, with earthy currant, anise, mineral and sage flavors. Rich and well focused, with pretty texture and finesse. To be released September 2000. Tasted twice, with consistent notes. Drink now through 2010.–J.L. • $NA • (5/31/2000) • **91**
Cabernet Sauvignon Stags Leap District Richard Chambers Vineyard 1996: Ripe and focused, with pretty extra flavor facets. The core of black cherry, currant, plum, cedar and anise builds to a complex finish. Best from 2001 through 2007.–J.L. • $65 • (11/15/1999) • **90**
Cabernet Sauvignon Stags Leap District Richard Chambers Vineyard 1995: Delivers a complex array of earthy currant, black cherry, wild berry and spice, yet is quite elegant and compact. Finishes with smooth, polished tannins and fine length, echoing cherry and plum on the finish. Drink through 2004.–J.L. • $65 • (10/31/1998) • **91**
Cabernet Sauvignon Stags Leap District Richard Chambers Vineyard 1994 • $53 Ⓐ • (10/31/1997) • **91**
Cabernet Sauvignon Stags Leap District Richard Chambers Vineyard 1993 • $38 Ⓐ • (11/30/1996) • **90**
Cabernet Sauvignon Stags Leap District Richard Chambers Vineyard 1992 • $35 Ⓐ • (12/15/1995) • **89**
Cabernet Sauvignon Stags Leap District Richard Chambers Vineyard 1991 • $43 Ⓐ • (12/31/1994) HR • **91**
Cabernet Sauvignon Stags Leap District Richard Chambers Vineyard 1990 • $38 Ⓐ • (11/15/1993) • **90**
Cabernet Sauvignon Stags Leap District Richard Chambers Vineyard 1989 • $36 • (11/15/1992) • **90**
Chardonnay Napa Valley Carneros District 1996 • $22 • (1/31/1998) • **87**
Diva Napa Valley 1991: Rich and seductive, redolent of fresh herbs and spice. A core of honey, hazelnut, peach, citrus and green apple weaves its way nicely here, lingering on the palate for a fresh, lengthy finish. Full-bodied yet delicate too. Drink now. • $50 • (9/15/1999) • **92**
Merlot Stags Leap District Reserve 1996: Smooth and polished, with moderately rich coffee, currant, herb and spice notes, firming up on the finish. Drink through 2006–J.L. • $40 • (10/15/1999) • **87**
Merlot Stags Leap District Reserve 1995 • $28 • (3/31/1998) • **87**
Merlot Stags Leap District Reserve 1994 • $28 • (12/31/1996) • **88**
Rosé Napa Valley 1992 • $25 • (11/30/1996) • **86**
Rosé Napa Valley 1991 • $25 • (12/31/1995) • **86**

ANDERSON'S CONN VALLEY | CALIFORNIA

Cabernet Sauvignon Napa Valley Estate Reserve 1997: Dense, complex and concentrated, with rich, earthy currant, black cherry, plum and anise. Finishes with gusty tannins, but it's well balanced.–J.L. • $NA • (8/31/1998) (BT) • **90-94**
Cabernet Sauvignon Napa Valley Estate Reserve 1996: Ripe, round and polished, with an attractive core of currant- and coffee-laced black cherry, cedar, oak and spice notes. Finishes with firm, tight, earthy tannins. Needs a little time. Drink through 2009–J.L. • $48 • (11/15/1999) • **90**
Cabernet Sauvignon Napa Valley Estate Reserve 1995: An elegant, understated style, with cedary tobacco flavors dominating the earthy currant ones. Pleasing. Tasted twice, with consistent notes. Drink through 2005.–J.L. • $24 Ⓐ • (11/15/1998) • **87**
Cabernet Sauvignon Napa Valley Estate Reserve 1994 • $27 Ⓐ • (10/15/1997) • **91**
Cabernet Sauvignon Napa Valley Estate Reserve 1993 • $35 • (11/15/1996) • **90**
Cabernet Sauvignon Napa Valley Estate Reserve 1992 • $29 Ⓐ • (11/15/1995) HR • **93**
Cabernet Sauvignon Napa Valley Estate Reserve 1991 • $30 • (11/15/1994) • **88**
Cabernet Sauvignon Napa Valley Estate Reserve 1990 • $25 Ⓐ • (11/15/1993) • **90**
Cabernet Sauvignon Napa Valley Estate Reserve 1989: Austere, with firm tannins and structure, the ripe, earthy cherry and berry character tilts toward the dry side. Altogether well balanced and pleasing to drink. (1989 California Cabernet retrospective tasting). Drink now through 2006.–J.L. • $25 • (8/31/1999) • **88**
Cabernet Sauvignon Napa Valley Estate Reserve 1988: An earthy, minerally style, it still has enough currant, black cherry, anise and spicy notes to balance things out. Finishes with dry, firm tannins, dashes of coffee and cedar. (1988 California Cabernet retrospective tasting). Drink now through 2002.–J.L. • $25 • (11/15/1998) • **87**
Éloge Napa Valley 1998: Elegant and complex, with a tasty band of currant, black cherry, earth, spice and cedary oak. A little rough-and-tumble now, but not out of line for a barrel sample.–J.L. • $NA • (8/31/1999) (BT) • **90-94**
Éloge Napa Valley 1993: Earthy cedar notes are followed by a well-focused mid-palate of plum and berry flavors. Chewy tannins on the finish. Tasted twice, with consistent notes. Drink through 2005.–J.L. • $60 • (10/31/1998) • **86**
Pinot Noir Napa Valley 1992 • $25 • (3/31/1995) • **85**
Pinot Noir Napa Valley Valhalla Vineyards 1996: Light in color, body and flavor, with pleasant plum, herb, cherry and smoky oak flavors that pick up a trace of orange peel. Drink now through 2002.–J.L. • $45 • (9/15/1999) • **86**
Pinot Noir Napa Valley Valhalla Vineyards 1995 • $40 • (1/31/1998) • **87**
Pinot Noir Napa Valley Valhalla Vineyards 1993 • $40 • (4/30/1996) • **86**
Pinot Noir Napa Valley Valhalla Vineyards 1989 • $25 • (2/28/1993) • **84**
Pinot Noir Russian River Valley Dutton Ranch 1996: Smells complex and offers attractive ripe plum, cherry, wild berry and pretty oak flavors that build on the finish. Drink now.–J.L. • $45 • (9/15/1999) • **87**

ANDRE | CALIFORNIA

Blush Pink Champagne California NV • $4 • (12/15/1997) • **79**
Brut California NV • $4 • (12/15/1997) • **83**
Extra Dry California NV • $4 • (12/15/1997) • **72**

ANDREW WILL | WASHINGTON

Cabernet Sauvignon Washington 1994 • $35 • (2/28/1997) • **88**
Cabernet Sauvignon Washington 1992 • $21 • (5/31/1995) • **88**
Cabernet Sauvignon Washington 1991 • $20 • (9/30/1994) • **85**
Cabernet Sauvignon Washington R 1996: Has a lively, bright core of black currant and mineral flavors that remain focused through a thin veil of fine-grained tannins. Needs cellaring to round things out. Best after 2001.–H.S. • $35 • (11/15/1999) • **88**
Cabernet Sauvignon Washington State Reserve 1994 • $NA • (2/28/1997) • **88**
Cabernet Sauvignon Washington Reserve 1991 • $22 • (9/30/1994) • **88**
Merlot Washington 1994 • $24 • (9/15/1996) • **87**
Merlot Washington 1993 • $21 • (6/15/1995) • **89**
Merlot Washington 1992 • $19 • (9/30/1994) • **90**
Merlot Washington Ciel du Cheval 1994 • $27 • (9/15/1996) • **89**
Merlot Washington Ciel du Cheval 1993 • $25 • (8/31/1995) • **89**
Merlot Washington Pepperbridge 1994 • $30 • (9/15/1996) • **88**
Merlot Washington Pepperbridge 1993 • $25 • (8/31/1995) • **86**
Merlot Washington Reserve 1993 • $28 • (9/30/1995) • **84**
Merlot Washington Sunshine 1991 • $19 • (9/30/1994) • **89**
Merlot Washington Sunshine Reserve 1992 • $21 • (9/30/1994) • **82**
Merlot Washington Sunshine Reserve 1991 • $21 • (9/30/1994) • **88**

ANDRUS | CALIFORNIA

Napa Valley Reserve 1996: A subtle, polished blend of ripe plum, cherry, currant and cedary oak flavors that are rich and concentrated, but also quite elegant and refined. From Pine Ridge Winery. Drink now through 2008.–J.L. • $95 • (8/31/1999) • **92**

ANGELINA | CALIFORNIA

Cabernet Sauvignon California Private Reserve 1997: Pleasant mineral and dried currant flavors. Turns dry on the finish.–J.L. • $7 • (9/30/1998) • **79**
Merlot California Private Reserve 1997: Yeasty and tart, with green bean and tar flavors overriding the plumminess. Tannic on the finish. • $7 • (9/15/1998) • **72**

ANGELINE | CALIFORNIA

Zinfandel California Old Vine Cuvée 1992 • $8 • (10/15/1995) • **83**

ANTARES | CALIFORNIA

Merlot California 1995 • $22 • (12/15/1997) • **88**

APEX | WASHINGTON

Cabernet Sauvignon Columbia Valley 1995: Crisp and refined, with subdued plum, herb and earth flavors that linger delicately on the finish. Tasted twice, with consistent notes. Drink now through 2002.–H.S. • $35 • (9/30/1999) • **82**
Cabernet Sauvignon Columbia Valley 1994 • $35 • (9/15/1997) • **90**
Cabernet Sauvignon Columbia Valley 1990 • $18 • (10/15/1993) • **88**
Cabernet Sauvignon Yakima Valley 1993 • $25 • (9/15/1996) • **88**
Chardonnay Columbia Valley 1998: On the light side, this supple wine has pleasant almond, pear and mineral flavors that linger delicately. Drink now through 2003.–H.S. • $20 • (5/15/2000) • **86**
Chardonnay Columbia Valley 1996: Fresh and straightforward, showing focused pear and spice flavors on a sturdy frame.–H.S. • $18 • (9/15/1998) • **87**
Chardonnay Yakima Valley Outlook Vineyard 1997: Lean in structure, becoming more generous on the spicy finish, with pinelike accents to the pear flavors. Drink now.–H.S. • $30 • (10/31/1998) • **86**
Gewürztraminer Yakima Valley Ice Wine 1991 • $14 • (4/15/1995) • **77**
Gewürztraminer Yakima Valley Late Harvest Ice Wine 1991 • $16 • (9/30/1994) • **86**
Merlot Columbia Valley 1995: Supple, velvety and generous with its pretty cherry and currant flavors on a background of fine-grained tannins, echoing on the finish. Has style and presence without being overbearing. Drink now through 2004.–H.S. • $35 • (9/15/1998) • **89**
Merlot Columbia Valley 1990 • $15 • (9/30/1993) • **84**
Merlot Yakima Valley 1992 • $18 • (9/30/1995) • **87**
Merlot Yakima Valley 1989 • $17 • (3/15/1993) • **83**
Pinot Noir Willamette Valley 1996: On the light side but smooth and ripe, this generous mouthful of berry, plum and vanilla flavors lingers enticingly on the harmonious finish. Drink now. 1999.–H.S. • $20 • (9/30/1998) • **88**
Pinot Noir Willamette Valley 1995 • $18 • (9/15/1997) • **85**
Riesling Yakima Valley LHR 1995 • $19 • (9/15/1996) • **78**

ARAUJO | CALIFORNIA

Cabernet Sauvignon Napa Valley Eisele Vineyard 1998: An impressive display of ripe, complex fruit, with pretty oak shadings. The core of currant, berry, spice and mineral is focused.–J.L. • $NA • (8/31/1999) (BT) • **90-94**
Cabernet Sauvignon Napa Valley Eisele Vineyard 1997: Ripe and smooth, an elegant, supple, harmonious wine with appealing cherry, berry and currant flavors. Finishes with ripe tannins.–J.L. • $NA • (8/31/1998) (BT) • **90-94**
Cabernet Sauvignon Napa Valley Eisele Vineyard 1996: Smooth and polished, with detailed flavors of ripe plum, black cherry, spice and light oak, this pedigreed red turns rich and elegant, with a long, complex aftertaste. Best from 2001 through 2008.–J.L. • $264 Ⓐ • (11/15/1999) HR • **94**
Cabernet Sauvignon Napa Valley Eisele Vineyard 1995: A sleek and elegant, rich and concentrated Cabernet, with sharply focused black cherry, currant, plum and wild berry flavors interspersed with cedary tobacco notes. Finishes with a burst of fruit and finely integrated tannins. It's quite delicious now, but it should be long-lived. Best from 2001 through 2010.–J.L. • $323 Ⓐ • (10/31/1998) CS • **95**
Cabernet Sauvignon Napa Valley Eisele Vineyard 1994 • $346 Ⓐ • (10/15/1997) HR • **96**
Cabernet Sauvignon Napa Valley Eisele Vineyard 1993 • $249 Ⓐ • (11/15/1996) CS • **93**
Cabernet Sauvignon Napa Valley Eisele Vineyard 1992 • $234 Ⓐ • (11/15/1995) CS • **96**
Cabernet Sauvignon Napa Valley Eisele Vineyard 1991 • $259 Ⓐ • (10/15/1994) CS • **90**
Sauvignon Blanc Napa Valley Eisele Vineyard 1996 • $22 • (4/30/1998) • **87**

Key: SS—Spectator Selection. CS—Cellar Selection. HR—Highly Recommended. $NA—Price not available. (BT)—Barrel tasting. Ⓐ—Auction Price.
For a key to the tasters' initials, see "How to Use These Listings."
Dates in parentheses represent the issues in which the ratings were published.

Syrah Napa Valley 1995: Smooth, rich and elegant, with polished currant, leather, anise, earth and mineral flavors that are complex and concentrated, sophisticated and long. Drink through 2008–J.L. • $50 • (4/30/1999) • **94**
Syrah Napa Valley Eisele Vineyard 1996: Wonderful depth, richness, texture and complexity to this, with tiers of leathery currant, earth, anise, sage and the hallmark mineral aftertaste. Drink now through 2007.–J.L. • $211 Ⓐ • (5/15/2000) • **93**

ARBIOS | CALIFORNIA

Cabernet Sauvignon Alexander Valley 1996: A muscular wine, packed with smoky oak and bacon flavors. The fruit comes through on the finish, with hints of coffee, black currant, licorice and herbs. Tannins are still tough, but firm and ripe. Best from 2002 through 2007. • $30 • (10/15/1999) • **87**
Cabernet Sauvignon Alexander Valley 1995 • $30 • (6/15/1998) • **88**

ARBOR CREST | WASHINGTON

Cabernet Franc Columbia Valley 1993 • $12 • (4/30/1995) • **82**
Cabernet Franc Washington 1994 • $12 • (9/15/1997) • **88**
Cabernet Franc Washington Cameo Reserve 1996: Firm in texture, with a modest tannic grip around a core of peppery blackberry and currant flavor. Best after 2001.–H.S. • $13 • (9/30/1999) • **85**
Cabernet Sauvignon Columbia Valley 1988 • $11 • (9/30/1991) • **87**
Cabernet Sauvignon Columbia Valley Bacchus Vineyard 1985 • $11 • (10/15/1989) • **80**
Cabernet Sauvignon Columbia Valley Bacchus Vineyard 1983 • $13 • (12/15/1987) • **77**
Cabernet Sauvignon Columbia Valley Cameo Reserve 1996: Ripe, round and generous. A lovely mouthful of fresh berry, black cherry and plum flavors shaded with hints of smoke and anise. Delicious. Drink now through 2002.–H.S. • $15 • (8/31/1999) • **88**
Cabernet Sauvignon Washington Dionysus Vineyard Block 16 1994 • $13 • (9/15/1997) • **87**
Cabernet Sauvignon Washington Dionysus Vineyard Block 16 1993 • $14 • (9/15/1996) • **87**
Cabernet Sauvignon Columbia Valley Dionysus Vineyard Block 16 1991 • $11 • (3/15/1994) • **83**
Cabernet Sauvignon Washington Dionysus Vineyard Block 16 Cameo Reserve 1995: Bright and jazzy up front, layering its berry, cherry, coffee and spice flavors in tiers of rich, supple texture. Fine-grained tannins wrap the focused flavors in a package that needs cellaring to reach its optimum. Drink through 2005–H.S. • $14 • (9/15/1998) • **89**
Cabernet-Merlot Washington 1997: Lean and lithe, with nicely layered blackberry and raspberry flavors, and hints of sassafras and tea on the spicy finish. Drink through 2004.–H.S. • $12 • (8/31/1999) • **87**
Cabernet Merlot Washington 1995 • $12 • (8/31/1997) • **85**
Cabernet-Merlot Columbia Valley 1994 • $12 • (9/15/1996) • **84**
Cabernet-Merlot Columbia Valley 1993 • $12 • (7/31/1995) • **88**
Cabernet-Merlot Columbia Valley 1992 • $11 • (8/31/1994) • **89**
Chardonnay Washington Cameo Reserve 1996: Bright in flavor and supple in texture, with nectarine, pear and hazelnut flavors that linger gently on the generous finish. Harmonious wine, artfully crafted. Drink now through 2001.–H.S. • $11 • (9/15/1998) • **88**
Dionysus 16 Columbia Valley 1995: Firm in texture, its dark berry and black cherry flavors glide impressively through this lithe wine. Shows intensity in a refined package. Drink through 2005–H.S. • $32 • (8/31/1999) • **89**
Grand Cépage Washington Cameo Reserve 1997: Smooth, graceful and muted in flavor, this Chardonnay blend is nicely proportioned to let its cream, tobacco and melon notes linger on the supple finish. Drink now through 2003.–H.S. • $10 • (8/31/1999) • **86**
Johannisberg Riesling Late Harvest Columbia Valley Select 1994 • $10/375 ml. • (9/15/1995) • **82**
Johannisberg Riesling Washington 1998: Light and simple, with an oxidized edge—like an apple that has been sitting out too long.–H.S. • $6 • (9/30/1999) • **77**
Johannisberg Riesling Washington Dionysus Vineyard 1997: Fresh and appealing for its sweet apple and melon flavors, picking up hints of tobacco on the finish. Drink now.–H.S. • $6 • (9/15/1998) • **80**
Merlot Columbia Valley 1991 • $10 • (6/15/1993) • **85**
Merlot Columbia Valley 1990 • $12 • (4/15/1992) • **88**
Merlot Columbia Valley 1988 • $9 • (8/31/1991) • **81**
Merlot Columbia Valley Cameo Reserve 1992 • $13 • (8/31/1995) • **88**
Merlot Columbia Valley Cameo Reserve 1991 • $13 • (9/30/1994) • **86**
Merlot Columbia Valley Rosebud Vineyard Cameo Reserve 1990 • $14 • (1/31/1993) • **86**

Merlot Columbia Valley Cameo Reserve 1989 • $12 • (3/31/1992) • **77**
Merlot Columbia Valley Cameo Reserve 1988 • $12 • (8/31/1991) • **83**
Merlot Columbia Valley Cameo Reserve 1987 • $11 • (6/15/1990) • **85**
Merlot Columbia Valley Bacchus Vineyard Cameo Reserve 1985 • $10 • (12/15/1987) • **83**
Merlot Washington 1997: Bright and flavorful, this is a jazzy red with pretty cherry and currant flavors shaded with spicy tones. Its fine tannins don't get in the way of the pleasure—and the price tag won't either. Drink now through 2002.–H.S. • $11 • (8/31/1999) • **86**
Merlot Washington 1995: Crisp at the core, with supple layers of plum and spicy oak flavors wrapped around the lean, chewy finish. Drink now through 2001.–H.S. • $11 • (9/15/1998) • **85**
Merlot Washington Dionysus Vineyard Block 16 Cameo Reserve 1995: Light, fragrant and spicy, with exotic pepper and floral overtones to the modest berry flavors lurking in the background. Drink now.–H.S. • $14 • (9/15/1998) • **82**
Merlot Washington Dionysus Vineyard Block 16 Cameo Reserve 1994 • $13 • (9/15/1997) • **85**
Merlot Washington Cameo Reserve 1993 • $13 • (9/15/1996) • **88**
Muscat Canelli Columbia Valley 1994 • $7 • (8/31/1995) • **85**
Pinot Gris Washington 1997: Fresh and bright, with pretty pear, melon and spice flavors on a refreshingly dry frame. Drink now.–H.S. • $11 • (9/30/1999) • **85**
Sauvignon Blanc Washington 1996 • $8 • (9/15/1997) • **85**
Sémillon Late Harvest Washington 1998: Sweet and refreshing, showing none of the intensity or honey character one would expect from a sweet Sémillon, but it has pretty pear and white fig flavors that soften on the finish. Drink now.–H.S. • $8 • (9/30/1999) • **83**

ARCADIAN | CALIFORNIA

Chardonnay Santa Maria Valley Bien Nacido Vineyard 1997: A curious mix of charred oak and tart, sour pineapple, though it straightens out on the finish, becoming more palatable. Drink now through 2003.–J.L. • $30 • (6/15/2000) • **84**
Chardonnay Santa Maria Valley Bien Nacido Vineyard 1996: Clean and spicy, with a crisp, flinty edge to the ripe peach, pear and nectarine flavors, and the acidity keeps the flavors fresh and lively. Impressive new wine. Drink now through 2002.–J.L. • $30 • (2/28/1999) • **91**
Pinot Noir Monterey Sleepy Hollow Vineyard 1997: Racy, with spicy wild berry, cherry, tart plum and raspberry character, it turns tight and firm on the finish, without being too tannic. Drink through 2004.–J.L. • $25 • (9/15/1999) • **87**

ARCHERY SUMMIT | OREGON

Pinot Noir Oregon 1993 • $25 • (10/31/1995) HR • **90**
Pinot Noir Oregon 100% Whole Cluster 1996 • $35 • (5/15/1998) • **86**
Pinot Noir Oregon Archery Summit Estate 1997: Light in structure, with an open texture to the modest blackberry and gentle smoke flavors. Has a minty, slightly bitter edge on the finish, which lingers impressively. Drink now through 2003.–H.S. • $75 • (5/15/2000) • **85**
Pinot Noir Oregon Archery Summit Estate 1996: A delicate, silky red, with pretty tea-leaf and chocolate overtones to the black cherry flavors hiding in the core. Drink now through 2001.–H.S. • $75 • (2/28/1999) • **87**
Pinot Noir Oregon Arcus Estate 1998: Smooth, ripe and generous with its fresh raspberry and black cherry flavors, which are harmoniously balanced with hints of spice and well-submerged tannins on the long finish. Has elegance and power. Drink now through 2007.–H.S. • $65 • (4/30/2000) • **92**
Pinot Noir Oregon Arcus Estate 1997: A pretty wine, with a modest level of richness to the cherry and spice flavors. Finishes smooth and toasty, lingering impressively for a light vintage. Drink now through 2001.–H.S. • $59 • (12/31/1999) • **88**
Pinot Noir Oregon Arcus Estate 1996: Nicely aromatic, with pretty plum, spice and floral flavors on a lithe frame. Ripe berry and chocolate notes emerge on the finish and echo enticingly, suggesting this is worth short-term cellaring to see what develops. Drink through 2002.–H.S. • $59 • (11/15/1998) • **88**
Pinot Noir Oregon Arcus Estate 1995 • $60 • (8/31/1997) • **91**
Pinot Noir Oregon Arcus Estate 1994 • $50 • (6/30/1996) • **87**
Pinot Noir Oregon Brick House Vineyard 1997: Firm and chewy, with a tannic bite that obscures some of the wild plum, berry and cinnamon flavors that linger on the finish. Needs cellaring. Best from 2001 through 2003.–H.S. • $49 • (4/30/1999) • **88**
Pinot Noir Oregon Brick House Vineyard 1996 • $40 • (5/15/1998) • **89**
Pinot Noir Oregon Chêne D'Oregon 1996 • $27 • (3/31/1998) • **88**
Pinot Noir Oregon Jeunesse 1997: Has lots of pretty flavors that linger elegantly. A light style but not fragile, it finishes with a flourish. Drink now through 2002.–H.S. • $27 • (4/30/1999) • **87**
Pinot Noir Oregon Jeunesse 1996 • $23 • (3/31/1998) • **85**
Pinot Noir Oregon Premier Cuvée 1997: Firm in texture, with more tannins than most '97s, but they're smooth and polished, letting the pretty oak-scented blackberry and cinnamon flavors come through and echo nicely on the finish. Drink now through 2003.–H.S. • $35 • (4/30/1999) • **88**
Pinot Noir Oregon Premier Cuvée 1996: On the light side, with a nice array of plum, berry, spice and tea leaf aromas and flavors. Finish echoes them all, and adds a hint of chocolate. Drink now through 2002.–H.S. • $35 • (11/15/1998) • **87**
Pinot Noir Oregon Premier Cuvée 1995 • $35 • (2/28/1997) • **87**
Pinot Noir Oregon Premier Cuvée 1994 • $30 • (6/30/1996) • **91**
Pinot Noir Oregon Red Hills Estate 1997: Has a lovely range of spicy, chocolate-scented cherry and plum flavors on a modest frame, echoing its flavors on the light but firm finish. This feels like it can develop more with short-term cellaring. Drink now through 2003.–H.S. • $65 • (12/31/1999) • **89**
Pinot Noir Oregon Red Hills Estate 1996: Firm in texture, with fine-grained tannins framing a lean, elegant wine that shades its sweet plum and berry flavors with hints of spice, cream and smoke. Drink through 2005–H.S. • $59 • (12/15/1998) • **89**
Pinot Noir Oregon Red Hills Estate 1995 • $60 • (8/31/1997) • **89**
Pinot Noir Oregon Red Hills Estate 1994 • $50 • (6/30/1996) • **89**
Vireton Oregon 1998: Rich and ripe, this lovely, round, fruit-forward mouthful of apricot-scented melon and spice flavors remains supple and appealing through the lightly floral finish. Drink now through 2001.–H.S. • $25 • (11/15/1999) • **89**
Vireton Oregon 1997: Bright, ripe and appealing for its Alsace-like pear and almond flavors, picking up a touch of melon on the soft finish. Mostly Pinot Gris. Drink now.–H.S. • $25 • (10/31/1998) • **88**
Vireton Oregon 1996 • $21 • (9/15/1997) • **85**

ARCIERO | CALIFORNIA

Arpeggio Paso Robles 1995 • $12 • (6/30/1998) • **80**
Cabernet Franc Paso Robles 1995 • $11 • (4/30/1998) • **75**
Cabernet Sauvignon Paso Robles 1995 • $11 • (6/30/1998) • **81**
Cabernet Sauvignon Paso Robles 1994 • $11 • (9/30/1997) • **85**
Cabernet Sauvignon Paso Robles 1993 • $9 • (12/15/1996) • **77**
Cabernet Sauvignon Paso Robles 1992 • $9 • (12/15/1995) • **82**
Cabernet Sauvignon Paso Robles 1991 • $9 • (12/15/1995) • **72**
Cabernet Sauvignon Paso Robles 1990 • $7 • (11/15/1994) • **78**
Cabernet Sauvignon Paso Robles 1989 • $NA • (11/15/1993) • **79**
Cabernet Sauvignon Paso Robles Reserve 1990 • $14 • (12/15/1995) • **78**
Chardonnay California 1996 • $9 • (5/15/1998) • **78**
Merlot Paso Robles 1993 • $12 • (3/31/1996) • **82**
Nebbiolo Paso Robles 1994 • $10 • (6/30/1998) • **72**
Nebbiolo Paso Robles 1993 • $11 • (2/28/1997) • **86**
Nebbiolo Paso Robles 1991 • $11 • (9/30/1994) • **79**
Petite Sirah Paso Robles 1989 • $8 • (6/15/1993) • **81**
Sangiovese Paso Robles 1995 • $13 • (6/30/1998) • **83**
Sangiovese Paso Robles 1994 • $14 • (2/28/1997) • **85**
Sauvignon Blanc California 1997 • $7 • (4/30/1998) • **79**
Zinfandel Paso Robles 1995 • $11 • (3/31/1998) • **87**
Zinfandel Paso Robles 1994 • $10 • (4/30/1997) • **86**
Zinfandel Paso Robles 1992 • $8 • (10/15/1995) • **83**
Zinfandel Paso Robles 1988 • $8 • (10/15/1992) • **77**

ARGONAUT | CALIFORNIA

Cabernet Sauvignon Sierra Foothills 1995 • $12 • (12/15/1997) • **79**
Fumé Blanc Sierra Foothills 1996 • $10 • (9/15/1997) • **83**

ARGYLE | OREGON

Brut Willamette Valley 1996: This Oregon sparkler is elegant, complex and layered with flavor. It has everything you want in a sparkling wine, including delicacy. The texture is fine-grained and flavors center around pear, toast and hints of exotic flowers and spices. Drink now.–H.S. • $22 • (4/30/2000) SS • **90**
Chardonnay Willamette Valley 1998: This young white is supple and ripe, appealing for its distinctive apricot, pear and gentle spice flavors that remain fresh and harmonious through the engaging finish. Oregon's top-scoring Chardonnay from the vintage. Drink now through 2003.–H.S. • $13 • (5/15/2000) SS • **89**

■ ■ ■ ■

ARGYLE

Chardonnay Willamette Valley 1997: Smooth and refined, with lively pear, apricot and vanilla flavors that suspend themselves nicely on the open-textured finish. Drink now through 2001.–H.S. • $13 • (4/30/1999) • **88**
Chardonnay Willamette Valley 1993 • $12 • (12/31/1996) HR • **88**
Chardonnay Willamette Valley Nuthouse 1997: Focused, distinctive and elegant, this is a beautifully formed, round, complex Oregon white, unfolding layers of nutmeg, melon, pear, peach and vanilla flavors that linger enticingly on the finish. Drink now through 2005.–H.S. • $21 • (12/31/1999) SS • **90**
Chardonnay Willamette Valley Nuthouse 1996: Smooth and supple, generous with its peach, fig and pineapple flavors on a round structure, finishing with pretty spicy notes that linger long. Drink now through 2001.–H.S. • $28 • (4/30/1999) • **90**
Chardonnay Willamette Valley Reserve 1997: This lovely, refined style of Chardonnay focuses on pretty pear and spice flavors that linger effortlessly on the airy finish. A particularly harmonious wine that lasts and lasts. Drink now through 2004.–H.S. • $28 • (12/31/1999) • **91**
Chardonnay Willamette Valley Reserve 1996: Bright and refreshing for its lively pear and citrus flavors, hinting at walnut and nutmeg on the round finish. Has concentration and depth, without weight. Drink now through 2001.–H.S. • $21 • (4/30/1999) • **90**
Pinot Noir Oregon Limited Reserve 1993 • $25 • (3/31/1996) • **87**
Pinot Noir Oregon Nuthouse Select Barrel 1994 • $30 • (12/31/1996) • **93**
Pinot Noir Willamette Valley 1998: Ripe, generous and harmonious, with blackberry, blueberry and plum flavors shining brightly through a thin veil of fine-grained tannin. Feels like it can develop for a few years. Drink now through 2008.–H.S. • $18 • (4/30/2000) • **90**
Pinot Noir Willamette Valley 1997: Light, almost fragile, with modest levels of pretty currant and cherry on a soft bed of tannins. Drink now through 2001.–H.S. • $15 • (4/30/1999) • **84**
Pinot Noir Willamette Valley 1996 • $14 • (5/15/1998) • **87**
Pinot Noir Willamette Valley 1993 • $10 • (10/31/1994) • **89**
Pinot Noir Willamette Valley Cowhouse 1996: Light and smooth, this delicate wine has wisps of spicy cherry and currant fruit, with a touch of tobacco on the firm finish. Drink now.–H.S. • $35 • (12/15/1998) • **82**
Pinot Noir Willamette Valley Limited Reserve 1994 • $30 • (12/31/1996) • **81**
Pinot Noir Willamette Valley Nuthouse 1997: Has riper flavors and more intensity than most '97 Pinots, showing lots of spicy, tobacco-scented plum and blackberry flavors that linger on the firm, elegant finish. Drink now through 2002.–H.S. • $35 • (4/30/2000) • **88**
Pinot Noir Willamette Valley Nuthouse 1996: Supple and flavorful. A juicy mixture of ripe plum, jazzy citrus and pretty vanilla and toast overtones on an elegant frame. Drink through 2003.–H.S. • $35 • (12/15/1998) • **88**
Pinot Noir Willamette Valley Nuthouse 1995 • $35 • (5/15/1998) • **85**
Pinot Noir Willamette Valley Reserve 1996: Light and smooth, with pretty plum and earth flavors nicely wrapped in a blanket of silky texture. Drink through 2002–H.S. • $35 • (12/15/1998) • **87**
Pinot Noir Willamette Valley Reserve 1995 • $30 • (10/31/1997) • **89**
Pinot Noir Willamette Valley Vintage Select 1995 • $14 • (12/31/1996) • **83**
Pinot Noir Willamette Valley Vintage Select 1994 • $12 • (3/31/1996) • **86**
Riesling Willamette Valley Dry Reserve 1998: Fresh and aromatic, prettier on the nose than on the palate. Finishes dry, echoing apple and floral flavors. Drink now.–H.S. • $12 • (5/15/2000) • **85**
Riesling Willamette Valley Dry Reserve 1997: Dry, with sappy green apple and citrus flavors that pick up nice floral hints on the finish. Drink now through 2002.–H.S. • $12 • (4/30/1999) • **86**
Riesling Willamette Valley Dry Reserve 1996 • $11 • (5/15/1998) • **87**

ARIES | CALIFORNIA

Cabernet Sauvignon Napa Valley 1990 • $11 • (10/31/1993) • **87**
Merlot Napa Valley Carneros 1989 • $11 • (11/30/1992) • **84**
Pinot Noir California 1995 • $10 • (5/15/1997) • **85**
Pinot Noir Napa Valley Carneros 1994 • $10 • (1/31/1996) • **86**
Pinot Noir Napa Valley Carneros 1992 • $10 • (2/28/1994) • **85**
Pinot Noir Napa Valley Carneros 1991 • $10 • (2/28/1993) • **84**
Pinot Noir Napa Valley Carneros Cuvée Vivace 1989 • $8 • (4/30/1991) • **70**
Pinot Noir North Coast 1997: Austere, a touch earthy, with a modest glimmer of plummy flavor and sharp, hard tannins. Drink now through 2001.–J.L. • $14 • (2/28/1999) • **83**

Key: SS—Spectator Selection. CS—Cellar Selection. HR—Highly Recommended. $NA—Price not available. (BT)—Barrel tasting. Ⓐ—Auction Price.
For a key to the tasters' initials, see "How to Use These Listings."
Dates in parentheses represent the issues in which the ratings were published.

ARIETTA | CALIFORNIA

Napa Valley 1997: Young and backward, though the earthy, meaty berry, anise, plum and currant flavors fold together nicely and may become even more complex and intriguing. Cellar short-term. Cabernet Franc and Merlot. Best from 2001 through 2008.–J.L. • $85 Ⓐ • (4/30/2000) • **89**

ARMIDA | CALIFORNIA

Merlot Russian River Valley 1994 • $16 • (7/31/1997) • **88**
Merlot Russian River Valley 1993 • $14 • (8/31/1996) • **81**
Merlot Russian River Valley 1990 • $14 • (5/31/1992) • **78**
Pinot Noir Russian River Valley 1992 • $13 • (3/31/1995) • **72**
Pinot Noir Russian River Valley 1991 • $12 • (2/28/1993) • **84**

ARNS | CALIFORNIA

Cabernet Sauvignon Napa Valley 1996: Firm, ripe and compact, with a rich, focused core of anise and currant-laced Cabernet fruit flavors, finishing with concentrated tannins and pretty spice and oak notes. Best from 2001 through 2009.–J.L. • $50 • (10/31/1999) • **92**
Cabernet Sauvignon Napa Valley 1995: Dark, ripe, rich and polished, with black cherry, chocolate, wild berry and spice. Gains complexity and nuance, but finishes with a touch of stemminess. Best from 2001 through 2008.–J.L. • $40 • (12/15/1998) • **91**
Cabernet Sauvignon Napa Valley 1994 • $35 • (10/31/1997) • **89**
Cabernet Sauvignon Napa Valley 1993 • $30 • (4/30/1997) • **93**

ARROWOOD | CALIFORNIA

Cabernet Sauvignon Sonoma County 1998: Complex, with its interplay of creamy, toasty oak and ripe, spicy currant and black cherry flavors.–J.L. • $NA • (8/31/1999) (BT) • **90-94**
Cabernet Sauvignon Sonoma County 1997: Hard-edged, firmly tannic, with a tight core of currant, dill and berry. Has the depth and concentration for excellence, even in this raw, unevolved form.–J.L. • $NA • (8/31/1998) (BT) • **90-94**
Cabernet Sauvignon Sonoma County 1996: Hints of dill and sage lead to a more centered core of currant, black cherry, plum and spice, and while it's elegant and polished, it's short on extra dimensions. Drink now through 2006.–J.L. • $41 • (10/15/1999) • **88**
Cabernet Sauvignon Sonoma County 1995: Supple, complex and harmonious, with an array of cedar, plum and currant, hints of coffee and anise, turning elegant. Drink now through 2002.–J.L. • $34 • (1/31/1999) • **88**
Cabernet Sauvignon Sonoma County 1994 • $55 Ⓐ • (10/15/1997) • **91**
Cabernet Sauvignon Sonoma County 1993 • $27 • (11/15/1996) SS • **92**
Cabernet Sauvignon Sonoma County 1992 • $36 Ⓐ • (11/15/1995) HR • **92**
Cabernet Sauvignon Sonoma County 1991 • $25 • (9/30/1994) SS • **91**
Cabernet Sauvignon Sonoma County 1990 • $24 • (10/31/1993) SS • **91**
Cabernet Sauvignon Sonoma County 1989: Presents a ripe, youthful core of plum, currant and cherry, fine, integrated tannins and good richness, depth and balance. Impressive now. (1989 California Cabernet retrospective tasting). Drink through 2005.–J.L. • $24 • (8/31/1999) • **91**
Cabernet Sauvignon Sonoma County 1988: Offers more up-front fruitiness than most 1988s, but shares the tannic dryness of the vintage on the finish. In between, there's plenty of ripe plum, black cherry, anise and cedary notes that stay focused. (1988 California Cabernet retrospective tasting). Drink now through 2003.–J.L. • $23 • (11/15/1998) • **88**
Cabernet Sauvignon Sonoma County 1987 • $22 • (12/15/1997) • **93**
Cabernet Sauvignon Sonoma County 1986 • $58 Ⓐ • (12/15/1996) • **83**
Cabernet Sauvignon Sonoma County 1985 • $46 Ⓐ • (12/15/1988) • **94**
Cabernet Sauvignon Sonoma County Réserve Spéciale 1995: Dark, ripe and intense, with a rich, supple, polished core of currant, blackberry, black cherry and spice. Holds its focus and gains complexity and nuance on the finish, where pretty toasty oak folds in nicely. Drink through 2008–J.L. • $75 • (11/15/1999) • **94**
Cabernet Sauvignon Sonoma County Réserve Spéciale 1994: Beautifully crafted, complex and concentrated, with a tightly focused core of earthy currant, black cherry, cedary oak and spicy nuances, turning long and full on the finish. Best from 2001 through 2010.–J.L. • $50 • (7/31/1998) • **94**
Cabernet Sauvignon Sonoma County Réserve Spéciale 1993 • $38 • (12/31/1996) • **92**
Cabernet Sauvignon Sonoma County Réserve Spéciale 1992 • $35 • (12/15/1995) HR • **92**

Cabernet Sauvignon Sonoma County Réserve Spéciale 1989 • $70/1.5 liter • (11/15/1993) • **88**

Chardonnay Sonoma County 1997: Ripe and very intense, with loads of exotic fruit flavors and layers of fig, nectarine and pear. Finishes with spicy oak. Drink now through 2001.–J.L. • $26 • (6/15/1999) • **91**

Chardonnay Sonoma County 1996: This delicious Chardonnay greets you with toasty, smoky oak before unveiling a rich core of concentrated pear, spice, vanilla, honey and citrus notes that parade across the palate and follow through to a long, complex aftertaste. Drink now through 2002.–J.L. • $24 • (9/30/1998) SS • **91**

Chardonnay Sonoma County Cuvée Michel Berthoud Réserve Spéciale 1997: Lots of complex, ripe, upfront spicy pear, melon and apple flavors that slowly unfold, revealing hints of hazelnut and nutmeg on a subtle finish. May benefit from short-term cellaring. Drink now through 2004.–J.L. • $40 • (11/15/1999) • **91**

Chardonnay Sonoma County Cuvée Michel Berthoud Réserve Spéciale 1996: Smooth, rich and harmonious, with pretty layers of ripe pear, fig, melon, toast, hazelnut and spice, finishing long and complex. Drink now through 2002.–J.L. • $37 • (2/28/1999) • **92**

Malbec Sonoma County 1995: Tight, firmly tannic, with tobacco leaf and cedar, hints of currant and berry, cherry and spice. Turns dry and austere, but if you love Malbec, here's a nice one. Best from 2001 through 2005.–J.L. • $37 • (3/31/1999) • **88**

Malbec Sonoma County 1993 • $28 • (4/30/1997) • **87**

Merlot Sonoma County 1995: Here's a California Merlot worth its salt. It's tight and firm, with a narrow band of spicy currant, plum and tobacco flavors that slowly fan out on the finish, revealing more depth and complexity. Give it a few more months in the bottle, then enjoy through 2004. –J.L. • $38 • (10/15/1998) HR • **90**

Merlot Sonoma County 1994 • $35 • (7/31/1997) • **92**

Merlot Sonoma County 1993 • $30 • (8/31/1996) • **89**

Merlot Sonoma County 1992 • $28 • (12/15/1995) • **89**

Merlot Sonoma County 1991 • $28 • (7/31/1994) HR • **90**

Merlot Sonoma County 1990 • $25 • (5/31/1993) • **89**

Pinot Blanc Russian River Valley Saralee's Vineyard 1997: Smooth and creamy, with complex fig, pear, melon and spicy citrus notes and a touch of anise. Drink now through 2001.–J.L. • $33 • (1/31/1999) • **87**

Pinot Blanc Russian River Valley Saralee's Vineyard 1996: Sleek, elegant and brimming with ripe, juicy peach, pear and nectarine flavors. Tightly focused from start to finish. Drink now through 2002.–J.L. • $33 • (12/15/1998) • **90**

Syrah Russian River Valley Saralee's Vineyard 1995: Dark, ripe, rich and concentrated, with exotic black cherry, plum and wild berry. Turns leathery and spicy, with supple tannins. Drink through 2006–J.L. • $40 • (2/28/1999) • **90**

Syrah Russian River Valley Saralee's Vineyard 1994 • $134 Ⓐ • (4/30/1997) • **92**

Viognier Russian River Valley Late Harvest Saralee's Vineyard Select 1994 • $28/375 ml. • (8/31/1996) • **88**

Viognier Russian River Valley Saralee's Vineyard 1998: Nice, with peach, apricot and vanilla notes, but soapy flavors detract from the finish. Drink now.–J.L. • $30 • (5/15/2000) • **84**

Viognier Russian River Valley Saralee's Vineyard 1997: Distinctively spicy, with a complex array of litchi, pear, melon, fig and exotic spices, offering depth and richness. Drink now through 2002.–J.L. • $30 • (2/28/1999) • **90**

White Riesling Alexander Valley Late Harvest Special Select Hoot Owl Creek Vineyards 1998: Sleek and elegant, with ripe, rich, sweet lemon, apple, floral and spicy notes that are smooth and polished. Long, lingering finish. Drink now through 2008.–J.L. • $40/375 ml. • (12/31/1999) • **95**

White Riesling Russian River Valley Late Harvest Oak Meadow Vineyard Special Select 1993 • $28/375 ml. • (4/30/1995) HR • **96**

White Riesling Russian River Valley Late Harvest Oak Meadow Vineyard Special Select 1991 • $20/375 ml. • (6/30/1993) • **87**

White Riesling Russian River Valley Late Harvest Select Preston Ranch H.S.S. 1998: Smooth, ripe and flavorful, with lots of sweet pear, spice, apple, citrus and floral notes. Quite elegant and tasty. Drink now through 2006.–J.L. • $35/375 ml. • (12/31/1999) • **90**

White Riesling Sonoma County Late Harvest 1998: Sweet and spicy, with true Riesling character. Hints of apricot and peach and floral notes are pure and appealing. Drink now through 2004.–J.L. • $15/375 ml. • (12/31/1999) • **88**

ARTERBERRY | OREGON

Pinot Noir Willamette Valley 1990 • $10 • (2/28/1993) • **79**

Pinot Noir Willamette Valley Weber Vineyards 1989 • $12 • (11/15/1991) • **85**

Pinot Noir Willamette Valley Winemaker Reserve 1991 • $7 • (3/15/1994) • **80**

Pinot Noir Willamette Valley Winemaker Reserve 1990 • $15 • (2/28/1993) • **79**

Pinot Noir Willamette Valley Winemaker Reserve 1989 • $12 • (11/15/1991) • **75**

Pinot Noir Willamette Valley Winemaker's Reserve 1988 • $14 • (1/31/1991) • **79**

Pinot Noir Yamhill County Red Hills Vineyard Winemaker's Reserve 1986 • $15 • (6/15/1988) • **74**

Pinot Noir Yamhill County Red Hills Vineyard Winemaker's Reserve 1985 • $16 • (6/15/1987) • **95**

Pinot Noir Yamhill County Red Hills Vineyard Winemaker's Reserve 1983 • $16 • (2/15/1990) • **86**

Pinot Noir Yamhill County Weber Vineyards Winemaker's Reserve 1987 • $14 • (2/15/1990) • **90**

ARTESA | CALIFORNIA

Chardonnay Carneros 1997: Bright, rich, focused, with ripe fig, lemon, pear, apricot and spice, turning even more complex, with layers of flavors on the finish. A new label from sparkling wine producer Codorniu Napa. Drink through 2005–J.L. • $20 • (10/15/1999) • **92**

Chardonnay Carneros Reserve 1997: Anise, pear, coconut and vanilla flavors fold together nicely in a ripe format. Tasted twice, with consistent notes. Drink now.–J.L. • $29 • (6/30/2000) • **85**

Chardonnay Napa Valley 1997: A touch woody, with cedar and oak flavors. The core of lemony pear and citrusy fruit is tightly focused and lingers on the finish, where it turns complex. Drink through 2004–J.L. • $20 • (10/15/1999) • **89**

Pinot Noir Carneros 1997: Smells and tastes earthy, with a coarse texture to the mineral and dried cherry flavors. Finishes with a tannic edge. Drink now through 2005.–J.L. • $22 • (5/31/2000) • **86**

Pinot Noir Russian River Valley 1997: Complex and mature-tasting, with dried plum, cherry and berryish fruit, anise, sage and spice tannins. Drink now through 2004.–J.L. • $21 • (11/30/1999) • **87**

Pinot Noir Santa Barbara County 1997: Earthy, with complex cola, dried cherry, sage and leaf notes. Delivers a tasty range of flavors, with mild tannins. Drink now through 2001.–J.L. • $21 • (11/30/1999) • **88**

Sauvignon Blanc Napa Valley 1997: Smooth, rich and elegant, with smoky pear, fig, melon and citrus flavors, it's tightly focused, long and complex. A new label from sparkling wine producer Codorniu Napa. Drink now through 2004.–J.L. • $15 • (10/15/1999) • **89**

ARTHUR, DAVID | CALIFORNIA

Cabernet Sauvignon Napa Valley 1996: Superrich Cabernet, plush, thick and concentrated, with layers of delicious currant, blackberry, black cherry, spice and pretty nutmeg flavors that are long and focused on the finish. Drink through 2008–J.L. • $45 • (5/15/1999) HR • **94**

Cabernet Sauvignon Napa Valley Elevation 1147 1996: Smooth, rich and perfumed, with a plush, complex array of chocolate, currant, black cherry, wild berry and spice and cedary, toasty oak. Finishes in a long, complex aftertaste that keeps pumping out the flavor. Drink through 2008–J.L. • $75 • (5/15/1999) • **95**

Chardonnay Napa Valley Reserve 1997: Clean and crisp, with bright young pear, apple, melon and citrus notes that are complex and concentrated. Drink now through 2002.–J.L. • $32 • (5/15/1999) • **88**

Chardonnay Napa Valley Reserve 1996 • $28 • (3/31/1998) • **86**

Meritagio Napa Valley 1996: Offers a lot of complex flavors, with a range of earthy, leathery currant, black cherry, anise, tar and cedar, finishing with firm but supple tannins. A blend of Cabernet Sauvignon, Cabernet Franc, Merlot, Petit Verdot and Sangiovese. Drink now through 2004.–J.L. • $38 • (5/15/1999) • **91**

Meritagio Napa Valley 1995 • $32 • (4/30/1998) • **88**

Meritagio Napa Valley 1992 • $25 • (8/31/1996) • **78**

ARTISAN | CALIFORNIA

Sangiovese North Coast Harvest 1996: Pleasant enough, with light cherry and vanilla flavors, and fairly smooth on the palate, but the finish is quite short. Drink now through 2001. • $14 • (2/28/1999) • **81**

ASHBY, HUNTER | CALIFORNIA

Zinfandel California 1995 • $12 • (3/31/1998) • **81**

ASHLAND | OREGON

Cabernet Franc Rogue Valley 1995 • $13 • (4/30/1997) • **86**

Cabernet Sauvignon Rogue Valley 1995: Distinctive and smoky, with some strong game and mineral-scented flavors. Supple black cherry tones hide in the background. Drink now through 2002.–H.S. • $11 • (4/30/1999) • **83**

ASHLAND

Cabernet Sauvignon Rogue Valley 1994 • $13 • (4/30/1997) • **87**
Cabernet Sauvignon Rogue Valley 1993 • $13 • (4/30/1997) • **85**
Cabernet Sauvignon Rogue Valley 1992 • $12 • (3/31/1996) • **85**
Cabernet Sauvignon Rogue Valley 1991 • $14 • (11/30/1994) • **87**
Cabernet-Merlot Rogue Valley 1995 • $10 • (4/30/1997) • **86**
Merlot Rogue Valley 1997: Firm, chewy and decidedly earthy, with modest berry flavors lurking under hard tannins.–H.S. • $14 • (5/15/2000) • **79**
Merlot Rogue Valley 1996: Light, smooth and pleasantly fruity, with pretty berry and mineral flavors on the finish. Drink now.–H.S. • $13 • (4/30/1999) • **85**
Merlot Rogue Valley 1995 • $12 • (3/31/1998) • **86**
Merlot Rogue Valley 1994 • $14 • (4/30/1997) • **82**
Merlot Rogue Valley 1992 • $12 • (3/31/1996) • **84**
Merlot Rogue Valley 1991 • $16 • (11/30/1994) • **83**
Millenium Rogue Valley 1997: Firm and flavorful, with a strong minty-herbal layer overtaking the modest cherry and spice right through to the polished finish. Drink now through 2002.–H.S. • $11 • (5/15/2000) • **82**
Pinot Gris Rogue Valley 1998: Distinctively spicy, with exotic overtones to the pretty melon and pineapple flavors. Drink now.–H.S. • $8 • (5/15/2000) • **87**

ASTRALE E TERRA | CALIFORNIA

Merlot Napa Valley 1996: Minty, with spice, bay leaf and herbal notes, holding that flavor profile while weaving in hints of plum, earth and currant. Finishes mildly tannic. Drink now through 2004.–J.L. • $32 • (8/31/1999) • **88**

ATLAS PEAK | CALIFORNIA

Cabernet Sauvignon Atlas Peak 1995: Light-textured, with spicy herb, tart cherry and wild berry flavors that carry through the crisp, slightly tannic finish. Drink now.–J.L. • $18 • (11/15/1998) • **84**
Cabernet Sauvignon Atlas Peak 1994 • $18 • (5/15/1998) • **75**
Cabernet Sauvignon Atlas Peak 1993 • $18 • (11/15/1996) • **87**
Cabernet Sauvignon Atlas Peak 1992 • $18 • (12/15/1995) • **89**
Cabernet Sauvignon Atlas Peak 1991 • $18 • (9/15/1995) • **86**
Cabernet Sauvignon Atlas Peak Consenso Vineyards 1996: Firm, with a core of mineral, tea and tart plum flavors, finishing with some rough, unripe edges. Slightly drying finish. Drink through 2004–J.L. • $30 • (10/15/1999) • **84**
Cabernet Sauvignon Atlas Peak Consenso Vineyards 1995: Dried cherry, leather, licorice and herbs lead the way in this oaky, lean-style wine. A bit rustic and finishes short. Drink through 2004 • $24 • (11/15/1998) • **82**
Cabernet Sauvignon Atlas Peak Consenso Vineyards 1994: Dull, with oak overriding the modest currant and cedar flavors. Never really shows its stuff. Tasted twice, with consistent notes.–J.L. • $22 • (9/30/1998) • **77**
Cabernet Sauvignon Atlas Peak Consenso 1993 • $22 • (11/15/1996) • **87**
Consenso Atlas Peak 1990 • $22 • (12/15/1995) • **87**
Consenso Atlas Peak 1989 • $22 • (3/31/1995) • **83**
Consenso Napa Valley 1990 • $22 • (11/15/1993) • **83**
Consenso Napa Valley 1989 • $22 • (3/31/1993) • **82**
Chardonnay Atlas Peak 1997: An elegant, understated style, with toasty, lemony flavors and tart pear notes built on a medium frame. Drink now.–J.L. • $16 • (7/31/1999) • **86**
Chardonnay Atlas Peak 1996 • $16 • (4/30/1998) • **86**
Chardonnay Atlas Peak 1995 • $16 • (3/31/1997) • **87**
Sangiovese Atlas Peak 1997: Muddled vegetal, leather and raspberry flavors struggle to find a focus.–J.L. • $16 • (5/15/2000) • **79**
Sangiovese Atlas Peak 1996: Marked by a dry, earthy edge, with appealing dried cherry, sage, wild berry and spice. Shows more complexity and finesse on the finish. Of medium weight. Drink now.–J.L. • $16 • (9/30/1998) • **84**
Sangiovese Atlas Peak 1995 • $16 • (5/15/1998) • **78**
Sangiovese Atlas Peak 1993 • $16 • (11/30/1995) • **84**
Sangiovese Atlas Peak 1992 • $16 • (2/28/1995) • **84**
Sangiovese Atlas Peak 1991 • $16 • (5/31/1994) • **83**
Sangiovese Atlas Peak Reserve 1997: Ripe and distinctive, with earthy cherry, wild berry, blackberry and spice. Complex aftertaste. Drink now through 2005.–J.L. • $30 • (1/31/2000) • **87**
Sangiovese Atlas Peak Reserve 1996: Quite spicy, with a firm core of bright cherry, anise, herb and subtle vanilla flavors. Finishes moderately, with tannins that are a bit coarse. Should smooth out in time. Drink now through 2005. • $30 • (2/28/1999) • **86**

Key: SS—Spectator Selection. CS—Cellar Selection. HR—Highly Recommended. $NA—Price not available. (BT)—Barrel tasting. Ⓐ—Auction Price. For a key to the tasters' initials, see "How to Use These Listings."
Dates in parentheses represent the issues in which the ratings were published.

Sangiovese Atlas Peak Reserve 1995: Smooth, ripe and polished, with appealing cherry, strawberry, plum and watermelon notes. Offers depth and complexity. Drink now.–J.L. • $24 • (9/30/1998) • **85**
Sangiovese Atlas Peak Reserve 1992 • $24 • (2/28/1995) • **88**
Sangiovese Napa Valley 1990 • $24 • (2/15/1993) • **85**
Sangiovese Napa Valley 1989 • $24 • (11/15/1991) • **86**
Sangiovese Napa Valley Reserve 1994 • $16 • (5/15/1997) • **87**

AU BON CLIMAT | CALIFORNIA

Aligoté California Mistral Vineyard 1996 • $12 • (3/31/1998) • **82**
Chardonnay Arroyo Grande Valley Talley Reserve 1997: A ripe, smooth and creamy Chardonnay, charming for its pretty pear, spice, fig and nutmeg flavors that are tightly focused and its flinty, pleasantly earthy aftertaste. Drink now through 2002.–J.L. • $25 • (6/30/1999) HR • **92**
Chardonnay Arroyo Grande Valley Talley Reserve 1996: Intense, with ripe, rich, creamy Chardonnay character, echoing pear, fig, melon and apple flavors. Long, complex aftertaste. Drink now through 2002 .–J.L. • $25 • (7/31/1998) • **92**
Chardonnay Arroyo Grande Valley Talley Vineyard Rincon 1998: Ripe and appealing for its up-front pear, apple and spicy citrus shadings, finishing with a touch of vanilla. Drink now through 2003.–J.L. • $25 • (6/30/2000) • **88**
Chardonnay Edna Valley Alban Vineyard 1997: Distinctive for its ripe core of juicy pineapple, pear, apricot and fig, with good intensity and richness. Drink now through 2002.–J.L. • $35 • (6/30/1999) • **92**
Chardonnay Edna Valley Alban Vineyard 1996 • $20 • (11/15/1997) • **90**
Chardonnay Santa Barbara County 1998: Tight and flinty, with spicy pear and nectarine notes, finishing with a twinge of green bitterness. Drink now through 2004.–J.L. • $18 • (1/31/2000) • **87**
Chardonnay Santa Barbara County 1997: Clean, ripe and fruity, with appealing fig, apricot, apple and melon notes that hold their focus on a long, fruity aftertaste. Drink now.–J.L. • $18 • (11/30/1998) • **88**
Chardonnay Santa Barbara County 1996 • $18 • (11/15/1997) • **88**
Chardonnay Santa Barbara County Le Bouge D'à côté 1996: Intense and a touch coarse, with nothing a little time in the bottle won't solve. The fruit flavors are ripe, complex and appealing, with earthy pear, spice and citrus notes. Drink now through 2001.–J.L. • $25 • (7/31/1998) • **88**
Chardonnay Santa Barbara County Nuits-Blanches 1996: Tight and flinty, with complex and concentrated pear, spice, cream and earthy citrus flavors. Deep and long. Drink now through 2002.–J.L. • $40 • (12/31/1998) • **90**
Chardonnay Santa Maria Valley Le Bouge D'à côté 1997: Tightly compact and richly flavored, with a focused core of tart pineapple, pear, apple and citrus. Finishes with a burst of energy and lots of richness. Drink now through 2002.–J.L. • $25 • (7/31/1999) • **92**
Chardonnay Santa Maria Valley Nuits-Blanches 1997: Smooth, ripe, rich and concentrated, with layers of fig, pineapple, spice, melon and apricot. Tightly focused, it's long and intricate on the finish. Drink now through 2005.–J.L. • $40 • (1/31/2000) • **91**
Chardonnay Santa Ynez Valley Sanford & Benedict Reserve 1996: Delicious, smooth, ripe and creamy, with pretty spice, nectarine, pear and fig flavors that are rich and concentrated, fanning out on the finish. Drink now through 2001.–J.L. • $35 • (11/30/1998) • **92**
Pinot Blanc Santa Barbara County Bien Nacido Reserve 1997: Smooth and rich, with a core of fig, grapefruit and melon. Turns tight and flinty on the finish, where the flavors linger. Drink now through 2002.–J.L. • $20 • (12/15/1998) • **89**
Pinot Blanc Santa Barbara County Bien Nacido Reserve 1996 • $20 • (2/28/1998) • **87**
Pinot Gris Santa Barbara County Bien Nacido Reserve 1997: Tight and flinty, with a core of citrus and spice, turning simpler on the finish. Drink now through 2001.–J.L. • $20 • (1/31/1999) • **86**
Pinot Noir Arroyo Grande Valley Picchο & Rincon 1996: Struggles to move into the fully ripened category, and as such is marked by cedary oak, blackberry, black cherry and spice. Drink through 2004–J.L. • $40 • (11/30/1998) • **87**
Pinot Noir Arroyo Grande Valley Rincon & Rosemary's 1997: Dark for the vintage, a touch spritzy, with blackberry, wild berry and raspberry flavors that turn quite tannic on the finish. Drink now through 2006.–J.L. • $40 • (8/31/1999) • **88**
Pinot Noir Arroyo Grande Valley Rincon & Rosemary's 1994 • $40 • (11/30/1996) • **90**
Pinot Noir Arroyo Grande Valley Rosemary's Talley Vineyard 1996: Lean and leathery, with hard-edged tannins. Best to wait in hopes the plum and berry flavors will appear. Best from 2000 through 2004.–J.L. • $50 • (12/15/1998) • **87**

Pinot Noir Arroyo Grande Valley Rosemary's Talley Vineyard 1993 • $40 • (12/31/1995) • **91**

Pinot Noir Arroyo Grande Valley Talley and Paragon Vineyards 1993 • $20 • (9/15/1995) • **87**

Pinot Noir Arroyo Grande Valley Talley Vineyard 1997: Firm and dark, with a compact, complex band of black cherry, dried berry, spice, plum and cedary oak. Give it time. Drink through 2006.–J.L. • $50 • (1/31/2000) • **91**

Pinot Noir California Isabelle 1997: Quite complex, with a supple range of dried cherry and wild berry flavors and tea, sage and cedary oak notes. Drink now through 2006.–J.L. • $50 • (1/31/2000) • **88**

Pinot Noir California Isabelle 1996: Ripe and spicy, with a smoky black cherry and wild berry core. Gains complexity on the finish, where it picks up hints of mushroom, anise, sage, tea and spice. Well-integrated tannins on the finish. Drink now through 2003.–J.L. • $50 • (11/30/1998) • **88**

Pinot Noir California Isabelle 1995 • $50 • (10/31/1997) • **88**

Pinot Noir California Isabelle 1994 • $50 • (12/31/1996) • **89**

Pinot Noir Central Coast 1995-96 • $18 • (8/31/1997) • **88**

Pinot Noir Central Coast Mistral Vineyard 1995 • $25 • (7/31/1997) • **90**

Pinot Noir Santa Barbara County 1989 • $16 • (9/30/1992) • **87**

Pinot Noir Santa Barbara County 1988 • $16 • (4/30/1991) • **80**

Pinot Noir Santa Barbara County 1987 • $16 • (12/15/1989) • **84**

Pinot Noir Santa Barbara County 1985 • $12 • (6/15/1988) • **73**

Pinot Noir Santa Barbara County La Bauge Au-dessus 1996: Starts out tight and earthy, but ripe cherry, loganberry and wild berry surface, giving added depth and dimension. Compact upon release; short-term cellaring should do the trick. Drink through 2002–J.L. • $25 • (9/30/1998) • **87**

Pinot Noir Santa Barbara County Bien Nacido Vineyard La Bauge 1995 • $30 • (8/31/1997) • **92**

Pinot Noir Santa Barbara County La Bauge Au-dessus 1994 • $25 • (2/28/1997) • **86**

Pinot Noir Santa Barbara County La Bauge Au-dessus Bien Nacido Vineyard 1993 • $25 • (9/15/1995) • **85**

Pinot Noir Santa Barbara County La Bauge Au-dessus Bien Nacido Vineyard 1991 • $25 • (2/28/1994) HR • **91**

Pinot Noir Santa Barbara County La Bauge Au-dessus Bien Nacido Vineyard 1990 • $30 • (2/28/1993) • **87**

Pinot Noir Santa Maria Valley 1997: Distinct for its sour cherry and tart wild berry flavors, this lighter, earthier style is best-suited for near-term consumption.–J.L. • $18 • (12/15/1998) • **84**

Pinot Noir Santa Maria Valley 1996 • $18 • (12/15/1997) • **84**

Pinot Noir Santa Maria Valley 1994 • $18 • (2/29/1996) • **88**

Pinot Noir Santa Maria Valley 1993 • $14 • (1/31/1995) • **86**

Pinot Noir Santa Maria Valley 1990 • $11 • (2/28/1993) • **86**

Pinot Noir Santa Maria Valley La Bauge Au-dessus 1997: Medium-weight, with attractive spice, black cherry, raspberry and strawberry notes, picking up hints of cola and herb. Mildly tannic. Drink now through 2004.–J.L. • $25 • (9/15/1999) • **87**

Pinot Noir Santa Maria Valley Rancho Vinedo Vineyard 1992 • $15 • (2/28/1994) • **86**

Pinot Noir Santa Maria Valley Rancho Vinedo Vineyard 1988 • $13 • (12/15/1989) • **83**

Pinot Noir Santa Ynez Valley 1989 • $30 • (9/30/1992) • **81**

Pinot Noir Santa Ynez Valley Benedict Vineyard 1987 • $30 • (12/15/1989) • **88**

Pinot Noir Santa Ynez Valley Sanford & Benedict Vineyard 1997: Tough and leathery, with glimpses of cherry, berry and spice that emerge to gain nuance and complexity on the finish. Needs a little time. Drink through 2005–J.L. • $35 • (8/31/1999) • **88**

Pinot Noir Santa Ynez Valley Sanford & Benedict Vineyard 1996: Delivers appealing earthy cherry and wild berry flavors—once you get past the firm, stemmy tannins. Needs time. Drink through 2006–J.L. • $35 • (12/15/1998) • **87**

Pinot Noir Santa Ynez Valley Sanford & Benedict Reserve 1995 • $35 • (10/31/1997) • **87**

Pinot Noir Santa Ynez Valley Sanford & Benedict Vineyard 1993 • $35 • (11/30/1996) • **89**

Pinot Noir Santa Ynez Valley Sanford & Benedict Vineyard 1991 • $35 • (2/28/1994) • **91**

AUDUBON | CALIFORNIA

Cabernet Sauvignon Napa Valley 1985 • $11 • (6/15/1988) • **77**

Zinfandel Amador County Picnic Hill Vineyard 1995 • $14 • (6/15/1998) • **70**

Zinfandel Sonoma County 1990 • $9 • (10/15/1992) • **81**

AURORA | OREGON

Pinot Noir Willamette Valley 1993 • $9 • (10/31/1995) • **85**

Pinot Noir Willamette Valley 1992 • $7 • (3/15/1994) • **79**

AUSTIN | CALIFORNIA

Pinot Noir Santa Barbara County 1993 • $14 • (2/29/1996) • **74**

Pinot Noir Santa Barbara County 1987 • $15 • (12/15/1989) • **77**

Pinot Noir Santa Barbara County 1983 • $25 • (12/15/1989) • **78**

Pinot Noir Santa Barbara County Artist Series 1988 • $10 • (12/15/1989) • **75**

Pinot Noir Santa Barbara County Bien Nacido Vineyard 1982 • $10 • (3/16/1985) • **88**

Pinot Noir Santa Barbara County Reserve 1991 • $16 • (2/28/1994) • **79**

Pinot Noir Santa Barbara County Sierra Madre Vineyards 1982 • $12 • (5/01/1984) • **87**

AUTUMN HILL | VIRGINIA

Cabernet Franc Monticello Flarepath Vineyard 1997: This soft red shows the berry and herb flavors typical of the varietal, with notes of chocolate and raisin that add a sweetness to the finish. Round and soft. Drink now through 2001.–T.M. • $15 • (12/15/1998) • **82**

Cabernet Franc Monticello Flarepath Vineyard 1995 • $12 • (4/30/1997) • **84**

Cabernet Sauvignon Monticello 1997: An incomplete red whose overt toasty, cedary oak flavors seem to overwhelm the light body and modest fruit. • $16 • (6/15/1999) • **77**

Cabernet Sauvignon Monticello 1995: This deeply colored red offers appealing black cherry flavors, but it's dominated by toasty, somewhat charred oak flavors and harsh tannins.–T.M. • $15 • (12/15/1998) • **79**

Chardonnay Monticello 1997: Starts off crisp and minerally, akin to Chablis, but the apple and butter notes broaden midpalate. It ends with firm acidity and a hint of spice. Drink now.–B.S. • $11 • (12/15/1998) • **82**

Chardonnay Monticello Barrel Select 1997: Offers some decent ripe pear and apple flavor, but it's a bit hollow in the middle.–K.M. • $13 • (5/31/1999) • **78**

Merlot Monticello 1997: This hints at black cherry and plum, but it's light and austere, with an astringent finish. Tasted twice, with consistent notes.–B.S. • $15 • (12/15/1998) • **75**

AUTUMN WIND | OREGON

Pinot Gris Yamhill County 1998: Light in texture, with a nice mineral note accenting the pear and melon character. Drink now.–H.S. • $15 • (12/31/1999) • **85**

Pinot Gris Yamhill County 1996 • $15 • (11/30/1997) • **88**

Pinot Noir Oregon 1995 • $10 • (12/15/1996) • **84**

Pinot Noir Oregon 1993 • $10 • (1/31/1996) • **80**

Pinot Noir Oregon 1992 • $10 • (11/30/1994) • **81**

Pinot Noir Oregon Reserve 1994 • $24 • (12/15/1996) • **88**

Pinot Noir Oregon Reserve 1993 • $20 • (1/31/1996) • **87**

Pinot Noir Oregon Reserve 1992 • $20 • (11/30/1994) • **80**

Pinot Noir Oregon Reserve 1990 • $20 • (1/31/1994) • **85**

Pinot Noir Oregon Reserve 1989 • $15 • (2/28/1993) • **73**

Pinot Noir Willamette Valley 1998: Supple in texture, on the light side, with pretty plum and floral flavors that mingle with a touch of mineral on the finish. Drink now through 2004.–H.S. • $20 • (4/30/2000) • **87**

Pinot Noir Willamette Valley 1997: Light in color and texture, with floral flavors and a hint of strawberry on the finish. Drink now.–H.S. • $20 • (4/30/1999) • **81**

Pinot Noir Willamette Valley 1996 • $15 • (5/15/1998) • **87**

Pinot Noir Willamette Valley 1988 • $12 • (4/15/1991) • **80**

Pinot Noir Willamette Valley 1987 • $15 • (2/15/1990) • **83**

Pinot Noir Yamhill County Estate Reserve 1997: Light and minty, with an herbal note at the center and light cherry notes on the finish. Drink through 2002–H.S. • $30 • (4/30/1999) • **83**

Pinot Noir Yamhill County Estate Reserve 1996 • $25 • (5/15/1998) • **90**

Pinot Noir Yamhill County Estate Reserve 1995 • $24 • (11/30/1997) • **80**

Sauvignon Blanc Oregon 1998: Ripe, round and spicy, with toast and honey overtones to the fig and pear flavors of this barrel-fermented white. Balanced and appealing from the start. Drink now through 2003.–H.S. • $12 • (3/31/2000) • **88**

Sauvignon Blanc Oregon 1997: Soft and round, with spicy oak flavors around a light core of pineapple and apple. Drink now.–H.S. • $12 • (6/30/1999) • **84**

AZALEA SPRINGS | CALIFORNIA

Merlot Napa Valley 1996: Firm in structure, with a complex range of ripe plum and earthy black cherry flavors that persist on the long finish. Tannins are firm but well integrated. Drink through 2005–J.L. • $30 • (9/15/1999) • **88**

Merlot Napa Valley 1995 • $30 • (3/31/1998) • **88**

Merlot Napa Valley 1994 • $24 • (5/15/1997) • **91**

Merlot Napa Valley 1992 • $22 • (12/15/1995) • **88**

Merlot Napa Valley 1991 • $22 • (9/15/1994) • **88**

BABCOCK | CALIFORNIA

Chardonnay Santa Barbara County 1997: Crisp and earthy at the outset, turning more complex with tangy nectarine, lemon-lime and other citrus flavors, holding its focus through the finish. Drink now through 2002.–J.L. • $18 • (12/15/1998) • **88**

Chardonnay Santa Barbara County Cuvée Lestat 1996: Smooth, rich and creamy, with pear, fig, honey, vanilla and spicy oak flavors that gain momentum and linger on the finish. Drink now.–J.L. • $35 • (12/15/1998) • **90**

Chardonnay Santa Barbara County Grand Cuvée 1998: Smooth, ripe and creamy, with rich floral, fig, tangering, nectarine and spicy notes, finishing in a long and complex aftertaste. Drink now through 2003.–J.L. • $35 • (6/30/2000) • **90**

Chardonnay Santa Barbara County Mt. Carmel Vineyard 1998: Ripe and full-bodied, with a range of tropical fruit, hints of guava and citrus, finishing with a subtle earthy note. Drink now through 2005.–J.L. • $35 • (6/30/2000) • **89**

Chardonnay Santa Maria Valley Bien Nacido Vineyard Block W Gravelly Vein 1996 • $30 • (5/31/1998) • **91**

Chardonnay Santa Ynez Valley Grand Cuvée 1997: Marked by distinctive earthy grapefruit and spice flavors before shifting focus to the fruit center. Once there, the earthy citrus builds into more pear and vanilla, adding complexity. Drink through 2004–J.L. • $30 • (6/30/1999) • **89**

Chardonnay Santa Ynez Valley Grand Cuvée 1996 • $30 • (6/30/1998) • **92**

Chardonnay Santa Ynez Valley Mt. Carmel Vineyard 1997: Fresh, snappy, a touch earthy and coarse, it needs a little time to soften, but the mineral and peach flavors are pure Santa Ynez Chardonnay. Drink through 2003–J.L. • $30 • (6/30/1999) • **88**

Chardonnay Santa Ynez Valley Mt. Carmel Vineyard 1996 • $30 • (6/30/1998) • **92**

Claret Santa Barbara County Cuvée Lestat 1996: Complex, with juicy cherry, plum and wild berry and a dash of cedary oak, but also some cellar-worthy tannins. A blend of Cabernet Franc, Cabernet Sauvignon and Merlot. Drink through 2006–J.L. • $35 • (1/31/1999) • **86**

Fathom Santa Barbara County 1997: Dark, rich and ripe, with noticeable oak flavors that quickly evolve into blackberry and spice notes. Polished on the finish. A blend of Cabernet Franc, Cabernet Sauvignon and Merlot. Drink now through 2003.–J.L. • $30 • (12/15/1999) • **87**

Pinot Gris Santa Barbara County 1996 • $15 • (5/15/1998) • **85**

Pinot Noir Santa Barbara County 1997: Marked by broad array of flavors, including spicy, earthy cola, wild berry, cherry and sage, this is a medium-bodied, crisp, trim style. Drink now through 2002.–J.L. • $22 • (12/15/1998) • **87**

Pinot Noir Santa Barbara County 1996 • $20 • (2/28/1998) • **86**

Pinot Noir Santa Barbara County 1995 • $30 • (12/31/1996) • **91**

Pinot Noir Santa Barbara County Bien Nacido Vineyard 1994 • $18 • (1/31/1996) • **84**

Pinot Noir Santa Barbara County Grand Cuvée 1998: Rich and concentrated, with a pretty array of dried black cherry, herb, tea and sage notes, turning dusty. Drink now through 2006.–J.L. • $50 • (6/30/2000) • **88**

Pinot Noir Santa Ynez Valley 1991 • $22 • (2/28/1993) • **79**

Pinot Noir Santa Ynez Valley Benedict Vineyard 1991 • $25/375 ml. • (2/28/1994) • **87**

Pinot Noir Santa Ynez Valley Casa Cassara Vineyard 1997: Rich, full-bodied and elegant, with a complex range of earthy mushroom, black cherry, cedar, spice and tar notes. Drink through 2005–J.L. • $30 • (9/15/1999) • **87**

Pinot Noir Santa Ynez Valley Estate Grown 1996 • $30 • (2/28/1998) • **90**

Pinot Noir Santa Ynez Valley Estate Grown 1993 • $30 • (12/31/1995) • **84**

Pinot Noir Santa Ynez Valley Estate Grown 1992 • $30 • (3/31/1995) • **85**

Key: SS—Spectator Selection. CS—Cellar Selection. HR—Highly Recommended. $NA—Price not available. (BT)—Barrel tasting. Ⓐ—Auction Price.
For a key to the tasters' initials, see "How to Use These Listings."
Dates in parentheses represent the issues in which the ratings were published.

Pinot Noir Santa Ynez Valley Grand Cuvée 1997: Dark and deceptively vibrant, with rich, complex, earthy cherry, berry and spice, a touch of leather and firm, tight tannins. Best to cellar short-term. Best from 2000 through 2007.–J.L. • $40 • (9/15/1999) • **90**

Pinot Noir Santa Ynez Valley Mt. Carmel Vineyard 1997: Tough, with a clayish, leathery edge to the dried cherry and berry, it slowly unfolds, but is quite reticent now. Best from 2001 through 2006.–J.L. • $35 • (9/15/1999) • **87**

Pinot Noir Santa Ynez Valley Sanford & Benedict Vineyard 1993 • $25 • (12/31/1995) • **83**

Pinot Noir Santa Ynez Valley Sanford & Benedict Vineyard 1992 • $25 • (11/30/1994) • **85**

Pinot Noir Santa Ynez Valley Selected Barrels Reserve 1989 • $35 • (2/28/1993) • **70**

Sangiovese Santa Ynez Valley Eleven Oaks 1997: Smooth and supple, with tasty plum, spice, currant and blackberry. Turns firm and complex on the finish, where creamy oak adds dimension. Drink now through 2004.–J.L. • $30 • (11/15/1999) • **88**

Sangiovese Santa Ynez Valley Eleven Oaks 1996: Complex, with pleasant cranberry, cherry and spice notes, picking up cedary oak and firm tannins on the finish. Drink now.–J.L. • $30 • (12/15/1998) • **86**

Sangiovese Santa Ynez Valley Eleven Oaks 1993 • $22 • (11/30/1995) • **85**

Sauvignon Blanc Santa Barbara County Eleven Oaks 1998: A racy style, with tart, expressive citrus, passion fruit and a touch of green kiwi that lingers. Braced by lively acidity. Drink now through 2005.–J.L. • $22 • (4/30/2000) • **86**

Sauvignon Blanc Santa Ynez Valley Eleven Oaks 1997: Quite tight, with a lemony core, this ultimately fans out nicely, serving up hints of grapefruit, almond, herbs and mineral. The finish is long and refreshing; the ensemble, refined. Drink now through 2002. • $22 • (5/15/1999) • **88**

Sauvignon Blanc Santa Ynez Valley Eleven Oaks 1996 • $20 • (3/31/1998) • **89**

Syrah Santa Barbara County Cuvée Lestat 1996: Dark, ripe and firmly tannic, with a core of fruit flavors built around spicy berry, mineral, leather and cedar. Tightens up on the finish, where the tannins make their presence known. Drink now through 2005.–J.L. • $35 • (11/30/1998) • **88**

Syrah Santa Barbara County Cuvée Lestat 1995 • $30 • (2/28/1997) • **85**

BACIO DIVINO | CALIFORNIA

Cabernet-Sangiovese-Petite Sirah-Merlot Napa Valley 1996: Delicious, ripe, rich and complex, with layers of juicy cherry, currant, blackberry, vanilla and spice. The long, intricate finish keeps pumping out the flavors. Drink now through 2007.–J.L. • $57 Ⓐ • (11/15/1999) • **94**

Cabernet-Sangiovese-Petite Sirah Napa Valley 1995: A curious mix of varietals, its up-front creamy, oak-driven currant and berry flavors are followed by chewy tannins. Hits a few rough spots on the finish but also shows pretty berry notes. Drink through 2006–J.L. • $72 Ⓐ • (10/31/1998) • **91**

BADGER MOUNTAIN | WASHINGTON

Cabernet Franc Columbia Valley 1997: Earthy, gamy notes add extra interest to this firm-textured wine. Finishes a bit short, but the flavors carry it. Drink now through 2002.–H.S. • $12 • (9/30/1999) • **84**

Cabernet Franc Columbia Valley 1994 • $12 • (9/30/1996) • **86**

Cabernet Franc Columbia Valley 1992 • $13 • (9/30/1994) • **84**

Cabernet Franc Columbia Valley Certified Organic Vineyard 1993 • $13 • (9/30/1995) • **85**

Cabernet Franc Columbia Valley Certified Organic Vineyard 1992 • $13 • (9/30/1995) • **85**

Cabernet Franc-Merlot Columbia Valley 1997: Pure, focused fruit shines through a thin veil of fine-textured tannins, offering blueberry, plum and hints of cola on the long, generous finish. Delicious. Drink through 2002.–H.S. • $12 • (8/31/1999) • **88**

Cabernet-Merlot Columbia Valley 1996: Open-textured, with plush, chewy tannins and a broad band of blueberry, currant and coffee flavors that slosh around on the generous finish. Approachable now. Drink through 2002–H.S. • $12 • (8/31/1998) • **86**

Cabernet-Merlot Columbia Valley 1995 • $12 • (9/15/1996) • **84**

Cabernet-Merlot Columbia Valley 1994 • $12 • (9/15/1996) • **85**

Chardonnay Columbia Valley 1997: Bright and fresh, with pretty apple and lime flavors that linger on the light, harmonious finish. Drink now through 2002.–H.S. • $9 • (6/30/1999) • **84**

Johannisberg Riesling Columbia Valley 1997: Raw-edged and off in flavor, leaning toward the brassy, leafy side instead of fruit.–H.S. • $7 • (9/15/1998) • **74**

Johannisberg Riesling Columbia Valley No Added Sulfites 1997: Fresh and soft, with appealing spice and apricot flavors on a light, airy frame. Drink now.–H.S. • $7 • (9/15/1998) • **82**
Merlot Columbia Valley 1997: Chewy tannins frame a modest range of blackberry and anise flavors that need time to soften. Best after 2000.–H.S. • $14 • (9/30/1999) • **83**
Merlot Columbia Valley 1995 • $14 • (12/31/1996) • **88**
Merlot Columbia Valley 1994 • $12 • (9/15/1996) • **85**
Mountain Blush Columbia Valley 1997: Very light coral in color, with varietal Gewürz aromas and flavors, finishing with a drying edge. Made from Gewürztraminer with some Cabernet Franc for color. Drink now.–H.S. • $7 • (9/30/1998) • **82**
Sevé White Columbia Valley 1997: Fresh and light, a nice mouthful of pear and citrus flavors. A blend: 40 percent Sémillon, 40 precent Chenin Blanc, 20 percent Gewürtraminer. Drink now.–H.S. • $7 • (9/15/1998) • **83**

BAILEYANA | CALIFORNIA

Chardonnay Edna Valley 1997: Refreshing, with ripe pineapple, pear and citrus flavors that remain focused and balanced on the finish. Drink now.–J.L. • $17 • (7/31/1999) • **87**
Chardonnay Edna Valley 1996: Rich, tropical fruit flavors, with sweet buttery notes. Intense yet lacking in finesse. Drink now. • $17 • (7/31/1998) • **82**
Chardonnay Monterey-San Luis Obispo Counties 1998: Offers vanilla, pear and oak notes of good richness. Drink now.–J.L. • $17 • (6/30/2000) • **84**
Pinot Noir Arroyo Grande Valley La Colline Vineyard 1997: Smooth and polished, with spicy, floral blackberry, black cherry, cola and anise flavors and a complex aftertaste. Drink now through 2006.–J.L. • $30 • (5/15/2000) • **87**
Pinot Noir Edna Valley 1996: Moderate depth and ripeness, with well-balanced cherry, cranberry, red currant and herb flavors that follow through on the firm finish. Drink through 2002–H.S. • $18 • (6/30/1999) • **86**
Pinot Noir Edna Valley Reserve 1997: Focused and flavorful, with a concentrated core of toasted oak, cherry and smoky wild berry flavors. Finishes with supple tannins. Best from 2000 through 2005.–J.L. • $30 • (9/15/1999) • **87**
Pinot Noir San Luis Obispo County 1998: Herbal, with some tart red currant flavors. Best from 2001 through 2003.–J.L. • $22 • (6/30/2000) • **82**
Sauvignon Blanc Edna Valley 1998: Round and a bit sweet-tasting, with a hint of citrus on the finish. Drink now.–J.L. • $12 • (5/15/2000) • **82**

BALCOM & MOE | WASHINGTON

Cabernet Sauvignon Washington 1996: Light and supple, with modest herb, mint and cherry flavors balancing nicely on the finish. Drink now through 2001.–H.S. • $19 • (9/30/1999) • **83**
Cabernet Sauvignon Washington 1994 • $14 • (9/15/1996) • **85**
Cabernet Sauvignon Washington 1992 • $14 • (9/30/1995) • **87**
Cabernet Sauvignon Washington 1991 • $14 • (9/30/1995) • **84**
Chardonnay Washington 1997: Tries to be fresh and fruity but misses, with a disconcerting tinny note and a coarse texture.–H.S. • $11 • (8/31/1999) • **77**
Merlot Washington 1997: Supple and generous, a pretty wine with spice-scented black cherry and herb flavors that linger gently on the finish. Drink now through 2002.–H.S. • $19 • (8/31/1999) • **87**
Merlot Washington 1994 • $14 • (9/15/1996) • **77**
Merlot Washington 1992 • $14 • (8/31/1995) • **87**

BALD MOUNTAIN | CALIFORNIA

Zinfandel Napa Valley 1992 • $11 • (10/15/1995) • **78**

BALLATORE | CALIFORNIA

Gran Spumante California NV • $7 • (12/15/1997) • **77**

BALLENTINE | CALIFORNIA

Cabernet Franc Napa Valley 1992 • $15 • (7/31/1995) • **82**
Merlot Napa Valley 1997: A touch woody and chunky, though the currant and blackberry flavors are pure and spicy on the finish, turning firm and charry. Best from 2001 through 2007.–J.L. • $20 • (5/15/2000) • **86**
Merlot Napa Valley 1995 • $18 • (4/30/1998) • **86**
Merlot Napa Valley 1994 • $18 • (7/31/1997) • **89**
Merlot Napa Valley 1992 • $18 • (7/31/1995) • **80**
Syrah Napa Valley 1997: Firm and full-bodied, with semisweet chocolate and cola notes that linger through the tannic finish. Best from 2001 through 2005.–J.L. • $22 • (5/15/2000) • **89**
Zinfandel Napa Valley 1997: Port-like and plummy, with leather and pepper notes. Drink now.–J.L. • $16 • (5/15/2000) • **82**
Zinfandel Napa Valley 1995 • $16 • (11/30/1997) • **88**
Zinfandel Napa Valley 1994 • $14 • (3/31/1997) • **88**
Zinfandel Napa Valley 1992 • $14 • (10/15/1995) • **85**

BANDIERA | CALIFORNIA

Cabernet Sauvignon California Coastal 1997: Pleasant, with soft grape, herb-tinged currant and cherry flavors. Easy drinking. Drink now.–J.L. • $9 • (10/15/1999) • **82**
Cabernet Sauvignon California Coastal 1996: Starts off with toasty coffee aromas, then feeds into a blend of herb and currant. Finishes a bit rough. Drink now. • $8 • (10/15/1998) • **80**
Cabernet Sauvignon California Coastal 1994 • $8 • (12/31/1996) • **82**
Cabernet Sauvignon Napa Valley 1993 • $8 • (11/30/1995) • **85**
Cabernet Sauvignon Napa Valley 1992 • $8 • (9/30/1995) • **83**
Cabernet Sauvignon Napa Valley 1991 • $7 • (9/30/1994) • **85**
Cabernet Sauvignon Napa Valley 1990 • $7 • (4/15/1994) • **87**
Cabernet Sauvignon Napa Valley 1989 • $7 • (10/31/1992) • **86**
Cabernet Sauvignon Napa Valley 1988 • $7 • (4/15/1992) • **80**
Cabernet Sauvignon Napa Valley Reserve 5 1995: A bit rustic, with ripe cassis and a vegetal core. Drink now. • $15 • (10/15/1998) • **78**
Cabernet Sauvignon Napa Valley Reserve 5 1993 • $12 • (11/30/1995) • **87**
Chardonnay California Coastal 1997: Pleasant, with straightforward pear, lemon and light earth flavors. Drink now.–H.S. • $8 • (11/30/1998) • **81**
Chardonnay California Coastal 1996 • $9 • (7/31/1997) • **86**
Merlot Napa Valley Reserve 1993 • $12 • (8/31/1996) • **77**
Sauvignon Blanc California Coastal 1997: Serves up modest pear and peach flavors; the finish is equally modest, though clean and refreshing. Drink now. • $7 • (2/28/1999) • **81**

BANNISTER | CALIFORNIA

Chardonnay Russian River Valley Porter-Bass Vineyards 1998: Oak notes dominate, with tangerine and apple flavors. Drink now.–J.L. • $28 • (6/15/2000) • **84**
Chardonnay Russian River Valley Porter-Bass Vineyard 1997: An initial earthy woodiness develops into a more mainstream core of spicy pear, apple and citrus. Turns complex on the finish. Drink now through 2002.–J.L. • $28 • (6/30/1999) • **89**
Chardonnay Russian River Valley Rochioli-Allen Vineyards 1998: Vanilla and oak overtones dominate, with tangerine and pear nuances. Drink now.–J.L. • $28 • (6/15/2000) • **86**
Chardonnay Russian River Valley Rochioli-Allen Vineyard 1997: Well balanced, with pretty pear, fig, apricot and apple flavors framed by pretty, smoky, toasty oak. Drink now through 2002.–J.L. • $28 • (6/30/1999) • **90**
Pinot Noir Anderson Valley Floodgate Vineyard 1996: Strives for delicacy and complexity, with a range of earth, spice, tea, cola and currant flavors. A touch of heat throws off the balance. Drink now.–J.L. • $24 • (12/31/1998) • **82**
Pinot Noir Anderson Valley Floodgate Vineyard 1995 • $20 • (8/31/1997) • **87**
Pinot Noir Russian River Valley 1995 • $20 • (8/31/1997) • **88**
Pinot Noir Russian River Valley 1994 • $18 • (5/31/1996) • **85**
Zinfandel Dry Creek Valley 1994 • $15 • (9/15/1996) • **85**
Zinfandel Dry Creek Valley 1992 • $12 • (1/31/1995) • **84**
Zinfandel Dry Creek Valley 1991 • $12 • (9/30/1993) • **83**
Zinfandel Dry Creek Valley Bradford Mountain Vineyard 1995 • $17 • (6/15/1998) • **85**
Zinfandel Dry Creek Valley Bradford Mountain Vineyard 1993 • $15 • (10/15/1995) • **86**
Zinfandel Russian River Valley Rochioli Vineyard 1994 • $18 • (4/30/1997) • **92**
Zinfandel Russian River Valley Rochioli Vineyard 1993 • $17 • (9/15/1996) • **85**

BARBOUR | CALIFORNIA

Cabernet Sauvignon Napa Valley 1996: Tight, with pretty oak shadings that lead to a core of ripe cherry, currant and blackberry flavor, this is a complex, concentrated wine that needs a few years of cellaring. Best from 2001 through 2007.–J.L. • $115 Ⓐ • (2/28/1999) • **91**
Cabernet Sauvignon Napa Valley 1995: Smooth and polished, with flavors tilting toward the herbal, cedary side of Cabernet, serving up currant, black cherry, anise and toasty oak notes. Finishes with round, supple tannins. Best from 2002 through 2010.–J.L. • $50 • (2/28/1999) • **92**

BARBOURSVILLE | VIRGINIA

Barbera Monticello Reserve 1997: A soft, berry-flavored red accented by a touch of earthiness, with a firm finish.–B.S. • $18 • (12/15/1998) • **79**

Brut Virginia NV: Effusive floral aromas and light flavors of banana and pear make this a pleasant but simple sparkler. • $15 • (11/15/1998) • **78**

Cabernet Franc Virginia 1997: This velvety red offers ripe, slightly candied flavors of cherry, plum and chocolate, with soft tannins and a sweet finish. Drink now.–T.M. • $19 • (5/31/2000) • **83**

Cabernet Franc Virginia 1996: This firm red show flavors of berry, cherry and herb, with vanilla notes that add a pleasant sweetness to the palate. The tannins are light but firm, making it a fine match for lighter dishes. Drink now through 2002.–T.M. • $15 • (12/15/1998) • **84**

Cabernet Franc Monticello 1995 • $15 • (4/30/1997) • **82**

Cabernet Franc Monticello 1993 • $12 • (12/31/1995) • **81**

Cabernet Sauvignon Monticello Reserve 1995: Mature in flavor, if still a bit tannic in texture, this medium-bodied red has cherry, herb and smoke flavors. • $20 • (11/15/1998) • **78**

Cabernet Sauvignon Monticello Reserve 1991 • $19 • (12/31/1995) • **80**

Cabernet Sauvignon Monticello Reserve 1983 • $15 • (2/29/1992) • **73**

Chardonnay Monticello 1997: There's good concentration in this lean yet enticing white. Vibrant acidity carries the apple and pear flavors to a moderate finish. Drink now.–B.S. • $12 • (12/15/1998) • **83**

Chardonnay Monticello Reserve 1998: Soft and ripe. Melon, pear and light herb flavors are lush, yet the wine retains a gentle delicacy, finishing with light vanilla and spice notes. Drink now.–T.M. • $15 • (5/31/2000) • **84**

Chardonnay Monticello Reserve 1997: Lovely aromas of toasty oak are well integrated with the apple and honey flavors and rich texture, all balanced by fresh acidity. It retains a sense of elegance, while the oak notes linger pleasantly. Drink now.–B.S. • $15 • (12/15/1998) • **86**

Dolcetto Monticello 1997: An attempt to put together tart, lean fruit flavors with buttery oak accents doesn't quite come off. • $20 • (10/31/1998) • **74**

Merlot Virginia 1998: This lively red from Virginia is jammy in aroma, with grapey and plummy flavors. Would make a good picnic wine; try it chilled. Drink now.–K.M. • $16 • (7/31/1999) • **82**

Octagon Monticello NV: A hearty, tannic red wine, with spicy, oaky accents and a good, firm texture but only modest fruit flavor. A blend of Merlot, Cabernet Sauvignon and Cabernet Franc. Drink now. • $22 • (10/31/1998) • **82**

Philéo Virginia NV: This lively, off-dry white offers well-defined Muscat flavors of orange, flowers and honey, with enough crisp acidity to balance the moderate sweetness. Brings you back for another sip. A blend of Muscat Canelli, Orange Muscat, Traminer, Riesling and Malvasia. Drink now.–T.M. • $16 • (12/15/1998) • **84**

Pinot Grigio Monticello 1997: Tart and simple, with modest green apple and lemon flavors. Finishes on an earthy note.–K.M. • $13 • (12/15/1998) • **75**

Pinot Noir Monticello 1993 • $12 • (5/31/1995) • **73**

Pinot Noir Monticello Reserve 1997: Good effort. Smoky and assertively flavored, with earth, berry and spice elements, this is an interesting Pinot Noir that's just shy on the fruit aspect to match the structure and oak treatment. Drink now.–B.S. • $25 • (6/15/1999) • **81**

Riesling Virginia 1998: Ripe and peachy, this dry white delivers plenty of appealing, straightforward Riesling character on a gentle, balanced framework. Finishes a little short. Drink now.–B.S. • $10 • (9/15/1999) • **83**

Sangiovese Monticello Reserve 1998: Soft and fruity, this gentle red shows lively cherry and berry flavors, with just enough tannin for grip. Drink now.–T.M. • $19 • (5/31/2000) • **83**

Sangiovese Monticello Reserve 1997: Light-bodied and lively, showing cherry and vanilla flavors and structured on the soft side. The aftertaste lingers. Drink now.–B.S. • $20 • (12/15/1998) • **81**

Traminer Aromatico Monticello Ivy Creek Vineyard 1997: Assertive, showing a soapy element to the floral and spice aromas and flavors typical of this varietal, in a light, crisp presentation.–B.S. • $15 • (12/15/1998) • **78**

Viognier Monticello Reserve 1998: A buttery white that tastes more like a Chardonnay blend, with pear and ripe apple flavors and a spicy aroma. Drink now.–K.M. • $18 • (10/15/1999) • **82**

Viognier Monticello Reserve 1997: An angular wine, with a buttery aroma and a resinous flavor. Ends on a toasty note.–K.M. • $16 • (12/15/1998) • **77**

Key: SS—Spectator Selection. CS—Cellar Selection. HR—Highly Recommended. $NA—Price not available. (BT)—Barrel tasting. Ⓐ—Auction Price.
For a key to the tasters' initials, see "How to Use These Listings."
Dates in parentheses represent the issues in which the ratings were published.

BAREFOOT | CALIFORNIA

Chenin Blanc California 1996 • $4 • (9/30/1997) • **72**

Sauvignon Blanc California NV • $5 • (7/31/1997) • **78**

White Zinfandel California NV • $6 • (9/15/1997) • **75**

Zinfandel California NV • $5 • (11/30/1996) • **77**

Bubbly California NV: Bright and fruity yet dry. Lacks the depth usually associated with bubbly. Drink now. • $8 • (11/30/1998) • **80**

BARGETTO, LAWRENCE J. | CALIFORNIA

Blanc de Noirs Santa Maria Valley 60th Anniversary 1933-1993 1991 • $11 • (12/31/1993) • **79**

Cabernet Sauvignon Central Coast Cyrpress 1991 • $9 • (11/15/1994) • **82**

Cabernet Sauvignon Napa Valley Komes Ranch 1988 • $15 • (11/15/1993) • **84**

Cabernet Sauvignon Santa Cruz Mountains Bates Ranch 1991 • $18 • (12/15/1996) • **79**

Cabernet Sauvignon Santa Cruz Mountains Bates Ranch 1990 • $16 • (12/15/1995) • **85**

Cabernet Sauvignon Santa Cruz Mountains Bates Ranch 1989 • $18 • (5/31/1995) • **77**

Cabernet Sauvignon Santa Cruz Mountains Bates Ranch 1988 • $15 • (11/15/1994) • **78**

Cabernet Sauvignon Santa Cruz Mountains Bates Ranch 1987 • $15 • (11/15/1993) • **83**

Cabernet Sauvignon Santa Cruz Mountains 1986 • $18 • (8/31/1992) • **84**

Chardonnay Central Coast 1997: Soft-textured, with pleasant citrus, lemon rind and mineral flavors. Drink now. • $10 • (2/28/1999) • **83**

Chardonnay Central Coast Cypress 1996 • $10 • (12/15/1997) • **85**

Chardonnay Santa Clara-Santa Cruz Counties Coastal Reserve 1996 • $15 • (3/31/1998) • **86**

Chardonnay Santa Cruz Mountains Regan Vineyard 1997: Lots of citrus flavors—lemon, mandarin orange and grapefruit. Firmly textured yet refreshing, serving up mineral and herb flavors on a long finish. Complex and quite tasty. Drink now through 2001. • $18 • (6/15/1999) • **88**

Chardonnay Santa Cruz Mountains Regan Vineyard 1996 • $18 • (12/15/1997) • **87**

Dolcetto Central Coast 1996 • $15 • (12/15/1997) • **85**

Dolcetto Central Coast 1995 • $15 • (12/31/1996) • **81**

Dolcetto Central Coast 1994 • $15 • (11/30/1996) • **79**

Gewürztraminer Monterey County 1996 • $11 • (7/31/1997) • **84**

Gewürztraminer Santa Cruz Mountains Dry 1996 • $12 • (6/15/1997) • **85**

Merlot California 1996: Soft and rich with a solid underlying structure. Hits most of the right notes, but a green streak detracts from the ripe plum and coffee flavors. Drink now.–H.S. • $18 • (9/15/1998) • **82**

Merlot California 1995 • $18 • (7/31/1997) • **79**

Merlot California 1994 • $17 • (8/31/1996) • **72**

Merlot California 1993 • $14 • (1/01/1996) • **78**

Merlot Central Coast 1989 • $13 • (12/31/1993) • **80**

Merlot San Ysidro 1992 • $14 • (6/15/1995) • **78**

Merlot Santa Cruz Mountains 1996: Licorice and oak seem to be the dominant characteristics of this austere wine. A hint of blackberry boosts the finish. Drink now through 2001. • $24 • (9/30/1998) • **82**

Pinot Grigio Central Coast 1996 • $15 • (9/15/1997) • **84**

Pinot Noir Carneros Madonna Vineyard 1985 • $13 • (9/15/1988) • **83**

Pinot Noir Central Coast Cypress 1989 • $10 • (9/30/1992) • **77**

Pinot Noir Santa Cruz Mountains 1994 • $20 • (3/31/1998) • **87**

Pinot Noir Santa Cruz Mountains 1993 • $18 • (11/30/1996) • **79**

Pinot Noir Santa Cruz Mountains 1992 • $23 • (12/31/1995) • **83**

Pinot Noir Santa Cruz Mountains 1989 • $15 • (2/28/1994) • **78**

Pinot Noir Santa Cruz Mountains Sessantesimo 1991 • $18 • (2/28/1994) • **87**

Pinot Noir Santa Maria Valley 1987 • $16 • (2/28/1991) • **81**

BARNETT | CALIFORNIA

Cabernet Sauvignon Napa Valley 1990 • $25 • (11/15/1993) • **83**

Cabernet Sauvignon Napa Valley 1989 • $18 • (11/15/1993) • **86**

Cabernet Sauvignon Spring Mountain 1997: Dark, rich and chocolaty, with ample black cherry, blackberry, pepper, sage and cedary oak all folding together. Turns quite tannic on the finish. Best from 2002 through 2012.–J.L. • $50 • (5/15/2000) • **90**

Cabernet Sauvignon Spring Mountain 1996: Intense, rich and marked by tannic, earthy currant flavors. The tannins bite down hard on the finish, so a little cellaring is advised. Best from 2001 through 2007.–J.L. • $45 • (4/30/1999) • **88**

Cabernet Sauvignon Spring Mountain 1993 • $32 • (8/31/1996) • **85**

Cabernet Sauvignon Spring Mountain 1992 • $32 • (5/31/1995) • **87**

Cabernet Sauvignon Spring Mountain District Rattlesnake Hill 1996: Dense, earthy and concentrated, with rich layers of currant, cedar, anise, mineral and sage, holding its focus and gaining depth and complexity. Has some tannins to shed. Best from 2001 through 2010.–J.L. • $60 • (4/30/1999) • **93**

Cabernet Sauvignon Spring Mountain Peacock Family Vineyard 1997: Very dark, rich and seductive, with chocolate-covered cherry, currant and plum notes that are plush and refined. Finishes with polished tannins. Best from 2002 through 2013.–J.L. • $60 • (5/15/2000) • **93**

Chardonnay Napa Valley-Carneros 1998: Dull, with gluey, green, unripe, herbal flavors. Napa Valley and Carneros (from Sonoma).–J.L. • $25 • (5/31/2000) • **78**

Chardonnay Napa Valley 1997: Openly spicy, with pretty ripe pear and apple flavors, picking up nutmeg, citrus and tangerine flavors that linger. Drink now through 2002.–J.L. • $25 • (5/15/1999) • **88**

Merlot Spring Mountain District 1997: Funky, with a tannic, mulchy edge to the potent spice flavors. Struggles to find a focus, even though it's dark and extracted. Best from 2001 through 2007.–J.L. • $30 • (5/15/2000) • **85**

Pinot Noir Santa Lucia Highlands 1998: Dark and a bit funky, with a mushroomy edge to the black cherry and wild berry flavors. Drink now through 2006.–J.L. • $25 • (5/15/2000) • **85**

Pinot Noir Santa Lucia Highlands 1997: Fairly exotic, tinged with cola, wild plum, cherry and herb flavors. Somewhat weighty on the palate, its flavors are deep yet also fan out nicely at present. Tannins are ripe and firm. Drink through 2004 • $25 • (9/15/1999) • **87**

Pinot Noir Santa Lucia Highlands 1996 • $20 • (1/31/1998) • **86**

Pinot Noir Carneros 1994 • $23 • (8/31/1996) • **80**

BARNWOOD | CALIFORNIA

Cabernet Sauvignon Santa Barbara County 1997: A blend of black cherry, cassis, herb, plum and licorice flavors supported by firm-textured tannins. Finishes harmoniously. Drink now through 2003. • $18 • (9/15/1999) • **84**

Cabernet Sauvignon Santa Barbara County 1996: A bit tart at first, it features bright cherry, vanilla and herb notes on a firm, tannic base. Moderate finish. Drink now. • $15 • (6/15/1999) • **85**

Merlot Santa Barbara County 1997: Pretty lean on the palate, with charry oak, anise and blackberry notes. Finishes dry. Drink now through 2003. • $18 • (10/15/1999) • **83**

Merlot Santa Barbara County Reserve 1997: Fairly smooth, with pretty berry and cherry notes. Tannins are ripe, though the texture is lean. Finishes long, with blackberry, spice and herb notes. Drink now through 2004. • $27 • (10/15/1999) • **86**

Merlot-Cabernet-Syrah Santa Barbara County Trio 1997: Licorice, blackberry and herb make an interesting blend in this lean-textured wine. Finishes a bit short, with rustic tannins. Drink now through 2004. • $NA • (11/15/1999) • **86**

Sauvignon Blanc Santa Barbara County 1998: Tart and appley, offering lean flavors. Drink now.–J.L. • $13 • (5/15/2000) • **80**

Sauvignon Blanc Santa Barbara County 1997: Firmly styled, with a core of citrus and herb flavors, this is a bit tight but nonetheless well made and refreshing. A tangy edge on the finish cries out for seafood. Drink now. • $10 • (5/15/1999) • **85**

BARON HERZOG | CALIFORNIA

Cabernet Sauvignon California 1997: Quite young and grapey, with soft tannins and hints of blackberry and herbs. A quaffer. Kosher. Drink now through 2002. • $13 • (10/15/1999) • **84**

Cabernet Sauvignon California 1996: Fairly soft, with pleasant grape, cherry and herb flavors and hints of vanilla oak. Finishes slightly bitter. Drink through 2003. • $13 • (2/28/1999) • **83**

Cabernet Sauvignon California 1994 • $13 • (11/30/1996) • **76**

Cabernet Sauvignon California 1992 • $9 • (12/31/1994) • **86**

Cabernet Sauvignon California Selection 1990 • $11 • (6/15/1993) • **75**

Cabernet Sauvignon Sonoma County 1989 • $11 • (3/31/1991) • **73**

Cabernet Sauvignon Sonoma County Special Reserve 1986 • $16 • (3/31/1991) • **74**

Chardonnay California 1997: Toasty oak, bright lemon and apple flavors turn creamy on the finish. Drink now.–J.L. • $13 • (7/31/1999) • **82**

Chardonnay California 1996 • $11 • (2/28/1998) • **84**

Chenin Blanc Clarksburg 1998: Quite fragrant, with floral and peach notes at the fore, this lovely white from California serves up attractive tangy acidity and citrus flavors to balance its fruity character, and an attractive price to balance your wine budget. Kosher. Drink now. • $7 • (10/15/1999) • **85**

Chenin Blanc Clarksburg 1997: Smooth, spicy and exotic. Sweet and lush, with tropical fruit and honey flavors. Drink now.–H.S. • $7 • (12/15/1998) • **85**

Chenin Blanc Clarksburg 1996 • $7 • (9/30/1997) • **80**

Johannisberg Riesling California Late Harvest 1989 • $8/375 ml. • (3/31/1991) • **86**

Sauvignon Blanc California 1998: A blend of peach, citrus, mineral and herb flavors couched in mild acidity. It's clean and fresh, fine for quaffing. Kosher. Drink now. • $9 • (8/31/1999) • **83**

Sauvignon Blanc California 1997: Fairly herbal and grassy, along with a bit of grapefruit and melon on the palate and the finish. Drink now. • $8 • (9/15/1998) • **81**

Sauvignon Blanc Shenandoah Valley 1996 • $9 • (10/15/1997) • **84**

Zinfandel California 1996: Focused on a nutty, oaky core with ripe cherry and spice flavors that focus on the finish, which turns gamy and tart. Drink now.–J.L. • $13 • (11/30/1998) • **81**

Zinfandel Lodi Old Vine 1998: Shows good depth to the chocolate, leather and black cherry flavors. Kosher. Drink now through 2004.–J.L. • $13 • (6/15/2000) • **85**

Zinfandel Lodi Old Vine 1997: Pleasant, with focused smoky plum and toasted oak flavors on a firm frame. Drink now.–J.L. • $13 • (6/15/1999) • **83**

Zinfandel Sonoma County Special Cuvée 1990 • $10 • (3/31/1993) • **86**

BARTHOLOMEW PARK | CALIFORNIA

Cabernet Sauvignon Sonoma Valley Alta Vista Vineyard 1995: Mineral, herb, tea flavors dominate. Pretty tight now, but might open with bottle time. Finishes a bit dry. Drink now through 2001. • $30 • (11/15/1998) • **80**

Cabernet Sauvignon Sonoma Valley Alta Vista Vineyard 1994 • $18 • (10/31/1997) • **86**

Cabernet Sauvignon Sonoma Valley Desnudos Vineyard 1995: An herbal style that nonetheless offers some pretty mint, coffee and cassis notes. Drink now through 2001. • $35 • (11/15/1998) • **82**

Cabernet Sauvignon Sonoma Valley Desnudos Vineyard 1994 • $20 • (10/31/1997) • **88**

Chardonnay Sonoma Valley Weiler Vineyard 1996 • $16 • (5/15/1998) • **81**

Merlot Sonoma Valley Alta Vista Vineyard 1995 • $18 • (3/31/1998) • **84**

Merlot Sonoma Valley Desnudos Vineyard 1995: Ripe and concentrated, but there is a layer of charred oak and herbal notes that overwhelm the mineral and black cherry flavors. Drink now.–J.L. • $30 • (10/15/1998) • **78**

Merlot Sonoma Valley Estate Vineyards 1995: Concentrated, showing layers of mineral, herb and black cherry. A minty note lingers on the lean finish. Drink now.–J.L. • $32 • (10/15/1998) • **83**

Merlot Sonoma Valley Weiler Vineyard 1995: Concentrated flavors of mineral and black cherry are marred by an herbal note. Tannic finish. Drink now.–J.L. • $25 • (10/15/1998) • **77**

Pinot Noir Sonoma Valley Estate Vineyards 1996: Rich strawberry flavors with traces of tea and herb soften on the fleshy, slightly hot finish. Lacks focus. Drink now.–J.L. • $23 • (8/31/1998) • **81**

Pinot Noir Sonoma Valley Estate Vineyards 1995 • $17 • (1/31/1998) • **87**

BATTAGLINI | CALIFORNIA

Zinfandel Russian River Valley Twin Pines 1997: Tangy, with chocolate, black cherry and raisin notes that show good intensity. Drink now through 2003.–J.L. • $22 • (6/15/2000) • **86**

Zinfandel Russian River Valley Twin Pines 1994 • $15 • (6/15/1998) • **81**

BAYLISS & FORTUNE | CALIFORNIA

Chardonnay Monterey County 1997: Tastes a touch sweet and manipulated, but the ripe pear and spicy, cedary oak flavors merit attention. Drink now.–J.L. • $12 • (2/28/1999) • **83**

Merlot Monterey County 1997: A modest range of ripe cherry flavors shuts down on a dry finish. Drink now through 2002.–J.L. • $13 • (2/28/1999) • **80**

Zinfandel Mendocino County 1998: Concentrated flavors of chocolate, ripe strawberry and currant and a twinge of smokiness linger nicely. Drink now through 2004.–J.L. • $13 • (5/31/2000) • **87**

Zinfandel Mendocino County 1997: A bright, cherry-flavored wine backed by hints of spice and herbs. Smooth and light-textured, it's made for quaffing. Drink now. • $13 • (2/28/1999) • **84**

BAYSTONE | CALIFORNIA

Chardonnay Russian River Valley 1998: Spicy oak dominates, with pear and apple notes. Drink now.–J.L. • $20 • (6/15/2000) • **81**

BAYVIEW CELLARS | CALIFORNIA

Cabernet Sauvignon Napa Valley 1992 • $16 • (9/15/1996) • **87**
Cabernet Sauvignon Napa Valley 1991 • $12 • (5/31/1995) • **83**
Charbono Napa Valley 1993: Restrained, with a hint of sage and blackberry. Moderately dry and powdery on the finish. Drink now through 2002. • $16 • (2/28/1999) • **81**
Charbono Napa Valley 1992 • $14 • (11/15/1995) • **86**
Merlot Napa Valley 1992 • $14 • (6/15/1996) • **82**
Sauvignon Blanc Napa Valley 1997: Somewhat understated for Napa Valley. This wine has firm, bright acidity and pretty grapefruit and mineral flavors. Could use more depth and focus. Drink now. • $14 • (3/31/1999) • **83**

BEAR CREEK | OREGON

Merlot Rogue Valley 1997: Firm and chewy, with a smoky ash note harmonizing with modest berry flavors. Best from 2001 through 2004.–H.S. • $30 • (5/15/2000) • **86**
Pinot Noir Rogue Valley 1997: Open-textured and appealing for its core of blackberry and currant flavor that echoes on the finish. Drink now through 2002.–H.S. • $30 • (4/30/2000) • **85**
Sauvignon Blanc Rogue Valley 1998: Smooth, polished and silky, with pretty floral, herb and fresh apple flavors that sail smoothly through the finish. Drink now.–H.S. • $15 • (5/15/2000) • **87**

BEARBOAT | CALIFORNIA

Chardonnay Russian River Valley 1996: Crisp and clean, with flinty pear, citrus and cream notes. Flavors of toasted oak and spice emerge on the finish. Drink now through 2001.–J.L. • $13 • (5/15/1999) • **86**
Pinot Noir Russian River Valley 1996: Light in weight, with herb, cherry and tea flavors and a dry finish.–J.L. • $17 • (6/30/1999) • **79**
Pinot Noir Russian River Valley 1995 • $25 • (2/28/1998) • **84**
Pinot Noir Russian River Valley 1994 • $NA • (1/01/1997) • **86**
Pinot Noir Russian River Valley 1992 • $16 • (3/31/1995) • **77**

BEAUCANON | CALIFORNIA

Cabernet Sauvignon Napa Valley 1992 • $12 • (11/30/1996) • **78**
Cabernet Sauvignon Napa Valley 1991 • $12 • (12/15/1995) • **79**
Cabernet Sauvignon Napa Valley 1990 • $11 • (2/28/1995) • **86**
Cabernet Sauvignon Napa Valley 1988 • $12 • (12/15/1992) • **70**
Cabernet Sauvignon Napa Valley 1986 • $15 • (12/31/1988) • **85**
Cabernet Sauvignon Napa Valley Jacques de Coninck 1996: Shows complexity, with well-focused layers of mineral, cedar, currant and leather flavors that hold through the long finish. A marked improvement over previous efforts. Drink now through 2006 .–J.L. • $55 • (10/15/1999) • **88**
Cabernet Sauvignon Napa Valley Reserve 1996: Firmly structured, with a range of currant, cedar and clay flavors. Tannins are tight but well integrated. Drink now through 2004.–J.L. • $14 • (10/15/1999) • **85**
Chardonnay Napa Valley Jacques de Coninck 1996 • $28 • (5/15/1998) • **89**
Chardonnay Napa Valley Reserve 1996 • $12 • (5/31/1998) • **84**
Merlot Napa Valley 1994 • $14 • (8/31/1996) • **79**
Merlot Napa Valley 1993 • $14 • (8/31/1996) • **81**
Merlot Napa Valley 1991 • $12 • (2/28/1995) • **77**
Merlot Napa Valley 1990 • $13 • (7/15/1993) • **81**
Merlot Napa Valley 1989 • $10 • (5/31/1992) • **73**
Merlot Napa Valley 1988 • $13 • (3/31/1991) • **84**
Merlot Napa Valley 1986 • $13 • (12/31/1988) • **78**
Merlot Napa Valley Reserve 1996: Simple, with drying tea and cherry notes. Somewhat vegetal at the end. • $15 • (10/15/1999) • **78**

BEAULIEU VINEYARD | CALIFORNIA

Beauzeaux California Signet Collection 1996: Plenty of ripe, plush, tender fruit flavors, with plum, black cherry, wild berry and spice, all supple and polished. Shows a lot of substance and depth. Zinfandel blend. Drink now through 2002.–J.L. • $16 • (9/30/1998) • **86**

Key: SS—Spectator Selection. CS—Cellar Selection. HR—Highly Recommended. $NA—Price not available. (BT)—Barrel tasting. Ⓐ—Auction Price. For a key to the tasters' initials, see "How to Use These Listings." **Dates in parentheses represent the issues in which the ratings were published.**

Beauzeaux Napa Valley Winemaker's Collection 1998: Serves up a pleasant band of dusty blackberry and wild berry before turning dry and tannic. Drink now through 2004.–J.L. • $20 • (5/31/2000) • **82**
Cabernet Sauvignon California Coastal 1997: Herbal, with a short range of black cherry and smoky oak flavors, turning crisp. Drink now.–J.L. • $12 • (8/31/1999) • **82**
Cabernet Sauvignon California Coastal 1995: A gentle sort of Cabernet, with modest tannins and a supple frame, spotlighting pretty, dark raspberry and root beer flavors, and hints of smoke on the finish. Quite a nice offering for so few dollars. Drink now.–H.S. • $9 • (10/31/1998) • **84**
Cabernet Sauvignon Napa Valley 1994 • $15 • (7/31/1997) • **85**
Cabernet Sauvignon Napa Valley Beautour 1994 • $11 • (10/15/1997) • **87**
Cabernet Sauvignon Napa Valley Beautour 1991 • $9 • (9/30/1994) • **82**
Cabernet Sauvignon Napa Valley Beautour 1990 • $8 • (11/15/1993) • **80**
Cabernet Sauvignon Napa Valley Beautour 1988 • $7 • (9/30/1990) • **79**
Cabernet Sauvignon Napa Valley Claret Special Release 1990 • $NA • (11/15/1992) • **79**
Cabernet Sauvignon Napa Valley Georges de Latour Private Reserve 1998: Complex and polished, with tightly focused currant, plum and berryish flavors, turning tannic.–J.L. • $NA • (8/31/1999) (BT) • **90-94**
Cabernet Sauvignon Napa Valley Georges de Latour Private Reserve 1996: Ripe, round and smooth, with a core of coffee, currant, sage, cedar and spice. Gains nuance and complexity on the finish, where the tannins are firm and integrated. Wonderful texture and polish. Drink now through 2008.–J.L. • $75 • (11/15/1999) • **92**
Cabernet Sauvignon Napa Valley Georges de Latour Private Reserve 1995: Complex and elegant, with ripe, round, plush, currant, cherry, berry and spice flavors, and a long, rich finish that gains nuances of ceder, anise, tobacco and mineral. Echoes toasty, spicy, vanilla-tinged oak on the aftertaste. Impressive finesse and polish.–J.L. • $70 • (10/31/1998) CS • **93**
Cabernet Sauvignon Napa Valley Georges de Latour Private Reserve 1994 • $62 Ⓐ • (10/15/1997) CS • **93**
Cabernet Sauvignon Napa Valley Georges de Latour Private Reserve 1993 • $46 Ⓐ • (11/15/1995) CS • **91**
Cabernet Sauvignon Napa Valley Georges de Latour Private Reserve 1992 • $35 Ⓐ • (12/15/1995) • **89**
Cabernet Sauvignon Napa Valley Georges de Latour Private Reserve 1991 • $51 Ⓐ • (12/15/1995) • **90**
Cabernet Sauvignon Napa Valley Georges de Latour Private Reserve 1990: A chunky and compacted Cabernet, with currant, mint and dark chocolate. Full-bodied, with chewy tannins and a long, fruity finish. Very ripe and rich. Tight and still closed. (Georges de Latour Private Reserve vertical tasting dated, as are all notes dated 2/29/00). Best after 2001.–J.S. • $60 Ⓐ • (2/29/2000) • **90**
Cabernet Sauvignon Napa Valley Georges de Latour Private Reserve 1989: Never very exciting, it's mature-tasting now, a touch earthy, herbal and diluted, with modest murky currant flavors. (1989 California Cabernet retrospective tasting).–J.L. • $28 • (8/31/1999) • **80**
Cabernet Sauvignon Napa Valley Georges de Latour Private Reserve 1988: A simple, moderately interesting BV, with a trim band of cedary currant, herb, anise and dried cherry; turns dry on the finish and, like many 1988s, may dry out soon. (1988 California Cabernet retrospective tasting). Drink now through 2001.–J.L. • $37 • (11/15/1998) • **84**
Cabernet Sauvignon Napa Valley Georges de Latour Private Reserve 1985: Superb BV. Dark, with lovely mint, berry, currant and eucalyptus character. Full-bodied and chewy, with a solid tannin structure and a long, minty dark chocolate aftertaste. Best after 2003.–J.S. • $70 Ⓐ • (2/29/2000) • **95**
Cabernet Sauvignon Napa Valley Georges de Latour Private Reserve 1984: Ripe and meaty, with loads of character. Full-bodied, with velvety tannins and a long, chewy finish. Still needs time to mellow, but very impressive. Best after 2001.–J.S. • $56 Ⓐ • (2/29/2000) • **91**
Cabernet Sauvignon Napa Valley Georges de Latour Private Reserve 1983: Delicious, with currant, plum and berry character. Medium-bodied, with well-integrated tannins and a short finish. Drying out. Drink now.–J.S. • $34 Ⓐ • (2/29/2000) • **84**
Cabernet Sauvignon Napa Valley Georges de Latour Private Reserve 1982: A bit herbal, with plum and dried fruit aromas. Full-bodied and chewy. Slightly rustic but impressive. Drink now.–J.S. • $47 Ⓐ • (2/29/2000) • **88**
Cabernet Sauvignon Napa Valley Georges de Latour Private Reserve 1981: Smells like iodine, peat and plums. Medium-bodied, with high acidity and raisin character. On the way down.–J.S. • $46 Ⓐ • (2/29/2000) • **78**
Cabernet Sauvignon Napa Valley Georges de Latour Private Reserve 1980: I expected a little more, but it's very good. A bit of a paradox—obviously ripe but with a slightly herbal note. Full-bodied, with velvety tannins and a solid, tight finish. Will still improve.–J.S. • $53 Ⓐ • (2/29/2000) • **89**

Cabernet Sauvignon Napa Valley Georges de Latour Private Reserve 1979: Much more mature-tasting and less compelling than it normally shows. Modest and mature cedar, dried plum and cherry lose intensity and richness on the finish. (1979 California Cabernet retrospective tasting). Drink now.–J.L. • $42 Ⓐ • (8/31/1999) • **86**

Cabernet Sauvignon Napa Valley Georges de Latour Private Reserve 1977: Chunky, well structured and better than expected. Excellent dark red color, with aromas of plum, cassis and berry and hints of wet earth. Full-bodied, with chewy tannins and a long, long finish. Still tight; needs time. Not at all dried out. Best from 2001 through 2006.–J.S. • $39 Ⓐ • (2/29/2000) • **90**

Cabernet Sauvignon Napa Valley Georges de Latour Private Reserve 1976: Rich, thick and Port-like, with tobacco, berry and raisin aromas and flavors. Full-bodied, with velvety tannins and an oily, fruity texture. Slightly monolithic. Drink now.–J.S. • $105 Ⓐ • (2/29/2000) • **87**

Cabernet Sauvignon Napa Valley Georges de Latour Private Reserve 1975: Has seen better days. Good dark garnet color, with aromas of raisin, asphalt and petrol. Medium- to full-bodied and chewy, but drying tannins and a slightly acidic, unclean and austere finish detracts from the overall quality.–J.S. • $38 Ⓐ • (2/29/2000) • **79**

Cabernet Sauvignon Napa Valley Georges de Latour Private Reserve 1974: A serious, chunky wine, but perhaps not up to its lofty reputation. Very good dark red, brick color, with fresh plum, milk chocolate and mint and hints of raisin. Medium- to full-bodied, with velvety tannins and a medium ripe fruit finish. Slightly dry and volatile. Drink now.–J.S. • $56 Ⓐ • (2/29/2000) • **87**

Cabernet Sauvignon Napa Valley Georges de Latour Private Reserve 1973: Barely alive, with herb and tea character and a dry, acidic finish.–J.S. • $36 Ⓐ • (2/29/2000) • **76**

Cabernet Sauvignon Napa Valley Georges de Latour Private Reserve 1963: A ghost of a wine, with ripe fruit character, but oxidized and tired. Brown sugar and Sherry flavors.–J.S. • $NA • (2/29/2000) • **75**

Cabernet Sauvignon Napa Valley Georges de Latour Private Reserve 1962: Tastes like an old Sherry, with cedar, popcorn and dried fruit character. Almost history.–J.S. • $NA • (2/29/2000) • **74**

Cabernet Sauvignon Napa Valley Georges de Latour Private Reserve 1961: Medium amber red in color. Drying out a bit, but with good berry, tobacco and mushroom character. Light finish. Drink now.–J.S. • $121 Ⓐ • (2/29/2000) • **82**

Cabernet Sauvignon Napa Valley Georges de Latour Private Reserve 1960: A lovely, soft, fruity wine. Medium-bodied, with rounded tannins and a delicious chocolate, berry and cream aftertaste. Drink now.–J.S. • $NA • (2/29/2000) • **87**

Cabernet Sauvignon Napa Valley Georges de Latour Private Reserve 1959: A bit musty and mushroomy, but with good berry, cherry and tobacco character. Medium-bodied, with dusty, chewy tannins. Starting to dry a bit. Drink now.–J.S. • $288 Ⓐ • (2/29/2000) • **86**

Cabernet Sauvignon Napa Valley Georges de Latour Private Reserve 1958: This big, Port-like wine is a blockbuster that betters the '51. Dark brick red with a ruby center, it has intense aromas of blackberry, tobacco and plum and hints of cigar box. Full-bodied and very ripe, with masses of chewy tannins and a long, long ripe fruit finish. Very smooth, thick and delicious. Drink now.–J.S. • $487 Ⓐ • (2/29/2000) • **97**

Cabernet Sauvignon Napa Valley Georges de Latour Private Reserve 1957: On the decline. Medium dark brick red, with an amber hue. Plums have hints of rhubarb and mineral. Medium-bodied, with elevated acidity and a crisp finish. A bit tart and thin, drying out a bit.–J.S. • $NA • (2/29/2000) • **79**

Cabernet Sauvignon Napa Valley Georges de Latour Private Reserve 1956: A bit earthy but holding on. Medium garnet red in color, with aromas of cedar, plum and tobacco and hints of redwood. Medium-bodied, with medium tannins and a tobacco, herb, berry and dust aftertaste. Drink now.–J.S. • $NA • (2/29/2000) • **84**

Cabernet Sauvignon Napa Valley Georges de Latour Private Reserve 1955: Very delicate, clean and fresh. Medium-bodied, with light to medium silky tannins and a berry, plum and tobacco aftertaste. Drink now.–J.S. • $259 Ⓐ • (2/29/2000) • **88**

Cabernet Sauvignon Napa Valley Georges de Latour Private Reserve 1954: A bit light but holding its own, with ripe fruit yet slightly oxidized. Aromas of orange, berry and leather. Medium-bodied, with fresh acidity, light tannins and a lively finish. Drink now.–J.S. • $NA • (2/29/2000) • **86**

Cabernet Sauvignon Napa Valley Georges de Latour Private Reserve 1953: Wonderful freshness, with currant, plum, game and berry character throughout. Medium-bodied, with well-integrated and velvety tannins. Long finish of berry, tobacco and cherry. A gorgeous, mellow wine. Drink now.–J.S. • $NA • (2/29/2000) • **91**

Cabernet Sauvignon Napa Valley Georges de Latour Private Reserve 1952: Very claretlike and graceful, with berry, tobacco, malt and cherry aromas and flavors. Medium-bodied, with well-integrated tannins and a fresh, lively finish, this harmonious old wine has good sweetness of fruit. Drink now.–J.S. • $NA • (2/29/2000) • **90**

Cabernet Sauvignon Napa Valley Georges de Latour Private Reserve 1951: Rich, youthful and complex. The prototype of the California blockbuster and long considered a classic, with lovely aromas of cassis, blackberry, mint and dark chocolate. Full-bodied and very chunky, with loads of fruit and a medium finish. Will age for decades more. Drink now.–J.S. • $1,466 • (2/29/2000) • **96**

Cabernet Sauvignon Napa Valley Georges de Latour Private Reserve 1950: A gamy, oily, mushroomy, earthy, funky red. Medium-bodied, with soft tannins and a buttery, oxidized finish. It's seen better days.–J.S. • $NA • (2/29/2000) • **79**

Cabernet Sauvignon Napa Valley Georges de Latour Private Reserve 1949: Impressive and well structured, with a good dark color and lovely mint, berry, plum and chocolate aromas and flavors. Full-bodied and velvety, with lots of ripe fruit (almost raisiny in character) and a long, fruity finish. Drink now.–J.S. • $NA • (2/29/2000) • **93**

Cabernet Sauvignon Napa Valley Georges de Latour Private Reserve 1948: This is history. Looks and tastes like day-old coffee grinds. Past its prime.–J.S. • $NA • (2/29/2000) • **50**

Cabernet Sauvignon Napa Valley Georges de Latour Private Reserve 1947: A very enjoyable old wine. Dark, with aromas of cherry, mint and spice that follow through to a medium-bodied palate. Slightly diluted midpalate, with herbal character throughout. Velvety tannins, a bit of volatile acidity and a long, fruity finish. Drink now.–J.S. • $NA • (2/29/2000) • **87**

Cabernet Sauvignon Napa Valley Georges de Latour Private Reserve 1946: Slightly one-dimensional but impressively fresh and clean. Great elegance. Clear and medium dark red, with an amber and brick edge. Pretty dried cherry and light vanilla aromas. Medium-bodied, with firm tannins and a fresh finish hinting of mint. Drink now.–J.S. • $NA • (2/29/2000) • **90**

Cabernet Sauvignon Napa Valley Georges de Latour Private Reserve 1945: A superb old wine. Dark red with a amber edge. Complex aromas of blackberry, mint and chocolate. Full-bodied and extremely well knit, with silky tannins and a long aftertaste. Harmonious. Drink now.–J.S. • $NA • (2/29/2000) • **94**

Cabernet Sauvignon Napa Valley Georges de Latour Private Reserve 1943: Promises more freshness on the nose than it delivers on the palate, but very good. Dark red, with wonderful cassis, berry and cherry aromas. Rather Port-like, full-bodied and chewy, with a slightly raised volatile acidity and maderized character on the aftertaste. Drink now.–J.S. • $NA • (2/29/2000) • **88**

Cabernet Sauvignon Napa Valley Georges de Latour Private Reserve 1942: A broad-shouldered, well-built old wine, with an amazingly youthful red color and loads of blackberry, cherry and dark chocolate character. Full-bodied, with a velvety texture and polished tannins. Medium finish. Drink now.–J.S. • $NA • (2/29/2000) • **90**

Cabernet Sauvignon Napa Valley Georges de Latour Private Reserve 1941: Fresh but rather light and faded. Apparently a great year in Napa. Light amber with a yellow edge. Strawberry, cherry, leather and cedar aromas, with a slight Sherry character. Light- to medium-bodied, with light, silky tannins and a fresh finish. Drink now.–J.S. • $NA • (2/29/2000) • **84**

Cabernet Sauvignon Napa Valley Georges de Latour Private Reserve 1939: A gorgeous old wine with loads of life left. Good dark amber color and lovely minty, fruity berry aromas. Medium- to full-bodied, with plenty of ripe fruit and velvety tannins. A real beauty. Drink now.–J.S. • $NA • (2/29/2000) • **95**

Cabernet Sauvignon Napa Valley Georges de Latour Private Reserve 1936: Still holding on, with a good dark amber color and aromas of leaf, meat and mushroom. Medium-bodied, with high acidity and a slightly maderized character, but still showing ripe fruit. Drink now.–J.S. • $2,875 Ⓐ • (2/29/2000) • **85**

Cabernet Sauvignon Napa Valley Rutherford 1995 • $14 • (4/30/1998) • **86**
Cabernet Sauvignon Napa Valley Rutherford 1994 • $15 • (7/31/1997) SS • **90**
Cabernet Sauvignon Napa Valley Rutherford 1993 • $15 • (12/15/1996) • **83**
Cabernet Sauvignon Napa Valley Rutherford 1992 • $12 • (11/30/1995) • **86**
Cabernet Sauvignon Napa Valley Rutherford 1991 • $13 • (10/15/1994) • **87**
Cabernet Sauvignon Napa Valley Rutherford 1990 • $11 • (10/31/1993) • **85**
Cabernet Sauvignon Napa Valley Rutherford 1989 • $11 • (3/31/1992) • **81**
Cabernet Sauvignon Napa Valley Rutherford 1988 • $15 • (7/15/1991) • **86**
Cabernet Sauvignon Napa Valley Rutherford 1987 • $12 Ⓐ • (12/15/1990) • **85**
Cabernet Sauvignon Napa Valley Rutherford 1986 • $12 • (9/15/1989) • **85**
Cabernet Sauvignon Napa Valley Rutherford 1970 • $NA • (6/01/1985) • **90**

BEAULIEU VINEYARD

Cabernet Sauvignon Rutherford Clone 4 Signet Collection 1995: Starts out with smoky, toasty oak, then folds in its spicy cherry, currant and plum. It's a shade tighter and richer than the BV Private Reserve, with a firmer tannin presence. Best to give it a little more time in the bottle. Best from 2001 through 2008.–J.L. • $100 • (10/31/1998) • **92**

Cabernet Sauvignon Rutherford Clone 6 Signet Collection 1996: Deliciously elegant, rich, vibrant and complex, with deep, sharply focused, ripe plum, black cherry, blackberry, spice and light cedary oak shadings. Best from 2001 through 2007.–J.L. • $100 • (11/15/1999) • **94**

Cabernet Sauvignon Rutherford Clone 6 Signet Collection 1994 • $100 • (11/15/1997) • **93**

Chardonnay California Beautour 1996 • $10 • (2/28/1998) • **87**

Chardonnay California Coastal 1997: Delicate, with pleasant crisp apple and pear flavors and a firm, refreshing finish, this is a lovely bottle of Chardonnay at a more than reasonable price. Drink now.–J.L. • $10 • (7/31/1999) • **85**

Chardonnay Carneros Centennial Release 1998: Soft, with vanilla and toast flavors. Drink now.–J.L. • $13 • (6/15/2000) • **83**

Chardonnay Carneros 1997: Soft and flavorful, with delicate peach, fig, citrus and herb. Finishes clean and elegant. Drink now.–J.L. • $13 • (7/31/1999) • **89**

Chardonnay Carneros 1996 • $14 • (5/15/1998) • **87**

Chardonnay Carneros Reserve 1998: Offers glimpses of peach, pear and tropical fruit, but then turns simple and dilute. Drink now.–J.L. • $25 • (6/15/2000) • **83**

Chardonnay Carneros Reserve 1997: Marked by a wonderful sense of harmony and finesse, offering ripe and polished pear, apple, ginger, spice and hazelnut flavors that turn elegant and linger, along with pretty smoky, toasty oak, on the finish. Drink this delicious California white now through 2003.–J.L. • $25 • (7/31/1999) SS • **93**

Chardonnay Carneros Reserve 1996: Spicy, with a slight Gewürztraminer edge to the ripe, exotic pineapple and tropical fruit flavors. Full-bodied, with a rich finish. Drink now through 2002.–J.L. • $25 • (7/31/1999) • **91**

Ensemble California Signet Collection 1994 • $25 • (7/31/1996) • **86**

Merlot California Coastal 1997: Simple, with a cedary edge to the toasted oak and cherry flavors. Drink now.–J.L. • $12 • (10/15/1999) • **80**

Merlot California Coastal 1995: Kind of smoky, with an herbal edge that's backed by currant and blackberry notes. The finish is bright, with a touch of bitterness. Drink now through 2002. • $10 • (7/31/1998) • **86**

Merlot Napa Valley 1996: Pleasant for its supple texture, earthy cherry and mineral flavors and lingering toasted oak notes. Finishes with delicate tannins. Drink now through 2003.–J.L. • $16 • (9/15/1999) • **86**

Merlot Napa Valley 1994 • $16 • (6/30/1997) • **84**

Merlot Napa Valley 1993 • $16 • (6/15/1996) • **82**

Merlot Napa Valley Beautour 1994 • $11 • (7/31/1997) • **84**

Merlot Napa Valley Beautour 1993 • $12 • (6/30/1996) • **82**

Merlot Napa Valley Beautour 1991 • $10 • (1/31/1995) • **82**

Petite Sirah Napa Valley Signet Collection 1995 • $NA • (9/30/1997) • **88**

Pinot Gris Central Coast Signet Collection 1996 • $14 • (9/30/1997) • **86**

Pinot Noir California Beautour 1996 • $10 • (3/31/1998) • **82**

Pinot Noir California Beautour 1995 • $11 • (1/31/1997) • **81**

Pinot Noir California Beautour 1994 • $10 • (12/31/1995) • **82**

Pinot Noir Napa Valley Beautour 1993 • $10 • (12/31/1995) • **81**

Pinot Noir Napa Valley Beautour 1992 • $9 • (3/31/1995) • **79**

Pinot Noir California Coastal 1997: Simple, with a green, tannic edge to the light strawberry flavors. Drink now.–J.L. • $10 • (9/15/1999) • **80**

Pinot Noir Carneros Centennial Release 1998: Tangy cherry and licorice notes mingle with earthy flavors. Drink now through 2002.–J.L. • $16 • (4/30/2000) • **83**

Pinot Noir Carneros Vin Gris Signet Collection 1996 • $10 • (9/30/1997) • **84**

Pinot Noir Carneros 1997: Light but flavorful, focused and simple, with strawberry, cherry and spice flavors that finish soft. Drink now.–J.L. • $16 • (9/15/1999) • **83**

Pinot Noir Carneros 1995 • $15 • (1/31/1998) • **86**

Pinot Noir Napa Valley Carneros 1994 • $12 • (3/31/1996) • **84**

Pinot Noir Napa Valley Carneros 1993 • $13 • (10/15/1995) • **86**

Pinot Noir Napa Valley Carneros 1992 • $13 • (3/31/1995) • **78**

Pinot Noir Carneros Reserve 1997: Silky in texture, with subtle cherry, berry and cola notes, turning earthy and picking up pretty tannins. Drink now through 2005.–J.L. • $30 • (9/15/1999) • **87**

Key: SS—Spectator Selection. CS—Cellar Selection. HR—Highly Recommended. $NA—Price not available. (BT)—Barrel tasting. Ⓐ—Auction Price. For a key to the tasters' initials, see "How to Use These Listings."
Dates in parentheses represent the issues in which the ratings were published.

Pinot Noir Carneros Reserve 1995 • $30 • (1/31/1998) SS • **91**

Pinot Noir Napa Valley Carneros Reserve 1994 • $19 • (3/31/1996) HR • **90**

Pinot Noir Napa Valley Carneros Reserve 1993 • $18 • (12/31/1995) • **83**

Pinot Noir Napa Valley Carneros Reserve 1992 • $18 • (5/15/1995) • **86**

Pinot Noir Napa Valley Carneros Reserve 1991 • $15 • (2/28/1994) • **85**

Pinot Noir Napa Valley Carneros Reserve 1990 • $17 • (2/28/1993) • **84**

Pinot Noir Napa Valley Carneros Reserve 1989 • $13 • (4/30/1991) • **85**

Pinot Noir Napa Valley Carneros Reserve 1988 • $10 • (4/15/1990) • **87**

Pinot Noir Napa Valley Carneros Reserve 1987 • $10 • (12/31/1988) • **90**

Sangiovese Bianco Napa Valley Signet Collection 1996 • $10 • (9/30/1997) • **80**

Sangiovese Napa Valley Signet Collection 1996: Austere, with dry, earthy tannins and wild berry and tart raspberry flavors that are moderately ripe, rendering a wine that's rather one-dimensional. Drink now.–J.L. • $16 • (11/15/1999) • **83**

Sangiovese Napa Valley Signet Collection 1995 • $16 • (9/15/1997) • **90**

Sangiovese Napa Valley Signet Collection 1994 • $25 • (7/31/1996) • **87**

Sauvignon Blanc California Coastal 1998: Ripe and aromatic, with litchi and fig notes, this California white is round in the mouth, with a hint of grapefruit tanginess that lingers on the finish. A flavorful and affordable version. Drink now through 2003.–J.L. • $9 • (5/31/2000) • **85**

Sauvignon Blanc California Coastal 1997: Fairly lightweight, this offers simple herb and citrus notes, then bows out quickly. Won't offend or excite. • $11 • (5/15/1999) • **79**

Sauvignon Blanc California Coastal 1996: Fairly hollow on the palate, with a vaguely peachy quality. Not much to speak about. • $7 • (8/31/1998) • **77**

Sauvignon Blanc Napa Valley 1997: Full-bodied, with melon, citrus, toast and spice flavors. Sits broadly on the palate, though it finishes short. Drink now. • $13 • (6/15/1999) • **84**

Sauvignon Blanc Napa Valley 1996 • $11 • (7/31/1997) • **87**

Syrah Dry Creek Valley Signet Collection 1995 • $25 • (9/30/1997) • **91**

Tapestry Reserve Napa Valley 1996: Tight in structure while plush in texture, offering rich plum, dark chocolate, cinnamon, spice and earth flavors that linger deliciously on the long, complex finish—this is one seductive California red. A blend of Cabernet Sauvignon, Merlot, Cabernet Franc and Petit Verdot. Drink now through 2005.–J.L. • $35 • (10/15/1999) SS • **92**

Tapestry Reserve Napa Valley 1995: This outstanding Cabernet blend shows a supple, elegant band of cherry, currant, anise, sage and tar notes, wrapped in a polished texture, with well-integrated tannins. The finish is long, complex and lingering. Given the suppleness of the tannins. it's drinkable now, or can be cellared through 2005. A blend of Cabernet Sauvignon, Merlot, Cabernet Franc, Petit Verdot.–J.L. • $30 • (11/30/1998) SS • **91**

Tapestry Reserve Napa Valley 1994 • $20 • (10/31/1997) SS • **91**

Tapestry Reserve Napa Valley 1993 • $20 • (12/15/1996) • **85**

Tapestry Reserve Napa Valley 1992 • $20 • (4/30/1996) • **88**

Tapestry Signet Collection Napa Valley 1991 • $20 • (12/15/1995) • **87**

Viognier Napa Valley Signet Collection 1996 • $16 • (1/01/1998) • **88**

Zinfandel California Beautour 1996 • $10 • (3/31/1998) • **85**

Zinfandel California Coastal 1997: Ripe berry, licorice and earth notes are straightforward and appealing. Drink now.–J.L. • $10 • (5/31/2000) • **84**

Zinfandel Napa Valley Centennial Release 1997: Dull, with prune and and tomato notes and a heavy finish. Drink now.–J.L. • $16 • (5/15/2000) • **80**

Zinfandel Napa Valley 1996 • $14 • (3/31/1998) • **85**

Zinfandel Napa Valley 1995 • $13 • (4/30/1997) SS • **91**

Zinfandel Napa Valley Signet Collection 1997: Delicious Zinfandel, BV's best to date. Ripe, with plush blackberry, cherry, currant and spice flavors that keep zooming along through a rich, concentrated aftertaste, picking up pretty, toasty oak. Drink now through 2004.–J.L. • $25 • (5/15/1999) HR • **93**

Zinfandel Napa Valley Signet Collection 1995 • $20 • (4/30/1997) • **91**

Zinfandel Napa Valley Signet Collection 1994 • $16 • (8/31/1996) • **88**

BEAUX FRERES | OREGON

Pinot Noir Willamette Valley Unfined and Unfiltered 1993 • $35 • (8/31/1995) HR • **90**

Pinot Noir Willamette Valley Unfined and Unfiltered 1992 • $82 Ⓐ • (3/15/1994) HR • **91**

Pinot Noir Willamette Valley Unfiltered 1991 • $34 • (3/15/1994) • **92**

Pinot Noir Yamhill County 1997: Much richer and grander than most 1997s, this impressive mouthful of plum, black cherry and toast flavors has firm but harmoniously integrated tannins that frame the long finish and promise a good future. Best from 2001 through 2007.–H.S. • $45 • (6/15/1999) • **90**

Pinot Noir Yamhill County 1995 • $50 • (4/30/1997) • **90**

Pinot Noir Yamhill County Belles Soeurs Shea Vineyard 1998: Smooth, silky and seductive. Delicious for its plum, berry and exotic spice flavors that swirl beautifully through the highly polished texture. Youthful, it's appealing already. New vineyard designation from Beaux Frères. Drink now through 2007.–H.S. • $40 • (4/30/2000) • **90**

Pinot Noir Yamhill County Belles Soeurs 1997: Has more intensity than most 1997s, offering black pepper and black cherry notes on a light frame, gently shaded with spicy oak. Drink now through 2003.–H.S. • $28 • (6/15/1999) • **87**

Pinot Noir Yamhill County Belles Soeurs The Beaux Frères Vineyard 1996 • $35 • (5/15/1998) • **88**

Pinot Noir Yamhill County The Beaux Frères Vineyard 1998: Rich and generous in flavor. A lush mouthful of blackberry, anise, vanilla and spice that lingers, balanced with a nice zing of citrusy acidity in the middle. Has layers of complexity without excess weight. Tasted twice, with consistent notes. Drink now through 2010.–H.S. • $70 • (5/15/2000) • **92**

Pinot Noir Yamhill County The Beaux Frères Vineyard 1996 • $50 • (5/15/1998) HR • **91**

Pinot Noir Yamhill County The Beaux Frères Vineyard 1994 • $40 • (6/30/1996) • **93**

BECKMEN | CALIFORNIA

Cabernet Sauvignon Santa Barbara County 1996: Rich and plush, with herbal, plum, cola, cedar, sage and spicy notes that linger on the mildly tannic finish. Drink now through 2003.–J.L. • $19 • (10/15/1999) • **87**

Cabernet Sauvignon Santa Barbara County 1995 • $20 • (3/31/1998) • **87**

Chardonnay Santa Barbara County 1996 • $16 • (5/15/1998) • **87**

Chardonnay Santa Barbara County Barrel Select 1996 • $20 • (6/15/1998) • **88**

Sauvignon Blanc Santa Barbara County 1998: Herbaceous, with lemon curd and vanilla aromas; slightly soapy flavors combine with tart acidity. Drink now through 2002.–J.L. • $12 • (5/15/2000) • **80**

Sauvignon Blanc Santa Barbara County 1997: Creamy yet bright on the palate, showing vivid lemon, lime, tangerine and grapefruit flavors. Finishes with a zingy edge, sporting fig and gooseberry essence. A fun one from this up-and-coming producer. Drink now. • $12 • (1/31/1999) • **89**

Sauvignon Blanc Santa Barbara County 1996 • $12 • (4/30/1998) • **85**

Syrah Santa Barbara County 1996: Rich and ripe, with jammy black currant, plum, anise, herb and blackberry flavors. Tannins are firm and ripe. Finishes long and clean. Drink now through 2006. • $20 • (11/30/1998) • **89**

Syrah Santa Barbara County 1995 • $18 • (12/15/1997) • **87**

BEDELL | NEW YORK

Cabernet Sauvignon North Fork of Long Island 1995: This inky wine is a showcase for sweet, smoky oak, but there's enough underlying blueberry and cassis flavors to balance. The tannins are firm but polished, and the beautiful oak lingers on the finish. Tasted twice, with consistent notes. Drink now through 2002.–T.M. • $22 • (6/30/1999) • **89**

Cabernet Sauvignon North Fork of Long Island 1993 • $18 • (12/31/1996) • **84**

Cabernet Sauvignon North Fork of Long Island 1988 • $15 • (6/30/1991) • **86**

Cupola North Fork of Long Island 1995: Rich and ripe. This generous, well-defined red is packed with plum and currant flavors, with firm tannins and toasty oak notes. A good match for grilled meats. Cabernet Sauvignon, Cabernet Franc and Merlot. Drink now through 2004.–T.M. • $25 • (5/31/2000) • **90**

Cupola North Fork of Long Island 1994: Soft and round, this gentle red shows ripe flavors of plum, herb and toast. Very smooth on the palate, without much structure or tannin. A little disappointing, though. Drink now.–T.M. • $25 • (6/30/1999) • **83**

Eis North Fork of Long Island NV: Very thick and rich, this golden wine displays cinnamon and burnt sugar flavors, a bit cloying on the finish, but impressive for their concentration. Drink now.–T.M. • $28/375 ml. • (5/31/2000) • **84**

Merlot North Fork of Long Island 1995: A serious style of Merlot. Inviting layers of fruit, smoke and spicy oak in the aromas and flavors are bound by very firm tannins and a tight finish. Drink now. • $17 • (10/31/1998) • **86**

Merlot North Fork of Long Island 1993 • $16 • (12/31/1996) • **87**

Merlot North Fork of Long Island 1987 • $18 • (3/31/1990) • **90**

Merlot North Fork of Long Island 1986 • $11 • (12/15/1988) • **88**

Merlot North Fork of Long Island Reserve 1995: Plush and lively, this dark red is packed with ripe blackberry and plum flavors, with pretty accents of toasty oak that never dominate the fruit. Tannins are ripe, and the wine has concentration without heaviness. Drink now through 2002.–T.M. • $28 • (6/30/1999) • **88**

Merlot North Fork of Long Island Reserve 1988 • $14 • (6/30/1991) • **90**

North Fork of Long Island Dessert 1992 • $24 • (4/15/1995) • **84**

Viognier North Fork of Long Island 1998: Shows the distinctive floral and spice aromas of Viognier, with buttery and slightly bitter accents on the palate. It's quite rich, but stays balanced. First Viognier from Bedell. Drink now.–T.M. • $18 • (5/31/2000) • **86**

BEDFORD THOMPSON | CALIFORNIA

Cabernet Franc Santa Barbara County 1997: Has dry tannins, with sweat and herb notes. Drink now.–J.L. • $20 • (6/15/2000) • **80**

Chardonnay Santa Barbara County 1998: Earthy, with funky notes and a bitterness on the finish.–J.L. • $18 • (6/15/2000) • **78**

Syrah Santa Barbara County 1997: Ginger and green bean notes show depth but are a bit raw on the finish. Drink now through 2003.–J.L. • $20 • (6/15/2000) • **82**

Syrah Santa Barbara County 1996: Starts off with bright cherry, currant, herb and smoke notes. Shows good structure, with firm, ripe tannins, good acidity and silky texture. Finishes just a little short. Drink now through 2004. • $20 • (2/28/1999) • **88**

Syrah Santa Barbara County 1995 • $20 • (11/15/1997) • **88**

Syrah Santa Barbara County 1994 • $18 • (9/30/1996) • **88**

Viognier Santa Barbara County 1997: Some pretty earthy aromas are followed by apricot, citrus and hazelnut flavors on the palate. Quite viscous and broadly textured, it's unusual yet interesting. Drink now. • $18 • (2/28/1999) • **87**

BEHRENS & HITCHCOCK | CALIFORNIA

Cabernet Sauvignon Napa Valley Inkgrade Vineyard 1995: Well focused on the earthy, lead pencil core of Cabernet flavor, but needs short-term cellaring to gain complexity and ripen the tannins. Earns points for the concept "Inkgrade." Drink through 2007–J.L. • $30 • (10/31/1998) • **87**

Cabernet Sauvignon Napa Valley Staglin Vineyard 1994 • $28 • (11/30/1997) • **92**

Cabernet Sauvignon Napa Valley TLK Ranch 1995: Complex, smooth and full of ripe berry, cherry and plummy Cabernet flavors that are pure and elegant. Displays good intensity, depth and concentration, and a long, rich aftertaste. Has the tannin to age. Drink through 2005–J.L. • $30 • (11/15/1998) • **91**

Merlot Napa Valley Oakville 1995 • $25 • (11/30/1997) • **88**

Zinfandel Napa Valley 1996: Gamy and a touch nutty, the firm band of berrylike flavor is a bit muddled, but the wine is still pleasing in its range of complex flavors. Drink now.–J.L. • $18 • (6/30/1999) • **86**

BEL ARBOR | CALIFORNIA

Cabernet Sauvignon California Vintner's Selection 1994 • $5 • (11/30/1996) • **78**

Cabernet Sauvignon California 1993 • $7 • (12/15/1995) • **84**

Cabernet Sauvignon California 1992 • $7 • (1/31/1995) • **78**

Cabernet Sauvignon California 1990 • $7 • (3/15/1993) • **82**

Cabernet Sauvignon California Founder's Selection 1990 • $7 • (11/15/1993) • **80**

Chardonnay California 1998: Simple, clean and light, with floral and herbal notes, but it shows just a modest hint of Chardonnay. Drink now.–J.L. • $6 • (7/31/1999) • **82**

Merlot California 1997: Simple cherry and oak flavors make this an easy quaff. Drink now. • $7 • (10/15/1999) • **80**

Merlot California Vintner's Selection 1994 • $6 • (6/30/1996) • **84**

Merlot California 1990 • $7 • (10/31/1992) • **84**

Zinfandel California Founder's Selection 1990 • $6 • (9/30/1992) • **85**

BELL | CALIFORNIA

Cabernet Sauvignon Rutherford Baritelle Vineyard 1994 • $50 • (4/30/1998) • **82**

Cabernet Sauvignon Rutherford Baritelle Vineyard 1992 • $50 • (7/31/1997) • **89**

Cabernet Sauvignon Rutherford Baritelle Vineyard 1991 • $40 • (12/15/1995) • **83**

Syrah Sierra Foothills Canterbury Vineyard 1997: Vanilla and coconut tones dominate the aromas. Good depth of flavor, with vanilla and berry notes that linger through the finish. Best from 2001 through 2004.–J.L. • $28 • (5/15/2000) • **86**

BELLE PENTE | OREGON

Pinot Gris Willamette Valley 1998: Smooth and generous. A silky mouthful of peach, orange and melon that lingers nicely. Drink now.–H.S. • $14 • (4/30/2000) • **88**

Pinot Noir Willamette Valley Murto Reserve 1997: Ripe for the vintage. Open-textured and generous with its black cherry and currant flavors, finishing with fine-grained tannins and a hint of smoke. The fruit persists. Drink now through 2003.–H.S. • $25 • (4/30/2000) • **87**

BELLE PENTE

Pinot Noir Willamette Valley Reserve 1996: Smooth, ripe and generous, it isn't a big wine, but its plum and currant flavors expand on the palate, picking up hints of cola and coffee on the finish. Drink now.–H.S. • $25 • (2/28/1999) • **87**

BELVEDERE | CALIFORNIA

Cabernet Sauvignon Alexander Valley Robert Young Vineyards Gifts of the Land 1985 • $16 • (1/31/1991) • **81**

Cabernet Sauvignon Alexander Valley Robert Young Vineyards 1984 • $13 • (7/15/1988) • **88**

Cabernet Sauvignon Alexander Valley Robert Young Vineyards 1983 • $12 • (5/15/1987) • **88**

Cabernet Sauvignon Alexander Valley Robert Young Vineyards 1982 • $18 • (12/01/1985) SS • **95**

Cabernet Sauvignon Dry Creek Valley 1995: Still quite young-tasting, this California Cab opens with bright, ripe cherry and plum flavors on a silky-smooth texture, with a gentle roundness, then finishes moderately with a hint of anise. Should evolve nicely; drink now through 2003. • $17 • (1/31/1999) SS • **89**

Cabernet Sauvignon Dry Creek Valley 1994 • $14 • (12/15/1997) • **82**

Cabernet Sauvignon Dry Creek Valley Preferred Stock 1994: This crisp, medium-weight Cabernet is fresh and lively, with plum and berry flavors. Mature, it's very good now, even with its firm, dry tannins, but can be further cellared. Drink now through 2004.–J.L. • $25 • (10/31/1998) • **86**

Cabernet Sauvignon Napa Valley York Creek Vineyard 1983 • $12 • (12/31/1987) • **79**

Cabernet Sauvignon Napa Valley York Creek Vineyard 1982 • $12 • (9/15/1986) • **72**

Cabernet Sauvignon Sonoma County 1992 • $12 • (3/31/1996) • **82**

Cabernet Sauvignon Sonoma County 1991 • $10 • (11/15/1994) • **82**

Cabernet Sauvignon Sonoma County Preferred Stock 1988 • $18 • (11/15/1993) • **84**

Chardonnay Alexander Valley 1996 • $14 • (5/15/1998) • **87**

Chardonnay Russian River Valley 1997: Toasty and creamy, with lemon, pear and fig notes, turning elegant and polished. Drink now through 2004.–J.L. • $17 • (2/29/2000) • **88**

Chardonnay Russian River Valley 1996 • $17 • (6/30/1998) • **87**

Chardonnay Sonoma County 1998: Easy to like, with butter, anise and apricot flavors. Drink now through 2001.–J.L. • $12 • (6/15/2000) • **86**

Chardonnay Sonoma County 1997: Hard to go wrong with this very good bottle from Sonoma. With its pleasant range of citrus, pear, fig and melon flavors and nice clean finish, it's comparable to many a Chardonnay selling at twice the price. Drink now.–J.L. • $11 • (1/31/1999) • **85**

Chardonnay Sonoma County 1996 • $11 • (3/31/1998) • **85**

Gewürztraminer Anderson Valley Floodgate Vineyard 1996 • $12 • (11/30/1997) • **83**

Merlot Alexander Valley Robert Young Vineyards 1986 • $13 • (6/30/1989) • **87**

Merlot Alexander Valley Robert Young Vineyards 1984 • $13 • (8/31/1988) • **90**

Merlot Alexander Valley Robert Young Vineyards 1983 • $12 • (12/31/1987) • **70**

Merlot Alexander Valley Robert Young Vineyards 1982 • $12 • (3/16/1986) • **94**

Merlot Dry Creek Valley 1996: Tight, with coffee and tobacco-laced berry flavor that's sharp with tannins. Drink now.–J.L. • $16 • (2/28/1999) • **80**

Merlot Dry Creek Valley 1995 • $13 • (3/31/1998) • **84**

Merlot Dry Creek Valley 1994 • $14 • (5/15/1997) • **80**

Merlot Dry Creek Valley Preferred Stock 1994 • $22 • (7/31/1997) • **89**

Merlot Sonoma County 1993 • $14 • (8/31/1996) • **77**

Merlot Sonoma County 1991 • $12 • (9/15/1994) • **82**

Muscat Canelli Alexander Valley Late Harvest 1990 • $10/375 ml. • (6/15/1992) • **80**

Petite Sirah Dry Creek Valley 1994: Firm, chewy and rough-textured, with just enough black cherry sneaking through to make it worth cellaring. Drink through 2005–H.S. • $21 • (11/30/1998) • **82**

Pinot Noir Los Carneros Winery Lake 1983 • $12 • (12/15/1987) • **73**

Pinot Noir Sonoma County Bacigalupi 1985 • $12 • (6/15/1988) • **73**

Zinfandel Dry Creek Valley 1997: Waxy crayon flavors dominate the earthy, peppery wild berry, finishing with a flat root beer flavor. Drink now.–J.L. • $17 • (6/15/2000) • **82**

Key: SS—Spectator Selection. CS—Cellar Selection. HR—Highly Recommended. $NA—Price not available. (BT)—Barrel tasting. (A)—Auction Price.
For a key to the tasters' initials, see "How to Use These Listings."
Dates in parentheses represent the issues in which the ratings were published.

Zinfandel Dry Creek Valley 1996: A light-edged wine, with spicy cherry and smoke flavors. It's almost sweet on the palate—a juicy, fruity wine. Drink now. • $17 • (1/31/1999) • **85**

Zinfandel Dry Creek Valley 1995 • $18 • (12/15/1997) • **87**

Zinfandel Dry Creek Valley 1994 • $14 • (3/31/1997) • **87**

Zinfandel Dry Creek Valley 1993 • $11 • (3/31/1996) • **84**

Zinfandel Dry Creek Valley 1991 • $10 • (3/31/1994) • **84**

Zinfandel Dry Creek Valley 1990 • $10 • (6/15/1993) • **74**

Zinfandel Dry Creek Valley 1989 • $9 • (5/15/1992) • **85**

BENESSERE | CALIFORNIA

Sangiovese Napa Valley 1996: Clean and ripe, with cherry, strawberry and cranberry notes that fade on the finish. Drink now.–J.L. • $25 • (12/15/1998) • **83**

Sangiovese Napa Valley 1995 • $25 • (9/15/1997) • **89**

BENHAM | CALIFORNIA

Sangiovese California 1992 • $9 • (11/30/1995) • **77**

BENICIA | CALIFORNIA

Cabernet Sauvignon Napa Valley Capitol Reserve NV • $12 • (11/30/1996) • **73**

Cabernet Sauvignon Napa Valley Diamond Mountain Capitol Reserve 1993 • $20 • (11/30/1996) • **72**

BENTON-LANE | OREGON

Pinot Noir Oregon 1998: Lighter than most '98 Oregon Pinots, with a distinct floral edge to the nice core of raspberry on a silky frame. Drink now.–H.S. • $16 • (4/30/2000) • **86**

Pinot Noir Oregon 1996 • $15 • (3/31/1998) • **87**

Pinot Noir Oregon 1994 • $14 • (3/31/1996) • **87**

Pinot Noir Oregon 1992 • $12 • (11/15/1994) • **88**

Pinot Noir Oregon Reserve 1996 • $30 • (3/31/1998) • **86**

Pinot Noir Oregon Reserve 1994 • $28 • (6/30/1996) • **87**

BENZIGER | CALIFORNIA

A Tribute Sonoma Mountain 1994 • $25 • (10/31/1997) • **87**

A Tribute Sonoma Mountain 1990 • $27 • (11/15/1994) • **84**

A Tribute Sonoma Mountain 1989 • $26 • (11/15/1992) • **88**

A Tribute Sonoma Mountain 1988 • $26 • (1/31/1992) • **88**

A Tribute Sonoma Mountain 1987 • $20 • (12/31/1990) • **85**

Brut Blanc de Blancs Carneros Late Disgorged 1990 • $10 • (11/30/1997) • **89**

Brut Carneros Imagery Series 1990 • $16 • (5/31/1995) • **87**

Cabernet Franc Alexander Valley Blue Rock Vineyard Imagery Series 1989 • $16 • (10/15/1993) • **85**

Cabernet Franc Alexander Valley Imagery Series 1995 • $20 • (12/15/1997) • **85**

Cabernet Franc Alexander Valley Imagery Series 1994 • $17 • (4/30/1997) • **91**

Cabernet Franc Alexander Valley Imagery Series 1992 • $16 • (2/28/1995) • **83**

Cabernet Sauvignon Alexander Valley Ash Creek Vineyards 1996: Smooth and polished, with a supple band of cherry, berry, stewed plum and spice, finishing with fleshy tannins. Drink through 2008–J.L. • $30 • (9/15/1999) • **88**

Cabernet Sauvignon Alexander Valley Ash Creek Vineyards Reserve 1995: Serves up lots of ripe berry, cherry, plum and spice, and then fills in the gaps with earthy tobacco and coffee notes. Finishes with crisp, lively tannins and good length. Drink through 2005–J.L. • $30 • (10/31/1998) • **88**

Cabernet Sauvignon Alexander Valley Blue Rock Vineyard 1996: Ripe, with bright black cherry and wild berry character, supple, well-integrated tannins and a long, lively aftertaste, finishing with vanilla-scented oak. Drink now through 2006.–J.L. • $30 • (4/30/1999) • **89**

Cabernet Sauvignon Sonoma County 1997: Solid, with firm, rich currant, anise, blackberry, sage and juniper berry, turning tannic. Drink now through 2005.–J.L. • $17 • (6/15/2000) • **86**

Cabernet Sauvignon Sonoma County 1996: Features concentrated black cherry, mineral, licorice and herb flavors, with toasted oak notes. Firm yet well-integrated tannins. Drink now through 2001.–J.L. • $16 • (2/28/1999) • **87**

Cabernet Sauvignon Sonoma County 1995 • $16 • (11/30/1997) • **87**

Cabernet Sauvignon Sonoma County 1992 • $13 • (9/15/1995) • **87**

Cabernet Sauvignon Sonoma County 1991 • $13 • (3/15/1994) • **88**

Cabernet Sauvignon Sonoma County 1990 • $13 • (9/30/1993) • **86**

Cabernet Sauvignon Sonoma County 1989 • $12 • (7/15/1992) • **84**

Cabernet Sauvignon Sonoma County 1988 • $12 • (11/15/1991) • **84**
Cabernet Sauvignon Sonoma County 1987 • $22 • (9/30/1990) SS • **93**
Cabernet Sauvignon Sonoma County 1986 • $10 • (7/31/1989) • **82**
Cabernet Sauvignon Sonoma County Five Bordeaux Varietals 1994 • $14 • (4/30/1997) SS • **90**
Cabernet Sauvignon Sonoma Mountain 1989 • $22 • (11/15/1994) • **84**
Cabernet Sauvignon Sonoma Mountain 1988 • $25 • (11/15/1991) • **85**
Cabernet Sauvignon Sonoma Mountain Reserve 1996: Enormously rich, deep, dense and concentrated, with cherry, currant, plum, anise and spice flavors that are woven neatly together, finishing long and intricate. Drink through 2008–J.L. • $35 • (10/31/1999) • **93**
Cabernet Sauvignon Sonoma Mountain Reserve 1995: Rugged in texture, with a minty, menthol edge to the currant and berry flavors, it's still a touch green and tannic. Tasted twice, with consistent notes. Drink through 2004–J.L. • $35 • (4/30/1999) • **87**
Cabernet Sauvignon Sonoma Mountain Reserve 1994 • $32 • (6/30/1998) • **88**
Cabernet Sauvignon Sonoma Valley 1986 • $17 • (4/30/1990) • **78**
Cabernet Sauvignon Sonoma Valley 1985 • $16 • (12/15/1988) • **83**
Cabernet Sauvignon Sonoma Valley Estate Bottled 1987 • $12 • (11/15/1990) • **85**
Cabernet Sauvignon Sonoma Valley Rancho Salina 1996: Pleasantly balanced, with ripe currant, plum and berry, touches of anise and cedary oak, finishing with mild, earthy but firm tannins. Drink now through 2002.–J.L. • $30 • (4/30/1999) • **88**
Chardonnay Carneros 1998: Pleasantly fruity, with spicy pear, apricot and cedar notes, turning simple. Drink now.–J.L. • $13 • (6/15/2000) • **83**
Chardonnay Carneros 1996: Ripe and spicy, with touches of fig, pear, anise and spice, holding its flavor and focus on a lingering finish. Drink now.–J.L. • $13 • (11/30/1998) • **87**
Chardonnay Carneros Reserve 1996 • $25 • (6/30/1998) • **91**
Chardonnay Carneros Sangiacomo Vineyards 1998: Sleek, with pretty pear, earth, hazelnut and fig flavors that are focused and lively, finishing with a spicy aftertaste. Drink now through 2004.–J.L. • $25 • (6/30/2000) • **88**
Chardonnay Carneros Sangiacomo Vineyards 1997: Rich and full-bodied, with a citrusy, leesy, yeasty edge to the pear and apple character. A little more time in the bottle should round out the flavors. Drink now through 2002.–J.L. • $25 • (4/30/1999) • **88**
Chardonnay Carneros Yamakawa Vineyards 1998: Stretches into rich tropical fruit flavors, with guava, pineapple, fig and spicy notes that linger. Drink now through 2004.–J.L. • $25 • (6/30/2000) • **88**
Chardonnay Carneros Yamakawa Vineyards 1997: Smooth and delicate, with subtle ripe pear, fig, citrus, nutmeg and spicy notes, finishing with a clean, fruity aftertaste. Drink now through 2004.–J.L. • $25 • (3/31/2000) • **86**
Chardonnay Carneros Yamakawa Vineyards Reserve 1996 • $25 • (5/31/1998) • **91**
Chardonnay Sonoma County Reserve 1997: Smooth, ripe and offering complex pear, fig, light oak and spicy flavors and a full-bodied aftertaste. Drink now through 2002.–J.L. • $25 • (9/15/1999) • **88**
Estate Tribute Sonoma Mountain 1995: Tightly focused, with pretty, complex black cherry, plum and currant flavors, hints of spice, herb and cedary oak. Lingering aftertaste has hints of tea and spice. Drink through 2005–J.L. • $25 • (11/15/1998) • **89**
Estate Tribute Sonoma Mountain 1993 • $22 • (4/30/1997) • **87**
Estate Tribute Sonoma Mountain 1992 • $20 • (10/15/1996) • **87**
Estate Tribute Sonoma Mountain 1991 • $20 • (3/31/1996) • **84**
Fumé Blanc Sonoma County 1998: Quite herbal. Also serves up a strong core of lime and other citrus flavors. Bright and refreshing at the end. Drink now. • $11 • (8/31/1999) • **84**
Fumé Blanc Sonoma County 1997: An attractive, solid California Sauvignon Blanc for current drinking, this delivers grapefruit, lemon and herb flavors couched in moderate body, finishing clean. The reasonable price rounds out the package. • $10 • (12/31/1998) • **84**
Fumé Blanc Sonoma County 1996 • $10 • (1/31/1998) • **87**
Merlot Sonoma County 1997: Smooth, flavorful and light-bodied, featuring cola, herb and black cherry flavors. Drink now.–J.L. • $18 • (10/15/1999) • **83**
Merlot Sonoma County 1996: Soft and forward but lacks focus, showing a slight green bell pepper edge to the cola, plum, cherry and spice flavors. Drink now.–J.L. • $16 • (12/31/1998) • **83**
Merlot Sonoma County 1995 • $17 • (11/30/1997) • **87**
Merlot Sonoma County 1994 • $15 • (10/15/1996) SS • **88**
Merlot Sonoma County 1993 • $14 • (3/31/1996) • **82**
Merlot Sonoma County 1992 • $14 • (2/28/1995) • **87**
Merlot Sonoma County 1991 • $14 • (9/15/1994) • **83**
Merlot Sonoma County 1990 • $14 • (10/15/1993) • **85**
Merlot Sonoma County 1989 • $14 • (5/31/1992) • **81**
Merlot Sonoma County 1988 • $12 • (11/15/1991) • **87**
Merlot Sonoma County Reserve 1995 • $35 • (6/30/1998) • **87**
Merlot Sonoma Mountain A Tribute 1994 • $25 • (5/31/1997) • **88**
Merlot Sonoma Valley 1987 • $12 • (3/31/1991) • **86**
Merlot Sonoma Valley 1986 • $16 • (7/31/1989) • **84**
Merlot Sonoma Valley Reserve 1996: Elegant and polished, with spicy cherry, anise, cedar and sage, finishing with tobacco and coffee notes that are supple. Drink now through 2005.–J.L. • $33 • (9/15/1999) • **87**
Petite Sirah Paso Robles Imagery Series 1994 • $18 • (7/31/1997) • **86**
Petite Sirah Paso Robles Shell Creek Vineyard Imagery Series 1993 • $16 • (11/30/1996) • **85**
Petite Sirah Paso Robles Shell Creek Vineyard Imagery Series 1989 • $16 • (10/15/1993) • **80**
Pinot Noir California 1997: Lightly fruity, soft and smooth in texture, with herb and strawberry flavors. Drink now.–J.L. • $21 • (6/15/2000) • **84**
Pinot Noir California 1996: Soft-textured, with pleasantly spicy strawberry, tea, cola and cherry flavors, finishing soft. Drink now through 2001–J.L. • $18 • (9/15/1999) • **86**
Pinot Noir California 1995 • $17 • (12/15/1997) • **87**
Pinot Noir California 1993 • $14 • (6/15/1996) • **88**
Pinot Noir California 1992 • $14 • (1/31/1995) • **86**
Pinot Noir California Reserve 1996: While not vineyard- or appellation-driven, this takes the best from several areas for a very complex and appealing wine, with a broad range of cherry, herb, plum, vanilla, anise, sage and spice, finishing with a long, complex aftertaste. Drink through 2005–J.L. • $33 • (9/15/1999) • **90**
Pinot Noir Sonoma County 1991 • $14 • (8/31/1994) • **87**
Pinot Noir Sonoma County 1990 • $14 • (2/28/1994) • **87**
Pinot Noir Sonoma County 1989 • $13 • (2/28/1993) • **85**
Pinot Noir Willamette Valley 1996: Light and elegant, with a firm backbone and fine-grained tannins supporting the pretty plum and berry flavors. Hints at tea and spice as the flavors echo on the finish. Drink now through 2003.–H.S. • $20 • (6/30/1999) • **87**
Riesling Santa Maria Valley Late Harvest Imagery Series Bien Nacido Vineyard 1994 • $16/375 ml. • (6/15/1996) • **89**
Sangiovese Dry Creek Valley Imagery Series 1995 • $18 • (3/31/1998) • **83**
Sangiovese Dry Creek Valley Larga Vista Vineyard Imagery Series 1994 • $20 • (10/15/1996) • **87**
Sangiovese Dry Creek Valley Larga Vista Vineyard Imagery Series 1993 • $16 • (6/15/1996) • **88**
Syrah California 1997: Straightforward but easy to like, with chocolate and black cherry notes. Drink now through 2002.–J.L. • $21 • (6/15/2000) • **85**
Syrah Central Coast 1996: Smooth and smoky with ripe black cherry, blackberry, mineral and toasted oak flavors. Drink now through 2004–J.L. • $18 • (9/15/1999) • **87**
Syrah Central Coast 1995: Pretty cherry, spice and blackberry notes lead the way. Tannins are ripe though a bit firm, giving structure but edging out the finish a bit. Good now, but might soften nicely in the bottle. Drink now through 2003. • $16 • (12/15/1998) • **86**
Syrah Central Coast Imagery Series 1994 • $19 • (5/15/1997) • **88**
Syrah Santa Maria Valley Bien Nacido Vineyard Imagery Series 1990 • $16 • (10/31/1993) • **70**
Zinfandel Port Dry Creek Valley Imagery Series 1994 • $20/500 ml. • (11/30/1996) • **78**
Zinfandel Port Dry Creek Valley Mayo Family & Carreras Vineyard Imagery Series 1990 • $22 • (10/15/1994) • **87**
Zinfandel Sonoma County 1997: Appealing for its complex berry, earth, spice and nutmeg flavors, holding its focus and gaining nuance. Drink now through 2004.–J.L. • $21 • (5/31/2000) • **85**
Zinfandel Sonoma County 1996: Ripe plum and raspberry flavors lead to notes of vanilla and caramel. Turns slightly green and dry on the finish. Drink now.–J.L. • $18 • (12/31/1998) • **84**
Zinfandel Sonoma County 1993 • $14 • (10/15/1995) • **85**
Zinfandel Sonoma County 1992 • $13 • (2/28/1995) • **86**
Zinfandel Sonoma County 1991 • $13 • (10/15/1994) • **87**
Zinfandel Sonoma County 1990 • $11 • (9/30/1993) • **85**
Zinfandel Sonoma County 1989 • $10 • (10/15/1992) • **83**
Zinfandel Sonoma County Old Vines 1995 • $17 • (5/15/1998) • **87**
Zinfandel Sonoma County Old Vines 1994 • $15 • (10/15/1996) • **89**

BERINGER | CALIFORNIA

Alluvium Knights Valley Red 1996: Supple and fruity up front, with ripe and chunky currant, plum, mineral and berryish flavors, it tightens up on the finish. Drink now through 2005.–J.L. • $30 • (9/15/1999) • **87**
Alluvium Knights Valley Red 1995: This delicious Merlot blend is tightly focused, with a firm tannic backbone and a well-defined core of black

cherry, plum and currant, picking up tea, herb and cedary notes. Finishes with fine, integrated tannins. Merlot, Cabernet Sauvignon, Cabernet Franc, Petit Verdot and Malbec. Drink now through 2005.–J.L. • $30 • (11/15/1998) SS • **90**

Alluvium Knights Valley Red 1994 • $25 • (3/31/1998) • **90**

Alluvium Knights Valley Red 1993 • $25 • (4/30/1997) • **90**

Alluvium Knights Valley White 1997: Rich and smoky, showing complex pear, fig, apricot and citrus notes, with a pleasant beam of acidity that keeps the flavors lively. Drink now.–J.L. • $16 • (4/30/2000) • **87**

Alluvium Knights Valley White 1996 • $16 • (3/31/1998) • **85**

Cabernet Franc Howell Mountain Third Century 1996: Supple and openly fruity, with rich, appealing, spicy cherry, wild berry and plum notes. Finishes with a touch of earth and cedar and polished tannins. Drink through 2008–J.L. • $75 • (12/15/1999) • **92**

Cabernet Sauvignon Howell Mountain Bancroft Vineyard 1998: Austere, with a tightly framed band of herb and cherry-laced flavors, picking up traces of dill and cedar before fanning out with oak.–J.L. • $NA • (8/31/1999) (BT) • **90-94**

Cabernet Sauvignon Howell Mountain Bancroft Ranch 1995: Tightly wound, with a core of herb-laced currant, spice, pencil lead and dusty berry, it's quite tannic and earthy now, but the finish reveals lots of complex flavors, so short-term cellaring is advised. Best from 2002 through 2007.–J.L. • $100 • (10/31/1999) • **93**

Cabernet Sauvignon Howell Mountain Bancroft Vineyard 1994 • $85 • (10/31/1997) • **97**

Cabernet Sauvignon Howell Mountain Tre Colline Vineyard 1995: Combines intensity with elegance. Ripe, detailed and complex, with pretty plum, currant, mineral, spice and coffee notes, picking up toasty oak and finishing long, rich and concentrated. Best from 2001 through 2009.–J.L. • $85 • (10/31/1999) • **92**

Cabernet Sauvignon Knights Valley 1994 • $20 • (7/31/1997) SS • **91**

Cabernet Sauvignon Knights Valley 1993 • $13 • (10/15/1996) • **87**

Cabernet Sauvignon Knights Valley 1992 • $15 • (8/31/1995) • **87**

Cabernet Sauvignon Knights Valley 1991 • $13 • (5/31/1994) • **87**

Cabernet Sauvignon Knights Valley 1990 • $13 • (11/15/1993) SS • **90**

Cabernet Sauvignon Knights Valley 1989 • $16 • (11/15/1992) • **85**

Cabernet Sauvignon Knights Valley 1988 • $16 • (11/15/1991) • **86**

Cabernet Sauvignon Knights Valley 1987 • $20 • (11/15/1990) HR • **90**

Cabernet Sauvignon Knights Valley 1985 • $20 • (5/31/1988) • **87**

Cabernet Sauvignon Knights Valley 1983 • $17 • (4/15/1987) • **83**

Cabernet Sauvignon Knights Valley 1982 • $22 • (4/15/1987) • **90**

Cabernet Sauvignon Knights Valley 1981 • $20 • (10/01/1985) • **86**

Cabernet Sauvignon Knights Valley 1980 • $20 • (2/16/1984) • **88**

Cabernet Sauvignon Knights Valley Appellation Collection 1996: Smooth, polished and concentrated, with a core of currant, cedar and plum flavors, finishing with mild tannins. Drink now through 2003.–J.L. • $25 • (10/15/1999) • **87**

Cabernet Sauvignon Knights Valley Appellation Collection 1995 • $22 • (6/15/1998) • **91**

Cabernet Sauvignon Napa Valley Chabot Vineyard 1994 • $85 • (10/31/1997) • **92**

Cabernet Sauvignon Napa Valley Chabot Vineyard 1993 • $100 • (6/15/1998) • **90**

Cabernet Sauvignon Napa Valley Chabot Vineyard 1992 • $100 • (12/15/1996) • **93**

Cabernet Sauvignon Napa Valley Chabot Vineyard 1989: Rich and chocolaty, with a band of mint, currant, anise, sage and cedar, finishing with firm, dry tannins and just a trace of nuttiness. Fine structure and complex flavors. (1989 California Cabernet retrospective tasting). Drink now through 2006.–J.L. • $35 • (8/31/1999) • **90**

Cabernet Sauvignon Napa Valley Chabot Vineyard 1988 • $35 • (11/15/1993) • **83**

Cabernet Sauvignon Napa Valley Chabot Vineyard 1987 • $35 • (12/15/1997) • **93**

Cabernet Sauvignon Napa Valley Chabot Vineyard 1985 • $31 • (11/15/1991) • **90**

Cabernet Sauvignon Napa Valley Chabot Vineyard 1984 • $55 Ⓐ • (9/15/1990) • **85**

Cabernet Sauvignon Napa Valley Marston Vineyard 1994 • $85 • (10/31/1997) • **92**

Key: SS—Spectator Selection. CS—Cellar Selection. HR—Highly Recommended. $NA—Price not available. (BT)—Barrel tasting. Ⓐ—Auction Price. For a key to the tasters' initials, see "How to Use These Listings." **Dates in parentheses represent the issues in which the ratings were published.**

Cabernet Sauvignon Napa Valley Private Reserve 1995: A tightly wound wine from a classic vintage, with a firm band of cedar and spice wrapped around a core of ripe plum, blackberry and black cherry. It fans out to reveal hints of olive and smoke, firming on the finish. Best from 2002 through 2011.–J.L. • $87 Ⓐ • (4/30/2000) CS • **92**

Cabernet Sauvignon Napa Valley Private Reserve 1994: A beautifully integrated, muscular young California Cabernet. Dark, dense and enormously complex and concentrated, with currant, black cherry, mineral, coffee, tar and anise aromas and flavors in spades, and ripe, rich tannins. Long, intensely flavorful aftertaste. Best from 2001 through 2009.–J.L. • $87 Ⓐ • (10/15/1998) CS • **95**

Cabernet Sauvignon Napa Valley Private Reserve 1993 • $69 Ⓐ • (5/31/1997) CS • **93**

Cabernet Sauvignon Napa Valley Private Reserve 1992 • $86 Ⓐ • (11/15/1995) CS • **95**

Cabernet Sauvignon Napa Valley Private Reserve 1991 • $93 Ⓐ • (3/31/1995) CS • **94**

Cabernet Sauvignon Napa Valley Private Reserve 1990 • $88 Ⓐ • (11/15/1994) CS • **92**

Cabernet Sauvignon Napa Valley Private Reserve 1989: Complex, and at an ideal drinking stage, with pretty plum, black cherry, currant, anise and spicy notes, finishing with firm, softening tannins and a nice dose of creamy oak. (1989 California Cabernet retrospective tasting). Drink now through 2007.–J.L. • $30 • (8/31/1999) • **91**

Cabernet Sauvignon Napa Valley Private Reserve 1988: Aging well, with earthy currant, anise, plum and cherry notes, it turns dry and leathery on the finish, yet manages to show a fleshy texture and bright fruit on the aftertaste. (1988 California Cabernet retrospective tasting). Drink now through 2002.–J.L. • $40 • (11/15/1998) • **88**

Cabernet Sauvignon Napa Valley Private Reserve 1987 • $112 Ⓐ • (12/15/1997) • **97**

Cabernet Sauvignon Napa Valley Private Reserve 1986 • $96 Ⓐ • (12/15/1996) • **89**

Cabernet Sauvignon Napa Valley Private Reserve 1985 • $111 Ⓐ • (12/15/1989) SS • **95**

Cabernet Sauvignon Napa Valley Private Reserve 1984 • $77 Ⓐ • (2/15/1989) CS • **94**

Cabernet Sauvignon Napa Valley Private Reserve 1983 • $19 • (4/15/1987) • **90**

Cabernet Sauvignon Napa Valley Private Reserve 1982 • $46 Ⓐ • (4/15/1987) • **94**

Cabernet Sauvignon Napa Valley Private Reserve 1981 • $18 • (4/15/1987) • **93**

Cabernet Sauvignon Napa Valley Private Reserve 1978: Dark, ripe and spicy, with a core of chocolate and currant, plum and cherry. Has reached a fine drinking plateau, with complex, concentrated flavors that are rich and sharply focused. Finishes with firm tannins, but it still shows lots of life. (1978 California Cabernet Retrospective tasting). Drink now through 2004.–J.L. • $25 • (11/15/1998) • **92**

Cabernet Sauvignon Napa Valley Private Reserve Lemmon-Chabot Vineyard 1981 • $34 • (4/15/1987) • **93**

Cabernet Sauvignon Napa Valley Private Reserve Lemmon-Chabot Vineyard 1980 • $20 • (8/01/1984) CS • **93**

Cabernet Sauvignon Napa Valley Private Reserve State Lane Vineyard 1980 • $15 • (8/01/1984) • **88**

Cabernet Sauvignon Napa Valley St. Helena Home Vineyard 1995: Wonderfully rich, smooth and polished, with chocolaty currant, black cherry, plum, herb and vanilla, it's tightly wound yet plush and concentrated. Drink through 2009–J.L. • $85 • (10/31/1999) • **94**

Cabernet Sauvignon Napa Valley State Lane Vineyard 1995: Ripe and juicy, with fleshy plum, black cherry, blackberry, earth and mushroom flavors, finishing with a nice focus and polished tannins that let the flavors ring true. Drink through 2009–J.L. • $85 • (10/31/1999) • **94**

Chardonnay Napa Valley 1996 • $15 • (1/31/1998) • **90**

Chardonnay Napa Valley Appellation Collection 1998: This starts with lots of smoky, toasty oak, but the fruit flavors fill in the gaps nicely, with ripe, focused pear, apple, citrus and melon notes that are elegant and lingering. Drink now through 2005.–J.L. • $16 • (2/29/2000) • **88**

Chardonnay Napa Valley Appellation Collection 1997: Elegant, with apple, toast and citrus notes, finishing with complex toasty oak flavors. Drink now.–J.L. • $16 • (12/31/1998) • **87**

Chardonnay Napa Valley Private Reserve 1998: Elegant, even understated, with a pretty core of hazelnut, ripe pear and citrus notes, if a bit shy on complexity and concentration. Tasted twice, with consistent notes. Drink now.–J.L. • $36 • (6/30/2000) • **87**

Chardonnay Napa Valley Private Reserve 1997: A tremendous effort in yet another great Chardonnay vintage in California. This wine is complex and concentrated, with lots of lovely ripe pear, nectarine, citrus and melon flavors, turning spicy with toasty oak notes. Drink now through 2002.–J.L. • $36 • (5/15/1999) HR • **93**

Chardonnay Napa Valley Private Reserve 1996 • $64 Ⓐ • (3/31/1998) HR • **95**

Chardonnay Napa Valley Sbragia Limited Release 1998: Ripe, rich and full-bodied, with layers of toasty pear, tangerine, butter and cream, holding its flavors on the long, complex aftertaste. Drink now through 2004.–J.L. • $40 • (6/30/2000) • **90**

Chardonnay Napa Valley Sbragia Limited Release 1997: Brilliant, tightly wound, richly flavored, with tiers of spicy pear, nutmeg, fig, melon and apricot that are sharply focused. Long, intense aftertaste. Drink now through 2003.–J.L. • $81 Ⓐ • (9/15/1999) • **93**

Chardonnay Napa Valley Sbragia Limited Release 1996: A big, ripe, rich and intense style, concentrated and full of exotic pear, fig, melon and toasty oak flavors. Another tremendous Chardonnay from Beringer (and winemaker Ed Sbragia), it's remarkably complex, turning elegant and supple on the finish. Bravo. Drink now through 2002 .–J.L. • $35 • (7/31/1998) HR • **94**

Gamay Beaujolais California 1996: A soft and flavorful red, à la Beaujolais, with ripe, juicy raspberry and black cherry flavors and hints of tea and vanilla. Its fruit flavors rev up in intensity on the finish. A tasty alternative, affordably priced. Drink now. • $7 • (9/30/1998) • **86**

Gamay Beaujolais California Nouveau 1997 • $7 • (2/28/1998) • **85**

Gamay Beaujolais California Nouveau 1996 • $7 • (2/28/1997) • **84**

Gamay Beaujolais California Nouveau 1995 • $8 • (2/29/1996) • **81**

Gamay Beaujolais California Nouveau 1994 • $8 • (1/01/1995) • **79**

Meritage Knights Valley 1992 • $13 • (11/15/1995) • **87**

Meritage Knights Valley 1991 • $13 • (9/15/1994) • **88**

Merlot California Founders' Estate 1997: Focused plum, berry and herb flavors ride on a supple though tightly knit frame. A new California appellation from Beringer. Drink now through 2003.–J.L. • $9 • (10/15/1999) • **85**

Merlot Howell Mountain Bancroft Ranch 1996: Supple and well proportioned, with earthy currant, cedar, spice, coffee and anise flavors, turning elegant and polished on the finish. Drink now through 2006.–J.L. • $75 • (9/15/1999) • **88**

Merlot Howell Mountain Bancroft Ranch 1995: A complex red from a reputable vineyard. Sharply focused, with a sense of elegance and finesse, this has a tight, tannic core of currant, anise, sage and spice, with pretty, vanilla-tinged oak shadings. Finishes with a long, integrated aftertaste. Drink through 2004–J.L. • $50 • (9/30/1998) CS • **92**

Merlot Howell Mountain Bancroft Ranch 1994 • $48 Ⓐ • (4/30/1998) • **89**

Merlot Howell Mountain Bancroft Ranch 1993 • $29 • (8/31/1996) • **89**

Merlot Howell Mountain Bancroft Ranch 1992 • $53 Ⓐ • (12/15/1995) SS • **92**

Merlot Howell Mountain Bancroft Ranch 1991 • $67 Ⓐ • (5/31/1994) CS • **90**

Merlot Howell Mountain Bancroft Ranch 1990 • $29 • (8/31/1993) • **90**

Merlot Howell Mountain Bancroft Ranch 1989 • $48 Ⓐ • (5/31/1992) • **91**

Merlot Howell Mountain Bancroft Ranch 1988 • $28 • (5/31/1992) • **90**

Merlot Howell Mountain Bancroft Ranch 1987 • $67 Ⓐ • (12/31/1990) • **91**

Nouveau California 1998: Soft-textured, with blackberry, black cherry, spicy vanilla notes and a touch of earthiness lingering on the soft finish. Drink now.–J.L. • $8 • (2/28/1999) • **84**

Pinot Noir Napa Valley Stanly Ranch 1994 • $20 • (12/31/1997) • **90**

Pinot Noir North Coast Appellation Collection 1996: Appealing for its modest cherry, plum and berry, turning simple with earthy brown sugar notes. Drink now.–J.L. • $16 • (8/31/1998) • **83**

Sauvignon Blanc Napa Valley 1996 • $9 • (1/31/1998) • **90**

Sauvignon Blanc Napa Valley Appellation Collection 1998: Good richness, dominated by buttery oak overtones and butterscotch flavors, with a hint of citrus. Drink now.–J.L. • $12 • (5/15/2000) • **85**

Sauvignon Blanc Napa Valley Appellation Collection 1997: A focused wine, smooth and silky on the palate, with a core of fresh pea, herb, grass, melon and grapefruit flavors. It's classy yet restrained, made in a bit of an older style, with subtlety as a hallmark. Drink now through 2001. • $11 • (1/31/1999) • **89**

Sauvignon Blanc-Sémillon Napa Valley Nightingale Botrytized Private Reserve 1994: Smooth, ultrarich and distinctive with its smoky fig, caramel, melon, toasted marshmallow and oaky flavors, this is a broad, complex, potent wine. Contains 17.1 percent residual sugar. Drink now through 2006.–J.L. • $22 • (12/15/1998) • **94**

Sémillon-Sauvignon Blanc Napa Valley Nightingale Founder's Reserve 1995: Truly exotic, loaded with caramel and nut as well as rich, creamy butterscotch, pear, fig, tobacco and smoky, toasty, roasted marshmallow flavors. Drink now through 2007.–J.L. • $30/375 ml. • (12/31/1999) • **94**

Viognier Napa Valley 1996: Decidedly spicy, with litchi, pear and orange blossom flavors that are rich, focused and long on the finish. Drink now through 2002.–J.L. • $28 • (12/15/1998) • **88**

Zinfandel Napa Valley 1992 • $9 • (9/15/1995) • **87**

Zinfandel Napa Valley 1991 • $8 • (8/31/1994) • **86**

Zinfandel Napa Valley 1990 • $9 • (9/30/1993) • **86**

Zinfandel Napa County 1989 • $9 • (10/15/1992) • **85**

Zinfandel North Coast 1994 • $12 • (8/31/1997) • **87**

Zinfandel North Coast 1993 • $10 • (2/28/1997) • **82**

Zinfandel North Coast 1992 • $10 • (12/31/1995) • **85**

Zinfandel North Coast 1988 • $9 • (2/29/1992) • **85**

Zinfandel North Coast Appellation Collection 1996: Barnyard and chocolate aromas, with cocoa, berry and oak flavors that linger. Drink now.–J.L. • $12 • (5/31/2000) • **83**

Zinfandel North Coast Appellation Collection 1995 • $12 • (6/15/1998) • **88**

BERNARDUS | CALIFORNIA

Chardonnay Monterey County 1997: An enticing California Chardonnay with a complex flavor profile of rich fig, pear, hazelnut and citrus couched in a smooth and creamy texture. A short term in the cellar should add the finishing touches. Try through 2003.–J.L. • $18 • (8/31/1999) SS • **90**

Chardonnay Monterey County 1996 • $18 • (6/30/1998) SS • **91**

Marinus Carmel Valley 1996: Firm, with a band of spicy currant, anise, cedary oak and hints of herb. Holds its focus, finishing with detailed tannins. Best from 2002 through 2009.–J.L. • $40 • (1/31/2000) • **88**

Marinus Carmel Valley 1995: Lean and a touch green, with cedary oak and hints of tobacco and currant. Strives for complexity and may deliver. Tasted twice, with consistent notes. A blend of Cabernet Sauvignon, Merlot, Cabernet Franc and Petit Verdot. Drink through 2006–J.L. • $36 • (1/31/1999) • **86**

Marinus Carmel Valley 1994 • $30 • (4/30/1997) • **90**

Marinus Carmel Valley 1993 • $24 • (8/31/1996) • **85**

Pinot Noir Santa Barbara County Bien Nacido Vineyard 1996: Light, with tarry orange blossom, dried cherry and spicy notes, this is elegant but on the simple side. Drink now.–J.L. • $42 • (2/28/1999) • **85**

Pinot Noir Santa Barbara County Bien Nacido Vineyard 1995 • $35 • (1/31/1998) • **91**

Pinot Noir Santa Maria Valley Bien Nacido Vineyard 1994 • $30 • (11/30/1996) • **90**

Pinot Noir Santa Barbara County Bien Nacido Vineyard 1993 • $25 • (1/31/1996) • **86**

Pinot Noir Santa Barbara County Bien Nacido Vineyard 1992 • $18 • (2/28/1995) • **86**

Sauvignon Blanc Monterey County 1998: Tight, flinty and restrained, almost to a fault, as the taut herb, artichoke and asparagus flavors are raw and coarse. Drink now through 2005.–J.L. • $14 • (4/30/2000) • **86**

Sauvignon Blanc Monterey County 1997: Tangy and sleek, boasting a refreshing medley of gooseberry, melon, citrus, fig, hay and fresh grass notes, this California white is really tasty and decently priced, too. It's elegant and refined, finishing long and clean. Drink now through 2002. • $14 • (1/31/1999) SS • **90**

Sauvignon Blanc Monterey County 1996 • $14 • (11/30/1997) • **87**

BETHEL HEIGHTS | OREGON

Pinot Blanc Willamette Valley 1998: Light and refreshing. A pretty mouthful of pear and green melon flavors that linger on the lively finish. Drink now.–H.S. • $12 • (3/31/2000) • **85**

Pinot Noir Willamette Valley 1997: Light and pretty, with a caramel and spice edge to the modest strawberry. Has a green tinge to the flavors on the finish. Drink now through 2002.–H.S. • $15 • (11/15/1999) • **84**

Pinot Noir Willamette Valley 1995 • $17 • (4/30/1997) • **87**

Pinot Noir Willamette Valley 1988 • $15 • (4/15/1991) • **87**

Pinot Noir Willamette Valley 1987 • $12 • (2/15/1990) • **86**

Pinot Noir Willamette Valley 1986 • $15 • (6/15/1988) • **86**

Pinot Noir Willamette Valley 1985 • $12 • (2/15/1990) • **79**

Pinot Noir Willamette Valley Eola Hills Cuvée 1996 • $12 • (5/15/1998) • **85**

Pinot Noir Willamette Valley Estate Grown 1997: Has a little more ripeness and heft than most 1997 Oregon Pinots, offering pretty currant and mineral flavors that finish with a light touch of tannin. Drink through 2005–H.S. • $22 • (11/15/1999) • **86**

Pinot Noir Willamette Valley Estate Grown 1996 • $20 • (5/15/1998) • **87**

Pinot Noir Willamette Valley Estate Grown 1992 • $16 • (11/30/1994) • **81**

Pinot Noir Willamette Valley Estate Grown 1991 • $15 • (6/30/1993) • **89**

Pinot Noir Willamette Valley Estate Grown 1990 • $15 • (2/28/1993) • **73**

Pinot Noir Willamette Valley Estate Grown First Release 1990 • $10 • (2/28/1993) • **85**

Pinot Noir Willamette Valley Estate Grown Flat Block Reserve 1992 • $24 • (11/30/1994) • **85**

Pinot Noir Willamette Valley Estate Grown Reserve 1990 • $24 • (2/28/1993) • **81**

Pinot Noir Willamette Valley Estate Grown Southeast Block Reserve 1992 • $24 • (11/30/1994) • **82**

BETHEL HEIGHTS

Pinot Noir Willamette Valley First Release 1994 • $10 • (1/31/1996) • **85**
Pinot Noir Willamette Valley Flat Block Reserve 1997: Crisp in texture, with modest berry flavors under a zingy layer of mineral and spice notes. Not generous, but it could broaden with time. Best from 2001 through 2004.–H.S. • $30 • (11/15/1999) • **83**
Pinot Noir Willamette Valley Flat Block Reserve 1993 • $24 • (1/31/1996) • **83**
Pinot Noir Willamette Valley Flat Block 1991 • $18 • (9/30/1993) • **78**
Pinot Noir Willamette Valley Reserve 1988 • $18 • (4/15/1991) • **86**
Pinot Noir Willamette Valley Southeast Block Reserve 1997: Firm in texture, with solid black cherry, earth and tobacco flavors that expand a bit on the generous finish. Balance favors the fruit. Drink now through 2004.–H.S. • $30 • (11/15/1999) • **86**
Pinot Noir Willamette Valley Southeast Block Reserve 1995 • $24 • (12/31/1997) • **87**
Pinot Noir Willamette Valley Southeast Block Reserve 1993 • $24 • (1/31/1996) • **79**
Pinot Noir Willamette Valley Southeast Block Reserve 1991 • $22 • (9/30/1993) • **81**
Pinot Noir Willamette Valley Unfiltered 1985 • $12 • (2/15/1990) • **86**
Pinot Noir Willamette Valley Wädenswil Block Reserve 1995 • $24 • (12/31/1997) • **81**

BETTINELLI | CALIFORNIA

Cabernet Sauvignon Napa Valley 1991 • $14 • (5/31/1995) • **82**
Merlot Napa Valley 1993 • $25 • (3/31/1996) • **88**

BIALE, ROBERT | CALIFORNIA

Petite Sirah Napa Valley Proprietor's Series Old Vineyards 1996: Pleasantly balanced, with ripe plum and black cherry tones accented by spicy, peppery notes. Polished tannins. Drink now through 2004.–J.L. • $35 • (12/31/1999) • **87**
Petite Sirah Napa Valley Old Vineyards 1995 • $35 • (4/30/1998) • **85**
Sangiovese Napa Valley Proprietor's Series Nonna's Vineyard 1997: A ripe, juicy style, with plenty of cherry, raspberry and cranberry flavors that are elegant and lively. Drink now through 2001.–J.L. • $30 • (11/15/1999) • **87**
Zinfandel Napa Valley Aldo's Vineyard 1997: Wonderful sense of harmony and finesse, packed with ripe, rich, polished cherry, plum and raspberry flavors that turn supple on the finish. Drink now through 2002.–J.L. • $30 • (6/15/1999) • **92**
Zinfandel Napa Valley Aldo's Vineyard 1996: Ripe, with a jammy wild berry edge, hints of cherry, sage, cedar and spice, turning spicier and elegant. Drink now through 2002.–J.L. • 48 Ⓐ • (1/31/1999) • **88**
Zinfandel Napa Valley Aldo's Vineyard Proprietor's Series 1994 • $19 • (5/15/1996) HR • **93**
Zinfandel Napa Valley Aldo's Vineyard Proprietor's Series 1993 • $18 • (10/15/1995) HR • **91**
Zinfandel Napa Valley Aldo's Vineyard Proprietor's Series 1992 • $14 • (10/15/1994) • **84**
Zinfandel Napa Valley Aldo's Vineyard Proprietor's Series 1991 • $15 • (9/30/1993) • **86**
Zinfandel Napa Valley Appellation Series 1997: A subtle, understated style, with ripe, dry raspberry and blackberry wrapped around firm, earthy tannins. Drink now through 2007.–J.L. • $26 • (12/15/1999) • **88**
Zinfandel Napa Valley Falleri Vineyards 1995 • $26 • (3/31/1997) • **88**
Zinfandel Napa Valley Old Crane Ranch 1996: Serves up ripe, jammy black cherry, blackberry, anise, sage and spice, turning fleshy and supple. Drink now through 2002.–J.L. • $48 Ⓐ • (1/31/1999) • **89**
Zinfandel Napa Valley Old Crane Ranch 1995 • $24 • (3/31/1997) • **85**
Zinfandel Napa Valley Old Vineyards Late Picked 1995 • $30 • (3/31/1997) • **88**
Zinfandel Napa Valley Proprietor Series Old Crane Ranch 1998: Candied, with coarse blackberry and cherry-laced fruit, turning dry and tannic. Drink now through 2004.–J.L. • $35 • (5/15/2000) • **82**
Zinfandel Napa Valley Two Vineyards 1995 • $24 • (3/31/1997) • **88**
Zinfandel Sonoma Valley Appellation Series 1997: Ripe, smooth and polished, with pretty, peppery cherry and wild berry, but it's shy of outstanding. Drink now through 2004.–J.L. • $26 • (11/30/1999) • **86**
Zinfandel Sonoma Valley Monte Rosso Vineyard 1997: Decidedly spicy, with lots of peppery notes. Turns supple and polished, with earthy berry, cherry, tar and cedar flavors. Finishes with firm but mild tannins. Drink now through 2002.–J.L. • $30 • (6/15/1999) • **88**
Zinfandel Sonoma Valley Monte Rosso Vineyard 1996: Supple and focused, with coffee-laced wild berry and blackberry flavors, picking up complex mint, sage and cedary notes. Drink now through 2002.–J.L. • $25 • (1/31/1999) • **90**
Zinfandel Sonoma Valley Valsecchi Vineyard 1996: Dark, ripe, rich and complex, brimming with juicy blackberry, black cherry and wild berry flavors that have a slight jammy edge. Drink now through 2003.–J.L. • $48 Ⓐ • (1/31/1999) • **90**

BIDWELL | NEW YORK

Cabernet Sauvignon North Fork of Long Island 1994: Fans of Pauillac will appreciate the flavors of lead pencil, mineral and earth in this rather tough, tannic red. Offers good concentration, if at the expense of finesse, and is still tight and firm. Drink through 2005–T.M. • $20 • (6/30/1999) • **86**
Cabernet Sauvignon North Fork of Long Island 1988 • $12 • (6/30/1991) • **82**
Cabernet Sauvignon North Fork of Long Island 1987 • $12 • (6/30/1991) • **81**
Chardonnay North Fork of Long Island Barrel Fermented 1997: Pear and apple flavors are clean and light in this smooth white. Leans toward refinement rather than exuberance, and turns soft and a bit nutty on the finish. Drink now.–T.M. • $15 • (6/30/1999) • **82**
Merlot North Fork of Long Island 1994: Maturing now, this thick, jammy red offers flavors of coffee, brown sugar and dried cherry. Plush on the palate but turning dry on the finish, it needs food to soften. Drink now through 2002.–T.M. • $20 • (6/30/1999) • **83**
Merlot North Fork of Long Island 1988 • $11 • (6/30/1991) • **85**
Merlot North Fork of Long Island Reserve 1987 • $16 • (3/31/1990) • **83**

BIGHORN RANCH | CALIFORNIA

Cabernet Sauvignon Napa County 1996: Flavorful and bright, this California red entices with its complex, up-front black cherry, raspberry, wild berry and spice, all on a medium-weight frame, with mild tannins. Drink now through 2007.–J.L. • $26 • (12/31/1999) HR • **88**
Chardonnay Carneros 1998: Pear, apple and licorice flavors precede a vanilla finish. To be released August 2000. Drink now.–J.L. • $22 • (6/30/2000) • **85**
Chardonnay Carneros 1997: Rich and full-bodied, with bright sweet cream, nut and lemony citrus flavors. Crisp finish. Drink now.–J.L. • $20 • (6/30/1999) • **86**
Chardonnay Carneros Camelback Vineyard 1998: Begins with a warm buttery depth, backed by pear and spicy vanilla notes. Drink now.–J.L. • $28 • (6/30/2000) • **85**
Chardonnay Napa Valley Reserve 1996 • $20 • (5/31/1998) SS • **91**

BILTMORE ESTATE | NORTH CAROLINA

Brut Blanc de Blancs North Carolina NV • $17 • (8/31/1997) • **80**
Cabernet Sauvignon America NV: Well focused, with pretty red cherry, currant and cranberry flavors mixed with spice and chocolate elements. Finishes with nice touches of herb and cinnamon. Drink now through 2001.–K.M. • $13 • (2/28/1999) • **83**
Cabernet Sauvignon America 1987 • $16 • (2/29/1992) • **84**
Cabernet Sauvignon North Carolina 1993 • $13 • (12/31/1995) • **81**
Cabernet Sauvignon North Carolina 1987 • $16 • (2/29/1992) • **76**
Cabernet Sauvignon North Carolina Château Biltmore 1997: Crisp and nicely concentrated, with red plum, currant and lovely cherry flavors. A good expression of Cabernet Sauvignon, ending on pleasant herb and chocolate notes. Drink now through 2001.–K.M. • $20 • (2/28/1999) • **86**
Cabernet Sauvignon North Carolina Château Biltmore 1993 • $20 • (12/31/1995) • **79**
Cabernet Sauvignon North Carolina George Washington Vanderbilt Centennial Release 1992 • $25 • (12/31/1995) • **83**
George Washington Vanderbilt Centennial North Carolina 1993 • $30 • (12/31/1995) • **83**
Vanderbilt Claret North Carolina 1995 • $20 • (8/31/1997) • **82**

BLACK ROCK | CALIFORNIA

Zinfandel Lake County 1996 • $15 • (6/15/1998) • **78**

BLACK SHEEP | CALIFORNIA

Zinfandel Sierra Foothills 1995 • $12 • (3/31/1998) • **85**

Key: SS—Spectator Selection. CS—Cellar Selection. HR—Highly Recommended. $NA—Price not available. (BT)—Barrel tasting. Ⓐ—Auction Price.
For a key to the tasters' initials, see "How to Use These Listings."
Dates in parentheses represent the issues in which the ratings were published.

BLACKJACK RANCH | CALIFORNIA

Chardonnay Central Coast 1998: Dull, with sour apple and mineral notes and a sparkle of lemon that livens up the finish. Drink now.–J.L. • $18 • (6/15/2000) • **81**
Chardonnay Santa Barbara County Reserve 1998: Earthy and a touch coarse, with extracted citrus, pear and juniper berry flavors. Finishes dry and tannic. Best from 2001 through 2005.–J.L. • $28 • (4/30/2000) • **85**
Chardonnay Santa Barbara County Reserve 1997: Lots of complex flavors, with rich smoky pear, fig and nutty notes that turn smooth and linger. Drink now.–J.L. • $28 • (2/28/1999) • **89**
Harmonie Santa Barbara County 1997: Smoky black currant and chocolate flavors have good depth and intensity, then turn slightly rough on the finish. Best from 2002 through 2004.–J.L. • $32 • (4/30/2000) • **86**
Pinot Noir San Luis Obispo County Laetitia Vineyard 1998: Earthy, with stewed plum, spicy cherry and dry, leathery notes. Rather dull. Drink now through 2005.–J.L. • $32 • (4/30/2000) • **80**

BLACKSTONE | CALIFORNIA

Chardonnay California 1997: Bright and citrusy, with apple and herb flavors, but it lacks dimension. Drink now.–J.L. • $10 • (7/31/1999) • **82**
Chardonnay Monterey County 1998: Crisp, with tart lemon flavors that are refreshing. Drink now.–J.L. • $10 • (6/30/2000) • **82**
Merlot California 1997: Shows a core of herbal plum and cherry flavors. Finishes with cedary notes and mild tannins. Drink now.–J.L. • $12 • (10/15/1999) • **81**
Merlot California 1995 • $11 • (11/30/1996) • **81**
Merlot California Barrel Reserve 1994 • $10 • (8/31/1996) • **77**
Merlot Napa County Grand Reserve 1994 • $14 • (8/31/1996) • **77**
Merlot Napa County Reserve 1993 • $10 • (4/30/1996) • **89**
Merlot Napa Valley 1997: Features lots of toasted oak flavors with complex plum, cherry and mineral notes that turn supple in texture, with integrated tannins on the finish. Drink now through 2003.–J.L. • $18 • (9/15/1999) • **88**
Merlot Sonoma County Grand Reserve 1994 • $18 • (7/31/1997) • **87**
Pinot Noir Santa Barbara County 1990 • $8 • (2/28/1993) • **81**
Zinfandel California Old Vine Cuvée 1994 • $12 • (11/30/1996) • **81**

BLOCKHEADIA RINGNOSII | CALIFORNIA

Petite Sirah Napa Valley 1994 • $25 • (5/15/1997) • **88**
Zinfandel Napa Valley 1994 • $20 • (5/15/1997) • **90**
Zinfandel Rutherford 1993 • $15 • (10/15/1995) • **85**
Zinfandel Rutherford 1992 • $15 • (2/28/1995) • **88**

BLOSSOM HILL | CALIFORNIA

Cabernet Sauvignon California 1993 • $5 • (12/15/1996) • **78**
Chardonnay California 1996: Simple and soft, with light, floral and earthy citrus flavors and a touch of celery. Drink now. • $5 • (7/31/1998) • **78**
Merlot California 1994 • $6 • (11/30/1996) • **77**

BOCAGE | CALIFORNIA

Cabernet Sauvignon Monterey Proprietor's Cuvée 1990 • $10 • (11/15/1994) • **70**
Merlot Monterey 1995: Ripe plum and black cherry here, with touches of charry oak and spice on the finish. Drink now.–J.L. • $9 • (9/30/1998) • **82**
Merlot Monterey Proprietor's Cuvée 1990 • $10 • (9/15/1994) • **84**
Merlot Monterey Proprietor's Cuvée 1989 • $10 • (10/31/1992) • **74**

BOEGER | CALIFORNIA

Barbera El Dorado 1997: Bright, with hints of Bing cherry, cassis and anise and a touch of tar at the end. Hangs in with a moderate finish. Soft and accessible. Drink now through 2001. • $14 • (11/15/1999) • **85**
Barbera El Dorado 1996: Full-bodied, with supple texture and pretty black cherry, blackberry, currant and spice notes. The finish is refreshing and tangy and lingers nicely on the palate. Drink now through 2002. • $14 • (4/30/1999) • **86**
Barbera El Dorado 1995 • $14 • (11/30/1997) • **84**
Barbera El Dorado 1993 • $12 • (11/15/1995) • **86**
Barbera El Dorado 1992 • $12 • (7/31/1995) • **84**
Barbera El Dorado 1991 • $11 • (10/31/1993) • **84**
Barbera El Dorado 1990 • $11 • (11/30/1992) • **81**
Barbera El Dorado 1989 • $10 • (10/31/1991) • **85**
Barbera El Dorado Vineyard Select 1997: Smoky oak leads the charge, followed by pretty plum, licorice, herb and spice flavors. Tannins are a bit rustic, but the wine drinks well, with a moderate finish. Drink now through 2002. • $20 • (11/15/1999) • **86**
Barbera El Dorado Vineyard Select 1996: Fairly smooth, with black cherry notes and a hint of bacon to round things out. Tannins are firm but supple, while the finish is fairly long, carried by bright acidity. Drink now through 2004. • $20 • (4/30/1999) • **87**
Barbera El Dorado Vineyard Select 1994 • $15 • (7/31/1997) • **87**
Cabernet Sauvignon El Dorado 1996: Smooth and herbal, with green pepper and plum flavors. Drink now through 2002 .–J.L. • $15 • (10/15/1999) • **81**
Cabernet Sauvignon El Dorado 1994 • $12 • (10/15/1997) • **85**
Cabernet Sauvignon El Dorado 1993 • $12 • (9/30/1997) • **80**
Cabernet Sauvignon El Dorado 1991 • $12 • (12/15/1995) • **78**
Cabernet Sauvignon El Dorado 1990 • $12 • (11/15/1994) • **83**
Cabernet Sauvignon El Dorado 1989 • $12 • (11/15/1992) • **83**
Cabernet Sauvignon El Dorado 1987 • $11 • (3/15/1991) • **85**
Cabernet Sauvignon El Dorado 1985 • $11 • (2/15/1989) • **77**
Cabernet Sauvignon El Dorado 1984 • $11 • (5/31/1988) • **81**
Cabernet Sauvignon El Dorado 1983 • $10 • (8/31/1987) • **82**
Cabernet Sauvignon Napa Valley Joseph A. Nichelini Vineyards 1989 • $12 • (11/15/1993) • **77**
Chardonnay El Dorado 1996: A pear and spice streak runs through, with a healthy dose of oak on the finish. Drink now. • $12 • (7/31/1998) • **83**
Majeure El Dorado Reserve 1994 • $15 • (9/30/1997) • **87**
Meritage El Dorado 1995: Smooth, featuring herb, jalapeño pepper and plum flavors. Drink now through 2003 .–J.L. • $15 • (10/15/1999) • **81**
Meritage Reserve El Dorado 1994 • $15 • (6/30/1998) • **84**
Meritage El Dorado 1993 • $15 • (10/15/1997) • **87**
Meritage El Dorado 1992 • $15 • (3/31/1996) • **77**
Meritage El Dorado 1991 • $15 • (12/15/1995) • **86**
Meritage El Dorado 1989 • $14 • (10/15/1992) • **83**
Merlot El Dorado 1996: Firm, with a narrow range of cherry, mineral and tea flavors and a slight green edge. Finishes with dry tannins. Drink now.–J.L. • $15 • (10/15/1999) • **80**
Merlot El Dorado 1995 • $15 • (11/30/1997) • **83**
Merlot El Dorado 1994 • $15 • (11/30/1996) • **80**
Merlot El Dorado 1993 • $14 • (8/31/1996) • **82**
Merlot El Dorado 1992 • $14 • (3/31/1995) • **86**
Merlot El Dorado 1991 • $13 • (10/15/1993) • **86**
Merlot El Dorado 1990 • $13 • (1/31/1993) • **78**
Merlot El Dorado 1988 • $13 • (3/31/1991) • **78**
Merlot El Dorado 1987 • $13 • (7/15/1990) • **81**
Merlot El Dorado 1986 • $13 • (1/31/1989) • **73**
Merlot El Dorado 1985 • $13 • (2/15/1988) • **82**
Merlot El Dorado 1982 • $10 • (10/01/1984) • **74**
Migliόre El Dorado Reserve 1995: Light in texture, with earthy, spicy flavors that linger. Barbera blend. Drink now.–H.S. • $15 • (7/31/1998) • **80**
Migliόre El Dorado Reserve 1994 • $14 • (2/28/1997) • **87**
Migliόre El Dorado Reserve 1993 • $14 • (11/30/1995) • **85**
Sauvignon Blanc El Dorado 1998: Light and refreshing, with lemongrass, citrus notes and a ripe pineapple flavor that lingers on the finish. Drink now through 2003.–H.S. • $13 • (3/31/2000) • **86**
Sauvignon Blanc El Dorado 1997 • $10 • (4/30/1998) • **88**
Sauvignon Blanc El Dorado 1996 • $9 • (6/30/1997) • **89**
Zinfandel El Dorado 1997: Smooth and soft, with a spicy core of cola, cherry and berry flavors. Drink now.–J.L. • $15 • (11/15/1999) • **84**
Zinfandel El Dorado 1996: Firm and chewy, with nicely focused blackberry and tar aromas and flavors. Mild tannins want hearty food. Drink now through 2002.–H.S. • $15 • (11/30/1998) • **86**
Zinfandel El Dorado Estate 1995 • $12 • (6/15/1998) • **81**
Zinfandel El Dorado 1994 • $10 • (4/30/1997) • **88**
Zinfandel El Dorado 1993 • $10 • (3/31/1996) • **76**
Zinfandel El Dorado 1992 • $10 • (10/15/1994) • **84**
Zinfandel El Dorado Walker Vineyard 1996: Soft and open-textured, with pretty plum and smoke aromas and flavors. Finishes with a light earthy bite. Drink now through 2002.–H.S. • $15 • (11/30/1998) • **85**
Zinfandel El Dorado Walker Vineyard 1995 • $15 • (5/15/1998) • **88**
Zinfandel El Dorado Walker Vineyard 1994 • $12 • (3/31/1997) • **88**
Zinfandel El Dorado Walker Vineyard 1993 • $12 • (10/15/1995) • **85**
Zinfandel El Dorado Walker Vineyard 1992 • $12 • (10/15/1994) • **87**
Zinfandel El Dorado Walker Vineyard 1991 • $10 • (9/30/1993) • **87**
Zinfandel El Dorado Walker Vineyard 1990 • $10 • (10/15/1992) HR • **90**
Zinfandel El Dorado Walker Vineyard 1989 • $10 • (9/30/1991) • **84**
Zinfandel El Dorado Walker Vineyard 1988 • $9 • (2/15/1991) • **85**

BOEGER

Zinfandel Napa Valley Joseph A. Nichelini Vineyards 1993 • $12 • (4/30/1997) • **87**
Zinfandel Napa Valley Joseph A. Nichelini Vineyards 1990 • $10 • (4/30/1993) • **81**
Zinfandel Napa Valley Joseph A. Nichelini Vineyards 1989 • $12 • (10/15/1992) • **80**
Zinfandel Napa Valley Joseph A. Nichelini Vineyards 1988 • $12 • (8/31/1991) • **85**

BOGLE | CALIFORNIA

Cabernet Sauvignon California 1997: Plush, with a beefy edge to the rich plum, dill, spice and currant flavors. Finishes firm. Good value. Drink now.–J.L. • $10 • (6/15/1999) • **85**
Cabernet Sauvignon California 1996: Serves up plum and blackberry notes while showing a little stewed-fruit and smoky notes around the edges. Moderate body and finish. • $10 • (11/15/1998) • **78**
Cabernet Sauvignon California 1995 • $8 • (12/15/1997) • **78**
Cabernet Sauvignon California 1994 • $7 • (11/30/1996) • **84**
Cabernet Sauvignon California 1993 • $7 • (11/30/1995) • **85**
Cabernet Sauvignon California 1992 • $7 • (5/15/1994) • **81**
Cabernet Sauvignon California 1990 • $6 • (11/15/1992) • **83**
Cabernet Sauvignon California 1989 • $7/1 liter • (11/15/1992) • **77**
Chardonnay California 1998: Watery, with apple and metallic notes, finishing pasty.–J.L. • $9 • (6/15/2000) • **78**
Chardonnay California 1997: Balanced mineral and mild citrus notes on a light frame. Drink now.–L. • $8 • (11/30/1998) • **80**
Chardonnay California 1996 • $7 • (11/30/1997) • **84**
Chenin Blanc Clarksburg 1998: Licorice and apple flavors are sweet and a bit watery. Drink now.–J.L. • $7 • (6/15/2000) • **82**
Chenin Blanc Clarksburg 1996 • $7 • (9/15/1997) • **83**
Fumé Blanc California 1996 • $7 • (7/31/1997) • **82**
Merlot California 1998: Shows camphor and candied cherry notes that are light, simple and straightforward. Drink now.–J.L. • $9 • (6/30/2000) • **81**
Merlot California 1997: Smooth, with toasted oak, herb and berry flavors that firm up on the finish. Drink now.–J.L. • $9 • (10/15/1999) • **81**
Merlot California 1996: A blend of oak, plum, cherry, smoke and spice flavors. Somewhat cloying on the finish, it tastes a bit manufactured, but is still pleasant. Drink now. • $9 • (7/31/1998) • **81**
Merlot California 1995 • $9 • (7/31/1997) • **83**
Merlot California 1994 • $9 • (8/31/1996) • **72**
Merlot California 1992 • $8 • (9/15/1994) • **83**
Merlot California 1991 • $8 • (7/15/1993) • **85**
Merlot California 1990 • $8 • (5/31/1992) • **82**
Merlot Clarksburg Reserve 1993: Earthy, with juniper berry and cherry-laced Merlot flavors that lack focus. Drink now.–J.L. • $18 • (10/15/1998) • **81**
Petite Sirah California 1997: Bogle does it again, earning this wine "best buy" status six of the last seven vintages. The '97 is ripe and juicy, with spicy blueberry and black currant flavors, finishing with peppery herbal tones and smoky, toasted oak notes. Drink now through 2001.–J.L. • $9 • (4/30/1999) • **87**
Petite Sirah California 1996: Ripe and rich, with a smooth texture, this effusive red brims with black cherry and blackberry aromas and flavors that unveil toast and vanilla tones on the long finish. Plush and polished, it's already approachable, and certainly fairly priced.–H.S. • $9 • (11/30/1998) • **88**
Petite Sirah California 1995 • $9 • (3/31/1998) • **85**
Petite Sirah California 1994 • $8 • (11/30/1996) • **78**
Petite Sirah California 1993 • $7 • (11/15/1995) • **86**
Petite Sirah California 1992 • $7 • (2/28/1995) • **85**
Petite Sirah California 1991 • $6 • (7/31/1993) • **88**
Petite Sirah Clarksburg 1988 • $7 • (10/31/1989) • **70**
Sauvignon Blanc California 1998: What a deal, from a habitual Best Buy producer. It's soft in texture, oozing with tropical fruit flavors—mango, passion fruit and pineapple. Refreshing acidity keeps the balance. Drink now through 2002.–H.S. • $7 • (3/31/2000) • **85**
Sauvignon Blanc California 1997: The light, pearlike flavors seem atypical of Sauvignon Blanc; the wine is lean and smooth but lacks the complexity one hopes for from this varietal. Drink now. • $8 • (2/28/1999) • **83**
Zinfandel California 1993 • $6 • (10/15/1995) • **83**
Zinfandel California 1992 • $7 • (5/15/1995) • **84**

> **Key:** SS—Spectator Selection. CS—Cellar Selection. HR—Highly Recommended. $NA—Price not available. (BT)—Barrel tasting. Ⓐ—Auction Price.
> For a key to the tasters' initials, see "How to Use These Listings."
> **Dates in parentheses represent the issues in which the ratings were published.**

Zinfandel California Old Vine Cuvée 1998: Plum, pepper and dried berry flavors are focused. Drink now through 2002.–J.L. • $11 • (6/15/2000) • **83**
Zinfandel California Old Vine Cuvée 1997: Joining Bogle's Petite Sirah of the same vintage as a Best Buy is this soft, rich, very ripe plum- and blackberry-flavored Zin, with pleasant notes of herbs and spices. Drink now through 2002.–J.L. • $10 • (5/15/1999) • **88**
Zinfandel California Old Vine Cuvée 1995 • $11 • (3/31/1998) • **82**
Zinfandel California Old Vine Cuvée 1994 • $9 • (2/28/1997) • **87**
Zinfandel California Old Vine Reserve 1994 • $18 • (5/15/1998) • **84**
Zinfandel Fiddletown Reserve 1997: Stewed berry, plum and funky overtones combine with dry tannins through the chocolaty finish. Drink now.–J.L. • $18 • (5/15/2000) • **84**

BON ANNO | CALIFORNIA

Fusione California NV: Earthy and gamy, with tart cherry flavors. Finishes dry. Sangiovese blend. • $10 • (2/28/1999) • **79**
Sangiovese Dry Creek Valley Riserva 1996: Pretty cherry and spice notes form the core of this light-textured wine. Finishes short and dry. Drink now. • $13 • (2/28/1999) • **82**

BONNY DOON | CALIFORNIA

Cabernet Franc California Pacific Rim 1994 • $10 • (11/30/1995) • **83**
Framboise Santa Cruz Mountains NV • $9/375 ml. • (7/31/1995) • **90**
Garnacha California NV • $12 • (12/15/1996) • **85**
Gewürztraminer Monterey County Pacific Rim 1996 • $12 • (11/30/1997) • **88**
Gewüztraminer Oregon Vin de Glacière 1990 • $15/375 ml. • (3/31/1992) • **90**
Grahm Crew Vin Rouge California 1989 • $8 • (10/31/1990) • **82**
Grahm Crew Vin Rouge California 1988 • $8 • (2/15/1990) • **83**
Grenache America Clos de Gilroy Cuvée St. Marcel NV • $9 • (8/31/1996) • **84**
Grenache California Clos de Gilroy 1994 • $8 • (11/15/1995) • **87**
Grenache California Clos de Gilroy 1993 • $8 • (4/15/1994) • **87**
Grenache California Clos de Gilroy 1992 • $8 • (2/15/1993) • **84**
Grenache California Clos de Gilroy 1991 • $8 • (7/31/1992) • **84**
Grenache California Clos de Gilroy 1990 • $8 • (2/15/1991) • **87**
Grenache California Clos de Gilroy Cuvée Tremblement de Terre 1989 • $8 • (2/15/1990) • **88**
Grenache California Clos de Gilroy 1988 • $7 • (2/15/1989) • **85**
Le Cigare Volant California 1996: Smells fruity, with hints of plum and wild berry, yet turns dry and tannic on the palate with less fruit evident. A blend of Syrah, Grenache, Cinsault and Mourvèdre. Drink now through 2002.–J.L. • $18 Ⓐ • (12/15/1998) • **85**
Le Cigare Volant California 1995 • $23 • (11/30/1997) • **88**
Le Cigare Volant California 1994 • $20 • (3/31/1997) • **87**
Le Cigare Volant California 1993 • $20 • (10/15/1995) • **85**
Le Cigare Volant California 1990 • $18 • (11/30/1992) • **87**
Le Cigare Volant California 1989 • $20 • (3/15/1992) • **80**
Le Cigare Volant California 1988 • $19 • (12/31/1990) • **86**
Le Cigare Volant California 1987 • $36 Ⓐ • (12/15/1989) • **85**
Le Cigare Volant California 1986 • $14 • (11/15/1988) • **92**
Le Cigare Volant California 1985 • $13 • (1/31/1988) • **90**
Le Cigare Volant California 1984 • $11 • (8/31/1986) • **87**
Le Gaucher California 1992 • $12 • (3/31/1994) • **82**
Le Sophiste Santa Cruz Mountains 1993 • $25 • (5/15/1995) • **87**
Malvasia Bianca Monterey Vin de Glacière 1991 • $15 • (12/15/1992) • **85**
Mourvèdre California Old Telegram 1995 • $30 • (11/30/1997) • **89**
Mourvèdre California Old Telegram 1993 • $20 • (12/15/1995) • **83**
Mourvèdre California Old Telegram 1991 • $20 • (3/31/1994) • **81**
Mourvèdre California Old Telegram 1990 • $20 • (2/15/1993) • **84**
Mourvèdre California Old Telegram 1988 • $20 • (12/31/1990) • **85**
Mourvèdre California Old Telegram 1986 • $14 • (11/15/1988) • **90**
Muscat California Vin de Glacière 1996 • $15/375 ml. • (10/31/1997) • **93**
Muscat California Vin de Glacière 1995 • $15 • (12/15/1996) • **92**
Muscat Canelli California Vin de Glacière 1994 • $15/375 ml. • (9/30/1995) HR • **94**
Muscat Canelli California Vin de Glacière 1990 • $15/375 ml. • (3/31/1992) • **91**
Muscat Canelli Monterey Vin de Glacière 1993 • $15 • (4/15/1995) • **82**
Muscat Canelli Monterey Vin de Glacière 1992 • $15/375 ml. • (11/15/1993) HR • **92**
Orange Muscat Monterey Vin de Glacière 1993 • $15 • (4/15/1995) • **83**
Pear eau-de-vie Washington Poire NV • $18/375 ml. • (3/31/1992) • **90**
Pinot Meunier California 1991 • $15 • (12/31/1993) • **87**
Pinot Noir California 1994 • $20 • (8/31/1996) • **87**
Pinot Noir Oregon Bethel Heights Vineyard 1985 • $18 • (6/15/1988) • **90**
Pinot Noir Oregon Bethel Heights Vineyard 1985 • $18 • (6/15/1987) • **82**

Pinot Noir Oregon Temperance Hill Vineyard 1985 • $18 • (6/15/1988) • **88**
Riesling America Critique of Pure Riesling NV • $20 • (11/30/1997) • **88**
Riesling American Pacific Rim NV: This well-priced Riesling from a California winemaker is made from a blend of grapes from California, Washington and Germany. The result is a tasty mouthful of focused lemon, apple and mineral notes. Drink now.–J.L. • $10 • (5/31/2000) • **85**
Riesling California-Washington Dry Pacific Rim NV • $9 • (10/31/1997) • **87**
Sparkling Pinot Meunier California Le Canard Froid 1993 • $9 • (12/31/1994) • **83**
Syrah Santa Cruz Mountains 1994 • $30 • (11/30/1996) • **88**
Syrah Santa Cruz Mountains 1988 • $25 • (2/15/1991) • **88**
Vin Gris de Cigare California 1998: An offbeat offering at a try-me price, this blush-style Mourvèdre blend is dry, with lots of forward strawberry, tea and apple skin flavors that finish crisp and refreshing. Drink now.–J.L. • $9 • (11/15/1999) • **87**
Zinfandel California Cardinal Zin 1996 • $15 • (6/15/1998) • **87**
Zinfandel California Cardinal Zin 1995 • $15 • (3/31/1997) • **87**

BONTERRA | CALIFORNIA

Cabernet Sauvignon Mendocino County 1993 • $12 • (3/31/1996) • **81**
Cabernet Sauvignon North Coast 1996: Showing a green side, but the follow-up features plum, currant and anise. Fairly smooth, if lightweight. Drink now. • $13 • (10/31/1998) • **83**
Cabernet Sauvignon North Coast 1995 • $13 • (9/30/1997) • **83**
Cabernet Sauvignon North Coast 1994 • $12 • (5/15/1997) • **82**
Chardonnay Mendocino County 1998: Toasty, with buttery, lemon flavors on a light frame. Drink now.–J.L. • $12 • (6/30/2000) • **82**
Chardonnay Mendocino County 1997: Pretty enough, with light citrus, apple and pear notes. Firm acidity gives structure, toasty oak frames the ensemble on the finish. Refreshing. Drink now. • $11 • (7/31/1999) • **85**
Chardonnay Mendocino County 1996 • $12 • (6/30/1998) • **87**
Merlot Mendocino County 1996: Lean yet smooth, offering layers of blackberry, cassis, herb, mint, smoke and anise. It's complex but also quite quaffable, finishing nicely, with firm, ripe tannins. Drink now through 2004. • $14 • (9/15/1999) • **87**
Organically Grown Grapes Mendocino County Red 1991 • $9 • (3/31/1994) • **83**
Organically Grown Grapes Mendocino County 1990 • $9 • (5/31/1993) • **83**
Sangiovese Mendocino County 1995 • $22 • (3/31/1998) • **79**
Sangiovese Mendocino County 1994 • $22 • (2/28/1997) • **79**
Sangiovese Mendocino County 1993 • $22 • (4/30/1996) • **85**
Syrah Mendocino County 1996: Firm and a bit lean, yet complex, with tightly wound blackberry, anise, and herb flavors wrapped in smoky oak. The finish is bright and long, with pretty cherry notes. Drink now through 2006. • $19 • (6/30/1999) • **88**
Syrah Mendocino County 1995 • $22 • (3/31/1998) • **88**
Syrah Mendocino County 1994 • $22 • (2/28/1997) • **88**
Syrah Mendocino County 1993 • $22 • (4/30/1996) • **86**
Viognier North Coast 1996 • $23 • (12/15/1997) • **87**

BONVERRE | CALIFORNIA

Cabernet Sauvignon California Lot Number 19 1994 • $9 • (11/30/1996) • **82**
Cabernet Sauvignon California Lot Number 9 1991 • $7 • (5/15/1994) • **83**
Merlot California Lot Number 11 1992 • $8 • (9/15/1994) • **76**
Zinfandel Napa Valley 1995 • $10 • (4/30/1997) • **83**

BOOKWALTER | WASHINGTON

Cabernet Sauvignon Columbia Valley 1997: Earthy, spicy notes add dimension to a core of black cherry and black currant in this supple, smooth-textured red. On the lighter side, but has plenty of flavor. Drink through 2003.–H.S. • $20 • (8/31/1999) • **87**
Cabernet Sauvignon Washington 1994 • $20 • (9/30/1997) • **91**
Cabernet Sauvignon Washington 1992 • $16 • (8/31/1995) • **89**
Cabernet Sauvignon Washington 1990 • $16 • (9/30/1994) • **88**
Cabernet Sauvignon Washington Reserve 1989 • $20 • (9/30/1994) • **88**
Cabernet Sauvignon Washington Vintner's Select 1996: Ripe and generous, with a funky, gamy edge to the broad, dark plum and currant flavors, shaded with considerable spice and vanilla. Approachable, but the fine-grained tannins need cellaring. Best from 2001 through 2005.–H.S. • $39 • (9/15/1998) • **90**
Cabernet Sauvignon Washington Vintner's Select 1994 • $38 • (9/30/1997) • **90**
Chardonnay Columbia Valley 1997: Fresh and appealing for its straight-ahead apple, pear and vanilla flavors, hinting at apricot on the generous finish. Drink now.–H.S. • $8 • (9/15/1998) • **86**
Chardonnay Idaho 1996: Light and fresh, with floral, peppery nectarine and earthy flavors that linger on the soft finish. Drink now.–H.S. • $8 • (11/15/1998) • **83**
Chardonnay Washington Vintner's Select 1997: Ripe and round but not fat, with pretty nectarine and lemon aromas and flavors that persist on the lively finish. Tasty now. Drink through 2003–H.S. • $18 • (6/30/1999) • **87**
Chenin Blanc Washington 1998: Silky, pretty and definitely sweet, with apple and lemon meringue flavors echoing on the soft finish. Drink now.–H.S. • $6 • (6/30/1999) • **87**
Chenin Blanc Washington 1997: Soft and fruity, balanced with enough acidity to make this a refreshing mouthful of melon and pear. Drink now.–H.S. • $5 • (9/15/1998) • **86**
Johannisberg Riesling Washington 1998: Here's an unbeatable value for fans of sweet whites. This one, from Washington, is distinctly honeyed, its appealing medley of leaf, floral and pear flavors remaining bright right through the soft finish. Drink now.–H.S. • $6 • (6/30/1999) • **87**
Johannisberg Riesling Washington 1997: Sweet, with appealing pear character that lasts through the soft finish. Drink now.–H.S. • $5 • (9/15/1998) • **82**
Lot #8 Red Washington NV: A bit firm for a non-vintage, but brimming with grapey, berrylike flavors. Has a tannic edge, but should be fine with a roasted bird. Drink now through 2002.–H.S. • $10 • (6/30/1999) • **83**
Merlot Columbia Valley Reserve 1997: Ripe in flavor, firm and spicy, offering a generous blend of black cherry, spice box, smoke and vanilla. Tannins are soft, not really in the way at all. Drink now through 2002.–H.S. • $25 • (8/31/1999) • **87**
Merlot Washington 1997: On the lean side, with herbal overtones to the modest blackberry, nutmeg and pepper flavors. Finishes with a richness that suggests it will be worth cellaring. Best after 2000.–H.S. • $15 • (6/15/1999) • **87**
Merlot Washington 1995 • $15 • (3/31/1998) • **85**
Merlot Washington 1994 • $15 • (3/31/1998) • **87**
Merlot Washington 1993 • $14 • (9/30/1995) • **87**
Merlot Washington 1992 • $12 • (9/30/1994) • **88**
Merlot Washington Vintner's Select 1996: Firm and chewy, with ripe blackberry and mineral flavors, finishing with tough tannins that need cellaring. Best after 2000.–H.S. • $29 • (12/15/1998) • **85**
Muscat Blanc-Riesling Washington Jocat 1998: Soft, sweet and appealing for its range of spicy pear, litchi and floral flavors that linger gently on the seductive finish. Drink now.–H.S. • $8 • (6/30/1999) • **88**
Riesling Washington Vintner's Select 1997: Sweet and generous, with enough tangy acidity to support the apricot, pineapple and pear flavors, all lingering on the round finish. Drink now.–H.S. • $8 • (9/15/1998) • **88**
Riesling Washington Vintner's Select 1996 • $8 • (10/15/1997) • **86**
Riesling-Muscat Blanc Washington Jocat 1997: Ripe fruit flavors remain jazzy and bright on the sweet finish, echoing pear and litchi. Drink now as a light dessert.–H.S. • $8 • (9/15/1998) • **87**
Red Washington NV: A solid red with pretty berry flavor and a touch of gaminess to give it extra character. A blend of Cabernet Sauvignon, Merlot, Pinot Noir and Sangiovese. Drink now.–H.S. • $10 • (9/15/1998) • **84**
White Riesling Washington Late Harvest 1994 • $8/375 ml. • (9/15/1995) • **85**

BOUCHAINE | CALIFORNIA

Cabernet Franc Sonoma Valley Limited Release 1995: Herbal at this stage, with hints of black currant on the finish. Could use more ripeness in the flavors and suppleness of texture. May improve with time. Drink through 2003 • $17 • (11/30/1998) • **82**
Cabernet Franc Sonoma Valley Limited Release 1994 • $14 • (7/31/1997) • **86**
Cabernet Franc Sonoma Valley Limited Release 1993 • $15 • (5/31/1998) • **82**
Cabernet Franc Sonoma Valley Limited Release 1991 • $14 • (2/28/1995) • **79**
Cabernet Franc Sonoma Valley Limited Release 1990 • $14 • (3/31/1993) • **83**
Chardonnay Carneros 1996: Tart pear and citrus-laced flavors here, with spicy, cedary oak folding in. A touch disjointed . Drink now through 2002.–J.L. • $18 • (1/31/1999) • **87**
Chardonnay Napa Valley Carneros 1998: Straightforward and round, with butter, licorice and peach pit flavors. Drink now.–J.L. • $20 • (6/30/2000) • **84**
Chardonnay Napa Valley Carneros Estate Reserve 1996: Plump and ripe, with hints of pear, apricot, citrus, earth and herb. The wine is smooth on the palate and elegant, and the moderate finish has a vanilla note. Drink now through 2002. • $25 • (6/30/1999) • **88**
Gewürztraminer Russian River Valley Dry 1996 • $12 • (3/31/1998) • **85**
Pinot Noir California Q.C. Fly 1993 • $9 • (12/31/1995) • **82**
Pinot Noir California Q.C. Fly 1992 • $9 • (3/31/1995) • **81**
Pinot Noir California Q.C. Fly 1991 • $8 • (2/28/1994) • **82**
Pinot Noir California Q.C. Fly 1990 • $8 • (9/30/1992) • **81**
Pinot Noir Carneros 1992 • $15 • (6/30/1995) • **86**

Pinot Noir Napa Valley 1982 • $20 • (6/30/1987) • **81**
Pinot Noir Napa Valley Carneros 1996: Brightly styled, with zingy cherry and herb notes. The finish is long, though the tannins are a bit coarse. Nonetheless, a pretty and refreshing wine. Drink now through 2002. • $19 • (9/15/1999) • **87**
Pinot Noir Napa Valley Carneros 1995: Lightly fruity, with hints of herb, tea and leather. Glimpses of cherry and cola emerge on the finish. For fans of delicate, very understated Pinot Noir. Drink now through 2001.–J.L. • $19 • (9/15/1998) • **84**
Pinot Noir Napa Valley Carneros 1994 • $17 • (1/31/1997) • **84**
Pinot Noir Napa Valley Carneros 1991 • $15 • (3/31/1995) • **82**
Pinot Noir Napa Valley Carneros 1990 • $15 • (2/28/1993) • **86**
Pinot Noir Napa Valley Carneros 1989 • $15 • (9/30/1992) • **84**
Pinot Noir Napa Valley Carneros 1988 • $15 • (7/31/1991) • **78**
Pinot Noir Napa Valley Carneros 1987 • $13 • (10/31/1990) • **82**
Pinot Noir Napa Valley Carneros 1986 • $12 • (5/31/1989) • **86**
Pinot Noir Napa Valley Carneros 1985 • $12 • (12/31/1988) • **82**
Pinot Noir Napa Valley Carneros Estate Bottled 1989 • $20 • (2/28/1993) • **75**
Pinot Noir Napa Valley Carneros Limited Release 1994 • $33 • (1/31/1998) • **87**
Pinot Noir Napa Valley Carneros Reserve 1995: Smooth, earthy in character, with hints of cherry and cola, turning simpler and a shade coarser on the finish. Drink now through 2001.–J.L. • $30 • (2/28/1999) • **86**
Pinot Noir Napa Valley Carneros Reserve 1994: Mature, with attractive dried cherry, strawberry, stewed plum and wild berry notes. Turns elegant and spicy on the finish, where the tannins are mild and well integrated. Drink now through 2001.–J.L. • $27 • (9/30/1998) • **87**
Pinot Noir Napa Valley Carneros Reserve 1993 • $25 • (11/30/1996) • **87**
Pinot Noir Napa Valley Carneros Reserve 1991 • $20 • (1/31/1995) • **88**
Pinot Noir Napa Valley Carneros Reserve 1990 • $20 • (4/30/1994) • **82**
Pinot Noir Napa Valley Carneros Reserve 1988 • $25 • (3/31/1992) • **83**
Pinot Noir Napa Valley Carneros Reserve 1987 • $20 • (10/31/1990) • **85**
Pinot Noir Napa Valley Los Carneros 1982 • $13 • (7/16/1985) • **87**
Pinot Noir Napa Valley Los Carneros Winery Lake Vineyard 1982 • $15 • (3/01/1986) CS • **91**
Pinot Noir Russian River Valley Limited Release 1991 • $17 • (6/30/1995) • **82**

BRANDBORG | CALIFORNIA

Charbono Napa Valley 1989 • $12 • (10/31/1991) • **85**
Pinot Noir Anderson Valley 1989 • $11 • (11/15/1991) • **86**
Pinot Noir Mendocino County 1992 • $13 • (3/31/1995) • **82**
Pinot Noir Mendocino County 1991 • $12 • (2/28/1994) • **84**
Pinot Noir Mendocino County 1990 • $11 • (2/28/1993) • **73**
Pinot Noir Santa Barbara County 1989 • $13 • (11/15/1991) • **87**
Pinot Noir Santa Maria Valley Bien Nacido Vineyard 1994 • $15 • (2/28/1997) • **86**
Pinot Noir Santa Maria Valley Bien Nacido Vineyard 1992 • $15 • (3/31/1995) • **86**
Pinot Noir Santa Maria Valley Bien Nacido Vineyard 1991 • $14 • (2/28/1994) • **84**
Pinot Noir Santa Maria Valley Bien Nacido Vineyard 1990 • $13 • (2/28/1993) • **78**
Zinfandel Napa Valley 1989 • $10 • (10/15/1992) • **84**

BRANDER | CALIFORNIA

Bouchet Tête de Cuvée Santa Ynez Valley 1993 • $22 • (12/15/1995) • **86**
Bouchet Tête de Cuvée Santa Ynez Valley 1990 • $18 • (11/15/1993) • **79**
Bouchet Tête de Cuvée Santa Ynez Valley 1989 • $20 • (3/31/1992) • **84**
Bouchet Tête de Cuvée Santa Ynez Valley 1988 • $20 • (7/15/1992) • **83**
Cabernet Franc Santa Ynez Valley High Density Vineyard 1993 • $35 • (4/30/1996) • **84**
Cuvée Natalie Santa Ynez Valley 1998: Delicious, with Riesling-like floral and spice notes mingling with pear, mineral and citrus flavors. Rich and complex. A blend of Sauvignon Blanc and Riesling. Drink now through 2003.–H.S. • $14 • (1/31/2000) • **90**
Cuvée Natalie Santa Ynez Valley 1996 • $14 • (6/30/1997) • **89**
Merlot Santa Ynez Valley 1997: Starts off with vegetal aromas, then kicks in with earthy, leathery, tarry notes. Plum and cedar stay in the background. Drink now. • $18 • (9/30/1998) • **79**

Key: SS—Spectator Selection. CS—Cellar Selection. HR—Highly Recommended. $NA—Price not available. (BT)—Barrel tasting. (A)—Auction Price.
For a key to the tasters' initials, see "How to Use These Listings."
Dates in parentheses represent the issues in which the ratings were published.

Merlot Santa Ynez Valley 1995 • $14 • (6/30/1997) • **78**
Merlot Santa Ynez Valley 1994 • $15 • (8/31/1996) • **78**
Merlot Santa Ynez Valley Reserve 1993 • $18 • (8/31/1996) • **83**
Merlot Santa Ynez Valley Three Flags 1989 • $12 • (5/31/1992) • **82**
Merlot Santa Ynez Valley Three Flags 1988 • $12 • (5/31/1992) • **81**
Sauvignon Blanc Santa Ynez Valley 1998: Racy, with onion skin, citrus, herb and tart nectarine flavors. Drink now.–J.L. • $12 • (5/15/2000) • **83**
Sauvignon Blanc Santa Ynez Valley 1997 • $11 • (6/15/1998) • **85**
Sauvignon Blanc Santa Ynez Valley 1996 • $11 • (7/31/1997) • **87**
Sauvignon Blanc Santa Ynez Valley au Naturel 1998: Vibrant and tangy. Not weighty, but it has tons of grass, lime, and gooseberry notes on a razor-sharp frame. Intense and focused, the finish just soars. Drink now through 2003.–H.S. • $30 • (1/31/2000) • **90**
Sauvignon Blanc Santa Ynez Valley au Naturel 1997: Intriguing aromas of gooseberry, fresh hay, melon and peach lead the way in this refreshing white. It's light-textured, but holds its own with bright acidity and complex citrus flavors that linger. Drink now through 2002. • $30 • (5/15/1999) • **89**
Sauvignon Blanc Santa Ynez Valley au Naturel 1996 • $25 • (5/31/1998) • **87**
Sauvignon Blanc Santa Ynez Valley Cuvée Nicolas 1997: A complex, racy, intensely flavored wine. Well oaked, but with ripe herb, grapefruit and grass notes, finishing with lemon peel. Drink now through 2003.–J.L. • $21 • (4/30/2000) • **87**
Sauvignon Blanc Santa Ynez Valley Cuvée Nicolas 1996 • $21 • (5/31/1998) • **87**

BRAREN PAULI | CALIFORNIA

Cabernet Sauvignon Dry Creek Valley 1990 • $13 • (10/31/1993) • **89**
Cabernet Sauvignon Dry Creek Valley Mauritson Vineyard 1989 • $12 • (11/15/1993) • **78**
Cabernet Sauvignon Mendocino Frost Reserve 1995: Juicy mineral, black cherry and gamy notes are intriguing, but it tightens on the finish. Needs some time. Drink through 2002–H.S. • $24 • (11/15/1998) • **80**
Cabernet Sauvignon Redwood Valley 1996: Soft, with light herb, cola and cherry notes. Dry and slightly tannic finish. Drink now.–H.S. • $16 • (11/15/1998) • **78**
Chardonnay Mendocino Busch Creek Vineyard 1996 • $13 • (12/15/1997) • **86**
Merlot Alexander Valley 1992 • $12 • (3/31/1996) • **84**
Merlot Alexander Valley 1991 • $13 • (9/15/1994) • **85**
Merlot Alexander Valley Mauritson Vineyard 1989 • $12 • (5/31/1992) • **77**
Merlot Alexander Valley Mauritson Vineyard 1987 • $11 • (3/31/1991) • **84**
Sauvignon Blanc Mendocino Busch Creek Vineyard 1996 • $9 • (11/15/1997) • **82**

BREAUX | VIRGINIA

Chardonnay Virginia Barrel Fermented 1998: Green apple flavors dominate this simple Chardonnay, and aren't enough for the overly toasty finish. Drink now.–T.M. • $18 • (1/01/2000) • **80**
Chardonnay Virginia Madeleine's 1998: Ripe and soft, with a warm apple pie aroma and a buttery note on the medium-bodied finish. Manages to stay lively. Drink now.–T.M. • $15 • (1/01/2000) • **82**

BRICK HOUSE | OREGON

Chardonnay Willamette Valley 1996 • $24 • (2/28/1998) • **88**
Chardonnay Willamette Valley Cuvée du Tonnelier 1997: Ripe, generous and smooth, with plump pear and peach flavors plus a thwack of smoky oak on the finish. Best after 2000.–H.S. • $28 • (4/30/1999) • **88**
Gamay Noir Willamette Valley 1997: Fresh, fruity and generous, with berry and floral aromas and flavors on an airy frame. Drink now.–H.S. • $18 • (6/15/1999) • **84**
Gamay Noir Willamette Valley 1994 • $13 • (3/31/1996) • **84**
Pinot Noir Willamette Valley 1996: Chewy at first but ultimately graceful, with lots of spice and toast flavors and plenty of black cherry character poking through to keep the balance. Drink through 2004–H.S. • $30 • (8/31/1998) • **90**
Pinot Noir Willamette Valley 1995 • $24 • (7/31/1997) • **85**
Pinot Noir Willamette Valley 1994 • $22 • (1/31/1996) • **91**
Pinot Noir Willamette Valley Cuvée du Tonnelier 1998: Smooth and generous with its currant and blackberry flavors, which extend into a lively, generous finish without losing any polish. Lip-smackingly tasty, with its characteristic cinnamon note, and elegantly proportioned. Drink now through 2008.–H.S. • $38 • (4/30/2000) • **91**
Pinot Noir Willamette Valley Cuvée du Tonnelier 1997: Bright and lively, with deep color for a '97 and a sparkle to the black cherry, currant and brewed tea flavors as they persist gently on the finish. Drink now through 2001.–H.S. • $36 • (4/30/1999) • **87**

Pinot Noir Willamette Valley Cuvée du Tonnelier 1996: Light in texture, with spicy flavors at the fore, centering on cinnamon, hinting at plum and orange peel on the rangy finish. Needs time to mesh. Drink through 2002–H.S. • $36 • (8/31/1998) • **89**

Pinot Noir Willamette Valley Cuvée du Tonnelier 1995 • $34 • (10/15/1997) • **87**

Pinot Noir Willamette Valley Les Dijonnais 1998: This wine is deep, dense, rich and concentrated. Powerful aromas of blackberry, raspberry, currant and plum melt into a supple, beautifully structured mouthfeel that lasts and lasts. Seductive now, but just wait. Best from 2001 through 2010.–H.S. • $38 • (4/30/2000) HR • **94**

BRIDGEVIEW | OREGON

Chardonnay Oregon 1997: A sturdy white, with slightly bitter metallic flavors hampering the modest fruit character.–H.S. • $7 • (4/30/1999) • **78**

Chardonnay Oregon 1996 • $6 • (6/15/1998) • **85**

Chardonnay Oregon Blue Moon 1998: Light and fresh, with pretty peach, pear and spicy-floral notes echoing on the open-textured finish. Drink now.–H.S. • $10 • (4/30/2000) • **85**

Chardonnay Oregon Blue Moon 1997: Strong sawed-wood flavors get in the way in this light, crisp Chardonnay, echoing resiny flavors on the finish.–H.S. • $10 • (2/28/1999) • **78**

Chardonnay Oregon Blue Moon 1996 • $10 • (6/30/1998) • **87**

Early Muscat Oregon 1997: Soft and fruity, with plenty of attractive pear and litchi flavors that persist on the finish with a nice hint of allspice. Drink now.–H.S. • $8 • (4/30/1999) • **86**

Early Muscat Oregon 1996 • $8 • (11/30/1997) • **88**

Gewürztraminer Oregon 1996 • $6 • (9/15/1997) • **86**

Merlot Oregon Black Beauty 1997: Smooth and light, soft-textured, with pleasant strawberry and currant notes on the gentle finish. Drink now.–H.S. • $20 • (4/30/1999) • **84**

Merlot Oregon Black Beauty 1996: Firm, a bit chewy, but packed with ripe blackberry, mineral and earth aromas and flavors. Picks up a hint of black pepper on the finish. Drink now through 2001.–H.S. • $25 • (4/30/1999) • **87**

Merlot Oregon Black Beauty 1994 • $12 • (7/31/1996) • **87**

Merlot Oregon Black Beauty 1993 • $11 • (3/31/1996) • **84**

Merlot Paso Robles Black Beauty 1996: Shows strong oak, plum and cherry flavors, but they don't seem very integrated. Woody finish. Drink now. • $17 • (7/31/1998) • **80**

Pinot Gris Oregon Cuvée Spéciale 1998: Light and refreshing, offering pretty pear, melon and delicate spice flavors that echo nicely on the finish. Drink now.–H.S. • $12 • (5/15/2000) • **85**

Pinot Gris Oregon Cuvée Spéciale 1997: Here's a charming young white at a try-me price. It's fresh and bright, offering up a jazzy mouthful of melon and nectarine flavors that persist prettily on the finish. Drink now.–H.S. • $10 • (4/30/1999) • **87**

Pinot Gris Oregon Cuvée Spéciale 1996 • $11 • (9/15/1997) • **86**

Pinot Noir Oregon 1998: A smooth Pinot, one that's generous in flavor while light in frame, focusing on raspberry and spice flavors that linger on the open-textured finish. Very good price and pretty good availability for its kind. Drink now.–H.S. • $11 • (5/15/2000) • **86**

Pinot Noir Oregon 1997: Light and fragrant, with pretty strawberry and floral aromas and flavors that start stronger than they finish. Drink now.–H.S. • $10 • (6/30/1999) • **81**

Pinot Noir Oregon 1996 • $11 • (11/15/1997) • **83**

Pinot Noir Oregon 1995 • $7 • (2/28/1997) • **85**

Pinot Noir Oregon 1994 • $6 • (3/31/1996) • **80**

Pinot Noir Oregon 10th Anniversary 1992 • $30 • (1/31/1996) • **81**

Pinot Noir Oregon Blue Moon 1998: Light and velvety, with pretty black cherry and spice flavors on a modest frame. Echoes pepper and floral notes on the finish. Drink now through 2006.–H.S. • $15 • (4/30/2000) • **87**

Pinot Noir Oregon Estate 10th Anniversary 1992 • $18 • (11/30/1994) • **84**

Pinot Noir Oregon Estate Bottled 1988 • $8 • (2/15/1990) • **88**

Pinot Noir Oregon Reserve 1996: Despite a grainy texture, this has plenty of ripe berry and black cherry flavors that persist on the finish. Give it time to soften. Drink through 2002–H.S. • $20 • (4/30/1999) • **86**

Pinot Noir Oregon Reserve 1995 • $16 • (10/15/1997) • **87**

Pinot Noir Oregon Reserve 1993 • $10 • (2/29/1996) • **83**

Pinot Noir Oregon Reserve 1992 • $10 • (1/31/1996) • **81**

Pinot Noir Oregon Reserve 1990 • $10 • (10/31/1994) • **83**

Pinot Noir Oregon Special Reserve 1987 • $12 • (2/15/1990) • **80**

Pinot Noir Oregon Winemaker's Reserve 1990 • $13 • (2/28/1993) • **70**

Pinot Noir Oregon Winemaker's Reserve 1989 • $13 • (2/28/1993) • **83**

Pinot Noir Oregon Winemaker's Reserve 1988 • $12 • (11/15/1991) • **87**

Pinot Noir Oregon Winemaker's Reserve 1987 • $15 • (2/15/1990) • **89**

Pinot Noir Rogue Valley Red Cedar Vineyard 1996: On the light side, but the crisp, clear plum and walnut flavors linger impressively on the finish. Still feels fresh. Drink now through 2003.–H.S. • $30 • (4/30/2000) • **87**

Pinot Noir Rogue Valley Reserve 1997: A bit rough for such a light wine, with nice blackberry flavors behind a layer of tannin. Best after 2001.–H.S. • $15 • (4/30/2000) • **81**

Pinot Noir Willamette Valley 1992 • $6 • (3/15/1994) • **79**

Pinot Noir Willamette Valley 1991 • $6 • (1/31/1993) • **83**

Pinot Noir Willamette Valley 1990 • $6 • (2/28/1993) • **75**

Riesling Oregon Blue Moon NV: This Oregon winery delivers good value in several varieties; this time with a softly sweet Riesling, offering pretty apple and spice flavors and a touch of honey on the round finish. Drink now.–H.S. • $7 • (5/15/2000) • **85**

Riesling Oregon Late Harvest 1992 • $25/375 ml. • (11/15/1994) • **88**

Rosé de Pinot Oregon 1996 • $12 • (11/15/1997) • **85**

BRIDGMAN, W.B. | WASHINGTON

Cabernet Sauvignon Columbia Valley 1996: Firm and ripe, with a peppery edge to the black cherry, blackberry and currant at the core. Needs to sort out the firm tannins. Best after 2000.–H.S. • $14 • (9/30/1999) • **86**

Cabernet Sauvignon Columbia Valley 1995: This crisp-style Cabernet shows a distinct personality, picking up a gamy, animal edge, finishing with modest intensity. Drink through 2002–H.S. • $14 • (9/15/1998) • **84**

Cabernet Sauvignon Columbia Valley 1993 • $12 • (9/15/1996) • **89**

Cabernet Sauvignon Yakima Valley 1991 • $11 • (7/31/1995) • **86**

Chardonnay Columbia Valley 1997: Fresh and lively, with apple, spice and earth flavors in equal measure that linger gently on the finish. Drink now.–H.S. • $11 • (9/30/1999) • **85**

Lemberger Columbia Valley 1995 • $9 • (9/15/1996) • **84**

Lemberger Yakima Valley 1997: Light and fresh, with pretty strawberry flavors that linger on the smooth finish. Drink now.–H.S. • $9 • (9/15/1998) • **84**

Merlot Columbia Valley 1997: Smooth and polished, this is appealing for its soft, spicy currant and berry flavors that linger on the gentle finish. Drink now through 2002.–H.S. • $16 • (2/29/2000) • **85**

Merlot Columbia Valley 1995 • $15 • (9/15/1997) • **87**

Merlot Columbia Valley 1994 • $15 • (9/15/1996) • **88**

Merlot Yakima Valley 1992 • $11 • (9/30/1995) • **86**

Syrah Columbia Valley 1997: Ripe and generous, with lots of red plum, black cherry and tar flavors that finish bright and with plenty of richness. Drink now through 2001.–H.S. • $16 • (9/30/1999) • **87**

Syrah Yakima Valley 1995 • $15 • (9/15/1997) • **86**

BRIDLEWOOD | CALIFORNIA

Pinot Noir Central Coast 1997: Light-bodied and smooth-textured, with cola, toasty oak, cherry and spice flavors that linger on the soft finish. Drink now through 2003 .–J.L. • $18 • (9/15/1999) • **83**

Syrah Central Coast 1997: Focused and complex, with a range of cola, mushroom, smoke and toasted oak flavors over a smooth frame. Finishes with firm but well-integrated tannins. Drink now through 2004.–J.L. • $18 • (11/15/1999) • **87**

BRIGGS, AUGUST | CALIFORNIA

Cabernet Sauvignon Napa Valley 1997: Tightly wound, with a firm band of earthy cedar, currant and cherry, picking up a touch of chocolate. Needs time and air. Tasted twice, with consistent notes. Drink now through 2007.–J.L. • $50 • (6/30/2000) • **88**

Cabernet Sauvignon Napa Valley 1996: Ripe, rich and concentrated, with complex currant, anise, sage, cedar and tarlike flavors, well-integrated tannins and a long, lingering aftertaste. August Briggs' first Cabernet. Drink now through 2005.–J.L. • $35 • (4/30/1999) • **91**

Cabernet Sauvignon Sonoma Mountain 1997: Tight and crisp, with sharp tannins preceding a core of leathery currant and plum flavors, turning bitter. A firm and chewy style that begs for short-term cellaring. Best from 2002 through 2007.–J.L. • $50 • (6/15/2000) • **83**

Chardonnay Carneros Leveroni Vineyards 1997: Ripe and peachy, with a sense of finesse, turning supple and elegant with a rich and spicy aftertaste of pear, fig and apricot. Drink now through 2002.–J.L. • $28 • (2/28/1999) • **91**

Chardonnay Carneros Leveroni Vineyards 1996 • $25 • (1/31/1998) • **92**

Chardonnay Russian River Valley 1998: Round, with vanilla, cream and pineapple flavors that finish a bit flat. Drink now through 2002.–J.L. • $28 • (5/15/2000) • **84**

BRIGGS, AUGUST

Chardonnay Russian River Valley 1997: Complex, with a pretty array of earthy pear, fig, melon and apricot, gaining richness and depth on the long, full finish. Drink now through 2002.–J.L. • $28 • (2/28/1999) • **91**

Chardonnay Russian River Valley 1996 • $25 • (1/31/1998) • **92**

Pinot Noir Carneros 1997: Firm and chunky, with mouthfilling spicy oak and black cherry flavors. Opens with aeration, with complex flavors on the firm finish. Drink now through 2002.–J.L. • $28 • (9/15/1999) • **87**

Pinot Noir Carneros 1995 • $25 • (7/31/1997) • **88**

Pinot Noir Napa Valley Dijon Clones 1997: Toasty oak, cherry notes and herb flavors are prominent. Light-bodied yet supple, with a mild finish. Drink now through 2001.–J.L. • $28 • (9/15/1999) • **84**

Pinot Noir Russian River Valley 1997: Delicate and subtle, with earthy cherry, tea and herb flavors. Firm finish. Drink now through 2002.–J.L. • $28 • (9/15/1999) • **85**

Pinot Noir Russian River Valley 1995 • $25 • (7/31/1997) • **87**

Zinfandel Napa Valley 1998: Adds flavor and dimension with toasty, cedary oak wrapped around spicy blackberry and wild berry, picking up a meaty, leathery edge that works in well. Drink now.–J.L. • $30 • (6/15/2000) • **88**

Zinfandel Napa Valley 1997: Pleasant vanilla overtones meld nicely with ripe flavors of black cherry, chocolate and plum. Drink now through 2004.–J.L. • $22 • (6/15/2000) • **88**

Zinfandel Napa Valley 1996 • $20 • (5/31/1998) • **83**

Zinfandel Napa Valley 1995 • $18 • (8/31/1997) • **91**

BRINDIAMO | CALIFORNIA

Cabernet Sauvignon California Limited Bottling 1991 • $8 • (11/15/1994) • **76**

Gioveto Limited Bottling South Coast 1993 • $14 • (8/31/1995) • **86**

Il Bacio Temecula 1990 • $13 • (11/30/1992) • **71**

Muscat Alexandria San Diego County Moscato Aromatico Limited Bottling 1994 • $6/F • (12/31/1995) • **80**

Nebbiolo South Coast Limited Bottling 1993 • $14 • (12/15/1995) • **85**

Pinot Noir Edna Valley Limited Bottling 1993 • $10 • (10/15/1995) • **84**

Pinot Noir Santa Barbara County Santa Maria Hills Vineyard Limited Bottling 1990 • $10 • (9/30/1992) • **77**

Rosso Vecchio South Coast Limited Bottling 1993 • $10 • (6/30/1995) • **86**

Rosso Vecchio South Coast Limited Bottling 1992 • $10 • (5/15/1995) • **80**

BROADLEY | OREGON

Pinot Noir Oregon 1990 • $10 • (2/28/1993) • **72**

Pinot Noir Oregon Claudia's Choice 1994 • $25 • (8/31/1996) • **94**

Pinot Noir Oregon Reserve 1995 • $15 • (7/31/1997) • **87**

Pinot Noir Oregon Reserve 1994 • $16 • (8/31/1996) • **88**

Pinot Noir Oregon Reserve 1992 • $13 • (10/31/1994) • **86**

Pinot Noir Oregon Reserve 1987 • $12 • (2/15/1990) • **88**

Pinot Noir Oregon Reserve 1986 • $12 • (6/15/1988) • **73**

Pinot Noir Willamette Valley Claudia's Choice 1997: Light in texture, with crisp tannins framing a core of earthy, gamy plum flavors that persist impressively on the finish. Has the pieces to age gracefully. Best after 2000.–H.S. • $35 • (9/30/1999) • **88**

Pinot Noir Willamette Valley Marcile Lorraine 1996: Lean and hard-edged, with hints of cinnamon and chocolate around a light core of currant flavor. Drink through 2002–H.S. • $26 • (4/30/1999) • **84**

Pinot Noir Willamette Valley Reserve 1997: Light and fragrant, showing a pretty trail of blackberry, nutmeg and vanilla flavors that linger attractively on the finish. Drink now through 2001.–H.S. • $23 • (6/15/1999) • **87**

Pinot Noir Willamette Valley Reserve 1996 • $18 • (5/15/1998) • **80**

BROMAN | CALIFORNIA

Cabernet Sauvignon Napa Valley 1994: Attractively ripe, rich and fruit-centered, with lush, lively black cherry, currant, plum and cedar notes. Holds a tight focus on the finish, where the tannins are mild. Best from 2001 through 2010.–J.L. • $45 • (3/31/2000) • **89**

Key: SS—Spectator Selection. CS—Cellar Selection. HR—Highly Recommended. $NA—Price not available. (BT)—Barrel tasting. (A)—Auction Price.
For a key to the tasters' initials, see "How to Use These Listings."
Dates in parentheses represent the issues in which the ratings were published.

BROPHY CLARK | CALIFORNIA

Pinot Noir Arroyo Grande Valley 1996: An earthy style, complete with claylike notes; lean, with a crisp core of black cherry, herb and leathery nuances. Has enough tannin to merit short-term cellaring. Try through 2002.–J.L. • $18 • (12/15/1998) • **87**

Pinot Noir Santa Maria Valley 1997: Mushroomy, with a leathery edge to the cherry and wild berry flavors, finishing with firm, integrated tannins. Best from 2000 through 2003.–J.L. • $18 • (9/15/1999) • **85**

Sauvignon Blanc Santa Barbara-San Luis Obispo Counties 1998: Mineral, citrus and apple flavors are tangy, but a bit sour. Drink now.–J.L. • $12 • (5/15/2000) • **80**

Sauvignon Blanc San Luis Obispo & Santa Barbara Counties 1997: Zippy acidity and brisk lemon and grapefruit flavors create a wake-up call for the palate, smoothing out on the moderate finish with hints of herb and freshly mowed grass. Drink now. • $12 • (3/31/1999) • **86**

Syrah Santa Ynez Valley 1997: Smooth, with a tangy core of earthy, gamy blueberry and bittersweet chocolate flavors. Mild tannins on the finish, where cherry and spice flavors persist. Drink now through 2004.–J.L. • $17 • (11/15/1999) • **86**

BROWN ESTATE | CALIFORNIA

Zinfandel Napa Valley 1997: Very ripe, intense and spicy, with complex black cherry, raspberry, plum and wild berry flavors that are all sharply focused. Rich finish. Drink now through 2004.–J.L. • $18 • (2/29/2000) • **91**

BROWN, STILLMAN | CALIFORNIA

Les Ramones California 1995 • $20 • (12/15/1997) • **86**

Zinfandel Santa Clara Valley Lion Oaks Ranch 1996 • $16 • (6/15/1998) • **87**

BRUCE, DAVID | CALIFORNIA

Cabernet Sauvignon Santa Clara Valley 1997: Struggles to find a focus, with herb, celery, mint and spice flavors overriding the cherry and berryish flavors. Drink now through 2007.–J.L. • $24 • (5/15/2000) • **86**

Chardonnay Santa Cruz Mountains 1997: Earthy, with pungent, dirty, cow-dung aromas and flavors. Tasted twice, with consistent notes.–J.L. • $18 • (5/15/2000) • **68**

Mr. Baggins California Red 1990 • $10 • (11/30/1992) • **80**

Mrs. Baggins California 1990 • $10 • (6/30/1992) • **84**

Petite Sirah California Vintner's Select 1991 • $12 • (10/15/1993) • **78**

Petite Sirah Central Coast 1998: Stale geranium aromas, turning earthy, with dried berry flavors that turn tannic. Drink now.–J.L. • $16 • (5/15/2000) • **81**

Petite Sirah Central Coast 1997: Dark, ripe and plush, with herb, black cherry, pepper and meaty notes, plus a dash of vegetable, finishing with supple tannins. Drink through 2004–J.L. • $16 • (3/31/1999) • **87**

Petite Sirah Central Coast 1996 • $15 • (12/31/1997) SS • **90**

Petite Sirah Central Coast Vintner's Select 1994 • $12 • (8/31/1996) • **86**

Petite Sirah Paso Robles Ranchita Canyon Vineyard 1997: Dark and intense, packed with rich wild berry, pepper, plum and anise flavors that saturate the palate. Drink now through 2004.–J.L. • $18 • (3/31/1999) • **91**

Petite Sirah Paso Robles Shell Creek Vineyard 1996 • $18 • (12/31/1997) • **93**

Pinot Noir Central Coast 1998: Serves up a modest range of dried cherry, sage, earth and berry, turning dry and cedary. Drink now.–J.L. • $18 • (5/15/2000) • **83**

Pinot Noir Central Coast 1997: Smooth, rich and polished, with a complex core of herb-laced black cherry, currant, plum and raspberry flavors that soar on the finish. This California red offers an attractive combination of high quality and reasonable price; should be fairly available, too. Drink through 2004–J.L. • $16 • (2/28/1999) SS • **90**

Pinot Noir Central Coast 1996 • $16 • (1/31/1998) • **87**

Pinot Noir Chalone 1997: Solid, with firm plum and black cherry, plus touches of mushroom and cedar, finishing with a gush of fruit and anise, supported by firm tannins. Drink now through 2007.–J.L. • $35 • (5/15/2000) • **88**

Pinot Noir Chalone 1996: Tight, and if a bit dry and tannic, there are also dried cherry, tea, mushroom, earth and sage flavors to fill out the palate and hold your interest. Finishes with an earthy mineral aftertaste. Drink through 2004–J.L. • $32 • (8/31/1998) • **87**

Pinot Noir Chalone 1995 • $30 • (12/15/1997) HR • **92**

Pinot Noir Chalone 1994 • $30 • (9/30/1996) • **89**

Pinot Noir Mendocino Vintner's Select 1990 • $12 • (2/28/1994) • **84**

Pinot Noir Russian River Valley 1997: Tight and firm, with complex black cherry, blackberry, raspberry and spice framed by smoky, toasty oak.–J.L. • $30 • (5/15/2000) • **88**
Pinot Noir Russian River Valley 1996: Simple, with modest dried cherry, plum, sage and herbal notes, finishing with more firm tannins and ample oak than it needs to support the fruit. Drink now.–J.L. • $30 • (8/31/1998) • **82**
Pinot Noir Russian River Valley Reserve 1995 • $25 • (12/31/1997) • **89**
Pinot Noir Russian River Valley Reserve 1994 • $25 • (12/31/1996) • **89**
Pinot Noir Russian River Valley Reserve 1993 • $25 • (12/31/1996) • **88**
Pinot Noir Santa Cruz Mountains 1997: Dark, ripe and rich, with a core of black cherry, mineral, earth and wild berry, well-focused, offering fine depth and a complex aftertaste. Drink now through 2008.–J.L. • $28 • (5/15/2000) • **87**
Pinot Noir Santa Cruz Mountains 1996: Tight, with a core of leather and anise-scented wild berry and cherry, turning complex and spicy on the finish. Drink through 2005–J.L. • $35 • (2/28/1999) • **89**
Pinot Noir Santa Cruz Mountains 1990 • $12 • (3/31/1997) • **91**
Pinot Noir Santa Cruz Mountains 1989 • $18 • (9/30/1992) • **75**
Pinot Noir Santa Cruz Mountains 1984 • $15 • (6/30/1987) • **81**
Pinot Noir Santa Cruz Mountains 1983 • $15 • (8/31/1986) • **78**
Pinot Noir Santa Cruz Mountains Estate Reserve 1993 • $35 • (12/31/1995) • **82**
Pinot Noir Santa Cruz Mountains Estate Reserve 1992 • $30 • (3/31/1995) • **88**
Pinot Noir Santa Cruz Mountains Estate Reserve 1990 • $20 • (3/31/1997) • **93**
Pinot Noir Santa Cruz Mountains Thirtieth Anniversary 1992 • $100 • (3/31/1995) • **91**
Pinot Noir Sonoma County 1997: Features tart black cherry, anise, herb and spice, with dry, slightly coarse, earthy tannins. Drink now through 2007.–J.L. • $24 • (5/15/2000) • **86**
Pinot Noir Sonoma County 1996: Tannic, earthy and gamy, this struggles to find focus with its minty berry and dry oak flavors. Perhaps short-term cellaring will work; try through 2001.–J.L. • $20 • (8/31/1998) • **80**
Pinot Noir Sonoma County 1995 • $18 • (1/31/1998) • **88**
Pinot Noir Sonoma County Vintner's Select 1993 • $12 • (12/31/1995) • **82**
Pinot Noir Sonoma County Vintner's Select 1992 • $12 • (3/31/1995) • **83**
Zinfandel Paso Robles Ranchita Canyon Vineyard 1995 • $15 • (3/31/1998) • **88**
Zinfandel San Luis Obispo-El Dorado Counties Vintner's Select 1994 • $13 • (3/31/1997) • **87**
Zinfandel San Luis Obispo County 1990 • $12 • (5/15/1992) HR • **90**

BRUCHER | CALIFORNIA

Pinot Noir Santa Barbara County 1992 • $16 • (3/31/1995) • **78**

BRUTOCAO | CALIFORNIA

Cabernet Sauvignon Mendocino 1990 • $13 • (5/15/1994) • **82**
Cabernet Sauvignon Mendocino 1988 • $13 • (3/31/1992) • **83**
Cabernet Sauvignon Mendocino 1986 • $13 • (3/31/1992) • **82**
Cabernet Sauvignon Mendocino Albert Vineyard 1993 • $13 • (12/15/1995) • **82**
Cabernet Sauvignon Mendocino Albert Vineyard 1992 • $13 • (7/31/1995) • **82**
Cabernet Sauvignon Mendocino Proprietor's Special Reserve 1991 • $35 • (7/31/1995) • **83**
Merlot Mendocino 1995 • $18 • (12/15/1997) • **86**
Merlot Mendocino 1994 • $15 • (12/15/1996) • **82**
Merlot Mendocino 1993 • $15 • (7/31/1995) • **78**
Merlot Mendocino 1992 • $15 • (9/15/1994) • **78**
Merlot Mendocino 1991 • $15 • (8/31/1993) • **87**
Merlot Mendocino 1988 • $13 • (5/31/1992) • **84**
Pinot Noir Anderson Valley Special Reserve 1993 • $20 • (3/31/1995) • **78**
Zinfandel Mendocino 1992 • $17 • (6/15/1994) • **84**
Zinfandel Mendocino Hopland Ranch 1994 • $14 • (4/30/1997) • **82**
Zinfandel Mendocino Hopland Ranch 1993 • $12 • (6/15/1995) • **84**
Zinfandel Mendocino Proprietor's Reserve 1991 • $17 • (9/30/1993) • **85**

BRYANT FAMILY | CALIFORNIA

Cabernet Sauvignon Napa Valley 1996: An immense, concentrated yet amazingly elegant and graceful red wine. Packed with rich, complex currant, plum, black cherry, blackberry and spice flavors, it turns floral and supple, with lovely vanilla-oak shadings, even as the tannins firm up on the finish. Best from 2001 through 2010.–J.L. • $440 Ⓐ • (10/15/1999) HR • **99**
Cabernet Sauvignon Napa Valley 1995: A classic Cabernet—dark, rich, plush and enormously extracted, packing in a range of currant, black cherry, coffee, vanilla, herb, tea and spicy flavors. Beautifully focused, long, rich and concentrated, it zooms on the finish. Awfully tempting now (you can drink it!), but cellaring should only broaden the flavors and add dimension. Drink through 2010–J.L. • $393 Ⓐ • (8/31/1998) CS • **97**
Cabernet Sauvignon Napa Valley 1994 • $409 Ⓐ • (11/30/1997) • **94**
Cabernet Sauvignon Napa Valley Pritchard Hill 1992 • $241 Ⓐ • (5/31/1996) • **89**

BUEHLER | CALIFORNIA

Cabernet Sauvignon California 1993 • $8 • (12/15/1995) • **79**
Cabernet Sauvignon Napa Valley 1996: Tightly wound with a rich core of black cherry, cassis and mineral flavors. Finishes with lots of ripe tannins. Drink through 2006–J.L. • $20 • (9/15/1999) • **87**
Cabernet Sauvignon Napa Valley 1995: Cedar and herbs provide an interesting opening here, with black currant, plum, vanilla and Bing cherry notes popping up on the finish. Drink through 2005 • $20 • (10/31/1998) • **86**
Cabernet Sauvignon Napa Valley 1994 • $20 • (7/31/1997) • **87**
Cabernet Sauvignon Napa Valley 1993 • $17 • (11/15/1996) • **87**
Cabernet Sauvignon Napa Valley 1992 • $14 • (12/15/1995) • **84**
Cabernet Sauvignon Napa Valley 1991 • $13 • (9/15/1994) • **86**
Cabernet Sauvignon Napa Valley 1990 • $12 • (11/15/1993) • **83**
Cabernet Sauvignon Napa Valley 1989 • $16 • (11/15/1992) • **79**
Cabernet Sauvignon Napa Valley 1987 • $21 • (7/31/1990) • **85**
Cabernet Sauvignon Napa Valley 1986 • $20 • (4/30/1989) • **85**
Cabernet Sauvignon Napa Valley 1985 • $14 • (4/30/1988) • **89**
Cabernet Sauvignon Napa Valley 1984 • $13 • (5/31/1987) • **92**
Cabernet Sauvignon Napa Valley 1983 • $12 • (7/16/1986) SS • **93**
Cabernet Sauvignon Napa Valley Estate 1996: Struggles to work past the green bean and herb notes into riper Cabernet flavors. Turns hard and tannic, with a dry, angular aftertaste. Short-term cellaring may help. Best from 2002 through 2008.–J.L. • $35 • (5/31/2000) • **83**
Cabernet Sauvignon Napa Valley Estate 1995: Balanced toward the fruity, supple side, with bright, ripe and juicy Cabernet flavors, lots of cherry and berry, and mild polished tannins. Drink now through 2004.–J.L. • $35 • (10/31/1998) • **88**
Cabernet Sauvignon Napa Valley Estate 1994 • $35 • (11/15/1997) • **90**
Cabernet Sauvignon Napa Valley Reserve 1991 • $25 • (9/30/1995) • **91**
Chardonnay Russian River Valley 1997: Firm, focused and packed with lemon, orange and a touch of grapefruit, all framed in toasty oak. The follow-up includes hints of peach, finishing moderately and brightly. Drink now through 2002. • $15 • (7/31/1999) • **88**
Chardonnay Russian River Valley 1996 • $15 • (4/30/1998) • **85**
Chardonnay Russian River Valley Reserve 1997: Seamless. Ripe, rich and creamy, with crème brûlée, toasty oak and a ripe pear core. Long, complex, deeply flavored aftertaste. Drink now.–J.L. • $30 • (7/31/1999) • **93**
Chardonnay Russian River Valley Reserve 1996 • $30 • (4/30/1998) • **90**
Pinot Noir Central Coast 1993 • $9 • (3/31/1995) • **79**
Zinfandel Napa Valley 1997: Medium-bodied, with simple, slightly green tea-like cherry and strawberry flavors that lose their focus. Drink now.–J.L. • $25 • (6/30/2000) • **83**
Zinfandel Napa Valley 1995 • $14 • (9/15/1997) • **80**
Zinfandel Napa Valley 1994 • $12 • (4/30/1996) • **87**
Zinfandel Napa Valley 1993 • $10 • (10/15/1995) • **84**
Zinfandel Napa Valley 1992 • $8 • (4/30/1994) • **88**
Zinfandel Napa Valley 1990 • $10 • (10/15/1992) • **77**
Zinfandel Napa Valley 1989 • $10 • (3/31/1992) • **83**
Zinfandel Napa Valley Estate 1996 • $25 • (5/31/1998) • **82**
Zinfandel Napa Valley Estate 1995 • $20 • (4/30/1998) • **89**
Zinfandel Napa Valley Reserve 1994 • $25 • (9/15/1996) • **85**

BUENA VISTA | CALIFORNIA

Brut Blanc de Blancs Carneros 1991 • $17 • (4/30/1998) • **88**
Brut Blanc de Blancs Carneros 1990 • $14 • (9/15/1996) • **86**
Cabernet Sauvignon Carneros 1995: With an interplay of herbs, cassis and oak, this somewhat tangy red still tastes quite young. Good now, should improve through 2005. • $16 • (10/31/1998) • **85**
Cabernet Sauvignon Carneros 1994 • $16 • (8/31/1997) • **88**
Cabernet Sauvignon Carneros 1993 • $NA • (1/01/1997) • **82**
Cabernet Sauvignon Carneros 1992 • $12 • (12/15/1995) • **80**
Cabernet Sauvignon Carneros 1991 • $12 • (10/15/1994) • **87**
Cabernet Sauvignon Carneros 1990 • $11 • (9/15/1993) • **82**
Cabernet Sauvignon Carneros 1989 • $9 • (11/15/1992) • **74**
Cabernet Sauvignon Carneros 1988: Better balanced than the Grand Reserve though it shares the same flavor profile, with herb, leather, weedy notes that override the Cabernet fruit. (1988 California Cabernet retrospective tasting). Drink now.–J.L. • $14 • (11/15/1998) • **82**
Cabernet Sauvignon Carneros 1987 • $11 • (10/15/1990) • **83**

■ ■ ■ ■

BUENA VISTA

Cabernet Sauvignon Carneros 1986 • $11 • (10/15/1989) • **91**
Cabernet Sauvignon Carneros 1985 • $10 • (11/15/1988) • **84**
Cabernet Sauvignon Carneros 1984 • $10 • (8/31/1987) • **94**
Cabernet Sauvignon Carneros 1982 • $11 • (9/16/1985) • **85**
Cabernet Sauvignon Carneros 1981 • $11 • (2/16/1985) • **89**
Cabernet Sauvignon Carneros Grand Reserve 1995: A bit lean on the palate, it nevertheless serves up some tasty blackberry, herb, anise and toasty oak. Tannins are firm; still young but should evolve nicely. Drink now through 2005. • $37 • (10/15/1999) • **86**
Cabernet Sauvignon Carneros Grand Reserve 1994: For fans of herbal Cabernets, here's an earthy style, with bell pepper, black cherry, anise and spicy Cabernet fruit flavors. Balanced, with fine tannins. Drink through 2004–J.L. • $26 • (10/31/1998) • **85**
Cabernet Sauvignon Carneros Grand Reserve 1993 • $26 • (8/31/1997) • **90**
Cabernet Sauvignon Carneros Grand Reserve 1992 • $24 • (9/15/1996) • **80**
Cabernet Sauvignon Carneros Grand Reserve 1990 • $24 • (10/15/1994) • **83**
Cabernet Sauvignon Carneros Grand Reserve 1988: Marked by earthy, weedy, vegetal notes, it struggles to find focus, shows little in the way of ripe Cabernet fruit. (1988 California Cabernet retrospective tasting).–J.L. • $24 • (11/15/1998) • **78**
Cabernet Sauvignon Carneros Private Reserve 1986 • $25 • (3/15/1991) • **89**
Cabernet Sauvignon Carneros Private Reserve 1985 • $18 • (10/15/1989) SS • **94**
Cabernet Sauvignon Carneros Private Reserve 1983 • $18 • (2/15/1988) • **90**
Cabernet Sauvignon Carneros Private Reserve 1982 • $19 • (2/15/1987) • **87**
Cabernet Sauvignon Carneros Private Reserve (Special Selection) 1981 • $18 • (7/01/1986) • **88**
Cabernet Sauvignon Carneros Special Selection 1978 • $18 • (6/01/1986) • **96**
Cabernet Sauvignon Sonoma County 1986 • $11 • (11/15/1989) • **90**
Cabernet Sauvignon Sonoma Valley 1978 • $30 • (6/01/1986) • **94**
Cabernet Sauvignon Sonoma Valley Special Selection 1978: Drying out, with chewy tannins gaining the upper hand. Still plenty of fruit, showing earthy currant, bay leaf, chocolate and berry flavors that hang with you on the finish. Tough call—it's still intense and concentrated, but the dryness on the finish is a concern. (1978 California Cabernet retrospective tasting). Drink now through 2002.–J.L. • $12 • (11/15/1998) • **88**
Chardonnay Carneros 1997: Medium in weight, with modest pear and vanilla notes that turn simple. Drink now through 2003.–J.L. • $15 • (4/30/2000) • **83**
Chardonnay Carneros 1996: Straightforward, with flinty citrus and toast flavors on a firm frame. Finishes with notes of pear and apple. Drink now.–J.L. • $14 • (12/31/1998) • **84**
Gamay Beaujolais Carneros 1988 • $8 • (7/15/1989) • **84**
Ingrid's Vineyard Late Harvest Carneros 1989 • $18 • (4/30/1991) • **87**
L'Année Carneros 1986 • $35 • (2/28/1991) • **87**
L'Année Carneros 1984 • $32/1.5 liter • (2/15/1988) • **88**
Merlot Carneros 1995: Rich and complex, with depth, concentration and distinctive spice, currant, smoke, plum and berry flavors that are tightly wound and sharply focused. Finishes with a plush wall of tannins, so this is no softie. Drink through 2004–J.L. • $18 • (10/15/1998) • **85**
Merlot Carneros 1994 • $12 • (5/15/1997) • **84**
Merlot Carneros 1993 • $13 • (6/30/1996) • **83**
Merlot Carneros 1992 • $13 • (5/15/1995) • **82**
Merlot Carneros 1991 • $12 • (12/31/1993) • **82**
Merlot Carneros 1990 • $11 • (10/31/1992) • **86**
Merlot Carneros 1989 • $11 • (5/31/1992) • **71**
Merlot Carneros 1985 • $11 • (6/30/1988) • **80**
Merlot Carneros Grand Reserve 1994 • $26 • (7/31/1997) • **88**
Merlot Carneros Grand Reserve 1989 • $20 • (5/31/1993) • **82**
Merlot Carneros Private Reserve 1988 • $17 • (5/31/1992) • **82**
Merlot Carneros Private Reserve 1987 • $18 • (3/31/1991) • **84**
Merlot Carneros Private Reserve 1986 • $17 • (10/31/1989) • **86**
Merlot Carneros Private Reserve 1984 • $15 • (2/15/1988) • **87**
Merlot Sonoma County 1987 • $11 • (7/31/1990) • **86**
Pinot Noir Carneros 1997: Lean and full of stewed apples, cinnamon and candied notes, with a drying finish. Drink now through 2003.–J.L. • $17 • (4/30/2000) • **82**
Pinot Noir Carneros 1996: Simple, with ripe cherry-berry flavors and oaky notes that lack focus. Finishes dry. Drink now.–J.L. • $16 • (2/28/1999) • **82**
Pinot Noir Carneros 1995 • $16 • (8/31/1997) • **86**
Pinot Noir Carneros 1994 • $12 • (11/30/1996) • **82**

Key: SS—Spectator Selection. CS—Cellar Selection. HR—Highly Recommended. $NA—Price not available. (BT)—Barrel tasting. Ⓐ—Auction Price. For a key to the tasters' initials, see "How to Use These Listings." **Dates in parentheses represent the issues in which the ratings were published.**

Pinot Noir Carneros 1993 • $10 • (10/15/1995) • **86**
Pinot Noir Carneros 1992 • $10 • (3/31/1995) • **77**
Pinot Noir Carneros 1991 • $10 • (2/28/1994) • **80**
Pinot Noir Carneros 1990 • $9 • (9/30/1992) • **81**
Pinot Noir Carneros 1989 • $7/5 liter • (7/31/1991) • **81**
Pinot Noir Carneros 1988 • $11 • (12/15/1990) • **82**
Pinot Noir Carneros 1983 • $14 • (8/31/1986) • **75**
Pinot Noir Carneros Grand Reserve 1996: Firm, with a core of strawberry, cherry, herb and toasted oak flavors that persist on the mildly tannic finish. Drink now through 2002.–J.L. • $26 • (9/15/1999) • **85**
Pinot Noir Carneros Grand Reserve 1995 • $26 • (11/15/1997) • **79**
Pinot Noir Carneros Grand Reserve 1994 • $20 • (2/29/1996) • **84**
Pinot Noir Carneros Grand Reserve 1991 • $20 • (10/31/1994) • **86**
Pinot Noir Carneros Grand Reserve 1990 • $16 • (2/28/1993) HR • **89**
Pinot Noir Carneros Limited Release 1996: Elegant, with floral plum, raspberry and wild berry flavors. Finishes with spicy oak and soft tannins. Drink now through 2005.–J.L. • $35 • (5/31/2000) • **87**
Pinot Noir Carneros Private Reserve 1987 • $14 • (6/30/1991) • **80**
Pinot Noir Carneros Private Reserve 1986 • $14 • (3/31/1990) • **85**
Pinot Noir Carneros Private Reserve 1984 • $15 • (2/15/1988) • **81**
Pinot Noir Carneros Private Reserve 1981 • $14 • (8/31/1986) • **88**
Sauvignon Blanc California 1998: Tangy, with green bean, herb and vanilla flavors. Drink now.–J.L. • $9 • (5/15/2000) • **84**
Sauvignon Blanc California 1997: Tangy lemon and grapefruit flavors, with a fine mineral edge, thread through this well-rounded, quaffable white, backed by hints of thyme and sage essence on the finish. It's affordably priced and made in a quantity that suggests availability. Drink now. • $9 • (1/31/1999) • **86**
Sauvignon Blanc California 1996 • $9 • (6/30/1997) • **88**
Zinfandel California 1998: Jammy strawberry, leather and plum flavors are straightforward, round and soft. Drink now through 2003.–J.L. • $9 • (5/31/2000) • **83**
Zinfandel California 1997: Plummy fruit flavors are bright but juicy, with a thread of spice. Picks up a touch of heat on the finish. Drink now.–J.L. • $9 • (12/31/1998) • **83**

BUFFALO RIDGE | CALIFORNIA

Zinfandel Central Coast French Camp Vineyard 1998: Tangy, with chocolate, berry and vanilla notes that carry through to the finish. Drink now through 2003.–J.L. • $12 • (5/31/2000) • **82**

BURGESS | CALIFORNIA

Cabernet Sauvignon Napa Valley Vintage Selection 1996: Tightly wound and focused, featuring a core of black cherry and toasted oak. Needs time. Best from 2000 through 2005.–J.L. • $26 • (9/15/1999) • **86**
Cabernet Sauvignon Napa Valley Vintage Selection 1995: Firm and chewy, with an olive character to the modest black cherry and anise flavors. Needs cellaring. Drink through 2004–H.S. • $24 • (10/31/1998) • **85**
Cabernet Sauvignon Napa Valley Vintage Selection 1994 • $22 • (11/30/1997) • **87**
Cabernet Sauvignon Napa Valley Vintage Selection 1993 • $22 • (5/15/1997) • **88**
Cabernet Sauvignon Napa Valley Vintage Selection 1992 • $22 • (11/15/1996) SS • **90**
Cabernet Sauvignon Napa Valley Vintage Selection 1991 • $20 • (12/15/1995) • **83**
Cabernet Sauvignon Napa Valley Vintage Selection 1990 • $18 • (10/15/1994) • **88**
Cabernet Sauvignon Napa Valley Vintage Selection 1989: Light and simple, with a modest band of ripe cherry and plummy Cabernet flavors, turning herbal and supple. (1989 California Cabernet retrospective tasting). Drink now.–J.L. • $20 • (8/31/1999) • **86**
Cabernet Sauvignon Napa Valley Vintage Selection 1988: Austere, but with enough spicy currant and wild berry to sustain it. Shows off a firm core of fruit and finishes with tight tannins, so you can drink it now or cellar short-term, through 2002. (1988 California Cabernet retrospective tasting).–J.L. • $18 • (11/15/1998) • **87**
Cabernet Sauvignon Napa Valley Vintage Selection 1987 • $20 • (10/15/1991) • **85**
Cabernet Sauvignon Napa Valley Vintage Selection 1986 • $20 • (7/15/1990) • **88**
Cabernet Sauvignon Napa Valley Vintage Selection 1985 • $24 • (7/15/1989) • **92**

Cabernet Sauvignon Napa Valley Vintage Selection 1984 • $17 • (7/31/1988) • **92**
Cabernet Sauvignon Napa Valley Vintage Selection 1983 • $17 • (10/15/1987) • **85**
Cabernet Sauvignon Napa Valley Vintage Selection 1982 • $16 • (10/15/1986) • **81**
Cabernet Sauvignon Napa Valley Vintage Selection 1981 • $16 • (9/16/1985) • **87**
Cabernet Sauvignon Napa Valley Vintage Selection 1980 • $16 • (5/01/1984) SS • **90**
Cabernet Sauvignon Napa Valley Vintage Selection 1979: Dry, earthy and tannic, with a fleeting glimpse of peppery plum and currant. (1979 California Cabernet retrospective tasting). Past its prime.–J.L. • $18 • (8/31/1999) • **78**
Cabernet Sauvignon Napa Valley Vintage Selection 1978: Holding up nicely, with attractive ripe plum, spice, currant and cedary notes, this is a tightly framed wine of excellent structure. (1978 California Cabernet retrospective tasting). Drink now through 2002.–J.L. • $14 • (11/15/1998) • **89**
Cabernet Sauvignon Napa Valley Vintage Selection 1974 • $55 • (11/15/1994) • **74**
Chardonnay Napa Valley 1998: Simple, with a sappy edge to the vanilla and ginger notes. Drink now.–J.L. • $18 • (6/15/2000) • **82**
Chardonnay Napa Valley 1997: Soft, rich and smooth, featuring creamy cheesecake flavors. Subtle fig and citrus notes add complexity. Drink now.–J.L. • $15 • (7/31/1999) • **87**
Merlot Napa Valley 1996: Still quite young, with firm tannins. Shows depth, with tangy blackberry notes, anise and plum flavors and lots of smoky oak. Needs time to soften and come together. Drink through 2006 • $22 • (11/30/1998) • **87**
Merlot Napa Valley 1995 • $22 • (4/30/1998) • **84**
Merlot Napa Valley 1994 • $20 • (11/30/1996) • **87**
Merlot Napa Valley 1993 • $20 • (5/31/1996) • **84**
Zinfandel Napa Valley 1996: Smooth and rich, this is a generous mouthful of blueberry, blackberry and vanilla flavors that linger beautifully on the finish. Tannins are fine-grained. Drink now through 2002.–H.S. • $15 • (11/30/1998) • **88**
Zinfandel Napa Valley 1994 • $13 • (4/30/1997) • **87**
Zinfandel Napa Valley 1993 • $12 • (11/30/1996) • **85**
Zinfandel Napa Valley 1992 • $11 • (10/15/1995) • **79**
Zinfandel Napa Valley 1991 • $12 • (10/15/1994) • **81**
Zinfandel Napa Valley 1990 • $12 • (9/30/1993) • **84**
Zinfandel Napa Valley 1989 • $10 • (10/15/1992) • **80**
Zinfandel Napa Valley 1988 • $12 • (7/31/1991) • **80**
Zinfandel Napa Valley 1987 • $10 • (5/31/1990) • **82**

BURRELL SCHOOL | CALIFORNIA

Cabernet Franc Napa Valley Aviemore Vineyard 1995 • $18 • (9/15/1997) • **87**

BUTTONWOOD | CALIFORNIA

Cabernet Franc Santa Ynez Valley 1994 • $15 • (3/31/1998) • **85**
Cabernet Sauvignon Santa Ynez Valley 1994 • $16 • (10/31/1997) • **83**
Marsanne Santa Ynez Valley 1996 • $12 • (1/31/1998) • **86**
Merlot Santa Ynez Valley 1996: Starts off with pretty spice and cedar notes, then kicks in with black currant and blackberry notes on the moderate finish. Tannins are firm. Drink now through 2003. • $18 • (10/15/1999) • **85**
Merlot Santa Ynez Valley 1995: Marked by a slightly weedy quality, it earns points for interesting cassis, coffee, spice and blackberry notes. Toasty oak rounds out the finish. Drink now through 2004. • $18 • (9/30/1998) • **85**
Merlot Santa Ynez Valley 1994 • $16 • (2/28/1998) • **87**
Merlot Santa Ynez Valley 1993 • $16 • (7/31/1997) • **87**
Sauvignon Blanc Santa Ynez Valley 1997: Peachy, with grassy, herbal overtones. Finishes with a menthol edge and bright acidity. Drink now. • $10 • (9/15/1998) • **83**
Sauvignon Blanc Santa Ynez Valley 1996 • $10 • (12/15/1997) • **86**

BYINGTON | CALIFORNIA

Alliage Sonoma County 1997: Smooth and polished, with pretty vanilla-scented oak and hints of cherry and plum, though it strays into herb and celery notes. Drink now through 2005.–J.L. • $19 • (6/15/2000) • **86**
Cabernet Sauvignon Alexander Valley Smith Reichel Vineyard 1994 • $18 • (11/30/1997) • **83**
Cabernet Sauvignon Alexander Valley Smith Reichel Vineyard 1993 • $17 • (9/15/1996) • **83**
Cabernet Sauvignon Alexander Valley Smith Reichel Vineyard 1992 • $15 • (12/15/1995) • **87**
Cabernet Sauvignon Napa Valley 1987 • $16 • (11/15/1991) • **86**
Cabernet Sauvignon Santa Cruz Mountains Bates Ranch 1995: Elegant and balanced, with leather, herb and earth nuances to the black cherry flavor. Smooth and flavorful finish. Drink now through 2003.–J.L. • $23 • (9/15/1999) • **88**
Cabernet Sauvignon Santa Cruz Mountains Bates Ranch 1992 • $22 • (12/15/1995) • **83**
Cabernet Sauvignon Santa Cruz Mountains Bates Ranch Special Reserve Vineyards 1993 • $20 • (9/15/1996) • **87**
Cabernet Sauvignon Santa Cruz Mountains Bates Ranch Vineyard 1997: Ripe and juicy, turning elegant and polished for such an immense wine, with a range of wild berry, black cherry, currant, cedar and tea. Firm and tannic on the finish. Best from 2002 through 2010.–J.L. • $24 • (1/31/2000) • **91**
Cabernet Sauvignon Santa Cruz Mountains Twin Mountains 1994 • $14 • (11/30/1997) • **82**
Chardonnay Napa Valley Twin Mountains 1996: A bit earthy, with a slight grassy twinge. The ripe pear and melon flavors are supple in texture, finishing with anise and oak on the aftertaste. Drink now through 2001–J.L. • $15 • (7/31/1998) • **88**
Chardonnay Santa Cruz Mountains 1998: Mint, butter and pear flavors have depth but are a bit hollow midpalate. Drink now.–J.L. • $16 • (6/15/2000) • **83**
Chardonnay Santa Cruz Mountains 1997: Ripe and concentrated, with a spicy edge to the pear, pineapple, mineral and toast flavors. Long and complex on the finish. Drink now.–J.L. • $20 • (7/31/1999) • **88**
Chardonnay Santa Cruz Mountains 1996 • $20 • (6/30/1998) • **90**
Chardonnay Santa Cruz Mountains Bald Mountain Vineyard Special Reserve Vineyards 1996: Smooth, ripe, rich and creamy, with sharply focused pear, anise, butter, fig and melon. Shows depth and richness, with a dash of hazelnut on the finish.–J.L. • $24 • (7/31/1998) • **90**
Chardonnay Santa Cruz Mountains Dirk Vineyard Special Reserve Vineyards 1996 • $24 • (6/30/1998) • **91**
Merlot Sonoma County Bradford Mountain 1994 • $18 • (5/15/1997) • **87**
Merlot Sonoma County Bradford Mountain 1993 • $15 • (7/31/1996) • **87**
Merlot Sonoma County Bradford Mountain 1991 • $15 • (9/15/1994) • **83**
Pinot Noir California 1988 • $15 • (4/30/1991) • **83**
Pinot Noir Central Coast 1995 • $18 • (2/28/1998) • **84**
Pinot Noir Napa Valley 1987 • $15 • (4/30/1991) • **74**
Pinot Noir Santa Barbara County Bien Nacido Vineyard 1991 • $15 • (3/31/1995) • **78**
Pinot Noir Santa Cruz Mountains Special Reserve Vineyards 1994 • $25 • (2/29/1996) • **88**
Pinot Noir Santa Cruz Mountains St. Charles Vineyard Special Reserve Vineyards 1993 • $30 • (2/29/1996) • **85**
Pinot Noir Willamette Valley 1995 • $20 • (2/28/1998) • **81**
Zinfandel Howell Mountain 1992 • $10 • (3/31/1996) • **86**
Zinfandel Paso Robles Sunny Slope Vineyard 1990 • $12 • (9/30/1993) • **85**
Zinfandel Santa Clara County Calle Cielo Vineyard 1992 • $15 • (10/15/1994) • **82**

BYNUM, DAVIS | CALIFORNIA

Cabernet Sauvignon Russian River Valley Hedin Vineyard Limited Edition 1994 • $20 • (12/15/1997) • **87**
Cabernet Sauvignon Sonoma County 1989 • $11 • (11/15/1992) • **81**
Cabernet Sauvignon Sonoma County 1987 • $11 • (11/15/1990) • **79**
Cabernet Sauvignon Sonoma County 1986 • $10 • (11/15/1989) • **84**
Chardonnay Russian River Valley Limited Edition 1998: Ripe, with cidery pineapple juice flavors that struggle to find focus. Drink now.–J.L. • $25 • (5/31/2000) • **82**
Chardonnay Russian River Valley McIlroy & Allen Vineyards Limited Edition 1997: Quite fragrant, with floral overtones and nectarine aromas. Light but elegant on the palate, with firm acidity and complex pear, apple and citrus flavors. Finishes long. Drink now. • $22 • (6/30/1999) • **90**
Eclipse Sonoma County 1994 • $28 • (4/30/1998) • **87**
Fumé Blanc Russian River Valley Shone Farm 1999: Intensely herbaceous and flinty. Lean but focused, with citrus precision to the flavors. Best from 2001 through 2005.–J.L. • $15 • (5/15/2000) • **87**
Merlot Russian River Valley Laureles 1997: Tough, with a chewy, tannic edge and a metallic note to the vague Merlot flavors. Drink now.–J.L. • $30 • (5/31/2000) • **80**
Merlot Russian River Valley Laureles Vineyard 1995: Racy, with black cherry, blackberry and enough bright flavors to keep it lively. It's tannic, too, so give it time in the cellar. Drink through 2004–J.L. • $24 • (9/30/1998) • **85**
Merlot Russian River Valley Laureles Vineyard 1994 • $22 • (5/15/1997) • **86**

Merlot Russian River Valley Laureles Vineyard 1991 • $20 • (9/15/1994) • **81**
Pinot Noir Russian River Valley 1998: Floral, with ripe black cherry and cola notes that are round and concentrated. Drink now through 2003.–J.L. • $25 • (6/30/2000) • **86**
Pinot Noir Russian River Valley 1996: Light and simple, with a glimmer of tea, cherry and cola and a smooth texture, though it shortens up quickly on the finish. Drink now.–J.L. • $18 • (9/30/1998) • **82**
Pinot Noir Russian River Valley 1994 • $14 • (11/30/1996) • **82**
Pinot Noir Russian River Valley 1993 • $12 • (12/31/1995) • **82**
Pinot Noir Russian River Valley 1991 • $17 • (2/28/1994) • **84**
Pinot Noir Russian River Valley 1990 • $18 • (2/28/1994) • **72**
Pinot Noir Russian River Valley Artist Series 1985 • $15 • (6/15/1988) • **82**
Pinot Noir Russian River Valley Le Pinot Rochioli Vineyard 1997: Elegant and complex, with pretty floral aromas and ripe cherry, cranberry and spicy notes, turning delicate. Drink now through 2004 .–J.L. • $50 • (2/29/2000) • **88**
Pinot Noir Russian River Valley Limited Edition 1995 • $28 • (12/15/1997) • **86**
Pinot Noir Russian River Valley Limited Edition 1994 • $24 • (2/28/1997) • **88**
Pinot Noir Russian River Valley Limited Edition 1992 • $21 • (9/15/1995) • **84**
Pinot Noir Russian River Valley Limited Release 1991 • $18 • (10/31/1994) • **88**
Pinot Noir Russian River Valley Limited Release 1990 • $18 • (9/30/1992) • **84**
Pinot Noir Russian River Valley Limited Release 1988 • $16 • (4/30/1991) • **86**
Pinot Noir Russian River Valley Limited Release 1986 • $14 • (3/31/1990) • **83**
Pinot Noir Russian River Valley Limited Release 1984 • $14 • (5/31/1988) • **89**
Pinot Noir Russian River Valley Rochioli Vineyard Le Pinot 1995: Displays good intensity and is firmly tannic, with a core of cherry, plum and wild berry that's quite appealing. Well balanced and worthy of short-term cellaring. Drink through 2003–J.L. • $40 • (9/30/1998) • **85**
Pinot Noir Russian River Valley Westside Road 1983 • $10 • (7/16/1986) • **71**
Sauvignon Blanc Russian River Valley Shone Farm Vineyard Selection 1996 • $11 • (6/30/1997) • **89**
Westside Road Sonoma County 1996: Weaves together ripe plum, earth, cedar, tar and black cherry, firming on the finish, where the flavors offer nuance. Merlot, Cabernet Sauvignon and Cabernet Franc. Drink now through 2007.–J.L. • $32 • (12/31/1999) • **87**
Zinfandel Russian River Valley 1992 • $12 • (10/15/1995) • **88**
Zinfandel Russian River Valley 1991 • $12 • (10/15/1994) • **87**
Zinfandel Russian River Valley 1990 • $12 • (10/15/1992) • **84**
Zinfandel Sonoma County Old Vines 1997: Appealing, with pretty, perfumed raspberry, plum and exotic flavors. Firms up on the finish, where the tannins are more evident. Drink now through 2004.–J.L. • $20 • (1/31/2000) • **87**
Zinfandel Sonoma County Old Vines 1995 • $16 • (12/15/1997) • **84**

BYRON | CALIFORNIA

Cabernet Sauvignon Central Coast 1985 • $14 • (12/15/1989) • **76**
Cabernet Sauvignon Santa Barbara County 1990 • $16 • (8/31/1992) • **85**
Cabernet Sauvignon Santa Barbara County 1989 • $16 • (11/15/1993) • **82**
Chardonnay Santa Maria Valley 1998: Crisp and flinty, with earthy citrus, nectarine and tart pear flavors on a tight beam. Drink now.–J.L. • $22 • (6/30/2000) • **88**
Chardonnay Santa Maria Valley 1997: Wonderfully rich and silky, with polished, focused pear, nectarine and toast, showing more nuances of flavor on the finish. Drink now.–J.L. • $17 • (7/31/1999) • **90**
Chardonnay Santa Maria Valley 1996: Clean and spicy, with plenty of ripe citrus, green pear, apple and melon flavors, finishing with a lingering tropical fruit aftertaste. Drink now through 2000 .–J.L. • $17 • (7/31/1998) • **88**
Chardonnay Santa Maria Valley Byron Vineyard 1996: Wonderful finesse, texture and polish. This delicious array of ripe, rich pear, fig, spice and citrus stays tightly focused on a long, lively, complex aftertaste. Drink now through 2002.–J.L. • $32 • (6/30/1999) • **93**
Chardonnay Santa Maria Valley Reserve 1996: Shows off ripe tangerine, citrus, pear and melon flavors that are rich and concentrated, though a bit awkward now; short-term cellaring is advised. Drink now through 2002.–J.L. • $24 • (4/30/1999) • **89**
Pinot Noir Santa Barbara County 1995 • $17 • (11/30/1997) SS • **90**
Pinot Noir Santa Barbara County 1994 • $17 • (2/29/1996) • **87**
Pinot Noir Santa Barbara County 1992 • $15 • (2/28/1994) • **83**
Pinot Noir Santa Barbara County 1986 • $12 • (3/31/1997) • **79**
Pinot Noir Santa Barbara County 1985 • $12 • (6/15/1988) • **81**
Pinot Noir Santa Barbara County Reserve 1994 • $24 • (6/30/1997) • **87**
Pinot Noir Santa Barbara County Reserve 1993 • $23 • (1/31/1997) • **88**
Pinot Noir Santa Barbara County Reserve 1992 • $23 • (3/31/1995) • **86**
Pinot Noir Santa Barbara County Reserve 1991 • $23 • (2/28/1994) • **88**
Pinot Noir Santa Barbara County Reserve 1990 • $20 • (3/31/1997) • **88**
Pinot Noir Santa Barbara County Reserve 1987 • $16 • (12/15/1989) • **85**
Pinot Noir Santa Barbara County Reserve 1986 • $12 • (6/15/1988) • **84**
Pinot Noir Santa Barbara County Sierra Madre Vineyards 1984 • $13 • (8/31/1986) • **85**
Pinot Noir Santa Maria Valley 1997: Medium-bodied, with a complex range of cola, tea, cherry and spicy flavors, finishing with mild tannins. Drink now.–J.L. • $20 • (9/15/1999) • **86**
Pinot Noir Santa Maria Valley 1996: Smooth and spicy, with a range of earthy cherry, cola, anise and sage. Good intensity and depth of flavor, finishing with a complex aftertaste. Given the tannin level, best to cellar short-term. Drink through 2004–J.L. • $18 • (8/31/1998) • **88**
Pinot Noir Santa Maria Valley Byron Vineyard 1996: Tightly wound, with a firm core of spice, earth, black cherry, currant, cedar and tar. Needs time to soften and evolve; cellar short-term. Best from 2001 through 2006.–J.L. • $40 • (9/15/1999) • **88**
Pinot Noir Santa Maria Valley Reserve 1995 • $25 • (1/31/1998) • **87**

CA' DEL SOLO | CALIFORNIA

Barbera Monterey 1998: Heavy on the bell pepper flavors, with simple, charry black cherry notes. Drink now.–J.L. • $15 • (4/30/2000) • **80**
Barbera Monterey 1996 • $15 • (12/15/1997) • **89**
Big House Red California 1998: Light, peppery and spicy, with hints of bell pepper around the core of tart cherry. Nice finish. Drink now.–J.L. • $10 • (5/15/2000) • **81**
Big House Red California 1992 • $8 • (10/15/1993) • **84**
Big House Red California 1991 • $8 • (11/30/1992) • **84**
Big House Red California 1990 • $8 • (6/30/1992) • **85**
Big House White California 1994 • $8 • (10/15/1995) • **86**
Big House White California 1993 • $8 • (4/15/1995) • **83**
Charbono California La Farfalla 1998: Strong barnyard nose, but it's dark and dense, with earth and mineral flavors and blackberry notes. A rustic wine that finishes tannic. Drink now through 2004.–J.L. • $15 • (4/30/2000) • **85**
Charbono California La Farfalla 1997: Quite dark in color, with firm, ripe tannins. Black cherry, anise and herb flavors blend nicely, while the finish is bright. Could use time to soften. Drink through 2005 • $15 • (6/15/1999) • **86**
Charbono California La Farfalla 1996 • $15 • (11/30/1997) • **83**
Charbono California La Farfalla 1994 • $10 • (8/31/1996) • **82**
Il Fiasco California 1997: Simple, with light cherry flavors. A pleasant quaffer that finishes short. Sangiovese blend. Drink now. • $15 • (6/15/1999) • **81**
Il Fiasco California 1996 • $15 • (12/15/1997) • **86**
Il Fiasco California 1995 • $15 • (12/31/1996) • **86**
Il Pescatore California 1996 • $15 • (3/31/1998) • **85**
Il Pescatore California 1993 • $12 • (4/15/1995) • **85**
Malvasia Bianca Monterey 1998: Smells like Muscat, with orange and floral overtones that turn intensely sour on the finish.–J.L. • $9 • (5/31/2000) • **77**
Malvasia Bianca Monterey 1994 • $9 • (9/30/1995) • **85**
Malvasia Bianca Monterey 1993 • $9 • (4/15/1995) • **85**
Sangiovese California 1998: Reminiscent of blueberry jam, but its drying tannins, sharp acidity and light body don't carry it.–J.L. • $12 • (5/15/2000) • **78**

CAFARO | CALIFORNIA

Cabernet Sauvignon Napa Valley 1996: Restrained, leading with rich, earthy mineral and leather flavors but falters slightly on the finish where the flavors lose focus. Finishes with mild tannins. Drink now through 2003. –J.L. • $37 • (10/15/1999) • **87**
Cabernet Sauvignon Napa Valley 1995: Open-textured, ripe and generous with its currant and spice flavors, picking up some nice hints of clove and anise on the round finish. Drink through 2003–H.S. • $35 • (10/31/1998) • **87**
Cabernet Sauvignon Napa Valley 1994 • $30 • (10/31/1997) • **89**
Cabernet Sauvignon Napa Valley 1993 • $28 • (10/15/1996) • **87**
Cabernet Sauvignon Napa Valley 1992 • $26 • (12/15/1995) • **88**
Cabernet Sauvignon Napa Valley 1991 • $28 • (9/15/1995) • **88**
Cabernet Sauvignon Napa Valley 1990 • $24 • (11/15/1993) • **84**
Cabernet Sauvignon Napa Valley 1989 • $25 • (11/15/1992) • **85**
Cabernet Sauvignon Napa Valley 1988: Tightly wound and well focused, with a rich core of currant, black cherry, olive, herb and cedary oak flavors. Well balanced, with a lingering aftertaste that echoes berry and

Key: SS—Spectator Selection. CS—Cellar Selection. HR—Highly Recommended. $NA—Price not available. (BT)—Barrel tasting. Ⓐ—Auction Price.
For a key to the tasters' initials, see "How to Use These Listings."
Dates in parentheses represent the issues in which the ratings were published.

spice. (1988 California Cabernet retrospective tasting). Drink now through 2004.–J.L. • $25 • (11/15/1998) • **88**
Cabernet Sauvignon Napa Valley 1987 • $20 • (11/15/1990) • **84**
Cabernet Sauvignon Napa Valley 1986 • $18 • (11/15/1989) • **93**
Cabernet Sauvignon Napa Valley Reserva 1994: A touch green and austere at first, the core of currant, black cherry, green olive and bell pepper fans out, and the texture is smooth and polished. Finishes long, with well-integrated tannins. Drink through 2008–J.L. • $48 Ⓐ • (10/15/1998) • **89**
Merlot Napa Valley 1996: Rich, smoky aromas are followed by dark cassis, blackberry, coffee, thyme and peppery notes. Firm on the palate, it should soften nicely in the bottle into a wine of depth and finesse. Best from 2002 through 2007. • $34 • (10/15/1999) • **89**
Merlot Napa Valley 1995: Lean, with a slight green edge to the adequately ripe cherry and currant flavors. Turns dry, with a stalky, herbal edge but enough complexity to merit short-term cellaring. Drink through 2005–J.L. • $30 • (11/30/1998) • **87**
Merlot Napa Valley 1994 • $30 • (11/15/1997) • **88**
Merlot Napa Valley 1988 • $20 • (11/15/1991) • **89**
Merlot Napa Valley 1987 • $18 • (12/31/1990) • **86**
Merlot Napa Valley 1986 • $18 • (12/31/1989) • **84**

CAIN | CALIFORNIA

Cabernet Sauvignon Napa Valley 1986 • $16 • (8/31/1990) • **85**
Cabernet Sauvignon Napa Valley 1985 • $16 • (4/15/1989) • **81**
Cabernet Sauvignon Napa Valley 1984 • $14 • (5/31/1988) • **79**
Cabernet Sauvignon Napa Valley 1983 • $14 • (8/31/1987) • **75**
Cabernet Sauvignon Napa Valley 1982 • $11 • (9/30/1986) • **78**
Cabernet Sauvignon Napa Valley Estate 1987 • $25 • (10/15/1990) • **92**
Cuvée Napa Valley 1997: This has concentration, but pronounced barnyard notes and dry tannins battle the black fruit flavors. Drink now through 2005.–J.L. • $24 • (6/30/2000) • **80**
Cuvée Napa Valley 1996: Complex interplay of racy, stalky currant, black cherry, leather and mineral leads to dry, earthy tannins on the finish. Best from 2001 through 2008.–J.L. • $24 • (1/31/2000) • **87**
Cuvée Napa Valley 1995: Shows racy Cabernet fruit flavors, a touch herbaceous, with pleasing cherry, berry and cedary oak notes. Finishes with firm, well-integrated tannins. Drink through 2005–J.L. • $22 • (10/31/1998) • **87**
Cuvée Napa Valley 1994 • $19 • (7/31/1997) • **85**
Cuvée Napa Valley 1993 • $18 • (12/15/1996) • **87**
Cuvée Napa Valley 1992 • $16 • (12/15/1995) • **83**
Cuvée Napa Valley 1991 • $15 • (12/31/1994) • **83**
Cuvée Napa Valley 1989 • $12 • (11/15/1993) • **84**
Cuvée Napa Valley 1988 • $12 • (3/31/1993) • **87**
Five Napa Valley 1998: A racy, spicy, herbal style, it backfills with currant, coffee, sage and spice, finishing with substantial if earthy tannins.–J.L. • $NA • (8/31/1999) (BT) • **90-94**
Five Napa Valley 1997: A touch stalky with a slight green bean edge, it slowly unfolds into more appealing Cabernet flavors, with currant, herb and cedary flavors. Has fine intensity and concentration.–J.L. • $NA • (8/31/1998) (BT) • **90-94**
Five Napa Valley 1996: Serves up a range of earthy, baked cherry pie-like flavors. Finishes with a gamy edge to the wood and tannins. Tasted three times, with consistent notes. Drink now through 2007.–J.L. • $66 • (5/15/2000) • **85**
Five Napa Valley 1995: Appetizingly earthy and leathery up front, it then unfolds a supple core of herb-accented cherry and currant flavors. Turns complex on the finish and the tannins are polished. Needs time in the bottle. A blend: 63 percent Cabernet Sauvignon, 23 percent Merlot, 9 percent Cabernet France, 4 percent Malbec, 1 percent Petit Verdot. Drink through 2008–J.L. • $67 Ⓐ • (10/31/1998) • **89**
Five Napa Valley 1994 • $45 • (10/31/1997) • **88**
Five Napa Valley 1992 • $40 • (12/15/1996) • **86**
Five Napa Valley 1991 • $40 • (12/15/1995) • **89**
Five Napa Valley 1990 • $34 • (9/15/1994) CS • **93**
Five Napa Valley 1987 • $30 • (12/15/1997) • **89**
Five Napa Valley 1986 • $72 Ⓐ • (12/15/1996) • **85**
Five Napa Valley 1985 • $26 • (6/15/1989) • **87**
Merlot Napa Valley 1986 • $14 • (2/28/1989) • **83**
Merlot Napa Valley 1984 • $12 • (9/30/1988) • **89**
Merlot Napa Valley 1982 • $11 • (2/01/1985) • **78**
Sauvignon Blanc Monterey Musqué Ventana Vineyard 1998: Clean and refreshing, with expressive grassy herb, melon, citrus, lemon peel and a touch of fig. Finishes with a twinge of bitterness. Drink now through 2005.–J.L. • $20 • (4/30/2000) • **87**
Sauvignon Blanc Monterey Ventana Vineyard Musqué 1997: Kicking off with a distinctive herb and gooseberry front, this offers both fresh acidity and classy smoothness on the palate. The finish is long, with subtle citrus and almond character. Resembles New Zealand in style more than California. Drink now through 2001. • $20 • (5/15/1999) • **88**
Sauvignon Blanc Monterey Ventana Vineyard Musqué 1996 • $17 • (1/31/1998) • **90**

CAKEBREAD | CALIFORNIA

Cabernet Sauvignon Napa Valley 1997: Complex, with a supple band of currant, blackberry and cherry. Turns dry and tannic, so be advised. Best after 2000.–J.L. • $30 • (6/15/2000) • **85**
Cabernet Sauvignon Napa Valley 1996: Lots of upfront ripeness and fruitiness, with an earthy clay edge to the ripe cherry and blackberry. Mildly tannic, this is not as lean as young Cakebread Cabernets usually are. Drink now through 2007.–J.L. • $35 • (11/15/1999) • **88**
Cabernet Sauvignon Napa Valley 1995: Shows meaty, slightly nutty flavors before unveiling its core of plum and currant. Has a touch of stemminess, but the pieces are here. Drink through 2006–J.L. • $30 • (10/31/1998) • **89**
Cabernet Sauvignon Napa Valley 1994 • $25 • (7/31/1997) SS • **92**
Cabernet Sauvignon Napa Valley 1993 • $23 • (12/15/1996) • **82**
Cabernet Sauvignon Napa Valley 1991 • $22 • (11/15/1994) • **88**
Cabernet Sauvignon Napa Valley 1990 • $21 • (9/15/1993) • **83**
Cabernet Sauvignon Napa Valley 1989: Holding together, if lacking depth and concentration, the earthy coffee, currant and anise flavors are balanced and appealing. (1989 California Cabernet retrospective tasting). Drink now through 2004.–J.L. • $20 • (8/31/1999) • **87**
Cabernet Sauvignon Napa Valley 1988: Tight, with firm tannins, and more fruit and flesh than most '88s; the currant, black cherry and plum flavors are well defined. Turns simple on the finish, where the flavors lose velocity. (1988 California Cabernet retrospective tasting). Drink now through 2004.–J.L. • $NA • (11/15/1998) • **87**
Cabernet Sauvignon Napa Valley 1987 • $25 • (10/15/1990) • **90**
Cabernet Sauvignon Napa Valley 1986 • $20 • (8/31/1989) • **90**
Cabernet Sauvignon Napa Valley 1985 • $20 • (4/15/1988) • **90**
Cabernet Sauvignon Napa Valley 1984 • $16 • (9/30/1987) • **87**
Cabernet Sauvignon Napa Valley 1983 • $16 • (11/30/1986) • **93**
Cabernet Sauvignon Napa Valley 1982 • $18 • (7/16/1986) • **70**
Cabernet Sauvignon Napa Valley 1979: Has aged nicely, with mature, complex aromas leading to dried cherry, mushroom, anise, sage and spice. At a great drinking age, with much to admire in flavor and texture. Drink now through 2004.–J.L. • $22 • (8/31/1999) • **89**
Cabernet Sauvignon Napa Valley Benchland Select 1995: Well integrated, harmonious if a bit rigid, the fruit flavors are pure and well focused, with layers of coffee, currant, black cherry and cedar. Turns complex on the finish, where the flavors mesh nicely. Tasted twice, with consistent notes. Drink through 2008–J.L. • $65 • (12/31/1998) • **90**
Cabernet Sauvignon Napa Valley Lot 2 1978: A big, thick, over-the-top style, but well done. Captures lots of rich, ripe, exotic Cabernet flavors, with hints of plum, raisin, black cherry, black olive and tar. A touch alcoholic, but still very well balanced, finishing with thick tannins and good length. (1978 California Cabernet retrospective tasting). Drink now.–J.L. • $12 • (11/15/1998) • **89**
Cabernet Sauvignon Napa Valley Lot 2 1974 • $100 • (11/15/1994) • **91**
Cabernet Sauvignon Napa Valley Reserve 1993 • $50 • (3/31/1998) • **87**
Cabernet Sauvignon Napa Valley Rutherford Reserve 1992 • $44 • (7/31/1997) • **87**
Cabernet Sauvignon Napa Valley Rutherford Reserve 1991 • $42 • (11/15/1996) • **89**
Cabernet Sauvignon Napa Valley Rutherford Reserve 1990 • $42 • (12/15/1995) • **87**
Cabernet Sauvignon Napa Valley Rutherford Reserve 1987 • $23 • (9/15/1993) HR • **91**
Cabernet Sauvignon Napa Valley Rutherford Reserve 1986 • $43 • (11/15/1991) • **89**
Cabernet Sauvignon Napa Valley Rutherford Reserve 1984 • $35 • (2/15/1990) • **85**
Cabernet Sauvignon Napa Valley Three Sisters 1996: Smooth and soft, with herb-laced cherry, blackberry, plum jam and cedar flavors, turning diffuse and simple. Drink now through 2004.–J.L. • $80 • (6/15/2000) • **87**
Cabernet Sauvignon Napa Valley Three Sisters 1995: Austere and tightly wound, with black cherry, blackberry, strawberry and spice. Turns quite tannic on the finish. Cellaring is advised. Tasted twice, with consistent notes. Drink through 2007–J.L. • $65 • (12/31/1998) • **89**

CAKEBREAD

Chardonnay Napa Valley 1998: Focused, with tart citrus, nectarine and cream flavors. Drink now.–J.L. • $30 • (6/15/2000) • **85**

Chardonnay Napa Valley 1997: Ripe and intense, with clean, juicy apple, pear, melon and fig flavors that are tightly wound and fan out nicely on the finish. Needs short-term cellaring. Try through 2003.–J.L. • $26 • (6/15/1999) • **90**

Chardonnay Napa Valley 1996 • $25 • (5/31/1998) • **88**

Chardonnay Napa Valley Reserve 1996: Tightly wound, with a firm band of citrus, pear, spice and grapefruit, it slowly unfolds to reveal layers of depth and complexity. Finishes rich. Drink now through 2002.–J.L. • $39 • (6/15/1999) • **91**

Merlot Napa Valley 1996: Ripe, firm and structured, with coffee, herb, currant and berry flavors that turn supple and fleshy, with polished tannins. Drink now through 2005.–J.L. • $30 • (10/15/1999) • **87**

Merlot Napa Valley 1995: Ripe, rich and flavorful, with a pretty array of black cherry, wild berry, spice and currant, finishing with spicy, cedary herbal notes. Impressive for its texture, balance and finesse. Drink now through 2004.–J.L. • $30 • (9/30/1998) • **88**

Merlot Napa Valley 1994 • $27 • (7/31/1997) • **89**

Pinot Noir Carneros 1995: Earthy, with a core of dried cherry and spicy plum flavors that taste a bit dry, turn leathery on the finish. Overly mature for a young wine from so wonderful a vintage. Drink now.–J.L. • $30 • (8/31/1998) • **84**

Pinot Noir Napa Valley Carneros 1994 • $25 • (11/30/1996) • **89**

Rubaiyat Napa Valley 1994 • $18 • (11/30/1996) • **82**

Rutherford Reserve Napa Valley 1988 • $39 • (11/15/1993) • **81**

Sauvignon Blanc Napa Valley 1998: Rich and spicy, with ripe fig, citrus, melon, herb and celery notes, turning complex. Drink now through 2002.–J.L. • $16 • (12/31/1999) • **88**

Sauvignon Blanc Napa Valley 1997: Firmly textured, with lemon-lime, grapefruit, grass and herb notes. Finishes with a hint of passion fruit. A tasty, refreshing wine. Drink now. • $15 • (11/30/1998) • **88**

Sauvignon Blanc Napa Valley 1996 • $14 • (1/31/1998) • **86**

Zinfandel Howell Mountain 1994 • $19 • (11/30/1996) • **89**

Zinfandel Howell Mountain 1992 • $17 • (9/15/1994) HR • **90**

CALDWELL, OLIVER | CALIFORNIA

Cabernet Sauvignon Napa Valley Aïda Vineyard 1996: Zeros in on the ripe, tight core of black cherry and blackberry, and keeps a vivid fruit profile. Firmly tannic but well integrated, and long and full on the finish. Drink through 2002–J.L. • $35 • (10/31/1998) • **88**

Petite Sirah Napa Valley Aïda Vineyard 1997: Dark but rather medium-weight for Petite, with spicy berry, cherry, anise, leather and earth notes. Drink now through 2006.–J.L. • $50 • (5/31/2000) • **87**

Petite Sirah Napa Valley Aïda Vineyard 1996: Dark, inky and complex, with tiers of earthy plum, leather, spice and cedar. Fans out at the end, where some toasty oak flavors fold in, but the finish is quite tannic, so be warned. Drink now through 2002.–J.L. • $40 • (12/15/1998) • **87**

Zinfandel Napa Valley Aïda Vineyard 1997: Pretty toasty, vanilla bean oak shadings round out the core of black cherry and wild berry, rendering a complex and intriguing wine. Drink now through 2007.–J.L. • $37 • (12/15/1999) • **92**

Zinfandel Napa Valley Aïda Vineyard 1996: A delicious wine, complex and concentrated, with ripe, peppery black cherry, wild berry and spicy nuances. Smooth and supple on the finish, where the tannins are rich and firm, turning creamy. Drink through 2004.–J.L. • $30 • (11/30/1998) • **92**

CALE | CALIFORNIA

Chardonnay Carneros Sangiacomo Vineyard 1997: Bright, with soft-textured sweet cream, pear and citrus flavors, finishing with delicate toasted oak notes. Drink now.–J.L. • $23 • (4/30/1999) • **88**

Chardonnay Carneros Sangiacomo Vineyard 1996 • $20 • (5/15/1998) • **88**

Merlot Sonoma Valley Serres Ranch Vintner's Reserve 1996: Delivers earthy, herbal flavors of mocha and charred oak on a fairly supple frame. Drink now through 2001.–H.S. • $25 • (2/28/1999) • **80**

Pinot Noir Carneros Sangiacomo Vineyard 1996 • $18 • (4/30/1998) • **82**

Key: SS—Spectator Selection. CS—Cellar Selection. HR—Highly Recommended. $NA—Price not available. (BT)—Barrel tasting. (A)—Auction Price. For a key to the tasters' initials, see "How to Use These Listings."
Dates in parentheses represent the issues in which the ratings were published.

CALERA | CALIFORNIA

Chardonnay Central Coast 1998: A wonderful value that is complex, ripe, bold and rich, layered with earth, pear, toast, fig and smoky oak flavors. It's smooth in texture, with a long, full aftertaste. Delicious now through 2008.–J.L. • $22 • (4/30/2000) SS • **91**

Chardonnay Central Coast 1997: Tight, tart and flinty, with a core of citrus, pear and earth notes that are clean and lively. Drink now through 2002.–J.L. • $16 • (12/31/1998) • **87**

Chardonnay Central Coast 1996 • $16 • (3/31/1998) • **90**

Chardonnay Mount Harlan 1996: Complex, with a range of tangerine, earth, spice and pear, turning elegant and polished on the finish. Drink now through 2002.–J.L. • $38 • (8/31/1999) • **89**

Pinot Noir Central Coast 1998: Clean and supple, with an earthy, herbal edge to the dried cherry, anise and sage notes, turning dry. Drink now through 2004.–J.L. • $24 • (1/31/2000) • **86**

Pinot Noir Central Coast 1997: Spicy, with an herbal streak running through the cherry notes. Turns complex and a bit tannic. Drink now through 2001.–J.L. • $16 • (12/31/1998) • **86**

Pinot Noir Central Coast 1996 • $16 • (1/31/1998) • **86**

Pinot Noir Central Coast 1995 • $16 • (11/30/1997) • **88**

Pinot Noir Central Coast 1994 • $16 • (2/29/1996) • **85**

Pinot Noir Central Coast 1993 • $15 • (12/31/1995) • **83**

Pinot Noir Central Coast 1992 • $15 • (2/28/1994) • **73**

Pinot Noir Central Coast 1991 • $14 • (2/28/1993) • **84**

Pinot Noir Central Coast 1990 • $14 • (3/31/1992) • **87**

Pinot Noir Central Coast 1989 • $14 • (11/15/1991) • **85**

Pinot Noir Central Coast 1987 • $14 • (2/15/1990) • **82**

Pinot Noir Central Coast Reserve 1993 • $20 • (7/31/1996) • **88**

Pinot Noir Mount Harlan 1993 • $35 • (12/31/1995) • **85**

Pinot Noir Mount Harlan Jensen 1994 • $38 • (7/31/1997) • **88**

Pinot Noir Mount Harlan Jensen 1993 • $38 • (3/31/1997) • **91**

Pinot Noir Mount Harlan Jensen 1992 • $40 • (1/01/1998) • **86**

Pinot Noir Mount Harlan Jensen 1991 • $34 • (3/31/1995) • **88**

Pinot Noir Mount Harlan Jensen 1990 • $38 • (2/28/1994) • **87**

Pinot Noir Mount Harlan Jensen 1989 • $35 • (2/28/1994) • **87**

Pinot Noir Mount Harlan Jensen 1988 • $35 • (11/15/1991) • **92**

Pinot Noir Mount Harlan Jensen 1987 • $30 • (4/30/1991) • **93**

Pinot Noir Mount Harlan Jensen 1986 • $45 • (5/31/1989) • **88**

Pinot Noir Mount Harlan Jensen 1985 • $25 • (6/15/1988) • **88**

Pinot Noir Mount Harlan Jensen 1983 • $22 • (8/31/1986) • **80**

Pinot Noir Mount Harlan Jensen 1982 • $23 • (1/01/1985) • **88**

Pinot Noir Mount Harlan Mills Vineyard 1996: A ripe and elegant California Pinot, with bright and juicy black cherry accented by anise, sage and tea notes. Firms up on the finish, where the tannins add backbone. Drink now through 2008.–J.L. • $55 • (1/31/2000) CS • **90**

Pinot Noir Mount Harlan Mills 1994 • $35 • (2/28/1998) • **88**

Pinot Noir Mount Harlan Mills 1993 • $35 • (6/30/1997) • **86**

Pinot Noir Mount Harlan Mills 1992 • $35 • (3/31/1997) • **91**

Pinot Noir Mount Harlan Mills 1990 • $30 • (3/31/1997) • **90**

Pinot Noir Mount Harlan Mills 1989 • $32 • (11/15/1992) • **91**

Pinot Noir Mount Harlan Mills 1988 • $30 • (11/15/1991) • **89**

Pinot Noir Mount Harlan Reed 1994 • $35 • (3/31/1998) • **88**

Pinot Noir Mount Harlan Reed 1992 • $35 • (3/31/1995) • **84**

Pinot Noir Mount Harlan Reed 1988 • $36 • (11/15/1991) • **85**

Pinot Noir Mount Harlan Reed 1987 • $35 • (4/30/1991) • **80**

Pinot Noir Mount Harlan Reed 1982 • $23 • (8/31/1986) • **75**

Pinot Noir Mount Harlan Selleck 1993 • $38 • (6/30/1997) • **85**

Pinot Noir Mount Harlan Selleck 1987 • $30 • (11/15/1991) • **92**

Pinot Noir Mount Harlan Selleck 1986 • $30 • (3/31/1990) • **85**

Pinot Noir San Benito County Selleck 1986 • $30 • (3/31/1997) • **89**

Pinot Noir Santa Barbara County Bien Nacido Vineyard 1985 • $13 • (6/15/1988) • **82**

Viognier Mount Harlan 1997: A delicious wine, rich and unctuous, with layers of fig, apple, melon and citrus. Finishes with a long, full-bodied aftertaste. Drink now through 2001.–J.L. • $30 • (12/15/1998) • **90**

CALLAGHAN | ARIZONA

Buena Suerte Cuvée Sonoita 1994 • $25 • (6/15/1997) • **83**

Buena Suerte Vineyard Sonoita 1994 • $20 • (8/31/1997) • **80**

Caitlin's Selection Sonoita 1995 • $30 • (6/15/1997) • **77**

Caitlin's Selection Sonoita 1994 • $25 • (6/15/1997) • **83**

Fumé Blanc Cochise County 1996 • $18 • (6/15/1997) • **83**

CALLAWAY | CALIFORNIA

Cabernet Sauvignon California 1996: On the light side, with pretty strawberry and delicate herb flavors on a supple frame. Drink now.–H.S. • $11 • (11/15/1998) • **83**
Cabernet Sauvignon California 1995 • $NA • (12/31/1997) • **86**
Cabernet Sauvignon California 1994 • $10 • (5/15/1997) • **78**
Cabernet Sauvignon California 1991 • $10 • (11/15/1994) • **79**
Cabernet Sauvignon California 1990 • $8 • (11/15/1993) • **79**
Cabernet Sauvignon California 1989 • $9 • (3/31/1993) • **80**
Cabernet Sauvignon California America's Cup 1989 • $10 • (11/15/1991) • **82**
Chardonnay California Calla-Lees 1997: Starts out with ripe pear and citrus flavors, but the acidity is a bit bright and the finish a tad bitter. Still enjoyable. Drink now. • $10 • (9/15/1998) • **83**
Chardonnay Temecula Calla-Lees 1996 • $10 • (9/15/1997) • **81**
Chenin Blanc California 1998: Redolent of fresh apple, with a hint of litchi, this off-dry wine is balanced by plenty of refreshing acidity. Fine either as an aperitif or with dinner. Drink now. • $8 • (6/15/1999) • **85**
Chenin Blanc Temecula 1997: Soft and pleasant for its melon and pear fruit. Finishes with a silky feel. Drink now.–H.S. • $8 • (12/15/1998) • **84**
Chenin Blanc Temecula Sweet Nancy Late Harvest NV • $22 • (2/29/1996) • **88**
Chenin Blanc Temecula Sweet Nancy Late Harvest 1991 • $25/375 ml. • (9/30/1995) • **79**
Dolcetto Temecula 1997: Quite smooth, with pretty cherry, blackberry, anise, spice and herb flavors. The finish is clean and crisp, with firm, ripe tannins. Drink now through 2003. • $15 • (11/15/1999) • **87**
Dolcetto Temecula 1996: A light cherry flavor permeates here. Somewhat thin, it's a bit like a restrained Beaujolais; try slightly chilled. • $16 • (2/28/1999) • **79**
Dolcetto Temecula 1995 • $15 • (9/15/1997) • **74**
Dolcetto Temecula 1994 • $15 • (11/30/1996) • **83**
Merlot California 1996: Soft in texture, with cherry and tea flavors. Turns herbal and earthy on the finish. Tannins are soft and integrated. Drink now.–J.L. • $13 • (11/30/1998) • **80**
Merlot Temecula Barrel Selection 1997: Toasty, showing lots of smoky oak, chocolate and coffee flavors but modest fruit. Drink now.–J.L. • $13 • (10/15/1999) • **81**
Pinot Gris Temecula 1997: With its faintly pink hue, this would make a refreshing summer quaff. Serves up pretty pear and applelike notes and is smooth-textured. Drink now. • $12 • (9/15/1998) • **85**
Pinot Gris Temecula 1996 • $12 • (9/15/1997) • **80**
Sauvignon Blanc Temecula 1998: A peachy, creamy version of this varietal. Lots of fruitiness, but lacking in substance. Not up to last year's effort. Drink now. • $9 • (5/31/1999) • **82**
Sauvignon Blanc Temecula 1997 • $8 • (5/15/1998) • **88**
Sauvignon Blanc Temecula 1996 • $8 • (1/31/1998) • **82**
Viognier Temecula 1997: Smooth and focused, with a core of honey, melon, citrus and spice accents. Finishes with a bright, refreshing edge. Drink now through 2001. • $15 • (12/31/1998) • **86**
Viognier Temecula 1996 • $15 • (9/30/1997) • **83**

CALLE CIELO | CALIFORNIA

Chardonnay Santa Cruz Mountains 1997: A bit heavy-handed with oak, giving it a mature, slightly candied edge, though with aeration it takes on more of a butterscotch flavor, adding to the ripe pear. Drink now through 2003.–J.L. • $24 • (12/31/1999) • **85**
Chardonnay Santa Cruz Mountains 1996 • $25 • (6/30/1998) • **90**
Chardonnay Santa Cruz Mountains Bald Mountain Vineyard 1998: Refreshing, with nutmeg and smoky lemon flavors that linger on the finish. Drink now.–J.L. • $28 • (6/30/2000) • **86**

CAMARADERIE | WASHINGTON

Cabernet Sauvignon Washington 1995: Crisp and more than a little tough, with an acrid edge to the fruit and earth flavors.–H.S. • $22 • (9/15/1998) • **77**
Cabernet Sauvignon Washington 1994 • $19 • (9/30/1997) • **84**
Cabernet Sauvignon Washington 1992 • $17 • (9/30/1995) • **82**

CAMBRIA | CALIFORNIA

Chardonnay Santa Maria Valley Katherine's Vineyard 1998: Round, with butter, anise and crème brûlée flavors that have good richness. Drink now.–J.L. • $18 • (6/15/2000) • **85**
Chardonnay Santa Maria Valley Katherine's Vineyard 1997: A tight band of ripe pear, citrus and pineapple leads to a spicy, cedary oak aftertaste. The fruit doesn't quite fill in all the gaps, but it's still pretty tasty. Drink now.–J.L. • $19 • (7/31/1999) • **87**
Chardonnay Santa Maria Valley Katherine's Vineyard 1996 • $18 • (4/30/1998) • **90**
Chardonnay Santa Maria Valley Reserve 1997: Clean and ripe, with a peachy edge to the citrus and nectarine, turning cedary. Drink now.–J.L. • $36 • (6/15/2000) • **86**
Chardonnay Santa Maria Valley Reserve 1996: Lots of ripe, juicy tropical fruit, with guava, nectarine, peach and pineapple flavors in a tightly framed, complex style. Long, clean, citrusy aftertaste. Drink now through 2003.–J.L. • $36 • (7/31/1999) • **90**
Pinot Noir Santa Maria Valley Julia's Vineyard 1997: Supple, showing tea, cherry and wild berry flavors with toasty oak nuances that linger on the lightly tannic finish. Drink now through 2003 .–J.L. • $24 • (9/15/1999) • **85**
Pinot Noir Santa Maria Valley Julia's Vineyard 1996 • $26 • (1/31/1998) • **87**
Pinot Noir Santa Maria Valley Julia's Vineyard 1995 • $26 • (1/01/1997) • **87**
Pinot Noir Santa Maria Valley Julia's Vineyard 1994 • $22 • (2/29/1996) • **89**
Pinot Noir Santa Maria Valley Julia's Vineyard 1993 • $18 • (2/28/1995) • **86**
Pinot Noir Santa Maria Valley Julia's Vineyard 1992 • $16 • (2/28/1994) • **87**
Pinot Noir Santa Maria Valley Julia's Vineyard 1991 • $16 • (2/28/1993) • **83**
Pinot Noir Santa Maria Valley Julia's Vineyard 1989 • $15 • (9/30/1992) • **80**
Pinot Noir Santa Maria Valley Julia's Vineyard 1988 • $16 • (12/15/1990) • **88**
Pinot Noir Santa Maria Valley Reserve 1996: Ripe, rich and concentrated, with a firm core of earthy cherry, cola, spice, anise and tea notes, holding a tight focus, turning supple on the finish. Drink now through 2004.–J.L. • $42 • (9/15/1999) • **88**
Pinot Noir Santa Maria Valley Reserve 1994 • $42 • (12/31/1996) • **88**
Pinot Noir Santa Maria Valley Reserve 1993 • $35 • (12/31/1995) • **85**
Pinot Noir Santa Maria Valley Reserve 1992 • $30 • (3/31/1995) • **86**
Sangiovese Santa Maria Valley Tepusquet Vineyard 1994 • $25 • (10/15/1996) • **88**
Sangiovese Santa Maria Valley Tepusquet Vineyard 1993 • $18 • (8/31/1995) • **86**
Syrah Santa Maria Valley Tepusquet Vineyard 1996: Smooth and racy, with herb-tinged cherry and berry flavors that turn elegant and supple. Drink now through 2002.–J.L. • $18 • (12/31/1998) • **87**
Syrah Santa Maria Valley Tepusquet Vineyard 1992 • $30 • (5/15/1995) • **88**
Viognier Late Harvest Santa Maria Valley 1997: Elegant, delicate and sweet, with bright peach, nectarine, citrus and spice, bracing acidity and a hint of orange peel. Drink now through 2004.–J.L. • $18/375 ml. • (12/31/1998) • **90**
Viognier Santa Maria Valley Tepusquet Vineyard 1997: Tart, with peach and nectarine flavors that are bright and lively. Finishes with a creamy flavor. Drink now through 2002.–J.L. • $18 • (12/31/1998) • **88**

CAMELOT | CALIFORNIA

Cabernet Sauvignon Central Coast 1992 • $11 • (11/15/1994) • **83**
Cabernet Sauvignon North Coast 1993 • $12 • (12/15/1995) • **87**
Chardonnay California 1997: Refreshing, with crisp green apple, pear and citrus flavors. Drink now.–J.L. • $13 • (6/15/1999) • **85**
Merlot California 1996: Light-bodied, with herbal black cherry flavors. Finishes firm and dry. Drink now.–J.L. • $13 • (8/31/1999) • **81**
Pinot Noir California 1997: Firm, featuring a range of herb, berry, toasty oak and spice flavors. Drink now through 2001 .–J.L. • $11 • (9/15/1999) • **84**
Pinot Noir California 1996: Earthy and leathery, showing cola, tea and dried berry flavors on a soft-textured background. Drink now.–J.L. • $11 • (9/15/1999) • **83**
Pinot Noir Central Coast 1994 • $12 • (2/29/1996) • **84**
Pinot Noir Central Coast 1993 • $12 • (3/31/1995) • **86**

CANARD | CALIFORNIA

Zinfandel Napa Valley 1997: Pleasant, with cassis, cinnamon and chocolate flavors that linger nicely on the softly tannic finish. Drink now through 2004.–J.L. • $22 • (6/15/2000) • **85**
Zinfandel Napa Valley 1990 • $12 • (4/30/1996) • **85**

CANEPA | CALIFORNIA

Chardonnay Alexander Valley Gauer Vineyard Adobe III 1998: A bit earthy, with round butter notes and apple flavors underscored by toasty oak. Drink now.–J.L. • $28 • (6/15/2000) • **84**
Chardonnay Alexander Valley Gauer Vineyard Adobe III 1997: Fairly rich in texture, offering pretty apple and melon notes framed in toasty oak. The

finish is moderate, couched in firm acidity. Well integrated and attractive. Drink now through 2002. • $28 • (7/31/1999) • **87**

Chardonnay Alexander Valley Gauer Vineyard Adobe III 1996 • $26 • (5/15/1998) • **88**

CANOE RIDGE | WASHINGTON

Cabernet Sauvignon Columbia Valley 1996: Ripe, rich and generous. A smooth, polished mouthful of blackberry, currant, herb and anise flavors that linger on the generous finish. Drink through 2006–H.S. • $25 • (6/15/1999) • **89**

Cabernet Sauvignon Columbia Valley 1995: Firm in texture up front, with smoothly balanced black cherry, nutmeg and pepper flavors gliding gently through the silky finish. Drink now through 2001.–H.S. • $22 • (10/15/1998) • **88**

Cabernet Sauvignon Columbia Valley 1994 • $20 • (9/15/1997) • **88**

Chardonnay Columbia Valley 1997: A lively wine, bright and silky, with pretty pear and vanilla flavors, hinting at sage on the balanced finish.–H.S. • $13 • (10/15/1998) • **87**

Chardonnay Columbia Valley 1996 • $12 • (9/15/1997) • **86**

Chardonnay Columbia Valley Reserve 1996: Ripe, round and complex, this smooth-textured wine has pretty citrus, pear and earthy flavors mingling on the elegant finish. Drink now through 2001.–H.S. • $20 • (10/15/1998) • **88**

Columbia Valley Red 1995 • $14 • (9/15/1997) • **86**

Merlot Columbia Valley 1997: Smooth and polished, with pretty black currant, black cherry and spice flavors that linger enticingly on the finish. Drink now through 2002.–H.S. • $21 • (8/31/1999) • **88**

Merlot Columbia Valley 1996: A smooth and spicy, a gentle swallow of cinnamon-scented plum and currant flavor, finishing soft, describes this Washington Merlot, impressive all-around for its quality, value and findability. And, it's drinkable now through 2001.–H.S. • $19 • (10/15/1998) SS • **88**

Merlot Columbia Valley 1995 • $18 • (9/15/1997) • **86**

Merlot Columbia Valley 1994 • $18 • (9/15/1996) • **84**

Merlot Columbia Valley 1993 • $14 • (9/30/1995) • **88**

Red Columbia Valley 1996: Ripe and smooth, this lovely mouthful of pretty currant and blackberry flavors is drinkable now, but finishes with enough intensity and roundness to warrant brief cellaring. A blend: 75 percent Cabernet Sauvignon, 25 percent Merlot. Drink now.–H.S. • $14 • (10/15/1998) • **88**

Red Table Wine Columbia Valley 1992 • $12 • (3/31/1995) • **86**

CANYON RIDGE | CALIFORNIA

Cabernet Sauvignon Central Coast 1995: Beefy, earthy flavors mingle with plum and vegetal notes. Finishes moderately. • $10 • (12/15/1998) • **75**

CANYON ROAD | CALIFORNIA

Cabernet Sauvignon California 1997: Straightforward, with lively, ripe grape flavors that carry through on the finish. Drink now. • $8 • (12/31/1998) • **83**

Cabernet Sauvignon California 1996: Starts off with a rubbery, charcoal-like flavor that gradually shifts to black cherry and herbs, bringing back into the ballpark. With moderate body, it's a fair wine. But this label—owned by Geyser Peak—usually does better. • $8 • (11/15/1998) • **75**

Cabernet Sauvignon California 1995 • $8 • (5/15/1997) • **86**

Cabernet Sauvignon California 1994 • $7 • (11/30/1996) • **79**

Cabernet Sauvignon California 1993 • $6 • (11/15/1995) • **85**

Cabernet Sauvignon California 1992 • $7 • (11/15/1994) • **83**

Cabernet Sauvignon California 1991 • $7 • (6/15/1993) • **81**

Cabernet Sauvignon Sonoma County Reserve 1995 • $18 • (9/30/1997) • **87**

Cabernet Sauvignon Sonoma County Reserve 1994 • $18 • (9/30/1997) • **84**

Chardonnay California 1998: A crisp, grassy style, with bright citrus, peach and herb flavors on a light frame. Refreshing and flavorful, though it finishes a bit short. Drink now. • $8 • (7/31/1999) • **84**

Chardonnay California 1997 • $8 • (6/30/1998) • **85**

Chardonnay California 1996 • $8 • (7/31/1997) • **78**

Merlot California 1997: Simple, with light cola, cherry and herb flavors. Finishes a bit short. Drink now. • $9 • (2/28/1999) • **80**

Key: SS—Spectator Selection. CS—Cellar Selection. HR—Highly Recommended. $NA—Price not available. (BT)—Barrel tasting. Ⓐ—Auction Price. For a key to the tasters' initials, see "How to Use These Listings."
Dates in parentheses represent the issues in which the ratings were published.

Merlot California 1996: Simple, with a focus on charred wood, green bean and plum flavors. Likeable for its soft, open texture. Drink now.–J.L. • $9 • (9/30/1998) • **79**

Merlot California 1994 • $7 • (6/15/1996) • **80**

Merlot California 1993 • $8 • (12/15/1995) • **84**

Sauvignon Blanc California 1999: Here's a nicely crisp Sauvignon Blanc at an easy-to-swallow price, showing flinty notes wrapped around herbal flavors with a refreshing citrus edge. Drink now.–J.L. • $8 • (5/15/2000) • **85**

Sauvignon Blanc California 1998: A blend of bright, lemony notes and subtle peach flavors, this has pucker power. Lean on the palate, with a squeaky-clean finish. Drink now. • $7 • (6/15/1999) • **84**

Sauvignon Blanc California 1997 • $7 • (5/15/1998) • **87**

Sauvignon Blanc California 1996 • $7 • (4/30/1997) • **85**

CAP ROCK | TEXAS

Cabernet Sauvignon Texas 1995 • $8 • (5/15/1998) • **84**

Cabernet Sauvignon Texas High Plains Reserve 1995 • $13 • (5/15/1998) • **83**

Diamond Royale Texas White 1996 • $7 • (2/28/1998) • **75**

Garnet Royale Texas 1996 • $7 • (3/31/1998) • **78**

Topaz Royale Texas White 1996 • $7 • (2/28/1998) • **70**

CAPIAUX | CALIFORNIA

Pinot Noir Sonoma Coast Hirsch Vineyard 1995 • $30 • (2/28/1998) • **83**

Pinot Noir Sonoma County Demonstene Vineyard 1995 • $25 • (2/28/1998) • **84**

Sauvignon Blanc Dry Creek Valley 1997: Framed by a bit too much toasty oak, nonetheless showing plenty of flavor, with layers of grapefruit, melon, herbs and spice. The ensemble is refreshing. Drink now. • $16 • (9/15/1998) • **86**

CARDINALE | CALIFORNIA

Meritage California 1992 • $60 • (11/15/1996) • **89**

Red Napa Valley-Sonoma Mountain 1998: Weaves together a complex band of ripe currant, plum and anise, with cedar, toasty oak and spice. Impressive.–J.L. • $NA • (8/31/1999) (BT) • **90-94**

Red Napa-Sonoma Counties 1996: Wonderful harmony and finesse, with layers of ripe, rich currant, black cherry, toasty oak, spice, coffee and cedar notes. Turns supple, elegant and spicy on the finish, where the flavors linger. 89 percent Cabernet Sauvignon, 11 percent Merlot. Best from 2001 through 2009.–J.L. • $100 • (11/15/1999) • **93**

Red Napa-Alexander Valleys 1995: Massages the intense tannins with supple currant and plum-laced flavors, shows off cedar, spice and mineral, too. Holds its focus through the long and complex finish. A blend of Cabernet Sauvignon and Merlot. Best from 2000 through 2008.–J.L. • $70 • (7/31/1998) • **92**

Red Napa-Dry Creek-Knights-Alexander Valleys 1993 • $60 • (1/31/1998) • **86**

CARMEL ROAD | CALIFORNIA

Chardonnay Monterey 1997: Packs in lots of complex flavors, with ripe fig, pear, melon, hazelnut and toasty oak notes, all woven together in a tightly knit frame. Drink now through 2005.–J.L. • $33 • (1/31/2000) • **93**

CARMENET | CALIFORNIA

Cabernet Franc Sonoma Valley Moon Mountain Vineyard 1992 • $20 • (4/30/1996) • **82**

Cabernet Sauvignon North Coast Dynamite 1997: Shows a range of black cherry, herb and earthy flavors. Soft and approachable on the focused finish. Drink now through 2003 .–J.L. • $20 • (9/15/1999) • **86**

Cabernet Sauvignon Sonoma County Moon Mountain Dynamite Cabernet 1992 • $15 • (9/15/1995) • **87**

Cabernet Sauvignon Sonoma Valley Dynamite Cabernet 1991 • $15 • (11/15/1993) • **85**

Chardonnay Sonoma Valley Carneros Sangiacomo Vineyard 1997: Bright, with juicy pippin apple, pear and citrus notes that are lean and focused. Crisp aftertaste. Drink now through 2001.–J.L. • $18 • (7/31/1999) • **88**

Chardonnay Sonoma Valley Carneros Sangiacomo Vineyard 1996 • $17 • (5/31/1998) • **89**

Meritage Sonoma Valley Moon Mountain Reserve 1996: Weaves together a complex array of coffee, currant, anise, sage and dried berry, firming up on the finish, where the flavors run deep and polished. Cabernet Sauvignon, Cabernet Franc and Petit Verdot. Best from 2001 through 2009.–J.L. • $39 • (11/15/1999) • **92**

Meritage Sonoma Valley Moon Mountain Estate Reserve 1995: Hits most of the right notes, with concentrated blackberry, currant, cedar, mineral and spice, finishing with firm, chewy tannins. Best from 2001 through 2007.–J.L. • $40 • (11/15/1998) • **90**
Meritage Moon Mountain Estate Vineyard Reserve Sonoma Valley 1994 • $40 • (11/15/1997) • **90**
Meritage Moon Mountain Estate Vineyard Sonoma Valley 1993 • $27 • (11/15/1997) • **87**
Meritage Moon Mountain Estate Vineyard Sonoma Valley 1992 • $25 • (11/30/1996) • **89**
Meritage Moon Mountain Estate Vineyard Sonoma Valley 1991 • $25 • (11/15/1996) • **88**
Meritage Moon Mountain Estate Vineyard Sonoma Valley 1990 • $25 • (11/15/1993) • **85**
Meritage Moon Mountain Estate Vineyard Sonoma Valley 1989 • $18 • (11/15/1992) • **86**
Meritage Moon Mountain Estate Vineyard Vin de Garde Sonoma Valley 1989 • $35 • (11/15/1993) • **83**
Merlot North Coast Dynamite 1997: Firm and structured, with a tight, balanced core of berry flavors. Needs time to soften. Best from 2000 through 2004.–J.L. • $20 • (10/15/1999) • **85**
Merlot Sonoma County Moon Mountain Dynamite 1995: Full-bodied, with bright blueberry notes framed in toasty oak. Finishes long, with hints of creamy vanilla and spice. Drink now through 2003. • $17 • (9/30/1998) • **87**
Merlot Sonoma Valley Carneros Sangiacomo Vineyard 1996: Ripe and complex, with appealing cherry, currant, anise, cedar and spice. Turns supple and polished. Drink now through 2005.–J.L. • $30 • (10/15/1999) • **87**
Merlot Washington Carmen B 1990 • $10 • (11/30/1992) • **86**
Red Sonoma Valley 1988 • $21 • (11/15/1991) • **87**
Red Sonoma Valley 1987 • $20 • (11/15/1990) • **89**
Red Sonoma Valley 1986 • $23 • (12/15/1996) • **74**
Red Sonoma Valley 1985 • $19 • (12/31/1988) • **91**
Red Sonoma Valley 1984 • $16 • (5/31/1987) • **93**
Red Sonoma Valley 1983 • $18 • (9/30/1986) • **84**
Red Sonoma Valley 1982 • $16 • (10/16/1985) • **93**
Sauvignon Blanc-Sémillon Edna Valley Paragon Vineyard Reserve 1997: A richly textured style, redolent of butterscotch, fig and green apple. It stops a bit short on the finish, but is clean and flinty at the end. Drink now. • $16 • (5/31/1999) • **86**
Sauvignon Blanc-Sémillon Edna Valley Reserve 1998: Sulphur intrudes upon the butter aromas and stewed apple flavors. Tasted twice, with consistent notes.–J.L. • $18 • (5/15/2000) • **76**
Zinfandel Contra Costa County Evangelho Vineyard Delta Zin Old Vines 1996 • $17 • (6/15/1998) • **82**

CARMODY MCKNIGHT | CALIFORNIA

Cabernet Sauvignon-Cabernet Franc-Merlot Paso Robles Cadenza 1996: Smooth and polished, with a range of plum and herb flavors turning crisp and firm. Drink now through 2004.–J.L. • $23 • (10/15/1999) • **83**
Chardonnay Paso Robles 1997: Features light lemon flavors couched in a fairly viscous texture. Hints of toast add interest, though it remains fairly simple. Finishes moderately. Drink now. • $15 • (5/31/1999) • **81**
Chardonnay Paso Robles 1996: Very pretty for its spice and mineral notes and tangerine and grapefruit rind flavors. Clean and refreshing. Drink now through 2000. • $15 • (7/31/1998) • **84**
Chardonnay Paso Robles Reserve 1997: Offers rich, ripe, round mouthfeel, with subtly complex toast, vanilla, citrus, pear and mineral flavors. Drink now through 2002.–J.L. • $17 • (6/30/1999) • **87**

CARNEROS CREEK | CALIFORNIA

Chardonnay Carneros Palombo Vineyard 1998: Smooth, ripe and creamy, an elegant and polished wine with pretty pear, apple and citrus notes. Drink now through 2003.–J.L. • $18 • (6/30/2000) • **87**
Chardonnay Carneros Palombo Vineyard 1997: Notes of tobacco, herb and sarsaparilla add complexity to the citrus and apple flavors. Smooth and rich on the finish, with a complex aftertaste. Drink now.–J.L. • $18 • (7/31/1999) • **89**
Chardonnay Carneros 1996 • $16 • (5/15/1998) • **87**
Merlot Napa Valley 1985 • $13 • (2/15/1988) • **84**
Merlot Napa Valley 1984 • $11 • (8/31/1987) • **87**
Merlot Napa Valley Truchard Vineyard 1983 • $10 • (10/01/1985) • **84**
Pinot Noir Carneros 1997: Focused and firm, with tart cherry and light oak flavors, finishing tannic with hints of coffee and herb. Drink now through 2001.–J.L. • $19 • (9/15/1999) • **85**
Pinot Noir Carneros 1996: Marked by toasty oak, the modest range of light cherry and berry struggles to the fore. On the finish, it manages to strike a nice balance between Pinot Noir fruit and oak. Drink now through 2001.–J.L. • $18 • (8/31/1998) • **85**
Pinot Noir Carneros 1995 • $19 • (12/31/1996) • **85**
Pinot Noir Carneros 1994 • $16 • (2/29/1996) • **87**
Pinot Noir Carneros 1993 • $13 • (9/15/1995) • **88**
Pinot Noir Carneros 1992 • $15 • (3/31/1995) • **86**
Pinot Noir Carneros 1991 • $15 • (1/31/1994) • **88**
Pinot Noir Carneros 1990 • $15 • (3/31/1997) • **89**
Pinot Noir Carneros 1989 • $15 • (3/31/1992) • **85**
Pinot Noir Carneros 1988 • $16 • (10/31/1990) • **83**
Pinot Noir Carneros 1987 • $15 • (2/15/1990) • **85**
Pinot Noir Carneros 1986 • $15 • (3/31/1997) • **82**
Pinot Noir Carneros 1985 • $13 • (4/15/1988) • **88**
Pinot Noir Carneros 1984 • $15 • (3/15/1987) • **92**
Pinot Noir Carneros 1983 • $13 • (8/31/1986) • **92**
Pinot Noir Carneros 25th Anniversary Signature Reserve 1995 • $40 • (2/28/1998) • **87**
Pinot Noir Carneros Côte de Carneros 1997: Firm, with a core of toasty oak surrounded by black cherry, spice and herb notes. Finishes firm and minty. Drink now through 2002 .–J.L. • $15 • (9/15/1999) • **84**
Pinot Noir Carneros Côte de Carneros 1996: Earthy, with dried flower and dried fruit flavors that quickly lose their modest appeal. Best soon.–J.L. • $15 • (8/31/1998) • **79**
Pinot Noir Carneros Fleur de Carneros 1994 • $10 • (11/30/1995) • **85**
Pinot Noir Carneros Fleur de Carneros 1993 • $10 • (1/31/1995) • **82**
Pinot Noir Carneros Fleur de Carneros 1992 • $10 • (2/28/1994) • **79**
Pinot Noir Carneros Fleur de Carneros 1991 • $9 • (2/28/1994) • **83**
Pinot Noir Carneros Fleur de Carneros 1990 • $9 • (2/28/1993) • **80**
Pinot Noir Carneros Fleur de Carneros 1989 • $9 • (4/30/1991) • **82**
Pinot Noir Carneros Fleur de Carneros 1988 • $10 • (2/15/1990) • **85**
Pinot Noir Carneros Las Lomas 1994 • $18 • (2/29/1996) • **86**
Pinot Noir Carneros Signature Reserve 1994 • $35 • (1/31/1997) • **91**
Pinot Noir Carneros Signature Reserve 1993 • $28 • (11/15/1995) • **88**
Pinot Noir Carneros Signature Reserve 1991 • $28 • (2/28/1993) • **81**
Pinot Noir Carneros Signature Reserve 1989 • $28 • (9/30/1992) • **80**
Pinot Noir Carneros Signature Reserve 1988 • $28 • (10/31/1990) • **89**
Pinot Noir Carneros Signature Reserve First Release 1987 • $28 • (10/31/1990) • **87**

CARPE DIEM | CALIFORNIA

Pinot Noir San Luis Obispo County 1994 • $20 • (9/15/1996) • **82**

CARTLIDGE & BROWNE | CALIFORNIA

Chardonnay California 1997: Soft in texture, with lemon and toast flavors. A pleasant quaff. Drink now. • $10 • (12/31/1998) • **80**
Chardonnay California 1996: A trim, bright-styled wine, with a tasty touch of pear and apple backed by a judicious note of oak. • $10 • (7/31/1998) • **84**
Pinot Noir California 1997: Offers modest flavors of tea and plum, with a spicy, earthy background.–J.L. • $13 • (12/31/1998) • **79**
Zinfandel California 1997: Straightforward, slightly cooked plum and pepper turn sharp-edged, with green notes and a touch of heat. Drink now.–J.L. • $10 • (12/31/1998) • **81**

CASCADE CREST | WASHINGTON

Cabernet-Merlot Washington 1995: Smooth and generous, with a streak of vegetal character running through the spice and mineral flavors.–H.S. • $19 • (12/31/1999) • **78**

CASCADE RIDGE | WASHINGTON

Cabernet Sauvignon Columbia Valley 1996: Dense, dark and chewy, with a crisp zing of acidity running through the smoky black cherry and chocolate flavors. Needs time to soften. Best after 2000.–H.S. • $15 • (11/30/1999) • **87**
Chardonnay Columbia Valley 1997: Feels a little stale, but it's distinctive for a dusky spice character that lingers on the finish. Firm in texture, with citrusy melon flavors. Tasted twice, with consistent notes. Drink now.–H.S. • $16 • (5/31/1999) • **81**
Merlot Columbia Valley 1996: Tight in texture, with an earthy streak adding interest and complexity to the ripe blackberry and spice flavors. Needs to soften, but the lean, zingy finish shows promise. Best after 2000.–H.S. • $19 • (11/30/1999) • **88**

CASE | California

Pinot Noir Monterey 1995: Marked by herb, tea and sage notes, with only a glimmer of wild berry and plum flavor. Turns dry and earthy on the finish, where the tannins weigh in. 1999. Drink now.–J.L. • $26 • (10/31/1998) • **85**

Pinot Noir Monterey 1994 • $25 • (2/28/1997) • **85**

CASTALIA | California

Pinot Noir Russian River Valley Rochioli Vineyard 1997: Ripe, with refreshing plum, cola, black cherry and spice and firm tannins. It has structure, depth and concentration, but needs a little time. Drink through 2006–J.L. • $28 • (9/15/1999) • **88**

Pinot Noir Russian River Valley Rochioli Vineyard 1996: Lacks focus; the spicy, earthy, oaky flavors override the moderately ripe plum and cherry ones. Finishes with dry tannins. Drink now.–J.L. • $23 • (8/31/1998) • **82**

Pinot Noir Russian River Valley Rochioli Vineyard 1995 • $23 • (5/31/1997) • **88**

Pinot Noir Russian River Valley Rochioli Vineyard 1994 • $20 • (11/15/1996) • **92**

Pinot Noir Russian River Valley Rochioli Vineyard 1993 • $18 • (3/31/1996) • **83**

CASTLE CREEK | California

Chardonnay California 1996 • $15 • (5/31/1998) • **87**

CASTLE ROCK | California

Cabernet Sauvignon Napa Valley 1993 • $15 • (9/30/1997) • **81**

Chardonnay Central Coast 1997: Light-bodied, with earthy mineral, citrus, pear and toast flavors. Finishes firm and lean. Drink now.–J.L. • $10 • (7/31/1999) • **84**

Chardonnay Central Coast Barrel Fermented 1998: For fans of overripe melon and oak flavors, this one comes together on a mushy frame. Drink now.–J.L. • $12 • (2/29/2000) • **81**

Chardonnay Central Coast Barrel Fermented 1997: Silky in texture, with a spicy floral edge to the cream, vanilla and fig flavors. Slightly rough on the finish. Drink now.–J.L. • $12 • (7/31/1999) • **85**

Chardonnay Napa Valley 1997: Smooth, featuring lemon and grapefruit flavors and finishing with soft apple and spice notes. Drink now.–H.S. • $14 • (7/31/1999) • **84**

Merlot Monterey County 1997: Soft, with an herbal edge to the plum character. Flavors persist on the slightly firm finish. Drink now. • $12 • (2/28/1999) • **82**

Merlot Monterey County Barrel Aged 1997: Young and grapey, this is supple, polished and ready to drink. Drink now through 2002.–H.S. • $12 • (10/15/1999) • **83**

Merlot Napa Valley 1993 • $13 • (8/31/1996) • **82**

Pinot Noir Russian River Valley 1996: Bright, showing focused berry and earthy mushroom flavors with background notes of caramel and toasted oak. Much better than previously reviewed. Drink now through 2002. • $15 • (2/28/1999) • **84**

Syrah California Cuvée 1998: Shows dill pickle flavors and lean melony notes.–J.L. • $10 • (5/15/2000) • **80**

Zinfandel Paso Robles 1998: Exotic spice and orange peel notes miss the mark.–J.L. • $9 • (5/31/2000) • **79**

CASTLE VINEYARDS | California

Merlot Carneros Sangiacomo El Novillero 1996: Firm and lean, with a slightly tart edge to the cherry, cassis and blackberry flavors. Finishes moderately; might flesh out somewhat in time. Best from 2001 through 2004. • $25 • (10/15/1999) • **84**

Merlot Sonoma Valley 1996: Blackberry, herb, bell pepper and tealike notes blend nicely. The texture is firm and the finish is moderate. Drink now through 2002. • $19 • (10/15/1998) • **85**

Merlot Sonoma Valley 1995: Firm, with bright cherry and underlying earthy, herbal flavors. Drink now.–J.L. • $18 • (10/15/1998) • **82**

Merlot Sonoma Valley 1993 • $17 • (6/30/1996) • **82**

Pinot Noir Carneros 1994 • $16 • (1/31/1996) • **84**

Key: SS—Spectator Selection. CS—Cellar Selection. HR—Highly Recommended. $NA—Price not available. (BT)—Barrel tasting. (A)—Auction Price. For a key to the tasters' initials, see "How to Use These Listings." **Dates in parentheses represent the issues in which the ratings were published.**

Pinot Noir Los Carneros Durell Vineyard 1997: Medium in weight, with cola and dill flavors, finishing with gritty tannins. Drink now.–J.L. • $30 • (4/30/2000) • **82**

Zinfandel Sonoma County 1996 • $16 • (6/15/1998) • **79**

Zinfandel Sonoma Valley 1993 • $15 • (10/15/1995) • **83**

CASTLEVIEW | California

Cabernet Sauvignon Napa Valley Private Reserve 1993 • $9 • (12/15/1995) • **84**

Merlot Napa Valley Private Reserve 1993 • $12 • (8/31/1996) • **74**

CASTORO | California

Cabernet Sauvignon Paso Robles 1995: Simple and medium-weight, with decent herb, cherry and toasted oak flavors, finishing with cedary tannins. Drink now.–J.L. • $12 • (11/15/1998) • **82**

Cabernet Sauvignon Paso Robles 1989 • $10 • (7/31/1992) • **84**

Cabernet Sauvignon Paso Robles Reserve 1995: Simple, woody flavors dominate the cherry and herb notes. Finishes dry and sour. Drink now.–H.S. • $15 • (11/15/1998) • **77**

Cabernet Sauvignon Paso Robles Reserve 1991 • $12 • (11/15/1994) • **82**

Cabernet Sauvignon Paso Robles Reserve 1990 • $12 • (11/15/1993) • **82**

Cabernet Sauvignon Paso Robles The Wine 1991 • $10 • (11/15/1994) • **83**

Chardonnay Paso Robles 1996: Well-structured, with a bright citrus and lemon-rind core, hints of butter and toast. Has a trace of bitterness on the finish. • $12 • (7/31/1998) • **81**

Dieci Anni Paso Robles 1991 • $16 • (11/15/1993) • **79**

Pinot Noir Santa Barbara County 1991 • $11 • (2/28/1994) • **77**

Pinot Noir Santa Barbara County 1990 • $11 • (2/28/1993) • **73**

Pinot Noir Santa Barbara County Reserve 1996: Ripe berry flavors are wound around an herbal core. Loses some focus on the slightly drying finish. Drink now.–J.L. • $16 • (8/31/1998) • **80**

Zinfandel Paso Robles 1996 • $13 • (6/15/1998) • **82**

Zinfandel Paso Robles 1995 • $13 • (6/15/1998) • **80**

Zinfandel Paso Robles 1992 • $10 • (10/15/1995) • **84**

Zinfandel Paso Robles 1990 • $8 • (10/15/1992) • **82**

Zinfandel Paso Robles The Wine 1991 • $9 • (10/15/1994) • **84**

CATERINA | Washington

Cabernet della Rosa Columbia Valley 1997: Light and on the dry side, with simple watermelon and citrus flavors. Drink now.–H.S. • $9 • (9/30/1998) • **83**

Cabernet Sauvignon Columbia Valley 1996: A gamy streak runs through the ripe black cherry flavors, meaning this won't please everyone, but it holds together on the finish, coming off more like olives. Drink through 2002–H.S. • $17 • (8/31/1998) • **86**

Cabernet Sauvignon Columbia Valley 1995 • $18 • (9/15/1997) • **87**

Cabernet Sauvignon Columbia Valley 1994 • $13 • (9/15/1996) • **86**

Cabernet Sauvignon Columbia Valley 1993 • $13 • (9/30/1995) • **89**

Cabernet Sauvignon Columbia Valley 1992 • $13 • (4/15/1995) • **85**

Cabernet Sauvignon Washington Wahluke Slope Vineyard Reserve 1995 • $30 • (10/15/1997) • **85**

Chardonnay Columbia Valley 1998: The ripe, exuberant style still feels a bit awkward, but the pear, lemon, floral and toast flavors are nicely balanced to come together with short-term cellaring. Drink through 2003–H.S. • $14 • (11/15/1999) • **88**

Chardonnay Columbia Valley 1997: Soft and charming, centered on fruit flavors. A lovely mouthful of apricot-scented pear and apple character.–H.S. • $14 • (9/15/1998) • **87**

Chardonnay Columbia Valley Reserve 1996 • $18 • (10/15/1997) • **89**

Johannisberg Riesling Columbia Valley Late Harvest 1994 • $10/375 ml. • (9/30/1995) • **76**

Merlot Columbia Valley 1996: Has a distinctly herbal edge to the pretty blueberry and plum flavors. Feels rich in texture, but needs time. Best from 2001 through 2005.–H.S. • $17 • (8/31/1998) • **88**

Merlot Columbia Valley 1995 • $18 • (9/15/1997) • **89**

Merlot Columbia Valley 1994 • $16 • (9/15/1996) • **87**

Merlot Columbia Valley 1993 • $13 • (9/30/1995) • **78**

Merlot Columbia Valley 1992 • $13 • (2/28/1995) • **86**

Merlot Columbia Valley 1991 • $13 • (9/30/1994) • **81**

Riesling Columbia Valley Late Harvest 1997: Sweet and smooth, with pretty tropical fruit and apricot flavors gliding gently through the finish. Drink now.–H.S. • $10/375 ml. • (9/15/1998) • **88**

Sauvignon Blanc Columbia Valley 1998: Bright, refreshing and fruity. A pretty wine with lime and apple flavors that persist enticingly on the sprightly finish. Drink now.–H.S. • $11 • (12/31/1999) • **87**

Sauvignon Blanc Columbia Valley 1997: Fresh and smooth, with nicely polished texture, apple and pineapple flavors. Finishes with a refreshing touch of citrus. Drink now.–H.S. • $11 • (9/15/1998) • **86**

Sauvignon Blanc Columbia Valley 1996 • $9 • (9/15/1997) • **87**

Wahluke Slope Reserve Red Columbia Valley 1994 • $25 • (9/15/1996) • **79**

CAYMUS | CALIFORNIA

Cabernet Sauvignon Napa Valley 1996: Attractive creamy, toasty oak upfront, with supple currant and black cherry folding in beneath. Though it remains complex on the finish, it comes up shy in depth and added dimensions compared with previous vintages. Grapes are from the sources normally used for the Special Selection, which was not made in '96. Drink now through 2007.–J.L. • $58 Ⓐ • (1/31/2000) • **90**

Cabernet Sauvignon Napa Valley 1995: A seductive style, with lots of spicy, vanilla-scented oak that leads to a rich, complex core of currant, black cherry, olive and plum. The tannins are smooth and polished; supple enough to drink now, yet substantial enough to cellar short-term. Drink through 2007–J.L. • $86 Ⓐ • (8/31/1998) • **92**

Cabernet Sauvignon Napa Valley 1994 • $87 Ⓐ • (5/31/1997) CS • **95**

Cabernet Sauvignon Napa Valley 1993 • $58 Ⓐ • (11/15/1996) SS • **91**

Cabernet Sauvignon Napa Valley 1992 • $55 Ⓐ • (9/30/1995) • **89**

Cabernet Sauvignon Napa Valley 1991 • $66 Ⓐ • (11/15/1994) SS • **93**

Cabernet Sauvignon Napa Valley 1990 • $65 Ⓐ • (12/15/1993) SS • **90**

Cabernet Sauvignon Napa Valley 1989 • $46 Ⓐ • (11/15/1992) • **88**

Cabernet Sauvignon Napa Valley 1988 • $20 • (1/31/1992) • **87**

Cabernet Sauvignon Napa Valley 1987 • $84 Ⓐ • (9/15/1990) • **93**

Cabernet Sauvignon Napa Valley 1986 • $91 Ⓐ • (3/15/1990) SS • **94**

Cabernet Sauvignon Napa Valley 1985 • $84 Ⓐ • (11/15/1988) • **90**

Cabernet Sauvignon Napa Valley 1984 • $86 Ⓐ • (12/31/1987) • **90**

Cabernet Sauvignon Napa Valley 1983 • $53 Ⓐ • (11/30/1986) CS • **94**

Cabernet Sauvignon Napa Valley 1982 • $60 Ⓐ • (4/01/1986) • **94**

Cabernet Sauvignon Napa Valley 1981 • $14 • (2/01/1986) • **93**

Cabernet Sauvignon Napa Valley 1980 • $56 Ⓐ • (2/01/1986) • **94**

Cabernet Sauvignon Napa Valley 1979 • $25 • (2/01/1986) • **90**

Cabernet Sauvignon Napa Valley 1978: Fading, but holding up better than the Special Selection. The plum and cherry flavors have a pleasant dried fruit, anise and earthy edge, and the tannins have all resolved, leaving an elegant, supple texture. (1978 California Cabernet retrospective tasting). Drink now.–J.L. • $67 Ⓐ • (11/15/1998) • **88**

Cabernet Sauvignon Napa Valley Cuvée 1986 • $48 Ⓐ • (8/31/1989) • **90**

Cabernet Sauvignon Napa Valley Cuvée 1985 • $12 • (7/15/1988) • **92**

Cabernet Sauvignon Napa Valley Cuvée 1984 • $12 • (8/31/1987) • **88**

Cabernet Sauvignon Napa Valley Special Selection 1995: Wow. This '95 Special Selection is a classic. Amazingly complex, it displays a wide range of flavors—including currant, wild berry, herb, sage, coffee and tobacco—gains in nuance, delicacy, elegance and finesse, and unveils pretty oak shadings on the finish. Drink now through 2009.–J.L. • $145 Ⓐ • (6/30/1999) CS • **97**

Cabernet Sauvignon Napa Valley Special Selection 1994 • $178 Ⓐ • (12/31/1997) CS • **95**

Cabernet Sauvignon Napa Valley Special Selection 1992 • $136 Ⓐ • (5/15/1996) CS • **92**

Cabernet Sauvignon Napa Valley Special Selection 1991 • $187 Ⓐ • (4/15/1995) CS • **99**

Cabernet Sauvignon Napa Valley Special Selection 1990 • $197 Ⓐ • (3/31/1994) CS • **98**

Cabernet Sauvignon Napa Valley Special Selection 1989 • $123 Ⓐ • (6/30/1993) CS • **93**

Cabernet Sauvignon Napa Valley Special Selection 1988: Pure Caymus, only on a slightly muted scale. The currant, plum, dried cherry, anise and spicy flavors are neatly layered, and the texture and tannins are smooth and polished. Shows fine balance and depth of flavor. (1988 California Cabernet retrospective tasting). Drink now through 2002.–J.L. • $99 Ⓐ • (11/15/1998) • **88**

Cabernet Sauvignon Napa Valley Special Selection 1987 • $168 Ⓐ • (12/15/1997) • **88**

Cabernet Sauvignon Napa Valley Special Selection 1986 • $185 Ⓐ • (12/15/1996) • **95**

Cabernet Sauvignon Napa Valley Special Selection 1985 • $283 Ⓐ • (4/30/1990) • **99**

Cabernet Sauvignon Napa Valley Special Selection 1984 • $168 Ⓐ • (7/15/1989) CS • **98**

Cabernet Sauvignon Napa Valley Special Selection 1983 • $97 Ⓐ • (5/31/1988) • **90**

Cabernet Sauvignon Napa Valley Special Selection 1982 • $134 Ⓐ • (11/30/1987) • **90**

Cabernet Sauvignon Napa Valley Special Selection 1981 • $109 Ⓐ • (11/30/1986) • **94**

Cabernet Sauvignon Napa Valley Special Selection 1980 • $122 Ⓐ • (3/16/1986) SS • **96**

Cabernet Sauvignon Napa Valley Special Selection 1979 • $201 Ⓐ • (6/01/1985) SS • **93**

Cabernet Sauvignon Napa Valley Special Selection 1978: Fading now after a long, glorious run. Nutty, with aldehydic notes, glimpses of plum, prune and cherry fade in and out, but the overall impression is that it's on its way out. (1978 California Cabernet retrospective tasting). Drink now.–J.L. • $30 • (11/15/1998) • **82**

Conundrum California 1998: Round and full, with creamy oak and lemon meringue notes and fresh fennel and pear flavors that lead to a long, rich finish. Sauvignon Blanc, Muscat, Chardonnay, Viognier and Sémillon. Drink now through 2003.–J.L. • $20 • (5/31/2000) • **88**

Conundrum California 1997: Smooth, ripe and creamy, this tasty blend of Chardonnay, Sauvignon Blanc, Sémillon, Viognier and Muscat delivers a harmonious medley of fruit flavors, with lingering notes of spicy pear, peach and nectarine, also fig, apricot and melon chiming in. Drink now.–J.L. • $20 • (12/31/1998) SS • **89**

Conundrum California 1996 • $20 • (12/15/1997) SS • **91**

Conundrum California 1994 • $17 • (10/15/1995) SS • **91**

Pinot Noir Napa Valley Special Selection 1990 • $18 • (2/28/1994) • **84**

Pinot Noir Napa Valley Special Selection 1989 • $18 • (9/30/1992) • **78**

Pinot Noir Napa Valley Special Selection 1988 • $18 • (11/15/1991) • **82**

Pinot Noir Napa Valley Special Selection 1987 • $14 • (12/15/1990) • **86**

Pinot Noir Napa Valley Special Selection 1986 • $15 • (12/31/1989) • **82**

Pinot Noir Napa Valley Special Selection 1985 • $15 • (12/31/1988) • **90**

Pinot Noir Napa Valley Special Selection 1984 • $13 • (2/15/1988) • **79**

Pinot Noir Napa Valley Special Selection 1982 • $13 • (8/31/1986) • **85**

Sauvignon Blanc Napa Valley 1998: On the oaky side, with a creamy texture and plenty of toast and coconut notes. Full-bodied, with hints of pear and herb flavors poking through. Drink now through 2003.–H.S. • $18 • (3/31/2000) • **86**

Sauvignon Blanc Napa Valley 1997: A ripe, oaky style, leaning toward butterscotch, fig and pear, with hints of lime on the finish. Richly textured and quite good, if lacking the focus and finesse of previous recent vintages. Drink now through 2002. • $14 • (2/28/1999) • **88**

Sauvignon Blanc Napa Valley 1996 • $14 • (1/31/1998) SS • **91**

Zinfandel Napa Valley 1992 • $13 • (9/30/1994) SS • **89**

Zinfandel Napa Valley 1991 • $11 • (9/30/1993) • **85**

Zinfandel Napa Valley 1990 • $10 • (10/15/1992) • **82**

Zinfandel Napa Valley 1989 • $10 • (11/15/1991) • **83**

Zinfandel Napa Valley 1988 • $9 • (10/15/1990) • **80**

Zinfandel Napa Valley 1987 • $14 • (10/31/1989) • **85**

Zinfandel Napa Valley 1986 • $15 • (12/15/1988) • **89**

Zinfandel Napa Valley 1985 • $15 • (12/31/1987) • **85**

Zinfandel Napa Valley 1984 • $15 • (5/15/1987) • **90**

Zinfandel Napa Valley 1983 • $16 • (12/31/1986) • **79**

Zinfandel Napa Valley 1982 • $16 • (5/16/1986) • **92**

Zinfandel Napa Valley 1981 • $16 • (12/01/1984) • **84**

Zinfandel California 1976 • $33 • (6/16/1985) • **79**

Zinfandel California Lot 31-J 1975 • $40 • (6/16/1985) • **77**

Zinfandel California 1974 • $29 • (6/16/1985) • **83**

CECCHETTI-SEBASTIANI | CALIFORNIA

Cabernet Franc Napa Valley 1996: Good mouthfeel, with herbal notes and cherry flavors that turn lean at the finish. Drink now through 2003.–J.L. • $28 • (5/15/2000) • **81**

Cabernet Sauvignon Alexander Valley 1989 • $10 • (11/15/1992) • **74**

Cabernet Sauvignon Alexander Valley 1988 • $11 • (8/31/1992) • **83**

Cabernet Sauvignon Napa Valley 1994: Bold, ripe and rustic, a touch cheesy, masking the currant, anise and dried cherry beneath. Best from 2002 through 2008.–J.L. • $50 • (4/30/2000) • **87**

Cabernet Sauvignon Napa Valley 1993 • $25 • (11/15/1996) • **89**

Cabernet Sauvignon Sonoma County 1983 • $13 • (9/30/1986) • **76**

Merlot Napa Valley 1996: Polished, with toasty oak, ripe plum and berry flavors that are supple and mildly tannic. Appealingly straightforward. Drink now through 2007 .–J.L. • $36 • (2/29/2000) • **87**

Merlot Napa Valley 1992 • $28 • (12/15/1996) • **87**

Merlot Sonoma County 1990 • $10 • (6/15/1993) • **78**

Merlot Sonoma County 1989 • $10 • (5/31/1992) • **83**

CEDAR BROOK | CALIFORNIA

Cabernet Sauvignon California 1994 • $9 • (9/15/1997) • **84**
Cabernet Sauvignon Napa Valley 1993 • $7 • (12/15/1995) • **84**
Cabernet Sauvignon Napa Valley 1992 • $8 • (11/15/1994) • **84**
Merlot California 1996: Tough tannins lend an astringency that mutes the core of cassis, blackberry and herb. The oak is toasty yet heavy. • $9 • (7/31/1998) • **80**
Merlot California 1995 • $9 • (7/31/1997) • **80**
Pinot Noir California 1995 • $9 • (7/31/1997) • **87**
Pinot Noir California 1993 • $7 • (11/15/1995) • **85**
Zinfandel California 1995 • $9 • (7/31/1997) • **79**

CEDAR MOUNTAIN | CALIFORNIA

Cabernet Sauvignon Livermore Valley Blanches Vineyard 1990 • $20 • (11/15/1993) • **83**
Merlot Livermore Valley 1995: Ripe but simple, with dill, eucalyptus and black cherry flavors. Finishes with ripe tannins and a sour note. Drink now.–J.L. • $22 • (10/15/1998) • **77**

CHADDSFORD | PENNSYLVANIA

Cabernet Franc Pennsylvania 1998: Browning in color with some tobacco leaf and bell pepper aromas and flavors that barely hang in on the wispy finish.–B.S. • $14 • (1/01/2000) • **76**
Cabernet Franc Pennsylvania 1996 • $NA • (3/31/1998) • **78**
Cabernet Franc Pennsylvania 1995 • $12 • (4/30/1997) • **77**
Cabernet Sauvignon Pennsylvania 1998: Smells like sour chocolate milk, then shows some herbaceous notes before finishing on a cloying, cherry cough syrup note.–B.S. • $17 • (1/01/2000) • **73**
Cabernet Sauvignon Pennsylvania 1996 • $13 • (5/15/1998) • **71**
Cabernet Sauvignon Pennsylvania Mica Ridge Vineyard 1998: Thin and a bit sharp, this light red offers tart cherry and herb flavors, with a smoky finish.–T.M. • $17 • (1/01/2000) • **79**
Chambourcin Pennsylvania 1998: This hybrid red variety shows clean, bright flavors of cherry and cranberry, with hints of smoke and toast. What it lacks in refinement it makes up in vivacity. Drink now through 2002.–T.M. • $16 • (5/31/2000) • **84**
Chambourcin Pennsylvania Proprietor's Reserve 1989 • $10 • (2/29/1992) • **80**
Chambourcin Pennsylvania Seven Valleys Vineyard 1995 • $16 • (8/31/1997) • **78**
Chambourcin Pennsylvania Seven Valleys Vineyard 1989 • $13 • (2/29/1992) • **81**
Chardonnay Pennsylvania 1997: A bit overdone, with pineapple flavors and a cloying sweetness.–K.M. • $13 • (10/15/1998) • **77**
Chardonnay Pennsylvania Barrel Select 1998: Notes of honey and smoke are rich and sweet in this ripe white, but tend to overwhelm the apple and melon flavors. Drink well chilled. Drink now.–T.M. • $19 • (5/31/2000) • **84**
Chardonnay Pennsylvania Philip Roth Vineyard 1997: This silky white offers soft flavors of cinnamon, vanilla and baked apple. It's a bit low in acidity for food, but has intriguing spicy notes on the finish. Drink now.–T.M. • $30 • (5/31/2000) • **83**
Dolcetto Pennsylvania 1997: Refreshing but lean, this is a light-bodied red wine with floral, grapey character, a green-apple texture and a tangy finish. • $15 • (10/31/1998) • **77**
Johannisberg Riesling Pennsylvania 1996 • $13 • (9/30/1997) • **75**
Merican Pennsylvania 1997: Balanced and harmonious, this red is supple on the palate but has enough tannin for grip, backing alluring flavors of toast, licorice, plum and berry. Cabernet Sauvignon, Cabernet Franc, Merlot and Carmine. Tasted twice, with consistent notes. Drink now through 2002.–T.M. • $33 • (5/31/2000) • **88**
Merican Pennsylvania 1995: Plum and coffee flavors are ripe but dominated by aggressive tannins in this muscular red. Try with hearty dishes. Drink now through 2003.–T.M. • $33 • (1/01/2000) • **85**
Pinot Grigio Pennsylvania 1998: This full-bodied white offers ripe melon and pear flavors, with a healthy dollop of vanilla oak and just enough acidity for balance. Drink now.–T.M. • $15 • (1/01/2000) • **84**
Pinot Noir Michigan Lake Erie Region 1988 • $28 • (2/28/1993) • **78**
Pinot Noir Pennsylvania 1998: This lively red marries ripe cherry and plum flavors with bright acidity and pleasing accents of spice and smoke. Drink now through 2002.–T.M. • $17 • (1/01/2000) • **84**
Pinot Noir Pennsylvania 1994 • $25 • (8/31/1997) • **73**
Pinot Noir Pennsylvania Lake Erie Region 1988 • $28 • (2/29/1992) • **82**
Proprietor's Reserve Pennsylvania White 1996 • $9 • (2/28/1998) • **79**

CHALK HILL | CALIFORNIA

Cabernet Sauvignon Chalk Hill 1996: Supple, it tilts toward the herb, olive and dill side of Cabernet, turning polished and complex on the finish. Drink now through 2006.–J.L. • $38 • (11/15/1999) • **88**
Cabernet Sauvignon Chalk Hill 1995: Pleasantly fruity if a bit dry, with moderate intensity and hints of plum and currant. Tannic on the finish. Drink now through 2002.–J.L. • $32 • (11/15/1998) • **85**
Cabernet Sauvignon Chalk Hill 1994 • $26 • (10/31/1997) • **89**
Cabernet Sauvignon Chalk Hill 1993 • $23 • (11/15/1996) • **88**
Cabernet Sauvignon Chalk Hill 1991 • $21 • (11/15/1994) • **85**
Cabernet Sauvignon Chalk Hill 1990 • $17 • (12/15/1993) • **86**
Cabernet Sauvignon Chalk Hill 1989 • $13 • (7/15/1992) • **75**
Cabernet Sauvignon Chalk Hill 1988 • $12 • (6/15/1991) • **87**
Cabernet Sauvignon Chalk Hill 1983 • $10 • (11/15/1986) • **78**
Chardonnay Chalk Hill 1997: An appetizing earthy note at the start makes way for a complex character, including hints of citrus, pear, hazelnut, vanilla and spice, that gains nuance and fans out on the finish. Drink now through 2002.–J.L. • $34 • (6/15/1999) HR • **92**
Chardonnay Chalk Hill 1996 • $28 • (6/15/1998) SS • **93**
Merlot Chalk Hill 1995: Starts out on the smoky, leathery side of Merlot, with hints of coffee, herb and cedar and traces of currant and berry Turns firm and tannic on the finish. Needs time to soften. Drink through 2005–J.L. • $36 • (11/30/1998) • **87**
Pinot Gris Chalk Hill Estate Vineyard Selection 1996: Smooth, ripe and peachy, with vanilla, nutmeg, anise and spicy nuances, finishing with richness and depth. Drink now through 2001.–J.L. • $22 • (4/30/1999) • **88**
Sauvignon Blanc Chalk Hill 1998: Earthy and a touch dull, with modest citrus and lemon flavors, turning pasty. Drink now.–J.L. • $29 • (5/15/2000) • **82**
Sauvignon Blanc Chalk Hill 1996: Fresh and lively, with bright grapefruit flavors and a firm, focused texture. The finish is long, with hints of mineral and herb. Distinctive and assertive. Drink now. • $19 • (6/15/1999) • **88**
Sémillon Chalk Hill Botrytized Estate Vineyard Selection 1994 • $40/375 ml. • (10/31/1997) HR • **97**

CHALONE | CALIFORNIA

Chardonnay Chalone 1998: Tight and flinty, with a beam of earthy citrus, mineral, pear and nectarine notes. Drink now through 2003.–J.L. • $31 • (6/30/2000) • **86**
Chardonnay Chalone 1997: A solid core of pear, apple and melon-laced flavors can stand a little more time in the bottle, as it is tight and restrained now. Drink through 2004.–J.L. • $31 • (7/31/1999) • **89**
Chardonnay Chalone 1996 • $27 • (5/31/1998) • **91**
Pinot Noir Chalone 1997: Tight, with creamy oak notes leading to a core of ripe cherry, plum and raspberry, finishing with an earthy, mushroomy flavor. Drink now through 2005.–J.L. • $31 • (9/15/1999) • **87**
Pinot Noir Chalone 1996: Smooth and supple, with a range of tea, spicy cherry, mushroom and berry notes, turning elegant and polished on the finish. Shortens up on the finish, but still delivers a lot of appealing flavors. Drink through 2005–J.L. • $27 • (10/31/1998) • **88**
Pinot Noir Chalone 1994 • $27 • (1/31/1998) • **88**
Pinot Noir Chalone 1992 • $26 • (3/31/1997) • **87**
Pinot Noir Chalone 1991 • $22 • (6/30/1995) • **88**
Pinot Noir Chalone 1990 • $30 • (3/31/1997) • **87**
Pinot Noir Chalone 1989 • $30 • (2/28/1993) • **77**
Pinot Noir Chalone 1986 • $32 • (3/31/1997) • **78**
Pinot Noir Chalone 1985 • $18 • (2/15/1990) • **85**
Pinot Noir Chalone 1984 • $19 • (12/15/1987) • **88**
Pinot Noir Chalone 1983 • $19 • (8/31/1986) • **89**
Pinot Noir Chalone 1981 • $19 • (12/16/1984) • **83**
Pinot Noir Chalone Gavilan 1992 • $14 • (10/31/1994) • **84**
Pinot Noir Chalone Gavilan 1991 • $13 • (2/28/1994) • **78**
Pinot Noir Chalone Reserve 1990 • $48 • (3/31/1997) • **88**
Pinot Noir Chalone Reserve 1989 • $32 • (3/31/1995) • **84**
Pinot Noir Chalone Reserve 1988 • $25 • (3/31/1995) • **84**
Pinot Noir Chalone Reserve 1987 • $20 • (2/28/1993) • **86**
Pinot Noir Chalone Reserve 1986 • $50 • (3/31/1997) • **85**
Pinot Noir Chalone Reserve 1981 • $28 • (8/31/1986) • **92**

Key: SS—Spectator Selection. CS—Cellar Selection. HR—Highly Recommended. $NA—Price not available. (BT)—Barrel tasting. (A)—Auction Price. For a key to the tasters' initials, see "How to Use These Listings."
Dates in parentheses represent the issues in which the ratings were published.

CHAMELEON | CALIFORNIA

Barbera Amador County 1997: Fresh, lively, with snappy flavors of blackberry, tart cherry, raspberry and anise, some nice earth notes. Drink now.–J.L. • $17 • (3/31/1999) • **88**
Barbera Amador County 1996 • $14 • (12/15/1997) • **85**
Sangiovese California 1995 • $NA • (1/01/1997) • **82**
Sangiovese North Coast 1998: Lean, if not thin, with simple, earthy, sour cherry flavors that stay in bounds. Drink now.–J.L. • $17 • (1/31/2000) • **82**
Sangiovese North Coast 1997: Tangy acids and rustic tannins make this a bit austere, but it shows off some pretty blackberry and herb flavors nonetheless. Perhaps it will smooth out with time. Drink through 2004 • $18 • (3/31/1999) • **84**
Sangiovese North Coast 1996 • $16 • (12/15/1997) • **85**

CHAMPOEG | OREGON

Chardonnay Willamette Valley Estate 1996: Crisp, earthy and a bit raw, this is distinctive for its floral edge to the citrusy pear flavors. Has more up front than on the finish. Drink now.–H.S. • $8 • (5/15/2000) • **85**
Pinot Gris Willamette Valley Estate 1997: Light and fragrant, with spicy melon aromas and flavors on a delicate frame. Drink now.–H.S. • $12 • (5/15/2000) • **83**
Pinot Gris Willamette Valley Estate 1996 • $12 • (5/15/1998) • **85**
Pinot Noir Willamette Valley 1991 • $12 • (11/30/1994) • **81**
Pinot Noir Willamette Valley Estate 1993 • $10 • (5/15/1998) • **84**
Pinot Noir Willamette Valley Reserve 1993: Though only recently released, this is a mature, velvety red, with modest yet lingering black cherry and earth aromas and flavors. Drink now.–H.S. • $18 • (5/15/2000) • **86**

CHANNING DAUGHTERS | NEW YORK

Chardonnay Long Island Brick Kiln 1996: Fresh, clean and appley, with just a hint of oak for support and flavor nuance. Mouthwatering acidity on the finish begs for food.–B.S. • $15 • (12/15/1998) • **85**
Chardonnay The Hamptons Long Island Scuttlehole 1997: Dull, earthy aromas turn nasty on the palate, with a sour/bitter taste that won't quit on the finish. Not recommended. Tasted three times, with consistent notes.–T.M. • $12 • (1/01/1999) • **58**
Merlot Long Island Sculpture Garden 1995 • $15 • (1/01/1998) • **75**
Sauvignon Blanc North Fork of Long Island Mudd Vineyard 1997: Seriously bad—maybe even a health hazard! An amazingly tart/bitter chemical taste begins in the back of the throat and won't let go. Not recommended. Tasted twice, with consistent notes.–T.M. • $14 • (1/01/1999) • **53**

CHAPPELLET | CALIFORNIA

Cabernet Sauvignon Napa Valley 1988 • $14 • (2/15/1993) • **85**
Cabernet Sauvignon Napa Valley 1983 • $22 • (2/15/1993) • **90**
Cabernet Sauvignon Napa Valley 1982 • $21 • (2/15/1993) • **74**
Cabernet Sauvignon Napa Valley 1981 • $23 • (2/15/1993) • **85**
Cabernet Sauvignon Napa Valley 1979 • $30 • (2/15/1993) • **89**
Cabernet Sauvignon Napa Valley 1978 • $41 • (2/15/1993) • **75**
Cabernet Sauvignon Napa Valley 1977 • $24 • (2/15/1993) • **86**
Cabernet Sauvignon Napa Valley 1976 • $31 • (2/15/1993) • **91**
Cabernet Sauvignon Napa Valley 1975 • $NA • (2/15/1993) • **81**
Cabernet Sauvignon Napa Valley 1974 • $18 Ⓐ • (11/15/1994) • **68**
Cabernet Sauvignon Napa Valley 1973 • $64 • (2/15/1993) • **77**
Cabernet Sauvignon Napa Valley 1972 • $41 • (2/15/1993) • **73**
Cabernet Sauvignon Napa Valley 1971 • $40 • (2/15/1993) • **78**
Cabernet Sauvignon Napa Valley 1970 • $95 • (2/15/1993) • **93**
Cabernet Sauvignon Napa Valley 1969 • $105 • (2/15/1993) • **90**
Cabernet Sauvignon Napa Valley Pritchard Hill Estates 1992 • $15 • (9/15/1995) • **86**
Cabernet Sauvignon Napa Valley Signature 1996: Understated, firmly structured and focused, with a complex range of cedar, currant, sage, anise and tobacco flavors that expand on the finish. Tannins are firm but integrated. Drink now through 2005.–J.L. • $27 • (10/15/1999) • **89**
Cabernet Sauvignon Napa Valley Signature 1995: Elegant, with understated cherry, cedar and currant flavors, turning spicy and firm on the finish, where dry tannins weigh in. Drink through 2006–J.L. • $24 • (4/30/1999) • **87**
Cabernet Sauvignon Napa Valley Signature 1994 • $22 • (12/31/1997) • **88**
Cabernet Sauvignon Napa Valley Signature 1993 • $22 • (5/15/1997) • **87**
Cabernet Sauvignon Napa Valley Signature 1992 • $20 • (3/31/1996) • **83**
Cabernet Sauvignon Napa Valley Signature 1991 • $20 • (11/15/1994) • **89**
Cabernet Sauvignon Napa Valley Signature 1990 • $25 • (11/15/1993) • **81**
Cabernet Sauvignon Napa Valley Signature 1989 • $27 • (3/31/1993) • **82**
Cabernet Sauvignon Napa Valley Signature Reserve 1987 • $18 • (12/15/1997) • **90**
Cabernet Sauvignon Napa Valley Signature Reserve 1986 • $20 • (2/15/1993) • **89**
Cabernet Sauvignon Napa Valley Signature Reserve 1985 • $25 • (2/15/1993) • **93**
Cabernet Sauvignon Napa Valley Signature Reserve 1984 • $24 • (2/15/1993) • **90**
Cabernet Sauvignon Napa Valley Signature Reserve 1980 • $35 • (2/15/1993) • **88**
Chardonnay Napa Valley 1998: Rich and flavorful, with a good dose of smoky, toasty oak framing the ripe pear, citrus and hazenut flavors. Drink now through 2003.–J.L. • $20 • (1/31/2000) • **90**
Chardonnay Napa Valley Signature 1998: A bit heavy-handed, turning earthy and a touch woody, with hints of pear and fig and a honeyed note. Drink now through 2003.–J.L. • $35 • (6/30/2000) • **86**
Chardonnay Napa Valley Signature 1997: Aromatically complex, with floral and grapey notes. Rich and fleshy, with ripe pear, apple and nutmeg flavors that fan out. Drink now through 2002.–J.L. • $26 • (7/31/1999) • **90**
Chardonnay Napa Valley Signature 1996 • $24 • (3/31/1998) • **90**
Chenin Blanc Napa Valley Dry 1996 • $11 • (5/15/1998) • **83**
Chenin Blanc Napa Valley Moelleux 1997: Earthy, if a touch cheesy, it nonetheless delivers the goods, with ripe apple, pear, fig and spice flavors. Drink now.–J.L. • $40/375 ml. • (2/29/2000) • **89**
Chenin Blanc Napa Valley Moelleux 1995: Sweet, with a sugary edge to the ripe peach, apricot and nectarine flavors, finishing with touches of orange peel and cream. Drink now through 2002.–J.L. • $34/375 ml. • (12/15/1998) • **91**
Merlot Napa Valley 1996: Smooth and herbal, with chocolate, berry, leather, sage and spice, turning supple and polished, with a lingering aftertaste. Drink now through 2004.–J.L. • $22 • (3/31/1999) • **88**
Merlot Napa Valley 1993 • $18 • (8/31/1996) • **85**
Merlot Napa Valley 1992 • $17 • (6/15/1995) • **84**
Merlot Napa Valley 1989 • $16 • (5/31/1992) • **68**
Merlot Napa Valley 1988 • $15 • (4/15/1992) • **85**
Merlot Napa Valley 1987 • $15 • (12/31/1990) • **89**
Merlot Napa Valley 1986 • $15 • (1/31/1990) • **80**
Merlot Napa Valley 1985 • $12 • (12/31/1988) • **78**
Sangiovese Napa Valley 1995 • $22 • (12/15/1997) • **87**

CHASE, S.E. | CALIFORNIA

Zinfandel St. Helena Hayne Vineyard 1998: Ripe, with jammy cherry, raspberry and wild berry. Turns herbal, with a touch of bitterness. Not what you might expect from this famous vineyard. Drink now through 2005.–J.L. • $32 • (5/15/2000) • **85**

CHASSEUR | CALIFORNIA

Chardonnay Russian River Valley Dutton 1996: Ultrarich and deeply concentrated, with a broad array of fig, pear, smoky-toasty oak, anise and nutmeg flavors that are long and complex on the finish. Drink now through 2002.–J.L. • $35 • (5/31/1999) • **93**
Chardonnay Sonoma County Dutton-Sangiacomo 1997: Wonderful complexity, finesse and balance, with supple layers of ripe fig, pear, spice and tangerine flavors kept alive by a seam of acidity. Turns smoky on the finish. Drink now through 2007.–J.L. • $35 • (4/30/2000) • **91**

CHATEAU BENOIT | OREGON

White Riesling Oregon Sweet Sophia 1995 • $14 • (4/30/1997) • **88**

CHATEAU BIANCA | OREGON

Chardonnay Oregon 1997: Lean and earthy at first, with a modest level of green apple and spice flavor that echoes nicely on the finish. Drink now.–H.S. • $9 • (4/30/2000) • **84**
Pinot Noir Oregon 1997: Earthy, gamy flavors predominate in this funky wine, with crisp tannins.–H.S. • $9 • (4/30/2000) • **77**
Pinot Noir Oregon Reserve 1996: Smooth, generous and supple, with dark cherry aromas and flavors and vaguely minty overtones. Finishes with a slight bite. Drink now through 2003.–H.S. • $19 • (4/30/2000) • **86**
Pinot Noir Oregon Winemaker's Reserve 1995 • $18 • (2/28/1997) • **79**
Pinot Noir Oregon Winemaker's Reserve 1993 • $9 • (1/31/1996) • **73**
Pinot Noir Oregon Winemaker's Reserve 1992 • $18 • (11/30/1994) • **82**

CHATEAU CHRISTINA | CALIFORNIA

Cabernet Sauvignon Carmel Valley 1994 • $25 • (11/15/1997) • **87**
Pinot Noir Monterey County 1996 • $25 • (2/28/1998) • **84**
Pinot Noir Monterey County 1995 • $20 • (9/30/1997) • **87**

CHATEAU DE BAUN | CALIFORNIA

Brut Rosé Sonoma County NV • $10 • (12/31/1994) • **73**
Brut Sonoma County NV • $10 • (12/31/1993) • **77**
Pinot Noir California Barrel Select Rouge 1991 • $5 • (3/31/1995) • **73**
Pinot Noir California Chateau Rouge Barrel Select 1990 • $5 • (2/28/1993) • **75**
Pinot Noir Russian River Valley 1994 • $12 • (11/30/1996) • **81**
Pinot Noir Russian River Valley 1993 • $10 • (12/31/1995) • **82**
Pinot Noir Russian River Valley 1992 • $10 • (12/31/1995) • **83**
Pinot Noir Sonoma County 1991 • $10 • (2/28/1994) • **82**
Symphony Russian River Valley Late Harvest Finale 1993 • $10/375 ml. • (7/31/1995) • **88**
Symphony Sonoma County Late Harvest Finale 1989 • $6/375 ml. • (11/15/1993) • **87**
Symphony Sonoma County Late Harvest Finale 1988 • $12/375 ml. • (4/30/1991) • **87**

CHATEAU FRANK | NEW YORK

Chardonnay Nassau County Old Brookville 1997: Apple, melon and vanilla flavors are clean, sweet and fresh in this straightforward white. Though not complex, it's well-balanced and draws you back for another sip. Drink now.–T.M. • $12 • (6/30/1999) • **83**
New York Sparkling Célèbre Crémant NV: This fruity, off-dry sparkler offers bright flavors of apples and pears, with a lively but gentle mousse and a clean finish. Drink now.–T.M. • $15 • (5/31/2000) • **82**

CHATEAU JULIEN | CALIFORNIA

Cabernet Sauvignon Monterey County Grand Reserve 1996: Simple, with tutti-frutti, cherry and watermelon notes and oak flavors. Finishes soft. Drink now. • $9 • (10/15/1998) • **75**
Cabernet Sauvignon Monterey County Grand Reserve 1992 • $7 • (11/30/1996) • **71**
Cabernet Sauvignon Monterey County Private Reserve 1992 • $18 • (11/30/1996) • **86**
Cabernet Sauvignon Monterey County Private Reserve 1989 • $20 • (8/31/1992) • **79**
Merlot Monterey County 1991 • $10 • (5/31/1993) • **84**
Merlot Monterey County 1989 • $9 • (5/31/1992) • **86**
Merlot Monterey County 1988 • $9 • (5/31/1992) • **72**
Merlot Monterey County Grand Reserve 1996: Somewhat green, though backed by plum and cassis flavors. The oak influence is charry and a bit resinous. Drink now.–J.L. • $11 • (9/30/1998) • **79**
Merlot Monterey County Grand Reserve 1995 • $10 • (4/30/1998) • **79**
Merlot Monterey County Grand Reserve 1994 • $9 • (6/30/1996) • **85**
Merlot Monterey County Private Reserve 1991 • $9 • (9/15/1994) • **85**
Merlot Santa Barbara County Bien Nacido Vineyard 1984 • $12 • (2/29/1988) • **76**

CHATEAU MONTELENA | CALIFORNIA

Cabernet Sauvignon Alexander Valley Sonoma 1978 • $58 Ⓐ • (11/15/1992) • **86**
Cabernet Sauvignon Alexander Valley Sonoma 1974 • $74 Ⓐ • (11/15/1994) • **88**
Cabernet Sauvignon Napa Valley Calistoga Cuvée 1997: Appealing for its ripe, supple plum, black cherry, tobacco, earth and cedar notes, it's only mildly tannic, with a mineral edge. Drink now through 2006.–J.L. • $25 • (4/30/2000) • **88**
Cabernet Sauvignon Napa Valley Calistoga Cuvée 1996: Smooth, rich and complex, with a range of currant, bell pepper, herb, sage and tea. Polished tannins. Drink now through 2005.–J.L. • $25 • (1/31/1999) • **88**
Cabernet Sauvignon Napa Valley Calistoga Cuvée 1995 • $18 • (10/31/1997) • **82**

Key: SS—Spectator Selection. CS—Cellar Selection. HR—Highly Recommended. $NA—Price not available. (BT)—Barrel tasting. Ⓐ—Auction Price.
For a key to the tasters' initials, see "How to Use These Listings."
Dates in parentheses represent the issues in which the ratings were published.

Cabernet Sauvignon Napa Valley Calistoga Cuvée 1994 • $18 • (11/15/1996) • **88**
Cabernet Sauvignon Napa Valley Calistoga Cuvée 1993 • $18 • (12/15/1995) • **86**
Cabernet Sauvignon Napa Valley Calistoga Cuvée 1992 • $15 • (11/15/1994) SS • **90**
Cabernet Sauvignon Napa Valley The Montelena Estate 1997: Barrel sample. Shows its grapey, youthful complexity. Very deep and polished, rich and flamboyant. Worth the effort to find when it's released. (Château Montelena vertical tasting, and all notes below from the 11/15/1999 issue).–J.L. • $NA • (11/15/1999) (BT) • **95-99**
Cabernet Sauvignon Napa Valley The Montelena Estate 1996: Openly fruity and seductive, with layers of cherry, currant and berry; extraordinary flavors and balance. Drink now through 2012.–J.L. • $NA • (11/15/1999) • **92**
Cabernet Sauvignon Napa Valley The Montelena Estate 1995: Not as dense and concentrated as the 1994, but still a tremendous wine. Elegant and rich, with currant, cherry, cookie dough and vanilla-scented oak. Drink through 2010–J.L. • $85 • (11/15/1999) • **92**
Cabernet Sauvignon Napa Valley The Montelena Estate 1994: Slowly unleashes a wonderful core of tightly bound, elegant currant and black cherry that turns creamy, deep and profound. Drink through 2014–J.L. • $40 • (11/15/1999) • **95**
Cabernet Sauvignon Napa Valley The Montelena Estate 1993: A very precocious wine, with lots of forward, supple plum, black cherry and berry flavor and a long, rich aftertaste. Drink through 2011–J.L. • $79 Ⓐ • (11/15/1999) • **94**
Cabernet Sauvignon Napa Valley The Montelena Estate 1972-1992 Anniversary 1992: Tight and a bit raw-tasting after the opulent 1991, but still solidly built, with compact berry- and cherry-laced flavor. Best from 2001 through 2010.–J.L. • $72 Ⓐ • (11/15/1999) • **92**
Cabernet Sauvignon Napa Valley The Montelena Estate 1991: Even more depth, focus, complexity and flavor than the 1990. Amazing length and detail. Drink now through 2011.–J.L. • $79 Ⓐ • (11/15/1999) • **97**
Cabernet Sauvignon Napa Valley The Montelena Estate 1990: Enormous complexity, depth, focus and richness, with tiers of Cabernet flavors. Drink now through 2010.–J.L. • $30 • (11/15/1999) • **94**
Cabernet Sauvignon Napa Valley 1989: Impressive, showing what happened when the grapes were left to hang after rains and a huge crop. Plenty of ripe, fleshy currant and black cherry flavors. Drink now through 2005.–J.L. • $49 Ⓐ • (11/15/1999) • **90**
Cabernet Sauvignon Napa Valley 1988: Lean, not very ripe-tasting or complete in terms of depth and length. Good, but nothing more. Drink now.–J.L. • $30 • (11/15/1999) • **82**
Cabernet Sauvignon Napa Valley 1987: Tight and perhaps even less flashy than usual, it is slow to reveal its complex range of earthy, cedary currant and black cherry. Drink now through 2008.–J.L. • $106 Ⓐ • (11/15/1999) • **93**
Cabernet Sauvignon Napa Valley 1986: Big and robust, with lots of rich fruit and substantial tannins. A real mouthful. Drink now through 2010.–J.L. • $99 Ⓐ • (11/15/1999) • **92**
Cabernet Sauvignon Napa Valley 1985: More subtle and subdued than the 1984, this is a wine of complexity and finesse, though the currant and black cherry flavor is tighter than I recall from previous tastings. Drink now through 2005.–J.L. • $100 Ⓐ • (11/15/1999) • **91**
Cabernet Sauvignon Napa Valley 1984: The ripest vintage since 1978, this is rich and opulent, with juicy black cherry and currant flavors, turning firm and tannic. Drink now through 2008.–J.L. • $84 Ⓐ • (11/15/1999) • **93**
Cabernet Sauvignon Napa Valley 1983: Tight and austere, very likable on its own terms, though lacking the body and rich flavors of the best Montelenas. Drink now through 2003.–J.L. • $18 • (11/15/1999) • **87**
Cabernet Sauvignon Napa Valley 1982: Very Bordeaux-like, earthy and minty, with a leathery aroma adding dimension to the core of currant. Quite rich for this difficult vintage. Drink now through 2006.–J.L. • $43 Ⓐ • (11/15/1999) • **92**
Cabernet Sauvignon Napa Valley 1981: Austere, with a touch of greenness. From an early harvest, this wine tastes like the grapes didn't hang long enough on the vine to develop deeper flavors. Drink now.–J.L. • $62 Ⓐ • (11/15/1999) • **86**
Cabernet Sauvignon Napa Valley 1980: A big, broad-shouldered wine that lacks fillings, with a band of cedary currant and berry and drying tannins. Drink now through 2004.–J.L. • $49 Ⓐ • (11/15/1999) • **89**
Cabernet Sauvignon Napa Valley 1979: Austere, quite like an aged Bordeaux, with smoky currant and meaty flavors, picking up black cherry and chocolaty notes and a touch of vanilla. Has enough tannin and richness for further cellaring. (1979 California Cabernet retrospective tasting). Drink now through 2007.–J.L. • $53 Ⓐ • (8/31/1999) • **91**

Cabernet Sauvignon Napa Valley 1978: A healthy ruby red in color, mature and complex, with wonderful depth, intensity and range of coffee and dried fruit flavors. About all you could ask for from a wine this age. Drink now through 2010.–J.L. • $110 Ⓐ • (11/15/1999) • **94**

Chardonnay Napa Valley 1997: Understated and not too showy now, though this is a wine that typically needs a year or two to develop. Restrained apple, pear and spice notes have a twinge of orange peel and citrus. Best from 2001 through 2010.–J.L. • $29 • (4/30/2000) • **87**

Chardonnay Napa Valley 1996: Here's an enticing Chardonnay in a crisp and elegant style, its bright flavor profile including tart tangerine, citrus and lemon flavors and with a leafy, peachy, hazelnut edge to the finish. It's enjoyable now or can be cellared. Drink now through 2002.–J.L. • $29 • (1/31/1999) SS • **90**

Zinfandel Napa Valley 1991 • $12 • (10/15/1994) • **84**

Zinfandel Napa Valley 1989 • $12 • (10/15/1992) • **80**

Zinfandel Napa Valley 1987 • $10 • (7/31/1990) • **69**

Zinfandel Napa Valley 1986 • $15 • (9/15/1989) • **80**

Zinfandel Napa Valley 1985 • $15 • (4/30/1988) • **90**

Zinfandel Napa Valley 1983 • $11 • (5/01/1986) • **84**

Zinfandel Napa Valley 1982 • $14 • (5/01/1984) • **91**

Zinfandel Napa Valley 1981 • $20 • (4/16/1984) • **80**

Zinfandel Napa & Alexander Valleys 1974 • $40 • (6/16/1985) • **92**

Zinfandel Napa Valley 1973 • $29 • (6/16/1985) • **90**

Zinfandel Napa Valley John Rolleri Vineyard 1984 • $18 • (5/15/1987) • **91**

Zinfandel Napa Valley The Montelena Estate 1992 • $12 • (7/31/1995) • **87**

Zinfandel North Coast 1976 • $25 • (6/16/1985) • **78**

CHATEAU POTELLE | CALIFORNIA

Cabernet Sauvignon Alexander Valley 1988 • $18 • (11/15/1992) • **87**

Cabernet Sauvignon Alexander Valley 1987 • $16 • (8/31/1991) • **83**

Cabernet Sauvignon Alexander Valley 1986 • $15 • (10/31/1990) • **84**

Cabernet Sauvignon Alexander Valley 1984 • $13 • (12/31/1988) • **83**

Cabernet Sauvignon Mount Veeder V.G.S. 1997: Tightly wound, firmly tannic, with tart wild berry, cherry and currant and a long, lingering aftertaste.–J.L. • $NA • (8/31/1998) (BT) • **90-94**

Cabernet Sauvignon Mount Veeder V.G.S. 1996 • $NA • (2/02/1997) (BT) • **90-94**

Cabernet Sauvignon Mount Veeder V.G.S. 1995: Austere, with a potent peppery edge to the anise and cherry flavors, turning quite tannic. Has enough concentrated earthy currant and sage flavors to be outstanding. Best from 2001 through 2010.–J.L. • $50 • (10/31/1999) • **90**

Cabernet Sauvignon Mount Veeder V.G.S. 1994: Has substantial tannins but also a smooth texture, given its size, with spice, cedar, wild berry and currant flavors that are elegant and focused. Drink now through 2004.–J.L. • $39 • (3/31/1999) • **90**

Cabernet Sauvignon Mount Veeder V.G.S. 1993: Dense, tight and chewy, with firm, gritty tannins, this is a big, dense, backward style with an uncertain future. If all goes well, the intense core of plum, earth, tar, pepper and cedar flavors will evolve into a complex, deeply flavored wine.–J.L. • $39 • (10/31/1998) • **88**

Cabernet Sauvignon Mount Veeder V.G.S. 1992 • $39 • (11/30/1996) • **88**

Cabernet Sauvignon Napa Valley 1991 • $18 • (10/15/1996) • **86**

Cabernet Sauvignon Napa Valley Cuvée 95 1990 • $16 • (10/15/1994) • **86**

Chardonnay Central Coast 1997: Racy, with a green, herbal, grassy, sweaty streak running through the flavors. Finishes with a slightly bitter edge. Drink now.–J.L. • $18 • (4/30/2000) • **83**

Chardonnay Central Coast 1996: Citrus and pear notes are pleasantly soft and flavorful. Finishes with modest length. Drink now.–J.L. • $18 • (7/31/1999) • **85**

Chardonnay Mount Veeder V.G.S. 1996: Smooth, rich and polished, with pretty vanilla, pear, nutmeg and hazelnut flavors that are firm, crisp and a touch earthy on the finish. Drink now through 2004.–J.L. • $38 • (10/15/1999) • **91**

Epice Mount Veeder 1997: Spicy and refreshing, with a grape flavor and a twinge of bitterness. Chardonnay, Viognier and Gewürztraminer. Drink now.–J.L. • $16 • (6/15/2000) • **84**

Sauvignon Blanc Napa Valley 1998: Tangy, with fig, grapefruit and earth notes and a crisp finish. Drink now through 2003.–J.L. • $13 • (5/15/2000) • **84**

Sauvignon Blanc Napa Valley 1997: Kicks off with a slightly earthy aroma, but the wine is clean on the palate, serving up subtle herb, nut, fresh pea and melon flavors. Finishes moderately. Drink now. • $12 • (5/15/1999) • **85**

Sauvignon Blanc Napa Valley 1996 • $11 • (4/30/1998) • **88**

Zinfandel Amador County 1996: A solid red, with generous black cherry, spice and coffee flavors that linger on the firm finish. Should be good with hearty food. Drink now through 2002.–H.S. • $16 • (11/30/1998) • **85**

Zinfandel Amador County Old Vines 1997: Firm, with hints of black fruit, herb and toasted oak, but not yet very expressive. Might open with cellaring. Drink now through 2004.–J.L. • $21 • (11/15/1999) • **84**

Zinfandel Mount Veeder V.G.S. 1997: Lighter than normal. An elegant, polished, understated style, with herb, anise and wild berry notes, finishing with soft tannins. Drink now through 2006.–J.L. • $43 • (3/31/2000) • **87**

Zinfandel Mount Veeder V.G.S. 1996: Ripe and elegant, with zesty wild berry, raspberry and cherry flavors and firm but well-integrated tannins, finishing with earthy, tarry notes.–J.L. • $38 • (5/15/1999) • **90**

Zinfandel Mount Veeder V.G.S. 1995 • $35 • (4/30/1998) • **91**

Zinfandel Mount Veeder V.G.S. 1994 • $32 • (3/31/1997) HR • **92**

Zinfandel Mount Veeder V.G.S. 1993 • $28 • (12/31/1995) • **88**

Zinfandel Mount Veeder V.G.S. 1992: Turning dry and showing a lot of toasty French oak, it's weighted toward the wood side, but slowly reveals more detailed cherry, currant, anise, plum and spice. An elegant, understated style. (Zinfandel retrospective tasting). Drink now.–J.L. • $28 • (6/30/1999) • **88**

Zinfandel Mount Veeder V.G.S. 1990: Wonderful fruit intensity, concentration and complexity, still displaying vibrant, youthful black cherry, wild berry, currant, plum and spice. Well focused on the finish, where the flavors linger, pure and true. Still has tannin, but it's ready. (Zinfandel retrospective tasting). Drink now through 2004.–J.L. • $27 • (6/30/1999) • **90**

CHATEAU SOUVERAIN | CALIFORNIA

Cabernet Sauvignon Alexander Valley 1997: Broad-shouldered, with herb, blackberry and earth notes wrapped in substantial tannins. Drink now through 2006.–J.L. • $20 • (6/15/2000) • **88**

Cabernet Sauvignon Alexander Valley 1996: Ripe and rich, with firm plum, herb, black cherry and spice flavors that are sharply focused, long and rich on the finish. Has the tannin for midterm cellaring. Drink now through 2006.–J.L. • $19 • (8/31/1999) • **88**

Cabernet Sauvignon Alexander Valley 1995 • $17 • (6/30/1998) HR • **89**

Cabernet Sauvignon Alexander Valley 1994 • $15 • (6/30/1997) SS • **89**

Cabernet Sauvignon Alexander Valley 1992 • $12 • (3/31/1995) • **85**

Cabernet Sauvignon Alexander Valley 1991 • $11 • (6/30/1994) • **85**

Cabernet Sauvignon Alexander Valley 1990 • $11 • (11/15/1993) SS • **90**

Cabernet Sauvignon Alexander Valley 1989: At a nice drinking stage, with ripe, complex, well-integrated cherry, currant, plum, spice and creamy oak flavors, finishing with firm tannins and good length. (1989 California Cabernet retrospective tasting). Drink now through 2004.–J.L. • $10 • (8/31/1999) • **88**

Cabernet Sauvignon Alexander Valley 1988 • $10 • (11/15/1991) • **85**

Cabernet Sauvignon Alexander Valley Barrel Aged 1993 • $13 • (10/15/1996) • **86**

Cabernet Sauvignon Alexander Valley Library Reserve 1995: Smooth, ripe and polished, with layers of currant, herb, cedar, tar and spice. Turns plush and firm on the finish. Available only through the winery. Drink through 2007–J.L. • $45 • (6/15/1999) • **91**

Cabernet Sauvignon Alexander Valley Library Reserve 1994: A delicious Cabernet, ripe, smooth and polished, with layers of currant, black cherry, plum, anise and toasty-cedary oak that even has a hint of chocolate. Well focused, with depth, richness and concentration. Drink now through 2005.–J.L. • $45 • (10/31/1998) • **91**

Cabernet Sauvignon Alexander Valley Library Reserve 1993 • $40 • (11/15/1996) • **91**

Cabernet Sauvignon Alexander Valley Private Reserve 1987 • $15 • (12/15/1997) • **87**

Cabernet Sauvignon Alexander Valley Reserve 1995: Smooth and supple, with polished cedar, black cherry, currant, sage and spice, picking up a trace of coffee on the finish. Drink now through 2004.–J.L. • $35 • (3/31/1999) • **88**

Cabernet Sauvignon Alexander Valley Winemaker's Reserve 1994 • $30 • (10/15/1997) • **93**

Cabernet Sauvignon Alexander Valley Winemaker's Reserve 1993 • $30 • (11/15/1996) • **90**

Cabernet Sauvignon Alexander Valley Winemaker's Reserve 1992 • $16 • (12/15/1995) • **89**

Cabernet Sauvignon Alexander Valley Winemaker's Reserve 1991 • $14 • (10/31/1994) HR • **91**

Cabernet Sauvignon Alexander Valley Winemaker's Reserve 1990 • $14 • (5/31/1994) • **89**

Cabernet Sauvignon Alexander Valley Winemaker's Reserve 1989: One corky bottle, but the second showed moderately ripe and polished cherry, currant and berryish flavors, turning a bit earthy and diluted on the finish. (1989 California Cabernet retrospective tasting). Drink now.–J.L. • $15 • (8/31/1999) • **85**

CHATEAU SOUVERAIN

Cabernet Sauvignon Alexander Valley Winemaker's Reserve 1988: A touch earthy and gamy, it slowly works its way into purer Cabernet flavors, with hints of cherry, berry and cedar. Turns dry and tannic on the finish, so drink soon, now through 2001. (1988 California Cabernet retrospective tasting).–J.L. • $17 • (11/15/1998) • **84**
Cabernet Sauvignon North Coast Vintage Selection 1980 • $13 • (9/16/1985) • **83**
Cabernet Sauvignon Sonoma County 1978 • $50 • (11/15/1992) • **82**
Cabernet Sauvignon Sonoma County Vintage Selection 1978 • $28 • (11/15/1992) • **83**
Cabernet Sauvignon Sonoma County Vintage Selection 1974 • $50 • (2/15/1990) • **84**
Chardonnay Russian River Valley Reserve 1997: Easy to like, with honeyed tangerine and cream flavors that finish with vanilla intensity. Drink now.–J.L. • $25 • (6/30/2000) • **86**
Chardonnay Russian River Valley Winemaker's Reserve 1996: Impressive texture marks this smooth, ripe and creamy wine, with hints of tropical fruit, ripe pear, fig and melon. Gains a pretty touch of smoky, toasty oak on the aftertaste, where the complex flavors linger. Drink now through 2002 .–J.L. • $20 • (7/31/1998) HR • **92**
Chardonnay Sonoma County 1998: A bit earthy, with vanilla and pear flavors that carry through to the slightly soapy finish. Drink now through 2001.–J.L. • $14 • (5/15/2000) • **84**
Chardonnay Sonoma County 1997: This California Chardonnay is a winner all around. It's firm and bright, offering a solid, snappy core of citrus and mineral along with pretty pear and apple flavors, all mingling on the long, zingy finish. And the price is right. Drink now through 2006. • $13 • (6/30/1999) SS • **90**
Chardonnay Sonoma County 1996 • $13 • (1/31/1998) SS • **90**
Merlot Alexander Valley 1996: Has a strong spice and bell pepper character along with the earthy cherry and wild berry flavors. Turns firm on the finish. Drink now through 2002.–J.L. • $18 • (12/31/1998) • **87**
Merlot Alexander Valley 1995 • $17 • (11/30/1997) • **87**
Merlot Alexander Valley 1994 • $13 • (7/31/1996) • **85**
Merlot Alexander Valley 1993 • $13 • (12/15/1995) • **86**
Merlot Alexander Valley 1992 • $12 • (6/30/1994) • **85**
Merlot Alexander Valley 1991 • $12 • (6/30/1994) • **87**
Merlot Alexander Valley 1990 • $10 • (5/31/1993) • **86**
Merlot Alexander Valley 1989 • $10 • (5/31/1992) • **89**
Merlot Sonoma County 1990 • $10 • (5/31/1992) • **86**
Merlot Sonoma County 1986 • $10 • (3/31/1989) • **74**
Pinot Noir Carneros Winemaker's Reserve 1993 • $16 • (3/31/1995) • **84**
Pinot Noir Carneros Winemaker's Reserve 1992 • $14 • (4/30/1994) • **85**
Pinot Noir Carneros Winemaker's Reserve 1991 • $15 • (2/28/1994) • **85**
Sauvignon Blanc Alexander Valley 1998: Fragrant, with hints of orange peel, melon, lemon and herbs, this California white is then silky on the palate, fanning out nicely and showing a classy touch of passion fruit on the long, racy finish. Very good wine, great price. Drink now through 2002. • $9 • (5/31/1999) • **88**
Sauvignon Blanc Alexander Valley 1997: Starts off with a lemony edge, followed by more bright citrus notes, a touch of passion fruit and herb and melon flavors that finish moderately. Quite refreshing. Drink now. • $9 • (11/30/1998) • **87**
Sauvignon Blanc Alexander Valley 1996 • $9 • (6/30/1997) • **88**
Zinfandel Dry Creek Valley 1997: Medium-bodied, with herbal, earthy chocolate and strawberry flavors, turning dry and austere on the finish. Drink now.–J.L. • $13 • (3/31/2000) • **84**
Zinfandel Dry Creek Valley 1996: Tight and trim, with a firm, narrow band of spice, wild berry, plum and pepper, remaining dry and tannic, with a tealike accent on the finish. Drink now through 2001.–J.L. • $12 • (5/15/1999) • **87**
Zinfandel Dry Creek Valley 1995 • $12 • (12/15/1997) SS • **89**
Zinfandel Dry Creek Valley 1994 • $10 • (9/15/1996) • **82**
Zinfandel Dry Creek Valley 1993 • $10 • (8/31/1995) • **87**
Zinfandel Dry Creek Valley 1992 • $9 • (8/31/1994) • **87**
Zinfandel Dry Creek Valley 1991 • $9 • (9/15/1993) • **87**
Zinfandel Dry Creek Valley 1990 • $8 • (10/15/1992) • **84**
Zinfandel Dry Creek Valley 1989 • $8 • (5/15/1992) • **82**
Zinfandel Dry Creek Valley Bradford Mountain Vineyard 1987 • $15 • (5/15/1990) • **85**

Key: SS—Spectator Selection. CS—Cellar Selection. HR—Highly Recommended. $NA—Price not available. (BT)—Barrel tasting. Ⓐ—Auction Price.
For a key to the tasters' initials, see "How to Use These Listings."
Dates in parentheses represent the issues in which the ratings were published.

CHATEAU ST. JEAN | CALIFORNIA

Brut Blanc de Blancs Sonoma County NV • $11 • (11/30/1994) SS • **88**
Brut Sonoma County NV • $11 • (12/31/1993) • **85**
Cabernet Franc Sonoma Valley Jeanette Vineyards 1989 • $24 • (7/15/1993) • **83**
Cabernet Franc Sonoma Valley St. Jean Estate Vineyard 1996: Firm, tight and spicy, with a complex, well-focused core of currant, plum and black cherry. Finishes with well-integrated tannins and pretty toasty oak shadings on the long, rich aftertaste. Drink now through 2006.–J.L. • $30 • (12/15/1999) • **92**
Cabernet Sauvignon Alexander Valley 1987 • $16 • (6/30/1991) SS • **92**
Cabernet Sauvignon Alexander Valley 1986 • $19 • (10/15/1989) • **90**
Cabernet Sauvignon Alexander Valley 1985 • $19 • (11/15/1988) • **86**
Cabernet Sauvignon Alexander Valley Reserve 1987 • $38 • (12/15/1997) • **90**
Cabernet Sauvignon Sonoma County 1997: Graceful, rich and concentrated, with pretty layers of currant, black cherry and toasty oak. Wonderful sense of harmony and finesse.–J.L. • $NA • (8/31/1998) (BT) • **90-94**
Cabernet Sauvignon Sonoma County 1989 • $18 • (6/30/1993) • **80**
Cabernet Sauvignon Sonoma County 1988 • $18 • (7/31/1992) • **87**
Cabernet Sauvignon Sonoma County 1981 • $15 • (11/30/1986) • **72**
Cabernet Sauvignon Sonoma County Cinq Cépages 1996: Dense, rich and complex describes this '96 California Cabernet—with its layers of currant, mineral, plum, cherry and toasty oak and its broad, intense and deeply flavorful finish. An extraordinary wine, scoring classic and well-priced. Drink through 2008–J.L. • $28 • (11/15/1999) SS • **95**
Cabernet Sauvignon Sonoma County Cinq Cépages 1995: An elegant California Cabernet, ripe and smooth, showcasing bright, complex black cherry, currant, plum and spicy notes, finishing with well-integrated tannins and the kind of fruit concentration that bodes well for short- to mid-range cellaring. Drink through 2005–J.L. • $24 • (10/31/1998) SS • **91**
Cabernet Sauvignon Sonoma County Cinq Cépages 1994 • $24 • (9/30/1997) SS • **91**
Cabernet Sauvignon Sonoma County Cinq Cépages 1993 • $22 • (11/15/1996) SS • **91**
Cabernet Sauvignon Sonoma County Cinq Cépages 1992 • $18 • (2/29/1996) • **89**
Cabernet Sauvignon Sonoma County Cinq Cépages 1991 • $18 • (11/15/1995) HR • **91**
Cabernet Sauvignon Sonoma County Cinq Cépages 1990 • $18 • (9/30/1994) • **87**
Cabernet Sauvignon Sonoma County Reserve 1995: Smooth and polished, if a bit shy on depth and concentration. Still, the currant, black cherry, sage, anise and cedar notes are supple and appealing. Drink now.–J.L. • $70 • (5/31/2000) • **89**
Cabernet Sauvignon Sonoma County Reserve 1994: This has lots of complex flavors, a firm structure and layers of ripe plum, black cherry, currant and spice, with spicy oak, anise and earthy mineral nuances. Best from 2001 through 2006.–J.L. • $60 • (11/15/1999) • **92**
Cabernet Sauvignon Sonoma County Reserve 1993: Gobs of ripe currant, plum and black cherry, cedar, anise, spice and toasty oak are molded into this delicious, complex and concentrated wine. Has already spent two years in bottle. Drink through 2007–J.L. • $47 • (11/15/1998) • **93**
Cabernet Sauvignon Sonoma County Reserve 1992 • $45 • (9/30/1997) • **92**
Cabernet Sauvignon Sonoma County Reserve 1991 • $39 • (11/15/1996) • **92**
Cabernet Sauvignon Sonoma County Reserve 1990 • $38 • (4/30/1996) CS • **95**
Cabernet Sauvignon Sonoma County Reserve 1989: Wonderful fruit definition, rich, focused, with layers of ripe black cherry, plum, currant, wild berry and cedar, turning supple and complex on the finish, where the flavors sail on. (1989 California Cabernet retrospective tasting). Drink now through 2007.–J.L. • $38 • (8/31/1999) • **92**
Cabernet Sauvignon Sonoma County Reserve 1988 • $38 • (10/15/1993) • **91**
Cabernet Sauvignon Sonoma Valley Glen Ellen Vineyards 1978: A touch nutty and quite tannic, nonetheless holding up well, with earthy, spicy, peppery currant and cedary flavors. Turns chewy on the finish; it appears the fruit will dry out before the tannins soften. (1978 California Cabernet retrospective tasting). Drink now through 2002.–J.L. • $17 • (11/15/1998) • **87**
Cabernet Sauvignon Sonoma Valley Wildwood Vineyards 1980 • $17 • (9/01/1985) • **82**
Cabernet Sauvignon Sonoma Valley Wildwood Vineyards 1979 • $17 • (7/01/1984) • **76**
Chardonnay Alexander Valley Belle Terre Vineyard 1997: Intense, with ripe and spicy pear, fig and apricot flavors, picking up touches of oak and nutmeg on the finish. Give it some time. Drink through 2005–J.L. • $24 • (4/30/1999) • **89**
Chardonnay Alexander Valley Belle Terre Vineyard 1996 • $22 • (5/15/1998) • **91**
Chardonnay Alexander Valley Robert Young Vineyard 1997: Spicy, with a core of ripe pear, nectarine and citrus and a background of light oak.

Turns smooth, with an herbal edge. Drink now through 2004.–J.L. • $24 • (5/31/2000) • **88**

Chardonnay Alexander Valley Robert Young Vineyard 1996: Generous with ripe, up-front fruit flavors, this late-release '96 is delicious for its medley of apple, peach, pear, nectarine flavors, tinged with nutmeg, turning smooth and silky on the finish, unobstructed by oak. Drink now through 2003.–J.L. • $24 • (4/30/1999) SS • **91**

Chardonnay Alexander Valley Robert Young Vineyard Reserve 1996: Smooth, ripe and creamy, with pretty fig, melon, apricot and light toasty, spicy oak, it turns complex and rich on the finish. Drink now through 2002.–J.L. • $33 • (6/15/1999) • **92**

Chardonnay Carneros Durell Vineyard 1997: Smooth, ripe and creamy, with spicy anise, ripe pear and fig and nice notes of nutmeg and hazelnut on the finish. Drink now through 2002.–J.L. • $24 • (6/30/1999) • **92**

Chardonnay Carneros Durell Vineyard 1996: Clean and fruity, with ripe, mature-tasting pear and apple flavors and touches of custard, anise and spice. Turns soft on the aftertaste. Drink now.–J.L. • $24 • (11/30/1998) • **89**

Chardonnay Sonoma County 1998: Serves up lots of creamy, complex flavors, ranging from spicy pear, apple and toasty oak to subtle anise and cedar notes. Drink now through 2004.–J.L. • $12 • (2/29/2000) • **87**

Chardonnay Sonoma County 1997: Ripe and creamy in texture, with snappy citrus and pear flavors and light oak shadings. Drink now.–J.L. • $13 • (12/31/1998) • **82**

Chardonnay Sonoma County 1996 • $13 • (12/31/1997) SS • **89**

Chardonnay Sonoma County Reserve 1997: Rich yet elegant, with smooth, complex and creamy pear, fig and hazelnut flavors that coat the palate, finishing with a burst of deep and refined flavor. First Chardonnay Reserve designation for St. Jean. Drink now through 2005.–J.L. • $40 • (4/30/2000) • **92**

Fumé Blanc Russian River Valley La Petite Étoile Vineyard 1998: Crisp and flinty, with a core of grapefruit, pear, passion fruit and sweet pea flavors that are rich and focused. Coarseness on the finish should subside with cellar time. Drink now through 2005.–J.L. • $14 • (4/30/2000) • **85**

Fumé Blanc Russian River Valley La Petite Étoile Vineyard 1997: Quite lemony at first, the follow-up features a blend of mineral, apple, grapefruit and spice flavors. It's refreshing and zippy on the palate, with staying power on the finish. Drink now through 2001. • $13 • (4/30/1999) • **87**

Fumé Blanc Russian River Valley La Petite Étoile Vineyard 1996 • $13 • (4/30/1998) • **86**

Fumé Blanc Sonoma County 1998: Here's a good value, in Sauvignon Blanc, offering nice balance among ripe fig, herb, citrus and melon flavors, turning elegant and lively. Drink now through 2003.–J.L. • $9 • (4/30/2000) • **87**

Fumé Blanc Sonoma County 1997: This California Sauvignon Blanc shows off lemon, lime, grapefruit and melon character, with good tangy acidity underscoring the somewhat viscous texture. A touch of hazelnut and an attractive hint of honey mark the supple finish. Nice wine, great price. Drink now through 2002. • $9 • (5/15/1999) • **88**

Fumé Blanc Sonoma County 1996 • $9 • (4/30/1998) • **85**

Johannisberg Riesling Late Harvest Alexander Valley Select 1988 • $20/375 ml. • (1/31/1993) • **88**

Johannisberg Riesling Late Harvest Alexander Valley Special Select Hoot Owl Creek Viney 1989 • $22/375 ml. • (1/31/1993) HR • **93**

Johannisberg Riesling Late Harvest Alexander Valley Special Select 1989 • $25/375 ml. • (11/15/1993) CS • **95**

Merlot Sonoma County 1997: A pure Merlot, with herb, tar, coffee and currant flavors. Supple and round, firm on the finish, with enough tannin to cellar short-term. Good value. Best from 2001 through 2007.–J.L. • $22 • (2/29/2000) • **88**

Merlot Sonoma County 1996: A firm yet supple texture easily supports the pretty black currant, cherry, tar, smoke and vanilla flavors. Has focus and finesse. Drink now through 2004. • $18 • (9/30/1998) • **88**

Merlot Sonoma County 1995 • $18 • (3/31/1998) • **87**

Merlot Sonoma County 1994 • $18 • (6/15/1997) • **90**

Merlot Sonoma County 1993 • $14 • (7/31/1996) SS • **90**

Merlot Sonoma County 1992 • $12 • (4/15/1995) • **86**

Merlot Sonoma County 1991 • $12 • (9/15/1994) • **84**

Merlot Sonoma County 1990 • $12 • (3/15/1994) • **85**

Merlot Sonoma County 1989 • $12 • (12/31/1993) • **80**

Merlot Sonoma County Reserve 1995: Complex, though not as deep and profound as previous efforts. Serves up a tasty array of ripe, spicy plum, blackberry, cherry and cedar notes. Finishes with integrated tannins. Drink now through 2007.–J.L. • $70 • (5/31/2000) • **88**

Merlot Sonoma County Reserve 1994: Wonderful richness and fruit definition, with spicy, toasty oak, ripe plum and black cherry, black olive, herb and sage flavors lingering on the long, complex aftertaste. Drink through 2006–J.L. • $60 • (8/31/1999) • **94**

Merlot Sonoma County Reserve 1993 • $35 • (5/15/1998) • **90**

Merlot Sonoma County Reserve 1992 • $35 • (6/15/1997) • **91**

Merlot Sonoma County Reserve 1991 • $32 • (2/29/1996) CS • **92**

Mourvèdre Sonoma Valley 1990 • $17 • (6/15/1993) • **83**

Pinot Noir Carneros Durell Vineyard 1997: Ripe, with a jammy wild berry, cola and black cherry core holding its richness and focus. Finishes with supple, polished tannins and a sense of finesse. Drink now through 2005.–J.L. • $30 • (11/30/1999) • **90**

Pinot Noir Carneros Durell Vineyard 1996: Smooth, ripe and well balanced, harmonious for a '96. Shows a nice core of supple plum and blackberry, with pretty toasty oak shadings. Best of all, it has a pleasant finish with lingering fruity flavors. Drink now.–J.L. • $30 • (8/31/1998) • **86**

Pinot Noir Carneros Durell Vineyard 1995 • $30 • (2/28/1998) • **85**

Pinot Noir Sonoma County 1998: Lightly herbal, with leather, cola, berry and cedar notes, turning simple. Drink now.–J.L. • $16 • (6/15/2000) • **85**

Pinot Noir Sonoma County 1997: Fleshy, with pleasant herb, dried fruit, anise, cherry and currant flavors. Finishes firm, with slightly dry tannins, but should soften with time. Try through 2002.–J.L. • $18 • (6/15/1999) • **85**

Pinot Noir Sonoma County 1994 • $18 • (1/31/1997) • **88**

Pinot Noir Sonoma County 1991 • $16 • (2/28/1994) • **86**

Pinot Noir Sonoma County 1990 • $19 • (2/28/1993) • **80**

Pinot Noir Sonoma Valley McCrea Vineyards 1983 • $12 • (9/30/1987) • **75**

CHATEAU STE. MICHELLE WASHINGTON

Cabernet Franc Columbia Valley Cold Creek Vineyard 1995 • $27 • (6/15/1998) • **89**

Cabernet Franc Columbia Valley Cold Creek Vineyard 1992 • $22 • (9/30/1995) • **85**

Cabernet Sauvignon Benton County Cold Creek Vineyards Chateau Reserve 1980 • $21 • (10/15/1989) • **85**

Cabernet Sauvignon Columbia Valley 1995: Firm in texture, with pretty blackberry and smoke flavors winding through its modest dimensions. Harmonious and polished, it's already appealing. Best after1999.–H.S. • $16 • (11/15/1998) • **87**

Cabernet Sauvignon Columbia Valley 1994 • $16 • (8/31/1997) SS • **89**

Cabernet Sauvignon Columbia Valley 1993 • $14 • (4/30/1996) • **89**

Cabernet Sauvignon Columbia Valley 1992 • $14 • (7/31/1995) • **86**

Cabernet Sauvignon Columbia Valley 1991 • $14 • (9/30/1994) • **88**

Cabernet Sauvignon Columbia Valley 1990 • $14 • (7/31/1994) • **87**

Cabernet Sauvignon Columbia Valley 1989 • $14 • (3/15/1993) • **88**

Cabernet Sauvignon Columbia Valley 1988 • $13 • (8/31/1991) • **84**

Cabernet Sauvignon Columbia Valley 1986 • $12 • (9/30/1990) • **88**

Cabernet Sauvignon Columbia Valley Canoe Ridge Estate Vineyard 1996: On the crisp side, this is not as supple as previous vintages. Shows fine-grained tannins and juicy acidity around a core of blackberry and cherry, which persist on the firm finish. Best after 2001.–H.S. • $22 • (9/30/1999) • **87**

Cabernet Sauvignon Columbia Valley Cold Creek Vineyard 1996: Rich, ripe and focused, this Washington Cabernet shows layers of currant, plum and vanilla flavors, with hints of pepper and bay leaf sneaking in on the long, supple finish. Fine-grained tannins. Best from 2001 through 2008.–H.S. • $25 • (2/29/2000) SS • **92**

Cabernet Sauvignon Columbia Valley Cold Creek Vineyard 1995: Firm in structure, but open-textured enough to let its currant, plum and gentle herb flavors cascade beautifully through the tasty finish. Has plenty of character. Needs a bit of cellaring to soften the edges. Best after 2000.–H.S. • $25 • (11/15/1998) • **89**

Cabernet Sauvignon Columbia Valley Cold Creek Vineyard 1993 • $26 • (8/31/1996) • **87**

Cabernet Sauvignon Columbia Valley Cold Creek Vineyard 1992 • $26 • (12/15/1995) SS • **92**

Cabernet Sauvignon Columbia Valley Cold Creek Vineyard 1991 • $22 • (1/31/1995) • **88**

Cabernet Sauvignon Columbia Valley Cold Creek Vineyard Limited Bottling 1987 • $20 • (8/31/1991) • **83**

Cabernet Sauvignon Columbia Valley Horse Heaven Vineyard 1995: Crisp at the core, with pretty black cherry and toast flavors wrapping around the chewy texture. Harmonious and well crafted. Drink through 2003–H.S. • $27 • (9/15/1998) • **88**

Cabernet Sauvignon Columbia Valley Horse Heaven Vineyard 1994 • $27 • (8/31/1997) • **90**

Cabernet Sauvignon Columbia Valley Horse Heaven Vineyard 1993 • $27 • (8/31/1996) • **87**

Cabernet Sauvignon Columbia Valley River Ridge Vineyard Limited Bottling 1987 • $18 • (8/31/1991) • **87**

Cabernet Sauvignon Columbia Valley Twentieth Vintage 1987 • $12 • (9/30/1990) • **85**

CHATEAU STE. MICHELLE

Cabernet Sauvignon Washington 1985 • $12 • (10/15/1989) • **85**
Cabernet Sauvignon Washington 1984 • $11 • (12/31/1988) • **89**
Cabernet Sauvignon Washington 1983 • $10 • (11/15/1987) • **81**
Cabernet Sauvignon Washington Cold Creek Vineyard Limited Bottling 1985 • $16 • (10/15/1989) • **82**
Cabernet Sauvignon Washington River Ridge Vineyard Limited Bottling 1985 • $17 • (11/30/1990) HR • **90**
Chardonnay Columbia Valley 1998: Bright and juicy, a snappy mouthful of lime-tinged pear and apple with a nice halo of spicy oak hovering in the background on the finish. Drink now through 2002.–H.S. • $13 • (6/30/2000) • **87**
Chardonnay Columbia Valley 1996: Fresh and appealing for its round texture and pretty pineapple, citrus and apple flavors that last impressively on the finish, with hints of spice echoing on the aftertaste. Earns points for price and availability, too. A Washington beauty. Drink now through 2001.–H.S. • $14 • (9/15/1998) HR • **89**
Chardonnay Columbia Valley Canoe Ridge Estate Vineyard 1997: On the lighter side for this vineyard; bright, youthful and appealing for its jazzy pear, spice and vanilla flavors that linger on the brisk, lively finish. Drink now through 2001.–H.S. • $20 • (9/15/1999) • **87**
Chardonnay Columbia Valley Canoe Ridge Estate Vineyard 1996: Light and lithe, a pretty mouthful of apple and nectarine flavors, with hints of mushroom and spice on the gentle finish. Deftly balanced and begs for drinking soon, now through 1999.–H.S. • $28 • (9/15/1998) • **89**
Chardonnay Columbia Valley Cold Creek Vineyard 1997: Ripe and intense, this outstanding Washington Chardonnay deftly balances its sharply focused core of vibrant pear, apple and citrus flavors against creamy, spicy overtones, the ensemble coming together harmoniously on the long finish. Drink now through 2004.–H.S. • $25 • (9/15/1999) SS • **92**
Chardonnay Columbia Valley Cold Creek Vineyard 1996: This Washington white is bright in flavor and focused tightly, showing pretty apple and pear notes, echoing spice and mint on the lively finish. Delicious now, so why wait? Enjoy through 2001.–H.S. • $26 • (9/15/1998) SS • **92**
Chardonnay Columbia Valley Indian Wells Vineyard 1996: Smooth and silky, this outstanding Washington white is a lovely mouthful of peach, spice, pear, honey and vanilla, wrapped up harmoniously and elegantly. It's tempting now, will be best from 1999 through 2002.–H.S. • $24 • (11/15/1998) SS • **91**
Chardonnay Columbia Valley Reserve 1997: This Washington offering is supple in texture, generous and beautifully proportioned to emphasize its honey- and spice-scented pear and sweet orange flavors that echo persistently on the long, long finish. Yummy. Drink now through 2004.–H.S. • $29 • (3/31/2000) SS • **92**
Chardonnay Columbia Valley Reserve 1996: Smooth and supple. A generous mouthful of honey-tinged apple and green fig flavors echoing with a tinge of lime on the finish. Goes for elegance over power. Drink now.–H.S. • $29 • (11/15/1998) • **90**
Chateau Reserve Ice Wine Columbia Valley 1995 • $30/375 ml. • (6/15/1997) • **95**
Ethos Reserve Columbia Valley 1995: Ripe and round, with firm tannins underpinning the smoky, gamy blackberry and currant flavors. Needs cellaring to smooth the edges. Best from 2001 through 2006.–H.S. • $29 • (5/31/1999) • **88**
Meritage Columbia Valley 1996: Has a tough edge to the spicy mushroom and cherry flavors, clamping down on the finish with some formidable tannins. Needs cellaring, but it shows promise. Best after 2002.–H.S. • $50 • (9/15/1999) • **87**
Meritage Columbia Valley 1995: Smooth and juicy, with black cherry and blackberry sliding gently over the supple structure, echoing fruit and chocolate on the finish. Stylish, with immediate appeal and more going on with each sip. A blend of Cabernet Sauvignon, Merlot, Cabernet Franc and Malbec. Drink now through 2002.–H.S. • $50 • (12/15/1998) • **91**
Meritage Columbia Valley Red 1994 • $50 • (9/15/1997) • **91**
Meritage Washington 1993 • $30 • (9/30/1996) • **88**
Merlot Columbia Valley 1997: Supple and appealing for its graceful style and cedar- and spice-scented berry and black cherry flavors. Finishes on the light side, but it's persistent. Drink now through 2002.–H.S. • $18 • (3/31/2000) • **88**
Merlot Columbia Valley 1996: Round and generous, with dark berry, tar, smoke and spice flavors that linger on the open-textured finish. Fine tannins can use some cellaring. Drink through 2004–H.S. • $18 • (1/31/1999) • **88**

Key: SS—Spectator Selection. CS—Cellar Selection. HR—Highly Recommended. $NA—Price not available. (BT)—Barrel tasting. Ⓐ—Auction Price. For a key to the tasters' initials, see "How to Use These Listings."
Dates in parentheses represent the issues in which the ratings were published.

Merlot Columbia Valley 1994 • $18 • (8/31/1997) • **85**
Merlot Columbia Valley 1993 • $15 • (5/31/1996) • **87**
Merlot Columbia Valley 1992 • $15 • (9/30/1995) • **83**
Merlot Columbia Valley 1990 • $14 • (4/15/1994) • **87**
Merlot Columbia Valley 1989 • $14 • (6/15/1993) • **85**
Merlot Columbia Valley 1988 • $15 • (3/31/1992) • **84**
Merlot Columbia Valley 1987 • $12 • (9/30/1990) • **84**
Merlot Columbia Valley 1986 • $12 • (9/30/1990) • **84**
Merlot Columbia Valley Canoe Ridge Estate Vineyard 1996: Lithe and polished, nicely proportioned with pretty black cherry and spice flavors that linger enticingly on the smooth finish. Drink now through 2003.–H.S. • $22 • (9/15/1999) • **88**
Merlot Columbia Valley Canoe Ridge Estate Vineyard 1995: Mouthfilling flavors on a supple, elegant frame make this immediately appealing. The cherry and tobacco character picks up a pretty peach note on the fine-grained finish. Best after1998.–H.S. • $29 • (11/15/1998) • **89**
Merlot Columbia Valley Canoe Ridge Estate Vineyard 1994 • $31 • (8/31/1997) • **90**
Merlot Columbia Valley Canoe Ridge Estate Vineyard 1993 • $28 • (6/15/1996) • **88**
Merlot Columbia Valley Cold Creek Vineyard 1994 • $29 • (8/31/1997) • **91**
Merlot Columbia Valley Cold Creek Vineyard 1993 • $28 • (6/15/1996) HR • **90**
Merlot Columbia Valley Cold Creek Vineyard 1987 • $19 • (6/15/1993) • **79**
Merlot Columbia Valley Cold Creek Vineyard Limited Bottling 1987 • $19 • (8/31/1991) • **81**
Merlot Columbia Valley Horse Heaven Vineyard 1995: Ripe and appealing for its firm-textured plum, cherry and spice flavors that expand and persist on the generous finish. Tannins are a bit grainy, but this feels like it has plenty of room to grow. Drink through 2005–H.S. • $31 • (9/15/1998) • **91**
Merlot Columbia Valley Horse Heaven Vineyard 1993 • $27 • (6/15/1996) • **88**
Merlot Columbia Valley Indian Wells Vineyard 1994 • $31 • (9/15/1997) • **87**
Merlot Columbia Valley Indian Wells Vineyard 1992 • $30 • (9/30/1995) • **90**
Merlot Columbia Valley Indian Wells Vineyard 1991 • $20 • (9/30/1994) • **88**
Merlot Columbia Valley Reserve 1995: Silky texture makes this immediately appealing as it shows off its pretty blackberry and plum flavors. The fruit swirls through the soft finish, echoing on the delicate aftertaste. A well-made wine that keeps its oak nicely in check. Drink now through 2004.–H.S. • $42 • (9/15/1998) • **90**
Merlot Columbia Valley Reserve 1994 • $42 • (9/15/1997) • **92**
Merlot Columbia Valley River Ridge Vineyard 1985 • $18 • (9/30/1990) • **89**
Merlot Washington 1983 • $10 • (12/31/1988) • **80**
Merlot Washington River Ridge Vineyard 1985 • $14 • (10/15/1989) • **87**
Merlot Washington River Ridge Vineyard Château Reserve 1983 • $15 • (12/31/1988) • **87**
Pinot Gris Columbia Valley Vineyard Select 1997: Light and fruity. A dry wine with pretty apple and peach flavors, turning slightly syrupy on the finish. Drink now.–H.S. • $14 • (12/31/1999) • **85**
Pinot Noir Columbia Valley Limited Bottling 1987 • $11 • (8/31/1991) • **79**
Riesling Columbia Valley Cold Creek Vineyard 1998: Soft, slightly sweet and appealing for its delicate nectarine and citrus flavors that linger on the smooth finish. Drink now.–H.S. • $12 • (11/15/1999) • **87**
Riesling Columbia Valley Vineyard Select 1997: Soft and pleasant, offering a nice mouthful of delicate pear and honey flavors that linger tastily on the finish. Drink now.–H.S. • $12 • (1/31/1999) • **85**
Sauvignon Blanc Columbia Valley 1998: Juicy and refreshing for its floral, pear and apple flavors, with a touch of herb on the finish. Drink now.–H.S. • $10 • (5/15/2000) • **85**
Sauvignon Blanc Columbia Valley Horse Heaven Vineyard 1997: Fresh and juicy, a light-textured wine with gentle herb notes among the citrus and apple flavors, lingering nicely on the finish. Drink now.–H.S. • $14 • (8/31/1999) • **87**
Sauvignon Blanc Columbia Valley Horse Heaven Vineyard 1996 • $15 • (6/30/1998) • **85**
Sémillon Columbia Valley 1997: How about a bargain on a change-of-pace white? Fresh-tasting and tightly packed, this lean Washington Sémillon displays a well-focused beam of spicy grapefruit and tobacco flavors that linger on the light finish. Drink now through 2002.–H.S. • $8 • (8/31/1999) • **86**
Sémillon Columbia Valley 1996: Bright in flavor and texture, with earthy tobacco notes adding interest to the melon flavors. Drink now.–H.S. • $8 • (12/15/1998) • **83**
Sémillon Late Harvest Columbia Valley Reserve 1995 • $20/375 ml. • (3/31/1998) • **92**
Sémillon Late Harvest Columbia Valley Reserve 1992 • $20/375 ml. • (4/30/1995) • **90**
Syrah Columbia Valley Reserve 1995: Ripe and satiny, layering its plum and blackberry flavors in a lovely swirl of spice and sweet leather on the fine-grained finish. Drink now through 2001.–H.S. • $27 • (9/15/1998) • **88**

White Riesling Columbia Valley Late Harvest Reserve 1997: Light in color but sweet and extraordinarily rich in flavor, piling on the apricot, walnut, vanilla, pear and spice. Starts off stronger than it finishes, but give it time. Drink now through 2009.–H.S. • $19/375 ml. • (9/30/1999) • **90**

White Riesling Columbia Valley Late Harvest Reserve 1996: Light and sweet, with pretty lime and meringue flavors and tart acidity on the finish. Needs time. Best from 2002 through 2006.–H.S. • $19/375 ml. • (6/30/1999) • **87**

White Riesling Late Harvest Columbia Valley Chateau Reserve 1991 • $9/375 ml. • (9/15/1995) HR • **93**

White Riesling Late Harvest Columbia Valley Horse Heaven Vineyard Chateau Reserve 1995 • $17/375 ml. • (2/28/1997) SS • **90**

White Riesling Late Harvest Columbia Valley River Ridge Vineyard Hand-Selected Cluster 1989 • $18 • (9/30/1991) • **82**

CHATEAU WOLTNER | CALIFORNIA

Chardonnay Howell Mountain 1997: Tight and flinty, with crisp pear, lemon and apple notes, good concentration and pure flavor, but lacking in extra dimensions. Drink now.–J.L. • $14 • (9/30/1998) • **85**

Chardonnay Howell Mountain 1996 • $13 • (11/30/1997) • **83**

Chardonnay Howell Mountain Frederique Vineyard 1998: Crisp, with tart grapefruit and lemon-lime notes, turning earthy. Drink now through 2005.–J.L. • $40 • (5/15/2000) • **86**

Chardonnay Howell Mountain Frederique Vineyard 1997: Clean and flinty, with rich pear, fig and melon, squeezing in a hint of citrus. Gains finesse and focus on the finish. Drink through 2004–J.L. • $40 • (6/15/1999) • **89**

Chardonnay Howell Mountain Frederique Vineyard 1996: Tight, tart and green around the edges, with modestly ripe peach, pear and nectarine. Shortens up on the finish, but perhaps with more time the flavors will stretch out. Drink now through 2001.–J.L. • $40 • (9/30/1998) • **86**

Chardonnay Howell Mountain St. Thomas Vineyard 1998: Tart and a touch green, with a lemony streak running through it. Turns earthy. Drink now.–J.L. • $23 • (5/31/2000) • **80**

Chardonnay Howell Mountain St. Thomas Vineyard 1997: Floral and grapey, with a slight grassy edge, this is a crisp, clean wine marked by mineral, citrus and tart pear. Needs time. Drink through 2004–J.L. • $23 • (7/31/1999) • **87**

Chardonnay Howell Mountain St. Thomas Vineyard 1996: A touch earthy, with mineral, citrus, pear and spice notes. No oak or malolactic flavor or texture dominates, so if you like your Chardonnay pure and unoaked, this one's for you. Drink now through 2001.–J.L. • $23 • (9/30/1998) • **86**

Chardonnay Howell Mountain Titus Vineyard 1998: Tart and lemony, with a strong citrus edge. For fans of Chablis-style California Chardonnay. To be released June 2000. Best from 2001 through 2005.–J.L. • $40 • (5/15/2000) • **85**

Chardonnay Howell Mountain Titus Vineyard 1997: Tight and juicy, with ripe, rich grapefruit, pear and lemon, picking up complex fig and light oak shadings. Impressive. Drink now through 2005.–J.L. • $40 • (6/15/1999) • **89**

Chardonnay Howell Mountain Titus Vineyard 1996: Young, tight and focused, with barely ripe peach, pear and citrus flavors. Holds its focus through the finish, revealing complex layers of flavor. Drink now through 2001.–J.L. • $40 • (9/30/1998) • **88**

Private Reserve Red Howell Mountain 1995: An austere style, the hints of cedar, tobacco, plum and currant tinged with significant tannins. Tasted three times, with consistent notes. Best from 2001 through 2009.–J.L. • $50 • (11/15/1998) • **85**

CHATOM | CALIFORNIA

Cabernet Sauvignon Calaveras County 1994 • $18 • (9/15/1997) • **81**

Cabernet Sauvignon Calaveras County 1993 • $16 • (11/30/1996) • **85**

Cabernet Sauvignon Calaveras County 1992 • $12 • (6/15/1995) • **84**

Cabernet Sauvignon Calaveras County 1991 • $12 • (11/15/1994) • **83**

Cabernet Sauvignon Calaveras County 1989 • $14 • (11/15/1992) • **84**

Merlot Calaveras County 1994 • $16 • (9/30/1997) • **80**

Merlot Calaveras County 1992 • $14 • (7/31/1995) • **74**

Merlot Calaveras County 1991 • $14 • (9/15/1994) • **85**

Sangiovese Calaveras County 1992 • $14 • (9/30/1994) • **70**

Sangiovese Calaveras County Gitano 1997: Medium-bodied, with dry, leathery black cherry, brown sugar and spice flavors, turning tannic. Drink now through 2004.–J.L. • $16 • (1/31/2000) • **81**

Sauvignon Blanc Calaveras County 1998: Decent weight, with vanilla and citrus flavors and a slightly raw mouthfeel. Drink now.–J.L. • $12 • (5/15/2000) • **82**

Syrah Calaveras County 1996: Quite spicy, and a bit hot on the palate. Shows some pretty cherry and herb flavors, but becomes somewhat muddled on the oaky, tannic finish. Drink now through 2002. • $23 • (5/31/1999) • **82**

Syrah Calaveras County 1995 • $20 • (9/30/1997) • **86**

Zinfandel Calaveras County 1997: Plum and mustard seed notes are tart and drying. Drink now.–J.L. • $14 • (5/31/2000) • **81**

Zinfandel Calaveras County 1994 • $9 • (9/15/1997) • **75**

Zinfandel Calaveras County 1993 • $9 • (4/30/1996) • **77**

Zinfandel Calaveras County 1992 • $8 • (7/31/1995) • **84**

Zinfandel Calaveras County 1991 • $8 • (10/15/1994) • **81**

Zinfandel Calaveras County 1989 • $8 • (9/30/1993) • **84**

CHAUFFE-EAU | CALIFORNIA

Cabernet Sauvignon Alexander Valley 1987 • $16 • (8/31/1992) • **85**

Cabernet Sauvignon Alexander Valley Smith-Reichel Vineyard 1996: An intriguing blend of herbal, mint, plum and black cherry flavor works well with mineral and tar notes. Rich, focused, with fine-grained tannins and a full-bodied finish. Drink through 2006–J.L. • $21 • (9/15/1999) • **89**

Cabernet Sauvignon Alexander Valley Smith-Reichel Vineyard 1995 • $19 • (6/30/1998) • **88**

Chardonnay Carneros Sangiacomo Vineyard 1996 • $20 • (6/15/1998) • **88**

Merlot Sonoma Valley Kunde Vineyards 1996: A little off-balance, with a hint of bitterness to the berry and herb notes. Firm, with a moderate finish. Drink now through 2002. • $19 • (10/15/1999) • **82**

Merlot Sonoma Valley Kunde Vineyards 1995 • $19 • (5/31/1998) • **86**

Merlot Sonoma Valley Kunde Vineyards 1992 • $17 • (9/30/1995) • **82**

Pinot Noir Carneros 1996 • $22 • (6/15/1998) • **85**

Pinot Noir Carneros 1993 • $19 • (3/31/1996) • **71**

CHEHALEM | OREGON

Cerise Ridgecrest Vineyards Oregon 1993 • $12 • (1/31/1996) • **77**

Cerise Ridgecrest Vineyards Oregon 1992 • $12 • (11/30/1994) • **82**

Cerise Willamette Valley Ridgecrest Vineyards NV • $12 • (12/31/1997) • **79**

Chardonnay Willamette Valley 1998: Crisp and enticing, with bright apple, peach and spice flavors that float through the racy finish. Drink now through 2003.–H.S. • $19 • (5/15/2000) • **88**

Chardonnay Willamette Valley 1997: A supple wine, light and pretty, with refreshing citrus and pear flavors, picking up a floral note on the finish. Drink now through 2001.–H.S. • $19 • (4/30/1999) • **85**

Chardonnay Willamette Valley 1996 • $17 • (5/15/1998) • **88**

Chardonnay Willamette Valley Ian's Reserve 1997: Ripe, supple and generous without being the least bit heavy, a refined white that offers spicy pear, honey and toast flavors on an elegant frame. Drink now through 2006.–H.S. • $32 • (9/30/1999) • **89**

Chardonnay Willamette Valley Reserve 1996 • $27 • (6/30/1998) • **88**

Pinot Gris Willamette Valley 1998: Bright and fresh, with lively apple, melon and mineral flavors that hold through the stony finish. Feels like it can develop more with age. Drink now through 2004.–H.S. • $14 • (12/31/1999) • **87**

Pinot Gris Willamette Valley 1997: Bright and ripe, with refreshingly crisp melon, peach and almond flavors that linger on the open-textured finish. Drink now.–H.S. • $14 • (11/15/1998) • **88**

Pinot Gris Willamette Valley Reserve 1998: Bright and appealing for its generous peach and tropical fruit aromas and flavors. Finishes soft and mildly spicy. Drink now.–H.S. • $19 • (4/30/2000) • **88**

Pinot Gris Willamette Valley Ridgecrest Vineyards 1996 • $14 • (9/15/1997) • **82**

Pinot Gris Willamette Valley Ridgecrest Vineyards Reserve 1997: Dry, almost austere, but it sounds pretty melon and citrus notes on the finish. Feels like it has room to fill out. Drink now through 2002.–H.S. • $19 • (4/30/1999) • **86**

Pinot Gris Willamette Valley Ridgecrest Vineyards Reserve 1996 • $19 • (5/15/1998) • **89**

Pinot Noir Oregon Ridgecrest Vineyards 1993 • $20 • (1/31/1996) • **82**

Pinot Noir Oregon Ridgecrest Vineyards 1992 • $20 • (11/30/1994) • **85**

Pinot Noir Oregon Ridgecrest Vineyards 1991 • $16 • (11/30/1994) • **88**

Pinot Noir Oregon Rion Reserve 1997: Bright and open-textured, with black cherry, vanilla and spice flavors that linger generously on the finish. Drink now through 2003.–H.S. • $38 • (4/30/2000) • **86**

Pinot Noir Oregon Ridgecrest Vineyards 1990 • $15 • (11/30/1994) • **85**

Pinot Noir Oregon Ridgecrest Vineyards Rion Reserve 1996: Light and appealing for its polished, supple texture, unusual for '96, with pretty tea and raspberry flavors echoing on the subtle finish. Drink now through 2001.–H.S. • $38 • (4/30/1999) • **87**

Pinot Noir Willamette Valley Rion Reserve 1995 • $34 • (10/15/1997) • **86**

Pinot Noir Willamette Valley Ridgecrest Vineyards Rion Reserve 1994 • $42 • (1/31/1997) • **91**

CHEHALEM

Pinot Noir Oregon Ridgecrest Vineyards Wadenswil Selection 1993 • $20 • (1/31/1996) • **79**

Pinot Noir Willamette Valley 3 Vineyard 1997: Light and velvety, with modest tannins around a delicate core of currant and spice flavors. Drink now through 2002.–H.S. • $18 • (9/30/1999) • **84**

Pinot Noir Willamette Valley 3 Vineyard 1996 • $18 • (5/15/1998) • **88**

Pinot Noir Willamette Valley 3 Vineyard 1995 • $15 • (2/28/1997) • **80**

Pinot Noir Willamette Valley Ridgecrest Vineyards 1997: A pretty, straightforward Pinot, with strawberry and plum aromas and flavors on a fine-textured frame. Drink now.–H.S. • $28 • (4/30/2000) • **84**

Pinot Noir Willamette Valley Ridgecrest Vineyards 1996: Has a wild, gamy side that adds interest to the light, supple mineral and orange peel flavors. Fine tannins don't get in the way of the berry flavors echoing on the finish. Drink now through 2001.–H.S. • $28 • (4/30/1999) • **86**

Pinot Noir Willamette Valley Ridgecrest Vineyards 1995 • $25 • (10/15/1997) • **80**

Pinot Noir Willamette Valley Ridgecrest Vineyards 1994 • $23 • (12/31/1996) • **88**

Pinot Noir Willamette Valley Stoller Vineyards 1997: Smooth and inviting for its spicy, slightly gamy black cherry flavors; the polished frame lets the flavors echo nicely on the round finish. Drink now through 2003.–H.S. • $28 • (9/30/1999) • **86**

CHERRY HILL WASHINGTON

Cabernet-Merlot Columbia Valley 1994 • $8 • (9/15/1996) • **86**

CHIMERE CALIFORNIA

Merlot Santa Barbara County 1992 • $16 • (7/31/1995) • **83**

Merlot Santa Barbara County Bien Nacido Vineyard 1994 • $18 • (5/31/1998) • **79**

Nebbiolo Santa Barbara County 1992 • $15 • (12/15/1995) • **77**

Pinot Noir Edna Valley 1995 • $18 • (5/15/1998) • **77**

Pinot Noir Santa Barbara County Bien Nacido Vineyard 1994 • $24 • (3/31/1997) • **88**

CHIMNEY ROCK CALIFORNIA

Cabernet Sauvignon Napa Valley 1996: Sleek and elegant, with ripe and spicy cherry, wild berry and strawberry flavors. Turns supple and polished on the finish. Drink through 2007–J.L. • $30 • (4/30/1999) • **90**

Cabernet Sauvignon Napa Valley 1995 • $28 • (5/15/1998) SS • **90**

Cabernet Sauvignon Napa Valley 1994 • $24 • (7/31/1997) • **90**

Cabernet Sauvignon Napa Valley Reserve 1997: Complex and well integrated, with layers of black cherry, currant, toasty oak and spice. Impressive balance and texture.–J.L. • $NA • (8/31/1998) (BT) • **90-94**

Cabernet Sauvignon Stags Leap District 1992 • $22 • (5/15/1996) • **83**

Cabernet Sauvignon Stags Leap District 1990 • $20 • (4/30/1994) • **85**

Cabernet Sauvignon Stags Leap District 1989 • $18 • (3/31/1993) • **76**

Cabernet Sauvignon Stags Leap District 1988 • $18 • (8/31/1992) • **87**

Cabernet Sauvignon Stags Leap District 1987 • $29 • (7/31/1991) SS • **90**

Cabernet Sauvignon Stags Leap District 1986 • $19 • (9/30/1989) • **87**

Cabernet Sauvignon Stags Leap District 1985 • $15 • (10/31/1988) • **88**

Cabernet Sauvignon Stags Leap District 1984 • $15 • (4/30/1988) • **87**

Cabernet Sauvignon Stags Leap District Reserve 1996: Firm and chunky up front, turning rich and complex, with layers of anise, currant, black cherry and cedar, finishing with enough tannin to merit short-term cellaring. Best from 2001 through 2008.–J.L. • $60 • (9/15/1999) • **88**

Cabernet Sauvignon Stags Leap District Reserve 1995: Showing a distinct smoky, toasty oak flavor at this point, with supple plum and berry flavors emerging. Needs more time to come together, but seems to lack the concentration and richness to merit a $60 price tag. Try through 2004.–J.L. • $60 • (10/31/1998) • **87**

Cabernet Sauvignon Stags Leap District Reserve 1994 • $50 • (10/15/1997) • **91**

Cabernet Sauvignon Stags Leap District Reserve 1993 • $40 • (11/30/1996) • **90**

Chardonnay Carneros 1996 • $17 • (5/31/1998) • **86**

Key: SS—Spectator Selection. CS—Cellar Selection. HR—Highly Recommended. $NA—Price not available. (BT)—Barrel tasting. Ⓐ—Auction Price. For a key to the tasters' initials, see "How to Use These Listings."
Dates in parentheses represent the issues in which the ratings were published.

Elevage Stags Leap District 1996: Smooth and supple, with polished currant, black cherry and berry flavors. Picks up cedary oak and anise notes on the firm finish. Drink now through 2006.–J.L. • $45 • (10/15/1999) • **87**

Elevage Stags Leap District 1995: An elegant, understated style, with ripe, spicy cherry, wild berry and plummy flavors, finishing with soft, fleshy tannins and pretty toasty oak shadings. Drink now through 2004.–J.L. • $45 • (10/31/1998) • **89**

Elevage Stags Leap District 1994 • $40 • (10/15/1997) • **88**

Elevage Stags Leap District 1993 • $40 • (11/30/1996) • **88**

Elevage Stags Leap District 1992 • $30 • (12/15/1995) • **88**

Elevage Stags Leap District 1991 • $30 • (11/15/1994) • **90**

Elevage Stags Leap District 1990 • $30 • (11/15/1993) • **88**

Fumé Blanc Napa Valley 1997: Somewhat sprightly in texture, serving up moderate mineral, hay, herb, citrus and melon flavors. Pleasant enough, just comes up a little short on the finish. Drink now. • $13 • (5/15/1999) • **84**

Fumé Blanc Napa Valley 1996 • $12 • (5/15/1998) • **83**

Reserve Stags Leap District Red 1992 • $30 • (12/15/1995) • **92**

CHINA BEND WASHINGTON

Nouveau Organic Red Wine Washington 1994 • $16 • (9/30/1995) • **81**

CHRISTINE WOODS CALIFORNIA

Pinot Noir Alexander Valley 1989 • $10 • (2/28/1993) • **69**

Pinot Noir Anderson Valley NV • $10 • (12/31/1995) • **80**

Pinot Noir Anderson Valley 1990 • $12 • (2/28/1993) • **72**

Pinot Noir Anderson Valley Estate Reserve 1997: Medium-bodied, with exotic spices and herbs and a touch of orange peel. The ripe plummy flavors turn earthy on the finish. Drink now through 2001. • $22 • (9/15/1999) • **84**

Pinot Noir Anderson Valley Estate Reserve 1993 • $16 • (2/28/1997) • **68**

Pinot Noir Anderson Valley Estate Reserve 1992 • $16 • (5/15/1995) • **79**

CHRISTOPHE CALIFORNIA

Cabernet Sauvignon California 1995: Light cherry and oak flavors are simple, here, in this lightweight wine. • $9 • (11/15/1998) • **75**

Cabernet Sauvignon Napa County 1994 • $9 • (5/15/1997) • **79**

Cabernet Sauvignon Napa County 1993 • $9 • (11/30/1996) • **82**

Cabernet Sauvignon Napa County 1992 • $9 • (12/15/1995) • **84**

Cabernet Sauvignon Napa County 1991 • $8 • (12/15/1995) • **75**

Cabernet Sauvignon Napa Valley 1990 • $9 • (7/15/1993) • **78**

Cabernet Sauvignon California 1989 • $7 • (8/31/1992) • **77**

Cabernet Sauvignon California 1988 • $9 • (3/31/1991) • **83**

Cabernet Sauvignon Napa Valley Reserve 1986 • $12 • (11/15/1990) • **78**

Cabernet Sauvignon Napa Valley Reserve 1985 • $13 • (11/15/1989) • **74**

Pinot Noir California 1995 • $9 • (2/28/1998) • **79**

Pinot Noir North Coast 1993 • $9 • (7/31/1996) • **79**

Pinot Noir Napa Valley Carneros 1992 • $8 • (3/31/1995) • **83**

Pinot Noir Sonoma County Reserve 1990 • $10 • (2/28/1993) • **75**

Pinot Noir Napa Valley Carneros Reserve 1989 • $9 • (9/30/1992) • **84**

CHRISTOPHER CREEK CALIFORNIA

Petite Sirah Russian River Valley 1996: Deep, dark and minerally, with flavors of black cherry, tar, grilled meat and herbs. Finishes with surprisingly supple tannins. Drink through 2004–J.L. • $18 • (3/31/1999) • **86**

Petite Sirah Russian River Valley 1995 • $18 • (3/31/1998) • **85**

Petite Sirah Russian River Valley 1988 • $11 • (10/15/1993) • **79**

Syrah Russian River Valley 1996: Tight, with firm tannins. Holds its cherry, anise and cedar flavors close to the vest, though they start to fan out nicely on the bright, moderate finish. Drink through 2005 • $18 • (12/31/1998) • **86**

Syrah Russian River Valley 1993 • $14 • (2/28/1997) • **84**

Syrah Russian River Valley 1992 • $14 • (5/15/1995) • **84**

Syrah Russian River Valley 1990 • $14 • (10/31/1993) • **86**

Syrah Russian River Valley Reserve 1997: Good richness, with fine intensity of cola and blackberry notes and lingering chocolate flavors. Drink now through 2004.–J.L. • $24 • (5/15/2000) • **87**

Zinfandel Dry Creek Valley 1998: Oaky, with the wood flavors dominating the berry and spice notes, finishing slightly sour.–J.L. • $22 • (6/15/2000) • **79**

CINNABAR CALIFORNIA

Cabernet Sauvignon Santa Cruz Mountains 1990 • $20 • (11/15/1994) • **84**

Cabernet Sauvignon Santa Cruz Mountains 1989 • $20 • (3/31/1993) • **82**

Cabernet Sauvignon Santa Cruz Mountains 1987 • $18 • (3/31/1991) • **84**

Cabernet Sauvignon Santa Cruz Mountains 1986 • $15 • (11/15/1989) • **93**
Cabernet Sauvignon Santa Cruz Mountains Saratoga Vineyard 1994 • $25 • (11/15/1997) • **88**
Cabernet Sauvignon Santa Cruz Mountains Saratoga Vineyard 1993 • $25 • (10/15/1996) • **89**
Cabernet Sauvignon Santa Cruz Mountains Saratoga Vineyard 1992 • $20 • (12/15/1995) • **88**
Cabernet Sauvignon Santa Cruz Mountains Saratoga Vineyard 1988 • $20 • (3/15/1992) • **82**
Chardonnay Santa Cruz Mountains Saratoga Vineyard 1996: Creamy texture is backed by a touch of tangy acidity. The wine sports a solid flint and mineral core, yet fans out to include melon, mango, pear and citrus flavors. Finishes clean. Drink now through 2002. • $23 • (6/30/1999) • **91**
Merlot Central Coast 1997: Light-textured, with hints of plum, earth, tar, coffee and herbs. Tannins are a bit coarse and the finish moderate. Drink now through 2002. • $18 • (10/15/1999) • **82**
Merlot Central Coast 1995 • $18 • (3/31/1997) • **85**

CIRRI | CALIFORNIA

Cabernet Sauvignon Alexander Valley 1992 • $10 • (12/15/1995) • **86**
Cabernet Sauvignon Alexander Valley 1991 • $10 • (11/15/1994) • **79**
Merlot Sonoma Valley 1992 • $10 • (3/31/1996) • **79**
Merlot Sonoma Valley 1991 • $11 • (9/15/1994) • **85**

CLAAR | WASHINGTON

Cabernet Sauvignon Columbia Valley 1996: On the smallish side for a Cabernet, but nicely turned, with pretty black cherry, currant and herb flavors in a soft package. Drink now through 2003.–H.S. • $15 • (6/30/1999) • **85**
Chardonnay Columbia Valley 1997: Supple, generous with its apple and honey flavors, hinting at almond, citrus and cream on the tangy finish. Drink now.–H.S. • $11 • (1/31/1999) • **87**
Riesling Columbia Valley Dry 1997: Earth, tobacco and stalk flavors cut through whatever fruit is present.–H.S. • $6 • (6/30/1999) • **73**
Riesling Columbia Valley Late Harvest 1996: Soft and frankly sweet, with earthy melon notes echoing on the finish. Drink now.–H.S. • $8 • (9/15/1998) • **80**

CLAIBORNE & CHURCHILL | CALIFORNIA

Chardonnay Edna Valley MacGregor Vineyard 1997: Quite earthy, with bright lemon flavors that border on canned fruit. The finish is fairly clean. • $18 • (7/31/1999) • **79**
Chardonnay Edna Valley MacGregor Vineyard 1996: Silky-textured, with a slightly earthy component that's followed by lemon, apple and pear flavors. Finishes a bit hot, but still quite interesting. Drink now. • $18 • (7/31/1998) • **87**
Gewürztraminer Central Coast Alsatian Style Dry 1997: Dry and appealingly floral, with orange-scented pear flavor at the core and a nutty note around the edges. Drink now.–H.S. • $12 • (7/31/1998) • **83**
Pinot Noir Edna Valley Runestone 1993 • $16 • (12/31/1995) • **78**
Pinot Noir Edna Valley MacGregor Vineyard 1992 • $15 • (12/31/1994) • **88**
Pinot Noir Edna Valley MacGregor Vineyard 1991 • $15 • (2/28/1994) • **82**
Pinot Noir Edna Valley MacGregor Vineyard 1990 • $12 • (2/28/1993) • **78**
Riesling Central Coast Alsatian Style Dry 1997: Dry and refreshing for its green apple and floral flavors, which are light in intensity. A straight-ahead Riesling for easy drinking. Drink now.–H.S. • $12 • (7/31/1998) • **85**

CLARK-CLAUDON | CALIFORNIA

Cabernet Sauvignon Napa Valley 1996: Herbal and earthy, the fruit tilts toward the just-ripe rather than the fully-ripe spectrum, with more sage, leather and tea than currant and cherry. Turns dry and tannic. Best from 2001 through 2005.–J.L. • $55 • (10/15/1999) • **86**
Cabernet Sauvignon Napa Valley 1995 • $67 Ⓐ • (6/15/1998) • **86**
Cabernet Sauvignon Napa Valley 1994 • $45 • (5/31/1997) • **92**
Cabernet Sauvignon Napa Valley 1993 • $50 • (12/15/1996) • **90**

CLAUDIA SPRINGS | CALIFORNIA

Chardonnay Anderson Valley 1996: Delicate and refreshing, with pretty sweet cream, pear and apple flavors. Softly textured, with a lingering finish. Drink now.–J.L. • $14 • (7/31/1998) • **84**
Chardonnay Anderson Valley Reserve 1996: Minerally, with a simple range of fruit flavors; pleasant peach, pear and earth notes linger on the finish. Drink now through 2000 .–J.L. • $20 • (7/31/1998) • **83**
Pinot Noir Anderson Valley 1996: Herb and ripe cherry flavors struggle to find focus but come together on the soft finish. Shows a touch of heat. Drink now.–J.L. • $18 • (8/31/1998) • **81**
Pinot Noir Anderson Valley 1991 • $13 • (2/28/1993) • **86**
Zinfandel Mendocino 1997: Smooth, with an array of pretty raspberry, currant, plum and herb flavors. Finishes with slightly earthy notes and mild tannins. Drink now.–J.L. • $15 • (11/15/1999) • **83**
Zinfandel Mendocino 1992 • $10 • (10/15/1994) • **81**
Zinfandel Mendocino Eaglepoint Vineyard 1997: Ripe, with smooth, concentrated black pepper, plum, raspberry and anise flavors. Fun and easy to drink, turning more complex on the finish. Drink now through 2004.–J.L. • $20 • (11/15/1999) • **87**
Zinfandel Mendocino Pacini Vineyard 1993 • $14 • (10/15/1995) • **85**
Zinfandel Redwood Valley Vassar Vineyard 1996 • $18 • (6/15/1998) • **81**

CLINE | CALIFORNIA

Carignane Contra Costa County 1994 • $12 • (11/30/1996) • **82**
Carignane Contra Costa County 1990 • $9 • (12/15/1992) • **86**
Carignane Contra Costa County Ancient Vines 1996: Fairly supple, with firm, ripe tannins, this wine shows black cherry, spice, vanilla and herb notes. Finishes moderately, almost plush. Drink now through 2002. • $18 • (1/31/1999) • **85**
Carignane Contra Costa County Ancient Vines 1995 • $18 • (12/15/1997) • **87**
Côtes d'Oakley Vin Blanc California 1998: Lots of fun in this bottle of white. It's rich and gooey, with fresh fennel, papaya, tangerine and melon flavors that are refreshing, not cloying. A blend of Marsanne, Roussanne, Viognier, Sémillon and others. Drink now through 2002.–J.L. • $9 • (2/29/2000) SS • **89**
Côtes d'Oakley Vin Blanc California 1997: Here's an interesting wine at a try-me price. Bracing acidity kicks off, followed by bright lemon, grapefruit, spice and melon flavors. Somewhat viscous in texture, this effusive white blend finishes on an almost sweet-and-sour note. A blend of Marsanne, Roussanne, Viognier, Palomino, Sémillon, Sauvignon Blanc, Muscat and Chenin Blanc. Drink now through 2002. • $9 • (12/31/1998) • **85**
Côtes d'Oakley Vin Rouge California 1996 • $9 • (3/31/1998) • **85**
Merlot California 1989 • $17 • (5/31/1992) • **75**
Mourvèdre Contra Costa County 1993 • $16 • (11/30/1996) • **82**
Mourvèdre Contra Costa County 1990 • $20 • (12/15/1995) • **81**
Mourvèdre Contra Costa County 1989 • $18 • (11/30/1991) • **86**
Mourvèdre Contra Costa County 1988 • $18 • (4/30/1990) • **91**
Mourvèdre Contra Costa County 1987 • $18 • (4/15/1989) • **82**
Mourvèdre Contra Costa County Ancient Vines 1996: Pretty cherry and currant flavors meet a healthy dose of oak in this somewhat weighty wine. Tannins and tangy acids shorten the finish a bit, but it's still quite pleasant. Drink now. • $18 • (1/31/1999) • **85**
Mourvèdre Contra Costa County Ancient Vines 1995 • $18 • (12/15/1997) • **87**
Mourvèdre Contra Costa County Reserve 1991 • $24 • (11/30/1996) • **88**
Mourvèdre Contra Costa County Reserve 1989 • $26 • (3/15/1992) • **78**
Oakley Cuvée Contra Costa County 1990 • $12 • (8/31/1995) • **85**
Oakley Cuvée Contra Costa County 1989 • $12 • (5/31/1991) • **88**
Oakley Cuvée Contra Costa County 1988 • $12 • (2/28/1990) • **90**
Roussanne Los Carneros 1998: Rich honeysuckle, melon and butter notes combine in a viscous package framed by oaky vanilla flavors. Tasted twice, with consistent notes. Drink now.–J.L. • $20 • (5/31/2000) • **86**
Roussanne Los Carneros 1997: Delicate on the palate, with a lean, firm core of lemon, pear and mineral flavors. Refreshingly clean on the finish, with a hint of mint and herb. Drink now. • $20 • (12/31/1998) • **87**
Syrah California 1998: Focused, with smoke, leather and spicy berry notes that remain concentrated through the firm finish. Great bang for the buck. Drink now through 2005.–J.L. • $10 • (5/31/2000) • **87**
Syrah Carneros 1997: Has good depth to the pleasant cracked pepper, blackberry and blueberry notes, but finishes with a slightly bitter note. Drink now through 2004.–J.L. • $20 • (11/15/1999) • **84**
Syrah Carneros 1995 • $18 • (9/30/1997) • **89**
Syrah Carneros 1994 • $17 • (1/31/1997) • **84**
Syrah Contra Costa County 1991 • $15 • (10/31/1993) • **84**
Vin Gris Côtes d'Oakley California 1996 • $9 • (9/30/1997) • **82**
Vin Rouge Côtes d'Oakley Contra Costa County 1991 • $8 • (12/31/1993) • **82**
Vin Rouge Côtes d'Oakley Contra Costa County 1990 • $8 • (11/15/1992) • **85**
Vin Rouge Côtes d'Oakley Contra Costa County 1989 • $8 • (5/31/1991) • **80**
Vin Rouge Côtes d'Oakley Contra Costa County 1988 • $9 • (4/30/1990) • **83**
Viognier Los Carneros 1997: Sits broadly on the palate, with a good dose of viscosity and a healthy dollop of acidity. Flavors are subtle, featuring peach, pear and lemon. Finishes with a fresh, minerally edge. Drink now through 2002. • $24 • (12/31/1998) • **87**
Viognier Los Carneros 1996 • $18 • (12/15/1997) • **84**

CLINE

Zinfandel California 1998: Milk chocolate, spice and plum flavors are round and easy to drink. Drink now through 2002.–J.L. • $10 • (6/15/2000) • **83**
Zinfandel California 1997: Have a yen for Zin? This one's very nice, and the price is right, too. It's rich and jammy-tasting, with harmonious plum, strawberry, spice and herb-laced flavors, finishing soft. Drink now through 2001 .–J.L. • $10 • (6/15/1999) • **86**
Zinfandel California 1996 • $10 • (11/15/1997) • **85**
Zinfandel Contra Costa County 1994 • $12 • (4/30/1996) • **87**
Zinfandel Contra Costa County 1993 • $12 • (9/15/1995) • **85**
Zinfandel Contra Costa County 1992: Tart, with earthy, tarry wild berry and raspberry fruit. Well focused, turning earthy on the aftertaste. Aging well. (Zinfandel retrospective tasting). Drink now through 2002.–J.L. • $10 • (6/30/1999) • **88**
Zinfandel Contra Costa County 1991 • $10 • (9/30/1993) • **84**
Zinfandel Contra Costa County 1990 • $10 • (10/15/1992) • **83**
Zinfandel Contra Costa County 1989 • $9 • (5/15/1991) • **86**
Zinfandel Contra Costa County Ancient Vines 1997: Solid, with a core of ripe black cherry, wild berry, raspberry and plum. Firms up on the finish, where the tannins weigh in. Drink now through 2007.–J.L. • $20 • (12/15/1999) • **89**
Zinfandel Contra Costa County Ancient Vines 1996: A ripe, full-bodied style, marked by an earthy, tarry edge to the rich berry and plummy Zinfandel fruit. Turns dry and tannic on the finish, so a short time in the cellar should help. Drink now through 2002.–J.L. • $18 • (12/15/1998) • **88**
Zinfandel Contra Costa County Ancient Vines 1995 • $18 • (3/31/1998) • **87**
Zinfandel Contra Costa County Big Break Vineyard 1997: Wonderful richness, complexity and finesse, with polished black cherry, wild berry, raspberry and spice. Finishes with a long, intricate aftertaste and firm tannins. Drink now through 2007.–J.L. • $28 • (12/15/1999) • **90**
Zinfandel Contra Costa County Big Break Vineyard 1996: Very ripe, with a slight jammy edge to the plum, wild berry, anise, sage and cedary oak flavors. Fills out on the palate, holds its flavors and keeps its focus even with its firm, drying tannins. Try through 2002.–J.L. • $24 • (12/15/1998) • **89**
Zinfandel Contra Costa County Big Break 1995 • $24 • (12/15/1997) • **84**
Zinfandel Contra Costa County Big Break 1994 • $22 • (9/30/1996) • **90**
Zinfandel Contra Costa County Big Break 1993 • $18 • (9/15/1995) • **87**
Zinfandel Contra Costa County Bridgehead 1997: Ripe, rich, plush and concentrated, with lots of currant, black cherry, anise, sage and tobacco notes. Complex aftertaste. Drink now through 2007.–J.L. • $28 • (12/15/1999) • **90**
Zinfandel Contra Costa County Bridgehead Vineyard 1996: A tarry style of Zin that's quite ripe, with just a glimmer of wild berry, stewed plum and cedary, spicy notes on the finish, where it turns a little bitter. Drink now through 2001.–J.L. • $24 • (12/15/1998) • **86**
Zinfandel Contra Costa County Bridgehead 1995 • $24 • (12/15/1997) • **84**
Zinfandel Contra Costa County Bridgehead 1994 • $22 • (9/30/1996) • **87**
Zinfandel Contra Costa County Bridgehead 1993 • $18 • (9/15/1995) • **87**
Zinfandel Contra Costa County Live Oak Vineyard 1997: Very ripe and jammy, with black cherry, wild berry, plum, tar and earth notes. Firms up on the finish, where it turns peppery. Drink now through 2007.–J.L. • $28 • (12/15/1999) • **87**
Zinfandel Contra Costa County Live Oak Vineyard 1996: A dark, intense, meaty style, with lots of tar, stewed plum, wild berry and mineral flavors. Turns thick and chewy on the finish, where the tannins are coarse and dry. Drink through 2004–J.L. • $24 • (12/15/1998) • **87**
Zinfandel Contra Costa County Live Oak 1995 • $24 • (11/15/1997) • **89**
Zinfandel Contra Costa County Reserve 1994 • $22 • (9/30/1996) • **89**
Zinfandel Contra Costa County Reserve 1993 • $16 • (9/15/1995) • **88**
Zinfandel Contra Costa County Reserve 1992 • $12 • (9/15/1994) • **89**
Zinfandel Contra Costa County Reserve 1991 • $14 • (9/30/1993) • **86**
Zinfandel Contra Costa County Reserve 1990 • $14 • (10/15/1992) • **82**
Zinfandel Contra Costa County Reserve 1989 • $12 • (12/31/1991) • **84**
Zinfandel Contra Costa County Reserve 1987 • $12 • (5/15/1990) • **87**
Zinfandel Russian River Valley Fulton Road 1997: Dark, rich and concentrated, with layers of black cherry, blackberry, raspberry and plum, finishing with mineral and detailed tannins. Drink through 2006–J.L. • $30 • (11/30/1999) • **88**

CLONINGER | CALIFORNIA

Cabernet Sauvignon Carmel Valley 1993 • $15 • (11/30/1996) • **75**
Cabernet Sauvignon Carmel Valley Quinn Vineyard 1996: Vegetal flavors take the lead here, with green bean and bell pepper up-front. Quite smooth on the palate, however. • $NA • (11/15/1998) • **77**
Cabernet Sauvignon Monterey 1992 • $11 • (11/30/1996) • **78**
Cabernet Sauvignon Monterey 1990 • $15 • (7/15/1993) • **82**
Pinot Noir Monterey 1993 • $16 • (2/28/1997) • **83**
Pinot Noir Monterey Jardini Vineyard 1997: Aromas of cinnamon and strawberry jam precede lean, earthy flavors. Drink now through 2002 .–J.L. • $22 • (4/30/2000) • **83**

CLOS DANIELLE | CALIFORNIA

Merlot Napa Valley 1993 • $10 • (5/15/1995) • **82**

CLOS DU BOIS | CALIFORNIA

Cabernet Franc Sonoma County Winemaker's Reserve 1993 • $20 • (9/15/1996) • **85**
Cabernet Sauvignon Alexander Valley Selection 1996: Herbal, oak-driven flavors open up to reveal a dark core of tarry black cherry. Finishes short and firm. Drink now through 2002.–J.L. • $18 • (5/31/1999) • **84**
Cabernet Sauvignon Alexander Valley Selection 1995 • $18 • (4/30/1998) • **88**
Cabernet Sauvignon Alexander Valley 1994 • $17 • (5/15/1997) • **85**
Cabernet Sauvignon Alexander Valley 1991 • $12 • (2/28/1994) • **86**
Cabernet Sauvignon Alexander Valley 1990 • $13 • (3/31/1993) • **87**
Cabernet Sauvignon Alexander Valley 1989 • $11 • (11/15/1992) • **80**
Cabernet Sauvignon Alexander Valley 1988 • $14 • (7/15/1991) • **77**
Cabernet Sauvignon Alexander Valley 1987 • $11 • (2/15/1990) • **86**
Cabernet Sauvignon Alexander Valley 1986 • $12 • (5/31/1989) • **86**
Cabernet Sauvignon Alexander Valley 1985 • $11 • (4/15/1988) • **87**
Cabernet Sauvignon Alexander Valley 1984 • $10 • (6/15/1987) • **87**
Cabernet Sauvignon Alexander Valley 1978: Mature, dominated by herbal and earthy flavors. There's a hint of dried fruit on the finish, but it turns diffuse and murky. (1978 California Cabernet retrospective tasting). Past its prime.–J.L. • $10 • (11/15/1998) • **78**
Cabernet Sauvignon Alexander Valley Briarcrest Vineyard 1996: Ripe and polished, with pretty toasty oak leading to a supple core of currant, black cherry and wild berry. Firms up on the finish but the flavors keep pouring through. Best from 2001 through 2008.–J.L. • $36 • (10/15/1999) • **92**
Cabernet Sauvignon Alexander Valley Briarcrest Vineyard 1995: Tightly wound, with a firm focus on black cherry and blackberry, this wine is complex, concentrated and firmly tannic, with a long, rewarding finish. Drink through 2007–J.L. • $30 • (11/15/1998) • **91**
Cabernet Sauvignon Alexander Valley Briarcrest Vineyard 1994 • $23 • (6/15/1998) • **89**
Cabernet Sauvignon Alexander Valley Briarcrest Vineyard 1993 • $21 • (7/31/1997) • **88**
Cabernet Sauvignon Alexander Valley Briarcrest Vineyard 1992 • $20 • (11/30/1995) • **89**
Cabernet Sauvignon Alexander Valley Briarcrest Vineyard 1991 • $18 • (11/15/1994) • **87**
Cabernet Sauvignon Alexander Valley Briarcrest Vineyard 1990 • $19 • (4/15/1994) • **89**
Cabernet Sauvignon Alexander Valley Briarcrest Vineyard 1989 • $19 • (8/31/1993) • **80**
Cabernet Sauvignon Alexander Valley Briarcrest Vineyard 1987 • $18 • (12/15/1997) • **91**
Cabernet Sauvignon Alexander Valley Briarcrest Vineyard 1986 • $17 • (8/31/1990) • **87**
Cabernet Sauvignon Alexander Valley Briarcrest Vineyard 1985 • $16 • (6/15/1989) • **86**
Cabernet Sauvignon Alexander Valley Briarcrest Vineyard 1984 • $16 • (7/15/1988) • **90**
Cabernet Sauvignon Alexander Valley Briarcrest Vineyard 1982 • $14 • (7/31/1987) • **91**
Cabernet Sauvignon Alexander Valley Briarcrest Vineyard 1980 • $13 • (4/16/1986) • **66**
Cabernet Sauvignon Alexander Valley Briarcrest Vineyard 1978: Holding up nicely, with complex, mature, even delicate fruit flavors. Black cherry, wild berry, plum, herb and spice flavors are graced by supple tannins that have softened. (1978 California Cabernet retrospective tasting). Drink now through 2002.–J.L. • $15 • (11/15/1998) • **88**
Cabernet Sauvignon Alexander Valley Reserve 1997: Herbal and tart, with vanilla and subtle black currant notes. Best from 2001 through 2003.–J.L. • $20 • (6/30/2000) • **83**

Key: SS—Spectator Selection. CS—Cellar Selection. HR—Highly Recommended. $NA—Price not available. (BT)—Barrel tasting. (A)—Auction Price.
For a key to the tasters' initials, see "How to Use These Listings."
Dates in parentheses represent the issues in which the ratings were published.

Cabernet Sauvignon Alexander Valley Winemaker's Reserve 1996: Distincitive for its spice, bay leaf and mint introduction, it turns rich and polished, with currant, toasty oak, stewed plum and spicy herb nuances. Holds its elegance. Drink now through 2007.–J.L. • $50 • (11/15/1999) • **92**
Cabernet Sauvignon Alexander Valley Winemaker's Reserve 1995: Smooth, ripe, supple and harmonious, with layers of plush currant, blackberry, sage, coffee, mineral, tea and spice. Keeps pumping out the flavors on a long, rich and polished finish. Drink through 2009–J.L. • $50 • (11/15/1998) • **92**
Cabernet Sauvignon Alexander Valley Winemaker's Reserve 1991 • $30 • (10/15/1994) CS • **92**
Cabernet Sauvignon Dry Creek Valley Proprietor's Reserve 1982 • $19 • (9/15/1987) • **88**
Cabernet Sauvignon Sonoma County 1996: Cherries, spice and herbs blend nicely here, although the oak sticks out a bit awkwardly. Finishes short. Drink now through 2003. • $15 • (11/15/1998) • **83**
Cabernet Sauvignon Sonoma County 1995 • $15 • (3/31/1998) • **84**
Cabernet Sauvignon Sonoma County 1994 • $13 • (11/15/1996) • **86**
Cabernet Sauvignon Sonoma County 1993 • $13 • (12/15/1995) • **82**
Cabernet Sauvignon Sonoma County Dry Creek 1974 • $NA • (2/15/1990) • **74**
Chardonnay Alexander Valley Alexander Valley Selection 1997: Firm, with a green, leafy quality dominating the citrus and toast flavors. Drink now.–J.L. • $15 • (4/30/1999) • **80**
Chardonnay Alexander Valley Alexander Valley Selection 1996 • $15 • (3/31/1998) • **89**
Chardonnay Alexander Valley Calcaire Vineyard 1998: Spicy, with complex pear, nectarine and tangerine flavors that are fresh and lively, if lacking in depth and extra dimensions. Drink now through 2002.–J.L. • $20 • (12/15/1999) • **87**
Chardonnay Alexander Valley Calcaire Vineyard 1997: Openly fruity, with complex pear, apple, licorice and vanilla flavors, this wine is elegant and polished, finishing with a hint of grapefruit. Drink now through 2001.–J.L. • $18 • (3/31/1999) • **89**
Chardonnay Alexander Valley Calcaire Vineyard 1996 • $18 • (4/30/1998) • **87**
Chardonnay Alexander Valley Reserve 1998: Offers a decent focus of golden delicious apples and pears, but the finish is lean and a touch bitter. Best from 2001 through 2002.–J.L. • $16 • (4/30/2000) • **82**
Chardonnay Dry Creek Valley Flintwood Vineyard 1997: Tight, flinty and simple, with spicy pear notes of modest depth and complexity. Drink now through 2002.–J.L. • $22 • (12/15/1999) • **84**
Chardonnay Dry Creek Valley Flintwood Vineyard 1996 • $17 • (5/15/1998) • **87**
Chardonnay Sonoma County 1998: A clean, crisp, grassy style, with ripe pear and peach flavors. Turns soft. Drink now.–J.L. • $14 • (7/31/1999) • **84**
Chardonnay Sonoma County 1997: Bright and citrusy, with a thread of mineral. Simple and refreshing. Drink now.–H.S. • $12 • (11/15/1998) • **82**
Chardonnay Sonoma County 1996 • $12 • (11/15/1997) • **84**
Malbec Alexander Valley L'Etranger Winemaker's Reserve 1991 • $19 • (3/31/1994) • **82**
Malbec Alexander Valley L'Etranger Winemaker's Reserve 1987 • $20 • (1/31/1991) • **87**
Marlstone Vineyard Alexander Valley 1996: Elegant and complex, with ripe, supple plum, currant, herb and berry, framed by soft tannins and herbal notes. Best from 2001 through 2007.–J.L. • $30 • (2/29/2000) • **88**
Marlstone Vineyard Alexander Valley 1995: Smells exotic and complex, with a broad range of dried cherry, currant, plum, anise, cedar and earth, holding its focus and finishing with a long, complex aftertaste. Cabernet Sauvignon, Merlot and Malbec. Drink through 2007–J.L. • $30 • (11/15/1998) • **91**
Marlstone Vineyard Alexander Valley 1994 • $25 • (5/15/1998) • **90**
Marlstone Vineyard Alexander Valley 1992 • $21 • (11/30/1995) • **89**
Marlstone Vineyard Alexander Valley 1991 • $18 • (1/31/1995) • **88**
Marlstone Vineyard Alexander Valley 1990 • $20 • (11/15/1993) • **88**
Marlstone Vineyard Alexander Valley 1989 • $20 • (3/31/1993) • **85**
Marlstone Vineyard Alexander Valley 1987 • $27 • (7/31/1991) HR • **90**
Marlstone Vineyard Alexander Valley 1986 • $24 • (8/31/1990) • **85**
Marlstone Vineyard Alexander Valley 1985 • $34 • (6/15/1989) • **81**
Marlstone Vineyard Alexander Valley 1984 • $20 • (5/15/1988) • **85**
Marlstone Vineyard Alexander Valley 1983 • $20 • (9/15/1987) • **88**
Marlstone Vineyard Alexander Valley 1982 • $16 • (9/30/1986) • **86**
Marlstone Vineyard Alexander Valley 1981 • $15 • (3/16/1986) • **96**
Marlstone Vineyard Alexander Valley 1978: Mature and fading, with dry, earthy tar notes, also mushroom and slightly sour notes. Not much fun. (1978 California Cabernet retrospective tasting). Past its prime.–J.L. • $16 • (11/15/1998) • **74**
Merlot Alexander Valley Alexander Valley Selection 1996: Medium-bodied, with a pleasant range of plum and berry flavors, finishing crisp but flavorful. Drink now through 2001.–J.L. • $20 • (8/31/1999) • **86**
Merlot Alexander Valley Alexander Valley Selection 1995 • $20 • (3/31/1998) • **86**
Merlot Alexander Valley Winemaker's Reserve 1993 • $28 • (9/15/1996) • **89**
Merlot Sonoma County 1996: Medium-bodied, with light currant and black cherry flavors accented by herbal notes, finishing slightly dry. Drink now.–J.L. • $17 • (8/31/1999) • **83**
Merlot Sonoma County 1995 • $17 • (3/31/1998) • **86**
Merlot Sonoma County 1994 • $17 • (11/30/1996) • **87**
Merlot Sonoma County 1993 • $16 • (6/15/1996) • **84**
Merlot Sonoma County 1992 • $15 • (1/31/1995) • **88**
Merlot Sonoma County 1991 • $15 • (4/15/1994) • **86**
Merlot Sonoma County 1990 • $15 • (6/15/1993) • **82**
Merlot Sonoma County 1989 • $15 • (5/31/1992) • **82**
Merlot Sonoma County 1988 • $15 • (5/31/1991) • **81**
Merlot Sonoma County 1987 • $12 • (4/15/1990) • **89**
Merlot Sonoma County 1986 • $11 • (10/15/1988) • **86**
Merlot Sonoma County 1985 • $10 • (10/31/1987) SS • **92**
Pinot Noir Sonoma County 1997: Soft but tightly structured, with herb, strawberry, dried cherry and tea flavors and pleasant toasted oak on the finish. Drink now.–J.L. • $15 • (6/15/1999) • **85**
Pinot Noir Sonoma County 1996 • $14 • (3/31/1998) • **85**
Pinot Noir Sonoma County 1990 • $12 • (2/28/1993) • **82**
Pinot Noir Sonoma County 1989 • $13 • (10/31/1991) • **78**
Pinot Noir Sonoma County 1988 • $12 • (4/30/1991) • **80**
Pinot Noir Sonoma County 1987 • $12 • (5/31/1990) • **73**
Pinot Noir Sonoma County 1986 • $11 • (10/15/1989) • **87**
Pinot Noir Sonoma County 1985 • $11 • (6/15/1988) • **70**
Pinot Noir Dry Creek Valley Proprietor's Reserve 1980 • $11 • (7/16/1984) • **86**
Sauvignon Blanc Sonoma County 1998: Somewhat herbal up front, with a crisp follow-up redolent of grapefruit, lemon and lime. Refreshing and brisk, with a bright, sleek texture. Drink now. • $9 • (6/15/1999) • **86**
Sauvignon Blanc Sonoma County 1997 • $9 • (6/30/1998) • **84**
Sauvignon Blanc Sonoma County 1996 • $8 • (6/30/1997) • **88**
Shiraz Alexander Valley Alexander Valley Selection 1996: Has some pleasant flavors but lacks concentration, with meaty cola and modest blueberry and tar notes. Drink now.–J.L. • $15 • (4/30/1999) • **83**
Tempranillo Alexander Valley Ageless NV: A blend of plummy, beefy flavors framed in toasty oak, it offers spice on the nose, though it comes up a bit short on the finish. Drink now through 2003. • $30 • (6/15/1999) • **83**
Zinfandel Sonoma County 1996: This Zin is quite zingy, with bright cherry and plum flavors and smoky oak overtones. Light in color, a bit thin on the finish. Drink now. • $14 • (2/28/1999) • **83**
Zinfandel Sonoma County 1995 • $14 • (6/15/1998) • **84**
Zinfandel Sonoma County 1994 • $13 • (11/30/1996) • **82**
Zinfandel Sonoma County 1993 • $13 • (10/15/1995) • **83**
Zinfandel Sonoma County 1992 • $13 • (10/15/1994) • **87**
Zinfandel Sonoma County 1991 • $13 • (9/30/1993) • **87**

CLOS DU LAC | CALIFORNIA

Muscat Amador County Vin Doux Naturel 1996 • $12/375 ml. • (11/30/1997) • **85**
Sauvignon Blanc Sierra Foothills 1997: Quite herbal—even a bit weedy; however, lemony flavors come to the fore on the bright and tangy finish. Drink now. • $11 • (5/31/1999) • **82**
Sauvignon Blanc Sierra Foothills 1996 • $10 • (7/31/1997) • **87**
Zinfandel Blanc Sierra Foothills 1997: Has a floral component up front, with a blend of apple, cinnamon and lemon notes. A bit thinly textured, this is a rare true white, rather than rosé-colored, white Zinfandel. Drink now. • $8 • (12/31/1998) • **83**
Zinfandel Shenandoah Valley Twin Rivers Vineyards 1996 • $12 • (3/31/1998) • **81**
Zinfandel Sierra Foothills Ghirardelli Vineyard 1996 • $16 • (6/15/1998) • **84**

CLOS DU VAL | CALIFORNIA

Ariadne Napa Valley White 1998: Simple, with honey, citrus and tart apple flavors. Drink now.–J.L. • $25 • (6/30/2000) • **80**
Ariadne Napa Valley White 1997: A richly textured wine that proudly touts its minerallike core, it then fans out on the palate to reveal layers of fig, melon and citrus, finishing fresh and clean. Drink now. • $25 • (10/15/1999) • **89**
Cabernet Sauvignon Napa Valley 1996: Trim, with good depth to the leathery cherry and cranberry flavors, with a firm herbal thread. Finishes with crisp tannins. Best from 2000 through 2006.–J.L. • $25 • (10/15/1999) • **87**
Cabernet Sauvignon Napa Valley 1995: Elegant and ripe, with black cherry and plummy Cabernet flavors of moderate depth, richness and concentration.

CLOS DU VAL

Finishes with a pretty burst of ripe fruit and firm but polished tannins. Drink now through 2004.–J.L. • $24 • (10/31/1998) • **88**

Cabernet Sauvignon Napa Valley 1994 • $24 • (3/31/1998) • **86**

Cabernet Sauvignon Napa Valley 1993 • $23 • (4/30/1997) • **83**

Cabernet Sauvignon Napa Valley 1990 • $12 • (6/30/1994) • **84**

Cabernet Sauvignon Napa Valley 1989 • $15 • (11/15/1992) • **83**

Cabernet Sauvignon Napa Valley 1979: Shows appealing ripe cherry, plum and currant up front, is well focused, a touch tannic and leathery, but overall holding quite nicely, finishing with complex herb and coffee notes. (1979 California Cabernet retrospective tasting). Drink now.–J.L. • $31 Ⓐ • (8/31/1999) • **87**

Cabernet Sauvignon Napa Valley 1974 • $52 Ⓐ • (11/15/1994) • **82**

Cabernet Sauvignon Napa Valley Joli Val 1988 • $13 • (7/31/1991) • **82**

Cabernet Sauvignon Napa Valley Joli Val 1986 • $13 • (12/15/1989) • **87**

Cabernet Sauvignon Napa Valley Reserve 1998: Firm, structured and focused, with a tight core of earthy currant, black cherry, light toasty oak and gritty tannins. Pointed in the right direction.–J.L. • $NA • (8/31/1999) (BT) • **90-94**

Cabernet Sauvignon Napa Valley Reserve 1996 • $NA • (2/02/1997) (BT) • **90-94**

Cabernet Sauvignon Napa Valley Reserve 1995: Elegant and refined, with a complex, spicy band of black cherry, currant, olive, pepper and plum notes, all neatly tapered on the long, lingering finish. Drink through 2007–J.L. • $65 • (11/15/1999) • **93**

Cabernet Sauvignon Napa Valley Reserve 1994: A rich and polished style, with pretty currant, coffee, anise, sage and cedary flavors that are elegantly understated, finishing with a smooth, supple aftertaste. Drinks well now, but has the intensity and richness for cellaring. Drink through 2006–J.L. • $53 • (10/31/1998) • **91**

Cabernet Sauvignon Napa Valley Reserve 1993 • $50 • (10/31/1997) • **91**

Cabernet Sauvignon Napa Valley Reserve 1992 • $45 • (12/31/1996) • **89**

Cabernet Sauvignon Napa Valley Reserve 1990 • $45 • (4/30/1995) • **89**

Cabernet Sauvignon Napa Valley Reserve 1988: Tasted from magnum. Ripe and full-bodied for an '88, this is one of the vintage's successes. Earthy, with clay, cedar, spice, currant and black cherry flavors, it turns supple and elegant and shows more depth and richness than most from this lean harvest. Has tannin to shed, but runs the risk of drying out. (1988 California Cabernet retrospective tasting). Drink now through 2002.–J.L. • $13 • (11/15/1998) • **88**

Cabernet Sauvignon Napa Valley Reserve 1987 • $45 • (12/15/1997) • **93**

Cabernet Sauvignon Napa Valley Reserve 1978: Starting to fray around the edges, this wine still possesses ripe cherry and currant-laced notes, complex flavors and aromas. Might hold together until 2006 or 2008 but we recommend drinking now. (1978 California Cabernet retrospective tasting).–J.L. • $47 Ⓐ • (11/15/1998) • **88**

Cabernet Sauvignon Rutherford Vineyard Georges III 1997: Supple and elegant, with pretty plum, black cherry, cedar, herb and spice flavors, turning supple. Drink now through 2007.–J.L. • $48 • (6/15/2000) • **87**

Cabernet Sauvignon Stags Leap District 1997: Marked by earthy currant, anise, sage, herb and cedar notes, picking up a mulchy flavor on the finish. Tannins are soft. Drink now through 2006.–J.L. • $48 • (6/15/2000) • **86**

Cabernet Sauvignon Stags Leap District 1991 • $20 • (9/30/1995) • **87**

Cabernet Sauvignon Stags Leap District 1990 • $18 • (11/15/1994) • **83**

Cabernet Sauvignon Stags Leap District 1989: Not quite ripe, medium-weight, with dry, earthy, simple, diluted cherry flavors. Never really takes off. (1989 California Cabernet retrospective tasting. Drink now.–J.L. • $18 • (8/31/1999) • **82**

Cabernet Sauvignon Stags Leap District 1988 • $18 • (3/31/1992) • **86**

Cabernet Sauvignon Stags Leap District 1987 • $17 • (6/30/1991) HR • **92**

Cabernet Sauvignon Stags Leap District 1986 • $NA • (12/15/1996) • **89**

Cabernet Sauvignon Stags Leap District 1985 • $32 • (6/15/1989) • **90**

Cabernet Sauvignon Stags Leap District 1984 • $16 • (4/15/1988) • **86**

Cabernet Sauvignon Stags Leap District 1983 • $15 • (9/15/1987) • **77**

Cabernet Sauvignon Stags Leap District 1982 • $13 • (7/01/1986) • **91**

Cabernet Sauvignon Stags Leap District 1981 • $NA • (2/01/1986) • **89**

Cabernet Sauvignon Stags Leap District 1980 • $14 • (2/01/1986) • **83**

Cabernet Sauvignon Stags Leap District 1979 • $16 • (2/01/1986) • **93**

Cabernet Sauvignon Stags Leap District 1978 • $45 • (11/15/1992) • **91**

Cabernet Sauvignon Stags Leap District Reserve 1979 • $25 • (9/01/1984) SS • **91**

Cabernet Sauvignon Stags Leap District Reserve 1978 • $NA • (11/15/1992) • **94**

Key: SS—Spectator Selection. CS—Cellar Selection. HR—Highly Recommended. $NA—Price not available. (BT)—Barrel tasting. Ⓐ—Auction Price.
For a key to the tasters' initials, see "How to Use These Listings."
Dates in parentheses represent the issues in which the ratings were published.

Chardonnay Carneros Single Vineyard 1998: An elegant, refreshing blend of citrus, pear, tangerine and nectarine, with vibrant acidity and a long, clean, refreshing aftertaste. Drink now through 2005.–J.L. • $21 • (4/30/2000) • **88**

Chardonnay Napa Valley Carneros 1997: Crisp, with a flinty edge to the moderately ripe pear, apple, fig and cedary oak flavors, finishing with a pleasantly fruity edge. Drink now through 2002.–J.L. • $17 • (4/30/1999) • **87**

Chardonnay Napa Valley Carneros 1996 • $17 • (4/30/1998) • **87**

Merlot Napa Valley 1997: Firm, leathery and a touch bitter, with a tough streak of Merlot fruit and only glimpses of dry currant and mineral. Quite tannic. Best from 2001 through 2006.–J.L. • $28 • (1/31/2000) • **80**

Merlot Napa Valley 1996: A light style, appealing for its elegance, but the cherry and berry are uncomplicated and lack richness and depth. Drink now through 2004.–J.L. • $28 • (10/15/1999) • **85**

Merlot Napa Valley 1995 • $28 • (4/30/1998) • **86**

Merlot Stags Leap District 1994 • $28 • (12/31/1996) • **88**

Merlot Stags Leap District 1993 • $21 • (7/31/1996) • **81**

Merlot Stags Leap District 1992 • $30 • (7/31/1995) • **84**

Merlot Stags Leap District 1991 • $21 • (5/31/1994) • **89**

Merlot Stags Leap District 1990 • $22 • (6/15/1993) • **86**

Merlot Stags Leap District 1989 • $21 • (5/31/1992) • **86**

Merlot Stags Leap District 1988 • $20 • (3/31/1991) • **89**

Merlot Stags Leap District 1987 • $17 • (3/31/1990) • **85**

Merlot Stags Leap District 1986 • $16 • (8/31/1989) • **86**

Merlot Stags Leap District 1985 • $16 • (4/30/1988) • **87**

Merlot Stags Leap District 1984 • $15 • (7/31/1987) • **88**

Merlot Stags Leap District 1983 • $14 • (6/16/1986) • **92**

Merlot Stags Leap District 1982 • $13 • (10/01/1985) • **80**

Merlot Stags Leap District 1981 • $14 • (2/16/1984) • **88**

Pinot Noir Napa Valley Carneros 1997: Woody, gamy flavors dominate the core of black cherry and spice. Finishes firm and dry. Drink now through 2001.–J.L. • $20 • (9/15/1999) • **81**

Pinot Noir Carneros 1995 • $20 • (12/15/1997) • **85**

Pinot Noir Napa Valley Carneros 1994 • $15 • (2/29/1996) • **83**

Pinot Noir Napa Valley Carneros 1990 • $13 • (3/31/1995) • **78**

Pinot Noir Napa Valley Carneros 1989 • $13 • (2/28/1994) • **81**

Pinot Noir Napa Valley Carneros 1988 • $14 • (9/30/1992) • **80**

Pinot Noir Napa Valley 1987 • $14 • (4/30/1991) • **84**

Pinot Noir Napa Valley 1986 • $16 • (2/15/1990) • **80**

Pinot Noir Napa Valley 1985 • $13 • (6/15/1988) • **80**

Pinot Noir Napa Valley 1984 • $12 • (9/30/1987) • **78**

Pinot Noir Napa Valley 1982 • $11 • (9/01/1984) • **75**

Reserve Napa Valley Red 1988 • $48 • (11/15/1993) • **88**

Reserve Stags Leap District Red 1987 • $45 • (7/15/1992) CS • **92**

Reserve Stags Leap District Red 1985 • $45 • (11/15/1990) • **94**

Reserve Stags Leap District Red 1982 • $28 • (11/15/1987) • **88**

Sangiovese Napa Valley Tre Grazie 1994 • $26 • (12/31/1996) • **86**

Zinfandel California 1998: Light, with simple coffee, leather and canned beef flavors. Turns dry and acrylic.–J.L. • $17 • (5/31/2000) • **75**

Zinfandel California 1996 • $15 • (6/15/1998) • **81**

Zinfandel California 1995 • $16 • (3/31/1998) • **84**

Zinfandel Napa-El Dorado-San Joaquin Counties 1997: Light and simple, with modest pepper, cranberry, tart cherry and spice flavors. Dry on the finish. Drink now.–J.L. • $17 • (11/15/1999) • **82**

Zinfandel Napa & El Dorado Counties 1996: A dry, earthy style, with spicy raspberry, sage and herbal flavors. Rather lacking in vibrancy for such a young wine. Turns tannic. Drink now through 2002.–J.L. • $15 • (2/28/1999) • **82**

Zinfandel Stags Leap District 1994 • $16 • (6/15/1998) • **85**

Zinfandel Stags Leap District 1993 • $16 • (3/31/1997) • **78**

Zinfandel Stags Leap District 1992 • $15 • (2/28/1997) • **88**

Zinfandel Stags Leap District 1991 • $15 • (7/31/1995) • **84**

Zinfandel Stags Leap District 1990 • $14 • (10/15/1994) • **74**

Zinfandel Stags Leap District 1989 • $14 • (9/30/1993) • **86**

Zinfandel Stags Leap District 1988 • $15 • (10/15/1992) • **85**

Zinfandel Stags Leap District 1987 • $16 • (5/31/1990) • **83**

Zinfandel Stags Leap District 1986 • $12 • (5/31/1989) • **87**

Zinfandel Stags Leap District 1985 • $12 • (4/30/1988) • **90**

Zinfandel Stags Leap District 1984 • $19 • (5/31/1987) • **81**

Zinfandel Stags Leap District 1981 • $18 • (5/16/1984) CS • **90**

Zinfandel Stags Leap District 1974 • $55 • (6/16/1985) • **77**

Zinfandel Stags Leap District 1973 • $50 • (6/16/1985) • **86**

Zinfandel Stags Leap District 1972 • $60 • (6/16/1985) • **90**

Zinfandel Stags Leap District Palisade Vineyard 1998: Smells spicy, almost with a salsa edge, with light, herbal cherry flavor. Drink now.–J.L. • $25 • (5/31/2000) • **82**

CLOS GARBO | OREGON

Pinot Noir Oregon 1993 • $18 • (5/15/1996) • **88**
Pinot Noir Oregon 1992 • $18 • (9/15/1994) • **89**

CLOS LACHANCE | CALIFORNIA

Cabernet Sauvignon Santa Cruz Mountains 1997: Tough, astringent and marked by bitter, green flavors. Slowly works its way into a range of coffee and currant, but it's tough sledding early on. Best from 2001 through 2007.–J.L. • $21 • (4/30/2000) • **83**
Cabernet Sauvignon Santa Cruz Mountains 1996: Soft, with pleasant flavors of coffee, herb, cherry and toast. The flavors are delicate but complex, lingering on the finish where the tannins are soft. Drink now through 2003 .–J.L. • $21 • (10/15/1999) • **85**
Cabernet Sauvignon Santa Cruz Mountains 1993 • $23 • (4/30/1996) • **86**
Cabernet Sauvignon Santa Cruz Mountains 1992 • $20 • (7/31/1995) • **88**
Chardonnay Napa Valley 1998: Weaves together ripe, spicy pear and apple flavors, with a baked apple pie and nutmeg aftertaste. Drink now through 2005.–J.L. • $18 • (4/30/2000) • **87**
Chardonnay Napa Valley 1997: Firm and lemony, with mineral notes to the fore. Crisp and zingy, with lingering flint, pear and apple flavors. Sleek. Drink now through 2003. • $18 • (7/31/1999) • **91**
Chardonnay Santa Cruz Mountains 1998: Has focus, with pineapple and apple flavors that linger. Drink now.–J.L. • $19 • (6/15/2000) • **84**
Chardonnay Santa Cruz Mountains 1997: Firmly structured, with bright acidity and feisty mineral and citrus flavors. Earthiness adds to the complexity. Bright, clean aftertaste. Drink now through 2003. • $19 • (6/30/1999) • **89**
Chardonnay Santa Cruz Mountains 1996 • $22 • (6/30/1998) • **88**
Chardonnay Santa Cruz Mountains Reserve 1997: Pretty pear and apple notes form the core of this delicate wine, which nonetheless sports rich body. Moderate acidity and a mineral edge leave a refreshing finish. Drink now through 2002. • $27 • (6/30/1999) • **90**
Chardonnay Santa Cruz Mountains Vintner's Reserve 1996 • $29 • (6/30/1998) • **90**
Merlot Central Coast 1997: Charry flavors, with green bean and coffee notes. Drink now through 2003.–J.L. • $17 • (6/15/2000) • **82**
Merlot Central Coast 1996: Light in texture and hue, the wine offers hints of cherry and herb framed in toasty oak. Finishes mild. Drink now through 2001. • $17 • (10/15/1999) • **81**
Pinot Noir Santa Cruz Mountains 1997: A light style but quite tasty, with ripe plum, cherry and strawberry notes and easygoing tannins that finish with touches of mushroom and earth. Drink now through 2004.–J.L. • $24 • (3/31/2000) • **87**
Pinot Noir Santa Cruz Mountains 1993 • $19 • (12/31/1995) • **85**
Zinfandel El Dorado 1997: Delicious, with juicy cherry flavors that explode in the mouth, along with marzipan, tea and dried flower notes. A wallop of flavor on a delicate frame. Drink now through 2006.–J.L. • $16 • (1/31/2000) • **90**

CLOS PEGASE | CALIFORNIA

Cabernet Sauvignon Napa Valley 1997: Serves up rich, chocolaty currant, blackberry and cedar flavors before the tannins weigh in, giving it a chewy aftertaste. Best from 2002 through 2010.–J.L. • $30 • (6/15/2000) • **87**
Cabernet Sauvignon Napa Valley 1996: Smooth and elegant, yet with plenty of structure and staying power. Flavors are well integrated, with black currant, blackberry, herbs, tobacco and chocolate in evidence. Finishes long, and should improve nicely in the cellar. Tasted twice, with consistent notes. Drink now through 2006. • $26 • (4/30/1999) • **91**
Cabernet Sauvignon Napa Valley 1994 • $23 • (10/31/1997) • **86**
Cabernet Sauvignon Napa Valley 1993 • $20 • (3/31/1996) • **87**
Cabernet Sauvignon Napa Valley 1992 • $19 • (10/15/1995) • **88**
Cabernet Sauvignon Napa Valley 1991 • $17 • (6/30/1994) • **88**
Cabernet Sauvignon Napa Valley 1990 • $17 • (11/15/1993) SS • **91**
Cabernet Sauvignon Napa Valley 1987 • $17 • (8/31/1992) • **82**
Cabernet Sauvignon Napa Valley 1986 • $17 • (9/30/1990) • **88**
Cabernet Sauvignon Napa Valley 1985 • $17 • (5/31/1988) • **86**
Chardonnay Carneros Mitsuko's Vineyard 1998: Nice entry, with ripe pear, peach, lemon and lime notes, holding its focus. Drink now.–J.L. • $19 • (6/15/2000) • **84**
Chardonnay Napa Valley Carneros Mitsuko's Vineyard 1997: Smooth, ripe and creamy, with elegant pear, vanilla, grapefruit and candied notes that finish with a dash of hazelnut. Drink now through 2004.–J.L. • $18 • (1/31/2000) • **88**
Chardonnay Napa Valley Carneros Mitsuko's Vineyard 1996: Elegant and intense, with cedary oak and ripe pear flavors that finish with a touch of spice and citrus. Drink now through 2001 .–J.L. • $19 • (7/31/1998) • **87**
Grenache California 1989 • $10 • (8/31/1991) • **84**
Hommage Artist Series Reserve Napa Valley 1996: Smooth, ripe and a bit understated, with supple cherry, currant, anise, sage and herb notes. The complex finish picks up hints of vanilla and cedar. Drink now through 2007.–J.L. • $60 • (11/15/1999) • **90**
Hommage Artist Series Reserve Cabernet Sauvignon Napa Valley 1995: Appealing for its elegant, up-front, supple fruitiness, with pretty plum, currant and black cherry notes, dashes of mint and sage and a complex, lingering finish, where the tannins are mild and integrated. Drink through 2006–J.L. • $50 • (11/15/1998) • **89**
Hommage Artist Series Reserve Cabernet Sauvignon Napa Valley 1994 • $40 • (9/30/1997) • **90**
Hommage Artist Series Reserve Cabernet Sauvignon Napa Valley 1993 • $35 • (11/15/1996) • **88**
Merlot Napa Valley 1991 • $16 • (9/15/1994) • **79**
Merlot Napa Valley 1990 • $16 • (6/15/1993) • **83**
Hommage California 1989 • $20 • (11/15/1993) • **83**
Hommage California 1988 • $25 • (10/15/1992) • **84**
Hommage California 1987 • $20 • (8/31/1991) HR • **90**
Hommage Napa Valley 1991 • $25 • (11/15/1994) • **86**
Hommage Napa Valley 1990 • $20 • (4/15/1994) • **87**
Merlot Napa Valley Carneros 1996: Tightly wound, with a firm band of currant, sage, anise and spice. It finishes with firm tannins and never really fans out its flavors, but it's compact and may be more forthcoming with a little more time in the bottle. Drink now through 2004.–J.L. • $23 • (10/15/1998) • **86**
Merlot Napa Valley Carneros 1995 • $23 • (11/30/1997) • **84**
Merlot Napa Valley 1993 • $19 • (2/29/1996) • **87**
Merlot Napa Valley 1992 • $17 • (9/30/1995) HR • **90**
Merlot Napa Valley 1989 • $15 • (10/31/1992) • **81**
Merlot Napa Valley 1988 • $15 • (11/15/1991) • **82**
Merlot Napa Valley 1986 • $16 • (7/15/1990) • **84**
Pegaso Napa Valley 1988 • $12 • (8/31/1992) • **82**
Petite Sirah Napa Valley 1988 • $15 • (10/31/1991) • **83**

CLOS ST. THOMAS | CALIFORNIA

Pinot Noir California 1993 • $9 • (3/31/1995) • **78**

CLOVERDALE RANCH | CALIFORNIA

Cabernet Sauvignon Alexander Valley Estate Cuvée 1994 • $15 • (9/15/1997) • **82**
Cabernet Sauvignon Alexander Valley Estate Cuvée 1991 • $12 • (11/15/1994) • **83**
Cabernet Sauvignon Alexander Valley Estate Cuvée 1989 • $11 • (3/31/1992) • **84**
Cabernet Sauvignon Alexander Valley Pellegrini Family Vineyards 1996: Mild tannins frame a smoky, oak-tinged wine. On the moderate finish, it serves up earth, tea and cherry flavors with a tangy edge. Drink now. • $17 • (2/28/1999) • **83**
Cabernet Sauvignon Alexander Valley Pellegrini Family Vineyards Estate Cuvée 1995 • $16 • (5/15/1998) • **80**
Cabernet Sauvignon Alexander Valley Pellegrini Family Vineyards 1993 • $13 • (11/15/1996) • **86**
Merlot Alexander Valley Estate Cuvée 1995 • $14 • (9/15/1997) • **88**

COBBLESTONE | CALIFORNIA

Chardonnay Monterey County Arroyo Seco 1997: Soft and rich in texture, with minerally pineapple flavors and buttery toasted oak notes. Keeps its focus on the finish. Drink now.–H.S. • $23 • (7/31/1999) • **87**
Chardonnay Arroyo Seco 1996 • $23 • (1/31/1998) • **87**

CODORNIU NAPA | CALIFORNIA

Blanc de Blancs Napa Valley 1991 • $20 • (11/30/1997) • **86**
Brut Napa Valley NV: A pretty, delicate wine, with fine bubbles and subtle toast, pear, citrus and herb flavors. The finish is long, with good acidity and hint of apple. A special release, primarily from the 1992 vintage, which spent an extra four years on the yeast before release. Drink now through 2002. • $40/1.5 liter • (10/15/1999) • **89**

CODORNIU NAPA

Brut Rosé Napa Valley NV: Light and toasty, with hints of tangerine, cherry, spice and citrus. Bright acidity and a good, clean finish. Drink now. • $18 • (12/15/1998) • **88**

Reserve Napa Valley 1991 • $23 • (11/30/1997) • **90**

COFFARO, DAVID | CALIFORNIA

Cabernet Sauvignon Dry Creek Valley Coffaro Estate Vineyard Old Vines 1995 • $19 • (10/31/1997) • **87**

Cabernet Sauvignon Dry Creek Valley Coffaro Estate Vineyard Old Vines 1994 • $16 • (9/15/1996) • **88**

Estate Cuvée Dry Creek Valley Coffaro Estate Vineyard Old Vines 1995 • $19 • (11/30/1997) • **88**

Estate Cuvée Dry Creek Valley Coffaro Estate Vineyard Old Vines 1994 • $16 • (9/15/1996) • **90**

Neighbors' Cuvée Coffaro Estate Vineyard Dry Creek Valley 1998: Pleasant, with dried cherry, plum and wild berry flavors that turn spicy and a bit muddled on the finish. Best from 2002 through 2007.–J.L. • $22 • (4/30/2000) • **86**

Zinfandel Dry Creek Valley Coffaro Estate Vineyard 1998: A glimpse of cherry and berry quickly turns dry, austere and simple. Drink now.–J.L. • $24 • (5/31/2000) • **80**

Zinfandel Dry Creek Valley 1997: Elegant, understated, with supple cherry, wild berry and spicy raspberry flavors that gain velocity and amplitude on the finish. May be better in a year or so. Try through 2002.–J.L. • $23 • (5/15/1999) • **88**

Zinfandel Dry Creek Valley Coffaro Estate Vineyard 1996 • $19 • (5/31/1998) • **90**

Zinfandel Dry Creek Valley Coffaro Estate Vineyard Old Vines 1995 • $17 • (2/28/1997) • **90**

Zinfandel Dry Creek Valley Coffaro Estate Vineyard Old Vines 1994 • $15 • (8/31/1996) • **91**

COHN, B.R. | CALIFORNIA

Cabernet Sauvignon North Coast 1994 • $14 • (9/15/1997) • **82**

Cabernet Sauvignon Sonoma Valley 1991 • $12 • (11/15/1994) • **83**

Cabernet Sauvignon Napa County Silver Label 1989 • $12 • (8/31/1992) • **82**

Cabernet Sauvignon Napa Valley Silver Label 1988 • $12 • (9/30/1991) • **87**

Cabernet Sauvignon Sonoma Valley Olive Hill Estate Vineyards Special Selection 1996: Packed with ripe, rich, concentrated cherry, currant, herb, anise, sage and spicy flavors, it's chunky and elegant. Drink now through 2007.–J.L. • $80 • (8/31/1999) • **93**

abernet Sauvignon Sonoma Valley Olive Hill Estate Vineyards Special Selection 1995 • $80 • (6/15/1998) • **90**

Cabernet Sauvignon Sonoma Valley Olive Hill Estate Vineyards 1997: Attractive for its ripe, up-front fruitiness, with plum, black cherry, anise and vanilla-scented oak, turning firm, rich and tannic on the finish. Best from 2002 through 2010.–J.L. • $38 • (2/29/2000) • **90**

Cabernet Sauvignon Sonoma Valley Olive Hill Estate Vineyards 1996: Ripe, intense and concentrated, with a rich array of cherry, berry, currant and plummy Cabernet flavors, turning supple and polished on the finish. Drink through 2009–J.L. • $35 • (8/31/1999) • **92**

CCabernet Sauvignon Sonoma Valley Olive Hill Estate Vineyards 1995: Austere in style, tight and cedary, with a trim band of currant, tar, sage and berry. It's dense and concentrated; absolutely needs time to soften and evolve. Best from 2002 through 2010.–J.L. • $35 • (7/31/1998) • **91**

Cabernet Sauvignon Sonoma Valley Olive Hill Vineyard 1994 • $43 Ⓐ • (2/28/1997) • **89**

Cabernet Sauvignon Sonoma Valley Olive Hill Vineyard 1993 • $32 • (4/30/1996) • **90**

Cabernet Sauvignon Sonoma Valley Olive Hill Vineyard 1991 • $28 • (4/15/1995) HR • **91**

Cabernet Sauvignon Sonoma Valley Olive Hill Vineyard 1990 • $25 • (11/15/1993) • **90**

Cabernet Sauvignon Sonoma Valley Olive Hill Vineyard 1989: Quite plush in texture, with attractive, ripe plum, wild berry, cherry and anise-laced flavors, holding a tight focus on the finish. Turns a touch dry, but overall quite complete.—1989 California Cabernet retrospective. Drink now through 2005.–J.L. • $NA • (8/31/1999) • **88**

Key: SS—Spectator Selection. CS—Cellar Selection. HR—Highly Recommended. $NA—Price not available. (BT)—Barrel tasting. Ⓐ—Auction Price. For a key to the tasters' initials, see "How to Use These Listings." **Dates in parentheses represent the issues in which the ratings were published.**

Cabernet Sauvignon Sonoma Valley Olive Hill Vineyard 1988: Ready to drink, with but a bit of dry tannin left to shed, this wine features ripe currant, herb, olive, toasty oak and spicy notes. Good length.—1988 California Cabernet retrospective.–J.L. • $25 • (11/15/1998) • **87**

Cabernet Sauvignon Sonoma Valley Olive Hill Vineyard 1987 • $25 • (12/15/1997) • **87**

Cabernet Sauvignon Sonoma Valley Olive Hill Vineyard 1986 • $31 Ⓐ • (12/15/1996) • **91**

Cabernet Sauvignon Sonoma Valley Olive Hill Vineyard 1985 • $16 • (11/15/1988) • **94**

Cabernet Sauvignon Sonoma Valley Olive Hill Vineyard 1984 • $15 • (6/30/1988) • **89**

Chardonnay Carneros Joseph Herman Vineyard Reserve 1996 • $24 • (5/15/1998) • **87**

Chardonnay Sonoma Valley 1996: A touch leafy, it works its way into spicy pear and apple flavors, with light oak shadings. Good, but lacks focus, and finishes with an earthy aftertaste. Drink now through 2001 .–J.L. • $14 • (7/31/1998) • **87**

Merlot Napa-Sonoma Counties 1992 • $14 • (11/15/1994) • **80**

Merlot Napa-Sonoma Counties 1990 • $14 • (10/31/1992) • **84**

Merlot Napa Valley Silver Label 1989 • $14 • (11/15/1991) • **82**

Merlot Sonoma Valley Olive Hill Estate Vineyard 1996: Ripe, smooth and complex, with pretty cherry, plum, blackberry, vanilla and spice, all neatly woven together and plush on the finish. Drink now through 2004.–J.L. • $28 • (9/15/1999) • **88**

Merlot Sonoma Valley Olive Hill Estate Vineyard 1995: Shows depth, richness and complexity, with firm, tight currant, anise, cedar, sage and herb notes that fan out nicely on the finish. Has the tannic strength to age. Drink now through 2004.–J.L. • $24 • (9/30/1998) • **88**

Merlot Sonoma Valley Olive Hill Vineyard 1994 • $20 • (6/30/1996) • **83**

Pinot Noir Sonoma Valley Olive Hill Vineyard 1997: Soft-textured, with anise, black cherry and spicy oak flavors that persist on the firm finish. Drink now through 2001 .–J.L. • $28 • (9/15/1999) • **83**

Pinot Noir Sonoma Valley Olive Hill Vineyard 1995 • $24 • (3/31/1997) • **84**

COL SOLARE | WASHINGTON

Columbia Valley 1996: This red blend from Washington displays remarkable density of flavor on a sleek frame. A smooth and generous wine, its black raspberry, cherry, currant and coffee flavors wrap themselves seductively in a blanket of fine-grained tannins. Lasts and lasts on the finish. From the partnership between Chateau Ste. Michelle and Italy's Marchesi Antinori. Contains 85 percent Cabernet Sauvignon, 15 percent Merlot. Best after 2001.–H.S. • $70 • (6/15/1999) HR • **92**

Columbia Valley 1995: Rich in flavor but remarkably light, with deftly balanced currant, blackberry and slightly herbal flavors in a supple if somewhat narrow frame. Elegant and graceful, with soft tannins. Drink now through 2005.–H.S. • $70 • (6/15/1999) • **89**

COLBY | CALIFORNIA

Chardonnay Napa Valley 1996: Somewhat silky on the palate, with hints of butterscotch, toasty oak, pear and spice and a mellow, moderately long finish. Drink now. • $14 • (7/31/1998) • **87**

COLD HEAVEN | CALIFORNIA

Pinot Noir Santa Barbara County Bien Nacido Vineyard 1996: Good intensity, depth and richness, with a broad array of ripe cherry, wild berry, cola and mint. Shortens up on the finish, where the tannins clamp down. Best to cellar short-term. Drink through 2002–J.L. • $25 • (9/30/1998) • **86**

Viognier Santa Barbara County Sanford & Benedict Vineyard 1997: Clean and refreshing, with spicy pear, apple and citrus notes that are rich and complex. Drink now through 2004.–J.L. • $25 • (1/31/2000) • **87**

Viognier Santa Ynez Valley 1998: Smooth and creamy, with tangerine, nectarine and ripe pear flavors, finishing with light spice and hazelnut. Drink now through 2004.–J.L. • $18 • (1/31/2000) • **87**

Viognier Santa Barbara County Sanford and Benedict Vineyard 1996 • $25 • (12/15/1997) • **86**

Viognier Santa Ynez Valley 1997: Spice, melon and tropical notes are couched in supple texture, but a bitter accent is compounded by a mineral finish. Good, though perhaps not to everyone's taste. From Morgan Clendenen. Drink now. • $18 • (12/31/1998) • **83**

Viognier Santa Ynez Valley Late Harvest Sanford & Benedict Vineyard 1997: Struggles to focus, with earthy tobacco flavors dominating the nice buttery pear. Turns oily. Drink now.–J.L. • $25 • (5/31/2000) • **81**

COLGIN | CALIFORNIA

Cabernet Sauvignon Napa Valley Herb Lamb Vineyard 1996: Big, ripe, rich and beefy, in a high-extract style delivering currant, bayleaf, black cherry and tar notes, this California collectible is complex, concentrated and firmly tannic, holding its focus. Best from 2001 through 2010.–J.L. • $520 Ⓐ • (10/31/1999) CS • **94**

Cabernet Sauvignon Napa Valley Herb Lamb Vineyard 1995: Dense and powerful, a majestic wine packed with earthy currant, black cherry, mineral, sage, coffee and spice flavors, and finishing with a remarkably rich, chewy aftertaste. Definitely cellar. Best from 2002 through 2010.–J.L. • $561 Ⓐ • (11/15/1998) • **94**

Cabernet Sauvignon Napa Valley Herb Lamb Vineyard 1994 • $515 Ⓐ • (7/31/1997) HR • **95**

Cabernet Sauvignon Napa Valley Herb Lamb Vineyard 1993 • $355 Ⓐ • (11/15/1996) • **96**

Cabernet Sauvignon Napa Valley Herb Lamb Vineyard 1992 • $348 Ⓐ • (10/15/1995) HR • **92**

COLLIER FALLS | CALIFORNIA

Zinfandel Dry Creek Valley Private Reserve 1998: A lighter style, attractive for its ripe, bright, peppery blackberry and black cherry pie flavors, turning juicy and spicy, with a nice touch of oak. Drink now through 2006.–J.L. • $24 • (6/30/2000) • **87**

Zinfandel Dry Creek Valley Private Reserve 1997: Deliciously complex, ripe, smooth and creamy, with spicy, peppery blackberry, black cherry, raspberry and wild berry flavors. Rich and concentrated on the finish. Drink now through 2002.–J.L. • $22 • (6/15/1999) • **90**

COLUMBIA | WASHINGTON

Cabernet Franc Yakima Valley Red Willow Vineyard David Lake Signature Series 1996: Firm, focused and generous with its plum and blueberry flavors, shaded with touches of smoke and spice. Appealing already. Drink through 2003–H.S. • $21 • (8/31/1999) • **88**

Cabernet Franc Yakima Valley Red Willow Vineyard David Lake Signature Series 1995 • $20 • (3/31/1998) • **87**

Cabernet Franc Yakima Valley Red Willow Vineyard David Lake Signature Series 1994 • $22 • (9/15/1997) • **89**

Cabernet Franc Yakima Valley Red Willow Vineyard Signature Series 1993 • $16 • (9/30/1995) • **87**

Cabernet Franc Yakima Valley Red Willow Vineyard Signature Series 1992 • $16 • (9/30/1994) • **87**

Cabernet Franc Yakima Valley Red Willow Vineyard Signature Series 1991 • $15 • (2/28/1993) • **86**

Cabernet Sauvignon Columbia Valley 1994: Ripe and round, its nicely supple texture surrounds a core of silky blackberry, currant and subtle herbal flavors that linger nicely on the finish. A fine curtain of tannin can use some cellar-time. Drink through 2006–H.S. • $15 • (8/31/1999) • **88**

Cabernet Sauvignon Columbia Valley 1993 • $13 • (9/15/1997) • **85**

Cabernet Sauvignon Columbia Valley 1992 • $13 • (3/31/1996) • **86**

Cabernet Sauvignon Columbia Valley 1991 • $13 • (9/30/1994) • **86**

Cabernet Sauvignon Columbia Valley 1990 • $13 • (11/30/1993) • **81**

Cabernet Sauvignon Columbia Valley 1989 • $16 Ⓐ • (10/15/1992) SS • **90**

Cabernet Sauvignon Columbia Valley 1988 • $10 • (3/31/1991) • **86**

Cabernet Sauvignon Columbia Valley 1986 • $10 • (10/15/1989) • **85**

Cabernet Sauvignon Columbia Valley Otis Vineyard Signature Series 1988 • $20 • (4/15/1992) • **89**

Cabernet Sauvignon Columbia Valley Red Willow Vineyard Signature Series 1988 • $20 • (4/15/1992) • **86**

Cabernet Sauvignon Columbia Valley Sagemoor Vineyard Signature Series 1989 • $18 • (3/31/1993) • **83**

Cabernet Sauvignon Columbia Valley Sagemoor Vineyard Signature Series 1988 • $20 • (4/30/1992) • **81**

Cabernet Sauvignon Columbia Valley Sagemoor Vineyards Signature Series 25th 1987 • $20 • (6/30/1994) • **89**

Cabernet Sauvignon Columbia Valley Sagemoor Vineyard Signature Series 1986 • $16 • (5/15/1991) • **85**

Cabernet Sauvignon Columbia Valley Sagemoor Vineyard 1985 • $15 • (10/15/1989) • **85**

Cabernet Sauvignon Columbia Valley Sagemoor Vineyards David Lake Signature Series 1994: Generous without being obvious, this harmonious wine subtly unfolds its berry and currant flavors. Vanilla and spice add pretty grace notes on the velvety finish. Very nice now, better from 2000 through 2005.–H.S. • $23 • (8/31/1998) • **90**

Cabernet Sauvignon Washington Bacchus Vineyard 1981 • $12 • (8/01/1984) • **86**

Cabernet Sauvignon Yakima Valley Otis Vineyard 1985 • $15 • (10/15/1989) • **91**

Cabernet Sauvignon Yakima Valley Otis Vineyard 1981 • $13 • (8/01/1984) • **83**

Cabernet Sauvignon Yakima Valley Otis Vineyard David Lake Signature Series 1995: A pretty wine, smooth and harmonious, with pretty raspberry and spice flavors that linger gently on the velvety finish. Drink now through 2001.–H.S. • $19 • (9/15/1999) • **87**

Cabernet Sauvignon Yakima Valley Otis Vineyard David Lake Signature Series 1994: Soft and creamy up front, displaying some pretty plum and currant flavors, turning tight and chewy on the finish. Best from 2001 through 2004.–H.S. • $23 • (8/31/1998) • **86**

Cabernet Sauvignon Yakima Valley Otis Vineyard David Lake Signature Series 1992 • $20 • (12/15/1996) • **90**

Cabernet Sauvignon Yakima Valley Otis Vineyard Signature Series 1993 • $23 • (4/30/1997) • **89**

Cabernet Sauvignon Yakima Valley Otis Vineyard Signature Series 1990 • $19 • (6/30/1994) • **85**

Cabernet Sauvignon Yakima Valley Otis Vineyard Signature Series 1989 • $18 • (6/15/1993) • **85**

Cabernet Sauvignon Yakima Valley Red Willow Vineyard 1985 • $15 • (10/15/1989) • **82**

Cabernet Sauvignon Yakima Valley Red Willow Vineyard 1981 • $35 • (10/15/1989) • **84**

Cabernet Sauvignon Yakima Valley Red Willow Vineyard David Lake Signature Series 1995: Light and silky, focusing its berry and earthy flavors into a long thread that keeps weaving through the firm finish. Drink now through 2002.–H.S. • $29 • (8/31/1999) • **87**

Cabernet Sauvignon Yakima Valley Red Willow Vineyard David Lake Signature Series 1994: Ripe and generous, a soft-texture mouthful of black cherry, currant and spice flavors, finishing with a chewy touch of tannin. Drink through 2005–H.S. • $23 • (8/31/1998) • **87**

Cabernet Sauvignon Yakima Valley Red Willow Vineyard David Lake Signature Series 1992 • $21 • (5/15/1996) • **87**

Cabernet Sauvignon Yakima Valley Red Willow Vineyard Signature Series 1993 • $23 • (4/30/1997) • **87**

Cabernet Sauvignon Yakima Valley Red Willow Vineyard Signature Series 1991 • $20 • (8/31/1995) • **88**

Cabernet Sauvignon Yakima Valley Red Willow Vineyard Signature Series 1989 • $18 • (5/31/1993) • **89**

Cabernet Sauvignon Yakima Valley Red Willow Vineyard Signature Series 25th 1987 • $20 • (6/30/1994) • **87**

Chardonnay Columbia Valley Woodburne Cuvée 1997: A bit on the earthy side, with leesy notes overriding otherwise-pretty apple and citrus flavors. Drink now through 2002.–H.S. • $14 • (9/30/1999) • **84**

Chardonnay Columbia Valley Woodburne Cuvée 1996: Crisp in texture, with spice and earth notes around a beam of bright citrus and apple. Drink now.–H.S. • $14 • (9/15/1998) • **85**

Chardonnay Yakima Valley Otis Vineyard David Lake Signature Series 1997: Polished, creamy and flavorful, this is a rich, harmonious white wine with spicy pear, lime, fig and vanilla flavors that linger effortlessly on the finish. A departure in style for this Washington winery, without the austerity that has characterized previous vintages. Drink now through 2003.–H.S. • $19 • (9/15/1999) HR • **91**

Chardonnay Yakima Valley Otis Vineyard David Lake Signature Series 1996 • $24 • (6/30/1998) • **90**

Chardonnay Yakima Valley Wyckoff Vineyard David Lake Signature Series 1997: Fresh and tangy, with distinctive floral, peppery notes around a lively core of apple and citrus flavors. Finishes gently but with persistent flavors. Drink now through 2002.–H.S. • $19 • (9/15/1999) • **89**

Chardonnay Yakima Valley Wyckoff Vineyard David Lake Signature Series 1996 • $24 • (6/15/1998) • **86**

Chenin Blanc Columbia Valley 1998: Lightly sweet, with pretty pear and leaf flavors on a modest frame. Drink now.–H.S. • $6 • (9/30/1999) • **83**

Gewürztraminer Yakima Valley 1996 • $7 • (9/15/1997) • **87**

Johannisberg Riesling Columbia Valley 1998: Starts off on the dry side, with more resiny flavors than floral or fruit, but finishes sweet, with a nice touch of pear. Drink now.–H.S. • $6 • (9/30/1999) • **83**

Merlot Columbia Valley 1994 • $13 • (2/28/1997) • **88**

Merlot Columbia Valley 1993 • $13 • (5/15/1996) • **85**

Merlot Columbia Valley 1992 • $13 • (5/31/1995) • **87**

Merlot Columbia Valley 1991 • $13 • (9/30/1994) • **87**

Merlot Columbia Valley 1990 • $13 • (6/15/1993) • **80**

Merlot Columbia Valley 1989 • $12 • (3/31/1992) • **80**

Merlot Columbia Valley 1988 • $10 • (3/31/1991) • **81**

Merlot Columbia Valley 1986 • $10 • (10/15/1989) • **84**

COLUMBIA

Merlot Washington 1981 • $25 • (10/15/1989) • **87**
Merlot Yakima Valley Milestone Merlot Signature Series 1992 • $20 • (9/30/1994) • **85**
Merlot Yakima Valley Red Willow Vineyard 1989 • $20 • (11/15/1991) • **89**
Merlot Yakima Valley Red Willow Vineyard David Lake Signature Series Milestone 1996: Highly aromatic but firm in texture, with a light layer of grainy tannins around a core of sweet black cherry and a hint of black pepper. Drink now through 2001.–H.S. • $24 • (9/15/1999) • **85**
Merlot Yakima Valley Red Willow Vineyard Milestone 1995: Supple and generous, almost plush in texture, with pretty raspberry and currant flavors that linger nicely on the light-textured, generous finish. Approachable now, best from 1999 through 2003.–H.S. • $23 • (8/31/1998) • **88**
Merlot Yakima Valley Red Willow Vineyard Milestone 1987 • $15 • (10/15/1989) • **80**
Merlot Yakima Valley Red Willow Vineyard Milestone David Lake Signature Series 1993 • $20 • (5/15/1996) • **87**
Merlot Yakima Valley Red Willow Vineyard Milestone Signature Series 1994 • $23 • (4/30/1997) • **85**
Merlot Yakima Valley Red Willow Vineyard Milestone Signature Series 1991 • $20 • (6/15/1993) • **84**
Merlot Yakima Valley Red Willow Vineyard Milestone Signature Series 1989 • $18 • (6/15/1992) • **88**
Merlot Yakima Valley Red Willow Vineyard Milestone Signature Series 1988 • $16 • (3/31/1991) • **82**
Peninsula Red Willow Vineyard Yakima Valley 1995: Has gorgeous plum, berry and spice aromas, but the flavors tighten up in a narrow band that persists nicely on the finish. Needs time to soften. Cabernet Sauvignon, Cabernet Franc and Merlot. Best after 2000.–H.S. • $65 • (11/30/1999) • **89**
Pinot Gris Yakima Valley 1996 • $10 • (9/30/1997) • **89**
Pinot Gris Yakima Valley Otis Vineyard 1997: Hard texture and metallic flavors intrude on this charmless white. Tasted twice, with consistent notes.–H.S. • $11 • (9/30/1999) • **71**
Pinot Noir Washington Woodburne Cuvée 1994 • $11 • (9/15/1996) • **84**
Pinot Noir Washington Woodburne Cuvée 1993 • $11 • (9/30/1995) • **85**
Pinot Noir Washington Woodburne Cuvée 1992 • $12 • (9/30/1994) • **82**
Pinot Noir Washington Woodburne Cuvée 1991 • $12 • (2/28/1993) • **72**
Pinot Noir Washington Woodburne Cuvée 1990 • $12 • (3/31/1992) • **77**
Pinot Noir Washington Woodburne Cuvée 1989 • $12 • (6/15/1992) • **84**
Pinot Noir Washington 1996 • $13 • (3/31/1998) • **84**
Pinot Noir Washington The Woodburne Collection 1987 • $10 • (3/31/1991) • **88**
Riesling Columbia Valley Cellarmaster's Reserve 1998: You can't beat this price for a very good quality Washington Riesling from a reputable producer. This version is soft and sweet, with pretty pear, cream and peach flavors that linger on the gentle finish. Drink now.–H.S. • $7 • (9/30/1999) • **86**
Riesling Columbia Valley Cellarmaster's Reserve 1997: Sweet but tangy, with pretty pineapple and apple character. Drink now.–H.S. • $8 • (9/15/1998) • **84**
Riesling Columbia Valley Cellarmaster's Reserve 1996 • $7 • (9/15/1997) • **86**
Sémillon Columbia Valley Reserve 1997: Gentle and smooth, with a spicy vanilla overlay to the round fig flavors. Has richness and depth, but manages to remain delicate. Can develop with age. Drink through 2002.–H.S. • $9 • (9/15/1999) • **88**
Sémillon Columbia Valley Sur Lie Reserve 1996: A dusky wine, smooth and appealing for its tobacco-scented fig and melon flavors. Drink now.–H.S. • $11 • (9/15/1998) • **85**
Syrah Yakima Valley 1996 • $14 • (3/31/1998) • **85**
Syrah Yakima Valley 1995 • $13 • (9/15/1997) • **87**
Syrah Yakima Valley Red Willow Vineyard 1994 • $24 • (9/15/1997) • **87**
Syrah Yakima Valley Red Willow Vineyard 1993 • $21 • (5/15/1996) • **88**
Syrah Yakima Valley Red Willow Vineyard 1992 • $20 • (9/30/1995) • **88**
Syrah Yakima Valley Red Willow Vineyard 1991 • $18 • (9/30/1994) • **83**
Syrah Yakima Valley Red Willow Vineyard 1990 • $20 • (12/31/1993) • **88**
Syrah Yakima Valley Red Willow Vineyard 1989 • $25 • (11/30/1992) • **87**
Syrah Yakima Valley Red Willow Vineyard 1988 • $25 • (5/15/1991) • **90**
Syrah Yakima Valley Red Willow Vineyard David Lake Signature Series 1996: Bright and clear in flavor, with just a nip of tannin to give grip to the pure blackberry and black cherry. Shaded with licorice and tar notes that linger on the elegant finish. Drink now through 2006.–H.S. • $30 • (11/30/1999) • **89**
Syrah Yakima Valley Red Willow Vineyard David Lake Signature Series 1995 • $24 • (1/31/1998) • **90**

Key: SS—Spectator Selection. CS—Cellar Selection. HR—Highly Recommended. $NA—Price not available. (BT)—Barrel tasting. Ⓐ—Auction Price.
For a key to the tasters' initials, see "How to Use These Listings."
Dates in parentheses represent the issues in which the ratings were published.

COLUMBIA CREST | WASHINGTON

Cabernet Sauvignon Columbia Valley 1996: Check out the deal on this Washington Cab. It's firm and chewy, but the ripe currant and blackberry flavors shine through and linger on the generous finish, and the tad-rough edges should smooth with a little cellar-time. Drink through 2006.–H.S. • $11 • (8/31/1999) • **88**
Cabernet Sauvignon Columbia Valley 1995: A solidly built, harmonious style, offering plenty of pretty black cherry and currant flavor alongside complementary herb and tobacco notes. Drink now through 2002.–H.S. • $11 • (7/31/1998) • **87**
Cabernet Sauvignon Columbia Valley 1994 • $11 • (9/15/1997) SS • **90**
Cabernet Sauvignon Columbia Valley 1993 • $9 • (9/30/1996) • **87**
Cabernet Sauvignon Columbia Valley 1992 • $9 • (7/31/1995) • **85**
Cabernet Sauvignon Columbia Valley 1991 • $9 • (9/30/1994) • **84**
Cabernet Sauvignon Columbia Valley 1990 • $10 • (11/30/1993) • **82**
Cabernet Sauvignon Columbia Valley 1989 • $8 • (10/15/1993) • **82**
Cabernet Sauvignon Columbia Valley 1988 • $9 • (7/31/1992) SS • **89**
Cabernet Sauvignon Columbia Valley 1987 • $10 • (8/31/1991) • **85**
Cabernet Sauvignon Columbia Valley Barrel Select 1991 • $15 • (5/31/1996) • **85**
Cabernet Sauvignon Columbia Valley Barrel Select 1990 • $15 • (9/30/1994) • **87**
Cabernet Sauvignon Columbia Valley Barrel Select 1989 • $15 • (6/30/1994) • **80**
Cabernet Sauvignon Columbia Valley Estate Series 1995: Firm in texture, a harmonious wine with a supple, round core of ripe blueberry and plum flavors, and hints of spice on the finish. Drink now.–H.S. • $20 • (9/15/1998) • **87**
Cabernet Sauvignon Columbia Valley Estate Series 1994 • $20 • (9/15/1997) • **85**
Cabernet Sauvignon Columbia Valley Estate Series 1993 • $18 • (2/28/1997) SS • **91**
Chardonnay Columbia Valley 1998: Bright in flavor, supple in texture, brimming with pineapple, cream and spice notes that harmonize nicely through the generous finish. Drink now through 2003.–H.S. • $9 • (6/30/2000) • **87**
Chardonnay Columbia Valley 1997: Here's a fresh and fragrant white delivering an enticing mouthful of apple and citrus flavors that echo on the harmonious finish. From one of Washington's biggest names; this vintage is lighter than usual, but the wine is a very good value, as usual. Drink now.–H.S. • $9 • (5/31/1999) • **85**
Chardonnay Columbia Valley 1996 • $9 • (6/15/1998) • **88**
Chardonnay Columbia Valley Estate Series 1998: Rich, long and generous, a complex, creamy wine dripping with pear, honey, nutmeg and clove, the flavors lingering enticingly. Delicious already. Drink now through 2003.–H.S. • $12 • (6/30/2000) SS • **90**
Chardonnay Columbia Valley Estate Series 1997: A smooth and generous offering from Washington, artfully balanced to showcase its profusion of pear, spice and coconut flavors that meld pleasantly with a hint of beeswax on the long, rich finish. A great value at this price and score, and availability should be good. Drink now through 2004.–H.S. • $11 • (8/31/1999) SS • **91**
Chardonnay Columbia Valley Estate Series 1996: Lighter style, offering plenty of nice pear and earthy mineral notes on a gentle frame. Finishes with pleasant sweetness. Drink now.–H.S. • $15 • (8/31/1998) • **87**
Chardonnay Columbia Valley Reserve 1997: Broad and generous if a bit overdone, with flavors that rely on oak, centering on spice, vanilla and butter, picking up hints of nectarine and pear on the supple finish. A bit hollow at the center, but the flavors are appealing. Drink now through 2002.–H.S. • $17 • (6/30/2000) • **88**
Chardonnay Columbia Valley Reserve 1996: Distinctly spicy and smoky, a silky-textured wine with lots of apple and pear flavors at the core. The finish unfolds gradually, leading to long echoes of the pretty flavors. Drink now.–H.S. • $17 • (9/15/1998) • **90**
Gamay Columbia Valley Beaujolais 1993 • $7 • (9/30/1994) • **85**
Gewürztraminer Columbia Valley 1998: Light and frankly sweet. Balanced, with a pleasantly bitter edge to the ripe pear, ginger and cream flavors. Drink now.–H.S. • $7 • (9/30/1999) • **84**
Gewürztraminer Columbia Valley 1997: Soft and off-dry, with lemony pear and honey flavors on a tight frame.–H.S. • $7 • (7/31/1998) • **83**
Johannisberg Riesling Columbia Valley 1998: Crisp and sweet at the same time, like a squeeze of fresh lime over a ripe peach, remaining tangy and tasty through the juicy finish. Picks up some nice mineral and floral hints at the end. Drink now through 2005.–H.S. • $7 • (9/15/1999) • **87**
Johannisberg Riesling Columbia Valley 1997: Off-dry, with simple apple and modest spice flavors. Drink now.–H.S. • $7 • (9/15/1998) • **81**
Johannisberg Riesling Columbia Valley 1996 • $7 • (6/30/1998) • **85**
Merlot Columbia Valley 1996: Smooth and spicy on the palate, this Washington red unfolds its dark cherry, licorice and herbal flavors on a bed of fine-grained tannins. A harmonious wine, its fruit echoing nicely on the finish. Drink now through 2004.–H.S. • $12 • (5/31/1999) SS • **88**

Merlot Columbia Valley 1995 • $15 • (6/15/1998) • **87**
Merlot Columbia Valley 1994 • $14 • (6/15/1997) SS • **90**
Merlot Columbia Valley 1993 • $10 • (5/31/1996) • **88**
Merlot Columbia Valley 1992 • $10 • (9/30/1994) • **87**
Merlot Columbia Valley 1991 • $10 • (4/15/1994) • **88**
Merlot Columbia Valley 1990 • $10 • (5/31/1993) • **85**
Merlot Columbia Valley 1989 • $10 • (2/29/1992) SS • **88**
Merlot Columbia Valley Barrel Select 1992 • $15 • (5/15/1996) • **88**
Merlot Columbia Valley Barrel Select 1991 • $15 • (9/30/1995) • **87**
Merlot Columbia Valley Barrel Select 1990 • $15 • (9/30/1994) • **86**
Merlot Columbia Valley Barrel Select 1989 • $15 • (5/31/1993) • **88**
Merlot Columbia Valley Barrel Select 1988 • $15 • (7/31/1992) • **87**
Merlot Columbia Valley Barrel Select 1987 • $15 • (5/31/1991) • **84**
Merlot Columbia Valley Estate Series 1995: Ripe, round and supple, balancing black cherry and dark plum flavors with spicy new oak and echoing vanilla and peach on the firm finish. Could develop more depth with short-term cellaring. Drink now.–H.S. • $22 • (9/30/1998) • **87**
Merlot Columbia Valley Estate Series 1994 • $NA • (9/15/1997) • **89**
Pinot Noir Willamette Valley Barrel Select 1992 • $15 • (3/31/1996) • **81**
Pinot Noir Willamette Valley Reserve 1996: Light and pretty, with spice-scented black cherry, anise and earth notes settling nicely on the gentle finish. Drink now.–H.S. • $19 • (9/30/1998) • **86**
Pinot Noir Willamette Valley Reserve 1995: Supple and harmonious, a gentle red with generous black cherry, berry and almond flavors, picking up floral hints on the finish. Drink now through 2001.–H.S. • $19 • (8/31/1998) • **87**
Reserve Columbia Valley 1995: Smooth, rich and aristocratic, this lovely red blend gently unfolds its blackberry, black currant, mineral and smoke flavors on a polished frame, serving up plenty of flavor on a refined foundation. Contains Merlot, Cabernet Sauvignon and Malbec. Drink now through 2005.–H.S. • $22 • (5/31/1999) HR • **92**
Reserve Columbia Valley 1994 • $22 • (9/30/1997) • **85**
Reserve Columbia Valley 1993 • $17 • (9/15/1996) • **87**
Reserve Columbia Valley 1992 • $18 • (7/31/1995) • **90**
Sauvignon Blanc Columbia Valley 1997: Fruity and appealing for its apple and spice flavors at the core, with just enough herbal and peppery notes to identify it as Sauvignon Blanc. Drink now.–H.S. • $8 • (5/31/1999) • **83**
Sauvignon Blanc Columbia Valley Estate Series 1997: Spicy and smooth, with some nice ripe fig and apple flavors balancing nicely with the prominent nutmeg and vanilla notes. Drink now.–H.S. • $10 • (9/15/1999) • **86**
Sauvignon Blanc Columbia Valley Estate Series 1996: Ripe, round style emphasizes the creamy texture, spicy flavors, and the touch of black fig character rolling through the finish. Drink now.–H.S. • $12 • (8/31/1998) • **88**
Sémillon Columbia Valley 1997: Light, dry and simple, with modest tobacco-scented pear flavors that, surprisingly, linger on the finish. Drink now.–H.S. • $7 • (9/15/1998) • **83**
Sémillon Columbia Valley Late Harvest 1995 • $21/375 ml. • (11/30/1997) • **83**
Sémillon Columbia Valley Late Harvest 1992 • $8/375 ml. • (4/30/1995) HR • **93**
Sémillon-Chardonnay Columbia Valley 1997: Has a strong Sémillon component, with all the tobacco and earth flavors you could want around a light core of fresh apple. Drink now.–H.S. • $8 • (8/31/1999) • **85**
Syrah Columbia Valley Reserve 1996: Ripe and generous with its plum, anise and coffee flavors, harmonious and balanced right through the fine-grained tannins. Marked by oak but not a huge wine, it's nicely focused and flavorful. Drink now through 2001.–H.S. • $24 • (9/15/1998) • **90**
Syrah Columbia Valley Reserve 1995 • $24 • (9/15/1997) • **89**
Syrah Columbia Valley Reserve 1994 • $17 • (9/15/1996) • **89**
White Riesling Columbia Valley Ice Wine Reserve 1995 • $26/375 ml. • (5/15/1997) • **87**

COMPASS | CALIFORNIA

Merlot California 1997: Simple, clean and pleasant, with flavors of strawberry and tea. Drink now.–J.L. • $10 • (10/15/1999) • **81**

CONCANNON | CALIFORNIA

Assemblage Livermore Valley Reserve 1996 • $15 • (5/15/1998) • **83**
Assemblage Reserve Livermore Valley 1995: A core of currant, cola and herb flavors permeates this wine, still a bit tight and with rustic tannins, but should soften nicely with time. Best from 2001 through 2004. • $19 • (9/30/1999) • **85**
Assemblage Reserve Central Coast 1993 • $17 • (11/15/1996) • **87**
Assemblage Reserve Central Coast 1992 • $15 • (12/15/1995) • **86**
Assemblage Livermore Valley 1991 • $15 • (11/15/1994) • **80**
Cabernet Sauvignon Central Coast 1995 • $10 • (9/30/1997) • **83**
Cabernet Sauvignon Central Coast Selected Vineyard 1996: Smooth and appealing for its plum, cherry and tobacco flavors, which linger nicely on the soft finish. Drink now through 2001.–H.S. • $10 • (11/15/1998) • **80**
Cabernet Sauvignon Central Coast Selected Vineyard 1994 • $10 • (11/30/1996) • **84**
Cabernet Sauvignon Central Coast Selected Vineyard 1993 • $10 • (11/30/1996) • **83**
Cabernet Sauvignon Central Coast Selected Vineyard 1992 • $10 • (11/15/1994) • **84**
Cabernet Sauvignon Livermore Valley 1983 • $12 • (6/15/1987) • **77**
Cabernet Sauvignon Livermore Valley 1981 • $12 • (12/16/1984) • **82**
Cabernet Sauvignon Livermore Valley Concannon Estate Vineyard 1991 • $10 • (11/15/1993) • **79**
Cabernet Sauvignon Livermore Valley Concannon Estate Vineyard 1989 • $10 • (11/15/1993) • **78**
Cabernet Sauvignon Livermore Valley Reserve 1995: Smooth and polished, here's a lush mouthful of raspberry-scented cherry and eucalyptus flavors, finishing gently. Drink now through 2002.–H.S. • $20 • (10/31/1998) • **86**
Cabernet Sauvignon Livermore Valley Reserve 1987 • $16 • (7/15/1991) • **83**
Cabernet Sauvignon Livermore Valley Reserve 1985 • $14 • (2/15/1989) • **87**
Chardonnay Central Coast Reserve 1997: Well balanced, with subtle pear and fig flavors on a medium frame. Focused on the finish, showing refreshing flinty notes. Drink now through 2001.–J.L. • $19 • (7/31/1999) • **87**
Chardonnay Central Coast Selected Vineyard 1997: This rich and softly textured white offers distinctive nut, apple, grapefruit, pear and spicy floral flavors that linger enticingly on the focused finish. A solid value at this price and score. Drink now through 2002.–J.L. • $11 • (7/31/1999) • **87**
Chardonnay Central Coast Selected Vineyards 1996: Offering appealing apple, pear and hazelnut flavors that are clean and refreshing, this simple, tasty white is perfect for summer sipping at a price that's hard to beat. Drink now.–J.L. • $10 • (7/31/1998) • **86**
Chardonnay Livermore Valley Reserve 1996: Ripe, with appealing pear, spice, fig and melon, picking up traces of citrus and spicy, toasty oak on the finish. A good value at this price. Drink now through 2001.–J.L. • $16 • (7/31/1998) • **87**
Merlot Alameda County Limited Vineyard Limited Bottling 1995: Starts nicely, with ripe black cherry and smoky, toasty herb notes. Falters slightly on the finish as the flavors turn dry. Drink now. • $15 • (8/31/1998) • **82**
Merlot Livermore Valley Beyer's Ranch Limited Bottling 1993 • $NA • (8/31/1996) • **84**
Petite Sirah Central Coast Reserve 1995: Ripe, smooth and darkly colored, with blackberry, black cherry and smoke flavors and soft, integrated tannins. Drink now through 2003.–J.L. • $23 • (11/15/1999) • **86**
Petite Sirah Central Coast Selected Vineyard 1991 • $10 • (2/28/1995) • **81**
Petite Sirah Livermore Valley 1987 • $11 • (8/31/1991) • **77**
Petite Sirah Livermore Valley Reserve 1985 • $15 • (8/31/1991) • **83**
Sauvignon Blanc Livermore Valley Selected Vineyard 1997 • $8 • (6/30/1998) • **86**
Sauvignon Blanc Livermore Valley 1996 • $8 • (4/30/1998) • **83**

CONN CREEK | CALIFORNIA

Anthology Napa Valley 1998: Supple and elegant, with ripe, polished cherry, currant and plum flavors, finishing with mild tannins.–J.L. • $NA • (8/31/1999) (BT) • **90-94**
Anthology Napa Valley 1996: Intense, with rangy, sprawling black cherry, plum and wild berry fruit that's in definite need of short-term cellaring to come together. Cabernet Sauvignon, Merlot and Cabernet Franc. Best from 2002 through 2010.–J.L. • $44 • (4/30/2000) • **88**
Anthology Napa Valley 1994 • $37 • (3/31/1998) • **90**
Anthology Napa Valley 1993 • $30 • (11/15/1996) • **93**
Anthology Napa Valley 1992 • $30 • (12/15/1995) • **90**
Anthology Napa Valley 1991 • $30 • (9/30/1994) CS • **93**
Cabernet Sauvignon Napa Valley 1981 • $14 • (12/16/1984) • **85**
Cabernet Sauvignon Napa Valley 1980 • $14 • (2/16/1984) • **86**
Cabernet Sauvignon Napa Valley 1974 • $250 • (11/15/1994) • **88**
Cabernet Sauvignon Napa Valley Barrel Select 1991 • $18 • (11/15/1994) • **85**
Cabernet Sauvignon Napa Valley Barrel Select 1988: A ripe '88 with lots of plum and blackberry, it's more complete than most, with good richness, depth and concentration. Finishes with a ripe, fruity aftertaste and enough richness to merit further cellaring. (1988 California Cabernet retrospective tasting). Drink through 2004.–J.L. • $15 • (11/15/1998) • **88**
Cabernet Sauvignon Napa Valley Barrel Select 1987 • $17 • (7/15/1991) • **87**
Cabernet Sauvignon Napa Valley Barrel Select 1986 • $18 • (2/28/1991) • **55**
Cabernet Sauvignon Napa Valley Barrel Select 1985 • $29 • (9/15/1990) • **90**
Cabernet Sauvignon Napa Valley Barrel Select 1983 • $15 • (12/31/1988) • **88**

■ ■ ■ ■

CONN CREEK

Cabernet Sauvignon Napa Valley Barrel Select Lot 79 1984 • $13 • (12/31/1988) • **86**

Cabernet Sauvignon Napa Valley Barrel Select Private Reserve 1986 • $40 • (12/15/1990) HR • **91**

Cabernet Sauvignon Napa Valley Barrel Select Private Reserve 1985 • $45 • (9/15/1990) • **91**

Cabernet Sauvignon Napa Valley Collins Vineyard Private Reserve 1984 • $28 • (3/31/1989) • **94**

Cabernet Sauvignon Napa Valley Limited Release 1996: Earthy, with a dirty, leathery flavor that muddles the modest cherry and currant within, so be advised. Drink now through 2005.–J.L. • $22 • (6/30/2000) • **82**

Cabernet Sauvignon Napa Valley Limited Release 1994 • $20 • (4/30/1998) • **84**

Cabernet Sauvignon Napa Valley Limited Release 1993 • $18 • (12/15/1996) • **84**

Cabernet Sauvignon Napa Valley Limited Release 1992 • $18 • (12/15/1995) • **88**

Cabernet Sauvignon Napa Valley Limited Release 1991 • $18 • (11/15/1994) • **88**

Cabernet Sauvignon Napa Valley Lot 1 1978: Shows off a lot of ripe plum, cherry and currant flavors, but also shades of oxidation, and the oak is still prevalent. Turns earthy, with a mushroom edge on the finish. (1978 California Cabernet retrospective tasting).–J.L. • $37 Ⓐ • (11/15/1998) • **87**

Cabernet Sauvignon Napa Valley Lot 2 1978: Dark, ripe and still showing plenty of ripe plum and berry up front, followed by hints of anise, sage, cedar and spice. Tannins have softened and there are hints of oxidation, but altogether it's a very complex and enticing wine that's aged well. (1978 California Cabernet retrospective tasting). Drink now through 2002.–J.L. • $13 • (11/15/1998) • **90**

Cabernet Sauvignon Napa Valley Reserve 1987 • $23 • (8/31/1992) • **87**

Merlot Napa Valley Barrel Select 1990 • $14 • (9/15/1994) • **84**

Merlot Napa Valley Barrel Select 1989 • $16 • (10/31/1992) • **80**

Merlot Napa Valley Barrel Select 1988 • $22 • (11/15/1991) • **86**

Merlot Napa Valley Collins Vineyard Barrel Select Limited Bottling 1987 • $22 • (12/31/1990) • **87**

Merlot Napa Valley Collins Vineyard 1985 • $14 • (3/31/1988) • **84**

Merlot Napa Valley Limited Release 1991 • $15 • (6/30/1996) • **83**

Triomphe Napa Valley 1987 • $26 • (7/15/1992) • **89**

Zinfandel Napa Valley Barrel Select 1988 • $10 • (10/15/1992) • **82**

Zinfandel Napa Valley Barrel Select 1987 • $10 • (11/15/1991) • **80**

Zinfandel Napa Valley Collins Vineyard 1983 • $10 • (12/15/1988) • **84**

CONSTANT | CALIFORNIA

Cabernet-Merlot-Cabernet Franc Napa Valley Diamond Mountain Vineyard 1996: Rich and elegant, with ripe, smooth, polished black cherry, cranberry, tart plum and spicy cedar nuances. Impressive for its subtle, polished nuances and delicate tannins. Drink through 2008.–J.L. • $100 • (11/15/1999) • **92**

Cabernet-Merlot-Cabernet Franc Napa Valley Diamond Mountain Vineyard 1995: Rich and elegant, it weaves together an appealing band of currant, plum, anise and spicy berry flavors, picking up cedary, dusty oak. Long, complex aftertaste. Best from 2001 through 2008.–J.L. • $95 • (11/15/1999) • **94**

COOK'S | CALIFORNIA

Brut America Imperial NV • $8 • (12/15/1997) • **81**

Cabernet Sauvignon California Captain's Reserve 1988 • $6 • (7/15/1992) • **80**

Extra Dry America Imperial NV • $8 • (12/15/1997) • **81**

Merlot California Captain's Reserve 1992 • $5 • (9/15/1994) • **81**

Merlot California Captain's Reserve 1989 • $6 • (5/31/1992) • **77**

Spumante America NV • $8 • (12/15/1997) • **84**

COOPER MOUNTAIN | OREGON

Chardonnay Willamette Valley 1997: Light and spicy, with an anise edge to the pretty apple and nectarine flavors that linger on the finish. Drink now.–H.S. • $13 • (4/30/1999) • **85**

Chardonnay Willamette Valley Reserve 1997: Bright and refreshing, with focused apple, pear and citrus flavors that last and last on the lively finish, with hints of spice and toast. Drink now through 2004.–H.S. • $18 • (3/31/2000) • **88**

Key: SS—Spectator Selection. CS—Cellar Selection. HR—Highly Recommended. $NA—Price not available. (BT)—Barrel tasting. Ⓐ—Auction Price. For a key to the tasters' initials, see "How to Use These Listings."
Dates in parentheses represent the issues in which the ratings were published.

Pinot Gris Willamette Valley 1997: Fresh and appealing for its pure peach and almond flavors, which charm regardless of the slightly coarse texture. Drink now.–H.S. • $15 • (7/31/1998) • **86**

Pinot Gris Willamette Valley 1996 • $12 • (7/31/1997) • **86**

Pinot Gris Willamette Valley Old Vines Reserve 1998: Has a distinctly green, earthy note mingling with the modest peach and melon. Earthy finish. Drink now.–H.S. • $20 • (3/31/2000) • **83**

Pinot Noir Willamette Valley 1998: Spice and floral notes swirl through the bright berry tones on a firm frame; a stylish wine and definitely one to cellar. Best from 2002 through 2007.–H.S. • $25 • (3/31/2000) • **89**

Pinot Noir Willamette Valley 1997: Light, with distinctly gamy overtones to the modest cherry flavors. Drink now through 2001.–H.S. • $14 • (6/15/1999) • **82**

Pinot Noir Willamette Valley 1996: Light in texture and flavor, with pretty cherry notes hovering around a soft core of currant and spice. Drink now through 2000.–H.S. • $15 • (7/31/1998) • **85**

Pinot Noir Willamette Valley 1995 • $13 • (7/31/1997) • **87**

Pinot Noir Willamette Valley 1994 • $15 • (2/28/1997) • **85**

Pinot Noir Willamette Valley 1993 • $13 • (1/31/1996) • **83**

Pinot Noir Willamette Valley 1990 • $14 • (2/28/1993) • **76**

Pinot Noir Willamette Valley 1988 • $13 • (4/15/1991) • **83**

Pinot Noir Willamette Valley 1987 • $13 • (2/15/1990) • **87**

Pinot Noir Willamette Valley Reserve 1997: Light and crisp, with a gamy edge to the modest strawberry flavors, finishing with a slight bite of tannin. Best from 2001 through 2004.–H.S. • $25 • (3/31/2000) • **82**

Pinot Noir Willamette Valley Reserve 1996: Firm in texture, with a light layer of blackberry and currant flavor combining with an earthy note on the chewy finish. Best after 2000.–H.S. • $26 • (4/30/1999) • **82**

Pinot Noir Willamette Valley Reserve 1995 • $25 • (7/31/1997) • **88**

Pinot Noir Willamette Valley Reserve 1994 • $30 • (2/28/1997) • **86**

Pinot Noir Willamette Valley Reserve 1993 • $19 • (1/31/1996) • **85**

Pinot Noir Willamette Valley Reserve 1988 • $20 • (4/15/1991) • **83**

Pinot Noir Willamette Valley Reserve Unfiltered 1990 • $20 • (2/28/1993) • **76**

White Pinot Noir Willamette Valley 1996 • $7 • (8/31/1997) • **87**

COOPER-GARROD | CALIFORNIA

Cabernet Franc Santa Cruz Mountains 1995 • $18 • (11/30/1997) • **81**

Cabernet Franc Santa Cruz Mountains 1994 • $18 • (4/30/1996) • **77**

Cabernet Franc Santa Cruz Mountains Premier Release 1992 • $16 • (2/28/1995) • **80**

Cabernet Sauvignon Santa Cruz Mountains 1995: Features rustic, earthy mineral flavors and a concentrated core of black cherry, sage and cedar that remains focused on the finish. Tannins are firm and well integrated. Best from 2000 through 2005.–J.L. • $28 • (10/15/1999) • **88**

Cabernet Sauvignon Santa Cruz Mountains 1994 • $25 • (11/30/1997) • **87**

Cabernet Sauvignon Santa Cruz Mountains 1992 • $20 • (3/31/1996) • **82**

Cabernet Sauvignon Santa Cruz Mountains Proprietor's Reserve 1995: A pretty, cherrylike core dominates this somewhat delicate Cabernet. Smoky oak, herb and blackberry flavors fan out on the finish, which has firm tannins. Drink now through 2006. • $35 • (11/15/1999) • **87**

Cabernet Sauvignon Santa Cruz Mountains Proprietor's Reserve 1993 • $35 • (11/30/1996) • **88**

Chardonnay Santa Cruz Mountains 1996: On solid ground, with traces of mineral and earth working their way into the pear and citrus notes. Finishes with a leafy edge. Drink now through 2000.–J.L. • $20 • (7/31/1998) • **85**

Chardonnay Santa Cruz Mountains Gravel Ridge Vineyard 1997: Clean and pure, with detailed flavors of pear, peach, apricot and spice. Turns slightly firm on the finish. Drink now.–J.L. • $20 • (7/31/1999) • **88**

COOPERS' LEGACY | CALIFORNIA

Merlot Sonoma County 1993 • $12 • (8/31/1996) • **79**

COPPOLA DIAMOND SERIES, FRANCIS | CALIFORNIA

Merlot California Blue Label 1997: Smooth, with herbal black cherry and currant flavors and integrated tannins. Drink now through 2003.–J.L. • $15 • (10/15/1999) • **82**

Zinfandel California Red Label 1997: Light and fruity, with strawberry, cherry and spicy, earthy notes. Drink now.–J.L. • $14 • (2/29/2000) • **82**

COPPOLA PRESENTS | CALIFORNIA

Bianco California 1997: A simple blend, with slightly sweet-tasting peach, mineral and floral flavors. Drink now.–J.L. • $12 • (12/31/1998) • **83**
Rosso California 1997: An up-front style featuring firm yet smooth tannins. Plum and raspberry flavors framed in smoky oak fan out nicely on the palate. Oddly enough, the finish tapers off quickly. A blend of Zinfandel, Syrah, Cabernet Sauvignon and Sangiovese. Drink now through 2002. • $10 • (6/15/1999) • **84**
Rosso California 1996: Fresh and open-textured, with just enough tannin backbone to make it sturdy enough for hearty food. A blend of Zinfandel, Cabernet Sauvignon, Sangiovese, Nebbiolo and Carignane. Drink now through 2002.–H.S. • $12 • (11/30/1998) • **86**

CORBETT CANYON | CALIFORNIA

Cabernet Sauvignon Alexander Valley Reserve 1989 • $9 • (11/15/1992) • **85**
Cabernet Sauvignon California Coastal Classic 1996: Simple, with pleasant herb and cherry notes. Drink now.–J.L. • $10 • (11/15/1998) • **79**
Cabernet Sauvignon California Coastal Classic 1994 • $6 • (11/30/1996) • **75**
Cabernet Sauvignon California Coastal Classic 1991 • $6 • (6/15/1993) • **80**
Cabernet Sauvignon California Coastal Classic 1989 • $7 • (11/15/1991) • **76**
Cabernet Sauvignon Napa Valley Reserve 1997: Lean, with a modest band of strawberry and herb flavors.–J.L. • $10 • (11/15/1999) • **78**
Cabernet Sauvignon Napa County Reserve 1994 • $9 • (11/30/1996) • **82**
Cabernet Sauvignon Napa Valley Reserve 1991 • $9 • (9/30/1994) • **82**
Cabernet Sauvignon Napa Valley Reserve 1990 • $9 • (9/15/1993) • **84**
Cabernet Sauvignon Santa Barbara-San Luis Obispo Counties Select 1985 • $10 • (5/31/1988) • **79**
Cabernet Sauvignon Sonoma County Reserve 1995: Straightforward, with toast, herb and ripe cherry flavors. Finishes lean. Drink now.–J.L. • $10 • (10/15/1998) • **79**
Cabernet Sauvignon Sonoma & Napa Counties Reserve 1989 • $9 • (11/15/1992) • **74**
Chardonnay Santa Barbara County Reserve 1997: Refreshing, toasty flavors are balanced by crisp citrus, pear and fig. Quaffable. Drink now.–H.S. • $9 • (11/30/1998) • **82**
Merlot California Coastal Classic 1994 • $7 • (7/31/1996) • **71**
Merlot California Coastal Classic 1992 • $7 • (9/15/1994) • **82**
Merlot California Coastal Classic 1991 • $6 • (11/30/1992) • **79**
Merlot California Coastal Classic 1989 • $7 • (11/15/1991) • **81**
Merlot California Reserve 1996: Soft and simple, with pleasant if diluted flavors of cherry, dill and vanilla. Drink now.–J.L. • $10 • (8/31/1998) • **79**
Merlot California Reserve 1994 • $9 • (7/31/1996) • **73**
Pinot Noir Central Coast Reserve 1989 • $10 • (11/15/1991) • **81**
Pinot Noir Santa Barbara County Coastal Classic 1990 • $7/1 liter • (2/28/1993) • **71**
Pinot Noir Santa Barbara County Reserve 1992 • $9 • (3/31/1995) • **82**
Pinot Noir Santa Barbara County Reserve 1991 • $9 • (2/28/1993) • **72**
Pinot Noir Santa Barbara County Reserve 1990 • $9 • (2/28/1993) • **73**
Pinot Noir Santa Maria Valley Sierra Madre Vineyard Reserve 1985 • $12 • (2/15/1988) • **81**
Zinfandel California Coastal Classic 1996 • $5 • (6/15/1998) • **78**

COREY CREEK | NEW YORK

Cabernet Franc North Fork of Long Island 1997: Bright and focused, this quaffable red offers attractive, sweet black cherry, toast and light herb flavors. Round and juicy, it has just enough tannin to match with lighter dishes. Drink now through 2001.–T.M. • $17 • (6/30/1999) • **85**
Chardonnay North Fork of Long Island 1998: Toasty oak flavors are prominent in this firm white, but there's just enough apple and citrus flavor for balance. Clean and refreshing. Drink now.–T.M. • $14 • (5/31/2000) • **83**
Chardonnay North Fork of Long Island Reserve 1998: Firm and polished, this well-structured white offers melon, honey and sweet vanilla flavors. Harmonious and lively on the finish. Drink now through 2002.–T.M. • $17 • (5/31/2000) • **88**
Chardonnay North Fork of Long Island Reserve 1997: Polished yet lively, this white offers focused pear, apple, melon, vanilla and light spicy flavors, balanced and clean. Not a showstopper, but will marry well with medium-weight dishes. Drink now through 2001.–T.M. • $17 • (6/30/1999) • **86**
Merlot North Fork of Long Island 1997: This lively red shows elegance and intensity. Black cherry, smoke and herb flavors are focused and firm. Drink now through 2002.–T.M. • $18 • (5/31/2000) • **86**
Merlot North Fork of Long Island 1994 • $17 • (12/31/1996) • **88**

CORISON | CALIFORNIA

Cabernet Sauvignon Napa Valley 1995: Starts with lots of anise, plum and wild berry, then tightens up, turning crisp. Needs short-term cellaring to develop a little more flesh and body. Drink through 2005.–J.L. • $40 • (10/31/1998) • **89**
Cabernet Sauvignon Napa Valley 1994 • $35 • (9/30/1997) • **87**
Cabernet Sauvignon Napa Valley 1993 • $30 • (10/15/1996) • **87**
Cabernet Sauvignon Napa Valley 1992 • $28 • (11/30/1995) CS • **92**
Cabernet Sauvignon Napa Valley 1991 • $26 • (10/15/1994) • **89**
Cabernet Sauvignon Napa Valley 1990 • $38 Ⓐ • (10/15/1993) HR • **91**
Cabernet Sauvignon Napa Valley 1989: Ripe cherry and berry-laced flavors turn dry, but the wine is well balanced and holds together nicely, finishing with a touch of austerity and herb and anise notes. (1989 California Cabernet retrospective tasting). Drink now.–J.L. • $20 • (8/31/1999) • **88**
Cabernet Sauvignon Napa Valley 1988: Solid, with ripe plummy currant, anise, mineral and sage flavors that are intense and firmly tannic, turning especially dry on the finish. Even though the fruit is ripe, the wine lacks the extra dimensions one hopes for from time. (1988 California Cabernet retrospective tasting). Drink now through 2002.–J.L. • $20 • (11/15/1998) • **84**
Cabernet Sauvignon Napa Valley 1987 • $20 • (12/15/1997) • **89**
Cabernet Sauvignon Napa Valley Kronos Vineyard 1996: Firm and focused, with ripe and intense cherry, currant and blackberry, turning supple and polished and holding its flavors for a long, complex aftertaste. Best from 2001 through 2009.–J.L. • $85 • (10/31/1999) • **91**
Cabernet Sauvignon Napa Valley Tenth Anniversary 1996: Marked by a supple, cedary core of spicy cherry, plum and currant, picking up complex anise, tar and oak, finishing with supple, polished tannins. A wine of richness and finesse. Drink now through 2007.–J.L. • $45 • (9/30/1999) • **90**

CORNERSTONE | CALIFORNIA

Cabernet Sauvignon Howell Mountain Beatty Ranch 1996: Dense, tight and concentrated, a bold expression, with rich currant, earth, mineral and sage, picking up spice and floral notes and revealing rich flavors on the firmly tannic finish. Best from 2002 through 2010.–J.L. • $45 • (10/31/1999) • **94**
Cabernet Sauvignon Howell Mountain Beatty Ranch 1994 • $35 • (10/31/1997) • **93**
Cabernet Sauvignon Howell Mountain Beatty Ranch 1993 • $33 • (4/30/1996) • **93**
Cabernet Sauvignon Howell Mountain Beatty Ranch 1992 • $33 • (12/15/1995) • **90**
Cabernet Sauvignon Howell Mountain Beatty Ranch 1991 • $33 • (11/15/1994) HR • **93**
Cabernet Sauvignon Howell Mountain Black Sears 1996: Supple and polished, with pretty oak leading to a core of ripe cherry and plum, it picks up earthy mineral, olive and clayish flavors, finishing long and complex. Best from 2002 through 2009.–J.L. • $44 • (10/31/1999) • **92**
Cabernet Sauvignon Napa Valley 1995: Decidedly earthy at first, but complex too, with the ripe berry and cherry needed to balance the initial earthiness, turning fleshy and elegant on the finish, where the tannins are well integrated. Drink through 2006.–J.L. • $39 • (11/15/1998) • **90**
Zinfandel Howell Mountain Beatty Ranch 1996: A big, ripe, expressive style, with loads of flavor, focused on black cherry, wild berry, raspberry, anise and cedar notes. Long, rich aftertaste. Drink now through 2007.–J.L. • $24 • (12/15/1999) • **91**
Zinfandel Howell Mountain Beatty Ranch 1994 • $20 • (2/28/1997) • **91**
Zinfandel Howell Mountain Cuvée Mysterieuses 1994 • $20 • (2/28/1997) • **91**

COSENTINO | CALIFORNIA

Cabernet Franc North Coast 1990 • $16 • (11/15/1992) • **83**
Cabernet Franc North Coast 1989 • $16 • (11/15/1992) • **78**
Cabernet Franc Napa County 1987 • $13 • (9/30/1989) • **75**
Cabernet Franc North Coast 1988 • $16 • (11/15/1991) • **80**
Cabernet Franc North Coast 1986 • $14 • (7/31/1988) • **92**
Cabernet Sauvignon Napa County 1990 • $15 • (11/15/1993) • **81**
Cabernet Sauvignon Napa County 1989 • $15 • (3/31/1992) • **86**
Cabernet Sauvignon Napa Valley 1997: Firm tannins support a blend of blackberry, currant, spice, cedar and herb flavors. Still a bit tight though, with a tangy, short finish. Best from 2002 through 2007. • $28 • (10/15/1999) • **87**
Cabernet Sauvignon Napa Valley 1996: An attractive, ripe and fruity style, with supple plum, black cherry and blackberry flavors and mild tannins. Should drink well early. Drink through 2004.–J.L. • $20 • (10/31/1998) • **88**

COSENTINO

Cabernet Sauvignon Napa Valley 1993 • $15 • (8/31/1996) • **84**
Cabernet Sauvignon Napa Valley 1991 • $16 • (10/31/1994) • **86**
Cabernet Sauvignon Napa Valley 1990 • $15 • (11/15/1993) • **86**
Cabernet Sauvignon Napa Valley Punched Cap Fermented Unfined 1992 • $16 • (9/15/1995) • **88**
Cabernet Sauvignon Napa Valley Reserve 1996: Disappointingly simple for a reserve in a great year. Fragrant cherry-berry flavors of modest depth and proportion turn diluted on the finish. Drink now through 2005.–J.L. • $75 • (5/31/2000) • **84**
Cabernet Sauvignon Napa Valley Reserve 1995: Smooth, ripe, rich and polished, with plush plum, currant, black cherry and wild berry, the flavors turning expansive and complex on the full-sail finish, where the tannins are well integrated. Drink through 2007.–J.L. • $50 • (10/31/1998) • **91**
Cabernet Sauvignon Napa Valley Reserve 1994 • $40 • (10/15/1997) • **89**
Cabernet Sauvignon Napa Valley Reserve 1993 • $35 • (11/15/1996) • **91**
Cabernet Sauvignon Napa Valley Reserve 1991 • $30 • (12/15/1995) • **90**
Cabernet Sauvignon Napa Valley Reserve 1990 • $25 • (11/15/1994) • **87**
Cabernet Sauvignon Napa Valley The Winemaster 1996: Distinctive for its core of coffee, herb and cedar notes, with currant and dried cherry filling in to give more depth and dimension. Drink now through 2006.–J.L. • $45 • (10/31/1999) • **87**
Cabernet Sauvignon Napa Valley The Winemaster 1989 • $20 • (11/15/1992) • **80**
Cabernet Sauvignon North Coast 1988 • $15 • (5/31/1991) • **88**
Cabernet Sauvignon North Coast 1987 • $16 • (6/30/1990) • **80**
Cabernet Sauvignon North Coast 1985 • $11 • (9/15/1988) • **84**
Cabernet Sauvignon North Coast Reserve 1988: Medium-weight, with a range of cherry, herb and olive flavors that are supple and understated, turning dry on the finish, where it's losing its intensity. (1988 California Cabernet retrospective tasting). Drink now through 2002.–J.L. • $20 • (11/15/1998) • **84**
Cabernet Sauvignon North Coast Reserve 1987 • $28 • (2/28/1991) • **86**
Cabernet Sauvignon North Coast Reserve 1986 • $18 • (5/15/1990) • **90**
Cabernet Sauvignon North Coast Reserve 1985 • $18 • (4/30/1989) • **81**
Cabernet Sauvignon North Coast Reserve 1984 • $14 • (3/31/1988) • **78**
Chardonnay Napa County 1998: Weaves together a mix of citrus offerings—orange and nectarine, along with canned pineapple and pithy notes. Drink now.–J.L. • $22 • (6/15/2000) • **82**
Chardonnay Napa Valley 1997: Snappy, refreshingly complex and detailed young wine, distinctive for its fresh apple, citrus, lemon-limelike flavors, finishing with a dash of hazelnut. Drink now through 2002.–J.L. • $18 • (5/15/1999) • **90**
Chardonnay Napa County 1996 • $18 • (5/15/1998) • **87**
Chardonnay Napa Valley The Sculptor Reserve 1997: Packs in lots of ripe, rich, fig, pear, melon and spice, picking up a trace of hazelnut on the finish, where the flavors linger. Drink now through 2003.–J.L. • $34 • (8/31/1999) • **90**
Chardonnay Napa Valley The Sculptor Reserve 1996 • $30 • (5/15/1998) • **90**
Gewürztraminer Napa Valley 1996 • $14 • (11/30/1997) • **85**
Il Chiaretto Classico Napa County 1994 • $12 • (11/30/1996) • **86**
M. Coz Meritage Napa Valley 1998: A very pretty barrel sample, rich in cherry, berry and currant flavors and framed by tasty, toasty oak, finishing with richness and a plush texture.–J.L. • $NA • (8/31/1999) (BT) • **90-94**
M. Coz Meritage Napa Valley 1996: Supple and elegant, with ripe and refined black cherry, currant and plummy Cabernet flavors, hints of floral and spice, finishing with ripe, round tannins. Drink now through 2009. –J.L. • $80 • (10/15/1999) • **91**
M. Coz Meritage Napa Valley 1995: A racy style, with earthy blackberry, cherry, currant and spice, turning simpler on the finish, with mild but well-integrated tannins. Drink through 2004.–J.L. • $75 • (10/31/1998) • **88**
M. Coz Meritage Napa Valley 1994 • $34 Ⓐ • (11/15/1997) • **91**
M. Coz Meritage Napa Valley 1993 • $45 • (11/15/1996) • **88**
M. Coz Meritage Napa Valley 1992 • $45 • (12/15/1995) • **92**
M. Coz Meritage Napa Valley 1991 • $45 • (11/15/1994) • **89**
M. Coz Meritage Napa Valley 1990 • $45 • (11/15/1993) • **92**
Cos Napa Valley 1989: Complex and complete, if lacking extra richness and depth. Ripe, with attractive, well-integrated cherry, plum, currant, berry, cedar, tar and spice flavors, turning dry and firm on the finish. (1989 California Cabernet retrospective tasting). Drink now through 2002.–J.L. • $45 • (8/31/1999) • **88**

Key: SS—Spectator Selection. CS—Cellar Selection. HR—Highly Recommended. $NA—Price not available. (BT)—Barrel tasting. Ⓐ—Auction Price. For a key to the tasters' initials, see "How to Use These Listings." **Dates in parentheses represent the issues in which the ratings were published.**

Cos Meritage Napa Valley 1988: Simple, with modest plum and black cherry flavors, it remains a rather unevolved wine. Finishes with herb and olive notes and slightly drying tannins. (Called Cos at the time this was bottled, the name was later changed to M. Coz when Château Cos d'Estournel contested.) A blend: 68 percent Cabernet Sauvignon, 14 percent Cabernet Franc, 11 percent Petit Verdot, 7 percent Merlot. (1988 California Cabernet retrospective tasting). Drink now through 2002.–J.L. • $45 • (11/15/1998) • **85**
Merlot California 1997: Strays toward the herbal side of Merlot, with pleasant herb-laced currant and plum flavors. Soft. Drink now.–J.L. • $20 • (10/15/1999) • **84**
Merlot Napa County 1997: Serves up ripe, spicy cherry and wild berry of modest depth and proportion, though the finish is more interesting. Drink now through 2004.–J.L. • $28 • (10/15/1999) • **86**
Merlot Napa County 1988 • $18 • (4/15/1991) • **82**
Merlot Napa County 1986 • $14 • (9/30/1988) • **85**
Merlot Napa County Reserve 1987 • $18 • (7/31/1990) • **80**
Merlot Napa Valley 1994 • $24 • (7/31/1996) • **87**
Merlot Napa Valley 1992 • $19 • (9/15/1994) • **88**
Merlot Napa Valley 1991 • $18 • (9/15/1994) • **77**
Merlot Napa Valley 1990 • $18 • (6/15/1993) • **84**
Merlot Napa Valley Oakville 1995 • $50 • (7/31/1997) • **92**
Merlot Napa Valley Oakville 1994 • $38 • (6/30/1996) • **87**
Merlot Napa Valley Oakville 1993 • $30 • (12/15/1995) • **89**
Merlot Napa Valley Oakville 1992 • $28 • (9/15/1994) • **89**
Merlot Napa Valley Reserve 1997: Good, but not very concentrated or flavorful. Those who prefer a light-style Merlot with herb and cherry flavors will find it serviceable. Drink now through 2004.–J.L. • $38 • (5/31/2000) • **84**
Merlot Napa Valley Reserve 1996: Supple and complex, with well-focused currant, plum, earth and cherry flavors, picking up pretty toasty oak and spice notes on the aftertaste. Drink now through 2004.–J.L. • $34 • (9/30/1998) • **88**
Merlot Napa Valley Reserve 1994 • $34 • (6/30/1997) • **91**
Merlot North Coast 1996: Smooth and engaging, with plump cherry, wild berry and spice. Fills in with a dash of sage and anise and well-integrated tannins. Drink through 2004.–J.L. • $25 • (10/15/1998) • **86**
Merlot Oakville Estate 1997: Smooth, ripe and polished, with supple tannins and pretty currant, anise, black cherry and vanilla scents, though it turns simple with modest tannins. Drink now through 2004.–J.L. • $75 • (10/15/1999) • **87**
Merlot Oakville Estate 1996: Packs in lots of flavor, though it is heavily tilted toward oak, with a core of plum, cherry and funky, earthy flavors. Give it time to smooth out. Drink through 2004.–J.L. • $60 • (9/30/1998) • **88**
Pinot Noir Carneros 1996 • $30 • (2/28/1998) • **84**
Pinot Noir Carneros 1994 • $25 • (2/29/1996) • **84**
Pinot Noir Carneros 1991 • $18 • (2/28/1994) • **82**
Pinot Noir Carneros Unfined & Unfiltered 1993 • $25 • (3/31/1995) • **84**
Pinot Noir Carneros Unfined & Unfiltered 1992 • $20 • (2/28/1994) • **89**
Pinot Noir Napa Valley 1996: Tart and lean, with stemmy, tealike cherry and berry flavors that turn to cola, tar and earth. Best now through 2002.–J.L. • $25 • (9/15/1998) • **82**
Pinot Noir Napa Valley 1995 • $25 • (12/31/1996) • **89**
Pinot Noir Napa Valley 1990 • $14 • (9/30/1992) • **83**
Pinot Noir Napa Valley LZ 1994 • $20 • (2/29/1996) • **87**
Pinot Noir Napa Valley Punched Cap Fermented Unfiltered & Unfined 1993 • $25 • (5/15/1995) • **86**
Pinot Noir Napa Valley Unfined & Unfiltered 1993 • $18 • (3/31/1995) • **83**
Pinot Noir Russian River Valley 1996 • $50 • (2/28/1998) • **89**
Pinot Noir Russian River Valley 1994 • $38 • (8/31/1996) • **88**
Pinot Noir Sonoma County 1997: Medium-bodied, with a core of ripe strawberry, mineral and spicy toasted oak flavors that finish firm and focused. Drink now through 2002.–J.L. • $30 • (9/15/1999) • **86**
Pinot Noir Sonoma County 1996: Tough, earthy and leathery, with a hint of greenness, some tea and stemmy notes. Shows off a touch of spice but not much fruit. Drink now through 2001.–J.L. • $20 • (9/15/1998) • **83**
Pinot Noir Sonoma County 1990 • $18 • (9/30/1992) • **83**
Pinot Noir Sonoma County 1989 • $13 • (6/30/1991) • **82**
The Novelist California Meritage 1998: Sweaty and cheesy, with a bitter, stemmy flavor. Tasted twice, with consistent notes.–J.L. • $18 • (5/31/2000) • **74**
The Novelist California Meritage 1997: Pretty herbal, with a solid grapefruit and grass core. Bright acidity in this old-style yet fairly complex wine. Finishes with a hint of ripe fig. Contains Sauvignon Blanc and Sémillon. Drink now through 2002. • $16 • (1/31/1999) • **87**
The Novelist California Meritage 1996 • $16 • (7/31/1997) • **87**
The Poet Meritage Napa Valley 1996: Fans of herb and cedar flavors will find the texture smooth and supple, with hints of sage and black cherry filling in the gaps. Drink now through 2005.–J.L. • $40 • (11/15/1999) • **87**

The Poet Meritage Napa Valley 1995: A clean, well-proportioned claret-style red, with spicy currant, berry, plum and cedary flavors, finishing with ripe, integrated tannins and a touch of raspberry. Nothing too fancy at this point, but it's well balanced and a year or two of cellaring should bring supple texture. A blend: 69 percent Cabernet Sauvignon, 21 percent Cabernet Franc, 8 percent Merlot, 2 percent Petit Verdot.–J.L. • $38 • (10/31/1998) • **88**
The Poet Meritage Napa Valley 1994 • $30 • (11/15/1997) • **89**
The Poet Meritage Napa Valley 1993 • $26 • (11/15/1996) • **91**
The Poet Meritage Napa Valley 1992 • $24 • (12/15/1995) • **87**
The Poet California Meritage 1990 • $23 • (5/15/1995) • **86**
The Poet California Meritage 1989 • $25 • (11/15/1993) • **79**
The Poet California Meritage 1988 • $27 • (5/31/1991) • **85**
The Poet California Meritage 1987 • $25 • (9/15/1990) • **85**
The Poet California Meritage 1986 • $22 • (7/31/1989) • **86**
The Poet California Meritage 1985 • $18 • (8/31/1988) • **79**
Zinfandel California Cigarzin 1998: Fair, but no cigar. Medium-bodied, with stewed cherry and earth notes, turning slightly green on the finish.–J.L. • $22 • (4/30/2000) • **79**
Zinfandel California Cigarzin 1997: Tastes sweet beyond ripeness, almost late-harvest in style, with jammy wild berry and cherry flavors. Drink now through 2002.–J.L. • $19 • (1/31/1999) • **88**
Zinfandel California Cigarzin 1996 • $16 • (3/31/1998) • **86**
Zinfandel California The Zin 1998: A trace of funk, with vegetal and stewed currant notes, but decent depth and round flavors. Drink now.–J.L. • $25 • (5/15/2000) • **80**
Zinfandel Russian River Valley The Zin Reserve 1998: Very ripe, with jammy, sweet-tasting blackberry Zinfandel flavors that are tight and one-dimensional. Finishes hot. Drink now through 2004.–J.L. • $50 • (5/15/2000) • **85**
Zinfandel California The Zin 1997: Elegant, with spicy, earthy, wild berry, cherry and tar, finishing with dusty tannins. Medium-weight, ready-to-drink style. Try now.–J.L. • $22 • (6/30/1999) • **87**
Zinfandel California The Zin 1995 • $23 • (3/31/1997) • **88**
Zinfandel Napa County-Sonoma County The Zin 1994 • $21 • (4/30/1996) • **90**
Zinfandel Sonoma County The Zin Unfined & Unfiltered 1993 • $18 • (9/15/1995) • **87**
Zinfandel Sonoma County The Zin 1992 • $16 • (7/31/1994) • **88**
Zinfandel Russian River Valley The Zin 1991 • $15 • (12/31/1992) • **89**
Zinfandel Sonoma County The Zin 1990 • $15 • (10/15/1992) • **88**

COSTA DE ORO | CALIFORNIA

Pinot Noir Santa Maria Valley Gold Coast Vineyard 1997: Firm, light-bodied, showing a modest range of tea and cherry flavors. Drink now through 2002.–J.L. • $17 • (9/15/1999) • **83**
Pinot Noir Santa Maria Valley Gold Coast Vineyard 1996: Tart, earthy and herbal flavors don't add much to the diluted style. Sour on the finish. Drink now.–J.L. • $17 • (9/30/1998) • **75**

COTES DE SONOMA | CALIFORNIA

Cabernet Sauvignon Sonoma County 1993 • $8 • (12/15/1995) • **83**
Cabernet Sauvignon Sonoma County 1990 • $7 • (10/31/1992) • **83**
Cabernet Sauvignon Sonoma County 1989 • $7 • (11/15/1991) • **83**
Deux Cépages Sonoma County 1990 • $6 • (11/15/1991) • **73**

COTTONWOOD CANYON | CALIFORNIA

Merlot Central Coast 1996: Pungent and vegetal, with a tarry edge. Not much fun. • $28 • (10/15/1999) • **72**
Merlot Central Coast 1995 • $26 • (5/15/1998) • **85**
Merlot Central Coast 1994 • $25 • (7/31/1997) • **90**
Pinot Noir Santa Barbara County 1991 • $29 • (12/31/1995) • **85**
Pinot Noir Santa Barbara County 1991 • $29 • (2/28/1997) • **80**
Pinot Noir Santa Barbara County 1990 • $20 • (2/28/1994) • **79**
Pinot Noir Santa Barbara County 1989 • $25 • (2/28/1993) • **88**
Pinot Noir Santa Barbara County Barrel Select 1991 • $38 • (12/31/1995) • **87**
Pinot Noir Santa Barbara County Barrel Select 1989 • $25 • (2/28/1993) • **82**
Pinot Noir Santa Maria-Sonoma Sharon's Vineyard 1996: Mature in color, but the flavor has lift, with tart cherry and earthy toasted oak over a soft, focused frame. Drink now.–J.L. • $32 • (6/15/1999) • **83**

COTURRI | CALIFORNIA

Cabernet Sauvignon Sonoma Valley Red The Founder's Series 1997: Showing quite a bit of mint and menthol, with an almost medicinal edge. Anise, blackberry and tealike notes add interest. Supple in texture, it has depth, character and a long finish. Not for everyone. Drink now through 2007. • $25 • (11/15/1999) • **88**
Merlot Sonoma Mountain 1994 • $22 • (7/31/1996) • **78**
Sangiovese Sonoma Valley Red The Founder's Series 1997: Richly textured, with a fine blend of black cherry, anise, herb, tea and classy oak. Firm, ripe tannins will make it last, adding depth and finesse. Finishes long. Drink now through 2005. • $25 • (11/15/1999) • **89**
Zinfandel Sonoma Mountain 1994 • $18 • (9/15/1996) • **88**
Zinfandel Sonoma Valley Chauvet Vineyards 1997: Sweet, with ripe, juicy wild berry, cherry, plum and spice, this is a well-made, tasty style of late-harvest Zin. Drink now.–J.L. • $20 • (6/30/1999) • **88**
Zinfandel Sonoma Valley Chauvet Vineyards 1990 • $17 • (10/15/1992) • **83**
Zinfandel Sonoma Valley P. Coturri Family Vineyards 1997: Off-dry, with a gamy, leathery edge, the sweet plum and wild berry flavors are focused and complex, with cedar and coffee notes. Drink now.–J.L. • $24 • (6/30/1999) • **88**

COUGAR RIDGE | CALIFORNIA

Cabernet Sauvignon Paso Robles 1996: Smooth-textured, with good body, though the flavors are a bit restrained. Finishes with hints of blackberry and herbs. Drink now. • $24 • (2/28/1999) • **82**

COULSON | CALIFORNIA

Chardonnay El Dorado Reserve 1996: Starts with delicate, lemony freshness and ripe apple flavors, but finishes with a yeasty note. Drink now.–T.G. • $13 • (7/31/1998) • **82**

COUNTERPOINT | CALIFORNIA

Cabernet Sauvignon Sonoma Mountain 1996: Tight, with complex cedary currant, anise, mineral, earth and sage, unfolding on the finish. One of Laurel Glen Vineyard's second labels. Drink through 2004.–J.L. • $20 • (5/15/1999) • **87**

COVEY RUN | WASHINGTON

Aligoté Yakima Valley Newhouse Vineyard 1997: This Washington version of a secondary white grape from Burgundy is round and fruity; a simple white with pretty apple and spice flavors. Drink now.–H.S. • $12 • (8/31/1999) • **83**
Cabernet Sauvignon Columbia Valley 1996: Ripe and generous, with focused berry and earthy mint flavors framed by very firm tannins. Needs cellaring to soften. Best after 2000.–H.S. • $12 • (9/30/1999) • **84**
Cabernet Sauvignon Columbia Valley 1995 • $13 • (9/15/1997) • **85**
Cabernet Sauvignon Columbia Valley 1993 • $12 • (9/15/1996) • **85**
Cabernet Sauvignon Yakima Valley 1993 • $7 • (9/30/1994) • **80**
Cabernet Sauvignon Yakima Valley 1992 • $11 • (3/31/1995) • **84**
Cabernet Sauvignon Yakima Valley 1990 • $9 • (3/15/1994) • **78**
Cabernet Sauvignon Yakima Valley 1989 • $12 • (3/15/1993) • **78**
Cabernet Sauvignon Yakima Valley 1988 • $11 • (4/30/1992) • **85**
Cabernet Sauvignon Yakima Valley 1986 • $10 • (10/15/1989) • **80**
Cabernet Sauvignon Yakima Valley Whiskey Canyon Vineyard 1995: Dense and gamy, an earthy wine, with tough tannins and decadent flavors lingering around the ripe blackberry notes on the finish. Best after 2001.–H.S. • $25 • (9/30/1999) • **85**
Cabernet Sauvignon Yakima Valley Whiskey Canyon 1993 • $23 • (4/30/1997) • **84**
Cabernet Sauvignon Yakima Valley Whiskey Canyon 1992 • $20 • (9/30/1995) • **79**
Cabernet Sauvignon Yakima Valley Whiskey Canyon 1991 • $20 • (9/30/1995) • **85**
Cabernet-Merlot Washington 1997: Light in texture and flavor, with pretty currant, blueberry and vanilla flavors that linger on the smooth finish. Drink now through 2002.–H.S. • $8 • (8/31/1999) • **86**
Cabernet-Merlot Washington 1995 • $11 • (4/30/1997) • **84**
Chardonnay Washington 1997: Fresh and open-textured, with pretty pear and resin flavors that linger gently on the finish. Drink now.–H.S. • $8 • (8/31/1999) • **85**
Chardonnay Washington 1996 • $10 • (6/15/1998) • **82**
Chardonnay Washington Celilo Vineyard 1996: Bright and spicy, striking a deft balance between its spicy oak notes and juicy core of vibrant peach and apple flavors. Drink now.–H.S. • $29 • (9/15/1998) • **88**
Chardonnay Yakima Valley Reserve 1996: Lean and sinewy, with racy acidity balanced against spicy peach and green apple flavors that persist nicely on the finish. Drink now through 2002.–H.S. • $12 • (8/31/1999) • **87**
Chardonnay Yakima Valley Whiskey Canyon Vineyard 1997: Youthful and exuberant, with pretty apple and peach flavors and a delicate touch of mint

to the fresh profile. Flavors last nicely on the finish. Drink now.–H.S. • $19 • (9/30/1999) • **87**

Chenin Blanc Columbia Valley 1996 • $8 • (9/15/1997) • **82**

Chenin Blanc Washington 1998: Strong leafy and minty aromas overshadow the light apple in this softly sweet sipper. Drink now.–H.S. • $6 • (9/30/1999) • **81**

Fumé Blanc Columbia Valley 1996: A fresh and tangy Sauvignon Blanc, tasty and affordable, its bright green pineapple, star fruit and citrus flavors bouncing around on the palate right through the zippy finish. A Sauvignon Blanc from Washington, it's a nice wine at a nice price. Ready to drink. –H.S. • $8 • (9/15/1998) • **87**

Fumé Blanc Washington 1997: Bright and fruity, this Sauvignon Blanc is ready to drink, offering apple and passion fruit flavors that linger on the juicy finish. It's a tasty white that won't break your budget when the occasion calls for multiple bottles.–H.S. • $7 • (8/31/1999) • **87**

Gewürztraminer Washington 1998: Bright and refreshing for its pear, orange and spice flavors on a soft frame. Stops short of being sweet. Drink now.–H.S. • $12 • (9/30/1999) • **85**

Gewürztraminer Washington Celilo Vineyard 1997: Crisp, bright and a little sweet, but not as spicy or flavorful as some. Has refinement and grace that suggest it would accompany food well. Drink now.–H.S. • $7 • (9/30/1999) • **83**

Gewürztraminer Washington Celilo Vineyard 1996: A zinger of an aromatic white wine, dry and generous with its apricot and grapefruit flavors. Drink now.–H.S. • $13 • (9/15/1998) • **88**

Johannisberg Riesling Columbia Valley 1996 • $6 • (9/15/1997) • **86**

Merlot Yakima Valley 1993 • $11 • (5/31/1995) • **83**

Merlot Yakima Valley 1992 • $11 • (5/15/1994) • **74**

Merlot Yakima Valley 1990 • $12 • (1/31/1993) • **82**

Merlot Yakima Valley 1989 • $11 • (6/15/1992) • **79**

Merlot Yakima Valley 1988 • $10 • (3/31/1991) • **87**

Merlot Yakima Valley Reserve 1995: Bright and crisp, with firm tannins and cherry flavors, shaded with hints of herb on the finish. Drink now.–H.S. • $20 • (12/15/1998) • **84**

Merlot Yakima Valley Reserve 1994 • $23 • (4/30/1997) • **82**

Merlot Yakima Valley Reserve 1993 • $15 • (9/30/1995) • **80**

Merlot Yakima Valley Reserve 1989 • $17 • (3/31/1992) • **83**

Merlot-Cabernet Columbia Valley 1994 • $10 • (9/15/1996) • **86**

Morio-Muskat Columbia Valley 1997: Light and sweet, with pretty pear and litchi flavors hovering around the finish. (3 percent residual sugar.) This variety is a hybrid blend of Sylvaner and Pinot Blanc. Drink now.–H.S. • $7 • (9/15/1998) • **84**

Morio-Muskat Washington 1998: Light and gently sweet. Not a dessert wine, but a pleasant sipper, with modest apple, citrus and spice flavors. Drink now.–H.S. • $7 • (9/30/1999) • **82**

Morio-Muskat Yakima Valley 1994 • $7 • (9/30/1995) • **81**

Riesling Columbia Valley Dry 1996 • $6 • (9/15/1997) • **88**

Riesling Washington 1998: Fruity and generous, juicy, with green apple, melon and mineral flavors that finish soft and elegant, this young white from Washington makes a big impression on the palate but only a small dent in the wallet. Drink now.–H.S. • $6 • (9/15/1999) • **85**

Riesling Washington Dry 1998: Says dry but it's pretty sweet, offset by some juicy, citrusy acidity. Modest in flavor, with some nice apple and floral notes. Drink now through 2001.–H.S. • $6 • (9/30/1999) • **83**

Riesling Washington Late Harvest Reserve 1997: Sweet and silky, with hints of apricot and spice to the core of pear flavor. Stands out for its polished texture.–H.S. • $10 • (9/15/1998) • **87**

Riesling Yakima Valley Ice Wine 1995 • $20/375 ml. • (4/30/1997) • **82**

Riesling Yakima Valley Ice Wine 1990 • $20 • (4/15/1995) • **83**

Riesling Yakima Valley Late Harvest Reserve 1998: Ripe, sweet and packed with flavor. Like biting into a ripe peach that's still crisp in texture. Finishes with juicy apple and apricot notes. Drink now through 2003.–H.S. • $8 • (9/30/1999) • **87**

White Riesling Columbia Valley Late Harvest 1996 • $9 • (9/15/1997) • **86**

White Riesling Columbia Valley Late Harvest 1995 • $8 • (9/15/1996) • **86**

White Riesling Yakima Valley Ice Wine 1990 • $20/375 ml. • (9/30/1994) • **90**

White Riesling Late Harvest Yakima Valley 1994 • $7 • (9/15/1995) • **91**

White Riesling Late Harvest Yakima Valley 1993 • $7 • (9/30/1994) • **88**

Key: SS—Spectator Selection. CS—Cellar Selection. HR—Highly Recommended. $NA—Price not available. (BT)—Barrel tasting. (A)—Auction Price. For a key to the tasters' initials, see "How to Use These Listings."
Dates in parentheses represent the issues in which the ratings were published.

COYNE, THOMAS | CALIFORNIA

Merlot El Dorado Quartz Hill Vineyard 1996: Firm and tough, but shows bright cherry flavors with notes of coffee and anise. Astringent on the finish. Drink now.–J.L. • $17 • (10/15/1998) • **81**

Merlot El Dorado Quartz Hill Vineyard 1990 • $13 • (6/30/1993) • **84**

Merlot Sonoma County 1996: Lean, but displays herb, cherry and mocha flavors that shut down on the austere finish. Drink now.–J.L. • $20 • (10/15/1998) • **80**

Merlot Sonoma County 1990 • $12 • (6/30/1993) • **84**

CRAIG, ROBERT | CALIFORNIA

Affinity Napa Valley 1997: Ripe date and plummy flavors turn lean and tannic in this young and chunky wine. May need time. Tasted twice, with consistent notes. Drink now through 2007.–J.L. • $44 • (6/30/2000) • **86**

Affinity Napa Valley 1996: A winner, this Bordeaux-style red blend is smooth and supple, with a tasty core of black cherry, currant, anise, sage, cedar and spice flavors that are rich and concentrated, long and lingering. A blend of Cabernet Sauvignon, Merlot and Cabernet Franc. Drink through 2007.–J.L. • $40 • (4/30/1999) CS • **92**

Affinity Napa Valley 1995 • $34 • (6/15/1998) CS • **91**

Affinity Napa Valley 1994 • $28 • (8/31/1997) HR • **94**

Affinity Napa Valley 1993 • $25 • (10/15/1995) • **87**

Cabernet Sauvignon Howell Mountain 1996: Supple and graceful, with elegant black cherry, currant, tar and anise, it unfolds to reveal layers of complexity and finesse, with a lingering aftertaste. Best from 2001 through 2008.–J.L. • $40 • (10/15/1999) • **91**

Cabernet Sauvignon Howell Mountain 1995: Captures ripe, rich, even polished Cabernet flavors, with distinct earth, mineral, plum, blackberry and currant. Fans out on the palate, with depth and concentration, all the while keeping a tight focus on the fruit and balance. Drink through 2007.–J.L. • $34 • (10/31/1998) • **91**

Cabernet Sauvignon Howell Mountain 1994 • $28 • (11/30/1997) • **90**

Cabernet Sauvignon Howell Mountain 1993 • $25 • (10/15/1995) • **89**

Cabernet Sauvignon Mount Veeder 1996: Deliciously rich and complex, with concentrated currant, black cherry, anise, berry and spice flavors, finishing with pleasant, well-integrated tannins. Drink now through 2007.–J.L. • $40 • (8/31/1999) • **92**

Cabernet Sauvignon Mount Veeder 1995: Tightly wound, with firm, chewy tannins built around a core of earthy currant, mineral, coffee, sage and cedar. You can drink this delicious wine now (decant it for an hour) or cellar short-term. Drink through 2008.–J.L. • $34 • (8/31/1998) • **91**

Cabernet Sauvignon Mount Veeder 1994 • $28 • (11/15/1997) • **94**

Cabernet Sauvignon Mount Veeder 1993 • $25 • (10/15/1995) • **90**

Cabernet Sauvignon Napa Valley 1992 • $20 • (10/15/1995) • **87**

Chardonnay Napa Valley Carneros 1998: Well oaked, with citrus and butterscotch flavors. Shows more oak than fruit. Drink now.–J.L. • $24 • (5/31/2000) • **84**

Chardonnay Napa Valley Carneros 1997: Smooth and creamy, with a pretty toasty oak and vanilla-scented edge. The rich core of pear, fig, apple and melon is bright, rich and concentrated, turning enormously complex. Drink now through 2002.–J.L. • $24 • (7/31/1999) • **93**

Syrah Paso Robles 1997: Smooth, plush and polished, with medium-rich smoke, meat, tart cherry, berry and Syrah-like fruit flavors, finishing with a solid dash of oak and cedar. Drink now through 2004.–J.L. • $24 • (9/30/1999) • **87**

Zinfandel Amador County 1997: Waxy and a touch beefy, it struggles to deliver much beyond a simple blend of dried berry and plum notes. Drink now through 2004.–J.L. • $24 • (5/31/2000) • **83**

CRANE CANYON | CALIFORNIA

Mourvèdre Sonoma Valley 1993 • $18 • (8/31/1995) • **86**

Pinot Noir Russian River Valley 1996: Cola and black cherry flavors rise to the fore in this lean-styled wine. Finishes a bit short and coarse, with a spicy edge. Drink now. • $24 • (8/31/1998) • **83**

Zinfandel Russian River Valley 1998: Full-bodied, with jammy, ripe black cherry and plum flavors and spice overtones on the long finish. Drink now through 2004.–J.L. • $24 • (5/31/2000) • **87**

Zinfandel Russian River Valley 1997: Bright and exuberant, with plum and spice bursting at the seams. Not a big wine, but it packs a lot of character on a jazzy frame, with flavors that last. Drink now through 2003.–H.S. • $20 • (11/30/1999) • **89**

Zinfandel Sonoma Valley 1993 • $18 • (10/15/1995) • **83**

CRESTON | CALIFORNIA

Cabernet Sauvignon Central Coast Winemaker's Selection 1985 • $17 • (12/15/1989) • **75**
Cabernet Sauvignon Central Coast Winemaker's Selection 1984 • $16 • (12/15/1987) • **71**
Cabernet Sauvignon Paso Robles 1994: Straightforward, soft and round, showing dried currant, herb and mocha flavors. Becomes tart on the finish. Drink now. • $15 • (11/15/1998) • **80**
Cabernet Sauvignon Paso Robles 1993 • $13 • (9/15/1997) • **84**
Cabernet Sauvignon Paso Robles 1992 • $10 • (12/15/1995) • **83**
Cabernet Sauvignon Paso Robles 1989 • $10 • (11/15/1993) • **85**
Cabernet Sauvignon Paso Robles 1988 • $10 • (11/15/1992) • **81**
Cabernet Sauvignon Paso Robles 1987 • $10 • (11/15/1991) • **79**
Cabernet Sauvignon Paso Robles Winemaker's Selection 1991 • $19 • (11/30/1996) • **85**
Cabernet Sauvignon Paso Robles Winemaker's Selection 1989 • $17 • (11/15/1994) • **83**
Cabernet Sauvignon Paso Robles Winemaker's Selection 1988 • $16 • (11/15/1992) • **80**
Cabernet Sauvignon Paso Robles Winemaker's Selection 1987 • $16 • (11/15/1991) • **82**
Cabernet Sauvignon San Luis Obispo 1990 • $10 • (11/15/1994) • **81**
Chardonnay Central Coast 1997: A strange mixture of charred and minerally notes, with bell pepper flavors.–J.L. • $20 • (6/15/2000) • **78**
Chardonnay Paso Robles 1996: Pretty hazelnut and pear flavors, though there is a leesy and slightly cheesy edge that might not please everyone. Drink now. • $13 • (7/31/1998) • **83**
Merlot Paso Robles 1995: Tart currant flavors and charred oak notes turn lean and slightly dry on the finish. Drink now.–J.L. • $16 • (9/30/1998) • **78**
Merlot Paso Robles 1991 • $13 • (12/31/1993) • **85**
Pinot Noir Paso Robles 1994 • $10 • (1/31/1996) • **82**
Pinot Noir Paso Robles 1993 • $10 • (12/31/1995) • **80**
Pinot Noir Paso Robles 1992 • $10 • (1/31/1994) • **83**
Pinot Noir Paso Robles 1991 • $10 • (2/28/1993) • **74**
Pinot Noir Paso Robles 1990 • $8 • (11/15/1991) • **70**
Pinot Noir San Luis Obispo County Petit d'Noir Maceration Carbonique 1988 • $8 • (12/15/1989) • **74**
Zinfandel Paso Robles 1995 • $13 • (6/15/1998) • **80**
Zinfandel Paso Robles 1991 • $10 • (9/30/1993) • **78**
Zinfandel Paso Robles 1990 • $10 • (10/15/1992) • **87**

CRICHTON HALL | CALIFORNIA

Chardonnay Napa Valley 1996: Tight, flinty, with appealing pear, hazelnut and anise notes, it turns a touch oaky with a twinge of wood bitterness that short-term cellaring may resolve. Try now through 2002.–J.L. • $22 • (1/31/1999) • **88**
Merlot Napa Valley 1996: Full-bodied, with firm tannins, this wine serves up layers of black currant, blackberry, mint and herbs. The finish is long, with a smoky licorice edge. Should smooth out nicely with time. Best from 2001 through 2005. • $26 • (9/15/1999) • **87**
Merlot Napa Valley 1993 • $22 • (6/15/1996) • **84**
Pinot Noir Napa Valley 1996: Light, muddled flavors of dried berries and tea, with an oaky flavor at the core, finishing a little dry. Drink now through 2001.–J.L. • $26 • (9/15/1999) • **82**
Pinot Noir Napa Valley 1993 • $22 • (1/31/1996) • **74**

CRISTOM | WASHINGTON

Chardonnay Columbia Valley Celilo Vineyard 1997: Bright and focused, with pretty pear and pineapple flavors, picking up hints of vanilla on the lively finish. Balanced enough to drink now, but could use time to settle down. Drink now through 2003.–H.S. • $20 • (9/30/1999) • **88**
Chardonnay Columbia Valley Celilo Vineyard 1996 • $20 • (5/15/1998) • **86**
Chardonnay Willamette Valley Germaine Vineyard 1997: Light and crisp, offering an earthy note to complement the modest apple and mineral flavors, which echo on the finish. Drink now through 2002.–H.S. • $19 • (9/30/1999) • **85**
Chardonnay Willamette Valley Germaine Vineyard 1996 • $20 • (5/15/1998) • **86**
Chardonnay Willamette Valley Mt. Hood Cuvée 1997: Bright and focused, with pretty pear and citrus flavors at the core, hinting at mineral on the edges. Drink now through 2002.–H.S. • $15 • (9/30/1999) • **85**
Pinot Gris Oregon-Washington 1996 • $11 • (10/31/1997) • **83**
Pinot Noir Willamette Valley 1993 • $17 • (1/31/1996) • **83**
Pinot Noir Willamette Valley 1992 • $15 • (11/30/1994) • **85**
Pinot Noir Willamette Valley Louise Vineyard 1997: Light and graceful, remarkably harmonious and supple, offering delicious cherry, spice and chocolate notes that linger enticingly on the finish. Drink now through 2002.–H.S. • $32 • (12/31/1999) • **88**
Pinot Noir Willamette Valley Louise Vineyard 1996: Firm in texture, with beautifully focused plum, currant, spice and mineral flavors in a harmonious package, all echoing nicely on the velvety finish. Drink now through 2002.–H.S. • $32 • (4/30/1999) • **90**
Pinot Noir Willamette Valley Marjorie Vineyard 1997: On the light side but well made, showing off pretty cherry, raspberry and tobacco notes that linger on the delicate finish. Drink now.–H.S. • $32 • (12/31/1999) • **87**
Pinot Noir Willamette Valley Marjorie Vineyard 1996: Very lean and tart, with a hard edge to the blackberry and cherry flavors. Remains crisp and picks up more flavor on the finish. Drink through 2003.–H.S. • $32 • (4/30/1999) • **87**
Pinot Noir Willamette Valley Marjorie Vineyard 1995 • $27 • (10/31/1997) • **85**
Pinot Noir Willamette Valley Marjorie Vineyard 1994 • $27 • (12/15/1996) • **93**
Pinot Noir Willamette Valley Mt. Jefferson Cuvée 1997: Very light in color, almost like rosé, with modest raspberry and leather notes on a firm, tight texture. Drink now through 2001.–H.S. • $20 • (9/30/1999) • **80**
Pinot Noir Willamette Valley Mt. Jefferson Cuvée 1996 • $20 • (5/15/1998) • **84**
Pinot Noir Willamette Valley Mt. Jefferson Cuvée 1995 • $17 • (7/31/1997) • **83**
Pinot Noir Willamette Valley Mt. Jefferson Cuvée 1994 • $17 • (7/31/1996) • **84**
Pinot Noir Willamette Valley Reserve 1997: Very light in texture, with pretty plum and toast aromas and flavors that echo nicely on the finish. Drink now.–H.S. • $30 • (12/31/1999) • **87**
Pinot Noir Willamette Valley Reserve 1996: Firm in texture, with slightly gritty tannins and pretty black cherry and earth flavors glowing through the finish. Drink through 2002.–H.S. • $30 • (4/30/1999) • **88**
Pinot Noir Willamette Valley Reserve 1995 • $27 • (10/31/1997) • **88**
Pinot Noir Willamette Valley Reserve 1994 • $27 • (12/15/1996) • **90**
Pinot Noir Willamette Valley Reserve 1993 • $26 • (1/31/1996) • **88**
Pinot Noir Willamette Valley Reserve 1992 • $24 • (11/30/1994) • **83**
Viognier Willamette Valley 1998: Ripe and exotic, with lavish pear, spice and tropical fruit flavors that never get fat and sloppy but finish with a sense of refinement. Distinctive and dripping with character. Drink now through 2003.–H.S. • $22 • (12/31/1999) • **88**
Viognier Willamette Valley 1996 • $20 • (10/31/1997) • **90**

CROCKER & STARR | CALIFORNIA

Cabernet Franc Napa Valley 1997: Wonderful grapey, floral perfume, turning supple and elegant, with an earthy, cedary edge to the tasty, ripe plum and cherry flavors. Mild tannins. Drink now through 2005.–J.L. • $27 • (12/15/1999) • **89**

CRONIN | CALIFORNIA

Cabernet Sauvignon Santa Cruz Mountains 1995: Dark, concentrated and tightly wound, with a core of cherry, mushroom and earth flavors, finishing with firm tannins. Best now through 2005.–J.L. • $23 • (9/15/1999) • **87**
Cabernet Sauvignon Santa Cruz Mountains 1994 • $23 • (4/30/1998) • **88**
Cabernet Sauvignon Santa Cruz Mountains 1992 • $20 • (1/01/1997) • **88**
Cabernet Sauvignon Santa Cruz Mountains 1991 • $17 • (4/30/1996) • **89**
Cabernet Sauvignon Santa Cruz Mountains 1990 • $17 • (2/28/1995) • **85**
Cabernet Sauvignon Santa Cruz Mountains 1989 • $17 • (3/15/1994) • **88**
Cabernet Sauvignon-Merlot San Mateo County Shaw & Cronin 1986 • $15 • (2/28/1991) • **88**
Cabernet Sauvignon-Merlot Santa Cruz Mountains 1988 • $17 • (3/31/1993) • **83**
Cabernet Sauvignon-Merlot Santa Cruz Mountains 1987 • $17 • (3/31/1992) • **84**
Cabernet Sauvignon-Merlot Stags Leap District Robinson Vineyard 1989 • $17 • (3/31/1993) • **90**
Cabernet Sauvignon-Merlot Stags Leap District Robinson Vineyard 1988 • $17 • (3/31/1992) • **88**
Cabernet Sauvignon-Merlot Stags Leap District Robinson Vineyard 1987 • $17 • (2/28/1991) • **89**
Cabernet Sauvignon-Merlot Stags Leap District Robinson Vineyard 1986 • $16 • (2/15/1990) • **88**
Chardonnay Alexander Valley Stuhlmuller Vineyard 1996: A tightly knit style, with smoky, nutty, honey-tinged flavors of fig and appleskin and a salt-mineral quality. Elegant and restrained, it promises to improve with bottle age. Try through 2002.–J.L. • $18 • (6/30/1999) • **88**
Chardonnay Santa Cruz Mountains 1996: Rich, toasty and minerally, featuring well-focused citrus and green apple flavors. Clean, crisp and tightly wound on the finish. Drink now through 2002.–J.L. • $20 • (6/30/1999) • **88**
Concerto Stags Leap District Robinson Vineyard 1995: Elegant and concentrated, with sharply defined wild berry, cherry and mineral flavors. Plush,

with well-integrated tannins on the long, complex finish. Drink through 2005.–J.L. • $25 • (9/15/1999) • **88**
Concerto Stags Leap District Robinson Vineyard 1994 • $23 • (4/30/1998) • **90**
Concerto Stags Leap District Robinson Vineyard 1993 • $18 • (8/31/1997) • **88**
Concerto Stags Leap District Robinson Vineyard 1992 • $17 • (4/30/1996) • **93**
Concerto Stags Leap District Robinson Vineyard 1991 • $17 • (2/28/1995) • **87**
Concerto Stags Leap District Robinson Vineyard 1990 • $17 • (3/15/1994) • **82**
Joe's Cuvée California 1990 • $27 • (3/15/1994) • **86**
Pinot Noir Santa Clara County 1989 • $17 • (2/28/1994) • **81**
Pinot Noir Santa Cruz Mountains 1994: Mature, with dried cherry and stewed plum flavors. At its peak, it turns dry, finishing with a mushroomy edge to the earth, tar, spice and cedary oak. Drink now.–J.L. • $23 • (9/30/1998) • **85**
Pinot Noir Santa Cruz Mountains 1993 • $22 • (4/30/1997) • **86**
Pinot Noir Santa Cruz Mountains Peter Martin Ray Vineyard 1992 • $22 • (4/30/1996) • **89**
Pinot Noir Santa Cruz Mountains Peter Martin Ray Vineyard 1991 • $20 • (3/31/1995) • **82**
Pinot Noir Santa Cruz Mountains Peter Martin Ray Vineyard 1990 • $20 • (4/30/1994) • **83**
Pinot Noir Santa Cruz Mountains Peter Martin Ray Vineyard 1988 • $27 • (3/31/1992) • **81**
Zinfandel Santa Clara County 1992 • $12 • (10/15/1995) • **85**
Zinfandel Sonoma Valley 1992 • $15 • (10/15/1995) • **91**

CUISINE CELLARS | CALIFORNIA

California Red NV: A rough-edged wine, with hints of black cherry and cassis. The charry finish is short. Contains Syrah, Zinfandel, Sangiovese. • $6 • (7/31/1998) • **79**
California White NV • $6 • (6/30/1998) • **82**
Chardonnay California 1996 • $9 • (6/30/1998) • **84**
Lighthearted Red California NV • $5 • (12/31/1996) • **80**
Merlot California 1996: Hints of blueberry, blackberry and cassis are framed by a smoke and oak edge, but this dries out on the finish. • $9 • (7/31/1998) • **83**
Rich Red California NV • $5 • (12/31/1996) • **84**

CULBERTSON | CALIFORNIA

Blanc de Noir California NV • $13 • (11/30/1997) • **85**
Brut California NV • $13 • (11/30/1997) • **86**
Brut Pinot Noir California Cuvée Rouge NV • $12 • (12/31/1992) • **82**
Cuvée de Frontignan California 1994 Artist Series NV • $10 • (5/31/1995) • **78**
Cuvée Rouge California NV • $14 • (12/31/1990) • **79**
Cuvée Rouge California 1994 Artist Series NV • $12 • (5/31/1995) • **84**
Demi-Sec California Cuvée de Frontignan NV • $12 • (5/15/1992) • **81**

CULLER | CALIFORNIA

Syrah Napa Valley 1997: Full of chocolate and blackberry aromas, this wine is fairly racy, with good intensity to the mocha and black cherry flavors. Drink now through 2005.–J.L. • $25 • (5/31/2000) • **85**

CUNEO CELLARS | WASHINGTON

Cana's Feast Columbia Valley 1992 • $25 • (5/15/1996) • **85**

CURTIS | CALIFORNIA

Cabernet Franc Santa Ynez Valley Kingsley Vineyard 1994 • $18 • (7/31/1997) • **88**
Cabernet Sauvignon Santa Ynez Valley La Cuesta Vineyard 1994 • $18 • (9/30/1997) • **77**
Merlot Santa Ynez Valley La Cuesta Vineyard 1994 • $20 • (5/15/1997) • **82**
Syrah Santa Ynez Valley Kalina Vineyard 1994 • $18 • (9/15/1997) • **88**

Key: SS—Spectator Selection. CS—Cellar Selection. HR—Highly Recommended. $NA—Price not available. (BT)—Barrel tasting. (A)—Auction Price.
For a key to the tasters' initials, see "How to Use These Listings."
Dates in parentheses represent the issues in which the ratings were published.

CUTLER CELLAR | CALIFORNIA

Cabernet Sauvignon Sonoma Valley 1990 • $19 • (11/15/1994) • **88**
Cabernet Sauvignon Sonoma Valley Batto Ranch 1986 • $17 • (11/15/1990) • **86**
Cabernet Sauvignon Sonoma Valley Batto Ranch 1985 • $20 • (7/31/1989) • **91**
Cabernet Sauvignon Sonoma Valley Batto Ranch 1987 • $17 • (3/31/1992) HR • **90**
Satyre Sonoma Valley 1989 • $20 • (12/15/1995) • **87**
Satyre Sonoma Valley 1987 • $20 • (7/15/1992) • **89**
Satyre Sonoma Valley 1986 • $20 • (2/28/1991) • **85**

CUVAISON | CALIFORNIA

Cabernet Sauvignon Napa Valley 1996: Marked by strong cedar and camphor aromas and flavors, turning dry and tannic. Whatever fruit is underneath struggles to emerge. Drink now.–J.L. • $30 • (5/31/2000) • **83**
Cabernet Sauvignon Napa Valley 1995: A ripe, smooth and polished style, with supple currant, earth, anise and cedary notes, finishing with fine tannins and good length. Drink through 2004.–J.L. • $28 • (10/31/1998) • **88**
Cabernet Sauvignon Napa Valley 1994 • $25 • (11/15/1997) • **89**
Cabernet Sauvignon Napa Valley 1993 • $28 • (11/15/1996) • **87**
Cabernet Sauvignon Napa Valley 1992 • $26 • (12/15/1995) • **88**
Cabernet Sauvignon Napa Valley 1991 • $22 • (11/15/1994) • **88**
Cabernet Sauvignon Napa Valley 1990 • $18 • (3/31/1994) • **85**
Cabernet Sauvignon Napa Valley 1989 • $22 • (2/15/1993) • **82**
Cabernet Sauvignon Napa Valley 1988 • $19 • (11/15/1991) • **82**
Cabernet Sauvignon Napa Valley 1987 • $18 • (12/15/1997) • **90**
Cabernet Sauvignon Napa Valley 1986 • $NA • (12/15/1996) • **89**
Cabernet Sauvignon Napa Valley 1985 • $40 • (3/31/1989) • **91**
Cabernet Sauvignon Napa Valley 1982 • $15 • (10/15/1987) • **90**
Cabernet Sauvignon Napa Valley 1981 • $11 • (11/30/1986) • **89**
Cabernet Sauvignon Napa Valley 1980 • $11 • (2/16/1985) • **85**
Cabernet Sauvignon Napa Valley 1978 • $14 • (5/16/1984) • **65**
Cabernet Sauvignon Napa Valley ATS 1994 • $50 • (4/30/1998) • **92**
Chardonnay Carneros Reserve 1996: Opens with appetizing earthy-oak flavors, then focuses attention on its intensely wound core of anise, mineral, pear and fig-laced flavors that are rich and concentrated. Draws you back for another sip. Drink now through 2002.–J.L. • $32 • (3/31/1999) HR • **92**
Chardonnay Napa Valley Carneros 1998: Earthy style, with a claylike edge to the modest pear and cedar notes. Drink now.–J.L. • $19 • (6/30/2000) • **85**
Chardonnay Napa Valley Carneros 1997: Elegant, with clean, bright, ripe pear, apple, melon, citrus and spicy hazelnut flavors. Drink now through 2004.–J.L. • $19 • (1/31/2000) • **88**
Chardonnay Napa Valley Carneros 1996 • $21 • (6/15/1998) • **88**
Chardonnay Napa Valley Carneros ATS Selection 1997: Earthy, with complex pear and hazelnut flavors that offer a touch of maturity. Butterscotch aftertaste. Drink now through 2004.–J.L. • $40 • (5/31/2000) • **88**
Chardonnay Napa Valley Carneros ATS Selection 1996: Smooth and creamy, with a focused core of fig, pear, apricot, honey and vanilla. Turns sleek and elegant on the finish. Drink now through 2002.–J.L. • $42 • (6/30/1999) • **92**
Chardonnay Napa Valley Carneros Reserve 1997: Racy, with a spicy pear, apple and hazelnut note, turning grassy. Drink now.–J.L. • $30 • (5/31/2000) • **84**
Meritage Reserve Napa Valley 1991 • $50 • (12/15/1995) • **86**
Merlot Napa Valley 1997: Firm and rich, with ample tannins wrapped around a core of cedar, pencil lead, currant and dried berry. Drink now through 2008.–J.L. • $31 • (6/15/2000) • **87**
Merlot Napa Valley 1996: Elegant, polished, medium-weight, with moderately rich minerally cherry and currant flavors, finishing with supple tannins. Drink now through 2006.–J.L. • $31 • (10/15/1999) • **87**
Merlot Napa Valley 1995: Smooth and plush, with a pretty array of coffee, currant, berry and plum. Finishes with a sense of elegance and grace and complex flavors that linger. Drink through 2004.–J.L. • $31 • (10/15/1998) • **88**
Merlot Napa Valley 1991 • $24 • (9/15/1994) • **83**
Merlot Napa Valley 1990 • $23 • (8/31/1993) • **87**
Merlot Napa Valley 1988 • $24 • (4/15/1991) • **86**
Merlot Napa Valley 1985 • $19 • (6/30/1988) • **89**
Merlot Napa Valley Anniversary Release 1984 • $14 • (8/31/1987) • **90**
Merlot Napa Valley ATS Selection 1995: Smooth, with an intriguing cherry cola flavor that runs through the cedar, anise, sage and mint notes, turning firm. Drink through 2006.–J.L. • $50 • (5/15/1999) • **87**
Merlot Napa Valley ATS Selection 1994: Smooth, with herb, leather and spicy stewed plum flavors, turning supple and polished, gaining nuance and complexity on the long, rich finish. Drink now through 2006.–J.L. • $50 • (1/01/1999) • **91**
Merlot Napa Valley Twenty-Fifth Anniversary Harvest 1994 • $30 • (12/31/1996) • **89**

Pinot Noir Napa Valley Carneros 1996: Smooth and spicy, with edgy wild berry, cherry and cedar notes that turn chunky and tannic. Drink now through 2002.–J.L. • $28 • (12/31/1998) • **87**
Pinot Noir Napa Valley Carneros 1995 • $30 • (1/31/1998) • **91**
Pinot Noir Napa Valley Carneros 1993 • $24 • (1/31/1996) • **76**
Pinot Noir Napa Valley Carneros 1992 • $22 • (3/31/1995) • **84**
Pinot Noir Napa Valley Carneros 1991 • $19 • (2/28/1994) • **85**
Pinot Noir Napa Valley Carneros Eris Vineyards 1997: A bit funky and muddled, with an earthy, mushroomy, cedary note weaving through the plum and black cherry flavors, though it turns tannic on the finish. Best to cellar short-term. Best from 2001 through 2007.–J.L. • $20 • (1/31/2000) • **86**
Pinot Noir Napa Valley Carneros Eris 1996: Offers enough cherry, berry and cola flavors to hold your interest, and a touch of oak adds dimension. Finishes with spicy mint and tea notes and mild tannins. Drink now through 2001.–J.L. • $21 • (9/15/1998) • **86**
Pinot Noir Napa Valley Carneros Eris 1995 • $19 • (12/15/1997) • **89**
Pinot Noir Napa Valley Carneros Eris 1994 • $15 • (2/28/1997) • **85**
Zinfandel Napa Valley 1986 • $10 • (3/15/1989) • **85**

D-CUBED CELLARS | CALIFORNIA

Zinfandel Howell Mountain 1997: Firm, ripe and intense, with earthy wild berry, black cherry, anise, sage and tarry notes; all adds up to complexity, with a long, deep finish. Drink now through 2007.–J.L. • $24 • (1/31/2000) • **91**
Zinfandel Howell Mountain 1996: A racy style that's tart and firm, with spicy wild berry, black pepper and bell pepper flavors that tighten up on the finish, where the tannins turn dry. Drink now through 2002.–J.L. • $20 • (11/30/1998) • **87**
Zinfandel Howell Mountain 1995 • $17 • (4/30/1997) • **89**
Zinfandel Howell Mountain 1994 • $15 • (4/30/1996) • **90**
Zinfandel Napa Valley 1998: Ripe and spicy, with a juniper berry edge to the cherry and raspberry notes that taste raisiny. Drink now.–J.L. • $22 • (5/31/2000) • **82**
Zinfandel Napa Valley 1997: Ripe, complex and concentrated, with black pepper, herb-tinged plum, cooked strawberry and spice. Finishes with soft, ripe tannins. Drink now through 2002.–J.L. • $18 • (6/15/1999) • **90**
Zinfandel Napa Valley 1996 • $17 • (5/31/1998) • **84**

DA VINCI | CALIFORNIA

Riesling Sierra Foothills NV • $7 • (12/31/1997) • **85**

DALLA VALLE | CALIFORNIA

Cabernet Sauvignon Napa Valley 1998: Smooth, ripe and polished, with firm, complex currant, plum, anise and cedary oak, finishing with a long, intricate aftertaste.–J.L. • $NA • (8/31/1999) (BT) • **90-94**
Cabernet Sauvignon Napa Valley 1996: Tight and focused, with a firm, structured core of currant, anise, cedar, cherry, mineral and plum flavors. An enormously complex and concentrated wine that needs time. Best from 2001 through 2009.–J.L. • $113 Ⓐ • (11/15/1999) • **95**
Cabernet Sauvignon Napa Valley 1995: This is a dark, sharply focused, richly flavored wine, brimming with pure cherry, currant, mineral, sage and spice. Has the tannic strength to age. Being mostly Cabernet, this contrasts nicely with Dalla Valle's Maya, a blend that's about 50 percent Franc. Best from 2001 through 2008.–J.L. • $101 Ⓐ • (11/15/1998) • **94**
Cabernet Sauvignon Napa Valley 1994 • $105 Ⓐ • (10/31/1997) CS • **93**
Cabernet Sauvignon Napa Valley 1993 • $84 Ⓐ • (11/15/1996) • **88**
Cabernet Sauvignon Napa Valley 1992 • $95 Ⓐ • (12/15/1995) CS • **92**
Cabernet Sauvignon Napa Valley 1991 • $99 Ⓐ • (11/15/1994) SS • **92**
Cabernet Sauvignon Napa Valley 1990 • $80 Ⓐ • (9/30/1993) HR • **93**
Cabernet Sauvignon Napa Valley 1989 • $41 Ⓐ • (11/15/1992) • **85**
Cabernet Sauvignon Napa Valley 1988 • $58 Ⓐ • (11/15/1991) • **85**
Cabernet Sauvignon Napa Valley 1986 • $NA • (12/15/1996) • **84**
Maya Napa Valley 1996: Wonderfully seductive. This year's version of this preeminent Cabernet blend is enormously rich and concentrated, beautifully fine-tuned and integrated, with bold, ripe, complex currant, black cherry, spice, earth, mineral and cedary oak. Best from 2001 through 2009.–J.L. • $420 Ⓐ • (11/15/1999) CS • **98**
Maya Napa Valley 1995: Dark, intense and deeply concentrated, with a sharp, tight beam of currant, blackberry and cherry, complex and spicy. The tannins are woven in, giving it seamless texture, and the finish pumps out lots of juicy fruit. A blend of Cabernet Sauvignon and Cabernet Franc. Drink through 2008.–J.L. • $458 Ⓐ • (11/15/1998) • **95**
Maya Napa Valley 1994 • $484 Ⓐ • (10/31/1997) HR • **95**
Maya Napa Valley 1993 • $407 Ⓐ • (11/15/1996) CS • **96**
Maya Napa Valley 1992 • $416 Ⓐ • (12/15/1995) • **94**
Maya Napa Valley 1991 • $368 Ⓐ • (11/15/1994) • **90**
Maya Napa Valley 1990 • $323 Ⓐ • (9/30/1993) • **89**
Maya Napa Valley 1989: Still immense, one of the biggest and most vibrant of the vintage, with layers of rich black cherry, currant, anise, cedar and plum notes, all well focused and lingering on the finish. (1989 California Cabernet retrospective tasting). Drink now through 2007.–J.L. • $259 Ⓐ • (8/31/1999) • **90**
Maya Napa Valley 1988 • $250 Ⓐ • (11/15/1991) • **86**
Pietre Rosse Napa Valley NV • $35 • (6/15/1996) • **82**
Pietre Rosse Napa Valley 1995 • $25 • (12/15/1997) • **86**
Sangiovese Napa Valley Pietre Rosse 1997: Dried cherry and berry flavors are tight, tannic and focused, offering depth, richness and complexity. Drink through 2003.–J.L. • $35 Ⓐ • (11/15/1999) • **88**
Sangiovese Napa Valley Pietre Rosse 1996: Openly fruity, with ripe, juicy black cherry and wild berry flavors, it's the best Pietre Rosse yet; all from Napa Valley grapes, unlike prior efforts which were blends from California and Italy. Only available in California and via the winery's mailing list. Drink now.–J.L. • $25 • (9/30/1998) • **85**
Zinfandel Napa Valley 1986 • $25 • (2/15/1991) • **84**

DANIELS, STEFAN | CALIFORNIA

Fumé Blanc Redwood Valley Cox Vineyards 1998: Of medium weight, with lemon, grapefruit and melon flavors mingling with spicy notes. Lingering finish. Drink now through 2002.–H.S. • $16 • (1/31/2000) • **86**
Syrah California Lockeford 1998: Distinctive, with prickly dill pickle, blackberry and ripe barnyard notes and firm tannins. Drink now through 2005.–J.L. • $20 • (5/31/2000) • **80**

DANTE | CALIFORNIA

Merlot California Special Selection 1997: Simple and smooth, with pleasant lightweight flavors of strawberry, cherry and herb. Drink now.–J.L. • $10 • (10/15/1999) • **82**
Sauvignon Blanc California Reserve Selection 1997: Starts off with an unusual hint of peach on the nose, but on the palate it is redolent of citrus, mostly grapefruit. Somewhat lean, it remains refreshing and light, sporting a moderate finish with a flinty edge. Good price. Drink now. • $8 • (6/15/1999) • **86**
Zinfandel California Reserve Selection 1997: A gentle Zin, with pretty plum, cherry, spice and a hint of vanilla. Tapers off quickly, but still quite quaffable. Drink now. • $10 • (6/15/1999) • **83**

DARK STAR | CALIFORNIA

Cabernet Sauvignon Paso Robles 1996: Shows some muscle, with chewy tannins and spicy black cherry and blackberry notes. It's a bright-styled wine that should calm down a bit with bottle age. Drink through 2006 • $19 • (10/31/1998) • **86**
Merlot Paso Robles 1996: Spice and plum flavors fold together nicely. Finishes with soft tannins. Drink now. • $18 • (12/15/1998) • **84**
Merlot Paso Robles Cougar Ridge Vineyards 1995 • $18 • (5/15/1998) • **80**
Ricordati Red Paso Robles 1996: Kicks off with bright cherry and plum flavors that carry through with a peppery edge. Tannins are mild, as is the finish. A blend: 64 percent Cabernet Sauvignon, 26 percent Merlot, 10 percent Cabernet Franc. Drink now through 2004. • $20 • (10/31/1998) • **85**
Zinfandel Paso Robles 1997: Tangy and a bit tart, with cranberry, chocolate and dried berry flavors. Drink now through 2002.–J.L. • $19 • (6/15/2000) • **85**
Zinfandel Paso Robles 1996: Smooth and generous, with cherry, currant and spice flavors that keep singing on the chewy finish. Best now through 2003.–H.S. • $18 • (11/30/1998) • **88**

DASHE | CALIFORNIA

Sangiovese Dry Creek Valley 1997: A light style, with simple cherry and herb flavors. Drying tannins flare up on the short finish. Drink now through 2002. • $18 • (11/15/1999) • **83**
Zinfandel Dry Creek Valley 1996: Ripe, teetering on jammy, with wild berry, raspberry, blackberry and spice, adding a complex, fruity finish. Drink now through 2004.–J.L. • $18 • (11/30/1998) • **87**
Zinfandel Russian River Valley 1997: Ripe and juicy, with tasty raspberry, black cherry, plum and spice, turning elegant, with crisp tannins. Drink now through 2002.–J.L. • $20 • (5/15/1999) • **89**

DAVIS FAMILY | CALIFORNIA

Sauvignon Blanc Sonoma County 1997: This citrusy, tart wine has an odd vegetal note running through flavors of toasted coconut and lime. Drink now through 2002.–H.S. • $18 • (1/31/2000) • **82**

DAYDREAM | CALIFORNIA

Cabernet Sauvignon Napa Valley 1994 • $24 • (11/30/1997) • **88**

DE LOACH | CALIFORNIA

Cabernet Sauvignon Dry Creek Valley 1984 • $11 • (12/15/1987) • **89**
Cabernet Sauvignon Dry Creek Valley 1983 • $11 • (9/30/1986) • **85**
Cabernet Sauvignon Dry Creek Valley 1981 • $11 • (4/01/1985) • **80**
Cabernet Sauvignon Russian River Valley 1995 • $18 • (5/31/1998) • **87**
Cabernet Sauvignon Russian River Valley 1993 • $15 • (12/15/1996) • **84**
Cabernet Sauvignon Russian River Valley 1992 • $15 • (12/15/1995) • **86**
Cabernet Sauvignon Russian River Valley 1991 • $15 • (11/15/1994) • **78**
Cabernet Sauvignon Russian River Valley 1990 • $16 • (3/31/1993) • **85**
Cabernet Sauvignon Russian River Valley 1989 • $16 • (11/15/1991) • **86**
Cabernet Sauvignon Russian River Valley O.F.S. 1996: Smooth and harmonious, with more depth and richness than you typically get from Russian River Cabernet, the fruit is focused around black cherry and currant, with a seductive toasty oak overlay. Drink through 2007.–J.L. • $36 • (10/15/1999) • **90**
Cabernet Sauvignon Russian River Valley O.F.S. 1995: Attractive with its ripe, fleshy cherry, wild berry and raspberry fruitiness and supple tannins; just lacks the concentration to score outstanding. Drink now through 2005.–J.L. • $30 • (9/15/1999) • **88**
Cabernet Sauvignon Russian River Valley O.F.S. 1994 • $28 • (9/30/1997) • **90**
Cabernet Sauvignon Russian River Valley O.F.S. 1993 • $25 • (1/31/1997) • **87**
Cabernet Sauvignon Russian River Valley O.F.S. 1992 • $25 • (9/30/1996) • **89**
Cabernet Sauvignon Russian River Valley O.F.S. 1991 • $25 • (9/30/1995) • **89**
Cabernet Sauvignon Russian River Valley O.F.S. 1987 • $22 • (12/15/1997) • **87**
Chardonnay California 1998: Offers modest lemon and orange peel flavors, turning slightly bitter. Drink now.–J.L. • $10 • (2/29/2000) • **82**
Chardonnay Russian River Valley 1998: Round and straightforward, with cardamom, oak and apricot flavors. Drink now.–J.L. • $18 • (6/15/2000) • **85**
Chardonnay Russian River Valley 1997: Firmly textured, with good acidity, serving up pretty apple, pear and citrus flavors. Finishes moderately, with a fresh, minerally taste. Drink now through 2001. • $18 • (6/30/1999) • **87**
Chardonnay Russian River Valley 1996 • $18 • (4/30/1998) • **86**
Chardonnay Russian River Valley Estate Bottled 1996 • $20 • (4/30/1998) • **89**
Chardonnay Russian River Valley O.F.S. 1998: Pear, tangerine and spicy oak notes have richness and good focus. Drink now.–J.L. • $30 • (6/15/2000) • **86**
Chardonnay Russian River Valley O.F.S. 1997: A ripe, oily, full-blown style, with rich fig, apricot, pear, spice and toasty oak. Well focused and complex through the finish. Drink now through 2002.–J.L. • $28 • (7/31/1999) • **90**
Chardonnay Russian River Valley O.F.S. 1996 • $28 • (6/30/1998) SS • **92**
Chardonnay Russian River Valley Olivet Ranch 1998: Cream, honey and spice flavors are ripe, with good intensity through the finish. Drink now.–J.L. • $20 • (6/15/2000) • **87**
Chardonnay Russian River Valley Olivet Ranch 1997: Clean and refreshing, with tightly wound citrus, apple and flinty pear flavors. Finishes long and pure. Drink now through 2002.–J.L. • $20 • (7/31/1999) • **87**
Chardonnay Sonoma County Sonoma Cuvée 1997: Generously open-textured, with restrained earth, green apple and pineapple flavors. Finishes crisp and refreshing, with lingering flinty fruit. Drink now through 2002.–J.L. • $13 • (7/31/1999) • **86**
Chardonnay Sonoma County Sonoma Cuvée 1996: Intense, with a core of pear and pineapple. Holds its fruitiness on the finish, where the pure flavors linger. Drink now through 2000.–J.L. • $13 • (7/31/1998) • **87**
Fumé Blanc Russian River Valley 1998: Round, with good concentration of herb, fig and vanilla notes. A hint of soapiness detracts from the finish. Drink now through 2002.–J.L. • $14 • (5/15/2000) • **84**
Fumé Blanc Russian River Valley 1997: A bright, firm wine with lemon-lime overtones backed by melon and herb flavors. Drink now. • $14 • (10/31/1998) • **85**

Key: SS—Spectator Selection. CS—Cellar Selection. HR—Highly Recommended. $NA—Price not available. (BT)—Barrel tasting. Ⓐ—Auction Price.
For a key to the tasters' initials, see "How to Use These Listings."
Dates in parentheses represent the issues in which the ratings were published.

Fumé Blanc Russian River Valley 1996 • $14 • (6/30/1997) • **88**
Gewürztraminer Russian River Valley Early Harvest 1996 • $12 • (7/31/1997) • **85**
Gewürztraminer Russian River Valley Late Harvest 1991 • $14/3 liter • (10/15/1992) • **86**
Gewürztraminer Russian River Valley Late Harvest 1989 • $10/375 ml. • (4/30/1991) • **88**
Merlot Russian River Valley 1997: Tart, with cherry and herb notes that turn firm on the finish. Best now through 2004.–J.L. • $18 • (10/15/1999) • **80**
Merlot Russian River Valley 1996: A mixed bag, with ripe berry and cherry flavors but also a firm, tannic edge and a waxy finish. Short-term cellaring may help. Drink through 2004.–J.L. • $18 • (9/30/1998) • **80**
Merlot Russian River Valley 1996: Ripe strawberry and tarry flavors, with a tealike accent. Finishes with notes of vanilla and slightly dry tannins. Drink now.–J.L. • $18 • (12/15/1998) • **80**
Merlot Russian River Valley 1995 • $16 • (6/30/1997) • **80**
Merlot Russian River Valley 1994 • $15 • (8/31/1996) • **84**
Merlot Russian River Valley 1993 • $14 • (9/30/1995) • **87**
Merlot Russian River Valley 1992 • $14 • (7/31/1994) • **86**
Petite Sirah Russian River Valley Flagstaff Ranch 1995: Lean, with tar, cedar, stem and wild berry notes. Some attractive floral notes emerge, but it's austere. De Loach's first Petite Sirah. Drink now through 2002.–J.L. • $20 • (12/15/1998) • **85**
Pinot Noir Russian River Valley 1997: Somewhat earthy on the nose, the wine unfolds slowly to reveal layers of herb and black cherry and a touch of spice. Smooth and supple, finishing moderately. Drink through 2003. • $18 • (9/15/1999) • **85**
Pinot Noir Russian River Valley 1995 • $15 • (12/31/1996) • **88**
Pinot Noir Russian River Valley 1994 • $25 • (2/29/1996) • **79**
Pinot Noir Russian River Valley 1992 • $13 • (3/31/1995) • **82**
Pinot Noir Russian River Valley 1991 • $13 • (2/28/1994) • **74**
Pinot Noir Russian River Valley 1990 • $13 • (9/30/1992) • **80**
Pinot Noir Russian River Valley 1986 • $12 • (5/31/1990) • **87**
Pinot Noir Russian River Valley 1985 • $12 • (6/15/1988) • **72**
Pinot Noir Russian River Valley 1983 • $10 • (3/01/1986) • **75**
Pinot Noir Russian River Valley 1982 • $10 • (8/31/1986) • **76**
Pinot Noir Russian River Valley O.F.S. 1997: Lightly fruity and herbal, with a modest range of spicy cherry and berry, and tealike tannins. Not what you might expect from a reserve-style wine. Drink now.–J.L. • $30 • (9/15/1999) • **83**
Pinot Noir Russian River Valley O.F.S. 1996 • $28 • (12/31/1997) • **89**
Pinot Noir Russian River Valley O.F.S. 1995 • $25 • (12/31/1996) • **89**
Pinot Noir Russian River Valley O.F.S. 1994 • $25 • (2/29/1996) • **89**
Pinot Noir Russian River Valley O.F.S. 1992 • $25 • (12/31/1995) • **88**
Pinot Noir Russian River Valley O.F.S. 1990 • $26 • (2/28/1993) • **82**
Pinot Noir Russian River Valley O.F.S. 1987 • $25 • (10/31/1990) • **82**
White Zinfandel Sonoma County 1996 • $8 • (9/15/1997) • **78**
Zinfandel California 1998: Medium-bodied and firm, with jammy blackberry and plum notes. Drink now through 2004.–J.L. • $10 • (4/30/2000) • **84**
Zinfandel Russian River Valley 1997: Crisp, a touch flinty, with a slight smoky edge to the tannic cherry and raspberry flavors, which linger and fan out nicely. Drink now through 2004.–J.L. • $18 • (2/28/1999) • **88**
Zinfandel Russian River Valley 1996 • $18 • (3/31/1998) • **85**
Zinfandel Russian River Valley 1995 • $15 • (2/28/1997) • **88**
Zinfandel Russian River Valley 1994 • $14 • (4/30/1996) • **86**
Zinfandel Russian River Valley 1993 • $13 • (10/15/1995) • **85**
Zinfandel Russian River Valley 1992: Earthy, tarry and showing its oak, it's smooth and elegant, with hints of dill and vanilla leading to the core of cherry and blackberry. The supple texture and complex aftertaste are most impressive. (Zinfandel retrospective tasting). Drink now through 2002. –J.L. • $NA • (6/30/1999) • **87**
Zinfandel Russian River Valley 1991 • $12 • (5/31/1993) • **83**
Zinfandel Russian River Valley 1990: Aging well; there's a slight gamy flavor that runs through the cherry and berry character. Starts to open with aeration, adding soft tannins and good length. (Zinfandel retrospective tasting). Drink now through 2001.–J.L. • $12 • (6/30/1999) • **88**
Zinfandel Russian River Valley 1989 • $11 • (9/30/1991) • **82**
Zinfandel Russian River Valley 1988 • $11 • (9/15/1990) • **78**
Zinfandel Russian River Valley 1987 • $10 • (9/15/1989) • **90**
Zinfandel Russian River Valley Barbieri Ranch 1998: Tastes muddled, with earth, cedar and blackberry flavors, turning tart and sharp. Drink now.–J.L. • $22 • (5/15/2000) • **80**
Zinfandel Russian River Valley Barbieri Ranch 1997: Smooth, rich and polished, with layers of plush cherry, raspberry and blackberry, tightly focused and long on the finish. Drink through 2004.–J.L. • $20 • (2/28/1999) • **90**

Zinfandel Russian River Valley Barbieri Ranch 1996 • $20 • (5/15/1998) • **86**
Zinfandel Russian River Valley Barbieri Ranch 1995 • $18 • (2/28/1997) • **88**
Zinfandel Russian River Valley Barbieri Ranch 1994 • $15 • (4/30/1996) • **85**
Zinfandel Russian River Valley Barbieri Ranch 1993 • $14 • (10/15/1995) • **88**
Zinfandel Russian River Valley Barbieri Ranch 1991 • $14 • (1/31/1993) • **82**
Zinfandel Russian River Valley Barbieri Ranch 1990 • $14 • (5/15/1992) • **82**
Zinfandel Russian River Valley Gambogi Ranch 1998: Juicy, with earthy, tarry berry and cherry flavors. Drink now.–J.L. • $22 • (5/15/2000) • **82**
Zinfandel Russian River Valley Gambogi Ranch 1997: A tart and spicy Zin, with wild berry, blackberry, anise and sage, tightly focused through the finish. Drink now through 2003.–J.L. • $20 • (2/28/1999) • **87**
Zinfandel Russian River Valley Gambogi Ranch 1996 • $20 • (3/31/1998) • **84**
Zinfandel Russian River Valley Gambogi Ranch 1995 • $18 • (2/28/1997) • **88**
Zinfandel Russian River Valley Gambogi Ranch 1994 • $15 • (4/30/1996) • **87**
Zinfandel Russian River Valley Gambogi Ranch 1993 • $14 • (10/15/1995) • **86**
Zinfandel Russian River Valley O.F.S. 1998: Muddled baked cherry, tea and cola flavors struggle to find a focus, turning simple and murky. Drink now.–J.L. • $35 • (5/15/2000) • **82**
Zinfandel Russian River Valley O.F.S. 1997: Starts with creamy, toasty oak, then works in ripe cherry, wild berry, raspberry and spice flavors that weave together nicely. Drink now through 2003.–J.L. • $30 • (2/28/1999) • **89**
Zinfandel Russian River Valley O.F.S. 1996 • $28 • (3/31/1998) • **90**
Zinfandel Russian River Valley O.F.S. 1995 • $25 • (2/28/1997) • **92**
Zinfandel Russian River Valley O.F.S. 1994 • $25 • (4/30/1996) • **88**
Zinfandel Russian River Valley Papera Ranch 1998: Earthy, with dry, dusty berry and cherry flavors. Drink now.–J.L. • $22 • (5/15/2000) • **82**
Zinfandel Russian River Valley Papera Ranch 1997: Clean, ripe and fruity, with a pretty, complex array of plum and blackberry, cedar and spice. Firm tannins. Drink now through 2004.–J.L. • $20 • (2/28/1999) • **88**
Zinfandel Russian River Valley Papera Ranch 1996 • $20 • (3/31/1998) • **87**
Zinfandel Russian River Valley Papera Ranch 1995 • $18 • (2/28/1997) • **90**
Zinfandel Russian River Valley Papera Ranch 1994 • $15 • (4/30/1996) • **87**
Zinfandel Russian River Valley Papera Ranch 1993 • $14 • (10/15/1995) • **86**
Zinfandel Russian River Valley Papera Ranch 1991 • $14 • (1/31/1993) • **85**
Zinfandel Russian River Valley Papera Ranch 1990 • $14 • (5/15/1992) • **81**
Zinfandel Russian River Valley Pelletti Ranch 1998: Offers enough complete ripeness to carry the cherry, wild berry and blackberry flavors through to the finish. Drink now.–J.L. • $22 • (5/15/2000) • **83**
Zinfandel Russian River Valley Pelletti Ranch 1997: Supple and balanced, with a pretty array of blackberry, wild berry, sage, cedar and spice, finishing with a burst of fruit. Drink now through 2004.–J.L. • $20 • (2/28/1999) • **90**
Zinfandel Russian River Valley Pelletti Ranch 1996 • $20 • (3/31/1998) • **86**
Zinfandel Russian River Valley Pelletti Ranch 1995 • $18 • (2/28/1997) • **90**
Zinfandel Russian River Valley Pelletti Ranch 1994 • $15/750 ml • (4/30/1996) • **86**
Zinfandel Russian River Valley Pelletti Ranch 1993 • $14 • (10/15/1995) • **88**
Zinfandel Russian River Valley Pelletti Ranch 1991 • $14 • (1/31/1993) • **86**
Zinfandel Russian River Valley Pelletti Ranch 1990 • $14 • (5/15/1992) • **87**
Zinfandel Russian River Valley Saitone Ranch 1998: A light style, with waxy strawberry and cherry fruit. Drink now.–J.L. • $22 • (5/15/2000) • **80**
Zinfandel Russian River Valley Saitone Ranch 1997: Smooth, ripe and creamy, with rich blackberry, raspberry, plum and strawberry flavors, gaining richness and depth. Drink now through 2003.–J.L. • $20 • (2/28/1999) • **89**
Zinfandel Russian River Valley Saitone Ranch 1996 • $20 • (3/31/1998) • **88**
Zinfandel Russian River Valley Saitone Ranch 1995 • $18 • (2/28/1997) • **89**
Zinfandel Russian River Valley Sonoma County 1992 • $12 • (6/15/1994) • **88**

DE LORIMIER | CALIFORNIA

Chardonnay Alexander Valley 1997: Solid, in a barrel-fermented style, with floral, fig, flinty mineral and toast flavors playing on the crisp finish. Drink now through 2002.–H.S. • $16 • (7/31/1999) • **85**
Chardonnay Alexander Valley 1996 • $16 • (3/31/1998) • **87**
Merlot Alexander Valley 1996: Ripe, with a mineral edge to the nice raspberry, plum and cherry, but the flavors aren't well focused. Finishes with tarry notes and powdery tannins. Drink now.–J.L. • $18 • (12/15/1998) • **82**
Mosaic Meritage Alexander Valley 1996: Firm, with an herbal bitterness that detracts from the currant and cherry flavors. Tannins are firm and ripe on the finish. Drink now through 2004.–J.L. • $25 • (11/15/1999) • **81**
Mosaic Meritage Alexander Valley 1995: Lean and spicy, with a piccolo-high minty note sailing over the supple black cherry and toasty oak. A blend of Cabernet Sauvignon, Merlot, Petit Verdot and Malbec. Drink now.–H.S. • $24 • (10/31/1998) • **85**
Mosaic Meritage Alexander Valley 1994 • $20 • (11/15/1997) • **86**
Mosaic Meritage Alexander Valley 1993 • $20 • (11/15/1996) • **89**
Mosaic Meritage Alexander Valley 1992 • $18 • (3/31/1996) • **85**
Mosaic Meritage Alexander Valley 1991 • $18 • (8/31/1995) • **85**
Mosaic Meritage Alexander Valley 1990 • $18 • (6/15/1994) • **77**
Mosaic Meritage Alexander Valley 1988 • $18 • (6/15/1993) • **81**
Mosaic Meritage Alexander Valley 1986 • $16 • (10/31/1989) • **84**
Mosaic Mertiage Alexander Valley 1987 • $18 • (3/31/1992) • **81**
Sauvignon Blanc Alexander Valley 1997: Offers floral, peachy flavors framed in tangy acidity with a flinty, lemony follow-up. A clean, refreshing white, a good price. Drink now. • $10 • (9/15/1998) • **86**
Sauvignon Blanc Alexander Valley 1996 • $10 • (11/30/1997) • **83**
Sauvignon Blanc Alexander Valley Late Harvest Lace 1994 • $16 • (11/30/1996) • **86**
Spectrum Alexander Valley 1997: A pretty wine, featuring hints of apple, spice, toast and citrus. Somewhat light on the palate, it finishes with a fresh, clean quality. A blend of Sauvignon Blanc, Sémillon and Viognier. Drink now. • $14 • (5/31/1999) • **86**
Spectrum Alexander Valley Meritage 1996 • $14 • (3/31/1998) • **87**

DE ROSE | CALIFORNIA

Cabernet Sauvignon Cienega Valley Cardillo Vineyard Special Reserve 1994: Insipid, with charred oak, almond, vanilla and cherry tones.–H.S. • $20 • (11/15/1998) • **75**
Zinfandel Cienega Valley Cedolini Family Vineyard 100 Year-Old Vines 1997: Sweet-tasting blackberry and vanilla flavors are overblown, finishing with heat. Drink now.–J.L. • $20 • (6/15/2000) • **83**
Zinfandel Cienega Valley Cedolini Family Vineyard Hillside Reserve 1993 • $19 • (9/15/1996) • **85**
Zinfandel Cienega Valley Cedolini Family Vineyard Hillside Reserve 1992 • $13 • (9/15/1996) • **82**

DEAVER | CALIFORNIA

Zinfandel Amador County 1995 • $15 • (5/31/1998) • **86**

DECHIEL | VIRGINIA

Merlot Monticello Unfiltered 1997: Tart cherry and sweet coffee flavors mingle in this firm red. Has personality, but needs food to come into balance. Drink now through 2002.–T.M. • $18 • (1/01/2000) • **84**

DECOY | CALIFORNIA

Migration Napa Valley Red 1997: Jammy blackberry notes mingle with flavors of smoky, roasted plum and dark chocolate. Give it a year to lose some of the edge off the tannin. Best from 2001 through 2004.–J.L. • $18 • (4/30/2000) • **86**
Migration Napa Valley Red 1996: Spicy, with well-rounded pepper, earth and crisp currant notes. Tannins are soft. Drink now.–J.L. • $15 • (12/31/1998) • **84**
Migration Napa Valley Red 1995 • $14 • (3/31/1998) • **85**
Migration Napa Valley Red 1994 • $12 • (2/28/1997) • **83**
Migration Napa Valley Red 1993 • $12 • (2/29/1996) SS • **90**
Migration Napa Valley White 1997: Delivers peaches-and-cream up front, then turns a bit tart on the finish, with a flinty, mineral edge. Drink now. • $10 • (1/31/1999) • **83**
Migration Napa Valley White 1996 • $10 • (1/31/1998) • **86**
Pinot Noir Anderson Valley 1996: A gentle, elegant, spicy new wine from Duckhorn Vineyards. Attractive, medium-weight, with cherry, berry, spice, tea and cedar. Drink now through 2001.–J.L. • $18 • (9/30/1998) • **86**

DEER PARK | CALIFORNIA

Cabernet Sauvignon Howell Mountain Beatty Ranch Reserve 1990 • $24 • (10/31/1994) • **88**
Cabernet Sauvignon Howell Mountain Beatty Ranch Reserve 1988 • $24 • (11/15/1992) • **87**
Petite Sirah Howell Mountain Parks/Muscatine Vineyards 1987 • $14 • (10/31/1991) • **82**
Zinfandel Howell Mountain Beatty Ranch 1995 • $17 • (6/15/1998) • **85**
Zinfandel Howell Mountain Beatty Ranch 1991 • $14 • (10/15/1995) • **83**
Zinfandel Howell Mountain Beatty Ranch 1990 • $14 • (10/15/1994) • **81**
Zinfandel Howell Mountain Beatty Ranch 1988 • $13 • (10/15/1992) • **83**
Zinfandel Howell Mountain Beatty Ranch 1987 • $14 • (8/31/1991) • **79**
Zinfandel Howell Mountain Beatty Ranch Reserve 1987 • $18 • (8/31/1991) • **85**
Zinfandel Napa Valley 1991 • $16 • (10/15/1995) • **83**

DEERFIELD RANCH | CALIFORNIA

Chardonnay North Coast 1996: Silky, subtle and elegant, with pretty, creamy oak notes and flavors of lemon and vanilla that linger on the palate. Moderate in intensity, but still very nice. Drink now. • $24 • (7/31/1998) • **86**

Sangiovese California 1995: A sturdy red, with straightforward cherry and vaguely floral flavors that balance nicely on the finish. Drink now through 1999.–H.S. • $18 • (7/31/1998) • **84**

Sauvignon Blanc Sonoma Valley Peterson Vineyard 1997: Pleasant, with a core of citrus, mineral and herb flavors. Has moderate body and a clean, refreshing finish. Drink now. • $15 • (5/31/1999) • **85**

Zin'abernet North Coast 1996 • $20 • (6/15/1998) • **79**

DEHLINGER | CALIFORNIA

Cabernet Franc Russian River Valley 1989 • $12 • (3/31/1992) • **75**

Cabernet Franc Russian River Valley 1988 • $13 • (4/30/1991) • **84**

Cabernet Sauvignon Russian River Valley 1996: Ripe and complex, medium weight, with attractive plum, wild berry, herb, cocoa and spicy notes, turning smooth and velvety. Drink now through 2007.–J.L. • $30 • (2/29/2000) • **88**

Cabernet Sauvignon Russian River Valley 1994 • $25 • (9/30/1997) • **91**

Cabernet Sauvignon Russian River Valley 1992 • $18 • (8/31/1996) • **86**

Cabernet Sauvignon Russian River Valley 1991 • $15 • (5/15/1995) • **88**

Cabernet Sauvignon Russian River Valley 1990 • $15 • (11/15/1994) • **80**

Cabernet Sauvignon Russian River Valley 1989 • $15 • (8/31/1993) • **79**

Cabernet Sauvignon Russian River Valley 1988 • $15 • (3/31/1992) • **83**

Cabernet Sauvignon Russian River Valley 1987 • $13 • (2/28/1991) • **88**

Cabernet Sauvignon Russian River Valley 1986 • $NA • (12/15/1996) • **91**

Cabernet Sauvignon Russian River Valley 1985 • $13 • (5/31/1989) • **74**

Cabernet Sauvignon Russian River Valley 1984 • $12 • (2/15/1988) • **76**

Cabernet Sauvignon Russian River Valley 1983 • $11 • (6/15/1987) • **85**

Cabernet Sauvignon Russian River Valley 1982 • $11 • (8/31/1986) • **73**

Chardonnay Russian River Valley 1996 • $20 • (6/30/1998) • **90**

Chardonnay Russian River Valley Late Bottled Reserve 1997: Smells complex and exotic, with ripe pineapple, butterscotch, fig and melon flavors, filling out on the palate and holding its focus, turning intricate. Drink now through 2005.–J.L. • $30 • (2/29/2000) • **92**

Chardonnay Russian River Valley Unfiltered 1997: Ripe, smooth and elegant, with creamy pear, fig, apple and melon notes that build on the finish. Gains depth and nuance, turning silky. Drink now through 2002.–J.L. • $22 • (6/30/1999) • **92**

Merlot Sonoma County 1986 • $13 • (7/31/1989) • **83**

Merlot Sonoma County 1985 • $11 • (4/30/1988) • **89**

Merlot Sonoma County 1984 • $12 • (6/15/1987) SS • **94**

Pinot Noir Russian River Valley 1997: This California Pinot is smooth, ripe and spicy, with bright and sharply focused black cherry, vanilla, cedar and spice flavors that fan out nicely, turning delicate and elegant, with a long, lively aftertaste. Drink now through 2008.–J.L. • $35 • (3/31/2000) HR • **91**

Pinot Noir Russian River Valley 1996: Pleasantly balanced and flavorful, with pretty plum, black cherry and wild berry notes. Holds its focus on the finish. Drink now.–J.L. • $32 • (10/31/1998) • **88**

Pinot Noir Russian River Valley 1995 • $28 • (12/31/1997) HR • **94**

Pinot Noir Russian River Valley 1994 • $24 • (12/31/1996) • **92**

Pinot Noir Russian River Valley 1993 • $20 • (11/30/1995) • **88**

Pinot Noir Russian River Valley 1992 • $18 • (12/31/1994) • **88**

Pinot Noir Russian River Valley 1991 • $17 • (2/28/1994) • **87**

Pinot Noir Russian River Valley 1990 • $18 • (3/31/1997) • **93**

Pinot Noir Russian River Valley 1989 • $17 • (3/31/1992) • **80**

Pinot Noir Russian River Valley 1987 • $14 • (2/15/1990) • **91**

Pinot Noir Russian River Valley 1986 • $13 • (5/31/1989) • **88**

Pinot Noir Russian River Valley 1985 • $12 • (2/15/1988) • **85**

Pinot Noir Russian River Valley 1984 • $11 • (6/30/1987) • **89**

Pinot Noir Russian River Valley 1983 • $10 • (8/31/1986) • **89**

Pinot Noir Russian River Valley 1982 • $10 • (10/01/1985) • **86**

Pinot Noir Russian River Valley Goldridge Vineyard 1996: Lots to admire in this ripe, forward, supple and tasty Pinot. The texture is polished and the core of black cherry, wild berry, plum and spice is accented by pretty vanilla-tinged oak. Elegant and mildly tannic. Drink now through 2001. –J.L. • $25 • (10/31/1998) • **89**

Pinot Noir Russian River Valley Goldridge Vineyard 1995 • $23 • (8/31/1997) • **91**

Pinot Noir Russian River Valley Goldridge Vineyard 1994 • $20 • (12/31/1996) • **92**

Pinot Noir Russian River Valley Goldridge Vineyard 20-Year-Old Vines 1994 • $32 • (12/31/1996) • **93**

Pinot Noir Russian River Valley Octagon Vineyard 1995: Rich and concentrated, with spicy cherry, wild berry, raspberry and plummy notes, this is a complete and impeccably balanced wine that's at an excellent stage and should drink well now through 2004.–J.L. • $35 • (10/31/1998) • **92**

Pinot Noir Russian River Valley Octagon Vineyard 1994 • $32 • (12/31/1996) • **92**

Pinot Noir Russian River Valley Reserve 1994 • $32 • (12/31/1996) • **95**

Pinot Noir Russian River Valley Reserve 1992 • $25 • (12/31/1994) HR • **91**

Pinot Noir Russian River Valley Reserve 1991 • $23 • (2/28/1994) HR • **91**

Pinot Noir Sonoma County Selection 1990 • $10 • (2/28/1993) • **81**

Syrah Russian River Valley 1995: Smooth, rich, plush and concentrated, with layers of juicy blackberry, cherry, plum, anise, currant and mineral, finishing with touches of oak and earthiness. Drink now through 2007.–J.L. • $28 • (4/30/1999) • **94**

Syrah Russian River Valley 1994 • $23 • (8/31/1997) • **92**

Syrah Russian River Valley 1993 • $18 • (5/31/1996) HR • **90**

Syrah Russian River Valley 1992 • $16 • (5/15/1995) HR • **93**

DEL DOTTO | CALIFORNIA

Cabernet Franc Napa Valley 1997: Offers a wonderful array of complex, elegant fruit flavors, accented by cedar, spice, coffee and tar notes. The core of black cherry, tobacco, vanilla, sage and blackberry is supple and polished. Drink now through 2007.–J.L. • $45 • (12/15/1999) • **91**

Cabernet Sauvignon Napa Valley 1996: Revs up with lots of complex flavors—pretty black cherry, currant, plum and spicy, toasty oak that fold together nicely, revealing depth, richness and concentration. Best from 2001 through 2010.–J.L. • $49 • (10/15/1999) • **92**

Cabernet Sauvignon Napa Valley 1995: A well-oaked style, with smoky vanilla flavors and a core of black cherry, plum and wild berry that's elegant and spicy, finishing with mild, well-integrated tannins. Impressive for its length and complexity. Drink through 2007.–J.L. • $43 • (11/15/1998) • **92**

Cabernet Sauvignon Napa Valley 1994 • $42 • (10/31/1997) • **92**

Cabernet Sauvignon Napa Valley 1993 • $30 • (4/30/1997) • **92**

Giovanni's Tuscan Reserve Napa Valley 1996: Tightly wound, revealing glimpses of complex cedar, anise, currant, olive and black cherry before turning austere and tannic. Best to cellar short-term. A blend of Cabernet Sauvignon and Sangiovese. Drink through 2007.–J.L. • $45 • (10/15/1999) • **88**

Giovanni's Tuscan Reserve Napa Valley 1995: Shows off spicy, toasty oak, but delivers the fruit too, with elegant, creamy black cherry, strawberry, anise, black olive and spice. Finishes with a long aftertaste and round, polished tannins. A blend of Cabernet Sauvignon and Sangiovese. Drink through 2004.–J.L. • $30/500 ml. • (11/15/1998) • **91**

Merlot Napa Valley 1997: A touch spritzy, with green olive, herb and cedar notes holding the upper hand. Drink now.–J.L. • $49 • (6/15/2000) • **80**

DELECTUS | CALIFORNIA

Cabernet Sauvignon Napa Valley 1996: Tightly framed, with a beam of crisp cherry and currant, picking up spice, anise and a touch of herb. Mildly tannic. Best from 2001 through 2008.–J.L. • $43 • (10/15/1999) • **88**

Cabernet Sauvignon Napa Valley 1995: Ripe and supple, with an elegant band of currant, chocolate, cherry, cedar, anise and spicy wood flavors. Holds its focus and keeps pumping out the flavors on a long, complex aftertaste. Drink through 2009.–J.L. • $42 • (7/31/1998) • **91**

Cabernet Sauvignon Napa Valley 1994 • $42 • (7/31/1997) • **88**

Cabernet Sauvignon Napa Valley Beckstoffer Vineyard Georges III 1997: Pleasantly balanced, with spicy currant and black cherry, framed by cedary oak. Losing velocity, turning simple. Drink now.–J.L. • $45 • (6/15/2000) • **85**

Meritage Napa Valley 1997: Light and simple, with cedary currant, cranberry and berryish notes that are vague; lacks complexity, depth and concentration, tasting rather ordinary. Drink now.–J.L. • $30 • (4/30/2000) • **82**

Merlot Napa Valley Stanton Vineyard 1997: Smooth and polished, with rich currant, chocolate, coffee, black cherry, cedar and tar notes. Finishes with a supple texture. Drink now through 2006.–J.L. • $39 • (1/31/2000) • **88**

Merlot Napa Valley Stanton Vineyard 1996: Ripe and juicy, with lots of spice, cherry, herbal and sage flavors that are supple and balanced, finishing with a pretty jalapeño pepper note. Drink now through 2002.–J.L. • $38 • (12/15/1998) • **87**

Key: SS—Spectator Selection. CS—Cellar Selection. HR—Highly Recommended. $NA—Price not available. (BT)—Barrel tasting. Ⓐ—Auction Price.
For a key to the tasters' initials, see "How to Use These Listings."
Dates in parentheses represent the issues in which the ratings were published.

DELICATO CALIFORNIA

Cabernet Sauvignon Napa Valley Carneros 1983 • $10 • (6/15/1987) • **72**
Merlot California 1997: Pleasant for its simple cherry and strawberry flavors and soft texture. Drink now.–J.L. • $5 • (10/15/1999) • **80**
Zinfandel California 1996: Simple, with charry oak, raspberry, dried berry and black cherry flavors, finishing soft. Drink now.–H.S. • $6 • (5/15/1999) • **82**

DELILLE WASHINGTON

Cabernet Sauvignon Yakima Valley Harrison Hill 1994 • $32 • (7/31/1997) • **92**
Chaleur Estate Columbia Valley White 1997: Herb and green pepper flavors peek through a layer of spicy oak in this smooth-textured wine. Has plenty of personality, though it is muted by the oak. Drink now.–H.S. • $20 • (9/30/1999) • **86**
Chaleur Estate Columbia Valley White 1996: Bright and focused, with herb and resin overtones to the fresh apple flavors. Drink now.–H.S. • $20 • (9/15/1998) • **82**
Chaleur Estate Yakima Valley Red 1996: Smooth and spicy, this round, velvety red has a core of plum and cherry. Refined and gentle, this should improve with short-term cellaring. Drink now through 2004.–H.S. • $32 • (9/30/1999) • **88**
Chaleur Estate Yakima Valley Red 1995: Smooth and inviting, spreading rich plum, currant, spice and coffee flavors over a deftly balanced framework of fine tannins. Impressive for its suppleness and elegance, folding in its flavors elegantly. Contains 66 percent Cabernet Sauvignon, 25 percent Merlot and 9 percent Cabernet Franc. Drink through 2005–H.S. • $38 • (8/31/1998) • **92**
Chaleur Estate Yakima Valley Red 1994 • $32 • (7/31/1997) • **89**
Chaleur Estate Yakima Valley Red 1993 • $28 • (8/31/1996) • **91**
Chaleur Estate Yakima Valley Red 1992 • $28 • (9/30/1995) • **85**
D2 Yakima Valley 1995: Light in texture, with subdued, almost earthy aromas, but pretty berry and vanilla flavors emerge on the smooth finish. Drink now.–H.S. • $28 • (9/30/1998) • **88**
D2 Yakima Valley 1994 • $22 • (7/31/1997) • **90**
D2 Yakima Valley 1993 • $18 • (8/31/1996) HR • **92**
Harrison Hill Yakima Valley 1996: Firm, polished and light in style, with a real sense of elegance as it unfolds its pretty plum, tobacco, berry and herb flavors, which linger on the gentle finish. Drink now through 2003.–H.S. • $32 • (9/30/1999) • **89**
Harrison Hill Yakima Valley 1995: Light, supple and smooth, with pretty chocolate and floral overtones to the berry notes at the center. Finishes gracefully. Drink now.–H.S. • $38 • (9/30/1998) • **89**

DEUX AMIS CALIFORNIA

Cabernet Sauvignon Dry Creek Valley 1987 • $14 • (11/15/1991) • **83**
Zinfandel Dry Creek Valley Rued Vineyards 1995 • $20 • (6/15/1998) • **87**
Zinfandel Sonoma County 1996: Somewhat earthy on the nose, soft on the palate, with hints of cherry and spice. Looks like it's aging fast. Drink now. • $15 • (5/15/1999) • **83**
Zinfandel Sonoma County 1995 • $15 • (5/31/1998) • **83**
Zinfandel Sonoma County 1994 • $14 • (4/30/1997) • **85**
Zinfandel Sonoma County 1993 • $12 • (10/15/1995) • **86**

DEVON CELLARS WASHINGTON

Dedication Yakima Valley 1992 • $19 • (7/31/1996) • **81**

DI BRUNO CALIFORNIA

Pinot Grigio Santa Barbara County Sanford & Benedict Vineyard 1996 • $14 • (5/15/1998) • **87**

DI STEFANO WASHINGTON

Cabernet Sauvignon Columbia Valley 1996: Fresh and bright, with pretty currant and plum flavors that ride smoothly over a bed of fine-grained tannins. Approachable now. Drink through 2003.–H.S. • $28 • (9/30/1999) • **87**
Cabernet Sauvignon Columbia Valley 1995: Lean and smooth, with spicy, earthy overtones to the licorice-scented black cherry flavors that linger tastily on the firm finish. Good now, best through 2001.–H.S. • $25 • (10/15/1998) • **87**
Cabernet Sauvignon Columbia Valley 1994 • $26 • (9/30/1997) • **92**
Cabernet Sauvignon Columbia Valley 1993 • $21 • (9/15/1996) • **91**
Cabernet Sauvignon Columbia Valley 1991 • $16 • (9/30/1994) • **84**
Fumé Blanc Willamette Valley 1997: Light and bright, with aggressively herbal green pea, citrus and melon flavors that linger on the lively finish. Drink now.–H.S. • $9 • (12/31/1999) • **87**
Fumé Blanc Willamette Valley 1996 • $9 • (10/31/1997) • **85**

DIAMOND CREEK CALIFORNIA

Cabernet Sauvignon Napa Valley Gravelly Meadow 1998: Marked by strong dill and earthy aromas, it's raw and peppery, if a bit stale.–J.L. • $NA • (8/31/1999) (BT) • **85-89**
Cabernet Sauvignon Napa Valley Gravelly Meadow 1997: Tightly focused, firm, tannic, rich and marked by sage, currant, black cherry, cedar and earth notes. This builds into a mouthful of Cabernet, but it needs a little time. Best from 2002 through 2012.–J.L. • $150 • (11/15/1999) • **93**
Cabernet Sauvignon Napa Valley Gravelly Meadow 1996: Austere in style, its character leans toward the earthy side of Cabernet, serving up the clay-tinged currant, plum and wild berry flavors of the vineyard before the tannins flex their muscles. Best from 2003 through 2010.–J.L. • $100 • (12/31/1998) CS • **91**
Cabernet Sauvignon Napa Valley Gravelly Meadow 1995 • $75 • (6/15/1998) • **96**
Cabernet Sauvignon Napa Valley Gravelly Meadow 1994 • $NA • (6/15/1998) • **93**
Cabernet Sauvignon Napa Valley Gravelly Meadow 1993 • $72 Ⓐ • (12/15/1995) • **86**
Cabernet Sauvignon Napa Valley Gravelly Meadow 1992 • $78 Ⓐ • (6/15/1998) • **92**
Cabernet Sauvignon Napa Valley Gravelly Meadow 1991 • $86 Ⓐ • (6/15/1998) • **92**
Cabernet Sauvignon Napa Valley Gravelly Meadow 1990 • $NA • (6/15/1998) • **88**
Cabernet Sauvignon Napa Valley Gravelly Meadow 1989 • $34 Ⓐ • (6/15/1998) • **89**
Cabernet Sauvignon Napa Valley Gravelly Meadow 1988: Lean and trim, with a narrow band of cedar, berry, currant and spice. Remains a tightly well-balanced wine that can age further. (1988 California Cabernet retrospective tasting). Drink now through 2003.–J.L. • $40 • (11/15/1998) • **87**
Cabernet Sauvignon Napa Valley Gravelly Meadow 1987 • $NA • (6/15/1998) • **89**
Cabernet Sauvignon Napa Valley Gravelly Meadow 1986 • $NA • (6/15/1998) • **92**
Cabernet Sauvignon Napa Valley Gravelly Meadow 1985 • $96 Ⓐ • (11/30/1987) • **89**
Cabernet Sauvignon Napa Valley Gravelly Meadow 1984 • $NA • (6/15/1998) • **90**
Cabernet Sauvignon Napa Valley Gravelly Meadow 1983 • $NA • (6/15/1998) • **88**
Cabernet Sauvignon Napa Valley Gravelly Meadow 1982 • $NA • (6/15/1998) • **88**
Cabernet Sauvignon Napa Valley Gravelly Meadow 1981 • $NA • (6/15/1998) • **84**
Cabernet Sauvignon Napa Valley Gravelly Meadow 1978: Characteristically more earthy (or gravelly) than the other Diamond Creek Cabs, still showing plenty of richness and flavor, with earthy currant, mineral, herb, sage and spice notes. Aging well and appears to have the concentration to go another five to 10 years. Will it get better? Doubtful, but it should hold for those who want to wait. (1978 California Cabernet retrospective tasting). Drink now through 2002.–J.L. • $13 • (11/15/1998) • **91**
Cabernet Sauvignon Napa Valley Gravelly Meadow 1976 • $NA • (6/15/1998) • **84**
Cabernet Sauvignon Napa Valley Gravelly Meadow 1975 • $NA • (6/15/1998) • **90**
Cabernet Sauvignon Napa Valley Gravelly Meadow 1974 • $NA • (6/15/1998) • **88**
Cabernet Sauvignon Napa Valley Gravelly Meadow-Lake 1992 • $NA • (6/15/1998) • **90**
Cabernet Sauvignon Napa Valley Gravelly Meadow-Lake 1991 • $50 • (11/15/1993) • **90**
Cabernet Sauvignon Napa Valley Gravelly Meadow Microclimate 1991 • $NA • (6/15/1998) • **90**
Cabernet Sauvignon Napa Valley Gravelly Meadow Special Select 1982 • $NA • (6/15/1998) • **80**
Cabernet Sauvignon Napa Valley Lake 1997: Dark, dense and marked by intense cedary notes, this is an enormous wine, quite rich and laden with black currant, anise, sage, leather, mineral and earth flavors. Needs time. Only available in 5-liter format, of which only 170 were made. Best from 2004 through 2014.–J.L. • $2000 • (5/31/2000) • **93**

■ ■ ■ ■

DIAMOND CREEK

Cabernet Sauvignon Napa Valley Lake 1996: This prestigious California red is ripe, smooth and elegant, with pretty black cherry, tart plum, herb and cedary oak notes that turn supple and polished. Displaying wonderful integration of fruit and tannins, it's tasty now—but it isn't for everyday drinking at this price. Best from 2002 through 2010.–J.L. • $345 Ⓐ • (12/31/1998) CS • **92**

Cabernet Sauvignon Napa Valley Lake 1994 • $230 Ⓐ • (6/15/1998) • **93**

Cabernet Sauvignon Napa Valley Lake 1992 • $311 Ⓐ • (6/15/1998) • **94**

Cabernet Sauvignon Napa Valley Lake 1990 • $192 Ⓐ • (6/15/1998) • **92**

Cabernet Sauvignon Napa Valley Lake 1987 • $NA • (6/15/1998) • **93**

Cabernet Sauvignon Napa Valley Lake 1984 • $NA • (6/15/1998) • **94**

Cabernet Sauvignon Napa Valley Lake 1978: An extraordinary wine, atypical for Diamond Creek with its lush, rich, fleshy texture and opulent fruit. Still young and vibrant, with complex currant, anise, plum and cherry flavors, this remains my favorite of the many Diamond Creek Cabernets. (1978 California Cabernet retrospective tasting). Drink now through 2005.–J.L. • $13 • (11/15/1998) • **97**

Cabernet Sauvignon Napa Valley Red Rock Terrace 1998: Firm, concentrated, a touch beefy, working its way into more complex flavors, with a firm aftertaste and chewy tannins.–J.L. • $NA • (8/31/1999) (BT) • **90-94**

Cabernet Sauvignon Napa Valley Red Rock Terrace 1997: Firm and concentrated, with mint, sage, currant and earthy berry flavors that slowly unfold. Needs time, but there's lots of richness and detail in this young wine. Best from 2002 through 2010.–J.L. • $150 • (11/15/1999) • **92**

Cabernet Sauvignon Napa Valley Red Rock Terrace 1996: A sleek and elegant bottling, its ripe, spicy Cabernet profile echoing focused berry, plum and currant flavors tinged with hints of tea, sage, cedar and earth. Finishes with supple tannins. At its best from 2002 through–J.L. • $86 Ⓐ • (12/31/1998) CS • **92**

Cabernet Sauvignon Napa Valley Red Rock Terrace 1995 • $75 • (6/15/1998) • **96**

Cabernet Sauvignon Napa Valley Red Rock Terrace 1994 • $NA • (6/15/1998) • **91**

Cabernet Sauvignon Napa Valley Red Rock Terrace 1993 • $67 Ⓐ • (12/15/1995) • **85**

Cabernet Sauvignon Napa Valley Red Rock Terrace 1992 • $77 Ⓐ • (6/15/1998) • **91**

Cabernet Sauvignon Napa Valley Red Rock Terrace 1991 • $25 • (6/15/1998) • **94**

Cabernet Sauvignon Napa Valley Red Rock Terrace 1990 • $NA • (6/15/1998) • **89**

Cabernet Sauvignon Napa Valley Red Rock Terrace 1989 • $29 Ⓐ • (1/31/1992) • **89**

Cabernet Sauvignon Napa Valley Red Rock Terrace 1988: Shows a shade more depth and flavor than the Gravelly Meadow, with earthy black cherry, leather, cedar and spice. Well balanced, this is one of a handful of 1988s that may have a future. Finishes with ripe, well-integrated tannins. (1988 California Cabernet retrospective tasting). Drink now through 2006. –J.L. • $40 • (11/15/1998) • **89**

Cabernet Sauvignon Napa Valley Red Rock Terrace 1987 • $NA • (6/15/1998) • **89**

Cabernet Sauvignon Napa Valley Red Rock Terrace 1986 • $67 Ⓐ • (6/15/1998) • **92**

Cabernet Sauvignon Napa Valley Red Rock Terrace 1985 • $82 Ⓐ • (11/30/1987) • **91**

Cabernet Sauvignon Napa Valley Red Rock Terrace 1984 • $77 Ⓐ • (6/15/1998) • **90**

Cabernet Sauvignon Napa Valley Red Rock Terrace 1983 • $NA • (6/15/1998) • **88**

Cabernet Sauvignon Napa Valley Red Rock Terrace 1982 • $NA • (6/15/1998) • **88**

Cabernet Sauvignon Napa Valley Red Rock Terrace 1981 • $NA • (6/15/1998) • **84**

Cabernet Sauvignon Napa Valley Red Rock Terrace 1978: Healthy color. Mature, but rich and enormously complex, with an array of earthy currant, anise, cedar and herb flavors, turning smooth and supple in texture. Drinks well now but can age further. (1978 California Cabernet retrospective tasting). Drink now through 2002.–J.L. • $125 Ⓐ • (11/15/1998) • **96**

Cabernet Sauvignon Napa Valley Red Rock Terrace First Pick 1977 • $NA • (6/15/1998) • **85**

Cabernet Sauvignon Napa Valley Red Rock Terrace Second Pick 1977 • $NA • (6/15/1998) • **84**

Key: SS—Spectator Selection. CS—Cellar Selection. HR—Highly Recommended. $NA—Price not available. (BT)—Barrel tasting. Ⓐ—Auction Price. For a key to the tasters' initials, see "How to Use These Listings." **Dates in parentheses represent the issues in which the ratings were published.**

Cabernet Sauvignon Napa Valley Red Rock Terrace 1976 • $NA • (6/15/1998) • **84**

Cabernet Sauvignon Napa Valley Red Rock Terrace 1975 • $NA • (6/15/1998) • **90**

Cabernet Sauvignon Napa Valley Red Rock Terrace 1974 • $140 • (11/15/1994) • **92**

Cabernet Sauvignon Napa Valley Red Rock Terrace Microclimate 3 1996: This impressive red is dense and concentrated, with a classy array of rich currant, black cherry, exotic spice, mineral and cedar flavors that are tightly focused and quite complex, ending in a long, rich aftertaste. Another outstanding DC Cab. Best from 2002 through 2012.–J.L. • $150 • (12/31/1998) CS • **94**

Cabernet Sauvignon Napa Valley Red Rock Terrace Microclimate 3 1991 • $50 • (11/15/1993) CS • **94**

Cabernet Sauvignon Napa Valley Red Rock Terrace Microclimate 2 1994 • $NA • (6/15/1998) • **93**

Cabernet Sauvignon Napa Valley Red Rock Terrace Special Select 1982 • $NA • (6/15/1998) • **82**

Cabernet Sauvignon Napa Valley Three Vineyard Blend 1990 • $NA • (6/15/1998) • **88**

Cabernet Sauvignon Napa Valley Three Vineyard Blend 1989 • $NA • (6/15/1998) • **87**

Cabernet Sauvignon Napa Valley Three Vineyard Blend 1985 • $NA • (6/15/1998) • **90**

Cabernet Sauvignon Napa Valley Three Vineyard Blend 1981 • $NA • (6/15/1998) • **84**

Cabernet Sauvignon Napa Valley Volcanic Hill 1998: Austere, with firm tannins and tight structure. Pure barrel sample; quite dry and tannic.–J.L. • $NA • (8/31/1999) (BT) • **90-94**

Cabernet Sauvignon Napa Valley Volcanic Hill 1997: Earthy, tannic and mushroomy, this renowned Diamond Creek red slowly emerges from its shell, unveiling tight currant, black cherry, anise, sage and cedar notes; there's a lot of substance in this young wine, so be patient. Best from 2002 through 2013.–J.L. • $150 • (11/15/1999) CS • **93**

Cabernet Sauvignon Napa Valley Volcanic Hill 1996: This year's version is ripe and intense, showing concentrated wild berry, currant, sage, anise and spice flavors, with a chalky accent adding interest. Tannins are tight and chewy. Needs cellaring. Best from 2004 through 2012.–J.L. • $100 • (12/31/1998) CS • **92**

Cabernet Sauvignon Napa Valley Volcanic Hill 1995 • $125 Ⓐ • (6/15/1998) • **94**

Cabernet Sauvignon Napa Valley Volcanic Hill 1994 • $NA • (6/15/1998) • **91**

Cabernet Sauvignon Napa Valley Volcanic Hill 1993 • $72 Ⓐ • (6/15/1998) • **88**

Cabernet Sauvignon Napa Valley Volcanic Hill 1992 • $72 Ⓐ • (6/15/1998) • **92**

Cabernet Sauvignon Napa Valley Volcanic Hill 1991 • $86 Ⓐ • (6/15/1998) • **93**

Cabernet Sauvignon Napa Valley Volcanic Hill 1990 • $NA • (6/15/1998) • **93**

Cabernet Sauvignon Napa Valley Volcanic Hill 1989: Dark and intense but not fully ripe, leaving it with cedary, earthy and mushroomy flavors and just glimpses of moderately ripe currant and cherry. Can still age, but it's not likely to improve. (1989 California Cabernet retrospective tasting). Drink now through 2005.–J.L. • $34 Ⓐ • (8/31/1999) • **87**

Cabernet Sauvignon Napa Valley Volcanic Hill 1988: Tight, tannic and earthy, but with a dense, compact core of mineral, currant, cedar and spice. An '88 you can wait on, as the fruit, while not overly ripe, is concentrated. (1988 California Cabernet retrospective tasting). Drink now through 2005.–J.L. • $40 • (11/15/1998) • **87**

Cabernet Sauvignon Napa Valley Volcanic Hill 1987 • $NA • (6/15/1998) • **87**

Cabernet Sauvignon Napa Valley Volcanic Hill 1986 • $71 Ⓐ • (6/15/1998) • **91**

Cabernet Sauvignon Napa Valley Volcanic Hill 1985 • $81 Ⓐ • (6/15/1998) • **90**

Cabernet Sauvignon Napa Valley Volcanic Hill 1984 • $78 Ⓐ • (6/15/1998) • **93**

Cabernet Sauvignon Napa Valley Volcanic Hill 1983 • $42 Ⓐ • (6/15/1998) • **88**

Cabernet Sauvignon Napa Valley Volcanic Hill 1982 • $70 Ⓐ • (6/15/1998) • **87**

Cabernet Sauvignon Napa Valley Volcanic Hill 1981 • $NA • (6/15/1998) • **88**

Cabernet Sauvignon Napa Valley Volcanic Hill 1980 • $NA • (6/15/1998) • **91**

Cabernet Sauvignon Napa Valley Volcanic Hill First Pick 1979 • $NA • (6/15/1998) • **93**

Cabernet Sauvignon Napa Valley Volcanic Hill 1979: Not showing the fruit complexity you often find in this wine; it starts out meaty and tight, working into currant and berry flavors. (1979 California Cabernet retrospective tasting). Drink now through 2002.–J.L. • $15 • (8/31/1999) • **88**

Cabernet Sauvignon Napa Valley Volcanic Hill 1978: Remains a dense, chewy, richly flavored wine, packed with earthy, leathery currant, spice and mineral flavors. Lingers long, with the kind of finish that suggests it could go another three, five, maybe 10 years with ease. (1978 California Cabernet retrospective tasting). Drink now through 2008.–J.L. • $154 Ⓐ • (11/15/1998) • **93**

Cabernet Sauvignon Napa Valley Volcanic Hill 1976 • $NA • (6/15/1998) • **88**

Cabernet Sauvignon Napa Valley Volcanic Hill 1975 • $NA • (6/15/1998) • **94**
Cabernet Sauvignon Napa Valley Volcanic Hill 1974 • $NA • (6/15/1998) • **86**
Cabernet Sauvignon Napa Valley Volcanic Hill 1973 • $NA • (6/15/1998) • **82**
Cabernet Sauvignon Napa Valley Volcanic Hill 1972 • $NA • (6/15/1998) • **90**
Cabernet Sauvignon Napa Valley Volcanic Hill Microclimate 1991 • $NA • (6/15/1998) • **92**
Cabernet Sauvignon Napa Valley Volcanic Hill Microclimate 4 1991 • $50 • (11/15/1993) CS • **93**
Cabernet Sauvignon Napa Valley Volcanic Hill Special Select 1982 • $NA • (6/15/1998) • **88**

DICKERSON | CALIFORNIA

Merlot Napa Valley 1994 • $16 • (11/30/1996) • **84**
Merlot Napa Valley Limited Release 1995 • $22 • (6/15/1998) • **86**
Merlot Napa Valley Limited Reserve 1993 • $16 • (8/31/1996) • **87**
Merlot Napa Valley Limited Reserve 1992 • $17 • (2/28/1995) HR • **90**
Ruby Cabernet Napa Valley 1994 • $10 • (11/15/1996) • **84**
Ruby Cabernet Napa Valley 1992 • $10 • (5/15/1995) • **85**
Ruby Cabernet Napa Valley 1988 • $9 • (2/28/1991) • **79**
Ruby Cabernet Napa Valley Limited Reserve 1993 • $9 • (12/15/1995) • **88**
Ruby Cabernet Napa Valley Limited Reserve 1991 • $11 • (11/15/1994) • **87**
Zinfandel Napa Valley Limited Reserve 1997: Pungent aromas and flavors of sweet camphor, with dry, lean tannins. Drink now.–J.L. • $27 • (5/31/2000) • **80**
Zinfandel Napa Valley Limited Reserve 1996: A lighter-style Zin, with delicate cherry and spice flavors. Pulls up a little short on the finish with some dryness, though a hint of anise lingers. Drink now through 2002. • $22 • (6/30/1999) • **83**
Zinfandel Napa Valley Limited Reserve 1995 • $22 • (6/15/1998) • **84**
Zinfandel Napa Valley Limited Reserve 1994 • $19 • (11/15/1996) • **84**
Zinfandel Napa Valley Limited Reserve 1993 • $17 • (12/31/1995) • **88**
Zinfandel Napa Valley Limited Reserve 1991: Shows off mintiness as the dominant flavor; ripe cherry and wild berry merge on the palate, but on the finish the mint, bay leaf and sage notes team up. If you like those flavors, you'll love this wine. (Zinfandel retrospective tasting). Drink now through 2002.–J.L. • $19 • (6/30/1999) • **88**

DOLCE | CALIFORNIA

Late Harvest Napa Valley 1995 • $55/375 ml. • (5/15/1998) • **90**
Late Harvest California 1994 • $55/375 ml. • (3/31/1998) HR • **95**
Late Harvest California 1993 • $50/375 ml. • (2/28/1997) • **92**
Late Harvest California 1992 • $50/375 ml. • (12/31/1995) • **90**
Late Harvest California 1991 • $NA • (1/01/1998) • **94**
Late Harvest California 1990 • $50/375 ml. • (11/15/1993) HR • **92**

DOMAINE ALFRED | CALIFORNIA

Pinot Noir Edna Valley Chamisal Vineyards 1998: Simple but pleasant, with ripe cherry, herb and spice notes. Drink now through 2004.–J.L. • $28 • (5/31/2000) • **85**
Pinot Noir Edna Valley Chamisal Vineyards Califa 1998: Firm and rich, a little rough around the edges, with a vegetal streak to the ripe cherry and wild berry. Drink now through 2006.–J.L. • $42 • (5/31/2000) • **86**

DOMAINE CARNEROS | CALIFORNIA

Blanc de Blancs Carneros Le Rêve 1993: Bright and tangy, with a toasty, lemony quality that leaves the palate refreshed. The finish is long, with a distinct mineral edge. Elegant, graceful and harmonious. Drink now. • $50 • (9/15/1999) • **91**
Brut Carneros NV • $17 • (12/31/1993) • **80**
Brut Carneros 1995: Fresh toast and citrus flavors make this a bright and refreshing wine. The moderate finish is redolent of tangy orange and herbs. Pretty and fresh. Drink now. • $19 • (10/15/1999) • **87**
Brut Carneros 2000 1994: Tightly wound, but showing a focused band of toast, citrus, pear and green apple notes on the midpalate. Bright and light in texture, it finishes long. Should improve with age; great price, too. Drink now through 2005. • $55/1.5 liter • (9/15/1999) • **92**
Brut Carneros 1993 • $18 • (6/15/1998) • **87**
Brut Carneros 1992 • $21 • (11/30/1997) • **87**
Brut Carneros 1991 • $20 • (12/31/1995) • **89**
Brut Carneros Blanc de Blancs 1991 • $24 • (11/15/1996) • **89**
Brut Carneros Blanc de Blancs 1990 • $25 • (9/15/1996) • **88**
Brut Carneros Taittinger NV • $18 • (12/31/1994) • **87**
Le Rêve Carneros 1992: A bright bubbly, with tangy lemon and mineral notes up front. It's firm and focused, yet made in a delicate style. Flavors fan out on the finish, with hints of gooseberry, mint, citrus, apple and pear. A complex wine with staying power. Drink now through 2002. • $35 • (7/31/1998) • **91**
Pinot Noir Carneros 1997: Smooth, ripe, rich and concentrated, with layers of ripe cherry, plum and wild berry, turning plush and polished. Drink now through 2005.–J.L. • $28 • (9/15/1999) • **89**
Pinot Noir Carneros 1996: Smooth, ripe, moderately rich and polished, with a pretty core of black cherry, plum and anise, turning plush and detailed on the finish, where mineral and leather nuances show up. Drink now through 2001.–J.L. • $22 • (8/31/1998) • **88**
Pinot Noir Carneros 1995 • $20 • (8/31/1997) • **88**
Pinot Noir Carneros 1994 • $20 • (2/29/1996) • **87**
Pinot Noir Carneros 1993 • $20 • (12/31/1995) • **90**
Pinot Noir Carneros The Famous Gate 1995 • $32 • (9/30/1997) • **88**
Pinot Noir Carneros The Famous Gate 1994 • $32 • (2/28/1997) • **88**
Pinot Noir Carneros The Famous Gate 1993 • $30 • (12/31/1995) • **87**

DOMAINE CHANDON | CALIFORNIA

Blanc de Noirs California Cuvée 390 NV • $14 • (9/15/1995) • **86**
Blanc de Noirs Carneros Cuvée 393 NV • $11 • (11/30/1997) • **88**
Blanc de Noirs Carneros Cuvée 394 NV: Tightly wound and lemony, sporting floral, honey and toast overtones. On the finish, its tangy character persists. Firm and assertive. Drink now through 2002. • $18 • (12/15/1998) • **87**
Blanc de Noirs Carneros Cuvée 396 NV: Firm and focused, with a crisp core of apple, citrus, pear and herb flavors. The finish is bright and long. Drink now. • $15 • (10/15/1999) • **87**
Brut Blanc de Noirs Carneros NV • $14 • (12/15/1995) • **89**
Brut Blanc de Noirs Napa-Sonoma Counties NV • $12 • (8/31/1992) • **82**
Brut California Classic 196 NV: Fresh and clean, with moderate citrus, green apple and herb notes. Drink now. • $15 • (10/15/1999) • **84**
Brut Napa County Cuvée NV • $12 • (12/31/1994) • **85**
Brut Napa County Cuvée 190 NV • $14 • (9/15/1995) • **87**
Brut Napa County étoile NV • $23 • (12/31/1991) • **85**
Brut Napa & Sonoma Counties Chandon Réserve NV • $16 • (12/31/1993) • **85**
Brut Napa & Sonoma Counties Cuvée 194 NV • $11 • (12/15/1997) • **88**
Brut Napa & Sonoma Counties étoile NV • $22 • (12/31/1993) • **85**
Brut Napa & Sonoma Counties Reserve NV • $16 • (12/31/1994) • **87**
Brut Napa Valley Chandon Réserve NV • $18 • (12/31/1992) • **86**
Brut Napa Valley étoile NV • $29 • (12/31/1997) • **88**
Brut Napa-Sonoma Cuvée Late Disgorged NV • $60/1.5 liter • (12/31/1997) • **91**
Brut Sonoma-Napa Counties Cuvée 195 NV: A fresh, lemony flavor dominates in this wine, which also displays toast and floral qualities. Bright and bubbly, it finishes with a tangy, minerally edge. Drink now through 2002. • $18 • (12/15/1998) • **87**
Cuvée 2000 Late Disgorged Napa County NV: An enjoyable blend of citrus, toast and herb flavors, set in a bright, firm texture. The finish is moderate, offering just a hint of a honeyed tone. Drink now. • $24 • (10/15/1999) • **87**
étoile Napa Valley NV: Toasty, doughy aromas and pretty fig, apple, melon and citrus offer an attractive blend in this somewhat weighty yet refreshing wine. The finish is long but clean. Drink now through 2001. • $31 • (12/15/1998) • **91**
étoile Rosé Napa-Sonoma Counties NV: A pleasant sparkler, with subtle cherry and floral character. On the finish, it serves up tangy lemon and lime flavors. Drink now. • $34 • (12/15/1998) • **87**
Fleur de Vigne California NV: Quite fruity, with pronounced peppermint and eucalyptus notes. A bit like Moscato d'Asti. Tangy and refreshing. A fun aperitif. Drink now. • $15 • (7/31/1998) • **83**
Napa Valley Club Cuvée NV • $17 • (6/15/1991) • **77**
Pinot Meunier Carneros 1997: Good depth to the red currant, cherry, cola and mushroom flavors, with a slight tartness on the finish. Drink now.–J.L. • $18 • (6/30/2000) • **86**
Pinot Noir Carneros 1997: Medium-weight, with light cherry, earth, spice and cola, finishing with crisp, earthy tannins. Drink now through 2005.–J.L. • $29 • (6/30/2000) • **86**
Réserve Cuvée 490 Napa County NV • $18 • (9/15/1996) SS • **90**
Réserve Cuvée 491 Napa County NV • $19 • (11/30/1997) • **86**
Réserve Cuvée Napa County 25th Anniversary NV • $24 • (6/15/1998) • **85**
Rosé Napa County Cuvée 291 Club Selection NV • $19 • (12/31/1995) • **87**

DOMAINE DANICA | CALIFORNIA

Zinfandel Sonoma County 1998: Flavors of chocolate, dried blackberry and vanilla are intense and finish sharply. Drink now through 2003.–J.L. • $33 • (5/15/2000) • **85**

DOMAINE DE LA TERRE ROUGE | CALIFORNIA

Blanc Sierra Foothills 1996 • $14 • (12/15/1997) • **80**
Marsanne-Viognier-Roussanne Sierra Foothills Enigma 1998: Serves up a complex band of spice, citrus, apricot and nectarine, with a slight bitter edge. Drink now.–J.L. • $18 • (11/30/1999) • **85**
Marsanne-Viognier-Roussanne Sierra Foothills Enigma 1997: Smooth and enticing, richly textured, showing pretty pear, hazelnut and mineral notes. Finishes long. Drink now. • $16 • (9/15/1998) • **88**
Mourvèdre Amador County 1997: Earthy and a touch leathery, with mineral, coffee ground, dried cherry, anise and wood flavors. Tilts toward bitterness. Drink now through 2004.–J.L. • $18 • (12/31/1999) • **85**
Muscat à Petits Grains Shenandoah Valley 1997: An odd blend of pine sap, maple syrup, spicy pear and tobacco notes. Drink now through 2004.–J.L. • $15 • (5/31/2000) • **84**
Noir California 1993 • $16 • (11/15/1997) • **86**
Noir Grande Année Sierra Foothills 1994: Plenty of ripe plum and wild berry flavors, with meaty cedar, anise, sage and herb notes. Finishes with firm, well-integrated tannins. Drink now through 2004.–J.L. • $20 • (9/30/1998) • **87**
Noir Sierra Foothills 1995: Pleasantly balanced, with supple dried cherry, earth, mineral, leather and spice. Finishes with a touch of anise and cedar. Grenache, Syrah, Mourvèdre. Drink now through 2004.–J.L. • $18 • (12/31/1999) • **87**
Noir Sierra Foothills 1992 • $15 • (2/28/1997) • **87**
Reserve Red California 1991 • $15 • (2/29/1996) • **86**
Sierra Foothills 1986 • $12 • (4/15/1989) • **89**
Syrah Amador County 1995 • $25 • (3/31/1998) • **88**
Syrah Amador County 1994 • $20 • (2/28/1997) • **88**
Syrah Amador County 1993 • $20 • (6/15/1996) • **89**
Syrah Shenandoah Valley Sentinel Oak Vineyard Pyramid Block 1996: Quite fragrant, with hints of herb, blackberry, vanilla and spice. Focused on the palate, with firm, ripe tannins, classy fruit and a moderate but bright finish. Should age nicely. Drink now through 2006. • $28 • (2/28/1999) • **88**
Tête-à-Tête Sierra Foothills 1997: Bright, grapey and attractive from the start, yet slows down a bit with rustic tannins. Still makes a good quaff. A blend of Grenache, Syrah and Mourvèdre. Drink now. • $12 • (2/28/1999) • **83**
Tête-à-Tête Sierra Foothills 1996 • $11 • (3/31/1998) • **86**
Viognier Shenandoah Valley 1998: Rich and focused, with layers of fig, citrus, honey, spice and apricot, turning complex and elegant. Drink now through 2004.–J.L. • $25 • (11/30/1999) • **88**
Viognier Shenandoah Valley 1997: A classy wine. Smooth on the palate, boating a touch of peach at the core. Good acidity keeps it firm on the finish, with hints of lemon and lime. Drink now. • $25 • (11/15/1998) • **88**
Viognier Shenandoah Valley 1996 • $25 • (12/15/1997) • **88**

DOMAINE DROUHIN | OREGON

Pinot Noir Oregon 1996: Firm and generous, nicely packed with berry and spice flavors, finishing with a gentle layer of tannins. Impressive for its fruit concentration in a light vintage. Drink now through 2002.–H.S. • $35 • (4/30/1999) • **87**
Pinot Noir Oregon 1995 • $39 Ⓐ • (2/28/1997) • **85**
Pinot Noir Oregon 1994 • $31 Ⓐ • (12/31/1996) • **88**
Pinot Noir Oregon 1993 • $30 • (8/31/1995) • **87**
Pinot Noir Oregon 1991 • $37 Ⓐ • (3/15/1994) • **86**
Pinot Noir Oregon 1990 • $30 • (1/31/1993) HR • **90**
Pinot Noir Oregon 1989 • $38 Ⓐ • (1/31/1992) • **87**
Pinot Noir Oregon 1988 • $32 • (5/31/1991) • **89**
Pinot Noir Oregon Laurène 1996: Gentle, refined style, offering a nice range of pretty plum, earth and toast aromas and flavors that linger on the silky frame. Coming together nicely in a decidedly Burgundian style. Drink now through 2006.–H.S. • $45 • (3/31/2000) • **88**
Pinot Noir Oregon Laurène 1995 • $45 • (5/15/1998) • **88**

Key: SS—Spectator Selection. CS—Cellar Selection. HR—Highly Recommended. $NA—Price not available. (BT)—Barrel tasting. Ⓐ—Auction Price.
For a key to the tasters' initials, see "How to Use These Listings."
Dates in parentheses represent the issues in which the ratings were published.

Pinot Noir Oregon Laurène 1994 • $45 • (7/31/1997) • **91**
Pinot Noir Oregon Laurène 1993 • $45 • (1/31/1996) • **88**
Pinot Noir Oregon Laurène 1992 • $40 • (11/30/1994) • **91**
Pinot Noir Oregon Non-Estate 1992 • $30 • (3/15/1994) • **85**

DOMAINE GRAND ARCHER | CALIFORNIA

Cabernet Sauvignon Sonoma County 1996: Big, with potent tannins, but also elegant, with dried cherry, wild berry and spice notes, finishing with earthy tannins and good length. Drink through 2006.–J.L. • $17 • (11/30/1998) • **87**
Cabernet Sauvignon Sonoma County 1995 • $16 • (3/31/1998) • **88**
Cabernet Sauvignon Sonoma County 1992 • $10 • (11/15/1994) • **87**
Chardonnay Sonoma County 1997: Smooth, ripe and creamy, if a touch sweet from ripe fruit, it serves up lots of vanilla, pear, fig and melon flavors. Drink now.–J.L. • $15 • (12/15/1998) • **88**
Chardonnay Sonoma County 1996 • $14 • (3/31/1998) • **89**
Merlot Sonoma County 1996: Light-bodied, with dusty, earthy, cherry flavors and a jalapeño pepper edge. Finishes simple and slightly dry. Drink now. –J.L. • $20 • (12/15/1998) • **80**
Merlot Sonoma County 1995 • $19 • (3/31/1998) • **88**
Merlot Sonoma County 1991 • $9 • (9/15/1994) • **82**
Sonoma County 1991 • $8 • (4/30/1994) SS • **89**
White Riesling Sonoma County 1996 • $11 • (3/31/1998) • **87**
Zinfandel Napa Valley 1996: Soft-textured, with ripe mineral, tar and black cherry flavors and soft tannins. Drink now.–H.S. • $21 • (5/15/1999) • **84**

DOMAINE SAINT GEORGE | CALIFORNIA

Cabernet Sauvignon California Select Reserve 1997: Mulchy, minty, charred flavors dominate the soft cherry notes. Finishes dry.–H.S. • $7 • (3/31/1999) • **78**
Cabernet Sauvignon California Select Reserve 1996: Shows a modest range of light, grapey cola flavors and soft tannins. • $8 • (12/15/1998) • **77**
Cabernet Sauvignon California Select Reserve 1994 • $6 • (11/30/1996) • **78**
Cabernet Sauvignon California Vintage Reserve 1992 • $6 • (11/15/1994) • **85**
Cabernet Sauvignon Dry Creek Valley Premiere Cuvée 1994: Offers ripe fruit and interesting earthy, piney, gamy flavors, finishes with integrated tannins. Drink now. • $12 • (12/15/1998) • **82**
Cabernet Sauvignon Dry Creek Valley STG Premiere Cuvée Wells Vineyard 1996: Firm and trim, showing modest cedar, pepper and currant flavors before moving into a greener mode, turning firmly tannic. Drink now.–J.L. • $12 • (10/15/1999) • **82**
Cabernet Sauvignon Dry Creek Valley Wells Vineyard Premiere Cuvée 1996: Quite minty at first, hinting at stewed fruits. Too much smoky, resinous oak, as it tempers the blackberry, currant and spice notes. Finish is a bit dry but may soften with time. Best from 2000. • $13 • (6/15/1999) • **84**
Cabernet Sauvignon Dry Creek Valley Wells Vineyard Premiere Cuvée 1995: Plush, with black cherry, mineral and rich green olive flavors that linger on the smooth and polished finish. Drink now through 2002.–J.L. • $14 • (3/31/1999) • **85**
Cabernet Sauvignon Russian River Valley Premiere Cuvée Reserve 1989 • $10 • (11/15/1994) • **83**
Cabernet Sauvignon Russian River Valley STG Premiere Cuvée Reserve 1996: Lean and trim, with a pretty band of bay leaf, cedar and currant flavors which turns firm and dry on the finish. Drink now.–J.L. • $15 • (10/15/1999) • **82**
Cabernet Sauvignon Russian River Valley STG Premiere Cuvée Reserve 1995: Shows herbal bay leaf, pickle barrel and cherry flavors that finish slightly hot and dry.–J.L. • $16 • (11/15/1999) • **76**
Cabernet Sauvignon Sonoma County 1988 • $6 • (11/15/1990) • **83**
Cabernet Sauvignon Sonoma County Premiere Cuvée Reserve 1989 • $9 • (11/15/1994) • **84**
Cabernet Sauvignon Sonoma County Premiere Cuvée Reserve 1988 • $8 • (11/15/1993) • **77**
Cabernet Sauvignon Sonoma County Vintage Reserve 1989 • $5 • (11/15/1992) • **74**
Chardonnay Chalk Hill Premiere Cuvée 1996: A touch bitter, with racy, smoky hazelnut and candied pear flavors that finish with a leafy edge. Drink now.–J.L. • $12 • (4/30/1999) • **86**
Merlot Alexander Valley Premiere Cuvée 1996: Lively, ripe and juicy, with a core of black cherry on a pleasantly earthy and herbal frame. Tannins are integrated and fine-grained. Drink now.–J.L. • $12 • (12/15/1998) • **85**
Merlot California Select Reserve 1997: Diluted, with tart, mulchy, herbal flavors, candied notes and drying tannins.–J.L. • $8 • (11/30/1998) • **72**
Merlot California Select Reserve 1995 • $6 • (11/30/1996) • **80**
Merlot Chalk Hill Premiere Cuvée Reserve 1989 • $11 • (12/31/1993) • **69**

Merlot Sonoma County Premiere Cuvée 1997: Simple and dilute, with weedy background flavors.–J.L. • $14 • (10/15/1999) • **77**
Pinot Noir Santa Barbara County STG Premiere Cuvée 1996: Light in color and texture, showing a range of tea, cola, tart cherry and earth flavors. Shows age prematurely. Drink now. • $13 • (2/28/1999) • **80**
Sauvignon Blanc California Select Reserve 1997: Fairly herbal, with hints of fresh-cut hay, fig, citrus and melon. The wine shows light texture, moderate body and a moderate finish. Not bad for the price. Drink now. • $7 • (5/31/1999) • **84**
Zinfandel California 1989 • $5 • (2/15/1991) • **77**

DOMAINE SANTA BARBARA | CALIFORNIA

Chardonnay Santa Barbara County 1996 • $14 • (5/31/1998) • **83**
Chardonnay Santa Barbara County Bien Nacido Vineyard 1997: Creamy texture and toasty oak are attractive. Flavors hint at orange, lemon, apple and pear, and bright acidity perks up the palate on the moderate finish. Drink now through 2001. • $25 • (7/31/1999) • **87**
Chardonnay Santa Barbara County Bien Nacido Vineyard 1996: Bright, with mango, citrus and toast notes. Has impressive intensity and a long, fruity finish. Drink now. • $20 • (7/31/1998) • **85**
Chardonnay Santa Barbara County Los Olivos Vineyard 1997: Rich butterscotch aromas are followed by mango, nectarine and citrus flavors. The oak is a bit heavy-handed, however, and the finish is a bit tart. Drink now through 2002. • $30 • (6/30/1999) • **87**
Chardonnay Santa Barbara County Los Olivos Vineyard 1996: Starts off with a bright hazelnut aroma, backed by pretty pear and spice flavors. Smooth finish. Drink now. • $19 • (7/31/1998) • **86**

DOMAINE SERENE | OREGON

Pinot Noir Willamette Valley Evenstad Reserve 1996: Supple in texture, with straightforward plum and berry on a light frame, the flavors echoing on the long, refined finish. Tannins are not intrusive. Drink now through 2003.–H.S. • $33 • (9/30/1999) • **88**
Pinot Noir Willamette Valley Evenstad Reserve 1995 • $33 • (2/28/1998) • **82**
Pinot Noir Willamette Valley Evenstad Reserve 1991 • $28 • (10/15/1994) • **83**
Pinot Noir Willamette Valley Reserve 1996: Bright and open-textured, with pretty black cherry, currant and spice flavors lingering on the finish after a solid start. Drink now through 2001.–H.S. • $23 • (4/30/1999) • **87**
Pinot Noir Willamette Valley Reserve 1992 • $18 • (10/15/1994) • **89**
Pinot Noir Willamette Valley Reserve 1991 • $18 • (10/15/1994) • **85**

DOMAINE STE. MICHELLE | WASHINGTON

Blanc de Blanc Columbia Valley NV: Distinctively spicy, this Washington bubbly is jazzy on on the palate, delivering pear, black pepper and yeast notes that persist on the creamy finish. Ready to drink, and it's a great value at this price and score.–H.S. • $11 • (9/15/1999) • **89**
Brut Columbia Valley Cuvée NV: A stylish wine, gentle and spicy, offering pretty peach and earth flavors on a well-balanced frame. Drink now.–H.S. • $11 • (9/15/1999) • **87**
Extra Dry Columbia Valley NV: A distinctive, lightly sweet bubbly, creamy and generous, with ripe melon and berry notes around a soft core of yeasty, earthy flavors. Drink now.–H.S. • $11 • (9/15/1999) • **86**

DOMINUS ESTATE | CALIFORNIA

Napa Valley Napanook Vineyard 1996: This impressive California Cabernet blend is Bordeaux-like in style, ripe and rich in flavor, with complex currant, earth, cherry and berry accented by plenty of spicy, peppery notes, and finishes with polished tannins. Tasted twice, with consistent notes. Best from 2001 through 2009.–J.L. • $106 Ⓐ • (8/31/1999) CS • **92**
Napa Valley Napanook Vineyard 1995 • $97 Ⓐ • (6/30/1998) • **87**
Napa Valley Napanook Vineyard 1994 • $148 Ⓐ • (7/31/1997) CS • **94**
Napa Valley Napanook Vineyard 1991 • $154 Ⓐ • (11/15/1995) CS • **93**
Napa Valley 1990 • $143 Ⓐ • (6/30/1994) SS • **91**
Napa Valley 1989: Mature, with a Bordeaux-like cedar, tobacco and black cherry core. Tannins are integrated, and it has enough fruit and tannin for another decade. (1989 California Cabernet retrospective tasting). Drink now through 2006.–J.L. • $69 Ⓐ • (8/31/1999) • **91**
Napa Valley 1988: Complex, with elegant flavors, currant, game, anise and spiciness, but one bottle showed a slight rubbery edge, while a second showed more fruit and leathery tannins. (1988 California Cabernet retrospective tasting). Drink now through 2003.–J.L. • $77 Ⓐ • (11/15/1998) • **87**
Napa Valley 1987 • $96 Ⓐ • (12/15/1997) • **92**
Napa Valley 1986 • $70 Ⓐ • (12/15/1996) • **88**
Napa Valley 1985 • $86 Ⓐ • (2/15/1990) • **84**
Napa Valley 1983 • $63 Ⓐ • (4/15/1989) • **86**

DORCICH | CALIFORNIA

Cabernet Sauvignon Santa Clara County 1991 • $18 • (7/31/1995) • **86**
Cabernet Sauvignon Santa Clara County 1990 • $20 • (7/31/1995) • **85**

DOS CABEZAS | ARIZONA

Chardonnay Cochise County Arizona 1996 • $28 • (6/15/1997) • **86**
Pinot Gris Cochise County 1997: Ripe-tasting, with vanilla, butterscotch and pineapple flavors. Doesn't quite hold together in the end.–K.M. • $16 • (12/15/1998) • **79**
Pinot Gris Cochise County Arizona Unfiltered 1996 • $20 • (8/31/1997) • **85**
Sauvignon Blanc Cochise County Unfiltered 1996 • $16 • (6/15/1997) • **84**
Viognier Cochise County 1997: Aromatic and a bit blunt, with flavors of orange peel and overripe apricot. Finishes on a spicy note.–K.M. • $18 • (12/15/1998) • **76**

DOUGLASS HILL | CALIFORNIA

Cabernet Franc Napa Valley 1995 • $16 • (4/30/1998) • **80**
Cabernet Sauvignon Napa Valley 1994 • $13 • (10/15/1997) • **88**
Cabernet Sauvignon Napa Valley 1992 • $15 • (12/15/1995) • **84**

DOVER CANYON | CALIFORNIA

Cabernet Sauvignon Paso Robles 1996: Juicy and mouthfilling, with black cherry, plum, mineral and spice flavors. Mild acidity keeps the ripe fruit balanced on the finish. Tannins are integrated. Drink now. • $18 • (11/30/1998) • **86**
Rhône Resêrve Central Coast 1997: An effusive blend of apricot, peach, mandarin orange and spice flavors typical of these varietals. Good acidity leaves it fresh and enticing, with a fairly long finish. Drink now. • $17 • (12/15/1998) • **88**
Zinfandel Paso Robles 1995 • $18 • (6/15/1998) • **86**
Zinfandel Paso Robles Cujo 1997: Quite earthy on the nose, but on the palate it shows pretty ripe cherry and plum notes. Tannins are soft, but the alcohol burns on the finish. Drink now. • $18 • (5/15/1999) • **82**
Zinfandel Paso Robles JanKris Vineyard 1996 • $18 • (6/15/1998) • **83**
Zinfandel Paso Robles Templeton Gap 1997: Kicks off with some earth tones, then smooths out in ripe berry and plum flavors. The finish is bright, with a nice touch of spice and firm but ripe tannins. Drink now through 2003. • $18 • (5/15/1999) • **86**

DRAXTON | CALIFORNIA

Merlot Alexander Valley Farrow Ranch 1996: Shows detailed currant and berry flavors, with touches of tobacco and mineral. Turns firm on the finish. Drink through 2004.–J.L. • $25 • (10/15/1999) • **85**
Sauvignon Blanc Alexander Valley 1998: Refreshingly straightforward, with honey notes and tart lemon flavors that dominate the finish. Drink now through 2002.–H.S. • $14 • (1/31/2000) • **86**

DREYER SONOMA | CALIFORNIA

Cabernet Sauvignon Sonoma County 1996: Powdery tannins make this a little rough, for now. The blackberry smoke, herb and currant flavors are nonetheless attractive, and more bottle age might round things out. Good price. Drink through 2005. • $11 • (10/15/1998) • **84**
Cabernet Sauvignon Sonoma County 1995 • $11 • (3/31/1998) • **87**
Cabernet Sauvignon Sonoma County 1993 • $10 • (11/30/1996) • **82**
Cabernet Sauvignon Sonoma County 1989 • $15 • (8/31/1992) • **79**
Chardonnay Sonoma County 1998: Tart, with lemon-lime flavors that refresh with bracing acidity. Drink now.–J.L. • $10 • (6/30/2000) • **83**
Chardonnay Sonoma County 1996 • $10 • (2/28/1998) • **82**

DRY CREEK | CALIFORNIA

Cabernet Franc Dry Creek Valley 1990 • $18 • (10/15/1993) • **83**
Cabernet Sauvignon Dry Creek Valley 1996: Attractive for its assertive, up-front fruitiness, with plum, wild berry, black cherry and anise notes.

Medium in body and richness, this mildly tannic wine is best enjoyed now through 2004.–J.L. • $19 • (10/31/1998) • **88**

Cabernet Sauvignon Dry Creek Valley 1994 • $17 • (11/30/1996) • **86**

Cabernet Sauvignon Dry Creek Valley 1993 • $16 • (11/30/1995) • **88**

Cabernet Sauvignon Dry Creek Valley 1992 • $16 • (10/15/1995) • **89**

Cabernet Sauvignon Dry Creek Valley 1974 • $55 • (11/15/1994) • **83**

Cabernet Sauvignon Dry Creek Valley 25th Anniversary 1994 • $30 • (3/31/1998) • **89**

Cabernet Sauvignon Dry Creek Valley Epoch 1997: Strives for complexity, though the cedary oak dominates the bright cherry and wild berry-scented Cabernet fruit. Finishes with supple tannins and a dry edge. Best now through 2009.–J.L. • $60 • (3/31/2000) • **87**

Cabernet Sauvignon Dry Creek Valley Reserve 1997: Shows off jammy cherry, spice and rye flavors. Turns simple and supple, with mild tannins. Drink now through 2005.–J.L. • $35 • (6/15/2000) • **87**

Cabernet Sauvignon Dry Creek Valley Reserve 1995 • $27 • (11/15/1997) • **86**

Cabernet Sauvignon Dry Creek Valley Reserve 1994 • $25 • (11/30/1996) • **87**

Cabernet Sauvignon Dry Creek Valley Reserve 1993 • $22 • (3/31/1996) • **83**

Cabernet Sauvignon Dry Creek Valley Reserve 1991 • $20 • (10/31/1994) • **89**

Cabernet Sauvignon Sonoma County 1997: Full-bodied, with an appealing range of currant, black cherry, herb, cedar, tar and tealike flavors. Some drying tannins on the finish. Drink now through 2004.–J.L. • $20 • (10/15/1999) • **87**

Cabernet Sauvignon Sonoma County 1995 • $19 • (10/31/1997) • **84**

Cabernet Sauvignon Sonoma County 1991 • $15 • (11/15/1993) • **87**

Cabernet Sauvignon Sonoma County 1989 • $14 • (3/31/1992) • **86**

Cabernet Sauvignon Sonoma County 1988 • $14 • (5/31/1991) • **81**

Cabernet Sauvignon Sonoma County 1987 • $13 • (12/15/1997) • **84**

Cabernet Sauvignon Sonoma County 1986 • $11 • (3/31/1989) • **88**

Cabernet Sauvignon Sonoma County 1985 • $11 • (5/31/1988) SS • **91**

Cabernet Sauvignon Sonoma County 1984 • $10 • (5/15/1987) • **85**

Cabernet Sauvignon Sonoma County Special Reserve 1980 • $13 • (5/01/1986) • **78**

Cabernet Sauvignon Sonoma County Vintner's Selection 1995: Openly fruity and supple in texture, with fleshy plum, black cherry and berryish notes, light oak and smooth tannins. Available only at the winery and through the mailing list. Drink now through 2004.–J.L. • $45 • (3/31/1999) • **88**

Chardonnay Dry Creek Valley Reserve 1998: Hazelnut, butter, citrus and vanilla notes show good concentration and a focused structure. Drink now.–J.L. • $22 • (6/15/2000) • **87**

Chardonnay Sonoma County 1996 • $15 • (6/30/1998) • **88**

Chardonnay Sonoma County Reserve 1997: Sleekly textured, with a firm minerallike core. Refined in style, offering delicate pear, herb and spice flavors. Light yet long on the finish. Clean and refreshing. Drink now through 2002. • $20 • (7/31/1999) • **89**

Chardonnay Sonoma County Reserve 1996 • $20 • (4/30/1998) • **87**

Chenin Blanc Clarksburg Dry 1998: A dry wine with a flinty quality. Somewhat lean, it nonetheless has a certain elegance. Finishes moderately, with hints of sweet pea and herbs. Drink now. • $9 • (10/15/1999) • **84**

Chenin Blanc Clarksburg Dry 1996 • $8 • (12/15/1997) • **86**

David S. Stare Vintner's Reserve Sonoma County 1984 • $18 • (5/31/1988) • **88**

David S. Stare Vintner's Selection Dry Creek Valley 1983 • $15 • (12/31/1986) • **74**

Fumé Blanc Dry Creek Valley Limited Edition DCV3 1998: Interesting and crisp, with lively pineapple, fresh pea and fresh cut grass notes that linger on the refreshing finish. Drink now through 2002.–H.S. • $16 • (1/31/2000) • **87**

Fumé Blanc Dry Creek Valley Reserve 1998: Floral, with fragrant orange overtones and tangy peach flavors. Drink now.–J.L. • $18 • (6/30/2000) • **85**

Fumé Blanc Dry Creek Valley Reserve 1997: A racy wine, with spicy, citrusy airs and a smoky, almost baconlike flavor that pairs well with the melony finish. Though bright, it is tempered by good viscosity and a flinty aftertaste. Drink now through 2002. • $16 • (5/15/1999) • **88**

Fumé Blanc Sonoma County 1998: This California white is a tasty choice for so few dollars, with lime, melon, hay and jalapeño notes that are crisp, clean and refreshing. Drink now through 2003.–H.S. • $12 • (1/31/2000) • **87**

Fumé Blanc Sonoma County 1997: Pretty grassy on the nose, with mild melon and grapefruit flavors following up. A little lightweight in texture, though the ensemble remains bright and pleasant. Drink now. • $12 • (5/15/1999) • **85**

Key: SS—Spectator Selection. CS—Cellar Selection. HR—Highly Recommended. $NA—Price not available. (BT)—Barrel tasting. Ⓐ—Auction Price. For a key to the tasters' initials, see "How to Use These Listings." **Dates in parentheses represent the issues in which the ratings were published.**

Fumé Blanc Sonoma County 1996 • $12 • (11/15/1997) • **88**

Meritage Sonoma County 1997: Focused, with pretty herb-tinged strawberry, raspberry, currant and anise flavors. Firms up on the finish. Drink now through 2005.–J.L. • $25 • (10/15/1999) • **86**

Meritage Dry Creek Valley 1995 • $25 • (4/30/1998) • **89**

Meritage Dry Creek Valley 1994 • $25 • (8/31/1997) • **88**

Meritage Dry Creek Valley 1993 • $20 • (11/30/1995) • **89**

Meritage Dry Creek Valley 1990 • $18 • (11/15/1994) • **89**

Meritage Dry Creek Valley 1988 • $24 • (10/15/1993) • **86**

Meritage Dry Creek Valley 1987 • $24 • (12/15/1997) • **89**

Meritage Dry Creek Valley 1986 • $22 • (9/15/1990) • **80**

Meritage Dry Creek Valley 1985 • $22 • (11/15/1989) • **89**

Merlot Dry Creek Valley 1992 • $15 • (6/15/1995) • **84**

Merlot Dry Creek Valley 1991 • $15 • (3/15/1994) • **84**

Merlot Dry Creek Valley 1990 • $14 • (3/31/1993) • **85**

Merlot Dry Creek Valley 1989 • $14 • (4/15/1992) • **86**

Merlot Dry Creek Valley 1988 • $15 • (3/31/1991) • **83**

Merlot Dry Creek Valley Bullock House Vineyard 1991 • $20 • (9/15/1994) • **85**

Merlot Dry Creek Valley Reserve 1997: Ripe and spicy, with a core of jammy wild berry and cherry-laced fruit that reminds you of Zinfandel. Mild tannins. Drink now.–J.L. • $35 • (6/15/2000) • **87**

Merlot Dry Creek Valley Reserve 1995: Tight and tannic, with a pleasant band of cedary currant, cherry, berry and spice. Best to cellar short-term to grow into its flavors and let the tannins subside. Best now through 2004.–J.L. • $30 • (9/30/1998) • **85**

Merlot Dry Creek Valley Reserve 1994 • $27 • (6/30/1997) • **88**

Merlot Dry Creek Valley Reserve 1993 • $22 • (8/31/1996) • **87**

Merlot Sonoma County 1997: Bright, with crisp raspberry, herb and berry notes that linger on the firm finish. Best now through 2004.–J.L. • $20 • (10/15/1999) • **82**

Merlot Sonoma County 1996: Dried cherry and cola notes are followed on the palate by plum, tar and licorice. Moderate finish. Drink now through 2002. • $19 • (9/30/1998) • **85**

Merlot Sonoma County 1995 • $19 • (3/31/1998) • **85**

Merlot Sonoma County 1994 • $17 • (6/30/1997) • **86**

Merlot Sonoma County 1986 • $15 • (3/31/1989) • **78**

Pinot Noir California 1998: Curious, with raisin and doughy notes wrapped in some chunky tannins. Drink now through 2003.–J.L. • $18 • (6/30/2000) • **84**

Pinot Noir Sonoma Valley 1997: A streak of herb, cola and sage runs through this racy wine, adding dimension to the core of black cherry and blackberry. Firm, tannic finish. Drink now through 2006.–J.L. • $24 • (1/31/2000) • **88**

Sauvignon Blanc Dry Creek Valley Reserve 1996 • $16 • (3/31/1998) • **86**

Sauvignon Blanc Sonoma County Late Harvest Soleil NV • $18/375 ml. • (4/30/1995) • **85**

Zinfandel Dry Creek Valley Old Vines 1991: Shows a nice balance between the ripe plum and cherry and the smooth, supple tannins. Elegant and pleasant to drink, with a long and fruity finish.—Zinfandel retrospective. Try through 2001.–J.L. • $12 • (6/30/1999) • **88**

Zinfandel Dry Creek Valley Old Vines 1990 • $11 • (10/15/1992) • **85**

Zinfandel Dry Creek Valley Old Vines 1988 • $11 • (2/15/1991) • **86**

Zinfandel Dry Creek Valley Reserve 1997: Ripe, with waxy blackberry, wild berry and olive flavors that are intense and lively, turning fruity. Finishes with crisp, lively tannins. Drink now through 2005.–J.L. • $30 • (6/15/2000) • **87**

Zinfandel Sonoma County Heritage Clone 1997: Cranberry and dried berry notes are lively, with dry tannin but good intensity. Drink now through 2003.–J.L. • $15 • (6/15/2000) • **85**

Zinfandel Sonoma County Old Vines 1996: Complex and well focused, with a pretty array of ripe plum, black cherry and wild berry flavors, firm, crisp tannins and good length. Drink now through 2002.–J.L. • $16 • (6/30/1999) • **88**

Zinfandel Sonoma County Old Vines 1995 • $16 • (5/15/1998) • **85**

Zinfandel Sonoma County Old Vines 1994 • $15 • (4/30/1997) • **89**

Zinfandel Sonoma County Old Vines 1993 • $15 • (9/15/1995) • **88**

Zinfandel Sonoma County Old Vines 1992 • $14 • (2/28/1995) • **83**

Zinfandel Sonoma County Reserve 1995 • $25 • (6/15/1998) • **88**

Zinfandel Sonoma County Reserve 1994 • $20 • (4/30/1997) • **89**

Zinfandel Sonoma County Reserve 1993 • $20 • (5/15/1996) • **83**

Zinfandel Sonoma County Reserve 1991: Shows a shade more depth than the Old Vines bottling. The core of plum, cherry and raspberry is impressive, with richness, fine balance and a long finish. (Zinfandel retrospective tasting). Drink now through 2001.–J.L. • $20 • (6/30/1999) • **88**

DUCK POND | WASHINGTON

Cabernet Sauvignon Columbia Valley Fries' Desert Wind Vineyard Wahluke Slope 1997: Firm and chewy, with modest blackberry and herb flavors in a nice but modest package. Picks up a floral note on the finish. Drink now through 2002.–H.S. • $12 • (3/31/2000) • **85**

Cabernet Sauvignon Columbia Valley Fries' Desert Wind Vineyard Wahluke Slope 1996: Light color, pretty flavors and a polished texture add up to an appealing wine for drinking now through 2001.–H.S. • $12 • (8/31/1998) • **83**

Cabernet Sauvignon Columbia Valley Fries Vineyard Wahluke Slope 1995 • $10 • (10/15/1997) • **86**

Chardonnay Columbia Valley 1997: Spicy, nutlike overtones add extra interest to the bright apple flavors in this lively, straightforward white from Washington. The price is right, and the availability is good. Drink now.–H.S. • $9 • (9/15/1998) • **85**

Chardonnay Columbia Valley 1996 • $8 • (9/30/1997) • **87**

Chardonnay Columbia Valley Fries' Desert Wind Vineyard Wahluke Slope 1998: From Washington comes this wallet-friendly Chardonnay, rich, round and spicy, with enticing nutmeg and pepper overtones to the core of pear and caramel flavors. Drink now through 2003.–H.S. • $9 • (11/15/1999) • **86**

Chardonnay Columbia Valley Wahluke Slope Reserve 1996: Shows more sappy, almost herbal flavors than fruit, but the flavors persist on a long and generous finish. Cellaring could bring out more. Try through 2003.–H.S. • $25 • (8/31/1999) • **88**

Chardonnay Oregon 1997: Soft and simple, with modest apple cider flavors that fade quickly.–H.S. • $10 • (12/15/1998) • **79**

Chardonnay Oregon Fries' Family Cellars 1998: Offering pretty pear and mineral flavors that linger on the round finish, this smooth, generous and supple Chardonnay exemplifies Oregon's strides with this variety, yet the price tag remains modest. Drink now through 2002.–H.S. • $10 • (5/15/2000) • **85**

Chardonnay Willamette Valley 1996 • $8 • (11/15/1997) • **85**

Merlot Columbia Valley 1995 • $12 • (4/30/1997) • **88**

Merlot Columbia Valley Fries' Desert Wind Vineyard Wahluke Slope 1997: Light and crisp, with a biting edge of tannin against modest raspberry and leather flavors. Needs food. Drink now through 2001.–H.S. • $12 • (9/30/1999) • **81**

Merlot Columbia Valley Fries' Desert Wind Vineyard Wahluke Slope 1996: Light and fruity. A wine of modest structure, with pretty black cherry and currant flavors, appealing in character. Drink now.–H.S. • $12 • (8/31/1998) • **85**

Merlot Columbia Valley Wahluke Slope Reserve 1995: Has firm tannins on the surface, but the ripe berry and spice flavors underneath are polished and glowing. Approachable now, despite the tannins. Best after 2000.–H.S. • $30 • (8/31/1999) • **87**

Pinot Gris Oregon 1997: Soft and appealing for its nectarine and melon flavors. Finishes with a touch of bitter almond. Drink now.–H.S. • $12 • (12/15/1998) • **80**

Pinot Gris Willamette Valley 1998: Bright in flavor, with ripe pear, orange and cream notes echoing on the raw-edged finish. Drink now.–H.S. • $10 • (3/31/2000) • **85**

Pinot Gris Willamette Valley 1996 • $12 • (12/31/1997) • **87**

Pinot Noir Willamette Valley 1996 • $8 • (2/28/1998) • **73**

Pinot Noir Willamette Valley 1995 • $8 • (2/28/1997) • **82**

Pinot Noir Willamette Valley 1993 • $8 • (3/31/1996) • **81**

Pinot Noir Willamette Valley Reserve 1994 • $25 • (2/28/1997) • **88**

Pinot Noir Willamette Valley Unfiltered 1992 • $7 • (9/15/1994) • **87**

Pinot Noir Yamhill County 1990 • $7 • (3/15/1994) • **70**

Syrah Columbia Valley Fries' Desert Wind Vineyard Wahluke Slope 1997: Very firm and chewy, a solid red without a lot of extra nuances, offering modest berry and spice flavors under a blanket of fine tannins. Drink now through 2004.–H.S. • $15 • (5/31/1999) • **83**

DUCK WALK | NEW YORK

Cabernet Sauvignon North Fork of Long Island Reserve 1995: Firm and focused. This clean, fresh red offers ripe plum and black cherry flavors, with notes of licorice and tobacco and firm tannins that add weight without sacrificing balance. A bit tough now, but should improve. Drink now through 2004.–T.M. • $19 • (6/30/1999) • **87**

Chardonnay North Fork of Long Island Reserve 1997: This smooth, well-knit wine is a showcase for the creamy vanilla flavors of oak. Apple and melon flavors are present but subdued, emerging on the finish. A nice match for sole or flounder. Drink now.–T.M. • $13 • (6/30/1999) • **85**

Merlot Long Island 1992 • $13 • (12/31/1996) • **77**

Merlot North Fork of Long Island Reserve 1997: Rich plum and chocolate notes are plump and chewy in this ripe red. Generous and juicy, balanced and quite long. Drink now through 2003.–T.M. • $19 • (5/31/2000) • **88**

Merlot North Fork of Long Island Reserve 1995: Good structure and balance give this red a food-friendly appeal. It has ripe plum and cassis flavors, with smoky, coffee-scented oak notes and firm tannins that need time to unwind. Best from 2001 through 2005.–T.M. • $19 • (6/30/1999) • **87**

Merlot North Fork of Long Island Special Vintner's Reserve 1997: This soft red is generous, with heavy coffee and chocolate flavors and notes of plum and prune. Has enough tannin for structure, but finishes a bit flat. Drink now through 2002.–T.M. • $27 • (5/31/2000) • **84**

Merlot North Fork of Long Island Special Vintner's Reserve 1995: Chewy and rustic. Sweet and sour cherry and herb flavors are accented by a charry oak note in this tough red.–T.M. • $NA • (5/31/2000) • **75**

Pinot Meunier Long Island 1994 • $13 • (12/31/1996) • **78**

DUCKHORN | CALIFORNIA

Cabernet Sauvignon Napa Valley 1998: Lots of ripe, rich, juicy black fruits, with black cherry, plum, wild berry and cherry notes that are long on the finish.–J.L. • $NA • (8/31/1999) (BT) • **90-94**

Cabernet Sauvignon Napa Valley 1997: Ripe, rich and racy, packed with earthy, tannic mint, cherry, currant and wild berry. Finishes with a chewy, tannic aftertaste, but nothing out of bounds for a wine this young.–J.L. • $NA • (8/31/1998) (BT) • **90-94**

Cabernet Sauvignon Napa Valley 1996: Well focused, elegant, with an earthy edge to the currant, black cherry, tar and anise, finishing with supple tannins. Drink through 2007.–J.L. • $43 Ⓐ • (9/15/1999) • **88**

Cabernet Sauvignon Napa Valley 1995: Complex but distinctive with its elegant core of earthy clay, currant and black cherry flavors. Long and supple on the finish. Drink through 2007.–J.L. • $35 • (10/31/1998) • **89**

Cabernet Sauvignon Napa Valley 1994 • $67 Ⓐ • (5/31/1997) • **90**

Cabernet Sauvignon Napa Valley 1993 • $26 • (11/15/1996) • **87**

Cabernet Sauvignon Napa Valley 1992 • $24 • (10/31/1995) SS • **90**

Cabernet Sauvignon Napa Valley 1990 • $65 Ⓐ • (7/31/1993) CS • **93**

Cabernet Sauvignon Napa Valley 1989: Firm, with an earthy, clayish flavor and a tobacco edge that runs through the mushroom, cherry and vaguely plummy notes. Pleasant enough, though it never quite comes into focus and turns dry and earthy on the finish. (1989 California Cabernet retrospective tasting). Drink now through 2002.–J.L. • $20 • (8/31/1999) • **87**

Cabernet Sauvignon Napa Valley 1988: Ripe, supple and very well balanced, with juicy black cherry, currant, spice and cedary notes. Finishes with supple tannins and good length. (1988 California Cabernet retrospective tasting). Drink now through 2004.–J.L. • $37 Ⓐ • (11/15/1998) • **88**

Cabernet Sauvignon Napa Valley 1987 • $60 Ⓐ • (12/15/1997) • **92**

Cabernet Sauvignon Napa Valley 1986 • $52 Ⓐ • (12/15/1996) • **94**

Cabernet Sauvignon Napa Valley 1985 • $65 Ⓐ • (6/15/1988) CS • **91**

Cabernet Sauvignon Napa Valley 1984 • $17 • (6/15/1987) • **87**

Cabernet Sauvignon Napa Valley 1983 • $53 Ⓐ • (7/01/1986) • **89**

Cabernet Sauvignon Napa Valley 1982 • $58 Ⓐ • (5/16/1985) • **86**

Cabernet Sauvignon Napa Valley 1978: Serves up lots of complex flavors without being too ripe. The core of currant, black cherry, cedar and spice is youthful and vibrant, complex and well integrated, finishing with a long, lively aftertaste. Shows no signs of going over the hill. (1978 California Cabernet retrospective tasting). Drink now through 2004.–J.L. • $11 • (11/15/1998) • **92**

Howell Mountain Red 1992 • $26 • (8/31/1996) • **88**

Howell Mountain Red 1991 • $25 • (11/15/1994) • **88**

Howell Mountain Red 1990 • $25 • (11/15/1993) • **86**

Howell Mountain Red 1989 • $50 Ⓐ • (11/15/1992) • **89**

Merlot Howell Mountain 1995: Firm, rich and flavorful, with hearty currant, black cherry, anise and mineral, finishing with firm tannins. Drink through 2007.–J.L. • $42 • (9/15/1999) • **89**

Merlot Howell Mountain 1994: Firm in oak and tannin, with earthy currant, wild berry and cherry. Needs time to soften, but it's well focused, intense and flavorful. Drink through 2006.–J.L. • $40 • (8/31/1998) • **89**

Merlot Howell Mountain 1993 • $35 • (7/31/1997) • **88**

Merlot Napa Valley 1997: Shows a strong cedary oak and earthy flavor at this stage, but also enough polished currant, anise and spice notes that firm up on the finish. Drink now through 2008.–J.L. • $36 • (3/31/2000) • **88**

Merlot Napa Valley 1996: Earthy, gamy and leathery in character, with underlying currant notes. Drink through 2005.–J.L. • $58 Ⓐ • (12/31/1998) • **87**

Merlot Napa Valley 1995 • $36 Ⓐ • (3/31/1998) • **88**

Merlot Napa Valley 1994 • $27 • (2/28/1997) SS • **90**

Merlot Napa Valley 1993 • $24 • (1/31/1996) HR • **90**

Merlot Napa Valley 1992 • $23 • (3/31/1995) • **88**

DUCKHORN

Merlot Napa Valley 1990 • $21 • (12/15/1992) SS • **89**
Merlot Napa Valley 1989 • $25 • (4/15/1992) • **82**
Merlot Napa Valley 1988 • $50 • (12/31/1990) • **86**
Merlot Napa Valley 1987 • $33 • (12/31/1989) • **91**
Merlot Napa Valley 1986 • $46 Ⓐ • (1/31/1989) • **86**
Merlot Napa Valley 1985 • $58 Ⓐ • (12/31/1987) CS • **93**
Merlot Napa Valley 1984 • $38 • (12/31/1986) SS • **94**
Merlot Napa Valley 1983 • $45 • (11/01/1985) CS • **94**
Merlot Napa Valley 1982 • $38 Ⓐ • (10/01/1985) • **81**
Merlot Napa Valley Estate Grown 1996: Supple, elegant and focused, with rich and complex earth, leathery currant, cherry and spicy flavors that are trim and polished. Drink now through 2007.–J.L. • $53 • (9/15/1999) • **91**
Merlot Napa Valley Estate Grown 1995: Dense, chewy, and richly flavored, highly extracted, too, with earthy currant, mineral, anise, sage, tea and spice—a full array of pretty aromas and flavors. Impressive for its richness, focus, balance and length. Best from 2001 through 2007.–J.L. • $50 • (8/31/1998) • **92**
Merlot Napa Valley Three Palms Vineyard 1996: Rich and complex, with a focused, full-bodied core of earth, currant, mineral, tar, cherry and spice, firming up on the finish. Wonderful depth and dimension that cellaring should reward. Drink through 2009.–J.L. • $47 • (9/15/1999) • **90**
Merlot Napa Valley Three Palms Vineyard 1995: Trim, even lean, but typical of this vineyard; for those who prefer an austere style. The mineral and currant are tight and so are the tannins. Drink through 2006.–J.L. • $45 • (8/31/1998) • **87**
Merlot Napa Valley Three Palms Vineyard 1991 • $46 Ⓐ • (9/15/1994) • **84**
Merlot Napa Valley Three Palms Vineyard 1990 • $83 Ⓐ • (8/31/1993) • **83**
Merlot Napa Valley Three Palms Vineyard 1989 • $49 Ⓐ • (5/31/1992) • **89**
Merlot Napa Valley Three Palms Vineyard 1988 • $98 Ⓐ • (11/15/1991) • **84**
Merlot Napa Valley Three Palms Vineyard 1987 • $121 Ⓐ • (7/31/1990) • **92**
Merlot Napa Valley Three Palms Vineyard 1986 • $55 Ⓐ • (7/31/1989) • **88**
Merlot Napa Valley Three Palms Vineyard 1985 • $63 • (6/30/1988) • **91**
Merlot Napa Valley Three Palms Vineyard 1984 • $75 • (7/31/1987) • **89**
Merlot Napa Valley Vine Hill Ranch 1987 • $18 • (7/31/1990) • **87**
Merlot Napa Valley Vine Hill Ranch 1986 • $18 • (7/31/1989) • **80**
Merlot Napa Valley Vine Hill Ranch 1985 • $16 • (6/30/1988) • **91**
Sauvignon Blanc Napa Valley 1998: Middle-of-the-road, with light, earthy herb, pear and spice, turning simple. Drink now.–J.L. • $18 • (4/30/2000) • **83**
Sauvignon Blanc Napa Valley 1997: Here's a tangy, mouthwatering white dishing up a harmonious blend of grapefruit, melon, lemon, lime and herb flavors. Bright in style, it finishes fresh, clean and long, with a slight mineral accent. Drink now through 2002. • $17 • (1/31/1999) HR • **88**
Sauvignon Blanc Napa Valley 1996 • $15 • (1/31/1998) HR • **90**

DUETTO | OTHER U.S.

Assemblage Red Mexico & USA 1996: Black cherry, plum, licorice and smoky oak flavors form the core of this slightly rustic wine. The finish is short, but the ensemble is pleasant. A blend of Cabernet Sauvignon, Merlot and Cabernet Franc. Drink now through 2002. • $30 • (10/31/1998) • **84**

DUMOL | CALIFORNIA

Chardonnay Russian River Valley Dutton Ranch 1996: A touch earthy and gamy, with a twinge of greenness and a distinct leesiness that detracts from the otherwise ripe core of pear and apple flavors. Drink now.–J.L. • $30 • (2/28/1999) • **82**
Pinot Noir Russian River Valley Dutton Ranch 1996: Elegant and even delicate, with ripe plum, smoky oak and leather and a slight bitterness, from tannins. Drink through 2002.–J.L. • $30 • (12/15/1998) • **86**

DUNCAN PEAK | CALIFORNIA

Cabernet Sauvignon Mendocino 1994 • $20 • (11/15/1997) • **88**
Cabernet Sauvignon Mendocino County 1997: Perfumed, with ripe cherry, wild berry, plum and spice notes. Turns polished and elegant on the finish. Best from 2002 through 2009.–J.L. • $31 • (4/30/2000) • **87**
Cabernet Sauvignon Mendocino County 1995: This one shows ripe fruit—blueberry, blackberry and plum—followed by a hint of anise. Starts out supple but comes up a little short on the rustic finish. Drink through 2005 • $NA • (11/15/1998) • **87**
Cabernet Sauvignon Mendocino County 1993 • $18 • (4/30/1996) • **86**
Cabernet Sauvignon Mendocino County 1992 • $16 • (11/15/1994) • **85**
Cabernet Sauvignon Mendocino County 1991 • $12 • (10/31/1993) • **88**
Cabernet Sauvignon Mendocino County 1989 • $10 • (11/15/1992) • **88**
Cabernet Sauvignon Mendocino County 1988: An oddball, with very ripe cherry and wild berry flavors and sharp, biting tannins that dry on the finish. Needs aeration. (1988 California Cabernet retrospective tasting).–J.L. • $18 • (11/15/1998) • **78**

DUNDEE SPRINGS | OREGON

Pinot Blanc Oregon 1998: Distinctly floral, this is a sturdy white with an aromatic streak of rose petal and a touch of stemminess running through the basic apple flavors. Drink now.–H.S. • $16 • (12/31/1999) • **83**
Pinot Gris Oregon Reserve 1998: Strong floral, peppery notes edge past the basic fruit flavors in this medium-weight white. Drink now.–H.S. • $16 • (3/31/2000) • **83**
Pinot Gris Oregon Reserve 1996 • $16 • (5/15/1998) • **83**
Pinot Noir Oregon 1998: Bright, ripe and focused. Jazzy, with raspberry, citrus and spice flavors that linger on the generous finish. Has concentration and raw content. Should soften in the cellar. Drink now through 2003.–H.S. • $30 • (3/31/2000) • **88**
Pinot Noir Oregon 1995 • $28 • (5/15/1998) • **83**
Pinot Noir Oregon Perry Bower Vineyard Reserve 1996: Light in texture and beautifully focused in flavor, offering a nice dose of currant and plum, with a hint of spice on the supple, elegant finish. Has none of the harshness found in some '96s. Drink now through 2005.–H.S. • $30 • (2/29/2000) • **89**
Pinot Noir Oregon Perry Bower Vineyards Reserve 1996 • $35 • (5/15/1998) • **87**
Pinot Noir Willamette Valley Reserve 1994 • $34 • (2/28/1997) • **89**

DUNHAM | WASHINGTON

Cabernet Sauvignon Columbia Valley I 1995 • $28 • (9/15/1997) • **89**
Cabernet Sauvignon Columbia Valley III 1997: Ripe, seductive and open-textured, wrapping its blueberry, plum and herb flavors around a smooth core of sweet tannins. Tempting now. Drink through 2002.–H.S. • $45 • (9/30/1999) • **88**

DUNN | CALIFORNIA

Cabernet Sauvignon Howell Mountain 1997: Earthy, racy, but quite complex and concentrated, with wild berry and floral aromas. An intense, deeply concentrated wine that packs in lots of flavor.–J.L. • $NA • (8/31/1998) (BT) • **90-94**
Cabernet Sauvignon Howell Mountain 1996: A classic Howell Mountain Cabernet. This is dark in color, impressively concentrated, with a very rich, firmly tannic core of mineral, cedar, currant, berry, plum and spice nuances, all sharply focused if a bit rustic and chewy at this youthful stage. Be patient. Best from 2002 through 2011.–J.L. • $50 • (10/15/1999) CS • **95**
Cabernet Sauvignon Howell Mountain 1995: Austerely styled, with firm tannins, this tightly wound California Cab unfolds slowly, revealing as it does its layers of dense flavors—currant, anise, mineral, sage and spice—before tightening up again on the finish. Will reward cellaring. Best from 2001 through 2007.–J.L. • $82 Ⓐ • (4/30/1999) CS • **93**
Cabernet Sauvignon Howell Mountain 1994 • $105 Ⓐ • (5/15/1998) CS • **91**
Cabernet Sauvignon Howell Mountain 1993 • $33 • (4/30/1997) • **90**
Cabernet Sauvignon Howell Mountain 1991 • $96 Ⓐ • (12/15/1995) CS • **91**
Cabernet Sauvignon Howell Mountain 1990 • $121 Ⓐ • (5/15/1994) • **89**
Cabernet Sauvignon Howell Mountain 1989: Dark and immense, still a youngster, with intense earthy currant, plum and black cherry flavors that are rich, yet for all their weight still quite elegant. Still has tannin to lose. Decant if you drink it now. (1989 California Cabernet retrospective tasting). Drink through 2010.–J.L. • $43 Ⓐ • (8/31/1999) • **92**
Cabernet Sauvignon Howell Mountain 1988: Among the best in depth, richness, concentration, complexity and length. Classic Dunn Howell Mountain in its core of rich, earthy currant, mineral and raspberry. Finishes with chewy tannins, but also the fruit to match. (1988 California Cabernet retrospective tasting). Drink now through 2008.–J.L. • $35 • (11/15/1998) • **89**
Cabernet Sauvignon Howell Mountain 1987 • $36 • (12/15/1997) • **97**
Cabernet Sauvignon Howell Mountain 1986 • $30 • (7/31/1990) CS • **95**
Cabernet Sauvignon Howell Mountain 1985 • $110 • (11/30/1991) • **88**
Cabernet Sauvignon Howell Mountain 1984 • $122 Ⓐ • (11/30/1991) • **96**
Cabernet Sauvignon Howell Mountain 1983 • $115 • (11/30/1991) • **91**
Cabernet Sauvignon Howell Mountain 1982 • $115 Ⓐ • (11/30/1991) • **94**

Key: SS—Spectator Selection. CS—Cellar Selection. HR—Highly Recommended. $NA—Price not available. (BT)—Barrel tasting. Ⓐ—Auction Price.
For a key to the tasters' initials, see "How to Use These Listings."
Dates in parentheses represent the issues in which the ratings were published.

Cabernet Sauvignon Howell Mountain 1981 • $160 • (11/30/1991) • **93**
Cabernet Sauvignon Howell Mountain 1980 • $180 • (11/30/1991) • **95**
Cabernet Sauvignon Howell Mountain 1979 • $200 • (11/30/1991) • **94**
Cabernet Sauvignon Napa Valley 1996: Tightly wound, with firm, crisp tannins wrapped around a core of currant, black cherry, wild berry, cedar, anise, sage and spice. Finishes with enough tannin to merit short-term cellaring. Best from 2002 through 2010.–J.L. • $45 • (10/15/1999) • **91**
Cabernet Sauvignon Napa Valley 1995: Tight, with an austere band of cedar, currant, mineral and sage, finishing with firm, earthy tannins. Needs some time. Drink through 2008.–J.L. • $39 • (1/01/1999) • **89**
Cabernet Sauvignon Napa Valley 1994 • $70 Ⓐ • (5/15/1998) • **88**
Cabernet Sauvignon Napa Valley 1993 • $33 • (11/15/1996) • **89**
Cabernet Sauvignon Napa Valley 1992 • $62 Ⓐ • (12/15/1995) • **88**
Cabernet Sauvignon Napa Valley 1991 • $45 Ⓐ • (11/15/1994) • **88**
Cabernet Sauvignon Napa Valley 1990 • $61 Ⓐ • (11/15/1993) CS • **92**
Cabernet Sauvignon Napa Valley 1989 • $41 Ⓐ • (4/30/1993) • **90**
Cabernet Sauvignon Napa Valley 1988 • $35 Ⓐ • (11/15/1991) • **87**
Cabernet Sauvignon Napa Valley 1987 • $74 Ⓐ • (11/15/1990) • **93**
Cabernet Sauvignon Napa Valley 1986 • $67 Ⓐ • (10/15/1989) CS • **95**
Cabernet Sauvignon Napa Valley 1985 • $65 Ⓐ • (9/15/1988) CS • **94**
Cabernet Sauvignon Napa Valley 1984 • $46 Ⓐ • (11/30/1987) • **90**
Cabernet Sauvignon Napa Valley 1983 • $51 Ⓐ • (10/31/1986) SS • **95**
Cabernet Sauvignon Napa Valley 1982 • $107 Ⓐ • (11/01/1985) SS • **97**

DUNNEWOOD | CALIFORNIA

Cabernet Sauvignon Alexander Valley Dry Silk Reserve Seven Arches Vineyard 1995: Earthy, with a core of herbal plum and cherry flavors. Finishes with crisp, dry tannins. Drink now.–J.L. • $13 • (10/15/1999) • **83**
Cabernet Sauvignon Alexander Valley Seven Arches Vineyard Gold Label Select 1992 • $10 • (2/29/1996) • **82**
Cabernet Sauvignon Napa Valley Dry Silk Reserve Seven Arches Vineyard 1995: Shows off smoky oak, cola and caramel flavors with background notes of cedar, plum and herb. Tannins are polished on the finish where the flavors pick up a touch of bitterness. Drink now through 2003.–J.L. • $13 • (10/15/1999) • **84**
Cabernet Sauvignon Napa Valley Napa Reserve 1986 • $11 • (6/15/1990) • **82**
Cabernet Sauvignon Napa Valley Reserve 1984 • $11 • (12/31/1988) • **85**
Cabernet Sauvignon North Coast Barrel Select 1991 • $8 • (11/15/1994) • **84**
Cabernet Sauvignon North Coast Barrel Select Coastal Series 1996: Coarse on the palate, with cherry and licorice notes. • $9 • (10/15/1998) • **76**
Chardonnay Carneros Dry Silk Reserve 1997: Rich and soft-textured, with toasty citrus, pear and apple flavors. Finishes smooth, with leafy notes. Drink now.–J.L. • $12 • (6/30/1999) • **86**
Merlot California Barrel Select 1990 • $6 • (4/15/1993) • **83**
Merlot North Coast Barrel Select 1994 • $10 • (11/30/1996) • **79**
Merlot North Coast Barrel Select 1992 • $7 • (9/15/1994) • **82**
Merlot North Coast Barrel Select Coastal Series 1996: Ripe flavors of herb, black cherry and mocha on a firm tannic frame. Drink now.–J.L. • $9 • (9/30/1998) • **80**
Pinot Noir North Coast Barrel Select Coastal Series 1996: Somewhat astringent, at first showing more oak and menthol than fruit. Beneath is a modest layer of black currant and spice. Drink now. • $7 • (9/15/1998) • **80**
Reserve Red California NV • $4 • (2/28/1989) • **76**
Zinfandel Mendocino Barrel Select Coastal Series 1995 • $9 • (6/15/1998) • **82**
Zinfandel Sonoma Valley Barrel Select 1992 • $10 • (2/28/1995) • **80**

DUNNING | CALIFORNIA

Cabernet Sauvignon Paso Robles Westside 1997: Supple and concentrated, featuring black cherry, berry and mineral flavors, finishing with smooth, ripe tannins. Drink now through 2004.–J.L. • $16 • (10/15/1999) • **87**
Cabernet Sauvignon Paso Robles Westside 1996: Somewhat tart, this serves up vegetal notes, with some black currant, smoke and spice. The finish is moderate, with fairly smooth tannins. Drink now through 2001. • $15 • (6/15/1999) • **83**
Cabernet Sauvignon Paso Robles Westside 1995 • $15 • (3/31/1998) • **87**
Cabernet Sauvignon Paso Robles Westside 1994 • $14 • (11/30/1996) • **86**
Chardonnay Paso Robles Westside 1997: Ripe and supple, displaying raspberry, strawberry, tea and toasted oak flavors, finishing firm and focused. Drink now through 2004.–J.L. • $15 • (9/15/1999) • **85**
Chardonnay Paso Robles Westside 1996 • $15 • (2/28/1998) • **84**
Merlot Paso Robles Westside 1996: Smoke, tar, licorice and black cherry mark this somewhat heavy-style, chewy wine. Touches of spice and herb lighten up the finish, however, for a good quaff. Drink now through 2002. • $18 • (9/15/1998) • **86**
Merlot Paso Robles Westside 1995 • $15 • (1/31/1998) • **87**

DURNEY | CALIFORNIA

Cabernet Sauvignon Carmel Valley 1993: Cola, cherry and tangy blackberry notes vie for attention. Still bright and firm, the wine is framed in smoky oak, with smooth tannins and a moderate finish. Drink now through 2003. • $25 • (6/15/1999) • **87**
Cabernet Sauvignon Carmel Valley 1990 • $17 • (11/15/1994) • **89**
Cabernet Sauvignon Carmel Valley 1981 • $13 • (9/01/1984) • **82**
Cabernet Sauvignon Carmel Valley Cachagua 1995: Soft and ripe but a bit dilute, showing herb, tobacco, black cherry, sage and earth flavors. Finishes with a touch of heat. A departure from the previously dry, tannic style. Drink now through 2002.–J.L. • $14 • (11/15/1999) • **82**
Cabernet Sauvignon Carmel Valley Dances On Your Palate 1992 • $21 • (11/30/1996) • **86**
Cabernet Sauvignon Carmel Valley Dances On Your Palate Cachagua 1993 • $13 • (11/30/1996) • **78**
Cabernet Sauvignon Carmel Valley Dances On Your Palate Private Reserve 1992 • $31 • (3/31/1996) • **86**
Cabernet Sauvignon Carmel Valley Private Reserve 1989 • $26 • (11/15/1994) • **83**
Cabernet Sauvignon Carmel Valley Private Reserve 1988 • $31 • (11/15/1994) • **82**
Cabernet Sauvignon Carmel Valley Private Reserve 1985 • $20/3 liter • (11/15/1992) • **86**
Cabernet Sauvignon Carmel Valley Private Reserve 1983 • $20 • (4/30/1991) • **86**
Carmel Valley Red NV • $7 • (11/15/1992) • **73**
Chardonnay Carmel Valley 1996: Smooth, with an oaky focus to the flavors, but finishes more subtly, with pretty hints of vanilla, citrus and pear. Drink now.–J.L. • $20 • (11/15/1999) • **85**
Johannisberg Riesling Carmel Valley Late Harvest Dances on Your Palate 1994 • $12/375 ml. • (11/30/1997) • **84**
Merlot Carmel Valley 1994 • $25 • (2/28/1998) • **80**
Merlot Carmel Valley Dances On Your Palate 1993 • $22 • (7/31/1997) • **87**
Pinot Noir Carmel Valley 1993 • $18 • (2/28/1998) • **76**
Pinot Noir Carmel Valley 1990 • $18 • (3/31/1995) • **80**
Pinot Noir Carmel Valley 1989 • $18 • (2/28/1994) • **80**
Pinot Noir Carmel Valley 1988 • $16 • (4/30/1991) • **80**
Pinot Noir Carmel Valley Dances On Your Palate 1992 • $24 • (12/31/1995) • **81**

DUTCH HENRY | CALIFORNIA

Merlot Napa Valley 1996: Soft and rich, with a flavorful core of tarry currant, black cherry, mint and earth flavors that hold on the polished finish. Drink now through 2003.–J.L. • $22 • (11/15/1999) • **85**
Pinot Noir Napa Valley 1998: Ripe and easy to drink, offering cinnamon notes and jammy cherry and currant flavors, framed by soft tannins at the finish. Drink now.–J.L. • $24 • (4/30/2000) • **86**
Zinfandel Napa Valley 1997: Flavors of dried berry and chocolate are wrapped with substantial tannins and a healthy alcohol punch. Drink now through 2005.–J.L. • $25 • (5/15/2000) • **85**

DUTTON-GOLDFIELD | CALIFORNIA

Chardonnay Russian River Valley Dutton Ranch 1998: Bright, crisp and lively, with a vibrant array of ripe pear, apple, papaya and spice notes that turn pleasantly earthy. Drink now through 2006.–J.L. • $28 • (2/29/2000) • **88**
Pinot Noir Russian River Valley Dutton Ranch 1998: Pleasant and polished, with ripe cherry, rhubarb and anise notes, it's solid if lacking in extra dimensions. Drink now through 2004.–J.L. • $33 • (2/29/2000) • **85**

DZUGAS | NEW YORK

Chardonnay North Fork of Long Island 1997: This firm white shows good concentration on the palate, with ripe flavors of melon and apple and a strong dose of toasty oak. Balanced and clean, it's a good match for poultry. Drink now.–T.M. • $12 • (6/30/1999) • **85**

E.B. FOOTE | WASHINGTON

Cabernet Sauvignon Columbia Valley 1995: Firm in texture, with a sour edge to the raspberry and black cherry, hinting at spices and resin as it comes together on the finish. Needs time; best from 2001 through 2005.–H.S. • $15 • (8/31/1998) • **83**
Cabernet Sauvignon Columbia Valley 1993 • $10 • (8/31/1996) • **79**
Cabernet Sauvignon Columbia Valley 1992 • $13 • (9/30/1994) • **85**

E.B. FOOTE

Cabernet Sauvignon Columbia Valley Cellar Reserve 1994: Strongly herbal, with beet and sage notes running through the modest berry flavors. Drink through 2002.–H.S. • $32 • (9/15/1998) • **82**

Cabernet-Merlot Columbia Valley 1996: Crisp and appealing for its bright berry and plum flavor, hinting at earth and spice on the finish. Drink through 2002.–H.S. • $15 • (6/30/1999) • **85**

Cabernet-Merlot Columbia Valley 1994 • $15 • (9/30/1997) • **89**

Chardonnay Columbia Valley 1997: Firm in texture, with a crisp, lemony underpinning to the light apple and spice flavors. Drink now through 2001. –H.S. • $12 • (6/30/1999) • **85**

Chardonnay Columbia Valley 1996: Light and smooth, with pretty pear and resin flavors that sustain themselves nicely on the finish. Drink now.–H.S. • $12 • (9/15/1998) • **86**

Merlot Columbia Valley 1997: Smooth and polished, with currant at the core and extra notes of caramel, coffee and smoky red pepper layering in on the finish. Drink now through 2003.–H.S. • $18 • (2/29/2000) • **86**

Merlot Columbia Valley 1995: A strong herb-and-olive component adds its voice to the chorus of ripe currant flavor in this open-textured Merlot. Finishes with firm tannins. Drink now.–H.S. • $15 • (9/15/1998) • **85**

Merlot Columbia Valley 1994 • $10 • (8/31/1996) • **88**

Merlot Columbia Valley 1993 • $8 • (9/30/1995) • **85**

Pinot Noir Washington NV • $7 • (9/30/1994) • **73**

Pinot Noir Washington La Center Vineyard 1993 • $8 • (9/30/1995) • **80**

EASTON | CALIFORNIA

Barbera Shenandoah Valley 1997: Has smooth, crisp tannins, with wild berry, vanilla and Dr. Pepper notes. Drink now.–J.L. • $18 • (2/29/2000) • **85**

Natoma Sierra Foothills 1998: Aromas of sweat and anise. Sour and lean, with just a vestige of fruit life.–J.L. • $14 • (5/15/2000) • **75**

Natoma White Sierra Foothills 1997: A mixture of apple, peach and vanilla notes; not varietally distinctive, but pleasant enough. Drink now. • $14 • (8/31/1998) • **83**

Zinfandel Fiddletown 1997: Firm and direct, with tobacco, cola and plum flavors that are well focused. Turns chunky on the finish. Drink now through 2004.–J.L. • $20 • (1/31/2000) • **86**

Zinfandel Fiddletown 1996: Complex and rustic, with ripe, juicy Zinfandel flavors, touches of prune, tar and earth, and firm tannins. A mouthful of wine. Drink now through 2002.–J.L. • $20 • (2/28/1999) • **88**

Zinfandel Fiddletown 1993 • $15 • (3/31/1996) • **77**

Zinfandel Shenandoah Valley 1997: Blueberry pie and herb notes are focused and pleasant, with the tannins kicking in on the finish. Drink now through 2004.–J.L. • $18 • (1/31/2000) • **86**

Zinfandel Shenandoah Valley 1996: A juicy style of Zin, with ripe wild berry, black cherry, plum and spice. Turns sleek and elegant, with earthy, supple tannins. Drink now through 2004.–J.L. • $18 • (12/31/1998) • **89**

EATON HILL | WASHINGTON

Cabernet Sauvignon Columbia Valley 1993 • $14 • (9/15/1996) • **85**

EBERLE | CALIFORNIA

Barbera Paso Robles Norman Vineyard 1992 • $18 • (11/15/1995) • **83**

Cabernet Sauvignon Paso Robles 1997: This California Cabernet delivers plummy, smoky fruit flavors that are ripe and lush and reveals complex anise, sage, mineral and leather notes before finishing in a long, rich aftertaste. A very good wine from an appellation making strides. Best from 2001 through 2008.–J.L. • $25 • (3/31/2000) SS • **89**

Cabernet Sauvignon Paso Robles 1996: Pleasant, with dried cherry and cinnamon qualities at the fore. Texture is a little coarse, with a slightly leathery finish, but the wine is enjoyable overall. Drink now through 2003. • $20 • (5/15/1999) • **84**

Cabernet Sauvignon Paso Robles 1995 • $18 • (11/15/1997) • **83**

Cabernet Sauvignon Paso Robles 1994 • $18 • (11/15/1997) • **86**

Cabernet Sauvignon Paso Robles 1991 • $16 • (4/15/1995) • **88**

Cabernet Sauvignon Paso Robles 1990 • $15 • (9/15/1994) • **84**

Cabernet Sauvignon Paso Robles 1989 • $15 • (11/15/1993) • **83**

Cabernet Sauvignon Paso Robles 1988 • $15 • (11/15/1992) • **86**

Cabernet Sauvignon Paso Robles 1987 • $22 • (11/15/1991) • **76**

Cabernet Sauvignon Paso Robles 1986 • $15 • (11/15/1989) • **85**

Cabernet Sauvignon Paso Robles 1985 • $12 • (2/15/1989) • **82**

Cabernet Sauvignon Paso Robles 1983 • $12 • (6/15/1987) • **79**

Cabernet Sauvignon Paso Robles 1982 • $10 • (9/30/1986) • **87**

Cabernet Sauvignon Paso Robles 1981 • $10 • (4/16/1985) • **87**

Cabernet Sauvignon Paso Robles Reserve 1995: Rustic tannins and plenty of oak form the backbone of this firmly structured wine, but a harmonious blend of black currant, blackberry anise, herb and cedar flavors shows depth and complexity. Finishes moderately. Best from 2001 through 2004. • $48 • (9/30/1999) • **88**

Cabernet Sauvignon Paso Robles Reserve 1991 • $35 • (11/15/1997) • **91**

Cabernet Sauvignon Paso Robles Reserve 1987 • $26 • (11/15/1993) • **86**

Chardonnay Paso Robles 1997: A ripe, intense mouthful of pineapple, pear, fig and herb. Finishes soft and flavorful. Drink now.–J.L. • $14 • (7/31/1999) • **87**

Côtes-du-Rôbles Red Paso Robles 1997: Pleasant and lightly textured, with subtle cherry and herb notes. A nice quaffer. Grenache blend. Drink now. • $14 • (5/15/1999) • **82**

Muscat Canelli Paso Robles 1997 • $11 • (3/31/1998) • **84**

Muscat Canelli Paso Robles 1994 • $9 • (9/30/1995) • **82**

Syrah Paso Robles 1991 • $16 • (10/31/1993) • **85**

Syrah Paso Robles Fralich Vineyard 1996: An earthy, leathery style, with meaty plum, bacon, black cherry and mineral, this covers a broad range of flavors even if it struggles to find a focus. Drink now through 2002.–J.L. • $18 • (4/30/1999) • **86**

Syrah Paso Robles Fralich Vineyard 1993 • $16 • (8/31/1995) • **89**

Syrah Paso Robles Fralich Vineyard 1992 • $16 • (7/31/1994) • **86**

Syrah Paso Robles Steinbeck Vineyard 1996: Ripe, with an earthy, mineral streak running through the cherry and berry flavors, turning earthy, dry and tannic. Drink now through 2002.–J.L. • $18 • (4/30/1999) • **83**

Syrah Paso Robles Steinbeck Vineyard 1995 • $16 • (5/15/1997) • **88**

Zinfandel Paso Robles 1989 • $12 • (10/15/1992) • **86**

Zinfandel Paso Robles Richard Sauret Vineyard 1996 • $18 • (6/15/1998) • **85**

Zinfandel Paso Robles Sauret Vineyard 1995 • $16 • (2/28/1997) • **90**

Zinfandel Paso Robles Sauret Vineyard 1994 • $16 • (4/30/1996) • **87**

Zinfandel Paso Robles Sauret Vineyard 1993 • $13 • (6/15/1995) • **86**

Zinfandel Paso Robles Sauret Vineyard 1992 • $13 • (10/15/1994) • **82**

Zinfandel Paso Robles Sauret Vineyard 1991 • $12 • (8/31/1993) HR • **89**

Zinfandel Paso Robles Sauret Vineyard 1990 • $12 • (12/31/1992) • **88**

Zinfandel Paso Robles Steinbeck Vineyard 1996 • $15 • (6/15/1998) • **83**

ECHELON | CALIFORNIA

Chardonnay Central Coast 1998: Pasty flavors detract from green apple undertones.–J.L. • $15 • (4/30/2000) • **79**

Chardonnay Central Coast 1997: Crisp and flavorful, with a range of grapefruit, lemon, tart pear and melon flavors, finishing with a pleasant earthy edge. New from Chalone Wine Group. Drink now.–J.L. • $12 • (10/31/1998) • **86**

Merlot Central Coast 1998: Ripe cherry flavors and a nice dose of toasty oak on a medium frame. Drink now.–J.L. • $15 • (6/30/2000) • **83**

Merlot Central Coast 1997: Crisp, with simple bright berry and herb flavors, finishing firm. Drink now.–J.L. • $15 • (8/31/1999) • **82**

Pinot Noir Central Coast 1998: Vanilla, cherry, clove and anise notes begin with intensity but fade on the finish. Drink now through 2002.–J.L. • $15 • (5/15/2000) • **85**

Pinot Noir Central Coast 1997: Crisp up front, and tannic, turning supple with appealing dried cherry, spice and wild berry flavors, hints of vanilla. Drink through 2002.–J.L. • $14 • (12/15/1998) • **86**

Syrah California 1998: Juicy black cherry and chocolate notes linger through the tangy finish of this medium-bodied wine. Drink now through 2004. –J.L. • $15 • (4/30/2000) • **87**

EDDY, TOM | CALIFORNIA

Cabernet Sauvignon Napa Valley 1995: Seductive. Smooth and polished, with currant, anise, cherry, sage and leather notes, finishing with a complex array of flavors, a touch of coffee. Drink through 2007.–J.L. • $60 • (4/30/1999) • **92**

Cabernet Sauvignon Napa Valley 1994 • $50 • (5/15/1998) • **90**

Cabernet Sauvignon Napa Valley 1993 • $40 • (10/31/1997) • **90**

Cabernet Sauvignon Napa Valley 1992 • $36 • (5/15/1996) • **88**

Cabernet Sauvignon Napa Valley 1991 • $32 • (4/30/1995) • **90**

Key: SS—Spectator Selection. CS—Cellar Selection. HR—Highly Recommended. $NA—Price not available. (BT)—Barrel tasting. (A)—Auction Price. For a key to the tasters' initials, see "How to Use These Listings."
Dates in parentheses represent the issues in which the ratings were published.

EDEN ROC | CALIFORNIA

Brut California NV • $5 • (12/31/1997) • **86**
Extra Dry California NV • $5 • (12/31/1997) • **83**

EDGEFIELD | OREGON

Black Rabbit Red Oregon 1997: A stylish wine, supple in texture, with earthy, gamy notes mingling with the black cherry flavors. A blend of Cabernet Sauvignon, Merlot, Pinot Noir, Zinfandel, Syrah. Drink now.–H.S. • $11 • (4/30/1999) • **85**
Black Rabbit Red Oregon 1996 • $11 • (5/15/1998) • **85**
Black Rabbit Red Oregon-Washington 1998: Light and refreshing, with pretty black cherry and spice flavors that linger on an open-textured finish. Cabernet Sauvignon, Merlot, Syrah and others. Drink now through 2002. –H.S. • $12 • (5/15/2000) • **86**
Chardonnay Oregon 1998: Light, bright and fruity, with pear, apple and spice flavors waxing on the nicely balanced finish. Drink now through 2003. –H.S. • $13 • (5/15/2000) • **86**
Chardonnay Willamette Valley 1996 • $11 • (5/15/1998) • **82**
Chardonnay Willamette Valley Vintage Select 1998: Fresh and appealing for its straightforward pear and apple character, finishing with a hint of flintiness. Drink now.–H.S. • $15 • (5/15/2000) • **83**
Chardonnay Willamette Valley Vintage Select 1996: Crisp and refined, offering pretty apple, pear and cream flavors plus a hint of spice on the delicate finish. Drink now.–H.S. • $15 • (4/30/1999) • **86**
Cuvée de L'Abri Rouge Columbia Valley 1995 • $18 • (5/15/1998) • **83**
Gewürztraminer Washington County 1996: Earthy, slightly bitter flavors mix with pear and spice notes to make this a bracing example of full-on, mostly dry Gewürz. Not for every taste. Drink now.–H.S. • $11 • (6/30/1999) • **86**
Pinot Gris Willamette Valley 1997: Light, open-textured and spicy, with pretty melon flavors at the center. Drink now.–H.S. • $11 • (4/30/1999) • **85**
Pinot Gris Willamette Valley 1996 • $11 • (10/31/1997) • **86**
Pinot Noir Willamette Valley 1998: On the light side but a bit firmer than most '98s, with soft tannins that at this point are more prominent than the delicate currant and berry. Best from 2001 through 2004.–H.S. • $13 • (5/15/2000) • **84**
Pinot Noir Willamette Valley Vintage Select 1998: Bright and spicy. A delicate wine with a distinctive streak of cinnamon and star anise running through the red cherry and raspberry flavors. Finishes with a touch of tobacco. Drink now through 2003.–H.S. • $18 • (5/15/2000) • **89**
Pinot Noir Willamette Valley Vintage Select 1996: Ripe in flavor, with a firm layer of chewy tannins surrounding the pretty black cherry and currant notes. Restrained on the finish. Drink through 2003.–H.S. • $15 • (6/15/1999) • **87**
Pinot Noir Willamette Valley Vintage Select 1995 • $18 • (10/15/1997) • **86**
Syrah Columbia Valley Chukar Ridge Vineyard 1995 • $18 • (5/15/1998) • **86**
White Riesling Yamhill County Vintage Select Hyland Vineyard 1998: Sweet, generous and deftly balanced to show off its pear, honey and apricot flavors without turning syrupy. Not an aperitif, however. Drink now.–H.S. • $12 • (5/15/2000) • **87**
White Riesling Yamhill County Vineyard Select Hyland Vineyards 1996 • $12 • (5/15/1998) • **87**
Zinfandel Columbia Valley The Pines Vineyard 1996: Crisp in texture, with a nice zip to the black cherry and chocolate flavors that persist on the finish. Drink through 2002.–H.S. • $20 • (6/30/1999) • **84**

EDGEWOOD | CALIFORNIA

Cabernet Franc Napa Valley 1992 • $16 • (7/31/1997) • **85**
Cabernet Sauvignon Napa Valley 1996: A fine blend of blackberry, herb, a hint of tobacco and cassis, all couched in toasty oak. The wine has finesse, with firm, ripe tannins, moderate body and a long finish. Best from 2002 through 2007. • $20 • (11/15/1999) • **88**
Cabernet Sauvignon Napa Valley 1995: A chewy wine, it serves up bright cherry flavors framed by toasty oak and herb notes. Tannins are a little rough, but it should soften with time. Drink through 2005. • $20 • (10/15/1998) • **85**
Cabernet Sauvignon Napa Valley 1994 • $20 • (4/30/1998) • **88**
Cabernet Sauvignon Napa Valley 1992 • $18 • (9/15/1996) • **82**
Chardonnay Napa Valley 1997: Elegant and creamy, with subtle, focused citrus, toasted oak and pear flavors. Drink now.–J.L. • $18 • (11/15/1999) • **88**
Malbec Napa Valley 1992 • $16 • (11/30/1996) • **83**
Merlot Napa Valley 1996: Tightly structured, with a range of moderately ripe plum, cinnamon, anise and toasted oak flavors that persist. Drink now through 2002.–J.L. • $20 • (10/15/1999) • **84**
Merlot Napa Valley 1995: Shows pleasant blackberry, smoke and spice along with a touch of bitterness. Finishes short with some resin notes. Drink now through 2001. • $20 • (9/30/1998) • **82**
Merlot Napa Valley 1994 • $20 • (3/31/1998) • **87**
Petite Sirah Napa Valley 1994 • $15 • (3/31/1998) • **85**
Petite Sirah Napa Valley 1992 • $14 • (11/30/1996) • **76**
Zinfandel Napa Valley 1996: Offers ripe berry, tobacco and cedary oak flavors that lean toward the mature side, turning dry and tannic. Drink now.–J.L. • $18 • (6/15/2000) • **85**
Zinfandel Napa Valley 1994 • $14 • (6/15/1998) • **81**
Zinfandel Napa Valley 1991 • $14 • (9/15/1996) • **84**

EDMEADES | CALIFORNIA

Chardonnay Anderson Valley 1997: Lively, with straightforward flavors of apple, pear and spicy oak. Drink now.–J.L. • $14 • (6/30/2000) • **82**
Chardonnay Anderson Valley 1996: Starts off with pretty hazelnut aromas, then kicks in with an elegant blend of citrus, pear, apple and peach flavors. The finish is long, with more fruit and minerals framed in toasty oak. Drink now through 2002. • $18 • (7/31/1999) • **91**
Gewürztraminer Anderson Valley 1996: Distinctly and decidedly Gewürz, with vivid pear, litchi and rose petal aromas and flavors that linger on the dry finish. Drink now.–H.S. • $16 • (11/30/1998) • **88**
Pinot Noir Anderson Valley 1997: The pleasant array of floral, raspberry and dried cherry doesn't quite come into focus, though there's sufficient depth and complexity to enjoy it now. Drink now through 2005.–J.L. • $17 • (5/15/2000) • **87**
Pinot Noir Anderson Valley 1996: Ripe, with juicy plum and strawberry flavors, it turns rich and complex on the finish, with lots of fruit notes. Drink now through 2002.–J.L. • $20 • (12/31/1998) • **88**
Pinot Noir Anderson Valley 1995 • $20 • (2/28/1998) • **87**
Pinot Noir Anderson Valley 1994 • $20 • (2/28/1997) • **86**
Pinot Noir Anderson Valley 1982 • $10 • (2/16/1985) • **89**
Pinot Noir Anderson Valley Anderson Crest Vineyard 1994 • $23 • (3/31/1996) • **85**
Pinot Noir Anderson Valley Dennison Vineyard 1993 • $20 • (9/15/1995) • **86**
Zinfandel Mendocino 1997: Very ripe and jammy, with sweet-tasting plum, cherry, wild berry and raspberry, finishing with crisp acidity and tannins. Drink through 2002.–J.L. • $19 • (5/15/1999) • **87**
Zinfandel Mendocino 1996 • $18 • (5/31/1998) • **87**
Zinfandel Mendocino 1995 • $19 • (4/30/1997) • **89**
Zinfandel Mendocino 1994 • $16 • (4/30/1996) • **88**
Zinfandel Mendocino Ciapusci Vineyard 1996: Lots of supple cherry and wild berry flavors that are plush with, spice, anise and cedar notes and mild tannins.–J.L. • $24 • (12/31/1998) • **88**
Zinfandel Mendocino Ciapusci Vineyard 1995 • $28 • (6/15/1998) • **88**
Zinfandel Mendocino Ciapusci Vineyard 1994 • $29 • (4/30/1996) • **85**
Zinfandel Mendocino Ciapusci Vineyard 1993 • $20 • (10/15/1995) • **86**
Zinfandel Mendocino Ciapusci Vineyard 1990 • $20 • (10/15/1992) • **86**
Zinfandel Mendocino Ridge 1997: Big and ripe, but there's a tough twinge of bitterness to the wild berry, raspberry and ripe Zinfandel fruit flavors. Let it breathe. Best from 2001 through 2007.–J.L. • $24 • (5/15/2000) • **86**
Zinfandel Mendocino Ridge Ciapusci Vineyard 1997: Very ripe and a touch jammy, with spicy cherry, licorice, cedar, sage and wild berry, turning smooth and polished. Label says 17 percent alcohol, so be advised. Drink now through 2007.–J.L. • $24 • (4/30/2000) • **91**
Zinfandel Mendocino Ridge Zeni Vineyard 1997: Offers enough ripe berry and raspberry flavors to hold your interest, turning dry and austere. Drink now through 2004.–J.L. • $25 • (5/15/2000) • **83**
Zinfandel Mendocino Zeni Vineyard 1996: Peppery, with earth, tar, raspberry and wild berry. A distinctive style, with firm, drying tannins. Drink now through 2004.–J.L. • $25 • (12/31/1998) • **88**
Zinfandel Mendocino Zeni Vineyard 1994 • $29 • (4/30/1996) • **84**
Zinfandel Mendocino Zeni Vineyard 1993 • $20 • (8/31/1995) • **88**
Zinfandel North Coast 1992 • $12 • (1/31/1995) • **86**

EDMUNDS ST. JOHN | CALIFORNIA

El Niño California 1992 • $11 • (6/30/1995) • **84**
Les Côtes Sauvages California 1995 • $20 • (11/30/1997) • **87**
Les Côtes Sauvages California 1992 • $16 • (6/30/1995) • **88**
Les Côtes Sauvages California 1989 • $19 • (7/15/1991) • **79**
Les Côtes Sauvages California 1986 • $14 • (4/15/1989) • **88**

■ ■ ■ ■

EDMUNDS ST. JOHN

Les Côtes Sauvages Cuvée Wahluke 90 America NV • $14 • (1/31/1994) • **86**
Les Fleurs du Chaparral Napa Valley 1987 • $15 • (8/31/1990) • **91**
Mourvèdre California L'Enfant Terrible 1994 • $12 • (8/31/1996) • **76**
Mourvèdre Napa Valley 1986 • $15 • (4/15/1989) • **87**
Port O'Call California New World Red 1989 • $10 • (8/31/1991) • **84**
Syrah California 1994 • $12 • (8/31/1996) • **86**
Syrah California 1987 • $18 • (12/15/1989) • **81**
Syrah El Dorado County Fenaughty Vineyard 1997: Grapey, with firm, ripe fruit flavors that echo cherry and berry, turning firm and tannic, picking up leather and mineral flavors. Drink now through 2003.–J.L. • $30 • (4/30/1999) • **87**
Syrah Sonoma Valley 1988 • $19 • (8/31/1991) • **85**
Syrah Sonoma County 1986 • $12 • (4/15/1989) • **91**
Syrah Sonoma Valley Durell Vineyard 1996: A rustic style that's earthy and gamy, with leather, pepper and mineral tones preceding a core of meaty plum and berryish flavors that turn tannic. Drink through 2006.–J.L. • $25 • (4/30/1999) • **87**
Syrah Sonoma Valley Durell Vineyard 1995 • $30 • (11/30/1997) • **88**
Syrah Sonoma Valley Durell Vineyard 1994 • $25 • (2/28/1997) • **87**
Syrah Sonoma Valley Durrell Vineyard 1991 • $20 • (12/31/1993) • **89**
Syrah-Grenache California Rocks and Gravel 1997: Tight and tough, with rustic tannins that barely allow the toast and hints of cherry, anise and herbs to shine through. Perhaps more bottle age will help it calm down and blossom. Best from 2001 through 2004. • $18 • (5/31/1999) • **83**
Zinfandel Amador County 1995 • $15 • (3/31/1997) • **87**
Zinfandel Amador County 1994 • $16 • (9/15/1996) • **86**
Zinfandel Amador County 1993 • $16 • (10/15/1995) • **86**
Zinfandel Mendocino County Pallini Rosso 1993 • $11 • (10/15/1995) • **83**
Zinfandel Napa Valley Amaronese 1988 • $12 • (10/15/1992) • **80**

EDNA VALLEY | CALIFORNIA

Chardonnay Edna Valley Paragon 1998: Tight and flinty, with medium-weight citrus and pear notes, its fruit shines through without too much oak. Drink now through 2003.–J.L. • $19 • (12/31/1999) • **87**
Chardonnay Edna Valley Paragon 1997: A clean, flavorful, fruit-centered style, with apple, pear and toast notes carrying through to the finish. Drink now through 2002.–J.L. • $18 • (7/31/1999) • **88**
Chardonnay Edna Valley Paragon 1996 • $17 • (5/15/1998) • **89**
Pinot Noir Edna Valley Paragon 1998: Very attractive. Pretty cherry, strawberry, vanilla and herb notes, with hints of spice and cedar. Drink now through 2004.–J.L. • $19 • (6/15/2000) • **87**
Pinot Noir Central Coast Paragon 1997: Dense, earthy and complex, with cola, black cherry, sage, mineral and berry flavors that coat the palate, turning tannic. Drink through 2005.–J.L. • $19 • (12/31/1999) • **87**
Pinot Noir Edna Valley Paragon 1995 • $17 • (1/31/1997) • **81**
Pinot Noir Edna Valley 1993 • $15 • (3/31/1995) • **73**
Pinot Noir Edna Valley 1992 • $15 • (3/31/1995) • **83**
Pinot Noir Edna Valley 1990 • $15 • (2/28/1993) • **84**
Pinot Noir Edna Valley 1986 • $15 • (12/15/1989) • **76**
Pinot Noir Edna Valley 1985 • $15 • (6/15/1988) • **78**
Pinot Noir Edna Valley 1984 • $10 • (12/15/1987) • **85**
Pinot Noir Edna Valley 1982 • $12 • (8/31/1986) • **80**
Pinot Noir Edna Valley Paragon Vineyard Reserve 1992 • $18 • (3/31/1995) • **86**
Pinot Noir Edna Valley Reserve 1988 • $18 • (2/28/1993) • **82**
Syrah Central Coast 1997: Intense, with ripe flavors of chocolate, black cherry and sage framed within a bed of soft tannin. Drink now through 2005.–J.L. • $17 • (6/15/2000) • **86**

EDWARDS, MERRY | CALIFORNIA

Pinot Noir Russian River Valley 1997: Firm, with ripe, fleshy cola, cherry, berry and herbal flavors, turning tight and tannic on the finish. Needs a little time. Drink through 2006.–J.L. • $28 • (9/15/1999) • **88**
Pinot Noir Russian River Valley Olivet Lane 1997: Complex, with a range of ripe cherry, earth, cedar and mushroom flavors, it firms up and shows its tannic weight on the finish. Drink through 2007.–J.L. • $42 • (9/15/1999) • **89**

Key: SS—Spectator Selection. CS—Cellar Selection. HR—Highly Recommended. $NA—Price not available. (BT)—Barrel tasting. Ⓐ—Auction Price.
For a key to the tasters' initials, see "How to Use These Listings."
Dates in parentheses represent the issues in which the ratings were published.

EHLERS GROVE | CALIFORNIA

Cabernet Sauvignon Mount Veeder 1997: Weaves together an attractive range of coffee, currant, plum and prune flavors, picking up earthy mushroom and wild berry. Drink now through 2007.–J.L. • $45 • (6/15/2000) • **88**
Cabernet Sauvignon Napa Valley 1993 • $11 • (12/15/1995) • **83**
Cabernet Sauvignon Napa Valley 1992 • $15 • (12/15/1995) • **88**
Chardonnay Napa Valley Carneros Reserve 1997: Lithe and silky, featuring rich, elegant pear, peach and nectarine flavors that linger on the long, pure, fruit-focused finish. Drink now.–J.L. • $30 • (7/31/1999) • **90**
Chardonnay Sonoma-Napa Counties Winery Reserve 1996 • $25 • (6/30/1998) • **88**
Dolcetto California 1997: Smoky notes hover around bright, pretty plum and black cherry. Quite rich for Dolcetto, this is full-bodied but balanced by fresh acidity. Finishes moderately, with a touch of anise. Drink now. • $18 • (6/15/1999) • **87**
Sauvignon Blanc Napa Valley Winery Reserve 1996 • $14 • (6/30/1997) • **88**
Zinfandel California 1997: Ripe, with soft, rich flavors of wild berry, plum, vanilla and earth that hold, with supple tannins. Drink now.–J.L. • $15 • (5/15/1999) • **83**

EISELE, VOLKER | CALIFORNIA

Cabernet Sauvignon Napa Valley 1997: Dark and supple, showing a mineral, tar and black cherry core. Toasted oak notes emerge on the finish. Tannins are big but integrated. Best now through 2005.–J.L. • $40 • (9/15/1999) • **87**
Cabernet Sauvignon Napa Valley 1996: Elegant and firmly textured, with tight berry, currant, dill and claylike flavors. Finishes tannic. Drink now through 2002.–J.L. • $32 • (6/15/1999) • **87**
Cabernet Sauvignon Napa Valley 1995: Smooth and spicy, with currant, tobacco, anise, sage and cedary flavors, turning elegant on the finish, where the tannins are polished and supple. Drink through 2007.–J.L. • $35 • (7/31/1998) • **88**
Cabernet Sauvignon Napa Valley 1994 • $30 • (10/31/1997) • **87**
Cabernet Sauvignon Napa Valley 1992 • $26 • (5/15/1997) • **88**

EKLUND | CALIFORNIA

Pinot Noir Carneros 1994 • $20 • (11/15/1997) • **83**

EL MOLINO | CALIFORNIA

Chardonnay Napa Valley 1996 • $38 • (6/30/1998) • **90**
Chardonnay Rutherford 1998: Spicy and floral, with pleasant pear, apple and mineral notes, turning simple. Drink now.–J.L. • $38 • (6/15/2000) • **86**
Chardonnay Rutherford 1997: Very rich and concentrated, with sharply focused layers of fig, pear, honey, vanilla and spice that fan out on the finish. Drink now through 2003.–J.L. • $38 • (6/15/1999) • **91**
Pinot Noir Carneros Abbott's Vineyard 1986 • $25 • (3/31/1997) • **84**
Pinot Noir Napa County 1990 • $30 • (3/31/1997) • **89**
Pinot Noir Napa County 1989 • $30 • (9/30/1992) • **82**
Pinot Noir Napa County 1988 • $30 • (11/15/1991) • **82**
Pinot Noir Napa County 1987 • $29 • (10/31/1991) • **85**
Pinot Noir Napa Valley 1996: Smooth and silky, with ripe black cherry, plum and berry flavors that are focused and complex on the finish, where the fruit persists. Drink now through 2004.–J.L. • $45 • (8/31/1999) • **88**
Pinot Noir Napa Valley 1995 • $38 • (1/31/1998) • **88**
Pinot Noir Napa Valley 1994 • $35 • (1/31/1997) • **89**
Pinot Noir Napa Valley 1993 • $35 • (5/31/1996) • **87**
Pinot Noir Napa Valley 1992 • $30 • (2/28/1995) HR • **91**
Pinot Noir Napa Valley 1991 • $30 • (2/28/1995) • **89**

ELAN | CALIFORNIA

Cabernet Sauvignon Atlas Peak 1995: Supple, with a range of peppery, earthy, mineral and tar flavors leading to a core of ripe plum, black cherry and herb. Finishes long, focused and flavorful. Drink now through 2005. –J.L. • $39 • (10/15/1999) • **89**
Cabernet Sauvignon Atlas Peak 1994: An elegant style, with mild, well-integrated tannins, its core of supple plum and berry flavor accented by bell pepper. Smoky, toasty oak precedes. Drink now through 2005.–J.L. • $34 • (10/31/1998) • **88**
Cabernet Sauvignon Atlas Peak 1992 • $30 • (11/30/1997) • **91**
Cabernet Sauvignon Napa Valley 1992 • $29 • (5/15/1997) • **86**

Merlot Atlas Peak 1995: Supple and complex if a touch green, with polished green olive, black cherry, herb and tea notes. Drink through 2007.–J.L. • $34 • (12/31/1999) • **86**

ELIZABETH | CALIFORNIA

Zinfandel Mendocino 1992 • $10 • (10/15/1994) • **86**
Zinfandel Mendocino 1990 • $10 • (10/15/1992) • **85**
Zinfandel Redwood Valley 1998: Grapey, with hints of green apple and coffee flavors on the finish. Drink now.–J.L. • $18 • (6/15/2000) • **83**
Zinfandel Redwood Valley 1996 • $14 • (6/15/1998) • **85**

ELK COVE | OREGON

Cabernet Sauvignon Willamette Valley Dundee Hills Vineyard Commander's Cabernet 1987 • $15 • (3/31/1991) • **80**
Chardonnay Willamette Valley 1996: Light and crisp, with pretty apple, peach and floral aromas and flavors on a modest frame. Flavors widen nicely on the finish.–H.S. • $13 • (11/15/1998) • **85**
Chardonnay Willamette Valley Clonal Selection Espiguette #352 1996 • $17 • (3/31/1998) • **86**
Gewürztraminer Willamette Valley Ultima 1996 • $25/375 ml. • (3/31/1998) • **88**
Oregon Sparkling 1996: Bright, light and refined, with pretty apple and cream aromas and flavors on a crisp frame. Remarkably refreshing. Drink now.–H.S. • $22 • (9/30/1999) • **88**
Pinot Gris Willamette Valley 1998: Ripe and rich, as aromatic and intense as a Viognier, with similar honeysuckle, pear and spice notes that last and last on the vibrant finish. As distinctive a Pinot Gris as Oregon has produced. Drink now.–H.S. • $15 • (10/15/1999) • **90**
Pinot Gris Willamette Valley 1997: Fresh and appealing for its citrusy melon and almond flavors, picking up a nice note of peach on the finish. Drink now.–H.S. • $14 • (11/15/1998) • **87**
Pinot Gris Willamette Valley 1996 • $14 • (10/31/1997) • **88**
Pinot Gris Willamette Valley Ultima 1992 • $20 • (5/31/1994) • **85**
Pinot Noir Oregon Estate 1997: Firm in texture, but there's a pretty band of sweet blackberry and currant flavors running through the finely balanced finish. Feels like it can gain depth. Drink now through 2003.–H.S. • $20 • (4/30/1999) • **89**
Pinot Noir Oregon La Bohème 1998: Strives for delicacy and achieves a lovely balance of juicy berry flavors and almost citrusy acidity, with the flavors extending into a long and lively finish. Picks up some nice hints of exotic spice as the flavors unfold. Drink through 2008.–H.S. • $30 • (4/30/2000) • **90**
Pinot Noir Oregon La Bohème 1997: A smooth, inviting, pretty wine, with ripe cherry and spice flavors that linger on the gentle finish. Unusually generous for the vintage, but still on the light side. Drink now through 2004.–H.S. • $28 • (11/15/1999) • **88**
Pinot Noir Oregon Roosevelt 1997: Firm in texture, almost crisp, with a nice beam of black cherry and tar flavors lingering on the finish. Needs to soften a bit. Drink through 2003.–H.S. • $40 • (11/15/1999) • **85**
Pinot Noir Oregon Roosevelt 1996: This wine sneaks up on you. Light in color, with pretty plum hues and aromas. Light on the palate, too, featuring modest currant and plum notes, finishing with delicacy as the flavors expand. Has a layer of scratchy tannins. Drink through 2003.–H.S. • $40 • (8/31/1998) • **88**
Pinot Noir Oregon Windhill 1998: Polished and seductive, a seamless wine with lovely bayleaf-scented raspberry, red currant and exotic spice flavors mingling on a plush texture, finishing with a tingle of acidity. Not a big, round wine, but it has plenty of offer. Drink now through 2007.–H.S. • $30 • (4/30/2000) • **90**
Pinot Noir Oregon Windhill 1997: Firm and a bit raucous, with wild berry and herb flavors, this is a solid wine with rough edges that might be smoothed by cellaring. Best from 2001 through 2003.–H.S. • $30 • (4/30/1999) • **85**
Pinot Noir Willamette Valley 1998: Dense, tight and chewy, packed with peppery, anise-scented black cherry and currant flavors. Finishes with more than a tinge of acidity. Needs time to settle down. Best from 2002 through 2008.–H.S. • $18 • (4/30/2000) • **88**
Pinot Noir Willamette Valley 1997: Light in texture, with modest raspberry and anise flavors that persist nicely on the finish. Drink now.–H.S. • $15 • (4/30/1999) • **85**
Pinot Noir Willamette Valley 1994 • $12 • (3/31/1996) • **85**
Pinot Noir Willamette Valley 1992 • $10 • (3/15/1994) • **83**
Pinot Noir Willamette Valley 1990 • $10 • (2/28/1993) • **83**
Pinot Noir Willamette Valley 1989 • $10 • (3/31/1992) • **88**
Pinot Noir Willamette Valley 1988 • $15 • (1/31/1991) • **78**
Pinot Noir Willamette Valley Dundee Hills Vineyard 1990 • $18 • (2/28/1993) • **75**
Pinot Noir Willamette Valley Dundee Hills Vineyard 1989 • $18 • (3/31/1992) • **84**
Pinot Noir Willamette Valley Dundee Hills Vineyard 1987 • $15 • (2/15/1990) • **81**
Pinot Noir Willamette Valley Dundee Hills Vineyard 1986 • $15 • (6/15/1988) • **78**
Pinot Noir Willamette Valley Dundee Hills Vineyard 1985 • $15 • (6/15/1987) • **85**
Pinot Noir Willamette Valley Estate Bottled 1987 • $15 • (2/15/1990) • **78**
Pinot Noir Willamette Valley Estate Bottled 1986 • $15 • (6/15/1988) • **87**
Pinot Noir Willamette Valley Estate Bottled Reserve 1990 • $22 • (2/28/1993) • **83**
Pinot Noir Willamette Valley Estate Reserve 1992 • $18 • (10/31/1994) • **88**
Pinot Noir Willamette Valley Estate Reserve 1991 • $18 • (3/15/1994) • **82**
Pinot Noir Willamette Valley La Bohème 1993 • $25 • (3/31/1996) • **84**
Pinot Noir Willamette Valley Reserve 1994 • $25 • (10/15/1996) • **77**
Pinot Noir Willamette Valley Reserve 1993 • $20 • (3/31/1996) • **79**
Pinot Noir Willamette Valley Reserve 1987 • $15 • (12/15/1990) • **85**
Pinot Noir Willamette Valley Reserve 1985 • $15 • (2/15/1990) • **79**
Pinot Noir Willamette Valley Reserve 1983 • $20 • (2/15/1990) • **79**
Pinot Noir Willamette Valley Wind Hill Vineyards 1990 • $18 • (2/28/1993) • **74**
Pinot Noir Willamette Valley Wind Hill Vineyards 1989 • $25 • (3/31/1992) • **82**
Pinot Noir Willamette Valley Wind Hills Vineyard 1988 • $18 • (1/31/1991) • **80**
Pinot Noir Willamette Valley Wind Hills Vineyard 1987 • $15 • (2/15/1990) • **75**
Pinot Noir Willamette Valley Wind Hills Vineyard 1986 • $15 • (6/15/1988) • **85**
Pinot Noir Willamette Valley Wind Hills Vineyard 1985 • $15 • (6/15/1987) • **91**
Pinot Noir Yamhill County 1995 • $18 • (2/28/1997) • **84**
Riesling Willamette Valley 1998: Light and appealing for its pretty pear and floral aromas and flavors. Drink now.–H.S. • $12 • (11/15/1999) • **83**
Riesling Willamette Valley Late Harvest Select 1998: Frankly sweet but not syrupy, this is a light-textured wine with lovely green apple, honey and citrus flavors that linger on the soft finish. Drink now.–H.S. • $12 • (5/15/2000) • **87**
Riesling Willamette Valley Ultima 1996 • $25/375 ml. • (3/31/1998) • **90**
Riesling Willamette Valley Ultima 1994 • $25/375 ml. • (11/30/1996) • **85**
Riesling Willamette Valley Ultima 1992 • $20/375 ml. • (11/30/1994) HR • **91**

ELK RUN | MARYLAND

Chardonnay Maryland 1998: Sweet but thin, this white shows smoky oak and slightly candied fruit flavors that turn a bit cloying on the finish.–T.M. • $12 • (5/31/2000) • **78**
Chardonnay Maryland Liberty Tavern Reserve 1998: Baked apple flavors dominate this medium-bodied Chardonnay that finishes with a touch of sweetness and mineral notes. Drink now.–K.M. • $15 • (1/01/2000) • **82**
Chardonnay Maryland Liberty Tavern Reserve 1997: Butter and peanutlike flavors dominate this white. Straightforward, but a little overdone. Drink now.–K.M. • $15 • (8/31/1999) • **82**
Pinot Noir Maryland 1998: This muscular red shows ripe fruit and firm tannins, but it's a bit heavy-handed. Best with food.–T.M. • $20 • (5/31/2000) • **79**

ELKE | CALIFORNIA

Pinot Noir Anderson Valley Donnelly Creek Vineyard 1997: Mature in color and flavor, with herb, tea, black cherry and wild berry flavors that turn elegant, with fine tannins. Drink now through 2005.–J.L. • $24 • (2/29/2000) • **87**

ELKHORN PEAK | CALIFORNIA

Pinot Noir Napa Valley Fagan Creek Vineyard 1995 • $26 • (12/15/1997) • **83**
Pinot Noir Napa Valley Fagan Creek Vineyard 1994 • $24 • (3/31/1997) • **78**
Pinot Noir Napa Valley Fagan Creek Vineyard 1993 • $21 • (12/31/1995) • **83**
Pinot Noir Napa Valley Fagan Creek Vineyard 1992 • $21 • (3/31/1995) • **79**

ELKTON VALLEY | OREGON

Pinot Noir Umpqua Valley 1994 • $9 • (3/31/1996) • **83**

ELLIOTT | CALIFORNIA

Cabernet Sauvignon Napa Valley 1994 • $24 • (11/15/1997) • **89**
Cabernet Sauvignon Napa Valley 1992 • $14 • (11/15/1996) • **86**

ELLISTON | CALIFORNIA

Cabernet Sauvignon Central Coast Sunol Valley Vineyard 1985 • $16 • (11/15/1991) • **74**
Cabernet Sauvignon Livermore Valley 1994 • $18 • (11/30/1997) • **76**
Captain's Claret California NV • $14 • (11/15/1994) • **82**
Captain's Claret Napa Valley 1992 • $14 • (8/31/1995) • **84**
Pinot Noir Santa Cruz Mountains Unfiltered Unfined 1993 • $22 • (12/31/1995) • **83**

ELYSE | CALIFORNIA

Cabernet Sauvignon Rutherford Morisoli Vineyard 1997: Wonderful harmony, finesse and elegance. Rich, with complex plum, cherry and light cedary oak flavors on the finish. Tannins are ripe and polished. Drink now through 2010.–J.L. • $60 • (4/30/2000) • **90**
Cabernet Sauvignon Napa Valley Morisoli Vineyard 1996: Big, ripe and tightly wound, with a range of black cherry, wild berry, currant, anise and prune notes. Turns elegant and polished on the finish. Drink now through 2008.–J.L. • $45 • (1/31/2000) • **92**
Cabernet Sauvignon Napa Valley Morisoli Vineyard 1993 • $30 • (11/15/1996) • **87**
Cabernet Sauvignon Napa Valley Morisoli Vineyard 1992 • $30 • (4/30/1996) • **89**
Cabernet Sauvignon Napa Valley Tietjen Vineyard 1996: This immense wine has wonderful complexity, depth and richness, with layers of ultrarich currant, black cherry, vanilla and chocolate. Long, intricate aftertaste. Best from 2001 through 2009.–J.L. • $37 • (1/31/2000) • **95**
Cabernet Sauvignon Napa Valley Tietjen Vineyard 1993 • $24 • (12/15/1996) • **85**
Jake's Cuveè Napa Valley 1997: Pleasing stewed plum and spicy dried cherry flavors hit the right notes. Grenache, Mourvèdre, Syrah and others. Drink now through 2005.–J.L. • $16 • (3/31/2000) • **85**
Nero Misto Napa Valley 1992 • $14 • (1/31/1995) • **84**
Nero Misto Napa Valley 1991 • $14 • (6/15/1993) • **86**
Nero Misto Napa Valley 1990 • $15 • (6/30/1992) • **86**
Syrah Napa Valley 1997: Smooth and polished, with a rich, focused core of meaty cherry, plum and berryish fruit, offset by hints of spice and leathery notes. Firms up on the finish. Drink now through 2007.–J.L. • $38 • (4/30/2000) • **90**
Zinfandel Howell Mountain 1994 • $16 • (4/30/1996) • **87**
Zinfandel Howell Mountain 1993 • $16 • (10/15/1995) • **85**
Zinfandel Howell Mountain 1992 • $14 • (10/15/1994) • **87**
Zinfandel Howell Mountain 1991 • $14 • (9/30/1993) • **85**
Zinfandel Napa Valley Coeur du Val 1994 • $14 • (4/30/1996) • **87**
Zinfandel Napa Valley Coeur du Val 1993 • $14 • (10/15/1995) • **83**
Zinfandel Napa Valley Coeur du Val 1992 • $14 • (10/15/1994) • **85**
Zinfandel Napa Valley Rutherford Bench-Morisoli Vineyard 1997: Wonderful layers of ripe, jammy wild berry, plum and blackberry flavors are plush and focused in this California Zin, finishing in a complex aftertaste. Tasted twice, with consistent notes. Bottles sold outside of California do not have the Rutherford Bench designation. Drink now through 2006.–J.L. • $28 • (1/31/2000) HR • **92**
Zinfandel Napa Valley Rutherford Bench-Morisoli Vineyard 1996: Juicy, with complex flavors of spicy wild berry, cherry and raspberry, tasting a touch sweet, with ripe, plush tannins. Drink now through 2001.–J.L. • $22 • (5/15/1999) • **88**
Zinfandel Napa Valley Rutherford Bench-Morisoli Vineyard 1994 • $16 • (8/31/1996) • **88**
Zinfandel Napa Valley Morisoli Vineyard 1993 • $16 • (10/15/1995) • **84**
Zinfandel Napa Valley Morisoli Vineyard 1992 • $14 • (10/15/1994) • **88**
Zinfandel Napa Valley Morisoli Vineyard 1991 • $14 • (9/30/1993) • **87**
Zinfandel Napa Valley Morisoli Vineyard 1990 • $13 • (10/15/1992) • **88**
Zinfandel Napa Valley Morisoli Vineyard 1989 • $13 • (8/31/1991) • **85**

EMILIO'S TERRACE | CALIFORNIA

Cabernet Sauvignon Napa Valley Reserve 1996: Dark, with classy cedary oak, blackberry, plum and currant, touches of spice and mineral and firm, well-integrated tannins. Built for cellaring, though with no track record, midterm cellaring is advised. Best from 2001 through 2007.–J.L. • $40 • (8/31/1999) • **92**

EMMOLO | CALIFORNIA

Merlot Napa Valley 1997: Starting out with dusty dill flavors, it works in earthy cherry, cedar and spice notes. Gains nuance on the finish. Drink now through 2004.–J.L. • $30 • (10/15/1999) • **85**
Merlot Napa Valley 1996: Serves up ripe, plump black cherry, plum and wild berry, with smooth, polished texture and tannins. Finishes with a burst of fruit. Drink now.–J.L. • $25 • (10/15/1998) • **87**
Sauvignon Blanc Napa Valley 1998: Lemon and green apple notes dominate here, matched with bright acidity and a fresh mineral edge. Light and refreshing. Drink now. • $14 • (9/30/1999) • **86**
Sauvignon Blanc Napa Valley 1997: Mild-mannered, with sweet pea, fig and light citrus notes. Moderate body and acid make it a pleasant quaff, if a little shy on intensity. Drink now. • $12 • (2/28/1999) • **83**
Sauvignon Blanc Napa Valley 1996 • $12 • (9/15/1997) • **84**

EOLA HILLS | OREGON

Cabernet Sauvignon Oregon 1996: Very firm and chewy, with enough plum and currant packed in among the tannins to make this worth cellaring to see what develops. Best after 2002.–H.S. • $13 • (5/31/1999) • **85**
Cabernet Sauvignon Oregon 1995 • $20 • (5/15/1998) • **89**
Cabernet Sauvignon Oregon 1992 • $9 • (11/30/1994) • **84**
Cabernet Sauvignon Oregon Visconti Vineyards 1992 • $15 • (3/31/1996) • **80**
Chardonnay Oregon 1997: Light and refreshing, with pretty pear and spice flavors that linger on the gentle finish. Drink now through 2001.–H.S. • $12 • (4/30/1999) • **85**
Chardonnay Oregon 1996 • $10 • (5/15/1998) • **86**
Chardonnay Oregon Reserve 1996: Odd flavors—more reminiscent of flower stalks and mint than fruit—followed by a long, appley finish with a pretty touch of spicy oak. Drink now through 2001.–H.S. • $16 • (4/30/1999) • **83**
Gamay Noir Oregon O'Connor Vineyards 1992 • $15 • (11/30/1994) • **80**
Gewürztraminer Late Harvest Oregon Vin d'Epice 1996 • $15/375 ml. • (5/15/1998) • **91**
Gewürztraminer Oregon Ultra Late Harvest Vin d'Epice 1992 • $15/375 ml. • (11/30/1994) • **89**
Merlot Oregon 1995 • $12 • (2/28/1997) • **87**
Merlot Oregon Reserve 1996: Firm in texture, with scratchy tannins but pretty plum, currant and spice flavors that echo on the lean finish. Best after 2001.–H.S. • $23 • (6/15/1999) • **83**
Pinot Gris Oregon 1997: Strongly spicy, with dusky overtones to the modest citrus and melon flavors. Drink now.–H.S. • $12 • (4/30/1999) • **82**
Pinot Noir Oregon 1997: Light and fragrant, with pretty strawberry and leaf aromas and flavors on a supple texture. Drink now through 2002.–H.S. • $12 • (6/30/1999) • **85**
Pinot Noir Oregon 1995 • $10 • (2/28/1997) • **82**
Pinot Noir Oregon 1989 • $10 • (2/28/1993) • **73**
Pinot Noir Oregon 1987 • $12 • (2/15/1990) • **76**
Pinot Noir Oregon 1986 • $12 • (2/15/1990) • **77**
Pinot Noir Oregon Illahe Hills Vineyard 1993 • $12 • (1/31/1996) • **80**
Pinot Noir Oregon Reserve 1996: Supple and harmonious, its flavors centering around plum and mineral, finishing with a hint of blueberry and a slight kick of tannin. Drink now through 2001.–H.S. • $23 • (4/30/1999) • **87**
Pinot Noir Oregon Temperance Hill Vineyard 1992 • $15 • (11/30/1994) • **83**
Sauvignon Blanc Late Harvest Oregon Vin d'Or 1996 • $15/375 ml. • (5/15/1998) • **90**

EOS | CALIFORNIA

Cabernet Sauvignon Paso Robles 1997: Medium-bodied, with concentrated plum flavors and focused black currant and herb notes. Drink now through 2004.–J.L. • $20 • (4/30/2000) • **86**
Chardonnay Paso Robles 1997: Shows a pleasant range of citrus, apple, pear, spice and toasted—almost sweet—oak flavors. Finishes clean and crisp. Drink now. • $15 • (5/31/1999) • **87**
Chardonnay Paso Robles Astraeus Vineyard 1996: Opens with pleasant peach and spice aromas, followed by brisk acidity on the palate. An impression of sweetness surprises, later framed by toasty oak. Drink now. • $15 • (7/31/1998) • **85**
Sauvignon Blanc Paso Robles 1997: Tangy and tart, with lemon and lime to the fore. Also has a bit of passion fruit and grassiness. Try with fillet of sole. Drink now. • $14 • (9/15/1998) • **83**

Key: SS—Spectator Selection. CS—Cellar Selection. HR—Highly Recommended. $NA—Price not available. (BT)—Barrel tasting. (A)—Auction Price. For a key to the tasters' initials, see "How to Use These Listings." **Dates in parentheses represent the issues in which the ratings were published.**

EQUINOX | CALIFORNIA

Blanc de Blanc Santa Cruz Mountains 1994: This creamy-textured wine starts off with a pretty blend of citrus and honey tones that fan out into layers of toasty hazelnut and pear. Finishes a little short, but still quite nice. Drink now. • $38 • (10/15/1999) • **88**

Blanc de Blanc Santa Cruz Mountains 1992: Hazelnut, toast and a bit of caramel are the enticing aromas in this creamy, smooth wine, while citrus, apple and honeyed flavors dominate the palate. Showing some age, it should be drunk pronto. Drink now. • $40 • (10/15/1999) • **89**

Blanc de Blanc Santa Cruz Mountains Cuvée de Chardonnay NV • $23 • (11/30/1996) • **75**

Blanc de Blanc Santa Cruz Mountains Reserve 1991 • $40 • (11/30/1996) • **78**

Brut Santa Cruz Mountains Harmony Cuvee NV: Rich, toasty aromas show more promise than what follows on the palate. The wine is showing age—it's quite honeyed up front yet tart on the finish. Drink now. • $27 • (10/15/1999) • **83**

ERATH | OREGON

Chardonnay Willamette Valley Brunker Hall Vineyards Reserve 1998: Light and refreshing, with a spicy, earthy edge to the apple and mineral flavors. Finishes smooth. Drink now through 2002.–H.S. • $35 • (3/31/2000) • **84**

Chardonnay Willamette Valley Reserve 1997: Crisp, almost raw-tasting, with tart apple and leafy flavors bouncing into the finish. Drink now through 2001.–H.S. • $27 • (4/30/1999) • **85**

Chardonnay Willamette Valley Reserve 1997: Tart, earthy flavors dominate this hard-edged white, which picks up some nice peach and honey notes on the finish. Maybe it just needs time.–H.S. • $20 • (12/31/1999) • **79**

Chardonnay Willamette Valley Reserve 1996 • $19 • (5/15/1998) • **87**

Gewürztraminer Willamette Valley Late Harvest 1995 • $18/375 ml. • (12/31/1996) • **92**

Pinot Blanc Willamette Valley 1998: Light, bright and intense, it's a jazzy mouthful of apple, spice and something reminiscent of oatmeal. Drink now.–H.S. • $13 • (12/31/1999) • **84**

Pinot Blanc Willamette Valley 1997: Light and tangy, with a citrus-peel edge to the melon and apple flavors. Drink now.–H.S. • $13 • (2/28/1999) • **83**

Pinot Gris Willamette Valley 1998: Earthy, nutty aromas and flavors add an odd whiff to this otherwise pleasant, medium-weight, dry white. Drink now.–H.S. • $14 • (10/15/1999) • **82**

Pinot Noir Willamette Valley 1993 • $12 • (1/31/1996) • **85**

Pinot Noir Willamette Valley Niederberger Vineyard Reserve 1992 • $25 • (1/31/1996) • **80**

Pinot Noir Willamette Valley Reserve 1997: Firm in texture, with chewy tannins and ripe cherry flavors. A streak of earthy, muddy flavor gets in the way. Drink now.–H.S. • $27 • (3/31/2000) • **80**

Pinot Noir Willamette Valley Reserve 1996: Firm and crisp, with a supple thread of blackberry and spice, finishing with an overlay of spicy oak. Lots of flavor for this vintage. Drink through 2003.–H.S. • $27 • (4/30/1999) • **88**

Pinot Noir Willamette Valley Reserve 1993 • $21 • (12/31/1996) • **85**

Pinot Noir Willamette Valley Twenty-Fifth Anniversary 1994 • $28 • (12/31/1996) • **82**

Pinot Noir Willamette Valley Vintage Select 1997: Light in color, with greenish berry and herb flavors that never quite loosen up. Tasted twice, with consistent notes.–H.S. • $20 • (3/31/2000) • **79**

Pinot Noir Willamette Valley Vintage Select 1996: Firm and focused, with ripe blackberry and currant flavors that persist nicely on the nubby-textured finish. Drink now through 2002.–H.S. • $20 • (4/30/1999) • **86**

Pinot Noir Willamette Valley Vintage Select 1994 • $17 • (12/31/1996) • **88**

Pinot Noir Willamette Valley Vintage Select 1993 • $16 • (1/31/1996) • **86**

Pinot Noir Willamette Valley Weber Vineyard Reserve 1994 • $35 • (5/15/1998) • **86**

Pinot Noir Willamette Valley Weber Vineyard Reserve 1993 • $28 • (1/31/1996) • **88**

ERIC ROSS | CALIFORNIA

Merlot Russian River Valley 1997: Firm and intense, with chunky currant, mineral, blackberry and oak notes. Needs time to simmer down. Best from 2001 through 2007.–J.L. • $25 • (3/31/2000) • **86**

Merlot Russian River Valley 1996: A peppery blend of licorice and woody oak flavors stand out, with black currants and herbs taking a back seat. Has depth but lacks great finesse. Drink now. • $24 • (10/15/1998) • **84**

Merlot Sonoma County 1995 • $22 • (3/31/1998) • **88**

Zinfandel Dry Creek Valley 1997: Firm, with stewed plum, berry and spice flavors, finishing with green notes and a little heat. Drink now.–J.L. • $17 • (5/15/2000) • **84**

Zinfandel Russian River Valley 1997: Aromatic, with cedar, blackberry pie and chocolate notes, turning crisp and spicy. Drink now.–J.L. • $24 • (6/15/2000) • **86**

Zinfandel Russian River Valley 1996: Focused, with lightly tart raspberry and plum flavors and hints of herbs. Lifts on the finish with a burst of tart fruit. Drink now.–J.L. • $16 • (2/28/1999) • **84**

Zinfandel Russian River Valley Occidental Vineyard 1996: Bright and juicy, showing tea- and anise-laced flavors of plum, blackberry and cherry. Drink now.–J.L. • $24 • (1/31/1999) • **85**

Zinfandel Russian River Valley Occidental Vineyard Old Vine 1997: Dark, tight and tart, with a greenish edge to the wild berry and blackberry flavors, firming up with dry tannins. Drink now through 2005.–J.L. • $28 • (3/31/2000) • **87**

Zinfandel Sonoma County Old Vine 1995 • $22 • (3/31/1998) • **88**

ESTANCIA | CALIFORNIA

Cabernet Sauvignon Alexander Valley 1992 • $10 • (11/15/1994) • **82**

Cabernet Sauvignon Alexander Valley 1991 • $9 • (10/31/1993) • **86**

Cabernet Sauvignon Alexander Valley 1990 • $9 • (6/15/1993) • **86**

Cabernet Sauvignon Alexander Valley 1989 • $10 • (11/15/1992) • **85**

Cabernet Sauvignon Alexander Valley 1988 • $9 • (5/31/1991) • **81**

Cabernet Sauvignon California 1996: This Cabernet is worth a second look—and not just for its value price. Fairly rich in texture, it offers a lot of smoky oak flavor, black currant and licorice notes and also harbors a pleasant herbal quality at the core. Finishing moderately, with mild tannins. • $12 • (1/31/1999) • **86**

Cabernet Sauvignon California 1995 • $13 • (5/31/1998) • **86**

Cabernet Sauvignon Sonoma-Napa Counties 1994 • $11 • (3/31/1997) • **88**

Cabernet Sauvignon Sonoma-Napa Counties 1993 • $10 • (12/15/1995) • **84**

Chardonnay Monterey County Pinnacles 1997: Ultraripe in style, with a bounty of pear, fig and tropical fruit flavors, this lovely white from California turns smooth and polished, with a pretty dash of toasty oak adding dimension. Not only a good value, it's ready to drink and widely available.–J.L. • $11 • (2/28/1999) • **88**

Chardonnay Monterey County Pinnacles 1996 • $11 • (6/30/1998) • **88**

Chardonnay Monterey Pinnacles 1998: Simple and straightforward in style, with pleasant pear, vanilla and spice notes that gain velocity, this young California white offers good value in an increasingly pricey category. Drink now.–J.L. • $12 • (5/31/2000) • **86**

Chardonnay Monterey Pinnacles Single Vineyard Reserve 1998: Green and a touch leafy, with sage, earthy pear, dry coconut and cedar notes. Drink now.–J.L. • $20 • (5/15/2000) • **82**

Chardonnay Monterey Reserve 1997: Smooth and creamy, with an elegant array of ripe pear, fig, melon, vanilla and anise flavors, turning to rich butterscotch and toast. Drink now through 2002.–J.L. • $19 • (7/31/1999) • **89**

Chardonnay Monterey Reserve 1996 • $19 • (6/30/1998) • **90**

Duo Alexander Valley 1997: Supple and polished, with a range of currant, coffee, sage and leather notes that turn dry and firm. Cabernet Sauvignon and Sangiovese. Drink now through 2005.–J.L. • $22 • (5/15/2000) • **85**

Duo Alexander Valley 1996: Rich and complex, with pretty plum, wild berry, cherry and spice, turning supple and polished on the finish. Contains Cabernet Sauvignon and Sangiovese. Drink now through 2003.–J.L. • $25 • (1/31/1999) • **89**

Duo Alexander Valley 1995 • $18 • (11/30/1997) • **88**

Fumé Blanc Monterey County Pinnacles 1997: Somewhat lean, with subtle peach, melon and herb notes. Soft on the palate, it finishes clean but lacks the focus of the '96. Drink now. • $10 • (5/15/1999) • **83**

Fumé Blanc Monterey County Pinnacles 1996: Here's a California Sauvignon Blanc in a softer style. This wine boasts a fine and varied collection of flavors, including fresh pea, fig, melon, grass, spice and vanilla. A bit shy on acidity, but very good overall and well worth the price. Drink now. • $10 • (9/15/1998) • **87**

Meritage Alexander Valley 1996: This Bordeaux-style red delivers complex and focused plum, currant, spice, cinnamon and cedar flavors that flow to a gentle finish with soft, integrated tannins. An elegant and enticing California bottling. A blend of Cabernet Sauvignon, Cabernet Franc and Merlot. Drink now through 2004.–J.L. • $30 • (10/15/1999) SS • **90**

Meritage Alexander Valley 1994 • $16 • (5/15/1997) SS • **92**

Meritage Alexander Valley 1993 • $15 • (3/31/1997) SS • **90**

Meritage Alexander Valley 1992 • $15 • (9/30/1995) • **89**

Meritage Alexander Valley 1991 • $14 • (9/15/1994) • **85**

Meritage Alexander Valley 1990 • $14 • (10/15/1993) SS • **90**

Meritage Alexander Valley 1989 • $14 • (11/15/1992) • **85**
Meritage Alexander Valley 1988 • $14 • (11/15/1991) • **83**
Meritage Alexander Valley 1987 • $12 • (1/31/1991) • **88**
Meritage Red Alexander Valley 1995: Ripe and flavorful, with bright cherry, currant, plum, sage and mineral flavors that are complex and focused. The tannins are a bit rough and chewy now, so cellar short-term. Drink through 2004.–J.L. • $22 • (10/15/1998) • **87**
Merlot Alexander Valley 1997: Shows the herbal side of Merlot but the plum and blackberry flavors are ripe and focused, finishing with soft tannins and notes of anise and toasted oak. Drink now through 2003.–J.L. • $15 • (10/15/1999) • **86**
Merlot Alexander Valley 1995 • $14 • (12/31/1997) • **85**
Merlot Alexander Valley 1994 • $13 • (11/30/1996) • **82**
Merlot Alexander Valley 1993 • $10 • (7/31/1996) • **88**
Merlot Alexander Valley 1992 • $10 • (11/15/1994) • **88**
Merlot Sonoma County 1996: Features plum, toasted oak and herbal notes on a soft-textured frame, but turns slightly dry on the finish. Drink now through 2003.–J.L. • $14 • (10/15/1999) • **84**
Pinot Noir Monterey County 1995 • $12 • (1/31/1997) • **83**
Pinot Noir Monterey County 1994 • $10 • (10/15/1995) • **84**
Pinot Noir Monterey County 1993 • $10 • (5/15/1995) • **84**
Pinot Noir Monterey Pinnacles 1998: Cinammon and stewed strawberry flavors are detracted by an earthy note. Drink now.–J.L. • $15 • (5/15/2000) • **80**
Pinot Noir Monterey Pinnacles 1997: Pleasant and soft-textured, with cherry, berry, cola and spicy notes that linger on the finish. Drink now through 2003.–J.L. • $14 • (9/15/1999) • **85**
Pinot Noir Monterey Pinnacles 1996 • $12 • (11/30/1997) • **87**
Pinot Noir Monterey Reserve 1997: Serves up an attractive range of black cherry, cola, raspberry and spicy notes. Finishing with a burst of fruit and dry tannins. Drink now through 2006.–J.L. • $22 • (5/15/2000) • **87**
Pinot Noir Monterey Reserve 1996: Elegant, with wonderfully ripe plum and black cherry flavors, supple, rounded tannins and a pretty focus, finishing with a rich, chocolaty taste. Drink now through 2005.–J.L. • $18 • (9/15/1999) • **88**
Pinot Noir Monterey Reserve 1995 • $18 • (8/31/1997) • **88**
Sangiovese Alexander Valley 1994 • $19 • (12/15/1996) • **83**
Sangiovese Alexander Valley 1993 • $20 • (11/30/1995) • **85**
Sangiovese Alexander Valley 1991 • $12 • (12/15/1993) • **83**

ESTATE BACCALA | CALIFORNIA

Merlot Alexander Valley 1984 • $10 • (2/28/1987) • **72**
Merlot Napa Valley 1996: Up front it's supple, with ripe strawberry and plum flavors and delicate herb notes, but the tannins firm up on the finish and there's a slightly bitter edge. Needs food. Drink now through 2002.–H.S. • $12 • (10/15/1999) • **84**
Merlot Napa Valley 1995: Smoke, toast and chocolate aromas lead the way. A little green on the palate, but shows pretty layers of herb, cassis and blackberry. Tannins are a touch astringent. Drink now through 2002. • $16 • (7/31/1998) • **84**
Merlot Napa Valley 1994 • $14 • (11/30/1997) • **88**
Merlot Napa Valley 1992 • $15 • (6/15/1996) • **74**
Merlot Napa Valley 1991 • $14 • (7/31/1994) • **86**
Merlot Napa Valley 1990 • $10 • (8/31/1993) HR • **90**
Zinfandel Mendocino County Old Vines 1996 • $16 • (6/15/1998) • **84**
Zinfandel Mendocino County Old Vines 1995 • $16 • (5/31/1998) • **85**
Zinfandel Mendocino County Old Vines 1994 • $15 • (12/15/1996) • **89**

ETUDE | CALIFORNIA

Cabernet Sauvignon Napa Valley 1996: This tight, crisp California Cabernet strings together a tasty ensemble of spicy, cedary currant, dried cherry and anise, finishing with a seamless band of tannins. Needs time. Best from 2003 through 2010.–J.L. • $50 • (4/30/2000) CS • **92**
Cabernet Sauvignon Napa Valley 1995: Sleek and elegant, with complex, detailed flavors of anise, cedar, currant and black cherry, it turns supple on the finish, where hints of olive and spice emerge. Drink now through 2008.–J.L. • $40 • (1/31/1999) • **92**
Cabernet Sauvignon Napa Valley 1994 • $43 Ⓐ • (9/30/1997) • **93**
Cabernet Sauvignon Napa Valley 1993 • $30 • (11/15/1996) • **90**

Key: SS—Spectator Selection. CS—Cellar Selection. HR—Highly Recommended. $NA—Price not available. (BT)—Barrel tasting. Ⓐ—Auction Price. For a key to the tasters' initials, see "How to Use These Listings."
Dates in parentheses represent the issues in which the ratings were published.

Cabernet Sauvignon Napa Valley 1992 • $30 • (11/30/1995) HR • **93**
Cabernet Sauvignon Napa Valley 1989: Hitting its stride. Intense, focused, with minty currant, cherry and cedary oak flavors, finishing with integrated tannins and good length. Just about there. (1989 California Cabernet retrospective tasting). Drink through 2008.–J.L. • $NA • (8/31/1999) • **89**
Cabernet Sauvignon Napa Valley 1987 • $41 Ⓐ • (12/15/1997) • **92**
Cabernet Sauvignon Napa Valley 1986 • $20 • (9/30/1989) • **92**
Cabernet Sauvignon Napa Valley 1985 • $48 Ⓐ • (12/15/1988) • **92**
Pinot Noir Carneros 1997: Lean, with a minty-menthol edge to the modest cherry and berryish flavors, turning firm and tannic. Give it time to see if anything develops. Drink through 2004.–J.L. • $35 • (9/15/1999) • **83**
Pinot Noir Carneros 1996: Dense, concentrated, firmly tannic, with an earthy, leathery, beefy edge to the ripe cherry, berry, plum and spicy notes. Finishes with complex flavors, and is quite concentrated. Short-term cellaring should bring the tannins into check. Drink through 2004.–J.L. • $30 • (8/31/1998) • **88**
Pinot Noir Carneros 1995 • $30 • (10/31/1997) • **88**
Pinot Noir Carneros 1994 • $27 • (12/15/1996) • **88**
Pinot Noir Carneros 1993 • $27 • (12/31/1995) • **84**
Pinot Noir Carneros 1992 • $24 • (1/31/1995) • **89**
Pinot Noir Carneros 1990 • $25 • (2/28/1993) • **88**
Pinot Noir Carneros 1989 • $20 • (11/15/1991) • **85**
Pinot Noir Carneros Rosé 1996 • $12 • (9/30/1997) • **83**
Pinot Noir Napa Valley 1988 • $20 • (12/15/1990) • **86**
Pinot Noir Napa Valley 1985 • $16 • (6/15/1988) • **83**

EVESHAM WOOD | OREGON

Pinot Noir Willamette Valley 1996: Light and pretty, with appealing plum, tea and spice flavors on a smooth frame. Drink now through 2001.–H.S. • $20 • (11/15/1998) • **85**
Pinot Noir Willamette Valley 1995 • $15 • (11/30/1997) • **81**
Pinot Noir Willamette Valley 1986 • $11 • (6/15/1988) • **84**
Pinot Noir Willamette Valley Cuvée J 1993 • $26 • (2/29/1996) • **86**
Pinot Noir Willamette Valley Unfiltered 1992 • $13 • (11/30/1994) • **80**
Pinot Noir Willamette Valley Unfiltered Cuvée J 1992 • $35 • (11/30/1994) • **86**

EXPRESSIONS | CALIFORNIA

Cabernet Sauvignon Napa Valley 1993 • $10 • (4/30/1996) • **87**
Cabernet Sauvignon North Coast 1994 • $10 • (9/30/1997) • **82**
Merlot Sonoma County 1995 • $13 • (2/28/1998) • **85**
Merlot Sonoma County 1994 • $12 • (6/15/1996) • **87**
Sangiovese California 1995 • $14 • (12/15/1997) • **79**
Sangiovese California 1994 • $12 • (4/30/1996) • **86**
Zinfandel Sonoma County 1993 • $12 • (4/30/1996) • **85**

EYRIE | OREGON

Chardonnay Willamette Valley 1996 • $18 • (1/31/1998) • **88**
Chardonnay Willamette Valley Reserve 1998: Light and simple, with herb and caramel notes sneaking past the modest apple flavors on the finish. Drink now.–H.S. • $30 • (5/15/2000) • **80**
Chardonnay Willamette Valley Reserve 1997: Light and bright, but a bitter note intrudes on the lime and apple flavors.–H.S. • $30 • (5/15/2000) • **77**
Pinot Gris Willamette Valley 1998: Ripe and round, a nice mouthful of peach, spice and almond notes that linger on the slightly raw finish. Drink now.–H.S. • $16 • (5/15/2000) • **87**
Pinot Gris Willamette Valley 1997: Bright and refreshing, generous with its melon and pear flavors, finishing soft and plump. Drink now.–H.S. • $18 • (4/30/1999) • **87**
Pinot Gris Willamette Valley 1996 • $16 • (2/28/1998) • **88**
Pinot Noir Oregon Reserve 1989 • $25 • (11/30/1994) • **86**
Pinot Noir Willamette Valley 1997: Very light in color, with light berry and root beer notes echoing on the delicate finish. Drink now.–H.S. • $20 • (4/30/1999) • **82**
Pinot Noir Willamette Valley 1996 • $20 • (2/28/1998) • **80**
Pinot Noir Willamette Valley 1991 • $14 • (11/30/1994) • **83**
Pinot Noir Willamette Valley 1990 • $18 • (2/28/1993) • **77**
Pinot Noir Willamette Valley 1987 • $20 • (2/15/1990) • **80**
Pinot Noir Willamette Valley 1986 • $20 • (6/15/1988) • **83**
Pinot Noir Willamette Valley 1985 • $19 • (2/15/1990) • **91**
Pinot Noir Willamette Valley 1984 • $15 • (8/31/1986) • **84**
Pinot Noir Willamette Valley 1983 • $30 • (2/15/1990) • **87**
Pinot Noir Willamette Valley Reserve 1995: Light color looks old already, with aromas and flavors to match. A fragile wine with orange peel, mush-

room and berry flavors on the smooth finish. Drink now.–H.S. • $37 • (4/30/1999) • **85**

Pinot Noir Willamette Valley Reserve 1994 • $40 • (2/28/1998) • **85**
Pinot Noir Willamette Valley Reserve 1989 • $18 Ⓐ • (2/28/1993) • **80**
Pinot Noir Willamette Valley Reserve 1987 • $19 Ⓐ • (2/15/1990) • **86**
Pinot Noir Willamette Valley Special Selection 1992 • $11 • (11/30/1994) • **84**
Pinot Noir Yamhill County Reserve 1990 • $32 • (2/28/1997) • **87**

FACELLI | WASHINGTON

Cabernet Sauvignon Columbia Valley 1994: Chewy, big-boned, a little rough in texture, with lots of mint flavor coursing through the ripe cherry and currant. Needs cellaring; best from 2001 through 2004.–H.S. • $25 • (8/31/1998) • **85**
Cabernet Sauvignon Columbia Valley 1993 • $25 • (9/15/1997) • **83**
Cabernet Sauvignon Columbia Valley 1992 • $20 • (9/30/1995) • **82**
Cabernet Sauvignon Columbia Valley 1991 • $25 • (7/31/1994) • **83**
Lemberger Yakima Valley 1994 • $12 • (9/15/1996) • **86**
Lemberger Yakima Valley Limited Bottling 1993 • $12 • (9/30/1995) • **85**
Merlot Columbia Valley 1995: Dark cherry and spice flavors have a hard edge of tannin and an acrid whiff that lowers the charm level on the finish.–H.S. • $20 • (9/15/1998) • **79**
Merlot Columbia Valley 1994 • $17 • (9/15/1997) • **87**
Merlot Columbia Valley 1992 • $15 • (9/30/1995) • **81**
Merlot Columbia Valley 1991 • $15 • (9/30/1994) • **83**
Pinot Noir Washington 1992 • $20 • (9/30/1994) • **85**

FALL CREEK | TEXAS

Cabernet Sauvignon Texas 1989 • $13 • (2/29/1992) • **75**
Cabernet Sauvignon Texas 1988 • $13 • (7/15/1991) • **78**
Carnelian Llano County 1988 • $13 • (7/15/1991) • **73**
Cascade Texas 1996 • $NA • (2/28/1998) • **73**
Chenin Blanc Texas 1996 • $NA • (2/28/1998) • **82**
Granite Reserve Texas 1996 • $9 • (5/15/1998) • **82**
Meritus Texas 1996: Good dark plum and sweet cherry flavors, but with pretty rough tannins. Finishes on a stewy note. Tasted twice, with consistent notes. A blend: 54 percent Merlot, 40 percent Cabernet Sauvignon, 6 percent Malbec. Drink now.–K.M. • $29 • (10/15/1998) • **78**
Merlot Texas 1996 • $NA • (12/31/1997) • **80**
Sauvignon Blanc Texas 1997: Here's a very good value in Sauvignon Blanc from an unexpected quarter. Smooth-textured and nicely fruity, it's an agreeable white wine whose pear and apple notes linger on the finish. Drink now. • $8 • (11/15/1998) • **85**
Sauvignon Blanc Texas 1996 • $NA • (12/31/1997) • **78**
Sweet Jo Texas 1996 • $NA • (12/31/1997) • **86**
Vintner's Cuvée Texas 1996 • $NA • (2/28/1998) • **78**

FANUCCHI | CALIFORNIA

Trousseau Gris Russian River Valley Wood Road Vineyard 1996 • $13 • (3/31/1998) • **82**
Zinfandel Russian River Valley Fanucchi Wood-Road Vineyard Old Vine 1997: Tightly wound, with firm, crisp tannins and a complex core of wild berry, raspberry and plum-laced Zinfandel flavors. Drink now through 2002.–J.L. • $39 • (6/30/1999) • **87**
Zinfandel Russian River Valley Old Vine 1996 • $33 • (3/31/1998) • **89**
Zinfandel Russian River Valley Old Vine 1995 • $26 • (4/30/1997) • **91**
Zinfandel Russian River Valley Old Vine 1994 • $22 • (10/15/1995) • **84**

FAR NIENTE | CALIFORNIA

Cabernet Sauvignon Napa Valley 1998: Firm, focused, elegant, with a spicy cherry and currant core and well-integrated tannins.–J.L. • $NA • (8/31/1999) (BT) • **90-94**
Cabernet Sauvignon Napa Valley 1997: Complex, with an intriguing interplay of ripe cherry, currant, plum, spice, anise and cedary oak. Wonderful finesse and polish, depth and concentration.–J.L. • $NA • (8/31/1998) (BT) • **95-99**
Cabernet Sauvignon Napa Valley 1996: Shopping for your cellar? Stash this California Cab away for the next two to ten years and you'll be rewarded. It's deliciously complex, with earth, cedar, plum, currant, black cherry and spice flavors, gaining depth and richness on the dry, firm finish.–J.L. • $77 • (6/15/1999) CS • **91**
Cabernet Sauvignon Napa Valley 1995 • $70 • (6/30/1998) HR • **92**
Cabernet Sauvignon Napa Valley 1994 • $55 • (2/28/1997) • **91**
Cabernet Sauvignon Napa Valley 1993 • $45 • (8/31/1996) • **86**
Cabernet Sauvignon Napa Valley 1992 • $45 • (11/15/1995) HR • **93**
Cabernet Sauvignon Napa Valley 1991 • $40 • (9/15/1994) • **89**
Cabernet Sauvignon Napa Valley 1990 • $36 • (9/15/1993) • **88**
Cabernet Sauvignon Napa Valley 1989: Supple texture, with mature, earthy, leathery flavors and just a touch of currant and cherry woven in with the cedary tobacco notes. (1989 California Cabernet retrospective tasting). Drink now.–J.L. • $36 • (8/31/1999) • **85**
Cabernet Sauvignon Napa Valley 1988: Well balanced for the vintage, with ripe, spicy currant, plum and cedar notes, turning supple and harmonious on the finish. Not a great Far Niente, but a pleasantly balanced one. (1988 California Cabernet retrospective tasting). Drink now through 2002.–J.L. • $36 • (11/15/1998) • **88**
Cabernet Sauvignon Napa Valley 1987 • $47 Ⓐ • (12/15/1997) • **91**
Cabernet Sauvignon Napa Valley 1986 • $58 Ⓐ • (9/30/1989) • **91**
Cabernet Sauvignon Napa Valley 1985 • $75 Ⓐ • (12/31/1988) • **90**
Cabernet Sauvignon Napa Valley 1984 • $25 • (10/15/1987) • **92**
Cabernet Sauvignon Napa Valley 1983 • $25 • (6/16/1986) HR • **93**
Cabernet Sauvignon Napa Valley 1982 • $25 • (9/16/1985) • **84**
Chardonnay Napa Valley 1998: Simple, with a pleasant core of earthy pear, melon, apple and spice. Best from 2001 through 2006.–J.L. • $44 • (4/30/2000) • **85**
Chardonnay Napa Valley 1997: Tight, with a flinty, mineral edge to the center of pear, nutmeg and hazelnut. Needs short-term cellaring to unfold. Drink through 2004.–J.L. • $44 • (4/30/1999) • **88**
Chardonnay Napa Valley 1996 • $40 • (6/30/1998) • **90**

FARALLON | CALIFORNIA

Cabernet Sauvignon North Coast 1997: Round and accessible, with vanilla and currant flavors that mingle with soft tannins at the finish. Drink now through 2004.–J.L. • $10 • (4/30/2000) • **85**
Chardonnay Central Coast 1998: A solid California Chardonnay at a modest price, delivering a mouthful of vanilla and lush tropical flavors that really persist on the finish, turning lemony. Drink now through 2004.–J.L. • $10 • (2/29/2000) • **88**
Chardonnay North Coast 1998: This tasty California Chardonnay is wallet-friendly too, with vanilla, butter, ripe pear and coconut flavors with good concentration and length. Drink now through 2001.–J.L. • $10 • (4/30/2000) • **85**
Merlot North Coast 1997: Ripe, with chocolate, dill and black cherry flavors. Intensity and soft tannins combine nicely with vanilla notes in the finish. Drink now through 2004.–J.L. • $10 • (6/30/2000) • **85**

FARELLA-PARK | CALIFORNIA

Cabernet Sauvignon Napa Valley 1996: Bitter, green and earthy. Quite disappointing. Lacks ripe fruit.–J.L. • $32 • (4/30/2000) • **74**
Cabernet Sauvignon Napa Valley 1991 • $25 • (2/28/1995) • **85**
Merlot Napa Valley 1996: Tastes green, unripe, bitter and metallic. Hard to swallow.–J.L. • $24 • (6/15/2000) • **72**
Merlot Napa Valley 1995: Attractive, with a good balance of licorice, tar, cassis, plum, spice and leather notes. Somewhat light on the palate, with a moderate finish. Drink now through 2002. • $24 • (9/15/1998) • **87**
Merlot Napa Valley 1990 • $20 • (2/28/1995) • **84**
Merlot Napa Valley 1988 • $18 • (8/31/1993) • **84**

FARRELL, GARY | CALIFORNIA

Cabernet Sauvignon Sonoma County 1987 • $16 • (10/31/1990) • **87**
Cabernet Sauvignon Sonoma County Hillside Selection 1995: A harmonious wine, on the light side, with pretty blackberry and herb notes and a touch of firm tannin on the finish. Drink now.–H.S. • $24 • (10/31/1998) • **86**
Cabernet Sauvignon Sonoma County Ladi's Vineyard 1994 • $20 • (11/15/1997) • **83**
Cabernet Sauvignon Sonoma County Ladi's Vineyard 1993 • $20 • (3/31/1997) • **88**
Cabernet Sauvignon Sonoma County Ladi's Vineyard 1992 • $20 • (7/31/1995) • **89**
Cabernet Sauvignon Sonoma County Ladi's Vineyard 1991 • $18 • (8/31/1994) • **87**
Cabernet Sauvignon Sonoma County Ladi's Vineyard 1990 • $18 • (11/15/1992) • **90**
Cabernet Sauvignon Sonoma County Ladi's Vineyard 1989 • $18 • (11/15/1992) • **81**

FARRELL, GARY

Cabernet Sauvignon Sonoma County Ladi's Vineyard 1988 • $18 • (8/31/1991) • **86**
Chardonnay Russian River Valley Allen Vineyard 1996 • $28 • (6/30/1998) • **93**
Chardonnay Russian River Valley Rochioli Vineyard 1997: Complex—from its initial toasty oak flavors and ripe pear, apple and spicy nuances to its rich butterscotch aftertaste. Drink now through 2002.–J.L. • $30 • (4/30/1999) • **91**
Chardonnay Santa Barbara County Bien Nacido Vineyard 1998: Racy, with an earthy grapefruit twinge to the cedary pineapple and citrus flavors. Straightens out on the finish, where it offers depth. Drink now through 2004.–J.L. • $28 • (5/15/2000) • **86**
Chardonnay Santa Barbara County Bien Nacido Vineyard 1996 • $22 • (4/30/1998) • **86**
Encounter Sonoma County 1996: Lean yet focused, this serves up a blend of blackberry, wild cherry, cedar and sage flavors. Tannins are firm but ripe, and the finish is moderate. Will improve with time. Best from 2002 through 2006. • $42 • (11/15/1999) • **87**
Merlot Russian River Valley 1997: Tight, with a firm band of currant, plum and wild berry that's sharply focused. Finishes with crisp tannins. Best from 2001 through 2007.–J.L. • $32 • (5/15/2000) • **87**
Merlot Russian River Valley 1996: Pretty plum and cedar notes on the nose are followed by blackberry and herbs on the palate. A bit lean, however, finishing somewhat tart. Drink now through 2003. • $24 • (10/15/1999) • **84**
Merlot Russian River Valley 1995 • $23 • (4/30/1998) • **88**
Merlot Russian River Valley Calypso Vineyard 1997: Lean and spicy, with racy black cherry, raspberry and spice and firm, dry tannins. Drink now through 2004.–J.L. • $24 • (5/15/2000) • **84**
Merlot Sonoma County Ladi's Vineyard 1996: Good intensity, with ripe plum, currant and herbal flavors that are clean and focused. Best to cellar short-term. Try now through 2002.–J.L. • $30 • (5/31/1999) • **88**
Merlot Sonoma County Ladi's Vineyard 1995: Firm and compact, with a narrow range of cedar, currant, herb and tar. Turns tannic and leathery on the finish. Definitely needs time to soften and evolve. Drink through 2006.–J.L. • $28 • (9/30/1998) • **86**
Merlot Sonoma County Ladi's Vineyard 1994 • $20 • (6/30/1997) • **87**
Merlot Sonoma County Ladi's Vineyard 1993 • $20 • (4/30/1996) • **87**
Merlot Sonoma County Ladi's Vineyard 1992 • $20 • (7/31/1995) • **83**
Merlot Sonoma County Ladi's Vineyard 1991 • $17 • (6/15/1994) • **88**
Merlot Sonoma County Ladi's Vineyard 1990 • $16 • (4/15/1993) • **88**
Pinot Noir Anderson Valley 1995 • $30 • (5/15/1997) • **86**
Pinot Noir Russian River Valley 1998: Fresh, with juicy, appealing, tart cherry and wild berry. Drink now through 2004.–J.L. • $30 • (5/15/2000) • **85**
Pinot Noir Russian River Valley 1996 • $23 • (6/30/1998) • **89**
Pinot Noir Russian River Valley 1995 • $20 • (5/15/1997) • **87**
Pinot Noir Russian River Valley 1994 • $19 • (7/31/1996) • **90**
Pinot Noir Russian River Valley 1991 • $18 • (2/28/1993) • **88**
Pinot Noir Russian River Valley 1990 • $16 • (12/31/1992) • **87**
Pinot Noir Russian River Valley 1989 • $16 • (7/31/1991) • **88**
Pinot Noir Russian River Valley 1988 • $16 • (10/31/1990) • **88**
Pinot Noir Russian River Valley 1986 • $15 • (6/15/1988) • **90**
Pinot Noir Russian River Valley 1984 • $12 • (4/15/1987) • **79**
Pinot Noir Russian River Valley 1983 • $12 • (8/31/1986) • **88**
Pinot Noir Russian River Valley Allen Vineyard 1997: Tight, with a medium-range band of spicy cherry, wild berry, strawberry, anise and spice, finishing with crisp tannins. Drink now through 2004.–J.L. • $40 • (11/30/1999) • **87**
Pinot Noir Russian River Valley Allen Vineyard 1995 • $40 • (12/31/1997) HR • **90**
Pinot Noir Russian River Valley Allen Vineyard 1994 • $40 • (11/15/1996) • **92**
Pinot Noir Russian River Valley Allen Vineyard 1992 • $32 • (11/30/1994) • **88**
Pinot Noir Russian River Valley Allen Vineyard 1991 • $32 • (2/28/1994) • **87**
Pinot Noir Russian River Valley Allen Vineyard 1990 • $28 • (3/31/1997) • **93**
Pinot Noir Russian River Valley Allen Vineyard 1988 • $25 • (10/31/1990) • **87**
Pinot Noir Sonoma County Howard Allen Vineyard 1987 • $20 • (2/15/1990) • **84**
Pinot Noir Sonoma County Howard Allen Vineyard 1986 • $15 • (3/31/1997) • **91**
Pinot Noir Russian River Valley Olivet Lane Vineyard 1994 • $30 • (6/30/1996) • **88**
Pinot Noir Russian River Valley Rochioli Vineyard 1997: Starts out earthy, with leather and mineral notes, but works its way into more complex plum and black cherry flavor. Finishes with enough tannin to consider short-term cellaring. Drink through 2006.–J.L. • $50 • (11/30/1999) • **88**
Pinot Noir Russian River Valley Rochioli Vineyard 1995 • $50 • (12/31/1997) • **92**
Pinot Noir Russian River Valley Rochioli Vineyard 1994 • $50 • (11/15/1996) • **94**

Key: SS—Spectator Selection. CS—Cellar Selection. HR—Highly Recommended. $NA—Price not available. (BT)—Barrel tasting. (A)—Auction Price.
For a key to the tasters' initials, see "How to Use These Listings."
Dates in parentheses represent the issues in which the ratings were published.

Pinot Noir Russian River Valley Stiling Vineyard 1997: Medium in weight and intensity, but well focused on the crisp, snappy cherry, raspberry, earth and wild berry flavors, firming up on the finish. Short-term cellaring is advised. Drink through 2006.–J.L. • $32 • (9/15/1999) • **88**
Pinot Noir Santa Barbara County Bien Nacido Vineyard 1997: Medium-weight, with ripe, supple cherry, plum and berry flavors that are tightly focused but seemingly unevolved at this stage. Give it time. Drink through 2005.–J.L. • $30 • (9/15/1999) • **86**
Pinot Noir Santa Barbara County Bien Nacido Vineyard 1996 • $28 • (6/30/1998) • **87**
Pinot Noir Santa Barbara County Bien Nacido Vineyard 1992 • $28 • (11/30/1994) • **85**
Pinot Noir Santa Barbara County Bien Nacido Vineyard 1990 • $24 • (9/30/1992) • **88**
Zinfandel Dry Creek Valley Bradford Mountain 1997: Smooth and elegant, with vibrant black cherry, wild berry and cedar notes, finishing with supple yet firm tannins. Drink through 2008.–J.L. • $30 • (11/30/1999) • **88**
Zinfandel Dry Creek Valley Grist Ranch 1995 • $20 • (6/15/1998) • **88**
Zinfandel Dry Creek Valley Maple Vineyard 1997: Serves up lots of ripe cherry, wild berry and raspberry flavors that are elegant, polished and of moderate depth. Drink now through 2004.–J.L. • $30 • (11/30/1999) • **86**
Zinfandel Russian River Valley 1995 • $20 • (8/31/1997) • **90**
Zinfandel Russian River Valley 1992: Bright and lively, with juicy cherry, raspberry and wild berry flavors. Turns elegant and polished on the finish, where the tannins are well integrated. (Zinfandel retrospective tasting). Drink now through 2001.–J.L. • $15 • (6/30/1999) • **89**
Zinfandel Russian River Valley 1991 • $15 • (4/30/1993) • **88**
Zinfandel Russian River Valley Collins Vineyard 1994 • $16 • (4/30/1996) • **88**
Zinfandel Russian River Valley Collins Vineyard 1993 • $15 • (7/31/1995) • **89**
Zinfandel Russian River Valley Collins Vineyard 1990 • $14 • (10/15/1992) • **88**
Zinfandel Sonoma County 1985 • $10 • (4/30/1988) • **91**
Zinfandel Sonoma County Old Vine Selection 1997: Serves up a range of black cherry, wild berry, raspberry and plum flavors, turning spicy and dry, with firm tannins. Drink now through 2005.–J.L. • $24 • (12/15/1999) • **88**
Zinfandel Sonoma County Old Vine Selection 1996 • $22 • (6/15/1998) • **86**

FATHOM | CALIFORNIA

Cabernet Franc Santa Ynez Valley 1992 • $17 • (2/28/1995) • **70**
Cabernet Sauvignon Santa Ynez Valley 1992 • $24 • (11/15/1994) • **86**
Merlot Santa Ynez Valley 1992 • $18 • (2/28/1995) • **84**

FATTORIA ENOTRIA | CALIFORNIA

Dolcetto Mendocino 1997: Soft, with simple plummy flavors and tobacco overtones that linger nicely on the finish. Drink now through 2003.–J.L. • $16 • (4/30/2000) • **84**

FENESTRA | CALIFORNIA

Cabernet Sauvignon Livermore Valley 1991 • $11 • (6/15/1995) • **79**
Cabernet Sauvignon Livermore Valley 1990 • $12 • (11/15/1993) • **82**
Cabernet Sauvignon Livermore Valley 1989 • $13 • (11/15/1992) • **79**
Cabernet Sauvignon Livermore Valley 1988 • $12 • (11/15/1991) • **85**
Cabernet Sauvignon Monterey Smith & Hook Vineyard 1989 • $14 • (11/15/1993) • **79**
Cabernet Sauvignon Monterey Smith & Hook Vineyard 1988 • $15 • (11/15/1992) • **86**
Cabernet Sauvignon Monterey Smith & Hook Vineyard 1987 • $14 • (11/15/1991) • **75**
Cabernet Sauvignon Monterey Smith & Hook Vineyard 1986 • $14 • (11/15/1993) • **83**
Cabernet-Merlot Livermore Valley 1990 • $35/1.5 liter • (12/15/1995) • **78**
Chardonnay Livermore Valley 1996: Emphasis is on the refreshing, zingy fruit, with sweet, but well-focused flavors of fresh pineapple. Well balanced, with hints of vanilla and toast. Drink now. • $15 • (7/31/1998) • **84**
Merlot Livermore Valley 1995: Simple and dilute, with light herb and cherry notes. Soft and herbal on the finish. Drink now.–J.L. • $14 • (10/15/1998) • **78**
Merlot Livermore Valley 1991 • $11 • (9/15/1994) • **83**
Merlot Livermore Valley 1990 • $13 • (9/15/1994) • **78**
Merlot Livermore Valley 1989 • $13 • (5/31/1992) • **87**
Merlot Livermore Valley Special Reserve 1989 • $40/1.5 liter • (5/31/1992) • **89**
Merlot Sonoma County 1986 • $11 • (10/15/1989) • **83**
Zinfandel Livermore Valley 1990 • $9 • (9/30/1993) • **80**
Zinfandel Livermore Valley 1989 • $9 • (10/15/1992) • **87**
Zinfandel Livermore Valley Special Reserve 1991 • $11 • (10/15/1995) • **78**

FERMENTATIONS & MORE | CALIFORNIA

Cabernet Sauvignon San Luis Obispo Silver Canyon Vineyard 1993 • $16 • (11/30/1996) • **70**
Zinfandel Paso Robles Benito Dusi Vineyard 1993 • $14 • (4/30/1996) • **88**

FERRARI-CARANO | CALIFORNIA

Cabernet Sauvignon Alexander Valley 1997: Dark, grapey and concentrated, on the tart side with wild berry, cherry and raspberry; reduced now, with firm tannins.–J.L. • $NA • (8/31/1998) (BT) • **90-94**
Cabernet Sauvignon Alexander Valley 1988 • $14 • (8/31/1992) • **84**
Cabernet Sauvignon Alexander Valley 1987 • $18 • (7/15/1991) • **84**
Cabernet Sauvignon Alexander Valley 1986 • $18 • (9/15/1990) • **80**
Cabernet Sauvignon Alexander Valley Reserve 1998: Ripe, rich, vibrant plum and black cherry abound in this wine, turning firm, earthy and spicy. Will be a component of either the Trésor Reserve, a blend, or the new Tre Monte Cabernet Sauvignon bottling.–J.L. • $NA • (8/31/1999) (BT) • **90-94**
Cabernet Sauvignon Alexander Valley Reserve 1988 • $40 • (11/15/1993) • **86**
Cabernet Sauvignon Alexander Valley Special Selection 1987 • $24 • (3/31/1993) • **83**
Cabernet Sauvignon Sonoma County 1996 • $NA • (2/02/1997) (BT) • **90-94**
Cabernet Sauvignon Sonoma County 1995: Firm, ripe and offering a wide range of flavors stretching from herb, mineral, sage and spice to currant, anise and tar, turning firmly tannic on the finish. Best from 2001 through 2008.–J.L. • $35 • (10/15/1999) • **88**
Cabernet Sauvignon Sonoma County 1994: Very good core of currant, black cherry and berry is ripe and flavorful, if a bit rough around the edges. Tannic finish needs about a year. Drink through 2004.–J.L. • $28 • (10/31/1998) • **87**
Cabernet Sauvignon Sonoma County 1993 • $23 • (11/15/1997) • **87**
Cabernet Sauvignon Sonoma County 1992 • $22 • (11/15/1996) • **89**
Cabernet Sauvignon Sonoma County 1991 • $16 • (9/15/1995) • **86**
Cabernet Sauvignon Sonoma County 1990 • $15 • (9/30/1994) • **89**
Chardonnay Alexander Valley 1998: Moderately ripe and rich, with a touch of peach, pear, fig and mineral flavors. Drink now.–J.L. • $25 • (6/15/2000) • **86**
Chardonnay Alexander Valley 1997: Here's a bottle of California's favorite white in a ripe and rich style. It's complex and concentrated, with lovely pear, apricot, tangerine and melon flavors that gain in opulence and pick up a pleasingly spicy note. Drink now through 2002.–J.L. • $23 • (6/15/1999) SS • **92**
Chardonnay Alexander Valley 1996: Elegant, even delicate in style, this northern Sonoma-grown Chardonnay shows a tasty mix of spicy pear, apple, melon and light oak shadings, finishes with a complex interplay of fruit and oak. Drink now through 2000.–J.L. • $21 • (7/31/1998) SS • **90**
Chardonnay Alexander Valley Tre Terre 1998: Elegant and spicy, with pear, nectarine, citrus and mineral notes, holding its focus on a lengthy finish. Drink now.–J.L. • $38 • (6/15/2000) • **87**
Chardonnay Alexander Valley Tre Terre 1997: Ripe, with smoky, toasty oak and a broad array of complex flavors, with layers of fig, pear, butterscotch and butter soaring on the finish. Drink now through 2002.–J.L. • $37 • (7/31/1999) • **92**
Chardonnay Alexander Valley Vineyards of TreMonte 1998: Simple, with passion fruit, mango and spicy pear, picking up a nutmeg edge. Drink now.–J.L. • $28 • (6/15/2000) • **86**
Chardonnay Alexander Valley Vineyards of TreMonte 1997: Well oaked, with lots of vanilla bean and toasty oak flavors that add a nice touch to the ripe, elegant core of pear and apple. Smoky aftertaste. Drink now through 2002. –J.L. • $42 • (6/30/1999) • **92**
Chardonnay Alexander Valley Vineyards of TreMonte 1996: Smooth, ripe, rich and creamy, with pretty apple, pear and spicy fig and vanilla-oak shadings. Turns elegant and holds its flavor on the long, lingering aftertaste. Drink now through 2001.–J.L. • $42 • (11/30/1998) • **92**
Chardonnay Napa-Sonoma Counties Reserve 1997: Ripe and spicy, with complex baked apple, pear and spice notes, finishing with smoky, toasty oak notes. Drink now.–J.L. • $32 • (6/15/2000) • **88**
Chardonnay Napa-Sonoma Counties Reserve 1996: This outstanding white from two of the variety's California hot-spots is sure to please as it serves up a wide array of smoky, toasty flavors that run deep and long, with complementary ripe fig, apricot, melon and spice in proportion and a long, rich aftertaste. Drink now through 2002.–J.L. • $32 • (6/30/1999) HR • **93**
Fumé Blanc Sonoma County 1998: Bright, with a core of grapefruit, lemon and herb. Refreshing, offering hints of fresh-cut hay and a pretty, long finish. Drink now. • $12 • (6/15/1999) • **89**
Fumé Blanc Sonoma County 1997: Peaches and fresh pea flavors embrace the palate in this light-bodied wine. On the finish are echoes of grapefruit and melon. Drink now. • $12 • (9/15/1998) • **86**
Fumé Blanc Sonoma County 1996 • $11 • (6/30/1997) • **87**
Fumé Blanc Sonoma County Reserve 1998: Struggles to find a focus, with earthy citrus, apple and sweet pea flavors of modest depth and proportion. Drink now.–J.L. • $18 • (5/15/2000) • **82**
Fumé Blanc Sonoma County Reserve 1997: Full-bodied, with zingy acidity, this richly textured white sports a broad spectrum of flavors, including melon, lemon, peach, grapefruit, fig, honey and herb, that mingle nicely. The finish is quite lemony and fairly long. Lovely now through 2002. • $18 • (1/31/1999) HR • **89**
Fumé Blanc Sonoma County Reserve 1996 • $18 • (1/31/1998) • **87**
Merlot Alexander Valley 1987 • $17 • (7/31/1990) • **84**
Merlot Alexander Valley 1986 • $15 • (6/30/1989) • **87**
Merlot Alexander Valley Vineyards of TreMonte 1996: A touch earthy, with tight tannins and a crisp band of cherry, berry, sage and spice. Finishes with complex notes. Drink now through 2004.–J.L. • $42 • (10/15/1999) • **86**
Merlot Sonoma County 1997: Crisp, with a light plum jam and cedary notes, finishing with a tannic bite. Drink now through 2005.–J.L. • $23 • (6/30/2000) • **85**
Merlot Sonoma County 1996: Simple, with grapey cherry and currant flavors that are firm. Offers modest depth. Drink now through 2002.–J.L. • $23 • (10/15/1999) • **83**
Merlot Sonoma County 1995: Offers pleasant cherry and berry flavors with a dash of spice, but then the tannins show up, turning it dry and chewy. Drink now through 2003.–J.L. • $23 • (9/30/1998) • **84**
Merlot Sonoma County 1994 • $23 • (9/30/1997) • **87**
Merlot Sonoma County 1993 • $23 • (6/30/1996) • **83**
Merlot Sonoma County 1992 • $20 • (9/30/1995) • **89**
Merlot Sonoma County 1991 • $17 • (5/31/1994) • **89**
Merlot Sonoma County 1990 • $15 • (7/15/1993) • **81**
Merlot Sonoma County 1989 • $15 • (5/31/1992) • **86**
Merlot Sonoma County 1988 • $18 • (8/31/1991) • **85**
Pinot Noir Napa & Sonoma Counties Rhonda's Reserve 1990 • $30 • (2/28/1993) • **82**
Reserve Red Sonoma County 1992 • $47 • (9/30/1997) • **91**
Reserve Red Sonoma County 1991 • $47 • (11/15/1996) • **90**
Reserve Red Sonoma County 1990 • $47 • (11/30/1995) • **91**
Reserve Red Sonoma County 1989 • $40 • (11/15/1994) • **85**
Sangiovese Alexander Valley Vineyards of TreMonte 1996: Somewhat muddled with its ripe plum, prune and anise flavors, it holds together but lacks the sharp focus usually found in this producer's wines. Drink now.–J.L. • $35 • (4/30/1999) • **85**
Sauvignon Blanc Alexander Valley Late Harvest Eldorado Gold 1989 • $17/375 ml. • (9/15/1991) • **88**
Sémillon-Sauvignon Blanc Dry Creek Valley Late Harvest Eldorado Gold 1996 • $23/375 ml. • (3/31/1998) • **89**
Sémillon-Sauvignon Blanc Dry Creek Valley Late Harvest Eldorado Gold 1994 • $18/375 ml. • (12/31/1995) • **91**
Sémillon-Sauvignon Blanc Sonoma County Late Harvest Eldorado Gold 1991 • $17/375 ml. • (4/15/1993) • **83**
Siena Sonoma County 1997: Generous, ripe and juicy plum, black cherry and cranberry flavors firm up, adding spice and tight tannins on the finish. A blend of Sangiovese, Cabernet Sauvignon and Malbec. Best from 2001 through 2008.–J.L. • $28 • (1/31/2000) • **88**
Siena Sonoma County 1996: Racy, with herb, black cherry, anise and cedary notes, this elegant, earthy-style red should improve with short-term cellaring. A blend of Sangiovese, Cabernet Sauvignon and Malbec. Drink now through 2004.–J.L. • $28 • (3/31/1999) • **87**
Siena Sonoma County 1995 • $28 • (12/31/1997) SS • **91**
Siena Sonoma County 1994 • $28 • (4/30/1997) • **89**
Siena Sonoma County 1993 • $24 • (11/30/1995) HR • **90**
Siena Sonoma County 1992 • $20 • (9/30/1995) • **89**
Siena Sonoma County 1991 • $20 • (11/15/1993) • **90**
Trésor Reserve Sonoma County 1995: Firm and tightly focused, with a beam of black cherry, plum and currant shaded by pretty toasty oak. Long, tapered finish. Best from 2001 through 2009.–J.L. • $65 • (6/30/2000) • **88**
Trésor Reserve Sonoma County 1994: Firm, dark, rich and focused, it's packed with earthy currant, anise, sage, cedar and tar, and fairly fills out the palate with waves of intense flavors. Finishes with a wall of tannins, so cellar short- to midterm. Best from 2001 through 2010.–J.L. • $65 • (10/15/1999) • **93**
Trésor Reserve Sonoma County 1993: Young-tasting, packed with ripe, rich, vibrant fruit, layers of plum, black cherry, currant and spice. A muscular

wine with firm tannins and lots of gorgeous fruit flavors. Has tannin to shed. Best from 2001 through 2007.–J.L. • $55 • (11/15/1998) • **92**
Zinfandel Dry Creek Valley 1992 • $15 • (9/30/1994) • **89**
Zinfandel Dry Creek Valley 1991 • $15 • (9/30/1993) • **85**
Zinfandel Dry Creek Valley 1990 • $15 • (1/31/1993) • **90**
Zinfandel Sonoma County 1996: Tight, with firm tannins and hints of dried strawberry jam and wild berry. Finishes firm, with oaky flavors. Drink through 2002.–J.L. • $17 • (6/15/1999) • **85**
Zinfandel Sonoma County 1995 • $18 • (5/15/1998) • **84**
Zinfandel Sonoma County 1994 • $18 • (3/31/1997) • **85**
Zinfandel Sonoma County 1993 • $14 • (8/31/1995) • **88**

FETZER | CALIFORNIA

Cabernet Sauvignon California Bel Arbors 1993 • $7 • (12/15/1995) • **84**
Cabernet Sauvignon California Reserve 1985 • $17 • (11/15/1989) • **87**
Cabernet Sauvignon California Valley Oaks 1997: Herb and sandalwood notes dominate the berry flavors. Finish is slightly bitter. Drink now.–J.L. • $10 • (6/30/2000) • **81**
Cabernet Sauvignon California Valley Oaks 1996: A light-style wine with cherry and cola flavors. Drink now. • $9 • (10/31/1998) • **81**
Cabernet Sauvignon California Valley Oaks 1995: Simple, with flavors of herb and currant supported by an oaky frame. Turns lean on the finish. Drink now.–J.L. • $9 • (10/15/1998) • **77**
Cabernet Sauvignon California Valley Oaks 1994 • $8 • (11/30/1996) • **84**
Cabernet Sauvignon California Valley Oaks 1993 • $8 • (12/15/1995) • **82**
Cabernet Sauvignon California Valley Oaks 1990 • $8 • (3/15/1993) • **83**
Cabernet Sauvignon California Valley Oaks 1989 • $8 • (8/31/1992) • **85**
Cabernet Sauvignon California Valley Oaks 1988 • $8 • (11/15/1991) • **82**
Cabernet Sauvignon Mendocino Barrel Select 1985 • $10 • (12/15/1988) • **85**
Cabernet Sauvignon Mendocino Special Reserve 1984 • $14 • (12/31/1988) • **85**
Cabernet Sauvignon Napa Valley Reserve Limited Release 1994: Serves up ripe, complex, spicy black cherry, plum and wild berry flavors, adding a touch of pepper, finishing with firm, chewy tannins. Drink through 2005–J.L. • $25 • (10/31/1998) • **88**
Cabernet Sauvignon Napa Valley Toga Red 1994 • $24 • (11/15/1997) • **82**
Cabernet Sauvignon Napa Valley Usibelli Vineyard Reserve 1994 • $24 • (11/15/1997) • **89**
Cabernet Sauvignon North Coast Barrel Select 1996: Starts with a decent depth of blackberry and plum notes, kicking in with fairly dry tannins and acidity. Drink now through 2004.–J.L. • $15 • (4/30/2000) • **83**
Cabernet Sauvignon North Coast Barrel Select 1995: Some smoke notes upon entry, followed up by black currant and licorice flavors. Not bad. Drink now. • $14 • (10/31/1998) • **82**
Cabernet Sauvignon North Coast Barrel Select 1994 • $14 • (9/30/1997) • **88**
Cabernet Sauvignon North Coast Barrel Select 1993 • $13 • (11/30/1996) • **87**
Cabernet Sauvignon North Coast Barrel Select 1992 • $12 • (12/15/1995) • **85**
Cabernet Sauvignon North Coast Barrel Select 1991 • $12 • (11/15/1994) • **83**
Cabernet Sauvignon California Barrel Select 1990 • $12 • (11/15/1993) • **87**
Cabernet Sauvignon California Barrel Select 1989 • $11 • (3/15/1993) • **87**
Cabernet Sauvignon California Barrel Select 1988: Distinctive for its spicy cherry and strawberry flavors, it's a simple, medium-weight wine that turns dry, tannic and oaky on the finish. (1988 California Cabernet retrospective tasting). Drink now.–J.L. • $11 • (11/15/1998) • **81**
Cabernet Sauvignon Sonoma County Reserve 1992 • $24 • (4/30/1997) • **86**
Cabernet Sauvignon Sonoma County Reserve 1989 • $24 • (12/15/1995) • **85**
Cabernet Sauvignon Sonoma County Reserve 1988: Very dry from start to finish. Only glimmers of cedary currant and spicy berry emerge. (1988 California Cabernet retrospective tasting). Drink now through 2001.–J.L. • $24 • (11/15/1998) • **85**
Cabernet Sauvignon Sonoma County Reserve 1987 • $22 • (12/15/1997) • **87**
Cabernet Sauvignon Sonoma County Reserve 1986 • $24 • (9/30/1991) • **88**
Cabernet Sauvignon Sonoma County Reserve 1985 • $24 • (8/31/1990) • **86**
Chardonnay California Sundial 1999: Grassy, with passion fruit and apple flavors that are refreshingly crisp. Drink now.–J.L. • $9 • (6/30/2000) • **83**
Chardonnay California Sundial 1997: Simple, clean and spicy, with bright pear, nectarine and citrus flavors that linger. Drink now.–J.L. • $8 • (7/31/1998) • **85**
Chardonnay California Sundial 1996 • $7 • (7/31/1997) • **80**

Key: SS—Spectator Selection. CS—Cellar Selection. HR—Highly Recommended. $NA—Price not available. (BT)—Barrel tasting. (A)—Auction Price.
For a key to the tasters' initials, see "How to Use These Listings."
Dates in parentheses represent the issues in which the ratings were published.

Chardonnay Mendocino County Barrel Select 1997: Crisp and focused, with pleasant peach, pear and apricot flavors. Drink now.–J.L. • $12 • (2/28/1999) • **84**
Chardonnay Mendocino Barrel Select 1996 • $12 • (3/31/1998) • **86**
Chardonnay Mendocino County Limited Release Reserve 1996: Complex, smooth, ripe and creamy, with spicy pear, apple and melon flavors, picking up a touch of toasty oak on the finish. Impressive for its balance and finesse. Drink now through 2001.–J.L. • $18 • (11/30/1998) • **89**
Fumé Blanc California Echo Ridge 1996 • $8 • (11/15/1997) • **77**
Gewürztraminer California 1997: Soft, off-dry and layered with pretty apple, spice and floral flavors that linger gently on the sweet finish, this pretty white offers a lovely change of pace at a no-risk price. 3.28 percent residual sugar. Drink now.–H.S. • $7 • (7/31/1998) • **85**
Gewürztraminer California 1996 • $7 • (11/30/1997) • **81**
Gewürztraminer Mendocino County Dry Beckstoffer Vinifera Vineyards Dry Reserve 1996 • $18 • (4/30/1998) • **88**
Merlot California Eagle Peak 1997: Simple and awkward, with cassis, cabbage and tea. Some will like its richness, but the vegetable flavors and lean finish make it hard to recommend. Ready now.–J.L. • $9 • (9/30/1998) • **78**
Merlot California Eagle Peak 1995 • $8 • (7/31/1997) • **81**
Merlot California Eagle Peak 1994 • $8 • (6/15/1996) • **85**
Merlot California Eagle Peak 1992 • $8 • (9/15/1994) • **81**
Merlot North Coast Limited Release Reserve 1995: Firm, with a narrow band of coffee-laced currant and berry flavors, clamping down on a tannic finish. Drink now through 2004.–J.L. • $23 • (2/28/1999) • **83**
Merlot North Coast Reserve 1995: Hints of tea, herb, sage and berry emerge, but they're buried deep beneath the tannins at this stage. Best after 2000.–J.L. • $22 • (10/15/1998) • **83**
Merlot Sonoma County Barrel Select 1997: Lean, featuring a range of herb and light coffee flavors. Plum flavors emerge on the light finish. Drink now.–J.L. • $13 • (10/15/1999) • **81**
Merlot North Coast Barrel Select 1996: Somewhat astringent, with light cherry, vanilla, beef and spice flavors. Drink now. • $14 • (9/30/1998) • **78**
Merlot Sonoma County Barrel Select 1995 • $14 • (2/28/1998) • **83**
Merlot North Coast Barrel Select 1994 • $12 • (6/30/1996) • **85**
Petite Sirah Mendocino County Eagle Point Ranch Reserve 1994 • $24 • (8/31/1997) • **86**
Pinot Noir California Barrel Select 1997: Light-bodied and firm, with a narrow band of toasted oak, spice and dried strawberry flavors. Drink now.–J.L. • $13 • (9/15/1999) • **82**
Pinot Noir California Barrel Select 1996 • $13 • (12/31/1997) • **83**
Pinot Noir California Barrel Select 1991 • $13 • (2/28/1994) • **88**
Pinot Noir California Reserve 1990 • $13 • (2/28/1993) • **85**
Pinot Noir Mendocino County Reserve 1986 • $18 • (10/31/1990) • **87**
Pinot Noir Mendocino County Special Reserve 1985 • $13 • (6/15/1988) • **78**
Pinot Noir North Coast Barrel Select 1994 • $13 • (2/29/1996) • **81**
Pinot Noir North Coast Barrel Select 1992 • $13 • (1/31/1995) • **82**
Pinot Noir Santa Barbara County Bien Nacido Vineyard Limited Release Reserve 1997: Soft-textured, with a spicy, earthy core of cherry, herb and cola flavors. Finishes with supple tannins. Drink now through 2004.–J.L. • $22 • (9/15/1999) • **86**
Pinot Noir Santa Barbara County Bien Nacido Vineyard Reserve 1996: Meaty, earthy, it works its way into some dried black cherry and berry flavors, turning dry and leathery. Drink now through 2001.–J.L. • $24 • (9/15/1998) • **82**
Pinot Noir Santa Barbara County Bien Nacido Vineyard Reserve 1995 • $24 • (5/15/1997) • **90**
Pinot Noir Santa Barbara County Bien Nacido Vineyards 1994 • $17 • (2/29/1996) • **82**
Pinot Noir Santa Barbara County Bien Nacido Vineyards 1992 • $24 • (1/31/1995) • **86**
Pinot Noir Sonoma County Barrel Select 1994 • $13 • (1/31/1997) • **84**
Pinot Noir Sonoma County Carneros Sangiacomo Vineyard Reserve 1994 • $24 • (12/31/1996) • **82**
Pinot Noir Sonoma County Olivet Lane Vineyard 1992 • $24 • (1/31/1995) • **87**
Cabernet Sauvignon Sonoma County Reserve 1986 • $NA • (12/15/1996) • **86**
Sauvignon Blanc California Echo Ridge 1998: Begins with floral and sweet hay aromas, then turns crisp and lemony, with peach notes on the finish. Drink now.–J.L. • $8 • (5/31/2000) • **84**
Sauvignon Blanc California Echo Ridge 1997: Tart and fairly austere, with grapefruit and lemon as its calling cards. Not for sipping, but should do fine with dinner. Drink now. • $9 • (9/15/1998) • **82**
Syrah California 1998: Straightforward, with asparagus and red currant flavors. Drink now through 2003.–J.L. • $11 • (6/15/2000) • **80**
Zinfandel California 1995 • $9 • (3/31/1998) • **86**

Zinfandel California 1989 • $7 • (11/30/1990) • **76**
Zinfandel California Barrel Select 1989 • $9 • (7/31/1992) • **84**
Zinfandel California Home Ranch 1996: Simple, with tea, herb, and bitter flavors and a thread of raspberry. Lightly tannic. Drink now.–J.L. • $9 • (11/30/1998) • **80**
Zinfandel El Dorado County Reserve 1993 • $13 • (3/31/1997) • **84**
Zinfandel Mendocino County Barrel Select 1997: Round and warm, with simple flavors of plum and currant liqueur. Drink now.–J.L. • $14 • (6/15/2000) • **84**
Zinfandel Mendocino County Barrel Select 1994 • $9 • (3/31/1997) • **82**
Zinfandel Mendocino County Barrel Select 1992 • $9 • (9/30/1994) • **86**
Zinfandel Mendocino County Barrel Select 1991 • $9 • (12/31/1993) • **86**
Zinfandel Mendocino County Reserve 1991 • $13 • (3/31/1994) • **87**
Zinfandel Mendocino County Reserve 1986 • $14 • (7/31/1990) • **83**
Zinfandel Mendocino Ricetti Vineyard 1985 • $14 • (10/15/1988) • **79**
Zinfandel Mendocino Ricetti Vineyard Reserve 1986 • $14 • (7/31/1990) • **74**
Zinfandel Mendocino Special Reserve 1985 • $14 • (12/15/1988) • **81**

FICKLIN | CALIFORNIA

Port California Tinta NV • $10 • (4/30/1991) • **78**
Port Madera County 1988 • $25 • (12/31/1997) • **88**
Tawny Port Madera County Aged 10 Years NV • $20 • (5/15/1996) • **87**

FIDDLEHEAD | CALIFORNIA

Pinot Noir Santa Maria Valley 1993 • $25 • (5/31/1996) • **88**
Pinot Noir Santa Maria Valley 1992 • $25 • (2/28/1995) • **88**
Pinot Noir Santa Maria Valley 1990 • $25 • (2/28/1994) • **82**
Pinot Noir Willamette Valley 1996: Smooth and generous, with depth to the pretty cherry and spice notes on a velvety background. Drink now.–H.S. • $36 • (11/15/1999) • **86**
Pinot Noir Willamette Valley 1995 • $36 • (11/30/1997) • **84**
Pinot Noir Willamette Valley 1994 • $34 • (5/31/1996) • **91**
Pinot Noir Willamette Valley 1992 • $29 • (2/28/1995) • **88**
Sauvignon Blanc Santa Ynez Valley 1997: A full-bodied wine, showing mature hazelnut and honey notes up front, followed by peach and zingy citrus flavors. Drying on the finish. Drink now. • $20 • (10/15/1999) • **86**

FIELD STONE | CALIFORNIA

Cabernet Sauvignon Alexander Valley 1996: Firm, with a core of tar, mineral and black currant flavors leading to a supple finish. Drink now. • $20 • (12/31/1998) • **84**
Cabernet Sauvignon Alexander Valley 1994: An herbal core fans out to include smoke, tar, currant and blackberry notes. Pulls up a bit short at the end, but still attractive. Drink now through 2002. • $18 • (7/31/1998) • **85**
Cabernet Sauvignon Alexander Valley 1993 • $17 • (9/30/1997) • **87**
Cabernet Sauvignon Alexander Valley 1992 • $16 • (11/30/1996) • **85**
Cabernet Sauvignon Alexander Valley 1991 • $14 • (11/15/1994) • **84**
Cabernet Sauvignon Alexander Valley 1989 • $14 • (11/15/1992) • **85**
Cabernet Sauvignon Alexander Valley 1987 • $14 • (2/28/1991) • **85**
Cabernet Sauvignon Alexander Valley 1983 • $11 • (10/15/1988) • **74**
Cabernet Sauvignon Alexander Valley Home Ranch Vineyard 1985 • $14 • (4/15/1989) • **70**
Cabernet Sauvignon Alexander Valley Hoot Owl Barrel Select 1990 • $16 • (5/15/1994) • **80**
Cabernet Sauvignon Alexander Valley Hoot Owl Reserve 1986 • $20 • (12/15/1990) • **85**
Cabernet Sauvignon Alexander Valley Hoot Owl Creek Vineyards 1985 • $20 • (3/31/1989) • **87**
Cabernet Sauvignon Alexander Valley Hoot Owl Creek Vineyards 1984 • $14 • (10/15/1988) • **82**
Cabernet Sauvignon Alexander Valley Staten Family Reserve 1994: A smoky blend of cassis, blackberry, licorice, pepper and herbs couched in a medium-bodied, even lean-textured, wine. Finishes fairly long. Drink now through 2003. • $28 • (7/31/1998) • **88**
Cabernet Sauvignon Alexander Valley Staten Family Reserve 1993 • $25 • (11/30/1997) • **86**
Cabernet Sauvignon Alexander Valley Staten Family Reserve 1991 • $23 • (11/30/1996) • **86**
Cabernet Sauvignon Alexander Valley Staten Family Reserve 1990 • $20 • (11/15/1994) • **84**
Cabernet Sauvignon Alexander Valley Staten Family Reserve 1989 • $20 • (11/15/1992) • **82**
Cabernet Sauvignon Alexander Valley Staten Family Reserve 1987 • $25 • (11/15/1991) • **72**
Cabernet Sauvignon Alexander Valley Turkey Hill Vineyard 1985 • $18 • (2/28/1991) • **84**
Cabernet Sauvignon Alexander Valley Turkey Hill Vineyard 1984 • $16 • (12/31/1988) • **88**
Cabernet Sauvignon Alexander Valley Turkey Hill Vineyard 1982 • $12 • (3/16/1986) • **78**
Cabernet Sauvignon Alexander Valley Vineyard Blend 1990 • $14 • (11/15/1993) • **84**
Chardonnay Carneros Staten Family Reserve 1996: Lightly textured, with peach, pineapple, pear and creamy toast nuances and a moderate, elegant finish. Drink now. • $20 • (6/30/1999) • **86**
Chardonnay Sonoma County 1998: Lean and watery, with citrus notes and a tinny finish.–J.L. • $16 • (6/15/2000) • **79**
Chardonnay Sonoma County 1997: Firm, with flavors of peach, pineapple, apple and mineral. Bright finish. Drink now through 2001. • $16 • (7/31/1999) • **85**
Chardonnay Sonoma County 1996 • $15 • (6/30/1998) • **87**
Gewürztraminer Sonoma County 1996 • $10 • (12/15/1997) • **84**
Petite Sirah Alexander Valley 1988 • $15 • (12/31/1990) • **85**
Petite Sirah Alexander Valley 1987 • $15 • (12/31/1990) • **84**
Petite Sirah Alexander Valley 1986 • $15 • (9/30/1989) • **79**
Petite Sirah Alexander Valley 1985 • $11 • (2/15/1989) • **83**
Petite Sirah Alexander Valley 1984 • $11 • (10/15/1988) • **88**
Petite Sirah Alexander Valley Old Vines 1990 • $17 • (6/15/1993) • **83**
Sauvignon Blanc Sonoma County 1997: Fairly rich, featuring fig, melon, herb and light citrus notes. Bright acidity is balanced by full body, while the flavors linger nicely on the palate. Drink now. • $12 • (6/15/1999) • **87**
Sauvignon Blanc Sonoma County 1996 • $15 • (10/15/1997) • **85**

FIELDBROOK | CALIFORNIA

Merlot Napa Valley Frediani Vineyard 1991 • $15 • (9/15/1994) • **84**
Pinot Noir Napa Valley Beard Vineyard 1992 • $18 • (10/31/1994) • **87**
Pinot Noir Napa Valley Beard Vineyard 1988 • $12 • (2/28/1993) • **77**
Sauvignon Blanc Redwood Valley Elizabeth Vineyard 1997 • $13 • (6/15/1998) • **83**
Sauvignon Blanc Redwood Valley Elizabeth Vineyard 1996 • $11 • (3/31/1998) • **86**
Zinfandel Mendocino County Pacini Vineyard 1997: Marked by bright cherry and plum flavors, this wine is fairly opulent and elegant. It moves along with spice and a touch of tar, which adds complexity. Finishes moderately. Serious fun. Drink now through 2003. • $18 • (5/15/1999) • **88**
Zinfandel Mendocino County Pacini Vineyard 50-year-old vines 1996 • $18 • (6/15/1998) • **82**
Zinfandel Mendocino County Pacini Vineyard 1995 • $13 • (4/30/1997) • **91**
Zinfandel Mendocino County Pacini Vineyard 1994 • $13 • (4/30/1997) • **87**
Zinfandel Mendocino County Pacini Vineyard 1993 • $12 • (10/15/1994) • **87**
Zinfandel Mendocino County Pacini Vineyard 1991 • $11 • (3/15/1993) • **84**
Zinfandel Mendocino County Pacini Vineyard Reserve 1992 • $12 • (10/15/1994) • **86**

FIFE | CALIFORNIA

Cabernet Sauvignon Napa Valley 1997: Ripe, supple and rich, with a lovely array of complex currant, black cherry, plum and spice. The long, intricate aftertaste has firm, polished tannins. A delicious wine at what these days is a comparatively good price for California Cabernet of this quality. Best from 2001 through 2009.–J.L. • $28 • (12/31/1999) SS • **91**
Cabernet Sauvignon Napa Valley Estate Vineyard 1995 • $24 • (5/15/1998) • **90**
Cabernet Sauvignon Spring Mountain District Reserve 1996: Supple, polished and elegant, with lots of coffee, currant, herb, spice and mineral flavors that are focused and rich on the finish, where the flavors linger. Best to cellar short-term. Drink through 2007.–J.L. • $40 • (11/15/1999) • **92**
Cabernet Sauvignon Spring Mountain District Reserve 1995: Dense, tight, massive and chewy, with a solid dose of oak and a core of currant, sage, anise, tar and mineral. At this stage, it's raw in texture, more like a barrel sample. The high tannin level suggests cellaring. Best from 2001 through 2010.–J.L. • $35 • (8/31/1998) • **88**
Cabernet Sauvignon Spring Mountain Reserve 1993 • $28 • (11/15/1996) • **90**
L'Attitude 39 Mendocino 1997: Smooth and polished, with a range of cherry, cola, wild berry, herb and spice, firming up on the finish. Drink now through 2005.–J.L. • $20 • (12/31/1999) • **87**
Max Cuvee Napa Valley 1997: Rich and complex, with a range of flavors including ripe plum, currant, coffee, anise, cedar and spice, finishing with

supple tannins. Contains Petite Sirah and Syrah, with tiny amounts of Zinfandel and Carignane. Drink now through 2005.–J.L. • $35 • (12/31/1999) • **88**

Max Cuvee Napa Valley 1996: Dark, dense and chewy, with tannic mineral, wild berry, sage and earth flavors, turning rustic; it opens with air to show more plush berry and spice flavors, so cellaring is advised. A blend of Petite Sirah, Zinfandel, Syrah, Carignane, Charbono. Drink through 2005.–J.L. • $30 • (4/30/1999) • **88**

Max Cuvee Napa Valley 1995 • $24 • (12/31/1997) • **89**

Max Cuvee Napa Valley 1994 • $19 • (7/31/1997) HR • **93**

Merlot Napa Valley 1997: Tight, with a trim band of currant, tobacco, cedar and spice. Finishes with firm tannins. Drink through 2005.–J.L. • $23 • (10/15/1999) • **86**

Merlot Napa Valley 1996: Rich and concentrated, it eases into some attractive vanilla-scented oak and cherry and wild berry flavors. Folds together nicely on the finish, where the texture softens. Drink through 2004.–J.L. • $21 • (10/15/1998) • **88**

Merlot Napa Valley 1995 • $20 • (12/31/1997) • **84**

Merlot Napa Valley Old Vines 1993 • $20 • (10/15/1996) • **86**

Petite Sirah Napa Valley 1994 • $16 • (7/31/1997) • **87**

Petite Sirah Napa Valley Alluvial Vineyard 1997: Smooth and polished for a young wine, with tasty plum, black cherry, earth, leather and mineral notes, firming on the finish. Drink now through 2006.–J.L. • $35 • (12/31/1999) • **87**

Petite Sirah Napa Valley Old Vines 1993 • $16 • (11/30/1996) • **88**

Petite Sirah Napa Valley Les Vieilles Vignes 1991 • $16 • (6/15/1993) • **87**

Petite Sirah Redwood Valley Redhead Vineyard 1996: Enormously tannic, but there's a glimmer of peppery wild berry, cherry, leather and sage. This is a dense wine that needs time. Drink now through 2004.–J.L. • $20 • (8/31/1998) • **85**

Petite Sirah Redwood Valley Redhead Vineyard 1995 • $19 • (12/31/1997) • **89**

Syrah Mendocino Old Yokayo Rancho Vineyard 1997: Nice focus on the peppery wild berry, cherry and earthy Syrah notes. Finishes with a complex interplay of flavors. Drink now through 2007.–J.L. • $30 • (12/31/1999) • **88**

Syrah Napa Valley Alluvial Vineyard 1997: Much to admire in this complex, textured Syrah. Serves up a range of spicy, meaty black cherry, raspberry and tar notes. Finishes with firm tannins. Best from 2001 through 2007.–J.L. • $35 • (12/31/1999) • **88**

Zinfandel Mendocino 1997: This California offering is ripe and plummy-tasting, with lots of complex cherry, wild berry and spice flavors that fan out nicely on the smooth, fleshy finish. Drink now through 2002.–J.L. • $17 • (6/15/1999) HR • **91**

Zinfandel Mendocino 1996 • $17 • (6/15/1998) • **87**

Zinfandel Mendocino County Uplands 1998: Up-front cherry and raspberry flavors are appealing. Turns simple and dry. Drink now.–J.L. • $17 • (5/31/2000) • **84**

Zinfandel Mendocino County Whaler Vineyard 1998: Simple, with candied berry and raspberry flavor that's soft and supple. Drink now.–J.L. • $20 • (5/31/2000) • **81**

Zinfandel Napa Valley Old Vines 1997: Tightly structured, with pretty plum, wild berry, blackberry and spice. Firm tannins have nice cedary oak shadings. Drink now through 2003.–J.L. • $20 • (6/15/1999) • **91**

Zinfandel Napa Valley Old Vines 1996 • $20 • (5/31/1998) • **84**

Zinfandel Napa Valley Old Vines 1995 • $19 • (9/30/1997) • **89**

Zinfandel Napa Valley Old Vines 1994 • $16 • (11/30/1996) • **88**

Zinfandel Napa Valley Les Vieilles Vignes 1992 • $16 • (9/15/1995) • **89**

Zinfandel Napa Valley Les Vieilles Vignes 1991 • $16 • (6/15/1993) • **85**

Zinfandel Redwood Valley Redhead Vineyard 1997: This tasty Zin is ripe and juicy, with spicy, peppery bell pepper and wild berry flavors. Firms up on the finish, where the tannins tighten up. Drink now through 2003.–J.L. • $24 • (6/15/1999) • **89**

Zinfandel Redwood Valley Redhead Vineyard 1996 • $20 • (6/15/1998) • **86**

Zinfandel Redwood Valley Redhead Vineyard 1995 • $19 • (9/30/1997) • **88**

Zinfandel Redwood Valley Redhead Vineyard 1994 • $19 • (3/31/1997) • **91**

Zinfandel Spring Mountain 1994 • $19 • (3/31/1997) • **91**

Key: SS—Spectator Selection. CS—Cellar Selection. HR—Highly Recommended. $NA—Price not available. (BT)—Barrel tasting. (A)—Auction Price.
For a key to the tasters' initials, see "How to Use These Listings."
Dates in parentheses represent the issues in which the ratings were published.

FILIPPI, JOSEPH | CALIFORNIA

Angelica Elena Limited Release Winemaker's Reserve Cucamonga Valley NV • $10/375 ml. • (6/15/1996) • **82**

Ruby Port California Limited Release Winemaker's Reserve NV • $9 • (6/15/1996) • **81**

White Grenache Cucamonga Valley Limited Release Winemaker's Reserve 1996 • $9 • (9/15/1997) • **59**

Zinfandel Cucamonga Valley Limited Release Winemaker's Reserve 1994 • $10 • (4/30/1996) • **76**

Zinfandel Cucamonga Valley Nouveau Winemaker's Reserve Limited Release 1996 • $11 • (6/15/1998) • **72**

FIRESTEED | OREGON

Pinot Noir Oregon 1997: Extremely light in color, with modest floral and berry flavors.–H.S. • $10 • (4/30/1999) • **79**

Pinot Noir Oregon 1996 • $10 • (11/30/1997) • **83**

Pinot Noir Oregon 1995 • $10 • (2/28/1997) • **81**

Pinot Noir Oregon 1994 • $10 • (1/31/1996) • **86**

Pinot Noir Oregon 1993 • $7 • (11/30/1994) • **83**

Pinot Noir Oregon 1992 • $9 • (9/30/1993) • **82**

FIRESTONE | CALIFORNIA

Cabernet Sauvignon Santa Barbara County 1978 • $20 • (11/15/1992) • **65**

Cabernet Sauvignon Santa Ynez Valley 1997: Plush, with earthy, herbal, charry oak notes, black cherry and currant flavors. With aeration, it shakes some of the charred qualities, so give it time. Drink through 2003.–J.L. • $14 • (10/15/1999) • **81**

Cabernet Sauvignon Santa Ynez Valley 1996: This wine is marred by vegetal, cooked flavors and a bitter finish. Slightly better than previously reviewed. • $13 • (1/31/1999) • **72**

Cabernet Sauvignon Santa Ynez Valley 1994 • $12 • (10/31/1997) • **85**

Cabernet Sauvignon Santa Ynez Valley 1993 • $12 • (9/15/1996) • **85**

Cabernet Sauvignon Santa Ynez Valley 1992 • $12 • (12/15/1995) • **83**

Cabernet Sauvignon Santa Ynez Valley 1991 • $12 • (11/15/1994) • **84**

Cabernet Sauvignon Santa Ynez Valley 1990 • $12 • (11/15/1993) • **81**

Cabernet Sauvignon Santa Ynez Valley 1989 • $12 • (11/15/1992) • **78**

Cabernet Sauvignon Santa Ynez Valley 1988 • $12 • (11/15/1991) • **75**

Cabernet Sauvignon Santa Ynez Valley 1987 • $11 • (5/31/1990) • **82**

Cabernet Sauvignon Santa Ynez Valley 1986 • $10 • (12/15/1989) • **81**

Cabernet Sauvignon Santa Ynez Valley Reserve 1990 • $20 • (11/15/1994) • **85**

Cabernet Sauvignon Santa Ynez Valley Reserve 1988 • $18 • (2/28/1991) • **84**

Cabernet Sauvignon Santa Ynez Valley Vintage Reserve 1990 • $20 • (2/15/1993) • **84**

Cabernet Sauvignon Santa Ynez Valley Vintage Reserve 1985 • $25 • (12/15/1989) • **67**

Cabernet Sauvignon Santa Ynez Valley Vintage Reserve 1979 • $12 • (3/16/1986) • **73**

Chardonnay Santa Ynez Valley 1997: Open-textured, with refreshing, ripe pear, fig, orange and herb flavors that persist on the soft finish. Drink now.–H.S. • $12 • (6/15/1999) • **87**

Chardonnay Santa Ynez Valley 1996: This one strikes a fairly complex pose, with spice, pear, apple, toast and hazelnut. The finish is bright and lemony. A refreshing wine. Drink now. • $13 • (7/31/1998) • **87**

Johannisberg Riesling Santa Barbara County Selected Harvest 1991 • $12/375 ml. • (12/15/1992) • **84**

Johannisberg Riesling Santa Barbara County Selected Harvest 1989 • $12/375 ml. • (4/30/1991) • **84**

Johannisberg Riesling Santa Ynez Valley Selected Harvest 1995 • $15/375 ml. • (11/30/1996) • **89**

Johannisberg Riesling Santa Ynez Valley Selected Harvest 1993 • $15/375 ml. • (6/15/1996) • **85**

Merlot Santa Ynez Valley 1993 • $13 • (3/31/1996) • **84**

Merlot Santa Ynez Valley 1992 • $12 • (11/15/1994) • **81**

Merlot Santa Ynez Valley 1991 • $12 • (12/31/1993) • **83**

Merlot Santa Ynez Valley 1990 • $13 • (11/30/1992) • **79**

Merlot Santa Ynez Valley 1989 • $12 • (8/31/1991) • **86**

Merlot Santa Ynez Valley 1988 • $11 • (3/31/1991) • **82**

Merlot Santa Ynez Valley Reserve 1995: Lean, with simple berry, green olive and bell pepper notes, finishing with firm tannins. Drink now.–J.L. • $25 • (10/15/1998) • **82**

Pinot Noir Santa Ynez Valley 1986 • $10 • (12/15/1989) • **77**

Prosperity Red Santa Ynez Valley NV • $5 • (3/31/1993) • **75**

Red Table Wine Santa Ynez Valley 1990 • $6 • (4/30/1992) • **74**

Reserve Santa Ynez Valley 1993 • $30 • (12/31/1996) • **84**
Sauvignon Blanc Santa Barbara County 1996 • $9 • (4/30/1998) • **86**
Sauvignon Blanc Santa Ynez Valley 1997: Leans toward grapefruit, lemon and herb flavors. Dried thyme weaves itself nicely into the profile, offering a mark of distinction. Finishes clean. Drink now through 2002. • $9 • (5/31/1999) • **84**
Vintage Reserve Santa Ynez Valley 1991 • $22 • (12/15/1995) • **89**
Zinfandel Cucamonga Valley Old Vines 1997: Ripe, with juicy blueberry and raspberry notes on a medium frame. Spicy finish. Drink now.–J.L. • $10 • (5/31/2000) • **84**

FISHER | CALIFORNIA

Cabernet Sauvignon Napa Valley Coach Insignia 1995: Smooth and polished—especially compared with Fisher's Wedding Vineyard bottling—this is a generous wine with pretty black cherry, plum and wild berry flavors, well-integrated tannins. Drink through 2006.–J.L. • $25 • (11/15/1998) • **88**
Cabernet Sauvignon Napa Valley Coach Insignia 1994 • $24 • (10/31/1997) • **87**
Cabernet Sauvignon Napa Valley Coach Insignia 1993 • $22 • (12/15/1996) • **85**
Cabernet Sauvignon Napa Valley Coach Insignia 1991 • $20 • (11/15/1994) • **84**
Cabernet Sauvignon Napa & Sonoma Counties Coach Insignia 1990 • $20 • (6/15/1993) • **86**
Cabernet Sauvignon Napa & Sonoma Counties Coach Insignia 1989 • $18 • (3/31/1992) • **82**
Cabernet Sauvignon Napa & Sonoma Counties Coach Insignia 1987 • $NA • (11/15/1997) • **78**
Cabernet Sauvignon Sonoma County Coach Insignia 1986 • $20 • (1/31/1990) • **87**
Cabernet Sauvignon Sonoma County Coach Insignia 1985 • $18 • (9/15/1988) • **91**
Cabernet Sauvignon Sonoma County Coach Insignia 1984 • $18 • (11/15/1987) • **90**
Cabernet Sauvignon Napa Valley Lamb Vineyard 1996: Firm, focused and concentrated, with rich, chunky, spicy currant, plum, herb, cedar and blackberry, turning complex with earthy, mineral flavors. Strikes a nice balance between its rustic properties and a sense of elegance. Drink through 2007.–J.L. • $60 • (9/30/1999) • **91**
Cabernet Sauvignon Napa Valley Lamb Vineyard 1994 • $53 Ⓐ • (10/31/1997) • **92**
Cabernet Sauvignon Napa Valley Lamb Vineyard 1993 • $45 • (11/15/1996) • **90**
Cabernet Sauvignon Napa Valley Lamb Vineyard 1989: Dark, ripe and intense, with a focused, up-front core of currant, coffee, cedar, anise and spice, ending with thick, chewy tannins. Turns austere on the finish. (1989 California Cabernet retrospective tasting). Drink now through 2009.–J.L. • $25 • (8/31/1999) • **90**
Cabernet Sauvignon Sonoma County 1983 • $13 • (6/15/1987) • **73**
Cabernet Sauvignon Sonoma County 1982 • $13 • (11/01/1985) • **88**
Cabernet Sauvignon Sonoma County 1981 • $12 • (12/01/1984) • **85**
Cabernet Sauvignon Sonoma County Wedding Vineyard 1995: This mountain-grown Cabernet is intense and concentrated, if a bit overpowering at this point. Lots of wild berry, currant, mineral and spice, along with chewy tannins. Earthy and oaky, its need some cellar time. Best from 2002 through 2008.–J.L. • $65 • (11/15/1998) • **89**
Cabernet Sauvignon Sonoma County Wedding Vineyard 1994 • $50 • (10/31/1997) • **88**
Cabernet Sauvignon Sonoma County Wedding Vineyard 1993 • $33 • (11/15/1996) • **90**
Cabernet Sauvignon Sonoma County Wedding Vineyard 1991 • $28 • (11/15/1994) • **88**
Chardonnay Russian River Valley O'Connor Vineyard 1998: Crisp, with a trim band of pippin apple, tart pear and earth notes, finishing with cedary oak. Drink now through 2003.–J.L. • $40 • (6/30/2000) • **87**
Chardonnay Sonoma County Coach Insignia 1998: Attractive for its ripe peach, pear, citrus and mineral flavors, holding its fruity edge. Drink now.–J.L. • $25 • (6/15/2000) • **87**
Chardonnay Sonoma County Coach Insignia 1997: Exotic, with smoky, spicy pear and fig flavors and an oily texture that remains impressively elegant and focused. Drink now.–J.L. • $25 • (7/31/1999) • **89**
Chardonnay Sonoma County Coach Insignia 1996: Tight, with spicy pear, apple, earth and sagelike flavors, it picks up a bit of funkiness and earthiness on the finish. Drink now through 2001.–J.L. • $22 • (9/15/1998) • **87**
Chardonnay Sonoma County Whitney's Vineyard 1998: Lots of up-front fruit, with spicy pear, apple and fig flavors that are supple and polished, turn elegant. Drink now through 2003.–J.L. • $36 • (6/30/2000) • **88**
Coach Insignia Napa County 1996: Intense and concentrated, with a rich core of earthy currant, leather, anise, mineral and sage. Takes time to open, but offers a lot of complex, concentrated fruit flavors. A blend of Cabernet Sauvignon, Cabernet Franc, Merlot. Best from 2001 through 2009.–J.L. • $30 • (2/28/1999) • **91**
Merlot Napa Valley RCF Vineyard 1996: Smooth, with herb and oak-laced Merlot flavors, offering currant, spice and wild berry and finishing with leathery tannins. Drink through 2006.–J.L. • $30 • (2/28/1999) • **87**
Merlot Napa Valley RCF Vineyard 1995: Shows off the cedar, tobacco and herb side of Merlot, with a glimmer of cherry and berry. Manages the tannins well, but slightly lacking in the middle. Drink now through 2002.–J.L. • $26 • (10/15/1998) • **84**
Merlot Napa Valley RCF Vineyard 1994 • $26 • (6/30/1997) • **84**
Merlot Napa Valley RCF Vineyard 1993 • $26 • (6/30/1996) • **84**
Merlot Napa Valley RCF Vineyard 1991 • $22 • (10/31/1993) • **84**

FISHER FAMILY | OREGON

Pinot Noir Willamette Valley 1995: On the crisp side, with racy, earthy flavors shaded with tasty flashes of blackberry, cherry and spice. Should be nice when it settles down. Best after 2000.–H.S. • $27 • (6/15/1999) • **87**

FLEUR DE CARNEROS CELLARS
CALIFORNIA

Pinot Noir Carneros 1996: A light, uncomplicated style, with moderately ripe and slightly green-tasting Pinot Noir flavors, notes of tea, sage and dried cherry. Drink now.–J.L. • $12 • (8/31/1998) • **83**
Pinot Noir Carneros 1995 • $12 • (3/31/1997) • **79**

FLORA SPRINGS | CALIFORNIA

Cabernet Sauvignon Napa Valley 1986 • $15 • (3/15/1990) • **85**
Cabernet Sauvignon Napa Valley 1985 • $15 • (7/31/1989) • **90**
Cabernet Sauvignon Napa Valley 1984 • $25 • (7/31/1988) • **71**
Cabernet Sauvignon Napa Valley 1983 • $20 • (12/15/1986) • **79**
Cabernet Sauvignon Napa Valley 1981 • $25 • (12/16/1984) • **82**
Cabernet Sauvignon Napa Valley Cellar Select 1988 • $24 • (2/29/1992) • **85**
Cabernet Sauvignon Napa Valley Cellar Select 1987 • $25 • (11/15/1990) • **91**
Cabernet Sauvignon Napa Valley Cypress Ranch 1995: A crisp style that slowly unfurls its currant and berry flavors, this is a Pope Valley appellation wine, lighter than the winery's efforts from Napa Valley proper. Drink through 2004.–J.L. • $15 • (10/31/1998) • **87**
Cabernet Sauvignon Napa Valley Reserve 1991 • $33 • (9/30/1994) CS • **97**
Cabernet Sauvignon Napa Valley Reserve 1990 • $33 • (2/28/1994) • **85**
Cabernet Sauvignon Napa Valley Reserve 1989 • $25 • (11/15/1992) • **88**
Cabernet Sauvignon Napa Valley Rutherford Reserve 1993 • $45 • (11/15/1996) • **90**
Cabernet Sauvignon Napa Valley Rutherford Reserve 1992 • $40 • (11/15/1995) HR • **96**
Cabernet Sauvignon Napa Valley St. Rutherford Vineyard 1996: Shows off mature cherry, berry and stewed plum character, with spicy notes, finishing with good length and polished tannins. Drink through 2006.–J.L. • $30 • (8/31/1999) • **88**
Cabernet Sauvignon Rutherford Hillside Reserve 1997: Still tasting sweet, as if the fermentation isn't complete, this is an enormously complex and concentrated wine, brimming with currant and black cherry.–J.L. • $NA • (8/31/1998) (BT) • **90-94**
Cabernet Sauvignon Rutherford Hillside Reserve 1996: Deliciously complex, rich and elegant, with ripe, polished and sophisticated currant, black cherry, anise, sage and spice, picking up pretty oak shadings. Lingering, rich aftertaste. Best from 2001 through 2008.–J.L. • $70 • (10/31/1999) • **92**
Cabernet Sauvignon Rutherford Hillside Reserve 1995: Smooth, plush and elegant, with pretty plum, currant and black cherry flavors, on the light side for this bottling. Drinks well now, with its well-integrated tannins, but is worthy of cellaring. Drink through 2007.–J.L. • $58 Ⓐ • (10/31/1998) • **90**
Cabernet Sauvignon Rutherford Hillside Reserve 1994 • $96 Ⓐ • (10/15/1997) HR • **96**
Chardonnay Napa Valley 1996 • $20 • (6/30/1998) • **91**
Chardonnay Napa Valley Barrel Fermented Reserve 1997: An up-front, ripe and fruity-style Chardonnay, with rich flavors of pear, fig, apple and melon. Picks up a hint of hazelnut and shows off juicy nectarine notes on the smooth, creamy finish. Drink now through 2001.–J.L. • $22 • (12/15/1998) SS • **91**
Chardonnay Napa Valley Lavender Hill Vineyard 1998: Serves up ripe pear, fig and vanilla flavors in a subtle package. Drink now.–J.L. • $30 • (5/31/2000) • **85**
Chardonnay Napa Valley Lavender Hill Vineyard 1996 • $23 • (6/30/1998) • **91**

FLORA SPRINGS

Chardonnay Napa Valley Reserve 1998: Simple, with muddled pear and vanilla flavors. Drink now.–J.L. • $23 • (5/31/2000) • **80**
Merlot Napa Valley 1997: Effusively fruity, with juicy plum, black cherry, wild berry and spice flavors that turn complex on the long, supple finish. Drink now through 2004.–J.L. • $20 • (9/30/1999) • **88**
Merlot Napa Valley 1996: Good, but earthy, with dry, leathery tannins, this only gives a glimpse of currant and berry flavors. Tasted twice, with consistent notes. Drink now through 2002.–J.L. • $18 • (10/15/1998) • **82**
Merlot Napa Valley 1994 • $14 • (6/30/1996) • **87**
Merlot Napa Valley 1993 • $12 • (9/30/1995) • **87**
Merlot Napa Valley 1988 • $15 • (8/31/1991) • **83**
Merlot Napa Valley 1987 • $17 • (7/31/1990) • **87**
Merlot Napa Valley 1985 • $15 • (6/30/1988) • **82**
Merlot Napa Valley Floréal 1991 • $12 • (10/31/1993) • **86**
Merlot Napa Valley Floréal 1990 • $14 • (11/30/1992) • **79**
Merlot Napa Valley Windfall Vineyard 1996: Ripe and juicy, with pretty plum, blackberry, cherry and spice, finishing with a leather-coffee-sage aftertaste that's rich and complex, with a cedary edge. Drink through 2006.–J.L. • $50 • (9/15/1999) • **90**
Merlot Napa Valley Windfall Vineyard 1995 • $40 • (3/31/1998) • **89**
Pinot Noir Carneros Lavender Hill Vineyard 1996 • $30 • (4/30/1998) • **88**
Pinot Noir Napa Valley Floréal 1989 • $12 • (9/30/1992) • **78**
Sangiovese Napa Valley 1998: Light, with pretty, spicy, herbal and charry notes intermingling with berry flavors. Finish is soft and lingering. Drink now through 2003.–J.L. • $16 • (1/31/2000) • **86**
Sangiovese Napa Valley 1996 • $15 • (5/15/1998) • **82**
Sangiovese Napa Valley 1995 • $15 • (4/30/1997) • **92**
Sangiovese Napa Valley 1993 • $15 • (2/28/1995) • **86**
Sauvignon Blanc Napa Valley 1998: Tangy, with herbaceous, buttery, earthy notes, turning soapy on the finish. Tasted twice, with consistent notes. Drink now through 2002.–J.L. • $10 • (5/15/2000) • **81**
Sauvignon Blanc Napa Valley 1996 • $15 • (3/31/1998) • **89**
Sauvignon Blanc Napa Valley Reserve 1997: Silky, offering a delicate blend of melon, citrus and herb flavors couched in firm, bright acidity. Drink now. • $14 • (6/15/1999) • **85**
Sauvignon Blanc Napa Valley Soliloquy 1998: Offers a glimmer of passion fruit, but turns simple and gluey. Drink now.–J.L. • $15 • (5/15/2000) • **83**
Trilogy Napa Valley 1996: An impressive red blend, tightly structured, with a rich array of currant, black cherry, anise, cedar, tar and spice flavors of remarkable harmony and finesse, ending in a long, complex aftertaste. A blend of Cabernet Sauvignon, Merlot and Cabernet Franc. Drink through 2009.–J.L. • $45 • (7/31/1999) CS • **94**
Trilogy Napa Valley 1995: Smooth, ripe and spicy, in a complex, elegant style with cherry, plum and berry flavors and attractive spicy nuances. Finishes with good length, fine, integrated tannins and a pretty dash of toasty oak. Drink through 2005.–J.L. • $37 Ⓐ • (10/31/1998) • **88**
Trilogy Napa Valley 1994 • $33 • (10/15/1997) • **90**
Trilogy Napa Valley 1993 • $30 • (11/15/1996) • **89**
Trilogy Napa Valley 1992 • $27 • (11/30/1995) CS • **92**
Trilogy Napa Valley 1991 • $25 • (11/15/1994) • **86**
Trilogy Napa Valley 1990 • $33 • (2/28/1994) • **85**
Trilogy Napa Valley 1989 • $33 • (11/15/1992) • **87**
Trilogy Napa Valley 1988: Good but not exceptional, as the core of fruit is simple, with tarry currant, sage and cedar flavors. Finishes with firm, dry tannins. (1988 California Cabernet retrospective tasting). Drink now through 2002.–J.L. • $33 • (11/15/1998) • **84**
Trilogy Napa Valley 1987 • $33 • (5/15/1991) • **90**
Trilogy Napa Valley 1986 • $33 • (2/15/1990) • **94**
Trilogy Napa Valley 1985 • $33 • (2/15/1989) • **87**
Trilogy Napa Valley 1984 • $30 • (2/29/1988) • **73**

FLOWERS | CALIFORNIA

Chardonnay Sonoma Coast 1997: A rich, resiny flavor gives this wine an earthy introduction. With aeration the core of pear, peach and nectarine emerges, finding focus on the long finish. Drink through 2004.–J.L. • $32 • (7/31/1999) • **91**
Chardonnay Sonoma Coast Camp Meeting Ridge 1997: Young and racy, packing in plenty of attractive ripe pear, nectarine, smoky oak and vanilla bean flavors, though the alcohol stands out a bit on the finish. Drink now through 2006.–J.L. • $74 Ⓐ • (2/29/2000) • **88**
Chardonnay Sonoma Coast Camp Meeting Ridge Moon Select 1997: Mature in color, with complex toasty oak, pear, fig, anise and hazelnut flavors. Bold yet dry and intense. Drink now through 2005.–J.L.• $48 • (4/30/2000) • **90**
Chardonnay Sonoma Coast Porter-Bass Vineyard 1997: Sharply focused, with brilliant flavors of ripe, tart pear, nectarine, peach, fig and spicy, buttery oak that gain depth and nuance. Drink now through 2003.–J.L. • $38 • (7/31/1999) • **93**
Perennial California 1998: Tastes better than it smells, tilting toward the dill and pickle side of Pinot Noir, though some cherry and berry emerge. Contains mostly Pinot Noir, with smaller amounts of Pinot Meunier and Zinfandel. Drink now through 2005.–J.L. • $25 • (2/29/2000) • **84**
Pinot Noir Carneros 1997: The cherry, earth, mushroom and wild berry flavors are intense and lively, firmly tannic but complex on the finish. Needs time to soften and evolve. Drink through 2006.–J.L. • $32 • (9/15/1999) • **89**
Pinot Noir Sonoma Coast Camp Meeting Ridge 1997: Lean and muscular, with a firm, trim band of spicy, earthy cherry, leather and cola, fanning out and turning complex. Best from 2001 through 2008.–J.L. • $94 Ⓐ • (3/31/2000) • **89**
Pinot Noir Sonoma Coast Camp Meeting Ridge Moon Select 1997: Tight and a touch earthy at first, but it opens to reveal chunky ripe plum, cherry, mushroom and cedar notes. Turns firm, with anise and tar. Tannic. Best from 2001 through 2008.–J.L. • $50 • (3/31/2000) • **90**
Pinot Noir Sonoma Coast Camp Meeting Ridge Vineyard 1996: Dark, ripe, complex and concentrated, with detailed black cherry, wild berry, plum, coffee and spicy notes fanning out on the finish, where the tannins are fine but firm. Drink through 2006.–J.L. • $40 • (2/28/1999) • **92**
Pinot Noir Sonoma Coast Camp Meeting Ridge Vineyard Moon Select 1996: Intense, with lively, complex, dense and chewy black cherry, plum, wild berry and spicy notes, deep and concentrated, finishing with a long aftertaste. Drink through 2006.–J.L. • $45 • (2/28/1999) • **94**
Pinot Noir Sonoma Coast Hirsch Vineyard 1997: Appealing for its up-front fruitiness, with ripe plum, blackberry, cherry and cedary oak, finishing with complex tannins. Best from 2001 through 2005.–J.L. • $42 • (8/31/1999) • **89**

FOG MOUNTAIN | CALIFORNIA

Merlot California 1997: Fleshy, with black cherry, mint and herb notes that finish short and slightly dry. Drink now. • $10 • (12/15/1998) • **80**

FOGARTY, THOMAS | CALIFORNIA

Brut Santa Cruz Mountains 1990 • $22 • (12/31/1995) • **87**
Cabernet Sauvignon Napa Valley 1996: Supple texture here, framed in firm, ripe tannins. Serves up layers of coffee, currant and black cherry highlighted by a bright herbal edge. Finishes long. Best from 2001 through 2008. • $28 • (10/15/1999) • **88**
Cabernet Sauvignon Napa Valley 1995: A classy wine. Starts off with fresh plummy aromas; on the palate, it's firm yet ripe, with a fine blend of black currant, anise and herb flavors. The finish is long and silky. Drink now through 2005. • $22 • (1/31/1999) • **88**
Cabernet Sauvignon Napa Valley 1985 • $15 • (7/15/1991) • **70**
Cabernet Sauvignon Napa Valley Vallerga Vineyards 1992 • $25 • (4/30/1996) • **90**
Chardonnay Monterey 1998: Ripe, smooth and rich, with complex fig, apricot, spice and pear flavors, turning elegant, if a bit short. Drink now through 2003.–J.L. • $18 • (3/31/2000) • **87**
Chardonnay Santa Cruz Mountains 1997: Ripe, rich and spicy, with a touch of butterscotch adding dimension to the complex pear, fig and vanilla flavors. Turns elegant and polished. Drink now through 2005.–J.L. • $20 • (1/31/2000) • **90**
Chardonnay Santa Cruz Mountains 1996: Tight and concentrated, with a band of pear, hazelnut and spicy oak that turns more complex with each sip. Drink now through 2002.–J.L. • $19 • (1/31/1999) • **92**
Chardonnay Santa Cruz Mountains Estate Reserve 1996: A well-oaked style that backs it up with ripe pear, citrus and apple flavors. Turns sleek and elegant, with smoky, toasty wood. Drink now through 2001.–J.L. • $28 • (11/30/1998) • **90**
Pinot Noir Napa Valley 1988 • $15 • (2/28/1991) • **86**
Pinot Noir Napa Valley Carneros 1985 • $15 • (6/15/1988) • **73**
Pinot Noir Santa Cruz Mountains 1997: Spicy and peppery, with a range of beefy, earthy plum and wild berry. Finishes with hints of mushroom and

Key: SS—Spectator Selection. CS—Cellar Selection. HR—Highly Recommended. $NA—Price not available. (BT)—Barrel tasting. Ⓐ—Auction Price.
For a key to the tasters' initials, see "How to Use These Listings."
Dates in parentheses represent the issues in which the ratings were published.

mineral and firm, leathery tannins. Drink now through 2005.–J.L. • $28 • (2/29/2000) • **86**

Pinot Noir Santa Cruz Mountains 1996: Richly flavored, with a complex range of black cherry, mushroom, wild berry and spice flavors and subtle nuances that linger. Drink now through 2003.–J.L. • $27 • (2/28/1999) • **88**

Pinot Noir Santa Cruz Mountains 1994 • $25 • (1/31/1997) • **80**

Pinot Noir Santa Cruz Mountains 1992 • $21 • (12/31/1995) • **84**

Pinot Noir Santa Cruz Mountains Estate 1993 • $22 • (9/15/1996) • **85**

Pinot Noir Santa Cruz Mountains Estate 1989 • $16 • (2/28/1993) • **74**

Pinot Noir Santa Cruz Mountains Estate 1988 • $15 • (2/28/1991) • **83**

Pinot Noir Santa Cruz Mountains Estate Reserve 1996: Smells complex, with cherry, herb and vanilla notes built on a lean frame, with firm acidity and tight tannins. Drinkable now, but worthy of cellaring. Drink through 2005.–J.L. • $35 • (9/15/1999) • **87**

Pinot Noir Santa Cruz Mountains Estate Reserve 1995 • $28 • (1/31/1998) • **87**

Pinot Noir Santa Cruz Mountains Reserve 1994 • $32 • (2/28/1997) • **87**

Sangiovese Santa Cruz Mountains Estate Reserve 1996: Dark, ripe, rich and concentrated, with layers of black cherry, spice, mineral, sage, anise and tar notes. Finishes with finesse and polished vanilla oak flavors. Tasted twice, with consistent notes. Drink now through 2002.–J.L. • $28 • (12/15/1998) • **88**

FOLEY | CALIFORNIA

Chardonnay Santa Barbara County Barrel Select 1997: Bright and juicy, with vivid mandarin, pear, melon and even a hint of fig, all well integrated with sweet oak. Zingy acidity carries the flavors to a long, refreshing finish. Drink now through 2003. • $28 • (6/30/1999) • **91**

Chardonnay Santa Maria Valley Bien Nacido Vineyard 1997: Zippy citrus and pear flavors weave a firm core. The wine is tight and bright, serving up a refreshing blend that finishes moderately. Drink now through 2001. • $24 • (6/30/1999) • **88**

Pinot Noir Santa Maria Valley Santa Maria Hills Vineyard 1997: Dark, ripe and intense, with rich cherry, raspberry and wild berry flavors that are focused and lively, finishing with fruity, spicy flavors. Drink through 2005.–J.L. • $28 • (8/31/1999) • **89**

Sauvignon Blanc Santa Barbara County 1998: Smoky, with toasty melon, citrus, fig and apricot flavors that are vibrant and rich, if a bit muddled on the finish. Drink now.–J.L. • $14 • (5/15/2000) • **86**

Sauvignon Blanc Santa Barbara County 1997: Fresh for its hints of sweet pea, honey and toast, this is a classy, elegant wine, richly styled, soft and silky, filled with fig, melon, citrus, hazelnut and herb notes. Long, heady finish. Drink now through 2003. • $14 • (5/15/1999) • **90**

FOLIE A DEUX | CALIFORNIA

Cabernet Sauvignon Napa Valley 1996: Lean and herbal, this wine opens to offer supple texture and a range of flavors that include thyme, sage, pepper and anise. Drink now through 2002. • $20 • (11/15/1998) • **85**

Cabernet Sauvignon Napa Valley 1995 • $18 • (10/31/1997) • **84**

Cabernet Sauvignon Napa Valley 1993 • $14 • (12/15/1995) • **85**

Cabernet Sauvignon Napa Valley 1988 • $18 • (8/31/1992) • **83**

Cabernet Sauvignon Napa Valley 1987 • $18 • (11/15/1990) • **92**

Cabernet Sauvignon Napa Valley 1986 • $17 • (4/15/1990) • **85**

Cabernet Sauvignon Napa Valley 1984 • $15 • (5/31/1988) • **88**

Cabernet Sauvignon Napa Valley Reserve 1995 • $22 • (11/30/1997) • **88**

Chardonnay California 1996: Smoky and toasty, with an intense core of lemon flavors and a creamy texture. Finish is long and concentrated, with lemon, green apple and flint notes. Drink now through 2003.–J.L. • $14 • (7/31/1999) • **88**

Chardonnay Napa County 1997: Nicely balanced flavors of citrus, apple, pear, spice and toast come together on a well-constructed, medium-bodied frame. Drink now.–J.L. • $20 • (7/31/1999) • **87**

Chardonnay Napa Valley Reserve 1996 • $25 • (5/15/1998) • **84**

Merlot Napa Valley 1988 • $18 • (3/31/1991) • **82**

Merlot Napa Valley Reserve 1995 • $22 • (11/30/1997) • **88**

Merlot Napa Valley Reserve 1993 • $25 • (8/31/1996) • **81**

Zinfandel Amador County 1997: Wild berry flavors turn dry and earthy, with spice and cola notes, finishing with a touch of astringency. Drink now through 2004.–J.L. • $18 • (3/31/2000) • **84**

Zinfandel Amador County Bowman Vineyard 1997: Elegant and ripe, with complex, intense cherry, wild berry, anise, sage and cedar flavors. Long, lingering aftertaste. Drink now through 2004.–J.L. • $24 • (6/15/1999) • **88**

Zinfandel Amador County D'Agostini Vineyard Old Vine 1997: Spicy, with dried raspberry and liqueur notes through the warm, dryly tannic finish. Drink now through 2004.–J.L. • $28 • (5/15/2000) • **85**

Zinfandel Amador County Harvey-Binz Vineyard 128 Year Old Vines 1997: Vanilla and oak overtones dominate this simple Zinfandel.–J.L. • $20 • (5/31/2000) • **77**

Zinfandel Amador County Old Vine 1996 • $18 • (6/15/1998) • **82**

Zinfandel Amador County Old Vine 1995 • $16 • (9/15/1997) • **88**

Zinfandel Fiddletown Eschen Vineyard Old Vine 1997: Very ripe and raisiny, with a tannic, peppery, earthy, leathery streak running through the core of racy Zinfandel flavors. Drink through 2004–J.L. • $22 • (6/15/1999) • **87**

Zinfandel Fiddletown Eschen Vineyard Old Vine 1996 • $22 • (6/15/1998) • **84**

FOPPIANO | CALIFORNIA

Cabernet Sauvignon Russian River Valley 1994 • $14 • (10/31/1997) • **82**

Cabernet Sauvignon Russian River Valley 1990 • $10 • (11/15/1994) • **80**

Cabernet Sauvignon Sonoma County 1989 • $10 • (3/15/1992) • **82**

Merlot Russian River Valley 1996: A strong cherrylike core distinguishes this wine, framed by toasty oak, spice and herbs. Tannins are a bit astringent, but the ensemble is quite enjoyable. Drink now through 2001. • $16 • (9/15/1998) • **86**

Merlot Russian River Valley 1994 • $12 • (8/31/1996) • **82**

Merlot Russian River Valley 1992 • $10 • (9/15/1994) • **83**

Petite Sirah Napa Valley Reserve La Grande Petite 1991 • $20 • (4/30/1995) • **80**

Petite Sirah Russian River Valley 1995 • $14 • (1/01/1998) • **87**

Petite Sirah Russian River Valley 1994 • $11 • (8/31/1997) • **86**

Petite Sirah Russian River Valley 1988 • $8 • (8/31/1990) • **86**

Petite Sirah Russian River Valley Centennial Harvest 1996: A fine effort from a longtime Petite Sirah producer. Concentrated, with firm flavors of chocolate, blackberry, licorice and espresso that linger on the brawny finish. Drink now through 2005.–J.L. • $48 • (6/15/2000) • **88**

Petite Sirah Russian River Valley Centennial Selection La Grande Anniversaire 1993 • $25 • (11/30/1996) • **88**

Petite Sirah Russian River Valley Reserve Le Grande Petite 1987 • $20 • (8/31/1990) • **79**

Petite Sirah Sonoma County 1997: A ripe and intense red from an underappreciated varietal, this wine offers rich plum, pepper, wild berry and leather notes, filling out on the palate and picking up a gamy edge. Altogether quite complete. Drink now through 2008.–J.L. • $18 • (3/31/2000) HR • **88**

Petite Sirah Sonoma County 1992 • $10 • (11/15/1995) • **82**

Petite Sirah Sonoma County 1991 • $11 • (2/28/1995) • **82**

Petite Sirah Sonoma County 1990 • $10 • (6/30/1992) • **87**

Pinot Noir Russian River Valley 1996 • $16 • (6/15/1998) • **82**

Zinfandel Dry Creek Valley 1994 • $11 • (8/31/1997) • **86**

Zinfandel Dry Creek Valley 1993 • $11 • (6/15/1995) • **81**

Zinfandel Dry Creek Valley 1991 • $10 • (9/30/1993) • **87**

Zinfandel Dry Creek Valley Proprietor's Reserve 1987 • $12 • (12/31/1990) • **86**

FORCHINI | CALIFORNIA

Zinfandel Dry Creek Valley Papa Nonno Old Vine Clone 1997: A bit rustic, with rich, ripe berry, tart cherry, orange peel, tar and herb flavors on a firm frame. Drink now.–J.L. • $17 • (6/15/1999) • **85**

FOREST GLEN | CALIFORNIA

Cabernet Sauvignon California Barrel Select 1995 • $10 • (6/30/1998) • **78**

Cabernet Sauvignon California Barrel Select 1994 • $10 • (10/31/1997) • **82**

Cabernet Sauvignon Sonoma County Barrel Select 1992 • $10 • (11/15/1994) • **83**

Cabernet Sauvignon Sonoma County 1991 • $10 • (4/30/1994) • **85**

Cabernet Sauvignon Sonoma County 1990 • $12 • (9/15/1993) • **83**

Chardonnay California 1996 • $10 • (3/31/1998) • **83**

Merlot California 1992 • $10 • (9/15/1994) • **82**

Merlot California Barrel Select 1997: Smoky, herbal and simple, finishing lean and dry.–J.L. • $10 • (10/15/1999) • **74**

Merlot California Barrel Select 1996 • $10 • (12/31/1997) • **86**

Merlot California Barrel Select 1995 • $10 • (2/28/1997) • **84**

Merlot Sonoma County Barrel Select 1994 • $10 • (5/31/1996) • **77**

Sangiovese California Barrel Select 1996: Good, but showcases oak at the expense of Sangiovese fruit, with mild cherry, spice and wild berry. Drink now.–H.S. • $10 • (9/30/1998) • **83**

Shiraz California Barrel Select 1996 • $10 • (6/15/1998) • **82**

Shiraz California Barrel Select 1995 • $10 • (9/15/1997) • **88**

FOREST VILLE | CALIFORNIA

Cabernet Sauvignon California 1993 • $6 • (11/30/1996) • **81**

Cabernet Sauvignon California 1992 • $6 • (11/15/1994) • **78**
Merlot California 1992 • $6 • (9/15/1994) • **79**
Zinfandel California 1993 • $6 • (10/15/1995) • **83**

FORIS | OREGON

Brut Oregon NV • $14 • (11/30/1997) • **87**
Cabernet Sauvignon Rogue Valley 1991 • $9 • (11/30/1994) • **82**
Cabernet Sauvignon Rogue Valley Reserve 1992 • $16 • (3/31/1996) • **87**
Cabernet Sauvignon Rogue Valley Reserve 1991 • $15 • (11/30/1994) • **83**
Cabernet Sauvignon Washington Klipsun Vineyard 1995: Firm in texture, with pretty blueberry, currant and herb flavors that linger on the finish, along with fine-grained tannins. Best after 2001.–H.S. • $25 • (5/31/1999) • **87**
Cabernet Sauvignon Washington Klipsun Vineyard 1994: Very firm and chewy, with coarse tannins around a modest core of currant and cherry flavors. Gets a little earthy on the finish, but stays in balance. Drink through 2003–H.S. • $19 • (12/15/1998) • **84**
Cabernet Sauvignon Washington Klipsun Vineyard 1993 • $13 • (1/31/1998) • **84**
Cabernet Sauvignon Washington Klipsun Vineyard 1992 • $16 • (9/30/1996) • **82**
Cabernet Sauvignon-Merlot-Cabernet Franc Oregon 1994 • $10 • (2/28/1997) • **76**
Cabernet Sauvignon-Merlot-Cabernet Franc Oregon-Washington 1997: Pure and focused, with lovely blackberry, currant and black cherry flavors on a lithe frame, focusing the fruit with hints of pepper and spice on the open-textured finish. Cabernet Sauvignon, Merlot and Cabernet Franc. Drink now through 2007.–H.S. • $12 • (5/15/2000) • **87**
Chardonnay Rogue Valley 1997: Light and refreshing. A simple wine with pretty apple and pear echoing on the finish. Drink now.–H.S. • $10 • (5/15/2000) • **85**
Chardonnay Rogue Valley 1996: The flavors are lovely, with just a hint of honey and spice to the core of apple and pear, but the texture still has enough of a raw edge to want a bit more cellaring. Drink through 2004.–H.S. • $10 • (3/31/2000) • **86**
Chardonnay Rogue Valley Siskiyou Terrace 1996: Has a strong floral character overshadowing the peppery fruit flavors, finishing with a touch of toast. Drink now.–H.S. • $19 • (4/30/1999) • **84**
Merlot Rogue Valley 1997: Firm, almost chewy in texture, with earthy raspberry flavors that linger on the finish. Needs to lose some tannin. Best from 2001 through 2003.–H.S. • $14 • (5/15/2000) • **85**
Merlot Rogue Valley 1996: Firm in texture, with wild berry, wild plum and herb flavors, chewy tannins on the finish and a future. Best from 2001 through 2005.–H.S. • $15 • (6/30/1999) • **86**
Merlot Rogue Valley 1995: Supple in texture and bright in flavor, this harmonious red has lovely boysenberry and vanilla flavors, hinting at olive on the finish. Modest tannins don't get in the way, and the flavors last. Drink now through 2001.–H.S. • $14 • (12/15/1998) • **88**
Merlot Rogue Valley 1993 • $15 • (3/31/1996) • **86**
Merlot Rogue Valley 1992 • $14 • (11/30/1994) • **86**
Merlot Rogue Valley Reserve 1992 • $25 • (3/31/1996) • **79**
Merlot Rogue Valley Rogue Reserve 1994 • $20 • (11/30/1996) • **85**
Merlot Washington Klipsun Vineyard 1994 • $17 • (11/30/1996) • **83**
Pinot Blanc Rogue Valley 1998: Bright, ripe and generous. A brilliant mouthful of pear, melon and mineral flavors that dance deftly through the open-textured finish. A real zinger. Drink now.–H.S. • $11 • (3/31/2000) • **89**
Pinot Blanc Rogue Valley 1997: Supple and spicy, with a citrusy tang to the pineapple and coconut-almond flavors. Drink now.–H.S. • $11 • (2/28/1999) • **84**
Pinot Gris Rogue Valley 1998: Ripe and spicy, with distinctive nutmeg and floral accents to the melon and pear. A beautiful example of what this grape can do when it expresses itself simply and plainly. Drink now.–H.S. • $11 • (3/31/2000) • **89**
Pinot Gris Rogue Valley 1997: Earthy, floral flavors add extra notes to the chorus of apple cider and melon flavors. Finish is a bit raucous. Drink now.–H.S. • $11 • (4/30/1999) • **83**
Pinot Noir Rogue Valley 1997: Firm in texture, with ripe currant and berry flavors on a light frame. Needs time to soften. Drink through 2002–H.S. • $14 • (6/30/1999) • **82**
Pinot Noir Rogue Valley 1995 • $11 • (2/28/1997) • **83**
Pinot Noir Rogue Valley 1994 • $11 • (4/30/1996) • **87**
Pinot Noir Rogue Valley 1993 • $11 • (3/31/1996) • **87**
Pinot Noir Rogue Valley 1992 • $10 • (11/30/1994) • **82**
Pinot Noir Rogue Valley Maple Ranch 1994 • $25 • (10/31/1996) • **85**
Pinot Noir Rogue Valley Siskiyou Terrace 1996: Soft and generous, with plum and spice flavors that linger on the finish, with a hint of bitterness. Drink now through 2001.–H.S. • $19 • (12/15/1998) • **85**
Ruby Oregon 1995 • $10/375 ml. • (12/31/1997) • **85**
Ruby Oregon 1993 • $10/375 ml. • (3/31/1996) • **87**

FORMAN | CALIFORNIA

Cabernet Sauvignon Napa Valley 1998: An earthy streak runs through this young, reduced wine. Rich and complex, with pretty new oak flavors adding to the ripe currant and cherry.–J.L. • $NA • (8/31/1999) (BT) • **90-94**
Cabernet Sauvignon Napa Valley 1997: Supple and concentrated, with tight currant, mint, sage and cedar. Gains depth and nuance, with a complex aftertaste. Drink now through 2008.–J.L. • $45 • (5/31/2000) • **90**
Cabernet Sauvignon Napa Valley 1996: An earthy, tarry, herbal streak runs through this otherwise firm, elegant and cedary wine, with mineral, spice, currant and plum notes. Earthy tannins on the long, complex finish. Drink through 2009–J.L. • $45 • (11/15/1999) • **92**
Cabernet Sauvignon Napa Valley 1995 • $49 Ⓐ • (6/30/1998) • **91**
Cabernet Sauvignon Napa Valley 1994 • $62 Ⓐ • (5/31/1997) • **92**
Cabernet Sauvignon Napa Valley 1993 • $27 Ⓐ • (4/30/1996) • **88**
Cabernet Sauvignon Napa Valley 1992 • $30 • (6/15/1995) CS • **93**
Cabernet Sauvignon Napa Valley 1991 • $46 Ⓐ • (3/15/1994) CS • **89**
Cabernet Sauvignon Napa Valley 1990 • $52 Ⓐ • (7/15/1993) • **89**
Cabernet Sauvignon Napa Valley 1989 • $34 Ⓐ • (7/15/1992) • **87**
Cabernet Sauvignon Napa Valley 1988: Starts out gamy, then works its way into more earthy currant, cedar and spice. A good effort, well balanced, with good depth and it's not too tannic but, like most '88s, it's drying on the finish. Contains 10 percent Merlot, 10 percent Cabernet Franc. (1988 California Cabernet retrospective tasting). Drink now through 2002.–J.L. • $34 Ⓐ • (11/15/1998) • **86**
Cabernet Sauvignon Napa Valley 1987 • $46 Ⓐ • (12/15/1997) • **90**
Cabernet Sauvignon Napa Valley 1986 • $50 Ⓐ • (6/15/1989) • **93**
Cabernet Sauvignon Napa Valley 1985 • $53 Ⓐ • (6/15/1988) • **92**
Cabernet Sauvignon Napa Valley 1984 • $17 • (4/30/1987) • **92**
Chardonnay Napa Valley 1997: Ripe and intense, with a tight core of pear, fig, spice and nutmeg, finishing with a citrus edge. Needs time. Tasted twice, with consistent notes. Drink through 2004.–J.L. • $29 • (4/30/1999) • **89**
Chardonnay Napa Valley 1996 • $27 • (11/30/1997) • **90**
Merlot Napa Valley 1997: Tightly wound, with a trim but complex band of cedar, cherry, currant and anise. Finishes with chewy tannins and a cedary edge. Best from 2002 through 2008.–J.L. • $32 • (4/30/2000) • **88**
Merlot Napa Valley 1996: Starts out earthy and gamy, with chewy, leathery tannins, and it's dense from start to finish, with glimpses of currant and black cherry, turning austere on the finish. Best from 2001 through 2006.–J.L. • $36 • (5/15/1999) • **88**
Merlot Napa Valley 1995 • $35 • (11/30/1997) • **85**
Merlot Napa Valley 1994 • $40 • (9/15/1997) • **89**

FOUNTAIN GROVE | CALIFORNIA

Cabernet Sauvignon California 1995: Pretty weedy, with herbal, vegetal flavors at the core. Short, and not particularly pleasant. • $NA • (8/31/1998) • **73**
Cabernet Sauvignon California 1994 • $10 • (9/15/1997) • **82**
Chardonnay California 1996: Rich, toasty, buttery flavors, with hints of citrus and green apple on the finish and an interesting floral note. Drink now.–T.G. • $10 • (7/31/1998) • **84**
Merlot California 1997: Simple and slightly firm, with light raspberry and herb flavors.–J.L. • $10 • (10/15/1999) • **79**
Merlot California 1996: Apple, cherry and strawberry flavors are a bit weedy. Charry finish. Drink now.–J.L. • $10 • (9/30/1998) • **78**
Petit Noir Russian River Valley 1995 • $8 • (7/31/1997) • **87**
Sauvignon Blanc California 1997: Brightly textured, with a core of melon, grapefruit and herbs. The finish, redolent of minerals and herbs, shows bright acidity and lingers. Good wine, good price. Drink now through 2001. • $9 • (5/31/1999) • **86**
Sauvignon Blanc California 1996 • $9 • (3/31/1998) • **88**
Sauvignon Blanc North Coast 1998: Refreshing and racy, with aromas of tangy apple and gunpowder. Better with food. Drink now through 2003.–J.L. • $10 • (4/30/2000) • **84**

Key: SS—Spectator Selection. CS—Cellar Selection. HR—Highly Recommended. $NA—Price not available. (BT)—Barrel tasting. Ⓐ—Auction Price.
For a key to the tasters' initials, see "How to Use These Listings."
Dates in parentheses represent the issues in which the ratings were published.

FOUR VINES | CALIFORNIA

Syrah Paso Robles 1997: Complex and concentrated, with a range of ripe plum, black cherry and toasty oak, all nicely focused. Supple finish. Drink now.–J.L. • $29 • (12/31/1999) • **87**

Zinfandel Paso Robles 1997: A refreshing, tangy and focused blend of cranberry, red currant, spice and raspberry flavors that linger on the finish. Drink now through 2004.–J.L. • $17 • (11/15/1999) • **85**

FOWLER | CALIFORNIA

Pinot Noir Central Coast 1997: Smooth and polished, supple for the vintage, with a modest range of dried cherry, anise, earth and barklike flavors. Drink through 2005.–J.L. • $25 • (9/15/1999) • **86**

Pinot Noir Central Coast 1996: Elegant and well balanced, with a modest core of spicy cherry, wild berry, subtle earth and tea notes. Finishes with modest tannins, so it's best to drink soon.–J.L. • $25 • (9/30/1998) • **82**

Pinot Noir Central Coast 1995 • $32 • (8/31/1997) • **88**

FOX CREEK | CALIFORNIA

Chardonnay Mendocino Ceago Vinegarden 1997: Ripe, clean and fruity, with plenty of pear, fig, apple and nectarine flavors that tilt toward the crisp side. Spicy, oaky aftertaste. Drink now through 2002.–J.L. • $30 • (7/31/1999) • **87**

FOX MOUNTAIN | CALIFORNIA

Cabernet Sauvignon Russian River Valley Reserve 1986 • $20 • (11/15/1992) • **87**

Cabernet Sauvignon Russian River Valley Reserve 1985 • $19 • (9/15/1989) • **75**

Cabernet Sauvignon Russian River Valley Reserve 1982 • $18 • (12/31/1987) • **77**

Cabernet Sauvignon Russian River Valley Reserve 1981 • $16 • (12/15/1986) • **79**

Cabernet Sauvignon Sonoma County Reserve 1987 • $15 • (11/15/1994) • **79**

Chardonnay California Limited Release 1996: Simple and sweet, with canned-fruit flavors. Flavors straighten out, become more palatable on the finish. Drink now.–T.G. • $12 • (7/31/1998) • **78**

Sauvignon Blanc Sonoma County Limited Release 1996 • $10 • (4/30/1998) • **85**

FOX RUN | NEW YORK

Blanc de Blancs Finger Lakes Méthode Champenoise NV • $NA • (5/15/1998) • **86**

Cabernet Franc Finger Lakes 1997: A focused red from New York with clean flavors of red plum, berry and appealing herbal notes on a firm frame. Medium-bodied, with red currant and coffee notes on the finish. Well done. Drink now through 2001.–K.M. • $13 • (10/15/1999) • **86**

Chardonnay Finger Lakes 1996 • $9 • (3/31/1998) • **84**

Chardonnay Finger Lakes Reserve 1998: Sweet and simple. This lush white shows plenty of sweet oak, with modest apple flavors and soft acidity. Drink now.–T.M. • $12 • (5/31/2000) • **80**

Chardonnay Finger Lakes Reserve 1997: Refreshing, with some nice crunchy apple flavors, and some ripe pear notes. Buttery and spicy notes chime in on the finish with a hint of lime. Drink now.–K.M. • $12 • (10/15/1999) • **84**

Chardonnay Finger Lakes Reserve 1996 • $12 • (3/31/1998) • **87**

Meritage Finger Lakes 1995 • $20 • (5/31/1997) • **80**

Pinot Noir Finger Lakes 1998: A candied strawberry aroma and flavor runs through this simple Pinot, finishing with a cough-syruplike note.–T.M. • $11 • (3/31/2000) • **79**

Pinot Noir Finger Lakes 1996: A light, lean red wine, with modest herb, smoke and cherry flavors, a soft texture and a short finish. Drink now. • $10 • (10/31/1998) • **78**

Pinot Noir Finger Lakes 1995 • $15 • (12/31/1997) • **83**

Pinot Noir Finger Lakes Reserve 1998: A silky texture carries smoke and dried cherry flavors on soft tannins. A bit candied, but with varietal character. Drink now.–T.M. • $20 • (5/31/2000) • **82**

Pinot Noir Finger Lakes Reserve 1997: A very dry, enjoyable Pinot Noir, with fresh, light cherry and smoke flavors, medium body and moderate tannins. Drink now. • $20 • (7/31/1999) • **85**

Port Finger Lakes NV: This sweet red shows simple chocolate and candied-cherry flavors, with quite a kick of alcohol on the finish.–T.M. • $20/375 ml. • (1/01/2000) • **78**

Riesling Finger Lakes 1998: A touch of sweetness perks up the apricot and nectarine flavors, while moderate acidity balances the whole package. Drink now.–B.S. • $9 • (3/31/2000) • **84**

Riesling Finger Lakes 1997: Lovely peach and apricot aromas and flavors highlight this spätlese-style Riesling, which offers a rich texture and a cleansing finish that balances the hint of sweetness. Drink now.–B.S. • $9 • (7/31/1999) • **84**

Riesling Finger Lakes 1996 • $9 • (3/31/1998) • **82**

Riesling Finger Lakes Dry 1998: Citrus and apple flavors are clean and well-defined in this round white. The finish is soft and generous. Drink now. –T.M. • $10 • (5/31/2000) • **83**

Riesling Finger Lakes Dry 1997: Apple, honey and a pine accent mark this firm, dry Riesling. Richly textured and delicate, it ends on a crisp appley note. Drink now.–B.S. • $10 • (7/31/1999) • **83**

Riesling Finger Lakes Dry 1996 • $10 • (3/31/1998) • **81**

Vintage Port Finger Lakes 1996 • $20/375 ml. • (6/15/1998) • **80**

FOXEN | CALIFORNIA

Cabernet Franc Santa Maria Valley Tinaquaic Vineyard 1994 • $24 • (5/31/1997) • **84**

Cabernet Franc Santa Maria Valley Tinaquaic Vineyard 1993 • $24 • (4/30/1996) • **90**

Cabernet Sauvignon Santa Barbara County 1994 • $24 • (11/15/1996) • **88**

Cabernet Sauvignon Santa Barbara County 1993 • $22 • (12/15/1995) • **86**

Cabernet Sauvignon Santa Barbara County 1992 • $20 • (10/31/1994) • **87**

Cabernet Sauvignon Santa Barbara County 1991 • $20 • (2/28/1994) HR • **90**

Cabernet Sauvignon Santa Barbara County 1990 • $20 • (11/15/1992) • **84**

Cabernet Sauvignon Santa Barbara County 1989 • $20 • (11/15/1991) • **91**

Cabernet Sauvignon Santa Barbara County 1988: Medium-bodied, a shade tart, with earthy mushroom aromas and a trim band of cherry- and blackberry-scented flavors. Turns simple on the finish. (1988 California Cabernet retrospective tasting). Drink now through 2001.–J.L. • $18 • (11/15/1998) • **82**

Chardonnay Santa Maria Valley 1997: Bright apple, lemon, pear and herb flavors have subtle earthy notes. Finishes long and complex. Drink now through 2002.–J.L. • $20 • (7/31/1999) • **89**

Chardonnay Santa Maria Valley 1996: Intense and lively, with a distinct earthiness that adds an attractive element to the core of fig, tropical fruit and spice. Turns complex and creamy on the aftertaste.–J.L. • $20 • (7/31/1998) • **88**

Chardonnay Santa Maria Valley Bien Nacido Vineyard 1996: Decidedly earthy but complex in its own way, with spicy pear, fig and a salted peanut quality that gives it a distinct personality. Drink now through 2002.–J.L. • $25 • (6/30/1999) • **87**

Chardonnay Santa Maria Valley Tinaquaic Vineyard 1996: Silky, complex and delicate, with a wide range of toast, pear, peach and spice flavors that come together on the long, focused finish. Drink now through 2002.–J.L. • $30 • (7/31/1999) • **91**

Merlot Santa Barbara County 1995 • $24 • (4/30/1998) • **88**

Merlot Santa Barbara County 1994 • $24 • (3/31/1997) • **84**

Merlot Santa Barbara County 1992 • $22 • (12/15/1995) • **84**

Merlot Santa Barbara County 1991 • $22 • (3/15/1994) • **88**

Merlot Santa Maria Valley Tinaquaic Vineyard 1993 • $24 • (4/30/1996) • **90**

Pinot Noir Santa Barbara County 1995 • $24 • (12/31/1996) • **86**

Pinot Noir Santa Maria 1996 • $24 • (1/31/1998) • **87**

Pinot Noir Santa Maria Valley 1994 • $20 • (1/31/1996) • **87**

Pinot Noir Santa Maria Valley 1993 • $20 • (11/15/1995) • **88**

Pinot Noir Santa Maria Valley 1992 • $30 • (11/30/1994) • **87**

Pinot Noir Santa Maria Valley 1991 • $20 • (1/31/1994) HR • **89**

Pinot Noir Santa Maria Valley 1990 • $20 • (9/30/1992) • **89**

Pinot Noir Santa Maria Valley 1987 • $16 • (12/15/1989) • **78**

Pinot Noir Santa Maria Valley Bien Nacido Vineyard 1997: Polished and flavorful, featuring a complex core of mineral-tinged cherry, cola, herb and mushroom flavors. Finishes smooth and focused. Drink now through 2004. –J.L. • $30 • (8/31/1999) • **88**

Pinot Noir Santa Maria Valley Bien Nacido Vineyard 1996: Earthy, with spicy cherry, cola and berry notes. Tight and tannic; best to cellar short-term to let it soften and evolve. Drink now through 2002.–J.L. • $30 • (8/31/1998) • **86**

Pinot Noir Santa Maria Valley Bien Nacido Vineyard 1995 • $30 • (7/31/1997) • **88**

Pinot Noir Santa Maria Valley Bien Nacido Vineyard 1993 • $26 • (11/15/1995) • **90**

Pinot Noir Santa Maria Valley Julia's Vineyard 1997: Ripe and rich, with a smoky, earthy background to the black cherry, mineral and tea flavors. Finishes firm, with dry tannins. Drink now through 2003.–J.L. • $30 • (9/15/1999) • **87**

Pinot Noir Santa Maria Valley Julia's Vineyard 1996: Smooth and supple, with racy cola, black cherry, cedar and spice and a lingering aftertaste. Drink through 2004.–J.L. • $25 • (8/31/1998) • **88**

Pinot Noir Santa Ynez Valley Sanford & Benedict Vineyard 1997: Fresh, bright and vibrant, with a range of cola, herb and cherry flavors, finishing firm and concentrated. Best now through 2004.–J.L. • $30 • (9/15/1999) • **87**

Pinot Noir Santa Ynez Valley Sanford & Benedict Vineyard 1996: This earthy, leathery style struggles to find its fruit focus. Hints of cherry and berry slowly emerge, but are still lost in the earthiness. Drink now through 2002.–J.L. • $30 • (9/30/1998) • **84**

Pinot Noir Santa Ynez Valley Sanford & Benedict Vineyard 1995 • $30 • (9/30/1997) • **88**

Pinot Noir Santa Ynez Valley Sanford & Benedict Vineyard 1993 • $30 • (11/15/1995) • **90**

Pinot Noir Santa Ynez Valley Sanford & Benedict Vineyard 1992 • $30 • (1/31/1995) • **87**

Pinot Noir Santa Ynez Valley Sanford & Benedict Vineyard 1991 • $30 • (2/28/1994) • **89**

Syrah Santa Ynez Valley Morehouse Vineyard 1997: Wonderful, plump, ripe cherry, raspberry and earthy currant flavors fan out on the finish, where they turn elegant and polished. Drink through 2008.–J.L. • $35 • (11/15/1999) • **90**

Syrah Santa Ynez Valley Morehouse Vineyard 1995 • $25 • (8/31/1997) • **92**

Syrah Santa Ynez Valley Morehouse Vineyard 1994 • $25 • (7/31/1996) • **88**

Viognier Santa Ynez Valley Rothberg Vineyard 1998: Quite rich and concentrated, with layers of fig, apricot, honey, nutmeg and spice. Holds its focus on the finish. Drink now through 2004.–J.L. • $25 • (11/30/1999) • **88**

Viognier Santa Ynez Valley Rothberg Vineyard 1997: A firm, bright wine, with a finely wound blend of flavors that includes lemon, lime, orange, pear and mineral. The finish is long and clean, the ensemble offers subtlety and finesse. Drink now through 2001. • $25 • (11/15/1998) • **89**

FOXHOLLOW | CALIFORNIA

Cabernet Sauvignon California Barrel Select 1994 • $9 • (10/31/1997) • **84**

Cabernet Sauvignon Paso Robles 1991 • $10 • (6/30/1994) • **82**

Chardonnay California Barrel Select 1996 • $9 • (12/15/1997) • **84**

Merlot California 1992 • $10 • (9/15/1994) • **81**

Merlot California Barrel Select 1996 • $9 • (12/15/1997) • **82**

FOXRIDGE | CALIFORNIA

Chardonnay Carneros 1997: Brightly textured, with pear, green apple and citrus notes. Finishes with toasty oak. Drink now. • $10 • (2/28/1999) • **83**

FRANCISCAN OAKVILLE ESTATE CALIFORNIA

Cabernet Sauvignon Napa Valley 1997: Smooth, with integrated herb, cherry and currant flavors. Firms on the finish, with a touch of greenness to the tannins. Best from 2001 through 2006.–J.L. • $25 • (4/30/2000) • **84**

Cabernet Sauvignon Napa Valley 1996: Shows lots of rustic, earthy, meaty, gamy flavors that are firm and focused, with a long, flavorful finish. Tannins are firm but ripe and integrated. Drink now through 2005.–J.L. • $20 • (11/15/1999) • **87**

Cabernet Sauvignon Napa Valley 1995: Supple and fruity, with creamy cherry, plum and berry notes that are elegant and polished, finishing with hints of coffee and spice. Drink through 2005.–J.L. • $17 • (8/31/1998) • **88**

Cabernet Sauvignon Napa Valley 1994 • $16 • (5/15/1997) • **88**

Cabernet Sauvignon Napa Valley 1993 • $15 • (12/15/1996) • **87**

Cabernet Sauvignon Napa Valley 1992 • $15 • (12/15/1995) • **87**

Cabernet Sauvignon Napa Valley 1991 • $13 • (11/15/1994) • **82**

Cabernet Sauvignon Napa Valley 1990 • $13 • (10/31/1993) • **88**

Cabernet Sauvignon Napa Valley 1989 • $13 • (5/15/1993) • **87**

Cabernet Sauvignon Napa Valley 1988 • $12 • (8/31/1992) • **81**

Cabernet Sauvignon Napa Valley 1987 • $12 • (2/15/1991) • **89**

Cabernet Sauvignon Napa Valley 1986 • $11 • (7/15/1990) • **84**

Cabernet Sauvignon Napa Valley 1985 • $11 • (5/15/1989) • **86**

Cabernet Sauvignon Napa Valley Library Selection 1987 • $20 • (12/15/1997) • **86**

Key: SS—Spectator Selection. CS—Cellar Selection. HR—Highly Recommended. $NA—Price not available. (BT)—Barrel tasting. Ⓐ—Auction Price. For a key to the tasters' initials, see "How to Use These Listings."
Dates in parentheses represent the issues in which the ratings were published.

Cabernet Sauvignon Napa Valley Reserve 1988 • $18 • (3/15/1993) • **81**

Cabernet Sauvignon Napa Valley Reserve 1985 • $15 • (5/31/1990) • **88**

Chardonnay Napa Valley 1997: Well proportioned, with a nice interplay of ripe pear, apple and melon and floral notes. Quite appealing though lacking the extra dimensions to be outstanding. Drink now through 2001.–J.L. • $17 • (7/31/1999) • **88**

Chardonnay Napa Valley 1996 • $15 • (6/30/1998) SS • **90**

Chardonnay Napa Valley Cuvée Sauvage 1996: An elegant, understated, richly flavored wine, with smoky, toasty oak, ripe fig and pear flavors that linger. Finishes with wonderful complexity. Drink now through 2002.–J.L. • $35 • (6/30/1999) • **92**

Magnificat Napa Valley 1996: Focused and elegant, with notes of leather and game running through the black cherry, plum, cedar, sage and tobacco flavors. Firm on the finish, where the flavors build, turning even more complex. Drink now through 2005.–J.L. • $35 • (10/15/1999) • **90**

Magnificat Napa Valley 1995: Ripe, with integrated flavors of black cherry, plum and wild berry. Finishes with spice, cedar, sage and mineral notes, and the tannins fold in nicely. Drink through 2006.–J.L. • $30 • (11/15/1998) • **89**

Magnificat Napa Valley 1994 • $25 • (11/30/1997) • **89**

Meritage Magnificat Napa Valley 1993 • $20 • (11/15/1996) • **91**

Meritage Magnificat Napa Valley 1991 • $20 • (12/15/1995) • **89**

Meritage Magnificat Napa Valley 1990 • $20 • (11/15/1994) • **85**

Meritage Magnificat Napa Valley 1989 • $18 • (11/15/1993) • **86**

Meritage Napa Valley 1988 • $18 • (7/15/1992) • **89**

Meritage Napa Valley 1987 • $17 • (4/30/1991) • **87**

Meritage Napa Valley 1986 • $15 • (7/31/1990) • **79**

Meritage Napa Valley 1985 • $16 • (3/31/1990) • **90**

Merlot Napa Valley 1996: A curious and complex style that stretches the band of flavors, with a range that goes from ripe cherry and currant to herb and bell pepper. Well-integrated tannins make it appealing now; best now through 2004.–J.L. • $17 • (10/15/1998) • **86**

Merlot Napa Valley 1994 • $17 • (10/15/1996) • **84**

Merlot Napa Valley 1993 • $16 • (12/15/1995) • **89**

Merlot Napa Valley 1990 • $12 • (7/15/1993) • **87**

Merlot Napa Valley 1989 • $12 • (5/31/1992) • **79**

Merlot Napa Valley 1987 • $13 • (6/15/1990) • **88**

Merlot Napa Valley 1986 • $12 • (7/31/1989) • **80**

Merlot Napa Valley Reserve 1991 • $25 • (1/31/1995) • **89**

Zinfandel Napa Valley 1994 • $15 • (10/15/1996) • **88**

Zinfandel Napa Valley 1993 • $11 • (6/15/1995) • **86**

Zinfandel Napa Valley 1992 • $12 • (10/15/1994) • **80**

Zinfandel Napa Valley 1991 • $10 • (9/30/1993) • **85**

Zinfandel Napa Valley 1990 • $10 • (7/31/1992) • **87**

Zinfandel Napa Valley 1989 • $10 • (7/31/1991) • **88**

Zinfandel Napa Valley 1988 • $9 • (5/31/1990) • **87**

FRANK, DR. KONSTANTIN | NEW YORK

Cabernet Finger Lakes NV • $15 • (10/31/1997) • **85**

Cabernet Sauvignon Finger Lakes 1995 • $22 • (6/15/1997) • **85**

Cabernet Sauvignon Finger Lakes 1993 • $22 • (6/30/1995) • **79**

Cabernet Sauvignon Finger Lakes 1991 • $22 • (6/30/1995) • **84**

Chardonnay Finger Lakes 1998: Generous and well structured. Ripe melon, vanilla and honey flavors run through this creamy-textured white, with enough acidity for liveliness. Drink now through 2002.–T.M. • $12 • (5/31/2000) • **87**

Chardonnay Finger Lakes Barrel Fermented 1996 • $11 • (5/15/1998) • **84**

Chardonnay New York Salmon Run 1998: Straightforward buttery aroma is followed by medium-weight apple and pear flavors. Decent zip on the finish. Drink now.–T.M. • $10 • (1/01/2000) • **83**

Gewürztraminer Finger Lakes 1998: A little reticent in its varietal character, yet showing good melon, litchi and spice notes, a medium body and a firm texture. A second bottle was dominated by a sulfur and rotten egg smell, so beware of bottle variation. Drink now.–B.S. • $13 • (11/15/1999) • **80**

Gewürztraminer Finger Lakes 1997: This shows characteristic Gewürz notes, but there's an off-putting sweaty, sour milk flavor that dominates. Not recommended. Tasted twice, with consistent notes.–T.M. • $13 • (12/15/1998) • **68**

Gewürztraminer Finger Lakes 1996: This wine wants to go somewhere, with buttery and apricot flavors, but it's hollow in the middle, cidery on the finish.–K.M. • $13 • (8/31/1998) • **76**

Johannisberg Riesling Finger Lakes Dry 1998: A white in the off-dry style rather than truly dry, focused and tasting of apricot on a lightweight frame. Good citrus note on the clean finish. Drink now.–B.S. • $10 • (11/15/1999) • **83**

Johannisberg Riesling Finger Lakes Dry 1997: This easy-to-like Riesling is generous in flavor, sweet in style and well balanced with acidity. Drink now. • $10 • (11/15/1998) • **83**

Johannisberg Riesling Finger Lakes Dry 1996 • $10 • (10/31/1997) • **81**

Johannisberg Riesling Finger Lakes Ice Wine 1995 • $30/375 ml. • (5/31/1997) • **88**

Johannisberg Riesling Finger Lakes Salmon Run NV: Easy to quaff. Slightly sweet, very fruity-tasting Riesling, with attractive pear, pineapple and apple flavors backed by good acidity. Drink now. • $9 • (11/15/1998) • **82**

Johannisberg Riesling Finger Lakes Salmon Run 1996 • $9 • (10/31/1997) • **84**

Johannisberg Riesling Finger Lakes Semi-Dry 1997: A sweeter style Riesling, with appealing but simple pear and honey flavors and a generous texture. Drink now. • $10 • (11/15/1998) • **81**

Johannisberg Riesling Finger Lakes Semi-Dry 1996 • $10 • (10/31/1997) • **83**

Johannisberg Riesling New York Salmon Run 1998: Attractive peach and citrus flavors lack focus and concentration, and the whole presentation is loosely knit. May firm up in time. Drink now.–B.S. • $9 • (11/15/1999) • **80**

Merlot Finger Lakes 1997: Lively, with an enticing spicy element and lovely flavors of blueberry and raspberry. A good, medium-bodied quaff. Drink now.–K.M. • $18 • (11/15/1999) • **83**

Pinot Gris Finger Lakes 1998: This juicy white offers pleasant, modest flavors of pears and citrus; it's round on the palate but has lively acidity. Drink now.–T.M. • $15 • (5/31/2000) • **83**

Pinot Noir Finger Lakes 1996: A basic red table wine, with light but agreeable cherry flavors and enough tannin and acidity to give it a crisp texture. • $19 • (10/31/1998) • **79**

Pinot Noir Finger Lakes 1995 • $19 • (8/31/1997) • **84**

Pinot Noir Finger Lakes 1992 • $18 • (5/15/1995) • **79**

Pinot Noir Finger Lakes 1990 • $18 • (5/15/1995) • **83**

Pinot Noir Finger Lakes 1985 • $15 • (6/15/1988) • **75**

Pinot Noir Finger Lakes Fleur de Pinot Noir NV: Mature-tasting, with stewy, leathery flavors, touches of spice and brown sugar on the finish.–K.M. • $12 • (8/31/1998) • **79**

Rkatsiteli Finger Lakes 1998: A soft, rich, inviting white, full of floral and peach nuances that end with a hint of earthiness. Drink now.–B.S. • $13 • (11/15/1999) • **82**

Rkatsiteli Finger Lakes 1997: This distinctive white resembles a Riesling in its crisp acidity, peach and pine flavors and racy texture. Very refreshing, with a core of fruit that keeps it lively. Drink now.–T.M. • $13 • (12/15/1998) • **85**

FRANK-ROMBAUER | CALIFORNIA

Cabernet Sauvignon Rutherford Frank-Rombauer Larkmead Cellars Reserve 1996: A jazzy style, with pretty oak shadings leading to a core of ripe cherry, berry, currant and spice that gains mocha-flavored nuances. Best from 2002 through 2010.–J.L. • $60 • (5/15/2000) • **89**

Cabernet Sauvignon Rutherford Frank-Rombauer Larkmead Cellars 1995: Dark and concentrated, with a firm core of claylike mineral, black cherry, blueberry and anise flavors. Very soft and rich on the complex finish, with vanilla oak and spice notes and grainy tannins. Drink now through 2005.–J.L. • $50 • (6/15/1999) • **90**

Chardonnay Napa Valley Frank-Rombauer Larkmead Cellars 1998: Very tasty, with pretty vanilla-scented oak leading to soft, ripe pear, apple, melon and fig notes. Turns elegant and polished. Drink now through 2004.–J.L. • $27 • (5/31/2000) • **89**

Chardonnay Napa Valley Frank-Rombauer Larkmead Cellars 1997: Refreshing, with concentrated lemon, peach, pear and custard flavors on a focused frame. Toasty and fruit-driven, with a pure, elegant finish. Drink now.–J.L. • $27 • (7/31/1999) • **88**

Merlot Napa Valley Frank-Rombauer Larkmead Cellars 1996: Smooth, ripe and plummy, with spicy berry, cherry, anise, herb and cedar notes that are elegant. Drink now through 2007.–J.L. • $29 • (5/31/2000) • **87**

Zinfandel Napa Valley Frank-Rombauer Larkmead Cellars 1997: Quite ripe and juicy, with a sweet-tasting, decadent edge to the plum and wild berry flavors, so be forewarned. Drink now through 2006.–J.L. • $23 • (5/31/2000) • **83**

FRANK-ROMBAUER LARKMEAD | CALIFORNIA

Cabernet Sauvignon Napa Valley 1993 • $50 • (5/15/1997) • **84**

Sangiovese Napa Valley 1992 • $23 • (5/15/1997) • **87**

FRANUS | CALIFORNIA

Cabernet Sauvignon Napa Valley 1996: Elegant, featuring a complex range of cedar, currant, anise and tobacco flavors that linger on the finish. Tannins are present, but smooth and integrated. Best now through 2006.–J.L. • $28 • (10/15/1999) • **89**

Cabernet Sauvignon Napa Valley 1995: Firm in texture, with ripe cherry and coffee flavors emerging through the grainy tannins. Flavors persist, suggesting it will benefit from cellaring. Drink through 2005.–H.S. • $28 • (10/31/1998) • **88**

Sauvignon Blanc Napa Valley Farella-Park Vineyard 1998: Bright in flavor and refined in texture, ultragrassy and herbal, with plenty of gooseberry flavors that come across clean and refreshing and linger enticingly. Drink now through 2002.–H.S. • $15 • (3/31/2000) • **89**

Zinfandel Contra Costa County Planchon Vineyard 1998: Tough and leathery, with a glimmer of cherry emerging before the tannins clamp down. Drink now.–J.L. • $19 • (5/31/2000) • **81**

Zinfandel Contra Costa County Planchon Vineyard 1997: A hearty style, with bold earthy cherry, currant, anise, sage and tar notes, turning elegant and sharply focused on the finish. Drink now through 2003.–J.L. • $18 • (5/31/1999) • **91**

Zinfandel Contra Costa County Planchon Vineyard 1996 • $NA • (6/15/1998) • **89**

Zinfandel Mount Veeder Brandlin Vineyard 1998: Beefy, with a leathery streak dominating the pepper and plum notes. Turns dry and tannic. Drink now through 2004.–J.L. • $NA • (6/15/2000) • **86**

Zinfandel Mount Veeder Brandlin Vineyard 1997: Chunky in style, with stewed plum, blackberry, earth, mineral and meaty sage flavors, finishing with a touch of heat and firm tannins. Best from 2001 through 2007.–J.L. • $24 • (6/30/2000) • **87**

Zinfandel Mount Veeder Brandlin Ranch 1995: Intense, with lots of wild berry, black cherry, spice, pepper and sage notes, turning tight and tannic on the finish. A year or more may soften the rough spots, but it's true to Mount Veeder Zinfandel. Drink now through 2003.–J.L. • $20 • (11/30/1998) • **88**

Zinfandel Mount Veeder Brandlin Ranch 1992 • $16 • (1/31/1995) • **88**

Zinfandel Mount Veeder Brandlin Ranch 1991 • $13 • (9/30/1993) • **86**

Zinfandel Napa Valley Hendry Vineyard 1993 • $14 • (10/15/1995) • **85**

Zinfandel Napa Valley Hendry Vineyard 1992 • $13 • (7/31/1994) • **88**

Zinfandel Napa Valley Hendry Vineyard 1991 • $13 • (9/30/1993) • **88**

Zinfandel Napa Valley Hendry Vineyard 1989 • $13 • (10/15/1992) • **83**

FRAZIER | CALIFORNIA

Cabernet Sauvignon Napa Valley Lupine Hill Vineyard 1997: Quite earthy, with leathery notes dominating the ripe, rich coffee, chocolate and black currant flavors. A controversial wine that's not for everyone. Drink now through 2005.–J.L. • $45 • (5/15/2000) • **84**

Cabernet Sauvignon Napa Valley Lupine Hill Vineyard 1996: Rich and well oaked, with broad, smooth, supple black cherry, wild berry, plum and currant flavors that are elegant and polished. Drink now through 2008. –J.L. • $36 • (11/15/1999) • **89**

Cabernet Sauvignon Napa Valley Lupine Hill Vineyard 1995: A plushly textured wine, with layers of black cherry, black currant, licorice, herb and cedar. Tannins are firm yet ripe; it finishes long and bright. Drink now through 2005. • $36 • (10/31/1998) • **88**

Merlot Napa Valley Lupine Hill Vineyard 1997: Concentrated, with rich chocolate, cola and vanilla flavors. Good length, with a touch of dryness to the tannins. Best from 2001 through 2006.–J.L. • $34 • (5/15/2000) • **88**

Merlot Napa Valley Lupine Hill Vineyard 1996: Smooth and polished, with pretty toasty oak, ripe plum, herb, currant and berryish notes, keeping its focus and turning supple. Mildly tannic. Drink now through 2005.–J.L. • $28 • (11/15/1999) • **88**

Merlot Napa Valley Lupine Hill Vineyard 1995 • $28 • (6/30/1998) • **85**

FREEMARK ABBEY | CALIFORNIA

Cabernet Sauvignon Napa Valley 1996: Shows a strong, cedary dill edge before working into smoother, more polished currant and cherry. Turns simple. Drink now.–J.L. • $26 • (5/31/2000) • **85**

Cabernet Sauvignon Napa Valley 1995: An herbal style of California Cabernet that's well-executed, with sage, black cherry, plum and currant notes. Most impressively, it unfolds into a smooth and polished texture, gaining length on the finish. Has well-integrated tannins, but given the up-front fruit, you can enjoy it now. Drink through 2004.–J.L. • $24 • (11/15/1998) SS • **89**

Cabernet Sauvignon Napa Valley 1994 • $18 • (10/31/1997) • **89**

■ ■ ■ ■

FREEMARK ABBEY

Cabernet Sauvignon Napa Valley 1993 • $18 • (11/15/1996) • **87**
Cabernet Sauvignon Napa Valley 1991 • $17 • (11/15/1994) • **85**
Cabernet Sauvignon Napa Valley 1990 • $16 • (11/15/1994) • **83**
Cabernet Sauvignon Napa Valley 1989 • $16 • (11/15/1993) • **81**
Cabernet Sauvignon Napa Valley 1988: Losing its fruit, turning dry and tannic, especially on the finish. What fruit there is appears muddled. (1988 California Cabernet retrospective tasting). Past its prime.–J.L. • $16 • (11/15/1998) • **78**
Cabernet Sauvignon Napa Valley 1987 • $16 • (12/15/1997) • **88**
Cabernet Sauvignon Napa Valley 1986 • $15 • (11/15/1990) • **83**
Cabernet Sauvignon Napa Valley 1985 • $19 Ⓐ • (10/31/1989) • **79**
Cabernet Sauvignon Napa Valley 1984 • $14 • (2/15/1989) • **84**
Cabernet Sauvignon Napa Valley 1983 • $12 • (2/15/1988) • **68**
Cabernet Sauvignon Napa Valley 1982 • $12 • (2/15/1987) • **84**
Cabernet Sauvignon Napa Valley 1981 • $11 • (10/01/1985) • **79**
Cabernet Sauvignon Napa Valley 1980 • $22 • (5/16/1984) • **84**
Cabernet Sauvignon Napa Valley 1979 • $11 • (1/01/1984) • **89**
Cabernet Sauvignon Napa Valley 1978: A pleasant surprise. Still offers plenty of ripe, plummy Cabernet fruit flavors, with nice herb, sage and spicy nuances and a smooth, supple texture. Only a hint of nutty oxidation creeps in on the finish. (1978 California Cabernet retrospective tasting). Drink now through 2002.–J.L. • $29 Ⓐ • (11/15/1998) • **89**
Cabernet Sauvignon Napa Valley 1974 • $50 • (11/15/1994) • **83**
Cabernet Sauvignon Napa Valley Cabernet Bosché Bosché Estate 1995: Not a grand wine, but a sophisticated one; rich, elegant and polished, with a pretty range of plum, cherry and currant, hints of sage, cedar and spice and a long, complex aftertaste. Best from 2001 through 2009.–J.L. • $50 • (10/31/1999) • **92**
Cabernet Bosché Bosché Estate Napa Valley 1994: A brilliant Bosche, ripe, rich and complex, with a supple, elegant texture and a wonderful array of flavors. Glides to a smooth, polished aftertaste, with complex currant, cherry, anise, cedar and spicy notes. Drink through 2006.–J.L. • $44 • (11/15/1998) • **91**
Cabernet Bosché Bosché Estate Napa Valley 1993 • $35 • (6/30/1998) CS • **92**
Cabernet Sauvignon Napa Valley Bosché 1992 • $32 • (9/30/1997) CS • **93**
Cabernet Sauvignon Napa Valley Bosché 1991 • $24 • (11/30/1996) • **90**
Cabernet Sauvignon Napa Valley Bosché 1989: Mature, with coffee, cedar and dried cherry flavors that are complex and elegant, finishing a tad dry, so it's best to drink soon. (1989 California Cabernet retrospective tasting). Drink now.–J.L. • $29 Ⓐ • (8/31/1999) • **86**
Cabernet Sauvignon Napa Valley Bosché 1988: Austere for Bosché, with dry tannins and a modest core of dried cherry and currant, framed by light sage, herb and oak notes. Turns earthy, with a slight medicinal note. (1988 California Cabernet retrospective tasting). Drink now.–J.L. • $25 • (11/15/1998) • **83**
Cabernet Sauvignon Napa Valley Bosché 1987 • $25 • (12/15/1997) • **88**
Cabernet Sauvignon Napa Valley Bosché 1986 • $40 Ⓐ • (7/31/1990) • **76**
Cabernet Sauvignon Napa Valley Bosché 1985 • $39 • (7/31/1989) • **90**
Cabernet Sauvignon Napa Valley Bosché 1984 • $20 • (4/30/1988) • **80**
Cabernet Sauvignon Napa Valley Bosché 1983 • $18 • (6/15/1987) • **80**
Cabernet Sauvignon Napa Valley Bosché 1982 • $15 • (5/16/1986) CS • **93**
Cabernet Sauvignon Napa Valley Bosché 1981 • $14 • (7/01/1985) • **89**
Cabernet Sauvignon Napa Valley Bosché 1980 • $24 • (2/01/1986) • **84**
Cabernet Sauvignon Napa Valley Bosché 1979: Drinks nicely though a shade past its prime; a dryness surrounds the dried cherry, stewed plum and spicy Cabernet flavors, finishing with drying tannins. (1979 California Cabernet retrospective tasting). Drink now.–J.L. • $12 • (8/31/1999) • **87**
Cabernet Sauvignon Napa Valley Bosché 1978: A touch oxidized and earthy, still there's plenty to enjoy here despite the nutty edge. Hints of ripe plum and currant turn dry on the finish, so it's best consumed soon. (1978 California Cabernet retrospective tasting).–J.L. • $13 • (11/15/1998) • **85**
Cabernet Sauvignon Napa Valley Bosché 1974 • $75 • (11/15/1994) • **85**
Cabernet Sauvignon Napa Valley Sycamore Vineyards 1994: Elegant in profile, with ripe cherry and currant offset by herb and sage. Well focused, firm enough to cellar yet supple enough to enjoy now. Best from 2001 through 2008.–J.L. • $42 • (10/15/1999) • **88**
Cabernet Sauvignon Napa Valley Sycamore Vineyards 1993: A terrific new release from Freemark Abbey, tight, with pretty plum, black cherry, herb and mineral flavors, and firm but polished tannins on the finish. Good fruit and concentration. Drink through 2005.–J.L. • $34 • (10/31/1998) • **89**

Key: SS—Spectator Selection. CS—Cellar Selection. HR—Highly Recommended. $NA—Price not available. (BT)—Barrel tasting. Ⓐ—Auction Price.
For a key to the tasters' initials, see "How to Use These Listings."
Dates in parentheses represent the issues in which the ratings were published.

Cabernet Sauvignon Napa Valley Sycamore Vineyards 1992 • $30 • (9/30/1997) • **89**
Cabernet Sauvignon Napa Valley Sycamore Vineyards 1991 • $22 • (11/30/1996) • **88**
Cabernet Sauvignon Napa Valley Sycamore Vineyards 1990 • $23 • (12/15/1995) • **88**
Cabernet Sauvignon Napa Valley Sycamore Vineyards 1989: Dark, firm and structured, with more richness, depth and flavor than the Bosché Vineyard. Shows off mature spice, currant, cedar and cherry flavors that are long and complex. Impressive. (1989 California Cabernet retrospective tasting). Drink now.–J.L. • $20 • (8/31/1999) • **88**
Cabernet Sauvignon Napa Valley Sycamore Vineyards 1988: Nicely balanced, fairly typical '88 for its modest range and depth of flavor. Offers simple herb, currant and spice notes, finishing on the simple side. (1988 California Cabernet retrospective tasting). Drink now through 2001.–J.L. • $25 • (11/15/1998) • **86**
Cabernet Sauvignon Napa Valley Sycamore Vineyards 1987 • $25 • (12/15/1997) • **84**
Cabernet Sauvignon Napa Valley Sycamore Vineyards 1986 • $25 • (11/15/1991) • **91**
Cabernet Sauvignon Napa Valley Sycamore Vineyards 1985 • $25 • (10/31/1989) • **88**
Cabernet Sauvignon Napa Valley Sycamore Vineyards 1984 • $20 • (12/15/1988) • **91**
Chardonnay Napa Valley 1998: Crisp, with good focus to the citrus, herbal and apple flavors. Drink now through 2001.–J.L. • $19 • (6/30/2000) • **85**
Chardonnay Napa Valley 1997: A crisp, flinty style, with moderate depth to the green apple and citrus flavors. Finishes with clean, complex mineral, apple and herb notes that linger. Drink now.–J.L. • $20 • (7/31/1999) • **87**
Chardonnay Napa Valley 1996 • $17 • (4/30/1998) • **88**
Chardonnay Napa Valley Carpy Ranch 1997: Round, with eucalyptus, pear, golden raisin and vanilla flavors. Drink now.–J.L. • $26 • (6/30/2000) • **85**
Chardonnay Napa Valley Carpy Ranch 1996 • $24 • (5/15/1998) • **88**
Johannisberg Riesling Napa Valley Edelwein Gold 1991 • $25/375 ml. • (10/15/1992) CS • **92**
Johannisberg Riesling Napa Valley Edelwein Gold 1989 • $22/375 ml. • (7/15/1990) • **92**
Merlot Napa Valley 1997: Gamy and medium in weight, turning earthy and green, with tea and herb notes. Drink now.–J.L. • $23 • (5/31/2000) • **80**
Merlot Napa Valley 1996: Pungently earthy and herbal, with a leathery streak running through the cherry and berryish flavors. Turns supple on the finish. Drink now through 2003.–J.L. • $28 • (10/15/1999) • **84**
Merlot Napa Valley 1995 • $21 • (4/30/1998) • **88**
Merlot Napa Valley 1994 • $18 • (12/31/1996) • **87**
Merlot Napa Valley 1993 • $16 • (8/31/1996) • **87**
Merlot Napa Valley 1992 • $15 • (3/31/1995) • **83**
Merlot Napa Valley 1991 • $15 • (4/15/1994) • **86**
Merlot Napa Valley 1989 • $15 • (7/15/1993) • **80**
Merlot Napa Valley 1985 • $10 • (12/31/1988) • **90**

FREESTONE | CALIFORNIA

Cabernet Sauvignon Napa Valley 1996: Medium-bodied, with sharp dill, cherry and herb notes. Finishes firm. Best after 2000. • $18 • (9/15/1999) • **82**
Cabernet Sauvignon Napa Valley 1994 • $15 • (10/15/1997) • **85**
Cabernet Sauvignon Napa Valley 1993 • $14 • (9/15/1996) • **82**
Merlot Napa Valley 1997: Firm, showing modest currant and herb flavors. Dry on the finish. Drink through 2002.–H.S. • $18 • (10/15/1999) • **80**
Sauvignon Blanc Napa Valley 1998: Struggles to find focus, with citrus and green vegetal notes. Drink now.–J.L. • $13 • (5/31/2000) • **80**
Sauvignon Blanc Napa Valley 1996 • $11 • (11/15/1997) • **86**

FREY | CALIFORNIA

Cabernet Sauvignon Redwood Valley Butow Vineyards 1997: Funky but interesting, with pretty flavors of violets, herbs and game, all wrapped around a core of peppery black fruit. Not for everyone. Tannic, too. Drink now.–H.S. • $10 • (11/15/1998) • **81**
Pinot Noir Mendocino 1991 • $11 • (2/28/1993) • **62**
Sauvignon Blanc Mendocino Late Harvest NV • $8 • (12/31/1995) • **72**
Syrah Mendocino Bulow Vineyard 1986 • $10 • (4/15/1989) • **82**
Zinfandel Mendocino 1993 • $8 • (10/15/1995) • **83**
Zinfandel Mendocino 1992 • $8 • (10/15/1994) • **84**
Zinfandel Mendocino 1990 • $8 • (10/15/1992) • **84**

FRICK | CALIFORNIA

Cabernet Sauvignon Dry Creek Valley 1994 • $20 • (9/15/1997) • **89**
Cabernet Sauvignon Dry Creek Valley 1993 • $16 • (11/30/1996) • **85**
Cinsaut Dry Creek Valley 1995 • $15 • (3/31/1998) • **85**
Merlot Dry Creek Valley 1995 • $20 • (3/31/1998) • **85**
Pinot Noir California 1981 • $12 • (8/31/1986) • **89**
Pinot Noir Santa Maria Valley 1984 • $12 • (2/28/1989) • **75**
Syrah Dry Creek Valley 1997: Distinctive, with lavender, blueberry and talc notes. Finishes with lean tannins. Drink now through 2005.–J.L. • $21 • (5/31/2000) • **82**
Syrah Dry Creek Valley 1996: Shows an unusual array of flavors—anise, rosemary, sage, black currant and eucalyptus—but they blend well and may integrate even better in a few years. Toasty oak and firm, ripe tannins round off the finish of this smooth and fairly elegant wine. Drink now through 2004. • $21 • (3/31/1999) • **88**
Syrah Dry Creek Valley 1995 • $21 • (3/31/1998) • **86**
Viognier Dry Creek Valley 1996 • $21 • (5/15/1998) • **83**
Zinfandel Dry Creek Valley 1993 • $14 • (4/30/1997) • **82**
Zinfandel Dry Creek Valley 1991 • $13 • (10/15/1994) • **79**
Zinfandel Russian River Valley 1990 • $13 • (9/30/1993) • **70**

FRITZ | CALIFORNIA

Cabernet Sauvignon Dry Creek Valley 1989 • $12 • (8/31/1992) • **86**
Chardonnay Russian River Valley Dutton Ranch 1998: Pretty peach and floral notes show good richness, with butter and lead pencil nuances on the finish. Drink now.–J.L. • $22 • (6/15/2000) • **86**
Chardonnay Russian River Valley Dutton Ranch 1997: Muted, almost dull for this vineyard, with a narrow range of toasty green apple flavors that turn earthy. Tasted twice, with consistent notes. Drink now through 2001.–J.L. • $20 • (7/31/1999) • **84**
Chardonnay Russian River Valley Dutton Ranch 1996 • $20 • (6/30/1998) • **91**
Chardonnay Russian River Valley Dutton Vineyard Ruxton Ranch 1996 • $26 • (6/30/1998) • **87**
Chardonnay Russian River Valley Dutton Vineyard Shop Block 1996 • $30 • (6/30/1998) • **91**
Chardonnay Russian River Valley Poplar Vineyard 1997: Earthy, with mushroom, oak and vague fruit aromas. More complex and tasty on the palate, though it lacks focus and turns muddled on the finish. Drink now.–J.L. • $22 • (4/30/2000) • **84**
Chardonnay Russian River Valley Poplar Vineyard 1996 • $22 • (6/30/1998) • **87**
Chardonnay Russian River Valley Ruxton Vineyard Dutton Ranch 1998: Buttery and warm, with honey and apricot flavors that show good richness. Drink now.–J.L. • $28 • (6/15/2000) • **87**
Chardonnay Russian River Valley Ruxton Vineyard Dutton Ranch 1997: Pleasant and open-textured, with subtle pear, fig and sweet cream flavors. Finishes bright and clean. Drink now.–J.L. • $26 • (7/31/1999) • **87**
Chardonnay Russian River Valley Shop Block Dutton Ranch 1998: Curious, with pronounced honey and barnyard flavors.–J.L. • $30 • (6/30/2000) • **78**
Chardonnay Russian River Valley Shop Block Dutton Ranch 1997: Elegant, with ripe, focused flavors echoing ripe pear, spice, apple and light oak. Drink now through 2004.–J.L. • $30 • (1/31/2000) • **88**
Merlot Dry Creek Valley 1997: Lean, with drying tannins, it ultimately fans out to feature some pretty cassis, anise and herb flavors. Finishes moderately. Best from 2001 through 2005. • $18 • (10/15/1999) • **84**
Sauvignon Blanc Dry Creek Valley Jenner Vineyard 1997: Smells of fresh-cut hay, with a follow-up that features hints of fresh pea, grapefruit, fig and herbs. This delicate wine packs a bit more punch on the finish, with a firm, lemony edge. Drink now. • $12 • (2/28/1999) • **85**
Sauvignon Blanc Dry Creek Valley Jenner Vineyard 1996 • $12 • (3/31/1998) • **87**
Sauvignon Blanc Dry Creek Valley Late Harvest 1995: Definitely sweet, a touch sweaty, the texture is also a bit coarse now, but should soften with time. The flavor profile is built around pear, fig, citrus and spice notes. Try through 2002.–J.L. • $20/375 ml. • (12/15/1998) • **89**
Sauvignon Blanc Russian River Valley Poplar Vineyard 1997: Quite lemony, this tangy wine also sports a serious grapefruit element. It's lean but very refreshing, finishing with a steely, clean aftertaste. Drink now. • $12 • (2/28/1999) • **86**
Sauvignon Blanc Russian River Valley Poplar Vineyard 1996 • $12 • (3/31/1998) • **89**
Zinfandel Dry Creek Valley 95-Year Old Vines Rogers' Reserve 1998: Ripe, with fleshy chocolate, cherry and vanilla notes. Drink now through 2003.–J.L. • $30 • (6/15/2000) • **86**
Zinfandel Dry Creek Valley 95-Year Old Vines Rogers' Reserve 1997: Firm, with jammy raspberry, tea and spice notes. Generous, but a little rustic and tannic on the finish. Best from 2001 through 2006.–J.L. • $30 • (1/31/2000) • **86**
Zinfandel Dry Creek Valley Eighty-Year-Old Vines Rogers' Reserve 1996 • $28 • (6/15/1998) • **86**
Zinfandel Dry Creek Valley Eighty-Year-Old Vines Rogers' Reserve 1994 • $18 • (10/15/1996) • **88**
Zinfandel Dry Creek Valley Eighty-Year-Old Vines 1993 • $12 • (10/15/1995) • **84**
Zinfandel Dry Creek Valley Eighty-Year-Old Vines 1992 • $11 • (10/15/1994) • **83**
Zinfandel Dry Creek Valley Eighty-Year-Old Vines 1991 • $11 • (9/30/1993) • **82**
Zinfandel Dry Creek Valley Eighty-Year-Old Vines 1990 • $10 • (10/15/1992) • **82**
Zinfandel Dry Creek Valley Eighty-Year-Old Vines 1989 • $10 • (3/31/1992) • **84**
Zinfandel Dry Creek Valley Eighty-Year-Old Vines 1988 • $10 • (7/31/1991) • **79**
Zinfandel Dry Creek Valley Old Vine 1998: Intense ripe plum and jammy cherry flavors. Finishes a bit hot. Drink now through 2004.–J.L. • $20 • (5/31/2000) • **86**
Zinfandel Dry Creek Valley Old Vine 1996 • $20 • (6/15/1998) • **88**

FROG'S LEAP | CALIFORNIA

Cabernet Sauvignon Rutherford 1996: Rich and full-bodied, with complex currant, spice, anise, sage and cedary notes, finishing with supple tannins. Drink now through 2007.–J.L. • $55 • (12/31/1999) • **88**
Cabernet Sauvignon Napa Valley 1997: Lean, trim and a touch earthy and cedary, with an herbal slant to the currant and black cherry. Finishes with firm tannins. Best from 2001 through 2007.–J.L. • $30 • (1/31/2000) • **86**
Cabernet Sauvignon Napa Valley 1996: Shows a flavorful range of leather, black cherry, mineral, tobacco and tar notes, finishing with complex flavors and firm tannins. Drink now through 2004.–J.L. • $27 • (9/15/1999) • **88**
Cabernet Sauvignon Napa Valley 1995: Plump, ripe and juicy, with pretty black cherry, berry, currant and spice framed by light, cedary oak. It all adds up to a nice mouthful of Cabernet, with mild, integrated tannins. Drink through 2005.–J.L. • $24 • (10/31/1998) • **88**
Cabernet Sauvignon Napa Valley 1994 • $20 • (11/15/1996) • **88**
Cabernet Sauvignon Napa Valley 1990 • $17 • (9/30/1993) • **88**
Cabernet Sauvignon Napa Valley 1989: Weaves together complex, medium-weight cherry, plum, cedar, anise and tar notes before turning tannic and dry. (1989 California Cabernet retrospective tasting). Drink now.–J.L. • $18 • (8/31/1999) • **86**
Cabernet Sauvignon Napa Valley 1988: Elegant and well balanced, with a pleasant band of black cherry, currant and berry. Finishes with integrated tannins and a pretty fruit note. (1989 California Cabernet retrospective tasting). Drink now.–J.L. • $15 • (11/15/1998) • **85**
Cabernet Sauvignon Napa Valley 1987 • $15 • (12/15/1997) • **84**
Cabernet Sauvignon Napa Valley 1986 • $14 • (12/31/1988) • **94**
Cabernet Sauvignon Napa Valley 1985 • $12 • (12/31/1987) • **82**
Cabernet Sauvignon Napa Valley 1984 • $12 • (3/31/1987) SS • **95**
Cabernet Sauvignon Napa Valley 1983 • $10 • (5/16/1986) • **85**
Chardonnay Carneros 1997: Medium-bodied, with well-focused lemon, lime and mineral flavors on a smooth frame. Finishes clean and pleasantly crisp. Drink now.–J.L. • $21 • (6/30/1999) • **87**
Chardonnay Carneros 1996 • $19 • (5/15/1998) • **85**
Chardonnay Napa Valley 1998: Crisp and flinty, with tart green apple, mineral, citrus and a touch of earthiness that adds dimension. Well made in this style. Drink now through 2004.–J.L. • $22 • (1/31/2000) • **86**
Leapfrögmilch Napa Valley 1997 • $16 • (6/30/1998) • **83**
Merlot Napa Valley 1997: Ripe, firm and focused, with a red currant and cherry core. Lingers on the finish, picking up spicy toasted oak notes. Tannins are firm but well integrated. Drink now through 2005.–J.L. • $27 • (11/15/1999) • **85**
Merlot Napa Valley 1996: Smooth and supple, with a rich, complex core of earthy currant, plum, black cherry and herb flavors, finishing with notes of toasted oak and well-integrated tannins. Drink now through 2003.–J.L. • $24 • (9/15/1999) • **87**
Merlot Napa Valley 1995: Tight, with an earthy streak running through the complex currant, berry and cherry fruit, though the flavors hold their focus. Drink now through 2001.–J.L. • $22 • (9/30/1998) • **86**
Merlot Napa Valley 1994 • $20 • (6/30/1997) • **87**
Merlot Napa Valley 1993 • $NA • (4/30/1996) • **87**
Merlot Napa Valley 1991 • $17 • (5/31/1994) • **88**
Merlot Napa Valley 1990 • $17 • (1/31/1993) • **84**
Sauvignon Blanc Napa Valley 1998: Light and zingy, dominated by grapefruit and lemon flavors. Bright and refreshing, with a hint of herb on the finish. Drink now. • $14 • (9/30/1999) • **86**
Sauvignon Blanc Napa Valley 1997: Attractively earthy on the nose, fanning out to include fresh pea, fig, melon and grapefruit flavors on the palate.

The blend is well integrated, though understated, coming up a little short on the finish. Drink now through 2001. • $13 • (5/15/1999) • **86**

Sauvignon Blanc Napa Valley 1996 • $13 • (6/30/1997) • **83**

Sauvignon Blanc Napa Valley Late Harvest Late Leap 1989 • $14/375 ml. • (10/31/1991) • **84**

Zinfandel Napa Valley 1997: Delicate, with a band of smoky strawberry and tea flavors. Finishes soft and focused, with pleasant spice and oak notes. Drink now.–J.L. • $17 • (11/15/1999) • **84**

Zinfandel Napa Valley 1996: Very ripe, quite minty, with sage and bay leaf leading to tar and wild berry flavors, turning supple and complex. Drink now through 2001.–J.L. • $17 • (5/15/1999) • **88**

Zinfandel Napa Valley 1995 • $16 • (6/15/1998) • **87**

Zinfandel Napa Valley 1994 • $15 • (3/31/1997) SS • **89**

Zinfandel Napa Valley 1992 • $13 • (10/15/1994) • **68**

Zinfandel Napa Valley 1991 • $13 • (9/30/1993) • **85**

Zinfandel Napa Valley 1990 • $12 • (10/15/1992) • **80**

Zinfandel Napa Valley 1989 • $12 • (11/15/1991) • **83**

Zinfandel Napa Valley 1988 • $12 • (12/15/1990) • **88**

Zinfandel Napa Valley 1987 • $11 • (3/15/1990) • **86**

Zinfandel Napa Valley 1986 • $10 • (12/15/1988) • **85**

G'SELL | CALIFORNIA

Chardonnay Alexander Valley Limited Reserve 1996: Toasty oak and pretty pear flavors blend well, but it finishes with a hint of bitterness. • $15 • (7/31/1998) • **83**

Zinfandel Sonoma County 1996 • $15 • (6/15/1998) • **82**

GABRIELLI | CALIFORNIA

Pinot Noir Anderson Valley Floodgate Vineyard 1995 • $18 • (9/30/1997) • **87**

Pinot Noir Mendocino 1997: Firm and lean, with berry and licorice notes. Unfolds with hints of cola and tea, finishing moderately with an herbal edge. Best from 2001 through 2004. • $18 • (9/15/1999) • **83**

Pinot Noir Mendocino County 1996: Somewhat herbal, with hints of cherry, smoke and spice. A pleasant quaff, though the finish pulls up short. Drink now. • $16 • (9/15/1998) • **83**

Pinot Noir Mendocino County 1995 • $14 • (1/31/1998) • **87**

Pinot Noir Mendocino County Weir Vineyard 1995 • $18 • (2/28/1998) • **84**

Pinot Noir Mendocino Reserve 1995 • $25 • (9/30/1997) • **88**

Sangiovese Mendocino 1995 • $14 • (11/30/1996) • **87**

Sangiovese Redwood Valley 1997: Firmly structured yet fairly smooth, this serves up a blend of black currant, tea and herbal, almost leaflike, notes. It works, however, and should improve in the bottle. Drink through 2005. • $20 • (1/31/1999) • **85**

Syrah Redwood Valley 1995 • $18 • (3/31/1998) • **86**

Syrah Redwood Valley Reserve 1997: Firm, with a dense core of blackberry, mineral, tar and herb. Finishes with firm tannins. Needs time to unfold. Best from 2001 through 2005.–J.L. • $30 • (11/15/1999) • **85**

Zinfandel Mendocino County 1995 • $14 • (3/31/1998) • **82**

Zinfandel Mendocino 1993 • $12 • (7/31/1995) • **86**

Zinfandel Mendocino 1992 • $12 • (10/15/1994) • **85**

Zinfandel Mendocino 1991 • $10 • (12/31/1993) • **85**

Zinfandel Mendocino 1990 • $10 • (10/15/1992) • **85**

Zinfandel Mendocino Reserve 1994 • $18 • (9/15/1997) • **84**

Zinfandel Mendocino Reserve 1992 • $18 • (10/15/1994) • **84**

Zinfandel Mendocino Reserve 1991 • $16 • (3/31/1994) • **84**

Zinfandel Mendocino Reserve 1990 • $16 • (10/15/1992) • **82**

Zinfandel Napa Valley Luvisi Vineyard 1997: Firm and lean, with a green edge to the berry flavors.–J.L. • $20 • (11/15/1999) • **76**

Zinfandel Redwood Valley Goforth Vineyard 1997: Stewed plum and earth flavors are a little unfocused and finish hot. Drink now.–J.L. • $18 • (5/31/2000) • **80**

Zinfandel Redwood Valley Goforth Vineyard 1995 • $18 • (6/15/1998) • **85**

GAINEY | CALIFORNIA

Cabernet Franc Santa Ynez Valley Limited Selection 1990 • $16 • (10/15/1993) • **88**

Cabernet Sauvignon Santa Barbara County 1987 • $13 • (11/15/1990) • **82**

Key: SS—Spectator Selection. CS—Cellar Selection. HR—Highly Recommended. $NA—Price not available. (BT)—Barrel tasting. Ⓐ—Auction Price.
For a key to the tasters' initials, see "How to Use These Listings."
Dates in parentheses represent the issues in which the ratings were published.

Cabernet Sauvignon Santa Barbara County Limited Selection 1989 • $20 • (11/15/1992) • **83**

Cabernet Sauvignon Santa Barbara County Limited Selection 1986 • $15 • (12/15/1989) • **89**

Cabernet Sauvignon Santa Maria Valley 1988 • $13 • (3/15/1992) • **77**

Cabernet Sauvignon Santa Ynez Valley 1989 • $13 • (11/15/1992) • **77**

Cabernet Sauvignon Santa Ynez Valley Limited Selection 1988 • $20 • (3/10/1992) • **75**

Chardonnay Santa Barbara County Limited Selection 1997: Struggles to find a focus, with subtle nutmeg, pear and earthy citrus flavors that are appealing if lacking in extra dimensions. Drink now through 2006.–J.L. • $28 • (2/29/2000) • **87**

Chardonnay Santa Barbara County Limited Selection 1996: An exotic yet elegant style, with an earthy streak running through the stream of ripe pear, fig, apricot and melon. Holds its flavor and gains finesse on the finish. Drink now through 2002.–J.L. • $25 • (7/31/1998) • **91**

Johannisberg Riesling Santa Ynez Valley 1996 • $10 • (11/30/1997) • **83**

Merlot Santa Barbara County 1989 • $14 • (5/31/1992) • **70**

Merlot Santa Barbara County 1988 • $13 • (4/15/1991) • **82**

Merlot Santa Ynez Valley 1990 • $14 • (7/15/1993) • **83**

Merlot Santa Ynez Valley Limited Selection 1996: Supple and seductive for its coffee, cola and cedar flavors. Shows lots of complex, concentrated black cherry, cassis and mineral notes and finishes with polished tannins. Drink through 2005.–J.L. • $25 • (9/15/1999) • **90**

Merlot Santa Ynez Valley Limited Selection 1990 • $20 • (10/15/1993) • **76**

Merlot Santa Ynez Valley Limited Selection 1988 • $20 • (2/29/1992) • **89**

Pinot Noir Santa Barbara County 1990 • $15 • (2/28/1994) • **87**

Pinot Noir Santa Barbara County 1986 • $15 • (12/15/1989) • **88**

Pinot Noir Santa Maria Valley 1989 • $18 • (9/30/1992) • **74**

Pinot Noir Santa Maria Valley Limited Selection 1997: Firm, ripe, with rich cherry, cola, spice and earth notes that are tightly bound and in need of short-term cellaring. Drink through 2005.–J.L. • $28 • (9/15/1999) • **87**

Pinot Noir Santa Maria Valley Limited Selection 1996: Serves up a range of black cherry, spice, herb, rhubarb and berry, finishing with pepper and anise, and fine but firm tannins. Drink through 2003.–J.L. • $25 • (8/31/1998) • **87**

Pinot Noir Santa Ynez Valley Limited Reserve 1991 • $30 • (2/28/1994) • **88**

Pinot Noir Santa Ynez Valley Limited Selection 1990 • $25 • (2/28/1994) • **85**

Pinot Noir Santa Ynez Valley Limited Selection 1989 • $25 • (2/28/1993) • **83**

Pinot Noir Santa Ynez Valley Limited Selection 1988 • $25 • (11/15/1991) • **86**

Pinot Noir Santa Ynez Valley Sanford and Benedict Vineyard 1993 • $30 • (4/30/1996) • **84**

Sauvignon Blanc Santa Ynez Valley Limited Selection 1998: Crisp, thin, with grapefruit and other citrus notes of modest proportion, finishing with a touch of melon. Drink now.–J.L. • $20 • (5/15/2000) • **84**

Sauvignon Blanc Santa Ynez Valley Limited Selection 1997: Introduces itself with plenty of butterscotch, then settles in with a band of well-integrated melon, fig, citrus, herb and mineral flavors. Smooth and rich, yet showing enough bright acidity to carry on for a long finish. Drink now through 2002. • $18 • (5/31/1999) • **90**

GALANTE | CALIFORNIA

Cabernet Sauvignon Carmel Valley Blackjack Pasture 1997: Dark and immense, unyieldingly hard and tannic, though it's not as overbearing as some. Some pleasing fruit flavors earn it a passing grade. Drink now through 2006.–J.L. • $40 • (3/31/2000) • **83**

Cabernet Sauvignon Carmel Valley Blackjack Pasture 1996: Packed with ripe plum and berry flavors backed by hints of anise and herbs. Tannins are a bit rustic, but should soften with time. Best from 2001 through 2006. • $35 • (4/30/1999) • **89**

Cabernet Sauvignon Carmel Valley Blackjack Pasture 1995: Tightly wound, this wine nonetheless shows complex, concentrated cassis and black currant flavors framed by herbs and toasty oak. Tannins are ripe and the finish is moderate. Should evolve nicely with time. Drink through 2005. • $30 • (11/15/1998) • **90**

Cabernet Sauvignon Carmel Valley Blackjack Pasture 1994 • $30 • (10/15/1996) • **86**

Cabernet Sauvignon Carmel Valley Rancho Galante 1997: Austere and tannic, with enough backbone for two wines, this is a crisp and tannic, muscular style. Drink now through 2006.–J.L. • $18 • (3/31/2000) • **82**

Cabernet Sauvignon Carmel Valley Rancho Galante 1996: Bright cherry and herb flavors announce this smooth-textured Cab. It's a bit tight now, but serves up pretty blackberry, spice and anise notes that linger on a moderate finish. Should evolve nicely in the bottle. Best from 2001 through 2006. • $18 • (5/15/1999) • **88**

Cabernet Sauvignon Carmel Valley Red Rose Hill 1997: Offers a touch of heat and tongue-gripping acidity, with plummy, bitter chocolate. Has depth of flavor, but tannins are a bit green. Drink now through 2003.–J.L. • $28 • (4/30/2000) • **84**

Cabernet Sauvignon Carmel Valley Red Rose Hill 1996: Rich and vibrant, with plush cherry, black currant and licorice notes. Tannins are slightly astringent but should smooth out nicely in the bottle. Finishes moderately, but remains distinctive. Drink now through 2006. • $25 • (4/30/1999) • **88**

Cabernet Sauvignon Carmel Valley Red Rose Hill 1995: Starts off with an unusual coffee-tea edge and a menthol follow-up. Black currant, cedar, cassis and herbs blend well, with firm tannins and a silky-textured finish. Different. Drink now through 2005. • $25 • (11/15/1998) • **88**

Cabernet Sauvignon Carmel Valley Red Rose Hill 1994 • $25 • (10/15/1996) • **85**

Merlot Carmel Valley 1996: Smoky oak, spice and cedar give way to solid, ripe black currant and anise flavors, framed by hints of herb and firm but ripe tannins. Tasty now, it should age well in the bottle. Try now through 2005. • $30 • (6/15/1999) • **88**

GALLERON | CALIFORNIA

Cabernet Sauvignon Napa Valley 1994 • $50 • (9/30/1997) • **91**

Cabernet Sauvignon Napa Valley 1993 • $40 • (11/15/1996) • **88**

Chardonnay Napa Valley Trio Vineyard 1998: Quite spicy, with a Muscat-like edge, the flavors are pure, with ripe apple and pear, turning crisp. Drink now through 2005.–J.L. • $40 • (5/15/2000) • **87**

GALLO, E. & J. | CALIFORNIA

Cabernet Sauvignon California NV • $5 • (8/31/1992) • **80**

Cabernet Sauvignon California Reserve NV • $6 • (11/15/1991) • **84**

Cabernet Sauvignon Northern Sonoma 1996: Enormously rich, detailed and concentrated, jam packed with layers of thick cherry, currant, anise, sage, tar and spice, this is a remarkably complex and satisfying wine that can be enjoyed now or cellared. Best from 2001 through 2008.–J.L. • $65 • (10/31/1999) • **94**

Cabernet Sauvignon Northern Sonoma Estate Bottled 1994: Elegant, refined, perfectly balanced, with ripe, fleshy cherry, currant, anise, cedar and spice, finishing with supple, well-integrated tannins. Drink through 2006–J.L. • $55 • (11/15/1998) • **92**

Cabernet Sauvignon Northern Sonoma Estate Bottled 1993 • $24 Ⓐ • (10/31/1997) • **90**

Cabernet Sauvignon Northern Sonoma Estate Bottled 1992 • $45 • (11/15/1996) • **92**

Cabernet Sauvignon Northern Sonoma Estate Bottled 1991 • $50 • (11/15/1994) HR • **91**

Cabernet Sauvignon Northern Sonoma Estate Bottled 1990 • $60 • (10/31/1993) CS • **93**

Chardonnay Northern Sonoma 1997: Complex, with an intriguing array of pear, fig, hazelnut and melon. Elegant aftertaste. Drink now through 2005.–J.L. • $45 • (5/15/2000) • **89**

Chardonnay Northern Sonoma Estate Bottled 1996: Deliciously fruity, elegant, ripe, rich and concentrated, with tiers of spicy pear, fig, apricot and melon, finishing with a complex spicy oak aftertaste. Drink now through 2002.–J.L. • $45 • (5/15/1999) • **93**

Classic Burgundy California NV • $11/1.5 liter • (5/15/1998) • **81**

Hearty Burgundy Limited Release California NV • $3 • (3/15/1988) • **80**

Zinfandel North Coast 1992 • $6 • (8/31/1995) • **82**

Zinfandel Northern Sonoma 1990 • $5 • (8/31/1994) • **88**

GALLO OF SONOMA | CALIFORNIA

Cabernet Sauvignon Alexander Valley Barrelli Creek Vineyard 1998: Fruity, medium- to full-bodied, with cherry and berryish flavors that are focused and bright.–J.L. • $NA • (8/31/1999) (BT) • **85-89**

Cabernet Sauvignon Alexander Valley Barrelli Creek Vineyard 1996: Dark, ripe and rich, with supple blackberry, anise, cedar, tar and wild berry flavors. Tannins are smooth and integrated. Drink now through 2007.–J.L. • $26 • (3/31/2000) • **88**

Cabernet Sauvignon Dry Creek Valley Frei Vineyard 1996: Puts the ripe black cherry, raspberry and currant flavors up front in a plush, rich style. Finishes with mocha, coffee and a minty edge. Drink now through 2008.–J.L. • $26 • (5/15/2000) • **87**

Cabernet Sauvignon Dry Creek Valley Frei Ranch Vineyard 1995: Trim and earthy, with complex and elegant leather, currant and cedar flavors that build on the focused finish. Tannins are well integrated. Drink now through 2005.–J.L. • $24 • (10/15/1999) • **88**

Cabernet Sauvignon Dry Creek Valley Frei Ranch Vineyard 1994: Impressive for its display of complex, up-front fruitiness, this '94 red is dark, ripe, plump and juicy, brimming with lively black cherry, plum and wild berry flavors and smooth, ripe tannins. Has a lot going for it, including an outstanding quality-to-price ratio. Drink now through 2004.–J.L. • $18 • (10/31/1998) SS • **91**

Cabernet Sauvignon Dry Creek Valley Frei Ranch Vineyard 1993 • $18 • (11/15/1997) • **87**

Cabernet Sauvignon Dry Creek Valley Frei Ranch Vineyard 1992 • $16 • (11/15/1995) • **89**

Cabernet Sauvignon Dry Creek Valley Stefani Vineyard 1998: Up-front fruitiness is appealing, and the toasty oak adds dimension, though the overall flavor profile is a bit muddled at this youthful stage.–J.L. • $NA • (8/31/1999) (BT) • **85-89**

Cabernet Sauvignon Dry Creek Valley Stefani Vineyard 1996: Has personality. Solid, dark and rich, with ripe plum, anise, cedar, mint and bay leaf, turning firm and tannic. Drink now through 2008.–J.L. • $26 • (6/15/2000) • **88**

Cabernet Sauvignon Dry Creek Valley Stefani Vineyard 1995: Quite tannic and muscular, with black currant, pepper and herb notes buried deep. Moderate finish features menthol and spice. Should soften in the cellar. Best from 2001 through 2005. • $24 • (11/15/1999) • **88**

Cabernet Sauvignon Dry Creek Valley Stefani Vineyard 1994: Bright and lively, with an earthy streak running through the wild berry, cherry and plummy Cabernet flavors. Has its share of tannin, but is balanced and flavorful, with a pretty, wild berry burst on the finish. Drink now through 2004.–J.L. • $18 • (10/31/1998) • **89**

Cabernet Sauvignon Sonoma County 1996: Fairly complex, with a core of blackberry, mint, herb, licorice and dill flavors couched in firm but ripe tannins. Focused and refined, it should evolve nicely in the bottle. Best from 2001 through 2006.–J.L. • $10 • (8/31/1999) • **87**

Cabernet Sauvignon Sonoma County 1994 • $10 • (10/31/1997) • **84**

Cabernet Sauvignon Sonoma County 1992 • $12 • (11/15/1995) • **87**

Cabernet Sauvignon Sonoma County 1991 • $12 • (3/31/1995) SS • **90**

Cabernet Sauvignon Sonoma County 1990 • $10 • (11/15/1994) • **86**

Chardonnay Dry Creek Valley Stefani Vineyard 1997: Shows off a tight, focused beam of citrus, pear, fig and appley flavors, finishing in a long, intricate aftertaste. Drink now through 2004.–J.L. • $20 • (6/30/2000) • **88**

Chardonnay Dry Creek Valley Stefani Vineyard 1996 • $16 • (5/31/1998) • **88**

Chardonnay Russian River Valley 1998: Ripe and lively, with pretty grapefruit, pear and fig flavors, if a touch coarse. Drink now through 2003.–J.L. • $12 • (3/31/2000) • **85**

Chardonnay Russian River Valley 1997: This is a really impressive Chardonnay at this price. Elegant, smooth and silky, not overbearing, it serves up pretty hazelnut, vanilla, pear and lemon flavors, with a long, refreshing finish complete with mineral overtones. Drink now through 2002. • $12 • (6/15/1999) • **89**

Chardonnay Russian River Valley 1996 • $11 • (6/30/1998) • **84**

Chardonnay Russian River Valley Laguna Ranch Vineyard 1997: Restrained on the nose, this tightly wound Chardonnay turns more complex and sophisticated on the palate, with a core of pear and nectarine flavors and a rich, buttery aftertaste that's long and focused. Drink now through 2006. –J.L. • $22 • (2/29/2000) SS • **91**

Chardonnay Russian River Valley Laguna Ranch Vineyard 1996 • $18 • (5/31/1998) SS • **91**

Chardonnay Sonoma County Gallo Family's 1998: Vibrant lemon and pineapple flavors are intensely focused, with smoky oak notes. Drink now.–J.L. • $11 • (6/30/2000) • **86**

Merlot Dry Creek Valley Frei Ranch Vineyard 1992 • $15 • (5/15/1995) • **82**

Merlot Dry Creek Valley Frei Ranch Vineyard 1991 • $15 • (9/15/1994) • **84**

Merlot Northern Sonoma 1993 • $15 • (4/30/1996) • **87**

Merlot Sonoma County 1997: Tightly wound, with firm tannins, this has a core of black currant and coffee framed in herbs and toasty oak. The finish is long, but it really needs some time in the bottle. Best from 2002 through 2005. • $12 • (9/15/1999) • **86**

Merlot Sonoma County 1996: Here's a mouthful of Merlot for but a few dollars. Concentrated flavors run in the earth, tobacco and tea spectrum, offset by a generous layer of black cherry and plum. Finishes with firm tannins, but the flavors linger on. Ready now, drink through 2000.–J.L. • $10 • (9/30/1998) • **86**

Pinot Noir Russian River Valley 1998: A little funky and earthy, with concentrated fresh cranberry flavors and a bitter, herbal edge. Drink now through 2003.–J.L. • $16 • (4/30/2000) • **82**

Pinot Noir Russian River Valley 1997: Fairly light on the palate, with cherry and herb flavors neatly intertwined. Tannins are firm, supporting a moderate, clean finish. Drink through 2003. • $12 • (9/15/1999) • **86**

GALLO OF SONOMA

Pinot Noir Russian River Valley 1996: Cola, tea and black cherry come to mind. Also has an herbal edge that is not unpleasant. A quaffer. Drink now. • $10 • (8/31/1998) • **82**

Valdiguié Alexander Valley Barrelli Creek Vineyard 1994 • $12 • (5/15/1997) • **82**

Zinfandel Alexander Valley Barrelli Creek Vineyard 1997: Disappointing, with earthy leather and bacon flavors and only a glimmer of berryish flavor. Tasted twice, with consistent notes. Drink now.–J.L. • $19 • (6/15/2000) • **80**

Zinfandel Alexander Valley Barrelli Creek Vineyard 1995 • $14 • (6/15/1998) SS • **90**

Zinfandel Dry Creek Valley 1997: Round, ripe and polished, a generous mouthful of blueberry, cherry and spice flavors that keep glowing through the supple finish. Has more flavor than aroma. Drink now through 2004. –H.S. • $12 • (11/30/1999) • **88**

Zinfandel Dry Creek Valley 1996: Shows a modest range of ripe, briary berry flavors on a soft frame, with hints of herb and spice. Drink now.–J.L. • $12 • (6/30/1999) • **86**

Zinfandel Dry Creek Valley Chiotti Vineyard 1997: A touch gamy, with an earthy mineral streak that runs through the wild berry, plum and anise flavors. Finishes with crisp tannins. Drink now through 2002.–J.L. • $18 • (6/15/1999) • **87**

Zinfandel Dry Creek Valley Chiotti Vineyard 1995 • $12 • (6/15/1997) • **90**

Zinfandel Dry Creek Valley Frei Ranch Vineyard 1996: Here's an outstanding California Zinfandel that's also reasonable in terms of price and availability. It's dark, ripe, rich and complex, with concentrated cherry, plum, blackberry, cedar and spice and a long, rich aftertaste. Drink now through 2006.–J.L. • $18 • (11/30/1999) SS • **90**

Zinfandel Dry Creek Valley Frei Ranch Vineyard 1995 • $14 • (6/15/1998) • **87**

Zinfandel Dry Creek Valley Frei Ranch Vineyard 1994 • $14 • (8/31/1997) • **84**

Zinfandel Dry Creek Valley Frei Ranch Vineyard 1993 • $14 • (4/30/1996) • **87**

Zinfandel Dry Creek Valley Frei Ranch Vineyard 1992 • $15 • (9/15/1995) • **85**

Zinfandel Dry Creek Valley Frei Ranch Vineyard 1991 • $14 • (2/28/1995) SS • **90**

Zinfandel Dry Creek Valley Frei Ranch Vineyard 1990: Smells fruity (berry and jam) and turns dry, with sage, wild berry, smoke and tar notes. Finishes with firm tannins. (Zinfandel retrospective tasting). Drink now through 2001.–J.L. • $14 • (6/30/1999) • **88**

Zinfandel Dry Creek Valley Stefani Vineyard 1996: Bright and lively, with zesty cherry and berry flavors that are fresh and snappy, along with creamy oak notes. Finishes with dashes of tar and cedar. Drink now through 2002.–J.L. • $18 • (5/15/1999) • **89**

Zinfandel Sonoma County 1995 • $10 • (11/15/1997) • **87**

GAN EDEN | CALIFORNIA

Black Muscat San Joaquin County 1995 • $10 • (5/15/1997) • **78**

Black Muscat San Joaquin County 1993 • $8 • (5/15/1995) • **80**

Cabernet Sauvignon Alexander Valley 1989 • $14 • (7/31/1995) • **83**

Cabernet Sauvignon Alexander Valley 1988 • $18 • (3/31/1993) • **77**

Cabernet Sauvignon Alexander Valley 1987 • $18 • (3/31/1991) • **90**

Cabernet Sauvignon Alexander Valley 1986 • $15 • (2/15/1989) • **86**

Gewürztraminer Monterey County Late Harvest 1993 • $9 • (9/30/1995) • **81**

Moscato Nero San Joaquin County 1995 • $10 • (9/15/1997) • **82**

GARRETSON | CALIFORNIA

Glimigrim Paso Robles NV: Strays into weird lima bean and vegetal flavors, but manages to rescue itself with a glimmer of ripe black berryish fruit that's crisp and lean. Syrah. Drink now.–J.L. • $12 • (4/30/2000) • **83**

Syrah Paso Robles The Aisling 1997: Tight and flavorful, with tart black cherry, plum, earth and anise notes that finish firm, but the tannins are soft. Drink now through 2004.–J.L. • $25 • (11/15/1999) • **88**

The Celeidh Rhône Rosé Central Coast NV: A refreshing, dry style, with mild red currant, strawberry, rose hip, spice and cinnamon flavors that linger on the finish. Made from Grenache, Mourvèdre, Syrah and Counoise. Drink now.–J.L. • $16 • (11/15/1999) • **87**

Key: SS—Spectator Selection. CS—Cellar Selection. HR—Highly Recommended. $NA—Price not available. (BT)—Barrel tasting. (A)—Auction Price. For a key to the tasters' initials, see "How to Use These Listings."
Dates in parentheses represent the issues in which the ratings were published.

GEHRS, DANIEL | CALIFORNIA

Cabernet Franc Santa Barbara County 1997: Cherry and cedar are spiked with notes of spice, with prettier flavors than aromas. Finishes firm and focused. Drink now through 2003.–J.L. • $15 • (12/15/1999) • **84**

Chardonnay Santa Barbara County 1998: Tight and earthy, with a band of citrus, pear and tart pineapple flavors unencumbered by oak. The first Chardonnay from this winery. Drink now through 2003.–J.L. • $19 • (12/31/1999) • **87**

Chenin Blanc Monterey County Carmel Vineyard Le Cheniere 1997: Firm and focused, unusually complex for this varietal, with an intense core of grapefruit, lemon and herb flavors. Brightly textured, it finishes long and refreshing. Drink now. • $10 • (1/31/1999) • **88**

Chenin Blanc Monterey County Carmel Vineyard Le Cheniere 1996 • $9 • (9/15/1997) • **86**

Fleetwood Cucamonga Valley 1996 • $9 • (9/30/1997) • **80**

Pinot Blanc Monterey County Carmel Vineyard 1997: Lemon and mineral notes lead the way here. The wine has body and weight, but finds balance in its tangy acidity. Finishes clean and fresh. Drink now. • $12 • (1/31/1999) • **85**

Pinot Blanc Monterey County Carmel Vineyard 1996 • $11 • (9/15/1997) • **82**

Pinot Noir Monterey County El Segundo Vineyard 1996 • $14 • (1/31/1998) • **85**

Pinot Noir Santa Barbara County 1997: Cola and coffee notes lead the way here, followed by a hint of eucalyptus. Plush-textured, it serves up layers of exotic spice, plum and cherry flavors, finishing harmoniously. Unusual and interesting. Drink through 2005. • $20 • (9/15/1999) • **88**

Sauvignon Blanc Monterey County Carmel Vineyard Fumé En Vogue 1997: Freshly mowed grass and asparagus aromas kick this off, in an older, brisk style. Remains quite attractive, however, with fresh pea, fig, melon and grapefruit flavors on the follow-up. Finishes long and bright. Drink now through 2001. • $11 • (2/28/1999) • **88**

Sauvignon Blanc Monterey County Carmel Vineyard Fumé En Vogue 1996 • $10 • (9/15/1997) • **81**

Syrah Paso Robles 1998: A bit funky, with chocolate and musty overtones. Drink now through 2002.–J.L. • $20 • (6/15/2000) • **81**

Syrah Paso Robles 1997: Richly fragrant, with ripe plum, smoke, vanilla and spice notes up front. On the palate, it's a classy blend of smooth-textured black cherry, herb and anise flavors, still tightly wound but positioned to unfold nicely with time. Tasted twice, with consistent notes. Best from 2001 through 2005. • $18 • (5/15/1999) • **91**

Viognier Santa Barbara County 1997: Quite viscous, this wine shows racy acidity backed by spice, melon and citrus flavors. Slightly tart on the finish, but still quite nice. Drink now. • $18 • (12/31/1998) • **86**

GEMELLO | CALIFORNIA

Zinfandel Mendocino 1993 • $16 • (10/15/1995) • **80**

Zinfandel Mendocino 60th Anniversary 1934-1994 1992 • $16 • (10/15/1995) • **82**

Zinfandel Mendocino County 1990 • $16 • (9/30/1993) • **84**

GEORIS | CALIFORNIA

Merlot Carmel Valley 1994 • $35 • (6/30/1997) • **80**

Merlot Carmel Valley 1992 • $28 • (8/31/1996) • **89**

Merlot Carmel Valley 1989 • $25 • (5/15/1993) • **87**

Merlot Carmel Valley 1987 • $27 • (3/31/1991) • **89**

Merlot Carmel Valley 1986 • $25 • (12/31/1990) • **77**

Merlot Carmel Valley 1985 • $20 • (4/15/1989) • **83**

GEYSER PEAK | CALIFORNIA

Cabernet Sauvignon Alexander Valley 1993 • $10 • (12/15/1995) • **83**

Cabernet Sauvignon Alexander Valley 1989 • $9 • (11/15/1992) • **82**

Cabernet Sauvignon Alexander Valley Bin 2 1995: Very dark, ripe and rich, almost with a Shiraz-like edge. Cedar, herb, black cherry, currant and mint notes turn elegant and polished on the finish. Best from 2001 through 2008.–J.L. • $100 • (11/15/1999) • **92**

Cabernet Sauvignon Alexander Valley Reserve 1998: Tight, a bit tart, with firm tannins gripping the earthy cherry and plum flavors. True barrel sample.–J.L. • $NA • (8/31/1999) (BT) • **85-89**

Cabernet Sauvignon Alexander Valley Reserve 1997: Smooth and cedary, with spice, floral, herb, cherry and mineral notes of modest depth and proportion. Mild tannins. Drink now through 2005.–J.L. • $40 • (6/15/2000) • **87**

Cabernet Sauvignon Alexander Valley Reserve 1996: Dark, ripe and focused, with a core of currant, mineral, black cherry and wild berry flavors that turn elegant and polished. Finishes with a cedary edge. Drink now through 2007.–J.L. • $32 • (11/15/1999) • **90**
Cabernet Sauvignon Alexander Valley Reserve 1995: Dark, ripe, rich and concentrated, with pretty black cherry, currant, anise and sage flavors, pretty toasty oak nuances, too. Gains complexity on the finish where the flavors fold together nicely. Drink through 2007.–J.L. • $28 • (10/31/1998) • **89**
Cabernet Sauvignon Alexander Valley Reserve 1994 • $28 • (5/31/1997) • **89**
Cabernet Sauvignon Alexander Valley Reserve 1993 • $20 • (12/15/1995) • **88**
Cabernet Sauvignon Alexander Valley Reserve 1991 • $20 • (3/15/1994) SS • **90**
Cabernet Sauvignon Alexander Valley Reserve 1990 • $15 • (6/15/1993) HR • **90**
Cabernet Sauvignon Alexander Valley Reserve 1989 • $14 • (11/15/1992) • **87**
Cabernet Sauvignon Alexander Valley Reserve 1987 • $14 • (12/15/1997) • **89**
Cabernet Sauvignon Alexander Valley Reserve 1986 • $15 • (9/30/1990) • **85**
Cabernet Sauvignon Alexander Valley Reserve 1985 • $15 • (5/15/1989) • **77**
Cabernet Sauvignon Sonoma County 1997: Forward, supple and medium weight, with a modest range of herb, cherry and berry that's straightforward. Drink now through 2006.–J.L. • $16 • (2/29/2000) • **86**
Cabernet Sauvignon Sonoma County 1996: Pleasant and balanced, with pretty dill, anise, black currant and plum flavors. Finishes firm, with hints of mineral. Drink now through 2004.–J.L. • $14 • (6/15/1999) • **87**
Cabernet Sauvignon Sonoma County 1995 • $15 • (10/31/1997) • **88**
Cabernet Sauvignon Sonoma County 1994 • $10 • (11/15/1996) • **86**
Cabernet Sauvignon Sonoma County 1991 • $10 • (3/15/1994) • **84**
Cabernet Sauvignon Sonoma County 1990 • $10 • (6/15/1993) • **81**
Chardonnay Alexander Valley Reserve 1997: Very attractive, ripe, creamy and elegant, with spicy pear, apple and pineapple flavors. Clean aftertaste. Drink now through 2005.–J.L. • $23 • (2/29/2000) • **89**
Chardonnay Alexander Valley Reserve 1996: Serves up lots of ripe, creamy pear, spice, fig and melon flavors, which linger on the elegant, polished finish. Drink now through 2001.–J.L. • $20 • (7/31/1998) • **89**
Chardonnay Russian River Valley 1998: This young California white is tight, crisp and focused, rich and concentrated, meshing ripe pear, fig and citrus with light oak shadings. Delivers lots of fruit and finesse for the price. Drink now through 2004.–J.L. • $16 • (12/31/1999) SS • **89**
Chardonnay Sonoma County 1998: Bright sour apple notes, with earthy citrus and spice flavors and a tingly acidity. Drink now through 2004.–J.L. • $12 • (2/29/2000) • **84**
Chardonnay Sonoma County 1997: Straightforward, with a modest range of citrus and toast flavors. Well balanced, with refreshing crispness. Drink now. • $14 • (12/31/1998) • **83**
Chardonnay Sonoma County 1996 • $14 • (6/15/1998) • **87**
Gewürztraminer California 1997 • $8 • (6/30/1998) • **74**
Gewürztraminer California 1996 • $8 • (11/30/1997) • **79**
Johannisberg Riesling California 1997 • $8 • (6/30/1998) • **82**
Johannisberg Riesling California 1996 • $8 • (5/15/1997) • **84**
Johannisberg Riesling California Soft 1995 • $7 • (6/15/1996) • **84**
Johannisberg Riesling Mendocino County Late Harvest Selected Dried Berry 1990 • $13/375 ml. • (8/31/1991) • **93**
Johannisberg Riesling Russian River Valley Late Harvest Selected Dried Berry 1991 • $16/375 ml. • (10/15/1992) HR • **90**
Malbec Alexander Valley 1991 • $10 • (3/31/1994) • **85**
Malbec Alexander Valley Trione Vineyards Winemaker's Selection 1993 • $18 • (3/31/1996) • **83**
Malbec Alexander Valley Winemaker's Selection 1995: Offers grapey Cabernet flavors accented by notes of sage and cedar, though it's not as complex as you might expect a "Winemaker's Selection" to be. Drink now through 2003.–J.L. • $20 • (10/31/1998) • **85**
Merlot Alexander Valley 1992 • $12 • (1/31/1995) • **85**
Merlot Alexander Valley 1991 • $13 • (6/15/1993) • **87**
Merlot Alexander Valley 1989 • $9 • (5/31/1992) • **79**
Merlot Alexander Valley Reserve 1996: Tightly structured, firm, with a chunky cedar- and cola-laced light berry character, it lacks focus and complexity. Drink through 2005.–J.L. • $32 • (10/15/1999) • **83**
Merlot Alexander Valley Reserve 1995: Offers ripe, complex, chewy plum, mineral, sage, tea and herbal flavors, turning deep and rich on the finish, where the flavors are focused and lively. Has the tannic strength to age. Drink through 2006.–J.L. • $32 • (7/31/1998) • **88**
Merlot Alexander Valley Reserve 1994 • $30 • (7/31/1997) • **86**
Merlot Sonoma County 1997: Tough and chewy, it struggles to work its way through the green, herbal flavors to a core of dry, tannic currant and berry. Dry, crisp aftertaste. Drink now through 2006.–J.L. • $16 • (4/30/2000) • **83**
Merlot Sonoma County 1996: Earthy, with a green edge to the light cherry flavor. Finishes slightly dry. Drink now.–J.L. • $17 • (12/31/1998) • **81**
Merlot Sonoma County 1995 • $16 • (5/31/1998) • **86**
Merlot Sonoma County 1994 • $16 • (2/28/1997) • **87**
Opulence California NV • $8 • (1/31/1987) • **80**
Petite Sirah Alexander Valley 1989 • $15 • (6/30/1992) • **79**
Petite Sirah Alexander Valley Winemaker's Selection 1997: Ruggedly tannic and drying. A glimpse of plum and cherry fights through the leathery flavors. Drink now through 2005.–J.L. • $20 • (5/31/2000) • **83**
Reserve Alexandre Alexander Valley 1997: Tight and angular, with firm tannins and an earthy core of black cherry, currant, cedar and herb, finishing with a touch of bitterness and tobacco. Tasted twice, with consistent notes. Best from 2001 through 2006.–J.L. • $45 • (4/30/2000) • **86**
Reserve Alexandre Alexander Valley 1996: Ripe, smooth and elegant, with a band of cherry, currant, wild berry and cranberry flavors. Turns supple and polished. Drink now through 2006.–J.L. • $45 • (11/15/1999) • **89**
Reserve Alexandre Alexander Valley 1995: Tight and well-oaked, with a complex array of cedar, plum, currant, anise, cherry and spice. Finishes with tight, chewy tannins, a dash of mineral and richness. Best from 2001 through 2008.–J.L. • $28 • (8/31/1998) • **90**
Reserve Alexandre Alexander Valley 1994 • $28 • (10/31/1997) • **91**
Reserve Alexandre Alexander Valley 1993 • $27 • (11/15/1996) • **88**
Reserve Alexandre Alexander Valley 1991 • $30 • (7/31/1994) CS • **91**
Reserve Alexandre Alexander Valley 1990 • $30 • (11/15/1993) • **90**
Reserve Alexandre Alexander Valley 1987 • $18 • (12/15/1997) • **92**
Reserve Alexandre Alexander Valley 1986 • $20 • (9/30/1990) • **89**
Reserve Alexandre Alexander Valley 1985 • $19 Ⓐ • (9/30/1989) • **88**
Reserve Alexandre Alexander Valley 1984 • $19 • (8/31/1988) • **89**
Reserve Alexandre Alexander Valley 1983 • $24 Ⓐ • (4/30/1987) • **80**
Riesling Sonoma County Late Harvest Trione Vineyards Reserve 1993 • $16/375 ml. • (7/31/1995) • **87**
Sauvignon Blanc Sonoma County 1999: This refreshing, racy and complex Sauvignon Blanc will wow you with grapefruit, jalapeño and lime notes and crisp, lively finish. Good price, too. Drink now through 2004.–J.L. • $9 • (4/30/2000) • **86**
Sauvignon Blanc Sonoma County 1998: Fresh fig and grapefruit come to mind in this effusively fruity wine that sports bright, refreshing acidity and a sleek, lean body. Hints of freshly mowed grass and minerals add complexity, and the finish is long and delightful. California grapes, Australia-style winemaking. Drink now. • $9 • (6/15/1999) SS • **90**
Sauvignon Blanc Sonoma County 1997 • $7 • (5/15/1998) • **88**
Sauvignon Blanc Sonoma County 1996 • $9 • (5/15/1997) • **87**
Shiraz Alexander Valley Bin 1 1995: Tight, tannic and firmly structured, with a core of earthy wild berry, black cherry, spice and cedar notes. Finishes with a tannic edge. Best from 2001 through 2008.–J.L. • $100 • (11/15/1999) • **89**
Shiraz Port Sonoma County Trione Vineyards Henry's Reserve 1993 • $15 • (12/31/1995) • **73**
Shiraz Sonoma County 1997: A bit raw and angular, with firm tannins, crisp acidity and tart plum, black cherry and cedar notes. A Merlot-style Syrah? Drink now.–J.L. • $16 • (4/30/2000) • **83**
Shiraz Sonoma County 1996: Somewhat restrained, with black cherry and herb flavors that are currently overshadowed by oak. Still, the wine offers a certain silkiness on the palate, and finishes with firm tannins and a hint of anise. Drink now through 2004. • $14 • (5/15/1999) • **86**
Shiraz Sonoma County 1995: Starts off with rich plum and earth tones. Somewhat meaty on the palate, with bright blackberry and mineral flavors. A very good wine, with potential for aging through 2005. • $15 • (12/31/1998) • **87**
Shiraz Sonoma County 1994 • $14 • (2/28/1997) • **87**
Shiraz Sonoma County Reserve 1997: Cola and chocolate overtones combine with substantial tannins and blackberry flavors. Best from 2001 through 2004.–J.L. • $35 • (5/15/2000) • **85**
Shiraz Sonoma County Reserve 1996: Struggles to find focus. Earthy, bitter, even a touch funky, with a strong dill flavor overriding the modest berry fruit. Tasted twice, with consistent notes. Drink now.–J.L. • $35 • (5/31/2000) • **80**
Shiraz Sonoma County Reserve 1994 • $32 • (9/30/1997) • **87**
Sparkling Shiraz-Cabernet Alexander Valley 1994: Ripe flavors and spicy overtones make this red sparkler attractive, featuring a colalike note on the creamy, well-modulated finish. Drink now.–H.S. • $20 • (3/31/2000) • **88**
Syrah Alexander Valley Reserve 1991 • $18 • (12/31/1993) HR • **91**
Syrah Alexander Valley Shiraz 1993 • $12 • (6/15/1996) • **89**
Zinfandel Cucamonga Valley De Ambrogio Ranch 100 Year Old Vines Winemaker's Selection 1997: Firm, chewy and almost bitey in texture, but it's brimming with ripe berry, plum and spice flavors that linger enticingly on the long finish. Has density and length, and should keep developing. Has the feel of old vines, with depth and character to burn. Drink now through 2004.–H.S. • $25 • (11/30/1999) • **91**

Zinfandel Sonoma County 1997: Crisp, with stemmy, plummy notes and a woody finish. Tasted twice, with consistent notes. Drink now.–J.L. • $16 • (5/15/2000) • **82**
Zinfandel Sonoma County 1996: Starts out lively, with a pretty array of plum, wild berry, cherry and spice, but turns tight and firm on the finish. Drink now through 2002.–J.L. • $14 • (5/15/1999) • **88**
Zinfandel Sonoma County 1995 • $16 • (6/15/1998) • **85**

GICOMA | CALIFORNIA

Cabernet Sauvignon Napa Valley Pointer Run Vineyards 1992 • $14 • (3/31/1996) • **78**

GIRARD | CALIFORNIA

Cabernet Sauvignon Napa Valley 1996: Complex and well balanced, though not especially rich, it's flavorful, with ripe cherry, currant, plum and cedary oak flavors that turn supple and polished. Drink now through 2006.–J.L. • $40 • (11/15/1999) • **89**
Cabernet Sauvignon Napa Valley 1995: Greeting you with dusty, cedary oak and a tightly wound, complex core of blackberry, black cherry, sage, herb and coffee notes, this California Cab is a bit awkward at this stage, but shows good potential for midterm cellaring. Finishes crisp and tannic. Best from 2001 through 2007.–J.L. • $30 • (2/28/1999) CS • **91**
Cabernet Sauvignon Napa Valley 1994 • $25 • (10/31/1997) • **88**
Cabernet Sauvignon Napa Valley 1993 • $22 • (11/15/1996) • **89**
Cabernet Sauvignon Napa Valley 1991 • $18 • (5/31/1994) • **86**
Cabernet Sauvignon Napa Valley 1990 • $16 • (11/15/1993) • **87**
Cabernet Sauvignon Napa Valley 1989 • $16 • (11/15/1992) • **82**
Cabernet Sauvignon Napa Valley 1988 • $16 • (11/15/1991) • **85**
Cabernet Sauvignon Napa Valley 1987 • $16 • (11/15/1990) • **86**
Cabernet Sauvignon Napa Valley 1986 • $16 • (11/15/1989) • **89**
Cabernet Sauvignon Napa Valley 1985 • $15 • (9/15/1988) • **88**
Cabernet Sauvignon Napa Valley 1984 • $11 • (11/30/1987) • **88**
Cabernet Sauvignon Napa Valley 1983 • $15 • (12/15/1986) • **71**
Cabernet Sauvignon Napa Valley 1982 • $13 • (2/16/1986) • **89**
Cabernet Sauvignon Napa Valley 1981 • $14 • (8/01/1985) • **89**
Cabernet Sauvignon Napa Valley Reserve 1995: May merit a higher rating in time, but for now it's elegant, with dusty, cedary oak and black cherry, wild berry, anise and olive notes. Very appealing, but falls shy of outstanding as it's missing those extra dimensions. Best from 2001 through 2007.–J.L. • $55 • (3/31/1999) • **89**
Cabernet Sauvignon Napa Valley Reserve 1994 • $40 • (11/15/1997) • **93**
Cabernet Sauvignon Napa Valley Reserve 1993 • $45 • (11/15/1996) • **88**
Cabernet Sauvignon Napa Valley Reserve 1992 • $31 Ⓐ • (12/15/1995) • **88**
Cabernet Sauvignon Napa Valley Reserve 1991 • $35 • (11/15/1994) • **87**
Cabernet Sauvignon Napa Valley Reserve 1990 • $25 • (4/15/1994) • **86**
Cabernet Sauvignon Napa Valley Reserve 1989 • $25 • (11/15/1993) • **84**
Cabernet Sauvignon Napa Valley Reserve 1988 • $25 • (11/15/1992) • **84**
Cabernet Sauvignon Napa Valley Reserve 1987 • $25 • (11/15/1991) • **88**
Cabernet Sauvignon Napa Valley Reserve 1986 • $19 Ⓐ • (11/15/1990) • **87**
Cabernet Sauvignon Napa Valley Reserve 1985 • $35 • (2/15/1990) • **86**
Cabernet Sauvignon Napa Valley Reserve 1984 • $25 • (12/15/1988) • **93**
Cabernet Sauvignon Napa Valley Reserve 1983 • $20 • (12/15/1987) • **86**
Chardonnay Napa Valley 1997: Toasty, flinty flavors unfold to richer, broader, more complex tones in this full-blown, opulent wine. Citrus, pear, fig and herb notes add dimension. Drink now.–J.L. • $28 • (7/31/1999) • **91**

GIRARDET | OREGON

Cabernet Sauvignon Umpqua Valley 1998: Dark and vibrant in flavor, packed with berry, herb and mineral that reverberate on the supple finish. Has a bit of tannin to lose. Best after 2001.–H.S. • $16 • (3/31/2000) • **87**
Cabernet Sauvignon Umpqua Valley 1995: On the light side, but has pretty raspberry and currant flavors—and a hint of volatility—that shine through the layer of modest tannins. Best from 1999 through 2003.–H.S. • $14 • (7/31/1998) • **85**
Chardonnay Oregon 1997: Smooth and polished, framing its floral and apple flavors with spicy, honey-scented aromas and a touch of bitterness. Drink now through 2002.–H.S. • $12 • (12/31/1999) • **85**
Pinot Noir Oregon Barrel Select 1997: Light in texture, with a smoky edge to the basic red cherry flavors, finishing with modest tannins. Drink now through 2002.–H.S. • $16 • (12/31/1999) • **83**
Pinot Noir Umpqua Valley 1987 • $12 • (2/15/1990) • **75**
Pinot Noir Umpqua Valley Barrel Select 1995: Light and soft, with pretty chocolate overtones to the modest berry and orange-peel flavors. Feels mature.–H.S. • $22 • (7/31/1998) • **83**
Pinot Noir Umpqua Valley Reserve 1996: Firm in texture, with focused black cherry and spice flavors that linger on the finish. Appealing now, but cellaring could add more suppleness. Drink now through 2003.–H.S. • $32 • (3/31/2000) • **87**

GLASS MOUNTAIN QUARRY | CALIFORNIA

Cabernet Sauvignon California 1996: Soft-textured, with light herbal flavors and cherry notes, finishing with soft tannins. Drink now.–J.L. • $10 • (5/15/1999) • **84**
Cabernet Sauvignon California 1992 • $10 • (12/15/1995) • **84**
Cabernet Sauvignon California 1990 • $9 • (6/15/1993) • **84**
Cabernet Sauvignon Napa Valley 1988 • $8 • (10/15/1991) • **85**
Chardonnay California 1997: Crisp and citrusy, with green apple, pear and leafy herb notes on the finish. Drink now.–J.L. • $10 • (4/30/1999) • **83**
Chardonnay California 1996: Soft, with pleasant fig, toast and nut flavors that linger on the finish. Drink now.–J.L. • $10 • (11/15/1998) • **84**
Petite Sirah Napa Valley 1988 • $8 • (10/31/1991) • **81**
Rubis du Val Napa Valley 1988 • $8 • (10/31/1991) • **82**

GLEN ELLEN | CALIFORNIA

Cabernet Franc Alexander Valley Imagery Series 1988 • $16 • (3/31/1992) • **86**
Cabernet Sauvignon California Proprietor's Reserve 1996: Ripe cherry and charred oak flavors on a soft, simple frame. Drink now.–J.L. • $6 • (10/15/1998) • **77**
Cabernet Sauvignon California Proprietor's Reserve 1995 • $6 • (10/31/1997) • **80**
Cabernet Sauvignon California Proprietor's Reserve 1994 • $6 • (11/30/1996) • **77**
Cabernet Sauvignon California Proprietor's Reserve 1993 • $6 • (12/15/1995) • **82**
Cabernet Sauvignon California Proprietor's Reserve 1991 • $6 • (11/15/1993) • **78**
Cabernet Sauvignon California Proprietor's Reserve 1989 • $7 • (11/15/1992) • **84**
Cabernet Sauvignon California Proprietor's Reserve 1988 • $6 • (11/15/1991) • **79**
Cabernet Sauvignon Sonoma Valley Benziger Family Selection 1984 • $14 • (10/15/1987) • **82**
Cabernet Sauvignon Sonoma Valley Imagery Series 1985 • $13 • (2/15/1989) • **86**
Chardonnay California Proprietor's Reserve 1997 • $6 • (6/30/1998) • **81**
Chardonnay California Proprietor's Reserve 1996: Simple, with tart apple and mineral flavors. Slightly herbal on the short finish. Drink now. • $6 • (7/31/1998) • **78**
Gamay California Beaujolais Proprietor's Reserve 1996: Simple, with light cherry and herb notes. Drink now. • $5 • (9/30/1998) • **78**
Merlot California Proprietor's Reserve 1997: Simple, with toasted oak notes to the light berry flavors.–J.L. • $7 • (10/15/1999) • **77**
Merlot California Proprietor's Reserve 1996: Simple coffee and currant flavors hide beneath an earthy veneer. Drink now. • $7 • (9/15/1998) • **77**
Merlot California Proprietor's Reserve 1994 • $6 • (7/31/1996) • **78**
Merlot California Proprietor's Reserve 1992 • $5 • (9/15/1994) • **82**
Merlot California Proprietor's Reserve 1991 • $7 • (4/15/1993) • **82**
Merlot California Proprietor's Reserve 1990 • $6 • (5/31/1992) • **79**
Petit Verdot Alexander Valley Imagery Series 1988 • $16 • (3/31/1992) • **88**
Riesling Santa Maria Valley Late Harvest Imagery Series 1989 • $10/375 ml. • (3/31/1992) • **79**
Sauvignon Blanc California Proprietor's Reserve 1996 • $5 • (4/30/1998) • **84**
Zinfandel California Proprietor's Reserve 1996 • $6 • (6/15/1998) • **70**

GLEN FIONA | WASHINGTON

Grenache Columbia Valley Noir 1995 • $16 • (9/30/1997) • **87**
Sauvignon Blanc-Sémillon Walla Walla County 1995 • $16/375 ml. • (10/15/1997) • **85**
Syrah Columbia Valley Bacchus Vineyard 1998: Fresh, ripe and inviting, this is already polished despite its youth, with exuberant plum flavors at the core and exotic fruit overtones. Has plenty to offer, but needs time to settle down. Best after 2000.–H.S. • $20 • (9/30/1999) • **88**

Key: SS—Spectator Selection. CS—Cellar Selection. HR—Highly Recommended. $NA—Price not available. (BT)—Barrel tasting. Ⓐ—Auction Price.
For a key to the tasters' initials, see "How to Use These Listings."
Dates in parentheses represent the issues in which the ratings were published.

Syrah Columbia Valley Bacchus Vineyard 1997: Youthful and exuberant, chewy with fine tannins and oozing with cherry and blackberry, layered with vanilla and peppery spices. Needs time to settle down. Drink through 2004.–H.S. • $20 • (9/15/1998) • **91**
Syrah Walla Walla County 1995 • $25 • (9/30/1997) • **88**
Syrah Walla Walla Valley 1997: Dark, dense and beautifully focused, packed with ripe blackberry, plum, black pepper and floral aromas and flavors that just don't quit on the long, firm finish, which shows just a hint of leather. Needs to shed some tannin. Best after 2000.–H.S. • $35 • (9/15/1999) • **91**

GLORIA FERRER | CALIFORNIA

Blanc de Noirs Carneros NV: Fairly supple, with ripe cherry, lemon and grapefruit flavors. Delivers pretty toast, orange peel and spice on the finish. Quite nice. Drink now through 2001. • $15 • (12/15/1998) • **88**
Blanc de Noirs Sonoma County Carneros NV • $15 • (11/30/1997) • **89**
Brut Carneros Carneros Cuvée Late Disgorged 1990: Firm and fresh on the palate, with lovely toast, lemon, orange, apple and pear flavors couched in a complex and classy structure. Bright on the finish, long and luxurious. Drink now. • $32 • (9/15/1999) • **91**
Brut Carneros Royal Cuvée Vintage Reserve 1991: Firm and tangy, with lemon and floral overtones. Toasty, doughy notes add interest, with the flavors carried along on tiny bubbles. Quite refreshing. Drink now. • $20 • (9/15/1999) • **88**
Brut Carneros Royal Cuvée Vintage Reserve 1990: A cleanly styled wine, marked by fresh lemons, apples, herbs and toast. Firm and bright, it tastes quite young considering the vintage. Should flesh out and gain complexity through 2002. • $20 • (11/30/1998) • **89**
Brut Rosé Carneros NV: Bright and toasty, with hints of Bing cherry and citrus. Fresh, lively and firmly structured, this packs a lingering, lemony finish. Available only at the winery. Drink now through 2001. • $20 • (12/15/1998) • **87**
Brut Rosé Sonoma County NV • $20 • (11/30/1997) • **90**
Brut Sonoma County NV: Toast and citrus aromas and flavors weave a pretty patchwork. Light and elegant, offering a fresh, fruity finish redolent of apples and pears. Drink now through 2001. • $15 • (12/15/1998) • **88**
Chardonnay Carneros 1998: Lemon and butter notes show focus, but middling depth. Drink now.–J.L. • $20 • (6/15/2000) • **83**
Chardonnay Carneros 1997: Bright and focused, with a tight core of pear, pineapple and citrus, adding touches of mineral and earthiness on the finish. Drink now through 2002.–J.L. • $20 • (7/31/1999) • **91**
Chardonnay Carneros 1996 • $19 • (5/15/1998) SS • **90**
Pinot Noir Carneros 1997: Light in color and body, with herbal cherry and strawberry, finishing with a cranberry edge. Drink now through 2002.–J.L. • $20 • (9/15/1999) • **85**
Pinot Noir Carneros 1996: A well-made wine that strives for complexity but comes up short. What's there is appealing—a lighter style of simple rhubarb and berry-laced flavors, finishing with hints of coffee and herb. Try now.–J.L. • $19 • (8/31/1998) • **85**
Pinot Noir Carneros 1995 • $19 • (2/28/1998) • **85**
Pinot Noir Carneros 1994 • $16 • (2/29/1996) • **79**
Pinot Noir Carneros 1993 • $16 • (12/31/1995) • **81**
Pinot Noir Carneros 1992 • $16 • (12/31/1995) • **86**
Pinot Noir Carneros 1991 • $15 • (2/28/1994) • **85**

GLORIA'S OLD VINES | CALIFORNIA

Cabernet Sauvignon Alexander Valley 1996: Neat and trim, with a band of cedar, currant, anise and berry, finishing with integrated tannins and a leathery note. Drink now through 2007.–J.L. • $45 • (3/31/2000) • **88**

GODSPEED | CALIFORNIA

Cabernet Sauvignon Mount Veeder 1994: A gentle wine with a lovely purity of Cabernet fruit character, its dark currant and blackberry flavors mingling with delicate spice and floral notes on the smooth, harmonious finish. Drink now through 2002.–H.S. • $14 • (11/15/1998) • **86**
Cabernet Sauvignon Mount Veeder 1991 • $15 • (12/15/1995) • **82**
Chardonnay Mount Veeder 1996: A bit of an oddball. Minerally seashell and sour notes detract from the otherwise crisp citrus flavors. Drink now. • $17 • (7/31/1998) • **75**

GODWIN | CALIFORNIA

Merlot Alexander Valley 1995 • $20 • (5/31/1998) • **84**

GOLDEN VALLEY | OREGON

Chardonnay Willamette Valley St. Herman's Vineyard Dijon Burgundian Clone 1997: Light and bracing, with citrus, green apple and hints of spice working their way into the finish nicely. Drink now.–H.S. • $13 • (5/15/2000) • **84**
Pinot Noir Willamette Valley St. Herman's Vineyard 1997: Light in texture, with modest berry and spice flavors under a thin layer of slightly scratchy tannin. Drink now through 2002.–H.S. • $13 • (4/30/2000) • **84**

GORDON BROTHERS | WASHINGTON

Cabernet Sauvignon Columbia Valley 1997: Supple in texture and light in flavor, with pretty blackberry and cherry notes sneaking through. Drink now.–H.S. • $18 • (3/31/2000) • **82**
Cabernet Sauvignon Columbia Valley 1996: Firm and fruity, with pretty raspberry and currant and a nice overlay of spice. Drink with hearty food. Drink through 2002.–H.S. • $18 • (12/15/1998) • **86**
Cabernet Sauvignon Columbia Valley 1994: A gentle style that lets the ripe currant, cherry and herb flavors float over a fine layer of modest tannins. Picks up a nice hint of chocolate on the finish. Drink now through 2002.–H.S. • $16 • (8/31/1998) • **86**
Cabernet Sauvignon Columbia Valley 1993 • $17 • (9/15/1997) • **82**
Cabernet Sauvignon Washington 1991 • $15 • (9/30/1995) • **85**
Cabernet Sauvignon Washington 1990 • $14 • (3/15/1994) • **77**
Cabernet Sauvignon Washington 1989 • $16 • (7/31/1992) • **83**
Cabernet Sauvignon Washington 1988 • $19 • (11/15/1991) • **89**
Chardonnay Columbia Valley 1998: Smooth and polished, this is generous with its pear and citrus flavors, sliding in a pretty spicy oak note on the long finish. Picks up a hint of honey that expands on the aftertaste. Drink now through 2003.–H.S. • $16 • (11/15/1999) • **90**
Chardonnay Columbia Valley 1997: A ripe and refreshing mouthful of pear, spice and floral flavors that linger, with a touch of pepper, on the finish. Lovely. Drink now.–H.S. • $16 • (10/15/1998) • **86**
Gewürztraminer Late Harvest Columbia Valley 1997: Lightly sweet, with honey-scented pear flavors and a floral hint on the finish. Drink now.–H.S. • $9/500 ml. • (9/30/1998) • **85**
Merlot Columbia Valley 1997: Firm in texture, this lean Merlot has nice black cherry and tar flavors under a fine-grained layer of chewy tannins. Best after 2001.–H.S. • $17 • (11/15/1999) • **86**
Merlot Columbia Valley 1995: Smooth and supple, a creamy-textured red with pretty plum, orange peel and vanilla aromas and flavors that spread nicely on the finish. Drink through 2001.–H.S. • $17 • (8/31/1998) • **87**
Merlot Columbia Valley 1994 • $19 • (9/15/1997) • **85**
Merlot Washington 1993 • $16 • (9/15/1996) • **82**
Merlot Washington 1992 • $15 • (9/30/1995) • **87**
Merlot Washington 1990 • $15 • (6/15/1993) • **78**
Tradition Columbia Valley 1996: Lean and herbal, this is distinctive for its bay leaf, mint and mineral overtones to the basic black cherry flavor, all of which echoes on the smooth finish. A blend of Merlot and Cabernet Sauvignon. Drink now through 2004.–H.S. • $30 • (11/15/1999) • **87**
Tradition Washington 1991 • $20 • (1/31/1995) • **88**

GOSSAMER BAY | CALIFORNIA

Cabernet Sauvignon California 1995 • $9 • (3/31/1998) • **85**
Zinfandel California 1995 • $9 • (2/28/1997) • **80**

GOTT, JOEL | CALIFORNIA

Zinfandel Amador County Dillian Ranch 1996: Impressive for its dense, ripe core of tarry and well-oaked black cherry, wild berry and herb flavors. Finishes with substantial tannins. Needs time to evolve. Try now through 2002.–J.L. • $18 • (6/30/1999) • **88**

GRACE FAMILY | CALIFORNIA

Cabernet Sauvignon Napa Valley 1997: Dark and ripe, rich and elegant, with a core of cedary currant, earth and berry, finishing with supple, polished tannins and good length. Available only in 1L-bottles by mailing list. Best from 2002 through 2012.–J.L. • $395 • (4/30/2000) • **92**
Cabernet Sauvignon Napa Valley 1995 • $475/1.5 liter • (6/15/1998) • **92**
Cabernet Sauvignon Napa Valley 1994 • $471 Ⓐ • (5/31/1997) CS • **94**
Cabernet Sauvignon Napa Valley 1993 • $291 Ⓐ • (5/15/1996) • **85**
Cabernet Sauvignon Napa Valley 1991 • $347 Ⓐ • (11/15/1994) • **88**

UNITED STATES

GRACE FAMILY

Cabernet Sauvignon Napa Valley 1990 • $311 Ⓐ • (8/31/1993) • **90**
Cabernet Sauvignon Napa Valley 1988 • $187 Ⓐ • (6/30/1991) • **92**
Cabernet Sauvignon Napa Valley 1987 • $386 Ⓐ • (6/30/1990) • **97**
Cabernet Sauvignon Napa Valley 1985 • $335 Ⓐ • (12/15/1988) • **93**
Cabernet Sauvignon Napa Valley 1984 • $307 Ⓐ • (4/15/1988) • **90**
Cabernet Sauvignon Napa Valley 1983 • $208 Ⓐ • (6/15/1987) • **85**

GRACELAND | CALIFORNIA

Cabernet Sauvignon Napa Valley Going Home 1994 • $23 • (10/31/1997) • **77**

GRAFF, RICHARD | CALIFORNIA

Mourvèdre Chalone 1992 • $16 • (1/31/1996) • **86**
Pinot Noir Central Coast 1994 • $18 • (1/31/1997) • **90**

GRAHAM, GREGORY | CALIFORNIA

Pinot Noir Carneros 1997: On the lighter side, with modest cedar, sage and a whiff of berry, turning dry and tannic. Lacks the ripe fruit for support. Drink now.–J.L. • $26 • (5/15/2000) • **82**
Pinot Noir Carneros 1994 • $22 • (3/31/1997) • **83**
Pinot Noir Carneros 1992 • $18 • (3/31/1995) • **86**
Syrah Napa Valley 1997: Light spice and meat notes struggle to focus. Could use more grapey flavors. Drink now.–J.L. • $24 • (4/30/2000) • **82**
Viognier Knights Valley 1998: Has floral and oak aromas and decent depth. Dominated by vanilla flavors that turn a bit pasty on the finish. Drink now.–J.L. • $27 • (5/15/2000) • **83**
Viognier Knights Valley 1996 • $24 • (4/30/1998) • **88**
Viognier Napa Valley 1996 • $22 • (4/30/1998) • **87**

GRAND CRU VINEYARDS | CALIFORNIA

Cabernet Sauvignon Alexander Valley Collector's Reserve 1986 • $22 • (5/15/1990) • **85**
Cabernet Sauvignon Alexander Valley Collector's Reserve 1985 • $18 • (7/15/1989) • **81**
Cabernet Sauvignon Alexander Valley Collector's Reserve 1982 • $15 • (9/30/1987) • **70**
Cabernet Sauvignon Alexander Valley Collector's Reserve 1980 • $15 • (11/01/1984) • **85**
Cabernet Sauvignon Sonoma County Premium Selection 1988 • $12 • (3/15/1992) • **84**
Cabernet Sauvignon Sonoma County Premium Selection 1987 • $12 • (11/15/1991) • **85**
Cabernet Sauvignon Sonoma County Premium Selection 1986 • $12 • (4/30/1990) • **79**
Chardonnay California Premium Selection 1996: Coconut and toast flavors dominate, but there are also some nice, tart apple and pear notes. No attempt to integrate the oak with the fruit, yet it has a silky texture, a long finish. Drink now.–T.G. • $8 • (7/31/1998) • **82**
Merlot California Premium Selection 1996 • $8 • (4/30/1998) • **83**
Merlot California Premium Selection 1992 • $8 • (9/15/1994) • **81**
Zinfandel California Premium Selection 1992 • $7 • (10/15/1995) • **78**

GREEN & RED | CALIFORNIA

Gamay Napa Valley 1996 • $14 • (3/31/1998) • **84**
Zinfandel California 1997: A blend of Lodi- and Calistoga-grown grapes, this is ripe, fruity, supple, with juicy plum, black cherry and wild berry notes, finishing with mild tannins. Drink now.–J.L. • $16 • (5/31/1999) • **89**
Zinfandel Napa Valley 1989 • $11 • (10/15/1992) • **81**
Zinfandel Napa Valley Chiles Mill Vineyard 1998: Struggles to find its focus. Leathery plum and wild berry flavors turn vegetal. Drink now.–J.L. • $22 • (5/31/2000) • **81**
Zinfandel Napa Valley Chiles Mill Vineyard 1997: Consistently a very good to outstanding bottle. The '97 is jammy-tasting, gushing with ripe black cherry, raspberry, boysenberry and spicy flavors that are rich and elegant, finishing with a zesty twist of pepper. Drink now through 2004.–J.L. • $20 • (5/15/1999) HR • **93**
Zinfandel Napa Valley Chiles Mill Vineyard 1996 • $18 • (5/31/1998) • **85**
Zinfandel Napa Valley Chiles Mill Vineyard 1995 • $17 • (4/30/1997) • **90**
Zinfandel Napa Valley Chiles Mill Vineyard 1994 • $16 • (4/30/1996) • **88**
Zinfandel Napa Valley Chiles Mill Vineyard 1992 • $14 • (7/31/1994) • **88**
Zinfandel Napa Valley Chiles Mill Vineyard 1991 • $12 • (9/30/1993) • **85**
Zinfandel Napa Valley Chiles Mill Vineyard 1990 • $12 • (3/15/1993) HR • **90**
Zinfandel Napa Valley Chiles Mill Vineyard Unfiltered 1993 • $15 • (9/30/1995) HR • **90**
Zinfandel Napa Valley Chiles Valley Vineyards 1998: Green and muddled. The berry notes struggle to work their way past the green bean, bell pepper and tomato flavors. Drink now.–J.L. • $20 • (5/31/2000) • **80**
Zinfandel Napa Valley Chiles Valley Vineyards 1997: Ripe and effusively fruity, with layers of plum, black cherry, raspberry, anise, sage and cedar, finishing with a long, rich aftertaste that keeps pumping out the fruit. Drink now through 2004.–J.L. • $18 • (5/15/1999) • **92**

GREENWOOD RIDGE | CALIFORNIA

Cabernet Sauvignon Anderson Valley 1995: Firm, but smoothly textured, this offers subtle cola, coffee, black currant, licorice, herb and cedar notes, with a slightly tart finish. Lovely. Drink now through 2005. • $32 • (10/31/1998) • **86**
Cabernet Sauvignon Anderson Valley 1994 • $36 • (11/15/1997) • **89**
Cabernet Sauvignon Anderson Valley 1992 • $18 • (9/15/1995) • **89**
Cabernet Sauvignon Anderson Valley 1991 • $14 • (11/15/1994) • **82**
Cabernet Sauvignon Anderson Valley 1989 • $12 • (8/31/1992) • **74**
Cabernet Sauvignon Anderson Valley Reserve 1990 • $16 • (6/15/1993) • **75**
Cabernet Sauvignon Anderson Valley Reserve 1989 • $16 • (11/15/1992) • **87**
Cabernet Sauvignon Mendocino 1988: Tight, a bit tart, with firm tannins and a core of chunky currant and black cherry. Finishes with hard tannins and a glimpse of olive. (1988 California Cabernet retrospective tasting). Drink now through 2002.–J.L. • $15 • (11/15/1998) • **85**
Cabernet Sauvignon Mendocino Ridge 1996: Elegant and well balanced, featuring cedar, tobacco and supple black cherry flavors, finishing with ripe tannins. Drink now through 2004 .–J.L. • $24 • (9/15/1999) • **88**
Chardonnay Anderson Valley Late Harvest 1993 • $18 • (6/15/1994) • **85**
Chardonnay Mendocino Ridge Du Pratt Vineyard 1998: Sweet-tasting and herbaceous, with vanilla and tropical fruit flavors that carry through to the finish. Drink now through 2002.–J.L. • $24 • (5/15/2000) • **83**
Chardonnay Mendocino Ridge DuPratt Vineyard 1997: Ripe, with rich fig, apple and a hint of butterscotch folded together nicely, this is plump and complex, if a bit cloying. Drink now through 2002.–J.L. • $22 • (4/30/1999) • **87**
Chardonnay Anderson Valley Du Pratt Vineyard 1996 • $22 • (3/31/1998) • **88**
Merlot Anderson Valley 1995 • $22 • (11/30/1997) • **89**
Merlot Anderson Valley 1994 • $20 • (2/28/1997) • **84**
Merlot Anderson Valley 1993 • $20 • (8/31/1996) • **89**
Merlot Anderson Valley 1992 • $20 • (4/15/1995) • **86**
Merlot Anderson Valley 1991 • $16 • (3/15/1994) • **78**
Merlot Anderson Valley 1989 • $16 • (11/15/1991) • **85**
Merlot Mendocino Ridge 1997: Supple, with a range of herb-tinged black cherry, chocolate, spice and toasted oak flavors that finish with smooth tannins. Drink now through 2003.–J.L. • $24 • (10/15/1999) • **86**
Merlot Mendocino Ridge 1996: Tightly wound, with a firm core of currant, black cherry and wild berry. Turns austere, tannic and hard on the finish, which has a greenish edge. Drink through 2004.–J.L. • $24 • (9/30/1998) • **84**
Pinot Noir Anderson Valley 1998: Cola and plum notes are framed nicely with vanilla overtones that linger through the finish. Drink now through 2002.–J.L. • $24 • (5/15/2000) • **86**
Pinot Noir Anderson Valley 1997: Light and soft-textured, with a spicy herbal thread running through the strawberry, quince and cherry flavors. Drink now through 2001.–J.L. • $22 • (9/15/1999) • **85**
Pinot Noir Anderson Valley 1996 • $22 • (2/28/1998) • **88**
Pinot Noir Anderson Valley 1995 • $19 • (12/31/1996) • **88**
Pinot Noir Anderson Valley 1994 • $16 • (1/31/1996) HR • **90**
Pinot Noir Anderson Valley 1990 • $15 • (3/31/1997) • **89**
Pinot Noir Anderson Valley 1989 • $14 • (6/30/1991) • **87**
Pinot Noir Anderson Valley Roederer Estate Vineyards 1993 • $15 • (3/31/1995) • **89**
Pinot Noir Anderson Valley Roederer Estate Vineyards 1992 • $15 • (10/31/1994) SS • **90**
Pinot Noir Mendocino County 1991 • $15 • (2/28/1993) • **87**

Key: SS—Spectator Selection. CS—Cellar Selection. HR—Highly Recommended. $NA—Price not available. (BT)—Barrel tasting. Ⓐ—Auction Price. For a key to the tasters' initials, see "How to Use These Listings."
Dates in parentheses represent the issues in which the ratings were published.

Sauvignon Blanc Mendocino 1997: Somewhat viscous but with good acidity, this serves up peach, melon and citrus flavors in a refreshing package. Drink now. • $11 • (10/31/1998) • **86**
Sauvignon Blanc Mendocino 1996 • $10 • (7/31/1997) • **82**
White Riesling Late Harvest Mendocino Ridge 1997: Sweet and earthy, with rich pear, fig and nectarine flavors that turn elegant and lively with zingy acidity. Drink now through 2004.–J.L. • $20/375 ml. • (12/31/1998) • **91**
White Riesling Mendocino Late Harvest 1989 • $18/375 ml. • (8/31/1991) • **89**
Zinfandel Mendocino 1996: Supple and generous, a harmonious wine that balances its plum and berry flavors on a nice edge of acidity, shading it all with a pretty layer of vanilla oak. Drink now through 2002.–H.S. • $16 • (11/30/1998) • **88**
Zinfandel Sonoma County 1991 • $13 • (5/31/1993) • **85**
Zinfandel Sonoma County 1990 • $13 • (7/31/1992) • **86**
Zinfandel Sonoma County 1989 • $12 • (10/15/1992) • **81**
Zinfandel Sonoma County 1988 • $11 • (5/15/1991) • **86**
Zinfandel Sonoma County Scherrer Vineyards 1998: Pleasant cherry and raspberry flavors turn earthy and tannic. Drink now.–J.L. • $21 • (5/15/2000) • **83**
Zinfandel Sonoma County Scherrer Vineyards 1997: Ripe and juicy, brimming with fresh blackberry, black cherry and wild berry flavors that turn spicy and peppery on the finish. Lacks some depth at midpalate, but overall quite complete. Drink now through 2005.–J.L. • $18 • (2/28/1999) • **88**
Zinfandel Sonoma County Scherrer Vineyards 1996 • $18 • (3/31/1998) • **86**
Zinfandel Sonoma County Scherrer Vineyards 1995 • $16 • (2/28/1997) • **89**
Zinfandel Sonoma County Scherrer Vineyards 1994 • $15 • (4/30/1996) • **90**
Zinfandel Sonoma County Scherrer Vineyards 1993 • $14 • (1/31/1995) • **87**
Zinfandel Sonoma County Scherrer Vineyards 1992 • $14 • (9/15/1994) • **88**
Zinfandel Sonoma County Scherrer Vineyards 1991: Still holding its fruit quite well, with plum, cherry and raspberry flavors that are ripe and lively. Finishes with a pretty floral aftertaste. (Zinfandel retrospective tasting). Drink now through 2002.–J.L. • $13 • (6/30/1999) • **88**

GRGICH HILLS | CALIFORNIA

Cabernet Sauvignon Napa Valley 1996: Tight and restrained, with a trim band of cedary currant, herb, sage and earth notes, firming on the finish. Best from 2001 through 2009.–J.L. • $45 • (4/30/2000) • **87**
Cabernet Sauvignon Napa Valley 1995: Wows you with finesse and elegance. Openly ripe and fruity, with supple, fleshy, plummy Cabernet flavors, hints of cedar and spice, finishing with a clean, polished aftertaste and supple tannins. Builds intensity on the aftertaste, so cellaring short-term is our advice. Drink through 2007.–J.L. • $45 • (11/15/1998) • **91**
Cabernet Sauvignon Napa Valley 1994 • $30 • (10/31/1997) • **88**
Cabernet Sauvignon Napa Valley 1993 • $28 • (11/15/1996) • **88**
Cabernet Sauvignon Napa Valley 1992 • $26 • (8/31/1996) • **79**
Cabernet Sauvignon Napa Valley 1991 • $24 • (12/15/1995) • **83**
Cabernet Sauvignon Napa Valley 1990 • $22 • (4/30/1995) • **87**
Cabernet Sauvignon Napa Valley 1989: Crisp, firmly tannic, with a tight band of black cherry, plum, sage, anise and spice, picking up the tannins on the finish. (1989 California Cabernet retrospective tasting). Drink now through 2002.–J.L. • $22 • (8/31/1999) • **86**
Cabernet Sauvignon Napa Valley 1988 • $22 • (11/15/1993) • **84**
Cabernet Sauvignon Napa Valley 1987 • $22 • (11/15/1992) • **87**
Cabernet Sauvignon Napa Valley 1986 • $20 • (12/15/1996) • **89**
Cabernet Sauvignon Napa Valley 1985 • $51 Ⓐ • (10/31/1990) • **90**
Cabernet Sauvignon Napa Valley 1984 • $53 Ⓐ • (4/30/1989) • **87**
Cabernet Sauvignon Napa Valley 1983 • $26 Ⓐ • (4/30/1988) • **90**
Cabernet Sauvignon Napa Valley 1982 • $17 • (4/15/1987) • **92**
Cabernet Sauvignon Napa Valley Yountville Selection 1994: Austere, with a focused band of earthy currant, cedar, tar and spice. Firms up on the finish, where the tannins are drying. Give it time in the cellar. Best from 2001 through 2010.–J.L. • $65 • (12/31/1998) • **91**
Cabernet Sauvignon Napa Valley Yountville Selection 1991 • $35 • (12/15/1995) • **89**
Chardonnay Napa Valley 1998: Tart and lemony, with focused herb and orange peel flavors. Drink now.–J.L. • $30 • (6/15/2000) • **85**
Chardonnay Napa Valley 1997: This is serious Chardonnay. Intense and bright, it's rich in pure varietal flavors, with tiers of pear, citrus, vanilla, honey and spice that build in complexity and gain nuance through the finish. Drink now or hold until 2004.–J.L. • $30 • (6/15/1999) CS • **91**
Chardonnay Napa Valley 1996: A pure, crisp expression of Chardonnay, with a citrus edge. Fans out on the aftertaste, with hints of pear and toasty oak. Has a track record for improving with age, so stash a couple of bottles. Best from 1999 through 2002.–J.L. • $30 • (7/31/1998) • **89**

Fumé Blanc Napa Valley 1997: Bright and lemony, cleans the palate with its refreshing acidity. Mineral, melon, grass and herb flavors add interest, finishing long and lean. Drink now. • $18 • (10/15/1999) • **88**
Fumé Blanc Napa Valley 1996 • $15 • (3/31/1998) SS • **90**
Johannisberg Riesling Napa Valley Late Harvest 1993 • $50/375 ml. • (4/30/1995) • **88**
Violetta Late Harvest Napa Valley 1995: Mature, with drying orange peel, apricot, pear, anise and toast. Turns dry and a bit tannic, with a tobacco edge. Riesling and Chardonnay. Drink now through 2004.–J.L. • $40/375 ml. • (12/31/1999) • **87**
Violetta Late Harvest Napa Valley 1994 • $26/375 ml. • (4/30/1997) • **95**
Zinfandel Alexander Valley 1986 • $19 • (5/15/1990) • **85**
Zinfandel Alexander Valley 1985 • $19 • (7/31/1989) • **84**
Zinfandel Alexander Valley 1984 • $19 • (3/15/1987) • **90**
Zinfandel Alexander Valley 1983 • $191 • (5/01/1986) • **85**
Zinfandel Alexander Valley 1982 • $18 • (5/16/1985) SS • **91**
Zinfandel Sonoma County 1997: Tight, with firm tannins and a complex core of raspberry, cherry, anise and sage. Drink now through 2005.–J.L. • $20 • (6/30/2000) • **86**
Zinfandel Sonoma County 1996: Earthy, gamy flavors dominate this tarry style of Zin. Serves up enough fruit to sustain it, with hints of cherry and berry. Drink now through 2002.–J.L. • $20 • (5/15/1999) • **87**
Zinfandel Sonoma County 1995 • $18 • (3/31/1998) • **88**
Zinfandel Sonoma County 1993 • $16 • (10/15/1996) • **85**
Zinfandel Sonoma County 1992 • $14 • (7/31/1995) • **84**
Zinfandel Sonoma County 1991 • $13 • (10/15/1994) • **84**
Zinfandel Sonoma County 1990 • $13 • (4/30/1994) • **85**
Zinfandel Sonoma County 1989 • $13 • (4/30/1993) • **85**
Zinfandel Sonoma County 1988 • $12 • (3/31/1992) • **85**
Zinfandel Sonoma County 1987 • $22 • (10/15/1990) • **84**
Zinfandel Sonoma County 1984 • $11 • (10/31/1988) • **86**
Zinfandel Sonoma County 1981 • $10 • (4/01/1984) • **80**

GRIFFIN, BARNARD | WASHINGTON

Cabernet Sauvignon Columbia Valley 1996: Firm and tannic, with spice, tobacco and sage overtones to the modest black cherry flavors. Needs cellaring. Best after 2001.–H.S. • $30 • (8/31/1999) • **85**
Cabernet Sauvignon Columbia Valley 1993 • $15 • (3/31/1996) • **88**
Cabernet Sauvignon Columbia Valley 1991 • $15 • (9/30/1995) • **86**
Cabernet Sauvignon Columbia Valley 1990 • $15 • (9/30/1994) • **78**
Cabernet Sauvignon Columbia Valley Mercer Vineyard Reserve 1996: Distinctly gamy, with a dark streak of anise weaving through the firm-textured plum and berry flavors. Best after 2000.–H.S. • $30 • (8/31/1999) • **85**
Cabernet Sauvignon Washington 1995: Crisp in texture, ripe in flavor, with solid black cherry and coffee notes shining through the light veil of tannin. Approachable now through 2000.–H.S. • $17 • (9/15/1998) • **85**
Cabernet-Merlot Columbia Valley 1992 • $10 • (8/31/1994) • **86**
Cabernet-Merlot Columbia Valley 1990 • $10 • (3/15/1994) • **88**
Cabernet-Merlot Washington Limited Release NV: Has some grainy tannins, but the ripe cherry and spice flavors have enough oomph to make this an appealing red. Drink now through 2001.–H.S. • $13 • (9/30/1999) • **84**
Chardonnay Washington 1997: Bright and fresh, with pretty pear and grapefruit flavors that linger delicately on the generous finish. Just a hint of oak. Drink now.–H.S. • $13 • (8/31/1999) • **86**
Chardonnay Washington 1996: A beguiling wine, ripe and juicy, with lively acidity to balance the generous nectarine, pear and honey flavors, all lingering nicely on the long finish. Drink now.–H.S. • $13 • (9/15/1998) • **89**
Fumé Blanc Columbia Valley 1998: This young Washington white delivers a lively mouthful of apple, lime, black pepper and a touch of herb, all lingering nicely on the bright finish. A juicy and refreshing Sauvignon Blanc with a lot to recommend it, including an affordable price. Drink now.–H.S.• $9 • (8/31/1999) • **87**
Fumé Blanc Columbia Valley 1997: Refreshing and bright, offering a mouthful of zingy pineapple and grapefruit flavors, this style packs a lot of character into the lively finish, where it unveils a tangy herbal note. A Sauvignon Blanc from Washington, it's a nice wine at a nice price. Enjoy now.–H.S. • $9 • (9/15/1998) • **87**
Merlot Columbia Valley 1997: Light and fresh, with crisp tannins framing a fresh core of black currant and sweet spice flavors. Drink now through 2002.–H.S. • $17 • (8/31/1999) • **85**
Merlot Columbia Valley 1996: Very firm and chewy, with a tart beam of jazzy blackberry flavor poking through the layer of fine-grained tannins. Drink through 2004.–H.S. • $17 • (9/15/1998) • **85**

Merlot Columbia Valley Reserve 1996: Firm around the edges but sleek and delicious at the core, with pretty blackberry, currant, vanilla and spice flavors that gleam through the finish. Drink through 2005.–H.S. • $30 • (8/31/1999) • **89**

Merlot Columbia Valley Reserve 1995: Supple and silky, almost sweet with its chocolate-scented plum and berry flavors, finishing with hints of nutmeg and clove. Fashioned to drink sooner rather than later, now through 2001.–H.S. • $27 • (9/15/1998) • **88**

Merlot Washington 1993 • $15 • (9/30/1995) • **85**

Merlot Washington 1992 • $15 • (12/31/1994) • **82**

Merlot Washington 1991 • $15 • (9/30/1994) • **78**

Sémillon Columbia Valley 1997: Bright and lively, immensely appealing for its melon, citrus and spice flavors that linger on the gentle finish.–H.S. • $8 • (9/15/1998) • **86**

GRIFFIN CREEK | OREGON

Merlot Rogue Valley 1997: Dark in color, not quite so dense on the palate, but it shows lots of pretty blackberry and tobacco flavors that linger on the soft finish. Drink now through 2002.–H.S. • $40 • (5/15/2000) • **87**

Merlot Rogue Valley 1996: Smooth, polished and distinctive for a minty-herbal streak running through the refined black cherry and anise flavors. Focused and elegant on the long finish. Drink now through 2005.–H.S. • $35 • (5/31/1999) • **91**

Pinot Gris Rogue Valley 1998: Ripe and rich, distinctive for its honeyed spicy pear and melon flavors, lingering enticingly on the generous finish. Drink now.–H.S. • $18 • (4/30/2000) • **89**

Pinot Gris Rogue Valley 1997: A jazzy new wine, crisp and racy, with youthfully exuberant nectarine, melon and citrus flavors that linger nicely. Drink now.–H.S. • $16 • (4/30/1999) • **88**

Pinot Noir Rogue Valley 1997: Lovely flavors and blackberry, currant and plum notes cascade onto a light, open-textured frame. Everything comes together harmoniously on the finish. Drink now through 2002.–H.S. • $35 • (6/15/1999) • **88**

Syrah Rogue Valley 1997: Supple and ripe, generous with its blackberry, plum, smoke and spice flavors that repeat on the polished finish, thinning out just a tad. Drink now.–H.S. • $NA • (4/30/1999) • **88**

Viognier Rogue Valley 1998: Soft and generous, a lovely mouthful of honeysuckle-scented pear, spice and citrus flavors that linger nicely on the gentle finish. Drink now through 2002.–H.S. • $30 • (9/30/1999) • **88**

GRISTINA | NEW YORK

Cabernet Franc North Fork of Long Island 1997: This brooding red is quite rich, dominated by gamy and smoky flavors, with firm tannins and a thick texture. A good match for hearty stews. Drink now through 2004.–T.M. • $20 • (5/31/2000) • **86**

Cabernet Sauvignon North Fork of Long Island 1995: A young, tannic, tough-textured Cabernet that will need time to mellow, but it has enough concentrated black cherry and currant flavor to fill out its frame and give it a sense of balance. Drink through 2005. • $15 • (11/15/1998) • **86**

Cabernet Sauvignon North Fork of Long Island 1993 • $16 • (5/31/1997) • **69**

Cabernet Sauvignon North Fork of Long Island 1988 • $14 • (6/30/1991) • **90**

Cabernet Sauvignon North Fork of Long Island Andy's Field 1995: Smooth and polished. This red is plush, if a bit subdued, offering ripe plum and black cherry flavors, with accents of toast, coffee and herb. The tannins are firm but in balance; the wine is rich and still closed. Drink now through 2003.–T.M. • $28 • (6/30/1999) • **86**

Chardonnay North Fork of Long Island Andy's Field 1998: This silky white offers spice, vanilla and apple flavors. Well integrated but a bit soft, clean and harmonious. Drink now.–T.M. • $22 • (5/31/2000) • **84**

Chardonnay North Fork of Long Island Andy's Field 1997: Bitter chocolate and coffee notes betray a heavy hand with oak in this rich but rather dull white. It does offer light apple and pear flavors, but the heavily toasted oak dominates the finish. Drink now.–T.M. • $22 • (6/30/1999) • **82**

Merlot North Fork of Long Island 1997: Ripe and rich. Dark flavors of plum, prune and coffee flow through this dense red, yet it remains focused and clean on the finish. Drink now through 2004.–T.M. • $17 • (5/31/2000) • **87**

Merlot North Fork of Long Island 1993 • $15 • (12/31/1996) • **82**

Key: SS—Spectator Selection. CS—Cellar Selection. HR—Highly Recommended. $NA—Price not available. (BT)—Barrel tasting. Ⓐ—Auction Price.
For a key to the tasters' initials, see "How to Use These Listings."
Dates in parentheses represent the issues in which the ratings were published.

Merlot North Fork of Long Island Andy's Field 1995: Lively blackberry, floral and licorice flavors give this a vibrant personality, but there's a bit too much charry, smoky oak influence for balance, so the finish turns dry. Best with hearty grilled dishes. Drink now through 2003.–T.M. • $27 • (6/30/1999) • **84**

Merlot North Fork of Long Island Andy's Field 1993 • $27 • (12/31/1996) • **87**

Pinot Noir North Fork of Long Island 1993 • $25 • (1/01/1996) • **84**

GROTH | CALIFORNIA

Cabernet Sauvignon Napa Valley 1996: Smooth and polished up front, with supple herb, chocolate and currant flavors, it tightens up on the finish, where it shows more tannic strength. Best from 2001 through 2008.–J.L. • $40 • (9/30/1999) • **89**

Cabernet Sauvignon Napa Valley 1995: An elegant, complex style that serves up a pretty array of cherry, plum, currant and sage flavors built around ripe, firm tannins. Can stand short-term cellaring. Drink through 2006. –J.L. • $45 Ⓐ • (10/31/1998) • **90**

Cabernet Sauvignon Napa Valley 1994 • $41 Ⓐ • (8/31/1997) • **88**

Cabernet Sauvignon Napa Valley 1993 • $29 Ⓐ • (11/15/1996) • **88**

Cabernet Sauvignon Napa Valley 1992 • $20 • (9/30/1995) CS • **91**

Cabernet Sauvignon Napa Valley 1991 • $18 • (10/15/1994) SS • **90**

Cabernet Sauvignon Napa Valley 1990 • $17 • (9/30/1993) SS • **90**

Cabernet Sauvignon Napa Valley 1989 • $17 • (11/15/1992) • **81**

Cabernet Sauvignon Napa Valley 1988 • $20 • (11/15/1991) • **75**

Cabernet Sauvignon Napa Valley 1987 • $58 Ⓐ • (10/31/1990) • **81**

Cabernet Sauvignon Napa Valley 1986 • $54 Ⓐ • (11/15/1989) HR • **92**

Cabernet Sauvignon Napa Valley 1985 • $57 Ⓐ • (11/15/1988) • **93**

Cabernet Sauvignon Napa Valley 1984 • $51 Ⓐ • (2/15/1988) • **86**

Cabernet Sauvignon Napa Valley 1983 • $26 Ⓐ • (8/31/1986) • **85**

Cabernet Sauvignon Napa Valley 1982 • $13 • (11/01/1984) • **84**

Cabernet Sauvignon Napa Valley Reserve 1996: Elegant and restrained, with a trim yet complex array of herb, black cherry, currant, olive and cedar notes that finish on the crisp side, with moderate tannins. Lacks the extra dimensions to rate outstanding. Tasted three times, with consistent notes. Drink now through 2005.–J.L. • $125 • (6/30/2000) • **89**

Cabernet Sauvignon Napa Valley Reserve 1995: Smooth, ripe and polished, delivering rich, complex layers of currant, herb, cedar, tar, black cherry and spice that unfurl across the palate into a long and supple finish. A classic California Cab from a great vintage, this wine will be at its best from 2000 through 2009.–J.L. • $115 Ⓐ • (8/31/1999) CS • **95**

Cabernet Sauvignon Napa Valley Reserve 1994 • $189 Ⓐ • (5/15/1998) CS • **96**

Cabernet Sauvignon Napa Valley Reserve 1992 • $166 Ⓐ • (4/30/1996) CS • **98**

Cabernet Sauvignon Napa Valley Reserve 1991 • $142 Ⓐ • (4/15/1995) CS • **95**

Cabernet Sauvignon Napa Valley Reserve 1990 • $107 Ⓐ • (11/15/1994) CS • **94**

Cabernet Sauvignon Napa Valley Reserve 1989: If you taste carefully you'll find hints of honeyed botrytis in this wine, evidence of noble rot. Otherwise, there are coffee, earthy currant, black olive and herbal notes. Drinking well for its style. (1989 California Cabernet retrospective tasting). Try now.–J.L. • $35 • (8/31/1999) • **86**

Cabernet Sauvignon Napa Valley Reserve 1988: Successful, with supple tannins and true-to-form Groth Vineyards & Winery flavors, a range of coffee, herb, currant, cedar and spice, finishing with touches of bay leaf, green bean, tobacco and mineral. Complete from start to finish. (1988 California Cabernet retrospective tasting). Drink now through 2004. –J.L. • $40 • (11/15/1998) • **88**

Cabernet Sauvignon Napa Valley Reserve 1987 • $25 • (12/15/1997) • **90**

Cabernet Sauvignon Napa Valley Reserve 1986 • $115 Ⓐ • (4/30/1991) • **91**

Cabernet Sauvignon Napa Valley Reserve 1985 • $476 Ⓐ • (4/15/1990) • **95**

Cabernet Sauvignon Napa Valley Reserve 1984 • $25 • (4/15/1989) • **84**

Cabernet Sauvignon Napa Valley Reserve 1983 • $25 • (12/15/1988) • **92**

Chardonnay Napa Valley 1998: Clean and spicy, with an elegant band of pear, apple, vanilla and light oak shadings, gaining nuance and subtlety. Drink now through 2005.–J.L. • $21 • (2/29/2000) • **87**

Chardonnay Napa Valley 1997: Clean and fruity on the palate, boasting a spicy range of pear, vanilla, nutmeg and subtle citrus flavors that are complex and lively, this is a very tasty version of California's most popular white variety. Drink now through 2001.–J.L. • $20 • (2/28/1999) SS • **90**

Chardonnay Napa Valley 1996 • $18 • (3/31/1998) • **88**

Merlot Napa Valley 1997: Tight and dense, with a rich core of mineral, currant and coffee notes, picking up a chocolate note on the tannic finish.

Best to cellar short-term. Best from 2001 through 2007.–J.L. • $40 • (6/30/2000) • **87**

Merlot Napa Valley 1994 • $27 • (6/30/1997) • **87**
Merlot Napa Valley 1992 • $20 • (9/30/1995) • **89**
Merlot Napa Valley 1991 • $17 • (9/15/1994) • **82**
Merlot Napa Valley 1990 • $15 • (8/31/1993) • **83**
Sauvignon Blanc Napa Valley 1998: Modest varietal character. Grassy, with a touch of sweet pea, herb, melon and spice, turning simple and light. Drink now.–J.L. • $14 • (4/30/2000) • **84**
Sauvignon Blanc Napa Valley 1997: A silky-textured wine, featuring subtle passionfruit, melon, grass and citrus flavors. Could use a little more zing, however. Drink now. • $14 • (11/30/1998) • **87**

GROVE STREET | CALIFORNIA

Cabernet Sauvignon California Barrel Reserve 1993 • $8 • (11/30/1996) • **79**
Cabernet Sauvignon California Vineyard Select 1992 • $7 • (11/15/1994) • **75**
Syrah California Baker 1998: A lip-smacking red at an affordable price. Straightforward in style, serving up intense, tangy raspberry flavors and a hint of pepper. Drink now through 2004.–J.L. • $9 • (5/15/2000) • **85**

GRUET | NEW MEXICO

Brut Blanc de Noirs New Mexico NV • $14 • (12/31/1997) • **79**
Brut New Mexico NV • $14 • (12/31/1997) • **87**
Brut Rosé New Mexico Grand Rosé NV • $28 • (12/31/1997) • **81**

GUENOC | CALIFORNIA

Cabernet Franc Lake County 1985 • $12 • (2/15/1989) • **70**
Cabernet Franc Napa Valley 1990 • $14 • (11/15/1993) • **83**
Cabernet Sauvignon California 1997: Chunky and herbal, with a core of black cherry and currant flavors. Firm on the finish. Drink now.–J.L. • $12 • (10/15/1999) • **81**
Cabernet Sauvignon California 1996: Simple herb, cherry and oak flavors on a moderate frame. Soft on the short finish. Drink now. • $12 • (2/28/1999) • **81**
Cabernet Sauvignon Guenoc Valley Premier Cuvée 1985 • $17 • (10/15/1990) • **84**
Cabernet Sauvignon Guenoc Valley Tephra Ridge Reserve 1997: Tight, a bit tart, and a bit awkward at this very early stage. The core of cherry and currant is firmly tannic.–J.L. • $NA • (8/31/1998) (BT) • **85-89**
Cabernet Sauvignon Guenoc Valley Tephra Ridge Vineyard Reserve 1996: A dry, tannic wine, with firm dried cherry, plum and currant notes, it picks up anise and cedar flavors on the finish. Best from 2001 through 2007.–J.L. • $31 • (11/15/1999) • **88**
Cabernet Sauvignon Guenoc Valley Tephra Ridge Reserve 1993 • $30 • (12/15/1995) • **86**
Cabernet Sauvignon Lake County 1994 • $15 • (11/15/1997) • **84**
Cabernet Sauvignon Lake County 1993 • $15 • (10/15/1996) • **85**
Cabernet Sauvignon Lake County 1992 • $15 • (12/15/1995) • **85**
Cabernet Sauvignon Lake County 1991 • $15 • (11/15/1994) • **85**
Cabernet Sauvignon Lake County 1990 • $11 • (4/15/1994) • **84**
Cabernet Sauvignon Lake County 1989 • $12 • (11/15/1992) • **77**
Cabernet Sauvignon Lake County 1987 • $12 • (7/15/1991) • **89**
Cabernet Sauvignon Lake County 1986 • $13 • (4/30/1991) • **78**
Cabernet Sauvignon Napa Valley Beckstoffer IV Vineyard Reserve 1996: Ripe and zesty, with wild berry, blackberry, raspberry and cherry flavors. On the lean side, but well crafted and crisply tannic. Drink through 2007.–J.L. • $40 • (9/30/1999) • **87**
Cabernet Sauvignon Napa Valley Beckstoffer IV Vineyard Reserve 1995: Intense, juicy and a touch tart, but with plenty of plum and wild berry flavors. Clamps down on the finish, where the tannins are firm. Best from 2001 through 2008.–J.L. • $41 • (12/31/1998) • **89**
Cabernet Sauvignon Napa Valley Beckstoffer IV Vineyard Reserve 1994 • $40 • (10/31/1997) • **93**
Cabernet Sauvignon Napa Valley Beckstoffer IV Vineyard Reserve 1993 • $40 • (11/15/1996) • **88**
Cabernet Sauvignon Napa Valley Beckstoffer IV Vineyard Reserve 1992 • $40 • (12/15/1995) • **90**
Cabernet Sauvignon Napa Valley Beckstoffer Vineyard Reserve 1991 • $35 • (9/30/1994) CS • **94**
Cabernet Sauvignon Napa Valley Beckstoffer Vineyard Reserve 1990 • $35 • (11/15/1993) HR • **92**
Cabernet Sauvignon Napa Valley Beckstoffer Vineyard Reserve 1989 • $30 • (3/31/1993) • **85**
Cabernet Sauvignon Napa Valley Beckstoffer Vineyard Reserve 1987 • $24 • (12/15/1997) • **91**
Cabernet Sauvignon Napa Valley Bella Vista Vineyard Reserve 1996: Dry, tight and tannic, with earthy cedar, ripe cherry, plum and berryish flavors, it's crisp and firm right through the finish. Best from 2001 through 2007. –J.L. • $33 • (10/31/1999) • **88**
Cabernet Sauvignon Napa Valley Bella Vista Vineyard Reserve 1995: Spicy, with bright, tart acidity and a distinct jalapeño pepper edge to the chunky, intense, now-unevolved fruit flavors. Time will favor it. Best from 2001 through 2008.–J.L. • $31 • (12/15/1998) • **87**
Cabernet Sauvignon Napa Valley Bella Vista Vineyard Reserve 1994 • $26 • (9/30/1997) • **90**
Cabernet Sauvignon Napa Valley Bella Vista Vineyard Reserve 1993 • $25 • (11/15/1996) • **88**
Cabernet Sauvignon Napa Valley Bella Vista Vineyard Reserve 1992 • $25 • (12/15/1995) • **90**
Cabernet Sauvignon Napa Valley Reserve 1998: Dense, with potent flavors, lots of mint, currant, cherry and spice, finishing with firm, substantial tannins.–J.L. • $NA • (8/31/1999) (BT) • **90-94**
Cabernet Sauvignon North Coast 1996: Crisp, with an elegant, narrow band of plum and berry flavor that persists on the trim finish. Drink now.–J.L. • $17 • (8/31/1999) • **85**
Cabernet Sauvignon North Coast 1995: Black currant and licorice flavors weave a dense pattern in this wine, but the resinous, slightly bitter finish falters. Drink now through 2002. • $16 • (10/15/1998) • **82**
Cabernet Sauvignon North Coast 1991 • $12 • (11/15/1994) • **82**
Cabernet Sauvignon North Coast 1988 • $12 • (8/31/1992) • **79**
Chardonnay California 1998: Tinny pineapple notes, with orange flavors on a watery frame. Drink now.–J.L. • $12 • (6/15/2000) • **80**
Chardonnay California 1997: A squeaky-clean style, with bright lemon flavors and a hint of herbs on the finish. Too tangy for sipping; needs food. Drink now. • $12 • (2/28/1999) • **82**
Chardonnay Guenoc Valley Genevieve Magoon Vineyard Estate Reserve 1997: Fresh and snappy, with spicy apple, pear, nutmeg and a hint of butterscotch filling out and lingering on the finish. Drink now through 2002.–J.L. • $25 • (6/30/1999) • **91**
Chardonnay Guenoc Valley Genevieve Magoon Vineyard Estate Unfiltered Reserve 1997: Rich and spicy, with neatly stacked tiers of fig, apricot, melon and oak and a complex, concentrated aftertaste. Drink now through 2002.–J.L. • $30 • (6/30/1999) • **93**
Chardonnay Guenoc Valley Genevieve Magoon Vineyard Reserve 1996 • $25 • (6/30/1998) • **90**
Chardonnay Guenoc Valley Genevieve Magoon Vineyard Unfiltered Reserve 1996 • $30 • (6/30/1998) • **92**
Chardonnay North Coast 1997: Marked by earthy grapefruit and citrus notes. Enough spicy pear and nectarine emerge to give it balance and breadth. Drink now.–J.L. • $16 • (12/15/1998) • **87**
Chardonnay North Coast 1996 • $16 • (5/15/1998) • **87**
Langtry Meritage Red Napa Valley 1996: Bright, firm, intense and marked by black cherry, blackberry and wild berry flavors, it's a solid, fruity style that comes up short on complexity and depth. Tasted twice, with consistent notes. Drink now through 2007.–J.L. • $48 • (11/15/1999) • **87**
Langtry Meritage Red North Coast 1995: A rustic, earthy, firmly tannic style, it takes some time to reveal its core of black cherry, plum and berry. Even after it opens up, it's ruggedly tannic; should be headed for the cellar. Drink through 2007.–J.L. • $48 • (11/15/1998) • **88**
Langtry Meritage Red Napa Valley 1994 • $41 • (9/30/1997) • **90**
Langtry Meritage Red California 1993 • $41 • (11/15/1996) • **88**
Langtry Meritage Red California 1992 • $35 • (12/15/1995) • **89**
Langtry Meritage Red California 1991 • $35 • (9/30/1994) HR • **91**
Langtry Meritage Red Lake County 1990 • $35 • (11/15/1993) HR • **91**
Langtry Meritage Red Lake County 1989 • $35 • (11/15/1992) • **88**
Langtry Meritage Red Lake-Napa Counties 1988 • $35 • (11/15/1991) • **86**
Langtry Meritage Red Lake-Napa Counties 1987 • $35 • (4/15/1991) • **88**
Langtry Meritage White Guenoc Valley 1998: Toasty oak, herb, ripe lemon, pineapple and melon flavors are well-balanced and generous. Full-bodied, with lively acidity and a long finish. Drink now through 2003.–H.S. • $23 • (3/31/2000) • **87**
Langtry Meritage White Guenoc Valley 1997: Fresh and lively, with hints of mint, grass, lemon and grapefruit. Firm texture, with a moderate, clean finish. A blend of Sauvignon Blanc and Sémillon. Drink now. • $21 • (11/30/1998) • **88**
Langtry Meritage White Guenoc Valley 1996 • $21 • (4/30/1998) • **87**
Meritage Red North Coast 1996: Firm, showing cola, currant, anise and cedar flavors, finishing with dry tannins. Best from 2000 through 2003.–J.L. • $20 • (10/15/1999) • **82**
Meritage Red California 1995: Tasty, tangy blackberry and currant notes lead off this tightly textured wine. Finishes a little short, but it's soundly made

and enjoyable. A blend of Cabernet Sauvignon, Cabernet Franc, Petit Verdot, Malbec and Merlot. Drink now through 2003. • $19 • (10/31/1998) • **85**

Meritage Red Lake County 1994 • $15 • (11/15/1997) • **86**

Meritage Red Lake County 1992 • $15 • (12/15/1995) • **88**

Meritage Red Lake County 1991 • $15 • (10/31/1994) SS • **89**

Meritage Red Lake County 1990 • $15 • (11/15/1993) SS • **91**

Meritage Red Lake County 1989 • $17 • (11/15/1992) • **83**

Merlot Guenoc Valley 1985 • $15 • (3/31/1989) • **85**

Merlot Lake-Napa Counties 1987 • $14 • (11/15/1991) • **86**

Merlot Lake-Napa Counties 1986 • $12 • (6/15/1990) • **80**

Petit Verdot Napa Valley 1993 • $18 • (11/30/1996) • **83**

Petite Sirah California 1996: Dry and a touch pruny, with sage, wild berry and spicy notes that firm up and turn tannic. Drink through 2005.–J.L. • $16 • (2/28/1999) • **84**

Petite Sirah California 1995 • $16 • (4/30/1998) • **87**

Petite Sirah Guenoc Valley 1988 • $10 • (8/31/1991) • **86**

Petite Sirah North Coast 1992 • $14 • (8/31/1996) • **89**

Petite Sirah North Coast 1990 • $13 • (9/30/1994) • **84**

Petite Sirah North Coast 1989 • $14 • (6/30/1992) • **82**

Port California 1994 • $25 • (2/28/1997) • **88**

Port California 1992 • $15 • (5/31/1995) • **89**

Sauvignon Blanc California 1998: Mild and unobtrusive, this wine shows a bit of lemon, grapefruit and melon, then fades quickly. Simple yet pleasant. Drink now. • $11 • (5/31/1999) • **81**

Sauvignon Blanc California 1997: Lightly styled, with hints of pear, grass, citrus and herbs. Firmly textured, pleasant and quaffable. Drink now. • $12 • (2/28/1999) • **83**

Sauvignon Blanc North Coast 1997: Citrus and melon notes blend nicely, framed by herbs, grass and a bit of toast. Medium-bodied, with moderate acidity. Drink now. • $14 • (1/31/1999) • **84**

Sauvignon Blanc North Coast 1996 • $14 • (4/30/1998) • **84**

Zinfandel California 1997: Firm, with plum and dried berry notes. Drink now through 2002.–J.L. • $13 • (6/15/2000) • **83**

Zinfandel California 1996: Somewhat earthy on the nose, this wine has notes of blackberry, spice, oak and tar, firm tannins and a texture that's a bit lean. Finishes bright, if a little dry. Drink now. • $11 • (2/28/1999) • **84**

Zinfandel California 1991 • $9 • (9/30/1993) • **86**

Zinfandel California 1990 • $10 • (9/30/1992) • **84**

Zinfandel California 1989 • $10 • (5/15/1992) • **85**

Zinfandel California 1988 • $8 • (9/15/1990) • **76**

GUGLIELMO | CALIFORNIA

Cabernet Sauvignon Monterey County 1989 • $8 • (11/15/1994) • **74**

Cabernet Sauvignon Santa Clara County Private Reserve 1986 • $12 • (11/15/1993) • **75**

Merlot Monterey County Private Reserve 1995 • $15 • (4/30/1998) • **86**

Merlot Napa Valley 1990 • $9 • (9/15/1994) • **78**

Petite Sirah Santa Clara Valley 1993 • $11 • (11/30/1996) • **86**

Pinot Noir Santa Clara Valley Private Reserve 1990 • $10 • (2/28/1993) • **75**

Sangiovese California 1994 • $10 • (11/30/1996) • **82**

Sangiovese California Private Reserve 1995 • $12 • (11/30/1997) • **77**

Zinfandel Santa Clara Valley Private Reserve 1991 • $9 • (10/15/1995) • **78**

Zinfandel Santa Clara Valley Private Reserve 1989 • $NA • (10/15/1994) • **79**

Zinfandel Santa Clara Valley Private Reserve 1988 • $9 • (9/30/1993) • **84**

GUILLIAMS | CALIFORNIA

Cabernet Sauvignon Spring Mountain District 1994: Herbal and earthy, with a core of tobacco and currant, finishing dry and hard.–H.S. • $24 • (11/15/1998) • **77**

Cabernet Sauvignon Spring Mountain 1993 • $20 • (12/15/1997) • **81**

Cabernet Sauvignon Spring Mountain 1991 • $17 • (12/15/1995) • **88**

Cabernet Sauvignon Napa Valley Spring Mountain District 1990 • $15 • (11/15/1994) • **86**

GUNDLACH BUNDSCHU | CALIFORNIA

Bearitage Sonoma Valley 1990 • $10 • (5/15/1993) • **81**

Key: SS—Spectator Selection. CS—Cellar Selection. HR—Highly Recommended. $NA—Price not available. (BT)—Barrel tasting. (A)—Auction Price. For a key to the tasters' initials, see "How to Use These Listings."
Dates in parentheses represent the issues in which the ratings were published.

Cabernet Franc Sonoma Valley Rhinefarm Vineyards 1994 • $14 • (12/15/1996) • **86**

Cabernet Franc Sonoma Valley Rhinefarm Vineyards 1989 • $12 • (2/29/1992) • **87**

Cabernet Franc Sonoma Valley Rhinefarm Vineyards 1987 • $12 • (9/15/1990) • **89**

Cabernet Sauvignon Sonoma Valley 1981 • $10 • (5/16/1985) • **85**

Cabernet Sauvignon Sonoma Valley Batto Ranch 1983 • $14 • (2/15/1988) • **74**

Cabernet Sauvignon Sonoma Valley Batto Ranch 1982 • $12 • (6/16/1985) • **89**

Cabernet Sauvignon Sonoma Valley Rhinefarm Vineyards 1996: Shows a range of complex mineral, black olive, earthy currant, anise, ripe black cherry and smoky, tarry flavors. Finishes with plush tannins. Drink now through 2005.–J.L. • $24 • (9/30/1999) • **88**

Cabernet Sauvignon Sonoma Valley Rhinefarm Vineyards 1994 • $20 • (1/01/1997) • **82**

Cabernet Sauvignon Sonoma Valley Rhinefarm Vineyards 1992 • $15 • (10/31/1995) • **87**

Cabernet Sauvignon Sonoma Valley Rhinefarm Vineyards 1991 • $15 • (10/31/1994) • **88**

Cabernet Sauvignon Sonoma Valley Rhinefarm Vineyards 1990 • $14 • (11/15/1993) • **83**

Cabernet Sauvignon Sonoma Valley Rhinefarm Vineyards 1989 • $15 • (11/15/1992) • **80**

Cabernet Sauvignon Sonoma Valley Rhinefarm Vineyards 1988: Has a lot going for it with its ripe, complex, concentrated spicy cherry and currant flavors. Fans out to show off herb, cedary oak and mineral flavors, with a long, full finish. (1988 California Cabernet retrospective tasting). Drink now through 2003.–J.L. • $24 • (11/15/1998) • **88**

Cabernet Sauvignon Sonoma Valley Rhinefarm Vineyards 1987 • $15 • (5/15/1991) • **85**

Cabernet Sauvignon Sonoma Valley Rhinefarm Vineyards 1985 • $12 • (3/31/1989) • **78**

Cabernet Sauvignon Sonoma Valley Rhinefarm Vineyards 1984 • $10 • (9/30/1988) • **84**

Cabernet Sauvignon Sonoma Valley Rhinefarm Vineyards 1974 • $40 • (11/15/1994) • **74**

Cabernet Sauvignon Sonoma Valley Rhinefarm Vineyards Reserve 1989 • $24 • (11/15/1993) • **84**

Cabernet Sauvignon Sonoma Valley Rhinefarm Vineyards Reserve 1986 • $25 • (8/31/1991) • **83**

Cabernet Sauvignon Sonoma Valley Rhinefarm Vineyards Reserve 1982 • $20 • (9/15/1987) • **71**

Cabernet Sauvignon Sonoma Valley Rhinefarm Vineyards Reserve 1981 • $20 • (11/30/1986) • **88**

Cabernet Sauvignon Sonoma Valley Rhinefarm Vineyards Vintage Reserve 1993 • $34 • (9/30/1997) • **85**

Cabernet Sauvignon Sonoma Valley Rhinefarm Vineyards Vintage Reserve 1992 • $30 • (11/15/1996) • **90**

Cabernet Sauvignon Sonoma Valley Rhinefarm Vineyards Vintage Reserve 1987 • $22 • (7/31/1992) • **89**

Chardonnay Sonoma Valley Carneros Sangiacomo Ranch 1997: Bright, crisp and clean, with a citrus rind and mineral core. Hints of herb on the finish, where the flavors continue to build. Drink now through 2003.–J.L. • $16 • (11/15/1999) • **87**

Chardonnay Sonoma Valley Carneros Sangiacomo Ranch 1996: Bright and lively, with intense citrus, pear and pineapple flavors that are crisp and refreshing. Finishes with herb and leaf notes. Drink now through 2001. –J.L. • $16 • (7/31/1998) • **87**

Chardonnay Sonoma Valley Rhinefarm Vineyards 1996: A grassy, herbaceous style that's a bit like Sauvignon Blanc, with a tangy, racy streak of citrus. Drink now.–J.L. • $14 • (7/31/1998) • **83**

Gewürztraminer Sonoma Valley Rhinefarm Vineyards 1997 • $12 • (6/30/1998) • **81**

Gewürztraminer Sonoma Valley Rhinefarm Vineyards 1996 • $10 • (7/31/1997) • **85**

Merlot Sonoma Valley Rhinefarm Vineyards 1996: Features black cherry, mineral and earthy herb flavors that tighten up on the finish and turn slightly bitter. Best now through 2004.–J.L. • $22 • (10/15/1999) • **84**

Merlot Sonoma Valley Rhinefarm Vineyards 1995: Austere, with a tightly wound core of currant, herb, anise and tobacco. Offers good intensity and concentration, yet has a core of firm tannins that may take some time to subside. Drink through 2002.–J.L. • $21 • (10/15/1998) • **86**

Merlot Sonoma Valley Rhinefarm Vineyards 1994 • $21 • (3/31/1997) • **88**

Merlot Sonoma Valley Rhinefarm Vineyards 1993 • $18 • (8/31/1996) • **84**

Merlot Sonoma Valley Rhinefarm Vineyards 1992 • $16 • (1/31/1995) • **88**

Merlot Sonoma Valley Rhinefarm Vineyards 1990 • $16 • (10/15/1993) • **85**

Merlot Sonoma Valley Rhinefarm Vineyards 1989 • $16 • (5/31/1992) • **80**
Merlot Sonoma Valley Rhinefarm Vineyards 1988 • $20 • (5/31/1991) • **81**
Merlot Sonoma Valley Rhinefarm Vineyards 1987 • $18 • (10/31/1989) SS • **93**
Merlot Sonoma Valley Rhinefarm Vineyards 1986 • $19 • (12/31/1988) • **91**
Merlot Sonoma Valley Rhinefarm Vineyards 1985 • $20 • (2/29/1988) SS • **92**
Merlot Sonoma Valley Rhinefarm Vineyards 1984 • $20 • (2/28/1987) • **88**
Merlot Sonoma Valley Rhinefarm Vineyards 1983 • $12 • (5/01/1986) HR • **92**
Merlot Sonoma Valley Rhinefarm Vineyards 1982 • $19 • (10/01/1985) • **88**
Pinot Noir Sonoma Valley Rhinefarm Vineyards 1997: Tight and lean, this serves up a spare fruit profile, hinting at cherries and herbs. The flavors linger, however, making it an enjoyable quaff. Drink through 2003. • $14 • (9/15/1999) • **84**
Pinot Noir Sonoma Valley Rhinefarm Vineyards 1996: Lean, a bit green and with stemmy tannins, it takes time for the barely ripe fruit to emerge. Decent but lacks ripe flavors and pizzazz.–J.L. • $16 • (9/15/1998) • **78**
Pinot Noir Sonoma Valley Rhinefarm Vineyards 1995 • $14 • (8/31/1997) • **86**
Pinot Noir Sonoma Valley Rhinefarm Vineyards 1994 • $14 • (11/30/1996) • **84**
Pinot Noir Sonoma Valley Rhinefarm Vineyards 1993 • $14 • (12/31/1995) • **85**
Pinot Noir Sonoma Valley Rhinefarm Vineyards 1992 • $14 • (3/31/1995) • **82**
Pinot Noir Sonoma Valley Rhinefarm Vineyards 1991 • $14 • (2/28/1994) • **78**
Pinot Noir Sonoma Valley Rhinefarm Vineyards 1989 • $14 • (10/31/1991) • **83**
Pinot Noir Sonoma Valley Rhinefarm Vineyards 1988 • $12 • (2/28/1991) • **88**
Pinot Noir Sonoma Valley Rhinefarm Vineyards 1986 • $14 • (6/15/1988) • **89**
Pinot Noir Sonoma Valley Rhinefarm Vineyards 1985 • $10 • (2/29/1988) • **81**
Sonoma Red #2 Sonoma Valley NV • $5 • (11/15/1989) • **77**
Zinfandel Sonoma Valley 1994 • $12 • (12/15/1996) • **88**
Zinfandel Sonoma Valley 1992 • $10 • (9/15/1994) SS • **92**
Zinfandel Sonoma Valley 1991 • $10 • (9/30/1993) • **85**
Zinfandel Sonoma Valley 1989 • $8 • (7/31/1991) • **84**
Zinfandel Sonoma Valley 1988 • $7 • (5/31/1990) • **88**
Zinfandel Sonoma Valley Morse Vineyard 1996 • $14 • (6/15/1998) • **80**
Zinfandel Sonoma Valley Rhinefarm Vineyards 1997: Jammy, peppery and herbal, finishing with earthy bitterness. Drink now.–J.L. • $20 • (6/15/2000) • **81**
Zinfandel Sonoma Valley Rhinefarm Vineyards 1996 • $16 • (6/15/1998) • **88**
Zinfandel Sonoma Valley Rhinefarm Vineyards 1994 • $16 • (3/31/1997) • **88**
Zinfandel Sonoma Valley Rhinefarm Vineyards 1993 • $14 • (10/15/1995) • **88**
Zinfandel Sonoma Valley Rhinefarm Vineyards 1990 • $9 • (9/30/1992) • **87**
Zinfandel Sonoma Valley Rhinefarm Vineyards 1989 • $12 • (7/31/1991) • **87**
Zinfandel Sonoma Valley Rhinefarm Vineyards 1988 • $10 • (12/15/1990) • **88**

GUSTAVO THRACE | CALIFORNIA

Zinfandel Napa Valley 1996: Has a bright sour cherry edge to the underlying plum, earth and spice notes. Finishes soft and flavorful. Drink now through 2003.–J.L. • $26 • (11/15/1999) • **82**

HACIENDA | CALIFORNIA

Antares Sonoma County 1987 • $28 • (11/15/1990) • **91**
Antares Sonoma County 1986 • $28 • (7/31/1989) • **91**
Cabernet Sauvignon California Clair de Lune 1992 • $8 • (11/15/1994) • **72**
Cabernet Sauvignon Sonoma County 1987 • $15 • (11/15/1992) • **81**
Cabernet Sauvignon Sonoma County 1986 • $15 • (11/15/1991) • **87**
Cabernet Sauvignon Sonoma County 1985 • $15 • (9/30/1990) • **83**
Cabernet Sauvignon Sonoma Valley 1983 • $11 • (5/31/1988) • **86**
Cabernet Sauvignon Sonoma Valley 1982 • $11 • (9/01/1985) • **63**
Cabernet Sauvignon Sonoma Valley Reserve 1985 • $18 • (11/15/1992) • **78**
Cabernet Sauvignon Sonoma Valley Reserve 1984 • $18 • (5/31/1991) • **87**
Cabernet Sauvignon Sonoma Valley Selected Reserve 1982 • $18 • (3/31/1987) • **86**
Chardonnay California Clair de Lune 1997: Simple, with flinty citrus flavors and a twinge of bitterness.–H.S. • $8 • (11/30/1998) • **78**
Merlot California Clair de Lune 1997: Simple ripe plum and oaky flavors in a supple frame. Finishes with coffee and spice notes. Drink now. • $8 • (9/15/1998) • **80**
Merlot California Clair de Lune 1996 • $7 • (3/31/1998) • **79**
Merlot California Clair de Lune 1992 • $8 • (9/15/1994) • **81**
Pinot Noir California Clair de Lune 1996: A layer of pleasant fruit is unfortunately masked by a heavy dose of drying, spicy oak flavors. Drink now.–J.L. • $8 • (8/31/1998) • **79**
Pinot Noir Sonoma Valley 1982 • $12 • (12/16/1984) • **85**
Pinot Noir Sonoma Valley Estate Reserve 1989 • $17 • (11/30/1992) • **81**
Pinot Noir Sonoma Valley Estate Reserve 1987 • $15 • (10/31/1990) • **78**
Pinot Noir Sonoma Valley Estate Reserve 1986 • $15 • (6/15/1988) • **80**
Pinot Noir Sonoma Valley Estate Reserve 1985 • $15 • (6/15/1988) • **86**

HAGAFEN | CALIFORNIA

Cabernet Franc Napa Valley 1996: Satisfying plum and spice flavors. Gobs of sweet oak, too—perhaps to a fault. Nonetheless, the wine is quite drinkable now, with firm, ripe tannins that should soften with time. Drink through 2006. • $18 • (11/30/1998) • **86**
Cabernet Sauvignon Napa Valley 1996: Filled with pretty cherry, anise and herb essence. Youthful tannins are ripe, while the finish is moderate, with hints of licorice and herb but just a touch of bitterness. Drink through 2005. • $24 • (10/15/1998) • **86**
Cabernet Sauvignon Napa Valley 1995 • $20 • (12/15/1997) • **85**
Cabernet Sauvignon Napa Valley 1993 • $20 • (12/15/1995) • **83**
Cabernet Sauvignon Napa Valley 1990 • $20 • (5/15/1994) • **77**
Cabernet Sauvignon Napa Valley 1989 • $20 • (12/15/1992) • **68**
Cabernet Sauvignon Napa Valley 1988 • $20 • (3/31/1991) HR • **88**
Cabernet Sauvignon Napa Valley 1987 • $20 • (4/30/1990) • **88**
Cabernet Sauvignon Napa Valley Reserve 1989 • $28 • (12/15/1995) • **84**
Cabernet Sauvignon Napa Valley Reserve 1988 • $28 • (3/31/1993) • **85**
Chardonnay Napa Valley 1996 • $14 • (2/28/1998) • **83**
Harmonia Napa Valley 1994 • $9 • (11/30/1995) • **77**
Johannisberg Riesling Napa Valley 1996 • $10 • (5/15/1997) • **87**
Pinot Noir Napa Valley 1996 • $13 • (2/28/1998) • **84**
Pinot Noir Napa Valley 1994 • $12 • (7/31/1996) • **77**
Pinot Noir Napa Valley 1991 • $11 • (2/28/1994) • **77**
Red Table Wine Napa Valley NV • $8 • (6/30/1992) • **75**

HAHN | CALIFORNIA

Cabernet Franc Santa Lucia Highlands 1995 • $12 • (9/15/1997) • **77**
Cabernet Franc Santa Lucia Highlands 1994 • $10 • (11/30/1996) • **85**
Cabernet Sauvignon Monterey 1989 • $10 • (6/15/1993) • **73**
Cabernet Sauvignon Monterey 1988 • $10 • (11/15/1992) • **80**
Cabernet Sauvignon Santa Lucia Highlands 1994 • $10 • (9/30/1997) • **79**
Cabernet Sauvignon Santa Lucia Highlands 1993 • $10 • (12/15/1996) • **83**
Cabernet Sauvignon Santa Lucia Highlands 1992 • $10 • (8/31/1995) • **83**
Cabernet Sauvignon Santa Lucia Highlands 1991 • $10 • (11/15/1994) • **80**
Cabernet Sauvignon Santa Lucia Highlands 1990 • $10 • (5/15/1994) • **80**
Chardonnay Monterey 1996 • $10 • (11/30/1997) • **78**
Merlot Monterey 1992 • $10 • (9/15/1994) • **81**
Merlot Monterey 1991 • $10 • (6/15/1993) • **84**
Merlot Monterey 1990 • $10 • (5/31/1992) • **83**
Merlot Monterey 1989 • $10 • (5/31/1992) • **86**
Merlot Santa Lucia Highlands 1995 • $NA • (3/31/1998) • **76**
Merlot Santa Lucia Highlands 1994 • $11 • (8/31/1996) • **78**
Merlot Santa Lucia Highlands 1993 • $10 • (12/15/1995) • **82**

HAMACHER | OREGON

Chardonnay Oregon Cuvée Forêts Diverses 1997: Light and appealing for its peach and pear flavors on an open-textured frame. Has an appealing transparency of flavors but no richness. Drink now through 2002.–H.S. • $22 • (4/30/2000) • **85**
Pinot Noir Oregon 1997: Tart, on balance, with a pleasant core of stewed plum and spice flavors, but the acidity tends to take over each sip.–H.S. • $33 • (4/30/2000) • **79**

HAMEL | CALIFORNIA

Syrah Russian River Valley Alegria Vineyard 1996: Firm, showing a tight core of wild berry, plum, sage and spice before the drying tannins set in. Drink now through 2002.–J.L. • $24 • (12/15/1998) • **86**
Syrah Russian River Valley Alegría Vineyard 1995 • $24 • (12/31/1997) • **92**
Syrah Sonoma County 1994 • $22 • (7/31/1997) • **88**

HANDLEY | CALIFORNIA

Blanc de Blancs Anderson Valley 1990 • $18 • (12/15/1995) • **88**
Brut Anderson Valley 1994: Light and lemony, with hints of grapefruit, apple and herbs. The wine is refreshing and delicate, finishing moderately. Firm acidity should keep it intact for a while. Drink now through 2003. • $26 • (10/15/1999) • **87**
Brut Anderson Valley 1993: Bright, fresh apple and floral aromas introduce this wine. On the palate it shows ginger, with layers of pear, apple and citrus. Quite refreshing on the nicely lingering finish. Drink now through 2003. • $20 • (12/15/1998) • **89**

HANDLEY

Brut Anderson Valley 1992 • $20 • (11/30/1997) • **89**
Brut Anderson Valley 1991 • $18 • (11/30/1996) • **80**
Brut Anderson Valley 1990 • $15 • (12/31/1995) • **87**
Brut Rosé Anderson Valley 1994 • $19 • (11/30/1997) • **86**
Brut Rosé Anderson Valley 1993 • $19 • (12/15/1996) • **87**
Brut Rosé Anderson Valley 1990 • $17 • (12/31/1994) • **85**
Chardonnay Anderson Valley 1996: Crisp and earthy, with nicely focused pear, mineral and green apple notes. Finishes with a touch of spice. Drink now through 2000. • $17 • (7/31/1998) • **84**
Chardonnay Dry Creek Valley Handley Vineyard 1996 • $17 • (5/31/1998) • **88**
Gewürztraminer Anderson Valley 1997: Bright and appealing for its pretty fruit character, offering apple and citrus and not a lot of spice. Finishes dry. Drink now.–H.S. • $12 • (11/30/1998) • **85**
Gewürztraminer Anderson Valley 1996 • $11 • (12/15/1997) • **89**
Pinot Gris Anderson Valley 1997: Light and pretty, with delicate pear and melon flavors that float on the finish. Drink now.–H.S. • $16 • (12/15/1998) • **84**
Pinot Meunier Anderson Valley Pinot Mystère 1996 • $19 • (1/31/1998) • **85**
Pinot Noir Anderson Valley 1997: Light, with herb-tinged strawberry and tea flavors that finish firm. Drink now through 2001.–J.L. • $20 • (9/15/1999) • **83**
Pinot Noir Anderson Valley 1996: Delicate cherry and earth tones combine to paint a pretty picture. A lighter style, slightly astringent on the finish. Drink now. • $19 • (9/15/1998) • **86**
Pinot Noir Anderson Valley 1995 • $20 • (1/31/1998) • **87**
Pinot Noir Anderson Valley 1994 • $15 • (2/29/1996) • **84**
Pinot Noir Anderson Valley 1993 • $15 • (12/31/1995) • **84**
Pinot Noir Anderson Valley 1992 • $14 • (10/31/1994) • **84**
Pinot Noir Anderson Valley 1991 • $13 • (6/15/1993) • **84**
Pinot Noir Anderson Valley Reserve 1996: Somewhat lean, with pretty blueberry, blackberry and herb flavors. Peppery on the finish, it's got elegance and lift, with firm yet ripe tannins. Drink now through 2003. • $28 • (6/30/1999) • **87**
Pinot Noir Anderson Valley Reserve 1995 • $28 • (2/28/1998) • **87**
Pinot Noir Anderson Valley Reserve 1994 • $24 • (9/15/1996) • **84**
Sauvignon Blanc Dry Creek Valley 1996 • $12 • (6/30/1997) • **86**
Sauvignon Blanc Dry Creek Valley Handley Vineyard 1997: Intensely tart—pure grapefruit juice comes to mind. Some herbal and mineral complexity plays a supporting role. Quite particular; should be dynamite with raw oysters. Drink now. • $12 • (2/28/1999) • **86**

HANNA | CALIFORNIA

Cabernet Sauvignon Alexander Valley 1997: Tight, with crisp, snappy wild berry and black cherry-laced fruit. Firm tannins. Drink now through 2005.–J.L. • $22 • (4/30/2000) • **86**
Cabernet Sauvignon Alexander Valley 1995 • $20 • (11/15/1997) • **86**
Cabernet Sauvignon Alexander Valley 1994 • $20 • (5/15/1997) • **82**
Cabernet Sauvignon Alexander Valley 1993 • $18 • (11/15/1996) • **88**
Cabernet Sauvignon Alexander Valley 1992 • $16 • (12/15/1995) • **84**
Cabernet Sauvignon Alexander Valley 1991 • $14 • (2/28/1995) • **85**
Cabernet Sauvignon Alexander Valley 1990 • $18 • (11/15/1993) • **87**
Cabernet Sauvignon Sonoma County 1988 • $16 • (11/15/1991) • **86**
Cabernet Sauvignon Sonoma County 1987 • $16 • (8/31/1990) • **80**
Cabernet Sauvignon Sonoma County 1986 • $16 • (7/31/1989) • **87**
Cabernet Sauvignon Sonoma Valley 1985 • $14 • (6/30/1988) • **86**
Chardonnay Russian River Valley 1997: Smoky and exotic, with intriguing flavors of herb, tobacco, tangerine and lemon on a ripe, rich frame. Flavors persist on the finish. Drink now.–J.L. • $16 • (7/31/1999) • **88**
Chardonnay Russian River Valley 1996 • $16 • (12/15/1997) • **88**
Merlot Alexander Valley 1995 • $21 • (12/31/1997) • **85**
Merlot Alexander Valley 1994 • $20 • (5/15/1997) • **88**
Merlot Alexander Valley 1993 • $16 • (6/15/1996) • **87**
Merlot Alexander Valley 1991 • $14 • (12/31/1993) • **82**
Merlot Alexander Valley 1990 • $14 • (12/15/1992) • **87**
Pinot Noir Russian River Valley 1992 • $14 • (1/31/1994) • **86**
Sauvignon Blanc Russian River Valley 1998: An earthy, herbal style on a medium frame that works because it's balanced with tangy citrus flavors. Finishes strong. Drink now through 2002.–H.S. • $12 • (1/31/2000) • **86**
Sauvignon Blanc Russian River Valley 1996 • $11 • (9/15/1997) • **86**

Key: SS—Spectator Selection. CS—Cellar Selection. HR—Highly Recommended. $NA—Price not available. (BT)—Barrel tasting. (A)—Auction Price.
For a key to the tasters' initials, see "How to Use These Listings."
Dates in parentheses represent the issues in which the ratings were published.

Sauvignon Blanc Russian River Valley Reserve 1997: With its hints of fresh hay, grapefruit, apples and herbs, this refreshing wine is firm and focused, graceful, multitiered and complex, if just a bit short on the finish. Drink now through 2001. • $22 • (4/30/1999) • **88**
Sauvignon Blanc Russian River Valley Reserve 1996 • $21 • (1/31/1998) • **88**
Zinfandel Alexander Valley Pourroy Vineyard 1995 • $20 • (4/30/1997) • **90**
Zinfandel Alexander Valley Pourroy Vineyard Reserve 1997: Plush and concentrated, with layers of ripe plum, black cherry, raspberry and cherry, this is a remarkably complex and well-crafted wine, finishing with pretty oak shadings. Drink now through 2003.–J.L. • $36 • (5/15/1999) • **91**
Zinfandel Alexander Valley Pourroy Vineyard Reserve 1996 • $35 • (5/31/1998) • **83**

HANSEL, WALTER | CALIFORNIA

Chardonnay Russian River Valley Hansel Family Vineyards 1997: Ultrarich and smoky, with broad layers of ripe fig, melon, pear and butterscotch. Finishes with mineral, anise, light oak and melon. Drink now through 2003.–J.L. • $27 • (7/31/1999) • **93**
Chardonnay Russian River Valley Hansel Family Vineyards 1996: Firm and focused, with layers of pear and melon backed by tangy citrus, mineral and sweet oak notes. A hint of earthiness adds interest, while bright acidity keeps the finish long and clean. Drink through 2003.–J.L. • $22 • (6/30/1999) • **91**
Pinot Noir Russian River Valley Hansel Family Vineyards 1996: Aromas of mint and black cherry are followed up by modest blackberry and toasty oak, finishing with moderate delicacy and length. Drink now. • $30 • (8/31/1998) • **84**

HANZELL | CALIFORNIA

Cabernet Sauvignon Sonoma Valley 1990 • $20 • (11/15/1994) • **83**
Cabernet Sauvignon Sonoma Valley 1989: Starts ripe, supple and polished, with hints of cherry and currant, but the tannins quickly move in to dominate the texture and aftertaste. (1989 California Cabernet retrospective tasting). Drink now through 2004.–J.L. • $23 • (8/31/1999) • **86**
Cabernet Sauvignon Sonoma Valley 1988 • $22 • (11/15/1992) • **82**
Cabernet Sauvignon Sonoma Valley 1987 • $22 • (11/15/1991) • **84**
Cabernet Sauvignon Sonoma Valley 1986 • $22 • (10/31/1990) • **90**
Cabernet Sauvignon Sonoma Valley 1982 • $20 • (3/31/1987) • **76**
Cabernet Sauvignon Sonoma Valley 1979: Ripe and pruny, tannic too, with a rawness to the texture. Holding up, but lacking in finesse. (1979 California Cabernet retrospective tasting). Drink now through 2004.–J.L. • $75 • (8/31/1999) • **85**
Chardonnay Sonoma Valley 1997: Crisp and lean, with a tight beam of tart apple and spice. Finishes with lively acidity and a lingering aftertaste that echoes pear and nutmeg. Best from 2002 through 2010.–J.L. • $42 • (4/30/2000) • **88**
Chardonnay Sonoma Valley 1996: Distinctive for its spicy grapefruit and citrus character, this is an intensely flavored, racy California Chardonnay, but rather than overpower the palate, it unfolds slowly, gaining complexity and nuance through the finish. Drink now through 2003.–J.L. • $35 • (3/31/1999) CS • **92**
Pinot Noir Sonoma Valley 1995: Mature, with an earthy streak running through the dried cherry and berryish flavors, turning firm and structured on the finish, where it becomes more complex. Drink now through 2004. –J.L. • $35 • (9/15/1999) • **87**
Pinot Noir Sonoma Valley 1994: Earthy, with a meaty streak along with hints of plum and dried cherry. Tight and backward, it needs time. Give it a year or two; drink through 2002.–J.L. • $30 • (9/15/1998) • **87**
Pinot Noir Sonoma Valley 1993 • $25 • (1/31/1998) • **87**
Pinot Noir Sonoma Valley 1992 • $23 • (1/31/1997) • **86**
Pinot Noir Sonoma Valley 1991 • $19 • (6/30/1995) • **86**
Pinot Noir Sonoma Valley 1990 • $21 • (3/31/1997) • **90**
Pinot Noir Sonoma County 1989 • $19 • (2/28/1994) • **87**
Pinot Noir Sonoma Valley 1988 • $19 • (2/28/1993) • **88**
Pinot Noir Sonoma County 1987 • $19 • (2/15/1992) • **84**
Pinot Noir Sonoma Valley 1986 • $19 • (3/31/1997) • **88**
Pinot Noir Sonoma Valley 1985 • $19 • (3/31/1990) • **82**
Pinot Noir Sonoma Valley 1984 • $17 • (5/31/1989) • **78**
Pinot Noir Sonoma Valley 1983 • $17 • (4/15/1988) • **70**
Pinot Noir Sonoma Valley 1981 • $17 • (8/31/1986) • **93**

HARGRAVE | NEW YORK

Cabernet Franc North Fork of Long Island 1988 • $14 • (6/30/1991) • **81**

Cabernet Franc North Fork of Long Island Lattice Label 1993: Library release. Maturing but still firm, this balanced red shows smoke, light earth and tobacco flavors but maintains a core of lively cherry. The tannins are firm but not astringent, and the finish is clean and still fresh. Drink now through 2002.–T.M. • $35 • (6/30/1999) • **87**
Cabernet Sauvignon North Fork of Long Island 1986 • $22 • (12/15/1988) • **87**
Cabernet Sauvignon North Fork of Long Island 1985 • $22 • (12/15/1988) • **82**
Cabernet Sauvignon North Fork of Long Island 1983 • $22 • (12/15/1988) • **86**
Cabernet Sauvignon North Fork of Long Island Reserve 1982 • $22 • (12/15/1988) • **70**
Cabernet Sauvignon North Fork of Long Island Vintner's Signature 1981 • $29 • (12/15/1988) • **78**
Chardonnay North Fork of Long Island Lattice Label Reserve 1998: Citrusy flavors are lively, but a waxy, plastic note mars the pleasure.–T.M. • $15 • (5/31/2000) • **72**
Fumé Blanc North Fork of Long Island Lattice Label 1998: This soft white offers sweet apple and light herbal flavors, smooth and simple. It's gentle on the palate, but lacks acidity.–T.M. • $11 • (5/31/2000) • **78**
Merlot North Fork of Long Island 1996: A good, basic red that has grapey flavors, a juicy texture and smoky overtones on the finish. Firm but not too tannic in texture. Drink now. • $12 • (10/31/1998) • **83**
Merlot North Fork of Long Island 1988 • $18 • (6/30/1991) • **81**
Merlot North Fork of Long Island 1985 • $19 • (12/15/1988) • **85**
Merlot North Fork of Long Island Lattice Label 1997: This rich, jammy red will appeal to fans of oak. It's oozing with chocolate, coffee and toast flavors, which somewhat overwhelm the ripe plum and cherry, but the structure is firm and clean. Drink now through 2003.–T.M. • $17 • (6/30/1999) • **86**
Merlot North Fork of Long Island Lattice Label 1993: Maturing now, this shows true varietal character, with cherry, light herb and licorice flavors. Balanced and clean. The tannins are beginning to turn a bit dry, but the wine will make a good match for rich dishes such as duck. Drink now. –T.M. • $38 • (6/30/1999) • **85**
Merlot North Fork of Long Island Lattice Label Reserve 1997: Floral, berry and herb aromas and flavors show delicacy in this light red, whose tannins are just firm enough for balance. Drink now.–T.M. • $24 • (5/31/2000) • **83**
Pinot Noir North Fork of Long Island Lattice Label 1997: This light red shows varietal character in its silky texture, spice and red berry flavors and firm tannins. The stemmy and charred wood flavors may soften with food. Drink now.–T.M. • $17 • (6/30/1999) • **81**

HARLAN ESTATE | CALIFORNIA

Napa Valley 1998: Lots of pizzazz and flavor, with creamy, toasty oak and ripe, rich cherry, currant, plum and anise, finishing with a plush texture. –J.L. • $NA • (8/31/1999) (BT) • **95-99**
Napa Valley 1997: Shows lots of complexity, with dark, ripe, rich currant, anise, cedar and spice, and frames it with spicy, toasty, cedary oak. This sample was 100 percent Cabernet Sauvignon. The finished wine will contain a small amount of Merlot and possibly Cabernet Franc.–J.L. • $NA • (8/31/1998) (BT) • **95-99**
Napa Valley 1996: Wow. This Bordeaux-style blend is amazingly potent and powerful, carried along by an impressively rich array of ultraripe currant, black cherry, plum, cedar and spice flavors that just don't stop. Best from 2002 through 2011.–J.L. • $125 • (11/15/1999) CS • **97**
Napa Valley 1995: A tremendous effort with all kinds of extra flavor dimensions, this Cabernet Sauvignon-Merlot blend is a big, ripe, complex and concentrated wine, with layers of spicy mint, currant, black cherry, cedar and tobacco, finishing with a long, integrated aftertaste. Firmly tannic. Best from 2001 through 2010.–J.L. • $420 Ⓐ • (11/15/1998) CS • **96**
Napa Valley 1994 • $454 Ⓐ • (5/15/1998) CS • **95**
Napa Valley 1993 • $277 Ⓐ • (10/15/1997) • **93**
Napa Valley 1992 • $285 Ⓐ • (11/15/1996) • **91**
Napa Valley 1991 • $334 Ⓐ • (11/30/1995) • **90**

HARMONY CELLARS | CALIFORNIA

Cabernet Sauvignon Paso Robles 1994 • $14 • (10/15/1997) • **87**
Cabernet Sauvignon Paso Robles 1993 • $13 • (11/15/1997) • **83**
Cabernet Sauvignon Paso Robles 1990 • $12 • (11/15/1993) • **77**
Cabernet Sauvignon Paso Robles 1989 • $12 • (11/15/1992) • **85**
Chardonnay San Luis Obispo 1996: Lots of smoky, toasty oak, with pretty honeysuckle, peach and coconut. Well focused, with concentrated flavors and a long finish. Drink now. • $14 • (7/31/1998) • **86**
Pinot Noir Paso Robles 1994 • $13 • (9/30/1997) • **88**
Pinot Noir Paso Robles 1990 • $11 • (2/28/1993) • **88**
Pinot Noir San Luis Obispo County 1995: Prunelike cherry flavors finish with tea and herb notes and a vinegary edge. Lacks finesse and freshness. Drink now.–J.L. • $14 • (8/31/1998) • **72**
Zinfandel Paso Robles 1998: Strawberry, plum and dried berry flavors have pleasant concentration. Drink now through 2004.–J.L. • $16 • (6/15/2000) • **84**

HARRIS, RANDALL | WASHINGTON

Merlot-Cabernet Washington 1995 • $10 • (4/30/1997) • **87**

HARRISON | CALIFORNIA

Cabernet Sauvignon Napa Valley 1997: Shows off richness, depth and complexity, even if it's tightly reined now. The core of blackberry, currant, mineral, cedar and sage is deep and concentrated. Best from 2003 through 2011.–J.L. • $56 • (4/30/2000) • **91**
Cabernet Sauvignon Napa Valley 1996: Delivers plenty of ripe, complex black cherry, currant, berry and mineral flavors and frames them with sage, cedary oak and spicy nuances. A complex and compelling style that's rich and lively, with a long, complex aftertaste. Drink through 2007.–J.L. • $42 • (10/31/1998) • **91**
Cabernet Sauvignon Napa Valley 1994 • $33 • (7/31/1997) HR • **93**
Cabernet Sauvignon Napa Valley 1993 • $33 • (9/15/1996) • **87**
Cabernet Sauvignon Napa Valley 1992 • $33 • (11/15/1995) • **90**
Cabernet Sauvignon Napa Valley 1991 • $32 Ⓐ • (11/15/1994) • **82**
Cabernet Sauvignon Napa Valley 1990 • $34 Ⓐ • (7/15/1993) • **87**
Cabernet Sauvignon Napa Valley 1989 • $30 • (4/15/1992) • **91**
Cabernet Sauvignon Napa Valley Reserve 1996: Complex, with an intriguing range of currant, black cherry, mocha and sage, but it comes up a little short on depth and richness. Drink now through 2007.–J.L. • $87 • (4/30/2000) • **87**
Cabernet Sauvignon Napa Valley Reserve 1994: Earthy in character, with dense currant, mineral and sage notes, an oaky edge and chewy tannins. Best from 2002 through 2010.–J.L. • $50 • (1/31/1999) • **88**
Cabernet Sauvignon Napa Valley Reserve 1990 • $40 • (10/15/1994) • **91**
Chardonnay Napa Valley 1996: An ultrarich style that's visibly unfined and unfiltered, with exotic, buttery pear, fig, apricot and spicy, toasty oak flavors. Zooms along on the finish. Drink now through 2002.–J.L. • $32 • (7/31/1998) • **92**
Chardonnay Napa Valley Christopher's Lot 1997: Shows off plenty of toasty, smoky oak flavors, with ripe, rich fig, apricot and honeysuckle. Finishes with a coarse texture. Drink now through 2004.–J.L. • $59 • (4/30/2000) • **88**
Merlot Napa Valley 1996: Ripe, rich and full bodied, with a pretty core of currant, black cherry, wild berry, mineral and spice, finishing firm and tannic. Needs time. Drink through 2007.–J.L. • $33 • (9/30/1999) • **89**
Merlot Napa Valley 1995: Supple and elegant, with ripe, spicy cherry, wild berry, strawberry and mint flavors, it offers finesse and polish, with a long, rich aftertaste. Drink now through 2004.–J.L. • $33 • (9/30/1998) • **89**
Merlot Napa Valley 1994 • $33 • (10/15/1996) • **87**
Merlot Napa Valley Millennium 2000 1997: Ripe and supple, with focused plum, wild berry, currant and spice flavors. Holds its focus and turns complex on the finish. Drink now through 2007.–J.L. • $40 • (12/31/1999) • **88**

HARRISON, WILLIAM | CALIFORNIA

Cabernet Sauvignon Napa Valley 1995: Firm on the palate, with tannins that are a touch drying. Flavors lean toward wild cherry, plum, spice, cedar and herb, all framed in toasty oak. Moderate finish. Drink through 2005. • $22 • (6/15/1999) • **87**

HART'S DESIRE | CALIFORNIA

Cabernet Sauvignon Alexander Valley Hidden Spring Vineyard 1996: Tight, firm and tannic, a bit hollow at midpalate, with modest black cherry and berry. Drink now.–J.L. • $20 • (4/30/2000) • **82**
Cabernet Sauvignon Alexander Valley Hidden Spring Vineyard 1995 • $20 • (6/30/1998) • **80**
Cabernet Sauvignon Napa Valley 1993 • $15 • (11/30/1996) • **79**
Cabernet Sauvignon Napa Valley Draper Vineyard 1995 • $17 • (11/15/1997) • **84**
Zinfandel Russian River Valley Ponzo Vineyard 1996: A bit earthy, with nice plum, cocoa and vanilla notes that linger through the finish. Drink now through 2004.–J.L. • $20 • (5/15/2000) • **86**
Zinfandel Russian River Valley Ponzo Vineyard 1995 • $18 • (3/31/1998) • **87**
Zinfandel Russian River Valley Ponzo Vineyard 1994 • $14 • (5/15/1996) • **85**

HARTFORD COURT | CALIFORNIA

Chardonnay Sonoma Coast Seascape Vineyard 1996: Rich and flavorful, with a complex core of pear, fig, melon and toasty oak. Well focused, with deep, concentrated flavors and a long, rich aftertaste that fans out and lingers. Drink now.–J.L. • $35 • (11/30/1998) • **89**

Pinot Noir Russian River Valley Arrendell Vineyard 1996: Tight, with firm tannins, hints of cola and black cherry, sage and spice, finishing with a spicy blackberry flavor. Needs a little time. Try through 2003.–J.L. • $35 • (11/30/1998) • **88**

Pinot Noir Russian River Valley Arrendell Vineyard 1995 • $45 • (2/28/1998) • **85**

Pinot Noir Russian River Valley Arrendell Vineyard 1994 • $42 • (2/29/1996) • **89**

Pinot Noir Russian River Valley Dutton Ranch-Sanchietti Vineyard 1996: Complex, with a pretty, focused array of black cherry, blackberry, vanilla, spice, cola and tea, finishing with crisp, well-integrated tannins. Drink now through 2004.–J.L. • $35 • (11/30/1998) • **88**

Pinot Noir Russian River Valley Dutton Ranch-Sanchietti Vineyard 1995 • $40 • (10/31/1997) • **87**

Pinot Noir Russian River Valley Dutton Ranch-Sanchietti Vineyard 1994 • $35 • (2/29/1996) • **86**

Pinot Noir Sonoma Coast 1996: Tight and compact, with complex black cherry, blackberry, herb, sage and spice, very neat. Short-term cellaring will let it soften and evolve. Try through 2002.–J.L. • $32 • (11/30/1998) • **88**

Pinot Noir Sonoma Coast 1995 • $32 • (12/15/1997) • **87**

Zinfandel Russian River Valley Dina's Vineyard 1998: Veers toward the tart side, with pepper, wild berry and cedar notes, turning firmly tannic. Drink now through 2005.–J.L. • $32 • (6/15/2000) • **86**

Zinfandel Russian River Valley Dina's Vineyard 1997: Lots to admire in this ripe, well-rounded Zin, with peppery cherry, cranberry, tart plum and cedar notes. A distinctive, complex style; Hartford Court's first Zin from this vineyard. Drink now through 2004.–J.L. • $NA • (5/31/1999) • **90**

Zinfandel Russian River Valley Fanucchi Vineyard 1998: Smooth, ripe, rich and polished, with jammy raspberry, blackberry, cherry and spice (white pepper). Long, intricate aftertaste. Drink now through 2006.–J.L. • $32 • (6/15/2000) • **90**

Zinfandel Russian River Valley Fanucchi-Wood Road Vineyard 1996: Firm, ripe and marked by plummy cherry and raspberry flavors, this wine combines ripe, rich, supple fruit with firm, structured tannins that turn soft and fleshy. Drink through 2002.–J.L. • $30 • (11/30/1998) • **88**

Zinfandel Russian River Valley Hartford Vineyard 1998: Tart, lean, tannic and well structured, with cinnamon, clove and wild berry flavors. Clamps down on the finish. Drink now through 2004.–J.L. • $32 • (6/15/2000) • **86**

Zinfandel Russian River Valley Hartford Vineyard 1997: Supple and juicy, with ripe, complex cherry, raspberry and wild berry flavors, picking up touches of plum and anise. Drink through 2006.–J.L. • $NA • (5/31/1999) • **92**

Zinfandel Russian River Valley Hartford Vineyard 1996: Folds together lots of ripe cherry, plum and blackberry flavor and finishes with dashes of cedar and spice. Firms up on the finish, so allow some time for the tannins to recede. Drink through 2004.–J.L. • $35 • (11/30/1998) • **87**

Zinfandel Russian River Valley Hartford Vineyard 1995 • $32 • (10/31/1997) • **90**

Zinfandel Russian River Valley Hartford Vineyard 1994 • $30 • (4/30/1996) • **92**

Zinfandel Russian River Valley Highwire Vineyard 1998: Tightly wound, with a firm band of cedar, wild berry, black cherry and earth notes, finishing with dry tannins. Drink now through 2006.–J.L. • $32 • (6/15/2000) • **87**

Zinfandel Russian River Valley High Wire 1997: Lots of complex, juicy fruit, with pretty plum, raspberry, black cherry and spicy notes, staying tightly focused and finishing with a long, crisp aftertaste. Drink now through 2004.–J.L. • $NA • (5/31/1999) • **90**

HARTWELL | CALIFORNIA

Cabernet Sauvignon Stags Leap District 1992 • $50 • (11/15/1995) • **90**

Cabernet Sauvignon Stags Leap District 1991 • $86 Ⓐ • (11/15/1994) • **92**

Cabernet Sauvignon Stags Leap District Grace Vineyard 1996: Smooth, ripe and polished, with a core of earthy currant, plum and wild berry, picking up pretty toasty, smoky oak. Long and supple. Drink through 2008.–J.L. • $65 • (6/15/1999) • **91**

Cabernet Sauvignon Stags Leap District Grace Vineyard 1994 • $63 • (11/30/1997) • **94**

Key: SS—Spectator Selection. CS—Cellar Selection. HR—Highly Recommended. $NA—Price not available. (BT)—Barrel tasting. Ⓐ—Auction Price.
For a key to the tasters' initials, see "How to Use These Listings."
Dates in parentheses represent the issues in which the ratings were published.

Cabernet Sauvignon Stags Leap District Sunshine Vineyard 1997: Solid, with chunky currant, blackberry and cherry flavors framed by toasty, cedary oak, finishing with complexity. Drink now through 2007.–J.L. • $95 • (6/30/2000) • **89**

Cabernet Sauvignon Stags Leap District Sunshine Vineyard 1996: Tightly wound, firm and crisp, with a complex core of plum, black cherry, blackberry, cedar and toasty oak. Finishes with a rich aftertaste and fine length. Best from 2001 through 2008.–J.L. • $55 • (9/15/1999) • **90**

Cabernet Sauvignon Stags Leap District Sunshine Vineyard 1995 • $90 Ⓐ • (5/15/1998) • **92**

Cabernet Sauvignon Stags Leap District Sunshine Vineyard 1994 • $63 Ⓐ • (11/30/1997) • **89**

Chardonnay Stags Leap District 1997: Smooth, ripe and creamy, with tiers of pear, fig, melon and citrus flavors that turn complex and linger. Drink now through 2002.–J.L. • $30 • (1/31/1999) • **90**

HAVENS | CALIFORNIA

Bourriquot Napa Valley 1995: Ripe, spicy, jammy aromas abound here. On the palate, pretty raspberry, plum, coffee and herb flavors marry nicely. Finish is a bit tart, but the essence lingers. A blend of Cabernet Franc and Merlot. Drink now through 2005. • $28 • (10/31/1998) • **88**

Merlot Napa Valley 1997: Dense, with a supple core of black cherry, tar and earth flavors framed by firm tannins. Best now through 2005.–J.L. • $22 • (10/15/1999) • **86**

Merlot Napa Valley 1996: A touch earthy, with a leathery note. Takes time to show its core of mineral, currant and herb flavors. Turns simple on the finish. Drink through 2003.–J.L. • $20 • (10/15/1998) • **84**

Merlot Napa Valley 1994 • $18 • (7/31/1996) • **85**

Merlot Napa Valley 1993 • $16 • (7/31/1996) • **86**

Merlot Napa Valley 1991 • $15 • (7/15/1993) HR • **90**

Merlot Napa Valley 1990 • $15 • (6/15/1993) • **87**

Merlot Napa Valley 1989 • $14 • (5/31/1992) • **84**

Merlot Napa Valley 1988 • $14 • (3/31/1991) • **82**

Merlot Napa Valley 1987 • $14 • (7/15/1990) • **89**

Merlot Napa Valley 1986 • $14 • (3/31/1990) • **72**

Merlot Napa Valley 1985 • $13 • (5/31/1988) • **84**

Merlot Napa Valley Carneros Reserve 1996: Intense, with concentrated, earthy currant and cherry flavors. Picks up nice oak shadings on the finish. Drink now through 2004.–J.L. • $28 • (10/15/1999) • **87**

Merlot Napa Valley Carneros Reserve 1995: Crisp and well balanced, with pleasant cherry and berry flavors that are young, vibrant, tight and unevolved. Best to cellar short-term. Drink through 2003.–J.L. • $28 • (9/30/1998) • **86**

Merlot Napa Valley Carneros Reserve 1993 • $24 • (7/31/1996) • **85**

Merlot Napa Valley Carneros Truchard Vineyard 1988 • $20 • (8/31/1991) • **76**

Merlot Napa Valley Carneros Truchard Vineyard Reserve 1990 • $20 • (6/15/1993) • **88**

Merlot Napa Valley Carneros Truchard Vineyard Reserve 1989 • $20 • (5/31/1992) • **82**

Syrah Carneros 1996: Smooth, ripe, plush and exotic, with complex meaty currant, mineral, sage and floral notes. Finishes with rugged tannins, but another year or two in the cellar should work. Drink through 2005.–J.L. • $24 • (3/31/1999) • **90**

Syrah Carneros 1995 • $20 • (11/30/1997) • **83**

HAWK CREST | CALIFORNIA

Cabernet Sauvignon California 1996: Light and vaguely spicy, with a note of orange peel on the tea- and sage-scented finish. Drink now.–H.S. • $12 • (10/31/1998) • **81**

Cabernet Sauvignon California 1995 • $12 • (3/31/1998) • **85**

Cabernet Sauvignon California 1994 • $10 • (12/15/1996) • **83**

Cabernet Sauvignon California 1991 • $9 • (3/31/1994) • **78**

Cabernet Sauvignon California 1990 • $9 • (4/30/1993) • **82**

Cabernet Sauvignon California 1989 • $9 • (3/15/1992) • **77**

Cabernet Sauvignon California Reserve 1995: Has ripe currant flavors and notes of cedar and herb, but is a bit clumsy. Drink now.–J.L. • $14 • (10/15/1998) • **79**

Chardonnay California 1997: Spicy, with crisp and refreshing citrus and pear flavors. Drink now.–H.S. • $10 • (11/30/1998) • **83**

Chardonnay California 1996 • $10 • (1/31/1998) • **86**

Chardonnay California Reserve 1996: Simple but pleasant, with bright citrus and apple flavors. Drink now.–H.S. • $12 • (11/15/1998) • **81**

Merlot California 1995 • $12 • (1/31/1998) • **83**

Merlot California Reserve 1995: This has juicy strawberry and cherry flavors over a light frame of tea and herbs. The concentrated flavors linger on the finish. Drink now.–J.L. • $14 • (9/30/1998) • **82**

HAWLEY | CALIFORNIA

Cabernet Sauvignon Dry Creek Valley 1997: Medium in weight, with a modest range of cedary currant, herb, cherry and spice plus a chocolate note. Mild tannins make it approachable now. Drink now through 2007.–J.L. • $33 • (4/30/2000) • **86**
Merlot Dry Creek Valley 1996: Clean, ripe and complex, with tart, earthy cherry, plum and wild berry flavors. Finishes with crisp, flinty tannins. Drink now through 2003.–J.L. • $28 • (10/15/1999) • **85**
Merlot Dry Creek Valley 1995 • $30 • (11/15/1997) • **83**
Viognier Dry Creek Valley 1997: Complex, with plenty of ripe, rich flavors of pear, fig, melon and apple that are focused, and elegant on the finish. Drink now.–J.L. • $24 • (12/15/1998) • **87**
Viognier Dry Creek Valley 1996 • $22 • (12/15/1997) • **83**

HAYWOOD | CALIFORNIA

Cabernet Sauvignon California 1991 • $8 • (11/15/1994) • **83**
Cabernet Sauvignon California Vintner's Select 1997: Firm tannins, with oak and a bit of fruit at the core. Finishes with a rustic, herbal edge. • $9 • (10/15/1999) • **78**
Cabernet Sauvignon California Vintner's Select 1996: Offers light cherry, herbal and oak flavors, finishes crisp. Drink now.–H.S. • $9 • (11/15/1998) • **79**
Cabernet Sauvignon California Vintner's Select 1995 • $8 • (11/15/1997) • **84**
Cabernet Sauvignon California Vintner's Select 1994 • $8 • (10/31/1997) • **82**
Cabernet Sauvignon California Vintner's Select 1993 • $8 • (12/15/1995) • **84**
Cabernet Sauvignon California Vintner's Select 1990 • $8 • (3/15/1993) • **82**
Cabernet Sauvignon California Vintner's Select 1989 • $8 • (3/15/1992) • **80**
Cabernet Sauvignon Sonoma Valley 1988 • $16 • (2/28/1991) • **82**
Cabernet Sauvignon Sonoma Valley 1986 • $19 • (11/15/1989) • **92**
Cabernet Sauvignon Sonoma Valley 1985 • $15 • (3/15/1988) • **91**
Cabernet Sauvignon Sonoma Valley 1984 • $13 • (10/31/1987) • **93**
Cabernet Sauvignon Sonoma Valley 1983 • $13 • (5/15/1987) • **77**
Cabernet Sauvignon Sonoma Valley 1981 • $11 • (9/01/1984) • **84**
Cabernet Sauvignon Sonoma Valley Los Chamizal Vineyards 1989 • $12 • (11/15/1994) • **84**
Cabernet Sauvignon Sonoma Valley Los Chamizal Vineyards 1988 • $16 • (11/15/1991) • **85**
Chardonnay California Vintner's Select 1997: Strikes a balance between simple floral and citrus flavors. Drink now.–J.L. • $8 • (11/30/1998) • **80**
Chardonnay California Vintner's Select 1996 • $8 • (11/15/1997) • **82**
Merlot California Vintner's Select 1997: Herbal, charred oak flavors, with hints of fruit. Dry, leathery tannins.–J.L. • $11 • (11/30/1998) • **74**
Merlot California Vintner's Select 1995 • $10 • (12/31/1997) • **84**
Spaghetti Red California NV • $6 • (2/15/1990) • **74**
Spaghetti Red Sonoma County NV • $5 • (4/30/1987) • **74**
Zinfandel Sonoma Valley 1986 • $11 • (9/15/1988) • **89**
Zinfandel Sonoma Valley Los Chamizal Vineyard 1997: Smooth and spicy, with pretty raspberry, cherry, anise, cedar and wild berry flavors that are tightly wound. Long, berry-flavored aftertaste. Drink now through 2007. –J.L. • $19 • (5/31/2000) • **88**
Zinfandel Sonoma Valley Los Chamizal Vineyard 1995 • $18 • (6/15/1998) • **87**
Zinfandel Sonoma Valley Los Chamizal Vineyard 1994 • $16 • (1/01/1998) • **88**
Zinfandel Sonoma Valley Los Chamizal Vineyard 1993 • $15 • (2/28/1997) • **88**
Zinfandel Sonoma Valley Los Chamizal Vineyard 1992 • $14 • (10/15/1995) • **84**
Zinfandel Sonoma Valley Los Chamizal Vineyard 1991 • $14 • (10/15/1994) • **84**
Zinfandel Sonoma Valley Los Chamizal Vineyard Rocky Terrace 1997: Spicy, toasty oak tames the racy anise, wild berry, cherry, tar and cedar notes. Gains nuance and complexity on the finish, where the creamy oak is polished. Drink now through 2007.–J.L. • $29 • (5/31/2000) • **89**
Zinfandel Sonoma Valley Los Chamizal Vineyard Rocky Terrace 1995 • $25 • (6/15/1998) • **90**
Zinfandel Sonoma Valley Los Chamizal Vineyard Rocky Terrace 1994 • $25 • (1/01/1998) • **89**
Zinfandel Sonoma Valley Los Chamizal Vineyard Rocky Terrace 1992 • $18 • (10/15/1994) • **88**
Zinfandel Sonoma Valley Los Chamizal Vineyards 1990 • $14 • (10/15/1992) • **83**
Zinfandel Sonoma Valley Los Chamizal Vineyards 1989 • $14 • (11/15/1991) • **85**
Zinfandel Sonoma Valley Los Chamizal Vineyards 1988 • $13 • (11/30/1990) • **89**

HEDGES | WASHINGTON

Cabernet-Merlot Three Vineyards Columbia Valley 1996: Firm in texture, even a bit rough, with some nice currant and blackberry flavor poking through on the finish and lingering nicely. That bodes well. Best after 2001.–H.S. • $20 • (9/15/1999) • **88**
Cabernet-Merlot Columbia Valley Three Vineyards 1995: Firm, chewy and jazzy, with bright berry and herb flavors. Packed with flavor, it needs cellaring to soften the tannins. Best from 2001 through 2005.–H.S. • $20 • (9/15/1998) • **87**
Cabernet Sauvignon Columbia Valley Three Vineyards at Red Mountain 1994 • $18 • (9/15/1996) • **90**
Cabernet-Merlot Washington 1996 • $11 • (12/15/1997) • **85**
Cabernet-Merlot Columbia Valley 1995 • $11 • (9/15/1996) HR • **87**
Cabernet-Merlot Columbia Valley 1994 • $10 • (5/15/1996) • **83**
Cabernet-Merlot Washington 1993 • $10 • (8/31/1994) • **87**
Cabernet-Merlot Washington 1992 • $10 • (12/31/1993) • **86**
Cabernet-Merlot Washington 1991 • $10 • (3/31/1993) • **88**
Cabernet-Merlot Columbia Valley 1990 • $9 • (6/15/1992) • **88**
Cabernet-Merlot Columbia Valley 1989 • $7 • (9/30/1991) • **89**
Cabernet-Merlot Washington 1997: Crisp and tasty, with pretty berry and herb flavors on a racy frame. Drink now through 2001.–H.S. • $10 • (1/31/1999) • **84**
Fumé-Chardonnay Columbia Valley 1998: This lively, fruity white from Washington blooms with apple, pear and spice flavors, hinting gently at mineral on the generous finish. An enticing mouthful at a hard-to-beat price. Drink now.–H.S. • $9 • (5/15/2000) • **86**
Fumé-Chardonnay Columbia Valley 1997: Fresh and tangy, lively with citrus and pear flavors that linger on the bright finish. Drink now.–H.S. • $10 • (9/15/1998) • **86**
Fumé-Chardonnay Washington-Oregon 1996 • $8 • (6/15/1997) • **86**
Red Mountain Reserve Columbia Valley 1995: Dark, dense and chewy, with tar, blackberry and cedar aromas and flavors on a firm frame. Flavors persist on the finish. Fine tannins need cellaring to soften. Try in 2000. –H.S. • $35 • (1/31/1999) • **87**
Red Mountain Reserve Columbia Valley 1994 • $30 • (9/15/1997) • **87**
Red Mountain Reserve Columbia Valley 1993 • $30 • (4/30/1997) • **92**
Red Mountain Reserve Columbia Valley 1991 • $23 • (9/30/1995) • **85**
Red Mountain Reserve Columbia Valley 1990 • $25 • (3/15/1994) • **84**
Red Mountain Reserve Columbia Valley 1989 • $25 • (3/31/1993) • **87**

HEITZ | CALIFORNIA

Cabernet Sauvignon Napa Valley 1995: Smooth, rich and polished, with pretty black cherry, currant, chocolate, anise, sage and cedar notes. Finishes with a complex aftertaste and firm tannins. Best from 2001 through 2009.–J.L. • $27 • (1/31/2000) • **90**
Cabernet Sauvignon Napa Valley 1994: Spicy and peppery, of medium weight, with a modest range of dried cherry and berry flavors that turn dry and austere. Good but not exciting. Drink now through 2004.–J.L. • $25 • (8/31/1999) • **84**
Cabernet Sauvignon Napa Valley 1993 • $21 • (5/15/1998) • **88**
Cabernet Sauvignon Napa Valley 1992 • $33 Ⓐ • (5/31/1997) • **89**
Cabernet Sauvignon Napa Valley 1991 • $19 • (4/30/1996) • **85**
Cabernet Sauvignon Napa Valley 1990 • $36 Ⓐ • (4/30/1995) HR • **90**
Cabernet Sauvignon Napa Valley 1989 • $22 Ⓐ • (7/31/1994) • **88**
Cabernet Sauvignon Napa Valley 1988 • $22 Ⓐ • (3/31/1993) • **88**
Cabernet Sauvignon Napa Valley 1987 • $40 Ⓐ • (4/15/1992) SS • **90**
Cabernet Sauvignon Napa Valley 1986 • $38 Ⓐ • (4/15/1991) • **88**
Cabernet Sauvignon Napa Valley 1985 • $38 Ⓐ • (5/15/1990) • **80**
Cabernet Sauvignon Napa Valley 1984 • $30 • (1/31/1990) • **89**
Cabernet Sauvignon Napa Valley 1983 • $20 • (1/31/1990) • **85**
Cabernet Sauvignon Napa Valley 1982 • $30 • (1/31/1990) • **80**
Cabernet Sauvignon Napa Valley 1981 • $30 • (1/31/1990) • **86**
Cabernet Sauvignon Napa Valley 1980 • $38 Ⓐ • (1/31/1990) • **88**
Cabernet Sauvignon Napa Valley 1979 • $12 • (1/31/1990) • **86**
Cabernet Sauvignon Napa Valley 1978 • $72 Ⓐ • (1/31/1990) • **90**
Cabernet Sauvignon Napa Valley 1977 • $48 • (1/31/1990) • **83**
Cabernet Sauvignon Napa Valley 1973 • $53 Ⓐ • (1/31/1990) • **78**
Cabernet Sauvignon Napa Valley 1970 • $41 Ⓐ • (1/31/1990) • **74**
Cabernet Sauvignon Napa Valley Bella Oaks Vineyard 1995: Medium in weight, with pretty black cherry, wild berry and plum notes. Turns elegant, with smooth tannins. Drink now through 2006.–J.L. • $45 • (6/15/2000) • **86**
Cabernet Sauvignon Napa Valley Bella Oaks Vineyard 1994: Medium ruby-red, medium-weight, with dried plum, red cherry and berryish notes that while

elegant and spicy never really frame a tight focus. Supple tannins make it ready now. Drink through 2003.–J.L. • $35 • (8/31/1999) • **87**

Cabernet Sauvignon Napa Valley Bella Oaks Vineyard 1993 • $28 • (5/15/1998) CS • **91**

Cabernet Sauvignon Napa Valley Bella Oaks Vineyard 1990 • $52 Ⓐ • (4/30/1995) • **85**

Cabernet Sauvignon Napa Valley Bella Oaks Vineyard 1989 • $23 • (7/31/1994) • **85**

Cabernet Sauvignon Napa Valley Bella Oaks Vineyard 1988 • $32 • (3/31/1993) • **81**

Cabernet Sauvignon Napa Valley Bella Oaks Vineyard 1987 • $50 Ⓐ • (6/30/1992) • **85**

Cabernet Sauvignon Napa Valley Bella Oaks Vineyard 1986 • $30 Ⓐ • (4/15/1991) • **89**

Cabernet Sauvignon Napa Valley Bella Oaks Vineyard 1985 • $67 Ⓐ • (5/15/1990) CS • **92**

Cabernet Sauvignon Napa Valley Bella Oaks Vineyard 1984 • $48 Ⓐ • (5/15/1989) • **86**

Cabernet Sauvignon Napa Valley Bella Oaks Vineyard 1983 • $20 • (4/30/1988) • **90**

Cabernet Sauvignon Napa Valley Bella Oaks Vineyard 1982 • $21 • (4/30/1987) • **91**

Cabernet Sauvignon Napa Valley Bella Oaks Vineyard 1978 • $60 Ⓐ • (2/16/1984) • **90**

Cabernet Sauvignon Napa Valley Bella Oaks Vineyard 1977 • $46 Ⓐ • (2/16/1984) • **89**

Cabernet Sauvignon Napa Valley Bella Oaks Vineyard 1976 • $35 • (2/16/1984) • **92**

Cabernet Sauvignon Napa Valley Fay Vineyard 1978 • $30 Ⓐ • (2/16/1984) • **80**

Cabernet Sauvignon Napa Valley Fay Vineyard 1977 • $26 Ⓐ • (2/16/1984) • **78**

Cabernet Sauvignon Napa Valley Martha's Vineyard 1992 • $79 Ⓐ • (5/31/1997) CS • **93**

Cabernet Sauvignon Napa Valley Martha's Vineyard 1991 • $75 Ⓐ • (4/30/1996) CS • **91**

Cabernet Sauvignon Napa Valley Martha's Vineyard 1990 • $87 Ⓐ • (4/30/1995) CS • **90**

Cabernet Sauvignon Napa Valley Martha's Vineyard 1989: Wonderful Martha's. Chocolate-covered cherry with mint character, well focused; not the depth or extra dimensions of a great year, but quite complete on its own terms. (1989 California Cabernet retrospective tasting). Drink now through 2005.–J.L. • $67 Ⓐ • (8/31/1999) • **90**

Cabernet Sauvignon Napa Valley Martha's Vineyard 1988 • $33 Ⓐ • (3/31/1993) • **87**

Cabernet Sauvignon Napa Valley Martha's Vineyard 1987 • $95 Ⓐ • (12/15/1997) • **92**

Cabernet Sauvignon Napa Valley Martha's Vineyard 1986 • $90 Ⓐ • (4/15/1991) CS • **95**

Cabernet Sauvignon Napa Valley Martha's Vineyard 1985 • $205 Ⓐ • (4/30/1990) • **98**

Cabernet Sauvignon Napa Valley Martha's Vineyard 1984 • $111 Ⓐ • (3/15/1989) SS • **97**

Cabernet Sauvignon Napa Valley Martha's Vineyard 1983 • $59 Ⓐ • (4/30/1988) • **90**

Cabernet Sauvignon Napa Valley Martha's Vineyard 1982 • $66 Ⓐ • (4/15/1987) CS • **94**

Cabernet Sauvignon Napa Valley Martha's Vineyard 1979: Pure Martha's with its minty currant flavors, there's a touch of maturity, with cedar, earth and just a trace of nuttiness. Still, quite complete and complex, with soft tannins. (1979 California Cabernet retrospective tasting). Drink now through 2004.–J.L. • $102 Ⓐ • (8/31/1999) • **90**

Cabernet Sauvignon Napa Valley Martha's Vineyard 1978: Classic Martha's—minty, spicy, elegant and aging exceptionally well. Shows off plenty of flavors, with currant, black cherry, anise, cedar and plum. (1978 California Cabernet retrospective tasting). Drink now through 2004.–J.L. • $107 Ⓐ • (11/15/1998) • **91**

Cabernet Sauvignon Napa Valley Martha's Vineyard 1977 • $88 • (1/31/1990) • **90**

Cabernet Sauvignon Napa Valley Martha's Vineyard 1976 • $111 Ⓐ • (2/16/1984) • **94**

Cabernet Sauvignon Napa Valley Martha's Vineyard 1975 • $83 Ⓐ • (2/16/1984) • **90**

Cabernet Sauvignon Napa Valley Martha's Vineyard 1974 • $435 Ⓐ • (11/15/1994) • **97**

Key: SS—Spectator Selection. CS—Cellar Selection. HR—Highly Recommended. $NA—Price not available. (BT)—Barrel tasting. Ⓐ—Auction Price. For a key to the tasters' initials, see "How to Use These Listings." **Dates in parentheses represent the issues in which the ratings were published.**

Cabernet Sauvignon Napa Valley MZ-1 NV • $NA • (1/31/1990) • **75**

Cabernet Sauvignon Napa Valley Trailside Vineyard 1994: An understated style, with a rustic array of herb, currant, berry, sage and tealike flavors. Turns tannic and dry on the finish. Best from 2001 through 2008.–J.L. • $49 • (10/15/1999) • **87**

Cabernet Sauvignon Napa Valley Trailside Vineyard 1993: Deliciously complex, with ripe, juicy currant, black cherry and spice flavors. There's also plenty of toasty, vanilla-laced oak, but it wears the wood well and finishes with minty chocolate notes that linger. This late-release Cabernet drinks well now. Drink through 2007.–J.L. • $48 • (8/31/1998) CS • **92**

Cabernet Sauvignon Napa Valley Trailside Vineyard 1992 • $48 • (9/30/1997) • **90**

Cabernet Sauvignon Napa Valley Trailside Vineyard 1991 • $45 • (11/15/1996) • **88**

Cabernet Sauvignon Napa Valley Trailside Vineyard 1990 • $45 • (10/15/1995) CS • **91**

Cabernet Sauvignon Napa Valley Trailside Vineyard 1989: Solid, fanning out with coffee, currant, chocolate and berry flavors, and firm, integrated tannins. Aging well. (1989 California Cabernet retrospective tasting). Drink now through 2004.–J.L. • $35 • (8/31/1999) • **88**

Grignolino Port Napa Valley 1992 • $13 • (9/30/1995) • **85**

Ryan's Red Napa Valley NV • $6 • (2/28/1989) • **74**

Zinfandel Napa Valley Heitz Vineyard 1989 • $9 • (9/30/1993) • **67**

Zinfandel Napa Valley Heitz Vineyard 1988 • $7 • (10/15/1992) • **78**

HELENA VIEW | CALIFORNIA

Cabernet Franc Napa Valley Johnston Vineyards 1992 • $21 • (11/30/1996) • **85**

Cabernet Sauvignon Napa Valley 1995: Pleasant, with tea, dried berry, licorice and vanilla flavors. However, quality doesn't equal the price tag. Drink now. • $32 • (11/15/1998) • **83**

Cabernet Sauvignon Napa Valley 1992 • $12 • (11/30/1996) • **87**

Cabernet Sauvignon Napa Valley 1991 • $12 • (11/30/1996) • **79**

Cabernet Sauvignon Napa Valley Moon Mountain 1992 • $8 • (11/30/1996) • **83**

Moon Mountain Harvest Moon Red Napa Valley 1994: Medium-bodied and softly textured, showing rounded cola, menthol, tea and light cherry flavors. Pleasant now, probably at its peak. Drink now. • $12 • (11/15/1998) • **83**

HELLACIOUS ACRES | CALIFORNIA

Zinfandel Howell Mountain 1997: Weird, with burnt plastic notes and charry meat flavors that are unappealing. Explains the vulture on the label.–J.L. • $25 • (5/15/2000) • **70**

HEMMETER, HAMILTON | CALIFORNIA

Pinot Noir Sonoma Valley 1996: A shade lighter than rosé, with a sweaty, stemmy aroma, but it tastes better than it smells, adding pleasant, simple cherry notes. • $14 • (8/31/1998) • **78**

HENDRY RANCH | CALIFORNIA

Chardonnay Napa Valley Hendry Blocks 9 & 21 1998: Oak overtones dominate, with tart citrus notes. Drink now.–J.L. • $24 • (6/15/2000) • **83**

Chardonnay Napa Valley Blocks 9 & 10 1997: Sleek, tight and flinty, with complex, concentrated citrus, pear, lemon and mineral flavors that are fresh and lively, with zingy acidity. Tasty now, but a good bet to improve with short-term cellaring. Best from 2001 through 2008.–J.L. • $20 • (4/30/2000) • **89**

Chardonnay Napa Valley Block 9 1996 • $22 • (5/31/1998) • **88**

Cabernet Sauvignon Napa Valley Block 8 1995 • $24 • (5/15/1998) • **90**

Zinfandel Mount Veeder Brandlin Vineyard 1994 • $17 • (1/31/1997) • **88**

Zinfandel Mount Veeder Brandlin Vineyard 1992 • $15 • (10/15/1995) • **86**

Zinfandel Napa Valley Block 7 1997: Subdued given its size, with restrained earth, oak, cola and black cherry flavors, turning firm and tannic on the finish. Best from 2001 through 2008.–J.L. • $20 • (3/31/2000) • **88**

Zinfandel Napa Valley Hendry Block 7 1994 • $17 • (1/31/1997) • **90**

Zinfandel Napa Valley Hendry Block 7 1992 • $14 • (10/15/1995) • **88**

HENRY ESTATE | OREGON

Cabernet Sauvignon Umpqua Valley 1992 • $12 • (3/31/1996) • **78**

Chardonnay Umpqua Valley 1996: This bright, juicy, tangy style of Chardonnay shows plenty of citrus, honey and pear flavors that linger on the finish. Drink now.–H.S. • $15 • (2/28/1999) • **85**

Gewürztraminer Umpqua Valley Dry 1996 • $9 • (2/28/1998) • **81**

Müller-Thurgau Umpqua Valley 1996 • $8 • (9/15/1997) • **83**
Pinot Gris Oregon 1997: Fresh and fruity, this brash mouthful of nectarine and honeydew flavors picks up a racy touch of lime on the finish. Drink now.–H.S. • $13 • (4/30/1999) • **87**
Pinot Noir Oregon Umpqua Cuvée 1996 • $10 • (2/28/1998) • **84**
Pinot Noir Oregon Umpqua Cuvée 1995 • $10 • (12/31/1996) • **82**
Pinot Noir Oregon Umpqua Cuveé 1994 • $9 • (12/31/1995) • **84**
Pinot Noir Oregon Umpqua Cuvée 1993 • $9 • (11/30/1994) • **79**
Pinot Noir Oregon Umpqua Cuveé 1992 • $9 • (11/30/1994) • **86**
Pinot Noir Umpqua Valley 1995 • $13 • (9/15/1997) • **85**
Pinot Noir Umpqua Valley 1993 • $10 • (9/30/1996) • **83**
Pinot Noir Umpqua Valley 1986 • $10 • (4/15/1991) • **81**
Pinot Noir Umpqua Valley 1985 • $12 • (6/15/1988) • **80**
Pinot Noir Umpqua Valley 1985 • $15 • (2/15/1990) • **85**
Pinot Noir Umpqua Valley Barrel Select 1995: Broader and richer than most '95s, this southern Oregon Pinot Noir shows dark cherry and spice flavors and fine-textured tannins. Drink now through 2002.–H.S. • $20 • (2/28/1999) • **85**
Pinot Noir Umpqua Valley Barrel Select 1994 • $24 • (2/28/1998) • **87**
Pinot Noir Umpqua Valley Barrel Select 1992 • $18 • (12/31/1995) • **88**
Pinot Noir Umpqua Valley Barrel Select 1991 • $18 • (11/30/1994) • **85**
Pinot Noir Umpqua Valley Barrel Select 1990 • $18 • (11/30/1994) • **88**
Pinot Noir Umpqua Valley Barrel Select 1988 • $15 • (2/28/1993) • **84**
Pinot Noir Umpqua Valley Estate Bottled 1990 • $11 • (11/30/1994) • **83**
Pinot Noir Umpqua Valley Winemakers Reserve 1990 • $25 • (10/31/1995) • **84**

HERON | CALIFORNIA

Chardonnay California 1998: Looking for a deal on Chardonnay? This one's pleasantly balanced, with a pretty core of ripe pear, apple and vanilla flavors, finishing with touches of citrus, lemon peel and light oak. Drink now.–J.L. • $10 • (4/30/2000) • **86**
Chardonnay North Coast 1997: This is very good California Chardonnay—elegant and refreshing, with supple lemon, spicy pear and fig grace notes; don't pass it by thinking the price is too good to be true. Drink now.–H.S. • $11 • (4/30/1999) • **87**

HERON HILL | NEW YORK

Seyval Blanc Finger Lakes Ingle Vineyard NV • $7 • (11/15/1997) • **82**

HERON LAKE | CALIFORNIA

Pinot Noir Wild Horse Valley 1994 • $24 • (2/29/1996) • **87**
Pinot Noir Wild Horse Valley 1990 • $12 • (12/31/1995) • **82**
Pinot Noir Wild Horse Valley Reserve 1996: Soft and supple, with attractive black cherry, anise, coffee, tea and herb flavors. The finish is a bit astringent, but the ensemble remains quite nice. • $24 • (12/31/1998) • **85**
Pinot Noir Wild Horse Valley Reserve 1994 • $26 • (2/28/1997) • **86**

HERZOG | CALIFORNIA

Cabernet Sauvignon Alexander Valley Special Edition 1996: Smooth, supple and complex, with pretty toasty vanilla-scented oak and lots of ripe cherry, berry, plum and currant flavors that fold together tightly on the elegant finish. Kosher. Drink now through 2006.–J.L. • $40 • (6/15/1999) • **92**
Cabernet Sauvignon Alexander Valley Special Edition 1995: Rich, ripe and creamy in texture, with pretty toasty oak and vanilla shadings. The core of fruit is dazzling, with ripe cherry, currant, plum and spice. Finishes with a long, clean aftertaste of smoky oak and Cabernet flavors. Tasted twice, with consistent notes. Kosher. Best now through 2006.–J.L. • $46 • (9/30/1998) • **93**
Cabernet Sauvignon Alexander Valley Special Reserve 1997: Has a quirky personality, showing coffee ground and bacony notes before revealing modest blackberry flavors. Kosher. Drink now through 2005.–J.L. • $26 • (6/30/2000) • **86**
Cabernet Sauvignon Alexander Valley Special Reserve 1996: Wonderful complexity, finesse and depth of flavor, with layers of earthy currant, plum, wild berry, spice and cedar. Long, elegant aftertaste. Kosher. Drink through 2007.–J.L. • $26 • (6/15/1999) • **92**
Cabernet Sauvignon Alexander Valley Special Reserve 1995: An herbaceous style, with racy green and bell pepper notes, spicy oak, herb and sage holding court over the slow-to-emerge, mainstream cherry and berry. Needs bottle time. Kosher. Drink through 2004.–J.L. • $25 • (10/31/1998) • **86**
Cabernet Sauvignon Chalk Hill Warnecke Vineyard Special Edition 1997: Lots of seductive oak flavors—vanilla, cedar and anise—but also a lot of pretty fruit, with blackberry, cherry and spice finishing in a complex aftertaste. Kosher. Drink now through 2008.–J.L. • $42 • (6/30/2000) • **88**
Cabernet Sauvignon Napa Valley Special Reserve 1997: Lots of smoky, toasty oak, though the spicy black cherry, currant and berryish flavors fill in the gaps nicely. Kosher. Drink now through 2005.–J.L. • $32 • (6/30/2000) • **88**
Cabernet Sauvignon Napa Valley Special Reserve 1996: Remarkable for its complexity, supple texture and richness of flavor, this Cab shows tiers of smoky, toasty oak, ripe plum, black cherry, wild berry and spice. The long, lingering aftertaste feels elegant. Kosher. Drink now through 2006.–J.L. • $30 • (6/15/1999) HR • **93**
Chardonnay Russian River Valley Special Reserve 1998: Shows off a waxy, cedary oak side that dominates the modest fruit flavors. Kosher. Drink now.–J.L. • $22 • (6/30/2000) • **81**
Chardonnay Russian River Valley Special Reserve 1997: Quite rich and complex, drawing on pear, citrus, hazelnut and mineral flavors, all framed in plenty of toasty oak. Good acidity carries it along nicely for a clean, long finish. A fine effort. Kosher. Drink now through 2002. • $21 • (6/15/1999) • **91**
Chardonnay Russian River Valley Special Reserve 1996: Smooth, ripe and creamy, with a complex array of rich pear, fig, vanilla and melon, picking up spicy, toasty oak and nutmeg flavors. Elegant and refined. An impressive new wine. Kosher. Drink now through 2001.–J.L. • $18 • (8/31/1998) • **88**

HESS COLLECTION, THE | CALIFORNIA

Cabernet Sauvignon Mount Veeder 1998: Very ripe, rich and flavorful, with tiers of plum, cherry, wild berry and spice, finishing with firm tannins and impressive length.–J.L. • $NA • (8/31/1999) (BT) • **95-99**
Cabernet Sauvignon Mount Veeder 1997: Shows off a racy, spicy, minty flavor, with a core of cherry and currant, finishing with firm, gritty tannins and a hint of bay leaf.–J.L. • $NA • (8/31/1998) (BT) • **90-94**
Cabernet Sauvignon Napa Valley 1996: Complex, with spicy berry, cherry and cedar and mint notes, turning earthy. Drink now through 2005. –J.L. • $29 • (6/30/2000) • **87**
Cabernet Sauvignon Napa Valley 1995: Smooth, lush and polished, with a pretty array of currant, black cherry, anise, earth, sage and tarry-leathery flavors building to and holding a sharp focus. Needs time, though. Best from 2001 through 2008.–J.L. • $25 • (5/15/1999) • **92**
Cabernet Sauvignon Napa Valley 1994 • $29 Ⓐ • (5/15/1998) • **88**
Cabernet Sauvignon Napa Valley 1993 • $20 • (5/15/1997) • **88**
Cabernet Sauvignon Napa Valley 1992 • $30 Ⓐ • (11/15/1995) SS • **94**
Cabernet Sauvignon Napa Valley 1991 • $18 Ⓐ • (11/15/1994) SS • **92**
Cabernet Sauvignon Napa Valley 1990 • $18 • (4/15/1994) CS • **90**
Cabernet Sauvignon Napa Valley 1989 • $17 • (2/15/1993) • **82**
Cabernet Sauvignon Napa Valley 1988: Fine balance for an '88, with ripe currant, olive, coffee, herb and tea notes, finishing with a nice balance of tannin and fruit. (1988 California Cabernet retrospective tasting). Drink now through 2004.–J.L. • $19 • (11/15/1998) • **87**
Cabernet Sauvignon Napa Valley 1987 • $58 Ⓐ • (12/15/1997) • **94**
Cabernet Sauvignon Napa Valley 1986 • $40 Ⓐ • (11/15/1989) • **90**
Cabernet Sauvignon Napa Valley 1985 • $51 Ⓐ • (11/15/1988) • **91**
Cabernet Sauvignon Napa Valley 1983 • $14 • (11/15/1987) • **82**
Cabernet Sauvignon Napa Valley Reserve 1994: Intense and tannic, definitely one for the cellar with its tightly wound band of currant, blackberry and earthy mineral nuances. Finishes with tight, firm tannins. Sold only at the winery. Drink through 2008.–J.L. • $45 • (10/31/1998) • **90**
Cabernet Sauvignon Napa Valley Reserve 1993 • $58 Ⓐ • (5/15/1998) • **90**
Cabernet Sauvignon Napa Valley Reserve 1992 • $39 • (11/15/1996) • **90**
Cabernet Sauvignon Napa Valley Reserve 1991 • $39 • (4/30/1996) • **91**
Cabernet Sauvignon Napa Valley Reserve 1990 • $38 • (11/15/1994) • **90**
Cabernet Sauvignon Napa Valley Reserve 1989: Tightly knit, firmly tannic, with mineral, black cherry, currant and berryish flavors, finishing with crisp, firm tannins. Lacks some concentration and depth. (1989 California Cabernet retrospective tasting). Drink now through 2004.–J.L. • $35 • (8/31/1999) • **87**
Cabernet Sauvignon Napa Valley Reserve 1988: Austere style, with lots of mint, herb, sage and tannin, without the suppleness and rich fruit to support it. Headed toward drying out; drink now. (1989 California Cabernet retrospective tasting).–J.L. • $37 • (11/15/1998) • **85**
Cabernet Sauvignon Napa Valley Reserve 1987 • $35 • (12/15/1997) • **94**
Cabernet Sauvignon Napa Valley Reserve 1986 • $52 Ⓐ • (9/15/1990) • **93**
Cabernet Sauvignon Napa Valley Reserve 1984 • $23 • (11/15/1988) • **92**
Cabernet Sauvignon Napa Valley Reserve 1983 • $23 • (9/15/1988) • **89**
Chardonnay Napa Valley 1997: Bright and inviting, the lively intensity of the complex grapefruit, melon, pear and spice flavors is nicely balanced by a

frame of pretty toast and cedary oak in this outstanding California white. Enjoy now through 2003.–J.L. • $18 • (8/31/1999) SS • **90**
Chardonnay Napa Valley 1996 • $18 • (6/30/1998) • **90**
Merlot Napa Valley 1995: Tight, with ripe plum, cedar, toasty oak and a hint of prune, finishing with a tannic edge. Drink now through 2004.–J.L. • $23 • (4/30/1999) • **87**
Merlot Napa Valley 1994 • $20 • (5/15/1998) • **88**
Merlot Napa Valley 1993 • $NA • (8/31/1997) • **86**
Merlot Napa Valley 1992 • $18 • (6/30/1996) • **88**
Merlot Napa Valley 1991 • $18 • (1/01/1996) • **83**
Merlot Napa Valley 1989 • $25 • (5/31/1992) • **86**
Zinfandel Napa Valley 1992 • $15 • (10/15/1995) • **87**

HESS SELECT | CALIFORNIA

Cabernet Sauvignon California 1997: Firm, with focused cola and blackberry flavors. Tannins clamp down on the finish. Best from 2001 through 2004.–J.L. • $13 • (4/30/2000) • **85**
Cabernet Sauvignon California 1996: Rich, ripe and focused, with balanced flavors of tart cherry and berry, herb and vanilla oak notes. Drink now through 2002.–J.L. • $11 • (3/31/1999) • **85**
Cabernet Sauvignon California 1995 • $10 • (4/30/1998) • **86**
Cabernet Sauvignon California 1994 • $10 • (1/31/1997) • **83**
Cabernet Sauvignon California 1993 • $10 • (11/30/1995) • **85**
Cabernet Sauvignon California 1992 • $10 • (11/15/1994) • **87**
Cabernet Sauvignon California 1991 • $9 • (2/28/1994) • **82**
Cabernet Sauvignon California 1990 • $10 • (11/15/1992) • **80**
Cabernet Sauvignon California 1988 • $10 • (3/31/1991) • **86**
Chardonnay California 1998: Good depth of citrus notes, but the flavors are pasty and a bit raw. Drink now.–J.L. • $11 • (4/30/2000) • **80**
Chardonnay California 1997: Soft, with creamy citrus and spice flavors finishing simple. Drink now.–J.L. • $10 • (4/30/1999) • **84**
Chardonnay California 1996 • $10 • (1/31/1998) • **87**
Pinot Noir Santa Barbara County Bien Nacido Vineyard 1994 • $13 • (5/15/1997) • **86**
Pinot Noir Santa Barbara County Bien Nacido Vineyard Q Block 1994 • $15 • (1/31/1997) • **78**
Pinot Noir Santa Barbara County Bien Nacido Vineyard Unfiltered 1993 • $14 • (12/31/1995) • **84**

HEWN, HANS | CALIFORNIA

California Red NV • $5 • (9/15/1997) • **84**
California White NV • $5 • (3/31/1998) • **80**

HICKOK | CALIFORNIA

Claret Napa Valley 1992 • $25 • (11/15/1997) • **86**

HIDDEN CELLARS | CALIFORNIA

Cabernet Sauvignon Mendocino County Mountanos Vineyard 1984 • $12 • (8/31/1988) • **88**
Chanson d'Or Bailey J. Lovin Vineyard Mendocino County 1989 • $15/375 ml. • (9/15/1991) • **84**
Chaucé Gris Mendocino 1996 • $9 • (3/31/1998) • **81**
Hillside Red Mendocino Old Vines 1997: Firmly structured, with a core of bright, spicy cherry and herbal complexity. Tannins are ripe and fairly smooth. It's a bit lean, but remains supple and versatile. An interesting blend. Drink now through 2005. • $13 • (2/28/1999) • **88**
Hillside Red Mendocino Old Vines 1995 • $11 • (3/31/1998) • **84**
Petite Sirah Mendocino 1997: Broad-shouldered, with cassis, chocolate, orange peel and tangy herbal notes. Firm, dry tannins in the finish. Drink now through 2005.–J.L. • $16 • (6/30/2000) • **86**
Petite Sirah Mendocino 1996: Simple, soft and flavorful, with plum and mineral notes and fleshy tannins that are firm and integrated. Drink now through 2003.–J.L. • $18 • (2/28/1999) • **85**
Petite Sirah Mendocino 1995 • $16 • (3/31/1998) • **86**
Petite Sirah Mendocino Eaglepoint Ranch 1997: Quite tannic, waxy and racy, with drying pepper and wild berry flavors. Drink now through 2004.–J.L. • $30 • (6/15/2000) • **82**
Petite Sirah Mendocino Eaglepoint Ranch Mendocino Heritage 1996: Intense, with ripe, juicy, complex layers of spicy raspberry, black cherry, anise and sage, turning plush and rich on the finish. Drink now through 2004.–J.L. • $28 • (3/31/1999) • **90**
Petite Sirah Mendocino Eaglepoint Ranch Mendocino Heritage 1995 • $25 • (4/30/1998) • **88**
Sauvignon Blanc Mendocino 1998: Tart, with simple pineapple and vanilla flavors. Drink now through 2002.–J.L. • $12 • (5/15/2000) • **81**
Sauvignon Blanc Mendocino 1997: Up front, it's redolent of butterscotch and vanilla. Flavors fan out toward fig, melon, grapefruit and fresh-cut hay, all lingering nicely on the finish. Fairly fat and forward. Drink now through 2002. • $13 • (5/15/1999) • **88**
Sauvignon Blanc Mendocino 1996 • $11 • (4/30/1998) • **85**
Sorcery Mendocino Heritage Mendocino 1997: Firm, with tarry berry, sage and cedar notes of moderate depth, turning dry and tannic. Drink now through 2004.–J.L. • $30 • (6/15/2000) • **84**
Sorcery Mendocino Mendocino Heritage 1996: Rich and detailed, with a wonderful array of concentrated currant, plum, wild berry and cherry flavors, finishing with firm tannins and a long, intricate aftertaste. A blend of Zinfandel, Petite Sirah and Syrah. Drink now through 2003.–J.L. • $28 • (5/31/1999) • **91**
Sorcery Red Mendocino Mendocino Heritage 1995 • $25 • (12/15/1997) • **85**
Syrah Mendocino 1997: Firm, with bitter chocolate, vegetal and vanilla flavors wrapped inside a solid framework of tannins. Drink now through 2003.–J.L. • $16 • (6/30/2000) • **81**
Syrah Mendocino 1996: A well-focused wine with silky tannins and finely meshed yet subtle herb, blackberry, pepper and sage notes. Plush and elegant yet restrained by its youth, it's a fine candidate for the cellar. Best from 2001 through 2006. • $18 • (2/28/1999) • **89**
Syrah Mendocino 1995 • $16 • (3/31/1998) • **87**
Syrah Mendocino Eaglepoint Ranch 1997: Cola, chocolate and black cherry flavors are soft and simple. Drink now through 2002.–J.L. • $30 • (6/15/2000) • **83**
Zinfandel Mendocino County 1992 • $10 • (10/15/1994) • **85**
Zinfandel Mendocino County 1991: Dry, tannic and earthy, with ripe cherry and plum flavors that quickly fade and a dry aftertaste. (Zinfandel retrospective tasting). Past its prime.–J.L. • $NA • (6/30/1999) • **80**
Zinfandel Mendocino County 1990 • $10 • (10/15/1992) • **85**
Zinfandel Mendocino County Pacini Vineyard 1989 • $10 • (2/29/1992) • **81**
Zinfandel Mendocino County Pacini Vineyard 1988 • $10 • (12/31/1990) • **85**
Zinfandel Mendocino Eaglepoint Ranch Mendocino Heritage 1996: Smooth, ripe and polished, with a wonderful array of plum, blackberry, black cherry, spice and hazelnut flavors. Finishes with a long, creamy aftertaste. Drink now through 2005.–J.L. • $28 • (2/28/1999) • **92**
Zinfandel Mendocino Ford & Hitzman Vineyards Mendocino Heritage 1996: Lots of complex flavors, ripe cherry, wild berry, toasty oak, all folding neatly together, finishing with firm tannins. Drink now through 2001.–J.L. • $32 • (6/30/1999) • **87**
Zinfandel Mendocino Ford & Hitzman Vineyards Mendocino Heritage 1995 • $30 • (3/31/1998) • **90**
Zinfandel Mendocino Hildreth Ranch Mendocino Heritage 1995 • $25 • (3/31/1998) • **88**
Zinfandel Mendocino McAdams Vineyard 1994 • $14 • (4/30/1997) • **89**
Zinfandel Mendocino McAdams Vineyard 1993 • $10 • (10/15/1995) • **83**
Zinfandel Mendocino Old Vines 1996: A full-bodied wine that sports plum, berry, spice and herb flavors. Tannins are firm, adding good structure to this low-keyed style of Zin—not effusive, but solid. Should improve nicely in the bottle. Drink through 2006. • $18 • (2/28/1999) • **88**
Zinfandel Mendocino Old Vines 1995 • $16 • (6/15/1998) • **80**
Zinfandel Mendocino Old Vines 1994 • $15 • (11/30/1996) • **84**
Zinfandel Mendocino Pacini Vineyard Mendocino Heritage 1997: Candied, with canned dried cherry, green bean and tinny earth flavors. Turns tannic. Drink now.–J.L. • $30 • (5/31/2000) • **81**
Zinfandel Mendocino Zaina & Hitzman Vineyards Mendocino Heritage 1997: Clumsy. Dried fruit, cherry and berry notes have hints of anise and sage, turning dry and tannic. Drink now.–J.L. • $30 • (5/31/2000) • **82**

HIGH PASS | OREGON

Cabernet Sauvignon Willamette Valley 1995: This firm, chewy red has a strong olive component but echoes some pretty berry notes. Best with hearty food. Drink through 2002.–H.S. • $12 • (12/15/1998) • **81**

Key: SS—Spectator Selection. CS—Cellar Selection. HR—Highly Recommended. $NA—Price not available. (BT)—Barrel tasting. Ⓐ—Auction Price. For a key to the tasters' initials, see "How to Use These Listings."
Dates in parentheses represent the issues in which the ratings were published.

Pinot Gris Willamette Valley 1998: Ripe and jazzy, with peach, almond and hints of spice on a generous frame. Drink now.–H.S. • $11 • (4/30/2000) • **87**
Pinot Noir Willamette Valley 1998: Youthful and bright, with focused raspberry and cherry flavors that persist on the supple finish. Lively acidity gives it a fresh balance. Drink now through 2005.–H.S. • $16 • (4/30/2000) • **87**
Pinot Noir Willamette Valley 1996: Soft and juicy, with a bit of an earthy tang to the modest plum flavors. Finishes with a pretty vanilla note. Drink now.–H.S. • $17 • (11/15/1998) • **83**
Pinot Noir Willamette Valley 1995 • $11 • (7/31/1997) • **88**
Pinot Noir Willamette Valley Bellpine NV: Racy cherry and tea-leaf flavors add interest to this simple, drink-me-now Pinot Noir.–H.S. • $9 • (11/15/1998) • **80**
Pinot Noir Willamette Valley Reserve 1995 • $15 • (7/31/1997) • **87**

HILL & THOMA WINEGROWERS | CALIFORNIA

Cabernet Sauvignon Napa Valley Clos Fontaine du Mont Reserve 1992 • $32 • (12/15/1995) • **87**
Cabernet Sauvignon Napa Valley Clos Fontaine du Mont Reserve 1991 • $32 • (12/31/1994) • **85**

HILL, WILLIAM | CALIFORNIA

Cabernet Sauvignon Napa Valley 1997: Tight and firm, with herbal leanings backed by anise, blackberry and cassis notes. Toasty oak frames the ensemble, which finishes moderately. Best from 2001 through 2008. • $20 • (10/15/1999) • **87**
Cabernet Sauvignon Napa Valley 1996: Packs a mouthful of tarry black cherry flavor onto firm structure, folding its fine-grained tannins into the finish with enough elegance to warrant cellaring. Drink through 2005.–H.S. • $16 • (11/15/1998) • **86**
Cabernet Sauvignon Napa Valley 1995 • $16 • (11/30/1997) • **86**
Cabernet Sauvignon Napa Valley 1994 • $14 • (9/30/1997) • **86**
Cabernet Sauvignon Napa Valley 1993 • $14 • (7/31/1997) • **87**
Cabernet Sauvignon Napa Valley 1992 • $14 • (12/15/1995) • **84**
Cabernet Sauvignon Napa Valley Aura 1996: Tightly framed, with cedary oak, mushroom, currant and plum flavors that firm up on the finish. Drink through 2008.–J.L. • $80 • (11/15/1999) • **88**
Cabernet Sauvignon Napa Valley Gold Label 1983 • $19 • (8/31/1987) • **89**
Cabernet Sauvignon Napa Valley Gold Label 1982 • $18 • (6/16/1986) SS • **94**
Cabernet Sauvignon Napa Valley Gold Label 1981 • $17 • (12/15/1984) • **88**
Cabernet Sauvignon Napa Valley Gold Label 1978: Hill's first, and in many ways his finest, this remains a ripe, intense, flavorful wine—if a bit past its prime. No longer exhibits the opulent fruit it did at age 10 or 12, but still quite flavorful, with meaty currant, anise, cedar and a touch of leather. (1978 California Cabernet retrospective tasting). Drink now.–J.L. • $16 • (11/15/1998) • **90**
Cabernet Sauvignon Napa Valley Reserve 1996: Ripe, with black olive, mineral, black cherry and sage notes. Focused finish is firmly tannic. Drink now.–J.L. • $36 • (9/30/1999) • **86**
Cabernet Sauvignon Napa Valley Reserve 1995: Tight and herbal, with a tough, leathery, cedary edge to the modest band of cherry and currant, it holds together but finishes starkly green. Drink through 2006.–J.L. • $27 • (2/28/1999) • **84**
Cabernet Sauvignon Napa Valley Reserve 1994 • $27 • (12/15/1997) • **88**
Cabernet Sauvignon Napa Valley Reserve 1992 • $24 • (12/15/1995) • **85**
Cabernet Sauvignon Napa Valley Reserve 1991 • $14 • (10/15/1994) • **84**
Cabernet Sauvignon Napa Valley Reserve 1990 • $24 • (11/15/1993) • **88**
Cabernet Sauvignon Napa Valley Reserve 1989 • $29 • (3/31/1993) • **87**
Cabernet Sauvignon Napa Valley Reserve 1988 • $26 • (11/15/1991) • **84**
Cabernet Sauvignon Napa Valley Reserve 1987 • $46 Ⓐ • (11/15/1990) SS • **95**
Cabernet Sauvignon Napa Valley Reserve 1986 • $29 • (11/15/1989) • **91**
Cabernet Sauvignon Napa Valley Reserve 1985 • $44 Ⓐ • (11/15/1988) • **92**
Cabernet Sauvignon Napa Valley Reserve 1984 • $18 • (4/15/1988) CS • **91**
Cabernet Sauvignon Napa Valley Silver Label 1989 • $14 • (3/31/1993) • **82**
Cabernet Sauvignon Napa Valley Silver Label 1987 • $14 • (11/15/1990) • **85**
Cabernet Sauvignon Napa Valley Silver Label 1985 • $12 • (4/30/1988) • **90**
Cabernet Sauvignon Sonoma County Silver Label 1988 • $14 • (11/15/1991) • **82**
Chardonnay Napa Valley 1997: A refreshing style, with ripe pear, lemon and hints of citrus flavors that persist on the clean, crisp finish. Drink now. –J.L. • $15 • (6/30/1999) • **87**
Chardonnay Napa Valley 1996 • $15 • (4/30/1998) • **87**
Chardonnay Napa Valley Reserve 1998: Ripe, with flavors of pear, anise and warm butter. Drink now.–J.L. • $22 • (6/30/2000) • **85**
Chardonnay Napa Valley Reserve 1997: Elegant, with delicate flavors of pear, apple and light toasted oak, some mineral notes. Drink now.–J.L. • $20 • (4/30/1999) • **87**
Chardonnay Napa Valley Reserve 1996 • $20 • (6/30/1998) • **87**
Merlot Napa Valley 1997: Simple, with a stalky green edge to the currant and berry flavors. Lacks focus. Drink now.–J.L. • $20 • (10/15/1999) • **82**
Merlot Napa Valley 1996: Herb and coffee-laced cherry flavors are supple and balanced, with mild tannins and a touch of olive. Drink now through 2002.–J.L. • $20 • (2/28/1999) • **84**
Merlot Napa Valley 1995 • $19 • (3/31/1998) • **86**
Merlot Napa Valley 1994 • $16 • (8/31/1996) • **82**
Merlot Napa Valley 1992 • $18 • (1/31/1995) • **82**
Merlot Napa Valley Premier Release 1991 • $15 • (9/15/1994) • **84**

HINMAN | OREGON

Cabernet Sauvignon Oregon 1997: On the light side for a Cabernet, but it show generous berry and mineral aromas and flavors that linger expectantly on the finish. Appealing now. Best from 2001 through 2004.–H.S. • $11 • (3/31/2000) • **85**
Pinot Gris Oregon 1997: Bright and refreshing for its pretty pear, citrus and almond flavors, finishing round and generous. Drink now.–H.S. • $11 • (12/15/1998) • **88**
Pinot Gris Oregon 1996 • $11 • (5/15/1998) • **78**
Pinot Noir Oregon 1997: Light and earthy, with a bitter, raw-herb edge to the modest raspberry and leather flavors.–H.S. • $11 • (9/30/1999) • **78**
Pinot Noir Oregon 1996 • $11 • (5/15/1998) • **83**
Pinot Noir Oregon 1994 • $10 • (1/31/1996) • **83**

HITCHING POST | CALIFORNIA

Pinot Noir Central Coast 1996 • $18 • (2/28/1998) • **84**
Pinot Noir Santa Barbara County 1994 • $14 • (12/31/1995) • **84**
Pinot Noir Santa Barbara County Highliner 1997: Ripe, with vibrant black cherry, berry and spicy Pinot Noir flavors, it's complex, elegant and concentrated, with a rich aftertaste. Drink through 2006.–J.L. • $40 • (9/15/1999) • **88**
Pinot Noir Santa Barbara County Sierra Madre and Gold Coast Vineyards 1993 • $14 • (12/31/1995) • **86**
Pinot Noir Santa Maria Valley 1994 • $18 • (9/15/1996) • **83**
Pinot Noir Santa Maria Valley 1993 • $16 • (10/15/1995) • **87**
Pinot Noir Santa Maria Valley Bien Nacido Vineyard 1997: Peppery and herbal, with flavors of leather, plum and cherry, with polished tannins on the finish. Drink now through 2003.–J.L. • $25 • (9/15/1999) • **86**
Pinot Noir Santa Maria Valley Bien Nacido Vineyard 1995 • $25 • (5/15/1997) • **88**
Pinot Noir Santa Maria Valley Bien Nacido Vineyard 1994 • $25 • (9/15/1996) • **89**
Pinot Noir Santa Maria Valley Bien Nacido Vineyard 1993 • $25 • (10/15/1995) • **88**
Pinot Noir Santa Maria Valley Julia's Vineyard 1997: Has some sharp edges to the herbal and spicy cherry notes, but finishes with a promising burst of focused berry flavors. Best now through 2004.–J.L. • $30 • (9/15/1999) • **86**
Pinot Noir Santa Maria Valley Sierra Madre & Riverbench Vineyards 1997: Elegant, with spicy herb, tea and black cherry, supple and polished, with a complex aftertaste. Drink now through 2003.–J.L. • $25 • (9/15/1999) • **86**
Pinot Noir Santa Maria Valley Sierra Madre & Riverbench Vineyards 1995 • $20 • (5/15/1997) • **87**
Pinot Noir Santa Ynez Valley Sanford & Benedict Vineyard 1997: Tight and subdued, with a restrained core of earthy black cherry and wild berry. Needs a little time to show its stuff. Drink through 2007.–J.L. • $30 • (9/15/1999) • **87**
Pinot Noir Santa Ynez Valley Sanford & Benedict Vineyard 1995 • $30 • (1/31/1998) • **90**
Pinot Noir Santa Ynez Valley Sanford & Benedict Vineyard 1994 • $30 • (1/31/1997) • **86**
Pinot Noir Santa Ynez Valley Sanford & Benedict Vineyard 1993 • $25 • (10/15/1995) • **88**
Syrah Santa Ynez Valley Fess Parker Vineyard 1996: Somewhat herbal, with hints of blackberry, black cherry and stewed plum. A touch of cola rounds off an otherwise drying finish. Drink now through 2004. • $18 • (11/30/1998) • **85**
Syrah Santa Ynez Valley Rodney's Vineyard 1997: An extreme style that's racy, with a vegetal streak running through the dried cherry, tomato and vinegar flavors.–J.L. • $20 • (12/31/1999) • **77**
Zinfandel California 1995 • $14 • (4/30/1997) • **87**

HOBBS, PAUL | CALIFORNIA

Cabernet Sauvignon Howell Mountain Liparita Vineyard 1995: Rough-and-tumble now, with firm, earthy tannins, time should help soften and bring into focus the earthy currant, sage, mineral and mint notes. Best from 2001 through 2006.–J.L. • $45 • (4/30/1999) • **87**

Cabernet Sauvignon Howell Mountain Liparita Vineyard 1994 • $45 • (10/31/1997) • **91**

Cabernet Sauvignon Howell Mountain Liparita Vineyard 1993 • $35 • (6/15/1997) • **88**

Cabernet Sauvignon Howell Mountain Liparita Vineyard 1992 • $35 • (5/15/1996) • **84**

Cabernet Sauvignon Napa Valley Carneros Hyde Vineyard 1996: Soft and polished, with delicate layers of earthy tobacco, cedar, tar and ripe berry and black cherry flavors that finish with an impressive push. Tannins are ripe and well integrated. Drink now through 2004.–J.L. • $45 • (11/15/1999) • **89**

Cabernet Sauvignon Napa Valley Carneros Hyde Vineyard 1994 • $40 • (10/31/1997) • **89**

Cabernet Sauvignon Napa Valley Carneros Hyde Vineyard 1993 • $30 • (11/30/1996) • **89**

Cabernet Sauvignon Napa Valley Carneros Hyde Vineyard 1992 • $30 • (12/15/1995) HR • **93**

Cabernet Sauvignon Napa Valley Carneros Hyde Vineyard 1991 • $30 • (10/31/1994) HR • **91**

Chardonnay Russian River Valley 1998: Lots of ripe, lively pear, nectarine and peach flavors, turning clean and spicy, with a touch of earthiness. Drink now through 2004.–J.L. • $35 • (6/15/2000) • **87**

Chardonnay Russian River Valley Walker Station Vineyard 1997: Loads of ripe, rich, complex, concentrated fruit flavors, with tiers of spicy green apple, pear, melon, fig and apricot. Holds its focus on a long, rich aftertaste. Drink now through 2002.–J.L. • $50 • (7/31/1999) • **93**

Chardonnay Sonoma Mountain Richard Dinner Vineyard 1997: A sleek, elegant, polished style, packed with rich, creamy pear, fig, spice, apricot and toasty oak flavors. Sharply focused and rich on the finish. Drink now through 2003.–J.L. • $45 • (7/31/1999) • **92**

Chardonnay Sonoma Mountain Richard Dinner Vineyard 1996 • $39 • (6/30/1998) • **91**

Chardonnay Sonoma Mountain Richard Dinner Vineyard Cuvée Augustina 1997: A touch earthy, with leafy pear and tangerine flavors, finishing with a cedary oak edge. Drink now.–J.L. • $60 • (6/15/2000) • **87**

Chardonnay Sonoma Mountain Richard Dinner Vineyard Cuvée Agustina 1996: Elegant, with a pretty medley of ripe pear, spice, fig and melon, picking up hints of hazelnut and toasty, buttery oak. Finishes with a long stream of complex flavors. Drink now through 2002.–J.L. • $60 • (4/30/1999) • **92**

Chardonnay Sonoma Valley Kunde Vineyard 1998: Complex, with ripe, rich pear, vanilla, hazelnut and spice notes, turning creamy and long on the finish. Drink now.–J.L. • $42 • (6/15/2000) • **88**

Chardonnay Sonoma Valley Kunde Vineyard 1997: Built on a frame of toasty oak, the core of pear, apricot, melon and fig flavors is rich and concentrated. Turns smoky and complex on the finish, where the spicy attributes are distinctive. Drink now through 2002.–J.L. • $36 • (7/31/1999) • **93**

Chardonnay Sonoma Valley Kunde Vineyard 1996 • $35 • (6/30/1998) • **91**

Merlot Napa Valley Michael Black Vineyard 1996: Medium-weight, with a band of cedary cherry and currant of moderate proportion, picking up more complexity on the finish. Drink through 2004.–J.L. • $38 • (10/15/1999) • **86**

Pinot Noir Napa Valley Carneros Hyde Vineyard 1995: Tart, a touch green and stemmy, with lots of earthy nuances and just a glimmer of cherry and strawberry. Drink now through 2001.–J.L. • $24 • (9/15/1998) • **81**

Pinot Noir Napa Valley Carneros Hyde Vineyard 1994 • $24 • (1/31/1997) • **89**

Pinot Noir Napa Valley Carneros Hyde Vineyard 1993 • $23 • (5/15/1996) • **84**

Pinot Noir Napa Valley Carneros Hyde Vineyard 1992 • $24 • (3/31/1995) • **81**

Pinot Noir Napa Valley Carneros Hyde Vineyard 1991 • $25 • (2/28/1994) • **86**

HOGUE | WASHINGTON

Cabernet Franc Yakima Valley Genesis 1994 • $14 • (1/31/1998) • **82**

Cabernet Sauvignon Columbia Valley 1993 • $15 • (11/15/1996) SS • **88**

Cabernet Sauvignon Columbia Valley 1992 • $15 • (9/15/1996) • **87**

Cabernet Sauvignon Columbia Valley 1991 • $14 • (6/15/1995) • **85**

Cabernet Sauvignon Columbia Valley Barrel Select 1996: A bit lighter and more refined than most, with pretty red plum and currant flavors that persist on the finish. Drink now through 2003.–H.S. • $15 • (8/31/1999) • **87**

Cabernet Sauvignon Columbia Valley Barrel Select 1995: Light for a Cabernet, with pretty herb, cola and cherry flavors on a sturdy frame. Drink now.–H.S. • $15 • (9/15/1998) • **82**

Cabernet Sauvignon Columbia Valley Barrel Select 1994 • $15 • (3/31/1998) • **86**

Cabernet Sauvignon Columbia Valley Barrel Select 1993 • $14 • (9/15/1997) • **84**

Cabernet Sauvignon Columbia Valley Champoux Vineyard Genesis 1996: Splendidly aromatic, very firm in texture, with a nice core of black cherry and eucalyptus flavors that keep forging on through the chewy finish. Needs cellaring to soften the edges a little. Best after 2002.–H.S. • $23 • (5/31/1999) • **88**

Cabernet Sauvignon Columbia Valley Genesis 1994 • $21 • (1/31/1998) • **81**

Cabernet Sauvignon Columbia Valley Proprietor's Selection 1996: Firm in texture, lively in flavor, with tasty currant, plum and spice flavors and a nice tinge of mint on the bordering-on-crisp finish. Best after 2001.–H.S. • $40 • (12/31/1999) • **89**

Cabernet Sauvignon Columbia Valley Reserve 1996: Lithe and spicy, with pretty cinnamon-scented berry and leather flavors wrapped in a layer of fine-grained tannins. Drink now through 2002.–H.S. • $30 • (9/30/1999) • **85**

Cabernet Sauvignon Columbia Valley Reserve 1995: Ripe and round, a generous wine with blackberry and currant flavors, softening on the finish. Drink now.–H.S. • $30 • (9/15/1998) • **85**

Cabernet Sauvignon Washington 1990 • $14 • (9/30/1994) • **85**

Cabernet Sauvignon Washington 1989 • $12 • (11/15/1991) • **84**

Cabernet Sauvignon Washington 1988 • $12 • (3/31/1992) • **88**

Cabernet Sauvignon Washington Reserve 1992 • $18 • (9/15/1997) • **87**

Cabernet Sauvignon Washington Reserve 1991 • $20 • (9/15/1996) • **82**

Cabernet Sauvignon Washington Reserve 1990 • $18 • (9/30/1995) • **90**

Cabernet Sauvignon Washington Reserve 1989 • $18 • (9/30/1994) • **86**

Cabernet Sauvignon Washington Reserve 1988 • $18 • (11/15/1991) • **89**

Cabernet Sauvignon Washington Reserve 1987 • $19 • (3/31/1991) • **88**

Cabernet Sauvignon Washington Reserve 1985 • $18 • (10/15/1989) • **81**

Cabernet-Merlot Columbia Valley 1997: On the lighter side, with herb-scented cherry and spice flavors on a simple frame. An amiable wine for current drinking.–H.S. • $9 • (5/31/1999) • **84**

Cabernet-Merlot Columbia Valley 1996: On the lighter side, with pretty raspberry and tobacco notes running through the spicy flavors. Drink now.–H.S. • $9 • (8/31/1998) • **84**

Cabernet-Merlot Columbia Valley 1995 • $10 • (9/15/1997) • **85**

Cabernet-Merlot Columbia Valley 1994 • $10 • (9/15/1996) • **81**

Chardonnay Columbia Valley 1998: Lean and lively, with a metallic edge to the pear and mineral flavors. Finishes with a nice touch of creaminess. Drink now.–H.S. • $10 • (6/30/2000) • **85**

Chardonnay Columbia Valley 1997: From Washington, here's a pretty Chardonnay at a budget-minded price. Light in texture, it offers bright green apple and spice flavors that linger nicely on the balanced finish. Drink now through 2001.–H.S. • $9 • (6/15/1999) • **87**

Chardonnay Columbia Valley Barrel Select 1998: Smooth, polished and brimming with pretty pear, nutmeg and vanilla flavors. Picks up nice peach notes on the long, charming finish. Drink now.–H.S. • $14 • (5/15/2000) • **88**

Chardonnay Columbia Valley Barrel Select 1997: Ripe and spicy on a crisp frame, this lively mouthful of apple, honey and citrus flavors drips more honey on the long, elegant finish. Drink now through 2003.–H.S. • $14 • (6/15/1999) • **90**

Chardonnay Columbia Valley Barrel Select 1996 • $14 • (3/31/1998) • **88**

Chardonnay Washington 1996 • $9 • (6/15/1998) • **88**

Chardonnay Yakima Valley Sunnyside Vineyard Genesis 1997: Unusually spicy and exotic for a Washington Chardonnay, offering layers of peach, mango, oak and smoke on a wide-open frame. On the oaky side, but it comes together with balance on the finish. Drink now through 2002.–H.S. • $20 • (5/31/1999) • **88**

Chardonnay Yakima Valley Crawford Vineyard Genesis 1996 • $19 • (1/31/1998) • **84**

Chenin Blanc Columbia Valley 1998: Soft and off-dry, with pretty melon and peach flavors that linger on the generous finish, this lovely Washington white provides tasty sipping that belies its affordable price. Ready now.–H.S. • $7 • (6/30/1999) • **86**

Chenin Blanc Columbia Valley 1997 • $7 • (6/30/1998) • **80**

Chenin Blanc Columbia Valley 1996 • $7 • (9/15/1997) • **85**

Chenin Blanc Columbia Valley Dry 1997 • $7 • (6/30/1998) • **81**

Chenin Blanc Columbia Valley Dry 1996 • $7 • (9/15/1997) • **84**

Key: SS—Spectator Selection. CS—Cellar Selection. HR—Highly Recommended. $NA—Price not available. (BT)—Barrel tasting. Ⓐ—Auction Price.
For a key to the tasters' initials, see "How to Use These Listings."
Dates in parentheses represent the issues in which the ratings were published.

Chenin Blanc Columbia Valley Dry Genesis 1997: Ripe and toasty, with fig, tobacco and earth flavors that linger on the polished finish, which has honey notes. Drink now through 2002.–H.S. • $13 • (6/30/1999) • **86**

Fumé Blanc Columbia Valley 1998: Fresh and appealing for its easy-drinking apple and lime flavors, finishing light and juicy. Drink now.–H.S. • $8 • (8/31/1999) • **85**

Fumé Blanc Columbia Valley 1997: Light and floral, with pretty apple and herb flavors that linger on the pleasantly balanced finish. Drink now.–H.S. • $8 • (10/31/1998) • **83**

Fumé Blanc Columbia Valley 1996 • $9 • (9/15/1997) • **87**

Gewürztraminer Columbia Valley 1998: Soft, bright and enticing, delivering textbook Gewürztraminer flavors of apple and rose petal, with a hint of litchi, on a fresh frame, this Washington offering is a reliable and delicious choice at a real value price. Drink now.–H.S. • $7 • (9/30/1999) • **86**

Gewürztraminer Columbia Valley 1997 • $7 • (6/30/1998) • **84**

Gewürztraminer Columbia Valley 1996 • $7 • (9/15/1997) • **84**

Gewürztraminer Washington Dry Genesis 1997: Dry and distinctly floral, with a decadent edge to the melon and apple. Drink now.–H.S. • $13 • (6/15/1999) • **80**

Johannisberg Riesling Columbia Valley 1998: Soft and ripe, offering a nice range of apricot and spice flavors that linger crisply on the fresh finish. Drink now through 2001.–H.S. • $7 • (9/15/1999) • **85**

Johannisberg Riesling Columbia Valley 1996 • $7 • (9/15/1997) • **84**

Johannisberg Riesling Columbia Valley Dry 1996 • $7 • (9/15/1997) • **82**

Johannisberg Riesling Washington 1997 • $7 • (6/30/1998) • **86**

Lemberger Columbia Valley 1994 • $10 • (9/15/1996) • **82**

Lemberger Columbia Valley 1992 • $9 • (9/30/1995) • **82**

Lemberger Columbia Valley Blue Franc Genesis 1996: Has lots of pretty plum and berry character on a light, supple frame. An earthy, burnt note on the nose is covered by the fruit after a few sips. Drink now through 2002.–H.S. • $13 • (6/15/1999) • **86**

Lemberger Columbia Valley Blue Franc Genesis 1995 • $12 • (1/31/1998) • **85**

Lemberger Yakima Valley 1993 • $9 • (9/30/1995) • **82**

Lemberger Yakima Valley 1991 • $10 • (12/31/1993) • **85**

Merlot Columbia Valley 1994 • $15 • (11/15/1996) SS • **89**

Merlot Columbia Valley 1993 • $15 • (9/15/1996) • **85**

Merlot Columbia Valley 1992 • $14 • (6/15/1995) • **86**

Merlot Columbia Valley 1991 • $14 • (9/30/1994) • **84**

Merlot Columbia Valley Barrel Select 1997: Firm and a bit chewy for the light cherry and herb flavors, finishing with a spicy edge. Drink now through 2002.–H.S. • $15 • (5/15/2000) • **85**

Merlot Columbia Valley Barrel Select 1996: Soft, supple and appealing for its smoky cherry and tobacco flavors. Finishes with soft, grainy tannins. Drink now.–H.S. • $15 • (6/15/1999) • **85**

Merlot Columbia Valley Barrel Select 1995 • $15 • (3/31/1998) • **85**

Merlot Columbia Valley Genesis 1995: Supple, spicy and silky, distinctive for the coffee and tobacco tones shading the subtle black cherry and currant flavors. Has a prunelike note on the rich finish. Drink now through 2003.–H.S. • $23 • (5/31/1999) • **88**

Merlot Columbia Valley Genesis 1994 • $21 • (1/31/1998) • **85**

Merlot Columbia Valley Reserve 1996: Firm in texture, but light enough to show off its pretty blackberry and delicate toasty flavors. Has some style, just needs time. Best after 2000.–H.S. • $30 • (9/30/1999) • **88**

Merlot Washington 1990 • $12 • (1/31/1993) • **86**

Merlot Washington 1989 • $12 • (10/15/1991) SS • **92**

Merlot Washington 1986 • $12 • (4/15/1989) • **85**

Merlot Washington 1985 • $12 • (11/15/1987) • **80**

Merlot Washington Reserve 1993 • $18 • (10/15/1997) • **85**

Merlot Washington Reserve 1992 • $20 • (9/15/1996) • **88**

Merlot Washington Reserve 1991 • $18 • (9/30/1995) • **89**

Merlot Washington Reserve 1990 • $18 • (9/30/1994) • **87**

Merlot Washington Reserve 1989 • $18 • (6/15/1993) • **88**

Merlot Washington Reserve 1988 • $18 • (11/15/1991) • **90**

Merlot Washington Reserve 1987 • $19 • (3/31/1991) • **89**

Pinot Gris Columbia Valley 1998: Bright, fresh and appealing; like biting into a juicy nectarine, with hints of melon and citrus. Drink now.–H.S. • $8 • (8/31/1999) • **87**

Pinot Gris Yakima Valley Genesis 1998: Has a raw edge, but the basic pear and melon flavors are pretty enough to carry it. Drink now.–H.S. • $13 • (12/31/1999) • **83**

Riesling Columbia Valley Late Harvest 1998: A frankly sweet wine sporting a crisp, lemony side to the light peach and apricot flavors, the ensemble gaining intensity on the balanced finish. This late-harvest Riesling isn't quite a dessert wine, but it's certainly sweet and flavorful. Good price, too. Drink now through 2003.–H.S. • $8 • (6/30/1999) SS • **89**

Riesling Yakima Valley Schwartzman Vineyard Genesis 1997: Lacks the freshness one usually expects from Riesling, with floral and fruit cocktail flavors.–H.S. • $13 • (6/15/1999) • **78**

Sauvignon Blanc Columbia Valley Genesis Burgess Vineyard 1998: An unusual style, offering herb and mineral notes that mingle with spicy oak character. Finishes soft and round. Needs time to come together. Best after 2000.–H.S. • $15 • (12/31/1999) • **84**

Sémillon Columbia Valley 1997: Washington strikes again—this time with this delicious and affordable Sémillon. It's a soft, broad white, offering a generous portion of fig, citrus and walnut flavors that persist nicely on the round finish. Drink now through 2004.–H.S. • $7 • (5/31/1999) • **85**

Sémillon Columbia Valley 1996 • $8 • (6/15/1998) • **86**

Sémillon Columbia Valley Genesis 1997: Lean, lithe and distinctive for its citrusy pear, fig and tobacco flavors. Finishes with a juicy balance (making it an ideal match for fish) and a touch of sweet oak. Drink now through 2003.–H.S. • $13 • (5/31/1999) • **88**

Sémillon Yakima Valley Genesis 1996 • $12 • (3/31/1998) • **85**

Sémillon-Chardonnay Columbia Valley 1997: Bright and appealing for its hay-scented fig and citrus flavors that hang on the finish. Pretty to drink sooner rather than later. Try now through 2000.–H.S. • $8 • (6/15/1999) • **85**

Sémillon-Chardonnay Columbia Valley 1996 • $9 • (3/31/1998) • **82**

Sémillon-Chardonnay Columbia Valley 1993 • $8 • (4/30/1995) • **85**

Syrah Columbia Valley Barrel Select 1997: Ripe and round, immensely appealing for its generous plum and blackberry flavors that persist on the long, beautifully balanced finish. Impressive for its balance and sense of refinement. Drink now through 2007.–H.S. • $15 • (9/15/1999) • **90**

Syrah Columbia Valley Genesis 1996: A generous, almost lavish mouthful of plum, black cherry, blackberry and spice flavors that remain rich and focused through the wide-open finish. Delicious now.–H.S. • $15 • (5/31/1999) • **91**

Syrah Columbia Valley Genesis 1995 • $14 • (1/31/1998) • **87**

White Riesling Late Harvest Columbia Valley 1997: Sweet, with tangy orange peel and floral notes around the peach and apple core.–H.S. • $7 • (9/15/1998) • **83**

White Riesling Late Harvest Columbia Valley 1996 • $7 • (9/15/1997) SS • **90**

White Riesling Late Harvest Columbia Valley 1994 • $6 • (8/31/1995) • **88**

White Riesling Late Harvest Columbia Valley 1993 • $6 • (9/30/1994) • **85**

HOMEWOOD | CALIFORNIA

Cabernet Sauvignon Alexander Valley 1990 • $14 • (11/30/1996) • **88**

Cabernet Sauvignon Alexander Valley 1989 • $14 • (11/15/1992) • **80**

Cabernet Sauvignon Alexander Valley 1988 • $13 • (11/15/1992) • **83**

Zinfandel Dry Creek Valley Quinn Vineyard 1993 • $12 • (4/30/1996) • **80**

Zinfandel Dry Creek Valley Quinn Vineyard 1992 • $10 • (3/31/1994) • **79**

Zinfandel Sonoma Valley 110-Year-Old Vines 1992 • $12 • (3/31/1994) • **83**

HONIG | CALIFORNIA

Cabernet Sauvignon Napa Valley 1997: Elegant and understated, with attractive ripe black cherry, plum, currant and herb-tinged flavors building momentum, gaining nuance. Drink now through 2007.–J.L. • $25 • (3/31/2000) • **88**

Cabernet Sauvignon Napa Valley 1996: A drink-me-now style that's ripe and plush, with complex oak, black currant, cherry, plum, cola and dill flavors that extend on the ripe, fleshy finish. Drink now through 2003 .–J.L. • $22 • (6/15/1999) • **88**

Cabernet Sauvignon Napa Valley 1995 • $22 • (5/15/1998) • **89**

Cabernet Sauvignon Napa Valley 1988 • $14 • (8/31/1992) • **83**

Sauvignon Blanc Napa Valley Reserve 1996 • $17 • (5/15/1998) • **84**

HOODSPORT | WASHINGTON

Cabernet Sauvignon Washington Limited Artist Edition 1994 • $21 • (9/15/1996) • **85**

Cabernet Sauvignon Yakima Valley Reserve 1996 • $17 • (3/31/1998) • **83**

Chardonnay Yakima Valley 1998: Bright and generous. A mouthful of pure pear and spice flavors on a wide-open frame. Not heavy, but nicely focused. Finishes smoothly. Drink now through 2003 .–H.S. • $11 • (3/31/2000) • **87**

Chardonnay Yakima Valley 1997: Ripe and supple, with pretty tropical fruit, fig and floral flavors that echo nicely on the finish. Drink now through 2002.–H.S. • $11 • (6/30/1999) • **86**

Chardonnay Yakima Valley Reserve 1998: Smooth and silky, with pretty pear and spice flavors mingling with floral and citrus touches on the finish. Drink now through 2003 .–H.S. • $11 • (3/31/2000) • **88**

HOODSPORT

Chenin Blanc Yakima Valley 1997: Light, dry and pretty for its apple, pear and floral flavors. Drink now.–H.S. • $9 • (6/30/1999) • **84**

Gewürztraminer Yakima Valley 1997: Smells and tastes strongly of rose petals, with light citrus and grape notes arriving to balance the finish. Barely off-dry. Drink now.–H.S. • $9 • (11/15/1998) • **86**

Johannisberg Riesling Yakima Valley 1998: Sweet and light, with a smooth texture and modest apple and cream flavors. Drink now.–H.S. • $9 • (9/30/1999) • **80**

Lemberger Washington 1992 • $8 • (9/30/1994) • **73**

Lemberger-Cab Yakima Valley 1997: Light in color and body but fragrant and flavorful, with pretty strawberry and floral aromas and flavors that linger impressively on the delicate finish. Drink now through 2002.–H.S. • $11 • (6/30/1999) • **88**

Lemberger-Cab Yakima Valley 1996 • $11 • (3/31/1998) • **83**

Lemberger-Cab Yakima Valley 1995 • $11 • (8/31/1997) • **86**

Lemberger-Cab Washington 1994 • $9 • (9/30/1996) • **85**

Lemberger-Cab Washington 1993 • $10 • (9/30/1995) • **77**

Merlot Washington 1994 • $11 • (9/15/1996) • **82**

Merlot Washington 1992 • $11 • (9/30/1994) • **80**

Merlot Yakima Valley 1997: On the light side, with pretty strawberry, raspberry and herbal-floral notes competing for attention on a smooth, delicately rounded frame. Sleek already. Drink through 2002.–H.S. • $17 • (6/30/1999) • **88**

Sauvignon Blanc Yakima Valley 1996 • $9 • (11/30/1997) • **85**

Sémillon Yakima Valley 1998: Smooth and supple, with lovely honey-scented pear, fig and tobacco flavors that linger on the generous finish. Drink now through 2003.–H.S. • $9 • (3/31/2000) • **88**

Sémillon Yakima Valley 1996: Soft and odd, with juniper and leaf notes that detract from the modest pear character.–H.S. • $9 • (8/31/1999) • **78**

HOP KILN | CALIFORNIA

Marty Griffin's Big Red Reserve Sonoma County NV • $8 • (9/15/1994) • **87**

Marty Griffin's Big Red Sonoma County 1994 • $10 • (9/15/1996) • **83**

Marty Griffin's Big Red Sonoma County 1992 • $9 • (2/28/1995) • **81**

Marty Griffin's Big Red Sonoma County 1991 • $8 • (9/15/1993) • **88**

Marty Griffin's Big Red Russian River Valley 1990 • $8 • (4/30/1993) • **81**

Marty Griffin's Big Red Russian River Valley 1988 • $8 • (11/30/1990) • **85**

Primitivo Russian River Valley 1995 • $22 • (3/31/1997) • **87**

Primitivo Russian River Valley 1992 • $18 • (2/28/1995) • **85**

Primitivo Russian River Valley 1985 • $12 • (3/15/1988) • **80**

Primitivo Russian River Valley Reserve 1985 • $12 • (6/15/1989) • **90**

Primitivo Sonoma County 1997: Tightly wound, with a crisp, tannic edge to the raspberry and blackberry flavors. Drink now.–J.L. • $22 • (6/30/1999) • **87**

Primitivo Sonoma County 1996 • $22 • (6/15/1998) • **84**

Primitivo Sonoma County 1994 • $18 • (10/15/1996) • **81**

Primitivo Sonoma County 1993 • $18 • (10/15/1995) • **86**

Primitivo Sonoma County 1991 • $15 • (9/15/1993) • **87**

Primitivo Sonoma County 1990 • $15 • (10/15/1992) • **85**

Primitivo Sonoma County 1988 • $14 • (12/31/1990) • **89**

Zinfandel Russian River Valley 1992 • $14 • (6/15/1995) • **86**

Zinfandel Russian River Valley 1988 • $12 • (12/15/1990) • **88**

Zinfandel Russian River Valley 1986 • $10 • (6/15/1989) • **85**

Zinfandel Russian River Valley M. Griffin Vineyards 1994 • $15 • (10/15/1996) • **85**

Zinfandel Sonoma County 1997: Lots of ripe, juicy cherry and wild berry flavors of medium weight, with a spicy aftertaste. Drink now through 2001.–J.L. • $18 • (5/15/1999) • **87**

Zinfandel Sonoma County 1996 • $16 • (6/15/1998) • **85**

Zinfandel Sonoma County 1995 • $16 • (3/31/1997) • **90**

Zinfandel Sonoma County 1991 • $12 • (10/15/1994) • **84**

Zinfandel Sonoma County 1990 • $12 • (10/15/1992) • **85**

HOPE FARMS | CALIFORNIA

Cabernet Sauvignon Paso Robles 1992 • $13 • (11/30/1996) • **85**

Cabernet Sauvignon Paso Robles 1990 • $9 • (11/15/1994) • **84**

Cabernet Sauvignon Paso Robles 1989 • $16 • (11/15/1993) • **84**

Claret Paso Robles 1991 • $10 • (11/15/1994) • **81**

Zinfandel Paso Robles NV • $7 • (9/30/1993) • **84**

Key: SS—Spectator Selection. CS—Cellar Selection. HR—Highly Recommended. $NA—Price not available. (BT)—Barrel tasting. (A)—Auction Price. For a key to the tasters' initials, see "How to Use These Listings."
Dates in parentheses represent the issues in which the ratings were published.

HOPKINS | CONNECTICUT

Chardonnay Western Connecticut Highlands 1997: There's a little layer of toast over the crisp apple flavors. Light-bodied, finishing bright and clean. Drink now.–T.M. • $15 • (3/31/2000) • **82**

Chardonnay Western Connecticut Highlands Ascot Reserve 1997: Elegant pear and snappy green apple run through this light-bodied, clean and fresh Chardonnay. Drink now.–T.M. • $18 • (3/31/2000) • **83**

HORIZON'S EDGE | WASHINGTON

Merlot Columbia Valley Reserve 1995: Crisp and firm in texture, with modest berry and anise flavors. Hints at tobacco and mint on the slightly chewy finish. Drink now.–H.S. • $19 • (9/15/1998) • **86**

Muscat Canelli Yakima Valley 1997: Off-dry, soft in texture, with pretty litchi and pear flavors in modest proportions. Drink now.–H.S. • $9 • (9/15/1998) • **84**

Muscat Canelli Yakima Valley Nouveaux Riche 1997: Pale in color and a bit fizzy, with perfumy flavors. Drink now.–H.S. • $9/375 ml. • (9/30/1998) • **80**

Muscat Canelli Yakima Valley Nouveaux Riche 1993 • $10/375 ml. • (9/30/1995) • **81**

HORTON | VIRGINIA

Cabernet Franc Orange County 1996: Meaty and leathery flavors and aromas are the hallmarks of this average wine. Also contains 17 percent Cabernet, 5 percent Touriga Nacional and 3 percent Tannat.–K.M. • $12 • (8/31/1998) • **77**

Cabernet Franc Orange County 1995: Stewy-tasting, with some plum and berry flavors, but ends up a bit dried out. Also contains Cabernet Sauvignon, Tannat and Tinta Cão.–K.M. • $12 • (8/31/1998) • **78**

Cabernet Franc Orange County 1994 • $12 • (4/30/1997) • **86**

Côtes d'Orange Orange County 1995: A mature, unusual red, with pronounced cherry, cola and spice flavors and earthy-foxy overtones. Not bad, but not our cup of tea. A blend of Grenache, Mourvèdre, Tinta Cão, Syrah, Touriga Nacional and Viognier. • $15 • (8/31/1998) • **78**

Dionysus Orange County 1995: Distinguished by coffeelike aromas and flavors, with some plum and berry notes. A thick, full-bodied red that finishes on a spicy note. A blend of Touriga Nacional, Tinta Cão and Cabernet Sauvignon.–K.M. • $25 • (8/31/1998) • **83**

Norton Orange County 1996: Fruity and lively, if overdone, with a distinctive charred note. Just doesn't hang together in the end. A blend of Norton, Cabernet Sauvignon and Mourvèdre.–K.M. • $11 • (8/31/1998) • **73**

Norton Orange County 1995: Leathery aromas and flavors dominate this red wine. Tired and overblown. A blend of Norton, Touriga Nacional, Mourvèdre and Cabernet Franc.–K.M. • $11 • (7/31/1998) • **74**

Port Orange County 1995: Shows plum and leather flavors, with a distinctive earthy note. Doesn't quite mesh in the end.–K.M. • $20 • (8/31/1998) • **77**

Viognier Orange County 1997: Cloying flavors and aromas make this awkward. Candied banana and insipid fruit-cocktail flavors dominate.–K.M. • $20 • (7/31/1998) • **74**

Viognier Orange County Reserve 1997: There's nothing resembling Viognier in this awkward, overblown wine. Shows almost no fruit.–K.M. • $30 • (8/31/1998) • **73**

HOSMER | NEW YORK

Chardonnay Cayuga Lake Limited Release 1997: Vanilla, pie crust and cooked fruit flavors are lush but a bit dull in this soft white. Gentle and harmonious. Drink now.–T.M. • $16 • (1/01/2000) • **82**

HOWELL MOUNTAIN VINEYARD | CALIFORNIA

Zinfandel Howell Mountain 1995 • $16 • (8/31/1997) • **89**

Zinfandel Howell Mountain 1994 • $15 • (2/28/1997) • **88**

Zinfandel Howell Mountain 1988 • $11 • (10/15/1992) • **74**

Zinfandel Howell Mountain Beatty Ranch 1997: Tight, firm and fleshy, with a complex array of sage, anise, mineral and spice. Finishes with a tightly focused core of flavorful tannins. Drink through 2004–J.L. • $NA • (6/15/1999) • **91**

Zinfandel Howell Mountain Black-Sears Vineyard 1997: What a mouthful of Zin. Brimming with ripe, plush, lush cherry, wild berry, cedar and spice, it's wall-to-wall Zinfandel, with amazing depth and complexity. Drink now through 2004.–J.L. • $NA • (6/15/1999) • **93**

Zinfandel Howell Mountain Old Vine 1997: Tightly focused, rich and complex, with peppery, earthy cherry, wild berry, anise, sage and cedar flavors. Finishes with firm but flavorful tannins. Drink now through 2003.–J.L. • $24 • (6/15/1999) • **91**

HUNTER, ROBERT | CALIFORNIA

Brut de Noirs Sonoma Valley 1992 • $25 • (11/30/1997) • **87**
Brut de Noirs Sonoma Valley 1991 • $25 • (9/15/1995) • **85**
Brut de Noirs Sonoma Valley Extended Tirage 1993: Toast, hazelnut and citrus flavors start this off, then fan out to include green apple and herbs, couched in creamy texture. Fresh, moderate finish. Drink now. • $28 • (9/15/1999) • **88**
Brut de Noirs Sonoma Valley Extended Tirage 1992 • $25 • (6/15/1998) • **88**

HUNTINGTON | CALIFORNIA

Cabernet Sauvignon Alexander Valley 1989 • $8 • (8/31/1992) • **68**
Cabernet Sauvignon California 1996: Simple, with light tea, cola, cherry and charred oak. Finishes slightly coarse. Drink now.–H.S. • $10 • (11/15/1998) • **78**
Merlot California 1996: Basic, with ripe, zingy black cherry and herb notes. Tannins are chewy. Drink now.–J.L. • $10 • (12/15/1998) • **81**
Merlot North Coast 1997: Simple, but it shows a pleasant range of currant and toasted oak flavors before finishing firm. Drink through 2003.–J.L. • $10 • (10/15/1999) • **82**
Sauvignon Blanc California 1997: Kicks off with herb and floral notes, then settles in on the palate with fig, melon and subtle citrus flavors. Not a blockbuster, it's a more delicate rendering of this grape. Clean, fresh finish. Drink now. • $9 • (5/31/1999) • **85**

HUSCH | CALIFORNIA

Cabernet Sauvignon Mendocino 1996: Tightly structured, featuring currant, wild berry and anise flavors that remain focused on the finish. Tannins are firm. Drink through 2004–J.L. • $17 • (10/15/1999) • **84**
Cabernet Sauvignon Mendocino La Ribera Vineyards 1994 • $15 • (10/15/1997) • **88**
Cabernet Sauvignon Mendocino La Ribera Vineyards 1993 • $15 • (9/30/1997) • **83**
Cabernet Sauvignon Mendocino La Ribera Vineyards 1992 • $8 • (11/15/1994) • **83**
Cabernet Sauvignon Mendocino La Ribera Vineyards 1991 • $14 • (3/31/1995) • **84**
Cabernet Sauvignon Mendocino La Ribera Vineyards 1990 • $14 • (8/31/1993) • **88**
Cabernet Sauvignon Mendocino La Ribera Vineyards 1989 • $8 • (11/15/1993) • **79**
Cabernet Sauvignon Mendocino La Ribera Vineyards 1988 • $12 • (6/30/1991) • **86**
Cabernet Sauvignon Mendocino La Ribera Vineyards 1987 • $12 • (12/15/1997) • **89**
Cabernet Sauvignon Mendocino La Ribera Vineyards 1986 • $12 • (2/15/1990) • **84**
Cabernet Sauvignon Mendocino La Ribera Vineyards 1984 • $10 • (12/31/1987) • **73**
Cabernet Sauvignon Mendocino North Field Select 1991 • $18 • (3/31/1995) • **81**
Cabernet Sauvignon Mendocino North Field Select 1990 • $18 • (11/15/1993) • **87**
Cabernet Sauvignon Mendocino North Field Select 1989 • $18 • (8/31/1993) • **87**
Cabernet Sauvignon Mendocino North Field Select 1988 • $18 • (8/31/1992) • **84**
Cabernet Sauvignon Mendocino North Field Select 1987 • $16 • (11/15/1990) • **87**
Cabernet Sauvignon Mendocino Reserve 1995: Shows modest depth, going for smoky cola and oak notes rather than currant or cherry flavors. Tannins are firm but not drying. Drink now through 2004.–J.L. • $27 • (10/15/1999) • **83**
Chardonnay Mendocino 1998: Toasty vanilla oak and apple flavors combine in a round and easy-drinking wine. Drink now through 2003.–J.L. • $13 • (4/30/2000) • **85**
Pinot Noir Anderson Valley 1994 • $16 • (11/30/1996) • **81**
Pinot Noir Anderson Valley 1993 • $15 • (12/31/1995) • **72**
Pinot Noir Anderson Valley 1992 • $14 • (11/30/1994) • **88**
Pinot Noir Anderson Valley 1991 • $14 • (4/30/1994) • **84**
Pinot Noir Anderson Valley 1990 • $14 • (2/28/1993) • **81**
Pinot Noir Anderson Valley 1989 • $14 • (11/15/1991) • **87**
Pinot Noir Anderson Valley 1988 • $13 • (12/15/1990) • **84**
Pinot Noir Anderson Valley 1987 • $13 • (2/15/1990) • **80**
Pinot Noir Anderson Valley 1986 • $13 • (10/15/1989) • **81**
Pinot Noir Anderson Valley 1985 • $10 • (6/15/1988) • **84**
Pinot Noir Anderson Valley Reserve 1992 • $24 • (2/28/1997) • **82**
Sauvignon Blanc Mendocino 1998: Soft and creamy, with pretty lemon-meringue flavors and a persistent finish. Drink now through 2002.–H.S. • $12 • (3/31/2000) • **85**
Sauvignon Blanc Mendocino La Ribera Vineyards 1997: Starts off with honey and citrus notes, remaining quite dry on the palate. Other flavors include fresh pea, grapefruit, herbs and minerals, all of which come together in a fresh, tangy finish. Drink now through 2002. • $11 • (5/31/1999) • **86**
Sauvignon Blanc Mendocino La Ribera Vineyards 1996 • $11 • (4/30/1998) • **83**

HYATT | WASHINGTON

Black Muscat Yakima Valley 1998: A delightful rosé brimming with watermelon, spice and berry flavors. Not too sweet but definitely not a dry wine, either. Drink now.–H.S. • $8 • (9/30/1999) • **84**
Black Muscat Yakima Valley 1994 • $7 • (3/31/1996) • **85**
Black Muscat Yakima Valley Ice Wine 1996 • $30/375 ml. • (10/15/1997) • **88**
Black Muscat Yakima Valley Royale 1993 • $7 • (9/30/1994) • **82**
Cabernet Sauvignon Yakima Valley 1993 • $12 • (9/15/1997) • **86**
Cabernet Sauvignon Yakima Valley 1991 • $13 • (3/31/1996) • **83**
Cabernet Sauvignon Yakima Valley Reserve 1996: Firm in texture, with pretty raspberry and red cherry flavors with spicy overtones. Best after 2000.–H.S. • $25 • (8/31/1999) • **85**
Cabernet Sauvignon Yakima Valley Reserve 1994 • $32 • (9/15/1997) • **88**
Cabernet Sauvignon Yakima Valley Reserve 1992 • $25 • (3/31/1996) • **84**
Cabernet Sauvignon Yakima Valley River's Bend Vineyard 1990 • $13 • (10/15/1993) • **82**
Cabernet-Merlot Yakima Valley 1997: A very good bottle for so few dollars, this easy-drinking red offers pretty raspberry, currant and spice notes on a modest scale, its flavors lingering pleasantly on the smooth finish. A nice, compact blend from Washington, containing more Merlot than Cabernet. Drink now through 2001.–H.S. • $10 • (8/31/1999) • **87**
Cabernet-Merlot Yakima Valley 1992 • $9 • (8/31/1994) • **84**
Merlot Columbia Valley 1991 • $11 • (5/15/1994) • **75**
Merlot Columbia Valley 1989 • $11 • (11/30/1992) • **87**
Merlot Washington 1996: Soft and ripe beneath a layer of prickly tannins, offering a generous dollop of blackberry, currant and smoke flavors. Best after 2000.–H.S. • $13 • (8/31/1999) • **87**
Merlot Yakima Valley 1993 • $11 • (3/31/1996) • **85**
Merlot Yakima Valley 1992 • $11 • (8/31/1995) • **88**
Merlot Yakima Valley 1990 • $13 • (6/15/1993) • **85**
Merlot Yakima Valley Reserve 1996: Firm in texture, with enough tannin to want cellaring to bring out the black cherry and anise flavors lurking behind. Finishes solid. Best after 2001.–H.S. • $25 • (8/31/1999) • **86**
Merlot Yakima Valley Reserve 1993 • $25 • (3/31/1996) • **84**
Riesling Yakima Valley 1998: Soft and pleasant, with modest apple and floral aromas and flavors that linger nicely on the finish. Drink now.–H.S. • $8 • (9/30/1999) • **83**
Riesling Yakima Valley Late Harvest 1994 • $9 • (3/31/1996) • **87**
Syrah Yakima Valley 1997: A solid red, firm in texture and generous with its spicy, bay leaf-scented blackberry flavors. Drink through 2003.–H.S. • $20 • (9/30/1999) • **85**

ICI/LA-BAS | OREGON

Pinot Noir Oregon Les Révélés 1997: Light in texture and a bit tight with tannin, but generous enough to balance, with leafy, slightly herbal berry flavors. Drink now.–H.S. • $35 • (4/30/2000) • **83**
Pinot Noir Oregon Les Révélés 1996: Very light in color, but offers plenty of flavor, centering on plum, currant and dark spices on a supple frame. Finish lasts impressively. Drink through 2002.–H.S. • $25 • (12/15/1998) • **87**
Pinot Noir Oregon Les Révélés 1995 • $25 • (10/31/1997) • **87**

IL CUORE | CALIFORNIA

Cabernet Sauvignon North Coast 1995 • $9 • (9/15/1997) • **84**
Rosso Classico California 1994 • $10 • (4/30/1997) • **85**

IL PODERE DELL'OLIVOS | CALIFORNIA

Barbera California 1995 • $12 • (12/15/1996) • **81**

Barbera California Ragazzo Legnoso Riserva 1993 • $18 • (10/15/1995) • **90**

Barbera Santa Barbara County Ragazzo Legnoso Riserva 1995 • $12 • (3/31/1998) • **86**

Barbera-Nebbiolo California Ragazzo Legnoso Riserva 1994 • $18 • (8/31/1996) • **81**

Borgo Buon Natale Primogénito Riserva Santa Maria Valley White 1998: Rich almond and honeyed toast notes mingle with lemon custard flavors. Lingering finish. Tocai Friulano, Pinot Grigio and Pinot Bianco. Drink now through 2003.–J.L. • $18 • (2/29/2000) • **87**

Fiano Central Coast 1996 • $18 • (3/31/1998) • **86**

Tocai Friulano Central Coast 1997: Smooth and silky, full of toasted nut, spicy pear, fresh herb, earth and citrus flavors, with a touch of bitterness. Drink now through 2002.–J.L. • $16 • (2/29/2000) • **85**

Tocai Friulano Central Coast 1996 • $15 • (3/31/1998) • **88**

INDIAN SPRINGS | CALIFORNIA

Cabernet Sauvignon Nevada County 1993 • $10 • (11/30/1996) • **82**

Cabernet Sauvignon Nevada County 1991 • $9 • (11/15/1994) • **82**

Cabernet Sauvignon Nevada County 1990 • $9 • (11/15/1993) • **80**

Merlot Nevada County 1992 • $12 • (9/15/1994) • **84**

Merlot Nevada County 1991 • $12 • (8/31/1993) • **84**

Merlot Nevada County Sierra Foothills 1990 • $12 • (6/15/1993) • **84**

Merlot Sierra Foothills 1989 • $10 • (11/30/1992) • **85**

Syrah Nevada County 1995 • $15 • (3/31/1998) • **86**

INDIGO HILLS | CALIFORNIA

Blanc de Blancs North Coast NV: A light, bright and refreshing blend of lemon, toast and green apple flavors. Not particularly complex, but thoroughly enjoyable. Good price, too. Drink now. • $12 • (10/15/1999) • **85**

Brut Chardonnay North Coast NV • $9 • (12/15/1997) • **88**

Cabernet Sauvignon Paso Robles 1995: Juicy, but shows more tomato, dill and charred oak than Cabernet flavors. Finishes slightly hot.–J.L. • $10 • (12/15/1998) • **78**

Chardonnay Mendocino County 1997: A refreshing white at a refreshing price, this California white is clean and lively, distinctive for its core of crisp and tangy citrus and tart pear flavors. Ready now, with good availability.–J.L. • $10 • (4/30/1999) • **86**

Chardonnay Mendocino County 1996 • $10 • (3/31/1998) • **85**

Chardonnay North Coast 1996: A soft white, woven together with focused tangerine, apple and pear flavors that finish with a subtle interplay of fruit and oak. Drink now.–J.L. • $10 • (12/15/1998) • **87**

Merlot California 1997: Shows pretty blueberry, currant, cherry and clay flavors. Finishes with soft tannins. Drink now through 2004.–J.L. • $15 • (11/15/1999) • **83**

Pinot Noir North Coast 1997: Ultimately simple, with pleasant strawberry, tea and clove flavors. Drink now.–J.L. • $12 • (4/30/1999) • **83**

Pinot Noir Mendocino County 1996: A simple red that lacks varietal distinction. Shows a modest range of earthy cherry notes and finishes slightly dry.–J.L. • $10 • (12/31/1998) • **79**

Pinot Noir North Coast 1995 • $10 • (12/31/1997) • **86**

Sauvignon Blanc Mendocino County 1996 • $10 • (3/31/1998) • **85**

Zinfandel North Coast 1995 • $10 • (3/31/1998) • **83**

INGLENOOK | CALIFORNIA

Classic Burgundy Premium Select California NV • $9/1.5 liter • (5/15/1998) • **81**

Sauvignon Blanc California Estate Cellars NV • $9/1.5 liter • (5/31/1998) • **80**

White Zinfandel California Premium Select Varietal NV • $9/1.5 liter • (5/15/1998) • **80**

Key: SS—Spectator Selection CS—Cellar Selection HR—Highly Recommended $NA—Price Not Available a—Auction Price (BT)—Barrel Tasting
For a key to the tasters' initials, see "How to Use These Listings."
Dates in parentheses indicate the issues in which the ratings were published.

INGLESIDE PLANTATION | VIRGINIA

Cabernet Franc Virginia 1995: Red plum, cedar and tobacco flavors dominate this straightforward red wine that ends on notes of rhubarb and mincemeat. On the light side.–K.M. • $12 • (2/28/1999) • **79**

Cabernet Franc Virginia 1993 • $12 • (4/30/1997) • **80**

Cabernet Sauvignon Virginia 1995: Tastes tired, with modest flavors of spice and dried cherry and a hint of vanilla.–K.M. • $12 • (2/28/1999) • **75**

Cabernet Sauvignon Virginia Chesapeake Claret NV: This is a stewy-tasting and muddled wine, with roasted tomato and herb flavors and a green finish.–K.M. • $9 • (2/28/1999) • **72**

Cabernet Sauvignon Virginia Special Reserve 1995: Cloying cough syrup flavors dominate this astringently textured, off-putting wine. Not recommended. Tasted twice, with consistent notes.–K.M. • $18 • (2/28/1999) • **63**

Merlot Virginia 1997: Interesting cherry and anise flavors give this red good zip and concentration. Finishes on a charry, almost resinous note. Drink now.–K.M. • $15 • (5/31/1999) • **82**

INTAGLIO | CALIFORNIA

Pinot Noir Russian River Valley Saralee's Vineyard 1992 • $14 • (3/31/1995) • **70**

IO | CALIFORNIA

Santa Barbara County Red 1996: Dark, rich and concentrated, with beefy plum, mineral, wild berry, currant and spice nuances, aided by cedary oak and spice notes. A wall-to-wall wine with depth and complexity. A blend of Syrah, Grenache and Mourvèdre. New from Ken Brown of Byron Winery. Best from 2001 through 2008.–J.L. • $40 • (11/15/1999) • **92**

IRON HORSE | CALIFORNIA

Blanc de Blancs Sonoma County Green Valley 1991: Bright and delicate, yet showing depth, with pear, lemon, herb and peppery notes. Ends with a tangy, citrusy finish. Quite fresh for its age. Drink now through 2001. • $30 • (11/30/1998) • **88**

Blanc de Blancs Sonoma County Green Valley LD 1990: Rich toast and hazelnut aromas up front lead to a refreshing, bright-textured wine showing hints of green apple, spice, pear and citrus. The finish is long and elegant. Only 1,000 bottles of 3L made. Tasted twice, with consistent notes. Drink now. • $600/3 liter • (9/15/1999) • **90**

Brut Rosé Sonoma County Green Valley 1993: A bright-textured wine with Bing cherry and herb notes. Races along the palate with exuberance, finishing with a tangy edge. Drink now through 2003. • $28 • (11/30/1998) • **87**

Brut Rosé Sonoma County Green Valley 1992 • $25 • (11/30/1997) • **88**

Brut Rosé Sonoma County Green Valley 1991 • $28 • (9/15/1996) • **86**

Brut Rosé Sonoma County Green Valley 1990 • $28 • (12/31/1994) • **84**

Brut Sonoma County Green Valley Classic Vintage 1994: Fresh citrus and toast aromas yield to pretty hazelnut, pear, mandarin orange and herb flavors. A complex wine couched in refined, tiny bubbles. Drink now through 2002. • $24 • (10/15/1999) • **88**

Brut Sonoma County Green Valley Classic Vintage 1993: A tangy, citrusy blend, with fresh-tasting lemon and apple flavors. Refreshing and elegant. Drink now through 2001. • $24 • (11/30/1998) • **88**

Brut Sonoma County Green Valley Classic Vintage 1992 • $20 • (11/30/1997) • **86**

Brut Sonoma County Green Valley 1991 • $24 • (12/31/1995) • **88**

Brut Sonoma County Green Valley 1990 • $24 • (12/31/1994) • **87**

Brut Sonoma County Green Valley LD 1991: Quite bright and loaded with complex flavors: green apple, pear, fresh pea, herb, anise, citrus and toast. All are intertwined elegantly, with a freshness that belies the wine's age. Drink now through 2002. • $60 • (9/15/1999) • **90**

Cabernet Sauvignon Alexander Valley 1994 • $19 • (11/30/1997) • **86**

Cabernet Sauvignon Alexander Valley 1981 • $14 • (12/16/1984) • **92**

Cabernet Sauvignon Alexander Valley Barrel Fermented 1994 • $19 • (11/30/1997) • **88**

Cabernet Sauvignon Alexander Valley Cuveé Joy 1994 • $25 • (11/15/1997) • **87**

Cabernet Sauvignon Alexander Valley T-T Vineyards 1996: Rich and focused, an elegant style featuring toasted oak, herb, tar and cherry flavors, turning firm on the finish. Drink now through 2004.–J.L. • $23 • (9/15/1999) • **88**

Cabernet Sauvignon Alexander Valley T-T Vineyards 1995: Tight and firm, with a waxy, claylike edge to the rustic currant and berry flavors, finishing with hard, gritty tannins. Time may help. Tasted twice, with consistent notes.–J.L. • $21 • (2/28/1999) • **78**

Cabernet Sauvignon Alexander Valley T-T Vineyards 1993 • $20 • (12/15/1996) • **78**
Cabernet Sauvignon Alexander Valley T-T Vineyards Reserve 1992 • $20 • (4/30/1996) • **82**
Cabernets Alexander Valley 1990 • $19 • (11/15/1993) • **88**
Cabernets Alexander Valley 1988 • $22 • (3/31/1992) • **85**
Cabernets Alexander Valley 1987 • $20 • (3/15/1991) • **86**
Cabernets Alexander Valley 1986 • $22 • (4/15/1990) • **90**
Cabernets Alexander Valley 1985 • $16 • (12/31/1988) • **88**
Cabernets Alexander Valley T-T Vineyards 1992 • $16 • (9/15/1996) • **83**
Cabernets Alexander Valley T-T Vineyards 1991 • $19 • (12/15/1995) • **87**
Cabernets Alexander Valley T-T Vineyards 1990 • $15 • (10/31/1994) • **86**
Cabernets Alexander Valley T-T Vineyards 1989 • $15 • (5/15/1994) • **86**
Chardonnay Sonoma County Green Valley 1998: Marked by candied nectarine and tangerine flavors, bright and lively. Drink now.–J.L. • $24 • (6/15/2000) • **85**
Chardonnay Sonoma County Green Valley 1997: Complex, clean and elegant, this open-textured wine has grapefruit, pear, spice, light cream and mineral notes that fan out. Drink now.–J.L. • $22 • (6/15/1999) • **88**
Chardonnay Sonoma County Green Valley 1996: Tight and a touch flinty, with fresh pear, fig, apricot and spice. Finishes with a touch of oak. Try to cellar short-term; best through 2001.–J.L. • $22 • (7/31/1998) • **88**
Chardonnay Sonoma County Green Valley Cuvée Joy 1997: Rich, with honeyed pear, fig and pineapple notes that are complex, firm and a touch coarse on the finish. Drink now through 2005.–J.L. • $30 • (2/29/2000) • **87**
Demi-Sec Sonoma County Green Valley 1990 • $20 • (11/30/1996) • **86**
Fumé Blanc Alexander Valley T-T 1998: Smooth and understated, with ripe, polished melon, fig, herb, spice and light oak. Gains richness on the finish. Drink now through 2005.–J.L. • $18 • (3/31/2000) • **88**
Fumé Blanc Alexander Valley T-T Vineyards 1997: Peaches, grapefruit and toasty oak form a trio in this viscous, almost sweet-tinged wine. The finish is long, with a minty, mineral edge. Made with 20 percent Viognier, which is quite forward. Drink now. • $18 • (9/15/1998) • **88**
Fumé Blanc Alexander Valley T-T Vineyards 1996 • $18 • (6/30/1997) • **87**
Merlot Alexander Valley T-T Vineyards 1994 • $18 • (12/15/1996) • **84**
Pinot Noir Sonoma County Green Valley 1998: Complex, with wild berry, black cherry and herb flavors, picking up a meat, clay, orange peel and mushroom edge. Drink now.–J.L. • $28 • (6/15/2000) • **87**
Pinot Noir Sonoma County Green Valley 1997: Moderate richness and depth to the ripe cherry, herb and toast flavors. Finishes with ripe tannins. Drink now through 2001.–J.L. • $24 • (6/30/1999) • **86**
Pinot Noir Sonoma County Green Valley 1996 • $23 • (1/31/1998) • **88**
Pinot Noir Sonoma County Green Valley 1995 • $19 • (12/15/1997) • **81**
Pinot Noir Sonoma County Green Valley 1994 • $18 • (8/31/1996) • **82**
Pinot Noir Sonoma County Green Valley 1993 • $18 • (12/31/1995) • **84**
Pinot Noir Sonoma County Green Valley 1992 • $19 • (10/31/1994) • **87**
Pinot Noir Sonoma County Green Valley 1987 • $19 • (10/31/1990) • **72**
Pinot Noir Sonoma County Green Valley 1986 • $18 • (6/15/1988) • **92**
Pinot Noir Sonoma County Green Valley 1985 • $18 • (6/15/1988) • **77**
Pinot Noir Sonoma County Green Valley 1982 • $10 • (10/01/1985) • **76**
Pinot Noir Sonoma County Green Valley Thomas Road Vineyard 1997: Light-bodied but balanced and flavorful, featuring baked black cherry, tea and toasted oak flavors. A bit hot on the firm finish. Drink now through 2001. –J.L. • $40 • (9/15/1999) • **87**
Pinot Noir Sonoma County Green Valley Thomas Road Vineyard 1996: Achieves a delicate balance between moderately ripe fruit and spicy, toasty oak; shows off hints of dried cherry, cola and spice, finishes with smooth, supple tannins. Drink now through 2002.–J.L. • $28 • (9/15/1998) • **87**
Russian Cuvée Sonoma County Green Valley 1994: Richly textured, with toasty hazelnut, pear, peach, green apple and citrus notes blending elegantly in well-balanced harmony. Firm acidity highlights the wine's substance and complexity. Finishes with both power and finesse. Drink now through 2002. • $25 • (10/15/1999) • **90**
Russian Cuvée Sonoma County Green Valley 1993: A complex and well-crafted California sparkling wine, impressive for an array of essences that includes wintergreen, mandarin orange, pear, hazelnut, spice and toast nuances. Finishes long, full and round. Drink now through 2002. • $24 • (11/30/1998) HR • **91**
Russian Cuvée Sonoma County Green Valley 1992 • $24 • (11/30/1997) • **87**
Sangiovese Alexander Valley T-T Vineyards 1996: Smooth and polished, with ripe plum, wild berry, spice and cedar notes. Holds together on the finish, where the flavors stay true. Drink now.–J.L. • $22 • (12/15/1998) • **86**
Sangiovese Alexander Valley T-T Vineyards 1995 • $18 • (3/31/1998) • **82**
Sangiovese Alexander Valley T-T Vineyards 1994 • $15 • (11/30/1996) • **88**
Sangiovese Alexander Valley T-T Vineyards 1993 • $18 • (4/30/1996) • **87**
Sauvignon Blanc Alexander Valley Cuvée Joy 1997: Floral, with some tropical and citrus undertones framed by subtle oak. Drink now.–J.L. • $18 • (6/30/2000) • **84**
Viognier Alexander Valley T-T Vineyards 1997: A fruity blend of apricot, citrus and spice flavors. Somewhat exotic, it coats the palate with good viscosity and balanced acidity to finish cleanly, with a mineral edge. Drink now through 2001. • $18 • (2/28/1999) • **88**
Vrais Amis Sonoma County Green Valley 1994: Quite lemony, with crisp, firm acidity, it also offers hints of toast, green apple and pear and serves up a long, bright finish. Refreshing now, it should age well, too. Drink now through 2004. • $29 • (10/15/1999) • **88**
Vrais Amis Sonoma County Green Valley 1993: A pretty, elegant wine, with subtle suggestions of jasmine, citrus, pear and spice. Moderate finish. Drink now through 2001. • $28 • (11/30/1998) • **87**
Vrais Amis Sonoma County Green Valley 1992 • $24 • (11/30/1997) • **89**
Vrais Amis Sonoma County Green Valley 1991 • $21 • (11/15/1996) • **87**
Vrais Amis Sonoma County Green Valley 1990 • $25 • (12/31/1995) • **88**
Wedding Cuvée Sonoma County Green Valley 1996: Toasty aromas and a pretty, cherrylike core make this salmon-colored bubbly fun and fanciful. Sports a moderate finish, with a clean, refreshing edge. Drink now. • $26 • (10/15/1999) • **87**
Wedding Cuvée Sonoma County Green Valley 1994 • $20 • (11/30/1997) • **87**
Wedding Cuvée Sonoma County Green Valley 1993 • $19 • (4/30/1996) • **87**
Wedding Cuvée Sonoma County Green Valley 1992 • $25 • (12/31/1995) • **84**
Wedding Cuvée Sonoma County Green Valley 1991 • $20 • (11/15/1994) • **87**
Wedding Cuvée Sonoma County Green Valley 1990 • $20 • (12/31/1993) • **86**

IRONSTONE | CALIFORNIA

Cabernet Franc California 1995 • $10 • (3/31/1998) • **83**
Cabernet Sauvignon California 1996: Smacks of simple cherry flavors, an herbal twist and a tangy edge. Finishes on the short side. • $10 • (11/15/1998) • **77**
Chardonnay California 1998: Lemony, with toasty pineapple flavors on a medium frame. Drink now.–J.L. • $9 • (6/30/2000) • **82**
Chardonnay California 1997: Pleasant citrus, mineral and toast flavors on a soft frame. Drink now.–H.S. • $10 • (11/30/1998) • **80**
Crown Jewel Meritage Library Collection California 1993: A pretty, light-style wine, with cherry, raspberry, cedar, anise and herb flavors. Finishes moderately, leaving a hint of spice and vanilla. Drink now through 2002. • $40 • (1/31/1999) • **85**
Merlot California Highlands 1995: Fairly focused, with cherry, spice and licorice flavors, yet it's a little astringent on the palate and finishes short. Drink now through 2001. • $10 • (9/30/1998) • **83**
Shiraz California 1997: Earthy, minty aromas are tinged with cherry, cola and tea notes on the palate in this straightforward presentation of Shiraz that gives its Aussie cousins real competition in the price/score ratio. Drink now through 2003.–J.L. • $9 • (5/15/2000) • **85**
Shiraz California 1995 • $11 • (3/31/1998) • **87**
Zinfandel California 1998: Muddled, with sour fruit flavors and lots of earthy notes.–J.L. • $9 • (5/31/2000) • **77**

J | CALIFORNIA

Brut Sonoma County 1994: Fresh and vibrant, this shows distinctive toast and tangy lemon-lime notes, crisp acidity. Refreshing apple and spice on the finish. Drink now through 2002. • $28 • (11/30/1998) • **88**
Chardonnay Russian River Valley 1997: Somewhat tropical, with honeyed hints of guava and melon. Its rich, creamy texture is balanced by bright, tangy acidity. Finishes with lemony verve and a clean mineral edge. Drink now through 2002. • $35 • (7/31/1999) • **89**
Pinot Gris Russian River Valley 1998: Tasty, rich and full-bodied, with subtle pear, honeydew melon and pippin apple notes that are fresh and clean. Drink now.–J.L. • $16 • (3/31/2000) • **88**
Pinot Noir Russian River Valley 1996: Lacks focus and depth, with light, simple cherry and berry flavor that quickly loses intensity. Drink now.–J.L. • $20 • (9/15/1998) • **78**
Pinot Noir Russian River Valley Nicole's Vineyard 1996: Light but focused, with bright black cherry, toasty oak and herb flavors turning firm on the finish. Drink now through 2002.–J.L. • $30 • (9/15/1999) • **83**
Pinot Noir Russian River Valley Nicole's Vineyard 1995: A lighter-styled wine, slightly waxy in texture, with light cherry and spice notes. A touch of anise on the finish adds interest. The first still-Pinot Noir from this sparkling wine producer. Drink now. • $33 • (10/31/1998) • **83**
Sonoma County Sparkling Wine 1995: A brightly textured wine with a refreshing blend of citrus, green apple, pear and mineral flavors that linger

delicately on the classy finish. Drink now through 2002. • $29 • (10/15/1999) • **89**

Sonoma County Sparkling Wine 1993: Finely tuned lemon, green apple, mineral and herb flavors mingle elegantly in this dry, classy sparkling wine, lingering on the palate, offering a bright, refreshing and extremely clean finish. Should improve for a while, too. A special release of this wine available in magnum format only. Drink now through 2003. • $72/1.5 liter • (9/15/1999) • **91**

Sonoma County Sparkling Wine 1991 • $26 • (11/30/1996) • **89**

Sonoma County Sparkling Wine 1990 • $23 • (11/30/1995) SS • **91**

JACOB FRANKLIN | CALIFORNIA

Petite Sirah Napa Valley Hayne Vineyard 1998: Dark, rich and detailed, with earthy, meaty mineral, leather, blackberry and stewed plum flavors that turn chewy. Second label for Elyse. Best from 2001 through 2010.–J.L. • $65 • (4/30/2000) • **91**

Sauvignon Blanc Napa Valley 1998: Rich and full, with herb, fig, pear and tart nectarine notes, kept alive by firm acidity and a touch of bitter lemon peel. Drink now.–J.L. • $24 • (4/30/2000) • **86**

JACUZZI | CALIFORNIA

Merlot Los Carneros Reserve 1997: Plush and smooth-textured, showing a range of chocolate, black cherry, blackberry, sage and other complex herbal notes. The finish is fairly long, with ripe, firm tannins. Drink now through 2005.–J.L. • $40 • (10/15/1999) • **87**

Zinfandel Contra Costa County Reserve 1995: Complex, ripe and juicy, with pretty berry, black cherry, anise, sage, cedar and spice. Finishes with firm, drying tannins but also a burst of fruit. Drink now through 2002.–J.L. • $38 • (12/15/1998) • **89**

Zinfandel Contra Costa County Reserve 1994 • $40 • (11/15/1997) • **88**

JADE MOUNTAIN | CALIFORNIA

Côtes du Soleil California 1994 • $8 • (8/31/1996) • **81**

La Provençale California 1995: Shows enough smoky, gamy, leathery flavors to throw a warning flag, but somehow manages to pull through with the plum, cherry, spice and wild berry needed to keep the balance. Not for everyone. Drink now through 2002.–J.L. • $17 • (9/30/1998) • **86**

La Provençale California 1994 • $15 • (8/31/1996) • **84**

La Provençale California 1992 • $14 • (6/30/1995) • **88**

La Provençale California 1990 • $12 • (3/15/1992) • **80**

Les Jumeaux California 1995 • $20 • (1/01/1998) • **83**

Les Jumeaux California 1994 • $18 • (8/31/1996) • **85**

Merlot Mount Veeder Paras Vineyard 1997: Despite rough edges, this wine may reward. The core of mineral, iodine, cedar, currant, berry and spice flavors is intense, rich and complex, if a bit gangly. Best from 2001 through 2006.–J.L. • $52 • (12/31/1999) • **87**

Merlot Napa Valley 1993 • $25 • (3/31/1996) • **87**

Merlot Napa Valley Caldwell Vineyard 1997: Medium-weight, with cedar, olive, herb, pickle and sage notes, this is pleasant if you like that flavor profile. Drink now through 2003.–J.L. • $34 • (12/31/1999) • **84**

Merlot Napa Valley Caldwell Vineyard 1995 • $30 • (3/31/1998) • **83**

Mourvèdre California 1997: Pleasant depth of ripe black currant flavor encased in slightly sharp acidity and tannins. Drink now through 2003.–J.L. • $17 • (5/15/2000) • **84**

Mourvèdre California 1995: Complex, with earthy, spicy cherry and wild berry and hints of plum. Loses its intensity on the finish, but drinks well now.–J.L. • $20 • (9/30/1998) • **85**

Mourvèdre California 1991 • $15 • (12/15/1995) • **74**

Mourvèdre California 1990 • $15 • (3/15/1992) • **81**

Mourvèdre California Unfiltered 1990 • $15 • (3/15/1992) • **83**

Syrah Mount Veeder 1995 • $40 • (3/31/1998) • **87**

Syrah Napa Valley 1993 • $18 • (8/31/1996) • **85**

Syrah Napa Valley 1992 • $18 • (6/30/1995) • **87**

Syrah Napa Valley Carneros Hudson Vineyard 1995: An earthy, meaty style that has enough funk to keep you on your toes, yet also enough ripe, smoky Syrah and mineral flavors. Walks the tightrope and keeps its balance. Drink now through 2004.–J.L. • $23 • (9/30/1998) • **86**

Key: SS—Spectator Selection CS—Cellar Selection HR—Highly Recommended $NA—Price Not Available a—Auction Price (BT)—Barrel Tasting
For a key to the tasters' initials, see "How to Use These Listings."
Dates in parentheses indicate the issues in which the ratings were published.

Zinfandel California 1991 • $13 • (10/15/1995) • **85**

JAFFURS | CALIFORNIA

Grenache Santa Barbara County 1995 • $18 • (1/01/1997) • **88**

Grenache Santa Barbara County Stolpman Family Vineyard 1998: Firm and snappy, with chunky cherry and currant flavors, turning spicy. Drink now through 2004.–J.L. • $19 • (5/31/2000) • **86**

Matilija Cuvée Santa Barbara County 1996: Coffee, tea and blackberry notes mingle nicely. A bit zippy for a red, but offers a pleasant, light-style quaff. Drink now. • $19 • (10/31/1998) • **85**

Syrah Santa Barbara County 1998: Firm, with concentrated, spicy overtones of black cherry and chocolate, herbal notes and a tight structure. Drink now through 2005.–J.L. • $22 • (5/31/2000) • **85**

Syrah Santa Barbara County 1997: Ripe and juicy, with fleshy cherry, wild berry, plum and spice flavors, subtle leather, mineral, sage and cedary notes chiming in, and a long, lingering finish. Drink now through 2004.–J.L. • $22 • (4/30/1999) • **89**

Syrah Santa Barbara County 1996 • $22 • (4/30/1998) • **86**

Syrah Santa Barbara County 1995 • $20 • (1/01/1997) • **88**

Syrah Santa Barbara County Bien Nacido Vineyard 1998: Fragrant, with a perfumed, floral spiciness that really jumps out of the glass, gamy overtones to the ripe black cherry and a toasty finish. Drink now through 2005. –J.L. • $28 • (5/31/2000) • **86**

Syrah Santa Barbara County Stolpman Family Vineyard 1998: Game, leather and chocolate notes show nice depth, wrapped in vanilla and oak flavors. Drink now through 2004.–J.L. • $30 • (5/31/2000) • **86**

Syrah Santa Barbara County Thompson Vineyard 1998: Chocolate, vanilla, black cherry and toasty oak flavors are framed by firm tannins. Drink now through 2005.–J.L. • $30 • (5/31/2000) • **86**

Syrah Santa Barbara County Thompson Vineyard 1996 • $25 • (4/30/1998) • **89**

Syrah Santa Barbara County Thompson Vineyard 1994 • $14 • (2/29/1996) • **91**

Viognier Santa Barbara County Bien Nacido Vineyard 1996 • $19 • (2/28/1998) • **88**

JAMES SCOTT | OREGON

Pinot Noir Willamette Valley 1992 • $15 • (5/31/1995) • **85**

Pinot Noir Willamette Valley Signature Reserve 1992 • $29 • (12/31/1995) • **84**

Pinot Noir Willamette Valley Signature Reserve 1991 • $28 • (1/31/1995) • **89**

JAMESPORT | NEW YORK

Cabernet Franc North Fork of Long Island 1997: Berry and herbal flavors are light but show varietal character in this supple red. Light but clean. Drink now.–T.M. • $17 • (1/01/2000) • **82**

Cabernet Franc North Fork of Long Island 1995: Lean and almost astringent, with only modest berry and cherry flavors.–K.M. • $15 • (8/31/1998) • **77**

Cabernet Sauvignon North Fork of Long Island North House 1987 • $10 • (6/30/1991) • **78**

Chardonnay North Fork of Long Island Cox Lane Vineyard 1997: Fresh, clean and straightforward. This light, silky white offers plenty of sweet vanilla oak flavor—a bit obvious but not unappealing—with light citrus and crisp acidity to keep it in balance. Drink now.–T.M. • $13 • (6/30/1999) • **84**

Mélange de Trois North Fork of Long Island 1993 • $16 • (12/31/1996) • **78**

Merlot North Fork of Long Island 1997: This generous red offers ripe, round flavors of plum, prune and chocolate that are fleshy but soft on the palate. Though lacking in structure, it has a sweet appeal. Drink now.–T.M. • $18 • (5/31/2000) • **86**

Merlot North Fork of Long Island 1995: Soft and round. Black cherry and coffee flavors are clean in this ripe, jammy red. The tannins are a bit soft for food, but the wine has a supple appeal. Drink now.–T.M. • $16 • (6/30/1999) • **82**

Merlot North Fork of Long Island 1994 • $20 • (12/31/1996) • **79**

Merlot North Fork of Long Island Reserve 1993 • $27 • (12/31/1996) • **77**

Riesling North Fork of Long Island Late Harvest 1998: Thick and very sweet, this honeyed white shows vanilla and dried pineapple flavors with a streak of lemony acidity that keeps things lively. Impressive concentration. Drink now through 2002.–T.M. • $45/375 ml. • (5/31/2000) • **86**

Sauvignon Blanc North Fork of Long Island 1998: This full-bodied white is firm and smooth, with melon and light pineapple flavors framed by buttery notes and a clean underlying acidity. Can stand up to food. Drink now.–T.M. • $13 • (5/31/2000) • **84**

Sauvignon Blanc North Fork of Long Island 1997: Light and silky, this white offers Key lime and vanilla flavors in a counterpoint of sweet and tart notes. It lacks the herbaceousness characteristic of the varietal, but remains lively and clean. Drink now.–T.M. • $12 • (6/30/1999) • **83**

JANKRIS | CALIFORNIA

Merlot Paso Robles 1992 • $12 • (9/15/1994) • **85**
Merlot Paso Robles 1991 • $11 • (8/31/1993) • **84**
Zinfandel Paso Robles 1993 • $9 • (10/15/1995) • **87**
Zinfandel Paso Robles 1992 • $10 • (10/15/1994) • **78**
Zinfandel Paso Robles 1991 • $9 • (9/30/1993) • **81**

JARVIS | CALIFORNIA

Cabernet Franc Napa Valley 1994 • $45 • (5/31/1997) • **87**
Cabernet Franc Napa Valley 1992 • $40 • (8/31/1995) • **86**
Cabernet Sauvignon Napa Valley 1994: Sleek and supple, with a range of currant and cherry flavors that build, gaining nuance and finesse and a touch of earthiness. Drink now through 2006.–J.L. • $58 • (5/15/1999) • **89**
Cabernet Sauvignon Napa Valley 1993 • $55 • (5/31/1997) • **88**
Cabernet Sauvignon Napa Valley 1992 • $72 Ⓐ • (8/31/1995) • **90**
Chardonnay Napa Valley 1996: Sleek and elegant, a touch earthy, with a core of pear, nectarine and fig-laced flavors that are well focused and lively. Drink now through 2002.–J.L. • $38 • (4/30/1999) • **88**
Lake William Napa Valley 1993 • $45 • (11/30/1996) • **90**
Merlot Napa Valley 1994 • $45 • (5/31/1997) • **88**

JC CELLARS | CALIFORNIA

Petite Syrah Napa Valley St. George Vineyard 1997: Dark, ripe and intense, packed with juicy wild berry, pepper, sage and spice flavors and built with firm tannins. Drink now through 2004.–J.L. • $35 • (6/15/1999) • **90**
Syrah Mendocino County Eagle Point Ranch 1997: Delicious. Ripe and complex, with smoke, meat, plum, wild berry and coffee-laced flavors. Turns supple and polished on the finish. Drink now through 2005.–J.L. • $25 • (6/15/1999) • **89**
Syrah Santa Barbara County Mesa Vineyard 1997: Openly fruity, with pretty plum, wild berry and black cherry. Finishes with an earthy edge and firm tannins. Drink now through 2004.–J.L. • $20 • (6/15/1999) • **88**
Zinfandel Napa Valley Baldoc Vineyard 1997: Tight and austere, even crisp and earthy, it needs time to grow out of its tannins and show more cherry and berry, even if it tilts toward the tart side. Cellar short-term. Drink through 2003.–J.L. • $35 • (6/15/1999) • **87**
Zinfandel Redwood Valley Rhodes Vineyard 1997: Very complex and elegant, with spicy, toasty oak adding dimension to the elegant cherry, raspberry and plum-laced Zinfandel flavors. Drink now through 2003.–J.L. • $26 • (6/15/1999) • **91**
Zinfandel Redwood Valley Rhodes Vineyard 1996 • $27 • (6/15/1998) • **91**
Zinfandel Russian River Valley Alegría Vineyard 1997: Bold, ripe and juicy, with complex spice, raspberry, black cherry and wild berry flavors, turning tight, with earthy tannins. Drink now through 2004.–J.L. • $30 • (5/31/1999) • **89**

JEFFERSON | VIRGINIA

Cabernet Franc Monticello 1998: A nice mix of lush and lively, this chewy red offers ripe plum and game flavors, with a vivid streak of acidity that perks up the finish. Drink now through 2003.–T.M. • $16 • (5/31/2000) • **87**
Cabernet Franc Virginia 1995 • $12 • (6/15/1997) • **72**
Cabernet Sauvignon Monticello 1998: Bright and juicy, this fruit-driven red is bursting with cherry, cranberry and plum flavors. Backed by vanilla oak, with soft tannins and bright acidity. Drink now through 2002.–T.M. • $17 • (5/31/2000) • **87**
Cabernet Sauvignon Monticello 1995 • $17 • (6/15/1998) • **72**
Chardonnay Monticello Fantaisie Sauvage 1998: This ambitious white shows lavish oak, with honey, butter and vanilla flavors. Ripe apple and melon peek through the framing, and there's enough acidity to keep it lively. Drink now.–T.M. • $27 • (5/31/2000) • **87**
Chardonnay Monticello Fantaisie Sauvage 1997: Crisp and well defined, with a slightly floral aroma and an interesting mix of mineral, lime and pear flavors, with quite a good slap of acidity. Has plenty of structure, and a refreshing tart note on the finish. Drink now.–K.M. • $25 • (3/31/1999) • **86**
Meritage Monticello 1995 • $28 • (6/15/1998) • **73**
Vidal Blanc Monticello Late Harvest 1997: Sweet and rich, with balanced flavors of apricot and peach, some honeyed notes as well. Creamy hazelnut flavors on the soft finish. Drink now.–K.M. • $15/375 ml. • (3/31/1999) • **86**

JEKEL | CALIFORNIA

Cabernet Franc Monterey 1990 • $13 • (7/31/1995) • **82**
Cabernet Sauvignon Arroyo Seco 1990 • $13 • (11/15/1994) • **84**
Cabernet Sauvignon Arroyo Seco 1989 • $13 • (4/30/1993) • **81**
Cabernet Sauvignon Arroyo Seco 1988 • $12 • (3/15/1993) • **80**
Cabernet Sauvignon Arroyo Seco 1986 • $13 • (11/15/1990) • **83**
Cabernet Sauvignon Arroyo Seco Sanctuary Estate 1992 • $13 • (12/15/1995) • **87**
Cabernet Sauvignon Monterey 1996: Starts off with an interesting hint of coffee on the nose, but winds down as its full-blown tannins put a damper on the tea, herb and blackberry flavors. Finishes moderately but might open with time. Best from 2001 through 2004. • $16 • (9/15/1999) • **83**
Cabernet Sauvignon Monterey 1984 • $12 • (7/31/1989) • **63**
Cabernet Sauvignon Monterey 1982 • $11 • (1/31/1987) • **71**
Cabernet Sauvignon Monterey Home Vineyard Private Reserve 1982 • $20 • (2/01/1986) • **69**
Cabernet Sauvignon Monterey Home Vineyard Private Reserve 1981 • $24 Ⓐ • (2/01/1986) • **76**
Cabernet Sauvignon Monterey Home Vineyard Private Reserve 1980 • $25 • (2/01/1986) • **63**
Cabernet Sauvignon Monterey Home Vineyard Private Reserve 1979 • $18 • (2/01/1986) • **77**
Cabernet Sauvignon Monterey Home Vineyard Private Reserve 1978 • $22 • (11/15/1992) • **68**
Chardonnay Monterey County Gravelstone 1996 • $15 • (5/31/1998) • **86**
Johannisberg Riesling Late Harvest Monterey County 1996: Sweet, yet balanced with the juicy acidity needed to keep the pear, apricot and honey flavors from becoming too sticky. Drink now through 2001.–H.S. • $18/375 ml. • (11/15/1998) • **87**
Meritage Arroyo Seco Sanctuary Estate 1992 • $13 • (12/15/1995) • **83**
Meritage Symmetry Arroyo Seco Sanctuary Estate 1989 • $20 • (11/15/1993) • **85**
Meritage Symmetry Arroyo Seco Sanctuary Estate 1987 • $25 • (3/31/1993) • **77**
Merlot Arroyo Seco Sanctuary Estate 1994 • $15 • (7/31/1997) • **84**
Merlot Arroyo Seco Sanctuary Estate 1993 • $13 • (8/31/1996) • **82**
Merlot Arroyo Seco Sanctuary Estate 1992 • $15 • (9/15/1994) • **83**
Merlot California 1995 • $15 • (6/15/1998) • **80**
Merlot Monterey 1997: Smooth in texture, with cherry and herb flavors. However, a vegetal note lingers on the moderate finish. Drink now through 2002. • $15 • (10/15/1999) • **82**
Merlot Monterey Sanctuary Estate Reserve 1996: Tight, lean and tart, with a green, herbal streak running through the core of modestly ripe berryish flavors. Drink now through 2003.–J.L. • $24 • (10/15/1999) • **81**
Monterey Sanctuary Estate Vineyard Red 1995: Features bright blackberry and cherry flavors, with herb and mint, but the oak takes over at the end. Tannins are moderate, though the acidity comes on a little strong. A blend of Cabernet Sauvignon, Merlot, Cabernet Franc, Malbec, Petit Verdot. Drink through 2005. • $26 • (6/15/1999) • **86**
Pinot Noir Monterey Gravelstone 1996: Simple, with sour cherry and charred flavors. Sharply astringent on the finish. Drink through 2001.–J.L. • $14 • (9/15/1998) • **77**
Pinot Noir Arroyo Seco Gravelstone 1994 • $15 • (3/31/1997) • **78**
Pinot Noir Arroyo Seco Gravelstone 1993 • $15 • (1/31/1996) • **82**
Pinot Noir Arroyo Seco 1992 • $14 • (2/28/1994) • **84**

JEPSON | CALIFORNIA

Blanc de Blanc Mendocino County Burnee Hill Vineyard 1991 • $16 • (11/30/1996) • **86**
Blanc de Blanc Mendocino County Burnee Hill Vineyard Estate Select NV: Tastes a bit oxidized, with hints of canned fruit up front. A lemony lilt on the finish evens things out a bit, leaving a certain freshness. Drink now. • $19 • (10/15/1999) • **84**
Chardonnay Mendocino County 1997: Soft in texture, featuring apple and pear flavors that turn crisp on the refreshing finish. Drink now through 2002.–J.L. • $15 • (7/31/1999) • **85**
Chardonnay Mendocino County Estate Select 1996: Somewhat chunky, with bold butterscotch, spice, citrus and apple notes. The oak stands out, though, along with a hint of bitterness on the finish. Drink now. • $15 • (7/31/1998) • **83**
Pinot Noir Sonoma County 1994 • $16 • (1/31/1997) • **78**
Sauvignon Blanc Mendocino County 1997: Somewhat steely, with a core of grapefruit and lemon flavors. Brisk and refreshing. Drink now. • $10 • (9/15/1998) • **86**

JEPSON

Sauvignon Blanc Mendocino County Estate Select 1996 • $9 • (6/30/1997) • **86**
Viognier Mendocino County 1997: Fairly simple, with pearlike character. A pleasant quaff. Drink now. • $14 • (9/15/1998) • **81**

JESSANDRA VITTORIA | CALIFORNIA

Santa Vittoria Sonoma Valley 1994 • $25 • (8/31/1996) • **83**

JESSUP | CALIFORNIA

Cabernet Sauvignon Napa Valley Atlas Peak Vineyards 1996: Rustic and firm, but flavorful, with dill, black cherry and berry flavors. Tar and mineral notes linger on the firm finish. Drink through 2005.–H.S. • $40 • (9/15/1999) • **86**
Cabernet Sauvignon Napa Valley Lauer Vineyard 1997: Delivers deep black currant, cola and plum flavors, along with substantial herbal undertones and drying tannins. Drink now through 2005.–J.L. • $45 • (6/30/2000) • **85**
Merlot Carneros 1998: Bright, with candied cherry and tart strawberry, turning earthy. Drink now.–J.L. • $30 • (6/15/2000) • **81**
Merlot Napa Valley 1997: Ripe, with lively, complex, Zinfandel-like plum and raspberry flavors accented by jasmine tea and cola notes. Flavors linger on the plush finish. Drink now through 2002.–J.L. • $30 • (10/15/1999) • **87**
Zinfandel Dry Creek Valley 1998: A quick glimpse of cherry-berry fruit fades, turning dry, pruny and earthy. Lacks concentration. Drink now.–J.L. • $28 • (6/15/2000) • **80**
Zinfandel Dry Creek Valley 1997: Ripe, jammy and sweet-tasting, with spicy plum, berry, cherry, herb and strawberry flavors. Smooth finish. Drink now.–J.L. • $24 • (6/30/1999) • **87**
Zinfandel Napa Valley Atlas Peak Vineyards 1996: A distinctive style with forward earth, leather, game, cola and spice notes on a soft frame. Flavorful, but won't appeal to everyone. Drink now.–J.L. • $23 • (6/30/1999) • **84**

JOHNS | WASHINGTON

Vintage Port Yakima Valley 1993 • $16 • (9/15/1996) • **80**

JOHNSON TURNBULL | CALIFORNIA

Cabernet Sauvignon Napa Valley Oakville 1994 • $22 • (4/30/1997) • **87**
Cabernet Sauvignon Napa Valley 1991 • $18 • (10/31/1994) • **89**
Cabernet Sauvignon Napa Valley 1990 • $16 • (3/31/1994) • **81**
Cabernet Sauvignon Napa Valley 1989 • $16 • (8/31/1993) • **85**
Cabernet Sauvignon Napa Valley 1988 • $16 • (11/15/1991) • **84**
Cabernet Sauvignon Napa Valley 1987 • $16 • (11/15/1990) • **80**
Cabernet Sauvignon Napa Valley 1985 • $15 • (7/15/1988) • **88**
Cabernet Sauvignon Napa Valley 1984 • $15 • (7/31/1987) • **73**
Cabernet Sauvignon Napa Valley 1983 • $13 • (9/15/1986) • **86**
Cabernet Sauvignon Napa Valley 1982 • $13 • (10/16/1985) • **86**
Cabernet Sauvignon Napa Valley 1981 • $12 • (4/16/1984) • **76**
Cabernet Sauvignon Napa Valley Vineyard Selection 67 1990 • $34 • (4/30/1994) • **87**
Cabernet Sauvignon Napa Valley Vineyard Selection 67 1989 • $16 • (11/15/1993) • **87**
Cabernet Sauvignon Napa Valley Vineyard Selection 67 1988 • $22 • (8/31/1993) • **86**
Cabernet Sauvignon Napa Valley Vineyard Selection 67 1987 • $22 • (6/30/1991) • **89**
Cabernet Sauvignon Napa Valley Vineyard Selection 67 1986 • $25 • (4/15/1990) • **86**
Cabernet Sauvignon Napa Valley Vineyard Selection 82 1986 • $25 • (8/31/1989) • **95**

JOLIESSE | CALIFORNIA

Cabernet Sauvignon California Reserve 1994 • $7 • (11/30/1996) • **73**
Merlot California Select 1996: Simple cherry and tar notes falter, turning herbal with dry, grainy tannins.–J.L. • $7 • (11/30/1998) • **77**

Key: SS—Spectator Selection CS—Cellar Selection HR—Highly Recommended
$NA—Price Not Available a—Auction Price (BT)—Barrel Tasting
For a key to the tasters' initials, see "How to Use These Listings."
Dates in parentheses indicate the issues in which the ratings were published.

JONES FAMILY | CALIFORNIA

Cabernet Sauvignon Napa Valley 1996: Packs in lots of delicious flavors, from the ripe, plump plum, blackberry, black cherry and spice notes to the pretty toasty, buttery oak shadings. Very complete, dark, complex and concentrated, though the tannins are fine and integrated. Drink through 2008.–J.L. • $50 • (11/15/1999) • **93**

JORDAN | CALIFORNIA

Cabernet Sauvignon Alexander Valley 1995: Elegant, with medium body, ripe cherry, currant, herb and spice flavors, and finishing with polished tannins. Drink now through 2005.–J.L. • $38 • (9/15/1999) • **88**
Cabernet Sauvignon Alexander Valley 1994 • $34 • (6/30/1998) • **88**
Cabernet Sauvignon Alexander Valley 1993 • $29 • (12/15/1997) • **87**
Cabernet Sauvignon Alexander Valley 1992 • $40 Ⓐ • (8/31/1996) • **83**
Cabernet Sauvignon Alexander Valley 1991 • $25 • (6/15/1995) • **84**
Cabernet Sauvignon Alexander Valley 1990 • $46 Ⓐ • (6/30/1994) • **87**
Cabernet Sauvignon Alexander Valley 1989 • $26 Ⓐ • (11/15/1993) • **80**
Cabernet Sauvignon Alexander Valley 1988 • $41 Ⓐ • (11/15/1992) • **85**
Cabernet Sauvignon Alexander Valley 1987 • $38 Ⓐ • (11/15/1991) HR • **90**
Cabernet Sauvignon Alexander Valley 1986 • $46 Ⓐ • (12/15/1996) • **82**
Cabernet Sauvignon Alexander Valley 1985 • $62 Ⓐ • (9/15/1989) • **88**
Cabernet Sauvignon Alexander Valley 1984 • $53 Ⓐ • (7/15/1988) • **86**
Cabernet Sauvignon Alexander Valley 1983 • $36 Ⓐ • (7/15/1987) • **81**
Cabernet Sauvignon Alexander Valley 1978: Smooth, supple and polished, with spicy black cherry, tea, herb, tar and cedary notes, this has held up well and shows no signs of deteriorating. Still, it's a lighter style of Cabernet, consistent with Alexander Valley. (1978 California Cabernet retrospective tasting). Drink now through 2002.–J.L. • $16 • (11/15/1998) • **87**

JORY | CALIFORNIA

Black Hand Mano Nera California 1995 • $15 • (4/30/1997) • **88**
Black Hand Mano Nera California 1993 • $13 • (4/30/1995) • **85**
Fumé Blanc Sierra County New Mexico 1996 • $15 • (5/15/1998) • **86**

JOULLIAN | CALIFORNIA

Cabernet Sauvignon Carmel Valley 1994 • $20 • (10/31/1997) • **80**
Cabernet Sauvignon Carmel Valley 1990 • $14 • (12/15/1995) • **83**
Cabernet Sauvignon Carmel Valley 1989 • $14 • (11/15/1994) • **81**
Cabernet Sauvignon Carmel Valley 1987 • $14 • (7/31/1991) • **81**
Merlot Carmel Valley Family Reserve 1994 • $25 • (4/30/1998) • **84**
Sauvignon Blanc Carmel Valley 1997: Starts off with hints of fresh-cut hay, melon and peach, couched in a velvety, plush-textured frame. On the moderate finish, a hint of tangy mineral remains, adding balance. Drink now. • $14 • (5/15/1999) • **87**
Sauvignon Blanc Carmel Valley Family Reserve 1996: Starts off with floral, sweet pea aromas, then takes off with grapefruit, melon and mineral flavors, all carried by fresh, brisk acidity. Finishes long. Drink now. • $17 • (9/15/1998) • **89**

JUDD'S HILL | CALIFORNIA

Cabernet Sauvignon Napa Valley 1996: Starts out a touch lean, but adds ripe black cherry, wild berry, cedar and plum notes. Holds its elegant focus. Drink now through 2005.–J.L. • $40 • (11/15/1999) • **88**
Cabernet Sauvignon Napa Valley 1995: Complex and elegant, with ripe plum, blueberry, spice and earthy mineral notes, tightening up on the finish, where the tannins offer a firm backbone. Drinkable now, better to cellar. Drink through 2007.–J.L. • $32 • (10/31/1998) • **90**
Cabernet Sauvignon Napa Valley 1994 • $30 • (5/15/1998) • **87**
Cabernet Sauvignon Napa Valley 1993 • $24 Ⓐ • (11/15/1996) • **88**
Cabernet Sauvignon Napa Valley 1992 • $26 • (12/15/1995) • **91**
Cabernet Sauvignon Napa Valley 1991 • $24 • (9/30/1994) SS • **93**
Cabernet Sauvignon Napa Valley 1989 • $20 • (4/15/1992) • **89**
Merlot Napa Valley Juliana Vineyards 1995: Bright, elegant and supple, with attractive black cherry, currant, strawberry and plum flavors. Well focused on the fruit, with ripe, well-integrated tannins and a long, rich, minty aftertaste. Drink now through 2004.–J.L. • $30 • (9/30/1998) • **88**
Merlot North Coast 1996: Smooth and spicy, with medium-bodied cherry, herb and currant flavors of modest proportion, finishing with a hint of strawberry. Drink now through 2003.–J.L. • $35 • (10/15/1999) • **85**

Pinot Noir Napa Valley 1996: A lighter, herbal style, with tea and stemmy notes and just a hint of cola and cherry. May gain with time in the bottle. Drink through 2002.–J.L. • $20 • (9/30/1998) • **84**

JUSTIN | CALIFORNIA

Cabernet Franc Paso Robles 1989 • $20 • (11/15/1992) • **86**
Cabernet Franc San Luis Obispo County 1993 • $20 • (5/31/1997) • **90**
Cabernet Franc San Luis Obispo County 1991 • $20 • (12/31/1994) • **87**
Cabernet Sauvignon Paso Robles Reserve 1997: Delicious. Serves up lots of complex, seductive flavors, with pretty toasty oak adding dimension to the tasty cherry, currant, plum and berry-laced fruit. Drink now through 2005.–J.L. • $25 • (12/31/1999) • **91**
Cabernet Sauvignon Paso Robles 1996: Silky, ripe tannins give this wine elegant structure. Blueberry, blackberry, anise, herb and smoky oak add interest and complexity, and the finish is long. Best from 2001 through 2005. • $20 • (9/30/1999) • **88**
Cabernet Sauvignon Paso Robles 1995: Firm in texture, nicely packed with black cherry and currant, and shades of tobacco and herb. A harmonious wine with lovely flavors that echo nicely on the finish. Approachable now. Drink through 2005.–H.S. • $20 • (11/15/1998) • **87**
Cabernet Sauvignon Paso Robles 1989 • $19 • (11/15/1992) • **81**
Cabernet Sauvignon Paso Robles 1988 • $19 • (11/15/1991) • **72**
Cabernet Sauvignon San Luis Obispo County Reserve 1994 • $20 • (3/31/1997) • **89**
Cabernet Sauvignon San Luis Obispo County 1993 • $20 • (4/30/1997) HR • **92**
Cabernet Sauvignon San Luis Obispo County 1992 • $18 • (12/15/1995) • **88**
Cabernet Sauvignon San Luis Obispo County Society Reserve 1991 • $19 • (11/15/1994) • **88**
Cabernet Sauvignon San Luis Obispo County 1990 • $19 • (11/15/1993) • **80**
Cabernet Sauvignon San Luis Obispo County Obtuse 1992 • $23 • (9/30/1995) • **84**
Chardonnay Paso Robles Reserve 1997: Focused and full-bodied describe this California Chardonnay, with its well-balanced profile of toasty, creamy, citrus-tinged peach and apricot flavors. The clean finish is harmonious and silky. Drink now.–J.L. • $20 • (6/30/1999) HR • **91**
Chardonnay San Luis Obispo County 1994 • $17 • (4/30/1997) • **89**
Isosceles Paso Robles 1996: Sleek and elegant, with a complex interplay of herb, green olive, black cherry and wild berry flavors. Supple and polished on the finish. Drink through 2006.–J.L. • $36 • (11/15/1999) • **88**
Isosceles Paso Robles 1994 • $33 • (10/31/1997) • **92**
Isosceles Reserve San Luis Obispo County 1993 • $28 • (1/31/1997) • **87**
Isosceles Reserve San Luis Obispo County 1992 • $25 • (12/15/1995) HR • **92**
Isosceles Reserve San Luis Obispo County 1991 • $23 • (11/15/1994) • **84**
Isosceles Reserve San Luis Obispo County 1990 • $23 • (11/15/1993) • **88**
Isosceles Reserve Paso Robles 1989 • $23 • (11/15/1992) • **86**
Justification Cabernet Franc-Merlot Paso Robles 1996: Quite grapey on the nose, with fresh, young grape flavors on the palate. Tastes more like Zinfandel than Cab Franc. The finish offers added complexity, soft tannins and hints of coffee, black currant and herbs. Drink now through 2003.• $25 • (10/15/1999) • **87**
Justification Merlot-Cabernet Franc Paso Robles 1997: Nice cherry, spice and oak flavors on a firm frame. Flavors echo nicely on the finish. Drink now through 2002.–J.L. • $NA • (12/15/1999) • **86**
Justification San Luis Obispo County 1992 • $20 • (5/15/1995) • **87**
Merlot Paso Robles 1994 • $20 • (6/30/1997) • **86**
Merlot San Luis Obispo County 1993 • $20 • (5/15/1997) • **89**
Merlot San Luis Obispo County 1992 • $20 • (12/31/1995) HR • **91**
Reserve Paso Robles Red 1988 • $23 • (11/15/1991) • **75**
Reserve Paso Robles Red 1987 • $NA • (12/15/1997) • **90**

KAHN | CALIFORNIA

Syrah Santa Ynez Valley 1996: Flavorful, with smoke, grape, anise and blackberry flavors and a smooth, rich texture. Nice first release for this producer. Drink now.–H.S. • $18 • (4/30/1999) • **87**

KALI-HART | CALIFORNIA

Chardonnay Monterey 1997: Bright and lively, with ripe, complex peach, nectarine, tangerine and light toasty oak notes. Excellent value. Talbott's second label. Drink now through 2004.–J.L. • $12 • (1/31/2000) • **87**

KALINDA | CALIFORNIA

Zinfandel Paso Robles 1991 • $9 • (10/15/1995) • **84**

KARL LAWRENCE | CALIFORNIA

Cabernet Sauvignon Napa Valley 1996: Concentrated, tightly structured and well balanced, with mineral, currant, black cherry, sage and cedar flavors that remain focused and complex on the finish. Tannins are firm and well integrated. Drink through 2006.–J.L. • $30 • (10/15/1999) • **90**
Cabernet Sauvignon Napa Valley 1994 • $28 • (9/30/1997) • **88**
Cabernet Sauvignon Napa Valley 1993 • $25 • (9/15/1996) • **88**

KARLY | CALIFORNIA

Cabernet Sauvignon El Dorado Stromberg Carpenter Vineyard 1991 • $15 • (11/15/1994) • **82**
Marsanne Amador County 1997: Light in texture, with nectarine and earth flavors lingering on the modest finish. Drink now.–H.S. • $20 • (11/30/1999) • **81**
Orange Muscat Amador County 1995 • $14/375 ml. • (11/30/1996) • **85**
Petite Sirah Amador County Not So Petite Sirah 1991 • $12 • (9/30/1994) • **83**
Petite Sirah Amador County 1989 • $12 • (3/15/1992) • **65**
Petite Sirah Amador County Not So Petite Sirah 1988 • $14 • (12/31/1990) • **81**
Sangiovese Amador County 1994 • $13 • (10/15/1996) • **87**
Sauvignon Blanc Amador County 1998: Rich and fragrant, with gooseberry and passion fruit aromas and just a hint of earthiness. The wine is a little hot on the palate, but still serves up plenty of fresh pea, melon and citrus flavors. Finishes on a minerally note. Drink now. • $10 • (5/31/1999) • **89**
Sauvignon Blanc Amador County 1997 • $10 • (5/15/1998) • **84**
Sauvignon Blanc Amador County 1996 • $10 • (6/30/1997) • **87**
Syrah Amador County 1996: Bright plum, cherry and herb notes blend nicely with a touch of earthiness in this medium-bodied wine. Tannins are a bit rough, however, and the finish is somewhat tart. Drink now through 2004. • $20 • (6/30/1999) • **85**
Syrah Amador County 1995 • $18 • (6/15/1998) • **87**
Syrah Amador County 1992 • $13 • (1/31/1995) • **85**
Zinfandel Amador County 1994 • $12 • (4/30/1996) • **79**
Zinfandel Amador County 1993 • $10 • (10/15/1995) • **82**
Zinfandel Amador County 1992 • $10 • (10/15/1994) • **82**
Zinfandel Amador County 1990 • $9 • (9/15/1993) • **86**
Zinfandel Amador County 1989 • $10 • (10/15/1992) • **74**
Zinfandel Amador County 1988 • $10 • (12/31/1990) • **83**
Zinfandel Amador County Buck's Ten Point 1997: Ripe, soft and pleasant, with modest depth to the earthy blackberry and cherry flavors. Drink now.–J.L. • $16 • (11/15/1999) • **83**
Zinfandel Amador County Pokerville 1995 • $8 • (3/31/1997) • **82**
Zinfandel Amador County Pokerville 1993 • $8 • (10/15/1995) • **87**
Zinfandel Amador County Pokerville 1990 • $6 • (9/15/1993) • **88**
Zinfandel Amador County Sadie Upton Vineyard 1992 • $14 • (1/31/1995) • **88**
Zinfandel Amador County Sadie Upton Vineyard 1991 • $15 • (10/15/1994) • **77**
Zinfandel Amador County Sadie Upton Vineyard 1989 • $15 • (3/31/1992) • **81**
Zinfandel Amador County Warrior Fires 1996: Austere, with an earthy, leathery streak running through the sage and wild berry flavors. Firms up on the finish with drying tannins. Drink through 2005.–J.L. • $20 • (12/31/1998) • **87**
Zinfandel Amador County Warrior Fires 1995 • $20 • (6/15/1998) • **89**
Zinfandel Amador County Warrior Fires 1994 • $20 • (3/31/1997) • **90**

KAZ | CALIFORNIA

Pinot Noir Sonoma County Ashton Vineyard 1995 • $19 • (4/30/1997) • **85**

KEEGAN | CALIFORNIA

Chardonnay Knights Valley 1997: Lots of rich, complex flavors—layers of fig, vanilla, toasty oak and apricot—fan out, turning polished and elegant. Drink now through 2005.–J.L. • $24 • (1/31/2000) • **91**
Pinot Noir Russian River Valley 1997: A bit funky, with earthy, leathery flavors presiding over modest green plum and tealike notes. Turns dry on the finish. Tasted twice, with consistent notes. Drink now through 2005.–J.L. • $28 • (5/15/2000) • **83**
Pinot Noir Russian River Valley 1996: Simple, with a modest band of dried cherry, oak, spice and vanilla, turning dry and leathery on the finish. Best soon.–J.L. • $26 • (8/31/1998) • **82**
Pinot Noir Russian River Valley 1994 • $18 • (7/31/1996) • **87**
Zinfandel Alexander Valley 1996: Ripe and elegant, with an earthy, tarry edge to the plummy, pruny Zinfandel flavors. Finishes with supple tannins and good length. Drink now through 2002.–J.L. • $24 • (5/15/1999) • **88**

KEENAN | CALIFORNIA

Cabernet Sauvignon Napa Valley 1995: Austere, with a crisp, concentrated band of earthy currant, cedar, tar and spicy flavors. Acidity and tannins dominate on the finish. Drink through 2007.–J.L. • $25 • (10/15/1999) • **87**
Cabernet Sauvignon Napa Valley 1992 • $20 • (12/15/1996) • **74**
Cabernet Sauvignon Napa Valley 1991 • $21 • (12/15/1995) • **85**
Cabernet Sauvignon Napa Valley 1989 • $18 • (11/15/1993) • **83**
Cabernet Sauvignon Napa Valley 1988 • $18 • (3/31/1992) • **85**
Cabernet Sauvignon Napa Valley 1987 • $19 • (5/31/1990) • **86**
Cabernet Sauvignon Napa Valley 1986 • $20 • (8/31/1989) • **93**
Cabernet Sauvignon Napa Valley 1985 • $15 • (3/31/1989) • **79**
Cabernet Sauvignon Napa Valley 1984 • $14 • (10/15/1987) SS • **94**
Cabernet Sauvignon Napa Valley 1983 • $11 • (2/15/1987) • **87**
Cabernet Sauvignon Napa Valley 1982 • $13 • (1/01/1986) • **91**
Cabernet Sauvignon Napa Valley 1980 • $14 • (1/01/1984) • **85**
Cabernet Sauvignon Napa Valley 1979: Tasted from magnum. Tastes raw and intense, high in acidity and tannin, with ripe, chewy, rugged plum, currant, earth, cedar and tarry flavors that finish with chewy tannins. This wine isn't fading, so further cellaring might help; a curious wine that seems suspended in time. (1979 California Cabernet retrospective tasting). Try through 2005.–J.L. • $13 • (8/31/1999) • **86**
Cabernet Sauvignon Napa Valley 1978 • $7 ⓐ • (11/15/1992) • **78**
Cabernet Sauvignon Spring Mountain Hillside Estate 1994: Flavors are multitiered and complex, showing black currant, cassis, anise and herbs. Tannins are a bit rustic. Drink through 2004. • $23 • (10/31/1998) • **87**
Chardonnay Napa Valley 1998: Smells stinky and sour, void of fresh fruit. Tasted twice, with consistent notes.–J.L. • $18 • (6/15/2000) • **71**
Chardonnay Napa Valley 1997: Compact, crisp and minerally, with citrus, pear and mild oak notes that linger on the finish. Needs time to unfold. Drink through 2003.–J.L. • $18 • (11/15/1999) • **86**
Chardonnay Napa Valley 1996: Crisp and clean, with attractive earthy pear, citrus and spice flavors and a lingering finish. Try through 2001.–J.L. • $20 • (7/31/1998) • **86**
Merlot Napa Valley 1996: Supple and concentrated plum, mineral and cassis notes are framed by fine-grained tannins. The flavors soar on the finish. Drink now through 2003.–J.L. • $25 • (9/15/1999) • **87**
Merlot Napa Valley 1995 • $30 • (4/30/1998) • **87**
Merlot Napa Valley 1994 • $NA • (3/31/1998) • **86**
Merlot Napa Valley 1993 • $25 • (6/30/1996) • **86**
Merlot Napa Valley 1992 • $17 • (9/30/1995) • **83**
Merlot Napa Valley 1990 • $18 • (7/15/1993) • **83**
Merlot Napa Valley 1989 • $18 • (5/31/1992) • **82**
Merlot Napa Valley 1988 • $18 • (5/31/1992) • **84**
Merlot Napa Valley 1987 • $20 • (3/31/1990) • **88**
Merlot Napa Valley 1986 • $18 • (6/30/1989) • **90**
Merlot Napa Valley 1985 • $19 • (5/31/1988) • **83**
Merlot Napa Valley 1984 • $30 • (7/31/1987) CS • **94**
Merlot Napa Valley Vintners Selection 1990 • $25 • (7/15/1993) • **88**
Zinfandel Napa Valley 1998: Muddled, with a stemmy, tannic edge to the moderately ripe cherry and berry. Turns dry and austere.–J.L. • $22 • (5/31/2000) • **79**

KELHAM MACLEAN | CALIFORNIA

Sauvignon Blanc Oakville 1998: Crisp and refreshing, with clean, polished, elegant grapefruit, passion fruit, tangerine and tart peach flavors. Wonderful balance and finesse tame the grape's aggressive tendencies. Drink now through 2002.–J.L. • $23 • (1/31/2000) • **88**

KEMPTON CLARK | CALIFORNIA

Zinfandel California Mad 1997: Shows a narrow range of tart blackberry and boysenberry flavors, turning lean with a minty edge. Drink now.–H.S. • $12 • (5/15/1999) • **84**
Zinfandel Cucamonga Valley Lopez Ranch 1997: Medium-weight, with blackberry, earth and spice flavors that linger on the soft finish, adding mild tannins. Drink now.–J.L. • $18 • (5/15/1999) • **87**

Key: SS—Spectator Selection CS—Cellar Selection HR—Highly Recommended $NA—Price Not Available a—Auction Price (BT)—Barrel Tasting
For a key to the tasters' initials, see "How to Use These Listings."
Dates in parentheses indicate the issues in which the ratings were published.

KENDALL-JACKSON | CALIFORNIA

Cabernet Franc California Vintner's Reserve 1992 • $15 • (1/31/1995) • **82**
Cabernet Sauvignon Alexander Valley Buckeye Vineyard Single Vineyard Series 1996: Ripe and concentrated with a tight core of mineral and smoky black cherry flavors. Finishes with firm tannins but loses intensity and focus. Drink now through 2004.–J.L. • $65 • (10/15/1999) • **86**
Cabernet Sauvignon Alexander Valley Buckeye Vineyard Single Vineyard Series 1995: Firm texture and pretty fruit flavors promise much in this well-modulated wine, which echoes its plum and black cherry flavors enticingly on the chewy finish. Best after 2000.–H.S. • $33 • (10/31/1998) • **87**
Cabernet Sauvignon Alexander Valley Buckeye Vineyard Single Vineyard Series 1994 • $24 • (8/31/1997) • **88**
Cabernet Sauvignon California Grand Reserve 1998: Ripe and plummy, with cherry, berry and spice, but in this tasting, lacking definition and depth.–J.L. • $75 • (8/31/1999) (BT) • **85-89**
Cabernet Sauvignon California Grand Reserve 1997: Dark, grapey, with spicy plum, currant and wild berry. Finishes with firm tannins and fine balance. Notably elegant at this early stage.–J.L. • $NA • (8/31/1998) (BT) • **90-94**
Cabernet Sauvignon California Grand Reserve 1996: Lots of up-front spicy and plummy flavors, turning elegant and refined. Finishes with a spicy richness and firm, supple tannins. Drink through 2007.–J.L. • $74 • (11/15/1999) • **90**
Cabernet Sauvignon California Grand Reserve 1995: A complex, well-structured, intensely flavored wine, with layers of currant, plum, black cherry and wild berry. Finishes with ripe, well-integrated tannins. Drink through 2005.–J.L. • $50 • (10/31/1998) • **90**
Cabernet Sauvignon California Grand Reserve 1994 • $39 • (7/31/1997) • **87**
Cabernet Sauvignon California Grand Reserve 1992 • $35 • (11/30/1995) • **91**
Cabernet Sauvignon California Grand Reserve 1991 • $30 • (11/15/1994) • **89**
Cabernet Sauvignon California Grand Reserve 1990 • $30 • (11/15/1993) • **90**
Cabernet Sauvignon California Proprietor's Grand Reserve 1988 • $23 • (3/15/1993) • **83**
Cabernet Sauvignon California Proprietor's Grand Reserve 1987 • $16 • (3/31/1992) • **87**
Cabernet Sauvignon California Proprietor's Reserve 1986 • $24 • (3/15/1990) • **85**
Cabernet Sauvignon California Proprietor's Reserve 1985 • $20 • (12/15/1988) • **95**
Cabernet Sauvignon California Vintner's Reserve 1996: Medium-bodied, with a smoky, rustic, barnyard streak to the black cherry and tar flavors. Finishes with leathery tannins. Drink now through 2003.–J.L. • $21 • (10/15/1999) • **83**
Cabernet Sauvignon California Vintner's Reserve 1995: Smooth and supple, with ripe wild berry, cola and cherry flavors, turning a bit earthy-metallic on the finish. Drink through 2003.–J.L. • $18 • (10/31/1998) • **83**
Cabernet Sauvignon California Vintner's Reserve 1994 • $16 • (2/28/1997) • **81**
Cabernet Sauvignon California Vintner's Reserve 1993 • $15 • (3/31/1996) • **85**
Cabernet Sauvignon California Vintner's Reserve 1992 • $14 • (4/30/1995) • **82**
Cabernet Sauvignon California Vintner's Reserve 1991 • $15 • (7/31/1994) • **83**
Cabernet Sauvignon California Vintner's Reserve 1990 • $13 • (11/15/1992) • **83**
Cabernet Sauvignon California Vintner's Reserve 1989 • $13 • (7/31/1992) • **84**
Cabernet Sauvignon California Vintner's Reserve 1987 • $14 • (11/15/1991) • **82**
Cabernet Sauvignon California Vintner's Reserve 1986 • $11 • (12/31/1988) • **85**
Cardinale Meritage California 1991 • $60 • (12/15/1995) • **91**
Cardinale Meritage California 1990 • $50 • (10/15/1994) HR • **91**
Cardinale Meritage California 1989 • $50 • (5/15/1994) • **88**
Cardinale Meritage California 1988 • $50 • (11/15/1993) • **85**
Cardinale Meritage California 1987 • $44 • (3/31/1992) HR • **95**
Cardinale Cabernet Sauvignon California 1986 • $65 ⓐ • (12/15/1996) • **78**
Cardinale Cabernet Sauvignon California 1985 • $45 • (11/15/1989) HR • **97**
Cardinale Cabernet Sauvignon California 1984 • $45 • (7/31/1987) • **84**
Cardinale Cabernet Sauvignon California 1983 • $50 • (10/16/1985) • **82**
Chardonnay Arroyo Seco Paradise Vineyard 1998: Light, with charry lemon notes and a muddled finish.–J.L. • $17 • (6/15/2000) • **77**
Chardonnay Arroyo Seco Paradise Vineyard Single Vineyard Series 1996 • $20 • (6/15/1998) • **88**
Chardonnay California Grand Reserve 1998: Watery and innocuous, with a hint of dilute citrus flavors. Drink now.–J.L. • $23 • (6/15/2000) • **80**
Chardonnay California Grand Reserve 1997: Ripe and polished, with creamy pear and hints of apple and spice, turning to citrus and spicy, anise-tinged oak. Drink now through 2001.–J.L. • $26 • (7/31/1999) • **88**
Chardonnay California Grand Reserve 1996 • $26 • (5/31/1998) • **89**

Chardonnay California Vintner's Reserve 1997: One of the better Vintner's Reserves of late, smooth, ripe and creamy, with complex pear, apple and spice notes that are supple and tender. Drink now.–J.L. • $15 • (11/30/1998) • **87**
Chardonnay California Vintner's Reserve 1996 • $15 • (11/30/1997) • **81**
Chardonnay Santa Maria Valley Camelot Vineyard Single Vineyard Series 1998: Round, with notes of melted butter, honey and cream. Drink now.–J.L. • $17 • (6/15/2000) • **84**
Chardonnay Santa Maria Valley Camelot Vineyard Single Vineyard Series 1997: Ripe and flavorful, with lots of spice, rich fig, pear and subtle honey notes. Turns smooth and creamy. Drink now through 2002.–J.L. • $19 • (7/31/1999) • **89**
Chardonnay Santa Maria Valley Camelot Vineyard Single Vineyard Series 1996: Brimming with complex flavors, this California Chardonnay offers a harmonious blend of ripe pear, nectarine, pineapple and spice, with smoky, toasty oak filling in the gaps nicely. Drink now through 2002.–J.L. • $19 • (7/31/1999) SS • **91**
Gewürztraminer California Vintner's Reserve 1996 • $10 • (11/30/1997) • **84**
Johannisberg Riesling California Vintner's Reserve 1996 • $11 • (7/31/1997) • **85**
Merlot Alexander Valley Buckeye Vineyard Single Vineyard Series 1996: Firm in structure, featuring red currant, toasted oak and herb flavors, finishing lean. Drink through 2004.–J.L. • $33 • (10/15/1999) • **84**
Merlot Alexander Valley Buckeye Vineyard Single Vineyard Series 1995: Firm and crisp, with austere tannins and a twinge of tealike greenness. Offers hints of currant and black cherry. Try now. • $29 • (10/15/1998) • **83**
Merlot California Grand Reserve 1995: Lean and a bit edgy, with crisp tannins and earthy currant, leather and herb notes, turning dry and tannic. Requires a leap of faith. Tasted twice, with consistent notes. Drink now through 2006.–J.L. • $47 • (2/29/2000) • **80**
Merlot California Grand Reserve 1994 • $39 • (6/30/1997) • **85**
Merlot California Grand Reserve 1993 • $42 • (6/30/1996) • **86**
Merlot California Grand Reserve 1992 • $30 • (9/30/1995) • **90**
Merlot California Grand Reserve 1991 • $30 • (9/15/1994) • **86**
Merlot California Vintner's Reserve 1997: Lean, with a strong toasted oak shade to the tart cherry, currant and herb flavors. Finishes lean, but the tannins are balanced, not drying. Drink now through 2003.–J.L. • $17 • (11/15/1999) • **82**
Merlot California Vintner's Reserve 1996: Ripe, juicy plum and currant flavors lack some focus. A touch herbal. Drink now.–J.L. • $19 • (12/15/1998) • **82**
Merlot California Vintner's Reserve 1994 • $18 • (2/28/1997) • **84**
Merlot California Vintner's Reserve 1993 • $NA • (8/31/1996) • **84**
Merlot California Vintner's Reserve 1992 • $15 • (9/15/1994) • **82**
Merlot California Vintner's Reserve 1991 • $14 • (10/15/1993) • **87**
Merlot California Vintner's Reserve 1990 • $14 • (1/31/1993) • **83**
Merlot California Vintner's Reserve 1989 • $14 • (5/31/1992) • **75**
Merlot California Vintner's Reserve 1988 • $14 • (11/15/1991) • **84**
Merlot Sonoma County The Proprietor's 1987 • $20 • (12/31/1990) • **87**
Pinot Noir California Grand Reserve 1996: Tight, with spicy strawberry, cherry, cola and tea flavors, finishing with light, grainy tannins. Drink now through 2002.–J.L. • $30 • (9/15/1999) • **86**
Pinot Noir California Grand Reserve 1994 • $30 • (2/28/1997) • **84**
Pinot Noir California Grand Reserve 1993 • $30 • (3/31/1995) • **88**
Pinot Noir California Proprietor's Grand Reserve 1992 • $30 • (10/31/1994) • **86**
Pinot Noir California Proprietor's Grand Reserve 1991 • $30 • (2/28/1994) • **82**
Pinot Noir California Vintner's Reserve 1997: Firm, with a narrow range of strawberry and tea flavors before the tannins clamp down.–J.L. • $16 • (9/15/1999) • **84**
Pinot Noir California Vintner's Reserve 1996 • $15 • (12/31/1997) • **83**
Pinot Noir California Vintner's Reserve 1994 • $14 • (11/15/1995) • **88**
Pinot Noir California Vintner's Reserve 1993 • $14 • (3/31/1995) • **83**
Pinot Noir California Vintner's Reserve 1992 • $13 • (2/28/1994) • **82**
Pinot Noir California Vintner's Reserve 1991 • $13 • (9/15/1993) • **80**
Pinot Noir California Vintner's Reserve 1990 • $13 • (2/28/1993) • **82**
Pinot Noir Santa Maria Valley Julia's Vineyard 1988 • $14 • (11/15/1991) • **82**
Riesling California Late Harvest Select 1993 • $15 • (7/31/1995) • **86**
Sauvignon Blanc California Grand Reserve 1997: A Chardonnay look-alike, with pronounced vanilla and butter notes and subtle peach flavors. Drink now through 2002.–J.L. • $20 • (5/31/2000) • **84**
Sauvignon Blanc California Grand Reserve 1996: Fairly tangy, with hints of vanilla on the nose. The flavors touch on sweet pea, fig and citrus, with a hint of fresh-mowed grass on the refreshing finish. Drink now. • $20 • (5/31/1999) • **86**
Sauvignon Blanc California Vintner's Reserve 1997: A medium-bodied wine that offers light citrus and herb notes, with hints of green apple and minerals on the clean and fresh finish. Drink now. • $11 • (5/31/1999) • **82**
Sauvignon Blanc California Vintner's Reserve 1996 • $11 • (12/15/1997) • **82**
Syrah California Grand Reserve 1992 • $20 • (7/31/1996) • **86**
Syrah California Grand Reserve 1991 • $20 • (9/30/1994) • **88**
Syrah California Proprietor's Grand Reserve 1990 • $16 • (2/15/1993) • **88**
Syrah California Vintner's Reserve 1996: Lean and focused, with a solid core of wild cherry, strawberry and herb flavors. Finishes clean and fairly long, with moderate acidity and ripe, firm tannins. Drink now through 2004. • $16 • (2/28/1999) • **87**
Syrah California Vintner's Reserve 1990 • $14 • (10/31/1993) • **83**
Syrah Sonoma Valley Durell Vineyard 1990 • $16 • (5/15/1995) • **85**
Syrah Sonoma Valley Durell Vineyard 1988 • $24 • (8/31/1991) • **89**
Syrah Sonoma Valley Durell Vineyard 1987 • $17 • (12/15/1989) • **90**
Syrah Sonoma Valley Durell Vineyard 1986 • $14 • (11/30/1988) • **92**
Zinfandel Anderson Valley DuPratt Vineyard 1990 • $20 • (9/30/1993) • **88**
Zinfandel Anderson Valley DuPratt Vineyard 1987 • $20 • (7/31/1991) HR • **90**
Zinfandel Anderson Valley DuPratt-DePatie Vineyard 1986 • $16 • (12/15/1989) • **85**
Zinfandel Anderson Valley DuPratt-DePatie Vineyard 1983 • $10 • (11/01/1985) • **76**
Zinfandel California Grand Reserve 1997: Round and simple, with plum flavors. Drink now.–J.L. • $25 • (6/15/2000) • **82**
Zinfandel California Grand Reserve 1996: Lightly fruity, with elegant cherry and wild berry flavors, a touch of pretty oak and modest tannins. Drink through 2001.–J.L. • $25 • (5/15/1999) • **87**
Zinfandel California Grand Reserve 1994 • $25 • (4/30/1997) • **90**
Zinfandel California Grand Reserve 1993 • $25 • (8/31/1996) • **82**
Zinfandel California Grand Reserve 1992 • $20 • (1/31/1995) • **84**
Zinfandel California Grand Reserve 1991 • $20 • (10/15/1994) • **86**
Zinfandel California Proprietor's Grand Reserve 1990 • $16 • (1/31/1993) • **89**
Zinfandel California Vintner's Reserve 1997: A restrained style, showing pepper, cherry, raspberry and tea notes. Finishes with smooth tannins. Drink now.–J.L. • $21 • (11/15/1999) • **84**
Zinfandel California Vintner's Reserve 1996: Pleasant and soft-textured, with a modest range of raspberry and wild berry flavors, finishing with integrated tannins. Drink now.–J.L. • $16 • (5/15/1999) • **83**
Zinfandel California Vintner's Reserve 1995 • $18 • (7/31/1997) • **82**
Zinfandel California Vintner's Reserve 1994 • $14 • (4/30/1996) • **83**
Zinfandel California Vintner's Reserve 1993 • $14 • (10/15/1995) • **83**
Zinfandel California Vintner's Reserve 1992 • $12 • (10/15/1994) • **83**
Zinfandel California Vintner's Reserve 1991 • $10 • (9/30/1993) • **84**
Zinfandel California Vintner's Reserve 1990 • $9 • (12/15/1992) • **78**
Zinfandel California Vintner's Reserve 1989 • $11 • (9/30/1991) • **84**
Zinfandel Mendocino Ciapusci Vineyard 1989 • $20 • (10/15/1992) • **82**
Zinfandel Mendocino Ciapusci Vineyard 1988 • $20 • (10/15/1992) • **77**
Zinfandel Mendocino Ciapusci Vineyard 1984 • $16 • (12/15/1989) • **86**
Zinfandel Mendocino County DuPratt Vineyard Proprietor's Grand Reserve 1990 • $23 • (10/15/1992) • **84**
Zinfandel Mendocino Zeni Vineyard 1990 • $20 • (10/15/1992) • **83**

KENNEDY, KATHRYN | CALIFORNIA

Cabernet Sauvignon Santa Cruz Mountains 1996: Tight, earthy and leathery, with tar, tobacco and earthy cherry and berry-laced fruit. Firms up on the finish, where the tannins have a strong presence. Best from 2001 through 2009.–J.L. • $110 • (12/15/1999) • **87**
Cabernet Sauvignon Santa Cruz Mountains 1995: Tight, lean and very concentrated, with a distinctive earthy, dusty blackberry flavor. Finishes with complexity and length. Best from 2001 through 2008.–J.L. • $110 • (12/15/1998) • **88**
Cabernet Sauvignon Santa Cruz Mountains 1993 • $70 • (10/31/1997) • **91**
Cabernet Sauvignon Santa Cruz Mountains 1992 • $63 • (7/31/1996) • **87**
Cabernet Sauvignon Santa Cruz Mountains 1991 • $54 • (11/15/1994) • **87**
Cabernet Sauvignon Santa Cruz Mountains 1990 • $54 • (6/15/1994) • **89**
Cabernet Sauvignon Santa Cruz Mountains 1989 • $54 • (3/31/1993) • **87**
Cabernet Sauvignon Santa Cruz Mountains 1988 • $60 • (11/15/1991) • **88**
Cabernet Sauvignon Santa Cruz Mountains 1987 • $45 • (12/15/1997) • **92**
Cabernet Sauvignon Santa Cruz Mountains 1986 • $37 • (3/15/1990) • **81**
Cabernet Sauvignon Santa Cruz Mountains 1985 • $33 • (12/15/1988) • **93**
Lateral California 1997: Rustic, with a barnyard edge to the complex leather, mushroom, currant, plum and sage flavors. Starts plush but firms up on the finish where the flavors continue to develop. Drink through 2005.–J.L. • $30 • (10/15/1999) • **88**
Lateral California 1996: Offers good ripe cherry, plum and wild berry character, turning supple and complex, with coffee, herb and cedar notes and firm, dry tannins. Drink now through 2002.–J.L. • $35 • (11/30/1998) • **86**
Lateral California 1995 • $26 • (4/30/1998) • **83**

KENNEDY, KATHRYN

Lateral California 1993 • $25 • (12/15/1995) • **86**
Lateral California 1991 • $18 • (11/15/1993) • **86**
Lateral California 1990 • $17 • (10/15/1992) • **88**
Lateral California 1989 • $17 • (11/15/1991) • **86**
Lateral California 1988 • $15 • (10/15/1990) • **87**
Syrah Santa Cruz Mountains Maridon Vineyard 1996: Packs in a lot of attractive ripe plum, wild berry, spice and black cherry, with a smooth, supple texture and long, rich aftertaste. Drink through 2006.–J.L. • $38 • (11/30/1998) • **91**

KENT, STEVEN | CALIFORNIA

Cabernet Sauvignon Livermore Valley Folkendt Vineyard 1996: Supple and full-bodied, with firm, ripe tannins and layers of coffee, black cherry, black currant, mint and herbs. The finish is moderate, tapering off with some elegance. Drink through 2004. • $45 • (9/30/1999) • **87**

KENWOOD | CALIFORNIA

Cabernet Sauvignon Sonoma County Artist Series 1995: Tight and on the austere side, with earthy cedar, clay and tobacco flavors dominating the currant and dried cherry fruit underneath. Needs time to grow into its flavors, as the tannins are firm. Best from 2001 through 2010.–J.L. • $65 • (12/15/1999) • **88**
Cabernet Sauvignon Sonoma Valley Artist Series 20th Anniversary 1994: Beautifully crafted, sleek and elegant, sharply focused on ripe, rich cherry, currant, plum and berry. Picks up pretty floral and spicy nuances and the tannins, while firm, are supple and integrated. Drink through 2007–J.L. • $65 • (11/15/1998) • **93**
Cabernet Sauvignon Sonoma Valley Artist Series 1993 • $50 • (10/31/1997) CS • **90**
Cabernet Sauvignon Sonoma Valley Artist Series 1992 • $31 ⓐ • (12/15/1996) • **91**
Cabernet Sauvignon Sonoma Valley Artist Series 1991 • $40 • (11/15/1994) • **89**
Cabernet Sauvignon Sonoma Valley Artist Series 1990 • $30 • (12/15/1993) • **86**
Cabernet Sauvignon Sonoma Valley Artist Series 1989: Firm, chunky and intense, with a meaty core of currant, mineral, cedar, earth and sage flavors, finishing with a still-immense core of tannins and good length, missing just finesse. (1989 California Cabernet retrospective tasting). Drink now through 2007.–J.L. • $38 ⓐ • (8/31/1999) • **89**
Cabernet Sauvignon Sonoma Valley Artist Series 1988: Firm, tight and tannic, an austere style, with a trim band of spicy, earthy currant and tobacco flavors. Still needs time to soften but may dry out, too. (1988 California Cabernet retrospective tasting). Drink now through 2002.–J.L. • $35 • (11/15/1998) • **86**
Cabernet Sauvignon Sonoma Valley Artist Series 1987 • $189 ⓐ • (12/15/1997) • **91**
Cabernet Sauvignon Sonoma Valley Artist Series 1986 • $58 ⓐ • (12/15/1996) • **90**
Cabernet Sauvignon Sonoma Valley Artist Series 1985 • $43 ⓐ • (2/15/1989) • **91**
Cabernet Sauvignon Sonoma Valley Artist Series 1984 • $36 ⓐ • (11/30/1987) • **93**
Cabernet Sauvignon Sonoma Valley Artist Series 1983 • $30 • (11/15/1986) CS • **92**
Cabernet Sauvignon Sonoma Valley Artist Series 1982 • $41 ⓐ • (11/01/1985) • **89**
Cabernet Sauvignon Sonoma Valley Artist Series 1981 • $53 ⓐ • (9/16/1984) SS • **89**
Cabernet Sauvignon Sonoma Valley Artist Series 1979: This wine has always had a cedary edge to the ripe cherry, mint and currant flavors, and it's still aging quite well if a shade past its peak. Turns quite tannic on the finish. (1979 California Cabernet retrospective tasting). Drink now through 2005.–J.L. • $20 • (8/31/1999) • **88**
Cabernet Sauvignon Sonoma County Artist Series 1978: Has aged well, and is now fully mature, with elegant currant, cedar, anise and sage. Starts to dry out on the finish, but held up well for more than an hour. (1978 California Cabernet retrospective tasting). Drink now through 2002.–J.L. • $20 • (11/15/1998) • **87**
Cabernet Sauvignon Sonoma County Yulupa 1996: Medium in weight, with herbal overtones to the black cherry, plum and light vanilla flavors. Firm but well-integrated tannins. Drink now through 2004.–J.L. • $14 • (6/15/1999) • **85**

Key: SS—Spectator Selection CS—Cellar Selection HR—Highly Recommended $NA—Price Not Available a—Auction Price (BT)—Barrel Tasting
For a key to the tasters' initials, see "How to Use These Listings."
Dates in parentheses indicate the issues in which the ratings were published.

Cabernet Sauvignon Sonoma Valley 1998: Racy, a touch green, with tealike and stemmy flavors. The berryish notes lack some definition and focus. –J.L. • $NA • (8/31/1999) (BT) • **85-89**
Cabernet Sauvignon Sonoma Valley 1997: Smooth, ripe and already plush in texture. Sharply focused, rich with currant, black cherry, herb and olive. Elegant and supple, long on the finish.–J.L. • $NA • (8/31/1998) (BT) • **90-94**
Cabernet Sauvignon Sonoma Valley 1996: Focused and rich-textured, with herb, mineral, cherry and tar flavors that keep going on the finish. Tannins are well integrated. Drink now through 2005.–J.L. • $21 • (9/15/1999) • **87**
Cabernet Sauvignon Sonoma Valley 1995: Light, with a cedar and tobacco edge to the medium-weight currant and cherry flavors. Picks up earthy mushroom notes on the finish. Drink through 2004.–J.L. • $18 • (10/31/1998) • **85**
Cabernet Sauvignon Sonoma Valley 1994 • $18 • (10/31/1997) • **88**
Cabernet Sauvignon Sonoma Valley 25th Anniversary Vintage 1993 • $16 • (12/15/1996) • **85**
Cabernet Sauvignon Sonoma Valley 25th Anniversary Vintage 1992 • $16 • (10/31/1995) • **86**
Cabernet Sauvignon Sonoma Valley 1991 • $16 • (11/15/1994) • **82**
Cabernet Sauvignon Sonoma Valley 1990 • $17 • (11/15/1993) • **84**
Cabernet Sauvignon Sonoma Valley 1989 • $15 • (11/15/1992) SS • **91**
Cabernet Sauvignon Sonoma Valley 1988: A nice wine, a shade on the dry, tannic side, with herb, currant, sage and cedary oak flavors. Best now, before it dries out. (1988 California Cabernet retrospective tasting).–J.L. • $10 • (11/15/1998) • **83**
Cabernet Sauvignon Sonoma Valley 1987 • $12 • (12/15/1997) • **88**
Cabernet Sauvignon Sonoma Valley 1986 • $NA • (12/15/1996) • **84**
Cabernet Sauvignon Sonoma Valley 1985 • $15 • (2/15/1989) • **91**
Cabernet Sauvignon Sonoma Valley 1984 • $12 • (5/31/1988) • **83**
Cabernet Sauvignon Sonoma Valley 1983 • $10 • (2/15/1988) • **85**
Cabernet Sauvignon Sonoma Valley Jack London Vineyard 1996: Somewhat rustic, with drying tannins up front, the smoky oak, blackberry, currant and herb flavors barrel through with muscle, nonetheless. This vineyard usually takes some time to come around; will be worth waiting for. Best from 2002 through 2010. • $30 • (10/15/1999) • **88**
Cabernet Sauvignon Sonoma Valley Jack London Vineyard 1995: Tight and trim, with a focused, austere band of spicy currant, cedar and cherry. Turns supple at midpalate and softens a bit on the finish, where the flavors spread out. Drink through 2005.–J.L. • $25 • (10/31/1998) • **89**
Cabernet Sauvignon Sonoma Valley Jack London Vineyard 1994 • $25 • (10/31/1997) • **88**
Cabernet Sauvignon Sonoma Valley Jack London Vineyard 1993 • $25 • (11/15/1996) • **88**
Cabernet Sauvignon Sonoma Valley Jack London Vineyard 1992 • $20 • (10/31/1995) • **87**
Cabernet Sauvignon Sonoma Valley Jack London Vineyard 1991 • $20 • (11/15/1994) • **83**
Cabernet Sauvignon Sonoma Valley Jack London Vineyard 1989 • $20 • (11/15/1992) • **89**
Cabernet Sauvignon Sonoma Valley Jack London Vineyard 1987 • $41 ⓐ • (12/15/1997) • **89**
Cabernet Sauvignon Sonoma Valley Jack London Vineyard 1986 • $NA • (12/15/1996) • **89**
Cabernet Sauvignon Sonoma Valley Jack London Vineyard 1985 • $21 • (10/15/1988) • **89**
Cabernet Sauvignon Sonoma Valley Jack London Vineyard 1984 • $21 • (11/30/1987) • **91**
Cabernet Sauvignon Sonoma Valley Jack London Vineyard 1983 • $21 • (2/15/1987) • **86**
Cabernet Sauvignon Sonoma Valley Jack London Vineyard 1980 • $25 • (5/16/1984) • **80**
Chardonnay Sonoma County 1998: Herbal, with penetrating citrus flavors, but soapy and raw. Drink now.–J.L. • $15 • (4/30/2000) • **80**
Chardonnay Sonoma County 1997: Pleasing. Marked by crisp, clean grapefruit, pear and apple notes, it fans out and turns refreshing. Drink now.–J.L. • $15 • (11/30/1998) • **87**
Chardonnay Sonoma County 1996 • $15 • (6/15/1998) • **87**
Chardonnay Sonoma County Yulupa 1997: A ripe, tropical blend, with hints of melon, mango and hazelnut. Firmly structured and bright on the finish, the wine is refreshing and clean. Part of Kenwood's restaurant-only Yulupa line of wines. Drink now through 2001. • $11 • (7/31/1999) • **87**
Chardonnay Sonoma Valley Reserve 1997: Tight, starting with smoky oak and working into complex pear, cedar, butterscotch and spice flavors that linger on the finish. Drink through 2002.–J.L. • $25 • (1/31/1999) • **87**
Chardonnay Sonoma County-Santa Maria Valley Reserve 1996: A racy style, with a grassy, Sauvignon Blanc-like edge and hints of oak, pear, cedar and

spice. The texture is a bit rough, unlike the rich, polished wine that emerged in 1995. Drink now through 2001.–J.L. • $22 • (7/31/1998) • **88**

Merlot Sonoma County 1997: Shows a range of polished black cherry, wild berry and earthy coffee flavors and finishes with supple tannins. Drink now through 2002.–J.L. • $21 • (10/15/1999) • **85**

Merlot Sonoma County 1996: Lacks a solid fruit core, but still serves up toasty oak, plum, licorice and herb flavors and a smoky finish. Drink now through 2002. • $20 • (9/30/1998) • **82**

Merlot Sonoma County 1992 • $16 • (7/31/1995) • **83**

Merlot Sonoma County 1991 • $16 • (9/15/1994) • **80**

Merlot Sonoma County 1990 • $16 • (6/15/1993) • **86**

Merlot Sonoma County 1989 • $15 • (1/31/1993) • **83**

Merlot Sonoma Valley Estate 1996: Ripe cherry and blackberry flavors lend a juicy, almost chewy air to this wine. The finish is a bit short, but the ensemble is quite attractive. Drink now through 2003. • $22 • (9/30/1998) • **85**

Merlot Sonoma Valley Jack London Vineyard 1997: Tight and firm, with dark, rich currant and dusty berry flavors and mineral, anise and sage notes that are complex yet restrained, finishing with solid tannins. Best from 2001 through 2010.–J.L. • $30 • (2/29/2000) • **88**

Merlot Sonoma Valley Jack London Vineyard 1996: A touch herbal, with cherry and berry notes, it turns dry, earthy and tannic on the finish. Give it time in the cellar. Drink through 2003.–J.L. • $25 • (9/30/1998) • **84**

Merlot Sonoma Valley Jack London Vineyard 1993 • $18 • (7/31/1996) • **81**

Merlot Sonoma County Jack London Vineyard 1992 • $18 • (9/30/1995) • **88**

Merlot Sonoma Mountain Jack London Vineyard 1991 • $18 • (6/30/1994) • **87**

Merlot Sonoma Mountain Jack London Vineyard 1990 • $18 • (6/15/1993) • **82**

Merlot Sonoma Valley Massara 1996: Fairly tight, with astringent tannins. Flavors come through, however, with cassis, blackberry and mint at the fore. Finishes with a hint of bitterness. Best from 2001 through 2005. • $25 • (10/15/1999) • **84**

Merlot Sonoma Valley Massara 1994 • $25 • (11/30/1997) • **85**

Merlot Sonoma Valley Massara Vineyards 1992 • $18 • (2/28/1995) • **84**

Pinot Noir Russian River Valley 1997: Fairly light in color and texture, with a blend of cherry and herb flavors couched in medium acidity. Finishes moderately, with hints of tea and earth. Drink now through 2002. • $17 • (9/15/1999) • **84**

Pinot Noir Russian River Valley 1996: Dry and earthy, with a glimmer of ripe cherry and berry-laced flavors, but it dries out on the finish, where it picks up floral notes. Drink now.–J.L. • $17 • (8/31/1998) • **82**

Pinot Noir Russian River Valley 1995 • $16 • (11/30/1997) • **82**

Pinot Noir Russian River Valley 1993 • $14 • (10/15/1995) • **84**

Pinot Noir Russian River Valley Olivet Lane 1996: Well proportioned, with a simple but appealing core of supple plum and black cherry flavors with light oak shadings. Drinks well now.–J.L. • $25 • (8/31/1998) • **85**

Pinot Noir Russian River Valley Olivet Lane 1993 • $22 • (10/15/1995) • **87**

Pinot Noir Sonoma Valley Jack London Vineyard 1997: Soft and supple, with a lush cherrylike core. The wine remains lean, however, finishing bright and clean, tinged with hints of herbs and anise. Drink now through 2003. • $20 • (9/15/1999) • **86**

Pinot Noir Sonoma Valley Jack London Vineyard 1996: Smooth, ripe and supple, with an appealing array of plum, blackberry, cherry and vanilla, finishing with a complex aftertaste that echoes fruit and smoky oak. Well made. Drink now through 2001.–J.L. • $20 • (9/15/1998) • **86**

Pinot Noir Sonoma Valley Jack London Vineyard 1992 • $18 • (3/31/1995) • **80**

Pinot Noir Sonoma Valley Jack London Vineyard 1990 • $18 • (9/30/1992) • **85**

Pinot Noir Sonoma Valley Jack London Vineyard 1989 • $15 • (10/31/1991) • **80**

Pinot Noir Sonoma Valley Jack London Vineyard 1984 • $15 • (5/31/1989) • **77**

Sauvignon Blanc Sonoma County 1998: Here's a tasty California white, starting off with hints of passion fruit and peach, then following through with pretty lemon-lime and herb flavors. It's fresh and light on the palate, with a long, flavorful finish. Good price and lots to go around. Drink now. • $11 • (9/30/1999) • **88**

Sauvignon Blanc Sonoma County 1997: Bright character of grass and lemon-lime balances subtle tones of melon and peach in this clean and firm California white, with the flavors fading pleasantly on the moderate finish. Nice for the price. Drink now. • $10 • (12/31/1998) • **85**

Sauvignon Blanc Sonoma County 1996 • $11 • (7/31/1997) • **88**

Sauvignon Blanc Sonoma County Reserve 1998: The peach, citrus and herb flavors carry through to the slightly tinny finish. Serve well chilled. Drink now through 2002.–J.L. • $15 • (5/31/2000) • **82**

Sauvignon Blanc Sonoma Valley Reserve 1997: Leans toward herb and grapefruit flavors up front. A lean, focused texture is complemented by a lemon-lime core that extends well into the bright, clean, mineral finish. Fairly elegant. Drink now through 2002. • $15 • (5/15/1999) • **87**

Sauvignon Blanc Sonoma Valley Reserve 1996 • $15 • (3/31/1998) • **88**

Zinfandel Geyserville Mazzoni 1997: Tight, with a narrow beam of earth, leather and dried berry flavors. Drink now.–J.L. • $20 • (5/31/2000) • **80**

Zinfandel Geyserville Mazzoni 1996: Quite earthy, and the fruit is mature, with leathery dried cherry and berryish flavors. Drink now through 2002.–J.L. • $20 • (5/15/1999) • **86**

Zinfandel Geyserville Mazzoni 1995 • $20 • (6/15/1998) • **87**

Zinfandel Geyserville Mazzoni 1994 • $20 • (4/30/1997) • **88**

Zinfandel Geyserville Mazzoni 1993 • $15 • (9/30/1995) • **89**

Zinfandel Lodi Old Vine 1997: Ripe, round and seductive, with pleasantly soft smoke, strawberry jam, spice and pepper flavors. Finishes with ripe tannins. Drink now through 2001.–J.L. • $11 • (6/15/1999) • **87**

Zinfandel Lodi Old Vine 1996: Rich and ripe-tasting, offering chunky plum and black cherry flavors and picking up cedar and tar notes that add dimension on the finish, this California Zinfandel is an impressive package at a reasonable price. Ready now.–J.L. • $10 • (5/31/1999) • **85**

Zinfandel Sonoma County 1997: Dried berry and leather notes show good depth and moderate tannins. Drink now through 2003.–J.L. • $15 • (6/15/2000) • **84**

Zinfandel Sonoma Valley 1997: Of medium weight, with mint, black cherry and charry notes and a tannic finish. Drink now through 2004.–J.L. • $15 • (1/31/2000) • **83**

Zinfandel Sonoma Valley 1996: Crisp, marked by earthy cherry, berry, tar and anise flavors, it finishes with a nice peppery edge and firm, drying tannins. Drink now through 2002.–J.L. • $15 • (12/15/1998) • **86**

Zinfandel Sonoma Valley 1995 • $15 • (6/15/1998) • **85**

Zinfandel Sonoma Valley 1994 • $14 • (4/30/1997) • **87**

Zinfandel Sonoma Valley 1992 • $12 • (7/31/1995) • **84**

Zinfandel Sonoma Valley 1991 • $12 • (10/15/1994) • **82**

Zinfandel Sonoma Valley 1990 • $12 • (9/30/1993) • **86**

Zinfandel Sonoma Valley 1988 • $14 • (12/31/1990) • **82**

Zinfandel Sonoma Valley 1987 • $15 • (10/31/1989) • **90**

Zinfandel Sonoma Valley 1985 • $15 • (5/15/1988) • **89**

Zinfandel Sonoma Valley 1984 • $16 • (9/15/1987) • **90**

Zinfandel Sonoma Valley 1983 • $16 • (11/15/1986) • **88**

Zinfandel Sonoma Valley 1982 • $16 • (7/16/1986) • **90**

Zinfandel Sonoma Valley Barricia 1994 • $20 • (4/30/1997) • **88**

Zinfandel Sonoma Valley Barricia 1993 • $16 • (1/01/1995) • **85**

Zinfandel Sonoma Valley Barricia Vineyard 1991 • $16 • (10/15/1994) • **84**

Zinfandel Sonoma Valley Barricia Vineyard 1990 • $12 • (10/15/1992) • **89**

Zinfandel Sonoma Valley Jack London Vineyard 1997: Firm and structured, with a tight band of earthy berry, sage, cedar, tar and spice, finishing with a nice touch of oak. Drink now through 2007.–J.L. • $20 • (2/29/2000) • **87**

Zinfandel Sonoma Valley Jack London Vineyard 1996: Medium-weight, with a pleasant array of spice, cedar, wild berry and black cherry flavors that are more subtle than powerful; still an elegant, complete wine. Drink now through 2002.–J.L. • $20 • (5/15/1999) • **87**

Zinfandel Sonoma Valley Jack London Vineyard 1995 • $20 • (3/31/1998) • **87**

Zinfandel Sonoma Valley Jack London Vineyard 1994 • $20 • (9/30/1996) • **85**

Zinfandel Sonoma Valley Jack London Vineyard 1993 • $14 • (10/15/1995) • **84**

Zinfandel Sonoma Valley Jack London Vineyard 1992 • $14 • (10/15/1994) • **82**

Zinfandel Sonoma Mountain Jack London Vineyard 1991 • $14 • (9/30/1993) • **86**

Zinfandel Sonoma Valley Jack London Vineyard 1990 • $14 • (10/15/1992) • **84**

Zinfandel Sonoma Valley Jack London Vineyard 1989 • $14 • (9/30/1991) • **83**

Zinfandel Sonoma Valley Jack London Vineyard 1987 • $12 • (12/15/1989) • **88**

Zinfandel Sonoma Valley Nuns Canyon 1997: Tough and chewy, with earthy, minty, leathery flavors dominating the rustic anise and metallic notes.–J.L. • $20 • (5/31/2000) • **78**

Zinfandel Sonoma Valley Nuns Canyon 1996: A touch earthy, with herb and sage overtones and a flavor core built around ripe cherry, blackberry, tea and spice. Mild tannins. Drink now through 2004.–J.L. • $20 • (1/31/1999) • **88**

Zinfandel Sonoma Valley Nuns Canyon 1995 • $20 • (6/15/1998) • **84**

Zinfandel Sonoma Valley Nuns Canyon 1994 • $20 • (4/30/1997) • **89**

Zinfandel Sonoma Valley Nuns Canyon 1993 • $16 • (4/30/1996) • **90**

Zinfandel Sonoma Valley Upper Weise 1997: Rustic, with chunky, chewy dried berry and raspberry, turning ruggedly tannic. Drink now through 2005.–J.L. • $20 • (5/31/2000) • **82**

Zinfandel Sonoma Valley Upper Weise 1996: Somewhat muted in flavor, with dried cherry and berryish tones, it's supple in texture if lacking in overt fruitiness. Drink now through 2001.–J.L. • $20 • (5/15/1999) • **86**

Zinfandel Sonoma Valley Upper Weise Ranch 1995 • $20 • (6/15/1998) • **84**

Zinfandel Sonoma Valley Upper Weise Ranch Old Vine 1994 • $20 • (4/30/1997) • **89**

KERR, J. | CALIFORNIA

Pinot Noir Santa Barbara County 1991 • $19 • (8/31/1994) • **85**
Pinot Noir Santa Barbara County 1990 • $19 • (3/31/1995) • **80**

KESTREL | CALIFORNIA

Merlot Sierra Foothills Limited Release 1996 • $17 • (5/31/1998) • **81**
Trinity Limited Release Amador County 1994 • $27 • (11/30/1997) • **85**

KESTREL | WASHINGTON

Cabernet Sauvignon Columbia Valley 1995: Distinctive for its spicy, bay leaf-scented berry and coffee flavors, harmonious in the way it wraps it all in a firm blanket of gentle tannins, finishing with style and grace. Drink now through 2007.–H.S. • $25 • (12/31/1999) • **91**
Chardonnay Columbia Valley 1996: Ripe and generous, a smooth-textured wine, with layers of rich pear, caramel, spice and honey flavors that echo enticingly on the long finish. Drink now through 2006.–H.S. • $18 • (12/31/1999) • **92**

KING ESTATE | OREGON

Cabernet Sauvignon Oregon 1994: On the light side for Cabernet, but the spicy thwack of oak tends to obscure the modest berry and herb flavors. Drink through 2003.–H.S. • $30 • (7/31/1998) • **81**
Cabernet Sauvignon Oregon 1992 • $30 • (4/30/1997) • **84**
Chardonnay Oregon 1997: Light, bright and fresh, with a polished texture. Apple, pear and toasty spice notes harmonize through the finish. Drink now through 2002.–H.S. • $14 • (4/30/2000) • **86**
Chardonnay Oregon 1996: A supple, generous, warm mouthful of pear, caramel, apple and leesy notes that linger on the round finish. Drink now through 2001.–H.S. • $14 • (4/30/1999) • **88**
Chardonnay Oregon Reserve 1997: Delicate and flavorful at the same time, offering honeyed pineapple and grapefruit notes that linger on a gentle frame. Drink now through 2002.–H.S. • $18 • (4/30/2000) • **87**
Chardonnay Oregon Reserve 1996: Bright and focused, smooth in texture, generous with its pear, spice and dark honey flavors that linger gently on the elegant finish. Drink now.–H.S. • $18 • (4/30/1999) • **89**
Pinot Gris Oregon 1998: Light, almost silky, with pretty melon and pineapple flavors that remain smooth and vibrant through the refreshing finish. Drink now.–H.S. • $14 • (4/30/2000) • **87**
Pinot Gris Oregon 1997: Bright and refreshing for its spicy melon and almond flavors and nicely lingering finish. Drink now.–H.S. • $13 • (4/30/1999) • **85**
Pinot Gris Oregon 1996 • $13 • (3/31/1998) • **80**
Pinot Gris Oregon Reserve 1998: Bright and appealing for its generous pear and melon flavors, which linger crisply. Drink now.–H.S. • $18 • (4/30/2000) • **87**
Pinot Gris Oregon Reserve 1997: A lovely white, smooth and round on the palate, delivering a generous portion of melon, spicy pear and caramel flavors that linger beautifully, drawing you back for another sip. Drink now.–H.S. • $18 • (4/30/1999) SS • **90**
Pinot Gris Oregon Reserve 1996 • $18 • (3/31/1998) • **87**
Pinot Noir Oregon 1996: Light in texture and flavor, with pretty caramel-scented raspberry notes echoing on the finish. Drink now.–H.S. • $18 • (4/30/1999) • **83**
Pinot Noir Oregon 1995 • $18 • (3/31/1998) • **86**
Pinot Noir Oregon 1994 • $18 • (2/28/1997) • **88**
Pinot Noir Oregon 1993 • $18 • (3/31/1996) • **87**
Pinot Noir Oregon 1992 • $18 • (11/30/1994) • **85**
Pinot Noir Oregon Reserve 1996: Smooth, ripe and appealing for its spicy blackberry and smoke aromas and flavors, which firm up and linger on the finish. Drink now through 2002.–H.S. • $35 • (4/30/1999) • **88**
Pinot Noir Oregon Reserve 1994 • $35 • (6/15/1997) • **91**
Zinfandel Oregon 1994: A supple, harmonious red with pretty plum and spice flavors that linger on the moderately chewy finish. Drink through 2001.–H.S. • $20 • (7/31/1998) • **85**

Key: SS—Spectator Selection CS—Cellar Selection HR—Highly Recommended $NA—Price Not Available a—Auction Price (BT)—Barrel Tasting
For a key to the tasters' initials, see "How to Use These Listings."
Dates in parentheses indicate the issues in which the ratings were published.

KIONA | WASHINGTON

Cabernet Sauvignon Washington 1996 • $15 • (1/31/1998) • **85**
Cabernet Sauvignon Washington 1995 • $15 • (8/31/1997) • **90**
Cabernet Sauvignon Washington 1993 • $15 • (9/15/1996) • **86**
Cabernet Sauvignon Washington 1991 • $12 • (9/30/1994) • **86**
Cabernet Sauvignon Washington 1990 • $12 • (7/31/1994) • **84**
Cabernet Sauvignon Yakima Valley 1992 • $20 • (1/01/1997) • **85**
Cabernet Sauvignon Yakima Valley 1991 • $18 • (9/30/1995) • **86**
Cabernet Sauvignon Yakima Valley 1990 • $18 • (8/31/1995) • **89**
Cabernet Sauvignon Yakima Valley 1989 • $15 • (7/31/1994) • **87**
Cabernet Sauvignon Yakima Valley Estate Bottled 1986 • $14 • (10/15/1989) • **89**
Cabernet Sauvignon Yakima Valley Reserve 1996: Firm in texture, noteworthy for its grace and well-modulated intensity, offering berry and herb flavors that linger on the harmonious finish. Drink now through 2004.–H.S. • $35 • (12/31/1999) • **89**
Cabernet Sauvignon Yakima Valley Reserve 1995: Jam-packed with flavor, jazzy, with spicy black cherry and currant flavors on a racy frame. Made for the cellar, it has fine-grained tannins and plenty of intensity. Best from 2002 through 2010.–H.S. • $30 • (5/31/1999) • **88**
Cabernet Sauvignon Yakima Valley Reserve 1994: Very ripe, Port-like flavors effuse black cherry, plum and chocolate. Feels almost sweet as it bulges with flavor, although the finish closes up. Drink through 2004.–H.S. • $18/375 ml. • (9/30/1998) • **86**
Cabernet Sauvignon Yakima Valley Reserve 1993 • $28 • (6/15/1998) • **87**
Cabernet Sauvignon Yakima Valley Tapteil Vineyard 1989 • $12 • (3/15/1993) • **89**
Cabernet Sauvignon Yakima Valley Tapteil Vineyard 1988 • $12 • (3/31/1992) • **85**
Cabernet-Merlot Washington 1997: Open-textured and generous, allowing plenty of black cherry, cinnamon and cola flavors to emerge. Drink now through 2002.–H.S. • $12 • (8/31/1999) • **86**
Chardonnay Columbia Valley 1997: Smooth, polished and deftly balanced, with pretty pear, honey and spice flavors that linger engagingly on the silky finish. Better than an earlier sample. Drink now through 2003.–H.S. • $18 • (6/30/1999) • **89**
Chardonnay Washington 1997: Chardonnay on your shopping list? How about this brightly styled, budget-minded version. It's aromatic and tasty, with pretty apple and guava aromas and flavors that persist appealingly on the open-textured finish. Drink now through 2002.–H.S. • $10 • (5/31/1999) • **87**
Chardonnay Yakima Valley Reserve 1996 • $18 • (6/15/1998) • **87**
Chenin Blanc Columbia Valley 1998: On the dry side, with light, juicy nectarine and melon flavors in modest proportions. Drink now.–H.S. • $7 • (8/31/1999) • **83**
Chenin Blanc Columbia Valley 1997: Light and delicately sweet, with grapefruit and apple flavors shining through the finish. Drink now.–H.S. • $6 • (9/30/1998) • **85**
Chenin Blanc Columbia Valley 1996 • $6 • (9/15/1997) • **83**
Chenin Blanc Late Harvest Yakima Valley Ice Wine 1993 • $19/375 ml. • (9/30/1994) • **80**
Chenin Blanc Late Harvest Yakima Valley Ice Wine 1989 • $20/375 ml. • (4/15/1995) • **68**
Gewürztraminer Late Harvest Yakima Valley 1997: Ripe and sweet, pillow-soft in texture, with lovely rose-scented pear and honey flavors that persist on the delicate finish. Drink now through 2002.–H.S. • $7/375 ml. • (9/30/1998) • **89**
Gewürztraminer Late Harvest Yakima Valley 1994 • $7/375 ml. • (9/30/1995) • **87**
Gewürztraminer Late Harvest Yakima Valley 1993 • $6/375 ml. • (9/30/1994) • **89**
Lemberger Washington 1997: Smooth and generous with its ripe fruit flavors, plus a strong earthy-gamy streak that persists on the finish. Not for everyone. Drink now.–H.S. • $10 • (6/15/1999) • **83**
Lemberger Washington 1995 • $10 • (9/15/1997) • **84**
Lemberger Yakima Valley 1994 • $10 • (9/15/1996) • **88**
Lemberger Yakima Valley 1993 • $10 • (9/30/1995) • **85**
Lemberger Yakima Valley 1992 • $10 • (9/30/1994) • **84**
Lemberger Yakima Valley 1990 • $10 • (9/30/1994) • **79**
Lemberger Yakima Valley 1989 • $9 • (5/15/1992) • **76**
Merlot Columbia Valley 1996: Ripe and focused, this firm-textured red has solid blackberry and plum flavors at the core, shaded with pretty hints of spice and toast. Drink now.–H.S. • $22 • (1/31/1999) • **87**
Merlot Columbia Valley 1994 • $18 • (9/15/1996) • **85**
Merlot Columbia Valley 1993 • $15 • (7/31/1996) • **85**

Merlot Columbia Valley 1992 • $12 • (9/30/1995) • **91**
Merlot Columbia Valley 1991 • $12 • (9/30/1994) • **87**
Merlot Columbia Valley 1990 • $12 • (6/15/1993) • **81**
Merlot Columbia Valley 1989 • $12 • (3/31/1992) • **86**
Merlot Columbia Valley 1988 • $12 • (5/31/1991) • **84**
Merlot-Cabernet Washington 1995 • $12 • (9/15/1996) • **85**
Muscat Yakima Valley Late Harvest 1994 • $7/375 ml. • (9/30/1995) • **82**
Muscat Yakima Valley Late Harvest 1993 • $7/375 ml. • (9/30/1994) • **89**
Red Columbia Valley 1997: On the light side, with pretty raspberry and spice flavors, this open-textured wine is appealing now for its freshness.–H.S. • $10 • (9/30/1998) • **85**
Vintage Rosé Washington 1997: On the dry side, this is generous with its straight-on guava and strawberry flavors. Finishes with a hint of green. Drink now.–H.S. • $6 • (9/30/1998) • **83**
White Riesling Columbia Valley 1998: Light and fragrant, delicately sweet and silky, offering nice peach and mineral flavors that recede gradually on the finish. Drink now.–H.S. • $7 • (9/30/1999) • **85**
White Riesling Columbia Valley 1997 • $7 • (6/30/1998) • **84**
White Riesling Columbia Valley 1996 • $6 • (9/15/1997) • **87**
White Riesling Columbia Valley Dry 1998: Fresh and appealing for its pretty apple and floral aromas and flavors on a lightly off-dry frame. Drink now. –H.S. • $6 • (6/30/1999) • **87**
White Riesling Columbia Valley Dry 1997: Aromatic and expressive, with pretty green apple, nectarine and floral aromas and flavors that linger enticingly on the finish. Picks up a nice hint of mineral. Drink now.–H.S. • $6 • (9/30/1998) • **88**
White Riesling Late Harvest Yakima Valley 1997: Frankly sweet, with pretty apricot, peach and pear flavors rolling smoothly through the long finish. Harmonious and tasty already. Drink now through 2001.–H.S. • $9 • (9/30/1998) • **90**
White Riesling Yakima Valley Late Harvest 1994 • $7/375 ml. • (9/15/1995) • **85**
White Riesling Yakima Valley Late Harvest 1991 • $6/375 ml. • (9/30/1994) • **86**

KISTLER | CALIFORNIA

Cabernet Sauvignon Sonoma Valley Kistler Estate Vineyard 1991 • $30 • (6/15/1995) HR • **90**
Cabernet Sauvignon Sonoma Valley Kistler Estate Vineyard 1990 • $30 • (2/28/1994) • **86**
Cabernet Sauvignon Sonoma Valley Kistler Estate Vineyard 1988 • $25 • (8/31/1992) • **86**
Cabernet Sauvignon Sonoma Valley Kistler Estate Vineyard 1987 • $33 • (2/28/1991) • **83**
Cabernet Sauvignon Sonoma Valley Kistler Estate Vineyard 1986 • $20 • (9/30/1989) • **84**
Cabernet Sauvignon Sonoma Valley Kistler Estate Vineyard 1985 • $17 • (5/31/1988) • **92**
Chardonnay Carneros Hudson Vineyard 1996: There's a wonderful range of ripe, exotic, complex flavors in this wine—tiers of concentrated earthy pear, citrus, fig and apricot—and it exhibits an elegance and finesse rarely achieved in California Chardonnay. Just wish there was more of it. Drink now through 2004.–J.L. • $48 • (6/30/1999) HR • **97**
Chardonnay Carneros Hyde Vineyard 1996: Intense, with complex earthy pear, fig, melon, citrus and hazelnut flavors that are remarkably elegant and sophisticated, long and lingering on the finish. Drink now through 2004.–J.L. • $45 • (3/31/1999) • **96**
Chardonnay Russian River Valley Dutton Ranch 1996: Starts out smoky and toasty, turning its focus to the ripe pear, fig, apricot and anise flavors, with a touch of hazelnut on the aftertaste. Drink now through 2002.–J.L. • $69 Ⓐ • (6/30/1999) • **93**
Chardonnay Russian River Valley Vine Hill Vineyard 1996: Tight and flinty, with rich pear, fig, anise, vanilla and hazelnut flavors that start out subtly and build to a rich, complex aftertaste. Drink now through 2002.–J.L. • $72 Ⓐ • (6/30/1999) • **93**
Chardonnay Sonoma Coast Camp Meeting Ridge 1996: Rich, smoky and exotic, with toasty oak, vanilla, fig, pear and hazelnut flavors that are deeply concentrated, long and complex on the finish. Drink now through 2004.–J.L. • $69 Ⓐ • (3/31/1999) • **97**
Chardonnay Sonoma Mountain McCrea Vineyard 1996: Tightly reined in, intense and deeply concentrated, with an elegant, bright core of pear, anise, hazelnut, citrus and honeyed notes, lingering long and lively on the finish. Drink now through 2004.–J.L. • $69 Ⓐ • (3/31/1999) • **96**
Chardonnay Sonoma Valley Durell Vineyard 1996: This is a delicious mouthful of Chardonnay. It's big, bold, rich and creamy, brimming with tiers of flavor—vanilla, pear, anise, fig and melon—and finishing with harmonious notes of smoke and nectarine. Drink now through 2002.–J.L. • $67 Ⓐ • (3/31/1999) HR • **95**
Chardonnay Sonoma Valley Kistler Vineyard 1996: Tight, rich and concentrated, with a pretty array of creamy oak, custard, citrus, pear and buttery oak flavors that fan out and gain nuance on the finish. Drink now through 2003.–J.L. • $50 • (6/30/1999) • **94**
Pinot Noir Russian River Valley Dutton Ranch 1987 • $15 • (3/31/1990) • **85**
Pinot Noir Russian River Valley Dutton Ranch 1986 • $14 • (6/15/1988) • **89**
Pinot Noir Russian River Valley Kistler Vineyard 1996: Deliciously rich and focused, with a bright core of ripe plum, black cherry, anise, cedar and spice. Impressively gains nuance and complexity on the finish, where the flavors sail on. Drink now through 2006.–J.L. • $55 • (6/30/1999) • **92**
Pinot Noir Russian River Valley Kistler Vineyard Cuvée Catherine 1994 • $45 • (3/31/1997) HR • **95**
Pinot Noir Russian River Valley Kistler Vineyard Cuvée Catherine 1992 • $40 • (12/31/1995) • **90**
Pinot Noir Sonoma Coast Camp Meeting Ridge 1994 • $38 • (6/30/1997) • **94**
Pinot Noir Sonoma Coast Cuvée Catherine 1996: Wonderful fruit purity. Ripe, rich and focused, with complex plum, raspberry, blueberry and spice, picking up light toasty oak on the finish. Shows enough tannic strength to merit short-term cellaring. Drink through 2006.–J.L. • $60 • (6/30/1999) • **92**
Pinot Noir Sonoma Coast Hirsch Vineyard 1995 • $50 • (6/30/1998) • **90**
Pinot Noir Sonoma Mountain McCrea Vineyard 1992 • $22 • (3/31/1995) • **88**

KNAPP | NEW YORK

Pinot Noir Finger Lakes 1992 • $13 • (11/15/1994) • **78**
Prism Finger Lakes 1993 • $NA • (6/30/1995) • **76**
Vignoles Finger Lakes Late Harvest 1991 • $17 • (6/30/1995) • **86**

KNIPPRATH | WASHINGTON

Cabernet Sauvignon Columbia Valley 1994 • $12 • (9/30/1997) • **88**
Lemberger Yakima Valley Pleasant Vineyards 1992 • $8 • (9/30/1994) • **81**
Merlot Washington 1995 • $13 • (10/15/1997) • **86**
Pinot Noir Columbia Valley 1994 • $10 • (11/30/1997) • **85**
Port Washington NV • $17 • (11/30/1997) • **84**

KNUDSEN ERATH | OREGON

Pinot Noir Willamette Valley 1993 • $12 • (3/31/1996) • **81**
Pinot Noir Willamette Valley 1992 • $10 • (3/15/1994) • **80**
Pinot Noir Willamette Valley 1991 • $10 • (3/15/1994) • **79**
Pinot Noir Willamette Valley 1990 • $12 • (2/28/1993) • **72**
Pinot Noir Willamette Valley 1988 • $11 • (5/31/1991) • **82**
Pinot Noir Willamette Valley 1987 • $11 • (2/15/1990) • **65**
Pinot Noir Willamette Valley 1986 • $10 • (6/15/1988) • **72**
Pinot Noir Willamette Valley Leland Vineyards Reserve 1987 • $24 • (2/15/1990) • **89**
Pinot Noir Willamette Valley Unfiltered Reserve 1991 • $22 • (11/30/1994) • **84**
Pinot Noir Willamette Valley Vintage Select 1992 • $16 • (2/28/1995) • **85**
Pinot Noir Willamette Valley Vintage Select 1991 • $16 • (1/31/1994) • **86**
Pinot Noir Willamette Valley Vintage Select 1987 • $16 • (3/15/1994) • **72**
Pinot Noir Willamette Valley Vintage Select 1986 • $15 • (6/15/1988) • **87**
Pinot Noir Willamette Valley Vintage Select 1985 • $NA • (9/30/1987) • **90**
Pinot Noir Yamhill County Vintage Select 1985 • $20 • (2/15/1990) • **75**
Pinot Noir Yamhill County Vintage Select 1983 • $35 • (2/15/1990) • **81**
White Riesling Willamette Valley Late Harvest 1994 • $8 • (3/31/1996) • **86**

KONGSGAARD | CALIFORNIA

Chardonnay Napa Valley 1997: Delicious California Chardonnay. Packs in lots of rich, supple, complex flavors, with a range of ripe fig, pear, apricot, melon and citrus, as well as a lively seam of acidity that keeps the flavors bright and lively. Subtle toasty oak adds dimension. Drink now through 2005.–J.L. • $96 Ⓐ • (1/31/2000) HR • **96**
Chardonnay Napa Valley 1996: Displays wonderful complexity and richness of flavors, with ripe, smooth fig, anise and pear woven together, finishing long and lively. Drink now through 2004.–J.L. • $82 Ⓐ • (3/31/1999) • **95**

KONRAD | CALIFORNIA

Barbera Amador County 1992 • $12 • (7/31/1995) • **85**
Charbono Mendocino 1992 • $11 • (11/15/1995) • **81**

Mélange à Trois Mendocino 1992 • $13 • (12/15/1995) • **85**
Mélange à Trois Mendocino 1991 • $12 • (3/15/1994) • **86**
Mélange à Trois Mendocino County 1989 • $16 • (7/15/1992) • **87**
Petite Sirah Mendocino 1991 • $12 • (9/30/1994) • **84**
Petite Sirah Port Mendocino Admiral's Quinta 1990 • $18 • (11/15/1993) • **74**
Zinfandel Mendocino 1992 • $10 • (10/15/1995) • **79**
Zinfandel Mendocino 1991 • $9 • (10/15/1994) • **80**
Zinfandel Mendocino County 1990 • $9 • (9/30/1993) • **88**
Zinfandel Mendocino County 1989 • $10 • (3/31/1992) • **84**

KORBEL | CALIFORNIA

Blanc de Noirs Russian River Valley Champagne Master's Reserve 1992: Starts off with pretty toast, dough and citrus aromas, then kicks into gear with complex hazelnut, fig, melon, cherry, lemon-lime and spice. Terrific price. Drink now. • $14 • (12/15/1998) • **90**
Blanc de Noirs California Cuvée Pinot Noir Champagne Master's Reserve 1991 • $15 • (11/30/1996) • **82**
Blanc de Noirs California Cuvée Master's Reserve 1990 • $15 • (5/31/1995) • **78**
Brut California NV: A fruity style, featuring apple and lemon flavors. Somewhat simple, yet pleasant and light on the palate. Drink now. • $11 • (10/15/1999) • **82**
Brut Rosé California Atlanta 1996 NV • $11 • (11/30/1996) • **86**
Brut Rosé California Jane Seymour NV • $13 • (5/15/1998) • **80**
Brut Rosé California Sinatra NV • $13 • (11/30/1997) • **80**
Brut Rosé California Whoopi Goldberg Artist Series NV: Tart and tangy, showing hints of cherry, watermelon and lemon. Pleasant and simple. Drink now. • $13 • (10/15/1999) • **81**
Cabernet Sauvignon Alexander Valley Heck Family Cellar Selection 1995: Emits pretty aromas of black currant, mushroom and smoke. A bit restrained at this point, the powdery tannins holding back blackberry, blueberry, anise and herb flavors. Better with more bottle age. Drink now through 2005. • $18 • (10/31/1998) • **87**
Cabernet Sauvignon Alexander Valley 1991 • $13 • (11/15/1994) • **73**
Chardonnay Champagne California NV: Pleasant enough, with bright apple and citrus flavors. Finishes clean and fresh. Drink now. • $13 • (10/15/1999) • **83**
Chardonnay Russian River Valley Heck Family Cellar Selection 1997: Tropical fruit, apple and spice flavors are tightly wound on a firm, elegant frame. Finishes with complex toast and fruit flavors. Drink now through 2001.–J.L. • $15 • (6/30/1999) • **88**
Chardonnay Russian River Valley Heck Family Cellar Selection 1996 • $15 • (3/31/1998) • **88**
Commemorative Cuvée Sonoma County NV: A bit sweet, though showing bright acidity. Green apple notes are a bit one-dimensional and there's slight oxidation; fun to quaff now. • $18 • (10/15/1999) • **82**
Kosher Champagne California NV: Pleasant and bright on the palate, with hints of toast and citrus. Finishes clean but short. Drink now. • $13 • (10/15/1999) • **83**
Le Premier Reserve Russian River Valley 1993: A lean style, with a lemony core. Fresh and clean, it harbors nice apple and herb flavors, if lacks the complexity of last year's release. Bright on the finish, it could improve in the bottle. Drink now. • $22 • (12/31/1998) • **85**
Le Premier Reserve California 1991 • $20 • (12/15/1997) HR • **91**
Natural' California NV: Toasty, zingy, lemony flavors in this bright, up-front wine wrap the palate in snappy acidity. Try with raw oysters. Drink now through 2002. • $12 • (12/15/1998) • **86**
Natural' Sonoma County 1996: Crisp apple and lemon notes form the core of this bright bubbly. It's refreshing and light-textured. Drink now through 2002. • $13 • (10/15/1999) • **86**
Rouge California NV: Smoky, earthy black currant and cassis flavors rise to the fore. Pleasant enough, but why bother with the bubbles? Drink now. • $12 • (12/15/1998) • **84**
Rouge Sonoma County NV: Red bubbly—a different animal. Pleasant enough, with tangy cherry and herb notes and a touch of astringent tannins. Drink now. • $13 • (10/15/1999) • **83**

Key: SS—Spectator Selection CS—Cellar Selection HR—Highly Recommended $NA—Price Not Available a—Auction Price (BT)—Barrel Tasting
For a key to the tasters' initials, see "How to Use These Listings."
Dates in parentheses indicate the issues in which the ratings were published.

KRAMER | OREGON

Chardonnay Willamette Valley Dijon Clone 1998: Distinctly floral, with aromas reminiscent of daisies and rose petals around a core of pear and citrus that comes through on the finish. Drink now through 2003.–H.S. • $20 • (4/30/2000) • **87**
Pinot Gris Willamette Valley 1997: Soft, almost syrupy, with earthy notes up front and modest fruit on the finish.–H.S. • $10 • (4/30/1999) • **79**
Pinot Gris Willamette Valley Estate Bottled 1996: On the crisp side, with pretty floral and apple flavors that persist on the finish.–H.S. • $12 • (11/15/1998) • **83**
Pinot Gris Willamette Valley Kimberley's Reserve 1998: Ripe and supple, a wine of delicacy and grace that features pear, vanilla and melon flavors that linger on the refreshing finish. Drink now.–H.S. • $18 • (5/15/2000) • **88**
Pinot Gris Willamette Valley Reserve 1996: Light, round and flavorful, with ripe nectarine and earth notes that linger on the open-textured finish. Drink now.–H.S. • $15 • (6/30/1999) • **85**
Pinot Noir Willamette Valley Estate Bottled 1996: Lean and chewy, very firm for a light-bodied wine, with modest berry and plum flavors lurking behind the chewy layers. Drink through 2002.–H.S. • $18 • (4/30/1999) • **81**
Pinot Noir Willamette Valley 1994 • $15 • (12/31/1996) • **81**
Pinot Noir Willamette Valley 1993 • $18 • (1/31/1996) • **87**
Pinot Noir Willamette Valley 1992 • $18 • (3/15/1994) • **84**
Pinot Noir Willamette Valley Estate Bottled 1991 • $18 • (2/28/1993) • **86**
Pinot Noir Willamette Valley Rebecca's Reserve 1998: Black cherry, currant and dark spice flavors vie for attention in this aromatic, focused, generous wine. Tannins are way in the background, making this tempting to consume early. Drink now through 2006.–H.S. • $30 • (4/30/2000) • **89**
Pinot Noir Yamhill County 1993 • $NA • (2/28/1997) • **73**
Pinot Noir Yamhill County 1991 • $14 • (2/28/1993) • **83**
Pinot Noir Yamhill County Reserve 1996: Silky and charming, with pretty blackberry and spice flavors that linger on the gentle finish. Drink now.–H.S. • $25 • (4/30/1999) • **84**
Pinot Noir Yamhill County Reserve 1992 • $22 • (1/31/1996) • **86**
Pinot Noir Yamhill County Reserve 1991 • $22 • (3/15/1994) • **82**
Riesling Willamette Valley Select Cluster 1992 • $12/375 ml. • (11/30/1994) • **77**

KRISTONE | CALIFORNIA

Blanc de Blancs California 1992 • $40 • (11/30/1997) • **90**
Blanc de Blancs California 1991 • $60 • (11/30/1995) • **87**
Blanc de Noirs California 1992 • $40 • (12/15/1997) • **82**
Blanc de Noirs California 1991 • $60 • (11/30/1995) • **91**
Brut Rosé California 1991 • $60 • (11/30/1995) • **90**
Brut Rosé California Late Disgorged 1991: Starts off on a doughy, almost cedary note, then serves up a blend of sour cherry, apple and citrus flavors. Unusual. Drink now. • $45 • (10/15/1999) • **82**

KRUG, CHARLES | CALIFORNIA

Cabernet Sauvignon Napa Valley Peter Mondavi Family 1996: Straightforward, with earthy black cherry, toasted oak and cedar flavors. Drink now.–J.L. • $16 • (9/15/1999) • **82**
Cabernet Sauvignon Napa Valley Peter Mondavi Family 1995: Black cherry, licorice and herb flavors framed in a whole lot of toasty oak—the ensemble is nice, if not totally balanced. Finish is moderate. Drink now through 2002. • $16 • (10/31/1998) • **84**
Cabernet Sauvignon Napa Valley Peter Mondavi Family 1994 • $14 • (8/31/1997) • **89**
Cabernet Sauvignon Napa Valley 1993 • $12 • (9/15/1996) • **83**
Cabernet Sauvignon Napa Valley 1992 • $12 • (12/15/1995) • **84**
Cabernet Sauvignon Napa Valley 1991 • $12 • (11/15/1994) • **81**
Cabernet Sauvignon Napa Valley 1990 • $12 • (10/31/1993) • **88**
Cabernet Sauvignon Napa Valley 1989 • $12 • (11/15/1992) • **77**
Cabernet Sauvignon Napa Valley 1988 • $12 • (3/15/1992) • **73**
Cabernet Sauvignon Napa Valley 1987 • $11 • (11/15/1991) • **79**
Cabernet Sauvignon Napa Valley 1986 • $11 • (2/28/1991) • **87**
Cabernet Sauvignon Napa Valley 1985 • $11 • (1/31/1990) • **77**
Cabernet Sauvignon Napa Valley 1965 • $35 • (7/16/1985) • **74**
Cabernet Sauvignon Napa Valley 1962 • $65 • (7/16/1985) • **84**
Cabernet Sauvignon Napa Valley 1961 • $125 • (7/16/1985) • **84**
Cabernet Sauvignon Napa Valley 1952 • $250 • (7/16/1985) • **86**
Cabernet Sauvignon Napa Valley 1951 • $250 • (7/16/1985) • **80**
Cabernet Sauvignon Napa Valley 1947 • $300 • (7/16/1985) • **89**
Cabernet Sauvignon Napa Valley 1944 • $NA • (7/16/1985) • **95**

Cabernet Sauvignon Napa Valley Vintage Selection 1994 • $35 • (10/31/1997) • **88**
Cabernet Sauvignon Napa Valley Vintage Selection 1993 • $35 • (6/30/1997) • **79**
Cabernet Sauvignon Napa Valley Vintage Selection 1991 • $28 • (12/15/1995) • **89**
Cabernet Sauvignon Napa Valley Vintage Selection 1988: Tasted from magnum. Tart, with crisp tannins and a narrow beam of black cherry and currant. Can age further, but given the sharp acidity and tannins and the lack of depth, don't expect it to improve. (1988 California Cabernet retrospective tasting). Drink now through 2002.–J.L. • $28 • (11/15/1998) • **84**
Cabernet Sauvignon Napa Valley Vintage Selection 1986 • $28 • (10/31/1992) HR • **92**
Cabernet Sauvignon Napa Valley Vintage Selection 1985 • $29 • (3/15/1992) • **89**
Cabernet Sauvignon Napa Valley Vintage Selection 1984 • $26 • (6/30/1990) • **87**
Cabernet Sauvignon Napa Valley Vintage Selection 1983 • $24 • (6/30/1990) • **81**
Cabernet Sauvignon Napa Valley Vintage Selection 1981 • $25 • (9/30/1990) • **90**
Cabernet Sauvignon Napa Valley Vintage Selection 1978 • $31 • (11/15/1992) • **78**
Cabernet Sauvignon Napa Valley Vintage Selection 1974 • $44 • (11/15/1994) • **81**
Cabernet Sauvignon Napa Valley Vintage Selection 1966 • $53 • (6/01/1985) • **87**
Cabernet Sauvignon Napa Valley Vintage Selection 1957 • $135 • (7/16/1985) • **81**
Chardonnay Carneros Peter Mondavi Family Reserve 1997: A clean, tangy wine, with lemony zest and subtle vanilla and pear hints on the finish. Light and refreshing. Drink now. • $21 • (11/15/1999) • **86**
Chardonnay Carneros Peter Mondavi Family Reserve 1996 • $20 • (5/15/1998) • **86**
Chardonnay Napa Valley Peter Mondavi Family 1998: Sour lemon flavors are focused and straightforward. Drink now.–J.L. • $15 • (6/30/2000) • **80**
Chardonnay Napa Valley Peter Mondavi Family 1996 • $15 • (5/31/1998) • **83**
Chenin Blanc Napa Valley Pineau 1996 • $13 • (10/15/1997) • **88**
Merlot Napa Valley Peter Mondavi Family 1996: Offers a focused core of rich black cherry, plum and earth flavors framed by spicy toasted oak notes. Ripe tannins make this easy to enjoy now.–J.L. • $16 • (12/15/1998) • **86**
Merlot Napa Valley Peter Mondavi Family 1995 • $15 • (7/31/1997) SS • **92**
Merlot Napa Valley Peter Mondavi Family 1994 • $14 • (11/30/1996) • **86**
Merlot Napa Valley 1993 • $14 • (8/31/1996) • **79**
Merlot Napa Valley 1992 • $14 • (3/31/1995) • **83**
Merlot Napa Valley 1991 • $13 • (9/15/1994) • **81**
Merlot Napa Valley 1990 • $14 • (6/15/1993) • **85**
Merlot Napa Valley 1989 • $13 • (5/31/1992) • **84**
Merlot Napa Valley Peter Mondavi Family Reserve 1994 • $23 • (4/30/1998) • **86**
Merlot Napa Valley Peter Mondavi Family Reserve 1993 • $22 • (2/28/1997) • **84**
Merlot Napa Valley Peter Mondavi Family Reserve 1992 • $22 • (8/31/1996) • **82**
Peter Mondavi Family Generations Napa Valley 1994 • $30 • (10/31/1997) • **87**
Peter Mondavi Family Generations Napa Valley 1993 • $30 • (6/30/1997) • **84**
Peter Mondavi Family Generations Napa Valley 1992 • $30 • (2/28/1997) • **84**
Peter Mondavi Family Generations Napa Valley 1991 • $30 • (9/15/1996) • **85**
Pinot Noir Napa Valley Carneros 1994 • $9 • (7/31/1996) • **83**
Pinot Noir Napa Valley Carneros 1993 • $9 • (12/31/1995) • **81**
Pinot Noir Napa Valley Carneros 1992 • $9 • (1/31/1995) • **82**
Pinot Noir Napa Valley Carneros 1991 • $9 • (2/28/1994) • **78**
Pinot Noir Napa Valley Carneros 1990 • $9 • (2/28/1993) • **78**
Pinot Noir Napa Valley Carneros 1989 • $10 • (2/15/1992) • **82**
Pinot Noir Napa Valley Carneros Peter Mondavi Family 1996: Velvety, with delicate berry nuances and herbal notes, turning spicy on the finish. Drink now through 2001.–J.L. • $16 • (9/15/1999) • **83**
Sangiovese Napa Valley Reserve 1996: Light, bright and fruity, with simple, pleasant cherry flavors. Drink now. • $16 • (12/31/1998) • **82**
Sangiovese Napa Valley Family Reserve 1993 • $16 • (9/15/1996) • **80**
Sangiovese Napa Valley Peter Mondavi Family Reserve 1995 • $16 • (5/15/1998) • **80**
Sangiovese Napa Valley Peter Mondavi Family Reserve 1993 • $22 • (2/28/1997) • **83**
Zinfandel Napa Valley Peter Mondavi Family 1996: Rich, smooth and smoky, with a spicy edge to the caramel, cherry and toasted oak notes. The flavors linger on the smooth finish. Drink now.–J.L. • $11 • (11/15/1999) • **85**
Zinfandel Napa Valley 1993 • $7 • (11/30/1996) • **81**
Zinfandel Napa Valley 1992 • $7 • (10/15/1994) • **81**
Zinfandel Napa Valley 1990 • $6 • (9/30/1993) • **74**
Zinfandel Napa Valley 1989 • $6 • (12/15/1990) • **83**

KUNDE | CALIFORNIA

Cabernet Sauvignon Sonoma Valley 1996: Rich and focused, showing ripe and earthy black cherry, currant and cedar flavors. Finishes with firm leathery tannins. Drink now through 2005.–J.L. • $20 • (9/30/1999) • **87**
Cabernet Sauvignon Sonoma Valley 1994 • $17 • (8/31/1997) • **82**
Cabernet Sauvignon Sonoma Valley 1993 • $15 • (10/15/1996) • **85**
Cabernet Sauvignon Sonoma Valley 1990 • $15 • (3/15/1993) • **88**
Cabernet Sauvignon Sonoma Valley Reserve 1995: Tart, but showing pretty cherry, smoke, blackberry and cedar notes. Somewhat lean, with mild tannins, it finishes moderately. Drink now through 2003. • $24 • (10/15/1999) • **85**
Cabernet Sauvignon Sonoma Valley Reserve 1994: Marked by a cedary edge and firm tannins, with a tight core of earthy currant flavor. Best from 2001 through 2007.–J.L. • $24 • (2/28/1999) • **87**
Cabernet Sauvignon Sonoma Valley Reserve 1993 • $24 • (11/15/1997) • **81**
Cabernet Sauvignon Sonoma Valley Reserve 1991 • $23 • (5/31/1996) • **85**
Cabernet Sauvignon Sonoma Valley Reserve 1990 • $23 • (11/15/1993) • **82**
Chardonnay Sonoma Valley 1998: Oak, pear and vanilla flavors have modest concentration. Drink now.–J.L. • $15 • (6/15/2000) • **84**
Chardonnay Sonoma Valley 1996 • $15 • (4/30/1998) • **87**
Chardonnay Sonoma Valley C.S. Ridge 1997: Elegant and perfumed, with spicy pear and citrus notes of modest depth and proportion. Drink now.–J.L. • $20 • (4/30/2000) • **85**
Chardonnay Sonoma Valley Kinneybrook 1997: Ripe, flavorful and complex with a range of citrus, fig, pear and earthy, minerally notes. Crisp and focused on the finish. Drink now through 2001.–J.L. • $20 • (8/31/1999) • **89**
Chardonnay Sonoma Valley Kinneybrook 1996: Ripe, rich and smoky, with a tight, complex band of fig, toast, pear and apricot flavors that fan out on the finish, gaining nuance and complexity. Drink through 2002.–J.L. • $20 • (12/15/1998) • **90**
Chardonnay Sonoma Valley Reserve 1996: Firm, tight and spicy, with a pretty, toasty oak overlay and creamy pear, spice, vanilla and apple notes. Could use short-term cellaring to round out the rough edges. Try through 2002.–J.L. • $22 • (9/15/1998) • **89**
Chardonnay Sonoma Valley Wildwood Vineyard 1997: A bit coarse and simple, with modest spicy Muscat-like fruit and a touch of ripe pear. Drink now.–J.L. • $20 • (4/30/2000) • **85**
Chardonnay Sonoma Valley Wildwood 1996: Ripe, rich and smoky, with tight pear, fig and hazelnut notes. Finishes with a crisp, intense aftertaste. Drink through 2001.–J.L. • $20 • (12/15/1998) • **88**
Claret Louis Kunde Founder's Reserve Sonoma Valley 1990 • $17 • (11/15/1993) • **88**
Claret Louis Kunde Founder's Reserve Sonoma Valley 1989 • $15 • (11/15/1992) • **90**
Fumé Blanc Sonoma Valley Magnolia Lane Vineyard 1998: Grassy, with racy, herbal, seedy grapefruit peel notes, turning earthy and funky. Drink now.–J.L. • $18 • (4/30/2000) • **81**
Merlot Sonoma Valley 1995 • $17 • (11/30/1997) • **82**
Merlot Sonoma Valley 1993 • $17 • (12/31/1995) • **88**
Merlot Sonoma Valley 1991 • $15 • (9/15/1994) • **77**
Muscat Canelli Sonoma Valley Late Harvest Louis Kunde Founder's Reserve 1995 • $11/375 ml. • (11/30/1996) • **88**
Sauvignon Blanc Sonoma Valley Magnolia Lane 1997: Firm, focused and lively, with a framework of bracing acidity supporting the array of citrus, fig, melon and herb flavors that linger through the finish, this California white offers an attractive combination of good drinking and good value. Ready now through 2002. • $11 • (1/31/1999) • **86**
Sauvignon Blanc Sonoma Valley Magnolia Lane 1996 • $11 • (10/15/1997) • **85**
Syrah Sonoma Valley 1997: Very fragrant and unusual, with pronounced black currant and apricot aromas. Rich and ripe, this concentrated Syrah has fine depth to the cocoa flavors. Good length. Drink now through 2004.–J.L. • $20 • (5/15/2000) • **88**
Syrah Sonoma Valley 1995 • $18 • (11/15/1997) • **88**
Viognier Sonoma Valley 1997: Leans toward peach and mineral flavors, which unfold in a spicy blend. The finish is a touch oily, but the ensemble remains refreshing. Drink now. • $18 • (12/31/1998) • **84**

Viognier Sonoma Valley 1996 • $18 • (12/15/1997) • **84**

Zinfandel Sonoma Valley 1997: Solid, chunky, somewhat unevolved, with earthy cherry, wild berry, raspberry, tar and spicy flavors, finishing with firm tannins. Best after 2000.–J.L. • $15 • (6/30/1999) • **88**

Zinfandel Sonoma Valley 1996 • $15 • (3/31/1998) • **85**

Zinfandel Sonoma Valley Robusto 1997: Tastes ripe and sweet but at the same time stripped, turning dry and earthy. Drink now.–J.L. • $30 • (4/30/2000) • **81**

Zinfandel Sonoma Valley Robusto 1995 • $24 • (7/31/1997) • **94**

Zinfandel Sonoma Valley The Shaw Vineyard Century Vines 1997: Very ripe, firm and dry, with earthy tannins wrapped around a core of spicy wild berry, blackberry and pepper notes. Best from 2001 through 2007.–J.L. • $24 • (4/30/2000) • **87**

Zinfandel Sonoma Valley The Shaw Vineyard Century Vines 1995 • $15 • (12/15/1997) • **85**

Zinfandel Sonoma Valley Century Vines 1994 • $14 • (11/15/1996) • **82**

Zinfandel Sonoma Valley The Shaw Vineyard Century Vines 1993 • $14 • (3/31/1996) • **85**

Zinfandel Sonoma Valley The Shaw Vineyard Century Vines 1992 • $14 • (10/15/1994) • **74**

Zinfandel Sonoma Valley The Shaw Vineyard Century Vines 1991 • $14 • (6/15/1994) • **82**

Zinfandel Sonoma Valley The Shaw Vineyard 1990 • $14 • (12/31/1992) • **84**

KUNIN | CALIFORNIA

Zinfandel Paso Robles Dante Dusi Vineyards 1998: Serves up an appealing array of ripe raspberry and cherry jam flavors. Finishes with anise and drying tannins. Drink now through 2004.–J.L. • $25 • (5/31/2000) • **86**

Zinfandel Paso Robles Westside 1998: Sweaty, with tangy dried berry flavors. Tasted twice, with consistent notes. Drink now.–D.S. • $18 • (6/15/2000) • **81**

KYNSI | CALIFORNIA

Chardonnay Santa Ynez Valley Sanford & Benedict Vineyard 1997: Peach pit and vanilla flavors here, finishing with a flinty, oaky note. Drink now. –J.L. • $25 • (6/30/2000) • **85**

Pinot Noir Edna Valley 1996: Pulls no punches, with intense layers of exotic spice, cola, tea, menthol and plum. The power begs for a bit more finesse, but the wine makes a strong statement nonetheless. Full-bodied, with a long finish. Drink through 2004. • $20 • (9/15/1999) • **87**

Pinot Noir Edna Valley 1995 • $18 • (3/31/1998) • **88**

Syrah San Luis Obispo 1996: Shows a pleasant range of grilled meat, plum, black cherry, spice and herb flavors. Not a blockbuster, but very pretty and elegant. Drink now.–J.L. • $20 • (11/15/1999) • **86**

Syrah San Luis Obispo County 1995 • $20 • (3/31/1998) • **86**

L'ECOLE NO. 41 | WASHINGTON

Apogee Pepper Bridge Vineyard Walla Walla Valley 1995 • $30 • (6/15/1998) • **89**

Apogee Pepper Bridge Vineyard Walla Walla Valley 1994 • $28 • (4/30/1997) • **90**

Cabernet Sauvignon Columbia Valley 1996: Ripe and supple, a huge mouthful of anise, smoke-tinged blackberry and black currant flavors that persist and seem to enlarge on the seductive finish. Dense and daring, this needs short-term cellaring to settle down. Best after 2000.–H.S. • $27 • (9/15/1999) • **92**

Cabernet Sauvignon Columbia Valley 1995 • $25 • (5/15/1998) • **90**

Cabernet Sauvignon Columbia Valley 1994 • $24 • (4/30/1997) • **90**

Cabernet Sauvignon Columbia Valley 1993 • $22 • (9/15/1996) • **87**

Cabernet Sauvignon Columbia Valley 1992 • $22 • (7/31/1995) • **88**

Cabernet Sauvignon Washington 1991 • $19 • (9/30/1994) • **87**

Cabernet Sauvignon Washington 1989 • $18 • (5/31/1993) • **88**

Cabernet Sauvignon Walla Walla Valley Windrow Vineyard 1995 • $30 • (5/15/1998) • **88**

Key: SS—Spectator Selection CS—Cellar Selection HR—Highly Recommended $NA—Price Not Available a—Auction Price (BT)—Barrel Tasting For a key to the tasters' initials, see "How to Use These Listings."
Dates in parentheses indicate the issues in which the ratings were published.

Chardonnay Columbia Valley 1998: Ripe, round and polished. Generous with its pear, honey and spice flavors, hinting at nutmeg and orange peel on the long, supple finish. Drink now through 2004.–H.S. • $19 • (5/15/2000) • **90**

Chardonnay Washington 1997: Smooth and generous with its creamy melon and nutmeg flavors, which linger pleasantly on the finish. Drink now.–H.S. • $20 • (8/31/1999) • **87**

Chardonnay Washington 1996 • $20 • (5/15/1998) • **87**

Merlot Columbia Valley 1997: Crisp and bright, with appealing blackberry flavors. Some hardness to the finish, although the fruit lingers nicely. Drink now through 2001.–H.S. • $27 • (9/15/1999) • **86**

Merlot Columbia Valley 1996: Soft and appealing for its pretty core of plum and currant, deftly balanced with a nice hint of spice and tannin on the persistent finish. Tasty now; try through 2003.–H.S. • $25 • (8/31/1998) • **89**

Merlot Columbia Valley 1995 • $24 • (7/31/1997) • **88**

Merlot Columbia Valley 1994 • $22 • (9/15/1996) • **89**

Merlot Columbia Valley 1993 • $19 • (8/31/1995) SS • **90**

Merlot Columbia Valley 1992 • $17 • (9/30/1994) • **87**

Merlot Washington 1990 • $17 • (4/15/1994) • **83**

Merlot Washington 1989 • $16 • (5/31/1993) • **82**

Merlot Washington 1987 • $13 • (11/30/1991) • **90**

Merlot Walla Walla Valley Seven Hills Vineyard 1997: Ripe, open-textured, with layers of blackberry, black cherry, tar and spice. Tannins fold in on the finish, marking this as one to cellar. Drink through 2004.–H.S. • $35 • (9/15/1999) • **90**

Merlot Walla Walla Valley Seven Hills Vineyard 1995 • $30 • (7/31/1997) • **91**

Merlot Walla Walla Valley Seven Hills Vineyard 1994 • $28 • (9/15/1996) • **90**

Merlot Walla Walla Valley Seven Hills Vineyard 1993 • $22 • (9/30/1995) • **91**

Sémillon Columbia Valley Barrel Fermented 1998: Bright and appealing for its citrusy pear flavors. Not as spicy and oaky as earlier vintages, but it picks up a hint of tobacco on the juicy finish. Drink now.–H.S. • $14 • (5/15/2000) • **88**

Sémillon Washington Barrel Fermented 1997: Round and generous, with pretty pineapple and tobacco flavors that remain focused through the nicely packed finish. Feels tightly wound, as if it might open up more with cellaring. Try through 2003.–H.S. • $14 • (8/31/1999) • **87**

Sémillon Washington 1996 • $14 • (5/15/1998) • **87**

Sémillon Washington Fries Vineyard Wahluke Slope 1997: Ripe and juicy, with exuberant pear, pineapple, tobacco and bay leaf aromas and flavors that persist on the smooth finish. Drink now through 2003.–H.S. • $22 • (8/31/1999) • **89**

Sémillon Washington Fries Vineyard Wahluke Slope 1996 • $22 • (5/15/1998) • **85**

L'ECOSSE | CALIFORNIA

Cabernet Franc Napa Valley Cuvée Hommage de Jeanne d'Arc 1995 • $22 • (4/30/1997) • **87**

Dolcetto Napa Valley 1996: Fresh and grapey, with ripe, juicy, complex plum, black cherry, wild berry and raspberry flavors. Holds its focus, with a lingering finish. Drink now through 2004.–J.L. • $24 • (11/15/1999) • **88**

L'ESCRIME | CALIFORNIA

Cabernet Sauvignon Napa Valley Prise De Fer Reserve 1997: Firm, with earthy tannins, cedar and currant. Turns dry, with mushroom and sage notes. Drink now through 2006.–J.L. • $27 • (6/15/2000) • **86**

L'UVAGGIO DI GIACOMO | CALIFORNIA

Barbera California la Pantera 1997: A fruity blend of black cherry and raspberry flavors, with a light peppery edge. Firm, ripe tannins and a slightly herbal finish balance things out. Quite enjoyable. Drink now through 2001. • $20 • (1/31/1999) • **87**

LA CREMA | CALIFORNIA

Chardonnay Russian River Valley Reserve 1997: A ripe, creamy, well-oaked style, with pretty pear, peach and nectarine flavors that turn elegant and polished on a long, supple aftertaste. Drink now through 2002.–J.L. • $27 • (7/31/1999) • **91**

Chardonnay Sonoma Coast Cold Coast Vineyards 1998: A bit of citrus tartness to this, combined with sweeter vanilla flavors. Drink now.–J.L. • $17 • (6/30/2000) • **81**

Chardonnay Sonoma Coast Cold Coast Vineyards 1997: Ripe and complex, with rich, focused citrus, pear and toasted oak flavors, and a long, creamy aftertaste. Drink now through 2002.–J.L. • $19 • (6/15/1999) • **88**
Chardonnay Sonoma Coast Reserve 1996: Intense, with rich and spicy pear, vanilla and earth notes, picking up touches of anise and cedary oak. Drink now through 2002.–J.L. • $27 • (2/28/1999) • **87**
Pinot Noir California 1992 • $12 • (2/28/1994) • **78**
Pinot Noir California 1991 • $12 • (2/28/1994) • **78**
Pinot Noir California 1986 • $12 • (12/31/1988) • **89**
Pinot Noir California 1985 • $11 • (9/30/1987) • **90**
Pinot Noir California 1984 • $11 • (3/15/1987) • **89**
Pinot Noir California Grand Cuvée 1993 • $19 • (3/31/1995) • **86**
Pinot Noir California Reserve 1993 • $11 • (3/31/1995) • **84**
Pinot Noir California Reserve 1992 • $20 • (2/28/1994) • **83**
Pinot Noir California Reserve 1991 • $20 • (2/28/1994) • **79**
Pinot Noir California Reserve 1990 • $17 • (2/28/1993) • **85**
Pinot Noir California Reserve 1986 • $22 • (5/31/1989) • **85**
Pinot Noir California Reserve 1985 • $18 • (12/31/1987) • **82**
Pinot Noir Russian River Valley Reserve 1997: Tight and crisp, with firm, detailed tannins, the core of cherry, strawberry and tealike notes will benefit from short-term cellaring as this is a well-balanced, concentrated young wine. Drink through 2007.–J.L. • $27 • (9/15/1999) • **88**
Pinot Noir Sonoma Coast Cold Coast Vineyards 1997: Delicate and balanced, with spicy, tea, cola and cherry flavors that linger on the soft finish. Drink now through 2002.–J.L. • $20 • (9/15/1999) • **86**
Pinot Noir Sonoma Coast Reserve 1996: Lean and a touch earthy, with spicy wild berry, black cherry, sage and cedar and dry tannins. Drink now through 2002.–J.L. • $27 • (2/28/1999) • **87**
Pinot Noir Sonoma Coast Reserve 1995 • $26 • (12/15/1997) • **88**
Pinot Noir Sonoma Coast 1995 • $21 • (1/01/1997) • **87**
Pinot Noir Sonoma County Reserve 1994 • $14 • (2/29/1996) • **87**
Pinot Noir Sonoma County 1994 • $17 • (3/31/1996) • **88**
Zinfandel Sonoma Coast Reserve 1995 • $24 • (12/15/1997) • **87**
Zinfandel Sonoma County Reserve 1997: Smooth and spicy, with crisp cherry, raspberry and wild berry flavors that are tart and lively, finishing with firm tannins. Drink now through 2003.–J.L. • $22 • (6/30/1999) • **88**
Zinfandel Sonoma County Reserve 1996: Tight, with a trim, attractive band of berry, cherry, cedar, sage and spice. Turns elegant and simple on the finish. Drink now through 2003.–J.L. • $22 • (2/28/1999) • **86**

LA CROSSE | CALIFORNIA

Cabernet Sauvignon Napa Valley 1993 • $8 • (12/15/1996) • **82**
Cabernet Sauvignon Napa Valley 1991 • $7 • (2/28/1995) • **77**
Cabernet Sauvignon Napa Valley 1989 • $6 • (12/15/1992) • **77**
Merlot Napa Valley 1994 • $9 • (7/31/1996) • **81**
Merlot Napa Valley 1993 • $8 • (5/15/1995) • **85**

LA FAMIGLIA DI ROBERT MONDAVI | CALIFORNIA

Barbera California 1996: A full-figured wine, but with firm structure. Bright cherry and blackberry flavors, with good acidity, taper to a tasty finish wrapped in spice and herbs. Drink now through 2003. • $18 • (4/30/1999) • **86**
Barbera California 1995 • $18 • (5/15/1998) • **84**
Barbera California 1994 • $18 • (4/30/1997) • **85**
Barbera California 1993 • $15 • (8/31/1995) • **85**
Pinot Grigio California 1996 • $16 • (5/15/1998) • **85**
Sangiovese Napa Valley 1996: A bit chewy on the palate, with moderate tannins, this wine serves up pretty cherry, herb and spice notes. The finish is clean and modest, with a zesty ending. (Bottle has a nice shape, but watch out; it's only 500ml.) Drink now through 2001. • $22/500 ml. • (4/30/1999) • **85**
Sangiovese California 1995 • $22 • (5/15/1998) • **83**
Sangiovese California 1994 • $22 • (4/30/1997) • **85**
Sangiovese California 1993 • $22 • (8/31/1995) • **83**

LA GARZA | OREGON

Cabernet Sauvignon Umpqua Valley 1995 • $15 • (5/15/1998) • **85**
Cabernet Sauvignon Umpqua Valley Reserve 1993 • $25 • (5/15/1998) • **84**
Riesling Umpqua Valley Bradley Vineyards Dry 1996 • $8 • (5/15/1998) • **82**

LA JOTA | CALIFORNIA

Cabernet Franc Howell Mountain 1997: Dark, firm and chunky, with earthy mineral, cedar, currant and sage. Long, spicy, minty cocoa aftertaste. Drink now through 2006.–J.L. • $48 • (6/15/2000) • **91**
Cabernet Franc Howell Mountain 1996: Spicy, complex, concentrated and aromatic, with pretty blackberry, spice, mineral, tobacco, sage and cedar flavors, turning smooth and polished. Drink now through 2003.–J.L. • $37 Ⓐ • (4/30/1999) • **91**
Cabernet Franc Howell Mountain 1995 • $36 • (3/31/1998) • **84**
Cabernet Franc Howell Mountain 1994 • $32 • (4/30/1997) • **88**
Cabernet Franc Howell Mountain 1993 • $28 • (4/30/1996) • **88**
Cabernet Franc Howell Mountain 1992 • $28 • (7/31/1995) • **89**
Cabernet Franc Howell Mountain 1991 • $28 • (12/31/1994) • **84**
Cabernet Franc Howell Mountain 1990 • $28 • (11/15/1993) • **80**
Cabernet Franc Howell Mountain 1988 • $28 • (8/31/1991) • **89**
Cabernet Franc Howell Mountain 1986 • $25 • (10/15/1989) • **81**
Cabernet Sauvignon Howell Mountain 1997: Tightly wound, quite tannic and earthy, but the core of fruit is dense and chewy. Will need a long, long time to come around, but has the raw ingredients.–J.L. • $48 • (8/31/1998) (BT) • **90-94**
Cabernet Sauvignon Howell Mountain 1990 • $41 Ⓐ • (11/15/1993) • **85**
Cabernet Sauvignon Howell Mountain 1989: Earthy and peppery, with a dill edge to the modest currant and cedary oak flavors. (1989 California Cabernet retrospective tasting). Drink now.–J.L. • $28 • (8/31/1999) • **82**
Cabernet Sauvignon Howell Mountain 1988: Ripe, chunky and well balanced, with smoke, earth, currant, mineral, herb and tobacco notes. The oak and tannins are well integrated, and the wine, while not especially complex or sophisticated, is holding up well and shows no signs of prematurely drying out. (1988 California Cabernet retrospective tasting). Drink now through 2005.–J.L. • $28 • (11/15/1998) • **87**
Cabernet Sauvignon Howell Mountain 1987 • $47 Ⓐ • (7/31/1990) SS • **95**
Cabernet Sauvignon Howell Mountain 1986 • $36 Ⓐ • (10/15/1989) • **85**
Cabernet Sauvignon Howell Mountain 1985 • $18 • (11/15/1988) • **91**
Cabernet Sauvignon Howell Mountain 1984 • $46 Ⓐ • (11/15/1987) • **84**
Cabernet Sauvignon Howell Mountain 1983 • $15 • (3/31/1987) • **90**
Cabernet Sauvignon Howell Mountain 16th Anniversary Release 1997: Spicy, fruity aromatics lead to a rich and supple wine with pretty currant, anise, cherry and blackberry flavors. Firms up on the finish, where a touch of chocolate emerges. Drink now through 2009.–J.L. • $75 • (6/30/2000) • **91**
Cabernet Sauvignon Howell Mountain 15th Anniversary Release 1996: A dark, rich, plush, concentrated Cabernet, its layers of currant, anise, sage, cedar, tar and mineral flavors building for a long, rich aftertaste. Best from 2001 through 2009.–J.L. • $82 Ⓐ • (4/30/1999) • **93**
Cabernet Sauvignon Howell Mountain 14th Anniversary Release 1995 • $78 Ⓐ • (6/30/1998) • **89**
Cabernet Sauvignon Howell Mountain 13th Anniversary Release 1994 • $46 • (4/30/1997) • **93**
Cabernet Sauvignon Howell Mountain 12th Anniversary Release 1993 • $72 Ⓐ • (4/30/1996) • **91**
Cabernet Sauvignon Howell Mountain 11th Anniversary Release 1992 • $42 • (1/01/1997) • **89**
Cabernet Sauvignon Howell Mountain 10th Anniversary Release 1991 • $38 • (6/15/1994) CS • **90**
Cabernet Sauvignon Howell Mountain Selection 1997: A touch earthy, with polished currant, herb, sage and mineral flavors that are elegant. Mildly tannic. Drink now through 2007.–J.L. • $34 • (6/30/2000) • **88**
Cabernet Sauvignon Howell Mountain Selection 1996: Ruggedly tannic, with an earthy streak running through the complex core of currant, mineral and cocoa flavors, finishing with a rich, tannic aftertaste. Best from 2001 through 2008.–J.L. • $34 • (4/30/1999) • **91**
Cabernet Sauvignon Howell Mountain Selection 1995 • $55 Ⓐ • (6/30/1998) • **86**
Cabernet Sauvignon Howell Mountain Selection 1994 • $77 Ⓐ • (5/15/1997) • **90**
Cabernet Sauvignon Howell Mountain Selection 1993 • $32 Ⓐ • (4/30/1996) • **87**
Cabernet Sauvignon Howell Mountain Selection 1992 • $18 • (6/15/1995) • **88**
Cabernet Sauvignon Howell Mountain Selection 1991 • $50 Ⓐ • (6/15/1994) • **79**
Petite Sirah Howell Mountain 1996: Rich, plush and concentrated, with layers of spicy plum, mint, mineral and spice that turn dense on the finish. Drink now through 2004.–J.L. • $28 • (3/31/1999) • **91**
Petite Sirah Howell Mountain 1995 • $28 • (4/30/1998) • **85**
Petite Sirah Howell Mountain 1994 • $24 • (1/01/1997) • **88**

Petite Sirah Howell Mountain 1992 • $18 • (2/28/1995) • **87**
Viognier Howell Mountain Barrel Fermented 1997: Intensely spicy, with a slight bitter accent to the fig, pear and melon flavors. Not quite as complex or compelling as the Cold Fermented bottling, but very good. Drink now through 2001.–J.L. • $24 • (2/28/1999) • **86**
Viognier Howell Mountain Barrel Fermented 1996 • $24 • (4/30/1998) • **88**
Viognier Howell Mountain Barrel Fermented 1993 • $24 • (1/31/1995) • **80**
Viognier Howell Mountain Cold Fermented 1997: Lean and tight, with a spicy core of nectarine and pear flavors, finishing with a green, leafy edge. Drink now through 2002.–J.L. • $24 • (2/28/1999) • **88**
Viognier Howell Mountain Cold Fermented 1993 • $24 • (1/31/1995) • **87**
Zinfandel Howell Mountain 1987 • $12 • (10/31/1989) • **83**
Zinfandel Howell Mountain 1986 • $10 • (10/31/1988) • **89**
Zinfandel Howell Mountain 1985 • $10 • (4/30/1988) • **85**
Zinfandel Howell Mountain 1984 • $10 • (11/15/1987) • **88**

LA ROUGETTE | CALIFORNIA

Pinot Noir Carneros Truchard Vineyard 1992 • $11 • (3/31/1995) • **86**

LA SIRENA | CALIFORNIA

Cabernet Sauvignon Napa Valley 1996: Smooth, ripe and supple, with appealing up-front cherry, plum, currant and spice nuances. Turns complex and elegant on the finish, with polished tannins. Drink through 2006.–J.L. • $75 • (11/15/1999) • **90**
Sangiovese Napa Valley 1994 • $24 • (7/31/1996) • **88**
Sangiovese Napa Valley Juliana Vineyard 1997: Light, with sweet-tasting oak flavors, herbal notes and a simple core of strawberry and cherry, turning bitter. Drink now through 2003.–J.L. • $28 • (5/15/2000) • **81**
Sangiovese Napa Valley Juliana Vineyards 1996: Dry, a touch earthy, with mature dried cherry and sage notes. Drink now.–J.L. • $25 • (2/28/1999) • **82**
Sangiovese Napa Valley Juliana Vineyards 1995: Smooth, ripe and polished, with a supple texture and plenty of plum, strawberry, black cherry and spice to hold your interest. Finishes with a complex aftertaste and good length. Drink now.–J.L. • $24 • (9/30/1998) • **86**

LAETITIA | CALIFORNIA

Arroyo Grande Valley Cuvée for the Millennium 1994: Honey and toast come to mind, followed by tangy lemon and subtle grapefruit flavors. This is a bright, tight wine; refreshing now, but with staying power, too. Drink through 2003. • $30 • (10/15/1999) • **86**
Brut San Luis Obispo County Sélect NV • $15 • (11/30/1997) • **84**
Chardonnay Arroyo Grande Valley 1998: A bit raw, with vanilla, butter and citrus flavors. Drink now.–J.L. • $18 • (6/15/2000) • **81**
Chardonnay Arroyo Grande Valley Estate 1997: Firm in texture and still tight, yet offering hints of pear, citrus and herb. Finishes moderately, with a bright mineral edge. Might open more with time in the bottle. Try through 2002. • $19 • (6/30/1999) • **87**
Chardonnay Arroyo Grande Valley Estate Reserve 1997: Full-bodied, with ripe tropical fruit, floral, fig and pear flavors that build on the silky finish. Drink now through 2002.–J.L. • $26 • (7/31/1999) • **89**
Chardonnay San Luis Obispo County La Colline Vineyard 1996: Ripe and flavorful, with complex oak, rich fruit and a lingering aftertaste. The core of fruit is built around ripe pear, peach and melon flavors. Drink now through 2001.–J.L. • $25 • (9/30/1998) • **90**
Chardonnay San Luis Obispo County Laetitia Vineyard 1996 • $25 • (6/30/1998) • **91**
Chardonnay San Luis Obispo County Reserve 1996 • $17 • (6/30/1998) • **88**
Crémant de Noirs San Luis Obispo County NV • $15 • (11/30/1997) • **86**
Pinot Blanc Arroyo Grande Valley 1998: Citrus and apple notes have focused flavors and decent depth. Drink now.–J.L. • $16 • (6/15/2000) • **84**
Pinot Noir Arroyo Grande Valley 1997: Smooth and polished, with supple black cherry, berry, spice, sage and tea, finishing with rounded tannins. Drink now through 2004.–J.L. • $23 • (9/15/1999) • **88**
Pinot Noir Arroyo Grande Valley Reserve 1997: Firm, with a core of cherry, citrus rind and herb notes, but the flavors are dominated by oak at this stage. Tightly structured, with well-integrated tannins. Drink now through 2004.–J.L. • $33 • (8/31/1999) • **88**
Pinot Noir San Luis Obispo County La Colline Vineyard 1996: Tightly wound, with good balance and concentration and hints of mineral, berry, mushroom and cola. Finishes with enough tannin to merit short-term cellaring. Drink through 2002.–J.L. • $30 • (9/30/1998) • **85**
Pinot Noir San Luis Obispo County Laetitia Vineyard 1996: Complex, with a nice interplay of toasty oak, ripe cherry and berry flavors. Turns elegant on the finish, with well-integrated tannins. Drink through 2001.–J.L. • $30 • (9/30/1998) • **86**
Pinot Noir San Luis Obispo County Laetitia Vineyard 1995 • $25 • (10/15/1997) • **88**
Pinot Noir San Luis Obispo County Les Galets Vineyard 1996: A touch earthy, with a mushroomy edge, this is the best of the '96 Laetitias, with concentrated dried cherry, berry and cola-laced flavors, fine balance and a long, persistent finish. Drink now through 2001.–J.L. • $30 • (9/30/1998) • **86**
Pinot Noir San Luis Obispo County Reserve 1996: Appealing for its supple texture and grace, this modestly flavored Pinot has hints of dried cherry, berry and tea. Turns simple on the finish. Drink now.–J.L. • $19 • (9/30/1998) • **83**
Pinot Noir San Luis Obispo County Reserve 1995 • $19 • (10/15/1997) • **87**
Pinot Noir San Luis Obispo County Tradition 1996: A bit hollow at midpalate, but has modest tea, sage, herb and dried cherry notes. Drink now.–J.L. • $15 • (9/30/1998) • **81**
Pinot Noir San Luis Obispo County Winemaker's Select Reserve 1996: Shows some substance and concentration, yet lacks the fruit definition of the great vintages. Serves up tasty, earthy cola, berry and spice, finishing with mild, supple tannins. Drink now.–J.L. • $30 • (9/30/1998) • **84**
San Luis Obispo County Elégance 1992 • $23 • (11/30/1997) • **86**
San Luis Obispo County Rosé Elégance 1993 • $25 • (11/30/1997) • **87**

LAIL | CALIFORNIA

J. Daniel Cuvée Napa Valley 1996: Wonderful, ripe, complex, intense fruit flavors, with lots of black cherry, plum, spice, cedar, anise and sage neatly woven together. Firms up on the finish, with well-integrated tannins. A blend of Merlot and Cabernet Sauvignon. Best from 2001 through 2009.–J.L. • $60 • (12/15/1999) • **92**
J. Daniel Cuvée Napa Valley 1995: Distinctive and austere in style, with a trim band of cedary oak, currant, anise and sage. Slowly works its way into more complex flavors, and once the tannins subside it should offer even more complexity. A blend of Merlot and Cabernet Sauvignon. New from Robin Lail, a former partner at Dominus. Drink through 2008.–J.L. • $60 • (9/30/1998) • **88**

LAKE SONOMA | CALIFORNIA

Cabernet Sauvignon Alexander Valley Heck Family Cellar Selection 1994: Lean, with cedary oak, mineral, tar and spicy notes. Remains focused on the finish, with soft tannins. Drink now.–J.L. • $17 • (2/28/1999) • **82**
Chardonnay Russian River Valley 1996: Rich and juicy, with ripe, buttery flavors and notes of toast, fig and Asian pear. Focused and refreshing, with a long, full finish. • $15 • (7/31/1998) • **86**
Cinsault Dry Creek Valley Vintner's Reserve 1991 • $16 • (2/15/1993) • **73**
Merlot Dry Creek Valley Yoakim Bridge Ranch 1991 • $14 • (3/31/1993) • **83**
Merlot Dry Creek Valley Yoakim Bridge Ranch 1990 • $14 • (5/31/1992) • **86**
Zinfandel Alexander Valley Heck Family Cellar Selection Old Vine 1996: Crisp cherry, cranberry and orange peel flavors are framed by smoky, bacon-tinged notes. Turns firm, with sweet oaky flavors on the finish. Drink now.–H.S. • $18 • (5/15/1999) • **83**
Zinfandel Dry Creek Valley 1996: Medium-weight, already mature, with modest flavors of dried plum, orange peel, baked fruit, spice and light herbs.–J.L. • $18 • (6/30/1999) • **78**
Zinfandel Dry Creek Valley 1995: Crisp acidity and a bright cherry flavor are the hallmarks of this wine. Smoke, licorice and herb notes linger on the finish. Showing a hint of age, however. Drink now. • $17 • (7/31/1998) • **85**
Zinfandel Dry Creek Valley 1990 • $10 • (9/30/1993) • **72**
Zinfandel Dry Creek Valley 1989 • $10 • (10/15/1992) • **84**
Zinfandel Dry Creek Valley Heck Family Cellar Selection 1997: Vanilla, plum and dried berry flavors have good concentration. Drink now through 2004.–J.L. • $15 • (6/15/2000) • **85**
Zinfandel Dry Creek Valley Saini Farms Heck Family Cellar Selection Old Vine 1997: Ripe and fruity, with complex black cherry, wild berry, raspberry and vanilla flavors, all well focused, long and tasty. Drink now through 2004.–J.L. • $20 • (6/15/2000) • **87**

Key: SS—Spectator Selection CS—Cellar Selection HR—Highly Recommended $NA—Price Not Available a—Auction Price (BT)—Barrel Tasting
For a key to the tasters' initials, see "How to Use These Listings."
Dates in parentheses indicate the issues in which the ratings were published.

LAKESPRING | CALIFORNIA

Cabernet Sauvignon Napa Valley 1993 • $12 • (3/31/1996) • **80**
Cabernet Sauvignon Napa Valley 1990 • $10 • (5/15/1994) • **87**
Cabernet Sauvignon Napa Valley 1987 • $17 • (10/15/1991) • **84**
Cabernet Sauvignon Napa Valley 1985 • $12 • (7/15/1988) • **92**
Cabernet Sauvignon Napa Valley 1983 • $11 • (12/15/1986) • **77**
Cabernet Sauvignon Napa Valley 1981 • $11 • (9/16/1984) • **87**
Cabernet Sauvignon Napa Valley Reserve Selection 1988 • $18 • (11/15/1992) • **74**
Cabernet Sauvignon Napa Valley Reserve Selection 1984 • $15 • (10/31/1988) SS • **92**
Cabernet Sauvignon Napa Valley Vintage Selection 1982 • $14 • (12/15/1986) • **94**
Chardonnay Alexander Valley 1996: Pear, cinnamon and peach notes blend nicely in this pleasant wine. Finishes with a mineral edge and just a touch of sweetness. Drink now. • $11 • (9/15/1998) • **84**
Elixia Late Harvest Napa Valley 1989 • $12/375 ml. • (3/31/1992) • **75**
Merlot Napa Valley 1994 • $14 • (3/31/1996) • **78**
Merlot Napa Valley 1987 • $14 • (6/15/1990) • **85**
Merlot Napa Valley 1986 • $14 • (3/31/1989) • **79**
Merlot Napa Valley 1985 • $15 • (3/31/1988) SS • **91**
Merlot Napa Valley 1984 • $12 • (5/15/1987) • **88**
Merlot Napa Valley 1983 • $11 • (5/16/1986) • **87**
Merlot Napa Valley 1982 • $10 • (10/01/1985) • **78**
Merlot Napa Valley Yount Mill Vineyard 1990 • $14 • (7/15/1993) • **88**
Merlot Napa Valley Yount Mill Vineyard 1988 • $15 • (2/29/1992) • **85**

LAKEWOOD | NEW YORK

Glaciovinum Delaware Finger Lakes 1993 • $9 • (4/15/1995) • **81**

LAMBERT BRIDGE | CALIFORNIA

Cabernet Sauvignon Dry Creek Valley 1994 • $20 • (11/15/1997) • **89**
Cabernet Sauvignon Sonoma County 1993 • $15 • (12/15/1995) • **86**
Cabernet Sauvignon Sonoma County 1992 • $15 • (12/15/1995) • **87**
Cabernet Sauvignon Sonoma County 1991 • $14 • (10/15/1994) • **84**
Cabernet Sauvignon Sonoma County 1984 • $10 • (4/15/1987) • **80**
Cabernet Sauvignon Sonoma County 1981 • $12 • (1/01/1985) • **75**
Chardonnay Dry Creek Valley Abbe Vineyards 1997: Pretty earth tones are followed up by rich mineral, green apple and spice notes. Focused, with moderate body and a long, toasty finish. Drink now through 2002. • $24 • (7/31/1999) • **89**
Chardonnay Sonoma County 1997: An elegant style featuring green apple, citrus, herb and toast flavors. Focused and firm on the finish. Drink now through 2001.–J.L. • $18 • (6/30/1999) • **87**
Chardonnay Sonoma County 1996: Complete and harmonious, with ripe pear, hazelnut, light oak and spicy apple flavors that are supple and focused, long and lingering. Drink now.–J.L. • $17 • (7/31/1998) • **88**
Crane Creek Cuvée Cabernet-Merlot-Cabernet Franc-Petit Verdot Dry Creek Valley 1995: Smooth and flavorful, with a crisp core of black cherry, plum, cedar and mineral. Well-integrated tannins. Drink now through 2005.–J.L. • $32 • (9/30/1999) • **86**
Crane Creek Cuvée Dry Creek Valley 1994 • $28 • (11/15/1997) • **91**
Crane Creek Cabernet Sauvignon Dry Creek Valley 1989 • $28 • (11/15/1992) • **80**
Merlot Dry Creek Valley 1994 • $18 • (12/15/1996) • **86**
Merlot Dry Creek Valley Tzabaco Vineyard 1994 • $24 • (6/30/1997) • **88**
Merlot Sonoma County 1997: Elegant, with ripe, medium-weight, polished currant, black cherry, sage and anise flavors, turning simple. Drink now through 2007.–J.L. • $22 • (6/30/2000) • **87**
Merlot Sonoma County 1996: Supple and concentrated, with a rich, complex core of mineral, tar, cassis and black cherry flavors and hints of herb. Finishes with ripe tannins. Drink now through 2003.–J.L. • $20 • (9/15/1999) • **87**
Merlot Sonoma County 1995 • $20 • (5/15/1998) • **85**
Merlot Sonoma County 1993 • $15 • (12/15/1995) • **86**
Merlot Sonoma County 1992 • $14 • (9/15/1994) • **87**
Merlot Sonoma County 1991 • $14 • (9/15/1994) • **79**
Merlot Sonoma County 1982 • $12 • (12/16/1984) • **79**
Merlot Sonoma County Library Reserve 1989 • $24 • (11/30/1992) • **85**
Petite Sirah Dry Creek Valley 1996: Lean, with a core of leathery plum and berry flavor that picks up a meaty edge. Turns dry and tannic, so it's best with food. Drink now through 2002.–J.L. • $19 • (12/15/1998) • **85**
Pinot Noir Oregon Muirfield Vineyards 1993 • $16 • (2/28/1995) • **82**
Sauvignon Blanc Dry Creek Valley 1997: A silky-textured wine, with hints of grapefruit, fresh peas, herbs, grass and spice. Shows good structure and balance, ending on a refreshing bright note. Drink now. • $12 • (1/31/1999) • **87**
Sauvignon Blanc Dry Creek Valley 1996 • $12 • (6/30/1997) • **87**
Viognier Dry Creek Valley 1997: A subtle style for this varietal, it nonetheless serves up delicate nectarine, apple and spice flavors. The texture is lean but still silky. Drink now. • $18 • (12/31/1998) • **87**
Zinfandel Dry Creek Valley 1997: Serves up lots of juicy berry flavors, with cherry, raspberry, blackberry and spicy notes, finishing with firm, dry tannins. Drink now through 2002.–J.L. • $20 • (5/15/1999) • **89**
Zinfandel Dry Creek Valley 1996 • $20 • (5/31/1998) • **87**
Zinfandel Dry Creek Valley 1995 • $15 • (3/31/1997) • **90**
Zinfandel Dry Creek Valley 1994 • $13 • (11/15/1996) • **85**
Zinfandel Dry Creek Valley 1992 • $11 • (10/15/1994) • **84**

LAMBORN FAMILY | CALIFORNIA

Zinfandel Howell Mountain 1990 • $12 • (10/15/1992) • **80**
Zinfandel Howell Mountain 1988 • $11 • (2/15/1991) • **89**
Zinfandel Howell Mountain 1987 • $10 • (3/15/1990) • **84**
Zinfandel Howell Mountain The Team Connection 1997: Nice balance between the spicy, earthy wild berry flavors and the rounded, earthy tannins. Drink now.–J.L. • $23 • (4/30/2000) • **86**
Zinfandel Howell Mountain The Family Connection 1996: Rustic, with earthy tannins, mint, loganberry and spicy notes, it's not for the meek. Drink now through 2002.–J.L. • $20 • (12/15/1998) • **82**
Zinfandel Howell Mountain The French Connection 1995 • $19 • (9/15/1997) • **90**
Zinfandel Howell Mountain The French Connection Unfiltered 1995 • $22 • (6/15/1998) • **85**
Zinfandel Howell Mountain The Queen's Vintage 1994 • $17 • (2/28/1997) • **88**
Zinfandel Howell Mountain The Hang Time Vintage 1993 • $15 • (11/30/1996) • **89**
Zinfandel Howell Mountain The Phoenix Vintage 1991 • $13 • (9/30/1993) • **82**

LAMOREAUX LANDING | NEW YORK

Cabernet Franc Finger Lakes 1997: Blunt flavors of cherry and chocolate are thick and simple in this slightly earthy red.–T.M. • $14 • (5/31/2000) • **76**
Chardonnay Finger Lakes Reserve 1997: Lively citrus and green apple flavors have zip, but light musty and vegetal notes detract from the pleasure.–T.M. • $20 • (5/31/2000) • **74**
Pinot Noir Finger Lakes 1998: A silky texture and bright cherry flavors have appeal, but strong charry and barnyard notes are off-putting.–T.M. • $14 • (1/01/2000) • **74**
Pinot Noir Finger Lakes 1993 • $12 • (9/30/1995) • **82**
Pinot Noir Finger Lakes 1991 • $12 • (11/15/1994) • **82**
Riesling Finger Lakes Dry 1998: This supple white offers clean apple and lime flavors, with light herbal accents and lively acidity. A good aperitif. Drink now.–T.M. • $10 • (5/31/2000) • **81**

LANCASTER | CALIFORNIA

Reserve Alexander Valley Red 1997: Smooth, ripe and plummy, with cherry, berry and vanilla notes. Turns elegant and supple, with light toasty oak. Drink now through 2008.–J.L. • $65 • (5/15/2000) • **88**
Reserve Alexander Valley Red 1995: Strives for complexity, but the fruit ripeness doesn't quite override the herbal flavors. A blend of Cabernet Sauvignon, Merlot, Malbec and Cabernet Franc. Drink now.–J.L. • $50 • (10/31/1998) • **84**

LANDMARK | CALIFORNIA

Chardonnay Russian River Valley Lorenzo 1998: Rich and full-bodied, with layers of ripe fig, lemon, spicy oak and apricot flavors. Drink now through 2004.–J.L. • $45 • (5/15/2000) • **90**
Chardonnay Russian River Valley Lorenzo 1997: Rich, creamy and loaded with complex flavors, this serves up concentrated pear, fig, tangerine, anise, butter and butterscotch flavors that zoom on and on. Delicious. Drink through 2004.–J.L. • $38 • (4/30/1999) • **94**
Chardonnay Russian River Valley Lorenzo 1996 • $35 • (6/30/1998) • **93**
Chardonnay Sonoma-Santa Barbara-Monterey Counties Damaris Reserve 1998: Very ripe and rich, this multicounty-sourced California Chardonnay reserve wakes up the taste buds with its layers of fig, tangerine, cedary oak and spice, culminating in a long, complex aftertaste. Drink now through 2004.–J.L. • $32 • (5/15/2000) SS • **92**

Chardonnay Sonoma-Santa Barbara-Monterey Counties Damaris Reserve 1997: Smooth and creamy, elegant and polished, with a subtle array of peach, pear, fig, nectarine and honey, finishing with a delicious aftertaste that echoes fruit. Drink now through 2004.–J.L. • $32 • (4/30/1999) • **93**

Chardonnay Sonoma County Damaris Reserve 1996 • $32 • (6/30/1998) • **92**

Chardonnay Sonoma-Santa Barbara-Monterey Counties Overlook 1998: Quite rich and concentrated, with a core of fig, pear, nectarine and spicy oak. Holds its focus, turning elegant and supple. Drink now through 2004.–J.L. • $22 • (1/31/2000) • **92**

Chardonnay Sonoma-Santa Barbara-Monterey Counties Overlook 1997: Ripe, smooth, rich and creamy, with layers of pear, vanilla, anise and fig flavors that are deep, complex and concentrated. Finishes with a long, delicious aftertaste. Drink now through 2004.–J.L. • $22 • (4/30/1999) SS • **92**

Chardonnay Sonoma County Overlook 1996 • $21 • (3/31/1998) SS • **92**

Pinot Noir Sonoma Coast Kastania 1997: Ripe and zesty, with lively cola, black cherry, earth and spice flavors; this is a tightly wound wine in need of short-term cellaring. Best from 2001 through 2009.–J.L. • $45 • (9/15/1999) • **89**

Pinot Noir Sonoma County Grand Detour 1995 • $30 • (9/15/1997) • **90**

Pinot Noir Sonoma County 1994 • $22 • (7/31/1996) • **90**

Pinot Noir Sonoma Mountain Van der Kamp Vineyard Grand Detour 1997: Remarkably smooth, supple and polished, with a pretty array of ripe black cherry, plum, wild berry and raspberry—a genuine fruit bowl. Finishes with a complex fruity aftertaste and fine tannins. Drink now through 2005.–J.L. • $34 • (9/15/1999) • **91**

Pinot Noir Sonoma Mountain Van der Kamp Vineyard Grand Detour 1996: A good '96, with a range of cherry, cola, rhubarb, tea and olive notes. Well balanced, with supple tannins and moderate richness. Drink now.–J.L. • $32 • (8/31/1998) • **86**

LANG & REED | CALIFORNIA

Cabernet Franc Napa Valley 1998: Fresh and snappy, with an herbal edge to the wild berry and cherrylike flavors, it turns stalky but then picks up a pretty strawberry note. Best from 2001 through 2008.–J.L. • $18 • (2/29/2000) • **87**

Cabernet Franc Napa Valley 1997: Ripe and supple, with a cedary edge to the tobacco, currant and berryish flavors, turning rich and polished on the finish. Drink through 2007.–J.L. • $18 • (1/31/1999) • **88**

Cabernet Franc Napa Valley 1996 • $18 • (3/31/1998) • **89**

Cabernet Franc Napa Valley 1993 • $20 • (3/31/1998) • **88**

Cabernet Franc Napa Valley Premier êtage 1996: Earthy cigar-box notes lead into appealing currant, wild berry and spicy flavors, finishing with firm tannins. Drink through 2005.–J.L. • $28 • (1/31/1999) • **87**

LANGE | OREGON

Chardonnay Willamette Valley Reserve 1996 • $20 • (5/15/1998) • **85**

Pinot Gris Willamette Valley 1996 • $12 • (5/15/1998) • **84**

Pinot Gris Willamette Valley Yamhill Vineyards Reserve 1996 • $16 • (5/15/1998) • **86**

Pinot Noir Willamette Valley 1994 • $18 • (2/28/1997) • **85**

Pinot Noir Willamette Valley 1993 • $35 • (1/31/1996) • **89**

Pinot Noir Willamette Valley 1992 • $14 • (11/30/1994) • **83**

Pinot Noir Willamette Valley Eola Hills 1990 • $20 • (2/28/1993) • **84**

Pinot Noir Willamette Valley Estate 1995 • $40 • (5/15/1998) • **83**

Pinot Noir Willamette Valley Freedom Hill Vineyard 1996: Firm in texture, with focused black currant and black cherry flavors that fill the mouth nicely. Drink now through 2001.–H.S. • $40 • (4/30/1999) • **84**

Pinot Noir Willamette Valley Reserve 1996: Light and pleasant, with simple currant and vanilla flavors that linger gently on the finish. Drink now.–H.S. • $28 • (4/30/1999) • **84**

Pinot Noir Willamette Valley Reserve 1995 • $40 • (5/15/1998) • **82**

Pinot Noir Willamette Valley Reserve 1994 • $40 • (2/28/1997) • **88**

Pinot Noir Willamette Valley Reserve 1992 • $30 • (11/30/1994) • **86**

Pinot Noir Willamette Valley Reserve 1991 • $30 • (3/15/1994) • **79**

Pinot Noir Willamette Valley Reserve 1990 • $25 • (2/28/1993) • **88**

Pinot Noir Willamette Valley Yamhill Vineyards 1996: Ripe and fruity, light-textured, with pretty berry and floral flavors that persist on the firm finish. Drink now.–H.S. • $40 • (4/30/1999) • **85**

Key: SS—Spectator Selection CS—Cellar Selection HR—Highly Recommended $NA—Price Not Available a—Auction Price (BT)—Barrel Tasting
For a key to the tasters' initials, see "How to Use These Listings."
Dates in parentheses indicate the issues in which the ratings were published.

LAS PIEDRAS | CALIFORNIA

Syrah South Coast 1997: Straightforward flavors of tart cherry, plum, vanilla and cinnamon linger on the firm finish. Drink now.–J.L. • $15 • (11/15/1999) • **83**

LATAH CREEK | WASHINGTON

Cabernet Sauvignon Washington 1993 • $12 • (7/31/1995) • **85**

Cabernet Sauvignon Washington Limited Bottling 1992 • $12 • (9/30/1994) • **77**

Cabernet Sauvignon Washington Limited Bottling 1990 • $12 • (6/15/1993) • **85**

Cabernet Sauvignon Washington Limited Bottling 1988 • $13 • (10/15/1991) • **91**

Cabernet Sauvignon Washington Limited Bottling 1987 • $13 • (10/15/1989) • **83**

Cabernet Sauvignon Washington 1986 • $13 • (10/15/1988) • **80**

Cabernet Sauvignon Washington Reserve 1991 • $20 • (9/15/1996) • **88**

Cabernet Sauvignon Washington Wahluke Slope Vineyards 1996: Bright and open in texture, with pretty plum and currant shining through a thin veil of fine-textured tannins. Drink now.–H.S. • $14 • (10/15/1998) • **87**

Cabernet Sauvignon Washington Wahluke Slope Vineyards 1995 • $13 • (9/30/1997) • **73**

Chardonnay Washington 1998: Ripe and exotic but not heavy, with delectable apricot, honey and spice overtones to the rich pear flavors. Offers plenty of character up front and a rich texture to build on. Drink through 2005.–H.S. • $11 • (11/15/1999) • **89**

Chardonnay Washington 1997: Light and smooth, with pretty apricot and apple flavors echoing on the open-textured finish.–H.S. • $11 • (10/15/1998) • **85**

Chardonnay Washington 1996 • $11 • (9/30/1997) • **89**

Chardonnay Washington Reserve 1998: Smooth and ripe, with pretty pear, floral and golden raisin flavors that linger enticingly on the polished finish, hinting at toast and spice on the aftertaste. Drink now through 2002.–H.S. • $16 • (11/15/1999) • **88**

Chardonnay Washington Reserve 1996 • $16 • (9/15/1997) • **88**

Johannisberg Riesling Washington 1998: Smooth and refreshing for its generous apple, pear and floral aromas and flavors. Creamy taste and texture on the finish. Drink now.–H.S. • $7 • (9/30/1999) • **86**

Johannisberg Riesling Washington 1997: Soft, bordering on sweet, with pretty pear and apricot flavors lingering on the finish. Drink now.–H.S. • $7 • (11/15/1998) • **86**

Johannisberg Riesling Washington 1996 • $7 • (10/15/1997) • **85**

Lemberger Washington 1997: Dark and rich, a supple wine with generous blueberry, plum and floral aromas and flavors that hang on nicely on the slightly chewy finish. Drink now through 2002.–H.S. • $9 • (9/30/1999) • **87**

Lemberger Washington 1995 • $9 • (9/15/1997) • **86**

Lemberger Washington 1994 • $8 • (9/15/1996) • **87**

Lemberger Washington 1992 • $8 • (12/31/1993) • **80**

Lemberger Washington 1991 • $8 • (4/30/1993) • **82**

Lemberger Washington 1990 • $9 • (1/31/1992) • **85**

Merlot Washington 1993 • $12 • (9/30/1995) • **85**

Merlot Washington Limited Bottling 1992 • $12 • (12/31/1993) • **82**

Merlot Washington Limited Bottling 1991 • $12 • (5/31/1993) • **87**

Merlot Washington Limited Bottling 1989 • $11 • (9/30/1991) HR • **91**

Merlot Washington Limited Bottling 1987 • $10 • (10/15/1989) • **90**

Merlot Washington 1986 • $10 • (5/31/1988) • **89**

Merlot Washington Wahluke Slope Vineyards 1995 • $14 • (9/15/1997) • **85**

Muscat Canelli Washington 1998: Aromatic, with litchi, pear and spice notes that continue through the sweet but refreshingly balanced, lightly citrusy finish. Drink now.–H.S. • $9 • (9/30/1999) • **86**

Muscat Canelli Washington 1997: Sweet and silky, with pretty litchi and spice flavors on a modest scale. Slurp it while it's fresh.–H.S. • $9 • (11/15/1998) • **85**

Muscat Canelli Washington 1996 • $8 • (10/15/1997) • **85**

Muscat Canelli Washington 1994 • $6 • (9/30/1995) • **80**

LAUREL GLEN | CALIFORNIA

Cabernet Sauvignon Sonoma Mountain 1998: Intense, well focused, with tiers of black cherry, currant and plum flavors, finishing with fine structure.–J.L. • $NA • (8/31/1999) (BT) • **90-94**

Cabernet Sauvignon Sonoma Mountain 1997: Tight, lean, even a bit tart, but the concentration is there, focused on currant and blackberry.–J.L. • $NA • (8/31/1998) (BT) • **90-94**

Cabernet Sauvignon Sonoma Mountain 1996: Tight and intense, with a firm, concentrated band of currant, anise, cedar, tar and spice notes. Needs time to soften and evolve. Best from 2002 through 2010.–J.L. • $40 • (10/31/1999) • **89**

Cabernet Sauvignon Sonoma Mountain 1995: Well crafted, if a bit on the austere side, well focused on a core of currant and black cherry, with light toast and cedary oak shadings. Finishes with firm, round tannins and a trace of mineral. Good structure. Best from 2001 through 2009.–J.L. • $35 • (11/15/1998) • **89**

Cabernet Sauvignon Sonoma Mountain 1994 • $46 Ⓐ • (8/31/1997) • **86**

Cabernet Sauvignon Sonoma Mountain 1993 • $40 Ⓐ • (2/28/1997) • **85**

Cabernet Sauvignon Sonoma Mountain 1992 • $42 Ⓐ • (12/15/1995) • **85**

Cabernet Sauvignon Sonoma Mountain 1991 • $46 Ⓐ • (11/15/1994) • **89**

Cabernet Sauvignon Sonoma Mountain 1990 • $46 Ⓐ • (11/15/1993) • **89**

Cabernet Sauvignon Sonoma Mountain 1989: Decidedly earthy, with dry, leathery notes, the currant and cherry flavors struggling to emerge, submitting in the end to the dryness of the tannins. (1989 California Cabernet retrospective tasting). Drink now through 2004.–J.L. • $28 • (8/31/1999) • **86**

Cabernet Sauvignon Sonoma Mountain 1988: Solid, with ripe, rich, concentrated currant, anise, mineral, sage and berry notes. Tightly wound, it's well balanced, and shows more depth and richness than most '88s. (1988 California Cabernet retrospective tasting). Drink now through 2004.–J.L. • $32 • (11/15/1998) • **88**

Cabernet Sauvignon Sonoma Mountain 1987 • $22 • (12/15/1997) • **93**

Cabernet Sauvignon Sonoma Mountain 1986 • $41 Ⓐ • (12/15/1996) • **91**

Cabernet Sauvignon Sonoma Mountain 1985 • $58 Ⓐ • (4/30/1988) • **91**

Cabernet Sauvignon Sonoma Mountain 1984 • $15 • (4/30/1987) • **87**

Cabernet Sauvignon Sonoma Mountain 1982 • $13 • (6/01/1986) • **83**

Cabernet Sauvignon Sonoma Mountain 1981 • $13 • (2/16/1985) SS • **93**

Cabernet Sauvignon Sonoma Mountain 1978 • $NA • (11/15/1992) • **92**

Cabernet Sauvignon Sonoma Mountain Counterpoint 1993 • $17 • (9/15/1996) • **87**

Cabernet Sauvignon Sonoma Mountain Counterpoint 1992 • $16 • (12/15/1995) • **88**

Cabernet Sauvignon Sonoma Mountain Counterpoint 1991 • $15 • (11/30/1993) SS • **90**

Cabernet Sauvignon Sonoma Mountain Counterpoint 1990 • $15 • (3/15/1993) • **87**

Cabernet Sauvignon Sonoma Mountain Counterpoint 1989 • $15 • (1/31/1992) • **85**

Cabernet Sauvignon Sonoma Mountain Counterpoint 1988 • $13 • (7/15/1991) • **83**

Cabernet Sauvignon Sonoma Mountain Counterpoint 1987 • $13 • (10/31/1989) • **94**

Cabernet Sauvignon Sonoma Mountain Counterpoint Cuvée 85-86 NV • $11 • (5/31/1988) • **89**

Cabernet Sauvignon Sonoma Mountain Reserve 1990 • $75/1.5 liter • (11/15/1993) • **88**

Reds California 1996: A smoky, charry blend of plum and cassis flavors. Somewhat rustic and chunky. Finishes a bit short. A blend of Zinfandel, Syrah, Petite Sirah, Grenache and Carignane. Drink now. • $7 • (7/31/1998) • **82**

Reds California 1994 • $7 • (10/15/1996) • **86**

Reds California 1993 • $7 • (11/30/1995) • **87**

LAUREL LAKE | NEW YORK

Cabernet Sauvignon North Fork of Long Island 1998: Sweet cherry and light vegetal flavors run through this thick, soft red. A bit rustic, but shows richness.–T.M. • $15 • (5/31/2000) • **79**

Chardonnay North Fork of Long Island Reserve 1998: This straightforward white is clean and well balanced, but remains fairly neutral through the waxy finish. Drink now.–T.M. • $15 • (5/31/2000) • **80**

Chardonnay North Fork of Long Island Reserve 1997: Shows good weight on the palate, with ripe flavors of pear, almond and vanilla and a soft, clean finish. The fruit character is a bit subdued, but the wine would match well with bigger dishes. Drink now through 2001.–T.M. • $14 • (6/30/1999) • **85**

Merlot North Fork of Long Island 1998: Soft and simple, this red offers cooked cherry flavors, with light vegetal notes. A bit cloying on the finish.–T.M. • $13 • (5/31/2000) • **77**

Merlot North Fork of Long Island 1996: Light and soft, this red offers light cherry, vanilla and herb flavors. Clean but without much concentration, with soft tannins and a short finish. Drink now.–T.M. • $13 • (6/30/1999) • **82**

LAUREL RIDGE | OREGON

Pinot Blanc Willamette Valley 1996: Soft and earthy, with peach and melon flavors dominating on the finish. Drink now.–H.S. • $10 • (11/15/1998) • **82**

Pinot Noir Willamette Valley 1996: Light in color and structure, with modest Pinot Noir fruit lurking under a fine layer of tannins. Drink now through 2002.–H.S. • $9 • (3/31/2000) • **82**

Pinot Noir Willamette Valley 1995 • $12 • (2/28/1998) • **85**

Pinot Noir Willamette Valley Estate Bottled 1996: Earthy, peppery aromas and flavors are more prominent than the modest fruit in this pleasant, light-colored and -textured red. Drink now.–H.S. • $12 • (3/31/2000) • **80**

Pinot Noir Willamette Valley Le Reserve du Vigneron 1996: Light in structure and firm in texture, with modest cherry and toast flavors that remain on the finish. Drink now through 2002.–H.S. • $16 • (3/31/2000) • **82**

Pinot Noir Willamette Valley Vintner's Reserve 1995 • $16 • (2/28/1998) • **86**

Pinot Noir Willamette Valley Vintner's Reserve 1994: A supple, generous wine with ripe plum and currant flavors glowing at the core. Has intensity without weight—a reminder of how flavorsome this vintage was for Oregon Pinot Noir. Drink now through 2003.–H.S. • $38 • (11/15/1998) • **89**

Riesling Willamette Valley 1996: Off-dry, with soft pear and floral flavors that linger smoothly on the finish. Drink now.–H.S. • $6 • (11/15/1998) • **83**

Riesling Willamette Valley Select Harvest 1995 • $8/375 ml. • (5/15/1998) • **88**

Sémillon-Chardonnay Willamette Valley 1996: Showing some age, with spicy, toasty notes offering more than the modest apple flavor. Develops richness on the finish. Drink now.–H.S. • $9 • (12/15/1998) • **87**

LAURIER | CALIFORNIA

Chardonnay Sonoma County 1996: Intense and ripe spicy pear, apple, citrus and light oak flavors. Focused, it turns a bit leafy and earthy on the finish. Drink now through 2002.–J.L. • $15 • (7/31/1998) • **88**

Pinot Noir Sonoma County 1996: Tight, with a firm tannic edge, and hints of dried cherry, leather, cola, tar and spice. Finishes with an earthy, gamy accent. Drink now through 2001.–J.L. • $18 • (9/15/1998) • **84**

Pinot Noir Sonoma County 1995 • $20 • (1/31/1997) • **84**

Pinot Noir Sonoma County 1994 • $15 • (3/31/1996) • **88**

Pinot Noir Sonoma County Green Valley 1986 • $10 • (6/15/1988) • **90**

Pinot Noir Sonoma County Green Valley 1981 • $10 • (2/16/1985) • **78**

LAVELLE | OREGON

Brut Willamette Valley 1997: Delicate coppery color and hints of berry character mark this as a Pinot Noir-centered sparkling wine, echoed on the round and vaguely spicy palate. Drink now.–H.S. • $18 • (4/30/2000) • **87**

Pinot Gris Willamette Valley 1997: Soft and supple, a pretty medley of pear, honey and peach flavors that linger delicately on the finish. Drink now.–H.S. • $13 • (2/28/1999) • **88**

Pinot Noir Willamette Valley Susan's Vineyard 1996: Light and pretty, polished, with a roséllike color, texture and range of flavors, picking up some additional earthy notes on the finish. Drink now.–H.S. • $11 • (2/28/1999) • **83**

Riesling Willamette Valley Susan's Vineyard 1997: Gently sweet, with mineral and earth notes adding interest to the modest apple flavors. Drink now.–H.S. • $8 • (2/28/1999) • **81**

LAWRENCE, DANIEL | CALIFORNIA

Chardonnay California Vineyard Select 1996: Simple, floral and earthy, with hints of citrus and herb. Drink now. • $12 • (7/31/1998) • **80**

Chardonnay Santa Cruz Mountains Vineyard Reserve 1996: Sweet citrus and ripe pineapple flavors turn awkward, finishing soft, with a note of bitterness. • $15 • (7/31/1998) • **79**

Syrah Alexander Valley Vineyard Reserve 1996 • $13 • (3/31/1998) • **86**

Zinfandel California Vineyard Select 1996 • $12 • (6/15/1998) • **75**

LAZY CREEK | CALIFORNIA

Chardonnay Anderson Valley 1996 • $10 • (5/15/1998) • **82**

Pinot Noir Anderson Valley 1997: Light-bodied and uncomplicated, with fresh tart cherry, spice and cola flavors, finishing crisp. Drink now.–H.S. • $15 • (9/15/1999) • **83**

Pinot Noir Anderson Valley 1996: Delicate flavors of dried cherry and tea linger on a soft frame. Ultimately it's simple, but pleasant and well rounded, too. Drink now.–J.L. • $14 • (9/15/1998) • **83**

Pinot Noir Anderson Valley 1991 • $12 • (2/28/1993) • **83**

LE DUCQ | CALIFORNIA

Napa Valley Red 1995: Well balanced, if a bit lean, with dusty cedar, chocolate and wild berry notes and firm, dry tannins. Turns complex, but needs

time to soften. Best from 2001 through 2008.–J.L. • $65 • (12/15/1998) • **89**
Napa Valley Red 1994 • $99 • (3/31/1998) • **85**
Napa Valley Red 1993 • $91 • (3/31/1998) • **86**

LEDSON | CALIFORNIA

Chardonnay Carneros Reserve 1997: Ultrarich and deeply concentrated, packed with layers of fig, smoky oak, pear, apricot, citrus and hazelnut flavors that are tightly wound, and long and sophisticated on the finish. Tasted twice, with consistent notes. Drink now through 2002.–J.L. • $27 • (7/31/1999) • **93**
Chardonnay Carneros Reserve 1996: Spicy, with a complex array of ripe pear, anise and hazelnut and nice oak aromas. Somewhat coarse in texture, but nothing a little time won't solve. Try now through 2002.–J.L. • $35 • (1/31/1999) • **90**
Chardonnay Sonoma County 1998: Pasty and floral, with stale pear and baked apple flavors. Drink now.–J.L. • $20 • (6/15/2000) • **82**
Chardonnay Sonoma County 1997: Silky, with complex earth, floral and sweet cream flavors that open to reveal subtle pear and apple notes. Complex and flavorful on the finish. Drink now.–J.L. • $20 • (7/31/1999) • **90**
Chardonnay Sonoma County Reserve 1998: Smooth, rich and full-bodied, with creamy pear, fig, butterscotch and citrus notes. Finishes with a pleasant earthy edge. Drink now through 2005.–J.L. • $27 • (6/15/2000) • **86**
Merlot Sonoma Valley 1996: Firm, and layered with lots of coffee, mineral, toasted oak and black cherry flavors that are tightly wound. Finishes firm but flavorful. Drink now through 2004.–J.L. • $25 • (9/15/1999) • **87**
Merlot Sonoma Valley 1995: Somewhat herbal, also showing ripe plum and blackberry and silky, smoky character. A bit lean, but nonetheless has depth. Should flesh out in a few years. Drink through 2005. • $25 • (11/30/1998) • **87**
Merlot Sonoma Valley Reserve 1996: Lavishly oaked, with smoky, toasty notes, the core of herb-laced currant and cherry flavor folds in nicely, giving depth and dimension. Drink now through 2005.–J.L. • $50 • (9/15/1999) • **89**
Merlot Sonoma Valley Reserve 1995: Features a minty, herbal quality up front, then settles into a wild blackberry mode, somewhat restrained, but tasty. Tannins are a little prickly, but might smooth out. Drink through 2005. • $45 • (11/30/1998) • **87**
Sauvignon Blanc Napa Valley 1997: Starts off with fig, floral and melon notes that give way to tangy citrus and mineral flavors. Brightly textured and refreshing, with a fairly long finish. Drink now. • $18 • (1/31/1999) • **85**

LEEWARD | CALIFORNIA

Cabernet Sauvignon Alexander Valley 1991 • $15 • (11/30/1993) • **81**
Cabernet Sauvignon Alexander Valley 1988 • $13 • (11/15/1992) • **78**
Cabernet Sauvignon Alexander Valley 1987 • $13 • (11/15/1990) • **84**
Cabernet Sauvignon Alexander Valley 1986 • $12 • (10/15/1989) • **79**
Cabernet Sauvignon Alexander Valley 1985 • $12 • (10/31/1987) • **83**
Chardonnay Central Coast 1996 • $11 • (12/15/1997) • **85**
Merlot Napa Valley 1995 • $18 • (12/15/1997) • **78**
Merlot Napa Valley 1993 • $15 • (2/29/1996) • **84**
Merlot Napa Valley 1992 • $15 • (9/15/1994) • **74**
Merlot Napa Valley 1991 • $15 • (9/15/1994) • **81**
Merlot Napa Valley 1989 • $14 • (11/15/1991) • **83**
Merlot Napa Valley 1985 • $10 • (5/15/1987) • **88**
Merlot San Ysidro 1996 • $15 • (5/15/1998) • **74**
Pinot Noir Santa Barbara County 1993 • $14 • (9/15/1995) • **86**
Pinot Noir Santa Barbara County 1990 • $14 • (2/28/1993) • **76**
Pinot Noir Santa Barbara County 1989 • $16 • (2/28/1993) • **82**
Pinot Noir Santa Barbara County Bien Nacido Vineyard 1997: Delicate, with a peppery edge to the tart cherry, dried strawberry and herb flavors, finishing soft. Drink now through 2001.–J.L. • $20 • (9/15/1999) • **84**
Pinot Noir Santa Barbara County Bien Nacido Vineyard Reserve 1997: Peppery, with a jalapeñolike edge, but the delicate cherry, strawberry and tea flavors are pleasant. Smooth finish. Drink now.–J.L. • $25 • (9/15/1999) • **85**

Key: SS—Spectator Selection CS—Cellar Selection HR—Highly Recommended $NA—Price Not Available a—Auction Price (BT)—Barrel Tasting
For a key to the tasters' initials, see "How to Use These Listings."
Dates in parentheses indicate the issues in which the ratings were published.

LENZ | NEW YORK

Cabernet Sauvignon North Fork of Long Island 1994: Maturing now, this brooding red shows good intensity, with mineral, tobacco and dried fruit flavors, firm tannins and a lingering, mineral-accented finish. Still tannic, but has the balance and underlying fruit to match well with food. Drink now through 2003.–T.M. • $20 • (6/30/1999) • **87**
Cabernet Sauvignon North Fork of Long Island 1993 • $20 • (12/31/1996) • **79**
Chardonnay North Fork of Long Island Gold Label 1996: Tiring now, this white tastes of toasted nuts and cooked fruit, with a rather metallic finish. This was the better of two samples. Past its prime.–T.M. • $25 • (5/31/2000) • **76**
Chardonnay North Fork of Long Island White Label 1996: Lush and soft, this ripe white shows a deep gold color and offers vanilla, butter and cooked apple flavors. It's ripe and rich, but is maturing now and fully ready to drink. Tasted twice, with consistent notes.–T.M. • $12 • (6/30/1999) • **80**
Gewürztraminer North Fork of Long Island 1996: This full-bodied white has cooked apple and bitter almond flavors, bold but a bit clumsy.–T.M. • $12 • (5/31/2000) • **79**
Merlot North Fork of Long Island 1995: Maturing now, this red offers cooked plum and cola flavors, with tough, underlying tannins that turn dry on the finish.–T.M. • $40 • (5/31/2000) • **78**
Merlot North Fork of Long Island 1993 • $25 • (12/31/1996) • **78**
Merlot North Fork of Long Island 1987 • $12 • (6/30/1991) • **80**
Merlot North Fork of Long Island 1986 • $12 • (12/15/1988) • **83**
Merlot North Fork of Long Island 1985 • $11 • (12/15/1988) • **84**
Merlot North Fork of Long Island 1984 • $12 • (12/15/1988) • **74**
Merlot North Fork of Long Island Vineyard Selections NV: This has ripe, juicy fruit flavors and a tannic, chewy texture, but the doughy, earthy aromas are a bit much at first whiff. Made from a blend of the 1995 and 1996 vintages. Drink now. • $13 • (10/31/1998) • **79**
Merlot-Cabernet Sauvignon North Fork of Long Island 1997: This soft red offers earth, mineral, licorice and light cherry flavors. Rather thick and dull, with round, soft tannins and a short finish. Drink now.–T.M. • $12 • (6/30/1999) • **81**

LEONETTI | WASHINGTON

Cabernet Sauvignon Columbia Valley 1995 • $91 Ⓐ • (6/15/1998) • **91**
Cabernet Sauvignon Columbia Valley 1994 • $45 • (6/15/1997) CS • **94**
Cabernet Sauvignon Columbia Valley 1992 • $83 Ⓐ • (6/15/1995) HR • **91**
Cabernet Sauvignon Columbia Valley 1986 • $20 • (10/15/1989) • **81**
Cabernet Sauvignon Walla Walla Valley Seven Hills Vineyard 1988 • $25 • (8/31/1991) • **91**
Cabernet Sauvignon Walla Walla Valley Seven Hills Vineyard 1985 • $22 • (10/15/1989) • **85**
Cabernet Sauvignon Walla Walla Valley Seven Hills Vineyard Reserve 1996: Firm and focused, a jazzy mouthful of spicy blackberry, black pepper and violet flavors that harmonize nicely on the graceful finish. Approachable now, but can age. Best after 2000.–H.S. • $75 • (9/15/1999) • **91**
Cabernet Sauvignon Walla Walla Valley Seven Hills Vineyard Reserve 1990 • $50 • (8/31/1995) • **90**
Cabernet Sauvignon Washington 1991 • $29 • (6/30/1994) CS • **95**
Cabernet Sauvignon Washington 1990 • $26 • (6/15/1993) CS • **96**
Cabernet Sauvignon Washington 1989 • $25 • (7/31/1992) HR • **96**
Cabernet Sauvignon Washington 1988 • $22 • (8/31/1991) • **87**
Cabernet Sauvignon Washington 1987 • $22 • (6/15/1990) • **91**
Cabernet Sauvignon Washington Reserve 1985 • $40 • (6/15/1991) • **84**
Merlot America 1996 • $50 • (6/15/1998) • **91**
Merlot Columbia Valley 1997: Dense in texture and distinctive in flavor, with floral, spicy, peppery notes swirling around the black cherry flavor at the core. Has more fruit and less obvious oak than previous vintages; as a result it feels a bit raucous now, but there's plenty of character packed into it. Drink now.–H.S. • $86 Ⓐ • (9/15/1999) • **91**
Merlot Columbia Valley 1995 • $40 • (11/30/1997) • **91**
Merlot Columbia Valley 1987 • $16 • (10/15/1989) • **88**
Merlot Washington 1994 • $96 Ⓐ • (7/31/1996) CS • **94**
Merlot Washington 1993 • $29 • (6/15/1995) SS • **91**
Merlot Washington 1992 • $25 • (5/15/1994) CS • **96**
Merlot Washington 1991 • $22 • (5/31/1993) HR • **92**
Merlot Washington 1990 • $22 • (6/15/1992) • **92**
Merlot Washington 1989 • $18 • (5/31/1991) HR • **93**
Merlot Washington 1988 • $17 • (4/15/1990) • **90**
Sangiovese Walla Walla Valley 1997: Smooth and ripe, with pretty raspberry and plum flavors and a nice floral note on the balanced, refined finish. Drink now through 2002.–H.S. • $45 • (9/30/1999) • **88**

Sangiovese Walla Walla Valley 1995 • $45 • (6/15/1997) • **90**
Select Red Walla Walla Valley 1990 • $28 • (6/15/1993) • **90**

LEWELLING | CALIFORNIA

Cabernet Sauvignon Napa Valley 1996: Ripe and focused, displaying herb, mineral, sage, tobacco and black cherry flavors; finishes ditto, with ripe tannins and focused flavors. Drink now through 2004.–J.L. • $34 • (9/30/1999) • **88**
Cabernet Sauvignon Napa Valley 1993 • $30 • (5/31/1998) • **88**

LEWIS | CALIFORNIA

Cabernet Sauvignon Napa Valley Reserve 1997: A bold, ripe, rich and polished Cabernet from an exciting Oakville producer, with layers of earthy currant, spice, mineral, plum and toasty, spicy oak. A wonderfully delicious young wine. Best from 2001 through 2009.–J.L. • $60 • (4/30/2000) CS • **93**
Cabernet Sauvignon Napa Valley Reserve 1996: Rich and polished, with pretty toasty oak notes leading to a supple texture and layers of black cherry, currant, coffee, berry and spice, finishing with smooth tannins. Drink through 2007.–J.L. • $48 Ⓐ • (3/31/1999) • **92**
Cabernet Sauvignon Napa Valley Reserve 1995 • $40 • (5/15/1998) HR • **93**
Cabernet Sauvignon Napa Valley Reserve 1994 • $56 Ⓐ • (6/15/1997) HR • **94**
Cabernet Sauvignon Napa Valley Oakville Ranch 1993 • $32 • (4/30/1996) • **88**
Cabernet Sauvignon Napa Valley Oakville Ranch 1992 • $30 • (11/30/1995) HR • **94**
Chardonnay Napa Valley Reserve 1998: Offers complex toasty, buttery notes, with hints of pear and hazelnut, turning to anise. Drink now.–J.L. • $45 • (6/15/2000) • **87**
Chardonnay Napa Valley Reserve 1997: Lots of everything—rich fig, citrus, melon, pear and hazelnut—and pretty oak flavors too, toasty and buttery, leaving a bold, complex aftertaste. Drink now through 2004.–J.L. • $39 • (3/31/1999) • **92**
Chardonnay Napa Valley Reserve 1996 • $32 • (5/15/1998) • **93**
Chardonnay Russian River Valley 1998: Ripe, rich and full-bodied, with layers of fig, apricot, pear and nutmeg, finishing with a rich and concentrated, if slightly coarse, aftertaste. Drink now through 2006.–J.L. • $40 • (2/29/2000) • **89**
Chardonnay Sonoma County 1998: Smooth, ripe, rich and creamy, with bright pear, nectarine, guava, tangerine and honey notes, holding its focus on a long, lively finish that turns creamy. Drink now through 2005. • $32 • (2/29/2000) • **91**
Merlot Napa Valley Reserve 1996: Features a core of ripe, juicy cherry, currant and berryish flavors framed by spicy, toasty oak, with a complex aftertaste. Drink through 2007.–J.L. • $60 • (8/31/1999) • **92**
Merlot Napa Valley Reserve 1995 • $45 • (5/31/1998) • **91**
Merlot Napa Valley Reserve 1994 • $40 • (6/15/1997) • **93**
Merlot Napa Valley Oakville Ranch 1993 • $32 • (1/31/1997) • **88**
Merlot Sonoma County 1997: Dark, rich and exotic, with oak-framed plum, currant and wild berry, this wine shows a measure of finesse and complexity, turning beefy and firm, with austere tannins. Best from 2001 through 2008.–J.L. • $37 • (2/29/2000) • **90**
Merlot Sonoma County 1996: Ripe, with complex spice, plum, herb, cedar and blackberry flavors, sharply focused and supple in texture. New Sonoma County appellation for this wine. Drink through 2005.–J.L. • $36 • (3/31/1999) • **90**
Syrah Napa County 1997: Wonderful California Syrah. The dark, ripe, plush, juicy and complex fruit flavors unfold in layers of plum, wild berry, chocolate and spice, and the long, intricate aftertaste is rich and full, with polished tannins. Best from 2001 through 2010.–J.L. • $40 • (3/31/2000) HR • **93**
Syrah Napa County 1996: Dark, ripe and intense, with spicy, minty notes leading to a core of chewy plum and wild berry. Finishes with a twinge of earthiness from tannin but also shows pretty oak. Drink now through 2004.–J.L. • $36 • (12/15/1998) • **89**

LIMERICK LANE | CALIFORNIA

Zinfandel Russian River Valley Collins Vineyard 1997: Clean and refreshing, with a pretty band of tart, spicy wild berry, raspberry, cherry and earth. Finishes with crisp tannins. Drink now through 2002.–J.L. • $22 • (6/15/1999) • **88**
Zinfandel Russian River Valley Collins Vineyard 1996 • $19 • (5/31/1998) • **87**
Zinfandel Russian River Valley Collins Vineyard 1995 • $18 • (6/30/1997) SS • **91**
Zinfandel Russian River Valley Collins Vineyard 1994 • $16 • (12/15/1996) HR • **90**
Zinfandel Russian River Valley Collins Vineyard 1993 • $14 • (10/15/1995) • **85**
Zinfandel Russian River Valley 1991 • $12 • (6/15/1993) • **88**
Zinfandel Russian River Valley 1990 • $13 • (10/15/1992) • **88**

LINCOURT | CALIFORNIA

Chardonnay Santa Barbara County 1998: A bit earthy, with tart citrus and vanilla flavors. Drink now.–J.L. • $18 • (6/15/2000) • **82**
Chardonnay Santa Barbara County 1997: A deep and concentrated wine, in an opulent style, with layers of rich fig, apricot, pear, spice and nectarine. Long and tasty, it's a very attractive Chardonnay from California's southern end. Drink now through 2002.–J.L. • $16 • (7/31/1999) SS • **92**
Pinot Noir Santa Barbara County 1997: Zesty, elegant and polished, with spicy cherry, wild berry, black cherry and anise, finishing with round, supple tannins. Drink through 2006.–J.L. • $16 • (9/15/1999) • **88**
Syrah Santa Barbara County 1998: Cola, black pepper and herb notes show decent focus within firm tannin. Drink now through 2004.–J.L. • $16 • (6/15/2000) • **82**

LINDEN | VIRGINIA

Cabernet Franc Virginia 1995 • $15 • (3/31/1998) • **75**
Cabernet Franc Virginia 1994 • $15 • (4/30/1997) • **79**
Cabernet Sauvignon Virginia 1995: An assertive Cabernet with obvious oak shadings to the generous cherry flavors—and plenty of tannin. Best after 2000. • $16 • (6/15/1999) • **82**
Cabernet Sauvignon Virginia 1994 • $16 • (5/15/1998) • **84**
Cabernet Sauvignon Virginia 1991 • $16 • (12/31/1995) • **88**
Cabernet Sauvignon Virginia 1990 • $16 • (9/30/1993) • **86**
Cabernet Sauvignon Virginia 1988 • $15 • (2/29/1992) • **84**
Chardonnay Virginia Reserve 1997: Toasty and honeyed aromas and flavors have allure, and a core of acidity keeps it fresh, bold and balanced. Drink now.–T.M. • $24 • (5/31/2000) • **84**
Fiery Run Red Virginia 1997: This ambitious red is thick and concentrated, with heavy oak flavors of coffee and chocolate, muscular tannins and ripe notes of plum and prune with herbal accents. Can stand up to hearty food. Cabernet Sauvignon, Cabernet Franc and Petit Verdot. Drink now through 2004.–T.M. • $22 • (5/31/2000) • **87**
Sauvignon Blanc Virginia Glen Manor 1998: This exuberant wine has the character of a tropical fruit cocktail. The flavors are intriguing, but lack depth and harmony.–T.M. • $16 • (5/31/2000) • **78**
Vidal Blanc Virginia Late Harvest 1996 • $16/375 ml. • (12/31/1997) • **84**

LION VALLEY | OREGON

Chardonnay Willamette Valley Shea Vineyards Reserve 1997: On the crisp side, with pretty lemon meringue, pear and toast flavors that become richer on the lingering finish. Drink now through 2002.–H.S. • $18 • (11/15/1999) • **87**
Pinot Noir Willamette Valley Shea Vineyards Reserve 1996: Soft and spicy, with mature, almost caramellike aromas and flavors around a light core of currant flavor. Drink now.–H.S. • $25 • (12/31/1999) • **81**
Pinot Noir Willamette Valley Shea Vineyards Unfiltered Reserve 1997: Light and firm, with a vinegar edge to the modest cherry and spice flavors. Unusual, but oddly appealing. Drink now through 2003.–H.S. • $27 • (11/15/1999) • **81**

LIONS PEAK | CALIFORNIA

Cabernet Sauvignon Paso Robles 1996: Juicy cherry flavors are focused and bright on a medium frame, with a spicy, toasty finish. Drink now through 2005.–J.L. • $20 • (6/30/2000) • **84**

LIPARITA | CALIFORNIA

Cabernet Sauvignon Howell Mountain 1996: Starts out tight, with a lean, cedary band of cherry and currant, but then the flavors open up, turning more supple and revealing more depth and complexity. Best from 2001 through 2008.–J.L. • $45 • (12/15/1999) • **89**
Cabernet Sauvignon Howell Mountain 1995: Tight, with a firm cedary edge to the ripe plum and berry flavors, turning elegant and rich on the finish. Drink through 2006.–J.L. • $37 • (1/31/1999) • **88**
Cabernet Sauvignon Howell Mountain 1994 • $32 • (5/15/1998) HR • **93**
Cabernet Sauvignon Howell Mountain 1993 • $32 • (10/15/1996) • **88**

LIPARITA

Cabernet Sauvignon Howell Mountain 1992 • $28 • (12/15/1995) • **84**
Cabernet Sauvignon Howell Mountain 1991 • $28 • (11/15/1994) • **86**
Cabernet Sauvignon Howell Mountain 1990 • $28 • (11/15/1993) • **89**
Chardonnay Carneros 1998: Light, with watery vanilla and earth flavors and a hint of baked apple. Drink now.–J.L. • $24 • (6/15/2000) • **81**
Chardonnay Carneros 1997: Sleek and elegant, with a tight band of citrus, pear and cedary oak, finishing with earthy nuances and a trace of bitterness. Drink now through 2003.–J.L. • $30 • (8/31/1999) • **88**
Chardonnay Howell Mountain 1996 • $24 • (5/15/1998) • **88**
Merlot Howell Mountain 1995: Crisp and a bit lean at first, with spicy, cedary oak and hints of currant, anise, plum and berry. More impressive on the finish, where the flavors fan out. Drink through 2004.–J.L. • $30 • (9/30/1998) • **88**
Merlot Howell Mountain 1994 • $28 • (5/15/1997) • **90**
Merlot Howell Mountain 1993 • $26 • (4/30/1996) • **88**
Merlot Howell Mountain 1991 • $24 • (9/15/1994) • **83**
Merlot Napa Valley 1996: Well oaked, with spicy currant, black cherry, herb, anise and cedar, turning supple and firm on the finish, with an earthy edge. Drink through 2006.–J.L. • $33 • (9/15/1999) • **87**
Sauvignon Blanc Howell Mountain 1996 • $18 • (6/30/1997) • **88**

LITTORAI | CALIFORNIA

Pinot Noir Anderson Valley One Acre 1995: Simple, with pleasant dried cherry, herb and light oak shadings, this holds its elegance and finesse through the finish. Drink now through 2002.–J.L. • $32 • (10/31/1998) • **87**
Pinot Noir Anderson Valley Savoy Vineyard 1995: Appealing for its tart cherry, wild berry and plum notes, with hints of mineral and gamy flavors. Well balanced. Drink through 2004.–J.L. • $32 • (10/31/1998) • **87**
Pinot Noir Sonoma Coast Hirsch Vineyard 1995: A lean and earthy style, finishing with tealike tannins. Perhaps time in the bottle will help. Drink through 2003.–J.L. • $32 • (10/31/1998) • **83**
Pinot Noir Sonoma Coast Hirsch Vineyard 1994 • $NA • (1/01/1997) • **88**

LIVINGSTON | CALIFORNIA

Cabernet Sauvignon Napa Valley Gemstone Vineyard 1997: Intense and concentrated, loaded with wild berry, currant, anise and sage. Rough and a bit raw in texture, it has the right stuff.–J.L. • $NA • (8/31/1998) (BT) • **90-94**
Cabernet Sauvignon Napa Valley Gonser Vineyard 1993 • $25 • (6/15/1997) • **83**
Cabernet Sauvignon Napa Valley Moffett Vineyard 1996: Crisp and tight, with a narrow range of flavors focused around a pretty beam of cherry and plum. Doesn't quite offer the depth and richness of the best, finishing with firm tannins, so cellar it short-term. Best from 2001 through 2009.–J.L. • $50 • (10/15/1999) • **88**
Cabernet Sauvignon Napa Valley Moffett Vineyard 1995: Crisp and austere, not quite as rich as it usually is, with bright, ripe black cherry, plum and currant notes that slowly fan out. Shows fruit and light oak complexities on the finish. Tasted twice, with consistent notes. Drink through 2008.–J.L. • $40 • (11/15/1998) • **89**
Cabernet Sauvignon Napa Valley Moffett Vineyard 1994 • $36 • (10/31/1997) HR • **94**
Cabernet Sauvignon Napa Valley Moffett Vineyard 1993 • $33 • (11/15/1996) • **89**
Cabernet Sauvignon Napa Valley Moffett Vineyard 1992 • $30 • (12/15/1995) • **89**
Cabernet Sauvignon Napa Valley Moffett Vineyard 1991 • $30 • (11/15/1994) • **89**
Cabernet Sauvignon Napa Valley Moffett Vineyard 1990 • $30 • (11/15/1993) HR • **91**
Cabernet Sauvignon Napa Valley Moffett Vineyard 1989: Sturdy, structured, with a tannic framework, turning earthy with mature currant and black cherry flavors. (1989 California Cabernet retrospective tasting). Drink now through 2004.–J.L. • $18 • (8/31/1999) • **85**
Cabernet Sauvignon Napa Valley Moffett Vineyard 1988: One of the better-balanced '88s. Impressive for its focused flavors, with ripe cherry, plum, currant, anise, sage and cedar, and mild, supple, well-integrated tannins. (1988 California Cabernet retrospective tasting). Drink now through 2005.–J.L. • $24 • (11/15/1998) • **88**

Key: SS—Spectator Selection CS—Cellar Selection HR—Highly Recommended
$NA—Price Not Available a—Auction Price (BT)—Barrel Tasting
For a key to the tasters' initials, see "How to Use These Listings."
Dates in parentheses indicate the issues in which the ratings were published.

Cabernet Sauvignon Napa Valley Moffett Vineyard 1987 • $31 ⓐ • (12/15/1997) • **94**
Cabernet Sauvignon Napa Valley Moffett Vineyard 1986 • $22 ⓐ • (11/30/1989) • **88**
Cabernet Sauvignon Napa Valley Moffett Vineyard 1985 • $22 ⓐ • (10/15/1988) • **85**
Cabernet Sauvignon Napa Valley Moffett Vineyard 1984 • $18 • (11/15/1987) • **86**
Cabernet Sauvignon Napa Valley Rockpile 1993 • $25 • (6/15/1997) • **87**
Cabernet Sauvignon Napa Valley Stanley's Selection 1995 • $22 • (3/31/1998) • **88**
Cabernet Sauvignon Napa Valley Stanley's Selection 1994 • $20 • (5/15/1997) • **84**
Cabernet Sauvignon Napa Valley Stanley's Selection 1993 • $20 • (12/15/1996) • **84**
Cabernet Sauvignon Napa Valley Stanley's Selection 1992 • $18 • (8/31/1995) • **87**
Cabernet Sauvignon Napa Valley Stanley's Selection 1991 • $20 • (11/15/1994) • **83**
Cabernet Sauvignon Napa Valley Stanley's Selection 1990 • $20 • (3/15/1993) • **88**
Cabernet Sauvignon Napa Valley Stanley's Selection 1989 • $26 • (7/15/1992) • **85**
Chardonnay Napa Valley 1997: Sharply focused, rich, charming and concentrated, with layers of vanilla, fig and pear, turning silky and complex. Tasted twice, with consistent notes. Drink now through 2002.–J.L. • $40 • (12/15/1999) • **93**
Chardonnay Napa Valley 1996 • $40 • (5/31/1998) • **92**
French Colombard California Premium Select NV • $8/1.5 liter • (5/15/1998) • **80**
Sangiovese Sonoma County 1996 • $20 • (5/15/1998) • **87**

LIVINGSTON MOFFETT | CALIFORNIA

Cabernet Sauvignon Napa Valley Stanley's Selection 1997: On the tart, lean side, with crisp cherry and wild berry flavors. Lacks depth, richness and concentration. Drink now through 2007.–J.L. • $25 • (6/15/2000) • **85**
Gemstone Vineyard Napa Valley 1998: Very spicy, with pretty floral and berryish flavors that are quite attractive, finishing with supple tannins.–J.L. • $75 • (8/31/1999) (BT) • **90-94**
Gemstone Vineyard Napa Valley 1997: Smooth, ripe, rich and complex, with a good dose of currant, sage, mint and wild berry. Firms up and turns tannic on the finish. Drink now through 2010.–J.L. • $75 • (5/15/2000) • **90**
Syrah Napa Valley Mitchell Vineyard 1997: Dark and firm, with a tight core of dried cherry, leather, coffee, anise and sage. Keeps its focus and finishes complex, with integrated tannins. The first Syrah from Livingston, which has now added Moffett to its name. Best from 2001 through 2007.–J.L. • $35 • (12/31/1999) • **88**

LLANO ESTACADO | TEXAS

Cabernet Sauvignon Texas 1988 • $12 • (2/29/1992) • **81**
Cabernet Sauvignon Texas High Plains 1992 • $12 • (1/31/1995) • **85**
Cabernet Sauvignon Texas High Plains Cellar Select 1994 • $19 • (11/30/1996) • **79**
Merlot Texas 1991 • $12 • (6/30/1993) • **81**
Merlot Texas Cellar Select 1995 • $19 • (11/30/1996) • **83**
Passionelle Texas Red 1997: The aromas lean toward a resiny note, yet there's good berry and spice notes and moderate concentration in this medium-bodied red. Made from Carignane. Drink now.–B.S. • $19 • (12/15/1998) • **82**
Port Texas High Plains Cellar Select NV • $20 • (12/31/1997) • **83**
Signature Edition Texas 1992 • $8 • (1/31/1995) • **83**
Viviano Noble Cepagé Texas 1994 • $40 • (9/30/1997) • **84**
Zinfandel Texas 1997: Full-bodied and firmly structured, this red's plummy fruit struggles against a vanilla element. Drink now.–B.S. • $13 • (12/15/1998) • **80**
Zinfandel Texas 1996 • $15 • (5/15/1998) • **81**

LOCKWOOD | CALIFORNIA

Cabernet Sauvignon Monterey 1996: A blend of ripe plum and berry notes framed in sweet oak. Tannins are firm but ripe and the finish is harmonious, showing hints of herb and dill. Drink now through 2004. • $17 • (9/15/1999) • **84**

Cabernet Sauvignon Monterey 1995: Cola, vanilla and black cherry notes are matched with a hint of stemminess. Fairly soft and accessible. Drink now through 2002. • $16 • (11/15/1998) • **82**
Cabernet Sauvignon Monterey 1994 • $15 • (5/31/1997) • **88**
Cabernet Sauvignon Monterey 1993 • $14 • (9/15/1996) • **85**
Cabernet Sauvignon Monterey 1992 • $14 • (9/30/1995) • **86**
Cabernet Sauvignon Monterey 1991 • $12 • (10/31/1993) • **88**
Cabernet Sauvignon Monterey Partners' Reserve 1996: Kicks off with a hint of cola, then moves on to feature plum, cassis, herb and tealike flavors. Tannins are moderate, as is the body, texture and finish. Pleasing now, it should get better. Drink through 2005. • $25 • (9/15/1999) • **87**
Cabernet Sauvignon Monterey Partners' Reserve 1995: Ripe and supple, with a pretty burst of blueberry and plum flavors that are smooth and polished, finishing with a pretty toasty oak interplay and mild, well-integrated tannins. Best from 2001 through 2007.–J.L. • $22 • (11/15/1998) • **90**
Cabernet Sauvignon Monterey Partners' Reserve 1994 • $21 • (11/15/1997) • **88**
Cabernet Sauvignon Monterey Partners' Reserve 1993 • $18 • (11/30/1996) • **83**
Cabernet Sauvignon Monterey Partners' Reserve 1991 • $16 • (11/15/1994) • **84**
Cabernet Sauvignon Monterey Partners' Reserve 1990 • $18 • (10/31/1993) • **88**
Chardonnay Monterey 1998: Soft, with bubblegum and tart lemon flavors that linger on the finish. Drink now.–J.L. • $16 • (6/15/2000) • **82**
Chardonnay Monterey 1997: Full-bodied, offering plenty of citrus, pear and apple flavors. The acidity is quite bright, providing balance but also lending a sharp edge to the finish. Drink now through 2002. • $16 • (6/30/1999) • **87**
Chardonnay Monterey 1996 • $16 • (3/31/1998) • **85**
Chardonnay Monterey Very Special Reserve 1997: Exotic, with apricot and spicy honey flavors wrapped within a vanilla finish. Drink now.–J.L. • $32 • (6/30/2000) • **87**
Chardonnay Monterey Very Special Reserve 1996: This California offering weaves a complex tapestry of flavors—ripe pear, fig, toasty oak and hazelnut with exotic floral and spicy nuances—all held together by lively acidity. Shows the bottle bouquet and positive effects of aging. Drink now.–J.L. • $32 • (5/15/2000) HR • **91**
Merlot Monterey 1995 • $17 • (11/30/1997) • **88**
Merlot Monterey 1994 • $17 • (2/28/1997) • **87**
Merlot Monterey 1993 • $16 • (8/31/1996) • **85**
Merlot Monterey 1992 • $15 • (9/15/1994) • **86**
Merlot Monterey 1991 • $12 • (5/31/1994) • **89**
Merlot Monterey Partners' Reserve 1995 • $25 • (3/31/1998) • **89**
Merlot Monterey Partners' Reserve 1994 • $25 • (6/30/1997) • **87**
Pinot Blanc Monterey 1996 • $12 • (4/30/1998) • **86**
Sangiovese Monterey 1996: Tightly wound, with hints of cherry and herb. A bit dry on the finish, but the modest fruit manages to hang in until the end. Drink now. • $16 • (12/31/1998) • **81**
Sangiovese Monterey 1995 • $16 • (12/15/1997) • **87**
Sauvignon Blanc Monterey 1998: Lean and dominated by oak, vanilla and lemon juice flavors. Drink now.–J.L. • $11 • (5/15/2000) • **81**
Sauvignon Blanc Monterey 1997: With its somewhat unusual cola and butterscotch aromas, this wine commands attention from the start, and its affordable price is noteworthy, too. On the palate, it's firm yet smooth and serves up a blend of citrus, hazelnut, grass, gooseberry and melon flavors. Finishes moderately, with freshness. Drink now through 2002. • $11 • (5/15/1999) • **89**
Sauvignon Blanc Monterey 1996 • $10 • (11/30/1997) • **85**
Syrah Monterey 1996: Smooth and supple, with rich black fruit and mineral notes that make it fun to drink, though the flavors are not well delineated. Tannins are ripe and integrated. Drink now.–J.L. • $15 • (4/30/1999) • **86**
Syrah Monterey 1995 • $16 • (4/30/1998) • **87**

LOGAN | CALIFORNIA

Chardonnay Monterey 1996: Shows off an earthy, gamy side before the ripe pear, citrus and spicy oak flavors work their way to the mainstream. Solid. Drink now.–J.L. • $17 • (7/31/1998) • **86**
Pinot Noir Monterey 1995 • $18 • (2/28/1998) • **84**
Pinot Noir Monterey 1994 • $18 • (1/31/1997) • **84**

LOHR, J. | CALIFORNIA

Cabernet Sauvignon California Cypress 1993 • $8 • (12/15/1995) • **82**
Cabernet Sauvignon California Cypress 1992 • $9 • (11/30/1995) • **86**
Cabernet Sauvignon California Cypress 1991 • $8 • (11/15/1994) • **82**
Cabernet Sauvignon California Cypress 1990 • $8 • (11/15/1993) • **86**
Cabernet Sauvignon California Cypress 1989 • $8 • (5/15/1993) • **83**
Cabernet Sauvignon California Cypress 1988 • $7 • (11/15/1991) • **80**
Cabernet Sauvignon Napa Valley Carol's Vineyard Reserve 1985 • $15 • (12/15/1988) • **89**
Cabernet Sauvignon Napa Valley Carol's Vineyard Reserve Lot 2 1985 • $18 • (9/30/1990) • **88**
Cabernet Sauvignon Paso Robles Seven Oaks 1996: Shows a light but focused core of toasted oak, cherry, strawberry and herb notes, with a firm, slightly drying finish. Drink now.–J.L. • $15 • (5/15/1999) • **84**
Cabernet Sauvignon Paso Robles Seven Oaks 1995 • $14 • (4/30/1998) • **85**
Cabernet Sauvignon Paso Robles Seven Oaks 1994 • $14 • (7/31/1997) • **87**
Cabernet Sauvignon Paso Robles Seven Oaks 1993 • $12 • (11/30/1995) • **87**
Cabernet Sauvignon Paso Robles Seven Oaks 1991 • $11 • (7/31/1994) • **84**
Cabernet Sauvignon Paso Robles Seven Oaks 1990 • $11 • (11/15/1993) • **88**
Cabernet Sauvignon Paso Robles Seven Oaks 1989 • $12 • (11/15/1992) • **89**
Cabernet Sauvignon Paso Robles Seven Oaks 1988 • $13 • (3/15/1992) • **83**
Cabernet Sauvignon Paso Robles Seven Oaks 1987 • $12 • (4/30/1991) • **86**
Cabernet Sauvignon Paso Robles VS 1991 • $22 • (11/30/1995) • **87**
Cabernet Sauvignon Paso Robles VS.1 1990 • $22 • (3/31/1995) • **88**
Chardonnay Monterey Riverstone 1997: Tastes of oak flavors; behind that the citrus, pear and cream notes emerge. There's enough fruit to merit recommendation. Drink now.–J.L. • $15 • (5/31/1999) • **84**
Chardonnay Monterey Riverstone 1996 • $14 • (6/15/1998) • **88**
Gamay Monterey Wildflower 1995 • $8 • (11/30/1996) • **86**
Gamay Monterey Wildflower 1993 • $8 • (9/15/1995) • **78**
Johannisberg Riesling Monterey Late Harvest Bay Mist 1993 • $10/375 ml. • (10/31/1995) HR • **93**
Merlot California Cypress 1996: Soft, medium-bodied, with sweet oak flavors and a layer of cherry. Tannins are drying. Drink now.–J.L. • $12 • (8/31/1998) • **79**
Merlot California Cypress 1995 • $11 • (7/31/1997) • **82**
Merlot California Cypress 1993 • $10 • (12/31/1995) • **86**
Merlot California Cypress 1992 • $9 • (6/15/1994) • **86**
Merlot California Cypress 1991 • $9 • (5/31/1993) • **82**
Merlot California Cypress 1989 • $9 • (2/29/1992) • **85**
Syrah Paso Robles South Ridge 1994 • $14 • (11/15/1997) • **86**
Syrah Paso Robles South Ridge 1993 • $14 • (8/31/1996) • **80**
Valdiguié Monterey Wildflower 1996 • $8 • (7/31/1997) • **86**

LOKOYA | CALIFORNIA

Cabernet Sauvignon Howell Mountain 1996: Dense, earthy and detailed, with firm, chewy tannins wrapped around a core of currant, dried plum, earth, anise and sage. Firms up on the finish, where the tannins are quite evident. Best from 2002 through 2010.–J.L. • $100 • (11/15/1999) • **92**
Cabernet Sauvignon Howell Mountain 1995: Tightly wound, tannic and firm, with exotic cherry-berry flavors and tannins that clamp down on the finish. Best to cellar, but with only 20 cases made, who has the wine? Available only at the winery.–J.L. • $100 • (12/15/1998) • **88**
Cabernet Sauvignon Mount Veeder 1996: Firm, tightly wound and austere, with a compact band of earth, mineral, currant, sage, tea and cherry. Turns tannic and concentrated on the finish, where the flavors sail on. Best from 2002 through 2010.–J.L. • $100 • (11/15/1999) • **94**
Cabernet Sauvignon Mount Veeder 1995: A big, ripe and firmly tannic style, dense, chunky and chewy, but wade past the tannins and you'll get a glimpse of a complex, concentrated wine. Definitely needs time. Best from 2002 through 2010.–J.L. • $199 Ⓐ • (11/15/1998) • **92**
Cabernet Sauvignon Napa Valley Diamond Mountain 1996: Enormously complex and detailed, with rich, concentrated, earthy currant, anise, mineral, sage, plum, cedar and spice. Unfolds gracefully, turning elegant and polished. Drink through 2009.–J.L. • $100 • (11/15/1999) • **95**
Cabernet Sauvignon Napa Valley Diamond Mountain 1995: Intense and tightly wound, with a slight earthy streak to the currant and black cherry, and nice leathery flavors, but once the tannins weigh in, it gets chewy. Best from 2002 through 2009.–J.L. • $158 Ⓐ • (11/15/1998) • **87**
Cabernet Sauvignon Rutherford 1998: Weaves together rich, complex cherry, currant, plum and spicy flavors, with pretty, toasty oak and elegant tannins. Beautifully crafted.–J.L. • $NA • (8/31/1999) (BT) • **90-94**
Cabernet Sauvignon Rutherford 1996: Smooth, ripe, rich and polished, with a wonderful array of juicy cherry, currant, plum, anise, herb, mineral and spice flavors, all wonderfully orchestrated. Finishes with supple tannins and pretty oak shadings. Best from 2001 through 2009.–J.L. • $115 Ⓐ • (11/15/1999) • **95**
Cabernet Sauvignon Rutherford 1995: This is a seductive and delicious California red, ripe and juicy, fruit-driven, with luscious currant, black cherry, wild berry and plummy Cabernet flavors that are sharply focused and long, complex and concentrated on the finish. Best from 2001 through 2009.–J.L. • $135 Ⓐ • (11/15/1998) HR • **97**

LOLONIS | CALIFORNIA

Cabernet Sauvignon Mendocino County 1994 • $15 • (10/31/1997) • **83**
Cabernet Sauvignon Mendocino County Lolonis Vineyards Private Reserve 1989 • $15 • (11/15/1991) • **86**
Cabernet Sauvignon Mendocino County Private Reserve 1994: Ripe, smooth and generous with its pretty currant and plum flavors, shading the finish with fine-grained tannins. Drink now through 2003.–H.S. • $25 • (10/31/1998) • **88**
Cabernet Sauvignon Mendocino County Private Reserve 1993 • $20 • (12/15/1997) • **85**
Cabernet Sauvignon Mendocino County Private Reserve 1989 • $16 • (8/31/1992) • **84**
Cabernet Sauvignon Mendocino County Private Reserve 1986 • $15 • (5/15/1990) • **83**
Cabernet Sauvignon Redwood Valley 1997: Firm, with orange peel, chocolate and pine overtones. Good intensity on the finish. Drink now through 2004.–J.L. • $19 • (6/30/2000) • **86**
Cabernet Sauvignon Redwood Valley 1996: Smooth, with toasted oak, cola, cherry and herb-laced flavors on a focused, compact frame. Drink now through 2005.–J.L. • $18 • (10/15/1999) • **86**
Cabernet Sauvignon Redwood Valley 1995: Smooth and juicy, with pretty blackberry and spice flavors, hinting at mushroom on the earthy finish. Drink now.–H.S. • $16 • (10/31/1998) • **82**
Chardonnay Redwood Valley 1998: Apple, pear and vanilla flavors are round and straightforward. Drink now.–J.L. • $16 • (6/15/2000) • **83**
Chardonnay Redwood Valley Private Reserve 1997: Very lemony, with a crisp acidity blending nicely with a creamy, toasty profile. Good, lingering finish. Drink now.–J.L. • $26 • (6/15/2000) • **86**
Chardonnay Redwood Valley Private Reserve 1996: Complex, with ripe pear, citrus and apple flavors that turn smooth and polished, with a pretty aftertaste that echoes the fruit. Drink through 2004.–J.L. • $25 • (1/31/1999) • **89**
Eugenia Late Harvest Private Reserve Mendocino County 1993 • $28 • (6/15/1997) • **88**
Fumé Blanc Redwood Valley 1998: Grassy, with melon and grapefruit flavors and a creamy, anise-scented finish. Drink now through 2002.–H.S. • $12 • (1/31/2000) • **84**
Fumé Blanc Redwood Valley 1997: A smooth blend of melon, citrus and herb flavor leads the way. The finish is moderate, with a fashionably flinty edge. Drink now. • $12 • (2/28/1999) • **86**
Merlot Mendocino County Private Reserve 1995 • $22 • (5/15/1998) • **84**
Merlot Mendocino County Private Reserve 1994 • $23 • (7/31/1997) • **87**
Merlot Mendocino County Private Reserve 1993 • $18 • (8/31/1996) • **88**
Merlot Redwood Valley Private Reserve 1996: Ripe and spicy, with pretty plum and cherry jam flavors, turning supple and polished on the finish. Drink now through 2007.–J.L. • $25 • (3/31/2000) • **87**
Petite Sirah Redwood Valley Orpheus Private Reserve 1996: Earthy, with a cheese rind edge to the dark, meaty plum and spice flavors. Mildly tannic, so drink now if you can look past the funkiness.–J.L. • $20 • (6/30/2000) • **83**
Petite Sirah Mendocino Orpheus Private Reserve 1994 • $16 • (3/31/1998) • **85**
Zinfandel Mendocino County 1995 • $16 • (6/15/1998) • **89**
Zinfandel Mendocino County 1994 • $12 • (4/30/1997) HR • **92**
Zinfandel Mendocino County 1992 • $10 • (10/15/1995) • **84**
Zinfandel Mendocino County 1991 • $10 • (10/15/1994) • **83**
Zinfandel Mendocino County 1990 • $10 • (9/30/1993) • **85**
Zinfandel Mendocino County Private Reserve 1994 • $19 • (12/31/1997) SS • **92**
Zinfandel Mendocino County Private Reserve 1993 • $17 • (4/30/1997) • **79**
Zinfandel Mendocino County Private Reserve 1992 • $16 • (10/15/1995) • **88**
Zinfandel Mendocino County Private Reserve 1991 • $16 • (10/15/1994) • **85**
Zinfandel Mendocino County Private Reserve 1990 • $13 • (10/15/1992) • **89**
Zinfandel Mendocino County Private Reserve Lot 1 Lolonis Vineyards 1989 • $12 • (8/31/1991) • **83**
Zinfandel Mendocino County Private Reserve Lot 2 Lolonis Vineyards 1989 • $8 • (10/15/1992) • **76**
Zinfandel Redwood Valley 1997: Ripe and generous, this effusive wine has appealing if somewhat Port-like plum, blackberry and spice flavors that linger nicely on the round finish. Drink now through 2003.–H.S. • $18 • (11/30/1999) • **89**
Zinfandel Redwood Valley 1996: Ripe and flavorful, with lots of complex earthy blackberry, tar, raisin and herbal notes, turning smooth and complex on the finish. Given the firm tannins, it's best to cellar short-term. Try through 2002.–J.L. • $17 • (12/15/1998) • **89**
Zinfandel Redwood Valley Private Reserve 1997: Simple if a bit muddled, with earthy, oaky flavors dominating the berryish fruit beneath. Turns dry and tannic. Rustic. Drink now.–J.L. • $30 • (4/30/2000) • **83**
Zinfandel Redwood Valley Private Reserve 1996: With lots of ripe and spicy cherry, wild berry, plum, sage, tar and anise, this is elegant and complex, rich in flavor without being heavy. Drink now through 2001.–J.L. • $25 • (5/15/1999) • **88**
Zinfandel Redwood Valley Private Reserve 1995 • $22 • (3/31/1998) • **87**

LONETREE | CALIFORNIA

Sangiovese Mendocino County 1997: Pretty cherry notes lead the way, backed by firm tannins and snappy acidity. Finishes moderately, with a fresh, herbal edge. Drink now through 2003. • $17 • (11/15/1999) • **85**
Sangiovese Mendocino County 1996: Distinct, with snappy wild berry, blackberry and spicy sage notes. Holds its fruit and focus on the finish. Drink now.–J.L. • $15 • (12/15/1998) • **86**
Sangiovese Mendocino County 1995 • $14 • (3/31/1998) • **82**
Syrah Mendocino County 1997: Tight and tannic, with a tough, chewy core of currant, leather, anise and sage, finishing with crisp acidity. Slightly better than when previously reviewed. Best from 2002 through 2008.–J.L. • $17 • (4/30/2000) • **85**
Syrah Mendocino County 1996: Leads off with attractive earth and forest floor aromas. Richly textured on the palate, with black cherry, herb and blackberry notes framed in plush, velvety tannins. Drink now through 2003. • $15 • (12/15/1998) • **90**
Syrah Mendocino County 1995 • $14 • (3/31/1998) • **87**
Zinfandel Mendocino County 1998: Tough going, with tobacco, wild berry and cherryish flavors, turning murky and simple. Drink now.–J.L. • $16 • (6/15/2000) • **83**
Zinfandel Mendocino County 1996 • $14 • (6/15/1998) • **88**

LONG | CALIFORNIA

Cabernet Sauvignon Napa Valley 1995 • $40 • (3/31/1998) • **90**
Cabernet Sauvignon Napa Valley 1994 • $35 • (1/31/1997) • **90**
Cabernet Sauvignon Napa Valley 1993 • $32 • (8/31/1996) • **84**
Cabernet Sauvignon Napa Valley 1990 • $30 • (8/31/1996) • **86**
Cabernet Sauvignon Napa Valley 1986 • $NA • (12/15/1996) • **86**
Cabernet Sauvignon Napa Valley 1984 • $38 • (12/15/1996) • **86**
Cabernet Sauvignon Napa Valley 1983 • $36 • (8/31/1987) • **72**
Chardonnay Napa Valley 1997: Crisp and refreshing, with ripe floral, apple, pear, citrus and hazelnut flavors. Has room to grow. Drink now through 2005.–J.L. • $35 • (5/31/2000) • **87**
Chardonnay Napa Valley 1996 • $31 • (5/31/1998) • **91**
Chardonnay Russian River Valley Seghesio Vineyards 1998: Marked by a metallic edge, with a tinny edge to the citrus and pear flavors. Largely uninspiring. Drink now.–J.L. • $22 • (5/31/2000) • **83**
Johannisberg Riesling Napa Valley Late Harvest 1994: Sweet and succulent. A golden wine with exotic tropical fruit overtones to honey, pear and floral flavors that extend into a long, silky finish. Beautifully balanced, this feels as though it can age for years. Drink now through 2010 .–H.S. • $19/500 ml. • (1/01/1999) • **91**
Johannisberg Riesling Napa Valley Late Harvest Botrytis 1996 • $25/500 ml. • (5/15/1998) • **92**
Johannisberg Riesling Napa Valley Late Harvest Botrytis 1990 • $18 • (9/15/1991) • **86**
Pinot Grigio Napa Valley 1996 • $18 • (10/15/1997) • **86**
Sangiovese Sonoma County Seghesio Vineyards 1995 • $20 • (7/31/1997) • **90**
Sauvignon Blanc North Coast 1997: Grapefruit, herb, fresh hay and fig notes blend nicely here. The wine is lightly textured and sports bright acidity on its moderate finish. Drink now through 2002. • $17 • (5/15/1999) • **87**
Sauvignon Blanc Sonoma County 1996 • $15 • (1/31/1998) • **85**

LONG MEADOW RANCH | CALIFORNIA

Cabernet Sauvignon Napa Valley 1996: Tightly wound but flavorful, with a band of earthy, cedary cherry, currant and black cherry fruit that's supple yet firm. Needs time. Best from 2001 through 2010.–J.L. • $50 • (12/15/1999) • **89**

Key: SS—Spectator Selection CS—Cellar Selection HR—Highly Recommended $NA—Price Not Available a—Auction Price (BT)—Barrel Tasting
For a key to the tasters' initials, see "How to Use These Listings."
Dates in parentheses indicate the issues in which the ratings were published.

LONGORIA | CALIFORNIA

Cabernet Franc Santa Ynez Valley Blues Cuvee 1995 • $21 • (3/31/1998) • **81**
Cabernet Franc Santa Ynez Valley Blues Cuvee 1993 • $20 • (11/30/1995) • **84**
Cabernet Sauvignon Santa Ynez Valley 1990 • $15 • (6/15/1993) • **83**
Chardonnay Santa Ynez Valley Santa Rita Cuvée 1998: Ripe, smooth and creamy, with layers of fig, spice, vanilla, honey and sage. Finishes firm and complex. Drink now through 2003.–J.L. • $25 • (4/30/2000) • **89**
Chardonnay Santa Ynez Valley Santa Rita Cuvée 1997: Bright and rich, with detailed peach and nectarine flavors and toasty, nutty notes. Complex, with a long finish that continues to push out the flavors. Drink now through 2002.–J.L. • $25 • (7/31/1999) • **92**
Chardonnay Santa Ynez Valley Santa Rita Cuvée 1996 • $25 • (6/30/1998) • **91**
Merlot Santa Ynez Valley 1997: Firm and tannic, a bit edgy and a twinge bitter. The core of smoky currant and spicy berry needs a little time to pull together. Best from 2001 through 2007.–J.L. • $23 • (3/31/2000) • **86**
Merlot Santa Ynez Valley 1996: Kicks off with hints of cedar, spice, black currant and black cherry. Tannins are coarse, however, leaving the finish short. Could smooth out with time. Drink through 2003. • $23 • (10/15/1999) • **83**
Merlot Santa Ynez Valley 1995 • $23 • (4/30/1998) • **87**
Merlot Santa Ynez Valley 1994 • $21 • (7/31/1997) • **88**
Merlot Santa Ynez Valley 1990 • $16 • (7/15/1993) • **85**
Pinot Noir Santa Maria Valley Bien Nacido Vineyard 1997: Complex, with rich cherry, spice, cola, anise and earth flavors, turning supple and polished on the finish. Drink now through 2006.–J.L. • $32 • (9/15/1999) • **88**
Pinot Noir Santa Maria Valley Bien Nacido Vineyard 1996: Smooth and polished, this tames the racier, vegetal flavors found in many wines from this appellation and instead claims a fruitier profile of plum and black cherry. Finishes with supple tannins. Drink now through 2002.–J.L. • $32 • (9/15/1998) • **87**
Pinot Noir Santa Maria Valley Bien Nacido Vineyard 1995 • $32 • (1/31/1998) • **88**
Pinot Noir Santa Maria Valley Bien Nacido Vineyard 1994 • $23 • (4/30/1996) • **86**
Pinot Noir Santa Maria Valley Bien Nacido Vineyard 1993 • $20 • (9/15/1995) • **86**
Pinot Noir Santa Ynez Valley Benedict Vineyard 1989 • $28 • (2/28/1993) • **86**

LORANE | OREGON

Chardonnay Oregon 1996 • $10 • (6/15/1998) • **83**
Pinot Noir Oregon 1996: Check out the deal on this elegant red. Light in color and aroma, it opens into pleasant spicy strawberry and tobacco flavors that emerge smoothly and linger on the finish. Drink now through 2002.–H.S. • $10 • (11/15/1999) • **85**
Pinot Noir Oregon 1995 • $10 • (6/15/1998) • **84**

LORENZA-LAKE | CALIFORNIA

Petite Sirah Napa Valley Blockheadia Ringnosii 1996 • $25 • (5/15/1998) • **88**
Zinfandel California Blockheadia Ringnosii 1998: Jammy strawberry and plum flavors, with vanilla and leather notes on a medium frame. Drink now.–J.L. • $17 • (5/31/2000) • **84**
Zinfandel California Blockheadia Ringnosii 1997: Very tasty, elegant and complex, with spicy cherry, raspberry and blueberry flavors that turn supple and polished on the finish. Drink now.–J.L. • $15 • (5/31/1999) • **89**
Zinfandel Napa Valley Blockheadia Ringnosii 1996 • $20 • (5/15/1998) • **88**
Zinfandel Russian River Valley Blockheadia Ringnosii 1998: Prickly, with a lean band of thin, spicy berry and cherry that fails to inspire. Drink now.–J.L. • $24 • (4/30/2000) • **82**

LOS ENCANTOS | CALIFORNIA

Cabernet Sauvignon Napa Valley Covenant Reserve 1992 • $14 • (2/29/1996) • **85**
Chardonnay Edna Valley Covenant Reserve 1996 • $16 • (11/30/1997) • **85**
Merlot California Covenant Reserve 1997: Disjointed, with stalky, sour cherry flavors and a sharp, acidic edge.–J.L. • $10 • (9/30/1998) • **70**
Pinot Noir Arroyo Grande Valley Covenant Reserve 1996 • $16 • (11/30/1997) • **84**
Pinot Noir Edna Valley Covenant Reserve 1994 • $14 • (1/31/1996) • **84**

LOS OLIVOS | CALIFORNIA

Pinot Noir Santa Barbara County 1993 • $20 • (2/29/1996) • **75**

LUNA | CALIFORNIA

Merlot Napa Valley 1997: Tight, with firm cherry, currant, mineral, coffee and leather notes. Turns firm and tannic on the finish. Best from 2001 through 2007.–J.L. • $28 • (1/31/2000) • **88**
Merlot Napa Valley 1996: Tight and concentrated, with rich and tannic tea, herb, cherry, leather and sage flavors that are closely bound, with crisp tannins. Drink now through 2004.–J.L. • $28 • (3/31/1999) • **90**
Sangiovese Napa Valley 1997: Tightly reined in and firmly tannic, with a candied, plummy black cherry core. A bit short on the finish. Drink now through 2005.–J.L. • $18 • (1/31/2000) • **85**
Sangiovese Napa Valley 1996 • $18 • (5/15/1998) • **87**

LYETH | CALIFORNIA

A Red Blend Alexander Valley 1992 • $18 • (8/31/1995) • **87**
A Red Blend Alexander Valley 1991 • $14 • (10/15/1994) SS • **89**
A Red Blend Alexander Valley 1990 • $13 • (6/30/1993) • **87**
Red Alexander Valley 1988 • $12 • (11/15/1992) • **84**
Red Alexander Valley 1987 • $15 • (10/15/1992) • **83**
Red Alexander Valley 1986 • $23 • (11/15/1990) • **88**
Red Alexander Valley 1985 • $23 • (5/31/1989) • **86**
Red Alexander Valley 1984 • $18 • (3/15/1988) • **91**
Red Alexander Valley 1983 • $17 • (6/30/1987) • **91**
Red Alexander Valley 1982 • $16 • (6/16/1986) • **86**
Cabernet Sauvignon California 1995: Pleasant cherry and oak flavors form the core of this medium-bodied wine, although they don't quite blend together; instead they run parallel to each other. The wood dominates the finish. • $13 • (11/15/1998) • **78**
Meritage California 1993 • $13 • (11/15/1995) • **86**
Meritage Red Napa County 1996: Pleasant for its soft texture and modest core of herbal-currant flavors. Remains soft on the finish, where the flavors turn simple. Drink now through 2002.–J.L. • $15 • (10/15/1999) • **83**
Meritage Reserve Napa-Sonoma Counties 1993 • $29 • (2/28/1997) • **87**

LYNMAR | CALIFORNIA

Chardonnay Russian River Valley Quail Hill Vineyard 1997: Attractive and fruit-driven, with spicy pear, apricot, apple and melon flavors that are rich, lively, long and complex. Tasty now. Drink now through 2006.–J.L. • $24 • (4/30/2000) • **90**
Chardonnay Russian River Valley Quail Hill Vineyard 1996: Ripe, rich and complex, with lots of smoky, toasty oak and ripe pear, apple and melon flavors to stand up to the wood. Finishes with a toasty oak and complex fruit aftertaste. Short-term cellaring is advised. Drink through 2002.–J.L. • $24 • (9/30/1998) • **90**
Chardonnay Russian River Valley Quail Hill Vineyard VV Cuvée 1997: Well crafted, with toast and vanilla-scented oak adding a nice round edge to the bright, lively pear, fig, melon and citrus notes. Finishes with a hazelnut accent. Drink now through 2006.–J.L. • $24 • (4/30/2000) • **89**
Pinot Noir Russian River Valley 1993 • $17 • (3/31/1996) • **83**
Pinot Noir Russian River Valley 1992 • $16 • (5/15/1995) • **88**
Pinot Noir Russian River Valley Quail Hill Vineyard 1996: Lean in style, with earthy tea and dried cherry flavors, finishing with a smoky, tarry aftertaste. Drink now through 2001.–J.L. • $30 • (11/30/1998) • **85**
Pinot Noir Russian River Valley Quail Hill Vineyard 1995 • $26 • (3/31/1998) • **87**
Pinot Noir Russian River Valley Quail Hill Vineyard 1994 • $26 • (3/31/1997) • **86**
Pinot Noir Russian River Valley Quail Hill Vineyard 1992 • $24 • (5/15/1995) • **90**
Pinot Noir Russian River Valley Quail Hill Vineyard Reserve 1996: Smooth, ripe and supple, with spicy cherry, raspberry, cola and tea notes, this silky-textured, complex, well-integrated wine has polished tannins and good length. Drink now through 2002.–J.L. • $45 • (9/30/1998) • **87**
Pinot Noir Russian River Valley Quail Hill Vineyard Reserve 1994 • $45 • (3/31/1997) • **91**

LYTTON SPRINGS | CALIFORNIA

Cabernet Sauvignon Mendocino County Private Reserve 1988 • $18 • (11/15/1991) • **80**
Cabernet Sauvignon Mendocino County Private Reserve 1987 • $18 • (9/15/1990) • **88**

Zinfandel Sonoma County 1994 • $18 • (4/30/1996) • **88**
Zinfandel Sonoma County 1992 • $16 • (8/31/1994) • **89**
Zinfandel Sonoma County 1989 • $15 • (8/31/1991) • **84**
Zinfandel Sonoma County 1988 • $12 • (7/31/1990) • **90**
Zinfandel Sonoma County 1987 • $12 • (5/31/1989) • **88**
Zinfandel Sonoma County 1986 • $10 • (10/15/1988) • **87**
Zinfandel Sonoma County Valley Vista Vineyard Private Reserve 1981 • $12 • (1/01/1985) • **85**

MACARI | NEW YORK

Bergen Road North Fork of Long Island Red 1997: Firm and polished, this red shows a nice balance of plum and cherry flavors with toast and light chocolate notes from oak, and a lingering, spicy finish. Cabernet Sauvignon, Merlot and Malbec. Tasted twice, with consistent notes. Drink now through 2002.–T.M. • $32 • (5/31/2000) • **88**
Cabernet Franc North Fork of Long Island 1997: Silky, pleasant texture, but behind the cherry and berry flavors are less appealing vegetal and charry notes, and it turns dry on the finish.–T.M. • $19 • (10/15/1999) • **77**
Chardonnay North Fork of Long Island 1997: Vibrant, with pear and peach flavors buoyed nicely on the firm structure. Tastes very dry, with a cleansing finish and a touch of spice. Should match well with food. Drink now. –B.S. • $12 • (12/15/1998) • **83**
Chardonnay North Fork of Long Island Barrel Fermented 1997: A pretty white, soft and a bit sweet, with plenty of vanilla and butter flavors backed by light apple and melon notes. Has just enough acidity for balance. Drink now.–T.M. • $17 • (6/30/1999) • **83**
Chardonnay North Fork of Long Island Barrel Fermented 1996: There's plenty of oak—toasty and coffee-flavored—but it dominates the light apple and pear flavors, and the wine finishes a bit tart and lemony. Tasted twice, with consistent notes.–T.M. • $14 • (12/15/1998) • **78**
Chardonnay North Fork of Long Island Reserve 1998: This lavishly oaked white is rich with toast, honey, modest apple and pear flavors and a soft, slightly dull finish. For fans of oak. Drink now.–T.M. • $22 • (5/31/2000) • **83**
Merlot North Fork of Long Island 1997: A fairly rich and herbal-tasting Merlot, with a nice texture and currant and red plum flavors, but it turns a bit heavy and charry on the finish. Drink now.–K.M. • $19 • (10/15/1999) • **83**
Merlot North Fork of Long Island 1996: Supple and stylish, this smooth-textured Merlot offers cedary, spicy oak aromas, almost-sweet fruit flavors with smoky undertones, and a lingering finish. Drink now through 2001. • $16 • (10/31/1998) • **88**
Pinot Blanc North Fork of Long Island 1998: Tasty, with apple, fig and nut flavors and a kiss of oak that lends vanilla and butterscotch. Round, lush and balanced, it finishes clean. Good aperitif. Drink now.–B.S. • $12 • (10/15/1999) • **85**
Rosé d'une Nuit North Fork of Long Island 1998: This rustic rosé has little fruit, with herbal and vegetal notes reminiscent of roasted peppers. Austere and a bit bitter on the finish.–T.M. • $12 • (10/15/1999) • **76**
Rosé d'une Nuit North Fork of Long Island 1997: Cherry and berry flavors are simple but vivid in this dry, exuberant rosé. Lively and crisp, turning slightly bitter on the finish. Drink now.–T.M. • $11 • (12/15/1998) • **80**
Sauvignon Blanc North Fork of Long Island 1997: Strongly herbal in aroma, crisp in texture, slightly austere in flavor, this is a lively Sauvignon Blanc. Drink now. • $12 • (11/15/1998) • **80**
Viognier North Fork of Long Island 1998: Fat and full-bodied, this Viognier offers typical peach and floral notes matched by vanilla and clove from new oak. Short finish. Drink now.–B.S. • $14 • (11/15/1999) • **82**

MACROSTIE | CALIFORNIA

Chardonnay Carneros 1998: Tight and a bit closed, with an earthy, cedary edge to the citrus and pear flavors. Finishes with a crisp edge. Drink now through 2004.–J.L. • $19 • (2/29/2000) • **87**
Chardonnay Carneros 1997: Tightly knit, with a complex core of cedar, pear, nutmeg and citrus, turning smooth and creamy on the finish, where the flavors fan out. Drink now through 2002.–J.L. • $18 • (4/30/1999) • **90**
Chardonnay Carneros 1996: Intense, with spicy, cedary oak and a solid core of ripe pear, melon and peach-laced flavors. Finishes with toasty, smoky oak and a bit of coarseness. Try now through 2002.–J.L. • $18 • (7/31/1998) • **87**

Key: SS—Spectator Selection CS—Cellar Selection HR—Highly Recommended
$NA—Price Not Available a—Auction Price (BT)—Barrel Tasting
For a key to the tasters' initials, see "How to Use These Listings."
Dates in parentheses indicate the issues in which the ratings were published.

Chardonnay Carneros Reserve 1997: Steely, with a tight, focused beam of ripe pear, apple and melon. Picks up a subtle buttery custard, with the flavors fanning out on the finish. Wonderful sense of balance and finesse. Drink now through 2005.–J.L. • $28 • (2/29/2000) • **90**
Chardonnay Carneros Reserve 1996: Crisp, with an earthy, oaky butterscotch edge to the ripe pear and pineapple flavors, it slowly gains complexity and nuance, finishing with a broad range of flavors. Grows on you. Drink now. –J.L. • $28 • (6/15/1999) • **90**
Merlot Carneros 1997: Firm, with subdued, earthy currant, anise, cedar and oak flavors that may benefit from short-term cellaring. Finishes with tealike tannins. Best from 2001 through 2006.–J.L. • $26 • (2/29/2000) • **87**
Merlot Carneros 1996: A silky, elegant, flavorful style, with hints of toast, currant, black cherry, leather, sage and spice, turning supple and polished. Drink now through 2004.–J.L. • $26 • (5/15/1999) • **89**
Merlot Carneros 1995 • $21 • (5/31/1998) • **87**
Merlot Carneros 1994 • $22 • (5/31/1997) • **84**
Merlot Carneros 1993 • $19 • (2/29/1996) • **86**
Merlot Carneros 1992 • $18 • (2/28/1995) • **87**
Merlot Carneros 1991 • $18 • (9/15/1994) • **82**
Pinot Noir Carneros 1997: Marked by green, stemmy notes, enough cherry, cola and berry emerge to sustain interest, but it tilts toward crispness. Drink now through 2003.–J.L. • $20 • (9/15/1999) • **85**
Pinot Noir Carneros 1996: Complex, with a pretty array of ripe plum, blackberry, spice and toasty oak notes, fanning out on the finish. Drink now through 2002.–J.L. • $19 • (9/15/1998) • **86**
Pinot Noir Carneros 1995 • $18 • (12/15/1997) • **88**
Pinot Noir Carneros 1994 • $17 • (8/31/1996) • **85**
Pinot Noir Carneros 1993 • $17 • (1/31/1996) • **87**
Pinot Noir Carneros 1992 • $16 • (2/28/1994) • **84**
Pinot Noir Carneros Reserve 1995 • $26 • (12/15/1997) • **88**
Pinot Noir Carneros Reserve 1994 • $25 • (11/15/1996) • **87**

MADDALENA | CALIFORNIA

Cabernet Sauvignon Alexander Valley Reserve 1986 • $10 • (3/31/1990) • **77**
Cabernet Sauvignon Alexander Valley Reserve 1985 • $11 • (6/30/1989) • **78**
Cabernet Sauvignon Sonoma County 1990 • $8 • (11/15/1994) • **76**
Cabernet Sauvignon Sonoma County 1988 • $8 • (3/31/1992) • **79**
Chardonnay Central Coast San Simeon Reserve 1996: Minerally, with a nice core of citrus, pear and toast. Delicate flavors linger on the crisp finish. Drink now. • $14 • (7/31/1998) • **84**
Chardonnay Monterey 1996: Starts with an awkward floral note, but straightens out with simple citrus and apple flavors. Drink now. • $10 • (7/31/1998) • **79**
Johannisberg Riesling Monterey County 1996 • $8 • (3/31/1998) • **81**
Merlot Central Coast San Simeon Collection 1990 • $9 • (9/15/1994) • **77**
Merlot Central Coast San Simeon Collection 1989 • $12 • (5/31/1992) • **73**
Merlot Central Coast San Simeon Reserve 1996: Marked by black cherry, licorice, spice and vanilla, the wine is made in a rustic style, with chunky tannins and bright acidity. Pretty oaky. Drink now. • $15 • (7/31/1998) • **83**
Muscat Canelli Central Coast 1996 • $8 • (3/31/1998) • **85**
Syrah Monterey 1997: Ripe black cherry, chocolate and subtle bell pepper notes are framed nicely, with round tannins. Drink now through 2005.–J.L. • $15 • (5/15/2000) • **87**

MADRIGAL | CALIFORNIA

Cabernet Sauvignon Napa Valley 1997: Tight and tannic, with chocolate, cherry and berry flavors framed by cedary oak and picking up a stalky green bean edge on the finish. Best from 2002 through 2010.–J.L. • $30 • (5/31/2000) • **85**
Cabernet Sauvignon Napa Valley 1996: Focused and polished, with well-defined flavors of ripe black cherry, herb, toasted oak and clay that carry through on the finish. Drink now through 2004.–J.L. • $30 • (10/15/1999) • **87**
Petite Sirah Napa Valley 1997: Enough ripe plum and wild berry flavor pushes through the potent wall of tannins. Finishes with leather, mineral and spice notes. Drink now through 2007.–J.L. • $25 • (5/31/2000) • **87**
Petite Sirah Napa Valley 1996: Firm and focused, showing rich black cherry, blueberry, pepper and spicy flavors wrapped in a tight core. Retains a degree of supple, mineral-tinged fruit flavors, with well-integrated tannins on the finish. Drink now through 2005.–H.S. • $25 • (3/31/1999) • **87**

MADRONA | CALIFORNIA

Cabernet Sauvignon El Dorado 1992 • $12 • (11/30/1996) • **73**
Cabernet Sauvignon El Dorado 1991 • $11 • (5/31/1995) • **81**

Cabernet Sauvignon El Dorado 1985 • $12 • (4/15/1992) • **82**
Chardonnay El Dorado 1996: Smoothly textured and well focused, with green apple, apricot and earthy orange peel notes. The intensity picks up on the long, concentrated finish. Drink now. • $12 • (7/31/1998) • **86**
Johannisberg Riesling El Dorado 1996 • $8 • (3/31/1998) • **80**
Zinfandel El Dorado 1998: Peppery, with ripe cassis flavors and a firm, focused structure. Drink now through 2004.–J.L. • $12 • (6/15/2000) • **87**
Zinfandel El Dorado 1995 • $10 • (12/15/1997) • **85**
Zinfandel El Dorado 1993 • $9 • (4/30/1996) • **83**
Zinfandel El Dorado 1992 • $9 • (10/15/1995) • **84**
Zinfandel El Dorado 1989 • $8 • (10/15/1992) • **64**
Zinfandel El Dorado Reserve 1997: Simple, with cola and bitter herb notes and an earthy, sour finish. Drink now.–J.L. • $18 • (5/31/2000) • **80**

MAISON DEUTZ | CALIFORNIA

Blanc de Noirs San Luis Obispo County NV • $12 • (11/30/1996) • **85**
Brut Rosé San Luis Obispo County NV • $18 • (11/30/1996) • **84**
Brut San Luis Obispo County Cuvée NV • $12 • (11/30/1996) • **85**
Brut San Luis Obispo County Reserve 1992 • $18 • (11/30/1996) • **88**
Brut San Luis Obispo County Reserve 1990 • $23 • (12/31/1994) • **85**

MAKOR | CALIFORNIA

Zinfandel California 1995 • $12 • (4/30/1997) • **90**

MARBLE CREST | WASHINGTON

Cabernet Sauvignon Columbia Valley 1993 • $8 • (9/30/1995) • **82**
Merlot Columbia Valley 1993 • $10 • (9/30/1995) • **80**

MARCASSIN | CALIFORNIA

Chardonnay Alexander Valley Gauer Ranch Upper Barn 1996: Enormously complex, rich and elegant, with exotic smoky fig, guava, pineapple, pear and nutmeg scents, bold and concentrated, long and delicious. Drink now through 2004.–J.L. • $50 • (3/31/1999) • **96**
Chardonnay Carneros Hudson Vineyards E Block 1996: Smooth, rich and intensely flavored, with a smoky, earthy edge to the ripe pear, flinty mineral and spicy nuances. Drink now through 2004.–J.L. • $50 • (3/31/1999) • **94**
Chardonnay Sonoma Coast Lorenzo Vineyard 1996: Ultrarich—the richest of Marcassin's three '96's—loaded with complex and concentrated pear, fig, anise, toasty oak and spicy flavors, bold and delicious. Drink now through 2005.–J.L. • $288 Ⓐ • (3/31/1999) • **96**
Chardonnay Sonoma Coast Marcassin Vineyard 1996: Enormous depth, richness and complexity here, with layers of ripe, complex pear, fig, melon, apricot, anise and mineral, finishing with a rich, buttery aftertaste that keeps pumping out the flavors. The first Chardonnay from Marcassin's Sonoma Coast vineyard. Drinks exceptionally well now. Try through 2007.–J.L. • $75 • (4/30/2000) • **97**
Pinot Noir Sonoma Coast Marcassin Vineyard 1996: The debut from estate-grown grapes, this is a ripe, lush, enormously complex and flavorful wine, brimming with sumptuous blackberry, black cherry, plum, sage, mineral, anise, wild berry and spice. Finishes with a long, elegant, detailed aftertaste. Wonderful now; try through 2007.–J.L. • $75 • (4/30/2000) • **96**

MARCELINA | CALIFORNIA

Cabernet Sauvignon Napa County 1993 • $20 • (12/15/1997) • **87**
Cabernet Sauvignon Napa Valley 1995: A leaner style, marked by herb and blackberry notes. Tannins are still coarse, and the ensemble finishes moderately with hints of anise and smoke. Best from 2001 through 2004. • $22 • (9/15/1999) • **86**
Chardonnay Napa Valley 1997: Very ripe and concentrated, with layers of rich pear, fig, apricot, honey and vanilla, all unfolding gracefully, if showing a touch of heat on the finish. Drink now through 2005.–J.L. • $22 • (2/29/2000) • **88**
Chardonnay Napa Valley 1996: Elegant and complex, with tasty pear, apple and spicy flavors that hold their focus through the finish and linger on. Drink now.–J.L. • $19 • (9/15/1998) • **88**

MARIAH | CALIFORNIA

Zinfandel Mendocino Ridge 1997: Earthy, with funky leather and barnyard flavors. Fruit is overpowered.–J.L. • $27 • (5/31/2000) • **78**
Zinfandel Mendocino Ridge 1996: Austere, with complex plum and berryish Zinfandel flavors. Finishes with firm, crisp tannins. Drink through 2003.–J.L. • $27 • (6/30/1999) • **88**

MARIETTA | CALIFORNIA

Cabernet Sauvignon Sonoma County 1987 • $10 • (2/28/1991) • **87**
Cabernet Sauvignon Sonoma County 1985 • $10 • (6/30/1990) • **83**
Cabernet Sauvignon Sonoma County 1984 • $10 • (12/31/1987) • **78**
Old Vine Red Sonoma County Lot No. Three NV • $5 • (4/16/1986) • **85**
Old Vine Red Sonoma County Lot No. Five NV • $5 • (12/31/1987) • **77**
Old Vine Red Sonoma County Lot No. Seven NV • $6 • (11/15/1989) • **82**
Old Vine Red Sonoma County Lot No. Eight NV • $6 • (5/31/1990) • **81**
Old Vine Red Sonoma County Lot No. Ten NV • $6 • (4/30/1992) • **79**
Old Vine Red Sonoma County Lot No. Eleven NV • $7 • (3/31/1993) • **79**
Old Vine Red Sonoma County Lot No. Fourteen NV • $8 • (4/30/1995) • **83**
Old Vine Red Sonoma County Lot No. Seventeen NV • $9 • (12/31/1996) • **83**
Petite Sirah Sonoma County 1988 • $10 • (3/15/1992) • **84**
Port Alexander Valley 1989 • $16 • (5/31/1995) • **86**
Syrah California 1997: What a find. A tight and firm Syrah, with a rich, focused core of plum, black cherry, earth, anise and wild berry flavors ending in a long, intricate aftertaste. Drink now through 2006.–J.L. • $16 • (2/29/2000) SS • **91**
Syrah California 1996: Redolent of cola, coffee, spice and black cherry on the nose, then a little chewy on the palate, with firm but ripe tannins. More berry and herb flavors follow through, lingering nicely on the finish. Has muscle and also finesse. Drink now through 2004. • $16 • (5/15/1999) • **88**
Zinfandel Geyserville 1996: Rich and supple, with ripe black cherry, plum, anise and mineral flavors. Finishes firm, but the tannins are well integrated. Drink now through 2002.–J.L. • $15 • (5/15/1999) • **89**
Zinfandel Geyserville 1995 • $14 • (6/15/1998) • **84**
Zinfandel Sonoma County 1992 • $11 • (9/15/1995) • **85**
Zinfandel Sonoma County 1988 • $8 • (12/31/1991) • **87**
Zinfandel Sonoma County Reserve 1985 • $10 • (12/31/1987) • **88**

MARK RIDGE | CALIFORNIA

Cabernet Sauvignon California 1994 • $NA • (11/30/1996) • **70**

MARK WEST | CALIFORNIA

Chardonnay Russian River Valley 1997: Soft and citrusy, with crisp, leafy green apple and pear flavors and spice notes. Drink now.–J.L. • $13 • (4/30/1999) • **86**
Chardonnay Russian River Valley 1996 • $15 • (5/15/1998) • **86**
Gewürztraminer Russian River Valley 1996 • $10 • (7/31/1997) • **82**
Gewürztraminer Russian River Valley Reserve 1997: Soft and floral, with pretty grapefruit and apple flavors finishing round and off-dry. Drink now.–H.S. • $15 • (11/30/1998) • **84**
Pinot Noir Russian River Valley 1997: A bit earthy up front, with black cherry, berry, herb, spice and tea notes on the follow-up. Tannins are firm, providing good structure, while the finish hints at anise. Best from 2001 through 2005. • $15 • (9/15/1999) • **86**
Pinot Noir Russian River Valley 1995 • $14 • (7/31/1997) • **87**
Pinot Noir Russian River Valley 1993 • $13 • (7/31/1996) • **82**
Pinot Noir Russian River Valley 1991 • $10 • (2/28/1994) • **84**
Pinot Noir Russian River Valley 1990 • $14 • (2/28/1993) • **82**
Pinot Noir Russian River Valley Ellis Vineyard 1986 • $14 • (3/31/1990) • **81**
Pinot Noir Russian River Valley Ellis Vineyard 1984 • $10 • (3/15/1987) • **84**
Sauvignon Blanc Russian River Valley 1997: Delicate, yet packed with flavor. Starts off with classic passion fruit and a hint of gooseberry, then the flavors extend to grapefruit, melon, pear, herbs and fresh-cut hay, all couched in a well-balanced frame with good acidity and elegant body. A terrific wine at a fabulous price. Tasted twice, with consistent notes. Drink now through 2002. • $10 • (5/15/1999) • **90**
Sauvignon Blanc Russian River Valley 1996 • $9 • (6/30/1997) • **87**
Sauvignon Blanc Russian River Valley Cohen Vineyard 1998: Focused, with tart lemon and toasty, spicy flavors. Lip-smacking on the finish. Drink now through 2002.–H.S. • $14 • (1/31/2000) • **85**
Zinfandel Sonoma County Robert Rue Vineyard 1987 • $17 • (5/15/1992) • **86**
Zinfandel Sonoma County Robert Rue Vineyard 1986 • $14 • (3/15/1990) • **83**
Zinfandel Sonoma County Robert Rue Vineyard 1985 • $14 • (7/31/1988) • **85**

MARKHAM | CALIFORNIA

Cabernet Sauvignon Napa Valley 1996: Bright, flavorful and smooth, with an herbal edge to the currant and tobacco flavors. Finishes with notes of toasted oak and mild tannins. Drink now through 2004.–J.L. • $22 • (10/15/1999) • **88**
Cabernet Sauvignon Napa Valley 1995: Ripe, with medium-weight currant, black cherry, anise, cedar and spice, finishing with firm, dry tannins. A bit chunky and backward; try through 2005.–J.L. • $21 • (10/31/1998) • **87**
Cabernet Sauvignon Napa Valley 1994 • $15 • (10/31/1997) SS • **92**
Cabernet Sauvignon Napa Valley 1993 • $15 • (11/15/1996) • **86**
Cabernet Sauvignon Napa Valley 1992 • $17 • (11/30/1995) • **88**
Cabernet Sauvignon Napa Valley 1991 • $17 • (11/15/1994) • **88**
Cabernet Sauvignon Napa Valley 1990 • $17 • (11/15/1993) SS • **90**
Cabernet Sauvignon Napa Valley 1989 • $17 • (11/15/1992) • **88**
Cabernet Sauvignon Napa Valley 1988 • $16 • (11/15/1992) • **80**
Cabernet Sauvignon Napa Valley 1987 • $15 • (12/15/1997) • **86**
Cabernet Sauvignon Napa Valley 1986 • $16 Ⓐ • (12/15/1996) • **87**
Cabernet Sauvignon Napa Valley 1985 • $17 • (4/15/1990) • **91**
Cabernet Sauvignon Napa Valley 1984 • $12 • (10/31/1988) • **87**
Cabernet Sauvignon Napa Valley 1983 • $26 • (7/31/1989) • **90**
Cabernet Sauvignon Napa Valley 1982 • $13 • (11/15/1987) • **92**
Cabernet Sauvignon Napa Valley Yountville Vineyard 1979: Earthy, with a waxy edge, and the plum and berryish flavors dropping out, leaving a dry aftertaste. (1979 California Cabernet retrospective tasting). Drink now. –J.L. • $22 • (8/31/1999) • **83**
Cabernet Sauvignon Napa Valley Yountville Vineyard 1978: A youthful, ripe and fleshy style that's aging very well. Has juicy cherry, plum and currant flavors, round, supple tannins, hints of mint, anise, sage and cedar, and a long, complex aftertaste. (1978 California Cabernet retrospective tasting). Drink now through 2006.–J.L. • $13 • (11/15/1998) • **91**
Chardonnay Napa Valley 1997: Ripe and flavorful, with an appealing range of refreshing peach, pear, fig and nutty toast flavors that carry through to the open-textured finish. Drink now.–J.L. • $15 • (7/31/1999) • **88**
Chardonnay Napa Valley 1996 • $16 • (5/15/1998) • **87**
Chardonnay Napa Valley Reserve 1997: Quite rich and concentrated, with tiers of nectarine, fig, pear and melon flavors that are tightly focused. A touch coarse and leafy now, but short-term cellaring should do the trick. Drink now through 2005.–J.L. • $30 • (11/15/1999) • **91**
Chardonnay Napa Valley Reserve 1996: Serves up lots of tasty fruit flavors, with tiers of pear, fig and apple, hints of custard, butterscotch and spicy oak. Finishes with a touch of grapefruit. Drink now through 2001.–J.L. • $30 • (5/15/1999) • **91**
Laurent Reserve Napa Valley 1990 • $25 • (12/31/1994) • **85**
Merlot Napa Valley 1997: Ripe and grapey, with lots of spicy plum, currant and cherry flavors that are up front and supple. Finishes with intriguing spicy notes and firm but polished tannins. Drink now through 2007.–J.L. • $17 Ⓐ • (2/29/2000) • **88**
Merlot Napa Valley 1996: Tight and complex, with cherry and wild berry flavors that turn elegant and spicy, finishing with supple tannins. Drink now through 2005.–J.L. • $20 • (3/31/1999) • **88**
Merlot Napa Valley 1995 • $18 • (5/15/1998) • **87**
Merlot Napa Valley 1994 • $18 • (12/31/1996) • **88**
Merlot Napa Valley 1993 • $16 • (12/15/1995) • **89**
Merlot Napa Valley 1992 • $17 • (4/15/1995) • **88**
Merlot Napa Valley 1991 • $16 • (5/31/1994) • **87**
Merlot Napa Valley 1990 • $15 • (5/31/1993) HR • **91**
Merlot Napa Valley 1989 • $15 • (5/31/1992) • **85**
Merlot Napa Valley 1988 • $14 • (4/15/1991) HR • **90**
Merlot Napa Valley 1987 • $14 • (10/15/1989) • **91**
Merlot Napa Valley 1985 • $11 • (4/30/1988) • **88**
Merlot Napa Valley Reserve 1996: Dark and ripe, with pretty toasty, vanilla-scented oak, black cherry and chocolate notes. Elegant and polished, with mild tannins. Drink now through 2006.–J.L. • $35 • (11/15/1999) • **89**
Merlot Napa Valley Reserve 1994 • $35 • (8/31/1997) • **91**
Muscat Napa Valley Blanc 1996 • $9/375 ml. • (5/15/1998) • **87**
Petite Sirah Napa Valley 1996: This is dark and firm, with tight, crisp tannins and a rich, intense core of blackberry, raspberry and black cherry in need of short-term cellaring. It finishes with detailed tannins and mineral and earth notes. A great version of this variety. Best from 2002 through 2010.–J.L. • $20 • (4/30/2000) SS • **91**
Petite Sirah Napa Valley 1995: Don't overlook this outstanding Rhône-style red from California, floral in character, overlaid with ripe, spicy plum, black cherry, pepper and raspberry. Turns smooth and rich on the finish, even with its firm tannins. Drink now through 2005.–J.L. • $17 • (2/28/1999) HR • **92**
Petite Sirah Napa Valley 1994 • $17 • (1/01/1998) • **88**
Petite Sirah Napa Valley 1993 • $17 • (8/31/1997) SS • **90**
Sauvignon Blanc Napa Valley 1998: This medium-bodied Napa Sauvignon Blanc won't disappoint with its nice grass and lemon notes and crisp finish. At this price and score, grab a few bottles to have on hand. Drink now through 2002.–H.S. • $10 • (1/31/2000) • **85**
Sauvignon Blanc Napa Valley 1997: Redolent of fresh peaches and herbs, the wine is firm on the palate, with a moderate, clean finish reminiscent of freshly mowed hay. Drink now. • $10 • (1/31/1999) • **85**
Sauvignon Blanc Napa Valley 1996 • $12 • (9/15/1997) SS • **90**
Zinfandel Napa Valley 1997: Tight, firm and tannic, with tart raspberry, stewed plum and blackberry and a dry, woody flavor on the finish, where the tannins pin you down. Drink now through 2005.–J.L. • $16 • (5/15/2000) • **84**
Zinfandel Napa Valley 1996: Ripe and juicy, with elegant plum and blackberry flavors, turning supple and tarry. Drink now.–J.L. • $17 • (5/15/1999) • **87**
Zinfandel Napa Valley 1995 • $16 • (5/31/1998) • **86**
Zinfandel Napa Valley 1994 • $17 • (8/31/1997) • **89**

MARQUAM HILL | OREGON

Gewürztraminer Willamette Valley Semi-Sweet 1996 • $8 • (6/30/1998) • **74**
Pinot Noir Willamette Valley 1993 • $12 • (2/28/1997) • **83**
Pinot Noir Willamette Valley 1991 • $14 • (2/28/1993) • **71**
Pinot Noir Willamette Valley Barrel Aged 1992 • $12 • (11/30/1994) • **80**
Riesling Willamette Valley Semi-Sweet 1997 • $8 • (6/30/1998) • **81**

MARTIN & WEYRICH | CALIFORNIA

Zinfandel Paso Robles Dante Dusi Vineyard Reserve 1997: Rather dull, with cedar and candied berry flavors and a drying finish. Drink now.–J.L. • $24 • (5/15/2000) • **80**
Zinfandel Paso Robles Uberroth Vineyard Reserve 1997: Heavy on the herbal side, with crisp berry flavors and spicy notes. Drink now.–J.L. • $24 • (5/31/2000) • **81**

MARTIN BROTHERS | CALIFORNIA

Cabernet Sauvignon Etrusco Paso Robles 1996: Shows bright cherry flavors backed by a firm herbal edge. Pleasant, but doesn't taste much of Cabernet—more like a Beaujolais with backbone. 85 percent Cabernet Sauvignon, 15 percent Sangiovese. Drink now through 2005. • $18 • (10/15/1998) • **84**
Cabernet Sauvignon Paso Robles 1989 • $12 • (11/15/1991) • **77**
Cabernet Sauvignon Paso Robles Etrusco 1995 • $18 • (10/31/1997) • **85**
Chardonnay Paso Robles in Botti 1996: Sweet, sour and bitter, with metallic flavors. Not a nice combination. Tasted twice, with consistent notes.—T.G. • $10 • (7/31/1998) • **69**
Etrusco Paso Robles 1993 • $16 • (12/15/1995) • **90**
Etrusco Paso Robles 1992 • $18 • (2/28/1995) • **79**
Etrusco Paso Robles 1991 • $18 • (6/30/1993) • **89**
Etrusco Paso Robles 1990 • $18 • (11/15/1992) • **85**
Gemelli Paso Robles NV • $25 • (10/15/1995) • **86**
Malvasia Bianca California Vin Santo 1990 • $15/5 liter • (3/15/1992) • **81**
Moscato Allegro California 1992 • $10 • (5/15/1993) • **77**
Moscato Frizzante California 1991 • $9 • (3/31/1992) • **88**
Nebbiolo California 1989 • $9 • (11/15/1991) • **76**
Nebbiolo California 1987 • $12 • (12/15/1989) • **75**
Nebbiolo California 1986 • $12 • (12/15/1989) • **75**
Nebbiolo California Vecchio 1992 • $20 • (12/15/1995) • **84**
Nebbiolo California Vecchio 1990 • $18 • (5/31/1993) • **83**
Nebbiolo Central Coast 1995 • $11 • (9/15/1997) • **81**
Nebbiolo Central Coast 1993 • $10 • (12/15/1995) • **84**
Nebbiolo Central Coast Vecchio 1994 • $20 • (9/15/1997) • **83**
Nebbiolo Paso Robles 1987 • $12 • (12/15/1989) • **85**
Sangiovese Central Coast Il Palio 1996 • $12 • (11/30/1997) • **83**
Sangiovese Paso Robles Il Palio 1997: The wine is full-bodied and sits well on the palate, with rich, plummy flavors up front. Finishes with hints of anise, blackberry and herb. Tangy acidity keeps it fresh. Drink now through 2002. • $15 • (11/15/1999) • **87**

Key: SS—Spectator Selection CS—Cellar Selection HR—Highly Recommended $NA—Price Not Available a—Auction Price (BT)—Barrel Tasting
For a key to the tasters' initials, see "How to Use These Listings."
Dates in parentheses indicate the issues in which the ratings were published.

Sangiovese Paso Robles Il Palio 1994 • $12 • (6/15/1996) • **84**
Sangiovese Paso Robles Il Palio 1992 • $12 • (5/31/1994) • **82**
Zinfandel Paso Robles La Primitiva 1995 • $12 • (4/30/1997) • **84**
Zinfandel Paso Robles La Primitiva 1994 • $11 • (4/30/1997) • **82**
Zinfandel Paso Robles La Primitiva 1993 • $10 • (10/15/1995) • **84**
Zinfandel Paso Robles La Primitiva 1992 • $10 • (6/15/1995) • **83**
Zinfandel Paso Robles La Primitiva 1991 • $10 • (10/15/1994) • **84**
Zinfandel Paso Robles Primitivo 1990 • $9 • (3/31/1993) • **82**
Zinfandel Paso Robles Ueberroth Vineyards 1996: Starts off with rich plum, licorice and spice aromas, but it's almost too juicy, packed with bright fruit and zingy acidity. Those who like effusive Zins won't be disappointed, however. Drink now through 2002. • $22 • (6/15/1999) • **86**
Zinfandel Port Paso Robles Primitivo Appassito 1990 • $12 • (3/15/1992) • **83**

MARTINELLI | CALIFORNIA

Chardonnay Russian River Valley Martinelli Road 1998: Smells like ripe pear and fig, but has a touch of bitterness from the toasty, charry oak. Drink now through 2005.–J.L. • $45 • (5/31/2000) • **87**
Gewürztraminer Russian River Valley Martinelli Vineyard 1996 • $12 • (3/31/1998) • **83**
Gewürztraminer Russian River Valley Martinelli Vineyard Dry Select 1996 • $18 • (3/31/1998) • **88**
Pinot Noir Russian River Valley 1994 • $25 • (9/30/1996) • **88**
Pinot Noir Russian River Valley Martinelli Vineyard 1997: Complex, with bright earthy cherry, raspberry and wild berry flavors, firming up with tannin on the finish. Needs a little time. Drink through 2007.–J.L. • $30 • (9/15/1999) • **87**
Pinot Noir Russian River Valley Martinelli Vineyard 1996: Lean and a bit tart, with dark berry, cherry and spice. Fans out a bit on the finish, where oak and spicy notes add dimension. Drink now through 2001.–J.L. • $25 • (9/15/1998) • **84**
Pinot Noir Russian River Valley Martinelli Vineyard 1995 • $25 • (5/31/1997) • **87**
Pinot Noir Russian River Valley Martinelli Vineyard Reserve 1998: Smooth and harmonious, with ripe, polished tannins and a pretty array of spicy plum, black cherry, anise and sage notes. Long, lively finish. Drink now through 2006.–J.L. • $45 • (5/31/2000) • **89**
Pinot Noir Russian River Valley Martinelli Vineyard Reserve 1997: Wonderful ripe, rich, focused plum, cherry, strawberry and spice flavors are wrapped in firm but supple tannins, finishing with a burst of fruitiness. Impressive. Drink now through 2006.–J.L. • $40 • (9/15/1999) • **90**
Pinot Noir Russian River Valley Martinelli Vineyard Reserve 1996: Simple, a touch earthy, with tea, dried cherry, herb and spice, it succeeds with its delicacy and finesse. Drink now.–J.L. • $36 • (9/15/1998) • **84**
Pinot Noir Russian River Valley Martinelli Vineyard Reserve 1995 • $36 • (1/31/1998) • **87**
Sauvignon Blanc Russian River Valley Martinelli Vineyard 1996 • $12 • (1/31/1998) • **87**
Zinfandel Russian River Valley Guiseppe & Louisa 1998: Ripe and lively, brimming with jazzy wild berry, raspberry, cherry and spice. Picks up a chocolaty edge, with toasty oak and heat. Drink now through 2005.–J.L. • $36 • (6/15/2000) HR • **91**
Zinfandel Russian River Valley Louisa and Giuseppe 1997: Thick, ripe and juicy, with layers of plum, black cherry, currant and cedary oak. Fills out on the palate, showing richness and depth, with anise and vanilla notes. A new bottling from Martinelli. Drink now through 2003.–J.L. • $25 • (6/15/1999) • **92**
Zinfandel Russian River Valley Jackass Hill 1994 • $25 • (9/30/1996) • **92**
Zinfandel Russian River Valley Jackass Vineyard 1997: Dark, rich and potent, with ripe, polished tannins and gobs of blackberry, black cherry, currant and spice. Finishes with broad, fleshy tannins. Drink now through 2004.–J.L. • $35 • (6/15/1999) • **92**
Zinfandel Russian River Valley Jackass Vineyard 1996 • $25 • (6/15/1998) • **89**
Zinfandel Russian River Valley Jackass Vineyard 1995 • $25 • (6/15/1997) • **91**
Zinfandel Russian River Valley Jackass Vineyard 1992 • $14 • (10/15/1994) • **88**
Zinfandel Russian River Valley Jackass Vineyard 1991 • $12 • (5/31/1993) • **81**
Zinfandel Russian River Valley Jackass Vineyard 1990: A big, ripe, jammy style that holds its balance, with ripe, almost raisiny flavors of tar and spice. Finishes with big but well-integrated tannins and floral, cherry and berry flavors. (Zinfandel retrospective tasting). Drink now through 2004.–J.L. • $13 • (6/30/1999) • **91**
Zinfandel Russian River Valley Martinelli Vineyard 1989 • $13 • (12/15/1992) • **81**
Zinfandel Russian River Valley Martinelli Vineyard 1988 • $11 • (4/30/1991) • **85**

MARTINE'S WINES | CALIFORNIA

Viognier California 1998: Sleek, elegant and spicy, with hints of pear, nectarine and peach, finishing with a sense of grace. Drink now through 2003.–J.L. • $15 • (11/30/1999) • **86**
Viognier California 1997: A pleasing, balanced blend of pear, peach and citrus flavors, this wine is smooth on the palate, with a clean, slightly flinty finish. Drink now. • $15 • (9/15/1998) • **87**

MARTINI, LOUIS M. | CALIFORNIA

Barbera California 1992 • $12 • (10/15/1996) • **82**
Barbera California 1991 • $12 • (10/15/1995) • **85**
Barbera Lake County 1995: Light, with fresh wild berry and cherry notes and mild tannins.–J.L. • $NA • (3/31/2000) • **79**
Barbera Lake County Heritage Collection 1994: Lean and earthy, with ripe cherry flavors lurking behind some chewy tannins. Try with hearty foods. Drink now through 2002.–H.S. • $12 • (11/30/1998) • **84**
Cabernet Sauvignon California 1995: Offering modest cherry and licorice flavors, this wine is framed in toasty oak. Tannins are a little rough; finish is moderate. Drink now through 2002. • $10 • (10/15/1998) • **82**
Cabernet Sauvignon California Special Selection 1974 • $45 • (11/15/1994) • **68**
Cabernet Sauvignon Napa Valley Reserve 1994: Spice and cedar notes open the way here. On the palate it's tight and a little bitter, showing hints of cassis, anise and toasty oak. Finishes short, with dusty tannins. Drink now through 2002. • $18 • (10/15/1998) • **83**
Cabernet Sauvignon Napa Valley Reserve 1993 • $18 • (11/15/1997) • **84**
Cabernet Sauvignon Napa Valley Reserve 1992 • $15 • (7/31/1997) • **86**
Cabernet Sauvignon Napa Valley Reserve 1991 • $15 • (9/15/1996) • **83**
Cabernet Sauvignon Napa Valley Reserve 1989 • $14 • (11/15/1994) • **81**
Cabernet Sauvignon Napa Valley Reserve 1988 • $14 • (11/15/1992) • **78**
Cabernet Sauvignon Napa Valley Reserve 1987 • $14 • (10/15/1990) • **87**
Cabernet Sauvignon North Coast 1996: Starts off with rich plum and herb aromas, but falters somewhat on the palate as the muscular tannins kick in. Complex blackberry, mint, earth and pepper notes take a back seat now, but may come to the fore in time. Best from 2001 through 2006. • $11 • (2/28/1999) • **85**
Cabernet Sauvignon North Coast 1993 • $11 • (9/15/1996) • **82**
Cabernet Sauvignon North Coast 1992 • $10 • (12/15/1995) • **82**
Cabernet Sauvignon North Coast 1990 • $8 • (11/15/1994) • **79**
Cabernet Sauvignon North Coast Special Selection 1980 • $12 • (12/15/1986) • **78**
Cabernet Sauvignon Sonoma County 1988 • $9 • (4/30/1991) • **81**
Cabernet Sauvignon Sonoma Valley Los Niños 1979: Earthy, cedary and nutty, this has lost its fruit and charm. (1979 California Cabernet retrospective tasting). Past its prime.–J.L. • $50 • (8/31/1999) • **78**
Cabernet Sauvignon Sonoma Valley Monte Rosso Vineyard Heritage Collection 1995: A lean style, with black cherry, currant, licorice, tar, coffee and chocolate notes all tightly packed in firmly textured tannins. The elegant ensemble could flesh out more with time. Drink through 2004. • $35 • (10/15/1998) • **88**
Cabernet Sauvignon Sonoma Valley Monte Rosso 1994 • $30 • (11/30/1997) • **87**
Cabernet Sauvignon Sonoma Valley Monte Rosso 1993 • $22 • (11/15/1996) • **86**
Cabernet Sauvignon Sonoma Valley Monte Rosso 1991 • $22 • (12/15/1995) • **78**
Cabernet Sauvignon Sonoma Valley Monte Rosso 1990 • $23 • (9/30/1994) • **85**
Cabernet Sauvignon Sonoma Valley Monte Rosso Vineyard Selection 1989: Firm and spicy, with good intensity and a core of cedar, mineral, earthy currant and berryish flavors. Finishes rather abruptly. (1989 California Cabernet retrospective tasting). Drink now through 2004.–J.L. • $22 • (8/31/1999) • **86**
Cabernet Sauvignon Sonoma County Monte Rosso Vineyard Selection 1988: Tight, tart and tannic; still, the black cherry, earth and mineral are well balanced and focused, and the acidity is zingy, giving it life and length. Finishes with crisp tannins. (1988 California Cabernet retrospective tasting). Drink now through 2002.–J.L. • $25 • (11/15/1998) • **87**
Cabernet Sauvignon Sonoma Valley Monte Rosso 1987 • $20 • (11/15/1990) HR • **93**
Cabernet Sauvignon Sonoma Valley Monte Rosso 1981 • $15 • (12/15/1986) • **90**
Chardonnay California 1998: Peachy, with a hint of marmalade, a toasty frame and a lingering finish. Drink now.–J.L. • $10 • (6/30/2000) • **84**
Chardonnay California 1996: Clean and understated, with green apple and citrus notes that linger. Drink now.–J.L. • $10 • (2/28/1999) • **83**

MARTINI, LOUIS M.

Chardonnay North Coast 1997: Here's a refreshing Chardonnay, a mouthful of crisp lemon and tangerine flavors accented with just a hint of oak, at a price that makes it easy to keep a couple of bottles on hand. Drink now. –J.L. • $10 • (2/28/1999) • **86**
Chardonnay Russian River Valley Reserve 1997: Very toasty flavors are followed by sweet-tasting cream, nectarine and citrus. Finishes firm. Drink now through 2001. • $18 • (7/31/1999) • **85**
Chardonnay Russian River Valley Reserve 1996: A blend of pear, apple and tropical fruit is rounded out by lemon curd and toast notes. Delicate quince flavors linger on the finish. Drink now. • $18 • (12/31/1998) • **87**
Folle Blanche Sonoma Valley Heritage Collection 1996 • $12 • (12/15/1997) • **83**
Gewürztraminer Russian River Valley Heritage Collection 1997: Ripe and jazzy, a spicy wine with a solid core of apple and grapefruit that lingers on the barely off-dry finish. Drink now.–H.S. • $12 • (11/30/1998) • **86**
Gewürztraminer Russian River Valley 1996 • $12 • (3/31/1998) • **88**
Merlot California 1997: Firm, with a narrow range of berry and earth notes that remain closed on the finish.–J.L. • $11 • (10/15/1999) • **78**
Merlot California 1996: Shows a modest range of cherry, plum and tea flavors on a medium-bodied frame. Tannins are soft. Drink now.–J.L. • $10 • (12/15/1998) • **82**
Merlot North Coast 1995 • $10 • (12/15/1997) • **80**
Merlot North Coast 1994 • $10 • (6/30/1996) • **83**
Merlot North Coast 1993 • $10 • (6/15/1996) • **81**
Merlot North Coast 1992 • $10 • (7/31/1995) • **81**
Merlot North Coast 1991 • $8 • (9/15/1994) • **82**
Merlot North Coast 1990 • $10 • (8/31/1993) • **79**
Merlot North Coast 1989 • $9 • (5/31/1992) • **74**
Merlot North Coast 1988 • $10 • (8/31/1991) • **85**
Merlot North Coast 1986 • $12 • (10/31/1989) • **79**
Merlot Russian River Valley Los Vinedos del Rio Commemorative Bottling 1995: A sleek wine, with a bright core of blackberry, blueberry and cassis flavors. On the finish, the tannins are firm and ripe. Drink now through 2004. • $35 • (9/30/1998) • **87**
Merlot Russian River Valley Los Vinedos del Rio Vineyard Selection 1991 • $20 • (8/31/1996) • **78**
Merlot Russian River Valley Los Vinedos del Rio 1990 • $20 • (9/15/1994) • **87**
Merlot Russian River Valley Los Vinedos del Rio 1988 • $22 • (5/31/1992) • **74**
Merlot Russian River Valley Los Vinedos del Rio 1986 • $20 • (3/31/1990) • **79**
Merlot Russian River Valley Los Vinedos del Rio 1984 • $12 • (2/15/1988) • **82**
Merlot Russian River Valley Los Vinedos del Rio 1981 • $10 • (10/01/1985) • **81**
Merlot Russian River Valley Reserve 1996: Trim, with a minty edge to the plum, cherry, tar and toasted oak flavors. Drink now through 2004.–J.L. • $18 • (10/15/1999) • **83**
Merlot Russian River Valley Reserve 1995: Cherries and herbs at the fore, framed by charry oak. On the finish, it's a little tart, with a hint of bitterness. Drink now. • $18 • (11/30/1998) • **81**
Merlot Russian River Valley Reserve 1992 • $15 • (8/31/1996) • **84**
Petite Sirah Napa Valley Reserve 1987 • $11 • (11/30/1991) • **85**
Petite Sirah Napa Valley Reserve 1986 • $12 • (10/31/1990) • **81**
Pinot Noir Napa Valley Carneros 1992 • $8 • (5/15/1995) • **86**
Pinot Noir Los Carneros 1993 • $8 • (1/31/1996) • **85**
Pinot Noir Los Carneros 1990 • $8 • (2/28/1994) • **79**
Pinot Noir Los Carneros 1988 • $8 • (7/15/1991) • **85**
Pinot Noir Los Carneros La Loma Vineyard 1990 • $16 • (2/28/1994) • **82**
Pinot Noir Napa Valley Carneros La Loma Vineyard 1988 • $18 • (3/31/1992) • **75**
Pinot Noir Napa Valley Carneros Las Amigas Vineyard Selection 1982 • $12 • (3/31/1990) • **85**
Sangiovese Dunnigan Hills Heritage Collection 1997: Soft, easy-drinking style, with smooth cherry, earth and olive notes. Drink now.–J.L. • $14 • (5/31/1999) • **83**
Sauvignon Blanc Napa County 1997: Bright grapefruit, fig, lemon, lime and melon notes blend nicely here. Creamy-textured, the wine has, nonethless, firm acidity. Finishes long, with hints of herbs and spice. Drink now. • $9 • (1/31/1999) • **87**
Zinfandel Paso Robles 1989 • $8 • (8/31/1991) • **83**
Zinfandel Sonoma County Heritage Collection 1995: Somewhat on the light side for Zin, this has pretty cherry and plum flavors backed by a hint of spice and oak. Finishes a little short. Drink now. • $12 • (2/28/1999) • **84**

Key: SS—Spectator Selection CS—Cellar Selection HR—Highly Recommended $NA—Price Not Available a—Auction Price (BT)—Barrel Tasting
For a key to the tasters' initials, see "How to Use These Listings."
Dates in parentheses indicate the issues in which the ratings were published.

Zinfandel Sonoma County Heritage Collection 1994 • $12 • (6/15/1998) • **81**
Zinfandel Sonoma Valley Heritage Collection 1993 • $12 • (3/31/1997) • **84**
Zinfandel Sonoma Valley Gnarly Vine 1996: Herbal and earthy, with a modest range of raspberry and plum flavors, finishing slightly dry. Drink now. –J.L. • $35 • (2/28/1999) • **81**
Zinfandel Sonoma Valley Monte Rosso Vineyard Gnarly Vine 1994 • $30 • (6/15/1998) • **84**
Zinfandel Sonoma Valley Monte Rosso Vineyard Gnarly Vine 1993 • $20 • (9/15/1996) • **86**
Zinfandel Sonoma Valley 1992 • $8 • (8/31/1995) • **84**
Zinfandel Sonoma-Napa Counties 1989 • $7 • (6/15/1993) • **73**
Zinfandel Sonoma-Napa Counties 1988 • $7 • (10/15/1992) • **79**

MARTINI & PRATI | CALIFORNIA

Barbera California 1994 • $10 • (11/30/1996) • **78**
Fuoco di Sant' Elmo California 1993 • $20 • (2/28/1997) • **85**
Pinot Bianco Monterey 1996 • $10 • (5/15/1998) • **87**
Sangiovese California 1994 • $10 • (12/15/1996) • **78**
Vino Grigio California 1996 • $10 • (5/15/1998) • **85**
Zinfandel Russian River Valley Reserve 1996: Ripe in flavor, solid in texture, this is a sturdy wine with blackberry and cola flavors. Firm tannins need cellaring. Drink through 2002.–H.S. • $20 • (11/30/1998) • **83**
Zinfandel California 1995 • $10 • (6/30/1998) • **83**
Zinfandel California 1993 • $13 • (4/30/1997) • **82**
Zinfandel Sonoma County 1991 • $7 • (10/15/1994) • **72**

MASON | CALIFORNIA

Merlot Napa Valley 1996: Crisp and medium-bodied, featuring herbal dried currant and cherry flavors. Turns slightly dry on the finish, where the flavors persist. Drink now through 2002.–J.L. • $20 • (8/31/1999) • **87**
Merlot Napa Valley 1995 • $20 • (6/15/1998) • **87**
Merlot Napa Valley 1994 • $20 • (7/31/1997) • **87**
Merlot Napa Valley 1993 • $20 • (4/30/1996) • **89**
Sauvignon Blanc Napa Valley 1998: A blend of peach, herb, floral and citrus. Silky in texture but with bright acidity, it finishes long, with hints of fresh-cut hay. Clean and refreshing. Drink now. • $14 • (9/30/1999) • **89**
Sauvignon Blanc Napa Valley 1997 • $14 • (5/31/1998) • **90**
Sauvignon Blanc Napa Valley 1996 • $12 • (7/31/1997) • **91**

MATANZAS CREEK | CALIFORNIA

Cabernet Sauvignon Sonoma Valley 1983 • $14 • (7/16/1986) • **75**
Cabernet Sauvignon Sonoma Valley 1982 • $14 • (8/01/1985) • **88**
Cabernet Sauvignon Sonoma Valley 1981 • $16 • (4/16/1984) • **84**
Chardonnay Sonoma Valley 1997: Smooth, ripe and spicy, this fruit-driven style has a flinty core of pear, nectarine, citrus and nutmeg. Oak doesn't play much of a role in this vibrant young wine. Drink through 2005.–J.L. • $31 • (11/15/1999) • **89**
Chardonnay Sonoma Valley 1996: Distinct for its spicy apple, melon and green pear notes. Turns elegant on the finish, with spice and light oak shadings. A little more bottle time should work in its favor.–J.L. • $30 • (12/15/1998) • **90**
Merlot Sonoma Valley 1996: A beautiful bottle of Merlot. Smooth and harmonious, the wine displays an elegant array of herb, currant, coffee, smoky oak and meaty notes, rich and polished, flowing over the palate into a long, complex aftertaste. Drink now through 2004.–J.L. • $47 • (5/31/1999) HR • **91**
Merlot Sonoma Valley 1995: Supple, with herb, currant and berry notes, finishing with clay, spice and cedary oak flavors. On solid ground, with intensity and concentration. A little more time in the bottle should do the trick. Drink now through 2004.–J.L. • $45 • (9/30/1998) • **87**
Merlot Sonoma Valley 1994 • $65 ⓐ • (6/15/1997) • **92**
Merlot Sonoma Valley 1993 • $41 ⓐ • (6/30/1996) • **88**
Merlot Sonoma Valley 1992 • $73 ⓐ • (4/15/1995) SS • **91**
Merlot Sonoma Valley 1991 • $29 • (9/15/1994) • **89**
Merlot Sonoma Valley 1990 • $28 • (5/15/1993) HR • **89**
Merlot Sonoma Valley 1989 • $28 • (4/15/1992) HR • **90**
Merlot Sonoma Valley 1988 • $28 • (8/31/1991) • **88**
Merlot Sonoma County 1987 • $25 • (6/15/1990) SS • **92**
Merlot Sonoma County 1986 • $20 • (6/30/1989) • **92**
Merlot Sonoma Valley 1985 • $18 • (5/31/1988) • **88**
Merlot Sonoma Valley 1984 • $15 • (6/30/1987) • **91**
Merlot Sonoma Valley 1982 • $14 • (10/01/1985) • **88**
Merlot Sonoma Valley 1981 • $13 • (4/16/1984) • **80**

Merlot Sonoma Valley Estate 1993: Complex and concentrated, with layers of currant, sage, tea, herb, coffee and spice. Finishes with depth and richness and a lingering aftertaste. Drink through 2004.–J.L. • $75 • (10/15/1998) • **90**
Merlot Sonoma Valley Journey 1994: Dark and sharply focused, with dense, chewy plum, currant and blackberry flavors, finishing with supple tannins and a cedary edge. Tasted twice, with consistent notes. Drink through 2007.–J.L. • $115 Ⓐ • (12/31/1998) • **88**
Merlot Sonoma Valley Journey 1992 • $125 • (2/28/1997) • **94**
Sauvignon Blanc Sonoma-Mendocino-Napa Counties 1998: Shows good citrus, mineral and herb notes. This was the best of four samples, with noticeable bottle variation. Drink now.–J.L. • $22 • (5/31/2000) • **85**
Sauvignon Blanc Sonoma County 1997: Zingy acidity meets citrus, melon and apple flavors here. The wine also carries a lot of oak and finishes long, with hints of mineral and herb. Bright and refreshing, it should gain complexity in the bottle. Drink now through 2005. • $18 • (3/31/1999) • **88**
Sauvignon Blanc Sonoma County 1996 • $18 • (4/30/1998) • **86**

MATTHEWS | WASHINGTON

Cabernet Sauvignon Washington Reserve 1994 • $30 • (8/31/1996) • **78**
Cabernet Sauvignon Yakima Valley Elerding Vineyard Reserve 1996: The ripe and generous flavors are centered around currant and blueberry, with hints of exotic spice and cedar. Has the richness and intensity to age well. Drink through 2005.–H.S. • $40 • (9/30/1998) • **90**
Cabernet Sauvignon-Merlot-Cabernet Franc Yakima Valley 1997: Smooth, ripe and appealing for its generous blackberry, spice and vanilla flavors swirling through the harmonious finish. Nice already. Drink through 2003.–H.S. • $35 • (9/30/1999) • **89**
Cabernet Sauvignon-Cabernet Franc-Merlot Yakima Valley 1996: Firm in texture, with fine-grained tannins surrounding a nice core of berry and plum flavors shaded by touches of cedar and herb. Drink now.–H.S. • $35 • (9/15/1998) • **88**
Merlot Washington Reserve 1993 • $NA • (9/30/1996) • **77**
Sémillon Yakima Valley Elerding Vineyards 1998: Soft, supple and generous with its butterscotch-scented pear and tobacco flavors. Finishes with plenty of flavor, nicely rounded with oak. Drink now through 2002.–H.S. • $15 • (9/30/1999) • **87**
Washington Red 1995 • $30 • (9/30/1997) • **85**
Washington Red 1994 • $21 • (8/31/1996) • **85**

MAXUS | CALIFORNIA

Brut California 1991: Toast, dough and citrus aromas blend well in this aged style that features hazelnut, herbs and coffee. The finish is long and hints at butterscotch. Drink now. • $20 • (11/30/1998) • **89**
English Cuvée California 1991: Rich, up-front aromatics include fresh toast and butterscotch. On the palate, hazelnut, lemon-lime and spice make an enticing blend. Quite mature, however. Drink now. • $22 • (11/30/1998) • **89**
Midnight Cuvée California 1991: Pleasant enough, with light herb and cherry notes. Refreshing but simple. • $20 • (11/30/1998) • **82**

MAYACAMAS | CALIFORNIA

Cabernet Sauvignon Napa Valley 1993: Smells and tastes like a mature Cabernet, with earthy, cedary flavors and hints of currant, anise and tar that turn tart on the finish. Tannins are firm. Drink through 2008.–J.L. • $35 • (12/31/1998) • **86**
Cabernet Sauvignon Napa Valley 1992: Tightly wound, with a narrow band of mineral, herb, currant and cherry. Shows fine depth and concentration, and the kind of austere tannins that merit short- to mid-range cellaring. Drink through 2008–J.L. • $30 • (10/31/1998) • **87**
Cabernet Sauvignon Napa Valley 1990 • $25 • (12/15/1995) • **85**
Cabernet Sauvignon Napa Valley 1989: Earthy, with herb, dill and cedary flavors holding the upper hand to rather modest cherry and berry. (1989 California Cabernet retrospective tasting). Drink now.–J.L. • $20 • (8/31/1999) • **80**
Cabernet Sauvignon Napa Valley 1987 • $41 • (12/15/1997) • **87**
Cabernet Sauvignon Napa Valley 1986 • $NA • (12/15/1996) • **88**
Cabernet Sauvignon Napa Valley 1985 • $50 Ⓐ • (1/31/1990) • **92**
Cabernet Sauvignon Napa Valley 1984 • $38 Ⓐ • (4/15/1989) • **80**
Cabernet Sauvignon Napa Valley 1983 • $20 • (9/15/1988) • **80**
Cabernet Sauvignon Napa Valley 1982 • $36 Ⓐ • (3/31/1987) • **77**
Cabernet Sauvignon California 1979: Dark, immense and detailed, an outstanding Mayacamas, with rich earthy currant, black cherry, mineral, anise, sage and cedar flavors, holding its flavor and focus. Could go another 10 years. (1979 California Cabernet retrospective tasting). Drink now through 2009.–J.L. • $18 • (8/31/1999) • **91**
Cabernet Sauvignon Napa Valley 1978: Mature, still with some chalky tannins, but has an immense, complex core of earthy tannins, currant, plum, pepper and mineral flavors. Impeccably balanced, it drinks exceptionally well. One of Mayacamas' great wines. (1978 California Cabernet retrospective tasting). Drink now through 2004.–J.L. • $101 Ⓐ • (11/15/1998) • **92**
Cabernet Sauvignon Napa Valley 1974 • $153 Ⓐ • (11/15/1994) • **88**
Pinot Noir Napa Valley 1988 • $14 • (2/28/1993) • **68**
Pinot Noir Napa Valley 1987 • $14 • (4/30/1991) • **80**
Pinot Noir Napa Valley 1986 • $14 • (3/31/1990) • **67**
Pinot Noir Napa Valley 1985 • $12 • (6/15/1988) • **72**
Pinot Noir Napa Valley 1984 • $12 • (12/31/1988) • **71**
Pinot Noir California 1981 • $12 • (8/31/1986) • **74**

MAYO | CALIFORNIA

Cabernet Sauvignon Dry Creek Valley 1995 • $18 • (9/30/1997) • **84**
Cabernet Sauvignon Sonoma Valley Los Chamizal Vineyard 1996: Elegant and plush, with intriguing black currant, dill, bay and cracked pepper flavors. Finishes with ripe, supple tannins. Drink now through 2004.–J.L. • $30 • (6/15/1999) • **88**
Cabernet Sauvignon Sonoma Valley Los Chamizal Vineyard 1995 • $24 • (3/31/1998) • **85**
Chardonnay Sonoma Valley 1997: Complex and concentrated, tight, displaying a pretty core of creamy pear, apple and melon flavors with a tart accent. Drink now through 2002.–J.L. • $20 • (1/31/1999) • **87**
Chardonnay Sonoma Valley 1996 • $17 • (5/15/1998) • **85**
Chardonnay Sonoma Valley Barrel Select 1997: This has intense, flinty pear and lemon flavors, with a toasty edge. Drink now.–J.L. • $25 • (12/31/1998) • **86**
Chardonnay Sonoma Valley Barrel Select 1996 • $22 • (5/15/1998) • **82**
Merlot Sonoma Valley 1995 • $20 • (6/15/1998) • **78**
Pinot Noir Carneros Sangiacomo Vineyard 1997: Supple and flavorful, featuring juicy black cherry, plum and spicy toasted oak notes, turning firm and tannic. Drink now through 2001. • $25 • (4/30/1999) • **87**
Pinot Noir Carneros 1996 • $20 • (2/28/1998) • **86**
Zinfandel Sonoma County Three Valley 1996 • $18 • (6/15/1998) • **80**

MAZZOCCO | CALIFORNIA

Cabernet Sauvignon Alexander Valley Claret Style 1988 • $18 • (3/15/1992) • **85**
Cabernet Sauvignon Alexander Valley Claret Style 1987 • $20 • (12/15/1997) • **88**
Cabernet Sauvignon Alexander Valley Claret Style 1986 • $20 • (7/31/1989) • **78**
Cabernet Sauvignon Sonoma County 1995: Firm, with an herbal edge to the mineral, clay, tart cherry and anise flavors, finishing with mild tannins and a slight bitterness. Drink now through 2004.–J.L. • $18 • (10/15/1999) • **83**
Cabernet Sauvignon Sonoma County 1994: Soft and supple, with a range of tea, cola and earthy currant flavors. Finishes with integrated tannins. Drink now.–J.L. • $18 • (12/31/1998) • **85**
Cabernet Sauvignon Sonoma County 1993 • $18 • (11/30/1997) • **81**
Cabernet Sauvignon Sonoma County 1992 • $18 • (4/30/1996) • **88**
Cabernet Sauvignon Sonoma County 1991 • $18 • (11/15/1994) • **88**
Cabernet Sauvignon Sonoma County 1989 • $15 • (6/15/1993) • **81**
Chardonnay Sonoma County Winemaker's Select 1997: Straightforward, with stewed apple and black licorice flavors. Drink now.–J.L. • $20 • (6/30/2000) • **84**
Chardonnay Dry Creek Valley Winemaker's Select 1996: Floral aromas lead into ripe pear, apple and spicy Chardonnay flavors, finishing with a complex, spicy aftertaste and pretty oak shadings. Drink now through 2002. –J.L. • $20 • (1/31/1999) • **90**
Chardonnay Sonoma County River Lane 1997: Ripe and fruity, with pretty pear, fig and melon flavors that are supple and delicate. Drink now through 2002.–J.L. • $15 • (1/31/1999) • **87**
Chardonnay Sonoma County River Lane 1996 • $15 • (12/15/1997) • **87**
Matrix Dry Creek Valley 1993 • $28 • (11/30/1997) • **84**
Matrix Dry Creek Valley 1992 • $28 • (8/31/1996) • **87**
Matrix Dry Creek Valley 1991 • $28 • (12/15/1995) • **87**
Matrix Sonoma County 1990 • $28 • (11/15/1994) • **82**
Matrix Sonoma County 1989 • $28 • (11/15/1993) • **86**
Matrix Sonoma County 1987 • $28 • (12/15/1997) • **87**

Merlot Dry Creek Valley 1995: Shows a solid cherry and raspberry core, backed by smoky oak and a hint of herb. Tannins are fairly ripe. Drink now through 2004. • $18 • (10/15/1998) • **87**
Merlot Dry Creek Valley 1994 • $18 • (11/30/1997) • **84**
Merlot Dry Creek Valley 1993 • $18 • (7/31/1996) • **88**
Merlot Dry Creek Valley 1992 • $15 • (5/31/1996) • **84**
Merlot Dry Creek Valley 1991 • $15 • (11/15/1994) • **78**
Merlot Dry Creek Valley 1989 • $14 • (6/15/1993) • **78**
Merlot Dry Creek Valley Estate Unfiltered 1989 • $14 • (5/31/1992) • **89**
Petite Sirah Dry Creek Valley 1993 • $21 • (8/31/1997) • **90**
Viognier Dry Creek Valley 1996 • $25 • (5/15/1998) • **82**
Zinfandel Alexander Valley 1995: Well proportioned, with a focused, complex band of earthy berry, tar, sage and spice, finishing with firm tannins. Drink now.–J.L. • $22 • (6/30/1999) • **87**
Zinfandel Alexander Valley 1994 • $20 • (4/30/1997) • **80**
Zinfandel Dry Creek Valley 1996: Shows a modest range of spicy plum, baked apple and cinnamon flavors, finishing firm and crisp. Drink now. –J.L. • $16 • (5/15/1999) • **83**
Zinfandel Dry Creek Valley Cuneo & Saini 1995: Medium-weight style, with ripe cherry and plum flavors of moderate depth and complexity. For fans of lighter- or claret-style Zin. Drink now.–J.L. • $22 • (6/30/1999) • **86**
Zinfandel Dry Creek Valley Cuneo & Saini 1994 • $20 • (4/30/1997) • **89**
Zinfandel Dry Creek Valley Cuneo & Saini 1993 • $20 • (10/15/1995) • **83**
Zinfandel Dry Creek Valley Quinn Vineyard 1996: Diluted and earthy, with dull berry flavors.–J.L. • $22 • (4/30/2000) • **73**
Zinfandel Dry Creek Valley Quinn Vineyard 1995 • $22 • (6/15/1998) • **79**
Zinfandel Sonoma County 1995 • $16 • (12/15/1997) • **81**
Zinfandel Sonoma County 1994 • $15 • (3/31/1997) • **82**
Zinfandel Sonoma County 1993 • $14 • (8/31/1995) • **86**
Zinfandel Sonoma County 1992 • $14 • (10/15/1994) • **86**
Zinfandel Sonoma County 1991 • $14 • (9/30/1993) • **88**
Zinfandel Sonoma Valley 1990 • $13 • (10/15/1992) • **87**
Zinfandel Sonoma County Traditional Style 1988 • $13 • (10/15/1990) • **89**
Zinfandel Sonoma County Traditional Style 1986 • $10 • (12/15/1988) • **90**

MCCOY, PETER | CALIFORNIA

Chardonnay Knights Valley Clos des Pierres 1996: Rich and creamy in texture and flavor yet tightly wound, with mineral-tinged fig and pear surfacing through all the butter and cream flavors. Drink now through 2002.–H.S. • $39 • (6/30/1999) • **87**
Chardonnay Sonoma County 1997: Subtle, with green apple, spice, herb and toast flavors. The firm finish picks up lovely spice and honey notes. Drink now.–H.S. • $25 • (6/15/1999) • **88**

MCCRAY RIDGE | CALIFORNIA

Merlot Dry Creek Valley Two Moon Vineyard 1997: Bright, with juicy cherry, wild berry, sage, earth and cedar notes, turning earthy and dry on the finish. Drink through 2006.–J.L. • $50 • (10/15/1999) • **86**
Merlot Dry Creek Valley Two Moon Vineyard 1996: Combines ripe, spicy cherry and wild berry flavors with supple, polished tannins and a sense of understated elegance and grace. Delicious enough to drink now or cellar through 2002.–J.L. • $35 • (10/15/1998) • **89**

MCCREA | WASHINGTON

Chardonnay Columbia Valley 1996: An earthy streak threads its way through the otherwise fresh apple and spice flavors. Drink through 2001.–H.S. • $20 • (9/15/1998) • **83**
Syrah-Grenache Columbia Valley Tierra del Sol NV: Gamy, tarry notes add extra dimension to this ripe, smooth-textured wine that features plum and anise flavors which echo and enlarge on the finish. Drink now through 2001.–H.S. • $14 • (9/15/1998) • **86**
Viognier Columbia Valley 1997: Smelling like a bowl full of melons and flowers, this enticingly rich and aromatic white wine fills the mouth with spicy, floral fruit flavors. Has a nice hint of pepper of the finish. Drink now.–H.S. • $18 • (9/15/1998) • **88**

Key: SS—Spectator Selection CS—Cellar Selection HR—Highly Recommended $NA—Price Not Available a—Auction Price (BT)—Barrel Tasting
For a key to the tasters' initials, see "How to Use These Listings."
Dates in parentheses indicate the issues in which the ratings were published.

MCDOWELL | CALIFORNIA

Bistro Red LVC Mendocino NV • $7 • (6/30/1992) • **79**
Cabernet Sauvignon California 1988 • $10 • (11/15/1991) • **78**
Cabernet Sauvignon McDowell Valley 1983 • $11 • (4/15/1988) • **76**
Cabernet Sauvignon McDowell Valley 1982 • $11 • (12/15/1986) • **89**
Cabernet Sauvignon McDowell Valley 1981 • $11 • (12/16/1984) • **78**
Cabernet Sauvignon Mendocino 1992 • $10 • (12/15/1995) • **85**
Cabernet Sauvignon Mendocino 1990 • $10 • (7/15/1993) • **82**
Cabernet Sauvignon Mendocino 1989 • $10 • (11/15/1992) • **75**
Les Vieux Cépages Les Trésor McDowell Valley 1990 • $13 • (10/15/1993) • **86**
Les Vieux Cépages Les Trésor McDowell Valley 1988 • $12 • (6/30/1992) • **75**
Les Vieux Cépages Les Trésor McDowell Valley 1987 • $14 • (8/31/1990) • **82**
Les Vieux Cépages Les Trésor McDowell Valley 1986 • $13 • (9/30/1989) • **86**
Marsanne Mendocino 1997: A bright wine, lively, with hints of orange, lemon and wintergreen. Finish is refreshing. • $16 • (11/15/1998) • **85**
Syrah McDowell Valley 1985 • $12 • (9/30/1989) • **90**
Syrah McDowell Valley 1982 • $10 • (1/31/1987) • **75**
Syrah McDowell Valley 1981 • $10 • (12/16/1984) • **90**
Syrah Mendocino Bistro Syrah 1992 • $10 • (7/31/1994) • **85**
Syrah McDowell Valley Bistro Syrah LVC 1991 • $9 • (3/31/1993) • **79**
Syrah McDowell Valley Bistro Syrah LVC 1990 • $9 • (6/30/1992) • **76**
Syrah McDowell Valley Les Vieux Cépages 1987 • $16 • (3/31/1991) • **74**
Syrah McDowell Valley Les Vieux Cépages 1986 • $14 • (8/31/1990) • **80**
Syrah Mendocino 1997: Here's a supple Syrah at a reasonable price, its smooth, round tannins framing black cherry and herb flavors. A hint of stemminess shows itself on the finish, adding complexity, and the oak nuances are pretty. Drink now through 2005. • $10 • (12/15/1998) • **88**
Syrah Mendocino 1996 • $10 • (12/15/1997) • **87**
Syrah Mendocino 1995 • $10 • (5/15/1997) • **87**
Syrah Mendocino 1993 • $10 • (10/15/1995) • **87**
Syrah Mendocino 1990 • $17 • (7/31/1994) • **82**
Syrah Mendocino McDowell Valley Estate 1995 • $16 • (4/30/1998) • **90**
Syrah Mendocino McDowell Valley Estate 1992 • $15 • (5/31/1996) • **84**
Viognier Mendocino 1997: Bright, spicy tangerine, peach and apple flavors sally forth for a heady blend in this very fruity wine. Quite opulent and fun to drink. Drink now. • $16 • (11/15/1998) • **87**
Viognier Mendocino 1996 • $15 • (12/15/1997) • **83**
Zinfandel McDowell Valley 1990 • $9 • (4/30/1993) • **79**
Zinfandel McDowell Valley 1989 • $9 • (10/15/1992) • **80**
Zinfandel McDowell Valley 1988 • $10 • (12/31/1990) • **80**

MCILROY | CALIFORNIA

Chardonnay Russian River Valley Aquarius Ranch 1996 • $18 • (6/30/1998) • **90**
Pinot Noir Russian River Valley Aquarius Ranch 1996: Lightweight, with touches of cherry, herb and oak. Pleasant enough as a quaffer, though slightly bitter at the end. Drink now. • $18 • (8/31/1998) • **80**
Red Russian River Valley 1993 • $15 • (12/15/1997) • **83**
Zinfandel Russian River Valley Porter-Bass Vineyard 1996 • $18 • (6/15/1998) • **86**
Zinfandel Russian River Valley Porter-Bass Vineyard 1995 • $18 • (1/01/1998) • **88**
Zinfandel Russian River Valley Porter-Bass Vineyard 1994 • $15 • (2/28/1997) • **82**

MCKENZIE-MUELLER | CALIFORNIA

Cabernet Sauvignon Napa Valley 1997: A bit of funkiness doesn't detract from the flavors of coffee, chocolate and roasted blackberry. Dry tannins will soften after a year or two. Best after 2002.–J.L. • $32 • (4/30/2000) • **85**

MCKINLAY | OREGON

Pinot Noir Willamette Valley 1990 • $15 • (2/28/1993) • **84**
Pinot Noir Willamette Valley 1988 • $13 • (4/15/1991) • **90**
Pinot Noir Willamette Valley Special Selection 1994 • $31 • (2/28/1997) • **86**
Pinot Noir Willamette Valley Special Selection 1993 • $23 • (1/31/1996) • **83**
Pinot Noir Willamette Valley Special Selection 1991 • $23 • (11/30/1994) • **86**

MEDICI | OREGON

Pinot Noir Willamette Valley 1995 • $20 • (5/15/1998) • **85**

Pinot Noir Willamette Valley Estate Reserve 1998: Rich, round and velvety, with ultraripe plum and currant aromas and flavors that expand on the spicy finish. Big and beautifully proportioned, opening nicely to show the flavors and promising more development. Best from 2001 through 2008.–H.S. • $32 • (4/30/2000) • **91**

MEEKER | CALIFORNIA

Cabernet Sauvignon Dry Creek Valley 1988 • $14 • (8/31/1992) • **85**
Cabernet Sauvignon Dry Creek Valley 1987 • $14 • (10/15/1991) • **87**
Cabernet Sauvignon Dry Creek Valley 1986 • $19 • (2/15/1990) • **72**
Cabernet Sauvignon Dry Creek Valley 1985 • $18 • (4/30/1989) • **76**
Cabernet Sauvignon Dry Creek Valley 1984 • $18 • (6/15/1988) • **78**
Cabernet Sauvignon Dry Creek Valley Gold Leaf Cuvée 1994 • $18 • (11/15/1997) • **88**
Cabernet Sauvignon Dry Creek Valley Gold Leaf Cuvée 1991 • $14 • (11/15/1994) • **78**
Cabernet Sauvignon Dry Creek Valley Gold Leaf Cuvée 1990 • $14 • (9/15/1993) • **82**
Cabernet Sauvignon Dry Creek Valley Red Table Wine Fourth Rack 1992 • $9 • (11/30/1996) • **83**
Cabernet Sauvignon Dry Creek Valley Red Table Wine Second Rack NV • $8 • (11/15/1994) • **79**
Cabernet Sauvignon Dry Creek Valley Scharf Family Vineyard 1990 • $14 • (11/15/1994) • **84**
Four Kings Sonoma County Scharf Family Vineyard Red 1994 • $20 • (11/15/1997) • **87**
Merlot Sonoma County Winemakers' Handprint Collection 1992 • $18 • (8/31/1996) • **87**
Petite Sirah Napa County Gold Leaf Cuvée 1994 • $18 • (1/01/1997) • **88**
Sauvignon Blanc Dry Creek Valley Late Harvest Gold Leaf Cuveé 1992 • $16 • (9/30/1995) • **88**
Zinfandel Dry Creek Valley 1991 • $8 • (9/30/1993) • **82**
Zinfandel Dry Creek Valley 1989 • $10 • (10/15/1992) • **80**
Zinfandel Dry Creek Valley 1988 • $10 • (8/31/1991) • **82**
Zinfandel Dry Creek Valley 1987 • $10 • (3/31/1990) • **85**
Zinfandel Dry Creek Valley Gold Leaf Cuvée 1994 • $14 • (2/28/1997) • **84**
Zinfandel Dry Creek Valley Gold Leaf Cuvée 1992 • $12 • (10/15/1994) • **80**
Zinfandel Dry Creek Valley Gold Leaf Cuvée 1991 • $11 • (9/30/1993) • **84**
Zinfandel Dry Creek Valley Gold Leaf Cuvée 1990: Intense, focused, complex and concentrated, with rich, chewy plum, wild berry, black cherry, spice, currant and cedar notes and a long, full, flavorful aftertaste. Still has tannin to shed, but the fruit is lovely. (Zinfandel retrospective tasting). Drink now through 2003.–J.L. • $10 • (6/30/1999) • **90**
Zinfandel Dry Creek Valley Gold Leaf Reserve 1989 • $14 • (10/15/1992) • **81**
Zinfandel Dry Creek Valley Red Table Wine Fifth Rack 1994 • $9 • (4/30/1997) • **80**
Zinfandel Dry Creek Valley Red Table Wine First Rack 1991 • $8 • (9/30/1993) • **86**
Zinfandel Sonoma County Sonoma Cuvée 1992 • $10 • (10/15/1994) • **84**

MELKA | CALIFORNIA

Cabernet Sauvignon Napa Valley CJ 1997: A touch earthy at first, with a trim core of currant, olive, herb and cedar notes. Finishes with firm, crisp tannins and good length. Best from 2002 through 2010.–J.L. • $28 • (4/30/2000) • **88**
Cabernet Sauvignon Napa Valley CJ 1996: Dense and minerally, with a core of tar, earth and black cherry flavors. Rustic but flavorful, with mild tannins. Drink now through 2005.–J.L. • $23 • (9/15/1999) • **86**

MENDELSON | CALIFORNIA

Muscat Canelli Napa Valley 1998: Sweet. Wonderful, spicy varietal character, with spice, spice and more spice, also ginger, orange peel, pear, anise and floral notes. Quite distinctive. Drink now through 2004.–J.L. • $35/375 ml. • (6/30/2000) • **91**
Pinot Gris Napa Valley 1998: Sweet, rich and aromatic, with complex peach, nectarine and apricot. Finishes with elegance and grace. Crisp acidity keeps the flavors jumping. Drink now through 2005.–J.L. • $35/375 ml. • (6/15/2000) • **92**
Pinot Gris Napa Valley 1997: Superrich and sugary, with layers of custard, vanilla, apricot, nutmeg and cumin notes. Long and sweet on the finish. Drink now through 2005.–J.L. • $35/375 ml. • (6/15/2000) • **91**
Pinot Gris Napa Valley 1996: Simply delicious. A wonderful sweet wine, rich, spicy, elegant, complex, with an amazing amount of flavor. At 17 percent alcohol, it's a shade light for white Port, but close. Drink now through 2006.–J.L. • $21/375 ml. • (2/28/1999) • **95**

MENDOCINO HILL | CALIFORNIA

Cabernet Sauvignon Mendocino County 1989 • $15 • (3/31/1993) • **88**
Cabernet Sauvignon Mendocino County Private Reserve 1992 • $14 • (9/15/1997) • **86**

MER SOLEIL | CALIFORNIA

Chardonnay Central Coast 1997: This wine is opulent, rich and creamy, with a core of nectarine, fig, citrus, pineapple and spice supported by firm, lively acidity, finishing long and full. Lovely Chardonnay from a growing California appellation. Drink now through 2005.–J.L. • $40 • (1/31/2000) HR • **93**
Chardonnay Central Coast 1996: An earthy note kicks this off, with a range of tangerine, nectarine and spicy fruit flavors following. Keeps its focus and gains complexity on the long, lingering aftertaste. Drink now through 2002.–J.L. • $36 • (12/15/1998) • **91**

MERIDIAN | CALIFORNIA

Cabernet Sauvignon California 1996: Pleasant, soft-textured and ripe, showing herb, anise and cherry flavors. Smooth and flavorful finish. Drink now through 2002.–J.L. • $11 • (10/15/1999) • **84**
Cabernet Sauvignon California 1995: Appealing for its medium-weight, ripe berry flavors, with hints of cherry and plum. A good value in a drink-now style.–J.L. • $11 • (10/31/1998) • **85**
Cabernet Sauvignon California 1994 • $11 • (9/30/1997) • **86**
Cabernet Sauvignon California Coastal Reserve 1995: Ripe-textured and tightly structured, with a range of tar, mineral, cola, black cherry and spice flavors. Finishes with slightly dry tannins and persistent flavors. Drink now through 2005.–J.L. • $22 • (10/15/1999) • **86**
Cabernet Sauvignon Paso Robles 1990 • $14 • (9/30/1993) • **87**
Cabernet Sauvignon Paso Robles 1989 • $14 • (7/31/1992) • **85**
Cabernet Sauvignon Paso Robles 1988 • $12 • (9/30/1991) SS • **92**
Chardonnay Edna Valley Coastal Reserve 1998: Ripe, creamy and elegant, with pretty pear, nectarine, hazelnut, citrus and subtle honey notes and a long, bright aftertaste. Drink now through 2005.–J.L. • $15 • (5/15/2000) • **88**
Chardonnay Edna Valley Coastal Reserve 1997: Clean and crisp, with a tangy edge to the ripe pear and peach notes, fanning out with creamy, smoky oak nuances. Drink now through 2002.–J.L. • $15 • (1/31/1999) • **88**
Chardonnay Edna Valley Coastal Reserve 1996 • $14 • (3/31/1998) SS • **92**
Chardonnay Santa Barbara County 1998: A nice all-around Chardonnay at an attractive price, this is medium in weight, with a core of earthy pear, fig and apple, finishing with light oak and a creamy note. Drink now.–J.L. • $11 • (4/30/2000) • **86**
Chardonnay Santa Barbara County 1997: Ripe, with sweet-tasting apple, pear, melon and apricot flavors, it's an elegant, polished, refreshing style. Drink now.–J.L. • $11 • (11/30/1998) • **87**
Chardonnay Santa Barbara County 1996 • $11 • (11/15/1997) • **87**
Merlot California 1994 • $15 • (11/30/1997) • **84**
Merlot California 1993 • $16 • (8/31/1996) • **82**
Pinot Noir Edna Valley Reserve 1991 • $16 • (4/30/1994) • **86**
Pinot Noir Santa Barbara County 1997: Delicate but focused, with a tight range of cherry, herb and toasted oak flavors. Well integrated on the finish, with earthy cherry notes. Drink now through 2002.–J.L. • $14 • (9/15/1999) • **84**
Pinot Noir Santa Barbara County 1996 • $14 • (12/15/1997) • **83**
Pinot Noir Santa Barbara County 1995 • $14 • (1/31/1997) • **88**
Pinot Noir Santa Barbara County 1994 • $14 • (3/31/1996) • **86**
Pinot Noir Santa Barbara-San Luis Obispo Counties 1993 • $14 • (9/15/1995) • **82**
Pinot Noir Santa Barbara County 1992 • $14 • (11/30/1994) • **83**
Pinot Noir Santa Barbara County 1991 • $14 • (2/28/1994) • **80**
Pinot Noir Santa Barbara County 1990 • $14 • (2/28/1993) • **80**
Pinot Noir Santa Barbara County Coastal Reserve 1996: Decidedly herbal, with spice, tea, black cherry and vanilla flavors folding in, turning dry and tannic. Drink through 2004.–J.L. • $20 • (2/28/1999) • **87**
Pinot Noir Santa Barbara County Riverbench Vineyard 1988 • $14 • (2/28/1991) • **86**
Pinot Noir Santa Barbara-San Luis Obispo Counties Reserve 1995 • $20 • (3/31/1998) • **91**
Pinot Noir Santa Barbara-San Luis Obispo Counties Reserve 1994 • $17 • (1/31/1997) • **84**

■ ■ ■ ■

MERIDIAN

Pinot Noir Santa Barbara-San Luis Obispo Counties Reserve 1993 • $16 • (11/30/1995) • **87**

Sauvignon Blanc California 1998: Simple, with dilute citrus and gooseberry flavors. Drink now.–J.L. • $8 • (5/15/2000) • **80**

Sauvignon Blanc California 1997 • $9 • (6/30/1998) • **83**

Sauvignon Blanc California 1996 • $9 • (9/15/1997) • **85**

Syrah Paso Robles 1996: Ripe and spicy Syrah, with rich pepper, meaty plum, cherry, earth and mineral notes, finishing with crisp, firm tannins. Drink now through 2004.–J.L. • $14 • (8/31/1998) • **88**

Syrah Paso Robles 1991 • $14 • (7/31/1994) • **83**

Syrah Paso Robles 1990 • $15 • (3/31/1993) • **85**

Syrah Paso Robles 1988 • $14 • (3/31/1991) HR • **91**

Zinfandel Paso Robles 1990 • $14 • (9/30/1993) • **86**

Zinfandel Paso Robles 1989 • $10 • (10/15/1992) • **85**

MERRYVALE | CALIFORNIA

Cabernet Sauvignon Napa Valley 1997: A firm, lean-textured wine, with a core of anise, blackberry, herb and currant flavors couched in toasty oak. A bit chunky on the finish, but should smooth out nicely. Best from 2002 through 2009. • $20 • (10/15/1999) • **87**

Cabernet Sauvignon Napa Valley Hillside 1996: Packs in lots of flavors, with tiers of currant, black cherry, plum and wild berry. Holds its focus on the long, complex aftertaste. Best from 2001 through 2008.–J.L. • $20 • (12/15/1998) • **90**

Cabernet Sauvignon Napa Valley 1994 • $27 • (10/31/1997) • **87**

Cabernet Sauvignon Napa Valley 1993 • $25 • (12/15/1996) • **83**

Cabernet Sauvignon Napa Valley 1992 • $24 • (12/15/1995) • **88**

Cabernet Sauvignon Napa Valley 1991 • $23 • (11/15/1994) • **87**

Cabernet Sauvignon Napa Valley 1990 • $20 • (6/30/1993) • **88**

Cabernet Sauvignon Napa Valley 1989 • $16 • (10/31/1992) SS • **92**

Cabernet Sauvignon Napa Valley 1988 • $18 • (7/15/1991) • **86**

Cabernet Sauvignon Napa Valley Reserve 1997: Weaves together complex, earthy cherry and currant flavors framed by toasty, cedary oak, with an elegant aftertaste. Tasted twice, with consistent notes. Drink now through 2008.–J.L. • $39 • (5/31/2000) • **88**

Cabernet Sauvignon Napa Valley Reserve 1996: Dense, ripe, rich and concentrated, focused on the core of spicy currant, plum and black cherry, this is a big, complex and richly flavored wine that's also firmly tannic, so cellar short-term. Best from 2001 through 2010.–J.L. • $35 • (10/15/1999) • **93**

Cabernet Sauvignon Napa Valley Reserve 1995: Has a lot going for it, including its price. Smooth, ripe and polished, with tiers of plum, black cherry, currant and berry, it's rich and focused, long and complex on the finish. A remarkable wine that combines depth, concentration and complexity. Drink through 2007.–J.L. • $40 Ⓐ • (10/31/1998) • **91**

Chardonnay Carneros Reserve 1997: Remarkably smooth and elegant, with ripe, rich pear, citrus, spice and light oak shadings. Turns sleek and polished on the finish. Drink now through 2003.–J.L. • $32 • (6/30/1999) • **93**

Chardonnay Napa Valley Reserve 1998: Aims for complexity but comes up shy, with elegant, light pear and toasty oak, turning simple. Drink now.–J.L. • $35 • (6/15/2000) • **86**

Chardonnay Napa Valley Reserve 1997: A touch earthy, with complex pear, fig, spice and hazelnut. Turns earthy again on the long finish. Drink through 2002.–J.L. • $32 • (7/31/1999) • **88**

Chardonnay Napa Valley Reserve 1996: Serves up lots of tasty, sharply focused Chardonnay flavors, with ripe, creamy pear, hazelnut, fig and toasty oak. Turns intricate and delicate on the finish, where the flavors are bright and lively. Drink now through 2002.–J.L. • $30 • (7/31/1998) • **92**

Chardonnay Napa Valley Silhouette 1997: Well crafted, with very ripe fruit and layers of fig, pear, spice and apricot notes and well-proportioned oak. Drink now through 2005.–J.L. • $48 • (4/30/2000) • **90**

Chardonnay Napa Valley Starmont 1998: Clean, ripe and fruity, weaving together complex pear, vanilla, citrus and apple flavors that are crisp and refreshing. Drink now through 2005.–J.L. • $20 • (4/30/2000) • **88**

Chardonnay Napa Valley Starmont 1997: Here's California Chardonnay in a smooth and polished style, delicious for its rich anise, fig, pear and nutmeg flavors that flow over the palate to a long, silky aftertaste. Drink now through 2001.–J.L. • $20 • (6/30/1999) SS • **90**

> **Key:** SS—Spectator Selection CS—Cellar Selection HR—Highly Recommended
> $NA—Price Not Available a—Auction Price (BT)—Barrel Tasting
> For a key to the tasters' initials, see "How to Use These Listings."
> **Dates in parentheses indicate the issues in which the ratings were published.**

Chardonnay Napa Valley Starmont 1996: A deliciously complex Chardonnay, layering flavors of pear, fig and hazelnut, and finishing with a lingering, intricate aftertaste. Smooth, ripe, rich and creamy, it's an outstanding wine, and reasonably priced. Drink now through 2002.–J.L. • $18 • (7/31/1998) SS • **91**

Chardonnay Russian River Valley Dutton Ranch 1998: Simple, with crisp green apple and grapefruit skin, giving it a slightly bitter twinge. Drink now.–J.L. • $35 • (6/15/2000) • **82**

Chardonnay Russian River Valley Dutton Ranch 1997: Intense, with a complex, tightly wound range of pear, fig, apricot and melon. Retains its austerity, with a flinty, citrusy edge on the finish. Drink through 2002.–J.L. • $30 • (7/31/1999) • **89**

Merlot Napa Valley 1994 • $28 • (6/30/1997) • **87**

Merlot Napa Valley 1993 • $25 • (7/31/1996) • **78**

Merlot Napa Valley 1992 • $24 • (9/30/1995) • **85**

Merlot Napa Valley 1991 • $28 • (9/15/1994) • **84**

Merlot Napa Valley 1990 • $18 • (12/15/1992) • **85**

Merlot Napa Valley 1989 • $16 • (5/31/1992) • **84**

Merlot Napa Valley Reserve 1997: Dark, deep and intense, with rich currant, anise, tar, cedar and mineral flavors. Finishes with plum and black cherry notes and firm tannins. Drink now through 2008.–J.L. • $39 • (2/29/2000) • **88**

Merlot Napa Valley Reserve 1996: Tight, trim and structured, with herb-scented coffee and currant notes, finishing with firm tannins. Best from 2001 through 2005.–J.L. • $32 • (9/15/1999) • **87**

Merlot Napa Valley Reserve 1995: Serves up plenty of juicy plum, currant and black cherry flavors, filling in the gaps with menthol and cedary oak. Nicely balanced, with a long, spicy aftertaste. Can stand short-term cellaring. Drink now through 2004.–J.L. • $32 • (9/30/1998) • **88**

Muscat de Frontignan Napa Valley Antigua NV • $12 • (11/30/1991) • **86**

Profile Napa Valley 1996: Round, smooth and spicy, with pretty, supple black cherry, plum, wild berry and mineral flavors. Turns mildly tannic, showing nice cedary, toasty oak. Drink through 2009.–J.L. • $75 • (11/15/1999) • **91**

Profile Napa Valley 1995: Young and vibrant, with a ripe, rich, lively core of currant, plum, anise, sage and cedar. This complex and concentrated wine is supported by a firm tannic backbone, but the flavors glide through on the finish. Cabernet, Merlot, Cabernet Franc.–J.L. • $65 • (11/15/1998) • **91**

Profile Napa Valley 1994: The core of currant and black cherry is marked by cedary oak and firm tannins, but it opens up to reveal rich, concentrated plum, currant, mineral, sage and oak. A complex, concentrated style. Drink through 2007.–J.L. • $48 Ⓐ • (10/31/1998) • **91**

Profile Napa Valley 1992 • $36 • (11/15/1996) • **88**

Profile Napa Valley 1991 • $36 • (12/15/1995) • **90**

Profile Napa Valley 1990 • $36 • (12/15/1995) • **78**

Profile Napa Valley 1989 • $30 • (6/30/1993) • **86**

Profile Napa Valley 1988 • $25 • (11/15/1992) • **85**

Profile Napa Valley 1987 • $25 • (11/15/1991) • **83**

Red Napa Valley 1986 • $24 • (10/15/1990) • **86**

Red Napa Valley 1985 • $25 • (11/15/1988) • **87**

Red Napa Valley 1984 • $24 • (10/31/1987) • **90**

Red Napa Valley 1983 • $20 • (2/15/1987) • **94**

Sauvignon Blanc Napa Valley 1998: Soft and fleshy, with supple herb, fig, citrus and honeysuckle notes. Drink now.–J.L. • $17 • (12/31/1999) • **87**

Sauvignon Blanc Napa Valley 1997: Fragrant, with hints of melon, lemon-lime, spice and herbs. The wine is lean yet clean, with balanced acidity and a hint of toast. Finishes a little short, but still quite nice. Drink now. • $17 • (5/15/1999) • **85**

Sauvignon Blanc Napa Valley 1996 • $17 • (4/30/1998) • **85**

Sauvignon Blanc Napa Valley Juliana Vineyard 1998: Tangy, with apples and anise overtones and a simple finish. Drink now through 2002.–J.L. • $22 • (5/15/2000) • **83**

Sauvignon Blanc Napa Valley Reserve 1998: Subdued, with earthy, sweet pea and citrus flavors. Drink now.–J.L. • $22 • (5/15/2000) • **84**

Solstice Late Harvest Alexander Valley 1989 • $24/375 ml. • (6/30/1993) • **85**

Vignette White Napa Valley 1997: Starts off with rich, ripe aromas redolent of fig and pear. Toasty oak and bright acidity follow up to create a refreshing blend on the palate. Finishes long, with hints of citrus and mineral. A blend of Sauvignon Blanc and Sémillon. Drink now through 2001. • $22 • (5/31/1999) • **88**

Vignette White Napa Valley 1996 • $22 • (4/30/1998) • **86**

MESSINA HOF | TEXAS

Cabernet Sauvignon Texas Barrel Reserve 1996: Quite thick and almost chalky-tasting, with menthol cherry flavors.–K.M. • $10 • (10/15/1998) • **73**

Cabernet Sauvignon Texas Barrel Reserve 1989 • $10 • (3/15/1993) • **84**

Cabernet Sauvignon Texas Private Reserve 1996: An assertively crisp and tannic Cabernet with a broad, sweet impression, apparently from oak. Not typical, but with enough lively cherry flavor to keep it interesting. Drink now. • $17 • (6/15/1999) • **82**

Cabernet Sauvignon Texas Private Reserve 1990 • $15 • (1/31/1995) • **81**

Gewürztraminer Texas 1998: This smells like tobacco, but tastes sweet and too much like nectarine juice.–B.S. • $8 • (11/15/1999) • **74**

Johannisberg Riesling Texas 1998: Fresh and young, this is simple in its peach and citrus notes, with a slight sweetness. Moderately rich and just delicious. Drink young and chilled.–B.S. • $17 • (6/15/1999) • **84**

Johannisberg Riesling Texas 1997: Quite sweet, slightly spritzy in texture and soft in balance. This is acceptable but simple. Drink now. • $8 • (11/15/1998) • **78**

Johannisberg Riesling Texas Late Harvest Angel 1998: A frankly sweet Riesling that delivers plenty of rich apricot and orange aromas and flavors up front, but falls short on the finish.–B.S. • $15 • (11/15/1999) • **78**

Merlot Texas Private Reserve 1996: Extremely aromatic, with smoke and plum flavors and a tannic finish that don't quite come together in the end.–K.M. • $10 • (10/31/1998) • **78**

Muscat Canelli Texas 1998: This off-dry white evokes raisin and floral aromas and flavors, with a dash of apricot. Well balanced, it should serve better as an aperitif. Drink now.–B.S. • $8 • (11/15/1999) • **83**

Muscat Canelli Texas Late Harvest 1995 • $17 • (1/01/1997) • **78**

Muscat Canelli Texas Late Harvest Glory 1997: Sweet and simple, with a candied grapefruit aroma and flavor.–B.S. • $15 • (11/15/1999) • **75**

Muscat Canelli Texas Late Harvest Glory 1996: Sweet and peachy, with nice apricot flavors and a touch of richness. Drink now.–K.M. • $15 • (10/15/1998) • **81**

Pinot Noir Texas Barrel Reserve 1996: A brownish-gray color, dull plummy flavors and an astringent texture make this severe in style. • $10 • (10/31/1998) • **74**

Pinot Noir Texas Private Reserve 1996: Mint, bay leaf and cherry vie for center stage in this awkward red. Light and short, it finishes on an astringent note.–B.S. • $17 • (6/15/1999) • **74**

Pinot Noir Texas Reflections 1991 • $10 • (2/28/1993) • **80**

Port Texas Papa Paulo 1993 • $20 • (1/01/1997) • **82**

Port Texas Papa Paulo Barrel Reserve NV: Tawny in color, this has stemmy, menthol aromas but shows fresher caramel and toffee notes on the palate. Moderately sweet, and just a touch hot on the finish. Drink now.–T.M. • $15 • (1/01/2000) • **80**

Sauvignon Blanc Texas Barrel Reserve 1997: An unusual, almost sweet style, with a soft texture and plenty of vanilla, cream and peach flavor. Practically a dessert. Drink now. • $8 • (11/15/1998) • **83**

Sémillon Texas Late Harvest 1995 • $17 • (1/01/1997) • **83**

Zinfandel Texas Barrel Reserve 1997: This has the spice, cherry and berry flavors of Zin, but it finishes short and astringent.–B.S. • $17 • (6/15/1999) • **75**

MICHAEL, PETER | CALIFORNIA

Chardonnay Knights Valley Belle Côte 1996: Elegant and understated at first, with delicate pear, tangerine and vanilla flavors that build into a more complex and concentrated wine, with hazelnut, citrus and fig. Drink now through 2002.–J.L. • $42 • (7/31/1998) • **93**

Chardonnay Napa County Clos du Ciel 1996: Distinctive for its rich, creamy tangerine flavors, with intense and lively pear, fig and citrus at the core, finishing with a complex, lingering aftertaste. Shows a remarkable amount of elegance and finesse for a wine that packs in so much flavor. Drink now through 2004.–J.L. • $76 Ⓐ • (7/31/1998) HR • **93**

Chardonnay Sonoma County Belle Côte 1998: Medium in weight, with spicy pear, tangerine and lemon tart and a nice dash of toasty oak. Drink now.–J.L. • $55 • (6/15/2000) • **87**

Chardonnay Sonoma County Belle Côte 1997: Lots of flavor, richness and finesse to this Chardonnay, with layers of ripe pear, citrus, fig, tangerine and melon unfolding gracefully. Turns elegant and polished on the finish, where the flavors show added depth and dimension. Drink now through 2003.–J.L. • $45 • (6/15/1999) HR • **93**

Chardonnay Sonoma County Cuvée Indigène 1998: Complex and elegant, with ripe, spicy pear, hazelnut, custard and toasty oak. Long, intricate aftertaste. Drink now.–J.L. • $NA • (6/15/2000) • **89**

Chardonnay Sonoma County La Carrière 1998: Tight and flinty, with bright, compact nectarine, pear and spice notes. Finishes with grapefruit and lemon notes. Drink now.–J.L. • $50 • (6/15/2000) • **88**

Les Pavots Knights Valley 1997: Dark, ripe, rich and focused, with tiers of currant, mineral, anise, sage and cedar, all folding neatly together, finishing with a chocolaty edge. Drink now through 2009.–J.L. • $85 • (6/15/2000) CS • **92**

Les Pavots Knights Valley 1996: This Cabernet blend is simply brimming with ripe, juicy, complex flavors of black cherry, currant, wild berry and plum. The wine is sharply focused, supple and elegant in texture and capped by a lingering, flavorful finish. Contains Cabernet Sauvignon, Merlot and Cabernet Franc. Drink through 2010.–J.L. • $123 Ⓐ • (6/30/1999) HR • **96**

Les Pavots Knights Valley 1995: A wine of enormous intensity, concentration and complexity, it's packed with crisp, firm currant, spice, cedar, tar and wild berry flavors, and the finish just goes on and on. Best on the aftertaste, where the flavors fold together ever so nicely. 73 percent Cabernet Sauvignon, 14 percent Merlot, 13 percent Cabernet Franc. Best from 2001 through 2010.–J.L. • $77 Ⓐ • (7/31/1998) • **93**

Les Pavots Knights Valley 1994 • $110 Ⓐ • (8/31/1997) CS • **94**

Les Pavots Knights Valley 1993 • $77 Ⓐ • (9/30/1996) CS • **90**

Les Pavots Knights Valley 1992 • $89 Ⓐ • (12/15/1995) • **90**

Les Pavots Knights Valley 1991 • $26 • (5/15/1995) • **87**

Les Pavots Knights Valley 1989 • $36 Ⓐ • (12/15/1992) • **79**

Les Pavots Knights Valley 1988 • $25 • (11/15/1991) • **90**

Sauvignon Blanc Napa County L'Après-Midi 1997: Rich and fragrant, redolent of ripe fig, melon, fresh hay, grapefruit, lemon and lime, the wine is complex, luscious and distinctive. Has great body, yet its tangy acidity carries the flavors beautifully over the palate. Finishes long, yet is clean and refreshing. Drink now through 2002. • $28 • (1/01/1999) • **92**

Sauvignon Blanc Napa County L'Après-Midi 1996: Quite lemony, with a silky texture, this wine also boasts a medley of melon, fig and grapefruit flavors. A polished effort, with plenty of oak yet lots of finesse, too. Drink now. • $30 • (7/31/1998) • **90**

MICHAEL-SCOTT | CALIFORNIA

Zinfandel Napa Valley Old Vine 1996 • $22 • (11/30/1997) • **87**

MICHEL-SCHLUMBERGER | CALIFORNIA

Cabernet Sauvignon Dry Creek Valley 1997: Tight, firmly tannic, with a lean band of currant, anise, cedar and spice, it's trim and compact on the finish. Best from 2001 through 2006.–J.L. • $NA • (10/15/1999) • **85**

Cabernet Sauvignon Dry Creek Valley 1996: Firm and focused, featuring black olive, currant, mineral and black cherry flavors. Tannins are firm. Drink now through 2006.–J.L. • $22 • (9/30/1999) • **86**

Cabernet Sauvignon Dry Creek Valley 1995: Fairly tight, with blackberry, anise, smoke and herb flavors waiting to emerge. Finishes on a bitter note, but might come around nicely. Drink through 2005. • $22 • (10/31/1998) • **85**

Cabernet Sauvignon Dry Creek Valley 1994: Features fine-textured flavors of black currant, cassis, anise, herb and black cherry. The finish is a bit bright, though the ensemble remains sound. Drink now through 2003. • $20 • (10/15/1998) • **87**

Cabernet Sauvignon Dry Creek Valley 1993 • $20 • (10/31/1997) • **86**

Cabernet Sauvignon Dry Creek Valley 1991 • $18 • (11/15/1994) • **81**

Cabernet Sauvignon Dry Creek Valley Reserve 1994: Still tight, with drying tannins. Hints of anise, blackberry, cedar and herbs add interest. Maybe more bottle age will soften it and flesh it out. Drink through 2004. • $45 • (9/30/1999) • **84**

Cabernet Sauvignon Dry Creek Valley Reserve 1990 • $35 • (11/15/1994) • **82**

Chardonnay Dry Creek Valley 1996: Flinty, with a lemony accent to the moderately ripe Chardonnay flavors and a minerally edge to the finish. Drink through 2004.–J.L. • $20 • (1/31/1999) • **87**

MIDNIGHT CELLARS | CALIFORNIA

Cabernet Franc Paso Robles Crescent 1995 • $15 • (5/31/1998) • **88**

Cabernet Sauvignon Paso Robles Nebula 1996: Supple, with lots of up-front toasted oak flavors leading to a core of black cherry, anise and cedar. Remains focused on the finish, where the tannins turn firm. Drink now through 2003.–J.L. • $18 • (10/15/1999) • **87**

Cabernet Sauvignon Paso Robles Nocturne 1995 • $16 • (6/30/1998) • **84**

Cabernet Sauvignon Paso Robles 1994 • $16 • (9/15/1997) • **85**

Cabernet Sauvignon Paso Robles Limited Reserve 1993 • $17 • (2/28/1998) • **87**

MIDNIGHT CELLARS

Chardonnay Central Coast 1996: A neat blend of hazelnut, pear, anise, spice and ginger flavors in a silky structure. Long finish. Drink now. • $16 • (7/31/1998) • **88**

Merlot Paso Robles Capricorn 1997: Shows off lots of cola, coffee and toasted oak flavors before moving into focused plum and black cherry. Finishes with plush tannins and slightly bitter notes. Drink now through 2002.–J.L. • $22 • (10/15/1999) • **86**

Merlot Paso Robles Eclipse 1995 • $19 • (4/30/1998) • **88**

Syrah Paso Robles Galaxy 1997: A curious style, with cocoa, malt and vanilla flavors; it has chocolate notes, but the charred oak and toasted popcorn overtones dominate. Drink now.–J.L. • $20 • (5/15/2000) • **84**

Zinfandel Paso Robles 1995 • $18 • (7/31/1997) • **82**

MIETZ | CALIFORNIA

Merlot Sonoma County 1996: A blend of tart berry, plum, herb and tar flavors, finishing firm. Drink now through 2003.–J.L. • $23 • (10/15/1999) • **83**

Merlot Sonoma County 1995 • $21 • (3/31/1998) • **87**

Merlot Sonoma County 1994 • $18 • (6/30/1996) • **82**

Merlot Sonoma County 1993 • $17 • (8/31/1996) • **81**

Merlot Sonoma County 1990 • $14 • (11/30/1992) • **81**

Merlot Sonoma County 1989 • $14 • (4/15/1992) • **91**

Zinfandel Sonoma County 1996 • $18 • (5/31/1998) • **84**

Zinfandel Sonoma County 1995 • $15 • (4/30/1997) • **88**

MILANO | CALIFORNIA

Cabernet Sauvignon Mendocino County Sanel Valley Vineyard 1993 • $13 • (11/30/1997) • **80**

Cabernet Sauvignon Mendocino County Sanel Valley Vineyard 1985 • $18 • (9/30/1989) • **80**

Cabernet Sauvignon Mendocino County Sanel Valley Vineyard 1982 • $13 • (12/15/1987) • **83**

Cabernet Sauvignon Mendocino County Sanel Valley Vineyards Vino di Famiglia NV • $25 • (11/30/1996) • **86**

Chardonnay Anderson Valley Late Harvest Marguerite Vineyards 1993 • $15/375 ml. • (11/30/1996) • **80**

Echo Bells Echo Vineyard Mendocino County 1994 • $30 • (11/30/1997) • **83**

Zinfandel Mendocino County Sanel Valley Vineyard 1994 • $12 • (4/30/1997) • **89**

Zinfandel Mendocino County Sanel Valley Vineyard 1993 • $10 • (10/15/1995) • **85**

Zinfandel Mendocino County Sanel Valley Vineyard 1990 • $8 • (9/15/1994) • **85**

Zinfandel Mendocino County Sanel Valley Vineyard 1988 • $8 • (4/30/1991) • **85**

MILL CREEK | CALIFORNIA

Cabernet Sauvignon Sonoma County 1997: Trim and compact, with a range of sweet toasted oak and black cherry flavors, finishing in a tight clamp of tannins. Drink now through 2006.–J.L. • $17 • (10/15/1999) • **84**

Cabernet Sauvignon Sonoma County 1995 • $17 • (3/31/1998) • **83**

Cabernet Sauvignon Sonoma County 1994 • $15 • (11/15/1997) • **81**

Cabernet Sauvignon Dry Creek Valley 1993 • $12 • (11/30/1996) • **83**

Cabernet Sauvignon Dry Creek Valley 1992 • $12 • (12/15/1995) • **85**

Cabernet Sauvignon Dry Creek Valley 1991 • $12 • (11/15/1994) • **83**

Cabernet Sauvignon Dry Creek Valley 1990 • $12 • (11/15/1993) • **74**

Cabernet Sauvignon Dry Creek Valley 1988 • $12 • (11/15/1991) • **78**

Chardonnay Dry Creek Valley 1997: Flavorful and supple, with focused lemon, green apple, pear and toasted oak notes. Drink now.–H.S. • $14 • (4/30/1999) • **88**

Chardonnay Dry Creek Valley 1996 • $13 • (11/30/1997) • **85**

Merlot Dry Creek Valley 1996: Firm, featuring tightly wound red currant, herb and toasted oak flavors and finishing with firm, fine-grained tannins. Drink now through 2004.–J.L. • $18 • (9/15/1999) • **86**

Merlot Dry Creek Valley 1995 • $18 • (11/30/1997) • **85**

Merlot Dry Creek Valley 1994 • $14 • (8/31/1996) • **86**

Merlot Dry Creek Valley 1993 • $14 • (8/31/1996) • **84**

Key: SS—Spectator Selection CS—Cellar Selection HR—Highly Recommended $NA—Price Not Available a—Auction Price (BT)—Barrel Tasting For a key to the tasters' initials, see "How to Use These Listings."
Dates in parentheses indicate the issues in which the ratings were published.

Merlot Dry Creek Valley 1991 • $12 • (9/15/1994) • **83**

Merlot Dry Creek Valley 1990 • $14 • (10/15/1993) • **84**

Merlot Dry Creek Valley 1989 • $12 • (3/31/1993) • **82**

Merlot Dry Creek Valley 1988 • $12 • (5/31/1992) • **77**

Merlot Dry Creek Valley 1987 • $12 • (11/15/1991) • **84**

Sauvignon Blanc Dry Creek Valley 1998: Sweet vanilla flavors, but a bit cloying, with lead pencil and paste notes on the finish. Drink now.–J.L. • $10 • (5/31/2000) • **80**

Sauvignon Blanc Dry Creek Valley 1997: Fairly tight, this hints at citrus, melon and herb flavors while serving up fresh acidity. Finishes clean. Drink now. • $10 • (5/15/1999) • **82**

Zinfandel Dry Creek Valley 1997: Soft, ripe and medium-bodied, with smoky vanilla and chocolate notes and light cherry flavors. Drink now.–H.S. • $19 • (5/15/1999) • **87**

MILLBROOK | NEW YORK

Arneis Central Coast Mistral Vineyard 1996 • $12 • (12/31/1997) • **82**

Cabernet Franc Hudson River Region Proprietor's Special Reserve 1995 • $19 • (3/31/1998) • **82**

Cabernet Franc New York 1997: A good, solid red, with plum and currant flavors. Nicely concentrated, with tobaccolike notes on the fairly short finish. Drink now.–K.M. • $19 • (11/15/1999) • **84**

Cabernet Sauvignon Hudson River Region Proprietor's Special Reserve 1993 • $17 • (12/31/1995) • **85**

Cabernet Sauvignon New York 1995 • $NA • (8/31/1997) • **85**

Chardonnay Central Coast Mistral Vineyard 1996 • $13 • (11/15/1997) • **83**

Chardonnay Hudson River Region Proprietor's Special Reserve 1997: This big-boned white is lush and oaky, but the canned-fruit flavors are a bit dull. This was the better of two samples.–T.M. • $18 • (5/31/2000) • **79**

Chardonnay Hudson River Region Proprietor's Special Reserve 1996 • $19 • (3/31/1998) • **85**

Chardonnay New York 1996 • $13 • (3/31/1998) • **85**

Fernão Pires Central Coast Mistral Vineyard 1996 • $12 • (8/31/1997) • **72**

Fiano Central Coast Mistral Vineyard 1996 • $12 • (7/31/1997) • **77**

Gamay Noir Hudson River Region 1996 • $11 • (8/31/1997) • **77**

Hunt Country Rosé Hudson River Region NV • $9 • (12/31/1997) • **77**

Merlot Central Coast Mistral Vineyard 1996 • $14 • (3/31/1998) • **81**

Moscato Bianco Central Coast Mistral Vineyard 1996 • $16 • (11/15/1997) • **85**

Pinot Grigio Central Coast Mistral Vineyard 1996 • $13 • (12/31/1997) • **79**

Pinot Noir Central Coast Mistral Vineyard 1996 • $14 • (12/31/1997) • **79**

Pinot Noir Central Coast Mistral Vineyard 1993 • $9 • (11/15/1994) • **80**

Pinot Noir Hudson River Region Proprietor's Special Reserve 1997: This round red offers ripe plum flavors, with firm, balanced tannins and appealing spicy, toasty accents. Can match with hearty foods. Drink now through 2003.–T.M. • $21 • (5/31/2000) • **84**

Pinot Noir Hudson River Region Proprietor's Special Reserve 1995 • $19 • (3/31/1998) • **81**

Pinot Noir Hudson River Region Proprietor's Special Reserve 1993 • $17 • (9/15/1996) • **80**

Pinot Noir New York 1995 • $14 • (8/31/1997) • **79**

Pinot Noir New York 1994 • $12 • (9/15/1996) • **77**

Roussanne Central Coast Mistral Vineyard 1996 • $12 • (7/31/1997) • **78**

Tocai Friulano Hudson River Region 1996 • $12 • (11/15/1997) • **83**

Verdelho Central Coast Mistral Vineyard 1996 • $12 • (7/31/1997) • **83**

Vernaccia Central Coast Mistral Vineyard 1996 • $NA • (11/15/1997) • **84**

MILLENNIUM | WASHINGTON

Columbia Valley 1995: Minty, minerally flavors weave through this lean red, centering around a core of pretty currant and berry. Tannins are firm but fine enough to drink now with food. Produced by Columbia Wine & Spirits. Drink now through 2002.–H.S. • $70 • (6/15/1999) • **87**

MILLSTREAM | CALIFORNIA

Cabernet Sauvignon California 1993 • $6 • (12/15/1995) • **84**

MILONE | CALIFORNIA

Viognier Sonoma County Slusser Vineyard 1997: Earthy aromas are followed by peach, lemon and mineral notes. Clean and dry on the slightly short finish. Drink now. • $18 • (12/31/1998) • **84**

MINER | CALIFORNIA

Cabernet Sauvignon Oakville 1997: Solid, with chunky coffee, toffee and oak flavors leading to a core of earthy currant, anise, mineral and sage, turning dry and austere. Needs time. Best from 2002 through 2010.–J.L. • $60 • (5/31/2000) • **89**

Cabernet Sauvignon Napa Valley Oakville 1996: Ripe and well oaked. Firm, chewy tannins are wrapped around the cedary, spicy wood flavors, with layers of ripe cherry, earth, currant, dusty berry and coffee. Cellar short-term. Best from 2001 through 2007.–J.L. • $50 • (7/31/1999) • **93**

Chardonnay Napa Valley 1998: Tries to rev up the flavors but can't. Offers simple but pleasant ripe pear, citrus and light oak, turning slightly bitter. Drink now.–J.L. • $28 • (5/31/2000) • **85**

Chardonnay Napa Valley 1997: Ripe, smooth and polished, with a wonderful band of smoky, toasty oak, ripe pear, fig, hazelnut and spice, turning sleek and elegant as it unveils hints of fruit and citrus, this delicious new Chardonnay is a welcome addition to California's repertoire. Drink now through 2002.–J.L. • $26 • (5/31/1999) HR • **94**

Chardonnay Napa Valley Oakville Ranch 1998: Rich, with spicy pear, apple, fig and melon notes. Has a pithy edge. Drink now.–J.L. • $35 • (6/15/2000) • **84**

Chardonnay Napa Valley Oakville Ranch 1997: A bold, ripe, luxurious style, brimming with ripe, juicy flavors and lots of pear, fig, anise, melon and nutmeg notes, all blending together beautifully, turning rich and complex. Drink now through 2003.–J.L. • $35 • (5/31/1999) • **93**

Chardonnay Napa Valley Wild Yeast 1998: Focused on buttery fig and lemon custard flavors, it's smooth and polished, finishing with a lemony edge. Drink now through 2003.–J.L. • $45 • (6/15/2000) • **87**

Chardonnay Napa Valley Wild Yeast 1997: Elegant, with a pretty band of spice, citrus, pear and hazelnut; there's a touch of coarseness to the texture, but nothing a little cellaring won't resolve. Try now through 2002.–J.L. • $45 • (5/31/1999) • **93**

Merlot Napa Valley Oakville Ranch 1996: Dark and immense, with leathery tannins, mineral and chewy currant flavors; a wine that needs short-term cellaring. Drink through 2005.–J.L. • $26 Ⓐ • (8/31/1999) • **88**

Pinot Noir Monterey County Pisoni Vineyard 1998: Has appealing cola and wild berry flavors, with a touch of oak and herb. Finishes soft and fleshy. Drink now through 2005.–J.L. • $50 • (5/15/2000) • **85**

Pinot Noir Monterey County Pisoni Vineyard 1997: Earthy, with a leathery edge to the cherry, plum and berry flavors. Needs a little time to round out the edges. Drink through 2005.–J.L. • $45 • (9/15/1999) • **87**

Sauvignon Blanc Napa Valley 1998: Ripe and lively, with delicious melon, citrus and herb flavors and a lingering, spicy finish. Drink now through 2002.–H.S. • $14 • (1/31/2000) • **87**

Viognier California 1997: Combines rich, earthy, creamy pear, fig and citrus, finishing with a slight bitter edge. Drink through 2004.–J.L. • $18 • (11/30/1999) • **86**

Zinfandel Napa Valley 1998: Smells and tastes beefy, with a spicy, salty edge to the modest Zinfandel flavors. Drink now.–J.L. • $22 • (5/31/2000) • **83**

Zinfandel Napa Valley 1997: Dry, tannic and candied, with strong oak flavors. Lacks concentration. Drink now.–J.L. • $12 Ⓐ • (5/15/2000) • **80**

MIRABELLE | CALIFORNIA

Brut North Coast NV: Opens up with pretty floral notes and light toast. The follow-through sports a bitter edge, albeit with hazelnut, pear and apple flavors. Drink now. • $14 • (11/30/1998) • **84**

MIRASSOU | CALIFORNIA

Blanc de Noirs Monterey Fifth Generation Cuvée 1991 • $14 • (12/31/1993) • **80**

Brut Monterey Fifth Generation Cuvée 1991 • $12 • (12/31/1995) • **84**

Brut Monterey Fifth Generation Cuvée 1990 • $12 • (7/31/1993) • **83**

Cabernet Sauvignon California Family Selection 1996: An herbal blend of cherry, anise and vegetal flavors. Fairly austere, the wine is lean and tight. • $12 • (11/15/1998) • **76**

Cabernet Sauvignon Central Coast Family Selection 1997: Soft, juicy and approachable, featuring plum, cola and herb notes and finishing with mild tannins. Drink now through 2003.–J.L. • $13 • (9/15/1999) • **84**

Cabernet Sauvignon Monterey County 1993 • $12 • (7/31/1997) • **83**

Cabernet Sauvignon Monterey County 1992 • $11 • (12/15/1996) • **85**

Cabernet Sauvignon Monterey County Fifth Generation Family Selection 1991 • $9 • (12/15/1995) • **74**

Cabernet Sauvignon Monterey County Fifth Generation Family Selection 1990 • $9 • (9/15/1993) • **81**

Cabernet Sauvignon Monterey County Fifth Generation Harvest Reserve 1991 • $12 • (12/15/1995) • **87**

Cabernet Sauvignon Monterey County Fifth Generation Harvest Reserve Limited Bottling 1990 • $12 • (11/15/1993) • **79**

Cabernet Sauvignon Monterey County Harvest Reserve 1992 • $15 • (11/15/1996) • **88**

Cabernet Sauvignon Monterey County Harvest Reserve 1988 • $13 • (11/15/1992) • **76**

Cabernet Sauvignon Monterey County Harvest Reserve 1987 • $13 • (11/15/1991) • **86**

Cabernet Sauvignon Monterey County Harvest Reserve 1986 • $13 • (7/31/1991) • **60**

Cabernet Sauvignon Monterey County Limited Bottling 1988: Well balanced, appealing if you like your Cabernet on the herbal, weedy side, though hints of plum and berry peek through. Dry, tannic finish. (1988 California Cabernet retrospective tasting). Drink now.–J.L. • $12 • (11/15/1998) • **80**

Cabernet Sauvignon Napa Valley Harvest Reserve 1995: Medium-weight, with ripe, spicy Cabernet flavors that echo plum and wild berry. Finishes with mild, integrated tannins. Drink now through 2003.–J.L. • $18 • (10/31/1998) • **86**

Cabernet Sauvignon Napa Valley Harvest Reserve 1985 • $12 • (11/15/1989) • **81**

Cabernet Sauvignon Napa Valley Harvest Reserve 1983 • $12 • (12/15/1986) • **67**

Cabernet Sauvignon Napa Valley Harvest Reserve 1982 • $12 • (4/16/1986) • **82**

Cabernet Sauvignon Napa Valley Harvest Reserve Limited Bottling 1994 • $18 • (5/15/1997) • **85**

Cabernet Sauvignon Stags Leap District Showcase Selection Harvest Reserve 1994 • $30 • (6/15/1998) • **80**

Chardonnay Monterey County Family Selection 1997: Clean and straightforward, with pleasant apple and citrus notes. Drink now.–J.L. • $12 • (12/31/1998) • **83**

Chardonnay Monterey County Family Selection 1996 • $12 • (12/31/1997) • **88**

Chardonnay Monterey County Harvest Reserve 1997: Tart, holding a tight beam of flavor, with citrus, green apple and pear notes that are elegant and refined. Drink now.–J.L. • $16 • (2/28/1999) • **87**

Chardonnay Monterey County Harvest Reserve 1996 • $16 • (5/15/1998) • **89**

Chardonnay Monterey County San Vicente Ranch Harvest Reserve 1997: Elegant and focused, with creamy citrus, fig, pear and complex toast flavors. Clean and refreshing, with pretty fruit and toast notes on the finish. Drink now.–J.L. • $22 • (7/31/1999) • **90**

Chardonnay Monterey County Showcase Selection Harvest Reserve 1997: Bold, ripe, rich and creamy, with layers of fig, nectarine, pear, melon and tropical fruit flavors that are complex and concentrated. Drink now through 2002.–J.L. • $29 • (5/15/1999) • **91**

Chardonnay Monterey County Showcase Selection Harvest Reserve 1996 • $28 • (6/30/1998) • **91**

Johannisberg Riesling Monterey Fifth Generation Select Harvest Reserve 1992 • $13 • (4/15/1994) • **85**

Merlot California Family Selection 1996: Shows coffee, mocha and tea flavors threaded with plum and cherry notes. Drink now.–J.L. • $13 • (2/28/1999) • **82**

Merlot Central Coast Family Selection 1991 • $10 • (6/15/1993) • **80**

Merlot Central Coast Fifth Generation Family Selection 1992 • $9 • (4/15/1995) • **84**

Merlot Central Coast Fifth Generation Family Selection 1991 • $9 • (9/15/1994) • **84**

Merlot Monterey County Family Selection 1990 • $10 • (3/31/1993) • **80**

Merlot Monterey County Harvest Reserve 1996: Crisp and firm, with a tight core of earthy black cherry and green bean flavors. Remains firm on the finish. Drink now through 2002.–J.L. • $18 • (10/15/1999) • **82**

Merlot Monterey County Harvest Reserve 1995: Lean and fleshy, with a stalky edge to the herb and berry notes. A solid effort that's ready now. Drink through 2002.–J.L. • $18 • (10/15/1998) • **83**

Merlot Monterey County Harvest Reserve Limited Bottling 1994 • $18 • (7/31/1997) • **85**

Petite Sirah Monterey County Family Selection 1996: Deeply colored, with juicy black fruit and mineral flavors, finishing with soft tannins and an herbal note. Drink now.–J.L. • $12 • (2/28/1999) • **86**

Petite Sirah Monterey County Family Selection 1989 • $8 • (3/15/1992) • **79**

Petite Sirah Monterey County Family Selection Commemorative Bottling 1990 • $9 • (3/31/1993) • **75**

Petite Sirah Monterey County Fifth Generation Family Selection 1993 • $11 • (11/30/1996) • **86**

Petite Sirah Monterey County Fifth Generation Family Selection 1991 • $9 • (2/28/1995) • **81**
Pinot Blanc Monterey County White Burgundy 1996 • $11 • (5/15/1998) • **82**
Pinot Blanc Monterey County White Burgundy Family Selection 1997: Quite minerallike on the nose. Lean yet very refreshing, leading off with lime and other citrus flavors. The finish is moderate and clean. Drink now. • $11 • (6/15/1999) • **86**
Pinot Noir Central Coast Family Selection 1995 • $11 • (12/15/1997) • **85**
Pinot Noir Monterey County 1994 • $11 • (1/31/1997) • **77**
Pinot Noir Monterey County 1990 • $8 • (9/30/1992) • **72**
Pinot Noir Monterey County Family Selection 1997: Light, almost dilute, with soft, sweet-tasting fruit notes and an earthy profile that lingers on the finish. Drink now.–J.L. • $12 • (4/30/2000) • **83**
Pinot Noir Monterey County Family Selection 1996: A light style of Pinot, with bright cherry and herb notes and hints of smoke and earth. Drink now. • $11 • (12/31/1998) • **82**
Pinot Noir Monterey County Family Selection 1990 • $8 • (2/28/1993) • **75**
Pinot Noir Monterey County Family Selection 1988 • $8 • (4/30/1991) • **81**
Pinot Noir Monterey County Fifth Generation Family Selection 1993 • $9 • (11/30/1996) • **84**
Pinot Noir Monterey County Fifth Generation Family Selection 1992 • $7 • (12/31/1995) • **80**
Pinot Noir Monterey County Fifth Generation Harvest Reserve 1993 • $15 • (9/15/1996) • **82**
Pinot Noir Monterey County Fifth Generation Harvest Reserve 1992 • $12 • (10/15/1995) • **86**
Pinot Noir Monterey County Fifth Generation Harvest Reserve Limited 1991 • $12 • (3/31/1995) • **83**
Pinot Noir Monterey County Harvest Reserve 1996: Serves up a modest band of spicy cherry and berry-laced flavors before the dry, tealike tannins fold in. Drink now.–J.L. • $16 • (9/30/1998) • **82**
Pinot Noir Monterey County Harvest Reserve 1995 • $16 • (2/28/1998) • **85**
Pinot Noir Monterey County Harvest Reserve 1989 • $13 • (9/30/1992) • **80**
Pinot Noir Monterey County Harvest Reserve 1988 • $13 • (4/30/1992) • **84**
Pinot Noir Monterey County Harvest Reserve 1986 • $12 • (4/30/1991) • **78**
Pinot Noir Monterey County Harvest Reserve Limited Bottling 1997: Charry oak notes mingle with spicy cherry flavors on a light frame. Drink now through 2003.–J.L. • $18 • (4/30/2000) • **82**
Pinot Noir Monterey County Harvest Reserve Limited Bottling 1994 • $16 • (1/31/1997) • **84**
Pinot Noir Monterey County Showcase Selection Harvest Reserve 1997: Pleasantly balanced, with ripe stewed plum and berry notes of modest depth and proportion. Drink now through 2005.–J.L. • $30 • (4/30/2000) • **84**
Zinfandel California 1989 • $5 • (4/30/1993) • **72**
Zinfandel California Dry Red Lot No. 3 NV • $5 • (7/31/1991) • **73**
Zinfandel California Lot No. 4 NV • $6 • (7/31/1991) • **81**
Zinfandel California Lot No. 6 NV • $6 • (9/15/1992) • **73**
Zinfandel Central Coast Fifth Generation Family Selection 1992 • $7 • (8/31/1995) • **83**
Zinfandel Santa Clara Valley Fifth Generation Harvest Reserve 1992 • $12 • (10/15/1995) • **83**
Zinfandel Santa Clara Valley Fifth Generation Harvest Reserve Limited Bottling 1991 • $12 • (10/15/1994) • **79**
Zinfandel Santa Clara Valley Harvest Reserve 1995 • $16 • (6/15/1998) • **82**
Zinfandel Santa Clara Valley Harvest Reserve 1990 • $13 • (3/15/1993) • **82**
Zinfandel Santa Clara Valley Harvest Reserve 1988 • $13 • (10/15/1992) • **85**

MISSION MOUNTAIN | WASHINGTON

Cabernet Sauvignon Columbia Valley 1994: Earthy flavors, with coffee and medicinal notes overpowering the fruit.–H.S. • $16 • (8/31/1998) • **70**
Cabernet Sauvignon Columbia Valley 1990 • $15 • (3/31/1995) • **79**
Merlot Columbia Valley Reserve 1995 • $25 • (1/31/1998) • **85**
Muscat Canelli Columbia Valley 1997: Light and sweet, a simple dessert wine with pretty apple and peach flavors. Drink now.–H.S. • $9 • (9/15/1998) • **82**

MISSION VIEW | CALIFORNIA

Cabernet Sauvignon Paso Robles 1994 • $13 • (11/30/1996) • **84**
Cabernet Sauvignon Paso Robles 1993 • $13 • (11/30/1996) • **79**
Cabernet Sauvignon Paso Robles 1990 • $12 • (11/15/1994) • **82**
Cabernet Sauvignon Paso Robles 1989 • $12 • (11/15/1992) • **85**
Cabernet Sauvignon Paso Robles 1988 • $12 • (11/15/1992) • **86**
Cabernet Sauvignon Paso Robles 1986 • $12 • (12/15/1989) • **72**
Classic Cuvee Paso Robles 1993 • $18 • (11/30/1996) • **84**
Merlot Paso Robles Limited Release 1992 • $14 • (6/15/1995) • **76**
Merlot Paso Robles Midnight Mischievous 1996: Simple, with decent cherry and herb notes. Finishes on the lean side. Drink now.–J.L. • $15 • (9/30/1998) • **79**
Pinot Noir Monterey County Limited Release 1990 • $14 • (2/28/1993) • **77**
Zinfandel Paso Robles 1993 • $12 • (1/01/1995) • **85**
Zinfandel Paso Robles 1990 • $11 • (9/30/1993) • **81**

MITCHELL, CHARLES B. | CALIFORNIA

Cabernet Sauvignon El Dorado 1994 • $12 • (11/30/1996) • **79**
Cabernet Sauvignon El Dorado 1993 • $10 • (11/30/1996) • **82**
Cabernet Sauvignon El Dorado Grand Reserve 1995 • $28 • (11/30/1997) • **86**
Cabernet Sauvignon El Dorado Reserve 1995 • $16 • (10/31/1997) • **82**
Cabernet Sauvignon El Dorado Reserve 1993 • $14 • (12/15/1995) • **80**
Cabernet Sauvignon El Dorado Vintner's Cuvée 1996: Licorice and black currant seem to dominate here. Finishes a bit short, with a blast of tannin that may subside with time. Drink through 2005. • $12 • (10/15/1998) • **83**
Cabernet Sauvignon El Dorado Vintner's Cuvée 1995 • $11 • (10/31/1997) • **85**
Merlot El Dorado Reserve 1996: Simple, with lots of charred oak flavor and little else. Drink now.–J.L. • $14 • (9/30/1998) • **76**
Port California NV • $15/500 ml. • (6/15/1996) • **83**
Sauvignon Blanc Napa Valley 1997: Fairly smooth, serving up melon and citrus flavors. It's pleasant, offering subtle herb notes on the moderate finish. Drink now. • $10 • (6/15/1999) • **84**
Sauvignon Blanc Sierra Foothills 1996 • $8 • (7/31/1997) • **87**
Sauvignon Blanc-Sémillon El Dorado Euphoria 1996 • $11 • (5/31/1998) • **80**
Vintage Cuvée Grand Reserve El Dorado 1996: Has an almost candylike cherry flavor and herbal overtones. Texture is somewhat coarse. • $30 • (10/15/1998) • **78**
Zinfandel El Dorado Old Vines 1998: Dilute, with cherry, cola and earth notes. Drink now.–J.L. • $17 • (5/31/2000) • **81**
Zinfandel El Dorado Special Selection 1996 • $15 • (6/15/1998) • **85**
Zinfandel El Dorado Vintners' Cuvee 1996 • $10 • (6/15/1998) • **76**
Zinfandel Sierra Foothills Special Selection 1995 • $14 • (7/31/1997) • **82**

MIURA | CALIFORNIA

Chardonnay Arroyo Grande Valley 1997: Flinty, focused on the crisp pear, apple and melon flavors, picking up subtle cedary oak notes and turning elegant and polished. Drink now through 2004.–J.L. • $44 • (10/15/1999) • **91**

MONDAVI, CK | CALIFORNIA

Cabernet Sauvignon California 1996 • $7 • (5/15/1998) • **75**
Cabernet Sauvignon California 1995 • $7 • (5/15/1997) • **84**
Cabernet Sauvignon California 1994 • $6 • (11/30/1996) • **79**
Cabernet Sauvignon California 1993 • $7 • (12/15/1995) • **80**
Chardonnay California 1997 • $7 • (6/30/1998) • **78**
Merlot California 1996: Simple and awkward, with tea and candied cherry flavors that fade on the dry finish. Drink now.–J.L. • $7 • (9/30/1998) • **77**
Merlot California 1995 • $8 • (5/15/1997) • **80**
Sauvignon Blanc California 1997 • $6 • (5/31/1998) • **81**
Zinfandel California 1996 • $7 • (6/15/1998) • **72**
Zinfandel California 1992 • $5 • (10/15/1994) • **81**
Zinfandel California 1991 • $5 • (10/15/1994) • **79**

MONDAVI, ROBERT | CALIFORNIA

Cabernet Sauvignon Napa Valley Vineyard 1998: Ripe, with juicy, complex cherry, berry, plum and anise flavors, showing fine depth and detailed tannins.–J.L. • $NA • (8/31/1999) (BT) • **90-94**
Cabernet Sauvignon Napa Valley 1997: Chunky and firmly tannic, but it packs in lots of ripe, chewy Cabernet character, with currant, anise, cedar and berry. Tightens on the finish. Best from 2001 through 2008.–J.L. • $29 • (6/30/2000) • **89**
Cabernet Sauvignon Napa Valley 1996: Wonderfully supple texture and great purity of fruit, with polished cherry, berry, sage, anise and leather notes that stay tightly focused and linger on the finish. Drink through 2006.–J.L. • $26 • (9/15/1999) • **89**

Key: SS—Spectator Selection CS—Cellar Selection HR—Highly Recommended $NA—Price Not Available a—Auction Price (BT)—Barrel Tasting
For a key to the tasters' initials, see "How to Use These Listings."
Dates in parentheses indicate the issues in which the ratings were published.

Cabernet Sauvignon Napa Valley 1995: A dense, well-oaked style, with plenty of anise, currant, chocolate, cedar and berry flavors to sustain it. Turns complex and supple on the finish, though it has the tannic strengh to cellar short-term. Drink now through 2004.–J.L. • $22 • (8/31/1998) SS • **90**
Cabernet Sauvignon Napa Valley 1994 • $22 • (11/15/1997) • **90**
Cabernet Sauvignon Napa Valley 1993 • $20 • (11/15/1996) • **88**
Cabernet Sauvignon Napa Valley 1990 • $62 Ⓐ • (10/31/1993) SS • **90**
Cabernet Sauvignon Napa Valley 1989: Mature and dry, with complex earth, herb, mint and spicy currant, it turns austere and tannic. (1989 California Cabernet retrospective tasting). Past its prime.–J.L. • $26 Ⓐ • (8/31/1999) • **84**
Cabernet Sauvignon Napa Valley 1988: Solid but fading. The currant, mint, spice and berry notes turn dry, and the tannins stick out on the finish, leaving a dry aftertaste. (1988 California Cabernet retrospective tasting). Drink now.–J.L. • $17 • (11/15/1998) • **85**
Cabernet Sauvignon Napa Valley 1987 • $20 • (12/15/1997) • **90**
Cabernet Sauvignon Napa Valley 1986 • $38 Ⓐ • (7/31/1989) • **93**
Cabernet Sauvignon Napa Valley 1985 • $30 Ⓐ • (12/15/1988) SS • **94**
Cabernet Sauvignon Napa Valley 1984 • $22 Ⓐ • (12/31/1987) • **80**
Cabernet Sauvignon Napa Valley 1983 • $26 • (4/15/1987) • **94**
Cabernet Sauvignon Napa Valley 1982 • $26 Ⓐ • (7/01/1985) • **90**
Cabernet Sauvignon Napa Valley 1981 • $27 • (12/16/1984) • **90**
Cabernet Sauvignon Napa Valley 1979: Fading, with simple dried cherry, mint, anise and spicy notes, turning dry. (1979 California Cabernet retrospective tasting). Drink now.–J.L. • $12 • (8/31/1999) • **84**
Cabernet Sauvignon Napa Valley 1978: Clearly on the downside, with oxidized flavors, it can still be enjoyed—just decant prior to drinking. Gives hints of dried cherry and plum, dashes of anise and sage. Drink up. (1978 California Cabernet retrospective tasting).–J.L. • $34 Ⓐ • (11/15/1998) • **82**
Cabernet Sauvignon Napa Valley 1977 • $NA • (7/16/1985) • **89**
Cabernet Sauvignon Napa Valley 1976 • $10 Ⓐ • (7/16/1985) • **84**
Cabernet Sauvignon Napa Valley 1975 • $18 Ⓐ • (11/30/1991) • **85**
Cabernet Sauvignon Napa Valley 1974 • $36 Ⓐ • (2/15/1990) • **85**
Cabernet Sauvignon Napa Valley 1973 • $NA • (7/16/1985) • **86**
Cabernet Sauvignon Napa Valley 1971 • $29 Ⓐ • (7/16/1985) • **87**
Cabernet Sauvignon Napa Valley 1970 • $58 Ⓐ • (11/30/1991) • **92**
Cabernet Sauvignon Napa Valley 1969 • $24 Ⓐ • (11/30/1991) • **91**
Cabernet Sauvignon Napa Valley 1968 • $81 • (11/30/1991) • **88**
Cabernet Sauvignon Napa Valley 1967 • $21 Ⓐ • (11/30/1991) • **79**
Cabernet Sauvignon Napa Valley 1966 • $110 • (11/30/1991) • **88**
Cabernet Sauvignon Napa Valley 30th Anniversary 1996: Weaves together a complex array of currant, earth, cedar, leather and anise, gaining richness and polish on the finish, turning firm and tannic. Sold only at the winery. Drink now through 2006.–J.L. • $150 • (6/30/2000) • **90**
Cabernet Sauvignon Napa Valley Oakville District 1994 • $28 • (6/30/1997) • **88**
Cabernet Sauvignon Napa Valley Oakville District 1993 • $28 • (11/15/1996) • **88**
Cabernet Sauvignon Napa Valley Oakville District 1992 • $28 • (12/15/1995) • **91**
Cabernet Sauvignon Napa Valley Reserve 1998: Elegant and refined, with detailed tannins giving structure to the core of earthy currant, spice and berryish flavors. Finishes with pretty oak nuances.–J.L. • $NA • (8/31/1999) (BT) • **90-94**
Cabernet Sauvignon Napa Valley Reserve 1997: A touch earthy and leathery, it quickly works its way into more complex and sophisticated flavors. Well integrated, supple in texture, actually quite elegant.–J.L. • $NA • (8/31/1998) (BT) • **90-94**
Cabernet Sauvignon Napa Valley Reserve 1996: Rich and complex yet restrained in style, with pretty coffee, currant, black cherry, spice and anise flavors that fan out nicely, this California Cabernet turns particularly elegant and polished on the long finish. Drink now through 2007.–J.L. • $72 Ⓐ • (11/15/1999) HR • **95**
Cabernet Sauvignon Napa Valley Reserve 1995: Ripe, dark, dense and earthy, with a rich core of currant, mineral and spice. Shows off pretty, toasty, spicy oak, too, all the while maintaining a tremendous sense of elegance and finesse. Best from 2002 through 2010.–J.L. • $61 Ⓐ • (7/31/1998) • **94**
Cabernet Sauvignon Napa Valley Reserve 1994 • $81 Ⓐ • (7/31/1997) CS • **94**
Cabernet Sauvignon Napa Valley Reserve 1993 • $54 Ⓐ • (11/30/1996) CS • **90**
Cabernet Sauvignon Napa Valley Reserve 1992 • $58 Ⓐ • (7/31/1995) CS • **91**
Cabernet Sauvignon Napa Valley Reserve 1991 • $77 Ⓐ • (11/15/1994) • **90**
Cabernet Sauvignon Napa Valley Reserve 1990 • $67 Ⓐ • (10/31/1993) HR • **91**
Cabernet Sauvignon Napa Valley Reserve 1989: With complex aromas and similarly complex cedar, currant, earth and mushroom flavors, it's very good, well balanced, dry and tannic, coming up a bit short on depth of flavor. Can age further, though the risk is the fruit will diminish. (1989 California Cabernet retrospective tasting). Drink now through 2004.–J.L. • $36 Ⓐ • (8/31/1999) • **87**
Cabernet Sauvignon Napa Valley Reserve 1988: Chunky, firmly tannic but well focused for the vintage, with earthy, leathery currant, cedar, mint and spice. Turns dry and tannic on the finish. (1988 California Cabernet retrospective tasting). Drink now through 2002.–J.L. • $41 Ⓐ • (11/15/1998) • **88**
Cabernet Sauvignon Napa Valley Reserve 1987 • $118 Ⓐ • (12/15/1997) • **93**
Cabernet Sauvignon Napa Valley Reserve 1986 • $64 Ⓐ • (12/15/1996) • **89**
Cabernet Sauvignon Napa Valley Reserve 1985 • $75 Ⓐ • (11/30/1991) • **94**
Cabernet Sauvignon Napa Valley Reserve 1984 • $55 Ⓐ • (11/30/1991) • **90**
Cabernet Sauvignon Napa Valley Reserve 1983 • $31 Ⓐ • (11/30/1991) • **82**
Cabernet Sauvignon Napa Valley Reserve 1982 • $41 Ⓐ • (11/30/1991) • **82**
Cabernet Sauvignon Napa Valley Reserve 1981 • $41 Ⓐ • (11/30/1991) • **85**
Cabernet Sauvignon Napa Valley Reserve 1980 • $53 Ⓐ • (11/30/1991) • **86**
Cabernet Sauvignon Napa Valley Reserve 1979: Mature and complex, with supple, elegant cherry, currant, mint and coffee notes, holding its elegance and finesse on the finish. (1979 California Cabernet retrospective tasting). Drink now through 2005.–J.L. • $58 Ⓐ • (8/31/1999) • **90**
Cabernet Sauvignon Napa Valley Reserve 1978 • $73 Ⓐ • (11/15/1992) • **91**
Cabernet Sauvignon Napa Valley Reserve 1977 • $42 Ⓐ • (11/30/1991) • **89**
Cabernet Sauvignon Napa Valley Reserve 1976 • $31 Ⓐ • (11/30/1991) • **84**
Cabernet Sauvignon Napa Valley Reserve 1975 • $50 Ⓐ • (7/16/1985) • **89**
Cabernet Sauvignon Napa Valley Reserve 1974 • $94 Ⓐ • (11/15/1994) • **87**
Cabernet Sauvignon Napa Valley Reserve 1973 • $46 Ⓐ • (11/30/1991) • **92**
Cabernet Sauvignon Napa Valley Reserve 1972 • $NA • (11/30/1991) • **78**
Cabernet Sauvignon Napa Valley Reserve 1971 • $125 • (11/30/1991) • **91**
Cabernet Sauvignon Napa Valley Unfiltered 1991 • $18 • (11/15/1994) SS • **90**
Cabernet Sauvignon Napa Valley Unfiltered 1970 • $46 Ⓐ • (7/16/1985) • **93**
Cabernet Sauvignon North Coast Coastal 1995 • $11 • (11/15/1997) • **85**
Cabernet Sauvignon North Coast Coastal 1994 • $11 • (12/31/1996) • **85**
Cabernet Sauvignon North Coast Coastal 1993 • $11 • (2/29/1996) • **85**
Cabernet Sauvignon North Coast Coastal 1991 • $11 • (9/30/1994) • **83**
Cabernet Sauvignon Oakville 1996: Firm, rich and supple, with a focused core of cherry, currant, anise, sage and cedar, and the oak in the background. The finish turns firm and mildly tannic. Drink through 2006.–J.L. • $45 • (9/15/1999) • **90**
Cabernet Sauvignon Stags Leap District 1996: Rich, earthy and complex, with mineral, sage, black cherry, olive and spice notes that turn supple and polished. Drink through 2008.–J.L. • $45 • (11/15/1999) • **90**
Chardonnay Carneros 1998: Mature-tasting, with ripe pear and apple flavors. Butter and peach nuances unfold through the finish. Drink now.–J.L. • $23 • (6/30/2000) • **86**
Chardonnay Carneros 1996: Flinty, with a compact range of pear, nectarine, anise and cedar flavors, it slowly unfolds to a spicy finish, but turns a bit astringent. Drink now through 2002.–J.L. • $23 • (4/30/1999) • **89**
Chardonnay Central Coast Coastal 1997: Citrus, apple and toast flavors here, turning crisp and leafy on the finish. Drink now.–J.L. • $10 • (12/15/1998) • **83**
Chardonnay Central Coast Coastal 1996 • $10 • (6/15/1998) • **84**
Chardonnay Napa Valley 1998: Crisp and clean, with tart, flinty citrus, pippin apple and light toasty oak shadings. Drink now.–J.L. • $20 • (6/15/2000) • **86**
Chardonnay Napa Valley 1997: Tight, crisp and a touch flinty, with mineral, citrus, pear and melon flavors. Finishes with light oak and attractive fruit. Drink now through 2001.–J.L. • $19 • (7/31/1999) • **88**
Chardonnay Napa Valley 1996: Ripe, rich and complex, with concentrated fruit flavors, lots of pretty spicy, toasty nuances and a core of rich pear, fig and melon. Lingering aftertaste. Drink now through 2002.–J.L. • $19 • (7/31/1998) • **90**
Chardonnay Napa Valley Reserve 1998: Offers enough fruit depth and purity to merit a very good rating, but the pear and citrus flavors are muted, even a touch flat on the finish. Disappointing knowing how great this wine can be. Drink now.–J.L. • $36 • (6/30/2000) • **87**
Chardonnay Napa Valley Reserve 1997: Fresh and snappy, with a citrusy edge to the ripe pear, melon, hazelnut and nutmeg, turning elegant and detailed. Drink now through 2003.–J.L. • $36 • (12/15/1999) • **91**
Chardonnay Napa Valley Reserve 1996: Ripe, with complex pear, fig and pineapple flavors that are smooth and polished, gaining nuance and elegance on the finish, where the flavors fan out. Drink now through 2002.–J.L. • $36 • (2/28/1999) • **92**
Fumé Blanc Napa Valley 1998: A short hit of tangerine and lime quickly fades. Drink now.–J.L. • $16 • (5/15/2000) • **82**
Fumé Blanc Napa Valley 1997: Bright and perky, with pretty grapefruit, melon and herb notes. The flavors blend nicely, yielding a refreshing and versatile wine that would be at home with any lighter-style cuisine. Drink now. • $13 • (5/15/1999) • **87**
Fumé Blanc Napa Valley 1996: Marked by hints of sweet pea, fig and melon, this has a bright, crisp and refreshing texture, finishes with a clean, lemony note. Drink now. • $12 • (8/31/1998) • **87**

MONDAVI, ROBERT

Fumé Blanc Napa Valley To-Kalon Vineyard I-Block 1998: Crisp, with lean citrus, onion skin and lime notes, turning tart. Drink now.–J.L. • $50 • (5/15/2000) • **82**

Fumé Blanc Napa Valley To-Kalon Vineyard Reserve 1997: Has nice subtle touches, with creamy oak overlaying the moderate range of herb, fig, sweet pea and hay notes. Drink now through 2003.–J.L. • $28 • (4/30/2000) • **86**

Fumé Blanc Napa Valley To-Kalon Vineyard Reserve 1996: Starts off with fresh herb and lemon-lime aromas. Well oaked, with fresh hay, fig and citrus flavors rounding off the ensemble, which is somewhat viscous at the end. Drink now. • $28 • (5/31/1999) • **86**

Johannisberg Riesling Central Coast Coastal 1996 • $9 • (3/31/1998) • **83**

Merlot Carneros 1996: Weaves together a supple, complex array of earthy currant, black cherry, herb, anise, tar and cedar, fanning out on the finish, revealing depth and nuance. Drink now through 2005.–J.L. • $35 • (9/15/1999) • **88**

Merlot Central Coast Coastal 1997: Good depth and weight, with ripe black cherry, herb and toasty oak notes. Well-integrated tannins. Nice wine for the price. Drink now.–J.L. • $11 • (11/30/1998) • **82**

Merlot Central Coast Coastal 1996 • $11 • (3/31/1998) • **84**

Merlot Napa Valley 1997: Minty, with pronounced currant and bay leaf flavors that are intense, if rustic and firmly tannic. Drink now through 2005.–J.L. • $24 • (6/30/2000) • **86**

Merlot Napa Valley 1995: Complex, with a spicy, minty dimension and supple plum, cherry and currant notes. Shows off more finesse and polish on the finish, where the flavors come together and fan out. Drink now through 2004.–J.L. • $22 • (9/30/1998) • **88**

Merlot Napa Valley 1994 • $22 • (4/30/1997) • **90**

Merlot Napa Valley 1993 • $19 • (5/31/1996) • **84**

Merlot Napa Valley 1992 • $19 • (8/31/1996) • **87**

Merlot Napa Valley 1991 • $21 • (6/15/1994) • **89**

Merlot Napa Valley 1990 • $21 • (3/31/1993) • **86**

Merlot Napa Valley 1989 • $21 • (5/31/1992) • **87**

Pinot Noir Carneros 1997: Smooth, ripe and juicy, with pretty black cherry, wild berry, herb, sage and spice, finishing with a complex interplay of flavors. Drink through 2006.–J.L. • $30 • (9/15/1999) • **88**

Pinot Noir Carneros 1996: Complex in flavor, with a range of herb, brown sugar and dried cherry, it turns austere, dry, and tannic, with a slight stemmy edge that's rather blunt. Try now through 2005.–J.L. • $26 • (8/31/1998) • **87**

Pinot Noir Carneros 1995 • $26 • (1/31/1998) • **87**

Pinot Noir Carneros 1994 • $26 • (12/31/1996) • **87**

Pinot Noir Carneros 1991 • $20 • (2/28/1994) • **83**

Pinot Noir Carneros Unfiltered 1992 • $24 • (3/31/1995) • **86**

Pinot Noir Central Coast Coastal 1997: Simple cherry flavors make for a pleasing quaff. Drink now. • $11 • (11/30/1998) • **81**

Pinot Noir Central Coast Coastal 1996 • $11 • (3/31/1998) • **84**

Pinot Noir Central Coast Coastal 1995 • $12 • (1/31/1997) • **84**

Pinot Noir Central Coast Coastal 1994 • $11 • (5/31/1996) • **82**

Pinot Noir Napa Valley 1997: Tightly strung, with a range of cherry, herb, spice and cedary oak. Needs a little time to soften and evolve. Drink through 2004.–J.L. • $19 • (9/15/1999) • **87**

Pinot Noir Napa Valley 1996: A touch earthy and leathery, but the texture is smooth and polished, and the hints of dried cherry and berry are appealing and, have some nuance. Finishes with mild tannins. Drink now through 2001.–J.L. • $19 • (9/15/1998) • **85**

Pinot Noir Napa Valley 1995 • $19 • (2/28/1998) • **85**

Pinot Noir Napa Valley 1994 • $17 • (1/31/1997) • **86**

Pinot Noir Napa Valley 1991 • $14 • (2/28/1994) • **85**

Pinot Noir Napa Valley 1990 • $18 • (3/31/1992) • **86**

Pinot Noir Napa Valley 1989 • $15 • (4/30/1991) • **86**

Pinot Noir Napa Valley 1988 • $13 • (2/15/1990) • **89**

Pinot Noir Napa Valley 1987 • $12 • (7/31/1989) • **88**

Pinot Noir Napa Valley 1985 • $11 • (6/15/1988) • **79**

Pinot Noir Napa Valley Carneros Unfiltered 1993 • $26 • (11/30/1995) • **89**

Pinot Noir Napa Valley Reserve 1997: Supple and elegant, with ripe plum, spice, anise, cedar and sage flavors fanning out, turning complex and refined. Drink through 2006.–J.L. • $50 • (9/15/1999) • **88**

Pinot Noir Napa Valley Reserve 1996: A successful '96 that strikes a nice balance between its moderately ripe, complex herb, cherry, berry and spicy flavors and its supple texture. Long, complex aftertaste. Drink now through 2002.–J.L. • $31 • (9/15/1998) • **87**

Pinot Noir Napa Valley Reserve 1995 • $31 • (8/31/1997) • **91**

Pinot Noir Napa Valley Reserve 1994 • $31 • (1/31/1997) • **89**

Pinot Noir Napa Valley Reserve 1993 • $30 • (5/31/1996) • **89**

Pinot Noir Napa Valley Reserve 1991 • $28 • (2/28/1994) • **89**

Pinot Noir Napa Valley Reserve 1990 • $30 • (3/31/1997) • **89**

Pinot Noir Napa Valley Reserve 1988 • $26 • (10/31/1990) • **82**

Pinot Noir Napa Valley Reserve 1986 • $22 • (3/31/1997) • **87**

Pinot Noir Napa Valley Reserve 1985 • $31 • (4/15/1989) SS • **92**

Pinot Noir Napa Valley Reserve 1983 • $25 • (11/15/1987) • **80**

Pinot Noir Napa Valley Reserve 1982 • $25 • (8/31/1986) • **78**

Pinot Noir Napa Valley Reserve 1981 • $17 • (8/31/1986) • **86**

Pinot Noir Napa Valley Reserve 1980 • $13 • (8/01/1984) • **81**

Pinot Noir Napa Valley Unfiltered 1993 • $16 • (9/15/1995) • **86**

Pinot Noir Napa Valley Unfiltered 1992 • $14 • (11/30/1994) • **84**

Pinot Noir Napa Valley Unfiltered Reserve 1992 • $29 • (3/31/1995) • **87**

Sauvignon Blanc North Coast Coastal 1997: Firm, bright and lemony, with herbal overtones, this tangy wine should go well with shellfish and other seafood. Drink now. • $9 • (6/15/1999) • **83**

Sauvignon Blanc North Coast Coastal 1996 • $9 • (4/30/1998) • **86**

Sauvignon Blanc Stags Leap District 1997: High-toned grapefruit flavors and zingy acidity mark this refreshing wine. The finish is long and clean, tasting of lemon and mineral. Drink now. • $18 • (9/30/1999) • **87**

Sauvignon Blanc Stags Leap District 1996: Although the texture is supple, the wine seems tangy and tart, with a tight, lemony edge. A brightly styled white that tacks a touch of honey onto its moderate finish. Drink now. • $18 • (4/30/1999) • **84**

Syrah Monterey County Coastal 1998: Serves up a wide range of flavors, from beefy to vegetal to ripe stewed plum, finishing with a smoky, gamy edge. Drink now through 2004.–J.L. • $15 • (6/15/2000) • **86**

Zinfandel Napa Valley 1997: Stylish in its presentation of ripe, rounded cherry, wild berry and plum fruit, though it lacks concentration, depth and extra facets. As such, it's ready now. Drink through 2006.–J.L. • $19 • (4/30/2000) • **87**

Zinfandel Napa Valley 1996 • $18 • (6/15/1998) • **87**

Zinfandel Napa Valley 1995 • $18 • (4/30/1997) SS • **92**

Zinfandel Napa Valley 1994 • $16 • (4/30/1996) • **91**

Zinfandel Napa Valley 1993 • $16 • (7/31/1995) • **86**

Zinfandel Napa Valley 1992 • $14 • (10/15/1994) SS • **92**

Zinfandel North Coast Coastal 1995 • $10 • (3/31/1998) • **85**

Zinfandel North Coast Coastal 1994 • $11 • (11/30/1996) • **82**

MONT ST. JOHN | CALIFORNIA

Cabernet Sauvignon Napa Valley 1987 • $14 • (11/15/1992) • **70**

Cabernet Sauvignon Napa Valley 1986 • $14 • (4/30/1991) • **87**

Cabernet Sauvignon Napa Valley 1983 • $15 • (7/31/1989) • **78**

Cabernet Sauvignon Napa Valley 1982 • $15 • (3/15/1989) • **82**

Cabernet Sauvignon Napa Valley Private Reserve 1980 • $12 • (5/16/1984) • **75**

Chardonnay Carneros 1996: Toasty oak and hazelnut lead the way, with a blend of citrus, tangerine and pear. Moderate finish. Drink now. • $15 • (7/31/1998) • **87**

Pinot Noir Carneros 1996: Pleasant ripe cherry, cola and tea flavors that don't quite come into focus. Softly textured, with a slightly hot finish. Drink through 2001.–J.L. • $16 • (8/31/1998) • **83**

Pinot Noir Carneros 1995 • $16 • (7/31/1997) • **86**

Pinot Noir Carneros 1993 • $15 • (12/31/1995) • **81**

Pinot Noir Carneros Madonna Estate 1997: Light, with sour cherry flavors and a strong green, herbal note that's a little overwhelming. Drink now.–J.L. • $18 • (4/30/2000) • **80**

Pinot Noir Napa Valley Carneros 1989 • $11 • (9/30/1992) • **85**

Pinot Noir Napa Valley Carneros 1988 • $14 • (4/30/1991) • **81**

Pinot Noir Napa Valley Carneros 1987 • $15 • (3/31/1990) • **76**

Pinot Noir Napa Valley Carneros 1985 • $15 • (10/15/1989) • **82**

Pinot Noir Napa Valley Carneros Madonna Vineyard 1985 • $11 • (6/15/1988) • **78**

MONTDOMAINE | VIRGINIA

Cabernet Franc Virginia 1993 • $12 • (4/30/1997) • **83**

Heritage Monticello 1988 • $14 • (2/29/1992) • **82**

Merlot Monticello Reserve 1987 • $15 • (2/29/1992) • **86**

Key: SS—Spectator Selection CS—Cellar Selection HR—Highly Recommended $NA—Price Not Available a—Auction Price (BT)—Barrel Tasting
For a key to the tasters' initials, see "How to Use These Listings."
Dates in parentheses indicate the issues in which the ratings were published.

MONTE CARASSO | CALIFORNIA

Sangiovese Napa Valley 1994 • $17 • (2/29/1996) • **84**

MONTE VOLPE | CALIFORNIA

Arneis Mendocino 1997: Quite tart. This lemony blend has pucker-power and could use a serious dose of seafood. Drink now. • $13 • (6/15/1999) • **80**
Barbera California 1995 • $14 • (5/15/1998) • **87**
Barbera California 1994 • $14 • (2/28/1997) • **85**
Barbera California 1992 • $9 • (11/15/1995) • **82**
Barbera Mendocino 1991 • $8 • (3/31/1993) • **87**
Dolcetto Mendocino 1996 • $20 • (6/30/1998) • **84**
Dolcetto Mendocino 1995 • $16 • (5/15/1997) • **85**
Nebbiolo Mendocino 1994 • $16 • (5/15/1997) • **85**
Nebbiolo Mendocino 1993 • $14 • (11/30/1996) • **84**
Peppolino Mendocino 1992 • $14 • (10/15/1995) • **85**
Pinot Bianco Mendocino 1997: Quite fruity, with tangerine, lemon-lime and applelike flavors. Viscous yet very bright, it's a fine quaffer. Drink now. • $12 • (1/31/1999) • **86**
Pinot Bianco Mendocino 1996 • $13 • (5/15/1998) • **81**
Pinot Grigio Mendocino 1997: Sweetness and tart acidity seem at odds and leave an unbalanced impression. Apple and peach flavors are pleasant enough, however. • $14 • (6/15/1999) • **79**
Sangiovese Mendocino 1997: Simple, with fruity black cherry and plummy flavors, turning a little green and crisp with hints of tobacco and oak. Drink now through 2002.–J.L. • $16 • (5/15/2000) • **85**
Sangiovese Mendocino 1995 • $16 • (4/30/1997) • **85**
Sangiovese Mendocino 1994 • $16 • (2/28/1997) • **84**
Sangiovese Mendocino 1992 • $14 • (9/30/1994) • **86**
Sangiovese Mendocino Riserva 1996: Pretty. A light-bodied wine that explores mint, tobacco, sour cherry and spice flavors, with a slightly drying finish. Drink now through 2003.–J.L. • $25 • (4/30/2000) • **83**
Sangiovese Mendocino Riserva 1995: Fairly lean, with subtle cherry and herb notes. The acidity is bright and the tannins are slightly drying. Could use a good bistecca to flesh it out. Drink now through 2002. • $25 • (3/31/1999) • **83**

MONTEREY PENINSULA | CALIFORNIA

Cabernet Sauvignon Monterey County 1991 • $12 • (12/15/1995) • **80**
Cabernet Sauvignon Monterey County 1986 • $10 • (11/15/1994) • **84**
Cabernet Sauvignon Monterey County 1985 • $12 • (11/15/1992) • **82**
Cabernet Sauvignon Monterey County 1982 • $11 • (3/31/1987) • **74**
Cabernet Sauvignon Monterey County Doctors' Reserve 1986 • $18 • (11/15/1994) • **86**
Cabernet Sauvignon Monterey County Doctors' Reserve 1985 • $25 • (11/15/1992) • **76**
Cabernet Sauvignon Monterey Doctors' Reserve 1984 • $18 • (11/15/1992) • **78**
Cabernet Sauvignon Monterey Doctors' Reserve Lot II 1982 • $14 • (6/15/1987) • **83**
Chardonnay Central Coast 1996 • $13 • (1/31/1998) • **86**
Pinot Noir Monterey County Sleepy Hollow Vineyard 1997: Medium in weight, with red currant, herb and cola flavors, but the finish is cut short by dryness. Drink now.–J.L. • $18 • (6/15/1999) • **83**
Pinot Noir Monterey County Sleepy Hollow Vineyard 1996: Light in color, light in flavor. Finishes with a bitter edge. • $18 • (8/31/1998) • **72**
Pinot Noir Monterey County Sleepy Hollow Vineyard 1995 • $17 • (2/28/1997) • **86**
Pinot Noir Monterey County Sleepy Hollow Vineyard 1992 • $12 • (1/31/1995) • **85**
Pinot Noir Monterey County Sleepy Hollow Vineyard 1989 • $12 • (2/28/1993) • **76**
Pinot Noir Monterey County Sleepy Hollow Vineyard 1987 • $18 • (2/28/1991) • **86**
Pinot Noir Monterey County Sleepy Hollow Vineyard Doctors' Reserve 1997: Shows a narrow range of toast and dried cherry flavors. Finishes dry. Drink now.–J.L. • $20 • (6/15/1999) • **80**
White Riesling Monterey County Late Harvest Sleepy Hollow 1989 • $15 • (6/30/1993) • **89**
Zinfandel Amador County Ferrero Ranch 1990 • $10 • (9/30/1993) • **80**
Zinfandel Amador County Ferrero Ranch Doctors' Reserve 1987 • $15 • (5/15/1991) • **83**
Zinfandel Amador County Ferrero Ranch Doctors' Reserve 1982 • $10 • (2/29/1988) • **83**
Zinfandel Amador County Ferrero Vineyard 1991 • $9 • (10/15/1994) • **80**
Zinfandel Mendocino M & M Vineyard 1994 • $15 • (4/30/1997) • **83**

MONTEREY VINEYARD | CALIFORNIA

Cabernet Sauvignon Monterey County 1997: Firm, with modest depth to the peppery core of oak and currant flavors. Drink now.–J.L. • $7 • (10/15/1999) • **83**
Cabernet Sauvignon Monterey County 1995 • $7 • (9/15/1997) • **82**
Cabernet Sauvignon Monterey County 1994 • $7 • (12/15/1996) • **79**
Cabernet Sauvignon Monterey County Classic 1994 • $7 • (11/30/1996) • **76**
Cabernet Sauvignon Monterey County Classic 1990 • $6 • (3/31/1993) • **80**
Cabernet Sauvignon Monterey County Classic 1989 • $6 • (3/15/1992) • **83**
Cabernet Sauvignon Monterey County Limited Release 1990 • $11 • (11/15/1994) • **84**
Cabernet Sauvignon Monterey County Limited Release 1985 • $10 • (8/31/1988) • **75**
Chardonnay Monterey County 1997: Subtle, tight and flinty, with a well-focused range of mouthwatering green apple flavors that finish crisp and refreshing. Ready now, it makes a nice summertime quaff, and the modest price invites you to imbibe freely. Drink now.–J.L. • $7 • (7/31/1999) • **85**
Chardonnay Monterey-San Joaquin-Napa Counties 1996: Simple, with flavors of spice, pear and apple. Has a nice focus on the finish. Drink now. • $7 • (7/31/1998) • **82**
Chardonnay Monterey-San Joaquin-Stanislaus Counties 1996 • $7 • (9/15/1997) • **84**
Classic Red Monterey County 1990 • $5 • (3/31/1993) • **76**
Merlot Monterey County 1992 • $6 • (9/15/1994) • **80**
Merlot Monterey County Classic 1989 • $6 • (2/29/1992) • **84**
Merlot Monterey County Classic 1988 • $6 • (12/31/1990) • **76**
Merlot Monterey County Limited Release 1994 • $15 • (4/30/1998) • **83**
Merlot Stanislaus-San Joaquin-Monterey Counties 1997: Simple and soft-textured, with cherry and cola flavors framed by herbal notes. Drink now.–J.L. • $7 • (10/15/1999) • **80**
Pinot Noir Monterey County 1997: Firm, with a narrow band of herb and cherry flavors. Drink now.–J.L. • $7 • (9/15/1999) • **81**
Pinot Noir Monterey County 1996: Starts off with decent cola, tea and strawberry flavors but lacks freshness, turning earthy and dry. Drink now.–J.L. • $7 • (8/31/1998) • **74**
Pinot Noir Monterey County 1995 • $7 • (9/15/1997) • **84**
Pinot Noir Monterey County Classic 1992 • $7 • (3/31/1995) • **77**
Pinot Noir Monterey County Classic 1991 • $6 • (2/28/1994) • **79**
Pinot Noir Monterey County Limited Release 1996: Simple, with sour cherry, orange rind, butter and toasted notes that turn bitter and tannic on the finish. Drink now.–J.L. • $15 • (9/15/1998) • **76**
Pinot Noir Monterey County Limited Release 1994 • $14 • (2/28/1997) • **81**
Pinot Noir Monterey County Limited Release 1990 • $9 • (2/28/1993) • **78**
Pinot Noir Monterey County Limited Release 1989 • $8 • (9/30/1992) • **71**
Pinot Noir Monterey County Limited Release 1988 • $9 • (2/28/1991) • **80**
Sauvignon Blanc Monterey County 1997: With its pretty melon, grapefruit and herb flavors and hints of gooseberry that crop up on the finish, this California white presents a clean, refreshing package; all the more enjoyable thanks to its painless price. Drink now. • $6 • (6/15/1999) • **86**
Sauvignon Blanc Monterey County 1996 • $6 • (4/30/1998) • **81**

MONTERRA | CALIFORNIA

Cabernet Sauvignon Monterey Promise 1995: Simple, with unripe flavors and woody notes on the finish. • $10 • (12/15/1998) • **74**
Cabernet Sauvignon Monterey 1991 • $7 • (11/15/1994) • **81**
Merlot Monterey 1995: Charred oak and herb flavors dominate the core of black cherry. Turns funky and metallic on the finish. Drink now.–J.L. • $10 • (9/30/1998) • **75**
Merlot Monterey Sand Hill 1992 • $10 • (2/29/1996) • **86**
Merlot Monterey 1991 • $7 • (5/31/1994) • **86**
Syrah Monterey Promise 1995: Starts off with cola and black cherry aromas, followed by licorice and herb notes. Texture is smooth, though it finishes on the bright side. Drink through 2002. • $10 • (11/30/1998) • **85**

MONTEVINA | CALIFORNIA

Aleatico Amador County 1993 • $8/375 ml. • (1/01/1995) • **78**
Barbera Amador County 1997: Smoky and peppery, with black currant, anise and blackberry flavors that hang nicely on the finish. Firmly structured, it drinks well now. Good price, too. Drink through 2003. • $12 • (11/15/1999) • **87**

MONTEVINA

Barbera Amador County 1996: Quite earthy on the nose, following up with ripe plum, raspberry, herb and spice flavors. Moderate finish has hints of anise and a touch of bitterness. Moderate tannins. Drink now through 2002. • $12 • (3/31/1999) • **86**
Barbera Amador County 1995 • $12 • (11/30/1997) • **86**
Barbera Amador County 1994 • $10 • (10/15/1996) • **84**
Barbera Amador County 1993 • $9 • (5/15/1996) • **84**
Barbera Amador County Reserve 1990 • $15 • (12/15/1992) • **82**
Barbera Amador County Terra d'Oro 1995 • $18 • (12/15/1997) • **81**
Barbera Amador County Terra d'Oro 1993 • $16 • (5/15/1996) • **86**
Cabernet Sauvignon California 1992 • $9 • (12/15/1995) • **83**
Cabernet Sauvignon California 1990 • $9 • (5/15/1993) • **80**
Cabernet Sauvignon California 1989 • $9 • (8/31/1992) • **78**
Cabernet Sauvignon California 1988 • $9 • (2/15/1990) • **77**
Matrimonio Amador County 1992 • $9 • (8/31/1995) • **84**
Montanaro Amador County 1992 • $8 • (8/31/1995) • **85**
Montanaro Amador County 1989 • $10 • (11/30/1992) • **80**
Nebbiolo Amador County Rosato 1996 • $8 • (9/15/1997) • **81**
Refosco Amador County 1995 • $8 • (9/15/1997) • **87**
Sangiovese Amador County 1997: Rustic tannins and simple cherry flavors make for a pleasant country wine. Try it with lunch. Drink now. • $12 • (11/15/1999) • **81**
Sangiovese Amador County 1996: Light and fragrant, aromatic, with strawberry and floral aromas and flavors. Finishes soft and simple. Drink now.–H.S. • $12 • (11/30/1998) • **82**
Sangiovese Amador County 1995 • $12 • (11/30/1997) • **84**
Sangiovese Amador County 1992 • $12 • (8/31/1995) • **86**
Sangiovese Amador County Terra d'Oro 1995 • $16 • (12/15/1997) • **81**
Sangiovese Amador County Terra d'Oro 1993 • $15 • (4/30/1996) • **80**
Zinfandel Amador County 1997: Features a modest range of cherry, herb and toasted oak flavors, with a thread of bitterness.–J.L. • $12 • (11/15/1999) • **79**
Zinfandel Amador County 1996 • $10 • (6/15/1998) • **82**
Zinfandel Amador County 1995 • $10 • (12/15/1997) • **81**
Zinfandel Amador County 1994 • $NA • (9/15/1996) • **79**
Zinfandel Amador County 1993 • $7 • (10/15/1995) • **83**
Zinfandel Amador County 1992 • $8 • (10/15/1995) • **84**
Zinfandel Amador County 1990 • $7 • (6/15/1994) • **83**
Zinfandel Amador County 1989 • $9 • (10/15/1992) • **72**
Zinfandel Amador County Brioso 1996 • $7 • (12/15/1997) • **82**
Zinfandel Amador County Brioso 1995 • $7 • (4/30/1997) • **84**
Zinfandel Amador County Brioso 1994 • $7 • (4/30/1996) • **83**
Zinfandel Amador County Brioso 1993 • $7 • (10/15/1995) • **83**
Zinfandel Amador County Brioso 1992 • $8 • (9/30/1993) • **83**
Zinfandel Amador County Brioso 1991 • $8 • (6/15/1993) • **77**
Zinfandel Amador County Brioso 1990 • $8 • (7/15/1992) • **86**
Zinfandel Amador County Reserve 1991 • $12 • (10/15/1994) • **82**
Zinfandel Amador County Reserve 1989 • $12 • (10/15/1992) • **87**
Zinfandel Amador County Terra d'Oro 1997: Muddled, with dried berry flavors and tart tannins, finishing with prune notes. Drink now.–J.L. • $22 • (5/31/2000) • **81**
Zinfandel Amador County Terra d'Oro 1996: Ripe cherry aromas and a hint of smoke start this off. On the tongue it's a little tight, with firm tannins holding back some of the spice and vanilla flavors. Might open up with a little more bottle age. • $16 • (5/15/1999) • **84**
Zinfandel Amador County Terra d'Oro 1995 • $16 • (6/15/1998) • **86**
Zinfandel Amador County Terra d'Oro 1993 • $15 • (4/30/1996) • **89**

MONTHAVEN | CALIFORNIA

Cabernet Sauvignon Napa Valley 1996: Pretty cassis, blackberry, tar, herb and smoke flavors highlight this Napa Cabernet with the un-Napalike price. There's lots of oak, too, and tannic strength, so give this bargain some time to smooth out. Best from 2001 through 2006. • $10 • (10/15/1999) • **85**
Cabernet Sauvignon Napa Valley 1995 • $10 • (3/31/1998) • **84**
Cabernet Sauvignon Napa Valley 1994 • $9 • (12/15/1996) • **81**
Cabernet Sauvignon Napa Valley 1993 • $8 • (3/31/1996) • **81**
Chardonnay Monterey 1996 • $10 • (6/30/1998) • **82**

Key: SS—Spectator Selection CS—Cellar Selection HR—Highly Recommended $NA—Price Not Available a—Auction Price (BT)—Barrel Tasting
For a key to the tasters' initials, see "How to Use These Listings."
Dates in parentheses indicate the issues in which the ratings were published.

Chardonnay Napa Valley 1997: Subtle flavors of pear, apple, citrus and toasted oak finish clean and refreshing. A soft, restrained wine that might be dominated by food. Drink now.–J.L. • $10 • (6/15/1999) • **85**
Chardonnay Napa Valley 1996 • $10 • (3/31/1998) • **84**
Malbec Napa Valley 1993 • $8 • (3/31/1996) • **81**
Sauvignon Blanc Napa Valley 1997: A surprisingly light style, considering it's from Napa. Fresh pea, herbs, melon and grapefruit reveal themselves subtly, lingering only moderately on the finish. Drink now. • $8 • (5/15/1999) • **83**
Sauvignon Blanc Napa Valley 1996 • $9 • (3/31/1998) • **86**
Syrah California 1995 • $10 • (7/31/1997) • **87**
Viognier California 1996: Starts off with grapefruit and pineapple aromas. On the palate, flavors turn to tangy, zesty lemon. Drink now. • $10 • (9/15/1998) • **85**
Zinfandel California 1996 • $10 • (6/15/1998) • **79**
Zinfandel Napa Valley 1995 • $10 • (3/31/1998) • **83**

MONTICELLO | CALIFORNIA

Cabernet Sauvignon Napa Valley Corley Select Reserve 1996: Tough and herbal, with chewy, drying tannins and not much fruit. Disappointing.–J.L. • $40 • (5/31/2000) • **76**
Cabernet Sauvignon Napa Valley Corley Select Reserve 1994: Smoke, mineral and cedar aromas lead off, followed by tartish blackberry and herb flavors. Drink now through 2002. • $35 • (10/31/1998) • **84**
Cabernet Sauvignon Napa Valley Corley Select Reserve 1993 • $35 • (6/30/1997) • **89**
Cabernet Sauvignon Napa Valley Corley Select Reserve 1992 • $28 • (12/15/1995) • **83**
Cabernet Sauvignon Napa Valley Corley Select Reserve 1991 • $25 • (12/15/1995) • **85**
Cabernet Sauvignon Napa Valley Corley Reserve 1990 • $25 • (11/15/1993) • **88**
Cabernet Sauvignon Napa Valley Corley Reserve 1989 • $19 Ⓐ • (11/15/1992) • **85**
Cabernet Sauvignon Napa Valley Corley Reserve 1987 • $25 • (11/15/1990) • **90**
Cabernet Sauvignon Napa Valley Corley Reserve 1986 • $33 Ⓐ • (3/15/1990) • **92**
Cabernet Sauvignon Napa Valley Corley Reserve 1985 • $35 • (7/31/1989) • **92**
Cabernet Sauvignon Napa Valley Corley Reserve 1984 • $21 Ⓐ • (11/30/1987) • **90**
Cabernet Sauvignon Napa Valley Corley Reserve 1982 • $15 • (12/16/1985) • **92**
Cabernet Sauvignon Napa Valley Jefferson Cuvée 1995: Smooth and generous, its spicy blackberry and cola flavors bumping past a background of fine-grained tannins. Drink now.–H.S. • $22 • (10/31/1998) • **85**
Cabernet Sauvignon Napa Valley Jefferson Cuvée 1993 • $18 • (7/31/1997) • **87**
Cabernet Sauvignon Napa Valley Jefferson Cuvée 1992 • $18 • (12/15/1995) • **89**
Cabernet Sauvignon Napa Valley Jefferson Cuvée 1989 • $15 • (11/15/1993) • **86**
Cabernet Sauvignon Napa Valley Jefferson Cuvée 1988 • $16 • (11/15/1991) • **85**
Cabernet Sauvignon Napa Valley Jefferson Cuvée 1987 • $14 • (9/30/1990) • **90**
Cabernet Sauvignon Napa Valley Jefferson Cuvée 1986 • $14 • (4/15/1989) • **89**
Cabernet Sauvignon Napa Valley Jefferson Cuvée 1985 • $36 Ⓐ • (2/29/1988) • **87**
Cabernet Sauvignon Napa Valley Jefferson Cuvée 1984 • $11 • (11/30/1987) • **90**
Cabernet Sauvignon Napa Valley Jefferson Cuvée 1983 • $10 • (11/30/1986) • **77**
Cabernet Sauvignon Napa Valley Jefferson Cuvée 1982 • $10 • (2/01/1986) • **91**
Chardonnay Napa Valley Corley Estate Reserve 1997: Lots of spicy nutmeg and hazelnut flavors, with ripe pear, peach and herb notes. Finishes with cedary oak. Drink now through 2004.–J.L. • $30 • (5/31/2000) • **87**
Chardonnay Napa Valley Corley Family Vineyards 1997: Crisp and flinty, with citrus and herb flavors. Reveals more toasty, minerally notes on the finish. Drink now through 2002.–J.L. • $18 • (7/31/1999) • **87**
Chardonnay Napa Valley Corley Wild Yeast Estate Reserve 1996: Concentrated earthy, resinous flavors evolve to more pleasant vanilla and lemon notes. Finishes crisp and citrusy but earthy, with a woody aftertaste. Best after 2000.–J.L. • $33 • (7/31/1999) • **85**
Merlot Napa Valley 1990 • $17 • (7/15/1993) • **86**
Merlot Napa Valley Corley Estate Reserve 1995: On the green side, with herb, sage and tea notes, some hints of cherry, but the tannins are potent, so be warned. Drink through 2004.–J.L. • $30 • (10/15/1998) • **82**
Merlot Napa Valley Corley Family Vineyards 1993 • $20 • (8/31/1996) • **85**
Merlot Napa Valley Corley Family Vineyards 1992 • $18 • (9/30/1995) • **88**
Pinot Noir Napa Valley 1994 • $18 • (1/31/1998) • **87**
Pinot Noir Napa Valley 1991 • $18 • (2/28/1994) • **81**

Pinot Noir Napa Valley 1990 • $18 • (9/30/1992) • **86**
Pinot Noir Napa Valley 1987 • $15 • (10/15/1989) • **85**
Pinot Noir Napa Valley 1986 • $12 • (6/15/1988) • **89**
Pinot Noir Napa Valley 1985 • $12 • (12/15/1987) • **89**
Pinot Noir Napa Valley Corley Estate Reserve 1995 • $32 • (1/31/1998) • **88**
Pinot Noir Napa Valley Corley Estate Reserve 1994 • $30 • (1/31/1998) • **87**
Pinot Noir Napa Valley Corley Family Vineyards 1997: Firm, with coffee, plum and toasted oak flavors that turn slightly drying on the finish. Drink now through 2001.–J.L. • $24 • (9/15/1999) • **84**
Pinot Noir Napa Valley Corley Family Vineyards 1995: A touch earthy, with smoke, leather and dried cherry in modest proportions. Turns simple on the finish. Drink now.–J.L. • $22 • (9/15/1998) • **82**
Pinot Noir Napa Valley Corley Family Vineyards 1993 • $18 • (1/31/1997) • **87**
Pinot Noir Napa Valley Corley Family Vineyards 1992 • $18 • (9/15/1995) • **88**
Pinot Noir Napa Valley Monticello Vineyards Estate Reserve 1993 • $30 • (11/30/1995) • **89**

MONTINORE | OREGON

Chardonnay Willamette Valley 1998: Smooth, pretty and light in texture, with apple and vanilla notes sliding through the polished finish. Drink now. –H.S. • $10 • (4/30/2000) • **85**
Chardonnay Willamette Valley Vintner's Cuvée 1996 • $5 • (7/31/1997) • **85**
Chardonnay Willamette Valley Winemaker's Reserve 1998: Crisp in texture, with racy pear, citrus and spice flavors that pick up floral nuances as they linger on the light finish. Drink now through 2003.–H.S. • $18 • (4/30/2000) • **87**
Gewürztraminer Late Harvest Willamette Valley 1993 • $6/375 ml. • (11/30/1994) • **85**
Gewürztraminer Willamette Valley 1996 • $5 • (7/31/1997) • **87**
Müller-Thurgau Willamette Valley 1996 • $5 • (7/31/1997) • **83**
Pinot Gris Willamette Valley 1996 • $8 • (7/31/1997) • **83**
Pinot Noir Oregon Vintner's Cuvée NV • $5 • (11/30/1994) • **73**
Pinot Noir Washington County 1989 • $12 • (2/28/1993) • **73**
Pinot Noir Washington County 1988 • $14 • (4/15/1991) • **88**
Pinot Noir Washington County 1987 • $13 • (2/15/1990) • **81**
Pinot Noir Willamette Valley NV • $7/1.5 liter • (2/28/1993) • **79**
Pinot Noir Willamette Valley 1997: Light and appealing for its bright, delicate strawberry and cherry flavors and smooth finish. Drink now.–H.S. • $10 • (4/30/2000) • **82**
Pinot Noir Willamette Valley 1995 • $9 • (7/31/1997) • **79**
Pinot Noir Willamette Valley 1994 • $8 • (4/30/1997) • **83**
Pinot Noir Willamette Valley 1993 • $10 • (1/31/1996) • **82**
Pinot Noir Willamette Valley 1992 • $12 • (11/30/1994) • **79**
Pinot Noir Willamette Valley 1990 • $12 • (2/28/1993) • **83**
Pinot Noir Willamette Valley Vintner's Cuvée 1996 • $5 • (7/31/1997) • **84**
Pinot Noir Willamette Valley Winemaker's Reserve 1995 • $14 • (2/28/1997) • **85**
Pinot Noir Willamette Valley Winemaker's Reserve 1994 • $NA • (2/28/1997) • **87**
Pinot Noir Willamette Valley Winemaker's Reserve 1992 • $18 • (11/30/1994) • **82**
Pinot Noir Willamette Valley Winemaker's Reserve 1990 • $18 • (11/15/1994) • **87**
Pinot Noir Willamette Valley Winemaker's Reserve 1989 • $20 • (2/28/1993) • **85**
White Riesling Late Harvest Willamette Valley 1996 • $5 • (7/31/1997) • **79**
White Riesling Late Harvest Willamette Valley 1993 • $6/375 ml. • (11/30/1994) • **84**
White Riesling Late Harvest Yamhill County 1989 • $7/375 ml. • (3/31/1991) • **84**
White Riesling Willamette Valley 1996 • $5 • (7/31/1997) • **72**

MONTPELLIER | CALIFORNIA

Cabernet Sauvignon California 1993 • $8 • (11/30/1996) • **83**
Cabernet Sauvignon California 1990 • $8 • (11/15/1994) • **83**
Cabernet Sauvignon California 1988 • $7 • (7/31/1991) • **83**
Merlot California 1996 • $8 • (3/31/1998) • **80**
Merlot California 1993 • $8 • (11/15/1995) • **83**
Merlot California 1992 • $8 • (9/15/1994) • **80**
Pinot Noir California 1993 • $8 • (12/31/1995) • **78**
Zinfandel California 1993 • $7 • (10/15/1995) • **83**

MOONDANCE | CALIFORNIA

Cabernet Sauvignon Napa Valley 1992 • $10 • (7/31/1995) • **82**

Merlot Napa Valley 1994 • $18 • (12/31/1996) • **85**
Merlot Napa Valley 1993 • $15 • (8/31/1996) • **83**
Merlot Napa Valley 1992 • $12 • (11/15/1994) • **87**
Merlot Napa Valley 1990 • $10 • (3/31/1993) • **86**
Moontage California NV • $7 • (12/31/1996) • **84**
Petite Sirah Napa Valley 1992 • $16 • (9/30/1995) • **88**
Sangiovese Alexander Valley 1993 • $13 • (11/30/1995) • **80**
Zinfandel Sonoma Valley 1992 • $12 • (10/15/1994) • **88**

MORAGA | CALIFORNIA

Red Bel Air 1994 • $55 • (5/15/1998) • **90**
Red Bel Air 1993 • $50 • (7/31/1997) • **91**
Red Bel Air 1990 • $50 • (11/15/1994) • **80**
Red Bel Air 1989 • $50 • (6/30/1993) • **87**

MORGAN | CALIFORNIA

Cabernet Sauvignon Carmel Valley 1991 • $15 • (11/15/1994) • **88**
Cabernet Sauvignon Carmel Valley 1990 • $14 • (11/15/1993) • **77**
Cabernet Sauvignon Carmel Valley 1989 • $15 • (8/31/1992) • **83**
Cabernet Sauvignon Carmel Valley 1988 • $19 • (11/15/1991) • **81**
Cabernet Sauvignon Carmel Valley 1987 • $16 • (9/30/1990) • **92**
Cabernet Sauvignon Carmel Valley 1986 • $16 • (9/15/1989) • **90**
Chardonnay Monterey County 1998: On the austere side, with a modest range of pear, herb, hay and citrusy bitterness on the finish. Drink now. –J.L. • $20 • (4/30/2000) • **85**
Chardonnay Monterey 1997: Focused and elegant, with a complex core of detailed citrus, pear, honey, toasted oak and spice flavors that remain concentrated on the long, refreshing finish. Drink now through 2001.–J.L. • $15 Ⓐ • (6/15/1999) • **91**
Chardonnay Monterey 1996 • $18 • (4/30/1998) SS • **90**
Chardonnay Monterey Reserve 1996: Intense, even racy, with complex pear, fig, citrus and vanilla notes that turn elegant and supple on the finish. Drink now through 2002.–J.L. • $25 • (3/31/1999) • **91**
Malvasia Bianca Monterey 1998: Smells wonderfully of grape and flowers, though it's tighter and leaner on the palate, with a grapefruit edge to the light pear flavors. Drink now.–J.L. • $12 • (1/01/2000) • **84**
Malvasia Bianca Monterey 1996 • $12 • (3/31/1998) • **86**
Pinot Noir California 1995 • $18 • (5/31/1997) • **87**
Pinot Noir California 1994 • $17 • (3/31/1997) • **78**
Pinot Noir California 1993 • $15 • (6/30/1995) • **83**
Pinot Noir California 1992 • $15 • (3/31/1995) • **85**
Pinot Noir California 1991 • $15 • (2/28/1993) • **81**
Pinot Noir California 1990 • $15 • (3/31/1997) • **85**
Pinot Noir California 1989 • $14 • (3/31/1992) • **85**
Pinot Noir California 1988 • $14 • (4/30/1991) • **75**
Pinot Noir California 1987 • $15 • (7/31/1989) • **81**
Pinot Noir California 1986 • $14 • (3/31/1997) • **70**
Pinot Noir Carneros Reserve 1993 • $27 • (2/28/1997) • **85**
Pinot Noir Carneros Reserve 1992 • $27 • (3/31/1995) • **87**
Pinot Noir Carneros Reserve 1991 • $23 • (2/28/1994) • **84**
Pinot Noir Carneros Reserve 1990 • $23 • (3/31/1997) • **86**
Pinot Noir Monterey County 1998: A disappointing effort from a usually reliable producer. A hint of cherry doesn't offset the sauerkraut overtones and musty flavors. Tasted twice, with consistent notes.–J.L. • $21 • (5/15/2000) • **77**
Pinot Noir Monterey 1997: Fairly herbal to start, but the flavors are pure—a blend of cherry and tea, with a touch of dill. Finishes clean and fresh, with firm tannins and toasty oak. Drink through 2002. • $20 • (9/15/1999) • **86**
Pinot Noir Monterey 1991 • $25 • (2/28/1994) • **81**
Pinot Noir Monterey County 1996: Light, with tea, herb and sage holding an upper hand over the berry flavor. Drink now.–J.L. • $20 • (9/30/1998) • **81**
Pinot Noir Monterey Paraiso Springs Vineyard 1997: Very delicate, with smooth, subtle cherry, cola and spicy oak flavors and a soft, flavorful finish. Drink now through 2002.–J.L. • $25 • (9/15/1999) • **86**
Pinot Noir Monterey Reserve 1997: Racy, refined, with spicy tea and cola, hints of cherry and wild berry, gaining momentum on the finish, where the tannins are firm. Drink through 2005.–J.L. • $32 • (8/31/1999) • **88**
Pinot Noir Monterey Reserve 1996: Smooth and spicy, with a core of ripe black cherry and a touch of vanilla, picking up hints of nutmeg, spice and cola that build on the finish, echoing fruit on the long, creamy aftertaste. Drink now through 2002.–J.L. • $30 • (8/31/1998) • **88**
Pinot Noir Monterey Reserve 1995 • $28 • (1/31/1998) • **90**
Pinot Noir Monterey Reserve 1994 • $27 • (2/28/1997) • **89**
Pinot Noir Monterey Reserve 1993 • $25 • (12/31/1995) • **86**

Pinot Noir Monterey Reserve 1992 • $27 • (3/31/1995) • **87**
Pinot Noir Monterey Reserve 1990 • $30 • (3/31/1997) • **89**
Sauvignon Blanc Monterey-Sonoma Counties 1998: Bright and zingy, with layers of grapefruit, lemon and herb. Will definitely clear the palate with its high acidity. Quite refreshing, nonetheless. Drink now. • $12 • (9/30/1999) • **88**
Sauvignon Blanc Sonoma & Monterey Counties 1997: Marked by a bit of smoke, spice and herbs, also serving up pretty melon, citrus, fresh pea and mineral notes. Somewhat fleshy on the palate, it has enough bright acidity to stay lively overall. Drink now through 2001. • $11 • (5/15/1999) • **87**
Sauvignon Blanc Sonoma-Monterey 1996 • $11 • (9/15/1997) • **86**
Syrah Monterey 1996: Earthy, a touch funky, soft in texture, with tar, black cherry and herb notes turning firm and leathery. Drink now.–J.L. • $20 • (4/30/1999) • **84**
Zinfandel Dry Creek Valley 1996: Elegant, finely balanced, with well-proportioned cherry, mint and wild berry flavors, finishing with firm tannins and a touch of earthiness. Ready now.–J.L. • $18 • (6/30/1999) • **87**
Zinfandel Dry Creek Valley 1995 • $15 • (6/15/1998) • **84**
Zinfandel Dry Creek Valley 1994 • $14 • (3/31/1997) • **83**
Zinfandel Dry Creek Valley Grist Vineyard 1996 • $19 • (6/15/1998) • **85**
Zinfandel Sonoma County 1993 • $14 • (10/15/1995) • **82**

MOROVINO | CALIFORNIA

Chardonnay Santa Barbara County 1996 • $16 • (6/15/1998) • **88**
Merlot Santa Barbara County 1995 • $18 • (12/15/1997) • **82**
Zinfandel Central Coast French Camp Vineyards 1994 • $14 • (10/15/1996) • **88**

MOSBY | CALIFORNIA

Nebbiolo Santa Barbara County 1995: Soft and light, with sour cherry, spice and tar notes and a tart finish. Drink now.–J.L. • $18 • (4/30/2000) • **82**
Nebbiolo Santa Barbara County Rosso di Nebbiolo 1991 • $12 • (9/30/1994) • **83**
Sangiovese Santa Barbara County Vigna Della Casa Vecchia 1996: Drying, with tart cherry flavors and herbal notes on a lean frame.–J.L. • $18 • (5/15/2000) • **77**
Sangiovese Santa Barbara County Vigna Della Casa Vecchia 1993 • $16 • (8/31/1995) • **79**

MOSHIN | CALIFORNIA

Pinot Noir Russian River Valley 1996: Shows promise on the nose, with spice and black cherry, but it falls short on the palate, as coarse tannins shut down the fruit. • $18 • (9/15/1998) • **79**
Pinot Noir Russian River Valley 1995 • $16 • (1/31/1998) • **87**
Pinot Noir Russian River Valley 1994 • $16 • (1/01/1997) • **84**
Pinot Noir Russian River Valley 1992 • $13 • (3/31/1995) • **83**
Pinot Noir Russian River Valley 1989 • $9 • (2/28/1993) • **75**
Pinot Noir Russian River Valley Barrel Select 1997: Light-bodied, with a delicate core of tea, strawberry and spice notes, finishing moderately. Drink now through 2001. • $18 • (9/15/1999) • **83**
Pinot Noir Russian River Valley Proprietor's Select 1995 • $24 • (1/31/1998) • **88**
Pinot Noir Russian River Valley Proprietor's Select 1994 • $30 • (8/31/1997) • **85**
Pinot Noir Russian River Valley Reserve 1991 • $25 • (3/31/1995) • **81**

MOSS CREEK | CALIFORNIA

Cabernet Sauvignon Napa Valley 1994: Offers plum and earth aromas that extend to the palate. Tannins are soft, framing a blend of mature herb, leather, cedar, mushroom and anise flavors. Drink now. • $45 • (10/15/1999) • **86**
Chardonnay Napa Valley 1997: Bitter, with a coarse, earthy, muddled personality.–J.L. • $22 • (6/30/2000) • **77**
Chardonnay Napa Valley 1996: Crisp, with a narrow band of green apple, tropical fruit and toasted oak flavors. Drink now.–J.L. • $22 • (8/31/1999) • **82**
Sauvignon Blanc Napa Valley 1997: Lean, with oak overtones and tart citrus flavors. Drink now.–J.L. • $18 • (5/31/2000) • **80**

Key: SS—Spectator Selection CS—Cellar Selection HR—Highly Recommended
$NA—Price Not Available a—Auction Price (BT)—Barrel Tasting
For a key to the tasters' initials, see "How to Use These Listings."
Dates in parentheses indicate the issues in which the ratings were published.

Sauvignon Blanc Napa Valley 1996: Fruity but weird, with lemon furniture polish notes. A little drying on the finish.–H.S. • $18 • (1/31/2000) • **79**
Zinfandel Napa Valley 1997: Refreshing and pretty, with delicate, spicy berry and cedar notes that linger. Drink now.–J.L. • $32 • (5/15/2000) • **85**
Zinfandel Napa Valley 1995: Supple and spicy, showing leathery plum, cola, strawberry and pepper flavors. Finishes with mild tannins. Drink now through 2001.–J.L. • $30 • (6/15/1999) • **86**

MOUNT EDEN | CALIFORNIA

Cabernet Sauvignon Santa Cruz Mountains 1994 • $30 Ⓐ • (5/15/1997) • **88**
Cabernet Sauvignon Santa Cruz Mountains 1993 • $18 • (4/30/1996) • **84**
Cabernet Sauvignon Santa Cruz Mountains 1992 • $16 • (5/31/1995) • **83**
Cabernet Sauvignon Santa Cruz Mountains 1989 • $25 • (11/15/1992) • **86**
Cabernet Sauvignon Santa Cruz Mountains 1988 • $26 • (11/15/1992) • **86**
Cabernet Sauvignon Santa Cruz Mountains 1987 • $28 • (4/30/1991) • **65**
Cabernet Sauvignon Santa Cruz Mountains 1986 • $25 Ⓐ • (8/31/1990) • **83**
Cabernet Sauvignon Santa Cruz Mountains 1985 • $25 Ⓐ • (11/15/1989) • **81**
Cabernet Sauvignon Santa Cruz Mountains 1984 • $29 Ⓐ • (10/31/1988) • **90**
Cabernet Sauvignon Santa Cruz Mountains 1981 • $17 Ⓐ • (11/01/1984) • **81**
Cabernet Sauvignon Santa Cruz Mountains 1979: Intense, firmly tannic still, with earthy, mushroomy cedar, currant and wild berry flavors that are holding together, if still a bit leathery. Amazing, as this is the best review I've given this wine in more than a decade. My only conclusion is that previous bottles were off. (1979 California Cabernet retrospective tasting). Drink now through 2006.–J.L. • $25 • (8/31/1999) • **86**
Cabernet Sauvignon Santa Cruz Mountains 1978 • $NA • (11/15/1992) • **84**
Cabernet Sauvignon Santa Cruz Mountains 1974 • $75 • (11/15/1994) • **88**
Cabernet Sauvignon Santa Cruz Mountains Kennedy Vineyard 1978 • $NA • (11/15/1992) • **85**
Cabernet Sauvignon Santa Cruz Mountains Lathweisen Ridge 1990 • $15 • (6/15/1993) • **88**
Cabernet Sauvignon Santa Cruz Mountains Lathweisen Ridge 1989: Tough, chewy and earthy, with tannins holding a significant upper hand over a modest strip of muddled Cabernet fruit, turning dry. Not going anywhere. (1989 California Cabernet retrospective tasting). Drink now.–J.L. • $12 • (8/31/1999) • **83**
Cabernet Sauvignon Santa Cruz Mountains Lathweisen Ridge 1988 • $12 • (4/30/1991) • **87**
Cabernet Sauvignon Santa Cruz Mountains Old Vine Cuvée 1989: Elegant, and avoids being overly tannic. Offers modest but pleasant and mature cedar and currant flavors that hold their focus. (1989 California Cabernet retrospective tasting). Drink now through 2005.–J.L. • $25 • (8/31/1999) • **87**
Cabernet Sauvignon Santa Cruz Mountains Old Vine Reserve 1996: Firm without being tight, it's complex and concentrated, with focused currant, wild berry and raspberry. Shows tannic strength on the finish. Best from 2002 through 2010.–J.L. • $45 • (12/31/1999) • **89**
Cabernet Sauvignon Santa Cruz Mountains Old Vine Reserve 1995: Tough and tannic, with earthy, herbal and mushroomy flavors that fairly dominate the core of currant, coffee and cedar flavors. Definitely needs time. Best from 2002 through 2010.–J.L. • $38 • (1/01/1999) • **88**
Cabernet Sauvignon Santa Cruz Mountains Old Vine Reserve 1994 • $36 • (3/31/1998) • **84**
Cabernet Sauvignon Santa Cruz Mountains Old Vine Reserve 1993 • $36 • (1/31/1997) • **88**
Cabernet Sauvignon Santa Cruz Mountains Old Vine Reserve 1992 • $35 • (6/15/1996) • **90**
Cabernet Sauvignon Santa Cruz Mountains Old Vine Reserve 1991 • $35 • (4/15/1995) • **88**
Cabernet Sauvignon Santa Cruz Mountains Old Vine Reserve 1990 • $36 Ⓐ • (11/15/1993) • **85**
Cabernet Sauvignon Santa Cruz Mountains Young Vine Cuvée 1987 • $12 • (4/15/1990) • **85**
Chardonnay Edna Valley MacGregor Vineyard 1997: Openly fruity, touching on exotic, with ripe and lively tropical fruit, Meyer lemon, butterscotch and toasted oak. Turns firm on the finish. Drink now.–J.L. • $17 • (6/15/1999) • **91**
Chardonnay Edna Valley MacGregor Vineyard 1996 • $16 • (3/31/1998) SS • **91**
Chardonnay Santa Cruz Mountains 1997: Crisp, a touch earthy and flinty, with a leafy edge to the ripe pear and apple flavors, it works its way into more complex nuances. Drink now through 2005.–J.L. • $45 • (12/31/1999) • **88**

Chardonnay Santa Cruz Mountains 1996: Tight and concentrated, with peach and citrus notes and a complex band of mineral, anise and spice. Slowly unfolds to reveal more elegance and complexity on the finish. Drink now through 2002.–J.L. • $38 • (12/31/1998) • **91**
Pinot Noir Edna Valley 1991 • $15 • (2/28/1994) • **83**
Pinot Noir Santa Cruz Mountains 1996: Light in color, with a rhubarb edge to the modestly concentrated ripe plum and cherry flavors. Drink now through 2002.–J.L. • $36 • (12/31/1998) • **86**
Pinot Noir Santa Cruz Mountains 1995 • $35 • (1/31/1998) • **87**
Pinot Noir Santa Cruz Mountains 1994 • $34 • (2/28/1997) • **90**
Pinot Noir Santa Cruz Mountains 1990 • $30 • (2/28/1994) • **86**
Pinot Noir Santa Cruz Mountains 1989 • $30 • (2/28/1994) • **85**
Pinot Noir Santa Cruz Mountains 1987 • $25 • (4/15/1990) • **79**
Pinot Noir Santa Cruz Mountains 1985 • $35 • (6/15/1988) • **90**
Pinot Noir Santa Cruz Mountains 1984 • $35 • (4/15/1988) • **86**
Pinot Noir Santa Cruz Mountains 1983 • $35 • (8/31/1986) • **77**

MOUNT KONOCTI | CALIFORNIA

Cabernet Franc Lake County Kelsey 1992 • $8 • (2/28/1995) • **84**
Cabernet Sauvignon Lake County 1993 • $10 • (12/15/1995) • **82**
Cabernet Sauvignon Lake County Kelsey 1992 • $10 • (11/15/1994) • **84**

MOUNT MAROMA | CALIFORNIA

Cabernet Sauvignon Napa Valley 1993 • $14 • (11/30/1996) • **80**

MOUNT PALOMAR | CALIFORNIA

Cabernet Sauvignon Temecula 1991 • $10 • (11/15/1994) • **74**
Cabernet Sauvignon Temecula 1990 • $12 • (7/15/1993) • **83**
Sangiovese Temecula Castelletto 1993 • $18 • (12/15/1996) • **82**
Sangiovese Temecula Castelletto 1992 • $18 • (8/31/1995) • **73**
Sangiovese Temecula Castelletto 1991 • $20 • (9/30/1994) • **82**

MOUNT VEEDER | CALIFORNIA

Cabernet Sauvignon Napa Valley 1996: There's wonderful richness, depth and complexity to this California Cabernet, with its layers of earthy currant, mushroom, cedar, clay, tar and leather. Made in a big, chewy and rustic style, it just needs short-term cellaring. Best from 2001 through 2009.–J.L. • $30 • (10/31/1999) SS • **91**
Cabernet Sauvignon Napa Valley 1995: Complex and intense without being overpowering, this wine has a pretty assortment of toasty oak, elegant plum and black cherry, and supple, harmonious tannins that linger long. Drinkable now, worthy of cellaring, too. Drink through 2007.–J.L. • $30 • (11/15/1998) • **90**
Cabernet Sauvignon Napa Valley 1994 • $25 • (8/31/1997) • **88**
Cabernet Sauvignon Napa Valley 1993 • $25 • (11/15/1996) • **87**
Cabernet Sauvignon Napa Valley 1992 • $25 • (12/15/1995) • **87**
Cabernet Sauvignon Napa Valley 1991 • $18 • (1/31/1995) • **85**
Cabernet Sauvignon Napa Valley 1990 • $15 • (10/31/1993) SS • **94**
Cabernet Sauvignon Napa Valley 1989: Firm, structured and tannic, with earthy clay, cedar and currant notes of moderate depth and complexity. (1989 California Cabernet retrospective tasting). Drink now through 2002.–J.L. • $13 • (8/31/1999) • **85**
Cabernet Sauvignon Napa Valley 1987 • $22 • (4/30/1991) • **85**
Cabernet Sauvignon Napa Valley 1986 • $20 • (11/15/1990) • **83**
Cabernet Sauvignon Napa Valley 1984 • $14 • (11/15/1988) • **83**
Cabernet Sauvignon Napa Valley 1983 • $14 • (10/31/1987) • **75**
Cabernet Sauvignon Napa Valley 1982 • $13 • (6/15/1987) • **64**
Cabernet Sauvignon Napa Valley 1981 • $13 • (7/16/1986) • **81**
Cabernet Sauvignon Napa Valley 1974 • $53 • (11/15/1994) • **85**
Cabernet Sauvignon Napa Valley Bernstein Vineyards 1980 • $12 • (5/16/1984) • **85**
Cabernet Sauvignon Napa Valley Bernstein Vineyards 1979: Very ripe and still quite chunky, with a peppermint flavor shading the plum and earthy cherry. Big, chewy, intense tannins remain in this rustic, mountain-grown wine. (1979 California Cabernet retrospective tasting). Drink now through 2007.–J.L. • $14 • (8/31/1999) • **88**
Cabernet Sauvignon Napa Valley Bernstein Vineyards 1978 • $31 • (11/15/1992) • **78**
Cabernet Sauvignon Napa Valley Mount Veeder Vineyards 1987 • $35 • (12/15/1997) • **87**
Cabernet Sauvignon Napa Valley Sidehill Ranch 1978: Distinct for its earthy, rustic, mushroomy flavors, the core of spicy currant, anise and sage is intense, still firmly tannic and aging well. Lacks the finesse and complexity of the best '78s, but is holding together nicely. (1978 California Cabernet retrospective tasting). Drink now through 2002.–J.L. • $14 • (11/15/1998) • **88**
Meritage Napa Valley 1989 • $24 • (6/15/1993) • **88**
Meritage Napa Valley 1988 • $24 • (7/15/1992) • **83**
Merlot Napa Valley 1994 • $22 • (6/30/1997) • **87**
Reserve Napa Valley 1995: Sharply focused, with a rich, complex core of black cherry, plum, wild berry and spice that unfolds to reveal layers of depth and complexity while offering a sense of elegance and finesse. Drink through 2008.–J.L. • $50 • (11/15/1999) • **92**
Reserve Napa Valley 1993 • $40 • (8/31/1997) • **90**
Reserve Napa Valley 1992 • $40 • (8/31/1996) • **88**
Reserve Napa Valley 1991 • $40 • (9/15/1995) • **84**
Reserve Napa Valley 1990 • $25 • (9/15/1994) CS • **92**
Zinfandel Napa Valley 1994 • $22 • (3/31/1997) • **86**
Zinfandel Napa Valley 1993 • $20 • (3/31/1996) • **83**

MOUNTAIN DOME | WASHINGTON

Brut Washington NV: Delicate, creamy, a fine-textured glass of fizz with perfumy overtones to its apple, citrus and vanilla flavors. Drink now.–H.S. • $11 • (9/15/1998) • **88**
Brut Rosé Washington NV: Dry, broad and creamy, but ultimately delicate enough to show its spice and strawberry flavors with finesse. Drink now.–H.S. • $16 • (9/15/1998) • **88**

MOUNTAIN SPIRIT | COLORADO

Chardonnay Colorado 1997: Not much life here. Tastes quite woody, with an overly charry note on the finish.–K.M. • $11 • (5/31/1999) • **71**

MUELLER | CALIFORNIA

Chardonnay Alexander Valley Gauer Ranch 1997: Bright and lively, with a beam of ripe pear, spice, apple and melon flavors that are clean and refreshing. Has a touch of cedary oak. Drink now through 2005.–J.L. • $24 Ⓐ • (4/30/2000) • **89**
Chardonnay Alexander Valley Gauer Ranch 1996: A ripe, complex and smoky style, loaded with fig, pear, apple, spice and toasty oak flavors. Even with all its richness and concentration, it manages to remain a wine of polish and finesse. Drink now through 2002.–J.L. • $20 • (9/15/1998) • **92**
Chardonnay Russian River Valley LB 1997: Smooth, ripe and creamy, with a wonderful core of peach, anise, fig and apricot. Very silky and polished, with a long, satisfying aftertaste. Drink now through 2002.–J.L. • $26 Ⓐ • (7/31/1999) • **93**
Chardonnay Russian River Valley LB 1996 • $18 • (6/30/1998) • **90**
Chardonnay Russian River Valley Oak Meadow Vineyard 1996: A subtle style that packs in lots of ripe, intense flavors, with a pretty array of rich pear, toasty oak, spice, mineral and citrus, turning complex with a hint of anise on the finish. Drink now through 2001.–J.L. • $18 • (7/31/1998) • **90**
Pinot Noir Russian River Valley Emily's Cuvée 1997: Smooth, ripe and supple, with rich cherry, plum and currant flavors that are complex and concentrated, finishing with a burst of fruitiness. Drink now through 2006.–J.L. • $27 • (9/15/1999) • **88**
Pinot Noir Russian River Valley Emily's Cuvée 1996: Opens from an initial austerity to reveal a trim band of earthy cherry, spice and vanilla, with a touch of blackberry and mild, well-integrated tannins. Drink through 2002.–J.L. • $25 • (12/15/1998) • **89**
Pinot Noir Russian River Valley Emily's Cuvée 1995 • $22 • (7/31/1997) • **91**
Pinot Noir Russian River Valley Emily's Cuvée 1994 • $20 • (4/30/1996) • **91**
Pinot Noir Russian River Valley Ranch 23 1997: Ripe and supple, with rich, complex black cherry, tea, herb and vanilla flavors, finishing with touches of raspberry and spice. Nicely tapered on the finish and not too tannic. Drink now through 2004.–J.L. • $27 • (9/15/1999) • **89**
Pinot Noir Russian River Valley Ranch 23 1996 • $25 • (6/30/1998) • **87**

MUMM CUVEE NAPA | CALIFORNIA

Brut Blanc de Blancs Napa Valley NV: Light pear and grapefruit aromas lead the way, backed by pretty green apple notes. Delicate, with a moderate finish. Drink now. • $18 • (12/15/1998) • **87**
Brut Blanc de Noirs Napa Valley NV: A racy style, with bright acidity and spice. Flavors include grapefruit, lemon-lime and wild cherry. The finish is lively, with a fresh mineral touch. Drink now through 2002. • $16 • (12/15/1998) • **88**

■ ■ ■ ■

MUMM CUVEE NAPA

Brut Napa Valley 21st Century Cuvée NV: Sleek on the palate, the wine is a bit lean yet offers a tangy blend of lemon, herb, green apple and pear flavors. Quite dry on the finish, it nonetheless makes a fine quaff. Drink now through 2002. • $25 • (10/15/1999) • **87**
Brut Napa Valley Carneros Winery Lake 1990 • $18 • (11/30/1995) • **89**
Brut Napa Valley Cuvée Napa NV • $14 • (12/31/1993) • **83**
Brut Napa Valley Prestige NV: This California sparkling wine is quite a value at this price and score. It's bright and tangy, with a core of lemon and lime flavors that fan out on the palate to yield a toasty, fresh finish with hints of apple and pear. Drink now. • $15 • (10/15/1999) SS • **88**
DVX Napa Valley 1995: A refreshing style of bubbly, with pretty citrus, apple, hazelnut and pear notes. The structure is focused and firm, showing elegance and depth and offering both bright acidity and creamy texture. Long finish. Drink now through 2003. • $35 • (10/15/1999) • **92**
DVX Napa Valley 1994: Toast, honey and citrus notes introduce this full-bodied bubbly, which serves up tangy layers of lemon, lime and grapefruit, with enticing hints of hazelnut and spice. A luscious style. Drink now through 2002. • $40 • (12/15/1998) • **92**
DVX Napa Valley 1993 • $40 • (11/30/1997) • **91**
DVX Napa Valley 1992 • $30 • (11/30/1996) HR • **92**
DVX Napa Valley 1991 • $30 • (12/31/1995) • **89**
DVX Napa Valley 1990 • $25 • (12/15/1994) SS • **91**

MURPHY-GOODE | CALIFORNIA

Cabernet Sauvignon Alexander Valley 1997: A wonderful value. Dark, firm and smoky, with complex, ripe, rich black cherry, plum, currant and spice notes. Finishes with mild tannins and good length. Best from 2001 through 2008.–J.L. • $19 • (3/31/2000) • **88**
Cabernet Sauvignon Alexander Valley 1996: Rich and soft, with an herb-tinged core of currant and berry flavors. Finishes with complex notes of mineral, herb and toasty oak. Fine-grained tannins. Drink through 2001.–J.L. • $19 • (2/28/1999) • **86**
Cabernet Sauvignon Alexander Valley 1995 • $19 • (3/31/1998) • **84**
Cabernet Sauvignon Alexander Valley 1988 • $16 • (11/15/1991) • **87**
Cabernet Sauvignon Alexander Valley Brenda Block Reserve 1997: Deep, ripe, rich and concentrated, with layers of complex currant, berry, cherry and plum framed by pretty toasty, smoky, vanilla-scented oak. All comes together on a long, lingering finish. Best from 2001 through 2010.–J.L. • $39 • (2/29/2000) • **93**
Cabernet Sauvignon Alexander Valley Brenda Block Reserve 1995: Impressive for its up-front fruitiness and complexity, with ripe, spicy cherry, plum and berry, toasty vanilla-scented oak and a long, complex aftertaste. Wonderful balance, medium-weight, with fine tannins. Drink now through 2004.–J.L. • $35 • (10/31/1998) • **90**
Cabernet Sauvignon Alexander Valley Brenda Block Reserve 1994 • $30 • (7/31/1997) • **89**
Cabernet Sauvignon Alexander Valley Goode-Ready 1989 • $10 • (6/15/1991) • **80**
Cabernet Sauvignon Alexander Valley Murphy Ranch 1994 • $18 • (11/15/1996) • **88**
Cabernet Sauvignon Alexander Valley Murphy Ranch 1993 • $16 • (11/15/1995) • **88**
Cabernet Sauvignon Alexander Valley Murphy Ranch 1992 • $15 • (5/15/1995) • **87**
Cabernet Sauvignon Alexander Valley Murphy Ranch 1991 • $15 • (11/15/1994) • **83**
Cabernet Sauvignon Alexander Valley Murphy Ranch 1990 • $15 • (10/15/1993) • **87**
Cabernet Sauvignon Alexander Valley Murphy Ranch 1989 • $16 • (11/15/1992) • **84**
Cabernet Sauvignon Alexander Valley Premier Vineyard 1987 • $17 • (5/31/1990) • **89**
Cabernet Sauvignon Alexander Valley Premier Vineyard 1986 • $16 • (11/15/1989) • **90**
Cabernet Sauvignon Alexander Valley Sarah Block Swan Song Reserve 1997: Lots to admire in this ripe, fruity, supple, deceptively complex wine. Offers layers of plum, black cherry, blackberry, cedar, tar and herb notes. Fun to drink now. Best from 2001 through 2009.–J.L. • $39 • (2/29/2000) • **89**

Key: SS—Spectator Selection CS—Cellar Selection HR—Highly Recommended $NA—Price Not Available a—Auction Price (BT)—Barrel Tasting For a key to the tasters' initials, see "How to Use These Listings."
Dates in parentheses indicate the issues in which the ratings were published.

Chardonnay Alexander Valley Island Block Reserve 1997: A touch leafy and tannic before moving into fruitier flavors, with ripe apple, pear and citrus notes. Drink now.–J.L. • $24 • (4/30/1999) • **88**
Chardonnay Alexander Valley Island Block Reserve 1996 • $24 • (5/15/1998) • **90**
Chardonnay Russian River Valley J & K Murphy Vineyard Reserve 1996 • $24 • (5/15/1998) • **89**
Chardonnay Sonoma County 1998: Tight and a touch tart, with flinty peach and nectarine flavors that finish with cedary oak. Drink now through 2004.–J.L. • $15 • (2/29/2000) • **85**
Chardonnay Sonoma County 1997: Starts crisp and toasty, but finishes with a modest range of pear and spice. Drink now.–J.L. • $15 • (12/31/1998) • **82**
Chardonnay Sonoma County 1996 • $15 • (2/28/1998) • **87**
Fumé Blanc Alexander Valley Reserve 1998: Minerally, with herb and citrus notes. Drink now.–J.L. • $17 • (6/15/2000) • **81**
Fumé Blanc Alexander Valley Reserve 1996 • $17 • (3/31/1998) • **88**
Fumé Blanc Sonoma County 1997: Firm and bright, with a core of grapefruit, lemon and herb flavors. Clean and fresh. Drink now through 2002. • $12 • (12/31/1998) • **86**
Fumé Blanc Sonoma County 1996 • $12 • (6/30/1997) • **88**
Fumé Blanc Sonoma County Dry 1998: Intriguing, with complex guava, mineral and toasty notes. It's light-bodied and steely, full of lovely flavors that linger. Drink now through 2003.–H.S. • $12 • (3/31/2000) • **87**
Merlot Alexander Valley 1997: Concentrated earth, barnyard, black cherry and coffee flavors are intriguing but stray from the norm. Finishes with supple tannins. Drink now through 2002.–J.L. • $18 • (10/15/1999) • **83**
Merlot Alexander Valley Murphy Ranches 1996: Hangs together, with spicy cherry, berry and plum notes. Turns elegant and manages the tannins better than most from this vintage. Drink now through 2004.–J.L. • $18 • (9/30/1998) • **85**
Merlot Alexander Valley Murphy Ranches 1995 • $18 • (6/30/1997) • **89**
Merlot Alexander Valley Murphy Ranches 1994 • $16 • (11/30/1996) • **84**
Merlot Alexander Valley Murphy Ranches 1993 • $16 • (12/15/1995) • **85**
Merlot Alexander Valley Murphy Ranches 1992 • $15 • (1/31/1995) • **83**
Merlot Alexander Valley Murphy Ranches 1991 • $15 • (3/15/1994) • **83**
Merlot Alexander Valley Murphy Ranch 1990 • $15 • (3/31/1993) • **83**
Merlot Alexander Valley Murphy Ranch 1989 • $15 • (5/31/1992) • **82**
Merlot Alexander Valley Premier Vineyard 1986 • $14 • (1/31/1989) • **90**
Pinot Blanc Russian River Valley 1997: Earthy in style, even rather neutral. Shy on fruit flavor. Drink now through 2001.–J.L. • $14 • (1/31/1999) • **81**
Pinot Blanc Sonoma County 1996 • $14 • (4/30/1998) • **84**
Pinot Noir Russian River Valley 1997: Lots of ripe, yummy plum, black cherry and wild berry flavors in this elegant, polished, fruit-driven wine. The winery's first Pinot Noir. Drink now through 2005.–J.L. • $30 • (2/29/2000) • **87**
Sauvignon Blanc Alexander Valley Fumé II The Deuce 1998: Buttery, with vanilla, pear and herb notes, but just a bit gluey on the finish. Drink now.–J.L. • $24 • (6/15/2000) • **83**
Sauvignon Blanc Alexander Valley Fumé II The Deuce 1997: A richly textured wine that serves up ripe melon, lemon and grapefruit flavors while also packing plenty of sweet oak. On the finish are hints of minerals and fresh-cut hay. The ensemble is elegant and smooth. Drink now through 2002. • $24 • (3/31/1999) • **88**
Sauvignon Blanc Alexander Valley Fumé II The Deuce 1996 • $24 • (3/31/1998) • **90**
Sauvignon Blanc Alexander Valley Reserve Fumé 1997: Shows off a creamy texture, contrasted by a flinty edge. Bright acidity carries modest citrus and apple flavors along to a moderate but clean finish. Drink now. • $17 • (4/30/1999) • **84**
Zinfandel Dry Creek-Alexander Valleys 1995 • $16 • (12/15/1997) • **88**
Zinfandel Sonoma County 1996 • $16 • (5/31/1998) • **88**
Zinfandel Sonoma County 86% Cuneo & Saini Vineyard 14% Capener Vineyard 1994 • $16 • (3/31/1997) • **88**
Zinfandel Sonoma County Liar's Dice 1997: Soft but flavorful, with light tea, strawberry and herb notes. Drink now.–J.L. • $16 • (11/15/1999) • **82**

MURRAY, ANDREW | CALIFORNIA

Espérance Santa Barbara County 1998: Austere and a bit tough, with complex spice, meat, leather, currant, tart dried cherry and floral notes. Turns a bit sour and tannic on the finish. Best from 2001 through 2009.–J.L. • $18 • (4/30/2000) • **86**
Roussanne Santa Barbara County 1998: Refreshing, with minty, herbal and flinty notes balanced by rich mango and pineapple flavors. Delicious and elegant. Drink now through 2002.–J.L. • $25 • (2/29/2000) • **87**
Syrah Santa Barbara County 1994 • $20 • (5/15/1997) • **84**

Syrah Santa Barbara County 1993 • $25 • (7/31/1996) • **85**

Syrah Santa Barbara County Hillside Reserve 1996: Intense, dark and marked by earth, mineral and wild berry flavors, picking up a chocolaty edge from oak. Finishes dry and firm, though it's not overly tannic. Best from 2001 through 2007.–J.L. • $25 • (12/31/1999) • **88**

Viognier Santa Barbara County 1998: A touch herbal, with spice, celery, ripe pear and apple notes that finish with a slightly sour, muscatlike edge. Drink now through 2004.–J.L. • $25 • (1/31/2000) • **84**

MURRIETA'S WELL | CALIFORNIA

Vendimia Livermore Valley Red 1996: A bit light in texture, the wine sports hints of licorice, blackberry, black currant and smoky oak. Dry on the finish, it nonetheless leaves an enjoyable aftertaste. Best from 2001 through 2005. • $30 • (11/15/1999) • **85**

Vendimia Livermore Valley Red 1995: A racy style that showcases mostly Cabernet. The berryish notes come through, along with a dash of bell pepper. Finishes with firm, dry tannins, so cellar short-term. A blend of Cabernet Sauvignon, Cabernet Franc, Merlot and Zinfandel. Drink through 2004.–J.L. • $28 • (10/31/1998) • **86**

Vendimia Livermore Valley Red 1993 • $28 • (4/30/1997) • **90**

Vendimia Livermore Valley Red 1991 • $28 • (5/31/1995) • **84**

Vendimia Livermore Valley Red 1990 • $28 • (11/15/1994) • **89**

Vendimia Livermore Valley White 1997: Features a melon and peach focus, framed with a refreshing mineral edge. Firmly textured, adding a clean finish. A blend of Sauvignon Blanc, Sémillon and Muscat. Drink now. • $22 • (5/15/1999) • **85**

Zinfandel Livermore Valley 1996: Medium-weight, with a streak of green bell pepper running through this otherwise simple Zin. Drink now.–J.L. • $28 • (6/30/1999) • **82**

Zinfandel Livermore Valley 1994 • $18 • (3/31/1997) • **90**

Zinfandel Livermore Valley 1991 • $16 • (10/15/1994) • **89**

Zinfandel Livermore Valley 1989 • $16 • (10/15/1994) • **83**

MUTT LYNCH | CALIFORNIA

Merlot Livermore Valley Merlot Over and Play Dead 1997: Ripe black currant mingles with leather, smoke and vanilla notes in a full-bodied format. Fine intensity through the finish. Drink now through 2006.–J.L. • $21 • (4/30/2000) • **86**

MYSTAL | CALIFORNIA

Merlot Napa Valley 1996: Firm and tannic but has a layer of dusty currant, black cherry and herbal tarry flavors. Firm and dry on the finish. Drink now through 2002.–J.L. • $30 • (8/31/1999) • **85**

MYSTIC CLIFFS | CALIFORNIA

Cabernet Sauvignon California 1995: This somewhat lean-styled wine starts off with vegetal notes—green beans come to mind. However, hints of cherry and anise pick up the baton and offer a more interesting, if moderate, finish. • $8 • (11/15/1998) • **78**

Chardonnay California 1997: A light style, with green apple and lemon flavors. Short finish. Drink now. • $8 • (2/28/1999) • **80**

Merlot California 1996: Simple and disjointed, with tart cherry, herb and wood flavors. Drink now.–J.L. • $8 • (9/30/1998) • **75**

Merlot Monterey County Winemaker's Select 1997: Tightly structured, with coffee, herb, toasted oak and black cherry flavors. Finishes with firm tannins and hints of spice. Drink now through 2005.–J.L. • $14 • (10/15/1999) • **82**

MYSTIC MOUNTAIN | OREGON

Chardonnay Willamette Valley 1997: Smooth and pretty, soft, with pear and citrus flavors, finishing with a hint of sweetness. Drink now.–H.S. • $16 • (4/30/1999) • **84**

NAKED MOUNTAIN | VIRGINIA

Cabernet Sauvignon Virginia Barrel Fermented 1996: Brown-colored, and the sour, stewy flavors make this undrinkable. Tasted twice, with consistent notes.–K.M. • $14 • (3/31/1999) • **53**

Chardonnay Virginia Barrel Fermented 1997: Buttery aromas are followed by a rich mix of fig and ripe pear flavors, with some tropical notes. A bit cloying on the spicyish finish. Drink now.–K.M. • $16 • (3/31/1999) • **83**

Riesling Virginia 1997: Simple, slightly sweet and straightforward, with a ripe peach flavor and some pine notes.–K.M. • $13 • (3/31/1999) • **79**

NALLE | CALIFORNIA

Cabernet Sauvignon Dry Creek Valley 1990 • $18 • (11/15/1993) • **85**

Cabernet Sauvignon Dry Creek Valley 1987 • $18 • (1/31/1991) • **89**

Zinfandel Dry Creek Valley 1997: Light and appealing for its delicate raspberry and toast flavors, aiming for elegance rather than exuberance. Drink now through 2002.–H.S. • $23 • (11/30/1999) • **86**

Zinfandel Dry Creek Valley 1996: An elegant, refined style that's smooth, ripe and spicy, with pretty black cherry and raspberry flavors, picking up tar, anise and cedary oak tones. Drink now through 2002.–J.L. • $21 • (11/30/1998) • **88**

Zinfandel Dry Creek Valley 1993 • $16 • (8/31/1995) • **87**

Zinfandel Dry Creek Valley 1992 • $15 • (10/15/1994) • **85**

Zinfandel Dry Creek Valley 1991 • $14 • (9/30/1993) • **86**

Zinfandel Dry Creek Valley 1990 • $14 • (10/15/1992) • **89**

Zinfandel Dry Creek Valley 1989 • $14 • (7/31/1991) • **85**

Zinfandel Dry Creek Valley 1988 • $25 • (7/31/1990) • **89**

Zinfandel Dry Creek Valley 1987 • $22 • (5/31/1989) SS • **92**

NAPA CREEK | CALIFORNIA

Cabernet Sauvignon Napa Valley 1991 • $12 • (11/15/1994) • **82**

Merlot Napa Valley 1988 • $13 • (3/31/1991) • **75**

Merlot Napa Valley 1987 • $14 • (6/15/1990) • **83**

Pinot Noir California Barrel Select 1995 • $NA • (3/31/1997) • **77**

NAPA RIDGE | CALIFORNIA

Cabernet Sauvignon Central Coast Coastal Oak Barrel 1997: Plush and flavorful, showing herb-tinged black cherry, cassis, tar and sweet oak nuances. Finishes with ripe tannins. Drink now through 2003.–J.L. • $11 • (10/15/1999) • **84**

Cabernet Sauvignon Central Coast 1996: What a deal on this up-front, pleasing, easy-to-drink California Cabernet, perfect to have on hand as your own house-red. It delivers plenty of Cabernet flavors, berry, cherry and currant notes, and soft, fleshy tannins. Enjoy now.–J.L. • $10 • (11/15/1998) • **86**

Cabernet Sauvignon Central Coast Oak Barrel 1995 • $9 • (10/15/1997) • **87**

Cabernet Sauvignon Central Coast Oak Barrel 1994 • $8 • (2/28/1997) • **87**

Cabernet Sauvignon Central Coast 1992 • $8 • (10/15/1995) • **87**

Cabernet Sauvignon Central Coast Oak Barrel 1991 • $8 • (11/15/1994) • **84**

Cabernet Sauvignon Napa Valley Reserve 1995: Rich and smoky, featuring black cherry and currant flavors laced with cedar, tar and herb notes. Flavors linger on the finish. Drink now through 2001.–J.L. • $17 • (8/31/1999) • **88**

Cabernet Sauvignon Napa Valley Reserve 1994 • $15 • (10/15/1997) • **87**

Cabernet Sauvignon Napa Valley Reserve 1992 • $15 • (10/15/1996) • **84**

Cabernet Sauvignon Napa Valley Reserve 1989 • $12 • (7/15/1993) • **85**

Cabernet Sauvignon North Coast Oak Barrel 1994 • $8 • (11/15/1996) • **87**

Cabernet Sauvignon North Coast Oak Barrel 1993 • $8 • (11/30/1995) • **87**

Cabernet Sauvignon North Coast Oak Barrel 1992 • $8 • (11/15/1994) • **79**

Cabernet Sauvignon North Coast Oak Barrel 1991 • $8 • (11/15/1993) • **77**

Cabernet Sauvignon North Coast 1989 • $6 • (11/15/1991) • **79**

Cabernet Sauvignon North Coast Reserve 1991 • $13 • (10/15/1995) • **87**

Cabernet Sauvignon North Coast Reserve 1990 • $13 • (11/15/1994) • **82**

Cabernet Sauvignon North Coast Reserve 1989 • $13 • (11/15/1993) • **87**

Chardonnay Central Coast Vines 1996 • $9 • (12/15/1997) • **85**

Chardonnay Napa Valley Reserve 1996: Very toasty and creamy, with smoky, baconlike flavors, from which focused citrus and pineapple emerge. Finishes with clean, complex, spicy fruit. Drink now through 2002.–J.L. • $17 • (6/30/1999) • **89**

Chardonnay North Coast Vines 1997: Smooth, ripe and creamy in texture, offering complex pear, apple, fig and nectarine flavors that are refreshing and finish clean, this is a tasty bottle of Chardonnay at a price that only adds to the charm. Drink now.–J.L. • $9 • (12/15/1998) • **87**

Chardonnay North Coast Vines 1996 • $9 • (5/31/1998) • **86**

Chardonnay-Sauvignon Blanc-Sémillon North Coast Triad Vines 1998: Buttery and herbaceous, offering apple and vanilla flavors. Drink now through 2002.–J.L. • $9 • (5/15/2000) • **83**

Chardonnay-Sauvignon Blanc-Sémillon North Coast Triad 1997: Tasty, though unusual, this blend from California is fairly rich and viscous, with up-front grapefruit and orange character followed by lots of spice and herb notes. Bright, with a little sweet oak on the finish. Drink now. • $9 • (1/31/1999) • **86**

Merlot North Coast 1993 • $10 • (6/30/1996) • **85**
Merlot North Coast 1992 • $9 • (3/31/1995) • **87**
Merlot North Coast 1991 • $10 • (9/15/1994) • **84**
Merlot North Coast 1990 • $7 • (6/15/1993) • **81**
Pinot Noir Carneros Reserve 1995 • $15 • (3/31/1998) • **84**
Pinot Noir North Coast Coastal 1997: Shows delicate flavors of strawberry and tea, faltering slightly on the finish, where the grainy tannins emerge. Drink now.–J.L. • $11 • (2/28/1999) • **82**
Pinot Noir North Coast Coastal 1996 • $11 • (6/30/1998) • **84**
Pinot Noir North Coast Coastal 1995 • $10 • (5/15/1997) • **89**
Pinot Noir North Coast 1994 • $8 • (1/31/1996) • **86**
Pinot Noir North Coast 1993 • $8 • (12/15/1994) • **84**
Pinot Noir North Coast 1991 • $6 • (2/28/1994) • **83**
Pinot Noir North Coast 1989 • $8 • (7/31/1991) • **82**
Sauvignon Blanc North Coast 1996 • $6 • (3/31/1998) • **86**
Zinfandel Central Coast 1995 • $9 • (12/15/1997) • **86**
Zinfandel Central Coast 1990 • $8 • (9/30/1993) • **76**
Zinfandel North Coast Coastal 1996: Somewhat low in fruit profile, with earth, juniper berry, tarry plum and cedar notes; a solid '96 lacking in extra dimensions. Drink now.–J.L. • $9 • (6/30/1999) • **83**

NAPA WINE CO. | CALIFORNIA

Cabernet Sauvignon Napa Valley 1996: Pleasantly balanced, with ripe currant, black cherry and cedary oak flavors. Turns a touch earthy on the firmly tannic finish. Drink now.–J.L. • $28 • (6/15/1999) • **88**
Pinot Blanc Napa Valley 1998: Apple and cornmeal flavors have good concentration and a firm finish. Drink now.–J.L. • $18 • (6/15/2000) • **84**
Sauvignon Blanc Napa Valley 1998: Racy and earthy, with sweaty geranium aromas and flavors that are more prominent than the modest Sauvignon character. Drink now.–J.L. • $18 • (4/30/2000) • **82**
Sauvignon Blanc Napa Valley 1997: Light in style, it nonetheless serves up plenty of bright fruit on the palate. Passion fruit and grapefruit are followed by hints of melon and freshly mowed hay. Moderate finish. Drink now. • $20 • (6/15/1999) • **87**

NAPANOOK | CALIFORNIA

Napa Valley 1997: Spicy, with cedary cherry, currant and berry notes, picking up tobacco and tar. Smooth and polished. Dominus' second label. Drink now through 2005.–J.L. • $30 • (5/31/2000) • **86**
Napa Valley 1996: A touch earthy and cedary, but plum and black cherry flavors emerge to fill in the gaps. Finishes with firm tannins, spice and leather notes. Best from 2001 through 2007.–J.L. • $30 • (8/31/1999) • **89**

NATHANSON CREEK | CALIFORNIA

Cabernet Sauvignon California NV • $6 • (11/15/1997) • **78**
Pinot Noir California NV • $14/1.5 liter • (5/15/1998) • **80**
Sauvignon Blanc California 1997: With a profile redolent of menthol, this stands out from the crowd at first. But it doesn't sport a similarly distinctive follow-through, remaining simple on the palate, with mild hints of citrus, melon and herbs. Drink now. • $5 • (5/31/1999) • **83**
Zinfandel California NV: Simple and diluted, with light cherry and herbal notes. • $6 • (6/30/1999) • **77**

NAVARRO | CALIFORNIA

Brut Anderson Valley NV • $17 • (5/31/1995) • **83**
Cabernet Sauvignon Mendocino 1994: Rustic, featuring earthy red currant and herb flavors. Tannins are firm and dry on the finish. Shows good concentration; will need some time to show its best. Best from 2001 through 2005.–J.L. • $24 • (10/15/1999) • **86**
Cabernet Sauvignon Mendocino 1992 • $19 • (11/15/1997) • **89**
Cabernet Sauvignon Mendocino 1991 • $18 • (11/15/1996) • **88**
Cabernet Sauvignon Mendocino 1990 • $17 • (10/15/1995) • **88**

Key: SS—Spectator Selection CS—Cellar Selection HR—Highly Recommended $NA—Price Not Available a—Auction Price (BT)—Barrel Tasting
For a key to the tasters' initials, see "How to Use These Listings."
Dates in parentheses indicate the issues in which the ratings were published.

Cabernet Sauvignon Mendocino 1989 • $16 • (11/15/1994) • **82**
Cabernet Sauvignon Mendocino 1988 • $16 • (10/15/1993) • **86**
Cabernet Sauvignon Mendocino 1987 • $16 • (11/15/1992) • **88**
Cabernet Sauvignon Mendocino 1986 • $16 • (10/15/1991) • **87**
Cabernet Sauvignon Mendocino 1985 • $14 • (11/15/1990) • **87**
Chardonnay Anderson Valley Première Reserve 1997: Openly fruity, with a range of peach, pear, apple and citrus flavors that are clean and elegant, turning subtle and polished. Drink now through 2002.–J.L. • $18 • (7/31/1999) • **89**
Chardonnay Anderson Valley Première Reserve 1996: Ripe and complex, with a nice interplay of spicy pear and apple, and light oak shadings on the finish. Intense and concentrated, it's drinkable now.–J.L. • $17 • (9/15/1998) • **88**
Chardonnay Mendocino 1997: Flavorful, with ripe pineapple and tangerine. Finishes firm and crisp. Drink now.–J.L. • $13 • (7/31/1999) • **85**
Chardonnay Mendocino 1996: Ripe, with clean apple, pear, spice and vanilla notes, hints of hazelnut and citrus. Fruit flavors linger long on the finish. Drink now.–J.L. • $13 • (9/15/1998) • **87**
Chenin Blanc Mendocino 1998: Strikes a fine balance between ripe fruit and a steely, tangy texture. Hints of orange peel, lemon, lime and melon linger on the palate for a zesty, refreshing quaff. Drink now. • $10 • (10/15/1999) • **86**
Gewürztraminer Anderson Valley Dry 1996 • $14 • (6/30/1998) • **89**
Gewürztraminer Anderson Valley Late Harvest Sweet 1998: A light style that's refreshing, with zesty peach, spice, litchi nut and Gewürz notes. Drink now through 2004.–J.L. • $12/375 ml. • (5/31/2000) • **84**
Gewürztraminer Anderson Valley Late Harvest Sweet Cluster Selected 1989 • $15/375 ml. • (3/15/1992) • **86**
Gewürztraminer North Coast Late Harvest Sweet 1991 • $14 • (12/31/1993) • **90**
Muscat Blanc Anderson Valley Dry 1996 • $14 • (6/30/1998) • **85**
Petits Villages Mendocino 1993 • $9 • (4/30/1995) • **83**
Pinot Noir Anderson Valley 1984 • $12 • (1/31/1988) • **91**
Pinot Noir Anderson Valley Clone 54 1992 • $12 • (11/30/1994) • **87**
Pinot Noir Anderson Valley Cuvée 90/91 NV • $9 • (2/28/1994) • **83**
Pinot Noir Anderson Valley Deep End Blend 1989 • $18 • (2/28/1993) • **88**
Pinot Noir Anderson Valley Méthode à l'Ancienne 1997: Lightly fruity, with simple cherry, berry and raspberry, finishing with light tannins. Drink now through 2005.–J.L. • $21 • (4/30/2000) • **85**
Pinot Noir Anderson Valley Méthode à l'Ancienne 1996: Tight and well structured, with earthy cherry, mushroom, cedar, bark and spice flavors that are well focused. Drink now through 2005.–J.L. • $18 • (12/31/1999) • **87**
Pinot Noir Anderson Valley Méthode à l'Ancienne 1995: Lightly fruity, with appealing plum, cherry and raspberry flavors, picking up spice and floral notes. Well balanced. Drink through 2002.–J.L. • $18 • (9/15/1998) • **87**
Pinot Noir Anderson Valley Méthode à l'Ancienne 1994 • $18 • (2/28/1998) • **88**
Pinot Noir Anderson Valley Méthode à l'Ancienne 1993 • $17 • (5/15/1997) SS • **90**
Pinot Noir Anderson Valley Méthode à l'Ancienne 1992 • $15 • (3/31/1996) • **85**
Pinot Noir Anderson Valley Méthode à l'Ancienne 1991 • $15 • (12/31/1994) • **86**
Pinot Noir Anderson Valley Méthode à l'Ancienne 1990 • $15/1.5 liter • (3/31/1997) • **88**
Pinot Noir Anderson Valley Méthode à l'Ancienne 1989 • $15 • (2/28/1993) • **87**
Pinot Noir Anderson Valley Méthode à l'Ancienne 1988 • $14 • (3/31/1992) • **89**
Pinot Noir Anderson Valley Méthode à l'Ancienne 1987 • $14 • (4/30/1991) • **85**
Pinot Noir Anderson Valley Méthode à l'Ancienne 1986 • $14/1.5 liter • (3/31/1997) • **88**
Pinot Noir Anderson Valley Méthode à l'Ancienne 1985 • $14 • (2/28/1989) • **85**
Pinot Noir Anderson Valley Méthode à l'Ancienne Unfiltered 1994 • $19 • (3/31/1998) • **87**
Pinot Noir Anderson Valley Table Wine 1993 • $10 • (12/31/1995) • **81**
Pinot Noir Mendocino 1997: Light, with ripe plum and black cherry presented in a very approachable style. Drink now through 2004.–J.L. • $13 • (12/31/1999) • **86**
Pinot Noir Mendocino 1996: Dark in color, ripe, with rich blackberry, cherry and plummy notes that are well focused, this is a solid effort in reasonably priced Pinot Noir. Drink now through 2002.–J.L. • $13 • (9/15/1998) • **87**
Pinot Noir Mendocino 1995 • $13 • (10/15/1997) • **88**
Pinot Noir Mendocino 1994 • $12 • (12/15/1996) • **87**
Sauvignon Blanc Mendocino Cuvée 128 1998: Full of lemon and herb notes, this Sauvignon Blanc has tart, lively flavors. Drink now through 2002.–J.L. • $13 • (5/15/2000) • **84**
Sauvignon Blanc Mendocino Cuvée 128 1997: Redolent of fresh apple and grapefruit, while on the palate it offers a blend of brightly textured citrus and herb flavors. A pretty and appealing wine with a fresh finish. Drink now through 2001. • $11 • (3/31/1999) • **87**
Sauvignon Blanc Mendocino Cuvée 128 1996 • $13 • (3/31/1998) • **90**

White Riesling Anderson Valley 1996: Crisp in texture, with pretty apricot and floral flavors on a steely frame, finishing barely off-dry.–H.S. • $12 • (12/15/1998) • **85**
White Riesling Anderson Valley Late Harvest Cluster Select Very Sweet 1997: Sweet, with a core of citrus-tinged pear, apricot, baked apple and spice. Finishes clean, with lively acidity, but lacks the extra dimensions often found in this wine. Drink now through 2006.–J.L. • $25/375 ml. • (5/31/2000) • **86**
White Riesling Anderson Valley Late Harvest Cluster Select Very Sweet 1994 • $20/375 ml. • (4/30/1997) • **87**
White Riesling Anderson Valley Late Harvest Sweet Cluster Selected 1994 • $14 • (10/31/1996) • **93**
White Riesling Anderson Valley Late Harvest Sweet Cluster Selected 1989 • $15 • (3/31/1992) • **83**
Zinfandel Mendocino 1993 • $15 • (3/31/1996) • **83**
Zinfandel Mendocino 1992 • $15 • (2/28/1995) • **85**
Zinfandel Mendocino 1991 • $14 • (3/31/1994) • **86**

NEVADA CITY | CALIFORNIA

Merlot Nevada County 1994 • $14 • (9/30/1997) • **84**
Merlot Nevada County 1989 • $14 • (5/31/1992) • **80**
Merlot Sierra Foothills 1991 • $14 • (9/15/1994) • **74**

NEW LAND | NEW YORK

Pinot Noir Finger Lakes Reserve 1993 • $15 • (6/30/1995) • **82**

NEWLAN | CALIFORNIA

Cabernet Sauvignon Napa Valley 1994 • $19 • (10/15/1997) • **87**
Cabernet Sauvignon Napa Valley 1993 • $19 • (9/15/1997) • **87**
Cabernet Sauvignon Napa Valley 1991 • $16 • (11/30/1995) • **89**
Cabernet Sauvignon Napa Valley 1990 • $26 • (2/28/1995) • **86**
Cabernet Sauvignon Napa Valley 1988 • $16 • (2/28/1995) • **84**
Cabernet Sauvignon Napa Valley 1987 • $15 • (11/15/1992) • **88**
Cabernet Sauvignon Napa Valley 1986 • $15 • (4/30/1991) • **89**
Cabernet Sauvignon Napa Valley 1985 • $15 • (3/31/1990) • **87**
Century Selection Napa Valley 1989 • $11 • (11/30/1992) • **78**
Johannisberg Riesling Napa Valley Late Harvest 1993 • $22 • (12/31/1995) • **94**
Johannisberg Riesling Napa Valley Late Harvest 1992 • $22/375 ml. • (4/30/1995) • **88**
Johannisberg Riesling Napa Valley Late Harvest 1991 • $20/375 ml. • (12/31/1993) • **89**
Pinot Noir Central Coast 1995 • $14 • (9/15/1997) • **83**
Pinot Noir Napa County School House Vieilles Vignes 1991 • $25 • (3/31/1995) • **79**
Pinot Noir Napa Valley 1996: Starts up with minty, herbal notes, followed by spice and cherry on the palate. Light-textured, it offers a moderate herbal finish. Drink now through 2002. • $20 • (9/15/1999) • **83**
Pinot Noir Napa Valley 1995 • $19 • (2/28/1998) • **85**
Pinot Noir Napa Valley 1994 • $19 • (12/15/1996) • **81**
Pinot Noir Napa Valley 1993 • $18 • (2/29/1996) • **87**
Pinot Noir Napa Valley 1992 • $18 • (3/31/1995) • **83**
Pinot Noir Napa Valley 1991 • $18 • (2/28/1994) • **80**
Pinot Noir Napa Valley 1989 • $18 • (2/28/1993) • **87**
Pinot Noir Napa Valley 1988 • $18 • (11/15/1991) • **81**
Pinot Noir Napa Valley 1987 • $16 • (3/31/1990) • **81**
Pinot Noir Napa Valley 1985 • $12 • (6/15/1988) • **88**
Pinot Noir Napa Valley Napa-Villages 1991 • $10 • (3/31/1995) • **81**
Pinot Noir Napa Valley Reserve 1995: Marked by up-front cinnamon, spice and earth aromas, it moves along in this exotic vein, adding cherry and plum flavors. But it's already showing age; a bit leathery and finishing dry. Drink now through 2002. • $25 • (9/15/1999) • **85**
Pinot Noir Napa Valley Reserve 1994 • $28 • (2/28/1997) • **83**
Pinot Noir Napa Valley Reserve 1993 • $28 • (5/15/1996) • **82**
Pinot Noir Napa Valley Reserve 1991 • $28 • (2/28/1994) • **84**
Pinot Noir Napa Valley Vieilles Vignes 1986 • $19 • (3/31/1990) • **76**
Pinot Noir Napa Valley Vieilles Vignes 1985 • $16 • (6/15/1988) • **80**
Zinfandel Alexander Valley Wallstrum Family Vineyards 1997: Spicy and lean, with jammy strawberry flavors and a warm, alcohol punch. Drink now through 2003.–J.L. • $22 • (5/31/2000) • **82**
Zinfandel Alexander Valley Wallstrum Family Vineyards 1996: Shows a modest range of earth, leather and plum flavors, with light spice and herb notes. Finishes dry. Drink now.–J.L. • $20 • (6/30/1999) • **83**
Zinfandel Napa Valley 1996: Fragrant, with ripe plum, blackberry, spice and smoke aromas. Has good follow-through with firm, ripe tannins and layers of berry and herb. Moderate finish. Drink now through 2003. • $18 • (5/15/1999) • **87**
Zinfandel Napa Valley 1995 • $16 • (12/15/1997) • **84**
Zinfandel Napa Valley 1994 • $16 • (4/30/1997) • **89**
Zinfandel Napa Valley 1992 • $14 • (10/15/1994) • **86**
Zinfandel Napa Valley 1991 • $15 • (3/31/1994) • **86**
Zinfandel Napa Valley 1990 • $13 • (9/30/1993) • **88**

NEWTON | CALIFORNIA

Cabernet Sauvignon Napa County 1991 • $NA • (1/01/1997) • **93**
Cabernet Sauvignon Napa Valley 1995: Tight and trim, with spicy cherry and wild berry, this austere, complex, concentrated wine fans out on the finish. Needs short-term cellaring. Best from 2001 through 2008.–J.L. • $35 • (12/15/1998) • **89**
Cabernet Sauvignon Napa Valley 1994 • $30 • (1/31/1998) • **89**
Cabernet Sauvignon Napa Valley 1993 • $25 • (5/31/1997) • **87**
Cabernet Sauvignon Napa Valley 1989 • $19 • (11/15/1993) • **84**
Cabernet Sauvignon Napa Valley 1988 • $17 • (11/15/1992) • **87**
Cabernet Sauvignon Napa Valley 1987 • $17 • (11/15/1991) • **87**
Cabernet Sauvignon Napa Valley 1986 • $16 • (5/31/1990) • **91**
Cabernet Sauvignon Napa Valley 1985 • $16 • (1/31/1989) • **89**
Cabernet Sauvignon Napa Valley 1984 • $14 • (9/30/1987) • **91**
Cabernet Sauvignon Napa Valley 1983 • $13 • (4/15/1987) SS • **96**
Cabernet Sauvignon Napa Valley 1981 • $13 • (12/16/1984) • **91**
Chardonnay Napa County Naturally Fermented 1997: Appealing with its up-front fruitiness, hints of apple, pear and spice and complex oak shadings, filling out on the palate to show depth and concentration. Drink now through 2002.–J.L. • $20 • (9/15/1998) • **89**
Chardonnay Napa & Sonoma County 1996 • $22 • (11/15/1997) SS • **91**
Chardonnay Napa Valley Unfiltered 1997: Rich and toasty, with a complex array of ripe pear, fig and nectarine. The finish has a good dose of toasty oak, giving it a butterscotch edge. Drink now through 2006.–J.L. • $NA • (4/30/2000) • **91**
Chardonnay Napa Valley Unfiltered 1996• $36 • (12/15/1998) • **93**
Claret Napa Valley 1996: A blend of black currant, cedar, herb and anise flavors couched in firm, ripe tannins and a moderate body. The finish lingers, tapering nicely. Drink now through 2004. • $NA • (9/30/1999) • **87**
Claret Napa Valley 1995 • $NA • (11/30/1997) • **87**
Claret Napa Valley 1994 • $16 • (2/28/1997) • **85**
Claret Napa Valley 1992 • $13 • (11/15/1994) • **88**
Claret Napa Valley 1991 • $12 • (6/15/1993) • **87**
Claret Napa Valley 1990 • $12 • (8/31/1992) • **83**
Claret Napa Valley 1988 • $11 • (3/15/1991) • **89**
Merlot Napa Valley 1997: Combines supple, polished black cherry, currant, anise and cedar notes with a deceptively firm tannic backbone. Tasty now. Best from 2001 through 2009.–J.L. • $41 • (3/31/2000) • **88**
Merlot Napa Valley 1996: Built around a tight core of coffee, currant, sage and mineral flavors, on the tannic side. Drink now through 2002.–J.L. • $33 • (12/15/1998) • **87**
Merlot Napa Valley 1995 • $NA • (1/31/1998) • **86**
Merlot Napa Valley 1994 • $24 Ⓐ • (5/15/1997) • **87**
Merlot Napa Valley 1989 • $20 • (5/31/1992) • **88**
Merlot Napa Valley 1987 • $17 • (7/31/1990) • **81**
Merlot Napa Valley 1986 • $15 • (12/31/1988) • **83**
Merlot Napa Valley 1985 • $14 • (3/31/1988) • **93**
Merlot Napa Valley 1983 • $12 • (2/28/1987) • **90**
Merlot Napa Valley 1982 • $12 • (10/01/1985) • **83**
Merlot Napa Valley 1981 • $13 • (12/16/1984) • **91**
Merlot Napa Valley Epic 1997: Pleasantly proportioned, with a nice balance of herb, sage and currant flavors. Firm on the finish, where the tannins are rich and tight. Best from 2002 through 2007.–J.L. • $NA • (4/30/2000) • **87**
Merlot Napa Valley Special Cuvée 1995: Marked by earthy, cedary flavors, it slowly finds a fruit focus with its clay and currant and its dry tannins. Needs time to soften, shed its tannins and expand its flavors; short-term cellaring is best. Drink through 2002.–J.L. • $23 • (9/30/1998) • **86**
Merlot Napa Valley Special Cuvée 1994 • $22 • (5/15/1997) • **87**
Pinot Noir Napa Valley Special Cuvée 1995 • $NA • (1/31/1998) • **86**

NEYERS | CALIFORNIA

Cabernet Franc Napa Valley 1987 • $16 • (11/15/1990) • **79**
Cabernet Sauvignon Napa Valley 1995 • $19 Ⓐ • (5/31/1998) • **88**
Cabernet Sauvignon Napa Valley 1988 • $15 • (11/15/1991) • **82**

NEYERS

Cabernet Sauvignon Napa Valley 1985 • $14 • (7/15/1989) • **83**
Cabernet Sauvignon Napa Valley 1984 • $13 • (4/30/1988) • **75**
Cabernet Sauvignon Napa Valley 1983 • $12 • (8/31/1987) • **79**
Chardonnay Carneros 1998: Lots of ripe, bold, complex pear, fig, apricot and buttery oak flavors stay rich and concentrated right through the finish. Drink now through 2002.–J.L. • $30 • (12/15/1999) • **91**
Chardonnay Carneros 1997: Ripe and complex, turning elegant and creamy, with lots of peach, pear, fig and nectarine flavors that are smooth and plush. Drink now through 2002.–J.L. • $28 • (1/31/1999) • **92**
Chardonnay Carneros 1996 • $25 • (11/15/1997) • **92**
Chardonnay Carneros El Novillero Vineyard 1998: Weaves together a complex array of flavors, with ripe, elegant pear, citrus, fig, melon and toasty oak, lingering on the finish. Drink now through 2002.–J.L. • $42 • (12/15/1999) • **90**
Chardonnay Carneros El Novillero Vineyard 1997: Intense and tightly wound, with a complex array of pear, peach, anise and spice, finishing with a burst of fruit and pretty, toasty oak notes. Drink now through 2002.–J.L. • $35 • (1/31/1999) • **92**
Chardonnay Napa Valley 1998: This California Chardonnay is packed with flavor, showing lots of up-front complexity in its layers of fig, vanilla, apricot, melon and spice. Holds its focus on the tasty finish. Drink now through 2002.–J.L. • $30 • (12/15/1999) SS • **91**
Chardonnay Napa Valley 1997: Bold, ripe and distinctive, with layers of plush, creamy, smoky pear, fig, apricot and melon, holding its focus on the finish. Drink through 2002.–J.L. • $28 • (1/31/1999) • **93**
Chardonnay Napa Valley 1996 • $25 • (11/15/1997) • **91**
Chardonnay Sonoma Coast Thieriot Vineyard 1998: Bright, crisp and lively, with a lemony edge to the tart pear, spice and nutmeg, finishing with bracing acidity. Drink now through 2005.–J.L. • $60 • (6/15/2000) • **87**
Chardonnay Sonoma Coast Thieriot Vineyard 1997: Packs in lots of richness and flavor, with a range of ripe fig, pear, anise, oak and spice. Sharply focused, deep and concentrated, finishing with a tangerine edge. Drink now through 2002.–J.L. • $48 • (7/31/1999) • **93**
Chardonnay Sonoma Coast Thieriot Vineyard 1996 • $35 • (11/15/1997) • **93**
Merlot Napa Valley 1997: Supple and harmonious, with appealing black cherry, currant, herb and spice. Finishes with a cedary oak edge and firm tannins. Drink through 2006.–J.L. • $30 • (10/15/1999) • **87**
Merlot Napa Valley 1996: Big and chewy, even rough around the edges, with firm, leathery tannins and a dry aftertaste. Hints of plum and currant emerge, but then the finish kicks in, turning dry and austere. Drink through 2004.–J.L. • $28 • (9/30/1998) • **87**
Merlot Napa Valley 1995 • $25 • (11/15/1997) • **91**
Merlot Napa Valley 1994 • $24 • (10/15/1996) • **86**
Merlot Napa Valley 1992 • $18 • (5/15/1995) • **84**
Merlot Napa Valley Neyers Ranch-Conn Valley 1997: A chunky, good extract, with firm, earthy anise, currant and cherry flavors that are tightly wound. Finishes with a tannic edge that merits short-term cellaring. Drink through 2007.–J.L. • $48 • (9/30/1999) • **88**
Merlot Napa Valley Neyers Ranch-Conn Valley 1996: Spicy, with currant, sage, tar and cedary oak flavors. Turns dry, austere and tannic on the finish. Best to give it time to soften. Drink through 2004.–J.L. • $42 • (9/30/1998) • **86**
Merlot Napa Valley Neyers Ranch-Conn Valley 1995 • $35 • (11/15/1997) • **91**
Syrah Napa Valley Hudson Vineyards 1998: Dark, with beefy, stewed plum, dried cherry, anise and cedar flavors. Turns rich and polished, with ripe tannins. Drink now through 2007.–J.L. • $55 • (6/15/2000) • **88**
Syrah Napa Valley Hudson Vineyards 1997: This espresso-style Syrah is dark, dense and detailed, with rich, plush wild berry, blackberry, pepper and spice. Has enormous structure and density and a long, tannic finish. Drink now through 2006.–J.L. • $48 • (6/15/1999) • **93**
Syrah Napa Valley Hudson Vineyards 1996: Ripe, rich and complex, with meaty plum, spice, mineral, cherry and berry flavors that fan out on the palate, keeping a tight focus and lingering long and full on the finish. Drink now through 2004.–J.L. • 24 ⓐ • (9/30/1998) • **89**
Zinfandel Contra Costa County Pato Vineyard 1997: Tight, with a tart edge to the ripe cherry, raspberry, wild berry and spice flavors. Finishes with firm, ripe, chewy tannins. Drink now through 2003.–J.L. • $30 • (6/15/1999) • **90**
Zinfandel Contra Costa County Pato Vineyard 1996 • $25 • (6/15/1998) • **87**
Zinfandel Contra Costa County Pato Vineyard 1995 • $20 • (6/30/1997) • **92**

Key: SS—Spectator Selection CS—Cellar Selection HR—Highly Recommended
$NA—Price Not Available a—Auction Price (BT)—Barrel Tasting
For a key to the tasters' initials, see "How to Use These Listings."
Dates in parentheses indicate the issues in which the ratings were published.

NICHELINI | CALIFORNIA

Cabernet Sauvignon Napa Valley 1991 • $17 • (11/30/1996) • **82**
Cabernet Sauvignon Napa Valley 1988 • $15 • (11/15/1993) • **81**
Cabernet Sauvignon Napa Valley Joseph A. Nichelini Vineyards 1989 • $12 • (6/15/1995) • **77**
Merlot Napa Valley 1992 • $20 • (3/31/1996) • **81**
Merlot Napa Valley Joseph A. Nichelini Vineyard 1994 • $18 • (3/31/1998) • **79**
Sauvignon Vert Napa Valley 1996 • $12 • (9/15/1997) • **82**
Zinfandel Napa Valley 1993 • $15 • (9/15/1997) • **87**
Zinfandel Napa Valley 1992 • $14 • (4/30/1997) • **88**
Zinfandel Napa Valley 1991 • $12 • (3/31/1996) • **87**
Zinfandel Napa Valley Centennial Vintage 1990 • $10 • (6/15/1995) • **79**
Zinfandel Napa Valley Joseph A. Nichelini Vineyards 1996: Charry, leathery and gamy flavors may not appeal to everyone, but the wine is well structured and works its way into some pleasing strawberry and tea notes. Drink now.–J.L. • $16 • (6/30/1999) • **83**
Zinfandel Napa Valley Joseph A. Nichelini Vineyard 1994 • $15 • (3/31/1998) • **87**

NICHOLS | CALIFORNIA

Chardonnay Arroyo Grande Valley La Colline Vineyard 1997: Silky, with concentrated baked apple, nectarine, mineral, toast and spice flavors that linger on the finish. Drink now through 2002.–J.L. • $30 • (7/31/1999) • **89**
Chardonnay Arroyo Grande Valley Talley Vineyard 1997: Marked by a crisp, flinty, earthy edge, this serves up a modest range of ripe pear and grapefruit flavors that, while pleasing, lack the extra dimensions of the best. Drink now through 2002.–J.L. • $30 • (6/30/1999) • **88**
Chardonnay Arroyo Grande Valley Talley Vineyard 1996: On the tart side, with a crisp lemon-lime streak. A lean and flinty style that's well made and well focused. Short-term cellaring is advised. Drink through 2002.–J.L. • $28 • (7/31/1998) • **88**
Chardonnay Central Coast Blend 1997: Focused, with light toast, vanilla, flinty apple and pear flavors that linger delicately on the finish. Best after 2000.–J.L. • $33 • (7/31/1999) • **88**
Chardonnay Central Coast Blend 1996 • $30 • (11/30/1997) • **89**
Chardonnay Central Coast Reserve 1996 • $33 • (2/28/1998) • **88**
Chardonnay Edna Valley Edna Ranch Vineyard 1997: Good intensity and richness, with ripe, spicy pear, fig and apricot. A touch earthy and oaky on the finish, but still quite complete. Drink now through 2002.–J.L. • $30 • (6/30/1999) • **89**
Chardonnay Edna Valley Paragon Vineyard 1997: Ripe, flavorful and complex, with baked apple, pear, spice and pretty oak shadings. Holds its focus on the long, creamy finish. Drink now through 2002.–J.L. • $30 • (7/31/1999) • **90**
Chardonnay Edna Valley Paragon Vineyard 1996 • $28 • (3/31/1998) • **87**
Chardonnay Santa Barbara County Bien Nacido Vineyard 1997: Exotic with its range of flavors, the core of pear and pineapple expands to spicy oak and nutmeg. Long, lingering finish. Drink now through 2002.–J.L. • $28 • (7/31/1999) • **89**
Chardonnay Santa Barbara County Bien Nacido Vineyard 1996 • $26 • (3/31/1998) • **87**
Chardonnay Santa Barbara County Bien Nacido Vineyard Soleil & Terroir 1997: Wonderful complexity and range of flavors—spicy pear, melon, apple, fig and apricot—and a long, complex aftertaste. Drink now through 2002.–J.L. • $24 • (6/30/1999) • **91**
Chardonnay Santa Barbara County Cottonwood Canyon Vineyard 1996 • $30 • (11/30/1997) • **91**
Pinot Blanc Arroyo Grande Valley La Colline Vineyard 1996 • $21 • (4/30/1998) • **86**
Pinot Noir Arroyo Grande Valley La Colline Vineyard 1997: Ripe, rich-textured and focused, showing a tight range of tart cherry, berry and tea flavors that linger on the plush finish. Drink now through 2002.–J.L. • $33 • (9/15/1999) • **87**
Pinot Noir Arroyo Grande Valley La Colline Vineyard 1996 • $33 • (2/28/1998) • **87**
Pinot Noir Central Coast Blend 1997: Quite exotic, with spice and menthol notes framing plum, berry and tea flavors. Leather and light earth tones add complexity and interest. Long finish. Drink through 2004. • $36 • (9/15/1999) • **87**
Pinot Noir Central Coast Blend 1996 • $36 • (2/28/1998) • **88**
Pinot Noir Central Coast Reserve 1997: Flavors reach out in several directions, with earth, mushroom, dried cherry, olive and plum, turning supple and polished on the finish. Drink now through 2004.–J.L. • $45 • (9/15/1999) • **87**

Pinot Noir Central Coast Reserve 1996 • $45 • (2/28/1998) • **89**
Pinot Noir Edna Valley Edna Ranch Vineyard 1997: Earthy and gamy, with flavors of cherry, sarsaparilla and herbs, finishing smooth. Drink now through 2002.–J.L. • $33 • (9/15/1999) • **86**
Pinot Noir Edna Valley Edna Ranch Vineyard Soleil & Terroir 1997: Exotic with its leathery, earthy flavors. Has a range of mineral, tar and black cherry, finishing firm. Drink now through 2003.–J.L. • $26 • (9/15/1999) • **85**
Pinot Noir Edna Valley Edna Ranch Vineyard Soleil & Terroir Reserve 1997: Rich and ripe, with a leathery edge to the earthy cherry and berry flavors. Focused, turning smooth on the finish, where the earthy flavors linger. Drink now through 2004.–J.L. • $28 • (9/15/1999) • **86**
Pinot Noir Edna Valley Paragon Vineyard 1997: Starts off with exotic spice and menthol notes, then offers plush berry, plum and tea flavors. Full on the palate, though a bit drying on the finish. Drink through 2004. • $30 • (9/15/1999) • **87**
Pinot Noir Edna Valley Paragon Vineyard 1996 • $28 • (2/28/1998) • **89**
Pinot Noir Monterey County Pisoni Vineyard 1997: Appealing ripe cherry, plum and wild berry flavors are neatly packaged, framed by firm tannins, but the texture beneath is supple. Drink now through 2005.–J.L. • $45 • (9/15/1999) • **87**
Pinot Noir Monterey County Pisoni Vineyards 1996 • $42 • (2/28/1998) • **89**
Pinot Noir Santa Barbara County Cottonwood Canyon Sharon's Vineyard 1997: Tea and spice flavors blend nicely with plum, cherry, cola and light leathery notes. Brightly textured, with some complexity, the wine finishes moderately. Drink through 2004. • $33 • (9/15/1999) • **87**
Pinot Noir Santa Barbara County Cottonwood Canyon Vineyard 1996 • $33 • (2/28/1998) • **87**
Pinot Noir Santa Barbara County Sierra Madre Vineyard 1995 • $32 • (2/28/1997) • **87**
Pinot Noir Santa Barbara County Sierra Madre Vineyard 1994 • $24 • (4/30/1996) • **89**
Pinot Noir Santa Barbara County Sierra Madre Vineyard 1993 • $24 • (12/31/1995) • **91**

NICHOL'S, DAVE | CALIFORNIA

Cabernet Sauvignon Napa Valley Stags Leap Hillside Personal Selection Reserve 1991 • $18 • (9/15/1996) • **83**
Cabernet Sauvignon Napa Valley Stags Leap Hillside Reserve 1993 • $18 • (9/15/1996) • **89**

NIEBAUM-COPPOLA | CALIFORNIA

Cabernet Franc Napa Valley 1997: Supple, polished, fragrant and spicy, with ripe, rich, complex layers of plum, black cherry, wild berry and raspberry. Finishes with mild, integrated tannins. Drink now through 2006.–J.L. • $32 • (12/15/1999) • **91**
Cabernet Franc Napa Valley Francis Coppola Family Wines 1996: Cedary, with elegant and understated spice, currant and berry notes that are clean and, though ultimately simple, pleasant. Drink through 2006.–J.L. • $26 • (1/31/1999) • **87**
Cabernet Franc Napa Valley Francis Coppola Family Wines 1995 • $20 • (12/15/1997) • **88**
Cabernet Franc Napa Valley Francis Coppola Family Wines 1991 • $14 • (1/31/1995) • **81**
Cabernet Franc Napa Valley Francis Coppola Family Wines 1990 • $12 • (3/31/1993) • **84**
Chardonnay Napa Valley Francis Coppola Family Wines 1997: Crisp and even flinty, with spades of grapefruit, tart apple and tangerine flavors that linger together with light oak. Finish is clean and refreshing. Drink now through 2001.–J.L. • $20 • (12/15/1998) • **88**
Merlot Napa Valley 1997: Medium in weight, with an attractive range of ripe cherry, plum and currant. Finishes with good length. Drink now through 2007.–J.L. • $40 • (4/30/2000) • **87**
Merlot Napa Valley Francis Coppola Family Wines 1996: Oozing with ripe, rich black cherry, blackberry, plum and jammy notes, turning elegant, polished and sophisticated, with a cedary note adding complexity on the finish. Drink now through 2004.–J.L. • $32 • (5/15/1999) • **90**
Merlot Napa Valley Francis Coppola Family Wines 1995 • $32 • (5/15/1998) • **88**
Merlot Napa Valley Francis Coppola Family Wines 1994 • $24 • (4/30/1997) • **92**
Merlot Napa Valley Francis Coppola Family Wines 1993 • $18 • (5/15/1996) • **89**
Merlot Napa Valley Francis Coppola Family Wines 1991 • $16 • (10/15/1993) • **86**
Rubicon Rutherford 1996: Restrained, with cedar, currant and herb notes, picking up a cocoa edge. Finishes with mild tannins and good length. Tasted twice, with consistent notes. Drink now through 2005.–J.L. • $90 • (6/15/2000) • **88**
Rubicon Rutherford 1995: A classy California red of impressive pedigree, this displays a rich character of earthy berry, cherry, cedar and spice, gaining complexity and finesse with supple, polished tannins. It's enjoyable now. 88 percent Cabernet Sauvignon, 6 percent Merlot, 6 percent Cabernet Franc.–J.L. • $80 • (6/15/1999) CS • **92**
Rubicon Rutherford 1994 • $65 • (6/15/1998) CS • **92**
Rubicon Rutherford 1993 • $55 • (5/15/1998) • **90**
Rubicon Rutherford 1992 • $50 • (5/31/1997) • **92**
Rubicon Rutherford 1991 • $40 • (9/15/1996) CS • **91**
Rubicon Napa Valley 1990 • $35 • (12/15/1995) • **90**
Rubicon Napa Valley 1989 • $30 • (11/15/1994) • **83**
Rubicon Napa Valley 1988 • $30 • (11/15/1994) • **83**
Rubicon Napa Valley 1987 • $30 • (12/15/1997) • **84**
Rubicon Napa Valley 1986 • $NA • (12/15/1996) • **85**
Rubicon Napa Valley 1985 • $29 • (11/15/1990) • **87**
Rubicon Napa Valley 1982 • $40 • (10/15/1989) • **88**
Rubicon Napa Valley 1981 • $35 • (11/15/1988) • **89**
Rubicon Napa Valley 1980 • $35 • (10/15/1987) • **92**
Rubicon Napa Valley 1979 • $25 • (2/28/1987) • **81**
Rubicon Napa Valley 1978 • $53 • (11/15/1992) • **88**
Rubicon Napa Valley 1977 • $NA • (2/28/1987) • **93**
Zinfandel Napa Valley Edizione Pennino 1997: Wonderful orchestration of Zinfandel fruit. Ripe, with juicy blackberry, black cherry, plum and raspberry. Turns plush, with polished tannins. Drink now through 2008.–J.L. • $32 • (4/30/2000) • **91**
Zinfandel Napa Valley Edizione Pennino 1996: Sleek and elegant, with wild berry, spice, menthol and cedary oak flavors, finishing with crisp tannins. Drink now through 2004.–J.L. • $26 • (1/31/1999) • **87**
Zinfandel Napa Valley Edizione Pennino 1995 • $24 • (3/31/1998) SS • **91**
Zinfandel Napa Valley Edizione Pennino 1994 • $20 • (3/31/1997) • **88**
Zinfandel Napa Valley Edizione Pennino 1993 • $16 • (10/15/1995) • **87**
Zinfandel Napa Valley Edizione Pennino 1992 • $15 • (10/15/1994) • **88**
Zinfandel Napa Valley Edizione Pennino 1991 • $14 • (10/15/1994) • **88**
Zinfandel Napa Valley Edizione Pennino 1990 • $14 • (9/30/1993) • **88**
Zinfandel Napa Valley Edizione Pennino 1989 • $14 • (9/30/1993) • **87**

NOCETO | CALIFORNIA

Sangiovese Shenandoah Valley 1995 • $12 • (10/15/1997) • **85**
Sangiovese Shenandoah Valley 1994 • $10 • (8/31/1996) • **87**
Sangiovese Shenandoah Valley 1993 • $10 • (8/31/1995) • **82**
Sangiovese Shenandoah Valley 1992 • $8 • (9/30/1994) • **77**
Sangiovese Shenandoah Valley 1991 • $8 • (7/31/1993) • **81**

NOMINEE | CALIFORNIA

Cabernet Sauvignon Napa Valley 1992 • $7 • (11/15/1994) • **75**
Cabernet Sauvignon Napa Valley 1991 • $7 • (7/15/1993) • **83**
Cabernet Sauvignon Paso Robles 1995 • $8 • (12/31/1997) • **82**
Cabernet Sauvignon Paso Robles 1994 • $8 • (11/30/1996) • **78**
Cabernet Sauvignon Paso Robles 1993 • $7 • (12/15/1995) • **83**
Chardonnay Paso Robles 1996: Simple, crisp, flinty lemon flavors are straightforward. Not a lot of personality, but a good wine in a lighter style. • $8 • (7/31/1998) • **82**
Merlot Napa Valley 1992 • $8 • (9/15/1994) • **83**

NORMAN | CALIFORNIA

Cabernet Sauvignon Paso Robles 1996: Serves up a fruity blend of blackberry, cherry and cassis flavors. The tannins are ripe and firm, while the wine remains lean-textured. Finishes with a touch of earthiness. Best from 2001 through 2006. • $17 • (10/15/1999) • **86**
Cabernet Sauvignon Paso Robles 1994 • $16 • (11/15/1997) • **86**
Cabernet Sauvignon Paso Robles 1993 • $16 • (12/15/1996) • **85**
Cabernet Sauvignon Paso Robles 1992 • $13 • (11/15/1994) • **87**
Cabernet Sauvignon Paso Robles No Nonsense Red 1992 • $9 • (11/15/1994) • **82**
Merlot Paso Robles 1996: Fairly austere and tight, with a narrow band of black cherry and cedar. Moderate finish. Drink through 2003. • $18 • (9/30/1998) • **84**
No Nonsense Red Paso Robles Claret 1996: A pretty wine, with berry and vanilla flavors on a polished frame, finishing smooth. 66 percent Cabernet Sauvignon, 13 percent Merlot, 21 percent Cabernet Franc. Drink now.–H.S. • $15 • (10/31/1998) • **85**

No Nonsense Red Paso Robles Claret 1995 • $14 • (10/31/1997) • **81**
No Nonsense Red Paso Robles Claret 1994 • $12 • (11/15/1996) • **86**
Pinot Noir Paso Robles William Cain Vineyard 1995 • $16 • (1/31/1998) • **86**
Sauvignon Blanc Paso Robles Morrow Vineyard 1997: Starts okay, but finishes with sour, vegetal flavors.–J.L. • $11 • (5/15/2000) • **74**
Sauvignon Blanc Paso Robles Morrow Vineyard 1996 • $12 • (3/31/1998) • **87**
Zinfandel Cucamonga Valley Old Vine 1998: Flavors of strawberry and spice finish with drying tannins. Drink now through 2004.–J.L. • $16 • (5/15/2000) • **84**
Zinfandel Paso Robles 1993 • $13 • (10/15/1995) • **90**
Zinfandel Paso Robles 1992 • $11 • (7/31/1994) • **88**
Zinfandel Paso Robles The Classic 1996: Ripe and juicy, with a wide array of plum, cherry, berry, tar, cedar and spicy nuances, turning smooth and creamy on the finish. Drink now.–J.L. • $15 • (5/31/1999) • **89**
Zinfandel Paso Robles The Classic 1995 • $16 • (6/15/1998) • **83**
Zinfandel Paso Robles The Classic 1994 • $13 • (4/30/1996) • **88**
Zinfandel Paso Robles The Monster 1997: A bold, ripe, juicy and complex Zin, brimming with ripe cherry, raspberry, wild berry and spicy nuances. It's a big wine, all right, but not the "monster" you might expect from the label. Drink now through 2003.–J.L. • $18 • (6/30/1999) • **88**
Zinfandel Paso Robles The Monster 1994 • $18 • (4/30/1997) • **90**

NORTHSTAR | WASHINGTON

Merlot Columbia Valley 1994 • $50 • (12/15/1997) • **88**

OAK FALLS | CALIFORNIA

Merlot California 1996: A pungent aroma of geraniums overwhelms the berry and cherry in the background. Drink now.–J.L. • $7 • (9/30/1998) • **75**
Merlot Napa Valley 1992 • $9 • (6/15/1995) • **80**
Merlot Napa Valley Private Reserve 1990 • $8 • (3/31/1993) • **82**
Zinfandel Amador County 1991 • $6 • (10/15/1995) • **82**

OAK KNOLL | OREGON

Chardonnay Willamette Valley 1996: Offers pretty pear and honey flavors on a chalky texture, with hints of citrus on the soft finish. Drink now.–H.S. • $14 • (5/31/1999) • **82**
Pinot Gris Willamette Valley 1998: Bright and effusive, with pretty citrus, melon and spice flavors lingering on the fresh finish. Drink now.–H.S. • $13 • (3/31/2000) • **88**
Pinot Gris Willamette Valley 1996 • $13 • (3/31/1998) • **82**
Pinot Gris Willamette Valley Vintage Reserve 1996: Has a floral, slightly stalky edge to the ripe melon and almond flavors. Finishes soft and generous. Drink now.–H.S. • $17 • (5/31/1999) • **80**
Pinot Noir Oregon Vintage Select 1983 • $20 • (2/15/1990) • **78**
Pinot Noir Oregon Vintage Select 1982 • $25 • (2/15/1990) • **77**
Pinot Noir Willamette Valley 1992 • $12 • (11/30/1994) • **83**
Pinot Noir Willamette Valley 1991 • $12 • (3/15/1994) • **83**
Pinot Noir Willamette Valley 1990 • $12 • (2/28/1993) • **80**
Pinot Noir Willamette Valley 1989 • $12 • (2/28/1993) • **70**
Pinot Noir Willamette Valley 1988 • $11 • (4/15/1991) • **81**
Pinot Noir Willamette Valley Five Mountains Vineyard 1997: A serious Pinot Noir in a light frame, with pretty currant flavors mingling with spice and toast on the finish. Drink now through 2004.–H.S. • $20 • (3/31/2000) • **86**
Pinot Noir Willamette Valley Silver Anniversary Reserve 1994 • $20 • (2/28/1997) • **87**
Pinot Noir Willamette Valley Vintage Reserve 1996: Crisp in texture, with bright currant and spice flavors that echo nicely on the finish. Needs to soften a bit. Best from 2001 through 2004.–H.S. • $30 • (3/31/2000) • **86**
Pinot Noir Willamette Valley Vintage Reserve 1994 • $34 • (2/28/1998) • **86**
Pinot Noir Willamette Valley Vintage Reserve 1992 • $24 • (1/31/1996) • **85**
Pinot Noir Willamette Valley Vintage Reserve 1990 • $20 • (3/15/1994) • **86**
Pinot Noir Willamette Valley Vintage Select 1989 • $18 • (2/28/1993) • **79**
Pinot Noir Willamette Valley Vintage Select 1988 • $18 • (5/31/1991) • **81**
Pinot Noir Willamette Valley Vintage Select 1987 • $18 • (2/15/1990) • **77**
Pinot Noir Willamette Valley Vintage Select 1985 • $15 • (6/15/1987) • **70**

Key: SS—Spectator Selection CS—Cellar Selection HR—Highly Recommended
$NA—Price Not Available a—Auction Price (BT)—Barrel Tasting
For a key to the tasters' initials, see "How to Use These Listings."
Dates in parentheses indicate the issues in which the ratings were published.

OAK RIDGE | CALIFORNIA

Cabernet Sauvignon California Classic Reserve 1997: Simple and soft, with grapey flavors and a vanilla note.–J.L. • $8 • (11/15/1999) • **74**

OAKENCROFT | VIRGINIA

Chardonnay Monticello 1997: A crisp, apple- and citrus-flavored white showing moderate richness midpalate, then firming up on the finish, where butterscotch nuances emerge. Drink now.–B.S. • $12 • (12/15/1998) • **82**
Merlot Monticello 1996: Exciting wine from Virginia. A really attractive Merlot whose bright fruit and mellow oak flavors melt in your mouth and linger on the finish due to a lush texture and good balance. Drink now. • $14 • (10/31/1998) • **88**

OAKFORD | CALIFORNIA

Cabernet Sauvignon Oakville 1996: A very seductive wine. Rich in flavor, finesse and polish, with ripe, juicy plum, blackberry, cherry, tar, tea, spice and pretty, toasty oak. Not overdone, but complex and elegant, with fine, detailed tannins. Drinkable now. Best from 2001 through 2008.–J.L. • $70 • (8/31/1999) • **92**
Cabernet Sauvignon Oakville 1995: Ripe and juicy, with bright, supple black cherry, currant and anise flavors that turn elegant and complex. Drink through 2007.–J.L. • $50 • (1/31/1999) • **90**
Cabernet Sauvignon Oakville 1994: The best Oakford to date and a good value for a '94. Smooth, ripe and polished, with a pretty array of well-integrated plum, black cherry, wild berry, anise and spice, it's a finesse style that doesn't overwhelm with extract and tannin. Drink through 2006.–J.L. • $45 • (10/31/1998) • **91**
Cabernet Sauvignon Napa Valley 1993 • $32 • (11/30/1997) • **86**
Cabernet Sauvignon Napa Valley 1992 • $30 • (11/15/1996) • **89**
Cabernet Sauvignon Napa Valley 1991 • $30 • (12/15/1995) • **88**
Cabernet Sauvignon Napa Valley 1990 • $25 • (11/15/1994) • **88**
Cabernet Sauvignon Napa Valley 1989 • $25 • (11/15/1994) • **88**
Cabernet Sauvignon Napa Valley 1988: Lean, with crisp, firm tannins, the core of currant, tobacco, herb and spice flavors is attractive, though it shortens up on the finish. Has the tannic strength to age further but, like most '88s, runs a risk of drying out. (1988 California Cabernet retrospective tasting). Drink now through 2002.–J.L. • $25 • (11/15/1998) • **86**
Cabernet Sauvignon Napa Valley 1987 • $25 • (11/15/1990) • **91**

OAKVILLE RANCH | CALIFORNIA

Cabernet Sauvignon Napa Valley 1997: Tightly wound, with a firm band of ripe cherry, plum and currant. Firms up on the finish, where the tannins are more evident. Best from 2002 through 2010.–J.L. • $50 • (5/15/2000) • **89**
Cabernet Sauvignon Napa Valley 1996: Lean and cedary, yet enough ripe plum and black cherry fills in the gaps to make it interesting, though it lacks richness and added depth. Mildly tannic. Drink now through 2004.–J.L. • $40 • (11/15/1999) • **88**
Cabernet Sauvignon Napa Valley 1995: Ripe, juicy, elegant Cabernet flavors here, with a band of black cherry, plum, currant and spice. Fans out and fills the palate, finishing with a lingering aftertaste, lively acidity and enough tannin to merit short-term cellaring. Drink through 2007.–J.L. • $35 • (11/15/1998) • **92**
Cabernet Sauvignon Napa Valley 1994 • $30 • (7/31/1997) • **88**
Cabernet Sauvignon Napa Valley 1993 • $28 • (11/15/1996) • **88**
Cabernet Sauvignon Napa Valley 1992 • $24 • (12/15/1995) • **90**
Cabernet Sauvignon Napa Valley 1991 • $27 a • (9/30/1994) • **89**
Cabernet Sauvignon Napa Valley 1990 • $23 • (10/15/1993) HR • **93**
Cabernet Sauvignon Napa Valley 1989 • $20 • (11/15/1992) • **90**
Cabernet Sauvignon Napa Valley Lewis Select 1991 • $28 • (9/30/1994) • **91**
Cabernet Sauvignon Napa Valley Reserve 1991 • $32 • (5/15/1995) HR • **92**
Chardonnay Napa Valley ORV 1996 • $32 • (5/15/1998) • **92**
Chardonnay Napa Valley Vista Vineyard 1998: Tight and restrained, with citrus, lemon and light cedary oak, finishing with a glimmer of tart pear and apple. Drink now through 2004.–J.L. • $35 • (5/15/2000) • **87**
Chardonnay Napa Valley Vista Vineyard 1997: Ripe, clean and spicy, with pear, nectarine, tangerine, apple and melon, it turns a bit on the finish, but nothing that short-term cellaring won't soften. Drink now through 2002.–J.L. • $30 • (4/30/1999) • **90**
Chardonnay Napa Valley Vista Vineyard 1996 • $26 • (5/31/1998) • **90**

Merlot Napa Valley 1995: Tight and tannic, with a hard edge to the core of mint and cherry. Best to let this one sit for a year or two, as the tannins are raw and biting. Drink through 2006.–J.L. • $35 • (9/30/1998) • **86**
Merlot Napa Valley 1994 • $28 • (7/31/1997) • **92**
Merlot Napa Valley 1993 • $26 • (11/30/1996) • **87**
Merlot Napa Valley 1992 • $24 • (5/15/1996) • **83**
Old Vine Field Blend Napa Valley 1993 • $18 • (11/30/1995) • **87**
Robert's Blend Napa Valley 1995: A touch tart and green now, atop a core of tart black cherry, currant and wild berry, finishing with tight, chewy tannins, traces of mineral and tobacco, and a lingering aftertaste. A blend of Cabernet Franc and Cabernet Sauvignon. Drink through 2007.–J.L. • $45 • (11/15/1998) • **89**
Robert's Blend Napa Valley 1994 • $45 • (3/31/1998) • **85**
Robert's Blend Napa Valley 1993 • $42 • (7/31/1997) • **88**

OAKWOOD | WASHINGTON

Cabernet Sauvignon Yakima Valley 1991: Offers nice mature flavors of plum and anise, with hints of pepper and cedar, but the grainy texture of the tannins means this will never be supple. Drink through 2004.–H.S. • $12 • (8/31/1998) • **86**
Cabernet Sauvignon Yakima Valley 1989 • $14 • (9/30/1995) • **87**
Cabernet Sauvignon Yakima Valley Reserve 1987 • $20 • (11/30/1993) HR • **92**
Cabernet-Petite Sirah-Lemberger-Merlot Yakima Valley Signature Red NV: Except for a raw-wood, almost medicinal aroma, this has plenty of charm, with its cherry, sarsaparilla and vanilla flavors. Light enough not to need cellaring. Drink now.–H.S. • $25 • (9/30/1999) • **81**
Lemberger Yakima Valley 1994: Ripe and generous, with a gamy edge to the plum and cranberry flavors as they linger on the gentle finish. Drink now. –H.S. • $10 • (8/31/1999) • **84**
Lemberger Yakima Valley 1993: Smooth and appealing for its ripe plum and anise flavors.–H.S. • $10 • (8/31/1998) • **85**
Lemberger Yakima Valley 1991 • $10 • (9/30/1995) • **78**
Merlot Yakima Valley 1995: On the lighter side, with pretty plum and spice flavors, finishing with a touch of exotic spice. Drink now.–H.S. • $18 • (8/31/1998) • **85**
Muscat Canelli Yakima Valley 1993 • $6 • (9/30/1995) • **85**
Riesling Yakima Valley Late Harvest 1995 • $10/375 ml. • (9/30/1996) • **88**

OASIS | VIRGINIA

Brut Virginia NV • $NA • (3/31/1998) • **78**
Brut Virginia Cuvée d'Or Celebration 2000 NV: Something quite solid from a little-known wine region. A satisfying, fruit-centered sparkling wine with plenty of crisp apple flavor and rather full body. Drink now. • $49 • (11/15/1998) • **84**
Cabernet Franc-Cabernet Sauvignon-Merlot Virginia Meritage 1997: Thin and fading, with only faint berry and cherry flavors and an astringent finish. Absurdly priced. Past its prime.–K.M. • $39 • (3/31/1999) • **74**
Cabernet Sauvignon Virginia 1995 • $20 • (5/15/1998) • **78**
Cabernet Sauvignon Virginia Reserve 1997: Some red berry flavors show up, but the finish dries out quickly. Not much fun.–K.M. • $20 • (3/31/1999) • **76**
Chardonnay Virginia Barrel Select 1997: Light and well balanced, this Chardonnay has flinty aromas, with hints of lemon, earth and apple. Drink now. • $19 • (6/15/1999) • **83**
Chardonnay Virginia Dogwood NV: Vanilla and honey aromas combine with a hint of apple on the palate in this rich yet subtly flavored white. Modest finish. 75 percent Chardonnay and 25 percent Seyval Blanc. Drink now. –B.S. • $10 • (12/15/1998) • **80**
Extra Dry Virginia NV • $16 • (5/15/1997) • **84**
Gewürztraminer Virginia Dry 1998: Floral and spice aromas are followed by an earthy flavor, with a hint of cherry candy at the end of this firm, straightforward white.–B.S. • $18 • (6/15/1999) • **79**
Meritage Virginia 1993 • $15 • (6/30/1995) • **77**
Merlot Virginia 1997: Thin, dried cherry flavors here, and a washed-out, tealike finish. Not recommended. Tasted twice, with consistent notes. –K.M. • $25 • (3/31/1999) • **67**
Merlot Virginia 1995 • $24 • (3/31/1998) • **78**
Merlot Virginia 1992 • $12 • (12/31/1995) • **74**
Riesling Virginia Semi-Dry 1997: Made in an Alsace style, this Riesling offers almond, pine forest and beeswax flavors. Medium-bodied, dry and moderately concentrated. Drink now.–B.S. • $18 • (6/15/1999) • **83**

OBESTER | CALIFORNIA

Pinot Noir Anderson Valley 1995 • $17 • (3/31/1997) • **72**
Pinot Noir Anderson Valley 1992 • $15 • (4/30/1994) • **78**
Sangiovese Mendocino County 1993 • $10 • (8/31/1995) • **83**
Sangiovese Mendocino County 1992 • $14 • (3/31/1994) • **79**
Zinfandel Mendocino 1995 • $15 • (6/15/1998) • **74**
Zinfandel Mendocino County 1991 • $11 • (6/15/1994) • **84**

OCEANA | CALIFORNIA

Merlot Central Coast 1997: Offers pleasant strawberry, black cherry and rhubarb notes, but turns tannic, firm and dry. Drink now.–J.L. • $10 • (11/30/1998) • **80**

OJAI | CALIFORNIA

Chardonnay Arroyo Grande Valley Talley Vineyard 1997: Though it takes time to unfold, the core of ripe pear, peach and melon is quite supple and appealing. Finishes with an earthy edge. Drink now through 2001.–J.L. • $20 • (6/30/1999) • **88**
Chardonnay Santa Barbara County Bien Nacido Vineyard 1996 • $20 • (12/15/1997) • **87**
Pinot Noir Santa Barbara County 1993 • $25 • (6/30/1995) • **86**
Pinot Noir Santa Barbara County Bien Nacido Vineyard 1997: Ripe and polished, with a range of earthy cherry, tea and cola flavors that finish smooth and rich. Drink now through 2002.–J.L. • $25 • (9/15/1999) • **86**
Pinot Noir Santa Barbara County Bien Nacido Vineyard 1996: A touch earthy and leathery, with subtle cherry and raspberry flavors that work their way into the mainstream. Finishes with well-integrated tannins and fine length. Drink now through 2001.–J.L. • $27 • (9/30/1998) • **86**
Pinot Noir Santa Barbara County Bien Nacido Vineyard Benjamin Lorenzo 1995 • $36 • (1/31/1998) • **91**
Pinot Noir Santa Lucia Highlands Pisoni Vineyard 1996: Elegant and spicy, with pretty, earthy, leathery notes, black cherry, wild berry and mineral flavors. Complex and concentrated. Drink now through 2002.–J.L. • $45 • (2/28/1999) • **88**
Syrah California 1996 • $18 • (4/30/1998) • **88**
Syrah California 1995 • $19 Ⓐ • (7/31/1997) • **89**
Syrah California 1994 • $15 • (9/30/1996) • **88**
Syrah California 1992 • $15 • (1/31/1995) • **84**
Syrah California 1991 • $15 • (12/31/1993) • **87**
Syrah California Roll Ranch Vineyard 1996: Very dark, rich and textured, with juicy plum and wild berry flavors and hints of spice, leather and mineral. Drink now through 2004.–J.L. • $23 • (12/31/1998) • **89**
Syrah Santa Barbara County Bien Nacido Vineyard 1996: Dark, but not as concentrated as the color suggests, with stewed plum and cherry flavors, beefy notes and a flash of mineral. Drink through 2004.–J.L. • $28 • (12/31/1998) • **87**
Syrah Santa Barbara County Bien Nacido Vineyard 1995 • $32 • (11/15/1997) • **91**
Syrah Santa Barbara County Stolpman Vineyard 1996: Intense, with spicy mineral, wild berry and black cherry flavors. Holds its focus, turning beefy and spicy. Drink through 2006.–J.L. • $23 • (12/31/1998) • **87**
Viognier California Roll Ranch Vineyard 1997: A tangy wine that serves up lots of lemon and mineral flavors. Firm and refreshing. Drink now. • $21 • (11/15/1998) • **85**
Viognier California Roll Ranch Vineyard 1996 • $20 • (12/15/1997) • **83**

OLD WORLD | CALIFORNIA

Zinfandel Dry Creek Valley Pena Creek Vineyard 1998: Elegant strawberry, nutmeg, cinnamon, steel and floral notes are on the lighter side, with a lingering finish. Drink now.–J.L. • $18 • (6/15/2000) • **86**
Zinfandel Russian River Valley Laughlin Vineyard 1998: Lovely blueberry, green pepper and earth flavors all come together on a light and delicate frame, with toasty oak. Drink now.–J.L. • $27 • (6/15/2000) • **87**

OLIVET LANE | CALIFORNIA

Chardonnay Russian River Valley Pellegrini Family Vineyards 1997: Ripe and elegant, with pineapple, pear and apple flavors. Finishes with detailed fruit and toast notes. Drink now through 2001.–J.L. • $15 • (6/30/1999) • **88**
Chardonnay Russian River Valley Pellegrini Family Vineyards 1996 • $14 • (5/15/1998) • **82**
Pinot Noir Russian River Valley 1993 • $13 • (12/31/1995) • **84**
Pinot Noir Russian River Valley 1992 • $12 • (2/28/1994) • **84**
Pinot Noir Russian River Valley 1991 • $10 • (2/28/1993) • **84**
Pinot Noir Russian River Valley 1988 • $9 • (6/30/1991) • **85**

OLIVET LANE

Pinot Noir Russian River Valley Pellegrini Family Vineyards 1997: Firm in texture, featuring flavors of herb, strawberry and cola. Finishes slightly dry, with lingering mint and herb flavors. Drink now.–J.L. • $20 • (6/15/1999) • **85**

Pinot Noir Russian River Valley Pellegrini Family Vineyards 1996 • $16 • (12/31/1997) • **84**

Pinot Noir Russian River Valley Pellegrini Family Vineyards 1995 • $15 • (1/31/1997) • **84**

Pinot Noir Russian River Valley Pellegrini Family Vineyards 1994 • $15 • (1/31/1996) • **86**

ONE VINEYARD | CALIFORNIA

Cabernet Sauvignon Napa Valley 1993 • $NA • (12/15/1997) • **86**

Cabernet Sauvignon Napa Valley 1989 • $18 • (3/31/1993) • **72**

Cabernet Sauvignon Napa Valley 1988 • $15 • (11/15/1992) • **77**

ONE WORLD WINERY | CALIFORNIA

Cabernet Sauvignon Russian River Valley 1991 • $15 • (5/15/1994) • **82**

Zinfandel Russian River Valley 1993 • $14 • (4/30/1996) • **70**

Zinfandel Russian River Valley 1992 • $11 • (4/30/1994) • **85**

OPTIMA | CALIFORNIA

Cabernet Sauvignon Alexander Valley 1996: Dark and leathery, with a mineral streak running through the black cherry and currant flavors. Finishes firm, with persistent flavors. Drink now through 2004.–J.L. • $35 • (9/15/1999) • **87**

Cabernet Sauvignon Alexander Valley 1995: Supple and harmonious, with a complex core of currant, herb, cherry and sage that weaves together nicely on the finish. Has a lot going for it, and short-term cellaring might do the trick. Drink through 2006.–J.L. • $30 • (12/15/1998) • **88**

Cabernet Sauvignon Alexander Valley 1994 • $28 • (8/31/1997) • **89**

Cabernet Sauvignon Alexander Valley 1992 • $25 • (12/15/1995) • **89**

Cabernet Sauvignon Alexander Valley 1991 • $25 • (2/28/1995) • **88**

Cabernet Sauvignon Alexander Valley 1990 • $27 • (6/15/1994) • **82**

Cabernet Sauvignon Sonoma County 1989 • $25 • (11/15/1992) • **88**

Cabernet Sauvignon Sonoma County 1987 • $22 • (12/15/1990) HR • **92**

Cabernet Sauvignon Sonoma County 1986 • $22 • (2/15/1990) • **91**

Cabernet Sauvignon Sonoma County 1985 • $19 • (12/15/1988) • **93**

Cabernet Sauvignon Sonoma County 1984 • $17 • (2/29/1988) • **90**

Chardonnay Carneros-Russian River Valley 1998: Spicy, with a Muscat edge to the citrus, orange and pear-laced flavors, finishing with a nice touch of light oak. Drink now.–J.L. • $30 • (4/30/2000) • **86**

Chardonnay Sonoma County 1997: Clean and refreshing, with crisp citrus, light nectarine, apple and toast flavors. Finishes with subtle hints of spice and mineral. Drink now through 2002.–H.S. • $30 • (6/30/1999) • **87**

Pinot Noir Carneros 1998: Has more ripeness than most from this vintage, with ripe cherry and berry and spicy cedar notes. Drink now through 2004.–J.L. • $40 • (5/15/2000) • **84**

Pinot Noir Russian River Valley 1998: Tight, with sour cherry and strawberry flavors and a touch of herb and cedar. Drink now through 2003.–J.L. • $45 • (5/15/2000) • **83**

Pinot Noir Russian River Valley 1997: Firmly textured, with a toasty core of black cherry, blackberry, herb and mint. The flavors linger nicely on the finish, which is clean, bright and complex, marked by ripe tannins. Drink through 2004. • $45 • (9/15/1999) • **87**

Pinot Noir Russian River Valley 1995 • $45 • (1/31/1997) • **84**

Pinot Noir Russian River Valley 1994 • $40 • (4/30/1996) • **87**

OPUS ONE | CALIFORNIA

Napa Valley 1998: Tight and grapey, dark in color, this is immense, if young and a bit unfocused. Still, the raw ingredients indicate this will be a very successful, potentially outstanding (Opus One vertical tasting—and all notes below).–J.L. • $NA • (2/29/2000) (BT) • **90-94**

Napa Valley 1997: Packed with wonderful perfumed currant, floral and spice notes atop a wall of berry, cherry and currant. Should be long-lived.–J.L. • $NA • (2/29/2000) (BT) • **95-99**

Napa Valley 1996: Wonderful finesse and complexity. Not the up-front opulent flavor of the '94 or '95, but seemingly deeper, with more finesse to the toasty clove, currant, black cherry and spice. Tannins are fine-grained. Best from 2002 through 2012.–J.L. • $132 ⓐ • (2/29/2000) • **96**

Napa Valley 1995: A shade more elegant and refined than the '94, yet sharing the delicious range of flavors, with bright black cherry, plum and floral notes. Turns smooth and polished. Best from 2003 through 2014.–J.L. • $142 ⓐ • (2/29/2000) • **95**

Napa Valley 1994: Like the '87, there's a wonderful sense of harmony and finesse to this graceful, elegant wine. Lots of complex flavors, with tiers of spicy currant and black cherry. Long, intricate aftertaste. Best from 2002 through 2014.–J.L. • $166 ⓐ • (2/29/2000) • **97**

Napa Valley 1993: Up front its supple in texture though firmly tannic, with grapey currant and black cherry. Turns firm, revealing its depth and concentration. Best from 2003 through 2012.–J.L. • $141 ⓐ • (2/29/2000) • **93**

Napa Valley 1992: Tightly wound, with firm tannins. The core of meaty currant, anise, cedar and spice tasted awkward, but all the ingredients are there for greatness. I expect this wine may take longer than most Opuses to reach its peak. Best from 2002 through 2010.–J.L. • $149 ⓐ • (2/29/2000) • **92**

Napa Valley 1991: This monumental wine has enormous richness, depth and polish, brimming with ripe, juicy plum, cherry, currant and cedary oak. Should be uncommonly long-lived. Delicious. Drink now through 2012. –J.L. • $174 ⓐ • (2/29/2000) • **97**

Napa Valley 1990: Dramatic, with its ripe, rich, plush core of exotic currant, anise, cedar, vanilla and berry notes that are enormously complex on the finish. Delicious. Drink now through 2010.–J.L. • $153 ⓐ • (2/29/2000) • **96**

Napa Valley 1989: An earthy style that's in sync with the rain-plagued vintage. Still, there's complexity within the earthy currant, cedar and spice notes, though it turns dry on the finish. Drink now through 2004.–J.L. • $136 ⓐ • (2/29/2000) • **87**

Napa Valley 1988: A very complete wine from a challenging vintage. Medium-weight, with cherry, herb, tea and coffee notes, finishing with mellow tannins. Drink now through 2003.–J.L. • $124 ⓐ • (2/29/2000) • **86**

Napa Valley 1987: Extra facets and dimensions abound in this deeply complex and flavorful wine. Impressive for its focus and finesse, though there's an underlying firmness and authority in the core of chewy currant, herb and anise flavors. Delicious. Drink now through 2007.–J.L. • $199 ⓐ • (2/29/2000) • **96**

Napa Valley 1986: Bordeaux-like in structure, this is an impressive showing. Firm tannins wrap around the currant, black cherry, anise, spice and cedar notes. Long, persistent finish. Drink now through 2006.–J.L. • $136 • (2/29/2000) • **94**

Napa Valley 1985: A wonderful showing. Very complex and intriguing, with harmony and grace. Mature, with currant, black cherry, dried fruit and spice notes and smooth, polished tannins. Drink now through 2006.–J.L. • $199 ⓐ • (2/29/2000) • **93**

Napa Valley 1984: Supple, very elegant and complex, with a meaty edge to the core of currant and black cherry flavors that turn dry and cedary. Drink now through 2004.–J.L. • $163 • (2/29/2000) • **89**

Napa Valley 1983: Tasted from magnum. A pleasant wine from a difficult vintage. Medium-weight, with dried fruit, herb and coffee notes, turning dry. Drink now.–J.L. • $135 ⓐ • (2/29/2000) • **84**

Napa Valley 1982: Tasted from magnum. A good wine from a challenging vintage, it leans toward the herbal side, with tarry dried fruit flavors and a dry finish. Drink now.–J.L. • $137 ⓐ • (2/29/2000) • **84**

Napa Valley 1981: Tasted from magnum. This light, simple wine has peaked, with coffee, herb and stewed plum flavors that turn dry. Drink now.–J.L. • $127 ⓐ • (2/29/2000) • **87**

Napa Valley 1980: Tasted from magnum. Bigger and riper than the 1979, though not as graceful or deep. Features subtle plum and cherry flavors. Drink now through 2004.–J.L. • $171 ⓐ • (2/29/2000) • **89**

Napa Valley 1979: Tasted from magnum. Wonderful range of mature, complex dried cherry, berry, herb, cedar, anise and olive. Offers depth, polish and grace, finishing with firm tannins. Lovely now. Drink now through 2006.–J.L. • $220 • (2/29/2000) • **91**

OREGON VINEYARDS | OREGON

Pinot Noir Oregon 1992 • $9 • (9/15/1994) • **83**

Pinot Noir Oregon Briggs Hill Vineyard 1997: Light and appealing for its modest strawberry and spice flavors. Second label for LaVelle Vineyards. Drink now through 2002.–H.S. • $18 • (4/30/2000) • **82**

Key: SS—Spectator Selection CS—Cellar Selection HR—Highly Recommended $NA—Price Not Available a—Auction Price (BT)—Barrel Tasting
For a key to the tasters' initials, see "How to Use These Listings."
Dates in parentheses indicate the issues in which the ratings were published.

O'REILLY'S | OREGON

Pinot Noir Oregon 1998: On the light side for a 1998, with pretty berry and mint flavors, but a streak of pickle barrel takes away some of the charm. Drink now through 2003.–H.S. • $13 • (5/15/2000) • **84**

ORFILA | CALIFORNIA

California Tawny Port NV • $13 • (5/31/1995) • **78**
Chardonnay San Diego-Monterey Counties Coastal California 1996: Soft and pleasant, with apple, pear, sweet vanilla and butter notes. Drink now. • $11 • (7/31/1998) • **83**
Merlot California 1992 • $15 • (5/15/1995) • **79**
Merlot California 1991 • $16 • (3/31/1995) • **79**
Merlot San Diego County 1991 • $25 • (3/31/1995) • **78**
Merlot San Diego County Ambassador's Reserve 1993 • $NA • (2/28/1997) • **85**
Merlot San Diego County Ambassador's Reserve 1992 • $25 • (3/31/1995) • **85**
Pinot Noir Arroyo Grande Valley Limited Bottling 1996: Dried cherry and gamy leather flavors are dominant in this lighter-style wine. The finish is a touch bitter. Drink now.–J.L. • $21 • (9/30/1998) • **79**
Sangiovese San Diego County Di Collina 1995 • $NA • (2/28/1997) • **87**
Syrah San Diego County Val De La Mer 1994 • $NA • (2/28/1997) • **87**

OSPREY'S DOMINION | NEW YORK

Cabernet Sauvignon North Fork of Long Island 1993 • $14 • (12/31/1996) • **86**
Cabernet Sauvignon North Fork of Long Island Reserve 1995: Fans of oak will love the flavors of sweet chocolate, vanilla and toast in this plush red. But there are notes of cherry and berry underneath, and the tannins are firm but gentle. Drink now through 2002.–T.M. • $25 • (6/30/1999) • **86**
Chardonnay North Fork of Long Island Reserve 1997: This lively white combines sweet vanilla notes, crisp citrusy acidity and flavors of banana and pineapple that linger on the finish. It's more exuberant than harmonious, but has the stuffing to match with food. Drink now through 2002.–T.M. • $20 • (6/30/1999) • **87**
Merlot North Fork of Long Island 1997: This ripe red shows good concentration, with toast and chocolate oak flavors matched with plum and tobacco notes. The tannins are firm, the texture thick and juicy, the finish clean. Drink now through 2003.–T.M. • $15 • (6/30/1999) • **86**
Merlot North Fork of Long Island 1993 • $14 • (12/31/1996) • **88**

PACIFIC ECHO | CALIFORNIA

Blanc de Blancs Anderson Valley 1995: Starts off with fresh floral and apple aromas. Fairly creamy on the palate, with a weighty mouthfeel despite the bubbles. Toasty, nutty flavors mingle with pear tones on the finish. Drink now through 2002. • $24 • (12/31/1998) • **88**
Brut Mendocino County NV: Tangy citrus and doughy aromas lead the way, followed by a creamy texture and a broad band of peach, pear, green apple and spice flavors. The finish is fresh, long and generous. Drink now through 2002. • $21 • (9/15/1999) • **90**
Brut Mendocino County Private Reserve 1992 • $30 • (6/30/1998) • **90**
Brut Rosé Anderson Valley 1996: Fragrant, with toasty, doughy, Bing cherry aromas. Weighty on the palate, featuring apple, citrus and herb flavors. Finishes long, with a clean mineral edge. Drink now. • $26 • (9/15/1999) • **89**
Brut Rosé Mendocino County NV • $24 • (6/30/1998) • **86**

PAGE MILL | CALIFORNIA

Cabernet Sauvignon Napa Valley V. & L. Eisele Vineyard 1990 • $18 • (3/31/1996) • **80**
Cabernet Sauvignon Napa Valley V. & L. Eisele Vineyard 1989 • $22 • (11/15/1993) • **74**
Cabernet Sauvignon Napa Valley V. & L. Eisele Vineyard 1988 • $18 • (11/15/1993) • **84**
Merlot Napa Valley O'Shaughnessy Vineyard 1997: Medium in weight, with dill-laced plum flavors of modest proportion and depth. Drink now.–J.L. • $21 • (4/30/2000) • **83**
Merlot Santa Maria Valley Bien Nacido Vineyard 1993 • $12 • (3/31/1996) • **80**
Pinot Noir Santa Maria Valley Bien Nacido Vineyard 1991 • $18 • (2/28/1994) • **86**
Pinot Noir Santa Barbara County Bien Nacido Vineyard 1990 • $18 • (2/28/1993) • **68**
Pinot Noir Santa Barbara County Bien Nacido Vineyard 1985 • $13 • (6/15/1988) • **87**
Port California Lewis 1995 • $20 • (10/15/1997) • **89**

PAGOR | CALIFORNIA

Cabernet Sauvignon California 1992 • $12 • (3/31/1996) • **73**
Merlot Santa Maria Valley 1984 • $11 • (4/30/1988) • **70**
Pinot Noir Santa Barbara County 1990 • $14 • (2/28/1993) • **65**
Pinot Noir Santa Barbara County 1987 • $11 • (12/15/1989) • **85**

PAHLMEYER | CALIFORNIA

Caldwell Vineyard Minty Cuvée Napa Valley 1990 • $NA • (12/15/1995) • **82**
Caldwell Vineyard Napa Valley 1990 • $54 Ⓐ • (10/15/1993) • **90**
Caldwell Vineyard Napa Valley 1989: Firm, minty and tannic, with a lean, angular band of currant, mineral, cedar and spice, returning to a firmly tannic finish. (1989 California Cabernet retrospective tasting). Drink now through 2005.–J.L. • $26 Ⓐ • (8/31/1999) • **87**
Caldwell Vineyard Napa Valley 1988: Firm, tight and tannic, with a leathery streak through the chewy currant, sage and mineral notes. A richly flavored wine that's among the best but, like the best, it turns dry and tannic on the finish, so drink it soon, now through 2004. Contains Cabernet Sauvignon, Cabernet Franc, Merlot, Petit Verdot, Malbec. (1988 California Cabernet retrospective tasting).–J.L. • $34 Ⓐ • (11/15/1998) • **87**
Caldwell Vineyard Napa Valley 1987 • $46 Ⓐ • (12/15/1997) • **86**
Caldwell Vineyard Napa Valley 1986 • $56 Ⓐ • (11/15/1989) • **89**
Chardonnay Napa Valley 1997: Ultrarich and ultraripe Chardonnay. A creamy, seamless wine, with sharply focused, deeply concentrated peach, pear and nectarine flavors. Turns even more complex on the finish, where pretty, toasty vanilla notes folds in. Drink now through 2004.–J.L. • $105 Ⓐ • (7/31/1999) HR • **96**
Chardonnay Napa Valley 1996 • $50 • (5/31/1998) • **90**
Jayson Napa Valley 1997: Dark, rich and plush, with complex, detailed currant, leather, mineral, sage and spice flavors that are broad and deep. Long, rich aftertaste. Merlot, Cabernet Sauvignon, Cabernet Franc, Petit Verdot and Malbec. Best from 2001 through 2007.–J.L. • $36 • (4/30/2000) • **91**
Jayson Napa Valley 1992 • $20 • (12/31/1994) • **88**
Merlot Napa Valley 1996: Impeccably balanced, remarkably complex and concentrated, with layers of currant, cedar, plum and blackberry. Turns plush and chocolaty on the finish, where the flavors soar on. Drink through 2006.–J.L. • $91 Ⓐ • (2/28/1999) • **92**
Merlot Napa Valley 1995 • $67 Ⓐ • (5/31/1998) • **90**
Merlot Napa Valley 1994 • $40 • (11/30/1996) • **89**
Merlot Napa Valley 1991 • $24 • (9/15/1994) • **85**
Merlot Napa Valley Caldwell Vineyard 1990 • $24 • (10/15/1993) • **85**
Napa Valley 1997: Dense and grapey, with rich, concentrated cherry, plum and currant, spice notes, a supple texture and a remarkably long and sophisticated finish.–J.L. • $NA • (8/31/1998) (BT) • **95-99**
Napa Valley 1996: Packs in layers of black cherry, anise, blackberry and plum, showing a sense of elegance and finesse. Firms up on the finish, where the tannins are tight and spicy. Best from 2001 through 2010.–J.L. • $134 Ⓐ • (11/15/1999) • **93**
Napa Valley 1995: Lots of ripe, juicy plum and black cherry up front, with hints of anise, sage and mineral. Finishes with well-integrated tannins and touches of tobacco and creamy oak. Drink through 2009.–J.L. • $73 Ⓐ • (10/31/1998) • **92**
Napa Valley 1994 • $83 Ⓐ • (11/30/1996) HR • **92**
Napa Valley 1993 • $36 • (5/31/1996) CS • **91**
Napa Valley 1992 • $53 Ⓐ • (12/15/1995) • **89**
Napa Valley 1991 • $56 Ⓐ • (11/15/1994) • **82**
Napa Valley 1986 • $39 • (12/15/1996) • **89**

PALMER | NEW YORK

Cabernet Franc North Fork of Long Island Proprietor's Reserve 1995: A French style of red that's quite firm and tannic, but balanced with acidity and generous enough in fruit flavor to keep your interest. A good dinner companion. Drink now through 2001. • $15 • (11/15/1998) • **86**
Cabernet Franc North Fork of Long Island Proprietor's Reserve 1994 • $14 • (12/31/1996) • **86**
Cabernet Franc North Fork of Long Island Proprietor's Reserve 1991 • $15 • (12/31/1995) • **79**
Cabernet Franc North Fork of Long Island Proprietor's Reserve 1989 • $13 • (11/15/1991) • **76**
Cabernet Sauvignon North Fork of Long Island 1995: Very serious, concentrated Cabernet, with ample but integrated tannins, ripe cherry and berry

flavors accented by chocolate and cedar, and a lingering finish. Drink now through 2002. • $13 • (11/15/1998) • **88**

Cabernet Sauvignon North Fork of Long Island 1993 • $13 • (12/31/1996) • **87**

Cabernet Sauvignon North Fork of Long Island 1988 • $14 • (6/30/1991) • **83**

Cabernet Sauvignon North Fork of Long Island 1986 • $10 • (12/15/1988) • **82**

Cabernet Sauvignon North Fork of Long Island Reserve 1997: This soft red has a lovely, velvety texture, with plum and vanilla flavors that are simple and a bit candied.–T.M. • $18 • (5/31/2000) • **79**

Chardonnay North Fork of Long Island Estate 1997: A lively combination of lemon and pineapple flavors with sweet vanilla notes gives this tender wine an assertive character. Though light, almost evanescent on the palate, its flavors linger on the finish. Drink now through 2001.–T.M. • $12 • (6/30/1999) • **84**

Chardonnay North Fork of Long Island Reserve 1997: Baked apple and vanilla flavors are lush and a bit sweet in this generous white. While not graceful, it has enough acidity to keep it fresh.–T.M. • $18 • (5/31/2000) • **79**

Gewürztraminer North Fork of Long Island 1997: A lovely Gewürztraminer, redolent of coconut, litchi and roses. Ripe and fat, yet with just enough acidity to bring everything to the harmonious conclusion with hints of grapefruit. Drink now.–B.S. • $15 • (12/15/1998) • **85**

Gewürztraminer North Fork of Long Island Select Harvest 1994 • $16/375 ml. • (6/15/1998) • **87**

Merlot North Fork of Long Island 1995: Smooth and firm. This polished red offers ripe black cherry, plum and light herb flavors, with toasty, earthy oak notes that leave a pleasant spicy finish. Tannins are a bit dry but should soften with food. Drink now through 2002.–T.M. • $20 • (6/30/1999) • **86**

Merlot North Fork of Long Island 1994 • $15 • (12/31/1996) • **84**

Merlot North Fork of Long Island 1989 • $13 • (7/31/1992) • **82**

Merlot North Fork of Long Island 1988 • $13 • (6/30/1991) • **86**

Merlot North Fork of Long Island 1986 • $10 • (12/15/1988) • **80**

Merlot North Fork of Long Island Reserve 1995 • $29 • (5/31/1998) • **85**

Pinot Blanc North Fork of Long Island 1997: Soft, with melon aromas and flavors. Finishes on an earthy note.–K.M. • $12 • (12/31/1998) • **79**

Pinot Blanc North Fork of Long Island Lieb Vineyards 1997: This shy white offers an appealing blend of delicacy and refreshment, with light floral and apple flavors that stay balanced and clean and bring you back for another sip. Drink now.–T.M. • $13 • (6/30/1999) • **83**

Pinot Blanc North Fork of Long Island Lieb Vineyards 1996: Dominated by green peach and green apple flavors, with a buttery note. A little muddled in the end.–K.M. • $12 • (8/31/1998) • **77**

Sauvignon Blanc North Fork of Long Island 1998: This straightforward white offers gentle apple and melon flavors, clean, soft and simple. Drink now.–T.M. • $15 • (5/31/2000) • **81**

Select Reserve Red North Fork of Long Island 1995: Rich and complex, a nicely balanced and fully flavored Bordeaux-style blend. It combines a firm texture, ripe plum and cherry flavors and smoky, oaky accents that linger on the finish. A blend of Cabernet Sauvignon, Merlot and Cabernet Franc. Drink now through 2001. • $25 • (11/15/1998) • **87**

Select Reserve White North Fork of Long Island 1997: This white has a lively mix of fruit flavors, with notes of melon, mango and banana. Round and generous on the palate, it makes a refreshing quaff. Easy to like. A blend of Chardonnay, Pinot Blanc, Sauvignon Blanc and Gewürztraminer. Drink now.–T.M. • $15 • (6/30/1999) • **84**

White Riesling North Fork of Long Island 1997: Slightly sweet, smooth in texture and simple in flavor. Easy to drink. • $12 • (11/15/1998) • **79**

PALOMA | CALIFORNIA

Merlot Napa Valley 1997: Supple and complex, an elegant, graceful style, with pretty currant, plum, wild berry, sage and cedar notes. Drink now through 2007.–J.L. • $39 • (12/31/1999) • **88**

Merlot Napa Valley 1996: Has a lot of stuffing, with concentrated currant, plum, mineral and black cherry flavors. Also shows off some pretty chocolate and vanilla-scented notes, with ripe, dense tannins. Takes time to open up. Drink through 2004.–J.L. • $30 • (10/15/1998) • **91**

Merlot Napa Valley 1995 • $26 • (12/15/1997) • **90**

Syrah Spring Mountain District 1997: Distinctive for its aromatic and peppery flavors, it's lean and trim on the palate, in need of a little more stuffing. Drink now through 2004.–J.L. • $30 • (12/31/1999) • **83**

Syrah Spring Mountain District Milagro 1996: Throws out lots of spicy plum, mint and wild berry flavors, turning firmly tannic on the finish, where the flavors are ripe and complex. Picks up a meaty note. Drink through 2005.–J.L. • $30 • (11/30/1998) • **88**

PANTHER CREEK | OREGON

Melon Willamette Valley Stewart Vineyard 1998: Bright and vibrant, appealing for its spicy pear and gently honeyed aromas and flavors, which echo on the juicy finish. Drink now.–H.S. • $20 • (4/30/2000) • **88**

Pinot Noir Willamette Valley 1994 • $15 • (10/15/1996) • **87**

Pinot Noir Willamette Valley 1988 • $15 • (4/15/1991) • **75**

Pinot Noir Willamette Valley 1987 • $17 • (4/15/1990) • **74**

Pinot Noir Willamette Valley Bednarik Vineyard 1996: Lithe and supple, its fine-grained tannins subdued enough to let the raspberry and cherry flavors emerge brightly on the finish. A delicate wine with charm, despite a touch of bitterness. Drink now through 2004.–H.S. • $36 • (8/31/1998) • **88**

Pinot Noir Willamette Valley Bednarik Vineyard 1995 • $33 • (11/30/1997) • **86**

Pinot Noir Willamette Valley Bednarik Vineyard 1994 • $36 • (10/15/1996) • **85**

Pinot Noir Willamette Valley Canary Hill Barn Block 1993 • $30 • (3/31/1996) • **85**

Pinot Noir Willamette Valley Canary Hill Vineyard 1992 • $35 • (11/30/1994) • **87**

Pinot Noir Willamette Valley Carter Vineyard 1993 • $30 • (3/31/1996) • **88**

Pinot Noir Willamette Valley Carter Vineyard 1992 • $30 • (11/30/1994) • **86**

Pinot Noir Willamette Valley Carter Vineyard 1990 • $30 • (2/28/1993) • **89**

Pinot Noir Willamette Valley Freedom Hill Vineyard 1996: Firm in texture, a soft-spoken wine with berry and currant flavors that persist on the floral-scented finish. Tannins need to soften. Drink through 2005.–H.S. • $36 • (8/31/1998) • **88**

Pinot Noir Willamette Valley Freedom Hill Vineyard 1995 • $33 • (12/31/1997) • **85**

Pinot Noir Willamette Valley Freedom Hill Vineyard 1994 • $36 • (10/15/1996) • **87**

Pinot Noir Willamette Valley Freedom Hill Vineyard 1993 • $30 • (3/31/1996) • **85**

Pinot Noir Willamette Valley Freedom Hill Vineyard Winemaker's Cuvée 1995 • $38 • (11/30/1997) • **88**

Pinot Noir Willamette Valley Reserve 1997: Light in structure, with a supple texture and nice black cherry and earth aromas and flavors that linger on the modest finish. Drink now.–H.S. • $27 • (3/31/2000) • **85**

Pinot Noir Willamette Valley Reserve 1996: Ripe flavors of black cherry and anise dance on a background of scratchy tannins; not a big wine, but one with a texture that needs time to refine. Drink through 2003.–H.S. • $25 • (8/31/1998) • **88**

Pinot Noir Willamette Valley Reserve 1995 • $25 • (11/30/1997) • **86**

Pinot Noir Willamette Valley Reserve 1994 • $25 • (10/15/1996) • **89**

Pinot Noir Willamette Valley Reserve 1993 • $21 • (1/31/1996) • **90**

Pinot Noir Willamette Valley Reserve 1990 • $18 • (2/28/1993) • **86**

Pinot Noir Willamette Valley Reserve Unfiltered 1992 • $20 • (11/30/1994) • **80**

Pinot Noir Willamette Valley Shea Vineyard 1996: Beneath the firm texture lurk solid currant and plum flavors, hinting at spice and orange peel on the silky finish. Give it some time. Drink through 2004.–H.S. • $36 • (8/31/1998) • **87**

Pinot Noir Willamette Valley Shea Vineyard 1995 • $33 • (11/30/1997) • **86**

Pinot Noir Willamette Valley Shea Vineyard 1994 • $36 • (10/15/1996) • **91**

Pinot Noir Willamette Valley Winemaker's Cuvée 1997: On the light side, with crisp plum and vanilla flavors that echo on the open-textured finish. Drink now through 2003.–H.S. • $32 • (12/31/1999) • **86**

Pinot Noir Willamette Valley Winemaker's Cuvée 1996: Lean and chewy, with racy blackberry and smoky flavors that remain lively through the finish. Drink through 2004.–H.S. • $30 • (8/31/1998) • **87**

Pinot Noir Willamette Valley Winemaker's Cuvée 1993 • $28 • (1/31/1996) • **89**

PAOLETTI | CALIFORNIA

Cabernet Sauvignon Napa Valley 1996: Firm, intense, rich and concentrated, with layers of ripe, spicy black cherry, currant, plum and mineral, adding a nice touch of toasty, spicy oak and a lingering aftertaste. Best from 2001 through 2008.–J.L. • $39 • (9/30/1999) • **90**

Cabernet Sauvignon Napa Valley 1995: Powdery tannins up front turn velvety on the finish, framing licorice, blackberry, cassis and herb flavors. Shows weight on the palate, with a smooth finish. Drink now through 2004. • $42 • (10/31/1998) • **87**

Cabernet Sauvignon Napa Valley 1994 • $30 • (12/15/1997) • **87**

Key: SS—Spectator Selection CS—Cellar Selection HR—Highly Recommended $NA—Price Not Available a—Auction Price (BT)—Barrel Tasting For a key to the tasters' initials, see "How to Use These Listings."
Dates in parentheses indicate the issues in which the ratings were published.

Cabernet Sauvignon Napa Valley Bella Novello 1997: Ripe and tightly textured, showing mineral, clay, cassis, red currant, cedar and sage flavors and finishing with modest tannins. Drink now through 2005.–J.L. • $28 • (10/15/1999) • **87**

Chardonnay Napa Valley 1998: Smells and tastes oxidized, with soapy, perfumed aromas and a touch of onion skin adding to the pear.–J.L. • $28 • (5/31/2000) • **77**

Chardonnay Napa Valley 1997: Quite massive in its rich texture and full-blown hazelnut, butterscotch, coconut, bacon and apricot flavors. Highly oak-influenced and atypical of the varietal and region. Tasty, fun and exotic. Drink now. • $28 • (6/30/1999) • **88**

La Forza Napa Valley 1995 • $30 • (3/31/1998) • **88**

Merlot Napa Valley 1996: Austere, with a strong cedary edge to the modest range of sage and plum flavors. Turns dry and sharp on the finish, where the dryness and tannins stand out. Best from 2001 through 2008.–J.L. • $36 • (4/30/2000) • **87**

Merlot Napa Valley 1995: Dark, dense and tannic, this hard-edged wine has firm, chewy tannins. Just enough ripe cherry and currant flavor emerges to suggest short-term cellaring. Drink through 2006.–J.L. • $32 • (9/30/1998) • **86**

PARADIGM | CALIFORNIA

Cabernet Sauvignon Oakville 1998: A racy style, with distinctive herbal notes adding to the core of currant and cherry. Lively finish.–J.L. • $NA • (8/31/1999) (BT) • **90-94**

Cabernet Sauvignon Oakville 1996: Dark, rich and seductive, with a pretty core of earthy cherry, currant and plum flavors, picking up traces of herb and sage on the finish. Wonderful sense of balance and finesse. Drink through 2008.–J.L. • $44 • (10/15/1999) • **91**

Cabernet Sauvignon Oakville 1995: Beautifully orchestrated, with a wonderful sense of harmony and finesse, and ripe, plush-textured currant, black cherry, anise, sage and cedar flavors that fan out and linger on the finish. Best from 2001 through 2009.–J.L. • $40 • (11/15/1998) • **93**

Cabernet Sauvignon Napa Valley Oakville 1994 • $30 • (9/30/1997) • **92**

Cabernet Sauvignon Napa Valley Oakville 1993 • $28 • (11/15/1996) • **89**

Cabernet Sauvignon Napa Valley 1992 • $28 • (12/15/1995) • **87**

Cabernet Sauvignon Napa Valley 1991 • $26 • (11/15/1994) • **90**

Merlot Napa Valley Oakville 1994 • $30 • (6/30/1997) • **92**

Merlot Oakville 1996: Bold, ripe and juicy, in a distinctive style with a leathery, sandalwood edge to the core of currant, plum and blackberry flavors, turning spicy, with supple tannins and a long finish. Drink now through 2004.–J.L. • $35 • (5/15/1999) • **93**

Merlot Oakville 1995: Touches of earth and leather, with a charred oak edge, introduce this tightly focused, firm and tannic, even a bit chunky, wine. The flavors are rich and supple, with tar, spice, currant and meaty flavors on the finish. Drink through 2005.–J.L. • $32 • (7/31/1998) • **91**

Zinfandel Oakville 1995 • $22 • (6/15/1998) • **89**

PARADISE RIDGE | CALIFORNIA

Blanc de Blanc Sonoma County Private Reserve 1995 • $19 • (5/15/1998) • **83**

Sauvignon Blanc Sonoma County Grandview Vineyard 1996 • $13 • (4/30/1998) • **82**

PARADISE VALLEY | ARIZONA

Cabernet Sauvignon Arizona 1994 • $8 • (12/15/1996) • **79**

PARADUXX | CALIFORNIA

Napa Valley 1997: Quite rich and focused, with ripe plum, blackberry, raspberry and wild berry. Long, complex aftertaste. Drink now through 2007.–J.L. • $35 • (4/30/2000) • **88**

Napa Valley 1996: Complex, with ripe, spicy plum, wild berry, earth and tar notes and gritty tannins that finally soften. Zinfandel, Cabernet Sauvignon, Merlot, Petit Verdot and Cabernet Franc. Drink now through 2004.–J.L. • $30 • (12/31/1998) • **87**

Napa Valley 1994 • $22 • (8/31/1997) • **84**

PARAISO SPRINGS | CALIFORNIA

Chardonnay Santa Lucia Highlands 1997: A fine balance of rich texture and subtle pear, fig and oak flavors that come together seamlessly on the long, complex finish. Drink now.–J.L. • $16 • (7/31/1999) • **91**

Chardonnay Santa Lucia Highlands 1996: Fairly tropical, with bright orange and lemon flavors to the fore. A bit blowsy, but balanced by its acidity. Fun. Better than previously reviewed. Drink now. • $16 • (9/15/1998) • **84**

Johannisberg Riesling Santa Lucia Highlands 1996 • $9 • (7/31/1997) • **87**

Johannisberg Riesling Santa Lucia Highlands Late Harvest 1993 • $20 • (7/31/1995) • **85**

Pinot Blanc Santa Lucia Highlands 1996 • $13 • (9/15/1997) • **88**

Pinot Blanc Santa Lucia Highlands Reserve 1996 • $23 • (5/15/1998) • **88**

Pinot Noir Carneros 1991 • $8 • (2/28/1994) • **77**

Pinot Noir Santa Lucia Highlands 1996: Pretty lightweight, yet it shows varietal character, with cherry, plum and herbs at the fore. Slightly oxidized, though. • $23 • (9/15/1998) • **78**

Pinot Noir Santa Lucia Highlands 1995 • $23 • (2/28/1998) • **85**

Pinot Noir Santa Lucia Highlands 1994: Tired, with a weedy edge. Some vanilla, cherry and plum flavors struggle through. Ends short. Past its prime. • $23 • (8/31/1998) • **74**

PARDUCCI | CALIFORNIA

Bono-Sirah Mendocino 1990 • $7 • (11/15/1992) • **82**

Cabernet Franc Mendocino County 1989 • $10 • (11/15/1991) • **85**

Cabernet Sauvignon Mendocino 1995 • $11 • (9/30/1997) • **81**

Cabernet Sauvignon Mendocino County 1992 • $8 • (11/15/1995) • **88**

Cabernet Sauvignon Mendocino County 1991 • $8 • (2/28/1995) • **84**

Cabernet Sauvignon Mendocino County 1989 • $8 • (4/15/1994) • **84**

Cabernet Sauvignon North Coast 1990 • $8 • (11/15/1994) • **79**

Cabernet Sauvignon North Coast 1988 • $8 • (11/15/1992) • **80**

Cabernet Sauvignon North Coast Vineyard Select 1996: Firm, with pronounced bell pepper flavors but enough texture and black cherry notes to keep it interesting. Better than previously reviewed. Drink now through 2003.–J.L. • $11 • (9/15/1999) • **82**

Cabernet-Merlot Mendocino County Cellarmaster Selection 1993 • $15 • (11/15/1995) • **88**

Cabernet-Merlot Mendocino County Cellarmaster Selection 1986 • $15 • (11/15/1992) • **80**

Cabernet-Merlot Mendocino County Cellarmaster Selection 1978 • $12 • (2/01/1986) • **75**

Charbono Mendocino Old Vines 1995: Pleasantly smoky, with tart cherry flavors and spicy, toasted oak notes. Finishes with grainy tannins. Drink now through 2003. • $10 • (3/31/1999) • **83**

Charbono Mendocino Old Vines 1994 • $10 • (3/31/1998) • **87**

Chardonnay Mendocino Old Vines 1996 • $10 • (11/30/1997) • **83**

Chardonnay Mendocino Vineyard Select 1997: Ripe, soft and open-textured, with simple toast and pear flavors. Finishes with nice crispness. Drink now.–J.L. • $10 • (5/31/1999) • **81**

Merlot California 1994 • $8 • (12/31/1995) • **88**

Merlot Mendocino County Vineyard Select 1997: Simple, with herbal and strawberry notes and a touch of earthiness. Turns dry on the finish. • $11 • (3/31/1999) • **78**

Merlot Mendocino Vineyard Select 1996: Pleasant plum and spice flavors turn rich with roasted oak notes. Finishes with grainy tannins. Drink now.–H.S. • $10 • (9/15/1998) • **82**

Merlot North Coast 1992 • $10 • (6/15/1994) • **85**

Merlot North Coast 1990 • $8 • (10/31/1992) • **82**

Merlot North Coast 1989 • $10 • (11/15/1991) • **85**

Merlot North Coast 1988 • $10 • (4/30/1991) • **78**

Petite Sirah California 1994 • $10 • (10/15/1996) • **87**

Petite Sirah California Old Vines 1995 • $10 • (3/31/1998) • **86**

Petite Sirah Mendocino County 1992 • $7 • (9/30/1995) • **86**

Petite Sirah Mendocino County 1991 • $7 • (2/28/1995) • **84**

Petite Sirah Mendocino County 1989 • $7 • (11/30/1992) • **80**

Petite Sirah Mendocino Vineyard Select 1996: Here's a rich red at an affordable price, from a winery doiing well with this variety in California. It shows good depth and an enticing array of floral, spice and blackberry flavors, turning firm and chewy with tannins. Drink now through 2003.–J.L. • $10 • (3/31/1999) • **86**

Pinot Noir Mendocino 1995 • $10 • (3/31/1997) • **74**

Pinot Noir Mendocino County 1994 • $8 • (1/31/1996) • **87**

Pinot Noir Mendocino County 1993 • $7 • (12/31/1995) • **79**

Pinot Noir Mendocino County 1992 • $7 • (1/31/1994) • **83**

Pinot Noir Mendocino County 1990 • $7 • (9/30/1992) • **85**

Pinot Noir Mendocino County 1988 • $8 • (4/15/1990) • **85**

Pinot Noir Mendocino County Cellarmaster Selection 1987 • $15 • (4/30/1991) • **84**

Pinot Noir Mendocino County Old Vines 1996 • $10 • (6/15/1998) • **83**

Pinot Noir Mendocino Vineyard Select 1997: Simple, with green herbal notes and muted cherry flavors.–J.L. • $10 • (8/31/1998) • **77**
Sauvignon Blanc Lake County Vineyard Select 1998: Herb and lemon notes are lively and tart, but turn simple and a bit green on the finish. Drink now.–J.L. • $9 • (5/31/2000) • **80**
Sauvignon Blanc Lake County Vineyard Select 1997: An interesting expression of Sauvignon Blanc, this California bottling serves up nontypical peachy aromas at the start, then comes in with bright acidity and fresh, clean grapefruit flavors on the palate. Well worth a try, at a no-risk price. Drink now. • $10 • (11/30/1998) • **85**
Sauvignon Blanc Mendocino 1996 • $8 • (6/30/1997) • **83**
Syrah Mendocino Old Vines 1995 • $10 • (3/31/1998) • **86**
Zinfandel Mendocino County 1994 • $8 • (11/30/1996) • **82**
Zinfandel Mendocino County 1993 • $7 • (10/15/1995) • **77**
Zinfandel Mendocino County 1992 • $6 • (10/15/1994) • **82**
Zinfandel Mendocino County 1991 • $6 • (9/15/1993) • **82**
Zinfandel Mendocino County 1990 • $6 • (9/30/1993) • **78**
Zinfandel Mendocino County Cellarmaster Selection 1990 • $12 • (10/15/1994) • **83**
Zinfandel Mendocino Old Vines 1996 • $10 • (5/31/1998) • **82**
Zinfandel Mendocino Vineyard Select 1997: Strawberry jam notes deteriorate on the bitter, tannic finish.–J.L. • $10 • (5/31/2000) • **77**
Zinfandel North Coast 1995 • $10 • (11/15/1997) • **78**
Zinfandel North Coast 1988 • $6 • (10/15/1992) • **74**

PARKER, FESS | CALIFORNIA

Chardonnay Santa Barbara County 1998: Ripe, with tropical, apricot, tangerine and lemon peel flavors that have good focus through the finish. Drink now.–J.L. • $16 • (6/15/2000) • **86**
Chardonnay Santa Barbara County American Tradition Reserve 1996: Tangy, with a band of earthy citrus, pear and vanilla flavors, it's an elegant style that remains complex and tasty through the finish. Drink now through 2001.–J.L. • $22 • (12/15/1998) • **89**
Chardonnay Santa Barbara County Marcella's Vineyard American Tradition Reserve 1996 • $24 • (6/30/1998) • **90**
Merlot Santa Barbara County 1995 • $18 • (11/30/1997) • **87**
Pinot Noir Santa Barbara County 1997: Bright and racy, with earthy cherry and wild berry flavors providing the centerpiece. Drink now through 2005.–J.L. • $30 • (6/15/2000) • **86**
Pinot Noir Santa Barbara County 1996: Light and fruity, with modest but appealing cherry, herb and berry flavors and mild, supple tannins. Drink now.–J.L. • $18 • (9/30/1998) • **83**
Pinot Noir Santa Barbara County 1994 • $16 • (2/29/1996) • **86**
Pinot Noir Santa Barbara County 1993 • $15 • (12/31/1994) • **86**
Pinot Noir Santa Barbara County American Tradition Reserve 1996: Light, supple and pleasantly balanced, with herb, dried cherry, cola and spice flavors and round, smooth tannins. Not especially complex, but well made and fun to drink now.–J.L. • $30 • (9/30/1998) • **85**
Pinot Noir Santa Barbara County American Tradition Reserve 1995 • $28 • (12/31/1996) • **84**
Pinot Noir Santa Barbara County American Tradition Reserve 1994 • $25 • (2/29/1996) • **88**
Pinot Noir Santa Barbara County American Tradition Reserve 1993 • $NA • (2/29/1996) • **86**
Syrah Santa Barbara County 1997: Straightforward, with red currant, cola and strawberry jam notes. Drink now through 2003.–J.L. • $18 • (6/15/2000) • **82**
Syrah Santa Barbara County 1995 • $18 • (11/15/1997) • **86**
Syrah Santa Barbara County 1994 • $18 • (11/30/1996) • **90**
Syrah Santa Barbara County 1992 • $15 • (9/30/1994) • **85**
Syrah Santa Barbara County American Tradition Reserve 1995: A decidedly spicy, herbal style, with a twinge of tomato and anise. A core of herb-flavored Syrah emerges, with hints of stewed plum and berry. Drink now through 2002.–J.L. • $30 • (12/15/1998) • **87**
Syrah Santa Barbara County American Tradition Reserve 1993 • $34 • (5/31/1996) • **87**
Viognier Santa Barbara County 1997: Well integrated and delicate, with a smooth texture and pretty, ripe mandarin orange, apple, spice and melon flavors. Firm on the palate. Very nice. Drink now through 2002. • $18 • (12/31/1998) • **89**

PASO ROBLES | CALIFORNIA

Zinfandel Paso Robles 1993 • $14 • (11/30/1996) • **85**

PATZ & HALL | CALIFORNIA

Chardonnay Carneros Hyde Vineyard 1997: This California Chardonnay is notable for its wonderful complexity and finesse, cascading its rich and supple pear, fig, hazelnut, citrus and spicy flavors on a smooth, creamy texture.–J.L. • $35 • (2/28/1999) HR • **93**
Chardonnay Carneros Hyde Vineyard 1996 • $35 • (1/31/1998) • **93**
Chardonnay Mendocino County Alder Springs Vineyard 1998: Serves up appealing baked apple, mineral and floral notes that turn earthy and simple on the finish. Drink now.–J.L. • $50 • (6/15/2000) • **85**
Chardonnay Mendocino County Alder Springs Vineyard 1997: Well oaked, with lots of toasty, spicy notes and a core of ripe pear, apple, melon and hazelnut nuances. Turns elegant and supple. Drink now through 2002.–J.L. • $50 • (6/15/1999) • **91**
Chardonnay Mount Veeder Carr Vineyard 1997: Sleek and elegant, rich and complex, with concentrated apple, pear, melon, fig and spicy nutmeg, this California Chardonnay shows the pedigree of the vineyard, gaining depth and nuance while showing delicacy and finesse. Drink now through 2002.–J.L. • $42 • (5/31/1999) HR • **95**
Chardonnay Mount Veeder Carr Vineyard 1996 • $42 • (6/30/1998) HR • **93**
Chardonnay Napa Valley 1998: Rich and intense, with full-bodied lemon, anise, pear and citrus, framed by toasty, smoky oak. Deep, complex aftertaste. Drink now through 2004.–J.L. • $32 • (6/15/2000) • **88**
Chardonnay Napa Valley 1997: Distinctive for its peach, pear and nectarine flavors, this enticing California white turns smooth and silky on the finish, where its elegance and finesse hold the spotlight. Drink now through 2002.–J.L. • $30 • (6/30/1999) HR • **92**
Chardonnay Napa Valley 1996 • $29 • (1/31/1998) HR • **94**
Chardonnay Russian River Valley 1996 • $29 • (1/31/1998) • **93**
Chardonnay Russian River Valley Dutton Ranch 1998: The tight band of earthy pear, spice and cedar notes gains complexity on the finish, though it remains crisp. Drink now through 2004.–J.L. • $35 • (5/15/2000) • **86**
Chardonnay Russian River Valley Woolsey Road Vineyard 1998: Crisp and citrusy, with ripe pear, fig and a bitter grapefruit edge, turning slightly sour. Drink now through 2004.–J.L. • $35 • (5/15/2000) • **85**
Chardonnay Sonoma Coast 1997: Lithe and elegant, with a pretty array of delicate lemon, citrus, tart pear and spice nuances. Turns sleek and polished on the long, complex aftertaste. Drink now through 2002.–J.L. • $30 • (6/15/1999) • **92**
Pinot Noir Carneros Hyde Vineyard 1997: Light in color and body, with pleasant strawberry and cherry notes of moderate depth and concentration, turning tannic. Drink now through 2002.–J.L. • $35 • (9/15/1999) • **86**
Pinot Noir Carneros Hyde Vineyard 1996 • $35 • (6/30/1998) • **88**
Pinot Noir Mendocino County Alder Springs Vineyard 1997: Spicy, cedary oak dominates the modest core of cherry and berryish fruit, with mild tannins. Drink now through 2005.–J.L. • $50 • (5/15/2000) • **85**
Pinot Noir Russian River Valley 1997: Tight, crisp, with toned-down cherry, earth, tea and strawberry notes, turning firmly tannic on the finish. Can use a little time. Drink through 2005.–J.L. • $30 • (9/15/1999) • **86**
Pinot Noir Russian River Valley 1996 • $29 • (6/30/1998) • **86**
Pinot Noir Russian River Valley 1995 • $27 • (12/31/1996) • **89**
Pinot Noir Santa Lucia Highlands Pisoni Vineyard 1997: Bright and juicy, with up-front cherry, raspberry and strawberry flavors, turning elegant and supple. Drink now through 2005.–J.L. • $50 • (5/15/2000) • **87**
Pinot Noir Sonoma County 1997: Tight, green edge to the tannins, with a permeating earthy tone to the vague berry and cherry character. Needs a little time. Drink through 2006.–J.L. • $30 • (9/15/1999) • **87**

PAUL, PATRICK M. | WASHINGTON

Cabernet Franc Walla Walla Valley 1988 • $12 • (2/29/1992) • **84**
Cabernet Franc Walla Walla Valley Reserve 1994 • $12 • (9/30/1996) • **87**
Cabernet Franc Walla Walla Valley Reserve 1992 • $14 • (9/30/1994) • **78**
Cabernet Franc Washington 1993 • $10 • (9/30/1995) • **89**
Cabernet Sauvignon Columbia Valley 1994 • $12 • (9/15/1996) • **78**
Merlot Columbia Valley 1994 • $12 • (9/15/1996) • **77**

Key: SS—Spectator Selection CS—Cellar Selection HR—Highly Recommended $NA—Price Not Available a—Auction Price (BT)—Barrel Tasting
For a key to the tasters' initials, see "How to Use These Listings."
Dates in parentheses indicate the issues in which the ratings were published.

PAUMANOK | NEW YORK

Assemblage Red North Fork of Long Island 1995 • $24 • (3/31/1998) • **85**
Assemblage Red North Fork of Long Island 1993 • $22 • (12/31/1995) • **88**
Cabernet Sauvignon North Fork of Long Island 1991 • $12 • (12/31/1995) • **75**
Cabernet Sauvignon North Fork of Long Island Grand Vintage 1995 • $19 • (3/31/1998) • **88**
Cabernet Sauvignon North Fork of Long Island Grand Vintage 1993 • $22 • (12/31/1995) • **88**
Cabernet Sauvignon North Fork of Long Island Tuthills Lane Vineyard 1995 • $29 • (3/31/1998) • **89**
Chardonnay North Fork of Long Island Barrel Fermented 1998: Lavish oak adds vanilla, honey and lanolin flavors, while crisp acidity keeps it lively. Citrus, green apple and pear mingle on the full-bodied palate. Drink now.–T.M. • $17 • (5/31/2000) • **86**
Chardonnay North Fork of Long Island Barrel Fermented 1997: Soft and blowsy. Candied apple aromas give way to round flavors of vanilla, apple and light citrus in this white. A pleasant snap of acidity on the finish just keeps it balanced. Drink now.–T.M. • $17 • (6/30/1999) • **81**
Merlot North Fork of Long Island 1997: Sweet flavors of milk chocolate and dried cherry are simple and straightforward in this light red. Likable but a bit cloying. Drink now.–T.M. • $18 • (5/31/2000) • **83**
Merlot North Fork of Long Island 1992 • $13 • (12/31/1995) • **81**
Merlot North Fork of Long Island 1991 • $13 • (12/31/1995) • **82**
Merlot North Fork of Long Island Grand Vintage 1995 • $19 • (5/31/1998) • **88**
Merlot North Fork of Long Island Grand Vintage 1993 • $19 • (12/31/1995) • **87**
Sauvignon Blanc North Fork of Long Island Late Harvest 1998: Sweet and rich, this offers flavors of dried pineapple and coconut, with light herbal accents and enough acidity to keep it lively. Drink now through 2003.–T.M. • $39/375 ml. • (5/31/2000) • **85**

PAVONA | CALIFORNIA

Pinot Blanc Monterey County Paraiso Springs Vineyard 1996 • $15 • (5/15/1998) • **84**
Pinot Blanc Monterey County Paraiso Springs Vineyard 1995 • $14 • (9/15/1997) • **87**
Pinot Noir Monterey County 1997: Marked by floral aromas, the wine is fairly silky on the palate, serving up a blend of bright cherry, plum, herb, tea and tar. Light in color, it has a moderate finish, somewhat tannic. Drink through 2004. • $18 • (9/15/1999) • **85**
Pinot Noir Monterey County Paraiso Springs Vineyard 1996: Fairly spicy—almost cinnamonlike. Simple cherry flavors follow up for a pleasant quaff. Drink now. • $18 • (8/31/1998) • **82**
Pinot Noir Monterey County Paraiso Springs Vineyard 1995 • $16 • (8/31/1997) • **82**
Pinot Noir Monterey County Paraiso Springs Vineyard 1994 • $15 • (4/30/1996) • **86**
Pinot Noir Monterey County Reserve 1997: Bricklike in color, it sports fruity, cherry and herb flavors that don't quite measure up to the oak. Somewhat exotic, it's quite developed for a young wine and probably won't get much better. Drink now. • $24 • (9/15/1999) • **83**
Zinfandel Paso Robles Twin Hills Vineyard 1994 • $18 • (6/15/1998) • **83**
Zinfandel Paso Robles Twin Hills Vineyard 1993 • $16 • (12/15/1997) • **86**

PEACHY CANYON | CALIFORNIA

Cabernet Sauvignon Central Coast 1994 • $20 • (12/15/1996) • **84**
Cabernet Sauvignon Central Coast 1993 • $20 • (12/15/1995) • **88**
Cabernet Sauvignon Central Coast 1992 • $18 • (11/15/1994) • **87**
Cabernet Sauvignon Paso Robles 1996: Bright, with raspberry, cherry and herb flavors, finishing crisp and flavorful, with integrated tannins. Drink early for its bright fruit, now through 2003.–J.L. • $20 • (9/15/1999) • **86**
Cabernet Sauvignon Paso Robles 1995 • $20 • (4/30/1998) • **86**
Cabernet Sauvignon Paso Robles 1991 • $18 • (11/15/1993) • **90**
Cabernet Sauvignon Paso Robles 1990 • $15 • (3/31/1993) • **85**
Merlot Paso Robles 1997: Tart, with lean tannin and vegetal and dried berry flavors.–J.L. • $23 • (6/15/2000) • **79**
Merlot Paso Robles 1996: Fruit-driven, with plenty of plum and black cherry notes. Fairly smooth and plush, it ends on a bright, toasty note. Drink now through 2004. • $23 • (10/15/1999) • **87**
Merlot Paso Robles 1995 • $23 • (4/30/1998) • **87**
Merlot Paso Robles 1993 • $22 • (3/31/1996) • **88**
Merlot Paso Robles 1992 • $22 • (7/31/1995) • **91**
Para Siempre Paso Robles 1995 • $28 • (5/15/1998) • **86**
Para Siempre Central Coast 1994 • $28 • (8/31/1997) • **86**
Para Siempre Central Coast 1993 • $28 • (3/31/1996) • **87**
Zinfandel Paso Robles Incredible Red Bin 108 1998: Stewed currant and strawberry flavors offer richness, but are a bit musty and mute. Drink now through 2001.–J.L. • $11 • (5/15/2000) • **80**
Zinfandel California Incredible Red Bin 106 1997: Charming for its bright, fresh strawberry, cherry, spice and pepper flavors that linger delicately on the finish. Drink now.–J.L. • $11 • (4/30/1999) • **86**
Zinfandel California Incredible Red Bin 105 NV: Smooth and ripe, a simple wine with pretty black cherry and berry flavors on a modest scale. Finishes soft. Drink now.–H.S. • $11 • (11/30/1998) • **83**
Zinfandel Paso Robles Incredible Red Bin 104 NV: Simple but juicy, with herbal strawberry and cherry flavors, hints of tea and sage. Finishes with soft tannins. Better than previously reviewed. Drink now.–J.L. • $11 • (2/28/1999) • **82**
Zinfandel Paso Robles Incredible Red Bin 103 NV • $10 • (6/30/1997) • **88**
Zinfandel Paso Robles Incredible Red Bin 102 NV • $10 • (3/31/1996) • **83**
Zinfandel Paso Robles 1995 • $30 • (11/15/1997) • **85**
Zinfandel Paso Robles 1989 • $10 • (12/31/1991) • **82**
Zinfandel Paso Robles Benito Dusi Ranch 1997: Firm in texture, with chunky black cherry, smoke and spice flavors that persist through the chewy finish. Best after 2000.–H.S. • $26 • (11/30/1999) • **87**
Zinfandel Paso Robles Dusi Ranch 1995 • $23 • (11/15/1997) • **87**
Zinfandel Paso Robles Dusi Ranch 1994 • $22 • (12/15/1996) • **87**
Zinfandel Paso Robles Dusi Ranch 1993 • $20 • (10/15/1995) • **88**
Zinfandel Paso Robles Dusi Ranch 1992 • $18 • (10/15/1994) • **85**
Zinfandel Paso Robles Eastside 1997: Watery, with earthy strawberry and oaky flavors that are muddled.–J.L. • $15 • (5/15/2000) • **78**
Zinfandel Paso Robles Eastside 1995 • $15 • (11/15/1997) • **84**
Zinfandel Paso Robles Eastside 1994 • $15 • (3/31/1997) • **84**
Zinfandel Paso Robles Eastside 1993 • $12 • (10/15/1995) • **87**
Zinfandel Paso Robles Especial 1997: Ripe and focused, really concentrated and silky, with blackberry, plum and spice flavors that linger nicely on the smooth finish. Drink now through 2003.–H.S. • $28 • (11/30/1999) • **89**
Zinfandel Paso Robles Especial 1995 • $25 • (11/15/1997) • **84**
Zinfandel Paso Robles Especial 1991 • $18 • (6/15/1994) • **85**
Zinfandel Paso Robles Especial 1990 • $14 • (8/31/1993) • **90**
Zinfandel Paso Robles Especial Reserve 1989 • $12 • (12/31/1991) • **89**
Zinfandel Paso Robles Lakeview Vineyard 1997: Watery, with waxy, wild berry cola flavors that are thin, turning dry.–J.L. • $21 • (5/15/2000) • **78**
Zinfandel Paso Robles Late Harvest Leona's Vineyard 1995 • $15/375 ml. • (12/31/1997) • **88**
Zinfandel Paso Robles Leona's Vineyard Second Crop 1995 • $23 • (11/15/1997) • **81**
Zinfandel Paso Robles Leona's Vineyard Second Crop 1994 • $22 • (12/15/1996) • **90**
Zinfandel Paso Robles Old Bailey Ranch 1995 • $23 • (11/15/1997) • **86**
Zinfandel Paso Robles Snow Vineyard 1997: Tanky, with a sour edge to the sage and berry, and there's a stamp of celery that's hard to overlook.–J.L. • $26 • (5/15/2000) • **77**
Zinfandel Paso Robles Westside 1997: Firm in texture, with a nice core of black cherry and spice flavors that hang on through the slightly chewy finish. Drink now through 2003.–H.S. • $19 • (11/30/1999) • **85**
Zinfandel Paso Robles Westside 1995 • $19 • (11/15/1997) • **86**
Zinfandel Paso Robles Westside 1994 • $18 • (12/15/1996) • **88**
Zinfandel Paso Robles Westside 1993 • $15 • (10/15/1995) • **86**
Zinfandel Paso Robles Westside 1992: A bit earthy, with sage and wild berry flavors, it's still youthful, firmly tannic and holding its fruit. Can be aged longer; may gain more dimensions. (Zinfandel retrospective tastng). Drink now through 2002.–J.L. • $12 • (6/30/1999) • **87**
Zinfandel Paso Robles Westside 1991 • $13 • (8/31/1993) • **84**
Zinfandel Paso Robles Westside 1990: Shows off ripe raspberry jam and berry aromas, turning dry and tannic on the finish. An elegant wine that's starting to dry on the aftertaste. (Zinfandel retrospective tastng). Drink now.–J.L. • $12 • (6/30/1999) • **87**
Zinfandel Paso Robles Westside Reserve 1996: Appealing ripe cherry and wild berry character has a touch of earthiness, finishing with dry tannins and a twinge of bitterness. Drink now through 2002.–J.L. • $23 • (6/30/1999) • **87**

PECONIC BAY | NEW YORK

Cabernet Sauvignon North Fork of Long Island 1994 • $19 • (12/31/1996) • **87**
Cabernet Sauvignon North Fork of Long Island 1988 • $13 • (6/30/1991) • **81**
Cabernet Sauvignon North Fork of Long Island 1987 • $13 • (6/30/1991) • **78**
Cabernet Sauvignon North Fork of Long Island 1986 • $11 • (12/15/1988) • **84**
Cabernet Sauvignon North Fork of Long Island 1985 • $11 • (12/15/1988) • **78**

PECONIC BAY

Chardonnay North Fork of Long Island Sandy Hill 1996: Smooth and polished, this shows vanilla and spicy oak notes, balanced by citrusy acidity, with light ripe apple and light melon flavors. Clean, but rather dominated by oak. Drink now.–T.M. • $22 • (6/30/1999) • **80**
Merlot North Fork of Long Island 1989 • $13 • (6/30/1991) • **78**
Merlot North Fork of Long Island Epic Acre 1995: Ripe and jammy, this plush red is packed with plum and coffee flavors up front, but seems to thin and fade on the finish, where charry oak flavors turn a bit dry. Drink now through 2002.–T.M. • $25 • (6/30/1999) • **83**
Merlot North Fork of Long Island Wesley Hall Vineyard 1994 • $19 • (12/31/1996) • **76**
White Riesling North Fork of Long Island 1996: This crisp, juicy white tastes like biting into a tree-ripened apple. The refreshing blend of sweet and tart flavors brings you back for another sip. A lively match for lighter fish dishes. Drink now.–T.M. • $11 • (6/30/1999) • **84**

PECOTA, ROBERT | CALIFORNIA

Cabernet Sauvignon Napa Valley Kara's Vineyard 1997: Elegant if leaning toward simple, with pleasant cherry, berry, cedar and herb notes of moderate depth and complexity. Drink now through 2006.–J.L. • $35 • (6/30/2000) • **86**
Cabernet Sauvignon Napa Valley Kara's Vineyard 1995 • $25 • (5/31/1998) • **90**
Cabernet Sauvignon Napa Valley Kara's Vineyard 1994 • $23 • (11/15/1996) • **88**
Cabernet Sauvignon Napa Valley Kara's Vineyard 1993 • $20 • (12/15/1995) • **86**
Cabernet Sauvignon Napa Valley Kara's Vineyard 1991 • $20 • (9/15/1994) HR • **91**
Cabernet Sauvignon Napa Valley Kara's Vineyard 1990 • $17 • (9/15/1993) • **86**
Cabernet Sauvignon Napa Valley Kara's Vineyard 1989 • $17 • (11/15/1992) • **78**
Cabernet Sauvignon Napa Valley Kara's Vineyard 1988: Pleasant, with ripe, spicy black cherry, wild berry and currant notes, this wine avoids being overly tannic and dry—as many '88s are. Finishes with an earthy mineral aftertaste. (1988 California Cabernet retrospective tasting). Drink now through 2002.–J.L. • $17 • (11/15/1998) • **86**
Cabernet Sauvignon Napa Valley Kara's Vineyard 1987 • $16 • (10/15/1990) • **90**
Cabernet Sauvignon Napa Valley Kara's Vineyard 1986 • $16 • (9/15/1989) • **86**
Cabernet Sauvignon Napa Valley Kara's Vineyard 1985 • $16 • (12/15/1988) • **89**
Cabernet Sauvignon Napa Valley Kara's Vineyard 1984 • $14 • (10/15/1987) • **91**
Merlot Napa Valley Steven André Vineyard 1997: Thin and tart, with simple, earthy berry flavors that turn dry. Drink now.–J.L. • $30 • (6/15/2000) • **80**
Merlot Napa Valley Steven André Vineyard 1996: Tight and oaky, with firm tannins but also a wonderful core of intensely flavored Merlot and tiers of plum, currant and berry. Drink now through 2004.–J.L. • $29 • (12/15/1998) • **91**
Merlot Napa Valley Steven André Vineyard 1995 • $25 • (3/31/1998) • **87**
Merlot Napa Valley Steven André Vineyard 1994 • $23 • (9/15/1996) • **88**
Merlot Napa Valley Steven André Vineyard 1993 • $20 • (12/15/1995) • **85**
Merlot Napa Valley Steven André Vineyard 1992 • $18 • (11/15/1994) • **87**
Merlot Napa Valley Steven André Vineyard 1991 • $18 • (10/31/1993) • **89**
Merlot Napa Valley Steven André Vineyard 1990 • $17 • (6/15/1993) • **86**
Merlot Napa Valley Steven André Vineyard 1989 • $17 • (11/15/1991) • **86**
Muscat Blanc Late Harvest Napa Valley Sweet Andrea Select 1990 • $16/375 ml. • (12/15/1992) • **81**
Muscat Canelli Napa Valley Moscato d'Andrea 1996 • $9/375 ml. • (11/30/1997) • **87**
Muscat Canelli Napa Valley Moscato d'Andrea 1994 • $11/375 ml. • (9/30/1995) • **84**
Muscat Canelli Napa Valley Moscato d'Andrea 1992 • $10/375 ml. • (5/15/1993) • **84**
Muscat Canelli Napa Valley Moscato d'Andrea 1991 • $10/375 ml. • (12/15/1992) • **83**
Sauvignon Blanc California 1997 • $11 • (3/31/1998) • **86**
Sauvignon Blanc Monterey County 1998: Shows hints of citrus, herbs and melon. It's light and fresh, with a moderate finish. A fine quaffer. Drink now. • $11 • (5/31/1999) • **84**
Syrah Monterey County 1997: Herbaceous and round, with cherry and green bean flavors that linger on the finish. Drink now through 2003.–J.L. • $24 • (6/15/2000) • **84**

Key: SS—Spectator Selection CS—Cellar Selection HR—Highly Recommended $NA—Price Not Available a—Auction Price (BT)—Barrel Tasting
For a key to the tasters' initials, see "How to Use These Listings."
Dates in parentheses indicate the issues in which the ratings were published.

PEDRONCELLI | CALIFORNIA

Cabernet Sauvignon Alexander Valley Morris Fay Vineyards 1996: Firm, featuring modest dusty red currant, sage and cedary oak flavors, finishing with firm, dry tannins. Drink through 2004.–J.L. • $13 • (10/15/1999) • **84**
Cabernet Sauvignon Alexander Valley Morris Fay Vineyards Single Vineyard Selection 1992 • $13 • (3/31/1996) • **84**
Cabernet Sauvignon Dry Creek Valley 1991 • $10 • (11/15/1994) • **75**
Cabernet Sauvignon Dry Creek Valley 1990 • $10 • (11/15/1993) • **73**
Cabernet Sauvignon Dry Creek Valley 1989 • $10 • (8/31/1992) • **75**
Cabernet Sauvignon Dry Creek Valley Raymond Burr Vineyards 1993 • $20 • (11/30/1997) • **80**
Cabernet Sauvignon Dry Creek Valley Raymond Burr Vineyards 1991 • $20 • (11/30/1996) • **80**
Cabernet Sauvignon Dry Creek Valley Reserve 1988: Simple, a touch murky, with mineral, leather and cherry flavors, it struggles to find focus. Finishes with dry, chewy tannins. (1988 California Cabernet retrospective tasting). Drink now through 2002.–J.L. • $15 • (11/15/1998) • **80**
Cabernet Sauvignon Dry Creek Valley Reserve 1986 • $14 • (11/15/1992) • **78**
Cabernet Sauvignon Dry Creek Valley Reserve 1985 • $14 • (3/31/1990) • **85**
Cabernet Sauvignon Dry Creek Valley Reserve 1982 • $13 • (10/15/1989) • **73**
Cabernet Sauvignon Dry Creek Valley Three Vineyards 1994 • $12 • (4/30/1997) • **82**
Cabernet Sauvignon Dry Creek Valley Three Vineyards Special Vineyard Selection 1997: Firm and dense, with black cherry and mineral flavors. Tannins are large on the finish and need time to resolve. Best from 2001 through 2005.–J.L. • $14 • (10/15/1999) • **85**
Cabernet Sauvignon Sonoma County 1988 • $10 • (10/15/1991) • **83**
Cabernet Sauvignon Sonoma County 1974 • $40 • (11/15/1994) • **78**
Chardonnay Dry Creek Valley F. Johnson Vineyard 1997: A polished, medium-weight wine, with lots of smoky, buttery sour cream aromas and flavors. Spicy tropical fruit notes gain focus on the finish. Drink now.–H.S. • $13 • (7/31/1999) • **85**
Chardonnay Dry Creek Valley Vintage Selection 1996 • $10 • (5/15/1998) • **83**
Fumé Blanc Dry Creek Valley 1996 • $9 • (4/30/1998) • **82**
Fumé Blanc Sonoma County Vintage Selection 1997: A pleasant, fruity wine, with hints of citrus and apple. Simple and enjoyable, with a moderate finish. Drink now. • $9 • (6/15/1999) • **84**
Merlot Dry Creek Valley 1991 • $10 • (9/15/1994) • **82**
Merlot Dry Creek Valley 1990 • $10 • (8/31/1993) • **83**
Merlot Dry Creek Valley Bench Vineyards Special Vineyard Selection 1996: Moderate cherry and anise flavors are beefed up by lots of oak extract. Drink now. • $13 • (9/30/1998) • **77**
Merlot Dry Creek Valley Benchlands 1994 • $12 • (8/31/1996) • **83**
Merlot Sonoma County 1989 • $13 • (2/29/1992) • **76**
Pinot Noir Dry Creek Valley 1993 • $9 • (12/31/1995) • **78**
Pinot Noir Dry Creek Valley 1992 • $9 • (3/31/1995) • **79**
Pinot Noir Dry Creek Valley 1991 • $9 • (1/31/1994) • **82**
Pinot Noir Dry Creek Valley 1990 • $9 • (2/28/1993) • **79**
Pinot Noir Dry Creek Valley 1989 • $9 • (3/31/1992) • **75**
Pinot Noir Dry Creek Valley 1988 • $8 • (2/28/1991) • **84**
Pinot Noir Dry Creek Valley F. Johnson Vineyard Single Vineyard Selection 1994 • $13 • (1/31/1997) • **83**
Primitivo Misto Sonoma County 1991 • $6 • (1/31/1995) • **75**
Zinfandel Dry Creek Valley 1991 • $8 • (10/15/1994) • **83**
Zinfandel Dry Creek Valley 1990 • $8 • (4/30/1993) • **80**
Zinfandel Dry Creek Valley 1989 • $8 • (10/15/1992) • **77**
Zinfandel Dry Creek Valley 1988 • $7 • (11/30/1990) • **84**
Zinfandel Dry Creek Valley Mother Clone Special Vineyard Selection 1998: Floral and juicy, with fairly intense plum, currant and cola notes that linger on the finish. Drink now through 2003.–J.L. • $14 • (6/15/2000) • **86**
Zinfandel Dry Creek Valley Mother Clone Special Vineyard Selection 1996 • $12 • (6/15/1998) • **84**
Zinfandel Dry Creek Valley Mother Clone Special Vineyard Selection 1993 • $11 • (10/15/1995) • **85**
Zinfandel Dry Creek Valley Pedroni-Bushnell Vineyard Single Vineyard Selection 1996: Medium-bodied, with a pleasant range of toasted oak, black cherry, tar and herb flavors. Finishes lean and dry. Drink now.–J.L. • $13 • (6/30/1999) • **86**
Zinfandel Dry Creek Valley Pedroni-Bushnell Vineyard Single Vineyard Selection 1994 • $12 • (3/31/1997) • **87**
Zinfandel Dry Creek Valley Pedroni-Bushnell Vineyard Single Vineyard Selection 1993 • $12 • (10/15/1995) • **84**
Zinfandel Sonoma County Vintage Selection 1997: Soft and simple, with ripe plum flavors and hints of mustard seed. Drink now.–J.L. • $10 • (6/15/2000) • **84**

PEIRANO ESTATE | CALIFORNIA

Zinfandel Lodi 1994 • $10 • (12/15/1996) • **79**
Zinfandel Lodi 1993 • $10 • (8/31/1995) • **87**
Zinfandel Lodi 1992 • $10 • (6/15/1995) • **86**

PEJU | CALIFORNIA

Cabernet Franc Napa Valley 1996: Vegetal and bell pepper flavors dominate. Finishes with a funky herbal and woody note.–J.L. • $25 • (12/15/1999) • **79**
Cabernet Franc Napa Valley 1994 • $25 • (5/31/1998) • **87**
Cabernet Sauvignon Napa Valley 1996: Balanced and soft-textured, with modestly concentrated earth, berry, coffee and herb flavors. Finishes with firm, dry tannins. Drink now through 2004.–H.S. • $38 • (9/15/1999) • **86**
Cabernet Sauvignon Napa Valley 1993 • $18 • (11/30/1996) • **88**
Cabernet Sauvignon Napa Valley 1992 • $18 • (12/15/1995) • **84**
Cabernet Sauvignon Napa Valley 1991 • $18 • (9/15/1995) • **85**
Cabernet Sauvignon Napa Valley 1989 • $15 • (8/31/1992) • **85**
Cabernet Sauvignon Napa Valley Estate Bottled 1995: Offers attractive ripe cherry, plum and minty Cabernet flavors that turn simple with fine tannins on the finish. Drink now through 2003.–J.L. • $55 • (10/31/1998) • **87**
Cabernet Sauvignon Napa Valley HB Vineyard 1994 • $55 • (10/31/1997) • **92**
Cabernet Sauvignon Napa Valley HB Vineyard 1993 • $35 • (11/30/1996) • **89**
Cabernet Sauvignon Napa Valley HB Vineyard 1992 • $35 • (12/15/1995) • **91**
Cabernet Sauvignon Napa Valley HB Vineyard 1991 • $35 • (9/15/1995) • **86**
Cabernet Sauvignon Napa Valley HB Vineyard 1990 • $35 • (11/15/1994) • **88**
Cabernet Sauvignon Napa Valley HB Vineyard 1989 • $30 • (8/31/1992) • **84**
Cabernet Sauvignon Napa Valley HB Vineyard 1988 • $30 • (8/31/1991) • **82**
Cabernet Sauvignon Napa Valley HB Vineyard 1987 • $20 • (11/15/1990) • **87**
Cabernet Sauvignon Napa Valley HB Vineyard 1986 • $20 • (11/15/1989) • **92**
Cabernet Sauvignon Napa Valley HB Vineyard Special Selection 1988 • $24 • (8/31/1992) • **87**
Cabernet Sauvignon Rutherford Reserve 1997: Complex, with a pretty array of currant, blackberry, vanilla, earth and mineral, turning supple and polished, with a long, engaging finish. Drink now through 2008.–J.L. • $85 • (6/30/2000) • **92**
Cabernet Sauvignon Napa Valley Reserve 1996: Deliciously complex, ripe, rich and flavorful, with tiers of black cherry, plum, wild berry and spice. Unfolds to reveal even more layers of complexity and finesse. Best from 2001 through 2008.–J.L. • $75 • (11/15/1999) • **95**
Chardonnay Napa Valley 1998: Lively, with fine focus to its tangerine, coconut and vanilla flavors. Drink now.–J.L. • $22 • (6/30/2000) • **86**
Chardonnay Napa Valley 1997: Complex, with elegant lemon, green apple and light toasted oak flavors. Drink now.–J.L. • $18 • (1/31/1999) • **87**
Chardonnay Napa Valley HB Vineyard 1996: Strays into the earthy side of Chardonnay and stays there, though hints of ripe pear and anise come to the fore. Drink now.–J.L. • $26 • (7/31/1998) • **83**
Chardonnay Napa Valley Late Harvest Select 1989 • $13/375 ml. • (3/15/1992) • **88**
Meritage Napa Valley 1992 • $24 • (11/15/1994) • **87**
Merlot Napa Valley 1997: Good concentration and length to the herb, berry and chocolate flavors, with slightly dry tannins on the finish. Drink now.–J.L. • $40 • (5/15/2000) • **87**
Merlot Napa Valley 1996: Offers a substantive core of earthy, leathery cherry, currant and plum. Firms up on the finish while keeping its focus. Drink now through 2005.–J.L. • $35 • (10/15/1999) • **87**
Merlot Napa Valley 1995: Distinctive, with full-bodied Merlot flavors—chocolate, cherry, oak and mint—that stay focused on the finish. Drink now through 2004.–J.L. • $35 • (9/30/1998) • **87**
Merlot Napa Valley 1994 • $30 • (7/31/1997) • **85**
Sauvignon Blanc Napa Valley Late Harvest Special Select 1992 • $14 • (6/15/1994) • **87**
Sauvignon Blanc Napa Valley Late Harvest Special Select 1991 • $15 • (1/31/1993) • **81**

PELICAN RANCH | CALIFORNIA

Syrah Paso Robles Meeker Vineyards 1998: Dominated by tart strawberry punch flavors and herbal notes.–J.L. • $17 • (5/31/2000) • **79**

PELLEGRINI | CALIFORNIA

Barbera Sonoma Valley Old Vines 1995 • $14 • (12/15/1996) • **80**
Barbera Sonoma Valley Old Vines 1994 • $11 • (11/30/1996) • **88**
Barbera Sonoma Valley Old Vines 1993 • $10 • (7/31/1995) • **81**
Cabernet Sauvignon Alexander Valley Cloverdale Ranch Estate Cuvée 1988 • $12 • (6/15/1991) • **82**
Carignane Alexander Valley Old Vines 1995 • $10 • (9/15/1997) • **84**
Carignane Alexander Valley Old Vines 1994 • $9 • (11/30/1996) • **85**
Côtes de Sonoma Deux Cépages Sonoma County 1991 • $6 • (3/31/1993) • **83**
Zinfandel Sonoma County Old Vines 1993 • $9 • (2/28/1995) • **81**

PELLEGRINI | NEW YORK

Cabernet Franc North Fork of Long Island 1995 • $24 • (6/15/1998) • **82**
Cabernet Sauvignon North Fork of Long Island 1994 • $15 • (6/15/1998) • **84**
Cabernet Sauvignon North Fork of Long Island 1993 • $15 • (12/31/1996) • **89**
Cabernet Sauvignon North Fork of Long Island 1991 • $15 • (11/15/1994) • **86**
Cabernet Sauvignon North Fork of Long Island Unfiltered 1995: This compact red offers a velvety texture and ripe, almost jammy notes of plum and chocolate. Elegant and harmonious though the tannins turn dry on the finish; best with food. Drink now through 2002.–T.M. • $16 • (5/31/2000) • **88**
Chardonnay North Fork of Long Island 1997: Butter and vanilla tones from oak dominate this smooth white, but the modest pear flavors are enlivened by a streak of lemony acidity. This was the better of two samples. Drink now.–T.M. • $13 • (5/31/2000) • **80**
Chardonnay North Fork of Long Island 1996: Round and soft. Vanilla, honey and ripe melon notes give a gentle richness on the palate, but there's not enough fruit to keep it lively. A pleasant quaff, but drink up.–T.M. • $13 • (6/30/1999) • **81**
Chardonnay North Fork of Long Island Eastend Select 1996 • $9 • (11/15/1997) • **85**
Encore Vintner's Pride North Fork of Long Island 1995: Velvety without being heavy, this red has a lovely texture and well-defined black cherry, chocolate and licorice flavors. The tannins are firm yet well integrated, the finish smoky and long. A blend of Cabernet Sauvignon, Merlot and Cabernet Franc. Tasted twice, with consistent notes. Drink now through 2003.–T.M. • $24 • (6/30/1999) • **88**
Encore Vintner's Pride North Fork of Long Island 1993 • $20 • (12/31/1996) • **85**
Encore Vintner's Pride North Fork of Long Island 1992 • $20 • (12/31/1995) • **81**
Finale North Fork of Long Island 1993 • $25 • (4/15/1995) • **78**
Merlot North Fork of Long Island 1995 • $17 • (5/31/1998) • **87**
Merlot North Fork of Long Island 1992 • $16 • (11/15/1994) • **84**
Merlot North Fork of Long Island Unfiltered 1997: Ripe and rich, this muscular red offers plum and cassis flavors over firm tannins, backed by toasty, smoky oak notes. Has lively acidity for balance and a spicy finish. Drink now through 2004.–T.M. • $17 • (5/31/2000) • **90**
Merlot North Fork of Long Island Unfiltered 1994 • $17 • (12/31/1996) • **86**

PEND D'OREILLE | IDAHO

Chardonnay Idaho 1997: Seems tinny, with green, vegetal notes and an oniony finish.–T.M. • $16 • (1/01/2000) • **75**
Merlot Columbia Valley 1997: Firm in texture and remarkably open in flavor, pouring out lovely berry, currant and delicate herb flavors right through the velvety finish. Delicious from the first sip. Drink now through 2006.–H.S. • $22 • (3/31/2000) • **89**

PEPI, ROBERT | CALIFORNIA

Cabernet Sauvignon Napa Valley Vine Hill Ranch 1991 • $18 • (12/15/1995) • **86**
Cabernet Sauvignon Napa Valley Vine Hill Ranch 1989 • $18 • (11/15/1994) • **85**
Cabernet Sauvignon Napa Valley Vine Hill Ranch 1988 • $18 • (11/15/1992) • **89**
Cabernet Sauvignon Napa Valley Vine Hill Ranch 1987 • $24 • (4/30/1991) HR • **90**
Cabernet Sauvignon Napa Valley Vine Hill Ranch 1986 • $18 • (10/31/1990) • **88**
Cabernet Sauvignon Napa Valley Vine Hill Ranch 1985 • $16 • (7/31/1990) • **85**
Cabernet Sauvignon Napa Valley Vine Hill Ranch 1984 • $21 • (8/31/1989) • **80**
Cabernet Sauvignon Napa Valley Vine Hill Ranch 1983 • $16 • (5/31/1988) • **89**
Cabernet Sauvignon Napa Valley Vine Hill Ranch 1982 • $14 • (3/31/1987) • **84**
Cabernet Sauvignon Napa Valley Vine Hill Ranch 1981 • $14 • (1/01/1986) CS • **93**
Cabernet Sauvignon-Sangiovese Napa Valley Due Baci 1997: Offers enough cedar, cherry and wild berry in an elegant style to sustain your interest. Drink now through 2003.–J.L. • $29 • (6/15/2000) • **85**
Cabernet Sauvignon-Sangiovese Napa Valley Due Baci 1995: A touch gamy, with firm, drying tannins and a glimpse of ripe plum and berry-laced flavor. Turns complex if a bit dry and leathery on the finish. Drink now through 2002.–J.L. • $25 • (12/15/1998) • **85**

PEPI, ROBERT

Sangiovese California Two-Heart Canopy 1996: Not quite focused and a touch earthy, with a simple core of spicy cherry and berry. Drink now.–H.S. • $17 • (9/30/1998) • **84**
Sangiovese California Two-Heart Canopy 1995 • $18 • (12/31/1997) • **84**
Sangiovese California Two-Heart Canopy 1994 • $18 • (9/15/1996) • **86**
Sangiovese Grosso Napa Valley Colline di Sassi 1991 • $20 • (11/30/1995) • **87**
Sangiovese Grosso Napa Valley Colline di Sassi 1990 • $25 • (2/15/1993) • **75**
Sangiovese Grosso Napa Valley Colline di Sassi 1989 • $25 • (10/31/1991) • **83**
Sangiovese Grosso Napa Valley Colline di Sassi 1988 • $25 • (11/10/1990) • **87**
Sangiovese Napa Valley Colline di Sassi 1996: Mature in color and flavor, with dried fruit, dusty, earthy tannins and hints of olive and tar on the finish. Drink now.–J.L. • $30 • (11/15/1999) • **82**
Sangiovese Napa Valley Colline di Sassi 1995: Ripe, with a spicy, leathery edge to the cherry and strawberry flavors. Turns dry and a bit stemmy on the finish. Drink now through 2001.–J.L. • $25 • (12/15/1998) • **84**
Sangiovese Napa Valley Colline di Sassi 1994 • $25 • (4/30/1997) • **88**
Sauvignon Blanc California Two-Heart Canopy 1998: Herbaceous and lemony, with slightly pasty buttery notes.–J.L. • $15 • (5/15/2000) • **79**
Sauvignon Blanc Howell Mountain 1997: Vanilla and oak flavors dominate this wine, which turns unpleasantly pasty and gummy on the finish. Tasted twice, with consistent notes.–J.L. • $20 • (5/15/2000) • **73**
Sauvignon Blanc Napa Valley Reserve 1996: Quite smooth, almost silky on the palate, with hints of hazelnut, herbs, citrus, fig and fresh pea. The flavors are well integrated and finish long, with a fresh, clean edge. Drink now through 2002. • $20 • (5/15/1999) • **88**
Sauvignon Blanc Napa Valley Two-Heart Canopy 1997: Somewhat understated, showing peach, lime and mineral character wrapped in a delicate veneer. A bit short on the finish. Drink now. • $14 • (5/15/1999) • **84**
Sauvignon Blanc Napa Valley Two-Heart Canopy 1996 • $15 • (12/15/1997) • **84**

PEPPERWOOD GROVE | CALIFORNIA

Cabernet Franc California 1995 • $7 • (7/31/1997) • **78**
Cabernet Franc California 1994 • $7 • (11/30/1996) • **81**
Cabernet Sauvignon California 1998: Dried berry and spice notes are light-bodied, and there's a hint of orange peel. Drink now.–J.L. • $7 • (6/30/2000) • **83**
Cabernet Sauvignon California 1996: Redolent of fresh green beans, grass and cooked asparagus, with a dash of maraschino cherry. It's a strange brew, but might interest analytic types. • $7 • (11/15/1998) • **72**
Cabernet Sauvignon California 1995 • $7 • (5/15/1997) • **82**
Cabernet Sauvignon California 1993 • $6 • (12/15/1995) • **78**
Cabernet Sauvignon California 1991 • $6 • (6/15/1993) • **77**
Cabernet Sauvignon California 1990 • $6 • (11/15/1992) • **74**
Chardonnay California 1997: Straightforward, with simple pear and apple notes. Shows slight oxidation.–J.L. • $7 • (2/28/1999) • **78**
Chardonnay California 1996 • $7 • (7/31/1997) • **84**
Merlot California 1997: Simple, herbal and chunky, with dry tannins and a bitter finish.–J.L. • $7 • (10/15/1999) • **72**
Merlot California 1996 • $7 • (12/15/1997) • **85**
Pinot Noir California 1997: Round and accessible, offering cola, licorice and chocolate flavors. Drink now through 2002.–J.L. • $7 • (5/15/2000) • **84**
Pinot Noir California 1996: Earthy strawberry and cola flavors pick up sweet, cooked accents on the finish. Drink now.–J.L. • $7 • (8/31/1998) • **79**
Pinot Noir California 1993 • $6 • (2/28/1995) • **83**
Pinot Noir California Cask Lot 1 1993 • $6 • (12/31/1995) • **83**
Pinot Noir California Cask Lot 1 1992 • $6 • (2/28/1994) • **78**
Pinot Noir California Cask Lot 2 1992 • $6 • (1/31/1994) • **86**
Pinot Noir California Cask Lot 3 1992 • $6 • (11/30/1994) • **84**
Pinot Noir Sonoma County 1994 • $8 • (7/31/1996) • **84**
Sauvignon Blanc California 1996 • $7 • (12/15/1997) • **78**
Syrah California 1998: A great value for Syrah lovers, this young red delivers spicy black cherry and pepper notes mingled with pleasant earthy flavors and soft tannins. Drink now through 2004.–J.L. • $7 • (4/30/2000) • **86**
Zinfandel California 1997: This easy-drinking Zinfandel is ripe and fruity, with mineral, blackberry and black cherry flavors on a supple frame, finishing with mild tannins. Its lightweight profile makes it a nice red for the warm weather season, and you can't beat the price. Drink now.–J.L. • $7 • (6/15/1999) • **85**
Zinfandel California 1996 • $7 • (6/15/1998) • **83**

Key: SS—Spectator Selection CS—Cellar Selection HR—Highly Recommended
$NA—Price Not Available a—Auction Price (BT)—Barrel Tasting
For a key to the tasters' initials, see "How to Use These Listings."
Dates in parentheses indicate the issues in which the ratings were published.

Zinfandel California 1994 • $7 • (11/30/1996) • **78**
Zinfandel California 1993 • $6 • (10/15/1995) • **83**

PER SEMPRE | CALIFORNIA

Cabernet Sauvignon Napa Valley 1994 • $35 • (1/31/1998) • **87**
Cabernet Sauvignon Napa Valley 1993 • $31 • (9/15/1996) • **84**
Cabernet Sauvignon Napa Valley Select Reserve 1994 • $43 • (1/31/1998) • **86**
Sangiovese Napa Valley Davide 1994 • $27 • (12/15/1996) • **87**

PERELLI-MINETTI, MARIO | CALIFORNIA

Cabernet Sauvignon Napa Valley 1994 • $NA • (3/31/1998) • **85**
Cabernet Sauvignon Napa Valley 1991 • $13 • (5/31/1996) • **86**
Cabernet Sauvignon Napa Valley 1990 • $15 • (11/15/1994) • **88**
Cabernet Sauvignon Napa Valley 1988 • $13 • (11/15/1992) • **86**
Cabernet Sauvignon Napa Valley 1987 • $12 • (4/30/1991) • **83**

PERRY CREEK | CALIFORNIA

Cabernet Sauvignon Sierra Foothills 1995: Shows cedar, tobacco and anise, on a rustic frame. Drink now. • $12 • (10/31/1998) • **80**
Merlot El Dorado 1996: Shows a touch of greenness but otherwise the spicy berry, plum and smoky notes ride on a plush frame. Drink now.–J.L. • $12 • (8/31/1998) • **84**
Mourvèdre Sierra Foothills Wenxell Vineyard 1996: A light-style wine, with hints of strawberries, cherries and herbs. Finishes moderately, with a touch of bitterness. Drink now. • $15 • (9/15/1998) • **83**
Viognier El Dorado 1997: Pleasant peach, apple and spice flavors sally forth from this tangy wine. Finishes brightly, with a touch of sweetness. Drink now. • $15 • (9/15/1998) • **84**
Zinfandel Sierra Foothills Cellar Select 1998: Heavy pepper notes and berry flavors are straightforward and focused. Drink now through 2003.–J.L. • $20 • (5/31/2000) • **84**
Zinfandel Sierra Foothills Zin Man 1998: Peppery, with herbal and tart berry flavors that turn dry. Drink now.–J.L. • $12 • (5/31/2000) • **81**
Zinfandel Sierra Foothills Zin Man 1997: Fleshy, but simple and dilute, with plum and berry flavors that finish firm. Drink now.–H.S. • $12 • (5/15/1999) • **82**
Zinfandel Sierra Foothills Zin Man 1996 • $12 • (6/15/1998) • **82**

PESENTI | CALIFORNIA

Zinfandel Late Harvest Paso Robles Dry Family Reserve 1993 • $7 • (11/30/1996) • **82**
Zinfandel Late Harvest Paso Robles Dry Family Reserve 1990 • $7 • (10/15/1994) • **72**
Zinfandel Paso Robles 1994 • $12 • (11/30/1996) • **86**
Zinfandel Paso Robles 1993 • $12 • (9/30/1995) • **88**
Zinfandel Paso Robles 1992 • $12 • (10/15/1994) • **78**

PETERSON | CALIFORNIA

Cabernet Sauvignon Dry Creek Valley 1992 • $16 • (9/15/1995) • **83**
Zinfandel Dry Creek Valley 1997: Excessively earthy, murky, musty, pungent and bitter. Tasted twice, with consistent notes.–J.L. • $17 • (6/15/2000) • **68**
Zinfandel Dry Creek Valley 1996: Fairly ripe, with cherry, berry earth and smoke flavors and a dry, slightly hot finish. Drink now.–H.S. • $16 • (5/15/1999) • **82**
Zinfandel Dry Creek Valley 1995 • $15 • (3/31/1997) • **87**
Zinfandel Dry Creek Valley 1994 • $15 • (3/31/1997) • **86**
Zinfandel Dry Creek Valley 1993 • $15 • (10/15/1995) • **84**
Zinfandel Dry Creek Valley Bradford Mountain Vineyard 1996: Quite spicy, but also a bit hot and drying on the palate. Has a rustic edge that may smooth out with time. Blackberry, cherry and herb notes leave their mark on the moderate finish. Drink now through 2003. • $18 • (5/15/1999) • **84**
Zinfandel Dry Creek Valley Bradford Mountain Vineyard 1995 • $18 • (6/15/1998) • **79**
Zinfandel Dry Creek Valley Bradford Mountain Vineyard 1994 • $18 • (4/30/1997) • **87**
Zinfandel Dry Creek Valley Tradizionale 1997: Elegant and light, with bay leaf and cinnamon notes and blueberry flavors. Drink now.–J.L. • $19 • (6/15/2000) • **83**
Zinfandel Dry Creek Valley Tradizionale 1996: Simple but flavorful, with smoky plum, herb and minty berry flavors, finishing firm. Drink now.–H.S. • $18 • (5/15/1999) • **82**

PEZZI KING | CALIFORNIA

Cabernet Sauvignon Dry Creek Valley 1997: A narrow band of cedar, currant and leather notes, turning a touch green and tannic. Drink now through 2006.–J.L. • $29 • (5/15/2000) • **83**

Cabernet Sauvignon Dry Creek Valley 1996: Dark-hued, with layers of black cherry, plum, herbs and anise framed in assertive, smoky, charry oak, all blending together harmoniously. The finish is a little tart, with firm tannins. Drink now through 2006. • $26 • (4/30/1999) • **90**

Cabernet Sauvignon Dry Creek Valley 1995 • $20 • (4/30/1998) • **88**

Cabernet Sauvignon Dry Creek Valley 1994 • $18 • (4/30/1997) • **89**

Chardonnay Sonoma County 1998: Racy, with spicy, toasty citrus, green pineapple and mint notes. A touch coarse. Drink now through 2003.–J.L. • $22 • (5/15/2000) • **86**

Chardonnay Sonoma County 1997: Ripe, smooth and focused, with apricot, lemon, lime and mineral flavors and a refreshing, herb-tinged finish. Drink now.–J.L. • $20 • (2/28/1999) • **88**

Chardonnay Sonoma County 1996 • $17 • (4/30/1998) • **89**

Fumé Blanc Dry Creek Valley 1998: Citrus and flint aromas, with a racy mouthfeel and concentrated grapefruit notes through the finish. Drink now through 2003.–J.L. • $16 • (5/15/2000) • **86**

Fumé Blanc Sonoma County 1997: Pear and sweet pea aromas lead off. On the palate, it remains rather lean, with light citrus and herb notes. Finishes clean, with a mineral edge. Drink now. • $15 • (3/31/1999) • **85**

Fumé Blanc Sonoma County 1996 • $15 • (9/15/1997) • **84**

Merlot Dry Creek Valley 1997: A solid effort. Dark and extracted, with herb, chocolate and blackberry flavors that are rich and focused, firming on the finish. Best from 2001 through 2008.–J.L. • $28 • (5/15/2000) • **88**

Merlot Dry Creek Valley Susie's Reserve 1997: Ripe and decidedly earthy, it weaves together enough ripe cherry, wild berry, sage, spice and cedar to hold your interest. Drink now through 2004.–J.L. • $28 • (12/31/1999) • **87**

Zinfandel Dry Creek Valley 1997: Smooth and spicy, with tasty cherry, plum and raspberry-laced flavors, a touch of spice and rounded tannins. Best from 2001 through 2007.–J.L. • $30 • (4/30/2000) • **87**

Zinfandel Dry Creek Valley 1996 • $25 • (6/15/1998) • **86**

Zinfandel Dry Creek Valley 1995 • $20 • (4/30/1997) • **92**

Zinfandel Dry Creek Valley 1994 • $18 • (9/15/1996) • **89**

Zinfandel Dry Creek Valley Maple Vineyard 1997: Zesty, with lively wild berry, black cherry, spice and nutmeg, picking up a touch of sweet berry fruit on the finish. Best from 2001 through 2008.–J.L. • $27 • (4/30/2000) • **88**

Zinfandel Dry Creek Valley SLR 1997: Ripe and zesty, with pretty blackberry, raspberry and wild berry. Turns peppery, with firm tannins and pretty earth notes. Drink now through 2003.–J.L. • $27 • (6/15/1999) • **88**

PFENIX | CALIFORNIA

Cabernet Pfeffer San Benito County 1996: Brightly flavored, with spicy cracked pepper, cranberry and dried strawberry notes. Tangy acidity and rustic tannins leave the finish a bit short. Drink now through 2003. • $20 • (3/31/1999) • **85**

PHANTOM HILL | OREGON

Pinot Noir Oregon Corral Creek Vineyard 1996 • $38 • (5/15/1998) • **86**

Pinot Noir Oregon Revelation Cuvée 1997: Firm in texture, with tight tannins wrapped around a vibrant core of blackberry and currant. Finishes with a layer of chewy spice. Best from 2001 through 2004.–H.S. • $39 • (4/30/1999) • **86**

Pinot Noir Willamette Valley 1997: Light in color, with pretty blackberry and peppery flavors that turn smooth and silky on the finish. Drink now through 2001.–H.S. • $25 • (4/30/1999) • **85**

Pinot Noir Willamette Valley 1996 • $24 • (5/15/1998) • **87**

PHELPS, JOSEPH | CALIFORNIA

Cabernet Sauvignon Napa Valley 1997: Wonderful balance of intense, ripe, complex currant, cherry, anise and sage-laced flavors that gain richness and depth on the finish, where the tannins firm up. Best from 2001 through 2009.–J.L. • $35 • (4/30/2000) • **88**

Cabernet Sauvignon Napa Valley 1996: Another outstanding red from Phelps, this one serving up lots of juicy ripe fruit, with layers of cherry, currant, blackberry and anise, turning supple and concentrated, with a rich aftertaste that keeps pumping out the flavors. Drink now through 2007.–J.L. • $30 • (5/15/1999) SS • **92**

Cabernet Sauvignon Napa Valley 1995 • $27 • (6/30/1998) SS • **91**

Cabernet Sauvignon Napa Valley 1994 • $24 • (2/28/1997) • **89**

Cabernet Sauvignon Napa Valley 1993 • $22 • (8/31/1996) • **86**

Cabernet Sauvignon Napa Valley 1992 • $20 • (9/30/1995) • **87**

Cabernet Sauvignon Napa Valley 1991 • $29 Ⓐ • (10/15/1994) • **89**

Cabernet Sauvignon Napa Valley 1990 • $18 • (6/15/1993) • **85**

Cabernet Sauvignon Napa Valley 1989 • $20 • (4/15/1992) • **78**

Cabernet Sauvignon Napa Valley 1988 • $23 • (11/15/1991) • **86**

Cabernet Sauvignon Napa Valley 1987 • $15 • (7/15/1991) • **75**

Cabernet Sauvignon Napa Valley 1985 • $14 • (5/15/1989) • **84**

Cabernet Sauvignon Napa Valley 1984 • $14 • (10/31/1988) • **91**

Cabernet Sauvignon Napa Valley 1983 • $13 • (8/31/1987) • **84**

Cabernet Sauvignon Napa Valley 1982 • $12 • (12/15/1986) • **82**

Cabernet Sauvignon Napa Valley 1981 • $11 • (9/01/1985) • **86**

Cabernet Sauvignon Napa Valley 1980 • $11 • (7/01/1984) • **89**

Cabernet Sauvignon Napa Valley Backus Vineyard 1996: Amazingly supple and plush, with elegant coffee, currant, black cherry and spice flavors, this is beautifully crafted, with fine tannins. Deceptively subtle and sophisticated. Best from 2001 through 2009.–J.L. • $95 • (10/31/1999) • **93**

Cabernet Sauvignon Napa Valley Backus Vineyard 1995: Minty, with sage notes leading to a supple, complex band of currant, coffee, cedar, olive and tar, this is rich and polished for such a young wine, finishing with mild tannins. Drink through 2008.–J.L. • $75 • (3/31/1999) • **91**

Cabernet Sauvignon Napa Valley Backus Vineyard 1994 • $70 Ⓐ • (10/15/1997) • **89**

Cabernet Sauvignon Napa Valley Backus Vineyard 1992 • $45 • (12/15/1995) • **89**

Cabernet Sauvignon Napa Valley Backus Vineyard 1991 • $35 • (10/15/1994) CS • **90**

Cabernet Sauvignon Napa Valley Backus Vineyard 1990 • $30 • (11/15/1993) • **88**

Cabernet Sauvignon Napa Valley Backus Vineyard 1989: A nice balance of flavors lets this succeed, if on a small scale. Has ripe cherry and plummy notes that eluded many Cabernets from this vintage, finishing with a dash of mint. (1989 California Cabernet retrospective tasting). Drink now through 2004.–J.L. • $31 • (8/31/1999) • **87**

Cabernet Sauvignon Napa Valley Backus Vineyard 1988: Earthy mineral, leather and currant flavors are medium-bodied and moderately rich. Supple texture, fine balance and length, with soft tannins. Doesn't have the extra depth and dimension of the best Backuses, but is very fine nonetheless. (1988 California Cabernet retrospective tasting). Drink now through 2004.–J.L. • $30 • (11/15/1998) • **88**

Cabernet Sauvignon Napa Valley Backus Vineyard 1987 • $48 Ⓐ • (7/15/1991) • **88**

Cabernet Sauvignon Napa Valley Backus Vineyard 1986 • $48 Ⓐ • (12/15/1996) • **84**

Cabernet Sauvignon Napa Valley Backus Vineyard 1985 • $58 Ⓐ • "(12/31/1988) • **91**

Cabernet Sauvignon Napa Valley Backus Vineyard 1984 • $41 Ⓐ • (12/31/1987) • **88**

Cabernet Sauvignon Napa Valley Backus Vineyard 1983 • $32 Ⓐ • (6/15/1987) • **85**

Cabernet Sauvignon Napa Valley Backus Vineyard 1981 • $15 • (4/16/1985) • **90**

Cabernet Sauvignon Napa Valley Backus Vineyard 1978: Firm, tight, intense and spicy, with rich, earth, mineral and currant flavors, hints of anise and cedar, and a full, complex aftertaste. Impressive for its structure and concentration; lingers long on the finish. (1978 California Cabernet retrospective tasting). Drink now through 2004.–J.L. • $17 • (11/15/1998) • **92**

Cabernet Sauvignon Napa Valley Eisele Vineyard 1991 • $45 • (10/15/1994) • **89**

Cabernet Sauvignon Napa Valley Eisele Vineyard 1989 • $36 Ⓐ • (6/15/1993) • **83**

Cabernet Sauvignon Napa Valley Eisele Vineyard 1986 • $73 Ⓐ • (8/31/1990) • **77**

Cabernet Sauvignon Napa Valley Eisele Vineyard 1985 • $83 Ⓐ • (5/31/1989) • **81**

Cabernet Sauvignon Napa Valley Eisele Vineyard 1984 • $65 Ⓐ • (3/15/1988) • **88**

Cabernet Sauvignon Napa Valley Eisele Vineyard 1983 • $25 • (8/31/1987) • **76**

Cabernet Sauvignon Napa Valley Eisele Vineyard 1982 • $31 Ⓐ • (12/15/1986) • **84**

Cabernet Sauvignon Napa Valley Eisele Vineyard 1981 • $30 • (11/16/1985) • **78**

Cabernet Sauvignon Napa Valley Eisele Vineyard 1979 • $30 • (2/16/1984) • **86**

Cabernet Sauvignon Napa Valley Eisele Vineyard 1978: This remains an extraordinary wine. Ripe, rich, deep, complex, flavorful—about all you could ask for in a Napa Valley Cabernet. Has aged exceptionally well, held its fruit, gained complexity, shows depth, refinement and polish, and the tannins are softening gracefully, in perfect balance with the wine. (1978

California Cabernet retrospective tasting). Drink now through 2004.–J.L. • $134 Ⓐ • (11/15/1998) • **94**

Chardonnay Los Carneros 1998: Firm, with a tight band of pear, hazelnut and citrus. Turns a touch coarse on the finish. Drink now through 2004.–J.L. • $24 • (4/30/2000) • **86**

Chardonnay Los Carneros 1997: Sleek and elegant, with a spicy edge to the pear, citrus and nectarine flavors, finishing with touches of oak and fig. Drink now through 2001.–J.L. • $22 • (4/30/1999) • **88**

Chardonnay Los Carneros 1996 • $20 • (5/31/1998) • **88**

Chardonnay Napa Valley Ovation 1997: Ripe and perfumed, with complex, elegant, even silky pear, apple, melon, nectarine and nutmeg flavors that unfold gracefully. Finishes with lots of flavor, polish and richness. Drink now through 2003.–J.L. • $40 • (5/31/1999) • **92**

Chardonnay Napa Valley Ovation 1996: Lots of ripe, juicy, spicy pear, apple, fig and melon flavors that are rich and concentrated. Sharply focused, with a sense of elegance and finesse, it carries through with a long, rich aftertaste echoing fruit and spicy oak. Drink now through 2002.–J.L. • $40 • (9/15/1998) • **93**

Gewürztraminer Anderson Valley 1996 • $15 • (12/15/1997) • **85**

Grenache Rosé California Vin du Mistral 1996 • $13 • (9/15/1997) • **86**

Insignia Napa Valley 1998: Sleek and elegant, with a tasty band of black cherry, currant, anise, cedar and spice. Gains momentum on the finish, where the tannins show considerable strength.–J.L. • $NA • (8/31/1999) (BT) • **90-94**

Insignia Napa Valley 1997: Wonderful fruit complexity and concentration, with smoky tar, black currant, cherry, anise, earth and cedar. Finishes with a wall of tannins, but they're friendly.–J.L. • $NA • (8/31/1998) (BT) • **95-99**

Insignia Napa Valley 1996: Ripe and polished, with deep, complex currant, herb, blackberry, cherry, sage, tea and spice flavors, all sharply focused and built on a frame of supple tannins. Tasty already. Best from 2001 through 2008.–J.L. • $96 Ⓐ • (8/31/1999) • **93**

Insignia Napa Valley 1995: A worthy successor to the stunning '94, this is dark and ripe, with exotic aromas and flavors—dense, earthy currant, black cherry, wild berry and plum with a cedary oak edge. Well-integrated tannins and pretty fruit flavors provide elegance. This renowned Cabernet blend is youthful and tight, will benefit from up to a decade of aging. Best from 2002 through 2010.–J.L. • $90 Ⓐ • (10/31/1998) CS • **93**

Insignia Napa Valley 1994 • $134 Ⓐ • (9/30/1997) CS • **96**

Insignia Napa Valley 1993 • $70 Ⓐ • (10/15/1996) HR • **90**

Insignia Napa Valley 1992 • $74 Ⓐ • (9/30/1995) CS • **90**

Insignia Napa Valley 1991 • $78 Ⓐ • (5/31/1995) CS • **90**

Insignia Napa Valley 1990 • $77 Ⓐ • (11/15/1994) • **86**

Insignia Napa Valley 1989: Complete and well balanced, if a shade on the tannic side, the mint, currant and cherryish flavors strive to gain a tight focus. There's enough flavor and finesse to enjoy it for another five years. (1989 California Cabernet retrospective tasting). Drink now through 2004.–J.L. • $35 • (8/31/1999) • **87**

Insignia Napa Valley 1988: Medium-bodied, a bit tart, with a green edge to the currant, herb, sage and tea flavors. Most of the tannins have resolved, so it's definitely ready. Finishes with tar, herb and green olive notes. A blend: 50 percent Cabernet Sauvignon, 30 percent Merlot, 20 percent Cabernet Franc. (1988 California Cabernet retrospective tasting). Drink now through 2002.–J.L. • $39 Ⓐ • (11/15/1998) • **87**

Insignia Napa Valley 1987 • $87 Ⓐ • (12/15/1997) • **96**

Insignia Napa Valley 1986 • $78 Ⓐ • (12/15/1996) • **92**

Insignia Napa Valley 1985 • $111 Ⓐ • (7/31/1989) CS • **93**

Insignia Napa Valley 1984 • $76 Ⓐ • (11/15/1988) • **91**

Insignia Napa Valley 1983 • $34 Ⓐ • (11/30/1987) • **90**

Insignia Napa Valley 1980 • $58 Ⓐ • (7/01/1984) CS • **90**

Insignia Napa Valley 1979: Still sleek and seductive, holding its core of minty black cherry, currant, mineral and anise flavors, and still with enough tannin to sustain it. Complex and supple finish. (1979 California Cabernet retrospective tasting). Drink now through 2006.–J.L. • $73 Ⓐ • (8/31/1999) • **92**

Insignia Napa Valley 1978: Mature, but aging quite well. Complex, with an intriguing array of flavors ranging from ripe, stewed plum to herb, sage, tobacco, cedar and spice. Turns elegant on the finish, where the tannins are soft and mellow. Judging from this and two other recent tastings, this wine is best enjoyed now through 2000. A blend: 50 Percent Cabernet Sauvignon, 30 percent Merlot and 20 percent Cabernet Franc.(1978 California Cabernet retrospective tasting).–J.L. • $25 • (11/15/1998) • **93**

Key: SS—Spectator Selection CS—Cellar Selection HR—Highly Recommended $NA—Price Not Available a—Auction Price (BT)—Barrel Tasting
For a key to the tasters' initials, see "How to Use These Listings."
Dates in parentheses indicate the issues in which the ratings were published.

Insignia Napa Valley 1974 • $155 • (11/15/1994) • **88**

Le Mistral California 1997: Ripe and plummy, with spice, earth, tar, black cherry and leather notes, turning complex and polished. Grenache, Syrah, Mourvèdre, Petite Sirah and Alicante Bouschet. Best from 2001 through 2007.–J.L. • $25 • (1/31/2000) • **90**

Merlot Napa Valley 1997: Rustic in style, with chunky, earthy currant, herb and berryish flavors that struggle to find focus and harmony. Perhaps short-term cellaring will work. Best from 2001 through 2007.–J.L. • $35 • (4/30/2000) • **86**

Merlot Napa Valley 1996: Firm, tight and concentrated, with a compact core of earthy plum, blueberry, sage, toast and spice, finishing with a spicy aftertaste. Drink now through 2005.–J.L. • $30 • (4/30/1999) • **88**

Merlot Napa Valley 1995: Intense and lively, with an appetizing touch of leather, and a smoky, meaty accent to the black cherry, currant and herbal flavors. Well focused through the complex, lingering finish. Still chunky in texture, it will benefit from short-term cellaring. Drink through 2006.–J.L. • $27 • (8/31/1998) SS • **91**

Merlot Napa Valley 1994 • $24 • (2/28/1997) • **89**

Merlot Napa Valley 1993 • $22 • (6/15/1996) • **83**

Merlot Napa Valley 1991 • $18 • (9/15/1994) • **83**

Merlot Napa Valley 1990 • $16 • (6/15/1993) • **83**

Merlot Napa Valley 1989 • $15 • (5/31/1992) • **88**

Merlot Napa Valley 1987 • $18 • (7/31/1990) • **80**

Merlot Napa Valley 1986 • $15 • (6/30/1988) • **84**

Sauvignon Blanc Napa Valley 1998: Firm and focused, with a squeaky-clean feel on the palate, this serves up bright grapefruit flavors backed by lemon, herb and pleasing mineral notes. Finishes long. Drink now. • $15 • (9/30/1999) • **89**

Sauvignon Blanc Napa Valley 1997: Fairly tight and firmly textured, but the flavors prove generous with layers of grapefruit, orange, lemon and lime. Finishes long, with a refreshing final statement of melon and herb. Drink now. • $14 • (9/15/1998) • **88**

Sauvignon Blanc Napa Valley 1996 • $14 • (3/31/1998) • **86**

Scheurebe Napa Valley Late Harvest 1990 • $13/375 ml. • (6/15/1992) • **81**

Scheurebe Napa Valley Late Harvest Special Select 1989 • $18/375 ml. • (4/30/1991) • **88**

Sémillon Napa Valley Late Harvest Délice du Sémillon 1989 • $13/375 ml. • (4/30/1991) • **89**

Syrah Napa Valley Vin du Mistral 1996: Dark and meaty, with complex, spicy currant, raspberry, anise, leather and coffee flavors. Chunky, with firm tannins. Drink now through 2007.–J.L. • $30 • (11/15/1999) • **89**

Syrah Napa Valley Vin du Mistral 1995: Racy, with a meaty, spicy accent to the dried cherry, sage and wild berry flavors. Finishes with a slight vegetal edge and firm tannins. Drink through 2005.–J.L. • $30 • (4/30/1999) • **87**

Syrah Napa Valley Vin du Mistral 1994 • $26 • (9/30/1997) • **92**

Syrah Napa Valley Vin du Mistral 1993 • $24 • (9/30/1996) • **89**

Syrah Napa Valley Vin du Mistral 1992 • $22 • (12/15/1995) HR • **92**

Syrah Napa Valley Vin du Mistral 1991 • $22 • (1/31/1995) • **88**

Syrah Napa Valley Vin du Mistral 1990 • $18 • (10/31/1993) • **81**

Syrah Napa Valley Vin du Mistral 1989 • $18 • (12/31/1992) • **81**

Syrah Napa Valley Vin du Mistral 1988 • $16 • (6/30/1992) • **87**

Syrah Napa Valley Vin du Mistral 1987 • $14 • (8/31/1991) • **81**

Syrah Napa Valley Vin du Mistral 1986 • $14 • (10/31/1990) • **88**

Vin du Mistral Le Mistral California 1993 • $15 • (12/15/1995) • **88**

Vin du Mistral Le Mistral California 1991 • $14 • (7/31/1993) • **84**

Vin du Mistral Le Mistral California 1990 • $14 • (11/30/1992) • **85**

Vin du Mistral Le Mistral California 1989 • $14 • (7/15/1991) • **85**

Viognier Napa Valley 1998: Ripe and vibrant, with rich, spicy litchi nut, pear, fig and apricot flavors that are well focused. Drink now through 2004.–J.L. • $30 • (1/31/2000) • **88**

Zinfandel Alexander Valley 1990 • $12 • (10/15/1992) • **88**

Zinfandel Alexander Valley 1989 • $12 • (10/15/1992) • **82**

Zinfandel Alexander Valley 1985 • $10 • (7/31/1987) • **74**

PHILIPPE-LORRAINE | CALIFORNIA

Cabernet Sauvignon Napa Valley 1997: Candied violet and cherry flavors dissipate quickly on a lean and drying frame. Drink now.–J.L. • $19 • (6/30/2000) • **80**

Cabernet Sauvignon Napa Valley 1990 • $11 • (9/15/1993) • **82**

Cabernet Sauvignon Napa Valley 1989 • $10 • (7/15/1992) • **84**

Merlot Napa Valley 1997: Ripe berry flavors turn dry and weedy on the finish.–J.L. • $21 • (6/30/2000) • **79**

Merlot Napa Valley 1989 • $15 • (5/31/1992) • **89**

PHILLIPS | CALIFORNIA

Chardonnay Lodi 1998: Watery, but full of buttery, toasty oak flavors. Drink now.–J.L. • $14 • (6/30/2000) • **82**

PHILLIPS, R.H. | CALIFORNIA

Alliance California 1992 • $9 • (4/30/1996) • **80**
Alliance California 1990 • $10 • (5/31/1993) • **80**
Alliance California 1989 • $10 • (11/30/1991) • **88**
Cabernet Sauvignon California 1992 • $7 • (5/15/1996) • **82**
Cabernet Sauvignon California 1991 • $8 • (5/15/1994) • **82**
Cabernet Sauvignon California 1990 • $8 • (11/15/1992) • **80**
Cabernet Sauvignon California 1989 • $8 • (7/31/1991) • **82**
Cabernet Sauvignon California Barrel Cuvée 1997: Leads off with smoky, toasty oak and bright plum flavors, with hints of earth and tar. Mildly tannic. Drink now through 2002.–J.L. • $9 • (10/15/1999) • **84**
Cabernet Sauvignon California Night Harvest NV • $4 • (11/30/1988) • **83**
Cabernet Sauvignon Dunnigan Hills Barrel Cuvée 1994 • $8 • (11/30/1996) • **80**
Cabernet-Syrah California Toasted Head 1996: Smoky and toasty, with a good dose of sweet black cherry and plum flavors. Finishes with chunky tannins. Drink now.–J.L. • $15 • (10/15/1999) • **86**
Cabernet-Syrah California Toasted Head 1995 • $15 • (6/15/1998) • **86**
Chardonnay Dunnigan Hills Barrel Cuvée 1998: Light-bodied, but with pretty citrus and peach notes and a focused finish. Drink now.–J.L. • $9 • (6/30/2000) • **83**
Chardonnay Dunnigan Hills Barrel Cuvée 1997: This ready-to-sip Chardonnay delivers tangy citrus flavors with melon and peach overtones that glide to a clean and refreshing finish. There's plenty to go around, and the price is as agreeable as the wine. • $8 • (1/31/1999) • **86**
Chardonnay Dunnigan Hills Barrel Cuvée 1996 • $8 • (9/15/1997) • **86**
Chardonnay Dunnigan Hills Toasted Head 1998: Toasty oak frames flavors of butter, herb, peach and mineral. Finishes a bit limp. Drink now.–J.L. • $14 • (6/15/2000) • **84**
Chardonnay Dunnigan Hills Toasted Head 1997: Ripe, with a supple band of pineapple, toasted oak, citrus and pear flavors. Finishes soft, but focused and refreshing. Drink now.–J.L. • $12 • (5/31/1999) • **87**
Chardonnay Dunnigan Hills Toasted Head 1996 • $12 • (6/30/1998) HR • **89**
Cuvée Rouge California Night Harvest NV • $4/500 ml. • (11/15/1992) • **80**
Mistura Dunnigan Hills Night Harvest 1994 • $6 • (8/31/1996) • **80**
Mourvèdre California EXP 1990 • $15/375 ml. • (10/15/1993) • **83**
Mourvèdre California EXP 1988 • $13/375 ml. • (4/30/1991) • **74**
Sauvignon Blanc Dunnigan Hills Night Harvest 1997 • $6 • (4/30/1998) • **84**
Sauvignon Blanc Dunnigan Hills Night Harvest 1996 • $6 • (6/30/1997) • **85**
Syrah California EXP 1993 • $10 • (12/31/1995) • **88**
Syrah California EXP 1989 • $15/500 ml. • (12/31/1992) • **86**
Syrah California EXP 1988 • $15 • (11/15/1991) HR • **91**
Syrah California Reserve 1987 • $13 • (12/31/1990) • **80**
Syrah Dunnigan Hills EXP 1997: Pleasant cherry and cola flavors almost get lost in the oak-dominated structure. Drink now.–J.L. • $14 • (5/15/2000) • **81**
Syrah Dunnigan Hills EXP 1995 • $12 • (9/30/1997) • **84**
Syrah Dunnigan Hills EXP 1994 • $12 • (4/30/1997) • **88**
Viognier Dunnigan Hills EXP 1997: Somewhat lean in texture, this carries the varietal pedigree of spice, melon, peach and citrus flavors. Bright on the finish and refreshing on the whole. Drink now through 2001. • $12 • (12/31/1998) • **87**
Viognier Dunnigan Hills EXP 1996 • $12 • (12/15/1997) • **84**

PHOENIX | CALIFORNIA

Cabernet Sauvignon Napa Valley 1997: Well focused and concentrated, with juniper, sage, tobacco, cherry and berry flavors. Finishes with integrated tannins. Drink now through 2003.–J.L. • $19 • (11/15/1999) • **86**
Cabernet Sauvignon Napa Valley 1995: Supple, with ripe and concentrated earth, mineral and black cherry flavors. A solid cedar note emerges on the finish. Drink now through 2001.–H.S. • $18 • (10/31/1998) • **84**
Cabernet Sauvignon Napa Valley 1992 • $16 • (11/30/1996) • **85**
Hillside Rogue Napa Valley 1992 • $16 • (4/30/1996) • **77**
Sangiovese Napa Valley Blood of Jupiter 1997: Bright raspberry, cherry and spice flavors lead the way in this juicy, fruity wine, which is tempered nicely by herbal notes, good acidity and firm tannins. Moderate finish. Fun to drink now through 2004. • $19 • (6/15/1999) • **88**
Zinfandel Napa Valley 1997: Ripe, with black cherry and herb flavors. Pleasant for its soft richness. Drink now.–J.L. • $17 • (6/30/1999) • **84**
Zinfandel Napa Valley 1996 • $15 • (6/30/1998) • **87**

PIEDMONT | VIRGINIA

Cabernet Sauvignon Virginia 1998: This round red shows plum, cherry and charry oak flavors that are bold but a bit rustic. Has the stuffing to match with rich dishes. Drink now.–T.M. • $20 • (5/31/2000) • **81**
Cabernet Sauvignon Virginia 1995: Smooth and ripe, with plum and currant flavors and minty notes. Tastes a little mature. Drink now.–K.M. • $18 • (10/15/1998) • **82**
Chardonnay Virginia Hunt Country NV: Rich and medium-bodied, with vanilla and nutmeg augmenting the apple and floral notes. Pleasant and balanced on the soft side, with a lingering finish. Drink now.–B.S. • $15 • (12/15/1998) • **84**
Chardonnay Virginia Native Yeast 1998: Honey and butter flavors are thick and a bit coarse in this oaky white, with melon and apple tart. Drink now.–T.M. • $25 • (5/31/2000) • **82**
Chardonnay Virginia Native Yeast 1997: Well made, full-bodied and thick, displaying fig, hazelnut and nutmeg aromas and flavors, with good concentration and balance. A touch astringent on the finish, perhaps due to the wood tannins, but harmonious overall.–B.S. • $30 • (12/15/1998) • **87**
Chardonnay Virginia Special Reserve 1998: This is lavishly oaked, but has the fruit for balance. Honey, vanilla, melon, pineapple and spice mingle on the full-bodied palate. Drink now through 2002.–T.M. • $20 • (5/31/2000) • **87**
Chardonnay Virginia Special Reserve 1997: Nicely sculpted, with apple and pear flavors and spicy notes. Pineapple and tropical flavors linger on the finish. Drink now.–K.M. • $20 • (8/31/1999) • **84**

PIETRA SANTA | CALIFORNIA

Dolcetto San Benito County 1996: Earthy, gamy notes are a bit more prominent than the berrylike flavor in this sturdy, simple red. Drink now.–H.S. • $10 • (7/31/1998) • **81**
Dolcetto San Benito County 1995 • $14 • (12/31/1996) • **85**
Sangiovese California Sassolino 1993 • $13 • (4/30/1996) • **83**
Sangiovese San Benito County 1996: Cinnamon and spice notes open this fruity, medium-bodied wine, while black cherry, anise and oak blend in nicely. Moderate, supple finish. Drink now through 2001. • $20 • (3/31/1999) • **85**
Sangiovese San Benito County 1993 • $19 • (2/29/1996) • **74**
Sangiovese San Benito County 1992 • $12/500 ml. • (2/28/1995) • **84**
Sassolino California 1995 • $15 • (6/30/1998) • **83**

PINDAR | NEW YORK

Cabernet Sauvignon North Fork of Long Island 1986 • $13 • (12/15/1988) • **86**
Cabernet Sauvignon North Fork of Long Island Reserve 1993 • $17 • (12/31/1996) • **82**
Cabernet Sauvignon North Fork of Long Island Reserve 1988 • $14 • (6/30/1991) • **85**
Merlot North Fork of Long Island 1995: Good concentration, with lively blackberry and black cherry flavors, but the toasty, smoky, coffee-scented oak notes tend to dominate now, and the tannins turn a bit dry on the finish. Drink through 2003.–T.M. • $19 • (6/30/1999) • **84**
Merlot North Fork of Long Island 1987 • $13 • (12/15/1990) • **80**
Merlot North Fork of Long Island 1986 • $13 • (12/15/1988) • **84**
Merlot North Fork of Long Island Reserve 1993 • $15 • (12/31/1996) • **85**
Merlot North Fork of Long Island Reserve 1988 • $14 • (6/30/1991) • **83**
Mythology North Fork of Long Island 1995: Smooth and balanced, this big Cabernet blend has good weight and concentration, but the flavors range from earth to toast to mushroom without much fruit, and the tannins turn a bit dry on the finish. Drink now through 2003.–T.M. • $37 • (6/30/1999) • **83**
Mythology North Fork of Long Island 1993 • $23 • (12/31/1996) • **86**
Mythology North Fork of Long Island 1988 • $20 • (6/30/1991) • **83**
Mythology North Fork of Long Island 1987 • $20 • (6/30/1991) • **81**

PINE RIDGE | CALIFORNIA

Andrus Reserve Diamond Mountain Napa Valley 1988 • $32 • (11/15/1991) • **82**
Andrus Reserve Howell Mountain 1988 • $15 • (11/15/1991) • **82**
Andrus Reserve Napa Valley 1995 • $85 • (6/30/1998) • **92**
Andrus Reserve Napa Valley 1994 • $85 • (7/31/1997) • **93**
Andrus Reserve Rutherford Cuvée Napa Valley 1988 • $19 • (11/15/1991) • **65**
Andrus Reserve Stags Leap District 1988 • $15 • (11/15/1991) • **82**
Cabernet Sauvignon Howell Mountain 1997: Firm and structured. Complex, elegant, spicy herb, earth and currant flavors have a chalky edge, with pret-

ty oak. Turns dry and tannic. Cellar short-term. Best from 2002 through 2010.–J.L. • $50 • (5/31/2000) • **88**

Cabernet Sauvignon Howell Mountain 1996: Dark, tight, dense and chewy, offering layers of mineral, currant, leather, blackberry and cedary oak flavors that are rich and concentrated, with a long, lingering aftertaste and firm, detailed tannins.–J.L. • $40 • (5/15/1999) • **93**

Cabernet Sauvignon Howell Mountain 1995 • $38 • (4/30/1998) • **88**

Cabernet Sauvignon Howell Mountain 1994 • $35 • (10/31/1997) • **90**

Cabernet Sauvignon Howell Mountain 1993 • $31 • (12/15/1995) • **88**

Cabernet Sauvignon Napa Valley Andrus Reserve 1991 • $60 • (11/15/1993) • **85**

Cabernet Sauvignon Napa Valley Andrus Reserve 1986 • $NA • (12/15/1996) • **80**

Cabernet Sauvignon Napa Valley Andrus Reserve 1984 • $38 • (6/30/1988) • **90**

Cabernet Sauvignon Napa Valley Andrus Reserve 1980 • $35 • (12/01/1984) CS • **93**

Cabernet Sauvignon Napa Valley Andrus Reserve Cuvée Duet 1985 • $60 ⓐ • (10/15/1988) • **83**

Cabernet Sauvignon Napa Valley Diamond Mountain 1986 • $NA • (12/15/1996) • **82**

Cabernet Sauvignon Napa Valley Rutherford Cuvée 1992 • $16 • (11/15/1995) SS • **91**

Cabernet Sauvignon Napa Valley Rutherford Cuvée 1991 • $17 • (11/15/1994) • **84**

Cabernet Sauvignon Napa Valley Rutherford Cuvée 1990 • $16 • (11/15/1993) • **84**

Cabernet Sauvignon Napa Valley Rutherford Cuvée 1987 • $16 • (3/15/1992) • **77**

Cabernet Sauvignon Napa Valley Rutherford Cuvée 1986 • $78 ⓐ • (12/15/1996) • **78**

Cabernet Sauvignon Napa Valley Rutherford Cuvée 1985 • $16 • (2/15/1989) • **88**

Cabernet Sauvignon Napa Valley Rutherford Cuvée 1984 • $14 • (8/31/1987) • **87**

Cabernet Sauvignon Napa Valley Rutherford Cuvée 1983 • $14 • (4/30/1987) • **81**

Cabernet Sauvignon Napa Valley Rutherford Cuvée 1982 • $13 • (10/01/1985) • **86**

Cabernet Sauvignon Napa Valley Rutherford Cuvée 1981 • $13 • (12/16/1984) • **93**

Cabernet Sauvignon Rutherford 1997: From Napa's reputable Rutherford appellation comes this ripe and elegant Cabernet, displaying spicy black cherry, currant, plum, anise and tar character, turning supple and polished. Drink now through 2008.–J.L. • $26 • (3/31/2000) SS • **89**

Cabernet Sauvignon Rutherford 1996: Tight, cedary oak leads to a plum and cherry core of moderate richness, depth and complexity. Drink through 2006.–J.L. • $25 • (12/31/1998) • **88**

Cabernet Sauvignon Rutherford 1995 • $24 • (3/31/1998) • **89**

Cabernet Sauvignon Rutherford 1994 • $22 • (10/31/1997) • **89**

Cabernet Sauvignon Stags Leap District 1997: Dark, ripe, rich and concentrated, this vibrant young wine is loaded with pretty currant, cedar, anise, wild berry and spice, fanning out and gaining depth and nuance. Has sufficient tannins to cellar. Best from 2002 through 2010.–J.L. • $50 • (1/31/2000) • **92**

Cabernet Sauvignon Stags Leap District 1996: Remarkably plush, rich and concentrated, with layers of ripe plum and black cherry that are sharply focused and intricate. Long, supple finish. Best from 2001 through 2008.–J.L. • $40 • (2/28/1999) • **92**

Cabernet Sauvignon Stags Leap District 1995 • $38 • (6/15/1998) • **90**

Cabernet Sauvignon Stags Leap District 1994 • $35 • (10/31/1997) • **92**

Cabernet Sauvignon Stags Leap District 1992 • $31 • (12/15/1995) • **90**

Cabernet Sauvignon Stags Leap District 1991 • $30 • (11/15/1994) • **88**

Cabernet Sauvignon Stags Leap District 1990 • $30 • (11/15/1993) • **83**

Cabernet Sauvignon Stags Leap District 1987 • $28 • (1/31/1992) • **85**

Cabernet Sauvignon Stags Leap District 1981 • $20 • (2/01/1985) • **88**

Cabernet Sauvignon Stags Leap District Pine Ridge Stags Leap Vineyard 1986 • $NA • (12/15/1996) • **78**

Cabernet Sauvignon Stags Leap District Pine Ridge Stags Leap Vineyard 1985 • $30 • (4/10/1989) • **80**

Cabernet Sauvignon Stags Leap District Pine Ridge Stags Leap Vineyard 1984 • $25 • (2/15/1988) • **91**

Key: SS—Spectator Selection CS—Cellar Selection HR—Highly Recommended $NA—Price Not Available a—Auction Price (BT)—Barrel Tasting
For a key to the tasters' initials, see "How to Use These Listings."
Dates in parentheses indicate the issues in which the ratings were published.

Cabernet Sauvignon Stags Leap District Pine Ridge Stags Leap Vineyard 1983 • $20 • (7/15/1987) • **79**

Cabernet Sauvignon Stags Leap District Pine Ridge Stags Leap Vineyard 1982 • $20 • (10/31/1986) CS • **91**

Chardonnay Napa Valley Carneros Dijon Clones 1998: Elegant and complex, with a supple, polished texture and delicate pear, fig, spice and apricot flavors that linger, this lovely Carneros white is a very good choice now through 2003.–J.L. • $25 • (12/15/1999) SS • **89**

Chardonnay Napa Valley Carneros Dijon Clones 1997: This California Chardonnay is smooth, rich and complex, its layers of ripe fig, melon, pear, anise and spice gaining nuance from light, toasty oak tones. An outstanding bottle to enjoy now through 2003.–J.L. • $24 • (1/31/1999) SS • **91**

Chardonnay Napa Valley Carneros Dijon Clones 1996 • $20 • (1/31/1998) • **90**

Chardonnay Napa Valley Knollside Cuvée 1996 • $18 • (2/28/1998) • **87**

Chardonnay Stags Leap District 1998: Simple, with an herbal, oaky edge to the modest grassy citrus notes. Good, but hardly worth the price. Drink now.–J.L. • $40 • (5/31/2000) • **83**

Chardonnay Stags Leap District 1997: Complex aromas lead to a tight, concentrated, flavorful wine, with hints of peach, pear, nectarine, guava and mineral. Finishes with a delicate, stony aftertaste that's clean and refreshing. Drink now through 2002.–J.L. • $35 • (5/15/1999) • **92**

Chardonnay Stags Leap District Dijon Clones 1996 • $34 • (5/15/1998) • **91**

Chenin Blanc California 1996 • $8 • (10/15/1997) • **85**

Chenin Blanc-Viognier California 1998: Delivering a mouthful of snappy pineapple, melon and pear, along with a dash of spice, this clean-tasting white blend offers refreshing drinking at a wallet-friendly price. Ready now.–J.L. • $11 • (9/30/1999) • **87**

Chenin Blanc-Viognier California 1997: How about trying this refreshing, fun-to-drink white blend? It's a fruity wine that sits broadly on the palate, rich in peach, apricot, apple and spice flavors, ending with a tangy, bright note. Drink now. • $10 • (1/31/1999) • **86**

Epitome Stags Leap District 1996: Smooth, ripe and complex, with layers of ripe cherry, blackberry, plum and currant. Turns silky and polished on the finish, where the flavors fan out nicely. Best from 2001 through 2008. –J.L. • $95 • (11/15/1999) • **91**

La Petite Vigne TSIFG Napa Valley White 1996 • $12 • (5/15/1998) • **85**

Merlot Napa Valley Carneros 1997: Firm and oaky, a tightly wound, compact, young and rich Merlot. Most impressive is the finish, where the currant, black cherry, wild berry and spicy oak add dimension. Needs time. Best from 2002 through 2010.–J.L. • $42 • (2/29/2000) • **89**

Merlot Napa Valley Carneros 1996: Elegant and complex, with a supple band of cedar, currant and black cherry, picking up black olive, sage and briar notes. Tannins are ripe and polished. Needs short-term cellaring. Drink through 2006.–J.L. • $35 • (2/28/1999) • **90**

Merlot Napa Valley Carneros 1995 • $33 • (3/31/1998) • **90**

Merlot Napa Valley Carneros 1994 • $29 • (6/30/1996) • **87**

Merlot Napa Valley Carneros 1993 • $28 • (5/15/1996) • **85**

Merlot Napa Valley Crimson Creek 1997: Smooth and polished, with an earthy, cedary band of plum and cherry. Firms up on the finish, where the tannins show more strength. Best from 2001 through 2007.–J.L. • $25 • (11/15/1999) • **87**

Merlot Napa Valley Crimson Creek 1996: Smooth and supple, with ripe, earthy plum, wild berry and black cherry flavors that fold together nicely. Finishes with a complex interplay of flavors and mild, well-integrated tannins. Drink now through 2004.–J.L. • $25 • (12/15/1998) • **90**

Merlot Napa Valley Crimson Creek 1995 • $35 • (3/31/1998) • **85**

Merlot Napa Valley Selected Cuvée 1994 • $19 • (7/31/1996) • **84**

Merlot Napa Valley Selected Cuvée 1993 • $18 • (5/15/1996) • **84**

Merlot Napa Valley Selected Cuvée 1991 • $17 • (9/15/1994) • **85**

Merlot Napa Valley Selected Cuvée 1989 • $17 • (5/31/1992) • **73**

Merlot Napa Valley Selected Cuvée 1988 • $17 • (8/31/1991) • **80**

Merlot Napa Valley Selected Cuvée 1987 • $15 • (4/15/1990) • **88**

Merlot Napa Valley Selected Cuvée 1986 • $15 • (6/30/1989) • **80**

Merlot Napa Valley Selected Cuvée 1985 • $13 • (2/15/1988) SS • **91**

Merlot Napa Valley Selected Cuvée 1984 • $18 • (5/15/1987) • **80**

Merlot Napa Valley Selected Cuvée 1983 • $13 • (12/16/1985) • **83**

Merlot Napa Valley Selected Cuvée 1982 • $13 • (10/01/1985) • **90**

Merlot Napa Valley Selected Cuvée 1981 • $13 • (3/16/1984) • **82**

PIPER SONOMA | CALIFORNIA

Blanc de Noirs Sonoma County NV • $16 • (12/15/1997) • **87**

Brut Rosé Sonoma County 1990 • $19 • (12/31/1995) • **84**

Brut Sonoma County NV • $15 • (12/15/1997) • **85**

PLAM | California

Cabernet Sauvignon California 1992 • $6 • (12/15/1995) • **82**
Cabernet Sauvignon Napa Valley 1992 • $30 • (11/15/1994) • **88**
Cabernet Sauvignon Napa Valley 1988 • $28 • (9/30/1991) • **79**
Cabernet Sauvignon Napa Valley 1986 • $24 • (9/15/1989) • **92**
Cabernet Sauvignon Napa Valley 1985 • $24 • (6/30/1988) • **91**
Merlot Napa Valley 1993 • $25 • (3/31/1996) • **78**

PLUM CREEK | Colorado

Merlot Colorado 1995 • $11 • (12/31/1997) • **80**
Merlot Colorado Redstone 1995: Cherry-cola and peppery flavors dominate this tannic red.–K.M. • $14 • (5/31/1999) • **76**
Merlot Colorado Redstone Reserve 1994 • $13 • (8/31/1997) • **84**
Riesling Colorado 1996 • $8 • (8/31/1997) • **73**
Sauvignon Blanc Colorado Whitecliff 1996 • $8 • (12/31/1997) • **76**

PLUMPJACK | California

Cabernet Sauvignon Napa Valley McWilliam's Mt. Eden Vineyard 1995 • $30 • (11/15/1997) • **92**
Cabernet Sauvignon Napa Valley McWilliam's Mt. Eden Vineyard Reserve 1995 • $65 • (11/15/1997) • **92**
Cabernet Sauvignon Oakville 1997: Stylish, with appealing ripe plum, cherry, cedar, anise, tobacco and sage notes. Holding its focus, with a long, intricate aftertaste. Best from 2001 through 2009.–J.L. • $44 • (6/15/2000) • **89**
Cabernet Sauvignon Oakville 1996: Supple and complex, with a pretty array of currant, anise, sage, cedar and tar notes. Complete if a bit chewy in tannin on the finish. Toasty oak smooths things out. Drink through 2008.–J.L. • $32 • (6/15/1999) • **90**
Chardonnay Napa Valley Reserve 1998: Tight and on the tart side, with crisp, mineral and lemon-lime, turning to pear and earth notes. Drink now.–J.L. • $32 • (6/15/2000) • **85**

PONTIN DEL ROZA | Washington

Cabernet Sauvignon Columbia Valley 1993 • $22 • (8/31/1996) • **84**
Merlot Columbia Valley 1993 • $11 • (8/31/1996) • **87**

PONZI | Oregon

Arneis Willamette Valley 1996 • $18/500 ml. • (10/31/1997) • **86**
Chardonnay Willamette Valley 1996 • $16 • (5/15/1998) • **88**
Chardonnay Willamette Valley Clonal Selection 1997: Light in texture, with bitter, pithy flavors reminiscent of grapefruit peel, along with pretty floral notes.–H.S. • $24 • (5/15/2000) • **79**
Chardonnay Willamette Valley Clonal Selection 1996 • $24 • (5/15/1998) • **89**
Pinot Gris Willamette Valley 1996 • $13 • (9/15/1997) • **87**
Pinot Noir Oregon Reserve 1992 • $30 • (10/15/1994) HR • **92**
Pinot Noir Willamette Valley 1997: Light and pretty, with simple berry and plum flavors on an airy frame. Has some fine tannins to lose. Drink now through 2002.–H.S. • $20 • (9/30/1999) • **85**
Pinot Noir Willamette Valley 1996: Unfolds its pretty plum and currant flavors over a gentle frame, lingering engagingly on the delicate finish. Drink now through 2001.–H.S. • $20 • (8/31/1998) • **88**
Pinot Noir Willamette Valley 1995 • $20 • (10/31/1997) • **86**
Pinot Noir Willamette Valley 1994 • $20 • (12/15/1996) • **88**
Pinot Noir Willamette Valley 1988 • $16 • (5/31/1991) • **76**
Pinot Noir Willamette Valley 1987 • $15 • (2/15/1990) • **88**
Pinot Noir Willamette Valley 1985 • $15 • (6/15/1987) • **90**
Pinot Noir Willamette Valley 20th Anniversary 1990 • $35 • (2/28/1993) • **91**
Pinot Noir Willamette Valley Reserve 1997: Bright and focused, with currant and black cherry flavors on a crisp frame. Impressive in how it echoes the fruit in this light vintage. Has a hint of toast and earth on the finish. Drink now through 2003.–H.S. • $48 • (2/29/2000) • **89**
Pinot Noir Willamette Valley Reserve 1996: Firm in texture, with pretty currant and plum flavors pulsing beneath a thin layer of gritty tannins. Finishes gracefully and shows more intensity than most '96 Oregon Pinot Noirs. A good bet for the cellar. Drink now through 2002.–H.S. • $48 • (4/30/1999) • **89**
Pinot Noir Willamette Valley Reserve 1995 • $48 • (10/31/1997) • **89**
Pinot Noir Willamette Valley Reserve 1994 • $35 • (12/15/1996) CS • **94**
Pinot Noir Willamette Valley Reserve 1991 • $25 • (1/31/1994) • **86**
Pinot Noir Willamette Valley Reserve 1990 • $25 • (2/28/1993) • **73**
Pinot Noir Willamette Valley Reserve 1988 • $25 • (4/15/1991) • **86**
Pinot Noir Willamette Valley Reserve 1987 • $20 • (2/15/1990) • **91**
Pinot Noir Willamette Valley Reserve 1986 • $15 • (6/15/1988) • **81**

POPE VALLEY | California

Cabernet Sauvignon Napa Valley 1990 • $14 • (11/15/1994) • **84**
Cabernet Sauvignon Napa Valley La Dolce DeVita Vineyard 1992 • $15 • (12/15/1995) • **87**
Port Napa Valley 1994 • $18 • (10/31/1995) • **88**
Zinfandel Napa Valley 1998: Perfumed, with charred overtones to the chocolate and black currant flavors. Drink now through 2002.–J.L. • $23 • (6/15/2000) • **83**

PORTER CREEK | California

Chardonnay Russian River Valley 1997: Light-bodied, showing focused flinty citrus, herb and toast notes. Elegant, minerally finish. Drink now through 2002.–J.L. • $16 • (6/30/1999) • **87**
Pinot Noir Russian River Valley Creekside Vineyard 1997: Tart, fresh and spicy, with a peppery edge to the black cherry and tea flavors. Hints of vanilla linger on the drying finish. Drink now through 2002.–H.S. • $20 • (9/15/1999) • **84**
Pinot Noir Russian River Valley Creekside Vineyard 1996: Marked by spice, herbs, cherry and currant notes, this is light in texture, with a vaguely waxy edge. Finishes with moderate length. Drink now. • $18 • (8/31/1998) • **83**
Pinot Noir Russian River Valley Hillside Vineyard 1997: Light and peppery, with a modest range of cherry and tea flavors, finishing firm. Drink now through 2002.–H.S. • $20 • (9/15/1999) • **83**
Pinot Noir Russian River Valley Hillside Vineyard 1996: Olive and herblike; somewhat bitter on the palate. Hints of black cherry attenuate abruptly, with a coarse finish. • $20 • (8/31/1998) • **79**

POWERS | Washington

Cabernet Sauvignon Columbia Valley 1993 • $12 • (9/30/1995) • **91**
Cabernet Sauvignon Columbia Valley Mercer Ranch Vineyard 1995: Firm in texture, with a silky core of blackberry and currant, shaded with touches of coffee and spice. Drink now.–H.S. • $16 • (9/15/1998) • **86**
Cabernet Sauvignon Columbia Valley Mercer Ranch Vineyard 1994 • $18 • (9/15/1996) • **88**
Cabernet Sauvignon Washington 1997: Fresh and lightly chewy, with pretty blackberry and currant flavors that linger nicely on the finish. Drink now through 2002.–H.S. • $10 • (8/31/1999) • **85**
Cabernet Sauvignon Washington 1996: Lithe and artfully balanced to show off its pretty plum, black cherry and minty-herbal flavors against a background of lively acidity. Drink through 2004.–H.S. • $11 • (9/15/1998) • **87**
Cabernet-Merlot Columbia Valley 1995 • $12 • (9/15/1997) • **86**
Cabernet-Merlot Columbia Valley 1994 • $10 • (5/15/1996) • **87**
Cabernet-Merlot Columbia Valley 1993 • $10 • (5/15/1996) • **91**
Cabernet-Merlot Columbia Valley 1992 • $8 • (10/15/1993) • **79**
Cabernet-Merlot Washington 1996: Firm in texture, with a lean beam of berry and spice flavor shining through a layer of fine-grained tannins. Drink through 2002.–H.S. • $11 • (8/31/1998) • **84**
Chardonnay Columbia Valley 1997: Fresh and lively, with apple and vanilla flavors on a crisp frame. Texture is a bit rough and unpolished. Drink now. –H.S. • $9 • (9/15/1999) • **85**
Chardonnay Columbia Valley 1996: Crisp and citrusy, with a metallic glint to the bright flavors. Drink now.–H.S. • $10 • (9/15/1998) • **82**
Chardonnay Columbia Valley Private Reserve 1996: A jazzy white wine with citrusy pear flavors. A disconcerting hint of bitterness from oak could settle down with short-term cellaring. Drink through 2001.–H.S. • $14 • (9/15/1998) • **83**
Fumé Blanc Columbia Valley 1997: Light and refreshing, with a smoky, peppery edge to the modest apple and citrus flavors. Drink now.–H.S. • $7 • (9/30/1999) • **84**
Fumé Blanc Columbia Valley 1996 • $8 • (9/15/1997) • **81**
Lemberger Columbia Valley Mercer Ranch Vineyard 1997: A ripe, round red, generous with its plum and berry flavors. Fine tannins don't get in the way as the flavors linger. Drink now.–H.S. • $9 • (8/31/1999) • **86**
Lemberger Columbia Valley Mercer Ranch Vineyard 1996: Firm in texture, almost chewy with fine-grained tannins, and its spicy black cherry and tar flavors have earthy overtones.–H.S. • $10 • (9/15/1998) • **83**
Lemberger Columbia Valley Mercer Ranch Vineyard 1995 • $10 • (12/31/1996) • **85**

POWERS

Merlot Columbia Valley 1997: Firm and generous, this lively mouthful of tarry blackberry and dark plum flavors is shaded with exotic spice overtones that linger nicely on the finish. Has more going for it than a sample reviewed earlier. Drink through 2005.–H.S. • $12 • (11/15/1999) • **88**
Merlot Columbia Valley 1995 • $18 • (9/15/1997) • **88**
Merlot Columbia Valley 1993 • $13 • (5/31/1996) • **85**
Merlot Columbia Valley 1992 • $12 • (9/30/1994) • **80**
Muscat Canelli Columbia Valley 1998: Sweet, bordering on syrupy, with modest apple and vaguely spicy flavors.–H.S. • $7 • (9/30/1999) • **78**
Muscat Canelli Columbia Valley 1997: Light, sweet and spicy, with hints of cinnamon and nutmeg adding extra interest to the delicate pear character. Drink now.–H.S. • $7 • (9/15/1998) • **84**
Muscat Canelli Columbia Valley 1996 • $7 • (9/15/1997) • **85**
Pinot Noir Columbia Valley 1996 • $9 • (9/15/1997) • **83**

POZZAN, MICHAEL | CALIFORNIA

Sangiovese Napa Valley Special Reserve 1996: Earth tones up front are backed by light cherry, herb and just a hint of chocolate. Light in texture and fairly smooth, with a lingering finish. Drink now through 2002. • $13 • (6/15/1999) • **86**

PRADEL, BERNARD | CALIFORNIA

Cabernet Sauvignon Howell Mountain Ranch 1991 • $21 • (9/15/1995) • **87**
Cabernet Sauvignon Napa Valley 1987 • $20 • (10/15/1990) • **86**
Cabernet Sauvignon Napa Valley 1986 • $12 • (1/31/1990) • **82**
Cabernet Sauvignon Napa Valley 1985 • $12 • (4/30/1989) • **91**
Cabernet Sauvignon Napa Valley 1984 • $11 • (2/29/1988) • **88**
Cabernet Sauvignon Napa Valley Limited Barrel Selection 1990 • $14 • (9/15/1995) • **85**
Cabernet Sauvignon Napa Valley Limited Barrel Selection 1989 • $18 • (8/31/1992) • **81**
Cabernet Sauvignon Napa Valley Limited Barrel Selection 1988 • $20 • (11/15/1991) • **80**

PRESTON | CALIFORNIA

Barbera Dry Creek Valley 1992 • $13 • (11/15/1995) • **89**
Barbera Dry Creek Valley 1990 • $13 • (11/30/1992) • **82**
Barbera Dry Creek Valley 1989 • $13 • (3/15/1992) • **86**
Cabernet Sauvignon Dry Creek Valley 1990 • $12 • (11/15/1994) • **88**
Cabernet Sauvignon Dry Creek Valley 1989 • $12 • (11/15/1993) • **81**
Cabernet Sauvignon Dry Creek Valley 1988 • $14 • (3/15/1992) • **80**
Cabernet Sauvignon Dry Creek Valley 1987 • $14 • (10/31/1990) • **88**
Cabernet Sauvignon Dry Creek Valley 1986 • $12 • (3/15/1990) • **87**
Cabernet Sauvignon Dry Creek Valley 1985 • $11 • (9/30/1988) • **86**
Cabernet Sauvignon Dry Creek Valley 1984 • $11 • (10/15/1987) • **91**
Cabernet Sauvignon Dry Creek Valley 1983 • $11 • (7/16/1986) • **86**
Cabernet Sauvignon Dry Creek Valley 1982 • $11 • (7/01/1985) • **84**
Estate Red Dry Creek Valley 1989 • $6 • (6/30/1990) • **77**
Estate Red Dry Creek Valley 1988 • $5 • (8/31/1989) • **82**
Faux Dry Creek Valley 1997: A delicate, easy-drinking style, with hints of cherry, spice and herbs, fresh and clean on the palate. Try now. • $11 • (5/15/1999) • **84**
Faux Dry Creek Valley 1996: Fragrant, with hints of plum, raspberry and mushroom. Finishes with a refreshing spicy edge. A blend of Mourvèdre, Carignane, Grenache, Syrah and Cinsault. Drink now. • $11 • (9/15/1998) • **86**
Faux Dry Creek Valley 1995 • $10 • (7/31/1997) • **85**
Faux Dry Creek Valley 1993 • $9 • (4/30/1995) • **85**
Faux Dry Creek Valley 1992 • $9 • (12/31/1993) • **83**
Faux-Castel Dry Creek Valley 1991 • $9 • (11/30/1992) • **85**
Faux-Castel Dry Creek Valley 1990 • $9 • (6/30/1992) • **82**
Gamay Dry Creek Valley 1997 • $12 • (3/31/1998) • **86**
Gamay Beaujolais Dry Creek Valley 1996 • $11 • (9/15/1997) • **87**
Gamay Beaujolais Dry Creek Valley 1995 • $9 • (2/29/1996) • **86**
Gamay Beaujolais Dry Creek Valley 1994 • $9 • (4/30/1995) • **87**
Gamay Beaujolais Dry Creek Valley 1988 • $7 • (2/15/1989) • **85**

Key: SS—Spectator Selection CS—Cellar Selection HR—Highly Recommended $NA—Price Not Available a—Auction Price (BT)—Barrel Tasting
For a key to the tasters' initials, see "How to Use These Listings."
Dates in parentheses indicate the issues in which the ratings were published.

Le Petit Faux Dry Creek Valley Blush 1996 • $10 • (9/15/1997) • **80**
Marsanne Dry Creek Valley 1997: Rich in flavor, offering layers of hazelnut, pear, apple and peach. Quite nice, even with the slight tartness on the finish. Drink now. • $18 • (11/15/1998) • **87**
Mourvèdre Dry Creek Valley 1997: Slightly peppery, earthy flavors combine with currant notes and drying tannins. Drink now.–J.L. • $16 • (5/15/2000) • **82**
Mourvèdre Dry Creek Valley Vineyard Select 1996: Light and lean, showing spice, smoky herb, game and cherry flavors. Drink now.–J.L. • $20 • (11/15/1999) • **80**
Muscat Canelli Late Harvest Dry Creek Valley Muscat Brûlée 1989 • $12/375 ml. • (3/15/1992) • **82**
Sauvignon Blanc Dry Creek Valley 1998: An exotic style, with passion fruit, herb and floral notes. Light in texture, balanced, with a harmonious finish. Drink now through 2002.–H.S. • $12 • (1/31/2000) • **88**
Sauvignon Blanc Dry Creek Valley Cuvée de Fumé 1997: Lean yet flavorful, with a grapefruit and herb theme that goes a long way toward the finish, punctuated by fig and fresh pea notes. Well balanced, with good acidity. Drink now through 2002. • $12 • (1/31/1999) • **87**
Sauvignon Blanc Dry Creek Valley Cuvée de Fumé 1996 • $12 • (12/15/1997) • **87**
Syrah Dry Creek Valley 1998: Dry and leathery, yet enough ripe plum, sage, mineral and black cherry fold in to give it depth and range of flavor. Drink now through 2005.–J.L. • $18 • (1/31/2000) • **87**
Syrah Dry Creek Valley 1997: Firm, with a tight core of blackberry, mineral and floral notes, it needs time to evolve and show more depth. Finishes firm. Drink now through 2005.–J.L. • $18 • (9/15/1999) • **87**
Syrah Dry Creek Valley 1994 • $20 • (5/15/1997) • **87**
Syrah Dry Creek Valley 1993 • $18 • (2/29/1996) • **88**
Syrah Dry Creek Valley 1992 • $18 • (5/15/1995) • **88**
Syrah Dry Creek Valley 1990 • $18 • (12/31/1992) • **85**
Syrah-Sirah Dry Creek Valley 1989 • $18 • (3/15/1992) • **78**
Syrah-Sirah Dry Creek Valley 1986 • $11 • (2/15/1989) • **90**
Syrah-Sirah Dry Creek Valley 1985 • $10 • (1/31/1988) • **91**
Vin Gris Dry Creek Valley 1998: Dry, with tea, herb and strawberry notes. Holds its focus and flavors through the finish. Drink now.–J.L. • $9 • (11/15/1999) • **85**
Viognier Dry Creek Valley 1997: A silky-textured wine sporting mandarin orange, lemon, lime and engaging mineral flavors. Finishes long and clean. Drink now. • $20 • (11/15/1998) • **87**
Viognier Dry Creek Valley 1996 • $20 • (8/31/1997) • **85**
Zinfandel Dry Creek Valley 1992 • $12 • (9/15/1994) SS • **89**
Zinfandel Dry Creek Valley 1991 • $12 • (9/30/1993) • **88**
Zinfandel Dry Creek Valley 1990 • $12 • (12/15/1992) • **87**
Zinfandel Dry Creek Valley 1989 • $11 • (10/15/1992) • **86**
Zinfandel Dry Creek Valley 1988 • $10 • (10/15/1990) • **86**
Zinfandel Dry Creek Valley 1987 • $10 • (3/15/1990) • **83**
Zinfandel Dry Creek Valley Old Vines Old Clones 1997: Focused, with a lean band of herb and berry flavors, but it suggests more depth beneath. Drink now.–J.L. • $16 • (11/15/1999) • **80**
Zinfandel Dry Creek Valley Old Vines Old Clones 1996 • $18 • (5/15/1998) • **88**
Zinfandel Dry Creek Valley Old Vines Old Clones 1995 • $15 • (2/28/1997) • **87**
Zinfandel Dry Creek Valley Old Vines Old Clones 1993 • $13 • (6/15/1995) • **88**

PRESTON PREMIUM WINES | WASHINGTON

Cabernet Franc Columbia Valley 1995 • $17 • (1/31/1998) • **80**
Cabernet Sauvignon Columbia Valley 1995 • $14 • (9/15/1997) • **85**
Cabernet Sauvignon Columbia Valley 1994 • $10 • (9/15/1996) • **79**
Cabernet Sauvignon Columbia Valley Reserve 1995: Expansive flavors of black cherry, plum, coffee and spice wrap themselves around a crisp structure. The fruit and tannin battle it out on the finish; try in a few years to see which won. Drink through 2005.–H.S. • $21 • (9/15/1998) • **89**
Cabernet Sauvignon Columbia Valley Reserve 1994 • $19 • (9/15/1997) • **89**
Cabernet Sauvignon Columbia Valley Reserve 1993 • $22 • (9/15/1996) • **91**
Cabernet Sauvignon Columbia Valley Western White Oak 1993 • $18 • (9/15/1996) • **88**
Cabernet Sauvignon Washington 1992 • $12 • (3/15/1994) • **82**
Cabernet Sauvignon Washington Oak Aged 1993 • $10 • (9/30/1995) • **89**
Cabernet Sauvignon Washington Oak Aged 1989 • $10 • (5/15/1991) • **85**
Cabernet Sauvignon Washington Preston Vineyard Oak Aged 1990 • $12 • (4/30/1992) • **76**
Cabernet Sauvignon Washington Preston Vineyard Reserve 1990 • $21 • (3/31/1992) • **91**
Cabernet Sauvignon Washington Preston Vineyard Selected Reserve 1987 • $14 • (10/15/1989) • **62**

Cabernet Sauvignon Washington Reserve 1992 • $27 • (9/30/1995) • **90**
Cabernet Sauvignon Washington Reserve 1991 • $28 • (10/15/1993) • **84**
Cabernet Sauvignon Washington Reserve 1989 • $24 • (8/31/1991) • **90**
Cabernet Sauvignon Washington Western White Oak Aged 1992 • $24 • (4/30/1996) • **81**
Cabernet Sauvignon Washington Western White Oak Aged 1991 • $18 • (10/15/1993) • **81**
Chardonnay Columbia Valley 1998: Ripe, focused and exuberant with its pear, vanilla, toast and citrus flavors that keep vibrating through the racy finish. Drink now through 2001.–H.S. • $10 • (8/31/1999) • **87**
Chardonnay Columbia Valley 1997: Soft and highly polished, with sweet oak flavors most prominent, weaving in hints of pear and citrus. Drink now.–H.S. • $10 • (1/31/1999) • **82**
Chardonnay Columbia Valley Reserve 1998: Smooth, creamy and generous with its spice- and toast-scented pear and lime flavors, which echo on the finely tuned finish. Drink now through 2003.–H.S. • $16 • (8/31/1999) • **88**
Gamay Columbia Valley Beaujolais Rosé 1997: Light and simple, this blast of strawberry candy flavor is not sweet, but crisp. Drink now.–H.S. • $8 • (9/30/1998) • **82**
Merlot Columbia Valley 1995 • $14 • (9/15/1997) • **80**
Merlot Columbia Valley 1994 • $10 • (9/15/1996) • **76**
Merlot Columbia Valley Reserve 1995: Already feels mature, almost gamy and earthy, with orange peel, tea and tobacco notes more prominent than fruit.–H.S. • $21 • (9/15/1998) • **80**
Merlot Columbia Valley Reserve 1994 • $19 • (9/15/1997) • **88**
Merlot Columbia Valley Reserve 1993 • $20 • (9/15/1996) • **88**
Merlot Columbia Valley Western White Oak 1995 • $16 • (1/31/1998) • **88**
Merlot Washington Bareback Riding Limited Edition 1992 • $18 • (6/15/1995) • **84**
Merlot Washington Oak Aged 1993 • $10 • (9/30/1995) • **83**
Merlot Washington Oak Aged 1988 • $7 • (8/31/1991) • **77**
Merlot Washington Reserve 1990 • $26 • (9/30/1993) • **80**
Platinum Red Columbia Valley NV • $22 • (9/15/1996) • **85**
Port Columbia Valley Tenrebac 1993 • $22 • (10/15/1997) • **87**

PRIDE | CALIFORNIA

Cabernet Franc Napa Valley 1992 • $18 • (12/31/1994) • **83**
Cabernet Franc Sonoma County 1997: Packs in lots of flavor, with ripe, juicy plum, spice, cedar, blackberry and cherry. Has finesse and polish, with a long, integrated, firmly tannic finish. Drink now through 2006.–J.L. • $34 • (12/15/1999) • **93**
Cabernet Franc Sonoma County 1995 • $24 • (12/15/1997) • **85**
Cabernet Franc Sonoma County 1993 • $20 • (4/30/1996) • **88**
Cabernet Sauvignon Napa Valley 1997: Dark and intense, with a solid, plush core of ripe, rich currant, black cherry, blackberry and light cedar notes. Jam-packed with flavors, it's an immense wine but beautifully balanced. Best from 2002 through 2012.–J.L. • $36 • (4/30/2000) • **94**
Cabernet Sauvignon Napa Valley 1995 • $24 • (11/30/1997) HR • **91**
Cabernet Sauvignon Napa Valley 1994 • $58 Ⓐ • (10/31/1997) • **90**
Cabernet Sauvignon Napa Valley 1993 • $22 • (9/15/1996) • **90**
Cabernet Sauvignon Napa Valley 1992 • $18 • (12/15/1995) • **87**
Cabernet Sauvignon Napa Valley 1991 • $18 • (5/15/1994) HR • **92**
Cabernet Sauvignon Napa Valley Reserve 1996: Ripe, rich and full-bodied, with a complex array of spicy currant, black cherry, earthy-leathery nuances and mineral flavors. Tightly wound, it's in need of short-term cellaring. Best from 2001 through 2010.–J.L. • $216 Ⓐ • (10/31/1999) • **94**
Cabernet Sauvignon Napa Valley Reserve 1995: Firm and tannic, with ripe, dense, compact black cherry, currant and blackberry flavor that's deeply concentrated and in need of time in the cellar to soften and evolve. Best from 2001 through 2010.–J.L. • $70 • (11/30/1998) • **93**
Cabernet Sauvignon Napa Valley Reserve 1994 • $65 • (3/31/1998) • **91**
Chardonnay Napa Valley 1998: Lots of bright, ripe, tasty Chardonnay fruit flavors in this, with pear, fig, apricot and melon echoing throughout. Keeps its fruity focus through the finish, while light oak adds a nice touch. Drink now through 2004.–J.L. • $NA • (12/31/1999) HR • **91**
Chardonnay Napa Valley 1997: A bit coarse in texture now, but the flavors ring true, with a flinty edge to the ripe pear, apple and nectarine, finishing with a light touch of cedary oak. Drink through 2004.–J.L. • $20 • (12/15/1998) • **91**
Chardonnay Napa Valley 1996 • $20 • (5/15/1998) • **91**
Merlot Napa Valley 1997: Wonderful ripe fruit is the hallmark of this lovely California Merlot, which displays rich and complex cherry, currant, anise, cedar and spice flavors. Gains in depth and nuance through the finish, where it keeps pumping out the flavors. Drink now through 2006.–J.L. • $30 • (9/30/1999) SS • **92**
Merlot Napa Valley 1996: Notable for its complexity, this lively Merlot boasts an attractive range of vanilla, berry, cherry, plum and currant flavors that fan out on the finish, showing a measure of finesse and polish. From a winery displaying ever-increasing skill with this variety. Drink through 2004.–J.L. • $24 • (9/30/1998) SS • **90**
Merlot Napa Valley 1995 • $24 • (9/30/1997) • **89**
Merlot Napa Valley 1994 • $20 • (6/30/1997) HR • **91**
Merlot Napa Valley 1993 • $20 • (12/15/1995) • **89**
Merlot Napa Valley 1992 • $18 • (1/31/1995) • **85**
Merlot Napa Valley 1991 • $18 • (3/15/1994) • **89**
Reserve Claret Napa Valley 1996: Smooth, ripe and polished, with a complex array of black cherry, currant, anise, cedar, sage and spice, finishing with a tight focus and a long, concentrated aftertaste. Tannins are firm but supple. A blend of Merlot, Cabernet and Petit Verdot. Drink through 2009.–J.L. • $80 • (12/15/1999) • **93**
Reserve Claret Napa Valley 1995: Tight, with a firm band of currant, chocolate, herb and coffee and chewy tannins framed by pretty, toasty oak, it's long and lively on the finish, turning tannic on the aftertaste. A blend of Merlot, Cabernet Sauvignon and Petit Verdot. Best from 2000.–J.L. • $70 • (11/30/1998) • **91**
Reserve Claret Napa Valley 1994 • $50 • (3/31/1998) • **92**
Reserve Claret Napa Valley 1993 • $50 • (9/30/1997) • **90**
Viognier Sonoma County 1998: Soft, ripe and wide open, a sunny wine, with pretty flavors reminiscent of vanilla, poached pear and subtle spice that linger on the gentle finish. Drink now.–H.S. • $32 • (11/30/1999) • **89**
Viognier Sonoma County 1997: Ripe tangerine, nectarine and a dollop of honey keep this elegant, complex wine alive and snappy. Drink now through 2002.–J.L. • $28 • (12/31/1998) • **88**

PRINCE MICHEL | VIRGINIA

Cabernet Franc Virginia de Virginia Reserve 1994 • $20 • (4/30/1997) • **85**
Cabernet Sauvignon America de Rapidan Cask 92 NV • $12 • (1/31/1995) • **83**
Cabernet-Merlot Virginia Reserve 1990 • $15 • (1/31/1993) • **87**
Chardonnay Virginia 1997: Restrained, with subtle shadings of apple and vanilla. The texture is rich, and the finish is slightly bitter.–B.S. • $13 • (12/15/1998) • **79**
Chardonnay Virginia 1996 • $13 • (5/31/1998) • **85**
Chardonnay Virginia Barrel Select 1997: A tasty white, displaying concentrated aromas and flavors of pear, vanilla custard, clove and just a hint of earth. Medium-bodied and lively, finishing slightly coarse. Drink now. –B.S. • $19 • (7/31/1999) • **83**
de Virginia Reserve 1991 • $16 • (1/31/1995) • **76**
Le Ducq Lot 87 America NV • $50 • (2/29/1992) • **79**
Le Ducq Lot 88 America NV • $65 • (1/31/1995) • **84**
Merlot America 1997: A juicy, grapey-tasting wine, with plum, cherry and spice flavors. There's a nice hint of raspberry on the finish. Drink now. –K.M. • $19 • (10/31/1998) • **84**
Merlot-Cabernet Virginia Reserve 1997: A smooth-textured, harmoniously balanced red that blends cherry, raspberry and earth flavors with firm tannins and a lingering, smoky finish. Drink now through 2001. • $19 • (6/15/1999) • **84**

PUGLIESE | NEW YORK

Brut Blanc de Blanc North Fork of Long Island 1997: Crisp and refreshing. This ebullient sparkler is bright with acidity, and its citrus and green apple flavors will stay lively with food. Drink now.–T.M. • $18 • (5/31/2000) • **84**
Brut Blanc de Blanc North Fork of Long Island 1996: Crisp and well focused, this nervy sparkler offers vivid flavors of lime, green apple, vanilla and light toast. The mousse is lively but gentle. Delicate enough for an aperitif, but rich enough for food. Drink now.–T.M. • $17 • (6/30/1999) • **85**
Cabernet Sauvignon North Fork of Long Island Reserve 1993 • $14 • (12/31/1996) • **84**
Chardonnay North Fork of Long Island Reserve 1998: This straightforward white offers light apple and herb flavors, with just enough acidity to keep it lively.–T.M. • $13 • (5/31/2000) • **77**
Chardonnay North Fork of Long Island Reserve 1997: Sweet, spicy notes of cinnamon and honey dominate this thick, soft white; though not unappealing, they don't quite taste natural, and while some ripe apple and banana flavors do emerge, the finish is cloying.–T.M. • $13 • (6/30/1999) • **78**
Merlot North Fork of Long Island Reserve 1995: Light and slightly dry, this lean red shows simple cherry and herb flavors, with a pleasant sweetness but not much depth.–T.M. • $14 • (6/30/1999) • **79**
Merlot North Fork of Long Island Reserve 1993 • $14 • (12/31/1996) • **83**

PUGLIESE

Vintage Port North Fork of Long Island Port Bello 1997: This smooth red is rich, with sweet chocolate and cherry flavors framed by firm tannins and fueled by high alcohol. A good winter-warmer. Drink now through 2004.–T.M. • $15/375 ml. • (5/31/2000) • **82**

PYRAMIDS | CALIFORNIA

Chardonnay Sonoma County 1997: Ripe and lively, with a vibrant core of toasty apple and citrus flavors. Finishes with clean flinty notes. Drink now.–J.L. • $20 • (7/31/1999) • **86**
Chardonnay Sonoma County 1996 • $16 • (6/15/1998) • **86**

QUADY | CALIFORNIA

Batch 88 Starboard Madera County NV: Sweet, with a hot edge to the green herb, fig, toffee and coffee flavors. Good. Drink now.–J.L. • $18 • (5/31/2000) • **83**
Black Muscat California Elysium 1998: Sweet and spicy, with modest cherry and strawberry flavors accented by a twist of lime. Some may find this quite appealing, while others may dismiss it as simple. Drink now.–J.L. • $17 • (5/31/2000) • **84**
Black Muscat California Elysium 1996 • $14 • (11/30/1997) • **88**
Black Muscat California Elysium 1995 • $15 • (11/30/1996) • **86**
Black Muscat California Elysium 1993 • $13 • (5/15/1995) • **87**
Black Muscat California Elysium 1992 • $12 • (11/15/1993) • **82**
Black Muscat California Elysium 1990 • $12 • (11/30/1991) • **86**
Black Muscat California Elysium 1989 • $12 • (10/15/1990) • **85**
Orange Muscat California Electra 1998: A spritzy white, with clean, refreshing orange, nectarine and tangerine flavors, turning elegant and fragrant. A nice change-of-pace wine at an attractive price. Drink now through 2004. –J.L. • $9 • (2/29/2000) • **88**
Orange Muscat California Electra 1996 • $8 • (4/30/1997) • **88**
Orange Muscat California Electra 1995 • $7 • (11/30/1996) • **85**
Orange Muscat California Electra 1993 • $9 • (4/30/1995) • **83**
Orange Muscat California Electra 1992 • $9 • (6/30/1993) • **86**
Orange Muscat California Electra 1991 • $10 • (6/15/1992) • **84**
Orange Muscat California Essencia 1998: Wonderful aromas and flavors to match, with lots of orange, nectarine, fig and tangerine flavors that are elegant and lively. Drink now through 2004.–J.L. • $17 • (2/29/2000) • **90**
Orange Muscat California Essensia 1995 • $14 • (10/31/1997) • **88**
Orange Muscat California Essensia 1994 • $15 • (11/30/1996) • **80**
Orange Muscat California Essensia 1993 • $13 • (5/15/1995) • **84**
Orange Muscat California Essensia 1990 • $12 • (11/30/1991) • **83**
Orange Muscat California Essensia 1989 • $12 • (10/15/1990) • **89**
Port Amador County LBV 1993 • $12 • (12/15/1997) • **87**
Port Amador County Starboard Batch 88 Rich Ruby 1988 • $15 • (11/30/1991) • **87**
Port Amador County Starboard Frank's Vineyard 1990 • $22 • (2/28/1997) • **88**
Port Amador County Starboard Frank's Vineyard 1989 • $19 • (11/30/1996) • **90**
Port California LBV 1991 • $9 • (5/31/1995) • **81**
Port California Starboard Batch 88 NV • $16 • (11/30/1996) • **85**
Starboard Lot A Amador County 1992: Big, ripe and brawny, with sweet plum, spice, hazelnut, tobacco, fig and chocolate flavors that firm up on the finish, where the tannins are quite evident. Well done. Best from 2003 through 2012.–J.L. • $28 • (5/31/2000) • **88**

QUAIL RIDGE | CALIFORNIA

Cabernet Sauvignon Napa Valley 1995 • $16 • (3/31/1998) • **85**
Cabernet Sauvignon Napa Valley 1992 • $15 • (4/30/1997) • **84**
Cabernet Sauvignon Napa Valley 1990 • $13 • (11/15/1994) • **85**
Cabernet Sauvignon Napa Valley 1989 • $16 • (6/15/1993) • **82**
Cabernet Sauvignon Napa Valley 1988 • $16 • (8/31/1992) • **80**
Cabernet Sauvignon Napa Valley 1987 • $16 • (9/30/1991) HR • **93**
Cabernet Sauvignon Napa Valley 1986 • $15 • (11/15/1990) • **89**
Cabernet Sauvignon Napa Valley 1985 • $15 • (7/31/1989) • **82**
Cabernet Sauvignon Napa Valley 1984 • $15 • (3/31/1989) • **88**
Cabernet Sauvignon Napa Valley 1982 • $13 • (9/16/1985) • **86**
Cabernet Sauvignon Napa Valley Reserve 1987 • $25 • (11/15/1992) • **87**

Key: SS—Spectator Selection CS—Cellar Selection HR—Highly Recommended
$NA—Price Not Available a—Auction Price (BT)—Barrel Tasting
For a key to the tasters' initials, see "How to Use These Listings."
Dates in parentheses indicate the issues in which the ratings were published.

Cabernet Sauvignon Napa Valley Volker Eisele Vineyard Reserve 1992 • $40 • (5/15/1997) • **82**
Cabernet Sauvignon Napa Valley V. & L. Eisele Vineyard Reserve 1989 • $30 • (12/15/1995) • **82**
Merlot California 1996: Fairly lean, with smoke, licorice, blackberry and cedar flavors bringing up the finish. Tannins are firm yet ripe. Drink through 2004. • $17 • (9/30/1998) • **85**
Merlot California 1994 • $19 • (7/31/1997) • **85**
Merlot Napa Valley 1991 • $14 • (12/15/1995) • **82**
Merlot Napa Valley 1990 • $15 • (9/15/1994) • **82**
Merlot Napa Valley 1989 • $15 • (7/15/1993) • **79**
Merlot Napa Valley 1988 • $15 • (5/31/1992) • **84**
Merlot Napa Valley 1987 • $15 • (6/15/1990) • **86**
Merlot Napa Valley 1985 • $14 • (3/31/1989) • **90**
Sauvignon Blanc Napa Valley 1996 • $10 • (3/31/1998) • **85**
Sauvignon Blanc Napa Valley Reserve 1996 • $15 • (1/31/1998) • **82**
Sauvignon Blanc Rutherford 1997: Fairly lean, this sports a dominant mineral edge that works well with the intertwining grapefruit, herb, grass and lemon notes. Refreshing. Drink now through 2001. • $10 • (5/15/1999) • **86**
Sauvignon Blanc Rutherford Reserve 1997: Pretty bright, with grapefruit and lemon flavors at the fore. A little weak on the midpalate, it rises to the occasion on the finish, with a clean, mineral edge. Drink now. • $15 • (5/15/1999) • **85**

QUATRO | CALIFORNIA

Cabernet Sauvignon Sonoma County 1994 • $18 • (8/31/1997) • **85**
Merlot Sonoma County 1996: Delivers a range of enjoyable mineral, plum and anise notes. Finishes slightly short. Drink now through 2002. • $13 • (2/28/1999) • **84**
Merlot Sonoma County 1994: Nice touches of spice, smoke, plums and cinnamon lead the way in this wine. The herbal core is followed by a hint of bitterness, however. Drink now. • $13 • (9/15/1998) • **83**
Pinot Noir Sonoma County 1995: Light smoke and beef notes announce this wine. On the palate, an herbal core dominates, finishing with hints of cherry and spice. Drink now. • $13 • (8/31/1998) • **82**
Pinot Noir Sonoma County 1994 • $13 • (2/28/1998) • **81**

QUILCEDA CREEK | WASHINGTON

Cabernet Sauvignon Washington 1995: Firm and chewy, a solid wine with appealing blackberry, plum and currant flavors poking through the thin veil of tannins draped over the finish. Flavors linger impressively. Drink through 2005.–H.S. • $47 • (9/15/1999) • **90**
Cabernet Sauvignon Washington 1994: Bright and flavorful, a generous mouthful of blueberry, blackberry and currant shaded with spicy oak notes on the persistent finish. Fine-grained tannins need cellaring. Drink through 2005.–H.S. • $63 ⓐ • (8/31/1998) • **92**
Cabernet Sauvignon Washington 1993 • $48 ⓐ • (8/31/1997) • **91**
Cabernet Sauvignon Washington 1992 • $31 • (9/15/1996) CS • **92**
Cabernet Sauvignon Washington 1990 • $24 • (5/15/1994) • **89**
Cabernet Sauvignon Washington 1989 • $24 • (10/15/1993) • **87**
Cabernet Sauvignon Washington 1988 • $75 ⓐ • (2/28/1993) HR • **89**
Cabernet Sauvignon Washington 1985 • $17 • (10/15/1989) • **74**
Cabernet Sauvignon Washington Reserve 1992 • $49 • (9/30/1995) • **95**
Merlot Washington 1993 • $45 • (12/31/1996) • **91**

QUINTANA | CALIFORNIA

Cabernet Sauvignon North Coast 1996: Simple, but offers flavors of black cherry, strawberry and smoky charred oak, some herbal notes as well. Made by Laurel Glen Vineyard. Drink now.–J.L. • $15 • (3/31/1999) • **83**

QUINTESSA | CALIFORNIA

Rutherford 1996: Tight and complex, with layers of spicy currant, earth, cedar, toast and anise. Firms up on the finish, with crisp acidity and mineral notes. Best from 2002 through 2010.–J.L. • $90 • (4/30/2000) • **91**
Rutherford 1995: An elegant, polished red, with a complex and neatly focused beam of currant, black cherry, spice and light, toasty oak, ending in a long, rich finish. A blend of Cabernet Sauvignon, Cabernet Franc and Merlot. From California. Drink through 2006.–J.L. • $90 • (1/31/1999) HR • **92**
Rutherford Napa Valley 1994 • $70 • (11/30/1997) • **91**

QUIVIRA | CALIFORNIA

Cabernet Cuvée Dry Creek Valley 1991 • $15 • (7/31/1995) • **82**
Cabernet Cuvée Dry Creek Valley 1990 • $15 • (11/15/1994) • **85**
Cabernet Cuvée Dry Creek Valley 1989 • $15 • (11/15/1992) • **84**
Cabernet Sauvignon Dry Creek Valley 1988 • $18 • (11/15/1991) • **84**
Cabernet Sauvignon Dry Creek Valley 1987 • $15 • (11/15/1990) • **87**
Dry Creek Cuvée Dry Creek Valley 1997: Tightly wound at present, its black cherry, spice, cola and toast flavors are still working their way to the surface. A little short on the finish, it should nonetheless flesh out with time. A blend of Grenache, Syrah, Mourvèdre and Zinfandel. Try now through 2003. • $13 • (5/15/1999) • **85**
Dry Creek Cuvée Dry Creek Valley 1995 • $13 • (7/31/1997) • **87**
Dry Creek Cuvée Dry Creek Valley 1994 • $13 • (8/31/1996) • **82**
Dry Creek Cuvée Dry Creek Valley 1993 • $12 • (6/30/1995) • **84**
Dry Creek Cuvée Dry Creek Valley 1992 • $12 • (9/30/1994) • **83**
Sauvignon Blanc Dry Creek Valley 1997: Somewhat lean on the palate, this serves up hints of wintergreen, herb, grapefruit, fresh melon and hay, finishing moderately but cleanly. Drink now through 2002. • $11 • (5/15/1999) • **86**
Sauvignon Blanc Dry Creek Valley 1996 • $10 • (4/30/1998) • **84**
Sauvignon Blanc Dry Creek Valley Fig Tree Vineyard 1998: Round and generous in flavor, centering on fig and vanilla, but a tart streak of limelike acidity pokes through on the finish. Drink now.–H.S. • $14 • (1/31/2000) • **82**
Sauvignon Blanc Dry Creek Valley Reserve 1996: Somewhat restrained, with a touch of grass and herbs at the fore. Mineral notes fill in at the end. Drink now. • $16 • (8/31/1998) • **81**
Zinfandel Dry Creek Valley 1998: Pronounced oak and vanilla overtones combine nicely with chocolate and berry flavors. Drink now through 2004. –J.L. • $18 • (5/31/2000) • **85**
Zinfandel Dry Creek Valley 1997: Supple, with a grapey tone to the cherry and berry character. An elegant, understated style with appealing flavors and mild, integrated tannins. Drink now through 2002.–J.L. • $18 • (5/15/1999) • **88**
Zinfandel Dry Creek Valley 1996 • $17 • (5/31/1998) • **85**
Zinfandel Dry Creek Valley 1995 • $16 • (8/31/1997) • **87**
Zinfandel Dry Creek Valley 1994 • $15 • (4/30/1996) • **88**
Zinfandel Dry Creek Valley 1993 • $14 • (4/30/1996) • **87**
Zinfandel Dry Creek Valley 1992: Aging quite nicely, holding its plummy cherry and wild berry flavors while maintaining a sense of elegance and finesse. Finishes with supple tannins and good length. (Zinfandel retrospective tasting). Drink now through 2002.–J.L. • $14 • (6/30/1999) • **88**
Zinfandel Dry Creek Valley 1991 • $13 • (9/30/1993) • **88**
Zinfandel Dry Creek Valley 1990: Complex and elegant, with a distinct red currant and cherry core. Well balanced, smooth and supple on the finish. Aging well. (Zinfandel Retrospective tasting). Try through 2002.–J.L. • $13 • (6/30/1999) • **88**
Zinfandel Dry Creek Valley 1989 • $13 • (7/31/1991) • **84**
Zinfandel Dry Creek Valley 1988 • $12 • (5/31/1990) • **88**
Zinfandel Dry Creek Valley 1987 • $11 • (7/31/1989) • **88**
Zinfandel Dry Creek Valley Reserve 1997: Refreshingly ripe, zesty and complex, with black cherry, wild berry and raspberry accented by peppery spice. Elegant and refined. Drink now through 2005.–J.L. • $25 • (12/31/1999) • **88**

QUPE | CALIFORNIA

Bien Nacido Cuvée Santa Barbara County 1996 • $16 • (8/31/1997) • **87**
Chardonnay Santa Barbara County Bien Nacido Vineyard 1998: A touch of raciness runs through this vibrant young wine, echoing spicy pear, grapefruit, citrus and melon. Drink now through 2004.–J.L. • $18 • (1/31/2000) • **88**
Chardonnay Santa Barbara County Bien Nacido Vineyard 1997: Focused, with subtle, creamy citrus, mineral and tropical flavors. Holds together on the finish, where citrus, toasted oak and herb-tinged flavors linger. Drink now.–J.L. • $18 • (6/15/1999) • **90**
Chardonnay Santa Barbara County Bien Nacido Vineyard 1996 • $18 • (11/15/1997) • **89**
Chardonnay Santa Barbara County Bien Nacido Vineyard Reserve 1998: Bright, zesty acidity keeps the core of ripe pear, tangerine and nectarine flavors lively, finishing with a nice touch of citrus. Drink now through 2002.–J.L. • $25 • (6/30/2000) • **88**
Chardonnay Santa Barbara County Bien Nacido Vineyard Reserve 1997: Elegant, ripe and juicy, with an earthy streak running through the pretty array of guava, pineapple, pear and fig flavors that linger. Drink now through 2001.–J.L. • $25 • (7/31/1999) • **91**
Chardonnay Santa Barbara County Bien Nacido Vineyard Reserve 1996: A concentrated, complex style, with pretty pear, citrus, nectarine and floral flavors, this is a tightly wound, deeply flavored young wine that should only get better with short-term cellaring. Drink now through 2001.–J.L. • $25 • (9/30/1998) • **90**
Chardonnay-Viognier Santa Barbara County Bien Nacido Cuvée 1998: A curious blend of two grapes—the spiciness of Viognier with the body of Chardonnay—with hints of tangerine and pear. Drink now through 2003.–J.L. • $16 • (1/31/2000) • **84**
Los Olivos Cuvée Santa Barbara County 1996: Quite earthy on the nose, but on the palate it's quite smooth and viscous. The flavors run from herbs to leather and black currant. Tannins are firm at the end. A blend of Syrah, Mourvèdre and Grenache. Drink now through 2003. • $18 • (11/30/1998) • **87**
Los Olivos Cuvée Santa Barbara County 1995 • $18 • (8/31/1997) • **88**
Los Olivos Cuvée Santa Barbara County 1994 • $18 • (9/15/1996) • **79**
Los Olivos Cuvée Santa Barbara County 1993 • $15 • (8/31/1995) • **88**
Los Olivos Cuvée Santa Barbara County 1989 • $15 • (8/31/1991) • **85**
Roussanne Edna Valley Alban Vineyard 1997: Offers complexity with its range of rose petal, citrus and nectarine, turning a bit soapy on the finish. Drink now through 2004.–J.L. • $25 • (2/29/2000) • **84**
Syrah Central Coast 1998: Trim and spicy, with a meaty, earthy edge to the ripe plum and berry flavors. Turns complex and enticing on the finish. Drink now through 2005.–J.L. • $14 • (1/31/2000) • **88**
Syrah Central Coast 1997: Smooth and complex, with layers of ripe plum, black cherry, stewed plum and spice, picking up anise, sage and cedar. Finishes with hints of leather, cedar and coffee. Drink now through 2004.–J.L. • $14 • (12/15/1998) • **89**
Syrah Central Coast 1996 • $13 • (12/15/1997) • **84**
Syrah Central Coast 1995 • $13 • (11/30/1996) • **88**
Syrah Central Coast 1993 • $11 • (8/31/1995) • **88**
Syrah Central Coast 1988 • $11 • (12/15/1989) • **90**
Syrah Santa Maria Valley Bien Nacido Hillside Estate 1997: Dark, rich and concentrated, with a complex array of black cherry, wild berry, anise, mineral, sage, tar and cedar. Long, rich aftertaste. Drink now through 2006.–J.L. • $35 • (1/31/2000) • **93**
Syrah Santa Barbara County Bien Nacido Hillside Estate 1996: Offers cherry-berry notes, with a meaty edge, before turning tannic. Drink through 2006.–J.L. • $35 • (12/31/1998) • **87**
Syrah Santa Barbara County Bien Nacido Hillside Estate 1995 • $35 • (12/31/1997) • **90**
Syrah Santa Barbara County Bien Nacido Hillside Select 1994 • $35 • (11/30/1996) • **90**
Syrah Santa Barbara County Bien Nacido Reserve 1997: Bold, ripe and spicy, with layers of black cherry, plum, earth, mineral and sage. Finishes with firm, rich tannins. Drink now through 2006.–J.L. • $25 • (1/31/2000) • **91**
Syrah Santa Barbara County Bien Nacido Reserve 1996: A real beauty, ripe, supple and complex, with a fleshy array of meaty plum, spice, oak and cedar. Holds its focus on the finish, where the flavors are vibrant, fan out and linger. Drink now through 2004.–J.L. • $25 • (8/31/1998) • **90**
Syrah Santa Barbara County Bien Nacido Reserve 1995 • $23/375 ml. • (8/31/1997) • **91**
Syrah Santa Barbara County Bien Nacido Reserve 1994 • $22 • (9/15/1996) • **88**
Syrah Santa Barbara County Bien Nacido Reserve 1993 • $17 • (8/31/1995) SS • **91**
Syrah Santa Barbara County Bien Nacido Vineyard 1989 • $20 • (8/31/1991) • **89**
Syrah Santa Barbara County Bien Nacido Vineyard 1987 • $20 • (2/28/1990) • **81**
Syrah Santa Barbara County Los Olivos Reserve 1993 • $20 • (8/31/1995) • **88**

RABBIT RIDGE | CALIFORNIA

Allure California 1995 • $7 • (3/31/1998) • **85**
Allure California 1991 • $7 • (6/30/1995) • **82**
Allure California 1990 • $8 • (10/15/1993) • **83**
Allure California 1989 • $7 • (5/31/1993) • **81**
Avventura Sonoma County Migliore di Vigneto Reserve 1994 • $30 • (5/15/1998) • **88**
Cabernet Sauvignon Russian River Valley Winemaker's Grand Reserve 1995: Tight, with a trim band of cherry, berry and spice flavors that struggle to excite and find a focus. Drink now through 2002.–J.L. • $50 • (9/15/1999) • **83**
Cabernet Sauvignon Russian River Valley Rabbit Ridge Ranch Winemaker's Grand Reserve 1994 • $40 • (3/31/1998) • **87**
Cabernet Sauvignon Sonoma County Rabbit Ridge Ranch Estate Reserve 1990 • $20 • (11/15/1994) • **86**

RABBIT RIDGE

Cabernet Sauvignon Sonoma County 1989 • $12 • (11/15/1994) • **77**
Cabernet Sauvignon Sonoma County 1988 • $12 • (8/31/1991) • **89**
Chardonnay Russian River Valley Rabbit Ridge Ranch Estate Reserve 1997: Rich and toasty, with a complex array of pear, fig, melon, smoke and citrus notes, turning smooth and polished. Drink now through 2002.–J.L. • $18 • (2/28/1999) • **91**
Chardonnay Russian River Valley Rabbit Ridge Ranch Estate Reserve 1996 • $18 • (4/30/1998) • **89**
Chardonnay Sonoma County 1996 • $12 • (5/15/1998) • **87**
Chardonnay Sonoma County Winemaker's Grand Reserve 1997: Remarkably complex and rich in flavor, with a broad array of fig, vanilla, smoky-toasty oak, pear and honey. Finishes with a burst of flavor and lots of finesse. Drink now through 2002.–J.L. • $30 • (5/31/1999) • **91**
Chardonnay Sonoma County Winemaker's Grand Reserve 1996: Smooth and ripe, with subtle pear, honey, vanilla, hazelnut and creamy notes, long and rich on the finish, where the toasty oak and Chardonnay fruit flavors fold together nicely. Drink now through 2002.–J.L. • $30 • (8/31/1998) • **91**
Dolcetto Napa Valley 1996: Smells a bit alcoholic and herbal. On the palate, light cherry notes are framed by woody flavors, some astringency and bright acids. • $12 • (2/28/1999) • **78**
Dolcetto Paso Robles 1995 • $12 • (6/30/1998) • **85**
Fumé Blanc Russian River Valley Rabbit Ridge Ranch Winemaker's Grand Reserve 1997: Fairly weighty on the palate, this wine packs grapefruit, herb, fig and floral notes, tightly intertwined yet balanced by firm acidity. The finish is smooth and long. Quite nice. Drink now through 2002. • $23 • (5/15/1999) • **88**
Merlot California Barrel Cuvée 1997: Dilute, with a slightly rubbery edge to the berry flavors.–J.L. • $9 • (10/15/1999) • **77**
Merlot California Barrel Cuvée 1996: Oak, blackberry and herb flavors ultimately kick in for a nice, simple quaff. Drink now through 2002. • $9 • (7/31/1998) • **84**
Merlot Carneros Sangiacomo Vineyard 1994 • $20 • (12/31/1996) HR • **91**
Merlot Carneros Sangiacomo Vineyard 1992 • $15 • (6/15/1995) • **86**
Merlot Carneros Sangiacomo Vineyard Reserve 1996: Pleasant for its supple texture, ripe berry and herb flavors. Finishes with ripe tannins. Drink now through 2002.–J.L. • $25 • (10/15/1999) • **85**
Merlot Carneros Sangiacomo Vineyard Reserve 1995 • $23 • (4/30/1998) • **89**
Merlot Sonoma County 1994 • $16 • (7/31/1996) • **84**
Merlot Sonoma County Winemaker's Grand Reserve 1996: Crisp and simple, with pleasant cherry, plum and light toasty oak flavors. Short-term cellaring may do the trick. Drink now through 2003.–J.L. • $32 • (10/15/1999) • **84**
Merlot Sonoma County Winemaker's Grand Reserve 1994 • $28 • (4/30/1997) • **90**
Montepiano California 1995 • $10 • (3/31/1998) • **85**
Mystique North Coast 1993 • $7 • (6/30/1995) • **85**
Nebbiolo California Barrique Riserva 1996: A spicy, cherrylike wine that sports a somewhat herbal edge, this nonetheless shows fullness on the palate and finishes fairly long, with hints of black cherry, blackberry and licorice. Drink now through 2005. • $20 • (2/28/1999) • **87**
Nebbiolo California Barrique Riserva 1994 • $18 • (12/31/1997) • **83**
Oddux Reserve Red California 1990 • $15 • (3/31/1993) • **78**
Petite Sirah Sonoma County 1990 • $10 • (3/31/1993) • **80**
Sangiovese Sonoma County Coniglio Selezione Reserve 1996: Serves up plush plum, blackberry, cherry and spice flavors and frames them with pretty vanilla-scented oak. Finishes with a complex interplay of fruit and wood. Drink now through 2001.–H.S. • $14 • (9/30/1998) • **87**
Sangiovese Sonoma County Coniglio Selezione Reserve 1995 • $13 • (5/15/1998) • **85**
Sangiovese Sonoma County Coniglio Selezione 1994 • $13 • (4/30/1997) HR • **92**
Sangiovese Sonoma County Coniglio Selezione 1993 • $13 • (11/30/1995) • **85**
Sangiovese California Coniglio Selezione 1992 • $12 • (8/31/1995) • **84**
Sauvignon Blanc Russian River Valley 1997 • $10 • (6/30/1998) • **86**
Sauvignon Blanc Russian River Valley 1996 • $9 • (6/30/1997) • **89**
Syrah Sonoma County Reserve 1995: Rich and concentrated, with a leathery streak to the black cherry and herb flavors. Finishes firm, but the tannins are integrated. Drink now through 2005.–J.L. • $20 • (9/15/1999) • **87**
Syrah Sonoma County Reserve 1994: A lean but classy style, with hints of blackberry, currant, smoke, herb and leather. Finishes long and clean, with ripe, but firm tannins. Drink now through 2002. • $20 • (11/15/1998) • **88**

Key: SS—Spectator Selection CS—Cellar Selection HR—Highly Recommended $NA—Price Not Available a—Auction Price (BT)—Barrel Tasting
For a key to the tasters' initials, see "How to Use These Listings."
Dates in parentheses indicate the issues in which the ratings were published.

Zinfandel Amador County 1997: A ripe, tarry-style Zin with mineral and gamy, leathery flavors over a plush core of plum and black cherry. Drink now.–J.L. • $12 • (5/15/1999) • **87**
Zinfandel Amador County 1996: A bit earthy on the nose, it follows up with black cherry, spice, anise and tar notes. Somewhat astringent, with perky acids, the wine demonstrates a forceful though rustic style. Drink now through 2002. • $12 • (2/28/1999) • **86**
Zinfandel California Barrel Cuvée 1997: From a reliable producer comes this soft and fleshy Zin, with earthy, toasty flavors, blackberry, black cherry and wild berry notes, finishing with mild tannins that make it enjoyable tonight. The cherry on top? It's affordably priced.–J.L. • $9 • (4/30/1999) • **86**
Zinfandel California Barrel Cuvée 1996: Ripe and round, with plum and cola flavors on a soft, rustic frame. Moderate tannins call for hearty food. Drink now.–H.S. • $9 • (11/30/1998) • **83**
Zinfandel California Barrel Cuvée 1995 • $9 • (11/15/1997) • **83**
Zinfandel Dry Creek Valley 1993 • $11 • (6/15/1995) • **85**
Zinfandel Dry Creek Valley 1992 • $11 • (10/15/1994) • **80**
Zinfandel Dry Creek Valley 1991 • $10 • (5/31/1993) • **87**
Zinfandel Dry Creek Valley 1990 • $10 • (10/15/1992) • **73**
Zinfandel Dry Creek Valley Olson Vineyard 1998: Nice balance to the ripe cherry and berryish notes, turning earthy and showing a touch of stemminess. Drink now.–J.L. • $25 • (6/15/2000) • **85**
Zinfandel Dry Creek Valley Olson Vineyard 1995 • $22 • (12/15/1996) • **88**
Zinfandel Dry Creek Valley Olson Vineyard 1994 • $16 • (4/30/1996) • **92**
Zinfandel Dry Creek Valley Olson Vineyard Reserve 1997: Effusively fruity, ripe, rich and complex, with tiers of sweet-tasting black cherry, wild berry, plum and spice flavors in a tight, complex package, with pretty, toasty oak on the aftertaste. Almost over-the-top with its sweet, ripe fruit. Drink now through 2004.–J.L. • $25 • (2/28/1999) • **91**
Zinfandel Dry Creek Valley Olson Vineyard Reserve 1996 • $23 • (5/31/1998) • **88**
Zinfandel Paso Robles Westside Vines 1996 • $16 • (6/15/1998) • **85**
Zinfandel Russian River Valley Hedin Vineyard Reserve 1997: An earthy style that's smooth, ripe and supple, with pretty blackberry, black cherry, cedar and spice flavors that are detailed with anise, sage and sandalwood notes. Drink now through 2004.–J.L. • $25 • (2/28/1999) • **91**
Zinfandel Russian River Valley Hedin Vineyard Reserve 1996 • $23 • (6/15/1998) • **86**
Zinfandel Russian River Valley Rabbit Ridge Ranch 1988 • $8 • (4/30/1991) • **86**
Zinfandel Russian River Valley Rabbit Ridge Ranch Estate Reserve 1997: Complex, with a tasty array of ripe plum, black cherry, wild berry and spice. Turns tight and tannic on the finish, but it should blossom with short-term cellaring.–J.L. • $35 • (5/15/1999) • **89**
Zinfandel Russian River Valley Rabbit Ridge Ranch Estate Reserve 1996 • $30 • (5/15/1998) • **87**
Zinfandel Russian River Valley Rabbit Ridge Ranch Estate Reserve 1995 • $25 • (6/15/1997) • **90**
Zinfandel Sonoma County 1998: Starts with attractive ripe berry and cherryish flavors, but then lightens up, finishing with a spicy floral aroma. Firmly tannic. Drink now through 2005.–J.L. • $15 • (6/15/2000) • **86**
Zinfandel Sonoma County 1997: Fresh, ripe and snappy, with pretty cherry, watermelon, wild berry and spice, firming up on the finish where the tannins weigh in, giving structure. Drink now through 2002.–J.L. • $15 • (5/15/1999) • **88**
Zinfandel Sonoma County 1996 • $14 • (6/15/1998) • **86**
Zinfandel Sonoma County 1995 • $13 • (3/31/1997) SS • **90**
Zinfandel Sonoma County 1994 • $10 • (3/31/1996) • **84**
Zinfandel Sonoma County 1989 • $10 • (8/31/1991) • **86**
Zinfandel Sonoma County OVZ Reserve 1997: Firm, dense and chewy, with a complex wall of tannins and flavors, offering layers of plum, black cherry, raspberry and wild berry and finishing with a tight, tannic aftertaste. Best to cellar short-term, but if not intimidated by tannins, try now. Drink through 2004.–J.L. • $30 • (5/15/1999) • **92**
Zinfandel Sonoma County OVZ Reserve 1996: Broad-shouldered, racy and a touch earthy, with murky wild berry, cherry and spice. Turns firmly tannic and tarry on the finish. Drink through 2004.–J.L. • $30 • (2/28/1999) • **86**
Zinfandel Sonoma County OVZ Reserve 1995 • $26 • (9/30/1997) • **92**
Zinfandel Sonoma County San Lorenzo Reserve 1994 • $23 • (8/31/1996) • **91**
Zinfandel Sonoma County San Lorenzo Reserve 1993 • $18 • (9/15/1995) HR • **93**
Zinfandel Sonoma County San Lorenzo Reserve 1991 • $14 • (9/30/1993) • **90**
Zinfandel Sonoma County Winemaker's Grand Reserve 1997: A sophisticated style, elegant and complex, with a pretty array of toasty, cedary oak overriding the concentrated core of raspberry, blackberry and wild berry. Neatly tapered on the finish. Drink now through 2004.–J.L. • $35 • (2/28/1999) • **91**

Zinfandel Sonoma County Winemaker's Grand Reserve 1996 • $32 • (6/15/1998) • **90**
Zinfandel Sonoma County Winemaker's Grand Reserve 1995 • $30 • (3/31/1998) • **91**

RADANOVICH | CALIFORNIA

Cabernet Sauvignon Sierra Foothills 1993 • $15 • (12/15/1996) • **77**
Cabernet Sauvignon Sierra Foothills Mariposa County 1989 • $18 • (12/15/1992) • **77**
Merlot Sierra Foothills Mariposa County 1991 • $15 • (9/15/1994) • **82**
Zinfandel Sierra Foothills 1993 • $10 • (4/30/1996) • **80**
Zinfandel Sierra Foothills Mariposa County 1989 • $11 • (12/15/1992) • **72**

RAFANELLI, A. | CALIFORNIA

Cabernet Sauvignon Dry Creek Valley 1998: Appealing array of berry, boysenberry and raspberry-tinged flavors that are crisp and lively. Lacking richness and concentration, though.–J.L. • $NA • (8/31/1999) (BT) • **85-89**
Cabernet Sauvignon Dry Creek Valley 1997: Brilliant fruit. Distinct for its earthy, racy wild berry and blackberry, and tight focus. Fine balance, firm tannins.–J.L. • $NA • (8/31/1998) (BT) • **90-94**
Cabernet Sauvignon Dry Creek Valley 1996: Dark, ripe and juicy, with a seamless, elegant band of black cherry, blackberry, plum, currant and spice, finishing with a burst of fruitiness. A more mellow, less tannic Rafanelli—at least this vintage. Drink now through 2007.–J.L. • $26 • (8/31/1999) • **90**
Cabernet Sauvignon Dry Creek Valley 1995: Tight, firm, with a touch of greenness, it unveils a core of plum, black cherry and currant before the tannins take over. Needs time. Best from 2001 through 2007.–J.L. • $22 • (11/15/1998) • **88**
Cabernet Sauvignon Dry Creek Valley 1994 • $20 • (9/30/1997) • **88**
Cabernet Sauvignon Dry Creek Valley 1993 • $18 • (9/15/1996) • **85**
Cabernet Sauvignon Dry Creek Valley 1992 • $17 • (9/30/1995) SS • **92**
Cabernet Sauvignon Dry Creek Valley 1991 • $15 • (9/15/1994) SS • **90**
Cabernet Sauvignon Dry Creek Valley 1990 • $15 • (9/15/1993) HR • **90**
Cabernet Sauvignon Dry Creek Valley 1989: Pleasantly earthy and tightly focused on a beam of black cherry and currant that's rich, deep and complex, finishing with firm, integrated tannins. Aging very well. (1989 California Cabernet retrospective tasting). Drink now through 2007.–J.L. • $12 • (8/31/1999) • **88**
Cabernet Sauvignon Dry Creek Valley 1988: Tightly wound, with earthy currant, mineral, leather and herbal notes up front, it's a solid effort if lacking in extra dimensions, turning simpler on the finish. Finishes with chewy, chunky tannins. (1988 California Cabernet retrospective tasting). Drink now through 2003.–J.L. • $13 • (11/15/1998) • **87**
Cabernet Sauvignon Dry Creek Valley 1987 • $NA • (12/15/1997) • **91**
Cabernet Sauvignon Dry Creek Valley 1986 • $NA • (12/15/1996) • **92**
Zinfandel Dry Creek Valley 1997: A touch tart and on the light side for this winery, with cranberry, cherry, strawberry and spice. Turns elegant, with mild tannins. Drink now through 2003.–J.L. • $21 • (11/30/1999) • **85**
Zinfandel Dry Creek Valley 1996: Smooth and pleasing, with attractive ripe plum, black cherry, raspberry and spice. Keeps its focus on a lingering finish. Firmly tannic; still, it'll be best soon. Best from 1999 through 2004.–J.L. • $18 • (11/30/1998) • **88**
Zinfandel Dry Creek Valley 1995 • $18 • (12/15/1997) SS • **90**
Zinfandel Dry Creek Valley 1994 • $16 • (6/30/1997) • **90**
Zinfandel Dry Creek Valley 1993 • $14 • (12/31/1995) • **88**
Zinfandel Dry Creek Valley 1992 • $13 • (10/15/1994) SS • **88**
Zinfandel Dry Creek Valley 1991: This is a formidable wine, dense, chewy, tannic and concentrated, with an intense core of earthy cherry and raspberry flavors. Turns dry on the finish, but has a lot of depth and richness. (Zinfandel retrospective tasting). Best now through 2004–J.L. • $13 • (6/30/1999) • **88**
Zinfandel Dry Creek Valley 1990: With a suspect cork, this is a meaty, smoky, concentrated, complex wine that displays mature, earthy Zinfandel flavors. Shows cherry and berry on the finish. Aging well, though the fruit is a little less bright. (Zinfandel retrospective tasting). Drink now through 2002.–J.L. • $12 • (6/30/1999) • **89**
Zinfandel Dry Creek Valley 1989 • $11 • (9/30/1991) • **85**
Zinfandel Dry Creek Valley 1988 • $10 • (9/15/1990) • **90**

RAINSONG | OREGON

Pinot Noir Oregon 1995 • $14 • (10/31/1997) • **82**

RAMEY | CALIFORNIA

Chardonnay Carneros Hudson Vineyard 1997: Rich and intense, though not as polished as the Hyde. The core of pear, apple, hazelnut and spice notes is complex and concentrated, and the finish folds in honey. Drink now through 2007.–J.L. • $48 • (3/31/2000) • **93**
Chardonnay Carneros Hyde Vineyard 1997: Amazing richness, complexity and finesse mark this ripe, polished, elegantly detailed California Chardonnay. Juicy pear, tangerine, citrus, hazelnut, fig and spice unfold gracefully, with subtle toast adding pretty shadings. Delicious. Drink now through 2007.–J.L. • $48 • (3/31/2000) HR • **97**
Chardonnay Napa Valley Carneros Hyde Vineyard 1996: Ripe and bold, with juicy pear, citrus, honey and hazelnut flavors and smooth, well-integrated oak flavors, most impressive on the finish, where the texture is silky. Drink through 2004.–J.L. • $45 • (1/31/1999) • **94**

RAMSAY | CALIFORNIA

Merlot Napa Valley 1992 • $14 • (9/15/1994) • **87**
Merlot Napa Valley 1991 • $14 • (6/15/1993) • **88**
Merlot Napa Valley 1989 • $12 • (4/15/1992) • **86**
Merlot Napa Valley Reserve 1996: A bit meaty, but also rich in plum, toasty oak, anise and herb notes. Tannins are a bit coarse, but should soften up with a little more time. Finishes slightly green. Try through 2000. • $25 • (9/15/1998) • **83**
Pinot Noir California Lot #8 1996 • $16 • (2/28/1998) • **83**
Pinot Noir California Lot #7 1995 • $12 • (2/28/1997) • **84**
Pinot Noir California 1994 • $15 • (3/31/1997) • **70**
Pinot Noir Carneros 1993 • $12 • (12/31/1995) • **86**
Pinot Noir Carneros 1992 • $12 • (3/31/1995) • **82**
Pinot Noir Carneros 1991 • $12 • (2/28/1994) • **81**
Sangiovese California 1993 • $14 • (2/29/1996) • **74**
Sangiovese California 1992 • $14 • (2/28/1995) • **82**

RAMSPECK | CALIFORNIA

Pinot Noir Napa Valley 1997: Marked by a strong current of leathery, gamy flavors, which underlies the supple cranberry and herb notes. Drink now. –J.L. • $18 • (4/30/1999) • **83**
Pinot Noir Napa Valley 1994 • $16 • (1/31/1996) • **88**

RANCHO SISQUOC | CALIFORNIA

Cabernet Sauvignon Santa Maria Valley 1996: Open-textured and generous with its smoky, anise-scented blackberry and dark currant flavors. Finishes with a firm layer of tannin. Best after1999.–H.S. • $20 • (11/15/1998) • **83**
Cabernet Sauvignon Santa Maria Valley 1994 • $18 • (9/15/1997) • **83**
Cabernet Sauvignon Santa Maria Valley 1993 • $18 • (11/30/1996) • **84**
Cabernet Sauvignon Santa Maria Valley 1992 • $15 • (12/15/1995) • **82**
Cabernet Sauvignon Santa Maria Valley 1991 • $15 • (11/15/1994) • **84**
Cabernet Sauvignon Santa Maria Valley 1990 • $14 • (11/15/1993) • **76**
Cabernet Sauvignon Santa Maria Valley 1989 • $14 • (11/15/1992) • **85**
Cabernet Sauvignon Santa Maria Valley 1986 • $10 • (12/15/1989) • **73**
Cabernet Sauvignon Santa Maria Valley 1974 • $NA • (11/15/1994) • **74**
Cellar Select Santa Maria Valley 1990 • $25 • (11/15/1993) • **88**
Cellar Select Santa Maria Valley 1989 • $25 • (11/15/1992) • **87**
Merlot Santa Maria Valley 1994 • $16 • (7/31/1997) • **88**
Merlot Santa Maria Valley 1991 • $13 • (9/15/1994) • **80**
Merlot Santa Maria Valley 1989 • $12 • (5/31/1992) • **81**
Sauvignon Blanc Santa Maria Valley 1997: Marked by lemon and herb notes, the wine is pleasant and somewhat delicate. Finishes bright. Drink now. • $12 • (5/31/1999) • **85**
Sauvignon Blanc Santa Maria Valley 1996 • $12 • (4/30/1998) • **88**

RANCHO ZABACO | CALIFORNIA

Chardonnay Dry Creek Valley 1997: Charred vanilla flavors dominate, with pear notes. Drink now.–J.L. • $16 • (6/15/2000) • **80**
Chardonnay Russian River Valley 1996: Bold, ripe and spicy, with rich apple, fig and pear. Turns complex, with spicy, toasty oak flavors that give depth and dimension. Drink now.–J.L. • $14 • (12/15/1998) • **88**
Zinfandel Dry Creek Valley 1996: Soft-textured, with ripe plum and raspberry and an earthy thread. Turns dry, with mild tannins. Drink now.–J.L. • $14 • (12/31/1998) • **84**

RANCHO ZABACO

Zinfandel Sonoma County Sonoma Heritage Vines 1997: Ripe, round and polished, this affordable Zinfandel is a nicely put-together amalgam of plum, berry and spice flavors wrapped in vanilla-scented oak. Finishes tangy and bright. Enjoy now through 2004.–H.S. • $12 • (11/30/1999) • **88**

RANDOM RIDGE | CALIFORNIA

Mount Veeder 1993 • $20 • (11/15/1996) • **86**
Sangiovese Mount Veeder 1993 • $27 • (2/29/1996) • **83**
Zinfandel Sonoma Valley Old Wave 1994 • $16 • (4/30/1997) • **88**
Zinfandel Sonoma Valley Old Wave 1993 • $14 • (10/15/1995) • **85**

RAPTOR RIDGE | OREGON

Pinot Noir Willamette Valley Shea Vineyard 1997: Rich, ripe and distinctive on the nose, with floral overtones to the black cherry and cinnamon flavors that narrow on the finish. Ends with a wee touch of vinegar, but that just adds to the interest. Drink now.–H.S. • $29 • (4/30/2000) • **86**

RASMUSSEN, KENT | CALIFORNIA

Cabernet Sauvignon Napa Valley 1988 • $20 • (11/15/1991) • **83**
Chardonnay Napa Valley 1997: Sleek and elegant, with a racy edge to the grapefruit, tart apple and melon notes, finishing with a crisp, clean aftertaste. Drink now through 2001.–J.L. • $25 • (5/15/1999) • **90**
Chardonnay Napa Valley 1996 • $23 • (5/31/1998) • **89**
Dolcetto Napa Valley 1990 • $20 • (3/15/1992) • **85**
Pinot Noir Carneros 1996: Starts off with smoky, plummy notes, but on the palate it shows a stemmy, slightly bitter edge. Regains speed on the finish with a cherry and cedar core couched in firm tannins. Color is light. Drink now through 2002. • $27 • (9/15/1999) • **84**
Pinot Noir Carneros 1995 • $26 • (1/31/1998) • **86**
Pinot Noir Carneros 1994 • $22 • (1/31/1997) • **84**
Pinot Noir Carneros 1993 • $20 • (12/31/1995) • **87**
Pinot Noir Carneros 1992 • $19 • (1/31/1995) • **87**
Pinot Noir Carneros 1991 • $18 • (2/28/1994) • **88**
Pinot Noir Carneros 1990 • $19 • (2/28/1993) • **86**
Pinot Noir Carneros 1988 • $22 • (10/31/1990) • **84**

RAVENSWOOD | CALIFORNIA

Cabernet Sauvignon Sonoma County 1993 • $15 • (12/15/1995) • **87**
Cabernet Sauvignon Sonoma County 1992 • $15 • (11/15/1994) • **86**
Cabernet Sauvignon Sonoma County 1991 • $14 • (11/15/1994) • **84**
Cabernet Sauvignon Sonoma County 1989 • $14 • (11/15/1992) • **84**
Cabernet Sauvignon Sonoma County 1988 • $14 • (3/15/1991) • **89**
Cabernet Sauvignon Sonoma County 1987 • $11 • (5/31/1990) • **84**
Cabernet Sauvignon Sonoma County 1986 • $12 • (12/31/1988) • **88**
Cabernet Sauvignon Sonoma County 1985 • $12 • (5/31/1988) • **83**
Cabernet Sauvignon Sonoma County 1984 • $12 • (9/10/1987) • **68**
Cabernet Sauvignon Sonoma County 1982 • $11 • (4/01/1986) SS • **95**
Cabernet Sauvignon Sonoma Valley Gregory 1994 • $20 • (2/28/1997) • **88**
Cabernet Sauvignon Sonoma Valley Gregory 1993 • $20 • (12/15/1995) • **89**
Cabernet Sauvignon Sonoma Valley Gregory 1990 • $18 • (4/30/1993) • **84**
Cabernet Sauvignon Sonoma Valley Gregory 1989 • $18 • (11/15/1992) • **85**
Cabernet Sauvignon Sonoma Valley Gregory 1988 • $18 • (11/15/1991) • **80**
Cabernet Sauvignon Sonoma Valley Olive Hill 1978 • $31 • (11/15/1992) • **80**
Chardonnay California Vintners Blend 1996: Simple and straightforward, with delicate notes of citrus, green apple and sweet pea. Drink now. • $10 • (7/31/1998) • **82**
Chardonnay Sonoma Valley Sangiacomo 1996: Leafy pear and cedary oak notes are followed by appealing flavors of smoky, toasty oak, hints of pear and melon. Drink now through 2002.–J.L. • $20 • (7/31/1998) • **87**
Icon Sonoma County 1996: Spicy, earthy-gamy character to this chunky, tannic wine, with hints of meaty blackberry and mineral, but it needs time to shed its tannins (one hopes) and show more appealing flavors. 92 percent Syrah, 8 percent Grenache. Best from 2001 through 2004.–J.L. • $20 • (3/31/1999) • **86**
Merlot Carneros Sangiacomo 1990 • $20 • (12/15/1992) • **88**
Merlot Carneros Sangiacomo 1989 • $18 • (11/15/1991) • **90**
Merlot Napa-Sonoma Counties Vintners Blend 1989 • $18 • (3/31/1991) • **84**
Merlot North Coast Vintners Blend 1992 • $10 • (9/15/1994) • **84**
Merlot North Coast Vintners Blend 1991 • $10 • (5/31/1993) • **83**
Merlot North Coast Vintners Blend 1990 • $10 • (5/31/1992) • **84**
Merlot Sonoma County 1994 • $18 • (6/30/1997) • **87**
Merlot Sonoma County 1993 • $18 • (7/31/1996) • **87**
Merlot Sonoma County 1992 • $15 • (2/28/1995) • **85**
Merlot Sonoma County 1990 • $15 • (6/15/1993) • **85**
Merlot Sonoma County 1989 • $15 • (5/31/1992) • **86**
Merlot Sonoma County 1987 • $18 • (1/31/1990) • **87**
Merlot Sonoma County 1986 • $18 • (12/31/1988) • **80**
Merlot Sonoma County 1984 • $11 • (2/28/1987) • **85**
Merlot Sonoma Valley Donnell 1996: Smooth, rich and polished, with focused plum, black cherry, blackberry and spice. Finishes with good length, fine tannin integration and attractive fruit flavors. Drink now through 2004.–J.L. • $21 • (10/15/1998) • **88**
Merlot Sonoma Valley Gregory 1994 • $30 • (2/28/1997) • **85**
Merlot Sonoma Valley Sangiacomo 1994 • $20 • (10/15/1996) • **88**
Merlot Sonoma Valley Sangiacomo 1992 • $20 • (6/15/1995) • **86**
Mountain Claret Sonoma County 1992 • $12 • (9/15/1995) • **84**
Pickberry Sonoma Mountain 1994 • $30 • (3/31/1997) • **90**
Pickberry Sonoma Mountain 1990 • $26 • (11/15/1993) • **86**
Pickberry Sonoma Mountain 1989 • $37 • (11/15/1992) • **89**
Pickberry Sonoma Mountain 1988 • $27 • (4/30/1991) • **82**
Pickberry Sonoma Mountain 1987 • $29 Ⓐ • (12/15/1997) • **87**
Pickberry Sonoma Mountain 1986 • $35 Ⓐ • (12/15/1996) • **87**
Rancho Salina Vineyards Sonoma Valley 1995: Earthy currant, leather, spice and cedary oak flavors are elegant and refined, if a bit stalky, with firm but supple and well-integrated tannins. A blend of Cabernet Franc, Cabernet Sauvignon and Merlot. Drink through 2008.–J.L. • $25 • (8/31/1998) • **89**
Rancho Salina Vineyards Sonoma Valley 1994 • $25 • (2/28/1997) • **87**
Zinfandel Alexander Valley 1994 • $14 • (3/31/1997) • **86**
Zinfandel Alexander Valley Big River 1996: Dry, with dusty cherry, wild berry, sage and herb notes, it fans out and shows off its complexity and range of flavors. Turns dry and tannic on the finish, so short-term cellaring is advised. Drink now through 2002.–J.L. • $20 • (11/30/1998) • **87**
Zinfandel Amador County 1997: Dry and simple, with earthy, leathery berry, anise, sage and dried fruit flavors, turning tannic. Drink now through 2004.–J.L. • $14 • (5/15/2000) • **84**
Zinfandel Dry Creek Valley Teldeschi 1997: Pretty aromas and a streamlined band of cherry, raspberry, plum and spice, with hints of vanilla and cedar lingering in the background. Not enough tannin to worry about. Drink now through 2007.–J.L. • $27 • (6/30/2000) • **88**
Zinfandel Lodi 1997: Bright and lively, with juicy plum, black cherry, wild berry, cedar, tar and spice. Turns silky, with well-integrated tannins and crisp acidity. Drink now through 2002.–J.L. • $14 • (6/30/1999) • **88**
Zinfandel Napa Valley 1997: Very ripe and racy, with zesty raspberry, wild berry, blackberry and spice notes that are bright and lively. Drink now through 2007.–J.L. • $13 • (4/30/2000) • **87**
Zinfandel Napa Valley Canard 1988 • $12 • (8/31/1991) • **75**
Zinfandel Napa Valley Canard 1986 • $11 • (3/15/1990) • **81**
Zinfandel Napa Valley Canard 1985 • $10 • (3/15/1989) • **85**
Zinfandel Napa Valley Dickerson 1997: Pleasant but unexciting, with trim cherry, wild berry and spice notes that fail to inspire. Given this vineyard's past efforts, this is disappointing. Drink now.–J.L. • $17 Ⓐ • (4/30/2000) • **84**
Zinfandel Napa Valley Dickerson 1996: Marked by ripe cherry, blackberry, spice and sage, this is an elegant wine with a minty edge and firm, dry tannins on the finish. Drink now through 2004.–J.L. • $24 • (2/28/1999) • **88**
Zinfandel Napa Valley Dickerson 1995 • $22 • (9/30/1997) • **89**
Zinfandel Napa Valley Dickerson 1994 • $20 • (3/31/1997) • **89**
Zinfandel Napa Valley Dickerson 1993 • $20 • (9/15/1995) • **89**
Zinfandel Napa Valley Dickerson 1992 • $18 • (9/15/1994) SS • **91**
Zinfandel Napa Valley Dickerson 1991 • $18 • (9/30/1993) • **87**
Zinfandel Napa Valley Dickerson 1990: This is a streamlined style, sleek, with sage, tea, spice and berry flavors that are very pretty, turning delicate on the finish. (Zinfandel retrospective tasting). Drink now through 2002. –J.L. • $16 • (6/30/1999) • **91**
Zinfandel Napa Valley Dickerson 1989 • $13 • (11/15/1991) • **87**
Zinfandel Napa Valley Dickerson 1988 • $13 • (8/31/1991) • **84**
Zinfandel Napa Valley Dickerson 1987 • $13 • (3/15/1990) • **86**

Key: SS—Spectator Selection CS—Cellar Selection HR—Highly Recommended
$NA—Price Not Available a—Auction Price (BT)—Barrel Tasting
For a key to the tasters' initials, see "How to Use These Listings."
Dates in parentheses indicate the issues in which the ratings were published.

Zinfandel Napa Valley Dickerson 1986 • $12 • (12/15/1988) • **88**
Zinfandel Napa Valley Dickerson 1985 • $11 • (12/31/1987) • **80**
Zinfandel North Coast Vintners Blend 1992 • $8 • (10/15/1994) • **83**
Zinfandel North Coast Vintners Blend 1991 • $8 • (5/31/1993) • **84**
Zinfandel North Coast Vintners Blend 1990 • $8 • (10/15/1992) • **81**
Zinfandel North Coast Vintners Blend 1989 • $8 • (7/31/1991) • **83**
Zinfandel North Coast Vintners Blend 1988 • $7 • (10/15/1990) • **81**
Zinfandel Russian River Valley Belloni 1997: Just enough dimension and depth to pique your interest, with wild berry, earth, spice and cedar notes fitting neatly together. Firmly tannic, so you can drink it now or cellar short-term. Best from 2001 through 2006.–J.L. • $27 • (4/30/2000) • **87**
Zinfandel Russian River Valley Wood Road/Belloni 1996: Smooth, with rich tar, wild berry, cola and earth notes, turning complex with supple tannins. Drink through 2003.–J.L. • $24 • (2/28/1999) • **88**
Zinfandel Russian River Valley Wood Road/Belloni 1995 • $22 • (9/30/1997) • **88**
Zinfandel Russian River Valley Wood Road/Belloni 1994 • $20 • (9/30/1996) • **88**
Zinfandel Russian River Valley Wood Road/Belloni 1993 • $20 • (9/15/1995) • **87**
Zinfandel Sonoma Valley Belloni 1992 • $18 • (9/15/1994) • **89**
Zinfandel Sonoma County Belloni 1991: Tasted from magnum. Ripe with a jammy berry flavor, this is a big, rich, enormously fruity wine, with cherry, raspberry, blackberry and spice flavors. (Zinfandel retrospective tasting). Drink now through 2004.–J.L. • $NA • (6/30/1999) • **90**
Zinfandel Sonoma County 1997: There's a touch of greenness to this medium-weight wine, with modest cherry, berry and mushroom flavors. Drink now.–J.L. • $16 • (4/30/2000) • **82**
Zinfandel Sonoma County 1994 • $15 • (3/31/1997) • **88**
Zinfandel Sonoma County 1993 • $15 • (9/15/1995) • **89**
Zinfandel Sonoma County 1992 • $12 • (8/31/1994) SS • **91**
Zinfandel Sonoma County 1987 • $11 • (3/15/1990) • **88**
Zinfandel Sonoma County Old Vine 1990 • $11 • (10/15/1992) • **89**
Zinfandel Sonoma County Old Vine 1989 • $11 • (12/31/1991) • **82**
Zinfandel Sonoma County Old Vine 1988 • $11 • (11/30/1990) • **87**
Zinfandel Sonoma Valley Barricia 1997: Medium in weight, with a spicy chili pepper edge to the ripe plum and berryish fruit. Drink now through 2003. –J.L. • $27 • (4/30/2000) • **86**
Zinfandel Sonoma Valley Cooke 1997: Lean and green, with tea, sage and tart blackberry fruit that tastes unripe. Drink now.–J.L. • $17 Ⓐ • (4/30/2000) • **82**
Zinfandel Sonoma Valley Cooke 1996: Lean and tart, with a narrow band of sage and berry, it unfolds to reveal more intensity, but it's best cellared short-term. Try through 2003.–J.L. • $19 Ⓐ • (2/28/1999) • **88**
Zinfandel Sonoma Valley Cooke 1995 • $22 • (9/30/1997) • **91**
Zinfandel Sonoma Valley Cooke 1994 • $20 • (9/30/1996) • **88**
Zinfandel Sonoma Valley Cooke 1993 • $20 • (9/15/1995) • **89**
Zinfandel Sonoma Valley Cooke 1992 • $18 • (10/15/1994) HR • **91**
Zinfandel Sonoma Valley Cooke 1991 • $18 • (9/30/1993) • **88**
Zinfandel Sonoma Valley Cooke 1990: Rich, dark, complex and smoky, with black cherry, plum and currant notes, a lush texture and a long, deep, concentrated aftertaste that keeps pumping out the flavors. Shows a good dose of alcohol, but holds its balance. (Zinfandel retrospective tasting). Drink now through 2004.–J.L. • $26 Ⓐ • (6/30/1999) • **92**
Zinfandel Sonoma Valley Cooke 1987 • $13 • (3/15/1990) • **84**
Zinfandel Sonoma Valley Kunde 1997: Sharp, with crisp acidity and firm tannins making it hard for the plum and berry flavors to shine. Drink now.–J.L. • $27 • (4/30/2000) • **83**
Zinfandel Sonoma Valley Monte Rosso 1996: Serves up ripe cherry, raspberry and strawberry flavors, with firm tannins and sage, tar and herbal notes. Drink now through 2003.–J.L. • $22 Ⓐ • (2/28/1999) • **88**
Zinfandel Sonoma Valley Monte Rosso 1995 • $22 • (9/30/1997) • **89**
Zinfandel Sonoma Valley Monte Rosso 1994 • $20 • (9/30/1996) • **90**
Zinfandel Sonoma Valley Monte Rosso 1993 • $20 • (9/15/1995) • **88**
Zinfandel Sonoma Valley Old Hill Vineyard 1997: Spicy and quite peppery, with firm tannins and a touch of leather. An austere style that needs short-term cellaring. Best from 2001 through 2008.–J.L. • $30 • (4/30/2000) • **86**
Zinfandel Sonoma Valley Old Hill Vineyard 1996: Tight, firmly tannic, with an austere band of spicy wild berry, sage and cherry, this opens up on the finish, so short-term cellaring is advised. Drink through 2004.–J.L. • $26 • (2/28/1999) • **88**
Zinfandel Sonoma Valley Old Hill Vineyard 1995 • $24 • (9/30/1997) • **92**
Zinfandel Sonoma Valley Old Hill Vineyard 1994 • $22 • (9/30/1996) • **87**
Zinfandel Sonoma Valley Old Hill Vineyard 1993 • $22 • (9/15/1995) • **90**
Zinfandel Sonoma Valley Old Hill Vineyard 1992: Shows off exotic, spicy aromatics and delivers a core of ripe plum and black cherry, with a twist of leather, anise and sage. Well balanced, gaining subtle nuances. (Zinfandel retrospective tasting). Drink now through 2002.–J.L. • $20 • (6/30/1999) • **88**
Zinfandel Sonoma Valley Old Hill Vineyard 1991 • $20 • (9/30/1993) • **87**
Zinfandel Sonoma Valley Old Hill Vineyard 1990 • $18 • (10/15/1992) • **89**
Zinfandel Sonoma Valley Old Hill Vineyard 1987 • $15 • (3/15/1990) • **87**
Zinfandel Sonoma Valley Old Hill Vineyard 1986 • $13 • (12/15/1988) • **92**
Zinfandel Sonoma Valley Old Hill Vineyard 1985 • $12 • (12/31/1987) • **87**

RAY, MARTIN | CALIFORNIA

Cabernet Sauvignon California Saratoga Cuvée 1996: Ripe and flavorful, with a tarry, earthy edge to the olive, plum and currant flavors. Smooth tannins, toasted oak and sage notes mark the finish. Drink through 2004.–J.L. • $25 • (10/15/1999) • **88**
Cabernet Sauvignon California Saratoga Cuvée 1995: Tightly wound, firmly tannic, distinctly herbal, with mint, currant, herb and mineral flavors, picking up hints of spice. Finishes with raw tannins. Definitely needs cellaring. Best from 2001 through 2009.–J.L. • $26 • (8/31/1998) • **88**
Cabernet Sauvignon California Saratoga Cuvée 1994 • $30 • (12/15/1997) • **88**
Cabernet Sauvignon California Saratoga Cuvée 1993 • $32 • (8/31/1996) • **86**
Cabernet Sauvignon California Saratoga Cuvée 1992 • $28 • (10/31/1995) • **89**
Cabernet Sauvignon Napa Valley 1993 • $32 • (8/31/1996) • **86**
Cabernet Sauvignon Napa Valley 1992 • $28 • (10/31/1995) • **86**
Cabernet Sauvignon Napa Valley 1991 • $28 • (11/15/1994) HR • **94**
Cabernet Sauvignon Napa Valley Diamond Mountain Vineyard 1996: Superrich and chocolaty, with a wonderful band of tasty currant, black cherry, wild berry, plum and spice. A truly exotic-flavored and personable wine that's complex and concentrated. Best from 2001 through 2010.–J.L. • $50 • (11/15/1999) • **95**
Cabernet Sauvignon Napa Valley Diamond Mountain 1995: Dark, ripe, rich and plush, with dense, chewy, complex currant, anise, mineral, cedar and spice. Tightly focused, deep and concentrated, with lots more anise, currant, tar and berry flavors on the amazingly long finish. Best from 2001 through 2010.–J.L. • $45 • (7/31/1998) • **95**
Cabernet Sauvignon Santa Cruz Mountains 1995: A racy, gamy style, with a range of herb, currant, sage and leathery flavors that are intense and concentrated, finishing with pepper and spice and full, chewy tannins. Needs time—lots of it. Best from 2003 through 2010.–J.L. • $45 • (8/31/1998) • **88**
Chardonnay California Mariage 1998: Openly fruity, with ripe, complex tangerine, pear, fig and citrus flavors that are bright and lively. Drink now through 2004.–J.L. • $18 • (5/15/2000) • **88**
Chardonnay California Mariage 1997: Complex in its interplay of smoky, toasty, spicy oak and vibrant pear, nectarine, pineapple, apple and nutmeg notes. Finishes long and lively. Drink now through 2002.–J.L. • $20 • (7/31/1999) • **90**
Chardonnay California Mariage 1996: Solid, with fresh, ripe pear, tangerine, nectarine and peach notes. Complex and elegant, with a clean, fruity aftertaste. Drink now through 2001.–J.L. • $25 • (7/31/1998) • **89**
Merlot Napa Valley Diamond Mountain Vineyard 1997: Spicy, with toasty oak and supple cherry, currant, anise, tar and cedar notes, holding a tight focus on the finish. Drink now through 2005.–J.L. • $60 • (9/30/1999) • **88**
Pinot Noir California 1995 • $28 • (2/28/1998) • **84**
Pinot Noir California 1994 • $28 • (11/15/1996) • **88**
Pinot Noir California La Montaña 1997: Toasty, with a range of spicy cola and cherry flavors on a smooth-textured frame, finishing with ripe tannins. Drink now through 2003.–J.L. • $20 • (9/15/1999) • **84**
Pinot Noir California Mariage 1996: A solid effort for '96, with a tight band of cherry, cola and spice and enough wood to merit short-term cellaring. Drink through 2001.–J.L. • $19 • (9/30/1998) • **84**
Pinot Noir Russian River Valley 1997: Tight, crisp, with green-tealike tannins atop the core of cola, cherry and blackberry flavors, finishing with a crisp edge. Drink through 2006.–J.L. • $35 • (9/15/1999) • **84**
Synthesis Diamond Mountain Vineyard Napa Valley 1997: A touch racy, with toasty, cedary oak and a core of currant, black cherry, anise and sage, firming and gaining focus on the finish. Merlot, Cabernet Franc and Cabernet Sauvignon. Best from 2001 through 2008.–J.L. • $60 • (3/31/2000) • **89**

RAYMOND | CALIFORNIA

Cabernet Sauvignon California Amberhill 1995 • $13 • (6/30/1998) • **77**
Cabernet Sauvignon California Amberhill 1994 • $10 • (11/15/1997) • **80**
Cabernet Sauvignon California Amberhill 1993 • $10 • (12/15/1996) • **81**
Cabernet Sauvignon California Amberhill 1991 • $8 • (11/15/1994) • **84**
Cabernet Sauvignon California Amberhill 1990 • $8 • (11/15/1994) • **78**
Cabernet Sauvignon Napa Valley 1992 • $17 • (11/30/1995) • **88**
Cabernet Sauvignon Napa Valley 1991 • $17 • (11/15/1994) • **88**

RAYMOND

Cabernet Sauvignon Napa Valley 1990 • $17 • (11/15/1993) • **88**
Cabernet Sauvignon Napa Valley 1989: Simple, pleasant, earthy coffee, currant and leathery notes are balanced and supple. (1989 California Cabernet retrospective tasting). Past its prime.–J.L. • $17 • (8/31/1999) • **83**
Cabernet Sauvignon Napa Valley 1988 • $18 • (8/31/1992) • **85**
Cabernet Sauvignon Napa Valley 1987 • $15 • (12/15/1997) • **88**
Cabernet Sauvignon Napa Valley 1986 • $16 • (5/31/1990) • **90**
Cabernet Sauvignon Napa Valley 1985 • $16 • (12/15/1989) • **84**
Cabernet Sauvignon Napa Valley 1984 • $28 • (2/15/1989) • **90**
Cabernet Sauvignon Napa Valley 1983 • $30 • (2/15/1988) • **89**
Cabernet Sauvignon Napa Valley 1982 • $22 • (11/15/1986) • **91**
Cabernet Sauvignon Napa Valley 1981 • $12 • (5/01/1985) • **77**
Cabernet Sauvignon Napa Valley 1980 • $12 • (1/01/1984) • **81**
Cabernet Sauvignon Napa Valley 1979: The texture is smooth and polished, but this herbal, dill-scented Cabernet needs food to take away the weedy edge. (1979 California Cabernet retrospective tasting). Drink now through 2001.–J.L. • $11 • (8/31/1999) • **82**
Cabernet Sauvignon Napa Valley 1978: Mature, but still quite rich, complex and supple, with an herbal, olive, currant and black cherry core, fine depth and concentration and a long, full-bodied aftertaste that pumps out flavor. (1978 California Cabernet retrospective tasting). Drink now through 2002.–J.L. • $10 • (11/15/1998) • **88**
Cabernet Sauvignon Napa Valley 1974 • $40 • (11/15/1994) • **78**
Cabernet Sauvignon Napa Valley Estates 1996: Quite cola-like at first, though the tannins temper it. Finishes with a smoky, jammy note. Drink now. • $15 • (10/31/1998) • **83**
Cabernet Sauvignon Napa Valley Estates 1995 • $15 • (5/31/1998) • **85**
Cabernet Sauvignon Napa Valley Estates 1994 • $14 • (5/31/1997) • **87**
Cabernet Sauvignon Napa Valley Estates 1993 • $12 • (3/31/1996) • **84**
Cabernet Sauvignon Napa Valley Generations 1996: Wonderful texture, polish and finesse, with a pretty core of currant, black cherry, plum and spice. Rounds out nicely on the complex finish, with a firm edge to the tannins. Drink now through 2008.–J.L. • $50 • (11/15/1999) • **92**
Cabernet Sauvignon Napa Valley Generations 1995: A well-oaked and complex style, with a pretty underlying band of berry, black cherry and plum. Drink through 2007.–J.L. • $45 • (10/31/1998) • **88**
Cabernet Sauvignon Napa Valley Generations 1994 • $38 ⓐ • (10/31/1997) SS • **93**
Cabernet Sauvignon Napa Valley Private Reserve 1992 • $26 • (11/15/1996) • **90**
Cabernet Sauvignon Napa Valley Private Reserve 1991 • $25 • (12/15/1995) • **84**
Cabernet Sauvignon Napa Valley Private Reserve 1990 • $25 • (10/31/1994) • **88**
Cabernet Sauvignon Napa Valley Private Reserve 1988 • $26 • (7/31/1993) • **88**
Cabernet Sauvignon Napa Valley Private Reserve 1987 • $20 • (12/15/1997) • **90**
Cabernet Sauvignon Napa Valley Private Reserve 1986 • $NA • (12/15/1996) • **82**
Cabernet Sauvignon Napa Valley Private Reserve 1985 • $30 • (7/15/1990) CS • **91**
Cabernet Sauvignon Napa Valley Private Reserve 1984 • $25 • (7/15/1989) • **87**
Cabernet Sauvignon Napa Valley Private Reserve 1983 • $18 • (6/30/1988) • **91**
Cabernet Sauvignon Napa Valley Private Reserve 1982 • $16 • (6/15/1987) • **88**
Cabernet Sauvignon Napa Valley Private Reserve 1981 • $16 • (8/31/1986) • **92**
Cabernet Sauvignon Napa Valley Reserve 1997: Here's an outstanding reserve Cabernet at a reasonable price. It's firm, focused and complex, leading off with a smoky, toasty core of oak notes and complementary flavors of ripe black cherry, currant, cedar and tar. Deliciously complex on the finish, where the flavors persist. Drink now through 2007.–J.L. • $29 ⓐ • (9/30/1999) SS • **90**
Cabernet Sauvignon Napa Valley Reserve 1996: Ripe in flavor and silky in texture, a pretty wine with black cherry, vanilla, chocolate and spice flavors that manage to remain restrained on the supple finish. Drink now through 2003.–H.S. • $20 • (11/15/1998) • **86**
Cabernet Sauvignon Napa Valley Reserve 1994 • $20 • (5/31/1997) • **89**
Cabernet Sauvignon Napa Valley Reserve 1993 • $17 • (4/30/1996) • **90**
Chardonnay California Amberhill 1996: Strays a bit from the main core of Chardonnay fruit, with racy, grassy, leesy flavors. Contains 10 percent Chenin Blanc.–J.L. • $9 • (7/31/1998) • **78**
Chardonnay Monterey Estates 1997: Soft and pleasant, with pineapple and citrus flavors and hints of toasted oak. Fruity and refreshing, with a nice earthy edge. Drink now.–J.L. • $13 • (6/15/1999) • **87**
Chardonnay Monterey Estates 1996 • $13 • (6/15/1998) • **84**

Key: SS—Spectator Selection CS—Cellar Selection HR—Highly Recommended SNA—Price Not Available a—Auction Price. (BT)—Barrel Tasting
For a key to the tasters' initials, see "How to Use These Listings."
Dates in parentheses indicate the issues in which the ratings were published.

Chardonnay Napa Valley Generations 1996 • $27 • (5/15/1998) • **91**
Chardonnay Napa Valley Reserve 1998: Ripe, with candied apple and peach flavors that show good intensity. Drink now through 2001.–J.L. • $15 • (6/15/2000) • **86**
Chardonnay Napa Valley Reserve 1996 • $15 • (5/15/1998) • **86**
Meritage Napa Valley 1989 • $35 • (11/15/1993) • **89**
Meritage Private Reserve Napa Valley 1991 • $40 • (12/15/1995) • **87**
Meritage Private Reserve Napa Valley 1990 • $40 • (10/31/1994) HR • **90**
Merlot California Amberhill 1996: Tastes of raspberry and candied cherry with an herbal, oaky edge. Cinnamon on the finish adds some interest. Drink now. • $13 • (7/31/1998) • **83**
Merlot Napa Valley 1992 • $17 • (11/15/1995) • **89**
Merlot Napa Valley Reserve 1996: Crisp but flavorful, featuring black cherry, currant and sage flavors, with smoky oak notes on the firm finish. Drink now through 2001.–J.L. • $22 • (8/31/1999) • **87**
Merlot Napa Valley Reserve 1995: Tight, tannic and built with a lean framework. Shows cherry and berry notes, but never fully comes together. Drink through 2003.–J.L. • $20 • (10/15/1998) • **83**
Merlot Napa Valley Reserve 1993 • $17 • (6/30/1996) • **83**
Pinot Noir Napa Valley 1992 • $17 • (9/15/1995) • **83**
Pinot Noir Napa Valley Reserve 1996: Medium-bodied, with cola, cherry, coffee and herbal flavors that persist, with supple tannins, on the finish. Drink through 2001.–J.L. • $22 • (9/15/1999) • **85**
Pinot Noir Napa Valley Reserve 1995 • $17 • (2/28/1998) • **81**
Sauvignon Blanc Napa Valley Reserve 1998: Flinty and herbaceous, with oak overtones and slightly sour apples. Drink now.–J.L. • $11 • (5/15/2000) • **80**
Sauvignon Blanc Napa Valley Reserve 1997: Intriguing on the nose, with hints of spice, honey, herbs and wintergreen. Fresh and bright in the mouth, with pretty citrus, mineral and melon flavors that linger nicely on a moderate finish. Drink now through 2001. • $11 • (5/15/1999) • **88**
Sauvignon Blanc Napa Valley Reserve 1996 • $11 • (4/30/1998) • **86**

REDWOOD CANYON | CALIFORNIA

Cabernet Sauvignon Napa Valley 1993 • $13 • (12/15/1995) • **84**

REGUSCI | CALIFORNIA

Cabernet Sauvignon Stags Leap District 1997: Serves up attractive, medium-weight black cherry, herb, anise and spicy currant flavors, though they trail off on the finish, where it turns simpler. Drink now through 2007.–J.L. • $42 • (4/30/2000) • **87**
Cabernet Sauvignon Stags Leap District 1996: Quite oaky but well done, very rich and concentrated, with layers of supple currant, black cherry and toasty oak, turning smooth and plush on the long, rich aftertaste. Best from 2001 through 2009.–J.L. • $42 • (9/15/1999) • **91**
Chardonnay Napa Valley Hillside Vineyard 1998: Stale, with a gluey pear and pasty edge. Drink now.–J.L. • $25 • (6/15/2000) • **80**
Chardonnay Napa Valley Hillside Vineyard 1997: Rich, complex and harmonious, with tiers of citrus, pear and creamy hazelnut notes built on a silky frame. Finishes with delicate flavors of fruit and spicy oak. Drink now through 2002.–J.L. • $25 • (2/28/1999) • **90**
Merlot Napa Valley 1996: Shows lots of oak-infused flavors of dill, chocolate, vanilla and hazelnut, but also complex black cherry and herbal notes, turning supple and crisp on the finish. Drink now through 2001.–J.L. • $38 • (2/28/1999) • **88**

REMICK RIDGE | CALIFORNIA

Cabernet Sauvignon Sonoma Valley 1992 • $19 • (5/31/1996) • **88**
Cabernet Sauvignon Sonoma Valley Limited 1995: Rich, with a range of gamy, leathery flavors which frame a core of black cherry, currant and earth notes. Tannins are ripe on the finish. Drink now through 2003.–J.L. • $24 • (9/15/1999) • **86**
Merlot Sonoma Valley Marcy's Vineyard 1994: Flavorful and polished, with tar, mineral and currant flavors, smooth on the finish. Drink now through 2002.–J.L. • $32 • (10/15/1999) • **85**
Merlot Sonoma Valley Marcy's Vineyard 1992 • $30 • (5/31/1996) • **88**

RENAISSANCE | CALIFORNIA

Cabernet Sauvignon North Yuba 1996: Starts bitter and woody, but works into more interesting earth and mineral flavors after lots of aeration. Still, it's extremely dry and tannic.–J.L. • $18 • (11/15/1999) • **76**

Cabernet Sauvignon North Yuba 1995: Firm, with flavors leaning toward sage and earth. Shows a layer of cherry before the tannins clamp down and dry out the flavors. Drink now.–J.L. • $13 • (10/15/1998) • **81**
Cabernet Sauvignon North Yuba 1994 • $13 • (10/31/1997) • **86**
Cabernet Sauvignon North Yuba 1993 • $15 • (11/30/1996) • **79**
Cabernet Sauvignon North Yuba 1991 • $12 • (12/15/1995) • **78**
Cabernet Sauvignon North Yuba 1990 • $14 • (11/15/1994) • **81**
Cabernet Sauvignon North Yuba 1988 • $12 • (11/15/1993) • **76**
Cabernet Sauvignon North Yuba 1986 • $21 • (11/15/1994) • **78**
Cabernet Sauvignon North Yuba Premiere Cuvée 1995: Dense, earthy and tannic, with a core of black cherry and herb notes. Finishes lean and firmly tannic. Needs time in hope that the tannins will soften. Best from 2001 through 2005.–J.L. • $39 • (10/15/1999) • **82**
Cabernet Sauvignon North Yuba Reserve 1994: A rustic wine, with chewy tannins, tar and licorice up front. Finishes with a hefty dose of black cherry, blackberry and cassis. Drink now through 2003. • $20 • (7/31/1998) • **86**
Cabernet Sauvignon North Yuba Reserve 1987 • $35 • (12/15/1995) • **88**
Cabernet Sauvignon North Yuba Reserve 1985 • $45 • (11/15/1992) • **82**
Chardonnay North Yuba 1997: Intriguing juniper berry, peach and citrus notes on a medium-bodied frame. Finishes crisp and minerally. Drink now.–J.L. • $15 • (6/30/1999) • **86**
Chardonnay North Yuba 1996: Fairly mineral-like in character, with an herbal note framed in toasty oak. Drink now. • $18 • (7/31/1998) • **82**
Claret Prestige North Yuba 1996: Lean and trim, showing cedar, anise and black cherry flavors, finishing with major-league, leathery tannins. Best from 2001 through 2005.–J.L. • $39 • (10/15/1999) • **82**
Merlot North Yuba 1994 • $18 • (12/15/1996) • **79**
Merlot North Yuba 1993 • $16 • (3/31/1996) • **74**
Sauvignon Blanc Late Harvest North Yuba Select 1991 • $13 • (5/15/1995) • **85**
Sauvignon Blanc Late Harvest North Yuba 1990 • $13/375 ml. • (12/31/1993) • **78**
Sauvignon Blanc North Yuba 1998: Sweaty and earthy aromas precede very tart lemon and herb flavors.–J.L. • $12 • (5/31/2000) • **78**
Sauvignon Blanc North Yuba 1996 • $10 • (11/30/1997) • **83**
Sauvignon Blanc North Yuba Barrel Select 1996 • $12 • (4/30/1998) • **88**

RENARD | CALIFORNIA

Syrah Napa Valley Arroyo Vineyards Cuvée Jacques 1997: Lively, with pronounced earthy and leathery flavors and ripe blackberry and violet aromas. Drink now through 2006.–J.L. • $25 • (5/31/2000) • **84**
Syrah Napa Valley Arroyo Vineyards Cuvee Lunettes 1996: Quite fragrant, with spice, herb and plum notes. On the palate, it's lean in texture yet packed with flavor—blackberry, cherry, more herbs, tea and a hint of stems all come to mind. The ensemble is elegantly balanced and finishes long. Drink now through 2005. • $22 • (5/31/1999) • **90**

RENWOOD | CALIFORNIA

Barbera Amador County 1996: Tart and spicy, with cherry, wild berry, mint, cedar and blackberry flavors that unfold and gain complexity and nuance on the finish. A juicy, complex style. Drink now through 2002.–J.L. • $18 • (12/15/1998) • **88**
Barbera Amador County 1995 • $16 • (11/30/1997) • **88**
Barbera Amador County 1992 • $16 • (7/31/1995) • **82**
Barbera Amador County Linsteadt Vineyard 1996: Ripe and spicy, with lively blackberry, cherry, plum and spice notes that are rich and concentrated. Has depth and complexity, turning long and zingy on the finish. Drink now.–J.L. • $23 • (12/15/1998) • **89**
Barbera Amador County Linsteadt Vineyard 1995 • $18 • (11/30/1997) • **87**
Late Bottled Vintage Port Shenandoah Valley 1989 • $18 • (5/31/1995) • **85**
Nebbiolo Amador County 1996: Pleasantly fruity. Distinct for its up-front cherry, raspberry and strawberry flavors. Finishes with a touch of anise and berry. Drink now.–J.L. • $20 • (12/15/1998) • **84**
Sangiovese Amador County Clockspring Vineyard 1996: A wine with character, it's earthy and even a touch gamy, slowly working in cherry and berry flavors and a dash of leather on the finish. Drink now through 2001.–J.L. • $17 • (12/15/1998) • **84**
Syrah Amador County 1995 • $22 • (9/30/1997) • **86**
Viognier Amador County 1996 • $22 • (12/15/1997) • **81**
Zinfandel Amador County 1991 • $12 • (3/31/1994) • **83**
Zinfandel Amador County Amador Ice 1994 • $20 • (4/30/1997) • **92**
Zinfandel Amador County Grandmère 1996: Ripe and racy, with a jammy wild berry and tar edge to the sage, dusty oak, cedar and spice. Finishes with gritty tannins. Drink now through 2005.–J.L. • $23 • (12/31/1998) • **88**
Zinfandel Amador County Grandmère 1994 • $23 • (10/15/1996) • **86**
Zinfandel Amador County Grandpère 1997: Dense and earthy, with gamy, bitter almond overtones to the otherwise appealing plum and black cherry flavors that linger on the finish. Best after 2000.–H.S. • $30 • (11/30/1999) • **87**
Zinfandel Amador County Grandpère 1996: Ripe, with an array of rustic wild berry, sage, tea, tar, anise and oak. Intense and tannic, but packed with flavor. Drink through 2004.–J.L. • $26 • (12/31/1998) • **89**
Zinfandel Amador County Grandpère 1995 • $23 • (11/15/1997) • **88**
Zinfandel Amador County Grandpère 1994 • $25 • (4/30/1997) • **88**
Zinfandel Shenandoah Valley Grandpère 1993 • $21 • (10/15/1995) • **87**
Zinfandel Shenandoah Valley Grandpère 1992: Impressive for its richness, focus, concentration and flavors, with tar, raspberry, plum and currant that fold together nicely on the finish. Not too tannic. (Zinfandel retrospective tasting). Drink now through 2003.–J.L. • $18 • (6/30/1999) • **91**
Zinfandel Shenandoah Valley Grandpère 1991 • $16 • (3/31/1994) • **86**
Zinfandel Amador County Jack Rabbit Flat 1997: Very ripe, smooth and layered, with juicy black cherry, plum, wild berry and cherry, finishing with a spicy edge and firm tannins. Drink now through 2007.–J.L. • $28 • (3/31/2000) • **88**
Zinfandel Amador County Jack Rabbit Flat Fox Creek Vineyard 1996: A smooth and polished offering of California Zinfandel, layered with ripe, rich flavors of blackberry and wild berry and creamy vanilla notes that fan out and turn supple. Drink now through 2005.–J.L. • $25 • (12/31/1998) SS • **90**
Zinfandel Amador County Jack Rabbit Flat Fox Creek Vineyard 1995 • $25 • (11/15/1997) • **89**
Zinfandel Amador County Old Vine 1997: Spicy, with dry notes of leather, berry and earth, turning even drier and earthier on the finish. Drink now.–J.L. • $19 • (5/15/2000) • **82**
Zinfandel Amador County Old Vine 1996: Ripe, with zesty berry, sage and menthol flavors on the palate, it's dry and tannic on the finish. Drink through 2002.–J.L. • $17 • (1/31/1999) • **87**
Zinfandel Amador County Old Vine 1994 • $17 • (4/30/1997) • **90**
Zinfandel Amador County Old Vine 1993 • $15 • (9/15/1995) • **89**
Zinfandel Fiddletown 1997: Racy if a touch volatile, with lots of wild berry and blackberry flavors that are ripe and spicy, finishing with a touch of alcohol. Drink now through 2007.–J.L. • $25 • (3/31/2000) • **87**
Zinfandel Fiddletown 1996: An earthy, gamy style that struggles to show ripe fruitiness, with hints of ripe berry and spice, but mostly drying, leathery tannins. Drink now through 2002.–J.L. • $23 • (12/15/1998) • **83**
Zinfandel Fiddletown Eschen Vineyard 1995 • $23 • (11/15/1997) • **89**
Zinfandel Fiddeltown Eschen Vineyard 1994 • $25 • (2/28/1997) • **89**
Zinfandel Fiddletown Old Vine 1993 • $22 • (4/30/1996) • **87**
Zinfandel Shenandoah Valley d'Agostini Bros. 1997: This is marked by a strong earth, menthol and game edge, with the fruit struggling to keep pace, so be forewarned. Best to cellar short-term in the hopes that the funkiness dissipates. Try through 2004.–J.L. • $30 • (12/15/1999) • **81**
Zinfandel Shenandoah Valley d'Agostini Bros. 1996: Serves up a pretty array of ripe, zesty Zinfandel flavors, with plum, wild berry, sage, cedar and spice, turning complex on the finish. Drink through 2004.–J.L. • $30 • (1/31/1999) • **89**

REVERIE | CALIFORNIA

Cabernet Franc Napa Valley 1995: Well oaked, firm and spicy, with a tight cedary band wrapped around a core of trim currant and spicy berry. Best from 2001 through 2006.–J.L. • $33 • (12/15/1999) • **87**
Cabernet Sauvignon Napa Valley 1996: Wonderful balance and sense of harmony, with layers of currant, cherry, coffee, cedar, herb and spice. Finishes with a tight focus and smooth, polished tannins that keep pumping out the fruit. Best from 2001 through 2010.–J.L. • $43 • (11/15/1999) • **92**
Cabernet Sauvignon Napa Valley 1995: Tightly wound, with a focused band of cedar, currant, plum and berry. Finishes with leathery, oaky flavors and drying tannins. Best from 2001 through 2006.–J.L. • $40 • (6/15/1999) • **88**
Special Reserve Napa Valley 1995: Dense, complex and concentrated, with an earthy band of cedar, currant, tar, tobacco and black cherry, this is a tightly wound, firmly tannic wine that will need short-term cellaring. Cabernet Sauvignon, Petit Verdot and Cabernet Franc. Best from 2001 through 2010.–J.L. • $75 • (6/15/1999) • **92**

REX HILL | OREGON

Cabernet Sauvignon Oregon Reserve 1994 • $30 • (5/15/1998) • **88**
Cabernet Sauvignon Oregon Reserve 1992 • $30 • (11/30/1994) • **85**
Chardonnay Oregon Reserve 1996: Smooth and silky, with pretty nutmeg- and vanilla-scented pear flavors, hinting at honey on the deft finish. Very nicely done. Drink now through 2003.–H.S. • $25 • (10/15/1999) • **88**

REX HILL

Chardonnay Willamette Valley 1996 • $14 • (5/15/1998) • **87**

Pinot Blanc Willamette Valley 1997: Soft and appealing for its straightforward melon and apple flavors. Drink now.–H.S. • $12 • (5/31/1999) • **83**

Pinot Blanc Willamette Valley Bellevue Cross Vineyards 1998: Fresh and appealing for its cantaloupe and apple flavors, weaving in a touch of earth and mineral on the finish. Drink now.–H.S. • $14 • (3/31/2000) • **85**

Pinot Gris Oregon Reserve 1998: Light and vibrant in flavor, with pretty citrus and melon notes echoing on the crisp finish. Drink now.–H.S. • $18 • (4/30/2000) • **86**

Pinot Gris Willamette Valley 1998: Light and juicy, with pretty melon and almond flavors that linger on the smooth finish. Drink now.–H.S. • $14 • (4/30/2000) • **85**

Pinot Gris Willamette Valley 1997: Has an earthy, sour edge to the apple cider flavors. –H.S. • $13 • (6/30/1999) • **76**

Pinot Gris Willamette Valley 1996 • $14 • (10/31/1997) • **82**

Pinot Noir Oregon 1985 • $15 • (2/15/1990) • **81**

Pinot Noir Oregon Archibald Vineyards 1990 • $22 • (3/15/1994) • **85**

Pinot Noir Oregon Archibald Vineyards 1985 • $30 • (2/15/1990) • **84**

Pinot Noir Oregon Dundee Hills 1996: Light in structure, firm in texture, with pretty currant and black cherry notes hovering over modestly chewy tannins. Drink now.–H.S. • $30 • (11/15/1998) • **85**

Pinot Noir Oregon Dundee Hills Vineyards 1989 • $22 • (2/28/1993) • **86**

Pinot Noir Oregon Dundee Hills Vineyards 1985 • $25 • (2/15/1990) • **74**

Pinot Noir Oregon Dundee Hills Vineyards 1983 • $35 • (2/15/1990) • **77**

Pinot Noir Oregon Jacob-Hart Vineyard 1997: Light and fragrant, a delicate red, with floral, currant and strawberry flavors that linger gently. Drink now.–H.S. • $40 • (2/29/2000) • **86**

Pinot Noir Oregon Kings Ridge 1997: Light in flavor, firm in texture, with modest black cherry notes persisting on the hard-edged finish. Drink now.–H.S. • $14 • (4/30/1999) • **80**

Pinot Noir Oregon Kings Ridge 1996 • $13 • (10/31/1997) • **80**

Pinot Noir Oregon Kings Ridge 1995 • $12 • (2/28/1997) • **79**

Pinot Noir Oregon Kings Ridge 1992 • $10 • (3/15/1994) • **81**

Pinot Noir Oregon Maresh Vineyard 1996: A lively wine, with generous raspberry, blackberry and vanilla flavors swirling around a firm frame. Dense color for a '96. Has a layer of fine-grained tannins to lose. Best after1999.–H.S. • $30 • (11/15/1998) • **87**

Pinot Noir Oregon Maresh Vineyard 1989 • $22 • (2/28/1993) • **84**

Pinot Noir Oregon Maresh Vineyard 1985 • $18 • (6/15/1988) • **79**

Pinot Noir Oregon Medici Vineyard 1985 • $28 • (2/15/1990) • **77**

Pinot Noir Oregon Reserve 1996: Packs a lot of earthy, tarry, anise-scented plum flavor into a lightish frame. Finishes a bit chewy. Tannins needs cellaring. Best after1999.–H.S. • $40 • (9/30/1998) • **84**

Pinot Noir Oregon Reserve 1994 • $40 • (2/28/1997) • **86**

Pinot Noir Oregon Reserve 1992 • $30 • (11/30/1994) • **82**

Pinot Noir Oregon Vino del Niño 1997: Light and bright, with pretty strawberry flavors on a delicate frame. Drink now.–H.S. • $8 • (11/15/1998) • **80**

Pinot Noir Oregon Wirtz Vineyards 1985 • $18 • (6/15/1988) • **82**

Pinot Noir Willamette Valley 1995 • $17 • (2/28/1997) • **85**

Pinot Noir Willamette Valley 1990 • $15 • (3/15/1994) • **79**

Pinot Noir Willamette Valley 1989 • $15 • (2/28/1993) • **77**

Pinot Noir Willamette Valley 1988 • $18 • (4/15/1991) • **88**

Pinot Noir Willamette Valley 1985 • $15 • (6/15/1988) • **79**

Sauvignon Blanc Willamette Valley 1997: Light and crisp, with citrus, apple and herb flavors mingling enticingly to the juicy finish. Drink now.–H.S. • $9 • (5/31/1999) • **87**

White Riesling Willamette Valley 1997: Dry, almost austere at first, with pretty white peach, floral and resiny flavors echoing on the crisp finish. Drink now through 2002.–H.S. • $10 • (4/30/1999) • **86**

White Riesling Oregon 1996 • $8 • (5/15/1998) • **83**

REY SOL | CALIFORNIA

Syrah Temecula 1995 • $16 • (6/15/1998) • **86**

Syrah Temecula 1994 • $10 • (8/31/1996) • **81**

Key: SS—Spectator Selection. CS—Cellar Selection. HR—Highly Recommended. $NA—Price not available. (BT)—Barrel tasting. Ⓐ—Auction Price.
For a key to the tasters' initials, see "How to Use These Listings."
Dates in parentheses represent the issues in which the ratings were published.

RIBOLI FAMILY | CALIFORNIA

Cabernet Sauvignon Rutherford 1997: Lean and tannic, it struggles to work through its austerity, with cedary oak, currant and earthy, woody flavors. Best from 2002 through 2010.–J.L. • $45 • (5/15/2000) • **86**

RICH, ANDREW | WASHINGTON

Cabernet Sauvignon Yakima Valley Les Vigneaux 1997: Has a lot of personality, though it might not appeal to everyone. Rich, dense and supple, the flavors include black cherry, game, mineral, mint and sage, on a solid frame. Needs cellaring. Best from 2002 through 2007.–H.S. • $18 • (8/31/1999) • **90**

Cabernet Sauvignon Yakima Valley Les Vigneaux 1996 • $16 • (5/15/1998) • **87**

Gewürztraminer Oregon Les Vigneaux 1998: Ripe, rich and deep, with layers of pineapple, honey, cream and spice swirling through the complex, generous finish. Drink now through 2005.–H.S. • $18/375 ml. • (5/15/2000) • **91**

Gewürztraminer Willamette Valley Les Vigneaux 1996 • $15/375 ml. • (11/30/1997) • **92**

Pinot Noir Rosé Willamette Valley Tabula Rasa 1996 • $10 • (11/15/1997) • **81**

Pinot Noir Yamhill County Les Vigneaux 1996 • $16 • (5/15/1998) • **80**

Tabula Rasa White Willamette Valley 1998: Bright and snappy, here's a crisp white with herbal notes among the apple and citrus flavors. Chenin Blanc and Sauvignon Blanc. Drink now.–H.S. • $10 • (5/15/2000) • **85**

Tabula Rasa White Willamette Valley 1997: Fresh and lean, with mineral-scented apple flavors lingering on the round finish. A blend of Chardonnay and Sauvignon Blanc. Drink now.–H.S. • $10 • (11/15/1998) • **82**

RICH PASSAGE | WASHINGTON

Merlot Washington 1994 • $13 • (9/15/1996) • **78**

Pinot Noir Oregon 1993 • $13 • (8/31/1996) • **83**

Pinot Noir Oregon Winemaker's Reserve 1991 • $13 • (11/30/1994) • **81**

Pinot Noir Oregon Winemaker's Reserve 1990 • $15 • (2/28/1993) • **79**

Pinot Noir Washington Morgan Vineyard 1990 • $12 • (2/28/1993) • **68**

RICHARDSON | CALIFORNIA

Cabernet Franc Sonoma Valley Giles Vineyard 1993 • $15 • (5/15/1996) • **83**

Cabernet Sauvignon Sonoma Valley 1985 • $12 • (11/30/1988) • **78**

Cabernet Sauvignon Sonoma Valley Horne Vineyard 1997: Dense and concentrated, with a core of mineral, grapey black cherry, plum and anise flavors. Finishes with large-scale, well-integrated tannins. Drink now through 2005.–J.L. • $27 • (10/15/1999) • **87**

Cabernet Sauvignon Sonoma Valley Horne Vineyard 1995 • $18 • (11/30/1997) • **83**

Cabernet Sauvignon Sonoma Valley Horne 1992 • $12 • (11/15/1994) • **81**

Cabernet Sauvignon Sonoma Valley Horne 1991 • $14 • (11/15/1993) • **89**

Cabernet Sauvignon Sonoma Valley Horne 1990 • $12 • (11/15/1993) • **73**

Cabernet Sauvignon Sonoma Valley Horne 1989 • $14 • (11/15/1991) • **78**

Merlot Carneros Sangiacomo 1993 • $18 • (8/31/1996) • **87**

Merlot Carneros Sangiacomo Vineyard 1998: Lean, with cassis, pepper and pine flavors that end with dry tannins. Drink now through 2004.–J.L. • $23 • (5/15/2000) • **81**

Merlot Carneros Sangiacomo Vineyard 1997: Shows a range of mineral, blueberry, cherry and anise flavors. Turns simple on the finish, with a slightly bitter edge. Drink now through 2003.–J.L. • $19 • (10/15/1999) • **82**

Merlot Carneros Sangiacomo Vineyard 1996: Darkly colored, with a firm but supple texture. Serves up layers of mint, blackberry, cassis, plum and herb flavors. Generous now, it harbors plenty of fruit for future drinking. Drink now through 2003. • $19 • (10/15/1998) • **88**

Merlot Carneros Sangiacomo Vineyard 1995 • $17 • (7/31/1997) • **88**

Merlot Carneros Sangiacomo Vineyard 1994 • $18 • (7/31/1996) • **82**

Merlot Sonoma Valley Los Carneros 1992 • $15 • (9/15/1994) • **87**

Merlot Sonoma Valley Los Carneros Gregory 1991 • $18 • (6/15/1993) • **86**

Merlot Sonoma Valley Los Carneros Gregory 1990 • $15 • (5/31/1992) • **89**

Merlot Sonoma Valley Los Carneros Gregory 1989 • $14 • (3/31/1991) • **83**

Merlot Sonoma Valley Los Carneros Sangiacomo 1990 • $15 • (5/31/1992) • **87**

Merlot Sonoma Valley Los Carneros Sangiacomo & Gregory Vineyards 1991 • $15 • (6/15/1993) • **85**

Pinot Noir Sonoma Valley Los Carneros Sangiacomo 1996 • $19 • (2/28/1998) • **84**

Pinot Noir Sonoma Valley Los Carneros Sangiacomo 1995 • $18 • (2/28/1997) • **86**

Pinot Noir Sonoma Valley Los Carneros Sangiacomo 1993 • $15 • (3/31/1995) • **84**

Pinot Noir Sonoma Valley Los Carneros Sangiacomo 1992 • $14 • (12/31/1995) • **74**
Pinot Noir Sonoma Valley Los Carneros Sangiacomo 1991 • $15 • (2/28/1993) • **80**
Pinot Noir Sonoma Valley Los Carneros Sangiacomo 1990 • $14 • (9/30/1992) • **81**
Pinot Noir Sonoma Valley Los Carneros Sangiacomo 1989 • $14 • (4/30/1991) • **86**
Pinot Noir Sonoma Valley Los Carneros Sangiacomo 1987 • $12 • (10/15/1989) • **88**
Pinot Noir Sonoma Valley Los Carneros Sangiacomo 1986 • $12 • (6/15/1988) • **87**
Synergy Sonoma Valley 1994 • $15 • (12/15/1995) • **86**
Synergy Sonoma-Napa Valleys 1989 • $15 • (5/31/1992) • **84**
Syrah Carneros 1998: A complex, intriguing nose, with spearmint, chocolate and nutmeg notes. Flavors don't quite follow through, with slightly dry tannins on the finish. Drink now through 2004.–J.L. • $23 • (5/15/2000) • **87**
Zinfandel Sonoma Valley NV • $9 • (7/31/1989) • **76**
Zinfandel Sonoma Valley 1995 • $16 • (4/30/1997) • **87**
Zinfandel Sonoma Valley Nora's Vineyard 1993 • $15 • (10/15/1995) • **84**
Zinfandel Sonoma Valley Nora's Vineyard 1992 • $12 • (8/31/1994) • **89**

RIDGE | CALIFORNIA

Cabernet Sauvignon Howell Mountain 1983 • $53 Ⓐ • (3/16/1986) • **83**
Cabernet Sauvignon Howell Mountain 1982 • $12 • (6/01/1985) • **88**
Cabernet Sauvignon Napa County York Creek 1991 • $16 • (11/15/1994) • **85**
Cabernet Sauvignon Napa County York Creek 1990 • $19 Ⓐ • (11/15/1993) • **88**
Cabernet Sauvignon Napa County York Creek 1987 • $21 • (11/15/1992) • **85**
Cabernet Sauvignon Napa County York Creek 1985 • $22 Ⓐ • (6/15/1989) • **78**
Cabernet Sauvignon Napa County York Creek 1984 • $33 Ⓐ • (2/15/1987) • **78**
Cabernet Sauvignon Napa County York Creek 1981 • $12 • (12/16/1984) • **89**
Cabernet Sauvignon Napa County York Creek 1978 • $33 • (11/15/1992) • **87**
Cabernet Sauvignon Napa County York Creek Spring House Vineyard 1981 • $12 • (2/16/1984) • **63**
Cabernet Sauvignon Santa Cruz Mountains 1993 • $NA • (12/15/1995) • **83**
Cabernet Sauvignon Santa Cruz Mountains 1992 • $16 • (11/15/1994) • **89**
Cabernet Sauvignon Santa Cruz Mountains 1991 • $16 • (10/15/1993) • **89**
Cabernet Sauvignon Santa Cruz Mountains 1990 • $14 • (2/15/1993) • **85**
Cabernet Sauvignon Santa Cruz Mountains 1989 • $12 • (3/31/1992) • **82**
Cabernet Sauvignon Santa Cruz Mountains 1986 • $15 • (10/31/1989) • **68**
Cabernet Sauvignon Santa Cruz Mountains 1985 • $12 • (6/15/1989) • **64**
Cabernet Sauvignon Santa Cruz Mountains 1984 • $12 • (6/15/1987) • **64**
Cabernet Sauvignon Santa Cruz Mountains Jimsomare 1985 • $16 • (2/15/1989) • **87**
Cabernet Sauvignon Santa Cruz Mountains Jimsomare 1984 • $16 • (10/31/1987) • **69**
Cabernet Sauvignon Santa Cruz Mountains Jimsomare 1983 • $10 • (11/30/1986) • **78**
Cabernet Sauvignon Santa Cruz Mountains Jimsomare & Monte Bello Vineyards 1981 • $12 • (1/01/1985) • **87**
Monte Bello Santa Cruz Mountains 1997: Fine intensity, focused, rich and concentrated, with currant, wild berry, anise and spice. Finishes with firm tannins and a sense of elegance.–J.L. • $NA • (8/31/1998) (BT) • **90-94**
Monte Bello Santa Cruz Mountains 1995: Wonderfully focused, if a bit tight now, the core of smoky currant, black cherry, blackberry and cedary-toasty oak is impressive, as is the seamless texture. This is a young and compact Cabernet blend that will benefit from cellaring. Best from 2001 through 2009.–J.L. • $100 • (10/31/1998) CS • **92**
Monte Bello Santa Cruz Mountains 1994 • $100 • (9/30/1997) • **93**
Monte Bello Santa Cruz Mountains 1993 • $80 • (10/15/1997) • **89**
Monte Bello Santa Cruz Mountains 1992 • $80 • (11/15/1996) CS • **91**
Monte Bello Santa Cruz Mountains 1991 • $75 • (11/15/1995) CS • **91**
Monte Bello Santa Cruz Mountains 1990 • $60 • (11/15/1993) • **89**
Monte Bello Santa Cruz Mountains 1989: Wonderful balance and supple texture, with complex currant, black cherry, anise, cedar, tar and rose petal notes. Rather defines elegance, grace and harmony. (1989 California Cabernet retrospective tasting). Drink now through 2006.–J.L. • $40 • (8/31/1999) • **92**
Cabernet Sauvignon Santa Cruz Mountains Monte Bello 1988: Starts out with earthy, gamy, leathery flavors, then turns supple and polished, with complex anise, currant, berry, mushroom and cedar notes. Shows more sweet-tasting fruit and balance than most '88s. (1988 California Cabernet retrospective tasting). Drink now through 2006.–J.L. • $65 Ⓐ • (11/15/1998) • **88**
Cabernet Sauvignon Santa Cruz Mountains Monte Bello 1987 • $74 Ⓐ • (11/15/1990) • **88**
Cabernet Sauvignon Santa Cruz Mountains Monte Bello 1986 • $73 Ⓐ • (9/15/1989) • **82**
Cabernet Sauvignon Santa Cruz Mountains Monte Bello 1985 • $120 Ⓐ • (7/15/1988) CS • **95**
Cabernet Sauvignon Santa Cruz Mountains Monte Bello 1984 • $116 Ⓐ • (9/15/1987) CS • **95**
Cabernet Sauvignon Santa Cruz Mountains Monte Bello 1982 • $28 Ⓐ • (11/30/1986) • **75**
Cabernet Sauvignon Santa Cruz Mountains Monte Bello 1981 • $19 Ⓐ • (8/01/1985) • **89**
Cabernet Sauvignon Santa Cruz Mountains Monte Bello 1980 • $42 Ⓐ • (4/01/1985) • **70**
Cabernet Sauvignon Santa Cruz Mountains Monte Bello 1978: Packed with rich, complex, concentrated flavors that are intense, youthful and vibrant. Shows loads of currant, plum, mushroom, tar and spice, finishing with a long aftertaste and still enough tannin to sustain it another five to 10 years. (1978 California Cabernet retrospective tasting). Drink now through 2004. –J.L. • $152 Ⓐ • (11/15/1998) • **92**
Cabernet Sauvignon Santa Cruz Mountains Monte Bello 1974 • $175 • (11/15/1994) • **94**
Cabernet Sauvignon Santa Cruz Mountains Monte Bello 1971 • $10 • (4/01/1986) • **85**
Chardonnay California 1997: Rich and full-bodied, featuring focused, spicy floral, pear, apple and peach flavors that turn clean and refreshing on the long, complex finish. Looking strictly at grape sources, this could carry the more specific Santa Cruz Mountains appellation. Drink now.–J.L. • $16 • (7/31/1999) • **91**
Chardonnay Santa Cruz Mountains 1998: Intense, with a pretty array of flavors ranging from tart fig to nectarine, finishing with touches of anise and cedar. Drink now through 2003.–J.L. • $28 • (6/30/2000) • **88**
Chardonnay Santa Cruz Mountains 1997: Tightly focused, combining rich, earthy Chardonnay flavors with elegance and grace. Shows lots of ripe pear, fig, mineral and citrus. Drink now through 2003.–J.L. • $28 • (7/31/1999) • **93**
Chardonnay Santa Cruz Mountains 1996 • $25 • (6/30/1998) • **92**
Geyserville Sonoma County 1998: Simple but pleasant, with cherry, berry and raspberry flavor that keeps its fruity profile. Drink now.–J.L. • $28 • (5/31/2000) • **85**
Geyserville California 1997: This hearty Zinfandel blend from Sonoma County is dense and earthy, delivering layers of complex cherry, wild berry, raspberry, cedar and spice, turning supple and polished, culminating in a long aftertaste. Drink now through 2005.–J.L. • $28 • (11/30/1999) SS • **92**
Geyserville Sonoma County 1996: This supple and harmonious Zinfandel blend opens with pretty, toasty oak, leading to spicy wild berry, cherry jam, plum and raspberry flavors that remain sharply focused on the long, lively finish. Drink now through 2004.–J.L. • $25 • (2/28/1999) SS • **93**
Geyserville Sonoma County 1995 • $25 • (11/15/1997) • **89**
Geyserville Sonoma County 1994 • $20 • (9/30/1996) SS • **91**
Geyserville Sonoma County 1993 • $20 • (9/15/1995) SS • **91**
Geyserville Sonoma County 1992 • $18 • (8/31/1994) • **86**
Geyserville Sonoma County 1991: Ripe, rich and concentrated, with complex black cherry, wild berry, raspberry and plum. Very complete and sophisticated, with a long, lingering finish. 50 percent Zinfandel, 30 percent Carignane, 20 percent Petite Sirah. (Zinfandel retrospective tasting). Drink now through 2004.–J.L. • $18 • (6/30/1999) • **91**
Geyserville Sonoma County 1990: Softening, a bit gamy and not as fruity as most of the '90s. Well balanced and pleasant to drink, with a core of earthy cherry and currant notes. (Zinfandel retrospective tasting). Drink now. –J.L. • $16 • (6/30/1999) • **87**
Geyserville Sonoma County 1989 • $14 • (11/15/1991) • **84**
Zinfandel Sonoma County Geyserville 1988 • $19 • (11/30/1990) SS • **90**
Zinfandel Sonoma County Geyserville 1987 • $15 • (10/31/1989) • **90**
Zinfandel Sonoma County Geyserville 1986 • $30 • (10/31/1988) • **79**
Zinfandel Sonoma County Geyserville 1985 • $34 Ⓐ • (9/15/1987) • **83**
Zinfandel Sonoma County Geyserville 1984 • $18 • (12/31/1986) • **79**
Zinfandel Sonoma County Geyserville 1982 • $32 • (9/16/1984) • **90**
Zinfandel Sonoma County Geyserville 1975 • $35 • (6/16/1985) • **67**
Zinfandel Sonoma County Geyserville 1974 • $44 • (6/16/1985) • **79**
Zinfandel Sonoma County Geyserville 1973 • $55 • (6/16/1985) • **80**
Lytton Springs Dry Creek Valley 1998: A touch earthy, with a mushroomy edge to dry berry and pepper notes. Turns dry and tannic. Drink now through 2005.–J.L. • $28 • (5/31/2000) • **84**
Lytton Springs California 1997: Smooth, rich and polished, with a pretty array of black cherry, blackberry, raspberry and plum. Elegant, fruity aftertaste. Drink now through 2004.–J.L. • $28 • (11/30/1999) • **89**
Lytton Springs Dry Creek Valley 1996 • $25 • (5/31/1998) • **88**

RIDGE

Lytton Springs Dry Creek Valley 1995 • $23 • (7/31/1997) SS • **92**
Lytton Springs Dry Creek Valley 1994 • $14 • (9/30/1996) • **87**
Lytton Springs Dry Creek Valley 1993 • $19 • (7/31/1995) SS • **91**
Zinfandel Dry Creek Valley Lytton Springs 1992 • $18 • (8/31/1994) SS • **90**
Zinfandel Dry Creek Valley Lytton Springs 1991: Impressive for its distinctive Zinfandel flavors, balance, suppleness and grace. The core of plum, raspberry, black cherry and spice is complex, with hints of coffee, cocoa and cedar. Long and delicious on the aftertaste. Zinfandel with 12 percent Petite Sirah, 5 percent Grenache and 3 percent Carignane. (Zinfandel retrospective tasting). Drink now through 2004.–J.L. • $26 Ⓐ • (6/30/1999) • **92**
Zinfandel Dry Creek Valley Lytton Springs 1990 • $15 • (10/15/1992) • **89**
Zinfandel Sonoma County Lytton Springs 1989 • $13 • (11/15/1991) • **82**
Zinfandel Sonoma County Lytton Springs 1988 • $12 • (11/30/1990) • **82**
Zinfandel Sonoma County Lytton Springs 1987 • $18 • (10/31/1989) • **91**
Zinfandel Sonoma County Lytton Springs 1986 • $25 • (10/15/1988) • **88**
Zinfandel Sonoma County Lytton Springs 1985 • $22 • (9/15/1987) • **81**
Zinfandel Sonoma County Lytton Springs 1984 • $17 • (11/15/1986) • **79**
Mataro California Bridgehead 1997: Appealing if lacking in extra facets, it's marked by tarry berry and dried cherry flavors. Turns austere and tannic. Drink now through 2004.–J.L. • $20 • (12/31/1999) • **86**
Mataro California Bridgehead Century-Old Vines 1995 • $18 • (8/31/1997) • **87**
Mataro California Evangelo Vineyards 1990 • $14 • (3/15/1992) • **73**
Mataro Contra Costa County Bridgehead 1996: Quite earthy, this wine nonetheless shows good cherry, plum and spice flavors. Tannins are smooth, with a smoky finish. Drink now. • $20 • (12/15/1998) • **86**
Mataro Contra Costa County Bridgehead 1993 • $16 • (12/15/1995) • **84**
Merlot Napa County York Creek 1991 • $18 • (11/15/1994) • **80**
Merlot Santa Cruz Mountains 1996: Lean yet supple, with a band of earth, cedar, cherry, currant and spice, finishing with smooth tannins and moderate length. Drink now through 2006.–J.L. • $40 • (10/15/1999) • **87**
Merlot Santa Cruz Mountains 1995: Austere and well crafted, with a tight range of currant, cedar and tobacco flavors and mild, well-integrated tannins. Drink now through 2004.–J.L. • $40 • (9/30/1998) • **88**
Merlot Santa Cruz Mountains Monte Bello Ridge 1994 • $40 • (6/30/1997) • **89**
Merlot Santa Cruz Mountains Monte Bello Ridge 1993 • $24 • (6/15/1996) • **88**
Merlot Santa Cruz Mountains Monte Bello Ridge 1992 • $16 • (1/31/1996) • **91**
Merlot Santa Cruz Mountains Monte Bello Ridge 1974 • $175 • (11/15/1994) • **84**
Merlot Sonoma County Bradford Mountain 1990 • $18 • (3/15/1994) HR • **89**
Merlot Sonoma County Bradford Mountain 1989 • $18 • (10/31/1992) • **82**
Merlot Sonoma County Bradford Mountain 1987 • $17 • (7/15/1990) • **75**
Merlot Sonoma County Bradford Mountain 1986 • $16 • (7/31/1989) • **64**
Petite Sirah California York Creek 1996: Firm, with chunky plum, wild berry, spice, earth and anise flavors wrapped in gritty tannins. Best from 2001 through 2007.–J.L. • $20 • (12/31/1999) • **88**
Petite Sirah California York Creek 1995: Offers a glimpse of dense, chewy plum and wild berry, pepper and spice before turning firmly tannic and chewy. From grapes grown in Spring Mountain District. Drink through 2004.–J.L. • $20 • (8/31/1998) • **87**
Petite Sirah Spring Mountain York Creek 1994 • $18 • (7/31/1997) • **88**
Petite Sirah Napa County York Creek 1991 • $18 • (9/30/1995) • **85**
Petite Sirah Napa County York Creek 1990 • $18 • (5/31/1994) • **83**
Petite Sirah Napa County York Creek 1988 • $16 • (3/15/1992) • **80**
Petite Sirah Napa County York Creek 1987 • $12 • (8/31/1991) • **76**
Petite Sirah Napa County York Creek 1984 • $10 • (1/31/1988) • **70**
Zinfandel California Pagani Ranch 1997: Dark, ripe, rich and concentrated, with chewy black cherry, blackberry, chocolate and cedar, finishing with chunky tannins. Drink now through 2006.–J.L. • $28 • (11/30/1999) • **90**
Zinfandel Sonoma Valley Pagani Ranch 1996: Ripe, earthy and a touch funky, with a twinge of dill to the ripe, raisiny fruit flavors that are rich and concentrated. Turns tannic. Drink now through 2004.–J.L. • $25 • (12/31/1998) • **88**
Zinfandel Sonoma Valley Pagani Ranch 1995 • $25 • (10/31/1997) SS • **92**
Zinfandel Sonoma Valley Pagani Ranch 1994 • $20 • (9/30/1996) • **90**
Zinfandel Sonoma Valley Pagani Ranch 1993 • $20 • (9/15/1995) CS • **90**
Zinfandel Sonoma Valley Pagani Ranch 1991 • $14 • (9/30/1993) • **86**
Zinfandel Sonoma Valley Pagani Ranch Late Picked 1992: A big, ripe, rich and supple style that packs in lots of black cherry, wild berry, currant, cedar and spice. Manages to hold its alcohol in check, even at the stated 15.8 percent. (Zinfandel retrospective tasting). Drink now through 2002. –J.L. • $NA • (6/30/1999) • **90**
Zinfandel California York Creek 1997: Lively, with zesty cherry, blackberry and raspberry plus hints of cedar and mushroom. Finishes with complex anise, tar and spice. Drink now through 2005.–J.L. • $28 • (11/30/1999) • **88**
Zinfandel Spring Mountain District York Creek Vineyards 1996: Tight, with a tarry edge to the smoky wild berry, wax and sage-laced Zin flavors. Firms up and turns tannic on the finish. Drink through 2005.–J.L. • $25 • (12/31/1998) • **87**
Zinfandel Spring Mountain York Creek 1995 • $23 • (11/15/1997) • **88**
Zinfandel Howell Mountain 1990 • $12 • (10/15/1992) • **80**
Zinfandel Howell Mountain 1989 • $12 • (3/31/1992) • **87**
Zinfandel Howell Mountain 1988 • $12 • (7/31/1991) • **82**
Zinfandel Howell Mountain 1987 • $10 • (5/31/1990) • **83**
Zinfandel Napa County York Creek 1985 • $11 • (12/31/1987) • **82**
Zinfandel Napa County York Creek 1984 • $11 • (3/15/1987) • **86**
Zinfandel Napa County York Creek 1982 • $22 • (7/16/1985) SS • **91**
Zinfandel Paso Robles 1990 • $10 • (10/15/1992) • **84**
Zinfandel Paso Robles 1989 • $10 • (11/15/1991) • **84**
Zinfandel Paso Robles 1987 • $10 • (3/15/1990) • **85**
Zinfandel Paso Robles Dusi Ranch 1996 • $20 • (5/31/1998) • **89**
Zinfandel Paso Robles Dusi Ranch 1995 • $20 • (4/30/1997) • **91**
Zinfandel Paso Robles Dusi Ranch 1994 • $16 • (9/30/1996) HR • **90**
Zinfandel Paso Robles Dusi Ranch 1993 • $14 • (9/30/1995) • **86**
Zinfandel Paso Robles Dusi Ranch 1992 • $14 • (8/31/1994) • **90**
Zinfandel Paso Robles Dusi Ranch 1991 • $12 • (9/15/1993) HR • **90**
Zinfandel Paso Robles Late Picked 1997: Very dark and ripe, with rich, complex layers of plum, black cherry, wild berry, tar and cedar, finishing with smooth, supple tannins. Drink now through 2002.–J.L. • $23 • (5/31/1999) • **91**
Zinfandel San Luis Obispo County Paso Robles 1998: Ripe and jammy on a modest frame, with black cherry, raspberry and vanilla, almost like a cobbler. Turns crisp and simple. Drink now.–J.L. • $23 • (5/31/2000) • **84**
Zinfandel Sonoma County 1994 • $14 • (9/30/1996) • **87**
Zinfandel Sonoma County 1993 • $12 • (9/15/1995) • **88**
Zinfandel Sonoma County 1991 • $10 • (8/31/1993) SS • **90**
Zinfandel Sonoma County 1990 • $9 • (12/31/1992) • **86**
Zinfandel Sonoma County 1989 • $9 • (3/31/1992) • **80**
Zinfandel Sonoma County 1988 • $9 • (2/15/1991) • **88**
Zinfandel Sonoma County Sonoma Station 1998: Thin, bordering on watery, with modest peppery and spicy notes but not much fruit. Drink now through 2004.–J.L. • $18 • (5/31/2000) • **82**
Zinfandel Sonoma County Sonoma Station 1997: Lots of fresh, lively plum and blueberry flavors lead into a crisp, tightly wound core of spice, cedar, earth and wild berry, finishing with firm tannins. Drink now through 2003.–J.L. • $18 • (5/15/1999) • **88**
Zinfandel Sonoma County Sonoma Station 1996 • $16 • (5/31/1998) • **88**
Zinfandel Sonoma County Sonoma Station 1995 • $18 • (4/30/1997) • **88**

RIO SECO | CALIFORNIA

Pinot Blanc Monterey San Bernabe Vineyard 1997: A fruity quality that accents mandarin orange and peach is balanced by a flinty edge. Toasty oak plays a role, too. Fresh and juicy. Drink now. • $15 • (9/15/1998) • **85**
Zinfandel Paso Robles Cherry Vineyard 1996: Big, ripe and generous, a jazzy mouthful of black cherry, beetroot and racy mineral flavors. The acidity is a bit sharp on the finish, but it has style. Best after 2000.–H.S. • $22 • (11/30/1998) • **87**

RISTOW | CALIFORNIA

Cabernet Sauvignon Napa Valley Quinta de Pedras Vineyard 1996: Tight, rich and intense, with a cedary band of currant, cherry, anise, sage and spice, finishing with firm, gritty tannins that need time. Best to cellar short-term. Best from 2001 through 2009.–J.L. • $45 • (10/31/1999) • **90**
Cabernet Sauvignon Napa Valley Quinta de Pedras Vineyard 1995: Impressive for its elegance and range of spicy black cherry, currant, olive and cedar notes. Finishes with ripe, polished tannins and fine length. A new wine from a vineyard off Silverado Trail near Signorello Vineyards.–J.L. • $40 • (11/15/1998) • **89**

RITCHIE CREEK | CALIFORNIA

Cabernet Sauvignon Napa Valley 1991 • $18 • (4/15/1995) • **85**
Cabernet Sauvignon Napa Valley 1978 • $22 • (11/15/1992) • **78**

Key: SS—Spectator Selection. CS—Cellar Selection. HR—Highly Recommended. $NA—Price not available. (BT)—Barrel tasting. Ⓐ—Auction Price. For a key to the tasters' initials, see "How to Use These Listings."
Dates in parentheses represent the issues in which the ratings were published.

RIVER ROAD | CALIFORNIA

Cabernet Sauvignon Napa County 1993 • $9 • (12/15/1995) • **83**

Chardonnay Sonoma County Proprietors Reserve 1996: Simple and earthy, with notes of citrus, apple and toast. A bit leesy on the finish, where the earthy notes compete with the fruit. Drink now.–T.G. • $10 • (7/31/1998) • **81**

Pinot Meunier Russian River Valley 1996: An herbal note modifies the ripe fruit flavors, finishing with a layer of vanilla and toast. Drink now.–J.L. • $14 • (8/31/1998) • **82**

RIVER RUN | CALIFORNIA

Syrah Monterey County Ventana Vineyard 1994 • $18 • (2/28/1997) • **86**

Zinfandel Paso Robles Beckwith Ranch Vineyard 1996 • $15 • (6/15/1998) • **84**

RIVERVIEW | NEW YORK

Merlot North Fork of Long Island Barrel Reserve 1993 • $16 • (6/15/1997) • **73**

ROBERT ALISON | CALIFORNIA

Cabernet Sauvignon California 1993 • $6 • (12/15/1995) • **81**

Cabernet Sauvignon California 1989 • $5 • (11/15/1992) • **78**

ROCHIOLI | CALIFORNIA

Cabernet Sauvignon Russian River Valley Neoma's Vineyard Reserve 1993 • $28 • (4/30/1996) • **86**

Cabernet Sauvignon Russian River Valley Neoma's Vineyard Reserve 1991 • $26 • (12/15/1995) • **87**

Cabernet Sauvignon Russian River Valley Neoma's Vineyard Reserve 1990 • $24 • (6/15/1993) • **86**

Chardonnay Russian River Valley 1998: Clean and spicy, with peach, nutmeg and vanilla, finishing with a mineral edge. Drink now.–J.L. • $29 • (6/15/2000) • **87**

Chardonnay Russian River Valley 1997: Supple and fruity, with ripe, up-front, elegant pear, apple and spice flavors that are focused and lively. Turns creamy. Drink now through 2002.–J.L. • $25 • (6/30/1999) • **90**

Chardonnay Russian River Valley 1996 • $24 • (5/31/1998) • **91**

Chardonnay Russian River Valley Allen Vineyard 1997: Rich and smoky, with a sharply defined core of fig, pear, melon, anise and nutmeg. The flavors run on and on, revealing more nuances with every sip. Tremendous depth and complexity. Drink now through 2004.–J.L. • $42 • (5/31/1999) • **95**

Chardonnay Russian River Valley Allen Vineyard 1996: A wonderful orchestration of fruit and oak, with a ripe, rich, tightly focused core of spicy pear, apple and hazelnut. Pretty smoke and toasted oak flavors fold in on the finish. Drink now through 2003.–J.L. • $38 • (7/31/1998) • **94**

Chardonnay Russian River Valley River Block 1998: Smooth and polished, with rich, creamy vanilla, pear, fig and spice notes, gaining nuance and depth on the finish. Drink now.–J.L. • $42 • (6/15/2000) • **89**

Chardonnay Russian River Valley River Block 1997: Ultraripe and rich, with layers of complex pear, vanilla, melon, fig, apricot and spice, this wine combines deeply concentrated flavors with a sense of elegance and finesse. Drink now through 2004.–J.L. • $38 • (5/31/1999) • **96**

Chardonnay Russian River Valley River Block 1996: Elegant and understated, with complex pear, hazelnut, honey and anise flavors that slowly build on the finish, revealing more depth and richness. Impressive for its fruit complexity. Drink now through 2004.–J.L. • $32 • (7/31/1998) • **93**

Chardonnay Russian River Valley South River Vineyard 1997: Ultrarich and toasty, with lots of oak, but enough ripe pear, fig and apricot flavors fold in to give added depth and dimension. Needs short-term cellaring. Drink now through 2002.–J.L. • $45 • (12/15/1999) • **92**

Chardonnay Russian River Valley South River Vineyard 1996: This greets you with spicy, toasty oak. The core of ripe, rich apple, pear, fig and melon flavors is sharply focused, complex and concentrated, gaining length and depth on the finish. Drink now through 2001.–J.L. • $42 • (12/15/1998) • **92**

Pinot Noir Russian River Valley 1997: Smooth, ripe and elegant, with pretty black cherry, herb, cedar and vanilla shadings. Supple, polished texture on the finish. Drink now through 2005.–J.L. • $36 • (9/15/1999) • **88**

Pinot Noir Russian River Valley 1996: Well proportioned, with a core of plum, cherry and berry, picking up some spicy, toasty oak and a hint of cola. Finishes with mild tannins. Drink now through 2001.–J.L. • $34 • (8/31/1998) • **87**

Pinot Noir Russian River Valley 1995 • $48 Ⓐ • (7/31/1997) • **92**

Pinot Noir Russian River Valley 1994 • $22 • (2/28/1997) • **91**

Pinot Noir Russian River Valley 1992 • $18 • (12/15/1994) • **88**

Pinot Noir Russian River Valley 1991 • $19 • (2/28/1994) SS • **90**

Pinot Noir Russian River Valley 1990 • $16 • (2/28/1993) • **80**

Pinot Noir Russian River Valley 1989 • $16 • (11/15/1991) • **84**

Pinot Noir Russian River Valley 1988 • $15 • (10/31/1990) • **85**

Pinot Noir Russian River Valley 1987 • $15 • (5/31/1990) • **89**

Pinot Noir Russian River Valley 1986 • $15 • (10/15/1989) • **87**

Pinot Noir Russian River Valley 1985 • $13 • (6/15/1988) • **92**

Pinot Noir Russian River Valley 1984 • $12 • (11/15/1987) • **84**

Pinot Noir Russian River Valley 1982 • $13 • (8/31/1986) • **89**

Pinot Noir Russian River Valley East Block 1997: Weaves together a complex range of tart blackberry and ripe cherry, plum and raspberry flavors. Turns elegant and polished, with complex nuances that linger. Gentle tannins make it attractive now. Drink through 2006.–J.L. • $65 • (11/30/1999) • **92**

Pinot Noir Russian River Valley East Block Reserve 1994 • $60 • (11/15/1996) • **95**

Pinot Noir Russian River Valley Little Hill 1997: Rich and focused, with complex, concentrated black cherry, currant and plum flavors that hold their focus and linger on the finish, where the tannins are mild. Drink now through 2004.–J.L. • $50 • (11/30/1999) • **90**

Pinot Noir Russian River Valley Little Hill Block 1996: Smooth and polished, with pretty black cherry, anise, mineral and spice, it finishes with attractive, complex flavors. Not a great Rochioli, but a very good one. Drink now through 2002.–J.L. • $40 • (9/15/1998) • **87**

Pinot Noir Russian River Valley Little Hill Block Reserve 1995 • $38 • (11/15/1997) • **89**

Pinot Noir Russian River Valley Reserve 1991 • $35 • (2/28/1994) SS • **92**

Pinot Noir Russian River Valley Reserve 1990 • $30 • (3/31/1997) • **92**

Pinot Noir Russian River Valley Three Corner Vineyard 1997: Tight and a touch earthy, but it turns complex, with elegant, mushroomy black cherry, wild berry and spice notes. Drink now through 2004.–J.L. • $45 • (11/30/1999) • **88**

Pinot Noir Russian River Valley Three Corner Vineyard 1996: A very good '96, with moderately ripe plum and cherry flavors, spicy vanilla-oak nuances and a clean, complex finish. Still, lacks the extra facets of the best from this vineyard. Drink now through 2002.–J.L. • $40 • (8/31/1998) • **87**

Pinot Noir Russian River Valley Three Corner Vineyard Reserve 1995 • $40 • (11/15/1997) • **89**

Pinot Noir Russian River Valley Three Corner Vineyard Reserve 1994 • $40 • (11/15/1996) • **94**

Pinot Noir Russian River Valley West Block 1997: Tight, firm, ripe and spicy, it turns fleshy, with a complex, intriguing range of black cherry, plum and raspberry. Finishes with firm, crisp tannins. Drink through 2006.–J.L. • $60 • (11/30/1999) • **93**

Pinot Noir Russian River Valley West Block 1996: Complex on a small scale, with bright black cherry, olive, coffee, toasty oak. Finishes with a complex aftertaste. Drink now.–J.L. • $50 • (8/31/1998) • **88**

Pinot Noir Russian River Valley West Block Reserve 1995 • $50 • (11/15/1997) • **89**

Pinot Noir Russian River Valley West Block Reserve 1994 • $48 • (11/15/1996) • **96**

Pinot Noir Russian River Valley West Block Reserve 1993 • $38 • (10/15/1995) • **89**

Pinot Noir Russian River Valley West Block Reserve 1992 • $36 • (12/15/1994) HR • **92**

Sauvignon Blanc Russian River Valley 1998: Strikes a nice balance between racy acidity and tamer Sauvignon Blanc grassy herb, citrus and passion fruit flavors. Finishes with a long, clean aftertaste. Drink now through 2003.–J.L. • $22 • (12/31/1999) • **88**

Sauvignon Blanc Russian River Valley 1997 • $14 • (6/30/1998) SS • **91**

Sauvignon Blanc Russian River Valley 1996 • $38 Ⓐ • (6/15/1997) • **90**

Sauvignon Blanc Russian River Valley Old Vines 1997: Effusively fragrant, with rich honeysuckle, fig, mint and herb notes. On the palate, it sings with grapefruit, melon and lemon-lime flavors, bright herbal notes and a long finish. Sleek, firm and elegant. Drink through 2002. • $22 • (12/31/1998) • **93**

Sauvignon Blanc Russian River Valley Old Vines Reserve 1996 • $20 • (11/30/1997) • **90**

Zinfandel Russian River Valley 1996 • $20 • (6/15/1998) • **89**

Zinfandel Russian River Valley Sodini Vineyard 1994 • $15 • (9/30/1996) • **89**

Zinfandel Russian River Valley Sodini Vineyard 1993 • $15 • (8/31/1995) • **88**

Zinfandel Russian River Valley Sodini Vineyard 1992 • $14 • (9/30/1994) • **91**

ROCKBRIDGE | VIRGINIA

Chardonnay Virginia 1998: This thick white shows opulent crème brûlée and honey flavors, with modest notes of apple and pear. Rich but a bit cloying on the finish. Drink now.–T.M. • $12 • (1/01/2000) • **81**

Chardonnay Virginia Reserve 1998: Pear and pineapple flavors are ripe and refreshing, while oak adds sweet vanilla accents. Balanced and polished. Drink now through 2002.–T.M. • $16 • (1/01/2000) • **85**

ROCKING HORSE | CALIFORNIA

Cabernet Sauvignon Rutherford Garvey Family Vineyard 1997: Shows off lots of complex toasted oak, cola and tar flavors before working into concentrated black cherry, plum, cedar and anise. Finishes with complex flavors and slightly dry tannins. Drink now through 2006.–J.L. • $30 • (10/15/1999) • **90**

Cabernet Sauvignon Rutherford Garvey Family Vineyard 1996: Young and ripe, with earth, black cherry, tar, cassis, toasted oak and herb flavors, finishing plush, with complex mineral notes. Drink through 2005.–J.L. • $26 • (9/15/1999) • **89**

Cabernet Sauvignon Napa Valley Garvey Family Vineyard 1994 • $24 • (11/30/1997) • **90**

Cabernet Sauvignon Napa Valley Garvey Family Vineyard 1993 • $20 • (4/30/1996) • **87**

Cabernet Sauvignon Napa Valley Hillside Cuvée 1991 • $18 • (3/15/1994) • **84**

Cabernet Sauvignon Napa Valley Hillside Cuvée 1989 • $17 • (3/31/1992) • **85**

Cabernet Sauvignon Stags Leap District Robinson Vineyard 1993 • $28 • (8/31/1996) • **83**

Cabernet Sauvignon Stags Leap District Robinson Vineyard 1992 • $24 • (4/15/1995) • **86**

Cabernet Sauvignon Stags Leap District Robinson Vineyard 1991 • $24 • (3/31/1994) HR • **90**

Cabernet Sauvignon Stags Leap District Robinson Vineyard 1990 • $22 • (2/15/1993) • **91**

Zinfandel Howell Mountain 1994 • $16 • (5/15/1997) • **88**

Zinfandel Howell Mountain Lamborn Vineyard Fat Lady Sings 1997: Dark, with tart, earthy blackberry, pepper and wild berry flavors propped up by firm acidity. The last vintage of this wine. Drink now through 2006.–J.L. • $24 • (6/30/2000) • **87**

Zinfandel Howell Mountain Lamborn Vineyard 1996: Tight and spicy, with lots of peppery wild berry flavor that turns tight and tannic on the finish, where it picks up a mushroomy edge. Drink through 2002.–J.L. • $18 • (11/30/1998) • **87**

Zinfandel Howell Mountain Lamborn Vineyard 1995 • $16 • (5/15/1998) • **85**

Zinfandel Howell Mountain Lamborn Vineyard 1993 • $15 • (4/30/1996) • **89**

Zinfandel Howell Mountain Lamborn Vineyard 1991: Has aged nicely, holding its fruit, with complex, earthy plum, wild berry, raspberry and spice. Long, complex aftertaste, too. (Zinfandel retrospective tasting). Drink now through 2002.–J.L. • $14 • (6/30/1999) • **88**

Zinfandel Howell Mountain Lamborn Vineyard 1989 • $13 • (10/15/1992) • **81**

Zinfandel Napa Valley 1997: Nice balance of ripe berry, plum, spice and cherryish fruit, turning elegant and polished, with mild tannins. Drink now through 2005.–J.L. • $18 • (6/30/2000) • **87**

Zinfandel Napa Valley Old Paint 1993 • $18 • (9/15/1996) • **84**

ROCKLAND | CALIFORNIA

Cabernet Sauvignon Napa Valley 1994 • $30 • (11/15/1996) • **93**

Cabernet Sauvignon Napa Valley 1993 • $30 • (5/15/1996) • **89**

Petite Sirah Napa Valley 1996: Massive, dense and earthy, with lots of tannin, wild berry, earth, sage, mineral and spice, finishing with a chewy aftertaste. Needs time, though. Drink now through 2006.–J.L. • $22 • (4/30/1999) • **91**

Petite Sirah Napa Valley 1995 • $22 • (4/30/1998) • **85**

Petite Sirah Napa Valley 1993 • $17 • (5/15/1996) • **89**

Key: SS—Spectator Selection. CS—Cellar Selection. HR—Highly Recommended. $NA—Price not available. (BT)—Barrel tasting. Ⓐ—Auction Price.
For a key to the tasters' initials, see "How to Use These Listings."
Dates in parentheses represent the issues in which the ratings were published.

ROEDERER ESTATE | CALIFORNIA

Brut Anderson Valley NV: A delicious California sparkler with rich and toasty aromas up front, and a follow-up that features focused and complex lemon, grapefruit, herb, green apple and pear flavors. It's bright and clean on the finish, quite refreshing. Drink now through 2002. • $19 • (9/15/1999) SS • **90**

Brut Anderson Valley L'Ermitage 1993: Rich toasty aromas lead off, introducing a muscularly structured California bubbly that features a fine blend of citrus, hazelnut, spice and green apple flavors. Despite its power, it has plenty of finesse, finishing crisp and clean, with a lingering touch of lemon-lime. Drink now through 2004. • $38 • (10/15/1999) HR • **93**

Brut Anderson Valley L'Ermitage 1992 • $33 • (11/30/1997) • **90**

Brut Anderson Valley L'Ermitage 1991 • $35 • (11/30/1996) • **91**

Brut Anderson Valley L'Ermitage 1990 • $35 • (12/31/1995) • **90**

Brut Rosé Anderson Valley NV: Fairly rich-textured, with toasty citrus and herb flavors and subtle cherry highlights. Tangy acidity paves the way for a long finish that's clean and refreshing. Drink now. • $24 • (10/15/1999) • **89**

ROLIN, NICOLAS | OREGON

Pinot Noir Willamette Valley 1994 • $27 • (2/28/1997) • **89**

ROLLING HILLS | CALIFORNIA

Tempranillo California Pagor 1997: Medium-bodied, full of black pepper and tobacco notes, with plummy flavors and a nice finish. Would be fun with tapas. Drink now through 2004.–J.L. • $10 • (4/30/2000) • **85**

ROMBAUER | CALIFORNIA

Cabernet Franc Napa Valley 1994 • $20 • (12/15/1997) • **79**

Cabernet Franc Napa Valley 1990 • $16 • (7/15/1993) • **87**

Cabernet Sauvignon Napa Valley 1996: Densely structured, with tightly wound black currant, blackberry, smoke, chocolate and herb notes. Firm yet smooth on the palate, with a finish that lets the flavors linger. Best from 2001 through 2008. • $30 • (11/15/1999) • **90**

Cabernet Sauvignon Napa Valley 1995: Elegant, with supple cedar, plum and black cherry flavors of polish and finesse. Drink now.–J.L. • $NA • (10/31/1998) • **88**

Cabernet Sauvignon Napa Valley 1994 • $27 • (11/15/1997) • **87**

Cabernet Sauvignon Napa Valley 1993 • $27 • (12/15/1996) • **85**

Cabernet Sauvignon Napa Valley 1991 • $20 • (12/15/1995) • **84**

Cabernet Sauvignon Napa Valley 1990 • $18 • (11/15/1994) • **86**

Cabernet Sauvignon Napa Valley 1989 • $15 • (11/15/1993) • **78**

Cabernet Sauvignon Napa Valley 1987 • $16 • (12/15/1997) • **85**

Cabernet Sauvignon Napa Valley 1986 • $18 • (4/15/1990) • **88**

Cabernet Sauvignon Napa Valley 1985 • $20 • (4/30/1989) • **85**

Cabernet Sauvignon Napa Valley 1984 • $14 • (2/15/1988) • **80**

Cabernet Sauvignon Napa Valley 1983 • $14 • (9/15/1987) • **73**

Cabernet Sauvignon Napa Valley 1982 • $13 • (2/16/1986) • **91**

Cabernet Sauvignon Napa Valley 1981 • $13 • (12/16/1984) • **88**

Cabernet Sauvignon Napa Valley Diamond Mountain Selection 1994 • $50 • (11/15/1997) • **90**

Chardonnay Carneros 1997: Smooth, ripe and creamy on the palate, this outstanding bottle of California Chardonnay presents a pretty array of complex pear, peach, vanilla, hazelnut and spicy nuances that are bright, rich and well focused through the finish. Drink now through 2001.–J.L. • $26 • (12/15/1998) SS • **92**

Chardonnay Carneros 1996 • $26 • (1/01/1998) • **91**

Le Meilleur du Chai Napa Valley 1992: A big style, earthy, with spicy anise, currant and berry flavors that are disjointed now; may need more time. A blend of Cabernet Sauvignon, Merlot and Cabernet Franc. Drink through 2004.–J.L. • $50 • (10/31/1998) • **87**

Le Meilleur du Chai Napa Valley 1990 • $40 • (8/31/1997) • **90**

Le Meilleur du Chai Napa Valley 1989 • $35 • (12/15/1995) • **84**

Le Meilleur du Chai Napa Valley 1987 • $35 • (11/15/1993) • **83**

Le Meilleur du Chai Napa Valley 1986 • $NA • (12/15/1996) • **83**

Le Meilleur du Chai Napa Valley 1985 • $48 • (10/31/1989) • **90**

Le Meilleur du Chai Napa Valley 1984 • $34 Ⓐ • (3/31/1989) • **94**

Merlot Napa Valley 1996: Supple and harmonious, with complex cherry, currant, herb, anise and sage flavors that fold together nicely. Supple tannins. Drink now through 2003.–J.L. • $26 • (5/31/1999) • **88**

Merlot Napa Valley 1995: Weaves together plenty of attractive currant, black cherry, plum and spice. Finishes with good length, nice oak nuances, firm

tannins and enough fruit to merit short-term cellaring. Drink through 2004.–J.L. • $25 • (9/30/1998) • **88**
Merlot Napa Valley 1994 • $25 • (6/30/1997) • **88**
Merlot Napa Valley 1993 • $20 • (7/31/1996) • **88**
Merlot Napa Valley 1991 • $20 • (3/15/1994) • **82**
Merlot Napa Valley 1990 • $16 • (7/15/1993) • **84**
Merlot Napa Valley 1989 • $16 • (11/15/1991) • **84**
Merlot Napa Valley 1987 • $14 • (2/15/1990) • **87**
Merlot Napa Valley 1986 • $14 • (7/31/1989) • **78**
Zinfandel Napa Valley 1996 • $20 • (5/31/1998) • **86**
Zinfandel Napa Valley 1995 • $20 • (6/15/1998) • **90**
Zinfandel Napa Valley 1994 • $20 • (3/31/1997) • **89**
Zinfandel Napa Valley 1993 • $18 • (7/31/1995) • **88**

ROSENBLUM | CALIFORNIA

Black Muscat California 1995 • $9/375 ml. • (11/30/1996) • **85**
Cabernet Sauvignon Napa Valley 1989 • $17 • (8/31/1992) • **80**
Cabernet Sauvignon Napa Valley George Hendry Vineyard 1990 • $14 • (11/15/1993) • **84**
Cabernet Sauvignon Napa Valley George Hendry Vineyard Reserve 1995 • $40 • (5/31/1998) • **88**
Cabernet Sauvignon Napa Valley George Hendry Vineyard Reserve 1991 • $30 • (11/15/1994) • **88**
Cabernet Sauvignon Napa Valley Holbrook Mitchell Vineyard 1997: Ripe and flavorful, with rich black cherry, plum, cedar and anise character. Finishes with firm, chunky tannins. Drink now through 2005.–J.L. • $35 • (9/30/1999) • **87**
Cabernet Sauvignon Napa Valley Holbrook Mitchell Vineyard 1996: Lean in structure, with blackberry and currant flavors shaded by earthy, spicy, tomatolike tones. Drink now.–H.S. • $32 • (10/31/1998) • **85**
Cabernet Sauvignon Napa Valley Holbrook Mitchell Vineyard 1995 • $30 • (4/30/1998) • **89**
Cabernet Sauvignon Napa Valley Holbrook Mitchell Vineyard 1991 • $14 • (10/31/1994) HR • **90**
Cabernet Sauvignon Napa Valley Yountville Vineyards 1994 • $20 • (11/30/1996) • **85**
Carignane Napa Valley Kenefick Ranch 1995 • $15 • (12/15/1997) • **87**
Carignane Napa Valley TLK Ranch 1994 • $11 • (11/30/1996) • **83**
Chardonnay Edna Valley 1998: Licorice, apple and vanilla flavors have moderate concentration. Drink now.–J.L. • $19 • (6/15/2000) • **82**
Chardonnay Edna Valley 1997: Pretty, with ripe pear and citrus notes. Well balanced, with good acidity. Added complexity appears on the long finish, which is bright, clean and tinged with herbal nuance. Drink now. • $23 • (6/30/1999) • **89**
Chardonnay Edna Valley 1996 • $24 • (12/15/1997) • **87**
Chardonnay Russian River Valley Lone Oak Vineyard Reserve 1998: Round, with ripe flavors of peach, pear and butter. Drink now.–J.L. • $24 • (6/15/2000) • **87**
Chardonnay Russian River Valley Lone Oak Vineyard Reserve 1997: Rich and spicy, with tiers of fig, nectarine, pear, apricot and toasty oak combining to give this wine a deeply concentrated flavor. Drink now through 2002.–J.L. • $28 • (4/30/1999) • **91**
Gewürztraminer California 1996 • $10 • (11/30/1997) • **86**
Holbrook Mitchell Trio Napa Valley 1996: Crisply styled, with tight acidity and tannins, and a narrow beam of good cherry and berry. Turns simple on the finish. 74 percent Cabernet Sauvignon, 18 percent Merlot, 8 percent Cabernet Franc. Drink now through 2002.–J.L. • $35 • (10/31/1998) • **85**
Holbrook Mitchell Trio Napa Valley 1995 • $35 • (4/30/1998) • **88**
Holbrook Mitchell Trio Napa Valley 1994 • $24 • (11/30/1996) • **88**
Holbrook Mitchell Trio Napa Valley 1993 • $23 • (12/15/1995) • **80**
Holbrook Mitchell Trio Napa Valley 1992 • $23 • (11/15/1994) • **85**
Holbrook Mitchell Trio Napa Valley 1991 • $22 • (11/15/1993) • **86**
Holbrook Mitchell Trio Napa Valley 1990 • $22 • (11/15/1992) • **87**
Merlot Napa Valley 1997: Light-bodied, with pleasant cherry, berry and tea flavors. Finishes with mild tannins. Drink now through 2002.–H.S. • $12 • (10/15/1999) • **84**
Merlot Napa Valley Holbrook Mitchell Vineyard 1989 • $20 • (5/31/1992) • **80**
Merlot Russian River Valley Lone Oak Vineyard 1997: Features ripe, juicy raspberry jam, black cherry and spice flavors. Turns simple, with mint and cedar. Drink now through 2004.–J.L. • $18 • (6/15/2000) • **86**
Merlot Russian River Valley Lone Oak Vineyard 1996: Chocolate, plum and herbal flavors with an earthy, tarry edge. Tannins are mildly drying and it shows some heat on the finish. Drink now.–J.L. • $21 • (12/15/1998) • **83**
Merlot Russian River Valley Lone Oak Vineyard 1995 • $20 • (3/31/1998) • **88**
Merlot Russian River Valley Lone Oak Vineyard 1990 • $15 • (7/15/1993) • **81**
Merlot Russian River Valley Lone Oak Vineyard 1989 • $14 • (5/31/1992) • **85**
Mourvèdre Contra Costa County Chateau La Paws Côte du Bone 1997: Leads off with enticing earth and plum aromas. On the palate, this silky wine serves up a fruity blend of raspberry, currant, cinnamon and spice flavors that linger nicely on the long yet clean finish. Delicious now for its freshness. • $10 • (1/31/1999) • **88**
Mourvèdre Contra Costa County Chateau La Paws Côte du Bone 1996 • $13 • (11/30/1997) • **85**
Mourvèdre Contra Costa County Chateau La Paws Côte du Bone 1995 • $10 • (11/30/1996) • **87**
Palomino Contra Costa County Fleur de Hoof 1996 • $8 • (3/31/1998) • **83**
Petite Sirah Napa Valley 1992 • $13 • (9/30/1995) • **86**
Petite Sirah Napa Valley Kenefick Ranch 1996: Supple and complex, with bright, chewy plum, wild berry, black cherry, plum and strawberry flavors that are rich, lively and long on the finish, even with this tannin level. Drink through 2005.–J.L. • $18 • (8/31/1998) • **90**
Petite Sirah Napa Valley Kenefick Ranch 1995 • $17 • (7/31/1997) • **88**
Petite Sirah Napa Valley Palisades Vineyard 1994 • $15 • (11/30/1996) • **87**
Petite Sirah Napa Valley Pickett Road 1998: Hits nice high notes, with black cherry, blackberry and cedar notes, turning dry and tannic. Drink now through 2004.–J.L. • $20 • (6/15/2000) • **87**
Pinot Noir Napa Valley George Hendry Vineyard 1990 • $12 • (2/28/1993) • **73**
Pinot Noir Russian River Valley Ellis Ranch 1991 • $10 • (2/28/1994) • **80**
Port California 1994 • $15 • (4/30/1997) • **88**
Sauvignon Blanc Napa Valley Late Harvest Concento d'Oro 1991 • $15/375 ml. • (11/30/1996) • **79**
Sémillon Livermore Valley Reserve 1997: Opens with a brisk nutty quality, with a nice follow-up of intricate mineral, grapefruit, herb and spice flavors. Quite elegant, with a long finish. Drink now through 2001. • $15 • (6/15/1999) • **89**
Sémillon Sonoma Valley 1996 • $14 • (9/15/1997) • **87**
Sémillon-Chardonnay Livermore Valley 1996 • $11 • (9/15/1997) • **84**
Sparkling Gewürztraminer Sonoma County 1996 • $15 • (5/15/1998) • **79**
Zinfandel Alexander Valley Harris Kratka Vineyard 1998: Refreshingly fruity, with pretty cherry, raspberry and blackberry flavors that are deftly balanced. Complex aftertaste. Drink now through 2005.–J.L. • $24 • (6/15/2000) • **87**
Zinfandel Alexander Valley Harris Kratka Vineyard 1997: Smooth, ripe and rich in flavor, with a complex array of black cherry, plum, wild berry and spice, finishing with a cascade of flavors. Drink now.–J.L. • $23 • (5/15/1999) • **91**
Zinfandel Alexander Valley Harris Kratka Vineyard 1996 • $22 • (6/15/1998) • **88**
Zinfandel Alexander Valley Harris Kratka Vineyard 1995 • $20 • (8/31/1997) • **92**
Zinfandel Alexander Valley Harris Kratka Vineyard 1994 • $16 • (9/30/1996) • **87**
Zinfandel Alexander Valley Harris Kratka Vineyard 1993 • $15 • (10/15/1995) • **83**
Zinfandel California Millennium Vintners Cuvée MM NV: Hot and a bit raw, with depth to the berry liqueur flavors. Drink now.–J.L. • $10 • (5/15/2000) • **80**
Zinfandel California Vintners Cuvée XVII NV: Ripe and juicy, lively and well balanced, with an appealing character of plum, cherry, berry and spice—quite enjoyable. Contains 10 percent Merlot. Drink now.–J.L. • $10 • (5/31/1999) • **86**
Zinfandel California Vintners Cuvée XVI NV • $10 • (6/15/1998) • **86**
Zinfandel California Vintners Cuvée XIV NV • $10 • (3/31/1997) • **88**
Zinfandel California Vintners Cuvée X NV • $8 • (10/15/1995) • **83**
Zinfandel California Vintners Cuvée IX NV • $8 • (10/15/1994) • **81**
Zinfandel California Vintners Cuvée VI NV • $8 • (9/30/1993) • **85**
Zinfandel California Vintners Cuvée V NV • $8 • (10/15/1992) • **82**
Zinfandel California Vintners Cuvée IV NV • $7 • (10/15/1992) • **84**
Zinfandel Contra Costa County 1998: Plum and strawberry flavors are round and straightforward. Drink now through 2004.–J.L. • $13 • (5/15/2000) • **84**
Zinfandel Contra Costa County 1996 • $15 • (5/15/1998) • **83**
Zinfandel Contra Costa County 1995 • $14 • (6/30/1997) • **89**
Zinfandel Contra Costa County 1994 • $11 • (4/30/1996) • **89**
Zinfandel Contra Costa County 1993 • $11 • (9/30/1995) • **86**
Zinfandel Contra Costa County 1992 • $10 • (10/15/1994) • **83**
Zinfandel Contra Costa County 1991 • $10 • (9/30/1993) • **90**
Zinfandel Contra Costa County 1990 • $10 • (10/15/1992) • **87**
Zinfandel Contra Costa County Carla's Vineyard 1997: Well crafted, with ripe, up-front cherry, wild berry, plum and spicy notes that are appealing, if lacking in extra depth. Drink now.–J.L. • $21 • (6/30/1999) • **87**
Zinfandel Contra Costa County Continente Vineyard 1997: Juicy, with ripe plum, tar, anise, sage and wild berry flavors that are supple and polished. Long, complex aftertaste. Drink now through 2004.–J.L. • $16 • (5/31/1999) • **90**

Zinfandel Contra Costa County Continente Vineyard Old Old Vine 1996 • $20 • (6/15/1998) • **83**
Zinfandel Contra Costa County Continente Vineyard Old Old Vine 1995 • $18 • (6/30/1997) • **88**
Zinfandel Contra Costa County Pato Vineyard Reserve 1996 • $19 • (6/15/1998) • **85**
Zinfandel Contra Costa County Pato Vineyard Reserve 1995 • $18 • (6/30/1997) • **88**
Zinfandel Dry Creek Valley Rockpile Vineyard 1996 • $18 • (6/15/1998) • **86**
Zinfandel Howell Mountain White Cottage Vineyard 1996 • $21 • (6/15/1998) • **86**
Zinfandel Mount Veeder Brandlin Ranch 1996 • $23 • (6/15/1998) • **91**
Zinfandel Mount Veeder Brandlin Ranch 1995 • $23 • (9/30/1997) • **89**
Zinfandel Mount Veeder Brandlin Ranch 1994 • $20 • (9/30/1996) • **92**
Zinfandel Mount Veeder Brandlin Ranch 1993 • $19 • (10/15/1995) • **87**
Zinfandel Mount Veeder Brandlin Ranch 1992 • $19 • (10/15/1994) • **86**
Zinfandel Mount Veeder Brandlin Ranch 1991: Earthy, with gamy Zinfandel flavors, turning cheesy on the finish. (Zinfandel retrospective tasting). Past its prime.–J.L. • $15 • (6/30/1999) • **78**
Zinfandel Napa Valley 1995 • $18 • (4/30/1998) • **89**
Zinfandel Napa Valley 1994 • $14 • (2/28/1997) • **84**
Zinfandel Napa Valley 1993 • $14 • (4/30/1996) • **87**
Zinfandel Napa Valley Ballentine Vineyard 1996 • $19 • (6/15/1998) • **84**
Zinfandel Napa Valley George Hendry Vineyard 1991: There's a shade more fruit to this than to the other Rosenblum Zins, with plum and blackberry flavors, turning dry and tannic on the finish. (Zinfandel retrospective tasting). Drink now.–J.L. • $30 • (6/30/1999) • **87**
Zinfandel Napa Valley George Hendry Vineyard 1989 • $13 • (10/15/1992) • **84**
Zinfandel Napa Valley Hendry Vineyard Reserve 1997: A streak of complex earthiness runs through this candied red cherry- and plum-laced wine, turning elegant and supple, with polished tannins. Best from 2001 through 2007.–J.L. • $30 • (3/31/2000) • **88**
Zinfandel Napa Valley Hendry Vineyard Reserve 1996 • $26 • (6/15/1998) • **88**
Zinfandel Napa Valley Hendry Vineyard Reserve 1995 • $25 • (4/30/1998) • **90**
Zinfandel Napa Valley Hendry Vineyard Reserve 1994 • $24 • (3/31/1997) • **89**
Zinfandel Napa Valley George Hendry Vineyard Reserve 1993 • $22 • (4/30/1996) • **90**
Zinfandel Napa Valley George Hendry Vineyard Reserve 1992 • $20 • (10/15/1994) • **86**
Zinfandel Napa Valley George Hendry Vineyard Reserve 1991: Austere, drying out and picking up a waxy flavor, it's not showing much in the way of fruit. Hints of dark berry emerge on the tannic finish. (Zinfandel retrospective tasting). Past its prime.–J.L. • $NA • (6/30/1999) • **84**
Zinfandel Napa Valley Hendry Vineyard Reserve 1988 • $14 • (4/30/1991) • **84**
Zinfandel Napa Valley Michael Marston Vineyard 1990 • $14 • (10/15/1992) • **84**
Zinfandel Paso Robles Richard Sauret Vineyard 1997: Lots of up-front, ripe, juicy cherry and wild berry flavors in a smooth, supple style. Drink now.–J.L. • $18 • (6/30/1999) • **86**
Zinfandel Paso Robles Richard Sauret Vineyard 1996 • $17 • (5/15/1998) • **88**
Zinfandel Paso Robles Richard Sauret Vineyard 1995 • $16 • (6/30/1997) • **88**
Zinfandel Paso Robles Richard Sauret Vineyard 1994 • $12 • (4/30/1996) • **87**
Zinfandel Paso Robles Richard Sauret Vineyard 1993 • $12 • (9/30/1995) • **88**
Zinfandel Paso Robles Richard Sauret Vineyard 1992 • $11 • (10/15/1994) • **87**
Zinfandel Paso Robles Richard Sauret Vineyard 1991: Tarry, earthy and gamy, this has lost its fruitiness. Finishes with drying, coarse tannins. (Zinfandel retrospective tasting). Past its prime.–J.L. • $11 • (6/30/1999) • **79**
Zinfandel Paso Robles Richard Sauret Vineyard 1990 • $10 • (10/15/1992) • **87**
Zinfandel Redwood Valley Rhodes Vineyard Annette's Reserve 1996 • $22 • (6/15/1998) • **89**
Zinfandel Redwood Valley Rhodes Vineyard Annette's Reserve 1995 • $19 • (12/15/1997) • **84**
Zinfandel Russian River Valley Alegria Vineyard 1997: Ripe and juicy, with lots of complex black cherry, wild berry, plum and raspberry, finishing with a supple texture and fine tannins. Drink now through 2006.–J.L. • $25 • (12/15/1999) • **90**
Zinfandel San Francisco Bay Carla's Vineyard 1998: Focused cola and plum flavors are nice, but the tannins get a little rough on the finish. Drink now through 2003.–J.L. • $22 • (5/15/2000) • **85**

Key: SS—Spectator Selection. CS—Cellar Selection. HR—Highly Recommended. $NA—Price not available. (BT)—Barrel tasting. (A)—Auction Price. For a key to the tasters' initials, see "How to Use These Listings."
Dates in parentheses represent the issues in which the ratings were published.

Zinfandel San Francisco Bay Continente Vineyard 1998: Pleasantly fruity, with tasty plum and wild berry flavors that turn murky on the finish. Drink now.–J.L. • $16 • (6/15/2000) • **85**
Zinfandel Sonoma County 1991: Drying out, with edgy tannins, there's a core of juicy plum and cherry that loses its intensity on the finish. (Zinfandel retrospective tasting). Drink now.–J.L. • $12 • (6/30/1999) • **84**
Zinfandel Sonoma County 1990 • $12 • (9/30/1992) HR • **90**
Zinfandel Sonoma County Old Vines 1995 • $18 • (6/30/1997) • **89**
Zinfandel Sonoma County Old Vines 1994 • $13 • (9/30/1996) • **88**
Zinfandel Sonoma County Old Vines 1993 • $13 • (9/30/1995) • **88**
Zinfandel Sonoma County Old Vines 1992 • $12 • (10/15/1994) • **85**
Zinfandel Sonoma County St. Peters Church Vineyard 1996 • $20 • (6/15/1998) • **89**
Zinfandel Sonoma Valley Cullinane Vineyard 1996 • $23 • (6/15/1998) • **87**
Zinfandel Sonoma Valley Samsel Vineyard Maggie's Reserve 1997: Intense and vibrant, with sharply focused black cherry, wild berry, raspberry and plum, finishing with tight tannins. Drink through 2006.–J.L. • $30 • (11/30/1999) • **88**
Zinfandel Sonoma Valley Samsel Vineyard Maggie's Reserve 1996 • $28 • (6/15/1998) • **88**
Zinfandel Sonoma Valley Samsel Vineyard Maggie's Reserve 1995 • $25 • (9/30/1997) • **92**
Zinfandel Sonoma Valley Samsel Vineyard Maggie's Reserve 1994 • $24 • (9/30/1996) • **89**
Zinfandel Sonoma Valley Samsel Vineyard Maggie's Reserve 1993 • $22 • (9/30/1995) • **89**
Zinfandel Sonoma Valley Samsel Vineyard Maggie's Reserve 1992 • $22 • (10/15/1994) • **87**
Zinfandel Sonoma Valley Samsel Vineyard Maggie's Reserve 1991 • $16 • (9/30/1993) • **91**
Zinfandel Sonoma Valley Samsel Vineyard Maggie's Reserve 1990 • $19 (A) • (10/15/1992) • **90**

ROSENTHAL-THE MALIBU ESTATE | CALIFORNIA

Cabernet Sauvignon California 1995: Smoky, with spicy, meaty cherry, wild berry and plummy flavors that are elegant and refined. Finishes with firm tannins and good length. Best from 2001 through 2006.–J.L. • $24 • (9/15/1999) • **87**
Cabernet Sauvignon California 1992 • $22 • (12/15/1995) • **89**
Cabernet Sauvignon California 1991 • $20 • (11/15/1994) • **91**
Cabernet Sauvignon Malibu-Newton Canyon 1996: Tight, with stewed plum, berry and vegetal notes, it's intense and tannic, with a red bell pepper aftertaste. Best from 2002 through 2010.–J.L. • $35 • (5/15/2000) • **84**
Cabernet Sauvignon Malibu-Newton Canyon 1994 • $25 • (5/15/1998) • **90**
Cabernet Sauvignon Malibu-Newton Canyon 1993 • $22 • (1/31/1997) • **84**
Chardonnay Malibu-Newton Canyon 1997: Intense and somewhat chunky, with toasty oak dominating the core of citrus, pear and baked apple flavors. Loses its focus on the finish, though it's very impressive for the first Chardonnay from this appellation and this winery. Drink now through 2002.–J.L. • $20 • (7/31/1999) • **87**
Merlot Malibu-Newton Canyon The Devon Vineyard 1996: Pleasantly earthy, with hints of cherry, currant and cranberry. Turns smooth and polished, with a complex finish. Drink now through 2004.–J.L. • $28 • (10/15/1999) • **87**

ROSS VALLEY | CALIFORNIA

Merlot Sonoma Valley 1992 • $13 • (8/31/1996) • **82**
Zinfandel Russian River Valley Tom and Kelly Parsons' Vineyard 1993 • $12 • (5/15/1996) • **83**
Zinfandel Sonoma County Tom and Kelley Parsons' Vineyard 1988 • $11 • (8/31/1991) • **83**

ROUND HILL | CALIFORNIA

Cabernet Sauvignon California 1995 • $8 • (5/31/1998) • **85**
Cabernet Sauvignon California 1993 • $8 • (4/30/1997) • **83**
Cabernet Sauvignon California 1992 • $7 • (12/15/1995) • **83**
Cabernet Sauvignon California 1991 • $7 • (11/15/1994) • **80**
Cabernet Sauvignon California 1990 • $7 • (5/31/1994) • **84**
Cabernet Sauvignon California 1989 • $6 • (12/15/1992) • **82**
Cabernet Sauvignon California House Lot 89 NV • $6 • (11/15/1992) • **80**
Cabernet Sauvignon California House Lot 8 NV • $6 • (7/31/1991) • **79**
Cabernet Sauvignon California House Lot 7 NV • $6 • (10/31/1990) • **79**
Cabernet Sauvignon California House Lot 6 NV • $5 • (10/15/1987) • **72**

Cabernet Sauvignon California House Lot 5 NV • $5 • (9/30/1986) • **76**
Cabernet Sauvignon Napa Valley 1993 • $12 • (2/28/1997) • **84**
Cabernet Sauvignon Napa Valley 1992 • $12 • (12/15/1995) • **85**
Cabernet Sauvignon Napa Valley 1988 • $9 • (11/15/1991) • **81**
Cabernet Sauvignon Napa Valley Reserve 1990 • $11 • (11/15/1994) • **84**
Cabernet Sauvignon Napa Valley Reserve 1989 • $11 • (11/15/1994) • **83**
Cabernet Sauvignon Napa Valley Reserve 1988 • $10 • (2/15/1993) • **75**
Cabernet Sauvignon Napa Valley Reserve 1987 • $11 • (11/15/1991) • **77**
Cabernet Sauvignon Napa Valley Reserve 1985 • $11 • (5/31/1988) • **86**
Cabernet Sauvignon Napa Valley Reserve 1984 • $10 • (10/31/1987) • **88**
Cabernet Sauvignon Napa Valley Signature Reserve 1990 • $20 • (9/15/1996) • **85**
Chardonnay California 1998: Dilute, with the suggestion of lemon-lime flavors.–J.L. • $8 • (6/30/2000) • **79**
Chardonnay California 1997: Simple, with a mineral and citrus focus. Drink now. • $7 • (2/28/1999) • **81**
Chardonnay California 1996: Decidedly citrusy, with grapefruit, spice and toast flavors on a light frame. Drink now.–J.L. • $8 • (11/15/1998) • **81**
Merlot California 1996: Plum and spice flavors are dominated by tarry oak. Finishes simple, with a green, bitter note. Drink now.–J.L. • $7 • (2/28/1999) • **80**
Merlot California 1995 • $9 • (12/31/1997) • **83**
Merlot California 1994 • $8 • (8/31/1996) • **82**
Merlot California 1993 • $8 • (8/31/1996) • **80**
Merlot California 1992 • $7 • (9/15/1994) • **77**
Merlot California 1990 • $7 • (1/31/1993) • **84**
Merlot Napa Valley 1994 • $12 • (4/30/1997) • **85**
Merlot Napa Valley 1993 • $14 • (8/31/1996) • **80**
Merlot Napa Valley Reserve 1991 • $11 • (9/15/1994) • **78**
Merlot Napa Valley Reserve 1990 • $11 • (6/15/1993) • **78**
Merlot Napa Valley Reserve 1989 • $11 • (5/31/1992) • **78**
Merlot Napa Valley Reserve 1988 • $11 • (11/15/1991) • **80**
Merlot Napa Valley Reserve 1986 • $11 • (12/31/1988) • **82**
Merlot Napa Valley Reserve 1985 • $10 • (5/31/1988) • **84**
Zinfandel California 1997: Simple, with delicate spice, cola and strawberry flavors and a soft finish.–J.L. • $8 • (11/15/1999) • **79**
Zinfandel Napa Valley 1993 • $10 • (3/31/1996) • **83**
Zinfandel Napa Valley 1992 • $8 • (10/15/1995) • **85**
Zinfandel Napa Valley 1990 • $6 • (10/15/1992) • **85**
Zinfandel Napa Valley 1989 • $6 • (3/31/1992) • **81**
Zinfandel Napa Valley 1988 • $7 • (2/15/1991) • **89**

ROWLAND | CALIFORNIA

Cabernet Sauvignon Napa Valley Red Triangle 1997: Tough, with an herbal green bean streak running through. Turns dirty. Not much hope for improvement.–J.L. • $22 • (5/31/2000) • **76**
Cabernet Sauvignon Napa Valley Red Triangle 1996: Unusual, with decadent, earthy herb, sage, plum and mineral flavors. Finishes with firm, well-integrated tannins. Drink now through 2006.–J.L. • $22 • (10/15/1999) • **86**
Pinot Noir Atlas Peak 1995: Firm but flavorful, with earthy tea, anise and herb notes balanced by tart cherry and vanilla flavors. Finishes with grainy tannins. Drink now through 2002.–H.S. • $22 • (4/30/1999) • **82**
Syrah Napa Valley Red Triangle 1998: Focused raspberry, spice and semisweet chocolate flavors, with drying tannins on the finish. Drink now through 2005.–J.L. • $22 • (5/31/2000) • **84**
Syrah Napa Valley Red Triangle 1997: Rustic and flavorful, with ripe and spicy blackberry, meaty mineral and smoky tea notes. Tannins are ripe and soft, letting the complex flavors push through on the finish. Drink now through 2002.–J.L. • $22 • (4/30/1999) • **87**

RUBISSOW-SARGENT | CALIFORNIA

Cabernet Sauvignon-Merlot Mount Veeder Les Trompettes 1992 • $22 • (11/15/1997) • **88**
Cabernet Franc-Merlot Mount Veeder Les Trompettes 1993: Tight, tart and earthy, with a narrow beam of berry flavor that turns sharp and tannic on the finish. Cellaring might help. Drink through 2006.–J.L. • $23 • (2/28/1999) • **82**
Cabernet Franc-Merlot Mount Veeder Les Trompettes 1990 • $18 • (11/15/1994) • **85**
Cabernet Franc-Merlot Mount Veeder Les Trompettes 1989 • $18 • (11/15/1994) • **79**
Cabernet Sauvignon Mount Veeder 1997: Awkward, with a slight vinegary edge to the murky currant, earth, herb and mineral, turning dry and tannic. Drink now through 2005.–J.L. • $30 • (6/15/2000) • **84**
Cabernet Sauvignon Mount Veeder 1996: Lean and tight, with crisp cherry, earthy and herbal flavors, finishing with light but firm tannins. Drink through 2005.–H.S. • $23 • (9/15/1999) • **85**
Cabernet Sauvignon Mount Veeder 1994: Earthy flavors and just a hint of berry highlight this ruggedly tannic wine. Drink through 2008.–J.L. • $21 • (2/28/1999) • **82**
Cabernet Sauvignon Mount Veeder 1993: A dark, firm and somewhat tannic wine that harbors licorice, black currant, black cherry, herb and spice flavors. Will perhaps soften with time. Drink through 2004. • $20 • (11/15/1998) • **86**
Cabernet Sauvignon Mount Veeder 1992 • $19 • (11/15/1997) • **88**
Cabernet Sauvignon Mount Veeder 1991 • $16 • (12/15/1995) • **84**
Cabernet Sauvignon Mount Veeder 1990 • $16 • (11/15/1994) • **84**
Cabernet Sauvignon Mount Veeder 1988 • $16 • (4/15/1992) • **87**
Merlot Mount Veeder 1997: Green and bitter, with sour cherry and ash flavors.–J.L. • $28 • (6/15/2000) • **77**
Merlot Mount Veeder 1996: Restrained and trim, with a narrow band of tea, earth, currant and herb flavors, finishing with dry tannins. Drink now through 2002. • $22 • (10/15/1999) • **81**
Merlot Mount Veeder 1994 • $21 • (7/31/1997) • **86**
Merlot Mount Veeder 1992 • $16 • (5/15/1996) • **85**
Merlot Mount Veeder 1990 • $15 • (9/15/1994) • **86**
Merlot Mount Veeder 1989 • $15 • (8/31/1993) • **76**
Merlot Mount Veeder 1988 • $15 • (5/31/1992) • **84**

RUDD ESTATE | CALIFORNIA

Cabernet Sauvignon Napa Valley Jericho Canyon Vineyard 1998: Firm, rich, detailed and focused, built around a core of earthy, cedary currant and blackberry flavors, finishing with a long, rich aftertaste.–J.L. • $NA • (8/31/1999) (BT) • **90-94**

RUNQUIST, J. | CALIFORNIA

Zinfandel Amador County Z Massoni Ranch 1996 • $18 • (6/15/1998) • **84**

RUSACK | CALIFORNIA

Anacapa Santa Ynez Valley 1997: Curious aromas of blackberry jam and jalapeño peppers. Despite the pungently vegetal overtones, it offers full-bodied wild berry flavors. Drink now through 2005.–J.L. • $32 • (4/30/2000) • **80**

RUSSELL, ERICH | CALIFORNIA

Merlot Sonoma County 1997: Firm and focused, with a tasty band of currant, cedar, anise and spice. Drink now.–J.L. • $23 • (6/15/2000) • **86**

RUSSIAN HILL | CALIFORNIA

Merlot Napa Valley 1996: Shows lots of roasted nut, caramel and toasted oak flavors, with hints of dill, black cherry and cassis. Firmly structured, with a flavorful finish and mild tannins. Drink now through 2004. • $20 • (10/15/1999) • **86**
Pinot Noir Russian River Valley Reserve 1998: Has pretty cherry and cinnamon notes, with overtones of earth and funk. Drink now through 2002.–J.L. • $30 • (5/15/2000) • **84**
Syrah Russian River Valley 1997: Chocolate, black cherry and cola notes are nicely integrated with roasted coffee flavors that linger on the moderately tannic finish. Drink now through 2004.–J.L. • $18 • (5/31/2000) • **85**
Zinfandel Russian River Valley Reserve 1997: Rich, with almost overripe flavors of black cherry and plum that linger. Drink now through 2004.–J.L. • $23 • (5/15/2000) • **87**

RUSTRIDGE | CALIFORNIA

Cabernet Sauvignon Napa Valley 1996: Has an herbal edge to the cherry, cranberry and currant flavors, finishing with mild tannins. Drink now through 2003.–J.L. • $30 • (10/15/1999) • **82**
Cabernet Sauvignon Napa Valley 1995: Powdery tannins tend to stunt the blackberry, coffee and herb flavors, but this still reveals harmony. Drink through 2004. • $22 • (10/15/1998) • **84**
Cabernet Sauvignon Napa Valley 1991 • $20 • (12/15/1995) • **87**
Cabernet Sauvignon Napa Valley 1990 • $30 • (12/15/1995) • **82**
Zinfandel Napa Valley 1996 • $18 • (6/15/1998) • **84**

■ ■ ■ ■

RUSTRIDGE

Zinfandel-Cabernet Napa Valley 1991 • $18 • (9/30/1993) • **82**

Merlot Napa Valley XVS Reserve 1992 • $21 • (6/15/1995) • **85**

RUTHERFORD ESTATE | CALIFORNIA

Cabernet Sauvignon Napa Valley 1992 • $7 • (11/30/1996) • **77**
Cabernet Sauvignon Napa Valley 1991 • $7 • (11/15/1994) • **81**
Merlot Napa Valley 1991 • $7 • (6/30/1994) • **84**
Pinot Noir Napa Valley 1992 • $7 • (1/31/1995) • **81**

RUTHERFORD GROVE | CALIFORNIA

Cabernet Sauvignon Napa Valley 1995: Smooth and ripe, with an interesting streak of exotic spices and fig flavors running through the open-textured blackberry and black cherry character. Harmonious. Drink now through 2002.–H.S. • $25 • (10/31/1998) • **87**
Cabernet Sauvignon Napa Valley 1993 • $20 • (11/30/1996) • **87**
Chardonnay Napa Valley 1997: Elegant, featuring grapefruit, mild toasted oak, light cinnamon and fig notes. Drink now through 2002.–J.L. • $25 • (11/15/1999) • **85**
Merlot Napa Valley 1996: Flavors run to earthy, with a sage and juniper edge, turning soft and seamless with ripe, lingering notes of cherry, plum and herb. Tannins are integrated. Drink now.–J.L. • $23 • (12/15/1998) • **85**
Merlot Napa Valley 1995 • $22 • (4/30/1998) • **85**
Petite Sirah Napa Valley Spring Creek Vineyard 1997: Ripe, smoky and meaty, with a dense core of tar, game, blueberry, blackberry and spice flavors and tame tannins. Complex and nicely balanced, this is something to sink your teeth into. Drink now through 2005.–J.L. • $23 • (11/15/1999) • **89**
Sangiovese Napa Valley 1996: Starts with a green, tealike edge but is filled in with cherry, plum and berry flavors, which give it weight, richness and complexity. Finishes with firm tannins and good length, with echoes of fruit on the aftertaste. Drink now through 2002.–J.L. • $27 • (9/30/1998) • **87**

RUTHERFORD HILL | CALIFORNIA

Cabernet Sauvignon Napa Valley 1991 • $14 • (11/15/1994) • **81**
Cabernet Sauvignon Napa Valley 1987 • $16 • (11/15/1992) • **85**
Cabernet Sauvignon Napa Valley 1986 • $14 • (2/28/1991) • **68**
Cabernet Sauvignon Napa Valley 1985 • $17 • (4/30/1990) • **82**
Cabernet Sauvignon Napa Valley 1984 • $13 • (8/31/1988) • **88**
Cabernet Sauvignon Napa Valley 1983 • $13 • (9/15/1987) • **83**
Cabernet Sauvignon Napa Valley 1982 • $13 • (11/15/1986) • **88**
Cabernet Sauvignon Napa Valley 1981 • $12 • (6/01/1986) • **90**
Cabernet Sauvignon Napa Valley 1980 • $12 • (10/16/1984) • **82**
Cabernet Sauvignon Napa Valley 1978 • $25 • (11/15/1992) • **78**
Cabernet Sauvignon Napa Valley Cask Lot 2 Limited Edition 1980 • $15 • (7/31/1987) • **92**
Cabernet Sauvignon Napa Valley XVS 1987 • $26 • (11/15/1992) • **86**
Cabernet Sauvignon Napa Valley XVS 1986 • $NA • (12/15/1996) • **75**
Cabernet Sauvignon Napa Valley XVS 1985 • $29 • (4/30/1989) • **88**
Chardonnay Napa Valley Carneros Reserve 1997: Very smooth and graceful, with a focused range of citrus-tinged pear, apple blossom and toast notes. Long, subtle, complex finish. Drink now.–J.L. • $32 • (7/31/1999) • **89**
Merlot Napa Valley 1991 • $16 • (9/15/1994) • **82**
Merlot Napa Valley 1989 • $14 • (5/31/1992) • **70**
Merlot Napa Valley 1988 • $15 • (5/31/1992) • **82**
Merlot Napa Valley 1987 • $14 • (3/31/1991) • **74**
Merlot Napa Valley 1986 • $13 • (6/15/1990) • **68**
Merlot Napa Valley 1985 • $12 • (1/31/1989) • **92**
Merlot Napa Valley 1984 • $11 • (4/30/1988) • **84**
Merlot Napa Valley 1983 • $10 • (8/31/1987) • **87**
Merlot Napa Valley 1982 • $11 • (5/16/1986) • **79**
Merlot Napa Valley 1981 • $10 • (10/01/1985) • **78**
Merlot Napa Valley Exceptional Vineyard Selections Reserve 1993 • $15 • (8/31/1996) • **77**
Merlot Napa Valley Reserve 1996: Appealing for its up-front cherry, anise and cedar flavors. Elegant and polished, finishing with round, supple tannins. Drink now through 2005.–J.L. • $44 • (10/15/1999) • **87**
Merlot Napa Valley Reserve 1995 • $40 • (5/15/1998) • **89**
Merlot Napa Valley Twentieth Anniversary 1994 • $15 • (8/31/1996) • **85**

Key: SS—Spectator Selection. CS—Cellar Selection. HR—Highly Recommended. $NA—Price not available. (BT)—Barrel tasting. (A)—Auction Price. For a key to the tasters' initials, see "How to Use These Listings." **Dates in parentheses represent the issues in which the ratings were published.**

RUTHERFORD RANCH | CALIFORNIA

Cabernet Sauvignon Napa Valley 1995: Medium-bodied and open-textured, with currant flavors and hints of cedar. Finishes with light tannins. Drink now.–J.L. • $12 • (6/15/1999) • **83**
Cabernet Sauvignon Napa Valley 1994: Marked by herbal, minty overtones, followed by black cherry, cassis and black pepper notes. Lean-textured, with a moderate finish. Drink now through 2002. • $12 • (9/15/1998) • **85**
Cabernet Sauvignon Napa Valley 1993 • $11 • (7/31/1997) • **82**
Cabernet Sauvignon Napa Valley 1992 • $11 • (11/15/1996) • **87**
Cabernet Sauvignon Napa Valley 1991 • $10 • (11/15/1994) • **86**
Cabernet Sauvignon Napa Valley 1987 • $13 • (4/30/1991) • **83**
Cabernet Sauvignon Napa Valley 1985 • $11 • (5/15/1990) SS • **92**
Cabernet Sauvignon Napa Valley 1984 • $13 • (5/31/1989) • **85**
Cabernet Sauvignon Napa Valley 1983 • $11 • (12/31/1987) • **83**
Cabernet Sauvignon Napa Valley 1982 • $11 • (6/15/1987) • **84**
Chardonnay Napa Valley 1997: Features crisp grapefruit, mild toasted oak and slightly bitter notes. Drink now.–J.L. • $11 • (11/15/1999) • **81**
Chardonnay Napa Valley 1996: Starts off with toasty notes that lead to a core of citrus and pineapple flavors. Drink now.–J.L. • $12 • (12/15/1998) • **83**
Merlot Napa Valley 1996: Smooth and polished, with delicate notes of vanilla, herb and ripe black cherry flavors, finishing with fine-grained tannins. Drink now through 2002.–H.S. • $13 • (9/15/1999) • **86**
Merlot Napa Valley 1995 • $13 • (1/31/1998) • **80**
Merlot Napa Valley 1994 • $12 • (12/15/1996) • **85**
Merlot Napa Valley 1992 • $10 • (4/15/1995) • **82**
Merlot Napa Valley 1990 • $9 • (3/31/1993) • **82**
Merlot Napa Valley 1988 • $12 • (8/31/1991) • **80**
Merlot Napa Valley 1986 • $12 • (12/31/1988) • **87**
Merlot Napa Valley 1985 • $11 • (4/30/1988) • **92**
Quintessence Meritage Napa Valley 1991 • $20 • (12/15/1995) • **86**
Quintessence Meritage Napa Valley 1989 • $NA • (11/15/1994) • **83**
Zinfandel Napa Valley 1992 • $8 • (8/31/1995) • **85**

RUTHERFORD VINTNERS | CALIFORNIA

Cabernet Sauvignon California Barrel Select 1993 • $8 • (12/15/1996) • **78**
Cabernet Sauvignon Lodi Barrel Select 1996: A real lightweight, with a bit of cherry and smoke on the palate. Vegetal on the finish. • $9 • (8/31/1998) • **76**
Cabernet Sauvignon Napa Valley Rutherford Bench 1992 • $8 • (12/15/1995) • **87**
Cabernet Sauvignon Sonoma County Barrel Select 1995 • $9 • (10/15/1997) • **86**
Chardonnay California Barrel Select 1997: Pleasant enough, though fairly simple, with hints of apple and oak followed by a lemony finish. Drink now. • $9 • (9/15/1998) • **81**
Chardonnay Lodi Barrel Select 1996 • $9 • (11/30/1997) • **85**
Merlot Stanislaus County Barrel Select 1996: Juicy, with rich toasted oak notes, spiced apple and ripe plum flavors all on a crisp structure. Drink now.–H.S. • $9 • (9/15/1998) • **84**
Zinfandel Lodi Barrel Select 1995 • $9 • (11/15/1997) • **85**

RUTZ | CALIFORNIA

Cabernet Sauvignon Napa Valley 1995: Features a core of mineral, green olive, sage and tart black cherry flavors that remain focused on the finish. Tannins are firm but well integrated. Drink now through 2003.–J.L. • $25 • (9/30/1999) • **86**
Cabernet Sauvignon Napa Valley 1994 • $26 • (11/30/1997) • **86**
Chardonnay Russian River Valley 1997: A complex blend, with pretty earth tones up front and creamy green apple, hazelnut and herb neatly intertwined. This classy wine grows on you, fans out nicely on the palate and lingers on the minerally finish. Drink now through 2002. • $20 • (7/31/1999) • **91**
Chardonnay Russian River Valley 1996 • $22 • (6/30/1998) • **88**
Chardonnay Russian River Valley Buena Tierra Vineyard 1997: Richly textured, with concentrated sweet cream, lemon and earth flavors. The long, complex finish features citrus, mineral and light toasty oak. Drink now through 2002.–J.L. • $25 • (7/31/1999) • **90**
Chardonnay Russian River Valley Dutton Ranch 1996 • $30 • (5/15/1998) • **89**
Chardonnay Russian River Valley Maison Grand Cru 1997: Shows a narrow range of toasty, flinty apple and lemon flavors. Firm finish. Drink now.–J.L. • $25 • (7/31/1999) • **83**
Chardonnay Russian River Valley Maison Grand Cru 1996 • $25 • (5/15/1998) • **86**

Chardonnay Russian River Valley Quail Hill Vineyard 1997: Complex and focused, with a tight range of earthy lemon, green apple and spicy toast notes. Rich in texture, with a long, flavorful finish. Drink now through 2002.–J.L. • $25 • (7/31/1999) • **90**

Pinot Noir California Maison Grand Cru 1996: Aims for complexity, but a little too much leather overrides the dried cherry and spice flavors. Turns dry on the finish. Drink soon, as the leather isn't likely to dissipate.–J.L. • $25 • (9/30/1998) • **83**

Pinot Noir Mendocino County Weir Vineyard 1995 • $35 • (12/15/1997) • **86**

Pinot Noir Monterey Sleepy Hollow Vineyard 1996: Smooth and creamy, with pretty vanilla, coffee, black cherry and plum flavors. Well focused, long and rich on the finish, with cola, spice and exotic nuances. Finishes with firm, dry, tealike tannins. Drink now through 2002.–J.L. • $28 • (8/31/1998) • **88**

Pinot Noir Russian River Valley 1996: A touch earthy, with a gamy, leathery edge to the berry and dried cherry flavors. Turns simple on the finish. Drink now.–J.L. • $20 • (9/15/1998) • **83**

Pinot Noir Russian River Valley 1995 • $20 • (12/15/1997) • **84**

Pinot Noir Russian River Valley 1994 • $NA • (11/15/1996) • **76**

Pinot Noir Russian River Valley Dutton Ranch 1994 • $25 • (8/31/1997) • **86**

Pinot Noir Russian River Valley Dutton Ranch 1993 • $24 • (1/31/1996) • **85**

Pinot Noir Russian River Valley Quail Hill Vineyard 1994 • $25 • (8/31/1997) • **85**

Pinot Noir Russian River Valley Quail Hill Vineyard 1993 • $24 • (1/31/1996) • **87**

RYAN, SETH | WASHINGTON

Cabernet Franc Yakima Valley 1994 • $16 • (9/30/1996) • **86**

Cabernet Sauvignon Yakima Valley 1993 • $21 • (9/15/1996) • **86**

Cabernet Sauvignon Yakima Valley 1992 • $24 • (9/15/1996) • **74**

Merlot Columbia Valley 1994 • $22 • (9/15/1996) • **81**

SADDLEBACK | CALIFORNIA

Cabernet Sauvignon Napa Valley 1996: Focused, with a complex core of plum, cherry, wild berry and spice. Finishes with detailed flavors and firm tannins. Cellar short-term. Drink through 2008.–J.L. • $32 • (6/15/1999) • **90**

Cabernet Sauvignon Napa Valley 1995: Packs in lots of flavor, with a range of currant, mineral, earth, sage and spice that's rich and concentrated, picking up hints of coffee and chocolate on the long, full finish. Drink now through 2008.–J.L. • $27 • (8/31/1998) • **91**

Cabernet Sauvignon Napa Valley 1994 • $23 • (9/30/1997) • **91**

Cabernet Sauvignon Napa Valley 1993 • $19 • (5/31/1996) • **92**

Cabernet Sauvignon Napa Valley 1992 • $17 • (12/15/1995) • **87**

Cabernet Sauvignon Napa Valley 1991 • $17 • (10/31/1994) HR • **90**

Cabernet Sauvignon Napa Valley 1990 • $15 • (11/15/1993) • **84**

Cabernet Sauvignon Napa Valley 1988 • $14 • (8/31/1992) • **73**

Cabernet Sauvignon Napa Valley Family Reserve 1989 • $25 • (11/15/1994) • **85**

Cabernet Sauvignon Napa Valley Family Reserve 1988 • $24 • (11/15/1993) • **81**

Chardonnay Napa Valley 1997: Bright and lemony, this firm-textured wine has a mineral core offset by pear and green apple flavors. The moderate finish is squeaky-clean. Drink now through 2002. • $18 • (7/31/1999) • **87**

Chardonnay Napa Valley 1996 • $18 • (12/31/1997) • **87**

SAGPOND | NEW YORK

Merlot Long Island 1994 • $14 • (12/31/1996) • **78**

Pinot Noir Long Island 1994 • $22 • (12/31/1996) • **79**

Pinot Noir Long Island 1993 • $18 • (9/15/1996) • **75**

ST. AMANT | CALIFORNIA

Port Amador County Late Bottled 1991 • $12 • (5/15/1996) • **86**

Port Amador County Reserve 1992 • $18 • (5/15/1996) • **88**

STE. CHAPELLE | IDAHO

Cabernet Sauvignon Idaho 73% Arena Valley Vineyard/27% Symms Old 1990 • $12 • (3/31/1994) • **74**

Cabernet Sauvignon Idaho Reserve 1988 • $20 • (2/29/1992) • **74**

Cabernet Sauvignon Washington 1993 • $10 • (11/15/1995) • **87**

Cabernet Sauvignon Washington 1992 • $10 • (1/31/1995) • **83**

Cabernet Sauvignon Washington 1989 • $10 • (3/15/1993) • **79**

Cabernet Sauvignon Washington 1988 • $10 • (2/29/1992) • **84**

Cabernet Sauvignon Washington 1986 • $10 • (8/31/1991) • **83**

Cabernet Sauvignon Washington Canyon 1992 • $7 • (1/31/1995) • **86**

Cabernet Sauvignon Washington Collectors Series 1988 • $16 • (10/15/1993) • **73**

Cabernet Sauvignon Washington Collectors Series 1981 • $18 • (10/15/1989) • **81**

Cabernet Sauvignon Washington Mercer Ranch Vineyard 1989 • $16 • (1/31/1994) • **80**

Fumé Blanc Idaho Dry 1996 • $8 • (5/31/1998) • **84**

Merlot Idaho 1992 • $10 • (9/15/1994) • **85**

Merlot Washington 1987 • $10 • (9/30/1990) • **73**

Merlot Washington Dionysus Vineyard 1986 • $12 • (5/31/1988) • **81**

Pinot Noir Idaho 1988 • $8 • (2/29/1992) • **74**

Syrah Idaho Reserve 1994 • $20 • (6/30/1996) • **84**

ST. CLEMENT | CALIFORNIA

Cabernet Sauvignon Howell Mountain 1996: Combines lots of ripe, complex fruit flavors with a sense of elegance and polish. The currant, black cherry, vanilla, sage and spice unfold gracefully. Available only at the winery. Best from 2001 through 2008.–J.L. • $50 • (10/15/1999) • **89**

Cabernet Sauvignon Howell Mountain 1995: The best of the new St. Clement Cabernets, this wine offers complex floral aromas and detailed currant, mineral, spice and sage. Flavors persist on the finish, where they fan out and linger. Drink through 2005.–J.L. • $45 • (10/31/1998) • **90**

Cabernet Sauvignon Howell Mountain White Cottage Ranch 1994 • $45 • (9/30/1997) • **92**

Cabernet Sauvignon Howell Mountain White Cottage Ranch 1993 • $45 • (11/15/1996) • **90**

Cabernet Sauvignon Napa Valley 1998: Pretty, but struggles to reach the extra depth of the best. The core flavors are built around cherry, currant and berry, with supple tannins.–J.L. • $NA • (8/31/1999) (BT) • **90-94**

Cabernet Sauvignon Napa Valley 1997: Beautifully crafted, impressive from the barrel. Dark, dense and concentrated, with a plush texture, and rich, currant, berry, chocolate and vanilla.–J.L. • $NA • (8/31/1998) (BT) • **90-94**

Cabernet Sauvignon Napa Valley 1996 • $28 • (2/02/1997) (BT) • **90-94**

Cabernet Sauvignon Napa Valley 1995: Complex, with a ripe, supple core of plum, black cherry, currant and wild berry flavor. Finishes with a burst of fruit, anise, sage and cedar. Elegant and well proportioned. Drink through 2005.–J.L. • $26 • (10/31/1998) • **90**

Cabernet Sauvignon Napa Valley 1994 • $27 • (7/31/1997) • **91**

Cabernet Sauvignon Napa Valley 1993 • $24 • (10/15/1996) • **88**

Cabernet Sauvignon Napa Valley 1992 • $24 • (10/31/1995) • **90**

Cabernet Sauvignon Napa Valley 1991 • $23 • (9/30/1994) SS • **90**

Cabernet Sauvignon Napa Valley 1990 • $22 • (10/31/1993) • **90**

Cabernet Sauvignon Napa Valley 1989: Nicely balanced, ripe, supple and polished, with attractive plum, currant, black cherry and spice, and rounded tannins. (1989 California Cabernet retrospective tasting). Drink now through 2004.–J.L. • $20 • (8/31/1999) • **87**

Cabernet Sauvignon Napa Valley 1988: Ripe and well balanced, with a modest band of plum, black cherry, spice and cedar notes that are focused and lingering on the finish. Turns crisp and tannic on the aftertaste. (1988 California Cabernet retrospective tasting). Drink now through 2002.–J.L. • $20 • (11/15/1998) • **87**

Cabernet Sauvignon Napa Valley 1987 • $34 Ⓐ • (12/15/1997) • **90**

Cabernet Sauvignon Napa Valley 1986 • $18 • (12/15/1996) • **87**

Cabernet Sauvignon Napa Valley 1984 • $15 • (10/15/1988) • **90**

Cabernet Sauvignon Napa Valley 1983 • $15 • (6/01/1986) • **89**

Cabernet Sauvignon Napa Valley 1982 • $14 • (3/16/1985) CS • **92**

Cabernet Sauvignon Napa Valley 1981 • $13 • (6/16/1984) SS • **89**

Cabernet Sauvignon Napa Valley 1979: Dry, tannic and earthy; the fruit is gone. (1979 California Cabernet retrospective tasting) Past its prime. –J.L. • $11 • (8/31/1999) • **75**

Chardonnay Napa Valley Carneros Abbott's Vineyard 1997: Smooth and spicy, with ripe pear, hazelnut, cedar and fig flavors, rich and concentrated. Holds its flavor and focus on the finish. Drink now through 2002.–J.L. • $20 • (4/30/1999) • **90**

Chardonnay Napa Valley Carneros Abbott's Vineyard 1996 • $20 • (5/31/1998) • **89**

Merlot Columbia Valley 1996: Youthful and fresh, with smooth-textured blueberry, tomato and currant flavors, shaded with vanilla and smoke on the oak-tinged finish. Packed with character. Drink now.–H.S. • $22 • (8/31/1998) • **89**

Merlot Columbia Valley 1995 • $22 • (9/30/1997) • **88**

Merlot Napa Valley 1997: Pretty integration of ripe plum, cherry, currant and chocolate flavors, with toasty, spicy oak, neatly tapered. Long, complex aftertaste. Drink now through 2008.–J.L. • $26 • (5/31/2000) • **90**

ST. CLEMENT

Merlot Napa Valley 1996: Tight, with a firm cedary edge to the supple core of currant, black cherry, sage, olive and toasty oak flavors. Drink now through 2005.–J.L. • $24 • (4/30/1999) • **88**
Merlot Napa Valley 1995 • $24 • (4/30/1998) • **88**
Merlot Napa Valley 1994 • $24 • (4/30/1997) • **89**
Merlot Napa Valley 1993 • $18 • (4/30/1996) • **87**
Merlot Napa Valley 1992 • $21 • (3/31/1995) • **88**
Merlot Napa Valley 1991 • $20 • (9/15/1994) • **83**
Merlot Napa Valley 1990 • $20 • (5/31/1993) • **88**
Merlot Napa Valley 1989 • $18 • (5/31/1992) • **87**
Merlot Napa Valley 1987 • $16 • (12/31/1990) • **85**
Merlot Napa Valley 1986 • $15 • (10/31/1989) • **74**
Merlot Napa Valley 1985 • $15 • (3/31/1989) • **91**
Merlot Napa Valley 1983 • $15 • (5/31/1988) • **81**
Oroppas Napa Valley 1997: Dark, rich and polished, with complex layers of black cherry, currant, anise, cedar and spice, all unfolding on the finish, where they gain depth and nuance. Tannins are in check. Best from 2002 through 2010.–J.L. • $40 • (5/15/2000) • **92**
Oroppas Napa Valley 1996: Elegant and refined, with a pretty core of spicy plum, black cherry and currant, picking up smoky, toasty oak nuances, finishing with a lingering aftertaste. Cabernet Sauvignon, Cabernet Franc and Merlot. Drink now through 2005.–J.L. • $35 • (10/31/1998) • **89**
Oroppas Napa Valley 1995 • $35 • (8/31/1997) • **93**
Oroppas Napa Valley 1994 • $30 • (11/15/1996) • **91**
Oroppas Napa Valley 1993 • $30 • (10/31/1995) HR • **92**
Oroppas Napa Valley 1992 • $25 • (9/30/1994) CS • **95**
Oroppas Napa Valley 1991 • $22 • (10/31/1993) HR • **94**
Sauvignon Blanc Napa Valley 1998: Ripe and polished, with a pretty array of fig, pear, citrus and melon, showing a touch of smoky, toasty oak on the finish. Drink now through 2003.–J.L. • $13 • (10/15/1999) • **88**
Sauvignon Blanc Napa Valley 1997: A refreshing wine, crisp and firm on the palate, with a strong streak of melon and citrus, then herb and lemon notes on the finish. Drink now. • $13 • (1/31/1999) • **85**
Sauvignon Blanc Napa Valley 1996 • $15 • (6/30/1997) • **88**

ST. FRANCIS | CALIFORNIA

Cabernet Franc Sonoma Valley 1989 • $14 • (11/15/1993) • **83**
Cabernet Sauvignon Sonoma County 1997: Soft-textured, with pleasant flavors of bay leaf, black cherry and herb. Finishes short, with mild tannins. Drink now through 2002.–J.L. • $15 • (10/15/1999) • **83**
Cabernet Sauvignon Sonoma County 1996: Smooth and supple, with ripe, fleshy cherry, herb, currant and bell pepper notes. Turns polished on the finish. An excellent value in a ready-to-drink style. Drink now.–J.L. • $12 • (10/31/1998) • **87**
Cabernet Sauvignon Sonoma County 1995 • $14 • (11/15/1997) • **85**
Cabernet Sauvignon Sonoma County 1994 • $10 • (10/15/1996) • **86**
Cabernet Sauvignon Sonoma County 1993 • $12 • (11/30/1995) • **85**
Cabernet Sauvignon Sonoma County 1992 • $10 • (11/15/1994) • **85**
Cabernet Sauvignon Sonoma County 1991 • $10 • (9/15/1993) • **84**
Cabernet Sauvignon Sonoma County 1990 • $10 • (9/30/1993) • **89**
Cabernet Sauvignon Sonoma County 1989 • $10 • (9/30/1993) • **84**
Cabernet Sauvignon Sonoma County 1988: Nice balance between the smoky, toasty oak and the supple core of black cherry and currant. Medium- to full-bodied, the flavors are appealing if lacking in depth and richness. (1988 California Cabernet retrospective tasting). Drink now through 2002. –J.L. • $10 • (11/15/1998) • **86**
Cabernet Sauvignon Sonoma County 1986 • $12 • (1/31/1990) • **89**
Cabernet Sauvignon Sonoma Valley Reserve 1996: Packs in lots of complex flavors, with toasty oak leading the way for ripe currant, chocolaty herb, cedar, spice and black cherry flavors. Quite rich and concentrated, it also manages to be delicate. Has enough tannin to cellar short-term. Best from 2001 through 2009.–J.L. • $39 • (10/15/1999) • **93**
Cabernet Sauvignon Sonoma Valley Reserve 1995: Dark-colored, stuffed to bursting with dense, ripe, rich and chewy Cabernet flavors, with tiers of plum, black cherry, chocolate and currant smoothing out on the finish where the flavors increase in depth and nuance. Delicious now, but worthy of cellaring. Drink through 2007.–J.L. • $29 • (10/31/1998) SS • **92**
Cabernet Sauvignon Sonoma Valley Reserve 1994 • $29 Ⓐ • (10/15/1997) SS • **93**

Key: SS—Spectator Selection. CS—Cellar Selection. HR—Highly Recommended. $NA—Price not available. (BT)—Barrel tasting. Ⓐ—Auction Price.
For a key to the tasters' initials, see "How to Use These Listings."
Dates in parentheses represent the issues in which the ratings were published.

Cabernet Sauvignon Sonoma Valley Reserve 1993 • $29 • (12/15/1996) • **90**
Cabernet Sauvignon Sonoma County Reserve 1992 • $24 • (11/30/1995) HR • **92**
Cabernet Sauvignon Sonoma County Reserve 1991 • $24 • (11/15/1994) • **88**
Cabernet Sauvignon Sonoma County Reserve 1990 • $24 • (9/30/1993) HR • **91**
Cabernet Sauvignon Sonoma Valley Reserve 1989: Still quite oaky, but the flavors are pretty, with toasty vanilla nuances. What makes it delicious, though, are the rich, complex layers of plum, berry, cherry and anise that marry so well with the oak. Turns a touch dry on the finish, but overall it's quite impressive. (1989 California Cabernet retrospective tasting). Drink now through 2004.–J.L. • $12 • (8/31/1999) • **91**
Cabernet Sauvignon Sonoma Valley Reserve 1988: Complex and supple for the vintage, this wine is marked by polished tannins and lots of herbal Cabernet flavors, hints of cherry and currant, coffee and sage. The finish echoes complex flavors. (1988 California Cabernet retrospective tasting). Drink now through 2002.–J.L. • $16 • (11/15/1998) • **88**
Cabernet Sauvignon Sonoma Valley Reserve 1986 • $20 • (11/30/1989) • **94**
Chardonnay Sonoma County 1998: Soft and round, with peach and floral notes. Drink now.–J.L. • $12 • (6/30/2000) • **82**
Chardonnay Sonoma County 1997: Crisp, with leafy green apple flavors, tinges of herb and cedar on the moderate finish. Drink now.–J.L. • $13 • (4/30/1999) • **82**
Chardonnay Sonoma County 1996 • $12 • (3/31/1998) • **85**
Chardonnay Sonoma Valley Reserve 1997: Plenty of smoky, toasty oak, pear, fig and hazelnut flavors in this smooth, rich and creamy California Chardonnay, turning richer and more complex on the finish, where the oak and fruit surge together. Drink through 2002.–J.L. • $20 • (6/15/1999) HR • **92**
Chardonnay Sonoma Valley Reserve 1996 • $22 • (3/31/1998) • **90**
Merlot Sonoma County 1997: Rich and supple, showing coffee, roasted nut, menthol and black cherry flavors that persist on the smooth finish. Drink through 2005.–J.L. • $25 • (10/15/1999) • **87**
Merlot Sonoma County 1996: Smooth and herbal, with coffee, cedar and hints of dried plum. Turns smoky, with a slightly charred edge. Drink through 2003.–J.L. • $20 • (12/31/1998) • **86**
Merlot Sonoma County 1995 • $23 • (3/31/1998) • **87**
Merlot Sonoma County 1994 • $18 • (11/30/1996) • **87**
Merlot Sonoma County 1993 • $18 • (7/31/1996) • **83**
Merlot Sonoma Valley 1992 • $17 • (2/29/1996) • **86**
Merlot Sonoma Valley 1991 • $18 • (7/31/1994) • **86**
Merlot Sonoma Valley 1990 • $18 • (5/31/1993) • **88**
Merlot Sonoma Valley 1989 • $14 • (5/31/1992) • **79**
Merlot Sonoma Valley 1988 • $16 • (11/15/1991) • **82**
Merlot Sonoma Valley 1987 • $14 • (6/15/1990) • **80**
Merlot Sonoma Valley 1986 • $14 • (6/30/1989) • **85**
Merlot Sonoma Valley 1985 • $12 • (10/15/1988) • **66**
Merlot Sonoma Valley 1984 • $12 • (10/31/1987) • **88**
Merlot Sonoma Valley 1983 • $11 • (7/31/1987) • **80**
Merlot Sonoma Valley 1982 • $11 • (10/01/1985) • **78**
Merlot Sonoma Valley Reserve 1996: A seductive style, with lots of smooth, creamy vanilla-scented oak and pretty, polished currant, black cherry and berryish flavors, finishing long and supple. Drink now through 2006.–J.L. • $39 • (9/15/1999) • **92**
Merlot Sonoma Valley Reserve 1995: A reliable choice for quality in California Merlot. Well oaked, in the winery's style, with toasty vanilla flavors that stand out, and cherry, plum and berry notes filling out the midpalate and continuing on the finish. A big, concentrated wine, it needs some time; drink through 2004.–J.L. • $29 • (9/30/1998) SS • **91**
Merlot Sonoma Valley Reserve 1994 • $29 • (6/15/1997) HR • **92**
Merlot Sonoma Valley Reserve 1993 • $26 • (8/31/1996) • **88**
Merlot Sonoma Valley Reserve 1992 • $24 • (7/31/1996) SS • **92**
Merlot Sonoma Valley Reserve 1991 • $24 • (9/15/1994) • **89**
Merlot Sonoma Valley Reserve 1990 • $24 • (5/31/1993) HR • **91**
Merlot Sonoma Valley Reserve 1989 • $24 • (5/31/1992) HR • **90**
Merlot Sonoma Valley Reserve 1988 • $24 • (11/15/1991) • **82**
Merlot Sonoma Valley Reserve 1986 • $28 • (1/31/1990) • **94**
Merlot Sonoma Valley Reserve 1985 • $15 • (12/31/1988) • **81**
Merlot Sonoma Valley Reserve 1984 • $16 • (2/15/1988) • **74**
Pinot Noir Sonoma Valley 1986 • $14 • (6/15/1988) • **74**
Zinfandel Sonoma County Old Vines 1997: Weaves together enough ripe plum, cherry and raspberry and frames it nicely with smoky, toasty oak. Finishes with a complex, if hot, aftertaste. Drink now through 2005.–J.L. • $24 • (5/15/2000) • **86**
Zinfandel Sonoma County Old Vines 1996 • $20 • (5/31/1998) • **88**
Zinfandel Sonoma County Old Vines 1995 • $22 • (8/31/1997) • **88**
Zinfandel Sonoma County Old Vines 1994 • $18 • (9/15/1996) HR • **89**

Zinfandel Sonoma Valley Old Vines 1993 • $18 • (10/15/1995) • **91**
Zinfandel Sonoma Valley Old Vines 1992 • $14 • (10/15/1994) • **87**
Zinfandel Sonoma Valley Old Vines 1990 • $12 • (10/15/1992) • **88**
Zinfandel Sonoma Valley Old Vines 1989 • $12 • (3/31/1992) • **76**
Zinfandel Sonoma Valley Pagani Vineyard Reserve 1997: This big, dark, massive yet plush wine is packed with rich, detailed plum, currant, spice, mineral, coffee and subtle earth nuances. Finishes with bold oak and chewy tannins. Not for lightweights. Drink now through 2004.–J.L. • $29 • (5/31/1999) • **92**
Zinfandel Sonoma Valley Pagani Vineyard Reserve 1996 • $28 • (6/15/1998) • **90**
Zinfandel Sonoma Valley Pagani Vineyard Reserve 1995 • $28 • (8/31/1997) • **92**
Zinfandel Sonoma Valley Pagani Vineyard Reserve 1994 • $24 • (9/15/1996) • **92**

STE. GENEVIEVE | TEXAS

Cabernet Sauvignon Escondido Valley NV • $5 • (5/15/1998) • **81**
Chardonnay Escondido Valley NV • $5 • (12/31/1997) • **78**
Gamay Nouveau Texas 1997 • $5 • (3/31/1998) • **80**
Pinot Noir Escondido Valley NV • $9/1.5 liter • (12/31/1997) • **81**
Sauvignon Blanc Escondido Valley NV • $5 • (12/31/1997) • **82**

SAINT GREGORY | CALIFORNIA

Pinot Noir Anderson Valley Reserve 1995: Showing age. Has hints of chocolate and spice, with ripe plum and cherry notes backed by herbal overtones. Smooth and medium-bodied, with a moderate finish. Drink through 2002. • $25 • (5/31/1999) • **87**
Pinot Noir Mendocino 1996: Ripe and silky, showing pretty berry, tea and spice flavors that carry through on the flavorful finish. Drink now through 2001 .–J.L. • $18 • (9/15/1999) • **85**
Pinot Noir Mendocino 1994 • $14 • (3/31/1997) • **84**
Pinot Noir Mendocino 1993 • $14 • (12/31/1995) • **81**
Pinot Noir Mendocino 1992 • $14 • (3/31/1995) • **81**
Pinot Noir Mendocino 1991 • $14 • (2/28/1994) • **84**
Pinot Noir Mendocino 1990 • $14 • (9/30/1992) • **86**

ST. INNOCENT | OREGON

Chardonnay Willamette Valley O'Connor Vineyard 1996: Light in texture and bright in flavor, offering jazzy lemon-scented apple and tart peach notes that linger on the finish. Drink now.–H.S. • $11 • (11/15/1998) • **86**
Chardonnay Willamette Valley Seven Springs Vineyards 1996: Light and refreshing, with pretty green apple and spice flavors, and some nice hints of resin on the bright finish. Drink now.–H.S. • $15 • (11/15/1998) • **84**
Pinot Blanc Willamette Valley Freedom Hill Vineyard 1998: Tangy, with generous spice and citrus overtones to the pear and apple flavors. Stylish and solid through the finish. Drink now.–H.S. • $14 • (3/31/2000) • **88**
Pinot Blanc Willamette Valley Freedom Hill Vineyard 1997: Bright and open-textured, with pretty flavors of pear and melon and a touch of almond. Finishes clear and pure. Drink now.–H.S. • $14 • (11/15/1998) • **88**
Pinot Gris Willamette Valley O'Connor Vineyard 1997: Almond and almond-blossom flavors add interesting tiers to this nicely concentrated white.–H.S. • $12 • (5/15/1999) • **86**
Pinot Gris Willamette Valley Vitae Springs Vineyard 1997: Fresh and open-textured, with pretty cantaloupe and mineral flavors that persist into the light finish. Drink now.–H.S. • $12 • (11/15/1998) • **86**
Pinot Noir Willamette Valley Freedom Hill Vineyard 1995 • $27 • (12/31/1997) • **89**
Pinot Noir Willamette Valley Freedom Hill Vineyard 1994 • $NA • (2/28/1997) • **85**
Pinot Noir Willamette Valley O'Connor Vineyard 1996: A good Pinot Noir in a lean style, with light berry flavors and considerable tannins. Drink now. –H.S. • $20 • (9/30/1998) • **81**
Pinot Noir Willamette Valley O'Connor Vineyard 1995 • $22 • (10/15/1997) • **85**
Pinot Noir Willamette Valley Seven Springs 1992 • $16 • (11/30/1994) • **85**
Pinot Noir Willamette Valley Seven Springs Vineyard 1995 • $27 • (12/31/1997) • **87**
Pinot Noir Willamette Valley Seven Springs Vineyard 1994 • $NA • (2/28/1997) • **88**
Pinot Noir Willamette Valley Temperance Hill Vineyard 1996: Light, with pretty loganberry and cinnamon notes shining through the fine-grained tannins. Tastes slightly cooked on the finish. Drink now.–H.S. • $18 • (9/30/1998) • **85**

ST. JOSEF'S | OREGON

Cabernet Sauvignon Oregon 1989 • $14 • (3/31/1996) • **83**
Cabernet Sauvignon Oregon 1988 • $12 • (3/31/1996) • **84**
Cabernet Sauvignon Oregon 1986 • $12 • (8/31/1991) • **68**
Cabernet Sauvignon Oregon 1985 • $15 • (3/31/1991) • **87**
Pinot Noir Oregon 1993 • $10 • (4/30/1996) • **72**
Pinot Noir Oregon 1985 • $16 • (2/15/1990) • **89**
Zinfandel Oregon 1990 • $10 • (3/31/1996) • **78**

ST. JULIAN | MICHIGAN

Cabernet Franc Michigan 1996: Firm, and nicely concentrated with plum flavors that are definitely on the herbal side. Not particularly complex, but a lot of up-front flavor and finishes on an appealing spicy note. Drink through 2001.–K.M. • $20 • (8/31/1998) • **83**
Chambourcin Lake Michigan Shore 1989 • $9 • (2/29/1992) • **76**
Chardonnay Michigan 1996: A serviceable Chardonnay with lemony, buttery flavors that could harmonize better. Has an attractive spiciness on the finish. Drink now. • $12 • (8/31/1998) • **82**
Merlot Michigan 1996: A jumbled mix of herbal, menthol and plummy flavors that finish on a somewhat sweet, spicy note.–K.M. • $20 • (8/31/1998) • **74**
Pinot Gris Michigan 1997: On the sweet side, with simple peach and apple flavors and a clean finish.–K.M. • $10 • (8/31/1998) • **79**
Riesling Michigan 1997: Sweet and peachy, with some green apricot notes but not much complexity.–K.M. • $10 • (8/31/1998) • **78**
Solera Light Cream Sherry Michigan NV • $12 • (2/29/1992) • **88**

ST. SUPERY | CALIFORNIA

Cabernet Sauvignon Napa Valley Dollarhide Ranch 1995: Soft, with a core of cherry, currant and anise notes wrapped in smoky tea and mocha flavors. Tannins are soft on the finish. Drink now through 2003. • $17 • (2/28/1999) • **86**
Cabernet Sauvignon Napa Valley Dollarhide Ranch 1993 • $15 • (3/31/1997) • **83**
Cabernet Sauvignon Napa Valley Dollarhide Ranch 1991 • $15 • (11/15/1996) • **88**
Cabernet Sauvignon Napa Valley Dollarhide Ranch 1990 • $14 • (5/15/1994) • **86**
Cabernet Sauvignon Napa Valley Dollarhide Ranch 1989 • $19 • (7/31/1994) • **86**
Cabernet Sauvignon Napa Valley Dollarhide Ranch 1988 • $14 • (9/30/1991) • **85**
Cabernet Sauvignon Napa Valley Dollarhide Ranch 1987 • $13 • (7/15/1990) • **85**
Cabernet Sauvignon Napa Valley Dollarhide Ranch Limited Edition 1997: Wonderfully proportioned, with ripe, chunky currant, plum and black cherry accented by light cedary oak, finishing with a chocolaty aftertaste. Drink now through 2007.–J.L. • $70 • (6/30/2000) • **90**
Cabernet Sauvignon Napa Valley Dollarhide Ranch Limited Edition 1991 • $25 • (11/15/1996) • **88**
Chardonnay Napa Valley 1998: Appealing for its straightforward fruitiness, with buttery pear, spice and apple, turning crisp. Drink now.–J.L. • $16 • (5/31/2000) • **86**
Chardonnay Napa Valley 1997: This California Chardonnay proffers a lively mix of bright flavors—tropical fruit, pear, fig and melon—and finishes with shades of nutmeg and oak that add dimension. Drink now through 2003.–J.L. • $15 • (12/31/1999) HR • **88**
Chardonnay Napa Valley Dollarhide Ranch 1996: Plenty of bright peach, pear, fig and toast flavors on a full-bodied, focused frame. Finishes moderately, with a tangy lift. Drink now.–J.L. • $14 • (7/31/1999) • **87**
Chardonnay Napa Valley Dollarhide Ranch Limited Edition 1998: Tight and flinty, with a core of spicy pear, citrus and herbs, finishing with dashes of spice and apple peel. Drink now.–J.L. • $25 • (5/15/2000) • **84**
Meritage Napa Valley 1995: A blend of cherry, herb, roasted coffee and sweet oak flavors, this is tight and a bit astringent. Carries bright cherry and vanilla on the finish. Drink through 2005. • $40 • (2/28/1999) • **86**
Meritage White Napa Valley 1997: Lemon and grapefruit flavors mingle nicely here, capped by subtle vanilla and herb notes. Fairly viscous on the palate, this Sauvignon Blanc blend remains fresh and clean, with tangy acidity and a flinty mineral essence. Drink through 2002. • $20 • (3/31/1999) • **88**
Merlot Napa Valley Dollarhide Ranch 1996: Tannins are a bit rustic, but ripe flavors still find their way through. Black cherry, anise, blackberry and herb

form the core of this wine, which remains lean on the moderate finish. Should improve. Best from 2001 through 2006. • $17 • (6/30/1999) • **86**

Merlot Napa Valley Dollarhide Ranch 1995: Pretty lightweight, with mild herb, cherry and smoke notes and a moderate finish. Drink now. • $17 • (9/15/1998) • **81**

Merlot Napa Valley Dollarhide Ranch 1993 • $17 • (8/31/1996) • **86**

Merlot Napa Valley Dollarhide Ranch 1992 • $15 • (5/15/1995) • **80**

Merlot Napa Valley Dollarhide Ranch 1991 • $14 • (12/31/1993) • **85**

Merlot Napa Valley Dollarhide Ranch 1990 • $14 • (11/30/1992) • **86**

Merlot Napa Valley Dollarhide Ranch 1989 • $14 • (5/31/1992) • **89**

Moscato California 1992 • $11 • (5/15/1993) • **76**

Sauvignon Blanc Napa Valley 1999: Crisp and lively, with very expressive citrus, passion fruit, sweet pea and herb notes. Clean, refreshing finish. Drink now through 2004.–J.L. • $14 • (5/31/2000) • **87**

Sauvignon Blanc Napa Valley 1998: Effusively fragrant, redolent of fig, peach and herb, this attractive white tastes rich and ripe, serving up layers of fresh grapefruit and melon with country charm, all carried along brightly by tangy acidity. Delicious. Drink now. • $12 • (6/15/1999) SS • **91**

Sauvignon Blanc Napa Valley Dollarhide Ranch 1997: Begins with herbal and floral aromas and hints of honey before unveiling a fine blend of melon, grapefruit and just the right amount of grassy character on the palate, where it shows good weight. The finish is refreshingly tangy. Drink now through 2003. • $13 • (3/31/1999) SS • **89**

Sauvignon Blanc Napa Valley Dollarhide Ranch 1996 • $10 • (6/30/1997) • **86**

SAINTSBURY | CALIFORNIA

Chardonnay Carneros 1997: Starts out earthy and leesy before opening into pure, ripe pear and apple flavors. The bright, clean aftertaste focuses on the fruit. Drink now through 2002.–J.L. • $19 • (7/31/1999) • **90**

Chardonnay Carneros 1996 • $17 • (5/15/1998) • **88**

Chardonnay Carneros Reserve 1997: A winner on all counts, this California Chardonnay shows enormous richness and concentration, yet maintains a remarkable sense of harmony and finesse as it gently layers its hazelnut, fig, pear, spice citrus and toasty oak flavors. Drink through 2006.–J.L. • $35 • (7/31/1999) CS • **93**

Pinot Noir Carneros 1997: Smooth and supple, with ripe plum, tea, tar and spice notes. Finishes with a clean cherry flavor. Drink now through 2002.–J.L. • $22 • (2/28/1999) • **88**

Pinot Noir Carneros 1996 • $20 • (1/31/1998) • **88**

Pinot Noir Carneros 1995 • $18 • (12/31/1996) • **88**

Pinot Noir Carneros 1992 • $16 • (2/28/1995) • **85**

Pinot Noir Carneros 1991 • $17 • (2/28/1994) • **87**

Pinot Noir Carneros 1990 • $15 • (3/31/1997) • **89**

Pinot Noir Carneros 1989 • $17 • (2/15/1992) • **85**

Pinot Noir Carneros 1988 • $20 • (12/15/1990) SS • **91**

Pinot Noir Carneros 1987 • $15 • (7/31/1989) • **86**

Pinot Noir Carneros 1986 • $14 • (6/15/1988) • **92**

Pinot Noir Carneros 1985 • $13 • (11/30/1987) • **92**

Pinot Noir Carneros 1984 • $12 • (12/15/1986) • **93**

Pinot Noir Carneros 1983 • $12 • (12/01/1985) • **93**

Pinot Noir Carneros Brown Ranch 1997: Wonderful color, richness, depth, polish and concentration; brimming with juicy plum, black cherry, spice, mushroom and mineral flavors, turning smooth and polished. Wine of the vintage so far. Drink now through 2006.–J.L. • $75 • (9/15/1999) • **92**

Pinot Noir Carneros Brown Ranch 1996: A new single-vineyard wine, this is ripe, supple and harmonious, with rich black cherry, plum and berry flavors and smooth, polished tannins. Drink now through 2002.–J.L. • $75 • (9/30/1998) • **91**

Pinot Noir Carneros Garnet 1997: Clean, ripe and spicy, with black cherry, wild berry, strawberry and tea. Delightful. Drink now.–J.L. • $15 • (2/28/1999) • **87**

Pinot Noir Carneros Garnet 1996 • $13 • (1/31/1998) • **87**

Pinot Noir Carneros Garnet 1995 • $13 • (12/31/1996) • **84**

Pinot Noir Carneros Garnet 1994 • $11 • (11/15/1995) • **85**

Pinot Noir Carneros Garnet 1993 • $11 • (12/15/1994) • **86**

Pinot Noir Carneros Garnet 1992 • $10 • (2/28/1994) • **84**

Pinot Noir Carneros Garnet 1991 • $10 • (12/31/1992) • **88**

Pinot Noir Carneros Garnet 1990 • $10 • (2/15/1992) • **86**

Pinot Noir Carneros Garnet 1989 • $9 • (12/15/1990) • **88**

Pinot Noir Carneros Garnet 1988 • $9 • (3/31/1990) • **84**

Pinot Noir Carneros Rancho 1981 • $NA • (11/30/1987) • **80**

Pinot Noir Carneros Reserve 1997: Seductive with its supple, ripe cherry, plum and berry flavors, smooth texture and polished vanilla-scented oak. Finishes with a long, complex aftertaste and the right amount of tannin. Drink through 2006.–J.L. • $38 • (9/15/1999) • **90**

Pinot Noir Carneros Reserve 1996: A complex and sophisticated California Pinot that combines pretty ripe cherry, plum and currant flavors with spicy, toasty oak, persisting for a long, rich, concentrated aftertaste. Drink through 2004.–J.L. • $35 • (8/31/1998) HR • **90**

Pinot Noir Carneros Reserve 1995 • $35 • (1/31/1998) HR • **93**

Pinot Noir Carneros Reserve 1994 • $35 • (12/31/1996) • **92**

Pinot Noir Carneros Reserve 1993 • $30 • (12/31/1995) • **88**

Pinot Noir Carneros Reserve 1992 • $30 • (12/15/1994) • **89**

Pinot Noir Carneros Reserve 1991 • $30 • (2/28/1994) • **88**

Pinot Noir Carneros Reserve 1990 • $30 • (3/31/1997) • **92**

SAKONNET | NEW ENGLAND

Cabernet Franc Rosé Southeastern New England 1996 • $10 • (12/31/1997) • **78**

Cabernet Franc Southeastern New England 1995: Sweet cherry and vanilla flavors are appealing in this supple red, but an underlying herbal note dominates the finish. Drink now.–T.M. • $20 • (5/31/2000) • **82**

Cabernet Franc Southeastern New England 1994 • $20 • (8/31/1997) • **82**

Chardonnay Southeastern New England 1998: This refreshing white offers polished flavors of melon and apple, with sweet oak accents and enough acidity to keep it lively. Drink now.–T.M. • $16 • (5/31/2000) • **85**

Fumé Vidal Southeastern New England 1998: Smooth and full-bodied, this gentle white offers vanilla and ripe apple flavors and a soft, slightly sweet finish. Drink now.–T.M. • $10 • (1/01/2000) • **80**

Gewürztraminer Southeastern New England 1998: Made in the dry style, this generous white shows distinctive rose petal and spicy aromas and ripe apple flavors. Clean, short finish. Drink now.–T.M. • $15 • (1/01/2000) • **83**

Gewürztraminer Southeastern New England 1997: This delicate white offers light peach and herb flavors that show varietal character, if in a minor key.–T.M. • $15 • (12/15/1998) • **78**

Mariner Red France-America NV • $9 • (1/01/1997) • **65**

Mariner White France-America NV • $9 • (8/31/1997) • **74**

Vidal Blanc Southeastern New England 1998: This generous white boasts lively apple and citrus flavors, with a good balance of fruit and acidity. It's refreshing and clean. Drink now.–T.M. • $10 • (5/31/2000) • **84**

SALISHAN | WASHINGTON

Cabernet Sauvignon Washington 1992 • $12 • (9/30/1995) • **78**

Pinot Noir Washington 1991 • $10 • (9/30/1995) • **83**

Pinot Noir Washington Lot 1 1992 • $6 • (8/31/1996) • **80**

Pinot Noir Washington Lot 1 1989 • $10 • (2/28/1993) • **77**

Pinot Noir Washington Silver Anniversary NV • $9 • (8/31/1996) • **81**

SALMON HARBOR | CALIFORNIA

Chardonnay Napa Valley Reserve 1998: Butterscotch overtones, with refreshing citrus flavors on a crisp frame. Drink now.–J.L. • $20 • (6/30/2000) • **82**

Syrah California 1996 • $12 • (6/15/1998) • **83**

SALVESTRIN | CALIFORNIA

Cabernet Sauvignon Napa Valley 1996: Ripe and focused, with a complex range of black currant, cedar, herb and anise flavors. Finishes with detailed flavors and integrated tannins. Drink now through 2005.–J.L. • $36 • (9/30/1999) • **88**

Cabernet Sauvignon Napa Valley 1994 • $26 • (3/31/1998) • **83**

SAN SABA | CALIFORNIA

Cabernet Sauvignon Monterey 1994 • $17 • (6/30/1998) • **75**

Cabernet Sauvignon Monterey 1990 • $15 • (11/15/1994) • **88**

Chardonnay Monterey 1996 • $20 • (5/31/1998) • **87**

Key: SS—Spectator Selection. CS—Cellar Selection. HR—Highly Recommended. $NA—Price not available. (BT)—Barrel tasting. (A)—Auction Price.
For a key to the tasters' initials, see "How to Use These Listings."
Dates in parentheses represent the issues in which the ratings were published.

SANFORD | CALIFORNIA

Chardonnay Santa Barbara County 1998: Sound, but lacking in extra dimensions. Medium in weight, with modest lemon, tart pear and citrus notes that are appealing. Drink now.–J.L. • $19 • (5/31/2000) • **86**
Chardonnay Santa Barbara County 1997: Tastes like there's a hint of botrytis to this California Chardonnay, tinging the concentrated ripe pear, fig, apricot and tangerine flavors with a honeyed complexity, all lingering on the finish. Drink now through 2001.–J.L. • $18 • (4/30/1999) SS • **90**
Chardonnay Santa Barbara County 1996 • $18 • (1/31/1998) • **88**
Chardonnay Santa Barbara County Barrel Select 1998: Tight and flinty, with a core of earthy pear, peach and nectarine, holding its focus, finishing with a lively aftertaste. Drink now through 2004.–J.L. • $30 • (6/30/2000) • **88**
Chardonnay Santa Barbara County Barrel Select 1996 • $30 • (6/30/1998) • **92**
Chardonnay Santa Ynez Valley 1996 • $26 • (6/30/1998) • **91**
Chardonnay Santa Ynez Valley Sanford & Benedict Vineyard 1998: Crisp and clean, with a flinty edge to the citrus flavors. Finishes with tart peach and a slight bitter grapefruit edge. Drink now.–J.L. • $28 • (5/31/2000) • **85**
Chardonnay Santa Ynez Valley Sanford & Benedict Vineyard 1997: Rich in fig and apricot flavors, it's a bold and complex style that also shows a remarkable amount of finesse and delicacy. Drink now through 2002. –J.L. • $27 • (7/31/1999) • **90**
Pinot Noir Carneros Vin Gris 1996 • $12 • (9/30/1997) • **87**
Pinot Noir Central Coast 1994 • $19 • (1/31/1997) • **86**
Pinot Noir Central Coast 1984 • $12 • (5/15/1987) • **85**
Pinot Noir Santa Barbara County 1997: A ripe, supple and harmonious red with an attractive range of plum, dried cherry, anise, sage and spice, holding its focus and bowing out with a long, rich aftertaste. Very impressive—among the best of the '97 California Pinots. Drink now through 2006. –J.L. • $23 • (9/15/1999) SS • **90**
Pinot Noir Santa Barbara County 1996 • $22 • (6/30/1998) • **87**
Pinot Noir Santa Barbara County 1995 • $20 • (10/31/1997) SS • **90**
Pinot Noir Santa Barbara County 1994 • $18 • (12/31/1995) • **88**
Pinot Noir Santa Barbara County 1992 • $18 • (1/31/1995) • **88**
Pinot Noir Santa Barbara County 1991 • $17 • (9/15/1993) • **87**
Pinot Noir Santa Barbara County 1990 • $17 • (11/30/1992) SS • **90**
Pinot Noir Santa Barbara County 1989 • $15 • (3/31/1992) • **85**
Pinot Noir Santa Barbara County 1988 • $15 • (6/30/1991) • **78**
Pinot Noir Santa Barbara County 1987 • $14 • (2/28/1991) • **76**
Pinot Noir Santa Barbara County 1986 • $14 • (12/15/1989) • **75**
Pinot Noir Santa Barbara County 1985 • $14 • (6/15/1988) • **74**
Pinot Noir Santa Barbara County Barrel Select 1986 • $20 • (12/15/1989) • **78**
Pinot Noir Santa Barbara County Barrel Select 1985 • $20 • (6/15/1988) • **75**
Pinot Noir Santa Barbara County Sanford & Benedict Vineyard 1997: Terrific fruit purity, depth and complexity, with concentrated black cherry, anise, berry, smoke, vanilla and cola woven into a supple texture with just enough tannin to know it will age. Drink now through 2006.–J.L. • $40 • (9/15/1999) • **91**
Pinot Noir Santa Barbara County Sanford & Benedict Vineyard Barrel Select 1996: Tightly wound and firmly tannic, but with lots of depth and substance. Offers a solid core of black cherry, cola, berry and spice flavors, which come through with intense tannins on the finish. Young and backward; needs time to soften. Drink through 2001.–J.L. • $36 • (9/30/1998) • **88**
Pinot Noir Santa Barbara County Sanford & Benedict Vineyard Barrel Select 1995 • $34 • (1/31/1998) • **91**
Pinot Noir Santa Barbara County Sanford & Benedict Vineyard Barrel Select 1992 • $30 • (1/31/1995) • **88**
Pinot Noir Santa Barbara County Sanford & Benedict Vineyard Barrel Select 1991 • $30 • (2/28/1994) • **88**
Pinot Noir Santa Barbara County Sanford & Benedict Vineyard Barrel Select 1990 • $30 • (3/31/1997) • **92**
Pinot Noir Santa Ynez Valley Barrel Select 1994 • $30 • (8/31/1996) HR • **91**
Pinot Noir Santa Ynez Valley Barrel Select 1993 • $30 • (12/31/1995) • **88**
Sauvignon Blanc Central Coast 1998: Medium in weight, with touches of herb, melon and mushroom. Turns simple. Drink now.–J.L. • $15 • (4/30/2000) • **84**
Sauvignon Blanc Central Coast 1997: A richly styled wine, redolent of fig, butterscotch, herb, fresh pea and tangy citrus flavors. Falters slightly on the finish, with a bitter edge, but still quite attractive on the whole. Drink now through 2002. • $14 • (5/15/1999) • **87**
Sauvignon Blanc Central Coast 1996 • $12 • (6/30/1997) • **89**

SANTA BARBARA | CALIFORNIA

Cabernet Sauvignon Santa Ynez Valley 1991 • $11 • (11/15/1994) • **75**
Cabernet Sauvignon Santa Ynez Valley 1990 • $11 • (11/15/1993) • **83**
Cabernet Sauvignon Santa Ynez Valley 1989 • $11 • (11/15/1992) • **79**
Cabernet Sauvignon Santa Ynez Valley 1988 • $12 • (11/15/1991) • **83**
Cabernet Sauvignon Santa Ynez Valley Reserve 1992 • $16 • (12/15/1995) • **86**
Cabernet Sauvignon Santa Ynez Valley Reserve 1991 • $16 • (11/15/1994) • **84**
Cabernet Sauvignon Santa Ynez Valley Reserve 1990 • $16 • (11/15/1993) • **83**
Cabernet Sauvignon Santa Ynez Valley Reserve 1989 • $16 • (11/15/1992) • **82**
Cabernet Sauvignon Santa Ynez Valley Reserve 1988 • $18 • (11/15/1991) • **83**
Cabernet Sauvignon Santa Ynez Valley Reserve 1987 • $18 • (11/15/1990) • **77**
Cabernet Sauvignon Santa Ynez Valley Reserve 1984 • $14 • (10/31/1987) • **81**
Cabernet Sauvignon Santa Ynez Valley Reserve 1974 • $16 • (12/15/1989) • **81**
Chardonnay Santa Barbara County 1997: Sleek and elegant, with a core of subtle pear and mineral flavors. The finish lingers, showing hints of citrus and spice. Drink now. • $15 • (6/30/1999) • **88**
Chardonnay Santa Barbara County 1996: Full-bodied, with a rich core of melon, peach, mineral and citrus qualities. Tangy finish. Drink now. • $15 • (7/31/1998) • **86**
Chardonnay Santa Ynez Valley Reserve 1996: Smooth, ripe and peachy, with complex pear, spice and apple notes, turning elegant and polished. Drink now through 2002.–J.L. • $24 • (1/31/1999) • **90**
Pinot Noir Santa Barbara County 1995 • $20 • (11/15/1997) • **88**
Pinot Noir Santa Barbara County 1994 • $15 • (2/29/1996) • **84**
Pinot Noir Santa Barbara County 1993 • $12 • (3/31/1995) • **83**
Pinot Noir Santa Barbara County 1991 • $11 • (2/28/1994) • **82**
Pinot Noir Santa Barbara County 1990 • $11 • (2/28/1993) • **87**
Pinot Noir Santa Barbara County 1989 • $11 • (7/31/1991) • **84**
Pinot Noir Santa Barbara County 1986 • $11 • (6/15/1988) • **80**
Pinot Noir Santa Barbara County Reserve 1995 • $40 • (11/15/1997) • **84**
Pinot Noir Santa Barbara County Reserve 1994 • $24 • (2/29/1996) • **82**
Pinot Noir Santa Barbara County Reserve 1993 • $20 • (12/31/1995) • **84**
Pinot Noir Santa Barbara County Reserve 1992 • $20 • (3/31/1995) • **86**
Pinot Noir Santa Barbara County Reserve 1991 • $20 • (2/28/1994) • **79**
Pinot Noir Santa Barbara County Reserve 1990 • $20 • (9/30/1992) • **89**
Pinot Noir Santa Barbara County Reserve 1989 • $20 • (11/15/1991) • **87**
Pinot Noir Santa Ynez Valley Reserve 1987 • $20 • (12/15/1989) • **89**
Sauvignon Blanc Late Harvest Santa Ynez Valley 1995 • $35/375 ml. • (5/15/1998) • **93**
Sauvignon Blanc Late Harvest Santa Ynez Valley 1994 • $18/375 ml. • (8/31/1996) • **83**
Sauvignon Blanc Late Harvest Santa Ynez Valley 1993 • $14/375 ml. • (5/15/1995) • **90**
Sauvignon Blanc Late Harvest Santa Ynez Valley Lafond Vineyard 1990 • $12 • (3/10/1992) • **72**
Sauvignon Blanc Santa Ynez Valley 1996 • $11 • (11/30/1997) • **81**
Syrah Santa Barbara County 1997: Quite bright and fruity, with wild cherry, blackberry and herb notes. The texture is a bit lean, and the tannins are still young. Moderate finish. Should smooth out in time. Drink through 2005. • $21 • (6/30/1999) • **87**
Syrah Santa Ynez Valley 1994 • $16 • (5/15/1996) • **85**
Zinfandel Central Coast Beaujour 1991 • $8 • (7/31/1992) • **84**
Zinfandel Late Harvest Santa Ynez Valley Essence 1993 • $20/375 ml. • (5/31/1995) • **87**
Zinfandel San Luis Obispo County Saucelito Canyon Vineyard 1990 • $11 • (10/15/1992) • **84**
Zinfandel San Luis Obispo County Saucelito Canyon Vineyard 1989 • $11 • (10/15/1992) • **82**
Zinfandel Santa Ynez Valley Beaujour 1994 • $9 • (2/28/1995) • **82**
Zinfandel Santa Ynez Valley Beaujour 1993 • $9 • (10/15/1994) • **84**
Zinfandel Santa Ynez Valley Beaujour 1992 • $9 • (3/15/1993) • **80**
Zinfandel Santa Ynez Valley Beaujour 1988 • $7 • (12/15/1989) • **80**
Zinfandel Santa Ynez Valley Lafond Vineyard 1993 • $14 • (4/30/1997) • **87**
Zinfandel Santa Ynez Valley Lafond Vineyard 1992 • $10 • (10/15/1994) • **85**
Zinfandel Santa Ynez Valley Lafond Vineyard 1991 • $10 • (9/30/1993) • **83**

SANTA CRUZ MOUNTAIN | CALIFORNIA

Cabernet Sauvignon Santa Cruz Mountains 1993: Opens with heady aromas of blackberry, cassis, cedar and spice. On the palate, it's still good, but not as exciting, with a vegetal hint on the finish. Drink now through 2002. • $19 • (10/15/1998) • **86**
Cabernet Sauvignon Santa Cruz Mountains 1979: Earthy and funky, with cedar, mushroom and pepper edge to the mature currant and wild berry flavors. Still tannic though the fruit is fading, so it's best soon. (1979 California Cabernet retrospective tasting). Drink now through 2004.–J.L. • $12 • (8/31/1999) • **84**
Cabernet Sauvignon Santa Cruz Mountains Bates Ranch 1991 • $18 • (11/15/1996) • **86**

SANTA CRUZ MOUNTAIN

Cabernet Sauvignon Santa Cruz Mountains Bates Ranch 1990 • $15 • (12/15/1995) • **85**

Cabernet Sauvignon Santa Cruz Mountains Bates Ranch 1989: Marked by dense, tannic, earthy flavors, tilting more toward cedar, bark and earth than ripe Cabernet fruit. Finishes with murky, mushroomy flavors. A highly stylized wine that's worth holding onto if it's in your cellar. Far from great, it still needs time. (1989 California Cabernet retrospective tasting). Drink through 2007.–J.L. • $15 • (8/31/1999) • **86**

Cabernet Sauvignon Santa Cruz Mountains Bates Ranch 1988 • $14 • (11/15/1993) • **87**

Cabernet Sauvignon Santa Cruz Mountains Bates Ranch 1987 • $NA • (12/15/1997) • **89**

Cabernet Sauvignon Santa Cruz Mountains Bates Ranch 1986 • $16 • (12/15/1996) • **89**

Cabernet Sauvignon Santa Cruz Mountains Bates Ranch 1983 • $27 • (6/15/1989) • **80**

Cabernet Sauvignon Santa Cruz Mountains Bates Ranch 1981 • $13 • (3/01/1985) • **88**

Cabernet Sauvignon Santa Cruz Mountains Bates Ranch 1978: Big, ripe, dense and chewy, finally hitting its stride at age 20. Packed with rich, earthy currant, mineral, sage and leathery aromas and flavors, it has taken this wine two decades to really come into balance. Some will still find it tannic, but those of us who've tasted this wine from its infancy will appreciate that it's finally matured. (1978 California Cabernet retrospective tasting). Drink now through 2008.–J.L. • $12 • (11/15/1998) • **91**

Chardonnay Santa Cruz Mountains S. Miller Vineyard 1997: An understated style that's crisp and minerally, showing hints of green apple and a slight bitterness on the finish. Best after 2000.–J.L. • $19 • (7/31/1999) • **83**

Chardonnay Santa Cruz Mountains S. Miller Vineyard 1996: Takes some getting used to, with earthy, leafy pear and spice notes, yet it's focused, with appealing Chardonnay fruit flavors, too. Drink now through 2001. –J.L. • $19 • (7/31/1998) • **87**

Duriff Paso Robles Shell Creek Vineyard 1997: Dark, with ripe, rich, exotic Asian spiciness. Earthy, ashy and charry notes have stewed plum and wild berry nuances. Drink now through 2006.–J.L. • $24 • (5/31/2000) • **88**

Duriff Santa Cruz Mountains 1992 • $14 • (11/30/1996) • **88**

Merlot California 1993 • $15 • (4/30/1996) • **86**

Merlot California 1991 • $14 • (7/31/1994) • **89**

Merlot California 1989 • $12 • (11/30/1992) • **83**

Merlot California 1983 • $10 • (10/01/1985) • **82**

Merlot San Ysidro San Ysidro Vineyard 1997: Herbaceous, with tart, lean tannin and vegetal flavors.–J.L. • $20 • (6/15/2000) • **79**

Merlot San Ysidro San Ysidro Vineyard 1996: Blackberry, cherry and currant flavors are packed in an herbal blend that comes on a little strong. Tannins are firm. Drink now through 2002. • $19 • (10/15/1998) • **81**

Pinot Noir Santa Cruz Mountains 1996: Medium in weight, bright and marked by pepper and wild berry flavors, enlivened by sharp acidity. Drink now through 2004.–J.L. • $30 • (5/15/2000) • **84**

Pinot Noir Santa Cruz Mountains 1992 • $25 • (9/15/1996) • **88**

Pinot Noir Santa Cruz Mountains 1990 • $18 • (2/28/1994) • **81**

Pinot Noir Santa Cruz Mountains 1989 • $15 • (2/28/1993) • **90**

Pinot Noir Santa Cruz Mountains 1985 • $15 • (6/15/1988) • **89**

Pinot Noir Santa Cruz Mountains Ciardella Vineyard 1997: Distinct for its white pepper flavors, it's lean and earthy, with a twinge of racy wild berry. For those who love white pepper in a Pinot. Drink now through 2005.–J.L. • $25 • (5/15/2000) • **83**

Pinot Noir Santa Cruz Mountains Estate Vineyard 1990 • $18 • (3/31/1997) • **84**

Pinot Noir Santa Cruz Mountains Estate Vineyard 1987 • $18 • (2/28/1994) • **84**

Pinot Noir Santa Cruz Mountains Estate Vineyard 1986 • $18 • (3/31/1997) • **84**

Pinot Noir Santa Cruz Mountains Jarvis Vineyard 1981 • $15 • (8/31/1986) • **89**

Pinot Noir Santa Cruz Mountains Matteson Vineyard 1996: Distinctive and flavorful, ripe and earthy, with a dill edge to the mineral, black cherry and mushroom flavors. Finishes long, smooth and rich. Drink now through 2006.–J.L. • $25 • (8/31/1999) • **88**

Pinot Noir Santa Cruz Mountains Matteson Vineyard 1995 • $18 • (1/31/1998) • **89**

Pinot Noir Santa Cruz Mountains Matteson Vineyard 1993 • $18 • (2/28/1997) • **88**

Pinot Noir Santa Cruz Mountains Matteson Vineyard 1992 • $16 • (4/30/1996) • **89**

Pinot Noir Santa Cruz Mountains Matteson Vineyard 1991 • $15 • (4/30/1996) • **88**

Pinot Noir Santa Cruz Mountains Matteson Vineyard 1990 • $15 • (2/28/1993) • **87**

Pinot Noir Santa Cruz Mountains Matteson Vineyard 1989 • $18 • (2/28/1993) • **87**

SANTINO | CALIFORNIA

Johannisberg Riesling Sonoma County Late Harvest Dry Berry Select 1989 • $18/375 ml. • (11/30/1991) • **92**

Muscat Canelli Amador County Moscato del Diavolo 1994 • $10/375 ml. • (11/30/1997) • **78**

Zinfandel California 1995 • $10 • (6/15/1998) • **84**

Zinfandel Amador County Aged Release 1990 • $9 • (9/30/1993) • **84**

Zinfandel Amador County Aged Release 1989 • $8 • (10/15/1992) • **81**

Zinfandel Amador County Aged Release 1988 • $7 • (2/29/1992) • **75**

Zinfandel Shenandoah Valley Grandpère Vineyards 1989 • $12 • (10/15/1992) • **83**

Zinfandel Shenandoah Valley Grandpère Vineyards 1988 • $12 • (8/31/1991) • **79**

SAPPHIRE HILL | CALIFORNIA

Chardonnay Russian River Valley 1998: A crisp, streamlined style, with ripe pear and nectarine flavors that stray into the bitter range on the finish. Drink now.–J.L. • $22 • (4/30/2000) • **85**

Chardonnay Russian River Valley 1997: Complex and smoothly structured, with subtle layers of toast, fig, pear and spice flavors that fan out on the finish. Drink now.–H.S. • $20 • (11/30/1998) • **87**

SARAH'S VINEYARD | CALIFORNIA

Chardonnay Monterey County Talbott Vineyard 1996: Elegant, with lots of ripe pear, spice, fig and vanilla flavors. Turns sleek and spicy. Drink now through 2002.–J.L. • $30 • (6/30/1999) • **91**

Chardonnay Santa Clara Valley 1998: A bit raw, with citrus, earth and peach pit flavors. Drink now.–J.L. • $45 • (6/15/2000) • **80**

Grenache California Cadenza 1988 • $NA • (4/15/1989) • **80**

L'Audace Santa Clara County 1988 • $30 • (11/15/1992) • **82**

Merlot San Luis Obispo County John Radike Vineyard 1997: Round and supple, but it lacks focus and the cherry, berry and plum flavors are not well defined. Drink through 2005.–J.L. • $40 • (10/15/1999) • **86**

Merlot San Luis Obispo County John Radike Vineyard 1991 • $30 • (3/31/1997) • **83**

Merlot San Luis Obispo County John Radike Vineyard 1987 • $30 • (5/31/1992) • **65**

Merlot Santa Clara Valley Viñuela Aguilar Vineyard 1997: Ripe, rich and exotic, with juicy plum, wild berry, raspberry and spice. Finishes with supple, integrated tannins. Drink now through 2005.–J.L. • $40 • (10/15/1999) • **87**

Pinot Noir Santa Clara County 1993 • $50 • (10/15/1995) • **92**

SATTUI, V. | CALIFORNIA

Cabernet Sauvignon Napa Valley 1991 • $14 • (11/15/1994) • **85**

Cabernet Sauvignon Napa Valley Julian Schwinger Reserve Stock 1992 • $50 • (4/30/1996) • **87**

Cabernet Sauvignon Napa Valley Mario's Reserve Stock 1991 • $35 • (11/15/1994) • **90**

Cabernet Sauvignon Napa Valley Morisoli Vineyard 1994 • $27 • (5/15/1997) • **88**

Cabernet Sauvignon Napa Valley Preston Vineyard 1993 • $24 • (10/15/1996) • **83**

Cabernet Sauvignon Napa Valley Preston Vineyard 1991 • $22 • (11/15/1994) • **87**

Cabernet Sauvignon Napa Valley Preston Vineyard 1988 • $20 • (11/15/1991) • **86**

Cabernet Sauvignon Napa Valley Preston Vineyard Reserve Stock 1988 • $35 • (11/15/1992) • **87**

Cabernet Sauvignon Napa Valley Preston Vineyard Reserve Stock 1987 • $35 • (11/15/1992) • **88**

Cabernet Sauvignon Napa Valley Suzanne's Vineyard 1993 • $18 • (10/15/1996) • **85**

Cabernet Sauvignon Napa Valley Suzanne's Vineyard 1991 • $16 • (11/15/1994) • **86**

Key: SS—Spectator Selection. CS—Cellar Selection. HR—Highly Recommended. $NA—Price not available. (BT)—Barrel tasting. (A)—Auction Price.
For a key to the tasters' initials, see "How to Use These Listings."
Dates in parentheses represent the issues in which the ratings were published.

Cabernet Sauvignon Napa Valley Suzanne's Vineyard 1989 • $15 • (11/15/1992) • **82**
Merlot Napa Valley 1994 • $20 • (11/30/1996) • **83**
Merlot Napa Valley 1989 • $16 • (9/15/1994) • **80**
Zinfandel Howell Mountain 1994 • $20 • (4/30/1997) • **89**
Zinfandel Howell Mountain 1993 • $18 • (4/30/1996) • **84**
Zinfandel Howell Mountain 1991 • $14 • (2/28/1995) • **86**
Zinfandel Napa Valley Suzanne's Vineyard 1994 • $14 • (4/30/1997) • **88**

SAUCELITO CANYON | CALIFORNIA

Zinfandel Arroyo Grande Valley 1998: Has heavy black pepper aromas, with intense berry and vegetable flavors. Drink now through 2003.–J.L. • $20 • (5/15/2000) • **84**
Zinfandel Arroyo Grande Valley 1997: Spicy, with pretty cherry, raspberry and blackberry flavors that are supple. Fun to drink. Try now.–J.L. • $20 • (6/30/1999) • **87**
Zinfandel Arroyo Grande Valley 1996 • $19 • (6/15/1998) • **87**
Zinfandel Arroyo Grande Valley 1995 • $17 • (4/30/1997) • **92**
Zinfandel Arroyo Grande Valley 1993 • $14 • (10/15/1995) SS • **91**
Zinfandel Arroyo Grande Valley 1992 • $12 • (8/31/1994) • **87**
Zinfandel Arroyo Grande Valley 1991 • $12 • (9/30/1993) • **88**
Zinfandel Arroyo Grande Valley 1990 • $13 • (10/15/1992) • **85**
Zinfandel Arroyo Grande Valley 1989 • $13 • (10/15/1992) • **89**

SAUSAL | CALIFORNIA

Cabernet Sauvignon Alexander Valley 1992 • $14 • (10/31/1995) • **88**
Cabernet Sauvignon Alexander Valley 1988 • $14 • (7/15/1993) • **80**
Cabernet Sauvignon Alexander Valley 1987 • $14 • (11/15/1992) • **79**
Cabernet Sauvignon Alexander Valley 1985 • $12 • (7/31/1989) • **74**
Sogno Della Famiglia Alexander Valley 1996: Elegant, with spicy cherry and wild berryish flavors, accents of cedar and light oak, turning complex. A blend of Zinfandel, Sangiovese, Cabernet Sauvignon. Drink now through 2002.–J.L. • $25 • (5/15/1999) • **88**
Zinfandel Alexander Valley 1996: You won't go wrong with this reasonable priced, ready-to-drink California Zin, offering ripe raspberry, black cherry and slightly smoky, earthy flavors that come together on a soft frame, with mild tannins.–J.L. • $10 • (5/15/1999) • **88**
Zinfandel Alexander Valley 1995 • $10 • (6/15/1998) • **84**
Zinfandel Alexander Valley 1994 • $10 • (4/30/1996) • **84**
Zinfandel Alexander Valley 1993 • $9 • (7/31/1995) • **88**
Zinfandel Alexander Valley 1992 • $9 • (1/31/1995) SS • **89**
Zinfandel Alexander Valley 1990 • $9 • (12/15/1992) • **82**
Zinfandel Alexander Valley 1989 • $9 • (3/31/1992) • **79**
Zinfandel Alexander Valley 1988 • $9 • (4/30/1991) • **82**
Zinfandel Alexander Valley Century Vines 1997: Soft tannins frame pleasant plum, prune and cola flavors. Drink now through 2003.–J.L. • $22 • (5/31/2000) • **86**
Zinfandel Alexander Valley Century Vines 1996: A touch nutty, with a stewed plum and loganberry flavor, it's tight, compact and worthy of short-term cellaring. Try through 2003.–J.L. • $20 • (5/15/1999) • **88**
Zinfandel Alexander Valley Century Vines 1995 • $18 • (6/15/1998) • **88**
Zinfandel Alexander Valley Century Vines 1993 • $15 • (3/31/1996) • **84**
Zinfandel Alexander Valley Private Reserve 1997: Marked by coffee, cola and toffee flavors, it's smooth and gamy, turning simpler on the finish. Drink now.–J.L. • $18 • (6/15/2000) • **84**
Zinfandel Alexander Valley Private Reserve 1996: Crisp, with tight black cherry and blackberry flavors. Elegant and fun to drink, finishing with firm tannins. Drink now through 2002.–J.L. • $16 • (5/15/1999) • **88**
Zinfandel Alexander Valley Private Reserve 1995 • $16 • (6/15/1998) • **88**
Zinfandel Alexander Valley Private Reserve 1994 • $14 • (3/31/1997) • **89**
Zinfandel Alexander Valley Private Reserve 1992 • $14 • (1/31/1995) • **87**
Zinfandel Alexander Valley Private Reserve 1991 • $14 • (10/15/1994) • **87**
Zinfandel Alexander Valley Private Reserve 1988 • $14 • (4/30/1991) • **88**
Zinfandel Alexander Valley Private Reserve 1984 • $10 • (2/15/1988) • **86**

SAVANNAH-CHANEL | CALIFORNIA

Cabernet Franc Santa Cruz Mountains 1996: Floral, with spice and wild berry flavors that linger on the firm and focused finish. Drink now through 2002.–J.L. • $28 • (12/15/1999) • **84**
Chardonnay Santa Cruz Mountains 1997: Creamy texture carries the pear, apple, mineral and light citrus flavors in an elegant manner. Fresh and light yet with substance, with a long, refreshing finish. Drink now through 2002. • $22 • (6/30/1999) • **88**
Pinot Noir Central Coast 1998: Definitely funky, with a range of earthy, sweaty notes leading to dried cherry and herb notes that somehow keep on track. Finishes dry and tannic. Drink now through 2006.–J.L. • $19 • (4/30/2000) • **81**
Pinot Noir Santa Lucia Highlands Sleepy Hollow Vineyard 1998: Struggles to find its focus, working through earthy, funky, mushroomy flavors that detract from the modest, earthy cherry and plum. Not quite clean-tasting, it turns dry on the finish. Drink now through 2005.–J.L. • $28 • (4/30/2000) • **81**
Syrah Paso Robles Meeker Vineyard 1998: Tangy raspberry and subtle chocolate nuances carry through nicely on the finish. Drink now through 2005.–J.L. • $20 • (5/31/2000) • **86**

SAXON BROWN | OREGON

Pinot Noir Willamette Valley 1997: Very light in color, with pretty spice and strawberry flavors that remain crisp and minty on the finish. Drink now.–H.S. • $32 • (2/29/2000) • **85**

SCHARFFENBERGER | CALIFORNIA

Blanc de Blancs Mendocino County 1991 • $23 • (11/30/1997) • **87**
Brut Blanc de Blancs Mendocino County Prestige Cuvée 1991 • $23 • (12/31/1995) • **90**
Brut Mendocino County NV • $18 • (11/30/1997) • **87**
Brut Rosé Mendocino County NV • $23 • (11/30/1997) • **87**
Brut Rosé Mendocino County 1992 • $23 • (11/30/1996) • **87**
Crémant Mendocino County Extra Dry NV • $17 • (12/31/1994) • **87**

SCHEID | CALIFORNIA

Cabernet Sauvignon Monterey 1994 • $18 • (3/31/1998) • **83**
Merlot Monterey 1995: An herbal style, with coffee bean notes, and a tartish finish. Drink now. • $22 • (10/15/1998) • **79**

SCHERRER | CALIFORNIA

Zinfandel Alexander Valley Old & Mature Vines 1997: Ripe and zesty, with plum, raspberry and black cherry. Turns supple and polished. Drink now through 2003.–J.L. • $25 • (11/30/1999) • **87**
Zinfandel Alexander Valley Old & Mature Vines 1996: Smooth, ripe and polished, with black cherry, wild berry, strawberry and spice. Elegant and supple finish, with a soft, fleshy texture. Drink now through 2002.–J.L. • $23 • (7/31/1998) • **89**
Zinfandel Alexander Valley Old & Mature Vines 1995 • $18 • (6/30/1997) • **89**
Zinfandel Alexander Valley Old & Mature Vines 1994 • $16 • (9/30/1996) • **86**
Zinfandel Alexander Valley Old & Mature Vines 1993 • $15 • (10/15/1995) • **87**
Zinfandel Alexander Valley Old Vines 1991 • $14 • (8/31/1993) • **87**
Zinfandel Alexander Valley Scherrer Vineyards 1992: Complex, with deep, inviting cherry, raspberry, plum and spice flavors that are well focused and hold their own. Finishes with nice toasty, smoky oak. (Zinfandel retrospective tasting). Drink now through 2002.–J.L. • $NA • (6/30/1999) • **90**
Zinfandel Alexander Valley Special Cuvée 1997: Ripe and jammy, with lively plum, berry and spicy notes, turning firm on the finish, where the tannins are tight. Drink now through 2003.–J.L. • $25 • (3/31/2000) • **86**
Zinfandel Alexander Valley The Shale Terrace 1997: Pleasing to drink, with elegant cherry and raspberry-laced fruit and moderate tannins. Drink now through 2003.–J.L. • $20 • (11/30/1999) • **85**
Zinfandel Alexander Valley The Shale Terrace 1996: Serves up lots of ripe, juicy plum, cherry and blackberry flavors, picking up mint, sage and spice notes while keeping a tight focus. Long on the finish. A new bottling from a section within Scherrer Vineyards. Drink now through 2004.–J.L. • $20 • (7/31/1998) • **89**

SCHNEIDER | NEW YORK

Cabernet Franc North Fork of Long Island 1995: Dressed for a night on the town, this full-bodied, concentrated red is wrapped in a stylish cloak of aromatic oak and firm, enveloping tannin. Invitingly well balanced. Drink now through 2002. • $22 • (11/15/1998) • **90**
Cabernet Franc North Fork of Long Island 1994 • $19 • (9/30/1997) • **86**
Chardonnay North Fork of Long Island 1998: This lively white offers spicy apple and melon flavors, with notes of vanilla and cream to smooth the finish. Clean and balanced. Drink now.–T.M. • $19 • (5/31/2000) • **84**
Chardonnay North Fork of Long Island 1997: Rich and viscous on the palate, this full-bodied white offers vanilla and honey flavors, with light notes of

melon and pear and just enough acidity for balance. Tasted twice, with consistent notes. Drink now.–T.M. • $19 • (6/30/1999) • **84**

Merlot North Fork of Long Island 1994 • $19 • (9/30/1997) • **89**

SCHOOL HOUSE | CALIFORNIA

Pinot Noir Spring Mountain 1995: An exotic style, with leather, mineral, spice, stewed plum and dried cherry flavors, picking up some mushroomy notes on the finish. Drink through 2002.–J.L. • $40 • (9/15/1998) • **84**

Pinot Noir Spring Mountain 1993 • $35 • (12/31/1995) • **77**

SCHRAMSBERG | CALIFORNIA

Blanc de Blancs Napa Valley 1996: Bright and refreshing, with a lemony, floral edge. The wine is crisp, still young, finishing clean and long, with hints of vanilla and herbs. Drink now through 2004. • $28 • (9/15/1999) • **88**

Blanc de Blancs Napa Valley 1994: Firmly structured, with a core of honeyed apple, pear and herb. The finish is clean and pretty, with tiny, graceful bubbles. Drink now. • $26 • (11/30/1998) • **88**

Blanc de Blancs Napa Valley 1993 • $25 • (11/30/1997) • **86**

Blanc de Blancs Napa Valley 1992 • $23 • (11/30/1996) • **86**

Blanc de Noirs Napa Valley 1995: Crisp and toasty, with a citrus and herbal core. Clean and refreshing, offering hints of hazelnut and floral notes on a moderate finish. Drink now through 2003. • $28 • (10/15/1999) • **87**

Blanc de Noirs Napa Valley 1992: Toasty, nutty flavors dominate here, eventually giving way to mature coffee, tea and herb essences. The finish is bright, however, with hints of pear and apple. Drink now. • $28 • (11/30/1998) • **90**

Blanc de Noirs Napa Valley 1990 • $26 • (11/30/1997) • **88**

Brut Napa Valley Reserve 1993: Richly textured and intensely flavored, exhibiting honey, pear and fig notes. Full-bodied and concentrated, ending in a long aftertaste of honey and grilled nuts. Good accompaniment to food. Drink now through 2003.–B.S. • $43 • (2/29/2000) • **90**

Brut Rosé Napa Valley Cuvée de Pinot 1996: Light, bright and refreshing, this wine offers lemon, apple and herb flavors, finishing moderately. Drink now. • $28 • (10/15/1999) • **85**

Brut Rosé Napa Valley Cuvée de Pinot 1995: Light and tangy, with lemony airs and a subtle cherrylike middle. The finish is moderate. Drink now. • $27 • (11/30/1998) • **85**

Brut Rosé Napa Valley Cuvée de Pinot 1994 • $25 • (11/30/1997) • **88**

Brut Rosé Napa Valley Cuvée de Pinot 1992 • $23 • (11/30/1996) • **89**

Brut Rosé Napa Valley Cuvée de Pinot 1990 • $23 • (12/31/1994) • **87**

Demi-Sec Napa Valley Crémant 1992 • $23 • (11/30/1996) • **86**

J. Schram Napa Valley 1992: An elegant blend of hazelnut, grapefruit, floral, herb and honey tones. This wine shows focus and finesse along with a certain smooth richness. The finish is long and satisfying. Drink now. • $65 • (11/30/1998) • **91**

J. Schram Napa Valley 1990 • $31 Ⓐ • (11/30/1997) • **92**

SCHUETZ OLES | CALIFORNIA

Zinfandel Napa Valley Korte Ranch 1997: Ripe and fruity—plum, cherry, raspberry and wild berry flavors turn dry and earthy, with a leathery edge. Drink now through 2005.–J.L. • $17 • (4/30/2000) • **86**

Zinfandel Napa Valley Korte Ranch 1993 • $14 • (10/15/1995) • **88**

Zinfandel Napa Valley Korte Ranch 1992 • $14 • (6/15/1995) • **89**

SCHUG | CALIFORNIA

Brut Carneros Rouge de Noir 1995 • $25 • (12/15/1997) • **78**

Cabernet Sauvignon Napa Valley 1994 • $18 • (12/15/1997) • **88**

Cabernet Sauvignon North Coast 1996: Smooth and smoky, with a range of currant, cola, cedar and spice flavors, finishing with mild tannins. Drink now through 2004.–J.L. • $18 • (10/15/1999) • **86**

Cabernet Sauvignon North Coast 1995: Earth, game and leather flavors dominate the straightforward black cherry ones. Concentrated and supple, but its flavors aren't for everyone. Drink now.–H.S. • $18 • (11/15/1998) • **80**

Key: SS—Spectator Selection. CS—Cellar Selection. HR—Highly Recommended. $NA—Price not available. (BT)—Barrel tasting. Ⓐ—Auction Price. For a key to the tasters' initials, see "How to Use These Listings."
Dates in parentheses represent the issues in which the ratings were published.

Cabernet Sauvignon Sonoma Valley Heritage Reserve 1997: Mint, leather, lavendar and blackberry syrup flavors are encased in a wall of dense tannins. Best from 2002 through 2005.–J.L. • $40 • (6/30/2000) • **84**

Cabernet Sauvignon Sonoma Valley Heritage Reserve 1996: Tightly structured, with a focused core of chocolate, mint, black cherry, exotic spice and toasted oak flavors that gain complexity on the long finish. The tannins, while firm, are well integrated. Drink now through 2005.–J.L. • $40 • (11/15/1999) • **91**

Cabernet Sauvignon Sonoma Valley Heritage Reserve 1995: Young and a bit oaky now, with pleasant cherry, berry and plummy Cabernet flavors. More complex, smoky, toasty currant flavors emerge slowly, as do notes of mineral and sage. Drink through 2004.–J.L. • $40 • (10/31/1998) • **88**

Cabernet Sauvignon Sonoma Valley Heritage Reserve 1994 • $30 • (12/15/1997) • **89**

Cabernet Sauvignon Sonoma Valley Heritage Reserve 1992 • $25 • (11/15/1994) • **86**

Chardonnay Carneros 1998: Citrus and spice notes are straightforward and focused on a medium frame. Drink now.–J.L. • $18 • (6/30/2000) • **83**

Chardonnay Carneros 1997: Brightly textured, with tropical notes; mango, melon and grapefruit come to mind. The finish is fresh, light and clean. Drink now. • $18 • (6/30/1999) • **87**

Chardonnay Carneros 1996 • $18 • (5/15/1998) • **90**

Chardonnay Carneros Heritage Reserve 1998: Pleasantly earthy, with elegant citrus, pear, spice, mushroom and light oak nuances. Finishes with fresh, lively acidity. Drink now through 2005.–J.L. • $25 • (4/30/2000) • **88**

Chardonnay Carneros Heritage Reserve 1997: Weaves together a tasty array of ripe peach, pear, fig and melon flavors that are bright and sharply focused. Full-bodied. Drink now through 2002.–J.L. • $25 • (7/31/1999) • **90**

Chardonnay Carneros Heritage Reserve 1996 • $25 • (5/15/1998) • **87**

Chardonnay North Coast 1996 • $14 • (6/30/1998) • **87**

Chardonnay Sonoma Valley 1998: Zingy lime and lemon flavors are crisp and refreshing, if a bit bitter. Drink now.–J.L. • $14 • (6/30/2000) • **82**

Chardonnay Sonoma Valley 1997: Mild, with flint, green apple, toast and herb flavors that remain tightly wound on the finish. Drink now.–J.L. • $14 • (7/31/1999) • **86**

Merlot Carneros Heritage Reserve 1996: Elegant and flavorful, with a complex range of tobacco, leather, currant and toasted oak flavors that are well focused and persistent. Drink now through 2002.–J.L. • $35 • (10/15/1999) • **86**

Merlot North Coast 1996: Chunky, with smoky, toasted oak edges to the berry flavors. Firmly tannic. Drink now through 2003.–J.L. • $18 • (10/15/1999) • **81**

Merlot North Coast 1995 • $20 • (12/31/1997) • **81**

Pinot Noir Carneros 1998: A bit earthy, with lavender and eucalyptus flavors that finish on a tart, tannic note. Drink now through 2003.–J.L. • $18 • (6/30/2000) • **80**

Pinot Noir Carneros 1997: Tight and firm, with bright acidity and a blend of wild cherry, herb and strawberry notes. Though lean, it fleshes out on the finish, showing some delicacy and length. Drink through 2004. • $18 • (9/15/1999) • **86**

Pinot Noir Carneros 1996 • $18 • (2/28/1998) • **83**

Pinot Noir Carneros 1995 • $18 • (2/28/1998) • **84**

Pinot Noir Carneros 1994 • $16 • (2/29/1996) • **87**

Pinot Noir Carneros 1993 • $16 • (12/31/1995) • **86**

Pinot Noir Carneros 1992 • $15 • (3/31/1995) • **78**

Pinot Noir Carneros 1991 • $15 • (3/31/1995) • **78**

Pinot Noir Carneros 1990 • $14 • (2/28/1994) • **78**

Pinot Noir Carneros Beckstoffer Vineyard 1990 • $16 • (3/31/1997) • **87**

Pinot Noir Carneros Beckstoffer Vineyard 1989 • $14 • (2/28/1993) • **74**

Pinot Noir Carneros Beckstoffer Vineyard 1988 • $13 • (9/30/1992) • **79**

Pinot Noir Carneros Beckstoffer Vineyard 1987 • $13 • (2/28/1991) • **81**

Pinot Noir Carneros Beckstoffer Vineyard 1986 • $13 • (3/31/1997) • **77**

Pinot Noir Carneros Heritage Reserve 1995 • $30 • (12/15/1997) • **87**

Pinot Noir Carneros Heritage Reserve 1994 • $25 • (10/15/1996) • **88**

Pinot Noir Carneros Heritage Reserve 1992 • $25 • (12/31/1995) • **86**

Pinot Noir Carneros Heritage Reserve 1991 • $25 • (12/15/1994) • **87**

Pinot Noir Napa Valley Heinemann Vineyard Reserve 1990 • $20 • (3/31/1997) • **84**

Pinot Noir Napa Valley Heinemann Vineyard Reserve 1989 • $18 • (2/28/1994) • **80**

Pinot Noir Napa Valley Heinemann Vineyard Reserve 1986 • $18 • (3/31/1997) • **74**

Pinot Noir Napa Valley Heinemann Vineyard Reserve 1985 • $15 • (11/15/1991) • **83**

Pinot Noir North Coast 1996: Light in color and flavor, with tart berry and earthy notes. Ready now. Drink now.–J.L. • $14 • (9/15/1998) • **82**

Pinot Noir North Coast 1994 • $14 • (10/15/1996) • **83**

Pinot Noir Sonoma Valley 1997: Light in color and texture, this offers pretty cherry, strawberry and herb flavors framed in firm tannins. The finish is moderate and bright and features a slightly waxy edge. Drink now through 2002. • $14 • (9/15/1999) • **85**

Rouge de Noirs Carneros 1992 • $20 • (12/31/1994) • **85**

Sauvignon Blanc North Coast 1998: Crisp and earthy, with citrus flavors that turn a bit pasty on the finish. Drink now through 2002.–J.L. • $12 • (5/15/2000) • **82**

Sauvignon Blanc North Coast 1997: Leans toward the herbal end of the spectrum, with cut-hay, olive, lemon and mineral notes to the fore. A quaffer. Drink now. • $12 • (5/15/1999) • **82**

Sauvignon Blanc North Coast 1996 • $12 • (9/15/1997) • **87**

SCIAMBRA | CALIFORNIA

Chardonnay Atlas Peak 1997: Creamy, displaying pleasant spicy clove, toasted oak, pear and melon flavors, finishing with a fruity aftertaste. Drink now. • $24 • (5/15/1999) • **87**

Chardonnay Napa Valley 1997: Medium-bodied, delivering fleshy citrus, apple and fig notes and finishing with complex toasted oak flavors. Drink now. • $22 • (5/15/1999) • **87**

SCOTLAND CRAIG | CALIFORNIA

Pinot Noir Atlas Peak 1995 • $22 • (1/31/1998) • **87**

Pinot Noir Russian River Valley Rochioli Vineyard 1993 • $35 • (12/31/1995) • **85**

SCREAMING EAGLE | CALIFORNIA

Cabernet Sauvignon Napa Valley 1996: Sharply defined, this hits all the right notes, with ripe, supple, seductive and detailed plum, berry, cherry, floral and spice flavors woven together. Picks up mineral, cedar, tar and anise on the long, elegant finish. Best from 2001 through 2010.–J.L. • $1,120 Ⓐ • (11/15/1999) • **96**

Cabernet Sauvignon Napa Valley 1995: Here's a delicious young California Cab, brimming with ripe, juicy, complex fruit flavors that echo black cherry, currant, berry and spice. Finishes with a bright, lively aftertaste that keeps the fruit aloft and the tannins fully integrated. Best from 2001 through 2008.–J.L. • $1,126 Ⓐ • (11/15/1998) CS • **96**

Cabernet Sauvignon Napa Valley 1994 • $1,244 Ⓐ • (10/31/1997) • **95**

Cabernet Sauvignon Napa Valley 1993 • $1,094 Ⓐ • (12/31/1996) • **91**

Cabernet Sauvignon Napa Valley 1992 • $1,079 Ⓐ • (2/29/1996) • **94**

SEA RIDGE COASTAL | CALIFORNIA

Cabernet Sauvignon California 1995: Fairly smooth, with hints of black currant, herbs and cola. Lean-textured, it finishes with touches of dill and resin. Drink now. • $10 • (8/31/1998) • **84**

Chardonnay California 1996 • $10 • (6/30/1998) • **78**

Merlot California 1996: Fairly complex, with ripe cherry, blackberry and herbal notes. Oak is a bit heavy, but the ensemble is attractive. Finishes moderately. Drink now through 2002. • $10 • (7/31/1998) • **86**

Pinot Noir California 1996: Maple-sugar candy and spice flavors dry out on the woody finish. Drink now.–J.L. • $10 • (8/31/1998) • **78**

Zinfandel California 1996: A bit herbal, the wine shows pleasant cherry notes, but fails to deliver the ripe, juicy promise inherent in this grape. Drink now. • $10 • (7/31/1998) • **78**

SEAVEY | CALIFORNIA

Cabernet Sauvignon Napa Valley 1996: Firm, tight and complex, with a rich, focused band of spicy currant, mineral, plum, cherry, cedar and anise, turning rich and flavorful on the finish. Best from 2001 through 2010. –J.L. • $48 • (10/31/1999) • **92**

Cabernet Sauvignon Napa Valley 1995: A solid effort. Ripe, rich and concentrated, with a dense, complex core of currant, anise, black cherry and spice, it fills out and finishes with a long, flavorful aftertaste echoing ripe Cabernet themes. Drink through 2004.–J.L. • $46 Ⓐ • (10/31/1998) • **92**

Cabernet Sauvignon Napa Valley 1994 • $30 • (12/31/1997) • **89**

Cabernet Sauvignon Napa Valley 1993 • $28 • (11/15/1996) • **88**

Cabernet Sauvignon Napa Valley 1992 • $28 • (7/31/1996) • **88**

Cabernet Sauvignon Napa Valley 1991 • $26 • (7/31/1995) • **89**

Cabernet Sauvignon Napa Valley 1990 • $43 Ⓐ • (8/31/1994) • **89**

Chardonnay Napa Valley 1997: Tight and flinty, with earthy grapefruit and pear flavors. Racy and complex. Drink now through 2002.–J.L. • $18 • (12/31/1998) • **88**

Merlot Napa Valley 1997: Rich and full-bodied, with ripe and chunky earthy currant and berry, finishing with firm tannins and a cedary oak edge. Drink now through 2005.–J.L. • $36 • (6/30/2000) • **87**

Merlot Napa Valley 1996: Complex, with its integration of ripe cherry, berry and plum flavors and pretty toasty, smoky oak, finishing in a long, rich aftertaste. Drink through 2004.–J.L. • $30 • (9/15/1999) • **88**

Merlot Napa Valley 1994 • $24 • (11/30/1997) • **91**

SEBASTIANI | CALIFORNIA

Barbera Sonoma County 1995: Light and fragrant, appealing for its smooth texture and modest plum and berry flavors, which linger on the pretty finish. Drink now.–H.S. • $20 • (11/30/1998) • **85**

Barbera Sonoma County 1994 • $14 • (7/31/1997) • **86**

Barbera Sonoma County 1989 • $10 • (3/31/1993) • **81**

Barbera Sonoma Valley 1992 • $14 • (7/31/1995) • **86**

Barbera Sonoma Valley 1987 • $11 • (4/30/1991) • **86**

Blanc de Noirs Sonoma County Five Star NV • $11 • (4/30/1990) • **77**

Brut Sonoma County Five Star NV • $11 • (4/30/1990) • **72**

Cabernet Franc California 1988 • $9 • (7/15/1991) • **77**

Cabernet Franc Sonoma County 1989 • $10 • (3/31/1993) • **88**

Cabernet Sauvignon California Proprietor's Reserve 1974 • $40 • (11/15/1994) • **68**

Cabernet Sauvignon North Coast 1986 • $13 • (3/31/1992) • **71**

Cabernet Sauvignon Sonoma County 1996: Rich, smoky and plush, showing off lots of toasty oak, coffee and cola flavors, complex black cherry, cedar and anise. Perks up on the smooth finish and carries the flavors through. Drink now through 2006.–J.L. • $15 • (9/30/1999) • **88**

Cabernet Sauvignon Sonoma County 1995: Muscular, with black currant, tar, anise and herb notes. It's got depth, though the tannins are somewhat drying. Should improve in the bottle. A fine value. Drink through 2004. • $15 • (10/15/1998) • **87**

Cabernet Sauvignon Sonoma County 1994 • $10 • (4/30/1997) • **87**

Cabernet Sauvignon Sonoma County 1992 • $10 • (11/15/1995) • **87**

Cabernet Sauvignon Sonoma County 1991 • $10 • (11/15/1994) • **85**

Cabernet Sauvignon Sonoma County 1990 • $10 • (11/15/1994) • **80**

Cabernet Sauvignon Sonoma County 1989 • $9 • (4/30/1993) • **82**

Cabernet Sauvignon Sonoma County 1988 • $8 • (11/15/1992) • **77**

Cabernet Sauvignon Sonoma County Reserve 1988: Seemingly unevolved, with tight, chewy currant and earth notes and firm tannins. Shows off currant, herb, cherry, cedar and sage flavors before turning dry. (1988 California Cabernet retrospective tasting). Drink now through 2002.–J.L. • $8 • (11/15/1998) • **83**

Cabernet Sauvignon Sonoma County Reserve 1986 • $13 • (1/31/1991) • **86**

Cabernet Sauvignon Sonoma County Reserve 1985 • $13 • (11/15/1990) • **86**

Cabernet Sauvignon Sonoma County Reserve 1978 • $25 • (11/15/1992) • **83**

Cabernet Sauvignon Sonoma Valley 1982 • $27 • (9/15/1986) • **75**

Cabernet Sauvignon Sonoma Valley 1981 • $25 • (8/01/1985) • **91**

Cabernet Sauvignon Sonoma Valley Cherryblock 1992 • $35 • (4/30/1997) • **89**

Cabernet Sauvignon Sonoma Valley Cherryblock 1987 • $14 • (7/15/1992) • **84**

Cabernet Sauvignon Sonoma Valley Cherryblock 1985 • $17 • (3/31/1990) • **89**

Cabernet Sauvignon Sonoma Valley Cherryblock Old Vines 1994: A dark, rich and complex style that captures ripe fruit flavors with a sense of elegance and grace, weaving black cherry, wild berry, anise, currant, spice and cedary notes into a supple and compelling wine. Tannins are well integrated and there's a flash of mineral on the aftertaste. Drink through 2008.–J.L. • $35 • (10/31/1998) • **90**

Cabernet Sauvignon Sonoma Valley Cherryblock Old Vines 1991 • $24 • (11/15/1994) • **88**

Cabernet Sauvignon Sonoma Valley Cherryblock Old Vines 1989 • $15 • (6/15/1993) • **82**

Cabernet Sauvignon Sonoma Valley Reserve 1982 • $11 • (12/31/1987) • **74**

Chardonnay California 1996 • $12 • (6/15/1998) • **88**

Chardonnay Russian River Valley Dutton Ranch 1996: A delicate, understated style, with lovely floral, light oak, ripe pear, fig, apple and melon flavors, which are supple and fleshy on the elegant finish. Drink now through 2001.–J.L. • $30 • (7/31/1998) • **91**

Chardonnay Sonoma County 1997: Mild-mannered, with a gentle core of pear and citrus flavors framed in moderate oak. Could use a bit more zest in the middle. Finishes short. Drink now. • $13 • (2/28/1999) • **83**

Merlot California Country NV • $5 • (5/31/1992) • **72**

Merlot Sonoma County 1996: A blend of cassis, blackberry and herb flavors, couched in subtle oak, with moderate body and ripe tannins. The finish is long, with a hint of bitterness, however. Drink through 2004. • $16 • (9/15/1999) • **86**

Merlot Sonoma County 1995 • $16 • (3/31/1998) • **87**
Merlot Sonoma County 1994 • $14 • (6/30/1996) • **82**
Merlot Sonoma County 1993 • $12 • (11/15/1995) • **87**
Merlot Sonoma County 1992 • $12 • (9/15/1994) • **79**
Merlot Sonoma County 1991 • $8 • (5/15/1993) • **84**
Merlot Sonoma County 1990 • $10 • (3/31/1993) • **82**
Merlot Sonoma County 1989 • $9 • (5/31/1992) • **85**
Merlot Sonoma Valley Town 1994 • $25 • (6/30/1997) • **89**
Mourvèdre California Old Vines 1993 • $14 • (8/31/1996) • **85**
Red Hill Vineyard Sonoma Valley 1989 • $14 • (11/15/1993) • **79**
Syrah Dry Creek Valley 1995 • $15 • (3/31/1998) • **89**
Syrah Sonoma County 1992 • $14 • (1/31/1995) • **86**
Wildwood Sonoma Valley 1987 • $15 • (8/31/1991) • **86**
Zinfandel Dry Creek Valley Cuneo-Saini Farms Old Vines 1994 • $12 • (10/15/1995) • **88**
Zinfandel Sonoma County 1991 • $8 • (10/15/1994) • **83**
Zinfandel Sonoma County 1989 • $7 • (3/31/1993) • **85**
Zinfandel Sonoma County 1988 • $6 • (9/15/1992) • **78**
Zinfandel Sonoma County Old Vines Cuvée 1996: Well oaked, with toasted grain notes and a ripe, supple core of blackberry, cherry and cedar. Drink now through 2003.–J.L. • $20 • (1/31/1999) • **88**
Zinfandel Sonoma County Old Vines Cuvée 1995 • $20 • (6/15/1998) • **82**
Zinfandel Sonoma Valley Domenici Vineyard Old Vines 1996: Ripe, supple and complex, with cherry, strawberry, anise and sage, it fans out and gains nuance on the finish. Drink now through 2003.–J.L. • $24 • (1/31/1999) • **88**
Zinfandel Sonoma Valley Domenici Vineyard Old Vines 1995 • $17 • (5/15/1998) • **87**

SEBASTOPOL | CALIFORNIA

Chardonnay Russian River Valley Dutton Ranch 1997: Earthy, with grapefruit, apple and toast flavors and a tight, citrusy finish. Drink now through 2001.–J.L. • $22 • (6/30/1999) • **86**
Chardonnay Russian River Valley Dutton Ranch 1996 • $24 • (5/15/1998) • **87**
Pinot Noir Russian River Valley Dutton Ranch 1997: Ripe and racy, with a range of black cherry, olive, sage, earth and cola. Turns spicy, with mild, integrated tannins. Drink now through 2004.–J.L. • $27 • (12/31/1999) • **88**
Pinot Noir Russian River Valley Dutton Ranch 1996: Pleasantly fruity, with dried cherry, berry, sage and spicy notes of moderate depth and proportion. Finishes with simple fruit flavors. Drink now.–J.L. • $25 • (9/15/1998) • **84**
Pinot Noir Russian River Valley Dutton Ranch 1995 • $24 • (1/31/1998) • **86**

SECRET HOUSE | OREGON

Pinot Noir Willamette Valley 1994 • $17 • (11/30/1996) • **89**

SEGHESIO | CALIFORNIA

Barbera California Noble Vines 1996 • $17 • (6/30/1998) • **84**
Barbera California Vitigno Piemontese 1995 • $15 • (11/30/1997) • **87**
Cabernet Sauvignon Sonoma County 1993 • $10 • (2/29/1996) • **84**
Cabernet Sauvignon Sonoma County 1992 • $9 • (11/15/1994) • **84**
Cabernet Sauvignon Sonoma County 1991 • $9 • (3/31/1994) • **83**
Cabernet Sauvignon Sonoma County 1990 • $9 • (6/15/1993) • **79**
Cabernet Sauvignon Sonoma County 1989 • $9 • (11/15/1992) • **82**
Carignane Alexander Valley Old Vine 1992 • $12 • (12/31/1993) • **84**
Omaggio Four Generations Sonoma County 1997: Bright, juicy and tight, with black cherry, currant and wild berry notes. Sharply focused, long and intense. Drink now through 2007.–J.L. • $45 • (5/15/2000) • **88**
Omaggio Four Generations Sonoma County 1995 • $30 • (12/31/1997) • **88**
Pinot Noir Russian River Valley 1995 • $14 • (2/28/1998) • **82**
Pinot Noir Russian River Valley 1994 • $12 • (2/28/1997) • **86**
Pinot Noir Russian River Valley 1991 • $9 • (2/28/1994) • **81**
Pinot Noir Russian River Valley 1990 • $9 • (2/28/1993) • **78**
Pinot Noir Russian River Valley 1988 • $9 • (10/31/1991) • **83**
Pinot Noir Russian River Valley Keyhole Ranch 1998: Medium in weight, with earthy cherry, cedar and sage notes that are decent, though lacking in focus and depth. Drink now.–J.L. • $25 • (5/15/2000) • **84**

Key: SS—Spectator Selection. CS—Cellar Selection. HR—Highly Recommended. $NA—Price not available. (BT)—Barrel tasting. (A)—Auction Price. For a key to the tasters' initials, see "How to Use These Listings."
Dates in parentheses represent the issues in which the ratings were published.

Pinot Noir Russian River Valley Keyhole Ranch 1997: Bright and rich, with a tight core of black cherry, cassis and spicy oak flavors. Tight and firm, but well integrated on the long finish. Drink now through 2003.–J.L. • $20 • (9/15/1999) • **87**
Pinot Noir Russian River Valley Reserve 1987 • $13 • (4/15/1990) • **83**
Pinot Noir Sonoma County 1993 • $12 • (11/15/1995) • **86**
Pinot Noir Sonoma County 1989 • $9 • (4/30/1992) • **79**
Sangiovese Alexander Valley Chianti Station Old Vine 1990 • $30 • (12/15/1992) • **86**
Sangiovese Alexander Valley Nonno's Clones 1996 • $15 • (6/30/1998) • **86**
Sangiovese Alexander Valley Vitigno Toscano 1995 • $15 • (10/15/1997) • **80**
Sangiovese Alexander Valley Vitigno Toscano 1992 • $14 • (5/31/1994) • **87**
Sangiovese Alexander Valley Vitigno Toscano 1991 • $14 • (12/15/1992) • **80**
Sonoma Red Lot 4 Sonoma County NV • $5 • (6/30/1990) • **75**
Sonoma Red Lot 3 Sonoma County NV • $4 • (5/31/1988) • **78**
Zinfandel Alexander Valley 1996 • $18 • (5/15/1998) • **87**
Zinfandel Alexander Valley Home Ranch 1997: A touch dry up front before moving into dried cherry and berry flavors, turning quite tannic. Drink now through 2002.–J.L. • $25 • (5/15/1999) • **87**
Zinfandel Alexander Valley Old Vine Reserve 1990 • $14 • (12/15/1992) • **83**
Zinfandel Alexander Valley Reserve 1988 • $12 • (8/31/1991) • **88**
Zinfandel Alexander Valley San Lorenzo 1997: Ripe, smooth and elegant, with spicy cherry, raspberry, wild berry and light oak; the tannins turn spicy. Drink now through 2002.–J.L. • $25 • (5/15/1999) • **87**
Zinfandel Alexander Valley San Lorenzo 1996 • $20 • (5/15/1998) • **86**
Zinfandel Alexander Valley San Lorenzo 1995 • $20 • (5/15/1998) • **88**
Zinfandel Dry Creek Valley 1993 • $12 • (10/15/1995) • **85**
Zinfandel Dry Creek Valley Cortina 1998: Brimming with spicy blackberry, cranberry and dried berry flavors, it holds together through the midpalate before turning dry and tannic. Drink now through 2005.–J.L. • $25 • (5/31/2000) • **87**
Zinfandel Sonoma County 1998: Hard and dry, with a tart berry edge to the modest fruit flavors. Finishes with a green tealike edge. Drink now through 2004.–J.L. • $15 • (5/31/2000) • **83**
Zinfandel Sonoma County 1995 • $10 • (4/30/1997) • **87**
Zinfandel Sonoma County 1994 • $10 • (9/15/1996) • **83**
Zinfandel Sonoma County 1993 • $9 • (10/15/1995) • **85**
Zinfandel Sonoma County 1992 • $9 • (9/15/1994) • **88**
Zinfandel Sonoma County 1991 • $8 • (9/30/1993) • **84**
Zinfandel Sonoma County 1990 • $8 • (10/15/1992) • **85**
Zinfandel Sonoma County 1989 • $8 • (7/31/1992) • **84**
Zinfandel Sonoma County 1988 • $7 • (9/30/1991) • **86**
Zinfandel Sonoma County Old Vine 1997: Ripe and juicy, with bright cherry, raspberry, plum and wild berry flavors, finishing with firm, dry tannins. Drink now through 2002.–J.L. • $25 • (5/15/1999) • **88**
Zinfandel Sonoma County Old Vine 1996 • $21 • (6/15/1998) • **90**
Zinfandel Sonoma County Old Vine 1995 • $20 • (4/30/1998) • **90**
Zinfandel Sonoma County Old Vine 1994 • $14 • (10/15/1996) • **88**
Zinfandel Sonoma County Sonoma 1997: Lush, complex and concentrated, with lots of appealing wild berry, blackberry, earth, sage and spicy flavors, finishing with a firm wall of tannins. Drink through 2005.–J.L. • $14 • (5/15/1999) • **87**
Zinfandel Sonoma County Sonoma 1996 • $13 • (5/15/1998) • **85**

SELBY | CALIFORNIA

Chardonnay Sonoma County 1997: Deliciously ripe and fruity, with lots of pear, spice, apple, melon, fig and nutmeg, turning long, rich and creamy on the finish. Drink now through 2001.–J.L. • $23 • (5/15/1999) • **92**
Chardonnay Sonoma County 1996 • $23 • (4/30/1998) • **90**
Merlot Sonoma County 1996: Earthy, minerally berry, cherry and herb flavors spread out on a ripe, supple frame. Finishes with ripe, integrated tannins. Drink now through 2002.–J.L. • $25 • (10/15/1999) • **86**
Merlot Sonoma County 1995: This is a little tough and tannic around the edges, and the core of currant, berry, leather and spice is tight and austere, so give it time. Drink through 2005.–J.L. • $25 • (9/30/1998) • **86**
Merlot Sonoma County 1994 • $23 • (5/15/1997) • **88**
Pinot Noir Russian River Valley 1996: Soft-textured, with delicate cola, tea, mushroom, spice and strawberry notes that linger. Drink now through 2001.–J.L. • $20 • (9/15/1999) • **85**
Pinot Noir Russian River Valley 1994 • $16 • (5/15/1996) • **85**
Syrah Sonoma County 1995: Silky and smoky, with a bay leaf edge to the rich black cherry, wild berry and toasted oak flavors. Smooth on the finish. Drink now through 2004.–J.L. • $20 • (9/15/1999) • **87**
Syrah Sonoma County 1994 • $20 • (4/30/1998) • **88**
Syrah Sonoma County 1993 • $20 • (2/28/1997) • **87**

Zinfandel Sonoma County Old Vines 1996: Lots of flavor and finesse, with a pretty array of cherry, plum, wild berry and vanilla, turning smooth and supple on the finish. Drink now through 2002.–J.L. • $20 • (5/15/1999) • **91**

Zinfandel Sonoma County Old Vines 1995 • $20 • (5/15/1998) • **85**

SELENE | CALIFORNIA

Merlot Carneros Hyde Vineyards 1996: Ripe and fleshy, if initially restrained in flavor; enough ripe cherry, berry, cedar, spice and nutmeg flavors emerge to fill out the gaps. Drink now through 2005.–J.L. • $28 • (10/15/1999) • **87**

Merlot Napa Valley 1996: Smooth and complex, with ripe plum, black cherry and pretty smoky oak flavors, turning perfumed and supple. Drink now through 2004.–J.L. • $30 • (12/31/1998) • **88**

Merlot Napa Valley 1995 • $28 • (12/31/1997) • **85**

Merlot Napa Valley 1994 • $26 • (11/30/1996) • **88**

Merlot Napa Valley 1993 • $25 • (6/15/1996) • **84**

Merlot Napa Valley 1992 • $25 • (8/31/1996) • **89**

Merlot Napa Valley 1991 • $22 • (7/31/1994) • **88**

Sauvignon Blanc Carneros Hyde Vineyard 1997: A richly textured wine, yet also one of restraint and finesse, this serves up ripe melon and fig flavors balanced by fresh grapefruit, sweet pea and herb notes. Has firm acidity, with silky viscosity. A delicious effort from a longtime devotee of the grape. Drink now through 2002. • $20 • (1/31/1999) • **90**

Sauvignon Blanc Carneros Hyde Vineyards 1996 • $20 • (11/30/1997) • **87**

SEQUOIA GROVE | CALIFORNIA

Cabernet Sauvignon Alexander Valley 1981 • $12 • (12/16/1984) • **87**

Cabernet Sauvignon Napa & Alexander Valleys 1983 • $13 • (2/15/1987) • **88**

Cabernet Sauvignon Napa & Alexander Valleys 1982 • $12 • (12/16/1985) • **83**

Cabernet Sauvignon Napa County 1986 • $16 • (9/30/1989) • **78**

Cabernet Sauvignon Napa County 1985 • $16 • (12/15/1988) • **86**

Cabernet Sauvignon Napa Valley 1996: Elegant and well focused, with a core of black cherry, mineral and toasted oak flavors and firm tannins. Drink now through 2004.–J.L. • $25 • (9/30/1999) • **87**

Cabernet Sauvignon Napa Valley 1995 • $22 • (6/15/1998) • **88**

Cabernet Sauvignon Napa Valley 1992 • $18 • (7/31/1995) SS • **90**

Cabernet Sauvignon Napa Valley 1991 • $18 • (11/15/1994) • **88**

Cabernet Sauvignon Napa Valley 1990 • $16 • (3/31/1994) SS • **90**

Cabernet Sauvignon Napa Valley 1989 • $16 • (11/15/1992) • **80**

Cabernet Sauvignon Napa Valley 1988 • $20 • (11/15/1992) • **87**

Cabernet Sauvignon Napa Valley 1987 • $19 • (11/15/1991) • **70**

Cabernet Sauvignon Napa Valley 1984 • $36 Ⓐ • (11/15/1987) • **82**

Cabernet Sauvignon Napa Valley 1981 • $12 • (3/01/1984) • **87**

Cabernet Sauvignon Napa Valley Estate 1988 • $25 • (11/15/1992) • **87**

Cabernet Sauvignon Napa Valley Estate 1987 • $31 • (11/15/1991) • **87**

Cabernet Sauvignon Napa Valley Estate 1986 • $28 • (9/30/1989) • **84**

Cabernet Sauvignon Napa Valley Estate 1985 • $30 • (8/31/1988) • **92**

Cabernet Sauvignon Napa Valley Reserve 1996: Firm, tight and marked by cedary currant, black cherry, olive and herbal flavors, turning tannic and austere on the finish. Best from 2002 through 2009.–J.L. • $40 • (10/31/1999) • **88**

Cabernet Sauvignon Rutherford Reserve 1995: Tightly wound, with firm, gripping tannins wrapped around the core of currant, black cherry and plummy berry flavors. Finishes with a flash of oak. Given a little time, it may be even better. Drink through 2008.–J.L. • $40 • (11/15/1998) • **89**

Cabernet Sauvignon Rutherford Estate Reserve 1994 • $37 • (3/31/1998) • **83**

Cabernet Sauvignon Rutherford Estate Reserve 1993 • $30 • (11/15/1996) • **88**

Cabernet Sauvignon Rutherford Estate Reserve 1992 • $30 • (7/31/1995) • **89**

Cabernet Sauvignon Napa Valley Estate Reserve 1991 • $26 • (7/31/1994) • **91**

Cabernet Sauvignon Napa Valley Estate Reserve 1990 • $25 • (12/15/1993) • **90**

Cabernet Sauvignon Napa Valley Estate Reserve 1989 • $25 • (10/31/1992) HR • **93**

Chardonnay Napa Valley Carneros 1997: Fresh, with snappy lemon and lime flavors, finishing with crisp pear, green apple and hints of cream that persist on the finish. Drink now.–H.S. • $18 • (4/30/1999) • **87**

Chardonnay Napa Valley Carneros 1996 • $18 • (5/15/1998) • **87**

Chardonnay Rutherford Estate Reserve 1997: A flavorful, crisp, clean, citrus-centered style, with a refreshing herb and pear-tinged finish that lingers. Drink now.–J.L. • $22 • (7/31/1999) • **88**

SEQUOIA RIDGE | CALIFORNIA

Cabernet Sauvignon California 1996: Soft and straightforward, with strawberry, cherry and toasty oak flavors. An easy, pleasant quaff. Drink now.–H.S. • $8 • (11/15/1998) • **81**

Merlot California 1996: Cherry notes are dominated by sweet oaky flavors that turn minty and herbal. Dry finish.–J.L. • $8 • (12/15/1998) • **77**

Zinfandel California 1996: Simple, with earthy herb and berry notes and firm tannins.–J.L. • $8 • (11/30/1998) • **78**

SEVEN HILLS | WASHINGTON

Cabernet Sauvignon Columbia Valley Klipsun Vineyard 1996: Dark in color, firm in texture and bright in flavor, offering currant and blackberry at the core and nice shadings of mint and vanilla. Drink through 2005.–H.S. • $25 • (9/30/1999) • **87**

Cabernet Sauvignon Columbia Valley Klipsun Vineyard 1994 • $22 • (7/31/1997) • **88**

Cabernet Sauvignon Columbia Valley Klipsun Vineyard 1993 • $20 • (9/15/1996) • **88**

Cabernet Sauvignon Columbia Valley Klipsun Vineyard 1992 • $20 • (7/31/1996) • **90**

Cabernet Sauvignon Columbia Valley Oregon Klipsun Vineyard 1991 • $20 • (10/15/1994) • **81**

Cabernet Sauvignon Oregon 1993 • $12 • (3/31/1996) • **82**

Cabernet Sauvignon Oregon 1991 • $10 • (10/15/1994) • **85**

Cabernet Sauvignon Walla Walla Valley Oregon 1990 • $20 • (9/30/1993) • **90**

Cabernet Sauvignon Walla Walla Valley Oregon 1989 • $20 • (3/31/1992) • **85**

Cabernet Sauvignon Walla Walla Valley Seven Hills Vineyard 1996: On the tough and earthy side, with gamy, leathery flavors weaving through the crisp berry and currant. Should come together with cellaring. Best after 2001.–H.S. • $25 • (9/30/1999) • **86**

Cabernet Sauvignon Walla Walla Valley Seven Hills Vineyard 1995 • $23 • (3/31/1998) • **87**

Cabernet Sauvignon Walla Walla Valley Seven Hills Vineyard 1991 • $22 • (10/15/1994) • **87**

Cabernet Sauvignon Walla Walla Valley Seven Hills Vineyard Reserve 1994: Firm at the core, with rich, supple texture and sage-accented flavors of currant and black cherry wrapped in a veil of spicy oak. Rich without extra weight, but it has a greenish edge on the finish. Drink through 2005. –H.S. • $40 • (9/15/1998) • **88**

Cabernet Sauvignon Walla Walla Valley Seven Hills Vineyard Reserve 1990 • $30 • (7/31/1996) • **91**

Merlot Columbia Valley 1995 • $20 • (8/31/1997) • **90**

Merlot Columbia Valley 1994 • $18 • (9/15/1996) • **87**

Merlot Columbia Valley Klipsun Vineyard 1995 • $24 • (8/31/1997) • **89**

Merlot Oregon 1997: Light and juicy, with pretty plum and spice flavors on a lean frame. Drink now.–H.S. • $16 • (9/30/1999) • **84**

Merlot Walla Walla Valley Oregon 1990 • $18 • (3/15/1993) • **88**

Merlot Walla Walla Valley Oregon Seven Hills Vineyard 1992 • $20 • (11/30/1994) • **84**

Merlot Walla Walla Valley Seven Hills Vineyard 1997: Dense and chewy, with lots of blackberry, tar and anise flavors opening up smoothly on the ripe, sweetly spicy finish. Tempting now. Best after 2000.–H.S. • $26 • (9/15/1999) • **89**

Merlot Walla Walla Valley Seven Hills Vineyard 1995 • $24 • (8/31/1997) • **85**

Merlot Walla Walla Valley Seven Hills Vineyard 1994 • $24 • (9/15/1996) • **86**

Merlot Walla Walla Valley Seven Hills Vineyard 1993 • $22 • (9/30/1995) • **88**

Pinot Gris Willamette Valley 1996 • $13 • (8/31/1997) • **83**

Pinot Gris Willamette Valley Coleman Vineyard 1998: Earthy, floral flavors overshadow the fruit in this medium-weight dry white.–H.S. • $12 • (10/15/1999) • **78**

Syrah Walla Walla Valley 1997: Ripe and generous, solidly packed with blackberry, plum and black pepper flavors that pick up a hint of bay leaf on the supple finish. Drink now through 2002.–H.S. • $28 • (9/30/1999) • **88**

White Riesling Columbia Valley 1994 • $7 • (9/30/1995) • **85**

SEVEN PEAKS | CALIFORNIA

Cabernet Sauvignon Central Coast 1997: Soft-textured, with good depth to the rich black cherry, currant, anise and smoky oak. Mild tannins on the finish. Drink now through 2002.–J.L. • $13 • (10/15/1999) • **85**

Cabernet Sauvignon Central Coast 1996: Smooth-textured, sporting tar, smoke and herb flavors on a modest frame. Drink now. • $12 • (12/31/1998) • **84**

SEVEN PEAKS

Cabernet-Shiraz Central Coast 1997: There's some initial richness to the milk chocolate and vanilla notes, then tart, austere tannins clamp down on the finish. Best from 2001 through 2004.–J.L. • $20 • (6/30/2000) • **81**

Cabernet-Shiraz Central Coast 1996: Rich and supple, offering a complex mouthful of juicy cassis, blackberry, tar, vanilla and mineral notes. Drink now.–J.L. • $16 • (12/31/1998) • **87**

Chardonnay California 1996 • $12 • (9/30/1997) • **87**

Chardonnay Central Coast 1998: Floral, with peach flavors that turn to vanilla and tart citrus on the finish. Drink now.–J.L. • $13 • (6/30/2000) • **83**

Chardonnay Central Coast 1997: Ripe and flavorful, with elegant apple, pear, apricot and toasty oak notes. Flavors persist on the clean, refreshing finish. Drink now.–J.L. • $14 • (2/28/1999) • **87**

Chardonnay Edna Valley Reserve 1997: Butter, pine and nectarine notes turn crisp on the finish. Drink now.–J.L. • $20 • (6/30/2000) • **82**

Chardonnay Edna Valley Reserve 1996 • $18 • (6/30/1998) • **88**

Merlot Central Coast 1997: Firm, with a tight range of herb, berry and mineral flavors, finishing with toasted oak notes. Drink now through 2004. –J.L. • $16 • (10/15/1999) • **84**

Pinot Noir Edna Valley 1997: Smooth and spicy, with fresh cherry, spice and tea flavors, turning simple on the finish. Drink now.–J.L. • $16 • (4/30/1999) • **83**

Shiraz Paso Robles 1997: Ripe and fat, with overtones of raw pastry dough and cassis. Some cinnamon notes on the dryly tannic finish. Best from 2002 through 2006.–J.L. • $20 • (6/30/2000) • **90**

Shiraz Paso Robles 1996: Ripe and lively, with chocolate and vanilla flavors threading the plum, cherry and charry, toasty oak notes. Packs a lot of juicy flavors on a supple frame. Drink now.–J.L. • $16 • (12/31/1998) • **85**

SHAFER | CALIFORNIA

Cabernet Sauvignon Napa Valley 1996: Ripe, rich and elegant, with a smoky currant, plum and black cherry character that's supple and well defined, finishing with mild, integrated tannins. Drink now through 2006.–J.L. • $38 • (8/31/1999) • **88**

Cabernet Sauvignon Napa Valley 1979: Quite rich, firm and concentrated, even tannic, but the fruit's quite impressive, with intense currant, cherry, coffee and cedar notes. (1979 California Cabernet retrospective tasting). Drink now through 2005.–J.L. • $13 • (8/31/1999) • **92**

Cabernet Sauvignon Stags Leap District 1995: Firm, focused, intense and concentrated, serving up plenty of ripe cherry, currant, plum and berry, finishing with rich, complex flavors and tannins. Wonderful focus and length; cellar short-term. Drink through 2007.–J.L. • $30 • (8/31/1998) • **93**

Cabernet Sauvignon Stags Leap District 1994 • $211 Ⓐ • (6/30/1997) • **88**

Cabernet Sauvignon Stags Leap District 1993 • $24 • (9/15/1996) • **86**

Cabernet Sauvignon Stags Leap District 1992 • $22 • (9/30/1995) CS • **91**

Cabernet Sauvignon Stags Leap District 1991 • $21 • (8/31/1994) HR • **90**

Cabernet Sauvignon Stags Leap District 1990 • $52 Ⓐ • (11/15/1993) • **90**

Cabernet Sauvignon Stags Leap District 1989 • $19 • (8/31/1992) • **86**

Cabernet Sauvignon Stags Leap District 1988 • $20 • (8/31/1991) • **88**

Cabernet Sauvignon Stags Leap District 1987 • $19 • (7/31/1990) • **92**

Cabernet Sauvignon Stags Leap District 1986 • $20 • (9/30/1989) SS • **93**

Cabernet Sauvignon Stags Leap District 1985 • $16 • (11/15/1988) • **88**

Cabernet Sauvignon Stags Leap District 1984 • $14 • (12/15/1987) SS • **93**

Cabernet Sauvignon Stags Leap District 1982 • $13 • (6/16/1985) • **90**

Cabernet Sauvignon Stags Leap District 1980 • $11 • (2/16/1984) • **73**

Cabernet Sauvignon Stags Leap District 1978: A real mouthful of Cabernet, time has worked in its favor. It still exhibits a rich core of currant and cherry and the tannins are a bit raw, but it's youthful for its age, with hints of anise, cedar and sage. Finishes with a long, complex aftertaste and a meaty edge. (1978 California Cabernet retrospective tasting). Drink now through 2004.–J.L. • $48 Ⓐ • (11/15/1998) • **92**

Cabernet Sauvignon Stags Leap District Hillside Select 1998: Dark, ripe and complex, with a wonderful core of rich, plush currant, mineral, spice, sage and tea notes and an amazingly long and intricate aftertaste.–J.L. • $NA • (8/31/1999) (BT) • **95-99**

Cabernet Sauvignon Stags Leap District Hillside Select 1997: A bit reduced, with floral and currant notes, this is a dense, chewy, complex young wine, overflowing with earthy currant, plum, black cherry and spice. Finishes with chewy but ripe and complex tannins.–J.L. • $NA • (8/31/1998) (BT) • **95-99**

Key: SS—Spectator Selection. CS—Cellar Selection. HR—Highly Recommended. $NA—Price not available. (BT)—Barrel tasting. Ⓐ—Auction Price. For a key to the tasters' initials, see "How to Use These Listings." **Dates in parentheses represent the issues in which the ratings were published.**

Cabernet Sauvignon Stags Leap District Hillside Select 1996: Tight, dense and concentrated, with tiers of spicy cherry, cedar, currant and plum that fan out nicely and run long and deep on the finish. Best from 2001 through 2008.–J.L. • $NA • (11/15/1999) • **93**

Cabernet Sauvignon Stags Leap District Hillside Select 1995: Ripe and plump, boasting a rich, supple core of plum and black cherry, with anise and wild berry flavors adding dimension. Shows excellent depth and focus, and the flavors linger on the finish. Drink through 2009.–J.L. • $213 Ⓐ • (10/31/1998) CS • **92**

Cabernet Sauvignon Stags Leap District Hillside Select 1994 • $250 Ⓐ • (10/15/1997) • **95**

Cabernet Sauvignon Stags Leap District Hillside Select 1993 • $110 Ⓐ • (10/31/1997) CS • **94**

Cabernet Sauvignon Stags Leap District Hillside Select 1992 • $133 Ⓐ • (11/15/1996) HR • **93**

Cabernet Sauvignon Stags Leap District Hillside Select 1991 • $91 Ⓐ • (11/15/1995) CS • **93**

Cabernet Sauvignon Stags Leap District Hillside Select 1990 • $153 Ⓐ • (12/15/1995) • **90**

Cabernet Sauvignon Stags Leap District Hillside Select 1989: Still firm and intense, with complex earthy mineral, currant, anise, cedar, tar and slightly nutty flavors, it's a big, muscular wine with ample tannins. (1989 California Cabernet retrospective tasting). Drink now through 2005.–J.L. • $35 • (8/31/1999) • **89**

Cabernet Sauvignon Stags Leap District Hillside Select 1988: Deep, rich and complex, with a supple array of spicy black cherry, plum and wild berry flavors and smooth, polished tannins. Gains on the finish, picking up chocolate and vanilla flavors. (1988 California Cabernet retrospective tasting). Drink now through 2006.–J.L. • $43 Ⓐ • (11/15/1998) • **89**

Cabernet Sauvignon Stags Leap District Hillside Select 1987 • $86 Ⓐ • (12/15/1997) • **96**

Cabernet Sauvignon Stags Leap District Hillside Select 1986 • $32 • (12/15/1996) • **90**

Cabernet Sauvignon Stags Leap District Hillside Select 1985 • $115 Ⓐ • (5/31/1990) CS • **91**

Cabernet Sauvignon Stags Leap District Hillside Select 1984 • $35 • (4/30/1989) • **89**

Cabernet Sauvignon Stags Leap District Hillside Select 1983 • $22 • (7/31/1988) • **84**

Chardonnay Napa Valley Carneros Red Shoulder Ranch 1998: Aims for complexity with its intense, lemony pear and spice nuances. Picks up a dash of nutmeg before turning simpler on the finish. Drink now through 2003.–J.L. • $35 • (5/31/2000) • **87**

Chardonnay Napa Valley Carneros Red Shoulder Ranch 1997: Rich and racy, with lots of distinctive peach, citrusy grapefruit and pear notes, finishing with even more intriguing tastes, it's lean and a touch coarse now, but filled with flavor. Drink through 2003.–J.L. • $35 • (5/15/1999) • **93**

Chardonnay Napa Valley Carneros Red Shoulder Ranch 1996 • $30 • (5/31/1998) HR • **92**

Firebreak Napa Valley 1996: Shows off a range of dry, earthy currant and berry-laced fruit. Turns austere and tannic on the finish. Drink now through 2002.–J.L. • $28 • (11/15/1999) • **84**

Firebreak Napa Valley 1995: Firm, tight and concentrated, with a complex core of currant, berry, cherry and spice. This Sangiovese blend gets a little backbone from 12 percent Cabernet. Finishes with good length. Drink now through 2001.–J.L. • $27 • (9/30/1998) • **87**

Firebreak Napa Valley 1994 • $25 • (7/31/1997) • **88**

Firebreak Stags Leap District 1993 • $24 • (2/29/1996) • **84**

Firebreak Stags Leap District 1992 • $22 • (11/30/1994) • **89**

Firebreak Stags Leap District 1991 • $20 • (12/15/1993) • **85**

Merlot Napa Valley 1997: Earthy initially, it builds in richness, with ripe, fleshy currant, black cherry, anise, sage and cedar notes, turning supple. Drink now through 2006.–J.L. • $35 • (9/15/1999) • **89**

Merlot Napa Valley 1996: Tight, with attractive plum, currant, berry and herbal notes, fanning out on the finish where it's complex and tannic. Drink now through 2003.–J.L. • $32 • (12/15/1998) • **88**

Merlot Napa Valley 1995 • $28 • (12/15/1997) • **86**

Merlot Napa Valley 1994 • $26 • (6/30/1997) • **85**

Merlot Napa Valley 1993 • $24 • (12/15/1995) • **88**

Merlot Napa Valley 1992 • $21 • (6/15/1995) • **88**

Merlot Napa Valley 1991 • $20 • (9/15/1994) • **83**

Merlot Napa Valley 1990 • $18 • (5/31/1992) HR • **91**

Merlot Napa Valley 1989 • $18 • (8/31/1991) • **87**

Merlot Napa Valley 1988 • $17 • (12/31/1990) • **83**

Merlot Napa Valley 1987 • $15 • (10/15/1989) • **92**

Merlot Napa Valley 1986 • $13 • (12/31/1988) • **91**

Merlot Napa Valley 1985 • $NA • (12/15/1987) HR • **90**
Merlot Napa Valley 1984 • $13 • (2/28/1987) • **87**
Merlot Napa Valley 1983 • $10 • (2/16/1986) • **93**

SHALE RIDGE | CALIFORNIA

Chardonnay Monterey 1997: Crisp, with a tight range of nectarine, grapefruit and pear flavors. Finishes ripe and flavorful. Drink now.–J.L. • $10 • (7/31/1999) • **86**
Chardonnay Monterey 1996 • $10 • (11/15/1997) • **83**
Merlot Monterey 1996 • $12 • (2/28/1998) • **84**

SHALESTONE | NEW YORK

Cabernet Sauvignon Finger Lakes 1995: A flavorful Cabernet that's lean in texture, with firm tannins and acidity. Has cherrylike, earthy flavors accented by spicy oak. Slightly austere, but appetizing. Drink now through 2001. • $15 • (11/15/1998) • **85**
Jem Finger Lakes Rosé NV: Bright as a cherry sourball, this rosé is very dry—nearly bitter—with crisp cranberry and herb flavors and firm tannins.–T.M. • $8 • (12/15/1998) • **77**
Merlot Finger Lakes 1995: An ambitious effort, with plenty of currant and cranberry flavors, but lacks a bit of flesh. Finishes with smoky accents. Drink now.–K.M. • $16 • (12/15/1998) • **83**
Red Legend Finger Lakes NV: Quite aromatic, with sweet cherry and cranberry aromas, but little depth. A blend of Cabernet Sauvignon, Merlot and Cabernet Franc.–K.M. • $11 • (12/15/1998) • **77**

SHEA | OREGON

Pinot Noir Willamette Valley Shea Vineyard Back Block 1998: Light and fragrant, with pretty cherry and spice notes floating on an open-textured frame, echoing nicely on the finish. Drink now through 2003.–H.S. • $36 • (5/15/2000) • **86**

SHENANDOAH | CALIFORNIA

Barbera Amador County Sobon Family Vineyards 1996 • $15 • (3/31/1998) • **84**
Black Muscat Amador County 1992 • $10 • (11/15/1993) • **84**
Cabernet Franc Amador County Varietal Adventure Series 1989 • $10 • (8/31/1991) • **87**
Cabernet Sauvignon Amador County 1996: Firmly textured but with supple tannins, this shows potential, with licorice, herbs, black currant, cassis and leather flavors still tightly wound. Finish shows a hint of bitterness, but still quite nice. Drink through 2005. • $13 • (11/15/1998) • **87**
Cabernet Sauvignon Amador County 1994 • $10 • (11/30/1996) • **86**
Cabernet Sauvignon Amador County 1992 • $10 • (11/15/1994) • **88**
Cabernet Sauvignon Amador County 1991 • $10 • (11/15/1994) • **79**
Cabernet Sauvignon Amador County 1990 • $10 • (11/15/1992) • **74**
Cabernet Sauvignon Amador County Artist Series 1987 • $10 • (2/28/1991) • **80**
Cabernet Sauvignon Amador County Artist Series 1986 • $12 • (10/31/1988) • **86**
Cabernet-Shiraz Amador County 1996: Earthy in character, with a focus on herbs and minerals, some berry flavor. Drink now. • $13 • (10/31/1998) • **82**
Cabernet-Shiraz Amador County 1993 • $10 • (12/15/1995) • **85**
Orange Muscat Amador County 1992 • $10 • (11/15/1993) • **84**
Orange Muscat Amador County 1990 • $10 • (6/15/1992) • **84**
Port Amador County 1989 • $8/375 ml. • (9/30/1995) • **81**
Sangiovese Amador County 1995 • $12 • (7/31/1997) • **81**
Sangiovese Amador County 1994 • $12 • (4/30/1996) • **84**
Sauvignon Blanc Amador County 1997 • $8 • (5/15/1998) • **86**
Sauvignon Blanc Amador County 1996 • $8 • (4/30/1997) • **88**
Serene Varietal Adventure Series Amador County 1989 • $8 • (3/31/1991) • **74**
Zinfandel Amador County Classico Varietal Adventure Series 1990 • $6 • (9/15/1992) • **82**
Zinfandel-Sirah Sierra Foothills Late Harvest 1991 • $8 • (10/15/1994) • **81**
Zinfandel Amador County Classico Varietal Adventure Series 1989 • $6 • (4/30/1991) • **82**
Zinfandel Amador County Sobon Family Vineyards Vintner's Selection 1995 • $15 • (12/15/1997) • **86**
Zinfandel Amador County Special Reserve 1997: Earthy and a bit awkward, with light cherry and plum flavors, a leather and berryish finish.–J.L. • $9 • (5/15/1999) • **82**
Zinfandel Amador County Special Reserve 1996 • $9 • (3/31/1998) • **85**
Zinfandel Amador County Special Reserve 1995 • $9 • (4/30/1997) • **84**
Zinfandel Amador County Special Reserve 1994 • $9 • (4/30/1996) • **87**
Zinfandel Amador County Special Reserve 1993 • $9 • (10/15/1995) • **87**
Zinfandel Amador County Special Reserve 1992 • $9 • (2/28/1995) • **83**
Zinfandel Amador County Special Reserve 1991 • $6 • (6/15/1993) • **76**
Zinfandel Amador County Special Reserve 1990 • $9 • (6/15/1993) • **78**
Zinfandel Amador County Special Reserve 1989 • $9 • (2/29/1992) • **84**
Zingiovese Amador County 1996: Crisp and hard-edged, with a jazzy core of bright blackberry and currant flavor, finishing with a layer of chewy tannins. A blend of Zinfandel and Sangiovese. Drink now.–H.S. • $12 • (11/30/1998) • **85**
Zingiovese Amador County 1993 • $10 • (5/15/1995) • **77**

SHENANDOAH | VIRGINIA

Cabernet Sauvignon Virginia 1997: Red plum and currant flavors dominate this medium-bodied red. Muddled finish, with tobacco and stewy notes. Drink now.–K.M. • $14 • (8/31/1999) • **81**
Chambourcin Virginia Founder's Reserve 1997: Smoky and peppery flavors dominate this medium-bodied and lively red. A good effort for this variety; finishes on a grapey note. Drink now.–K.M. • $17 • (10/15/1999) • **84**
Chardonnay Virginia 1997: This Chardonnay has apple, pear and butter notes. Spicy notes linger on the finish. Drink now.–K.M. • $13 • (8/31/1999) • **82**
Chardonnay Virginia Founder's Reserve 1997: Got to like this for its chutzpah. This wine has flavors of crème brûlée, baked apple and bread dough, with a buttery-mapley note that lingers on the finish. Drink now.–K.M. • $16 • (8/31/1999) • **85**
Merlot Virginia Lot 95 NV: Fruity, with plum, berry and cherry flavors, some chocolaty notes on the finish, but a bit awkward in the end. Drink now.–K.M. • $17 • (8/31/1999) • **81**

SHERWIN FAMILY | CALIFORNIA

Cabernet Sauvignon Spring Mountain District 1996: Combines elegance with a tightly wound core of currant, cedar, coffee, olive and sage flavors, turning bright with black cherry notes. Tannins firm up on the finish. Best from 2003 through 2012.–J.L. • $52 • (2/29/2000) • **92**

SHOOTING STAR | CALIFORNIA

Cabernet Franc Lake County 1997: Has malty, vanilla overtones and overripe plum flavors, finishing with some heat. Drink now.–J.L. • $12 • (5/15/2000) • **81**
Cabernet Franc Clear Lake 1995 • $10 • (11/30/1997) • **87**
Cabernet Franc Clear Lake 1994 • $9 • (9/15/1996) • **87**
Cabernet Franc Clear Lake 1992 • $9 • (12/31/1994) • **84**
Cabernet Franc Clear Lake 1991 • $9 • (10/15/1993) • **85**
Cabernet Sauvignon Clear Lake 1996: Bright, focused flavors on a firm frame call for short-term cellaring or drinking with hearty food. Has lovely currant, plum and coffee flavors, hinting at vanilla and spice on the finish. Best after 2000.–H.S. • $14 • (10/31/1998) • **88**
Chardonnay California 1997: Refreshing for its citrus and pear flavors, with a spicy, racy, jalapeño-like edge. Well focused and well balanced, with a complex finish. Drink now through 2001.–J.L. • $14 • (6/30/1999) • **88**
Chardonnay California 1996: Solid if unexciting. The core of spicy pear and light oak is tasty, though somewhat one-dimensional and simple. Drink now through 2000.–J.L. • $14 • (7/31/1998) • **83**
Chardonnay Carneros 1997: Smooth in texture, with a band of sweet cream flavors running through the earthy apple and pear. Finishes soft, light and refreshing. Drink now.–J.L. • $12 • (7/31/1999) • **86**
Chardonnay Santa Barbara County 1997: Rich, creamy and sweet-tasting, with citrus and fig flavors. A bit abrupt at the finish. Drink now.–H.S. • $13 • (4/30/1999) • **85**
Grenache Washington Côte de Columbia 1997: Smooth and appealing for its distinctive dusky spice notes around a supple core of pretty black cherry. Great now, while it's fresh.–H.S. • $10 • (6/30/1999) • **86**
Grenache Washington Côte de Columbia 1996: Smooth in texture, with vibrant cherry and spice flavors that glide gently through the silky finish. Drink now.–H.S. • $9 • (8/31/1998) • **88**
Grenache Washington Côte de Columbia 1995 • $10 • (4/30/1997) • **87**
Grenache Washington Côte de Columbia 1994 • $9 • (9/30/1995) • **85**
Lemberger Washington Blue Franc 1998: Fresh and juicy, with pretty blackberry and cherry flavors lingering appealingly on a soft frame. Drink now.–H.S. • $11 • (3/31/2000) • **87**
Lemberger Washington Blue Franc 1997: Firm in texture and round in structure, with gamy black cherry and anise flavors that smooth out nicely on the finish. Drink now through 2002.–H.S. • $11 • (6/30/1999) • **86**

SHOOTING STAR

Lemberger Washington Blue Franc 1996: Light in texture, with smooth plum and berry flavors on a supple frame. Geared to drink soon, but more distinctive than most Lembergers.–H.S. • $10 • (9/15/1998) • **86**
Lemberger Washington Blue Franc 1995 • $9 • (4/30/1997) • **84**
Merlot Lake County 1997: Ripe and polished, with rich currant, black cherry, plum and cedary oak that fold together quite nicely. Drink now through 2004.–J.L. • $15 • (10/15/1999) • **86**
Merlot Clear Lake 1996: A ripe, juicy style, with a core of herb and mint to balance the plum and raspberry flavors. Toasty, smoky oak aromas round things off nicely, with a plush finish hinting at licorice. Drink now. • $14 • (7/31/1998) • **89**
Merlot Clear Lake 1994 • $12 • (7/31/1996) • **89**
Merlot Clear Lake 1992 • $10 • (6/30/1994) • **87**
Pinot Noir Carneros 1997: Light in color and flavor, with earthy cherry and cola notes, turning tannic. Drink now.–J.L. • $14 • (4/30/1999) • **81**
Pinot Noir Mendocino 1994 • $10 • (1/31/1997) • **82**
Pinot Noir Mendocino 1993 • $10 • (2/28/1995) • **86**
Sauvignon Blanc Lake County 1996 • $9 • (11/30/1997) • **81**
Syrah Lake County 1998: Straightforward and round, with caramel and toffee flavors. Finishes with lingering black cherry notes and moderate tannins. Drink now through 2003.–J.L. • $12 • (5/31/2000) • **84**
Syrah Lake County 1997: Well oaked, with sweet blueberry, toasted oak and vanilla notes, finishing with ripe tannins and lingering flavors. Drink now.–J.L. • $12 • (4/30/1999) • **85**
Syrah Lake County 1996 • $12 • (4/30/1998) • **88**
Zinfandel Lake County 1996 • $11 • (5/31/1998) • **86**
Zinfandel Lake County 1995 • $11 • (2/28/1997) • **83**
Zinfandel Lake County 1994 • $9 • (4/30/1996) • **89**
Zinfandel Lake County 1993 • $9 • (2/28/1995) • **87**
Zinfandel Mendocino 1995 • $10 • (4/30/1997) • **88**
Zinfandel Mendocino Zin Gris Pacini Vineyard 1994 • $8 • (10/15/1995) • **78**

SHOWKET | CALIFORNIA

Sangiovese Napa Valley 1997: Ripe and flavorful, with a supple texture and complex plum, black cherry, wild berry and spice flavors. Finishes with a nice toasty oak edge and good length. Drink now through 2005.–J.L. • $35 • (11/15/1999) • **89**

SHYPOKE | CALIFORNIA

Charbono Napa Valley 1996: Full of eucalyptus and tar notes, with heavy herb and juniper flavors on a lean frame. Slightly bitter finish. Drink now through 2002.–J.L. • $15 • (4/30/2000) • **83**

SIDURI | CALIFORNIA

Pinot Noir Anderson Valley Rose Vineyard 1995 • $40 • (5/31/1997) • **92**
Pinot Noir Anderson Valley Rose Vineyard 1994 • $30 • (1/31/1996) • **89**
Pinot Noir California 1998: Tart, lean and dry, with trim, earthy berry and cedar notes. Drink now.–J.L. • $26 • (4/30/2000) • **83**
Pinot Noir Carneros 1996: A complete and satisfying Pinot Noir, with moderately ripe cherry, berry, tea, sage and spice flavors that fan out nicely on the finish. Shows off some pretty light oak on the aftertaste. Has filled out nicely. Better than when previously reviewed. Drink through 2002. –J.L. • $30 • (8/31/1998) • **88**
Pinot Noir Oregon 1997: Light in color, crisp and sharply focused, with a beautiful beam of pure blackberry, blueberry and currant running through to the elegant finish. Drink now through 2002.–H.S. • $29 • (4/30/1999) • **88**
Pinot Noir Oregon 1996 • $28 • (5/15/1998) • **88**
Pinot Noir Oregon 1995 • $20 • (11/30/1996) • **91**
Pinot Noir Oregon Archery Summit Vineyard 1997: Spicy, toasty, chocolaty flavors overpower the thread of black cherry that weaves through this oak-centered red. Has a definite style and some power. Best after 2001.–H.S. • $48 • (9/30/1999) • **86**
Pinot Noir Santa Lucia Highlands Pisoni Vineyard 1997: Ripe, smooth and polished, with a slight earthy edge to the black cherry, plum and raspberry flavors. Drink through 2005.–J.L. • $42 • (8/31/1999) • **88**

Key: SS—Spectator Selection. CS—Cellar Selection. HR—Highly Recommended. $NA—Price not available. (BT)—Barrel tasting. (A)—Auction Price. For a key to the tasters' initials, see "How to Use These Listings." **Dates in parentheses represent the issues in which the ratings were published.**

Pinot Noir Sonoma Coast Hirsch Vineyard 1998: Smoky, with a meaty edge to vague dried berry and dried cherry flavors. Dry, tannic aftertaste. Drink now.–J.L. • $46 • (4/30/2000) • **85**
Pinot Noir Sonoma Coast Hirsch Vineyard 1997: Medium-weight, ripe and spicy, with good intensity and hints of plum and berry, turning herbal and stemmy. Drink now through 2002.–J.L. • $42 • (9/15/1999) • **85**
Pinot Noir Sonoma Coast Hirsch Vineyard 1996: Complex for its interplay of spicy, toasty oak and supple, elegant black cherry, spice and wild berry flavors. Holds its focus and flavors on the finish. Slightly better than when previously reviewed. Drink now through 2002.–J.L. • $40 • (10/31/1998) • **87**
Pinot Noir Sonoma Coast Hirsch Vineyard 1995 • $40 • (5/31/1997) • **88**
Pinot Noir Sonoma Mountain Van der Kamp Vineyard Old Vines 1997: Almost light enough in color to be a rosé of Pinot, this is nonetheless appealing for its snappy wild berry, watermelon and raspberry flavors. Finishes with firm tannins. Drink through 2003.–J.L. • $40 • (2/28/1999) • **87**
Pinot Noir Sonoma Mountain Van der Kamp Vineyard 1996 • $40 • (4/30/1998) • **86**

SIERRA VISTA | CALIFORNIA

Cabernet Sauvignon El Dorado 1989 • $11 • (11/15/1992) • **76**
Cabernet Sauvignon El Dorado 1988 • $11 • (4/15/1992) • **84**
Cabernet Sauvignon El Dorado Five Star Reserve 1991 • $22 • (11/15/1994) • **86**
Chardonnay El Dorado 1996 • $16 • (1/31/1998) • **84**
Fleur De Montagne Red El Dorado 1997: A interesting blend of bright fruit—cherries and raspberries come to mind—and herbs like sage and thyme. Finish is moderate and clean. A blend of Syrah, Grenache, Mourvèdre and Cinsault. Drink now through 2001. • $14 • (11/15/1998) • **86**
Fleur De Montagne Red El Dorado 1996 • $14 • (12/15/1997) • **89**
Syrah El Dorado 1995 • $10 • (12/15/1997) • **86**
Syrah El Dorado Red Rock Ridge 1996: Somewhat drying on the palate, with herb and tar notes. A core of blackberry and currant surfaces, however, leading to a pleasant finish. Drink now through 2002. • $18 • (2/28/1999) • **81**
Viognier El Dorado 1996 • $20 • (2/28/1998) • **86**
Zinfandel El Dorado 1996 • $13 • (6/15/1998) • **85**
Zinfandel El Dorado 1990 • $9 • (10/15/1992) • **73**
Zinfandel El Dorado 1989 • $9 • (3/31/1992) • **78**
Zinfandel El Dorado Five Star Reserve 1995 • $22 • (6/15/1998) • **82**
Zinfandel El Dorado Herbert Vineyard 1996: Ripe and generous, a big mouthful of black cherry and game character, finishing with a touch of spice and leather. Drink through 2003.–H.S. • $15 • (11/30/1998) • **85**
Zinfandel El Dorado Reeves Vineyard 1996: A smooth, somewhat dense wine sporting a peppery core, with black currant and plum flavors that fan out. Tannins are smooth and ripe, with a good, long finish. Drink now through 2004. • $15 • (1/31/1999) • **88**
Zinfandel El Dorado Reeves Vineyard Special Reserve 1985 • $12 • (4/30/1988) • **73**

SIGNORELLO | CALIFORNIA

Cabernet Sauvignon Napa Valley 1997: Lean and potent, with dry, gritty tannins overriding the dry plum and anise flavors, finishing with crisp tannins. Drink now through 2008.–J.L. • $48 • (6/30/2000) • **85**
Cabernet Sauvignon Napa Valley 1996: Elegantly styled and well balanced, with ripe black cherry, currant, plum, cedar and spice flavors that fan out and gain depth and nuance. Drink now through 2004.–J.L. • $35 • (11/15/1999) • **89**
Cabernet Sauvignon Napa Valley 1995: Dark, ripe and intense, with spicy currant, plum and blackberry flavors, picking up pretty, spicy oak, anise and tobacco notes. Remains remarkably elegant and spicy for all its dark fruit flavors. Has the tannic strength to age. Drink through 2008.–J.L. • $30 • (7/31/1998) • **93**
Cabernet Sauvignon Napa Valley 1994 • $30 • (11/15/1997) • **88**
Cabernet Sauvignon Napa Valley Founder's Reserve 1996: Wonderful sense of harmony, finesse and balance, with ripe, bright black cherry, plum and currant flavors, hints of herb and spice, a long, supple finish. Tempting now, but worthy of cellaring. Drink through 2007.–J.L. • $75 • (9/15/1999) • **92**
Cabernet Sauvignon Napa Valley Founder's Reserve 1995: Ripe and plummy, with a firm tannic backbone and plenty of black cherry, smoky, toasty oak, anise, earth and tarry nuances that are rich and focused. Finishes with a long, complex, intricate aftertaste echoing currant, coffee and spice. Best from 2001 through 2010.–J.L. • $55 • (7/31/1998) • **93**
Cabernet Sauvignon Napa Valley Founder's Reserve 1994 • $55 • (9/30/1997) • **90**
Cabernet Sauvignon Napa Valley Founder's Reserve 1993 • $32 • (5/15/1996) • **88**

Cabernet Sauvignon Napa Valley Founder's Reserve 1992 • $32 • (9/15/1995) CS • **90**

Cabernet Sauvignon Napa Valley Founder's Reserve 1991 • $30 • (9/30/1994) • **90**

Cabernet Sauvignon Napa Valley Founder's Reserve 1990 • $30 • (10/15/1993) • **92**

Cabernet Sauvignon Napa Valley Founder's Reserve 1989 • $25 • (7/15/1992) • **85**

Cabernet Sauvignon Napa Valley Founder's Reserve 1988 • $25 • (5/15/1991) • **92**

Chardonnay Napa Valley 1998: Ripe and polished, with pretty pear, buttery oak, nutmeg and cedar. Finishes with a slight bitter edge. Drink now through 2004.–J.L. • $38 • (6/15/2000) • **87**

Chardonnay Napa Valley 1997: Lots of ripe, complex fruit, and the smooth, creamy texture lets the fig, nutmeg, citrus and anise flavors flow together. Drink now through 2002.–J.L. • $30 • (6/30/1999) • **91**

Chardonnay Napa Valley 1996: Sharply focused, ripe, rich and lively, with complex, concentrated pear, apple, spice and peach flavors. A bright and lively style that finishes with vanilla and hazelnut. Drink now through 2002.–J.L. • $30 • (7/31/1998) • **92**

Chardonnay Napa Valley Founder's Reserve 1996: Intense, supple and complex, this Chardonnay offers creamy texture with ripe, rich pear, fig, melon and apricot flavors that are sharply focused. It's long and full-bodied on the finish, where vanilla and hazelnut notes chime in. Drink now through 2002.–J.L. • $48 • (7/31/1998) HR • **93**

Chardonnay Napa Valley Hope's Cuvée 1997: Wonderful richness, depth and concentration, with a delicious array of ripe pear, fig, melon, toasty oak and anise. The complex aftertaste keeps pumping out the flavors. Drink now through 2002.–J.L. • $60 • (7/31/1999) • **93**

Chardonnay Napa Valley Hope's Cuvée 1996: A complex mouthful of Chardonnay, with toasty fig, pear, melon, apricot and hazelnut flavors that fan out and gain nuance and depth on the finish. Drink now through 2002.–J.L. • $60 • (12/15/1998) • **92**

Il Taglio Napa Valley 1991 • $10 • (3/31/1994) • **86**

Merlot Napa Valley 1990 • $25 • (3/15/1994) • **82**

Petite Sirah Napa Valley 1990 • $15 • (10/15/1993) • **84**

Petite Sirah Napa Valley 110-Year-Old Vines 1996: Dark, dense, rich and chewy, with firm notes of wild berry, stewed plum and sage, turning dry and tannic. Drink through 2007.–J.L. • $25 • (1/31/1999) • **88**

Pinot Noir Carneros Las Amigas Vineyard 1997: Intense and spicy, with a pretty array of black cherry, plum, cola and wild berry, picking up some pretty oak and finishing with firm tannins. Drink through 2005.–J.L. • $45 • (8/31/1999) • **88**

Pinot Noir Carneros Las Amigas Vineyard 1996: Smooth, ripe, rich and complex, with plush black cherry, wild berry and vanilla, this impresses with its focused, bright Pinot Noir flavors and generous dose of spicy, toasty oak. Finishes with fine, well-integrated tannins. Drink through 2004.–J.L. • $45 • (8/31/1998) • **89**

Pinot Noir Carneros Las Amigas Vineyard 1995 • $48 • (3/31/1998) • **88**

Pinot Noir Carneros Las Amigas Vineyard 1994 • $35 • (1/31/1997) • **85**

Pinot Noir Napa Valley 1988 • $25 • (2/28/1991) • **85**

Pinot Noir Napa Valley Founder's Reserve 1992 • $28 • (3/31/1995) • **87**

Pinot Noir Napa Valley Founder's Reserve 1991 • $28 • (2/28/1994) • **87**

Pinot Noir Napa Valley Founder's Reserve 1990 • $25 • (2/28/1993) • **82**

Pinot Noir Napa Valley Founder's Reserve 1989 • $25 • (11/15/1991) • **78**

Pinot Noir North Coast 1994 • $22 • (1/31/1997) • **85**

Pinot Noir North Coast Founder's Reserve 1993 • $28 • (12/31/1995) • **86**

Pinot Noir Russian River Valley Martinelli Vineyard 1997: Tightly wound and tart, with a firm band of earthy cherry, berry and spice, turning tannic. Drink through 2005.–J.L. • $45 • (9/15/1999) • **86**

Pinot Noir Russian River Valley Martinelli Vineyard 1996: Has some substance, with chunky, tannic, black cherry and wild berry flavors, hints of earth and spice, a dash of oak. Drink through 2002.–J.L. • $45 • (9/15/1998) • **86**

Sémillon Napa Valley 1997: Bright and lemony, this leaves a clean slate on the palate despite its full body. The finish is moderate, showing a flinty mineral quality offset by dried herb. Drink now through 2002. • $22 • (6/30/1999) • **88**

Sémillon Napa Valley 1996: Hints of creamy caramel, toast, fresh pea and fig are offset by a steely mineral side that finishes long. An unusual style. Drink now. • $20 • (9/15/1998) • **88**

Syrah Napa Valley 1996: A solid, beefy style, with ripe stewed plum, sage, anise and berry notes. Finishes with firm, drying tannins and good length. Drink now through 2002.–J.L. • $30 • (12/15/1998) • **88**

Zinfandel Napa Valley 1997: Tough and chewy, with a leathery streak running through the bramble berry flavors, turning earthy and bitter. Drink now through 2006.–J.L. • $28 • (5/15/2000) • **83**

Zinfandel Napa Valley 1993 • $18 • (9/15/1995) • **86**

Zinfandel Napa Valley 1990 • $15 • (6/15/1993) • **75**

Zinfandel Russian River Valley 1996: A twinge of greenness weaves through otherwise ripe cherry and wild berry flavors. Well balanced and tasty, with mild, firm tannins. Drink through 2003.–J.L. • $25 • (12/15/1998) • **88**

SILVAN RIDGE | OREGON

Early Muscat Oregon Semi-Sparkling 1998: Sweet, fragrant and delightful for its distinctly allspice and nutmeg-scented pear and litchi flavors. Finishes light, sweet and delicately crackling. Drink now.–H.S. • $13 • (11/15/1999) • **89**

Early Muscat Oregon Semi-Sparkling 1997: Light, delicate and sweet, with disarmingly gorgeous pear, melon, litchi and floral flavors that keep singing on the harmonious finish. Drink now.–H.S. • $12 • (4/30/1999) • **90**

Early Muscat Oregon Semi-Sparkling 1995 • $12 • (2/28/1997) • **86**

Early Muscat Oregon Semi-Sparkling 1994 • $12 • (3/31/1996) • **90**

Early Muscat-Huxelrebe Oregon Late Harvest 1995 • $16 • (2/28/1997) • **85**

Merlot Oregon 1994 • $25 • (11/30/1996) • **86**

Merlot Rogue Valley 1996: Firm in texture, with an aromatic core of black cherry and game notes. Finishes with a graceful lightness. Drink now.–H.S. • $19 • (5/31/1999) • **85**

Merlot Rogue Valley 1995 • $22 • (5/15/1998) • **84**

Merlot Walla Walla Valley Seven Hills Vineyard 1994 • $28 • (1/31/1997) • **88**

Pinot Gris Oregon 1998: Ripe and generous, a lovely mouthful of pear, apricot and floral flavors that linger aromatically on the finish. Has more character than most Pinot Gris. Drink now.–H.S. • $13 • (3/31/2000) • **89**

Pinot Gris Oregon 1996: Smooth and exotic, with earthy melon and almond flavors that remain funky on the finish. Drink now.–H.S. • $14 • (12/15/1998) • **81**

Pinot Noir Willamette Valley 1996: Light in structure and firm in texture, with modest black cherry and toast flavors that echo on the finish. Drink now through 2002.–H.S. • $18 • (3/31/2000) • **83**

Pinot Noir Willamette Valley 1995 • $19 • (5/15/1998) • **82**

Pinot Noir Willamette Valley 1994 • $22 • (10/31/1996) • **88**

Pinot Noir Willamette Valley 1993 • $19 • (1/31/1996) • **84**

Pinot Noir Willamette Valley 1992 • $19 • (11/30/1994) • **82**

Pinot Noir Willamette Valley Bockelman Vineyard 1994 • $30 • (10/15/1996) • **89**

Pinot Noir Willamette Valley Eola Springs Vineyard 1996: Light in texture, with firm tannins wrapped around a pure core of currant and plum. The flavors echo nicely on the finish. Drink through 2003.–H.S. • $26 • (12/15/1998) • **85**

Pinot Noir Willamette Valley Hoodview Vineyard 1995 • $22 • (5/15/1998) • **85**

Pinot Noir Willamette Valley Visconti Vineyard 1994 • $26 • (10/15/1996) • **86**

SILVER HORSE | CALIFORNIA

Cabernet Sauvignon Paso Robles 1993 • $13 • (3/31/1996) • **79**

Cabernet Sauvignon Paso Robles 1990 • $10 • (11/15/1994) • **82**

Pinot Noir Paso Robles 1994 • $13 • (2/29/1996) • **81**

Zinfandel Paso Robles 1992 • $12 • (2/28/1995) • **84**

SILVER LAKE | WASHINGTON

Cabernet Sauvignon Columbia Valley 1995: Firm in texture, with tightly packed currant and berry flavors that persist on the finish, poking through a thin veil of tannin. Drink through 2002.–H.S. • $13 • (9/15/1998) • **86**

Cabernet Sauvignon Columbia Valley 1994 • $13 • (9/30/1997) • **83**

Cabernet Sauvignon Columbia Valley 1993 • $11 • (9/15/1996) • **83**

Cabernet Sauvignon Columbia Valley 1991 • $13 • (9/30/1994) • **80**

Cabernet Sauvignon Columbia Valley Reserve 1995: Ripe and generous, with exuberantly grapey, earthy flavors that sort of float away and turn wispy on the finish. Drink now through 2003.–H.S. • $20 • (9/30/1999) • **84**

Cabernet Sauvignon Columbia Valley Reserve 1994: Generous flavors of blackberry, currant and purple plum glide nicely on an open frame. Fine-textured tannins don't get in the way, letting the flavors expand on the finish. Drink now through 2003.–H.S. • $12 • (8/31/1998) • **89**

Cabernet Sauvignon Columbia Valley Reserve 1993 • $16 • (9/30/1997) • **88**

Cabernet Sauvignon Columbia Valley Reserve 1992 • $25 • (9/30/1996) • **85**

Cabernet Sauvignon Columbia Valley Reserve 1989 • $16 • (9/30/1994) • **86**

Cabernet-Merlot Columbia Valley 1997: Light in texture, with modest blackberry and toast flavors. Drink now.–H.S. • $12 • (9/30/1999) • **80**

SILVER LAKE

Cabernet-Merlot Columbia Valley 1996: Crisp in texture, with nice, ripe currant and blueberry flavors that finish with enough generosity to balance the texture smoothly. Drink now through 2002.–H.S. • $12 • (8/31/1998) • **85**
Cabernet-Merlot Columbia Valley 1995 • $9 • (9/30/1997) • **85**
Chardonnay Columbia Valley 1997: Straightforward and pleasant for its apple and cola flavors on a soft, easy-drinking frame. Drink now.–H.S. • $12 • (8/31/1999) • **83**
Chardonnay Columbia Valley 1996: Light and tangy, a lively wine with citrus and star fruit flavors lingering on the polished frame. Drink now.–H.S. • $12 • (9/15/1998) • **86**
Chardonnay Columbia Valley Reserve 1997: A simple, earthy white with modest apple and spice flavors.–H.S. • $16 • (8/31/1999) • **79**
Fumé Blanc Columbia Valley 1996: Melon flavors are nice, but the overtones of decaying flowers and herbs won't please everyone.–H.S. • $8 • (9/15/1998) • **79**
Fumé-Chardonnay Columbia Valley 1997: Sprightly, appealing for its nicely balanced apple, herb and citrus flavors on a fresh, open-textured frame. Drink now.–H.S. • $8 • (8/31/1999) • **85**
Hervé Cuvée Selipsky Columbia Valley Founder's Series 1997: Open and generous white, beautifully balanced to show its pear, citrus and delicately herbal flavors as they linger elegantly. Drink now.–H.S. • $16 • (8/31/1999) • **89**
Johannisberg Riesling Columbia Valley 1997: Sweet and refreshing for its open-textured peach and pine flavors, which persist nicely on the balanced finish. Drink now.–H.S. • $7 • (9/15/1998) • **86**
Merlot Columbia Valley 1995: Soft and supple, with a gamy edge to the ripe blackberry and currant flavors, finishing with a generous dollop of coffee. Drink now through 2002.–H.S. • $13 • (8/31/1998) • **87**
Merlot Columbia Valley 1994 • $13 • (9/30/1997) • **88**
Merlot Columbia Valley 1993 • $13 • (9/15/1996) • **87**
Merlot Columbia Valley 1990 • $16 • (9/30/1994) • **86**
Merlot Columbia Valley Reserve 1995: Earthy, minty and lightly gamy flavors run through this firm-textured wine, offering balancing black cherry notes on the finish. Best after 2001.–H.S. • $20 • (9/30/1999) • **83**
Merlot Columbia Valley Reserve 1994: Ripe, earthy and gamy, distinctive for its funky flavors, all wrapped in a blanket of smooth tannins. Approachable now, best from 2000 through 2003.–H.S. • $18 • (8/31/1998) • **85**
Merlot Columbia Valley Reserve 1993 • $16 • (9/30/1997) • **86**
Merlot Columbia Valley Reserve 1992 • $25 • (9/30/1996) • **85**
Merlot Columbia Valley Sentinel Peak 1993 • $8 • (9/30/1995) • **78**
Pinot Noir Willamette Valley Reserve 1993 • $13 • (10/15/1996) • **87**
Pinot Noir Willamette Valley Reserve 1992 • $13 • (3/31/1996) • **84**
Red Reserve Columbia Valley 1992 • $25 • (9/15/1996) • **85**
Red Reserve Columbia Valley 1990 • $16 • (9/30/1995) • **84**
Reserve Columbia Valley 1993 • $16 • (9/30/1997) • **87**
Riesling Columbia Valley Dry 1997: Dry and a bit raw, with jazzy apple and apricot flavors plus a hint of white pepper on the finish. Drink now.–H.S. • $7 • (9/15/1998) • **85**
Riesling Columbia Valley Ice Wine 1989 • $25/375 ml. • (4/15/1995) • **85**
Riesling Columbia Valley Late Harvest 1997: Sweet and supple, a subtle wine with nicely defined tiers of apple, pear, honey and floral flavors that linger gently. Drink now.–H.S. • $8 • (9/15/1998) • **87**
Riesling Columbia Valley Late Harvest 1994 • $8 • (9/30/1996) • **86**
Sentinel Peak Columbia Valley 1993 • $7 • (9/30/1995) • **79**

SILVER OAK | CALIFORNIA

Cabernet Sauvignon Alexander Valley 1995: Serves up lots of supple and complex currant, cedar, toasty oak, tobacco and anise flavors that are rich and focused, smooth and polished, firming up on the finish. Drink through 2008.–J.L. • $72 Ⓐ • (10/15/1999) CS • **90**
Cabernet Sauvignon Alexander Valley 1994: Combines ripe, rich, complex fruit with a sense of finesse and harmony. The core of anise, currant, sage and cedar unfolds to reveal more depth and complexity. Finishes with a long, satisfying aftertaste. Drink now through 2006.–J.L. • $90 Ⓐ • (10/31/1998) • **89**
Cabernet Sauvignon Alexander Valley 1993 • $70 Ⓐ • (9/30/1997) CS • **90**
Cabernet Sauvignon Alexander Valley 1992 • $87 Ⓐ • (11/15/1996) • **90**
Cabernet Sauvignon Alexander Valley 1991 • $86 Ⓐ • (11/15/1995) HR • **91**
Cabernet Sauvignon Alexander Valley 1990 • $83 Ⓐ • (11/15/1994) • **89**

Key: SS—Spectator Selection. CS—Cellar Selection. HR—Highly Recommended. $NA—Price not available. (BT)—Barrel tasting. Ⓐ—Auction Price.
For a key to the tasters' initials, see "How to Use These Listings."
Dates in parentheses represent the issues in which the ratings were published.

Cabernet Sauvignon Alexander Valley 1989 • $48 Ⓐ • (11/15/1993) • **82**
Cabernet Sauvignon Alexander Valley 1988 • $38 • (10/31/1992) HR • **91**
Cabernet Sauvignon Alexander Valley 1987 • $102 Ⓐ • (12/15/1997) • **93**
Cabernet Sauvignon Alexander Valley 1986 • $89 Ⓐ • (12/15/1996) • **92**
Cabernet Sauvignon Alexander Valley 1985 • $112 Ⓐ • (10/31/1989) • **86**
Cabernet Sauvignon Alexander Valley 1984 • $92 Ⓐ • (12/15/1988) • **85**
Cabernet Sauvignon Alexander Valley 1983 • $21 • (11/30/1987) • **82**
Cabernet Sauvignon Alexander Valley 1982 • $19 • (2/15/1987) • **90**
Cabernet Sauvignon Alexander Valley 1981 • $19 • (9/30/1986) • **92**
Cabernet Sauvignon Alexander Valley 1980 • $18 • (3/01/1985) • **90**
Cabernet Sauvignon Alexander Valley 1979 • $16 • (2/16/1984) • **81**
Cabernet Sauvignon Alexander Valley 1978: Hanging on, but fading, with just a glimmer of fruit left. Marked by herb, cherry and currant notes, the spicy American oak stands out on the finish, where the tannins have faded. (1978 California Cabernet retrospective tasting). Drink now.–J.L. • $16 • (11/15/1998) • **86**
Cabernet Sauvignon Napa Valley 1995: Wonderful sense of balance, harmony and finesse, with ripe, polished cedary currant, plum and black cherry. Finishes with supple tannins and a whiff of dill. Drink now through 2009. –J.L. • $75 • (4/30/2000) • **91**
Cabernet Sauvignon Napa Valley 1994: Complex and sophisticated, with layers of concentrated currant, herb, coffee, sage, mineral and spice flavors that fan out and linger on the finish. A wonderfully textured wine with a strong dose of American oak. Drink through 2008.–J.L. • $103 Ⓐ • (10/31/1998) • **91**
Cabernet Sauvignon Napa Valley 1993 • $85 Ⓐ • (10/15/1997) • **88**
Cabernet Sauvignon Napa Valley 1992 • $98 Ⓐ • (11/15/1996) CS • **93**
Cabernet Sauvignon Napa Valley 1991 • $91 Ⓐ • (11/15/1995) • **90**
Cabernet Sauvignon Napa Valley 1990 • $270 Ⓐ • (11/15/1994) CS • **91**
Cabernet Sauvignon Napa Valley 1989 • $60 Ⓐ • (11/15/1993) • **86**
Cabernet Sauvignon Napa Valley 1987 • $105 Ⓐ • (12/15/1997) • **87**
Cabernet Sauvignon Napa Valley 1986 • $91 Ⓐ • (12/15/1996) • **92**
Cabernet Sauvignon Napa Valley 1985 • $139 Ⓐ • (10/31/1989) • **88**
Cabernet Sauvignon Napa Valley 1984 • $227 Ⓐ • (12/15/1988) • **88**
Cabernet Sauvignon Napa Valley 1983 • $77 Ⓐ • (11/30/1987) • **87**
Cabernet Sauvignon Napa Valley 1982 • $62 Ⓐ • (2/15/1987) CS • **96**
Cabernet Sauvignon Napa Valley 1981 • $19 • (9/15/1986) • **75**
Cabernet Sauvignon Napa Valley 1980 • $18 • (3/1/1985) • **80**
Cabernet Sauvignon Napa Valley 1979 • $18 • (3/1/1984) • **83**
Cabernet Sauvignon Napa Valley Bonny's Vineyard 1991 • $101 Ⓐ • (9/15/1996) CS • **93**
Cabernet Sauvignon Napa Valley Bonny's Vineyard 1987 • $125 Ⓐ • (12/15/1997) • **95**
Cabernet Sauvignon Napa Valley Bonny's Vineyard 1986 • $100 • (12/15/1996) • **94**
Cabernet Sauvignon Napa Valley Bonny's Vineyard 1985 • $125 Ⓐ • (11/15/1990) • **83**
Cabernet Sauvignon Napa Valley Bonny's Vineyard 1984 • $170 Ⓐ • (10/15/1989) • **84**
Cabernet Sauvignon Napa Valley Bonny's Vineyard 1982 • $35 • (9/15/1987) • **66**
Cabernet Sauvignon Napa Valley Bonny's Vineyard 1979 • $30 • (6/16/1984) • **81**
Cabernet Sauvignon North Coast 1974 • $99 Ⓐ • (11/15/1994) • **83**

SILVER RIDGE | CALIFORNIA

Cabernet Sauvignon California Barrel Select 1994 • $10 • (10/31/1997) • **82**
Cabernet Sauvignon Napa Valley 1989 • $10 • (11/15/1994) • **84**
Cabernet Sauvignon Napa Valley Barrel Select 1992 • $10 • (11/30/1996) • **83**
Chardonnay California 1996 • $10 • (6/30/1998) • **83**
Merlot California 1992 • $12 • (9/15/1994) • **80**
Merlot California Barrel Select 1996 • $15 • (3/31/1998) • **82**
Merlot California Barrel Select 1992 • $10 • (8/31/1996) • **81**
Pinot Noir California Barrel Select 1996 • $10 • (12/31/1997) • **83**
Syrah California Barrel Select 1996: Light cherry and herb flavors are no match for full-on tannins and an oaky finish. • $10 • (9/15/1998) • **77**

SILVERADO HILL CELLARS | CALIFORNIA

Cabernet Sauvignon Napa Valley 1995: Simple and sweet, with juicy, sour cherry and butterscotch flavors. A bit too candied.–J.L. • $13 • (7/31/1998) • **78**
Cabernet Sauvignon Napa Valley 1992 • $15 • (11/15/1996) • **87**
Chardonnay Napa Valley Art Cuvée 1996 • $10 • (6/15/1998) • **70**

Chardonnay Napa Valley Le Mélange Supérieur 1996: Earthy, sour and bitter, with rancid butter and toast notes. Avoid. Tasted twice, with consistent notes. • $13 • (7/31/1998) • **65**

Chardonnay Napa Valley Traditional Cuvée 1996: Softly textured, with subtle, pleasant flavors of citrus, butter and toast. Flavors are focused and linger on the finish. Drink now. • $10 • (7/31/1998) • **84**

SILVERADO VINEYARDS | CALIFORNIA

Cabernet Sauvignon Napa Valley 1996: Here's a well-balanced '96 Cabernet that's drinkable now. It's smooth and spicy, with bell pepper and chili pepper accents to the core of cherry and currant-laced fruit flavors, showing even more complexity on the finish. Drink through 2005.–J.L. • $28 • (11/15/1999) SS • **89**

Cabernet Sauvignon Napa Valley 1995: Cherry, plum and berry flavors hold the fort, accented by a green bean note. Finishes with mild, dry tannins. Drink through 2003.–J.L. • $25 • (10/31/1998) • **87**

Cabernet Sauvignon Napa Valley 1993 • $20 • (8/31/1996) • **87**

Cabernet Sauvignon Napa Valley 1992 • $19 • (3/31/1995) SS • **90**

Cabernet Sauvignon Napa Valley 1988: Ripe, full-bodied and well balanced, with a slight weedy edge to the otherwise ripe and pure plum, black cherry and blackberry flavors. Finishes with complex nuances, hints of cedar and earth, along with rather firm tannins. Can age further; drink through 2004. (1988 California Cabernet retrospective tasting).–J.L. • $18 • (11/15/1998) • **87**

Cabernet Sauvignon Napa Valley 1987 • $14 • (12/15/1997) • **92**

Cabernet Sauvignon Napa Valley 1986 • $13 • (12/15/1996) • **91**

Cabernet Sauvignon Napa Valley 1985 • $13 • (11/15/1988) SS • **91**

Cabernet Sauvignon Napa Valley 1984 • $12 • (11/30/1987) • **89**

Cabernet Sauvignon Napa Valley 1983 • $12 • (12/31/1986) • **92**

Cabernet Sauvignon Napa Valley 1982 • $12 • (9/30/1986) • **82**

Cabernet Sauvignon Napa Valley 1981 • $10 • (12/16/1984) • **91**

Cabernet Sauvignon Napa Valley Limited Reserve 1995: A bold, dramatic expression of Cabernet, as this wine usually is. Packed with rich, complex currant, black cherry, plum, anise and spicy nuances, hints of tar, cedar, sage and vanilla, and finishing with a lingering aftertaste and finely honed tannins. Drink through 2007.–J.L. • $76 Ⓐ • (11/15/1998) • **95**

Cabernet Sauvignon Napa Valley Limited Reserve 1994 • $96 Ⓐ • (11/30/1997) HR • **93**

Cabernet Sauvignon Napa Valley Limited Reserve 1993 • $81 Ⓐ • (2/28/1997) • **90**

Cabernet Sauvignon Napa Valley Limited Reserve 1991 • $77 Ⓐ • (11/15/1994) CS • **93**

Cabernet Sauvignon Napa Valley Limited Reserve 1990 • $86 Ⓐ • (10/31/1993) CS • **97**

Cabernet Sauvignon Napa Valley Limited Reserve 1987 • $38 • (12/15/1997) • **96**

Cabernet Sauvignon Napa Valley Limited Reserve 1986 • $73 Ⓐ • (12/15/1996) • **97**

Cabernet Sauvignon Napa Valley Stags Leap District 1991 • $17 • (4/30/1994) SS • **93**

Cabernet Sauvignon Napa Valley Stags Leap District 1990 • $17 • (6/30/1993) HR • **90**

Cabernet Sauvignon Napa Valley Stags Leap District 1989 • $19 • (8/31/1992) • **81**

Cabernet Sauvignon Napa Valley Stags Leap District 1988 • $18 • (3/31/1991) • **86**

Cabernet Sauvignon Stags Leap District Disney Family Vineyard 1998: Supple and polished, with an elegant band of cherry, currant, plum and anise and, most importantly, a long aftertaste. A potential component of the new Disney Family Vineyard bottling.–J.L. • $NA • (8/31/1999) (BT) • **90-94**

Cabernet Sauvignon Stags Leap District Disney Family Vineyard 1996: Lots of supple herb, green olive, currant, black cherry and spice flavors spread out, turning rich and detailed on the finish. Drink now through 2007.–J.L. • $50 • (11/15/1999) • **90**

Chardonnay Napa Valley 1998: Simple, with modest floral and fruity flavors that lack focus. Drink now.–J.L. • $19 • (6/15/2000) • **81**

Chardonnay Napa Valley Limited Reserve 1998: Disappointingly simple, with modest floral and spicy fruit flavors that fail to find focus or added richness and depth. Drink now through 2004.–J.L. • $38 • (6/15/2000) • **82**

Chardonnay Napa Valley Limited Reserve 1997: A crisp, flinty style, with a pretty band of intense pear, spice, fig and melon. Gains nuance, with hints of toast and earth. Drink now through 2003.–J.L. • $NA • (7/31/1999) • **90**

Chardonnay Napa Valley Limited Reserve 1996: Distinctive for its clean, tangy core of pineapple, apple and spicy citrus notes, this bottling isn't the rich blockbuster it's been in the past, but it's complex and concentrated, with a lively aftertaste. Drink now through 2001.–J.L. • $36 • (11/30/1998) • **88**

Merlot Napa Valley 1996: Tilted toward the minty, bay leaf side of Merlot, with a range of herb and currant flavors of modest proportion. Drink through 2005.–J.L. • $24 • (10/15/1999) • **82**

Merlot Napa Valley 1995: Clean and well balanced, with a pleasant, concentrated core of currant, plum and berry, picking up oak and herb notes on the finish, where it turns tannic and chewy. Drink through 2004.–J.L. • $22 • (9/30/1998) • **87**

Merlot Napa Valley 1994 • $20 • (2/28/1997) • **85**

Merlot Napa Valley 1992 • $18 • (1/31/1995) • **85**

Merlot Napa Valley 1991 • $17 • (9/15/1994) • **85**

Merlot Napa Valley Limited Reserve 1992 • $45 • (8/31/1996) • **89**

Merlot Stags Leap District 1990 • $17 • (6/15/1993) • **87**

Merlot Stags Leap District 1989 • $16 • (4/15/1992) • **87**

Merlot Stags Leap District 1988 • $16 • (5/31/1991) • **86**

Merlot Stags Leap District 1987 • $14 • (4/15/1990) • **92**

Merlot Stags Leap District 1986 • $12 • (8/31/1989) • **91**

Merlot Stags Leap District 1984 • $13 • (12/15/1987) • **78**

Sangiovese Napa Valley 1996: Simple, with clean cherry, strawberry and vanilla flavors that are attractive. Drink now.–J.L. • $20 • (12/15/1998) • **82**

Sangiovese Napa Valley 1995 • $20 • (12/15/1997) • **84**

Sangiovese Napa Valley 1994 • $20 • (2/28/1997) • **82**

Sauvignon Blanc Napa Valley 1998: Oak and apple flavors intermingle with mineral notes that turn sour on the finish. Drink now.–J.L. • $13 • (5/15/2000) • **80**

Sauvignon Blanc Napa Valley 1997: Bright and refreshing, its mouthful of passion fruit, grapefruit, herb and lemon-lime flavors dancing around on the palate, zingy yet balanced. An effusive, racy white for drinking now through 2002. • $12 • (11/30/1998) SS • **89**

Sauvignon Blanc Napa County 1996 • $11 • (11/30/1997) • **84**

Sauvignon Blanc-Chardonnay-Sémillon Late Harvest Napa Valley Limited Reserve NV • $25/375 ml. • (4/30/1995) • **90**

SIMI | CALIFORNIA

Altaire North Coast 1992 • $9 • (7/31/1993) • **78**

Cabernet Sauvignon Alexander Valley 1997: Grapey, with a smooth texture and bright cherry, plum and wild berry flavors. Finishes with smoky, toasty oak and firm tannins.–J.L. • $NA • (8/31/1998) (BT) • **90-94**

Cabernet Sauvignon Alexander Valley 1996 • $NA • (2/02/1997) (BT) • **95-99**

Cabernet Sauvignon Alexander Valley 1995: Smooth, ripe and polished, with lots of pretty plum, currant, black cherry and spicy Cabernet flavors to admire. The tannins are ripe and polished, too. Drink now through 2003. –J.L. • $22 • (10/31/1998) • **89**

Cabernet Sauvignon Alexander Valley 1994 • $18 • (10/31/1997) • **88**

Cabernet Sauvignon Alexander Valley 1993 • $17 • (11/15/1996) • **88**

Cabernet Sauvignon Alexander Valley 1992 • $15 • (10/15/1995) • **89**

Cabernet Sauvignon Alexander Valley 1989 • $14 • (6/15/1993) • **77**

Cabernet Sauvignon Alexander Valley 1988 • $15 • (7/31/1992) • **84**

Cabernet Sauvignon Alexander Valley 1981 • $20 • (11/01/1985) • **79**

Cabernet Sauvignon Alexander Valley 1980 • $28 • (7/01/1984) • **81**

Cabernet Sauvignon Alexander Valley 1979 • $28 • (4/01/1984) SS • **91**

Cabernet Sauvignon Alexander Valley Reserve 1998: Racy, with spicy cherry, currant and berry flavors that are openly elegant and tasty, if seemingly a bit shy on concentration.–J.L. • $NA • (8/31/1999) (BT) • **85-89**

Cabernet Sauvignon Alexander Valley Reserve 1995 • $NA • (9/15/1996) (BT) • **90-94**

Cabernet Sauvignon Alexander Valley Reserve 1992 • $40 • (11/15/1996) CS • **93**

Cabernet Sauvignon Alexander Valley Reserve 1991 • $35 • (10/15/1995) HR • **92**

Cabernet Sauvignon Alexander Valley Reserve 1988: Clean, ripe and well focused, with currant, black cherry, wild berry and cedar flavors. Holds its flavors on the finish, where the tannins are well integrated. (1988 California Cabernet retrospective tasting). Drink now through 2003.–J.L. • $32 • (11/15/1998) • **87**

Cabernet Sauvignon Alexander Valley Reserve 1987 • $28 • (12/15/1997) • **92**

Cabernet Sauvignon Alexander Valley Reserve 1986 • $NA • (12/15/1996) • **91**

Cabernet Sauvignon Alexander Valley Reserve 1985 • $46 Ⓐ • (8/31/1990) SS • **94**

Cabernet Sauvignon Alexander Valley Reserve 1981 • $30 • (12/15/1988) • **86**

Cabernet Sauvignon Alexander Valley Reserve 1980 • $NA • (6/01/1986) • **87**

Cabernet Sauvignon Alexander Valley Reserve 1979 • $NA • (2/01/1986) • **77**

Cabernet Sauvignon Alexander Valley Reserve 1978 • $17 • (2/01/1986) • **69**

Cabernet Sauvignon Alexander Valley Reserve 1974 • $54 • (2/15/1990) • **85**

Cabernet Sauvignon Alexander Valley Special Reserve 1974 • $54 • (11/15/1994) • **82**

SIMI

Cabernet Sauvignon Mendocino-Sonoma-Napa Counties Reserve 1982 • $50 • (4/15/1989) • **90**
Cabernet Sauvignon Sonoma County 1996: Soft and medium-weight, with modest pepper and plum flavors and a lingering finish, but it really never takes off. Drink now.–J.L. • $21 • (9/15/1999) • **84**
Cabernet Sauvignon Sonoma County Centennial Edition 1990 • $14 • (11/15/1994) • **84**
Cabernet Sauvignon Sonoma County 1987 • $17 • (5/15/1991) • **89**
Cabernet Sauvignon Sonoma County 1985 • $21 • (9/30/1989) • **91**
Cabernet Sauvignon Sonoma County 1984 • $20 • (10/31/1988) • **86**
Cabernet Sauvignon Sonoma County 1982 • $15 • (11/15/1986) • **90**
Cabernet Sauvignon Sonoma County Reserve 1995: Remarkably complex and concentrated, with a dark, plush, focused core of ripe plum, black cherry, blackberry and spice. Turns rich on the long finish. Drink through 2008.–J.L. • $45 • (11/15/1999) • **93**
Cabernet Sauvignon Sonoma County Reserve 1994: A brilliant Cabernet from a great vintage, this is ripe, rich and complex, with a distinctive flavor
profile of earthy currant, herb, coffee, black cherry and spice. Finishes with ripe, bold, rich tannins and a wonderful aftertaste that keeps pumping out the fruit. Drink through 2006.–J.L. • $47 • (11/30/1998) CS • **93**
Chardonnay Carneros 1997: Soft, rich and elegant, with a toasty, buttery core to the citrus, peach and green apple flavors. Clean and refreshing on the finish. Drink now.–J.L. • $22 • (7/31/1999) • **90**
Chardonnay Carneros 1996: A sleek, elegant style that delivers a lot of complex flavors ranging from ripe pear to spicy, toasty oak, to fig, melon and nutmeg. Wonderful balance, polish and finesse. Drink now through 2001.–J.L. • $21 • (7/31/1998) • **91**
Chardonnay Russian River Valley Goldfields Vineyard Reserve 1996: Wonderful complexity, with rich, elegant layers of fig, pear, vanilla, citrus and nutmeg. Very concentrated and long on the finish. Simply delicious. Drink now through 2004.–J.L. • $30 • (5/31/1999) • **92**
Chardonnay Sonoma County 1997: Refreshing, with tightly drawn citrus, pear and mineral flavors and a hint of tropical fruit. Well balanced. Finishes firm, but the flavors linger. Drink now through 2002.–J.L. • $19 • (6/30/1999) • **88**
Chardonnay Sonoma County 1996: Appealing green apple, pear, honeysuckle and spicy apricot flavors emerge from behind a green note up front for a long, rich aftertaste. Drink now through 2001.–J.L. • $17 • (7/31/1998) • **90**
Pinot Noir Carneros 1997: Smooth, with a core of cherry, anise and herbs. The wine is delicate; the tannins firm but supple. On the finish, it shows some length, ending on clean mineral and herb notes. Drink through 2004. • $21 • (9/15/1999) • **87**
Pinot Noir Carneros 1994 • $18 • (3/31/1997) • **84**
Pinot Noir Russian River Valley 1997: Diluted, with modest strawberry notes under toasted oak tones. Very simple and light. Drink now through 2001. –J.L. • $21 • (9/15/1999) • **81**
Sauvignon Blanc Sonoma County 1997: Sweet pea and fig notes introduce this wine; the follow-up includes touches of lemon, melon and herb. It's firm, with bright acidity, finishing moderately. Drink now through 2001. • $13 • (5/15/1999) • **85**
Sauvignon Blanc Sonoma County 1996 • $12 • (4/30/1998) • **84**
Sendal White Sonoma County 1996: Lemony, with hints of melon and grass, the wine strikes a nice balance between elegance and assertiveness. Bright finish. A blend of Sauvignon Blanc and Sémillon. Drink now. • $20 • (11/30/1998) • **87**
Shiraz Sonoma County 1995 • $17 • (9/30/1997) • **87**
Zinfandel Dry Creek Valley 1997: Stays off the course of true Zin through the mulchy, pruny, waxy aftertaste. Drink now through 2004.–J.L. • $22 • (5/15/2000) • **81**

SINE QUA NON | CALIFORNIA

Against the Wall California 1996: Wonderful flavors, richness and complexity, with layers of spicy cherry, currant, earthy leather, mineral, sage and cedary oak. Long, rich, soothing aftertaste. 92 percent Syrah and 8 percent Grenache. Drink now through 2008.–J.L. • $115 Ⓐ • (1/01/1999) • **92**
Impostor McCoy California 1997: Lots to admire—ripe, rich currant, meat and smoke flavors, hints of anise and mineral plus coffee and toffee notes. Finishes smooth and polished. Syrah, with 5 percent Grenache. Drink now through 2007.–J.L. • $59 • (5/31/2000) • **92**
Queen of Spades Santa Barbara County 1994 • $31 • (11/30/1996) • **92**
Red Handed California 1995 • $36 • (12/15/1997) • **92**
The Other Hand California 1995 • $86 Ⓐ • (12/31/1997) • **84**

Key: SS—Spectator Selection. CS—Cellar Selection. HR—Highly Recommended. $NA—Price not available. (BT)—Barrel tasting. Ⓐ—Auction Price. For a key to the tasters' initials, see "How to Use These Listings." **Dates in parentheses represent the issues in which the ratings were published.**

SINEANN | WASHINGTON

Cabernet Sauvignon Columbia Valley Block One Vineyard 1996: Ripe and generous, this is a gorgeous mouthful of black cherry and mint flavors, folding in a touch of spicy oak on the rich finish. An amiable wine already. Drink now through 2002.–H.S. • $30 • (5/31/1999) • **88**
Cabernet Sauvignon Columbia Valley Block One Vineyard 1995 • $30 • (9/15/1997) • **86**
Merlot Columbia Valley 1997: Firm and focused, this lively red has spicy blackberry and mint flavors. Chewy tannins turn hard on the finish, but this has the density to develop in the cellar. Best after 2001.–H.S. • $20 • (6/15/1999) • **86**
Merlot Columbia Valley Oregon 1998: Smooth, polished and distinctive for its herbal, spicy nuances to the rich blackberry and cherry flavors. The seductive, elegant style sneaks up on you, then delivers pretty flavors on the long finish. Drink now through 2005.–H.S. • $23 • (5/15/2000) • **90**
Pinot Gris Willamette Valley 1998: Supple and generous, with flavors centering on melon, spice and almond. Nicely balanced, finishing soft and inviting. Drink now.–H.S. • $14 • (5/15/2000) • **87**
Pinot Noir Willamette Valley 1998: Generous, polished and nicely focused to show off its lovely blackberry, currant and delicate pepper flavors. Hints at cola on the long finish. Drink now through 2004.–H.S. • $34 • (5/15/2000) • **89**
Zinfandel Columbia Valley Old Vine 1997: Smooth, bright, generous and appealing for its earthy berry and plum flavors. Drink now through 2001.–H.S. • $20 • (6/30/1999) • **86**
Zinfandel Columbia Valley Old Vine 1994 • $15 • (9/30/1996) • **88**
Zinfandel Columbia Valley Oregon Old Vine 1998: Firm and chewy, with a nice layer of pretty raspberry and blackberry fruit. Has a bite of tannin on the finish. Best after 2001.–H.S. • $30 • (5/15/2000) • **86**

SINSKEY, ROBERT | CALIFORNIA

Cabernet Sauvignon Stags Leap District 1989 • $22 • (11/15/1992) • **89**
Claret Carneros 1990 • $28 • (5/15/1994) • **87**
Claret Carneros 1989 • $28 • (2/15/1993) • **85**
Claret Carneros 1988 • $28 • (11/15/1991) • **89**
Claret Stags Leap District 1996: Tightly structured, with a firm band of cedar, currant, spice and anise notes. Holding its focus, with tannins to shed. Best from 2001 through 2007.–J.L. • $36 • (11/15/1999) • **88**
Claret Stags Leap District 1994: Dense and closed, with earthy currant, mineral, tar and leathery flavors that are a bit diffuse. Finishes with chewy tannins and tarry, smoky flavors; time may give a boost. A blend of Cabernet Sauvignon, Merlot and Cabernet Franc. Drink through 2008.–J.L. • $40 • (8/31/1998) • **88**
Claret Stags Leap District 1993 • $30 • (5/15/1998) • **89**
Claret Stags Leap District 1991 • $28 • (11/15/1994) • **88**
Merlot Los Carneros 1995 • $30 • (5/15/1998) • **87**
Merlot Los Carneros Reserve 1994: Clean, ripe, rich and complex, with lots of dark cherry, plum, anise, sage and mineral flavors, picking up hints of tar and spice. Has a nice sense of balance and proportion, finishing with supple, well-integrated tannins. 20 percent Cabernet Franc, 4 percent Cabernet Sauvignon. Drink now through 2004.–J.L. • $33 • (10/15/1998) • **87**
Merlot Napa Valley Los Carneros 1992 • $18 • (4/30/1996) • **85**
Merlot Napa Valley Los Carneros 1990 • $18 • (12/31/1993) • **86**
Merlot Napa Valley Los Carneros 1989 • $18 • (5/31/1992) • **83**
Merlot Napa Valley 1987 • $18 • (3/31/1991) • **88**
Merlot Napa Valley 1986 • $17 • (10/15/1989) • **83**
Pinot Noir Los Carneros 1997: Bright, with a tight range of cherry, currant and herb flavors. Firms up on the finish. Drink now through 2003. –J.L. • $25 • (9/15/1999) • **84**
Pinot Noir Napa Valley Carneros 1996: Dry and earthy, with a leathery streak that runs through the modest core of cherry and berry. Turns dry and finishes with a colalike aftertaste. Drink now through 2002.–J.L. • $24 • (8/31/1998) • **86**
Pinot Noir Carneros 1995 • $22 • (9/30/1997) • **87**
Pinot Noir Napa Valley Los Carneros 1992 • $19 • (3/31/1995) • **83**
Pinot Noir Napa Valley Los Carneros 1991 • $19 • (2/28/1994) • **82**
Pinot Noir Napa Valley Los Carneros 1990 • $18 • (9/30/1992) • **85**
Pinot Noir Napa Valley Los Carneros 1988 • $18 • (2/28/1991) • **81**

Pinot Noir Napa Valley Carneros 1987 • $14 • (3/31/1990) • **86**
Pinot Noir Napa Valley Carneros 1986 • $12 • (6/15/1988) • **79**
Pinot Noir Napa Valley Carneros Reserve 1995: Well balanced, with appealing, juicy ripe cherry, plum and spicy nuances, it holds its flavors and focus through the finish, where it shows a leathery note and firm tannins. Drink through 2002.–J.L. • $40 • (9/15/1998) • **86**
Pinot Noir Napa Valley Los Carneros Reserve 1990 • $32 • (11/30/1992) • **80**

SIRITA | CALIFORNIA

Merlot Napa Valley 1997: Firm and dense, with a tight range of herb and currant flavors. Finishes with solid tannins. A new wine from Master Sommelier Larry Stone. Drink through 2003.–J.L. • $24 • (10/15/1999) • **87**
Merlot Sonoma County 1997: Concentrated, with a grapey edge to the black cherry, clay, chocolate and anise flavors. Tannins are firm and integrated. From Master Sommelier Larry Stone. Drink through 2006.–J.L. • $26 • (10/15/1999) • **85**

SKETCHBOOK | CALIFORNIA

Syrah Mendocino 1997: Fairly lean, with cola, chocolate and leather notes framed by tart tannin. Drink now through 2003.–J.L. • $30 • (6/15/2000) • **84**

SKEWIS | CALIFORNIA

Pinot Noir Anderson Valley Floodgate Vineyard 1996: Starts smooth, with ripe cherry and herbal mushroom flavors turning tart and focused on the finish. Drink now through 2002.–H.S. • $29 • (4/30/1999) • **87**
Pinot Noir Russian River Valley Montgomery Vineyard 1997: Serves up a pretty stream of spicy wild berry and black cherry fruit accented by spice and cedar notes. Turns firm and crisp on the finish. Drink now through 2007.–J.L. • $40 • (4/30/2000) • **87**

SKY | CALIFORNIA

Zinfandel Mount Veeder 1996: A refreshing, crisp, peppery Zin, with raspberry, apricot, currant and herb flavors that turn pretty on the finish. Drink now.–J.L. • $20 • (11/15/1999) • **84**
Zinfandel Mount Veeder 1995: Ripe and spicy, with a distinctive pickle barrel note to the berry flavors, finishing with a tough edge of tannin. Needs time. Drink through 2002.–H.S. • $20 • (11/30/1998) • **83**
Zinfandel Mount Veeder 1990 • $16 • (9/30/1993) • **88**
Zinfandel Mount Veeder 1989 • $13 • (10/15/1992) • **87**
Zinfandel Napa Valley 1988 • $12 • (8/31/1991) • **78**
Zinfandel Napa Valley 1987 • $17 • (10/15/1990) • **90**

SMITH & HOOK | CALIFORNIA

Cabernet Sauvignon Santa Lucia Highlands 1994 • $18 • (9/30/1997) • **85**
Cabernet Sauvignon Santa Lucia Highlands 1993 • $18 • (11/15/1996) • **87**
Cabernet Sauvignon Santa Lucia Highlands 1992 • $18 • (12/15/1995) • **83**
Cabernet Sauvignon Santa Lucia Highlands 1991 • $18 • (11/15/1994) • **86**
Cabernet Sauvignon Santa Lucia Highlands 1990 • $18 • (3/31/1994) • **87**
Cabernet Sauvignon Santa Lucia Highlands 1988 • $15 • (11/15/1991) • **80**
Cabernet Sauvignon Santa Lucia Highlands Masterpiece Edition 1994 • $35 • (11/30/1997) • **86**
Cabernet Sauvignon Santa Lucia Highlands Masterpiece Edition 1992 • $30 • (12/15/1995) • **88**
Cabernet Sauvignon Monterey 1983 • $14 • (11/15/1987) • **78**
Cabernet Sauvignon Monterey 1981 • $14 • (12/16/1984) • **90**
Cabernet Sauvignon Napa County 1985 • $12 • (9/30/1989) • **88**
Cabernet Sauvignon Napa County 1982 • $17 • (6/15/1987) • **79**
Merlot Santa Lucia Highlands 1995 • $19 • (12/15/1997) • **83**
Merlot Santa Lucia Highlands 1994 • $18 • (12/15/1996) • **80**
Merlot Santa Lucia Highlands 1993 • $18 • (8/31/1996) • **83**
Merlot Santa Lucia Highlands 1992 • $18 • (7/31/1995) • **85**
Merlot Santa Lucia Highlands 1991 • $18 • (9/15/1994) • **78**
Merlot Santa Lucia Highlands 1990 • $18 • (9/15/1994) • **81**
Merlot Santa Lucia Highlands 1989 • $15 • (5/31/1992) • **70**
Merlot Santa Lucia Highlands 1988 • $15 • (5/31/1992) • **80**
Merlot Napa County 1987 • $15 • (12/31/1990) • **83**
Merlot Napa County 1986 • $20 • (8/31/1989) • **86**
Viognier Arroyo Seco 1996 • $18 • (2/28/1998) • **84**

SMITH WINES, W.H. | CALIFORNIA

Pinot Noir Sonoma Coast 1997: Light in color and in weight, with herb, cherry, wild berry and simple spicy notes, finishing with tame tannins. Drink now through 2002.–J.L. • $31 Ⓐ • (2/28/1999) • **85**
Pinot Noir Sonoma Coast 1996 • $26 • (2/28/1998) • **79**
Pinot Noir Sonoma Coast Hellenthal Vineyard 1998: A very impressive '98. Rich, earthy and pleasantly decadent, with lots of plum, black cherry, anise, leather, mineral and sage unfolding on the long, rich, complex aftertaste. Drink now through 2007.–J.L. • $48 • (6/15/2000) • **91**
Pinot Noir Sonoma Coast Hellenthal Vineyard 1997: Firm, with cedary oak flavors overriding the core of herb-laced black cherry and forest floor-type flavors, turning tannic. Drink now through 2002.–J.L. • $36 • (2/28/1999) • **86**
Pinot Noir Sonoma Coast Hellenthal Vineyard 1996 • $36 • (12/15/1997) • **84**
Pinot Noir Sonoma Coast Hellenthal Vineyard 1995 • $32 • (7/31/1997) • **93**
Pinot Noir Sonoma Coast Hellenthal Vineyard 1994 • $28 • (11/15/1996) • **87**
Pinot Noir Sonoma Coast Hellenthal Vineyard Young Vines 1994 • $22 • (4/30/1996) • **91**
Pinot Noir Sonoma Coast Little Billy 1997: Light all around—in color, body and depth—with an herbal edge to the cherry and berry notes. Drink now. –J.L. • $18 • (2/28/1999) • **83**

SMITH-MADRONE | CALIFORNIA

Cabernet Sauvignon Napa Valley 1996: Misses the mark, with bitter green bean, dirt and metallic flavors.–J.L. • $30 • (5/31/2000) • **72**
Cabernet Sauvignon Napa Valley 1993 • $20 • (12/15/1996) • **83**
Cabernet Sauvignon Napa Valley 1992 • $17 • (12/15/1996) • **82**
Cabernet Sauvignon Napa Valley 1985 • $19 • (4/15/1990) • **74**
Cabernet Sauvignon Napa Valley 1984 • $14 • (12/31/1988) • **92**
Cabernet Sauvignon Napa Valley 1980 • $13 • (1/01/1984) • **83**
Chardonnay Napa Valley 1998: Smells and tastes like canned corn and potatoes, with a starchy, vegetal edge.–J.L. • $22 • (5/31/2000) • **74**

SMOKING DUCK | CALIFORNIA

Cabernet Sauvignon California 1997: Subtle bell pepper notes harmonize with blackberry, coffee and vanilla in a medium-bodied format. Drink now through 2004.–J.L. • $12 • (4/30/2000) • **85**

SNOQUALMIE | WASHINGTON

Cabernet Sauvignon Columbia Valley 1989 • $11 • (3/15/1994) • **87**
Cabernet Sauvignon Columbia Valley 1987 • $10 • (9/30/1990) • **90**
Cabernet Sauvignon Columbia Valley Reserve 1996: Firm in texture, with broad currant and black cherry surrounded by hints of sage and spicy oak, which echo on the finish. A bit chewy now. Best after 2000.–H.S. • $22 • (5/31/1999) • **88**
Cabernet-Merlot Columbia Valley 1996: Polished and supple, this pretty red blend from Washington delivers generous blackberry, currant and bay leaf aromas and flavors that extend into a smooth, plush finish. Shows considerable refinement and depth for so reasonable a price. Drink now through 2004.–H.S. • $11 • (5/31/1999) • **89**
Cabernet-Merlot Columbia Valley 1992 • $8 • (2/28/1995) • **85**
Merlot Columbia Valley Reserve 1996: Firm in texture, with crisp tannins, a solid core of black cherry and dried cherry and a delicate layer of herbal flavors. Impressive finish. Drink through 2005.–H.S. • $22 • (5/31/1999) • **89**
Merlot Columbia Valley Reserve 1987 • $12 • (9/30/1990) • **91**
Muscat Canelli Columbia Valley 1994 • $8 • (9/30/1995) • **82**

SNOWDEN | CALIFORNIA

Cabernet Sauvignon Napa Valley 1997: Dark, ripe, rich and racy. Still malolactic, but brimming with juicy, grapey Cabernet fruit, with lots of fresh, complex berry, cherry, currant and floral notes. Elegant finish.–J.L. • $NA • (8/31/1998) (BT) • **90-94**
Cabernet Sauvignon Napa Valley 1995: Momentum builds slowly in this firm, tight California Cabernet, with gritty tannins leading the way to a core of currant and black cherry flavors that fan out to reveal extra nuance and depth, finishing with herb and tea notes. Needs cellar time. Best from 2002 through 2010.–J.L. • $57 Ⓐ • (10/31/1999) HR • **93**
Cabernet Sauvignon Napa Valley 1994: Tough, tight and on the austere side; definitely one for the cellar. The flavors are dense and concentrated, but also quite backward. Given some air time, the plum and cherry emerge,

with a slight green edge. Best from 2001 through 2009.–J.L. • $40 • (11/15/1998) • **91**
Cabernet Sauvignon Napa Valley 1993 • $35 • (7/31/1997) • **92**

SOBON ESTATE | CALIFORNIA

Cabernet Franc Shenandoah Valley 1990 • $12 • (8/31/1992) • **81**
Cabernet Sauvignon Shenandoah Valley 1988 • $14 • (8/31/1992) • **78**
Cabernet Sauvignon Shenandoah Valley 1987 • $15 • (11/30/1990) • **83**
Primitivo Shenandoah Valley 1997: Rich and concentrated, with ripe black cherry, blackberry and herb flavors. Well focused, with a complex finish and ripe tannins. Drink now through 2002.–J.L. • $18 • (5/31/1999) • **87**
Rhône Rouge Shenandoah Valley 1992 • $8 • (5/15/1995) • **86**
Roussanne Shenandoah Valley 1998: Round and richly layered, with pineapple, citrus and melon flavors coming together nicely on the sappy finish. Drink now through 2003.–H.S. • $15 • (11/30/1999) • **86**
Roussanne Shenandoah Valley 1997: Bright citrus fruit flavors—especially lemon and grapefruit—are followed by apple and pear. Could use a bit more balance, but finishes on a clean, flinty note. Drink now. • $15 • (9/15/1998) • **87**
Syrah Shenandoah Valley 1996 • $13 • (6/15/1998) • **87**
Syrah Shenandoah Valley 1995 • $12 • (9/15/1997) • **80**
Syrah Shenandoah Valley 1993 • $10 • (9/30/1995) • **82**
Syrah Shenandoah Valley 1991 • $12 • (1/31/1995) • **82**
Syrah Shenandoah Valley 1990 • $12 • (12/31/1992) • **86**
Viognier Shenandoah Valley 1998: Bright, almost crisp in texture, with pretty almond and floral aromas and flavors that echo nicely on the tight finish. Drink now.–H.S. • $15 • (11/30/1999) • **84**
Viognier Shenandoah Valley 1997: Shows a distinctly pearlike profile, backed by moderate acidity and a clean, mineral finish. Drink now. • $15 • (11/15/1998) • **85**
Viognier Shenandoah Valley 1996 • $15 • (2/28/1998) • **87**
Zinfandel Amador County Vintners Selection 1996 • $15 • (6/15/1998) • **83**
Zinfandel Fiddletown 1996 • $15 • (6/15/1998) • **77**
Zinfandel Fiddletown 1995 • $15 • (8/31/1997) • **88**
Zinfandel Fiddletown Lubenko 1994 • $14 • (9/15/1996) • **78**
Zinfandel Fiddletown Lubenko 1993 • $14 • (3/31/1996) • **83**
Zinfandel Fiddletown Lubenko 1992 • $14 • (6/15/1995) • **82**
Zinfandel Shenandoah Valley 1992 • $10 • (10/15/1995) • **81**
Zinfandel Shenandoah Valley 1988 • $10 • (11/30/1990) • **88**
Zinfandel Shenandoah Valley Cougar Hill 1997: Gamy and earthy, with bitter berry flavors and an overly bitter finish.–J.L. • $15 • (6/15/2000) • **78**
Zinfandel Shenandoah Valley Cougar Hill 1996 • $15 • (6/15/1998) • **78**
Zinfandel Shenandoah Valley Cougar Hill 1995 • $15 • (4/30/1997) • **86**
Zinfandel Shenandoah Valley Cougar Hill 1994 • $14 • (9/15/1996) • **81**
Zinfandel Shenandoah Valley Cougar Hill 1993 • $14 • (3/31/1996) • **83**
Zinfandel Shenandoah Valley Old Vines Sobon Estate 1990 • $16 • (9/30/1993) • **78**
Zinfandel Shenandoah Valley Rocky Top 1997: An earthy, smoky style that's smooth and flavorful. Well focused and firm, it leans toward an oak-framed center. Slightly dry on the finish. Drink through 2004.–J.L. • $15 • (11/15/1999) • **85**
Zinfandel Shenandoah Valley Rocky Top 1996 • $15 • (5/31/1998) • **88**
Zinfandel Shenandoah Valley Rocky Top 1995 • $15 • (8/31/1997) • **88**
Zinfandel Shenandoah Valley Rocky Top 1993 • $14 • (3/31/1996) • **85**
Zinfandel Shenandoah Valley Rocky Top 1992 • $14 • (2/28/1995) • **82**
Zinfandel Sierra Foothills 1990 • $10 • (9/30/1993) • **81**
Zinfandel Sierra Foothills 1989 • $10 • (7/31/1992) • **86**

SOKOL BLOSSER | OREGON

Cabernet Sauvignon Yamhill County 1994 • $30 • (1/31/1998) • **86**
Cabernet Sauvignon Yamhill County 1992 • $30 • (1/31/1998) • **83**
Evolution No. 9 Oregon NV: Soft and aromatic, appealing for its pretty floral, spice and litchi overtones to the basic pear and apple character. Lap it up while it's fresh. Contains Pinot Gris, Müller-Thurgau, Riesling and several other grapes. Drink now.–H.S. • $15 • (12/31/1999) • **87**
Pinot Gris Willamette Valley 1998: Soft and fragrant, with pretty melon and green apple flavors that linger on the finish. Drink now.–H.S. • $16 • (12/31/1999) • **86**

Key: SS—Spectator Selection. CS—Cellar Selection. HR—Highly Recommended. $NA—Price not available. (BT)—Barrel tasting. (A)—Auction Price.
For a key to the tasters' initials, see "How to Use These Listings."
Dates in parentheses represent the issues in which the ratings were published.

Pinot Noir Oregon 1993 • $7 • (11/30/1994) • **78**
Pinot Noir Willamette Valley 1997: Has an earthy, minty edge to the basic cherry flavor, finishing with moderate intensity. Drink now through 2003.–H.S. • $20 • (9/30/1999) • **85**
Pinot Noir Willamette Valley 1994 • $15 • (10/15/1996) • **82**
Pinot Noir Willamette Valley Red Hills Vineyard 1985 • $NA • (9/30/1987) • **92**
Pinot Noir Yamhill County 1993 • $14 • (1/31/1996) • **81**
Pinot Noir Yamhill County 1992 • $13 • (10/31/1995) • **85**
Pinot Noir Yamhill County 1991 • $10 • (11/30/1994) • **80**
Pinot Noir Yamhill County 1990 • $13 • (2/28/1993) • **81**
Pinot Noir Yamhill County 1989 • $13 • (2/28/1993) • **83**
Pinot Noir Yamhill County Hyland Vineyards 1986 • $15 • (6/15/1988) • **79**
Pinot Noir Yamhill County Hyland Vineyards 1985 • $15 • (6/15/1987) • **86**
Pinot Noir Yamhill County Hyland Vineyards 1983 • $14 • (8/31/1986) • **82**
Pinot Noir Yamhill County Hyland Vineyards Reserve 1985 • $18 • (6/15/1988) • **86**
Pinot Noir Yamhill County Hyland Vineyards Reserve 1983 • $30 • (2/15/1990) • **67**
Pinot Noir Yamhill County Red Hills 1986 • $15 • (6/15/1988) • **77**
Pinot Noir Yamhill County Red Hills 1985 • $15 • (6/15/1987) • **80**
Pinot Noir Yamhill County Red Hills Reserve 1985 • $30 • (2/15/1990) • **74**
Pinot Noir Yamhill County Redland 1994 • $NA • (2/28/1997) • **87**
Pinot Noir Yamhill County Redland 1993 • $25 • (10/15/1996) • **84**
Pinot Noir Yamhill County Redland 1992 • $25 • (2/29/1996) • **86**
Pinot Noir Yamhill County Redland 1991 • $23 • (11/15/1994) • **88**
Pinot Noir Yamhill County Redland 1989 • $24 • (2/28/1993) • **83**
Pinot Noir Yamhill County Redland 1988 • $13 • (4/15/1991) • **82**
Pinot Noir Yamhill County Redland 1987 • $13 • (2/15/1990) • **66**
Pinot Noir Yamhill County Redland Winemaker's Reserve 1997: Light and simple, with pretty berry and chocolate notes floating on the soft finish. Drink now.–H.S. • $40 • (12/31/1999) • **83**
Pinot Noir Yamhill County Redland Winemaker's Reserve 1996: Light and velvety, with a nice thread of plum and toast on a firm layer of fine-grained tannins. Drink now through 2002.–H.S. • $30 • (9/30/1999) • **87**
Sémillon-Chardonnay Oregon NV • $9 • (11/30/1995) • **81**
White Riesling Columbia Valley Sweet Reserve 1995 • $12 • (10/31/1996) • **76**

SOLEO | CALIFORNIA

California White 1996 • $5 • (9/15/1997) • **87**

SOLITUDE | CALIFORNIA

Pinot Noir Carneros Sangiacomo Vineyard 1994 • $18 • (3/31/1997) • **79**
Pinot Noir Carneros Sangiacomo Vineyard 1993 • $18 • (1/31/1996) • **84**
Pinot Noir Carneros Sangiacomo Vineyard 1991 • $18 • (2/28/1994) • **75**
Pinot Noir Russian River Valley Rochioli Vineyard 1994 • $25 • (2/28/1997) • **84**
Pinot Noir Sonoma County 1992 • $17 • (3/31/1995) • **84**

SONOMA CREEK | CALIFORNIA

Cabernet Sauvignon California 1994 • $11 • (11/30/1996) • **80**
Cabernet Sauvignon Napa Valley Reserve 1991 • $15 • (11/15/1994) • **84**
Cabernet Sauvignon Sonoma County 1997: Looking for a value in California Cabernet? This firm-textured wine has anise, blackberry and coffee notes framed by toasty oak, with supple tannins that give good structure, and the flavors resonate on the finish. Drink now through 2004. • $12 • (11/15/1999) • **87**
Cabernet Sauvignon Sonoma County 1991 • $15 • (11/15/1993) • **78**
Cabernet Sauvignon Sonoma Mountain Van der Kamp Vineyard 1995: Juicy, ripe black cherry and herb notes swirl around the palate. Not much complexity, but the tannins are integrated and the flavors are bright and tasty. Drink now.–J.L. • $26 • (11/15/1998) • **84**
Cabernet Sauvignon Sonoma Valley 1991 • $15 • (11/15/1994) • **82**
Cabernet Sauvignon Sonoma Valley 1988 • $12 • (11/15/1991) • **74**
Cabernet Sauvignon Sonoma Valley Rancho Salina Vineyard 1996: Oak dominates while ripe fruit takes a back seat. Blackberry, cassis and herb are trying to show their stuff, supported by firm tannins. The wine will probably flesh out nicely in time. Best from 2002 through 2008. • $25 • (11/15/1999) • **87**
Cabernet Sauvignon Sonoma Valley Rancho Salina Vineyard 1994 • $28 • (10/31/1997) • **90**
Cabernet Sauvignon Sonoma Valley Reserve 1996: Sweet oak and bright fruit make this fun to drink now. Tannins are firm and muscular; the wine has staying power. The plush plum, black cherry, cedar and spice notes should

evolve nicely. Good price, too. Drink now through 2006. • $20 • (11/15/1999) • **89**

Chardonnay Sonoma County 1998: Buttery, toasty popcornlike nuances are soft and appealing. Drink now.–J.L. • $12 • (6/30/2000) • **83**

Meritage Sonoma County 1994 • $18 • (10/31/1997) • **82**

Merlot Sonoma County 1997: Cedary, with dried blueberry flavors and a drying cinnamon finish. Drink now.–J.L. • $14 • (6/30/2000) • **83**

Merlot Sonoma Valley Sangiacomo Vineyard 1994 • $28 • (7/31/1997) • **88**

Merlot Sonoma Valley Sangiacomo Vineyard 1992 • $25 • (11/15/1994) • **85**

Pinot Noir Carneros 1992 • $10 • (3/31/1995) • **77**

Pinot Noir Sonoma County 1995 • $12 • (7/31/1997) • **85**

Pinot Noir Sonoma County 1993 • $10 • (12/31/1995) • **83**

Zinfandel California 1994 • $11 • (12/15/1996) • **79**

Zinfandel Sonoma County 1994 • $14 • (12/15/1996) • **81**

Zinfandel Sonoma County 1992 • $10 • (10/15/1994) • **78**

Zinfandel Sonoma Valley 1990 • $9 • (10/15/1992) • **78**

SONOMA-CUTRER | CALIFORNIA

Chardonnay Russian River Valley The Cutrer 1997: Marked by tart green apple and pineapple flavors, it's crisp and lean, turning simple and earthy. Drink now through 2004.–J.L. • $30 • (5/31/2000) • **83**

Chardonnay Sonoma Coast Les Pierres 1996: Intense, ripe and concentrated, with a flinty, earthy edge to the core of pear, anise and mineral notes, turning elegant. Drink now through 2002.–J.L. • $35 • (3/31/1999) • **89**

Chardonnay Sonoma Coast Russian River Ranches 1998: A touch candied, with earthy, tart apple flavors that turn sour. Drink now.–J.L. • $18 • (5/31/2000) • **82**

Chardonnay Sonoma Coast Russian River Ranches 1997: Tight and crisp, with a flinty edge to the narrow band of pear, spice and apricot, slowly unfolding to reveal more nuance and complexity. Drink through 2004.–J.L. • $19 Ⓐ • (4/30/1999) • **90**

Chardonnay Sonoma Coast Russian River Ranches 1996 • $17 • (3/31/1998) • **89**

Chardonnay Sonoma Valley Les Pierres 1997: Complex up front, with ripe pear, fig and melon flavors accented by a touch of citrus, but then loses intensity for a lean finish. Drink now.–J.L. • $30 • (5/31/2000) • **86**

SONOMA-LOEB | CALIFORNIA

Cabernet Sauvignon Alexander Valley 1988 • $10 • (2/29/1992) • **82**

Chardonnay Sonoma County 1998: Ripe, rich and toasty, with lots of fig, apricot, vanilla and hazelnut. Finishes with spicy, creamy notes. Drink now.–J.L. • $20 • (6/15/2000) • **87**

Chardonnay Sonoma County 1997: Elegant, ripe and fruity, with a creamy array of pear, spice, melon, fig and apricot. Turns smooth and silky on the finish, where the flavors linger. Drink now through 2002.–J.L. • $12 Ⓐ • (7/31/1999) • **91**

Chardonnay Sonoma County 1996 • $10 Ⓐ • (11/30/1997) • **89**

Chardonnay Sonoma County Private Reserve 1998: Ripe and creamy, with complex, spicy pear, vanilla, anise and smoky fig, turning long and detailed. Drink now.–J.L. • $35 • (6/15/2000) • **88**

Chardonnay Sonoma County Private Reserve 1997: Smooth, ripe and creamy, with cedary oak, ripe pear, apple and a touch of vanilla. Pleasantly earthy aftertaste. Drink now through 2002.–J.L. • $16 Ⓐ • (7/31/1999) • **91**

Chardonnay Sonoma County Private Reserve 1996: Starts out with toasty oak flavors, then delivers attractive ripe pear, apple, fig and melon notes that are rich and elegant, finishing with a long, spicy aftertaste. Drink now through 2002.–J.L. • $30 • (11/30/1998) • **93**

SOOS CREEK | WASHINGTON

Cabernet Sauvignon Columbia Valley 1996: Tough and tannic, but the berry and cherry flavors emerge with plenty of style and persist impressively on the round finish. Give it time to soften. Best after 2001.–H.S. • $25 • (9/15/1999) • **90**

Cabernet Sauvignon Columbia Valley 1995 • $21 • (5/15/1998) • **87**

Cabernet Sauvignon Columbia Valley 1994 • $19 • (8/31/1997) • **86**

Cabernet Sauvignon Columbia Valley 1993 • $17 • (2/28/1997) • **88**

Cabernet Sauvignon Columbia Valley 1992 • $16 • (9/15/1996) • **88**

Cabernet Sauvignon Columbia Valley 1991 • $15 • (4/30/1996) • **84**

Cabernet Sauvignon Columbia Valley 1989 • $15 • (10/15/1993) • **86**

SOQUEL | CALIFORNIA

Cabernet Sauvignon Santa Cruz Mountains 1996: Trim and focused, with earthy cherry, berry, mineral, tar and herb notes. Firm, but should improve with cellaring. Best from 2000 through 2006.–J.L. • $25 • (9/15/1999) • **87**

Cabernet Sauvignon Santa Cruz Mountains 1994 • $22 • (10/31/1997) • **87**

Cabernet Sauvignon Santa Cruz Mountains 1991 • $20 • (4/15/1994) • **86**

Cabernet Sauvignon Santa Cruz Mountains 1990 • $16 • (3/31/1993) • **88**

Cabernet Sauvignon Santa Cruz Mountains Partners' Reserve 1995: Firm in texture, on the chewy side, with pretty spice, cedar and modest cherry flavors that linger gently on the finish. Needs cellaring to open the tight core of flavors. Best after 2001.–H.S. • $40 • (11/15/1998) • **85**

Cabernet Sauvignon Santa Cruz Mountains Partners' Reserve 1994 • $40 • (12/15/1997) • **80**

Cabernet Sauvignon Santa Cruz Mountains Special Reserve 1992 • $22 • (5/31/1998) • **83**

Cabernet Sauvignon Santa Cruz Mountains Special Reserve 1989 • $25 • (8/31/1992) • **85**

Cabernet Sauvignon Stags Leap District 1992 • $20 • (5/31/1998) • **83**

Cabernet Sauvignon Stags Leap District 1991 • $18 • (5/15/1994) • **83**

Cabernet Sauvignon Stags Leap District 1990 • $20 • (2/29/1996) • **80**

Cabernet Sauvignon Stags Leap District 1989 • $16 • (2/15/1993) • **85**

Chardonnay Monterey County 1996 • $16 • (6/30/1998) • **87**

Chardonnay Santa Cruz Mountains 1997: Richly textured, serving up a blend of ripe pear, light citrus and herb flavors couched in firm acidity. The finish is moderate, fresh and clean. Drink now. • $20 • (6/30/1999) • **88**

Chardonnay Santa Cruz Mountains 1996 • $20 • (6/30/1998) • **89**

Merlot Santa Cruz Mountains 1997: Firm in structure, with a tight range of mineral, cherry and earth flavors, finishing tannic. Drink now through 2004.–J.L. • $25 • (10/15/1999) • **84**

Merlot Santa Cruz Mountains Partners' Reserve 1996: Still young and a bit coarse, it nonetheless displays a complex core of black currant, black cherry, tar and herb flavors. Should evolve nicely with time. Drink through 2004. • $30 • (10/15/1998) • **87**

Pinot Noir Santa Cruz Mountains 1991 • $16 • (2/28/1994) • **80**

Pinot Noir Santa Cruz Mountains 1990 • $18 • (9/30/1992) • **86**

Pinot Noir Santa Cruz Mountains Longridge Vineyard 1994 • $25 • (2/29/1996) • **85**

Pinot Noir Santa Cruz Mountains Special Reserve 1994 • $25 • (3/31/1996) • **83**

Pinot Noir Santa Cruz Mountains Special Reserve 1993 • $25 • (12/31/1995) • **81**

Zinfandel Alexander Valley 1991 • $8 • (6/15/1993) • **79**

SPARROW LANE | CALIFORNIA

Zinfandel Howell Mountain Beatty Ranch 1996 • $22 • (6/15/1998) • **86**

Zinfandel North Coast 1994 • $15 • (4/30/1997) • **84**

Zinfandel North Coast 1993 • $12 • (10/15/1995) • **88**

SPELLETICH | CALIFORNIA

Bodog Red Napa Valley 1997: Shows off the racy, spicy wild berry and raspberry flavors of Zin, anchored by the currant and tannic side of Cabernet. Zinfandel, Sangiovese, Cabernet, Syrah, Merlot and others. Drink now through 2006.–J.L. • $23 • (5/31/2000) • **88**

Zinfandel Napa Valley Adella 1997: Ripe and spicy, with wild berry, plum and cherry-laced flavors that are on the lighter side. Drink now.–J.L. • $20 • (6/30/2000) • **83**

SPENKER | CALIFORNIA

Zinfandel Lodi 1996 • $15 • (6/15/1998) • **60**

Zinfandel Lodi 1995 • $14 • (7/31/1997) • **90**

SPOTTSWOODE | CALIFORNIA

Cabernet Sauvignon Napa Valley 1998: Features a pure fruit profile marked by ripe plum, black cherry, wild berry and spice, with supple tannins and minimal oak at this stage. Fine balance.–J.L. • $NA • (8/31/1999) (BT) • **90-94**

Cabernet Sauvignon Napa Valley 1997: Openly fruity, supple, with plum and cherry-laced flavors, this is a notably harmonious and well-balanced young wine.–J.L. • $NA • (8/31/1998) (BT) • **90-94**

Cabernet Sauvignon Napa Valley 1996: Delicious, sporting an elegant array of plum, black cherry, currant, herb and olive notes. Ripe, smooth and polished, flowing across the palate to a rich finish that lingers on and on. Drink now through 2008.–J.L. • $73 Ⓐ • (10/31/1999) CS • **93**

Cabernet Sauvignon Napa Valley 1995: An outstanding effort. Ripe, with supple, polished tannins and a wonderful core of mouthfilling currant, black cherry, berry and spice flavors. Lushly textured to the long finish, where it tightens up. Approachable now, but better if cellared. Best from 2001 through 2007.–J.L. • $69 Ⓐ • (10/31/1998) CS • **93**

Cabernet Sauvignon Napa Valley 1994 • $81 Ⓐ • (10/15/1997) • **92**

Cabernet Sauvignon Napa Valley 1993 • $51 Ⓐ • (11/15/1996) • **90**

Cabernet Sauvignon Napa Valley 1992 • $78 Ⓐ • (11/30/1995) CS • **90**

Cabernet Sauvignon Napa Valley 1991: This big, muscular red reflects its tannic vintage, with deep, smoky flavors of plum, spice and tar. It's still a bit tough. (Spottswoode vertical tasting—and all listings below from the 12/31/1998 issue). Best after 2001.–T.M. • $81 Ⓐ • (12/31/1998) • **94**

Cabernet Sauvignon Napa Valley 1990: Still young and firm, this delivers spicy plum and chocolate flavors; it's polished, balanced and intense. Approachable now; best after 2000.–T.M. • $103 Ⓐ • (12/31/1998) • **90**

Cabernet Sauvignon Napa Valley 1989: A tannic wine from a tannic vintage, this has ripe plum and black cherry flavors with light earthy notes; it's firm and a bit austere. Drink now through 2008.–T.M. • $52 Ⓐ • (12/31/1998) • **88**

Cabernet Sauvignon Napa Valley 1988: Ripe, supple and well balanced, with a tightly focused band of currant, black cherry, anise, tar and cedar. Finishes with well-integrated tannins and just a hint of dryness. (1988 California Cabernet retrospective tasting). Drink now through 2002. –J.L. • $61 Ⓐ • (11/15/1998) • **88**

Cabernet Sauvignon Napa Valley 1987: Rich and sweet, this luscious red offers ripe plum, raisin and chocolate flavors, with full, soft tannins and great depth. Drink now through 2010.–T.M. • $112 Ⓐ • (12/31/1998) • **95**

Cabernet Sauvignon Napa Valley 1986: This has everything: deep color, rich, ripe aromas and bold fruit flavors, a velvety texture, depth and balance. It's delicious now but will improve for years. Drink now through 2016.–T.M. • $85 Ⓐ • (12/31/1998) • **96**

Cabernet Sauvignon Napa Valley 1985: This brawny red offers rich aromas of plum and cedar, with plum and mint flavors bracketed by full tannins and crisp acidity. It's balanced and should still improve in the bottle. Approachable now; best after 2000.–T.M. • $95 Ⓐ • (12/31/1998) • **92**

Cabernet Sauvignon Napa Valley 1984: Thick and rather hard, this shows ripe plum and chocolate flavors that are a bit overshadowed by firm tannins, but the cedary finish suggests it's at its peak now. Drink now. –T.M. • $84 Ⓐ • (12/31/1998) • **88**

Cabernet Sauvignon Napa Valley 1983: Another difficult vintage, and based on this bottle, the wine has not aged well, showing herbal and slightly vegetal flavors with a dry, cedary finish. Drink now.–T.M. • $18 • (12/31/1998) • **82**

Cabernet Sauvignon Napa Valley 1982: Spottswoode made a fine debut in a difficult vintage, but this bottle—the only one of a different provenance—was austere and tired, showing mature cedar and tobacco flavors and a dry finish. Drink now.–T.M. • $45 Ⓐ • (12/31/1998) • **84**

Sauvignon Blanc Napa Valley 1996 • $18 • (6/15/1997) • **87**

SPRING MOUNTAIN | CALIFORNIA

Cabernet Sauvignon Napa Valley 1985 • $20 • (10/15/1989) • **85**

Cabernet Sauvignon Napa Valley 1984 • $15 • (3/15/1989) • **89**

Cabernet Sauvignon Napa Valley 1983 • $15 • (9/30/1987) • **80**

Cabernet Sauvignon Napa Valley 1982 • $15 • (12/15/1986) • **87**

Miravalle-Alba-Chevalier Napa Valley Red 1995: Tight, rich and concentrated, with an earthy side to the currant and cherry, herb and cedar. The best effort from this revived Napa Valley winery. 100 percent Cabernet Sauvignon. Drink through 2006.–J.L. • $40 • (10/31/1998) • **89**

Miravalle-Alba-Chevalier Napa Valley Red 1993 • $30 • (11/15/1996) • **87**

Miravalle-La Perla-Chevalier Napa Valley Red 1996: Weaves together a complex array of currant, cherry, herb, coffee, mushroom, anise and sage flavors that remain focused. Though the tannins are strong and unyielding, you get a glimpse of fleshiness. Best from 2001 through 2010.–J.L. • $45 • (11/15/1999) • **90**

Miravalle-La Perla-Chevalier Napa Valley White 1998: Has more flavor and richness than most from this vintage, offering bright, ripe tangerine, nectarine and lemon notes. 100 percent Sauvignon Blanc. Drink now.–J.L. • $25 • (5/15/2000) • **85**

Key: SS—Spectator Selection. CS—Cellar Selection. HR—Highly Recommended. $NA—Price not available. (BT)—Barrel tasting. Ⓐ—Auction Price. For a key to the tasters' initials, see "How to Use These Listings."
Dates in parentheses represent the issues in which the ratings were published.

Miravalle-La Perla-Chevalier Napa Valley White 1997: Pretty toast notes up front, after which the wine shows firm texture and bright acidity. Flavors lean toward herb, fresh-cut grass, melon, fig and just a hint of grapefruit. Finishes long. A blend of Sauvignon Blanc, Chardonnay and Muscat Blanc. Drink now through 2003. • $20 • (5/31/1999) • **88**

Napa Valley 1994 • $36 • (4/30/1998) • **90**

SPRINGHILL | OREGON

Pinot Gris Willamette Valley 1998: Light and bright, with citrus and apple flavors that remain lively through the finish. Drink now.–H.S. • $14 • (5/15/2000) • **85**

Pinot Noir Oregon Barrel Select 1992 • $15 • (11/30/1994) • **85**

Pinot Noir Willamette Valley 1997: Lean, with pickle barrel notes running through the light, slightly astringent blackberry flavors. Drink now.–H.S. • $18 • (4/30/2000) • **82**

Pinot Noir Willamette Valley 1996 • $20 • (5/15/1998) • **87**

Pinot Noir Willamette Valley 1990 • $8 • (11/30/1994) • **78**

Pinot Noir Willamette Valley Barrel Select 1997: Lean and tight, with firm tannins and a modest level of blackberry and anise flavor. Best from 2001 through 2003.–H.S. • $20 • (4/30/2000) • **80**

Pinot Noir Willamette Valley Reserve 1996 • $35 • (5/15/1998) • **87**

Pinot Noir Willamette Valley Reserve 1995 • $25 • (7/31/1997) • **90**

Pinot Noir Willamette Valley Reserve 1993 • $20 • (1/31/1996) • **85**

Riesling Willamette Valley 1998: Soft, with the sweetness nicely balanced by citrusy acidity, finishing with a squeeze of lime. Drink now.–H.S. • $9 • (5/15/2000) • **84**

Riesling Willamette Valley 1996 • $9 • (5/15/1998) • **84**

Riesling Willamette Valley Late Harvest Select Cluster Botrytized 1994 • $12 • (1/31/1996) • **83**

STAG HOLLOW | OREGON

Pinot Noir Oregon Celebré 1995 • $21 • (2/28/1998) • **85**

Pinot Noir Oregon Celebré 1994 • $32 • (4/30/1997) • **88**

Pinot Noir Oregon Vendage Sélection 1996: Lovely balance of ripe plum and berry flavors, with a velvety texture and hints of spice on the warm finish. Has style, clarity and more than a little seductiveness. Drink now through 2003.–H.S. • $28 • (4/30/2000) • **89**

Pinot Noir Oregon Vendange Sélection 1995 • $28 • (6/15/1998) • **86**

Pinot Noir Oregon Vinnae 1997: A pretty wine, with raspberry and cherry fruit shining through a frame of modest, fine-textured tannin. Flavors last on the finish. Drink now through 2002.–H.S. • $24 • (4/30/2000) • **86**

STAGLIN | CALIFORNIA

Cabernet Sauvignon Rutherford 1996: Smooth, ripe and spicy, with a pretty array of anise, plum, cherry and strawberry tones, finishing with a focused core of flavors and firm tannins. Drink through 2008.–J.L. • $50 • (8/31/1999) • **90**

Cabernet Sauvignon Rutherford 1995: This California Cabernet is elegant and supple, with a pretty array of currant, blackberry, cherry, toasty oak and spice flavors. Finishes with firm but polished tannins, and a long, rich aftertaste punctuated by mineral, cedar and spice. Drinkable now, but worthy of cellaring. Best from 2001 through 2009.–J.L. • $43 • (8/31/1998) HR • **92**

Cabernet Sauvignon Rutherford 1994 • $40 • (6/15/1997) • **90**

Cabernet Sauvignon Napa Valley 1993 • $30 • (4/30/1996) • **89**

Cabernet Sauvignon Napa Valley 1992 • $28 • (12/15/1995) • **91**

Cabernet Sauvignon Napa Valley 1991 • $48 Ⓐ • (11/15/1994) • **89**

Cabernet Sauvignon Napa Valley 1989: Revs up just enough richness to grab your attention, with supple chocolate, currant, coffee and black cherry flavors that are focused and pleasing before they bow to the earthy, drying tannins. (1989 California Cabernet retrospective tasting). Drink now through 2004.–J.L. • $24 • (8/31/1999) • **87**

Cabernet Sauvignon Napa Valley 1988: One of the better efforts in this group. Has richness, with complex currant, black cherry, berry and a dash of mint, and sustains its flavors on the finish, with body and flesh. Has firm, crisp tannins and seems complete overall, if short. (1988 California Cabernet retrospective tasting). Drink through 2003.–J.L. • $20 • (11/15/1998) • **88**

Chardonnay Napa Valley 1997: A nonmalolactic, low-oak style that's tight, crisp and concentrated, with spicy pear, hints of peach, vanilla and mineral, finishing clean. Drink through 2004.–J.L. • $40 • (2/28/1999) • **88**

Sangiovese Napa Valley Stagliano 1994 • $34 • (4/30/1996) • **87**

Sangiovese Napa Valley Stagliano 1993 • $34 • (2/28/1995) • **88**

Sangiovese Rutherford Stagliano 1996: Shows more finesse and polish than most California Sangiovese, with spicy cherry, plum and wild berry. Finishes with mild, well-integrated tannins. Drink now through 2001.–J.L. • $40 • (9/30/1998) • **87**

STAG'S LEAP WINE CELLARS | CALIFORNIA

Cabernet Sauvignon Napa Valley 1995 • $40 Ⓐ • (4/30/1998) • **87**
Cabernet Sauvignon Napa Valley 1994 • $24 • (5/15/1997) • **88**
Cabernet Sauvignon Napa Valley 1993 • $22 • (10/15/1996) • **88**
Cabernet Sauvignon Napa Valley 1991 • $18 • (3/31/1994) • **87**
Cabernet Sauvignon Napa Valley 1990 • $18 • (5/15/1993) SS • **91**
Cabernet Sauvignon Napa Valley 1989 • $18 • (9/30/1992) • **83**
Cabernet Sauvignon Napa Valley 1988 • $18 • (6/15/1991) • **90**
Cabernet Sauvignon Napa Valley 1987 • $18 • (8/31/1990) • **75**
Cabernet Sauvignon Napa Valley 1986 • $18 • (6/15/1989) • **82**
Cabernet Sauvignon Napa Valley 1985 • $56 Ⓐ • (9/15/1988) • **90**
Cabernet Sauvignon Napa Valley 1984 • $15 • (7/15/1987) • **83**
Cabernet Sauvignon Napa Valley 1981 • $15 • (12/16/1984) • **82**
Cabernet Sauvignon Napa Valley Fay 1996: Firm, tight and tannic, this is a tightly wound '96 that needs patience, as the chunky core of currant, spice, coffee, mineral and earth notes needs time to soften and evolve. Drink through 2005.–J.L. • $100 • (11/15/1999) • **88**
Cabernet Sauvignon Napa Valley Fay 1995: Lots of cedar, coffee and toasty oak before the currant, plum, black cherry and meaty flavors unfold, filling in the gaps rather nicely. Complex and concentrated, yet delicate and polished, with fine tannins and a long, rich, complex aftertaste that keeps pumping flavor. Drink through 2006.–J.L. • $70 • (10/31/1998) • **93**
Cabernet Sauvignon Napa Valley Fay 1994 • $50 • (3/31/1998) CS • **92**
Cabernet Sauvignon Napa Valley Fay 1993 • $40 • (11/15/1996) • **91**
Cabernet Sauvignon Napa Valley Fay 1992 • $56 Ⓐ • (12/15/1995) CS • **91**
Cabernet Sauvignon Napa Valley Fay 1991 • $83 Ⓐ • (12/31/1994) • **88**
Cabernet Sauvignon Napa Valley Fay 1990 • $30 • (3/31/1994) • **88**
Cabernet Sauvignon Napa Valley S.L.V. 1996: Dense, rich and earthy, with complex mineral, currant, anise and sage flavors that unfold gracefully and persist on the firm finish. Best from 2001 through 2010.–J.L. • $100 • (11/15/1999) • **92**
Cabernet Sauvignon Napa Valley S.L.V. 1995: Decidedly supple and elegant, with ripe, rich, polished layers of currant, black cherry, vanilla, herb, anise and spice, and gentle, ripe, elegant tannins. Finishes with hints of coffee, cedar and sage. A rewarding wine. Best from 2001 through 2007.–J.L. • $70 • (11/15/1998) • **93**
Cabernet Sauvignon Napa Valley S.L.V. 1994 • $50 • (11/30/1997) CS • **91**
Cabernet Sauvignon Napa Valley S.L.V. 1993 • $40 • (11/15/1996) • **90**
Cabernet Sauvignon Napa Valley S.L.V. 1992 • $48 Ⓐ • (12/15/1995) • **88**
Cabernet Sauvignon Napa Valley S.L.V. 1990 • $61 Ⓐ • (3/31/1994) HR • **89**
Cabernet Sauvignon Napa Valley SLV~FAY 1989: Earthy, with a mulchy, dill flavor running through the dried cherry and cedary anise notes. Not a great wine, but drinking well; no point in holding any longer. This vintage is the only SLV~FAY bottling. (1989 California Cabernet retrospective tasting). –J.L. • $25 • (8/31/1999) • **83**
Cabernet Sauvignon Napa Valley S.L.V. 1988: Smooth and polished in texture, with complex currant, coffee, cedar and herbal notes. Well balanced and well focused, with a complex, lingering aftertaste and integrated tannins. (1988 California Cabernet retrospective tasting). Drink now through 2004.–J.L. • $NA • (11/15/1998) • **88**
Cabernet Sauvignon Napa Valley S.L.V. 1987 • $58 Ⓐ • (11/15/1990) • **77**
Cabernet Sauvignon Napa Valley S.L.V. 1986 • $58 Ⓐ • (12/15/1996) • **91**
Cabernet Sauvignon Napa Valley S.L.V. 1985 • $73 Ⓐ • (10/31/1988) • **90**
Cabernet Sauvignon Napa Valley Stag's Leap Vineyards 1984 • $48 Ⓐ • (11/30/1987) • **81**
Cabernet Sauvignon Napa Valley Stag's Leap Vineyards 1983 • $18 • (11/15/1986) • **77**
Cabernet Sauvignon Napa Valley Stag's Leap Vineyards 1982 • $17 • (10/01/1985) • **69**
Cabernet Sauvignon Napa Valley Stag's Leap Vineyards 1981 • $48 Ⓐ • (9/16/1984) CS • **90**
Cabernet Sauvignon Napa Valley Stag's Leap Vineyards 1979: Mature, with complex ripe cherry, coffee, herb, cedar and spice, turning supple and a touch dry on the finish. Later vintages of this bottling are called SLV. (1979 California Cabernet retrospective tasting). Drink now.–J.L. • $41 Ⓐ • (8/31/1999) • **88**
Cabernet Sauvignon Napa Valley Stag's Leap Vineyards 1974 • $95 • (2/15/1990) • **83**
Cabernet Sauvignon Napa Valley Stag's Leap Vineyards 1973 • $NA • (4/01/1986) • **82**
Cabernet Sauvignon Napa Valley Stag's Leap Vineyards Lot 2 1978 • $83 Ⓐ • (11/15/1992) • **88**
Cabernet Sauvignon Stags Leap District Fay 1997: A subtle style, supple, with currant, herb, sage and anise. Turns complex on the finish, where the flavors linger.–J.L. • $NA • (8/31/1998) (BT) • **90-94**
Cask 23 Napa Valley 1998: Intriguing array of blueberry, wild berry, oak, spice and cherry, with wonderful harmony and finesse, polish and texture.–J.L. • $NA • (8/31/1999) (BT) • **95-99**
Cask 23 Napa Valley 1995: A tremendous effort, ultrarich, supple, complex and concentrated. Delivers a wave of plush currant, black cherry, black olive, sage and spicy flavors that glide across the palate with smooth, silky tannins that have become the trademark of this wine. Contains 95 percent Cabernet, with a touch of Merlot. Drink through 2010.–J.L. • $110 Ⓐ • (11/15/1998) • **94**
Cask 23 Napa Valley 1994 • $134 Ⓐ • (3/31/1998) CS • **93**
Cask 23 Napa Valley 1993 • $112 Ⓐ • (3/31/1997) • **88**
Cask 23 Napa Valley 1992 • $121 Ⓐ • (12/15/1995) CS • **94**
Cask 23 Napa Valley 1991 • $157 Ⓐ • (12/31/1994) CS • **92**
Cask 23 Napa Valley 1990 • $117 Ⓐ • (10/31/1993) CS • **92**
Cask 23 Napa Valley 1987 • $115 Ⓐ • (12/15/1997) • **87**
Cask 23 Napa Valley 1986 • $115 Ⓐ • (12/15/1996) • **88**
Cask 23 Napa Valley 1985 • $372 Ⓐ • (11/30/1989) • **96**
Cabernet Sauvignon Napa Valley Stag's Leap Vineyards Cask 23 1984 • $144 Ⓐ • (12/31/1988) • **90**
Cabernet Sauvignon Napa Valley Stag's Leap Vineyards Cask 23 1983 • $166 Ⓐ • (10/15/1988) • **82**
Cabernet Sauvignon Napa Valley Stag's Leap Vineyards Cask 23 1978: Still has plenty of ripe fruit flavors, but also a dryness on the finish. The core is built around ripe plum, currant, herb and berry. Tannins have softened nicely, making for a complex and mellow wine that finishes with a slight metallic edge. (1978 California Cabernet retrospective tasting). Drink now through 2001.–J.L. • $188 Ⓐ • (11/15/1998) • **88**
Cabernet Sauvignon Napa Valley Stag's Leap Vineyards Cask 23 1977 • $58 Ⓐ • (1/01/1983) CS • **91**
Chardonnay Napa Valley 1998: On the simple side, with a modest range of pear and citrus, turning earthy. Drink now.–J.L. • $26 • (6/15/2000) • **83**
Chardonnay Napa Valley 1996 • $24 • (4/30/1998) • **89**
Chardonnay Napa Valley Beckstoffer Ranch 1996 • $28 • (5/15/1998) • **91**
Chardonnay Napa Valley Reserve 1997: Well focused on high-toned fruit flavors, with elegant, rich citrus, lemon, pear and green apple. The remarkably delicate and complex aftertaste weaves in a pretty band of toasty oak. Drink now through 2002.–J.L. • $45 • (7/31/1999) • **92**
Chardonnay Napa Valley Reserve 1996 • $37 • (5/15/1998) • **91**
Merlot Napa Valley 1995: Elegant in texture, it serves up a range of coffee, herb, tobacco and mineral flavors woven into the center of currant and berry. Finishes with chewy tannins and less focus than it began with. Drink through 2004.–J.L. • $26 • (10/15/1998) • **87**
Merlot Napa Valley 1994 • $26 • (6/30/1997) • **88**
Merlot Napa Valley 1992 • $24 • (12/15/1995) • **88**
Merlot Napa Valley 1991 • $22 • (5/31/1994) • **86**
Merlot Napa Valley 1990 • $22 • (3/31/1993) • **87**
Merlot Napa Valley 1985 • $26 Ⓐ • (5/31/1988) • **86**
Merlot Napa Valley 1984 • $15 • (5/15/1987) • **78**
Merlot Napa Valley 1982 • $14 • (10/01/1985) • **78**
Merlot Napa Valley 1981 • $14 • (4/16/1984) • **82**
Petite Sirah Napa Valley 1993 • $18 • (10/15/1996) • **85**
Petite Sirah Napa Valley 1992 • $18 • (9/30/1995) • **83**
Petite Sirah Napa Valley 1991 • $19 • (2/28/1995) • **85**
Petite Sirah Napa Valley 1987 • $12 • (8/31/1990) • **87**
Stag's Leap Vineyards Cask 23 Napa Valley 1974 • $288 Ⓐ • (11/15/1994) • **94**
Sauvignon Blanc Napa Valley 1998: Appley, with vanilla, citrus and herb flavors. Drink now.–J.L. • $20 • (6/15/2000) • **82**
Sauvignon Blanc Napa Valley 1996 • $15 • (4/30/1998) • **88**
Sauvignon Blanc Napa Valley Rancho Chimiles 1998: Lean, with pronounced citrus and cat pee notes. Drink now.–J.L. • $22 • (6/15/2000) • **80**
White Riesling Napa Valley 1996 • $13 • (11/30/1997) • **83**

STAGS' LEAP WINERY | CALIFORNIA

Cabernet Sauvignon Napa Valley 1991 • $20 • (11/15/1994) • **85**
Cabernet Sauvignon Napa Valley 1989 • $19 • (3/15/1993) • **86**
Cabernet Sauvignon Napa Valley 1987 • $18 • (6/30/1991) • **89**
Cabernet Sauvignon Napa Valley 1984 • $14 • (7/15/1988) • **90**
Cabernet Sauvignon Napa Valley 1981 • $14 • (3/01/1985) • **86**
Merlot Napa Valley 1996: Smoky toasted oak works in nicely with earthy cassis and currant flavors. Firm and mildly tannic finish, where the flavors turn complex. Drink now through 2003.–J.L. • $29 • (9/15/1999) • **88**
Merlot Napa Valley 1994 • $25 • (6/30/1997) • **82**

STAGS' LEAP WINERY

Merlot Napa Valley 1990 • $20 • (6/15/1993) • **78**
Merlot Napa Valley 1989 • $17 • (5/31/1992) • **88**
Merlot Napa Valley 1987 • $17 • (11/15/1991) • **85**
Merlot Napa Valley 1986 • $17 • (12/31/1990) • **84**
Merlot Napa Valley 1981 • $12 • (2/16/1985) • **83**
Petite Sirah Napa Valley 1990 • $17 • (9/30/1994) • **81**
Petite Sirah Napa Valley 1988 • $15 • (11/30/1992) • **88**
Petite Sirah Napa Valley 1987 • $14 • (10/31/1991) • **82**
Petite Sirah Napa Valley 1980 • $10 • (3/01/1985) • **84**
Petite Sirah Napa Valley Stags' Leap Reserve 1993 • $45 • (4/30/1998) • **88**
Petite Syrah Napa Valley 1996: Tight and a touch tart, with leathery berry, dried cherry and sage notes that turn dry. Lacks the concentration for cellaring. Drink now through 2006.–J.L. • $28 • (6/15/2000) • **86**

STALEY, PHILIP | CALIFORNIA

Grenache Russian River Valley Staley Vineyard 1995 • $13 • (3/31/1998) • **83**
Mourvèdre Russian River Valley Staley Vineyard 1995 • $15 • (3/31/1998) • **85**
Rue Rivage Russian River Valley 1994 • $10 • (3/31/1998) • **84**
Sangiovese Dry Creek Valley Somers Vineyard 1995 • $20 • (3/31/1998) • **83**
Syrah Russian River Valley Staley Vineyard 1995 • $18 • (3/31/1998) • **85**
Zinfandel Dry Creek Valley Somers Vineyard 1996: Focused, with minerally, earthy notes and a core of blackberry and pepper flavors. Finishes a bit dry. Drink now through 2002.–J.L. • $16 • (5/15/1999) • **85**
Zinfandel Dry Creek Valley Somers Vineyard 1995: Shows lean, mature dusty currant, cherry, herb and spice flavors. Tart and narrow on the finish. Drink now through 2001.–J.L. • $18 • (6/30/1999) • **84**

STANDING STONE | NEW YORK

Cabernet Franc Finger Lakes 1997: This perfumed red shows strawberry and sweet cherry flavors, with accents of cola and herbs, and slightly dry tannins that are firm yet a bit clumsy. Drink now through 2001.–T.M. • $16 • (9/15/1999) • **84**
Chardonnay Finger Lakes 1998: This lush white offers ripe melon and honey flavors. Soft and gentle on the palate, it's sweet and generous. Drink now.–T.M. • $14 • (5/31/2000) • **84**
Chardonnay Finger Lakes 1997: Good Chardonnay flavors of pear, butter and spice, with a touch of sweetness on the finish. Pleasant and easygoing. Drink now.–K.M. • $13 • (7/31/1999) • **84**
Gewürztraminer Finger Lakes 1998: The rose petal, litchi and spice exude varietal character in this open, medium-bodied white. Finishes on the crisp side. Drink now.–B.S. • $16 • (11/15/1999) • **82**
Gewürztraminer Finger Lakes 1997: Classic Gewürztraminer flavors of rose and litchi combine with a rich texture and a balanced structure for an appealing presentation. Drink now.–B.S. • $13 • (10/15/1999) • **87**
Gewürztraminer Finger Lakes 1996 • $11 • (3/31/1998) • **87**
Pinnacle Finger Lakes 1998: Chocolate and cherry flavors are soft and a bit candied in this round red. Generous, but it lacks backbone.–T.M. • $18 • (5/31/2000) • **78**
Pinnacle Finger Lakes 1997: A vibrant and focused red with flavors of cherry and red currant, with some appealing herbal notes mixed in. A blend of Cabernet Sauvignon, Cabernet Franc and Merlot. Drink now.–K.M. • $18 • (7/31/1999) • **86**
Riesling Finger Lakes 1998: Noticeably sweet yet balanced, with floral and apricot notes, a soft texture and a mouthwatering finish. Try as an aperitif. Drink now.–B.S. • $10 • (11/15/1999) • **83**
Riesling Finger Lakes 1997: Good complexity here, with lime, peach and a hint of pine, all held together by crisp, balancing acidity. A touch of sulphur dioxide, but it should dissipate with a few months' bottle age. Drink now through 2001.–B.S. • $10 • (9/15/1999) • **86**
Riesling Finger Lakes 1996 • $9 • (3/31/1998) • **84**
Riesling Finger Lakes Dry 1998: Lovely aromas of rose, apricot and citrus mark this rich, round Riesling that is more off-dry than dry. The structure is soft, yet it's hard to deny the delicious flavors. Drink now.–B.S. • $11 • (11/15/1999) • **85**
Riesling Finger Lakes Dry 1997: Lovely ripe apricot character is complemented by moderate acidity and a rich texture. Dry, it tails off quickly and the finish is slightly austere. Drink now.–B.S. • $11 • (9/15/1999) • **82**
Riesling Finger Lakes Dry 1996 • $11 • (3/31/1998) • **86**

Key: SS—Spectator Selection. CS—Cellar Selection. HR—Highly Recommended. $NA—Price not available. (BT)—Barrel tasting. Ⓐ—Auction Price. For a key to the tasters' initials, see "How to Use These Listings."
Dates in parentheses represent the issues in which the ratings were published.

STANGELAND | OREGON

Chardonnay Willamette Valley Estate Reserve 1994 • $18 • (4/30/1997) • **81**
Pinot Noir Willamette Valley 1995 • $12 • (2/28/1997) • **82**
Pinot Noir Willamette Valley Estate Reserve 1994 • $18 • (2/28/1997) • **77**
Pinot Noir Willamette Valley Rob Roy Red NV • $8 • (1/31/1996) • **82**

STARR | OREGON

Pinot Gris Willamette Valley Fox Ridge Vineyard 1997: Crisp in texture, with a raw edge to the apple and nectarine flavors. Needs food. Drink now. –H.S. • $10 • (6/30/1999) • **84**
Pinot Noir Willamette Valley 1996 • $14 • (5/15/1998) • **83**
Pinot Noir Willamette Valley Bert's Blend Reserve 1997: Light and fragrant, with pretty tobacco and fig notes around the modest berry flavors. Fine tannins don't get in the way on the finish. Drink now through 2001.–H.S. • $30 • (6/15/1999) • **87**
Pinot Noir Willamette Valley Bert's Blend Reserve 1996 • $28 • (6/15/1998) • **89**

STATON HILLS | WASHINGTON

Cabernet Sauvignon Columbia Valley Unfiltered 1993 • $18 • (9/15/1997) • **86**
Cabernet Sauvignon Washington 1992 • $12 • (6/15/1996) • **87**
Cabernet Sauvignon Washington 1989 • $14 • (1/31/1995) • **87**
Cabernet Sauvignon Washington 1988 • $15 • (3/31/1992) • **81**
Cabernet Sauvignon Washington 1987 • $13 • (3/31/1991) • **86**
Cabernet Sauvignon Washington 1986 • $12 • (10/15/1989) • **80**
Cabernet Sauvignon Washington Estate 1987 • $20 • (2/29/1992) • **79**
Cabernet Sauvignon Washington Estate 1986 • $20 • (3/31/1991) • **83**
Cabernet Sauvignon Washington Reserve 1987 • $22 • (3/31/1992) • **85**
Cabernet Sauvignon Washington Reserve 1986 • $22 • (8/31/1991) • **83**
Cabernet Sauvignon Yakima Valley 1992 • $14 • (11/30/1996) • **86**
Fumé Blanc Yakima Valley 1996: Light and earthy, with peppery anise and pear flavors. Drink now.–H.S. • $9 • (10/15/1998) • **83**
Merlot Washington 1992 • $13 • (6/15/1996) • **85**
Merlot Washington 1988 • $15 • (3/31/1992) • **82**
Merlot Washington 1987 • $14 • (8/31/1991) • **79**
Merlot Washington Reserve 1987 • $22 • (10/15/1992) • **87**
Phoenix Lot #2 Yakima Valley 1992 • $30 • (9/30/1997) • **78**
Phoenix Yakima Valley 1992 • $18 • (6/15/1996) • **82**
Pinot Noir Oregon 1990 • $10 • (11/30/1994) • **79**
Pinot Noir Oregon 1988 • $15 • (2/28/1993) • **78**
Pinot Noir Oregon 1987 • $13 • (4/15/1991) • **84**
Pinot Noir Oregon 1987 • $13 • (2/15/1990) • **75**

STAUB, RUSTY | CALIFORNIA

Cabernet Sauvignon California 1992 • $10 • (12/15/1995) • **83**

STEELE | CALIFORNIA

Cabernet Franc Clear Lake 1997: Fleshy, with ripe plum, tobacco and berry flavors, finishing with a clean herbal edge. Drink now through 2002.–J.L. • $16 • (12/15/1999) • **86**
Cabernet Franc Clear Lake 1994 • $15 • (4/30/1997) • **86**
Cabernet Sauvignon Anderson Valley 1995: Dark, ripe and deeply flavored, with an array of currant, cedar, spice and cherry, finishing with a complex aftertaste. Best from 2001 through 2007.–J.L. • $26 • (2/28/1999) • **90**
Cabernet Sauvignon Anderson Valley 1994 • $24 • (12/15/1997) • **91**
Cabernet Sauvignon Anderson Valley 1993 • $22 • (4/30/1996) • **90**
Chardonnay California Steele Cuvée 1998: Crisp, with a tight, focused band of citrus and pear notes, turning simple and earthy. Drink now through 2004.–J.L. • $18 • (5/15/2000) • **85**
Chardonnay California Steele Cuvée 1997: Lots of up-front fruit and spice make this white distinctive, with tiers of fig, pear, melon, apricot and nutmeg cascading to a long finish with an intricate aftertaste. Even better than last year's version, also a Spectator Selection. Drink now through 2001.–J.L. • $18 • (5/15/1999) SS • **91**
Chardonnay California Steele Cuvée 1996 • $19 • (5/31/1998) SS • **90**
Chardonnay Carneros Durell Vineyard 1998: Earthy, with a pasty edge to the ripe pear and grapefruit flavors. Drink now through 2004.–J.L. • $28 • (5/15/2000) • **87**
Chardonnay Carneros Durell Vineyard 1997: Perfumed, with an elegant array of pear, fig, spice, vanilla and melon notes that turn elegant and delicate on the finish. Drink now through 2002.–J.L. • $26 • (5/15/1999) • **92**

Chardonnay Carneros Durell Vineyard 1996 • $24 • (6/30/1998) • **93**
Chardonnay Carneros Sangiacomo Vineyard 1997: Lots of rich, smooth, creamy pear, fig and vanilla flavors combine to give this wine depth and distinction, finishing with a complex, spicy aftertaste. Drink now through 2002.–J.L. • $24 • (5/15/1999) • **90**
Chardonnay Carneros Sangiacomo Vineyard 1996 • $24 • (5/15/1998) • **90**
Chardonnay Mendocino DuPratt Vineyard 1997: An understated style that's tight, unfolding to reveal an attractive core of spice, earth, oak and pear flavors that are smooth and elegant. Drink now through 2002.–J.L. • $27 • (7/31/1999) • **91**
Chardonnay Mendocino DuPratt Vineyard 1996 • $26 • (6/30/1998) • **92**
Chardonnay Mendocino Lolonis Vineyard 1998: Ripe and spicy, with pretty nectarine, tangerine, pear and nutmeg notes, if a touch coarse. Drink now. –J.L. • $28 • (5/15/2000) • **87**
Chardonnay Mendocino Lolonis Vineyard 1997: Smooth, ripe, rich and loaded with complex pear, fig, melon, spice and pretty oak shadings. Finishes with long, complex aftertaste where the flavors interweave. Drink now through 2001.–J.L. • $28 • (5/15/1999) • **91**
Chardonnay Mendocino Lolonis Vineyard 1996 • $26 • (6/30/1998) • **93**
Chardonnay Santa Barbara County Bien Nacido Vineyard 1997: Elegant and creamy, with a core of vanilla, fig, pear and spice flavors. Gains depth and nuance on the finish, which shows anise and nutmeg. Drink through 2002. –J.L. • $27 • (6/30/1999) • **92**
Chardonnay Santa Barbara County Bien Nacido Vineyard 1996 • $26 • (5/31/1998) • **92**
Chardonnay Santa Barbara County Goodchild Vineyard 1997: Exotic in its presentation of smoky, toasty oak. The fruit flavors underneath are ripe and full-bodied, turning rich with fig, apricot, baked pie and custard. Drink now through 2002.–J.L. • $27 • (7/31/1999) • **91**
Chardonnay Santa Barbara County Goodchild Vineyard 1996 • $26 • (5/31/1998) • **92**
Chardonnay Sonoma Valley Parmelee-Hill Vineyard 1998: Smooth, ripe and creamy, with pretty pear, coconut, spice and hazelnut flavors. Drink now through 2004.–J.L. • $26 • (5/15/2000) • **88**
Chardonnay Sonoma Valley Parmelee-Hill Vineyard 1997: Very rich and complex, with concentrated fig, apricot and smoky, toasty oak. The long, tasty aftertaste keeps pumping out the flavors. Drink now through 2002.–J.L. • $27 • (6/30/1999) • **92**
Chardonnay Sonoma Valley Parmelee-Hill Vineyard 1996 • $26 • (6/30/1998) • **90**
Fumé Blanc Lake County Dry 1998: Buttery, with pleasant vanilla and herb notes and a lingering finish. Drink now through 2002.–J.L. • $14 • (5/31/2000) • **85**
Merlot Clear Lake 1997: Dark, firm and concentrated, with pretty plum, currant and blackberry flavors. Turns smooth and polished. Drink now through 2007.–J.L. • $22 • (3/31/2000) • **89**
Merlot Clear Lake 1996: Ripe, round and supple, with attractive plum, black cherry and berry notes. Finishes with firm, well-integrated tannins. Steele's first Merlot. Drink through 2004.–J.L. • $25 • (10/15/1998) • **87**
Pinot Blanc Santa Barbara County Bien Nacido Vineyard 1998: Floral, with mineral, vanilla and apple flavors. Tasted twice, with consistent notes. Drink now.–J.L. • $16 • (6/15/2000) • **83**
Pinot Blanc Santa Barbara County Bien Nacido Vineyard 1996 • $15 • (2/28/1998) SS • **92**
Pinot Gris Anderson Valley Romani Family Vineyard 1996 • $18 • (4/30/1998) • **87**
Pinot Noir Anderson Valley 1996: Ripe and plush, with complex layers of rich plum, cherry, light vanilla-scented oak, herb and spice, turning supple. Drink through 2002.–J.L. • $24 • (2/28/1999) • **89**
Pinot Noir Anderson Valley 1995 • $22 • (10/15/1997) • **88**
Pinot Noir Anderson Valley 1994 • $22/750 ml. • (4/30/1997) • **88**
Pinot Noir Carneros 1997: Elegant and polished, with complex, earthy cherry, wild berry, mushroom, tar and spice nuances. Drink now through 2004.–J.L. • $19 • (12/31/1999) • **88**
Pinot Noir Carneros 1996: An earthy yet complex style, with mushroom, dried cherry and leather notes. Shows more funk and personality than the best Steeles from 1996, but it's a challenging bottle that's fun to drink now –J.L. • $19 • (9/30/1998) • **87**
Pinot Noir Carneros 1995 • $18 • (10/15/1997) SS • **90**
Pinot Noir Carneros 1993 • $18 • (9/15/1995) HR • **90**
Pinot Noir Carneros 1992 • $16 • (2/28/1994) • **87**
Pinot Noir Carneros 1991 • $18 • (2/15/1993) HR • **90**
Pinot Noir Carneros Durell Vineyard 1996: Intensely varietal, bordering on stewed plum and tomato, with lots of anise and spice, some offbeat meaty flavors. Straightens out on the finish. Drink now through 2002.–J.L. • $26 • (2/28/1999) • **87**
Pinot Noir Carneros Durell Vineyard 1995 • $24 • (10/31/1997) • **88**
Pinot Noir Carneros Durell Vineyard 1993 • $19 • (9/15/1995) • **88**
Pinot Noir Carneros Durell Vineyard 1992 • $20 • (2/28/1994) • **87**
Pinot Noir Carneros Sangiacomo Vineyard 1997: Ripe, rich and smoky, with complex plum, black cherry, cedar and spice, holding its focus on the finish. Drink through 2005.–J.L. • $25 • (12/31/1999) • **88**
Pinot Noir Carneros Sangiacomo Vineyard 1996: Supple, complex and harmonious, with pretty toasty oak and plenty of ripe cherry, strawberry and spice nuances, which the finish weaves together in an elegant, flavorful fashion. Drink now through 2001.–J.L. • $25 • (9/30/1998) • **89**
Pinot Noir Carneros Sangiacomo Vineyard 1995 • $24 • (10/15/1997) • **90**
Pinot Noir Carneros Sangiacomo Vineyard 1994 • $22 • (4/30/1997) • **91**
Pinot Noir Carneros Sangiacomo Vineyard 1993 • $22 • (9/15/1995) • **88**
Pinot Noir Carneros Sangiacomo Vineyard 1991 • $22 • (2/28/1993) • **88**
Pinot Noir Mendocino DuPratt Vineyard 1997: Dark, rich and peppery, with a core of wild berry, black cherry, herb and cedar. Firm enough for short-term cellaring. Drink through 2005.–J.L. • $28 • (12/31/1999) • **88**
Pinot Noir Mendocino DuPratt Vineyard 1996: Smooth and spicy, with an elegant band of earthy cherry, wild berry and raspberry and perfumed aromas. Just needs time. Drink through 2002.–J.L. • $28 • (2/28/1999) • **89**
Pinot Noir Mendocino DuPratt Vineyard 1995 • $28 • (10/15/1997) • **92**
Pinot Noir Mendocino DuPratt Vineyard 1994 • $26 • (4/30/1997) • **91**
Pinot Noir Mendocino DuPratt Vineyard 1992 • $26 • (2/28/1994) • **86**
Pinot Noir Santa Barbara County Bien Nacido Vineyard 1997: Supple, ripe and polished, with well-focused cherry, cola, vanilla and spice, turning smooth and focused. Drink now through 2004.–J.L. • $26 • (8/31/1999) • **88**
Pinot Noir Santa Barbara County Bien Nacido Vineyard 1996: Ripe, smooth and polished, this is a wonderful drink-me-now style, with earthy cola, black cherry, herb and sage notes. Finishes with a complex aftertaste and well-integrated tannins. Drink now.–J.L. • $28 • (9/30/1998) • **88**
Pinot Noir Santa Barbara County Bien Nacido Vineyard 1995 • $38 • (10/31/1997) • **93**
Pinot Noir Santa Barbara County Bien Nacido Vineyard 1994 • $20 • (4/30/1996) • **90**
Pinot Noir Santa Barbara County Bien Nacido Vineyard 1993 • $22 • (9/15/1995) • **86**
Syrah Clear Lake 1997: Deep in color but basic, with meaty, plummy notes of modest depth. Drink now through 2004.–J.L. • $18 • (4/30/2000) • **85**
Syrah Clear Lake 1996: Firm and beefy, with plum and wild berry flavors. Turns leathery and chunky, with big tannins. Drink through 2004.–J.L. • $16 • (12/31/1998) • **87**
Viognier Clear Lake Dorn Vineyard 1996 • $16 • (12/15/1997) • **86**
Zinfandel Clear Lake Catfish Vineyard 1996 • $18 • (5/31/1998) • **87**
Zinfandel Clear Lake Catfish Vineyard 1994 • $18 • (10/31/1997) • **91**
Zinfandel Clear Lake Catfish Vineyard 1993 • $13 • (9/30/1995) • **89**
Zinfandel Clear Lake Catfish Vineyard 1992 • $13 • (9/15/1994) HR • **90**
Zinfandel Clear Lake Catfish Vineyard 1991 • $13 • (9/30/1993) • **90**
Zinfandel Mendocino DuPratt Vineyard 1997: Ripe and spicy, with vibrant black cherry and blackberry accented by pepper, sage and exotic berry flavors. Finishes with tealike tannins. Drink now through 2007.–J.L. • $21 • (2/29/2000) • **88**
Zinfandel Mendocino DuPratt Vineyard 1996: Firm and chunky, with earthy wild berry, raspberry and cherry flavors that turn rustic, minty and tannic. Drink through 2005.–J.L. • $20 • (12/31/1998) • **87**
Zinfandel Mendocino DuPratt Vineyard 1995 • $20 • (10/31/1997) • **89**
Zinfandel Mendocino DuPratt Vineyard 1994 • $18 • (2/28/1997) HR • **93**
Zinfandel Mendocino DuPratt Vineyard 1993 • $18 • (4/30/1996) • **91**
Zinfandel Mendocino Pacini Vineyard 1997: Firm and restrained, with ripe berry, plum, spice and peppery notes, it's focused and lean on the finish, with tight tannins. Drink now through 2006.–J.L. • $18 • (3/31/2000) • **88**
Zinfandel Mendocino Pacini Vineyard 1996 • $20 • (5/31/1998) • **90**
Zinfandel Mendocino Pacini Vineyard 1995 • $16 • (10/31/1997) • **88**
Zinfandel Mendocino Pacini Vineyard 1994 • $15 • (4/30/1996) • **88**
Zinfandel Mendocino Pacini Vineyard 1993 • $14 • (9/30/1995) • **87**
Zinfandel Mendocino Pacini Vineyard 1992 • $13 • (10/15/1994) • **82**
Zinfandel Mendocino Pacini Vineyard 1991 • $13 • (9/30/1993) • **84**

STELTZNER | CALIFORNIA

Cabernet Sauvignon Stags Leap District 1996: Rich, with a focused band of currant, cedar, cherry and spice, turning firm and concentrated. Best from 2001 through 2007.–J.L. • $25 • (10/31/1999) • **88**
Cabernet Sauvignon Stags Leap District 1994 • $21 • (3/31/1998) • **83**
Cabernet Sauvignon Stags Leap District 1991 • $18 • (3/31/1995) • **85**
Cabernet Sauvignon Napa Valley Stags Leap District 1988 • $19 • (11/15/1992) • **82**

Cabernet Sauvignon Napa Valley Stags Leap District 1987 • $25 • (11/15/1991) • **86**
Cabernet Sauvignon Napa Valley Stags Leap District 1986 • $NA • (12/15/1996) • **87**
Cabernet Sauvignon Napa Valley Stags Leap District 1985 • $16 • (11/15/1988) • **92**
Cabernet Sauvignon Napa Valley Stags Leap District 1984 • $33 • (3/31/1988) • **91**
Cabernet Sauvignon Napa Valley Stags Leap District 1983 • $NA • (6/30/1987) • **88**
Cabernet Sauvignon Napa Valley Stags Leap District 1982 • $14 • (6/30/1987) • **93**
Cabernet Sauvignon Napa Valley Stags Leap District 1981 • $NA • (6/30/1987) • **91**
Cabernet Sauvignon Napa Valley Stags Leap District 1980 • $NA • (6/30/1987) • **88**
Cabernet Sauvignon Napa Valley Stags Leap District 1979 • $NA • (6/30/1987) • **89**
Cabernet Sauvignon Napa Valley Stags Leap District 1977 • $NA • (6/30/1987) • **88**
Cabernet Sauvignon Stags Leap District 1978: Youthful, a wine that combines ripe Cabernet fruit with a touch of elegance, showing bright black cherry, plum, currant and anise flavors, a smooth, polished texture, and finishing with firm tannins that give it structure and strength. A touch of heat on the finish. (1978 California Cabernet retrospective tasting). Drink now through 2002.–J.L. • $14 • (11/15/1998) • **90**
Cabernet Sauvignon Stags Leap District Barrel Select Reserve 1994 • $35 • (3/31/1998) • **84**
Cabernet Sauvignon Stags Leap District Commemorative 1991 • $45 • (3/31/1995) • **85**
Claret Stags Leap District 1993 • $11 • (12/15/1995) • **77**
Claret Stags Leap District 1992 • $11 • (3/31/1995) • **84**
Claret Stags Leap District 1991 • $10 • (2/28/1994) • **84**
Claret Stags Leap District 1990 • $11 • (11/15/1992) • **88**
Merlot Stags Leap District 1994 • $20 • (7/31/1997) • **87**
Merlot Stags Leap District 1993 • $19 • (8/31/1996) • **83**
Merlot Stags Leap District 1992 • $19 • (3/31/1995) • **82**
Merlot Stags Leap District 1991 • $17 • (9/15/1994) • **83**
Merlot Stags Leap District 1990 • $20 • (8/31/1993) • **85**
Merlot Stags Leap District 1989 • $15 • (11/15/1991) • **85**
Sauvignon Blanc Napa Valley 1996 • $9 • (7/31/1997) • **81**

STEMMLER, ROBERT | CALIFORNIA

Cabernet Sauvignon Sonoma County 1982 • $15 • (4/01/1985) • **66**
Pinot Noir Sonoma County 1996: Medium-bodied, with light cherry flavors framed by mushroom, tea and earth notes. Firm finish. Drink now through 2001.–H.S. • $26 • (6/30/1999) • **84**
Pinot Noir Sonoma County 1995 • $26 • (11/30/1997) • **86**
Pinot Noir Sonoma County 1994 • $22 • (2/28/1997) • **80**
Pinot Noir Sonoma County 1993 • $20 • (11/30/1996) • **79**
Pinot Noir Sonoma County 1992 • $20 • (12/31/1995) • **84**
Pinot Noir Sonoma County 1991 • $20 • (3/31/1995) • **78**
Pinot Noir Sonoma County 1990 • $20 • (2/28/1994) • **80**
Pinot Noir Sonoma County 1989 • $20 • (2/28/1993) • **71**
Pinot Noir Sonoma County 1988 • $20 • (2/28/1993) • **71**
Pinot Noir Sonoma County 1987 • $19 • (10/31/1990) • **82**
Pinot Noir Sonoma County 1986 • $18 • (6/15/1988) • **84**
Pinot Noir Sonoma County 1985 • $18 • (9/30/1987) • **79**
Pinot Noir Sonoma County 1984 • $16 • (8/31/1986) • **90**
Pinot Noir Sonoma County 1983 • $15 • (3/16/1985) SS • **93**

STEPHAN | CALIFORNIA

Chardonnay Paso Robles L'Aventure 1998: Taut, with a tart, green edge you can't ignore. Still, it's a flinty, stylistic wine that's atypical for California Chardonnay. Needs food. Best from 2001 through 2006.–J.L. • $55 • (2/29/2000) • **86**

Key: SS—Spectator Selection. CS—Cellar Selection. HR—Highly Recommended. $NA—Price not available. (BT)—Barrel tasting. (A)—Auction Price. For a key to the tasters' initials, see "How to Use These Listings."
Dates in parentheses represent the issues in which the ratings were published.

STEPHEN ROSS | CALIFORNIA

Chardonnay Edna Valley Edna Ranch 1998: Medium in weight, with spicy pear, light oak, cedar and nutmeg, turning vapid. Drink now through 2004.–J.L. • $19 • (5/15/2000) • **84**
Chardonnay Edna Valley Edna Ranch 1997: Pure and focused, with a core of citrus, pear, peach and toast flavors. Long, rich, complex, minerally finish. Drink now through 2002.–J.L. • $19 • (7/31/1999) • **90**
Chardonnay Edna Valley Edna Ranch 1996: Tightly wound and sharply focused, with an intense core of citrus, pear, apple and guava, showing a touch of elegance and finesse.–J.L. • $18 • (7/31/1998) • **89**
Chardonnay Edna Valley Linda's Vineyard 1997: Tightly wound, showing a range of concentrated apple, pear, spice and nut flavors on a silky background. Finishes long, focused and complex. Drink now through 2003.–J.L. • $19 • (7/31/1999) • **90**
Chardonnay Edna Valley Linda's Vineyard 1996: Ripe and clean, with a pleasant range of spicy melon and pear flavors. Picks up a little more depth and complexity on the finish, while maintaining its elegance. Drinks well now.–J.L. • $18 • (7/31/1998) • **87**
Chardonnay Santa Maria Valley Bien Nacido Vineyard 1998: Clean, with moderately ripe pear, melon, nectarine and citrus flavors that are appealing if simple. Drink now.–J.L. • $24 • (5/15/2000) • **85**
Chardonnay Santa Maria Valley Bien Nacido Vineyard 1997: Rich and full-bodied, with tightly focused, complex flavors of pear, peach and nectarine that come together on a silky, complex finish. Drink now through 2002.–J.L. • $20 • (7/31/1999) • **91**
Pinot Noir Arroyo Grande Valley La Colline Vineyard 1996 • $20 • (2/28/1998) • **85**
Pinot Noir Edna Valley Edna Ranch 1997: A bit beefy at first, with a follow-up that includes exotic menthol, cola and herb notes. Full-bodied, it also serves up plum and berry flavors framed in firm but ripe tannins. Finishes moderately. Best from 2001 through 2004. • $22 • (9/15/1999) • **87**
Pinot Noir Edna Valley Edna Ranch 1996 • $22 • (1/31/1998) • **87**
Pinot Noir Edna Valley Edna Ranch 1995 • $18 • (2/28/1997) • **91**
Pinot Noir Santa Maria Valley Bien Nacido Vineyard 1997: Ripe, smoky and flavorful, showing a tight range of tea, cherry and herb tones that linger on the firm finish. Drink through 2004.–J.L. • $25 • (9/15/1999) • **87**
Pinot Noir Santa Maria Valley Bien Nacido Vineyard 1996 • $24 • (1/31/1998) • **88**
Zinfandel Sonoma Valley Monte Rosso Vineyard 1997: Medium in weight, with attractive spice, pepper, wild berry and cherry flavors that are elegant if tilting toward simple. Drink now.–J.L. • $22 • (4/30/2000) • **86**

STERLING | CALIFORNIA

Cabernet Sauvignon Central Coast Vintner's Collection 1997: Sage, thyme and black currant aromas precede flavors of chocolate and plum. The finish is a bit raw. Drink now through 2003.–J.L. • $13 • (4/30/2000) • **85**
Cabernet Sauvignon Napa Valley 1997: Tight if a touch austere, with a trim band of cedary currant, anise and spice. Turns elegant and even delicate on the finish, where the tannins are dry and firm. Drink through 2009.–J.L. • $22 • (2/29/2000) • **88**
Cabernet Sauvignon Napa Valley 1996: Chunky at this stage, showing currant, dried berry, toasted oak and herb flavors and finishing with mild tannins. Drink through 2005.–J.L. • $16 • (10/15/1999) • **87**
Cabernet Sauvignon Napa Valley 1995 • $14 • (4/30/1998) HR • **88**
Cabernet Sauvignon Napa Valley 1994 • $14 • (12/15/1996) • **84**
Cabernet Sauvignon Napa Valley 1993 • $14 • (9/15/1996) • **84**
Cabernet Sauvignon Napa Valley 1992 • $14 • (11/30/1995) • **85**
Cabernet Sauvignon Napa Valley 1991 • $14 • (11/15/1994) • **82**
Cabernet Sauvignon Napa Valley 1990 • $14 • (11/15/1993) • **83**
Cabernet Sauvignon Napa Valley 1989: Herbal, even a touch weedy, though the texture is smooth and the tannins are mature, with modest cherry flavors. Not a good cellar candidate to begin with. (1989 California Cabernet retrospective tasting). Past its prime.–J.L. • $18 • (8/31/1999) • **83**
Cabernet Sauvignon Napa Valley 1988: Firmly tannic, turning dry, with glimmers of cherry, currant, herb, olive and cedar. Turns simple on the finish, where the tannins stick out. (1988 California Cabernet retrospective tasting). Drink now through 2002.–J.L. • $15 • (11/15/1998) • **83**
Cabernet Sauvignon Napa Valley 1987 • $14 • (5/15/1990) • **91**
Cabernet Sauvignon Napa Valley 1986 • $18 • (3/31/1989) • **91**
Cabernet Sauvignon Napa Valley 1985 • $17 • (5/15/1988) • **89**
Cabernet Sauvignon Napa Valley 1983 • $18 • (2/15/1987) • **81**
Cabernet Sauvignon Napa Valley 1982 • $16 • (5/16/1986) • **66**
Cabernet Sauvignon Napa Valley 1981 • $20 • (8/01/1985) • **88**
Cabernet Sauvignon Napa Valley 1980 • $28 • (2/16/1984) • **84**

Cabernet Sauvignon Napa Valley 1979: Simple earth, plum and berry flavors, turning dry. (1979 California Cabernet retrospective tasting). Past its prime. –J.L. • $13 • (8/31/1999) • **81**

Cabernet Sauvignon Napa Valley 1978: Elegant and understated, aging very well, with complex herb, currant, cherry, tea and spice flavors that are well focused and bright. Finishes with a long, lingering aftertaste. (1978 California Cabernet retrospective tasting).–J.L. • $13 • (11/15/1998) • **89**

Cabernet Sauvignon Napa Valley 1974 • $37 Ⓐ • (11/15/1994) • **82**

Cabernet Sauvignon Napa Valley Diamond Mountain Ranch 1997: Nicely proportioned, with a trim band of cedar, currant, anise and black cherry, turning chunky and tannic. Best from 2002 through 2009.–J.L. • $40 • (6/15/2000) • **87**

Cabernet Sauvignon Napa Valley Diamond Mountain Ranch Vineyard 1996: Austere, with a cedary edge to the cherry, currant and berryish flavors, it's well crafted, turning supple and elegant, with coffee and cedar notes. Drink through 2007.–J.L. • $25 • (10/15/1999) • **87**

Cabernet Sauvignon Napa Valley Diamond Mountain Ranch Vineyard 1995: Tight and smoky, with firm, earthy tannins, it works in some mineral, currant, sage and cedar notes. Turns complex and leathery on the finish. Best from 2001 through 2006.–J.L. • $25 • (11/30/1998) • **88**

Cabernet Sauvignon Napa Valley Diamond Mountain Ranch Vineyard 1994 • $18 • (10/31/1997) • **85**

Cabernet Sauvignon Napa Valley Diamond Mountain Ranch Vineyard 1993 • $18 • (11/15/1996) • **88**

Cabernet Sauvignon Napa Valley Diamond Mountain Ranch Vineyard 1992 • $17 • (10/31/1995) • **88**

Cabernet Sauvignon Napa Valley Diamond Mountain Ranch Vineyard 1991 • $18 • (11/15/1994) • **86**

Cabernet Sauvignon Napa Valley Diamond Mountain Ranch 1990 • $18 • (11/15/1993) • **81**

Cabernet Sauvignon Napa Valley Diamond Mountain Ranch 1989 • $18 • (11/15/1992) • **79**

Cabernet Sauvignon Napa Valley Diamond Mountain Ranch 1987 • $16 • (11/15/1990) • **91**

Cabernet Sauvignon Napa Valley Diamond Mountain Ranch 1986 • $17 Ⓐ • (12/15/1996) • **80**

Cabernet Sauvignon Napa Valley Diamond Mountain Ranch 1985 • $21 • (5/31/1989) • **88**

Cabernet Sauvignon Napa Valley Diamond Mountain Ranch 1984 • $16 • (2/15/1988) • **84**

Cabernet Sauvignon Napa Valley Diamond Mountain Ranch 1983 • $15 • (11/30/1986) • **74**

Cabernet Sauvignon Napa Valley Diamond Mountain Ranch 1982 • $15 • (11/16/1985) CS • **94**

Cabernet Sauvignon Napa Valley Reserve 1997: Still quite grapey, with fermentation aromas, it's tart and focused, with black cherry, blackberry, cedar and spice.–J.L. • $NA • (8/31/1998) (BT) • **90-94**

Cabernet Sauvignon Napa Valley Reserve 1996: Ripe, smooth and harmonious, showing layers of currant, cedar, coffee, anise and blackberry, this outstanding California red unfolds to reveal a supple texture, then firms up nicely on the finish. Competitively priced in this category at this score, too. Drink through 2009.–J.L. • $50 • (10/31/1999) CS • **94**

Cabernet Sauvignon Napa Valley Reserve 1984 • $47 • (3/31/1989) CS • **92**

Cabernet Sauvignon Napa Valley Reserve 1983 • $24 Ⓐ • (6/15/1987) • **86**

Cabernet Sauvignon Napa Valley Reserve 1980 • $28 • (11/01/1984) CS • **90**

Cabernet Sauvignon Napa Valley Reserve 1978 • $36 Ⓐ • (11/15/1992) • **90**

Cabernet Sauvignon Napa Valley Reserve 1974 • $67 Ⓐ • (11/15/1994) • **83**

Chardonnay Napa Valley 1997: Bold and refreshing, with ripe fig, apple, pear and melon flavors and spicy, toasty oak, all folding together on the complex finish. Drink now through 2001.–J.L. • $15 • (12/15/1998) • **88**

Chardonnay Napa Valley 1996 • $14 • (1/31/1998) • **87**

Chardonnay Napa Valley Carneros Winery Lake Vineyard 1998: Offers attractive floral notes but is relatively simple, with ripe pear, sweet pea and herb notes. Drink now.–J.L. • $24 • (4/30/2000) • **86**

Chardonnay Napa Valley Carneros Winery Lake Vineyard 1996 • $18 • (5/31/1998) • **86**

Chardonnay Napa Valley Diamond Mountain Ranch Vineyard 1996 • $18 • (5/31/1998) • **87**

Dolcetto Napa Valley 1994 • $10 • (1/01/1995) • **80**

Merlot Central Coast Vintner's Collection 1997: Trim, with a crisp, modest band of currant and spice. Drink now through 2004.–J.L. • $13 • (4/30/2000) • **84**

Merlot Napa Valley 1997: Firm in structure, with tight, cedary currant, earth and cherry notes, turning dry. A style that will appeal to left-bank Bordeaux lovers. Drink now through 2006.–J.L. • $20 • (2/29/2000) • **87**

Merlot Napa Valley 1996: Quite tannic, but that can't stop the layers of licorice, blackberry, herb and mint that blend nicely through the moderate finish. Needs some time to settle down and soften up. Best from 2001 through 2005. • $16 • (9/15/1999) • **86**

Merlot Napa Valley 1995 • $14 • (4/30/1998) • **86**

Merlot Napa Valley 1994 • $14 • (3/31/1997) • **87**

Merlot Napa Valley 1993 • $14 • (3/31/1996) • **82**

Merlot Napa Valley 1991 • $14 • (9/15/1994) • **74**

Merlot Napa Valley 1990 • $14 • (6/15/1993) • **82**

Merlot Napa Valley 1989 • $15 • (5/31/1992) • **82**

Merlot Napa Valley 1988 • $15 • (4/15/1991) • **83**

Merlot Napa Valley 1987 • $13 • (6/15/1990) • **83**

Merlot Napa Valley 1986 • $14 • (3/31/1989) • **85**

Merlot Napa Valley 1985 • $14 • (3/31/1988) • **87**

Merlot Napa Valley 1984 • $12 • (4/30/1987) • **93**

Merlot Napa Valley 1983 • $11 • (6/01/1986) • **91**

Merlot Napa Valley 1982 • $12 • (10/01/1985) • **83**

Merlot Napa Valley 1981 • $11 • (3/01/1984) • **83**

Merlot Napa Valley Carneros Winery Lake Vineyard 1997: Fails to inspire. Trim and compact, with modest berry, tea and cola flavors that turn tannic. Drink now through 2005.–J.L. • $30 • (6/15/2000) • **84**

Merlot Napa Valley Carneros Winery Lake Vineyard 1995: Packs in plenty of ripe plum, currant, sage and spice flavors, picking up anise and coffee notes along with a pleasant earthiness on the finish. Drink through 2005.–J.L. • $35 • (9/30/1998) • **87**

Merlot Napa Valley Carneros Winery Lake 1987 • $25 • (12/31/1990) • **90**

Merlot Napa Valley Diamond Mountain Ranch 1997: Soft, with ripe plum, currant, anise and cedar notes that taste muted. Drink now through 2007.–J.L. • $30 • (6/15/2000) • **86**

Merlot Napa Valley Diamond Mountain Ranch Vineyard 1995: Shows a measure of polish and finesse, with spicy, toasty oak integrated into the core of coffee, currant and dried cherry. Focused and well balanced, with ripe tannins. Drink through 2004.–J.L. • $35 • (9/30/1998) • **87**

Merlot Napa Valley Diamond Mountain Ranch Vineyard 1994 • $NA • (6/30/1997) • **88**

Merlot Napa Valley Three Palms Vineyard 1997: A stylish if understated wine, with rich, cedary currant and cherry notes, picking up mineral, anise and herb flavors before the tannins tighten. Cellar short-term. Best from 2002 through 2010.–J.L. • $50 • (2/29/2000) • **88**

Merlot Napa Valley Three Palms Vineyard 1995: Tough, tight and tannic, with just a glimmer of currant and cherry peeking through. Finishes with tobacco, tar, coffee and cedar notes, turning dry and hard; best to cellar short-term. Drink through 2004.–J.L. • $20 • (9/30/1998) • **86**

Merlot Napa Valley Three Palms Vineyard 1994 • $NA • (6/30/1997) • **85**

Merlot Napa Valley Three Palms Vineyard 1992 • $22 • (3/31/1996) • **83**

Merlot Napa Valley Three Palms Vineyard 1990 • $26 Ⓐ • (4/15/1994) • **85**

Pinot Noir Napa Valley Carneros Winery Lake Vineyard 1998: Lightly fruity, with simple plum and cherry flavors, finishing with touches of herb and tea. Drink now.–J.L. • $25 • (6/30/2000) • **83**

Pinot Noir Napa Valley Carneros Winery Lake Vineyard 1997: Flavorful but uncomplicated, with black cherry, tea and light oak flavors. On the firm side, with a moderately tannic finish. Drink through 2004.–J.L. • $20 • (9/15/1999) • **85**

Pinot Noir Napa Valley Carneros Winery Lake Vineyard 1996: A tough-edged '96, with hard tannins. In the middle are black cherry and cola flavors, turning dry and leathery. Drink now through 2002.–J.L. • $16 • (9/15/1998) • **84**

Pinot Noir Napa Valley Carneros Winery Lake Vineyard 1995 • $16 • (12/15/1997) • **84**

Pinot Noir Napa Valley Carneros Winery Lake Vineyard 1994 • $18 • (2/29/1996) • **82**

Pinot Noir Napa Valley Carneros Winery Lake Vineyard 1993 • $18 • (12/31/1995) • **82**

Pinot Noir Napa Valley Carneros Winery Lake Vineyard 1992 • $15 • (3/31/1995) • **73**

Pinot Noir Napa Valley Carneros Winery Lake 1991 • $18 • (2/28/1993) • **78**

Pinot Noir Napa Valley Carneros Winery Lake 1990 • $14 • (3/31/1997) • **82**

Pinot Noir Napa Valley Carneros Winery Lake 1989 • $14 • (3/31/1992) • **87**

Pinot Noir Napa Valley Carneros Winery Lake 1988 • $14 • (4/30/1991) • **87**

Pinot Noir Napa Valley Carneros Winery Lake 1987 • $18 • (12/31/1989) • **86**

Pinot Noir Napa Valley Carneros Winery Lake 1986 • $18 • (3/31/1997) • **90**

Reserve Napa Valley 1995: Deliciously complex, this Cabernet blend delivers a pretty array of ripe currant, black cherry, sage, cedar and spice notes, revealing its depth and gaining nuance on a long, intricate aftertaste that keeps pumping out flavor. Drink through 2008.–J.L. • $50 • (4/30/1999) CS • **94**

Reserve Napa Valley 1994 • $40 • (12/15/1997) • **88**

STERLING

Reserve Napa Valley 1993 • $40 • (11/15/1996) • **88**
Reserve Napa Valley 1992 • $40 • (12/15/1995) • **87**
Reserve Napa Valley 1991 • $30 • (11/15/1994) • **90**
Reserve Napa Valley 1990 • $30 • (11/15/1994) • **87**
Reserve Napa Valley 1989: Medium-weight, with mature and dry currant, plum and spicy flavors, turning drier and tannic on the finish. A shade past its peak. (1989 California Cabernet retrospective tasting). Drink now.–J.L. • $35 • (8/31/1999) • **86**
Reserve Napa Valley 1988 • $40 • (3/31/1992) • **85**
Reserve Napa Valley 1987 • $43 • (12/15/1997) • **90**
Reserve Napa Valley 1986 • $41 • (12/15/1996) • **90**
Reserve Napa Valley 1985 • $42 • (7/15/1989) SS • **96**
Reserve Napa Valley 1979: Elegant and seductive in its own way, with mature dried cherry, olive, herb and spicy nuances, soft and drying tannins. Drink now. (1989 California Cabernet retrospective tasting).–J.L. • $28 • (8/31/1999) • **86**
Sangiovese Atlas Peak 1993 • $14 • (11/30/1995) • **82**
Sauvignon Blanc North Coast 1998: Vibrant acidity is followed by tangy grapefruit and lemon notes. The moderate body rounds it out, while the medium finish is fresh and herb-tinged. Drink now. • $12 • (6/15/1999) • **85**
Sauvignon Blanc North Coast 1997: Somewhat floral, with hints of hay, sweet pea and melon. Finishes moderately, with a touch of citrus. Drink now. • $12 • (11/30/1998) • **82**
Sauvignon Blanc North Coast 1996 • $8 • (10/15/1997) • **85**
Three Palms Vineyard Napa Valley 1988 • $19 • (11/15/1992) • **85**
Three Palms Vineyard Napa Valley 1987 • $23 • (11/15/1990) • **87**
Three Palms Vineyard Napa Valley 1986 • $22 • (12/31/1989) • **86**
Three Palms Vineyard Napa Valley 1985 • $22 • (12/31/1988) • **93**

STEVENOT | CALIFORNIA

Barbera Sierra Foothills 1996: Light and chunky, with firm texture and simple berry and earth flavors. Drink now.–H.S. • $15 • (11/30/1998) • **82**
Cabernet Franc Sierra Foothills 1995 • $15 • (11/30/1997) • **78**
Cabernet Sauvignon Amador County Grand Reserve 1988 • $10 • (11/15/1992) • **83**
Cabernet Sauvignon Calaveras County Grand Reserve 1984 • $15 • (12/31/1987) • **75**
Cabernet Sauvignon Calaveras County Reserve 1993 • $12 • (11/15/1996) • **87**
Cabernet Sauvignon Calaveras County Reserve 1992 • $10 • (7/31/1995) • **82**
Cabernet Sauvignon Calaveras County Reserve 1991 • $11 • (11/15/1994) • **84**
Cabernet Sauvignon Calaveras County Reserve 1990 • $10 • (7/31/1993) • **86**
Cabernet Sauvignon Calaveras County Reserve 1989 • $10 • (3/15/1993) • **82**
Cabernet Sauvignon California 1991 • $8 • (4/30/1993) • **83**
Cabernet Sauvignon California 1990 • $8 • (11/15/1992) • **79**
Cabernet Sauvignon California 1989 • $8 • (11/15/1992) • **79**
Cabernet Sauvignon Sierra Foothills 1996: Simple and soft, with mild herb and cherry flavors. Finishes with oak notes.–J.L. • $12 • (11/15/1999) • **78**
Cabernet Sauvignon Sierra Foothills 1993 • $7 • (12/15/1995) • **83**
Chardonnay Calaveras County Shaw Ranch 1997: Rich lemon flavors are focused and framed by spicy nuances. Drink now.–J.L. • $18 • (6/30/2000) • **84**
Chardonnay Calaveras County Shaw Ranch 1996 • $20 • (5/31/1998) • **85**
Chardonnay Sierra Foothills 1998: Elegant, with vibrant pear and tangerine notes and an earthy accent on the finish. Drink now through 2003.–J.L. • $10 • (3/31/2000) • **84**
Chardonnay Sierra Foothills 1997: Clean and ripe, with tasty pear and mineral flavors, turning pretty on the finish, this California Chardonnay is an easy-drinking choice that's easy-on-the-wallet. Drink now through 2004.–J.L. • $10 • (2/29/2000) • **85**
Chardonnay Sierra Foothills 1996 • $10 • (11/30/1997) • **88**
Merlot California Reserve 1995 • $12 • (7/31/1997) • **86**
Merlot North Coast Reserve 1991 • $10 • (3/31/1993) • **75**
Merlot North Coast Reserve 1990 • $10 • (11/30/1992) • **80**
Merlot North Coast Reserve 1989 • $10 • (5/31/1992) • **83**
Merlot Sierra Foothills 1997: Fruit flavors struggle to find focus among hard-edged leafy flavors and dry tannins.–J.L. • $13 • (10/15/1999) • **78**
Merlot Sierra Foothills Reserve 1992 • $11 • (9/15/1994) • **77**
Sangiovese Calaveras County Reserve 1994 • $12 • (12/15/1996) • **80**
Sangiovese Sierra Foothills 1996: Ripe and sturdy, generous with its sweet berry and plum flavors. The finish is smooth and polished. Drink now through 2001.–H.S. • $15 • (11/30/1998) • **85**
Sauvignon Blanc Calaveras County 1996 • $10 • (3/31/1998) • **88**
Sauvignon Blanc Calaveras County 1995 • $9 • (10/31/1996) • **89**
Sauvignon Blanc Sierra Foothills 1998: Herb and citrus notes combine in a crisp format. Drink now.–J.L. • $10 • (5/15/2000) • **84**
Syrah Sierra Foothills 1996: Some pleasant light cherry and spice flavors here, though the texture is coarse and somewhat astringent. Drink now. • $15 • (9/15/1998) • **80**
Zinfandel Calaveras County Reserve 1991 • $10 • (6/15/1994) • **73**
Zinfandel Calaveras County Reserve 1990 • $10 • (6/15/1993) • **77**
Zinfandel California 1989 • $6 • (4/30/1993) • **79**
Zinfandel Sierra Foothills 1997: Has flavors of raspberry and strawberry extract, with pepper notes. Drink now through 2003.–J.L. • $11 • (5/15/2000) • **83**
Zinfandel Sierra Foothills 1996: Soft and juicy, with light strawberry and cinnamon flavors. Slightly bitter on the finish. Drink now.–H.S. • $10 • (11/30/1998) • **82**
Zinfandel Sierra Foothills Reserve 1993 • $8 • (10/15/1995) • **80**

STEWART | WASHINGTON

Cabernet Sauvignon Columbia Valley 1993 • $10 • (9/15/1996) • **85**
Cabernet Sauvignon Columbia Valley 1988 • $11 • (8/31/1991) • **79**
Gewürztraminer Late Harvest Yakima Valley 1994 • $9/375 ml. • (9/30/1995) • **88**

STONE CELLARS | WASHINGTON

Cabernet Sauvignon Columbia Valley 1993 • $5 • (5/31/1995) • **83**
Merlot Columbia Valley 1993 • $6 • (5/31/1995) • **83**

STONE CREEK | CALIFORNIA

Cabernet Sauvignon California Special Selection 1996: Firm in texture, with chewy smoke and plum flavors showing through the fine-grained tannins on the finish. Best from 2001 through 2004.–H.S. • $7 • (10/31/1998) • **80**
Cabernet Sauvignon California Special Selection 1995 • $7 • (11/15/1997) • **83**
Cabernet Sauvignon California Special Selection 1994 • $7 • (12/31/1996) • **82**
Cabernet Sauvignon California Special Selection 1989 • $7 • (11/15/1993) • **72**
Cabernet Sauvignon Napa Valley Chairman's Reserve 1990 • $10 • (11/15/1993) • **68**
Cabernet Sauvignon Napa Valley Limited Bottling 1986 • $10 • (6/15/1990) • **85**
Cabernet Sauvignon Napa Valley Special Selection 1986 • $10 • (11/15/1991) • **80**
Cabernet Sauvignon North Coast Chairman's Reserve 1996: Modest in scope but pretty in flavor, with plum and coffee tones lurking under the mild tannins. Drink through 2002.–H.S. • $16 • (10/31/1998) • **82**
Cabernet Sauvignon Sonoma County Chairman's Reserve 1995 • $16 • (10/15/1997) • **87**
Chardonnay California Special Selection 1997: Light and simple, with earthy apple flavors.–H.S. • $7 • (11/30/1998) • **75**
Chardonnay California Special Selection 1996 • $7 • (5/31/1998) • **84**
Merlot California Special Selection 1996: Simple and pleasant, with herbs, cola and a dash of currant. Drink now. • $8 • (9/15/1998) • **80**
Merlot California Special Selection 1995 • $8 • (7/31/1997) • **80**
Merlot California Special Selection 1990 • $8 • (11/30/1992) • **80**
Merlot California Special Selection 1989 • $6 • (5/31/1992) • **79**
Merlot Columbia Valley 1989 • $7 • (5/31/1991) • **86**
Merlot Columbia Valley 1988 • $6 • (9/30/1990) • **78**
Merlot Sonoma County Chairman's Reserve 1994 • $17 • (7/31/1997) • **77**
Merlot Washington Special Selection 1993 • $8 • (5/15/1996) • **84**
Pinot Noir Sonoma County Chairman's Reserve 1996 • $14 • (11/30/1997) • **83**
Zinfandel California 1991 • $6 • (9/30/1994) • **85**
Zinfandel California Special Selection 1995 • $7 • (4/30/1997) • **84**
Zinfandel California Special Selection 1991 • $7 • (10/15/1995) • **83**

STONE HILL | MISSOURI

Norton Missouri 1992 • $NA • (10/31/1995) • **85**
Port Missouri 1992 • $NA • (10/31/1995) • **83**

Key: SS—Spectator Selection. CS—Cellar Selection. HR—Highly Recommended. $NA—Price not available. (BT)—Barrel tasting. (A)—Auction Price.
For a key to the tasters' initials, see "How to Use These Listings."
Dates in parentheses represent the issues in which the ratings were published.

STONE WOLF | OREGON

Chardonnay Oregon 1997: Delicate and refined, this very pretty white has lemon-tinged pear, spice and vanilla flavors that weave neatly through the lean, lithe structure. Finish echoes nicely. Drink now through 2002.–H.S. • $15 • (11/15/1999) • **89**

Pinot Noir Willamette Valley Barrel Select Cuvee 1998: Flavorful and velvety, with rich cherry, spice and slightly earthy flavors glowing behind a veil of slightly chewy tannins. Needs time to settle down. Best from 2002 through 2006.–H.S. • $19 • (4/30/2000) • **88**

STONECROFT | OREGON

Pinot Noir Willamette Valley 1998: Crisp in texture, gentle and harmonious, with blackberry, anise and herb flavors lingering on the focused finish. Drink now through 2005.–H.S. • $18 • (3/31/2000) • **88**

STONEGATE | CALIFORNIA

Cabernet Franc Napa Valley 1990 • $NA • (11/15/1993) • **81**

Cabernet Sauvignon Napa Valley 1996: Soft-textured, with plush tannins giving structure nonetheless. Pretty plum, cherry and currant flavors fan out on the palate, with a touch of herbs tempering the fruit. Moderate finish. Drink now through 2004. • $23 • (5/15/1999) • **87**

Cabernet Sauvignon Napa Valley 1991 • $18 • (12/15/1995) • **82**

Cabernet Sauvignon Napa Valley 1990 • $14 • (11/15/1994) • **81**

Cabernet Sauvignon Napa Valley 1989 • $15 • (11/15/1993) • **80**

Cabernet Sauvignon Napa Valley 1988 • $14 • (11/15/1992) • **84**

Cabernet Sauvignon Napa Valley 1987 • $14 • (3/31/1992) • **82**

Cabernet Sauvignon Napa Valley 1986 • $NA • (12/15/1996) • **84**

Cabernet Sauvignon Napa Valley 1985 • $17 • (8/31/1990) • **86**

Cabernet Sauvignon Napa Valley 1984 • $13 • (2/15/1989) • **86**

Cabernet Sauvignon Napa Valley 1981 • $12 • (11/15/1986) • **78**

Cabernet Sauvignon Napa Valley 1978 • $27 • (11/15/1992) • **87**

Chardonnay Napa Valley 1998: Pear, herb, butter and cedar shaving notes are round, with good concentration. Drink now.–J.L. • $18 • (6/30/2000) • **84**

Chardonnay Sonoma County 1997: Distinctive for its herbal, spicy, toasted oak flavors and hints of fig and pear, all on a delicate frame. Drink now.–H.S. • $18 • (5/15/1999) • **85**

Meritage Reserve Napa Valley 1988 • $17 • (11/15/1993) • **85**

Meritage Reserve Napa Valley 1987 • $17 • (11/15/1993) • **86**

Merlot Napa Valley 1989 • $17 • (10/31/1992) • **86**

Merlot Napa Valley 1988 • $17 • (5/31/1992) • **81**

Merlot Napa Valley 1986 • $15 • (4/15/1990) • **84**

Merlot Napa Valley Pershing Vineyard 1987 • $17 • (3/31/1991) • **83**

Merlot Napa Valley Spaulding Vineyard 1987 • $17 • (3/31/1991) • **86**

Merlot Napa Valley Spaulding Vineyard 1984 • $15 • (12/31/1988) • **85**

Merlot Napa Valley Spaulding Vineyard 1982 • $14 • (2/28/1987) • **84**

Merlot Napa Valley Spaulding Vineyard 1980 • $12 • (10/01/1985) • **68**

Reserve Napa Valley 1989 • $24 • (12/15/1995) • **88**

Sauvignon Blanc Napa Valley 1998: Lean and tart, with herbaceous citrus notes. Drink now.–J.L. • $15 • (5/31/2000) • **81**

Sauvignon Blanc-Sémillon Late Harvest Napa Valley 1989 • $13/375 ml. • (4/30/1991) • **87**

Sémillon-Sauvignon Blanc Late Harvest Napa Valley 1990 • $10/375 ml. • (3/31/1992) • **83**

STONEHEATH | CALIFORNIA

Nebbiolo California Riserva 1996: Starts off with bright cherry aromas, tempered somewhat on the palate by tough tannins. Flavors carry through to the moderate finish, nonetheless, with a blend of herb, coffee, and spice. Drink now through 2003. • $18 • (2/28/1999) • **84**

STONEHEDGE | CALIFORNIA

Cabernet Sauvignon Napa Valley 1995 • $15 • (10/31/1997) • **86**

Cabernet Sauvignon Napa Valley Winemaker's Reserve 1994 • $10 • (11/30/1996) • **77**

Cabernet Sauvignon Napa Valley Winemaker's Reserve 1993 • $10 • (3/31/1996) • **79**

Cabernet Sauvignon Napa Valley Winemaker's Reserve 1992 • $10 • (11/30/1995) • **89**

Chardonnay California 1997: Here's an applaudable value in California's most popular white. It's firm yet supple, with a solid core of apple and lemon flavors, and the finish is smooth and clean. Ready to drink. • $10 • (9/15/1998) • **86**

Chardonnay California 1996 • $10 • (11/30/1997) • **82**

Malbec Napa Valley 1994 • $15 • (11/30/1996) • **84**

Malbec Napa Valley 1993 • $15 • (3/31/1996) • **79**

Sauvignon Blanc California 1996 • $8 • (5/31/1998) • **86**

Zinfandel California Century Vine 1997: Sweet-tasting berry flavors turn earthy and muddled.–J.L. • $10 • (5/31/2000) • **75**

Zinfandel Napa Valley 1995 • $15 • (6/15/1998) • **78**

Zinfandel Napa Valley 1994 • $13 • (11/15/1997) • **89**

STONESTREET | CALIFORNIA

Cabernet Sauvignon Alexander Valley 1998: Enormous oak presence, toasty and smoky, with rich, elegant, complex fruit and integrated tannins.–J.L. • $45 • (8/31/1999) (BT) • **90-94**

Cabernet Sauvignon Alexander Valley 1997: Dark, rich, intense and tannic, with roasted coffee, currant and toasty oak flavors. Hard and unyielding now, but has a solid core of fruit and oak.–J.L. • $NA • (8/31/1998) (BT) • **90-94**

Cabernet Sauvignon Alexander Valley 1996: Supple, elegant and well defined, with pretty black cherry, plum and wild berry character that's complex, if lacking the extra depth of the best. Drink now through 2006.–J.L. • $37 • (9/15/1999) • **88**

Cabernet Sauvignon Alexander Valley 1995: Complex, intense and well integrated, with ripe, rich fruit, lots of currant, anise, earth, mineral and spice, picking up leather and meat notes on the finish. Has the tannic strength to age. Best from 2001 through 2008.–J.L. • $34 • (8/31/1998) • **91**

Cabernet Sauvignon Alexander Valley 1994 • $35 • (10/31/1997) • **91**

Cabernet Sauvignon Alexander Valley 1993 • $30 • (9/15/1996) • **84**

Cabernet Sauvignon Alexander Valley 1992 • $25 • (10/31/1995) HR • **91**

Cabernet Sauvignon Alexander Valley 1991 • $22 • (5/15/1995) • **88**

Cabernet Sauvignon Alexander Valley 1990 • $20 • (11/15/1994) • **87**

Cabernet Sauvignon Alexander Valley 1989 • $24 • (11/15/1992) • **84**

Cabernet Sauvignon Alexander Valley 1988 • $24 • (8/31/1992) • **82**

Cabernet Sauvignon Alexander Valley Alexander Mountain Estate Three Block 1995: Elegant and complex, offering layers of cedar, black cherry and wild berry with spicy nuances, turning sleek and earthy on the finish, where the tannins are mild but firm. Best from 2001 through 2007.–J.L. • $60 • (2/28/1999) • **92**

Cabernet Sauvignon Alexander Valley Christopher's Vineyard Alexander Mountain Estate 1996: Firm for a '96, with earthy tannins and a tasty core of ripe plum, currant and cherry flavors accented by a touch of sage and spice. Drink through 2008.–J.L. • $60 • (11/15/1999) • **90**

Chardonnay Alexander Valley Upper Barn 1996: Elegant, with spicy, toasty oak, picking up complex pear, tart apple, citrus and subtle earthy nuances. Drink now through 2002.–J.L. • $60 • (2/28/1999) • **92**

Chardonnay Sonoma County 1997: A remarkably complex California Chardonnay, with its layers of spicy, toasty, cedary oak and bounty of pretty pear, fig, apricot and citrus flavors that are long and lively on the finish.–J.L. • $24 • (6/15/1999) SS • **93**

Chardonnay Sonoma County 1996: Distinct for its smoky, toasty oak and rich array of ripe pear, fig and melon. Delicious from start to finish. Drink now through 2002. Drink now.–J.L. • $24 • (1/01/1999) • **92**

Legacy Alexander Valley 1996: Openly ripe and fruity, with complex aromas and flavors. The texture is smooth and polished, giving the core of currant, cherry, coffee, cedar and spice a gentle ride until the finish, where the tannins firm up. A blend of Cabernet Sauvignon, Merlot and Cabernet Franc. Best from 2002 through 2008.–J.L. • $85 • (7/31/1999) • **93**

Legacy Alexander Valley 1995: Tight, rich and concentrated, with tiers of coffee, currant, anise, sage and berry, it slowly unfolds to reveal its treasures. Finishes with well-integrated tannins and fine length. Best from 2001 through 2007.–J.L. • $65 • (11/15/1998) • **91**

Legacy Alexander Valley 1994 • $106 Ⓐ • (10/15/1997) HR • **93**

Legacy Alexander Valley 1993 • $40 • (9/30/1996) • **90**

Legacy Alexander Valley 1992 • $35 • (9/30/1995) CS • **92**

Legacy Alexander Valley 1991 • $35 • (11/15/1994) • **91**

Legacy Alexander Valley 1990 • $35 • (11/15/1993) • **85**

Merlot Alexander Valley 1996: Supple, with polished cherry, currant, anise, tar and toasty oak, folding together nicely on the finish. Drink now through 2004.–J.L. • $37 • (9/15/1999) • **87**

Merlot Alexander Valley 1995: The flavor core is built around dry coffee, herb and currant. Turns austere on the dry, firm and tannic finish. Drink now through 2004.–J.L. • $37 • (9/30/1998) • **86**

Merlot Alexander Valley 1994 • $30 • (6/30/1997) • **88**

Merlot Alexander Valley 1993 • $30 • (6/30/1996) • **86**

Merlot Alexander Valley 1992 • $22 • (5/15/1995) SS • **90**
Merlot Alexander Valley 1991 • $24 • (9/15/1994) • **85**
Merlot Alexander Valley 1990 • $20 • (9/15/1994) • **82**
Merlot Alexander Valley 1989 • $24 • (5/31/1992) • **88**
Pinot Noir Russian River Valley 1997: Earthy, with stemmy cola, herb and cherry flavors that are disjointed and quite tannic on the finish. Drink now through 2005.–J.L. • $33 • (9/15/1999) • **84**
Pinot Noir Russian River Valley 1995 • $30 • (12/15/1997) • **89**
Pinot Noir Russian River Valley 1994 • $30 • (2/29/1996) • **87**
Pinot Noir Russian River Valley 1990 • $30 • (9/30/1992) • **84**
Pinot Noir Sonoma County 1993 • $25 • (12/31/1995) • **87**
Pinot Noir Sonoma County 1992 • $20 • (3/31/1995) • **86**
Pinot Noir Sonoma County 1991 • $30 • (2/28/1994) • **89**
Pinot Noir Sonoma County Reserve 1992 • $34 • (12/15/1994) • **89**
Sauvignon Blanc Alexander Valley Alexander Mountain Estate 1997: Bright and lemony, with hints of grapefruit, herb, mineral and subtle melon notes. Has a lean edge, but shows a more supple, viscous quality on the finish. Drink now through 2002. • $20 • (5/15/1999) • **88**
Sauvignon Blanc Alexander Valley Pinnacle Block Alexander Mountain Estate 1996: A full-textured, somewhat oily wine, with hints of gooseberry, herb, lemon and grapefruit. Toasty butterscotch notes add to the complexity. Distinctive. Drink now. • $24 • (7/31/1998) • **88**

STONEWALL | VIRGINIA

Chardonnay Virginia 1997: Bright and focused, showing apple, pear and vanilla character, with moderate concentration. Subtle finish. Drink now. –B.S. • $10 • (12/15/1998) • **82**

STONY HILL | CALIFORNIA

Chardonnay Napa Valley 1998: Tart, with green pineapple and pippen apple flavors, finishing with sour lemony notes. Drink now.–J.L. • $24 • (6/15/2000) • **85**
Chardonnay Napa Valley 1997: For fans of crisp, lean Chardonnay. Tart, with a green streak to the pippen apple, mineral and citrus notes. Drink now. –J.L. • $24 • (6/15/2000) • **84**

STORRS | CALIFORNIA

Chardonnay Santa Cruz Mountains 1997: Shows light, spicy flavors of citrus, herb and pear that stand out on the slightly coarse finish. Drink now.–H.S. • $18 • (7/31/1999) • **83**
Zinfandel California Ben Lomond Mountain Beauregard Ranch 1992 • $15 • (10/15/1995) • **82**
Zinfandel California Ben Lomond Mountain Beauregard Ranch 1990 • $15 • (10/15/1992) • **82**
Zinfandel California Ben Lomond Mountain Beauregard Ranch 1989 • $13 • (10/15/1992) • **81**
Zinfandel Santa Clara Valley Lion Oak Vineyard 1996: Ripe and spicy, with plum, cola and herb flavors. The finish is firm and a bit abrupt. Drink now through 2001.–J.L. • $25 • (6/15/1999) • **85**
Zinfandel Santa Cruz Mountains 1996: Rich and concentrated, with dark, smoky berry, cola, orange peel, plum and spice flavors. Plush and fleshy on the finish. Drink now through 2001.–J.L. • $20 • (6/15/1999) • **88**

STORY | CALIFORNIA

Zinfandel Shenandoah Valley 1992 • $10 • (10/15/1995) • **83**
Zinfandel Shenandoah Valley 1991 • $10 • (9/30/1993) • **86**
Zinfandel Shenandoah Valley 1990 • $8 • (9/30/1993) • **83**
Zinfandel Shenandoah Valley 1989 • $9 • (9/30/1993) • **82**
Zinfandel Shenandoah Valley Picnic Hill Vineyard Old Vines 1993 • $16 • (10/15/1995) • **84**
Zinfandel Shenandoah Valley Private Reserve 1992 • $16 • (10/15/1995) • **82**
Zinfandel Shenandoah Valley Private Reserve 1984 • $14 • (4/30/1991) • **79**

Key: SS—Spectator Selection. CS—Cellar Selection. HR—Highly Recommended. $NA—Price not available. (BT)—Barrel tasting. (A)—Auction Price. For a key to the tasters' initials, see "How to Use These Listings." **Dates in parentheses represent the issues in which the ratings were published.**

STORYBOOK MOUNTAIN | CALIFORNIA

Zinfandel Howell Mountain 1992 • $14 • (10/15/1995) • **83**
Zinfandel Howell Mountain 1991 • $15 • (10/15/1994) • **87**
Zinfandel Napa Mayacamas Range 1998: Tart, with a green streak running through the tart berry and cherry. Turns peppery and tannic. Drink now through 2005.–J.L. • $20 • (5/31/2000) • **86**
Zinfandel Napa Valley 1992 • $14 • (10/15/1995) • **86**
Zinfandel Napa Valley 1991 • $14 • (9/30/1993) • **87**
Zinfandel Napa Valley 1990 • $14 • (3/15/1993) • **83**
Zinfandel Napa Valley 1989 • $15 • (3/31/1992) • **80**
Zinfandel Napa Valley 1988 • $13 • (12/31/1990) • **75**
Zinfandel Napa Valley 1987 • $12 • (12/15/1989) • **88**
Zinfandel Napa Valley 1986 • $11 • (12/15/1988) • **88**
Zinfandel Napa Valley 1985 • $10 • (12/31/1987) • **90**
Zinfandel Napa Valley Eastern Exposures 1998: Tough-edged, with green bean and beef flavors that are muddled on the almost sweet finish.–J.L. • $30 • (5/31/2000) • **78**
Zinfandel Napa Valley Eastern Exposures 1997: Firm, ripe and tannic, with a tasty core of black cherry, wild berry and tart plum, holding its focus and structure, picking up a peppery note. Drink now through 2007.–J.L. • $25 • (12/15/1999) • **88**
Zinfandel Napa Valley Eastern Exposures 1995 • $19 • (5/31/1998) • **87**
Zinfandel Napa Valley Eastern Exposures 1994 • $19 • (4/30/1997) • **88**
Zinfandel Napa Valley Eastern Exposures 1992 • $17 • (10/15/1995) • **89**
Zinfandel Napa Valley Estate Reserve 1992 • $25 • (3/31/1997) • **90**
Zinfandel Napa Valley Estate Reserve 1991 • $25 • (10/15/1995) • **86**
Zinfandel Napa Valley Estate Reserve 1989 • $20 • (6/15/1993) • **71**
Zinfandel Napa Valley Estate Reserve 1988 • $20 • (3/31/1992) • **84**
Zinfandel Napa Valley Estate Reserve 1987 • $25 • (12/31/1990) • **89**
Zinfandel Napa Valley Estate Reserve 1986 • $27 • (5/15/1990) • **82**
Zinfandel Napa Valley Estate Reserve 1985 • $29 • (5/31/1989) • **88**
Zinfandel Napa Valley Estate Reserve 1984 • $22 • (4/30/1988) • **92**
Zinfandel Napa Valley Estate Reserve 1983 • $22 • (7/31/1987) • **81**
Zinfandel Napa Valley Mayacamas Range 1997: Tight, with a crisp band of earthy cherry, wild berry, anise, sage and tea. Turns firm, with tight tannins. Best from 2001 through 2006.–J.L. • $20 • (4/30/2000) • **86**
Zinfandel Napa Valley Mayacamas Range 1996 • $17 • (5/31/1998) • **88**
Zinfandel Napa Valley Mayacamas Range 1994 • $15 • (4/30/1997) • **90**
Zinfandel Napa Valley Reserve 1998: Hollow, with dry, lean, leathery fruit flavors, finishing with dill and bell pepper notes.–J.L. • $40 • (5/31/2000) • **77**

STRATFORD | CALIFORNIA

Cabernet Sauvignon California 1990 • $12 • (11/15/1992) • **81**
Cabernet Sauvignon California 1985 • $10 • (11/30/1988) • **83**
Cabernet Sauvignon Napa Valley 1993 • $10 • (12/15/1995) • **81**
Cabernet Sauvignon Napa Valley 1987 • $12 • (4/30/1990) • **85**
Cabernet Sauvignon Napa Valley Partners' Reserve 1988 • $16 • (3/15/1992) • **68**
Cabernet Sauvignon Napa Valley Partners' Reserve 1987 • $16 • (4/30/1991) • **90**
Chardonnay California 1996 • $12 • (5/15/1998) • **85**
Dolcetto Napa Valley 1994 • $9 • (11/15/1995) • **83**
Merlot California 1991 • $12 • (7/15/1993) • **84**
Merlot California 1990 • $10 • (5/31/1992) • **85**
Merlot California 1987 • $13 • (10/31/1989) • **83**
Merlot California 1986 • $10 • (1/31/1989) • **78**
Merlot Sierra Foothills 1996 • $14 • (6/15/1998) • **84**
Zinfandel California 1991 • $8 • (6/15/1993) • **83**

STRAUS | CALIFORNIA

Merlot Napa Valley 1991 • $17 • (5/15/1995) • **85**
Merlot Napa Valley 1990 • $16 • (8/31/1993) • **85**
Merlot Napa Valley 1989 • $15 • (11/15/1991) • **81**
Merlot Napa Valley 1988 • $14 • (12/31/1990) • **82**
Merlot Napa Valley 1987 • $12 • (2/15/1990) • **90**
Merlot Napa Valley 1986 • $11 • (2/28/1989) • **93**
Merlot Napa Valley 1985 • $10 • (2/15/1988) • **81**

STRONG, RODNEY | CALIFORNIA

Cabernet Sauvignon Northern Sonoma Alexander's Crown Vineyard 1996: Quite oaky and tannic, though with short-term cellaring it may smooth out and let the plum and cherry play a more prominent role. Lots of dill and wood flavors. Best from 2001 through 2007.–J.L. • $25 • (3/31/2000) • **85**

Cabernet Sauvignon Northern Sonoma Alexander's Crown Vineyard 1995: Cedary oak flavors mute the mature, ripe plum and currant flavors that turn diffuse on the finish. Drink now.–J.L. • $24 • (10/31/1998) • **82**

Cabernet Sauvignon Northern Sonoma Alexander's Crown Vineyard 1994 • $23 • (3/31/1998) • **86**

Cabernet Sauvignon Northern Sonoma Alexander's Crown Vineyard 1993 • $22 • (8/31/1997) • **88**

Cabernet Sauvignon Northern Sonoma Alexander's Crown Vineyard 1992 • $20 • (9/15/1996) • **87**

Cabernet Sauvignon Northern Sonoma Alexander's Crown Vineyard 1991 • $20 • (12/15/1995) • **86**

Cabernet Sauvignon Northern Sonoma Alexander's Crown Vineyard 1990 • $20 • (11/15/1993) • **86**

Cabernet Sauvignon Northern Sonoma Alexander's Crown Vineyard 1988 • $18 • (9/30/1992) HR • **91**

Cabernet Sauvignon Alexander Valley Alexander's Crown Vineyard 1987 • $17 • (7/15/1991) • **89**

Cabernet Sauvignon Alexander Valley Alexander's Crown Vineyard 1985 • $17 • (5/31/1991) • **87**

Cabernet Sauvignon Alexander Valley Alexander's Crown Vineyard 1984 • $12 • (4/30/1989) • **80**

Cabernet Sauvignon Alexander Valley Alexander's Crown Vineyard 1982 • $12 • (10/31/1988) • **80**

Cabernet Sauvignon Alexander Valley Alexander's Crown Vineyard 1981 • $12 • (11/30/1987) • **77**

Cabernet Sauvignon Alexander Valley Alexander's Crown Vineyard 1980 • $11 • (4/16/1985) • **86**

Cabernet Sauvignon Alexander Valley Alexander's Crown Vineyard 1979 • $12 • (4/16/1984) • **79**

Cabernet Sauvignon Alexander Valley Alexander's Crown Vineyard 1978 • $12 • (1/01/1984) • **80**

Cabernet Sauvignon Sonoma County Alexander's Crown Vineyard 1974 • $50 • (11/15/1994) • **74**

Cabernet Sauvignon Alexander Valley Reserve 1988 • $30 • (11/15/1992) • **84**

Cabernet Sauvignon Alexander Valley Reserve 1987 • $28 • (9/30/1991) HR • **92**

Cabernet Sauvignon Northern Sonoma Reserve 1995: Firm, trim and focused, showing a tight, complex range of cedar, currant, tar and toasted oak; the flavors linger on the mildly tannic finish. Drink now through 2004.–J.L. • $40 • (10/15/1999) • **87**

Cabernet Sauvignon Northern Sonoma Reserve 1994: With its very good core of currant and cherry flavors and firm, chewy tannins, this needs time in the bottle to gain harmony and focus. Drink through 2004.–J.L. • $35 • (10/31/1998) • **86**

Cabernet Sauvignon Northern Sonoma Reserve 1993 • $30 • (9/30/1997) • **87**

Cabernet Sauvignon Northern Sonoma Reserve 1992 • $30 • (11/15/1996) • **89**

Cabernet Sauvignon Northern Sonoma Reserve 1991 • $30 • (12/15/1995) • **86**

Cabernet Sauvignon Northern Sonoma Reserve 1990 • $30 • (6/15/1994) • **88**

Cabernet Sauvignon Sonoma County 1996: Features herbal, earthy flavors, with blackberry notes peeking through. Ripe-textured, and the flavors linger. Drink now through 2005. • $16 • (9/15/1999) • **85**

Cabernet Sauvignon Sonoma County 1994 • $12 • (4/30/1997) • **82**

Cabernet Sauvignon Sonoma County 1993 • $11 • (12/15/1995) • **86**

Cabernet Sauvignon Sonoma County 1992 • $10 • (6/15/1995) • **83**

Cabernet Sauvignon Sonoma County 1991 • $10 • (11/15/1994) • **82**

Cabernet Sauvignon Sonoma County 1990 • $11 • (11/15/1993) • **81**

Cabernet Sauvignon Sonoma County 1989 • $10 • (9/30/1992) • **84**

Cabernet Sauvignon Sonoma County 1988 • $10 • (11/15/1991) • **80**

Cabernet Sauvignon Sonoma County 1987 • $10 • (6/30/1991) • **85**

Chardonnay Chalk Hill 1998: A touch tinny, with a sour pineapple edge to the tart apple flavors. Drink now through 2004.–J.L. • $16 • (5/31/2000) • **82**

Chardonnay Chalk Hill 1997: Firm and ripe, with citrus and peach flavors backed by bright acidity. The finish is clean, with a flinty mineral edge. Drink now. • $17 • (7/31/1999) • **86**

Chardonnay Chalk Hill Chalk Hill Vineyard 1996 • $16 • (2/28/1998) • **87**

Chardonnay Northern Sonoma Chalk Hill Vineyard Reserve 1997: Earthy, with dried apricot, fig, toasty oak and herbal flavors, it's rich and full-bodied, if lacking in finesse. Drink now through 2005.–J.L. • $30 • (5/15/2000) • **86**

Chardonnay Sonoma County Chalk Hill Vineyard Reserve 1996: Clean, with spicy peach, nectarine and melon flavors, finishing with a hint of cedar and vanilla-tinged oak. Drink now through 2001.–J.L. • $30 • (2/28/1999) • **87**

Chardonnay Sonoma County 1998: Curious aromas of cornmeal and ripe melon. Lively pear flavors turn a bit soapy on the finish. Drink now.–J.L. • $13 • (4/30/2000) • **83**

Chardonnay Sonoma County 1997: Spicy, with citrus and toast flavors and a slight earthy note. Drink now.–J.L. • $12 • (12/31/1998) • **82**

Chardonnay Sonoma County 1996 • $12 • (11/15/1997) • **83**

Merlot Russian River Valley River West Vineyard 1985 • $12 • (2/28/1989) • **79**

Merlot Sonoma County 1997: Oak dominates, with black currant and herb flavors. Drink now through 2003.–J.L. • $16 • (6/15/2000) • **81**

Merlot Sonoma County 1996: Firm, with a core of plum, cherry and currant flavors balanced by an earthy note. Smooth on the finish. Drink now.–J.L. • $16 • (12/15/1998) • **85**

Merlot Sonoma County 1995 • $16 • (4/30/1998) • **83**

Merlot Sonoma County 1994 • $12 • (3/31/1997) • **84**

Merlot Sonoma County 1993 • $16 • (8/31/1996) • **87**

Merlot Sonoma County 1992 • $14 • (2/28/1995) • **84**

Pinot Noir Russian River Valley 1997: Fresh and fragrant, with pretty floral and cherry aromas. Well balanced, with plush tannins, strawberry flavors, moderate acidity and a medium finish rounded out with pretty herb notes. Drink now through 2003. • $16 • (9/15/1999) • **85**

Pinot Noir Russian River Valley 1996: Shows a shade more depth and complexity than do many '96s, with earthy cherry, wild berry, leather and spice. Holds its focus and depth on the finish. Drink now.–J.L. • $17 • (9/15/1998) • **85**

Pinot Noir Russian River Valley River East Vineyard 1994 • $16 • (11/15/1996) • **85**

Pinot Noir Russian River Valley River East Vineyard 1993 • $16 • (12/31/1995) • **87**

Pinot Noir Russian River Valley River East Vineyard 1992 • $14 • (3/31/1995) • **83**

Pinot Noir Russian River Valley River East Vineyard 1991 • $14 • (2/28/1994) • **87**

Pinot Noir Russian River Valley River East Vineyard 1990 • $14 • (9/30/1992) • **82**

Pinot Noir Russian River Valley River East Vineyard 1985 • $10 • (2/28/1991) • **83**

Pinot Noir Russian River Valley River East Vineyard 1980 • $10 • (7/01/1984) • **78**

Sauvignon Blanc Northern Sonoma Charlotte's Home 1998: Showing moderate acidity, this leans toward grass, citrus, peach and melon flavors. Smooth and clean, it ends on a fresh mineral note. Drink now. • $10 • (8/31/1999) • **86**

Sauvignon Blanc Northern Sonoma Charlotte's Home 1997 • $10 • (6/30/1998) • **88**

Sauvignon Blanc Northern Sonoma Charlotte's Home 1996 • $10 • (6/30/1997) • **88**

Symmetry Alexander Valley 1996: Smells better than it tastes. Tight and tannic, with a dark color, currant and plum fruit and pretty, toasty, cedary oak, finishing with firm tannins. Drink now through 2008.–J.L. • $50 • (5/15/2000) • **86**

Zinfandel Northern Sonoma Old Vines 1997: Tart and earthy, with camphor, dried cherry and wax notes.–J.L. • $16 • (5/31/2000) • **76**

Zinfandel Northern Sonoma Old Vines 1996: Tart plum, spice and earth flavors linger on the slightly dry, waxy finish. Drink now.–J.L. • $16 • (12/31/1998) • **82**

Zinfandel Northern Sonoma Old Vines 1995 • $16 • (5/15/1998) • **86**

Zinfandel Northern Sonoma Old Vines 1994 • $14 • (4/30/1997) • **82**

Zinfandel Northern Sonoma Old Vines 1993 • $14 • (3/31/1996) • **84**

Zinfandel Russian River Valley River West Vineyard Old Vines 1992 • $14 • (7/31/1995) • **86**

Zinfandel Russian River Valley River West Vineyard Old Vines 1991 • $14 • (4/30/1994) • **82**

Zinfandel Russian River Valley River West Vineyard Old Vines 1990 • $14 • (12/15/1992) • **86**

Zinfandel Russian River Valley River West Vineyard Old Vines 1988 • $15 • (10/15/1992) • **89**

Zinfandel Russian River Valley River West Vineyard Old Vines 1987 • $14 • (8/31/1991) • **82**

Zinfandel Russian River Valley River West Vineyard Old Vines 1980 • $12 • (11/15/1987) • **68**

Zinfandel Russian River Valley River West Vineyard Old Vines 1979 • $10 • (3/15/1987) • **71**

STUHLMULLER | CALIFORNIA

Chardonnay Alexander Valley 1998: Spicy and herbal, with cedar and pear flavors that are ripe if simple and lacking focus. Drink now.–J.L. • $22 • (6/15/2000) • **84**

Chardonnay Alexander Valley 1997: Well-focused spice and subtle tropical, pear, tangerine, apple, salt-mineral and hazelnut flavors, with a silky texture. Soft and subtle on the finish. Drink now through 2002.–J.L. • $21 • (6/30/1999) • **89**

Chardonnay Alexander Valley 1996: Fresh, with complex, concentrated spicy apple, pear, citrus and melon notes. Firm and tightly wound. Cellar short-term. New, from a vineyard that's been selling grapes to Cronin, which has made a vineyard-designated wine from this property.–J.L. • $21 • (7/31/1998) • **90**

SULLBERG, MICHAEL | CALIFORNIA

Cabernet Sauvignon California Lot 66 Reserve 1994 • $7 • (9/15/1997) • **80**

Cabernet Sauvignon California Lot 75 1995: Tastes like a vegetable stew, with celery, green bean and asparagus in the lead. Finishes with hints of plum and oak. • $8 • (10/15/1998) • **75**

Cabernet Sauvignon Central Coast 1992 • $6 • (12/15/1995) • **84**

Cabernet Sauvignon Napa Valley 1991 • $7 • (11/15/1994) • **79**

Merlot California Barrel Reserve 1991 • $7 • (9/15/1994) • **81**

Merlot California Lot 82 Reserve 1997: Fairly smooth, with a black currant and cherry core. Finishes on the herbal side. Drink now. • $8 • (10/15/1998) • **82**

Merlot-Cabernet Mount Veeder Cuvée Reserve NV • $6 • (12/15/1995) • **80**

Pinot Noir Anderson Valley 1992 • $6 • (3/31/1995) • **81**

Zinfandel California Old Vine Reserve 1990 • $5 • (10/15/1994) • **79**

SULLIVAN | CALIFORNIA

Cabernet Sauvignon Napa Valley 1993 • $26 • (11/30/1997) • **86**

Cabernet Sauvignon Napa Valley 1991 • $23 • (11/15/1994) • **85**

Cabernet Sauvignon Napa Valley 1989 • $23 • (11/15/1992) • **85**

Coeur de Vigne Private Reserve Napa Valley 1993 • $40 • (11/30/1997) • **88**

Coeur de Vigne Private Reserve Napa Valley 1991 • $30 • (11/15/1994) • **82**

Coeur de Vigne Private Reserve Napa Valley 1989 • $25 • (8/31/1992) • **82**

Meritage Coeur de Vigne Napa Valley 1988 • $25 • (7/15/1992) • **83**

Merlot Napa Valley 1994 • $35 • (2/28/1997) • **77**

Merlot Napa Valley 1991 • $23 • (9/15/1994) • **83**

Merlot Napa Valley 1990 • $20 • (6/15/1993) • **87**

Merlot Napa Valley 1989 • $20 • (4/15/1992) HR • **92**

SUMMERFIELD | CALIFORNIA

Chardonnay California Vintner's Reserve 1996: Simple, with pleasant notes of peach and almond and a soft finish. Drink now. • $9 • (7/31/1998) • **83**

Merlot California Vintner's Reserve 1995 • $8 • (11/30/1996) • **85**

SUMMERS RANCH | CALIFORNIA

Charbono Napa Valley Villa Andriana Vineyard 1997: Fun and easy to like, featuring ripe grapey flavors and hints of vanilla and spice in a smooth, supple package. Drink now.–H.S. • $18 • (4/30/1999) • **84**

Chardonnay Napa Valley 1996 • $20 • (5/15/1998) • **83**

Merlot Knights Valley 1996: Fairly smooth on the palate, with pretty blackberry flavors and herbal notes. Supple finish, with a hint of bitterness. Drink now. • $28 • (10/15/1999) • **85**

Merlot Knights Valley 1995 • $24 • (4/30/1998) • **88**

Merlot Knights Valley 1992 • $21 • (2/29/1996) • **87**

SUMMIT LAKE | CALIFORNIA

Cabernet Sauvignon Howell Mountain Emily Kestrel 1992 • $25 • (11/30/1996) • **87**

Zinfandel Howell Mountain 1995 • $16 • (6/15/1998) • **84**

Zinfandel Howell Mountain 1994 • $16 • (6/15/1998) • **82**

Zinfandel Howell Mountain 1992 • $13 • (3/31/1996) • **83**

Zinfandel Howell Mountain 1991 • $12 • (10/15/1995) • **87**

Zinfandel Howell Mountain 1989 • $9 • (8/31/1993) • **84**

Zinfandel Howell Mountain 1988 • $11 • (10/15/1992) • **82**

Zinfandel Howell Mountain 1987 • $11 • (2/15/1991) • **87**

Zinfandel Howell Mountain 1986 • $11 • (3/15/1990) • **84**

SUNSET | CALIFORNIA

Zinfandel Potter Valley 1997: Very light and pleasant, with candied strawberry flavors and a spicy, herbal band. Drink now.–J.L. • $13 • (6/15/2000) • **83**

SUNSTONE | CALIFORNIA

Cabernet Sauvignon Santa Barbara County 1994 • $18 • (10/31/1997) • **79**

Cabernet Sauvignon Santa Ynez Valley 1993 • $18 • (11/30/1996) • **77**

Chardonnay Santa Barbara County 1997: Pleasant peach, tropical and mineral flavors on a soft frame. Finishes with green apple and slightly bitter flavors. Drink now.–J.L. • $15 • (7/31/1999) • **85**

Chardonnay Santa Barbara County 1996: Starts off with earth and mineral aromas. Firm and lemony on the palate, with a solid core of nectarine, fresh pea, mineral and herb flavors. Crisp, complex finish. Drink now through 2001.–J.L. • $18 • (7/31/1998) • **87**

Chardonnay Santa Barbara County Reserve 1997: Earthy aromas are contrasted by tropical echoes of melon, pineapple and a touch of coconut on the palate. Bright acidity perks it up nicely, leaving a tangy finish. Drink now. • $19 • (6/30/1999) • **86**

Equinox Santa Barbara County 1994 • $21 • (12/15/1996) • **84**

Merlot Santa Barbara County 1997: Offers smoky oak, black cherry, herb and blackberry flavors. A bit dry on the palate, it nonetheless finishes moderately, with a hint of earthiness. Drink through 2004. • $20 • (10/15/1999) • **84**

Merlot Santa Barbara County 1996: Lots of licorice followed by black cherry and herbs. A slight earthiness adds interest. Drink now through 2002. • $20 • (9/30/1998) • **85**

Merlot Santa Barbara County 1995: Cherries, herbs and a gamy note blend well in this light-styled wine. Finishes moderately, and is quite quaffable. Drink now. • $20 • (9/15/1998) • **84**

Merlot Santa Barbara County 1994 • $18 • (8/31/1996) • **80**

Merlot Santa Barbara County Reserve 1997: Serves up subtle coffee and chocolate aromas, followed by earthiness. Black cherry and currant dominate on the palate. There's plenty of oak, though the tannins are a bit rustic and the finish is slightly bitter. Drink now. • $25 • (10/15/1999) • **86**

Merlot-Cabernet Franc-Cabernet Santa Barbara County Eros 1997: Rich and plush, with a decidedly herbal core of concentrated plum, black cherry, cola and sage flavors. Tannins are ripe, and ready for drinking. Drink now through 2003.–J.L. • $28 • (10/15/1999) • **87**

Syrah Santa Barbara County 1995 • $24 • (6/15/1998) • **87**

SUTTER HOME | CALIFORNIA

Cabernet Sauvignon California 1991 • $6 • (11/15/1994) • **81**

Cabernet Sauvignon California 1990 • $6 • (9/15/1993) • **81**

Cabernet Sauvignon California 1989 • $6 • (10/15/1991) • **83**

Cabernet Sauvignon California 1988 • $5 • (11/15/1990) • **81**

Cabernet Sauvignon Napa Valley Centennial Selection Reserve 1990 • $12 • (10/31/1993) • **87**

Cabernet Sauvignon Napa Valley Reserve 1992 • $12 • (11/15/1996) • **87**

Cabernet Sauvignon Napa Valley Reserve 1991 • $12 • (11/15/1994) • **82**

Chardonnay California 1997: Soft and simple, with a core of lemon and light cream notes. Drink now.–H.S. • $6 • (4/30/1999) • **82**

Gewürztraminer California 1996 • $6 • (11/30/1997) • **80**

Merlot California 1996 • $6 • (7/31/1997) • **77**

Merlot California 1992 • $6 • (9/15/1994) • **79**

Merlot California 1991 • $6 • (8/31/1993) • **78**

Merlot Rosé California 1997 • $6 • (6/30/1998) • **82**

Moscato California 1996 • $6 • (9/15/1997) • **80**

Muscat Alexandria California 1994 • $5 • (9/30/1995) • **84**

Pinot Noir California 1997: Spicy; tight in structure, with delicate berry, currant and herb flavors and a mild finish. A good effort. Drink now.–J.L. • $6 • (6/15/1999) • **84**

Sauvignon Blanc California 1996 • $5 • (7/31/1997) • **85**

Sauvignon Blanc Monterey County Signature Series 1997 • $14 • (5/31/1998) • **88**

Zinfandel Amador County 1973 • $NA • (6/16/1985) • **86**

Zinfandel Amador County 1972 • $NA • (6/16/1985) • **85**

Zinfandel Amador County 1970 • $NA • (6/16/1985) • **80**

Key: SS—Spectator Selection. CS—Cellar Selection. HR—Highly Recommended. $NA—Price not available. (BT)—Barrel tasting. (A)—Auction Price.
For a key to the tasters' initials, see "How to Use These Listings."
Dates in parentheses represent the issues in which the ratings were published.

Zinfandel Amador County Centennial Selection Reserve 1990 • $10 • (10/15/1994) • **83**

Zinfandel Amador County Reserve 1989 • $10 • (10/15/1992) • **79**

Zinfandel Amador County Reserve 1988 • $10 • (3/31/1992) • **84**

Zinfandel Amador County Signature Series 1995: Ripe and soft, with dried strawberry, plum and cherry flavors accented by delicate spice and earth notes. Drink now through 2001.–J.L. • $12 • (4/30/1999) • **84**

Zinfandel California 1996: Light-bodied, with hints of dried strawberry and herb, finishing short with dry tannins. Pleasant but simple.–J.L. • $5 • (5/15/1999) • **79**

Zinfandel California 1994 • $10 • (4/30/1997) • **81**

Zinfandel California 1993 • $5 • (4/30/1996) • **77**

Zinfandel California 1992 • $5 • (10/15/1994) • **75**

Zinfandel California 1991 • $5 • (4/30/1993) • **82**

Zinfandel California 1990 • $5 • (9/15/1992) • **77**

Zinfandel California 1989 • $5 • (5/15/1991) • **85**

Zinfandel California 1988 • $5 • (3/31/1991) • **72**

SWAN, JOSEPH | CALIFORNIA

Cabernet Sauvignon Sonoma Mountain Steiner Vineyard 1990 • $18 • (11/15/1993) • **84**

Chardonnay Russian River Valley Estate 1997: Leans toward the earthy side but straightens out, holding on to its core of elegant spice, pear and citrusy Chardonnay flavors. Drink now through 2002.–J.L. • $23 • (6/30/1999) • **88**

Chardonnay Russian River Valley Estate 1996: A twinge of earthiness interrupts the flow of ripe pear and apple, but it fills out at midpalate, where the texture is creamy. Finishes with spice and vanilla notes. Drink now through 2002.–J.L. • $25 • (7/31/1998) • **88**

Côtes du Rosa Russian River Valley 1991 • $10 • (11/30/1992) • **88**

Mourvèdre Russian River Valley 1997: Pronounced aromas and flavors of white pepper mingle with earth, black cherry and pretty floral notes. Drink now through 2003.–J.L. • $18 • (5/15/2000) • **85**

Pinot Gris Russian River Valley Saralee's Vineyard 1997: Fairly leesy and complex, with hints of toast, apple and pear and a mineral finish. Not typical of the varietal, it makes a good alternative to Chardonnay. Drink now. • $17 • (9/15/1998) • **87**

Pinot Noir Russian River Valley 1994 • $30 • (6/30/1997) • **88**

Pinot Noir Russian River Valley 1993 • $14 • (12/31/1995) • **82**

Pinot Noir Russian River Valley 1992 • $22 • (12/31/1995) • **87**

Pinot Noir Russian River Valley 1991 • $20 • (3/31/1995) • **83**

Pinot Noir Russian River Valley 1990 • $20 • (3/31/1997) • **94**

Pinot Noir Russian River Valley 1988 • $20 • (6/30/1991) • **79**

Pinot Noir Russian River Valley 1986 • $20 • (3/31/1997) • **87**

Pinot Noir Russian River Valley 1985 • $18 • (6/15/1988) • **89**

Pinot Noir Russian River Valley 1982 • $17 • (8/31/1986) • **82**

Pinot Noir Russian River Valley Estate 1996: A touch earthy and tilting toward the crisp side up front, it nonetheless has a sense of plum and wild berry and then picks up wonderful richness with raspberry and anise, turning delicious. Long, complex aftertaste. Drink through 2006.–J.L. • $30 • (9/15/1999) • **90**

Pinot Noir Russian River Valley Estate 1995: Tough, with dry, earthy and leathery tannins. Slowly reveals a core of cherry and berry, and it will benefit from short-term cellaring to let the tannins mellow. Finishes with spice and mineral notes. Drink through 2002.–J.L. • $32 • (9/15/1998) • **87**

Pinot Noir Sonoma Mountain Steiner Vineyard 1996: Tight, firmly tannic, with a green-tealike edge to the barely ripe Pinot Noir fruit flavors. Can stand cellaring to soften and shed the greenness. Drink through 2003.–J.L. • $22 • (9/15/1998) • **84**

Pinot Noir Sonoma Mountain Steiner Vineyard 1995 • $18 • (7/31/1997) • **87**

Pinot Noir Sonoma Mountain Steiner Vineyard 1994 • $17 • (4/30/1996) • **86**

Pinot Noir Sonoma Mountain Steiner Vineyard 1993 • $15 • (3/31/1995) • **84**

Pinot Noir Sonoma Mountain Steiner Vineyard 1992 • $16 • (2/28/1995) • **88**

Pinot Noir Sonoma Mountain Wolfspierre Vineyard 1996: Elegant, ripe and spicy, with pretty black cherry and strawberry flavors, hints of sage, mineral and vanilla. Finishes with mild, supple tannins. Drink now through 2001.–J.L. • $17 • (9/15/1998) • **86**

Pinot Noir Sonoma Mountain Wolfspierre Vineyard 1995 • $16 • (1/01/1997) • **88**

Pinot Noir Sonoma Mountain Wolfspierre Vineyard 1992 • $14 • (3/31/1995) • **86**

Zinfandel California 1973 • $NA • (6/16/1985) • **84**

Zinfandel California 1969 • $NA • (6/16/1985) • **83**

Zinfandel Russian River Valley Anniversary Selection 1997: Decidedly minty, with bay leaf, pepper and sage notes, but the ripe, juicy wild berry fills in the gaps quite nicely. Drink now through 2007.–J.L. • $30 • (2/29/2000) • **88**

Zinfandel Russian River Valley Frati Ranch 1996: A touch earthy, showing a mushroomy edge up front before revealing its dried fruit flavors, with hints of plum, raspberry, spice and cedar that linger. Drink now through 2002. –J.L. • $25 • (5/15/1999) • **88**

Zinfandel Russian River Valley Frati Ranch 1995 • $24 • (6/15/1998) • **91**

Zinfandel Russian River Valley Frati Ranch 1993 • $18 • (10/15/1995) • **90**

Zinfandel Russian River Valley Frati Ranch 1992: A ripe, jammy style that's aging nicely. Offers lots of ripe, juicy plum and wild berry flavors and has a sense of finesse and polish on the finish, where the tannins are fine. (Zinfandel retrospective tasting). Drink now through 2002.–J.L. • $16 • (6/30/1999) • **91**

Zinfandel Russian River Valley Lone Redwood Ranch 1997: Spritzy. Elegant, racy cherry and wild berry flavors have black cherry and raspberry nuances. Drink now through 2005.–J.L. • $20 • (2/29/2000) • **86**

Zinfandel Russian River Valley V.H.S.R. Vineyard 1993 • $15 • (10/15/1995) • **85**

Zinfandel Russian River Valley V.H.S.R. Vineyard 1992 • $15 • (10/15/1994) HR • **92**

Zinfandel Russian River Valley Zeigler Vineyard 1997: Firm, with earthy tannins holding a grip on the racy wild berry, raspberry and blackberry. Turns dry and austere on the finish. Drink now through 2007.–J.L. • $25 • (2/29/2000) • **87**

Zinfandel Russian River Valley Zeigler Vineyard 1996: Smooth, ripe and spicy, with a pretty array of black cherry, raspberry, tar, anise and cedar, firming up on the finish. Drink now through 2002.–J.L. • $23 • (5/15/1999) • **88**

Zinfandel Russian River Valley Zeigler Vineyard 1995 • $20 • (6/15/1998) • **90**

Zinfandel Sonoma County Ziegler Vineyard 1993 • $15 • (10/15/1995) • **81**

Zinfandel Sonoma County Ziegler Vineyard 1987 • $16 • (9/15/1990) • **86**

Zinfandel Sonoma County 1989 • $13 • (10/15/1992) • **80**

Zinfandel Sonoma County 1988 • $16 • (8/31/1991) • **82**

Zinfandel Sonoma County 1987 • $16 • (7/31/1990) • **86**

Zinfandel Sonoma County 1986 • $16 • (3/15/1990) • **89**

Zinfandel Sonoma County 1985 • $17 • (3/15/1989) • **82**

Zinfandel Sonoma Valley Stellwagen Vineyard 1997: Ripe and juicy, with spicy cherry, wild berry, cola and raspberry jam notes. The most polished and balanced of the Swan '97s. Drink now through 2008.–J.L. • $23 • (2/29/2000) • **89**

Zinfandel Sonoma Valley Stellwagen Vineyard 1996: An earthy style that opens into a complex array of plum, berry, cherry, anise and spice. Finishes with drying, earthy tannins. Drink now through 2002.–J.L. • $18 • (6/30/1999) • **87**

Zinfandel Sonoma Valley Stellwagen Vineyard 1995 • $20 • (6/15/1998) • **90**

Zinfandel Sonoma Valley Stellwagen Vineyard 1993 • $16 • (10/15/1995) • **88**

Zinfandel Sonoma Valley Stellwagen Vineyard 1992 • $14 • (10/15/1994) • **77**

Zinfandel Sonoma Valley Stellwagen Vineyard 1989 • $14 • (10/15/1992) • **80**

Zinfandel Sonoma Valley Stellwagen Vineyard 1987 • $13 • (9/15/1990) • **86**

SWANSON | CALIFORNIA

Alexis Napa Valley 1997: Weaves together a complex array of rich black cherry, ripe plum, wild berry and floral notes, all sharply focused, finishing with firm tannins and wonderful length. Best from 2002 through 2010.–J.L. • $45 • (1/31/2000) • **93**

Alexis Napa Valley 1996: Remarkably complex, with an intriguing array of cedary oak, tar, berry, currant and cherry flavors that gain depth and finesse on the finish. A blend of Syrah, Cabernet Sauvignon and Cabernet Franc. Drink now through 2006.–J.L. • $40 • (2/28/1999) • **92**

Alexis Napa Valley 1995 • $40 • (12/15/1997) HR • **92**

Alexis Napa Valley 1994 • $33 • (3/31/1997) • **91**

Cabernet Sauvignon Napa Valley 1997: Smooth and polished, with currant, cedar, herb and tobacco notes. Rich aftertaste and firm tannins. Best from 2001 through 2009.–J.L. • $40 • (6/15/2000) • **88**

Cabernet Sauvignon Napa Valley 1996: Bold, ripe, smooth and polished, with a pretty array of anise-scented black cherry, plum and wild berry, rich and plush, with depth and complexity. A wonderful value. Drink through 2007.–J.L. • $30 • (10/31/1999) • **91**

Cabernet Sauvignon Napa Valley 1995: Complex, with a pretty interplay of ripe cherry and plummy Cabernet flavor and mineral notes. Turns a bit minty and earthy on the finish, where leather and tobacco notes add dimension. Supple texture. Best from 2001 through 2010.–J.L. • $26 • (7/31/1998) • **91**

Cabernet Sauvignon Napa Valley 1994 • $24 • (7/31/1997) • **91**

Cabernet Sauvignon Napa Valley 1993 • $22 • (8/31/1996) • **83**

Cabernet Sauvignon Napa Valley 1992 • $22 • (12/15/1995) • **90**

Cabernet Sauvignon Napa Valley 1991 • $20 • (11/15/1994) • **89**

Cabernet Sauvignon Napa Valley 1990 • $23 • (11/15/1993) • **89**

Cabernet Sauvignon Napa Valley 1988 • $23 • (11/15/1992) • **82**

SWANSON

Cabernet Sauvignon Napa Valley 1987 • $25 • (12/15/1997) • **88**
Chardonnay Napa Valley Carneros 1996 • $26 • (5/31/1998) • **88**
Merlot Napa Valley 1997: This California Merlot is smooth, ripe, rich and complex, if a bit understated in its fruit profile, as layers of earth, clay-laced currant, anise and black cherry mingle with light oak and coffee. Delicious. Drink now through 2008.–J.L. • $27 • (1/31/2000) SS • **91**
Merlot Napa Valley 1996: Lean yet smooth, with herb, chocolate, dill, currant and berry notes and leathery tannins. Drink now through 2003.–J.L. • $26 • (2/28/1999) • **86**
Merlot Napa Valley 1995 • $24 • (9/30/1997) • **89**
Merlot Napa Valley 1994 • $22 • (5/15/1997) • **89**
Merlot Napa Valley 1993 • $18 • (8/31/1996) • **85**
Merlot Napa Valley 1992 • $16 • (7/31/1995) • **86**
Merlot Napa Valley 1991 • $15 • (5/31/1994) • **84**
Merlot Napa Valley 1990 • $16 • (5/31/1992) • **82**
Sangiovese Napa Valley 1997: Distinct for its minty menthol edge. A lean yet complex and flavorful wine that gains nuance and finesse on the finish. Drink through 2004.–J.L. • $24 • (11/15/1999) • **88**
Sangiovese Napa Valley 1996: Pleasingly supple, with ripe plum and cherry notes of modest proportion, but not especially varietal. Drink now.–J.L. • $24 • (2/28/1999) • **83**
Sangiovese Napa Valley 1995 • $24 • (12/15/1997) • **87**
Sangiovese Napa Valley 1994 • $22 • (4/30/1997) • **88**
Sangiovese Napa Valley 1993 • $18 • (6/15/1996) • **88**
Sangiovese Napa Valley 1992 • $18 • (11/30/1994) SS • **90**
Sangiovese Napa Valley 1991 • $16 • (5/31/1994) • **84**
Sangiovese Napa Valley Rosato 1998: A sophisticated rosé. Pretty, with plum, strawberry and creamy vanilla notes and a lingering spicy edge. Full-bodied yet refreshing. Drink now.–J.L. • $14 • (1/31/2000) • **88**
Sangiovese Napa Valley Rosato 1996 • $12 • (9/15/1997) • **83**
Sémillon Napa Valley Late Harvest 1996: Delicious, with soft, sweet, rich apricot, apple, fig, hazelnut and pear flavors that fan out and linger on the finish. Drink now through 2010.–J.L. • $33/375 ml. • (2/29/2000) • **95**
Sémillon Napa Valley Late Harvest 1992 • $25/375 ml. • (12/31/1995) • **97**
Sémillon Napa Valley Late Harvest 1991 • $25/375 ml. • (5/15/1995) • **88**
Sémillon Napa Valley Late Harvest 1988 • $25/375 ml. • (6/30/1993) • **80**
Syrah Napa Valley 1997: Marked by cedar, blackberry, cherry and anise flavors, turning soft and herbal, with mild tannins. Drink now through 2005.–J.L. • $40 • (6/15/2000) • **86**
Syrah Napa Valley 1996: A well-oaked style with vanilla and toasty notes leading to supple, spicy wild berry, blackberry, anise and sage flavors that are complex and lingering. Tempting now, but worthy of cellaring, too. Drink now through 2005.–J.L. • $40 • (3/31/1999) • **90**
Syrah Napa Valley 1995 • $40 • (3/31/1998) • **88**
Syrah Napa Valley 1994 • $33 • (4/30/1997) • **93**
Syrah Napa Valley 1993 • $30 • (2/29/1996) • **89**
Syrah Napa Valley 1992 • $25 • (1/31/1995) • **87**
Zinfandel Napa Valley 1988 • $12 • (3/31/1993) • **86**

SWEDENBURG | VIRGINIA

Cabernet Sauvignon Virginia 1995: A weak, overly mature Cabernet, with a thin, brownish hue and tired flavors. Not recommended. Tasted twice, with consistent notes. • $14 • (12/31/1998) • **62**
Chantilly Virginia White 1997: This round white offers crisp apple and pear flavors, with good weight on the palate, but a slight rubbery note detracts. Best with assertively flavored food. Made from Seyval Blanc.–T.M. • $7 • (12/15/1998) • **79**
Chardonnay Virginia 1997: The aromas are slightly candied, like toffee and candy apple. The dilute flavors have an earthy edge and turn a little sour on the finish.–B.S. • $10 • (12/15/1998) • **74**
Riesling Virginia 1997: Pleasant, light and simple white wine, with peach and apple flavors and decent balance. • $8 • (11/15/1998) • **79**
Virginia Rosé C'est la vie 1997: This dry rosé is balanced and crisp, with light berry flavors and lively yet not excessive acidity. Straightforward, clean and refreshing. Drink now.–T.M. • $8 • (12/15/1998) • **83**

SWEDISH HILL | NEW YORK

Optimus Finger Lakes 1991 • $15 • (11/15/1994) • **75**
Vignoles Finger Lakes Late Harvest 1992 • $11 • (6/30/1995) • **83**

SYLVESTER | CALIFORNIA

Cabernet Sauvignon Paso Robles Kiara Reserve 1995: Straightforward, with dill, tea, cherry and charred oak notes. Soft on the finish. Drink now.–J.L. • $14 • (10/15/1998) • **80**
Cabernet Sauvignon Paso Robles Kiara Reserve 1988 • $9 • (7/15/1993) • **82**
Merlot Paso Robles Kiara Reserve 1996: A watery, cherrylike wine. Simple. Drink now. • $12 • (9/30/1998) • **71**
Merlot Paso Robles Kiara Reserve Italian Bottling 1996: Focusing on cherry and charred oak notes. Simple and tannic on the finish. Drink now.–J.L. • $17 • (10/15/1998) • **75**

SYLVIANE | CALIFORNIA

Cabernet Sauvignon Napa Valley Le Ducq Vineyards 1995 • $30 • (4/30/1998) • **87**
Merlot Napa Valley 1995: Lean and trim, with a narrow band of currant, sage, spice and cedar, turning greenish on the finish. Drink through 2002. –J.L. • $30 • (10/15/1998) • **82**
Merlot Napa Valley 1994 • $30 • (3/31/1998) • **86**

T VINE | CALIFORNIA

T Napa Valley 1997: Ripe and complex, with a pretty array of juicy plum, currant and cherry. Turns elegant and refined, finishing with tasty toasty oak and earthy mineral nuances. Best from 2001 through 2008.–J.L. • $35 • (5/31/2000) • **91**
Zinfandel Napa Valley 1992 • $10 • (10/15/1995) • **83**

TABLAS CREEK | CALIFORNIA

Tablas Blanc Paso Robles 1998: Subtle, with moderately ripe and complex litchi, tangerine and hazelnut flavors, finishing with richness and depth. A blend of Roussanne, Viognier and Marsanne. Drink now.–J.L. • $27 • (11/30/1999) • **87**
Tablas Blanc Paso Robles 1997: Silky-textured, offering a mineral-like note on the palate followed by hints of apricot, citrus and hazelnut. The total effect is one of integration. Finishes moderately. A blend of Marsanne, Viognier and Roussanne. A first release from Château de Beaucastel's American effort. Drink now. • $35 • (12/15/1998) • **89**
Tablas Rouge Paso Robles 1997: Ripe, with spicy, pleasantly integrated cherry and earthy berry notes. Turns complex and tannic on the finish. Mourvèdre, Grenache, Syrah and Cournoise. Drink now through 2005.–J.L. • $32 • (12/31/1999) • **87**

TABLAS HILLS | CALIFORNIA

Cuvée Blanc Paso Robles 1996: Smooth, with a hint of butterscotch on the nose, this serves up an array of pear, apple, orange, lemon and mineral notes. A blend of Viognier and Roussanne. Drink now. • $20 • (11/15/1998) • **87**
Cuvée Rouge Paso Robles 1996: Simple cherry and herb flavors and soft tannins make this a pleasant, easy-drinking wine. Ready now. • $21 • (12/15/1998) • **83**
Cuvée Rouge Paso Robles 1995 • $20 • (1/01/1998) • **82**

TABULA RASA | WASHINGTON

Columbia Valley Red 1995 • $10 • (11/30/1996) • **86**

TAFT STREET | CALIFORNIA

Cabernet Sauvignon California 1995 • $12 • (4/30/1998) • **84**
Cabernet Sauvignon California 1994 • $11 • (9/15/1997) • **84**
Cabernet Sauvignon California 1992 • $10 • (12/15/1995) • **85**
Cabernet Sauvignon Sonoma County 1991 • $11 • (3/15/1994) • **81**
Cabernet Sauvignon Sonoma County Cask Selection 1997: Medium-bodied, with a pleasant streak of herb through the cherry and plum flavors. Finishes with firm tannins. Drink now.–J.L. • $15 • (10/15/1999) • **83**
Chardonnay Russian River Valley 1998: Soft and buttery, with vanilla notes and ripe, creamy pear flavors in a medium-bodied format, turning smoky. Drink now through 2002.–J.L. • $10 • (4/30/2000) • **86**

Key: SS—Spectator Selection. CS—Cellar Selection. HR—Highly Recommended. $NA—Price not available. (BT)—Barrel tasting. (A)—Auction Price.
For a key to the tasters' initials, see "How to Use These Listings."
Dates in parentheses represent the issues in which the ratings were published.

Chardonnay Sonoma County 1997: Mineral, pear, fig, spice and citrus flavors flow through the smooth, thick texture, while floral and herbal notes add dimension. Drink now.–J.L. • $10 • (6/15/1999) • **86**

Chardonnay Sonoma County 1996: Well focused, with a pear and mineral core, its moderate body and medium balance lend elegance, while the finish is clean and refreshing. A solid Chardonnay offering real value. Drink now. • $10 • (7/31/1998) • **86**

Merlot Central Coast 1997: Shows off a pleasant range of ripe plum, berry, herb and smoky coffee flavors that linger on the finish. Tannins are soft and approachable. Drink now.–J.L. • $14 • (8/31/1999) • **87**

Merlot Sonoma County 1995 • $14 • (4/30/1998) • **77**

Merlot Sonoma County 1994 • $14 • (7/31/1997) • **83**

Merlot Sonoma County 1993 • $13 • (8/31/1996) • **83**

Merlot Sonoma County 1992 • $11 • (1/31/1995) • **81**

Merlot Sonoma County 1991 • $11 • (7/15/1993) • **83**

Merlot Sonoma County 1990 • $12 • (5/31/1992) • **89**

Merlot Sonoma County 1989 • $12 • (5/31/1992) • **85**

Merlot Sonoma County 1985 • $10 • (5/31/1988) • **83**

Merlot Sonoma County Cask Selection 1997: A chunky, rustic, flavorful wine with herb and black cherry notes. Tannins are firm and drying on the finish. Drink through 2004.–J.L. • $14 • (10/15/1999) • **82**

Sauvignon Blanc Russian River Valley 1997: A well-balanced wine, with hints of herb, pear, melon and citrus. Finish is moderate and clean. Drink now. • $9 • (10/31/1998) • **85**

Sauvignon Blanc Russian River Valley 1996 • $9 • (3/31/1998) • **84**

Sauvignon Blanc Russian River Valley Cask Selection 1998: Lemon-lime, grapefruit, melon and tangy acids make this affordable California white a delightful quaff, while also lending substance and structure. It finishes moderately, with a fresh, flinty accent to the aftertaste. Drink now. • $10 • (9/30/1999) • **88**

Zinfandel Sonoma County 1997: Straightforward, featuring light berry, herb and spice notes.–J.L. • $12 • (11/15/1999) • **79**

Zinfandel Sonoma County 1996 • $13 • (3/31/1998) • **87**

TAGARIS | WASHINGTON

Cabernet Sauvignon Columbia Valley 1995 • $15 • (9/30/1997) • **86**

Cabernet Sauvignon Columbia Valley 1994 • $13 • (9/15/1996) • **87**

Cabernet-Merlot Columbia Valley 1996: Firm and chewy, with rich currant and black cherry flavors lurking behind the mint notes and tannic texture. Needs cellaring. Best after 2001.–H.S. • $15 • (6/15/1999) • **87**

Chardonnay Columbia Valley 1996: Lean, racy and sleek, with vibrant green apple, spice and lime flavors that ricochet on the finish. Drink now through 2004.–H.S. • $10 • (6/30/1999) • **86**

Fumé Blanc Columbia Valley 1997: Finishes with pretty nectarine notes, although some earthy, slightly bitter flavors run through it. Drink now.–H.S. • $9 • (6/15/1999) • **80**

Fumé Blanc Columbia Valley 1996 • $8 • (9/30/1997) • **87**

Johannisberg Riesling Columbia Valley 1998: Light and fruity, with grapey, floral flavors that linger nicely on the mostly dry finish. Drink now.–H.S. • $7 • (6/30/1999) • **86**

Johannisberg Riesling Columbia Valley 1993 • $6 • (9/30/1995) • **77**

Johannisberg Riesling Columbia Valley Reserve 1994 • $6 • (9/30/1995) • **87**

Merlot Columbia Valley 1997: Offers nice layers of ripe berry, cinnamon and gentle herb flavors on a velvety frame. Finishes with the flavors and tannins mingling and echoing nicely. Drink now through 2005.–H.S. • $15 • (5/15/2000) • **88**

Merlot Columbia Valley 1996: Firm in texture and generous in character, with layers of spicy black currant and blackberry flavors that linger on the lean, focused finish. Should become more supple with cellaring. Best after 2000.–H.S. • $15 • (6/15/1999) • **87**

Merlot Columbia Valley 1995 • $15 • (9/30/1997) • **87**

Merlot Columbia Valley 1994 • $13 • (9/15/1996) • **89**

TALBOTT | CALIFORNIA

Chardonnay Monterey Cuvée Cynthia 1996: Ripe, lush and concentrated, with a leafy celery edge to the spicy pear, toasty oak and nutmeg-scented flavors. Drink now through 2002.–J.L. • $45 • (2/28/1999) • **92**

Chardonnay Monterey Diamond T Estate 1996: Ripe and buttery, with spicy pear, tangerine, nectarine and honey notes, gaining complexity and nuance, with toasty oak. Drink now through 2004.–J.L. • $25 • (1/31/2000) • **89**

Chardonnay Monterey Sleepy Hollow Vineyard 1997: Deep, ripe, rich and concentrated, with layers of fig, pear, apple and melon, gaining a nice oaky touch of hazelnut and cedar. Finishes with a burst of fruit. Drink now through 2005.–J.L. • $35 • (6/30/2000) SS • **92**

Chardonnay Monterey Sleepy Hollow Vineyard 1996: Impresses with its rich, complex array of pear, peach, spice and nectarine flavors, gaining in intensity and richness before finishing with a flinty mineral aftertaste. Just lovely. Drink now through 2002.–J.L. • $35 • (2/28/1999) HR • **92**

TALISMAN | CALIFORNIA

Pinot Noir Carneros 1996: A tough, tannic young wine that may evolve into a gentler mode, but for now the core of cola, black cherry and minty flavor is hard-edged. Try through 2002.–J.L. • $28 • (12/15/1998) • **83**

Pinot Noir Carneros 1995: An overly minty style, with menthol dominating the flavor profile. Missing are the cherry and berry flavors. Drink now through 2001.–J.L. • $25 • (9/30/1998) • **77**

TALLEY | CALIFORNIA

Chardonnay Arroyo Grande Valley 1998: Tight, with an earthy, claylike edge to the narrow beam of pear, mineral and light oak. Drink now through 2003.–J.L. • $22 • (6/30/2000) • **88**

Chardonnay Arroyo Grande Valley 1997: Intense and sharply focused, with a ripe band of pear, green fig, apple and melon flavors that are fleshy and supple. Drink now through 2002.–J.L. • $22 • (8/31/1999) • **89**

Chardonnay Arroyo Grande Valley 1996: From one of this appellation's first growers comes this supple and creamy Chardonnay, with rich, attractive pear, vanilla, spice and citrus flavors that linger on the elegant, delicate finish. Drink now through 2001.–J.L. • $20 • (7/31/1998) SS • **90**

Chardonnay Arroyo Grande Valley Rincon Vineyard 1997: Ripe and buttery, with smooth, rich, creamy fig, pear, melon, citrus and apple notes. Turns trim and tight on the finish, where the focus narrows. Drink now through 2004.–J.L. • $32 • (11/15/1999) • **92**

Chardonnay Arroyo Grande Valley Rincon Vineyard 1996: Aromatically complex, with yeast, oak and earth aromas. A supple, elegant, concentrated center of ripe pear, fig and melon flavors come together on the finish. Drink through 2002.–J.L. • $30 • (7/31/1998) • **93**

Chardonnay Arroyo Grande Valley Rosemary's Vineyard 1997: Elegant and refined, this is a rich, ripe yet subtle young wine, with a pretty core of pear, fig, spice, melon and apple flavors that turn delicate on the finish. Drink now through 2005.–J.L. • $35 • (11/15/1999) • **93**

Chardonnay Arroyo Grande Valley Rosemary's Vineyard 1996: Smooth, ripe, rich and creamy, with pretty pear, nectarine, peach, fig and melon flavors, all sharply focused and deeply concentrated. Wonderful texture, balance and finesse. Drink through 2002.–J.L. • $30 • (7/31/1998) • **93**

Chardonnay Edna Valley Oliver's Vineyard 1998: Lively, with ripe tangerine, citrus, pear and flinty apple notes that are refreshing. Drink now through 2003.–J.L. • $20 • (5/15/2000) • **87**

Chardonnay Edna Valley Oliver's Vineyard 1997: Smooth, rich and creamy, with polished pear, citrus, fig, melon and apricot flavors that fan out, gaining complexity and nuance. Drink now through 2002.–J.L. • $20 • (4/30/1999) • **91**

Chardonnay Edna Valley Oliver's Vineyard 1996 • $18 • (12/31/1997) SS • **92**

Pinot Noir Arroyo Grande Valley 1997: Starts out smooth and polished, with herb, cherry, strawberry and spice, picking up traces of plum and more spice. Finishes firm. Drink now through 2004.–J.L. • $28 • (9/15/1999) • **87**

Pinot Noir Arroyo Grande Valley 1996: Austere, with a tight ring of tannin wrapped around the core of earthy, slightly stemmy wild berry and black cherry, it slowly unfolds to reveal a solid core of intense, concentrated fruit Drink now through 2003.–J.L. • $25 • (8/31/1998) • **87**

Pinot Noir Arroyo Grande Valley 1994 • $22 • (12/31/1996) • **88**

Pinot Noir Arroyo Grande Valley 1993 • $22 • (9/15/1996) • **87**

Pinot Noir Arroyo Grande Valley 1992 • $20 • (3/31/1995) • **82**

Pinot Noir Arroyo Grande Valley 1990 • $17 • (9/30/1992) • **87**

Pinot Noir Arroyo Grande Valley 1989 • $17 • (10/31/1991) • **75**

Pinot Noir Arroyo Grande Valley Rincon Vineyard 1997: Smooth, ripe, rich and polished, with a pretty core of plum and black cherry, offering hints of sage and anise. Drink now through 2008.–J.L. • $40 • (5/15/2000) • **89**

Pinot Noir Arroyo Grande Valley Rincon Vineyard 1996: Tightly wound, with firm, intense currant, plum and black cherry flavors. Has a lot going for it; just needs time to soften. Drink through 2004.–J.L. • $32 • (8/31/1998) • **88**

Pinot Noir Arroyo Grande Valley Rincon Vineyard 1995 • $30 • (12/15/1997) • **92**

Pinot Noir Arroyo Grande Valley Rincon Vineyard 1994 • $32 • (12/31/1996) • **91**

Pinot Noir Arroyo Grande Valley Rincon Vineyard 1993 • $30 • (12/31/1995) • **85**

Pinot Noir Arroyo Grande Valley Rosemary's Vineyard 1997: Complex for its array of smoky, meaty nuances and core of black cherry fruit, finishing with spice and cedar notes. Drink now through 2007.–J.L. • $45 • (5/15/2000) • **88**

Pinot Noir Arroyo Grande Valley Rosemary's Vineyard 1996: Ultrarich and concentrated, packed with ripe, rich, supple plum, black cherry, currant and berry, rounded out with spice and pretty, toasty oak. Drink now through 2004.–J.L. • $36 • (8/31/1998) • **92**
Pinot Noir Arroyo Grande Valley Rosemary's Vineyard 1995 • $32 • (12/15/1997) • **93**
Pinot Noir Arroyo Grande Valley Rosemary's Vineyard 1994 • $32 • (12/31/1996) • **93**
Pinot Noir Arroyo Grande Valley Rosemary's Vineyard 1993 • $30 • (12/31/1995) • **90**

TALUS | CALIFORNIA

Cabernet Sauvignon California 1995: Light cherry and oak flavors combine with a somewhat waxy texture to produce a simple, pleasant wine. Drink now. • $9 • (10/31/1998) • **80**
Cabernet Sauvignon California 1994 • $9 • (9/15/1997) • **78**
Cabernet Sauvignon California 1993 • $8 • (12/15/1995) • **84**
Chardonnay California 1996: Supple and fruity, with easygoing, ripe and clean pear, apple, citrus and melon flavors. Drink now.–J.L. • $9 • (7/31/1998) • **83**
Merlot California 1997: Simple, featuring herb, currant and cedar notes. Drink now.–J.L. • $9 • (10/15/1999) • **80**
Merlot California 1996: Simple, with well-oaked, light cherry and herb notes. Turns green and drying on the finish. Drink now.–T.G. • $8 • (8/31/1998) • **79**
Merlot California 1995 • $9 • (7/31/1997) • **82**
Merlot California 1994 • $8 • (6/30/1996) • **82**
Pinot Noir California 1995 • $10 • (7/31/1997) • **85**
White Zinfandel California 1996 • $7 • (9/15/1997) • **77**
Zinfandel California 1997: Light and simple, with an almost-candied element followed by plums and canned cherries. • $8 • (6/30/1999) • **78**
Zinfandel California 1995 • $7 • (7/31/1997) • **82**
Zinfandel California 1994 • $8 • (11/30/1996) • **82**
Zinfandel California 1993 • $7 • (3/31/1996) • **82**

TAMAS, IVAN | CALIFORNIA

Cabernet Sauvignon Livermore Valley 1992 • $7 • (12/15/1995) • **80**
Cabernet Sauvignon Livermore Valley Le Clan des Quatre Vineyards 1991 • $8 • (11/15/1993) • **77**
Cabernet Sauvignon Livermore Valley Reserve 1994: Soft, herbal and tart, with odd notes of watermelon and cherry turning dry. Drink now.–H.S. • $15 • (2/28/1999) • **80**
Cabernet Sauvignon Livermore Valley Reserve 1993: A soft style, with flavors of coffee and plum that linger on the moderate finish. Drink now.–J.L. • $14 • (9/30/1998) • **81**
Cabernet Sauvignon Livermore Valley Reserve 1992 • $14 • (9/15/1997) • **86**
Chardonnay Central Coast 1997: Light and elegant, with refreshing pear, citrus and light toast flavors that persist on the soft finish, it's a pleasant mouthful of California's most popular white—at a price that's hard to beat these days. Drink now.–J.L. • $9 • (6/30/1999) • **86**
Chardonnay Central Coast 1996: Bright and simple, with pleasant, earthy citrus notes. Drink now.–T.G. • $9 • (7/31/1998) • **82**
Chardonnay Central Coast Reserve 1997: Pretty, subtle, light-bodied and smooth, featuring delicate nectarine, citrus and pear flavors. Clean, soft and pleasant on the finish. Drink now.–J.L. • $18 • (6/30/1999) • **87**
Zinfandel Livermore Valley 1993 • $9 • (4/30/1997) • **82**
Zinfandel Livermore Valley Beyer Ranch Vineyard 1998: Plum jam and dried berry flavors show good depth if a bit of mustiness on the finish. Drink now through 2002.–J.L. • $14 • (6/15/2000) • **84**
Zinfandel Livermore Valley Beyer Ranch 1995: Earthy, herbal plum flavors finish with a salty mineral edge and signs of oxidation. • $10 • (2/28/1999) • **76**
Zinfandel Livermore Valley Beyer Ranch 1994 • $9 • (6/15/1998) • **83**

TANNER, LANE | CALIFORNIA

Pinot Noir Santa Barbara County 1992 • $20 • (3/31/1995) • **84**

Key: SS—Spectator Selection. CS—Cellar Selection. HR—Highly Recommended. $NA—Price not available. (BT)—Barrel tasting. (A)—Auction Price.
For a key to the tasters' initials, see "How to Use These Listings."
Dates in parentheses represent the issues in which the ratings were published.

Pinot Noir Santa Barbara County 1991 • $20 • (2/28/1993) • **75**
Pinot Noir Santa Barbara County Benedict Vineyard 1989 • $25 • (11/15/1991) • **85**
Pinot Noir Santa Barbara County Sanford & Benedict Vineyard 1993 • $30 • (1/31/1997) • **85**
Pinot Noir Santa Barbara County Sanford & Benedict Vineyard 1992 • $30 • (3/31/1995) • **82**
Pinot Noir Santa Barbara County Sanford & Benedict Vineyard 1991 • $25 • (2/28/1994) • **88**
Pinot Noir Santa Barbara County Sierra Madre Vineyard 1990 • $22 • (9/30/1992) • **84**
Pinot Noir Santa Barbara County Sierra Madre Vineyard Hitching Post 1987 • $25 • (2/28/1993) • **81**
Pinot Noir Santa Maria Valley 1997: Solid, focused, with a mushroomy edge to the cherry and herb flavors. Tight on the finish, but the tannins are integrated. Drink now through 2002.–J.L. • $22 • (9/15/1999) • **87**
Pinot Noir Santa Maria Valley Bien Nacido Vineyard 1997: Shows a delicate range of cinnamon, strawberry and earthy tea flavors, finishing soft. Drink now through 2002.–J.L. • $25 • (9/15/1999) • **84**
Pinot Noir Santa Maria Valley Bien Nacido Vineyard 1996: Lean and spicy, it opens to rhubarb, black cherry, spice and berry notes, with hints of mineral, sage and cedary oak. Given the firm tannins, cellar short-term. Drink through 2004.–J.L. • $25 • (8/31/1998) • **87**
Pinot Noir Santa Maria Valley Bien Nacido Vineyards 1995 • $30 • (12/31/1996) • **85**
Pinot Noir Santa Maria Valley Bien Nacido Vineyards 1994 • $20 • (2/29/1996) • **86**
Pinot Noir Santa Maria Valley Bien Nacido Vineyards Picked Under A Blue Moon 1993 • $22 • (12/31/1995) • **84**
Pinot Noir Santa Maria Valley Julia's Vineyard 1997: Ripe, with an earthy, leathery edge to the wild berry, cherry and mineral flavors. Slightly dry on the finish. Drink now through 2003.–J.L. • $25 • (9/15/1999) • **85**
Pinot Noir Santa Maria Valley Julia's Vineyard 1996: A touch on the green, tannic side, yet also offers tea, black cherry and spicy berry. Finishes with a dry, tannic edge. Drink through 2003.–J.L. • $20 • (8/31/1998) • **86**
Pinot Noir Santa Maria Valley Sierra Madre Vineyard 1996: Clean, crisp and spicy, with tart black cherry, spice and tea, it slowly evolves into a more supple-textured wine, and the finish is focused and lively. Drinks well now but should benefit from short-term cellaring.–J.L. • $25 • (8/31/1998) • **88**
Pinot Noir Santa Maria Valley Sierra Madre Plateau 1995 • $25 • (1/31/1997) • **82**
Pinot Noir Santa Maria Valley Sierra Madre Plateau 1994 • $20 • (2/29/1996) • **88**

TANTALUS | CALIFORNIA

Cabernet Sauvignon Sonoma County 1994: Firm, with well-focused black cherry, olive, anise and tar flavors. Finishes with moderate length and mild tannins. Drink now through 2001. • $18 • (2/28/1999) • **84**
Meritage Sonoma County 1991 • $16 • (7/31/1995) • **83**
Meritage Sonoma County 1989 • $15 • (7/15/1992) • **86**

TARARA | VIRGINIA

Cabernet Frederick County 1989 • $12 • (2/29/1992) • **82**
Cabernet Sauvignon Virginia 1997: Sweet cherry and red berry flavors dominate this medium-bodied red, with a strong minty note. Finishes with some bittersweet chocolate notes. Drink now.–K.M. • $16 • (10/15/1999) • **83**
Chardonnay Virginia 1997: Light on aroma and flavor, with modest apple and vanilla. Light-bodied and simple.–B.S. • $13 • (12/15/1998) • **78**
Meritage Virginia 1997: A bit muddled with dark plum and stewed flavors and chocolaty notes on the drying finish. A blend of Cabernet Sauvignon, Merlot and Cabernet Franc.–K.M. • $19 • (10/15/1999) • **78**
Pinot Noir Virginia 1997: This shows berry and spice notes, with modest varietal character, moderate intensity and light body. The finish is a little coarse.–B.S. • $15 • (6/15/1999) • **78**
Vidal Blanc Virginia 1997: Light and lean, an off-dry style, showing modest peach and pear aromas and flavors that tail off quickly.–B.S. • $13/375 ml. • (7/31/1999) • **78**

TARIUS | CALIFORNIA

Pinot Noir Chalone 1997: Well oaked, with toasty vanilla notes. Enough plum and cherry flavor folds in underneath to give dimension and depth. Drink now through 2006.–J.L. • $36 • (1/31/2000) • **88**

Pinot Noir Santa Lucia Highlands Pisoni Vineyard 1997: Firm, with a band of coffee, currant and cherry and a touch of vanilla-scented oak. A well-dressed young Pinot that needs a little time. Drink through 2005.–J.L. • $39 • (1/31/2000) • **87**

Zinfandel Alexander Valley Demonstene Vineyard 1997: Light and refreshing, with sweet-tasting blueberry, plum and curry flavors that linger on the finish. Drink now through 2004.–J.L. • $27 • (1/31/2000) • **86**

TAY | CALIFORNIA

Cabernet Sauvignon Napa Valley 1993 • $35 • (4/30/1996) • **92**

TEFFT | WASHINGTON

Cabernet Sauvignon Columbia Valley 1996: Firm in texture, with fine tannins and modest berry, cinnamon and black pepper notes ringing on the light finish. Drink now through 2002.–H.S. • $20 • (9/30/1999) • **84**

Cabernet Sauvignon Yakima Valley 1995: Dense and chewy. Front-loaded with plenty of black cherry and anise flavor, adding a mouthful of chewy tannins to the finish. Needs time; best from 2001 through 2010.–H.S. • $22 • (7/31/1998) • **86**

Cabernet Sauvignon Yakima Valley 1994 • $25 • (11/30/1997) • **85**

Cabernet Sauvignon Yakima Valley 1993 • $23 • (9/15/1996) • **84**

Cabernet Sauvignon Yakima Valley 1992 • $20 • (9/30/1995) • **91**

Cabernet Sauvignon Yakima Valley 1991 • $13 • (9/30/1994) • **79**

Cabernet Sauvignon Yakima Valley Winemakers Reserve 1995: Firm in texture, this crisp red has a distinctive anise tinge to the blackberry and pepper flavors, which linger appealingly. Approachable now. Best after 2001.–H.S. • $20 • (6/15/1999) • **88**

Cabernet Sauvignon Yakima Valley Winemakers Reserve 1994 • $30 • (11/30/1997) • **83**

Merlot Columbia Valley NV: A bit coarse and rustic, but the black cherry and slightly herbal flavors have enough pizzazz to carry it. Drink now.–H.S. • $15 • (7/31/1998) • **83**

Merlot Columbia Valley 1991 • $13 • (6/15/1993) • **88**

Merlot Yakima Valley 1997: Sleek and spicy, with pretty nutmeg-scented berry and cherry flavors lingering on the smooth finish. Drink now.–H.S. • $15 • (8/31/1999) • **85**

Merlot Yakima Valley 1995 • $16 • (11/30/1997) • **87**

Merlot Yakima Valley 1994 • $16 • (9/15/1996) • **85**

Merlot Yakima Valley 1993 • $14 • (9/30/1995) • **83**

Merlot Yakima Valley Winemaker's Reserve 1997: Coarse in texture, with a core of black cherry flavor that peeks through some rough edges of tannin. Best after 2000.–H.S. • $17 • (9/30/1999) • **82**

Pinot Grigio Columbia Valley 1998: Bright, vivid flavors of apple, melon and spice balance appealingly on a light frame. A refreshing wine to enjoy as an aperitif or with a first course. Drink now.–H.S. • $9 • (6/30/1999) • **87**

Pinot Grigio Columbia Valley Crystal Pheasant Vineyard 1997: Bright, crisp and light-textured, with floral, citrusy pear flavors on a sleek frame. Drink now for its freshness.–H.S. • $8 • (7/31/1998) • **85**

Proprietor's Red Columbia Valley NV • $10 • (9/30/1995) • **85**

Red Table Wine Yakima Valley NV • $10 • (9/30/1994) • **83**

Sangiovese Yakima Valley 1997: Has a strong floral streak running through the lively raspberry and vanilla flavors. Firm but not overly tannic. Drink now through 2001.–H.S. • $20 • (9/30/1999) • **84**

Syrah Yakima Valley 1997: Smoky, tarry aromas distinguish this crisp red, slightly chewy from tannin. It picks up some berry flavor on the light finish, but it's not a typically big Syrah. Best after 2000.–H.S. • $22 • (9/30/1999) • **81**

TELDESCHI | CALIFORNIA

Moscato Dry Creek Valley Frontignan NV • $11 • (12/31/1995) • **87**

Zinfandel Dry Creek Valley 1991 • $15 • (7/31/1996) • **85**

Zinfandel Sonoma County 1990 • $10 • (10/15/1995) • **84**

TERNHAVEN | NEW YORK

Cabernet Sauvignon North Fork of Long Island 1995: This delicate red has a distinctive and appealing liveliness, with vivid blackberry and vanilla flavors, firm yet not aggressive tannins and a pretty floral finish. A nice combination of finesse and intensity. Drink now through 2003.–T.M. • $18 • (6/30/1999) • **86**

Merlot North Fork of Long Island 1995: Rich and velvety in texture, this jammy red shows flavors of plum, chocolate and toast, with a disconcerting dill pickle note that mars the pleasure. The finish is quite dry.–T.M. • $20 • (6/30/1999) • **79**

TERRA | CALIFORNIA

Cabernet Franc Napa Valley 1990 • $15 • (2/28/1995) • **82**

Cabernet Sauvignon Napa Valley 1990 • $13 • (1/01/1994) • **79**

Merlot Napa Valley 1988 • $14 • (5/31/1992) • **84**

TERRA ROSA | CALIFORNIA

Cabernet Sauvignon North Coast 1995 • $11 • (8/31/1997) • **87**

Cabernet Sauvignon North Coast 1994 • $11 • (10/15/1996) • **82**

Cabernet Sauvignon North Coast 1992 • $10 • (4/30/1995) SS • **88**

Cabernet Sauvignon Napa Valley 1990 • $9 • (9/30/1993) • **89**

Cabernet Sauvignon Sonoma County 1989 • $9 • (7/15/1992) • **86**

Red Napa Valley 1988 • $12 • (11/15/1990) • **85**

Red Napa Valley 1987 • $14 • (7/31/1990) • **86**

TERRA VIN | CALIFORNIA

Vigil Vineyard Napa Valley NV • $11 • (2/29/1996) • **88**

TERRACES | CALIFORNIA

Cabernet Sauvignon Napa Valley 1996: Sharply focused, with a ripe, rich, complex beam of currant, black cherry, herb, olive, anise, cedar and spice, finishing with firm but supple tannins and a lingering aftertaste. Best from 2001 through 2009.–J.L. • $50 • (10/31/1999) • **92**

Cabernet Sauvignon Napa Valley 1995: Smooth and creamy even with its core of firm tannins, this wine unveils an appealing array of vanilla, currant, plum, anise, sage and cedary notes and, again, the tannins weigh in strongly. Best from 2001 through 2007.–J.L. • $50 • (4/30/1999) • **92**

Cabernet Sauvignon Napa Valley 1994: Dill, cedar and anise flavors precede currant and black cherry flavors of depth, richness and complexity. Needs time to soften. Drink through 2009.–J.L. • $50 • (10/31/1998) • **91**

Cabernet Sauvignon Napa Valley 1993 • $40 • (11/30/1997) • **91**

Cabernet Sauvignon Napa Valley 1992 • $40 • (2/28/1997) • **88**

Cabernet Sauvignon Napa Valley 1991 • $40 • (10/31/1995) • **88**

Cabernet Sauvignon Napa Valley 1990 • $40 • (11/15/1994) • **86**

Cabernet Sauvignon Napa Valley 1989 • $40 • (11/15/1993) • **89**

Cabernet Sauvignon Napa Valley 1988 • $40 • (3/31/1993) • **88**

Cabernet Sauvignon Napa Valley 1987 • $38 • (12/15/1997) • **90**

Cabernet Sauvignon Napa Valley 1986 • $NA • (12/15/1996) • **89**

Zinfandel Napa Valley 1997: Trim and on the austere side, with dried cherry and dried berry flavors of moderate depth and proportion. Drink now through 2004.–J.L. • $25 • (12/15/1999) • **86**

Zinfandel Napa Valley 1995 • $20 • (12/15/1997) • **92**

Zinfandel Napa Valley 1994 • $20 • (2/28/1997) • **90**

Zinfandel Napa Valley 1993 • $20 • (9/15/1996) • **87**

Zinfandel Napa Valley 1992 • $16 • (10/15/1995) • **88**

Zinfandel Napa Valley 1991 • $13 • (10/15/1994) • **87**

Zinfandel Napa Valley 1990 • $15 • (6/15/1994) • **84**

Zinfandel Napa Valley 1989 • $13 • (3/31/1993) • **87**

Zinfandel Napa Valley 1988 • $13 • (2/29/1992) • **86**

Zinfandel Napa Valley 1987 • $13 • (2/15/1991) • **89**

Zinfandel Napa Valley Hogue Vineyard 1985 • $13 • (10/31/1988) • **87**

TESSERA | CALIFORNIA

Cabernet Sauvignon California 1996: Simple, with charry toasted oak and light cherry flavors. Finishes firm, with an herbal note.–J.L. • $10 • (11/15/1999) • **79**

Cabernet Sauvignon California 1995 • $10 • (6/30/1998) • **84**

Cabernet Sauvignon California 1994 • $9 • (11/30/1996) • **80**

Chardonnay California 1996: Clean and lively, with pleasant citrus-laced pear and apple flavors. Drink now.–J.L. • $10 • (7/31/1998) • **81**

Merlot California 1996: Smoothly textured, with tangy cherry flavors up front, but not much behind it. Ends on a woody note. Drink now. • $10 • (7/31/1998) • **80**

Merlot California 1995 • $10 • (2/28/1997) • **86**

Merlot California 1994 • $9 • (6/30/1996) • **86**

Zinfandel California Old Vine 1996 • $10 • (6/15/1998) • **78**

Zinfandel California Old Vine 1995 • $10 • (12/31/1996) • **85**

TESTAROSSA | CALIFORNIA

Chardonnay California George Troquato Signature Reserve 1997: Serves up a wide range of spicy, fruity flavors, with pear, fig, apple, melon, citrus and apricot. Holds its focus, turning elegant and complex. Drink now through 2004.–J.L. • $39 • (12/31/1999) • **91**

Chardonnay California George Troquato Signature Reserve 1996: Wonderful ripeness, richness and complexity, with layers of pear, hazelnut, fig, apricot and citrus notes. Full-bodied and concentrated. Drink now through 2005. –J.L. • $39 • (11/15/1999) • **93**

Chardonnay Chalone 1997: Strikes a fine balance between the ripe peach, mineral and light toasty oak flavors and the beam of citrus-supported acidity. Drink now through 2003.–J.L. • $30 • (4/30/2000) • **89**

Chardonnay Chalone 1996: A wine of elegance and finesse, with ripe, spicy pear, fig and toasty oak, picking up a tinge of earthy mushroom on the aftertaste, where it gains nuance and dimension. Drink through 2002.–J.L. • $28 • (11/30/1998) • **90**

Chardonnay Chalone Michaud Vineyard 1997: Fresh, crisp and a touch earthy, with grapefruit, pear, hazelnut and cedary oak flavors that turn complex on the finish. Drink now through 2003.–J.L. • $39 • (7/31/1999) • **91**

Chardonnay Santa Lucia Highlands Sleepy Hollow Vineyard 1997: Rich and oaky, with firm, buttery, cedary flavors dominating the core of pear, apple, melon, anise and spice. Complex finish. Drink now through 2004.–J.L. • $32 • (12/31/1999) • **89**

Chardonnay Santa Maria Valley 1998: Rich and creamy, with tightly focused citrus, nectarine, tangerine and subtle tropical notes. Finishes with bright acidity. Drink now through 2004.–J.L. • $26 • (6/30/2000) • **88**

Chardonnay Santa Maria Valley 1997: Ripe and vibrant, with complex, concentrated pear, spice, vanilla, honey and pineapple flavors, all sharply focused and long and rich on the finish. Drink now through 2004.–J.L. • $26 • (12/31/1999) • **91**

Chardonnay Santa Maria Valley 1996: A wine with a wonderful sense of harmony and finesse. Deliciously rich and smoky, with a smooth, creamy texture and lots of fig, vanilla and apricot, showing hints of anise and citrus on the finish. Drink now through 2001.–J.L. • $24 • (11/30/1998) • **92**

Chardonnay Santa Maria Valley Bien Nacido Vineyard 1997: Brilliant fruit. Ripe, generous, supple and complex, with lots of fresh, ripe pear, peach, fig, tangerine and spice nuances. Finishes with a pretty array of toasty oak. Drink now through 2006.–J.L. • $32 • (11/15/1999) • **94**

Chardonnay Santa Maria Valley Bien Nacido Vineyard 1996: A tremendous wine, ripe, complex and concentrated, rich and sharply focused, brimming with pear, fig, apricot and spicy fruit flavors. The finish goes on and on. Drink now through 2002.–J.L. • $28 • (11/30/1998) • **93**

Pinot Blanc Chalone 1996: Tight, tart and flinty, with a rich, complex core of pear, peach and hazelnut. Picks up a slight nutty edge on the finish. Drink now through 2002.–J.L. • $21 • (12/15/1998) • **88**

Pinot Noir Santa Lucia Highlands Pisoni Vineyard 1997: Ripe and supple, with a core of cedar, cherry, raspberry, anise and smoked meat flavors that turn rich, supple and quite elegant. Drink through 2004.–J.L. • $36 • (8/31/1999) • **89**

Pinot Noir Santa Lucia Highlands Sleepy Hollow Vineyard 1997: Deliciously ripe, bold and deeply flavored, with layers of plum, black cherry, blackberry and spice. Long, complex, intricate finish. Drink now through 2007.–J.L. • $32 • (1/31/2000) • **92**

Pinot Noir Santa Maria Valley 1997: A medium-weight mix of ripe cherry, plum, herb and tea flavors, turning silky, with a modest tannic bite. Drink now through 2003.–J.L. • $26 • (9/15/1999) • **87**

Viognier Chalone 1997: Subtle and understated, with hints of grapefruit, guava, litchi and macadamia nut flavors. Drink now through 2004.–J.L. • $28 • (11/30/1999) • **86**

Viognier Chalone 1996: Shows off an earthy side, then folds in ripe, rich, creamy pear, fig and melon flavors that linger on, gaining spicy notes. Drink now through 2001.–J.L. • $28 • (12/15/1998) • **89**

THACKREY, SEAN H. | CALIFORNIA

Mourvèdre California Taurus 1989 • $24 • (8/31/1991) • **86**
Mourvèdre California Taurus 1988 • $24 • (9/30/1990) • **86**

Key: SS—Spectator Selection. CS—Cellar Selection. HR—Highly Recommended. $NA—Price not available. (BT)—Barrel tasting. Ⓐ—Auction Price. For a key to the tasters' initials, see "How to Use These Listings."
Dates in parentheses represent the issues in which the ratings were published.

Orion California Rossi Vineyard Old Vines 1996: Openly ripe and grapey, this is dark, rich and concentrated, with hints of currant, anise, sage and spice. Packs in lots of flavor and a wall of tannins, with a long, rich aftertaste. Drink through 2008.–J.L. • $60 • (12/31/1998) • **91**

Orion California Rossi Vineyard Old Vines 1995 • $45 • (3/31/1998) • **88**
Petite Sirah Napa Valley Marston Vineyard Sirius Old Vines 1989 • $24 • (8/31/1991) • **87**
Petite Sirah Napa Valley Sirius Doomed Vines 1992 • $24 • (11/30/1996) • **91**

Pleiades VII California Old Vines NV: Serves up fresh, effusive grape, plum and herb flavors, striking a fine balance between fruity and firm. Supple and smooth. A ripe one that's ready to quaff; drink now. • $18 • (2/28/1999) • **86**

Pleiades Old Vines V California NV • $15 • (11/30/1996) • **88**
Pleiades Old Vines California NV • $15 • (12/15/1995) • **88**
Pleiades Old Vines California 1991 • $20 • (10/31/1993) • **84**
Pleiades California NV • $15 • (6/30/1992) • **83**
Syrah California Orion 1994 • $38 • (11/30/1996) • **91**
Syrah California Orion 1992 • $30 • (12/15/1995) • **91**
Syrah Napa Valley Orion 1990 • $62 Ⓐ • (10/31/1993) • **83**
Syrah Napa Valley Orion 1989 • $45 • (12/31/1991) • **90**
Syrah Napa Valley Orion 1988 • $30 • (9/30/1990) • **89**
Syrah Napa Valley Orion 1987 • $34 Ⓐ • (9/30/1989) • **92**
Syrah Napa Valley Orion 1986 • $26 • (4/15/1989) • **83**
Syrah Napa Valley Rossi Vineyard Orion 1993 • $30 • (4/30/1996) • **91**

THOMAS | OREGON

Pinot Noir Willamette Valley 1996: Light and crisp, with mature mushroom and dried orange peel notes around hints of cherry, finishing with more intensity than the light texture would suggest. Drink now through 2001.–H.S. • $26 • (4/30/1999) • **84**

Pinot Noir Willamette Valley 1994 • $27 • (7/31/1997) • **90**
Pinot Noir Willamette Valley 1991 • $17 • (11/15/1994) • **91**

THOMAS, PAUL | WASHINGTON

Cabernet Sauvignon Columbia Valley 1993 • $9 • (3/31/1995) • **87**
Cabernet Sauvignon Columbia Valley 1992 • $10 • (9/30/1994) • **78**

Cabernet Sauvignon Washington 1997: Light in color and weight, with pretty strawberry and spice flavors. Not much that says Cabernet, but a nice drink. Try now.–H.S. • $9 • (9/30/1999) • **81**

Cabernet Sauvignon Washington 1995 • $8 • (6/15/1997) • **85**
Cabernet Sauvignon Washington 1994 • $10 • (3/31/1996) • **84**
Cabernet Sauvignon Washington 1989 • $12 • (3/31/1992) • **80**
Cabernet Sauvignon Washington 1986 • $14 • (9/30/1990) • **84**
Cabernet Sauvignon Washington 1985 • $20 • (10/15/1989) • **88**
Cabernet Sauvignon Washington Reserve 1995 • $15 • (9/15/1997) • **88**
Cabernet Sauvignon Washington Reserve 1988 • $15 • (3/15/1994) • **80**
Cabernet Sauvignon Washington Reserve 1987 • $16 • (3/31/1992) • **86**
Cabernet-Merlot Columbia Valley 1993 • $9 • (3/31/1995) • **87**
Cabernet-Merlot Columbia Valley 1992 • $10 • (8/31/1994) • **87**
Cabernet-Merlot Columbia Valley 1991 • $10 • (12/31/1993) • **80**

Cabernet-Merlot Washington 1997: Light in color; a simple red with pretty strawberry and mint flavors. Drink now.–H.S. • $9 • (9/30/1999) • **81**

Cabernet-Merlot Washington 1995 • $10 • (6/15/1997) • **84**
Cabernet-Merlot Washington 1994 • $10 • (6/15/1996) • **84**

Chardonnay Columbia Valley Reserve 1997: Light and spicy, with a tarry, smoky, slightly bitter edge to the modest apple character.–H.S. • $10 • (9/30/1999) • **79**

Johannisberg Riesling Columbia Valley Select Harvest 1994 • $6 • (9/30/1995) • **85**

Johannisberg Riesling Washington 1997: Soft and lightly sweet, with pretty pear and floral flavors. Drink now.–H.S. • $6 • (9/15/1998) • **81**

Lemberger Columbia Valley 1995: Supple and generous with its currant and black cherry flavors, open-textured and easy to slurp. Drink now.–H.S. • $8 • (9/15/1998) • **85**

Merlot Columbia Valley 1993 • $9 • (6/15/1995) • **78**
Merlot Columbia Valley 1992 • $9 • (4/30/1995) • **87**

Merlot Washington 1997: Very light, just a little darker than a rosé, with modest berry and floral flavors on a delicate frame. Drink now.–H.S. • $9 • (9/30/1999) • **82**

Merlot Washington 1996: Firm in texture, with enough pretty currant and spice flavors to balance the chewy, fine tannins. Drink through 2003.–H.S. • $13 • (8/31/1998) • **85**

Merlot Washington 1995 • $13 • (9/15/1997) • **84**
Merlot Washington 1987 • $16 • (9/30/1990) • **89**

Merlot Washington Reserve 1990 • $15 • (5/15/1994) • **79**
Merlot Washington Reserve 1989 • $15 • (3/31/1992) • **79**
Rattlesnake Red Washington 1995 • $10 • (9/15/1997) • **85**
Riesling Columbia Valley 1998: Soft and sweet, with a welcome apricot edge to the pretty apple flavors. Drink now.–H.S. • $6 • (9/30/1999) • **83**

THORNTON | CALIFORNIA

Brut California NV: Fresh and clean, with hints of lemon and herbs. Finishes moderately, with bright acidity. Drink now. • $11 • (10/15/1999) • **82**
Brut California Reserve 1992: Unusual in its mild-mannered approach, serving up some floral, honey and citrus. Quite understated. Drink now. • $25 • (12/15/1998) • **81**
Côte Red Limited Bottling South Coast 1996: Earthy, spicy aromas are followed by bright cherry, plum and strawberry on the palate. Finish is a bit drying, though the fruit hangs in nicely. Drink now through 2002. • $15 • (12/15/1998) • **86**
Cuvée de Frontignan California NV: Simple and peachlike. An easy quaffer. Drink now. • $11 • (10/15/1999) • **80**
Cuvée de Frontignan California Artist Series NV • $12 • (11/30/1996) • **78**
Cuvée Rouge California Artist Series NV • $12 • (11/30/1996) • **86**
Gioveto Limited Bottling South Coast 1994 • $16 • (11/30/1996) • **88**
Pinot Noir San Luis Obispo County Coastal Reserve 1994 • $18 • (2/29/1996) • **72**
Zinfandel Cucamonga Valley Old Vine Limited Bottling 1996: Ripe, juicy flavors of blackberry, black licorice and sarsaparilla laced with spicy, leathery notes. Firm tannins. Drink now.–H.S. • $17 • (11/30/1998) • **83**
Zinfandel South Coast Limited Bottling 1994 • $12 • (3/31/1996) • **85**

THUNDER MOUNTAIN | CALIFORNIA

Cabernet Sauvignon Cienega Valley Miller Vineyards Doc's 1997: Strives for complexity with its deep color and lavish oak. Teeters on going overboard, with very ripe, rich, plush currant, black cherry, stewed plum and berryish notes. Best from 2003 through 2010.–J.L. • $48 • (4/30/2000) • **90**
Cabernet Sauvignon Santa Cruz Mountains Bates Ranch 1997: Very dark and ripe, a high-extract style with layers of rich stewed plum, wild berry, cherry and spice. Packs a full load of fruit and oak. Best from 2004 through 2012.–J.L. • $48 • (4/30/2000) • **91**
Cabernet Sauvignon Santa Cruz Mountains Bates Ranch 1996: Sharp and focused, with concentrated mushroom-tinged berry flavors, and toasted oak and coffee notes that linger on the finish. Best from 2001 through 2006.–J.L. • $39 • (9/15/1999) • **88**
Cabernet Sauvignon Santa Cruz Mountains Bates Ranch 1995 • $35 • (11/15/1997) • **85**
Cabernet Sauvignon Santa Cruz Mountains Beauregard Ranch 1995: A bit tart, with bright cherry and blackberry tones. Herb and anise persevere on the squeaky-clean finish. A lean style. Drink now through 2002. • $45 • (10/31/1998) • **83**
Chardonnay Cienega Valley DeRose Vineyard 1998: Deep yellow gold, this moderately rich and extracted wine is framed by plenty of toasty oak. Flavors of toasty pineapple, macaroon, vanilla and coconut turn dry. Drink now through 2005.–J.L. • $34 • (4/30/2000) • **87**
Chardonnay Santa Cruz Mountains Bald Mountain Vineyard 1997: Complex earth tones have honey, fig, melon, herb and pear notes. This full-bodied wine pulls no punches, delivering gobs of flavor couched in plush oak. The finish is long and seductive. A big, beautiful wine. Drink now through 2002.–J.L. • $29 • (7/31/1999) • **93**
Chardonnay Santa Cruz Mountains Bald Mountain Vineyard 1996 • $29 • (6/30/1998) • **91**
Chardonnay Santa Cruz Mountains Matteson Vineyard 1996 • $29 • (6/30/1998) • **92**
Merlot Cienega Valley 1998: Flat and dull, with earthy, leathery flavors and only a glimmer of dried cherry and plum.–J.L. • $32 • (4/30/2000) • **78**
Star Ruby Santa Cruz Mountains Bates Ranch 1996: Smooth and flavorful, with mature cola, cherry, mushroom and herb flavors, finishing with polished tannins. Drink now through 2004.–J.L. • $49 • (9/15/1999) • **87**

TITUS | CALIFORNIA

Cabernet Sauvignon Napa Valley 1994 • $22 • (4/30/1998) • **87**
Cabernet Sauvignon Napa Valley 1992 • $19 • (12/15/1995) • **85**
Zinfandel Napa Valley 1997: Medium in weight, with a simple band of cherry and strawberry. Drink now.–J.L. • $17 • (6/30/2000) • **84**
Zinfandel Napa Valley 1996 • $17 • (5/31/1998) • **83**

TOBIN JAMES | CALIFORNIA

Cabernet Franc San Luis Obispo County Quasar 1995 • $18 • (3/31/1998) • **78**
Cabernet Franc San Luis Obispo County Constellation 1994 • $14 • (11/30/1996) • **86**
Cabernet Sauvignon Paso Robles James Gang Reserve 1996: Herbal, but smooth and ripe-textured, with stewed fruit flavors. Flavorful, but lacks finesse. Drink now through 2004.–J.L. • $20 • (10/15/1999) • **83**
Cabernet Sauvignon San Luis Obispo County Morning Star 1995 • $14 • (3/31/1998) • **83**
Cabernet Sauvignon San Luis Obispo County Super Star 1994 • $14 • (11/30/1996) • **79**
Cabernet Sauvignon San Luis Obispo County Star Light 1993 • $14 • (3/31/1996) • **84**
Cabernet Sauvignon San Luis Obispo County Twilight 1991 • $12 • (11/15/1993) • **86**
Cabernet Sauvignon Paso Robles Private Stash 1990 • $12 • (11/15/1992) • **84**
Cabernet Sauvignon Paso Robles Private Stash 1989 • $12 • (8/31/1992) • **88**
Chardonnay Paso Robles Summer Sunshine 1996 • $13 • (12/31/1997) • **80**
Chateau Le Cacheflo Central Coast NV • $8 • (11/30/1996) • **80**
Chateau Le Cacheflo Paso Robles NV • $6 • (7/31/1993) • **82**
Dessert Zinfandel Paso Robles James Gang Reserve 1996 • $16/375 ml. • (12/31/1997) • **89**
Merlot Paso Robles 7th Heaven 1996: Modest flavors of bright cherry, currant and berry laced with hints of herb. Drink now.–J.L. • $16 • (10/15/1998) • **82**
Merlot Paso Robles Midnight Star 1995 • $16 • (3/31/1998) • **83**
Merlot Paso Robles Lucky Star 1994 • $15 • (12/31/1996) • **84**
Merlot San Luis Obispo County Made in the Shade 1992 • $14 • (3/31/1995) • **84**
Merlot Paso Robles Full Moon 1991 • $14 • (6/15/1993) • **86**
Pinot Noir Monterey County Elegance 1995 • $16 • (1/31/1998) • **87**
Pinot Noir Monterey County High Noon 1994 • $14 • (2/28/1997) • **82**
Pinot Noir Santa Barbara County Black Tie 1992 • $13 • (3/31/1995) • **84**
Pinot Noir Santa Barbara County Sunshine 1990 • $14 • (11/30/1992) • **86**
Syrah Paso Robles Bulls Eye 1996: Shows hints of blueberry, black cherry, spice and earth flavors, all blending harmoniously. The texture is velvety, with a finish that's moderate and somewhat herbal. Drink now through 2002. • $15 • (2/28/1999) • **87**
Syrah Paso Robles Bodacious 1995 • $14 • (3/31/1998) • **82**
Syrah Paso Robles Smokey 1994 • $13 • (11/30/1996) • **88**
Syrah Paso Robles High Five 1992 • $13 • (8/31/1995) • **87**
Zinfandel Late Harvest Paso Robles James Gang Reserve 1994 • $16 Ⓐ /375 ml. • (11/30/1996) • **85**
Zinfandel Late Harvest Paso Robles Solar Flair 1991 • $11 • (10/15/1994) • **85**
Zinfandel Paso Robles Ballistic 1996: Pepper, spice, dried strawberry and plum flavors here, finishing with orange peel and earthy, herbal notes. Slightly dry tannins. Drink now. • $15 • (2/28/1999) • **83**
Zinfandel Paso Robles Big Time 1991 • $12 • (6/15/1993) • **82**
Zinfandel Paso Robles Blue Moon Reserve 1991 • $14 • (6/15/1993) • **84**
Zinfandel Paso Robles Blue Moon Reserve 1990 • $12 • (12/15/1992) • **84**
Zinfandel Paso Robles Commemorative 1997: Simple, with juicy cherry and vanilla flavors framed by oak notes. Drink now.–J.L. • $30 • (5/15/2000) • **82**
Zinfandel Paso Robles Flag Ship 1993 • $14 • (4/30/1996) • **84**
Zinfandel Paso Robles James Gang Reserve 1997: Funky, earthy notes and ripe berry flavors turn muddled.–J.L. • $22 • (5/31/2000) • **77**
Zinfandel Paso Robles James Gang Reserve 1996: A bright, juicy, lively, medium-weight style, with attractive cherry, plum and berry flavors that are clean, focused and long. Ready now.–J.L. • $22 • (6/30/1999) • **87**
Zinfandel Paso Robles James Gang Reserve 1995 • $20 • (3/31/1998) • **87**
Zinfandel Paso Robles James Gang Reserve 1994 • $20 • (10/15/1996) • **87**
Zinfandel Paso Robles James Gang Reserve 1993 • $20 • (4/30/1996) • **81**
Zinfandel Paso Robles Solar Flair 1992 • $10 • (10/15/1994) • **84**
Zinfandel Paso Robles Solar Flair 1991 • $12/375 ml. • (1/31/1993) • **87**
Zinfandel Paso Robles Wild Child 1994 • $18 • (4/30/1997) • **88**

TOGNI, PHILIP | CALIFORNIA

Ca' Togni Napa Valley 1992 • $20/375 ml. • (8/31/1996) • **88**
Cabernet Sauvignon Napa Valley 1997: Definitely an earthy, beefy and leathery red, but that's just part of the story as its mineral, currant, berry and cedar notes grow in complexity and turn elegant, yet retain a hearty, rustic edge. Drink now through 2010.–J.L. • $65 • (5/31/2000) CS • **91**
Cabernet Sauvignon Napa Valley 1996: Distinctive for its coffee bean, herbal and complex berry flavors, this wine is intense, with a chewy core of currant and blackberry flavors. Best to cellar short-term, although it's less

rustic and backward at this stage than in previous vintages. Best from 2001 through 2008.–J.L. • $81 Ⓐ • (5/15/1999) • **93**
Cabernet Sauvignon Napa Valley 1994 • $89 Ⓐ • (11/15/1996) • **90**
Cabernet Sauvignon Napa Valley 1993 • $48 Ⓐ • (5/31/1996) • **87**
Cabernet Sauvignon Napa Valley 1992 • $76 Ⓐ • (11/15/1994) CS • **91**
Cabernet Sauvignon Napa Valley 1991 • $72 Ⓐ • (11/15/1993) • **90**
Cabernet Sauvignon Napa Valley 1990 • $68 Ⓐ • (11/15/1992) • **92**
Cabernet Sauvignon Napa Valley 1989 • $30 • (8/31/1992) • **84**
Cabernet Sauvignon Napa Valley 1988: Wine of the vintage? Has more ripeness, richness, depth, detail and concentration than any other in this tasting. Serves up a wide range of chunky currant, wild berry, herb and olive and even a touch of green bean, but also some exotic spice qualities. Best of all, the finish is rich, focused and complex. (1988 California Cabernet retrospective tasting). Drink now through 2005.–J.L. • $26 • (11/15/1998) • **90**
Cabernet Sauvignon Napa Valley 1987 • $24 • (12/15/1997) • **93**
Cabernet Sauvignon Napa Valley 1986 • $NA • (12/15/1996) • **89**
Cabernet Sauvignon Napa Valley Tanbark Hill Vineyard 1988 • $24 • (6/30/1991) • **87**

TOPAZ | CALIFORNIA

Rouge de Trois Napa Valley 1991 • $17 • (12/15/1995) • **84**
Rouge de Trois Napa Valley 1990 • $16 • (6/30/1993) • **82**
Rouge de Trois Napa Valley 1988 • $15 • (11/15/1991) • **87**
Sauvignon Blanc-Sémillon Late Harvest Napa Valley Special Select 1994 • $25/375 ml. • (11/30/1996) • **91**
Sauvignon Blanc-Sémillon Late Harvest Napa Valley Special Select 1991 • $19/375 ml. • (6/15/1994) • **87**
Sauvignon Blanc-Sémillon Late Harvest Napa Valley Special Select 1989 • $19/375 ml. • (8/31/1991) • **90**

TOPEL | CALIFORNIA

Cabernet Sauvignon Mendocino Hidden Vineyard Reserve 1997: Firm, with herbal and chunky black currant flavors. Dry tannins on the finish. Best from 2001 through 2005.–J.L. • $46 • (6/30/2000) • **83**
Cabernet Sauvignon Mendocino Proprietor's Reserve 1993 • $40 • (4/30/1998) • **84**

TOPOLOS | CALIFORNIA

Cabernet Sauvignon Sonoma County 1992 • $18 • (11/15/1994) • **83**
Pinot Noir Sonoma Mountain Dry Farmed 1992 • $12 • (2/28/1994) • **79**
Riserva Sonoma County 1991 • $18 • (11/15/1993) • **79**
Zinfandel California 1996 • $9 • (6/15/1998) • **78**
Zinfandel Napa County 1993 • $9 • (10/15/1995) • **83**
Zinfandel Russian River Valley Bella Lisa 1996 • $16 • (6/15/1998) • **83**
Zinfandel Russian River Valley Pagani Ranch Old Vines Reserve 1995 • $30 • (6/15/1998) • **86**
Zinfandel Russian River Valley Piner Heights Old Vines 1995 • $17 • (6/15/1998) • **83**
Zinfandel Russian River Valley Rossi Ranch 86-Year-Old Vines 1996 • $27 • (6/15/1998) • **83**
Zinfandel Sonoma County 1992 • $9 • (10/15/1994) • **84**
Zinfandel Sonoma County 1991 • $9 • (9/30/1993) • **81**
Zinfandel Sonoma County Piner Heights Old Vines 1994 • $13 • (10/15/1995) • **83**
Zinfandel Sonoma County Piner Heights Old Vines 1993 • $13 • (10/15/1995) • **84**
Zinfandel Sonoma County Rossi Ranch 1991 • $15 • (9/30/1993) • **85**
Zinfandel Sonoma County Rossi Ranch 1990 • $10 • (10/15/1992) • **84**
Zinfandel Sonoma County Rossi Ranch 1989 • $10 • (10/15/1992) • **84**
Zinfandel Sonoma County Rossi Ranch 80-Year-Old Vines 1992 • $15 • (10/15/1994) • **78**
Zinfandel Sonoma County Rossi Ranch 80-Year-Old Vines Late Picked 1993 • $18 • (10/15/1995) • **83**
Zinfandel Sonoma County Ultimo 1991 • $18 • (9/30/1993) • **84**
Zinfandel Sonoma County Ultimo 1988 • $12 • (5/15/1992) • **77**
Zinfandel Sonoma County Ultimo Old Vines 1993 • $20 • (10/15/1995) • **86**

Key: SS—Spectator Selection. CS—Cellar Selection. HR—Highly Recommended. $NA—Price not available. (BT)—Barrel tasting. Ⓐ—Auction Price.
For a key to the tasters' initials, see "How to Use These Listings."
Dates in parentheses represent the issues in which the ratings were published.

Zinfandel Sonoma County Ultimo Old Vines 1992 • $18 • (10/15/1994) • **83**

TORII MOR | OREGON

Chardonnay Oregon 1998: Crisp, bright and focused, with an earthy edge to the fresh apple and melon flavors. Drink now through 2002.–H.S. • $16 • (3/31/2000) • **86**
Pinot Noir Oregon 1998: Smooth, silky and moderately generous with its blackberry and citrus flavors, finishing with a crisp note that balances the flavors and texture. Drink now through 2003.–H.S. • $22 • (3/31/2000) • **88**
Pinot Noir Oregon 1997: Ripe and more generous than most '97s, with a black cherry note and hints of game and smoke on the finish. Drink now through 2002.–H.S. • $20 • (9/30/1999) • **87**
Pinot Noir Oregon 1996: On the light side, with cherry and tobacco flavors that feel tightly wrapped in the background. Needs cellaring. Drink through 2003.–H.S. • $20 • (8/31/1998) • **86**
Pinot Noir Polk County Temperance Hill Vineyard 1997: Fresh and vibrant, with a bit of raw edge but plenty of raspberry flavors, and an herbal note adding interest on the firm finish. Drink now through 2003.–H.S. • $37 • (9/30/1999) • **88**
Pinot Noir Washington County Quail Hill Vineyard 1998: Dark, dense and ripe, brimming with intense blackberry, cherry, currant and spice flavors, beautifully balanced with a zing of acidity on the finish. Has more up front than on the finish, but it's a beauty. Drink now through 2005.–H.S. • $100 • (3/31/2000) • **92**
Pinot Noir Yamhill County 1995 • $18 • (6/15/1997) • **86**
Pinot Noir Yamhill County 1994 • $19 • (2/28/1997) • **88**
Pinot Noir Yamhill County Balcombe Vineyard 1997: Bright and juicy, with floral, berry and currant flavors that persist on the slightly scratchy finish. Drink now.–H.S. • $34 • (9/30/1999) • **85**
Pinot Noir Yamhill County Eason Vineyard 1996: Soft and grainy, with cherry and toast flavors against a background of fine tannins. Flavors persist nicely on the polished finish. Drink through 2003.–H.S. • $30 • (8/31/1998) • **87**
Pinot Noir Yamhill County Four Winds Vineyard 1998: Firm, fresh and generous, here's a jazzy mouthful of ripe cherry, spice and citrus flavors that linger on the finish. Drink now through 2005.–H.S. • $27 • (3/31/2000) • **89**
Pinot Noir Yamhill County Olson Vineyard 1997: Fresh, ripe and supple, a light style showing a lot of black cherry, raspberry and spice flavor that lingers on the open-textured finish. Drink now through 2005.–H.S. • $39 • (5/15/2000) • **87**
Pinot Noir Yamhill County Olson Vineyard Reserve 1996: Ripe and generous. A round wine that offers lots of delicious pure fruit character on a polished frame. Plum, prune and blackberry flavors echo on the harmonious finish. Drink now through 2002.–H.S. • $49 • (4/30/1999) • **90**
Pinot Noir Yamhill County Reserve 1995 • $37 • (11/30/1997) • **88**
Pinot Noir Yamhill County Reserve 1994 • $36 • (2/28/1997) • **91**
Pinot Noir Yamhill County White Rose Vineyard 1996: Light and open-textured, with pretty rose petal nuances to the currant and strawberry flavors, hinting at coffee on the long, supple finish. Needs to lose some tannin. Drink through 2005.–H.S. • $30 • (8/31/1998) • **90**

TORRES, MARIMAR | CALIFORNIA

Chardonnay Russian River Valley Don Miguel Vineyard 1997: From a vineyard of distinction comes this sleek and spicy Chardonnay, with pretty aromas and flavors of ripe pear, pippin apple and pineapple. It's supple and elegant on the palate, finishes long and rich. Drink now through 2002.–J.L. • $25 • (7/31/1999) SS • **92**
Chardonnay Sonoma County Green Valley Don Miguel Vineyard 1996: Sleek and elegantly styled, offering ripe, creamy pear, vanilla, apple and honey notes, this complex Chardonnay holds its focus through a long, lingering aftertaste that picks up pretty oak shadings. Delicious. Drink now through 2001.–J.L. • $23 • (11/30/1998) SS • **90**
Pinot Noir Russian River Valley Don Miguel Vineyard 1997: Complex, if tilting toward the earthy, mushroomy side of Pinot Noir; notes of cherry, spice, cola and cedar fill in the gaps. Finishes with mild, integrated tannins. Drink through 2005.–J.L. • $30 • (9/15/1999) • **87**
Pinot Noir Sonoma County Green Valley Don Miguel Vineyard 1996: Ripe, with smoky oak and earthy, slightly funky streaks to match the blackberry and cherry flavors. Picks up complex, concentrated tea, sage and cola notes. Give the tannins time to mellow. Drink through 2004.–J.L. • $28 • (11/30/1998) • **87**
Pinot Noir Sonoma County Green Valley Don Miguel Vineyard 1995 • $25 • (2/28/1998) SS • **91**
Pinot Noir Sonoma County Green Valley Don Miguel Vineyard 1994 • $25 • (11/15/1996) • **87**

Pinot Noir Sonoma County Green Valley Don Miguel Vineyard 1993 • $25 • (12/31/1995) • **84**
Pinot Noir Sonoma County Green Valley Don Miguel Vineyard 1992 • $25 • (3/31/1995) • **86**
Pinot Noir Sonoma County Green Valley Don Miguel Vineyard Vineyard Selection 1992 • $35 • (4/30/1996) • **87**

TOTIER CREEK | VIRGINIA

Cabernet Franc Virginia Monticello 1995 • $13 • (4/30/1997) • **79**

TOTT'S | CALIFORNIA

Blanc de Noir California Reserve Cuvée NV • $7 • (12/31/1997) • **71**
Brut California Reserve Cuvée NV • $7 • (12/31/1997) • **87**
Extra Dry California Reserve Cuvée NV • $7 • (12/31/1997) • **81**

TRAIL RIDGE | COLORADO

Cabernet Franc Colorado 1994 • $15 • (3/31/1998) • **83**
Chardonnay Colorado 1996 • $12 • (12/31/1997) • **73**
Merlot Colorado Reserve 1994 • $16 • (12/31/1997) • **79**

TRAVIS | CALIFORNIA

Zinfandel Lodi 1997: Cooked vegetable and sulfurous flavors mar this otherwise rich, softly textured wine. • $11 • (6/15/1999) • **76**

TREANA | CALIFORNIA

Central Coast 1997: Weaves together an attractive range of flavors, with ripe cherry, herb, anise, berry, sage and tea, turning smooth and supple. Cabernet, Syrah, Merlot, Sangiovese and Petite Sirah. Drink now through 2007.–J.L. • $35 • (4/30/2000) • **87**
Central Coast 1996: Smooth and polished, with a green tealike edge to the dried cherry, plum, sage, herb and wild berry flavors, finishing with mild tannins. A blend of Cabernet, Syrah, Merlot, Sangiovese and Petite Sirah. Drink now through 2002.–J.L. • $32 • (12/15/1998) • **88**
Viognier-Marsanne Central Coast Mer Soleil Vineyard 1997: Succeeds in rendering a wine of complexity and individuality, with elegant pear, citrus, tangerine and nectarine flavors. Drink now.–J.L. • $25 • (11/30/1999) • **87**

TREFETHEN | CALIFORNIA

Cabernet Sauvignon California Eshcol 1994 • $10 • (11/30/1996) • **85**
Cabernet Sauvignon California Eshcol 1993 • $10 • (11/30/1996) • **78**
Cabernet Sauvignon Napa Valley 1996: Tightly drawn, showing only a narrow beam of cherry, earth and mineral flavors. Firm on the finish. Drink through 2004.–J.L. • $27 • (9/15/1999) • **83**
Cabernet Sauvignon Napa Valley 1994 • $24 • (11/15/1997) • **87**
Cabernet Sauvignon Napa Valley 1993 • $23 • (12/15/1996) • **83**
Cabernet Sauvignon Napa Valley 1992 • $21 • (2/29/1996) • **87**
Cabernet Sauvignon Napa Valley 1991 • $19 • (12/15/1995) • **84**
Cabernet Sauvignon Napa Valley 1990 • $19 • (11/15/1995) • **87**
Cabernet Sauvignon Napa Valley 1989 • $18 • (7/31/1994) • **84**
Cabernet Sauvignon Napa Valley 1988: Medium-weight, with light menthol, cedar and only a glimmer of cherry and currant flavors. Simple. (California Cabernet retrospective tasting). Drink now.–J.L. • $16 • (11/15/1998) • **81**
Cabernet Sauvignon Napa Valley 1987 • $16 • (12/15/1997) • **88**
Cabernet Sauvignon Napa Valley 1986 • $16 • (10/31/1989) • **84**
Cabernet Sauvignon Napa Valley 1984 • $14 • (5/31/1988) • **88**
Cabernet Sauvignon Napa Valley 1983 • $12 • (7/15/1987) • **90**
Cabernet Sauvignon Napa Valley 1982 • $11 • (3/16/1986) • **63**
Cabernet Sauvignon Napa Valley 1981 • $11 • (12/16/1984) SS • **88**
Cabernet Sauvignon Napa Valley 1974 • $37 • (11/15/1994) • **78**
Cabernet Sauvignon Napa Valley Hillside Selection 1985 • $30 • (11/15/1990) • **80**
Cabernet Sauvignon Napa Valley Library Selection 1983 • $30 • (10/15/1990) • **80**
Cabernet Sauvignon Napa Valley Reserve 1995: Complex cedar, mint, herb and fruit aromas turn tight and firm, with plum, black cherry and smoky oak notes. Finishes with simple, crisp tannins and good length. A real stretch at the price, though. Drink now through 2006.–J.L. • $60 • (6/15/2000) • **84**
Cabernet Sauvignon Napa Valley Reserve 1991 • $40 • (11/15/1996) • **86**
Cabernet Sauvignon Napa Valley Reserve 1989 • $30 • (7/31/1994) • **86**
Cabernet Sauvignon Napa Valley Reserve 1986 • $NA • (12/15/1996) • **80**
Chardonnay Napa Valley 1997: A flinty, minerally style, with a pretty core of apple and citrus built on a light, clean frame. Drink now through 2002. –J.L. • $21 • (7/31/1999) • **87**
Chardonnay Napa Valley 30th Anniversary Cuvée 1996: Pleasant, if understated, with attractive ripe pear and apple flavors, touches of lemon and grapefruit and a clean, fruity aftertaste. Drink through 2002–J.L. • $30 • (11/30/1998) • **87**
Eshcol Red Napa Valley NV • $9 • (11/15/1994) • **80**
Eshcol Red Napa Valley NV • $9 • (6/15/1993) • **79**
Eshcol Red Napa Valley NV • $6 • (2/15/1991) • **79**
Merlot Napa Valley 1994 • $24 • (11/30/1997) • **87**
Pinot Noir Napa Valley 1986 • $13 • (7/31/1989) • **68**
Pinot Noir Napa Valley 1985 • $12 • (6/15/1988) • **74**
Riesling Napa Valley Dry 1996 • $12 • (11/30/1997) • **84**

TRENTADUE | CALIFORNIA

Cabernet Sauvignon Dry Creek Valley 1989 • $10 • (11/15/1993) • **77**
Merlot Alexander Valley 1995: Ripe, bright, forward berry and cherry flavors with traces of herb and spice. Finishes with a bit of heat. Drink now.–J.L. • $18 • (9/30/1998) • **80**
Old Patch Red Sonoma County 1994 • $12 • (6/15/1998) • **79**
Sangiovese Alexander Valley 1994: Has a crispness and freshness that's balanced with some mature red wine flavors, offering hints of blackberry and tar on the finish. Drink now.–H.S. • $18 • (7/31/1998) • **86**
Zinfandel Sonoma County 1993 • $11 • (10/15/1995) • **83**
Zinfandel Sonoma County 1992 • $10 • (10/15/1994) • **88**

TRIA | CALIFORNIA

Cabernet Franc Dry Creek Valley 1993 • $24 • (5/15/1996) • **83**
Claret Dry Creek Valley 1993 • $24 • (5/31/1996) • **87**
Labyrinth California 1995 • $18 • (5/31/1998) • **86**
Labyrinth California 1994 • $18 • (11/15/1997) • **86**
Pinot Noir Carneros 1997: Firm and spicy, with a core of tarry black cherry flavors, picking up herb and toasted oak and turning mildly tannic. Drink now through 2001.–J.L. • $20 • (9/15/1999) • **85**
Pinot Noir Carneros 1996: Quite tannic and earthy, with muddled Pinot Noir flavors that slowly straighten out. Drink now.–J.L. • $22 • (8/31/1998) • **79**
Pinot Noir Monterey 1997: Soft and rich, with green tea, spice and strawberry flavors. Finishes firm. Drink now.–J.L. • $14 • (9/15/1999) • **85**
Pinot Noir Monterey 1996: Dry and earthy, with a slightly bitter edge to the ripe plum and wild berry flavors. Finishes with dried blackberry notes and a tannic edge. Drink through 2002.–J.L. • $20 • (8/31/1998) • **85**
Port Monterey County Souzao 1994 • $15 • (4/30/1997) • **86**
Syrah Dry Creek Valley 1994 • $20 • (4/30/1997) • **88**
Syrah Dry Creek Valley 1993 • $20 • (5/15/1996) • **89**
Syrah Sonoma County 1996: Shows firm tannins and a trim, tart band of berry, cedar, anise and cherry that lacks the extra dimensions found in earlier vintages. Good but nothing more. Drink now through 2001.–J.L. • $20 • (4/30/1999) • **83**
Syrah Sonoma County 1995 • $20 • (11/15/1997) • **84**
Zinfandel Dry Creek Valley 1997: Smooth and supple, offering ripe, grapey plum, wild berry, black cherry and spicy nuances, finishing with firm, crisp tannins. Drink now through 2003.–J.L. • $18 • (5/15/1999) • **88**
Zinfandel Dry Creek Valley 1996 • $18 • (5/31/1998) • **88**
Zinfandel Dry Creek Valley 1995 • $16 • (3/31/1997) • **86**
Zinfandel Dry Creek Valley 1994 • $16 • (5/15/1996) • **83**
Zinfandel Napa Valley 1996 • $16 • (5/31/1998) • **84**
Zinfandel Napa Valley 1995 • $16 • (3/31/1997) • **87**
Zinfandel Napa Valley 1994 • $16 • (5/15/1996) • **89**

TRIBAUT | CALIFORNIA

Blanc de Noirs California NV • $9 • (5/31/1995) • **81**
Blanc de Noirs Monterey County NV • $10 • (1/31/1992) • **82**
Brut Blanc de Blancs California Special Cuvée NV: Butter and toast on the nose, followed by bright, lemony flavors. It's clean and light. Drink now. • $9 • (11/30/1998) • **84**
Brut Blanc de Noirs California Special Cuvée NV: Nicely toasty, with lemon, apple, pear and butterscotch notes in the supporting cast, this sparkling wine is quite focused, and it leaves a long, clean and refreshing aftertaste. A good price for all that it offers. Drink now through 2002. • $9 • (11/30/1998) • **87**

TRIBAUT

Brut California NV • $9 • (5/31/1995) • **81**
Rosé Monterey County NV • $13 • (1/31/1992) • **77**

TRINCHERO, M. | CALIFORNIA

Cabernet Sauvignon Napa Valley 1995: Front-loaded with fruit, with attractive plum, currant, cedar, anise and sage, but at this early stage it's a bit overdone with oak; best to cellar and let the formidable tannins on the finish subside. Drink through 2009.–J.L. • $30 • (8/31/1998) • **88**
Cabernet Sauvignon Napa Valley Founder's Estate 1996: A touch green, with olive and herb flavors and a smooth texture. The core of cherry and currant is appealing, but it's short on depth. From the owners of Sutter Home. Drink now through 2002.–J.L. • $30 • (6/15/1999) • **87**
Cabernet Sauvignon Napa-Santa Barbara Counties Coastal Selection 1996: Rustic in texture, this one serves up blackberry, tar, tobacco and herb flavors that fan out on the moderate, resinous finish. Drink now through 2003. • $13 • (11/15/1999) • **84**
Chardonnay Napa Valley 1996: Elegant, with pretty toasty oak nuances and a core of lemon, pear and spice. Gains points for its delicacy, but could use a shade more depth and richness. Clean and refreshing on the finish. An impressive new wine from Sutter Home's new ultrapremium brand.–J.L. • $25 • (7/31/1998) • **88**
Chardonnay Napa Valley Founder's Estate 1997: Crisp and clean, featuring bright lemon and green apple flavors. Finishes with lingering toasty notes. Drink now.–J.L. • $25 • (7/31/1999) • **87**
Merlot California Coastal Selection 1997: A lean style, with licorice and blackberry notes. The finish is somewhat resinous, ending on a bitter note. Drink now. • $12 • (11/15/1999) • **83**

TROUT GULCH | CALIFORNIA

Pinot Noir Santa Cruz Mountains 1997: Smooth and supple, with a core of oak-tinged cherry flavors. Finishes soft and ripe, with earthy notes. Drink now through 2002. • $16 • (9/15/1999) • **84**
Pinot Noir Santa Cruz Mountains 1995 • $16 • (2/28/1998) • **83**
Pinot Noir Santa Cruz Mountains 1994 • $16 • (1/31/1998) • **87**

TRUCHARD | CALIFORNIA

Cabernet Sauvignon Napa Valley Carneros 1996: Seductive with its elegant band of toasty oak, cedar, currant, black cherry and spice, it turns supple and polished on the finish, where the flavors linger. Best from 2001 through 2009.–J.L. • $32 • (10/15/1999) • **92**
Cabernet Sauvignon Napa Valley Carneros 1995: Here's a delicious, complex, youthful Cabernet. Explore all the currant, black cherry, coffee, cedar, anise and blackberry flavors and mild, supple tannins. Drink through 2005.–J.L. • $27 • (11/15/1998) • **91**
Cabernet Sauvignon Napa Valley Carneros 1994 • $24 • (9/30/1997) • **91**
Cabernet Sauvignon Napa Valley Carneros 1993 • $22 • (11/15/1996) • **90**
Cabernet Sauvignon Napa Valley Carneros 1992 • $20 • (3/31/1996) • **88**
Cabernet Sauvignon Napa Valley Carneros 1991 • $18 • (11/15/1994) • **87**
Cabernet Sauvignon Napa Valley Carneros 1990 • $18 • (11/15/1993) • **87**
Cabernet Sauvignon Napa Valley Carneros 1989 • $18 • (12/15/1992) • **87**
Cabernet Sauvignon Napa Valley Carneros Reserve 1995: Ripe, smooth and focused, with flavors built around a core of black cherry, olive, anise, herb, chocolate and coffee, this is rich and concentrated, with a long, flavorful finish. Drink through 2007.–J.L. • $55 • (10/31/1999) • **93**
Cabernet Sauvignon Napa Valley Carneros Reserve 1994: Rich, complex and flavorful, with tiers of currant, sage, mineral, anise and cherry flavors that slowly unfold to reveal even more depth and concentration. The finish goes on and on. The first reserve wine from Truchard. Drink now through 2006.–J.L. • $48 • (10/15/1998) • **91**
Chardonnay Napa Valley Carneros 1998: Elegant and restrained, with a core of citrus, ripe pear, cedary oak and nutmeg. Turns trim and flinty. Tasted twice, with consistent notes. Best from 2001 through 2006.–J.L. • $28 • (4/30/2000) • **89**
Chardonnay Napa Valley Carneros 1997: A solid offering vintage after vintage, this wine is smooth, ripe, rich and concentrated, with tiers of fig, pear, melon, apple and hazelnut, turning creamy and rich on the finish, with an aftertaste that goes on and on. Drink now through 2002.–J.L. • $25 • (4/30/1999) HR • **94**
Chardonnay Napa Valley Carneros 1996 • $24 • (4/30/1998) • **92**
Merlot Napa Valley Carneros 1996: Strays initially into the earthier spectrum of Merlot, with pungent leather, coffee, chocolate and currant flavors, turning firm and decadent on the finish. Drink through 2008.–J.L. • $26 • (9/30/1999) • **89**
Merlot Napa Valley Carneros 1995 • $24 • (5/15/1998) • **91**
Merlot Napa Valley Carneros 1994 • $22 • (6/30/1997) • **89**
Merlot Napa Valley Carneros 1993 • $20 • (4/30/1996) • **89**
Merlot Napa Valley Carneros 1992 • $18 • (9/30/1995) • **87**
Merlot Napa Valley Carneros 1991 • $18 • (6/30/1994) • **87**
Merlot Napa Valley Carneros 1990 • $18 • (7/15/1993) • **85**
Merlot Napa Valley Carneros 1989 • $18 • (5/31/1992) • **81**
Pinot Noir Napa Valley Carneros 1997: Ripe and polished, with a complex band of cola, black cherry, spice and wild berry, holding its focus and turning supple on the long finish. Remarkably elegant. Drink now through 2005.–J.L. • $28 • (9/15/1999) • **89**
Pinot Noir Napa Valley Carneros 1996: Smooth, ripe and polished, this well-made '96 offers cola, berry, cherry and spice, shows off a nice dose of oak, but best of all it's well balanced. Turns complex on the finish. Drink now through 2001.–J.L. • $25 • (8/31/1998) • **87**
Pinot Noir Napa Valley Carneros 1995 • $23 • (8/31/1997) • **91**
Pinot Noir Napa Valley Carneros 1994 • $21 • (2/28/1997) • **91**
Pinot Noir Napa Valley Carneros 1993 • $18 • (11/30/1995) • **88**
Pinot Noir Napa Valley Carneros 1992 • $18 • (2/28/1994) • **84**
Pinot Noir Napa Valley Carneros 1991 • $18 • (2/28/1993) • **82**
Pinot Noir Napa Valley Carneros 1990 • $18 • (9/30/1992) • **86**
Pinot Noir Napa Valley Carneros 1989 • $18 • (10/31/1991) • **90**
Syrah Napa Valley Carneros 1997: Dark, rich, intense and spicy, with peppery currant, blackberry and spice, fanning out with dense mineral, coffee and tea. Has the tannic strength to age. Best from 2001 through 2008.–J.L. • $30 • (11/15/1999) • **92**
Syrah Napa Valley Carneros 1996: Ripe and plump, showing juicy cherry, plum and wild berry with rich, supple tannins, finishing with complex meat and leather notes. Drink now through 2004.–J.L. • $23 Ⓐ • (8/31/1998) • **89**
Syrah Napa Valley Carneros 1995 • $24 • (7/31/1997) • **90**
Syrah Napa Valley Carneros 1994 • $21 • (8/31/1996) • **91**
Syrah Napa Valley Carneros 1993 • $18 • (5/15/1995) HR • **92**
Syrah Napa Valley Carneros 1992 • $16 • (7/31/1994) • **84**
Zinfandel Napa Valley Carneros 1998: Medium in weight, with stemmy, herbaceous cherry and tart berry notes that are barely ripe. Finishes with a green, tannic edge. Drink now through 2005.–J.L. • $24 • (5/31/2000) • **83**
Zinfandel Napa Valley Carneros 1997: Dense and plush, with a mint, sage and bay leaf edge to the rich core of wild berry, cherry, raspberry and spice. Finishes with a gush of fruit and spice. Quite exotic and distinctive. Drink now through 2004.–J.L. • $20 • (5/31/1999) • **92**
Zinfandel Napa Valley Carneros 1996 • $18 • (5/31/1998) • **91**
Zinfandel Napa Valley Carneros 1994 • $15 • (3/31/1996) • **88**

TUALATIN | OREGON

Chardonnay Willamette Valley 1997: Generous, supple and appealing for its pretty pear, peach and spice flavors. Picks up a hint of toasty oak character on the long, gentle finish. Drink now through 2004.–H.S. • $14 • (4/30/2000) • **88**
Gewürztraminer Willamette Valley Late Harvest 1997: Sweet, focused and brimming with spice, honey and floral flavors around a nice core that echoes apricot and pineapple. Drink now through 2005.–H.S. • $12/375 ml. • (6/30/1999) • **90**
Müller-Thurgau Willamette Valley 1996 • $7 • (11/15/1997) • **85**
Muscat Willamette Valley Semi-Sparkling 1998: Bright and appealing for its delicacy and sweet spiciness, with a varied palette of fruit flavors—litchi, peach and guava—that trips smoothly through the dancing finish. Drink now.–H.S. • $15 • (4/30/2000) • **89**
Muscat Willamette Valley Semi-Sparkling 1997: Bright, open-textured and refreshingly straightforward, echoing pretty pear and litchi notes on the finish. Drink now.–H.S. • $14 • (4/30/1999) • **87**
Pinot Blanc Oregon 1998: Bright, juicy and pretty, with melon, apple and citrus flavors that linger on the finish. Drink now.–H.S. • $14 • (3/31/2000) • **87**
Pinot Blanc Willamette Valley 1997: Ripe and round, generous with its apple, melon and spice flavors, finishing with a supple feel. Drink now.–H.S. • $15 • (2/28/1999) • **86**
Pinot Noir Oregon 1990 • $8 • (2/28/1993) • **80**

Key: SS—Spectator Selection. CS—Cellar Selection. HR—Highly Recommended. $NA—Price not available. (BT)—Barrel tasting. Ⓐ—Auction Price.
For a key to the tasters' initials, see "How to Use These Listings."
Dates in parentheses represent the issues in which the ratings were published.

Pinot Noir Willamette Valley 1995 • $13 • (10/31/1997) • **84**
Pinot Noir Willamette Valley 1992 • $10 • (10/15/1994) • **87**
Pinot Noir Willamette Valley 1987 • $14 • (2/15/1990) • **79**
Pinot Noir Willamette Valley 1986 • $14 • (6/15/1988) • **85**
Pinot Noir Willamette Valley Barrel Aged 1994 • $10 • (1/31/1996) • **87**
Pinot Noir Willamette Valley Barrel Aged 1993 • $10 • (12/31/1995) • **83**
Pinot Noir Willamette Valley Barrel Selected Private Reserve 1994 • $20 • (12/31/1996) • **75**
Pinot Noir Willamette Valley Barrel Selected Private Reserve 1993 • $25 • (3/31/1996) • **84**
Pinot Noir Willamette Valley Barrel Selected Private Reserve 1992 • $20 • (10/15/1994) • **90**
Pinot Noir Willamette Valley Private Reserve 1985 • $14 • (2/15/1990) • **84**
White Riesling Willamette Valley 1996 • $7 • (11/15/1997) • **81**

TUCKER | WASHINGTON

Chenin Blanc Yakima Valley 1997: Light and crisp, with a fresh lime edge to the pretty melon flavors. Drink now.–H.S. • $7 • (9/30/1998) • **86**
Gewürztraminer Yakima Valley 1997: Distinctly spicy and floral, with peppery overtones to the sweet pear and grapefruit flavors. Drink now. –H.S. • $7 • (9/15/1998) • **85**
Muscat Canelli Yakima Valley 1997: Fresh, youthful and lightly sweet, with pretty pear, pine and litchi flavors swirling around. Drink now.–H.S. • $8 • (9/15/1998) • **85**
Muscat Canelli Yakima Valley 1993 • $7 • (9/30/1995) • **83**
Pinot Noir Yakima Valley 1989 • $8 • (2/28/1993) • **72**

TUDAL | CALIFORNIA

Cabernet Sauvignon Napa Valley 1992 • $18 • (12/15/1995) • **83**
Cabernet Sauvignon Napa Valley 1990 • $17 • (2/28/1994) • **88**
Cabernet Sauvignon Napa Valley 1989 • $17 • (11/15/1992) • **74**
Cabernet Sauvignon Napa Valley 1988 • $17 • (11/15/1992) • **80**
Cabernet Sauvignon Napa Valley 1986 • $15 • (12/15/1989) • **91**

TULOCAY | CALIFORNIA

Cabernet Sauvignon Napa Valley 1986 • $12 • (6/30/1990) • **70**
Cabernet Sauvignon Napa Valley 1978 • $NA • (11/15/1992) • **78**
Cabernet Sauvignon Napa Valley Cliff Vineyard 1994 • $22 • (11/30/1997) • **87**
Cabernet Sauvignon Napa Valley Cliff Vineyard 1993 • $18 • (11/15/1996) • **86**
Cabernet Sauvignon Napa Valley Cliff Vineyard 1991 • $12 • (11/15/1994) • **86**
Cabernet Sauvignon Napa Valley Cliff Vineyard 1990 • $12 • (11/15/1994) • **74**
Cabernet Sauvignon Napa Valley Cliff Vineyard 1988: Earthy, with a claylike flavor, this wine is complex, with mineral, sage, currant and spicy notes. Firms up on the finish, where the tannins are tight. (1988 California Cabernet retrospective tasting). Drink now through 2004.–J.L. • $16 • (11/15/1998) • **86**
Cabernet Sauvignon Napa Valley De Celles Vineyard 1993 • $18 • (12/15/1996) • **84**
Cabernet Sauvignon Napa Valley De Celles Vineyard 1991 • $12 • (11/15/1994) • **87**
Cabernet Sauvignon Napa Valley Egan Vineyard 1988: Pleasant, with ripe cherry, currant, anise and spice, finishing with a cedary edge and firm but balanced tannins. (1988 California Cabernet retrospective tasting). Drink now through 2004.–J.L. • $16 • (11/15/1998) • **85**
Cabernet Sauvignon Napa Valley Egan Vineyard 1987 • $17 • (2/15/1991) • **74**
Pinot Noir Napa Valley Haynes Vineyard 1992 • $15 • (11/30/1995) • **87**
Pinot Noir Napa Valley Haynes Vineyard 1989 • $16 • (3/31/1992) • **76**
Pinot Noir Napa Valley Haynes Vineyard 1988 • $15 • (3/31/1992) • **75**
Pinot Noir Napa Valley Haynes Vineyard 1985 • $18 • (2/28/1991) • **83**
Zinfandel Napa Valley Casanova Vineyard 1997: Has weight, but the chunky flavors of pepper and black currant are hot and a bit raw. Drink now through 2003.–J.L. • $24 • (5/15/2000) • **82**

TURLEY | CALIFORNIA

Petite Sirah Napa Valley Aïda Vineyard 1996: Young and grapey, with a deep, saturated color and appealing ripe berry and cherry flavors, finishing with big, ripe tannins. Drink through 2004.–J.L. • $28 • (8/31/1998) • **90**
Petite Sirah Napa Valley Aïda Vineyard 1995 • $79 Ⓐ • (7/31/1997) • **88**
Petite Sirah Napa Valley Aïda Vineyard 1993 • $72 Ⓐ • (9/30/1995) • **90**
Petite Sirah Napa Valley Hayne Vineyard 1996: Ultradark in color, packed with rich, deep, dense currant, plum and wild berry flavors, it turns plush and concentrated on the finish, where it pumps out the flavors on a long, rich aftertaste. Drink through 2009.–J.L. • $38 • (8/31/1998) • **92**
Petite Sirah Napa Valley Hayne Vineyard 1995 • $30 • (7/31/1997) • **91**
Zinfandel Alexander Valley Vineyard 101 1997: Lots of ripe, juicy cherry, berry, plum and jam notes. Turns plush and fleshy on the finish, where the tannins are smooth and polished. Drink through 2005.–J.L. • $32 • (6/15/1999) • **91**
Zinfandel Alexander Valley Vineyard 101 1996: Ripe and complex, with pretty, spicy, toasty oak and a pretty core of juicy plum, blackberry, cherry and spice. Deliciously fruity and complex on the finish. Tasty now for its fruit, yet mildly tannic, so you can age it short-term. A new wine from Turley's estate vineyard near Geyserville. Drink now through 2004.–J.L. • $35 • (7/31/1998) • **91**
Zinfandel California Old Vines 1997: Effusively fruity, with juicy cherry, plum and wild berry flavors that are very ripe and plush. Finishes with firm tannins. Drink through 2004.–J.L. • $53 Ⓐ • (6/15/1999) • **91**
Zinfandel California Old Vines 1996: A ripe, jammy style, with lots of fresh strawberry, black cherry and raspberry flavors that are rich, supple and focused. Finishes with a long, fruity aftertaste and hints of anise and sage. Drink now through 2004.–J.L. • $20 • (7/31/1998) • **90**
Zinfandel Contra Costa County Duarte Vineyard 1997: Very ripe and jammy, with layers of plum, black cherry, wild berry and spice. Finishes with a cedary edge and drying tannins. Drink now through 2004.–J.L. • $28 • (6/15/1999) • **89**
Zinfandel Contra Costa County Duarte Vineyard 1996: Ripe, almost sweet, with a range of plum, sage and blackberry. Turns earthy and dry on the aftertaste, with a slight candied flavor. Drink now through 2002.–J.L. • $22 • (7/31/1998) • **86**
Zinfandel Dry Creek Valley Grist Vineyard 1997: Smooth, ripe and jammy, with layers of plum, cherry, wild berry and blackberry. Finishes with firm, drying tannins. Drink now through 2004.–J.L. • $35 • (6/15/1999) • **91**
Zinfandel Dry Creek Valley Grist Vineyard 1996: Ripe, almost raisiny, with dry, earthy sage, wild berry and black cherry flavors. A mouthful of Zin. Finishes with firm tannins. Drink now through 2002.–J.L. • $32 • (7/31/1998) • **89**
Zinfandel Dry Creek Valley Grist Vineyard 1995 • $30 • (7/31/1997) • **93**
Zinfandel Howell Mountain Black-Sears Vineyard 1996: Marked by distinctive spice, mint and pepper flavors built around a core of plum and blackberry. Finishes with a long, lingering aftertaste and remarkably plush, polished tannins. Drink now through 2004.–J.L. • $26 • (7/31/1998) • **91**
Zinfandel Howell Mountain Black-Sears Vineyard 1995 • $96 Ⓐ • (7/31/1997) HR • **95**
Zinfandel Howell Mountain Black-Sears Vineyard 1994 • $24 • (4/30/1996) • **93**
Zinfandel Lodi Spenker Ranch 1997: Very ripe, with jammy, tarry, earthy, cedary flavors that are rich and intense. Complex finish. Drink now through 2004.–J.L. • $96 Ⓐ • (6/15/1999) • **89**
Zinfandel Napa Valley Aïda Vineyard 1997: Very ripe and earthy, with complex berry, cherry and plum notes. Finishes with a tannic edge that pumps out the flavor. Drink through 2004.–J.L. • $40 • (6/15/1999) • **90**
Zinfandel Napa Valley Aïda Vineyard 1996: A big, ripe, massive style that packs in lots of flavor, with tiers of mineral, spice, blackberry, black cherry and currant. Finishes with firm but supple tannins and a long, full, lingering aftertaste that keeps pumping out the flavor. A highly individual style. Drink now through 2005.–J.L. • $25 • (7/31/1998) • **94**
Zinfandel Napa Valley Aïda Vineyard 1995 • $25 • (7/31/1997) • **90**
Zinfandel Napa Valley Aïda Vineyard 1994 • $20 • (4/30/1996) • **90**
Zinfandel Napa Valley Aïda Vineyard 1993 • $20 • (9/30/1995) • **93**
Zinfandel Napa Valley Hayne Vineyard 1996: Here's a big, ripe mouthful of Zinfandel from a winery specializing in the variety. You can feel the energy in this seductive wine—dense, chewy and jam-packed with rich, concentrated plum, black cherry, blackberry and spice character. From a 90-year-old vineyard. Drink now through 2004.–J.L. • $105 Ⓐ • (7/31/1998) CS • **95**
Zinfandel Napa Valley Hayne Vineyard 1995 • $35 • (7/31/1997) • **94**
Zinfandel Napa Valley Hayne Vineyard 1994 • $27 • (4/30/1996) HR • **96**
Zinfandel Napa Valley Hayne Vineyard 1993 • $22 • (9/30/1995) HR • **95**
Zinfandel Napa Valley Moore "Earthquake" Vineyard 1996: Spot-on Napa Zinfandel, with lots of cherry, blackberry, spice, pepper and oak. Tightly focused, finely balanced and quite pleasurable. Drink now through 2002.–J.L. • $30 • (7/31/1998) • **91**
Zinfandel Napa Valley Moore "Earthquake" Vineyard 1995 • $30 • (7/31/1997) • **93**
Zinfandel Napa Valley Moore "Earthquake" Vineyard 1994 • $25 • (4/30/1996) HR • **94**
Zinfandel Napa Valley Moore "Earthquake" Vineyard 1993 • $20 • (9/30/1995) • **90**

Zinfandel Napa Valley Tofanelli Vineyard 1997: Juicy, with ripe plum, cherry, wild berry and spice. The long, lingering aftertaste echoes the berry flavors. Drink now through 2003.–J.L. • $30 • (6/15/1999) • **90**

Zinfandel Napa Valley Tofanelli Vineyard 1996: A potent, powerful wine with rough edges, it nonetheless delivers a ripe, juicy, tannic core of black cherry, wild berry, plum and cedar. Finishes with firm, chewy tannins. Another new vineyard for Turley. Drink through 2004.–J.L. • $28 • (7/31/1998) • **92**

Zinfandel Napa Valley Whitney Tennessee Vineyard 1996: Hits the right notes, with pretty blackberry, black cherry, pepper and spice. The flavors zoom along, revealing depth, richness and concentration. Has the tannic strength to cellar short-term. The last Whitney Tennessee bottling for Turley. Drink now through 2004.–J.L. • $86 Ⓐ • (7/31/1998) • **92**

Zinfandel Napa Valley Whitney Tennessee Vineyard 1995 • $25 • (7/31/1997) • **90**

Zinfandel Napa Valley Whitney Vineyard 1994 • $22 • (4/30/1996) • **91**

Zinfandel Oakley Duarte Vineyard 1995 • $22 • (7/31/1997) HR • **95**

TURNBULL | CALIFORNIA

Syrah Napa Valley Oakville 1995 • $25 • (4/30/1998) • **88**

TURNING LEAF | CALIFORNIA

Cabernet Sauvignon California 1996: Straightforward and appealing for its pretty currant and spice flavors, supple texture. Drink now.–H.S. • $8 • (11/15/1998) • **82**

Cabernet Sauvignon California 1995 • $8 • (12/15/1997) • **85**

Cabernet Sauvignon San Luis Obispo County Coastal Reserve 1996: Tart cranberry flavors fade quickly into the background as herbal notes take over and turn dry. Drink now.–J.L. • $10 • (6/30/2000) • **81**

Cabernet Sauvignon Sonoma County Sonoma Reserve 1994: The oh-so-low price on this Sonoma Cabernet may make you do a double take. The wine is concentrated and accessible, delivering dill, mocha, plum and mineral flavors that linger and become more complex on the finish. Drink now.–J.L. • $10 • (9/30/1998) • **85**

Cabernet Sauvignon Sonoma County Sonoma Reserve 1993 • $10 • (2/28/1997) • **87**

Chardonnay California 1996: Marked by a leesy, slightly sour edge to the modest pear and melon flavors. Average; not as good as last year's model. Drink now.–J.L. • $7 • (7/31/1998) • **77**

Chardonnay Sonoma County Coastal Reserve 1997: Charry lemon notes are thin and dull.–J.L. • $10 • (6/30/2000) • **77**

Chardonnay Sonoma County Sonoma Reserve 1996: Soft, smooth and ever-so-slightly sweet, this tasty Chardonnay has an enticing nutty, creamy character, with an earthy quality tinging the pear and apple flavors. A good buy from a great vintage, and ready now.–J.L. • $10 • (4/30/1999) • **86**

Merlot California 1997: Offers simple berry and herb flavors that linger on the modest finish. Drink now.–J.L. • $8 • (10/15/1999) • **80**

Merlot California 1996: Tutti-frutti flavors and a layer of earth add up to a rather simple wine. Drink now.–J.L. • $7 • (8/31/1998) • **72**

Merlot California 1995 • $8 • (12/15/1997) • **84**

Merlot Sonoma County Sonoma Reserve 1997: Shows a range of earthy herb, mineral, coffee and black cherry flavors that persist on the firm finish. Drink now through 2003.–J.L. • $10 • (10/15/1999) • **84**

Merlot Sonoma County Sonoma Reserve 1995: Ripe and round, with an earthy layer to the raspberry, black cherry, tea and herb flavors. Finishes with astringency, so drink now to enjoy the fruit.–J.L. • $10 • (9/30/1998) • **83**

Merlot Sonoma County Sonoma Reserve 1994 • $10 • (7/31/1997) • **86**

Pinot Noir California Reserve 1996: Light and peppery, with simple Pinot Noir flavors that offer hints of dried cherry and spice. Drink now.–J.L. • $10 • (8/31/1998) • **79**

Pinot Noir Sonoma County Sonoma Reserve 1995 • $8 • (12/15/1997) • **84**

Pinot Noir Sonoma County Sonoma Reserve 1994 • $10 • (1/31/1997) • **83**

Zinfandel California 1996 • $8 • (12/15/1997) • **87**

Zinfandel Sonoma County Sonoma Reserve 1994 • $10 • (12/31/1996) • **87**

Key: SS—Spectator Selection. CS—Cellar Selection. HR—Highly Recommended. $NA—Price not available. (BT)—Barrel tasting. Ⓐ—Auction Price.
For a key to the tasters' initials, see "How to Use These Listings."
Dates in parentheses represent the issues in which the ratings were published.

TYEE | OREGON

Pinot Noir Willamette Valley 1994 • $20 • (7/31/1997) • **87**
Pinot Noir Willamette Valley 1989 • $12 • (2/28/1993) • **68**
Pinot Noir Willamette Valley 1988 • $13 • (2/28/1993) • **63**

UNALII | CALIFORNIA

Chardonnay Sonoma County 1998: Tightly wound, with a trim band of pear, citrus, herb and cedar notes. Turns light and simple. Drink now through 2004.–J.L. • $15 • (4/30/2000) • **84**

Chardonnay Sonoma County 1997: Well focused, with pretty flavors of citrus and fig and elegant pineapple notes woven together with a light spiciness. Drink now.–H.S. • $14 • (4/30/1999) • **88**

Chardonnay Sonoma County 1996 • $14 • (1/31/1998) • **87**

Merlot Napa Valley 1997: Neat and tight, with complex, well-focused flavors of earthy currant, cedary oak, plum and blackberry. Lively aftertaste. Drink now through 2007.–J.L. • $32 • (3/31/2000) • **89**

Syrah Mendocino 1996: A meaty, earthy wine—almost chewy in texture. Behind the tannins lie rich cassis and blackberry flavors. Has depth along with its slightly quirky personality. Drink now through 2001. • $16 • (9/15/1998) • **87**

Zinfandel Lodi 1997: Round and full-bodied, with dried berry flavors and earthy and oaky nuances. Drink now through 2004.–J.L. • $14 • (5/31/2000) • **83**

UVE CELLARS | CALIFORNIA

Vin Santo Napa Valley 1992 • $20 • (11/30/1996) • **85**
Vin Santo Napa Valley 1991 • $19/375 ml. • (12/31/1995) • **89**

VALLEJO, M.G. | CALIFORNIA

Cabernet Sauvignon California 1994 • $7 • (10/31/1997) • **81**
Cabernet Sauvignon California 1992 • $6 • (11/30/1995) • **85**
Cabernet Sauvignon California 1990 • $6 • (11/15/1992) • **80**
Cabernet Sauvignon California Harvest Select 1991 • $6 • (11/15/1994) • **79**
Cabernet Sauvignon California Harvest Select 1990 • $7 • (6/15/1993) • **78**

Chardonnay California 1996: Pleasantly soft on the palate, with focused pear and citrus flavors and light oak shadings. Drink now.–H.S. • $8 • (12/15/1998) • **83**

M.G.V. Red California NV • $3 • (5/31/1990) • **74**

Merlot California 1996: Light-bodied and simple, with modest berry flavors. Finishes with herbal notes.–J.L. • $8 • (10/15/1999) • **77**

Merlot California 1994 • $8 • (7/31/1996) • **80**
Merlot California 1991 • $6 • (11/30/1992) • **84**
Merlot California 1990 • $6 • (5/31/1992) • **80**
Merlot California Harvest Select 1992 • $6 • (9/15/1994) • **82**
Merlot California Harvest Select 1991 • $7 • (6/15/1993) • **79**

Pinot Noir California 1996: Pretty light, but with some pleasant cherry and herb flavors. Finishes short. Drink now. • $8 • (9/15/1998) • **80**

Pinot Noir California 1995 • $7 • (2/28/1998) • **82**
Pinot Noir California 1994 • $7 • (12/15/1996) • **76**
Pinot Noir California Harvest Select 1994 • $8 • (1/31/1996) • **80**

VALLEY OF THE MOON | CALIFORNIA

Chardonnay Sonoma County 1998: Round and soft, with pear, butter and pineapple flavors. Drink now.–J.L. • $17 • (6/15/2000) • **83**

Chardonnay Sonoma County 1997: Delivers bright flavors of tangerine and tropical fruit and spicy notes that linger. Goes for delicacy, if slightly rough around the edges. Drink now. • $20 • (2/28/1999) • **85**

Cuvée de la Luna Reserve Sonoma County 1996: Serves up a core of black cherry, pepper and earth notes. Finishes with tangy edge, tar and toasted oak, ripe tannins. Drink now through 2003.–J.L. • $25 • (10/15/1999) • **85**

Pinot Blanc Sonoma County 1997: A bit sweet-tasting, with orange rind and vanilla flavors. Drink now through 2002.–J.L. • $20 • (5/31/2000) • **82**

Pinot Blanc Sonoma County 1996: A firm-textured, appealing blend of hazelnut, pear and apple flavors. Finishes with a refreshing lemony edge. Drink now. • $20 • (9/15/1998) • **87**

Sangiovese Sonoma County 1997: Strong tobacco essence, intriguing when mixed with the spicy, leathery, cherry, minty and cedary notes. Finish is slightly drying. Drink now through 2002.–J.L. • $25 • (5/15/2000) • **85**

Sangiovese Sonoma County 1996: Starts off with bright cherry aromas, offering bright texture and smoke, anise and berry flavors. Tannins are a bit rustic, but should smooth out with time. Finishes long. Drink now through 2004. • $25 • (6/15/1999) • **87**

Syrah Sonoma County 1997: For fans of earthy-style Syrah, with tarry notes on the finish. Some hollowness midpalate. Drink now through 2004.–J.L. • $30 • (5/31/2000) • **80**

Syrah Sonoma Valley 1995: This dark-hued wine starts off with spicy black cherry and cassis aromas. Has tangy acidity for a red and offers a refreshing blend of fruit and herbs on the palate. A first release. Drink now. • $25 • (9/15/1998) • **87**

Zinfandel Sonoma Valley 1997: Beefy, with drying, chewy tannins that mask the earthy berry flavors. Drink now through 2004.–J.L. • $20 • (5/31/2000) • **81**

Zinfandel Sonoma Valley 1996: Tight and bright, with cherry, spice and oak flavors leading the way. Tannins are a bit rustic, closing down the finish prematurely. Still, the fruit is ripe and the ensemble remains attractive. Drink now through 2002. • $25 • (2/28/1999) • **86**

Zinfandel Sonoma Valley Reserve 1990 • $10 • (10/15/1994) • **80**

VALLEY VIEW | OREGON

Anna Maria Reserve Rogue Valley 1995 • $18 • (5/15/1998) • **86**

Anna Maria Reserve Rogue Valley 1994 • $20 • (10/31/1997) • **85**

Anna Maria Reserve Rogue Valley 1992 • $20 • (11/30/1994) • **77**

Anna Maria Reserve Rogue Valley 1990 • $27 • (5/15/1994) • **87**

Anna Maria Vintners Reserve Rogue Valley 1994 • $20 • (5/15/1998) • **90**

Cabernet Franc Rogue Valley Anna Maria 1994 • $20 • (10/31/1997) • **87**

Cabernet Sauvignon Rogue Valley 1996: Light in flavor and chewy in texture, with a pretty spice halo around the fine berry flavors. Drink now. –H.S. • $12 • (4/30/1999) • **85**

Cabernet Sauvignon Rogue Valley 1995 • $12 • (10/31/1997) • **86**

Cabernet Sauvignon Rogue Valley 1992 • $10 • (7/31/1996) • **78**

Cabernet Sauvignon Rogue Valley 1991 • $6 • (5/15/1994) • **75**

Cabernet Sauvignon Rogue Valley Anna Maria 1990 • $18 • (5/15/1994) • **86**

Cabernet Sauvignon Rogue Valley Barrel Select 1991 • $13 • (11/30/1994) • **84**

Cabernet Sauvignon Rogue Valley Barrel Select 1989 • $13 • (6/15/1992) • **83**

Chardonnay Rogue Valley 1997: Unusually earthy and spicy, with a nice whiff of fresh apple wafting through the finish. Drink now.–H.S. • $9 • (4/30/1999) • **84**

Chardonnay Rogue Valley Anna Maria 1996 • $15 • (5/15/1998) • **87**

Fumé Blanc Rogue Valley Anna Maria 1998: A light and refreshing mouthful of bright apple flavor. Picks up a floral, peppery note on the open-textured finish. Drink now.–H.S. • $12 • (12/31/1999) • **86**

Fumé Blanc Rogue Valley Anna Maria 1997: Light and crisp, with lemon and pear notes on a lean frame. Drink now.–H.S. • $12 • (2/28/1999) • **80**

Merlot Oregon 1983 • $10 • (5/31/1988) • **78**

Merlot Rogue Valley 1996: Smooth and silky, with distinctly gamy flavors running through the ripe black fruit notes. Finishes with a hint of anise. Drink now through 2002.–H.S. • $12 • (5/31/1999) • **86**

Merlot Rogue Valley 1995 • $12 • (10/31/1997) • **86**

Merlot Rogue Valley 1991 • $10 • (11/30/1994) • **78**

Merlot Rogue Valley Anna Maria 1995: Exotic, with pretty spice and cedar-scented blackberry flavors on a light frame, and lots of lovely mineral and earth notes emerging on the finish. Drink now.–H.S. • $26 • (2/28/1999) • **88**

Merlot Rogue Valley Anna Maria 1992 • $18 • (3/31/1996) • **85**

Merlot Rogue Valley Anna Maria Old Stage 1994 • $30 • (10/31/1997) • **85**

Merlot Rogue Valley Jazz Label 1992 • $10 • (11/30/1994) • **85**

Pinot Gris Rogue Valley Anna Maria 1998: A generous mouthful of melon, apple and wildflower honey flavors on a medium frame, echoing the flavors on the open-textured finish. Drink now.–H.S. • $15 • (12/31/1999) • **88**

Rogue Red Oregon NV • $4 • (2/15/1988) • **74**

Syrah Rogue Valley Anna Maria 1997: A lighter style of Syrah, with pretty berry flavors and a hint of black pepper that lingers on the modest finish. Drink now.–H.S. • $28 • (12/31/1999) • **84**

VAN ASPEREN | CALIFORNIA

Cabernet Sauvignon Napa Valley 1995: Medium in weight, with an elegant band of mild herb, berry and black cherry flavors. Finishes with soft, fleshy tannins. Drink now.–J.L. • $18 • (6/15/1999) • **86**

Cabernet Sauvignon Napa Valley Signature Reserve 1994: Austere out of the gate, with firm tannins, it slowly unveils its complex cedar, anise, currant and black cherry flavors. Drink now through 2003.–J.L. • $28 • (1/31/1999) • **86**

Chardonnay Napa Valley 1998: Watery, bitter citrus notes turn muddled on the finish.–J.L. • $13 • (6/30/2000) • **79**

Chardonnay Napa Valley 1997: Fresh and crisp, with pretty citrus, pear and toast notes. The finish is clean and focused. Drink now.–J.L. • $13 • (6/15/1999) • **87**

Zinfandel Napa Valley 1997: Brimming with sweet-tasting oak notes and strawberry flavors. Medium-bodied, with a racy finish. Drink now through 2003.–J.L. • $18 • (5/31/2000) • **84**

Zinfandel Napa Valley 1995 • $10 • (6/15/1998) • **84**

VAN DUZER | OREGON

Chardonnay Oregon 1997: Light and bright, a crisp style, with floral and lemon flavors, finishing on a slightly herbal note. Drink now through 2001.–H.S. • $14 • (4/30/1999) • **85**

Chardonnay Willamette Valley 1998: Refreshing for its juicy nectarine and other citrus flavors on a light frame, remaining flavorful through the finish. Drink now through 2003.–H.S. • $16 • (3/31/2000) • **87**

Pinot Gris Willamette Valley 1997: Smooth and generous, with melon, almond and exotic spice aromas and flavors that persist on the open-textured finish. Drink now.–H.S. • $18 • (5/31/1999) • **87**

Pinot Noir Oregon 1997: Light, with distinctive, tea-shaded blueberry and black cherry flavors that linger smoothly on the finish. Drink now through 2002.–H.S. • $14 • (4/30/1999) • **86**

Pinot Noir Oregon Appellation Selection 1992 • $10 • (3/31/1996) • **87**

Pinot Noir Oregon Domain Hill & Mayes Reserve 1991 • $15 • (11/30/1994) • **83**

Pinot Noir Oregon Eola Selection 1996 • $13 • (5/15/1998) • **87**

Pinot Noir Oregon Eola Selection 1994 • $13 • (2/28/1997) • **84**

Pinot Noir Oregon Eola Selection 1993 • $14 • (9/30/1996) • **81**

Pinot Noir Oregon Reserve 1994 • $18 • (10/31/1997) • **88**

Pinot Noir Oregon Reserve 1989 • $16 • (6/15/1992) • **87**

Pinot Noir Willamette Valley 1998: Light in texture but remarkably generous in flavor, showing lovely black cherry, spice and vanilla notes that linger on the supple finish. Drink now through 2004.–H.S. • $18 • (3/31/2000) • **86**

Pinot Noir Willamette Valley Reserve 1990 • $16 • (3/15/1994) • **74**

Riesling Oregon Reserve 1996 • $8 • (5/15/1998) • **82**

VENDANGE | CALIFORNIA

Cabernet Sauvignon California 1991 • $6 • (11/15/1994) • **76**

Cabernet Sauvignon California 1990 • $6 • (8/31/1992) • **73**

Cabernet Sauvignon California Autumn Harvest NV • $12/1.5 liter • (5/15/1998) • **80**

Merlot California Autumn Harvest 1992 • $7 • (9/15/1994) • **78**

Merlot California 1990 • $6 • (5/31/1992) • **80**

Pinot Noir California Autumn Harvest 1993 • $6 • (3/31/1995) • **76**

Pinot Noir California 1990 • $6 • (2/28/1994) • **78**

Sauvignon Blanc California Autumn Harvest 1997: Pleasant enough, with light melon and citrus flavors and moderate body. Clean on the finish, with a bright mineral edge. Can't beat the price. Drink now. • $4 • (5/31/1999) • **83**

Sauvignon Blanc California Autumn Harvest 1996 • $6/1.5 liter • (5/15/1998) • **80**

Zinfandel California Autumn Harvest 1993 • $6 • (10/15/1994) • **79**

Zinfandel California 1991 • $7 • (12/31/1993) • **78**

Zinfandel California 1989 • $6 • (7/31/1992) • **84**

VENEZIA | CALIFORNIA

Bianco Nuovo Mondo Meritage Alexander Valley 1997: Enticing aromas of freshly mowed grass and herb are followed by a core of mineral, pear, melon and citrus flavors. Light-textured finish. Drink now through 2001. • $20 • (6/30/1999) • **88**

Bianco Nuovo Mondo Meritage White Alexander Valley 1996: Richly textured, with a thick, plush mouthfeel. Flavors range from grapefruit and fresh pea to fig and melon, while it also sports the grassy overtones common to Sauvignon Blanc. Also contains Sémillon. Drink now through 2002. • $20 • (12/31/1998) • **89**

Cabernet Sauvignon Alexander Valley 1993 • $20 • (4/30/1996) • **88**

Cabernet Sauvignon Alexander Valley Meola Vineyards 1996: A touch green, with a tart, cedary edge to the currant and black cherry flavors. Turns simple on the finish. Drink now through 2004.–J.L. • $24 • (12/31/1998) • **85**

Cabernet Sauvignon Alexander Valley Meola Vineyards 1995: Lots of ripe, spicy plum, cherry and berry here, with cedary oak flavors, too. With good length and mild tannins, it's ready now through 2003.–J.L. • $20 • (10/31/1998) • **87**

Cabernet Sauvignon Alexander Valley Meola Vineyards 1994 • $25 • (5/15/1997) • **91**

VENEZIA

Chardonnay Alexander Valley Big River Ranch 1996: Elegant, with an earthy edge to ripe peach and nectarine flavors that turn dry and flinty. Drink through 2002.–J.L. • $20 • (12/31/1998) • **88**

Chardonnay Napa Valley Regusci Vineyards 1997: Well oaked, if a bit heavy-handed, with rich fig, melon, apricot and spicy notes. Drink now through 2003.–J.L. • $20 • (3/31/2000) • **87**

Sangiovese Alexander Valley Nuovo Mondo 1997: Light and fruity, a touch on the simple side but pleasant, with dried ripe cherry and berryish flavors. Drink now.–J.L. • $24 • (11/15/1999) • **83**

Sangiovese Alexander Valley Trione Vineyards Hoffman Ranch 1995 • $24 • (12/15/1997) • **85**

Sangiovese California Nuovo Mondo 1995 • $24 • (2/28/1997) • **78**

Sangiovese Mendocino County Eagle Point Ranch 1995 • $24 • (7/31/1997) • **88**

Sangiovese North Coast Nuovo Mondo 1996: Fairly supple in texture, with smooth tannins. Remains subtle in the flavor department, however, with hints of cherry, plum and herb. Tangy finish. Drink now through 2004. • $24 • (12/31/1998) • **84**

Sangiovese Russian River Valley Alegría Vineyard 1996: Austere, with crisp tannins and a trim, narrow band of anise-laced dried berry flavor. Turns dry and tannic. Drink now through 2001.–J.L. • $24 • (3/31/1999) • **82**

Sangiovese Russian River Valley Alegría Vineyard 1995 • $24 • (7/31/1997) • **87**

Sangiovese Russian River Valley Van Noy Vineyards 1996: A touch gamy, with murky berry and cherry flavors that turn tannic. A good wine that lacks varietal distinction and turns hot on the finish. Drink now through 2001.–J.L. • $24 • (3/31/1999) • **83**

Viognier Alexander Valley Sonoma Moment 1997: A spicy style, with plenty of citrus, pear, tart apple and melon notes that turn elegant on the finish. Drink now.–J.L. • $24 • (12/15/1998) • **87**

VENGE | CALIFORNIA

Cabernet Sauvignon Napa Valley Family Reserve 1992 • $35 • (8/31/1996) • **88**

Merlot Napa Valley 1996: Tight, vibrant and detailed, with rich cherry, currant and berryish flavors, hints of clay and mineral, picking up a trace of coffee on the tannic finish. Drink through 2006.–J.L. • $35 • (9/30/1999) • **89**

Merlot Napa Valley 1995 • $28 • (3/31/1998) • **88**

Merlot Napa Valley Family Reserve 1997: Ripe, rich and complex, with an intriguing range of black cherry, currant, cedar, tar and wild berry. Firms up on the finish, where the tannins weigh in. Best from 2001 through 2010.–J.L. • $35 • (2/29/2000) • **91**

Sangiovese Oakville Penny Lane Vineyard Family Reserve 1997: Elegant, with velvety, ripe and spicy cherry flavors, sage and cedar notes and a lingering finish. Drink now through 2002.–J.L. • $24 • (5/15/2000) • **86**

VENTANA | CALIFORNIA

Chardonnay Monterey Gold Stripe 1997: Firm yet fruity, showing peach, citrus and apple flavors. Bright acidity is refreshing and balances the almost-sweet fruit. Fairly long on the finish. Drink now. • $12 • (6/15/1999) • **85**

Chardonnay Monterey Gold Stripe 1996 • $12 • (12/15/1997) • **86**

Chardonnay Monterey J. Douglas Meador Winegrower's Grand Reserve 1996 • $25 • (5/15/1998) • **85**

Chardonnay Monterey Reserve 1997: Quite fruity, with hints of peach, pear and orange. Bright acidity keeps it refreshing, though it doesn't speak with particular varietal distinction. Still fun to drink. Drink now. • $18 • (7/31/1999) • **85**

Chardonnay Monterey Reserve 1996 • $18 • (12/31/1997) • **84**

Chenin Blanc Monterey Dry 1997: Ripe and exotic, a lush mouthful of tropical fruit, melon and spice flavors that linger enticingly on the soft finish. Drink now.–H.S. • $8 • (12/15/1998) • **87**

Chenin Blanc Monterey Dry 1996 • $8 • (9/30/1997) • **84**

Meritage Magnus Monterey 1986 • $20 • (10/31/1989) • **79**

Merlot Monterey 1996 • $13 • (5/15/1998) • **77**

Riesling Monterey Dry 1997: Soft and appealing for its modest nectarine and earth flavors. Drink now.–H.S. • $8 • (12/15/1998) • **81**

Riesling Monterey Dry 1996 • $8 • (7/31/1997) • **87**

Sauvignon Blanc Monterey 1997: A bit austere, but with a clean, fresh mineral and grapefruit core. Drink now. • $10 • (9/15/1998) • **84**

Sauvignon Blanc Monterey 1996 • $10 • (7/31/1997) • **88**

VIA FIRENZE | CALIFORNIA

Charbono Napa Valley 1994: Dark-colored, with pleasant plum and spice aromas, but falters somewhat on the palate with drying tannins. A simple quaffer. Drink now. • $13 • (4/30/1999) • **81**

Dolcetto Napa Valley 1995: A little lean on the palate, this offers light cherry and herb flavors while finishing with some astringency. Simple yet pleasant. New from Canandaigua. Drink now. • $15 • (3/31/1999) • **83**

Nobella Napa Valley 1994: This features tart cherry and herb notes, with a good dose of toasty, vanilla oak flavors, turning a bit dry and bitter on the finish. Contrary to its misleading label, it's anything but Tuscan; it's a California blend of Bordeaux varietals. New from Canandaigua. Drink now through 2003. • $19 • (3/31/1999) • **84**

Sangiovese Mendocino 1996: Offers light cherry and strawberry flavors, with firm tannins and a mild-mannered finish. Light on color. Drink now. • $15 • (4/30/1999) • **82**

VIADER | CALIFORNIA

Napa Valley 1998: Serves up a wide range of appealing, elegant flavors, with spicy currant, black cherry, blackberry and herbal notes. This represents only the Cabernet Sauvignon in Viader's Cabernet blend.–J.L. • $NA • (8/31/1999) (BT) • **90-94**

Napa Valley 1997: Ripe, round, rich and complex, with well-focused plum, cherry, currant and spice. A deceptively elegant and understated style. Finishes with a long, fruity aftertaste. This sample was 100 percent Cabernet Sauvignon. The finished wine will contain Cabernet Franc as well.–J.L. • $NA • (8/31/1998) (BT) • **90-94**

Napa Valley 1996: Complex, elegant, spicy and balanced. Tightly wound, with an earthy, green olive edge to the spicy plum and currant notes. Contains Cabernet Sauvignon and Cabernet Franc. Best from 2001 through 2008.–J.L. • $45 • (12/15/1998) • **88**

Napa Valley 1995 • $33 • (1/31/1998) HR • **92**

Napa Valley 1994 • $30 • (5/31/1997) • **93**

Napa Valley 1993 • $29 • (5/15/1996) • **89**

Napa Valley 1992 • $28 • (7/31/1995) • **88**

Napa Valley 1991 • $28 • (11/15/1994) HR • **91**

Napa Valley 1990 • $25 • (7/15/1993) HR • **91**

Napa Valley 1989 • $43 Ⓐ • (11/15/1992) • **90**

VIANO | CALIFORNIA

Cabernet Sauvignon California Reserve Selection 1993: Firm, with cedar, tobacco, dried cherry and currant flavors. Dries a bit on the finish. Drink now.–H.S. • $13 • (10/31/1998) • **82**

Cabernet Sauvignon California Reserve Selection 1988 • $10 • (11/15/1994) • **81**

Zinfandel Contra Costa County Reserve Selection 1993 • $9 • (4/30/1997) • **90**

Zinfandel Contra Costa County Sand Rock Hill Reserve Selection 1995: Packs sweet oak, black cherry and ripe plum flavors in a well-balanced, harmonious blend. Elegant and full-bodied, yet delicate. Quite nice. Drink now through 2002. • $12 • (1/31/1999) • **89**

Zinfandel Contra Costa County Sand Rock Hill Reserve Selection 1994 • $10 • (12/15/1997) • **90**

Zinfandel Contra Costa County Sand Rock Hill Reserve Selection 1992 • $9 • (10/15/1995) • **89**

Zinfandel Contra Costa County Sand Rock Hill Reserve Selection 1991 • $8 • (10/15/1994) • **80**

Zinfandel Contra Costa County Sand Rock Hill Reserve Selection 1989 • $8 • (6/15/1993) • **81**

Zinfandel Late Harvest Contra Costa County Reserve Selection 1989 • $9 • (12/31/1995) • **76**

Zinfandel Port Contra Costa County Vintage Old Vines Reserve Selection NV • $10 • (2/28/1997) • **86**

VIANSA | CALIFORNIA

Cabernet Sauvignon Napa Valley Reserve 1994 • $30 • (11/30/1997) • **89**

Cabernet Sauvignon Napa & Sonoma Counties Reserve 1988 • $23 • (11/15/1993) • **78**

Cabernet Sauvignon Sonoma Valley Grand Reserve 1983 • $35 • (10/15/1988) • **88**

Cabernet Sauvignon Sonoma Valley Reserve 1983 • $18 • (10/15/1988) • **88**

Key: SS—Spectator Selection. CS—Cellar Selection. HR—Highly Recommended. $NA—Price not available. (BT)—Barrel tasting. Ⓐ—Auction Price.
For a key to the tasters' initials, see "How to Use These Listings."
Dates in parentheses represent the issues in which the ratings were published.

Cabernet Sauvignon Napa & Sonoma Counties 1988 • $17 • (11/15/1992) • **76**
Cabernet Sauvignon Napa & Sonoma Counties 1986 • $20 Ⓐ • (7/31/1990) • **77**
Cabernet Sauvignon Napa & Sonoma Counties 1985 • $13 • (9/15/1989) • **72**
Cabernet Sauvignon Napa & Sonoma Counties 1984 • $13 • (7/31/1988) • **85**
Cabernet Sauvignon Napa & Sonoma Counties 1983 • $15 • (11/30/1986) • **88**
Nebbiolo California Northern California 1990 • $15 • (11/30/1992) • **81**
Ossidiana Napa Valley 1994 • $70 • (11/30/1997) • **87**
Prindelo California 1996 • $28 • (11/30/1997) • **89**
Prindelo Sonoma Valley 1993 • $20 • (10/15/1995) • **92**
Prindelo Sonoma Valley 1991 • $16 • (12/31/1993) • **82**
Riserva Anatra Rosso Napa-Sonoma Counties 1989 • $18 • (11/15/1993) • **80**
Sangiovese California Piccolo Toscano 1995 • $18 • (12/31/1997) • **80**

VICHON | CALIFORNIA

Cabernet Sauvignon California Coastal Selection 1994 • $11 • (11/30/1996) • **79**
Cabernet Sauvignon California Coastal Selection 1992 • $9 • (1/31/1995) • **87**
Cabernet Sauvignon California Coastal Selection 1991 • $11 • (9/30/1994) • **82**
Cabernet Sauvignon California Coastal Selection 1990 • $9 • (11/15/1993) • **82**
Cabernet Sauvignon California Coastal Selection 1989 • $10 • (11/15/1992) • **84**
Cabernet Sauvignon Napa Valley 1993 • $20 • (8/31/1996) • **87**
Cabernet Sauvignon Napa Valley 1992 • $16 • (12/15/1995) • **87**
Cabernet Sauvignon Napa Valley 1991 • $16 • (4/30/1994) • **81**
Cabernet Sauvignon Napa Valley 1990 • $16 • (8/31/1993) HR • **89**
Cabernet Sauvignon Napa Valley 1989 • $16 • (11/15/1992) • **89**
Cabernet Sauvignon Napa Valley 1988 • $16 • (5/15/1991) • **84**
Cabernet Sauvignon Napa Valley 1985 • $14 • (11/15/1988) • **91**
Cabernet Sauvignon Napa Valley 1983 • $12 • (11/30/1986) • **91**
Cabernet Sauvignon Napa Valley 1982 • $13 • (7/16/1986) • **89**
Cabernet Sauvignon Napa Valley 1981 • $14 • (12/16/1984) • **89**
Cabernet Sauvignon Stags Leap District 1992 • $31 • (3/31/1996) • **84**
Cabernet Sauvignon Stags Leap District 1991 • $28 • (12/15/1995) • **88**
Cabernet Sauvignon Stags Leap District 1990 • $24 • (11/15/1993) HR • **91**
Cabernet Sauvignon Stags Leap District 1989 • $24 • (8/31/1993) • **83**
Cabernet Sauvignon Stags Leap District 1988 • $24 • (11/15/1991) • **90**
Cabernet Sauvignon Stags Leap District 1987 • $17 • (7/31/1990) • **87**
Cabernet Sauvignon Stags Leap District 1986 • $21 • (10/31/1989) • **91**
Cabernet Sauvignon Stags Leap District 1985 • $20 • (1/31/1989) • **93**
Merlot California Coastal Selection 1994 • $11 • (8/31/1996) • **84**
Merlot California Coastal Selection 1993 • $10 • (7/31/1996) • **84**
Merlot California Coastal Selection 1992 • $10 • (1/31/1995) • **83**
Merlot Napa Valley 1993 • $21 • (7/31/1996) • **83**
Merlot Napa Valley 1992 • $18 • (1/31/1996) • **90**
Merlot Napa Valley 1991 • $19 • (9/15/1994) • **84**
Merlot Napa Valley 1990 • $18 • (6/30/1993) • **89**
Merlot Napa Valley 1989 • $17 • (4/15/1992) • **88**
Merlot Napa Valley 1988 • $16 • (12/31/1990) • **81**
Merlot Napa Valley 1987 • $16 • (2/15/1990) • **91**
Merlot Napa Valley 1986 • $16 • (8/31/1989) • **86**
Merlot Napa Valley 1985 • $14 • (12/15/1987) • **88**
Zyrah California 1993 • $13 • (8/31/1996) • **85**

VICTOR HUGO | CALIFORNIA

Petite Sirah Paso Robles Shell Creek Vineyard 1997: Violet, earth, candied blueberry and orange rind notes are wrapped up in a chewy, solid frame, finishing slightly tannic. Drink now through 2007.–J.L. • $15 • (6/15/2000) • **85**
Zinfandel Paso Robles Templeton Hills Vineyard 1997: Jammy, with crisp plum and strawberry notes and an earthy edge. Drink now.–J.L. • $16 • (5/31/2000) • **82**

VIGIL | CALIFORNIA

Cabernet Franc Napa Valley 1995 • $20 • (11/30/1997) • **89**
Cabernet Sauvignon Napa Valley NV • $12 • (12/15/1995) • **84**
Cabernet Sauvignon Napa Valley 1994 • $18 • (10/31/1997) • **81**
Terra Vin California 1996: Menthol and charry oak notes soften into flavors of tar, herb, tart cherry and berry. Finishes slightly dry. Zinfandel blend. Drink now.–J.L. • $10 • (6/30/1999) • **84**
Terra Vin California 1995 • $12 • (1/01/1998) • **82**
Terra Vin Napa Valley Reserve 1996 • $20 • (6/15/1998) • **87**
Valiente Napa Valley Meritage 1996: Fairly floral on the nose and initially smooth on the palate despite its firmly structured tannins. The coffee, cola, tar and blackberry flavors blend well, but the finish is rustic and slightly bitter. A blend of Cabernet Sauvignon, Merlot, Carignane, Malbec, Petit Verdot. Drink through 2005. • $20 • (2/28/1999) • **85**
Valiente Napa Valley Claret 1995 • $20 • (12/31/1997) • **87**
Vigilánte Red Numero Tres California NV: Firm in texture, with chewy tannins and a lean core of blueberry and currant echoing through the finish. A blend of Syrah, Blue Portuguese, Carignane and others. Drink now.–H.S. • $9 • (11/30/1998) • **85**
Zinfandel California Tres Condados 1997: Strange, with lavender, talc and pepper notes that struggle to find focus.–J.L. • $14 • (5/31/2000) • **78**
Zinfandel California Tres Condados 1996 • $13 • (6/15/1998) • **82**
Zinfandel California Tres Condados 1995 • $14 • (12/15/1997) • **85**
Zinfandel Howell Mountain 1995 • $16 • (11/30/1997) • **79**
Zinfandel Howell Mountain Beatty Ranch 1997: Marked by a potent mint and menthol flavor, so if you like that in your Zin, you'll be delighted. There are attractive wild berry and cherry notes and firm, crisp tannins. Finishes with a cedary flavor. Drink through 2003.–J.L. • $28 • (6/30/1999) • **85**
Zinfandel Lodi Mohr-Fry Ranch Old Vines 1998: Herbal, with mineral and earth flavors dominating the cherry notes.–J.L. • $18 • (5/31/2000) • **78**
Zinfandel Lodi Mohr-Fry Ranch Old Vines 1997: Minty, with bay leaf flavors, opening into more complex currant, black cherry, plum and cedary oak. Finishes with a nice touch of fruit and spice. Drink now through 2002.–J.L. • $18 • (6/30/1999) • **88**
Zinfandel Lodi Mohr-Fry Ranch Old Vines 1996 • $16 • (6/15/1998) • **86**

VILLA ANDRIANA | CALIFORNIA

Bianco di Palisades Napa Valley 1996 • $9/500 ml. • (3/31/1998) • **83**
Charbono Napa Valley 1996 • $16 • (3/31/1998) • **87**

VILLA MT. EDEN | CALIFORNIA

Cabernet Sauvignon California 1995 • $12 • (4/30/1998) • **82**
Cabernet Sauvignon California 1994 • $12 • (10/15/1997) • **86**
Cabernet Sauvignon California Cellar Select 1993 • $9 • (9/15/1996) • **82**
Cabernet Sauvignon California Cellar Select 1991 • $10 • (5/15/1994) • **82**
Cabernet Sauvignon California Cellar Select 1990 • $10 • (3/31/1993) • **83**
Cabernet Sauvignon California Cellar Select 1989 • $10 • (3/31/1993) • **85**
Cabernet Sauvignon California Cellar Select 1988 • $8 • (7/15/1992) • **85**
Cabernet Sauvignon Mendocino Signature Series 1996: Elegant and juicy, with a smooth band of plum, cherry, currant and wild berry. Gains richness and nuance on the long, tasty finish. Drink through 2007.–J.L. • $52 • (11/15/1999) • **92**
Cabernet Sauvignon Mendocino Signature Series 1995: Here's proof positive that Mendocino can make great Cabernet. This is a dense, chewy, complex and concentrated wine brimming with currant, black cherry, herb, mineral and sage notes tightly framed by spicy, cedary, toasty oak. Finishes with a long, full aftertaste. Drink through 2008.–J.L. • $45 • (11/15/1998) • **94**
Cabernet Sauvignon Mendocino Signature Series 1994 • $50 • (10/31/1997) • **92**
Cabernet Sauvignon Mendocino Signature Series 1993 • $45 • (4/30/1997) • **88**
Cabernet Sauvignon Mendocino Signature Series 1992 • $45 • (3/31/1995) HR • **92**
Cabernet Sauvignon Napa Valley 1987 • $13 • (2/15/1991) • **88**
Cabernet Sauvignon Napa Valley 1986 • $13 • (2/15/1991) • **84**
Cabernet Sauvignon Napa Valley 1982 • $10 • (4/15/1988) • **71**
Cabernet Sauvignon Napa Valley 1980 • $22 Ⓐ • (1/01/1984) • **86**
Cabernet Sauvignon Napa Valley 1978 • $45 • (11/15/1992) • **85**
Cabernet Sauvignon Napa Valley 1974 • $95 • (11/15/1994) • **90**
Cabernet Sauvignon Napa Valley Grand Reserve 1998: Marked by ripe berryish flavors and firm tannins, with black cherry, plum and floral notes, finishing with a burst of fruit.–J.L. • $NA • (8/31/1999) (BT) • **90-94**
Cabernet Sauvignon Napa Valley Grand Reserve 1996: Mature-tasting and a touch dry, with firm currant, black cherry, cedar and leaf notes. Finishes with dry, earthy tannins. Drink now through 2007.–J.L. • $20 • (1/31/2000) • **87**
Cabernet Sauvignon Napa Valley Grand Reserve 1995: Supple and elegant, with pleasing coffee, cedar, currant and spicy berry flavors that are woven together. Turns firm and tart on the finish, with sharp acidity. Drink through 2006.–J.L. • $20 • (2/28/1999) • **87**
Cabernet Sauvignon Napa Valley Grand Reserve 1993 • $16 • (9/15/1996) • **82**
Cabernet Sauvignon Napa Valley Grand Reserve 1992 • $16 • (4/30/1996) • **88**
Cabernet Sauvignon Napa Valley Grand Reserve 1991 • $14 • (3/31/1995) • **83**
Cabernet Sauvignon Napa Valley Grand Reserve 1990 • $16 • (11/15/1993) • **86**
Cabernet Sauvignon Napa Valley Grand Reserve 1989 • $14 • (10/31/1992) • **84**
Cabernet Sauvignon Napa Valley Grand Reserve 1988 • $12 • (7/15/1992) • **87**
Cabernet Sauvignon Napa Valley Reserve 1983 • $13 • (10/15/1990) • **90**

VILLA MT. EDEN

Cabernet Sauvignon Napa Valley Reserve 1981 • $17 • (2/01/1986) • **81**
Cabernet Sauvignon Napa Valley Reserve 1980 • $25 • (10/01/1984) • **89**
Chardonnay California 1997: Soft, with simple pear, ripe apple, lemon and spice notes. Drink now.–J.L. • $10 • (2/29/2000) • **81**
Chardonnay California 1996: Solid, with a modest core of ripe pear and melon flavors. A bit cloying on the finish, which has a hint of oak. Drink now.–J.L. • $12 • (7/31/1998) • **84**
Chardonnay Monterey County Coastal 1998: Dirty overtones detract from green apple flavors.–J.L. • $10 • (4/30/2000) • **79**
Chardonnay Santa Maria Valley Bien Nacido Vineyard Grand Reserve 1997: Clean and refreshing, with a zesty core of ripe pear, apple, fig and melon, picking up a trace of citrus on the finish. Drink now through 2001.–J.L. • $18 • (7/31/1999) • **88**
Chardonnay Santa Maria Valley Bien Nacido Vineyard Grand Reserve 1996: Smooth, ripe, rich and creamy. A supple, elegant, complex wine, with tiers of toasty, spicy oak, hints of pear, nectarine and peach, and a long, refreshing finish. Drink now through 2002.–J.L. • $20 • (9/15/1998) • **91**
Chardonnay Santa Maria Valley Bien Nacido Vineyard Signature Series 1997: Ultraripe, rich and creamy, with layers of juicy fig, pear, nectarine and peach flavors. Holds its tight focus on the lingering finish. Drink now through 2002.–J.L. • $31 • (7/31/1999) • **92**
Chardonnay Santa Maria Valley Bien Nacido Vineyards Signature Series 1996 • $35 • (5/31/1998) HR • **95**
Merlot California Coastal 1997: Firm, with coffee, vanilla and black currant notes encased in dry tannins. Best from 2001 through 2004.–J.L. • $10 • (4/30/2000) • **85**
Merlot Napa Valley Grand Reserve 1994 • $16 • (6/30/1996) • **85**
Merlot Napa Valley Grand Reserve 1993 • $16 • (12/31/1995) • **86**
Merlot Napa Valley Grand Reserve 1991 • $15 • (5/31/1994) • **88**
Merlot Napa Valley Grand Reserve 1990 • $15 • (3/31/1993) • **88**
Pinot Blanc Santa Maria Valley Bien Nacido Vineyard Grand Reserve 1996 • $20 • (2/28/1998) • **86**
Pinot Noir California 1997: Coarse, with stewed cherry and strawberry flavors and an earthy finish. Drink now.–J.L. • $12 • (4/30/2000) • **82**
Pinot Noir California 1996 • $12 • (12/31/1997) • **85**
Pinot Noir California Cellar Select 1994 • $8 • (1/31/1996) • **82**
Pinot Noir California Cellar Select 1993 • $8 • (3/31/1995) • **83**
Pinot Noir Carneros Grand Reserve 1991 • $14 • (2/28/1994) • **86**
Pinot Noir Napa Valley 1988 • $12 • (2/28/1991) • **82**
Pinot Noir Santa Maria Valley Bien Nacido Vineyard 1995 • $20 • (10/31/1997) • **89**
Pinot Noir Santa Maria Valley Bien Nacido Vineyard Grand Reserve 1997: Well crafted and smooth, with a caramel edge to the pretty cherry flavors. Drink now through 2001.–J.L. • $20 • (9/15/1999) • **85**
Pinot Noir Santa Maria Valley Bien Nacido Vineyard Grand Reserve 1996 • $20 • (1/31/1998) • **88**
Pinot Noir Santa Maria Valley Bien Nacido Vineyard Grand Reserve 1994 • $12 • (1/31/1996) • **86**
Pinot Noir Santa Maria Valley Bien Nacido Vineyard Grand Reserve 1993 • $14 • (3/31/1995) • **84**
Sauvignon Blanc Late Harvest Napa Valley 1989 • $13/375 ml. • (4/30/1991) • **83**
Sauvignon Blanc Mendocino Coastal 1998: Grapefruit and grass notes combine in a racy, crisp package. Drink now.–J.L. • $10 • (5/31/2000) • **83**
Syrah California Coastal 1998: Pleasant, with soft red currant and herb flavors. Drink now through 2002.–J.L. • $10 • (6/15/2000) • **84**
Syrah California Grand Reserve 1995 • $20 • (4/30/1998) • **89**
Zinfandel California 1995 • $12 • (11/30/1997) • **85**
Zinfandel California Cellar Select 1994 • $9 • (11/30/1996) • **82**
Zinfandel California Cellar Select 1993 • $8 • (9/15/1995) • **88**
Zinfandel California Cellar Select 1992 • $8 • (10/15/1994) • **84**
Zinfandel California Cellar Select 1991 • $8 • (8/31/1993) • **86**
Zinfandel California Cellar Select 1990 • $8 • (9/15/1992) • **84**
Zinfandel California Cellar Select 1989 • $8 • (9/15/1992) • **86**
Zinfandel Napa Valley Mead Ranch Vineyard Grand Reserve 1997: A rustic, chunky style, with a coarse edge to the wild berry, dried plum, cedary oak and gritty tannins. Drink now through 2005.–J.L. • $21 • (6/15/2000) • **86**
Zinfandel Sonoma Valley Monte Rosso Vineyard Grand Reserve 1997: Full of ripe wild berry, black cherry and toasty oak flavors, this is an assertive style that's young and vibrant, with a touch of heat and firm tannins on the finish. Drink now through 2007.–J.L. • $21 • (3/31/2000) • **87**

Key: SS—Spectator Selection. CS—Cellar Selection. HR—Highly Recommended. $NA—Price not available. (BT)—Barrel tasting. Ⓐ—Auction Price.
For a key to the tasters' initials, see "How to Use These Listings."
Dates in parentheses represent the issues in which the ratings were published.

Zinfandel Sonoma Valley Monte Rosso Vineyard Grand Reserve 1996: Flavorful, with ripe, rich wild berry, plum and floral notes and spicy nuances. Turns plush and complex on the finish, with heat and cedary oak. Drink now through 2004.–J.L. • $20 • (2/28/1999) • **91**
Zinfandel Sonoma Valley Monte Rosso Vineyard Grand Reserve 1995 • $20 • (12/15/1997) • **84**
Zinfandel Sonoma Valley Monte Rosso Vineyard Grand Reserve 1994 • $16 • (1/31/1997) • **88**
Zinfandel Sonoma Valley Monte Rosso Vineyard Grand Reserve 1993 • $16 • (9/15/1995) • **88**

VINE CLIFF | CALIFORNIA

Cabernet Sauvignon Oakville Estate 1996: Sharply focused, ripe, rich and perfumed, with firm currant, black cherry, currant, leather and cedary oak. Turns firm and tannic on the finish, where it shows depth and concentration. Drink through 2006.–J.L. • $44 • (11/15/1999) • **94**
Cabernet Sauvignon Napa Valley 1995: A classy style, with ripe, complex, concentrated cherry, plum and berry flavors and pretty, toasty oak shadings. Shows depth and richness while maintaining a sense of elegance. Should only get better. Drink through 2008.–J.L. • $38 • (10/31/1998) • **92**
Cabernet Sauvignon Napa Valley Oakville Estate 1994 • $36 • (10/15/1997) • **90**
Cabernet Sauvignon Napa Valley Oakville Estate 1993 • $30 • (11/15/1996) • **90**
Cabernet Sauvignon Napa Valley 1992 • $30 • (5/15/1996) • **83**
Cabernet Sauvignon Napa Valley 1991 • $25 • (4/30/1995) • **88**
Cabernet Sauvignon Napa Valley 1990 • $41 Ⓐ • (11/15/1993) • **85**
Chardonnay Napa Valley 1998: Well focused, with an elegant array of bright, ripe pear, tangerine and buttery oak. Clean, refreshing aftertaste. Drink now through 2004.–J.L. • $34 • (5/15/2000) • **87**
Chardonnay Napa Valley 1997: Tightly focused, bright and lively, with a pretty, neatly woven tapestry of pear, spice, nutmeg and citrus. Drink now through 2002.–J.L. • $34 • (6/30/1999) • **92**
Chardonnay Napa Valley 1996 • $25 • (4/30/1998) HR • **93**
Chardonnay Napa Valley Proprietress Reserve 1997: Clean and fruity, with ripe pear, fig, melon and hazelnut notes. Creamy oak nuances gain depth and richness on the finish. Drink now.–J.L. • $44 • (11/15/1999) • **90**
Merlot Napa Valley 1997: Dry and earthy, its high-density tannins still masking the rich, extracted currant and blackberry buried beneath. Needs time. Best from 2002 through 2007.–J.L. • $35 • (5/15/2000) • **88**
Merlot Napa Valley 1996: Tight, structured, with firm tannins and a band of cherry, cedar, plum and spice, finishing with leathery tannins that need cellar time. Drink through 2007.–J.L. • $35 • (9/15/1999) • **88**
Merlot Napa Valley 1995 • $27 • (4/30/1998) • **88**

VINEYARD 29 | CALIFORNIA

Cabernet Sauvignon Napa Valley 1996: Marked by herb, chocolate, bell pepper and currant flavors, this turns supple and polished, finishes with a leathery currant flavor. Drink through 2007.–J.L. • $134 Ⓐ • (9/30/1999) • **88**
Cabernet Sauvignon Napa Valley 1994 • $163 Ⓐ • (9/30/1997) • **90**
Cabernet Sauvignon Napa Valley 1993 • $105 Ⓐ • (3/31/1996) • **88**
Cabernet Sauvignon Napa Valley 1992 • $96 Ⓐ • (9/15/1996) • **86**

VINUM | CALIFORNIA

Cabernet Franc Placer County Clos Du Lac Vineyard 1998: Pleasant ripeness to the currant and cola tones and weedy notes, but lean on the finish. Drink now through 2003.–J.L. • $20 • (5/15/2000) • **82**
Mourvèdre El Dorado County 1998: Pleasant depth of black cherry and cola flavors, with intense vanilla notes through the finish. Drink now through 2003.–J.L. • $20 • (5/15/2000) • **86**
Pointe Blanc California 1998: Apple and mineral flavors are crisp and straightforward. Chenin Blanc, Viognier and Roussanne. Drink now.–J.L. • $15 • (6/15/2000) • **83**
Pointe Blanc California 1997: Tight and tangy, showing a broad range of citrus flavors—lemon, orange and grapefruit. Finishes a bit short, however, with a hint of tart apple. A blend of Chenin Blanc, Roussanne and Viognier. Drink now. • $14 • (1/31/1999) • **83**
Viognier San Benito County Vista Verde Vineyard 1998: Fairly rich, with peach, floral and vanilla flavors that turn just a touch earthy on the finish. Drink now.–J.L. • $20 • (5/31/2000) • **85**

VISTA DEL REY | CALIFORNIA

Zinfandel Paso Robles 1996 • $16 • (6/15/1998) • **79**
Zinfandel Paso Robles 1995 • $15 • (6/15/1998) • **85**

VITA NOVA | CALIFORNIA

Cabernet Franc Santa Barbara County 1994 • $8 • (11/30/1996) • **81**

Cabernet Sauvignon-Sangiovese Santa Barbara County Reservatum 1995: A distinctly celerylike aroma is followed by black cherry, herbs and charred oak on the palate. Moderate body and medium weight. However, one expects more refinement from the folks who also make Au Bon Climat. • $18 • (11/15/1998) • **79**

Merlot-Sangiovese Central Coast 1994 • $16 • (6/15/1996) • **83**

Reservatum Santa Barbara County 1986 • $20 • (12/15/1989) • **87**

VOILA! | CALIFORNIA

Mélange Red Napa Valley 1994: A bit weedy on the nose, but chock-full of plummy, tarry anise, prune and herb flavors on the palate. An unusual wine, it finishes long, with a nod to the herbal spectrum. Drink now through 2002. • $18 • (7/31/1998) • **86**

VON STRASSER | CALIFORNIA

Cabernet Sauvignon Diamond Mountain 1997: Austere, tightly wound and firmly tannic, with a chewy core of currant, anise, sage and cedar. Definitely needs time in the cellar for the tannins to soften. Best from 2004 through 2012.–J.L. • $50 • (4/30/2000) • **88**

Cabernet Sauvignon Napa Valley Diamond Mountain 1996: Dark, rich and chewy, with a potent core of complex, earthy mineral, currant, cedar, spice and tar notes. Sharply focused, with wonderful balance and finesse, it shows the tannic strength for short-term cellaring. Drink through 2009.–J.L. • $29 Ⓐ • (11/15/1999) • **92**

Cabernet Sauvignon Napa Valley Diamond Mountain 1995: Delicious Cabernet. Ripe, plummy, with complex cedar, black cherry, spice and herbal menthol notes, it zooms along the palate and shows remarkable texture and suppleness on the finish. Has firm, polished tannins. Best from 2002 through 2011.–J.L. • $36 • (7/31/1998) • **93**

Cabernet Sauvignon Napa Valley Diamond Mountain 1994 • $31 Ⓐ • (10/31/1997) • **92**

Cabernet Sauvignon Napa Valley Diamond Mountain 1993 • $28 • (4/30/1996) • **89**

Cabernet Sauvignon Napa Valley Diamond Mountain 1992 • $29 Ⓐ • (2/28/1995) • **88**

Cabernet Sauvignon Napa Valley Diamond Mountain 1991 • $25 • (3/31/1994) • **88**

Cabernet Sauvignon Napa Valley Diamond Mountain 1990 • $25 • (11/15/1993) • **87**

Chardonnay Napa Valley 1997: Spicy, with a Muscat-like edge that works into ripe pear and apple flavors. Crisp, fruity aftertaste. Drink now through 2002.–J.L. • $36 • (7/31/1999) • **87**

Chardonnay Napa Valley 1996 • $30 • (5/31/1998) • **90**

Reserve Napa Valley 1997: A big, chewy, tannic bruiser, with gobs of blackberry, plum and black cherry. Watch out for the tannins. Petit Verdot, Cabernet Sauvignon and Merlot. Best from 2003 through 2010.–J.L. • $100 • (4/30/2000) • **87**

VOSS | CALIFORNIA

Merlot Napa Valley 1997: Framed by cedary, toasty oak, the core of currant and black cherry is chunky and well focused, if somewhat short at midpalate. Drink now through 2006.–J.L. • $20 • (3/31/2000) • **87**

Merlot Napa Valley 1996: Lean and tannic, with a core of cherry and berry, turning dry on the finish. Drink now.–J.L. • $19 • (10/15/1998) • **81**

Merlot Napa Valley 1995 • $18 • (4/30/1998) • **88**

Merlot Napa Valley 1994 • $18 • (7/31/1997) • **88**

Merlot Napa Valley 1993 • $16 • (5/31/1996) • **75**

Merlot Napa Valley 1992 • $15 • (4/15/1995) • **83**

Merlot Napa Valley 1991 • $18 • (9/15/1994) • **75**

Sauvignon Blanc Napa Valley 1998: Quite fragrant—its aromas a blend of passion fruit, fig and fresh-mowed hay. On the palate, this California white is full-bodied yet light, its flavors ripe and fresh, adding lemon and grapefruit to the equation. Delicious and fun. Drink now. • $15 • (9/30/1999) HR • **90**

Sauvignon Blanc Napa Valley 1997: Vibrant aromas of gooseberry and passion fruit herald a fresh, fruity white that's downright fun to drink. The flavors are interestingly complex, with layers of grapefruit, lemon and lime that play long on the finish. Ready to drink and more than fairly priced for this quality. Tasted twice, with consistent notes. • $13 • (11/30/1998) SS • **91**

Sauvignon Blanc Napa Valley 1996 • $12 • (6/30/1997) • **87**

Sauvignon Blanc Napa Valley Botrytis 1997: An elegant style, moderately rich and concentrated, with creamy fig, pear, vanilla and spice notes. Drink now through 2005.–J.L. • $18/375 ml. • (2/29/2000) • **88**

Sauvignon Blanc Napa Valley Botrytis 1996 • $19/375 ml. • (5/15/1998) • **85**

Shiraz Napa Valley 1996: Tight, firm and tannic, with a complex core of wild berry, cherry and anise framed by toasty, spicy oak, turning dry. Best from 2001 through 2007.–J.L. • $24 • (3/31/2000) • **87**

Shiraz Napa Valley 1995: Dark and chewy, with an earthy, leathery edge to the plum and mineral flavors. Turns complex and fans out on the finish, but needs time to shed tannins. Drink through 2006.–J.L. • $25 • (2/28/1999) • **89**

Zinfandel Alexander Valley 1994 • $14 • (3/31/1997) • **84**

Zinfandel Alexander Valley 1992 • $13 • (1/31/1995) • **77**

Zinfandel Alexander Valley 1991 • $13 • (5/31/1993) • **88**

WAGNER | NEW YORK

Cabernet Franc Finger Lakes 1997: Cassis and tobacco leaf aromas give way to a crisply textured wine, with ripe black cherry notes and firm acidity on the finish. Drink now.–T.M. • $14 • (3/31/2000) • **84**

Cabernet Sauvignon Finger Lakes 1995: A charred character is the hallmark of this rough wine, overriding the faint red cherry flavors.–K.M. • $15 • (2/28/1999) • **76**

Chardonnay Finger Lakes Barrel Fermented 1998: Light-bodied Chardonnay, with some earth and pear notes. Finishes on a simple buttery note. Drink now.–T.M. • $8 • (3/31/2000) • **82**

Gewürztraminer Finger Lakes Dry 1998: A lively Gewürztraminer, delivering its litchi and rose flavors in a slightly dilute presentation. Turns to menthol on the finish.–B.S. • $8 • (4/30/2000) • **78**

Gewürztraminer Finger Lakes Dry 1997: Dominated by lemon-lime flavors, with some decent acidity, and a pinelike aroma.–K.M. • $8 • (2/28/1999) • **79**

Gewürztraminer Finger Lakes Semi-dry 1998: Slightly sweet, with candied aromas and flavors evoking marzipan, nectarine and mint. Round and simple, getting a little washed out on the finish.–B.S. • $8 • (4/30/2000) • **79**

Johannisberg Riesling Finger Lakes Ice Wine 1990 • $15/375 ml. • (4/15/1995) • **76**

Johannisberg Riesling Finger Lakes Ice Wine 1989 • $14/375 ml. • (1/31/1992) • **85**

Melody Finger Lakes 1999: This juicy white offers simple, slightly candied apple and orange flavors, but stays fresh and clean through the finish.–T.M. • $6 • (5/31/2000) • **79**

Merlot Finger Lakes 1997: A silky texture carries light berry and herb flavors, kept fresh by a lively acidity. A charry note mars the finish.–T.M. • $14 • (5/31/2000) • **77**

Pinot Noir Finger Lakes Reserve 1995: Shows good varietal character, with pleasant cherry, berry and spice flavors. On the light side but still lively, with pleasant tea and spice notes on the finish. Drink now.–K.M. • $18 • (2/28/1999) • **85**

Ravat Blanc Finger Lakes Ice Wine 1990 • $14/375 ml. • (4/15/1995) • **79**

Riesling Finger Lakes Dry 1998: Crisp and austere in aroma and flavor, this dry Riesling shows richness midpalate, where the subtle peach and apple notes emerge. Lean, citrusy finish. Drink now.–B.S. • $8 • (3/31/2000) • **83**

Riesling Finger Lakes Dry 1997: Shows a smoky aroma and flavor, with some faint peach flavors, too. Quite tart on the finish.–K.M. • $8 • (2/28/1999) • **73**

Riesling Finger Lakes Ice Wine 1998: A classy dessert wine, exhibiting sweet-tasting floral, apricot and vanilla that's deftly integrated with the vibrant structure. Just a hint of earth on the long finish. Drink now through 2004.–B.S. • $18/375 ml. • (4/30/2000) • **89**

Riesling Finger Lakes Semi-dry 1998: Earth and mineral notes mingle with apple and melon in this focused, lively white. Off-dry, it has a citrus and herbal finish. Drink now.–B.S. • $8 • (3/31/2000) • **80**

Seyval Blanc Finger Lakes Barrel Fermented 1997: Has a green apple aroma, but tastes more of onion skin and celery. Finish is a tad dilute.–T.M. • $7 • (3/31/2000) • **78**

Seyval Blanc Finger Lakes Barrel Fermented 1996: A bit angular, with some onion and herbal flavors, and a bit rough in the end.–K.M. • $6 • (2/28/1999) • **76**

Vidal Blanc Finger Lakes Ice Wine 1998: Smells great, like grilled nuts and honey, then an earthy note emerges on the palate. Sweet, with tart acidity as a counterpoint. Drink now through 2003.–B.S. • $18/375 ml. • (4/30/2000) • **84**

Vignoles Finger Lakes 1999: This juicy, off-dry white serves up lively orange and floral notes reminiscent of Muscat, but with more body and generosity. A refreshing quaff. Drink now.–T.M. • $7 • (5/31/2000) • **83**

Vignoles Finger Lakes Ice Wine 1998: Very sweet and bracing at the same time, showing intense rhubarb, honey and green leaf flavors. Thick, yet stays fresh and clean on the finish. Drink now through 2003.–B.S. • $18/375 ml. • (4/30/2000) • **88**
Vignoles Finger Lakes Ice Wine 1997: This simple sweet wine has appealing orange peel and anise flavors. Drink now.–K.M. • $12/375 ml. • (2/28/1999) • **84**

WALLA WALLA VINTNERS | WASHINGTON

Cabernet Franc Walla Walla Valley Spring Valley Vineyard 1997: A firm, focused red, with solid blackberry and black pepper flavors and a nice floral edge to the finish. Not a rough wine. Drink now through 2002.–H.S. • $25 • (9/30/1999) • **87**
Cabernet Franc Yakima Valley 1995 • $14 • (12/15/1997) • **88**
Cabernet Sauvignon Columbia Valley 1995 • $20 • (12/15/1997) • **91**
Cabernet Sauvignon Walla Walla County Windrow Vineyard 1997: Ripe, supple and generous with its black cherry, currant and spicy oak flavors, smoothly integrated on the long, fine-textured finish. Has the stuff to age well. Drink now through 2009.–H.S. • $32 • (12/31/1999) • **90**
Cabernet Sauvignon Washington 1995 • $22 • (12/15/1997) • **88**
Merlot Walla Walla Valley Spring Valley Vineyard 1997: Earthy, gamy, tobacco-scented flavors permeate this firm-textured wine. At the core, focused currant and black cherry flavors prevail, with a minty note on the finish. Needs cellaring. Best after 2000.–H.S. • $25 • (9/30/1999) • **88**
Merlot Washington 1995 • $18 • (12/15/1997) • **90**
Merlot Yakima Valley Pleasant Vineyard 1997: Light in color, with pretty strawberry and currant flavors that linger on the velvety finish, suggesting this could deepen with age. Drink now through 2002.–H.S. • $25 • (9/30/1999) • **86**
Washington State Cuvée Washington 1996: Generous, supple and spicy, with a sweet streak of coffee and leather wending its way through the rich mouthful of blueberry, plum and red currant. Artfully balanced. Cabernet Sauvignon, Merlot and Cabernet Franc. Drink through 2004.–H.S. • $18 • (8/31/1998) • **90**

WASHINGTON HILLS | WASHINGTON

Cabernet Sauvignon Columbia Valley Varietal Select 1997: Don't pass up this well-crafted and affordably priced Cabernet from Washington. It's crisp and bright, with juicy blackberry and cherry flavors that keep glowing on the nicely balanced finish, and the tannins are not intrusive. Drink now through 2003.–H.S. • $10 • (9/15/1999) • **86**
Cabernet Sauvignon Columbia Valley Varietal Select 1994 • $10 • (9/15/1996) • **85**
Cabernet Sauvignon Columbia Valley Varietal Select 1993 • $9 • (9/30/1995) • **86**
Cabernet-Merlot Columbia Valley 1992 • $8 • (8/31/1994) • **83**
Cabernet-Merlot Columbia Valley Varietal Select 1997: Light and herbal, with a strong mint and sage edge to the strawberry and currant flavors. Tannins are modest. Drink now through 2002.–H.S. • $10 • (9/30/1999) • **82**
Cabernet-Merlot Columbia Valley Varietal Select 1995 • $12 • (9/15/1997) • **84**
Cabernet-Merlot Columbia Valley Varietal Select 1994 • $10 • (9/15/1996) • **85**
Cabernet-Merlot Columbia Valley Varietal Select 1993 • $9 • (9/30/1995) • **83**
Chardonnay Columbia Valley Varietal Select 1997: Bright and fruity in style, with modest pear and spice flavors that expand gently on the lithe finish, this Washington Chardonnay drinks very nicely now, and is quite a bargain, too.–H.S. • $8 • (9/15/1998) • **86**
Chenin Blanc Columbia Valley Dry Varietal Select 1998: Fresh and fruity, a lovely mouthful of ripe apple and citrus flavors that remain lively on the soft finish. Drink now.–H.S. • $6 • (9/30/1999) • **86**
Chenin Blanc Columbia Valley Dry Varietal Select 1996 • $6 • (9/15/1997) • **85**
Gewürztraminer Columbia Valley Varietal Select 1998: Light and sappy, with a resiny edge to the modest apple and spice flavors. Finishes sweet. Drink now.–H.S. • $6 • (9/30/1999) • **81**
Gewürztraminer Columbia Valley Varietal Select 1997: On the light side, off-dry, an aromatic wine with pretty pear and grapefruit flavors, hinting at rose petal at the edges. Drink now.–H.S. • $6 • (9/15/1998) • **85**
Johannisberg Riesling Columbia Valley Varietal Select 1996 • $6 • (10/15/1997) • **87**

Key: SS—Spectator Selection. CS—Cellar Selection. HR—Highly Recommended. $NA—Price not available. (BT)—Barrel tasting. Ⓐ—Auction Price.
For a key to the tasters' initials, see "How to Use These Listings."
Dates in parentheses represent the issues in which the ratings were published.

Merlot Columbia Valley 1992 • $9 • (9/30/1994) • **81**
Merlot Columbia Valley Varietal Select 1997: Herbal, cooked aromas and dry, peppery flavors are not immediately appealing, but the nice core of light cherry flavor could emerge with cellaring. Best after 2001.–H.S. • $11 • (9/30/1999) • **82**
Merlot Columbia Valley Varietal Select 1995 • $13 • (9/15/1997) • **81**
Merlot Columbia Valley Varietal Select 1994 • $10 • (9/15/1996) • **84**
Merlot Columbia Valley Varietal Select 1993 • $9 • (9/30/1995) • **85**
Merlot Washington Varietal Select 1996: Light in color and texture, a simple red with pretty leather and cherry notes. Drink now.–H.S. • $11 • (9/15/1998) • **82**
Riesling Columbia Valley Dry Varietal Select 1997: Light, dry and refreshing for its refined apple, spice and floral flavors that linger appealingly on the finish. Drink now.–H.S. • $6 • (9/15/1998) • **86**
Sauvignon Blanc Columbia Valley 1998: Bright and juicy, a mouthful of citrus, apple and guava flavors that linger on the open-textured finish. Drink now.–H.S. • $8 • (5/15/2000) • **83**
Sauvignon Blanc Columbia Valley Varietal Select 1997: Soft and fruity, with simple apple and citrus flavors. Drink now.–H.S. • $6 • (9/15/1998) • **81**
Sémillon Columbia Valley Varietal Select 1998: Round and spicy, generous with its ripe fig, melon and herbal flavors, picking up a nice hint of nutmeg on the focused finish. Drink now through 2002.–H.S. • $8 • (9/30/1999) • **86**
Sémillon Columbia Valley Varietal Select 1996: Light and pleasant for its melon and pear flavors, with hints of tobacco on the finish.–H.S. • $7 • (9/15/1998) • **82**
Sémillon-Chardonnay Columbia Valley 1998: Smooth and gentle, its pretty spice, apple and fig flavors in modest proportions yet persisting nicely on the finish. Drink now through 2001.–H.S. • $8 • (9/30/1999) • **85**
White Riesling Columbia Valley Late Harvest Varietal Select 1997: Sweet and ripe, with peach, pear and floral notes that remain generous through the soft finish. Drink now.–H.S. • $7 • (9/15/1998) • **85**
White Riesling Columbia Valley Late Harvest Varietal Select 1996 • $8 • (10/15/1997) • **85**
White Riesling Columbia Valley Late Harvest Varietal Select 1995 • $8 • (9/15/1996) • **88**
White Riesling Columbia Valley Varietal Select 1998: Fresh, like biting into raw fruit, offering pretty melon and mineral flavors on a sweet, smooth frame. Drink now.–H.S. • $6 • (9/30/1999) • **84**
White Riesling Columbia Valley Varietal Select 1997: Fresh and fruity, with a pine cone overtone to the apple and pear flavors. Drink now.–H.S. • $6 • (9/15/1998) • **83**
White Riesling Columbia Valley Varietal Select Special Harvest 1993 • $7 • (9/30/1995) • **81**
White Riesling Late Harvest Columbia Valley Varietal Select 1998: Sweet, bright and refreshing. Not typical of a dessert wine, but it offers ripe apricot and peach flavors that linger on the soft finish. Drink now through 2001.–H.S. • $8 • (9/30/1999) • **83**

WATERBROOK | WASHINGTON

Cabernet Franc Columbia Valley 1994 • $20 • (12/31/1996) • **89**
Cabernet Sauvignon Columbia Valley 1996: A layer of fine tannins surrounds a core of pretty violet-scented blackberry and black currant flavors that linger nicely. Deserves cellaring. Best after 2001.–H.S. • $24 • (8/31/1999) • **87**
Cabernet Sauvignon Columbia Valley 1995 • $24 • (5/15/1998) • **88**
Cabernet Sauvignon Columbia Valley 1994 • $20 • (12/15/1996) • **92**
Cabernet Sauvignon Columbia Valley 1993 • $18 • (12/15/1995) • **88**
Cabernet Sauvignon Columbia Valley 1992 • $16 • (4/15/1995) SS • **91**
Cabernet Sauvignon Columbia Valley 1991 • $15 • (9/30/1994) • **88**
Cabernet Sauvignon Columbia Valley 1989 • $13 • (10/15/1993) • **86**
Cabernet Sauvignon Columbia Valley 1988 • $14 • (4/15/1992) • **85**
Chardonnay Columbia Valley 1998: A bright and zingy style, this Washington white is lively on the palate, with citrus, mineral and pear flavors. Finishes with a nice lime bite that lingers on the racy finish. Drink now through 2003.–H.S. • $10 • (5/15/2000) SS • **89**
Chardonnay Columbia Valley 1997: Immediately appealing and imminently drinkable, this light and tangy Washington white shows a thread of sweet cream weaving through the modest apple flavors. Won't disappoint, and won't break the budget.–H.S. • $11 • (1/31/1999) • **86**
Chardonnay Columbia Valley 1996 • $11 • (1/31/1998) • **87**
Mélange Columbia Valley 1997: Smooth, almost silky, with distinctive overtones of exotic spice and peach to the light core of black cherry flavor. Finish lingers gently. Drink now through 2006.–H.S. • $12 • (11/15/1999) • **87**

Merlot Columbia Valley 1996: A little chewy with tannins, but a veritable spice box of aromas and flavors; exotic, with cinnamon, allspice and star anise overtones to the basic black cherry. The finish lingers. Drink now.–H.S. • $19 • (8/31/1999) • **89**
Merlot Columbia Valley 1995 • $22 • (5/15/1998) • **86**
Merlot Columbia Valley 1994 • $20 • (12/15/1996) HR • **91**
Merlot Columbia Valley 1993 • $18 • (5/15/1996) • **90**
Merlot Columbia Valley 1992 • $15 • (9/30/1995) • **90**
Merlot Columbia Valley 1991 • $14 • (12/31/1993) • **86**
Merlot Columbia Valley 1990 • $15 • (6/15/1993) • **84**
Merlot Columbia Valley 1989 • $14 • (4/30/1992) HR • **94**
Merlot Columbia Valley Reserve 1995: Ripe flavors of plum and berry and a velvety texture entice, while the harmonious finish delivers nice touches of smoke and spice. Better than when previously reviewed. Drink now through 2003.–H.S. • $32 • (6/15/1999) • **88**
Merlot Columbia Valley Reserve 1992 • $22 • (5/31/1995) • **89**
Sauvignon Blanc Columbia Valley 1998: Soft and appealing for its pretty pear and floral flavors, which come together for a snappy finish. Drink now.–H.S. • $8 • (5/15/2000) • **86**
Sauvignon Blanc Columbia Valley 1997: Ripe and polished, with the spicy note of barrel fermentation adding an extra fillip to the melon and citrus flavors.–H.S. • $13 • (9/15/1998) • **87**
Sauvignon Blanc Columbia Valley 1996 • $11 • (9/15/1997) • **86**
Viognier Columbia Valley 1998: Ripe and generous, not as exuberant as some Viogniers but nicely tuned to show off its melon, spice, cream and floral flavors and let them linger gently on the finish. Drink now.–H.S. • $18 • (8/31/1999) • **90**
Viognier Columbia Valley 1997: Ripe and generous, built to contain rather than explode the flavors, so it focuses its peach, melon, apricot and exotic spice flavors into a bright beam. Delicious now.–H.S. • $18 • (9/15/1998) • **89**

WATTLE CREEK | CALIFORNIA

Cabernet Sauvignon Alexander Valley 1995: Layers of black currant, anise, plum, leather and smoke are tightly intertwined. Tannins are powdery. Moderate finish. Drink now through 2004. • $30 • (10/15/1998) • **87**
Chardonnay Alexander Valley 1997: Showing moderate body and a core of pear, citrus and toasty oak flavors, this is firm and focused. On the finish, it offers bright acidity, with a lemony aftertaste. Drink now through 2002. • $19 • (6/15/1999) • **88**
Chardonnay Alexander Valley 1996: Smooth though somewhat restrained, this wine shows pretty pear and citrus flavors in a delicate vein. Drink now. • $19 • (9/15/1998) • **86**
Sauvignon Blanc Alexander Valley 1998: Flint, earth and citrus notes combine in a tart, tangy package. Tasted twice, with consistent notes. Drink now through 2002.–J.L. • $18 • (5/15/2000) • **81**
Sauvignon Blanc Alexander Valley 1997: Peaches and passion fruit strike a pose here, followed by hints of melon and citrus. The ensemble is a bright, fine balance of tangy acidity and full, fresh body. • $16 • (9/15/1998) • **89**
Sauvignon Blanc Alexander Valley 1996 • $16 • (9/15/1997) • **89**
Shiraz Alexander Valley 1995: Rich and juicy, with a good dose of acidity. Pretty cherry, strawberry and herb flavors are the hallmarks. Firmly structured, it's good now and should age well. Drink through 2004. • $24 • (10/31/1998) • **87**

WEDELL | CALIFORNIA

Chardonnay Edna Valley 1996: Simple, earthy citrus and tropical fruit flavors, with toasty oak, turning candied on the finish. Drink now.–J.L. • $23 • (12/15/1998) • **80**

WEINSTOCK | CALIFORNIA

Cabernet Sauvignon Paso Robles 1997: A fruity style, showing off bright cherry and grape flavors. Mild tannins make this a fine candidate for early quaffing. Kosher. Drink now. • $11 • (10/15/1999) • **84**
Cabernet Sauvignon Sonoma County 1994 • $10 • (11/30/1996) • **72**
Cabernet Sauvignon Sonoma County 1992 • $9 • (5/31/1995) • **85**
Gamay Sonoma County 1989 • $8 • (3/31/1991) • **75**
Pinot Noir Sonoma County Winemaker Selection Reserve 1989 • $13 • (11/15/1991) • **79**

WEISINGER'S | OREGON

Cabernet Sauvignon Rogue Valley Layne Vineyard Vintage Select 1990 • $23 • (11/30/1994) • **79**
Chardonnay-Sémillon Rogue Valley NV • $11 • (5/15/1998) • **86**
Chardonnay-Sémillon Rogue Valley 1997: Fresh, bright and lively, with a pretty mouthful of lime, nectarine and spice flavors that linger on the slightly raw finish. Drink through 2002.–H.S. • $12 • (6/30/1999) • **87**
Mescolare Oregon NV: Light in texture and jazzy in flavor, with cherry, strawberry, mint and spice flavors that linger on the open-textured finish. Cabernet Sauvignon, Pinot Noir and Nebbiolo. Drink now.–H.S. • $17 • (5/15/2000) • **86**
Petite Pompadour Pompadour Vineyard Rogue Valley 1997: A solid, firm-textured red, with pretty plum and raspberry flavors echoing nicely on the finish. Cabernet Franc, Cabernet Sauvignon, Merlot and Malbec. Drink now through 2002.–H.S. • $19 • (5/15/2000) • **85**
Petite Pompadour Pompadour Vineyard Rogue Valley 1996: Firm and chewy, with an earthy-gamy streak running through the black cherry and herb flavors. Needs time to soften. Best after 2001.–H.S. • $19 • (6/30/1999) • **85**
Petite Pompadour Pompadour Vineyard Rogue Valley 1995 • $17 • (5/15/1998) • **87**
Petite Pompadour Rogue Valley Pompadour Vineyard 1993 • $15 • (12/31/1996) • **81**
Petite Pompadour Rogue Valley Pompadour Vineyard 1992 • $15 • (3/31/1996) • **86**
Petite Pompadour Rogue Valley 1992 • $15 • (11/30/1994) • **78**
Pinot Noir Rogue Valley 1992 • $15 • (1/31/1996) • **86**

WELLINGTON | CALIFORNIA

Cabernet Franc Mount Veeder 1990 • $13 • (11/15/1992) • **80**
Cabernet Sauvignon Mount Veeder Random Ridge 1996: Full-bodied, with plenty of toasty oak framing a blend of herb, mint, cassis and blackberry flavors. The finish is long, with firm, ripe tannins and just a hint of anise. Best from 2001 through 2005. • $20 • (9/30/1999) • **88**
Cabernet Sauvignon Mount Veeder Random Ridge 1994: Woody, with hints of tea, chocolate and berry emerging from a solid foundation. Drink now. • $18 • (11/15/1998) • **79**
Cabernet Sauvignon Mount Veeder Random Ridge 1993 • $16 • (11/15/1996) • **87**
Cabernet Sauvignon Mount Veeder Random Ridge 1992 • $16 • (12/15/1995) • **83**
Cabernet Sauvignon Mount Veeder Random Ridge 1991 • $16 • (11/15/1994) • **84**
Cabernet Sauvignon Mount Veeder Random Ridge 1990 • $16 • (10/15/1993) • **86**
Cabernet Sauvignon Sonoma County Mohrhardt Ridge Vineyard 1996: An herbal style featuring tar, green bean and earthy notes as well as a concentrated core of black cherry, currant and mineral. Finishes firmly tannic. Improves with aeration, so give it time. Best from 2001 through 2006.–J.L. • $16 • (10/15/1999) • **86**
Cabernet Sauvignon Sonoma County Mohrhardt Ridge Vineyard 1995: Black cherry, currant and anise flavors are followed by rich, concentrated mineral and iodine notes, all folding into a plush, ripe frame. For fans of mineral flavors. Drink now through 2001.–H.S. • $15 • (10/31/1998) • **85**
Cabernet Sauvignon Sonoma County Mohrhardt Ridge Vineyard 1994 • $15 • (11/15/1997) • **87**
Cabernet Sauvignon Sonoma County Mohrhardt Ridge Vineyard 1993 • $14 • (11/15/1996) • **87**
Cabernet Sauvignon Sonoma County Mohrhardt Ridge Vineyard 1992 • $14 • (12/15/1995) • **84**
Cabernet Sauvignon Sonoma County Mohrhardt Ridge Vineyard 1991 • $14 • (11/15/1994) • **85**
Cabernet Sauvignon Sonoma County Mohrhardt Ridge Vineyard 1990 • $14 • (9/15/1993) • **83**
Cabernet Sauvignon Sonoma County Mohrhardt Ridge Vineyard 1989 • $14 • (8/31/1992) • **85**
Cabernet Sauvignon Sonoma Valley Glen Lyon Vineyard 1993 • $14 • (12/15/1995) • **84**
Chardonnay Sonoma County 1997: Mineral, citrus and apple notes form the core. Flinty mineral flavors persist on the firm finish. Drink now. • $14 • (7/31/1999) • **84**
Chardonnay Sonoma County 1996 • $13 • (6/30/1998) • **86**
Criolla Sonoma Valley Old Vines 1991 • $7 • (6/15/1993) • **85**
Criolla Sonoma Valley Old Vines 1990 • $7 • (3/31/1992) • **85**
Merlot Sonoma County 1992 • $15 • (11/15/1995) • **86**
Merlot Sonoma County 1991 • $11 • (9/15/1994) • **85**
Merlot Sonoma Valley 1997: Charry oak notes almost drown out the crisp, modest black cherry. Finishes with slightly burnt, sour notes. Drink now.–J.L. • $18 • (4/30/2000) • **83**

Merlot Sonoma Valley 1995 • $16 • (12/15/1997) • **80**
Merlot Sonoma Valley 1994 • $15 • (12/15/1996) • **84**
Merlot Sonoma Valley 1993 • $15 • (8/31/1996) • **83**
Random Ridge Mount Veeder 1989 • $16 • (11/15/1992) • **86**
Sauvignon Blanc Sonoma Mountain Herron Vineyard 1998: Medium-bodied, with herb, citrus and earth notes. Drink now through 2003.–J.L. • $14 • (4/30/2000) • **83**
Syrah Russian River Valley 1997: Fine concentration of earthy, leathery fruit and game notes, finishing with dry tannins. Best from 2001 through 2004.–J.L. • $17 • (5/15/2000) • **85**
Syrah Russian River Valley Alegría Vineyard 1996: Somewhat austere at first, with astringent tannins, but the blackberry, blueberry and herb flavors stretch out nicely after a little time in the glass. Drink through 2002. • $17 • (9/15/1998) • **86**
Syrah Russian River Valley Alegría Vineyard 1995 • $16 • (3/31/1998) • **88**
Syrah Russian River Valley Alegría Vineyard 1994 • $15 • (9/15/1996) • **84**
Syrah Russian River Valley Alegría Vineyard 1993 • $12 • (9/30/1995) • **89**
Victory Reserve Sonoma County 1994: A sleekly styled wine, sporting cassis, anise and cedar flavors. It's well balanced, with firm but ripe tannins and a moderate finish. 49 percent Cabernet Sauvignon, 30 percent Merlot, 21 percent Cabernet Franc. Drink now through 2002. • $24 • (10/15/1998) • **87**
Victory Sonoma County Reserve 1991 • $20 • (9/15/1996) • **86**
Viognier Sonoma County 1997: Almost sweet-tasting, its richness backed by peach, spice and mineral flavors. Finishes clean, though a little short. Drink now. • $18 • (12/31/1998) • **85**
Zinfandel Russian River Valley 1996 • $14 • (5/31/1998) • **85**
Zinfandel Sonoma County 1994 • $10 • (8/31/1996) • **88**
Zinfandel Sonoma County Old Vines 1993 • $9 • (10/15/1995) • **72**
Zinfandel Sonoma County 100-Year-Old Vines 1997: Dark, with chewy, earthy, extracted blackberry and vanilla notes and a drying finish. Drink now through 2003.–J.L. • $24 • (5/15/2000) • **83**
Zinfandel Sonoma Valley 100-Year-Old Vines 1995 • $20 • (6/15/1998) • **87**
Zinfandel Sonoma Valley 100-Year-Old Vines 1994 • $18 • (2/28/1997) • **83**
Zinfandel Sonoma Valley 100-Year-Old Vines 1993 • $15 • (10/15/1995) • **87**
Zinfandel Sonoma Valley 100-Year-Old Vines 1992 • $13 • (10/15/1994) • **87**
Zinfandel Sonoma Valley Casa Santinamaria 1996 • $16 • (5/31/1998) • **86**
Zinfandel Sonoma Valley Casa Santinamaria 1995 • $16 • (3/31/1997) • **86**
Zinfandel Sonoma Valley Casa Santinamaria 1994 • $15 • (8/31/1996) • **87**
Zinfandel Sonoma Valley Casa Santinamaria 1993 • $12 • (10/15/1995) • **86**
Zinfandel Sonoma Valley Casa Santinamaria 1992 • $10 • (10/15/1994) • **84**

WENTE | CALIFORNIA

Blanc de Blancs Arroyo Seco NV • $14 • (12/31/1993) • **82**
Blanc de Noir Arroyo Seco NV • $14 • (12/31/1993) • **85**
Brut Arroyo Seco Grande Brut NV • $12 • (12/31/1993) • **82**
Cabernet Sauvignon Livermore Valley 1997: Ripe plum and earth tones are accented by toasty oak nuances and supported by a hearty frame. Drink now through 2005.–J.L. • $12 • (6/30/2000) • **84**
Cabernet Sauvignon Livermore Valley 1996: Tutti-frutti cherry flavors swim in a simple, lightweight wine. • $21 • (11/15/1998) • **73**
Cabernet Sauvignon Livermore Valley 1995 • $11 • (10/15/1997) • **85**
Cabernet Sauvignon Livermore Valley 1993 • $8 • (11/15/1995) • **85**
Cabernet Sauvignon Livermore Valley 1991 • $10 • (11/15/1994) • **82**
Cabernet Sauvignon Livermore Valley 1990 • $9 • (11/15/1993) • **81**
Cabernet Sauvignon Livermore Valley Charles Wetmore Reserve 1995: A fruit-juicy wine with a healthy dollop of charry oak. Redolent of Bing cherry and smoke, with a short finish and firm tannins. • $11 • (11/15/1998) • **79**
Cabernet Sauvignon Livermore Valley Charles Wetmore Vineyard Reserve 1990 • $16 • (8/31/1994) • **86**
Cabernet Sauvignon Livermore Valley Charles Wetmore Vineyard Reserve 1989 • $18 • (11/15/1993) • **85**
Cabernet Sauvignon Livermore Valley Charles Wetmore Vineyard Reserve 1987 • $18 • (4/30/1991) • **86**
Cabernet Sauvignon Livermore Valley Charles Wetmore Vineyard Reserve 1986 • $12 • (10/15/1990) • **82**
Chardonnay Arroyo Seco Riva Ranch Reserve 1996: Delivers more flavor than grace, with ripe tangerine and peachy flavors leading to a toasty oak layer. Drink now.–J.L. • $13 • (12/15/1998) • **85**

Key: SS—Spectator Selection. CS—Cellar Selection. HR—Highly Recommended. $NA—Price not available. (BT)—Barrel tasting. Ⓐ—Auction Price.
For a key to the tasters' initials, see "How to Use These Listings."
Dates in parentheses represent the issues in which the ratings were published.

Chardonnay Central Coast 1996: This California white is ready to drink, with pleasant fig, pear and citrus flavors that come together subtly on a soft frame. A very nice wine, and its price tag invites you to give it a try.–J.L. • $9 • (12/15/1998) • **85**
Merlot Livermore Valley 1996: A smoky, oaky wine, it serves up cassis, tea and licorice flavors. While not totally harmonious, it's still quite tasty, and has a good price, too. Drink now through 2002. • $10 • (9/30/1998) • **84**
Merlot Livermore Valley Crane Ridge 1993 • $13 • (8/31/1996) • **84**
Merlot Livermore Valley Crane Ridge 1991 • $12 • (9/15/1994) • **84**
Merlot Livermore Valley Crane Ridge 1990 • $12 • (12/31/1993) • **84**
Merlot Livermore Valley Crane Ridge Reserve 1996: A tight band of plum and black cherry flavors leads the way, backed up by smoky oak and a smooth texture. Finishes with an herbal grip. Drink now through 2003. • $15 • (9/30/1998) • **85**
Pinot Noir Arroyo Seco Reliz Creek Reserve 1995: Color is light and browning, with thin, peppery, weedy flavors. Misses the mark by a wide margin. Best to avoid.–J.L. • $15 • (9/15/1998) • **70**
Pinot Noir Arroyo Seco Reliz Creek Reserve 1994 • $15 • (3/31/1997) • **78**
Sauvignon Blanc Central Coast 1998: A bit funky, with herb and grapefruit notes that carry through to the slightly green finish. Drink now.–J.L. • $9 • (5/31/2000) • **80**
Sauvignon Blanc Livermore Valley 1997: Features a silky texture, with tangy acidity to balance it. Pretty grass, herb, grapefruit and melon flavors fan out, with a fresh, clean finish. Drink now through 2002. • $10 • (5/15/1999) • **87**
Sauvignon Blanc Livermore Valley 1996 • $8 • (3/31/1998) • **88**
Zinfandel Livermore Valley Raboli Vineyards 1985 • $10 • (12/15/1989) • **77**

WESTBEND | NORTH CAROLINA

Cabernet Sauvignon North Carolina 1994 • $14 • (6/15/1998) • **72**
Cabernet Sauvignon North Carolina 1993 • $14 • (4/30/1997) • **82**
Cabernet Sauvignon North Carolina 1992 • $14 • (4/30/1997) • **82**
Cabernet Sauvignon North Carolina 1990: Library release. Eerie, molasses in color, with muddled brown sugar and unpleasant, murky herbal notes. Past its prime.–B.S. • $NA • (1/01/2000) • **71**
Chambourcin North Carolina 1997: Ambitious from its dark purple color to its overtly sweet, smoky nose, this has a grapey exuberance, with sweet black cherry and cracked pepper flavors. A good picnic wine. Drink now. –B.S. • $11 • (1/01/2000) • **81**
Chardonnay North Carolina 1997: Straightforward, with caramel and smoke flavors and buttery notes on the finish. Drink now.–K.M. • $11 • (1/01/2000) • **81**
Chardonnay North Carolina Barrel Fermented 1997: Heavy-handed, with oaky flavors and apple notes. Finishes with a touch of bitter almond. –K.M. • $17 • (1/01/2000) • **79**
Chardonnay North Carolina Silver Creek Vineyards 1996 • $13 • (5/31/1998) • **84**
Riesling North Carolina 1998: Fresh and slightly sweet, but there's a metallic or plastic note that detracts from the overall presentation.–B.S. • $9 • (3/31/2000) • **75**
Sauvignon Blanc North Carolina 1996: This thick, heavy-handed white could almost pass for a barrel-fermented Chardonnay. Deep gold in color, with butter and vanilla aromas but very little fruit flavor. • $10 • (6/15/1999) • **75**
Vidal Blanc North Carolina 1997: This viscous white is marred by burnt, bitter flavors; it lacks fruit and finesse.–T.M. • $12/375 ml. • (1/01/2000) • **72**
Vidal Blanc North Carolina 1994 • $35 • (6/15/1998) • **86**
Vidal Blanc North Carolina Botrytis 1993 • $24/375 ml. • (1/01/1997) • **82**
White Gamay North Carolina 1996: An innocuous rosé, with only modest strawberry and watermelon flavors.–K.M. • $8 • (8/31/1998) • **75**

WESTPORT RIVERS | NEW ENGLAND

Chardonnay Southeastern New England 1998: This full-bodied white offers heavily oaked flavors of toast, hazelnuts and butter, with ripe flavors of melon and pear as well, and enough lemony acidity for balance. An ambitious wine that needs food to show its best. Tasted twice, with consistent notes. Drink now through 2002.–T.M. • $17 • (5/31/2000) • **87**
Chardonnay Southeastern New England Noble 1994 • $15/375 ml. • (1/31/1997) • **84**
Chardonnay Southeastern New England Silver Label 1997: Buttery-tasting, but a tart, almost tinny flavor makes it a bit unbalanced in the end.–K.M. • $16 • (5/31/1999) • **76**
Johannisberg Riesling Southeastern New England 1997: This is fresh and lively, offering citrus and floral aromas and flavors, with a dry and tangy impression in a light-bodied style. Drink now.–B.S. • $15 • (6/15/1999) • **82**

Signature Reserve North Fork of Long Island 1994: A cloying red wine, with an overt green bell pepper flavor to it.–K.M. • $22 • (8/31/1998) • **71**

WESTREY | OREGON

Chardonnay Willamette Valley Reserve 1997: Light and earthy, with floral and apple flavors that finish with a rough edge. Drink now through 2001.–H.S. • $18 • (3/31/2000) • **81**
Pinot Noir Willamette Valley 1997: Light, fruity and appealing for its bright berry and distinctly herbal flavors, including a minty note on the finish. Drink now through 2002.–H.S. • $15 • (3/31/2000) • **85**
Pinot Noir Willamette Valley Croft Vineyard Reserve 1997: Light and appealing, with earthy black cherry flavors that float easily over the solid finish. Drink now through 2003.–H.S. • $20 • (3/31/2000) • **86**
Pinot Noir Willamette Valley Reserve 1995 • $26 • (10/31/1997) • **83**

WHEELER | CALIFORNIA

Cabernet Franc California 1994 • $19 • (7/31/1997) • **76**
Cabernet Sauvignon California 1995 • $15 • (5/15/1997) • **85**
Cabernet Sauvignon Dry Creek Valley 1989 • $13 • (6/15/1993) • **81**
Cabernet Sauvignon Dry Creek Valley 1988 • $15 • (8/31/1992) • **83**
Cabernet Sauvignon Dry Creek Valley 1987 • $14 • (11/15/1991) • **84**
Cabernet Sauvignon Dry Creek Valley 1986 • $12 • (8/31/1990) • **83**
Cabernet Sauvignon Dry Creek Valley 1985 • $12 • (7/15/1989) • **76**
Cabernet Sauvignon Dry Creek Valley 1984 • $11 • (4/15/1988) • **75**
Cabernet Sauvignon Dry Creek Valley Norse Vineyard Private Reserve 1985 • $18 • (11/15/1990) • **83**
Cabernet Sauvignon Dry Creek Valley Norse Vineyard Private Reserve 1984 • $15 • (7/31/1989) • **60**
Cabernet Sauvignon Dry Creek Valley Norse Vineyard Reserve 1991 • $12 • (11/15/1994) • **84**
Malbec California 1994 • $19 • (7/31/1997) • **86**
Merlot Dry Creek Valley 1992 • $12 • (4/15/1995) • **79**
Quintet California 1990 • $8 • (5/31/1993) • **76**
RS Reserve California 1989 • $11 • (10/31/1991) • **77**
RS Reserve California 1988 • $10 • (8/31/1990) • **83**
Sangiovese California 1994 • $19 • (4/30/1997) • **80**
Zinfandel California 1994 • $15 • (4/30/1997) • **78**
Zinfandel Dry Creek Valley 1992 • $11 • (8/31/1995) • **87**
Zinfandel Dry Creek Valley 1991 • $12 • (9/30/1993) • **80**

WHIDBEY ISLAND | WASHINGTON

Cabernet Sauvignon Yakima Valley 1996: Earthy, with a sharp edge to the berry flavors, a touch of astringency on the otherwise juicy finish.–H.S. • $15 • (9/15/1998) • **78**
Cabernet Sauvignon Yakima Valley 1995 • $14 • (9/15/1997) • **86**
Lemberger Yakima Valley 1995 • $10 • (9/15/1997) • **79**

WHITCRAFT | CALIFORNIA

Chardonnay Santa Maria Valley Bien Nacido Vineyard 1996 • $22 • (11/30/1997) • **89**
Petite Sirah Santa Barbara County 1995 • $22 • (7/31/1997) • **86**
Pinot Noir Russian River Valley Olivet Lane Vineyard 1992 • $30 • (2/28/1994) • **90**
Pinot Noir Russian River Valley Olivet Lane Vineyard 1991 • $25 • (2/28/1993) • **81**
Pinot Noir Santa Maria Valley Bien Nacido Vineyard 1997: Builds up with supple cherry, earth and berry flavors, with hints of spice and mushroom, then firms up on the finish, where the tannins are quite evident. Drink now through 2004.–J.L. • $25 • (9/15/1999) • **87**
Pinot Noir Santa Maria Valley Bien Nacido Vineyard 1996 • $35 • (1/31/1998) • **88**
Pinot Noir Santa Maria Valley Bien Nacido Vineyard 1995 • $35 • (12/31/1996) • **88**
Pinot Noir Santa Maria Valley Bien Nacido Vineyard 1994 • $30 • (12/31/1995) • **93**
Pinot Noir Santa Maria Valley Bien Nacido Vineyard 1993 • $30 • (12/31/1994) • **88**
Pinot Noir Santa Maria Valley Bien Nacido Vineyard 1992 • $30 • (2/28/1994) • **88**
Pinot Noir Santa Maria Valley Bien Nacido Vineyard 1991 • $25 • (2/28/1993) • **83**
Pinot Noir Santa Maria Valley Bien Nacido Vineyard 1990 • $25 • (2/28/1993) • **88**
Pinot Noir Santa Maria Valley Bien Nacido Vineyard N Block 1996 • $40 • (2/28/1998) • **79**
Pinot Noir Santa Maria Valley Bien Nacido Vineyard N Block 1994 • $40 • (5/15/1996) • **89**
Pinot Noir Santa Maria Valley Bien Nacido Vineyard N Block 1993 • $35 • (12/31/1995) • **87**
Pinot Noir Santa Maria Valley Bien Nacido Vineyard Q Block 1996 • $40 • (1/31/1998) • **88**
Pinot Noir Santa Maria Valley Bien Nacido Vineyard Q Block 1995 • $40 • (12/31/1996) • **88**
Pinot Noir Santa Maria Valley Bien Nacido Vineyard Q Block 1994 • $35 • (12/31/1995) • **88**
Pinot Noir Santa Maria Valley Bien Nacido Vineyard Q Block 1993 • $35 • (12/31/1994) • **89**
Pinot Noir Santa Maria Valley Bien Nacido Vineyard Q Block 1992 • $40 • (2/28/1994) • **88**
Pinot Noir Sonoma Coast Hirsch Vineyard 1996 • $40 • (2/28/1998) • **82**
Pinot Noir Sonoma Coast Hirsch Vineyard 1995 • $40 • (12/31/1996) • **87**
Pinot Noir Sonoma Coast Hirsch Vineyard 1994 • $40 • (5/15/1996) • **92**

WHITE COTTAGE | CALIFORNIA

Cabernet Sauvignon Howell Mountain 1996: A subtle, supple style from Howell Mountain, with polished cherry, currant, herb and cedary notes, holding tight focus on the finish, where the tannins turn elegant. Drink through 2008.–J.L. • $40 • (10/15/1999) • **90**
Cabernet Sauvignon Howell Mountain 1995: Elegant for Howell Mountain, with ripe, complex currant, black cherry, mineral, sage and cedary oak flavors, picking up touches of clay and toasty oak. Forward and appealing now, this appears to be a midrange wine. Drink through 2005.–J.L. • $40 • (11/15/1998) • **90**
Cabernet Sauvignon Howell Mountain 1994 • $96 Ⓐ • (10/15/1997) • **93**
Merlot Howell Mountain 1996: Relatively simple, with a modest range of earth, cedary currant and spice notes, turning somewhat diluted. Drink now through 2004.–J.L. • $33 • (10/15/1999) • **82**

WHITE HALL | VIRGINIA

Cabernet Franc Virginia 1995 • $18 • (4/30/1997) • **79**

WHITE HERON | WASHINGTON

Chantepierre Washington 1992 • $10 • (9/30/1995) • **80**
Chantepierre Washington 1990 • $10 • (9/30/1994) • **83**
Chantepierre Washington 1989 • $10 • (3/15/1993) • **70**
Chantepierre Washington 1988 • $11 • (4/15/1992) • **80**
Pinot Noir Washington 1990 • $7 • (9/30/1994) • **81**

WHITE OAK | CALIFORNIA

Cabernet Franc Alexander Valley 1992 • $17 • (12/31/1994) • **85**
Cabernet Franc Alexander Valley 1989 • $12 • (11/15/1992) • **84**
Cabernet Sauvignon Alexander Valley 1992 • $14 • (12/15/1995) • **85**
Cabernet Sauvignon Alexander Valley 1991 • $14 • (11/15/1994) • **84**
Cabernet Sauvignon Alexander Valley 1990 • $14 • (11/15/1993) • **87**
Cabernet Sauvignon Alexander Valley 1988 • $14 • (11/15/1992) • **85**
Cabernet Sauvignon Alexander Valley Myers Limited Reserve 1985 • $18 • (7/31/1989) • **85**
Cabernet Sauvignon Sonoma County 1987 • $14 • (2/29/1992) • **85**
Chardonnay Sonoma County Myers Limited Reserve 1996 • $20 • (5/15/1998) • **87**
Myers Limited Reserve Sonoma County 1997: Fresh and grapey, featuring cassis, black cherry, wild berry, tar and herb, finishing with firm, well-integrated tannins. Drink now through 2005.–J.L. • $22 • (10/15/1999) • **86**
Sauvignon Blanc Napa Valley 1997: A full-bodied wine, redolent of fig, fresh pea, melon, hay and citrus. Weighty on the palate, it nonetheless finishes with a fresh, clean edge. Drink now through 2002. • $12 • (5/15/1999) • **87**
Zinfandel Alexander Valley 1994 • $15 • (4/30/1997) • **89**
Zinfandel Alexander Valley 1993 • $15 • (10/15/1995) • **88**
Zinfandel Alexander Valley 1990 • $10 • (12/15/1992) • **75**
Zinfandel Alexander Valley Church Vineyard 1992 • $14 • (10/15/1994) • **82**
Zinfandel Dry Creek Valley Saunders Vineyard 1992 • $16 • (10/15/1994) • **85**
Zinfandel Dry Creek Valley Saunders Vineyard 1991 • $16 • (9/15/1993) • **89**
Zinfandel Dry Creek Valley Saunders Vineyard 1990 • $13 • (10/15/1992) • **91**

Zinfandel Sonoma County 1994 • $13 • (4/30/1997) • **86**
Zinfandel Sonoma County 1992 • $9 • (10/15/1994) • **85**
Zinfandel Sonoma County 1991 • $10 • (9/15/1993) • **87**
Zinfandel Sonoma County 1989 • $10 • (2/29/1992) • **87**
Zinfandel Sonoma County Limited Reserve 1993 • $13 • (10/15/1995) • **85**
Zinfandel Sonoma County Limited Reserve 1992 • $13 • (10/15/1994) • **86**
Zinfandel Sonoma County Limited Reserve 1991 • $13 • (9/15/1993) • **88**
Zinfandel Sonoma Valley 1993 • $9 • (10/15/1995) • **87**

WHITE ROCK | CALIFORNIA

Chardonnay Napa Valley 1998: Pear and butter flavors are nice, though muddled by some soapy aromas and flavors. Drink now.–J.L. • $24 • (5/31/2000) • **82**
Chardonnay Napa Valley 1997: Perfumed, with flavors of ripe fruit, nutmeg, cinnamon, pear, fig and melon, this is complex and elegant, with a long, spicy finish. Drink now through 2001.–J.L. • $23 • (4/30/1999) • **89**
Chardonnay Napa Valley 1996 • $20 • (5/15/1998) • **87**
Claret Napa Valley 1996: Understated, with cedary oak leading to a modest range of well-integrated currant, spice, herb, tobacco and olive flavors. Finishes with mild tannins. Drink now through 2007.–J.L. • $32 • (4/30/2000) • **87**
Claret Napa Valley 1995: Complex, with dusty, cedary oak and ripe plum, tobacco, mineral and sage notes, finishing with firm but gentle tannins. A blend of Cabernet Sauvignon, Cabernet Franc, Petit Verdot, Malbec. Drink through 2006.–J.L. • $31 • (4/30/1999) • **87**
Claret Napa Valley 1994: Ripe and generous, with nicely modulated berry and leather flavors that keep swirling through the polished finish. Approachable style. Drink now through 2004.–H.S. • $28 • (10/31/1998) • **87**
Claret Napa Valley 1992 • $24 • (5/15/1997) • **87**
Claret Napa Valley 1991 • $22 • (12/15/1995) • **85**
Claret Napa Valley 1990 • $19 • (4/15/1994) • **88**
Claret Napa Valley 1989 • $18 • (11/15/1993) • **83**
Claret Napa Valley 1988 • $18 • (11/15/1993) • **84**
Claret Napa Valley 1986 • $18 • (10/31/1989) • **80**

WHITEHALL LANE | CALIFORNIA

Cabernet Franc Napa Valley 1990 • $15 • (7/15/1993) • **86**
Cabernet Franc Napa Valley 1989 • $18 • (8/31/1992) • **79**
Cabernet Franc Napa Valley 1988 • $19 • (11/15/1990) • **88**
Cabernet Sauvignon California NV • $7 • (10/15/1988) • **70**
Cabernet Sauvignon California Le Petit NV • $9 • (3/31/1990) • **81**
Cabernet Sauvignon Napa Valley NV • $6 • (12/31/1987) • **77**
Cabernet Sauvignon Napa Valley 1997: Smooth and ripe, floral and spicy in character, this Napa red displays tiers of juicy plum, blackberry and black cherry flavors that are complex and vibrant. Quite appealing now; will be even better with cellaring. Best from 2001 through 2007.–J.L. • $28 • (11/15/1999) SS • **91**
Cabernet Sauvignon Napa Valley 1996: A touch earthy, with attractive plum, cherry and berry flavors, it's a medium-weight wine of modest concentration, finishing with simple Cabernet notes. Drink now through 2002.–J.L. • $22 • (10/31/1998) • **87**
Cabernet Sauvignon Napa Valley 1995 • $20 • (4/30/1998) • **88**
Cabernet Sauvignon Napa Valley 1994 • $18 • (11/15/1996) • **89**
Cabernet Sauvignon Napa Valley 1992 • $15 • (10/15/1995) • **87**
Cabernet Sauvignon Napa Valley 1991 • $14 • (11/15/1994) • **88**
Cabernet Sauvignon Napa Valley 1990 • $13 • (12/15/1993) • **88**
Cabernet Sauvignon Napa Valley 1988 • $18 • (11/15/1991) • **87**
Cabernet Sauvignon Napa Valley 1987 • $18 • (9/15/1990) • **84**
Cabernet Sauvignon Napa Valley 1986 • $33 Ⓐ • (8/31/1989) • **89**
Cabernet Sauvignon Napa Valley 1985 • $16 • (11/15/1988) • **93**
Cabernet Sauvignon Napa Valley 1984 • $14 • (12/31/1987) • **84**
Cabernet Sauvignon Napa Valley 1983 • $14 • (11/30/1986) • **77**
Cabernet Sauvignon Napa Valley 1982 • $12 • (2/16/1985) • **86**
Cabernet Sauvignon Napa Valley Leonardini Vineyard 1996: Weaves together a complex array of ripe plum, black cherry, cedar, currant and spice. Turns supple and polished, with a long, rich, elegant and refined aftertaste. Drink now through 2008.–J.L. • $60 • (11/15/1999) • **94**

Key: SS—Spectator Selection. CS—Cellar Selection. HR—Highly Recommended. $NA—Price not available. (BT)—Barrel tasting. Ⓐ—Auction Price.
For a key to the tasters' initials, see "How to Use These Listings."
Dates in parentheses represent the issues in which the ratings were published.

Cabernet Sauvignon Napa Valley Leonardini Vineyard 1995: An ultrarich, deeply concentrated, richly flavored wine, loaded with complex currant, spice and black cherry, hints of plum, framed by toasty, smoky oak. A plush, chewy but polished style, thick and flavorful from start to finish. Drink through 2010.–J.L. • $50 • (11/15/1998) • **92**
Cabernet Sauvignon Napa Valley Morisoli Vineyard 1992 • $28 • (10/15/1995) HR • **93**
Cabernet Sauvignon Napa Valley Morisoli Vineyard 1991 • $36 • (5/31/1995) • **89**
Cabernet Sauvignon Napa Valley Morisoli Vineyard Reserve 1993 • $30 • (11/15/1996) • **91**
Cabernet Sauvignon Napa Valley Reserve 1996: Has a wonderful sense of harmony. Ripe, rich and deeply concentrated, with layers of juicy plum, black cherry, plum and spice, with a pretty, toasty oak and blackberry aftertaste. Best from 2001 through 2009.–J.L. • $48 • (11/15/1999) • **93**
Cabernet Sauvignon Napa Valley Reserve 1995: A surprise star of the vintage. Big and ripe, wonderfully supple and seductive, with layers of juicy plum, black cherry, currant and blackberry that saturate the palate. Finishes with a long, richly flavored, fruity aftertaste and beautifully integrated tannins. Drink through 2005.–J.L. • $40 • (11/15/1998) HR • **95**
Cabernet Sauvignon Napa Valley Reserve 1992 • $23 • (10/15/1995) HR • **92**
Cabernet Sauvignon Napa Valley Reserve 1991 • $26 • (5/31/1995) • **89**
Cabernet Sauvignon Napa Valley Reserve 1990 • $23 • (2/28/1995) • **88**
Cabernet Sauvignon Napa Valley Reserve 1989 • $19 • (11/15/1993) • **89**
Cabernet Sauvignon Napa Valley Reserve 1988: Marked by spicy, minty aromas and flavors, it has a core of ripe plum and currant flavors, turning smooth and fleshy on the finish, where the tannins are supple. Medium in weight and depth. (1988 California Cabernet retrospective tasting). Drink now.–J.L. • $20 • (11/15/1998) • **87**
Cabernet Sauvignon Napa Valley Reserve 1987 • $28 • (11/15/1991) • **90**
Cabernet Sauvignon Napa Valley Reserve 1986 • $30 • (11/15/1990) • **77**
Cabernet Sauvignon Napa Valley Reserve 1985 • $30 • (11/30/1989) • **88**
Cabernet Sauvignon Rutherford Morisoli Vineyard Reserve 1994 • $62 Ⓐ • (9/30/1997) • **92**
Chardonnay Carneros 1998: Butterscotch, nectarine, citrus and anise notes have good intensity and a modest finish. Drink now.–J.L. • $20 • (6/15/2000) • **84**
Chardonnay Napa Valley 1997: Ripe and juicy, with appealing pear, apple, spice, citrus and toast flavors that linger on the clean finish. Drink now.–J.L. • $16 • (7/31/1999) • **88**
Johannisberg Riesling Napa Valley Late Harvest 1994 • $12/375 ml. • (12/31/1995) • **88**
Meritage Napa Valley 1991 • $15 • (11/15/1994) • **85**
Merlot Knights Valley 1992 • $17 • (5/15/1995) • **88**
Merlot Knights Valley 1991 • $15 • (9/15/1994) • **86**
Merlot Knights Valley 1987 • $16 • (7/15/1990) • **77**
Merlot Knights Valley 1984 • $14 • (12/31/1987) • **87**
Merlot Knights Valley 1983 • $12 • (10/01/1985) • **85**
Merlot Knights Valley 1982 • $10 • (6/01/1985) CS • **92**
Merlot Knights Valley Reserve 1986 • $15 • (7/31/1989) • **72**
Merlot Knights Valley Summers Ranch 1990 • $16 • (6/15/1993) • **86**
Merlot Knights Valley Summers Ranch 1989 • $18 • (4/15/1992) • **84**
Merlot Knights Valley Summers Ranch 1988 • $18 • (3/31/1991) • **82**
Merlot Napa Valley 1997: Firm and complex, with earthy, leathery currant, anise, mineral and sage flavors. Firms up and gains richness on the finish. Best from 2001 through 2008.–J.L. • $24 • (11/15/1999) • **88**
Merlot Napa Valley 1996: Smooth, ripe and polished, with a complex array of ripe plum, herb and chocolate. Firms up on the finish, where the tannins are ripe and well integrated. Drink now through 2004.–J.L. • $22 • (12/15/1998) • **89**
Merlot Napa Valley 1995 • $20 • (11/15/1997) SS • **92**
Merlot Napa Valley 1994 • $18 • (11/30/1996) • **86**
Merlot Napa Valley 1993 • $18 • (12/15/1995) • **86**
Merlot Napa Valley Leonardini Vineyard 1997: Big and firm, muscular in style, with chunky currant, blackberry, cherry, sage and tar notes, picking up a touch of coffee and spice. Turns tannic, so give it time. Best from 2001 through 2008.–J.L. • $44 • (11/15/1999) • **89**
Merlot Napa Valley Leonardini Vineyard 1996: Complex, with ripe, rich plum, black cherry, currant and spice Merlot flavors. Turns smooth and supple on the finish, where the tannins are ripe and well integrated. Lots of flavor and finesse. Drink now through 2003.–J.L. • $40 • (9/30/1998) • **89**
Merlot Napa Valley Leonardini Vineyard Reserve 1995 • $36 • (9/30/1997) • **90**
Merlot Napa Valley Leonardini Vineyard Reserve 1994 • $30 • (11/30/1996) • **92**
Merlot Napa Valley Leonardini Vineyard Reserve 1993 • $28 • (12/15/1995) • **88**
Pinot Noir Alexander Valley 1990 • $12 • (2/28/1994) • **82**
Pinot Noir Alexander Valley 1988 • $14 • (10/31/1990) • **82**

Pinot Noir Napa Valley 1987 • $12 • (10/15/1989) • **88**
Primavera California NV • $8 • (10/15/1992) • **74**
Sauvignon Blanc Rutherford 1998: Complex, with ripe melon, grass, fig and apple notes that are full-bodied and long on the finish. Drink now.–J.L. • $14 • (6/30/2000) • **87**
Sauvignon Blanc Rutherford 1997: This has up-front fruit—with peach, kiwi, grapefruit and melon overtones. Tangy acidity and just a touch of grassiness make it refreshing as well. Drink now. • $13 • (9/15/1998) • **86**
Sauvignon Blanc Rutherford Bommarito Vineyard 1996 • $12 • (6/30/1997) • **88**
Zinfandel Napa Valley 1995 • $20 • (9/30/1997) • **89**
Zinfandel Napa Valley 1994 • $16 • (8/31/1996) • **89**

WHITETHORN | CALIFORNIA

Pinot Noir Carneros 1995: A simple, cherry-flavored wine. Fading fast, however. Drink now. • $20 • (9/15/1998) • **77**
Pinot Noir Carneros Hyde Vineyard 1996: Strawberry flavors mingle nicely with cola and herb notes, with slightly firm tannins on the finish. Drink now through 2001.–J.L. • $32 • (9/15/1999) • **86**
Pinot Noir Carneros Hyde Vineyard 1995: Smoky, with a tarry edge, its fruit character is light and simple, with grapey flavors, hints of dried cherry and plum. Drink now through 2001.–J.L. • $29 • (11/15/1998) • **85**

WIEMER, HERMANN J. | NEW YORK

Brut Finger Lakes Cuvée 2000 1997: Compact, this elegant sparkling wine cleanses the palate with fresh acidity, carrying the apple and honey flavors to a crisp conclusion. Great aperitif. Drink now.–B.S. • $25 • (1/01/2000) • **84**
Chardonnay Finger Lakes 1997: Interesting flavors of quince and gooseberry, not normally associated with Chardonnay, yet the wine's purity, vibrance and elegant structure make it pleasant in its own way. Drink now.–B.S. • $12 • (12/15/1998) • **83**
Johannisberg Riesling Finger Lakes Dry 1997: This fresh, balanced wine shows true Riesling character, with peach, pine and floral notes that have good intensity and linger on the finish. Dry, with a clean, lingering finish. Drink now.–T.M. • $9 • (12/15/1998) • **85**
Johannisberg Riesling Finger Lakes Late Harvest 1990 • $13 • (9/15/1994) • **87**
Johannisberg Riesling Finger Lakes Late Harvest Select 1997: Creamy-tasting and fairly rich, with notes of orange, lime and custard. A bit heavy on the finish, but still enjoyable. A nice fat-tasting dessert wine. Drink now through 2001.–K.M. • $NA/375 ml. • (12/31/1998) • **86**
Johannisberg Riesling Finger Lakes Reserve 1997: Very dry and quite austere, this white is crisp, even tart, with light lemon and herb flavors. Has intensity and needs food to show its best. Drink now.–T.M. • $16 • (12/15/1998) • **83**
Johannisberg Riesling Finger Lakes Semi-Dry 1996: This white walks the line between sweet and sour, with dried apricot, citrus and light petrol notes characteristic of Riesling. Lively in texture, with a clean finish. Drink now. –T.M. • $10 • (12/15/1998) • **82**

WILD HOG HILL | CALIFORNIA

Pinot Noir Russian River Valley Saralee's Vineyard 1997: Medium-weight, with delicate tea, cola and dried strawberry flavors, finishing with ripe, round tannins. Drink now through 2003.–H.S. • $24 • (9/15/1999) • **85**
Pinot Noir Sonoma Coast 1997: Medium-weight, racy, with cherry, berry and cola notes and simple, spicy tannins. Drink now.–J.L. • $22 • (3/31/1999) • **87**
Pinot Noir Sonoma County 1990 • $14 • (2/28/1993) • **82**

WILD HORSE | CALIFORNIA

Cabernet Sauvignon Paso Robles 1996: A supple wine that shows layers of coffee, spice, plum, currant and herb. The finish lingers nicely with hints of earth and anise. It's smooth and accessible now, should last awhile. • $16 • (2/28/1999) • **88**
Cabernet Sauvignon Paso Robles 1995: Pretty lean on the palate, with light blackberry and coffee notes. Though the texture is refined, oak seems to be the dominant flavor. • $16 • (11/15/1998) • **82**
Cabernet Sauvignon Paso Robles 1987 • $13 • (4/30/1991) • **88**
Cabernet Sauvignon Paso Robles 1985 • $11 • (6/30/1988) • **70**
Cabernet Sauvignon San Luis Obispo County 1994 • $16 • (12/15/1996) • **86**
Chardonnay Central Coast 1998: Lively, with tart lemon and pineapple flavors. Refreshingly crisp. Drink now through 2004.–J.L. • $16 • (2/29/2000) • **83**
Chardonnay Central Coast 1997: Clean on the palate, with bright, lemony flavors. Finishes moderately, with a hint of toast. Drink now. • $14 • (2/28/1999) • **83**
Chardonnay Central Coast 1996: Ripe, creamy pear and melon-scented Chardonnay flavors combine with toasty oak. Turns complex and elegant on the finish, where the fruit shines through. Drink now through 2000. –J.L. • $16 • (7/31/1998) • **88**
Dolcetto Central Coast 1994 • $14 • (12/31/1996) • **86**
Malvasia Bianca Monterey 1998: Lively, with soft green apple, litchi and peach flavors. A fun wine that would pair well with a spicy dish. Drink now.–J.L. • $14 • (2/29/2000) • **86**
Malvasia Bianca Monterey 1997: Fragrant and spicy up front, the wine is dry but filled with lush fruit. Peach, apple and litchi are backed by almost-searing acidity. Fun. Drink now. • $13 • (6/15/1999) • **86**
Malvasia Bianca Monterey 1996 • $13 • (3/31/1998) • **87**
Malvasia Bianca Monterey 1993 • $13 • (4/15/1995) • **84**
Merlot Central Coast 1989 • $15 • (5/31/1992) • **76**
Merlot Central Coast 1986 • $11 • (7/31/1989) • **77**
Merlot Paso Robles 1997: Shows a modest range of pretty raspberry and strawberry flavors, with hints of herb. Well balanced, with integrated tannins. Drink now through 2004.–J.L. • $19 • (10/15/1999) • **85**
Merlot Paso Robles 1996: Cassis, black cherry and leather come to mind. Tannins are a bit rough, and the finish is moderate with a hint of spice. Drink through 2002. • $17 • (9/30/1998) • **83**
Merlot Paso Robles 1995 • $16 • (12/31/1997) • **85**
Merlot Paso Robles Cheval Sauvage 1990 • $28 • (3/31/1993) • **87**
Merlot San Luis Obispo 1991 • $14 • (2/28/1995) • **85**
Negrette Cienega Valley 1992 • $16 • (1/31/1995) • **85**
Pinot Blanc Monterey County 1998: A Chardonnay look-alike, with vanilla, butter and pear flavors that linger on the finish. Drink now through 2002.–J.L. • $14 • (5/31/2000) • **83**
Pinot Blanc Monterey County 1997: Crisp and clean on the palate, delicate, with hints of honeysuckle, melon and citrus. Finishes with a flinty note. Drink now. • $13 • (9/15/1998) • **87**
Pinot Blanc Monterey County 1996 • $13 • (4/30/1998) • **87**
Pinot Noir Central Coast 1997: A touch earthy and cedary, this lean, trim wine has spicy cherry, earth and leather flavors that shorten up on the finish. Drink now through 2005.–J.L. • $20 • (1/31/2000) • **85**
Pinot Noir Central Coast 1996 • $18 • (2/28/1998) • **85**
Pinot Noir Central Coast 1995 • $18 • (1/31/1997) • **87**
Pinot Noir Central Coast 1993 • $12 • (2/28/1995) • **85**
Pinot Noir Central Coast 1992 • $14 • (1/31/1995) • **84**
Pinot Noir Central Coast 1991 • $16 • (2/28/1994) • **87**
Pinot Noir Central Coast 1990 • $13 • (3/31/1997) • **88**
Pinot Noir Central Coast Cheval Sauvage 1994 • $35 • (9/30/1997) • **88**
Pinot Noir Paso Robles Cheval Sauvage 1993 • $35 • (12/31/1996) • **92**
Pinot Noir Paso Robles Cheval Sauvage 1990 • $28 • (2/28/1993) • **90**
Pinot Noir Paso Robles 1987 • $14 • (10/15/1989) • **90**
Pinot Noir Santa Barbara County 1990 • $14 • (2/28/1993) • **86**
Pinot Noir Santa Barbara County 1988 • $14 • (4/30/1991) • **79**
Pinot Noir Santa Barbara County 1987 • $14 • (3/31/1990) • **82**
Pinot Noir Santa Barbara County 1986 • $12 • (3/31/1997) • **84**
Pinot Noir Santa Barbara County 1985 • $13 • (6/15/1988) • **86**
Pinot Noir Santa Barbara County Cheval Sauvage 1990 • $25 • (2/28/1994) • **88**
Pinot Noir Santa Barbara County Cheval Sauvage 1989 • $28 • (2/28/1993) • **85**
Sauvignon Blanc Edna Valley Late Harvest 1994 • $14/375 ml. • (12/31/1996) • **91**
Syrah Central Coast 1994 • $16 • (3/31/1997) • **89**
Zinfandel California 1996: Medium in weight, with pleasant flavors of herb, currant and berry and a spicy finish. Drink now.–J.L. • $13 • (6/15/1999) • **84**
Zinfandel Paso Robles 1997: Aromas of kirsch, plum and cola precede peppery, high-alcohol flavors. Drink now through 2004.–J.L. • $14 • (4/30/2000) • **84**
Zinfandel Paso Robles 1989 • $11 • (9/30/1993) • **85**
Zinfandel Paso Robles Unbridled 1990 • $16 • (9/15/1994) • **88**

WILDHURST | CALIFORNIA

Cabernet Sauvignon Clear Lake 1997: Has a tart green edge to the pleasant currant, cedar and black cherry flavors. Drink through 2003.–J.L. • $14 • (10/15/1999) • **82**
Cabernet Sauvignon Clear Lake 1991 • $9 • (11/15/1993) • **76**
Cabernet Sauvignon Clear Lake 1990 • $10 • (7/31/1992) • **83**
Cabernet Sauvignon Clear Lake Private Reserve 1993 • $16 • (10/31/1997) • **84**
Merlot Clear Lake 1994 • $12 • (7/31/1996) • **80**
Merlot Clear Lake 1991 • $8 • (3/31/1993) • **84**

Merlot Lake County Reserve 1992 • $15 • (9/15/1994) • **84**
Merlot Lake County Reserve 1991 • $15 • (10/15/1993) • **87**
Pinot Noir Mendocino County 1992 • $9 • (2/28/1994) • **74**
Sauvignon Blanc Clear Lake 1997: Somewhat herbal on the nose, though on the palate it serves up ripe fig, pear and apple. Light-textured, the wine finishes moderately, with a hint of citrus and honey. Drink now. • $9 • (5/31/1999) • **86**
Zinfandel Clear Lake 1997: Earthy and hot, this shows some simple cherry flavors but lacks balance and focus. • $14 • (5/15/1999) • **79**
Zinfandel Clear Lake 1996 • $14 • (6/15/1998) • **80**
Zinfandel Clear Lake 1992 • $9 • (10/15/1994) • **80**
Zinfandel Clear Lake 1991 • $7 • (9/30/1993) • **86**
Zinfandel Clear Lake 1990 • $7 • (7/15/1992) • **85**

WILLAKENZIE | OREGON

Chardonnay Willamette Valley 1996: A pretty wine, favoring grace over power, with spicy pear and hazelnut notes echoing on the smooth finish. Drink through 2001.–H.S. • $15 • (4/30/1999) • **88**
Gamay Noir Willamette Valley 1996 • $16 • (5/15/1998) • **87**
Gamay Noir Yamhill County 1995 • $15 • (2/28/1997) • **87**
Pinot Blanc Oregon 1998: Ripe, round and generous, with lovely pear, apricot and mineral aromas and flavors that remain juicy and lively through the finish. Has depth and distinction. Drink now.–H.S. • $16 • (3/31/2000) • **90**
Pinot Blanc Oregon 1996 • $14 • (11/30/1997) • **86**
Pinot Blanc Willamette Valley 1997: Light and smooth, with distinctively spicy citrus-peel notes around the soft melon flavors. Drink now.–H.S. • $13 • (2/28/1999) • **85**
Pinot Gris Oregon 1996 • $14 • (11/30/1997) • **89**
Pinot Gris Willamette Valley 1997: Soft and spicy, a pretty mouthful of melon and allspice flavors, finishing with a refreshing tang of citrus that lingers. Drink now.–H.S. • $15 • (4/30/1999) • **88**
Pinot Meunier Willamette Valley 1998: Rich and supple, this has lovely blackberry and plum flavors on a velvety frame, and the fruit persists on the finish. Drink now through 2003.–H.S. • $20 • (5/15/2000) • **87**
Pinot Meunier Willamette Valley 1997: Light and crisp, with pretty, focused berry flavors and a hint of smoke on the finish. Tannins are not intrusive. Drink now through 2002.–H.S. • $19 • (6/15/1999) • **86**
Pinot Meunier Willamette Valley 1996 • $16 • (5/15/1998) • **87**
Pinot Noir Willamette Valley 1997: Soft and open-textured, with fragrant raspberry, cherry and smoky notes that echo gently on the finish. Drink now through 2002.–H.S. • $20 • (4/30/1999) • **86**
Pinot Noir Willamette Valley 1996 • $18 • (5/15/1998) • **86**
Pinot Noir Willamette Valley 1995 • $18 • (10/31/1997) • **88**
Pinot Noir Willamette Valley Aliette 1997: Light, supple in texture and especially appealing for its bright currant and blackberry flavors that linger on the delicate finish. Remarkable for its persistence and delicacy. Drink now through 2002.–H.S. • $30 • (4/30/1999) • **88**
Pinot Noir Willamette Valley Aliette 1996 • $25 • (5/15/1998) • **90**
Pinot Noir Willamette Valley Aliette 1995 • $25 • (10/31/1997) • **87**
Pinot Noir Willamette Valley Dijon Clone 777 1998: Rich and velvety, aromatic with red cherry, plum and floral aromas that carry through to the smooth-textured palate. A harmonious wine that balances its rich flavors with a subtle frame. Drink through 2008.–H.S. • $30 • (4/30/2000) • **90**
Pinot Noir Willamette Valley Dijon Clone 113 1997: Vibrant and intense for a '97, showing lots of exuberant blackberry, currant and plum flavors on a supple, elegant frame. Fine tannins can use cellaring. Drink through 2005. –H.S. • $30 • (4/30/1999) • **89**
Pinot Noir Willamette Valley Dijon Clone 115 1997: Has a strong minty-herbal edge to the pretty raspberry and currant flavors that linger on the firm, slightly chewy finish. Best from 2001 through 2003.–H.S. • $30 • (4/30/1999) • **83**
Pinot Noir Willamette Valley Pierre Léon 1997: Light and crisp, with pretty blackberry and plum flavors that remain focused through the finish, where the fruit notes echo nicely. Drink now through 2003.–H.S. • $30 • (4/30/1999) • **87**
Pinot Noir Willamette Valley Pierre Léon 1996 • $22 • (5/15/1998) • **88**
Pinot Noir Willamette Valley Pierre Léon 1995 • $21 • (10/31/1997) • **86**

Key: SS—Spectator Selection. CS—Cellar Selection. HR—Highly Recommended. $NA—Price not available. (BT)—Barrel tasting. (A)—Auction Price.
For a key to the tasters' initials, see "How to Use These Listings."
Dates in parentheses represent the issues in which the ratings were published.

WILLAMETTE VALLEY | OREGON

Cabernet Sauvignon Oregon Founders' Reserve 1992 • $17 • (3/31/1996) • **82**
Cabernet Sauvignon Oregon Karina's Vineyard OVB 1992 • $27 • (12/31/1996) • **85**
Cabernet Sauvignon Oregon OVB 1992 • $25 • (3/31/1996) • **84**
Chardonnay Oregon 1998: Generous and fruity, this pretty mouthful of pear and citrus flavors is shaded with spicy oak notes. Drink now.–H.S. • $14 • (4/30/2000) • **87**
Chardonnay Oregon 1997: A crisp Chardonnay, light and bright, with pretty lime and nectarine flavors. Drink now through 2001.–H.S. • $14 • (4/30/1999) • **87**
Chardonnay Oregon 1996 • $10 • (5/15/1998) • **87**
Chardonnay Oregon Estate Founders' Reserve 1996 • $22 • (5/15/1998) • **86**
Chardonnay Oregon Founders' Reserve 1996 • $18 • (5/15/1998) • **89**
Gewürztraminer Oregon 1996 • $8 • (11/15/1997) • **87**
Merlot Oregon Whittaker Vineyards 1992 • $25 • (11/30/1994) • **85**
Muscat Willamette Valley Frizzanté Semi-Sparkling 1997: Light and sweet. A lovely, bright mouthful of pear and litchi flavors that remain refreshing through the finish. Drink now.–H.S. • $12/500 ml. • (4/30/1999) • **88**
Oregon Blossom Oregon 1996 • $7 • (11/30/1997) • **79**
Pinot Gris Oregon 1998: Crisp and lively, juicy with lime and melon flavors, finishing on the tart side. Needs food. Drink now.–H.S. • $14 • (5/15/2000) • **86**
Pinot Gris Willamette Valley 1997: Light and sprightly, with green apple, melon and guava flavors that linger on the crisp finish. Drink now.–H.S. • $14 • (4/30/1999) • **86**
Pinot Gris Oregon 1996 • $13 • (11/15/1997) • **87**
Pinot Noir Oregon 1998: The supple, spicy style emphasizes nutmeg and mineral overtones to the solid black cherry flavors. Not a big wine, but it's graceful and inviting. Drink now through 2005.–H.S. • $16 • (4/30/2000) • **87**
Pinot Noir Oregon 1997: Firm and appealing for its pretty black cherry and caramel notes that echo on the round finish. Drink now through 2001.–H.S. • $15 • (4/30/1999) • **84**
Pinot Noir Oregon 1995 • $13 • (2/28/1997) • **79**
Pinot Noir Oregon 1994 • $12 • (1/31/1996) • **84**
Pinot Noir Oregon 1993 • $12 • (3/31/1996) • **86**
Pinot Noir Oregon 1992 • $12 • (11/30/1994) • **79**
Pinot Noir Oregon 1991 • $15 • (1/31/1994) • **83**
Pinot Noir Oregon Burger Vineyard Reserve 1991 • $25 • (10/15/1994) • **88**
Pinot Noir Oregon Commemorative Release 1992 • $9 • (1/31/1994) • **82**
Pinot Noir Oregon Founders' Reserve 1996: Light and fragrant, this delicately framed Pinot Noir has pretty plum and currant flavors that linger gently on the finish. Texture is supple, making it approachable now. Drink through 2002.–H.S. • $25 • (12/15/1998) • **86**
Pinot Noir Oregon Founders' Reserve 1995 • $18 • (2/28/1997) • **85**
Pinot Noir Oregon Founders' Reserve 1994 • $18 • (4/30/1996) • **87**
Pinot Noir Oregon Founders' Reserve 1993 • $18 • (1/31/1996) • **86**
Pinot Noir Oregon Founders' Reserve 1991 • $15 • (1/31/1994) • **83**
Pinot Noir Oregon Nectar Founders' Reserve 1993 • $14 • (11/30/1994) • **83**
Pinot Noir Oregon OVB 1994 • $30 • (4/30/1996) • **90**
Pinot Noir Oregon OVB 1993 • $25 • (1/31/1996) • **86**
Pinot Noir Oregon Whole Berry Fermented 1996 • $13 • (10/31/1997) • **84**
Pinot Noir Oregon Whole Berry Fermented 1994 • $12 • (3/31/1996) • **85**
Pinot Noir Oregon Whole Berry Fermented 1993 • $12 • (11/30/1994) • **83**
Pinot Noir Oregon Whole Cluster 1999: On the light side and ebulliently fruity, with aromas and flavors of black cherry, rose petal and anise seed echoing on the soft finish. Reminiscent of good Beaujolais. Enjoy now, while it's fresh.–H.S. • $15 • (4/30/2000) • **85**
Pinot Noir Oregon Whole Cluster 1998: Amazingly ripe and generous, this smooth mouthful of black cherry and exotic spice flavors is already showing some depth. Drink now.–H.S. • $15 • (4/30/1999) • **85**
Pinot Noir Willamette Valley Founders' Reserve 1992 • $16 • (10/15/1994) • **84**
Pinot Noir Willamette Valley Joe Dobbes Signature Cuvée 1996: Bright and jazzy. A lively mouthful of raspberry, plum and red cherry flavors on a sleek frame, finishing supple and generous. Has more intensity and life than most '96s. Joe Dobbes is winemaker. Drink now through 2003.–H.S. • $48 • (4/30/1999) • **89**
Pinot Noir Willamette Valley Karina Vineyard 1997: The light, compact style emphasizes pretty black cherry and spice flavors on a smooth, polished frame. Drink now.–H.S. • $39 • (5/15/2000) • **85**
Port Oregon Quinta Reserva Pinot Noir 1993 • $18 • (3/31/1996) • **83**
Riesling Oregon 1998: Light and sweet, not a late-harvest style, but emphasizing vaguely leafy apple and floral flavors. Pleasant, but lacks intensity. Drink now.–H.S. • $8 • (5/15/2000) • **82**

Riesling Oregon 1997: Soft and floral, with iris and rose petal notes overshadowing the citrusy fruit. Finishes with a nice balance. Drink now.–H.S. • $8 • (11/15/1999) • **84**
Riesling Oregon 1996 • $8 • (11/15/1997) • **84**
Riesling Oregon Dry 1996 • $8 • (11/15/1997) • **89**
Viognier Willamette Valley Late Harvest 1997: A stunner. Rich, ripe and generous, with tiers of nectarine, pineapple, honey and caramel flavors that remain rich and harmonious. Has a hint of pepper on the deftly balanced finish. Drink now through 2004.–H.S. • $20/375 ml. • (6/30/1999) • **93**

WILLIAMS SELYEM | CALIFORNIA

Chardonnay Russian River Valley 1996: Bold, superripe and oily. Rich in banana, fig, pear and spicy vanilla flavors, it's a mouthful from start to finish. Drink now through 2003.–J.L. • $35 • (7/31/1999) • **93**
Chardonnay Russian River Valley Allen Vineyard 1997: Ripe, with appealing fig, citrus, apple and spice, gaining richness and polish on the finish. Drink now through 2003.–J.L. • $46 • (6/15/2000) • **88**
Chardonnay Sonoma Coast Hirsch Vineyard 1997: Subtle and polished, with toasty, creamy oak. Hints of pear, honey, spice and peach pick up a touch of oak. Drink now.–J.L. • $43 • (6/15/2000) • **88**
Pinot Noir Anderson Valley Ferrington Vineyard 1996: Dark and ripe, brimming with complex plum, black cherry and raspberry flavors that are rich and sharply focused. Drink through 2004.–J.L. • $50 • (2/28/1999) • **91**
Pinot Noir Anderson Valley Ferrington Vineyard 1995 • $40 • (10/31/1997) • **90**
Pinot Noir Anderson Valley Ferrington Vineyard 1994 • $38 • (10/31/1997) • **91**
Pinot Noir Anderson Valley Ferrington Vineyard 1993 • $35 • (10/31/1997) • **91**
Pinot Noir Anderson Valley Ferrington Vineyard 1992 • $30 • (12/15/1994) • **92**
Pinot Noir Russian River Valley 1995 • $59 Ⓐ • (10/31/1997) • **90**
Pinot Noir Russian River Valley 1994 • $28 • (10/31/1997) • **89**
Pinot Noir Russian River Valley 1993 • $23 • (10/31/1997) • **85**
Pinot Noir Russian River Valley 1992 • $25 • (10/31/1997) • **89**
Pinot Noir Russian River Valley 1991 • $23 • (10/31/1997) • **93**
Pinot Noir Russian River Valley 1990 • $20 • (10/31/1997) • **91**
Pinot Noir Russian River Valley 1989 • $18• (10/31/1997) • **89**
Pinot Noir Russian River Valley 1988 • $46 Ⓐ • (10/31/1997) • **90**
Pinot Noir Russian River Valley Allen Vineyard 1997: Light in color, though blessed with ripe, pleasant black cherry, blackberry, strawberry, cedar and herb notes that gain complexity and nuance. Drink now through 2007.–J.L. • $60 • (1/31/2000) • **89**
Pinot Noir Russian River Valley Allen Vineyard 1996: Ripe and rich, with creamy oak and lots of plum, blackberry and cherry character, turning tannic and sophisticated. Drink through 2006.–J.L. • $55 • (2/28/1999) • **90**
Pinot Noir Russian River Valley Allen Vineyard 1995 • $134 Ⓐ • (10/31/1997) • **93**
Pinot Noir Russian River Valley Allen Vineyard 1994 • $42 • (10/31/1997) • **92**
Pinot Noir Russian River Valley Allen Vineyard 1993 • $40 • (10/31/1997) • **88**
Pinot Noir Russian River Valley Allen Vineyard 1992 • $38 • (10/31/1997) • **93**
Pinot Noir Russian River Valley Allen Vineyard 1991 • $86 Ⓐ • (10/31/1997) • **95**
Pinot Noir Russian River Valley Allen Vineyard 1990 • $30 • (10/31/1997) • **90**
Pinot Noir Russian River Valley Allen Vineyard 1989 • $27 • (10/31/1997) • **89**
Pinot Noir Russian River Valley Allen Vineyard 1988 • $25 • (10/31/1997) • **91**
Pinot Noir Russian River Valley Allen Vineyard 1987 • $20 • (10/31/1997) • **90**
Pinot Noir Russian River Valley Cohn Vineyard 1993 • $35 • (10/31/1997) • **88**
Pinot Noir Russian River Valley Olivet Lane Vineyard 1997: Dark, ripe and distinct for its rich, exuberant black cherry and blackberry flavors, it turns supple and polished, with a long, full finish. Drink now through 2005. –J.L. • $45 • (11/30/1999) • **92**
Pinot Noir Russian River Valley Olivet Lane 1995 • $36 • (10/31/1997) • **93**
Pinot Noir Russian River Valley Olivet Lane 1994 • $34 • (10/31/1997) • **88**
Pinot Noir Russian River Valley Olivet Lane 1993 • $28 • (10/31/1997) • **88**
Pinot Noir Russian River Valley Olivet Lane 1992 • $28 • (10/31/1997) • **88**
Pinot Noir Russian River Valley Olivet Lane 1991 • $28 • (10/31/1997) • **92**
Pinot Noir Russian River Valley Olivet Lane 1990 • $25 • (10/31/1997) • **87**
Pinot Noir Russian River Valley Olivet Lane 1989 • $25 • (10/31/1997) • **89**
Pinot Noir Russian River Valley Riverblock Vineyard 1997: Firm, dark, rich and concentrated, with layers of ripe plum, black cherry, blackberry and spice. Delicious aftertaste. Best from 2001 through 2009.–J.L. • $55 • (1/31/2000) • **93**
Pinot Noir Russian River Valley Riverblock Vineyard 1995 • $36 • (12/31/1997) • **90**
Pinot Noir Russian River Valley Riverblock Vineyard 1994 • $35 • (10/31/1997) • **91**
Pinot Noir Russian River Valley Rochioli Vineyard 1997: Silky-smooth in texture, bright, rich and concentrated, with lively black cherry and plummy flavors. Wonderfully perfumed aromatics add complexity and dimension. The last Rochioli Vineyard bottling. Tasty now. Best from 2001 through 2007.–J.L. • $125 • (1/31/2000) • **93**
Pinot Noir Russian River Valley Rochioli Vineyard 1996: Boasts a complex, intriguing array of ripe plum, cherry, cola, spice and anise, not especially dense but distinctive and elegant, long on the finish. Drink now through 2004.–J.L. • $78 • (2/28/1999) • **90**
Pinot Noir Russian River Valley Rochioli Vineyard 1995 • $65 • (12/31/1997) • **94**
Pinot Noir Russian River Valley Rochioli Vineyard 1994 • $60 • (10/31/1997) • **93**
Pinot Noir Russian River Valley Rochioli Vineyard 1993 • $60 • (10/31/1997) • **88**
Pinot Noir Russian River Valley Rochioli Vineyard 1992 • $50 • (10/31/1997) • **97**
Pinot Noir Russian River Valley Rochioli Vineyard 1991 • $45 • (10/31/1997) • **95**
Pinot Noir Russian River Valley Rochioli Vineyard 1990 • $230 Ⓐ • (10/31/1997) • **89**
Pinot Noir Russian River Valley Rochioli Vineyard 1989 • $40 • (10/31/1997) • **92**
Pinot Noir Russian River Valley Rochioli Vineyard 1988 • $40 • (10/31/1997) • **95**
Pinot Noir Russian River Valley Rochioli Vineyard 1987 • $35 • (10/31/1997) • **88**
Pinot Noir Russian River Valley Rochioli Vineyard 1986 • $35 • (10/31/1997) • **92**
Pinot Noir Russian River Valley Rochioli Vineyard 1985 • $30 • (10/31/1997) • **90**
Pinot Noir Sonoma Coast 1997: Starts out gamy and a touch peppery, but doesn't stray too far from its core of dense, ripe plum, black cherry and raspberry-laced fruit. Finishes with firm tannins. Best from 2001 through 2006.–J.L. • $35 • (11/30/1999) • **91**
Pinot Noir Sonoma Coast 1995 • $30 • (10/31/1997) • **88**
Pinot Noir Sonoma Coast 1994 • $30 • (10/31/1997) • **89**
Pinot Noir Sonoma Coast 1993 • $26 • (10/31/1997) • **91**
Pinot Noir Sonoma Coast 1991 • $24 • (10/31/1997) • **90**
Pinot Noir Sonoma Coast 1990 • $22 • (10/31/1997) • **87**
Pinot Noir Sonoma Coast 1989 • $22 • (10/31/1997) • **87**
Pinot Noir Sonoma Coast 1988 • $18 • (5/31/1990) • **92**
Pinot Noir Sonoma Coast Coastlands Vineyard 1997: Distinct with its pepper notes. Firm, complex and concentrated, with black cherry and wild berry flavors moving to the forefront. Has enough tannin to cellar short-term. Best from 2001 through 2008.–J.L. • $55 • (1/31/2000) • **92**
Pinot Noir Sonoma Coast Coastlands Vineyard 1995 • $40 • (12/31/1997) • **92**
Pinot Noir Sonoma Coast Coastlands Vineyard 1994 • $38 • (10/31/1997) • **92**
Pinot Noir Sonoma Coast Hirsch Vineyard 1996: Firm, with chewy tannins and a core of flavors built around wild berry, black cherry, sage, mineral and spice. Drink through 2006.–J.L. • $45 • (2/28/1999) • **88**
Pinot Noir Sonoma Coast Hirsch Vineyard 1995 • $40 • (10/31/1997) • **94**
Pinot Noir Sonoma Coast Hirsch Vineyard 1994 • $36 • (10/31/1997) • **92**
Pinot Noir Sonoma Coast Precious Mountain Vineyard 1996: Elegant, with delicate, complex strawberry, plum, raspberry and vanilla shadings and modest tealike tannins. New from this winery. Drink now through 2003. –J.L. • $65 • (2/28/1999) • **89**
Pinot Noir Sonoma Coast Summa Vineyard 1993 • $40 • (10/31/1997) • **85**
Pinot Noir Sonoma Coast Summa Vineyard 1991 • $35 • (10/31/1997) • **96**
Pinot Noir Sonoma Coast Summa Vineyard 1988 • $25 • (10/31/1997) • **86**
Pinot Noir Sonoma County 1994 • $23 • (10/31/1997) • **87**
Pinot Noir Sonoma County 1987 • $16 • (10/31/1997) • **88**
Pinot Noir Sonoma County 1986 • $16 • (3/31/1997) • **90**
Pinot Noir Sonoma County 1985 • $15 • (10/31/1997) • **87**
Pinot Noir Sonoma County 1984 • $15 • (10/31/1997) • **82**
Pinot Noir Sonoma County 1983 • $14 • (10/31/1997) • **85**
Pinot Noir Sonoma County 1982 • $12 • (10/31/1997) • **90**
Pinot Noir Sonoma County 1981 • $12 • (10/31/1997) • **88**
Zinfandel Mendocino County 1994 • $17 • (2/28/1997) • **88**
Zinfandel Russian River Valley 1992 • $30 • (4/30/1996) • **89**
Zinfandel Russian River Valley 1991 • $20 • (9/30/1994) • **92**
Zinfandel Russian River Valley Leno Martinelli Vineyard 1985 • $10 • (7/31/1988) • **79**

WILLIAMSBURG | VIRGINIA

Chardonnay Virginia Act 12 of Sixteen Nineteen 1998: Floral aromas are distinctive, but the cooked apple flavors are sweet and rather cloying in this thick white.–T.M. • $15 • (5/31/2000) • **77**

Chardonnay Virginia Acte 12 of Sixteen Nineteen 1996: Mature and mellow, displaying soft, buttery pear and fig notes, lively acidity and balance. Sandalwood and vanilla accents linger on the finish. Drink now.–B.S. • $NA • (12/15/1998) • **83**

Chardonnay Virginia Glebe Vineyard 1997: Big, bold and in your face, with plenty of butter, clove, nutmeg and peach character. All up front, with a broad structure, it finishes short. Drink now.–B.S. • $NA • (12/15/1998) • **83**

Chardonnay Virginia John Adlum 1997: Rich in texture but lacking in fruit flavor, this has an odd floral and earthy character. • $10 • (6/15/1999) • **72**

Chardonnay Virginia Ratcliffe Vineyard 1998: Vanilla and apple flavors are pleasant but a bit candied in this straightforward, silky white. Finishes clean.–T.M. • $24 • (5/31/2000) • **79**

Chardonnay Virginia Vintage Reserve 1997: Straightforward, in a rich, buttery style, this Chardonnay delivers pineapple and nutmeg flavors that give way to oaky notes on the finish. Drink now.–B.S. • $NA • (12/15/1998) • **81**

Gabriel Archer Reserve Virginia 1997: This soft red shows light plum and rather vegetal flavors. Rustic and a bit dull.–T.M. • $21 • (5/31/2000) • **76**

Governor's White Virginia NV: A bit muddled, with a mix of sweet apple and apricot flavors.–K.M. • $7 • (12/15/1998) • **75**

Plantation Blush Virginia NV: Odd-colored, more orange than pink, but shows conventional "blush" flavors of cherry and strawberry, both quite sweet and crisply tart.–T.M. • $7 • (12/15/1998) • **77**

Two Shilling Red Virginia NV: This medium-bodied red has a juicy aroma and sweet cherry and fruit flavors. Finishes on a cinnamon note.–K.M. • $7 • (12/15/1998) • **79**

Vidal Blanc Virginia Late Harvest Dominion Wine Cellars 1996: Aromas and flavors of orange peel and spice make this interesting. Balanced and straightforward, with a clean finish. Drink now.–K.M. • $14/375 ml. • (12/31/1998) • **84**

WILRIDGE | WASHINGTON

Cabernet Sauvignon Yakima Valley Crawford Vineyard 1995 • $19 • (9/30/1997) • **83**

Cabernet Sauvignon Columbia Valley Crawford Vineyard 1994 • $19 • (9/15/1996) • **80**

Cabernet Sauvignon Columbia Valley Crawford Vineyard 1991 • $19 • (9/30/1994) • **86**

Cabernet Sauvignon Yakima Valley Klipsun Vineyards 1997: Firm in texture, bright in flavor, featuring pretty berry and plum notes around a spicy core. Has more up front than on the finish. Drink now through 2005.–H.S. • $29 • (12/31/1999) • **86**

Cabernet Sauvignon Yakima Valley Klipsun Vineyard 1996: Earthy, gamy notes slide in among the ripe currant and herb flavors, making this distinctive if not to every taste. Drink through 2004.–H.S. • $24 • (9/15/1998) • **86**

Cabernet Sauvignon Yakima Valley Klipsun Vineyard 1995 • $19 • (9/30/1997) • **87**

Cabernet Sauvignon Columbia Valley Klipsun Vineyard 1994 • $19 • (9/15/1996) • **84**

Cabernet Sauvignon Columbia Valley Klipsun Vineyard 1993 • $19 • (9/30/1995) • **88**

Cabernet Sauvignon Columbia Valley Klipsun Vineyard 1992 • $19 • (9/30/1995) • **87**

Melange Yakima Valley 1996: Ripe and generous, a powerful mouthful of blackberry, currant, herb and a touch of exotic spices making this an attention-grabber. Has richness and extra dimensions of flavor that need time to evolve. Cabernet Sauvignon with 4 percent Merlot. Drink through 2005.–H.S. • $19 • (9/15/1998) • **90**

Merlot Yakima Valley Crawford Vineyard 1995 • $19 • (9/30/1997) • **85**

Merlot Columbia Valley Crawford Vineyard 1994 • $19 • (9/15/1996) • **81**

Merlot Yakima Valley Klipsun Vineyards 1997: Bright and pretty, with lively blackberry, blueberry and bay leaf aromas and flavors, and a fine layer of tannin on the finish. Drink now through 2004.–H.S. • $29 • (12/31/1999) • **88**

Key: SS—Spectator Selection. CS—Cellar Selection. HR—Highly Recommended. SNA—Price not available. (BT)—Barrel tasting. (A)—Auction Price. For a key to the tasters' initials, see "How to Use These Listings." **Dates in parentheses represent the issues in which the ratings were published.**

Merlot Yakima Valley Klipsun Vineyards 1996: Bright in flavor, firm in texture, with lovely blackberry, currant and chocolate notes persisting impressively on the finish. Approachable now, but the tannins will benefit from cellaring. Best from 2000.–H.S. • $29 • (9/15/1998) • **88**

Merlot Yakima Valley Klipsun Vineyards 1995 • $19 • (9/30/1997) • **87**

Merlot Columbia Valley Klipsun Vineyards 1994 • $19 • (9/15/1996) • **79**

Merlot Columbia Valley Klipsun Vineyards 1993 • $19 • (9/30/1995) • **86**

Merlot-Cabernet Franc-Cabernet Columbia Valley Melange 1997: Youthful and lively, raw in texture, with sturdy berry and herb flavors that pick up a pleasantly earthy note on the finish. Drink now through 2003.–H.S. • $29 • (12/31/1999) • **85**

Pinot Noir Willamette Valley Corral Creek Vineyard 1997: Supple and spicy, with coffee notes around the soft core of cherry and mint flavors. Drink now.–H.S. • $29 • (12/31/1999) • **84**

WILSON DANIELS | CALIFORNIA

Chardonnay California 1996: Has a bitter edge, with canned pineapple and smoky oak flavors.–H.S. • $14 • (11/30/1998) • **78**

Pinot Noir Carneros 1995 • $18 • (2/28/1998) • **84**

WINDEMERE | CALIFORNIA

Cabernet Sauvignon Napa Valley 1991 • $16 • (3/31/1996) • **82**

Cabernet Sauvignon Napa Valley 1989 • $16 • (8/31/1992) • **83**

Cabernet Sauvignon Napa Valley Diamond Mountain 1990 • $14 • (8/31/1993) • **88**

Chardonnay Edna Valley MacGregor Vineyard 1996: Zingy acidity and bright lemon flavors give this wine pucker-power. A bit meaty and earthy, it finishes with a touch of honey. Struggles for balance. Drink now. • $18 • (7/31/1998) • **81**

Zinfandel Paso Robles Benito Dusi Vineyard 1993 • $15 • (3/31/1996) • **86**

WINDSOR | CALIFORNIA

Cabernet Sauvignon North Coast 1995: Smooth, almost velvety in texture, with pretty currant, tobacco and spice notes of moderate intensity. Nice. Drink now through 2001.–H.S. • $13 • (10/31/1998) • **83**

Cabernet Sauvignon North Coast Preference Vineyard Private Reserve 1995: Soft in texture and modest in flavor, with tobacco and cedar notes ringing louder than the cherry flavor. Aimed for early drinking.–H.S. • $11 • (11/15/1998) • **82**

Cabernet Sauvignon Russian River Valley River West Vineyard 1987 • $20 • (11/15/1992) • **87**

Cabernet Sauvignon Sonoma County Signature Series 1988 • $26 • (11/15/1992) • **83**

Chardonnay Russian River Valley Signature Series 1996 • $16 • (6/30/1998) • **87**

Merlot California Private Reserve 1996: Pleasant ripe currant and cherry flavors are laid over a soft layer of toasty oak and vanilla notes. Drink now.–J.L. • $12 • (9/30/1998) • **82**

Merlot Russian River Valley Signature Series 1987 • $25 • (5/31/1992) • **84**

Merlot Sonoma County Signature Series 1995: Soft, ripe plum notes are wrapped in a coating of pleasantly nutty, toasted oak flavors. Finishes with slightly green tannins. Drink now.–H.S. • $24 • (9/15/1998) • **84**

Pinot Noir California Signature Series 1993 • $15 • (12/31/1995) • **82**

Pinot Noir Sonoma County Private Reserve 1993 • $14 • (12/31/1995) • **84**

Zinfandel Alexander Valley Signature Series 1995 • $15 • (6/15/1998) • **81**

Zinfandel Mendocino County Private Reserve 1996: Firm, showing flavors of earthy raspberry, tea and herb that turn slightly stalky on the finish. Might improve with time.–J.L. • $14 • (2/28/1999) • **79**

Zinfandel Russian River Valley Old Vines Private Reserve 1996: Moderate in body, with nutty orange peel, plum and baked fruit flavors, finishing slightly dry. • $14 • (2/28/1999) • **83**

WINDWALKER | CALIFORNIA

Cabernet Sauvignon El Dorado 1996: Dry and tannic, with simple fruit and herb flavors. • $11 • (11/15/1998) • **74**

Cabernet Sauvignon El Dorado 1994 • $11 • (4/30/1998) • **79**

Chardonnay El Dorado 1996: Citrus and heavy-handed butterscotch flavors have pleasant focus, but finish abruptly. The finish shows some spice.–T.G. • $11 • (7/31/1998) • **80**

Merlot El Dorado 1996: Firm, with mineral, charred oak and dried currant flavors. Drying on the finish. Drink now.–J.L. • $12 • (9/30/1998) • **80**

Sauvignon Blanc El Dorado 1997 • $8 • (5/15/1998) • **83**

Sauvignon Blanc El Dorado 1996 • $8 • (3/31/1998) • **82**

WINDWARD | CALIFORNIA

Pinot Noir Paso Robles 1994 • $19 • (8/31/1997) • **85**
Pinot Noir Paso Robles Monopole 1997: Tightly focused, with a core of dried cherry, earthy berry, spice and herb flavors, finishing clean and firm. Drink through 2004.–H.S. • $25 • (9/15/1999) • **86**
Pinot Noir Paso Robles Monopole 1995 • $25 • (2/28/1998) • **83**
Pinot Noir Paso Robles Monopole Barrel Select Gold Label 1996: Light cherry, plum and herb flavors lock in with floral notes and a hint of bitterness at the end. Fairly smooth, however. • $55 • (9/15/1998) • **83**

WINEGLASS CELLARS | WASHINGTON

Cabernet Sauvignon Yakima Valley Elerding Vineyard 1996: Ripe and exotic, with seductive blackberry, raspberry, cola and coffee flavors that spread across a generous, almost-plush texture. Already appealing. Drink through 2006.–H.S. • $35 • (6/15/1999) • **90**
Cabernet Sauvignon Yakima Valley Elerding Vineyard 1995: Ripe and generous, a lush mouthful of bright berry, plum and spice flavors, all swirling attractively though the tightly packed finish. Balances freshness and complexity nicely. Drink through 2002.–H.S. • $30 • (9/15/1998) • **89**
Cabernet Sauvignon Yakima Valley Elerding Vineyard 1994 • $28 • (11/30/1997) • **85**
Merlot Yakima Valley 1995 • $16 • (11/30/1997) • **86**
Merlot Yakima Valley 1994 • $16 • (9/15/1996) • **83**
Merlot Yakima Valley Reserve 1995: Supple and plush, with a lavish layer of spice and toast to complement the fresh plum at the center. An expansive wine, poised for drinking now through 2001.–H.S. • $21 • (9/15/1998) • **87**
Merlot Yakima Valley Reserve 1994 • $25 • (9/15/1997) • **84**
Pinot Noir Oregon 1994 • $21 • (5/15/1996) • **91**

WING CANYON | CALIFORNIA

Cabernet Sauvignon Mount Veeder 1996: Austere, with trim, tannic wild berry, black cherry and cedar notes. Turns tight and tannic on the finish. Best from 2002 through 2008.–J.L. • $28 • (1/31/2000) • **87**

WITNESS TREE | OREGON

Chardonnay Oregon 1997: Crisp, brisk style offers modest apple and spice flavors, with a touch of astringency on the finish. Drink now through 2002.–H.S. • $13 • (10/15/1999) • **83**
Chardonnay Willamette Valley Vintage Select 1997: Has a chalky, slightly astringent texture, but the pretty apple and floral notes echo on the finish. Drink now.–H.S. • $22 • (10/15/1999) • **81**
Pinot Noir Oregon 1989 • $14 • (2/28/1993) • **82**
Pinot Noir Willamette Valley 1997: Light and crisp, with pretty blackberry notes under a layer of biting tannins and herbal tones. Needs time. Best after 2000.–H.S. • $18 • (9/30/1999) • **83**
Pinot Noir Willamette Valley 1995 • $17 • (5/15/1998) • **83**
Pinot Noir Willamette Valley 1994 • $16 • (7/31/1996) • **85**
Pinot Noir Willamette Valley Benchmark 1996: Ripe and plummy, both in color and in flavor, with a veil of fine-grained tannins around a rich layer of nicely articulated fruit, which persists on the refined finish. Drink now through 2003.–H.S. • $40 • (9/30/1999) • **89**
Pinot Noir Willamette Valley Estate Bottled 1992 • $13 • (3/15/1994) • **83**
Pinot Noir Willamette Valley Vintage Select 1997: Chewy in texture, with ripe cherry and earth flavors lurking beneath a layer of fine-grained tannins, echoing lightly on the finish. Best after 2000.–H.S. • $34 • (9/30/1999) • **87**
Pinot Noir Willamette Valley Vintage Select 1994 • $30 • (6/30/1996) • **87**
Pinot Noir Willamette Valley Vintage Select 1993 • $25 • (10/31/1995) • **88**

WOLFE, THURSTON | WASHINGTON

Black Muscat Washington 1992 • $9 • (9/30/1994) • **85**
Grenache Columbia Valley 1994 • $10 • (9/30/1996) • **84**
Lemberger Columbia Valley Blue Franc 1996: A thick wine layered with exotic spices, including allspice, nutmeg and cinnamon, around a core of modest black cherry and smoke.–H.S. • $12 • (8/31/1998) • **83**
Lemberger Columbia Valley RW Reserve 1994 • $10 • (9/30/1996) • **85**
Lemberger Columbia Valley RW Reserve 1992 • $10 • (9/30/1994) • **77**
Pinot Gris Washington 1997: Nectarine and melon flavors bounce to the fore in this raw-boned, medium-weight wine. Drink now.–H.S. • $12 • (9/15/1998) • **84**
Port Columbia Valley JTW's 1992 • $17 • (9/30/1995) • **85**
Port Washington JTW's Port 1991 • $10 • (6/15/1995) • **87**
Sweet Rebecca Late Harvest Yakima Valley 1992 • $10 • (9/30/1994) • **85**
Zinfandel Columbia Valley 1992 • $12 • (9/30/1994) • **85**

WOLFFER ESTATE SAGPOND VINEYARDS
NEW YORK

Chardonnay The Hamptons Long Island 1997: Shows some fuller, nutty notes on the nose, but verges on cidery on the palate, finishing tart.–T.M. • $13 • (1/01/2000) • **77**
Chardonnay The Hamptons Long Island 1996: Plush and soft, this round white offers hazelnut, nutmeg and ripe melon flavors, well integrated and deep. Though quite oaky in character, it has enough acidity to balance. Drink now.–T.M. • $13 • (6/30/1999) • **83**
Chardonnay The Hamptons Long Island Estate Selection 1997: There's an intriguing earth and grilled hazelnut note in this ambitious Chardonnay, before the mature, baked apple flavor takes over. Medium-bodied. Drink now.–T.M. • $27 • (1/01/2000) • **85**
Chardonnay The Hamptons Long Island La Ferme Martin 1998: This austere white offers toasty and smoky oak flavors, backed by modest apple and firm acidity. Its structure makes this a good match with food. Drink now.–T.M. • $13 • (5/31/2000) • **81**
Chardonnay The Hamptons Long Island Reserve 1997: Buttery aroma and baked apple flavors here, but there's enough acidity to keep it interesting. Drink now.–T.M. • $17 • (1/01/2000) • **81**
Merlot The Hamptons Long Island 1997: A medium-bodied red, with cherry and herb flavors and tobaccolike notes on the finish, which has good length. Drink now.–K.M. • $18 • (11/15/1999) • **83**
Merlot The Hamptons Long Island 1996: Soft and rather delicate, yet still fruity and quite refreshing, this balanced red shows ripe cherry, spice and light chocolate flavors with soft tannins and a pretty, floral finish. Not a blockbuster, but it brings you back for another sip. Drink now through 2001.–T.M. • $18 • (6/30/1999) • **85**
Merlot The Hamptons Long Island Estate Selection 1995: Soft and smooth, this polished red offers well-focused floral, berry and cherry flavors, with smoky accents and well-integrated yet very firm tannins. A nice balance of delicacy and firmness. Drink now through 2002.–T.M. • $NA • (6/30/1999) • **86**
The Hamptons Long Island Blush 1998: This pale pink wine offers light, fresh strawberry flavors. Clean and crisp, it's simple but balanced and refreshing. A good aperitif. Drink now.–T.M. • $11 • (6/30/1999) • **82**

WOODBRIDGE | CALIFORNIA

Cabernet Sauvignon California 1997: Starts off with a pronounced licorice quality, framed in smoky oak. The wine shows moderate body, with currant and spice fanning out on an herbal finish. Drink through 2006. • $8 • (10/15/1999) • **84**
Cabernet Sauvignon California 1996: An odd assortment of flavors: smoke, black currant, burnt rubber and herbs. A certain firmness and tannic edge seems to hold it together, however. • $8 • (11/15/1998) • **74**
Cabernet Sauvignon California 1994 • $8 • (5/31/1997) • **83**
Cabernet Sauvignon California 1992 • $7 • (11/15/1994) • **82**
Cabernet Sauvignon California 1991 • $8 • (11/15/1993) • **80**
Cabernet Sauvignon California 1990 • $8 • (10/31/1992) • **81**
Cabernet Sauvignon California 1988 • $6 • (2/28/1991) • **81**
Cabernet Sauvignon California Barrel Aged 1992 • $7 • (12/15/1995) • **83**
Cabernet Sauvignon California Lot No. 295 1995 • $8 • (11/15/1997) • **79**
Cabernet Sauvignon California Twin Oaks 1995 • $9 • (6/30/1998) • **80**
Chardonnay California 1998: Light and toasty, with apple and pear notes finishing slightly bitter. Drink now.–J.L. • $8 • (6/30/2000) • **80**
Chardonnay California 1997: Pleasant but simple, with tangerine and toast flavors. Drink now.–H.S. • $8 • (11/30/1998) • **80**
Chardonnay Monterey County Lot No. 196 1996 • $8 • (3/31/1998) • **81**
Port Lodi Portocinco Limited Edition 1992 • $15 • (4/30/1997) • **91**
Sauvignon Blanc California 1997: Made in a grassy, herbal style, although it finishes with hints of ripe melon. Light-textured, with moderate body. Drink now. • $7 • (2/28/1999) • **83**
Sauvignon Blanc California Lot No. 396 1996 • $7 • (3/31/1998) • **84**
White Zinfandel California 1996 • $5 • (9/15/1997) • **76**
Zinfandel California 1996 • $NA • (1/01/1998) • **74**
Zinfandel California 1995 • $6 • (7/31/1997) • **85**

Zinfandel California 1992 • $6 • (10/15/1994) • **77**
Zinfandel California 1991 • $6 • (6/15/1993) • **79**
Zinfandel California 1990 • $7 • (7/15/1992) • **84**
Zinfandel California Barrel Aged 1993 • $5 • (8/31/1995) • **82**
Zinfandel California Lot No. 496 1996 • $7 • (3/31/1998) • **79**

WOODSIDE | CALIFORNIA

Cabernet Sauvignon Santa Cruz Mountains 1990 • $24 • (11/15/1993) • **75**
Chardonnay Santa Cruz Mountains 1996: Awkward, with a bitterness to the simple apple and butter flavors. Drink now.–T.G. • $17 • (7/31/1998) • **78**
Chardonnay Santa Cruz Mountains Estate Reserve 1996: Simple and pleasant, with hints of apple, citrus and toasty oak. Drink now.–T.G. • $21 • (7/31/1998) • **81**
Zinfandel Santa Cruz Mountains Vineyard Hill Vineyards 1991 • $14 • (10/15/1994) • **77**

WOODWARD CANYON | WASHINGTON

Cabernet Sauvignon Columbia Valley 1996: Beautifully focused, generous with its ripe currant and blackberry flavors, shaded nicely with sage and spice notes, finishing with a deceptively full complement of fine-grained tannins. Drink through 2006.–H.S. • $45 • (9/15/1999) • **91**
Cabernet Sauvignon Columbia Valley 1994 • $34 • (7/31/1997) • **92**
Cabernet Sauvignon Columbia Valley 1991 • $29 • (7/31/1994) HR • **93**
Cabernet Sauvignon Columbia Valley 1989 • $27 • (5/15/1992) HR • **92**
Cabernet Sauvignon Columbia Valley 1988 • $24 • (4/15/1992) • **93**
Cabernet Sauvignon Columbia Valley 1987 • $35 • (4/15/1992) • **95**
Cabernet Sauvignon Columbia Valley 1986 • $35 • (4/15/1992) • **87**
Cabernet Sauvignon Columbia Valley 1985 • $30 • (4/15/1992) • **86**
Cabernet Sauvignon Columbia Valley 1984 • $27 • (4/15/1992) • **81**
Cabernet Sauvignon Columbia Valley 1983 • $30 • (4/15/1992) • **88**
Cabernet Sauvignon Columbia Valley 1982 • $28 • (4/15/1992) • **83**
Cabernet Sauvignon Columbia Valley 1981 • $30 • (4/15/1992) • **85**
Cabernet Sauvignon Columbia Valley Dedication Series #13 1993 • $30 • (6/15/1996) • **88**
Cabernet Sauvignon Columbia Valley Dedication Series #12 1992 • $27 • (8/31/1995) CS • **90**
Cabernet Sauvignon Columbia Valley Dedication Series #10 1990 • $27 • (7/31/1993) HR • **91**
Cabernet Sauvignon Columbia Valley Old Vines 1995: Ripe and succulent, complex, with chocolate, earth and woodsy overtones to the slender beam of plum and berry at the center. A nicely balanced wine that seems to have reached its best. Drink now through 2001.–H.S. • $45 • (10/15/1998) • **89**
Cabernet Sauvignon Washington Artist Series #6 1997: Supple, generous and nicely focused to show off its raspberry, red cherry and herb flavors, hinting at cream and vanilla on the polished finish. Delicious now. Best from 2001 through 2007.–H.S. • $33 • (5/15/2000) • **89**
Cabernet Sauvignon Washington Canoe Ridge Vineyard 1992 • $20 • (5/31/1995) • **90**
Cabernet Sauvignon Washington Canoe Ridge Vineyard Artist Series #5 1996: Ripe and generous, this soft-textured mouthful has currant, blackberry and black cherry flavors that linger enticingly and share mouth-space with a spicy oak note that becomes stronger on the polished finish. Drink through 2005.–H.S. • $30 • (5/31/1999) • **91**
Cabernet Sauvignon Washington Canoe Ridge Vineyard Artist Series #4 1995: A smooth and silky Washington Cab, its dark plum, blackberry and vanilla flavors tumbling over the palate, finishing with sweet ripeness wrapped in polished, fine-grained tannins. Folds some pretty oak into the mix on the aftertaste. Delicious now. Drink through 2005.–H.S. • $28 • (8/31/1998) SS • **92**
Cabernet Sauvignon Washington Canoe Ridge Vineyard Artist Series #2 1993 • $25 • (6/15/1996) • **90**
Cabernet Sauvignon-Merlot-Cabernet Franc Washington Special Selection 1993: Still fresh after five years, with its supple core of currant and blueberry flavor and hints of cedar and herb all wrapped in a veil of fine tannins. Persists nicely on the finish. Drink through 2004.–H.S. • $75 • (9/15/1998) • **90**
Charbonneau Walla Walla County 1994 • $38 • (7/31/1997) • **90**
Charbonneau Walla Walla County 1989 • $30 • (5/15/1992) • **88**
Charbonneau Walla Walla County 1988 • $NA • (4/15/1992) • **95**
Charbonneau Walla Walla County 1987 • $30 • (12/31/1990) • **89**
Charbonneau Walla Walla County 1985 • $30 • (4/15/1992) • **86**
Chardonnay Columbia Valley 1997: Crisp, and distinctive for its layers of spice and earth notes around a fine core of pear and citrus flavors. Light on its feet, but offers plenty of Chardonnay fruit that lasts impressively on the elegant finish before a hint of oak flavor sneaks in. Drink now through 2003.–H.S. • $28 • (5/31/1999) • **90**
Chardonnay Columbia Valley Reserve 1997: A layer of distinctly earthy flavor runs through this firm Chardonnay, but enough citrusy pear peeks through to make this worth holding onto. Drink now.–H.S. • $34 • (5/31/1999) • **89**
Chardonnay Idaho Arena Valley Vineyard 1996: A fresh and open-textured wine, its rich mouthful of spicy pear and apricot flavors hinting at earth and floral notes on the vanilla-tinged finish. Has impressive length, too. Drink now.–H.S. • $30 • (11/15/1998) • **90**
Chardonnay Walla Walla Valley 1998: This beautifully balanced, elegant expression of Chardonnay holds a lot back but shows layers of spicy pear, orange, citrus and mineral flavors lurking beneath the surface. Drink now through 2005.–H.S. • $34 • (5/15/2000) • **89**
Chardonnay Washington 1996: Supple and spicy, with a pretty core of apple and grapefruit flavor, lingering on the jazzy finish. Turns crisp with succeeding sips. A good Chardonnay for delicate food. Drink now.–H.S. • $28 • (9/15/1998) • **89**
Chardonnay Washington Celilo Vineyard 1996: Misses the vibrant freshness and crispness of the vineyard, but it's still smooth and has nice apple and tobacco flavors, folding in a touch of earthiness on the finish.–H.S. • $34 • (9/15/1998) • **85**
Chardonnay Washington Conner Lee Vineyard 1998: Ripe and generous, this rich, round Chardonnay has spicy pear and toasty, gently honeyed flavors that linger on the beautifully balanced finish. Drink now through 2003.–H.S. • $25 • (5/15/2000) • **90**
Merlot Columbia Valley 1997: Ripe and chewy, with pretty cherry, spice, chocolate and leather notes weaving through a firm-textured, artfully balanced frame. Tempting already. Drink through 2002.–H.S. • $30 • (9/30/1999) • **88**
Merlot Columbia Valley 1996: Firm in texture, with pepper and blackberry notes poking through a layer of fine tannins. Finish persists, suggesting this just needs time. Best from 2001 through 2005.–H.S. • $30 • (8/31/1998) • **89**
Merlot Columbia Valley 1995 • $30 • (9/30/1997) • **88**
Merlot Columbia Valley 1994 • $27 • (6/15/1996) HR • **91**
Merlot Columbia Valley 1993 • $23 • (9/30/1995) • **89**
Merlot Columbia Valley 1992 • $21 • (9/30/1994) • **86**
Merlot Columbia Valley 1991 • $22 • (11/15/1993) • **84**
Red Columbia Valley NV • $14 • (7/31/1997) • **88**

WORDEN | WASHINGTON

Cabernet Sauvignon Washington Cascade Crest Winemakers Reserve 1996: Lighter and more supple than most Cabernets, this features ripe plum and spice flavors amidst the fine-grained tannins. Drink now.–H.S. • $25 • (12/31/1999) • **87**
Cabernet Sauvignon-Merlot Washington 1995: Soft, almost plush, with straightforward black cherry and smoky flavors winding through the generous finish.–H.S. • $19 • (9/15/1998) • **85**
Cabernet Sauvignon-Merlot Washington Cascade Collection 1994 • $15 • (9/15/1997) • **90**
Cabernet Sauvignon-Merlot Washington 1993 • $15 • (9/15/1996) • **85**
Cabernet Sauvignon-Merlot Washington 1992 • $12 • (9/30/1995) • **84**
Cabernet Sauvignon-Merlot Washington 1991 • $12 • (8/31/1994) • **83**
Cabernet Sauvignon-Merlot Washington 1990 • $10 • (7/31/1992) • **73**
Cabernet Sauvignon-Merlot Washington 1989 • $10 • (2/29/1992) • **86**
Claret Washington 1994 • $10 • (9/15/1996) • **81**
Claret Washington 1993 • $8 • (9/30/1995) • **79**
Cascade Claret Washington 1992 • $9 • (9/30/1994) • **87**
Gewürztraminer Washington 1997: Muddled flavors of rose petal and citrus peel come up against a hard edge of metallic acidity. Not pleasant.–H.S. • $7 • (9/15/1998) • **73**
Gewürztraminer Washington Late Harvest 1992 • $8 • (9/30/1994) • **83**
Johannisberg Riesling Washington Cascade Collection 1997: Light and barely sweet, with pretty apple and peach flavors shaded by nice hints of sweet pea and pine. Drink now.–H.S. • $7 • (9/15/1998) • **86**
Lemberger Washington Crawford Vineyard Winemaker's Reserve 1997: Very light in color, with a spicy, leathery edge to the modest raspberry flavors. Drink now.–H.S. • $14 • (9/15/1998) • **81**

Key: SS—Spectator Selection. CS—Cellar Selection. HR—Highly Recommended. $NA—Price not available. (BT)—Barrel tasting. (A)—Auction Price.
For a key to the tasters' initials, see "How to Use These Listings."
Dates in parentheses represent the issues in which the ratings were published.

Merlot Washington Crawford Vineyard Winemaker's Reserve 1996: Light in texture, with pretty strawberry and spice flavors that linger gently as the low-tannin finish picks up a hint of chocolate. Drink now.–H.S. • $16 • (9/15/1998) • **86**

Merlot Washington 1993 • $8 • (9/30/1995) • **81**

Merlot Washington 1992 • $12 • (5/15/1994) • **76**

Riesling Washington Cascade Crest 1998: Soft and fragrant, with subtle, pretty apple, floral and pear flavors that linger enticingly. Drink now.–H.S. • $9 • (12/31/1999) • **85**

WRIGHT, KEN | OREGON

Chardonnay Oregon 1996: Fresh and open-textured, with appealing orange-scented pear and spice flavors up front, echoing spice and citrus on the finish. Drink now.–H.S. • $20 • (10/31/1998) • **87**

Pinot Blanc Willamette Valley 1998: Lithe and generous on a racy frame, offering apple, pear, spice and honey notes that harmonize nicely and linger on the smooth finish. Drink now.–H.S. • $18 • (4/30/2000) • **88**

Pinot Noir Willamette Valley 1996: Youthful and polished, with pretty cherry and raspberry flavors that pick up hints of cola and spice on the smooth finish. Feels elegant now. Drink through 2001.–H.S. • $21 • (8/31/1998) • **88**

Pinot Noir Willamette Valley 1995 • $21 • (11/30/1997) • **86**

Pinot Noir Willamette Valley 1994 • $21 • (8/31/1996) SS • **90**

Pinot Noir Willamette Valley Abbey Heights 1994 • $28 • (8/31/1996) • **90**

Pinot Noir Willamette Valley Abbey Heights Whistling Ridge 1994 • $28 • (8/31/1996) • **92**

Pinot Noir Willamette Valley Abbey Ridge Vineyard 1996: Light in texture, with firm tannins and light, pretty plum and currant flavors that linger delicately on the crisp finish. Drink now through 2001.–H.S. • $30 • (8/31/1998) • **87**

Pinot Noir Willamette Valley Arcus Vineyard 1998: Bright, crisp and focused, this vibrant wine offers a cascade of blueberry, blackberry and vanilla-spice notes that linger on the juicy finish. Drink now through 2006.–H.S. • $35 • (3/31/2000) • **92**

Pinot Noir Willamette Valley Canary Hill Vineyard 1998: Bright, juicy, distinctive for the floral, citrusy edge to the core of blackberry and spice flavors. Everything lingers nicely on the long finish. Drink now through 2006.–H.S. • $35 • (3/31/2000) • **90**

Pinot Noir Willamette Valley Canary Hill Vineyard 1997: Light in structure and firm in texture, with pretty raspberry and spice notes coming together nicely on the finish. Best from 2001 through 2004.–H.S. • $30 • (1/01/2000) • **87**

Pinot Noir Willamette Valley Canary Hill Vineyard 1996: Bright, smooth and ravishing for its up-front raspberry and strawberry flavors, shaded with delicate tobacco and nutmeg nuances. Finishes gently, with plenty of flavor echoing. Drink through 2005.–H.S. • $30 • (8/31/1998) • **91**

Pinot Noir Willamette Valley Canary Hill Vineyard 1995 • $28 • (11/30/1997) • **86**

Pinot Noir Willamette Valley Canary Hill Vineyard 1994 • $28 • (8/31/1996) • **84**

Pinot Noir Willamette Valley Carter Vineyard 1998: Broad and generous, densely packed with flavors of black cherry and currant and a touch of earth, nicely balanced by a refined thread of acidity. Drink now through 2006.–H.S. • $35 • (3/31/2000) • **91**

Pinot Noir Willamette Valley Carter Vineyard 1997: Bright and intense, with pretty black cherry and licorice notes swirling around on a velvety texture. Finishes with a twang of tartness. Has more depth and length than most '97s. Drink now through 2003.–H.S. • $30 • (1/01/2000) • **89**

Pinot Noir Willamette Valley Carter Vineyard 1996: Light and focused, with pretty raspberry and spice flavors persisting on the gleaming finish. Packs lots of character into a lean, lithe package. Nice now; better with some cellaring. Drink through 2002.–H.S. • $30 • (8/31/1998) • **89**

Pinot Noir Willamette Valley Carter Vineyard 1995 • $28 • (11/30/1997) • **85**

Pinot Noir Willamette Valley Carter Vineyard 1994 • $28 • (8/31/1996) • **91**

Pinot Noir Willamette Valley Freedom Hill Vineyard 1997: Fresh, ripe and generous for the vintage, with lovely raspberry and cherry flavors mingling with spice and gentle herbs on the finish. Drink now through 2004.–H.S. • $30 • (1/01/2000) • **88**

Pinot Noir Willamette Valley Freedom Hill Vineyard 1995 • $28 • (11/30/1997) • **88**

Pinot Noir Willamette Valley Guadalupe Vineyard 1998: Especially youthful, with a gamy edge to the dense blackberry and currant flavors, all balancing on a sharp edge of acidity. Finishes balanced and refined, but needs time to come together. Best from 2001 through 2007.–H.S. • $35 • (3/31/2000) • **90**

Pinot Noir Willamette Valley Guadalupe Vineyard 1997: Offers lovely Pinot flavors on a light frame, centering on black cherry and toast notes that linger on the generous finish. Drink now through 2003.–H.S. • $30 • (1/01/2000) • **86**

Pinot Noir Willamette Valley Guadalupe Vineyard 1996: Firm in texture, with juicy blackberry and currant flavors that persist on the chewy finish. Needs time to resolve the tannins. Try through 2004.–H.S. • $30 • (8/31/1998) • **88**

Pinot Noir Willamette Valley Guadalupe Vineyard 1995 • $28 • (11/30/1997) • **87**

Pinot Noir Willamette Valley McCrone Vineyard 1998: Smooth and polished, generous with its spicy berry and cherry flavors that grow with each sip. Finish echoes cinnamon and nutmeg. Needs time to settle down, but it's a winner. Best after 2001.–H.S. • $35 • (4/30/2000) • **90**

Pinot Noir Willamette Valley McCrone Vineyard 1996: Light and airy, with pretty plum and spice flavors that linger appealingly on the slightly chewy finish. Drink through 2002.–H.S. • $30 • (8/31/1998) • **87**

Pinot Noir Willamette Valley Nysa Vineyard 1998: Ripe and focused, with a layer of chewy tannins around a lovely core of black cherry, tobacco and spice flavors. Balanced and generous on the finish. Drink now through 2005.–H.S. • $35 • (3/31/2000) • **90**

Pinot Noir Willamette Valley Shea Vineyard 1998: One of Oregon Pinot Noir specialist Ken Wright's new releases, this has a purity of flavor and a graceful balance that are totally disarming. A seductive wine, its pretty raspberry, black cherry and floral aromas and flavors linger enticingly on the open-textured finish. Best from 2001 through 2008.–H.S. • $35 • (3/31/2000) CS • **93**

Pinot Noir Willamette Valley Shea Vineyard 1997: Light and refreshing, a stylishly delicate wine, with pretty raspberry and earth notes lingering on the firm finish. Drink now through 2003.–H.S. • $30 • (1/01/2000) • **87**

Pinot Noir Willamette Valley Shea Vineyard 1996: Soft, supple and generous with its blueberry, currant and cherry wood aromas and flavors, all in a gentle frame that already feels elegant. Finishes with enough intensity to merit cellaring. Drink through 2003.–H.S. • $30 • (8/31/1998) • **89**

Pinot Noir Willamette Valley Shea Vineyard 1995 • $28 • (11/30/1997) • **88**

Pinot Noir Willamette Valley Shea Vineyard 1994 • $28 • (8/31/1996) • **90**

Pinot Noir Willamette Valley Wahle Vineyard 1998: Bright and generous, this is a remarkably elegant wine, almost crisp in texture up front, unfolding its berry, spice and sassafras flavors on a supple frame. Drink now through 2005.–H.S. • $35 • (3/31/2000) • **91**

YAKIMA RIVER | WASHINGTON

Cabernet Sauvignon Columbia Valley 1992 • $14 • (7/31/1996) • **87**

Cabernet Sauvignon Columbia Valley 1988 • $15 • (3/31/1992) • **74**

Cabernet Sauvignon Yakima Valley 1995: Smooth and velvety, with spicy cherry and leather notes on a round frame. Drink now through 2002.–H.S. • $16 • (8/31/1999) • **85**

Cabernet Sauvignon Yakima Valley 1994: Ripe and round, with a funky, earthy edge to the blackberry and spice flavors. Drink now through 2003.–H.S. • $15 • (8/31/1998) • **82**

Cabernet Sauvignon Yakima Valley 1993 • $15 • (7/31/1997) • **81**

Cabernet Sauvignon Yakima Valley 1991 • $13 • (3/31/1996) • **79**

Cabernet Sauvignon Yakima Valley 1990 • $15 • (4/15/1995) • **84**

Cabernet Sauvignon Yakima Valley Winemaker's Reserve 1994: Earthy, slightly sour at first, but with enough pretty raspberry flavor to give some immediate appeal. Drink now.–H.S. • $30 • (8/31/1998) • **80**

Cabernet Sauvignon Yakima Valley Winemaker's Reserve 1989 • $25 • (9/30/1994) • **83**

Johannisberg Riesling Yakima Valley 1997: Off-dry, with stale apple and floral flavors on a modest frame.–H.S. • $7 • (9/15/1998) • **77**

Lemberger Rendezvous Yakima Valley 1989 • $8 • (3/31/1992) • **81**

Lemberger Yakima Valley Rendezvous 1996 • $10 • (7/31/1997) • **84**

Lemberger Yakima Valley Rendezvous 1995 • $10 • (7/31/1996) • **73**

Merlot Columbia Valley 1988 • $15 • (4/15/1992) • **83**

Merlot Yakima Valley 1994: Light, smooth and decidedly earthy, nice but with a hint of vinegar sneaking in amid the modest leather and spice notes. Drink now.–H.S. • $18 • (8/31/1998) • **80**

Merlot Yakima Valley 1993 • $15 • (7/31/1997) • **81**

Merlot Yakima Valley 1992 • $12 • (5/15/1996) • **86**

Merlot Yakima Valley 1991 • $15 • (6/15/1995) • **88**

Merlot Yakima Valley 1990 • $15 • (9/30/1994) • **85**

Port Yakima Valley Johns 1994 • $17 • (9/15/1997) • **87**

Port Yakima Valley Johns Vintage Port 1992 • $16 • (6/15/1995) • **82**

White Riesling Yakima Valley Late Harvest 1996 • $10 • (9/15/1997) • **78**

YAMHILL VALLEY | OREGON

Pinot Blanc Oregon 1998: Bright and generous, delivering a lovely range of apple, floral and mineral flavors that echo on the ripe finish. Drink now. –H.S. • $14 • (3/31/2000) • **87**
Pinot Blanc Oregon 1996 • $17 • (11/15/1997) • **87**
Pinot Gris Oregon 1998: Crisp and bright, offering nicely focused pear, mineral and floral flavors. Finishes a bit tight. Drink now.–H.S. • $12 • (3/31/2000) • **85**
Pinot Noir Oregon 1985 • $16 • (6/15/1987) • **86**
Pinot Noir Oregon 1983 • $17 • (8/31/1986) • **92**
Pinot Noir Willamette Valley 1997: Light, almost crisp, with currant and cola flavors on an airy frame. Drink now through 2001.–H.S. • $17 • (3/31/2000) • **83**
Pinot Noir Willamette Valley 1995 • $17 • (2/28/1997) • **85**
Pinot Noir Willamette Valley 1992 • $11 • (11/30/1994) • **83**
Pinot Noir Willamette Valley 1988 • $12 • (1/31/1991) • **76**
Pinot Noir Willamette Valley 1983 • $35 • (2/15/1990) • **87**
Pinot Noir Willamette Valley Estate Reserve 1988 • $18 • (11/15/1991) • **78**
Pinot Noir Willamette Valley Reserve 1997: Bright and simple, with a firm texture and nice black cherry flavors that last on the finish. Drink now. –H.S. • $29 • (3/31/2000) • **86**
Pinot Noir Willamette Valley Reserve 1994 • $35 • (11/15/1997) • **86**
Pinot Noir Willamette Valley Reserve 1991 • $22 • (11/30/1994) • **82**

YORK CREEK | CALIFORNIA

Meritage Spring Mountain District 1995: Tight and firm, with a compact focus on the chunky currant, mineral, plum and blackberry flavors, it slowly unfolds to reveal more nuances. Should reward patience in the cellar. Made by Cathy Corison. Best from 2002 through 2009.–J.L. • $40 • (1/31/2000) • **89**

YORK MOUNTAIN | CALIFORNIA

Cabernet Sauvignon San Luis Obispo County 1990 • $14 • (12/15/1995) • **85**
Cabernet Sauvignon San Luis Obispo County 1989 • $14 • (11/15/1994) • **71**
Cabernet Sauvignon San Luis Obispo County 1988 • $12 • (11/15/1992) • **83**
Cabernet Sauvignon San Luis Obispo County 1987 • $12 • (11/15/1992) • **84**
Cabernet Sauvignon San Luis Obispo County 1986 • $14 • (11/15/1992) • **84**
Cabernet Sauvignon San Luis Obispo County 1985 • $15 • (12/15/1989) • **83**
Cabernet Sauvignon San Luis Obispo County Carver Vineyard 1993 • $18 • (5/15/1998) • **77**
Cabernet Sauvignon San Luis Obispo County Reserve 1990 • $16 • (12/15/1995) • **82**
Chardonnay San Luis Obispo County 1996: Odd, with heavy mineral notes and traces of citrus and herb. Drink now. • $14 • (7/31/1998) • **78**
Merlot San Luis Obispo County 1993 • $12 • (8/31/1996) • **70**
Merlot San Luis Obispo County 1991 • $12 • (9/15/1994) • **79**
Merlot San Luis Obispo County 1990 • $12 • (9/15/1994) • **77**
Merlot San Luis Obispo County 1989 • $13 • (5/31/1992) • **84**
Merlot San Luis Obispo County 1986 • $10 • (12/15/1989) • **80**
Pinot Noir San Luis Obispo County 1993 • $14 • (2/28/1997) • **81**
Pinot Noir San Luis Obispo County 1992 • $10 • (12/31/1995) • **78**
Pinot Noir San Luis Obispo County 1991 • $10 • (12/31/1995) • **73**
Pinot Noir San Luis Obispo County 1990 • $10 • (3/31/1995) • **82**
Pinot Noir San Luis Obispo County 1989 • $9 • (2/28/1993) • **76**
Pinot Noir San Luis Obispo County William Cain Vineyard 1995: A bright cherry core is flanked by hints of cola, tea and spice. Finishes a bit dry and short. Drink now.–J.L. • $14 • (8/31/1998) • **82**
Pinot Noir San Luis Obispo County William Cain Vineyard 1994 • $14 • (5/15/1998) • **82**
Pinot Noir San Luis Obispo Stephen's 1995: Strawberry, cherry, vanilla and tea flavors blend pleasantly on a soft frame. Drink now.–J.L. • $18 • (8/31/1998) • **83**
Zinfandel San Luis Obispo County 1997: Spicy and racy, with superripe plum and berry flavors that really fan out. Finishes a bit hot, with a dash of clove. Drink now through 2003.–J.L. • $16 • (5/31/2000) • **84**
Zinfandel San Luis Obispo County 1991 • $9 • (10/15/1995) • **83**

Key: SS—Spectator Selection. CS—Cellar Selection. HR—Highly Recommended. $NA—Price not available. (BT)—Barrel tasting. Ⓐ—Auction Price. For a key to the tasters' initials, see "How to Use These Listings."
Dates in parentheses represent the issues in which the ratings were published.

Zinfandel San Luis Obispo County 1990 • $9 • (6/15/1994) • **82**
Zinfandel San Luis Obispo County 1989 • $8 • (9/30/1993) • **78**
Zinfandel San Luis Obispo County 1988 • $9 • (10/15/1992) • **74**

YORKVILLE | CALIFORNIA

Cabernet Franc Mendocino 1994 • $13 • (9/15/1997) • **84**
Eleanor of Aquitaine White Mendocino 1997: Kicks off with hints of butterscotch, then carries forth pretty grapefruit, mineral and herb flavors. The blend is tight yet well integrated, with an elegant, long finish. A blend of Sauvignon Blanc and Sémillon. Drink now through 2001. • $16 • (5/31/1999) • **88**
Sauvignon Blanc Mendocino 1997: Melon, herb and citrus flavors are carried along nicely by tangy acidity. The wine is tight and firm; not necessarily a sipper, but a fine match for seafood. Drink now through 2002. • $10 • (5/15/1999) • **85**
Sémillon Mendocino 1997: Tart and grapefruitlike, this is quite firm and tight on the tongue. Needs oysters or the equivalent. Drink now. • $12 • (6/15/1999) • **81**

YOUNGBERG HILL | OREGON

Pinot Noir Willamette Valley 1996 • $24 • (6/15/1998) • **78**

ZABACO | CALIFORNIA

Pinot Noir Russian River Valley 1995 • $10 • (1/31/1998) • **84**
Sauvignon Blanc Sonoma County 1996 • $9 • (4/30/1998) • **84**
Zinfandel Sonoma County 1995: Medium-bodied, with ripe black cherry and hints of tea and pepper, finishing with firm tannins. Drink now.–J.L. • $10 • (5/15/1999) • **85**
Zinfandel Sonoma County 1994 • $10 • (2/28/1997) • **86**

ZACA MESA | CALIFORNIA

Cabernet Sauvignon Central Coast 1988 • $12 • (11/15/1991) • **58**
Cabernet Sauvignon Central Coast Reserve 1987 • $25 • (11/15/1991) • **83**
Cabernet Sauvignon Santa Barbara County American Reserve 1983 • $13 • (3/31/1987) • **87**
Cabernet Sauvignon Santa Barbara County Reserve 1986 • $23 Ⓐ • (12/15/1988) • **80**
Cabernet Sauvignon Santa Barbara County Reserve 1985 • $15 • (10/15/1988) • **79**
Chardonnay Santa Barbara County Chapel Vineyard 1998: Round, with honeysuckle, peach, butter and vanilla flavors. Drink now.–J.L. • $20 • (6/30/2000) • **85**
Chardonnay Santa Barbara County Zaca Vineyards 1998: Clean and refreshing, with crisp pear, melon, apple, grapefruit and spicy notes. Drink now through 2003.–J.L. • $15 • (3/31/2000) • **85**
Chardonnay Santa Barbara County Zaca Vineyards 1997: Opens up with fresh apple and pear notes. Has a lot of oak but also ripe papaya and tangy citrus flavors. Finishes with refreshing zest. Drink now. • $14 • (2/28/1999) • **87**
Chardonnay Santa Barbara County Zaca Vineyards 1996 • $14 • (5/15/1998) • **89**
Cuvee Z Santa Barbara County 1997: Impressive for its range of complex flavors, it blends together dried cherry, wild berry, spice and cranberry, with hints of sage and cedar. Finishes with mild yet firm tannins. Grenache, Mourvèdre, Syrah, Cinsault and Counoise. Drink now through 2004.–J.L. • $17 • (12/31/1999) • **88**
Cuvee Z Santa Barbara County 1996 • $15 • (12/15/1997) • **86**
Cuvee Z Santa Barbara County 1995 • $15 • (4/30/1997) • **88**
Cuvee Z Santa Barbara County 1994 • $14 • (4/30/1996) • **85**
Cuvee Z Santa Barbara County 1993 • $14 • (4/30/1995) • **85**
Cuvee Z Santa Barbara County 1992 • $14 • (9/30/1994) • **78**
Pinot Noir Santa Barbara County Alumni Winemaker Series Lane Tanner 1993 • $18 • (3/31/1995) • **84**
Pinot Noir Santa Barbara County American Reserve 1984 • $13 • (2/15/1987) • **93**
Pinot Noir Santa Barbara County Reserve 1990 • $16 • (2/28/1993) • **74**
Pinot Noir Santa Barbara County Reserve 1989 • $16 • (9/30/1992) • **73**
Pinot Noir Santa Barbara County Reserve 1988 • $16 • (10/31/1990) • **86**
Pinot Noir Santa Barbara County Reserve 1987 • $15 • (12/15/1989) • **82**
Pinot Noir Santa Barbara County Reserve 1986 • $15 • (6/15/1988) • **91**
Pinot Noir Santa Barbara County Sierra Madre Vineyard 1990 • $16 • (8/31/1994) • **82**

Roussanne Santa Barbara County Zaca Vineyards 1997: Bright peach, apple and citrus flavors are supported by tangy acidity. Very fruity, with a silky, velvety finish. Drink now. • $16 • (12/31/1998) • **87**
Roussanne Santa Barbara County Zaca Vineyards 1996: A blend of tropical fruits comes to mind—papaya, mango, oranges and lemons. Lingers nicely on the finish, with tangy acidity. Drink now. • $16 • (9/15/1998) • **88**
Syrah Santa Barbara County 1990 • $12 • (12/31/1992) • **83**
Syrah Santa Barbara County 1989 • $12 • (8/31/1991) • **83**
Syrah Santa Barbara County Alumni Winemaker Series Bob Lindquist 1993 • $18 • (2/29/1996) • **88**
Syrah Santa Barbara County Alumni Winemaker Series Bob Lindquist 1992 • $18 • (1/31/1995) • **90**
Syrah Santa Barbara County B3 Black Bear Block 1996: Plenty of dark blackberry and black cherry flavors that are bright and focused, with crisp acidity and firm tannins. Drink now through 2006.–J.L. • $35 • (5/15/2000) • **87**
Syrah Santa Barbara County Chapel Vineyard 1992 • $19 • (1/31/1995) • **85**
Syrah Santa Barbara County Zaca Vineyards 1996: Dark, ripe and rich, brimming with snappy, fresh wild berry and black cherry. Finishes with firm tannins and a touch of earth. Drink now through 2007.–J.L. • $20 • (12/31/1999) • **87**
Syrah Santa Barbara County Zaca Vineyards 1995 • $20 • (11/15/1997) • **88**
Syrah Santa Barbara County Zaca Vineyards 1994 • $20 • (2/28/1997) • **89**
Syrah Santa Barbara County Zaca Vineyards 1993 • $13 • (11/30/1995) SS • **94**
Z Gris Santa Barbara County 1998: A full-bodied rosé, with ripe berry, spice and orange rind flavors. Complex finish. Drink now.–J.L. • $9 • (11/15/1999) • **87**
Z Gris Santa Barbara County 1996 • $8 • (9/15/1997) • **85**

ZD WINES | CALIFORNIA

Cabernet Sauvignon California 1982 • $12 • (7/16/1986) • **66**
Cabernet Sauvignon Napa Valley 1995 • $32 • (5/15/1998) • **91**
Cabernet Sauvignon Napa Valley 1994 • $30 • (7/31/1997) • **88**
Cabernet Sauvignon Napa Valley 1990 • $20 • (11/15/1992) • **86**
Cabernet Sauvignon Napa Valley 1989 • $20 • (11/15/1992) • **78**
Cabernet Sauvignon Napa Valley 1988 • $20 • (4/30/1991) • **86**
Cabernet Sauvignon Napa Valley 1987 • $16 • (2/15/1991) • **78**
Cabernet Sauvignon Napa Valley 1985 • $14 • (5/15/1989) • **81**
Cabernet Sauvignon Napa Valley Estate Bottled 1987 • $40 • (1/31/1991) • **90**
Cabernet Sauvignon Napa Valley Reserve 1995: Smooth, ripe, rich and polished, with currant, cherry, coffee, prune and tobacco flavors, turning silky and supple on the long, rich aftertaste. Drink through 2009.–J.L. • $60 • (4/30/1999) • **92**
Cabernet Sauvignon Napa Valley Reserve 1994 • $55 • (5/15/1998) • **90**
Cabernet Sauvignon Napa Valley Reserve 1993 • $40 • (3/31/1997) • **88**
Cabernet Sauvignon Napa Valley Reserve 1992 • $34 • (4/30/1996) • **88**
Chardonnay California 1997: Racy, with a citrus edge to the core of pear and sweet pea flavors, it turns diffuse on the finish but holds its flavors. Light oak in the background. Drink now through 2001.–J.L. • $26 • (4/30/1999) • **89**
Chardonnay California 1996: Crisp, with a core of citrus, pear, nectarine, herb and spice. The texture is a bit raw, but the wine is concentrated. Drink now.–J.L. • $25 • (7/31/1998) • **88**
Chardonnay Napa Valley Reserve 1997: Ripe, bold and creamy describes this California Chardonnay, with its rich character of fig, pear, vanilla, melon and spice. Picks up tropical fruit notes, with pineapple and guava singing on the finish. Drink now through 2003.–J.L. • $45 • (12/15/1999) HR • **93**
Merlot Napa Valley 1997: Tight and cedary, with a green streak running through the earthy mushroom and taut plum and berryish notes. Give it time in the hopes it will improve. Best from 2001 through 2007.–J.L. • $30 • (4/30/2000) • **84**
Pinot Noir Carneros 1996: Dry, earthy and leathery, it's struggling to find a fruit focus and thus seems wanting in character. Give it some air, and dried cherry and berry emerge. Drink now.–J.L. • $27 • (9/15/1998) • **82**
Pinot Noir Carneros 1995 • $25 • (11/15/1997) • **84**
Pinot Noir Napa Valley Carneros 1991 • $20 • (2/28/1994) • **78**
Pinot Noir Napa Valley Carneros 1990 • $20 • (9/30/1992) • **83**
Pinot Noir Napa Valley Carneros 1989 • $16 • (11/15/1991) • **82**
Pinot Noir Napa Valley Carneros 1988 • $17 • (6/30/1991) • **82**
Pinot Noir Napa Valley Carneros 1985 • $14 • (7/31/1989) • **79**
Pinot Noir Napa Valley 1982 • $13 • (8/31/1986) • **75**

ZELLERBACH ESTATES | CALIFORNIA

Cabernet Sauvignon Alexander Valley 1988 • $10 • (10/31/1990) • **82**
Cabernet Sauvignon California 1991 • $9 • (3/31/1994) • **78**
Cabernet Sauvignon Sonoma County 1978 • $NA • (11/15/1992) • **84**
Merlot Napa Valley 1993 • $14 • (6/15/1996) • **75**

ZIA | CALIFORNIA

Cabernet Sauvignon Napa Valley 1992 • $24 • (4/30/1996) • **90**

ZILLAH OAKES | WASHINGTON

Cabernet Franc Yakima Valley 1993 • $10 • (9/30/1995) • **79**
Muscat Canelli Yakima Valley 1994 • $8 • (8/31/1995) • **87**
Riesling Yakima Valley Late Harvest 1993 • $9 • (9/15/1995) • **84**

ZINGARO | CALIFORNIA

Zinfandel Mendocino 1997: Earthy plum and dried berry notes finish a bit hot. Drink now.–J.L. • $14 • (5/31/2000) • **80**

ZOOM | CALIFORNIA

Zinfandel Contra Costa County 104-Year-Old Vines 1998: A bit offbeat yet authentic, it mixes sweet-tasting cherry and plum flavors with a juniper berry edge. Turns tannic. Drink now.–J.L. • $24 • (6/15/2000) • **86**
Zinfandel Contra Costa County 103-Year-Old Vines 1997: Tastes muddled, with murky cherry and berry flavors that seem a bit cooked. Turns tarry. Drink now.–J.L. • $23 • (6/30/1999) • **80**
Zinfandel Contra Costa County 102-Year-Old Vines 1996 • $20 • (5/31/1998) • **88**
Zinfandel Dry Creek Valley 42-Year-Old Vines 1998: Clean, with pleasant, upfront berry and cranberry flavors that are simple. Drink now.–J.L. • $24 • (6/15/2000) • **83**
Zinfandel Napa Valley 33-Year-Old Vines 1998: Intense aromas of blueberry extract. Shows good depth and a zippy mouthfeel, with raisiny flavors and firm tannins. Drink now through 2001.–J.L. • $24 • (6/15/2000) • **87**
Zinfandel Paso Robles 30-Year-Old Vines 1998: Concentrated, with intense blackberry, chocolate and tobacco notes that show excellent length and richness. Drink now through 2004.–J.L. • $24 • (6/15/2000) • **89**
Zinfandel Paso Robles 29-Year-Old Vines 1997: Ripe and rich, with plum, spice, herb and black cherry flavors framed by toasted oak. Finishes with ripe tannins and slightly green notes. Drink now through 2002.–J.L. • $23 • (6/30/1999) • **87**

Winery Index